ENGLISH
DICTIONARY &
THESAURUS

GEDDES &
GROSSET

Published 2007 by Geddes & Grosset,
David Dale House, New Lanark, ML11 9DJ,
Scotland

© 2007 Geddes & Grosset

World maps created and supplied by Lovell Johns Limited, Oxfordshire, England

ISBN: 978 1 84205 600 4

Printed and bound in India

Contents

Elements of the Dictionary

headword

pronunciation guide with stress marks

other part-of-speech forms of the root word

plural forms

part of speech

subject label

alternative pronunciation

homographs

variant forms

variant forms

cross references

alfresco /æl'freskɔ:/ or /al-/ *adj* taking place outside in the open.—*also adv.*

alga /'ælgə/ *n* (*pl* **algae**) any of a group of chiefly aquatic lower plants classified according to colour.—**algal** *adj.*

algarroba, algaroba /,ælgə'rɔ:bə/ *n* the carob tree and bean; St John's bread.

algebra /'ældʒəbrə/ *n* the branch of mathematics dealing with the properties and relations of numbers; the generalization and extension of arithmetic.—**algebraic, algebraical** *adj.*—**algebraist** *n.*

Algerian /æl'dʒiːriən/ *adj* pertaining to Algeria or Algiers. • *n* a native of Algeria or Algiers.

Algerine /ældʒə'riːn/ *adj* Algerian.

-algia /'ældʒə/ or /-dʒiə/ *n suffix* pain.—**algic** *adj.*

algid /'ældʒid/ *adj* cold, chilly.

ALGOL /'ælgɒl/ *acronym* (*comput*) a high-level programming language used for solving general problems in science and mathematics.

algology /æl'gɒlədʒi/ *n* the study of algae.—**algologist** *n.*

Algonquian /æl'gɒŋkwiən/ or /-kiən/ *n* a group of eastern North American Indian languages; a member of a North American Indian people who speaks one of these languages. • *adj* of or pertaining to these peoples or their languages.

algor /'ælgɔr/ *n* the rigor or chill on the onset of fever.

algorism /'ælgərizəm/ *n* the arabic (decimal) numeration; arithmetic.—**algorismic** *adj.*

algorithm /'ælgəriðəm/ *n* (*math*) any method or procedure for computation.—**algorithmic** *adj.*—**algorithmically** *adv.*

alias /'eiliəs/ *adv* otherwise called. • *n* (*pl* **aliases**) an assumed name.

alibi /'æli,bai/ *n* (*pl* **alibis**) (*law*) the plea that a person charged with a crime was elsewhere when it was committed; (*inf*) any excuse.

alien /'eiliən/ *adj* foreign; strange; distasteful to, counter to. • *n* a person from another country, place, etc; a person of foreign birth who has not been naturalized; a being from outer space.

alienable /-əbəl/ *adj* (*law*) (*property*) that may be transferred.—**alienability** *n.*

alienage /'eiliənidʒ/ *n* the state or legal status of an alien.

alienate /'eiliəneit/ *vt* to render hostile or unfriendly; to make less affectionate or interested.

alienation /,eiliən'eiʃən/ *n* estrangement; transference; diversion to another purpose; mental derangement.

alienee /,eiliən'iː/ *n* (*law*) one to whom property is transferred.

alienism /'eiliənizəm/ *n* the study and treatment of mental alienation.—**alienist** *n.*

alienor /-ɔr/ or /-ɔr/ *n* (*law*) one who transfers property to another.

aliform /'eili,fɔrm/ *adj* wing-shaped.

alight¹ /ə'lait/ *vi* (**alighting, alighted** *or* **alit**) to come down, as from a bus; to land after flight.

alight² *adj* on fire; lively.

align /ə'lain/ *vt* to place in a straight line, to bring into agreement, etc. • *vi* to line up.—**alignment** *n.*

alignment /-mənt/ *n* the act of laying out or adjusting by a line; the ground plan of a railway or road.

alike /ə'laik/ *adj* like one another. • *adv* equally; similarly.

aliment /'æləmənt/ *n* food; the necessaries of life generally; an allowance for support by decree of court. • *vt* to make provision for the maintenance of; to make provision for the support of parents or children respectively.—**alimental** *adj.*

alimentary /,æli'məntəri/ *adj* pertaining to nourishment, food.

alimentary canal *n* the tube extending within the body from the mouth to the anus through which food passes and is absorbed.

alimentation /,ælimən'teiʃən/ *n* the act of giving nourishment; the function of the alimentary canal.

alimony /'æli,mɔːni/ *n* (*pl* **alimonies**) an allowance for support made by one spouse to the other, *esp* a man to his wife or former wife, pending or after a legal separation or divorce.

aliped /'æli,ped/ *adj* having wing-like limbs, as the bat.

aliphatic /,æli'fætik/ *adj* (*chem*) of fat.

aliquant /'æləkwənt/ or /-kwɒnt/ *adj* (*math*) being a part of a number that does not divide it without a remainder, as 8 is the aliquant part of 25.—*also n.*

aliquot /'æləkwɒt/ or /-kwɒt/ *adj* (*math*) being a part of a number

of quantity that will divide it without a remainder, as 8 is the aliquot part of 24.—*also n.*

alive /ə'laiv/ *adj* having life; active, alert; in existence, operation, etc.

alizarin /ə'lizərin/ *n* a red colouring matter found in madder but now produced from anthracene.

alkahest /'ælkə,hest/ *n* the supposed universal solvent of the alchemists.—*also* **alcahest**.

alkali /'ælkəlai/ *n* (*pl* **alkalis, alkalies**) (*chem*) any salt or mixture that neutralizes acids.—**alkaline** *adj.*

alkalify /'ælkəli,fai/ *vb* (**alkalifying, alkalified**) *vt* to form or convert into alkali. • *vi* to become an alkali.

alkalimeter /,ælkə'limətər/ *n* an instrument used to determine the relative strength of alkalis.

alkalimetry /-mətri/ *n* the process of determining the strength of an alkaline mixture or liquid.—**alkalimetric** *adj.*

alkaline /'ælkə,lain/ or /-,lain/ *adj* pertaining to, or having the properties of, an alkali.—**alkalinity** *n.*

alkalize /-,laiz/ *vt* to convert into an alkali or render alkaline.—**alkalizable** *adj.*

alkaloid /-,loid/ *n* a body or substance containing alkaline properties; (*pl*) nitrogenous compounds met with in plants in combination with organic acids. • *adj* resembling an alkali in its properties.

alkanet /'ælkə,net/ *n* a rich red dye; the plant the root of which yields it.

all /ɔːl/ *adj* the whole amount or number of; every one of. • *adv* wholly; supremely, completely; entirely. • *n* the whole number, quantity; everyone; everything.

alla breve /,ɒlə'brevi/ *adv* (*mus*) in quick time, with one breve to a measure.

Allah /'ælə/ or /'ɒlə/ *n* the Muslim name of God.

all along *adv* throughout.

all but *adv* almost.

all clear /'ɒl,kliːr/ *n* a signal indicating that a danger has passed or that it is safe to proceed.

allantoid /ə'læn,tɔːid/ *adj* of or pertaining to the allantois; (*bot*) sausage-shaped. • *n* the allantois.—**allantoidal** *adj.*

allantois /ə'læn,tɔːis/ *n* (*pl* **allantoides**) a membranous appendage of most vertebrate embryos.

allay /'ælei/ or /ə-/ *vt* to lighten, alleviate; to pacify or make calm.

allegation /,ælə'geiʃən/ *n* the act of alleging; assertion; declaration; that which is asserted or alleged; that which is offered as a plea, an excuse, or justification; the statement as yet unproved of a party to a suit.

allege /ə'ledʒ/ *vt* to assert or declare, *esp* without proof; to offer as an excuse.

allegedly /ə'ledʒədli/ *adv* asserted without proof.

allegiance /ə'liːdʒəns/ *n* the obligation of being loyal to one's country, etc; devotion, as to a cause.

allegorical /,ælə'gɒrikəl/ or /-'gɒr-/, **allegoric** *adj* pertaining to, consisting of, or in the nature of allegory; figurative.—**allegorically** *adv.*

allegorize /'æləgə,raiz/ or /,æləgə,raiz/ *vt* to put in the form of an allegory.—**allegorization** *n.*

allegory /'æləgɒri/ or /-,gɒri/ *n* (*pl* **allegories**) a fable, story, poem, etc in which the events depicted are used to convey a deeper, *usu* moral or spiritual, meaning.—**allegorist** *n.*

allegretto /,ælə'gretɔ/ *adv* (*mus*) moderately fast. • *n* (*pl* **allegrettos**) a piece of music played in this way.

allegro /ə'legrɔ/ *adv* (*mus*) fast. • *n* (*pl* **allegros**) a piece of music played in this way.

allele /æ'liːl/ *n* (*genetics*) either of a pair of contrasting characteristics one or the other of which is found unmixed in descendants of a cross between parental forms respectively possessing them.—*also* **allelomorph**.—**allelic** *adj.*—**allelism** *n.*

alleluia /,ælə'luːjə/ or /-,lei-/ *see* **hallelujah**.

allemande /,ælə'mænd/ or /-'mãnd/ *n* a German national dance in three-quarter time.

allergen /'ælərdʒən/ *n* a substance inducing an allergic reaction.

allergenic /-,dʒenik/ *adj* causing an allergic reaction.

allergy /'ælərdʒi/ *n* (*pl* **allergies**) an abnormal reaction of the body to substances (certain foods, pollen, etc) normally harmless; antipathy.—**allergic** *adj.*

and the Thesaurus

guide word

new part of speech

page number

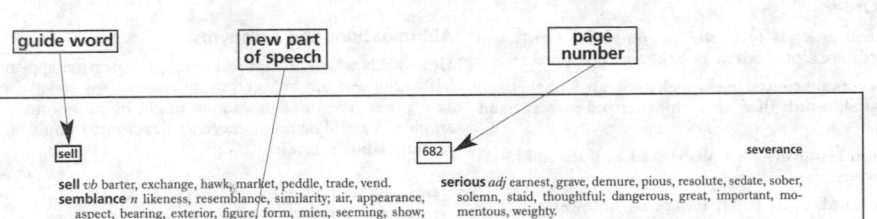

sell *vb* barter, exchange, hawk, market, peddle, trade, vend.

semblance *n* likeness, resemblance, similarity; air, appearance, aspect, bearing, exterior, figure, form, mien, seeming, show; image, representation, similitude.

seminal *adj* important, original, germinal, radical, rudimental, rudimentary, unformed.

seminary *n* academy, college, gymnasium, high school, institute, school, university.

send *vb* cast, drive, emit, fling, hurl, impel, lance, launch, project, propel, throw, toss; delegate, depute, dispatch; forward, transmit; bestow, confer, give, grant.

senile *adj* aged, doddering, superannuated; doting, imbecile.

senior *adj* elder, older; higher.

seniority *n* eldership, precedence, priority, superiority.

sensation *n* feeling, sense, perception; excitement, impression, thrill.

sensational *adj* exciting, melodramatic, startling, thrilling.

sense *vb* appraise, appreciate, estimate, notice, observe, perceive, suspect, understand. • *n* brains, intellect, intelligence, mind, reason, understanding; appreciation, apprehension, discernment, feeling, perception, recognition, tact; connotation, idea, implication, judgment, notion, opinion, sentiment, view; import, interpretation, meaning, purport, significance; sagacity, soundness, substance, wisdom.

senseless *adj* apathetic, inert, insensate, unfeeling; absurd, foolish, ill-judged, nonsensical, silly, unmeaning, unreasonable, unwise; doltish, foolish, simple, stupid, witless, weak-minded.

sensible *adj* apprehensible, perceptible; aware, cognizant, conscious, convinced, persuaded, satisfied; discreet, intelligent, judicious, rational, reasonable, sagacious, sage, sober, sound, wise; observant, understanding; impressionable, sensitive.

sensitive *adj* perceptive, sentient; affected, impressible, impressionable, responsive, susceptible; delicate, tender, touchy.

sensual *adj* animal, bodily, carnal, voluptuous; gross, lascivious, lewd, licentious, unchaste.

sentence *vb* condemn, doom, judge. • *n* decision, determination, judgment, opinion, verdict; doctrine, dogma, opinion, tenet; condemnation, conviction, judgment; period, proposition.

sententious *adj* compendious, compact, concise, didactic, laconic, pithy, pointed, succinct, terse.

sentiment *n* judgment, notion, opinion; maxim, saying; emotion, tenderness; disposition, feeling, thought.

sentimental *adj* impressible, impressionable, over-emotional, romantic, tender.

sentinel *n* guard, guardsman, patrol, picket, sentry, watchman.

separate *vb* detach, disconnect, disjoin, disunite, dissever, divide, divorce, part, sever, sunder; eliminate, remove, withdraw; cleave, open. • *adj* detached, disconnected, disjoined, disjointed, dissociated, disunited, divided, parted, severed; discrete, distinct, divorced, unconnected; alone, segregated, withdrawn.

separation *n* disjunction, disjuncture, dissociation; disconnection, disseverance, disseveration, disunion, division, divorce; analysis, decomposition.

sepulchral *adj* deep, dismal, funereal, gloomy, grave, hollow, lugubrious, melancholy, mournful, sad, sombre, woeful.

sepulchre *n* burial place, charnel house, grave, ossuary, sepulture, tomb.

sequel *n* close, conclusion, denouement, end, termination; consequence, event, issue, result, upshot.

sequence *n* following, graduation, progression, succession; arrangement, series, train.

sequestrated *adj* hidden, private, retired, secluded, unfrequented, withdrawn; seized.

seraphic *adj* angelic, celestial, heavenly, sublime; holy, pure, refined.

serene *adj* calm, collected, placid, peaceful, quiet, tranquil, sedate, undisturbed, unperturbed, unruffled; bright, calm, clear, fair, unclouded.

serenity *n* calm, calmness, collectedness, composure, coolness, imperturbability, peace, peacefulness, quiescence, sedateness, tranquility; brightness, calmness, clearness, fairness, peace, quietness, stillness.

serf *n* bondman, servant, slave, thrall, villein.

serfdom *n* bondage, enslavement, enthralment, servitude, slavery, subjection, thraldom.

series *n* chain, concatenation, course, line, order, progression, sequence, succession, train.

serious *adj* earnest, grave, demure, pious, resolute, sedate, sober, solemn, staid, thoughtful; dangerous, great, important, momentous, weighty.

sermon *n* discourse, exhortation, homily, lecture.

serpentine *adj* anfractuous, convoluted, crooked, meandering, sinuous, spiral, tortuous, twisted, undulating, winding.

servant *n* attendant, dependant, factotum, helper, henchman, retainer, servitor, subaltern, subordinate, underling; domestic, drudge, flunky, lackey, menial, scullion, slave.

serve *vb* aid, assist, attend, help, minister, oblige, succour; advance, benefit, forward, promote; content, satisfy, supply; handle, officiate, manage, manipulate, work.

service *vb* check, maintain, overhaul, repair. • *n* labour, ministration, work; attendance, business, duty, employ, employment, office; advantage, benefit, good, gain, profit; avail, purpose, use, utility; ceremony, function, observance, rite, worship.

serviceable *adj* advantageous, available, beneficial, convenient, functional, handy, helpful, operative, profitable, useful.

servile *adj* dependent, menial; abject, base, beggarly, cringing, fawning, grovelling, low, mean, obsequious, slavish, sneaking, sycophantic, truckling.

servility *n* bondage, dependence, slavery; abjection, abjectness, baseness, fawning, meanness, obsequiousness, slavishness, sycophancy.

servitor *n* attendant, dependant, footman, lackey, retainer, servant, squire, valet, waiter.

servitude *n* bondage, enslavement, enthralment, serfdom, service, slavery, thraldom.

set¹ *vb* lay, locate, mount, place, put, stand, station; appoint, determine, establish, fix, settle; risk, stake, wager; adapt, adjust, regulate; adorn, stud, variegate; arrange, dispose, pose, post; appoint, assign, predetermine, prescribe; estimate, prize, rate, value; embarrass, perplex, pose; contrive, produce; decline, sink; congeal, concern, consolidate, harden, solidify; flow, incline, run, tend; (*with about*) begin, commence; (*with apart*) appropriate, consecrate, dedicate, devote, reserve, set aside; (*with aside*) abrogate, annul, omit, reject; reserve, set apart; (*with before*) display, exhibit; (*with down*) chronicle, jot down, record, register, state, write down; (*with forth*) display, exhibit, explain, expound, manifest, promulgate, publish, put forward, represent, show; (*with forward*) advance, further, promote; (*with free*) acquit, clear, emancipate, liberate, release; (*with off*) adorn, decorate, embellish; define, portion off; (*with on*) actuate, encourage, impel, influence, incite, instigate, prompt, spur, urge; attack, assault, set upon; (*with out*) display, issue, publish, proclaim, prove, recommend, show; (*with right*) correct, put in order; (*with to rights*) adjust, regulate; (*with up*) elevate, erect, exalt, raise; establish, found, institute; (*with upon*) assail, assault, attack, fly at, rush upon. • *adj* appointed, established, formal, ordained, prescribed, regular, settled; determined, fixed, firm, obstinate, positive, stiff, unyielding; immovable, predetermined; located, placed, put. • *n* attitude, position, posture; scene, scenery, setting.

set² *n* assortment, collection, suit; class, circle, clique, cluster, company, coterie, division, gang, group, knot, party, school, sect.

setback *n* blow, hitch, hold-up, rebuff; defeat, disappointment, reverse.

set-off *n* adornment, decoration, embellishment, ornament; counterbalance, counterclaim, equivalent.

settle *vb* adjust, arrange, compose, regulate; account, balance, close up, conclude, discharge, liquidate, pay, pay up, reckon, satisfy, square; allay, calm, compose, pacify, quiet, repose, rest, still, tranquillize; confirm, decide, determine, make clear; establish, fix, set; fall, gravitate, sink, subside; abide, colonize, domicile, dwell, establish, inhabit, people, place, plant, reside; (*with on*) determine on, fix on, fix upon; establish. • *n* bench, seat, stool.

settled *adj* established, fixed, stable; decided, deep-rooted, steady, unchanging; adjusted, arranged; methodical, orderly, quiet; common, customary, everyday, ordinary, usual, wonted.

set-to *n* combat, conflict, contest, fight.

sever *vb* divide, part, rend, separate, sunder; detach, disconnect, disjoin, disunite.

several *adj* individual, single, particular; distinct, exclusive, independent, separate; different, divers, diverse, manifold, many, sundry, various.

severance *n* partition, separation.

superscript numeral identifies homographs

usage details

commas separate synonyms

semicolons separate the different senses of the headword

How to Use the Dictionary

Alphabetical Order

Strict alphabetical order is followed. All compound words and hyphenated words are alphabetized as if they are one word.

Headwords that contain contractions, such as St, are alphabetized as would the whole word; thus St is alphabetized just as Saint would be.

Abbreviations and acronyms are alphabetized as if the abbreviation is a whole word.

Capitalized headwords come before lower case headwords.

Numerals take precedence over letters.

Variations

Variant spellings appear in bold type and in brackets next to the headword.

Other terms, of a different part of speech, that are related to the headword are given at the end of an entry in bold preceded by a dash.

Inflected forms of verbs and plural forms of nouns appear in bold and in brackets following the headword.

e.g.:

eat /iːt/ *vt* (**eating, ate,** *pp* **eaten**) to take into the mouth, chew and swallow as food; to have a meal; to consume, to destroy bit by bit; (*also with* *into*) to corrode; (*inf*) to bother, cause anxiety to; (*with* **up**) to consume completely; (*inf*) to listen or absorb avidly; (*inf*) to preoccupy. • *vi* (*with* **out**) to eat away from home, *esp* in a restaurant. • *n* (*pl: inf*) food.—**eater** *n*.

Parts of Speech

Parts of speech are indicated in italic by the abbreviations shown on page 8, and the bold headword .

Other parts of speech after the main headword are indicated by a full point (.) and •.

e.g.:

bang /bæŋ/ *n* a hard blow; a sudden loud sound. • *vt* to hit or knock with a loud noise; (*door*) to slam. • *vi* to make a loud noise; to hit noisily or sharply; • *adv* with a bang, abruptly; successfully; (*inf*) precisely.

Senses and Definitions

Within entries synonyms are separated by commas (,). Different senses are separated by semicolons (;). Parts of speech are separated by full points (.).

Homographs

Words of different origins but with the same spelling are given separate, numbered entries.

e.g.:

bank[1] /bæŋk/ *n* a mound or pile; the sloping side of a river; elevated ground in a lake or the sea; a row or series of objects, as of dials, switches. • *vti* to form into a mound; to cover (a fire) with fuel so that it burns more slowly; (*aircraft*) to curve or tilt sideways.

bank[2] *n* an institution that offers various financial services, such as the safekeeping, lending and exchanging of money; the money held by the banker or dealer in a card game; any supply or store for the future, such as a *blood bank*. • *vti* (*cheques, cash, etc*) to deposit in a bank; to work as a banker.

Abbreviations and Acronyms

Headwords which are abbreviations or acronyms appear with the label *abbr* and are followed by an equals sign (=). Where doubt arises over how the abbreviation might be pronounced – for example if it could be pronounced as an acronym would, as a word – pronunciation is given.

e.g.:

HC *abbr* = Holy Communion; House of Commons.
HCF *abbr* = highest common factor.
HIV /ˈeɪtʃˈaɪˈviː/ *abbr* = human immunodeficiency virus, the virus that causes Aids.

Pronunciation

Pronunciation is given using the International Phonetic Alphabet (IPA) between oblique strokes (//).

Where pronunciation differs from foreign pronunciation of some foreign words this pronunciation is also given and labelled.

e.g.:

hors d'oeuvre /ˌɔːˈdɜːrv/, *Fr.* /ɑːrˈdœvr/ *n* (*pl* **hors d'oeuvre, hors d'oeuvres**) an appetizer served at the beginning of a meal.

Where variations occur, for example on the end syllable of a word, this is indicated by a hyphen followed by the variation.

e.g.:

horse /hɒrs/ *n* a four-legged, solid-hoofed herbivorous mammal with a flowing mane and a tail, domesticated for carrying loads or riders, etc; cavalry; a vaulting horse; a frame with legs to support something.
horseflesh /-fleʃ/ *n* horses; the flesh of a horse, *esp* for eating.
horsehair /-hɛr/ *n* hair from the mane or the tail of a horse, used for padding, etc.

Pronunciation is not given for compound word headwords if the words appear elsewhere in the dictionary.

Primary and secondary stress marks precede the relevant symbols, *see* Key to Phonetics section on page 7.

Register

Level of registers are indicated by the following labels: formal, informal, slang, derogatory, dialect, offensive. *See* Abbreviations.

Key to Phonetic Symbols

Vowels

1. i: as in **see** /si:/
2. i as in **cosy** /kʊ:zi/
3. ɪ as in **pit** /pɪt/
4. ɛ as in **ten** /tɛn/
5. æ as in **absence** /æbsəns/
6. ɑ as in **arm** /ɑrm/
7. ɒ as in **hot** /hɒt/
8. ɔ as in **abort** /ə'bɔrt/
9. o: as in **roam** /ro:m/
10. ʊ as in **put** /pʊt/
11. u: as in **root** /ru:t/
12. ə as in **ago** /ə'go:/
13. ɐ as in **cup** /kɐp/
14. eɪ as in **page** /peɪdʒ/
15. əɪ as in **light** /ləɪt/
16. aɪ as in **my** /maɪ/
17. aʊ as in **now** /naʊ/
18. ɐʊ as in **house** /hɐʊs/
19. ɔɪ as in **oil** /ɔɪl/

Consonants

1. p as in **pet** /pɛt/
2. b as in **black** /blæk/
3. t as in **teak** /ti:k/
4. d as in **den** /dɛn/
5. k as in **cat** /kæt/
6. g as in **got** /gɒt/
7. tʃ as in **chin** /tʃɪn/
8. dʒ as in **juice** /dʒu:s/
9. f as in **foil** /fɔɪl/
10. v as in **voice** /vɔɪs/
11. θ as in **thick** /θɪk/
12. ð as in **them** /ðɛm/
13. s as in **so** /so:/
14. z as in **zoo** /zu:/
15. ʃ as in **she** /ʃi:/
16. ʒ as in **vision** /'vɪʒən/
17. h as in **how** /haʊ/
18. m as in **man** /mæn/
19. n as in **no** /no:/
20. ŋ as in **ring** /rɪŋ/
21. l as in **lip** /lɪp/
22. r as in **red** /rɛd/
23. j as in **yes** /jɛs/
24. w as in **wet** /wɛt/

Foreign Sounds

1. y as in French *couture* /kʊ'tyr/. Pronounce /i:/ with the lips rounded as for English /u:/.
2. ø as in French *berceuse* /ˌbɛr'søz/. Pronounce /ø/ as the initial sound /e/ in /eɪ/ with the lips rounded as in English /u:/.
3. œ as in French *chef-d'oeuvre* /ʃe'dœvr/. Pronounce /eɪ/ with the lips rounded, like /o:/.
4. a as in French *cabochon* /kabɒʃo:/. Pronounce /a/ with the tongue between the positions of English /æ/ and /ɑ/.
5. ɒ as in French *agent provocateur* /a'ʒã:prɒvɒkaˌtœr/. It is pronounced with the tongue a little forward, with lips rounded as in /ɔ/.
6. x as in Gaelic *loch* /lɒx/. Pronounce /k/ without closing the air passage completely, so that the air comes out with friction.
7. ʀ as in French *rouge* /ʀu:ʒ/. It resembles the German *ach* but is produced further back in the throat.
8. ɾ as in Spanish *banderilla* /ˌbandɛ'ri:ljɑ/. Pronounce ɾ by trilling the tip of the tongue.

/:/ denotes a long vowel as in **peak** /pi:k/
/ ̃/ denotes a vowel is nasalized as in French **bon** /bɔ̃:/
/'/ denotes a primary stress preceding the relevant syllable as in **about** /ə'bɐʊt/
/ˌ/ denotes secondary stress preceding the relevant syllable as in **abattoir** /ˌæbə'twɑr/
(ə) The "ə" in parenthesis denotes optional pronunciation as is heard in some varieties of English.
/-/ Hyphens preceding and/or following parts of a repeated transcription indicate that only the transcribed part changes.

Abbreviations

abbr	abbreviation		*naut*	nautical
adj	adjective		*neut*	neuter
adv	adverb		*news*	news media
anat	anatomy		*nf*	noun feminine
approx	approximately		*npl*	noun plural
arch	archaic		*n sing*	noun singular
archit	architecture		NT	New Testament
astrol	astrology		*obs*	obsolete
astron	astronomy		*orig*	original, originally, origin
Austral	Australia, Australasia		OT	Old Testament
aux	auxiliary		*p*	participle
biol	biology		*pers*	person, personal
bot	botany		*philos*	philosophy
Brit	Britain, British		*photog*	photography
c	circa, about		*pl*	plural
cap	capital		*poet*	poetical
cent	century		*poss*	possessive
chem	chemical, chemistry		*pp*	past participle
compar	comparative		*prep*	preposition
comput	computing		*pres t*	present tense
conj	conjunction		*print*	printing
demons	demonstrative		*pron*	pronoun
derog	derogatory, derogatorily		*pr p*	present participle
dimin	diminutive		*psychol*	psychology
econ	economics		*pt*	past tense
eg	*exempli gratis*, for example		RC	Roman Catholic
elect	electricity		*reflex*	reflexive
esp	especially		*Scot*	Scotland
fig	figuratively		*sing*	singular
geog	geography		*sl*	slang
geol	geology		*superl*	superlative
geom	geometry		*theat*	theatre
gram	grammar		*TV*	television
her	heraldry		*TM*	trademark
hist	history		UK	United Kingdom
ie	*id est*, that is		US	United States
imper	imperative		*USA*	United States of America
incl	including		*usu*	usually
inf	informal		*var*	variant
interj	interjection		*vb*	verb
math	mathematics		*vb aux*	auxiliary verb
mech	mechanics		*vi*	intransitive verb
med	medicine		*vt*	transitive verb
mil	military		*vti*	transitive or intransitive verb
mus	music		*vulg*	vulgar, vulgarly
myth	mythology		*zool*	zoology
n	noun			

DICTIONARY

A

A /eɪ/ *abbr* = ampere(s).

Å *abbr* = ångström(s).

a /ə/ or /eɪ/ *adj* the indefinite article; one; any; per.

A[1] *adj* (*inf*) in perfect condition; physically fit; excellent.

AA *abbr* = Alcoholics Anonymous; anti-aircraft; Automobile Association.

AAA *abbr* = Automobile Association of America; Amateur Athletics Association.

aardvark /ˈɑrdvɑrk/ *n* a nocturnal African mammal with a long snout that feeds on termites.

aardwolf /ˈɑrdwulf/ *n* (*pl* **aardwolves** /ˈɑːrdˌwulvz/) the earth wolf, a South African carnivore like a hyena.

ab- /əb/ or /æb/ *prefix* away, from, apart.

ab /æb/ *prep* from, as in *ab initio*.

abaca /ˈæbəkə/ *n* Manila hemp.

aback /əˈbæk/ *adv* **taken aback** startled.

abacus /ˈæbəkəs/ *n* (*pl* **abaci, abacuses**) a frame with sliding beads for doing arithmetic.

Abaddon /əˈbædən/ *n* a destroying angel, the devil; hell.

abaft /əˈbæft/ *adv, prep* (*naut*) behind.

abalone /ˈæbəˈloːni/ *n* an edible mollusc having an ear-shaped shell lined with mother-of-pearl.

abandon /əˈbændən/ *vt* to leave behind; to desert; to yield completely to an emotion or urge. • *n* freedom from inhibitions.—**abandonment** *n*.

abandoned /əˈbændənd/ *adj* (*behaviour*) showing abandon, unrestrained.—**abandonedly** *adv*.

abase /əˈbeɪs/ *vt* to degrade, humiliate.—**abasement** /əˈbeɪsmənt/ *n*.

abash /əˈbæʃ/ *vt* to cause a feeling of shame, embarrassment or confusion.—**abashment** /-mənt/ *n*.

abashed /əˈbæʃt/ *adj* ashamed, embarrassed.

abate /əˈbeɪt/ *vti* to make or become less; (*law*) to end.—**abatement** *n*.

abatis /ˈæbətɪs/ *n* (*pl* **abatis, abatises** /ˈæbətiː/) a defence work of fallen trees with the branches towards the enemy.

abattoir /ˈæbəˌtwɑr/ *n* a slaughterhouse.

abbacy /ˈæbəsi/ *n* (*pl* **abbacies** /ˈæbəsiːs/) the office or rights of an abbot.

abbatial /əˈbeɪʃəl/ *adj* of an abbey or abbot.

abbé /ˈæˈbeɪ/ *n* a French ecclesiastic.

abbess /ˈæbəs/ *n* the woman who heads a convent of nuns.

abbey /ˈæbi/ *n* a building occupied by monks or nuns; a church built as part of such a building; the community of monks or nuns.

abbot /ˈæbət/ *n* the head of an abbey of monks.

abbreviate /əˈbriːviˌeɪt/ *vt* to make shorter, *esp* to shorten (a word) by omitting letters.

abbreviation /əˌbriːviˈeɪʃən/ *n* the process of abbreviating; a shortened form of a word.

ABC[1] /ˌeɪbiːˈsiː/ *n* the alphabet; the basic facts of a subject.

ABC[2] *abbr* = American Broadcasting Corporation; Australian Broadcasting Corporation.

abdicate /ˈæbdɪˌkeɪt/ *vti* to renounce an official position or responsibility, etc.—**abdication** *n*.

abdomen /ˈæbdəmən/ *n* the region of the body below the chest containing the digestive organs; the belly; (*insects, etc*) the section of the body behind the thorax.—**abdominal** /æbˌdɒmənl/ *adj*.—**abdominally** *adv*.

abducent /æbˈduːsənt/ or /əb-/, /-ˈdjuːs/ *adj* (*anat*) (*limb, etc*) drawn from its natural position.

abduct /əbˈdʌkt/ *vt* to carry off (a person) by force; (*anat*) to draw (a limb, etc) from its natural position.—**abduction** *n*.—**abductor** *n*.

abeam /əˈbiːm/ *adv* (*naut*) at right angles to a ship's length, abreast.

abecedarian /ˌeɪbiːsiːˈdɛrɪən/ *adj* of the ABC, elementary; arranged alphabetically. • *n* one learning the ABC, a beginner, a learner.

abed /əˈbed/ *adv* in bed.

abelmosk /ˈeɪblmɒsk/ *n* an Asian herb of the mallow family yielding musk.

aberrant /əˈbɛrənt/ *adj* deviating from that regarded as normal or right.—**aberrance, aberrancy** /æˈbɛrənsi/ *n*.

aberration /ˌæbəˈreɪʃən/ *n* a deviation from the normal; a mental or moral lapse.

abet /əˈbet/ *vt* (**abetting, abetted**) to encourage or assist, *esp* to do wrong.—**abetment** *n*.—**abetter,** (*esp law*) **abettor** *n*.

abeyance /əˈbeɪəns/ *n* (*usu preceded by* **in**) (*law, etc*) suspended temporarily.

abhor /əbˈhɔr/ *vt* (**abhorring, abhorred**) to detest, despise.

abhorrence /əbˈhɒrəns/ *n* detestation.

abhorrent /əbˈhɒrənt/ *adj* detestable.

abide /əˈbaɪd/ *vt* (**abiding, abode** *or* **abided**) to endure; to put up with.

abiding /əˈbaɪdɪŋ/ *adj* permanent.—**abidingly** *adv*.

abigail /ˈæbɪɡeɪl/ *n* a lady's maid.

ability /əˈbɪlɪti/ *n* (*pl* **abilities**) the state of being able being able; power to do; talent; skill.

ab initio /ˌæbɪˈnɪʃɪoː/ (*Latin*) from the beginning.

abiogenesis /ˌeɪbaɪoːˈdʒɛnəsɪs/ *n* spontaneous generation.—**abiogenetic** *adj*.

abject /ˈæbdʒekt/ *adj* wretched; dejected.—**abjection** *n*.—**abjectly** *adv*.

abjure /əbˈdʒʊr/ *vt* to renounce.—**abjuration** *n*.—**abjurer** *n*

ablactation /ˌæblækˈteɪʃən/ *n* the act of weaning a child from the breast.

ablate /æbˈleɪt/ (**ablating, ablated**) *vb* to remove surgically; (*astrophysics*) to melt or vaporize when entering the earth's atmosphere; (*geol*) to erode, to waste or wear away.—**ablation** *n*.

ablative /ˈæblətɪv/ *adj* (*gram*) expressing source, instrumentality, etc; (*astrophysics*) ablating. • *n* one of the cases of Latin nouns, expressing chiefly separation and instrumentality and sometimes place.

ablative absolute *n* a particular construction in Latin of a noun and a participle in the ablative case, agreeing in gender and number, and forming a clause by themselves, but unconnected gramatically with the rest of the sentence.

ablaut /ˈæblɐʊt/ *n* (*linguistics*) a vowel permutation, the change of a root vowel in the derivation of a word, as *do, did* or *sing, sang, sung, song*.

ablaze /əˈbleɪz/ *adj* burning, on fire.

-able /əbəl/ *adj suffix* capable of, as in suitable.

able /ˈeɪbəl/ *adj* having the competence or means (to do); talented; skilled.—**ably** *adv*.

able-bodied /ˈeɪbəlˌbɒdiːd/ *adj* fit, strong.

able-bodied seaman *n* a trained seaman in the (merchant) navy.—*also* able seaman.

abloom /əˈbluːm/ *adv* in bloom, blooming.

ablution /əˈbluːʃən/ *n* (*usu pl*) a washing or cleansing of the body by water; the ritual cleansing of vessels or hands.—**ablutionary** *adj*.

ably /ˈeɪbli/ *adv* in an able manner.

ABM /ˌeɪbiːˈem/ *abbr* = antiballistic missile.

abnegate /ˈæbnəˌɡeɪt/ *vt* to deny oneself (a right, etc); to renounce.—**abnegation** *n*.

abnormal /æbˈnɔrml/ *adj* unusual, not average or typical; irregular.—**abnormality** *n*.—**abnormally** *adv*.

abnormality /ˌæbnɔrˈmælɪti/ *n* (*pl* **abnormalities**) deformity; irregularity; difference or departure from a regular type or rule.

aboard /əˈbɔrd/ *adv* on or in an aircraft, ship, train, etc.—*also prep*.

abode[1] /əˈboːd/ *n* a home, residence.

abode[2] *see* abide.

abolish /əˈbɒlɪʃ/ *vt* to bring to an end, do away with.—**abolisher** *n*.—**abolishment** *n*.

abolition /ˌæbəˈlɪʃən/ *n* the act of abolishing; (*with cap*) in UK, the ending of the slave trade (1807) or slavery (1833), in US, the emancipation of the slaves (1863).

abolitionist /ˌæbəˈlɪʃənɪst/ *n* one who is in favour of the repeal or abolition of some existing law or custom; (*often with cap*) one in favour of abolition.

abomasum /ˌæbəˈmeɪsəm/ *n* (*pl* **abomasa**) the fourth stomach of a ruminant animal.—**abomasal** *adj*.

A-bomb /ˈeɪbɒm/ *n* atomic bomb.

abominable /əˈbɒmɪnəbl/ *adj* despicable, detestable; (*inf*) very unpleasant.—**abominably** *adv*.

abominable snowman *n* a huge creature of legend resembling a man or an animal, said to be found in the Himalayas.—*also* **yeti**.

abominate /əˈbɒmɪˌneɪt/ *vt* to abhor; to regard with feelings of disgust or hatred.—**abominator** *n*.

abomination /əˌbɒmɪˈneɪʃən/ *n* detestation; a loathsome person or thing.

aboriginal /ˌæbəˈrɪdʒənəl/ *adj* existing in a place from the earliest times; of aborigines. • *n* the species of animals or plants presumed to have originated within a given area.

aborigine /ˌæbəˈrɪdʒɪnɪ/ *n* any of the first known inhabitants of a region; (*with cap*) one of the original inhabitants of Australia before the arrival of European settlers.

abort /əˈbɔːt/ *vti* to undergo or cause an abortion; to terminate or cause to terminate prematurely. • *n* the premature termination of a rocket flight, etc.

abortion /əˈbɔːʃən/ *n* the premature expulsion of a foetus, *esp* if induced on purpose.

abortionist /əˈbɔːʃənɪst/ *n* a person who performs abortions, *esp* illegally.

abortive /əˈbɔːtɪv/ *adj* failing in intended purpose; fruitless; causing abortion.—**abortively** *adv*.

aboulia /əˈbuːlɪə/ or /-ˈbjuː-/ *see* **abulia**.

abound /əˈbaʊnd/ *vi* to be in abundance; to have in great quantities.

about /əˈbaʊt/ *prep* on all sides of; near to; with; on the point of; concerning. • *adv* all around; near; to face the opposite direction.

about-turn, about-face *n* a complete reversal in direction or opinion, etc. • *vi* to make an about-turn.

above /əˈbʌv/ *prep* over, on top of; better or more than; beyond the reach of; too complex to understand. • *adv* in or to a higher place; in addition; (*text*) mentioned earlier.

aboveboard /əˈbʌvˌbɔːd/ *adj, adv* without trickery; in open sight.

abracadabra /ˌæbrəkəˈdæbrə/ *n* a cabbalistic word used as a charm, a spell; gibberish.

abradant /æˈbreɪdənt/ *adj* having the property of rubbing away. • *n* a substance employed for abrading or scouring.

abrade /əˈbreɪd/ *vt* to wear or rub away; to remove as by friction or abrasion; to corrode, as by acids.—**abrader** *n*.

abranchiate /eɪˈbræŋkiːɪt/ or /-kieɪt/, **abranchial** *adj* (*zool*) devoid of gills. • *n* an animal without gills.

abrasion /əˈbreɪʒən/ *n* the act or process of rubbing away by friction, etc; a scraped area, *esp* on the body.

abrasive /əˈbreɪsɪv/ *adj* causing abrasion; harsh, irritating. • *n* a substance or tool used for grinding or polishing, etc.—**abrasively** *adv*.

abreact /ˌæbrɪˈækt/ *vt* (*psychoanal*) to remove (a complex) by acting it out or talking it out.—**abreaction** *n*.—**abreactive** *adj*.

abreast /əˈbrɛst/ *adv* side by side and facing the same way; informed (of); aware.

abridge /əˈbrɪdʒ/ *vt* to shorten by using fewer words but keeping the substance.

abridgment, abridgement /əˈbrɪdʒmənt/ *n* the state of being contracted or curtailed; a shortened version of a text; an epitome.

abroach /əˈbroːtʃ/ *adj, adv* letting out; broached, pierced so as to let the liquor run.

abroad /əˈbrɔːd/ *adv* in or to a foreign country; over a wide area; out in the open; in circulation, current.

abrogate /ˈæbrəˌgeɪt/ *vt* to repeal, cancel.—**abrogator** *n*.

abrogation /ˌæbrəˈgeɪʃən/ *n* the act of abrogating; the repeal or annulling of a law.

abrupt /əˈbrʌpt/ *adj* sudden; unexpected; curt.—**abruptly** *adv*.—**abruptness** *n*.

abruption /æbˈrʌpʃən/ or /əb-/ *n* a separation with violence; a sudden or abrupt termination.

abscess /ˈæbsɛs/ *n* an inflamed area of the body containing pus.

abscissa /əbˈsɪsə/ *n* (*pl* **abscissas, abscissae**) (*geom*) one of the two coordinates fixing the position of a point.

abscission /əbˈsɪʒən/ *n* the act of severance; (*bot*) the shedding of parts; the breaking off in a sentence, leaving the rest to be implied.

abscond /əbˈskɒnd/ *vi* to hide, run away, *esp* to avoid punishment for a wrongdoing.

abseil /ˈæbseɪl/ or /-zaɪl/ *vi* to descend a rock face by means of a double rope attached to a higher point.—**abseiling** *n*.

absence /ˈæbsəns/ *n* the state of not being present; the time of this; a lack; inattention.

absent /ˈæbsənt/ *adj* not present; not existing; inattentive.—**absently** *adv*.

absent /æbˈsɛnt/ *vt* to keep (oneself) away.

absentee /ˌæbsənˈtiː/ *n* a person who is absent, as from work or school.

absenteeism /ˌæbsənˈtiːɪzəm/ *n* persistent absence from work, school, etc.

absently /ˈæbsəntli/ *adv* in an abstracted manner.

absent-minded /ˌæbsəntˈmaɪndəd/ *adj* inattentive; forgetful.

absinthe, absinth /ˈæbsɪnθ/ *n* a potent, green, brandy-based liqueur flavoured with wormwood.

absit omen /ˌæbsɪtˈoːmɛn/ *interj* (*Latin*) may the foreboding caused by some unlucky word or event not come to pass.

absolute /ˈæbsəˌluːt/ or /ˌæbsəˈluːt/ *adj* unrestricted, unconditional; complete; positive; perfect, pure; not relative; (*monarch, ruler, etc*) authoritarian, despotic; (*inf*) utter, out-and-out.

absolutely /ˈæbsəˌluːtli/ or /ˌæbsəˈluːtli/ *adv* completely; unconditionally; (*inf*) I completely agree, certainly.

absolution /ˌæbsəˈluːʃən/ *n* forgiveness; remission of sin or its penalty.

absolutism /ˈæbsəluːˌtɪzəm/ *n* the state of being absolute; the principle or system of absolute government.—**absolutist** *n, adj*.

absolve /əbˈzɒlv/ or /-ˈsɒlv/ *vt* to clear from guilt or blame; to give religious absolution to; to free from a duty, obligation, etc.

absolver /əbˈzɒlvər/ or /-ˈsɒl-/ *n* one who absolves, or pronounces absolution.

absorb /əbˈzɔːb/ *vt* to take in; to soak up; to incorporate; to pay for (costs, etc); to take in (a shock) without recoil; to occupy one's attention or interest completely.—**absorber** *n*.—**absorptive** *adj*.

absorbable /əbˈzɔːbeɪbəl/ *adj* capable of being absorbed.—**absorbability** *n*.

absorbefacient /əbˈzɔːbɪˌfeɪʃənt/ or /-sənt/ *adj* inducing or causing absorption. • *n* something that causes absorption.

absorbent /əbˈzɔːbənt/ *adj* capable of absorbing moisture, etc.—**absorbency** *n*.

absorbent cotton *n* raw cotton that has been bleached and sterilized for use as a dressing, etc.—*also* **cotton wool**.

absorbing /əbˈzɔːbɪŋ/ *adj* engrossing.—**absorbingly** *adv*.

absorption /əbˈzɔːpʃən/ *n* the process or act of absorbing; the state of being absorbed; entire preoccupation of the mind.—**absorptive** *adj*.

absorption lines *npl* dark lines in the spectrum produced by the absorption of cool vapours through which the light has passed.

absorptivity /əbˈzɔːpˌtɪvɪti/ *n* the power of absorption; (*physics*) the rate of absorption of radiation by a material.

abstain /əbˈsteɪn/ *vi* to keep oneself from some indulgence, *esp* from drinking alcohol; to refrain from using one's vote.

abstainer /-ər/ *n* one who abstains, especially from intoxicants.

abstemious /æbˈstiːmiəs/ *adj* sparing in consuming food or alcohol.—**abstemiously** *adv*.—**abstemiousness** *n*.

abstention /əbˈstɛnʃən/ *n* the act of holding off or abstaining; the withholding of a vote.—**abstentious** *adj*.—**abstentionist** *n*.

abstergent /æbˈstɜːdʒənt/ *adj* possessing cleansing or purging properties. • *n* that which cleanses or purges; a detergent.

abstinence /ˈæbstɪnəns/ *n* an abstaining or refraining, *esp* from food or alcohol.

abstinent /ˈæbstɪnənt/ *adj* refraining from over-indulgence, *esp* with regard to food and drink. • *n* an abstainer.—**abstinently** *adv*.

abstract /ˈæbstrækt/ *adj* having no material existence; theoretical; (*art*) non-representational. • *n* (*writing, speech*) a summary or condensed version. • *vt* to remove or extract; to separate; to summarize.

abstract noun /-naʊn/ *n* the name of a state or quality considered apart from the object to which it belongs.

abstracted /əbˈstræktəd/ *adj* not paying attention.—**abstractedly** *adv*.—**abstractedness** *n*.

abstraction /əbˈstrækʃən/ *n* preoccupation, inattention; an abstract concept.—**abstractive** *adj*.

abstractionism /əbˈstrækʃəˌnɪzəm/ *n* the theory and art of the abstract, *esp* non-representational painting.—**abstractionist** *adj, n*.

abstruse /əbˈstruːs/ *adj* obscure; hidden; difficult to comprehend; profound.—**abstrusely** *adv*.—**abstruseness** *n*.

absurd /əbˈsərd/ or /-ˈzərd/ *adj* against reason or common sense; ridiculous.—**absurdly** *adv*.

absurdity /əbˈsərdɪtɪ/ or /-ˈzərd-/ *n* (*pl* **absurdities**) the state of being absurd; that which is absurd.

abulia *n* /əˈbuːlɪə/ *n* (*psychol*) loss of willpower.—*also* **aboulia**.—**abulic** *adj*.

abundance /əˈbʌndəns/ *n* a plentiful supply; a considerable amount.

abundant /əˈbʌndənt/ *adj* plentiful; rich (in).—**abundantly** *adv*.

abuse /əˈbjuːz/ *vt* to make wrong use of; to mistreat; to insult, attack verbally. • *n* misuse; mistreatment; insulting language; immoderate or illegal use of drugs or other stimulants.—**abuser** *n*.

abusive /əˈbjuːsɪv/ *adj* insulting.—**abusively** *adv*.—**abusiveness** *n*.

abut /əˈbʌt/ *vi* (**abutting, abutted**) to adjoin, border or lean (on, against).

abutment /-mənt/, **abuttal** /-əl/ *n* that which borders upon something else; the solid structure that supports the extremity of a bridge or arch.

abutter /əˈbʌtər/ *n* (*law*) the owner of an adjoining property.

abuzz /əˈbʌz/ *adv* filled with buzzing sounds; active, alive.

abysm /əˈbɪzm/ *n* (*arch*) an abyss, a gulf.

abysmal /əˈbɪzməl/ *adj* extremely bad, deplorable.—**abysmally** *adv*.

abyss /əˈbɪs/ *n* a bottomless depth; anything too deep to measure; hell.

abyssal /əˈbɪsəl/ *adj* pertaining to oceanic depths.

AC, ac *abbr* = alternating current.

Ac (*chem symbol*) actinium.

a/c *abbr* = account; account current.

ac- /ək/ *prefix* the form of *ad-* before *c, k, g*.

acacia /əˈkeɪʃə/ *n* a genus of shrubby or arboreous leguminous plants of warmer regions with white or yellow flowers, several species of which yield gum.

academic /ˌækəˈdemɪk/ *adj* pertaining to a school, college or university; scholarly; purely theoretical in nature. • *n* a member of a college or university; a scholarly person.

academically /ˈækədemɪkəlɪ/ *adv* theoretically, unpractically.

academician /ˌækədəˈmɪʃən/ or /əˌkædəˈmɪʃən/ *n* a member of an Academy.

academy /əˈkædəmɪ/ *n* (*pl* **academies**) a school for specialized training; (*Scot*) a secondary school; (*with cap*) a society of scholars, writers, scientists, etc.

Acadian /əˈkeɪdɪən/ *n* one of the settlers in the former French colony of Acadia in Canada, or a descendant in the Maritime Provinces of Canada, southeast Quebec, or eastern Maine. • *adj* of Acadia, a region of Canada, Nova-Scotian.

acanthine /əˈkænθɪn/ or /-ˌθaɪn/, /ˌθiːn/ *adj* pertaining to or resembling the plant acanthus. • *n* ornamentation in the shape of the acanthus leaf.

acanthus /əˈkænθəs/ *n* (*pl* **acanthuses, acanthi**) a genus of herbaceous plants with sharp-toothed leaves; (*archit*) ornamentation adopted in the capitals of the Corinthian and Composite orders, and resembling the foliage of the acanthus.

a cappella /ˌpkəˈpɛlə/ or /ˌækə-/ *adv* (*mus*) after the style of church or chapel music, without accompaniment.

acarid /ˈækərɪd/ *n* a tick or mite of the *Acarina* order of insects, etc, in which the divisions of head, thorax and abdomen are not apparent.—*also adj*.

acarpellous, acarpelous /eɪˈkɑrpələs/ *adj* (*bot*) without carpels.

acarpous /eɪˈkɑrpəs/ *adj* (*bot*) not producing fruit; sterile or barren.

acatalectic /eɪˌkætəlɛkˈtɪk/ *adj* (*verse*) with a complete number of syllables, not catalectic. —*also n*.

acaudal /eɪˈkɔdəl/, **acaudate** /eɪˈkɔˌdeɪt/ *adj* (*zool*) without a tail.

acaulescent /eɪˌkɔˈlɛsənt/ *adj* (*bot*) stemless or with a very short stem.—**acaulescence** *n*.

acc. *abbr* = according; account; accusative.

Acadian /əˈkeɪdɪən/ *see* Akkadian.

accede /ækˈsiːd/ *vi* to take office; to agree or assent to (a suggestion).

accelerando /əkˌseləˈrændoː/ or /əˌtʃɛl-/ *adv, adj* (*mus*) with gradual increase of speed. • *n* (*pl* **accelerandos**) a piece of music played in this way.

accelerate /əkˈseləˌreɪt/ *vti* to move faster; to happen or cause to happen more quickly; to increase the velocity of (a vehicle, etc).—**accelerative, acceleratory** *adj*.

acceleration /əkˌseləˈreɪʃən/ *n* the act of accelerating or condition of being accelerated; the rate of increase in speed or change in velocity; the power of accelerating.

accelerator /əkˈseləˌreɪtər/ *n* a device for increasing speed; a throttle; (*physics*) an apparatus that imparts high velocities to elementary particles.

accent /ˈæksent/ *n* emphasis on a syllable or word; a mark used to indicate this; any way of speaking characteristic of a region, class, or an individual; the emphasis placed on something; rhythmic stress in music or verse. • *vt* to express the accent, or denote the vocal division of a word by stress or modulation of the voice; to pronounce; to mark or accent a word in writing by use of a sign; to dwell upon or emphasize, as a passage of music.

accentuate /ækˈsentʃʊˌeɪt/ *vt* to emphasize.

accentuation /ækˌsentʃʊˈeɪʃən/ *n* the act of accentuating by stress or accent; speaking or writing with emphasis or distinction.

accept /əkˈsept/ *vt* to receive, *esp* willingly; to approve; to agree to; to believe in; to agree to pay.

acceptable /əkˈseptəbəl/ or *adj* satisfactory; welcome; tolerable.—**acceptability** *n*.—**acceptably** *adv*.

acceptance /əkˈseptəns/ *n* the act of accepting; the act of being accepted or received with approbation; agreement; the subscription to a bill of exchange; the bill accepted or the sum contained in it.

acceptation /ˌæksepˈteɪʃən/ *n* the act of accepting or state of being accepted or acceptable; the meaning or sense of a word or statement in which it is to be understood.

accepter, acceptor /əkˈseptər/ *n* one who accepts; the person who accepts a bill of exchange.

access /ˈækses/ *n* approach, or means of approach; the right to enter, use, etc. • *vt* (*comput*) to retrieve (information) from a storage device; to gain access to.

accessible /əkˈsesəbəl/ *adj* able to be reached; open (to).—**accessibility** *n*.—**accessibly** *adv*.

accession /əkˈseʃən/ *n* the act of reaching or assuming a rank or position.—**accessional** *adj*.

accessory /əkˈsesərɪ/ *adj* additional; extra. • *n* (*pl* **accessories**) a supplementary part or item, *esp* of clothing; a person who aids another in a crime.—**accessorial** *adj*.

acciaccatura /əˈtʃækəˌtʊrə/ *n* (*pl* **acciaccaturas, acciaccature**) a half-note or grace note below the principal note, struck at the same time as the principal note and immediately released while the latter is held.

accidence /ˈæksɪdəns/ *n* (*linguistics*) the part of grammar that deals with the inflections of words, which are accidents, not essentials; a book containing the rudiments of grammar; the rudiments themselves.

accident /ˈæksɪdənt/ *n* an unexpected event; a mishap or misfortune, *esp* one resulting in death or injury; chance.

accidental /ˌæksɪˈdentəl/ *adj* occurring or done by accident; nonessential; (*mus*) a sign prefixed to a note indicating a departure from the key signature.—**accidentally** *adv*.

accidie /ˈæksɪˌdɪ/ *n* sloth, torpor, apathy.

accipiter /əkˈsɪpɪtər/ *n* a generic name for birds of prey, as the common hawk.

accipitrine /-aɪn/ *adj* hawk-like, rapacious.

acclaim /əˈkleɪm/ *vt* to praise publicly (the merits of a person or thing); to welcome enthusiastically. • *vi* to shout approval. • *n* a shout of welcome or approval.

acclamation /ˌækləˈmeɪʃən/ *n* a shout of applause or other demonstration of hearty approval, loud united assent; an outburst of joy or praise; the adoption of a resolution *viva voce*; a mode of papal election.—**acclamatory** *adj*.

acclimatize /əˈklaɪməˌtaɪz/ *vt* to adapt to a new climate or environment. • *vi* to become acclimatized.—**acclimatization** *n*.

acclivity /əˈklɪvɪtɪ/ *n* (*pl* **acclivities**) an ascent or upward slope of the earth; the talus of a rampart.—**acclivitous** *adj*.

accolade /ˈækəˌleɪd/ *n* praise; approval; an award; a ceremonial touch on the shoulder with a sword to confer knighthood.

accommodate /əˈkɒməˌdeɪt/ *vt* to provide lodging for; to oblige; supply; to adapt, harmonize.

accommodating /-ɪŋ/ *adj* obliging, willing to help.—**accommodatingly** *adv*.

accommodation /əˌkɒməˈdeɪʃən/ *n* lodgings; the process of adapting; willingness to help.

accommodation bill *n* a bill or note endorsed by one or more parties to enable the drawer to raise money upon it.

accommodation ladder *n* a ladder or stairway suspended at the gangway of a ship.

accommodative /ə'kɒmə,deɪtɪv/ *adj* disposed or tending to accommodate.

accompaniment /ə'kʌmpənɪmənt/ *n* an instrumental part supporting a solo instrument, a voice, or a choir; something that accompanies.

accompanist, accompanyist /ə'kʌmpənɪst/ *n* one who plays a musical accompaniment.

accompany /ə'kʌmpəni/ *vt* (**accompanying, accompanied**) (*person*) to go with; (*something*) to supplement.

accomplice /ə'kɒmplɪs/ *n* a partner, *esp* in committing a crime.

accomplish /ə'kɒmplɪʃ/ *vt* to succeed in carrying out; to fulfil.

accomplished /-plɪʃd/ *adj* done; completed; skilled, expert; polished.

accomplishment /-plɪʃmənt/ *n* a skill or talent; the act of accomplishing; something accomplished.

accord /ə'kɔrd/ *vi* to agree; to harmonize (with). • *vt* to grant. • *n* consent; harmony.

accordance /ə'kɔrdəns/ *n* agreement; conformity.

accordant /ə'kɔrdənt/ *adj* corresponding; of the same mind.

according /ə'kɔrdɪŋ/ *prep* as stated by or in; (*with* **to**) in conformity with; (*with* **as**) depending on whether. • *adj* agreeing, harmonious.

accordingly /-li/ *adv* consequently; therefore; suitably.

accordion /ə'kɔrdiən/ *n* a portable keyboard instrument with manually operated folding bellows that force air through metal reeds.—**accordionist** *n*.

accost /ə'kɒst/ *vt* to approach and speak to, often to accuse of crime or to solicit sexually.

account /ə'kaʊnt/ *n* a description; an explanatory statement; a business record or statement; a credit arrangement with a bank, department store, etc; importance, consequence. • *vt* to think of as; consider. • *vi* to give a financial reckoning (to); (*with* **for**) to give reasons (for); (*with* **for**) to kill, dispose of.

accountable /ə'kaʊntəbəl/ *adj* liable; responsible; explainable.—**accountability** *n*.—**accountably** *adv*.

accountancy /ə'kaʊntənsi/ *n* the profession or practice of an accountant.

accountant /ə'kaʊntənt/ *n* one whose profession is auditing business accounts.

account book *n* a book for the entering of accounts, or in which particulars of sales, purchases, etc, are kept.

accounting /ə'kaʊntɪŋ/ *n* the maintaining or auditing of detailed business accounts; accountancy.

accoutre, accouter /ə'kuːtər/ *vt* to dress; to equip; to array in military dress; to furnish with accoutrements.—**accoutrement, accouterment** *n*.

accoutrements, accouterments /ə'kuːtərmənts/ or /-'kuːtrə-/ *npl* equipage; dress; military equipment.

accredit /ə'krɛdɪt/ *vt* to give credit or authority to; to have confidence in; to authorize; to stamp with authority; to believe and accept as true.—**accreditation** /-teɪʃən/ *n*.

accredited /-əd/ *adj* authorized officially; accepted as valid; certified as being of a prescribed quality.

accrescent /ə'krɛsənt/ *adj* (*bot*) increasing; growing.

accrete /ə'kriːt/ *vi* to adhere, to grow together; to be added. • *vt* to cause to grow or unite. • *adj* (*bot*) grown into one.

accretion /ə'kriːʃən/ *n* an increase by natural growth; the addition of external parts; the growing together of parts or members naturally separate.—**accretive, accretionary** *adj*.

accrue /ə'kruː/ *vi* (**accruing, accrued**) to come as a natural increase or addition; (*money, etc*) to accumulate or be added periodically.—**accrual, accrument** *n*.

accumbent /ə'kʌmbənt/ *adj* (*bot*) reclining or recumbent; (*hist*) of the Roman style of reclining on a couch at meals.—**accumbency** *n*.

accumulate /ə'kjuːmjʊ,leɪt/ *vti* to collect together in increasing quantities, to amass.

accumulation /ə,kjuːmʊ'leɪʃən/ *n* the act of accumulating or amassing; the addition of interest to principal; the mass accumulated.

accumulative /ə'kjuːmjʊlətɪv/ *adj* cumulative; acquisitive.

accumulator /ə'kjuːmjʊ,leɪtər/ *n* a rechargable battery; (*horseracing*) a bet that accumulates in value over successive races; (*comput*) a storage register.

accuracy /'ækjʊrəsi/ *n* (*pl* **accuracies**) the quality of being accurate; exactness or correctness.

accurate /'ækjərət/ *adj* conforming with the truth or an accepted standard; done with care, exact.—**accurately** *adv*.

accursed, accurst /ə'kərsəd/ or /ə'kərst/ *adj* under or subject to a curse; ill-fated, doomed to destruction; detestable; execrable.

accusation /,ækjuː'zeɪʃən/ *n* the act of accusing or being accused; an allegation; the charge of guilt brought against a person.

accusative /ə'kjuːzətɪv/ *n* (*gram*) the case expressing the direct object of a word.

accusatorial /ə,kjuːzə'tɔriəl/, **accusatory** /ə'kjuːzə,tɔri/ *adj* accusing, or containing an accusation; (*of legal procedure*) in which prosecutor and judge are not the same (opposite to inquisitorial).

accuse /ə'kjuːz/ *vt* to charge with a crime, fault, etc; to blame.—**accuser** *n*.—**accusingly** *adv*.

accused /ə'kjuːzd/ *n* (*law*) (*with* **the**) the defendant in court facing a criminal charge.

accuser /-zər/ *n* one who accuses; one who formally charges an offence against another.

accustom /ə'kʌstəm/ *vt* to make used (to) by habit, use, or custom.

accustomed /ə'kʌstəmd/ *adj* usual, customary; used to.

ace /eɪs/ *n* the one spot in dice, playing cards, dominoes, etc; a point won by a single stroke, as in tennis; an expert. • *adj* (*inf*) excellent.

-acea /'eɪʃə/ *n suffix* forming the plural names for orders of animals, *eg* Crustacea, Crustaceae.

-aceae /'eɪsiːiː/ *n suffix* forming plural names for families of plants, *eg* Rosaceae.

acedia /ə'siːdiə/ *n* an abnormal condition of the mind, characterized by lassitude, listlessness, and general indifference.

acentric /eɪ'sɛntrɪk/ *adj* away from the centre; having no centre.

acephalous /ə'sɛfələs/ *adj* headless; without a leader; an ovary of a plant that has its style springing from the base instead of the apex.

acerbic /ə'sərbɪk/ *adj* bitter and harsh to the taste; astringent.

acerbity /ə'sərbɪti/ *n* (*pl* **acerbities**) sharpness of speech or manner; (of taste) bitterness.

acerose /'æsər,oːz/ *adj* (*bot*) like a needle, very narrow, rigid, and tapering to a point.

acervate /əsər,vɪt/ or /-,veɪt/ *adj* growing in closely compacted clusters.

acet-, aceto- /ə'siːt/ or /'sɛt/, /'æsɛt/ *prefix* vinegar.

acetabulum /,æsə'tæbjuləm/ *n* (*pl* **acetabula, acetabulums**) the cavity of the hip bone into which the femur fits; one of the cup-like suckers on the arms of the cuttlefish; the posterior sucker of the leech; the saucer-shaped fructification of certain lichens; the receptacle of various fungi; a cup to hold vinegar.

acetanilide /,æsət'ænɪlaɪd/, **acetanilid** /-,lɪd/ *n* a pungent white powder, formed by the action of acetyl choride on aniline, used in medicine as an antipyretic.

acetate /'æsə,teɪt/ *n* a salt or ester of acetic acid; a fabric made from cellulose acetate.

acetic /ə'siːtɪk/ *adj* of acetic acid or vinegar.

acetic acid *n* a clear liquid with a strong acid taste and sharp smell, present in a dilute form in vinegar.

acetify /ə'sɛtə,faɪ/ or /-'siːt-/ *vt* (**acetifying, acetifed**) to turn into vinegar.—**acetification** *n*.—**acetifier** *n*.

acetometer /'æsɪ,tɒmətər/ *n* an instrument for gauging the strength or purity of vinegar or acetic acid.

acetone /'æsə,toːn/ *n* a clear flammable liquid used as a solvent.

acetous /'æsətəs/, **acetose** /-,toːs/ *adj* of the nature of vinegar; sour; causing acetification.

acetylene /əsɛtɪ'liːn/ *n* a gas that burns with a hot flame, used for welding, etc.

Achates /ə'kɒtiːz/ *n* a faithful friend, from Aeneas's friend in Virgil's *Aeneid*.

ache /eɪk/ *n* a dull, continuous pain. • *vi* to suffer a dull, continuous mental or physical pain; (*inf*) to yearn.—**achy** *adj*.

achieve /ə'tʃiːv/ *vt* to perform successfully, accomplish; to gain, win.—**achievable** *adj*.—**achiever** *n*.

achievement /ə'tʃiːvmənt/ *n* a thing achieved, *esp* by great effort, courage, determination, etc; accomplishment; (*her*) an escutcheon in memory of a distinguished feat.

Achilles' heel *n* a person's vulnerable or weak point.

Achilles' tendon *n* a tendon attaching the heel to the calf muscles.

achlamydeous /,æklə'mɪdiəs/ *adj* having neither calyx nor corolla.

achromatic /,ækroː'mætɪk/ *adj* colourless; transmitting light without decomposing it.—**achromatically** *adv*.—**achromaticity, achromatism** *n*.

achromatize /əɪˈkroːməˌtaɪz/ vt to deprive of the power of transmitting colour; to render achromatic.—**achromatization** n.

acicula /əˌsɪkjuˈlə/ n (pl **aciculae**) a spine or prickle.

acicular /əˌsɪkjulər/ adj needle-shaped.

aciculate /əˌsɪkjuˌlɪt/ or /-ˌleɪt/, **aciculated** /-ɪd/ adj in the shape of a needle; acicular.

acid /ˈæsɪd/ adj sharp, tart, sour; bitter. • n a sour substance; (chem) a corrosive substance that turns litmus red; (sl) LSD.—**acidly** adv.

acid house /-ˌhaʊs/ n a party where people dance to House music; the style of popular music played.

acidic /əˈsɪdɪk/ adj containing a large proportion of the acid element; opposed to basic.

acidifier /ɒˈsɪdɪˌfaɪər/ or /-ˌfaɪr/ n a substance having the property of imparting an acid quality.

acidify /əˈsɪdɪˌfaɪ/ vti (**acidifying, acidified**) to make or become acid.—**acidification** n.

acidimeter /ˌæsəˈdɪmətər/ n an instrument for measuring the strength of acids.—**acidimetric** /æˈsɪdɪˌmetrɪk/ adj.—**acidimetrically** /-ˌkəli/ adv.—**acidimetry** n.

acidity /əˈsɪdɪti/ n (pl **acidities**) the quality or condition of being acid.

acidosis /ˌæsɪˈdoːsɪs/ n an acid condition of the blood.—**acidotic** adj.

acid rain /-ˌreɪn/ n rain made acidic by air pollution from power stations, etc.

acid test /-ˌtest/ n a crucial or conclusive test.

acidulate /əˈsɪdjuˌleɪt/ vt to render slightly acid. • adj acidulous.—**acidulation** n.

acidulous /əˈsɪdjuləs/, **acidulent** /æˈsɪdjulənt/ adj somewhat acid; tart; peevish.

acierate /æˈsiːərˌeɪt/ vt (**acierating** /-ɪŋ/, **acierated** /-ɪd/) to change into steel.—**acieration** n.

acinaciform /æˌsəˈnæsəˌfɔrm/ adj (bot) resembling a scimitar in shape, as an acinaciform leaf or pod.

aciniform /əˈsɪnəˌfɔrm/ adj grape-like; clustered like grapes.

-acious /ˈeɪʃəs/ adj suffix forming adjectives meaning full of, inclined to, as mendacious.

-acity /ˈæsɪti/ n suffix forming corresponding nouns of quality, as mendacity.

acknowledge /əkˈnɒlɪdʒ/ vt to admit that something is true and valid; to show that one has noticed or recognized.

acknowledgment, acknowledgement /-mənt/ n the act of acknowledging; the admission or recognition of a truth; confession; the expression of appreciation of a favour or benefit conferred; a printed recognition by an author of others' works used or referred to; a receipt.

aclinic line /əˈklɪnɪk/ n the imaginary point near the equator where the magnetic needle has no dip, the magnetic equator.

acme /ˈækmi/ n the peak or highest point; the height of perfection.

acne /ˈækni/ n inflammation of the skin glands producing pimples.

acolyte /ˈækəˌlaɪt/ n an assistant or follower, esp a priest.

aconite /ˈækəˌnaɪt/, **aconitum** /-nɪtəm/ n the plant wolf's-bane or monk's-hood; the drug prepared from the plant.—**aconitic** adj.

acorn /ˈeɪˈkɔrn/ n the nut of the oak tree.

acotyledon /ˌeɪˌkɒtˈliːdn/ n (bot) a plant with seeds (spores) that have no cotyledons (seed lobes).—**acotyledonous** adj.

acoustic /əˈkuːstɪk/, **acoustical** /-kəl/ adj of the sense of hearing or sound; of acoustics; (mus) not amplified, eg a guitar.—**acoustically** adv.

acoustician /ˌækuːsˈtiːʃən/ n one skilled in the study of acoustics.

acoustics /əˈkuːstɪks/ npl (room, concert hall, etc) properties governing how clearly sounds can be heard in it; (in sing) the physics of sound.—**acoustician** n.

acquaint /əˈkweɪnt/ vt to make (oneself) familiar (with); to inform; (with **with**) to introduce (to).

acquaintance /əˈkweɪntəns/ n a person whom one knows only slightly.

acquainted /əˈkweɪntəd/ adj having personal knowledge; (with **of, with**) familiar, known.

acquiesce /ˌæˈkwiˌɛs/ vi (with **in**) to comply with readily, or put up no opposition to.

acquiescence /ˌæˈkwiˌɛsəns/ n compliance; assent.—**acquiescent** adj.

acquire /əˈkwaɪr/ vt to gain by one's own efforts; to obtain.—**acquirable** adj.

acquirement /ˌæˈkwaɪrˌmənt/ n the act of acquiring; that which is acquired; mental attainment.

acquisition /əˌkwɪˈzɪʃən/ or /ˈækwəˌzɪʃən/ n the act of gaining; acquiring; someone or something that is acquired, often of special worth or talent.

acquisitive /əˈkwɪzətɪv/ adj eager or greedy for possessions.—**acquisitively** adv.—**acquisitiveness** n.

acquit /əˈkwɪt/ vt (**acquitting, acquitted**) to free from an obligation; to behave or conduct (oneself); to declare innocent.

acquittal /əˈkwɪtl/ n the act of releasing or acquitting, the state of being acquitted; a judicial discharge from accusation; the performance (of duty).

acquittance /əˈkwɪtəns/ n a discharge or release from debt or other liability; a receipt barring a further demand.

acre /ˈeɪkər/ n land measuring 4840 square yards.

acreage /ˈeɪkərɪdʒ/ n area measured in acres.

acrid /ˈækrɪd/ adj sharp and bitter of taste or smell; caustic, critical in attitude or speech.—**acridity** n.—**acridly** adv.

acrimony /ˈækrɪˌmoːni/ n (pl **acrimonies**) bitterness of manner or language.—**acrimonious** adj.—**acrimoniously** adv.

acro- /æˈkroː/ or /ˈækrə/ prefix topmost, extreme.

acrobat /ˈækrəˌbæt/ n a skilful performer of spectacular gymnastic feats.—**acrobatic** adj.—**acrobatically** adv.

acrobatics /ˌækrəˈbætɪks/ npl acrobatic feats.

acrocarpous /ˌækrəˈkɑrpəs/ adj (bot) having (like the mosses) the fruit at the end of the primary axis.

acrogen /ˈækrəˌdʒən/ n (bot) a nonflowering plant increasing by growth from the top, as ferns and mosses.—**acrogenic, acrogenous** adj.

acrolith /ˈækrəˌlɪθ/ n a sculptured figure, with head and extremities of stone and the rest of wood.

acromegaly /ˌækrəˈmɛgəli/ n a hormonal disease resulting in overdeveopment of the extremities.—**acromegalic** adj.

acronycal, acronical /əˈkrɒnəˌkəl/ adj (astron) (stars) rising at sunset and setting at sunrise.

acronym /ˈækrənɪm/ n a word formed from the initial letters of other words (as laser).

acrophobia /ˌækrəˈfoːbɪə/ n dread of heights.—**acrophobe** n.—**acrophobic** adj, n.

acropolis /əˈkrɒːpələs/ n the highest part or citadel of a Grecian city; the citadel itself.

acrospire /ˈækrəspɔɪr/ n (bot) the sprout of a seed.

across /əˈkrɒs/ prep from one side to the other of; on or at an angle; on the other side of. • adv crosswise; from one side to the other.

across-the-board /-ðəˌbɔrd/ adj (wage increase, cut, etc) applying equally to all; (horseracing) winning a bet if the horse comes first, second or third.

acrostic /əˈkrɒstɪk/ n a poem or word puzzle in which certain letters of each line spell a complete word, etc.—**acrostically** adv.

acrylic /əˈkrɪlɪk/ adj of or derived from acrylic acid. • n an acrylic fibre or resin.

act /ækt/ vi to perform or behave in a certain manner; to perform a specific function; to have an effect; to perform on the stage; (with **up**) (inf) to misbehave; to malfunction. • vt to portray by actions, esp on the stage; to pretend, simulate; to take the part of, as a character in a play. • n something done, a deed; an exploit; a law; a main division of a play or opera; the short repertoire of a comic, etc; something done merely for effect or show.

act of God n a direct and unforeseeable act of nature that could not reasonably have been guarded against.

acting /-ɪŋ/ n the art of an actor. • adj holding an office or position temporarily.

actinia /ækˈtɪnɪə/ n (pl **actiniae, actinias**) any of a genus of sea anemones that resemble flowers when the tentacles of the mouth are spread out.

actiniform /ækˈtɪnɪˌfɔrm/, **actinoid** /ækˈtɪnɔɪd/ adj having the form of rays; star-shaped.

actinism /ækˈtɪnɪzm/ n the property of light by which chemical changes are caused, as in photography.—**actinic** adj.—**actinically** adv.

actinium /ækˈtɪnɪəm/ n a radioactive element occurring as a decay product of uranium.

actinozoan /ækˌtɪnoːˈzoːən/ see **anthozoan**.

action /ˈækʃən/ n the process of doing something; an operation; a movement of the body, gesture; a land or sea battle; a lawsuit; the unfolding of events in a play, novel, etc; (inf) (with **the**) the centre of (social) activity.

actionable /-əbəl/ adj providing grounds for legal action.—**actionably** adv.

action painting *n* expressionist art produced by daubing, dribbling, splashing, throwing, etc, paint on to the canvas.

activate /ˈæktɪˌveɪt/ *vt* to make active; to set in motion; to make radioactive.—**activation** *n*.—**activator** *n*.

active /ˈækˈtɪv/ *adj* lively, physically mobile; engaged in practical activities; energetic, busy; (*volcano*) liable to erupt; capable of producing an effect; radioactive; (*armed forces*) in full-time service. • *n* (*gram*) the verb form having as its subject the doer of the action.—**actively** *adv*.—**activeness** *n*.

active service, active duty *n* full-time service in a military force, *esp* during a war.

activist /ˈæktɪvɪst/ *n* an advocate of direct or militant action, *esp* in politics.—**activism** *n*.

activity /ækˈtɪvɪti/ *n* (*pl* **activities**) the state of being active; energetic, lively action; specific occupations (*indoor activities*).

actor /ˈæktər/ *n* a person who acts in a play, film, etc.—**actress** *nf*.

actual /ˈækˈtʃʊəl/ *adj* real; existing in fact or reality.

actuality /ˌækˌtʃʊˈwælɪti/ or /-ˌʃuː-/ *n* (*pl* **actualities**) the state of being real or actual; that which is in full existence; reality

actualize /ˈækˈtʃʊəˌlaɪz/ or /-ˈʃuːə-/ *vt* to realize in action; to describe realistically; to make actual.—**actualization** *n*.

actually /ˈæktʃʊəli/ or /ˈækfəli/ *adv* as an existing fact, really; strange though it seems.

actuary /ˈæktʃʊˌeri/ *n* (*pl* **actuaries** /-riz/) a person who calculates insurance risks, premiums, etc.—**actuarial** *adj*.

actuate /ˈæktʃʊeɪt/ *vt* to move or incite to action; to put in motion; to impel, influence.—**actuation** *n*.—**actuator** *n*.

acuity /əˈkjuːəti/ *n* sharpness of thought or vision.

aculeate /əˈkjuːliət/ *adj* pointed; (*zool*) equipped with a sting; (*bot*) having aculei or sharp prickles.

aculeus /əˈkjuːliːəs/ *n* (*pl* **aculei**) a prickle.

acumen /əˈkjuːmən/ or /ˈækjəmən/ *n* sharpness of mind, perception.

acuminate /əˈkjuːmɪnət/ *adj* ending in a sharp point. • *vt* /-ˌneɪt/ (**acuminating, acuminated**) to sharpen.—**acumination** *n*.

acupuncture /ˈækjuːˌpʌŋktʃər/ *n* the insertion of the tips of fine needles into the skin at certain points to treat various common ailments.—**acupuncturist** *n*.

acute /əˈkjuːt/ *adj* perceptive; sharp-witted; (*hearing*) sensitive; (*pain*) severe; very serious; (*angles*) less than 90 degrees; (*disease*) severe but not long lasting.—**acutely** *adv*.—**acuteness** *n*.

acute accent *n* a mark (´) over a vowel in certain languages to indicate emphasis or special quality.

-acy /əsi/ *n suffix* forming nouns of state or quality, *eg* piracy.

ad- /əd/ or /æd/ *prefix* to, as in *adhere*.

ad[1] /æd/ *abbr* = advertisement.

ad[2] *prep* to, as in *ad absurdum*.

AD, A.D. /ˌeɪˈdiː/ *abbr* = *anno domini* (in the year of Our Lord) in dates of the Christian era, indicating the number of years since the birth of Christ.

ad absurdum /æd ˌæbˈzɜrdəm/ or /-sɜr-/ (*Latin*) to absurdity.

adactylous /eɪˈdæktələs/ *adj* without toes or fingers.

adage /ˈædɪdʒ/ *n* a proverb, old saying.

adagio /əˈdæːʒioː/ or /-ˈdʒioː/ *adv* (*mus*) slowly, gracefully. • *n* (*pl* **adagios**) a slow movement.

adamant /ˈædəmənt/ *adj* inflexible, unyielding. • *n* adamantine, an extremely hard substance.

adamantine /ˌædəˈmæntaɪn/ *adj* made of adamantine; impenetrable, very hard. • *n* an extremely hard substance; the diamond (—*also* **adamant**).

Adamite /ˈædəmˌaɪt/ *n* a child of Adam; a member of a sect who went naked; a nudist.—**Adamitic** *adj*.

Adam's apple /ˈædəmzˌæpəl/ *n* the hard projection of cartilage in the front of the neck.

Adam's needle /-niːdəl/ *n* a popular name of the yucca.

adapt /əˈdæpt/ *vti* to make or become fit; to adjust to a new purpose or circumstances.—**adaptability** *n*.—**adaptable** *adj*.—**adapter** *n*.

adaptation /ˌædæpˈteɪʃən/ *n* the process or condition of being adapted; something produced by modification; a version of a literary composition rewritten for a different medium.

adaptor /əˈdæptər/ *n* a device that allows an item of equipment to be put to new use; a device for connecting parts of differing size and shape; an electrical plug using one socket for different appliances.

adaxial /ædˈæksiəl/ *adj* towards the axis.

ADC /ˌeɪdiːˈsiː/ *abbr* = aide-de-camp.

add /æd/ *vt* to combine (two or more things together); to combine numbers or amounts in a total; to remark or write further. • *vi* to perform or come together by addition.

addax /ˈædæks/ *n* (*pl* **addaxes, addax**) a large North African antelope with twisted horns.

addendum /əˈdendəm/ *n* (*pl* **addenda**) a thing to be added; supplementary text appended to a book, etc.

adder /ˈædər/ *n* the venomous viper.

adder's-tongue /ˈædərzˌtʌŋ/ *n* a kind of fern whose spike resembles the tongue of a snake.

addict /ˈædɪkt/ *n* a person who is dependent upon a drug. • *vt* to devote or give oneself up to; to practise sedulously (*usu* pejorative).—**addiction** *n*.—**addictive** *adj*.

addition /əˈdɪʃən/ *n* the act or result of adding; something to be added; an extra part.

additional /əˈdɪʃənəl/ *adj* added, extra; supplementary.—**additionally** *adv*.

additive /ˈædɪtɪv/ *adj* produced by addition. • *n* a substance added (to food, etc) to improve texture, flavour, etc.

addle /ˈædəl/ *vb* (**addling, addled**) *vt* to make corrupt, putrid or confused. • *vi* to become addled. • *adj* rotten.

addle-headed, addle-pated *adj* stupid, weak-brained; muddled.

address /əˈdres/ *vt* to write directions for delivery on (a letter, etc); to speak or write directly to; to direct one's skills or attention (to); (*golf*) to adjust one's stance and aim before hitting the ball; • *n* a place where a person or business resides, the details of this on a letter for delivery; a speech, *esp* a formal one; (*comput*) a specific memory location where information is stored.—**addressable** *adj*.

addressee /ˌædreˈsiː/ *n* a person or company to whom a letter is addressed.

Addressograph /əˈdresəˌgræf/ *n* (*trademark*) an addressing machine.

adduce /əˈdjuːs/ *vt* to offer as an example or evidence.

adducent /æˈduːsənt/ or /ə-/, /-ˈdjuːs-/ *adj* bringing forward or together.

adducible, adduceable /əˈdjuːsəbəl/ *adj* capable of being adduced.

adduct /əˈdʌkt/ *vt* to pull towards; (*of muscles*) to draw to a common centre.—**adduction** *n*.—**adductive** *adj*.

adductor muscle /əˈdʌktər/ *n* a muscle that draws certain parts to a common centre.

ademption /əˈdempʃən/ *n* (*law*) the revocation of a grant; the lapse of a legacy.

aden- /ˈædən/, **adeno-** /ˈædnoː/ *prefix* gland.

adenitis /ˌædnˈaɪtɪs/ *n* inflammation of a gland.

adenoids /ˈædəˌnɔɪdz/ *npl* enlarged masses of tissue in the throat behind the nose.—**adenoidal** *adj*.

adenoma /ˌædˈnoːmə/ *n* (*pl* **adenomas, adenomata**) a gland-like benign tumour.

adept /ˈædept/ or /əˈdept/ *adj* highly proficient. • *n* a highly skilled person.—**adeptly** *adv*.—**adeptness** *n*.

adequacy /ˈædəkwəsi/ *n* adequateness; sufficiency for a particular purpose.

adequate /ˈædəkwət/ *adj* sufficient for requirements; barely acceptable.—**adequately** *adv*.—**adequateness** *n*.

à deux /æˈdɜː/ *Fr.* /adø/ for two; intimate.

adhere /ədˈhɪr/ *vi* to stick, as by gluing or suction; to give allegiance or support (to); to follow.

adherence /ədˈhɪrəns/ *n* the act or state of adhering; unwavering attachment.

adherent /ədˈhɪrənt/ *adj* sticking, attached. • *n* a supporter of a political party, idea, etc.

adhesion /ədˈhiːʒən/ *n* the action or condition of adhering; the attachment of normally separate tissues in the body.

adhesive /ədˈhiːsɪv/ or /-zɪv/ *adj* sticky; causing adherence. • *n* a substance used to stick, such as glue, paste, etc.—**adhesiveness** *n*.

ad hoc /ædˈhɒk/ *adj* for a particular purpose.

ad hominem /ædˈhɒmɪˌnem/ (*Latin*) to the man, personal.

adiabatic /ˌeɪdiəˈbætɪk/ or /ˌeɪdaɪə-/ *adj* (*physics*) not gaining or losing heat.—**adiabatically** *adv*.

adiaphorous /ˌædiːˈæfərəs/ or /ˌædaɪˈæ-/ *adj* (*theol*) tolerant in nonessential points of religion; morally indifferent; (*med*) neither helping nor harming.

adieu /əˈdjuː/ *n* (*pl* **adieux, adieus**) farewell, goodbye; good wishes at parting.

ad infinitum /ˌædˌɪnfɪˈnaɪtəm/ *adv* without end, forever.

ad interim /æd'ɪntərɪm/ *adv* (*Latin*) for the meantime.

adipocere /'ædɪpəˌsiːr/ *n* a fatty substance resulting from decomposition of animal bodies in moist places.—**adipocerous** *adj*.

adipose /'ædɪˌpoːs/ or /-poːz/ *adj* of, like or containing animal fat; fatty.—**adiposity** *n*.

adit /'ædɪt/ *n* an entrance or passage; an entrance to a mine more or less horizontal.

adjacent /ə'dʒeɪsənt/ *adj* nearby; adjoining, contiguous.—**adjacency** *n*.

adjective /'ædʒəktɪv/ *n* a word used to add a characteristic to a noun or pronoun.—**adjectival** *adj*.—**adjectivally** *adv*.

adjoin /ə'dʒɔɪn/ *vt* to unite or join. • *vi* to lie next to.

adjoining /-ɪŋ/ *adj* beside, in contact with.

adjourn /ə'dʒɜrn/ *vt* to suspend (a meeting) temporarily. • *vi* (*inf*) to retire (to another room, etc).—**adjournment** *n*.

adjournment /-mənt/ *n* the act of adjourning; the postponement of a meeting.

adjudge /ə'dʒʌdʒ/ *vt* (**adjudging, adjudged**) to decide or award judicially; to sentence; to determine in a controversy, to adjudicate.—**adjudgment, adjudgement** *n*.

adjudicate /ə'dʒuːdɪˌkeɪt/ *vt* (*law*) to hear and decide (a case). • *vi* to serve as a judge (in or on).—**adjudicator** *n*.

adjudication /əˈdʒuːdɪˈkeɪʃən/ *n* the act of determining judicially; a judicial sentence; a court's decision.

adjunct /'ædʒʌŋkt/ *n* something joined or added but inessential.—**adjunctive** *adj*.

adjuration /ˌædʒə'reɪʃən/ *n* the solemn charging on oath; the oath used.

adjure /ə'dʒɜr/ or /ə'dʒʊr/ *vt* to command on oath under pain of a penalty; to charge solemnly, request earnestly.

adjust /ə'dʒʌst/ *vt* to arrange in a more proper or satisfactory manner; to regulate or modify by minor changes; to decide the amount to be paid in settling (an insurance claim). • *vi* to adapt oneself.—**adjustable** *adj*.—**adjuster** *n*.

adjustment /-mənt/ *n* the act of adjusting; arrangement.

adjutancy /'ædʒətənsi/ *n* (*pl* **adjutancies**) the office of an adjutant.

adjutant /'ædʒətənt/ *n* a military staff officer who assists the commanding officer.

adjutant general *n* (*pl* **adjutants general**) the chief staff officer of an army, through whom all orders, etc, are received and issued by the general commanding.

adjuvant /'ædʒəvənt/ *adj* assisting, helpful. • *n* a helper, an auxiliary.

ad-lib /æd'lɪb/ *vti* (**ad-libbing, ad-libbed**) (*speech, etc*) to improvise. • *n* an ad-libbed remark. • *adv* spontaneously, freely.—**ad-libber** *n*.

adman /'ædmæn/ *n* (*pl* **admen**) (*inf*) a person who works in the advertising business.

admass /'ædmæs/ or /-mɒs/ *n* the public targeted by or influenced by advertising.

admeasure /əd'meʒər/ *vt* (**admeasuring, admeasured**) to measure dimensions; to apportion.

admeasurement /-mənt/ *n* a measurement by a rule; adjustment of proportions; dimensions.

admin /ˌəd'mɪn/ *n* (*inf*) administration.

administer /əd'mɪnɪstər/ *vt* to manage, direct; to give out as a punishment; to dispense (medicine, punishment, etc); to tender (an oath, etc).

administrate /əd'mɪnɪˌstreɪt/ *vti* to manage or control the affairs of a business, institution, etc.

administration /ədˌmɪnɪ'streɪʃən/ *n* management; the people who administer an organization; the government; (*with cap*) the executive officials of a government, their policies, and term of office.

administrative /əd'mɪnɪˌstreɪtɪv/ *adj* of management; executive.—**administratively** *adv*.

administrator /əd'mɪnɪˌstreɪtər/ *n* a person who manages or supervises; (*law*) one appointed to settle an estate.

admirable /'ædmərəbəl/ *adj* deserving of admiration or approval.—**admirably** *adv*.

admiral /'ædmərəl/ *n* the commanding officer of a fleet; a naval officer of the highest rank.

admiralty /-ti/ *n* (*pl* **admiralties**) the department of a government having authority over naval affairs; the building in which naval affairs are transacted; the office of an admiral.

admiration /ˌædmɪ'reɪʃən/ *n* a feeling of pleasurable and often surprised respect or approval; an admired person or thing.

admire /əd'maɪr/ *vt* to regard with honour, approval and pleasure; to express admiration for.—**admirer** *n*.—**admiring** *adj*.—**admiringly** *adv*.

admissible /əd'mɪsɪbəl/ *adj* that may be admitted or allowed.—**admissibility, admissibleness** *n*.

admission /əd'mɪʃən/ *n* an entrance fee; a conceding, confessing, etc; a thing conceded, confessed, etc.—**admissive** *adj*.

admit /əd'mɪt/ *vb* (**admitting, admitted**) *vt* to allow to enter or join; to concede or acknowledge as true. • *vi* to give access; (*with* **of**) to allow or permit.

admittance /əd'mɪtəns/ *n* the act of admitting; the right to enter.

admittedly /əd'mɪtədli/ *adv* acknowledged as fact, willingly conceded.

admix /æd'mɪks/ *vt* to mix with something else; to add as an extra ingredient.

admixture /-tʃər/ *n* a mixture, a compound of substances mixed together.

admonish /əd'mɒnɪʃ/ *vt* to remind or advise earnestly; to reprove gently.

admonition /ˌædmə'nɪʃən/ *n* a friendly reproof or warning.—**admonitory** *adj*.

adnate /'ædˌneɪt/ *adj* (*bot*) with organic cohesion of unlike parts.

ad nauseam /æd'nɔːzɪˌəm/ or /-zɪˌæm/ *adv* to a sickening degree.

ado /ə'duː/ *n* fuss, excitement, *esp* over trivial matters.

adobe /ə'doːbi/ *n* a brick made of sun-dried clay; clay for making adobe bricks; a building using such bricks.

adolescence /ˌædə'lesəns/ *n* the period of life between puberty and maturity; youth.

adolescent /ˌædə'lesənt/ *adj* pertaining to the stage between childhood and maturity; (*inf*) immature. • *n* an adolescent person.

adopt /ə'dɒpt/ *vt* to take legally into one's family and raise as one's child; to select and pursue, *eg* a course of action; to take as one's own.—**adoption** *n*.

adoptive /ə'dɒptɪv/ *adj* made or related by adoption.

adorable /ə'dɔrəbəl/ *adj* worthy of being adored; extremely charming.—**adorably** *adv*.

adoration /ˌædə'reɪʃən/ *n* worship, homage; profound regard.

adore /ə'dɔr/ *vt* to worship; to love deeply.—**adoringly** *adv*.

adorn /ə'dɔrn/ *vt* to decorate; to make more pleasant or attractive.—**adornment** *n*.

ad rem /æd'rem/ *adj, adv* to the point or purpose.

adrenal /ə'driːnəl/ *adj* of or near the kidney. • *n* an adrenal gland.

adrenal gland *n* one of two glands situated above the kidneys that secretes adrenaline.

adrenaline /ə'drenəlɪn/ *n* a hormone that stimulates the heart rate, blood pressure, etc in response to stress and that is secreted by the adrenal glands or manufactured synthetically.

adrift /ə'drɪft/ *adj, adv* afloat without mooring, drifting; loose; purposeless.

adroit /ə'drɔɪt/ *adj* skilful and clever, sharp-witted.—**adroitly** *adv*.—**adroitness** *n*.

adscititious /ˌædsɪ'tɪʃəs/ *adj* taken in addition; added from without; additional, supplementary.

adsorb /əd'sɔrb/ *vti* to accumulate on a surface, to collect by adsorption.—**adsorbable** *adj*.

adsorbent /-ənt/ *n* an adsorbing substance.

adsorption /æd'sɔrpʃen/ *n* the action of a solid in condensing and holding a gas upon it.

adulate /'ædʒuˌleɪt/ *vt* to flatter excessively or basely.—**adulator** *n*.—**adulatory** *adj*.

adulation /'ædʒu'leɪʃən/ *n* excessive flattery.—**adulatory** *adj*.

adult /ə'dʌlt/ or /'ædʌlt/ *adj* fully grown; mature; suitable only for adults, as in pornography, etc. • *n* a mature person, etc.—**adulthood** *n*.

adulterant /ə'dʌltərənt/ *adj* adulterating. • *n* the person or thing that adulterates.

adulterate /ə'dʌltəˌreɪt/ *vt* to make impure or inferior, etc by adding an improper substance.—**adulteration** *n*.—**adulterator** *n*.

adulterer /ə'dʌltərər/ *n* a person who commits adultery.—**adulteress** *nf*.

adulterine /ə'dʌltəˌraɪn/ *adj* resulting from adulterous intercourse; fake, spurious; illegal.

adulterous /ə'dʌltərəs/ *adj* guilty of adultery.

adultery /ə'dʌltəri/ *n* (*pl* **adulteries**) sexual intercourse between a married person and someone other than their legal partner.

adumbral /'ædəm,brəl/ *adj* overshadowing; shady.

adumbrate /'ædəm,breɪt/ *vt* to foreshadow; to overshadow; to give a faint semblance of.—**adumbration** *n.*—**adumbrative** *adj.*

ad valorem /,ædvə'lɔrem/ *adj, adv* according to value; (*customs, duties*) levied on the value of goods as sworn to by the owner.

advance /əd'væns/ *vt* to bring or move forward; to promote; to raise the rate of; (*money*) to lend. • *vi* to go forward; to make progress; to rise in rank, price, etc. • *n* progress; improvement; a rise in value; payment beforehand; (*pl*) friendly approaches, *esp* to please. • *adj* in front; beforehand.

advanced /əd'vænst/ *adj* in front; old; superior in development or progress.

advancement /əd'vænsmənt/ or /-vɒns-/ *n* promotion to a higher rank; progress in development.

advantage /əd'væntɪdʒ/ *n* superiority of position or condition; a gain or benefit; (*tennis*) the first point won after deuce. • *vt* to produce a benefit or favour to.

advantageous /,ædvən'teɪdʒəs/ *adj* producing advantage, beneficial.—**advantageously** *adv.*

advent /'ædvent/ *n* an arrival or coming; (*with cap*) (*Christianity*) the coming of Christ; the four-week period before Christmas.

Adventist /,æd'ventɪst/ *n* a person who believes in Christ's second coming to set up a kingdom on earth.—**Adventism** *n.*

adventitious /,ædven'tɪʃəs/ *adj* happening by chance; casual; fortuitous; accidental; produced out of normal and regular order; growing in an abnormal position.—**adventitiously** *adv.*—**adventitiousness** *n.*

Advent Sunday *n* the Sunday nearest (before or after) to St Andrew's Day (30 November).

adventure /əd'ventʃər/ *n* a strange or exciting undertaking; an unusual, stirring, often romantic, experience.

adventure playground *n* a children's playground equipped with materials and objects for building, climbing, hiding in, etc.

adventurer /-ər/ *n* a person who seeks adventure; someone who seeks money or power by unscrupulous means.—**adventuress** *nf.*

adventurous /-əs/ *adj* inclined to incur risk; full of risk; rash; enterprising; daring.—**adventurously** *adv.*

adverb /'ædvərb/ *n* a word that modifies a verb, adjective, another adverb, phrase, clause or sentence and indicates how, why, where, etc.—**adverbial** *adj.*—**adverbially** *adv.*

adversary /'ædvər,seri/ *n* (*pl* **adversaries**) an enemy or opponent.

adversative /əd'vərsətɪv/ *adj* (*words*) denoting opposition or contrariety; expressing opposition.

adverse /əd'vərs/ or /'æd-/ *adj* hostile; contrary or opposite; unfavourable.—**adversely** *adv.*

adversity /əd'vərsiti/ *n* (*pl* **adversities**) trouble, misery, misfortune.

advert[1] /əd'vərt/ *vt* to refer (to); to turn attention (to).

advert[2] /'ædvərt/ *n* (*inf*) an advertisement.

advertence /æd'vərtəns/, **advertency** /-si/ *n* attention; heedfulness.—**advertent** *adj.*

advertently /æd'vərtəntli/ *adv* in an intentional manner.

advertise, advertize /'ædvər,taɪz/ *vt* to call public attention to, *esp* in order to sell something, by buying space or time in the media, etc. • *vi* to call public attention to things for sale; to ask (for) by public notice.—**advertiser, advertizer** *n.*

advertisement, advertizement /,əd'vərtɪzmənt/ or /'ædvər,taɪzmənt/ *n* advertising; a public notice, *usu* paid for by the provider of a good or service.

advertising, advertizing /'ædvər,taɪzɪŋ/ *n* the promotion of goods or services by public notices; advertisements; the business of producing adverts.

advice /əd'vaɪz/ *n* recommendation with regard to a course of action; formal notice or communication.

advisable /əd'vaɪzəbəl/ *adj* prudent, expedient.—**advisability** *n.*

advise /əd'vaɪz/ *vt* to give advice to; to caution; to recommend; to inform. • *vi* to give advice.—**adviser, advisor** *n.*

advised /əd'vaɪzd/ *adj* acting with caution; deliberate; judicious.—**advisedly** *adv.*

advisory /əd'vaɪzəri/ *adj* having or exercising the power to advise; containing or giving advice.

advocaat /,ædvə'kɒt/ *n* a sweet egg-based liqueur.

advocacy /'ædvəkəsi/ *n* (*pl* **advocacies**) the function of an radynamic *adj.*

advocate /'ædvəkət/ or /'æd'vəkeɪt/ *n* a person who argues or defends the cause of another, *esp* in a court of law; a supporter. • *vt* to plead in favour of, to recommend.

adynamia /,ædaɪ'neɪmiə/ or /,ædɪ'neɪ-/ *n* want of vital power, prostration, weakness.—**adynamic** *adj.*

adze, adz /ædz/ *n* a type of axe with a blade at right angles to the handle for cutting and shaping wood.

aedile /'iːdaɪl/ *n* a Roman magistrate who exercised supervision over the temples, public and private buildings, the markets, public games, sanitation, etc, hence a municipal officer.—*also* **edile**.

aegis /'iːdʒɪs/ *n* protection, sponsorship.—*also* **egis**.

Aeolian /eɪ'oːliən/ *adj* pertaining to Aeolis in Asia Minor or to the Aeolic race; of Aeolus, the Greek god of winds.

aeolian harp *n* a stringed instrument, the wires of which are set in motion and sounded by the wind.

Aeolic /i'ɒlɪk/ *adj* of Aeolis. • *n* the Aeolic dialect of ancient Greece.

aeon /'iːən/ or /'iː,ɒn/ *n* a period of immense duration; an age.—*also* **eon**.

aeonian /i'oːniən/ *adj* everlasting.—*also* **eonian**.

aerate /'ɛreɪt/ *vt* to supply (blood) with oxygen by respiration; to supply or impregnate with air; to combine or charge a liquid with gas.—**aeration** *n.*

aerator /-ər/ *n* an apparatus for making aerated waters.

aerial /'ɛriəl/ *adj* belonging to or existing in the air; of aircraft or flying. • *n* a radio or TV antenna.

aerialist /'ɛriəlɪst/ *n* a trapeze or high-wire artist.

aerie /'ɛri/ or /'iːri/ *see* **eyrie**.

aeriform /'ɛrəfɔrm/ *adj* having the form of air; gaseous; like air; unsubstantial.

aerify /'ɛrəfaɪ/ *vt* (**aerifying, aerified**) to combine with air.—**aerification** *n.*

aero- /'ɛroː/ *prefix* aviation; air vessel.

aerobatics /,ɛrə'bætɪks/ *npl* stunts performed while flying an aircraft.

aerobe /'ɛroːb/, **aerobium** /ɛr'oːbiəm/ *n* (*pl* **aerobes, aerobia**) a microbe that cannot live without air.

aerobic /ɛ'roːbɪk/ *adj* (*exercise*) that conditions the heart and lungs by increasing the efficient intake of oxygen by the body.

aerobics /-s/ *npl* aerobic exercises.

aerodrome /'ɛrə,droːm/ *n* an airfield.

aerodynamics /,ɛroːdaɪ'næmɪks/ *n* the study of the forces exerted by air or other gases in motion, *esp* around solid bodies such as aircraft.—**aerodynamic** *adj.*—**aerodynamically** *adv.*

aerofoil /'ɛrə,fɔɪl/ *n* a wing, the lifting surface of an aeroplane.

aerogram, aerogramme /'ɛrə,græm/ *n* a radio telegraphic message.

aerolite /'ɛrə,laɪt/ *n* a stone falling from the air, a meteorite.

aerology /ɛ'rɒlədʒi/ *n* the science that deals with the air and the atmosphere.—**aerologic, aerological** *adj.*—**aerologist** *n.*

aerometer /ɛ'rɒmətər/ *n* an instrument for weighing the air.—**aerometric** *adj.*

aerometry /ɛr'ɒmətri/ *n* the branch of physics concerned with air, pneumatics.

aeronaut /,ɛrə'nɒt/ *n* an aviator; the pilot or navigator of an aircraft.

aeronautical /,ɛrə'nɒtɪkəl/, **aeronautic** /,ɛrə'nɒtɪk/ *adj* of or pertaining to aeronautics or an aeronaut.—**aeronautically** *adv.*

aeronautics /-ɪks/ *n* the science dealing with the operation of aircraft; the art or science of flight.

aeroplane /'ɛrə,pleɪn/ *n* a power-driven aircraft.—*also* **airplane**.

aerosol /'ɛrə,sɒl/ *n* a suspension of fine solid or liquid particles in gas, *esp* as held in a container under pressure, with a device for releasing it in a fine spray.

aerospace /'ɛroː,speɪs/ *n* the earth's atmosphere and the space beyond. • *adj* technology for flight in aerospace.

aerostat /'ɛrəstæt/ *n* a balloon; a balloonist.

aerostatics /-tɪks/ *n* (*used as sing*) the science that studies the equilibrium of bodies sustained in air; the science of air navigation.—**aerostatic, aerostatical** *adj.*

aerostation /'ɛrəsteɪʃən/ *n* ballooning.

aeruginous /i'ruːdʒɪnəs/ *adj* of or like verdigris or copper rust.

aery /'eɪəri/ or /'iri/, /'ɛri/, /'ɪri/ *see* **eyrie**.

Aesculapian /,iːskuˈleɪpiən/ or /,ɛ-/ *adj* of or pertaining to Aesculapius, the Roman god of medicine, or to medicine.

aesthete /'ɛsθi:t/ *n* a person who is or pretends to be highly sensitive to art and beauty.—*also* **esthete**.

aesthetic /ɛs'θetɪk/, **aesthetical** /ɛs'θetɪkəl/ *adj* of or pertaining to aesthetics; concerned with beauty rather than practicality.—*also* **esthetic, esthetical**.—**aesthetically, esthetically** *adv*.

aestheticism /ɛs'θetɪˌsɪzm/ *n* the cult of the beautiful, *esp* a fantastic art movement at the end of the 19th century.—*also* **estheticism**.

aesthetics /ɛs'θetɪks/ *n* the philosophy of art and beauty.—*also* **esthetics**.

aestival /'ɛstɪvəl/ *adj* of or occurring in summer.—*also* **estival**.

aestivation /ˌɛstɪ'veɪʃən/ or /ˌi:s-/ *n* (*bot*) the arrangement of petals in a flower bud; (*zool*) the spending of the dry season in a dormant state.—*also* **estivation**.

aet., aetat. *abbr* = *aetatis*, of, at, the age of.

aetiology /ˌi:ti'ɒlədʒi/, **aetiological** /-kəl/, **aetiologist** /-ɪst/ *see* **etiology**.

af- /əf/ *prefix* the form of *ad-* before *f*.

afar /ə'fɑr/ *adv* at, to, or from a great distance.

affable /'æfəbəl/ *adj* friendly; approachable.—**affability** *n*.—**affably** *adv*.

affair /ə'fɛr/ *n* a thing done or to be done; (*pl*) public or private business; (*inf*) an event; a temporary romantic or sexual relationship.

affaire (de coeur) /æ'fɛr/ *n* a love affair.

affect[1] /ə'fɛkt/ *vt* to have an effect on; to produce a change in; to act in a way that alters or affects the feelings of.

affect[2] *vt* to pretend or feign (an emotion); to incline to or show a preference for.

affect[3] /'æfɛkt/ *n* an emotion, feeling or desire associated with a certain stimulus.

affectation /ˌæfɛk'teɪʃən/ *n* a striving after or an attempt to assume what is not natural or real; pretence.

affected /ə'fɛktəd/ *adj* (*manner, etc*) assumed artificially.—**affectedly** *adv*.—**affectedness** *n*.

affecting /ə'fɛktɪŋ/ *adj* having power to excite the emotions; moving; pathetic.—**affectingly** *adv*.

affection /ə'fɛkʃən/ *n* tender feeling; liking.—**affectional** *adj*.

affectionate /ə'fɛkʃənət/ *adj* showing affection, loving.—**affectionately** *adv*.

affective /ə'fɛktɪv/ *adj* arousing the emotions, emotional.—**affectivity, affectiveness** *n*.

afferent /'æfərənt/ *adj* conveying inwards or to a part.

affettuoso /əˌfetu'o:so:/ *adv* (*mus*) with feeling, tender, pathetic.

affiance /ˌæfi:'ɒns/ or /ə'faɪəns/ *vt* to promise in marriage, betroth. • *n* faith, trust; a marriage contract.

affiche /ə'fitʃ/ *n* a paper affixed to a wall, a poster.

affidavit /ˌæfɪ'deɪvɪt/ *n* a statement written on oath.

affiliate /ə'fɪliːˌeɪt/ *vt* to connect as a subordinate member or branch; to associate (oneself with). • *vi* to join. • *n* an affiliated person, club, etc.—**affiliation** *n*.

affinity /ə'fɪnɪti/ *n* (*pl* **affinities**) attraction, liking; a close relationship, *esp* by marriage; similarity, likeness; (*chem*) a tendency in certain substances to combine.

affirm /ə'fɜrm/ *vt* to assert confidently or positively; to confirm or ratify; (*law*) to make an affirmation.

affirmation /ˌæfər'meɪʃən/ *n* affirming; an assertion; a solemn declaration made by those declining to swear an oath, *eg* on religious grounds.

affirmative /ə'fɜrmətɪv/ *adj* confirming; indicating agreement. • *n* a positive word or statement, *eg* yes.—**affirmatively** *adv*.

affix /ə'fɪks/ *vt* to fasten; to add, *esp* in writing; to attach.

afflatus /ə'fleɪtəs/ *n* a breath or blast of wind; poetic or divine inspiration; creative power.

afflict /ə'flɪkt/ *vt* to cause persistent pain or suffering to; to trouble greatly.—**afflictive** *adj*.

affliction /ə'flɪkʃən/ *n* persistent pain, suffering; a cause of this.

affluence /'æfluəns/ *n* an abundant supply, as of thoughts, words, riches; wealth.

affluent /-ənt/ or *adj* rich, well provided for.—**affluently** *adv*.

affluenza /'æflu:wɒnzɒ/ *n* a psychological disease resulting from an excess of affluence.

afflux /'æflʌks/ *n* a flowing towards; an increase; an influx.

afford /ə'fɔrd/ *vt* to be in a position to do or bear without much inconvenience; to have enough time, money, or resources for; to supply, produce.

afforest /ə'fɒrəst/ or /-fɑr-/, /æ-/ *vt* to plant trees to cover with forest.—**afforestation** *n*.

affranchise /ə'fræntʃaɪz/ *vt* to free from an obligation or slavery; to enfranchise.—**affranchisement** *n*.

affray /ə'freɪ/ *n* a noisy fight.

affreightment /ə'freɪtmənt/ *n* the hire of a ship for the transportation of goods or freight.

affright /ə'fraɪt/ *vt* (*arch*) to frighten, to terrify; to alarm; to confuse.

affront /ə'frʌnt/ *vi* to insult or offend openly or deliberately. • *n* such an insult or offence.

affusion /ə'fju:ʒən/ *n* the act of pouring upon, *esp* in baptism.

Afghan /'æfgæn/ *adj* pertaining to Afghanistan. • *n* a native of Afghanistan.—*also* **Afghani**.

aficionado /əfiˌʃɒnɒdo:/ or /əˌfɪsjə'nɒdo:/ *n* (*pl* **aficionados**) a devotee of a particular sport, activity, etc.

afield /ə'fi:ld/ *adv* far away from home; to or at a distance; astray.

afire /ə'faɪr/ *adj, adv* on fire.

aflame /ə'fleɪm/ *adj, adv* flaming, ablaze, in a glow.

afloat /ə'flo:t/ *adj* floating; at sea, on board a ship; debt-free; flooded.—*also adv*.

afoot /ə'fut/ *adj, adv* on foot; astir; on the move; in operation.

afore /ə'fɔr/ *adv, prep* in front, before; previously.

aforementioned /ə'fɔrˌmɛnʃənd/ *adj* mentioned previously.

aforesaid /-ˌsɛd/ *adj* referred to previously.

aforethought /-θɒt/ *adj* premeditated.

a fortiori /ˌeɪfɔrti'ɔri/ (*Latin*) with stronger reason, more conclusively.

afraid /ə'freɪd/ *adj* full of fear or apprehension; regretful.

afreet /'æfri:t/ *n* (*Arabian myth*) an evil demon.

afresh /ə'frɛʃ/ *adv* anew, starting again.

African /'æfrɪkən/ *adj* pertaining to Africa. • *n* a native of Africa.

African violet *n* any of various African plants popular as houseplants, with purple, pink or white flowers and velvet-textured leaves.

Afrikaans /ˌæfrɪ'kɒns/ *n* a language derived from Dutch used in South Africa.

Afrikander, Africander /ˌæfrɪ'kɒndər/ *n* (any of) a breed of southern African beef cattle.

Afrikaner /ˌæfrɪ'kɒnər/ *n* a South African native white, *esp* of Dutch descent.

Afro /'æfro:/ *n* (*pl* **Afros**) a bushy hairstyle.

Afro- /'æfro:/ *prefix* Africa or African.

Afro-American /ˌæfro:ə'mɛrɪkən/ *n* a Black American. • *adj* of or relating to Black Americans, or their culture, history, etc.

afrormosia /ˌæfrɔr'mo:zɪə/ *n* a hard wood similar to teak, used in furniture.

aft /æft/ *adv* at, near, or towards the stern of a ship or rear of an aircraft.

after /'æftər/ *prep* behind in place or order; following in time, later than; in pursuit of; in imitation of; in view of, in spite of; according to; about, concerning; subsequently. • *adv* later; behind. • *conj* at a time later than. • *adj* later, subsequent; nearer the stern of a ship or aircraft.

afterbirth /-ˌbərθ/ *n* the placenta expelled from the womb after giving birth.

afterbrain /-ˌbreɪn/ *n* that portion of the brain behind the hindbrain, the medulla oblongata.

afterburner /-ˌbərnər/ *n* a device in a jet engine used to provide extra thrust by igniting additional fuel.

aftercare /-ˌkɛr/ *n* care following hospital treatment, etc.

afterdamp /-ˌdæmp/ *n* the carbonic acid found in coal mines after an explosion of fire damp; choke damp.

aftereffect /-əˌfɛkt/ *n* an effect that occurs some time after its cause.

afterglow /-ˌglo:/ *n* the glow in the sky after sunset.

afterimage /-ˌɪmɪdʒ/ *n* the image that remains momentarily after the eye has been withdrawn from a bright object.

afterlife /-ˌlaɪf/ *n* life after death.

aftermath /-ˌmæθ/ *n* the result, *esp* an unpleasant one.

aftermost /-ˌmo:st/ *adj* hindmost; farthest aft, nearest to the stern.

afternoon /-ˌnu:n/ *n* the time between noon and sunset or evening.—*also adj*.

afternote /-ˌnoːt/ *n* the second or unaccented note, which takes its time from the first or accented note.

afterpains /-ˌpeɪnz/ *npl* pains after childbirth.

aftershave /-ˌʃeɪv/ *n* lotion for use after shaving.

aftertaste /-ˌteɪst/ *n* the taste that remains after eating or drinking.

afterthought /-ˌθɒt/ *n* a thought or reflection occurring later.

afterwards /-wərdz/, **afterward** /-ˌwərd/ *adv* at a later time.

afterwit /-ˌwɪt/ *n* wisdom that comes too late.

Ag (*chem symbol*) silver.

ag- /əg/ *prefix* the form of *ad-* before *g*.

aga /ˈɑːgə/ *n* in Turkey, a commander or chief officer; a title of respect.—*also* **agha**.

again /əˈgeɪn/ or /əˈgɛn/ *adv* once more; besides; on the other hand.

against /əˈgeɪnst/ or /əˈgɛnst/ *prep* in opposition to; unfavourable to; in contrast to; in preparation for; in contact with; as a charge on.

agalloch /əˈgæləʃ/ *n* a fragrant resinous heartwood.—*also* **eaglewood**.

agama /əˈgeɪmə/ *n* a short-tongued lizard found in India and Africa.

agami /əˈgæmi/ *n* a South American bird allied to the cranes; a trumpeter bird.

agamic /əˈgæmɪk/ *adj* (*biol*) produced without sexual action, asexual.—**agamically** *adj*.

agamogenesis /ˌægəˌmoːˌdʒɛnəsɪs/ *n* (*biol*) asexual reproduction.—**agamogenetic** *adj*.—**agamogenetically** *adv*.

agapanthus /ˌægəˈpænθəs/ *n* an ornamental plant with bright blue flowers.

agape /əˈgeɪp/ *adj* open-mouthed.

Agape /ˈægəˌpeɪ/ *n* the love feast of the early Christians at communion time.

agar /ˈeɪgɑr/ *n* a preparation of seaweed used for jelly, glue and bacteria culture.

agaric /ˈægərɪk/ *n* a mushroom or other fungus of the genus *Agaricus*.

agate /ˈægət/ *n* stone with striped or clouded colouring used as a gemstone.

agave /əˈgeɪvi/ *n* a genus of plants of which the chief species is the century plant.

age /eɪdʒ/ *n* the period of time during which someone or something has lived or existed; a stage of life; later years of life; a historical period; a division of geological time; (*inf: often pl*) a long time. • *vti* (**ageing** *or* **aging, aged**) to grow or make old, ripe, mature, etc.

aged /eɪdʒd/ *adj* very old; of a specified age. • *n* (*with* **the**) the elderly.

ageism /ˈeɪdʒɪzəm/ *n* discrimination on grounds of age.—*also* **agism**.—**ageist, agist** *adj*.

ageless /ˈeɪdʒləs/ *adj* timeless; appearing never to grow old.

age-long /-lɒŋ/ *see* **age-old**.

agency /ˈeɪdʒənsi/ *n* (*pl* **agencies**) action; power; means; a firm, etc empowered to act for another; an administrative government division.

agenda /əˈdʒɛndə/, **agendum** /-dəm/ *n* (*pl* **agendas, agendums**) a list of items or matters of business that need to be attended to.

agenesis /eɪˈdʒɛnəsɪs/ *n* imperfect development of the body.—**agenetic** *adj*.

agent /ˈeɪdʒənt/ *n* a person or thing that acts or has an influence; a substance or organism that is active; one empowered to act for another; a government representative; a spy.

agent general *n* the official representative of a Canadian province or Australian state in a foreign country or region.

agent provocateur *Fr.* /aˈʒɑ̃ːpʀɒvəkaˌtœr/ *n* (*pl* **agents provocateurs**) a person hired to tempt or provoke suspected persons into illegal acts so to incriminate themselves.

age-old /ˈeɪdʒˌoːld/ *adj* ancient.—*also* **age-long**.

agglomerate /əˈglɒməˌreɪt/ *vti* to gather into a heap; to accumulate; to collect into a mass. • *n* a heap or mass; a rock consisting of volcanic fragments.—**agglomeration** *n*.—**agglomerative** *adj*.

agglutinate /əˈgluːtɪˌneɪt/ *vti* to stick or fuse together; to form words into compounds. • *adj* glued together.—**agglutination** *n*.—**agglutinative** *adj*.

agglutination /-ˈneɪʃən/ *n* the act or condition of being united or joined together; the formation of words by combination, not inflexion.

aggrandize /əˈgrændaɪz/ *vt* to increase the power, rank, wealth, or reputation of.—**aggrandizement** *n*.

aggravate /ˈægrəˌveɪt/ *vt* to make worse; (*inf*) to annoy, irritate.—**aggravation** *n*.

aggravated /-ɪd/ *adj* (*law*) denoting a grave form of a specified offence.

aggravating /-ɪŋ/ *adj* making worse or more heinous; (*inf*) annoying, irritating.

aggregate /ˈægrəˌgeɪt/ *vt*, /ˈægrəgət/ *adj* formed of parts combined into a mass or whole; taking all units as a whole. • *n* a collection or sum of individual parts; sand, stones, etc mixed with cement to form concrete. • *vt* to collect or form into a mass or whole; to amount to (a total).—**aggregation** *n*.

aggression /əˈgrɛʃən/ *n* an unprovoked attack; a hostile action or behaviour.

aggressive /əˈgrɛsɪv/ *adj* boldly hostile; quarrelsome; self-assertive, enterprising.—**aggressively** *adv*.—**aggressiveness** *n*.

aggressor /əˈgrɛsər/ *n* a person or country that attacks first.

aggrieve /əˈgriːv/ *vt* to pain; to injure; to have a grievance; to bear heavily upon; to oppress.—**aggrieved** *adj*.—**aggrievedly** *adv*.

aggro *n* /ˈægro/ (*sl*) aggression.

agha /ˈægə/ *see* **aga**.

aghast /əˈgæst/ *adj* utterly horrified.

agile /ˈædʒaɪl/ or /ˈædʒəl/ *adj* quick and nimble in movement; mentally acute.—**agility** /əˈdʒɪləti/ *n*.

agio /ˈædʒioː/ *n* (*pl* **agios**) the premium on changing paper money into cash or for exchanging one currency for another.—**agiotage** *n*.

agism /ˈeɪdʒɪzəm/ *see* **ageism**.

agitate /ˈædʒɪˌteɪt/ *vt* to shake, move; to disturb or excite the emotions of. • *vi* to stir up public interest for a cause, etc.—**agitation** *n*.—**agitator** *n*.

agitato /ˌædʒɪˈtɒtoː/ *adj, adv* (*mus*) in a hurried or agitated manner.

agitator /ˈædʒɪˌteɪtər/ *n* one who starts or keeps up a political or other agitation; an implement for stirring.

aglet /ˈæglət/ *n* a tag (of a shoelace, etc); a spangle, a metallic ornament; a catkin.—*also* **aiglet**.

aglow /əˈgloː/ *adj* radiant with warmth or excitement.

AGM /ˈeɪˌdʒiːˈem/ *abbr* = Annual General Meeting.

agnail /ˈægneɪl/ *n* a sore under or near the nail, a hangnail.

agnate /ˈægneɪt/ *adj* related by the father's side or with the same male ancestor. • *n* a relative by the father's side.—**agnatic** *adj*.

agnomen /ægˈnoːmən/ *n* (*pl* **agnomina**) the fourth name of a person in ancient Rome; an additional name or epithet, as *Milton, the poet*.—**agnominal** *adj*.

agnostic /ægˈnɒstɪk/ *n* one who believes that knowledge of God is impossible. • *adj* pertaining to the agnostics or their teachings; expressing ignorance.—**agnostically** *adv*.—**agnosticism** *n*.

Agnus Dei /ˌægnʊsˈdeiiː/ or /ˌænjʊs-/ *n* a figure of a lamb bearing a banner or cross, symbolic of Christ and associated emblematically with St John the Baptist; the lamb and flag; a medal of wax or precious metal stamped with the figure of the Agnus Dei and blessed by the pope for distribution on Low Sunday.

ago /əˈgoː/ *adv* in the past. • *adj* gone by; past.

agog /əˈgɒg/ *adj, adv* in agitation or expectation; eager, on the lookout.

agonic /əˈgɒnɪk/ or /-eɪ-/ *adj* making no angle.

agonistic /ˌægəˈnɪstɪk/ *adj* of athletic contests; athletic; polemic; melodramatic; strained; unnatural.

agonize /ˈægəˌnaɪz/ *vti* to suffer or cause to suffer agony; to strive.—**agonizingly** *adv*.

agony /ˈægəni/ *n* (*pl* **agonies**) extreme mental or physical suffering.

agony aunt *n* a person who replies to readers' problem letters in an agony column.

agony column *n* the column of a newspaper devoted to advertisements relating to lost friends, etc; a column in a magazine containing readers' letters with helpful replies to problems.

agoraphobia /ˌægərəˈfoːbiə/ *n* abnormal fear of crossing open places.—**agoraphobic** *adj, n*.

agouti /əˈguːti/ *n* (*pl* **agoutis, agouties**) a rodent similar to the guinea pig found in the West Indies and South America.

AGR *abbr* = advanced gas-cooled reactor.

agraphia /eɪˈgræfiə/ *n* the inability to write due to mental illness.

agrarian /əˈgreriən/ *adj* of or relating to fields, or their cultivation; of or relating to farmers or agricultural life. • *n* an advocate of redistribution of property in land.

agrarianism /-ˌɪzəm/ *n* the principle of a uniform division of land; agitation with respect to land tenure.

agree /ə'griː/ vb (**agreeing, agreed**) vi to be of similar opinion; to consent or assent (to); to come to an understanding about; to be consistent; to suit a person's digestion; (gram) to be consistent in gender, number, case, or person. • vt to concede, grant; to bring into harmony; to reach terms on.

agreeable /-əbəl/ adj likeable, pleasing; willing to agree.—**agreeableness** n.—**agreeably** adv.

agreement /-mənt/ n harmony in thought or opinion, correspondence; an agreed settlement between two people, etc.

agrestic /ə'grɛstɪk/ adj rustic; uncouth.

agriculture /,ægrɪ'kʌltʃər/ n the science or practice of producing crops and raising livestock; farming.—**agricultural** adj.—**agriculturally** adv.—**agriculturist, agriculturalist** n.

agrimony /'ægrɪ,moːni/ n (pl **agrimonies**) a yellow-flowered plant.

agronomics /,ægrə'nɒmɪks/ n (used as sing) the part of economics concerned with the management and distribution of farming lands.—**agronomic, agronomical** adj.

agronomy /ə'grɒnəmi/ n the science of land cultivation and management, husbandry.—**agronomist** n.

agrostology /,ægrəs'tɒlədʒi/ n the branch of botany that treats of the grasses.

aground /ə'graund/ adj, adv on or onto the shore.

aguardiente /,əgwɑr'djenteɪ/ n an inferior Spanish brandy.

ague /'eɪgjuː/ n malaria, an intermittent fever; the cold fit of the intermittent fever.—**aguish** adj.

ah /ɒ/ interj an exclamation of sudden emotion.

AH abbr = anno Hegirae (in the year of the Hegira) used in dates of the Muslim era.

aha /ɒ'hɒ/ or /ə'hɒ/ interj an exclamation of satisfaction, triumph or mockery.

ahead /ə'hɛd/ adj in or to the front; forward; onward; in advance; winning or profiting.—also adv.

ahem /ə'həm/ or /ə'hɛm/ interj an exclamation to call attention.

ahoy /ə'hɔɪ/ interj a term used in hailing a vessel.

A.I. abbr = artificial insemination; artificial intelligence.

ai /'ɒi/ n (pl **ais**) a South American three-toed sloth.

aid /eɪd/ vti to help, give assistance to. • n anything that helps; a specific means of assistance, eg money, equipment; a helper.

AID abbr = Agency for International Development; artificial insemination (by) donor.

aide /eɪd/ n an aide-de-camp; assistant.

aide-de-camp /,eɪddə'kɑ̃/ n (pl **aides-de-camp**) a military officer serving as an assistant to a senior officer.

aide-mémoire /,eɪdmɛ'mwɑr/, Fr. /ɛdmeɪ'mwaʀ/ n (pl **aides-mémoire**) a summarized document; a memorandum, etc, as an aid to the memory.

AIDS, Aids /eɪdz/ n (acronym for acquired immune deficiency syndrome) a condition caused by a virus, HIV, in which the body loses its immunity to infection.

AIDS-related complex /'eɪdzrɪ,leɪtɪd-/ n a condition in which mild symptoms of AIDS (eg fever, weight loss) precede development of the full-blown disease.

aiglet see **aglet**.

aigrette, aigret /eɪ'grɛt/ or /'eɪgrɛt/ n a small white heron; a plume arranged in imitation of the feathers of the heron, worn on helmets and as a hat decoration.

aiguille /eɪ'gwiːl/ n a sharp peak of rock.

aiguillette /,eɪgwi'lɛt/ n an ornamental tag or lace worn on uniforms and liveries.

AIH abbr = artificial insemination (by) husband.

ail /eɪl/ vt to give or cause pain. • vi to feel pain; to be afflicted with pain.

aileron /'eɪlə,rɒn/ n a hinged section on the wing of an aircraft used for lateral control.

ailing /'eɪlɪŋ/ adj unwell.

ailment /-mənt/ n a slight illness.

ailurophobia /eɪ,lurə'fɒːbiə/ or /aɪ-/ n cat fear; a morbid dread of cats and a consciousness of their presence even when they are not in sight.—**ailurophobe** n.

aim /eɪm/ vti to point or direct towards a target so as to hit; to direct (one's efforts); to intend. • n the act of aiming; purpose, intention.

aimless /'eɪmləs/ adj without purpose or object.—**aimlessly** adv.—**aimlessness** n.

ain't /eɪnt/ (inf) = am not, is not, are not, has not, have not.

air /ɛr/ n the mixture of invisible gases surrounding the earth; the earth's atmosphere; empty, open space; a light breeze; aircraft, aviation; outward appearance, demeanour; a pervading influence; (mus) a melody; (pl) an affected manner. • vt to expose to the air for drying, etc; to expose to public notice; (clothes) to place in a warm place to finish drying.

airbag /'ɛrbæg/ n a safety device in a motor vehicle that automatically inflates to protect the occupants in the event of an accident.

air base n a base for military aircraft.

air bath n a lengthened exposure of the body to the action of the air and sun; an arrangement for drying articles by exposing them to air of any regulated temperature.

air bed n an inflatable mattress usu of plastic or rubber.

airborne /-bɔrn/ adj carried by or through the air; aloft or flying.

air box n a tube for conveying fresh air to a mine; a flue supplying air to a furnace; a chamber behind the fire box of a furnace to assist combustion by supply of air.

air brake n a brake operated by compressed air.

air brick n a brick with holes in the sides through which air for ventilation can pass.

airbrush /'ɛrbrʌʃ/ n a device for spraying paint by compressed air.

airbus n a jet aircraft designed for short-distance intercity flights.

air conditioning n regulation of air humidity and temperature in buildings, etc.

air-cooled /'ɛrkuːld/ adj cooled by having air passed over, into, or through.

air course n a ventilating passage in a mine.

air cover n protection for ground forces given by fighter aircraft; the aircraft giving this protection.

aircraft /'ɛrkræft/ n (pl **aircraft**) any machine for travelling through air.

aircraft carrier n a warship with a large flat deck, for the carrying, taking off and land of aircraft.

aircrew /'ɛrkruː/ n the crew of an aircraft.

air cushion n an inflatable cushion usu of plastic or rubber.

air drop /'ɛrdrɒp/ n a dropping by parachute of troops and supplies.

Airedale /'ɛrdeɪl/ n a large rough-coated terrier.

airfield /'ɛrfiːld/ n a field where aircraft can take off and land.

air force the aviation branch of a country's armed forces.

air gas n an illuminating gas made from air charged with the vapour of petroleum, naphtha, etc.

airgun /'ɛrgʌn/ n a gun that fires pellets by compressed air.

airhead /-hɛd/ n (sl) a stupid person.

air hostess n a stewardess on a passenger aircraft.

airing /'ɛrɪŋ/ n exposure to the open air for drying or freshening; exercise in the open air; exposure to public view.

airless /'ɛrləs/ adj stuffy; sultry.—**airlessness** n.

air letter n a sheet of light writing paper that is folded and sealed for sending by airmail.

airlift /-lɪft/ n the transport of cargo, troops, passengers, etc by air, esp in an emergency.—also vt.

airline /-laɪn/ n a system or company for transportation by aircraft; a beeline.

airliner /-,laɪnər/ n a large passenger aeroplane.

airlock /-lɒk/ n a blockage in a pipe caused by an air bubble; an airtight compartment giving access to a pressurized chamber.

airmail /-meɪl/ n mail transported by aircraft.

airman /-mən/ n (pl **airmen**) a male civilian or military pilot, etc.—**airwoman** nf (pl **airwomen**).

airmiss /-mɪs/ n the near collision of aircraft in flight.

airplane /-pleɪn/ see **aeroplane**.

air plant n a plant that derives its nourishment from the air, an epiphyte.

airplay /-pleɪ/ n the playing of a recording over radio or TV.

air pocket n a patch of rarefied air causing aircraft to drop abruptly.

airport /-pɔrt/ n a place where aircraft can land and take off, with facilities for repair, etc.

air pump n a machine for exhausting the air from a receiver; the pump used to exhaust the water and gases from the condenser of a steam engine.

air raid n an attack by military aircraft on a surface target.

airs /'ɛrz/ npl affected behaviour for the purpose of impressing others.

airship /'ɛrʃɪp/ n a self-propelled steerable aircraft that is lighter than air.

airsick /-sɪk/ *adj* nauseated due to the motion of an aircraft.

airspace /-speɪs/ *n* the space above a nation over which it maintains jurisdiction.

airspeed /-spiːd/ *n* the speed of an aircraft relative to the outside air.

airstrip /-strɪp/ *n* an area of land cleared for aircraft to land on; a runway.

airtight /-taɪt/ *adj* too tight for air or gas to enter or escape; (*alibi, etc*) invulnerable.

airtime /-taɪm/ *n* (*radio, TV*) the time alotted to a programme, item, commercial, etc; the time at which the broadcast begins.

air-to-air /ˈɛrtuːˈɛr/ *adj* (*weaponry, communications, etc*) activated between aircraft in flight.

air valve *n* a valve regulating the supply of air to a boiler or pipe.

air vesicle *n* a dilatation of the trachea of certain insects enabling them to ascend or descend by its inflation or expiration; a vesicle filled with air in certain fishes, connected with the swim bladder.

airway /ˈɛrweɪ/ *n* an aircraft route; a ventilation passage, as in a mine; a passage for air into the lungs; (*med*) a device to maintain the airway of an unconscious person.

airworthy /-ˌwɜrði/ *adj* safe to fly.—**airworthiness** *n*.

airy /ˈɛri/ *adj* (**airier, airiest**) open to the air; breezy; light as air; graceful; lighthearted; flippant.—**airily** *adv*.—**airiness** *n*.

aisle /aɪl/ *n* a passageway, as between rows of seats; a side part of a church.

ait /eɪt/ *n* a small island in a river or lake.—*also* **eyot**.

aitch /eɪtʃ/ *n* the letter H.

aitchbone /ˈeɪtʃboːn/ *n* the rump bone; the cut of meat lying over it.

ajar /əˈdʒɑr/ *adv* partly open, as a door.

AK *abbr* = Alaska.

aka, a.k.a. *or* **AKA** /ˌeɪˌkeɪˈeɪ/ *abbr* = *also* known as.

akimbo /əˈkɪmboː/ *adv* having the hands on the hips and the elbows bent outwards.

akin /əˈkɪn/ *adj* related; essentially similar, compatible.

Akkadian /əˈkeɪdiən/ *n* an ancient Babylonian language preserved in cuneiform inscriptions. • *adj* of Akkad or Accad, the Babylonian city.—*also* **Accadian**.

al- /æl/ *or* /əl/ *prefix* the form of *ad-* before *l*.

-al /əl/ *adj suffix* of, of the nature of, as in *mortal, colossal*. • *n suffix esp* of verbal action, as in *approval*.

AL *abbr* = Alabama.

Al (*chem symbol*) = aluminium.

Ala. *abbr* = Alabama.

à la /ˈælə/ *or* /ˈɒlə/ *prep* in the style of.

alabaster /ˈæləˌbæstər/ *or* /ˌæləˌbæstər/ *n* a type of soft, chalky stone used in ornaments.—**alabastrine** *adj*.

à la carte /ˌæləˈkɑrt/ *or* /ˌɒlə-/ *adj* (*menu*) with dishes listed and priced as separate items.

alack /əˈlæk/ *interj* an exclamation of blame, sorrow, or surprise.

alacrity /əˈlækrɪti/ *n* promptness, eager readiness.—**alacritous** *adj*.

alameda /ˌæləˈmiːdə/ *n* a public promenade planted with trees.

à la mode /ˌæləˈmoːd/ *or* /ˌɒlə-/ *adv* in the fashion. • *adj* fashionable.

alamode *n* a thin, light, glossy black silk.

alar /ˈeɪlər/ *adj* of wings; winged; winglike; wing-shaped.—*also* **alary**.

alarm /əˈlɑrm/ *n* a signal warning of danger; an automatic device to arouse from sleep or to attract attention; the fear arising from the expectation of danger. • *vt* to give warning of danger; to fill with apprehension or fear.

alarm clock *n* a clock with an apparatus that can be set to ring loudly at a particular time.

alarming /-ɪŋ/ *adj* frightening, disconcerting.—**alarmingly** *adv*.

alarmist /-ɪst/ *n* one who keeps prophesying danger, a panic-monger.—**alarmism** *n*.

alarum /əˈlærəm/ *n* (*arch*) an alarm.

alary /ˈeɪləri/ *or* /ˈæləri/ *see* **alar**.

alas /əˈlæs/ *interj* expressive of misery, unhappiness, grief, etc.

alate /ˈeɪˌleɪt/ *adj* having wings or winglike side appendages.

alb /ælb/ *n* a white priestly vestment reaching to the feet, worn at the celebration of the Eucharist in the RC Church and in some Anglican churches.

albacore /ˈælbəˌkoːr/ *n* a large species of mackerel or tunny found in the Atlantic and Pacific Oceans.

albata an alloy imitating silver; German silver.

albatross /ˈælbəˌtrɒs/ *n* any of various large web-footed seabirds; a heavy burden, as of debt, guilt, etc; (*golf*) a score of three under par.

albeit /ɒlˈbiːət/ *conj* although, even though, notwithstanding.

albescent /ælˈbɛsənt/ *adj* shading into white; whitish; becoming white.—**albescence** *n*.

albino /ælˈbaɪnoː/ *n* (*pl* **albinos**) a person lacking normal coloration, so that they have white skin and pink eyes; an animal or plant with abnormal pigmentation.

Albion /ˈælbiən/ *n* (*arch*) Britain.

album /ˈælbəm/ *n* a book with blank pages for the insertion of photographs, autographs, etc; a long-playing record, cassette, or CD.

albumen /ˈælbjuːmɪn/ *n* the white of an egg.

albumenize /-ˌaɪz/ *vt* to coat (paper) with an albuminous solution.

albuminoid /-ˌnɔɪd/ *adj* like albumen. • *n* a class of organic compounds that form the chief part of the organs and tissues of animals and plants; proteids.

albuminous /ælˈbjuːmɪnəs/ *adj* like, or containing, albumin.

albuminuria /ælˌbjuːmɪˈniəriə/ *or* /-ˈnjʊr-/ *n* the presence of albumin in the kidneys and the urine.

alburnum /ælˈbɜrnəm/ *n* the white and softer part of wood between the bark and the heartwood; sapwood.

alcahest *see* **alkahest**.

Alcaic /ælˈkeɪɪk/ *n* a kind of lyric verse form consisting of four lines of four feet devised by the 7th-century BC Greek poet Alcaeus.—*also adj*.

alcaide /ælˈkaɪd/ *or* /-ˈkeɪd/ *n* the commander of a castle in Spain; the warder of a Spanish jail.

alcalde /ɒlˈkɒldi/, **alcade** *n* a magistrate or justice in Spain or Portugal.

alcazar /ˈælkəˌzɑr/ *or* /ælˈkæzər/ *n* a Spanish or Moorish palace or castle.

alchemist /ˈælkəmɪst/ *n* one who studies or practises alchemy.

alchemize /-maɪz/ *vt* to transmute.

alchemy /ˈælkəmi/ *n* (*pl* **alchemies**) chemistry as practised during medieval times, with the aim of transmuting base metals into gold.—**alchemic, alchemical** *adj*.—**alchemist** *n*.

alcohol /ˈælkəhɒl/ *n* a liquid, generated by distillation and fermentation, that forms the intoxicating agent in wine, beer and spirits; a liquid containing alcohol; a chemical compound of this nature.

alcoholic /ˌælkəˈhɒlɪk/ *adj* of or containing alcohol; caused by alcohol. • *n* a person suffering from alcoholism.

alcoholism /ˈælkəˌhɒlɪzəm/ *n* a disease caused by excessive consumption of alcohol.

alcoholize /-aɪz/ *vt* to subject to the influence of alcohol; to rectify (spirits of wine).—**alcoholization** *n*.

alcoholometer /-ˌhɒləmətər/ *n* an instrument for determining the strength of spirits.

Alcoran /ˌælkoːˈrɒn/ *or* /-ˈræn/ *n* the Koran, the Muslim bible.

alcove /ˈælˌkoːv/ *n* a recess off a larger room.

aldehyde /ˈældəˌhaɪd/ *n* a volatile fluid with a suffocating smell, obtained from alcohol.

al dente /ælˈdɛnteɪ/ *or* /æl-/ *adj* cooked but still firm to the teeth.

alder /ˈɒldər/ *n* a genus of plants growing in moist land and related to the birch.

alderman /ˈɒldərmən/ *n* (*pl* **aldermen**) in US, a member of certain municipal councils; (*formerly*) in England and Wales, a senior councillor.—**aldermanic** *adj*.

ale /eɪl/ *n* beer.

aleatory /ˈeɪliəˌtɔri/ *adj* depending on dice or chance.

alee /əˈliː/ *adj, adv* (*naut*) on the lee, to leeward.

alegar /ˈæləgər/ *or* /ˈɒl-/ *n* vinegar made from ale.

alehouse /ˈeɪlˌhɐʊs/ *n* a place where ale is sold.

alembic /əˈlɛmbɪk/ *n* an apparatus formerly used in distilling.

Alençon /əˈlɛnˌsɒn/ *or* /ˈsən/, *Fr.* /alɑ̃sɔ̃ː/ *n* a fine lace made at Alençon in France.

alert /əˈlɜrt/ *adj* watchful; active, brisk. • *n* a danger signal. • *vt* to warn of impending danger, put in a state of readiness.—**alertly** *adv*.—**alertness** *n*.

alexandrine /ˌæləgzændrɪn/ *or* /-ˌdriːn/ *n* a heroic verse of six iambic feet, or twelve syllables.—*also adj*.

alexia /əˈlɛksiə/ *n* the inability to read, due to mental illness.

alexin /əˈlɛksɪn/ *n* a disease-resisting protein in blood serum.

alfalfa /ælˈfælfə/ *n* a deep-rooted leguminous plant grown widely for hay and forage.—*also* **lucerne**.

alfresco /ælˈfreskoː/ or /ɑl-/ *adj* taking place outside in the open.—*also adv.*

alga /ˈælgə/ *n* (*pl* **algae**) any of a group of chiefly aquatic lower plants classified according to colour.—**algal** *adj.*

algarroba, algaroba /ˌælgəˈroːbə/ *n* the carob tree and bean; St John's bread.

algebra /ˈældʒəbrə/ *n* the branch of mathematics dealing with the properties and relations of numbers; the generalization and extension of arithmetic.—**algebraic, algebraical** *adj.*—**algebraist** *n.*

Algerian /ælˈdʒiːriən/ *adj* pertaining to Algeria or Algiers. • *n* a native of Algeria or Algiers.

Algerine /ˌældʒəˈriːn/ *adj* Algerian.

-algia /ˈældʒə/ or /-dʒiə/ *n suffix* pain.—**algic** *adj.*

algid /ˈældʒɪd/ *adj* cold, chilly.

ALGOL /ˈælˌgɒl/ *acronym* (*comput*) a high-level programming language used for solving general problems in science and mathematics.

algology /ælˈgɒlədʒi/ *n* the study of algae.—**algologist** *n.*

Algonquian /ælˈgɒŋkwiən/ or /-kiən/ *n* a group of eastern North American Indian languages; a member of a North American Indian people who speaks one of these languages. • *adj* of or pertaining to these peoples or their languages.

algor /ˈælgɔr/ *n* the rigor or chill on the onset of fever.

algorism /ˈælgərizəm/ *n* the arabic (decimal) numeration; arithmetic.—**algorismic** *adj.*

algorithm /ˈælgərɪðəm/ *n* (*math*) any method or procedure for computation.—**algorithmic** *adj.*—**algorithmically** *adv.*

alias /ˈeɪliəs/ *adv* otherwise called. • *n* (*pl* **aliases**) an assumed name.

alibi /ˈælɪˌbaɪ/ *n* (*pl* **alibis**) (*law*) the plea that a person charged with a crime was elsewhere when it was committed; (*inf*) any excuse.

alien /ˈeɪliən/ *adj* foreign; strange; distasteful to, counter to. • *n* a person from another country, place, etc; a person of foreign birth who has not been naturalized; a being from outer space.

alienable /-əbəl/ *adj* (*law*) (*property*) that may be transferred.—**alienability** *n.*

alienage /ˈeɪliənɪdʒ/ *n* the state or legal status of an alien.

alienate /ˈeɪliəneɪt/ *vt* to render hostile or unfriendly; to make less affectionate or interested.

alienation /ˌeɪliənˈeɪʃən/ *n* estrangement; transference; diversion to another purpose; mental derangement.

alienee /ˌeɪliənˈiː/ *n* (*law*) one to whom property is transferred.

alienism /ˈeɪliənizəm/ *n* the study and treatment of mental alienation.—**alienist** *n.*

alienor /-ər/ or /-ɔr/ *n* (*law*) one who transfers property to another.

aliform /ˈeɪlɪˌfɔrm/ *adj* wing-shaped.

alight[1] /əˈlɔɪt/ *vi* (**alighting, alighted** *or* **alit**) to come down, as from a bus; to land after a flight.

alight[2] *adj* on fire; lively.

align /əˈlaɪn/ *vt* to place in a straight line, to bring into agreement, etc. • *vi* to line up.—**alignment** *n.*

alignment /-mənt/ *n* the act of laying out or adjusting by a line; the ground plan of a railway or road.

alike /əˈlaɪk/ *adj* like one another. • *adv* equally; similarly.

aliment /ˈælɪmənt/ *n* food; the necessaries of life generally; an allowance for support by decree of court. • *vt* to make provision for the maintenance of; to make provision for the support of parents or children respectively.—**alimental** *adj.*

alimentary /ˌælɪˈmentəri/ *adj* pertaining to nourishment, food.

alimentary canal *n* the tube extending within the body from the mouth to the anus through which food passes and is absorbed.

alimentation /ˌælɪmənˈteɪʃən/ *n* the act of giving nourishment; the function of the alimentary canal.—**alimentative** *adj.*

alimony /ˈæləˌmoːni/ *n* (*pl* **alimonies**) an allowance for support made by one spouse to the other, *esp* a man to his wife or former wife, pending or after a legal separation or divorce.

aliped /ˈælɪˌped/ *adj* having wing-like limbs, as the bat.

aliphatic /ˌælɪˈfætɪk/ *adj* (*chem*) of fat.

aliquant /ˈælɪkwənt/ or /-kwɒnt/ *adj* (*math*) being a part of a number that does not divide it without a remainder, as 8 is the aliquant part of 25.—*also n.*

aliquot /ˈælɪkwət/ or /-kwɒt/ *adj* (*math*) being a part of a number

of quantity that will divide it without a remainder, as 8 is the aliquot part of 24.—*also n.*

alive /əˈlaɪv/ *adj* having life; active, alert; in existence, operation, etc.

alizarin /əˈlɪzərɪn/ *n* a red colouring matter found in madder but now produced from anthracene.

alkahest /ˈælkəˌhest/ *n* the supposed universal solvent of the alchemists.—*also* **alcahest.**

alkali /ˈælkəlaɪ/ *n* (*pl* **alkalis, alkalies**) (*chem*) any salt or mixture that neutralizes acids.—**alkaline** *adj.*

alkalify /ˈælkəlɪˌfaɪ/ *vb* (**alkalifying, alkalified**) *vt* to form or convert into alkali. • *vi* to become an alkali.

alkalimeter /ˌælkəˈlɪmətər/ *n* an instrument used to determine the relative strength of alkalis.

alkalimetry /-mətri/ *n* the process of determining the strength of an alkaline mixture or liquid.—**alkalimetric** *adj.*

alkaline /ˈælkəˌlaɪn/ or /-ˌlaɪn/ *adj* pertaining to, or having the properties of, an alkali.—**alkalinity** *n.*

alkalize /-ˌlaɪz/ *vt* to convert into an alkali or render alkaline.—**alkalizable** *adj.*

alkaloid /-ˌlɔɪd/ *n* a body or substance containing alkaline properties; (*pl*) nitrogenous compounds met with in plants in combination with organic acids. • *adj* resembling an alkali in its properties.

alkanet /ˈælkəˌnet/ *n* a rich red dye; the plant the root of which yields it.

all /ɒl/ *adj* the whole amount or number of; every one of. • *adv* wholly; supremely, completely; entirely. • *n* the whole number, quantity; everyone; everything.

alla breve /ˌɒləˈbreve/ *adv* (*mus*) in quick time, with one breve to a measure.

Allah /ˈælə/ or /ˈɒlə/ *n* the Muslim name of God.

all along *adv* throughout.

allantoid /əˈlænˌtoːɪd/ *adj* of or pertaining to the allantois; (*bot*) sausage-shaped. • *n* the allantois.—**allantoidal** *adj.*

allantois /əˈlænˌtoːɪs/ *n* (*pl* **allantoides**) a membranous appendage of most vertebrate embryos.

allay /əˈleɪ/ or /ə-/ *vt* to lighten, alleviate; to pacify or make calm.

all but *adv* almost.

all clear /ˌɒlˈklɪr/ *n* a signal indicating that a danger has passed or that it is safe to proceed.

allegation /ˌæləˈgeɪʃən/ *n* the act of alleging; assertion; declaration; that which is asserted or alleged; that which is offered as a plea, an excuse, or justification; the statement as yet unproved of a party to a suit.

allege /əˈledʒ/ *vt* to assert or declare, *esp* without proof; to offer as an excuse.

allegedly /əˈledʒədli/ *adv* asserted without proof.

allegiance /əˈliːdʒəns/ *n* the obligation of being loyal to one's country, etc; devotion, as to a cause.

allegorical /ˌæləˈgɒrɪkəl/ or /-ˈgɑr-/, **allegoric** *adj* pertaining to, consisting of, or in the nature of allegory; figurative.—**allegorically** *adv.*

allegorize /ˈæləgəˌraɪz/ or /ˌæləgɒˌraɪz/ *vt* to put in the form of an allegory.—**allegorization** *n.*

allegory /ˈæləˌgɒri/ or /-ˌgɑri/ *n* (*pl* **allegories**) a fable, story, poem, etc in which the events depicted are used to convey a deeper, *usu* moral or spiritual, meaning.—**allegorist** *n.*

allegretto /ˌæləˈgretoː/ *adv* (*mus*) moderately fast. • *n* (*pl* **allegrettos**) a piece of music played in this way.

allegro /əˈlegroː/ *adv* (*mus*) fast. • *n* (*pl* **allegros**) a piece of music played in this way.

allele /æˈliːl/ *n* (*genetics*) either of a pair of contrasting characteristics one or the other of which is found unmixed in descendants of a cross between parental forms respectively possessing them.—*also* **allelomorph.—allelic** *adj.*—**allelism** *n.*

alleluia /ˌæləˈluːjə/ or /ˌɒleɪ-/ *see* **hallelujah.**

allemande /ˌæləˈmænd/ or /-ˈmɑnd/ *n* a German national dance in three-quarter time.

allergen /ˈælərdʒən/ *n* a substance inducing an allergic reaction.

allergenic /-ˌdʒenɪk/ *adj* causing an allergic reaction.

allergy /ˈælərdʒi/ *n* (*pl* **allergies**) an abnormal reaction of the body to substances (certain foods, pollen, etc) normally harmless; antipathy.—**allergic** *adj.*

allerion /ə'lɛrɪən/ *n* (*her*) an eagle displayed without feet or beak.

alleviate /ə'li:vɪeɪt/ *vt* to lessen or relieve (pain, worry, etc).—**alleviation** *n*.—**alleviator** *n*.

alleviative /ə'li:vɪˌeɪtɪv/ *adj* tending to alleviate. • *n* that which alleviates.

alley /'æli/ *n* a narrow street between or behind buildings; a bowling lane.

all fours *adv* on hands and knees.

All-hallowe'en /ˌɒl'hæloːˌwiːn/ *n* Hallowe'en.

All-hallows /ˌɒl'hæloːz/ *npl* All Saints' Day, celebrated on 1 November, in honour of all the saints.

alliaceous /ˌæli'eɪʃəs/ *adj* of the nature or property of garlic or the onion.

alliance /ə'laɪəns/ *n* a union by marriage or treaty for a common purpose; an agreement for this; the countries, groups, etc in such an association.

allied /æ'laɪd/ or /ə'laɪd/ *see* **ally**.

alligator /'æliˌgeɪtər/ *n* a large reptile similar to the crocodile but having a short, blunt snout.

alligator pear *n* the avocado.

all in *adj* (*price, etc*) all-inclusive.

all-in *adj* (*inf*) exhausted.

all-inclusive /ˌɒlɪn'kluːzɪv/ *adj* including everything.

alliteration /əˌlɪtə'reɪʃən/ *n* the repetition of the same sound at the beginning of two or more words in a phrase, etc.—**alliterative** *adj*.

allocate /'æləˌkeɪt/ *vt* to distribute or apportion in shares; to set apart for a specific purpose.

allocation /ˌælə'keɪʃən/ *n* the act of alloting, allocating, or assigning; an allotment or assignment; an allowance made on an account.

allocution /ˌæləkju:ʃən/ *n* a formal address, *esp* as one delivered by the Pope to his clergy or to the Church generally.

allodial /æ'loːdɪəl/ *adj* freehold; not feudal. • *n* land thus held.

allodium /-əm/, **allod** *n* (*pl* **allodia, allods**) freehold estate; land that is the absolute property of the owner.

allogamy /ə'lɒgəmi/ *n* (*biol*) cross-fertilization.—**allogamous** *adj*.

allograph /'æləˌgræf/ *n* a signature by one person on behalf of another, opposite of autograph.—**allographic** *adj*.

allomorphism /ˌælə'mɔrfɪzəm/ *n* (*chem*) the property in certain substances of assuming a different form while remaining the same in constitution.

all one *adj, n* in effect the same.

allopath /'æləpæθ/, **allopathist** /ə'lɒpəθɪst/ *n* one who favours or practises allopathy.

allopathy /ə'lɒpəθi/ *n* the orthodox medical practice of treating disease by inducing an action opposite to the disease it is sought to cure, opposite of homoeopathy.—**allopathic** *adj*.—**allopathically** *adv*.

allophone /'æləˌfoːn/ *n* a phonetic term describing any of various possible contextual or environmental variants of the same phoneme.—**allophonic** *adj*.

allot /ə'lɒt/ *vt* (**allotting, allotted**) to distribute, allocate.

allotment /-mənt/ *n* allotting; a share allotted; a small area of land rented for cultivation.

allotropy /ə'lɒtrəpi/, **allotropism** *n* the capability shown by certain chemical elements to assume different forms, each characterized by peculiar qualities, as the occurrence of carbon in the form of the diamond, charcoal and plumbago respectively.—**allotropic** *adj*.—**allotropically** *adv*.

allottee /əˌlɒt'iː/ *n* one to whom an allotment or share is granted or assigned; a plot-holder.

all out /'ɔl'aʊt/ *adv* with maximum capacity.

all-out *adj* using maximum effort.

all-over /'ɔl'oːvər/ *adj* covering the whole surface.

allow /ə'laʊ/ *vt* to permit; to acknowledge, admit as true; (*money*) to give, grant as an allowance at regular intervals; to estimate as an addition or deduction. • *vi* to admit the possibility (of).

allowable /ə'laʊəbəl/ *adj* permissible.—**allowably** *adv*.

allowance /ə'laʊəns/ *n* an amount or sum allowed or given at regular times; a discount; a portion of income not subject to income tax; permission; admission, concession.

alloy /æ'lɔɪ/ *n* a solid substance comprising a mixture of two or more metals; something that degrades the substance to which it is added. • *vt* to make into an alloy; to degrade or spoil by mixing with an inferior substance.

all-purpose /'ɒlˌpɜrpəs/ *adj* suitable for many uses.

all right *adv* good enough, acceptable; without doubt. • *adj* satisfactory; safe, well; agreeable. • *interj* (*used to express consent*).—*also* **alright**.

all-round /'ɒlˌraʊnd/ *adj* efficient in all respects, *esp* sport.

All Saints' Day *n* (*Christian Church*) 1 November, a festival in honour of all the saints.

All Souls' Day /-soːlz-/ *n* (*RC Church*) the day, celebrated 2 November, in honour of the departed.

allspice /'ɒlˌspaɪs/ *n* an aromatic spice made from the berry of a West Indian tree.

all-star /'ɒlˌstɑr/ *adj* made up entirely of outstanding performers.

all there *adj* (*sl*) not mentally wanting.

all-time /'ɒlˌtaɪm/ *adj* unsurpassed until now.

all told *adv* with all counted; all in all.

allude /ə'luːd/ *vi* to refer indirectly to.

allure /ə'lʊr/ *vt* to entice, charm. • *n* fascination; charm.—**allurement** *n*.

alluring /-ɪŋ/ *adj* attractive.

allusion /ə'luːʒən/ *n* alluding; an implied or indirect reference.—**allusive** *adj*.

allusive /ə'luːsɪv/ *adj* having reference to something not definitely expressed.—**allusively** *adv*.—**allusiveness** *n*.

alluvion /ə'luːvɪən/ *n* the wash of the sea or river against a shore; land added to a shore or riverbank by the action of the water; an overflow.

alluvium /ə'luːvɪəm/ *n* (*pl* **alluviums, alluvia**) earth, sand, gravel, etc deposited by moving water.—**alluvial** *adj*.

ally /æ'laɪ/ *vti* (**allying, allied**) to join or unite for a specific purpose; to relate by similarity of structure, etc. • *n* (*pl* **allies**) a country or person joined with another for a common purpose.

Almagest /'ælməˌdʒɛst/ *n* the great astronomical treatise of Ptolemy of the 2nd century ad; (*without cap*) other similar treatises.

alma mater /'ælmə'mɒtər/ or /'ɒl-/, /-'meɪt-/ *n* one's school, college, or university.

almanac /'ælməˌnæk/ or /'ɒl-/ *n* a calendar with astronomical data, weather forecasts, etc.

almanack /'ælməˌnæk/ or /'ɒl-/ *n* (*arch*) an almanac.

almandine /'ælmənˌdiːn/ or /-daɪn/ *n* a violet-red variety of garnet, tinged sometimes with blue or yellow.

almighty /ɒl'maɪti/ *adj* all-powerful. • *n* (*with cap*) God, the all-powerful.—**almightily** *adv*.—**almightiness** *n*.

almond /'ɒmənd/ or /'ɒl-/ *n* the edible kernel of the fruit of a tree of the rose family; the tree bearing this fruit. • *adj* (*eyes, etc*) oval and pointed at one or both ends.

almoner /'ɒlmənər/ *n* (*formerly*) one who dispenses or distributes alms or charity; an alms purse; a pouch or purse which in early times was suspended from the girdle.

almost /'ɒlmoːst/ *adv* all but, very nearly but not quite all.

alms /ɒmz/ *npl* money, food, etc given to the poor.

almshouse /-haʊz/ *n* a house endowed by private or public charity and appropriated to the use of the poor.

aloe /'æˌloː/ *n* (*pl* **aloes**) a succulent plant with tall spikes of flowers.

aloes /'æˌloːz/ *n* (*used as sing*) the bitter juice of the aloe plant used in medicine.

aloft /ə'lɒft/ *adv* in the air, flying; high up.

alone /ə'loːn/ *adj* isolated; without anyone or anything else; unassisted; unique. • *adv* exclusively.

along /ə'lɒŋ/ *adv* onward, forward; over the length of; in company and together with; in addition. • *prep* in the direction of the length of; in accordance with.

alongside /-saɪd/ *prep* close beside. • *adv* at the side.

aloof /ə'luːf/ *adv* at a distance; apart. • *adj* cool and reserved.—**aloofness** *n*.

alopecia /ˌælə'peɪʃə/ *n* baldness; loss of hair through skin disease.

aloud /ə'laʊd/ *adv* with a normal voice; loudly; spoken.

alow /ə'loː/ *adv* (*naut*) to or in a lower part; below.

alp /ælp/ *n* a mountain peak.

alpaca /æl'pækə/ *n* a Peruvian llama with long fine wool; a fabric made of this wool.

alpenglow /'ælpənˌgloː/ *n* a peculiar purple glow on the snow on the Alps seen just before sunrise and after sunset.

alpenhorn /-ˌhɔrn/ *n* a long and nearly straight horn used by the mountaineers of the Alps.

alpenstock /-ˌstɒk/ *n* a stout staff with an iron spike, used by mountain climbers.

alpha /'ælfə/ *n* the first letter of the Greek alphabet.

alphabet /'ælfə,bet/ *n* the characters used in a language arranged in conventional order.

alphabetical /'ælfə,betikəl/, **alphabetic** *adj* pertaining to an alphabet; in the order of the alphabet.—**alphabetically** *adv*.

alphabetize /'ælfəbə,taiz/ *vt* to arrange in alphabetical order.—**alphabetization** *n*.

alphanumeric /,ælfənu:'merik/ or /-nju:-/, **alphameric** /,ælfə'merik/ *adj* containing letters of the alphabet and numerals.—**alphanumerically, alphamerically** *adv*.

alpha particle *n* a particle of helium given off by radium.

alpha ray *n* radiation of alpha particles.

alpine /æl'pain/ *adj* (*with cap*) of the Alps; of high mountains. • *n* a mountain plant, *esp* a small herb.

alpinist /'ælpinist/ *n* a mountaineer who climbs in the Alps or in areas of similar mountains.—**alpinism** *n*.

Alps /ælps/ *npl* a high mountain range in south central Europe.

already /ɒl'redi/ *adv* by or before the time specified; before the time expected.

alright /ɒl'rait/ *adv* a frequent spelling of all right.

Alsatian /æl,seiʃən/ *n* a German shepherd; a native of Alsace.

also /'ɒlsəu/ *adv* in addition, besides.

also-ran /-,ræn/ *n* a defeated contestant in a race, an election, etc.

alt /ælt/ *n* (*mus*) the high notes above the treble staff.

Altaic /æl'teiik/ *adj* pertaining to the Altaic mountain regions, partly bounding Russia and China. • *n* the language of the region.

altar /'ɒltər/ *n* a table, etc for sacred purposes in a place of worship.

altarage *n* the offerings placed upon the altar to be devoted to the church, or appropriated by the priest as stipend.

altar cloth /-,klɒθ/ *n* a general term for the coverings of the altar.

altar ledge /-,ledz/ *n* a step or ledge behind the altar of a church, slightly raised above it for holding lights, flowers, and other symbolical ornaments; a retable.

altarpiece /-,pi:s/ *n* a painting, decorative screen, or other work of art, placed over or behind an altar.

altarscreen /-,skri:n/ *n* a screen or partition separating the altar from the choir; a reredos.

altar slab /-,slæb/ *n* the top of an altar; the consecrated part of an altar (the mensa).

altarwise /-,waiz/ *adv* placed in the usual position of an altar, with the ends towards the north and south, and the front to the west.

altazimuth /,æl'tæzəməθ/ *n* an instrument for determining the altitudes and azimuths of the stars and planets.

alter /'ɒltər/ *vti* to make or become different in a small way; to change.—**alterable** *adj*.—**alterability** *n*.

alteration /,ɒltər'eiʃən/ *n* the act of altering or changing; the change or modification effected.

alterative /'ɒltə,reitiv/ or /-tərətiv/ *adj* producing change; having the power to alter. • *n* a medicine that restores the healthy functions of the body.

altercate /'ɒltər,keit/ *vi* to contend in words; to wrangle; to dispute with anger or heat.

altercation /,ɒltər'keiʃən/ *n* an angry or heated quarrel.

alter ego /'ɒltər,i:gəu/ or /'æl-/ *n* one's other self; a constant companion.

alternant /'ɒltərnənt/ *adj* alternating; composed of alternate layers.

alternate¹ /'ɒltərneit/ *vt* to do or use by turns. • *vi* to act, happen, etc by turns; to take turns regularly.—**alternation** *n*.

alternate² *adj* occurring or following in turns.—**alternately** *adv*.

alternate angles *npl* the internal angles made by two lines with a third on opposite sides of it.

alternating current *n* an electric current that reverses its direction at regular intervals.

alternation /,ɒltər'neiʃən/ *n* the act of alternating, or state of being alternate; reciprocal succession; antiphonal singing or reading.

alternative /,ɒltər'neitiv/ *adj* presenting a choice between two things. • *n* either of two possibilities.—**alternatively** *adv*.

alternative comedy *n* a form of comedy that avoids conventional humour (e.g. racist and sexist jokes), characterized by aggressively delivered and blackly humourous stand-up routines that *usu* challenge political and social orthodoxy.

alternative medicine *n* any technique of medical treatment without use of drugs, *eg* osteopathy, acupuncture, dieting.

alternator /,ɒltər'neitər/ or /,æl-/ *n* an electric generator that produces alternating current.

althaea, althea /æl'θi:ə/ *n* a genus of plants including the marshmallow and the hollyhock.

althorn /'ælt,hɔːn/ *n* a musical instrument of the saxhorn class, frequently used in military bands.

although /ɒl'ðəu/ or /ɒl'θəu/ *conj* though; in spite of that.

altimeter /æl'timitər/ *n* an instrument for measuring altitude.

altimetry /-tri/ *n* the art of measuring altitudes by the use of the altimeter.—**altimetrical** *adj*.

altissimo /æl'tisiməu/ or /ɒl-/ *adj* (*mus*) of the part or notes situated above F in alt.

altitude /'ælti,tu:d/ or /-,tju:d/ *n* height, *esp* above sea level.—**altitudinal** *adj*.

alto /'æltəu/ or /'ɒltəu/ *n* (*pl* **altos**) the range of the highest male voice; a singer with this range; a contralto. • *adj* high.

alto clef /-klɛf/ *n* the C clef placed on the third line of the staff.

altogether /,ɒltə'geðər/ or /'ɒltəgeðər/ *adv* in all; on the whole; completely.

alto-relievo, alto-rilievo /,æltəurə'li:vəu/ *n* (*pl* **alto-relievos, alto-rilievos**) high relief; figures or other objects that stand out boldly from the background, and having more than half their thickness projecting.

altruism /'ɒl,tru:izəm/ or /'æl-/ *n* unselfish concern for or dedication to the interests or welfare of others.—**altruist** *n*.—**altruistic** *adj*.—**altruistically** *adv*.

aludel /'ælju:,del/ *n* one of the pear-shaped glass or earthenware pots, open at both ends, used in sublimation.

alum /ə'lʌm/ *n* a double sulphate formed of aluminium and some other element, usually an alkali metal.

alumina /ə'lu:minə/ *n* the single oxide of aluminium, the most abundant of the earths; a notable constituent of common clay, alumina is largely used in dyeing and calico printing as a mordant.

aluminiferous /ə,lu:mi'nəfərəs/ *adj* containing or yielding alum, alumina, or aluminium.

aluminium, aluminum /ə'lu:minəm/ *n* a silvery-white malleable metallic element notable for its lightness.

aluminous /ə'lu:minəs/ *adj* of, containing or resembling alum or alumina.

alumna /ə'lʌmnə/ *n* (*pl* **alumnae**) a female graduate or pupil of a university or college.

alumnus /ə'lʌmnəs/ *n* (*pl* **alumni**) a former pupil or student.—**alumna** *nf* (*pl* **alumnae**).

alum root /'æləm,ru:t/ *n* a popular name given to certain astringent roots of saxifrages.

alum schist /-,ʃist/ *n* a thin-bedded fissile rock from which alum is procured.

alunite /'æljə,nait/ or /-jə-/ *n* subsulphate of alumina and potash.

alveolar /æl'viɒlər/ *adj* of tooth sockets.

alveolate /æl'viɒleit/ *adj* with deep pits or cells resembling the honeycomb.—**alveolation** *n*.

alveolus /æl'viɒləs/ *n* (*pl* **alveoli**) a small pit, cell, cavity, or socket; the socket in which a tooth is fixed; the cell of a honeycomb.

alvine /æl'vain/ *adj* pertaining or belonging to the intestines or belly.

always /'ɒlweiz/ *adv* at all times; in all cases; repeatedly; forever.

Alzheimer's disease /'ɒlts,haimərz/ or /'ɒls-/, /'ælts-/, /'æls-/ *n* a degenerative disorder of the brain resulting in progressive senility.

am /æm/ *see* **be**.

a.m. /'ei'ɛm/ *abbr* = *ante meridiem*, before noon.

amadou /'æmə,du:/ *n* a styptic and a tinder prepared by steeping the solid portions of a fungus affecting trees in a solution of saltpetre; German tinder.

amah /'ɒmə/ *n* an East Indian nurse or female servant.

amalgam /ə'mælgəm/ *n* an alloy of mercury and another metal; a mixture.

amalgamate /ə'mælgə,meit/ *vt* to combine, unite.

amalgamation /ə,mælgə'meiʃən/ *n* the act or process of compounding mercury with another metal; the separation of precious metals from the mother rock by means of quicksilver; the blending or mixing of different elements or things; the union or consolidation of two or more companies or businesses into one concern, a merger.

amanuensis /ə,mænju:'ensis/ *n* (*pl* **amanuenses**) one who is employed to write at the dictation or direction of another; a secretary.

amaranth /'æmə,rænθ/ *n* an imaginary flower said by poets to be unfading; a plant of the genus *Amarantus*; a colour mixture in which magenta is the chief ingredient; red colouring added to some foods.

amaranthine /'æmə,rænθaɪn/ *adj* pertaining to the amaranth; never-fading, like amaranth; purplish.

amaryllis /,æmə'rɪlɪs/ *n* a genus of bulbous flowering plants to which the belladonna lily and narcissus belong.

amass /ə'mæs/ *vt* to bring together in a large quantity; to accumulate.—**amasser** *n*.—**amassment** *n*.

amateur /'æmətʃər/ or /-'tər/ *n* one who engages in a particular activity as a hobby, and not as a profession. • *adj* of or done by amateurs.—**amateurism** *n*.

amateurish /'æmətərɪʃ/ or /,æmə'tʃərɪʃ/, /-'tərɪʃ/ *adj* lacking expertise.—**amateurishiy** *adv*.—**amateurishness** *n*.

amatol /'æmə,tɒl/ or /-,tɔl/, /-,toːl/ *n* a high explosive.

amatory /'æmə,tɔri/, **amatorial** /-əl/*adj* relating to or expressive of love.

amaurosis /,æmə'roːsɪs/ *n* loss or decay of sight due to partial, periodic, or complete paralysis of the optic nerve.—**amaurotic** *adj*.

amaze /ə'meɪz/ *vt* to fill with wonder, astonish.—**amazing** *adj*.—**amazingly** *adv*.

amazement /ə'meɪzmənt/ *n* the state of being amazed; astonishment; perplexity arising from sudden surprise.

Amazon /'æmə,zɒn/ *n* (*Greek myth*) a race of women warriors; a tall strong athletic woman.—**Amazonian** *adj*.

amazon ant *n* a species of ant found in Europe and America, which seizies the neuters of other species in the pupa stage and brings them up with their own larvae.

amazonite /'æmɐzənaɪt/ *n* the amazon stone gemstone.

amazon stone *n* a beautiful green feldspar found near the Amazon.

ambary, ambari /æm'bɑri/ *n* (*pl* **ambaries, ambaris**) a plant of Asia that produces a jute-like fibre; the fibre.

ambassador /æm'bæsədər/ *n* the highest-ranking diplomatic representative from one country to another; an authorized messenger.—**ambassadorial** *adj*.—**ambassadress** *nf*.

ambassador extraordinary *n* an ambassador sent on a special mission.

ambassador plenipotentiary *n* an ambassador sent with full powers to make a treaty.

amber /'æmbər/ *n* a hard yellowish fossil resin, used for jewellery and ornaments, etc; the colour of amber; a yellow traffic light used to signal "caution".

ambergris /-grɪs/ or /-,grɪs/ *n* a waxy substance found in tropical seas, which is secreted by sperm whales and is used in perfumery as a fixative.

amberoid, ambroid /-ɔɪd/ *n* pressed amber; synthetic amber.

amber tree *n* the common name for various species of African evergreen shrubs with fragrant leaves.

ambidextrous /,æmbi'dekstrəs/ *adj* able to use the left and the right hand equally well.—**ambidexterity** *n*.

ambience, ambiance /'æmbiəns/ or /'æmbiɑ̃s/, *Fr.* /ɑ̃mbi'ɑ̃s/ *n* surrounding influence, atmosphere.

ambient /'æmbiənt/ *adj* surrounding.

ambiguity /,æmbə'gjuːiti/ *n* (*pl* **ambiguities** /-ɪz/) double or dubious significance; vagueness.

ambiguous /æm'bɪgjuːəs/ *adj* capable of two or more interpretations; indistinct, vague.—**ambiguously** *adv*.—**ambiguousness** *n*.

ambit /'æmbɪt/ *n* a circuit or compass; the line or sum of the lines by which a figure is bounded; the perimeter; sphere of action.

ambition /æm'bɪʃən/ *n* desire for power, wealth and success; an object of ambition.

ambitious /-ʃəs/ *adj* having or governed by ambition; resulting from or showing ambition; requiring considerable effort or ability.—**ambitiously** *adv*.

ambivalent /æm'bɪvələnt/ *adj* having mixed feelings toward the same object.—**ambivalence** *n*.

amble /'æmbəl/ *vi* to walk in a leisurely way. • *n* an easy pace. — **ambler** *n*.

amblyopia /,æmbi'oːpiə/ *n* dimness of vision; amaurosis.—**amblyopic** *adj*.

ambo /'æmboː/ *n* (*pl* **ambos, ambones**) a pulpit; a reading desk.

amboyna, amboina /æm,bɔɪnə/ *n* a beautifully mottled and curled variegated wood used in cabinet work.

ambrosia /æm'broːʒə/ *n* (*Classical myth*) the food of the gods; anything exquisitely pleasing to taste or smell; a genus of weeds allied to wormwood.—**ambrosial, ambrosian** *adj*.

ambrotype /'æmbroː,taɪp/ *n* (*photog*) a process by which the light parts of a photograph are produced in silver, the dark parts showing as a background through the clear glass.

ambry /'æmbri/ *n* (*pl* **ambries** /-iːz/) a recess in a church wall for sacred vessels; a repository for arms; a cupboard for money tools, etc.

ambsace /'eɪmz,eɪts/ or /'æmz-/ *n* two ones, the lowest throw at dice; bad luck.

ambulacrum /,æmbjuː'leɪkrəm/ *n* (*pl* **ambulacra**) a perforation in the shell of echinoderms through which the tube feet are protruded.—**ambulacral** *adj*.

ambulance /'æmbjuːləns/ *n* a special vehicle for transporting the sick or injured.

ambulance chaser /-,tʃeɪʒər/ *n* one who attempts to profit from disaster.

ambulant /'æmbjuːlənt/ *adj* (*patient*) able to walk, not bed-ridden; moving from place to place.

ambulate /'æmbjuː,leɪt/ *vi* to walk about; to move about; to wander.—**ambulation** *n*.

ambulatory /-lə,tɔri/ *adj* of or pertaining to walking; movable; temporary; capable of walking. • *n* (*pl* **ambulatories**) a place for walking in; a covered way.

ambuscade /,æmbəs'keɪd/ *n* a strategic disposition of troops in ambush.

ambush /'æmbuʃ/ *n* the concealment of soldiers, etc to make a surprise attack; the bushes or other cover in which they are hidden. • *vti* to lie in wait; to attack from an ambush.

ambush marketing *n* the practice of taking advantage of another's official event to advertise one's own products.—*also* **ambushing**.

ameba /ə'miːbə/ *see* **amoeba**.

ameer /ə'mɪr/ *see* **amir**.

ameliorate /ə'miːliə,reɪt/ *vti* to make or become better.—**ameliorative** *adj*.—**ameliorator** *n*.

amelioration /-iə,reɪʃən/ *n* the making or growing better; improvement.

amen /ɒ'men/ or /'eɪ-/ *interj* may it be so!

amenable /ə'menəbəl/ *adj* easily influenced or led, tractable; answerable to legal authority.—**amenability** *n*.—**amenably** *adv*.

amend /ə'mend/ *vt* to remove errors, *esp* in a text; to modify, improve; to alter in minor details.—**amendable** *adj*.—**amender** *n*.

amendatory /ə'mendə,tɔri/ *adj* tending to amend; corrective.

amende honorable /ə,mɑ̃dɒnɒ'ræblə/ *n* (*pl* **amendes honorables**) a public apology and reparation; a punishment formerly inflicted in France on traitors and the sacrilegious.

amendment /ə'mendmənt/ *n* the act of amending, correction; an alteration to a document, etc.

amends /ə'mendz/ *npl* (*used as sing*) compensation or recompense for some loss, harm, etc.

amenity /ə'meniti/ or /ə'miːniti/ *n* (*pl* **amenities**) pleasantness, as regards situation, convenience, or service.

amenorrhoea, amenorrhea /eɪ,menə'riːə/ *n* abnormal absence of menstruation.

ament /ə'ment/, **amentum** /-əm/ *n* (*pl* **aments, amenta**) a catkin, as of the willow.

amentia /ə'menʃə/ *n* want of reason; mental deficiency.

amerce /ə'mərs/ *vt* to punish by an arbitrary fine.—**amerceable** *adj*.—**amercement** *n*.

Amerenglish /'æmər,ɪŋlɪʃ/ or /,æmər'ɪŋlɪʃ/ *n* the English language as spoken in the United States.

American /ə'merikən/ *adj* belonging to or characteristic of America. • *n* an inhabitant of the US.

Americanism /ə'merikə,nɪzəm/ *n* a form of expression peculiar to the US; a custom peculiar to the US; attachment to the US.

Americanize /ə'merikə,naɪz/ *vt* to render American; to assimilate to the political and social institutions of the US.—**Americanization** *n*.

americium /,æmə'rɪʃiəm/ or /-'rɪs-/ *n* a white radioactive metallic element derived from plutonium.

Amerindian /,æmə'rɪndiən/, **Amerind** /,æmə'rɪnd/ *n* an American Indian.—**Amerindic** *adj*.

ametabolic /eɪ,metə'bɒlɪk/ *adj* (*certain insects*) not undergoing metamorphosis.

amethyst /'æmεθɪst/ *n* a gemstone consisting of bluish-violet quartz; the colour of an amethyst.—**amethystine** *adj*.

amiable /'eimiəbəl/ *adj* friendly in manner, congenial.—**amiability** *n*.—**amiably** *adv*.

amianthus /ˌæmi'ænθəs/ *n* earth or mountain flax, a fibrous variety of asbestos.—**amianthine, amianthoid, amianthoidal** *adj*.

amicable /'æmikəbəl/ *adj* friendly; peaceable.—**amicability, amicableness** *n*.—**amicably** *adv*.

amice /'æmis/ *n* a square of white linen formerly worn on the head but now worn about the neck and shoulders by celebrant priests while saying Mass; a pilgrim's cloak.

amicus curiae /ə'mikus'kjuri,ai/ or /ə'mi:kəs'kjuri,ai/ *n* (*pl* **amici curiae**) (*law*) a friend of the court; a disinterested adviser.

amid /ə'mid/, **amidst** /əmidst/ *prep* in or to the middle of; during.

amide /'æmaid/ or /'eim-/ *n* any of several compounds produced by the replacement of a hydrogen atom of ammonia by an acid radical or metal atom.

amidships /ə'midʃips/ *adv* in the middle of a ship.

amine /æ'mi:n/ or /ə-/ *n* any of several organic compounds formed by replacing hydrogen atoms of ammonia by one or more univalent hydrocarbon radicals.

amino acid *n* any of a group of organic acids that occur in proteins.

amir /ə'mir/ *n* (*formerly*) the Muslim ruler of Afghanistan.—*also* **ameer**.

amiss /ə'mis/ *adj* wrong, improper. • *adv* in an incorrect manner.

amity /'æmiti/ *n* (*pl* **amities**) friendship.

ammeter /'æmi:tər/ *n* an instrument for measuring electric current in amperes.

ammo /'æmo:/ *n* (*sl*) ammunition.

ammonal /ə'mo:nəl/ *n* a highly explosive compound.

ammonia /ə'mo:niə/ or /-'mo:niə/ *n* a pungent colourless gas composed of nitrogen and hydrogen.

ammoniac[1] /ə'mo:ni,æk/ *n* a gum resin.—*also* **gum ammoniac**.

ammoniacal /ˌæmə'niəkəl/, **ammoniac**[2] *adj* of, pertaining to, like or containing ammonia.

ammonite /'æmo:,nait/ *n* a fossil shell, twisted like a ram's horn; snakestone.—**ammonitic** *adj*.

ammonium /æ'mo:niəm/ *n* the hypothetical base of ammonia.

ammunition /ˌæmju'niʃən/ *n* bullets, shells, rockets, etc; any means of attack or defence; facts and reasoning used to prove a point in an argument.

amnesia /æm'ni:ʒə/ *n* a partial or total loss of memory.—**amnesiac, amnesic** *n, adj*.

amnesty /'æmnəsti/ *n* (*pl* **amnesties**) a general pardon, *esp* of political prisoners; a pardon granted for a limited time. • *vt* (**amnestying, amnestied**) to pardon (an offence).

amniocentesis /ˌæmni,o:sen'ti:sis/ *n* the extraction by hollow needle of a sample of amniotic fluid from the womb to test for foetal abnormalities.

amnion /'æmniən/ *n* (*pl* **amnions, amnia**) the thin innermost membrane surrounding the foetus in the womb of mammals, birds, and reptiles.—**amniotic** *adj*.

amoeba /ə'mi:bə/ *n* (*pl* **amoebae** /ə,mi:bai/, **amoebas** /ə'mi:bəz/) a unicellular microorganism found in water, damp soil and the digestive tracts of animals.—*also* **ameba**.—**amoebic, amebic** *adj*.

amoebaean, amoebean /'æmi:biən/ *adj* (*verse form*) alternately answering.

amok /ə'mɛk/ *adj, adv* **run amok** to run about armed, in a state of frenzy, attacking all that come in the way; indiscriminate slaughter; headstrong violence.—*also* **amuck**.

among /ə'mʌŋ/, **amongst** /ə'mʌŋst/ *prep* in the number of, surrounded by; in the group or class of; within a group, between; by the joint efforts of.

amontillado /əˌmɒnti'lɑ:do:/, *Sp.* /əˌmɒnti:'jɒdo:/ *n* (*pl* **amontillados**) a dry fashion of light-coloured sherry.

amoral /ei'mɒrəl/ or /-'mɒrəl/ *adj* neither moral nor immoral; without moral sense.—**amorality** *n*.—**amorally** *adv*.

amoretto /ˌæmə'reto:/, **amorino** /ˌɑmə'ri:no:/ *n* (*pl* **amoretti, amorini**) (*art*) a figure of cupid and representations of children.—*also* **putto**.

amorist /'æmərist/ *n* an amateur in love, a philanderer.

amoroso /ˌæmə'ro:so:/ *adj* (*mus*) in a tender, amatory style.

amorous /'æmərəs/ *adj* displaying or feeling love or desire.—**amorously** *adv*.—**amorousness** *n*.

amor patriae /æˌmur'pætri,pi/ *n* love of one's country.

amorphous /ə'mɔrfəs/ *adj* lacking a specific shape, shapeless; unrecognizable, indefinable.—**amorphism** *n*.

amortization /ˌæmərti'zeiʃən/ *n* the extinction of a debt by means of a sinking fund; the act of alienating lands to a corporation in mortmain.—**amortizement** *n*.

amortize /'æmərtaiz/ or /ə'mɔr-/ *vt* to put money aside at intervals for gradual payment of (a debt, etc).—**amortization** *n*.

amount /ə'maunt/ *vi* to be equivalent (to) in total, quantity or significance. • *n* the total sum; the whole value or effect; a quantity.

amour /æ'mur/ *n* a love affair; an intrigue.

amour propre /æˌmur'prɒpr/ *n* self-love, vanity; self-respect.

amp /æmp/ *n* an ampere; (*inf*) an amplifier.

ampelopsis /ˌæmpi'lɒpsis/ *n* kinds of vine creeper, incl the Virginia creeper.

amperage /'æmpəridʒ/ or /æm'pir-/ *n* the strength of an electric current measured in amperes.

ampere /'æmper/ *n* the standard SI unit by which an electric current is measured.

ampersand /'æmpər,sænd/ *n* the sign (&) meaning "and".

amphetamine /æm'fetə,mi:n/ or /-min/ *n* a drug used *esp* as a stimulant and to suppress appetite.

amphi- /'æmfi/ *prefix* of both kinds; on both sides; around.

amphibian /æm'fibiən/ *n* an animal living on land but breeding in water; an aircraft that can take off and land on water or land; a vehicle that can travel on land and through water.

amphibious /æm'fibiəs/ *adj* living on both land and in water; (*mil*) involving both sea and land forces.

amphibology /æmˌfi'bɒlədʒi/, **amphiboly** /-li/ *n* (*pl* **amphibologies, amphibolies**) an ambiguous phrase, as a sentence that may be construed in two distinct ways, as "The duke yet lives that Henry shall depose"; a quibble.

amphibrach /'æmfə,bræk/ *n* (*verse*) a foot of three syllables, the middle long, the first and last short.—**amphibrachic** *adj*.

amphimacer /æm'fiməsər/ *n* (*verse*) a foot of three syllables, the middle short, the first and last long.

amphimixis /ˌæmfə'miksis/ *n* (*pl* **amphimixes**) a mingling of male and female gametes in sexual reproduction.

amphioxus /ˌæmfi'ɒksəs/ *n* (*pl* **amphioxi, amphioxuses**) the name of the lancelet, a fish with a body tapering at both ends, the lowest in organization of the vertebrates.

amphipod /'æmfə,pɒd/ *n* any of the *Amphipoda* order of crustaceans having feet for both walking and swimming, including the sandhoppers and sand fleas.

amphiprostyle /ˌæmfə'prɒstail/ or /æmfi'prɔ,stail/ *adj* (*archit*) with a portico at both ends. • *n* a building of this kind, *esp* a temple.—**amphiprostylar** *adj*.

amphisbaena /ˌæmfis'bi:nə/ *n* (*pl* **amphisbaenae, amphisbaenas**) a fabled serpent with a head at each end; a kind of lizard or worm.—**amphisbaenic** *adj*.

amphitheatre, amphitheater /ˌæmfi'θi:ətər/ *n* an oval or circular building with rising rows of seats around an open arena.

amphora /'æmfərə/ *n* (*pl* **amphorae, amphoras**) a two-handled vessel of oblong shape, used by the ancients for holding wine, etc; a Greek and Roman liquid measure, the former 9 gallons, the latter 6 gallons.

ample /'æmpəl/ *adj* large in size, scope, etc; plentiful.—**amply** *adv*.

amplification /'æmpləfə'keiʃən/ *n* the act of amplifying or expanding; enlargement.

amplifier /'æmplə,fair/ *n* a device that increases electric voltage, current, or power, or the loudness of sound.

amplify /'æmplə,fai/ *vt* (**amplifying, amplified**) to expand more fully, add details to; (*electrical signals, etc*) to strengthen.

amplitude /'æmplə,tu:d/ or /-,tju:d/ *n* largeness of extent, scope; abundance; the maximum deviation of an oscillation from the mean or zero.

amplitude modulation *n* (the transmitting of information by) the modulation of the amplitude of a radio carrier wave in accordance with the amplitude of the signal carried.

ampoule, ampul, ampule /'æm,pul/ or /-,pel-/ *n* a small sealed glass vessel containing liquid, *esp* for injection.

ampulla /æm'pulə/ *n* (*pl* **ampullae**) an ancient vessel which contained unguents for the bath; a drinking vessel; a vessel for consecrated oil or chrism used in church rites and at the coronation of sovereigns.—**ampullar, ampullary** *adj*.

amputate /'æmpju,teit/ *vt* to cut off, *esp* by surgery.—**amputation** *n*.

amuck /ə'mɛk/ *see* **amok**.

amulet /'æmjulət/ *n* something worn as a charm against evil.

amuse /ə'mju:z/ *vt* to entertain or divert in a pleasant manner; to cause to laugh or smile.—**amusing** *adj*.

amusement /-mənt/ *n* that which amuses; the state of being amused; an entertainment; a pastime.

amusement arcade *n* an indoor or roofed area with mechanical games for entertainment.

amusement park *n* an outdoor area with fairground entertainments.

amygdalate /ə'mɪgdəleɪt/ *adj* of or belonging to the almond.

amygdalin /ə'mɪgdə,lɪn/ *n* a white crystalline substance obtained from the kernels of almonds.

amygdaloid /ə'mɪgdə,lɔɪd/ *adj* almond shaped. • *n* an igneous rock containing almond-shaped nodules of some mineral.

amyl /'eɪmaɪl/ or /'æmɪl/ *n* (*formerly*) the alcohol radical of many chemical compounds.

amylaceous /,æmɪ'leɪʃəs/ *adj* of starch, starchy.

amylase /'æmɪ,leɪz/ *n* an enzyme that breaks down starch and glycogen.

amylene /'æmɪ,li:n/ *n* a hydrocarbon obtained by the removal of water from amyl alcohol.

amyl nitrite *n* a drug inhaled to relieve spasms.

amyloid /'æmɪ,lɔɪd/ *n* a starchy food.

amylopsin /,æmɪ'lɒpsɪn/ *n* a pancreatic ferment converting starch into sugar.

an- /ən/ or /æn/ *prefix* the form of *ad-* before *n*.

-an /ən/, **-ain** /eɪn/, **-ane** /æn/ *adj suffix* of, of the nature of, as in *suburban, certain, humane*.

an /æn/ *adj* the indefinite article ("a"), used before words beginning with the sound of a vowel except "u".

ana- /'ænə/ *prefix* up, anew, again.

-ana /'ænə/, **-iana** *n suffix* sayings of, publications about, as *Shakespeariana*, etc.

Anabaptist /,ænə'bæptɪst/ *n* one who believes in the rebaptizing of adults on their profession of faith; one who holds the invalidity of infant baptism; (*pl*) the sect of Baptists.—**Anabaptism** *n*.

anabas /'ænəbəs/ *n* a genus of Indian fishes allied to the perch, remarkable for their power of living a long time out of water and of travelling on land.

anabasis /ə'næbəsɪs/ *n* (*pl* **anabases**) the name given to Xenophon's account of the expedition of Cyrus the Younger (401BC); an inland military expedition.

anabatic /,ænə'bætɪk/ *adj* (*of wind*) caused by upward current of air.

anabiosis /,ænə'bio:sɪs/ *n* a coming to life again, resuscitation.

anableps /'ænəbleps/ *n* (*pl* **anableps**) a genus of the perch family found in Guiana, remarkable for the structure of its eye.

anabolic steroid /,ænə'bɒlɪk'stɪrɔɪd/ or /'steraɪd/ *n* any of various synthetic steroid hormones that promote rapid muscle growth.

anabolism /ə'næbə,lɪzəm/ *n* constructive metabolism, in which simple molecules synthesize into more complex ones.—**anabolic**.

anabranch /'ænə,bræntʃ/ *n* a stream that leaves a river and rejoins it lower down.

anachronism /ə'nækrə,nɪzəm/ *n* a person, custom, or idea regarded as out of date or out of its period.—**anachronistic** *adj*.—**anachronistically** *adv*.

anacoluthia /,ænəkə'lu:θiə/ *n* want of grammatical sequence, *esp* in a sentence.—**anacoluthic** *adj*.

anacoluthon /,ænəkə'lu:θɒn/ *n* (*pl* **anacolutha**) a sentence in which one part belongs to a different construction from the other.

anaconda /,ænə'kɒndə/ *n* a large South American semiaquatic snake that kills its prey by constriction.

Anacreontic /ə,nækri'ɒntɪk/ *adj* after the manner of Anacreon, the Greek poet (6th century BC); amatory, erotic. • *n* a poem in praise of love and wine.

anacrusis /,ænə'kru:sɪs/ *n* (*pl* **anacruses**) (*linguistics*) an unstressed syllable at the beginning of a verse.—**anacrustic** *adj*.

anadiplosis /,ænədɪ'plo:sɪs/ *n* (*rhetoric*) the repetition of the last word of a line or clause at the beginning of the next.

anadromous /ə'nædrəməs/ *adj* (*fish*) ascending from the sea to freshwater rivers to deposit spawn, as the salmon, etc.

anaemia /ə'ni:miə/ *n* a condition in which the blood is low in red cells or in haemoglobin, resulting in paleness, weakness, etc. —*also* **anemia**.

anaemic /ə'ni:mɪk/ *adj* suffering from anaemia; weak; pale; listless.—*also* **anemic**.

anaerobe /'ænə,ro:b/ or /ə,nɛro:b/, **anaerobium** /-biəm/ *n* (*pl* **anaerobes, anaerobia**) a microbe that can live without air.

anaerobiosis /,ænəro:bi'o:sɪs/ *n* life devoid of oxygen.—**anaerobic** *adj*.—**anaerobically** *adv*.

anaesthesia /,ænəs'θi:ziə/ or /-ʒə/ *n* a partial or total loss of the sense of pain, touch, etc.—*also* **anesthesia**.

anaesthetic /,ænəs'θetɪk/ *n* a drug, gas, etc used to produce anaesthesia, as before surgery. • *adj* of or producing anaesthesia. —*also* **anesthetic**.

anaesthetist /ə'nɛsθətɪst/ or /ə'ni:-/ *n* a person trained to give anaesthetics.—*also* **anesthetist**.

anaesthetize /ə'nɛsθə,taɪz/ or /ə'ni:-/ *vt* to administer an anaesthetic.—*also* **anesthetize**.—**anaesthetization, anesthetization** *n*.

anaglyph /'ænəglɪf/ *n* an ornament or work of art carved in low relief, as distinguished from intaglio.—**anaglyphic, anaglyphical, anaglyptic, anaglyptical** *adj*.

anagnorisis /ə'nægnərɪsɪs/ *n* (*pl* **anagnorises**) the denouement in a drama.

anagoge, anagogy /,ænə'go:dʒi/ *n* an allegorical or mystical interpretation, a hidden sense.—**anagogic, anagogical** *adj*.—**anagogically** *adv*.

anagram /'ænə,græm/ *n* a word or sentence formed by rearranging another word or sentence.—**anagrammatic, anagrammatical** *adj*.—**anagrammatically** *adv*.

anagrammatize /,ænə'græmə,taɪz/ *vt* to make into an anagram. • *vi* to construct anagrams.—**anagrammatism** *n*.—**anagrammatist** *n*.

anal /'eɪnəl/ *adj* of or situated near the anus.

analects /'ænəlekts/, **anelecta** /,ænə'lektə/ *npl* literary passages or extracts selected from published works by different authors.—**analectic** *adj*.

analeptic /,ænə'leptɪk/ *adj* restorative. • *n* a restorative drug.

analgesia /,ænəl'dʒi:ziə/ or /-siə/ *n* insensibility to pain without loss of consciousness.

analgesic /,ænəl'dʒi:zɪk/ or /-sɪk/ *adj* relieving pain. • *n* a pain-relieving drug.

analogism /,ænə'lɒdʒɪzəm/ *n* a reasoning from the cause to the effect; study and examination of matters and things by reference to their analogies.—**analogist** *n*.

analogize /ə'nælə,dʒaɪz/ *vt* to reason or expound by reference to analogy, to draw comparisons. • *vi* to treat or investigate by use of analogy.

analogous /ə'næləgəs/ *adj* corresponding in certain respects (to).—**analogously** *adv*.

analogue, analog /'ænə,lɒg/ *n* a word or thing analogous to something else.

analogy /ə'nælədʒi/ *n* (*pl* **analogies**) a similarity or correspondence in certain respects between two things.—**analogical, analogic** *adj*.

analysable, analyzable *adj* capable of being resolved by, or that may be subjected to, analysis.

analysand /ə'nælɪ,sænd/ *n* anyone undergoing psychoanalysis.

analyse, analyze /'ænə,laɪz/ *vt* to separate (something) into its constituent parts to investigate its structure and function, etc; to examine in detail; to psychoanalyse.

analysis /ə'næləsɪs/ *n* (*pl* **analyses** /-ɪsi:s/) the process of analysing; a statement of the results of this; psychoanalysis.

analyst /'ænəlɪst/ *n* a person who analyses; a psychoanalyst.

analytic /,ænə'lɪtɪk/, **analytical** /-kl/ *adj* pertaining to analysis.—**analytically** *adv*.

anamnesis /,ænəm'ni:sɪs/ *n* (*pl* **anamneses** /-si:z/) recollection; a patient's case history.—**anamnestic** *adj*.—**anamnestically** *adv*.

anamorphosis /,ænə'mɔrfəsɪs/ *n* (*pl* **anamorphoses** /-si:z/) the irregular and distorted representation of an object as viewed directly, but which is corrected and reduced to its proper proportion when regarded from a different point of view, or reflected by a curved mirror; the abnormal or monstrous development of a portion of a plant or flower; a gradual progression from one type to another.

ananas /ə'nænəs/ *n* a genus of tropical plants to which the pineapple belongs.

anandrous /ə,nændrəs/ *adj* without stamens.

ananthous /ə'nænθəs/ *adj* without flowers.

anapaest, anapest /'ænə,pest/ *n* a foot comprising two short syllables and one long syllable.—**anapaestic, anapestic** *adj*.

anaphora /ə'næfərə/ n (*rhetoric*) the repetition at the beginning of the succeeding clauses of sentences of the word or words used in beginning the first; that part of the Eucharistic service which starts with the Sursum Corda; the oblique ascension of a star.—**anaphoric** adj.—**anaphorically** adv.

anaphrodisia /æn,æfrə'dɪzɪə/ n impotence of the sexual organs; absence of venereal desire.

anaphrodisiac /æn,æfrə'dɪːzɪˌæk/ adj tending to diminish sexual desire. • n a remedy that produces such an effect.

anaphylaxis /,ænəfɪ'læksɪs/ n excessive sensitivity to a substance or germ due to prior inoculation with it, an allergy.—**anaphylactic** adj.—**anaphylactically** adv.

anaplasty /,ænə'plæstɪ/ n the repairing of wounds by the transplantation of adjacent healthy tissue, plastic surgery.—**anaplastic** adj.

anarchism /'ænərˌkɪzəm/ n lawlessness; confusion; anarchy; the doctrines of the anarchists.

anarchist /'ænərkɪst/ n a person who believes that all government is unnecessary and should be abolished.—**anarchistic** adj.

anarchy /'ænərkɪ/ n the absence of government; political confusion; disorder, lawlessness.—**anarchic, anarchical** adj.

anarthrous /æn'ɑrθrəs/ adj without the article; destitute of joints; without articulated limbs.

anasarca /ænə'sɑrkə/ (*med*) dropsy.—**anasarcous** adj.

anastigmat /æ'næstɪgˌmæt/ n a lens corrected of astigmatism.—**anastigmatic** adj.

anastomosis /ə,næstə'mo:sɪs/ n (*pl* **anastomoses**) a cross-connection of arteries, rivers, etc.—**anastomotic** adj.

anastrophe /ə'næstrəfɪ/ n (*rhetoric*) an inversion of the sequence of words in a sentence, as "echoed the hills", for "the hills echoed".

anathema /ə'næθəmə/ n (*pl* **anathemas**) anything greatly detested; an ecclesiastical curse or denunciation accompanied by excommunication.

anathematize /ə'næθəməˌtaɪz/ vt to pronounce a decree of excommunication against. • vi to curse.—**anathematization** n.

anatomist /ə'nætəmɪst/ n one possessing a knowledge of anatomy by dissection.

anatomize /ə'nætəˌmaɪz/ vt to dissect; to study the structure of; to analyse.—**anatomization** n.

anatomy /ə'nætəmɪ/ n (*pl* **anatomies**) the science of the physical structure of plants and animals; the structure of an organism.—**anatomical** adj.—**anatomically** adv.

anbury /'ænbərɪ/ n (*pl* **anburies**) a soft wart or tumour on horses and cattle; a disease in turnips.

ANC /'eɪ'en'si:/ abbr = African National Congress.

-ance /əns/ n suffix denoting quality or action, as in *arrogance, penance*.

ancestor /'æn,sestər/ or /-səs-/ n one from whom a person is descended, a forefather; an early animal or plant from which existing types are descended; something regarded as a forerunner.—**ancestress** nf.

ancestral /æn'sestrəl/ adj belonging to, or connected with, one's ancestors; derived from one's progenitors; lineal.

ancestry /'ænsestrɪ/ n (*pl* **ancestries**) ancestors collectively; lineage.

anchor /'æŋkər/ n a heavy metal implement that lodges at the bottom of the sea or a river to hold a ship in position; something that gives support or stability. • vt to fix by an anchor; to secure firmly.

anchorage /'æŋkərɪdʒ/ n a safe anchoring place for ships; the charge for anchoring.

anchorite /'æŋkəraɪt/ n one who voluntarily secludes him or herself from society and lives a solitary life devoted to religious or philosophic meditation; a recluse; a hermit.—**anchoress** nf.

anchorman /'æŋkərˌmæn/ n (*pl* **anchormen**) (*sport*) the last man in a team to compete and whose contribution is vital; the compere of a television broadcast.

anchor stock n the crossbar at the top of the shank, at right angles to the arms.

anchor watch n the watch on board ship when at anchor; the seamen on this watch.

anchovy /'æn,tʃoːvɪ/ or /'æantʃəvɪ/, /æn'tʃoːvɪ/ n (*pl* **anchovies, anchovy**) a small Mediterranean fish resembling a herring with a very salty taste.

anchovy pear n a West Indian fruit like the mango, used as a pickle.

anchylose /'æŋkəˌloːs/ or /-ˌloːz/ see **ankylose**.

anchylosis /-ˌloːsɪs/ see **ankylosis**.

ancien régime /ɑ̃,sjæ̃reɪ'ʒiːm/, *Fr.* /ɑ̃sjæ̃ʀeɪ'ʒiːm/ n (*pl* **anciens régimes**) the old order, *esp* that ruling France before the Revolution.

ancient /'eɪnʃənt/ adj very old; dating from the distant past; of the period and civilizations predating the fall of the Roman Empire; old-fashioned. • n a person who lived in the ancient period; (*pl*) the members of the classical civilizations of antiquity, *esp* of Greece and Rome.

Ancient of Days n (*Bible*) God, as described in the Book of Daniel.

ancillary /æn'sɪlərɪ/ adj subordinate (to); auxiliary; supplementary. • n (*pl* **ancillaries**) a subordinate or auxiliary person or thing.

ancipital /æn'sɪpɪtəl/, **ancipitous** /-ɪtəʃ/ adj (*biol*) two-edged and sharp.

ancon, ancone /'æŋkən/ n (*pl* **ancones** /æn'koʊniːz/ or /æŋ-/) (*archit*) a bracket or projection for the support of a cornice; the elbow.—**anconal, anconeal** adj.

and /ænd/ or /ənd/ conj in addition to; together with; plus; increasingly; as a consequence, afterwards; expressing contrast.

andalusite /,ændə'luːsaɪt/ n a silicate of alumina.

andante /æn'dɒnteɪ/ or /-'dænteɪ/ adj (*mus*) moderately slow; naturally and easily. • n a movement written and to be played in andante time.

andantino /æn,dɒn'tiːno:/ or /,ændæn-/ adj rather slower than andante. • n (*pl* **andantinos**) a movement slower than an andante.

andesite /'ændɪ,zaɪt/ n a silicate of alumina, soda, and lime.

andiron /'ænd,aɪrn/ npl metal standards used for open fires to support the logs; fire dogs.

androgen /'ændrədʒən/ n a male sex hormone.—**androgenic** adj.

androgenous /æn'drɒdʒənəs/ adj (*biol*) having only male offspring.

androgynous /æn'drɒdʒɪnəs/ adj combining both sexes or bearing both male and female organs; hermaphroditical.—**androgyne** n.—**androgyny** n.

android /'ændrɔɪd/ n (*science fiction*) a robot in human form.—*also adj*.

androsphinx /'ændrə,sfɪks/ n (*pl* **androsphinxes, androsphinges**) a sphinx with the body of a lion and the head of a man.

anecdotal /'ænək,do:təl/ adj relating to anecdotes; (*evidence, etc*) obtained from experience, not scientific.

anecdote /'ænək,do:t/ or /-ɛk-/ n a short entertaining account about an amusing or interesting event or person.

anemia /ə'niːmɪə/ see **anaemia**.

anemic /ə'niːmɪk/ see **anaemic**.

anemograph /ə'nɛmə,græf/ n an instrument for registering the force or direction of the wind.

anemography /ə'nɛmə,grəfɪ/ n the scientific description of winds, and the measurement and registration of their force and direction.—**anemographic** adj.—**anemographically** adv.

anemology /,ænə'mɒlədʒɪ/ n the science and literature of the winds.

anemometer /,ænə'mɒmətər/ n an instrument for measuring the force or speed of the wind.

anemone /ə'nɛmənɪ/ n a plant of the buttercup family.

anemophilus /,ænə'mɒfɪləs/ adj (flowers etc) fertilized by pollen carried by the wind, wind-pollinated.—**anemophily** n.

anemoscope /ə'nɛmə,sko:p/ n an apparatus for exhibiting the direction of the wind.

anent /ə'nɛnt/ prep, adv (*Scot*) with regard or respect to; concerning.

aneroid /'ænə,rɔɪd/ adj having no liquid, as quicksilver. • n a barometer shaped like a watch, the action depending on the varying pressure of the atmosphere on the top of an elastic metal box.

aneroid barometer n a barometer that measures air pressure by its effect on the flexible lid of a box containing a partial vacuum.

anesthesia /,ænəs'θiːʒə/ or /-ʒɪə/, see **anaesthesia**.

anesthetic /,ænəs'θetɪk/ see **anaesthetic**.

anesthetist /ə'nɛsθətɪst/ or /ə,niː-/ see **anaesthetist**.

anesthetize /ə'nɛsθə,taɪz/ or /ə,niː-/ see **anaesthetize**.

aneurysm, aneurism /'ænju,rɪzəm/ n the permanent abnormal swelling of an artery.

anew /ə'nuː/ or /-'njuː/ adv afresh; again, once more; in a new way or form.

anfractuous /æn'fræktʃuːəs/ adj winding, intricate.—**anfractuosity** n (*pl* **anfractuosities**).

angary /'æŋgəri/ *n* a belligerent's right to seize and use neutral property, for which it pays indemnity.

angel /'eɪndʒəl/ *n* a messenger of God; an image of a human figure with wings and a halo; a very beautiful or kind person; (*inf*) one who gives financial backing to an enterprise.

angel cake *n* a small round cake with a round fruit on the top.

Angeleno /ˌændʒə'liːnoː/ or *n* (*pl* **Angelenos**) (*inf*) an inhabitant of the city of Los Angeles.

angelfish /'eɪndʒəlˌfɪʃ/ *n* (*pl* **angelfish, angelfishes**) a species of shark with large pectoral fins, which give to it a winged appearance.

angelic /'ændʒɛlɪk/, **angelical** /-əl/ *adj* belonging to or resembling an angel in nature or function.—**angelically** *adv*.

angelica /-ɪkə/ *n* the candied stalks of a fragrant plant used *esp* in cake decoration.

Angelus /'ændʒələs/ *n* (*RC Church*) a devotional exercise commemorating the Incarnation, during which the Ave Maria is twice repeated, said morning, noon, and night; the bell that is rung to announce the time of such devotions.

anger /'æŋgər/ *n* strong displeasure, often because of opposition, a hurt, etc. • *vti* to make or become angry.

angina /æn'dʒaɪnə/ *n* sharp stabbing pains in the chest, *usu* caused by angina pectoris.

angina pectoris /'pɛktərɪs/ *n* a heart disease causing a spasmodic gripping pain in the chest.

angiology /ˌændʒi'ɒlədʒi/ *n* the branch of anatomy that deals with the blood vessels and lymphatics.

angioma /ændʒi'oːmə/ *n* (*pl* **angiomas, angiomata**) a tumour caused by the enlargement of a blood vessel.—**angiomatous** *adj*.

angiosperm /'ændʒiəˌspərm/ *n* (*bot*) a plant having its seeds protected by a covering.—**angiospermous** *adj*.

angle[1] /'æŋgəl/ *n* a corner; the point from which two lines or planes extend or diverge; a specific viewpoint; an individual method or approach (*eg* to a problem). • *vt* to bend at an angle; to move or place at an angle; to present information, news, etc from a particular point of view.

angle[2] *vi* to fish with a hook and line; to use hints or artifice to get something.—**angler** *n*.

angler /'æŋglər/ *n* one who fishes with rod and line; the name of a fish with filamentary appendage that attracts smaller fish on which it feeds.

Anglican /'æŋglɪkən/ *adj* belonging to or of the Church of England and other churches in communion with it. • *n* a member of the Anglican Church; a ritualist.

Anglicanism /-ɪzəm/ *n* the principles and ritual of the Anglican Church.

Anglicism /'æŋglɪˌsɪzəm/ *n* a form of speech, an English idiom; a principle or mannerism peculiar to England.

anglicize /'æŋglɪˌsaɪz/ *vt* to make or to render into English; to accord with English manners and customs.—**anglicization** *n*.

angling /'æŋglɪŋ/ *n* the art or act of fishing with rod and line.

Anglo- /'æŋgloː/ or *prefix* English, British.

Anglo-American /'æŋgloːə'mɛrɪkən/ *adj* pertaining to England and the United States conjointly, as to commerce or population. • *n* an American citizen of English descent.

Anglo-Canadian *adj* pertaining to England and Canada, as to commerce or population.

Anglo-Catholic /'kəθɒlɪk/ *adj* Catholic according to the teachings and ritual of the English Church; in the strictest Catholic sense; high church. • *n* a member of the English Church, popularly a ritualist or high churchman, who repudiates the term "Protestant".

Anglo-Catholicism /kə'θɒlɪsɪzəm/ *n* the principles and ritual of the Anglican Church interpreted in their strictest Catholic sense.

Anglo-French /'frɛntʃ/ *adj* English and French. • *n* the old French language introduced into England by the Normans.

Anglo-Indian /'ɪndiən/ *adj* pertaining to England and India conjointly. • *n* one of English descent born or residing in India.

Anglo-Irish /'aɪrɪʃ/ *adj* pertaining to England and Ireland, or to the English settled in Ireland and their descendants; having the father or mother of English or Irish race. • *npl* English born or resident in Ireland.

Anglomania /-'meɪniə/ *n* a predilection carried to excess for every-

thing that is English, in the sense of being peculiar to England.

Anglo-Norman /-'nɔrmən/ *adj* common to England and Normandy. • *n* one of the Norman settlers in England after the Conquest (AD 1066).

Anglophile /'æŋgloːˌfaɪl/ *n* a person who loves England or anything English.—*also* **Anglophil**.

Anglophobe /'æŋgləˌfoːb/ *n* one who hates or fears England and the English.

Anglophobia /ˌæŋglə'foːbiə/ *n* an intense aversion or fear of everything English.—**Anglophobe** *n*.

Anglo-Saxon /'æŋglə'sæksən/ *adj* pertaining to the Saxon settlers in England prior to the Conquest, or to their language. • *n* one of the Saxon settlers in England as distinguished from those on the Continent; Old English, the language of the settlers; (*pl*) the English race.

angora /æn'gɔrə/ *n* a long-haired variety of cat, rabbit or goat; fabric made from the hair of angora goats or rabbits.

angostura bark /ˌæŋgə'stʊrə/ *n* a bitter aromatic bark used for medicinal purposes.

angostura bitters *npl* a bitter flavouring made from the bark of a South American tree.

angry /'æŋgri/ *adj* (**angrier, angriest**) full of anger; inflamed. —**angrily** *adv*.

angst /æŋgst/ *a* feeling of anxiety, fear or remorse.

angstrom, ångström /'æŋstrəm/ or /'ɒŋ-/ *n* one hundred millionth of a centimetre, a unit used in measuring the length of light waves.

anguilliform /æn'gwɪləˌfɔrm/ *adj* shaped like an eel or a serpent.

anguine /'æŋgwɪn/ *adj* snakelike.

anguish /'æŋgwɪʃ/ *n* agonizing physical or mental distress.

angular /'æŋgjʊlər/ *adj* having one or more angles; forming an angle; measured by an angle; stiff and clumsy in manner, thin and bony.

angularity /æŋgjʊ'lærɪti/ *n* (*pl* **angularities**) the quality of being angular in any sense.

angulate /'æŋgjʊlɪt/ *adj* constructed of angles; having the form of an angle.

angulation /ˌæŋgjʊ'leɪʃən/ *n* the exact measurement of angles; an angular shape.

anhydride /æn'haɪdraɪd/ *n* an oxygen compound formed by substituting an acid radicle for the whole of the hydrogen in one or two molecules of water.

anhydrite /æn'haɪdraɪt/ *n* anhydrous sulphate of lime.

anhydrous /æn'haɪdrəs/ *adj* without water, applied to minerals in which the water of crystallization is not present.

ani /'æni/ *n* (*pl* **anis** /'æniːz/) a tropical American bird of the cuckoo family.

aniconic /ˌænɪ'kɒnɪk/ or /-kɔn-/ *adj* (*idols*) not of human or animal form.

anil /'ænɪl/ *n* the indigo plant; a dye yielded by it.

anile /'ænaɪl/ *adj* resembling an old woman; aged.—**anility** *n*.

aniline /'ænɪˌlɪn/ or /-ˌliːn/, /-ˌlaɪn/ *n* a base used in the formation of many rich dyes obtained from coal tar but more extensively from benzole. • *adj* of or pertaining to aniline.

animadversion /ˌænɪmæd'vɔrʒən/ *n* the act of observing; capacity for perception; censure; criticism; stricture.

animadvert /ˌænɪmæd'vɔrt/ *vi* to give the mind to; to pass comment or stricture upon, to criticize.

animal /'ænɪməl/ *n* any living organism except a plant or bacterium, typically able to move about; a lower animal as distinguished from man, *esp* mammals; a brutish or bestial person. • *adj* of or like an animal; bestial; sensual.

animalcule /ˌænɪ'mælkjuːl/, **animalculum** *n* (*pl* **animalcules, animalcula**) one of a class of minute or microscopic organisms abounding in water and infusions.—**animalcular** *adj*.

animalism /'ænɪməˌlɪzəm/ *n* the state of being animal, or actuated by animal instincts or appetites; the theory that regards humankind as merely animal; sensuality.—**animalist** *n*.—**animalistic** *adj*.

animality /ˌænɪ'mælɪti/ *n* the state or quality of being an animal, or possessing animal characteristics, animal nature.

animalize /'ænɪməˌlaɪz/ *vt* to make animal; to impart animal life, form, and attributes; to sensualize or bestialize; to convert into animal substance by assimilation.—**animalization** *n*.

animal kingdom *n* beings endowed with animal life and regarded collectively, one of the three great divisions of nature.

animal liberation *n* freeing animals from captivity and exploitation (*eg* in laboratories) by humans, action *esp* associated with organizations such as the Animal Liberation Front.

animal magnetism *n* another name for mesmerism; attractiveness, *esp* to the opposite sex.

animal rights *n* a movement that seeks to extend certain rights, such as freedom from captivity and exploitation by humans, to animals.

animal spirits *npl* vivacity; liveliness of disposition.

animal worship *n* the worship of animals as symbols of deities, as among the ancient Egyptians, Hindus, etc.

animate /ˈænɪmət/ *adj*, /ˈænɪˌmeɪt/ *vt* to give life to; to liven up; to inspire, encourage. • *adj* alive; lively.

animated /ˈænɪˌmeɪtəd/ *adj* lively, full of spirit.

animated cartoon *n* a film made by photographing a series of drawings, giving the illusion of movement.

animation /ˌænɪˈmeɪʃən/ *n* liveliness; movement; the skill of making animated films.

animato /æˈniːmɒˌtoː/ *adv, adj (mus)* with vigour.

animator, animater /ˈænɪmeɪtər/ *n* an artist who draws and produces animated cartoons.

animé /ˈænɪˌmeɪ/ *n* an amber-coloured resin, resembling copal, obtained from a tropical American tree and used in varnish.

animism /ˈænɪˌmɪzəm/ *n* in primitive religion, the belief that natural effects are due to spirits and that inanimate objects have spirits; the belief in a human apparitional soul, having the form and appearance of the body, existing after death as semi-human.—**animist** *n*.—**animistic** *adj*.

animosity /ˌænəˈmɒsɪti/ *n* (*pl* animosities) strong dislike; hostility.

animus /ˈænɪməs/ *n* an actuating spirit; a bitter or hostile feeling (against); hostility.

anion /ˈænˌaɪɒn/ *n* the element in a body decomposed by voltaic action, which is evolved at the positive pole or anode.—**anionic** *adj*.

anise /ˈænɪs/ *n* the common name for a plant (indigenous in Egypt) yielding the seeds used in aniseed.

aniseed /ˈænɪˌsiːd/ *n* the seed of the anise plant, used as a flavouring.

anisette /ˌænɪˈsɛt/ *n* a liqueur prepared from aniseed.

ankh /æŋk/ *n* an Egyptian cross with a loop or handle at the top, the symbol of life.—*also* **crux ansata**.

ankle /ˈæŋkəl/ *n* the joint between the foot and leg, the part of the leg between the foot and calf.

anklet /ˈæŋklət/ *n* an ornamental chain worn round the ankle.

ankylose /ˈæŋkɪˌloːz/ *vt* to consolidate or join by bony growth; to stiffen as a joint. • *vi* to grow together; to become stiff.—*also* **anchylose**.

ankylosis /ˌæŋkɪˈloːsɪs/ *n* (*zool*) the joining or consolidation of parts formerly or normally separate or movable by means of bony growth; (*med*) the stiffening of a joint by fibrous bands or union of bones.—*also* **anchylosis**.—**ankylotic, anchylotic** *adj*.

anna /ˈænə/ *n* an Indian coin, one sixteenth of a rupee.

annals /ˈænəlz/ *npl* a written account of events year by year; historical records; periodical reports or records of a society.—**annalist** *n*.—**annalistic** *adj*.

annates /ˈæneɪts/ *npl* (*RC Church*) the sum paid to the pope by an abbot or bishop on his appointment to a benefice or see and consisting of the first year's revenue of the living, now chiefly supplied by Peter's Pence.

anneal /əˈniːl/ *vt* to fix by heat; to temper and render malleable; to bake or fuse.—**annealer** *n*.

annelid /ˈænəlɪd/ *n* any of a class of invertebrates which includes the worms, whose bodies are composed of numerous segments or ring-like divisions.—**annelidan** *adj*.

annex /ˈænɛks/ *vt* to attach, *esp* to something larger; to incorporate into a state the territory of (another state).

annexation /ˌænɛkˈseɪʃən/ *n* the act of annexing; that which is annexed.—**annexational** *adj*.—**annexationism** *n*.—**annexationist** *n*.

annexe /ˈænɛks/ *n* an extension to a main building; something added, a supplement.

annihilate /əˈnaɪəˌleɪt/ *vt* to destroy completely; (*inf*) to defeat convincingly, as in an argument.—**annihilable** *adj*.—**annihilative** *adj*.—**annihilator** *n*.

annihilation /əˌnaɪəˈleɪʃən/ *n* the act of annihilating; nonexistence.

anniversary /ˌænɪˈvɜrsəri/ *n* (*pl* anniversaries) the yearly return of the date of some event; a celebration of this.—*also adj*.

Anno Domini /ˌænoːˈdɒmɪˌni/ or /-ˌnaɪ/ *adv* (*abbr* AD) in the year of our Lord, dating from the birth of Christ. • *n* (*inf*) advancing age.

annotate /ˈænoːˌteɪt/ or /-nə-/ *vti* to provide with explanatory notes.—**annotative** *adj*.—**annotator** *n*.

annotation /ˌænoːˈteɪʃən/ or /-nə-/ *n* the act of noting or commenting upon; a note, remark, or criticism made in a book.

announce /əˈnaʊns/ *vt* to bring to public attention; to give news of the arrival of; to be an announcer for. • *vi* to serve as an announcer.

announcement /-mənt/ *n* the act of announcing; that which is announced; a proclamation.

announcer /-ər/ *n* a person who reads the news, etc on the radio or TV.

annoy /əˈnɔɪ/ *vt* to vex, tease, irritate, as by a repeated action.—**annoyingly** *adv*.

annoyance /əˈnɔɪəns/ *n* the act of annoying or causing vexation; the state of being annoyed; the thing or act that annoys.

annual /ˈænjʊəl/ *adj* of or measured by a year; yearly; coming every year; living only one year or season. • *n* a plant that lives only one year; a periodical published once a year.—**annually** *adv*.

annuitant /əˈnjuːɪtənt/ *n* one who is in receipt of, or is entitled to receive, an annuity.

annuity /əˈnjuːɪti/ or /əˈnuː-/ *n* (*pl* annuities) an investment yielding fixed payments, *esp* yearly; such a payment.

annul /əˈnʌl/ *vt* (**annulling, annulled**) to do away with; to deprive of legal force, nullify.

annular /æˈnjʊlər/ or /-jə-/ *adj* ring-like; in the form of a ring or annulus. • *n* the ring of light surrounding the moon's body in an annular eclipse of the sun.

annulate /ˈænjʊlət/ *adj* ringed; having ring-like bands or circles.

annulation /ˌænjʊˈleɪʃən/ *n* a ring-like formation.

annulet /æˈnjuːlət/ *n* a small ring; (*archit*) a small fillet encircling a column.

annulment /əˈnʌlmənt/ *n* the act of reducing to nothing; abolition; invalidation.

annulose /æˈnjʊləs/ *adj* composed of a succession of rings; segmented.

annunciate /əˈnʌnsɪˌeɪt/ *vt* to make known officially or publicly; to announce, proclaim.—**annunciation** *n*.—**annunciative, annunciatory** *adj*.

annunciation /əˌnʌnsɪˈeɪʃən/ *n* (*Bible*) the intimation of the Incarnation made by the angel Gabriel to the Virgin Mary (Luke 1:28-33); the Church festival (Lady Day, 25 Mar) commemorating this.

annunciator /əˈnʌnsɪˌeɪtər/ *n* a signalling apparatus; an indicator connected with bells and telephones, to show where attendance is required.

anode /ˈænoːd/ *n* the positive electrode by which electrons enter an electric circuit.

anodyne /ˈænəˌdaɪn/ *n* a drug that relieves pain; anything that relieves pain or soothes.

anoestrus /æˈniːstrəs/ *n* the period of sexual inactivity in mammals between periods of estrus.—*also* **anestrus**.—**anoestrous, anestrous** *adj*.

anoint /əˈnɔɪnt/ *vt* to rub with oil; to apply oil in a sacred ritual as a sign of consecration.—**anointment** *n*.

anomalistic year /əˌnɒməˈlɪstɪk/ *n* the time occupied by the earth in passing through its orbit (365 days, 6 hours, 13 minutes, 48 seconds), from perihelion to perihelion.

anomalous /əˈnɒmələs/ *adj* deviating from the common order, abnormal.

anomaly /əˈnɒməli/ *n* (*pl* anomalies) abnormality; anything inconsistent or odd.—**anomalistic** *adj*.—**anomalistically** *adv*.

anon /əˈnɒn/ *adv* soon; at another time; (*arch*) anonymous.

anonym /ˈænənɪm/ *n* an unnamed person; an assumed name.

anonymous /əˈnɒnɪməs/ *adj* having or providing no name; written or provided by an unnamed person; lacking individuality.—**anonymity** *n*.—**anonymously** *adv*.

anopheles /əˈnɒfəˌliːz/ *n* (*pl* anopheles) any of a genus of mosquitos, which transmits the microbe of malaria.

anorak /ˈænəˌræk/ *n* a waterproof jacket with a hood.

anorexia /ˌænəˈrɛksɪə/ *n* loss of appetite.—**anorexic** *adj*.

anorexia nervosa /nərˈvoːsə/ *n* the psychological condition causing fear of becoming overweight and reluctance to eat even to the point of starvation and death.

anosmia /ænˈɒzmɪə/ *n* the inability to smell.—**anosmatic, anosmic** *adj*.

another /ə'nʌðər/ *adj* a different or distinct (thing or person); an additional one of the same kind; some other.—*also pron.*

ansate /'æn.seɪt/ *adj* with a handle, as a vase.

Anschluss /'ænʃlus/ *n* the union of Nazi Germany with Austria in 1938; the annexation of one territory by another for the benefit of the more powerful.

anserine /'ænsə.raɪn/ or /-rɪn-/, **anserous** /'ænsə.rəs/ *adj* of, relating to or resembling a goose; stupid as a goose.

answer /'ænsər/ *n* a spoken or written reply or response; the solution to a problem; a reaction, response. • *vt* to speak or write in reply; to satisfy or correspond to (*eg* a specific need); to justify, offer a refutation of. • *vi* to reply; to act in response (to); to be responsible (for); to conform (to).

answerable /'ænsərəbəl/ *adj* capable of being refuted; (*with* **for** *or* **to**) responsible, accountable.—**answerability** *n*.—**answerableness** *n*.

answering machine *n* an apparatus that records incoming telephone calls.

-ant /-ənt/ *adj suffix* as in *repentant*. • *n suffix* denoting agent, as in *celebrant*.

ant /ænt/ *n* any of a family of small, generally wingless insects of many species, all of which form and live in highly organized groups.

anta /'æntə/ *n* (*pl* **antae**) (*archit*) a square pilaster at either corner of a building, or at either side of a door.

antacid /ænt'æsɪd/ *n* a substance that counters excessive acidity.

antagonism /æn'tægə.nɪzəm/ *n* antipathy, hostility; an opposing force, principle, etc.

antagonist /æn'tægənɪst/ *n* an adversary; an opponent.

antagonistic /æn.tægə'nɪstɪk/ *adj* acting in opposition; opposed.—**antagonistically** *adv*.

antagonize /æn'tægə.naɪz/ *vt* to arouse opposition in.—**antagonization** *n*.

antalkali /ænt'ælkəlaɪ/ *n* (*pl* **antalkalis, antalkalies**) a substance that counteracts the presence of alkali in the system; an acid.—**antalkaline** *adj, n*.

Antarctic /ænt'ɑrktɪk/ or /-'ɑrtɪk/ *adj* of the South Pole or its surroundings. • *n* the Antarctic regions; the Antarctic Ocean.

ant bear *n* the aardvark.

ant bird *n* one of an extensive group of South American birds.

ant cow *n* an aphid or similar insect collected by ants for the sweet secretion in its body.

ante /'ænti/ *n* a player's stake in poker; (*inf*) money contributed as a share in a joint project.

ante- *prefix* in front of; earlier than.

anteater /'ænt.i:tər/ *n* an ant-eating animal, as the pangolin.

antecede /.ænti'si:d/ *n* to precede or go before in time or space.

antecedence /-'si:dəns/ *n* precedence; going before; priority.

antecedent /-'si:dənt/ *adj* prior in time, previous. • *n* a preceding event or happening; (*pl*) ancestry; (*pl*) the previous events of a person's life.

antechamber /'ænti.tʃeɪmbər/ *n* an anteroom.

antedate /.ænti'deɪt/ *vt* to carry back to an earlier period; to anticipate. • *n* a date *esp* on a document earlier than the actual date.

antediluvian /.æntidɪ'lu:viən/ *adj* of or pertaining to the world before the Flood; belonging to very ancient times; antiquated, primitive. • *n* one who lived before the Flood; an old-fashioned person.

antelope /'æntə.loʊp/ *n* (*pl* **antelopes, antelope**) any of the family of fast-running and graceful deer-like animals of Africa and Asia.

ante meridiem /.æntimə'rɪdiəm/ *n* (*abbr* a.m.) the period between midnight and noon.—**antemeridian** *adj*.

antenatal /.ænti'neɪtəl/ *adj* occurring or present before birth.

antenna /æn'tɛnə/ *n* (*pl* **antennae**) either of a pair of feelers on the head of an insect, crab, etc; (*pl* **antennas**) a metal device for transmitting and receiving radio waves.

antennule /æn'tɛnju:l/ *n* a little antenna.

antependium /.ænti'pɛndiəm/ *n* (*pl* **antependia**) a covering for the front of an altar.

antepenult /-pə'nʌlt/ *n* the last but two, *usu* of syllables.

antepenultimate /-pɪ'nʌltəmət/ *adj* pertaining to the last but two. • *n* that which is last but two, antepenult.

anterior /æn'ti:riər/ *adj* at or towards the front; earlier; previous.

anteroom /'ænti.ru:m/ *n* an outer room leading into a larger or main room.

anthelion /æn'θi:liən/ *n* (*pl* **anthelia**) (*meteorol*) a luminous halo, opposite the sun, formed around the shadow of the head of the observer, as projected on a cloud or fog bank.

anthem /'ænθəm/ *n* a religious choral song; a song of praise or devotion, as to a nation.

anther /'ænθər/ *n* the part of a flower's stamen containing pollen.—**antheral** *adj*.

anthill /'ænθɪl/ *n* a mound thrown up by ants or termites in digging their nests.

anthologize /æn'θɒlə.dʒaɪz/ *vt* to compile or include in an anthology.

anthology /æn'θɒlədʒi/ *n* (*pl* **anthologies**) a collection of poetry or prose.—**anthological** *adj*.—**anthologist** *n*.

anthozoan /.ænθə'zoʊən/ *n* any of a class of radiated soft marine zoophytes, which includes the sea anemones, corals, etc.—*also* **actinozoan**.

anthracene /'ænθrə.si:n/ *n* a complex hydrocarbon obtained from coal tar, the source of a red dye.

anthracite /'ænθrə.saɪt/ *n* a hard coal that gives off a lot of heat and little smoke.—**anthracitic** *adj*.

anthrax /'ænθræks/ *n* (*pl* **anthraxes**) a contagious bacterial disease of cattle and sheep, etc that can be transmitted to people.

anthropo- /'ænθrəpə/ or /-pə/ *prefix* man.

anthropocentric /.ænθrəpoʊ'sɛntrɪk/ or /.ænθrɒpoʊ-/ *adj* centring in man.—**anthropocentrism** *n*.

anthropoid /'ænθrə.pɔɪd/ *adj* resembling man. • *n* one of the higher apes resembling man.—**anthropoidal** *adj*.

anthropology /.ænθrə'pɒlədʒi/ *n* the scientific study of human beings, their origins, distribution, physical attributes and culture.—**anthropological** *adj*.—**anthropologist** *n*.

anthropometry /-'pɒmətri/ *n* the measurement of the human body; the branch of anthropology relating to such measurement of persons at various ages and in different tribes, races, occupations, etc.—**anthropometric, anthropometrical** *adj*.—**anthropometrist** *n*.

anthropomorphism /-pə'mɔrfɪzəm/ *n* the ascription of human behaviour to other animals or to things.—**anthropomorphic** *adj*.—**anthropomorphist** *n*.

anthropomorphize /-pə'mɔrfaɪz/ *vt* to invest with human qualities.

anthropomorphous /-pə'mɔrfəs/ *adj* in the form of a human being.

anthropophagi /-'pɒfədʒi/ *npl* (*sing* **anthropophagus**) cannibals, men-eaters.

anti- /'ænti/ or /'æntaɪ/ *prefix* opposed to; against.

anti-aircraft /.ænti'ɛrkræft/ *adj* for use against aircraft.

antiar /'ænti.ɑr/ *n* the upas tree of Java; a poison obtained from one species of it.

antibiotic /.æntibaɪ'ɒtɪk/ *n* any of various chemical, fungal or synthetic substances used against bacterial or fungal infections.

antibody /'ænti.bɒdi/ *n* (*pl* **antibodies**) a protein produced by an organism in response to the action of a foreign body, such as the toxin of a parasite, that neutralizes its effects.

antic /'æntɪk/ *n* a ludicrous action intended to amuse.

Antichrist /'ænti.kraɪst/ *n* (*Bible*) an opponent of Christ, *esp* the great personal opponent expected to appear before the end of the world (1 John 2:22).

Antichristian /'ænti.krɪstʃən/ or /'ænti.krɪstʃiən/ *n* one who is an opponent of the Christian religion. • *adj* pertaining to Antichrist; opposed to the Christian religion.

anticipant /æn'tɪsɪpənt/ *adj* operating beforehand. • *n* one who looks forward.

anticipate /æn'tɪsɪ.peɪt/ *vt* to give prior thought and attention to; to use, spend, act on in advance; to foresee and take action to thwart another; to expect. • *vi* to speak, act, before the appropriate time.

anticipation /æn.tɪsɪ'peɪʃən/ *n* the act of taking beforehand; expectation; hope; preconception.

anticlerical /.ænti'klɛrɪkəl/ *adj* opposed to the power of the clergy or church, *esp* in secular affairs. • *n* a person opposed to the power of the church.—**anticlericalism** *n*.

anticlimax /.ænti'klaɪmæks/ or /'æntaɪ-/ *n* a sudden drop from the important to the trivial; an ending to a story or series of events that disappoints one's expectations.—**anticlimactic** *adj*.—**anticlimactically** *adv*.

anticlinal /.ænti'klaɪnl/ *adj* (*strata*) inclining or folding with the convex side upwards; inclined in opposite directions.

anticlockwise /.ænti'klɒkwaɪz/ *see* **counterclockwise**.

anticoagulant /ˌæntɪkoːˈægjʊlənt/ n a substance that inhibits blood clotting.

anticyclone /ˌæntɪˈsaɪkloːn/ n a body of air rotating about an area of high atmospheric pressure.—**anticyclonic** adj.

antidepressant /ˌæntɪdəˈpresənt/ n any of various drugs used to alleviate mental depression.—also adj.

antidote /ˈæntɪˌdoːt/ n a remedy that counteracts a poison; something that counteracts harmful effects.

antifebrile /æntaɪˈfibrəl/ or /-ˈfebrəl/, /ˌænti:-/, /-tɪ-/ adj capable of allaying fever. • n a medicine for allaying fever.

antifreeze /ˈæntɪˌfriːz/ n a substance used, as in a car radiator, to prevent freezing up.

antigen /ˈæntɪdʒən/ or /-ˌdʒən/ n a substance introduced into the blood to stimulate production of antibodies.—**antigenic** adj.—**antigenically** adv.

antihero /ˈæntɪˌhiːroː/ n (pl **antiheroes**) a leading character in a book, film, etc who lacks the conventional heroic attributes.

antihistamine /ˌæntɪˈhɪstəmiːn/ or /-mɪn/ n any of a group of drugs that inhibit the action of histamines, used in treating allergic conditions.

antilog /ˈæntɪˌlɒg/ n an antilogarithm.

antilogarithm /ˌæntɪˈlɒgəˌrɪðəm/ n a number which a logarithm represents.—**antilogarithmic** adj.

antilogy /ænˈtɪlədʒi/ n (pl **antilogies**) a contradiction.

antimacassar /ˌæntɪməˈkæsər/ n an ornamental covering for chairbacks, etc, to prevent their being soiled (formerly by macassar oil, once used as a pomade).

antimasque /ˈæntɪˌmæsk/ n a droll or grotesque interlude between parts of a more serious nature in a masque.

antimatter /ˈæntɪˌmætər/ n matter composed of antiparticles.

antimere /ˈæntɪˌmɪr/ n (biol) one of two or more corresponding parts or organs on opposite sides of animals.—**antimeric** adj.—**antimerism** n.

antimonic /ˈæntɪˈmoːnɪk/, **antimonous** /ˈæntɪˈmoːnəs/ adj relating to, composed of, or obtained from antimony.

antimony /ˈæntɪˌmoːni/ n (pl **antimonies**) a brittle metallic element used in making alloys.—**antimonial** adj, n.

antinomy /ænˈtɪnəmi/ n (pl **antinomies**) contradiction in law or authorities or conclusions; the opposition of one law or part of a law to another.—**antinomic** adj.—**antinomically** adv.

antiparallel /ˌæntɪˈpærəˌlel/ or /ˌænti-/, /-ti:-/ adj running parallel, but in an opposite direction. • n one of two or more lines making equal angles with two other lines, but in contrary order.

antiparticle /ˈæntɪˌpɑrtɪkəl/ n an elementary particle with the same mass as its corresponding particle but having an equal and opposite electric charge, resulting in mutual destruction when brought into contact.

antipathetic /ˌæntɪpəˈθetɪk/, **antipathetical** /ˌæntɪpəˈθetɪkəl/ adj possessing or causing a natural antipathy or aversion (to).—**antipathetically** adv.

antipathy /ænˈtɪpəθi/ n (pl **antipathies**) a fixed dislike; aversion; an object of this.

antiperiodic /ˌæntɪˌpɪriˈɒdɪk/ adj preventive of a return in periodic or intermittent disease. • n a medicine for periodic diseases.

antipersonnel /ˌæntɪˌpərsəˈnel/ adj (weapon) used to destroy people rather than objects.

antiperspirant /ˌæntɪˈpərspɪrənt/ n a substance used to stem excessive perspiration.

antiphlogistic /ˌæntɪfləˈdʒɪstɪk/ adj efficacious in counteracting fever or inflammation. • n any remedy that checks inflammatory symptoms.

antiphon /ˈæntɪˌfɒn/ n a verse or sentence sung by one choir in response to another, as in church services; an anthem.

antiphonal /ænˈtɪfənəl/ adj characterized by responsive singing; sung alternately. • n a collection of antiphons.—**antiphonally** adv.

antiphonary /ænˈtɪfəˌneri/ n (pl **antiphonaries**) a book of responses used in church services; an antiphonal. • adj antiphonal or responsive.

antiphony /ænˈtɪfəni/ n (pl **antiphonies**) the alternate or responsive rendering of psalms or chants by a dual choir; a musical setting of sacred verses arranged for alternate singing.

antiphrasis /ænˈtɪfrəsɪs/ n (rhetoric) the use of words in a sense opposite to the true one.

antipodes /ænˈtɪpəˌdiːz/ npl the regions on the earth's surface opposite each other; (with cap preceded by the) Australia and New Zealand.—**antipodean** adj.

antipope /ˈæntɪˌpoːp/ n one who usurps or is elected to the papal office in opposition to a pope canonically elected; a rival pope.

antipyretic /ˌæntɪpaɪˈretɪk/ adj preventive of, or remedial to fever. • n a fever-allaying drug.—**antipyresis** n.

antipyrine /-ˈpaɪˌriːn/ or /-ˈpaɪrɪn/ n a drug obtained from coal tar and used to relieve neuralgia, etc, and to reduce heat in fevers.

antiquarian /ˌæntɪˈkwerɪən/ adj connected with the study of antiquities. • n an antiquary.

antiquary /ˈæntɪˌkweri/ n (pl **antiquaries**) a person who studies or collects antiquities.

antiquated /ˈæntɪˌkweɪtəd/ adj old-fashioned; obsolete.

antique /ænˈtiːk/ adj from the distant past; old-fashioned. • n a relic of the distant past; a piece of furniture, pottery, etc dating from an earlier historical period and sought after by collectors.

antiquity /ænˈtɪkwɪti/ n (pl **antiquities**) the far distant past, esp before the Middle Ages; (pl) relics dating from the far distant past.

antirrhinum /ˌæntɪˈraɪnəm/ n snapdragon.

antisabbatarian /ˌæntɪˌsæbəˈterɪən/ adj opposed to the observance of the Sabbath.—also n.

antiscorbutic /ˌæntɪskərˈbjuːtɪk/ n a remedy against scurvy.—also adj.

anti-Semite /ˌæntɪˈsemaɪt/ n one who is hostile toward or discriminates against Jews as a religious or racial group.—**anti-Semitic** adj.—**anti-Semitism** n.

antiseptic /ˌæntɪˈseptɪk/ n a substance that destroys or prevents the growth of disease-producing microorganisms. • adj destroying harmful organisms; very clean; (inf) unexciting.—**antiseptically** adv.

antiserum /ˈæntɪˌsiːrəm/ n (pl **antiserums, antisera**) blood serum containing antibodies.

antisocial /ˌæntɪˈsoːʃəl/ adj avoiding the company of other people, unsocial; contrary to the interests of society in general.

antispasmodic /-spæzˈmɒdɪk/ adj counteractive to or curative of spasms. • n a medicine having such an effect.

antistatic /-ˈstætɪk/ adj (material, agent) counteracting the effects of static electricity.

antistrophe /ænˈtɪstrəfi/ n a stanza or movement of a Greek chorus alternating with the strophe, sung in moving to the right.—**antistrophic** adj.

antithesis /ænˈtɪθəsɪs/ n (pl **antitheses**) a contrast or opposition, as of ideas; the exact opposite.—**antithetical, antithetic** adj.

antitoxin /ˌæntɪˈtɒksɪn/ n a substance that acts against a specific toxin in the body; a serum containing an antitoxin, injected into a person to prevent disease.—**antitoxic** adj.

antitrade /ˈæntɪˌtreɪd/ or /ˌænti-/ n a tropical wind blowing steadily in an opposite direction to the trade wind.

antitrust /ˌæntɪˈtrʌst/ adj (laws, regulations) restricting or opposing the activities of cartels and monopolies.

antitype /ˈæntɪˌtaɪp/ n that which a type or symbol stands for; that which preceded the type and of which the type is the representation.

antivenin /ˌæntɪˈvenɪn/ n an antidote to snake poison.

antivivisectionist /-ˌvɪvɪˈsekʃəˌnɪst/ n a person who opposes scientific experimentation on live animals.

antler /ˈæntlər/ n the branched horn of a deer or related animal.—**antlered** adj.

antlion n a neuropterous insect whose larva constructs a pitfall for ants and other insects.

antonomasia /ˌæntənəˈmeɪʒə/ n (rhetoric) the use of an attribute or epithet, or style of dignity or office, in place of the proper noun, eg "the Stagirite" for Aristotle, or the reverse, of a proper noun for a common noun, eg "some mute inglorious Milton".—**antonomastic** adj.—**antonomastically** adv.

antonym /ˈæntənɪm/ n a word that has the opposite meaning to another.

antrum /ˈæntrəm/ n (pl **antra**) (anat) a cavity, esp in the upper jawbone.

anurous /ænˈjuːrəs/ adj (zool) tailless.

anus /ˈeɪnəs/ n the excretory orifice of the alimentary canal.

anvil /ˈænvɪl/ n the heavy iron block on which metal objects are shaped with a hammer.

anxiety /ænˈzaɪəti/ n (pl **anxieties**) the condition of being anxious; eagerness, concern; a cause of worry.

anxious /ˈænkʃəs/ adj worried; uneasy; eagerly wishing; causing anxiety.—**anxiously** adv.—**anxiousness** n.

any /ˈeni/ adj one out of many, some; every.

anybody /-ˌbɐdi/ or /-ˌbɒdi/ *pron* any person; an important person.

anyhow /-ˌhaʊ/ *adv* in any way whatever; in any case.

any more, anymore /-ˈmɔr/ *adv* now; nowadays.

anyone /-ˌwʌn/ *pron* any person; anybody.

anything /-θɪŋ/ *pron* any object, event, fact, etc. • *n* a thing, no matter what kind.

anyway /-ˌweɪ/ *adv* in any manner; at any rate; haphazardly.

anywhere /-ˌwer/ *adv* in, at, or to any place.

Anzac /ˈænˌzæk/ *abbr* = Australian and New Zealand Army Corps. • *n* a member of this corps.—*also adj.*

aorist /ˈeɪərɪst/ *n* (*gram*) an indeterminate past tense of the verb expressing completed action. • *adj* indefinite; pertaining to the aorist tense.—**aoristic** *adj.*—**aoristically** *adv.*

aorta /eɪˈɔrtə/ *n* (*pl* **aortas, aortae**) the main artery that carries blood from the heart to be distributed through the body.—**aortic, aortal** *adj.*

aoudad /ˈaʊˌdæd/ or /ˈaʊˌdæd/ *n* a wild sheep-like animal of North Africa, somewhat resembling the chamois.

ap- /æp/ *prefix* the form of *ad-* before *p.*

apace /əˈpeɪs/ *adv* at a swift pace.

apache /əˈpæʃ/ *Fr.* /aˈpaʃ/ *n* a Parisian street ruffian, a hooligan.

Apache /əˈpætʃi/ *n* (*pl* **Apaches, Apache**) a tribe of North American Indians.

apagoge /æpəˈgoːgi/ or /-ˈgɔg/ *n* (*logic*) the establishing of a proposition by demonstrating the untenability of its opposite.—**apagogic, apagogical** *adj.*—**apagogically** *adv.*

apanage /ˈæpənɪdʒ/ *see* **appanage.**

apart /əˈpɑrt/ *adv* at a distance, separately, aside; into two or more pieces.

apartheid /əˈpɑrtaɪt/ or /-teɪt/, /-taɪd/ *n* a policy of racial segregation implemented in South Africa.

apartment /əˈpɑrtmənt/ *n* a room or rooms in a building; a flat.

apathetic /ˌæpəˈθetɪk/ *adj* devoid of or insensible to feeling or emotion.—**apathetically** *adv.*

apathy /ˈæpəθi/ *n* lack of feeling; lack of concern, indifference.—**apathetic** *adj.*—**apathetically** *adv.*

apatite /ˈæpəˌtaɪt/ *n* a crystalline phosphate of lime.

ape /eɪp/ *n* a chimpanzee, gorilla, orangutan, or gibbon; any monkey; a mimic. • *vt* to imitate.

apeak /əˈpiːk/ *adv* (*naut*) nearly vertical in position.

apeman /ˈeɪpˌmæn/ *n* (*pl* **apemen**) an extinct creature supposedly intermediate in development between apes and man.

aperçu /ˌæpərˈsuː/, *Fr.* /apɛrˈsu/ *n* a first view; a rapid survey; a brief outline.

aperient /əˈpɪriənt/ *adj* gently laxative; opening the bowels. • *n* a mild laxative medicine.

aperiodic /ˌeɪpɪriˈɒdɪk/ *adj* without periodicity.—**aperiodically** *adv.*—**aperiodicity** *n.*

aperitif, apéritif /əˌperiˈtiːf/, *Fr.* /apeɪriːˈtiːf/ *n* an alcoholic drink taken before a meal as an appetizer.

aperture /ˈæpərˌtʃər/ *n* an opening; a hole; a slit; in optical instruments, the (diameter of the) opening allowing or controlling the amount of light or radiation to enter.

apery /ˈeɪpəri/ *n* (*pl* **aperies**) mimicry.

apetalous /eɪˈpetələs/ *adj* without petals or corolla.—**apetaly** *n.*

apex /ˈeɪpeks/ *n* (*pl* **apexes, apices**) the highest point, the tip; the culminating point; the vertex of a triangle.

aphaeresis /əˈfirəsɪs/ or /-ˈfe-/ *n* (*pl* **aphaereses**) (*linguistics*) the removal of a letter or syllable from the beginning of a word.—*also* **apheresis.**

aphagia /əˈfeɪdʒə/ *n* the inability to swallow.

aphasia /əˈfeɪʒə/ or /-ziə/ *n* loss of the power of speech or the appropriate use of words due to disease or injury of the brain.—**aphasic** *adj.*

aphelion /æpˈhiːliən/ or /əˈfiːliən/ *n* (*pl* **aphelia**) that point in the orbit of a planet or a comet which is farthest from the sun.

apheliotropic /əˌfiːliəˈtrɒpɪk/ *adj* (*bot*) turning from the sun.

apheresis /əˈferəsɪs/ or /əˈfirəsɪs/ *see* **aphaeresis.**

aphesis /ˈæfɪsɪs/ *n* (*linguistics*) the gradual loss of an unaccented vowel at the beginning of a word, as in "squire" for "esquire".—**aphetic** *adj.*—**aphetically** *adv.*

aphid /ˈeɪfɪd/ or /ˈæfɪd/ *n* any of various small insects, such as the greenfly, that suck the juice of plants.

aphis /ˈeɪfɪs/ or /ˈæfɪs/ *n* (*pl* **aphides**) an aphid.

aphonia /əˈfoːnɪə/, **aphony** /-i/ *n* dumbness, loss of voice.—**aphonic** *adj.*

aphorism /ˈæfəˌrɪzəm/ *n* a brief, wise saying; an adage.—**aphoristic** *adj.*

aphrodisiac /ˌæfroˈdiːziæk/ or /ˌæfrəˈdɪziˌæk/ *adj* arousing sexually. • *n* a food, drug, etc that excites sexual desire.

aphtha /ˈæfθə/ or /ˈæp-/ *n* (*pl* **aphthae**) the small round white ulcers infesting the interior of the mouth; thrush.

aphyllous /əˈfɪləs/ *adj* (*bot*) without leaves.—**aphylly** *n.*

apian /ˈeɪpiən/ *adj* of, pertaining to, or like bees.

apiarian /ˌeɪpiˈeriən/ *adj* of or relating to beekeeping.

apiarist /ˈeɪpiərɪst/ *n* a beekeeper.

apiary /ˈeɪpiˌeri/ *n* (*pl* **apiaries**) a place with hives where bees are kept.

apical /ˈæpɪkəl/ or /ˈeɪpɪ-/ *adj* of, pertaining to, belonging to, or at the apex.—**apically** *adv.*

apices /ˈæpəˌsiːz/, /ˈeɪpə-/ *see* **apex.**

apiculate /əˈpɪkjʊlɪt/ or /-ˌleɪt/ *adj* terminated abruptly by a point, as leaves.

apiculture /ˈeɪpɪˌkʌltʃər/ *n* beekeeping.—**apicultural** *adj.*—**apiculturist** *n.*

apiece /əˈpiːs/ *adv* to, by, or for each one.

apish /ˈeɪpɪʃ/ *adj* like an ape in manners; foolish; imitative.—**apishness** *n.*

apivorous /eɪˈpɪvərəs/ *adj* feeding on bees.

aplacental /ˌeɪpləˈsentəl/ *adj* without a placenta.

aplanatic /ˌæpləˈnætɪk/ *adj* (*physics*) free from, or correcting, spherical or chromatic aberration.—**aplanatically** *adv.*

aplastic /əˈplæstɪk/ *adj* without plasticity; not easily moulded.

aplomb /əˈplɒm/ *n* poise; self-possession.

apnea, apnoea /æpˈniːə/ *n* partial suspension of breathing; suffocation.—**apnoeic** *adj.*

apo- /ˈæpə/ or /ˈæpoː/ *prefix* off, from, away; un-; quite.

apocalypse /əˈpɒkəlɪps/ *n* a cataclysmic event, the end of the world; revelation, *esp* that of St John; (*with cap*) the last book of the New Testament.—**apocalyptic** *adj.*—**apocalyptically** *adv.*

apocarpous /ˌæpəˈkɑrpəs/ *adj* (*bot*) having the carpels of the ovary separate or distinct.

apochromat /ˈæpəkrəˌmæt/ or /ˌæpə-/ *n* a highly achromatic lens.—**apochromatic** *adj.*

apocopate /əˈpɒkəˌpeɪt/ *vt* to cut off or drop the last letter or syllable of a word.—**apocopation** *n.*

apocope /əˈpɒkəpi/ *n* (*linguistics*) the cutting off or deletion of the last letter or syllable of a word.

Apocrypha /əˈpɒkrɪfə/ *npl* (*used as sing*) books of the Old Testament, *eg* Ecclesiasticus, accepted as an authentic part of the Holy Scriptures by the RC Church but not by Protestants.

apocryphal /əˈpɒkrɪfəl/ *adj* doubtful; untrue; invented; (*with cap*) of the Apocrypha.—**apocryphally** *adv.*

apodal /ˈæpədəl/ *adj* without feet.

apodeictic, apodictic /ˌæpəˈdɪktɪk/ *adj* clearly established, unquestionable true.—**apodeictically, apodictically** *adv.*

apodosis /əˈpɒdəsɪs/ *n* (*pl* **apodoses**) (*gram*) the latter portion, or consequent clause, of a conditional sentence.

apogamy /əˈpɒgəmi/ *n* the absence of sexual reproduction; asexual reproduction.—**apogamic** *adj.*—**apogamous** *adj.*

apogee /ˈæpəˌdʒi/ *n* the point in the orbit of the moon or any planet where it is most distant from the earth; the highest point.

apolitical /ˌeɪpəˈlɪtɪkəl/ *adj* uninterested or uninvolved in politics.

Apollo /əˈpɒloː/ *n* (Greek, Roman myth) a sun god and god of music; (*pl* **Apollos**) a young handsome man.

apologetic /əˌpɒləˈdʒetɪk/ *adj* expressing an apology; contrite; presented in defence.—**apologetically** *adv.*

apologetics /-ɪks/ *n* (*used as sing*) the defence and vindication of the principles and laws of Christian belief.

apologia /ˌæpəˈloːdʒiə/ *n* a written defence of one's principles or conduct.

apologist /əˈpɒlədʒɪst/ *n* a person who makes an apology; a defender of a cause.

apologize /əˈpɒləˌdʒaɪz/ *vi* to make an apology.

apologue /ˈæpəˌlɒg/ *n* a moral fable; a fiction or allegory embodying a moral application, as *Aesop's Fables.*

apology /əˈpɒlədʒi/ *n* (*pl* **apologies**) an expression of regret for wrongdoing; a defence or justification of one's beliefs, etc; (*with* **for**) a poor substitute.

apophthegm /ˈæpəˌθem/ or /ˈæpəfˌθem/ *n* a pithy saying embodying a wholesome truth or precept, a maxim.—*also* **apothegm.**

apophyge /ə'pɒfə,dʒiː/ *n* (archit) the small hollow curve of a column where it springs from the base or top of the shaft.

apoplectic /ˌæpə'plɛktɪk/ *adj* of, causing, or exhibiting symptoms of apoplexy; (*inf*) furious.

apoplexy /'æpə,plɛksi/ *n* a sudden loss of consciousness and subsequent partial paralysis, *usu* caused by a broken or blocked artery in the brain.

aport /ə'pɔrt/ *adv* (*naut*) on or towards the port or left side of a ship.

aposiopesis /ˌæpə,saɪə'piːsɪs/ *n* (*pl* **aposiopeses**) (*rhetoric*) a sudden breaking off in speech for effect, *eg* "Bertrand is —what I dare not name".—**aposiopetic** *adj*.

apostasy /ə'pɒstəsi/ *n* (*pl* **apostasies**) abandonment of one's religion, principles or political party.

apostate /-teɪt/ *n* a person who commits apostasy.

apostatize /-tə,taɪz/ *vi* to abandon one's faith, church or party; to change one's religion for another.

a posteriori /ˌeɪpɒˌstiri'ɔraɪ/ *adj* (*logic*) inductively, from effect to cause, founded on observation of facts, effects or consequences.

apostil /ə'pɒstɪl/ *n* a marginal note.

apostle /ə'pɒsəl/ *n* the first or principal supporter of a new belief or cause; (*with cap*) one of the twelve disciples of Christ.

apostle spoon *n* a spoon having a figure of one of the Apostles at the top of the handle.

Apostles' Creed *n* the shortest of the three creeds, so named as containing a summary of apostolic doctrine.

apostolate /ə'pɒstələt/ *n* the dignity or office of an apostle, now restricted to that of the pope.

apostolic /ˌæpə'stɒlɪk/ *adj* of or relating to the Apostles or their teachings; of or relating to the pope as successor to the Apostle St Peter.

Apostolic Church, Apostolic See *n* the Christian church as founded and governed by the Apostles on their doctrine and order. The name originally applied to the Churches of Rome, Antioch, Ephesus, Alexandria and Jerusalem.

Apostolic succession *n* the regular and uninterrupted transmission of ministerial authority by bishops from the Apostles.

apostrophe[1] /ə'pɒstrəfi/ *n* a mark (') showing the omission of letters or figures, *also* a sign of the possessive case or the plural of letters and figures; a breaking off in speech to appeal to someone dead or absent.—**apostrophic** *adj*.

apostrophe[2] *n* (*rhetoric*) a digression made in a speech or address, *esp* one directed at a person.

apostrophize /-ˌfaɪz/ *vt* to address by apostrophe; to omit a letter or letters; to mark an omission by the sign ('). • *vi* to make an apostrophe or short digressive address in speaking.

apothecaries' weight *n* a system of weights used for dispensing drugs, comprising the pound (12 oz), the ounce (8 drachms), the drachm (3 scruples), the scruple (20 grains), and the grain.

apothecary /ə'pɒθə,kɛri/ *n* (*pl* **apothecaries**) (*arch*) one who prepares and dispenses medicines and drugs, a pharmacist.

apothecium /ˌæpə'θiːsiəm/ *n* (*pl* **apothecia**) the shield-like receptacle of lichens.—**apothecial** *adj*.

apothegm /'æpə,θɛm/ *see* **apophthegm**.

apotheosis /ə,pɒθi'oːsɪs/ *n* (*pl* **apotheoses**) deification; glorification of a person or thing; the supreme or ideal example.

apotheosize /ə'pɒθiə,saɪz/ *vt* to exalt to the rank of a god; to deify.

appal, appall /ə'pɒl/ *vt* (**appals** or **appalls, appalling, appalled**) to fill with terror or dismay.

appalling /-ɪŋ/ *adj* shocking, horrifying.—**appallingly** *adv*.

appanage /'æpənɪdʒ/ *n* provision for the younger sons of kings, etc; a perquisite; a dependency; an attribute.—*also* **apanage**.

apparatus /ˌæpə'rætəs/ or /-'reɪt-/ *n* (*pl* **apparatus, apparatuses**) the equipment used for a specific task; any complex machine, device, or system.

apparel /ə'pɛrəl/ or /-pær-/ *n* clothing, dress. • *vt* (**apparelling, apparelled** or **appareling, appareled**) to dress; to clothe.

apparent /ə'pɛrənt/ or /-pær-/ *adj* easily seen, evident; seeming, but not real.—**apparently** *adv*.

apparition /ˌæpə'rɪʃən/ *n* an appearance or manifestation, *esp* something unexpected or unusual; a ghost.

appassionato /ə,pɒsiə'nɒtoː/, *It.* /a,pasjə'naːtə/ *adj, adv* (*mus*) with passion.

appeal /ə'piːl/ *vi* to take a case to a higher court; to make an earnest request; to refer to a witness or superior authority for vindication, confirmation, etc; to arouse pleasure or sympathy. • *n* the referral of a lawsuit to a higher court for rehearing; an earnest call for help; attraction, the power of arousing sympathy; a request for public donations to a charitable cause.—**appealable** *adj*.—**appealer** *n*.—**appealing** *adj*.

appear /ə'piːr/ *vi* to become or be visible; to arrive, come in person; to be published; to present oneself formally (before a court, etc); to seem, give an impression of being.

appearance /-əns/ *n* the act or occasion of appearing; that which appears; external aspect of a thing or person; outward show, semblance.

appease /ə'piːz/ *vt* to pacify; to allay; to conciliate by making concessions.—**appeasement** *n*.

appellant /ə'pɛlənt/ *n* a person who makes an appeal to a higher court.

appellate /-lət/ *adj* pertaining to appeals; dealing with appeals. • *n* the person appealed against or called upon to appear.

appellation /ˌæpə'leɪʃən/ *n* the name, title or designation by which a person or thing is called or known; the act of appealing.

appellative /ə'pɛlətɪv/ *n* (*gram*) a common, as distinguished from a proper, name; the designation of a class. • *adj* serving to distinguish, as a name or denomination of a group or class; common, as a noun.

appellee /ˌæpə'liː/ or /ə,pɛli/ *n* the person appealed against; the defendant in an appeal.

append /ə'pɛnd/ *vt* to attach; to add, *esp* to the end as a supplement, etc.

appendage /ə'pɛndɪdʒ/ *n* something appended; an external organ or part, as a tail.

appendant /ə'pɛndənt/ *adj* attached or annexed; attached in a subordinate capacity to another. • *n* that which is appended or added.

appendicectomy, appendectomy /ˌæpen'dɛktəmi/ *n* (*pl* **appendicectomies, appendectomies**) surgical removal of the appendix that grows from the intestine.

appendicitis /ə,pɛndɪ'saɪtɪs/ *n* inflammation of the appendix that grows from the intestine.

appendicle /ə'pɛndɪkəl/ *n* a small appendage.

appendix /ə'pɛndɪks/ *n* (*pl* **appendixes, appendices**) a section of supplementary information at the back of a book, etc; a small tube of tissue that forms an outgrowth of the intestine.—*also* **vermiform appendix**.

apperception /ˌæpər'sɛpʃən/ *n* (*psychol*) perception with consciousness of self.—**apperceptive** *adj*.

appertain /ˌæpər'teɪn/ *vi* to belong or pertain to, as by relation or custom.

appetence /'æpətəns/, **appetency** /'æpətənsi/ *n* (*pl* **appetences, appetencies**) desire, craving; affinity.

appetite /'æpə,taɪt/ *n* sensation of bodily desire, *esp* for food; (*with* **for**) a strong desire or liking, a craving.

appetizer /-,taɪzər/ *n* a food or drink that stimulates the appetite; something that whets one's interest.

appetizing /-,taɪzɪŋ/ *adj* stimulating the appetite.—**appetizingly** *adv*.

applaud /ə'plɒd/ *vt* to show approval, *esp* by clapping the hands; to praise.

applause /ə'plɒz/ *n* approval expressed by clapping; acclamation.

apple /'æpəl/ *n* a round, firm, fleshy, edible fruit.

apple brandy *n* a liqueur distilled from cider.

applecart *n* upset the applecart to spoil one's plans.

applejack /'æpəl,dʒæk/ *n* apple brandy.

apple-pie bed *n* a bed made with the sheets folded so that one's legs cannot get down.

apple-pie order *n* perfect order.

apple sauce /'æpəl,sɒs/ *n* a sauce of stewed apples *usu* served with pork; (*sl*) nonsense, flattery.

appliance /ə'plaɪəns/ *n* a device or machine, *esp* for household use.

applicable /ə'plɪkəbəl/ *adj* that may be applied; appropriate, relevant (to).—**applicability** *n*.

applicant /'æplɪkənt/ *n* a person who applies, *esp* for a job.

application /ˌæplɪ'keɪʃən/ *n* the act of applying; the use to which something is put; a petition, request; concentration, diligent effort; relevance or practical value.

applicative /'æplɪ,keɪtɪv/ *adj* capable of being applied.

applicator /'æplɪ,keɪtər/ *n* a device for applying something.

applicatory /'æplɪkə,tɔri/ *adj* fit to be applied.

applied /ə'plaɪd/ *adj* practical.

appliqué /'æplɪkeɪ/ *n* ornamental fabricwork applied to another fabric. • *vt* (**appliquéing, appliquéed**) to decorate with appliqué.

apply /ə'plaɪ/ *vb* (**applying, applied**) *vt* to bring to bear; to put to practical use; to spread, lay on; to devote (oneself) with close attention. • *vi* to make a formal, *esp* written, request; to be relevant.

appoggiatura /ə‚pɒdʒə'tʊərə/ *n* (*pl* **appoggiaturas, appoggiatura**) (*mus*) a grace note immediately preceding a principal note with which it is connected, and taking its time from the latter.

appoint /ə'pɔɪnt/ *vt* to fix or decide officially; to select for a job; to prescribe.

appointed /ə‚pɔɪntəd/ *adj* equipped; furnished.

appointee /ə‚pɔɪn'tiː/ or /‚æpɔɪn'tiː/ *n* a person appointed.

appointment /ə'pɔɪntmənt/ *n* an appointing; a job or position for which someone has been selected; an arrangement to meet.

apportion /ə'pɔrʃən/ *vt* to divide into shares; allot.—**apportionable** *adj*.—**apportioner** *n*.—**apportionment** *n*.

appose /ə'poːz/ *vt* to apply; to place opposite or in juxtaposition.

apposite /'æpəzɪt/ *adj* (*remarks*) especially pertinent, appropriate.—**appositably** *adv*.

apposition /‚æpə'zɪʃən/ *n* the act of adding; addition by application, or placing together; (*gram*) the placing of a second noun in the same case in juxtaposition to the first, which it characterizes or explains, as St Mark, the Evangelist.—**appositional** *adj*.

appraisal /ə'preɪzəl/, **appraisement** /ə'preɪzmənt/ *n* the act of appraising or valuing, *esp* the putting of a price upon with a view to sale; a valuation.

appraise /ə'preɪz/ *vt* to estimate the value or quality of.—**appraiser** *n*.

appreciable /ə'priːʃəbəl/ *adj* capable of being perceived or measured; fairly large.—**appreciably** *adv*.

appreciate /ə'priːʃiˌeɪt/ *vt* to value highly; to recognize gratefully; to understand, be aware of; to increase the value of. • *vi* to rise in value.

appreciation /ə‚priːʃi'eɪʃən/ *n* gratitude, approval; sensitivity to aesthetic values; an assessment or critical evaluation of a person or thing; a favourable review; an increase in value.—**appreciative** *adj*.

apprehend /‚æprɪ'hɛnd/ *vt* to arrest, capture; to understand, to perceive.

apprehension /‚æprɪ'hɛnʃən/ *n* anxiety; the act of arresting; understanding; an idea.

apprehensive /‚æprɪ'hɛnsɪv/ *adj* uneasy; anxious.—**apprehensively** *adv*.

apprentice /ə'prɛntɪs/ *n* one being taught a trade or craft; a novice. • *vt* to take on as an apprentice.—**apprenticeship** *n*.

apprise, apprize /ə'praɪz/ *vt* to give notice to; to inform.

approach /ə'proːtʃ/ *vi* to draw nearer. • *vt* to make a proposal to; to set about dealing with; to come near to. • *n* the act of approaching; a means of entering or leaving; a move to establish relations; the final descent of an aircraft.

approachable /ə'proːtʃəbəl/ *adj* within approaching distance; easy to approach; inviting friendship.—**approachability** *n*.—**approachably** *adv*.

approbation /‚æprə'beɪʃən/ *n* formal approval; sanction.

appropriate /ə'proːprɪət/ *adj* fitting, suitable. • *vt* to take for one's own use, *esp* illegally; (*money, etc*) to set aside for a specific purpose.—**appropriately** *adv*.—**appropriateness** *n*.

appropriation /ə‚proːprɪ'eɪʃən/ *n* the act of setting apart or reserving for one's own use; a sum of money set aside for a particular purpose.

approval /ə'pruːvəl/ *n* the act of approving; favourable opinion; official permission.

approve /ə'pruːv/ *vt* to express a good opinion of; to authorize. • *vi* (*with* **of**) to consider to be favourable or satisfactory.

approx. *abbr* = approximate(ly).

approximate /ə'prɒksɪmət/ *adj* almost exact or correct. • *vt* to come near to; to be almost the same as. • *vi* to come close. —**approximately** *adv*.

approximation /ə‚prɒksɪ'meɪʃən/ *n* a close estimate; a near likeness.

appulse /ə'pɒlz/ *n* a coming towards; (astron) the near approach of a planet to a conjunction with the sun or any fixed star.—**appulsive** *adj*.

appurtenance /ə'pərtɪnəns/ *n* that which belongs or relates to something else; an adjunct or appendage; that which belongs it, is accessory to; an estate or property.—**appurtenant** *adj, n*.

Apr. *abbr* = April.

APR. *abbr* = annual percentage rate.

après-ski /‚æpreɪ'skiː/, *Fr.* /a'prɛ-/ *n* social activity after skiing. —*also adj*.

apricot /'æprɪˌkɒt/ or /'eɪprɪ-/ *n* a small, oval, orange-pink fruit resembling the plum and peach.

April /'eɪprəl/ *n* the fourth month of the year, having 30 days.

April Fool *n* the victim of a trick played on 1 April, **April Fool's Day**.

a priori /‚eɪpraɪ'ɔraɪ/ (*Latin*) deductively, from cause to effect.

apron /'eɪprən/ *n* a garment worn to protect clothing often tied at the waist; anything resembling the shape of an apron used for protection; the paved surface on an airfield where aircraft are parked, etc.

apropos /‚æprə'poː/ or /'æprəˌpoː/ *adv* at the right time; opportunely; appropriately. • *adj* appropriate. • *prep* (*with* **of**) regarding, in reference to.

apse /æps/ *n* a domed or vaulted recess, *esp* in a church.

apsis /'æpsɪs/ *n* (*pl* **apsides** /'æpsəˌdiːz/) (*astron*) one of two points in the orbit of a planet situated at the furthest or the least distance from the central body or sun; the imaginary line connecting these points.—**apsidal** *adj*.

apt /æpt/ *adj* ready or likely (to); suitable, relevant; able to learn easily.—**aptness** *n*.

apteral /'æptərəl/ *adj* (*archit*) without side columns.

apterous /'æptərəs/ *adj* without wings.

apterygial /‚æptə'rɪdʒɪəl/ *adj* lacking wings or fins.

apteryx /'æptərɪks/ *n* the kiwi, a New Zealand bird with rudimentary wings and no tail.

aptitude /'æptɪˌtuːd/ or /-ˌtjuːd/ *n* suitability; natural talent, *esp* for learning.

apyretic /‚eɪpaɪ'rɛtɪk/ *adj* without fever, or with intermission of fever.

aq *abbr* = aqua.

aqua *n* /'ækwə/ or /ɒ-/ (*pl* **aquae** /'eɪkwi/, **aquas** /'ækwəz/) water as used in pharmacy.

aquaculture /-ˌkɛltʃər/ or /ɒkwə-/ *n* the cultivation and breeding of fish and other marine organisms.—*also* **aquiculture**. —**aquacultural** *adj*.—**aquaculturist** *n*.

aqua fortis *n* /-'fɔrtɪs/ or /‚pkwə/ impure nitric acid.

aqualung /'ækwəˌlʌŋ/ *n* portable diving gear comprising air cylinders connected to a face mask.

aquamarine /‚ækwəmə'riːn/ *n* a variety of bluish-green beryl used as a gemstone; its colour.

aquaplane /'ækwəˌpleɪn/ *n* a plank towed at high speed. • *vi* to ride on one.

aqua regia /‚ækwə'riːdʒɪə/ *n* a mixture of nitric and hydrochloric acids, capable of dissolving gold.

aquarelle /‚ækwə'rɛl/ or /‚ɒkwə'rɛl/ *n* a style of painting in Chinese ink and thin watercolours; a painting so executed. —**aquarellist** *n*.

aquarium /ə'kwɛrɪəm/ *n* (*pl* **aquariums, aquaria**) a tank, pond, etc for keeping aquatic animals or plants; a building where collections of aquatic animals are exhibited.

Aquarius /ə'kwɛrɪəs/ *n* (*astrol*) the eleventh sign of the zodiac, the water-carrier, operative 20 January–18 February.—**Aquarian** *adj, n*.

aquatic /ə'kwætɪk/ or /ə'kwɒtɪk/ *adj* of or taking place in water; living or growing in water.

aquatics /ə'kwætɪks/ or /ə'kwɒtɪks/ *npl* water sports.

aquatint /'ækwətɪnt/ *n* a style of etching resembling a watercolour drawing in Indian ink or in sepia; an engraving produced by this process. • *vt* to etch or engrave in aquatint.

aqua vitae /‚ækwə'viːtaɪ/ *n* unrectified alcohol; brandy and other ardent spirits.

aqueduct /'ækwəˌdʌkt/ *n* a large pipe or conduit for carrying water; an elevated structure supporting this.

aqueous /'eɪkwɪəs/ *adj* of, like, or formed by water.

aqueous humour *n* a limpid fluid of the eye, filling the space between the crystalline lens and the cornea.

aquiculture /'ækwɪˌkɛltʃər/ or /'ɒk-/ *n* hydroponics; another name for aquaculture.—**aquicultural** *adj*.—**aquiculturist** *n*.

aquilegia /‚ækwə'liːdʒə/ *n* columbine.

aquiline /'ækwɪˌlaɪn/ *adj* of or like an eagle; (*nose*) hooked, like an eagle's beak.

ar- /ər/ *prefix* the form of *ad-* before *r*.

-ar /ər/ *adj suffix* of, belonging to, as in *angular, popular*.

Ar (*chem symbol*) argon.

Arab /'ærəb/ or /'ɛrəb/ n a native of Arabia; one of the Arabic races spread over the African and Syrian deserts. • adj pertaining to Arabia or the Arabs.

arabesque /ˌærə'bɛsk/ or /ɛrə-/ n a decorative design incorporating organic motifs, such as leaves and flowers, in an intricate pattern; (ballet) a posture in which the dancer balances on one leg with one arm extending forwards and the other arm and leg extending backwards.

Arabian /ə'reɪbiən/ adj of Arabia, Arab. • n an Arab.

Arabian camel n a camel with a single hump.

Arabic /'ærəbɪk/ or /'ɛrə-/ n the Arabian language. • adj of or pertaining to the Arabic language and the countries in which it is spoken.

Arabic numeral n one of the numbers 0, 1, 2, 3, 4, 5, etc.

arable /'ærəbəl/ or /ɛr-/ adj (land) suitable for ploughing or planting crops.—also n.

arachnid /ə'ræknɪd/ n any of a class of animals including spiders, scorpions, mites and ticks.—**arachnidan** adj, n.

arachnoid /-ˌnɔɪd/ adj pertaining to spiders; resembling the web of a spider. • n the enveloping membrane of the brain and spinal cord, between the dura mater and the pia mater.

aragonite /ə'rægəˌnɔɪt/ or /'ærəgə-/ n a variety of carbonate of lime.

arak /ə'ræk/ see arrack.

Aramaic /ˌærə'meɪɪk/ or /ˌɛrə-/ n the language of Palestine at the time of Christ.

araneid /ə'reɪnɪˌɪd/ n a member of the Arachnida order, the spider family.

araucaria /ˌærɒ'keriə/ n one of a genus of coniferous trees, found principally in South America and Australia, which includes the monkey puzzle.

arbalest /'arbəˌlɛst/ n a crossbow with a drawing mechanism.

arbiter /'arbɪtər/ n a person having absolute power of decision or absolute control.

arbitrage /'arbɪtrɒdʒ/ or /-trɑdʒ/ n the rapid purchase and resale of stocks to maximize price discrepancy, often using confidential knowledge.—also **index arbitrage.**

arbitrament /'arbɪtrəmənt/ n an arbiter's judgment; an authoritative decision.

arbitrary /'arbəˌtreri/ adj not bound by rules; despotic, absolute; capricious, unreasonable.—**arbitrarily** adv.—**arbitrariness** n.

arbitrate /'arbɪˌtreɪt/ vi to act as an arbitrator. • vt to submit to an arbiter; to act as an arbiter upon.

arbitration /ˌarbɪ'treɪʃən/ n the settlement of disputes by arbitrating.

arbitrator /ˌarbɪ'treɪtər/ n a person chosen to settle a dispute between contending parties.

arbor[1] /'arbər/ see arbour.

arbor[2] n the main support of a machine; an axis, a spindle.

arboraceous /ˌarbə'reɪʃəs/ adj pertaining to, or of the nature of, a tree or trees; living on or among trees.

arboreal /ar'bɔriəl/ adj of or living in trees.

arboreous /ær'bɔriəs/ adj wooded.

arborescent /ˌarˌbə'rɛsənt/ adj growing or formed like a tree.—**arborescence** n.

arboretum /ˌarbə'ri:təm/ n (pl **arboreta, arboretums**) a botanical tree garden where rare trees are cultivated and exhibited.

arboriculture /'arbərɪˌkʌltʃər/ n the cultivation of trees and shrubs, forestry.

arborization, arborisation /ˌarbəri'zeɪʃən/ n a tree-like appearance.

arbor vitae /ˌarbər'vi:taɪ/ n an evergreen tree extensively cultivated in gardens, etc.

arbour /'arbər/ n a place shaded by trees, foliage, etc; a bower.—also **arbor.**

arbutus /ar'bju:təs/ n (pl **arbutuses**) one of a genus of tree-like evergreen shrubs to which the strawberry tree belongs.

arc /ark/ n a portion of the circumference of a circle or other curve; a luminous discharge of electricity across a gap between two electrodes or terminals. • vi to form an electric arc.

ARC /ˌeɪ'ar'si:/ abbr = AIDS-related complex.

arcade /ar'keɪd/ n a series of arches supported on columns; an arched passageway; a covered walk or area lined with shops.

Arcadia /ar'keɪdiə/, **Arcady** /ar'keɪdi/ n (poet) ideal countryside.

Arcadian /ar'keɪdiən/ adj of or pertaining to Arcadia, a department of Greece, or its inhabitants; rurally simple. • n an inhabitant of Arcadia.

arcane /ar'keɪn/ adj secret or esoteric.

arcanum /ar'keɪnəm/ n (pl **arcana**) a secret, a mystery; a valuable elixir.

arch[1] /artʃ/ n a curved structure spanning an opening; the curved underside of the foot. • vti to span or cover with an arch; to curve, bend into an arch.

arch[2] adj (criminal, etc) principal, expert; clever, sly; mischievous.—**archly** adv.—**archness** n.

Archaean /ar'ki:ən/ adj of the earliest geological period or strata.—also **Archean.**

archaeology /ˌarkɪɒ'lədʒɪ/ n the study of past human societies through their extant remains.—also **archeology.**—**archaeological, archeological** adj.—**archaeologist, archeologist** n.

archaeopteryx /ˌarkɪ'ɒptərɪks/ n oldest fossil bird.

archaic /ar'keɪɪk/ adj belonging to ancient times; (language) no longer in common use.

archaism /'arkeɪɪzəm/ or /-ki:ɪzəm/ n an archaic word or phrase.—**archaistic** adj.

archaize /'arkaɪz/ vti to affect the archaic; to make archaic.—**archaizer** n.

archangel /'arkeɪndʒəl/ n a principal angel.—**archangelic** adj.

archbishop /'artʃ'bɪʃəp/ n a bishop of the highest rank.

archbishopric /-rɪk/ n the jurisdiction, office or see of an archbishop.

archdeacon /-'di:kən/ n a clergyman ranking next under a bishop.

archdeaconry /-'di:kənri/ n (pl **archdeaconries**) the office, rank, jurisdiction, or residence of an archdeacon.

archdiocese /-'daɪəsəsz/ or /-'daɪɒsɪs/, /-'daɪəsi:z/ n the diocese of an archbishop.—**archdiocesan** adj.

archducal /-'du:kəl/ or /-'dju:kəl/ adj of or pertaining to an archduchess, an archduchy or an archduke.

archduchess /-'dʌtʃəs/ n a daughter of the emperor of Austria; the wife or widow of an archduke.

archduchy /-'dʌtʃi/ n (pl **archduchies**) the territory or rank of an archduke or an archduchess.

archduke /-'du:k/ or /-'dju:k/ n a prince of the imperial house of Austria.

Archean see Archaean.

archegonium /ˌarkə'goʊniəm/ n (pl **archegonia**) (bot) the pistillidium or female organ of the higher cryptogams (ferns, etc).

archenemy /ˌartʃ'ɛnəmi/ n (pl **archenemies**) a principal enemy; Satan.

archeology see archaeology.

archer /'artʃər/ n a person who shoots with a bow and arrow.

archerfish /'artʃər,fɪʃ/ n (pl **archerfish, archerfishes**) a scaly-finned fish of the Java seas, which catches insects by darting drops of water upon them.

archery /'artʃəri/ n the art or sport of shooting arrows from a bow.

archetype /'arkɪ,taɪp/ n the original pattern or model; a prototype.—**archetypal, archetypical** adj.

archfiend /'artʃ,fi:nd/ n a chief fiend; Satan.

archidiaconal /ˌarkɪdaɪ'ækənəl/ adj of or pertaining to an archdeacon or to his office.

archidiaconate /ˌarkɪdaɪ'ækəneɪt/ n the office of an archdeacon.

archiepiscopal /ˌarkɪə'pɪskəpəl/ adj of or pertaining to an archbishop or to his office.

archiepiscopate /ˌarkɪə'pɪskəpət/ or /-,peɪt/, /-si/, **archiepiscopacy** /-si/ n the rule or dignity of an archbishop.

archil /'arkɪl/ see orchil.

archimagus, archimage /'arkɪ,meɪdʒ/ n the high priest of the Persian magi or fire-worshippers; a chief magician.

archimandrite /ˌarkɪ'mænd,raɪt/ n (Greek Orthodox Church) the abbot of a monastery, or an abbot-general having the charge and superintendence of several monasteries.

Archimedean screw n an instrument for raising water, consisting of a flexible tube wound spirally around or within a cylinder in the form of a screw. When placed in an inclined position, with the lower end immersed in water, by the revolution of the screw the water is raised to the upper end.

archipelago /arkɪ'pɛlə,goʊ/ n (pl **archipelagoes, archipelagos**) a sea filled with small islands; a group of small islands.—**archipelagic, archipelagian** adj.

architect /'arkɪ,tɛkt/ n a person who designs buildings and supervises their erection; someone who plans something.

architectonic /ˌɑrkɪtekˈtɒnɪk/ *adj* pertaining to design or construction; skilled in architecture; expert in constructing; of the systematizing of knowledge.—**architectonically** *adv*.

architectonics /-nɪks/ *n* (*used as sing*) the science of architecture; structure.

architecture /ˈɑrkɪˌtektʃər/ *n* the art, profession, or science of designing and constructing buildings; the style of a building or buildings; the design and organization of a computer's parts.—**architectural** *adj*.—**architecturally** *adv*.

architrave /ˌɑrkɪˈtreɪv/ *n* an epistyle, the lowest division of an entablature, the part resting immediately on a column; the parts round a door or window.

archives /ɑrˈkaɪvs/ *npl* the location in which public records are kept; the public records themselves.—**archival** *adj*.

archivist /ˈɑrkɪvɪzst/ *n* a keeper of public records.

archivolt /ˈɑrkɪvɒlt/ *n* the undercurve of an arch or the moulding on it.

archpriest /ˈɑrtʃˌpriːst/ *n* a chief priest; a rural dean.

archway /ˈɑrtʃˌweɪ/ *n* an arched or vaulted passage, *esp* that leading into a castle.

arc light *n* light produced by a current of electricity passing between two carbon points placed a short distance from each other.

Arctic, arctic /ˈɑrktɪk/ or /ˈɑrtɪk/ *adj* of, near, or relating to the North Pole or its surroundings; (*inf*) very cold, icy. • *n* (*usu cap with* **the**) the area north of the Arctic Circle; (*without cap*) an arctic boot.

Arctic char *n* a freshwater fish of northern North America, similar to salmon.

Arctic Circle *n* an imaginary circle around the Arctic regions parallel to the equator.

Arctic cotton *n* a northern sedge whose flower heads have long white cottony hairs.

Arctic fox *n* a small species of fox, whose fine fur is used for muffs, trimmings, etc.

Arctic hare *n* a large hare of northern Canada and Greenland, whose coat is brown in summer and white in winter.

Arctic Ocean *n* the ocean that washes the northern coasts of Europe, Asia and North America.

Arctic poppy *n* a northern plant with four-petalled golden flowers.

arcuate /ˈɑrkjuːət/ or /-ˌeɪt/ *adj* bent or curved in the form of a bow.

arcuation /ˌɑrkjuːˈweɪʃən/ *n* the act of bending; the state of being bent or curved; a method of propagating trees by bending branches to the ground and covering portions of them with earth.

arc welding *n* welding using an electric arc.

ardent /ˈɑrdənt/ *adj* passionate; zealous.—**ardency** *n*.—**ardently** *adv*.

ardent spirits *npl* alcoholic beverages, as brandy, whisky, etc.

ardour, ardor /ˈɑrdər/ *n* warmth of feeling; extreme intensity.

arduous /ˈɑrdʒuːəs/ *adj* difficult, laborious; steep, difficult to climb. —**arduously** *adv*.—**arduousness** *n*.

are[1] /ɑr/, /er/ *see* be.

are[2] *n* a metric unit of measure equal to 100 square metres.

area /ˈerɪə/ *n* an expanse of land; a total outside surface, measured in square units; a specific part of a house, district, etc; scope or extent.

areca /ˈærəkə/ or /əˈriːkə/ *n* a genus of lofty palms, including the tree from which the betelnut and the astringent juice Catechu are obtained.

arena /əˈriːnə/ *n* an area within a sports stadium, etc where events take place; a place or sphere of contest or activity.

arenaceous /ˌærɪˈneɪʃəs/ or /-ˌerɪ-/ *adj* sandy; abounding in, or having the properties of, sand.

aren't /ɑrnt/ = are not.

areola /əˈrɪələ/ *n* (*pl* **areolae, areolas**) a very small area; an interstice in tissue; the coloured circle or halo surrounding the nipple of the breast.—**areolar, areolate** *adj*.—**areolation** *n*.

arête /æˈret/ *n* the sharp ridge or spur of a mountain.

argali /ˈɑrgəli/ *n* (*pl* **argalis, argali**) a large wild Asiatic sheep, remarkable for its huge curved horns.

argent /ˈɑrdʒənt/ *n* (*her*) silver, represented in a drawing or engraving of a coat of arms by a plain white surface, symbolic of purity, beauty, etc. • *adj* made of or resembling silver; silvery white; bright like silver.

argentiferous /ˌɑrdʒənˈtɪfərəs/ *adj* producing or containing silver.

argentine /ˈɑrdʒənˌtaɪn/ or /-ˌtiːn/ *adj* pertaining to or resembling silver; silvery. • *n* a silvery-white slaty variety of calcite; white metal coated with silver, imitation silver.

argil /ˈɑrdʒɪl/ *n* clay, *esp* potter's clay or earth.

argillaceous /ˌɑrdʒəˈleɪʃəs/ *adj* of or containing clay, clayey.

argilliferous /ˌɑrdʒələˈfərəs/ *adj* producing or containing clay.

argillite /ˈɑrdʒɪˌlaɪt/ *n* clay-slate.—**argillitic** *adj*.

argol /ˈɑrgɒl/ *n* a deposit of crude tartar on the sides of wine vessels; crude tartar from which cream of tartar is prepared.

argon /ˈɑrgɒn/ *n* an inert gaseous element.

argosy /ˈɑrgəsi/ *n* (*pl* **argosies**) a large, richly laden merchant ship.

argot /ˈɑrgoː/ or /ˈɑrgət/ *n* the special vocabulary of any set of persons, as of lawyers, criminals, etc.—**argotic** *adj*.

arguable /ˈɑrgjuːəbl/ *adj* debatable; able to be asserted; plausible.—**arguably** *adv*.

argue /ˈɑrgjuː/ *vb* (**arguing, argued**) *vt* to try to prove by reasoning; to debate, dispute; to persuade (into, out of). • *vi* to offer reasons for or against something; to disagree, exchange angry words.—**arguer** *n*.

argufy /ˈɑrgjəfaɪ/ *vi* (**argufying, argufied**) (*sl*) to argue tediously, to wrangle.

argument /ˈɑrgjʊmənt/ or /-gjə-/ *n* a disagreement; a debate, discussion; a reason offered in debate; an abstract, summary.

argumentation /ˌɑrgjʊmenˈteɪʃən/ *n* systematic reasoning; argument, discussion.

argumentative /ˌɑrgjʊˈmentətɪv/ *adj* prone to arguing.—**argumentatively** *adv*.—**argumentativeness** *n*.

argy-bargy /ˈɑrgiˈbɑrgi/ (*pl* **argy-bargies**) *n* a tedious discussion. • *vi* to argue at length.

aria /ˈɑrɪə/ *n* a song for one voice accompanied by instruments, *eg* in opera.

Arian /ˈerɪən/ or /ˈæ-/ *adj* pertaining to the doctrines of the Arian sect, which held that Christ is not divine.—**Arianism** *n*.

arid /ˈærəd/ or /ˈærɪd/ *adj* very dry, parched; uninteresting; dull.—**aridity** *n*.—**aridly** *adv*.

Aries /ˈeriːz/ or /ˈær-/, /-ˈiːz/ *n* (*astrol*) the first sign of the zodiac, the Ram, operative 21 March–21 April.—**Arian** *adj*, *n*.

arietta /ˌɑriˈetə/ or /ˌæri-/, /ˌeri-/ *n* a short aria, song or air.

aright /əˈraɪt/ *adv* correctly.

aril /ˈærərl/ *n* (*bot*) an accessory covering or appendage of certain seeds.

arioso /ˌɑriˈoːˌsoː/ *adj, adv* (*mus*) like an air; in a smooth melodious style.

arise /əˈraɪz/ *vi* (**arising, arose**, *pp* **arisen**) to get up, as from bed; to rise, ascend; to come into being, to result (from).

arista /əˈrɪstə/ *n* (*pl* **aristae** /əˈrɪsti/) the awn or beard of grasses; a bristle.

aristate /əˈrɪsteɪt/ *adj* bearded; having a beard or bristle, as certain grasses.

aristocracy /ˌæriˈstɒkrəsi/ or /ˈeri-/ *n* (*pl* **aristocracies** /-siːz/) (a country with) a government dominated by a privileged minority class; the privileged class in a society, the nobility; those people considered the best in their particular sphere.

aristocrat /ˈærəstəˌkræt/ or /əˈrɪstəˌkræt/ *n* a member of the aristocracy; a supporter of aristocratic government; a person with the manners or taste of a privileged class.

aristocratic /ˌærəstəˈkrætɪk/ or /əˌrɪstəˈkrætɪk/ *adj* relating to or characteristic of the aristocracy; elegant, stylish in dress and manners.—**aristocratically** *adv*.

Aristotelian /ˌærɪstəˈtiliən/ or /əˌrɪstə-/ *adj* pertaining to, or characteristic of, Aristotle (384—322 BC) or his philosophy.

arithmetic /əˈrɪθˌmətiːk/ or /əˈrɪ-/ *n* (*math*) computation (addition, subtraction, etc) using real numbers; calculation.—**arithmetic, arithmetical** *adj*.—**arithmetically** *adv*.

arithmetician /-ˈtɪʃən/ *n* one skilled in the science of numbers.

ark /ɑrk/ *n* (*Bible*) the boat in which Noah and his family and two of every kind of creature survived the Flood; a place of safety.

Ark, Holy Ark *n* (*Judaism*) an enclosure in a synagogue for the scrolls of the Torah.

Ark of the Covenant *n* (*Judaism*) the most sacred symbol of God's presence among the Hebrew people.

arm[1] /ɑrm/ *n* the upper limb from the shoulder to the wrist; something shaped like an arm, as a support on a chair; a sleeve; power, authority; an administrative division of a large organization.

arm[2] *n* (*usu pl*) a weapon; a branch of the military service; (*pl*) heraldic bearings. • *vt* to provide with weapons, etc; to provide with something that protects or strengthens, etc; to set a fuse ready to explode. • *vi* to prepare for war or any struggle.

armada /ɑr'mɒdə/ *n* a fleet of warships or aircraft.

armadillo /ˌɑrmə'dɪloː/ *n* (*pl* **armadillos** /-z/) a small animal from South America with a body covering of small bony plates.

Armageddon /ˌɑrmə'gedən/ *n* (*Bible*) the site of the last decisive battle between good and evil; any great decisive battle.

armament /'ɑrməmənt/ *n* (*often pl*) all the military forces and equipment of a nation; all the military equipment of a warship, etc; the process of arming or being armed for war.

armature /ɑrmətʃər/ *n* a piece of iron connecting the poles of a magnet or electromagnet to preserve and increase the magnetic force; the revolving part of a dynamo; arms, armour, that which serves as a means of defence; iron bars or framework used to strengthen a building; a framework supporting clay, etc, in sculpture or modelling.

armchair /'ɑrmtʃer/ *n* a chair with side rests for the arms. • *adj* lacking practical experience.

armed forces *npl* the military forces of a nation.—*also* **armed services**.

armful /'ɑrmfʊl/ *n* as much as the arms can hold.

armhole /'ɑrmhoːl/ *n* an opening for the arm in an item of clothing.

armiger /'ɑrmidʒər/ *n* one entitled to use heraldic bearings, an esquire.—**armigerous** *adj*.

armillary /'ɑrmiləri/ *adj* of or resembling a bracelet; consisting of circles or rings.

armillary sphere *n* a skeleton celestial globe showing the relative positions of the stars, etc.

Arminianism /ɑr'miniəˌnizəm/ *n* a Christian Protestant doctrine that denies Calvin's doctrine of predestination.—**Arminian** *adj, n*.

armistice /'ɑrməstəs/ or /'ɑrmitis/ *n* a truce, preliminary to a peace treaty.

armlet /ɑrmlət/ *n* an ornamental or protective band worn around the arm; a badge worn on the arm; a small arm of the sea.

armorial /ɑr'mɔriəl/ *adj* pertaining to armour or the arms or escutcheon of a family. • *n* a book or dictionary of heraldic devices and the names of persons entitled to use them.

armour, armor /'ɑrmər/ *n* any defensive or protective covering.

armoured, armored /'ɑrmərd/ *adj* covered or protected with armour; equipped with tanks and armour vehicles.

armourer, armorer /'ɑrmərər/ *n* the custodian of the arms of a battleship, etc; (formerly) a maker of arms or armour; one who had charge of the armour of another.

armour plate, armor plate *n* a plate of iron or steel affixed to a ship or tank as part of a casing for protection against shellfire.

armoury, armory /'ɑrməri/ *n* (*pl* **armouries, armories**) an arsenal; a place where armour or ammunition is stored.

armpit /'ɑrmˌpit/ *n* the hollow underneath the arm at the shoulder.

arms /ɑrmz/ *see* **arm**[2].

army /'ɑrmi/ *n* (*pl* **armies** /'ɑrmiːz/) a large organized body of soldiers for waging war, *esp* on land; any large number of persons, animals, etc.

army worm *n* the larva of a moth that devastates grain and other crops, *esp* destructive in North America; the larva of a European small two-winged fly.

arnica /'ɑrnikə/ *n* a genus of perennial herbs, *esp* mountain tobacco, whose roots and flowers are used to make a tincture for treating bruises.

aroma /ə'roːmə/ *n* a pleasant smell; a fragrance.

aromatherapy /əˌroːmə'θerəpi/ *n* the massage of fragrant oils into the skin to relieve tension and promote wellbeing.

aromatic /ˌerə'mætik/ *adj* giving out an aroma; fragrant, spicy; odoriferous. • *n* a plant, herb or drug yielding a fragrant smell.—**aromatically** *adv*.

aromatize /ə'roːməˌtaiz/ *vt* to render fragrant, to perfume, to scent.—**aromatization** *n*.

arose *see* **arise**.

around /ə'raʊnd/ *prep* on all sides of; on the border of; in various places in or on; approximately, about. • *adv* in a circle; in every direction; in circumference; to the opposite direction.

arousal /ə'raʊzəl/ *n* the act of awakening or stimulating; the state of being awakened or stimulated.

arouse /ə'raʊz/ *vt* to wake from sleep; to stir, as to action; to evoke.

arpeggio /ɑr'pedʒioː/ *n* (*pl* **arpeggios** /-z/) (*mus*) the playing of notes of a chord in rapid succession, instead of simultaneously; a passage or chord so played.

arquebus /'ɑrkwəbəs/ *n* an old-fashioned handgun fired from a forked rest.—*also* **harquebus**.

arrack /'ærək/ *n* an alcoholic spirit distilled in some Asian countries from rice, molasses, the juice of the date palm, etc.—*also* **arak**.

arraign /ə'rein/ *vt* to put on trial; to indict, accuse; to censure publicly; to impeach.—**arraigner** *n*.—**arraignment** *n*.

arrange /ə'reindʒ/ *vt* to put in a sequence or row; to settle, make preparations for; (*mus*) to prepare a composition for different instruments other than those intended. • *vi* to come to an agreement; to make plans.—**arranger** *n*.

arrangement /ə'reindʒmənt/ *n* the act of putting in proper form or order; that which is ordered or disposed; the method or style of disposition; a preparatory measure; preparation; settlement; classification; adjustment; adaptation; (*pl*) plans.

arrant /'erənt/ *adj* notorious; unmitigated; downright, thorough; shameless.

arras /'ærəs/ or /'ɛres/ *n* a tapestry; hangings made of a rich figured fabric.

array /ə'rei/ *n* an orderly grouping, *esp* of troops; an impressive display; fine clothes; (*comput*) an ordered data structure that allows information to be easily indexed. • *vt* to set in order, to arrange; to dress, decorate.—**arrayal** *n*.

arrears /ə'riːrz/ *npl* overdue debts; work, etc still to be completed.

arrest /ə'rest/ *vt* to stop; to capture, apprehend *esp* by legal authority; to check the development of a disease; to catch and hold the attention of. • *n* a stoppage; seizure by legal authority.

arrestee /ə'resti/ *n* one who has been arrested.

arrester /ə'restər/ *n* one who or that which stops or seizes, or causes to be detained.

arresting /ə'restiŋ/ *adj* striking or attracting to the mind or eye; impressive.—**arrestingly** *adv*.

arrière-pensée *Fr*. /'ærjer pã'sei/ *n* (*pl* **arrière-pensées**) a mental reservation.

arris /'æris/ or /'ɛris/ *n* (*pl* **arris, arrises**) (*archit*) the line or sharp edge in which two curved or straight surfaces, forming an exterior angle, meet each other.

arrival /ə'raivəl/ *n* arriving; a person or thing that has arrived.

arrive /ə'raiv/ *vi* to reach any destination; to come; (*with* **at**) to reach agreement, a decision; to achieve success, celebrity.

arriviste /ˌæri'viːst/ *n* an ambitious person, a self-seeker.

arrogance /'ærəgəns/ or /'ɛr-/ *n* an exaggerated assumption of importance.

arrogant /'ærəgənt/ or /'æ-/ *adj* overbearing; aggressively self-important.—**arrogantly** *adv*.

arrogate /'ærəgeit/ *vt* to assume or lay claim to unduly or presumptuously.—**arrogation** *n*.—**arrogative** *adj*.—**arrogator** *n*.

arrondissement /æˌrɒdiːs'mã/ *n* a subdivision of a French department; a municipal subdivision of Paris, etc.

arrow /'æroː/ or /ɛ-/ *n* a straight, pointed weapon, made to be shot from a bow; a sign used to indicate direction or location.

arrowhead /-ˌhed/ *n* the head or barb of an arrow; an aquatic plant so named from the shape of its leaves.

arrowroot /-ˌruːt/ or /-ˌrʊt/ *n* a starch obtained from the rootstocks of several species of West Indian plants.

arrowwood /-ˌwʊd/ *n* a wood once used for arrows by American Indians.

arroyo /ə'rɔioː/ *n* a watercourse or rivulet; the dry bed of a small stream.

arse /ɑrs/ *n* (*vulg*) the buttocks.

arsenal /'ɑrsənəl/ *n* a workshop or store for weapons and ammunition.

arsenate /'ɑrsəˌneit/ or /-ˌnit/ *n* a salt formed by combination of arsenic acid with any base.

arsenic /'ɑrsəˌnik/ *n* a soft grey metallic element, highly poisonous.

arsenical /ɑr'senikəl/ *adj* pertaining to or containing arsenic.

arsenious, arsenous /ɑr'siniəs/ *adj* pertaining to or containing arsenic.

arsenite /'ɑrsəˌnait/ *n* a salt of arsenious acid.

arsis /'ɑrsis/ *n* (*poet*) the part of a metrical foot where the accent is placed.

arson /'ɑrsən/ *n* the crime of using fire to destroy property deliberately.—**arsonist** *n*.

art[1] /ɑrt/ *n* human creativity; skill acquired by study and experience; any craft and its principles; the making of things that have form and beauty; any branch of this, as painting, sculpture, etc; drawings, paintings, statues, etc; (*pl*) the creative and nonscientific branches of knowledge, *esp* as studied academically.

art[2] (*arch*) the second person singular indicative mood and present tense of the verb to be.

art deco /-'dɛkoː/ *n* a style of design and architecture popular in the 1920s and 1930s and characterized by bold geometrical lines.

artefact /'ɑrtə,fækt/ *see* **artifact**.

artel /ɑr'tɛl/ *n* a workers' guild in the former USSR.

artemisia /ɑrtə'miːʒə/ or /-'miːʃə/, *n* a large genus of plants to which the common wormwood belongs, yielding a volatile oil (the chief ingredient of absinthe).

arterial /ɑr'tiːrɪəl/ *adj* pertaining to an artery or the arteries; contained in an artery; (*blood*) oxygenated, of a lighter red colour than venous blood; (*road*) major, with many branches.

arterialize /-,aɪz/ *vt* to convert as venous blood into arterial blood by exposure to oxygen in the lungs.—**arterialization** *n*.

arteriosclerosis /ɑr,tiːrɪoːsklə'roːsəs/ *n* (*med*) hardening of the walls of the arteries due to the action of fatty deposits, which impairs blood circulation.—**arteriosclerotic** *adj*.

artery /'ɑrtəri/ *n* (*pl* **arteries**) a tubular vessel that conveys blood from the heart; any main channel of transport or communication.

artesian well /ɑr'tiːʒən/ *n* a well in which water rises to the surface by internal pressure.

artful /'ɑrtful/ *adj* skilful at attaining one's ends; clever, crafty.—**artfully** *adv*.—**artfulness** *n*.

arthritis /ɑr'θraɪtɪs/ *n* painful inflammation of a joint.—**arthritic** *adj*.

arthropod /'ɑrθrə,pɒd/ *n* a member of the largest group of invertebrate animals with jointed legs, such as the butterfly, spider, crab, centipede.

artichoke /'ɑrti,tʃoːk/ *n* a thistle-like plant with a scaly flower head, parts of which are eaten as a vegetable.

article /'ɑrtəkəl/ *n* a separate item or clause in a written document; an individual item on a particular subject in a newspaper, magazine, etc; a particular or separate item; (*gram*) a word placed before a noun to identify it as definite or indefinite.

articled /-d/ *adj* apprenticed to, as an articled clerk to a solicitor.

articular /ɑr'tɪkjuːlər/ or /-jə-/ *adj* of a joint or structural components in a joint.

articulate /ɑr'tɪkjuːlət/ *adj* capable of distinct, intelligible speech, or expressing one's thoughts clearly; jointed. • *vti* to speak or express clearly; to unite or become united (as) by a joint.—**articulatedly** *adv*.—**articulateness** *n*.

articulated lorry, articulated truck *n* a large vehicle composed of a tractor and one or more trailers connected by flexible joints for greater manoeuvrability.—*also* **trailer truck**.

articulation /ɑr,tɪkjuː'leɪʃən/ *n* the act of jointing; the act of speaking distinctly; a distinct utterance; the state of being articulated; a joint or juncture between bones; the point of separation of organs or parts of a plant; a node or joint of the stem, or the space between two nodes.—**articulatory** *adj*.

articulator /ɑr'tɪkjuː,leɪtər/ or /-jə-/ *n* one who pronounces distinctly; any organ of the mouth, etc, that moves to produce speech sounds.

artifact /'ɑrtə,fækt/ *n* a product of human craftsmanship, *esp* a simple tool or ornament.—*also* **artefact**.

artifice /'ɑrtə,fɪs/ *n* a clever contrivance or stratagem; a trick, trickery.

artificer /ɑr'tɪfəsər/ or /'ɑrtəfə-/ *n* a skilled or artistic worker; a maker or constructor; an inventor.

artificial /,ɑrtə'fɪʃəl/ *adj* lacking natural qualities; man-made.—**artificiality** *n*.—**artificially** *adv*.

artificial insemination *n* injection of semen into the womb by artificial means so that conception takes place without sexual intercourse.

artificial intelligence *n* (*comput*) the ability to imitate intelligent human behaviour.

artificial respiration *n* the forcing of air into and out of the lungs of somebody whose breathing has stopped.

artillery /ɑr'tɪləri/ *n* (*pl* **artilleries**) large, heavy guns; the branch of the army that uses these.

artisan /'ɑrti,zæn/ or /-,sæn/ *n* a skilled workman.

artist /'ɑrtɪst/ *n* one who practises fine art, *esp* painting; one who does anything very well.—**artistic** *adj*.

artiste /ɑr'tiːst/ *n* a professional, *usu* musical or theatrical, entertainer.

artistic /ɑr'tɪstɪk/ *adj* pertaining to art or to artists; characterized by aesthetic feeling or conformity to the principles of a school of art or design.—**artistically** *adv*.

artistry /'ɑrtɪstri/ *n* artistic quality, ability, work, etc.

artless /'ɑrtləs/ *adj* simple, natural; without art or skill.—**artlessly** *adv*.—**artlessness** *n*.

art nouveau /,ɑrt'nuːvoː/ or /,ɑr-/ *n* a style of art and decoration that developed in the late 19th century, characterized by flowing curves and designs in imitation of nature.

arty /'ɑrti/ *adj* (**artier, artiest**) (*inf*) having a pretentious or affected interest in art.

arty-crafty, artsy-craftsy *adj* (*inf*) relating to arts and crafts, *esp* when affecting a simple, traditional style.

arum /'ɛrəm/ *n* a genus of plants with small flowers within a hood-shaped leaf.

arundinaceous /ə,rʌndɪ'neɪʃəs/ *adj* pertaining to or resembling a reed or cane.

-ary /'ɛri/ or /əri/ *adj suffix, n suffix* connected with, as *dictionary*.

Aryan /'ɛriən/ *n* a member of the Indo-European race; according to Nazi belief, a Caucasian, *esp* of the Nordic type, with no Jewish blood. • *adj* pertaining to the Aryans, or to their language.

As (*chem symbol*) arsenic.

as[1] /æz/ *adv* equally; for instance; when related in a certain way. • *conj* in the same way that; while; when; because. • *prep* in the role or function of.

as[2] /æs/ *n* (*pl* **asses**) a Roman weight equivalent to the libra or pound; a Roman copper coin.

ASA /'eɪ'es'eɪ/ *abbr* = (*Brit*) Amateur Swimming Association; (*US*) American Standards Association.

asafoetida, asafetida /,æsə'fetədə/ or /-'fiːtədə/ *n* a foul-smelling gum resin obtained from the roots of several large umbelliferous plants and used in medicine.

ASAP, a.s.a.p. /eɪ'sæp/ or /'æsæp/ *abbr* = as soon as possible.

asbestos, asbestus /æs'bestəs/ or /æz-/ *n* a fine fibrous mineral used for making incombustible and chemical-resistant materials.

asbestosis /,æsbes'toːsis/ or /,æz-/ *n* (*med*) a disease of the lungs caused by the inhalation of asbestos fibres.

ascend /ə'send/ *vti* to go up; to succeed to (a throne).

ascendancy, ascendency /ə'sendənsi/ *n* governing or dominating influence; power; sway.

ascendant, ascendent /-dənt/ *adj* rising upwards; dominant.

ascender /ə'sendər/ *n* one who ascends; the top part of letters such as b, d, h.

ascension /ə'senʃən/ *n* the act of ascending or rising.—**ascensional** *adj*.

Ascension *n* the ascent of Christ into heaven after the Resurrection.

Ascension Day *n* a movable feast commemorating the Ascension, celebrated on the Thursday next but one before Whit Sunday.—*also* **Holy Thursday**.

ascent /ə'sent/ *n* an ascending; an upward slope; the means of, the way of ascending.

ascertain /,æsər'teɪn/ *vt* to acquire definite knowledge of, to discover positively.—**ascertainable** *adj*.

ascetic /ə'setɪk/ *adj* self-denying, austere. • *n* a person who practises rigorous self-denial as a religious discipline; any severely abstemious person.—**ascetically** *adv*.—**asceticism** *n*.

ascidian /ə'sɪdiən/ *n* a type of mollusc with a leathery tunic resembling a double-necked bottle, a sea squirt.—*also* **sea squirt**.

ascidium /-əm/ *n* (*pl* **ascidia**) (*bot*) a pitcher-shaped or flask-shaped organ peculiar to certain plants, as the pitcher plants.

ASCII /'æski/ *acronym* (*comput*) = American Standard Code for Information Interchange, a standard code of 128 alphanumeric characters for storing and exchanging information.

ascomycete /,æsko'maɪ,sɪt/ or /-,maɪ'siːt/ *n* one of a family of the fungi, including most of the lichens, which form free spores within elongated spore cases.—**ascomycetous** *adj*.

ascorbic acid /ə'skɔrbɪk/ *n* vitamin C, found *esp* in citrus fruit and fresh green vegetables.

ascribe /ə'skraɪb/ *vt* to attribute, impute or refer; to assign.—**ascribable** *adj*.—**ascription, adscription** *n*.

ascus /'æskəs/ *n* (*pl* **asci**) the spore case of lichens and fungi.

asdic /'æzdɪk/ *n* an apparatus for locating submarines; an echo sounder; sonar.

asepsis /eɪ'sɛpsɪs/ or /ə-/ *n* an absence of disease or putrefaction; a surgical method aiming at this.—**aseptic** *adj*.

asexual /eɪ'sɛkʃuəl/ *adj* lacking sex or sexual organs; (*reproduction*) produced without the union of male and female germ cells.—**asexuality** *n*.—**asexually** *adv*.

ash[1] /æʃ/ *n* a tree with silver-grey bark; the wood of this tree.

ash[2] *n* powdery residue of anything burnt; fine, volcanic lava.

ashamed /ə'ʃeɪmd/ *adj* feeling shame or guilt.—**ashamedly** *adv*.

ash can /'æʃ.kæn/ *n* a container for household refuse, a garbage can.

ashen /'æʃən/ *adj* like ashes, *esp* in colour; pale.

Ashkenazi /,æʃkə'nɒzi/ *n* (*pl* **Ashkenazim**) a Jew from Germany or eastern Europe.

ashlar, ashler /'æʃlər/ *n* a squared stone used in building; masonry of this; thin slabs of building stone squared for facing walls.

ashlaring /-ɪŋ/ *n* a wall faced with ashlar; a low wall of a garret, built close to where the rafters reach the floor.

ashore /ə'ʃɔr/ *adv* to or on the shore; to or on land.—*also adj*.

ashram /'æʃrəm/ *n* a Hindu religious retreat.

ashtray /'æʃtreɪ/ *n* a small receptacle for tobacco ash and cigarette stubs.

Ash Wednesday *n* the first day of Lent; a special day set apart for fasting.

ashy /'æʃi/ *adj* (**ashier, ashiest**) of ashes; ash-coloured, pale.

Asian /'eɪʒən/ *adj* of or relating to the continent of Asia, its inhabitants or languages.—*also n*.

Asiatic cholera *n* a virulent form of cholera.

aside /ə'saɪd/ *adv* on or to the side; in reserve; away from; notwithstanding. • *n* words uttered and intended as inaudible, *esp* as spoken by an actor to the audience and supposedly unheard by the other actors on the stage.

asinine /'æsə.naɪn/ *adj* silly, stupid.—**asininity** *n*.

ask /æsk/ or /ɒsk/ *vt* to put a question to, inquire of; to make a request of or for; to invite; to demand, expect. • *vi* to inquire about.—**asker** *n*.

askance, askant /ə'skæns/ or /ə'skænt/ *adv* with a sideways glance; with distrust.

askew /ə'skju:/ *adv* to one side; awry.—*also adj*.

aslant /ə'slænt/ *adv* not at right angles; obliquely. • *prep* slantingly across, athwart.

asleep /ə'slip/ *adj* sleeping; inactive; numb. • *adv* into a sleeping condition.

asocial /eɪ'soːʃəl/ *adj* not capable of or avoiding social contact; antisocial.

asp /æsp/ *n* a small poisonous snake.

asparagus /ə'spɛrəgəs/ or /-'spær-/ *n* a plant cultivated for its edible young shoots.

aspartame /'æspər.teɪm/ *n* an artificial sweetener derived from an amino acid.

aspect /'æs.pɛkt/ *n* the look of a person or thing to the eye; a particular feature of a problem, situation, etc; the direction something faces; view; (*astrol*) the position of the planets with respect to one another, regarded as having an influence on human affairs.

aspen /'æspən/ *n* a species of poplar with leaves that have tremble in the slightest breeze. • *adj* (*arch*) quivering.

aspergillus /,æspər'dʒɪləs/ *n* (*pl* **aspergilli**) a genus of microscopic fungi, to which several of the moulds belong.

asperity /ə'spɛrəti/ *n* (*pl* **asperities**) hardship, severity; sharpness of temper.

asperse /ə'spɜrs/ *vt* to slander; (*rare*) to besprinkle, to bespatter.—**asperser** *n*.—**aspersive** *adj*.

aspersions /ə'spɜrʒənz/ or /-ʃənz/ *n pl* slander; an attack on a person's reputation.

aspersorium /,æspər'sɔriəm/ *n* (*pl* **aspersoria, aspersoriums**) a vessel containing holy water for sprinkling; a brush or metallic instrument used for sprinkling the water.

asphalt /'æs.fɔlt/ or /'æʃ-/ or /'æʃ-/ *n* a hard, black bituminous substance, used for paving roads, etc. • *vt* to surface with asphalt.—**asphaltic** *adj*.

asphodel /'æsfə.dɛl/ *n* one of several plants of the lily family; (*poet*) the daffodil; (*poet*) an immortal, unfading flower that bloomed in the meadows of Elysium (possibly the narcissus).

asphyxia /æs'fɪksiə/ *n* unconsciousness due to lack of oxygen or excess of carbon dioxide in the blood.

asphyxiate /-si.eɪt/ *vt* to suffocate.—**asphyxiation** *n*.—**asphyxiator** *n*.

aspic /'æs.pɪk/ *n* a savoury jelly used to coat fish, game, etc.

aspidistra /,æspɪ'dɪstrə/ *n* an Asian plant with broad leaves, grown as a house plant.

aspirant /'æspɪrənt/ or /ə'spaɪrənt/ *n* someone who aspires to something.

aspirate[1] /'æspərət/ *n* the sound of *h*.

aspirate[2] /'æspə.reɪt/ *vt* to pronounce with an *h*; to suck out using an aspirator.

aspiration /,æspɪ'reɪʃən/ *n* strong desire; ambition; the act of aspirating; the act of breathing; the withdrawal of air or fluid from a body cavity.—**aspiratory** *adj*.

aspirator /'æspɪ.reɪtər/ *n* a device used to suck (air, fluid, etc) from a (body) cavity.

aspire /ə'spaɪr/ *vi* to desire eagerly; to aim at high things.—**aspirer** *n*.—**aspiring** *adj*.

aspirin /'æspɪ.rɪn/ or /-.prɪn/ *n* (*pl* **aspirin, aspirins**) acetylsalicylic acid, a pain-relieving drug.

asquint /ə'skwɪnt/ *adv, adj* with a squint, to or out of the corner of the eye; obliquely.

ass /æs/ *n* a donkey; a silly, stupid person; (*sl*) the arse, the buttocks.

assagai /'æsə.gaɪ/ *see* **assegai**.

assai /æ'saɪ/ *adv* (*mus*) very, more, extremely.

assail /ə'seɪl/ *vt* to attack violently either physically or verbally.—**assailable** *adj*.—**assailer** *n*.—**assailment** *n*.

assailant /-ənt/ *n* an attacker.

assassin /ə'sæsɪn/ *n* a murderer, *esp* one hired to kill a leading political figure, etc.

assassinate /-.eɪt/ *vt* to kill a political figure, etc; to harm (a person's reputation, etc).—**assassination** *n*.

assault /ə'sɒlt/ *n* a violent attack; (*law*) an unlawful threat or attempt to harm another physically. • *vti* to make an assault (on); to rape.—**assaulter** *n*.

assault course *n* an obstacle course used for military training.

assay /ə'seɪ/ or /'æseɪ/ *n, vb* the analysis of the quantity of metal in an ore or alloy, *esp* the standard purity of gold or silver; a test. • *vt* (**assaying, assayed**) to subject to analysis; to determine the quantity or proportion of one or more of the constituents of a metal.—**assayable** *adj*.—**assayer** *n*.

assegai, assagai /'æsə.gaɪ/ *n* (*pl* **assegais, assagais**) (*S Africa*) a light hardwood javelin or spear for casting or stabbing.

assemblage /ə'sɛmblɪdʒ/ *n* a gathering of persons or things; (*art*) a form of collage.

assemble /-bəl/ *vti* to bring together; to collect; to fit together the parts of; (*comput*) to translate using an assembler.

assembler /-blər/ *n* (*comput*) a program that converts low-level mnemonic symbols into machine code.

assembly /-bli/ *n* (*pl* **assemblies**) assembling or being assembled; a gathering of persons, *esp* for a particular purpose; the fitting together of parts to make a whole machine, etc.

assembly line *n* a series of machines, equipment and workers through which a product passes in successive stages to be assembled.

assemblyman /ə'sɛmblimən/ *n* (*pl* **assemblymen**) a member of a legislative assembly.—**assemblywoman** *nf* (*pl* **assemblywomen**)

assent /ə'sɛnt/ *vi* to express agreement to something. • *n* consent or agreement.—**assentor, assenter** *n*.

assentation /,əsɛn'teɪʃən/ *n* compliance with the opinion of another, in flattery or obsequiousness.

assert /ə'sɜrt/ *vt* to declare, affirm as true; to maintain or enforce (*eg* rights).—**assertible** *adj*.

assertion /ə'sɜrʃən/ *n* an asserting; a statement that something is a fact, *usu* without evidence.

assertive /ə'sɜrtɪv/ *adj* self-assured, positive, confident; dogmatic.—**assertively** *adv*.—**assertiveness** *n*.

assess /ə'sɛs/ *vt* to establish the amount of, as a tax; to impose a tax or fine; to value, for the purpose of taxation; to estimate the worth, importance, etc of.—**assessable** *adj*.

assessment /-mənt/ *n* the act of assessing or determining an amount to be paid; an official valuation of property, or income, for the purpose of taxation; the specific sum levied as tax, or assessed for damages.

assessor /-ər/ *n* a person appointed to assess property or persons for taxation; an expert appointed to assist a judge or magistrate as an adviser on special points of law.—**assessorial** *adj*.

asset /'æset/ *n* anything owned that has value; a desirable thing; (*pl*) all the property, accounts receivable, etc of a person or business; (*pl*) (*law*) property usable to pay debts.

asset-stripping *n* the practice of buying a company in order to sell off its assets at a profit.—**asset-stripper** *n*.

asseverate /ə'sevə‚reɪt/ *vt* to declare solemnly; to affirm or aver positively.—**asseveration** *n*.

asshole /'æs‚hoːl/ *n* (*sl*) a stupid person; (*vulg*) the anus.

assibilate /ə'sɪbə‚leɪt/ *vt* (*phonetics*) to pronounce with a hissing sound; to alter to a sibilant.—**assibilation** *n*.

assiduity /‚æsɪ'dʒuːɪtɪ/ or /-'djuːɪtɪ/ *n* (*pl* **assiduities**) close application, steady attention; diligence; (*usu pl*) constant attentions.

assiduous /ə'sɪdʒʊəs/ or /-djʊəs/ *adj* persistent or persevering; diligent.—**assiduously** *adv*.—**assiduousness** *n*.

assign /ə'saɪn/ *vt* to allot; to appoint to a post or duty; to ascribe; (*law*) to transfer (a right, property, etc).—**assignable** *adj*. —**assigner** *n*.

assignat /'æsɪɡ‚næt/ *n* a money or currency bond secured on state lands, issued by the French Revolutionary Government (1789–96).

assignation /‚æsɪɡ'neɪʃən/ *n* the act of assigning; a meeting, *esp* one made secretly by lovers.

assignee /‚æsaɪ'niː/ *n* (*law*) one to whom an assignment of anything is made, either in trust or for his or her own use and enjoyment.

assignment /ə'saɪnmənt/ *n* the act of assigning; something assigned to a person, such as a share, task, etc.

assignor /-ər/ *n* (*law*) one who assigns or transfers an interest.

assimilate /ə'sɪmə‚leɪt/ *vt* to absorb; to digest; to take in and understand fully; to be ascribed; to be like.—**assimilable** *adj*. —**assimilation** *n*.

assimilative /ə'sɪmə‚leɪtɪv/, **assimilatory** /-‚tɔrɪ/ *adj* having the power of assimilating, or causing assimilation, tending to produce assimilation.

assist /ə'sɪst/ *vti* to support or aid.—**assister** *n*.

assistance /ə'sɪstəns/ *n* help; furtherance; aid; succour; support.

assistant /-tənt/ *n* one who or that which assists; a helper; an auxiliary; a subordinate. • *adj* helping; lending aid; auxiliary.

assize /ə'saɪz/ *n* (*pl* **assizes**) a court or session of justice for the trial by jury of civil or criminal cases; (*usu pl*) (*formerly*) the sessions held periodically in each county of England by judges of the Supreme Court; (*usu pl*) the time or place of holding the assize.

associable /ə'soːʃɪəbəl/ or /-ʃəbəl/ *adj* capable of being joined or associated; liable to be affected by sympathy with kindred parts or organs.

associate /ə'soːʃɪ‚eɪt/ or /-sɪ-/ *vt* ; /ə'soːʃət/ or /-'sɪət/ *n, adj* to join as a friend, business partner or supporter; to bring together; to unite; to connect in the mind. • *vi* to combine or unite with others; to come together as friends, business partners or supporters. • *adj* allied or connected; having secondary status or privileges. • *n* a companion, business partner, supporter, etc; something closely connected with another; a person admitted to an association as a subordinate member.

association /ə'soːsi'eɪʃən/ *n* an organization of people joined together for a common aim; the act of associating or being associated; a connection in the mind, memory, etc.

association football *n* football played with a round ball that is not handled, soccer.

associationism *n* (*psychol*) the mental connection existing between an object and the ideas related to it.

associative /ə'soːʃɪ‚eɪtɪv/ *adj* tending to or characterized by association; (*math*) having elements whose result is the same despite the grouping.

assonance /'æsənəns/ *n* a correspondence in sound between words or syllables.—**assonant** *adj, n*.—**assonantal** *adj*.

assort /ə'sɔrt/ *vt* to arrange in groups according to kind. • *vi* to agree in kind.—**assortative, assortive** *adj*.—**assorter** *n*.

assorted /-ɪd/ *adj* distributed according to sorts; miscellaneous.

assortment /-mənt/ *n* a collection of people or things of different sorts.

asst *abbr* = assistant.

assuage /ə'sweɪdʒ/ *vt* to soften the intensity of; to soothe.—**assuager** *n*.—**assuagement** *n*.—**assuasive** *adj*.

assume /ə'suːm/ or /-'sjuːm/ *vt* to take on, to undertake; to usurp; to take as certain or true; to pretend to possess.—**assumable** *adj*.—**assumer** *n*.

assuming /ə'suːmɪŋ/ or /-juː-/ *adj* presumptuous.

assumption /ə'sʌmpʃən/ *n* something taken for granted; the taking on of a position, *esp* of power; (*with cap*) the ascent of the Virgin Mary into heaven; (*RC Church*) the Christian feast in remembrance of this, celebrated 15 August.—**assumptive** *adj*.

assurance /ə'ʃʊrəns/ *n* a promise, guarantee; a form of life insurance; a feeling of certainty, self-confidence.

assure /ə'ʃʊr/ or /ə‚ʃər/ *vt* to make safe or certain; to give confidence to; to state positively; to guarantee, ensure.—**assurable** *adj*.—**assurer** *n*.

assured /ə'ʃʊrd/ or /ə‚ʃərd/ *adj* certain; convinced; self-confident.—**assuredness** *n*.

assuredly /ə'ʃʊrədlɪ/ or /ə‚ʃərədlɪ/ *adv* certainly.

assurgent /ə'sərdʒənt/ *adj* ascending, rising; (*bot*) rising in a curve.

Assyrian /ə'sɪrɪən/ *adj* pertaining to Assyria, an ancient kingdom of Mesopotamia, or to its inhabitants or language. • *n* the language spoken in Assyria; an inhabitant of Assyria.

Assyriology /ə‚sɪrɪ'plədʒɪ/ *n* the science or study of the extinct language and the antiquities of Assyria.—**Assyriologist** *n*.

astatic /eɪ'stætɪk/ or /ə-/ *adj* having a tendency not to stand still; unstable.—**astatically** *adv*.—**astaticism** *n*.

astatine /'æstə‚tiːn/ *n* a radioactive element.

aster /'æstər/ *n* a kind of plant with round composite flowers; a Michaelmas daisy.

-aster /'æstər/ *n suffix* petty imitation, as in *poetaster*.

asteriated /æs'tɪrɪ‚eɪtɪd/ *adj* (*crystal, etc*) radiated; having the form of a star.

asterisk /'æstərɪsk/ *n* a sign (*) used in writing or printing to mark omission of words, a footnote or other reference, etc. • *vt* to mark with an asterisk.

asterism /'æstə‚rɪzəm/ *n* a group or cluster of stars; three asterisks placed in the form of a triangle (***) or (***) to direct attention to a particular passage; the star-like appearance in certain crystals.

astern /ə'stərn/ *adv* behind a ship or aircraft; at or towards the rear of a ship, etc; backward.

asternal /eɪ'stərnəl/ *adj* (*anat*) (*ribs*) not joined to the sternum or breastbone.

asteroid /'æstərɔɪd/ *n* any of the small planets between Mars and Jupiter. • *adj* star-like; star-shaped.—*also* **asteroidal**.

asthenia /æs'θiːnɪə/ *n* debility, weakness.—**asthenic** *adj*.

asthma /'æzmə/ *n* a chronic respiratory condition causing difficulty with breathing.—**asthmatic** *adj*.—**asthmatically** *adv*.

asthmatic /æz'mætɪk/ *adj* of or suffering from or good for asthma. • *n* an asthmatic person.—**asthmatically** *adv*.

astigmatism /ə'stɪɡmə‚tɪzəm/ *n* a defective condition of the eye or lens causing poor focusing.—**astigmatic** *adj*.—**astigmatically** *adv*.

astir /ə'stər/ *adv* moving or bustling about; out of bed.

astomatous /eɪ'stɒmətəs/ *adj* (*biol*) lacking a mouth; without breathing pores.

astonish /ə'stɒnɪʃ/ *vt* to fill with sudden or great surprise.—**astonishing** *adj*.—**astonishment** *n*.

astound /ə'staʊnd/ *vt* to astonish greatly.—**astounding** *adj*. —**astoundingly** *adv*.

astraddle /ə'strædəl/ *adv* astride, straddling.

astragal /'æstrəɡəl/ *n* (*archit*) a small moulding or bead of semi-circular form; a ring of moulding round the top or bottom of a column.

astragalus /ə'stræɡələs/ *n* (*pl* **astragali**) the ball of the ankle joint; the lower bone into which the tibia articulates.

Astrakhan /'æstrə‚kæn/ *n* the dark curly fleece of lambs from Astrakhan in Russia; a cloth with a curled pile made from or imitating this.

astral /'æstrəl/ *adj* of or from the stars.

astray /ə'streɪ/ *adv* off the right path; into error.

astride /ə'straɪd/ *adv* with a leg on either side. • *prep* extending across.

astringent /ə'strɪndʒənt/ *adj* that contracts body tissues; stopping blood flow, styptic; harsh; biting. • *n* an astringent substance.—**astringency** *n*.

astro- /'æstro:/ *prefix* (*astrophysics*) of a star or stars.

astrodome /'æstrə‚doːm/ *n* a large sports stadium covered with a domed translucent roof.

astrolabe /'æstrə,leɪb/ or /-trə-/ *n* an instrument formerly used for taking altitudes of the sun and stars.

astrology /ə'strɒlədʒi/ *n* the study of planetary positions and motions to determine their supposed influence on human affairs.—**astrologer, astrologist** *n*.—**astrological** *adj*.—**astrologically** *adv*.

astrometry /ə'strɒmətri/ *n* the art by which the apparent relative magnitude of the stars is determined.—**astrometric, astrometrical** *adj*.

astronaut /'æstrə,nɒt/ *n* one trained to make flights in outer space.

astronautics /,æstrə'nɒtɪks/ *npl* (*used as sing*) the scientific study of space flight and technology.

astronomical, astronomic /,æstrə'nɒmɪkəl/ *adj* enormously large; of or relating to astronomy.—**astronomically** *adv*.

astronomical clock *n* a clock that keeps sidereal time.

astronomical year *n* a year the length of which is determined by astronomical observations.

astronomy /ə'strɒnəmi/ *n* the scientific investigation of the stars and other planets.—**astronomer** *n*.

astrophotography /,æstrofə'tɒɡrəfi/ *n* photography of the heavenly bodies.—**astrophotographic** *adj*.

astrophysics /,æstro'fɪzɪks/ *n* (*used as sing*) the branch of astronomy that deals with the physical and chemical constitution of the stars.—**astrophysical** *adj*.—**astrophysicist** *n*.

astute /ə'stuːt/ or /-'stjuːt-/ *adj* clever, perceptive; crafty, shrewd.—**astutely** *adv*.—**astuteness** *n*.

asunder /ə'sʌndər/ *adv* apart in direction or position; into pieces.

asylum /ə'saɪləm/ *n* a place of safety, a refuge; (*formerly*) an institution for the blind, the mentally ill, etc.

asymmetric /,eɪsə'metrɪk/, **asymmetrical** /,eɪsə'metrɪkəl/ *adj* lacking symmetry.—**asymmetrically** *adv*.

asymmetry /eɪ'sɪmətri/ or /æ'sɪm-/ *n* a lack of symmetry or proportion between the parts of a thing.

asymptote /'æsɪmp,toːt/ or /'æsɪm,toːt/ *n* (*geom*) the line that continually approaches nearer to a given curve without ever meeting it.—**asymptotic, asymptotical** *adj*.

asyndeton /ə'sɪndətən/ *n* (*pl* **asyndetons, asyndeta**) (*gram*) a figure of speech in which conjunctions are omitted, as "I came, I saw, I conquered"; such a figure.

At (*chem symbol*) astatine.

at- /æt/ *prefix* the form of *ad-* before *t*.

at /æt/ *prep* on; in; near; by; used to indicate location or position.

at. no. *abbr* = atomic number.

ataraxia /,ætə'ræksiə/, **ataraxy** /'ætə,ræksi/ *n* impassivity; peace of mind.

atavism /'ætə,vɪzəm/ *n* the appearance in plants or animals of characteristics typical in more remote ancestors; reversion to a more primitive type.—**atavistic** *adj*.—**atavistically** *adv*.

ataxia /ə'tæksiə/ *n* irregularities in the functions of the body, *esp* muscular coordination, or in the course of a disease.—**ataxic, atactic** *adj*.

ate /ɔɪt/ *see* **eat**.

-ate /eɪt/ or /ət/ *adj suffix* having or furnished with, as *foliate*. • *n suffix* forming the equivalent of *pp*, as in *associate*.

atelier /,ætəl'jeɪ/ *n* a workshop; the studio of a painter or sculptor.

a tempo, a tempo primo /æ'tempoː/ *n* (*mus*) a direction to a musician to restore the original time after acceleration or retardation.

a tempo giusto *n* (*mus*) a direction to a performer to sing or play in strict time.

Athanasian Creed /,æθə'neɪʃən/ *n* one of the three creeds thus named as containing an exposition of the doctrines of the Trinty and incarnation of Christ, which Athanasius, bishop of Alexandria (c.296–373), defended.

atheism /'eɪθi,ɪzəm/ *n* belief in the nonexistence of God.—**atheist** *n*.—**atheistic, atheistical** *adj*.

atheling /'æθəlɪŋ/ *n* an Anglo-Saxon title of honour conferred on royal children and young nobles.

athenaeum, atheneum /,æθə'niːəm/ or /-'neɪəm/ *n* a public institution, club or building devoted to the purposes or study of literature, science and art; a literary club; (*with cap*) the temple of Athena in ancient Athens, where scholars met.

Athenian /ə'θiːniən/ *adj* pertaining to Athens, the capital of Greece. • *n* a native or citizen of Athens.

athermanous /eɪ'θɜrmənəs/ *adj* resisting the passage of heat; nonconducting.—**athermany** *n*.

atherosclerosis /,æθəroː,skləˈroːsɪs/ *n* (*pl* **atheroscleroses**) a degenerative disease of the arteries characterized by deposition of fatty material on the inner arterial walls.—**atherosclerotic** *adj*.

athirst /ə'θɜrst/ *adj* thirsty; eager (for).

athlete /'æθliːt/ *n* a person trained in games or exercises requiring skill, speed, strength, stamina, etc.

athlete's foot *n* a fungal infection of the feet.

athletic /æθ'letɪk/ *adj* of athletes or athletics; active, vigorous.—**athletically** *adv*.—**athleticism** *n*.

athletics /æθ'letɪks/ *n* (*used as sing or pl*) running, jumping, throwing sports, games, etc.

athwart /ə'θwɔrt/ *prep* across, from side to side. • *adv* crosswise; obliquely; across the course or direction of a ship; adversely (to).

atilt /ə'tɪlt/ *adv* in the position or with the action of a person making a thrust; tilted.

-ation /'eɪʃən/ *n suffix* denoting action or its result, as in *flirtation, vacation*.

atlantes /ət'læntiːz/ *see* **atlas**².

Atlantic /ət'læntɪk/ *adj* of, near or relating to the Atlantic Ocean.

Atlantic salmon *n* a salmon of the coastal North Atlantic Ocean and its tributaries.

atlas¹ /'ætləs/ *n* a book containing maps, charts and tables.

atlas² *n* (*pl* **atlantes**) (*archit*) a figure or half-figure of a man, used in place of a column or pilaster to support an entablature.—*also* **telamon**.

ATM /,eɪtiːem/ *abbr* = automated teller machine.

atmo- /ætmə/ or /ætmɒ/ *prefix* vapour, air, atmosphere.

atmometer /æt'mɒmətər/ *n* an instrument for measuring the rate and amount of evaporation from a moist surface.—**atmometry** *n*.

atmosphere /'ætməs,fɪr/ *n* the gaseous mixture that surrounds the earth or the other stars and planets; a unit of pressure equal to the pressure of the atmosphere at sea level; any dominant or surrounding influence; special mood or aura.—**atmospheric, atmospherical** *adj*.

atmospherics /,ætməs'fɪrɪks/ or /'fɛrɪks/ *n pl* interference in radio reception, etc caused by atmospheric disturbances.

atoll /'ætɒl/ *n* a coral reef enclosing a central lagoon.

atom /'ætəm/ *n* the smallest particle of a chemical element; a tiny particle, bit.

atomic /ə'tɒmɪk/ *adj* pertaining to or consisting of atoms; extremely minute.—**atomically** *adv*.

atomic bomb *n* a bomb whose explosive power derives from the atomic energy released during nuclear fission or fusion.—*also* **A-bomb**.

atomic energy *n* the energy derived from nuclear fission.

atomicity /,ætə'mɪsɪti/ *n* the number of atoms in a molecule of an element; equivalence; the combining capacity of an element, valency.

atomic theory *n* the theory that elemental bodies consist of ultimate atoms of definite weight, and that atoms of different elements unite chemically with each other in fixed proportions.

atomic weight *n* the weight of the atom of any element as compared with another taken as a standard, *usu* hydrogen, taken as 1.

atomism /'ætə,mɪzəm/ *n* the doctrine of atoms, atomic theory.—**atomist** *n*.—**atomistic, atomistical** *adj*.

atomize /,ætə'maɪz/ *vt* to reduce to a fine spray or minute particles.—**atomization** *n*.

atomizer /'ætə,maɪzər/ *n* a device for atomizing liquids, *usu* perfumes or cleaning agents.

atonal /eɪ'toːnəl/ *adj* (*mus*) avoiding traditional tonality; not written in any established key.—**atonality** *n*.—**atonally** *adv*.

atone /ə'toːn/ *vi* to give satisfaction or make amends (for).—**atonable, atoneable** *adj*.—**atoner** *n*.

atonement /ə'toːnmənt/ *n* satisfaction, reparation; (*Christianity*: *with cap*) the reconciliation of humankind with God through Christ's self-sacrifice.

atonic /ə'tɒnɪk/ *adj* (*word, etc*) unaccented; lacking tone, or vital energy. • *n* an unaccented word or syllable; a medicine to allay excitement.—**atonicity** *n*.

atony /'ætəni/ *n* lack of tone; debility; weakness of any organ.

atop /ə'tɒp/ *adv* on or at the top.

atrip /ə'trɪp/ *adv* (*naut*) (*anchor*) just clear of the ground.

atrium /'eɪtrɪəm/ *n* (*pl* **atria** /'eɪtrɪə/, **atriums** /'eɪtrɪəms/) an auricle of the heart; the unroofed courtyard of a Roman house; an entrance hall that rises up several storeys, often with a glass roof.

atrocious /ə'trəʊʃəs/ *adj* extremely brutal or wicked; (*inf*) very bad, of poor quality.—**atrociously** *adv*.

atrocity /ə'trɒsɪti/ *n* (*pl* **atrocities**) a cruel act; something ruthless, wicked, repellent.

atrophy /'ætrəfi/ *n* (*pl* **atrophies**) a wasting away or failure to grow of a bodily organ. • *vti* (**atrophying, atrophied**) to cause or undergo atrophy.

atropine, atropin /'ætrəpiːn/ or /'ætrəpɪn/ *n* a crystalline alkaloid of a very poisonous nature extracted from the deadly nightshade (belladonna), having the singular property of producing dilatation of the pupil of the eye.

attacca /'ætəkə/ *n* (*mus*) a direction to a performer at the end of a movement to follow on with the next without pause.

attach /ə'tætʃ/ *vt* to fix or fasten to something; to appoint to a specific group; to ascribe, attribute. • *vi* to become attached; to adhere.—**attachable** *adj*.—**attacher** *n*.

attaché /ætæ'ʃeɪ/ or /ætə'ʃeɪ/ *n* a technical expert on a diplomatic staff.

attaché case *n* a flat case for carrying documents, etc.

attached /ə'tætʃt/ *adj* fixed; feeling affection for.

attachment /ə'tætʃmənt/ *n* a fastening; affection, devotion; something attached; a device or part fixed to a machine, implement, etc; the act of attaching or being attached.

attack /ə'tæk/ *vt* to set upon violently; to assault in speech or writing; to invade, as of a disease. • *vi* to make an assault. • *n* an assault; a fit of illness; severe criticism; an enthusiastic beginning of a performance, task, undertaking, etc.—**attacker** *n*.

attain /ə'teɪn/ *vt* to succeed in getting or arriving at; to achieve. • *vi* to come to or arrive at by growth or effort.—**attainable** *adj*.—**attainability** *n*.

attainder /ə'teɪndər/ *n* loss of estate and civil rights following conviction for high treason.

attainment /ə'teɪnmənt/ *n* something attained; an accomplishment.

attaint /ə'teɪnt/ *vt* to subject to attainder; to infect; to stain, to disgrace.

attar /'ætər/ *n* a fragrant essential oil extracted from rose petals and used in making perfume.

attempt /ə'tempt/ *vt* to try to accomplish, get, etc. • *n* an endeavour or effort to accomplish; an attack, assault.—**attemptable** *adj*.—**attempter** *n*.

attend /ə'tend/ *vt* to take care of; to go with, accompany; to be present at. • *vi* to apply oneself (to); to deal with, give attention to.—**attender** *n*.

attendance /ə'tendəns/ *n* attending; the number of people present; the number of times a person attends.

attendant /ə'tendənt/ *n* a person who serves or accompanies another; someone employed to assist or guide. • *adj* accompanying, following as a result; being in attendance.

attention /ə'tenʃən/ *n* the application of the mind to a particular purpose, aim, etc; awareness, notice; care, consideration; (*usu. pl*) an act of civility or courtesy; (*usu. pl*) indications of admiration or love; (*mil*) a soldier's formal erect posture.

attentive /ə'tentɪv/ *adj* observant, diligent; courteous.—**attentively** *adv*.—**attentiveness** *n*.

attenuate /ətenjʊeɪt/ *vt* to make thin; to weaken; to reduce the force or severity of. • *vi* to become thin; to weaken.—**attenuation** *n*.

attest /ə'test/ *vt* to state as true; to certify, as by oath; to give proof of. • *vi* to testify, bear witness (to).—**attestable** *adj*.—**attestation** *n*.—**attester, attestor** *n*.

attestation /ætə'steɪʃən/ *n* the act of attesting; testimony or evidence given on oath or by official declaration; swearing in.

attic /'ætɪk/ *n* the room or space just under the roof; a garret.

Attic *adj* pertaining to Attica in Greece; classical; elegant. • *n* a dialect of ancient Athens.

Attic order *n* a square column of any of the five Greek orders of architecture.

atticism /'ætəsɪzəm/ *n* an elegant expression; (*with cap*) a peculiarity of style or idiom characterizing the Attic rendering of the Greek language.

Attic salt, Attic wit *n* delicate wit.

attire /ə'taɪr/ *vt* to clothe; to dress up. • *n* dress, clothing.

attitude /'ætɪtjuːd/ or /'ætɪtjuːd/ *n* posture, position of the body; a manner of thought or feeling; behaviour; the position of an aircraft or spacecraft in relation to certain reference points.—**attitudinal** *adj*.

attitudinize /ætɪ'tuːdɪnaɪz/ or /ætɪ'tjuː-/ *vi* to assume affected postures, to pose for effect.—**attitudinizer** *n*.

attorn /ə'tɜːn/ *vti* to transfer; to make legal acknowledgment of a new landlord.—**attornment** *n*.

attorney /ə'tɜːni/ *n* (*pl* **attorneys**) one legally authorized to act for another; a lawyer.

attorney general *n* (*pl* **attorneys general, attorneys generals**) the chief law officer of of a state or nation acting as its legal representative and advising the chief executive on legal matters.

attract /ə'trækt/ *vt* to pull towards oneself; to get the admiration, attention, etc of. • *vi* to be attractive.—**attractable** *adj*.—**attractor** *n*.

attraction /ə'trækʃən/ *n* the act of attraction; the power of attracting, *esp* charm; (*physics*) the mutual action by which bodies tend to be drawn together.

attractive /ə'træktɪv/ *adj* pleasing in appearance, etc; arousing interest; able to draw or pull.—**attractively** *adv*.—**attractiveness** *n*.

attribute /ə'trɪbjuːt/ *vt* to regard as belonging to; to ascribe, impute (to). • *n* a quality, a characteristic of.—**attributable** *adj*.

attribution /ætrɪ'bjuːʃən/ *n* the act of attributing, *esp* a work of art, etc to a particular creator; a designation; a function.—**attributional** *adj*.

attributive /ə'trɪbjʊtɪv/ *adj* expressing an attribute; (*gram*) qualifying. • *n* a word joined to and describing a noun; an adjective or adjective phrase.—**attributively** *adv*.

attributive *adj* pertaining to, of the nature of, or expressing, an attribute; (*gram*) qualifying. • *n* a word denoting an attribute; a word joined to and describing a noun; an adjective or adjectival phrase.

attrition /ə'trɪʃən/ *n* a grinding down by or as by friction; a relentless wearing down and weakening; natural wastage or reduction of a workforce by not employing replacements for those who resign or leave.—**attritional** *adj*.—**attritive** *adj*.

attune /ə'tjuːn/ or /ə'tuːn/ *vt* to bring (a person or thing) into harmony with; to adapt.

at. wt. *abbr* = atomic weight.

atypical /eɪ'tɪpɪkəl/ *adj* not according to type; without definite typical character.—**atypically** *adv*.

Au (*chem symbol*) gold.

aubade /oʊ'bɑːd/ *n* a musical announcement of dawn; a sunrise song.

auberge *Fr.* /oʊ'bɛərʒ/ *n* an inn.

aubergine /'oʊbərʒiːn/ *n* a plant producing a smooth, dark-purple fruit; this fruit used as a vegetable.—*also* **eggplant**.

aubrietia, aubretia /ɒ'briːʃə/ *n* a small purple-flowered perennial plant.

auburn /'ɒbərn/ *adj* reddish brown.

au contraire *Fr.* /oːkõː'trɛr/ *adv* on the contrary.

au courant *Fr.* /oːkuː'rɑ̃/ *adj* well-informed, *esp* in current affairs.

auction /'ɒkʃən/ *n* a public sale of items to the highest bidder. • *vt* to sell by or at an auction.

auction bridge *n* a form of bridge in which the players contract to take a certain number of tricks, with extra tricks counting towards game.

auctioneer /ɒkʃə'niːr/ *n* one who conducts an auction.

audacious /ɒ'deɪʃəs/ *adj* daring, adventurous; bold; rash; insolent.—**audaciously** *adv*.—**audaciousness** *n*.

audacity /ɒ'dæsɪti/ *n* (*pl* **audacities**) boldness; daring; spirit; presumptuousness; impudence; effrontery.

audible /'ɒdɪbəl/ *adj* heard or able to be heard.—**audibility** *n*.—**audibly** *adv*.

audience /'ɒdɪəns/ *n* a gathering of listeners or spectators; the people addressed by a book, play, film, etc; a formal interview or meeting, *esp* one in which one's views are heard.

audile /'ɒdaɪl/ *adj* received through hearing.

audio /'ɒdioʊ/ *n* sound; the reproduction, transmission or reception of sound.

audio frequency *n* a frequency audible to the human ear.

audiometer /ɒdi'ɒmɪtər/ *n* an instrument for gauging the power of hearing.—**audiometric** *adj*.—**audiometrically** *adv*.—**audiometry** *n*.

audiotypist /ˌɔdio:'taɪpɪst/ *n* a typist who works from a recording.

audiovisual /-'vɪʒʊəl/ *adj* using both sound and vision, as in teaching aids.

audit /'ɔdɪt/ *n* the inspection and verification of business accounts by a qualified accountant. • *vt* to make such an inspection.

audition /ɔ'dɪʃən/ *n* a trial to test a performer. • *vti* to test or be tested by audition.

auditor /'ɔdɪtər/ *n* a person qualified to audit business accounts.—**auditorial** *adj.*

auditorium /ˌɔdɪ'tɔriəm/ *n* (*pl* **auditoriums** /ˌɔdɪ'tɔriəms/, **auditoria**) the part of a building allotted to the audience; a building or hall for speeches, concerts, etc.

auditory /'ɔdɪˌtɔri/ *adj* of or relating to the sense of hearing.

au fait /o:'feɪ/ *adj* fully informed about; competent.

au fond *Fr.* /o:'fõ:/ fundamentally.

auf Wiedersehen *Ger.* /aʊf'vi:dərˌzeɪən/ *interj, n* till we meet again.

Aug. *abbr* = August.

auger /'ɔgər/ *n* a tool for boring holes, a large gimlet.

aught /ɔt/ *n* anything; any part. • *adv* (*arch*) in any degree, in any way; at all.—*also* **ought**.

augite /'ɔdʒaɪt/ *or* /'ɔg-/ *n* a variety of pyroxene of a black or dark green colour.—**augitic** *adj.*

augment /ɔg'mɛnt/ *vti* to increase.—**augmentable** *adj.*—**augmenter, augmentor** *n.*

augmentation /ˌɔgmɛn'teɪʃən/ *n* enlargement, addition, increase; (*mus*) the increase in time value of the notes of a theme; (*her*) an additional charge to a coat of arms bestowed as a mark of honour.

augmentative /ɔg'mɛntətɪv/ *adj* having the quality or power of augmenting; (*gram*) increasing in force the idea of a word. • *n* a word or affix that expresses with greater force the idea conveyed by the term from which it is derived, opposite of diminutive.

au gratin /ˌo:'græ'tæ̃/ *adj* topped with breadcrumbs or breadcrumbs and cheese, and cooked until crisp.

augur /'ɔgər/ *vti* to prophesy; to be an omen (of).—**augural** *adj.*

augury /'ɔgjəri/ *n* (*pl* **auguries**) the art or practice of foretelling events by reference to natural signs or omens; an omen; prediction; presage.

August /'ɔgəst/ *n* the eighth month of the year, having 31 days.

august /ɔ'gʌst/ *adj* imposing; majestic.

Augustan /ɔ'gʌstən/ *adj* of or pertaining to Augustus Caesar, emperor of Rome, or his reign, during which Roman literature gained its highest point; of or pertaining to the period of the highest stage of literary excellence in other countries.

auk /ɔk/ *n* a northern sea bird with short wings used as paddles.

au lait /o:'le/ *adj* with milk.

auld lang syne /ˌo:ld læŋ'saɪn/ *or* /ˌɒld læŋ'saɪn/ *n* days of old; long ago.

au naturel /ˌo:nætʃə'rel/ *adj, adv* in the natural state; cooked plainly; raw; nude.

aunt /ɑnt/ *or* /ænt/ *n* a father's or mother's sister; an uncle's wife.

auntie, aunty /'ænti/ *or* /'ɒnti/ *n* (*pl* **aunties** /'ænti:z/) (*inf*) aunt.

au pair /o:'peər/ *n* a person, *esp* a girl, from abroad who performs domestic chores, child-minding, etc in return for board and lodging.

aura /'ɔrə/ *n* (*pl* **auras, aurae**) a particular quality or atmosphere surrounding a person or thing.

aural /'ɔrəl/ *adj* of the ear or the sense of hearing.—**aurally** *adv.*

aural *adj* of the air or an aura.

au revoir /o:rə'vwɑr/ *n* goodbye for the present.

aureate /'ɔriət/ *adj* golden; gilded; golden yellow.

aureole /'ɔriˌo:l/, **aureola** /'ɔriˌo:lə/ *n* (*art*) a halo, radiance, or luminous cloud encircling the figures of Christ, the virgin and the saints in sacred pictures; anything resembling an aureole.

auric /o:'ri:k/ *adj* of or pertaining to gold.

auricle /'ɔrɪkəl/ *n* the external part of the ear; either of the two upper chambers of the heart.

auricula /ɔr'ɪkjʊlə/ *n* (*pl* **auriculas, auriculae**) a species of primrose with leaves the shape of a bear's ear.

auricular /ɔr'ɪkjʊlər/ *adj* of or received by the ear; shaped like an ear; spoken privately; relating to the auricles of the heart.

auriculate /ɔr'ɪkjʊlət/ *adj* ear-shaped; having ears or ear-like appendages.

auriferous /ɔr'ɪfərəs/ *adj* gold-bearing; yielding or containing gold.

aurochs /'ɔrɒks/ *n* (*pl* **aurochs**) an extinct wild ox of North Africa, Europe and Asia.

aurora /ə'rɔrə/ *n* (*pl* **auroras** /ə'rɔrəs/, **aurorae** /ə'rɔri/) either of the luminous bands seen in the night sky in the polar regions.—*also* **northern lights**.

aurora australis /-ɒ'streɪlɪs/ *n* the aurora seen at the South Pole.

aurora borealis /-ˌbɒri'ælɪs/ *n* the aurora seen at the North Pole.

aurous /'ɔrəs/ *adj* of or bearing gold.

auscultate /'ɒskəlˌteɪt/ *vt* to examine by auscultation.—**auscultator** *n.*—**auscultatory** *adj.*

auscultation /ˌɒskəl'teɪʃən/ *n* a listening to the sounds of the heart, lungs, etc in the chest for medical diagnosis.

auspex /'ɒsˌpeks/ *n* (*pl* **auspices** /'ɔspɪsɪz/) one who divined by observation of birds in ancient Rome.

auspice /'ɒspɪs/ *n* (*pl* **auspices** /'ɔspɪsɪz/) an omen; (*pl*) sponsorship; patronage.

auspicious /ɒ'spɪʃəs/ *adj* showing promise, favourable.—**auspiciously** *adv.*

Aussie /'ɒzi/ *or* /'ɒsi/ *n* (*sl*) an Australian.

austere /ɒ'sti:r/ *adj* stern, forbidding in attitude or appearance; abstemious; severely simple, plain.—**austerely** *adv.*—**austereness** *n.*

austerity /ɒ'steriti/ *n* (*pl* **austerities** /'ɒspəsəs/)being austere; economic privation.

austral /'ɒstrəl/ *adj* southern; (*with cap*) Australian.

Australasian /ˌɒstrə'leɪʒən/ *adj* of or pertaining to Australasia (Australia, New Zealand and adjacent islands). • *n* a native or inhabitant of Australasia.

Australian /ɒ'streɪliən/ *adj* of or pertaining to Australia. • *n* a native or inhabitant of Australia.

Australoid /'ɒstrəlɔɪd/ *adj* of the variety of human population that includes the Australian aborigines. • *n* an Australoid person.

autarchy /'ɒtɑrki/ *n* (*pl* **autarchies** /'ɒtɑrki:z/) absolute or autocratic rule or sovereignty; a country governed in such a way; autarky.—**autarchic, autarchical** *adj.*

autarky /'ɒtɑrki/ *n* (*pl* **autarkies** /'ɒtɑrki:z/) self-sufficiency, *esp* in the economic sphere; the policy of encouraging economic self-sufficiency.—**autarkic, autarkical** *adj.*

authentic /ɒ'θentik/ *adj* genuine, conforming to truth or reality; trustworthy, reliable.—**authentically** *adv.*—**authenticity** *n.*

authenticate /ɒ'θentiˌkeɪt/ *vt* to demonstrate the authenticity of; to make valid; to verify.—**authentication** *n.*—**authenticator** *n.*

author /'ɒθər/ *n* a person who brings something into existence; the writer of a book, article, etc. • *vt* to be the author of.—**authoress** *nf.*—**authorial** *adj.*

authoritarian /əˌθɒrɪ'teriən/ *or* /-θɔr-/, /ɒ-/ *adj* favouring strict obedience; dictatorial. • *n* a person advocating authoritarian principles.—**authoritarianism** *n.*

authoritative /ə'θɒrɪˌteɪtɪv/ *or* /-θɔr-/, /ɒ-/ *adj* commanding or possessing authority; accepted as true; official.—**authoritatively** *adv.*

authority /ə'θɒrɪti/ *or* /-ˌθɔr/, /ɒ-/ *n* (*pl* **authorities** /ə'θɒrəti:z/) the power or right to command; (*pl*) officials with this power; influence resulting from knowledge, prestige, etc; a person, writing, etc cited to support an opinion; an expert.

authorize /'ɒθəˌraɪz/ *vt* to give authority to, to empower; to give official approval to, sanction.—**authorization** *n.*

Authorized Version /'ɒθəˌraɪzd'vərzən/ *n* the version of the Bible published by the sanction of James I of England in 1611 and appointed to be read in churches.—*also* **King James Bible, King James Version**.

authorship /'ɒθərʃɪp/ *n* the writing profession; the origin (of book).

autism /'ɒtɪzəm/ *n* (*psychiatry*) a mental state, *usu* of children, marked by disregard of external reality.—**autistic** *adj.*

auto /'ɒto:/ *n* (*pl* **autos** /'ɒto:z/) (*inf*) an automobile.

auto- /'ɒto:/ *or* /'ɔto:/ *prefix* self; by oneself or itself.

autobahn /'ɒto:ˌbɒn/ *n* a German, Austrian or Swiss motorway.

autobiography /ˌɒto:baɪ'ɒgrəfi/ *n* (*pl* **autobiographies** /ˌɒtəbaɪ'ɒgrəfi:z/) the biography of a person written by himself or herself.—**autobiographer** *n.*—**autobiographical** *adj.*

autocephalous /ˌɒto:'sefələs/ *adj* having its own head; independent.

autochondriac /ˌɒto:'kɒndriˌæk/ *n* a person who is preoccupied with his or her car.

autochthon /ɒ'tɒkθən/ *n* (*pl* **autochthons, autochthones**) an earliest known inhabitant, an aboriginal.

autochthonous /-nəs/, **autochthonal** /-nəl/ *adj* pertaining to primitive inhabitants; indigenous, native to the soil.—**autochthonism, autochthony** *n*.

autoclave /'ɒtə,kleɪv/ *n* a strong container used for chemical reactions at high temperatures and pressures; a device for sterilizing implements using steam at high pressure.

autocracy /ɒ'tɒkrəsi/ *n* (*pl* **autocracies**) government by one person with absolute power.

autocrat /'ɒtə,kræt/ *n* an absolute ruler; any domineering person.—**autocratic** *adj*.—**autocratically** *adv*.

autocross /'ɒtə:,krɒs/ *n* cross-country motor racing.

Autocue /'ɒtə:kju:/ *n* (*trademark*) a prompting device used in TV, etc, which provides speakers with a script that remains invisible to the audience.—*also* **Teleprompter**.

auto-da-fé /,ɒtə:dæ'feɪ/ or /,ɒtə:z-/, *Fr.* /'autədɐ'fe/ *n* (*pl* **autos-da-fé**) a public judgment by the Spanish Inquisition upon prisoners tried for heresy and other offences against the religious or civil law; the subsequent execution of such sentences by burning.

autoeroticism /,ɒtəʊ'rɒtɪ,sizəm/, **autoerotism** /-'erə,tizəm/ *n* self-produced sexual emotion.—**autoerotic** *adj*.

autogamy /ɒ'tɒɡəmi/ *n* self-fertilization.—**autogamous** *adj*.

autogenesis /,ɒtə:'dʒenəsɪs/, **autogeny** /,ɒtə:'dʒeni/ *n* spontaneous generation.—**autogenetic** *adj*.

autogenous /ɒ'tɒdʒənəs/ *adj* self-generated; produced independently.

autogyro, autogiro /,ɒtə:'dʒaɪrəʊ/ *n* (*pl* **autogyros, autogiros**) an aircraft like a helicopter but with unpowered rotor blades.

autograph /'ɒtə,ɡræf/ *n* a pers on's signature. • *vt* to write one's signature in or on.—**autographic** *adj*.—**autographically** *adv*.

autography /ɒ'tɒɡrəfi/ *n* one's own handwriting; a lithographic process by which copies of writings or drawings are reproduced in facsimile.

autolysis /ɒ'tɒlɪsɪs/ *n* the destruction of cells of a body by the action of its own serum.—**autolytic** *adj*.

automaker /'ɒtə:,meɪkər/ *n* a manufacturer of automobiles.

automat /'ɒtə:,mæt/ *n* a vending machine; in US, a restaurant equipped with slot machines for dispensing food and drink.

automate /'ɒtə,meɪt/ *vt* to control by automation; to convert to automatic operation.

automated telling machine *n* a device that provides cash and other banking services automatically when activated by a plastic card issued to customers; a cash dispenser.—*also* **autoteller**.

automatic /,ɒtə'mætɪk/ *adj* involuntary or reflexive; self-regulating; acting by itself. • *n* an automatic pistol or rifle.—**automatically** *adv*.

automatic pilot *n* a device that can maintain an aircraft or ship on a previously set course.—*also* **autopilot**.

automatic transmission *n* a system in a motor vehicle for changing gears automatically.

automation /,ɒtə'meɪʃən/ *n* the use of automatic methods, machinery, etc in industry.

automatism /ɒ'tɒmə,tizəm/ *n* automatic action; involuntary action; mechanical routine; the doctrine that assigns all animal functions to the active operation of physical laws.—**automatist** *n*.

automaton /ə'tɒmə,tɒn/ *n* (*pl* **automatons, automata**) any automatic device, *esp* a robot; a human being who acts like a robot.

automatous /ə'tɒmətəs/ *adj* spontaneous; of the nature of an automaton.

automobile /'ɒtəmə,bi:l/ *n* a *usu* four-wheeled vehicle powered by an internal combustion engine.—*also* **motor car**.

automotive /,ɒtə'mo:tɪv/ *adj* relating to motor vehicles.

autonomy /ɒ'tɒnəmi/ *n* (*pl* **autonomies**) freedom of self-determination; independence, self-government.—**autonomous** *adj*.

autopilot /'ɒtə:,paɪlət/ *n* automatic pilot.

autoplasty /-,plæsti/ *n* the process of repairing lesions by application of tissue removed from another part of the same body.—**autoplastic** *adj*.

autopsy /'ɒ,tɒpsi/ *n* (*pl* **autopsies**) a post-mortem examination to determine the cause of death.

autoroute /'ɒtə:,ru:t/ *n* a French motorway.

autostrada /'ɒtə:,strædə/ *n* an Italian motorway.

autosuggestion /,ɒtə:sə'dʒestʃən/ or /-səɡ'dʒest/ *n* (*psychoanal*) self-applied suggestion.—**autosuggestive** *adj*.

autoteller *see* **automated telling machine**.

autotoxin /,ɒtə'tɒksɪn/ *n* a poisonous substance produced by changes within an organism.—**autotoxic** *adj*.

autumn /'ɒtəm/ *n* the season between summer and winter.—*also* fall.

autumnal /ɒ'tʌmnəl/ *adj* belonging or peculiar to autumn; produced or gathered in autumn; pertaining to the period of life when middle age is past. • *n* a plant that flowers in autumn.

aux. /ɒks/ *abbr* = auxiliary.

auxiliary /ɒɡ'zɪljəri/ or /-'zɪləri/ *adj* providing help, subsidiary; supplementary. • *n* (*pl* **auxiliaries**) a helper; (*gram*) a verb that helps form tenses, moods, voices, etc of other verbs, as *have, be, may, shall*, etc.

AV /'eɪ'vi:/ *abbr* = ad valorem; audiovisual; Authorized Version.

avadavat /,ævədə'væt/ *n* a small Asian finch-like bird, kept as a caged bird for its song.

avail /ə'veɪl/ *vti* to be of use or advantage to. • *n* benefit, use or help.

available /ə'veɪləbəl/ *adj* ready for use; obtainable, accessible.—**availability** *n*.—**availably** *adv*.

avalanche /'ævə,lænʃ/ *n* a mass of snow, ice, and rock tumbling down a mountainside; a sudden overwhelming accumulation or influx.

avalanche lily *n* a plant of the lily family with a large yellow flower found near the snow line on mountains.

avant-garde /ˌævɒnt'ɡɑrd/, *Fr.* /ævɑ̃'ɡɑrd/ *n* (*arts*) those ideas and practices regarded as in advance of those generally accepted. • *adj* pertaining to such ideas and practices and their creators.—**avant-gardism** *n*.

avarice /'ævərɪs/ *n* greed for wealth.—**avaricious** *adj*.—**avariciously** *adv*.

avast /ə'væst/ *interj* (*naut*) stop! cease! hold!

avatar /'ævə,tɑr/ *n* (*Hinduism*) the descent to earth of a deity in an incarnate form; manifestation or embodiment; transference of personality.

avdp. *abbr* = avoirdupois.

ave /'ɒveɪ/ *interj* hail; farewell. • *n* an Ave Maria; a salutation.

Ave, ave *abbr* = avenue.

Ave Maria /'ɒveɪmə'ri:ə/ *n* (*RC Church*) Hail Mary.

avenge /ə'vendʒ/ *vt* to get revenge for.—**avenger** *n*.

avens /'ævənz/ *n* (*pl* **avens**) the popular name of plants to which the herb bennet belongs.

aventurine /ə'ventʃə,ri:n/ *n* a brown, gold-spangled kind of Venetian glass; a variety of micaceous quartz or feldspar.

avenue /'ævə,nju:/ *n* a street, drive, etc, *esp* when broad; means of access; the way to an objective.

aver /ə'vɜr/ *vt* (**averring, averred**) to state as true; to assert.—**averment** *n*.

average /'ævrɪdʒ/ *n* the result of dividing the sum of two or more quantities by the number of quantities; the usual kind, amount, quality, etc. • *vt* to calculate the average of; to achieve an average number of.

averse /ə'vɜrs/ *adj* unwilling; opposed (to).

aversion /ə'vɜrʒən/ or /-ʃən/ *n* antipathy; hatred; something arousing hatred or repugnance.

avert /ə'vɜrt/ *vt* to turn away or aside from; to prevent, avoid.—**avertible, avertable** *adj*.

avian /'eɪvɪən/ *adj* of or pertaining to birds.

aviary /'eɪvɪ,eri/ *n* (*pl* **aviaries**) a building or large cage for keeping birds.

aviate /'eɪvɪət/ *vi* to pilot or travel in an aircraft.

aviation /,eɪvɪ'eɪʃən/ *n* the art or science of flying aircraft.

aviator /'eɪvɪ,eɪtər/ *n* a pilot, *esp* in the early history of flying.

aviculture /'eɪvɪ,kʌltʃər/ *n* the breeding and rearing of birds.—**aviculturist** *n*.

avid /'ævɪd/ *adj* eager, greedy.—**avidly** *adv*.

avidity /ə'vɪdɪti/ *n* greediness; eagerness; strong appetite.

avifauna *n* /'eɪvɪ,fɒnə/ (*pl* **avifaunae**) the birds of a region regarded collectively.—**avifaunal** *adj*.

avionics /,eɪvɪ'ɒnɪks/ *n* (*used as sing*) the application of electronics in aviation.—**avionic** *adj*.

avocado /,ævə'kɒdo:/ *n* (*pl* **avocados**) a thick-skinned, pear-shaped fruit with yellow buttery flesh.

avocet /'ævə,set/ *n* one of several species of wading birds, characterized by very long legs and an extremely slender curved bill.

avoid /ə'vɔɪd/ *vt* to keep clear of, shun; to refrain from.—**avoider** *n*.

avoidable *adj* able to be avoided.

avoidance /ə'vɔɪdəns/ *n* the act of annulling or making void; the act of shunning; the state of being vacant.

avoirdupois /ˌævərdə'pɔɪz/ *n* the system of weights based on the pound of 16 ounces; (*inf*) excess weight.

avow /ə'vau/ *vt* to declare confidently; to acknowledge.—**avowed** *adj*.—**avowedly** *adv*.—**avower** *n*.

avowal /ə'vauəl/ *n* an open declaration; a frank acknowledgment; a confession.

avulsion /ə'vʌlʃən/ *n* a separation by violence; the sudden removal of land, without change of ownership, caused by a flood, etc.

avuncular /ə'vʌŋkjulər/ *adj* like an uncle.

await /ə'weɪt/ *vti* to wait for; to be in store for.

awake /ə'weɪk/ *vb* (**awaking, awoke** *or* **awaked,** *pp* **awoken** *or* **awaked**) *vi* to wake; to become aware. • *vt* to rouse from sleep; to rouse from inaction. • *adj* roused from sleep, not asleep; active; aware.

awaken /ə'weɪkən/ *vti* to awake.

awakening /-ɪŋ/ *n* the act of rousing from sleep; a revival of religion, or activity of a particular religious sect. • *adj* rousing; exciting; alarming.

award /ə'wɔrd/ *vt* to give, as by a legal decision; to give (a prize, etc); to grant. • *n* a decision, as by a judge; a prize.

aware /ə'weɪr/ *adj* realizing, having knowledge; conscious; fully conversant with and sympathetic towards (*ecologically aware*).—**awareness** *n*.

awash /ə'wɒʃ/ *adj* filled or overflowing with water.

away /ə'weɪ/ *adv* from a place; in another place or direction; off, aside; far. • *adj* absent; at a distance.

awe /ɒ/ *n* a mixed feeling of fear, wonder and dread. • *vt* to fill with awe.

aweather /ə'weðər/ *adv* (*naut*) on the weather side, or towards the wind. • *n* opposed to the alee.

aweigh /ə'weɪ/ *adj, adv* (*naut*) (*anchor*) atrip, just drawn out of the ground and hanging perpendicularly.

awesome /'ɒsəm/ *adj* inspiring awe; (*inf*) marvellous, terrific.

awestricken /'ɒstrɪkən/, **awestruck** /'ɒstrek/ *adj* struck with awe.

awful /'ɒfəl/ *adj* very bad; unpleasant. • *adv* (*inf*) very.—**awfulness** *n*.

awfulize *vt* to envisage a situation as being worse than it is.—*also* **catastrophize**.

awfully /'ɒfəli/ *or* /'ɒfli/ *adv* in an awful manner; excessively; (*inf*) very.

awhile /ə'waɪl/ *adv* for a short time.

awkward /'ɒkwərd/ *adj* lacking dexterity, clumsy; graceless; embarrassing; embarrassed; inconvenient; deliberately obstructive or difficult to deal with.—**awkwardly** *adv*.—**awkwardness** *n*.

awl /ɒl/ *n* a small pointed tool for boring or piercing, used by shoemakers, etc.

awn /ɒn/ *n* the beard or bristle-like appendage of the outer glume of wheat, barley, and numerous grasses.

awning /'ɒnɪŋ/ *n* a structure, as of canvas, extended above or in front of a window, door, etc to provide shelter against the sun or rain.

awoke /ə'wo:k/ *see* **awake**.

AWOL /'eɪwɒl/ *acronym* = absent without leave.

awry /ə'raɪ/ *adv* twisted to one side. • *adj* contrary to expectations, wrong.

axe, ax /æks/ *n* (*pl* **axes**) a tool with a long handle and bladed head for chopping wood, etc. • *vt* to trim, split, etc with an axe.

axial /'æksɪəl/ *adj* of, forming or round an axis.—**axially** *adv*.

axil /'æksɪl/ *n* (*bot*) the angle formed by the upper side of an organ or branch with the stem or trunk to which it is attached.

axile /'æksɪl/ *or* /-ˌsaɪl/ *adj* (*bot*) of, lying or situated in, or attached to, an axis.

axilla /æk'sɪlə/ *n* (*pl* **axillae, axillas**) the armpit, or cavity in the junction of the arm and shoulder; the axil of a leaf.

axillary /æk'sɪləri/ *adj* of or pertaining to the armpit; (*bot*) pertaining to, springing from, or situated in, the axil. • *n* (*pl* **axillaries**) a feather from the axilla of a bird.

axiom /'æksɪəm/ *n* a widely held or accepted truth or principle.

axiomatic /ˌæksɪə'mætɪk/ *adj* pertaining to, or of the nature of, an axiom.—**axiomatically** *adv*.

axis[1] /'æksɪs/ *n* (*pl* **axes**) a real or imaginary straight line about which a body rotates; the centre line of a symmetrical figure; a reference line of a coordinate system; (*with cap*) a partnership, alliance, *esp* of Germany and Italy, 1936 to the end of World War II.—**axial** *adj*.

axis[2] *n* (*pl* **axises**) a small deer of India and Asia with slender antlers.

axle /'æksəl/ *n* a rod on or with which a wheel turns; a bar connecting two opposite wheels, as of a car.

axletree /-ˌtri/ *n* a bar connecting the opposite wheels of a carriage, on the rounded ends of which the wheels revolve.

axolotl /'æksəˌlɒtəl/ *n* a Mexican amphibian like the salamander, having gills.

ay[1], **aye**[1] /eɪ/ *or* /aɪ/ *adv* (*arch*) for ever, always; continually.

ay[2], **aye**[2] /aɪ/ *adv, interj* yes; even so; indeed. • *n* (*pl* **ayes**) an affirmative answer or vote in a parliamentary division; the members so voting.

ayah /'aɪjə/ *n* a native Indian nurse or lady's maid.

Ayatollah /ˌaɪjə'tɒːlə/ *n* a Shiite Muslim leader; a title of respect.

aye-aye /'aɪaɪ/ *n* a small nocturnal quadruped, native to Madagascar and allied to the lemurs.

azalea /ə'zeɪlɪə/ *n* a flowering shrub-like plant.

azan /ɒ'zɒn/ *n* the call to public prayers in Islamic countries.

azedarach /ə'zɛdəræk/ *n* an Asian tree, the bark or root of which was formerly used as a drug.

Azilian /ə'zɪlɪən/ *adj* of a Mesolithic geological stage characterized by bone harpoon heads and painted stone pebbles.

azimuth /'æzɪməθ/ *n* (*astron*) a vertical arc from the zenith to the horizon; the angular distance of this from the meridian.—**azimuthal** *adj*.

azoic /ə'zoːɪk/ *or* /-eɪ-/ *adj* without life; (*geol*) without fossils, older than the lowermost series of rocks containing traces of organic life.

azote /ə'zoːt/ *or* /-æ-/ *n* an old name for nitrogen.

AZT /'eɪ'zed'tiː/ *abbr* = azidothymidine, a drug that has been effective in prolonging life and alleviating symptoms in some AIDS sufferers.—*also called* **zidovudine**.

Aztec /'æztek/ *adj* pertaining to the Aztec race that ruled Mexico before the Spanish conquest. • *n* a member of the Aztec race.

azure /'æʒər/ *or* /-zjər/ *adj* sky-blue.

azurite /'æʒəˌraɪt/ *n* blue carbonate of copper; blue malachite or chessylite; lazulite.

azygous /'eɪzaɪgəs/ *adj* (*anat*) single, as a muscle or vein; not one of a pair.

B

B *abbr* = boron.

b *abbr* = born; billion.

BA /ˈbiːˈeɪ/ *abbr* = Bachelor of Arts; British Airways; British Academy.

Ba *abbr* = barium.

baa /bɒ/ *n* the bleat of a sheep. • *vi* to bleat as a sheep.

baba /ˈbɒbə/ *n* a small sponge cake soaked in (*usu* rum) flavoured syrup.

Babbitt metal /ˈbæbɪt/ *n* any of a number of anti-friction alloys originally based on copper, tin and antimony, used in crank and axle bearings, etc.

Babbittry /ˈbæbɪtri/ *n* (*US derog*) businessman's or middle-class person's standards or blinkered outlook.—**Babbitt** *n*.

babble /ˈbæbəl/ *vi* to make sounds like a baby; to talk incoherently, endlessly or senselessly; to give away secrets; to murmur, as a brook. • *n* incoherent talk; chatter; a murmuring sound.—**babbler** *n*.

babe /beɪb/ *n* a baby; a naive person; (*sl*) a girl or young woman, especially an attractive one.

Babel /ˈbeɪbəl/ or /ˈbæbəl/ *n* (*Bible*) the tower in Shinar (Genesis 11); a lofty structure; a confused and meaningless sound of voices; a scene of confusion and noise.

babirusa, babiruossa, babirussa /ˈbɒbəˌruːsə/ *n* the wild hog of Eastern Asia.

baboon /bæˈbuːn/ or /bə-/ *n* a large, short-tailed monkey.

babul /bəˈbuːl/ *n* the rind of the East Indian acacia.

baby /ˈbeɪbi/ *n* (*pl* **babies**) a newborn child or infant; a very young animal; (*sl*) a girl or young woman; a personal project. • *vt* (**babying, babied**) to pamper.—*also adj.*—**babyish** *adj*.

baby boom *n* a sharp rise in the birth rate.

baby-boomer *n* a person born in the period immediately after World War II when the birthrate increased sharply (*baby boom*).

baby break *n* a period, often five years, when a parent raises children before returning to work.

baby burst *n* a sudden fall in birth rate.

baby carriage *n* a perambulator.

baby grand *n* a small grand piano.

Babylonian /ˌbæbəˈloːniən/ *adj* of or pertaining to the ancient kingdom of Babylonia; magnificent; luxurious. • *n* an inhabitant of Babylonia; its language.

baby-sit /ˈbeɪbiˌsɪt/ *vti* (**baby-sitting, baby-sat**) to look after a baby or child while the parents are out.—**baby-sitter** *n*.

baby snatcher *n* (*inf*) one who marries or has a liaison with a much younger person; a person who steals a baby.

baby wipe *n* a disposable paper towel, ready moistened.

baccalaureate /ˌbækəˈlɔːriət/ *n* the university degree awarded to a Bachelor of Arts etc; a commencement address.

baccarat /ˈbækəˌrɒ/ or /ˌbækəˈrɒ/, /bɒ-/ *n* a card game where players bet against the banker.

baccate /ˈbækeɪt/ *adj* having many berries; berry-shaped.

bacchanal /ˌbækəˈnɒl/ or /ˌbɒk-/ *n* a priest of Bacchus, the god of wine; a drunken reveler; a drunken feast.—**bacchanalian** *adj*.

bacchanalia /ˌbækəˈneɪliə/ or /ˌbɒk-/ *npl* drunken revels.

bacchant /ˈbækənt/ *n* (*pl* **bacchants, bacchantes**) a priest or votary of Bacchus; a drunkard.—**bacchante** *nf* (*pl* **bacchantes**).

Bacchic /ˈbækɪk/ or /ˈbɒkɪk/ *adj* pertaining to Bacchus or the feasts in his honour; riotous, or mad with drink.

bacciferous /bækˈsɪfərəs/ *adj* bearing or producing berries.

bacciform /ˈbæksəˌfɔrm/ *adj* berry-shaped.

baccivorous /bækˈsɪvərəs/ *adj* eating or subsisting on berries.

bachelor /ˈbætʃələr/ or /ˈbætʃlər/ *n* an unmarried man; a person who holds a degree from a college or university.—**bachelorhood** *n*.

bachelor flat *n* a flat that has one large room serving as a bedroom and living room, together with a kitchenette and bathroom.

bachelor's buttons *npl* the popular name for a double-flowered buttercup with blossoms resembling buttons.

bacillary /bəˈsɪləri/ or /ˈbæsəˌlɛri/, **bacillar** *adj* of, like, caused by, or consisting of bacilli; rod-shaped.

bacilliform /bəˈsɪləˌfɔrm/ *adj* rod-shaped, like a bacillus.

bacillus /bəˈsɪləs/ *n* (*pl* **bacilli** /bəsɪlˈaɪ/) any of a genus of rod-shaped bacteria; (*loosely*) bacteria in general.

back¹ /bæk/ *n* the rear surface of the human body from neck to hip; the corresponding part in animals; a part that supports or fits or makes firm the back of anything; the part farthest from the front; (*sport*) a player or position behind the front line. • *adj* at the rear; (*streets, etc*) remote or inferior; (*pay, etc*) of or for the past; backward. • *adv* at or towards the rear; to or towards a former condition, time, etc; in return or requital; in reserve or concealment. • *vti* to move or go backwards; to support; to bet on; to provide or be a back for; to supply a musical backing for a singer; (*with* **down**) to withdraw from a position or claim; (*with* **off**) to move back (or away, etc); (*with* **out**) to withdraw from an enterprise; to evade keeping a promise, etc; (*with* **up**) to support; to move backwards; to accumulate because of restricted movement; (*comput*) to make a copy (of a data file, etc) for safekeeping.

back² *n* a large shallow cistern or vat used by brewers, etc, for liquids.

backache /ˈbækeɪk/ *n* an ache or pain in the back.

back bacon *n* round, lean bacon cut from a pork loin.

backbencher /-bentʃər/ *n* in UK, Australia, etc, a member of parliament who does not hold office.

backbite /-baɪt/ *vt* (**backbiting, backbit**, *pp* **backbitten** *or* **backbit**) to talk spitefully or ill of behind a person's back.—**backbiter** *n*.—**backbiting** *n*.

backboard /ˈbækbɔrd/ *n* a board at the back of a cart; a board worn at the back to support the back; a thin wooden backing used for picture frames, mirrors, etc.

backbone /-boːn/ *n* the spinal column; main support; strength, courage.

backbreaking /-breɪkɪŋ/ *adj* arduous; physically exhausting.

back channel *n* a person who acts as a secret intermediary, *esp* in diplomacy.

backchat /-tʃæt/ *n* (*inf*) cheeky repartee.

backcomb /-koːm/ *vt* (*hair*) to comb towards the roots to give body.

backdate /-deɪt/ *vt* to declare valid from some previous date.

backdoor /-dɔːr/ *adj* indirect, concealed, devious.

backdown /-daʊn/ *n* the act of backing down; the withdrawal of a claim, etc.

backdrop /-drɒp/ *n* a curtain, often scenic, at the back of a stage; background.

back end /-ɛnd/ *n* (*dial*) autumn.

backer /-ər/ *n* a patron; one who bets on a contestant.

backfire /-faɪr/ *vi* (*cars*) to ignite prematurely causing a loud bang from the exhaust; to have the opposite effect from that intended, *usu* with unfortunate consequences.—*also n*.

backgammon /ˈbækˌgæmən/ or /bækˈgæmən/ *n* a board game played by two people with pieces moved according to throws of the dice.

background /-graʊnd/ *n* the distant part of a scene or picture; an inconspicuous position; social class, education, experience; circumstances leading up to an event.

backhand /-hænd/ *n* (*tennis, etc*) a stroke played with the hand turned outwards.

backhanded /ˈbækˌhændəd/ or /bækˈhændəd/ *adj* backhand; (*compliment*) indirect, ambiguous.—*also adv*.—**backhandedly** *adv*.

backhander /-ˌhændər/ *n* a backhanded stroke; (*inf*) a backhanded remark; (*sl*) a bribe.

backing /-ɪŋ/ *n* support; supporters; a lining to support or strengthen the back of something; musical accompaniment to a (*esp* pop) singer.

backlash /-læʃ/ *n* a violent and adverse reaction; a recoil in machinery.

backlist /-lɪst/ *n* books published in past years that are still in print.

backlog /-lɒg/ *n* an accumulation of work, etc still to be done.

back number *n* a former issue (of a magazine, etc); an out-of-date person.

backpack /-pæk/ *n* a rucksack; an equipment pack carried on the back of an astronaut, etc. • *vi* to travel, hike, etc wearing a backpack.

back pay /-peɪ/ *n* an increase in wages or salary paid retrospectively.

back-pedal /-ˌpedəl/ *vi* (**back-pedalling, back-pedalled** *or* **back-pedaling, back-pedaled**) to work the pedals of a bicycle backwards; to modify or withdraw one's original argument or action.

back-seat driver /'siːt/ *n* a passenger in a car who irritates the driver with persistent unwanted advice.

backside /'bæksaɪd/ *n* (*inf*) buttocks.

backslide /-slaɪd/ *vi* (**backsliding, backslid,** *pp* **backslid** *or* **backslidden**) to return to one's (bad) old ways.—**backslider** *n*.

backspace /-speɪs/ *vi* to move a typewriter carriage or cursor of a word processor back one space.

backspin /-spɪn/ *n* (*sport*) a backward spin in a ball to slow it down.

backstage /'bæksteɪdʒ/ *or* /bæk'steɪdʒ/ *adv* behind the stage of a theatre in areas hidden from the audience; (*inf*) away from public view.—*also adj*.

backstairs /-'sterz/ *npl* stairs in the back part of a house; stairs for private use. • *adj* indirect; underhand; secret; intriguing.

backstay /-steɪ/ *n* (*naut*) a long rope extending from the masthead to the side of a ship, supporting the mast.

backstitch /-stɪtʃ/ *n* an overlapping stitch. • *vt* to sew with this stitch.

backstroke /-stroːk/ *n* (*swimming*) a stroke using backward circular sweeps of the arms whilst lying face upwards.

backsword /-sord/ *n* a sword with one sharp edge, a broadsword; a stick with a basket handle used in the game of singlestick.

back-to-back *adj* facing in opposite directions, often with the backs touching.

backtrack /'bɒktræk/ *vi* to return along the same path; to reverse or recant one's opinion, action, etc.

backup /-ʌp/ *n* an alternate or auxiliary; support, reinforcement; (*comput*) a copy of a data file, etc.

backward /-wərd/ *adj* turned toward the rear or opposite way; shy; slow or retarded. • *adv* backwards.—**backwardness** *n*.

backwards /-ˌwərdz/ *adv* towards the back; with the back foremost; in a way opposite the usual; into a less good or favourable state or condition; into the past.

backwash /-wɒʃ/ *n* water receding from the action of an oar, propeller, etc; the consequences of an event.

backwater /-wɒtər/ *n* a pool of still water fed by a river; a remote, backward place.

backwoods /-wʊdz/ *npl* uncleared forest land; an isolated, thinly populated area.—**backwoodsman** *n* (*pl* **backwoodsmen**).

backyard /-'jɑrd/ *n* a yard at the back of a house.

baclava /ˌbɒklə'vɒ/ *see* **baklava**.

bacon /'beɪkən/ *n* salted and smoked meat from the back or sides of a pig; **to bring home the bacon** to succeed; to help materially; **to save one's bacon** to have a narrow escape.

bacteria /bæk'tiːriə/ *npl* (*sing* **bacterium**) microscopic unicellular organisms *usu* causing disease.—**bacterial** *adj*.

bactericide /bæk'tɪrɪˌsaɪd/ *n* a substance that destroys bacteria.—**bactericidal** *adj*.

bacteriology /bækˌtɪri'ɒlədʒi/ *n* the scientific study of bacteria.—**bacteriological** *adj*.—**bacteriologist** *n*.

bacteriolysis /bækˌtiːri'ɒləsɪs/ *n* destruction of bacteria by a serum.—**bacteriolytic** *adj*.

bacterium /bæk'tiːriəm/ *see* **bacteria**.

Bactrian camel *n* a camel with two humps.

bad[1] /bæd/ *adj* (**worse, worst**) not good; not as it should be; inadequate or unfit; rotten or spoiled; incorrect or faulty; wicked; immoral; mischievous; harmful; ill; sorry, distressed.—**badness** *n*.

bad[2] *see* **bid**.

bad blood *n* enmity, hostility.

bad debt *n* a debt that is not recoverable.

baddie, baddy /'bædi/ *n* (*pl* **baddies**) (*inf*) a villain.

badderlocks /'bædərˌlɒks/ *n* a large dark-green edible seaweed.

bade /beɪd/ *see* **bid**.

badge /bædʒ/ *n* an emblem, symbol or distinguishing mark.

badger /'bædʒər/ *n* a hibernating, burrowing black and white mammal related to the weasel. • *vt* to pester or annoy persistently.

badinage /'bædɪˌnɒʒ/ *n* light or playful raillery or banter.

badlands /ˌbædlændz/ *npl* barren, dry, heavily eroded areas of land in northwestern North America.

badly /'bædli/ *adv* (**worse, worst**) poorly; inadequately; unsuccessfully; severely; (*inf*) very much.

badminton /'bædmɪntən/ *n* a court game for two or four players played with light rackets and a shuttlecock volleyed over a net.

badmouth *vt* (*sl*) to speak ill of; to slander.

baffle /'bæfəl/ *vt* to bewilder or perplex; to frustrate; to make ineffectual. • *n* a plate or device used to restrict the flow of sound, light or fluid.—**bafflement** *n*.—**baffling** *adj*.

bag /bæg/ *n* a *usu* flexible container of paper, plastic, etc that can be closed at the top; a satchel, suitcase, etc; a handbag; a purse; game taken in hunting; a bag-like shape or part; (*derog*) an old, unpleasant or ugly woman; (*inf: in pl*) plenty (of). • *vti* (**bagging, bagged**) to place in a bag; to kill in hunting; (*inf*) to get; to make a claim on; to hang loosely.

bagasse /bə'gæs/ *n* sugar-cane refuse after crushing, used as a fuel.

bagatelle /ˌbægə'tɛl/ *n* something of little value; a piece of light music *usu* for piano; a board game in which balls struck with a cue or by a spring are aimed at holes or pinned spaces.

bagel /'beɪgəl/ *n* a ring-shaped bread roll, hard and glazed on the outside, soft in the centre.

bagful /'bægfʊl/ *n* (*pl* **bagfuls**) as much as will fill one bag.

baggage /'bægɪdʒ/ *n* suitcases; luggage; **bag and baggage** with one's entire possessions; entirely.

bagging /'bægɪŋ/ *n* the act of putting into bags; a coarse cloth or other material used for bags; filtration through canvas bags.

baggy /'bægi/ *adj* (**baggier, baggiest**) hanging loosely in folds.—**baggily** *adv*.—**bagginess** *n*.

bag lady *n* (*pl* **bag ladies**) a homeless woman who wanders the streets carrying her possessions in shopping bags or carrier bags.

bagman /'bægmæn/ *n* (*pl* **bagmen**) (*formerly*) a travelling salesman who carried his wares in saddlebags; a person who collects or distributes illegally obtained money for another.

bagnio /'bænjoː/ *n* (*pl* **bagnios**) a brothel; a bath house; an oriental prison.

bagpipe /'bægpaɪp/ *n* (*often pl*) a musical instrument consisting of an air-filled bag fitted with pipes.

bail[1] /beɪl/ *n* money lodged as security that a prisoner, if released, will return to court to stand trial; such a release; the person pledging such money. • *vt* to free a person by providing bail; (*with* **out**) to help out of financial or other difficulty; (*government, bank, etc*) to assist a floundering business.—**bailable** *adj*.

bail[2] *vti* (*usu with* **out**) to scoop out (water) from (a boat).

bail[3] *n* (*cricket*) either of two wooden crosspieces that rest on the three stumps; a bar separating horses in an open stable; a metal bar that holds the paper against the roller of a typewriter.

bailee /beɪ'liː/ *n* (*law*) the person to whom goods are delivered in trust.

bailey /'beɪli/ *n* the outer wall of a castle; a castle yard.

Bailey bridge /'beɪli/ *n* a prefabricated bridge of steel easily and quickly assembled for temporary use.

bailie /'beɪli/ *n* (*Scot*) a municipal officer corresponding to an alderman.

bailiff /'beɪlɪf/ *n* in UK, the agent of a landlord or landowner; a sheriff's officer who serves writs and summonses; a minor official in some US courts, *usu* a messenger or usher.

bailiwick /'beɪlɪwɪk/ *n* the district within which a bailiff has jurisdiction; a person's special sphere of knowledge or activity or jurisdiction.

bailment /'beɪlmənt/ *n* (*law*) a delivery of goods in trust to another; the action of becoming surety for one in custody.

bailor /'beɪlər/ *n* (*law*) one who delivers goods in trust.

bail-out *n* assistance by a bank, government, etc, to help (a company) in financial trouble.

bailsman /'beɪlzmən/ *n* (*pl* **bailsmen**) one who gives bail for another.

bain-marie /ˌbæmæ'riː/ *n* (*pl* **bains-marie**) a vessel that holds hot water for cooking or warming food.

bairn /bɛrn/ n (Scot) a child.

bait /beɪt/ n food attached to a hook to entice fish or make them bite; any lure or enticement. • vt to put food on a hook to lure; to set dogs upon (a badger, etc); to persecute, worry or tease, esp by verbal attacks; to lure, to tempt; to entice.

baize /beɪz/ n a coarse, green woollen fabric used to cover snooker tables.

bake /beɪk/ vt (pottery) to dry and harden by heating in the sun or by fire; (food) to cook by dry heat in an oven. • vi to do a baker's work; to dry and harden in heat; (inf) to be very hot. • n all the food baked at one time or baking; a party or picnic featuring one baked item, eg a clambake.

baked beans npl cooked haricot beans canned in tomato sauce.

bakehouse /'beɪkhəʊs/ n a bakery.

Bakelite /'beɪkə̩laɪt/ n (trademark) a hard synthetic resin used for dishes, etc.

baker /'beɪkər/ n a person who bakes and sells bread, cakes, etc.

baker's dozen n thirteen.

bakery /'beɪkəri/ n (pl **bakeries**) a room or building for baking; a shop that sells bread, cakes, etc; baked goods.

baking powder n a leavening agent containing sodium bicarbonate and an acid-forming substance.

baking soda n sodium bicarbonate.

baklava /̩bæklə'vɒ/ or /'bæklɒvə/ n a cake made with thin, flaky pastry, honey and nuts.—also **baclava**.

baksheesh /'bækʃiːʃ/ n a present of money as a bribe or tip to expedite service.

balaclava (helmet) /̩bælə'klɒvə/ n a woollen hood that covers the ears and neck.

balalaika /̩bælə'laɪkə/ n a Russian, three-stringed guitar with a triangular body.

balance /'bæləns/ n a device for weighing, consisting of two dishes or pans hanging from a pivoted horizontal beam; equilibrium; mental stability; the power to influence or control; a remainder.—**in the balance** a state of uncertainty.—**on balance** having considered all aspects or factors. • vt to weigh; to compare; to equalize the debit and credit sides of an account. • vi to be equal in power or weight, etc; to have the debits and credits equal.—**balanceable** adj.—**balancer** n.

balance of payments n the difference between a country's total receipts from abroad and total payments abroad over a given period.

balancer /'bælənsər/ n one who or that which keeps anything in equilibrium; an acrobat; (pl) halter.

balance sheet n a statement of assets and liabilities.

balance wheel n a wheel that regulates the speed of a clock or watch.

balas /'bæləs/ n a variety of spinel ruby of a pale rose-red colour.

balata /'bælətə/ n dried gum from a South American tree, used as a substitute for guttapercha.

balcony /'bælkəni/ n (pl **balconies**) a projecting platform from an upper storey enclosed by a railing; an upper floor of seats in a theatre, etc, often projecting over the main floor.—**balconied** adj.

bald /bɒld/ adj lacking a natural or usual covering, as of hair, vegetation, or nap; (tyre) having little or no tread; (truth) plain or blunt; bare, unadorned.—**baldly** adv.—**baldness** n.

baldachin /'bɒldəkɪn/ n a canopy, esp over a throne or altar; a rich brocade fabric used for this.

balderdash /'bɒldər̩dæʃ/ n nonsense.

balding /'bɒldɪŋ/ adj becoming bald.

baldric /'bɒldrɪk/ n a broad belt, often richly ornamented, worn round the waist, or over one shoulder and across the breast.

bale¹ /beɪl/ n a large bundle of goods, as raw cotton, compressed and bound. • vt (hay etc) to make into bales. • vi (with **out**) to parachute from an aircraft, usu in an emergency.

bale² n a great evil; woe.

baleen /bə'liːn/ n whalebone.

baleful /'beɪlfʊl/ adj evil; harmful; deadly; ominous.—**balefully** adv.—**balefulness** n.

balk see **baulk**.

ball¹ /bɒl/ n a spherical or nearly spherical body or mass; a round object for use in tennis, football, etc; a throw or pitch of a ball; a missile for a cannon, rifle, etc; any rounded part or protuberance of the body; (pl: sl) testicles; nonsense. • interj (pl) (sl) nonsense! • vti to form into a ball; (vulg sl) to have sexual intercourse with.

ball² n a formal social dance; (inf) a good time.—**ballroom** n.—**ballroom dancing** n.

ballad /'bæləd/ n a narrative song or poem; a slow, sentimental, esp pop, song.—**balladeer** n.—**balladry** n.

ballade /bæ'lɒd/ n a poem of (usu) three eight-line stanzas and an envoy, all with the same rhymes and refrain.

balladmonger /'bæləd̩mʌŋgər/ n a dealer in ballads; an inferior poet, a poetaster.

ballast /'bæləst/ n heavy material carried in a ship or vehicle to stabilize it when it is not carrying cargo; crushed rock or gravel, etc used in railway tracks.

ball bearing n a device for lessening friction by having a rotating part resting on small steel balls; one of these balls.

ball boy n (tennis) a boy who retrieves balls that go out of play.—**ball girl** nf.

ballcock n a device that uses a floating ball to regulate the flow of water in a cistern, tank, etc.

ballerina /̩bælə'riːnə/ n a female ballet dancer.

ballet /'bæleɪ/ or /bæ'leɪ/ n a theatrical representation of a story, set to music and performed by dancers; the troupe of dancers.

balletomane /bə'lɛtoˌmeɪn/ n an enthusiastic lover of ballet.—**balletomania** n.

ballistic /bə'lɪstɪk/ adj relating to the flight of projectiles.

ballistic missile n a missile whose trajectory is initially guided then ballistic.

ballistics /bə'lɪstɪks/ n (used as sing) the scientific study of projectiles and firearms.

ballonet /̩bælə'nɛt/ n a small balloon; a subdivision of a balloon's or an airship's gasbag for controlling descent.

balloon /bə'luːn/ n a large airtight envelope that rises up when filled with hot air or light gases, often fitted with a basket or gondola for carrying passengers; a small inflatable rubber pouch used as a toy or for decoration; a balloon-shaped line enclosing speech or thoughts in a strip cartoon. • vti to inflate; to swell, expand; to travel in a balloon.—**balloonist** n.

balloon jib, balloon sail n (naut) a light triangular sail used by yachts in a slight breeze.

ballooning n the art or practice of managing balloons or making balloon ascents.

ballot /'bælət/ n a paper used in voting; the process of voting; the number of votes cast; the candidates offering themselves for election. • vi (**balloting, balloted**) to vote.—**balloter** n.

ballot box n a secure container for ballot papers.

ballpoint pen n a pen with a tiny ball, which rotates against an inking cartridge, as its writing tip.

ball valve n a valve that is opened or shut by the rising or falling of a ball.

ballyhoo /'bælɪˌhuː/ or /̩bælɪ'huː/ n vulgar, noisy publicity or advertisement.

ballyrag /'bælɪˌræg/ vb (**ballyragging, ballyragged**) vt to hustle, to jeer at. • vi to indulge in horseplay.—also **bullyrag**.

balm /bɒm/ n a fragrant ointment used in healing and soothing; anything comforting and soothing.

balm of Gilead n any of various fragrant resins, as that of the evergreen terebinth tree of Arabia or the balsam fir; a North American poplar with broad heart-shaped leaves.

balmoral /bæl'mɒrəl/ n a laced boot; a Scottish bonnet of wool; a petticoat.

balmy /'bɒmi/ adj (**balmier, balmiest**) having a pleasant fragrance; soothing; (weather) mild, warm.

balneology /̩bælni'ɒlədʒi/ n the science of therapeutic baths and their effect.—**balneological** adj.—**balneologist** n.

baloney /bə'loːni/ n (inf) foolish talk; nonsense.—also **boloney**.

balsa /'bɒlsə/ n lightweight wood from a tropical American tree.

balsam /'bɒlsəm/ n a fragrant, resinous substance; the tree yielding it.—**balsamic** adj.

balsam fir n a North American evergreen pine with flat needles and yielding balsam.

balsamiferous /̩bɒlsəˌmɪfərəs/ adj producing or yielding balsam.

Baltimore oriole n an American bird nearly related to the starlings with bright orange and black plumage.

baluster /'bæləstər/ n any of the small posts of a railing, as on a staircase.—**balustered** adj.

balustrade /ˈbæləˌstreɪd/ *n* an ornamental row of balusters joined by a rail.

bambino /bæmˈbiːnoː/ *n* (*pl* **bambinos, bambini**) a child or baby; (*RC Church*) a figure of the infant Christ wrapped in swaddling clothes, exhibited in churches from Christmas to Epiphany.

bamboo /bæmˈbuː/ *n* (*pl* **bamboos**) any of various, often tropical, woody grasses, used for furniture.

bamboo shoots *npl* the edible shoots of certain bamboos.

bamboozle /bæmˈbuːzəl/ *vt* (*inf*) to deceive; to mystify.—**bamboozlement** *n*.—**bamboozler** *n*.

ban[1] /bæn/ *n* a condemnation, an official prohibition. • *vt* (**banning, banned**) to prohibit, *esp* officially; to forbid.

ban[2] *n* (*feudal*) a public proclamation or summons to arms.

banal /bəˈnæl/ *adj* trite, commonplace.—**banally** *adv*.

banality /bəˈnælɪti/ *n* (*pl* **banalities**) anything trite or trivial; a commonplace remark, etc.

banana /bəˈnɑːnə/ *n* a herbaceous plant bearing its fruit in compact, hanging bunches.

banana republic *n* (*derog*) a small country, *esp* in Central America, that is dominated by foreign interests.

banana skin *n* (*inf*) an unforeseen occurrence that causes embarrassment.

banana split *n* ice cream served on a lengthwise sliced banana and topped with syrup, nuts, cream, etc.

banausic /bəˈnɔːsɪk/ *adj* merely mechanical; mean, illiberal.

band[1] /bænd/ *n* a strip of material used for binding; a stripe; (*radio*) a range of wavelengths.

band[2] *n* a group of people with a common purpose; a group of musicians playing together, an orchestra. • *vti* to associate together for a particular purpose.

bandage /ˈbændɪdʒ/ *n* a strip of cloth for binding wounds and fractures. • *vt* to bind a wound.

bandanna, bandana /bænˈdænə/ *n* a large coloured handkerchief.

B and B, B & B *abbr* = bed and breakfast.

bandbox *n* a light box of pasteboard, etc, for holding collars or hats.

bandeau /ˈbændoː/ or /-ˈdoː/ *n* (*pl* **bandeaux**) a band for the hair; a fitting band inside a hat.

banderilla /ˌbændəˈriːjə/ or /-ˈriːljə/ *n* a barbed dart, used by a banderillero in bullfights to exasperate the bull.

banderillero *n* (*pl* **banderilleros**) a bullfighter's assistant.

banderole, banderol /ˈbændəˌroːl/ *n* a long narrow flag with a cleft end; a streamer; a small flag carried at the head of a lance or mast; a scroll or band with an inscription.—*also* **bannerol**.

bandicoot /ˈbændɪˌkuːt/ *n* a large rat, native to India and Sri Lanka, very destructive to rice fields and gardens; the name given to rat-like marsupials of several species found in Australia and Tasmania.

bandit /ˈbændɪt/ *n* (*pl* **bandits, banditti**) a robber.—**banditry** *n*.

bandmaster /ˈbændˌmæstər/ *n* the conductor of a musical, *esp* brass, band

bandoleer, bandolier /ˌbændəˈliːr/ *n* a soldier's broad shoulder belt worn over the chest with pockets or loops for holding ammunition.

bandore, bandora /bænˈdɑːr/ or /ˈbændɑːr/ *n* an ancient stringed instrument that resembles a zither.—*also* **pandora, pandore**.

band saw *n* a power-operated saw consisting of a motorized, toothed steel belt.

bandsman /ˈbændzmən/ *n* (*pl* **bandsmen**) a player in a musical, *esp* brass, band.

bandstand /ˈbændˌstænd/ *n* a platform for a musical band, usually outside with a roof.

bandwagon /ˈbændˌwægən/ *n* a wagon for carrying a band in a parade; a movement, idea, etc that is (thought to be) heading for success.

bandwidth /ˈbændwɪdθ/ *n* the range of frequencies within a given waveband for radio or other types of transmission.

bandy[1] /ˈbændi/ *vt* (**bandying, bandied**) to pass to and fro; (*often with* **about**) (*rumours, etc*) to spread freely; to exchange words, *esp* angrily.

bandy[2] *adj* (**bandier, bandiest**) having legs curved outwards at the knee.

bandy-legged /-lɛgɪd/ or /-lɛgd/ *adj* bandy.

bane /beɪn/ *n* a person causing distress or misery; something bringing destruction or death; a poison.—**baneful** *adj*.

baneberry /ˈbeɪnˌberi/ or /-bəri/ *n* (*pl* **baneberries**) a plant of the buttercup family bearing white or red poisonous berries; its berry.—*also* **herb Christopher, cohosh**.

bang[1] /bæŋ/ *n* a hard blow; a sudden loud sound. • *vt* to hit or knock with a loud noise; (*door*) to slam. • *vi* to make a loud noise; to hit noisily or sharply. • *adv* with a bang, abruptly; successfully; (*inf*) precisely.

bang[2] *n* (*pl*) hair cut straight across the forehead to form a fringe; false hair so worn. • *vt* to cut the hair across the forehead to form a fringe.

bang[3] *see* **bhang**.

banger /ˈbæŋgər/ *n* an exploding firework; (*sl*) a sausage; (*sl*) an old car.

bangle /ˈbæŋgəl/ *n* a bracelet worn on the arm or ankle.

banian /ˈbænjən/ *see* **banyan**.

banish /ˈbænɪʃ/ *vt* to exile from a place; to drive away; to get rid of.—**banishment** *n*.

banister /ˈbænɪstər/ *n* the railing or supporting balusters in a staircase.—*also* **bannister**.

banjo /ˈbændʒoː/ *n* (*pl* **banjos, banjoes**) a stringed musical instrument with a drum-like body and a long fretted neck.—**banjoist** *n*.

bank[1] /bæŋk/ *n* a mound or pile; the sloping side of a river; elevated ground in a lake or the sea; a row or series of objects, as of dials, switches. • *vti* to form into a mound; to cover (a fire) with fuel so that it burns more slowly; (*aircraft*) to curve or tilt sideways.

bank[2] *n* an institution that offers various financial services, such as the safekeeping, lending and exchanging of money; the money held by the banker or dealer in a card game; any supply or store for the future, such as a *blood bank*. • *vti* (*cheques, cash, etc*) to deposit in a bank; to work as a banker.

bank account *n* money deposited in a bank and credited to the depositor.

bank bill *n* a note or a bill of exchange of a bank payable on demand or at a future specified time.

bankbook *n* a book at certain banks in which a record is kept of deposits and withdrawals of money into a personal account.

bank discount *n* a deduction made according to the current rate of interest.

banker /-ər/ *n* a person who runs a bank; the keeper of the bank at a gaming table.

banker's card *see* **cheque card**.

bank holiday *n* (*Brit*) in UK, a weekday when banks are officially closed; a day observed as a public holiday.

banking /-kɪŋ/ *n* the activity or occupation of running a bank. • *adj* of or concerning a bank.

banknote *n* a promissory note issued by a bank, which serves as money.

bank rate *n* the rate at which a central bank will discount bills.

bankrupt /ˈbæŋkrəpt/ *n* a person, etc legally declared unable to pay his debts; one who becomes insolvent. • *adj* judged to be insolvent; financially ruined; devoid of resources, ideas, etc. • *vt* to make bankrupt.—**bankruptcy** *n*.

banksia /ˈbæŋksiə/ *n* any of an Australian genus of flowering shrubs with evergreen leaves.

banner /ˈbænər/ *n* a flag or ensign; a headline running across a newspaper page; a strip of cloth bearing a slogan or emblem carried between poles in a parade.

banneret /ˈbænərət/ or /-ˈrɛt/ *n* (*hist*) an order of knighthood conferred on the field of battle for distinguished service or a deed of valour; the person on whom the degree was conferred and who ranked between a baron and a knight.

bannerette /ˈbænəˌrɛt/ *n* a little banner or flag.

bannerol /ˈbænəˌroːl/ *see* **banderole**.

bannister /ˈbænɪstər/ *see* **banister**.

bannock /ˈbænək/ *n* (*Scot*) a round flat cake, made of oatmeal or barley and unsweetened and baked on a griddle.

banns /bænz/ *npl* public declaration of intention, *esp* in church, to marry.

banquet /ˈbæŋkwət/ *n* a feast; an elaborate and sometimes formal dinner in honour of a person or occasion. • *vt* (**banqueting, banqueted**) to hold a banquet.—**banqueter** *n*.

banquette /bæŋ'kɛt/ *n* a cushioned bench; a step along the inside of a parapet on which soldiers stood to fire upon the enemy; the footway of a bridge when raised above the carriageway.

banshee /'bænʃiː/ *n* (*folklore*) a female fairy whose wail portends a death in the family.

bantam /'bæntəm/ *n* a dwarf breed of domestic fowl; a small, aggressive person; (*boxing*) a bantamweight.

bantamweight /-ˌweit/ *n* a boxing weight (112–118 lbs; 51–53.5 kg) between featherweight and flyweight.

banter /'bæntər/ *vt* to tease good-humouredly.—**banterer** *n*.

Bantu /'bæntuː/ *n* (*pl* **Bantu, Bantus**) one of a group of Southern African peoples or their language.

banyan /'bænjən/ *n* an Indian fig tree with vast, rooting branches.—*also* **banian**.

banzai /'bɒnˈzaɪ/ or /bænˈzaɪ/ *interj* a Japanese greeting or salute.

baobab /'beɪoːˌbæb/ *n* an African tree with an enormously thick trunk.

bap /bæp/ *n* a large soft bread roll.

baptism /'bæptɪzəm/ *n* the sprinkling of water on the forehead, or complete immersion in water, as a rite of admitting a person to a Christian church; any initiating experience.—**baptismal** *adj*.—**baptismally** *adv*.

Baptist /'bæptɪst/ *n* a member of a Protestant Christian denomination holding that the true church is of believers only, who are all equal, that the only authority is the Bible, and that adult baptism by immersion is necessary.

baptistry /'bæptɪstri/, **baptistery** /'bæptɪstəri/ *n* (*pl* **baptistries, baptisteries**) the part of a church where baptism takes place.

baptize /'bæptaɪz/ or /bæpˈtaɪz/ *vt* to christen, to name.—**baptizer** *n*.

bar[1] /bar/ *n* a straight length of wood or metal; a counter where alcoholic drinks or other refreshments are served; a place with such a counter; an oblong piece, as of soap; anything that obstructs or hinders; a band or strip; a strip or bank of sand or mud near and in line with the shore or across a river or harbour; (*mil*) a badge signifying a second award; (*with cap*) barristers or lawyers collectively; the legal profession; (*mus*) a vertical line dividing a staff into measures; (*mus*) a measure. • *vt* (**barring, barred**) to secure or fasten as with a bar; to exclude or prevent; to oppose. • *prep* except for.

bar[2] *n* a unit of atmospheric pressure.

barathea /ˌbærəˈθiːə/ *n* a type of fine woollen material.

barb /barb/ *n* the sharp backward point of a fish-hook, etc; one of the sharp parts combined to form barbed wire; a pointed or critical remark; a beard-like growth. • *vt* to provide with a barb.—**barbed** *adj*.

barbarian /barˈberiən/ *n* an uncivilized, primitive person; a cruel vicious person.—*also adj*.

barbaric /barˈberik/ or /barˈbærik/ *adj* of or suitable for barbarians.—**barbarically** *adv*.

barbarism /'barbərizəm/ *n* a barbarous act; the state of being a barbarian; an expression or word that is tasteless or not standard; an object or act that offends.

barbarity /barˈberəti/ or /-ˈbæriti/ *n* (*pl* **barbarities**) savage cruelty; a vicious act.

barbarize /'barbəˌraiz/ *vti* to make or become barbarous.

barbarous /'barbərəs/ *adj* uncivilized, cruel, coarse.—**barbarously** *adv*.

Barbary ape *n* a tailless macaque monkey of North Africa and Gibraltar.

barbate /'barbeit/ *adj* tufted, bearded.

barbecue /'barbəˌkjuː/ *n* a metal frame for grilling food over an open fire; an open-air party where barbecued food is served. • *vt* (**barbecuing, barbecued**) to cook on a barbecue.

barbed wire /barbd/ *n* wire with barbs at close intervals.—*also* **barbwire**.

barbel /'barbəl/ *n* a freshwater fish with beard-like filaments at its mouth; such a filament.—**barbelled** *adj*.

barbell /'barˌbɛl/ *n* a metal rod with weights at each end, used in weightlifting.

barber /'barbər/ *n* a person who cuts hair and shaves beards.

barberry /'barˌbɛri/ or /-ˌbəri/ *n* (*pl* **barberries**) a thorny shrub with yellow flowers; its red berry.

barbershop /'barbərˌʃɒp/ *n* the business premises of a barber.

barbet /'barbət/ *n* a tropical bird with tufts of feathers at the base of the bill.

barbette /barˈbɛt/ *n* a raised platform for guns to fire over a parapet; a type of armoured turret in a warship.

barbican /'barbikən/ *n* a defensive tower over the gate or drawbridge of a castle or fortification.

barbitone /'barbitoːn/, **barbital** /'barbiˌtɒl/ *n* a habit-forming, toxic, hypnotic and sedative drug.

barbiturate /barˈbitʃurət/ or /-ˌreit/ *n* a sedative drug.

barbule /'barbjuːl/ *n* a minute barb; a filament fringing the barb of a feather.

barbwire /'barbˌwaiər/ *see* **barbed wire**.

barcarole, barcarolle /'barkəˌroːl/ *n* a Venetian gondolier's song; an instrumental piece resembling this.

bar code /'barkoːd/ or /ˌbarˈkoːd/ *n* a striped pattern on a package, book cover, etc, containing information about the price that can be read by a computer for stock control, etc.

bard /bard/ *n* a poet.—**bardic** *adj*.

bare /ber/ *adj* without covering; unclothed, naked; simple, unadorned; mere; without furnishings. • *vt* to uncover; to reveal.—**bareness** *n*.

bareback /'berˌbæk/ *adj* on a horse with no saddle.—*also adv*.

barefaced /'berfeist/ *adj* with the face shaven or uncovered; shameless.—**barefacedly** *adv*.

barefoot /'berfʊt/, **barefooted** /-id/ *adj* with the feet bare.—*also adv*.

barège, barege /bəˈreiʒ/ *n* a thin gauze-like fabric, *usu* of silk and worsted.

barehanded /'berˌhændid/ *adj* without using weapons.

barely /'berli/ *adv* openly; merely, scarcely.

bargain /'bargən/ *n* an agreement laying down the conditions of a transaction; something sold at a price favourable to the buyer; **into the bargain** as well; in addition. • *vt* to make a bargain, to haggle; (*with* **for**) to expect or hope for.

barge /bardʒ/ *n* a flat-bottomed vessel, used to transport freight along rivers and canals; a large boat for excursions or pleasure trips. • *vi* to lurch clumsily; (*with* **in**) to interrupt (a conversation) rudely; (*with* **into**) to enter abruptly.

bargeboard /-bord/ *n* a board placed at a gable to conceal the roof timbers.

barge couple *n* either of a pair of beams bounding a gable, mortised and tenoned together and used for strengthening a building.

barge course *n* the tiling that projects beyond the principal rafters in a building; a wall coping constructed of bricks set on edge.

bargee /barˈdʒiː/ *n* the owner of or one employed on a barge; a bargeman.

barilla /bəˈrilə/ *n* an alkali made from kinds of marine plant or seaweed.

barite /'bereit/ *see* **barytes**.

baritone /'beriˌtoːn/ or /bæri-/ *n* the adult male voice ranging between bass and tenor; a singer with such a voice.—*also adj*.

barium /'beriəm/ or /'bæ-/ *n* (*chem*) a white metallic element.

barium sulphate /-ˌsʌlfeit/ *n* a white insoluble fine heavy powder which is opaque to X-rays, swallowed by a patient before X-ray of the alimentary canal.

bark[1] /bark/ *n* the harsh or abrupt cry of a dog, wolf, etc; a similar sound, such as one made by a person. • *vi* to make a loud cry like a dog; to speak or shout sharply or angrily.

bark[2] *n* the outside covering of a tree trunk. • *vt* to remove the bark from; to scrape; to skin (the knees, etc).

bark[3] *see* **barque**.

barkentine /'barkənˌtiːn/ *see* **barquentine**.

barker /'barkər/ *n* one who or that which barks; a person who shouts his wares, etc, *usu* at a fairground.

barking /'barkiŋ/ *n* the process of stripping bark from trees; the process of tanning leather or dyeing with bark.

barley /'barli/ *n* a grain used in making beer and whisky, and for food.

barleycorn /'barliˌkorn/ *n* a grain of barley; (*formerly*) a measure of length, one-third of an inch (0.85 cm).

barley sugar /'barliˌʃugər/ *n* a transparent amber-coloured sweet.

barm /barm/ *n* the froth on fermenting liquor used as leaven in breadmaking, yeast.

barmaid /'barmeid/ *n* a female serving alcohol in a bar.

barman /'barmən/ *n* (*pl* **barmen**) a man serving alcohol in a bar.

Barmecide /'bɑrməˌsaɪd/, **Barmedcidal** *adj* like the Barmecide's feast in *The Arabian Nights*; imaginarily satisfying; unreal, illusory.

bar mitzvah /bɑr'mɪtzvə/ *n* (*Judaism*) the ceremony marking the thirteenth birthday of a boy, who then assumes full religious obligations; the boy himself.

barn /'bɑrn/ *n* a farm building used for storing grain, hay, etc, and sheltering animals.

barnacle /'bɑrnəkəl/ *n* a marine crustacean that attaches itself to rocks and ship bottoms.

barnacle goose *n* a wild European grey-winged goose that breeds in the Arctic.

Barnard's star *n* a red dwarf star in the constellation Ophiuchus that has the largest proper motion known.

barn dance *n* a social dance featuring several dance forms (as square dancing).

barn owl *n* any of a genus of owl with brownish plumage above and white plumage below.

barn raising *n* (*US*) a gathering of people who share the work of putting up the framework of a neighbour's barn, often followed by a party.

barnstorm /'bɑrnstɔrm/ *vi* to tour (rural areas) as an actor, or making speeches in a political campaign, or demonstrating flying stunts.—**barnstormer** *n*.

barograph /'bærəˌgræf/ *n* a self-recording aneroid barometer.—**barographic** *adj*.

barogram /'bærəˌgræm/ *n* the record traced by a barograph.

barometer /bə'rɒmɪtər/ *n* an instrument for measuring atmospheric pressure and imminent changes in the weather; anything that marks change.—**barometric** *adj*.—**barometrically** *adv*.

baron /'bærən/ or /'bɛrən/ *n* a member of a rank of nobility, the lowest in the British peerage; a powerful businessman.—**baroness** *nf*.

baronage /'bærənɪdʒ/ or /'bɛr-/ *n* the whole body of barons; the dignity or rank of a baron.

baronet /'bɛrənət/ or /ˌbɛrə'nɛt/, /bær-/ *n* the lowest hereditary title of honour in Britain.

baronetage /-ɪdʒ/ *n* the collective body of baronets; the dignity or rank of a baronet.

baronetcy /-si/ *n* (*pl* **baronetcies**) the dignity or rank of a baronet.

baronial /bə'roːnɪəl/ *adj* pertaining to or suitable for a baron or barons.

barony /'bærəni/ *n* (*pl* **baronies**) the rank or lands of a baron; (*Scot*) a large manor; (*Ir*) a division of a county.

baroque /bə'roːk/ *adj* extravagantly ornamented, *esp* in architecture and decorative art.

baroscope /'bærəskoːp/ *n* an instrument for indicating variations in the pressure of the atmosphere without actual measurement of its weight.—**baroscopic** *adj*.

barouche /bə'ruːʃ/ *n* a 19th-century roomy four-wheeled carriage for four with a folding top.

barque /bɑrk/ *n* (*poet*) a ship; a three-masted vessel with the foremast and main mast square-rigged and the mizzen fore-and-aft.—*also* **bark**.

barquentine, barquantine /'bɑrkənˌtiːn/ *n* a three-masted vessel with the foremast square-rigged and the main mast and mizzenmast fore-and-aft or schooner-rigged.—*also* **barkentine**.

barrack /'bærək/ or /'bɛr-/ *vti* to criticize loudly or shout at a player, team or speaker; to jeer; to shout support for.—**barracker** *n*.

barracks /'bærəks/ or /'bɛr-/ *n* (*used as sing*) a building for housing soldiers.

barracuda /ˌbɛrə'kuːdə/ or /'bær-/ *n* (*pl* **barracuda, barracudas**) a fierce fish with edible flesh.

barrage /bə'rɒʒ/ *n* a man-made dam across a river; heavy artillery fire; (*of protests, questions, etc*) continuous and heavy delivery.

barrage balloon /bə'rɒʒbəˌluːn/ *n* a large balloon anchored to the ground and trailing cables or nets, used as a defence against low-flying enemy aircraft.

barranca /bə'rænkə/, **barranco** /-koː/ *n* (*pl* **barrancas, barrancos**) a deep mountain gully or ravine.

barratry /'bærətri/ *n* the defrauding or injury of a ship's owner, freighter or insurer by the master or crew; the practice of inciting and encouraging lawsuits or litigation.—**barrator** *n*.—**barratrous** *adj*.

barre /bɑr/ *n* a horizontal rail used for ballet practice.

barred *see* **bar**[1].

barrel /'bærəl/ or /'bɛr-/, /'bɑrəl/ *n* a cylindrical container, *usu* wooden, with bulging sides held together with hoops; the amount held by a barrel; a tubular structure, as in a gun. • *vt* (**barrelling, barrelled** *or* **barreling, barreled**) to put into barrels.

barrel-chested *adj* having a large rounded chest.

barrel organ *n* a mechanical piano or organ played by a revolving cylinder with pins that operate the keys or valves to produce sound.

barren /'bærən/ or /'bɛr-/ *adj* infertile; incapable of producing offspring; unable to bear crops; unprofitable; (*with* **of**) lacking in.

barricade /ˌbærɪ'keɪd/ or /ˌbɛrɪ-/ *n* a barrier or blockade used in defence to block a street; an obstruction. • *vt* to block with a barricade.

barrier /'bærɪər/ or /'bɛr-/ *n* anything that bars passage, prevents access, controls crowds, etc, such as a fence; obstruction; hindrance.

barrier reef *n* an exposed coral reef separated from the shore by a navigable channel.

barring /'bɑrɪŋ/ *prep* excepting; leaving out of account.

barrister /'bærɪstər/ or /'bɛr-/ *n* a qualified lawyer who has been called to the bar in England.

barrow[1] /'bæroː/ or /'bɛr-/ *n* a wheelbarrow or hand-cart used for carrying loads.

barrow[2] *n* a prehistoric burial mound.

Barsac /'bɑrsæk/ *n* a French white wine.

bar sinister *n* (*her*) in error for **bend sinister**, the badge of illegitimacy.

Bart *abbr* = baronet.

barter /'bɑrtər/ *vt* to trade commodities or services without exchanging money. • *vi* to haggle or bargain. • *n* trade by the exchanging of commodities.—**barterer** *n*.

bartizan /'bɑrtɪzən/ or /ˌbɑrtɪ'zæn/ *n* an overhanging turret at the top of a tower or wall.

barytes /bə'raɪtiːz/ *n* a white crystalline mineral of great weight, consisting mainly of barium sulphate.—*also* **barite, heavy spar.**

baryon /'bærɪˌɒn/ *n* an elementary particle (nucleon or hyperon) with a mass greater than or equal to that of the proton.

basal /'beɪsəl/ *adj* pertaining to, at or forming the base; fundamental. • *n* a basal part.—**basally** *adv*.

basalt /'bæsɒlt/ *n* hard, compact, dark-coloured igneous rock.—**basaltic** *adj*.

bascule /'bæskjuːl/ *n* a mechanical arrangement on the seesaw principle by which the lowering of one end raises the other; a kind of drawbridge so operated.

base[1] /beɪs/ *n* the bottom part of anything; the support or foundation; the fundamental principle; the centre of operations (*eg* military); (*baseball*) one of the four corners of the diamond. • *vt* to use as a basis; to found (on); (*with* **at, in**) to place, to station.—**basal** *adj*.

base[2] *adj* low in morality or honour; worthless; menial.—**basely** *adv*.—**baseness** *n*.

baseball /'beɪsbɒl/ *n* the US national game, involving two teams that score runs by hitting a ball and running round four bases arranged in a diamond shape on the playing area.

baseborn /'beɪsbɔrn/ *adj* (*arch*) of low or mean birth; illegitimate; mean.

baseless /'beɪsləs/ *adj* without a base; unfounded.

baseline /'beɪslaɪn/ *n* the line at each end of a games court marking the limit of play; (*baseball*) the line between any two consecutive bases; a measured line in a survey area from which triangulations are calculated.

baseman /-mən/ *n* (*pl* **basemen**) (*baseball*) a fielder placed at the first, second, and third bases respectively.

basement /'beɪsmənt/ *n* the part of a building that is partly or wholly below ground level.

base metal *n* any metal other than the precious metals.

bash /bæʃ/ *vt* (*inf*) to hit hard; to dent by striking. • *n* (*inf*) a heavy blow; (*inf*) a try or attempt; (*sl*) a party.

bashful /-fʊl/ *adj* easily embarrassed, shy.—**bashfully** *adv*.—**bashfulness** *n*.

bashibazouk /ˌbæʃɪbə'zuːk/ *n* a volunteer or irregular in the Turkish army.

BASIC /'beɪsɪk/ *n* (*comput*) a simple programming language: *Beginners' All-purpose Symbolic Instruction Code*.

basic /'beɪsɪk/ *adj* fundamental; simple. • *n* (*often pl*) a basic principle, factor, etc; the rudiments.—**basically** *adv*.

basicity /beɪ'sɪsɪtɪ/ *n* the state of being a base; (*chem*) the power of an acid to unite with one or more atoms of a base.

basic slag *n* the phosphates of lime and oxidized impurities left as a brittle powder in steelmaking and used as a fertilizer.

basidium /bə'sɪdɪəm/ *n* (*pl* **basidia**) the cell to which the spores of certain fungi are attached.—**basidial** *adj*.

basify /'beɪsɪfaɪ/ *vt* (**basifying, basified**) to convert into a base, make basic.

basil /'bæzəl/ *n* a plant with aromatic leaves used for seasoning food.

basilar /'bæsɪlər/, **basilary** *adj* (*anat*) pertaining to or situated at the base, *esp* of the skull.

basilica /bə'sɪlɪkə/ or /'bæzɪl-/ *n* a church with a broad nave, side aisles, and an apse; (*RC Church*) a church with special ceremonial rites.—**basilican** *adj*.

basilisk /'bæzɪlɪsk/ *n* a fabulous creature dealing death by its gaze, sometimes identified with the cockatrice; a lizard with an inflatable crest. • *adj* pertaining to the basilisk; penetrating or malignant.

basin /'beɪsən/ *n* a wide shallow container for liquid; its contents; any large hollow, often with water in it; a tract of land drained by a river.

basinet /'bæsɪnət/ *n* a light steel helmet of medieval times, often with a visor.

basis /'beɪsɪs/ *n* (*pl* **bases**) a base or foundation; a principal constituent; a fundamental principle or theory.

bask /bæsk/ *vi* to lie in sunshine or warmth; to enjoy someone's approval.

basket /'bæskət/ *n* a container made of interwoven cane, wood strips, etc; the hoop through which basketball players throw the ball to score.

basketball /-ˌbɒl/ *n* a game in which two teams compete to score by throwing the ball through an elevated net basket or hoop; this ball.

basket hilt *n* the hilt of a sword shaped like a basket.

basking shark *n* a large shark of northern seas, which is harmless and has the habit of basking at the surface in the sun.

basque /bæsk/ *n* a woman's jacket with a short skirt.

Basque /bæsk/ or /bɒsk/ *n* one of a people inhabiting the western Pyrenees; their language.

bas-relief /ˌbɒrɪ'liːf/ or /ˌbæs-/ *n* a low relief; a form of relief in which the figures stand out very slightly from the ground.—*also* **basso-rilievo**.

bass[1] /bæs/ *n* (*mus*) the range of the lowest male voice; a singer or instrument with this range. • *adj* of, for or in the range of a bass.

bass[2] *n* (*pl* **bass**) any of numerous freshwater food and game fishes.

bass clef /beɪs/ *n* (*mus*) the character C placed at the beginning of the bass staff.

basset[1] /'bæsət/, **basset hound** *n* a smooth-haired hound with short legs.

basset[2] *vi* (**basseting, basseted**) (*geol*) to crop out at the surface. • *n* an outcrop.

basset horn *n* a tenor clarinet.

bassinet /ˌbæsə'nɛt/ *n* a wickerwork or wooden cradle with a hood; a pram.

bassist /'beɪsɪst/ *n* a player of the double bass.

basso /'bæsoː/ *n* (*pl* **bassos, bassi**) one who sings bass.

bassoon /bə'suːn/ *n* an orchestral, deep-toned woodwind instrument.—**bassoonist** *n*.

basso profundo /-proːˈfʊndoː/ *n* (*pl* **basso profundos**) the lowest bass voice; a singer with such a voice.

basso-rilievo /-rɪ'ljeɪvoː/ *n* (*pl* **basso-rilievos**) a bas-relief.

bass viol /bæs/ *n* a large stringed instrument of the violin class for playing bass, the violoncello.

bast /bæst/ *n* the tough inner fibrous bark of various trees, especially of the lime; rope or matting made from this bark.

basta /'bæstɒ/ *interj* enough!

bastard /'bæstərd/ *n* a person born of unmarried parents; (*offensive*) an unpleasant person; (*inf*) a person (can be positive or derogatory); (*inf*) a difficult task, situation, etc. • *adj* illegitimate (by birth); false; not genuine.—**bastardy** *n*.

bastardize /'bæstərdaɪz/ *vt* to declare illegitimate; to falsify or corrupt.—**bastardization** *n*.

baste[1] /beɪst/ *vt* to drip fat over (roasting meat, etc).

baste[2] *vt* to sew with long loose stitches as a temporary seam.

bastinado /ˌbæstɪ'neɪdoː/ *n* (*pl* **bastinadoes**) a caning of the soles of the feet as a form of torture. • *vt.* (**bastinadoing, bastinadoed**) to torture in this way.

bastion /'bæstiən/ *n* a tower at the corner of a fortification; any strong defence; one who strongly upholds or supports a principle, etc.—**bastioned** *adj*.

basuco /bɒ'zuːkoː/ *n* the dregs of cocaine after refining, which are packaged and sold in Colombia.

bat[1] /bæt/ *n* a wooden club used in cricket, baseball, etc; a batsman; a paddle used in table tennis. • *vb* (**batting, batted**) *vt* to hit as with a bat. • *vi* to take one's turn at bat.

bat[2] *n* a nocturnal, mouse-like flying mammal with forelimbs modified to form wings.

bat[3] *vt* (**batting, batted**) (*one's eyelids*) to wink or flutter.

batch /bætʃ/ *n* the quantity of bread, etc produced at one time; one set, group, etc; an amount of work for processing by a computer in a single run.

bate /beɪt/ *vt* to lessen or reduce; to deduct.

bateau /bæ'toː/ or /'bæto:/ *n* (*pl* **bateaux**) a light boat used *esp* on Canadian rivers.

bath /bæθ/ *n* water for washing the body; a bathing; a bathtub; (*pl*) a building with baths for public use; a municipal swimming pool. • *vti* to give a bath to; to bathe.

bath chair *n* a wheeled chair for invalids.

bathe /beɪð/ *vt* to dampen with any liquid. • *vi* to have a bath; to go swimming; to become immersed.—**bather** *n*.

bathometer /bə'θɒmətər/ *n* an apparatus for measuring depths.

bathos /'beɪθɒs/ *n* anticlimax; descent from the elevated to the ordinary in speech or writing.

bathrobe /'bæθˌroːb/ *n* a loose-fitting garment of absorbent fabric for use after bathing or as a dressing gown.

bathroom /-ruːm/ *n* a room with a bath or shower and usually a lavatory and washbasin.—*also* **lavatory**.

bathtub /-tʊb/ *n* a *usu* fixed tub for bathing.

bathymetry /bæ'θɪmɪtrɪ/ *n* the art or science of sounding or of measuring sea depths.—**bathymetric** *adj*.—**bathymetrically** *adv*.

bathyscaphe /'bæθɪˌskæf/ *n* a submersible vessel for deep-sea observation and exploration.

bathysphere /-ˌsfɪːr/ *n* a hollow steel sphere for descending to great depths in the sea.

batik /bə'tiːk/ *n* a method of printing coloured designs on fabric; fabric produced by this method.

batiste /bæ'tiːst/ or /bə-/ *n* a kind of cambric; a fabric like cambric.

batman /'bætmən/ *n* (*pl* **batmen**) (*mil*) in UK, an officer's servant.

baton /bə'tɒn/ *n* a staff serving as a symbol of office; a thin stick used by the conductor of an orchestra to beat time; a hollow cylinder carried by each member of a relay team in succession; a policeman's truncheon.

batrachian /bə'treɪkiən/ *n* one of the amphibians, which includes frogs and toads. • *adj* of or pertaining to frogs or toads.

batsman /'bætsmən/ *n* (*pl* **batsmen**) (*cricket, baseball*) the player whose turn it is to bat.

battalion /bə'tælɪən/ *n* an army unit consisting of three or more companies; a large group.

batten[1] /'bætən/ *n* a strip of wood or metal; a strip of wood put over a seam between boards. • *vt* to fasten or supply with battens.

batten[2] *vt* to make fat by rich living; to fertilize or enrich. • *vi* to grow or become fat; to thrive at the expense of others.

batter /'bætər/ *vt* to beat with repeated blows; to wear out with heavy use; to criticize strongly and at length. • *vi* to strike heavily and repeatedly. • *n* a mixture of flour, egg, and milk or water used in cooking.—**batterer** *n*.

battering ram /'bætərɪŋˌræm/ *n* (*hist*) a military machine for breaching the walls of besieged places, consisting of a large beam with an iron head resembling the head of a ram.

battery /'bætərɪ/ *n* (*pl* **batteries**) a set of heavy guns; a small unit of artillery; an electric cell that supplies current; an unlawful beating; an arrangement of hens' cages designed to increase egg laying.

battle /'bætəl/ *n* a combat or fight between two opposing individuals or armies; a contest; any struggle towards a goal. • *vti* to fight; to struggle.—**battler** *n*.

battle-axe, battle-ax /-ˌæks/ *n* (*pl* **battle-axes**) an old-fashioned two-headed axe; (*inf*) a domineering woman.

battle cruiser *n* a heavy-gunned ship with higher speed and lighter armour than a battleship.

battle cry *n* a war cry; a slogan used to rally supporters of a political campaign, etc.

battledore /'bætəl,dɔr/ *n* a wooden bat used in washing, baking, etc; a bat used in **battledore and shuttlecock**, a forerunner of badminton.

battlefield /'bætəl,fi:ld/ *n* the land on which a battle is fought.

battlement /-mənt/ *n* a parapet or wall with indentations, from which to shoot.

battle royal *n* (*pl* **battles royal**) a fight with many combatants; a general engagement; a melee.

battleship /-ʃɪp/ *n* a large, heavily armoured warship.

battue /bæ'tu:/ *or* /-'tju:/ *n* (*hunting*) the driving up of game by beaters towards the guns; wholesale slaughter.

batty /'bæti/ *adj* (**battier, battiest**) (*inf*) crazy; eccentric.—**battiness** *n*.

bauble /'bɒbəl/ *n* a showy toy; a shining ball hung on a Christmas tree as a decoration; a worthless trifle or ornament.

baud /bɒd/ *n* (*comput*) a unit used in measuring the speed of electronic data transmissions.

baulk /bɔk/ *vt* to obstruct or foil. • *vi* to stop and refuse to move and act.—*also* **balk**.

bauxite /'bɒksaɪt/ *n* aluminium ore.

bawd /bɒd/ *n* a woman who runs a brothel; a prostitute.

bawdy /'bɒdi/ *adj* (**bawdier, bawdiest**) humorously indecent; obscene, lewd.—**bawdily** *adv*.—**bawdiness** *n*.

bawl /bɒl/ *vti* to shout; to weep loudly. • *n* a loud shout; a noisy weeping.—**bawler** *n*.—**bawling** *n*.

bay[1] /beɪ/ *n* a type of laurel tree.

bay[2] *n* a wide inlet of a sea or lake; an inward bend of a shore.

bay[3] *n* an alcove or recess in a wall; a compartment used for a special purpose.

bay[4] *vti* to bark (at). • *n* the cry of a hound or a pursuing pack.—**at bay** the position of one forced to turn and fight.

bay[5] *adj* reddish brown. • *n* a horse of this colour.

bayberry /'beɪ,beri/ *n* (*pl* **bayberries**) any of various shrubs, *esp* the wax myrtle of North America; the grey waxy berry of the wax myrtle; a West Indian tree with fragrant leaves used in bay rum.

bay leaf *n* the leaf of the laurel dried and used as a flavouring for food.

bayonet /,beɪə'nɛt/ *n* a blade for stabbing attached to the muzzle of a rifle. • *vt* (**bayoneting, bayoneted** *or* **bayonetting, bayonetted**) to kill or stab with a bayonet.

bayou /'baɪu:/ *n* in the southern US, the marshy inlet or outlet of a lake or river.

bay rum *n* a perfumed cosmetic obtained from the leaves of the bayberry.

bay window *n* a window projecting from the outside wall of a house.

bazaar /bə'zɑr/ *n* a marketplace; a street full of small shops; a benefit sale for a church, etc.

bazooka /bə'zu:kə/ *n* a portable anti-tank weapon that fires rockets from a long tube.

BBC *abbr* = British Broadcasting Corporation.

BC *abbr* = Before Christ.

BD *abbr* = Bachelor of Divinity.

bdellium /'dɛlɪəm/ *n* a fragrant gum used medicinally and as a perfume; the African and Asian tree yielding it.

be- /bɪ/ *prefix* all over, thoroughly, as in *bespatter*; to make, as in *bedim*; to call, as in *bedevil*; to form a transitive verb from an intrasitive, as *bewail*.

Be (*chem symbol*) beryllium.

be /bi:/ *vi* (*pr t* **am, are, is**, *pt* **was, were**, *pp* **been**) to exist; to live; to take place.

beach /bi:tʃ/ *n* a flat, sandy shore of the sea. • *vi* to bring (a boat) up on the beach from the sea.

beachcomber /-,ko:mər/ *n* a person who hangs about the shore on the lookout for wreckage or plunder; a long curling wave rolling in from the ocean.—**beachcombing** *n*.

beachhead /-hɛd/ *n* an area of seashore captured from the enemy by an advance force in preparation for a full-scale landing of troops and equipment.

beach music *n* a style of pop music originating on the coast of South Carolina, based on soul music and rhythm and blues.

beacon /'bi:kən/ *n* a light, *esp* on a high place, tower, etc, for warning or guiding. • *vi* to guide, to act as a beacon.

bead /bi:d/ *n* a small ball pierced for stringing; (*pl*) a string of beads; (*pl*) a rosary; a bubble or droplet of liquid; the sight of a rifle.—**beaded** *adj*.

beading /-ɪŋ/ *n* moulding or edging in the form of a series of beads; a wooden strip, rounded on one side, used for trimming.—*also* **beadwork**.

beadle /'bi:dəl/ *n* an officer of a parish or church; a mace-bearer; (*formerly*) an officer in a law court.

beady /'bi:di/ *adj* (**beadier, beadiest**) (*eyes*) small, round and bright, sometimes calculating or unfriendly.—**beadily** *adv*.—**beadiness** *n*.

beagle /'bi:gəl/ *n* a small hound with short legs and drooping ears.

beak /bi:k/ *n* a bird's bill; any projecting part; the nose.—**beaked** *adj*.

beaker /'bi:kər/ *n* a large drinking cup, or the amount it holds; a cylindrical vessel with a pouring lip used by chemists and pharmacists.

beam /bi:m/ *n* a long straight piece of timber or metal; the crossbar of a balance; a ship's breadth at its widest point; a slender shaft of light, etc; a radiant look, smile, etc; a steady radio or radar signal for guiding aircraft or ships. • *vt* (*light, etc*) to send out; to smile with great pleasure.

beamy /-i/ *adj* (**beamier, beamiest**) emitting rays of light; resembling a beam in size and weight; (*ship*) broad; (*inf*) having broad hips.

bean /bi:n/ *n* a plant bearing kidney-shaped seeds; a seed or pod of such a plant; any bean-like seed.

bean bag /-bæg/ *n* a small cloth bag filled with dried beans and used in games; a larger cloth bag filled with plastic granules and used for sitting on.

bean curd *n* soft cheese made from soya milk.—*also* **tofu**.

beanfeast *n* (*inf*) an annual dinner given by an employer for his employees; (*inf*) any festive meal.

bean sprout *n* the shoot of the mung bean used in Chinese cooking.

bear[1] /bɛr/ *vb* (**bearing, bore**, *pp* **borne**) *vt* to carry; to endure; to support, to sustain; to conduct (oneself); to produce or bring forth; (*with* **out**) to show to be true, confirm. • *vi* to be productive; (*with* **down**) to press or weigh down; to overwhelm; (*with* **on** *or* **upon**) to have reference to, be relevant to; (*with* **out**) to confirm the truth of; (*with* **up**) to endure with courage; (*with* **with**) to listen to patiently.

bear[2] *n* (*pl* **bears, bear**) a large mammal with coarse black, brown or white fur, short legs, strong claws and feeding mainly on fruit and insects; a gruff or ill-mannered person; a teddy bear; a speculator who sells stock in anticipation of a fall in price so that he may buy them back at a lower price.

bearable /-əbəl/ *adj* endurable.—**bearably** *adv*.

bear baiting /-,beɪtɪŋ/ *n* the former sport of setting dogs to attack captive bears.

beard /'bi:rd/ *n* hair covering a man's chin; similar bristles on an animal or plant. • *vt* to defy, oppose openly.—**bearded** *adj*.

beardless /'bi:rdləs/ *adj* without a beard; youthful.

bearer /'bɛrər/ *n* a person who bears or presents; a person who carries something (a coffin, etc).

bear garden *n* (*formerly*) a place where bears were kept for sport; any scene or place of tumult or disorder.

bear hug /'bɛr,hʌg/ *n* (*wrestling*) a hold in which the opponent's arms and chest are pinned in a tight embrace; any tight embrace.

bearing /'bɛrɪŋ/ *n* demeanour; conduct; a compass direction; (*with* **on, upon**) relevance; a machine part on which another part slides, revolves, etc; (*usu pl*) one's position, orientation.

bearing rein *n* a short fixed rein for holding up the head of a horse.—*also* **checkrein**.

bearish /'bɛrɪʃ/ *adj* resembling a bear in qualities; rude, surly.—**bearishly** *adv*.—**bearishness** *n*.

bear's breech /'bɛrz,bri:tʃ/ *n* one of two tall plants of the acanthus genus with purple-tinged white flowers.

bear's ear /-,ɪr/ *see* **auricula**.

bearskin /'bɛrskɪn/ *n* the skin of a bear used as a garment, rug, etc; a tall furry cap worn by a guardsman in the British army.

beast /bi:st/ *n* a large, wild, four-footed animal; a brutal, vicious person; (*inf*) something difficult, an annoyance.

beastings /'bi:stɪŋz/ *see* **beestings**.

beastly /'bi:stli/ *adj* (**beastlier, beastliest**) (*inf*) disagreeable. • *adv* (*inf*) very (*beastly cold*).

beat /bi:t/ *vb* (**beating, beaten**, *pp* **beat**) *vt* to strike, dash or pound repeatedly; to flog; to overcome or counteract; to win against, to arrive first; to find too difficult for; (*mus*) to mark (time) with a baton, etc; (*eggs, etc*) to mix by stirring vigorously; (*esp wings*) to move up and down; (*a path, way, etc*) to form by repeated trampling; (*sl*) to baffle; (*with* **up**) (*inf*) to cause grievous bodily harm to by severe and repeated blows and kicks. • *vi* to hit, pound, etc repeatedly; to throb; (*naut*) to sail against the wind. • *n* a recurrent stroke, pulsation, as in a heartbeat or clock ticking; rhythm in music or poetry; the area patrolled by a police officer.—**beatable** *adj*.

beaten /'bi:tən/ *adj* defeated; (*metal*) shaped or formed by pounding; (*a path*) formed by constant trampling.

beater /'bi:tər/ *n* an implement for beating, such as an attachment for an electric food mixer; one who rouses game birds from cover.

beatific /ˌbiə'tıfık/ *adj* showing great happiness; making blessed.—**beatifically** *adv*.

beatify /bi'ætıˌfaı/ *vt* (**beatifying, beatified**) (*RC Church*) to declare that one who has died is among the blessed in heaven; to make blissfully happy.—**beatification** *n*.

beating /'bi:tıŋ/ *n* the act of striking or thrashing; throbbing or pulsation; a defeat.

beatitude /bi:'ætıˌtu:d/ or /-ˌtju:d/ *n* blessedness; heavenly happiness; (*with cap*) (*Bible*) one of Christ's eight sayings in the Sermon on the Mount (Matthew 5).

beau *Fr.* /bo:/ *n* (*pl* **beaus, beaux**) a woman's suitor or sweetheart.

Beaufort scale *Fr.* /'bo:fərt/ *n* an international system of indicating wind strength, from 0 (calm) to 12 (hurricane).

beau geste *Fr.* /bo:'ʒest/ *n* (*pl* **beaux gestes**) a fine gesture; a gesture that appears noble but is meaningless.

beau ideal *Fr.* /ˌbo:i:dei'æl/ *n* (*pl* **beaux ideals**) ideal excellence, a standard of perfection.

beaujolais *Fr.* /'bo:ʒəˌlei/ *n* (*often with cap*) a popular fruity red or white wine from Burgundy in France.

beau monde *Fr.* /bo:'mɒnd/ *n* the fashionable world.

beaut /bju:t/ *adj* (*sl*) good. • *n* (*sl*) beauty.

beauteous /'bju:tiəs/ *adj* (*poet*) beautiful.

beautician /bju:'tıʃən/ *n* one who works in a beauty salon offering cosmetic treatments.

beautiful /'bju:tıˌful/ *adj* having beauty; very enjoyable.—**beautifully** *adv*.

beautify /'bju:tıˌfaı/ *vti* (**beautifying, beautified**) to make or become beautiful.—**beautification** *n*.

beauty /'bju:ti/ *n* (*pl* **beauties**) the combination of qualities in a person or object that cause delight or pleasure; a very attractive woman or girl; good looks; a very fine specimen.

beauty salon, beauty parlour, beauty shop *n* an establishment that offers cosmetic beauty treatments.

beauty sleep *n* sleep taken before midnight, supposed to be more restorative than that taken later.

beauty spot *n* a scenic location; a small birthmark or artificial patch on the cheek, regarded as a mark of beauty.

beaver[1] /'bi:vər/ *n* a large semi-aquatic dam-building rodent; its fur; a hat made from beaver fur. • *vi* (*often with* **away**) to work hard (at).

beaver[2] *n* the lower or moveable part of a helmet's face guard.

beaver dam *n* a dam of mud and sticks built by beavers across a narrow body of water.

bebop /'bi:bɒp/ *see* **bop**.

becalm /bi:'kɑm/ *vt* to make calm; to make (a ship) motionless from lack of wind.—**becalmed** *adj*.

became /bi'keim/ or /bı-/ *see* **become**.

because /bi'kɒz/ or /-'kʌz/ *conj* since; for the reason that.

because of *prep* by reason of.

beccafico /ˌbekə'fiko:/ *n* (*pl* **beccaficos**) a small bird of the warbler family, eaten as a delicacy in Italy.

béchamel sauce /ˌbeiʃə'mel/ *n* a thick, rich white sauce.

bêche-de-mer /beʃdə'mər/ *n* (*pl* **bêches-de-mer**) the trepang, a sea slug dried and eaten as a food in China; a form of pidgin English used in the islands of the Pacific.—*also* **beach-la-mar**.

beck[1] /bek/ *n* a wave or nod with the finger or head.

beck[2] *n* a brook, a mountain stream.

becket /'bekət/ *n* (*naut*) a rope loop, a hook, or a bracket for securing sails, tackle, etc.

beckon /'bekən/ *vti* to summon by a gesture.—**beckoner** *n*.—**beckoning** *adj*.

becloud /bi'klaud/ or /bı-/ *vt* to obscure by clouds, to dim.

become /bi'kʌm/ *vb* (**becoming, became,** *pp* **become**) *vi* to come or grow to be. • *vt* to be suitable for.

becoming /-ıŋ/ *adj* appropriate; seemly; suitable to the wearer.—**becomingly** *adv*.

becquerel /'bekəˌrel/ *n* the SI unit of radiation activity.

bed /bed/ *n* a piece of furniture for sleeping on; the mattress and covers for this; a plot of soil where plants are raised; the bottom of a river, lake, etc; any flat surface used as a foundation; a stratum. • *vt* (**bedding, bedded**) to put to bed; to embed; to plant in a bed of earth; to arrange in layers.

BEd *abbr* = Bachelor of Education.

bed and breakfast /bed ənd 'brekfəst/ *n* overnight accommodation and breakfast the following morning, as offered in hotels and guesthouses, etc.—**bed-and-breakfast** *adj*.

bedaub /bi'dɒb/ *vt* to smear all over.

bedbug /'bedˌbʌg/ *n* a bloodsucking wingless insect that infests dirty bedding.

bedchamber /-ˌtʃeimbər/ *n* a bedroom.

bedclothes /-klo:ðz/ *npl* sheets, blankets, etc for a bed.

bedding /-ıŋ/ *n* bedclothes; litter (straw, etc) for animals; a bottom layer, foundation.

bedding plant *n* a young plant suitable for a garden bed.

bedeck /bi'dek/ *vt* to cover with finery, to adorn.

bedevil /bi'devəl/ *vt* (**bedevilling, bedevilled** *or* **bedeviling, bedevilled**) to plague or bewilder.—**bedevilment** *n*.

bedew /bi'du:/ or /-'dju:/ *vt* to moisten, to sprinkle.

bedfellow /'bedˌfelo:/ *n* a sharer of a bed; an associate, ally, etc, *esp* a temporary one.

bedim /bi'dim/ *vt* (**bedimming, bedimmed**) to make dim.

bedizen /bi'daizən/ or /-'dizən/ *vt* to adorn or dress gaudily.—**bedizenment** *n*.

bedlam /'bedləm/ *n* (*arch*) a madhouse; uproar.

Bedouin /'bedu:ın/ *n* (*pl* **Bedouins, Bedouin**) an Arab desert nomad; a gypsy.

bedpan /'bedpæn/ *n* a vessel used as a lavatory by a bedridden person; a warming pan.

bedplate /-pleit/ *n* the base plate or frame or platform on which a machine is fixed.

bedraggle /bi'drægəl/ or /bı-/ *vt* to make untidy or dirty by dragging in the wet or dirt.—**bedraggled** *adj*.

bedridden /'bedˌridən/ *adj* confined to bed through illness.

bedrock /-rɒk/ *n* solid rock underlying soil, etc; the base or bottom; fundamentals.

bedroom /-ru:m/ *n* a room for sleeping in. • *adj* suggestive of sexual relations; (*area, suburb, etc*) inhabited by commuters.

bedside /-said/ *n* the space beside a bed. • *adj* situated or conducted at the bedside; suitable for someone bedridden.

bedsitter, bedsit, bedsitting room *n* a single room with sleeping and cooking facilities.

bedsore /-sɔr/ *n* an ulcerous sore caused by pressure, common in bedridden persons.

bedspread /-spred/ *n* a covering for a bed, *usu* decorative.

bedstead /-sted/ *n* a frame for the spring and mattress of a bed.

bedstraw /-strɒ/ *n* a plant of the madder family used formerly as straw for stuffing beds.

bee[1] /bi:/ *n* a social, stinging four-winged insect that is often kept in hives to make honey; any of numerous insects that also feed on pollen and nectar and are related to wasps.

bee[2] /bi/ *n* a social meeting for work on behalf of a neighbour or a charitable object.

bee[3] /bi/ *n* (*naut*) strips of wood bolted each side of a bowsprit, through which the fore topmast stays are reeved.

beebread /-ˌbred/ *n* a brown bitter substance consisting of the pollen of flowers collected and stored by bees as food for larvae.

beech /bi:tʃ/ *n* a tree with smooth silvery-grey bark; its wood.

beechmast /'bi:tʃmæst/ *n* beechnuts collectively.

beechnut /-net/ *n* the triangular nut of the beech, which yields an oil.

bee-eater *n* any of the numerous species of bee-eating birds.

beef /bi:f/ *n* (*pl* **beefs**) the meat of a full-grown cow, steer, etc; (*inf*) muscular strength; (*inf*) a complaint, grudge; (*pl* **beeves**) cows, ox, steers, etc bred for their meat. • *vt* (*with* **up**) to add weight, strength or power to.

beefburger *n* a flat grilled or fried cake of minced beef.

beefcake /-keik/ *n* (*sl*) muscular men displayed provocatively, *esp* in photographs.

beefeater /-ˌi:tər/ *n* an eater of beef; (*inf*) in UK, a yeoman of the royal guard, attending the sovereign on state occasions.

beef tea *n* stewed beef juice.

beefy /'bi:fi/ *adj* (**beefier, beefiest**) brawny, muscular.

beehive /'bi:haɪv/ *n* a container for keeping honeybees; a scene of crowded activity.

beekeeper /-ˌki:pər/ *n* one who keeps bees for producing honey.—**beekeeping** *n*.

beeline /-laɪn/ *n* the straight course pursued by a bee returning laden to the hive; a direct line or course.

Beelzebub /bi'ɛlzə,bʌb/ *n* the devil, Satan; a fallen angel, next in power to Satan.

bee moth *n* a moth that lays its eggs in beehives, and whose larvae feed upon the wax.

been /bi:n/ *see* **be**.

beep /bi:p/ *n* the brief, high-pitched sound of a horn or electronic signal. • *vi* to make or cause to make this sound.

beer /bi:r/ *n* an alcoholic drink made from malt, sugar, hops and water fermented with yeast.

beery /'bi:ri/ *adj* (**beerier, beeriest**) smelling or tasting of beer.

beestings /'bi:stɪŋz/ *npl* the first milk given by a cow after calving.—*also* **biestings, beastings**.

beeswax /'bi:zwæks/ *n* wax secreted by bees, refined and used for polishing.

beeswing /-wɪŋ/ *n* a gauze-like crust that occurs in port and some other wines, indicative of age.

beet /bi:t/ *n* a red, edible root used as a vegetable, in salads, etc; a source of sugar.

beetle[1] /'bi:təl/ *n* any of an order of insects having hard wing covers.

beetle[2] *n* a heavy wooden mallet for driving wedges, etc; a club for beating linen, etc, in washing. • *vt* to use a beetle on; to beat with a heavy wooden mallet.

beetle[3] *vi* to be prominent; to jut out, overhang, as a cliff.—**beetling** *adj*.

beetroot /'bi:tru:t/ *n* (*pl* **beetroot**) the fleshy root of beet used as a vegetable, in salads, etc.—*also* **red beet**.

beeves /bi:vz/ *see* **beef**.

beezer /'bi:zər/ *n* (*sl*) a fellow; (*sl*) a nose.

befall /bi'fɒl/ *vti* (**befalling, befell,** *pp* **befallen**) to happen or occur to.

befit /bi'fɪt/ *vt* (**befitting, befitted**) to be suitable or appropriate for; to be right for.—**befittingly** *adv*.

befog /bi'fɒg/ *vt* (**befogging, befogged**) to involve in a fog, to confuse.

befool /bi'fu:l/ *vt* to make a fool of.

before /bi'fɔr/ *prep* ahead of; in front of; in the presence of; preceding in space or time; in preference to; rather than. • *adv* beforehand; previously; until now. • *conj* earlier than the time that; rather than.

beforehand /-hænd/ *adv* ahead of time; in anticipation.

befoul /bi'faul/ *vt* to make foul, to soil.—**befouler** *n*.—**befoulment** *n*.

befriend /bi'frɛnd/ *vt* to be a friend to, to favour.

befuddle /bi'fʌdəl/ *vt* to confuse, stupefy, often with drink.

beg /bɛg/ *vti* (**begging, begged**) to ask for money or food; to ask earnestly; to implore.

began /bi'gæn/ *see* **begin**.

beget /bi'gɛt/ *vt* (**begetting, begot** *or* **begat,** *pp* **begotten** *or* **begot**) to become the father of; to cause.—**begetter** *n*.

beggar /'bɛgər/ *n* a person who begs or who lives by begging; a pauper; (*inf*) a person. • *vt* to reduce to poverty; (*description*) to render inadequate.

beggarly /-li/ *adj* like, or in the condition of, a beggar; poor; mean, contemptible.—**beggarliness** *n*.

beggary /'bɛgəri/ *n* the state of a beggar; extreme poverty; beggars collectively.

begin /bi'gɪn/ *vti* (**beginning, began,** *pp* **begun**) to start doing, acting, etc; to originate.

beginner /bi'gɪnər/ *or* /bɪ-/ *n* one who has just started to learn or do something; a novice.

beginning /-ɪŋ/ *n* source or origin; commencement.

begird /bi'gɜrd/ *or* /bɪ-/ *vt* (**begirding, begirded** *or* **begirt**) to gird round, to encompass, surround.

begone /bi'gɒn/ *interj* go away! be off!

begonia /bə'go:njə/ *or* /-niə/ *n* a tropical plant cultivated for its showy petalless flowers and ornamental lopsided leaves.

begorra /bə'gɒrə/ *interj* by God.

begot /bi'gɒt/, **begotten**/-'gɒtən/ *see* **beget**.

begrime /bi'graɪm/ *vt* to make grimy, to soil deeply.

begrudge /bi'grʌdʒ/ *vt* to grudge; to envy.—**begrudgingly** *adv*.

beguile /bi'gaɪl/ *vt* (**beguiling, beguiled**) to cheat or deceive; to charm; to fascinate.—**beguilement** *n*.—**beguiler** *n*.—**beguilingly** *adv*.

beguine /bi'gi:n/ *n* a West Indian dance in bolero rhythm; the music for this.

begum /'beigəm/ *n* a Muslim queen or lady of high rank.

begun /bi'gʌn/ *see* **begin**.

behalf /bi'hæf/ *n* **in** *or* **on behalf of** in the interest of; for.

behave /bi'heɪv/ *vti* to act in a specified way; to conduct (oneself) properly.

behaviour, behavior /bi'heɪvjər/ *n* way of behaving; conduct or action.—**behavioural, behavioral** *adj*.

behaviourism, behaviorism /-,ɪzəm/ *n* the doctrine that human action is governed by external stimuli.—**behaviourist, behaviorist** *adj, n*.—**behaviouristic, behavioristic** *adj*.

behead /bi'hɛd/ *vt* to cut the head off.

beheld /bi'hɛld/ *see* **behold**.

behemoth /bə'hi:məθ/ *or* /'bɪə,məθ/ *n* (*Bible*) an enormous animal described in Job, possibly the hippopotamus.

behest /bi'hɛst/ *n* a command; a precept.

behind /bi'haɪnd/ *prep* at the rear of; concealed by; later than; supporting. • *adv* in the rear; slow; late.

behindhand /-hænd/ *adj, adv* late, in arrears.

behold /bi'ho:ld/ *vb* (**beholding, beheld**) *vt* to look at; to observe. • *vi* to see.—**beholder** *n*.

beholden /-ən/ *adj* indebted to; bound under an obligation.

behoof /bi'hu:f/ *or* /bɪ-/ *n* advantage; interest; profit; use; behalf.

behove, behoove /bi'hu:v/ *vt* to be necessary or fit for, to be incumbent.

beige /beɪʒ/ *n* a very light brown.

being /'bi:ɪŋ/ *n* life; existence; a person or thing that exists; nature or substance.

bejewel /bi'dʒu:əl/ *vt* (**bejewelling, bejewelled** *or* **bejeweling, bejeweled**) to ornament or furnish with jewels.

bel /bɛl/ *n* a unit equal to 10 decibels.

belabour, belabor /bi'leɪbər/ *vt* to beat soundly, to thump; to criticize severely.

belated /bi'leɪtəd/ *adj* coming late.—**belatedly** *adv*.

belay /bɪ'leɪ/ *vti* (**belaying, belayed**) to secure (a rope) by winding it round a spike, piton; to secure by a rope.

belch /bɛltʃ/ *vti* to expel gas from the stomach by the mouth; to eject violently from inside.—*also n*.

beleaguer /bə'li:gər/ *vt* to besiege, to blockade; to harass.

belemnite /'bɛləm,naɪt/ *n* a pointed fossil internal bone or shell of an extinct family of cuttlefish.

bel esprit /ˌbɛlɛ'spri:/ *n* (*pl* **beaux esprits**) a person of wit or genius.

belfry /'bɛlfri/ *n* (*pl* **belfries**) the upper part of a tower, in which bells are hung.

Belgian /'bɛldʒən/ *adj* of or pertaining to Belgium or its inhabitants. • *n* a native or inhabitant of Belgium.

Belial /'bi:liəl/ *n* a demon or devil; a fallen angel.

belie /bə'laɪ/ *vt* (**belying, belied**) to show to be a lie; to misrepresent; to fail to live up to (a hope, promise).—**belier** *n*.

belief /bə'li:f/ *n* a principle or idea considered to be true; religious faith.

believe /bəli:v/ *vt* to accept as true; to think; to be convinced of. • *vi* to have religious faith.—**believable** *adj*.—**believer** *n*.

believing /-ɪŋ/ *adj* trustful.

belittle /bi'lɪtəl/ *vt* (*a person*) to make feel small; to disparage.—**belittlement** *n*.—**belittler** *n*.—**belittlingly** *adv*.

bell[1] /bɛl/ *n* a hollow metal object which rings when struck; anything bell-shaped; the sound made by a bell.

bell[2] *n* the cry of a stag in rut. • *vi* to make this cry.

belladonna /ˌbɛlə'dɒnə/ *n* the deadly nightshade plant, whose flowers, leaves and stalk are poisonous.

bellbird /'bɛlbərd/ *n* an American bird whose note resembles a bell; an Australian bird with a similar call.

bell buoy *n* a buoy with a warning bell activated by wave movement.

belle /bɛl/ *n* a pretty woman or girl.

belles-lettres /bɛl'lɛtr/ *n* (*used as sing*) artistic literature, including poetry, essays, etc.—**belletrist** *n*.—**belletristic** *adj*.

bellfounder *n* a person who casts bells.—**bellfoundry** *n*.

bellhop, bellboy /'bɛlhɒp/ *n* one who carries luggage, runs errands, etc in a hotel or club.

bellicose /'bɛli,ko:s/ *adj* war-like; ready to fight.—**bellicosity** *n*.

belligerent /bə'lɪdʒərənt/ *adj* at war; of war; war-like; ready to fight or quarrel.—**belligerence** *n*.—**belligerently** *adv*.

bell jar *n* a protective glass cover in the shape of a bell.

bellman /'belmən/ *n* (*pl* **bellmen**) one who uses a bell for public announcement, a town crier.

bell metal *n* an alloy of copper and tin, used for the manufacture of bells.

bellow /'belo:/ *vi* to roar; to make an outcry. • *vt* to utter loudly. • *n* the roar of a bull; any deep roar.

bellows /'belo:z/ *n* (*used as pl or sing*) a device for creating and directing a stream of air by compression of its collapsible sides.

bellpull *n* a rope or handle for a bell.

bell punch *n* a punch with a signal bell used for punching tickets and checking the number of fares issued.

bellpush *n* a button that operates a bell.

bellwether /'bel,weðər/ *n* the leading sheep of a flock with a bell round its neck.

belly /'beli/ *n* (*pl* **bellies**) the lower part of the body between the chest and the thighs; the abdomen; the stomach; the underside of an animal's body; the deep interior, as of a ship. • *vti* (**bellying, bellied**) to swell out; to bulge.

bellyache /-,eɪk/ *n* (*inf*) a pain in the stomach. • *vi* (*sl*) to complain constantly.

bellyband /-,bænd/ *n* a band that encircles the belly of a horse, a saddle girth.

bellybutton /-,bʌtən/ *n* (*inf*) the navel.

belly dance *n* a solo dance performed by a woman with sinuous, provocative movements of the belly and hips.—**belly dancer** *n*.

belly-flop /-flɒp/ *vt* (**belly-flopping, belly-flopped**) to dive in such a way that the body lands almost flat against the water.—**belly flop** *n*.

bellyful /-,fʊl/ *n* (*sl*) as much as one can tolerate of something.

belong /bi'lɒŋ/ *vi* to have a proper place; to be related (to); (*with* **to**) to be a member; to be owned; (*inf*) to fit in socially.

belongings /-ɪŋz/ *npl* personal effects, possessions.

beloved /bə'lʌvəd/ or /-'lʌvd/ *adj* dearly loved. • *n* one who is dearly loved.

below /bə'lo:/ *prep* lower than; unworthy of. • *adv* in or to a lower place; south of; beneath; later (in a book, etc).

belt /belt/ *n* a band of leather, etc worn around the waist; any similar encircling thing; a belt as an award for skill, *eg* in boxing, judo; a continuous moving strap passing over pulleys and so driving machinery; a distinctive region or strip; (*sl*) a hard blow. • *vt* to surround, attach with a belt; to thrash with a belt; (*sl*) to deliver a hard blow; (*sl*) to hurry; (*with* **out**) (*sl*) to sing or play loudly; (*with* **up**) to fasten with a belt. • *vi* (*with* **up**) (*inf*) to wear a seat belt; (*sl:often imper*) to be quiet.

Beltane /'belteɪn/ *n* a Celtic festival formerly observed in Scotland on old May Day and in Ireland on June 21 by the kindling of huge bonfires.

beluga /bə'lu:gə/ *n* a large sturgeon; its caviar; a white whale.

belvedere /'belvə,di:r/ *n* a raised turret or summerhouse for viewing scenery.

bema /'bi:mə/ *n* the inner part of the chancel in a Greek church; a speaker's platform; a platform in a synagogue from which services are led.

bemire /bə'maɪr/ *vt* to soil with mire; to be stuck in mud.

bemoan /bi'mo:n/ *vti* to lament.

bemuse /bə'mju:z/ *vt* to muddle; to preoccupy.—**bemused** *adj*.—**bemusement** *n*.

ben /ben/ *n* (*Scot*) a mountain.

bench /bentʃ/ *n* a long hard seat for two or more persons; a long table for working at; the place where judges sit in a court of law; the status of a judge; judges collectively; (*sport*) the place where reserves, etc, sit during play.

bencher /'bentʃər/ *n* a member of the governing body of the Inns of Court, usually a judge or a Queen's Counsel.

bench mark *n* a surveyor's mark for making measurements; something that serves as a standard.

bench warrant *n* a warrant issued by a court or judge for someone's arrest.

bend /bend/ *vb* (**bending, bent**) *vt* to form a curve; to make crooked; to turn, *esp* from a straight line; to adapt to one's purpose, distort. • *vi* to turn, *esp* from a straight line; to yield from pressure to form a curve; (*with* **over** *or* **down**) to curve the body; to give in. • *n* a curve, turn; a bent part; (*pl: used as sing or pl*) decompression sickness in divers.—**bendable** *adj*.

bender /'bendər/ *n* one who or that which bends; (*sl*) a bout of drinking.

bend sinister *n* (*her*) a bar or band drawn from the upper corner of the shield at the left (sinister) to the opposite base at the right (dexter), a sign of illegitimacy.

beneath /bə'ni:θ/ *prep* underneath; below; unworthy. • *adv* in a lower place; underneath.—*also adj*.

benedict /'benə,dɪkt/ *n* a newly married man, *esp* if previously a confirmed bachelor.

benedicite *n* a blessing, a grace; (*with cap*) a Christian hymn or canticle sung at morning prayer when the Te Deum is not used.

Benedictine /,benə'dɪkti:n/ *adj* of or relating to the order of St Benedict. • *n* a monk of the Benedictine order; a kind of liqueur made from herbs and spices.

benediction /,benə'dɪkʃən/ *n* a blessing; an invocation of a blessing, *esp* at the end of a church service.—**benedictory** *adj*.

Benedictus /,benə'dɪktʊs/ *n* the Song of Zacharias (Luke 1) used as a canticle after the second lesson at morning prayer when the Jubilate is not sung.

benefaction /,benə'fækʃən/ *n* the act of doing good; the money or help given.

benefactor /'benə,fæktər/ *n* a patron.—**benefactress** *nf*.

benefice /'benəfɪs/ *n* a church office yielding an income to a clergyman.

beneficence /bə'nefəsəns/ *n* active kindness, the act of doing good; a benefaction.

beneficent /-sənt/ *adj* generous; conferring blessings.—**beneficence** *n*.—**beneficently** *adv*.

beneficial /,benə'fɪʃəl/ *adj* advantageous.—**beneficially** *adv*.

beneficiary /,benə'fɪʃieri/ *n* (*pl* **beneficiaries**) a person who receives or will receive benefit, as from a will, etc.

benefit /'benəfɪt/ *n* advantage; anything contributing to improvement; (*often pl*) allowances paid by a government, insurance company, etc; a public performance, bazaar, etc, the proceeds of which are to help some person or cause. • *vb* (**benefiting, benefited**) *vt* to help. • *vi* to receive advantage.

benefit of clergy *n* a sanctioning by the church; (*hist*) exemption from trial by a secular court.

benefit society, benefit association *n* an association for mutual insurance against sickness, etc.

benevolence /bə'nevələns/ *n* inclination to do good; kindness; generosity; (*formerly*) a royal tax levied under the guise of a gratuity to the sovereign.—**benevolent** *adj*.—**benevolently** *adv*.

Bengali /ben'gɒli/ or /-'gæli/ *n* a native or inhabitant of the Bengal province of India; the language spoken in Bengal. • *adj* of or pertaining to Bengal, its inhabitants or language.

Bengal light /'beŋgɒl/ *n* a firework used also for signals, giving a steady bright blue light.

benighted /bə'naɪtəd/ or /bɪ-/ *adj* overtaken by night; in moral darkness or ignorance.

benign /bə'naɪn/ *adj* favourable; kindly; gentle or mild; (*med*) not malignant.—**benignly** *adv*.

benignant /bə'nɪgnənt/ *adj* kind; benign.—**benignancy** *n*.

benignity /-nɪti/ *n* (*pl* **benignities**) kindliness.

benison /'benɪzən/ *n* (*arch*) a benediction or blessing.

benne /'beni/ *n* the sesame, an Asian annual cultivated for its seeds, which yield a valuable oil.

bent[1] /bent/ *see* **bend**.

bent[2] *n* aptitude; inclination of the mind. • *adj* curved or crooked; (*with* **on**) strongly determined; (*sl*) dishonest.

bent[3] *n* a kind of coarse stiff grass; a withered grass stalk; a heath.

benthos /'benθɒs/ *n* the flora and fauna at the bottom of the sea; the sea bottom itself.—**benthic, benthonic** *adj*.

bentwood /'bentwʊd/ *adj* (*furniture*) made of wood that is bent and shaped by heat.

benumb /bi'nʌm/ *vt* to make numb.—**benumbed** *adj*.

benzene /'benzi:n/ *n* a mixture of hydrocarbons from petroleum used as a solvent, in the manufacture of plastics, and as motor fuel.

benzine /'benzi:n/, **benzol** /ben'zɒl/ *n* a volatile mixture of lighter hydrocarbons from petroleum, used as a solvent and as motor fuel.

benzoin /'benzo:ɪn/ *n* a resin of the benjamin tree of Sumtra, used chiefly in cosmetics, perfumes and incense.—**benzoic** *adj*.

bequeath /bi'kwi:θ/ or /-'kwi:ð/ *vt* (*property, etc*) to leave by will; to pass on to posterity.—**bequeathal** *n*.—**bequeather** *n*.

bequest /bi'kwɛst/ *n* act of bequeathing; something that is bequeathed, a legacy.

berate /bi'reɪt/ *vt* to scold severely.

berberine /'bərbər,in/ *n* an alkaloid used in dyeing and medicine, and obtained as a bitter yellow substance from the barberry and other plants.

berceuse *Fr.* /bɛr'səz/ *n* (*pl* **berceuses**) a cradle song; a tender or soothing musical composition.

bereave /bi'ri:v/ *vt* to deprive (of) a loved one through death.— **bereaved** *adj*.—**bereavement** *n*.

bereft /bɪ'rɛft/ *adj* deprived; bereaved.

beret /bə'reɪ/ or /be-/ *n* a flat, round, brimless, soft cap.

berg /bərg/ *n* an iceberg.

bergamot /'bərgə,mɒt/ *n* a variety of lemon, the rind of which yields a valuable oil used in perfumery; the oil of the bergamot; a variety of pear; a variety of mint; a coarse kind of tapestry.

bergschrund /'bɛrkʃrunt/ *n* a crevasse between a glacier and the side of its valley.

beriberi /,beri'beri/ *n* a disease of the nervous system, due to lack of vitamin B.

berkelium /bər'ki:liəm/ or /'bərkli:əm/ *n* a radioactive metallic element derived from americium.

berlin /bər'lɪn/ *n* a fine dyed knitting wool; an 18th-century four-wheeled carriage with a hood behind.

berm, berme /bərm/, *Fr.* /bermə/ *n* a ledge between a ditch and rampart; a narrow shelf along a slope; a shoulder of a road.

Bermuda grass /bər'mju:də/ *n* a valuable variety of pasture grass.

Bermuda shorts *npl* close-fitting knee-length shorts.

Bermuda-rigged *adj* (*naut*) rigged with a high tapering mainsail.

berry /be'ri/ *n* (*pl* **berries**) any small, juicy, stoneless fruit (*eg* blackberry, holly berry). • *vti* (**berrying, berried**) to bear, produce or gather berries.

berserk /bə'zərk/ or /bər-/ *adj* frenzied; destructively violent.— *also adv*.

berth /bərθ/ *n* a place in a dock for a ship at mooring; a built-in bed, as in a ship or train; (*inf*) a job. • *vt* to put into or furnish with a berth; to moor a ship. • *vi* to occupy a berth.

bertha /'bərθə/ *n* a wide lace collar.

Bertillon system /'bərtə,lɒn/, *Fr.* /bɛrti'jõ:/ *n* a method of identifying criminals by body measurements.

beryl /beril/ *n* a (*usu* green) precious stone.

beryllium /bə'rɪliəm/ *n* a hard lightweight silvery-white metallic element used in making alloys.

beseech /bi'si:tʃ/ *vt* (**beseeching, beseeched** *or* **besought**) to implore, to entreat; to beg earnestly for.

beset /bi'set/ *vt* (**besetting, beset**) to surround or hem in; to attack from all sides; to harass.

besetting /-ɪŋ/ *adj* constantly harassing.

beside /bi'saɪd/ *prep* at, by the side of, next to; in comparison with; in addition to; aside from; **beside oneself** extremely agitated.

besides /-z/ *prep* other than; in addition; over and above. • *adv* in addition; also; except for that mentioned; moreover.

besiege /bi'si:dʒ/ *vt* to hem in with armed forces; to close in on; to overwhelm, harass, etc.

besmear /bi'smi:r/ *vt* to smear with sticky stuff; to soil.

besmirch /bi'smərtʃ/ *vt* to sully; to make dirty, to soil.

besom /'bi:zəm/ *n* a broom made of twigs; (*Scot*) a naughty or silly woman.

besotted /bi'sɒtəd/ *adj* muddled with drunkenness or infatuation; dull, stupid.—**besottedly** *adv*.

besought /bi'sɒt/ *see* **beseech**.

bespangle /bi'spæŋəl/ *vt* to adorn with spangles; to dot or sprinkle with something that glitters.

bespatter /bi'spætər/ *vt* to soil by spattering; to spot with mud; to asperse with calumny.

bespeak /bi'spi:k/ *vt* (**bespeaking, bespoke**, *pp* **bespoken** *or* **bespoke**) to speak for beforehand; to order or arrange in advance; to be evidence of; to indicate, as by signs or marks.

bespoke /bi'spo:k/ *adj* (*clothes*) custom-made; (*tailor*) making such clothes.

besprent /bi'sprent/ *adj* (*poet*) sprinkled; scattered.

besprinkle /bi'sprɪŋkəl/ *vt* to sprinkle over (with).

best /bɛst/ *adj* (*superl of* **good**) most excellent; most suitable, desirable, etc; largest; above all others. • *n* one's utmost effort; the highest state of excellence. • *adv* (*superl of* **well**) in or to the highest degree. • *vt* to defeat, outdo.

bestial /'bi:stiəl/ or /'bes-/ *adj* brutal; savage.—**bestially** *adv*.

bestiality /,bi:sti'æliti/ or /,best-/ *n* (*pl* **bestialities**) brutal or brutish behaviour; a brutal or savage action or practice; sexual intercourse by a person with an animal.

bestialize /'bi:stiəl,aɪz/ or /,best-/ *vt* to make like a beast; to degrade to the level of a brute.

bestiary /'bi:sti,eri/ or /,best-/ *n* (*pl* **bestiaries**) a medieval treatise on beasts.

bestir /bi'stər/ *vt* (**bestirring, bestirred**) to put into brisk or vigorous action; to rouse, exert (oneself).

best man *n* the principal attendant of the bridegroom at a wedding.

bestow /bi'sto:/ *vt* to present as a gift or honour.—**bestowal** *n*.—**bestower** *n*.

bestrew /bi'stru:/ *vt* (**bestrewing, bestrewed**, *pp* **bestrewed** *or* **bestrewn**) to strew or scatter over; to lie scattered over.

bestride /bi'straɪd/ *vt* (**bestriding, bestrode**, *pp* **bestridden**) to stand, sit on or mount with the legs astride.

best seller /,best'selər/ *n* a book or other commodity that sells in vast numbers; the author of such a book.—**best-selling** *adj*.

bet /bɛt/ *n* a wager or stake; the thing or sum staked; a person or thing likely to bring about a desired result; (*inf*) belief, opinion. • *vti* (**betting, bet** *or* **betted**) to declare as in a bet; to stake (money, etc) in a bet (with someone).

beta /'beɪtə/ *n* the second letter of the Greek alphabet; (*astron*) the second star in a constellation; (*chem*) the second of two or more isomerous modifications of the same compound; (*biol*) the second subspecies or permanent variety of a species.

beta blocker *n* a drug that subdues cardiac activity, used in the treatment of high blood pressure.

betake /bi'teɪk/ *vt* (**betaking, betook**, *pp* **betaken**) to have recourse (to), to resort; to take oneself (to), to go.

beta particle *n* an electron or positron ejected from the nucleus of an atom during radioactive disintegration.

beta ray *n* a stream of penetrating rays emitted by radioactive substances.

beta wave *n* an electrical rhythm of the brain associated with normal waking consciousness.

betel /'bi:təl/ *n* an Asian pepper, the leaves of which are mixed with betel nuts and chewed as a stimulant or narcotic.

bête noir /,beɪt'nwar/, *Fr.* /bɛt'nwaʀ/ *n* (*pl* **bêtes noires**) pet hate.

betel nut *n* the seed of the betel palm.

betel palm *n* a palm tree of tropical Asia with feathery leaves and scarlet or orange fruit.

bethel /'beθəl/ *n* a hallowed spot; a seamen's church; in UK, a nonconformist chapel.

betide /bi'taɪd/ *vt* to happen to, to befall. • *vi* to come to pass.

betimes /bi'taɪmz/ *adv* (*arch*) in good time; before it is too late; early; soon.

bêtise /beɪ'ti:z/ *n* folly; an ill-chosen remark.

betoken /bi'to:kən/ *vt* to signify, to indicate by signs; to augur, to foreshadow.

betony /'betəni/ *n* (*pl* **betonies**) a purple-flowered woodland plant formerly used in medicine and as a dye.

betook *see* **betake**.

betray /bi'treɪ/ or /bi-/ *vt* to aid an enemy; to expose treacherously; to be a traitor to; to reveal unknowingly.—**betrayal** *n*.— **betrayer** *n*.

betroth /bi'tro:ð/ *vt* to promise in marriage.

betrothal /-əl/ *n* the state of being engaged to marry; a mutual promise for future marriage made between a man and a woman.

betrothed /bi'tro:ðd/ or /-ðəd/ *adj* affianced, engaged to be married. • *n* a fiancé or fiancée.

better[1] /'betər/ *adj* (*compar of* **good**) more excellent; more suitable; improved in health; larger. • *adv* (*compar of* **well**) in a more excellent manner; in a higher degree; more. • *n* a person superior in position, etc; a more excellent thing, condition, etc. • *vt* to outdo; to surpass.

better[2] *n* someone who bets.

betterment /-mənt/ *n* an improvement.

between /bi'twi:n/ *prep* the space, time, etc separating (two things); (*bond, etc*) connecting from one or the other.

betweentimes /-,taɪmz/, **betweenwhiles** /-hwaɪlz/ *adv* at or during intervals.

betwixt /bi'twɪkst/ *prep* between; in the space that separates.

bevel /'bevəl/ *n* an angle other than a right angle; the inclination that one surface makes with another when not at right angles; a tool for setting of angles. • *vb* (**bevelling, bevelled** *or* **beveling, beveled**) *vt* to cut on the slant. • *vi* to slant or incline.

bevel gear *n* a gear in which the axis or shaft of the driving wheel forms an angle with the shaft of the wheel driven.

beverage /ˈbevərɪdʒ/ *n* a drink, *esp* one other than water.

bevy /ˈbevi/ *n* (*pl* **bevies**) a flock of quails; a large group (*esp* of girls).

bewail /bɪˈweɪl/ *vt* to mourn or weep aloud for, to lament. • *vi* to express grief.—**bewailer** *n*.—**bewailing** *n*.

beware /bɪˈweɪr/ *vti* to be wary or careful (of).

bewilder /bɪˈwɪldər/ *vt* to perplex; to confuse hopelessly.—**bewilderingly** *adv*.—**bewilderment** *n*.

bewitch /bɪˈwɪtʃ/ *vt* to cast a spell over; to fascinate or enchant.

bewitching /-ɪŋ/ *adj* fascinating, enchanting, captivating, alluring.—**bewitchingly** *adv*.

bey /beɪ/ *n* a Turkish title of respect; a title similar to Mr; (*formerly*) a governor of a province or district in the Turkish dominions.

beyond /bɪˈjɒnd/ *prep* further on than; past; later than; outside the reach of (*beyond help*). • *adv* further away. • *n* (*with* **the**) life after death.

bezant /ˈbezənt/ or /bɪˈzænt/ *n* a gold coin of Byzantium or Constantinople, issued in the Middle Ages and current in Europe until the fall of the Eastern Empire, 1472; (*her*) a small circle of gold representing the coin.

bezel /ˈbezəl/ *n* the sloping edge of a chisel; the rim that holds a gem in its setting; the groove in which the glass of a watch is fitted.

bezique /bəˈziːk/ *n* a game of cards for two, three, and four persons using two decks of cards with sixes and cards below omitted.

bezoar /ˈbiːzɔr/ or /ˈbiːzɔːɑr/ *n* a calcareous concretion found in the intestines of certain animals.

bhang /bæŋ/ *n* the dried leaves of Indian hemp, chewed or smoked as an intoxicant or narcotic, hashish.—*also* **bang**.

bhp *abbr* = brake horsepower.

Bi (*chem symbol*) bismuth.

bi- /baɪ/ *prefix* having two; doubly; happening twice during; every two; using two or both; joining or involving two; having twice the amount of acid or base.

biannual /baɪˈænjuəl/ *adj* occurring twice a year.—**biannually** *adv*.

bias /ˈbaɪəs/ *n* a slanting or diagonal line, cut or sewn across the grain in cloth; a weight inside a bowl in a game of bowls slanting its course when rolled; partiality; prejudice. • *vt* (**biasing**, **biased** *or* **biassing**, **biassed**) to prejudice.

biathlon /baɪˈæθlɒn/ *n* (*sport*) an athletic event combining cross-country skiing and rifle shooting.

biauriculate /baɪɔːˈrɪkjuːlɪt/, **biauricular** /-lər/ *adj* having two auricles, as the heart of the higher vertebrates; (*bot*) having two ear-like projections at the base, as a leaf.

biaxial /baɪˈæksɪəl/ *adj* having two (optic) axes.—**biaxially** *adv*.

bib¹ /bɪb/ *n* a cloth or plastic cover tied around a baby or child to prevent food spillage on clothes; the upper part of dungarees or an apron.

bib² *vi* (**bibbing**, **bibbed**) (*arch*) to drink, to tipple.

bib³ *n* a kind of fish, whiting pout.

bibelot /ˈbɪb,lo:/ *n* a trinket, a knickknack.

Bible /ˈbaɪbəl/ *n* the sacred book of the Christian Church; the Old and New Testaments; (*without cap*) an authoritative book on a particular subject.

biblical /ˈbɪblɪkəl/ *adj* of or referring to the Bible.—**biblically** *adv*.

Biblicist /ˈbɪblɪsɪst/ *n* a biblical scholar; a fundamentalist.—**Biblicism** *n*.

biblio- /ˈbɪblioː/ or /-ə/ *prefix* book or books.

bibliography /ˌbɪbliˈɒgrəfi/ *n* (*pl* **bibliographies**) a list of writings on a given subject or by a given author; the study of the history of books and book production. —**bibliographer** *n*.—**bibliographic** *adj*.—**bibliographical** *adj*.

bibliolatry /ˌbɪbliˈɒlətri/ *n* book worship; excessive reverence for the letter of the Bible.—**bibliolater** *n*.—**bibliolatrous** *adj*.

bibliomania /ˌbɪblioˈmeɪniə/ *n* a mania for acquiring rare and curious books.—**bibliomaniac** *adj*, *n*.

bibliophile, **bibliophil** /ˈbɪblio,faɪl/ *n* a book lover.—**bibliophilistic** *adj*.—**bibliophism** *n*.

bibliopole /ˈbɪblio,po:l/, **bibliopolist** /-ɪst/ *n* a bookseller, *esp* one who deals in rare works.—**bibliopolic** *adj*.—**bibliopoly** *n*.

bibliotheca /ˌbɪblioˈθiːkə/ *n* (*pl* **bibliothecas**, **bibliothecae**) a library; a list of books.

bibulous /ˈbɪbjuːləs/ *adj* readily absorbing or imbibing fluids; spongy; addicted to drink.—**bibulously** *adv*.—**bibulousness** *n*.

bicameral /baɪˈkæmərəl/ *adj* (*legislature*) having two chambers.

bicarbonate /baɪˈkɑrbəneɪt/ or /-nət/ *n* sodium bicarbonate.

bicentenary /ˌbaɪsənˈtenəri/ or /-ˈtiːnəri/ *adj* occurring every two hundred years. • *n* (*pl* **bicentenaries**) a two hundredth anniversary or its celebration.

bicentennial /ˌbaɪsenˈteniəl/ *adj* lasting or occurring every two hundred years. • *n* a bicentenary, the two hundredth anniversary of an event, or its celebration.

bicephalous /baɪˈsefələs/, **bicephalic** /ˌbaɪsəˈfælɪk/ *adj* (*biol*) two-headed.

biceps *n* /ˈbaɪˌseps/ (*pl* **biceps, bicepses**) the muscle with two points of origin, *esp* the large muscle in the upper arm.

bichloride /baɪˈkloːraɪd/ *n* (*chem*) a compound of two or more atoms of chlorine combined with a base; dichloride.

bicipital /baɪˈsɪpətl/ *adj* (*anat*) having two heads, as a biceps muscle; dividing into two parts at either extremity.

bicker /ˈbɪkər/ *vi* to squabble, quarrel.—*also n*.—**bickerer** *n*.

bicoastal /baɪˈkoːstəl/ *adj* pertaining to both the west and east coasts of the United States.

biconcave /baɪˈkɒŋkeɪv/ or /baɪˈkɒŋkeɪv/ *adj* hollow on both sides.—**biconcavity** *n*.

biconvex /baɪˈkɒŋveks/ *adj* rounded on both sides.

bicorn /ˈbaɪˌkɔrn/, **bicornuate** *adj* having two horns.

bicuspid /baɪˈkʌspɪd/ *adj* having two points or prominences.—*also* **bicuspidate**. • *n* one of the two double-pointed teeth forming the first pair of molars on either side of the jaw, above and below.

bicycle /ˈbaɪˌsɪkəl/ *n* a vehicle consisting of a metal frame on two wheels, driven by pedals and having handlebars and a seat. • *vti* to ride or travel on a bicycle.—**bicyclist, bicycler** *n*.

bid¹ /bɪd/ *n* an offer of an amount one will pay or accept; (*cards*) a statement of the number of tricks that a player intends to win. • *vi* (**bidding, bid**) to make a bid.—**bidder** *n*.

bid² *vt* (**bidding, bade** *or* **bid**, *pp* **bidden** *or* **bid**) to command or ask; to summon; (*farewell, etc*) to express.

biddable /ˈbɪdəbəl/ *adj* docile, obedient; worth bidding on.—**biddability** *n*.—**biddably** *adv*.

bidding /-ɪŋ/ *n* an order; command; an invitation; the act of offering a price at auction.

biddy¹ /ˈbɪdi/ *n* (*pl* **biddies**) (*inf*) a woman, *esp* an old or meddlesome one.

biddy² *n* (*pl* **biddies**) (*dial*) a fowl or chicken.

bide /baɪd/ *vb* (**biding, bided** *or* **bode**) *vi* to wait; to dwell. • *vt* to endure, suffer; to wait for.

bidentate /baɪˈdenˌteɪt/ *adj* having two teeth, or two tooth-like processes.

bidet /biːˈdeɪ/ *n* a low, bowl-shaped bathroom fixture with running water for bathing the crotch and anus.

biennial /baɪˈeniəl/ *adj* lasting two years; occurring every two years. • *n* a plant that lasts for two years.—**biennially** *adv*.

bier /biːr/ *n* a portable framework on which a coffin is put.

biestings /ˈbiːstɪŋz/ *see* **beestings**.

bifacial /baɪˈfeɪʃəl/ *adj* having two faces or fronts; (*leaves*) having upper and lower surfaces that are dissimilar; having opposite surfaces alike.

bifarious /baɪˈferiəs/ *adj* (*bot*) two-fold; two-rowed; pointing in two ways.

biff /bɪf/ *n* (*sl*) a blow. • *vt* to hit, strike.

bifid /ˈbaɪˌfɪd/ *adj* divided by a deep cleft, partially divided into two.—**bifidity** *n*.—**bifidly** *adv*.

bifilar /baɪˈfɪlər/ *adj* two-threaded; fitted with two threads.—**bifilarly** *adv*.

bifocal /baɪˈfoːkəl/ *adj* (*spectacles*) having two different focuses.

bifocals /ˈbaɪˌfoːkəlz/ *npl* spectacles with bifocal lenses for near and distant vision.

bifoliate /baɪˈfoːlieɪt/ *adj* (*bot*) having two leaves.

bifurcate /ˈbaɪfərˌkeɪt/ or /baɪˈfərkeɪt/, /-kət/ *vti* to divide into two branches.—**bifurcation** *n*.

big /bɪg/ *adj* (**bigger, biggest**) large; of great size; important; influential; grown-up; pregnant; generous; boastful.—**bigness** *n*.

bigamist /ˈbɪgəmɪst/ *n* a person guilty of bigamy.

bigamy /ˈbɪgəmi/ *n* (*pl* **bigamies**) the act of marrying a second time when one is already legally married.—**bigamous** *adj*.—**bigamously** *adv*.

big bang theory /ˈbɪgˌbæŋ/ *n* (*astron*) the theory that the universe originated in a cataclysmic explosion and is still expanding.

big brother *n* an older brother; a person who fills that protective role; (*with caps*) a ruthless and sinister dictator, corporation, etc that wields absolute power.

big business *n* large corporations and enterprises collectively, *esp* when regarded as exploitative.

big cat *see* **cat**.

big deal *n* an important achievement. • *interj* (*sl*) an expression of scorn or contempt.

big dipper *n* a roller coaster; (*with caps*) the seven main stars in the constellation Ursa Major.

big dry *n* a period of drought longer than normal.

big game *n* large animals or fish hunted for sport; an important, *usu* risky objective.

biggin[1] /'bɪgɪn/ *n* a close-fitting child's hood or cap.

biggin[2] *n* a small building; a cottage.

bighead /ˌbɪgˌhɛd/ *n* (*inf*) a boastful or conceited person.—**big-headed** *adj*.

bighorn /'bɪgˌhɔrn/ *n* (*pl* **bighorns, bighorn**) the wild sheep of the Rocky Mountains.

bight /baɪt/ *n* a loop or bend of a rope, in distinction from the ends; a bend in a coastline forming an open bay; a small bay between two headlands.

bigmouth /'bɪgˌmaʊθ/ *n* (*inf*) a loud-mouthed, bragging or indiscreet person.

big name *n* a famous person, *esp* in entertainment.

bigot /'bɪgət/ *n* an intolerant person who blindly supports a particular political view or religion.—**bigoted** *adj*.

bigotry /'bɪgətri/ *n* (*pl* **bigotries**) the state or condition of a narrow-minded, intolerant person; blind and obstinate attachment to a particular creed, party or opinion; intolerance; fanaticism.

big screen *n* (*inf*) the cinema (industry).

big shot *n* (*inf*) an important person.

big stick *n* the threat of force.

big time /'bɪgˌtaɪm/ *n* the top level in any profession.

big top *n* a large circus tent.

bigwig /'bɪgwɪg/ *n* (*inf*) an important person.

bijou /'biːˌʒuː/ or /biˈʒuː/ *n* (*pl* **bijoux**) a jewel; any small and elegantly finished article. • *adj* (*often derog*) small and elegant.

bijouterie /biːˈʒuːtəri/ *n* bijoux collectively, jewellery.

bijugate /'haɪdʒuːˌgeɪt/, **bijugous** /-dʒuːˌgəs/ *adj* (*bot*) having two pairs of leaflets; having two heads in profile, one of which overlaps the other.

bike /baɪk/ *n* (*inf*) a bicycle; a motorcycle.

bikini /bɪˈkiːni/ *n* (*pl* **bikinis**) a scanty two-piece swimsuit for women.

bilabiate /baɪˈleɪbiˌeɪt/ *adj* (*bot*) having two lips, as a flower.

bilateral /baɪˈlætərəl/ *adj* having two sides; affecting two parties reciprocally.—**bilaterally** *adv*.

bilberry /'bɪlbɛri/ *n* (*pl* **bilberries**) an edible dark-blue berry.

bilbo /'bɪlˌboː/ *n* (*pl* **bilboes**) a rapier or sword; (*pl*) a long bar of iron with sliding shackles for the feet and a lock at the end, formerly used as fetters.

bile /baɪl/ *n* a gall, a thick bitter fluid secreted by the liver; bad temper.

bilge /bɪldʒ/ *n* the lowest part of a ship's hull; filth that collects there.

bilge keel *n* a piece of timber secured edgeways under the bottom of a vessel to prevent heavy rolling.

bilge water *n* foul water in a ship's bilge.

bilharzia /bɪlˈhɑrtsiə/ *n* a tropical disease caused by a parasitic worm.

biliary /'bɪliˌɛri/ or /'bɪljəri/ *adj* of or pertaining to the bile; conveying bile.

bilingual /baɪˈlɪŋgwəl/ or /-gjuːəl/ *adj* written in two languages; able to speak two languages.—**bilingualism** *n*.—**bilingually** *adv*.

bilious /'bɪljəs/ or /'bɪliəs/ *adj* suffering from or caused by disorder of the bile; peevish.—**biliously** *adv*.—**biliousness** *n*.

bilirubin /ˌbɪliˈruːbɪn/ *n* an orange or yellow pigment in the bile.

biliverdin /ˌbɪliˈvɜrdɪn/ *n* a green pigment in the bile, the oxidized form of bilirubin.

bilk /bɪlk/ *vt* to deceive or defraud, as by evading a payment; to leave in the lurch; (*cribbage*) to spoil the score of an opponent. • *n* a swindler; the act of spoiling the score of an opponent at cribbage.—**bilker** *n*.

bill[1] /bɪl/ *n* a bird's beak.

bill[2] *n* a statement for goods supplied or services rendered, the money due for this; a list, as a menu or theatre programme; a poster or handbill; a draft of a proposed law, to be discussed by a legislature; a bill of exchange; a piece of paper money; (*law*)

a written declaration of charges and complaints filed. • *vt* to make out a bill of (items); to present a statement of charges to; to advertise by bills; (*a performer*) to book.

billabong /'bɪləˌbɒŋ/ *n* an Australian word for a pond or a stagnant pool connected to a river.

billboard /'bɪlˌbɔrd/ *n* a large panel designed to carry outdoor advertising; a hoarding.

billet[1] /'bɪlət/ *n* a written order to provide lodging for military personnel; the lodging; a position or job. • *vt* (**billeting, billeted**) to assign to lodging by billet.

billet[2] *n* a small stick or log of wood, as for fuel; (*archit*) a moulding ornament, resembling a billet of wood.

billet-doux /ˌbɪlɛˈduː/ or /ˌbɪli-/ *n* (*pl* **billets-doux**) a love letter.

billfold /'bɪlˌfoːld/ *n* a notecase or wallet.

billhook /'bɪlˌhʊk/ *n* a small curved cutting tool with a hooked point.

billiards /'bɪljərdz/ *n* a game in which hard balls are driven by a cue on a felt-covered table with raised, cushioned edges.

billing /'bɪlɪŋ/ *n* the order in which actors' names are listed.

billingsgate /'bɪlɪŋzˌgeɪt/ *n* coarse or profane language; virulent abuse.

billion /'bɪljən/ *n* (*pl* **billions, billion**) a thousand millions, the numeral 1 followed by 9 zeros; in UK, a million million, a trillion.—**billionaire** *n*.—**billionth** *adj, n*.

bill of exchange *n* a written order to pay a certain sum of money to the person named.

bill of fare *n* a menu.

bill of health *n* a ship's certificate of health; a report on a situation or condition, *usu* favourable.

bill of lading *n* a receipt issued to a shipper by a carrier, listing the goods received for shipment.

bill of rights *n* a charter or summary of basic human rights.

bill of sale *n* a written statement transferring ownership by sale.

billon /'bɪljən/ *n* an alloy of gold and silver, with a large proportion of copper or other base metal, used in coinage of low value.

billow /'bɪloː/ *n* a large wave; any large swelling mass or surge, as of smoke. • *vi* to surge or swell in a billow.—**billowy** *adj*.

billposter /'bɪlˌpoːstər/ *n* a person who pastes up bills.

billsticker /'bɪlˌstɪkər/ *n* a billposter.

billy /'bɪli/, **billycan** /-ˌkæn/ *n* (*pl* **billies, billycans**) (*Austral*) a can used as a kettle by campers.

billy-goat *n* a male goat.

bilobate /baɪˈloːˌbeɪt/, **bilobed** /'baɪloːbd/ *adj* divided into two lobes or segments, with two lobes.

bilocular /baɪˈlɒkjuːlər/, **biloculate** /baɪlɒkjuːˌleɪt/ *adj* divided into, or containing, two cells.

biltong /'bɪltɒŋ/ *n* (*S Africa*) strips of meat, salted and dried in the sun.

bimanous /baɪˈmeɪnəs/ *adj* (*zool*) having two hands.

bimbo /'bɪmboː/ *n* (*pl* **bimbos, bimboes**) (*sl*) an attractive, but brainless, young woman, often one who has an affair with a prominent person.

bimetallic /ˌbaɪməˈtælɪk/ *adj* of or containing two metals; of or based on bimetallism.

bimetallism /baɪˈmɛtəlɪzəm/ *n* a monetary system using both gold and silver as a standard currency at a fixed relative value.—**bimetallist** *n*.

bimonthly /baɪˈmʌnθli/ *adj* every two months; loosely twice a month.

bin /bɪn/ *n* a box or enclosed space for storing grain, coal, etc; a dustbin. • *vt* (**binning, binned**) to put or store in a bin; (*inf*) to discard, throw away.

binary /'baɪnəri/ or /-ɛri/ *adj* made up of two parts; double; denoting or of a number system in which the base is two, each number being expressed by using only two digits, specifically 0 and 1.

binary star *n* a double star or sun whose members revolve round their common centre of gravity.

binate /'baɪˌneɪt/ *adj* (*bot*) occurring in twos or growing in pairs.—**binately** *adv*.

binaural /baɪˈnɔrəl/ *adj* of or used with both ears; (*sound*) transmitted from two sources.—**binaurally** *adv*.

bind /baɪnd/ *vb* (**binding, bound**) *vt* to tie together, as with rope; to hold or restrain; to encircle with a belt, etc; to fasten together the pages of (a book) and protect with a cover; to obligate by duty, love, etc; (*with* **over**) to compel, as by oath or legal restraint; (*often with* **up**) to bandage. • *vi* to become tight or stiff; to stick together; to be obligatory; (*sl*) to complain. • *n* anything that binds; (*inf*) a difficult situation.

binder /'baɪndər/ *n* a folder for keeping loose papers together; a bookbinder; something used to bind; a sheaf-binding machine.

bindery /'baɪndəri/ *n* (*pl* **binderies**) a bookbinder's workshop.

binding /'baɪndɪŋ/ *n* the covering of a book holding the pages together.

bindweed /'baɪnd,wiːd/ *n* a common name for twining plants belonging to the genus Convolvulus.

bine /baɪn/ *n* the slender stem of a twining plant, *esp* hop; one of these plants.

binge /bɪndʒ/ *n* (*inf*) a heavy drinking session; immoderate indulgence in anything.

bingo /'bɪŋgoʊ/ *n* a game of chance in which players cover numbers on their cards according to the number called aloud. • *interj*, *n* a cry of delight, surprise or success.

binnacle /'bɪnəkəl/ *n* a turret-shaped box containing a ship's compass.

binocular /baɪ'nɒkjʊlər/ or /bɪ-/ *adj* for or using both eyes.

binoculars /bɪ'nɒkjʊlərz/ *npl* a viewing device for use with both eyes, consisting of two small telescope lenses joined together.

binomial /baɪ'noʊmɪəl/ *n* (*math*) an expression or quantity consisting of two terms connected by the sign plus (+) or minus (-). • *adj* consisting of two terms; pertaining to binomials; (*biol*) using two names, *esp* of classification by genus and species.—**binomially** *adv*.

binomial theorem *n* the general algebraic formula, discovered by Newton, by which any power of a binomial quantity may be found with performing the progressive multiplication.

binturong /'bɪntu,rɒŋ/ or /'bɪntju:,rɒn/ *n* a prehensile-tailed civet of India.

binucleate /baɪ'nu:kli,eɪt/, **binucleated, binuclear** *adj* having two nuclei.

bio- /'baɪoʊ/ *prefix* life.

biochemistry /-'kemɪstri/ *n* the chemistry of living organisms.—**biochemical** *adj*.—**biochemist** *n*.

biodegradable /-dɪ'greɪdəbəl/ *adj* readily decomposed by bacterial action.

bioengineering /-,endʒɪ'nɪrɪŋ/ *n* the application of engineering principles in the biological and medical sciences.—**bioengineer** *n*.

biofeedback /-'fi:d,bæk/ *n* the practice of monitoring and recording involuntary mental and physiological processes (*eg* brainwaves) in order to attempt to bring them under conscious control.

biogenesis /,baɪoʊ'dʒenəsɪs/ *n* the theory that only living matter can produce living matter; the science of life development.—**biogenetic** *adj*.—**biogenetically** *adv*.

biography /baɪ'ɒgrəfi/ *n* (*pl* **biographies**) an account of a person's life written by another; biographical writings in general.—**biographer** *n*.—**biographical** *adj*.

biology /baɪ'ɒlədʒi/ *n* the study of living organisms.—**biological** *adj*.—**biologically** *adv*.—**biologist** *n*.

biometry /baɪ'ɒmətri/, **biometrics** *n* (used as sing) the statistics of biology or probable duration of life.—**biometric, biometrical** *adj*.—**biometrically** *adv*.—**biometrician** *n*.

bionics /baɪ'ɒnɪks/ *n* the study of electronically operated mechanical systems that function like living organisms.—**bionic** *adj*.

bionomics /,baɪoʊ'nɒmɪks/ *n* (*used as sing*) ecology.—**bionomic, bionomical** *adj*.—**bionomist** *n*.

biophysics /baɪoʊ'fɪzɪks/ *n* the application of physics to biology.—**biophysical** *adj*.—**biophysicist** *n*.

bioplasm /'baɪoʊ,plæzəm/ *n* living germinal matter, living protoplasm.—**bioplasmic** *adj*.

biopsy /'baɪ,ɒpsi/ *n* (*n* **biopsies**) the removal of parts of living tissue for medical diagnosis.

biorhythm /'baɪoʊ,rɪðəm/ *n* a cyclical pattern in physiological activity said to determine a person's intellectual, emotional and physical moods and behaviour.—**biorhythmic** *adj*.

biosphere /'baɪoʊ,sfɪːr/ *n* the regions of the earth's surface and atmosphere inhabited by living things.

biosynthesis /,baɪoʊ'sɪnθəsɪs/ *n* (*pl* **biosyntheses**) the formation of chemical compounds by living organisms.—**biosynthetic** *adj*.—**biosynthetically** *adv*.

biotechnology /,baɪoʊtek'nɒlədʒi/ *n* the commercial and industrial application of biological processes, such as the use of microorganisms to dye cloth.

biotic /baɪ'ɒtɪk/ *adj* of life or specific life conditions.

biotin /'baɪətɪn/ *n* a factor of the vitamin B group found in liver and egg yolk.

biparous /'bɪpərəs/ *adj* producing two at once in time or place; (*zool*) producing offspring in pairs; (*bot*) having two branches.

bipartisan /baɪ'partɪzən/ *adj* of, representing or supported by two political parties.—**bipartisanship** *n*.

bipartite /baɪ'par,taɪt/ *adj* having two parts; involving two.—**bipartition** *n*.

biped /'baɪ,ped/ *n* an animal having two feet.—*also adj*.—**bipedal** *adj*.

bipinnate /baɪ'pɪn,eɪt/ *adj* (*bot*) having lobes that are lobed themselves.—**bipinnately** *adv*.

biplane /'baɪ,pleɪn/ *n* an aeroplane with two sets of wings.

bipod /'baɪ,pɒd/ *n* a stand with two legs for supporting a weapon, etc.

bipolar /baɪ'poːlər/ *adj* having two poles or opposite extremities; of or affecting both the earth's poles; having or expressing two directly opposite ideas or qualities.—**bipolarity** *n*.

biquadratic /,baɪkwɒd'rætɪk/ *adj* (*math*) pertaining to the fourth power. • *n* the fourth power, arising from the multiplication of a square number or quantity by itself.

birch /bɜːtʃ/ *n* a tree with a smooth white bark and hard wood; a bundle of birch twigs used for thrashing. • *vt* to flog.—**birchen** *adj*.

bird /bɜːd/ *n* any class of warm-blooded, egg-laying vertebrates with a feathered body, scaly legs, and forelimbs modified to form wings; (*sl*) a woman; (*sl*) time in prison; **for the birds** useless, worthless, unimportant; **get** *or* **give the bird** (*inf*) to boo an entertainer off the stage.

birdbrain /'bɜːd,breɪn/ *n* (*inf*) a stupid or frivolous person.—**bird-brained** *adj*.

bird of passage *n* a migratory bird; a transient person.

bird of prey *n* a meat-eating bird (as a hawk, owl, falcon, etc) that hunts other animals for food.

birdie /'bɜːdi/ *n* (*inf*) a small bird; (*golf*) a score of one stroke under par for a hole.

birdlime /'bɜːd,laɪm/ *n* a viscous substance used for snaring small birds; a thing that snares. • *vt* to smear or trap with birdlime.

birdseed /'bɜːd,siːd/ *n* a mixture of seeds for feeding wild or caged birds.

bird's-eye /'bɜːdz,aɪ/ *adj* seen from above; dappled to resemble the eye of a bird. • *n* any of several plants with flowers resembling a bird's eye.

bird watcher *n* one who makes a study of birds in the wild.—**bird watching** *n*.

bireme /'baɪri:m/ *n* an ancient galley with two tiers of oars.

biretta /bɪ'retə/ *n* a square cap with three corners worn by Roman Catholic clergy.

Biro /'baɪroʊ/ *n* (*trademark*) (*pl* **Biros**) a ball-point pen.

birr /bɜːr/ *vi* to make a whirring sound, like that of a spinning wheel. • *n* a whirring sound.

birth /bɜːθ/ *n* the act of being born; childbirth; the origin of something; lineage, ancestry.

birth control *n* the use of contraceptive drugs or devices to limit reproduction.

birth rate /-reɪt/ *n* the number of births per thousand of population per year.

birthday /'bɜːθdeɪ/ *n* the day of birth; the anniversary of the day of birth.

birthmark /'bɜːθmark/ *n* a patch or blemish on the body dating from birth.

birthright /-raɪt/ *n* privileges or property that a person is believed entitled to by birth.

birthstone /-stoːn/ *n* a gem symbolizing the month of one's birth.

bis /bi:s/ or /bɪs/ *adv* twice; (*mus*) for a second time; encore.

biscuit /'bɪskət/ *n* a small, flat, dry, sweet or plain cake baked from dough.—*also* **cookie**. • *adj* pale brown in colour.

bise /biːz/ *n* a piercing dry northeast wind prevalent in Switzerland.

bisect /baɪ'sekt/ *vt* to split into two equal parts; (*geom*) to divide into two equal parts.—**bisection** *n*.

bisector /-ər/ *n* a line bisecting.

bisexual /baɪ'sekʃʊəl/ *adj* sexually attracted to both sexes; having the characteristics of both sexes. • *n* a person sexually attracted to both sexes.—**bisexualism, bisexuality** *n*.

bishop /'bɪʃəp/ *n* a high-ranking clergyman governing a diocese or church district; a chessman that can move in a diagonal direction.

bishopric /'bɪʃəprɪk/ *n* the office, dignity or jurisdiction of a bishop; a diocese.

bismuth /'bɪzməθ/ *n* one of the elements, a light reddish-coloured metal of brittle texture.—**bismuthal, bismuthic** *adj*.

bison /'baɪsən/ or /'baɪzən/ *n* (*pl* **bison**) a wild ox of Europe and America.—*also* **buffalo**.

bisque[1] /bɪsk/ *n* a thick cream soup made from shellfish.

bisque[2] *n* an unglazed white porcelain, used for statuettes, etc, biscuit porcelain.

bisque[3] *n* (*croquet, tennis, golf*) a stroke allowed to an inferior player or side.

bissextile /bɪs'sɛkstɪl/ or /-taɪl/, /təl/ *n* a leap year. • *adj* pertaining to a leap year.

bister /'bɪstər/ *see* **bistre**.

bistort /'bɪstɔrt/ *n* a herb with twisted roots, snakeweed.

bistoury /'bɪstu:ri/ *n* (*pl* **bistouries** /-i:z/) a surgeon's knife, a scalpel.

bistre /'bɪstər/ *n* a warm brown pigment made from wood soot. • *adj* of this colour.—*also* **bister**.

bistro /'bi:stro:/ or /'bɪs,tro:/ *n* (*pl* **bistros**) a small restaurant.

bisulcate /baɪ'sʌl,keɪt/ *adj* having two furrows or grooves; cloven-footed.

bisulphate, bisulfate /baɪ'sʌl,feɪt/ *n* a salt of sulphuric acid in which half of its hydrogen is replaced by a positive element.

bisulphite, bisulfite /baɪ'sʌl,faɪt/ *n* a salt of sulphurous acid, half the hydrogen of which is replaced by the base.

bit part *n* a small acting role in a play, film, etc.

bit[1] /bɪt/ *n* a small amount or piece; in US, a small coin worth one eighth of a dollar; a small part in a play, film, etc, a bit part.—**a bit** slightly, rather.

bit[2] *n* a metal mouthpiece in a bridle used for controlling a horse; a cutting or boring attachment for use in a brace, drill, etc. • *vt* (**bitting, bitted**) to put a bridle upon; to put the bit in the mouth of.

bit[3] *n* (*comput*) a unit of information in binary notation equivalent to either of two digits, 0 or 1.

bit[4] *see* **bite**.

bitch /bɪtʃ/ *n* a female dog or wolf; (*sl*) a spiteful woman; (*inf*) an unpleasant or difficult situation. • *vi* (*inf*) to grumble; to act spitefully; (*with* **up**) to make a mess of, to ruin.

bite /baɪt/ *vb* (**biting, bit**, *pp* **bitten**) *vt* to grip or tear with the teeth; to sting or puncture, as an insect; to cause to smart; to take the bait. • *vi* to press or snap the teeth (into, at, etc); (*with* **back**) to stop oneself from saying something offensive, embarrassing, etc. • *n* the act of biting with the teeth; a sting or puncture by an insect.

biting /'baɪtɪŋ/ *adj* severe; critical, sarcastic.—**bitingly** *adv*.—**bitingness** *n*.

bitt /bɪt/ *n* (*usu pl*) (*naut*) a post of wood or iron to which cables are made fast. • *vt* to put round the bitts.

bitter /'bɪtər/ *adj* having an acrid or sharp taste; sorrowful; harsh; resentful; cynical; (*weather*) extremely cold.—**bitterly** *adj*.—**bitterness** *n*.

bitter end *n* final extremity.

bittern[1] /'bɪtərn/ *n* a wading bird of the heron family, with a booming cry.

bittern[2] *n* the liquid that remains after cystallization of common salt from sea water or the brine of salt springs.

bitters /'bɪtərz/ *npl* liquor in which herbs or roots are steeped.

bittersweet /'bɪtər,swi:t/ *n* the woody nightshade, the roots and leaves of which when chewed produce first a bitter then a sweet taste; a variety of apple. • *adj* simultaneously sweet and bitter; pleasantly sad.

bitty /'bɪti/ *adj* (**bittier, bittiest**) small, tiny; made up of scraps of something.

bitumen /bɪ'tju:mən/ or /-tu:-/ *n* any of several substances obtained as residue in the distillation of coal tar, petroleum, etc, or occurring naturally as asphalt.—**bituminous** *adj*.

bituminize /bɪtju:mə,naɪz/ or /-tu:-/ *vt* to make into or mix with bitumen.—**bituminization** *n*.

bivalent /'baɪ,veɪlənt/ *adj* (*chem*) having a valency of two; (*genetics*) having two homologous chromosomes; (*logic*) having two truth values. • *n* an element, one of the atoms of which can replace two atoms of hydrogen; (*genetics*) a pair of homologous chromsomes.—**bivalency** *n*.

bivalve /'baɪ,vælv/ *n* any mollusc having two valves or shells hinged together, as a clam.—**bivalvular** *adj*.

bivouac /'bɪvə,wæk/ *n* a temporary camp, *esp* one without tents or other cover. • *vi* (**bivouacking, bivouacked**) to spend the night in a bivouac.

biweekly /baɪ'wi:kli/ *adj* every two weeks; twice a week. • *n* (*pl* **biweeklies**) a periodical published every two weeks.

bizarre /bɪ'zɑr/ *adj* odd, unusual.

Bk (*chem symbol*) berkelium.

blab /blæb/ *vti* (**blabbing, blabbed**) to reveal (a secret); to gossip. • *n* a gossip.—**blabber** *n*.

black /blæk/ *adj* of the darkest colour, like coal or soot; having dark-coloured skin and hair; without light; wicked; sad, dismal; sad sullen; angry; (*coffee, etc*) without milk. • *n* black colour; (*often with* **cap**) of the black-skinned population, *usu* of African origin; Australian Aborigine; black clothes, *esp* when worn in mourning; (*chess, draughts*) black pieces.—**in the black** without debts, in credit. • *vt* to make black; to blacken; (*shoes*) to polish with blacking; to boycott; (*with* **out**) (*lights*) to extinguish, obliterate; (*broadcast*) to prevent transmission. • *vi* (*with* **out**) to lose consciousness or vision.—**blackly** *adv*.—**blackness** *n*.

black-and-blue *adj* livid with bruises.

black and white *n* writing, print; a line drawing; a photograph not in colour. • *adj* black-and-white.

black-and-white *adj* (*film, photography*) in black and white, not colour; (*ideas, etc*) highly simplistic.

black art *n* black magic, witchcraft.

blackball /-,bɔl/ *vt* to ostracize.

black belt *n* a black belt awarded to an expert of the highest skill in judo or karate; a person who holds a black belt.

blackberry /'blæk,beri/ or /-bəri/ *n* (*pl* **blackberries**) a woody bush with thorny stems and berry-like fruit; its black or purple edible fruit (—*also* **bramble**). • *vt* to gather blackberries.

blackbird /-,bɜrd/ *n* any of various birds, the male of which is almost all black.

blackboard /-,bɔrd/ *n* a black or dark green board written on with chalk.

black book *n* a record of offenders; **in someone's black books** in disfavour; **little black book** (*sl*) an address book with names and telephone numbers of women.

black box *n* a flight recorder on an aircraft.

black bread *n* rye bread.

black bryony *n* a European climbing plant with small green flowers and poisonous red berries.

blackcap /'blæk,kæp/ *n* the popular name of several black-crested birds.

blackcock /-,kɒk/ *n* the male of the European black grouse or black game.

black comedy *n* a comedy with a tragic theme.

Black Death *n* the name given to the bubonic plague that ravaged Europe and Asia in the 14th century.

black duck *n* a wild duck of North America, mainly dark brown with a purple patch on its wings.

black economy *n* undeclared economic activity.

blacken /'blækən/ *vt* to make black; to defame.

black eye *n* (*inf*) discoloration around the eye caused by a blow; (*sl*) shame.

blackfish /-,fɪʃ/ *n* (*pl* **blackfish, blackfishes**) a female salmon immediately after spawning; a common name for several species of British and American fish.

black flag *n* the flag of a pirate with a skull and crossbones emblazoned upon it.

blackfly *n* (*pl* **blackflies**) any of various dark insects, *esp* a North American fly that sucks the blood of mammals.

black frost *n* a severe frost without a rime that damages vegetation.

blackguard /'blægərd/ or /-,ɑrd/ *n* a villain, scoundrel.—**blackguardism** *n*.—**blackguardly** *adj*.

blackhead /'blæk,hed/ *n* a small spot or pimple clogging a pore in the skin.

black hole /'blæk,ho:l/ *n* a hypothetical, invisible region in space.

black ice /'blæk,aɪs/ *n* a thin transparent coating of ice on roads or other surfaces.

blacking /'blækɪŋ/ *n* black shoe polish.

blackish /'blækɪʃ/ *adj* rather black.—**blackishly** *adv*.—**blackishness** *n*.

blackjack (oak) *n* a dark shrubby oak of North America.
blackjack[1] /'blæk,dʒæk/ *n* a gambling game with cards in which players try to obtain points better than the banker's but not more than 21.—*also* **pontoon, twenty-one, vingt-et-un.**
blackjack[2] *n* a large leather vessel or drinking cup; a short leather club with a flexible handle. • *vt* to hit with a blackjack.
black lead *n* plumbago, graphite.
blackleg /-,lɛg/ *n* a person who takes a striker's place, a scab; a person who endeavours to obtain money by cheating at races or cards, a rook; a disease affecting sheep and cattle. • *vti* (**black-legging, blacklegged**) to act or injure, as a blackleg.
black letter *n* the old English or Gothic type used in early manuscripts and the first printed books. • *adj* written or printed in black letter.
blacklist /-lɪst/ *n* a list of those censored, refused employment, regarded as suspicious politically or generally not to be trusted. • *vt* to put on such a list.
black magic *n* sorcery, witchcraft.
blackmail /'blæk,meɪl/ *vt* to extort money by threatening to disclose discreditable facts. • *n* the crime of blackmailing.—**blackmailer** *n*.
Black Maria *n* a prison van, a patrol wagon.
black market *n* the illegal buying and selling of goods, *esp* banned goods, *eg* drugs, or when rationing is in force.—**black marketeer, black marketer** *n*.
black mass *n* a travesty of the Mass used by Satanists.
blackout /'blæk,aʊt/ *n* the darkness when all lights are switched off; temporary loss of consciousness or electricity; a breakdown of communications between a spacecraft and ground control; a closing down of radio or TV broadcasting due to strike action or government ban.
black power *n* a movement of black people whose goal is political, social and economic equality with whites.
black pudding *n* a dark sausage with a large proportion of blood.
Black Rod *n* in UK, the usher belonging to the order of the Garter and the House of Lords, so called from the black rod of the office.
black sheep *n* a person regarded as disreputable or a disgrace by their family.
Blackshirt *n* a fascist, *esp* a member of Mussolini's Italian Fascist party.
blacksmith /'blæk,smɪθ/ *n* a metal worker, *esp* one who shoes horses.
black spot *n* an area where traffic accidents frequently happen; a difficult or dangerous place; a disease affecting leaves, *esp* of roses.
blackthorn /-,θɔrn/ *n* the sloe; a walking stick cut from the stem of the sloe.
black widow *n* a poisonous spider found in America, the female of which devours its mate.
bladder /blædər/ *n* a sac that fills with fluid, *esp* one that holds urine flowing from the kidneys; any inflatable bag.
bladderwort /-,wərt/ *n* any of a genus of water plants, some of which trap insects.
bladderwrack /-,ræk/ *n* a type of seaweed with trailing fronds containing small air bladders.
blade /bleɪd/ *n* the cutting edge of a tool or knife; the broad, flat surface of a leaf; a straight, narrow leaf of grass; the flat part of an oar or paddle; the runner of an ice skate.—**bladed** *adj*.
blah[1] /blɒ/ *n* (*sl*) nonsense, exaggeration; a blunder.
blah[2] *adj* (*sl*) boring; mediocre.
blain /bleɪn/ *n* an inflamed sore, a blister.
blame /bleɪm/ *vt* to hold responsible for; to accuse. • *n* responsibility for an error; reproof.—**blamable, blameable** *adj*.
blameful /'bleɪmfʊl/ *adj* meriting blame; guilty.—**blamefully** *adv*.—**blamefulness** *n*.
blameless /-ləs/ *adj* innocent; free from blame.—**blamelessly** *adv*.—**blamelessness** *n*.
blameworthy /-,wərði/ *adj* deserving blame.—**blameworthiness** *n*.
blanch /'blæntʃ/ *vt* to whiten or bleach; to make pale; (*vegetables, almonds, etc*) to scald. • *vi* to turn pale.
blancmange /blə'mɒndʒ/ *n* a dessert made from gelatinous or starchy ingredients (as cornflour) and milk.
bland /blænd/ *adj* mild; gentle; insipid.—**blandly** *adv*.—**blandness** *n*.

blandish /'blændɪʃ/ *vti* to flatter in order to coax; to cajole.
blandishment /-mənt/ *n* (*usu pl*) a winning expression or action, an artful caress, cajolery.
blank (cartridge) *n* a powder-filled cartridge without a bullet.
blank /blæŋk/ *adj* (*paper*) bearing no writing or marks; vacant; (*mind*) empty of thought; (*look*) without expression; (*denial, refusal*) utter, complete; (*cheque*) signed but with no amount written in. • *n* an empty space, *esp* one to be filled out on a printed form; an empty place or time.—**blankly** *adv*.—**blankness** *n*.
blank cheque, blank check *n* a signed cheque with the amount left blank to be filled by the payee; complete freedom of action.
blank verse *n* unrhymed verse.
blanket /'blæŋkət/ *n* a large, soft piece of cloth used for warmth, *esp* as a bed cover; (*of snow, smoke*) a cover or layer. • *adj* applying to a wide variety of cases or situations. • *vt* to cover.
blare /blɛr/ *vti* to sound harshly or loudly. • *n* a loud, harsh sound.
blarney /'blɑrni/ *n* wheedling talk, flattery. • *vt* (**blarneying, blarneyed**) to influence or talk over by soft wheedling speeches; to humbug with flattery.
Blarney Stone *n* a stone in the wall of Blarney Castle, Cork, on kissing which a person is said to become an adept in flattery.
blasé /blɒ'zeɪ/ or /'blɒzeɪ/ *adj* bored, indifferent; sated with pleasure.
blaspheme /blæs'fiːm/ or /'blæsfiːm/ *vt* to speak irreverently of (God, a divine being or sacred things). • *vi* to utter blasphemy.—**blasphemer** *n*.
blasphemous /'blæsfəməs/ *adj* impious, grossly insulting (to God, etc).
blasphemy /'blæsfəmi/ *n* (*pl* **blasphemies**) impious speaking; speaking irreverently of God, a divine being or sacred things.
blast /blæst/ *n* a sharp gust of air; the sound of a horn; an explosion; an outburst of criticism. • *vt* to wither; to blow up, explode; to criticize sharply. • *vi* to make a loud, harsh sound; to set off explosives, etc; (*with* **off**) to be launched.
blasted /'blæstəd/ *adj* withered; (*inf*) damned.
blastema /blæs'tiːmə/ *n* (*pl* **blastemas, blastemata**) (*biol*) the point of growth of an organ as yet unformed, from which it is developed.—**blastemal, blastemic, blastematic** *adj*.
blast furnace *n* a smelting furnace using compressed air.
blasto- /'blæstə/ or /-tə/ *prefix* bud; germination.
blastoderm /-,dərm/ *n* a layer of embryonic cells in an egg from which an organism is formed.—**blastodermic** *adj*.
blastoff /'blæst,ɒf/ *n* the launch of a space vehicle or rocket; the time when this takes place.
blastogenesis /,blæstə'dʒenəsɪs/ *n* reproduction by budding.—**blastogenic, blastogenetic** *adj*.
blatant /'bleɪtənt/ *adj* noisy; glaringly conspicuous.—**blatancy** *n*.—**blatantly** *adv*.
blather /'blæðər/ *see* **blether**.
blatherskite /-,skaɪt/ *n* a blethering or blustering person.
blaze[1] /bleɪz/ *n* an intensive fire; a bright light; splendour; an outburst (of emotion). • *vi* to burn brightly; to shine with a brilliant light; to be excited, as with anger.
blaze[2] *n* a white mark on the face of a horse or other quadruped; a white mark cut on a tree to serve as a guide. • *vt* to mark, as trees, by removing a portion of the bark; to indicate, as a path or boundary, by blazing trees; **blaze a trail** to act as a pioneer.
blaze[3] *vt* to proclaim, to publish widely.
blazer /'bleɪzər/ *n* a lightweight jacket, often in a bright colour representing membership of a sports club, school, etc.
blazon /'bleɪzən/ *vt* to proclaim publicly; to adorn; to describe (heraldic or armorial bearings) in technical terms. • *n* the terminology of coats of arms.—**blazoner** *n*.—**blazonment** *n*.
blazonry /-ri/ *n* (*pl* **blazonries**) a heraldic device; the art of describing and explaining coats of arms; decoration, as with heraldic devices; a bright display.
bldg. *abbr* = building.
bleach /bliːtʃ/ *vti* to make or become white or colourless. • *n* a substance for bleaching.—**bleachable** *adj*.—**bleacher** *n*.
bleachers /-ərz/ *npl* the unroofed seats at a baseball field or sports ground.
bleaching powder *n* a white powder, chloride of lime, used for bleaching.
bleak[1] /bliːk/ *adj* cold; exposed; bare; harsh; gloomy; not hopeful.—**bleakly** *adv*.—**bleakness** *n*.
bleak[2] *n* (*pl* **bleak, bleaks**) a small European river fish with brilliant silvery scales.

blear /blɪr/ *adj* (*eyes*) sore or dim with inflammation. • *vt* to make (eyes) sore or watery; to dim or blur.

bleary /'blɪːri/ *adj* (**blearier, bleariest**) (*eyesight*) dim with water or tears; obscure, indistinct.—**blearily** *adv.*—**bleariness** *n.*

bleary-eyed /-,aɪd/ *adj* with eyes dulled by tears or tiredness; dull.

bleat /bliːt/ *vi* to cry as a sheep, goat or calf; to complain. • *n* a bleating cry or sound.—**bleater** *n.*—**bleatingly** *adv.*

bleb /blɛb/ *n* a small blister; a bubble in water or glass.

bleed /bliːd/ *vb* (**bleeding, bled**) *vi* to lose blood; to ooze sap, colour or dye; to die for a country or an ideal; to sympathize (often ironically). • *vt* to remove blood or sap from; (*inf*) to extort money or goods from.

bleeder /'bliːdər/ *n* one who bleeds, *esp* blood from another; (*inf*) a person with haemophilia; (*sl*) an annoying person.

bleep /bliːp/ *vi* to emit a high-pitched sound or signal (*eg* a car alarm). • *n* a small portable electronic radio receiver that emits a bleep to convey a message.—*also* **bleeper**.

blemish /'blɛmɪʃ/ *n* a flaw or defect, as a spot. • *vt* to mar; to spoil.

blench /blɛntʃ/ *vi* to flinch; to blanch.

blend /blɛnd/ *vt* (*varieties of tea, etc*) to mix or mingle; to mix so that the components cannot be distinguished. • *vi* to mix, merge; to shade gradually into each other, as colours; to harmonize. • *n* a mixture.

blende /blɛnd/ *n* any of various minerals composed mainly of metallic sulphides; a yellow to brownish-black zinc ore, sphalerite.

blender /'blɛndər/ *n* something or someone that blends; an electrical device for preparing food.—*also* **liquidizer**.

blenny /'blɛni/ *n* (*pl* **blennies, blenny**) a small elongated spiny-finned sea fish.

blepharitis /,blɛfə'raɪtɪs/ *n* inflammation of the eyelids.—**blepharitic** *adj.*

blesbok /'blɛs,bɒk/ *n* (*pl* **blesboks, blesbok**) a South African white-faced antelope.

bless /blɛs/ *vt* (**blessing, blessed** *or* **blest**) to consecrate; to praise; to call upon God's protection; to grant happiness; to make the sign of the cross over.

blessed /'blɛsəd/ *or* /blɛst/ *adj* holy, sacred; fortunate; blissful; beatified.—**blessedly** *adv.*—**blessedness** *n.*

blessing /'blɛsɪŋ/ *n* a prayer or wish for success or happiness; a cause of happiness; good wishes or approval; a grace said before or after eating.

blest /blɛst/ *see* **bless**.

blet /blɛt/ *n* a decayed spot in fruit.

blether /'blɛðər/ *vi* (*inf*) to talk foolishly. • *n* (*inf*) foolish talk; one who talks it.—*also* **blather**.

blew /bluː/ *see* **blow²**.

blight /blaɪt/ *n* any insect, disease, etc that destroys plants; anything that prevents growth or destroys; somone or something that spoils. • *vt* to destroy; to frustrate.

blimp /blɪmp/ *n* a small, nonrigid airship; any airship; a soundproof cover for a camera.

blind /blaɪnd/ *adj* sightless; unable to discern or understand; not directed by reason; (*exit*) hidden, concealed; closed at one end. • *n* something that deceives; a shade for a window; (*sl*) a drinking bout. • *vti* to make sightless, to deprive of insight; to dazzle (with facts, a bright light, etc); to deceive.—**blindly** *adv.*—**blindness** *n.*

blind alley *n* a street closed at one end; an occupation or inquiry that leads to nothing.

blind date *n* a date between two individuals who have never met before; either individual on a blind date.

blinder /-ər/ *n* a horse's blinkers.

blindfish /-,fɪʃ/ *n* (*pl* **blindfish, blindfishes**) a diminutive fish of a pale colour and with rudimentary eyes, which inhabits underground waters.

blindfold /-,foːld/ *n* a cloth or bandage used to cover the eyes. • *adj* having the eyes covered, so as not to see; reckless. • *vt* to cover the eyes with a strip of cloth, etc; to hamper sight or understanding; to mislead.

blind man's buff *n* a game in which a blindfold person tries to catch and identify others.

blind spot *n* a point on the retina of the eye that is insensitive to light; a place where vision is obscured; a subject on which someone is ignorant.

blindstorey, blindstory /'blaɪnd,stɔri/ *n* (*pl* **blindstoreys, blindstories**) (*archit*) the storey below the clerestory, admitting no light.

blindworm /-,wɜrm/ *n* the slowworm, a small, slender limbless lizard with very small eyes.

blini, blinis /'blɪni/ *npl* (*sing* **blin**) buckwheat pancakes.

blink /blɪŋk/ *vi* to open and close the eyes rapidly; (*light*) to flash on and off; (*with* **at**) to ignore. • *vt* (*with* **at**) to be amazed or surprised. • *n* a glance, a glimpse; a momentary flash.

blinker /-ər/ *n* one who blinks; that which obscures the sight or mental perception; (*pl*) a screen for a horse's eye, to prevent it from seeing sideways; (*sl*) the eyes.

blip /blɪp/ *n* a trace on a radar screen; a recurring sound; a temporary setback. • *vi* (**blipping, blipped**) to make a blip.

bliss /blɪs/ *n* supreme happiness; spiritual joy.—**blissful** *adj.*—**blissfully** *adv.*

blister /'blɪstər/ *n* a raised patch on the skin, containing water, as caused by burning or rubbing; a raised bubble on any other surface. • *vti* to cause or form blisters; to lash with words.

blistering /'blɪstərɪŋ/ *adj* (*criticism*) scornful, cruel.

BLit, BLitt *abbr* = Bachelor of Literature.

blithe /blaɪθ/ *or* /'blaɪð/ *adj* happy, cheerful, gay.—**blithely** *adv.*—**blitheness** *n.*

blithering /'blɪðərɪŋ/ *adj* (*inf*) stupid, idiotic.

blithesome /'blaɪðsəm/ *or* /'blaɪθ-/ *adj* blithe, merry.—**blithesomely** *adv.*—**blithesomeness** *n.*

blitz /blɪts/ *n* heavy aerial bombing; any sudden destructive attack; a determined effort. • *vt* to subject to a blitz.

blitzkrieg /'blɪts,kriːg/ *n* warfare in which blitz is employed; any swift combined action.

blizzard /'blɪzərd/ *n* a severe storm of wind and snow.

bloat /bloːt/ *vti* to swell as with water or air; to puff up, as with pride; to cure or dry (fish) in smoke.—**bloated** *adj.*

bloater /'bloːtər/ *n* a herring or mackerel smoked and partially dried, but not split open.

blob /blɒb/ *n* a drop of liquid; a round spot (of colour, etc).

bloc /blɒk/ *n* a group of parties, nations, etc united to achieve a common purpose.

block /blɒk/ *n* a solid piece of stone or wood, etc; a piece of wood used as a base (for chopping, etc); a group or row of buildings; a number of things as a unit; the main body of a petrol engine; a building divided into offices; an obstruction; a child's building brick; (*sl*) the head. • *vt* to impede or obstruct; to shape; (*often with* **out**) to sketch roughly. • *vi* to obstruct an opponent in sports.—**blocker** *n.*

blockade /blɒ'keɪd/ *n* (*mil*) the obstruction of an enemy seaport by warships; any strategic barrier. • *vt* to obstruct in this way.—**blockader** *n.*

blockage /'blɒkɪdʒ/ *n* an obstruction.

blockbuster /'blɒk,bʌstər/ *n* (*sl*) a very heavy bomb of great penetrative power; a conspicuously powerful or effective person or thing; one who engages in blockbusting.

blockbusting /-,bʌstɪŋ/ *n* the practice of persuading house owners to sell their houses quickly by convincing them that property values will drop.

blockhead /'blɒk,hɛd/ *n* a dolt, a stupid person.

blockhouse /'blɒk,haʊs/ *n* a small fort, *usu* of timber; a log house; a concrete fortification with loopholes for observation or firing from.

block letter *n* a handwritten capital letter similar to a printed letter.

block vote *n* at a conference, a total vote represented by one delegate.

bloke /bloːk/ *n* (*inf*) a man.

blond, blonde /blɒnd/ *adj* having light-coloured hair and skin; light-coloured. • *n* a blond person.—**blondness, blondeness** *n.*

blonde lace *n* a silk lace.

blood /blʌd/ *n* the red fluid that circulates in the arteries and veins of animals; the sap of a plant; the essence of life; kinship; descent; hatred; anger; bloodshed; guilt of murder.

blood-and-thunder *adj* melodramatic. • *n* a sensational story or play.

blood bank *n* a place where blood is taken from blood donors and stored.

blood bath *n* a massacre.

blood brother *n* one of two men or boys pledged to treat the other as a brother, as confirmed by the ceremonial mingling of blood.

blood cell *n* a red or white cell present in the blood.

blood count *n* the determination of the numbers of red and white corpuscles in a sample of blood.

bloodcurdling /ˈblʌdˌkərdlɪŋ/ *adj* exciting terror, horrifying, chilling.

blood donor *n* a person who donates his or her blood for transfusion.

blooded /ˈblʌdɪd/ *adj* having a specific kind of blood (*hot-blooded*); of fine breed; initiated.

blood group *n* any of the classes of human blood.—*also* **blood type**.

blood heat *n* the normal heat of the human blood in health (37°C, 98.4°F).

bloodhound /ˈblʌdˌhaʊnd/ *n* a large breed of hound used for tracking; a detective.

bloodless /ˈblʌdlɪs/ *adj* without blood or slaughter; unfeeling.—**bloodlessly** *adv*.—**bloodlessness** *n*.

bloodletting /ˈblʌdˌletɪŋ/ *n* phlebotomy; bloodshed, *eg* a massacre.

blood money *n* money obtained at the cost of another's life; the reward paid for the discovery or capture of a murderer; compensation paid to the next of kin of a person slain by another.

blood poisoning *n* septicaemia.

blood pressure *n* the pressure of the blood in the arterial system.

blood pudding *n* blood sausage.

blood-red /blʌdˈred/ *adj* red as blood.

blood relation, blood relative *n* a person related by descent, not marriage.

bloodroot /ˈblʌdruːt/ *n* a woodland plant of eastern North America with white flowers and a red root.

blood sausage *n* a dark sausage with a large proportion of blood.

bloodshed /ˈblʌdʃed/ *n* killing.

bloodshot /ˈblʌdˌʃɒt/ *adj* (*eye*) suffused with blood, red and inflamed.

blood sport *n* any sport in which an animal is hunted and killed.

bloodstain /ˈblʌdˌsteɪn/ *n* a stain made by blood.

bloodstained /ˈblʌdˌsteɪnd/ *adj* stained with blood; responsible for killing.

bloodstock /ˈblʌd ˌstɒk/ *n* thoroughbred horses collectively.

bloodstone /ˈblʌdˌstoːn/ *n* a dark green quartz flecked with red jasper; heliotrope.

bloodstream /ˈblʌdˌstriːm/ *n* the flow of blood through the blood vessels in the human body.

bloodsucker /ˈblʌdˌsʌkər/ *n* an animal that sucks blood, a leech; a person who sponges or preys on another, an extortionist.—**bloodsucking** *adj, n*.

blood test *n* an examination of a blood specimen to ascertain blood group, alcohol intake, etc.

bloodthirsty /ˈblʌdˌθɜːsti/ *adj* (**bloodthirstier, bloodthirstiest**) eager for blood, cruel, warlike.—**bloodthirstiness** *n*.

blood type *see* **blood group**.

blood vessel *n* in the body, a vein, artery, or capillary.

bloody /ˈblʌdi/ *adj* (**bloodier, bloodiest**) stained with or covered in blood; bloodthirsty; cruel, murderous; (*sl*) as an intensifier (*a bloody good hiding*). • *vt* (**bloodying, bloodied**) to cover with blood.—**bloodily** *adv*.—**bloodiness** *n*.

Bloody Mary *n* (*pl* **Bloody Marys**) a drink made with vodka and tomato juice.

bloody-minded /ˈblʌdˌmaɪndəd/ *adj* (*inf*) deliberately obstructive.—**bloody-mindedness** *n*.

bloom[1] /bluːm/ *n* a flower or blossom; the period of being in flower; a period of most health, vigour, etc; a youthful, healthy glow; the powdery coating on some fruit and leaves. • *vi* to blossom; to be in one's prime; to glow with health etc.

bloom[2] *n* a rough mass of incandescent iron for hammering or rolling into bars. • *vt* to make (iron) into bloom.

bloomer /ˈbluːmər/, **blooper** /ˈbluːpər/ *n* (*inf*) a stupid mistake.

bloomers /ˈbluːmərz/ *npl* (*inf*) baggy knickers.

blooming /ˈbluːmɪŋ/ *adj* blossoming, flowering; flourishing; (*sl*) confounded, bloody.—**bloomingly** *adv*.

blossom /ˈblɒsəm/ *n* a flower, *esp* one that produces edible fruit; a state or time of flowering. • *vi* to flower; to begin to develop.—**blossomy** *adj*.

blot /blɒt/ *n* a spot or stain, *esp* of ink; something that diminishes or spoils the beauty of; a blemish in reputation. • *vt* (**blotting, blotted**) to spot or stain; to obscure; to disgrace; to absorb with blotting paper.

blotch /blɒtʃ/ *n* a spot or discoloration on the skin; any large blot or stain. • *vt* to cover with blotches.—**blotched** *adj*.—**blotchily** *adv*.—**blotchy** *adj*.

blotter /ˈblɒtər/ *n* a piece of blotting paper.

blotting paper *n* absorbent paper used to dry freshly written ink.

blotto /ˈblɒtoː/ *adj* (*sl*) very drunk.

blouse /blaʊz/ *or* /blaʊs/ *n* a shirt-like garment worn by women.

blow[1] /bloː/ *n* a hard hit, as with the fist; a sudden attack; a sudden misfortune; a setback.

blow[2] *vb* (**blowing, blew**, *pp* **blown**) *vi* to cause a current of air; to be moved or carried (by air, the wind, etc); (*mus*) to make a sound by forcing in air with the mouth; (*often with* **out**) to burst suddenly; to breathe hard; (*with* **out**) to become extinguished by a gust of air; (*gas or oil well*) to erupt out of control; (*with* **over**) to pass without consequence. • *vt* to move along with a current of air; to make a sound by blowing; to inflate with air; (*a fuse, etc*) to melt; (*inf*) to spend (money) freely; (*sl*) to leave; (*sl*) to divulge a secret; (*sl*) to bungle; (*often with* **up**) to burst by an explosion; (*with* **out**) to extinguish by a gust; (*storm*) to dissipate (itself) by blowing; (*with* **over**) to pass over or pass by; (*with* **up**) to enlarge a photograph; (*with* **up**) (*inf*) to lose one's temper.

blow[3] *vi* (**blowing, blew**, *pp* **blown**) to blossom, to flower. • *n* a mass of blossom; the state or condition of flowering.

blow-by-blow /ˈbloːbaɪˈbloː/ *adj* told or shown in great detail.

blow-dry /ˈbloːˌdraɪ/ *vi* (**blow-drying, blow-dried**) to style recently washed hair with a hand-held drier.

blower /ˈbloːər/ *n* one who blows; a braggart; a device for producing a stream of gas or air.

blowfly /ˈbloːˌflaɪ/ *n* (*pl* **blowflies**) a fly that lays its eggs in rotting meat.

blowhole /ˈbloːˌhoːl/ *n* a nostril of a whale; a vent for the escape of gas, air, etc; a hole in ice used for breathing by whales, seals, etc; a hole of gas in metal capturing during the solidifying process.

blowlamp /ˈbloːlæmp/, **blowtorch** /-ˌtɔːtʃ/ *n* a gas-powered torch that produces a hot flame for welding, etc.

blown /bloːn/ *adj* swollen or bloated.

blowout /ˈbloːˌaʊt/ *n* (*inf*) a festive social event; a bursting of a container (as a tyre) by pressure on a weak spot; an uncontrolled eruption of a gas or oil well.

blowpipe /ˈbloːˌpaɪp/ *n* a tube through which a current of air or gas is driven upon a flame to concentrate its heat on a substance, *eg* glass, to fuse it; a long tube of cane or reed used to discharge arrows by the force of the breath.

blowup /ˈbloːˌʌp/ *n* an explosion; an enlarged photograph; (*sl*) an angry outburst.

blowy /ˈbloːi/ *adj* (**blowier, blowiest**) breezy, windy.

blowzy, blowsy /ˈbloːzi/ *adj* (**blowzier, blowziest** *or* **blowsier, blowsiest**) (*esp a woman*) fat and ruddy, slatternly.—**blowzily, blowsily** *adv*.—**blowziness, blowsiness** *n*.

blubber[1] /ˈblʌbər/ *vi* to weep loudly.

blubber[2] *n* whale fat; excessive fat on the body.

bludgeon /ˈblʌdʒən/ *n* a short, heavy stick used for striking. • *vti* to strike with a bludgeon; to bully or coerce.

blue /bluː/ *adj* (**bluer, bluest**) of the colour of the clear sky; depressed; (*film*) indecent, obscene. • *n* the colour of the spectrum lying between green and violet; (*with* **the**) the sky, the sea; (*pl: with* **the**) (*inf*) a depressed feeling; (*pl: with* **the**) a style of vocal and instrumental jazz; a representative in a sport of a university, *esp* Oxford or Cambridge; the badge worn or honour bestowed; in UK, a member or adherent of the Tory party. • *vt* (**blueing** *or* **bluing, blued**) to make or dye blue; to dip in blue liquid; (*sl*) to squander.

blue baby *n* one born with a heart condition causing a blueness of the skin.

bluebell /ˈbluːˌbel/ *n* any of several plants with a one-sided cluster of blue bell-shaped flowers.

bluebird /ˈbluːˌbərd/ *n* any of various small songbirds prevalent in North America.

blue blood *n* royal or aristocratic descent.

bluebonnet /ˈbluːˌbɒnɪt/ *n* a Scottish cap of blue cloth; a name given to the Scottish troops before the Union, 1707; a Scotsman.

bluebook *n* a governmental official report, etc, bound in blue paper covers; a directory of socially prominent persons; a booklet in which students answer examination questions.

bluebottle /ˈbluːˌbɒtəl/ *n* a large fly; (*inf*) a policeman.

blue cheese *n* cheese with veins of blue mould.

blue chip *adj* (*stocks, shares*) providing a reliable return.

blue-collar /ˌbluːˈkɒlər/ *adj* of or pertaining to manual workers.

blue devils *npl* low spirits; mental depression; delirium tremens.

bluegrass /ˈbluːˌɡræs/ *n* any of several rich pasture grasses with bluish green blades, *esp* in Kentucky; improvisatory country music played on unamplified instruments.

blue gum *n* a lofty eucalyptus tree of Australia, valuable for its timber and essential oil.

blueing /ˈbluːɪŋ/ *n* the process of imparting a blue tint; the indigo, etc, used by washerwomen.—*also* **bluing**.

bluejacket /ˈbluːˌdʒækət/ *n* a seaman in the British or US navy.

blue jay *n* a crested jay of eastern and central North America with a large tail and blue, black and white plumage.

blue mould *n* a minute fungus that attacks bread and other foodstuffs.

bluenose /ˈbluːnoːz/ *n* (*US sl*) a puritanical person.

blue peter *n* a small blue flag with a white square in the centre, hoisted when a ship is about to sail.

blueprint /ˈbluːˌprɪnt/ *n* a blue photographic print of plans; a detailed scheme, template of work to be done; basis or prototype for future development.

blue ribbon *n* in UK, the broad ribbon of a dark blue colour worn by members of the order of the Garter; a prized distinction; a mark of success; a thin blue strip worn as a badge of teetotalism.

blue rinse *n* a rinse giving a blue tint to grey hair.

blue-rinse *adj* (*inf*) describing mature, assured, social women and their background.

blues /bluːz/ *npl* (*used as sing or pl*) depression, melancholy; a type of melancholy folk music originating among Black Americans.

bluestocking /-ˌstɒkɪŋ/ *n* a woman of literary tastes or occupation.

bluestone /-ˌstoːn/ *n* a grey sandstone used for building, etc; copper sulphate in crystalline form.

blue whale *n* a rorqual, the largest mammal known.

bluey /ˈbluːiː/ *n* (*Austral*) a bushman's bundle.

bluff[1] /blʌf/ *adj* rough in manner; abrupt, outspoken; ascending steeply with a flat front. • *n* a broad, steep bank or cliff.—**bluffness** *n*.

bluff[2] *vti* to mislead or frighten by a false, bold front.• *n* deliberate deception.—**bluffer** *n*.

bluff[3] *n* a steep cliff or bank.

bluing /ˈbluːɪŋ/ *see* **blueing**.

blunder /ˈblʌndər/ *vi* to make a foolish mistake; to move about clumsily. • *n* a foolish mistake.—**blunderer** *n*.—**blundering** *adj*.—**blunderingly** *adv*.

blunderbuss /-ˌbʌs/ *n* (*hist*) a short gun or firearm with a wide bore, firing many balls; a clumsy person.

blunge /blʌndʒ/ *vt* (*pottery*) to mix clay with water.

blunt /blʌnt/ *adj* not having a sharp edge or point; rude, outspoken, unsubtle. • *vti* to make or become dull.—**bluntly** *adv*.—**bluntness** *n*.

blur /blɜːr/ *n* a stain, smear; an ill-defined impression. • *vti* (**blurring, blurred**) to smear; to make or become indistinct in shape, etc; to dim.—**blurred** *adj*.—**blurredly** *adv*.—**blurry** *adj*.

blurb /blɜːrb/ *n* a promotional description, as on a book cover; an exaggerated advertisement.

blurt /blɜːrt/ *vt* (*with* **out**) to utter impulsively.

blush /blʌʃ/ *n* a red flush of the face caused by embarrassment or guilt; any rosy colour. • *vi* (*with* **for, at**) to show embarrassment, modesty, joy, etc involuntarily, by blushing; to become rosy.

blusher /ˈblʌʃər/ *n* a cosmetic that gives colour to the cheeks.

blush wine *n* rose wine, a blend of red and white wines.

bluster /ˈblʌstər/ *vi* to make a noise like the wind; to bully. • *n* a blast, as of the wind; bullying or boastful talk, often to hide shame or embarrassment.—**blusterer** *n*.—**blustery** *adj*.—**blusteringly, blusterously** *adv*.

Blvd *abbr* = Boulevard.

B-movie *n* (*cinema*) a film made as a supporting feature, *esp* in the 1940s and 1950s.

BMus *abbr* = Bachelor of Music.

bn *abbr* = battalion; billion.

BNA *abbr* = (*hist*) British North America.

BO *abbr* = (*inf*) body odour.

boa /ˈboːə/ *n* any of various large South American snakes that crush their prey; a long fluffy scarf of feathers.

boa constrictor *n* the largest boa, remarkable for its length and power of destroying its prey by constriction.

boar /bɔːr/ *n* a male pig, a wild hog.

board[1] /bɔːrd/ *n* meals, *esp* when provided regularly for pay; a long, flat piece of sawed wood, etc; a flat piece of wood, etc for some special purpose; pasteboard; a council; a group of people who supervise a company; the side of a ship (*overboard*). • *vt* to provide with meals and lodging at fixed terms; to come onto the deck of (a ship); to get on (a train, bus, etc). • *vi* to provide with meals, or room and meals, regularly for pay; (*with* **up**) to cover with boards; **to take on board** to appoint to a position; to adopt new ideas.

boarder /ˈbɔːrdər/ *n* one who is provided with board.

board game *n* a game as chess, chequers, etc, played by moving pieces on a marked board.

boarding /ˈbɔːrdɪŋ/ *n* light timber collectively; a covering of planks; the act of supplying, or state of being supplied with, food and lodging for a stipulated sum; the act of entering a ship or aircraft.

boarding house *n* a house for paying guests.

boarding school *n* a school where some or all of the pupils are boarded.

boardroom /ˈbɔːrdˌruːm/ *n* a room where meetings of a company's board are held.

board rule *n* a figured scale for finding the number of square feet in a board without calculation.

boardwalk /ˈbɔːrdˌwɔːk/ *n* mainly in the US, a footway of boards, *esp* by the sea.

boarish /ˈbɔːrɪʃ/ *adj* coarse; brutal; cruel.

boart *see* **bort**.

boast[1] /boːst/ *vi* to brag. • *vt* to speak proudly of; to possess with pride. • *n* boastful talk.—**boaster** *n*.—**boastingly** *adv*.

boast[2] *vt* to dress stone with a broad chisel and mallet; to dress a block in outline for a statue, etc, prior to more detailed or delicate work.

boastful /ˈboːstfʊl/ *adj* given to boasting.—**boastfully** *adv*.—**boastfulness** *n*.

boat /boːt/ *n* a small, open, waterborne craft; (*inf*) a ship. • *vi* to travel in a boat, *esp* for pleasure.

boatbill(ed heron) /-ˌbɪldˈherən/ *n* a South American wading bird with a boat-shaped bill.

boater /-ər/ *n* a stiff flat straw hat.

boathook /-ˌhʊk/ *n* a hooked pole for drawing a boat to land, fending off, etc.

boathouse /-ˌhaʊs/ *n* a shed for boats.

boating /-ɪŋ/ *n* rowing, sailing, etc, for pleasure.

boatman /-mən/ *n* (*pl* **boatmen**) a person who works on, deals in, or operates boats.

boat people *npl* refugees fleeing by boat.

boatswain /ˈboːsən/ *n* a ship's officer in charge of hull maintenance and related work.—*also* **bosun**.

boat train *n* a train for steamer or ferry passengers.

bob /bɒb/ *vb* (**bobbing, bobbed**) *vi* to move abruptly up and down, often in water; to nod the head; to curtsey. • *vt* (*hair*) to cut short. • *n* a jerking motion up and down; the weight on a pendulum, plumb line, etc; a woman's or girl's short haircut.

bobbery *n* (*pl* **bobberies**) a rumpus, a row, a noisy disturbance; a pack of hunting dogs.

bobbin /ˈbɒbɪn/ *n* a reel or spool on which yarn or thread is wound.

bobbinet /ˈbɒbɪˌnet/ *n* a machine-made cotton netting or lace in imitation of pillow lace.

bobble /ˈbɒbəl/ *n* a small woolly ball used for ornament or trimming; a bobbing movement; (*inf*) a mistake; a fumble. *vti* to bob up and down; to make a mistake; to fumble with (a ball).

bobby /ˈbɒbi/ *n* (*pl* **bobbies**) (*sl*) a policeman.

bobby pin *n* (*US*) a clip for holding hair in position; (*Brit*) a hairgrip, kirby grip.

bobcat /ˈbɒbˌkæt/ *n* (*pl* **bobcats, bobcat**) a medium-sized feline of eastern North America with a black-spotted reddish-brown coat and a short tail.

bobolink /ˈbɒbəˌlɪŋk/ *n* an American migratory songbird.—*also* **reedbird, ricebird**.

bobsleigh /ˈbɒbˌsleɪ/ *n* a long racing sledge for two or more people. • *vi* to ride or race on a bobsleigh.

bobstay /'bɒb,steɪ/ n (naut) a rope holding the bowsprit down to the stem.

bobtail /'bɒb,teɪl/ n a short tail or a tail cut short; an animal with a docked tail; the rabble (rag-tag and bobtail). • adj with a docked tail.—**bobtailed** adj.

Boche /bɒʃ/ n (pl **Boche**) (sl) a German, esp a soldier.

bock /bɒk/ n a variety of lager beer of double strength; a glass of beer.

bode /bo:d/ vt to be an omen of.

bodega /bo:'deɪgə/ n a shop selling wine and sometimes groceries, esp in a Spanish-speaking country.

bodice /'bɒdɪs/ n the upper part of a woman's dress.

bodiless /'bɒdi:ləs/ adj without a body, incorporeal.—**bodilessness** n.

bodily /'bɒdɪli/ adj physical; relating to the body. • adv in the flesh; as a whole; altogether.

bodkin /'bɒdkɪn/ n a large blunt needle, a tool for piercing holes; a pin for fastening hair; a small dagger.

body /'bɒdi/ n (pl **bodies**) the whole physical substance of a person, animal, or plant; the trunk of a person or animal; a corpse; the principal part of anything; a distinct mass; substance or consistency, as of liquid; a richness of flavour; a person; a distinct group of people. • vt (**bodying, bodied**) to give shape to.

body bag n a large plastic sack, usu zipped, to carry a corpse from the scene of a disaster.

bodybuilding /-,bɪldɪŋ/ n strengthening and enlarging the muscles through exercise and diet for competitive display.— **bodybuilder** n.

bodyguard /-,gɑrd/ n a person or persons assigned to guard someone.

body language n gestures, unconscious bodily movements, etc, that function as a means of communication.

body politic n the collective body of people living under an organized political government.

body-snatcher n (formerly) one who stole corpses from graves for dissection by anatomists.

body stocking n a woman's tight-fitting garment that covers the torso and sometimes the legs.

body warmer n a sleeveless, quilted outer garment.

bodywork /'bɒdi,wɜrk/ n the outer shell of a motor vehicle.

Boeotian /bi'o:ʃən/ adj pertaining to Boeotia in central Greece, noted for its moist and heavy atmosphere; dull, stupid. • n an inhabitant of Boeotia; a dull, stupid person.

Boer /bɔr/ or /'bo:r/, /bur/ n a Dutch-descended South African.— also adj.

boffin /'bɒfɪn/ n (inf) a military research scientist.

boffo /'bɒfo:/ adj (sl) wonderful, amazing.

bog /bɒg/ or /bɒg/ n wet, spongy ground; quagmire. • vb (**bogging, bogged**) vt to sink or submerge in a bog or quagmire. • vi to sink or stick in a bog.—**boggy** adj.

bogey[1] /'bo:gi/ n (pl **bogeys**) (golf) one stroke more than par on a hole.

bogey[2] n (pl **bogeys**) a goblin; a cause of worry.—also **bogy** (pl **bogies**).

bogeyman /'bo:gi,mæn/ n (pl **bogeymen**) an imaginary monster commonly used to frighten children.

boggle /'bɒgəl/ vi to be surprised; to hesitate (at). • vt to confuse (the imagination, mind, etc).

bogie /'bo:gi/ n an assembly of four or six wheels on a rail carriage.

bogle /'bo:gəl/ n a goblin, a spectre; a scarecrow.

bogus /'bo:gəs/ adj counterfeit, spurious.

bogy /'bo:gi/ or /'bugi/ see **bogey**[2].

bohea n a black China tea of the lowest quality.

Bohemian /bo:'hi:miən/ adj of or pertaining to Bohemia in Czechoslovakia; unconventional. • n an inhabitant of Bohemia; a person who disregards social conventions or evinces a wild or roving disposition; a gipsy.

Bohemianism /-,ɪzəm/ n the life or habits of a person, usu artistic or literary, who by natural inclination leads a free and easy unconventional existence.

boil[1] /bɔɪl/ vi to change rapidly from a liquid to a vapour by heating; to bubble when boiling; to cook in boiling liquid; to be aroused with anger; (with **down**) to reduce by boiling; to condense; (with **over**) to overflow when boiling; to burst out in anger. • vt to heat to boiling point; to cook in boiling water.—**boilable** adj.

boil[2] n an inflamed, pus-filled, painful swelling on the skin.

boiler /'bɔɪlər/ n a container in which to boil things; a storage tank in which water is heated and steam generated; a device for providing central heating and hot water.

boilersuit /-su:t/ n coveralls.

boiling point n the temperature at which a liquid boils; the point at which a person loses his temper; the point of crisis.

boisterous /'bɔɪstərəs/ adj wild, noisy; stormy; loud and exuberant.—**boisterously** adv.

bola, bolas /'bo:lə/ n a South American hunting implement consisting of two or more balls of iron or stone attached to the ends of a leather cord, used to entangle the legs of an animal.

bold /bo:ld/ adj daring or courageous; fearless; impudent; striking to the eye. • n boldface type.—**boldly** adv.—**boldness** n.

boldface type /-,feɪs/ n type characters with thickened, heavy strokes.

bole[1] /bo:l/ n the trunk or stem of a tree.

bole[2] n friable clay or clayey shale, usu coloured by oxide of iron.

bolection /bo:'lekʃən/ n (archit) a raised moulding on a panel.

bolero /bo:'lɛro:/ n (pl **boleros**) a lively Spanish dance; the music accompanying such a dance; a short jacket-shaped bodice.

boletus /bo:'leɪtəs/ n (pl **boletuses, boleti**) any of a large genus of thick-stemmed fungi containing edible or poisonous species.

bolide /'bo:,laɪd/ or /-,lɪd/ n a large meteor that explodes on coming into contact with air, a fire ball.

boll /bo:l/ n the pod of a plant, esp of cotton or flax.

boll weevil n an American weevil that infests cotton bolls.

bollard /'bɒlərd/ n a strong post on a wharf around which mooring lines are secured; one of a line of posts closing off a street to traffic; an illuminated marker on a traffic island.

bolometer /bo:'lɒmətər/ n an instrument for measuring radiation.—**bolometric** adj.—**bolometrically** adv.

boloney /bə'lo:ni/ see **baloney**.

Bolshevik /'bo:lʃə,vɪk/ or /'bɒl-/ n (pl **Bolsheviks, Bolsheviki**) a Russian communist; a revolutionary; an opponent of an existing social order.

Bolshevism /-,vɪzm/ n the doctrines and practices of the Bolsheviks; the communist form of government adopted in Russia in March 1917.—**Bolshevist** adj, n.

bolshie, bolshy /'bo:lʃi/ adj (sl) left-wing; rebellious. • n (pl **bolshies**) (often with cap) a Bolshevik; a revolutionary.

bolster /'bo:lstər/ n a long narrow pillow; any bolster-like object or support. • vt (often with **up**) to support or strengthen.— **bolsterer** n.—**bolsteringly** adv.

bolt[1] /bo:lt/ n a bar used to lock a door, etc; an arrow for a crossbow; a flash of lightning; a threaded metal rod used with a nut to hold parts together; a roll (of cloth, paper, etc); a sudden dash. • vt to lock with a bolt; to eat hastily; to say suddenly; to blurt (out); to abandon (a party, group, etc). • vi (horse) to rush away suddenly • adv erectly upright.—**bolter** n.

bolt[2] vt to sift or separate coarser from finer particles; to examine with care, to investigate; to separate.—also **boult**.—**bolter** n.

bolthole /-,ho:l/ n an escape route; a safe and secret hiding place; a person's private refuge.

boltrope /-,ro:p/ n (naut) a rope to which the edges of sails are sewn.

bolus /'bo:ləs/ n (pl **boluses**) a medicine in the form of a soft rounded mass, larger than an ordinary pill, to be swallowed at once; anything disagreeable, which must be accepted.

bomb /bɒm/ n a projectile containing explosives, incendiary material, or chemicals used for destruction; (with **the**) the hydrogen or atomic bomb; (sl) a lot of money. • vt to attack with bombs. • vi to fail, to flop.

bomb site /bɒmsaɪt/ n an area devastated by bombing; a vacant area cleared after a bombing raid.

bombard /bɒm'bard/ vt to attack with bombs or artillery; to attack verbally.—**bombardment** n.

bombardier /,bɒmbər'di:r/ n the crew member who releases the bombs in a bomber; in Britain and Canada, a noncommissioned artillery officer.

bombardier beetle n any of various coleopterous insects that, when irritated, expel a fluid from the abdomen with a slight report.

bombast /'bɒm,bæst/ n pretentious or boastful language.— **bombastic** adj.—**bombastically** adv.

bombazine /,bɒmbə'zi:n/ or /'bɒmbə,zi:n/ n a twilled fabric of which the warp is silk and the weft worsted.

bombe /bɒm/, *Fr.* /bõ:b/ *n* a frozen dessert moulded into a round shape.

bomber /'bɒmər/ *n* a person who bombs; an aeroplane that carries bombs.

bomber jacket *n* a waist-length bloused jacket with a zip and cuffed sleeves.

bombshell /'bɒm,ʃɛl/ *n* a shocking surprise.

bombsight /'bɒmsaɪt/ *n* a manual or electronic device for aiming bombs.

bombycid /'bɒmbə,sɪd/ *n* any of a family of moths, including the silkworm moth.

bona fide /'boːnə,faɪd/ or /'boːnə-/, /,boːnəˈfaɪdɪ/ *adj* in good faith; genuine or real.

bona fides /'boːnəˈfaɪ,diz/ or /-,faɪdz/ *n* good faith; honourable dealing.

bonanza /bəˈnænzə/ *n* a rich vein of ore; any source of wealth; unexpected good fortune or luck.

bonbon /'bɒn,bɒn/ *n* a small piece of candy, a sweet.

bond /bɒnd/ *n* anything that binds, fastens, or unites; (*pl*) shackles; an obligation imposed by a contract, promise, etc; the status of goods in a warehouse until taxes are paid; an interest-bearing certificate issued by the government or business, redeemable on a specified date; surety against theft, absconding, etc. • *vt* to join, bind, or otherwise unite; to provide a bond for; to place or hold (goods) in bond; to put together bricks or stones so that they overlap to give strength. • *vi* to hold together by means of a bond.—**bondable** *adj*.—**bonder** *n*.

bondage /'bɒndɪdʒ/ *n* slavery, captivity.

bondstone /'bɒnd,stoːn/ *n* a long stone runing through a wall and so binding it.

bone /boːn/ *n* the hard material making up the skeleton; any constituent part of the skeleton; (*pl*) the skeleton; the essentials or basics of anything. • *vti* to remove the bones from, as meat; (*with* **up**) (*inf*) to study hard.—**boneless** *adj*.

bone black *n* a black pigment made partly from charcoal obtained by roasting animal bones.

bone china *n* china made from clay mixed with bone ash.

bone-dry /'boːnˈdraɪ/ *adj* completely dry.

bonehead /'boːn,hed/ *n* (*sl*) a fool.

bone meal *n* fertilizer or feed made of crushed or ground bone.

bone of contention *n* a source of strife.

bonesetter *n* one who treats fractures or dislocated limbs without medical qualification to do so.

bonfire /'bɒn,faɪr/ *n* an outdoor fire.

bongo[1] /'bɒŋgoː/ *n* (*pl* **bongos**) either of a pair of small drums of different pitch struck with the fingers.

bongo[2] *n* (*pl* **bongo, bongos**) a large striped African antelope.

bonhomie /,bɒnɒˈmi/, *Fr.* /bɒnɒˈmi/ *n* good-heartedness; a frank good-natured manner.—**bonhomous** *adj*.

bonito /boːˈnitoː/ or /bə-/ *n* (*pl* **bonitos, bonito**) one of several species of warm-sea game fishes allied to the tuna.

bon mot /'boːnˈmoː/, *Fr.* /boːnˈmoː/ *n* (*pl* **bons mots**) a witty saying, a fitting remark.

bonne *Fr.* /bɒn/ *n* a French nursemaid.

bonnet /'bɒnət/ *n* a hat with a chin ribbon, worn by women and children; a case or covering, *usu* of sheet metal, placed over a motor.—*also* **hood**.

bonny, bonnie /'bɒni/ *adj* (**bonnier, bonniest**) healthy, attractive looking.

bonsai /'bɒn,saɪ/ or /bɒnˈsaɪ/ *n* (*pl* **bonsai**) a miniature tree or shrub that has been dwarfed by selective pruning; the art of cultivating bonsai.

bonspiel /'bɒn,spiːl/ or /-,spəl/ *n* (*Scot*) a curling match between players of different clubs.

bontebok /'bɒntə,bɒk/ *n* (*pl* **bonteboks, bontebok**) a pied antelope of South Africa.

bon ton /boːnˈtoːn/ *n* the style of persons in high life; good breeding; fashionable society; height of fashion.

bonus /'boːnəs/ *n* (*pl* **bonuses**) an amount paid over the sum due as interest, dividend, or wages.

bon vivant /bõvi:ˈvã/ *n* (*pl* **bons vivants**) a gourmet.

bon voyage /,bɒnvɔɪˈɒdʒ/, *Fr.* /bõvwɒˈjɒʒ/ or /-vɔɪˈjɒʒ/ *n*, *interj* an expression used to wish travellers a pleasant trip.

bony /'boːni/ *adj* (**bonier, boniest**) of or resembling bones; having large or prominent bones; full of bones.

bonze /bɒnz/ *n* a Buddhist monk.

boo /buː/ *interj* an expression of disapproval. • *n* (*pl* **boos**) hooting. • *vb* (**booing, booed**) *vi* to low like an ox; to groan. • *vt* to hoot at.

boob /buːb/ *n* a stupid awkward person; a blunder.

booby /'buːbi/ *n* (*pl* **boobies**) a foolish person; the loser in a game.

booby prize *n* a prize of little value for the lowest score.

booby trap *n* a trap for playing a practical joke on someone; a camouflaged explosive device triggered by an unsuspecting victim.

boodle /'buːdəl/ *n* money paid for votes or undue political influence; graft; lot, caboodle.

boogie /'buːgi/ or /'buːgi/ *vi* (**boogieing, boogied**) to dance to pop music or jazz. • *n* fast, rhythmic music for dancing.

boogie-woogie /,buːgiˈwʊgi/ or /,buːgiˈwuːgi/ *n* a style of jazz piano.

boohoo /,buːˈhuː/ *vi* (**boohooing, boohooed**) to weep noisily or to pretend to do so. • *n* (*pl* **boohoos**) the sound of noisy weeping.

book /bʊk/ *n* a bound set of printed or blank pages; a literary composition of fact or fiction; the script or libretto of a play or musical; (*pl*) written records of transactions or accounts; a book or record of bets. • *vt* to make a reservation in advance; to note a person's name and address for an alleged offence. • *vi* to make a reservation.

bookcase /-,keɪs/ *n* a piece of furniture with shelves for books.

book club *n* an organization that sells books to its members at cheaper prices, *usu* by mail order.

book end /-,end/ *npl* a prop at the end of a row of books to keep them upright.

bookie /-i/ *n* (*inf*) a bookmaker.

bookish /-ɪʃ/ *adj* fond of reading.—**bookishness** *n*.**book learning** *n* theoretical, not practical, knowledge.—**book-learned** *adj*.

bookkeeping /-,kiːpɪŋ/ *n* the systematic recording of business accounts.—**bookkeeper** *n*.

booklet /-lɪt/ *n* a small book, *usu* with a paper cover; a pamphlet.

bookmaker /-,meɪkər/ *n* a person who takes bets on horse races, etc and pays out winnings; a manufacturer or publisher of books.

bookman /-mən/ *n* (*pl* **bookmen**) a literary man, a scholar; one who works in publishing.

bookmark(er) /-,markər/ *n* a thing to mark a place in a book.

bookplate /-,pleɪt/ *n* a label in a book with the owner's name on it.

bookseller /-,selər/ *n* a person who sells books.

bookstall /-stɒl/ *n* a stall for the sale of books, magazines, etc.

bookworm /-,wɜrm/ *n* an insect that feeds on books; a person who reads a lot.

Boolean algebra *n* (*math*) a system of symbolic logic used in the manipulation of sets and other mathematical entities, and in computing science.

boom[1] *n* a spar on which a sail is stretched; a barrier across a harbour; a long pole carrying a microphone.

boom[2] *vi* to make a deep, hollow sound. • *n* a resonant sound, as of the sea.

boom[3] *vi* to flourish or prosper suddenly. • *n* a period of vigorous growth (*eg* in business, sales, prices).

boomer /'buːmər/ *n* the male of the great kangaroo; one who starts or promotes a boom; (*sl*) a migratory worker.

boomerang /'buːmə,ræŋ/ *n* a curved stick that, when thrown, returns to the thrower; an action that unexpectedly rebounds and harms the agent.—*also vi*.

boom town /'buːm,taʊn/ *n* a town that suddenly grows and increases in economic prosperity.

boon[1] /buːn/ *n* something useful or helpful; a blessing; a favour.

boon[2] *adj* bountiful; convivial, jolly; specially friendly (**boon companion**).

boondocks /'buːn,dɒks/ *npl* (*sl*) a wild, inhospitable area; a dull, provincial region.—**boondock** *adj*.

boor /'bʊr/ *n* an ill-mannered or coarse person.—**boorish** *adj*.—**boorishly** *adv*.—**boorishness** *n*.

boost /buːst/ *vt* (*sales, etc*) to increase; to encourage, to improve; to push; to help by advertising or promoting. • *n* a push.

booster /-ər/ *n* a thing or person that increases the effectiveness of another mechanism; the first stage of a rocket, which usually breaks away after launching; a substance that increases the effectiveness of medication.

boosterism /-ˌɪzəm/ *n* the practice of boosting an image or product commercially.

booster shot, booster injection *n* a supplementary dose of medicine, *esp* a vaccine.

boot[1] /buːt/ *n* a strong covering for the foot and lower part of the leg; (*sl: with* **the**) dismissal from employment; the rear compartment of a car used for holding luggage, etc.—*also* **trunk**. • *vt* to kick; to get rid of by force; (*comput*) to bring a program from a disc into the memory.

boot[2] *n* (*arch*) advantage, use; **to boot** as well. • *vi* (*arch*) to avail.

bootblack /ˈbuːtˌblæk/ *n* one who shines shoes.

booted *adj* wearing boots.

bootee /buːˈtiː/ *n* a knitted or soft shoe for a baby.

booth /buːθ/ *n* a stall for selling goods; a small enclosure for voting; a public telephone enclosure.

bootjack /ˈbuːtˌdʒæk/ *n* an appliance for drawing off boots.

bootleg /-ˌleg/ *vt* (**bootlegging, bootlegged**) to smuggle illicit alcohol; to deal in illegally made records and tapes of live music, etc.—**bootlegger** *n*.

bootless /-ləs/ *adj* useless, unavailing.—**bootlessly** *adv*.—**bootlessness** *n*.

bootlicker /-ˌlɪkər/ *n* a person who ingratiates himself or herself to gain favour, a toady.

boots /buːts/ *n* (*pl* **boots**) in UK, the servant in an hotel who cleans the boots of the guests.

boots and saddles *n* a cavalry signal to mount.

booty /ˈbuːti/ *n* (*pl* **booties**) spoils obtained as plunder.

booze /buːz/ *vi* (*inf*) to drink alcohol excessively. • *n* alcohol.—**boozer** *n*.

boozy /ˈbuːzi/ *adj* (**boozier, booziest** (*sl*) addicted to drink; drunk.—**boozily** *adv*.

bop /bɒp/ *n* a style of 1940s jazz music.—*also* **bebop**.

bora /ˈbɔːrə/ or /ˈbɒrə/ *n* a fierce dry northeast wind that blows on the coasts of the Adriatic Sea.

boracic /bəˈræsɪk/ *see* **boric**.

boracic acid *see* **boric acid**.

borage /ˈbɒrədʒ/ *n* a blue-flowered herb used in salads, etc.

borax /ˈbɒræks/ *n* a mineral composed of the sodium salt compounded of boracic acid chiefly from the dried beds of certain lakes, used in the manufacture of glass, enamel, antiseptics, soaps, etc; (*sl*) shoddy merchandise.

Bordeaux /bɔrˈdoː/ *n* any of several red, white or rosé wines from around Bordeaux in France.

bordello /bɔrˈdɛloː/ *n* (*pl* **bordellos**) a brothel.

border /ˈbɔrdər/ *n* the edge, rim, or margin; a dividing line between two countries; a narrow strip along an edge. • *vi* (*with* **on, upon**) to be adjacent; to approach, to verge on. • *vt* to form a border.

bordereau *Fr.* /bɔrdəˈroː/ *n* (*pl* **bordereaux**) a memorandum of contents, a docket.

borderer /ˈbɔrdərər/ *n* a dweller on a frontier.

borderland /ˈbɔrdərˌlænd/ *n* land forming a border or frontier; an uncertain or debatable district; an intermediate state.

borderline /ˈbɔrdərˌlaɪn/ *n* a boundary. • *adj* on a boundary; doubtful, indefinite.

bordure /ˈbɔrdjur/ *n* (*her*) a border round a shield.

bore[1] /bɔr/ *vt* to drill so as to form a hole; to weary, by being dull or uninteresting. • *n* a hole made by drilling; the diameter of a gun barrel; a dull or uninteresting person.

bore[2] *see* **bear**[1].

bore[3] *n* a tidal wave that breaks in the estuaries of some rivers and, impeded by a narrowing channel, rises in a ridge and courses along with great force and noise.

boreal /ˈbɔriəl/ *adj* of or pertaining to the north, or to the north wind; situated on the northern side; of a northern character.

Boreas /-əs/ *n* the north wind personified.

boredom /ˈbɔrdəm/ *n* tedium.

boric /ˈbɒrɪk/ *adj* of or yielding boron.—*also* **boracic**.

boric acid *n* a white solid acid used in manufacturing and as a mild antiseptic.

boring /ˈbɔrɪŋ/ *adj* dull, tedious; making holes.

born /bɔrn/ *pp* of **bear**[1]. • *adj* by birth, natural.

born-again /ˈbɔrnəˈgen/ *adj* having undergone a revival of personal faith or conviction.

borne /bɔrn/ *see* **bear**[1].

bornite /ˈbɔrˌnaɪt/ *n* a valuable ore of copper.

boron /ˈbɔrˌɒn/ *n* a nonmetallic element found in borax.

borough /ˈbərə/ *n* a self-governing, incorporated town; an administrative area of a city, as in London or New York.

borough English *n* (*formerly*) a custom existing in some parts of England by which an estate descended to the youngest son instead of the eldest, or, if there were no son, to the youngest brother.

borrow /ˈbɒrə/ or /ˈbɑr-/ *vt* to obtain (an item) with the intention of returning it; (*an idea*) to adopt as one's own; (*loan, money*) to obtain from a financial institution at definite rates of interest.—**borrower** *n*.

borscht /bɔrʃt/, **borsch** *Russ.* /bɑrʃtʃ/ *n* a type of soup (orig from Russia) made with beetroot.

borstal system /ˈbɔrstəlˌsɪstəm/ *n* (*often cap*) (*formerly*) a reformatory system by which the sentence depended on the prisoner's conduct; now called a youth custody centre.

bort /bɔrt/, **bortz** *n* an imperfect or inferior diamond used for polishing other stones; a fragment of diamond made in the cutting.—*also* **boart**.

borzoi /ˈbɔrˌzɔɪ/ *n* (*pl* **borzois**) a tall hound with a long, silky coat and a long head, a Russian wolfhound.

boscage, boskage /ˈbɒskɪdʒ/ *n* ground covered with trees and shrubs; thickets; a wooded landscape.

bosh /bɒʃ/ *n* (*inf*) nonsense.—*also* **interj**.

bosk /bɒsk/ *n* a small wood, a thicket.

bosky /ˈbɒski/ *adj* (**boskier, boskiest**) wooded, bushy.—**boskiness** *n*.

bosom /ˈbuzəm/ *n* the breast of a human being, *esp* a woman; the part of a dress that covers it; the seat of the emotions. • *adj* (*friend*) very dear, intimate.

boss[1] /bɒs/ *n* (*inf*) the manager or foreman; a powerful local politician. • *vt* to domineer; to be in control.

boss[2] *n* a protuberant part; a stud or knob, an ornamental projection of a ceiling. • *vt* to ornament with studs or knobs.

bossa nova /ˌbɒsəˈnoːvə/ *n* a dance from Brazil similar to the samba; the music for this.

bossy /ˈbɒsi/ *adj* (**bossier, bossiest**) (*inf*) domineering, fond of giving orders.—**bossily** *adv*.—**bossiness** *n*.

bosun /ˈboːsən/ *see* **boatswain**.

bot /bɒt/ *n* the larva of the botfly, which infests horses, cattle, sheep, etc; (*pl*) the disease that it causes.—*also* **bott**.

botanical /bəˈtænɪkəl/, **botanic** *adj* pertaining to plants and botany.—**botanically** *adv*.

botanize /ˈbɒtəˌnaɪz/ *vi* to study plants, *esp* on a field trip.—**botanizer** *n*.

botany /ˈbɒtəni/ *n* (*pl* **botanies**) the study of plants.—**botanist** *n*.

botch /bɒtʃ/ *n* a poorly done piece of work. • *vt* to mend or patch clumsily; to put together without sufficient care.—**botcher** *n*.

botchy /ˈbɒtʃi/ *adj* (**botchier, botchiest**) clumsily made or done; marked with botches.—**botchily** *adv*.—**botchiness** *n*.

botfly /ˈbɒtˌflaɪ/ *n* (*pl* **botflies**) any of many winged insects with larvae parasitic on humans and livestock.

both /boːθ/ *adj, pron* the two together; the one and the other. • *conj* together equally.—*also adv*.

bother /ˈbɒðər/ *vt* to perplex or annoy; to take the time or trouble. • *n* worry; trouble; someone who causes problems, etc.

botheration /ˌbɒðəreɪˈʃən/ *n* bother.—*also interj*.

bothersome /ˈbɒðərsəm/ *adj* causing bother.

bothy /ˈbɒθi/ *n* (*pl* **bothies**) (*Scot*) a small cottage or hut, *esp* a hut or barrack serving as farm servants' quarters; a shelter for climbers on mountains.

bo tree /ˈboːˌtriː/ *n* the peepul, the sacred tree of the Buddhists.

botryoidal /ˌbɒtriˈɔɪdəl/ *adj* resembling a bunch of grapes.—**botryoidally** *adv*.

bott /bɒt/ *see* **bot**.

bottle green *adj* dark green.

bottle[1] /ˈbɒtəl/ *n* a glass or plastic container for holding liquids; its contents; (*sl*) courage, nerve. • *vt* to put in bottles; to confine as if in a bottle.

bottle[2] *n* (*dial*) a quantity of hay or grass bundled up.

bottleneck /-ˌnek/ *n* a narrow stretch of a road where traffic is held up; a congestion in any stage of a process.

bottlenose /-ˌnoːz/ *n* a dolphin with a sharp protruding beak; a moderately large toothed whale with a prominent beak.

bottom /ˈbɒtəm/ *n* the lowest or deepest part of anything; the base or foundation; the lowest position (*eg* in a class); the buttocks; (*naut*) the part of a ship's hull below water; the seabed. • *vt* to be based or founded on; to bring to the bottom, to get to the bottom of. • *vi* to become based; to reach the bottom; (*with* **out**) to flatten off after dropping sharply.

bottomlands /-ˌlændz/ *npl* rich flat low-lying land along watercourses in the western states of the US.

bottomless /-ləs/ *adj* very deep; without limit.

bottom line *n* the crux; the line at the bottom of a financial report that shows the net profit or loss; the final result.—**bottom-line** *adj*.

bottomry /ˈbɒtəmri/ *n* (*pl* **bottomries**) the borrowing of money by the owner on the security of his or her ship. • *vt* to pledge (a ship) thus.

botulism /ˈbɒtʃʊˌlizəm/ *n* a type of severe food poisoning.

bouclé, boucle /buːˈkleɪ/ *n* a type of looped yarn or fabric.

boudoir /buːˈdwɑr/ *n* a woman's bedroom.

bouffant /buːˈfɒnt/ *adj* puffed out; (*of hair*) backcombed.

bougainvillea, bougainvillaea /ˌbuːgənˈvɪliə/ *n* a tropical plant with large rosy or purple bracts.

bough /baʊ/ *n* a branch of a tree.

bought /bɒt/ *see* **buy**.

bougie /ˈbuːˌdʒi/ *or* /-ˌʒi/ *n* a wax candle; (*med*) a slender flexible tube for inserting into the gullet, etc; a catheter.

bouillabaisse /ˌbuːjəˈbeɪs/ *n* a French fish stew.

bouillon /ˈbuːˌjõ/ *or* /-ˌljɒn/, /ˈbuˌljɒn/, *Fr.* /buːˈjõ/ *n* a clear seasoned stock or broth.

boulder /ˈbɒːldər/ *n* a large stone or mass of rock rounded by the action of erosion.

boule[1] /ˈbuːl/ *n* an imitation gemstone.

boule[2] /ˈbuːli/ *n* in ancient Athens, a higher popular assembly; (*with cap*) the lower house of the modern Greek legislative assembly.

boule[3] /ˈbuːl/ *see* **boulle**.

boules /ˈbuːl/ *n* (*used as sing*) a French game similar to bowls played with small, hard balls.

boulevard /ˈbuːləˌvɑrd/ *n* a broad, often tree-lined road.

boulevardier *Fr.* /buːlvɑrˈdjeɪ/ *n* a frequenter of a boulevard, *esp* a Parisian; a man about town.

bouleversement *Fr.* /buːlvɛrsˈmɑ̃/ *n* an overturning, overthrow.

boulle /ˈbuːl/ *n* decorative inlaying for cabinetwork, consisting of brass or other metal, tortoiseshell, etc, worked into scrolls or other patterns, the articles so ornamented.—*also* **boule, buhl**.

boult *see* **bolt**[2].

bounce /baʊns/ *vi* to rebound; to jump up suddenly; (*sl: cheque*) to be returned because of lack of funds; (*with* **back**) to recover easily, *eg* from misfortune or ill health. • *vt* to cause a ball to bounce; (*sl*) to put (a person) out by force; (*sl*) to fire from a job. • *n* a leap or springiness; capacity for bouncing; sprightliness; boastfulness, arrogance.

bouncer /ˈbaʊnsər/ *n* (*sl*) a man hired to remove disorderly people from nightclubs, etc.

bouncing /ˈbaʊnsɪŋ/ *adj* big, healthy, etc.

bouncy /ˈbaʊnsi/ *adj* able to spring or bound; elastic; vigorous, lively.—**bouncily** *adv*.—**bounciness** *n*.

bound[1] /baʊnd/ *see* **bind**.

bound[2] *n* (*usu pl*) the limit or boundary. • *vt* to limit, confine or surround; to name the boundaries of.

bound[3] *n* a jump or leap. • *vi* to jump or leap.

bound[4] *adj* (*with* **for**) intending to go to, on the way to.

boundary /ˈbaʊndəri/ *or* /-dəri/ *n* (*pl* **boundaries**) the border of an area; the limit; (*cricket*) the limit line of a field; a stroke that goes beyond the boundary line.

bounden /ˈbaʊndən/ *adj* (*duty*) obligatory.

bounden duty *n* a moral obligation.

bounder /ˈbaʊndər/ *n* one who or that which bounds; (*inf*) an insolent, ill-bred man, who makes himself disagreeable to those whom he meets.

boundless /ˈbaʊndləs/ *adj* unlimited, vast.—**boundlessly** *adv*.—**boundlessness** *n*.

bounteous /ˈbaʊntiəs/ *adj* giving freely, bountiful, generous; plentiful.—**bounteously** *adv*.—**bounteousness** *n*.

bountiful /ˈbaʊntəˌfʊl/ *adj* generous in giving.—**bountifully** *adv*.—**bountifulness** *n*.

bounty /ˈbaʊnti/ *n* (*pl* **bounties**) generosity in giving; the gifts given; a reward or premium.

bouquet /buːˈkeɪ/ *or* /bo:-/ *n* a bunch of flowers; the perfume given off by wine.

bouquet garni /buːˈkeɪgɑrˈni:/ *n* (*pl* **bouquets garnis**) herbs tied in a small bundle used for flavouring stews, soups, sauces, etc.

bourbon /ˈburbən/ *or* /ˈbʊrbõ/ *n* a whisky distilled in the US from corn mash.

bourdon /ˈburdən/ *n* the bass drone of the bagpipe; a bass stop of an organ.

bourgeois /burˈʒwɒ/ *n* (*pl* **bourgeois**) a member of the bourgeoisie or middle class; a conventional and unimaginative individual. • *adj* smug, respectable, conventional; mediocre.

bourgeoisie /ˌburʒwɒˈzi:/ *n* the class between the lower and upper classes, mostly composed of professional and business people.—*also* **middle class**.

bourn, bourne[1] /bɔrn/ *or* /burn/ *n* a small stream, a rivulet.

bourn, bourne[2] *n* (*arch*) a boundary; a destination, goal; a realm.

bourrée /buːˈreɪ/ *n* (*mus*) a composition of a lively character, similar to the gavotte; the music for this.

bourse /burs/ *n* a stock exchange for the transaction of business; (*with cap*) the stock exchange of Paris.

bouse /bɒus/ *or* /baʊz/ *vi* (*naut*) to pull or haul hard.—*also* **bowse**.

boustrophedon /ˌbɒustrəˈfiːdən/, /ˌbuː-/ *n* an ancient mode of writing lines alternately from left to right and from right to left.—**boustrophedonic** *adj*.

bout /baʊt/ *n* a spell, a turn, a period spent in some activity; a contest or struggle, *esp* boxing or wrestling; a time of illness.

boutique /buːˈtiːk/ *n* a small shop, usually selling fashionable clothing and accessories.

boutonniere, boutonnière /ˌbuːtəˈniːr/ *n* a buttonhole; a spray of flowers worn in it.

bouzouki /buːˈzuːki/ *n* (*pl* **bouzoukis**) a Greek stringed instrument similar to the mandolin.

bovine /ˈbɒːˌvaɪn/ *adj* relating to cattle; dull; sluggish. • *n* an ox, cow etc.

bow[1] /baʊ/ *vi* to bend the knee or to lean the head (and chest) forward as a form of greeting or respect or shame; (*with* **before**) to accept, to submit; (*with* **out**) to withdraw or retire gracefully. • *vt* to bend downwards; to weigh down; to usher in or out with a bow. • *n* a lowering of the head (and chest) in greeting.

bow[2] /bo:/ *n* a weapon for shooting arrows; an implement for playing the strings of a violin; a decorative knot of ribbon, etc. • *vti* to bend, curve.

bow[3] /baʊ/ *n* the forward part of a ship.—**bow compass** /bo:/ *n* (*geom*) a compass with jointed legs.

bowdlerize /ˈbaʊdlərˌaɪz/ *vt* to expurgate, to remove indelicate words from.—**bowdlerism** *n*.—**bowdlerization** *n*.

bowel /ˈbaʊəl/ *n* the intestine; (*pl*) entrails; (*pl*) the deep and remote part of anything.

bower[1] /ˈbaʊər/ *n* an arbour, a shady recess; (*poet*) dwelling.

bower *n* (*naut*) an anchor carried at the bow of a ship.

bower[3] *n* (*cards*) one of the two highest cards in some card games, or the second and third highest (when the joker is used).

bowerbird /-ˌbɔrd/ *n* one of various Australian birds belonging to the starling family.

bowhead /ˈbo:ˌhed/ *n* an Arctic whale with a large mouth; Greenland whale.

bowie knife /ˈbo:iˌnaɪf/ *or* /ˈbo:-/ *n* a long hunting knife, a sheath knife.

bowing /ˈbo:ɪŋ/ *n* a playing upon an instrument of the violin class with a bow; the particular style of execution.

bowl[1] /bo:l/ *n* a wooden ball having a bias used in bowling; (*pl*) a game played on a smooth lawn with bowls. • *vti* to play the game of bowls; (*cricket*) to send a ball to a batsman; to dismiss (a batsman) by hitting the wicket with a bowled ball; (*with* **over**) to knock over; (*inf*) to astonish.

bowl[2] *n* a deep, rounded dish; the rounded end of a pipe; a sports stadium.

bow-legged /ˈbo:ˌlegəd/ *adj* having legs that curve outwards between the thigh and the ankle; bandy.

bowler[1] /ˈbo:lər/ *n* a person who plays bowls; (*cricket*) the player who delivers the ball.

bowler[2] *n* a stiff felt hat.—*also* **derby**.

bowline /ˈbo:lən/ *n* (*naut*) a knot used in making a fixed end loop; (*naut*) a rope from the weather side of a square sail to the bow to keep the ship near the wind.

bowling /ˈbo:lɪŋ/ *n* a game in which a heavy wooden ball is bowled along a bowling alley at ten wooden skittles; the game of bowls.

bowling alley *n* a long narrow wooden lane, *usu* one of several in a building designed for them.

bowling green *n* a smooth lawn for bowls.

bowman[1] /'bɔːmən/ *n* (*pl* **bowmen**) an archer.

bowman[2] /'baumən/ *n* (*pl* **bowmen**) (*naut*) the oarsman nearest the bow.

bowsaw *n* a saw with a blade under tension for cutting curves.

bowse *see* **bouse**.

bowsprit /'bɔːˌsprɪt/ or *n* a large boom or spar running out from the stem of a (sailing) ship to carry its sails forward.

bowstring /'bɔːˌstrɪŋ/ *n* the string of a bow.

bow tie /'bɔːˌtaɪ/ *n* a necktie tied in the shape of a bow.

bow window /bɔː'wɪndəʊ/ *n* a curved bay window.

bow-wow /'bauwau/ or /-'wau/ *n* a dog's bark; a child's name for a dog. • *vi* to bark like a dog.

bowyer /'bɔːjər/ *n* a maker or seller of archery bows.

box[1] /bɒks/ *n* a container or receptacle for holding anything; (*theatre*) a compartment with seats; (*inf*) a television set. • *vt* to put into a box; to enclose; (*with* **in**) to restrict.

box[2] *vt* to hit using the hands or fists. • *vi* to fight with the fists. • *n* a blow on the head or ear with the fist.

box[3] *n* an evergreen shrub or small tree yielding a hard close-grained wood; the wood. • *adj* of box or boxwood.

boxcar /-ˌkɑr/ *n* an enclosed freight car.

boxer /'bɒksər/ *n* a person who engages in boxing; a breed of dog with smooth hair and a stumpy tail.

boxer shorts *npl* loose underpants that resemble the pants worn by boxers.

box girder *n* a girder constructed from rectangular metal plates.

boxing /'bɒksɪŋ/ *n* the skill or sport of fighting with the fists.

Boxing Day the weekday following December 25, Christmas, when traditionally presents were given to tradesmen, employees, etc.

box office *n* a theatre ticket office; the popularity of a play, film, actor.—**box-office** *adj*.

box pleat *n* a double pleat in cloth made by two facing folds.

boxwood /'bɒksˌwʊd/ *n* the hard wood of the box tree; the tree itself.

boy /bɔɪ/ *n* a male child; a son; a lad; a youth. • *interj* an exclamation of surprise or joy.

boyar /bɔː'jɑr/ *n* (*formerly*) a Russian landed proprietor of an old aristocratic order abolished by Peter I.

boycott /'bɔɪˌkɒt/ *vt* to refuse to deal with or trade with in order to punish or coerce.—*also n*.

boyfriend /'bɔɪˌfrɛnd/ *n* a male friend with whom a person is romantically or sexually involved.

boyhood /-ˌhʊd/ *n* the time, or state, of being a boy.

boyish /-ɪʃ/ *adj* like a boy; puerile; with the appeal of a boy.—**boyishly** *adv*.—**boyishness** *n*.

Boy Scout *n* a scout; (*without cap*) (*inf*) a man with a strong sense of duty.

boysenberry /'bɔɪzənˌbɛri/ or /'bɔɪsən-/ *n* (*pl* **boysenberries**) (the fruit of) a hybrid shrub developed by crossing the loganberry and various blackberries and raspberries.

BP, B/P *abbr* = blood pressure.

Bq (*symbol*) bequerel.

Br *abbr* = British; (*chem symbol*) bromine; brother.

br'er /brər/ *n* (*dial*) brother.

bra /brɑ/ *n* a brassiere.

brace /breɪs/ *n* a prop; a support to stiffen a framework; a hand tool for drilling; (*pl* **brace**) a pair, *esp* of game; (*pl*) straps for holding up trousers; a dental appliance for straightening the teeth. • *vt* to steady.

brace and bit *n* a revolving tool for boring.

bracelet /'breɪslət/ *n* an ornamental chain or band for the wrist; (*pl*: *sl*) handcuffs.

bracer[1] /'breɪsər/ *n* something that braces; a pick-me-up.

bracer[2] *n* a wrist guard in archery.

brachial /'breɪkɪəl/ or /'breɪ-/ *adj* of, pertaining to, or like the arm.

brachiate /'breɪkɪət/ or /'breɪ-/, /-eɪt/ *adj* having arms; (*bot*) having branches in pairs, nearly horizontal and each pair at right angles to the next.—**brachiation**.

brachiopod /'breɪkɪˌʊˌpɒd/ or /'breɪ-/ *n* an animal like a mollusc with two spirally coiled armlike appendages, one on each side of the mouth.

brachy- /'breɪki/ *prefix* short.

brachycephalic /ˌbrækɪsə'fælɪk/, **brachycephalous** /ˌbrækɪsə'fələs/ *adj* (*anat*) having the skull short in proportion to its breadth, short-headed.—**brachycephaly** *n*.

brachylogy /brə'kɪlədʒi/ *n* (*pl* **brachylogies**) conciseness; a condensed expression.—**brachylogous** *adj*.

brachypterous /brə'kɪptərəs/ *adj* (*insects*) short-winged.

brachyuran /ˌbrækɪjʊrən/ *adj* of or belonging to a group of ten-footed crustaceans, including the crabs, marked by an undeveloped abdomen.—*also* **brachyurous**. • *n* a member of this group.

bracing /'breɪsɪŋ/ *adj* refreshing, invigorating.—**bracingly** *adv*.

bracken /'brækən/ *n* a large, coarse fern; a wide area of these growing on hills or moorland.

bracket /'brækət/ *n* a projecting metal support for a shelf; a group or category of people classified according to income; (*pl*) a pair of characters (), [], {}, used in printing or writing as parentheses. • *vt* to support with brackets; to enclose by brackets; (*people*) to group together.

brackish /'brækɪʃ/ *adj* somewhat salty; nauseating.—**brackishness** *n*.

bract /brækt/ *n* a modified leaf growing from a flower stem or enveloping a head of flowers.—**bracteal** *adj*.

bracteate /'bræktɪeɪt/ *adj* (*plant*) furnished with bracts. • *n* a plate or dish made of a thin beaten precious metal and decorated.

brad /bræd/ *n* a slender flat nail with a projection on one side.

bradawl /-ˌpl/ *n* a small boring tool for making holes for brads.

brady- /'breɪdi/ *prefix* slow.

brae /breɪ/ *n* (*Scot*) a hillside; sloping ground.

brag /bræg/ *vti* (**bragging, bragged**) to boast. • *n* a boast or boastful talk.—**bragger** *n*.

braggadocio /ˌbrægə'dɔːtʃɪo/ or /-'dɔːʃo/ *n* (*pl* **braggadocios**) bragging talk, empty boasting; a boaster, braggart.

braggart /'brægərt/ *n* a loud arrogant boaster.

Brahma[1] /'brɒmə/ *n* (*Hinduism*) a supreme god; divine essence.

Brahma[2] *n* a useful variety of large domestic fowl with feathered legs.

Brahman[1] /'brɒmən/ *n* (*pl* **Brahmans**) (*Hinduism*) a member of the highest caste, formerly consisting only of priests; Brahma.—**Brahmanic, Brahmanical** *adj*.

Brahman[2] *n* (*pl* **Brahmans, Brahman**) a breed of Indian cattle with a large hump used in crossbreeding beef cattle.

Brahmani /'brɒməni/ *n* (*pl* **Brahmanis**) a female Brahman.

Brahmanism /'brɒmənˌɪzəm/ *n* the religion or doctrines of the Brahmans.—**Brahmanist** *n*.

Brahmin /'brɒmɪn/ *n* a Brahman; a member of an upper-class New England family.

braid /breɪd/ *vt* to interweave three or more strands (of hair, straw, etc); to make by such interweaving. • *n* a narrow band made by such interweaving for decorating clothing; a plait.—**braider** *n*.

brail /breɪl/ *n* (*naut*) one of certain ropes used to gather up the foot and leeches of a sail prior to furling. • *vt* (*usu with* **up**) to haul in by the brails.

Braille /breɪl/ *n* printing for the blind, using a system of raised dots that can be understood by touch.—*also adj*.

brain /breɪn/ *n* nervous tissue contained in the skull of vertebrates that controls the nervous system; intellectual ability; (*inf*) a person of great intelligence; (*often pl*) the chief planner of an organization or enterprise. • *vt* to shatter the skull of; (*sl*) to hit on the head.

brainchild /-ˌtʃaɪld/ *n* (*pl* **brainchildren**) the result of creative thought; a clever and original idea or plan.

brain death *n* the irreversible cessation of brain activity, but not of the heartbeat, widely accepted as a criterion of death.

brain drain *n* the loss of highly skilled scientists, technicians, academics, etc through emigration.

brainless /-ləs/ *adj* (*inf*) stupid.—**brainlessness** *n*.

brainpan /-ˌpæn/ *n* the cranium.

brainstorm /-ˌstorm/ *n* a violent mental disturbance; a brain wave.

brainteaser /-ˌtiːzər/ *n* a mathematical puzzle; a difficult problem.

brainwash /-wɒʃ/ *vt* to change a person's ideas or beliefs by physical or mental conditioning, *usu* over a long period.—**brainwasher** *n*.—**brainwashing** *n*.

brain wave *n* an electrical impulse in the brain; (*inf*) a bright idea.

brainy /ˈbreɪni/ *adj* (**brainier, brainiest**) (*inf*) having a good mind; intelligent.—**braininess** *n*.

braise /breɪz/ *vt* (*meat, vegetables, etc*) to sauté lightly and cook slowly in liquid with the lid on.

brake[1] /breɪk/ *n* a device for slowing or stopping the motion of a wheel by friction. • *vt* to retard or stop by a brake. • *vi* to apply the brake on a vehicle; to become checked by a brake.

brake[2] *n* bracken.

brake[3] *n* a place overgrown with brushwood, etc; a thicket.

brake horsepower *n* the rate of work of an engine measured in terms of its resistance to a brake.

brakeman /ˈbreɪkmən/ *n* (*pl* **brakemen**) a person in charge of a brake; a guard on a train; the person at the back of a bobsled team.

brake shoe *n* that part of a brake which presses against the wheel.

bramble /ˈbræmbəl/ *n* a prickly shrub or vine, *esp* of blackberries and raspberries.—**brambly** *adj*.

brambling /ˈbræmblɪŋ/ *n* a migratory European finch with bright plumage.

bran /bræn/ *n* the husks of grain separated by sieving from the flour; a food containing these.

branch /brɑːntʃ/ *n* an offshoot extending from the trunk or bough of a tree or from the parent stem of a shrub; a separately located subsidiary or office of an enterprise or business; a part of something larger, *eg* a road or railway. • *vi* to possess branches; to divide into branches; to come out (from a main part) as a branch; (*with* **out**) to extend or enlarge one's interests, activities, etc.

branchia /ˈbræŋkiə/ *n* (*pl* **branchiae**) a respiratory organ of fishes and some amphibians, a gill.—**branchial** *adj*.

branchiate /ˈbræŋkieɪt/ *adj* having permanent gills.

branchio- /ˈbræŋkiə/ *prefix* gills.

branchiopod /-ˌpɒd/ *n* one of a group of crustaceans, including the water flea, the gills of which are situated on the feet.

brand /brænd/ *n* an identifying mark on cattle, imprinted with hot iron; a burning piece of wood; a mark of disgrace; a trademark; a particular make (of goods). • *vt* to burn a mark with a hot iron; to fix in the memory; to denounce.

brandish /ˈbrændɪʃ/ *vt* (*a weapon, etc*) to wave or flourish in a threatening manner.—**brandisher** *n*.

brandling /ˈbrændlɪŋ/ *n* a small brownish-red earthworm used as bait by freshwater anglers.

brand name *n* the name by which a certain commodity is known.—**brand-name** *adj*.

brand-new /ˈbrændˌnjuː/ *adj* entirely new and unused.

brandy /ˈbrændi/ *n* (*pl* **brandies**) an alcoholic liquor made from distilled wine or fermented fruit juice.

brant /brænt/ *n* the brent goose, the smallest species of the wild goose.

brash[1] /bræʃ/ *adj* bold; loud-mouthed; reckless.—**brashly** *adv*.—**brashness** *n*.

brash[2] *n* broken, loose and angular fragments of rock underlying alluvial deposits; small broken pieces of ice; hedge clippings.

brash[3] *n* acid eructation, a fit of sickness; a rash; a burst of rain.

brasilin /ˈbræzəˌlɪn/ or /brəˈzɪlɪn/ *see* **brazilin**.

brass /brɑːs/ *n* an alloy of copper and zinc; (*inf*) impudence; nerve; cheek; money; (*often pl*) the brass instruments of an orchestra or band; (*sl*) officers or officials of high rank.

brassard, brassart /ˈbræsˌɑːd/ *n* an identifying armband or badge; armour for the upper arm.

brass band *n* a band that uses brass and percussion instruments.

brasserie /ˌbræsəˈriː/ *n* a bar in which drinks and often food are served; a small and *usu* cheap restaurant.

brassica /ˈbræsɪkə/ *n* any of a group of plants that includes cabbages, turnips and mustards.—**brassicaceous** *adj*.

brassie /ˈbræsi/ *n* (*golf*) a wooden club orig with a brass sole, now No.2 wood.

brassiere /brəˈzɪːr/ *n* a woman's undergarment for protecting and supporting the breasts, a bra.

brass tacks *npl* (*inf*) basic facts.

brassy /ˈbræsi/ *adj* (**brassier, brassiest**) like brass; brazen, cheeky.—**brassily** *adv*.—**brassiness** *n*.

brat /bræt/ *n* an ill-mannered, annoying child.

bratpack /-pæk/ *n* a group of precociously young actors, writers, etc.

brattice /ˈbrætɪs/ *n* (*mining*) a wooden partition or separating wall in a level or shaft to form an air passage. • *vt* to divide by a brattice.

bratwurst /ˈbrætwɜːst/ *n* a type of seasoned German sausage made from pork.

bravado /brəˈvɑːdəʊ/ *n* (*pl* **bravadoes, bravados**) pretended confidence; swaggering.

brave /breɪv/ *adj* showing courage; not timid or cowardly; fearless; handsome; of excellent appearance. • *vt* to confront boldly; to defy. • *n* a North American Indian warrior.—**bravely** *adv*.

bravery /ˈbreɪvəri/ *n* (*pl* **braveries**) the quality of being brave; courage, fearlessness; finery, magnificence.

bravo /ˈbrɑːvəʊ/ *interj* well done! • *n* (*pl* **bravoes, bravos**) a cry or shout of "bravo!"

bravura /brəˈvjʊərə/ *n* bold daring; dash; (*mus*) a passage requiring spirit and technical brilliance.

brawl /brɔːl/ *n* a loud quarrel; a noisy fight. • *vi* to quarrel loudly.—**brawler** *n*.

brawn /brɔːn/ *n* strong, well-developed muscles; physical strength; pickled pork.

brawny /-ni/ *adj* (**brawnier, brawniest**) muscular, tough.—**brawnily** *adv*.—**brawniness** *n*.

bray[1] /breɪ/ *n* the sound of a donkey; any harsh sound. • *vi* (**braying, brayed**) to make similar sounds.—**brayer** *n*.

bray[2] *vt* (**braying, brayed**) to pound or beat fine or small.

brayer /-ər/ *n* (*print*) a hand roller used to rub down and temper ink.

braze[1] /breɪz/ *vt* to solder with an alloy of brass and zinc.—**brazer** *n*.

braze[2] /breɪz/ *vt* to cover or ornament with brass; to colour like brass.

brazen /ˈbreɪzən/ *adj* made of brass; shameless. • *vt* (*usu with* **out**) to face a situation boldly and shamelessly.—**brazenness** *n*.

brazier[1] /ˈbreɪzjər/ or /-ʒər/ *n* a metal container for hot coals.

brazier[2] *n* a worker in brass.

brazil /brəˈzɪl/ *n* brazilwood; a dye of various tints of *esp* red and orange obtained from brazilin.

brazilin /ˈbrɑːzəˌlɪn/ or /brəˈzɪlɪn/ *n* the colouring substance extracted from brazilwood.—*also* **brasilin**.

brazil nut *n* a large three-cornered nut, the seed of a tall tree of Brazil.

brazilwood /brəˈzɪlwʊd/ *n* a very heavy wood of a red colour from various species of Central and South American trees.

breach /briːtʃ/ *n* a break or rupture; violation of a contract, promise, etc; a break in friendship. • *vt* to make an opening in.

breach of promise *n* the breaking of a promise to marry.

breach of the peace *n* a public disturbance.

bread /bred/ *n* a dough, made from flour, yeast and milk, that is baked; nourishment; (*sl*) money; **bread and butter** (*inf*) one's livelihood. • *vt* to coat meat, fish, etc with breadcrumbs before cooking.

bread-and-butter /-ənˈbʌtər/ *adj* (*job*) providing a basic income; (*issues, etc*) fundamental, basic; (*letter*) thanking for hospitality.

breadbasket /-ˌbæskət/ *n* a basket for holding bread; (*sl*) the stomach; a source of food.

breadboard /-ˌbɔːd/ *n* a wooden board for cutting bread on; board used for constructing experimental electric circuits.

breaded /-əd/ *adj* coated with breadcrumbs.

breadfruit /-fruːt/ *n* (*pl* **breadfruits, breadfruit**) the fruit of a tree growing in the Pacific islands, which, when roasted, is eaten as bread.

breadline /-laɪn/ *n* a queue for bread ration; **on the breadline** poverty-stricken, only just able to subsist.

breadth /bredθ/ *n* measurement from side to side, width; extent; liberality (*eg* of interests).

breadthways /-ˌweɪz/, **breadthwise** /-ˌwaɪz/ *adv* from side to side.

breadwinner /ˈbredˌwɪnər/ *n* the principal wage-earner of a family.

break /breɪk/ *vb* (**breaking, broke**, *pp* **broken**) *vt* to smash or shatter; to tame; (*rules*) to violate; to discontinue; to cause to give up a habit; (*fall*) to lessen the severity of; to ruin financially; (*news*) to impart; to decipher or solve; (*with* **down**) to crush or destroy; to analyse; (*with* **in**) to intervene; to train. • *vi* to fall apart; (*voice*) to assume a lower tone at puberty; to cut off relations with; to suffer a collapse, as of spirit; (*news*) to become public in a sudden and sensational way; (*with* **down**) to fail completely; to succumb emotionally; (*with* **even**) to suffer neither profit nor loss (after taking certain action); (*with* **in**) to force a way in; (*with* **out**) to appear, begin; to erupt; to throw off restraint, escape; (*with* **up**) to disperse; to separate; to collapse. • *n* a breaking; an interruption; a gap; a sudden change, as in weather; a rest or a short holiday; an escape; (*snooker, billiards*) a continuous run of points; (*sl*) a fortunate opportunity.

breakable /'breɪkəbəl/ *adj* able to be broken. • *n* a fragile object.

breakage /'breɪkədʒ/ *n* the action of breaking; something broken.

breakaway /'breɪkəweɪ/ *n* secession, disassociation.

break dancing /'breɪkdænsɪŋ/ *n* dancing that involves acrobatic movements.

breakdown /'breɪkdaʊn/ *n* a mechanical failure; failure of health; nervous collapse; an analysis.

breakdown truck *n* a vehicle for towing away smashed or damaged cars, etc.

breaker[1] /'breɪkər/ *n* a large wave that crashes onto the shore, reef, etc.

breaker[2] *n* (*naut*) a small cask for holding water.

breakeven /ˌbreɪk'iːvən/ *n* the point at which costs are covered but no profit is made.

breakfast /'brɛkfəst/ *n* the first meal of the morning; the food consumed. • *vi* to have breakfast.

break-in /'breɪkˌɪn/ *n* the unlawful entering of premises, *esp* by thieves.

breakneck /'breɪknɛk/ *adj* dangerously steep or fast.

break of day *n* dawn.

break-out /'breɪkˌaʊt/ *n* an escape, *esp* from prison.

breakthrough /'breɪkˌθruː/ *n* the action of breaking through an obstruction; an important advance or discovery.

break-up /'breɪkʌp/ *n* separation; collapse; dispersal.

breakwater /'breɪkˌwɔtər/ *n* a barrier that protects a harbour or area of coast against the force of the waves.

bream[1] /briːm/ *n* (*pl* **bream**) a freshwater fish.

bream[2] *vt* (*naut*) to clear (a ship's bottom) of shells, seaweed, etc, by heating and scraping.

breast /brɛst/ *n* the chest; one of the two mammary glands; the seat of the emotions. • *vt* to oppose, confront; to arrive at the top of; to confess (*make a clean breast of*).

breastbone /'brɛstboːn/ *n* (*anat*) the flat narrow bone in the centre of the chest that connects the ribs, the sternum.

breast-feed /'brɛstfiːd/ *vt* (**breast-feeding, breast-fed**) to allow a baby to suck milk from the breast.

breastplate /'brɛstpleɪt/ *n* armour covering the front of the body; a part of the vestment of a Jewish high priest.

breaststroke /'brɛstˌstroːk/ *n* a swimming stroke in which both arms are brought out sideways from the chest.

breastwork /brɛstˌwɜrk/ *n* a hastily constructed work thrown up breast-high for defence; the parapet of a building.

breath /brɛθ/ *n* the inhalation and exhalation of air in breathing; the air taken into the lungs; life; a slight breeze; (*scandal*) a hint.

Breathalyzer, Breathalyser /brɛθəlaɪzər/ *n* (*trademark*) a device for measuring the amount of alcohol in a person's breath.

breathe /briːð/ *vi* to inhale and exhale, to respire air; to take a rest or pause; to exist or live; to speak or sing softly; to whisper. • *vt* to emit or exhale; to whisper or speak softly.

breather /'briːðər/ *n* a pause during exercise to recover one's breath.

breathing /'briːðɪŋ/ *n* respiration; air in gentle motion; a gentle influence; a pause; (*phonetics*) an accent (') whether an initial vowel is aspirated or not.

breathing space *n* a pause in which to recover, get organized or get going.

breathless /'brɛθləs/ *adj* out of breath; panting; gasping; unable to breathe easily because of emotion.—**breathlessly** *adv*.—**breathlessness** *n*.

breathtaking /'brɛθˌteɪkɪŋ/ *adj* very exciting.

breathy /'brɛθi/ *adj* (**breathier, breathiest**) (*voice*) not clear sounding.—**breathily** *adv*.—**breathiness** *n*.

breccia /'brɛtʃiə/ *n* a rock of angular fragments cemented by lime, etc.—**brecciated** *adj*.

bred *see* **breed**.

bree /briː/ *n* (*Scot*) broth; juice or liquor in which something has been steeped or boiled.

breech /briːtʃ/ *n* the back part of a gun barrel.

breech delivery, breech birth *n* the birth of a baby buttocks or feet first.

breeches /-əz/ *npl* trousers extending just below the knee.

breeches buoy *n* a lifebuoy on a hawser to take people off a wreck.

breeching /-ɪŋ/ *n* the harness that passes round a horse's hindquarters; a strong rope to check the recoil of a gun.

breechloader /-loːdər/ *n* a gun loaded at the breach.—**breechloading** *adj*.

breed /briːd/ *vb* (**breeding, bred**) *vt* to engender; to bring forth; (*dogs*) to raise; to give rise to. • *vi* to produce young; to be generated. • *n* offspring; lineage or race; species (of animal).—**breeder** *n*.

breeder reactor *n* a nuclear reactor that produces more fissile material than it consumes.

breeding /'briːdɪŋ/ *n* the bearing of offspring; one's education and training; refined behaviour.

breeze[1] /briːz/ *n* a light gentle wind; something easy to do. • *vi* (*inf*) to move quickly or casually.

breeze[2] *n* sifted ashes and cinders used in burning bricks; house sweepings, refuse.

breeze block *n* a lightweight building brick composed mainly of the ashes of coal and coke.

breezy /'briːzi/ *adj* (**breezier, breeziest**) windy; nonchalant; light-hearted, cheerful.—**breezily** *adv*.—**breeziness** *n*.

brent (goose) /brɛnt/ *n* the smallest species of the wild goose.—*also* **brant**.

brethren /'brɛðrən/ *see* **brother**.

Breton /'brɛtən/ *adj* of or relating to Brittany, its people or language. • *n* an inhabitant of Brittany; the Celtic language of Brittany.

breve /briːv/ *n* a mark (^) used to indicate a short vowel; (*mus*) the longest note now used, equal to two whole notes (two semibreves or four minims).

brevet /brə'vɛt/ *n* (*mil*) a commission to an officer in the army conferring a higher rank but without increase of pay; a warrant; a licence. • *adj* conferred by brevet; nominal, honorary. • *vt* (**brevetting, brevetted** *or* **breveting, breveted**) to confer brevet rank on.—**brevetcy** *n*.

brevi- /'brɛvɪ/ *prefix* short.

breviary /'briːvɪəri/ *or* /'briːˌvɪəri/, /'brɛv-/ *n* (*pl* **breviaries**) (*RC Church*) a book containing the daily offices and prayers.

brevirostrate /'brɛvɪˈrɒsˌtreɪt/ *adj* (*birds*) short-billed.

brevity /'brɛvɪti/ *n* (*pl* **brevities**) briefness; conciseness.

brew /bruː/ *vt* to make (beer, ale, etc) from malt and hops by boiling and fermenting; to infuse (tea, etc); to plot, scheme. • *vi* to be in the process of being brewed; to be about to happen. • *n* a brewed drink.

brewage /-ədʒ/ *n* something made by brewing; the brewing process.

brewer /'bruːər/ *n* a person who brews, *usu* beer.

brewery /'bruːəri/ *n* (*pl* **breweries**) a place where beer, etc is brewed.

briar /'braɪər/ *see* **brier**.

bribe /braɪb/ *n* money or gifts offered illegally to gain favour or influence; the gift to achieve this. • *vt* to offer or give a bribe to.—**bribable** *adj*.—**briber** *n*.

bribery /-əri/ *n* (*pl* **briberies**) the giving or taking of bribes.

bric-a-brac /'brɪkəˌbræk/ *n* curios, ornamental or rare odds and ends.

brick /brɪk/ *n* a baked clay block for building; a similar shaped block of other material. • *vt* to lay or wall up with brick.

brickbat /-bæt/ *n* a piece of brick, *esp* one used as a weapon; an unfavourable remark.

bricklayer /'brɪkleɪər/ *n* a person who lays bricks.

brick red *n* a greyish red colour.—**brick-red** *adj*.

brickwork /'brɪkwɜrk/ *n* a structure formed of bricks.

bridal /'braɪdəl/ *adj* relating to a bride or a wedding.

bride /braɪd/ *n* a woman about to be married or recently married.

bridegroom /'braɪdgruːm/ *or* /-grʊm/ *n* a man about to be married or recently married.

bridesmaid /'braɪdzmeɪd/ *n* a young girl or woman attending the bride during a wedding.

bridge[1] /brɪdʒ/ *n* a structure built to convey people or traffic over a river, road, railway line, etc; the platform on a ship where the captain gives directions; the hard ridge of bone in the nose; an arch to raise the strings of a guitar, etc; a mounting for false teeth. • *vt* to be or act as a bridge; to be a connecting link between.—**bridgeable** *adj*.

bridge² *n* a card game for two teams of two players based on whist.

bridgeboard /'brɪdʒ,bɔrd/ *n* a notched board into which the ends of the steps of wooden stairs are fastened.

bridgehead /-hed/ *n* a defensive work covering the end of a bridge nearest the enemy; a foothold in enemy territory.

bridge loan *n* a temporary loan made to cover a short period before more permanent financing is arranged.

bridgework /-wərk/ *n* a false tooth or teeth secured to the natural teeth.

bridging /-ɪŋ/ *n* a piece of wood between two beams to keep them apart.

bridging loan *n* a loan, *usu* short-term, advanced to cover the gap between the settlement of two transactions, *esp* between buying a new house and selling the old one.

bridle /'braɪdəl/ *n* the headgear of a horse, controlling its movements; a restraint or check; (*naut*) a mooring cable. • *vt* to put a bridle on (a horse); to restrain or check. • *vi* to draw one's head back as an expression of anger, scorn, etc.— **bridler** *n*.

bridle path *n* a trail suitable for horse riding.

bridoon /brɪ'duːn/ *n* the light snaffle and rein of a military bridle.

brie /briː/ *n* creamy white soft cheese.

brief /briːf/ *n* a summary of a client's case for the instruction of a barrister in a trial at law; an outline of an argument, *esp* that setting out the main contentions; (*pl*) men's or women's close-fitting underpants or knickers. • *vt* to provide with a precise summary of the facts. • *adj* short, concise.—**briefly** *adv*.—**briefness** *n*.

briefcase /'briːfkeɪs/ *n* a flat case for carrying documents, etc.

brier /'braɪr/ *n* a plant with a thorny or prickly woody stem; a mass of these; a tobacco pipe made from the root of the brier.—*also* **briar**.—**briery, briary** *adj*.

brig /brɪg/ *n* a two-masted square-rigged vessel; a naval prison, *esp* on a ship.

brigade /brɪ'geɪd/ *n* an army unit, smaller than a division, commanded by a brigadier; a group of people organized to perform a particular function.

brigadier /,brɪgə'diːr/ *n* an officer commanding a brigade and ranking next below a major general.

brigand /'brɪgənd/ *n* a bandit, *usu* one of a roving gang.

brigantine /'brɪgən,tiːn/ *n* a small two-masted vessel, square-rigged on the foremast only and with raking masts.

bright /braɪt/ *adj* clear, shining; brilliant in colour or sound; favourable or hopeful; intelligent, illustrious.—**brightly** *adv*.—**brightness** *n*.

Bright's disease *n* a kidney disease characterized by the presence of albumin in the urine.

brighten /'braɪtən/ *vti* to make or become brighter.—**brightener** *n*.

brill /brɪl/ *n* (*pl* **brill, brills**) a European flatfish resembling the turbot.

brilliance /'brɪljəns/ *n* intense radiance, lustre, splendour.

brilliancy /-si/ *n* the quality of being brilliant; shining quality, lustrousness, shining brightness.

brilliant /'brɪljənt/ *adj* sparkling, bright; splendid; very intelligent.—**brilliantly** *adv*.

brilliantine /'brɪljən,tiːn/ *n* a cosmetic oil giving a gloss to the hair; a shiny fabric of cotton and mohair.

brim /brɪm/ *n* the rim of a hollow vessel; the outer edge of a hat. • *vti* (**brimming, brimmed**) to fill or be filled to the brim; (*with* **over**) to overflow.

brimful /'brɪm,fʊl/ *adj* completely full; overflowing.

brimstone /'brɪmstoːn/ *n* sulphur; a yellow butterfly.

brindled /'brɪndəld/ *adj* streaked brown or grey, or with flecks of a darker colour.

brine /braɪn/ *n* salt water; the sea.

bring /brɪŋ/ *vt* (**bringing, brought**) to fetch, carry or convey "here" or to the place where the speaker will be; to cause to happen (*eg* rain, relief), to result in; to lead to an action or belief; to sell for; (*with* **about**) to induce, to effect; (*with* **down**) to cause to fall by or as if by shooting; (*with* **forth**) to give birth to; (*with* **forward**) to present something for consideration; to transfer a total figure from the bottom of a page to the top of the next page; (*with* **in**) to yield a profit or return; to return a verdict in court; to introduce (a legislative bill); to earn (an income); (*with* **off**) to achieve a success, often against odds; accomplish; (*with* **out**) to cause to appear; to produce (a play) or publish (a book); to

demonstrate clearly, expose to view; to help someone with encouragement; (*with* **over**) to convince a person to change their loyalties; (*with* **round**) to convince a person to change their opinion; to get someone to agree or give support; to restore a person to consciousness, revive; (*with* **up**) to educate, rear a child; to raise (a matter) for discussion; to vomit.—**bringer** *n*.

brink /brɪŋk/ *n* the verge of a steep place; the edge of the sea; the point of onset; the threshold of danger.

brinkmanship /'brɪŋkmənʃɪp/, **brinksmanship** *n* the pursuing of a policy, *esp* in international relations, that brings serious risk of danger in order to gain advantage.

briny /'braɪni/ *adj* (**brinier, briniest**) salty. • *n* the sea.—**brininess** *n*.

brio /'briːoː/ *n* vivacity.

brioche /'briːɒʃ/ or /briː'oːʃ/ *n* a small, slightly sweet, bread roll.

briony /'braɪəni/ *see* **bryony**.

briquette, briquet /brɪ'ket/ *n* a compacted brick *usu* of fine compressed material, *esp* charcoal.

brisk /brɪsk/ *adj* alert; quick; vigorous; sharp in tone.—**briskly** *adv*.—**briskness** *n*.

brisket /'brɪskət/ *n* meat from the breast of an animal.

brisling /'brɪzlɪŋ/ or /'brɪs-/ *n* a small fish like a sardine.

bristle /'brɪsəl/ *n* a short, coarse hair. • *vi* to stand up, as bristles; to have the bristles standing up; to show anger or indignation; to be thickly covered (with).

bristly /'brɪsli/ *adj* (**bristlier, bristliest**) covered with bristles; rough.—**bristliness** *n*.

Bristol board *n* a thick smooth white pasteboard.

brit /brɪt/ *n* the young of the herring and sprat; small animals upon which whales feed.

Brit /brɪt/ *n* (*inf*) a British person.

Brit. *abbr* = Britain; British.

Britannia /brɪ'tænjə/ *n* Britain or its former empire personified as a female warrior carrying a trident and wearing a helmet.

Britannia metal *n* a white metal alloy of tin, copper, antimony and bismuth, resembling pewter.

Britannic /brɪ'tænɪk/ *adj* of Britain; British.

Briticism /'brɪtə,sɪzəm/ *n* a word, phrase, etc, peculiar to or characteristic of British English.

British /'brɪtɪʃ/ *adj* of or pertaining to Great Britain or its inhabitants; pertaining to the ancient Britons. • *n* the people of Britain; the language of the ancient Britons.

Britisher /-ər/ *n* a British subject.

Britishism /-,ʃɪzəm/ *n* a Briticism.

Briton /'brɪtən/ *n* a native of Great Britain, *esp* before the Anglo-Saxon conquest.

brittle /'brɪtəl/ *adj* easily cracked or broken; fragile; sharp-tempered.—**brittleness** *n*.

britzka /'brɪtskə/, **britzska** /'brɪtʃkə/ *n* an open carriage with a hooded top and space for reclining.

bro /broː/ *n* (*inf*) mate, buddy.

broach /broːtʃ/ *vt* (*a topic*) to introduce for discussion; to pierce (a container) and draw out liquid.

broad /brɔd/ *adj* of large extent from side to side; wide; spacious; giving an overall view or idea; (*humour*) coarse; strongly marked in dialect or pronunciation. • *n* (*sl*) a woman.—**broadly** *adv*.—**broadness** *n*.

broad arrow *n* an arrow with a broad barbed head; a UK government mark to distinguish its property, formerly used on prison clothing.

broad bean *n* a plant widely grown for its large flat edible seed.

Broad Church *n* a section or party intermediate between the High and the Low Church of England; any group that opposes rigid dogma.—**Broad-Church** *adj*.

broad seal *n* the official seal of a nation.

broadcast /-kæst/ *n* a programme on radio or television. • *vti* (**broadcasting, broadcast**) to transmit on radio or television; to make known widely; to scatter seed.—**broadcaster** *n*.

broadcloth /-klɒθ/ *n* a fine woollen cloth with a smooth finished surface.

broaden /'brɔdən/ *vti* to grow or make broad; to widen.

broadloom /'brɔdluːm/ *adj* (*carpets*) woven on a wide loom.

broad-minded /brɔd'maɪndɪd/ *adj* tolerant; liberal in outlook.—**broad-mindedly** *adv*.—**broad-mindedness** *n*.

broadsheet /'brɔdʃiːt/ *n* a large sheet of paper printed on one side only; a large format newspaper, approx 15 by 24 inches (38 by 61cms).

broadside /'brɒdsaɪd/ *n* the entire side of a ship above the water-line; a simultaneous volley from one side of a warship; a sheet printed on one side containing information of a popular nature or an attack on some public person; any verbal or written attack.

broad-spectrum /-'spɛktrəm/ *adj* efficacious against a wide range (of diseases, microorganisms).

broadsword /'brɒdsɔrd/ *n* a cutting sword with a broad straight blade.

Brobdingnagian /brɒbdɪŋ'nægiən/ *adj* resembling one of the giant inhabitants of the land of Brobdingnag in Swift's *Gulliver's Travels*; gigantic.

brocade /bro:'keɪd/ *n* a heavy fabric woven with raised patterns, orig in gold and silver. • *vt* to work with a raised pattern.

brocatelle, brocatel /ˌbrɒkə'tɛl/ *n* a figured brocade of silky texture; a variegated marble from Italy and Spain.

broccoli /'brɒkəli/ *n* (*pl* **broccoli**) a kind of cauliflower with loose heads of tiny green buds.

broch /brɒk/ or *Scot.* /brɒx/ *n* (*Scot*) a dry-built circular tower of the Iron Age.

brochette /brɒ'ʃɛt/ or /brə'ʃɛt/ *n* (food cooked on) a skewer or small spit.

brochure /'bro:ʃʊr/ or /-'ʃər/, /'bro:ʃər/ *n* an advertising booklet.

brock /brɒk/ *n* (*dial*) a badger.

brogan /'bro:gən/ *n* a sturdy ankle-high work shoe.

brogue /bro:g/ *n* a sturdy shoe; a dialectical accent, *esp* Irish.

broil[1] /brɔɪl/ *vti* to cook by exposure to direct heat; to grill.

broil[2] *n* a noisy quarrel, a tumult. • *vi* to be heated with passion.

broiler /'brɔɪlər/ *n* a pan, grill, etc for broiling; a bird fit for broiling.

broke /bro:k/ *pt* of **break**. • *adj* (*inf*) hard up, having no money.

broken /'bro:kən/ *pp* of **break**. • *adj* splintered, fractured; violated; ruined; tamed; disconnected, interrupted; overwhelmed by sorrow or ill fortune; (*speech*) imperfect.—**brokenly** *adv*.—**brokenness** *n*.

broken-down /-daʊn/ *adj* extremely infirm; worn out.

brokenhearted *adj* grief-stricken; very sad.

broken-winded *adj* (*horse*) having the heaves.

broker /'bro:kər/ *n* an agent who negotiates contracts of purchase and sale (as of commodities or securities); a power broker; a stockbroker.

brokerage /'bro:kərɪdʒ/ *n* a broker's business; the commission charged by a broker.

bromate /'bro:meɪt/ *n* a salt of bromic acid.

brome (grass) /bro:m/ *n* any of a genus of oat-like grasses with drooping clusters of spikelets.

bromic acid *n* a compound of bromine and oxygen.

bromide /bro:maɪd/ *n* a compound of bromine; a sedative; (*sl*) a bore; a trite remark.

bromine /bro:mi:n/ *n* an evil-smelling nonmetallic element related to chlorine and iodine.—**bromic** *adj*.

bronchi /'brɒŋ.kaɪ/ *see* **bronchus**.

bronchia /'brɒŋkɪə/ *npl* (*sing* **bronchium**) the bronchial tubes.

bronchial /-əl/ *adj* of or pertaining to the bronchial tubes.

bronchial tube *n* either of the two main branches of the windpipe.

bronchitis /brɒŋ'kaɪtɪs/ *n* inflammation of the lining of the bronchial tubes.—**bronchitic** *adj*.

bronchopneumonia /ˌbrɒŋko:nə'mo:njə/ or /-nu:'mo:/, /nju:'mo:/ *n* diffuse inflammation of the lungs and bronchi.

bronchus /'brɒŋkəs/ *n* (*pl* **bronchi**) one of the two principal branches of the windpipe or trachea.

bronco /'brɒŋko:/ *n* (*pl* **broncos**) a wild or half-tamed horse of North America.

broncobuster /-ˌbɛstər/ *n* a cowboy who breaks in broncos.—**broncobusting** *n*.

brontosaur, brontosaurus /ˌbrɒntə'sɔrəs/ *n* (*pl* **brontosauruses**) a large plant-eating dinosaur.—**brontosaurian** *adj*.

Bronx cheer *n* (*inf*) (*mainly US*) a rude sound made with the lips; a raspberry.

bronze /brɒnz/ *n* a copper and tin alloy, sometimes other elements; any object cast in bronze; a reddish-brown colour. • *adj* made of, or like, or of the colour of bronze; (*skin*) tanned.—**bronzy** *adj*.

Bronze Age *n* the age succeeding the Stone Age, the ornaments and weapons of that period being made of bronze.

brooch /bro:tʃ/ *n* an ornament held by a pin or a clasp.

brood /bru:d/ *vi* to incubate or hatch (eggs); to ponder over or worry about. • *n* a group having a common nature or origin, *esp* the children in a family; the number produced in one hatch.

broody /'bru:di/ *adj* (**broodier, broodiest**) contemplative, moody; (*inf*) wanting to have a baby.—**broodily** *adv*.—**broodiness** *n*.

brook[1] /brʊk/ *n* a freshwater stream.

brook[2] *vt* to tolerate.—**brookable** *adj*.

brooklet /-lət/ *n* a small brook.

broom[1] /bru:m/ *n* a bundle of fibres or twigs attached to a long handle for sweeping.

broom[2] *n* a shrub bearing large yellow flowers.

broomstick /'bru:mstɪk/ or /brʊm-/ *n* the handle of a broom.

Bros *abbr* = Brothers.

brose /bro:z/ *n* (*Scot*) a kind of porridge made by pouring boiling water or milk or meat liquor on oatmeal.

broth /brɒθ/ *n* a thin or thick soup made by boiling meat, etc in water.

brothel /'brɒθəl/ *n* a house where prostitutes work.

brother /'brɛðər/ *n* a male sibling; a friend who is like a brother; a fellow member of a group, profession or association; a lay member of a men's religious order; (*pl* **brethren**) used chiefly in formal address or in referring to the members of a society or sect.

brotherhood /-hʊd/ *n* the state or quality of being a brother, brotherliness; a fraternity, an association.

brother-in-law /-ɪnlɔ/ *n* (*pl* **brothers-in-law**) the brother of a husband or wife; the husband of a sister.

brotherly /-li/ *adj* like a brother; kind; affectionate.—**brotherliness** *n*.

brougham /'bru:əm/ or /bru:m/, /'bro:əm/ *n* a light closed four-wheeled carriage for one or two horses.

brought /brɒt/ *see* **bring**.

brouhaha /'bru:hɒˌhɒ/ *n* a fuss; uproar.

brow /braʊ/ *n* the forehead; the eyebrows; the top of a cliff; the jutting top of a hill.

browbeat /'braʊbi:t/ *vt* (**browbeating, browbeat**, *pp* **browbeaten**) to intimidate with threats, to bully.

brown /braʊn/ *adj* having the colour of chocolate, a mixture of red, black and yellow; tanned. • *n* a brown colour. • *vti* to make or become brown, *esp* by cooking.—**brownish** *adj*.—**brownness** *n*.

brown bear *n* a large wild bear of a brownish colour that lives in forests in temperate areas of Asia, North America and Europe.

brown bread *n* bread made from wholemeal flour.

brown coal *n* lignite.

brownie /'braʊni/ *n* a square of flat, rich chocolate cake; a friendly helpful elf; (*with cap*) a member of the junior branch of the Girl Scout or Guide movement.

Brownie point *n* a credit gained by having scored some success.

brown rice *n* unpolished rice.

brown study *n* a reverie.

brown sugar *n* sugar that is unrefined or partially refined.

browned-off *adj* (*sl*) fed up, depressed.

Brownian movement *n* a rapid whirling movement frequently seen in microscopic particles suspended in water or other liquids.

Browning /'braʊnɪŋ/ *n* an automatic or semi-automatic gas-operated rifle; an automatic machine gun.

brownshirt /-ʃɔrt/ *n* (*often cap*) a member of the Nazi Party; a storm trooper.

brownstone /'braʊnsto:n/ *n* a kind of sandstone; a house built of this.

browse /braʊz/ *vti* to nibble, to graze; to examine (a book) at one's leisure or casually.—**browser** *n*.

brucellosis /ˌbru:sə'lo:sɪs/ *n* an infectious disease of livestock, *esp* cattle, which can be passed to human beings.

bruin /'bru:ɪn/ *n* the brown bear personified.

bruise /bru:z/ *vt* to injure and discolour (body tissue, surface of fruit) without breaking the skin; to break down (as leaves and berries) by pounding; to inflict psychological pain on. • *vi* to inflict a bruise; to undergo bruising. • *n* contusion of the skin; a similar injury to plant tissue; an injury, *esp* to the feelings.

bruiser /'bru:zər/ *n* a tough, pugnacious man; a boxer.

bruit /bru:t/ *n* a report; a rumour; fame. • *vt* to report; to noise abroad.

brumal /'bru:məl/ *adj* of or like winter, wintry.

brume /bru:m/ *n* fog, mist; a thick vapour.—**brumous** *adj*.

brunch /brʌntʃ/ *n* breakfast and lunch combined.

brunette, brunet /bruːˈnet/ *adj* having dark-brown or black hair, often with dark eyes. • *n* a brunette person.

brunt /brʌnt/ *n* the main force or shock of a blow; the hardest part.

brush[1] /brʌʃ/ *n* a device made of bristles set in a handle, used for grooming the hair, painting or sweeping; a short unfriendly meeting or exchange of words; a fox's bushy tail; a light stroke or graze, made in passing. • *vt* to groom or sweep with a brush; to remove with a brush; (*with* **aside**) to ignore, to regard as little account; (*with* **up**) to refresh one's memory of or skill in a subject; to wash and tidy oneself. • *vi* to touch lightly or graze; (*with* **up**) to smarten one's appearance.—**brusher** *n*.

brush[2] *n* brushwood.

brush-off /-ɒf/ *n* a curt dismissal.

brush-up /-ʌp/ *n* a smartening of one's appearance; refreshment of memory or skill.

brushwood /ˈbrʌʃwʊd/ *n* rough, close bushes; a thicket, a coppice; small wood or twigs suitable for the fire.

brushwork /ˈbrʌʃwɜːk/ *n* a particular or characteristic style of painting.

brusque /bresk/ or /brʊsk/, /bruːsk/ *adj* blunt and curt in manner.—**brusquely** *adv*.—**brusqueness** *n*.

Brussels carpet *n* a strong kind of woollen carpet.

Brussels lace *n* a fine, expensive lace with a floral pattern made orig in Brussels.

Brussels sprout *n* a plant of the cabbage family with a small edible green head.

brut /bruːt/ *adj* (*wines*) dry, unsweetened.

brutal /ˈbruːtəl/ *adj* inhuman; savage, violent; severe.—**brutally** *adv*.

brutality /bruːˈtæləti/ *n* (*pl* **brutalities**) the quality of being brutal; pitiless cruelty; a brutal act.

brutalize /ˈbruːtəˌlaɪz/ *vt* to treat brutally; to degrade.—**brutalization** *n*.

brute /bruːt/ *n* any animal except man; a brutal person; (*inf*) an unpleasant or difficult person or thing. • *adj* (*force*) sheer, physical.

brutish /ˈbruːtɪʃ/ *adj* brutal; stupid; savage, violent; coarse.—**brutishly** *adv*.—**brutishness** *n*.

bryology /braɪˈɒlədʒi/ *n* the scientific study of mosses.—**bryological** *adj*.—**bryologist** *n*.

bryony /ˈbraɪəni/ *n* (*pl* **bryonies**) any of several climbing plants of Europe and North Africa; black bryony; white bryony.—*also* **briony**.

bryozoan /ˌbraɪəˈzoʊən/ *n* any small animal belonging to the class Polyzoa, forming moss-like colonies by budding.

BSc /ˌbiːesˈsiː/ *abbr* = Bachelor of Science.

Bt. *abbr* = Baronet.

bub /bʌb/ *n* (*inf*) a boy; brother.

bubble /ˈbʌbəl/ *n* a film of liquid forming a ball around air or gas; a tiny ball of gas or air in a liquid or solid; a transparent dome; a scheme that collapses. • *vi* to boil; to rise in bubbles; to make a gurgling sound.

bubble and squeak *n* meat and vegetables fried together.

bubble bath *n* perfumed crystals or liquid added to a bath to soften the water and produce foam; a bath to which this has been added.

bubble gum *n* chewing gum that can be blown into large bubbles.

bubbly /ˈbʌbli/ *adj* (**bubblier, bubbliest**) having bubbles, effervescent; cheerful, high-spirited. • *n* (*inf*) champagne.

bubo /ˈbjuːboː/ or /buː-/ *n* (*pl* **buboes**) an inflamed swelling in the groin or armpit.—**bubonic** *adj*.

bubonic plague *n* a highly infectious often fatal disease contracted from fleas from infected rats.

bubonocele /bjuːˈbɒnəsiːl/ *n* a rupture or hernia in the groin.

buccal /ˈbʌkəl/ *adj* pertaining to the cheek or the mouth.

buccaneer /ˌbʌkəˈniːr/ *n* a sea robber, a pirate. • *vi* to be a pirate.

buccinator /ˈbʌksɪneɪtər/ *n* a flat muscle of the cheek, also called the trumpeter's muscle from its use in blowing wind instruments.

Buchmanism *see* **Oxford Group**.

buck /bʌk/ *n* the male of animals such as the deer, hare, rabbit, antelope; (*inf*) a dashing young man; (*sl*) a dollar. • *vti* (*horse*) to rear upwards quickly; (*inf*) to resist; (*with* **up**) (*inf*) to make or become cheerful; to hurry up.

buckaroo /ˌbʌkəˈruː/ or /ˌbʌkəˈruː/ *n* (*pl* **buckaroos**) a cowboy.

buckbean /ˈbʌkbiːn/ *n* a water plant with pinkish flowers.

buckboard /ˈbʌkbɔːd/ *n* a light four-wheeled carriage with a flexible board bearing the seats.

bucket /ˈbʌkət/ *n* a container with a handle for carrying liquid or substances in small pieces; (*comput*) a direct-access storage area from which data can be retrieved; (*inf*) a wastepaper bin. • *vt* to drive fast or recklessly; to pour with rain.

bucket seat *n* a single, contoured seat with an adjustable back as in a car, etc.

bucket shop *n* (*sl*) a dishonest brokerage firm; a business that sells cheap airline tickets.

buckeye /ˈbʌkaɪ/ *n* a North American tree with white or reddish flowers growing in clusters, the American horse chestnut; its nut; a native of Ohio.

buckjumper *n* (*Austral*) a vicious untrained horse that endeavours to throw its rider by arching its back and drawing its feet together.

buckle /ˈbʌkəl/ *n* a fastening or clasp for a strap or band; a bend or bulge. • *vti* to fasten with a buckle; to bend under pressure, etc; (*with* **down**) (*inf*) to apply oneself diligently.

buckler /ˈbʌklər/ *n* a small shield; protection. • *vt* to defend.

bucko /ˈbʌkoː/ *n* (*pl* **buckoes**) (*naut: sl*) a swaggering bully; (*Irish*) a young man.

buckpasser /ˈbʌkˌpæsər/ *n* (*inf*) one who regularly shifts the blame or responsibility to someone else.

buckram /ˈbʌkrəm/ *n* a coarse linen or cotton cloth stiffened with dressing. • *adj* made of, or resembling, buckram; stiff, precise. • *vt* (**buckraming, buckramed**) to stiffen with or bind in buckram.

buckshee /ˈbʌkˌʃiː/ *n* (*sl*) an extra allowance, a windfall. • *adj, adv* free, for nothing.

buckshot /ˈbʌkʃɒt/ *n* shot of a large size for shooting game.

buckskin /ˈbʌkskɪn/ *n* a soft leather of deerskin, etc; (*pl*) breeches or shoes made of this; (*hist*) a native American. • *adj* made of buckskin.

buckthorn /-θɔrn/ *n* any of several shurbs or trees with small greenish flowers, black berries and thorny branches.

bucktooth /-ˌtuːθ/ *n* (*pl* **buckteeth**) (*derog*) a projecting front tooth.

buckwheat /-wiːt/ *n* a plant cultivated for its triangular seeds, which are ground into meal and used as a cereal.

bucolic /bjuːˈkɒlɪk/ *adj* pastoral; rustic. • *n* a pastoral poem; a rustic.—**bucolically** *adv*.

bud[1] /bʌd/ *n* an embryo shoot, flower, or flower cluster of a plant; an early stage of development. • *vi* (**budding, budded**) to produce buds; to begin to develop.

bud[2] *n* (*inf*) buddy.

Buddha /ˈbuːdə/ or /ˈbʊdə/ *n* one who has arrived at the state of perfect enlightenment; an image of Siddharta Gautama, founder of Buddhism.

Buddhism /ˈbuːdɪzəm/ or /ˈbʊd-/ *n* a system of ethics and philosophy based on teachings of Buddha.

Buddhist /-dɪst/ *n* a follower of Buddhism.

budding /ˈbʌdɪŋ/ *n* being in an early stage of development; promising or showing promise.

buddle /ˈbʌdəl/ *n* an inclined trough in which ore is separated from earth by the action of running water. • *vt* to wash ore in a buddle.

buddleia /ˈbʌdliə/ *n* a shrub with lilac or yellow flowers.

buddy /ˈbʌdi/ *n* (*pl* **buddies**) (*inf*) a friend; a term of informal address; one who helps and supports another, *esp* an AIDS sufferer. • *vi* (**buddying, buddied**) to help as a buddy.

budge[1] /bʌdʒ/ *vti* to shift or move.

budge[2] *n* lambskin dressed with the wool outwards.

budgerigar /ˈbʌdʒərɪˌɡɑr/ *n* a small Australian parrot bred as a cage bird in many varieties of different colours.

budget /ˈbʌdʒət/ *n* an estimate of income and expenditure within specified limits of a country, a business, etc; the total amount of money for a given purpose; a stock or supply; **on a budget** restricting one's expenditure. • *vb* (**budgeting, budgeted**) *vi* to make a budget. • *vt* to put on a budget; to plan; (*with* **for**) to allow for or save money for a purpose or aim.—**budgetary** *adj*.

budgie /ˈbʌdʒi/ *n* (*inf*) a budgerigar.

buff /bʌf/ *n* a heavy, soft, brownish-yellow leather; a dull brownish yellow; (*inf*) a devotee, fan; (*inf*) a person's bare skin. • *adj* made of buff; of a buff colour. • *vt* to clean or shine, orig with leather or a leather-covered wheel.

buffalo /'bʌfələo:/ *n* (*pl* **buffalo, buffaloes** *or* **buffalos**) a wild ox; a bison.

buffer[1] /'bʌfər/ *n* anything that lessens shock, as of collision; something that serves as a protective barrier; a temporary storage area in a computer.

buffer[2] *n* (*sl*) a good-tempered somewhat foolish person; an elderly man.

buffer zone, buffer state *n* an area intended to separate; a neutral area.

buffet car *n* a railway coach where light refreshments are served.

buffet[1] /'bʌfət/ *n* a blow with the hand or fist. • *vb* (**buffeting, buffeted**) *vt* to hit with the hand or fist; to batter (as of the wind). • *vi* to make one's way *esp* under difficult conditions.— **buffeter** *n*.

buffet[2] /bə'feɪ/ *or* /bʌ'feɪ/, /bʊ'feɪ/ *n* a counter where refreshments are served; a meal at which guests serve themselves food.

buffeting *n* repeated battering.

buffo /'bʌfoː/ *n* (*pl* **buffi, buffos**) a comic actor, *esp* in an opera. • *adj* comic; burlesque.

buffoon /bə'fuːn/ *n* a clown, a jester; a silly person.

buffoonery *n* ridiculous behaviour.

bug[1] /bʌg/ *n* a continuing source of irritation.

bug[2] *n* an insect with sucking mouth parts; any insect; (*inf*) a germ or virus; (*sl*) a defect, as in a machine; (*sl*) a hidden microphone; an obsession, an enthusiasm. • *vt* (**bugging, bugged**) (*sl*) to plant a hidden microphone; (*sl*) to annoy, anger, etc.

bugbear /'bʌgbɛər/ *n* an object that causes great fear and anxiety.

buggy /'bʌgi/ *n* (*pl* **buggies**) a light four-wheeled, one-horse carriage with one seat; a small pushchair for a baby; a small vehicle.

bughouse /bʌg,haʊs/ *n* (*sl*) a mental home. • *adj* crazy.

bugle[1] /'bjuːgəl/ *n* a valveless brass instrument like a small trumpet, used *esp* for military calls. • *vti* to signal by blowing a bugle.— **bugler** *n*.

bugle[2] *n* an elongated glass bead, *usu* black.

bugle[3] *n* bugleweed.

bugleweed /-wiːd/ *n* a plant of Europe and Asia with spikes or clusters of small blue or white flowers.

bugloss /'bjuː,glɒs/ *n* any of various plants with hairy leaves and stems.

buhl /buːl/ *see* **boulle**.

build /bɪld/ *vb* (**building, built**) *vt* to make or construct, to establish, base; (*with* **up**) to create or develop gradually. • *vi* to put up buildings; (*with* **up**) to grow or intensify; (*health, reputation*) to develop. • *n* the way a thing is built or shaped; the shape of a person; the physical appearance or weight or size of a person.— **builder** *n*.

building /-ɪŋ/ *adj* the skill or occupation of constructing houses, boats, etc; something built with walls and a roof.

building society *n* a company that pays interest on deposits and issues loans to enable people to buy their own houses.— *also* **savings and loan association**.

built-in /,bɪlt'ɪn/ *adj* incorporated as an integral part of a main structure; inherent.

built-up /,bɪltʌp/ *adj* made higher, stronger, etc with added parts; having many buildings on it, *eg* built-up area.

bulb /bʌlb/ *n* the underground bud of plants such as the onion and daffodil; a glass bulb in an electric light; a rounded shape.— **bulbous** *adj*.

bulbiferous /bʌl'bɪfərəs/ *adj* (*plants*) producing bulbs.

bulbil /'bʌl,bɪl/ *n* (*bot*) a small bulb formed at the side of an old one; a small solid or scaly bud, which detaches itself from the stem, becoming an independent plant.

bulbul /'bʊlbʊl/ *n* an Eastern songbird; (*poet*) the Persian nightingale.

bulge /bʌldʒ/ *n* a swelling; a rounded projected part; a significant rise in numbers (of population). • *vti* to swell or bend outward.— **bulgy** *adj*.

bulimia /buː'liːmɪə/ *n* insatiable hunger, voracity.

bulimia nervosa /- nər'voːsə/ *n* an illness characterized by bouts of compulsive eating followed by self-induced vomiting.

bulk /bʌlk/ *n* magnitude; great mass; volume; the main part; **in bulk** in large quantities. • *adj* total, aggregate; (*goods*) not packaged.

bulk buying *n* the large-scale buying of one commodity *usu* at a cost reduction; the purchase by one country of the total output of a product of another country.

bulk carrier *n* a ship carrying as cargo one unpackaged commodity.

bulkhead /bʌlk'hɛd/ *n* a wall-like partition in the interior of a ship, aircraft or vehicle.

bulky /bʌlki/ *adj* (**bulkier, bulkiest**) large and unwieldy.— **bulkily** *adv*.— **bulkiness** *adj*.

bull[1] /bʊl/ *n* an adult male bovine animal; a male whale or elephant; a speculator who buys in anticipation of reselling at a profit; the bull's-eye; (*sl*) nonsense; bullshit. • *adj* male; rising in price.

bull[2] *n* an official edict issued by the pope, with the papal seal on it.

bull[3] *n* a ludicrous inconsistency in language.— *also* **Irish bull**.

bulla /'bʊlə/ *n* (*pl* **bullae**) a lead seal on a papal document; a blister.— **bullous** *adj*.

bullace /'bʊləs/ *n* a wild European species of plum cultivated as the damson.

bullate /'bʊlət/ *or* /-eɪt/, /bʌl-/ *adj* blistered; puffy.

bulldog /,bʊldʊg/ *n* a variety of dog of strong muscular build, remarkable for its courage and ferocity, formerly used for baiting bulls; a short-barrelled pistol with a large calibre. • *adj* characterized by the courage of a bulldog; tenacious.

bulldog clip *n* a spring clip with a powerful grip.

bulldoze /'bʊldoːz/ *vt* to demolish with a bulldozer; (*inf*) to force.

bulldozer /bʊl,doːzər/ *n* an excavator with caterpillar tracks for moving earth.

bullet /'bʊlət/ *n* a small metal missile fired from a gun or rifle.

bulletin /'bʊlətɪn/ *n* an announcement; a short statement of news or of a patient's progress.

bulletin board *n* a board on which notices are posted.

bulletproof /'bʊlətpruːf/ *adj* providing protection against bullets.

bullfight /'bʊl,faɪt/ *n* a combat between armed men and a bull or bulls.

bullfighting /-ɪŋ/ *n* the sport of goading and then killing bulls, popular in Spain, etc.— **bullfighter** *n*.

bullfinch /-,fɪntʃ/ *n* a common brightly coloured European songbird.

bullfrog /-,frɒg/ *n* a large North American frog found in marshy places, remarkable for its loud bellowing croak.

bullheaded /-,hɛdəd/ *adj* stubborn; stupid.— **bullheadedly** *adv*.— **bullheadedness** *n*.

bullion /'bʊljən/ *n* gold or silver in mass before coinage.

bull-necked /-,nɛkt/ *adj* having a short thick neck.

bullock /'bʊlək/ *n* a gelded bull; steer.

bullring /-rɪŋ/ *n* an arena for bullfighting.

bull's-eye /'bʊlz,aɪ/ *n* (*darts, archery*) the centre of a target; something resembling this; a direct hit; a large round peppermint boiled sweet.

bullwhip /-wɪp/ *n* a whip with a long lash for driving cattle. • *vt* (**bullwhipping, bullwhipped**) to whip with this.

bullshit /'bʊl,ʃɪt/ *n* (*vulg sl*) nonsense; exaggeration, pretentious talk. • *vti* (**bullshitting, bullshitted**) (*vulg sl*) to claim knowledge that is lacking; to talk boastfully.— **bullshitter** *n*.

bull terrier *n* a dog bred by a cross between the bulldog and the terrier.

bully /'bʊli/ *n* (*pl* **bullies**) a person, adult or child, who hurts or intimidates others weaker than himself or herself. • *vb* (**bullying, bullied**) *vt* to intimidate, oppress or hurt. • *vi* (*with* **off**) (*hockey*) to cross sticks in a bully-off to start a match. • *adj* (*inf*) very good, as in *bully for you*.

bully beef *n* canned corned beef.

bully boy *n* a hoodlum, a ruffian, *usu* one hired to beat up someone.

bullyrag /-,ræg/ *see* **ballyrag**.

bulrush /'bʊlrʌʃ/ *n* a tall marsh plant.

bulwark /'bʊlwərk/ *or* /-wɔːk/ *n* a defensive wall or rampart; (*naut*) a fence-like structure projecting above the deck of a ship; an object or person acting as a means of defence.

bum /bʌm/ *n* (*inf*) a tramp; an idle person; (*inf*) a devotee, as of skiing or tennis; (*sl*) buttocks or anus. • *adj* broken; useless. • *vti* (**bumming, bummed**) to beg, to sponge; to live as a vagabond; (*with* **around**) to be idle, to loaf about.

bumble /'bʌmbəl/ *vi* to do or say something clumsily or in a confused way; to stumble.— **bumbler** *n*.

bumblebee /-,biː/ *n* a large, furry bee.

bumboat /'bʌm,boːt/ *n* a boat used for conveying provisions, fruit, etc, for sale to vessels lying off shore.

bummer /'bʌmər/ *n* a worthless person who sponges on others; a low politician; an unpleasant experience, *esp* due to drug taking.

bump /bʌmp/ *vi* to knock with a jolt. • *vt* to hurt by striking or knocking; (*inf*) to refuse a booked passenger a seat on a flight because of overbooking by the airline; (*with* **into**) to collide with; (*inf*) to meet by chance; (*with* **off**) (*sl*) to kill, murder; (*with* **up**) (*inf*) to increase prices, size or bulk. • *n* a jolt; a knock; the noise made by a bump or a collision; a swelling or lump; one of the bulges on the head supposedly indicating a special faculty.

bumper /'bʌmpər/ *n* a shock-absorbing bar fixed to the front and rear of a motor vehicle; a brimming glass for a toast. • *adj* exceptionally large.

bumpkin /'bʌmpkɪn/ *n* an awkward or simple country person.

bumptious /'bʌmpʃəs/ *adj* offensively conceited or self-assertive.—**bumptiously** *adv*.—**bumptiousness** *n*.

bumpy /'bʌmpi/ *adj* (**bumpier, bumpiest**) having many bumps; rough; jolting, jerky.—**bumpily** *adv*.—**bumpiness** *n*.

bum steer *n* (*sl*) false or deceptive information or advice.

bun /bʌn/ *n* a roll made of bread dough and currants, spices and sugar; a bun-shaped coil of hair at the nape of the neck.

bunch /bʌntʃ/ *n* a cluster; a number of things growing or fastened together; (*inf*) a group of people. • *vi* to group together. • *vt* to make into a bunch.—**bunchy** *adj*.—**bunchiness** *n*.

buncombe /'bʌŋkəm/ *see* **bunkum**.

bund[1], **Bund** /bund/ or /bunt/ *n* (*pl* **bunds, Bünde**) a league, a confederacy.

bund[2] /bund/ *n* an embankment to protect land against inundation.

bundle /'bʌndəl/ *n* a number of things fastened together; a fastened package; (*sl*) a large sum of money. • *vt* to put together in bundles; to push hurriedly into.—**bundler** *n*.

bung /bʌŋ/ *n* a cork or rubber stopper. • *vt* to close up with or as with a bung; (*sl*) to throw, toss.

bungalow /'bʌŋɡə.loː/ *n* a one-storey house.

bungle /'bʌŋɡəl/ *n* a mistake or blunder; something carried out clumsily. • *vt* to spoil something through incompetence or clumsiness.—**bungler** *n*.—**bungling** *adj*, *n*.

bunion /'bʌnjən/ *n* a lump on the side of the first joint of the big toe.

bunk[1] /bʌŋk/ *n* a narrow, shelf-like bed; a bunk bed.

bunk[2] *n* (*sl*) a hurried departure.

bunk[3] *n* (*sl*) buncombe.

bunk bed *n* one of two or three single beds arranged one above the other in a compact unit.

bunker /'bʌŋkər/ *n* a large storage container, *esp* for coal; a sand pit forming an obstacle on a golf course; an underground shelter.

bunkhouse /'bʌŋkhəʊs/ *n* (*US*) a building where workers *esp* on a ranch are housed temporarily.

bunkum /'bʌŋkəm/ *n* idle or showy speech; nonsense.—*also* **buncombe**.

bunny /'bʌni/ *n* (*pl* **bunnies**) a pet name for a rabbit; (**girl**) a nightclub waitress dressed to resemble a rabbit.

Bunsen burner /'bʌnsən'bɜːnər/ *n* a burner that mixes gas and air to produce a smokeless flame of great heat.

bunt[1] /bʌnt/ *vti* (*animal*) to butt; (*baseball*) to tap (the ball) within the infield. • *n* this stroke.

bunt[2] *n* a species of fungus that produces the smut disease in wheat.

bunt[3] *n* the bulge of a sail, net, etc.

bunting[1] /-ɪŋ/ *n* a cotton fabric used for making flags; a line of pennants and decorative flags.

bunting[2] *n* a bird allied to the finches and sparrows.

buntline /'bʌntlaɪn/ *n* (*naut*) one of the ropes attached to the foot rope of a square sail to draw the sail up to the yard.

buoy /bɔɪ/ or /'buːi/ *n* a bright, anchored, marine float used for mooring and for making obstacles. • *vt* to keep afloat; (*usu with* **up**) to hearten or raise the spirits of; to mark with buoys.

buoyancy /'bɔɪənsi/ *n* ability to float or rise; cheerfulness; resilience.

buoyant /'bɔɪənt/ *adj* able to float; light, elastic; not easily depressed, cheerful.—**buoyantly** *adv*.

bur /bɜr/ *n* a prickly seed-case of a plant; a person hard to shake off; a rough edge left after drilling or cutting; a burr. • *vt* (**burring, burred**) to pick burs off.

burble /'bɜːbəl/ *vi* to make a gurgling sound; to speak incoherently, *esp* from excitement.—**burbler** *n*.

burbot /'bɜːbət/ *n* (*pl* **burbot, burbots**) a freshwater fish like the eel.

burden[1] /'bɜːdən/ *n* a load; something worrisome that is difficult to bear; responsibility. • *vt* to weigh down, to oppress.

burden[2] *n* the chorus or refrain of a song; a topic dwelt on in speech or writing.

burdensome /-səm/ *adj* onerous; oppresive; heavy.—**burdensomely** *adv*.

burdock /'bɜːdɒk/ *n* a large wayside weed with prickly flowers and rough broad leaves.

bureau /'bjʊəroː/ *n* (*pl* **bureaus, bureaux**) a writing desk; a chest of drawers; a branch of a newspaper, magazine or wire service in an important news centre; a government department.

bureaucracy /bjʊə'rɒkrəsi/ *n* (*pl* **bureaucracies**) a system of government where the administration is organized in a hierarchy; the government collectively; excessive paperwork and red tape.

bureaucrat /'bjʊərə.kræt/ or /-roː-/, /-kræt/ *n* an official in a bureaucracy, *esp* one who adheres inflexibly to this system.—**bureaucratic** *adj*.—**bureaucratically** *adv*.

burette, buret /bjʊ'rɛt/ *n* a graduated glass tube, *usu* with a tap, for measuring the volume of liquids.

burg /bɜrɡ/ *n* a town; (*formerly*) a fortified town.

burgee /bər'dʒiː/ *n* a swallow-tailed flag or pennant flown on the mast of a yacht to show membership of a club or of a merchant vessel to show ownership.

burgeon /'bɜːdʒən/ *vt* to start to increase rapidly; (*plant*) to bloom copiously.

burger /'bɜrɡər/ *n* (*inf*) hamburger.

burgess /'bɜːdʒəs/ *n* in UK, a citizen or freeman of a borough; (*formerly*) a member of parliament for a borough or university; in US, a representative sent by a town to the colonial legislative body of Virginia or Maryland.

Burgh /'bɜrə/ *n* (*Scot*) a borough.—**burghal** *adj*.

burgher /'bɜrɡər/ *n* a citizen or freeman of a burgh or borough; a prosperous person of the middle classes.

burglar /'bɜrɡlər/ *n* a person who trespasses in a building with the intention of committing a crime, such as theft.

burglary /-ləri/ *n* (*pl* **burglaries**) the act or crime of breaking into a house or any building with intent to commit a felony, *esp* theft.

burgle /'bɜrɡəl/, **burglarize** /'bɜrɡlə.raɪz/ *vti* to commit burglary (in or on).

burgomaster /'bɜrɡə.mæstər/ *n* the chief magistrate of a municipal town in Holland, Belgium or Germany.

burgonet /'bɜrɡə.nɛt/ *n* a kind of steel cap or helmet of the 16th century.

Burgundy /'bɜrɡəndi/ *n* (*pl* **Burgundies**) a dryish wine, red or white, made in the Burgundy region of eastern France; a similar wine produced elsewhere; a dark purplish red colour.

burial /'bɛriəl/ *n* the act of burying; interment of a dead body.

burial ground *n* a graveyard.

burin /'bjʊrɪn/ *n* a chisel used for engraving metal, wood or marble; (*archaeol*) a primitive tool with a chisel-shaped head.

burke /bɜrk/ *vt* to murder by suffocation; to dispose of quietly; to hush up.

burl /bɜrl/ *n* a small knot or lump in thread or cloth; a knot in wood; a wood veneer with knots in it. • *vt* to pick knots, etc, from, as in finishing cloth.

burlap /'bɜrlæp/ *n* a coarse fabric made of jute, hemp, etc, used for bagging or in upholstery.

burlesque /bɜrlɛsk/ *n* a caricature; a literary or dramatic satire. • *vti* (**burlesquing, burlesqued**) to make fun of, to caricature. • *adj* of or like burlesque; mockingly imitative.

burly /'bɜrli/ *adj* (**burlier, burliest**) heavily built; sturdy.—**burliness** *n*.

burn[1] /bɜrn/ *vb* (**burning, burned** *or* **burnt**) *vt* to destroy by fire; to injure by heat. • *vi* to be on fire; to feel hot; to feel passion; (*inf*) to suffer from sunburn; (*with* **off**) to clear ground by burning all vegetation; to get rid of (surplus gas, energy) by burning or using up; (*with* **out**) (*fire*) to go out; (*person*) to lose efficiency through exhaustion, excess or overwork. • *n* a scorch mark or injury caused by burning.

burn[2] *n* (*Scot*) a small stream, a brook.

burner *n* the part of a lamp or stove that produces a flame.

burnet /bər'nɛt/ *n* a brown-flowered plant of the rose family.

burning /'bɜrnɪŋ/ *adj* intense, passionate; urgent.—**burningly** *adj*.

burning glass *n* a double convex lens used to focus the sun's rays on combustible substances to ignite them.

burnish /'bɜrnɪʃ/ *vt* to make shiny by rubbing; to polish. • *n* lustre; polish.—**burnishable** *adj*.—**burnisher** *n*.

burnous, burnoose /bər'nuːs/ or /'bɜrnuːs/ *n* a long, hooded cloak worn by Arabs.

burnt /bɜrnt/ *see* **burn**.

burnt offering *n* something offered and burnt upon an altar as a sacrifice or an atonement for sin.

burnt sienna *n* an orange-reddish pigment used in painting.

burp /bɜrp/ *vi* to belch. • *vt* to pat a baby on the back to cause it to belch. • *n* a belch.

burr¹ /bɜr/ *see* **bur**.

burr² *n* a whirring sound; a gruff pronunciation of the letter *r*. • *vti* to pronounce with a burr.

burrito /bəˈriːtoː/ *n* a tortilla baked with a savoury filling.

burro /ˈbɜroː/ *n* (*pl* **burros**) a donkey.

burrow /ˈbɜroː/ *n* an underground hide or tunnel dug by a rabbit, badger or fox, etc for shelter. • *vi* to dig a burrow; to live in a burrow; to hide (oneself); to grope into the depths of one's pockets.—**burrower** *n*.

burry /ˈbɜri/ *adj* (**burrier, burriest**) full of or covered in burs; rough; prickly.

bursa /ˈbɜrsə/ *n* (*pl* **bursae, bursas**) (*anat*) a sac or sac-like cavity, *esp* between joints, full of a fluid that lessens friction.—**bursal** *adj*.

bursar /ˈbɜrsər/ *n* a treasurer; a person in charge of the finances of a college or university; a student holding a bursary.—**bursarial** *adj*.

bursary /-ri/ *n* (*pl* **bursaries**) a scholarship awarded to a student.—**bursarial** *adj*.

burst /bɜrst/ *vb* (**bursting, burst**) *vt* to break open; to cause to explode. • *vi* to emerge suddenly; to explode; to break into pieces; to give vent to. • *n* an explosion; a burst; a volley of shots; a sudden increase of activity; a spurt.—**burster** *n*.

burton /ˈbɜrtən/ *n* (*naut*) a tackle formed of two or more blocks or pulleys; **go for a burton** to die; to be no longer useful.

bury /ˈberi/ *vt* (**burying, buried**) (*bone, corpse*) to place in the ground; to inter; to conceal, to cover; to blot out of the mind; **bury the hatchet** to make peace; to be reconciled.

bus /bʌs/ *n* (*pl* **buses, busses**) a motor coach for public transport. • *vti* (**busing, bused** *or* **bussing, bussed**) to transport or travel by bus; (*US*) to take by bus children from one area to another, *esp* to balance racial numbers.

busby /ˈbʌzbi/ *n* (*pl* **busbies**) a tall, fur hat, *esp* one worn by a guardsman.

bush¹ /bʊʃ/ *n* a low shrub with many branches; a cluster of shrubs forming a hedge; woodland; (*with* **the**) uncultivated land, *esp* in Africa, Australia, New Zealand, Canada; a thick growth, *eg* of hair; a fox's tail or brush.

bush² *n* a metal lining of a hole in which an axle turns to reduce wear by friction.—*also* **bushing**. • *vt* to furnish with a bush.

bushbaby /-beibi/ *n* (*pl* **bushbabies**) a small tree-dwelling nocturnal lemur from Africa.

bushed /bʊʃt/ *adj* (*inf*) tired, exhausted.

bushel¹ /ˈbʊʃl/ *n* a dry measure containing eight gallons (*UK*) or 64 pints (*US*); a vessel of such a capacity; a large quantity.

bushel² *vt* (**bushelling, bushelled** *or* **busheling, busheled**) to patch or repair, *esp* clothes.—**busheller, busheler** *n*.

bushfire /ˌbʊʃˈfair/ *n* a fire, often widespread, in bush or scrubland.

bushing /ˈbʊʃɪŋ/ *see* **bush**².

bushman /ˈbʊʃmən/ *n* (*pl* **bushmen**) a woodsman; (*Austral*) a settler in the bush or newly opened country; (*with cap*) one of a tribe of South African aboriginals near the Cape of Good Hope.

bushmaster /-ˌmæstər/ *n* a large deadly South American snake with brown and grey markings.

bushranger /-ˌreindʒər/ *n* a frontiersman; (*Austral: formerly*) a criminal who escaped and lived a lawless life in the bush.

bush telegraph *n* a means of communicating news by drumbeat across a large area; (*inf*) a means of spreading gossip.

bushwhack /ˈbʊʃˌwæk/ *vi* (*US, Austral*) to work one's way through the bush; to ambush.—**bushwhacker** *n*.

bushy /ˈbʊʃi/ *adj* (**bushier, bushiest**) covered with bushes; (*hair*) thick.—**bushiness** *n*.

business /ˈbɪznəs/ *n* trade or commerce; occupation or profession; a firm; a factory; one's concern or responsibility; a matter; the agenda of a business meeting.

businesslike /-ˌlaik/ *adj* efficient, methodical, practical.

businessman /-mæn/ *n* (**businessmen**) a person who works for an industrial or commercial company, *esp* as an executive.—**businesswoman** *nf* (*pl* **businesswomen**).

busing *see* **bussing**.

busker /ˈbʌskər/ *n* a street entertainer.—**busking** *n*.

buskin /ˈbʌskɪn/ *n* a half boot or high shoe; a high boot once worn by tragic actors to increase their height; a tragic drama.

busman's holiday *n* a holiday spent doing what one usually does at work.

buss /bʌs/ *n* a smacking kiss. • *vt* to kiss.

bussing /-ɪŋ/ *n* the transport of children to a school in another district to achieve racially balanced classes.—*also* **busing**.

bust¹ /bʌst/ *n* the chest or breast of a human being, *esp* a woman; a sculpture of the head and chest.

bust² /bʌst/ *vti* (**busting, busted** *or* **bust**) (*inf*) to burst or break; to make or become bankrupt or demoted; to hit; to arrest. • *n* (*inf*) a failure; financial collapse; a punch; a spree; an arrest.

bustard /ˈbʌstərd/ *n* any of a genus of large swift-running birds of Europe and Africa.

buster /ˈbʌstər/ *n* a person or thing that busts; something very large; a frolic; a violent wind; (*with cap*) (*inf*) boy, man, a form of address.

bustle¹ /ˈbʌsl/ *vi* to move or act noisily, energetically or fussily. • *n* noisy activity, stir, commotion.—**bustler** *n*.—**bustling** *adj*.

bustle² *n* a pad placed beneath the skirt of a dress to cause it to puff up at the back.

bust-up /ˈbʌstəp/ *n* (*inf*) a fight or quarrel; a noisy brawl; the permanent ending of a relationship.

busy /ˈbɪzi/ *adj* (**busier, busiest**) occupied; active; crowded; full; industrious; (*painting*) having too much detail; (*room, telephone*) engaged, in use. • *vt* (**busying, busied**) to occupy; to make or keep busy (*esp* oneself).—**busily** *adv*.—**busyness** *n*.

busybody /ˈbɪziˌbɒdi/ *n* (*pl* **busybodies**) a meddlesome person.

but /bʌt/ *prep* save; except. • *conj* in contrast; on the contrary, other than. • *adv* only; merely; just. • *n* an objection.

butane /ˈbjuːteɪn/ *or* /bjuːˈteɪn/ *n* an inflammable gas used as a fuel.

butch /bʊtʃ/ *adj* (*sl*) tough; aggressively male; (*often of a woman*) male-looking.

butcher /ˈbʊtʃər/ *n* a person who slaughters meat; a retailer of meat; a ruthless murderer. • *vt* to slaughter; to murder ruthlessly; to make a mess of or spoil.

butcher's-broom *n* a low-growing evergreen shrub with rigid branched stems and spiny leaves.

butcherbird /-ˌbɜrd/ *n* any of a genus of shrikes that suspend their slaughtered prey from thorns.

butchery /ˈbʊtʃəri/ *n* (*pl* **butcheries**) the preparation of meat for sale; slaughter.

butler /ˈbʌtlər/ *n* a manservant, *usu* the head servant of a household, etc.

butt¹ /bʌt/ *vti* to strike or toss with the head or horns, as a bull, etc; (*with* **in**) to interfere, to enter into unasked. • *n* a push with the head or horns.—**butter** *n*.

butt² *n* a large cask for wine or beer.

butt³ *n* a mound of earth behind targets; a person who is the target of ridicule or jokes; (*pl*) the target range.

butt⁴ *n* the thick or blunt end; the stump; (*sl*) a cigarette; fag end; (*sl*) the buttocks. • *vti* to join end to end.

butte /bjuːt/ *n* an abrupt isolated hill or ridge.

butter /ˈbʌtər/ *n* a solidified fat made from cream by churning. • *vt* to spread butter on; (*with* **up**) (*inf*) to flatter.

butter bean *n* a variety of lima bean cultivated for its large flat pale edible seeds.

buttercup /-ˌkʌp/ *n* any of various plants with yellow, glossy, cup-shaped flowers.

butterfingers /-ˌfɪŋgərz/ *n* (*used as sing*) a person who lets (a ball, etc) slip through his or her fingers.—**butterfingered** *adj*.

butterfly /-ˌflai/ *n* (*pl* **butterflies**) an insect with a slender body and four *usu* brightly coloured wings; a swimming stroke.

buttermilk /-ˌmɪlk/ *n* the sour liquid that remains after separation from the cream in buttermaking.

butternut /-ˌnʌt/ *n* a North American tree of the walnut family; its large oily nut; its hard wood; the colour of the butternut, a brownish grey, the colour of the Confederate uniform in the American Civil War; one who wore the uniform of the Confederate army.

butterscotch /-ˌskɒtʃ/ *n* a sauce made of melted butter and brown sugar; a kind of hard toffee made from this; its flavour; a brownish-yellow colour.

butterwort /-ˌwɜrt/ *n* a violet-flowered bog plant with leaves that secrete a viscid fluid to entrap small insects.

buttery¹ /ˈbʌtəri/ *adj* like or tasting of butter; insincere.

buttery² *n* (*pl* **butteries**) a storeroom for wine or food.

buttock /ˈbʌtək/ *n* either half of the human rump.

button /'bʌtən/ *n* a disc or knob of metal, plastic, etc used as a fastening; a badge; a small button-like sweet; an electric bell push; a knob at the point of a fencing foil. • *vti* to fasten with a button or buttons.

buttonhole /-ˌhoːl/ *n* the slit through which a button is passed; a single flower in the buttonhole. • *vt* to make buttonholes; to sew with a special buttonhole stitch; (*person*) to keep in conversation.

buttonhook /-ˌhʊk/ *n* a tool for fastening buttons on shoes or gloves.

buttress /'bʌtrəs/ *n* a projecting structure for strengthening a wall. • *vt* to support or prop.

butyraceous /ˌbjuːtə'reɪʃəs/ *adj* like butter in consistency, appearance or properties.

butyrate /'bjuːtəˌreɪt/ *n* a salt of butyric acid.

butyric acid /'bjuːtəˌrɪk/ *n* a colourless liquid obtained from butter, also present in cod-liver oil and sweat glands.

buxom /'bʌksəm/ *adj* plump and healthy; (*woman*) big-bosomed.—**buxomness** *n*.

buy /baɪ/ *vt* (**buying, bought**) to purchase (for money); to bribe or corrupt; to acquire in exchange for something; (*inf*) to believe; (*with* **off**) to pay (someone) to ensure that some undesired action is not taken; (*with* **out**) to purchase a controlling interest in or share of; to secure the release of (e.g. a person from the army) by payment; (*with* **up**) to purchase the total supply of something; to acquire a controlling interest in. • *n* a purchase.

buyer /baɪr/ *n* a person who buys; a customer; an employee who buys on behalf of his or her employer, *esp* a company or store.

buyer's market *n* a market in which, because the supply exceeds the demand, the buyers control the price.

buzz /bʌz/ *vi* to hum like an insect; to gossip; to hover (about). • *vt* spread gossip secretly; (*inf*) to telephone. • *vi* (*with* **off**) to go away. • *n* the humming of bees or flies; a rumour; (*sl*) a telephone call; (*sl*) a thrill, a kick.

buzzard /'bʌzərd/ *n* a large bird of prey of the hawk family.

buzzer /'bʌzər/ *n* a device producing a buzzing sound.

buzz saw *n* a circular saw.

buzzword /'bʌzˌwɜrd/ *n* (*inf*) a vogue or jargon word; a word or phrase that was once a technical or specialist term and which has suddenly become popular, often used mainly for effect.—*also* **fuzzword**.

bwana /'bwɒnə/ *n* (*E Africa*) an employer, a boss; (*with cap*) a form of address.

by *prep* beside; next to; via; through the means of; not later than. • *adv* near to; past; in reserve, aside.

by-, bye- /baɪ/ *prefix* subordinate, side, secret.

by and by *adv* presently, before long; later; eventually; in the future.—**by-and-by** *n*.

by and large *adv* on the whole.

by-blow /'baɪˌbloː/ *n* a side blow; a bastard.

bye /baɪ/ *n* something subordinate or incidental; an odd man in a knockout competition; (*cricket*) a run scored without the ball being hit by the batsman; (*golf*) holes left after a match is decided; (*lacrosse*) a goal.

bye-bye[1] /'baɪˌbaɪ/ or /ˌbaɪ'baɪ/ *interj* (*inf*) goodbye.

bye-bye[2] *n* sleep; bed.

by-election, bye-election /'baɪɪˌlekʃən/ *n* an election held other than at a general election.

bygone /'baɪˌgɒn/ *adj* past. • *n* (*pl*) past offences or quarrels.

bylaw, bye-law /'baɪˌlɒ/ *n* a rule or law made by a local authority or a company.

by-line /'baɪlaɪn/ *n* a line under a newspaper article naming its author.

bypass /-pæs/ *n* a main road built to avoid a town; a channel redirecting the flow of something around a blockage; (*med*) an operation to redirect the flow of blood into the heart. • *vt* (**bypassing, bypassed**) to go around; to avoid, to act by ignoring the usual channels.

bypath /-pæθ/ *n* a secluded path.

byplay /-pleɪ/ *n* action or dumb show aside from the main action.

byproduct, by-product /-ˌprɒdəkt/ *n* something useful produced in the process of making something else.

byre /baɪr/ *n* a shed for cows.

byroad /'baɪˌroːd/ *n* an unfrequented or side road.

byssus /'bɪsəs/ *n* (*pl* **byssuses, byssi**) a tuft of long soft silky filaments by which certain molluscs attach themselves to rocks; a fine linen used by the ancient Egyptians for wrapping mummies.

bystander /'baɪˌstændər/ *n* a chance onlooker.

byte /baɪt/ *n* (*comput*) a set of eight bits treated as a unit.

by the by, by the bye *adv* incidentally.

by the way *adv* incidentally.

byway /'baɪweɪ/ *n* a side road; a specialist or abstruse interest or area of study.

byword /'baɪˌwɜrd/ *n* a well-known saying; a perfect example; an object of derision.

Byzantine /'bɪzænˌtiːn/ or /-taɪn/ *adj* of or pertaining to Byzantium, the ancient capital of the Eastern Roman Empire; (*archit*) in the style of the Eastern Empire. • *n* an inhabitant of Byzantium.

C

C *abbr* = Celsius, centigrade; (*math*) third known quantity; (*roman numerals*) 100; (*chem symbol*) = carbon.

c. *abbr* = carat; cent(s); century.

c. *abbr* = *circa*, about.

© (*symbol*) = copyright.

CA *abbr* = Chartered Accountant.

Ca (*chem symbol*) = calcium.

CAA *abbr* = Civil Aviation Authority.

cab /kæb/ *n* a taxicab; the place where the driver sits in a truck, crane, etc.

cabal /kə'bæl/ *n* a conspiracy, a secret plot; a small group of people united in perpetrating this; a clique. • *vi* (**caballing, caballed**) to form a cabal, to plot.

cabala, cabbala /kə'bɒlə/ or /'kæbələ/ *n* a mystic interpretation of Scripture by Jewish rabbis; occult lore.—*also* **kabala, kabbala.—cabalism, cabbalism** *n*.—**cabalist, cabbalist** *n*.— **cabalistic, cabbalistic** *adj*.

caballero /ˌkæbə'ljɛroː/ *n* (*pl* **caballeros**) a Spanish knight or gentleman; a horseman; a Spanish dance.

cabaret /'kæbəˌreɪ/ *n* entertainment given in a restaurant or nightclub.

cabbage /'kæbədʒ/ *n* a garden plant with thick leaves formed *usu* into a compact head, used as a vegetable.

cabbage rose *n* a large full rose.

cabby, cabbie /'kæbi/ *n* (*pl* **cabbies**) (*inf*) a person who drives a cab for hire.

caber /'keɪbər/ *n* a rough pole, *usu* cut from a tree, tossed as a trial of strength at Highland games.

cabin /'kæbɪn/ *n* a small house, a hut; a room in a ship; the area where passengers sit in an aircraft.

cabin cruiser *n* a powerful motorboat with living accommodation.

cabinet /'kæbɪnət/ *n* a case or cupboard with drawers or shelves; a case containing a TV, radio, etc; (*often with cap*) a body of official advisers to a government; the senior ministers of a government.

cabinetmaker /-ˌmeɪkər/ *n* a person who makes fine furniture.

cable /'keɪbəl/ *n* a strong thick rope often of wire strands; an anchor chain; an insulated cord that carries electric current; a cablegram; a bundle of insulated wires for carrying cablegrams, TV signals, etc; (*naut*) a cable length. • *vti* to send a message by cablegram.

cable car /-ˌkɑr/ *n* a car drawn by a moving cable, as up a steep incline.

cablegram /-ˌgræm/ *n* a message transmitted by telephone line, submarine cable, satellite, a cable.

cable-laid /-ˌleɪd/ *adj* (*rope*) composed of three triple strands.

cable length *n* (*naut*) (*UK*) a unit of length, about 100 fathoms, 608 feet or one tenth of a nautical mile, (*US*) 120 fathoms, 720 feet.

cable stitch *n* a pattern of knitting stitches resembling a cable.

cable television *n* TV transmission to subscribers by cable.

cabman /'kæbmən/ *n* (*pl* **cabmen**) the driver of a cab.

cabochon /'kæbəˌʃɒn, *Fr* /kabɔ'ʃõː/ *n* a precious stone polished but not faceted.

caboodle /kə'buːdəl/ *n* (*sl*) a lot, a set (*the whole caboodle*).

caboose /kə'buːs/ *n* a kitchen on a ship's deck; (*US*) the guard's car at the rear of a freight train.

cabriolet /ˌkæbrioː'leɪ/ *n* a covered carriage with two or four wheels drawn by one horse; a car body with a folding hood and fixed sides.

cacao /kæ'kæoː/ or /-'keɪoː/ *n* a tropical tree; its seed, from which cocoa and chocolate are obtained.

cachalot /'kæʃəˌlɒt/ or /-ˌloːt/ *n* the sperm whale.

cache /kæʃ/ *n* a secret hiding place; a store of weapons or treasure; a store of food left for use by travellers, etc. • *vt* to place in a cache.

cache (memory) *n* a small high-speed memory for easy access and frequent reference to computer data.

cachepot /'kæʃˌpoː/ or /-ˌpɒt/ *n* an ornamental pot to hold a flowerpot.

cachet /kæ'ʃeɪ/ or /'kæʃeɪ/ *n* a mark of authenticity; any distinguishing mark; prestige.

cachexia /kə'keksiə/, **cachexy** /-ksi/ *n* (*med*) a bad state of general health, weakness.—**cachectic** *adj*.

cachinnate /'kækəˌneɪt/ *vi* to laugh loudly and unrestrainedly.—**cachinnation** *n*.

cachou[1] /'kæʃuː/ *see* **catechu.**

cachou[2] *n* a lozenge for sweetening the breath.

cachucha /kə'tʃuːtʃə/ *n* a quick Spanish dance; the music for it.

cacique /kə'siːk/ *n* a West Indian or American Indian chief; a political boss.

cackle /'kækəl/ *n* the clucking sound of a hen; shrill or silly talk or laughter. • *vi* to utter with a cackle.

caco- /'kækoː/ *prefix* bad.

cacodemon, cacodaemon /ˌkækə'diːmən/ *n* an evil spirit.

cacodyl /'kækəˌdɪl/ or /-daɪl/ *n* an evil-smelling compound of arsenic and methyl.

cacoethes /ˌkækoː'iːθiːz/ *n* a bad habit or propensity of the body or mind; an uncontrollable urge.—**cacoethic** *adj*.

cacography /kə'kɒgrəfi/ *n* bad handwriting or spelling, the opposite of calligraphy and orthography.—**cacographic** *adj*.

cacophonous /kə'kɒfənəs/ *adj* harsh, ill-sounding, discordant.

cacophony /kə'kɒfəni/ *n* (*pl* **cacophonies**) an ugly sound, a discord.

cactus /'kæktəs/ *n* (*pl* **cactuses, cacti**) a plant with a thick fleshy stem that stores water and is often studded with prickles.

cad /kæd/ *n* (*inf*) a man who behaves in an ungentlemanly or dishonourable way.—**caddish** *adj*.—**caddishly** *adv*.—**caddishness** *n*.

cadastre, cadaster /kə'dæstər/ *n* a register of the real estate of a district or county as a basis for taxation.—**cadastral** *adj*.

cadaver /kə'dævər/ *n* a dead body.—**cadaveric** *adj*.

cadaverous /-əs/ *adj* gaunt, haggard; pallid, livid.—**cadaverousness** *n*.

caddie, caddy /'kædi/ *n* (*pl* **caddies**) a person who carries a golfer's clubs.—*vi* (**caddying, caddied**) to perform as a caddie.

caddis /'kædɪs/ *n* the larva of the mayfly used as bait.

caddy /'kædi/ *n* (*pl* **caddies**) a small box or tin for storing tea.

cade /keɪd/ *n* a lamb, etc, bred by hand.

cadence /'keɪdəns/ *n* a falling of the voice; the intonation of the voice; rhythm; measured movements as in marching.

cadent /kə'dɛnt/ *adj* rhythmic; falling.

cadenza /kə'dɛnzə/ *n* (*mus*) an ornamental flourish at the close of a movement.

cadet /kə'dɛt/ *n* a student at an armed forces academy, police college, etc; a school pupil in a school army training corps.

cadge /kædʒ/ *vti* to beg or obtain by begging.—**cadger** *n*.

cadi /'kɒdi/ or /'keɪ-/ *n* a minor Mohammedan judge.

cadmium /'kædmiəm/ *n* a whitish metallic element.

cadre /'kædrə/ or /'kɒ-, /-dreɪ/ *n* a permanent nucleus or framework of a political or military unit.

caduceus /kə'duːsiəs/ or /-'djuː-/, /-ʃiəs/, /-ʃəs/ *n* (*pl* **caducei**) the winged wand of Hermes (Mercury) entwined with two serpents, the emblem of the medical profession; an ancient herald's wand.

caducity /-sɪti/ or /-'djuː-/ *n* the quality or condition of being caducous; senility.

caducous /-kəs/ *adj* (*biol*) (*parts of a plant*) falling off quickly or before maturity; fleeting; perishable.

caecum /'siːkəm/ *n* (*pl* **caeca**) the pouch at the beginning of the large intestine containing the vermiform appendix.—*also* **cecum.—caecal** *adj*.

Caesar /'siːzər/ *n* the title of Roman emperors, *esp* Julius Caesar (*c*. 100–44 bc); (*without cap*) any ruler.

Caesarean section, Cesarean section /sə'zɛriən'sɛkʃən/ *n* the removal of a child from the womb by a surgical operation involving the cutting of the abdominal wall.

caesium /'siːziəm/ *n* a rare silvery alkaline metal.—*also* **cesium.**

caesura /sɪ'zjuːrə/ or /-'dʒuːrə/ *n* (*pl* **caesuras, caesurae**) a natural pause in the rhythm of a verse line.—**caesural** *adj*.

cafe, café /'kæfeɪ/ *n* a small restaurant, a coffee bar, a nightclub, etc.

café au lait /-oːˈleɪ/ *n* coffee with milk; a light brown colour.

café noir /-ˈnwɑr/, *Fr.* /kafeɪˈnwɑr/ *n* coffee without milk.

cafeteria /ˌkæfəˈtiːriə/ *n* a self-service restaurant.

cafetière /kæfitiˈɛr/ *n* a *usu* glass coffee pot with a plunger to press down coffee grounds.

caffeine /'kæfiːn/ or /kæfˈiːn/ *n* a stimulant present in coffee and tea.—**caffeinic** *adj*.

caftan /'kæftæn/ *n* a long-sleeved, full-length, voluminous garment originating in the Middle East.—*also* **kaftan.**

cage /keɪdʒ/ *n* a box or enclosure with bars for confining an animal, bird, prisoner, etc; a car for raising or lowering miners. • *vt* to shut in a cage, to confine.

cagey, cagy /'keɪdʒi/ *adj* (**cagier, cagiest**) (*inf*) wary, secretive, not frank.—**cagily** *adv*.—**caginess** *n*.

cahier /kɒˈjeɪ/ *n* sheets of paper put loosely together, a notebook.

cahoots /kəˈhuːts/ *npl* partnership; **in cahoots** in league or partnership.

CAI *abbr* = Computer-Aided Instruction.

caiman /'keɪmən/ *n* (*pl* **caimans**) an alligator of South and Central America.—*also* **cayman.**

caique, caïque /kaɪˈiːk/ *n* a skiff or light rowing boat used on the Bosphorus in Turkey.

cairn /kɛrn/ *n* a stone mound placed as a monument or marker.

cairngorm /'kɛrngɔrm/ *n* (a gemstone of) a yellow or brown variety of quartz or rock crystal.

caisson /'keɪsɒn/ *n* a watertight chamber used for carrying out underwater repairs or construction work; an apparatus for floating or lifting a vessel.

caitiff /'keɪtɪf/ *n* (*arch*) a coward; a rascal. • *adj* (*arch*) base, despicable, cowardly.

cajole /kəˈdʒoːl/ *vti* to persuade or soothe by flattery or deceit.—**cajoler** *n*.—**cajolingly** *adv*.

cajolery, cajolement *n* (*pl* **cajoleries, cajolements**) the action or practice of cajoling; persuasion by false arts.

Cajun /'keɪdʒən/ *n* an inhabitant of Louisiana descended from 18th-century French-Canadians who were expelled by the British; the dialect spoken by Cajuns.

cake /keɪk/ *n* a mixture of flour, eggs, sugar, etc baked in small, flat shapes or a loaf; a small block of compacted or congealed matter. • *vti* to encrust; to form into a cake or hard mass.

cakewalk /'keɪkˌwɒk/ *n* an elaborate step dance; a task accomplished without difficulty.

Cal *abbr* = Calorie.

cal *abbr* = calendar; calibre; calorie.

Calabar bean /'kæləˌbɑr/ *n* a West African plant; its poisonous bean.

calabash /'kæləˌbæʃ/ *n* the fruit of the calabash tree of tropical America, used when dried as a vessel for liquids, etc.

calaboose /'kæləˌbuːs/ *n* (*US inf*) a jail.

calamanco /'kæləˌmæŋkoː/ *n* (*pl* **calamancoes, calamancos**) a glossy woollen fabric, brocaded or checkered.

calamander /'kæləˌmændər/ *n* a fine variety of Indian ebony of a very hard texture.

calamari /'kæləˌmɑri/ *n* squid eaten as a food.

calamary /'kæləˌmɛri/ *n* (*pl* **calamaries**) squid.

calamine /'kæləˌmaɪn/ *n* a zinc oxide powder used in skin lotions, etc for its soothing effect.

calamint /'kæləˌmɪnt/ *n* an aromatic herb of the mint family.

calamite /'kæləˌmaɪt/ *n* a fossil plant resembling a horsetail.

calamitous /kəˈlæmɪtəs/ *adj* producing or resulting from calamity; disastrous.—**calamitously** *adv*.—**calamitousness** *n*.

calamity /kæˈlæmɪti/ *n* (*pl* **calamities**) a disastrous event, a great misfortune; adversity.

calamus /'kæləməs/ *n* (*pl* **calami**) any of a genus of palms producing the rattan canes; the sweet flag.

calando /kəˈlændoː/ *adv* (*mus*) gradually; slower and softer.

calash /kəˈlæʃ/ *n* a light carriage with low wheels and a folding removable top; (*Canada*) a two-wheeled single-seater carriage; a hood formerly adopted by women.—*also* **caleche.**

calcar /'kælˌkɑr/ *n* (*pl* **calcaria**) a tube or spur at the base of a petal or sepal; a furnace used in glass-making.

calcareous /'kælkɛriəs/ *adj* of the nature of, or containing, lime.—**calcareousness** *n*.

calceiform /'kælsɪˌfɔrm/ or /kælˈsiː-/, **calceolate** /-əlat/ *adj* (*bot*) slipper-shaped.

calceolaria /ˌkælsiəˌlɛriə/ *n* any of a genus of South American ornamental plants with slipper-shaped flowers.

calcic /'kælsɪk/ *adj* of or containing calcium.

calciferous /kælˈsɪfərəs/ *adj* containing or yielding carbonate of lime.

calcify /'kælsəfaɪ/ *vb* (**calcifying, calcified**) *vt* to convert into lime. • *vi* to harden by conversion into lime.

calcimine /-ˌmaɪn/ *n* a white or tinted wash for walls or ceilings.—*also* **kalsomine.**

calcination /ˌkælsəˈneɪʃən/ *n* the act or process of reducing to powder by heat.

calcine /'kælˌsaɪn/ or /-sɪn/ *vt* to reduce a substance to chalky powder by the action of heat; to burn to ashes. • *vi* to undergo calcination.

calcite /'kælˌsaɪt/ *n* crystallized carbonate of lime.—**calcitic** *adj*.

calcium /'kælsiəm/ *n* the chemical element prevalent in bones and teeth.

calcium carbide *n* a fusion of coal or coke with lime in an electrical furnace, which, with water, produces acetylene gas.

calcium carbonate *n* a compound occurring naturally in limestone, chalk, and in bones and shells.

calcsinter /'kælkˌsɪntər/ *n* a crystalline deposit from lime springs.

calcspar /-ˌspɑr/ *n* calcite, a crystalline carbonate of lime.

calculate /'kælkjuˌleɪt/ *vti* to reckon or compute by mathematics; to suppose or believe; to plan.—**calculable** *adj*.

calculated /-ˌleɪtəd/ *adj* adapted or suited (to); deliberate, cold-blooded, premeditated.—**calculatedly** *adv*.

calculating /-ˌleɪtɪŋ/ *adj* shrewd, scheming.—**calculatingly** *adv*.

calculation /-ˌleɪʃən/ *n* the act of calculating; the result obtained from this; an estimate.—**calculational** *adj*.

calculator /-ˌleɪtər/ *n* a device, *esp* a small, electronic, hand-held one, for doing mathematical calculations rapidly; one who calculates.

calculous /-ləs/ *adj* stony; gritty.

calculus /-ləs/ *n* (*pl* **calculi, calculuses**) an abnormal, stony mass in the body; (*math*) a mode of calculation using symbols.

caldera /kælˈdɛrə/ or /kɒl-/ *n* a deep caldron-like cavity on the summits of extinct volcanoes.

caldron /'kɒldrən/ *see* **cauldron.**

caleche /kəˈleʃ/ *see* **calash.**

Caledonian /ˌkæləˈdoːniən/ *adj* pertaining to Caledonia, the ancient name of Scotland; Scottish. • *n* a native of Scotland.

calefacient /ˌkæləˈfeɪsiənt/ or /-ʃiənt/, /-ʃənt/ *adj* producing or exciting heat. • *n* a heat-producing substance.—**calefaction** *n*.

calendar /'kæləndər/ *n* a system of determining the length and divisions of a year; a chart or table of months, days and seasons; a list of particular, scheduled events.

calendar month *n* a solar month reckoned according to the calendar, as distinguished from the lunar month.

calender[1] /'kæləndər/ *n* a press with rollers for finishing the surface of cloth, paper, etc. • *vt* to press in a calender.—**calenderer** *n*.

calender[2] *n* a mendicant dervish.

calends /'kæləndz/ *npl* in the Roman calendar, the first day of each month.—*also* **kalends.**

calendula /kəˈlɛndjulə/ *n* any of a genus of plants, including the marigold, from which a medical tincture is obtained.

calenture /'kæləntʃər/ *n* a tropical fever with delirium.

calf[1] /kæf/ *n* (*pl* **calves**) the young of a cow, seal, elephant, whale, etc; the leather skin of a calf.

calf[2] *n* (*pl* **calves**) the fleshy back part of the leg below the knee.

calf love *n* puppy love; an immature infatuation.

calfskin /'kæfskɪn/ *n* the skin of a calf made into leather.

calibrate /'kæləˌbreɪt/ *vt* to measure the calibre of a gun; to adjust or mark units of measurement on a measuring scale or gauge.—**calibration** *n*.—**calibrator** *n*.

calibre, caliber /'kæləbər/ *n* the internal diameter of a gun barrel or tube; capacity, standing, moral weight.

calico /'kæləˌkoː/ *n* (*pl* **calicoes, calicos**) a kind of cotton cloth. • *adj* made of this.

calif /'keɪlɪf/ or /'kæ-/ *see* **caliph.**

califate /'kælɪfət/ or /-ˌfeɪt/ *see* **caliphate.**

californium /ˌkæləˈfɔrniəm/ *n* an artificial radioactive metallic element.

calipash /'kæləpæʃ/ or /kæləˈpæʃ/ *n* the part of a turtle belonging to the upper shell, enclosing a dull greenish gelatinous edible substance.

calipee /'kæləpi/ or /kælə'piː/ *n* the part of a turtle belonging to the lower shell, enclosing a light yellow gelatinous edible substance.

caliper /'kæləpər/ *see* **calliper**.

caliph /'keɪlɪf/ or /'kæ-/ *n* the former title assumed by the successors of Mohammed as rulers; title of a Turkish sultan.—*also* **calif**.

caliphate /'kælɪfət/ or /-ˌfeɪt/ *n* the office, dignity or government of a caliph.—*also* **califate**.

calisthenics /ˌkælɪs'θenɪks/ *npl* light gymnastic exercises.—*also*—**callisthenics**.—**calisthenic, callisthenic** *adj*.

calix /'keɪlɪks/ or /'kæl-/ *n* (*pl* **calices**) a chalice; a cup-like cavity or organ.

calk[1] /kɒk/ *see* **caulk**.

calk[2] *n* the part of a horseshoe that projects downwards to prevent slipping; a semicircular piece of iron nailed to the heel of a boot.

call /kɒl/ *vi* to shout or cry out; to pay a short visit; to telephone; (*with* **in**) to pay a brief or informal visit; (*with* **on**) to pay a visit; to ask, to appeal to. • *vt* to summon; to name; to describe as specified; to awaken; to give orders for; (*with* **down**) to invoke; (*with* **in**) to summon for advice or help; to bring out of circulation; to demand payment of (a loan); (*with* **off**) to cancel; (*an animal*) to call away in order to stop, divert; (*with* **out**) to cry aloud; to order (workers) to come out on strike; to challenge to a duel; to summon (troops) to action; (*with* **up**) to telephone; to summon to military action, as in time of war; to recall. • *n* a summons; the note of a bird; a vocation, *esp* religious; occasion; a need; a demand; a short visit; the use of a telephone; a cry, a shout.

calla (lily) /'kælə/ *n* an ornamental plant of the arum family with a large white spathe that enfolds a yellow spadix.

callant /kælənt/, **callan** /-ən/ *n* (*Scot*) a lad, a youth.

call box *n* a telephone booth; a roadside box containing a telephone for making emergency calls.

callboy /'kɒlˌbɔɪ/ *n* a prompter's attendant who tells actors when to go on.

caller[1] /-ər/ *n* one who calls, *esp* by telephone; one who pays a brief visit.

caller[2] *adj* (*Scot*) (*food*) cool, fresh; in season; (*fish*) recently caught.

call girl /-ˌgərl/ *n* (*inf*) a prostitute who makes appointments by telephone.

calligraphy /kə'lɪgrəfi/ *n* handwriting; beautiful writing.—**calligrapher, calligraphist** *n*.—**calligraphic** *adj*.—**calligraphically** *adv*.

calling /'kɒlɪŋ/ *n* the act of summoning; a summons or invitation; a vocation, trade or profession; the state of being divinely called.

calliope /kə'laɪəpi/ *n* a steam organ; (*with cap*) the muse of epic poetry.

calliper /'kælɪpər/ *n* a metal framework for supporting a crippled or weak leg; paper thickness measured in microns; (*pl*) a two-legged measuring instrument. • *vt* to measure with or use callipers.—*also* **caliper**.

callisthenics /ˌkælɪs'θenɪks/ *see* **calisthenics**.

call loan *n* a loan subject to recall without notice.

callosity /kə'lɒsɪti/ *n* (*pl* **callosities**) the state or quality of being hardened; a callus.

callous /'kæləs/ *adj* (*skin*) hardened; (*person*) unfeeling.—**calloused** *adj*.—**callously** *adv*.—**callousness** *n*.

callow /'kæloʊ/ *adj* inexperienced, undeveloped.—**callowness** *n*.

call sign *n* a signal identifying a particular radio transmitter.

call-up /'kɒlˌʌp/ *n* a summons to military service.

callus /'kæləs/ *n* (*pl* **calluses**) a hardened, thickened place on the skin.

calm /kɒm/ or /kɒlm/ *adj* windless; still, unruffled; quiet, peaceful. • *n* the state of being calm; stillness; tranquillity. • *vti* to become or make calm.—**calmly** *adv*.—**calmness** *n*.

calmative /'kɒmətɪv/ or /'kælm-/ *adj* (*med*) sedating. • *n* a sedative.

calomel /'kæləˌmel/ *n* a preparation of mercury used as a purgative.

caloric /kə'lɒrɪk/ *adj* of or pertaining to heat or calories.—**calorically** *adv*.

calorie /'kæləri/ *n* a unit of quantity of heat also called a kilocalorie; a measure of food energy.—*also* **calory**.

calorific /kə'lərɪfɪk/ *adj* heat-producing; (*inf*) causing fat.—**calorifically** *adv*.

calorimeter /ˌkælə'rɪmətər/ *n* an instrument for measuring quantities of heat.—**calorimetric, calorimetrical** *adj*.—**calorimetry** *n*.

calory /'kæləri/ *see* **calorie**.

calotte /kə'lɒt/ *n* a small plain skullcap of satin, etc, worn by priests.

calotype /'kælətəɪp/ *n* a photographic process in which the image is received on paper prepared with iodide of silver.

caloyer /'kæləjər/ *n* a Greek monk of the order of St Basil.

calpac, calpack /'kælˌpæk/ *n* a tall brimless sheepskin cap worn by Turks and Armenians.—*also* **kalpak**.

caltrop, caltrap, calthrop /'kæltrəp/ any of various plants with prickly fruit; an iron instrument with four spikes, placed in ditches, etc, to hinder the advance of troops.

calumet /'kæljʊˌmet/ *n* the tobacco pipe of the North American Indians, smoked as a symbol of peace or to ratify treaties.

calumniate /kə'lʌmniˌeɪt/ *vt* to accuse falsely and maliciously. • *vi* to utter calumnies.—**calumniation** *n*.—**calumniator** *n*.

calumny /'kæləmni/ *n* (*pl* **calumnies**) a slander; a lie, a false accusation.—**calumnious** *adj*.—**calumniously** *adv*.

calvados /'kælvəˌdɒs/ *n* apple brandy distilled in Normandy in France.

calvary /'kælvəri/ *n* (*pl* **calvaries**) a place or representation of the crucifixion of Christ; an experience of intense mental suffering; (*with cap*) the place where Christ was crucified.

calve /kæv/ *vti* to give birth to a calf; (*glacier, iceberg*) to break up and release ice.

calves /kævz/ *see* **calf**.

Calvinism /'kælvɪnˌɪzəm/ *n* the doctrines of John Calvin (1509–64) the French theologian and reformer, *esp* those relating to predestination and election.—**Calvinist** *n*.—**Calvinistic** *adj*.

calvities /'kælvɪʃɪˌiːz/ *n* (*med*) baldness.

calx /kælks/ *n* (*pl* **calxes, calces**) the powder left when a metal or mineral has been subjected to great heat.

calycine /'keɪləˌsaɪn/, **calycinal** /-əl/ *adj* having a calyx; of or on the calyx.

calycle /'kælɪkəl/, **calyculus** /-'kjuːləs/ *n* (*pl* **calycles, calyculi**) a whorl of small bracts forming a secondary calyx below the true one.

calypso /kə'lɪpsoʊ/ *n* (*pl* **calypsos**) a West Indian folk song that comments on current events or personalities.

calyptra /kə'lɪptrə/ *n* (*bot*) the hood-like covering of the spore case of mosses.—**calyptrate** *adj*.

calyx /'keɪlɪks/ or /'kælɪks/ *n* (*pl* **calyxes, calyces**) the outer series of leaves that form the cup from which the petals of a flower spring.

cam /kæm/ *n* a device to change rotary to reciprocating motion.

camas /'kæməs/ *n* North American plant of the lily plants with edible bulbs, once consumed by some Native American peoples.

camaraderie /ˌkɒmə'rɒdəri/ or /ˌkæmə'rædəri/, /ˌkæmə'rɒdəri/ *n* friendship, comradeship.

camarilla /ˌkæmə'rɪlə/, *Sp.* /ˌkɑmɑ'riːljə/ *n* a political clique, a cabal.

camber /'kæmbər/ *n* a slight upward curve in the surface of a road, etc. • *vti* to curve upwards slightly.—**cambered** *adj*.

cambist /'kæmbɪst/ *n* an expert in exchanges; a dealer in bills of exchange.

cambium /'kæmbiəm/ *n* (*pl* **cambiums, cambia**) the formative layer of cellular tissue that lies between the young wood and the bark of exogenous trees.—**cambial** *adj*.

Cambrian /'kæmbriən/ *adj* of Wales; (*geol*) of the earliest Palaeozoic period, before the Silurian. • *n* the strata underlying the Silurian rocks, now classed with them.

cambric /'kæmbrɪk/ or /'kæm-/ *n* a fine white linen or cotton cloth.

camcorder *n* a portable video recorder with built-in sound recording facilities.

came /keɪm/ *see* **come**.

camel /'kæməl/ *n* a large four-footed, long-necked animal with a humped back; a fawny-beige colour.—*also adj*.

cameleer /'kæməˌliːr/ *n* a camel driver.

camellia /kə'miːliə/ *n* an oriental evergreen shrub with showy blooms.—*also* **japonica**.

camelopard /'kæmələˌpɑrd/ or /kə'mel'-/ *n* the giraffe.

camel's hair, camelhair *n* the hair of a camel; cloth from this; its fawn-tan colour; the hair from a squirrel's tail used as a paintbrush.—**camel's-hair, camelhair** *adj*.

Camembert /'kæməmbər/ *n* a soft white cheese originating in Normandy.

cameo /'kæmioʊ/ *n* (*pl* **cameos**) an onyx or other gem carved in relief, often showing a head in profile; an outstanding bit role, *esp* in a motion picture; a short piece of fine writing.

camera /ˈkæmrə/ or /-ərə/ n the apparatus used for taking still photographs or television or motion pictures; a judge's private chamber; **in camera** in private, esp of a legal hearing exluding the public; **off camera** outside the area being filmed; **on camera** being filmed, before the camera.

cameraman /-ˌmæn/ n (pl **cameramen**) a film or television camera operator.

camera obscura /-ɒbˈskjuːrə/ n a darkened chamber or box in which, by means of lenses, external objects are exhibited on paper, glass, etc.

camera-ready /-ˌrɛdi/ adj (printing) ready for photographic platemaking.

camera-shy /-ˌʃaɪ/ adj unwilling to, or against, being filmed or photographed.

camion /ˈkæmiən/, Fr. /kaˈmjɔ̃/ n a heavy truck, a wagon.

camise /kəˈmiːs/ n a light loose robe, a chemise.

camisole /ˈkæmɪˌsoːl/ n a woman or girl's loose sleeveless underbodice.

camlet /ˈkæmlət/ n a kind of light cloth.

camomile /ˈkæməˌmaɪl/ see **chamomile**.

Camorra /kəˈmɒrə/ n a secret terrorist organization in southern Italy; a lawless clique.

camouflage /ˈkæməˌflɒʒ/ n a method (esp using colouring) of disguise or concealment used to deceive an enemy; a means of putting people off the scent. • vt to conceal by camouflage.

camp[1] /kæmp/ n the ground on which tents or temporary accommodation is erected; the occupants of this, such as holiday-makers or troops; the supporters of a particular cause. • vi to lodge in a camp; to pitch tents.—**camping** n.

camp[2] adj (sl) theatrical, exaggerated; effeminate; homosexual. • vi (with **up**) to make or give an exaggerated display of camp characteristics.

campaign /kæmˈpeɪn/ n a series of military operations; a series of operations with a particular objective, such as election of a candidate or promotion of a product; organized course of action. • vi to take part in or conduct a campaign.—**campaigner** n.

campanile /ˌkæmpəˈniːleɪ/ n a bell tower detached from the body of a church.

campanology /ˌkæməˈnɒlədʒi/ n the art of bell ringing.—**campanologist** n.

campanula /kæmˈpænjʊlə/ n a plant with bell-shaped flowers.

campanulate /kæmˈpænjʊlət/ adj (flower) bell-shaped.

camper /ˈkæmpər/ n one who lives in a tent; a person on a camping holiday; a vehicle equipped with all domestic facilities.

campfire /ˈkæmpˌfaɪr/ n an outdoor fire at a camp; a social gathering around such a fire.

camp follower n a civilian, esp a prostitute, who provides unofficial services to military personnel; a person who is sympathetic to the aims of a particular group but is not a member.

camphene /ˈkæmfiːn/ or /kæmˈfiːn/ n rectified oil of turpentine.

camphor /ˈkæmfər/ n a solid white transparent essential oil with a pungent taste and smell used to repel insects, as a stimulant in medicine, etc.—**camphoric** adj.

camphorate /ˈkæmfəˌreɪt/ vt to saturate or treat with camphor.

camphor tree n a species of laurel that yields camphor.

campion /ˈkæmpiən/ n any of various wild plants of the pink family, the commonest having red or white flowers.

camp meeting n an oudoor religious meeting.

campsite /ˈkæmpˌsaɪt/ n a camping ground, often with facilities for holiday-makers.

campstool /-ˌstuːl/ n a folding stool or seat.

campus /ˈkæmpəs/ n (pl **campuses**) the grounds, and sometimes buildings, of a college or university.

camshaft /ˈkæmʃæft/ n the rotating shaft to which cams are fitted to lift valves in engines.

Can abbr = Canada; Canadian.

can[1] /kæn/ vt (pt **could**) to be able to; to have the right to; to be allowed to.

can[2] n a container, usu metal, with a separate cover in which petrol, film, etc is stored; a tin in which meat, fruit, drinks, etc are hermetically sealed; the contents of a can; (sl) jail; (sl) a lavatory; **in the can** (film) shot and edited and ready for showing; (inf) accomplished, agreed, tied up. • vti (**canning, canned**) to preserve (foods) in a can.—**canner** n.

Canada balsam /ˈkænədəˌbɒlsəm/ n a resin obtained from a species of fir.

Canada goose /-ˌguːs/ n a large grey goose with a black head and neck and a white throat patch.

Canada jay n a large common jay in North America.

Canada lily n a lily of eastern North America with large yellow, orange or spotted flowers.

Canada mayflower n a woodland lily of eastern North America with white flowers and red berries.

Canadarm /kænəˈdarm/ n (Trademark) a mechanical arm on a spacecraft, used to release, retrieve and repair satellites and other equipment.

Canadian /kəˈneɪdiən/ adj of or pertaining to Canada. • n a native of Canada.

Canadianism /kəˈneɪdiəˌnɪzəm/ n a form of expression peculiar to Canada; a custom peculiar to Canada.

Canadianize /kəˈneɪdiəˌnaɪz/ vt to render Canadian; to assimilate to the political and social institutions of Canada. — **Canadianization** n.

canaille /kəˈneɪl/, Fr. /kaˈnaj/ n a rabble, the lowest orders.

canal /kəˈnæl/ n an artificial waterway cut across land; a duct in the body. • vt (**canalling, canalled** or **canaling, canaled**) to provide with canals.

canalize, canalise /ˈkænəˌlaɪz/ vt to provide with a canal or channel. • vi to flow in or into a channel; to establish new channels or outlets.—**canalization, canalisation** n.

canapé /ˈkænəˌpeɪ/ n a small piece of pastry, bread or toast with a savoury spread or topping.

canard /kəˈnɑrd/ n a false report, an absurd story, a baseless rumour.

canary /kəˈnɛri/ n (pl **canaries**) a small finch, usu greenish to yellow in colour, kept as a songbird.

canasta /kəˈnæstə/ n a card game played with two packs of cards, for two to six players.

cancan /ˈkænkæn/ n an energetic dance performed by women, involving high kicks and the lifting of frothy petticoats.

cancel /ˈkænsəl/ vt (**cancelling, cancelled** or **canceling, canceled**) to cross out; to obliterate; to annul, suppress; (reservation, etc) to call off; to countermand; (with **out**) to make up for.—**canceller, canceler** n.

cancellation, cancelation /ˌkænsəˈleɪʃən/ n the act of cancelling; annulment; something that has been cancelled; the mark made by cancelling.

cancellous /ˈkænsələs/, **cancellate** /-lət/, **cancellated** /-tɪd/ adj (med) marked with cross lines or ridges.

cancer /ˈkænsər/ n the abnormal and uncontrollable growth of the cells of living organisms, esp a malignant tumour; an undesirable or dangerous expansion of something.—**cancerous** adj.

Cancer /ˈkænsər/ n (astron) the Crab, a northern constellation; (astrol) the 4th sign of the zodiac, operative 21 June–21 July.—**Cancerian** adj.

cancroid /ˈkænˌkrɔɪd/ or /ˈkæn-/ adj resembling a cancer; like a crab.

candela /ˌkænˈdiːlə/ or /-ˈdɛlə/ n a unit of luminous intensity.

candelabrum /ˌkændəˈlæbrəm/ n (pl **candelabra**) a branched and ornamented candlestick or lampstand.

candescent /kænˈdɛsənt/ adj glowing; white-hot.—**candescence** n.

candid /ˈkændɪd/ adj frank, outspoken; unprejudiced; (photograph) informal.—**candidly** adv.—**candidness** n.

candidate /ˈkændɪdeɪt/ or /-ˌdət/n a person who has nomination for an office or qualification for membership or award; a student taking an examination.—**candidacy** n.—**candidature** n.

candid camera n a small camera for photographing people unexpectedly or unknowingly.

candied /ˈkændiːd/ adj preserved in or encrusted with sugar.

candle /ˈkændəl/ n a stick of wax with a wick that burns to give light. • vt to check the freshness of eggs by examining in front of a light.

candlelight /-ˌlaɪt/ n the light produced by a candle or candles.

Candlemas (Day) n the Feast of the Purification of the Virgin Mary (2 February).

candlepower /-ˌpaʊr/ n a unit of measurement of the intensity of a light source, measured in candelas.

candlestick /-stɪk/ n a holder for one or more candles.

candlewick /-wɪk/ n a cotton fabric with raised pattern of tufted yarn.—**also adj.**

candour, candor /ˈkændər/ n sincerity, openness, frankness.

candy /'kændi/ *n* (*pl* **candies**) a solid confection of sugar or syrup with flavouring, fruit, nuts, etc, a sweet. • *vb* (**candying, candied**) *vt* to preserve by coating with candy; to encrust with crystals. • *vi* to become candied.

candyfloss /-ˌflɒs/ *n* a confection of spun sugar.—*also* (*US*) **cotton candy**.

candy-striped *adj* (*cloth*) with narrow stripes of colour on a white background.

candytuft /-ˌtʌft/ *n* a plant with pink, white or purple tufted flowers.

cane /keɪn/ *n* the slender, jointed stem of certain plants, as bamboo; a plant with such a stem, as sugar cane; (*usu with* **the**) a stick of this used for corporal punishment; strips of this used in furniture making etc or for supporting plants; a walking stick. • *vt* to thrash with a cane; to weave cane into; (*inf*) to beat, eg in a game.

canebrake /'keɪnbreɪk/ *n* a thicket of canes.

canella /kə'nelə/ *n* an aromatic and tonic bark of a West Indian tree.

canescent /kə'nesənt/ *adj* (*biol*) growing white, hoary.

cane sugar *n* sugar made from sugar cane.

cangue /kæŋ/ *n* (*formerly*) a square wooden collar worn as a punishment by criminals in China.

canine /'keɪnaɪn/ *adj* of or like a dog; of the family of animals that includes wolves, dogs and foxes; pertaining to a canine tooth. • *n* a dog or other member of the same family of animals; in humans, a pointed tooth next to the incisors.

canister /'kænɪstər/ *n* a small box or container *usu* of metal for storing tea, flour, etc; a tube containing tear gas which explodes and releases its contents on impact.

canker /'kæŋkər/ *n* an erosive or spreading sore; a foot disease in horses; an ear disease in cats and dogs; a fungal disease of trees; a corrupting influence.—**cankerous** *adj*.

cankerworm /-wɜrm/ *n* a caterpillar destructive to trees or plants.

canna /'kænə/ *n* a showy American tropical plant.

cannabin /'kænəˌbɪn/ *n* a narcotic resin extracted from hemp.

cannabis /'kænəbɪs/ *n* a narcotic drug obtained from the hemp plant; the hemp plant.—*also* **hashish, marijuana.**—**cannabic** *adj*.

canned /kænd/ *adj* stored in sealed tins; recorded for reproduction; (*sl*) drunk.

canned hunt *n* (*sl*) an organized big-game hunt carried out within an area from which the quarry cannot escape.

cannel (coal) /'kænəl/ *n* a hard bituminous coal burning with a clear bright flame.

cannelloni /ˌkænə'lo:ni/ *npl* stuffed pasta tubes.

cannelure /ˈkænəljʊr/ or /-luːr/ *n* a groove or fluting.

cannery /'kænəri/ *n* (*pl* **canneries**) a building, etc, where foods are canned.

cannibal /'kænəbəl/ *n* a person who eats human flesh; an animal that feeds on its own species. • *adj* relating to or indulging in this practice.—**cannibalism** *n*.—**cannibalistic** *adj*.

cannibalize /-ˌlaɪz/ *vti* to strip (old equipment) of parts for use in other units.—**cannibalization** *n*.

cannikin /'kænɪkɪn/ *n* a small can.

cannon /'kænən/ *n* (*pl* **cannon**) a large mounted piece of artillery; an automatic gun on an aircraft; (*pl* **cannons**) (*billiards*) a carom. • *vi* to collide with great force (with into); to rebound; (*billiards*) to make a carom.

cannonade /ˌkænən'eɪd/ *n* a heavy, continuous artillery attack. • *vti* to attack with cannon.

cannonball /'kænənˌbɒl/ *n* the heavy, round shot fired from a cannon; (*tennis*) a low, fast service stroke. • *vi* to move along at great speed.

cannoneer /ˌkænəniːr/ *n* an artilleryman.

cannon fodder *n* soldiers regarded as expendable in war.

cannonry /'kænənri/ *n* (*pl* **cannonries**) artillery.

cannot /kæ'nɒt/ or /kə-/, /'kænɒt/ = can not.

cannula /'kænjulə/ *n* (*pl* **cannulas, cannulae**) (*med*) a small tube for inspecting or withdrawing fluids.

canny /'kæni/ *adj* (**cannier, canniest**) knowing, shrewd; cautious, careful; thrifty.—**cannily** *adv*.—**canniness** *n*.

canoe /kə'nuː/ *n* a narrow, light boat propelled by paddles.—*also* *vi* (**canoeing, canoed**).—**canoeist** *n*.

canola /kə'no:lə/ *n* the seeds of a variety of the rape plant, used to make cooking oil.

canon /'kænən/ *n* a decree of the Church; a general rule or standard, criterion; a list of the books of the Bible accepted as genuine; the works of any author recognized as genuine; a list of

canonized saints; a member of a cathedral chapter; a part of the mass containing words of consecration; (*mus*) a round.

canoness /'kænənəs/ *n* (*RC Church*) one of a number of women living under canon law but not compelled to take religious vows.

canonical /kə'nɒnɪkəl/ *adj* pertaining to a rule or canon; according to or established by ecclesiastical laws; belonging to the canon of scripture. • *n* (*pl*) the official dress of the clergy.—**canonically** *adv*.

canonical hour *n* (*RC Church*) one of the hours appointed by ecclesiastical law for daily prayer: matins with lauds, prime, sext, nones, vespers, and compline.

canonist /'kænənɪst/ *n* an expert in canon law.—**canonistic** *adj*.

canonize /'kænəˌnaɪz/ *vt* (*RC Church*) to officially declare (a person) a saint.—**canonization** *n*.

canon law *n* rules or laws relating to faith, morals and discipline that regulate church government, as laid down by popes and councils.

canonry /'kænənri/ *n* (*pl* **canonries**) the office of a cathedral canon.

canoodle /kə'nuːdəl/ *vti* (*sl*) to cuddle, to fondle.

canopy /'kænəpi/ *n* (*pl* **canopies**) a tent-like covering over a bed, throne, etc; any roof-like structure or projection; the transparent cover of an aeroplane's cockpit; the tops of trees in a forest; the sky regarded as a covering. • *vt* (**canopying, canopied**) to cover with or as with a canopy.

cans /kænz/ *npl* (*sl*) headphones.

cant[1] /kænt/ *n* insincere or hypocritical speech; language specific to a group (eg thieves, lawyers); cliched talk, meaningless jargon. • *vi* to talk in or use cant.

cant[2] *n* an inclination or tilt; a slanting surface, bevel. • *vti* to slant, to tilt; to overturn by a sudden movement.

can't /kænt/ = can not.

cantabile /kæn'tæbiˌleɪ/ *adv* (*mus*) in a lyrical flowing style.

Cantabrigian /ˌkæntə'brɪdʒiən/ *n* a student or graduate of Cambridge University; an inhabitant of Cambridge.—*also adj*.

cantaloupe, cantaloup /'kæntəlo:p/ *n* a variety of melon with orange flesh.

cantankerous /kæn'tæŋkərəs/ *adj* ill-natured, bad-tempered, quarrelsome.—**cantankerously** *adv*.—**cantankerousness** *n*.

cantata /kæn'tætə/ or /tɒtə-/ *n* (*mus*) a composition for voices of a story or religious text.

cantatrice *Fr.* /kɑntɑ'trɪːs/, *It.* /ˌkɑntɑ'triːtʃe/ *n* a female singer, *esp* one who sings in operas.

canteen /kæn'tiːn/ *n* a restaurant attached to factory, school, etc, catering for large numbers of people; a flask for carrying water; (a box containing) a set of cutlery.

canter /'kæntər/ *n* a horse's three-beat gait resembling a slow, smooth gallop.—*also vti*.

Canterbury bell /'kæntərbəri/ *n* a large variety of campanula with handsome bell-shaped blossoms.

cantharides /kæn'θærɪˌdiːs/ *npl* (*sing* **cantharis**) (*med*) a diuretic preparation made from dried Spanish flies, formerly considered an aphrodisiac.—*also* **Spanish fly**.

canthus /'kænθəs/ *n* (*pl* **canthi**) the angle made by the meeting of the eyelids.

canticle /'kæntɪkəl/ *n* a song taken from the Bible (eg the Magnificat).

cantilever /'kæntˌliːvər/ *n* a projecting beam that supports a balcony, etc.

cantilever bridge *n* a bridge supported by cantilevers springing from piers.

cantle /'kæntəl/ *n* a corner; a piece; the rising rear part of a saddle.

canto /'kæntoː/ *n* (*pl* **cantos**) a division of a long poem.

canton /'kæntɒn/ *n* a political and administrative division of Switzerland.—**cantonal** *adj*.

Cantonese /ˌkæntə'niːz/ *n* (*pl* **Cantonese**) a Chinese language deriving from Canton; an inhabitant or native of Canton.—*also adj*.

cantonment /kæn'tɒnmənt/ *n* a part of a town or village alloted to a body of troops; in India, a permanent military station.

cantor /'kæntər/ or /-tɔr/ *n* a singer of liturgical solos in a synagogue; the leader of singing in a church choir.

cantorial /-'tɔːriəl/ *adj* of or pertaining to a precentor's or the north side of the choir of a church.

cantrip /'kæntrɪp/ *n* a prank, a piece of mischief; a magic spell.

canvas /'kænvəs/ *n* a strong coarse cloth of hemp or flax, used for tents, sails, etc, and for painting on; a ship's sails collectively; a tent or tents; an oil painting on canvas.

canvasback /-ˌbæk/ *n* (*pl* **canvasbacks, canvasback**) a North American duck esteemed for the delicacy of its flesh.

canvass /ˈkænvəs/ *vti* to go through (places) or among (people) asking for votes, opinions, orders, etc.—*also n*.— **canvasser** *n*.

canyon /ˈkænjən/ *n* a long, narrow valley between high cliffs.

canzone *It.* /kɑnˈtsɔnɛ/, **canzona** /-ˌnɒ/ *n* (*pl* **canzoni, canzone**) a song or air resembling the madrigal; an instrumental piece in the style of a madrigal.

canzonet, canzonette /ˌkænzəˈnɛt/ *n* a short light song.

caoutchouc /kauˈtʃuk/ *n* rubber.—*also adj*.

cap /kæp/ *n* any close-fitting headgear, visored or brimless; the special headgear of a profession, club, etc; the top of a mushroom or toadstool; a cap-like thing, as an artificial covering for a tooth; a top, a cover; a percussion cap in a toy gun; a type of contraceptive device; (*sport*) the head gear presented to a player chosen for a team. • *vt* (**capping, capped**) to put a cap on; to cover (the end of); to award a degree at a university; to seal (an oil or gas well); to equal, outdo or top; to limit the level of a tax increase, etc; (*sport*) to choose a player for a team.

capability /ˌkeɪpəˈbɪləti/ *n* (*pl* **capabilities**) the quality of being capable; an undeveloped faculty.

capable /ˈkeɪpəbəl/ *adj* able or skilled to do; competent, efficient; susceptible (of); adapted to.—**capably** *adv*.

capacious /kəˈpeɪʃəs/ *adj* able to hold a great deal; roomy.—**capaciousness** *n*.

capacitance /kəˈpæsɪtəns/ *n* (a measure of) the ability of a system to store an electric charge.

capacitate /-ˌteɪt/ *vt* to make capable; to enable; to qualify.—**capacitation** *n*.

capacitor /-tər/ *n* a device for storing electric charge.

capacity /kəˈpæsɪti/ *n* (*pl* **capacities**) the power of holding or grasping; cubic content; mental ability or power; character; the position held; legal competence; the greatest possible output or content.

cap-a-pie /ˌkæpəˈpiː/ *adv* from head to foot.

caparison /kəˈpærɪsən/ *n* an ornamental covering for a horse; rich clothing. • *vt* to cover (a horse) with rich clothing; to adorn with rich dress.

cape[1] /keɪp/ *n* a headland or promontory running into the sea.

cape[2] *n* a sleeveless garment fastened at the neck and hanging over the shoulders and back.

capelin, caplin /ˈkæplɪn/ *n* a small sea fish of the smelt family, largely used as bait for cod.

caper[1] /ˈkeɪpər/ *vi* to skip about playfully, to frolic. • *n* a playful leap or skip; (*sl*) an escapade; (*sl*) a criminal activity.

caper[2] *n* a low, prickly Mediterranean shrub; its pickled flower buds, used in cooking (eg caper sauce).

capercaillie /kæpərˈkeɪli/, **capercailzie** /-lzi/ *n* the largest Old World grouse.

capetian /kəˈpiːʃən/ *adj* of or pertaining to the dynasty founded by Hugh Capet, who ascended the French throne in 1987.

capias /ˈkæpɪəs/ or /ˈkeɪp-/ *n* (*law*) a writ for arrest.

capillarity /ˌkæpɪˈlerɪti/ *n* (*pl* **capillarities**) the power possessed by porous bodies of drawing up a fluid; surface tension.

capillary /ˈkæpɪˌleri/ *adj* of or as fine as a hair; (*tube, pipe*) of a hair-like calibre; (*anat*) of the capillaries. • *n* (*pl* **capillaries**) one of the very fine blood vessels connecting arteries and veins.

capital[1] /ˈkæpɪtəl/ *adj* of or pertaining to the head; (*offence*) punishable by death; serious; chief, principal; leading, first-class; of, or being the seat of government; of capital or wealth; relating to a large letter, upper case; (*inf*) excellent. • *n* a city that is the seat of government of a country; a large letter; accumulated wealth used to produce more; stock or money for carrying on a business; a city, town, etc pre-eminent in some special activity.—**capitally** *adv*.

capital[2] *n* the head or top part of a column or pillar.

capital gain *n* the profit made on the sale of an asset.

capital goods *npl* goods (eg machinery) used to produce other goods.

capitalism /ˈkæpɪtəˌlɪzəm/ *n* the system of individual ownership of wealth; the dominance of such a system.

capitalist /-lɪst/ *n* a person who has money invested in business for profit; a supporter of capitalism. • *adj* of or favouring capitalism.—**capitalistic** *adj*.

capitalize /-ˌlaɪz/ *vti* (*with* **on**) to use (something) to one's advantage; to convert into money or capital; to provide with capital; to write in or print in capital letters.—**capitalization** *n*.

capitally /-li/ *adv* in a capital manner; excellently.

capital punishment *n* the death penalty for a crime.

capitate /ˈkæpɪteɪt/ *adj* (*bot*) shaped like a head; head-like.

capitation /ˌkæpɪˈteɪʃən/ *n* a direct, uniform tax imposed on each person, a tax per head.

capitol /ˈkæpɪtəl/ *n* (*with* **the**) the building where the US Congress meets; the temple of Jupiter on the Capitoline in Rome.

capitular /kəˈpɪtjʊlər/ *adj* of or pertaining to a chapter. • *n* a member of a cathedral chapter.

capitulary *n* (*pl* **capitularies**) a statue passed in a chapter, as of knights or canons; (*pl*) the body of statues of a chapter or of an ecclesiastical council.

capitulate /kəˈpɪtʃjʊleɪt/ *vi* to surrender on terms; to give in.—**capitulation** *n*.—**capitulatory** *adj*.

capo /ˈkeɪpɔ/ *n* (*pl* **capos**) a device attached across the fingerboard of a guitar to raise the pitch of the strings.

capon /ˈkeɪpɒn/ *n* a castrated cockerel fattened for eating.

caponize /-pənaɪz/ *vt* to make a cock a capon by castration.

caporal /ˈkæpərəl/ or /ˈkæpɔˌræl/ *n* a French tobacco.

capote /kəˈpoːt/ *n* a long coarse cloak; a long mantle for women.

cappuccino /ˌkæpəˈtʃinoː/ *n* (*pl* **cappuccinos**) frothy, milky coffee *usu* served sprinkled with chocolate powder.

capreolate /ˈkæprɪɔˌlət/ *adj* (*bot*) furnished with tendrils.

capriccio /kəˈpriːtʃiɔ/ *n* (*pl* **capriccios, capricci**) a light musical composition in a fantastic, whimsical style.

capriccioso /kəˌpriːtʃiˈoːsoː/ *adv* (*mus*) in a free, fantastic style.

caprice /kəˈpriːs/ *n* a passing fancy; an impulsive change in behaviour, opinion, etc; a whim.

capricious /kəˈprɪʃəs/ or /-ˈpriː-/ *adj* unstable, inconstant; unreliable.—**capriciously** *adv*.—**capriciousness** *n*.

Capricorn /ˈkæprɪˌkɔrn/ *n* (*astron*) the Goat, a southern constellation; (*astrol*) the tenth sign of the zodiac, operative 21 December–19 January.—**Capricornean** *adj*.

caprification /ˌkæprɪfɪˈkeɪʃən/ *n* a process of accelerating the ripening of the fig by puncturing it.

caprine /ˈkæpraɪn/ *adj* of, pertaining to, or like a goat.

capriole /ˈkæprɪˌoːl/ *n* a leap of a horse made without advancing; a caper. • *vi* to execute a capriole, to kick up the heels.

capsaicin /kæpˈseɪəsɪn/ *n* an alkaloid extracted from several species of capsicum.

capsicum /ˈkæpsɪkəm/ *n* a tropical plant with bell-shaped fruits containing hot or mild seeds; the fruit of this plant used as a vegetable.—*also* **red** *or* **green pepper**.

capsize /ˈkæpsaɪz/ or /kæpˈsaɪz/ *vti* to upset or overturn.

capstan /ˈkæpstən/ *n* an upright drum around which cables are wound to haul them in; the spindle in a tape recorder that winds the tape past the head.

capsulate, capsulated /ˈkæpsəˌleɪt/ *adj* furnished with or enclosed in a capsule.—**capsulation** *n*.

capsule /ˈkæpsəl/ or /-sjəl/ *n* a small gelatin case enclosing a drug to be swallowed; a metal or plastic container; (*bot*) a seed case; the orbiting and recoverable part of a spacecraft.—**capsular** *adj*.

capsulize /-aɪz/ *vt* to present (information) in a concise or condensed form.—**capsulization** *n*.

captain /ˈkæptən/ *n* a chief, leader; the master of a ship; the pilot of an aircraft; a rank of army, naval and marine officer; the leader of a team, as in sports; a leading employer in industry; a policeman responsible for a precinct. • *vt* to be captain of.—**captaincy** *n*.

captaincy, captainship *n* (*pl* **captaincies, captainships**) the rank, post, or commission of a captain.

caption /ˈkæpʃən/ *n* a heading in a newspaper, to a chapter, etc; a legend or title describing an illustration; a subtitle. • *vti* to provide with a caption.

captious /-ʃəs/ *adj* ready to find fault or take offence; carping, quibbling.—**captiously** *adv*.

captivate /ˈkæptəˌveɪt/ *vt* to fascinate; to charm.—**captivating** *adj*.—**captivation** *n*.—**captivator** *n*.

captive /ˈkæptɪv/ *n* one kept confined; a prisoner; a person obsessed by an emotion. • *adj* taken or kept prisoner; unable to avoid being addressed (*a captive audience*); unable to refuse (a product) through a lack of choice (*a captive market*); captivated.

captivity /kæpˈtɪvɪti/ *n* (*pl* **captivities**) the state of being a captive; a period of imprisonment.

captor /ˈkæptər/ *n* a person or animal who takes a prisoner.

capture /-tʃər/ vt to take prisoner; (fortress, etc) to seize; to catch; to gain or obtain by skill, attraction, etc, to win. • n the act of taking a prisoner or seizing by force; anything or anyone so taken.

capuche /kə'puːtʃ/ or /-puːʃ/ n a monk's hood or cowl; the hood of a cloak.

capuchin /'kæpjuːtʃɪn/ or /-puː-/, /-ʃɪn/ n a monkey with hair resembling a cowl; a pigeon with cowl-like feathers; a woman's cloak and hood; (with cap) a Franciscan monk of the mendicant order.

capybara /ˌkæpə'bɑrə/ n a large South American rodent that lives mostly in water.

car /kɑr/ n a self-propelled motor vehicle, an automobile, a motorcar; the passenger compartment of a train, airship, lift, cable railway, etc; a railway carriage.

carabineer, carabinier /ˌkærəbə'nɪr/ see **carbineer**.

carabiner /ˌkærə'bɪnər/ or /'kærə-/ n (climbing) a type of shackle with a snap link, used to secure a rope.

caracal /'kærəkæl/ or /'kærə-/ n a kind of lynx; its fur.

caracole, caracol /'kærəkoːl/ or /'kærə-/ vi (horse) to make a half turn to the right or left. • n a half turn, right or left; a spiral staircase.

carafe /kə'ræf/ n an open-topped bottle for serving water or wine at table.

carageen /'kærəgɪn/ see **carrageen**.

caramel /'kerəmel/ or /'kɑrməl/ n burnt sugar, used in cooking to colour or flavour; a type of sweet tasting of this.

caramelize /'kerəməlaɪz/ or /'kærə-/, /'kɑrmə-/ vti to turn or be turned into caramel.

carapace /'kerəpeɪs/ or /'kærə-/ n the upper shell of the tortoise, turtle, crab, etc.

carat /'kerət/ or /'kæ-/ n a measure of weight for precious stones; a measure of the purity of gold.—also **karat**.

caravan /'kerəvæn/ or /'kærə-/ n a large enclosed vehicle equipped to be lived in and may be towed by a car.—also US **trailer**; a band of merchants travelling together for safety. • vi (**caravanning, caravanned**) to travel with a caravan, esp on holiday.

caravanserai /ˌkerə'vænsəraɪ/, **caravansary** /-səri/ n (pl **caravanserais, caravansaries**) in the East, a large inn surrounding a spacious courtyard, where caravans rest at night.

caravel, caravelle /'kærə,vel/ n an ancient small light fast Spanish ship with broad bows, a narrow high poop, four masts and lateen sails.—also **carvel**.

caraway /'kærə,weɪ/ n a biennial plant with pungent aromatic seeds used as a flavouring.

carbide /'kɑr,baɪd/ n a compound of carbon with another element, esp calcium carbide.

carbine /'kɑrbaɪn/ n a light, semiautomatic or automatic rifle.

carbineer /'kɑrbəniːr/ n a mounted soldier armed with a carbine.—also **carabineer, carabinier**.

carbo-, carb- /'kɑrboː/ prefix carbon.

carbohydrate /ˌkɑrboː'haɪdreɪt/ n a compound of carbon, hydrogen and oxygen, esp in sugars and starches as components of food. • npl starchy foods.

carbolic acid /kɑr'bɒlɪk/ n phenol.

carbolize /'kɑrbə,laɪz/ vt to sterilize with carbolic acid.

carbon /'kɑrbən/ n a nonmetallic element, a constituent of all organic matter; a duplicate made with carbon paper.

carbon-12 n an isotope of carbon, used as the standard for atomic weight.

carbon-14 n a radioisotope used in medicine as a tracer and in carbon dating.

carbonaceous /ˌkɑrbə'neɪʃəs/ adj pertaining to, composed of or resembling carbon.

carbonado /ˌkɑrbə'neɪdoː/ or /-nɑ-/ n (pl **carbonadoes, carbonados**) a piece of meat cut crossways for grilling.

carbonate /'kɑrbəneɪt/ n a salt of carbonic acid. • vt to treat with carbon dioxide, as in making soft, fizzy drinks.—**carbonated** adj.

carbon copy n a copy of typed or written material made by using carbon paper; (inf) an exact copy of something or someone.

carbon dating n a scientific method of dating material by measuring the amount of carbon-14 it contains.

carbon dioxide n a gas formed by combustion and breathing and absorbed by plants.

carbonic /'kɑrbɒnɪk/ adj of or obtained from carbon.

carbonic acid n a weakly acidic solution of carbon dioxide in water.

carboniferous /ˌkɑrbə'nɪfərəs/ adj coal-bearing, yielding carbon; (with cap) of or relating to strata of the Palaeozoic Age from which coal is derived.

carbonize /'kɑrbə,naɪz/ vt to convert into carbon or a carbon residue.—**carbonization** n.

carbon monoxide n a colourless, odourless, highly poisonous gas.

carbon paper n a sheet of paper covered with a dark, waxy pigment inserted between sheets of paper for making copies of writing or typing.

carborundum /ˌkɑrbə'rɛndəm/ n (trademark) a compound of carbon and silicon used for polishing and grinding.

carboy /'kɑrbɔɪ/ n a, usu cushioned, container of glass, plastic or metal for the safe transportation of liquids.

carbuncle /'kɑr,bʌŋkəl/ n a red, knob-shaped gemstone, esp a garnet; a large inflamed boil; a pimple.—**carbuncular** adj.

carburet /'kɑrbə,reɪt/ or /-rɛt/, /-bə-/ vt (**carburetting, carburetted** or **carbureting, carbureted**) to combine with carbon.

carburetor, carburettor /'kɑrbə,reɪtə/ n a device in an internal-combustion engine for making an explosive mixture of air and fuel vapour.

carburize /'kɑrbə,raɪz/ or /-bə-/ vt to combine with carbon.—**carburization** n.

carcanet /'kɑrkə,net/ n (arch) a collar of jewels.

carcass /'kɑrkəs/ n the dead body of an animal; a framework, skeleton or shell; (derog) the body of a living person.

carcinogen /kɑr'sɪnədʒən/ n a substance that produces cancer.—**carcinogenic** adj.

carcinoma /ˌkɑrsɪ'noːmə/ n (pl **carcinomas, carcinomata**) a tumour caused by a cancer.

card[1] /kɑrd/ n a small piece of cardboard; a piece of this with a figure or picture for playing games or fortune-telling; a piece of this filed in a card index; a membership card; a piece of card with a person or firm's name, address or with an invitation, greeting, message, etc; (inf) an entertaining or eccentric person; a small piece of plastic identifying a person for banking purposes, eg a cheque card, credit card; (pl) card games; (pl) card playing; (pl) employees insurance and tax documents held by the employer.

card[2] n a toothed instrument for combing cotton, wool or flax fibres off. • vt (wool, etc) to comb.

cardamom, cardamum, cardamon /'kɑrdəməm/ n a tropical Asian plant the seed pods of which are used as a spice.

cardboard /'kɑrdbɔrd/ n thick stiff paper, often with a clay coating, for boxes, cartons, etc. • adj made of this; lacking substance; makeshift.

card-carrying adj being an official member of a political party, organization, etc.

card catalogue n a catalogue, each item of which is entered on a separate card.

card file n a filing system in which each item is entered separately on a single card.

cardi- /'kɑrdi/ or /-dɪ/, /-də/ prefix heart.

cardiac /'kɑrdi,æk/ adj relating to the heart. • n a person suffering a disorder of the heart; a drug to stimulate the heart.

cardiac arrest n heart failure.

cardialgia /ˌkɑrdi'ældʒiə/ or /-dʒə/ n heartburn.—**cardialgic** adj.

cardigan /'kɑrdɪgən/ n a knitted sweater that fastens up the front.

cardinal /'kɑrdɪnəl/ adj of chief importance, fundamental; of a bright red. • n an official appointed by the Pope to his councils; bright red.—**cardinally** adv.

cardinalate /-leɪt/, **cardinalship** /-ʃɪp/ n the office, rank, or dignity of a cardinal; the body of cardinals.

cardinal numbers npl numbers that express how many (1, 2, 3, 4 etc).

cardinal points npl the four chief points of the compass: north, south, east, west.

cardinal virtues npl justice, prudence, temperance, and fortitude.

cardio- /'kɑrdi,oː/ prefix heart.

cardiogram /'kɑrdio,græm/ n an electrocardiogram.

cardiograph /-,græf/ n a device for recording heart movements; an electrocardiograph.

cardiology /ˌkɑrdi'ɒlədʒi/ n the branch of medicine concerned with the heart and its diseases.—**cardiological** adj.—**cardiologist** n.

cardiopulmonary /ˌkɑrdio'pʌlmə,neri/ or /-pʊl/ adj concerned with or affect the heart and lungs.

cardiovascular /-'væskjulər/ adj of or pertaining to the heart and the blood vessels.

carditis /kɑr'daɪtɪs/ n inflammation of the muscular tissue of the heart.

cardoon /kɑrˈduːn/ *n* a plant related to and resembling the artichoke and used as a vegetable in Spain and France.

cards /kɑrds/ *see* **card**[1].

cardsharp(er) /kɑrdˈʃɑrp(ər)/ *n* a person who cheats at cards.

care /kɛr/ *n* anxiety; concern; serious attention, heed; consideration; charge, protection; the cause or object of concern or anxiety. • *vt* to feel concern; to agree, like, or be willing (to do something); **care of** at the address of, c/o; **in, into care** (*person*) taken charge of by a local authority by court order. • *vi* (*usu with* **for** *or* **about**) to feel affection or regard; to have a desire (for); to provide for, have in one's charge.

careen /kəˈriːn/ *vt* to bring (a ship) over on one side for calking, cleansing, or repairing. • *vi* to incline to one side, as a ship under press of sail.

career /kəˈriːr/ *n* progress through life; a profession, occupation, *esp* with prospects for promotion. • *vi* to rush rapidly or wildly.

careerist /-ɪst/ *n* a person who is ambitious to advance in a chosen profession.

career woman *n* a woman primarily interested in her job and in furthering her career.

carefree /kɛrˈfriː/ *adj* without cares, lively, light-hearted.

careful /ˈkɛrfʊl/ *adj* painstaking; cautious; thoughtful.—**carefully** *adv.*—**carefulness** *n.*

careless /ˈkɛrləs/ *adj* not careful; unconcerned, insensitive; carefree.—**carelessly** *adv.*—**carelessness** *n.*

carer /ˈkɛrər/ *n* one who takes on (professionally) the care of a dependent person.

caress /kəˈrɛs/ *n* any act or expression of affection; an embrace. • *vt* to touch or stroke lovingly.—**caresser** *n.*—**caressingly** *adv.*

caret /ˈkærət/ *n* a mark (^) showing where something omitted in text is to be inserted.

caretaker /ˈkɛrˌteɪkər/ *n* a person put in charge of a place or thing; (*government*) one temporarily in control.

careworn /ˈkɛrwɔrn/ *adj* showing signs of care stress, worry, etc.

cargo /ˈkɑrgoː/ *n* (*pl* **cargoes, cargos**) the load carried by a ship, truck, aircraft, etc; freight.

Carib /ˈkɛrɪb/ *n* (*pl* **Caribs, Carib**) a member of an Indian people of the Lesser Antilles and neighbouring parts of the South American coast, or of their descendants; their language. • *adj* of or pertaining to the Carib people or language.

Caribbean /ˌkɛrəˈbiən/ or /kəˈrɪbiən/ *adj* of or pertaining to the Caribbean Sea and its islands. • *n* the Caribbean Sea.

caribou /ˈkɛrɪˌbuː/ or /ˈkærə-/ *n* (*pl* **caribou, caribous**) a large North American reindeer.

caricature /ˈkærɪkətʃər/ *n* a likeness made ludicrous by exaggeration or distortion of characteristic features. • *vt* to make a caricature of, to parody.—**caricaturist** *n.*

caries /ˈkɛˌriːz/ *n* (*pl* **caries**) decay of bones or teeth.

carillon /ˈkærələn/ or /-ɒn/ *n* a chime of bells diatonically tuned and played by hand or machinery; a simple air adapted for playing on a set of bells.

carina /kəˈriːnə/ *n* (*pl* **carinae, carinas**) a keel; the two lower petals of a papilionaceous flower (as the furze) partially joined; the keel of the breastbone of birds.

carinate /ˈkærɪˌneɪt/, **carinated** /-ɪd/ *adj* shaped like a keel.

caring /ˈkɛrɪŋ/ *adj* compassionate; of or dealing with people's welfare, *usu* professionally.

carious /ˈkɛriəs/ *adj* affected with caries; decayed.

carjacking /ˈkɑrˌdʒækɪŋ/ *n* the violent hijacking and theft of a car, possibly involving the abduction or kidnapping of the driver or passenger.

carling /ˈkɑrlɪŋ/ *n* a ship's timber running fore and aft from one transverse deck beam to another, serving as a foundation for the planks of the deck.

Carlovingian /ˌkɑrləvɪnjiən/ *see* **Carolingian**.

carmagnole /ˈkɑrmənˌjoːl/ *n* a popular song and dance of the time of the French Revolution; a costume adapted by the revolutionists; a bombastic report from the French armies during the Revolution.

Carmelite /ˈkɑrməˌlaɪt/ *n* a member of a mendicant order founded on Mount Carmel in the 12th century, a white friar; a variety of pear; a kind of fine woollen cloth. • *adj* of or belonging to the order of Carmelites.

carminative /kɑrˈmɪnətɪv/ or /ˈkɑr-/ *n* a medicine that expels wind and relieves colic and flatulence. • *adj* expelling wind.

carmine /ˈkɑrmaɪn/ *n* a rich crimson pigment; the essential colouring principle of cochineal.

carnage /ˈkɑrnɪdʒ/ *n* great slaughter.

carnal /ˈkɑrnəl/ *adj* of the flesh; sexual; sensual; worldly.—**carnality** *n.*—**carnally** *adv.*

carnal knowledge *n* sexual intercourse.

carnation /kɑrˈneɪʃən/ *n* a garden flower, the clove pink.

carnelian /kɑrˈniːljən/ *see* **cornelian**.

carnet /ˈkɑrneɪ/ *n* a customs permit or licence, *esp* for a vehicle; a book of tickets, etc.

carnival /ˈkɑrnəvəl/ *n* public festivities and revelry; a travelling fair with sideshows, etc.

carnivore /ˈkɑrnəˌvɔr/ *n* a flesh-eating mammal.

carnivorous /kɑrˈnɪvərəs/ *adj* (*animals*) feeding on flesh; (*plants*) able to trap and digest insects.

carob /ˈkɛrəb/ or /ˈkær-/ *n* an edible, sugary pod of a Mediterranean tree.

carol /ˈkɛrəl/ or /ˈkæ-/ *n* a joyful song or hymn; a Christmas hymn. • *vi* (**carolling, carolled** or **caroling, caroled**) to sing carols; to sing with happiness.

Caroline /ˈkɛrəlaɪn/ or /ˈkærə/, **Carolean** /-liːən/ *adj* belonging to the period of Charles I or Charles II.

Carolingian /ˌkɛrəˈlɪndʒiən/ or /ˈkærə-/ *adj* of or pertaining to the medieval Frankish dynasty that once ruled France. • *n* a member of this dynasty.—*also* **Carlovingian**.

Carolinian /ˌkɛrəˈlɪniən/ or /ˈkærə-/ *adj* of or pertaining to either North or South Carolina.

carom /ˈkɛrəm/ or /ˈkærəm/ *n* (*billiards*) a shot in which the cue ball hits two others successively. • *vi* to make a carom.—*also* **cannon**.

carotid (artery) /kəˈrɒtɪd/ *n* one of the two principal arteries, one on either side of the neck, which convey blood from the aorta to the head.—**carotidal** *adj.*

carousal /kəˈrɑːzəl/ or /ˈkærə-/ *n* a feast or festival; a noisy drinking bout or revel.

carouse /kəˈrɑːuz/ *vi* to drink and have fun.—**carousal** *n.*—**carouser** *n.*

carousel /ˈkærəˌsɛl/ or /ˌkærəˈsɛl/ *n* a merry-go-round; a revolving circular platform, as in an airport luggage conveyor.

carp[1] /kɑrp/ *vi* to find fault, complain.

carp[2] *n* (*pl* **carp, carps**) a brown and yellow freshwater fish.

carpal /ˈkɑrpəl/ *adj* pertaining to the carpus or wrist.

car park *n* a parking lot.

carpe diem /ˌkɑrpeɪˈdiːɛm/ (*Latin*) seize the day; take advantage of a present opportunity.

carpel /ˈkɑrpəl/ *n* a simple pistil, or one of the parts of a compound pistil or ovary of a flower.—**carpellary** *adj.*

carpellate /-ˌleɪt/ *adj* having a carpel.

carpenter /ˈkɑrpəntər/ *n* a person skilled in woodwork, *esp* in house building.—**carpentry** *n.*

carpenter bee *n* a bee that makes nests in wood.

carpentry /ˈkɑrpəntri/ *n* the art of cutting, framing, and joining timber; work done by a carpenter.

carpet /ˈkɑrpət/ *n* a woven fabric for covering floors; any thick covering. • *vt* to cover with carpet; (*inf*) to issue a reprimand, to have on the carpet to rebuke.

carpetbag /-ˌbæg/ *n* a carrying bag formerly made of carpeting.

carpetbagger /-ˌbægər/ *n* an outsider, *esp* a nonresident who meddles in politics.

carpeting /-ɪŋ/ *n* cloth for carpets; carpets in general.

carpet sweeper *n* a mechanical device for removing dirt, etc, from a carpet.

carphone *n* a cellular telephone fitted in and operated from a car.

carpology /kɑrˈpɒlədʒi/ *n* the branch of botany that treats of the structure of fruits in general.—**carpological** *adj.*—**carpologist** *n.*

carpophore /ˈkɑrpəfɔr/ *n* (*bot*) a slender prolongation of the axis that bears the carpels.

carport /ˈkɑrpɔrt/ *n* an open-sided shelter for a car extending from the side of a house.

carpus /ˈkɑrpəs/ *n* (*pl* **carpi**) the bones between the forearm and the hand, forming the wrist in man and the corresponding bones in other animals.

carrack /ˈkɛrək/ or /ˈkæ-/ *n* a large round-built vessel formerly used by the Portuguese and Spaniards in the East Indian and American trade.

carrageen, carragheen /'kɛrə,giːn/ or /'kærə-/ n a seaweed very common on the rocks of the Irish coast that, when dried and bleached, is known as Irish moss and is used for blancmanges, soup, etc.—*also* **carageen**.

carrel /'kɛrəl/ or /'kærəl/ n a small study room or cubicle, *esp* in a library.

carriage /'kɛrɪdʒ/ or /'kærədʒ/ n the act of carrying, transport; the cost of this; deportment, bearing; behaviour; a rail coach or compartment; a wheeled coach drawn by horses; a frame with wheels to carry a gun; the moving part of a typewriter.

carriage dog n the spotted Dalmatian.

carrick bend /'kɛrɪk/ or /'kæ-/ n (*naut*) a particular kind of knot for splicing two hawsers together.

carrick bitt n (*naut*) one of the bitts supporting the windlass.

carrier /'kɛrɪər/ or /'kær-/ n one who carries or transports goods, *esp* for hire; a device for carrying; a person or animal transmitting an infectious disease without being affected by it; an aircraft carrier; a plastic or paper bag with handles for holding things; a portable seat for a baby, a carrycot.

carrier pigeon n a homing pigeon used to carry messages.

carrier wave n an electromagnetic wave that can be modulated in frequency, amplitude, etc, to transmit (radio, TV, etc) signals.

carrion /'kɛrɪən/ or /'kær-/ n the dead putrefying flesh of an animal.

carrion crow n the common crow of Europe.

carronade /,kɛrə'neɪd/ n a short cannon of large bore for close range, formerly used in the navy.

carron oil n a mixture of linseed oil and lime water used as a liniment for burns.

carrot /'kɛrət/ or /'kæ-/ n a plant grown for its edible, fleshy orange root; an inducement, often illusory.

carroty /'kærəti/ adj orange-red in colour.

carry /'kɛri/ or /'kæ-/ vb (**carrying, carried**) vt to convey or transport; to support or bear; to involve, have as a result; to hold (oneself); to extend or prolong; to gain by force; to win over; to stock; to be pregnant; (*with* **away**) to delight; to arouse to extreme enthusiasm; to remove violently; (*with* **forward**) (*book-keeping*) to transfer (a total) to the next column, page, etc; (*with* **off**) to cause to die; to remove by force, capture; (*situation*) to handle successfully; (*with* **out**) to perform (a task, etc); to accomplish; (*with* **over**) to carry forward; (*with* **through**) to complete. • vi (*with* **away**) to be filled with joy or emotion; (*with* **on**) to persevere; to conduct a business, etc; (*inf*) to have an affair; (*inf*) to cause a fuss; (*with* **through**) to enable to survive; to persist.

carryall /'kɛrɪɔːl/ or /'kæri-/ n an overnight or holdall bag.

carrycot /'kɛrɪkɒt/ or /'kæri-/ n a baby carrier, a portable cot.

carry-out /-ɐʊt/ n food or drink sold by a restaurant but consumed elsewhere.—*also adj*.

carsick /'kɑrsɪk/ adj ill or queasy from the motion of a moving vehicle.—**carsickness** n.

cart /kɑrt/ n a two-wheeled vehicle drawn by horses; any small vehicle for carrying loads. • vt to carry in a cart; (*inf*) to transport with effort.

cartage /'kɑrtɪdʒ/ n conveyance in a cart; the charge made for this.

carte blanche /'kɑrt'blɑnʃ/, Fr. /kart'blɑ̃ʃ/ n (*pl* **cartes blanches**) full authority to act as one thinks best.

cartel /kɑr'tɛl/ n an association of business firms to coordinate production, prices, etc to avoid competition and maximize profits; a union of political parties to achieve common aims.

Cartesian /kɑr'tiːʒən/ or /-iːzɪən/ adj pertaining to the French philosopher René Descartes (1596–1650) or his philosophy. • n a follower of Descartes or his philosophy.

Carthaginian /,kɑrθə'dʒɪnɪən/ adj pertaining to ancient Carthage, a city of North Africa.

Carthusian /kɑr'θjuːzɪən/ or /-'θuː:ʒən/ n one of an order of monks founded (1086) by St Bruno in the Grande Chartreuse, France.

cartilage /'kɑrtəlɪdʒ/ n tough, elastic tissue attached to the bones of animals; gristle.—**cartilaginous** adj.

cartload /'kɑrtloːd/ n the amount a cart will hold.

cartogram /'kɑrtə,græm/ n a map showing statistical information in diagrammatic form.

cartography /kɑr'tɒgrəfi/ n the drawing and publishing of maps.—**cartographer** n.—**cartographic, cartographical** adj.

carton /'kɑrtən/ n a cardboard box or container.

cartoon /kɑr'tuːn/ n a humorous picture dealing with current events; a comic strip; an animated cartoon; a full-size preparatory sketch for reproduction on a fresco, etc.—**cartoonist** n.

cartouche, cartouch /kɑr'tuːʃ/ n a cartridge; a canvas cartridge case; an ornament in the form of an unrolled scroll; on Egyptian monuments, etc, an oval figure containing the name or title of a sovereign or deity.

cartridge /'kɑrtrɪdʒ/ n the case that contains the explosive charge and bullet in a gun or rifle; a sealed case of film for a camera; the device containing the stylus on the end of the pick-up arm of a record player.

cartridge belt n a belt with loops for holding spare cartridges.

cartridge clip n a detachable container for cartridges in an automatic firearm.

cartulary /'kɑrtʃə,lɛri/ n (*pl* **cartularies**) a collection or register of charters.—*also* **chartulary**.

cartwheel /'kɑrtwiːl/ n an acrobatic handspring in which the body revolves with the weight on each hand in turn and the legs spread like the spokes of a wheel.

caruncle /'kær,ɒŋkəl/ or /kə'rɛŋkəl/ n a small fleshy excrescence on a bird's head, as the comb or wattle of a fowl; an appendage surrounding the hilum of a seed.—**caruncular, carunculate** adj.

carve /kɑrv/ vt to shape by cutting; to adorn with designs; to cut up (meat, etc); (*with* **up**) to cut into pieces or shares; (*sl*) to share out illegal proceeds; to slash someone with a knife or razor.

carvel /'kɑrvəl/ *see* **caravel**.

carvel-built /-,bɪlt/ adj (*vessel*) with the outer boards or plates meeting flush, not overlapping.

carving /-ɪŋ/ n a figure or design carved from wood, stone, etc; the act of carving.

caryatid /,kæ,rɪætɪd/ n (*pl* **caryatids, caryatides**) a figure of a woman in long robes supporting an entablature.—**caryatic, caryatidic, caryatidal, caryatidean** adj.

caryophyllaceous /,kærɪo'fɪleɪʃəs/ adj (*flowers*) belonging to the pink family.

caryopsis /,kær'ɪɒpsɪs/ n (*pl* **caryopses, caryopsides**) a small dry fruit with the thin pericarp adherent to the seed, as in wheat, etc.

casaba /kə'sɒbə/ n a variety of winter melon with a yellow rind and sweet flesh.—*also* **cassaba**.

Casanova /,kæsə'noːvə/ or /,kæsə-/ n a man of amorous reputation.

cascade /kæs'keɪd/ n a small, steep waterfall; a shower, as of sparks, etc. • vti to fall in a cascade.

cascara /kæs'kɑrə/ n Californian bark used as an aperient; a bark canoe.

cascarilla /,kæskə'rɪlə/ n the bark of a West Indian shrub, possessing aromatic and bitter properties; the shrub itself, from which is obtained a white bitter crystalline substance, cascarillin.

case[1] /keɪs/ n a covering; a suitcase; its contents; the binding covering a book.

case[2] n an instance; a state of affairs; a condition, circumstance; a lawsuit; an argument for one side; (*sl*) a character; a person of a specific type; (*med*) a patient under treatment; (*gram*) the relationship between nouns, pronouns and adjectives in a sentence; **in case** in order to prevent, lest.

case-harden /'keɪs,hɑrdən/ vt to make the surface (of iron or steel) harder than the interior.

case-hardened /-dənd/ adj with a hard surface; made callous.

case history n a record of a person's medical background, etc.

casein /'keɪsiːn/ or /'keɪsiːɪn/ n a protein in the curd matter of milk.

case knife n a sheath knife.

case law n law as settled by precedent.

casemate /'keɪsmeɪt/ n a bomb-proof vault or battery in a fortification; an armoured enclosure for a gun in a warship; a hollow moulding.

casement /'keɪsmənt/ n a window or its frame with a side hinge for opening.

caseous /'keɪsɪəs/ adj like cheese, cheesy.

casern, caserne /kə'zɜrn/ n a lodging or barrack for soldiers in a garrison town.

case study n an analysis arrived at from studying more than one case history.

casework /'keɪs,wɜrk/ n social work based on the close monitoring of individuals or families.—**caseworker** n.

cash[1] /kæʃ/ n money in coins or notes; immediate payment, as opposed to that by cheque or on credit. • vt to give or get cash for; (*with* **in**) to exchange something for money; (*inf*) to gain an advantage or seize an opportunity to profit from; (*sl*) to die. • vi (*with* **in**) to exploit for profit; to take advantage of.—**cashable** adj.

cash[2] *n* (*pl* **cash**) the name of various Eastern coins of low value.

cash and carry *n, adj* (a policy of) selling for cash without delivery of goods.

cash-book *n* a book in which a register is kept of money received or paid out.

cash crop *n* a crop grown for market not for consumption.

cashew /'kæʃuː/ or /kæ'ʃuː/ *n* the small, edible nut of a tropical tree.

cash flow *n* money which is paid into and out of a business during its operations.

cashier[1] /kæʃiːr/ *n* a person in charge of the paying and receiving of money in a bank, shop, etc.

cashier[2] *vt* to dismiss (an officer) from military service; to discharge.

cashmere /'kæʃˌmiːr/ *n* a fine wool from Kashmir goats; a material made from this.

cash on delivery *n* delivery to be paid for to a postman or carrier.

cash register *n* an automatic or electronic machine that shows and records the amount placed in it.

casimere *see* **cassimere**.

casing /'keɪsɪŋ/ *n* any protective or outer covering; the material for this.

casino /kə'siːnoː/ *n* (*pl* **casinos**) a room or building where gambling takes place.

cask /kæsk/ *n* a barrel of any size, *esp* one for liquids; its contents.

casket /'kæskɪt/ *n* a small box or chest for jewels, etc; a coffin.

casque /kæsk/ *n* (*poet*) a helmet.

cassaba /kə'sɒbə/ *see* **casaba**.

cassava /kə'sɑːvə/ *n* a plant of tropical America and Africa cultivated for its tuberous roots, which yield a nutritious starch from which cassava bread and tapioca are made.

casserole /'kæsɭəˌroːl/ *n* a covered dish for cooking and serving; the food so cooked and served. • *vt* to cook in a casserole.

cassette /kə'set/ *n* a case containing magnetic tape or film for loading into a tape recorder or camera.

cassia /'kæsiə/ or /'kæʃə/ *n* one of several tropical leguminous plants, the leaves of several species of which constitute the drug senna.

cassimere /'kæsəˌmiːr/ *n* a thin twilled woollen cloth used for men's garments.—*also* **casimere**.

cassiterite /kə'sɪtəˌraɪt/ *n* a native tin dioxide; the principal ore of tin.

cassock /'kæsək/ *n* a long close-fitting black garment worn by certain clergy and by choristers.

cassowary /'kæsəˌweri/ *n* (*pl* **cassowaries**) a large running bird resembling the ostrich, inhabiting Australia and New Guinea.

cast /kæst/ *vb* (**casting, cast**) *vt* to throw or fling; to throw off or shed; to record; to direct; to shape in a mould; to calculate; to select actors, etc for a play; to throw a fishing line into the water. • *vi* to throw, hurl; (*with* **off**) to untie a ship from its moorings; (*knitting*) to loop off stitches from a needle without letting them unravel; (*with* **on**) to loop the first row of stitches onto a needle. • *n* act of casting; a throw; a plaster form for immobilizing an injured limb; a mould for casting; type or quantity; a tinge of colour; the actors assigned roles in a play; the set of actors; a slight squint in the eye.

castanets /ˌkæstə'nets/ *npl* hollow shell-shaped pieces of wood held between the fingers and rattled together, *esp* to accompany Spanish dancing.

castaway /'kæstəweɪ/ *adj* shipwrecked; discarded. • *n* a shipwrecked person.

cast down *adj* depressed.

caste /kæst/ *n* any of the Hindu hereditary social classes; an exclusive social group.

castellan /'kæstələn/ *n* the governor of a castle.

castellated /-leɪtəd/ *adj* having turrets and battlements, as a castle.

caster /'kæstər/ *see* **castor**.

castigate /'kæstɪˌgeɪt/ *vt* to chastise; to punish; to correct.—**castigation** *n*.

casting vote /'kæstɪŋ/ *n* the deciding vote used by the chairman of a meeting when the votes on each side are equal.

cast iron /'kæst'aɪrən/ *n* an iron-carbon alloy melted and run into moulds.

cast-iron *adj* made of cast iron; untiring; rigid, unadaptable.

castle /'kæsəl/ *n* a fortified building; a chess piece.—*also* **rook**.

castoff /'kæstɒf/ *n* a rejected item; a rough estimate of the number of pages of a finished book, etc.

cast-off *adj* laid aside or rejected.—**castoff** *n*.

castor /'kæstər/ *n* a small container with a perforated top for sprinkling salt, sugar, etc; a small swivelled wheel on a table leg, etc.—*also* **caster**.

castoroil /'kæstər/ *n* a vegetable oil used as a cathartic and lubricant.

castrate /'kæstreɪt/ *vt* to remove the testicles of, to geld.—**castration** *n*.—**castrator** *n*.

castrato /kæs'trɒtoː/ *n* (*pl* **castrati, castratos**) a male castrated in childhood to prevent a change of voice at the age of puberty; an artificial male soprano.

casual /'kæʒʊəl/ or /'kæʒjʊəl/ *adj* accidental, chance; unplanned; occasional; careless, offhand; unmethodical; informal. • *n* someone who works occasionally; (*pl*) informal or leisure clothing, shoes.—**casually** *adv*.—**casualness** *n*.

casualty /'kæʒʊəlti/ *n* (*pl* **casualties**) a person injured or killed in a war or in an accident; something damaged or destroyed.

casuarina /ˌkæsjʊ'riːnə/ *n* a tree of Australia and southeast Asia having jointed branches.

casuist /'kæʒjuːɪst/ or /'kæʒuːɪst/ *n* one who studies or resolves cases of conscience; one skilled in casuistry.—**casuistic, casuistical** *adj*.—**casuistically** *adv*.

casuistry /'kæʒuːɪstri/ *n* (*pl* **casuistries**) the study or application of rules of right and wrong; sophistical or equivocal reasoning, *esp* on moral matters.

casus belli /'kæsəs'beli/ or /ˌkeɪsəs-/ *n* (*pl* **casus belli**) an act or occurrence justifying war.

CAT /kæt/ (*acronym*) computerized axial tomography.—*also* **computer-aided** *or* **computer-assisted tomography**; the production of detailed three-dimensional images from scans of cross-sections of internal organs (**CAT scans**) using a computer-controlled X-ray machine (**CAT scanner**).

cat /kæt/ *n* a small, domesticated feline mammal kept as a pet; a wild animal related to this; lions, tigers, etc.—*also* **big cat**; (*inf*) a spiteful woman; (*sl*) a man.

cata- /'kætə/ *prefix* down; wrongly; thoroughly.

catabolism /kə'tæbəˌlɪzəm/ *n* a downward series of changes by which complex bodies are broken down into simpler forms.—**catabolic** *adj*.—**catabolically** *adv*.

catabolize /-aɪz/ *vti* to subject to or undergo catabolism.

catachresis /ˌkætə'kriːsɪs/ *n* (*pl* **catachreses**) misapplication of words; formation of words on a false analogy.—**catachrestic** *adj*.—**catachrestically** *adv*.

cataclysm /'kætəˌklɪzəm/ *n* a violent disturbance or disaster.—**cataclysmic** *adj*.

catacomb /'kætəˌkoːm/ *n* (*usu pl*) an underground burial place.

catadromous /kə'tædrəməs/ *adj* going down to the sea to spawn.

catafalque /'kætəˌfɒlk/ *n* a temporary structure erected, *usu* in a church, to support the coffin on the occasion of a lying in state.

Catalan /'kætəˌlæn/ *adj* of or pertaining to Catalonia, a province of Spain, or to its inhabitants or language. • *n* an inhabitant of Catalonia; the language of Catalonia.

catalectic /'kætəˌlektɪk/ *adj* (*poetry*) lacking a syllable in the last foot.

catalepsy /'kætəˌlepsi/ *n* (*pl* **catalepsies**) a state of temporary rigidity and unconsciousness.—**cataleptic** *adj*.

catalogue, catalog /'kætəˌlɒg/ *n* a list of books, names, etc in systematic order. • *vti* to list, to make a catalogue of.—**cataloger, cataloguer** *n*.

catalogue raisonné /'kætəˌlɒg'reɪzɒˌneɪ/, *Fr.* /kata'lɒgʀɛzɔ'neɪ/ *n* a catalogue of books, paintings, etc, classed according to their subjects.

catalpa /kə'tælpə/ *n* an American tree with trumpet-shaped flowers.

catalyse /'kætəˌlaɪz/ *vt* to accelerate or retard (a chemical reaction) by catalysis.—**catalyser** *n*.

catalysis /kə'tælɪsɪs/ *n* (*pl* **catalyses**) the acceleration or retardation of a chemical reaction by the action of a catalyst. —**catalytic** *adj*.

catalyst /'kætəlɪst/ *n* a substance which accelerates or retards a chemical reaction without itself undergoing any permanent chemical change; a person or thing which produces change.

catalytic converter *n* a filter device in vehicles to reduce pollution from exhaust produced by combustion, eg carbon monoxide, nitrogen oxide, etc.

catamaran /ˌkætəmə'ræn/ *n* a (sailing) boat with twin hulls; a raft of logs.

catamenia /ˌkætəˈmiːniə/ n menstruation.—**catamenial** adj.

catamite /ˈkætəmɔɪt/ n a boy kept by a sodomite.

catamount /ˈkætəmaʊnt/, **catamountain** /-eɪn/ n the wild cat; the puma, cougar, or mountain lion.

cataplasm /ˌkætəˈplæzəm/ n a poultice.

cataplexy /ˈkætəˌpleksɪ/ n (pl cataplexies) a sudden shock to the nerves causing paralysis.

catapult /ˈkætəpʊlt/ or /-pʌlt/ n a slingshot; a device for launching aircraft from the deck of an aircraft carrier. • vt to shoot forwards as from a catapult.

cataract /ˈkætəˌrækt/ n a waterfall, esp a large sheet one; a disease of the eye causing dimming of the lens and loss of vision.

catarrh /kəˈtɑr/ n inflammation of a mucous membrane, esp in the nose and throat, causing a flow of mucus.—**catarrhal** adj.

catarrhine /ˈkætəˌraɪn/ adj of or pertaining to a group of monkeys and apes of the Old World, which have the nostrils close together and pointing downwards.

catastrophe /kəˈtæstrəfɪ/ n a great disaster.—**catastrophic** adj.—**catastrophically** adv.

catastrophize /-aɪz/ vt to envisage a situation as being worse than it is.—also **awfulize**.

catatonia /ˌkætəˈtɒnɪə/ n a form of schizophrenia in which a trance-like state is punctuated by periods of hyperactivity.—**catatonic** adj.

Catawba /kəˈtɒbə/ n (pl **Catawba, Catawbas**) a member of a North American Indian people formerly of North and South Carolina; a light red variety of American grape; a light wine made from this grape.

catbird /ˈkætbərd/ n a kind of American thrush.

catboat /-boːt/ n a small boat with one sail on a single mast near the bows.

cat burglar n a burglar who enters by climbing.

catcall /-ˌkɒl/ n a shrill whistle or cry used to express disapproval. • vt to express disapproval by a catcall.

catch /kætʃ/ vb (**catching, caught**) vt to take hold of, to grasp; to capture; to ensnare or trap; to be on time for; to detect; to apprehend; to become infected with (a disease); to attract (the eye); (inf) to see, hear, etc; to grasp (a meaning); (with out) (inf) to detect (a person) in a mistake; (cricket) to catch a ball hit by a batsman before it touches the ground, making him "out". • vi to become entangled; to begin to burn; (with on) (inf) to become popular; to understand; (with up) to reach or come level with (eg a person ahead); to make up for lost time, deal with a backlog. • n the act of catching; the amount or number caught; a device for fastening; someone worth catching; a hidden difficulty.

catch-all /ˈkætʃˌɒl/ adj, n (something) intended to cover all eventualities.

catcher /-ər/ n (baseball) the player who stands behind the batter to catch the ball.

catching /-ɪŋ/ adj infectious; attractive.

catchment /-mənt/ n the collecting or the drainage of water.

catchment area n the area from which a body of water is fed, eg a river or reservoir; a geographic area served by a particular institution.

catchpenny /-ˌpenɪ/ n (pl **catchpennies**) an article of little value got up attractively to effect a quick sale.

catch phrase /-freɪz/ n a well-known phrase or slogan, esp one associated with a particular group or person.

catchpole /-ˌpoːl/ n a sheriff's officer; a constable in medieval England.

catch-22 /-twentiˈtuː/ n a predicament from which a victim is powerless to escape due to conditions beyond his or her control.

catchup /-əp/ see **ketchup**.

catchweight /-ˌweɪt/ n a weight left to the choice of an owner of a horse. • adv without being handicapped.

catchword /-wərd/ n a guide word; a word or expression, briefly popular, representative of a person or point of view; a cue in the theatre.

catchy /ˈkætʃɪ/ adj (**catchier, catchiest**) easily remembered, as a tune.—**catchiness** n.

catechetic /ˌkætəˈketɪk/, **catechetical** /-əl/ adj instructing orally; proceeding by question and answer; of catechism.—**catechetically** adv.

catechin /ˈkætətʃɪn/ or /-kɪn/ n a tannic acid extracted from catechu.

catechism /ˈkætəˌkɪzəm/ n a simple summary of the principles of religion in question and answer form, used for instruction; continuous questioning.—**catechismal** adj.

catechize /ˈkætəˌkaɪz/ vt to instruct by question and answer.—**catechization** n.—**catechist, catechizer** n.

catechu /ˈkætətʃuː/ n a brown astringent substance obtained from tropical plants and used in the arts and as a medicine.—also **cachou, cutch**.

catechumen /ˌkætəˈkjuːmən/ n one who is under religious instruction prior to receiving baptism; a beginner in the first principles of knowledge.

categorical /ˌkætəˈgɒrɪkəl/ or /-gɒr-/ adj unconditional, absolute; positive, explicit.—**categorically** adv.

categorical imperative n (philos) in Kantian ethics, the absolute and unconditional command of moral law.

categorize /ˈkætəgəˌraɪz/ vt to place in a category.—**categorization** n.

category /ˈkætəgɒrɪ/ n (pl **categories**) a class or division of things.

catena /kəˈtiːnə/ n (pl **catenae, catenas**) a series of notions; things connected with each other like the links of a chain; a systematic arrangement of selections from authors to illustrate a doctrine.

catenary /ˈkætəˌneri/ n (pl **catenaries**) a curve formed by a hanging chain. • adj of or resembling a chain.—also **catenarian**.

catenate /ˈkætəneɪt/ vt (biol) to link together.—**catenation** n.

catenulate /ˈkətenjuːleɪt/ adj (bot) consisting of little links.

cater /ˈkeɪtər/ vi (with for or to) to provide with what is needed or desired, esp food and service, as for parties.—**caterer** n.

cateran /ˈkætərən/ n a kern; a Highland or Irish irregular soldier; a Highland freebooter.

caterpillar /ˈkætərˌpɪlər/ n the worm-like larvae of a butterfly or moth; the ribbed band in place of wheels on a heavy vehicle; a vehicle (eg tank, tractor) equipped with such tracks.

caterwaul /-ˌwɒl/ vi to make a howling noise like a cat. • n such a cry.

catfish /ˈkætfɪʃ/ n (pl **catfish, catfishes**) a large, usu freshwater, fish with whisker-like feelers around the mouth.

catgut /ˈkætgʌt/ n a strong cord made from animal intestines, used for the strings of musical instruments, sports rackets, and surgical ligatures.

catharsis /kəˈθɑrsɪs/ n (pl **catharses**) emotional relief given by art, esp tragedy; (med) purgation; (psychoanal) relief obtained by the uncovering of buried repressions, etc.

cathartic /-tɪk/ adj bringing about catharsis; purgative. • n a purgative medicine.—**cathartically** adv.

cathead /ˈkæthɛd/ n a beam projecting from a ship's bows to which the anchor is secured.

cathedra /ˈkæθiːdrə/ or /kəˈθiːdrə/ n (pl **cathedrae**) a bishop's throne in the cathedral of his diocese; an official or professional chair.

cathedral /kəˈθiːdrəl/ n the chief church of a diocese. • adj having or belonging to a cathedral.

Catherine wheel /ˈkæθərɪn/ n a rotating firework.—also **pinwheel**.

catheter /ˈkæθətər/ n a flexible tube inserted into the bladder for drawing off urine.

catheterize /-ˌraɪz/ vt to insert a catheter into.—**catheterization** n.

cathode /ˈkæθoːd/ n (elect) the negative terminal; the electrode by which current leaves.—**cathodal** adj.—**cathodic, cathodical** adj.

cathode rays /-reɪz/ n (one of the electrons in) a stream of electrons emitted by a cathode in a vacuum tube.

cathode-ray tube n a vacuum tube in which electron beams are directed onto a fluorescent screen to produce luminous images, as used in television sets.

Catholic /ˈkæθlɪk/ or /-əl-/ n a member of the Roman Catholic Church. • adj relating to the Roman Catholic Church; embracing the whole body of Christians.—**Catholicism** n.

catholic /ˈkæθlɪk/ or /-əl-/ adj universal, all-embracing; broadminded, liberal; general, not exclusive.

Catholic Epistles npl the Epistles of the Apostles addressed to believers generally, ie James 1 and 2, Peter 1, 2 and 3, John, and Jude.

Catholicism /kəˈθɒlɪˌsɪzəm/ n the belief of, or adherence to, the Catholic Church or faith, esp to that of the Roman Catholic Church.

catholicity /ˌkæθəˈlɪsɪtɪ/ n the quality of being catholic; universality, comprehensiveness; accordance with Catholic, esp Roman Catholic, church doctrine.

catholicize /kəˈθɒlɪˌsaɪz/ vt to convert to the Roman Catholic Church.—**catholicization** n.

catholicon /-ɪˌkɒn/ or /-ɪkən/ n a universal remedy, a panacea.

cathouse /ˈkætˌhɛʊs/ n (inf) a brothel.

cation /ˈkætˌaɪən/ or /-aɪɒn/ n a positively charged ion.—**cationic** adj.

catkin /ˈkætkɪn/ n a hanging spike of small flowers, eg on birch, willow and hazel trees.

cat-like /-ˌlaɪk/ adj like a cat; stealthy, noiseless.

catmint /-ˌmɪnt/, **catnip** /-ˌnɪp/ n a strongly-scented plant attractive to cats.

catnap /ˈnæp/ n a short, light or intermittent sleep, a snooze, a doze.—also vi (**catnapping, catnapped**).

cat-o'-nine-tails /ˌkætəˈnaɪnˌteɪlz/ n (pl **cat-o'-nine-tails**) a whip with nine lashes of knotted cord, formerly used as a punishment in the army and navy.

catoptric /kəˈtɒpˌtrɪk/, **catoptrical** /-əl/ adj of or pertaining to mirrors or reflected light.

Cat scan, Cat scanner see CAT.

cat's cradle n a game of making designs with string looped over the fingers.

cat's-eye /ˈkætsˌaɪ/ n a hard semi-transparent variety of quartz.

cat's-paw /ˈkætsˌpɒ/ n a person used as a tool by another, a dupe; (naut) a light breeze that slightly ripples the surface of the water.

catsup /ˈkætsəp/ see **ketchup**.

cattery /ˈkætəri/ n (pl **catteries**) a place for boarding or breeding cats.

cattle /ˈkætəl/ npl domesticated bovine mammals such as bulls and cows.

cattle-grid /-grɪd/ n a grid of metal bars over a hole in a road that allows the passage of people and vehicles, but not cattle or other livestock.

cattleman /-mən/ or /-ˌmæn/ n (pl **cattlemen**) one who tends or drives cattle; a breeder of cattle.

cattle prod /-prɒd/ n an electrified prod for driving cattle.

catty[1] /ˈkæti/ adj (**cattier, cattiest**) (inf) spiteful, mean.—**cattily** adv.—**cattiness** n.

catty[2] n (pl **catties**) an East Indian weight equal to one and a third pounds; a name applied to a Chinese kin or pound; a Siamese coin.

catwalk /ˈkætˌwɒk/ n a narrow, raised pathway on a stage, bridge, etc; fashion modelling (with **the**).

Caucasian /kɒˈkeɪʒən/ adj of the light-skinned racial group of humankind; of or relating to the Caucasus Mountains. • n a Caucasian person.—**Caucasoid** adj.

Caucasus /ˈkɒkəsəs/ n a mountain range in the southwest USSR (with **the**).—also **Caucasus Mountains**.

caucus /ˈkɒkəs/ n (pl **caucuses**) a private meeting of leaders of a political party or faction, usu to plan strategy.

caudal /ˈkɒdəl/ adj of or pertaining to a tail.—**caudally** adv.

caudate /ˈkɒdeɪt/, **caudated** /-ɪd/ adj having a tail; having a tail-like appendage.

caudex /ˈkɒdɛks/ n (pl **caudices, caudexes**) the main trunk or axis of a plant.

caudle /ˈkɒdəl/ n a warm drink made of wine or ale, spiced or sugared, and mixed with bread, eggs, etc.

caught /kɒt/ see **catch**.

caul /kɒl/ n the membrane covering a foetus; part of this covering the head of some infants at birth.

cauldron /ˈkɒldrən/ n a large kettle or boiling pot; a state of violent agitation.—also **caldron**.

caulescent /kɒˈlɛsənt/ adj having a true stem or stalk.

caulicle /ˈkɒlɪkəl/ n a small or rudimentary stem.

cauliflower /ˈkɒlɪflaʊr/ n a kind of cabbage with an edible white flower-head used as a vegetable.

cauliflower ear n a thickening condition of the ear, common to boxers, caused by repeated blows.

cauline /ˈkɒˌlaɪn/ adj of, on or belonging to a stem.

caulk /kɒk/ vt to make (a boat) watertight by stopping up the seams with pitch.—also **calk**.—**caulker, calker** n.

causal /ˈkɒzəl/ adj forming or being a cause; involving, expressing or implying a cause.—**causally** adv.

causality /kɒˈzælɪti/ n (pl **causalities**) the relationship between cause and effect.

causation /-ˈzeɪʃən/ n causality; the act of causing something to happen.—**causational** adj.

causative /ˈkɒzəˌtɪv/ adj that causes; effective as a cause; expressing causation.

cause /kɒz/ n that which produces an effect; reason, motive, purpose, justification; a principle for which people strive; a lawsuit. • vt to bring about, to effect; to make (to do something).—**causer** n.

cause célèbre /ˈkɒzsəˈlɛb/ or /koːz-/, /seɪ-/, /-ˈlɛbrə/, Fr /koːzseɪˈlɛˌbʀ/ n (pl **causes célèbres**) a famous lawsuit, trial or celebrated issue.

causeless /kɒzləs/ adj without cause; groundless.

causerie /ˌkoːzəˈriː/ n a discursive conversational article; an informal chat.

causeway /ˈkɒzˌweɪ/ n a raised road across wet ground or water.

caustic /ˈkɒstɪk/ adj burning tissue, etc by chemical action; corrosive; sarcastic, cutting. • n a caustic substance.—**caustically** adv.—**causticness, causticity** n.

caustic potash n potassium hydroxide, a white substance acting as a powerful bleach, much used in medicine and manufacturing.

caustic soda n sodium hydroxide, a white solid substance, largely used in soap making.

cauterize /ˈkɒtərˌaɪz/ vt to burn with a caustic substance or a hot iron so as to destroy dead tissue, stop bleeding, etc; to deaden.—**cauterization** n.

cautery /ˈkɒtəri/ n (pl **cauteries**) a burning or searing; an instrument or drug used for such a purpose.

caution /ˈkɒʃən/ n care for safety, prudence; a warning, esp a formal one, to a suspect or accused person. • vt to warn (against), to admonish.

cautionary /-ˌɛri/ adj of a warning nature.

cautious /ˈkɒʃəs/ adj careful, circumspect.—**cautiously** adv.—**cautiousness** n.

cavalcade /ˌkævəlˈkeɪd/ n a procession of riders on horseback; a dramatic sequence or procession.

cavalier /ˌkævəˈliːr/ adj free and easy, careless; offhand, brusque. • n a horseman; a lady's escort; (with cap) a royalist in the English Civil War.—**cavalierly** adv.

cavalry /ˈkævəlri/ n (pl **cavalries**) combat troops originally mounted on horseback.

cavatina /ˌkævəˈtiːnə/ n (pl **cavatine**) a short simple melody.

cave /keɪv/ n a hollow place inside the earth open to the surface. • vti (with **in**) to collapse or make collapse; (inf) to yield, submit.—**cave-in** n.

caveat /ˈkeɪvɪˌæt/ n (law) a process to suspend proceedings; a warning.

caveat emptor /-ˈɛmpˌtɔr/ (Latin) let the buyer beware.

cavefish n (pl **cavefish, cavefishes**) a fish belonging to the family Amblyopsidae, species of which inhabit cave streams of the US.

caveman /ˈkeɪvˌmæn/ n (pl **cavemen**) a prehistoric cave dweller; (inf) a person who acts in a primitive or crude manner.

cavern /ˈkævərn/ n a large cave.—**cavernous** adj.

cavetto /kəˈvɛtoː/ n (pl **cavetti**) (archit) a round concave moulding.

caviar, caviare /ˈkævɪˌɑr/ n salted roe of the sturgeon or other large fish.

cavil /ˈkævəl/ vi (**cavilling, cavilled** or **caviling, caviled**) to make trifling objections, to find fault. • n a trifling objection.—**caviller** n.

caving /ˈkeɪvɪŋ/ n the sport of exploring caves.—**caver** n.

cavity /ˈkævɪti/ n (pl **cavities**) a hole; a hollow place, esp in a tooth.

cavort /kəˈvɔrt/ vi to frolic, prance.

cavy /ˈkeɪvi/ n (pl **cavies**) one of several kinds of small rodent including the guinea pig.

caw /kɒ/ n the cry of the crow, rook, or raven. • vi to utter this cry.

cay /keɪ/ n a small low island.

cayenne /kaɪˈɛn/, **cayenne pepper** n a hot red pepper made from capsicum.

cayman /ˈkeɪmən/ see **caiman**.

Cayuse /ˈkaɪˌuːs/ or /keɪ-/ n (pl **Cayuse, Cayuses**) a member of an American Indian tribe of Oregon and Washington; their language.

CB abbr = Citizens' Band.

CBC abbr = Canadian Broadcasting Corporation.

CD abbr = compact disc; corps diplomatique.

Cd (chem symbol) = cadmium.

cd abbr = candela.

Cdn. abbr = Canadian.

CD-ROM /ˈsiːˈdiːˈrɒm/ abbr = compact disc read only memory: a CD used for distributing text and images in electronic publishing, for computer software, and for permanent storage of computer data.

CDV abbr = CD-video; compact video disc.

Ce (*chem symbol*) = cerium.

cease /si:s/ *vti* to stop, to come to an end; to discontinue.

ceasefire /'si:sfaɪr/ *n* a period of truce in a war, uprising, etc.

ceaseless /-ləs/ *adj* without ceasing; incessant.—**ceaselessly** *adv*.

cecum /'si:kəm/ *see* **caecum**.

cedar /'si:dər/ *n* a large coniferous evergreen tree; its wood.—**cedarwood** *n*.

cede /si:d/ *vt* to yield to another, give up, *esp* by treaty; to assign or transfer the title of.—**ceder** *n*.

cedilla /sə'dɪlə/ *n* a character written under a c in certain languages (ç) to indicate that it is pronounced as an (s) not (k).

ceil /si:l/ *vt* to overlay or cover the inner surface of a roof; to furnish with a ceiling.

ceiling /'si:lɪŋ/ *n* the inner roof of a room; the lining of this; any upper limit; the highest altitude a particular aircraft can fly.

celadon /'selə,dɒn/ *n* a soft pale sea-green colour; porcelain or fine earthenware of such a colour. • *adj* having the colour of celadon.

celandine /'selən,daɪn/ *n* one of several kinds of wild plant with star-shaped yellow flowers.

celebrant /'seləbrənt/ *n* one who celebrates, *esp* the principal officiating priest in offering mass or celebrating the Eucharist.

celebrate /'selə,breɪt/ *vt* to make famous; to praise, extol; to perform with proper rites; to mark with ceremony; to keep (festival).—**celebrant** *n*.

celebrated /-əd/ *adj* famous.

celebration /-'breɪʃən/ *n* the act of celebrating; an observance or ceremony to celebrate anything.

celebrity /sə'lebrəti/ *n* (*pl* **celebrities**) fame; a famous or well-known person.

celeriac /sə'lerɪæk/ *n* a variety of celery with a turnip-like root.

celerity /sə'lerɪti/ *n* quickness, dispatch.

celery /'seləri/ *n* (*pl* **celeries**) a vegetable with long juicy edible stalks.

celesta, celeste /sə'lestə/ *n* a kind of glockenspiel with a keyboard.

celestial /sə'lestəl/ *adj* in or of the sky; heavenly; divine.—**celestially** *adv*.

celestite /'seləs,taɪt/ *n* native strontium sulphate.

celiac /'si:li,æk/ *see* **coeliac**.

celibacy /'seləbəsi/ *n* (*pl* **celibacies**) the unmarried state; complete sexual abstinence.

celibate /'seləbət/ *n* a person who remains unmarried, *esp* one who has taken religious vows; a person who abstains from sexual intercourse.—*also adj*.

cell /sel/ *n* a small room for one in a prison or monastery; a small cavity as in a honeycomb; a device that converts chemical energy into electricity; a microscopic unit of living matter; a small group of people bound by common aims within an organization or political party.—**cellular** *adj*.

cellar /'selər/ *n* a basement; a stock of wines.

cellarage /'selərədʒ/ *n* cellars collectively; the space occupied by cellars; a charge for storage in cellars.

cellarer /-ər/ *n* an official in a monastery who superintends the cellar and distribution of provisions; an official of the chapter who has charge of the temporals.

cellarete, cellaret /,selə'ret/ *n* a case for holding bottles of wine or liquor.

cellnet *n* a portable radio telephone used in cellular radio.

cello /'tʃelo:/ *n* (*pl* **cellos**) the violoncello, a large four-stringed bass instrument of the violin family, held between the knees.—**cellist** *n*.

cellophane /'selə,feɪn/ *n* a thin transparent paper made from cellulose, used for wrapping.

cellphone /'selfo:n/ *n* (*trademark*) a cellular telephone, a portable mobile telephone operated by cellular radio.

cellular /'selju:lər/ *adj* of, resembling or containing cells; (*textiles*) of an open texture.

cellular radio *n* a computer-controlled radio communications system for Cellphones, etc, using a network of transmitters serving small zones called cells, as users move between cells the transmitters/receivers are transferred automatically.

cellule /'selju:l/ *n* a small cell or cavity.

cellulite /'selju:,laɪt/ *n* a form of fat on the hips, thighs and buttocks that causes puckering of the skin surface.

celluloid /'selju:,lɔɪd/ *n* a type of plastic made from cellulose nitrate and camphor; a plastic coating on film; cinema film.

cellulose /'selju:,lo:s/ or /-lo:z/ *n* a starch-like carbohydrate forming the cell walls of plants, used in making paper, textiles, film, etc.

cellulose acetate *n* a compound used in the manufacture of artificial textiles, film, and varnishes.

celsius /'selsiəs/ *adj* pertaining to a thermometer scale with a freezing point of 0 degrees and a boiling point of 100 degrees.

Celt /kelt/ or /selt/ *n* a member of an ancient people who inhabited pre-Roman Britain, Gaul and Spain.

celt /selt/ *n* a prehistoric edged instrument or weapon of stone or bronze, resembling a chisel or blade of an axe, found in ancient tumuli.

Celtic /'keltɪk/ or /'seltɪk/ *adj* of or relating to the Celts; the language of the Celts, including Scots or Irish Gaelic, Manx, Welsh, Cornish and Breton.

Celticist, Celtist *n* a student of Celtic antiquities, languages, etc.

cement /sə'ment/ *n* a powdered substance of lime and clay, mixed with water, etc to make mortar or concrete, which hardens upon drying; any hard-drying substance. • *vt* to bind or glue together with or as if with cement; to cover with cement.—**cementer** *n*.

cementation /,simen'teɪʃən/ or /,semən-/ *n* the act of cementing; a process for converting iron into steel, glass into porcelain, etc.

cemetery /'semə,teri/ or /-tri/ *n* (*pl* **cemeteries**) a place for the burial of the dead.

cenobite /'senə,baɪt/ or /'sinə-/ *see* **coenobite**.

cenotaph /'senə,tæf/ *n* a monument to a person who is buried elsewhere.—**cenotaphic** *adj*.

Cenozoic /,sinə'zo:ɪk/ or /,senə-/ *adj* of the third geological period, Tertiary.

cense /sens/ *vt* to perfume with incense.

censer /'sensər/ *n* a covered cup-shaped vessel pierced with holes in which incense is burned.

censor /'sensər/ *n* an official with the power to examine literature, films, mail, etc and remove or prohibit anything considered obscene, objectionable, etc. • *vt* to act as a censor.—**censorable** *adj*.—**censorial** *adj*.—**censorship** *n*.

censorious /sen'sɔri:əs/ *adj* expressing censure; fault-finding.—**censoriously** *adv*.—**censoriousness** *n*.

censure /'senʃər/ *n* an expression of disapproval or blame. • *vt* to condemn as wrong; to reprimand.—**censurable** *adj*.

census /'sensəs/ *n* (*pl* **censuses**) an official count of the population, including details of age, sex, occupation, etc; any official count.

cent /sent/ *n* a hundredth of a dollar; (*inf*) a negligible amount of money.

centaur /'sen,tɔr/ *n* a fabulous monster, half man, half horse; an expert horseman; (*astron*) a southern constellation.

centaury /'sen,tɔri/ *n* (*pl* **centauries**) a medicinal herb.

centavo /sen'tævo:/ *n* (*pl* **centavos**) the hundredth part of a dollar or peso in use in the South American republics.

centenarian /,sentə'neri:ən/ *n* one who is one hundred years old or more.—*also adj*.

centenary /,senti'nəri/ or /sen'tenəri/ *n* (*pl* **centenaries**) a hundredth anniversary or its celebration. • *adj* of a hundred years.

centennial /sen'tenɪəl/ or /-jəl/ *adj* happening every hundred years. • *n* a centenary.

center /'sentər/ *see* **centre**.

centerboard /-,bɔrd/ *see* **centreboard**.

centerfold /-,fo:ld/ *see* **centrefold**.

centerpiece /'sentər,pi:s/ *see* **centrepiece**.

centesimal /sen'tesiməl/ *adj* counting or counted by hundredths. • *n* a hundredth part.

centi- /'senti/ *prefix* one hundredth.

centiare, centare /sen'ter/ *n* a square metre, equal to the hundredth part of an are.

centigrade /'senti,greɪd/ *adj* Celsius.

centigram, centigramme /-,græm/ *n* one hundredth of a gram.

centilitre, centiliter /,li:tər/ *n* one hundredth of a litre.

centime *Fr.* /'sã'ti:m/ *n* a small french coin, the hundredth part of a franc.

centimetre, centimeter /'senti,mi:tər/ *n* one hundredth of a metre.

centimetre-gram-second /-'græm'sækənd/ *n* a unit system in which the centimetre, the gram and the mean solar second are taken respectively as the units of length, mass, and time (*usu abbr* **cgs units**).

centipede /'senti,pi:d/ *n* a crawling creature with a long body divided into numerous segments each with a pair of legs.

centner /'sentnər/ *n* a weight divisible first into a hundred parts and then into smaller parts; in some European countries the commercial name for a hundredweight.

cento /'sɛntoː/ n (pl **centos**) a literary or musical composition formed by selections from various authors or composers and arranged in a new order.

central /'sɛntrəl/ adj in, at, from or forming the centre; main, principal; important.—**centrally** adv.—**centrality** n.

central bank n a national bank that handles government transactions as opposed to private business.

central heating n a system of heating by pipes from a central boiler or other heat source.

centralism /-ˌlɪzəm/ n the policy or process of bringing under central control.—**centralist** adj, n.

centralize /'sɛntrəˌlaɪz/ vt to draw to the centre; to place under the control of a central authority, esp government.—**centralization** n.

central nervous system n in vertebrates, the brain and spinal cord which coordinates an animal's activity.

central processing unit n (comput) the part of a computer that performs logical and arithmetical operations on data in accordance with program instructions.

centre /'sɛntər/ n the approximate middle point or part of anything, a pivot; interior; point of concentration; a place where a particular activity goes on (shopping centre); source; political moderation; (sport) a player at the centre of the field, etc, a centre-forward. • adj of or at the centre. • vt (**centring, centred**) to place in the centre; to concentrate; to be fixed; (football, hockey) to kick or hit the ball into the centre of the pitch.—also **center**.

centre bit n a carpenter's tool turning upon a centre, for boring holes.

centreboard n a keel so constructed that it may be raised within the hull of a vessel or lowered, extensively used by racing craft; a yacht with this.—also **centerboard**.

centrefold n a colour illustration spread across the two facing pages in the middle of a newspaper or magazine.—also **centerfold**.

centre of gravity n that point of a body through which the resultant of all the forces acting upon it in consequence of the earth's attraction will pass.

centrepiece /'sɛntərˌpiːs/ n a central ornament or decoration.—also **centerpiece**.

centric, centrical /'sɛntrɪk/ adj placed in the centre; central.—**centricity** n.

centrifugal /sɛntrɪˈfjuːgəl/ or /-ˈtrɪfjəgəl/ adj moving away from the centre of rotation.—**centrifugally** adv.

centrifugal force n an imaginary force which acts outwards on a rotating body or one moving along a curved path.

centrifuge /'sɛntrɪˌfjuːdʒ/ n a device used to separate milk, blood, etc, by rotating at very high speed.—**centrifugation** n.

centripetal /sɛnˈtrɪpətəl/ adj tending to move towards the centre.—**centripetally** adv.

centrist /'sɛntrɪst/ n a person of moderate political opinions, etc.—**centrism** n.

centrobaric /ˌsɛntroːˈbærɪk/ adj relating to the centre of gravity or to the method of its determination.

centroid /'sɛntrɔɪd/ n the centre of mass or gravity of a body.

centurion /sɛnˈtʃʊriən/ or /-ˈtʃɜr-/ n an officer commanding a hundred Roman soldiers.

century /'sɛntʃəri/ n (pl **centuries**) a period of a hundred years; a set of a hundred; (cricket) 100 runs made by a batsman in a single innings; a company of a Roman legion.

century plant n a name of the American aloe, from the supposition that it flowered once only in a hundred years.

cep /sɛp/ n an edible woodland fungus with a shiny brown cap and a white underside.

cephalagia /səˈfæləˌdʒiə/ n a headache.

cephalic /səˈfælɪk/ adj of the head.

cephalic index n the relation of the length of the head to its breadth.

cephalization /ˌsɛfəlɪˈzeɪʃən/ n the tendency in animal development to localize important parts or organs in or near the head.

cephalopod /'sɛfələˌpɒd/ n a marine mollusc, such as an octopus, characterized by a well-developed head and eyes and a ring of sucker-bearing tentacles.—**cephalopodan** n, adj.

cephalothorax /ˌsɛfæloːˈθɔrˌæks/ n (pl **cephalothoraxes, cephalothoraces**) the anterior part of the body in the higher crustaceans, spiders, etc.

ceraceous /səˈræʃəs/ adj resembling wax.

ceramic /səˈræmɪk/ adj of earthenware, porcelain, or brick. • n something made of ceramic; (pl) the art of pottery.

ceramics n sing work executed wholly or partly in clay and baked; the art of pottery.—**ceramist, ceramicist** n.

cerastes /səˈræstiːz/ n (pl **cerastes**) the horned viper.

cerate /'sɪrˌeɪt/ or /'sɪrɪt/ n a thick ointment of wax, etc.

ceratodus /sɪˈrætədəs/ or /ˌserəˈtoːdəs/ n (pl **ceratoduses**) a genus of Australian fishes containing the barramunda, or native salmon.

cere¹ /sɪr/ n a wax-like membrane at the base of the bill of many birds, as the parrot.

cere² vt to cover or close with cerecloth.

cereal /'sɪriəl/ n a grass grown for its edible grain, eg wheat, rice; the grain of such grasses; a breakfast food made from such grains. • adj of corn or edible grain.

cerebellum /ˌserəˈbɛləm/ n (pl **cerebellums, cerebella**) a part of the brain below and behind the cerebrum which coordinates voluntary movements.—**cerebellar** adj.

cerebral /'serəbrəl/ or /səˈriːbrəl/ adj of or relating to the cerebrum; intellectual.—**cerebrally** adv.

cerebral hemisphere n one of the two lateral halves of the cerebrum.

cerebral palsy n a disability caused by brain damage before, during or immediately after birth resulting in poor muscle coordination.

cerebrate /'serəˌbreɪt/ vi to use the brain; to think.

cerebration /'serəˌbreɪʃən/ n the conscious or unconscious action of the brain; thought or thinking.

cerebrospinal /səˈriːˌbroːˈspaɪnəl/ adj of the brain and spinal cord.

cerebrum /'serəbrəm/ or /səˈriːbrəm/ n (pl **cerebrums, cerebra**) the front part of the brain of vertebrates; the dominant part of the brain in man, associated with intellectual function; the brain as a whole.

cerecloth /'sɪːrkloθ/ n a cloth saturated with wax or some gummy substance, used for wrapping embalmed bodies in.

cerement /'sɪːrmənt/ n a grave cloth or shroud; (pl) grave clothes.

ceremonial /ˌserəˈmoːniəl/ adj of or with ceremony; formal. • n a set of rules for ceremonies.—**ceremonially** adv.

ceremonialism /-niəˌlɪzm/ n adherence to, or fondness for, ceremonial observance; ritualism.—**ceremonialist** n.

ceremonious /-niəs/ adj observant of ceremony; marked by formality; overpolite.—**ceremoniously** adv.

ceremony /'serəˌmoːni/ n (pl **ceremonies**) a sacred rite; formal observance or procedure; behaviour that follows rigid etiquette.

cerise /səˈriːz/ or /-ˈriːs/ n a light and clear red.—also adj.

cerium /'sɪːriəm/ n a grey metallic element used in various metallurgical and nuclear applications.

cero- /'sɪroː/ or /'seroː/, /-ə/ prefix wax.

cert abbr = certified; certificate; (sl) certainty.

certain /'sɜrtən/ adj sure, positive; unerring, reliable; sure to happen, inevitable; definite, fixed; some; one; unnamed, unspecified.

certainly /-tənli/ or /-tənli/ adv without doubt; yes.

certainty /-tənti/ n (pl **certainties**) something undoubted, inevitable; the condition of being certain.

certificate /sərˈtɪfɪkɪt/ n a document formally attesting a fact; a testimonial of qualifications or character.—**certificated** adj.

certified public accountant n an accountant who has qualified by passing official examinations; a chartered accountant.

certify /'sɜrtɪfaɪ/ vt (**certifying, certified**) to declare in writing or attest formally; to endorse with authority.—**certification** n.

certiorari /ˌsɜrʃioːˈrari/ n a writ issuing from a superior court calling for the records of an inferior court, or to remove a case from a court below.

certitude /'sɜrtəˌtuːd/ or /-ˌtjuːd/ n freedom from doubt.

cerulean /səˈruːliən/ adj deep blue.

cerumen /səˈruːmən/ n wax of the ear.—**ceruminous** adj.

ceruse /'sɪːruːs/ or /sɪˈruːs/ n white lead used as a pigment and from which a cosmetic is prepared.

cervical /'sɜrvɪkəl/ adj of the neck of the womb.

cervical smear n (med) a sample of cells taken from the cervix for detection of cancer; the taking of the sample.

cervine /'sɜrvaɪn/ adj of or pertaining to the deer family; of a tawny or fawn colour.

cervix /'sɜrvɪks/ n (pl **cervixes, cervices**) the neck of the womb.

cesium /'siziəm/ see **caesium**.

cespitose /'sespɪˌtoːs/ adj (bot) growing in tufts.

cess¹ /ses/ vt to impose a tax; to assess. • n a rate or tax, esp the land tax.

cess[2] *n* (*Irish*) luck or fortune.

cessation /se'seɪʃən/ *n* a stoppage; a pause.

cession /'seʃən/ *n* a giving up, a surrender; something ceded.

cessionary /'seʃə,nerɪ/ *n* (*pl* **cessionaries**) (*law*) a giving or yielding up.

cesspool /'sespuːl/, **cesspit** /-pɪt/ *n* a covered cistern for collecting liquid waste or sewage; (*fig*) a place of sin and depravity.

cestoid /'sestɔɪd/ *adj* of or pertaining to the Cestoda, an order of parasitic flat worms to which the tapeworms belong. • *n* a flat intestinal worm.

cetacean /sə'teɪʃən/ *n* a member of an order of aquatic, *usu* marine, mammals that includes whales, dolphins and porpoises. • *adj* belonging to this order.—*also* **cetaceous**.

ceteris paribus /'setərɪs'pærɪ,bus/ (*Latin*) other things being equal.

Cf (*chem symbol*) californium.

cf. *abbr* = compare (*Latin* confer).

CFC *abbr* = chlorofluorocarbon.

CGM *abbr* = Computer Graphics Metafile, a file format for graphics which uses mainly vector notation.

cgs *abbr* = centimetre-gram-second.

ch. *abbr* = chapter; church; (*chess*) check.

cha-cha(-cha) /'tʃɒtʃɒ/ *n* a ballroom dance orig from Latin America; the music for this.

chablis /ʃæ'bliː/ or /ʃə-/, /'ʃæbli/ *n* (*often with cap*) a dry white wine from Chablis, France.

chacma *n* a South African baboon.

chaconne /ʃə'kɒn/, *Fr.* /ʃɑ'kən/ *n* an old Spanish dance; the music for such a dance.

chad /tʃæd/ *n* (*comput*) the little scraps of paper or cardboard left by the punching of holes in computer cards or paper tape.

chafe /tʃeɪf/ *vti* to restore warmth by rubbing; to make or become sore by rubbing; to irritate; to feel irritation, to fret.

chafer /'tʃeɪfər/ *n* any of various large beetles.

chaff[1] /tʃæf/ *n* husks of grain separated from the seed by threshing or winnowing; cut hay or straw; worthless stuff.

chaff[2] *vt* to banter; to make a game of. • *vi* to use bantering language. • *n* good-natured teasing, banter.

chaffer /'tʃæfər/ *vi* to bargain, haggle. • *n* the act of bargaining.

chaffinch /'tʃæfɪntʃ/ *n* a European songbird.

chaffy /'tʃæfi/ *adj* resembling, or full of, chaff; anything light or worthless.

chafing dish /'tʃeɪfɪŋ/ *n* a vessel for heating or cooking food on a table; a small portable grate for coals.

chagrin /ʃə'grɪn/, *Brit.* /'ʃægrɪn/ *n* annoyance; vexation; disappointment.

chain /tʃeɪn/ *n* a series of connected links or rings; a continuous series; a series of related events; a bond; a group of shops, hotels, etc owned by the same company; a unit of length equal to 66 feet; a range of mountains; a group of islands; (*pl*) anything that restricts or binds; fetters. • *vt* to fasten with a chain or chains.

chain gang *n* a group of prisoners chained together.

chain mail *n* flexible armour formed of metal links interwoven.

chain reaction *n* a process in which a chemical, atomic or other reaction stimulates further reactions, eg combustion or nuclear fission; a series of events, each of which stimulates the next.

chain saw *n* a power-driven saw with teeth linked as in a chain.

chain-smoke /'tʃeɪn,smoːk/ *vti* to smoke (cigarettes) one after the other.—**chain-smoker** *n*.

chain stitch *n* an embroidery stitch that resembles the links of a chain.

chain store *n* one of a series of retail stores owned by one company.

chair /tʃer/ *n* a separate seat for one, with a back and legs; a seat of authority; a chairman; a professorship; the electric chair. • *vt* to preside as chairman of.

chair lift /-,lɪft/ *n* a series of seats suspended from a cable for carrying sightseers or skiers uphill.

chairman /-mən/ *n* (*pl* **chairmen**) a person who presides at a meeting; the president of a board or committee.—**chairwoman** *nf* (*pl* **chairwomen**).—*also* **chairperson**.

chaise /ʃeɪz/ *n* a light two-wheeled carriage; any carriage.

chaise longue /,ʃeɪz'lɒŋ/ or /-'laʊndʒ/ *n* (*pl* **chaise longues**, **chaises longues**) a couch-like chair with a long seat.

chalcedony /kæl'sedəni/ *n* (*pl* **chalcedonies**) a form of quartz used as a gemstone.

chalco- /'kælkoː/ or /-kə/ *prefix* copper.

chalcopyrite /,kælkə'paɪrəɪt/ *n* a copper ore.

Chaldean, Chaldaean /kæl'diːən/ *adj* pertaining to Chaldea, or ancient Babylon, or its language. • *n* the language of ancient Babylon.

chalet /ʃæl'eɪ/ *n* a Swiss hut; any similar building used in a holiday camp, as a ski lodge, etc.

chalice /'tʃælɪs/ *n* a large cup with a base; a communion cup.

chalk /tʃɒk/ *n* calcium carbonate, a soft white limestone; such a stone or a substitute used for drawing or writing. • *vt* to write, mark or draw with chalk; (*with* **up**) (*inf*) to score, get, achieve; to charge or credit.

chalky /'tʃɒki/ *adj* (**chalkier, chalkiest**) containing or resembling chalk.—**chalkiness** *n*.

challenge /'tʃælɪndʒ/ *vt* to summon to a fight or contest; to call in question; to object to; to hail and interrogate; to demand proof of identity. • *n* the act of challenging; a summons to a contest; a calling in question; a problem that stimulates effort.—**challenger** *n*.—**challenging** *adj*.

challis /'ʃæli/ or /ʃæ'liː/ *n* a light all-wool fabric.

chalybeate /kə'lɪbiət/ or /-'lɪbieɪt/ *adj* (*water*) impregnated with iron.

chamber /'tʃeɪmbər/ *n* a room, *esp* a bedroom; a deliberative body or a division of a legislature; a room where such a body meets; a compartment; a cavity in the body of an organism; part of a gun cylinder holding the cartridge; (*pl*) a judge's office.

chamberlain /'tʃeɪmbərlɪn/ *n* an official in charge of the household of a monarch or nobleman; a steward, treasurer or factor of a municipal corporation.

chambermaid /'tʃeɪmbər,meɪd/ *n* a woman employed to clean bedrooms in a hotel, etc.

chamber music *n* music for performance by a small group, as a string quartet.

chamber of commerce *n* (*often cap*) an organization of representatives from local businesses formed to promote and protect their interests.

chamber pot *n* a vessel for urine.

chameleon /kə'miːliən/ *n* a lizard capable of changing colour to match its surroundings; a person of variable moods or behaviour; an adaptable person.—**chameleonic** *adj*.

chamfer /'tʃæmfər/ *n* a flat surface made in wood or metal by paring off an angle, a bevel. • *vt* to groove, channel or flute.—**chamferer** *n*.

chamois /'ʃæmwɒ/ *n* (*pl* **chamois**) a small antelope found in Europe and Asia; a piece of chamois leather.

chamois leather, chammy (leather) *n* a soft, pliable leather formerly made from chamois skin, and now obtained from sheep, goats and deer; a piece of this for polishing.—*also* **shammy (leather)**.

chamomile /'kæmə,maɪl/ or /-,miːl/ *n* an aromatic plant with daisy-like flowers used medicinally for its soothing property and as a hair lightener, and in making camomile tea.—*also* **camomile**.

champ[1] /tʃæmp/ *vti* to munch noisily, chomp; **champ at the bit** to be impatient.

champ[2] *n* (*inf*) a champion.

champagne /ʃæm'peɪn/ *n* a sparkling white wine; a pale straw colour.

champaign /ʃæm'peɪn/ *n* flat open country, a level expanse. • *adj* level, open.

champerty /'tʃæmpərti/ *n* (*pl* **champerties**) (*law*) the maintenance of a party in a suit on condition that, if successful, the property is shared; the offence of aiding another's lawsuit in order to share in gains from it.—**champertous** *adj*.

champignon /ʃæm'pɪnjən/, *Fr.* /ʃɑ̃pi'njoʊn/ *n* an edible mushroom that grows in circular clusters.

champion /'tʃæmpiən/ *n* a person who fights for another; one who upholds a cause; a competitor successful against all others. • *adj* first-class; (*inf*) excellent. • *vt* to defend; to uphold the cause of.

championship /-ʃɪp/ *n* the act of championing; the process of determining a champion; a contest held to find a champion.

champlevé /ʃɑ̃lə'veɪ/ *n* enamel bearing indentations filled with colour.—*also adj*.

chance /tʃæns/ *n* a course of events; fortune; an accident, an unexpected event; opportunity; possibility; probability; risk. • *vti* to risk; to happen; to come upon unexpectedly. • *adj* accidental, not planned.

chancel /'tʃænsəl/ n the part of a church around the altar, for the clergy and the choir.

chancellery, chancellory /'tʃænsələri/ or /-sləri/ n (pl **chancelleries, chancellories**) a chancellor's department or office; an office attached to an embassy.

chancellor /'tʃænsələr/ n a high government official, as, in certain countries, a prime minister; in some universities, the president or other executive officer.—**chancellorship** n.

chance-medley /'tʃæns,medli/ n (law) justifiable homicide in self-defence; inadvertency.

chancery /'tʃænsəri/ n (pl **chanceries**) originally in England, next to Parliament the highest court of justice, since 1873 a division of the High Court of Justice; the office for public records; in US a court of equity.

chancre /'ʃæŋkər/ n a syphilitic ulcer.—**chancrous** adj.

chancy /'tʃænsi/ adj (**chancier, chanciest**) (inf) risky, uncertain.—**chancily** adv.

chandelier /,ʃændə'li:r/ n an ornamental hanging frame with branches for holding lights.

chandler /'tʃændlər/ n a dealer or merchant, esp in candles, oil, soap, etc.

chandlery /-ri/ n (pl **chandleries**) a chandler's shop or stock.

change /tʃeɪndʒ/ vt to make different, to alter; to transform; to exchange; to put fresh clothes on. • vi to become different, to undergo alteration; to put on fresh clothes; to continue one's journey by leaving one station, etc, or mode of transport and going to and using another. • n alteration, modification; substitution; variety; a fresh set, esp clothes; money in small units; the balance of money returned when given in a larger denomination as payment.—**changer** n.

changeable /'tʃeɪndʒəbəl/ adj able to be changed; altering rapidly between different conditions; inconstant.—**changeability** n.—**changeably** adv.

changeful /'tʃeɪndʒfəl/ adj often changing.

changeless /-ləs/ adj constant, immutable.—**changelessly** adv.—**changelessness** n.

changeling /-lɪŋ/ n a child secretly left in place of another.

change of life n (inf) the menopause.

changeover /-ʊ:,vər/ n a complete change of system, method, state, attitude, etc.

channel[1] /'tʃænəl/ n the bed or the deeper part of a river, harbour, etc; a body of water joining two larger ones; a navigable passage; a means of passing or conveying or communicating; a band of radio frequencies reserved for a particular purpose, eg television station; a path for an electrical signal; a groove or line along which liquids, etc may flow. • vt (**channelling, channelled** or **channeling, channeled**) to form a channel in; to groove; to direct.

channel[2] n a projection from a ship's side to spread the shrouds and keep them clear of the bulwarks.

chanson /'ʃɑ̃sɔ̃/ n (pl **chansons**) a song.

chant /tʃænt/ vti to sing; to recite in a singing manner; to sing or shout (a slogan) rhythmically. • n sacred music to which prose is sung; sing-song intonation; a monotonous song; a rhythmic slogan, esp as sung or shouted by sports fans, etc.

chanter /'tʃæntər/ n a person who chants; the tenor or treble pipe of a bagpipe on which the melody is played.

chanterelle /,tʃæntə'rel/ n an edible yellow mushroom.

chantey /'ʃænti/, **chanty** /'tʃɒnti/ n (pl **chanteys, chanties**) a shanty.

chanticleer /,tʃæntɪ'kli:r/ or /,tʃɒn-/, /,ʃæn-/, /ʃɒn-/ n a rooster.

chantry /'tʃæntri/ n (pl **chantries**) a chapel endowed for the saying or singing mass daily for the soul of the founder; such an endowment.

chaology /'keɪɒlədʒi/ n the study of chaos theory.—**chaologist** n.

chaos /'keɪɒs/ n utter confusion, muddle.

chaos theory n (physics) the theory that the behaviour of dynamic systems is haphazard rather than mathematical.

chaotic /keɪ'ɒtɪk/ adj completely without order or arrangement.—**chaotically** adv.

chap[1] /tʃæp/ vti (**chapping, chapped**) (skin) to make or become split or rough in cold weather. • n a chapped place in the skin.

chap[2] n (inf) a man.

chap[3] /tʃɒp/ or /tʃæp/ n (usu pl) one of the jaws or its fleshy covering; the mouth of a channel.

chaparejos /,tʃæpə'reɪɒ:s/ or /,ʃæp-/ npl a cowboy's leather leg coverings.—also **chaps**.

chaparral /,ʃæpə'ræl/ or /,tʃæp-/ n a dense thicket.

chapatti, chapati /tʃə'pɒti/ or /-'pæti/ n (pl **chapattis, chapatis**) in Indian cookery, flat unleavened bread.

chapbook /'tʃæpbʊk/ n a small book of ballads, romances, etc, formerly hawked by a chapman.

chape /tʃeɪp/ n the metal tip of a scabbard; the part attaching a scabbard to a belt.

chapeau /ʃæ'po:/ n (pl **chapeaux, chapeaus**) a hat or head covering.

chapel /'tʃæpəl/ n a building for Christian worship, not as large as a church; an association or trade union of printers in a printing office.

chaperon, chaperone /'ʃæpə,ro:n/ n a woman who accompanies a girl at social occasions for propriety. • vt to attend as a chaperon.—**chaperonage** n.

chapfallen /'tʃæp,fɒlən/ adj with the jaw hanging down, dejected, dispirited.—also **chopfallen**.

chapiter /'tʃæpɪtər/ n (archit) the upper part or capital of a column.

chaplain /'tʃæplən/ n a clergyman serving in a religious capacity with the armed forces, or in a prison, hospital, etc.—**chaplaincy** n.

chaplet /'tʃæplət/ n a wreath or garland encircling the head; a rosary; a round moulding carved into beads, olives, etc.—**chapleted** adj.

chapman /'tʃæpmən/ n (pl **chapmen**) formerly a merchant or trader; a hawker.

chaps /tʃæps/ or /ʃæps/ npl chaparejos.

chapter /'tʃæptər/ n a main division of a book; the body or meeting of canons of a cathedral or members of a monastic order; a sequence of events; an organized branch of a society or association.

chapterhouse n a room for the meetings of a cathedral chapter.

char[1] /tʃɑr/ n a charwoman. • vti (**charring, charred**) to work as a charwoman.

char[2] vb (**charring, charred**) vt to burn to charcoal or carbon. • vti to scorch.

char[3] n (pl **char, chars**) a red-bellied fish allied to the salmon.—also **charr**.

character /'kærəktər/ n the combination of qualities that distinguishes an individual person, group or thing; moral strength; reputation; disposition; a person of marked individuality; an eccentric; (inf) a person; a person in a play or novel; a guise, role; a letter or mark in writing, printing, etc.

characterful /-fʊl/ adj full of character, unusual.

characteristic /,kærəktə'rɪstɪk/ adj marking or constituting the particular nature (of a person or thing). • n a characteristic or distinguishing feature.—**characteristically** adv.

characterize /'kærɪktə,raɪz/ vt to describe in terms of particular qualities; to designate; to be characteristic of, mark.—**characterization** n.

characterless /-ləs/ adj ordinary, undistinguished.

charade /ʃə'reɪd/ n a travesty; an absurd pretence; (usu pl) a game of guessing a word from the acted representation of its syllables and the whole.

charcoal /'tʃɑrko:l/ n the black carbon matter obtained by partially burning wood and used as fuel, as a filter or for drawing.

chard /tʃɑrd/ n a type of beet with edible leaves and stalks.

charge /tʃɑrdʒ/ vt to ask as the price; to record as a debt; to load, to fill, saturate; to lay a task or trust on; to burden; to accuse; to attack at a run; to build up an electric charge (in). • n a price charged for goods or service; a build-up of electricity; the amount which a receptacle can hold at one time; the explosive required to fire a weapon; trust, custody; a thing or person entrusted; a task, duty; accusation; an attack.

chargeable /'tʃɑrdʒəbəl/ adj liable to be charged.—**chargeability** n.

charge account n an account with a store, etc, to which the cost of goods are charged for later payment.

charge card n a type of credit card issued by a chain store or other organization.

chargé d'affaires /,ʃɑrʒeɪdæ'fer/ n (pl **chargés d'affaires**) an ambassador's deputy; a minor diplomat.

charger /'tʃɑrdʒər/ n a cavalry horse; a device for charging a battery.

charily /'tʃerəli/ adv reluctantly; cautiously.

chariness /-ɪnəs/ n a being chary.

chariot /'tʃærɪət/ n a two-wheeled vehicle driven by two or more horses in ancient warfare, races, etc.—**charioteer** n.

charisma, charism /kə'rɪzmə/ n (pl **charismata, charisms**) personal quality enabling a person to influence or inspire others; a God-given power or gift.—**charismatic** adj.

charitable /'tʃærɪtəbəl/ or /'tʃɛrɪ-/ *adj* of or for charity; generous to the needy, benevolent; lenient in judging others, kindly.— **charitableness** *n.*—**charitably** *adv.*

charity /'tʃærɪti/ or /'tʃɛrɪ-/ *n* (*pl* **charities**) leniency or tolerance towards others; generosity in giving to the needy; a benevolent fund or institution.

charity shop *n* a shop that sells used clothing and other items to raise money for charity.

charivari /ˌʃɑrɪ'vɑri/ *n* a mock serenade of discordant music; hurly-burly.—*also* **shivaree**.

charlatan /'ʃɑrlətən/ *n* a person who pretends to be what he or she is not; one who professes knowledge dishonestly, *esp* of medicine.—**charlatanism, charlatanry** *n.*

charleston /'tʃɑrlstən/ *n* a lively dance with sidekicks from the knee.

charlock /'tʃɑrlɒk/ *n* wild mustard.

charlotte /'tʃɑrlət/ *n* a pudding of stewed fruit covered with breadcrumbs.

charlotte russe /'ruːs/ *n* whipped cream custard enclosed in a sponge cake.

charm /tʃɑrm/ *n* an alluring quality, fascination; a magic verse or formula; something thought to possess occult power; an object bringing luck; a trinket on a bracelet. • *vt* to delight, captivate; to influence as by magic.—**charmer** *n.*

charming /'tʃɑrmɪŋ/ *adj* delightful, attractive.—**charmingly** *adv.*

charnel house /'tʃɑrnəlˌhɛʊs/ *n* a vault containing corpses or bones.

charpoy /'tʃɑrpɔɪ/ *n* a light portable Indian bedstead.

charqui /'tʃɑrki/ *n* beef cut into strips and sun-dried.

charr /tʃɑr/ *see* **char³**.

chart /tʃɑrt/ *n* a map, *esp* for use in navigation; an information sheet with tables, graphs, etc; a weather map; a table, graph, etc; (*pl with* **the**) a list of the most popular music recordings. • *vt* to make a chart of; to plan (a course of action).

charter /'tʃɑrtər/ *n* a document granting rights, privileges, ownership of land, etc; the hire of transportation. • *vt* to grant by charter; to hire.

chartered accountant *n* an accountant who has qualified by passing the official examinations; a certified public accountant.

Chartism /'tʃɑrtɪzəm/ *n* a democratic reforming movement in England for the extension of political power to the working class, embodied in the People's Charter of 1838.—**Chartist** *adj, n.*

Chartreuse /ʃɑr'trɒz/, *Fr.* /ʃɑr'trøz/ *n* (*trademark*) a yellowish green liqueur; (*without cap*) its colour.

charwoman /'tʃɑrˌwʊmən/ *n* (*pl* **charwomen**) a woman employed to clean a house.

chary /'tʃɛri/ *adj* (**charier, chariest**) cautious; sparing; (*with* **of**) unwilling to risk.

chase¹ /tʃeɪs/ *vt* to pursue; to run after; to drive (away); to hunt; (*inf: usu with* **up**) to pursue in a determined manner. • *n* pursuit; a hunt; a quarry hunted; a steeplechase.

chase² *Fr.* /tʃæs/ *n* a frame for securing a page of type; a groove; that part of a cannon in front of the trunnions.

chase³ *vt* to work or emboss precious metals; to cut a screw.

chaser /'tʃeɪsər/ *n* a horse used in steeplechasing; a person that chases; (*inf*) a drink taken after another, as in beer after a whisky.

chasm /'kæzəm/ *n* a deep cleft, an abyss, a gaping hole; a wide difference in opinions, etc.—**chasmal, chasmic** *adj.*

chassé /'ʃæseɪ/ *n* a rapid gliding step in dancing. • *vi* to perform a chassé.

chasseur /ʃæ'sər/ *n* a French light-armed foot or cavalry soldier.

chassis /'tʃæsi/ or /'ʃæsi/ *n* (*pl* **chassis**) the frame, wheels, engine of a car, aeroplane or other vehicle.

chaste /tʃeɪst/ *adj* pure, abstaining from unlawful sexual intercourse; virgin; modest; restrained, unadorned.—**chastely** *adv.*—**chasteness** *n.*

chasten /'tʃeɪsən/ *vt* to correct by suffering, discipline; to restrain.—**chastener** *n.*

chastise /tʃæs'taɪz/ or /'tʃæstaɪz/ *vt* to punish; to beat; to scold.— **chastisement** *n.*

chastity /'tʃæstɪti/ *n* sexual abstinence; virginity; purity.

chasuble /'tʃæzʊbəl/ or /'tʃæzjʊ-/, /-sʊ-/ *n* a rich sleeveless vestment worn over the alb by a priest celebrating mass.

chat /tʃæt/ *vti* (**chatting, chatted**) to talk in an easy or familiar way; (*with* **up**) (*inf*) to talk in a flirtatious way with another person. • *n* informal conversation.

chateau, château /ʃæ'tɒ:/ or /'ʃætɒ:/ *n* (*pl* **chateaus, châteaux**) a castle or large country estate in France.

chatelaine /'ʃætəˌleɪn/ *n* the lady of a country house; a bunch of chains to which are attached keys, etc, worn at the waist by ladies.

chatoyant /ʃə'tɔɪənt/ *adj* changing in colour or lustre.—**chatoyancy** *n.*

chatroom /tʃæ'trʊm/ *n* (*comput*) on the Internet, a function on a website that allows several Internet users to type messages to each other in real time, simultaneously.

chat show *n* a television or radio programme with informal interviews and conversation.

chattel /'tʃætəl/ *n* (*usu pl*) goods, possessions; (*law*) personal property except freehold.

chatter /'tʃætər/ *vi* to talk aimlessly and rapidly; (*animal, etc*) to utter rapid cries; (*teeth*) to rattle together due to cold or fear. • *n* idle rapid talk; the sound of chattering.— **chatterer** *n.*

chatterbox /-ˌbɒks/ *n* an incessant talker.

chatty /'tʃæti/ *adj* (**chattier, chattiest**) talkative, full of gossip.—**chattily** *adv.*—**chattiness** *n.*

chauffeur /'ʃoːfər/ or /ʃoː'fər/ *n* a person who drives a car for someone else. • *vt* to drive as a chauffeur.—**chauffeuse** *nf.*

chauvinism /'ʃoːvəˌnɪzəm/ *n* aggressive patriotism; excessive devotion to a belief, cause, etc, *as in* male chauvinism, a man's belief in the superiority of men over women.—**chauvinist** *n.*—**chauvinistic** *adj.*

chaw /tʃɒ/ *vt* (*dial*) to chew, to munch, *esp* tobacco. • *n* a plug of tobacco.

cheap /tʃiːp/ *adj* low-priced, inexpensive; good value; of little worth, inferior; vulgar.—**cheaply** *adv.*—**cheapness** *n.*

cheapen /'tʃiːpən/ *vti* to make or become cheap; to lower the value, worth or reputation of.

cheap-jack /'tʃiːpˌdʒæk/ *n* (*inf*) a person who sells cheap or worthless goods. • *adj* worthless, inferior.

cheapskate /-skeɪt/ *n* (*inf*) a mean or dishonourable person.

cheat /tʃiːt/ *vti* to defraud, to swindle; to deceive; to play unfairly. • *n* a fraud, deception; a person who cheats.—**cheater** *n.*

check /tʃek/ *vti* to bring or come to a stand; to restrain or impede; to admonish, reprove; to test the accuracy of, verify; (*with* **in**) to sign or register arrival at a hotel, work, an airport, etc; (*with* **out**) to settle the bill and leave a hotel; to investigate. • *n* repulse; stoppage; a pattern of squares; a control to test accuracy; a tick against listed items; a bill in a restaurant; (*US*) a cheque; (*chess*) a threatening of the king; a money order to a bank.—*also* **check**.

checkbook /'tʃekˌbʊk/ *see* **chequebook**.

check digit *n* (*comput*) a digit added to data digits to test accuracy and check for corruption.

checker¹ /'tʃekər/ *see* **chequer**.

checker² *n* a cashier in a supermarket.

checkerboard /-ˌbɔrd/ *n* a draughtboard.

checkered /'tʃekərd/ *see* **chequered**.

check list /'tʃeklɪst/ *n* a list of items, used for reference or verification.

checkmate /-meɪt/ *n* (*chess*) the winning position when the king is threatened and unable to move; utter defeat. • *vt* (*chess*) to place in checkmate; to defeat, foil.

checking account *n* a bank account, *usu* with no interest, from which money is withdrawn by cheques or cash cards; a current account.

checkout /-ɛʊt/ *n* a place where traffic may be halted for inspection; the place in a store where goods are paid for.

checkpoint /-pɔɪnt/ *n* a place where visitors' passports or other official documents may be examined.

checkrein /-ˌreɪn/ *see* **bearing rein**.

checkroom /-ruːm/ *n* a temporary repository for luggage, coats, etc.

checkup /-ˌɛp/ *n* a thorough examination; a medical examination, *usu* repeated at intervals.

Cheddar, cheddar /'tʃedər/ *n* a type of hard, white or yellow cheese originally made in Cheddar, England.

cheek /tʃiːk/ *n* the side of the face below the eye; (*sl*) buttock; impudence.

cheeky /'tʃiːki/ *adj* (**cheekier, cheekiest**) disrespectful, impudent.—**cheekily** *adv.*—**cheekiness** *n.*

cheep /tʃiːp/ *n* the frail squeak of a young bird. • *vi* to make such a sound.

cheer /tʃiːr/ *n* a shout of applause or welcome; a frame of mind, spirits; happiness. • *vt* to gladden; to encourage; to applaud.

cheerful /'tʃɪrfʊl/ *adj* in good spirits; happy.—**cheerfully** *adv.*—**cheerfulness** *n*.

cheerleader /-ˌliːdər/ *n* a person who leads organized cheering, *esp* at a sports event.

cheerless /-ləs/ *adj* dismal, depressing.

cheers /tʃɪrz/ *interj (inf)* an expression used in offering a toast, as a form of farewell or thanks.

cheery /'tʃɪri/ *adj* (**cheerier, cheeriest**) lively, genial, merry.—**cheerily** *adv.*—**cheeriness** *n*.

cheese /tʃiːz/ *n* the curds of milk pressed into a firm or hard mass; a boss or important person (*big cheese*).

cheeseburger /'tʃiːzˌbɜrgər/ *n* a hamburger with melted cheese on top.

cheesecake /-keɪk/ *n* a cake made with cottage or cream cheese; (*sl*) attractive women or men displayed as sex objects in photographs, etc.

cheesecloth /-klɒθ/ *n* a thin cotton fabric.

cheeseparing /-'pɛrɪŋ/ *adj* niggardly, mean.

cheesy /-i/ *adj* (**cheesier, cheesiest**) like cheese.—**cheesiness** *n*.

cheetah /'tʃiːtə/ *n* a large spotted cat, similar to a leopard.

chef /ʃɛf/ *n* a professional cook.

chef-d'oeuvre /ʃeɪˈdəːvr/, *Fr.* /ʃɛˈdœˌvr/ *n* (*pl* **chefs-d'oeuvre**) a masterpiece.

cheiro-, chiro- /'kaɪrou/ or /-rə/ *prefix* hand.

chela /'kiːlə/ *n* (**chelae**) a claw-like pincer of the crab, etc.—**cheliferous** *adj*.

chelonian /kə'loːniən/ *n* any of the order of reptiles, including turtles and tortoises.—*also adj*.

chemical /'kɛmɪkəl/ *n* a substance used in, or arising from, a chemical process. • *adj* of, used in, or produced by chemistry.—**chemically** *adv*.

chemical engineering *n* the branch of engineering dealing with the design, construction, and manufacture of plant used in industrial chemical processes.

chemical warfare *n* warfare in which poison gases and other chemicals are used.

chemin de fer /ʃəˌmædə'fɛr/ *n* a gambling game, a kind of baccarat.

chemise /ʃə'miːz/ *n* a woman's undergarment; a loose-fitting dress.

chemisette /ʃɛmɪ'zɛt/ *n* a short bodice worn over the breast; lace, etc, filling the neck opening of a dress.

chemist /'kɛmɪst/ *n* a pharmacy; a manufacturer of medicinal drugs; a person skilled in chemistry.

chemistry /'kɛməstri/ *n* (*pl* **chemistries**) the science of the properties of substances and their combinations and reactions; chemical structure.

chemotherapy /ˌkiːmoːˈθɛrəpi/ *n* the treatment of disease, *esp* cancer, by drugs and other chemical agents.

chenille /ʃə'niːl/ *n* silk or worsted cord.

cheque /tʃɛk/ *see* **check**.

chequebook *n* a book containing blank cheques to be drawn on a bank.—*also* **checkbook**.

chequer /'tʃɛkər/ *n* a pattern of squares.—*also* **checker**; a flat counter used in the game of checkers.—*also* **draughtsman**; (*pl*) a game for two players who each move twelve round flat pieces over a checkerboard.—*also* **draughts**.

chequered *adj* marked with a variegated pattern; having a career marked by fluctuating fortunes.—*also* **checkered**.

cherish /'tʃɛrɪʃ/ *vt* to tend lovingly, foster; to keep in mind as a hope, ambition, etc.—**cherisher** *n*.

cheroot /ʃə'ruːt/ *n* a cigar cut square at each end.

cherry /'tʃɛri/ *n* (*pl* **cherries**) a small red, pitted fruit; the tree bearing it; a bright red colour.

cherry picker *n* a crane, *usu* on a truck, with a long elbow-jointed arm carrying a platform that can be raised and lowered.

chersonese /'kɜrsəˌniːs/ *n* (*poet*) a peninsula.

chert /tʃɜrt/ *n* an impure flint-like quartz or hornstone.—**cherty** *adj*.

cherub /'tʃɛrəb/ *n* (*pl* **cherubim**) an angel of the second order; a winged child or child's head; (*pl* **cherubs**) an angelic, sweet child.—**cherubic** *adj*.

chervil /'tʃɜrvɪl/ *n* an aromatic herb used for flavouring.

Cheshire cheese /'tʃɛʃiːr/ or /-ɜr/ *n* a mild flavoured cheese, originally made in Cheshire, England.

chess[1] /tʃɛs/ *n* a game played by two people with 32 pieces on a chessboard.

chess[2] *n* one of the flooring planks of a pontoon bridge.

chessboard /'tʃɛsbɔrd/ *n* a board chequered with 64 squares in two alternate colours, used for playing chess or draughts.

chessman /-mæn/ *n* (*pl* **chessmen**) any of the 16 pieces used by each player in chess.

chest /tʃɛst/ *n* a large strong box; the part of the body enclosed by the ribs, the thorax.

chesterfield /'tʃɛstərˌfiːld/ *n* a large, stuffed couch with straight ends; a man's overcoat.

chestnut /'tʃɛsnʌt/ *n* a tree or shrub of the beech family; the edible nut of a chestnut; the wood of the chestnut; a horse with chestnut colouring; (*inf*) an old joke. • *adj* of the colour of a chestnut, a deep reddish brown.

chest of drawers *n* a piece of furniture containing several drawers.

chesty /'tʃɛsti/ *adj* (**chestier, chestiest**) (*inf*) prone to chest infections; having a large chest or bosom.—**chestily** *adv*.—**chestiness** *n*.

cheval-de-frise /ʃəˌvældə'friːz/ *n* (*pl* **chevaux-de-frise**) a fence constructed of a bar armed with long spikes.

cheval glass /ʃə'væl/ *n* a full-length mirror which can swivel in its frame.

chevalier /ˌʃəvə'liːr/ or /ˌʃə'væljeɪ/ *n* a knight; a horseman; a member or knight of an honourable order; the lowest title or rank of the old French nobility; a gallant.

chevet /ʃə'veɪ/ *n* an apse; a group of apses.

cheviot /'tʃɛviət/ or /'ʃ-/ *n* a rough cloth made from the wool of sheep bred on the Cheviot Hills along the border between England and Scotland.

chevron /'ʃɛvrən/ or /-rɒn/ *n* the V-shaped bar on the sleeve of a uniform, showing rank.

chevrotain /'ʃɛvrəˌteɪn/ or /-tɪn/ *n* a small musk deer.

chew /tʃuː/ *vt* to grind between the teeth, to masticate; (*with* **over**) to ponder, think over; (*with* **up**) to spoil by chewing. • *n* the act of chewing; something to chew, as a sweet or tobacco.—**chewable** *adj*.—**chewer** *n*.

chewing gum *n* a flavoured gum made from chicle, for chewing.

chewed-up *adj* (*sl*) made nervous or worried.

chewy /'tʃuːi/ *adj* (**chewier, chewiest**) needing to be chewed.

chez /ʃeɪ/ *prep* at the home of.

chi /kaɪ/ *n* the 22nd letter of the Greek alphabet.

Chianti /ki'ænti/ *n* a dry red or white wine from Italy.

chiaroscuro /kiˌɑrəˈsjuːroː/ or /-ˈskjɜroː/ *n* (*pl* **chiaroscuros**) the effects of light and shade; the treatment of this in painting, drawing, or engraving; the use of contrast and relief in literature. • *adj* pertaining to such treatment.—**chiaroscurism** *n*.—**chiaroscurist** *n*.

chiasma, chiasm /kaɪ'æzmə/ *n* (*pl* **chiasmas, chiasmata, chiasms**) the central body of nervous matter formed by the junction and the crossing of the fibres of the optic nerves.—**chiasmal** *adj*.—**chiasmic** *adj*.

chiasmus /kaɪ'æzməs/ *n* (*pl* **chiasmi**) a figure of speech by which the order of words in the first of two parallel clauses is reversed in the second, eg "to stop too fearful and too faint to go".—**chiastic** *adj*.

chibouk, chibouque /tʃɪ'buːk/ *n* a long Turkish tobacco pipe.

chic /ʃiːk/ *n* elegance, style. • *adj* stylish.

chicane /ʃɪ'keɪn/ *n* a hand at bridge without trumps; a barrier or obstacle on a motor-racing course; chicanery.

chicanery /ʃɪ'keɪnəri/ *n* (*pl* **chicaneries**) underhand dealing, trickery; verbal subterfuge.

Chicano /tʃɪ'kɒnoː/ or /-'kænoː/ *n* (*pl* **Chicanos**) a Mexican-American.—*also adj*.

chick /tʃɪk/ *n* a young bird; (*sl*) a young attractive woman or girl.

chickadee /'tʃɪkəˌdiː/ *n* the American blackcap titmouse.

chickaree /'tʃɪkəˌriː/ *n* the American red squirrel.

chicken /'tʃɪkən/ *n* a young, domestic fowl; its flesh. • *adj* cowardly, timorous. • *vi* (*with* **out**) (*inf*) to suffer a failure of nerve or courage.

chicken feed *n* poultry food; (*inf*) a trifling amount of money.

chicken-hearted /-ˌhɑrtɪd/, **chicken-livered** *adj* cowardly.

chickenpox /-ˌpɒks/ *n* a contagious viral disease that causes a rash of red spots on the skin.

chicken wire *n* light wire netting with a hexagonal mesh.

chickpea /'tʃɪkˌpiː/ *n* (the seed eaten as a vegetable of) an Asian leguminous plant.

chickweed /-wiːd/ *n* a small white-flowered plant of the pink family.

chicle /'tʃɪkəl/ or /-liː/ *n* the milky gum of a tropical American tree used to make chewing gum.

chicory /'tʃɪkəri/ n (pl **chicories**) a salad plant; its dried, ground, roasted root used to flavour coffee or as a coffee substitute.

chide /tʃaɪd/ vt (**chiding, chided** or **chid**; pp **chided, chid** or **chidden**) to rebuke, scold.—**chider** n.—**chidingly** adv.

chief /tʃiːf/ adj principal, most important. • n a leader; the head of a tribe or clan.

chiefly /'tʃiːfli/ adv especially; mainly; for the most part.

chieftain /'tʃiːftən/ n the head of a Scottish clan; a chief.

chiffchaff /'tʃɪftʃæf/ n a European warbler.

chiffon /ʃə'fɒn/ n a thin gauzy material. • adj made of chiffon; (pie filling, etc) having a light fluffy texture.

chiffonier, chiffonnier /ˌʃɪfə'niːr/ n a high chest of drawers; a wide, low cupboard.

chignon /'ʃiːnjɔ̃/ n a mass of hair worn in a roll at the back of the head, a bun.

chigoe /'tʃɪgoː/ n a species of West Indian and South American flea that burrows beneath the skin of the feet, causing irritation and ulcers.—also **jigger**.

chihuahua /tʃə'wɒwɒ/ n a tiny dog with erect ears, originally from Mexico.

chilblain /'tʃɪlbleɪn/ n an inflamed swelling on the hands, toes, etc, due to cold.

child /tʃaɪld/ n (pl **children**) a young human being; a son or daughter; offspring; an innocent or immature person.

child abuse n physical, mental or sexual maltreatment of a child by parents or any other adult.

childbearing /'tʃaɪldˌbeərɪŋ/ n pregnancy and childbirth.—also adj.

childbirth /-ˌbɜːrθ/ n the process of giving birth to children.

child care /-ˌkeər/ n care by an authority of homeless children or those from a disturbed home background.

childe /tʃaɪld/ n a term formerly applied to the scions of knightly houses before their admission into knighthood; a youth of noble birth.

childhood /'tʃaɪldhʊd/ n the period between birth and puberty in humans.

childish /'tʃaɪldɪʃ/ adj of, like or suited to a child; foolish.—**childishly.—childishness** n.

child labour n illegal employment of children below a certain age.

childless adj having no children.

child-like /'tʃaɪldlaɪk/ adj like a child; innocent, simple, candid.

children /'tʃɪldrən/ see **child**.

child's play n an easy task.

chili /'tʃɪli/ n (pl **chilies**) the hot-tasting pod of some of the capsicums, dried and used as flavouring.

chiliad /'kɪliˌæd/ n a thousand; a thousand years.—**chiliadal, chiliadic** adj.

chiliasm /'kɪliˌæzəm/ n the doctrine of the milennium.—**chiliast** n.—**chiliastic** adj.

chili con carne /'tʃɪlikɒn'kɑːrni/ n a spicy stew of minced beef, beans, onions and tomatoes flavoured with chilli powder or chillies.

chill /tʃɪl/ n a sensation of coldness; an illness caused by exposure to cold and marked by shivering; anything that dampens or depresses. • adj shivering with cold; feeling cold; unemotional, formal. • vti to make or become cold; to harden by cooling; to depress.

chillum /'tʃɪləm/ n the bowl of a hookah; a hookah; smoking.

chilly /'tʃɪli/ adj (**chillier, chilliest**) cold; unfriendly.—**chilliness** n.

chilopod /'kaɪloˌpɒd/ or /-lə-/ n any of an order of the class Myriopoda, containing the centipedes.

chime[1] /tʃaɪm/ n the harmonious sound of a bell; accord; harmony; (pl) a set of bells or metal tubes, etc tuned in a scale; their ringing. • vi to ring (a bell); (with in) (inf) to join in in agreement; to interrupt a conversation; (with with) to agree. • vt to indicate the hour by chiming, as a clock.

chime[2], **chimb** n the rim formed by the ends of the staves of a cask.

chimera, chimaera /kaɪ'miːrə/ or /kɪ-/ n (Greek myth) a firebreathing monster with body parts from various different animals; a fantastic hybrid; an impossible fancy.

chimere /tʃɪ'mɪr/ or /ʃɪ-/ n a loose silk robe worn by an Anglican bishop, either sleeveless or with lawn sleeves.

chimeric /kaɪ'merɪkəl/ or /kɪ-/, **chimerical** /-kəl/ adj merely imaginary; fantastic, visionary; unreal.—**chimerically** adv.

chimney /'tʃɪmni/ n (pl **chimneys**) a passage for smoke, hot air or fumes, a funnel; a chimney stack; the vent of a volcano; a vertical crevice in rock large enough to enter and climb.

chimneypiece n a mantelpiece.

chimneypot n a pipe extending a chimney at the top.

chimney stack n the chimney above roof level.

chimney sweep n a person who removes soot from chimneys.

chimp /tʃɪmp/ n (inf) chimpanzee.

chimpanzee /ˌtʃɪmpæn'ziː/ n an African anthropoid ape.

chin /tʃɪn/ n the part of the face below the mouth.

china /'tʃaɪnə/ n fine porcelain; articles made from this.

china clay n kaolin.

Chinatown /'tʃaɪnəˌtaʊn/ n the Chinese quarter of any city.

chinch /tʃɪntʃ/ n a tropical American insect destructive to corn crops; a bedbug.

chinchilla /tʃɪn'tʃɪlə/ n a small South American rodent with soft grey fur; a breed of domestic cat; a breed of rabbit.

chine /tʃaɪn/ n the backbone or spine of an animal; a piece of the backbone of an animal with adjacent parts cut for cooking; a ridge; a rocky ravine or large fissure in a cliff.

Chinese /tʃaɪ'niːz/ adj of or pertaining to China. • n (pl **Chinese**) an inhabitant of China.

Chinese chequers n a board game played with marbles.

Chinese gooseberry see **kiwi fruit**.

Chinese lantern n a collapsible paper lantern.

Chinese puzzle n an intricate puzzle based on fitting boxes within boxes; any very difficult puzzle or complex problem.

Chinese restaurant syndrome n an ailment characterized by chest pain, dizziness, flushing, allegedly caused by consuming in quantity monosodium glutamate often found in Chinese food.

Chinese white n a white pigment; white zinc oxide.

chink[1] /tʃɪŋk/ n a narrow opening; a crack or slit.

chink[2] n the sound of coins clinking together.

chino /'tʃiːnoː/ n (pl **chinos**) a strong, hardwearing twilled cotton; (pl) trousers made of this cloth.

chinoiserie /ʃiːnˌwɒzə'riː/ n (an object or objects in) a style of decoration copying Chinese motifs.

Chinook /ʃə'nʊk/ n a jargon of native and foreign words used on the northwest Pacific coast by Indians and whites.

chinook n a warm dry southwesterly wind of the eastern slopes of the Rocky Mountains; a warm moist wind blowing onto the northwest coast of America.

chinquapin /'tʃɪŋkəpɪn/ n the dwarf chestnut of the US; its nut.

chintz /tʃɪnts/ n a glazed cotton cloth printed with coloured designs.

chintzy /'tʃɪntsi/ adj (**chintzier, chintziest**) of or describing furniture, decor, etc covered in chintz; cheap; tasteless in a flowery way.

chinwag /'tʃɪnwæg/ vi (**chinwagging, chinwagged**) (sl) to talk, to gossip. • n (sl) a chatty conversation, a gossip.

chip /tʃɪp/ vt (**chipping, chipped**) to knock small pieces off; to shape or make by chipping. • n a small piece cut or broken off; a mark left by chipping; a thin strip of fried potato, french fry; a potato chip; a counter used in games; a tiny piece of semiconducting material, such as silicon, printed with a microcircuit and used as part of an integrated circuit.

chipboard /'tʃɪpbɔːrd/ n a thin stiff material made from compressed wood shavings and other waste pieces combined with resin.

chipmunk /'tʃɪpmʌŋk/ n a small, striped, squirrel-like animal of North America.

Chippendale /'tʃɪpənˌdeɪl/ adj of the light style of furniture introduced in the middle of the 18th century by the furniture maker and designer, Thomas Chippendale (1718–79).

chipper /'tʃɪpər/ adj active; lively, cheerful.

chip shot n a short, lofted approach shot in golf.

chiro-, cheiro- /'kaɪroː/ prefix hand.

chirography /kaɪ'rɒgrəfi/ n the art of writing, calligraphy; judgment of character by the handwriting.—**chirographer** n.—**chirographic, chirographical** adj.

chiromancy /'kaɪroːˌmænsi/ n palmistry.—**chiromancer** n.

chiropody /kɪ'rɒpədi/ or /ʃɪ-/ n the care and treatment of the feet.—**chiropodist** n.

chiropractic /ˌkaɪroː'præktɪk/ n the manipulation of joints, esp of the spine, to alleviate nerve pressure as a method of curing disease.—**chiropractor** n.

chirp /tʃɜːrp/ n the sharp, shrill note of some birds or a grasshopper. • vi to make this sound.—**chirper** n.

chirpy /'tʃɜːrpi/ adj (**chirpier, chirpiest**) lively, cheerful.—**chirpily** adv.—**chirpiness** n.

chirr /tʃər/ n the shrill rasping sound of a grasshopper. • vi to make this sound.—*also* **churr**.

chirrup /'tʃərəp/ vi (*birds*) to twitter; to make a clicking sound to a horse. • n a chirruping sound.—**chirruper** n.—**chirrupy** adj.

chisel /'tʃɪzəl/ n a tool with a square cutting end. • vt (**chiselling, chiselled** or **chiseling, chiseled**) to cut or carve with a chisel; (*sl*) to defraud.—**chiseller** n.

chit[1] /tʃɪt/ n a voucher or a sum owed for drink, food, etc; a note; a requisition.

chit[2] n a child; (*derog*) an impudent girl.

chitchat /'tʃɪtʃæt/ n gossip, trivial talk.

chitin /'kaɪtɪn/ n the white horny substance that forms the outer covering of many invertebrate animals.—**chitinoid** adj.—**chitinous** adj.

chiton /'kaɪtən/ n in ancient Greece, a knee-length tunic; a full-length woman's dress; a genus of molluscs.

chitterlings /'tʃɪtər.lɪŋz/, **chitlins** /'tʃɪtlɪnz/, **chitlings** /'tʃɪtlɪŋz/ npl the small edible entrails of pigs.

chivalrous /'ʃɪvəlrəs/ adj relating to chivalry; war-like; high-spirited; brave, gallant; generous to the weak.—**chivalrously** adv.

chivalry /'ʃɪvəlri/ n (*pl* **chivalries**) the medieval system of knighthood; knightly qualities, bravery, courtesy, respect for women.—**chivalric** adj.—**chivalrous** adj.—**chivalrously** adv.

chive /tʃaɪv/, **chives** /tʃaɪvz/ n a plant whose onion-flavoured leaves are used in cooking and salads.

chivvy, chivy /'tʃɪvi/ vt (**chivvying, chivvied** or **chivying, chivied**) to annoy, harass, nag.

chloral (hydrate) /'klɔrəl/ n a bitter white crystalline compound used as a sedative or anaesthetic.

chlorate /'klɔreɪt/ n a salt of chloric acid.

chlor-, chloro- /'klɔrə/ prefix green.

chloric /'klɔrɪk/ adj pertaining to or containing chlorine.

chloric acid n an acid containing hydrogen, oxygen, and chlorine.

chloride /'klɔraɪd/ n any compound containing chlorine.—**chloridic** adj.

chloride of lime n a compound of chlorine with lime used in bleaching.

chlorinate /'klɔrə.neɪt/ vt to treat or combine with chlorine; to disinfect with chlorine.—**chlorination** n.

chlorine /klɔr'iːn/ or /'klɔr-/ n a nonmetallic element, a yellowish-green poisonous gas used in bleaches, disinfectants, and in industry.

chloro-, chlor- /'klɔrə/ prefix green.

chlorofluorocarbon /ˌklɔrəˈfluːrəˌkɑrbən/ n any of various compounds containing carbon, chlorine, fluorine and hydrogen, used in refrigerants, aerosol propellants, etc, and thought to be harmful to the earth's atmosphere.

chloroform /'klɔrəˌfɔrm/ n a colourless volatile liquid formerly used as an anaesthetic.

chlorophyll, chlorophyl /'klɔrəfɪl/ n the green photosynthetic colouring matter in plants.

chlorosis /klə'roːsɪs/ or /klɔr-/ n a disease affecting young women, characterized by anaemia.—**chlorotic** adj.

chock /tʃɒk/ n a block of wood or other material used as a wedge. • vt to secure with a chock.

chock-a-block /'tʃɑkəˌblɒk/ adj completely full.—*also* **chock-full**.

chocolate /'tʃɒklət/ or /'tʃɒkələt/ n a powder or edible solid made of the roasted, pounded cacao bean; a drink made by dissolving this powder in boiling water or milk; a sweet with a centre and chocolate coating. • adj flavoured or coated with chocolate; dark reddish brown.—**chocolaty** adj.

chocolate-box adj sweetly pretty; oversentimental.

choice /tʃɔɪs/ n act of choosing; the power to choose; selection; alternative; a thing chosen; preference; the best part. • adj of picked quality, specially good.—**choicely** adv.—**choiceness** n.

choir /'kwaɪr/ n an organized group of singers, *esp* of a church; the part of a church before the altar used by them.

choirboy /'kwaɪrˌbɔɪ/ n one of the young trebles in a choir.

choirmaster /-ˌmæstər/ n one who trains and conducts the singers in a choir.

choke /tʃoːk/ vti to stop the breath of, stifle; to throttle; to suffocate; to block (up); to check, *esp* emotion, to choke back or up. • n a fit of choking; a choking sound; a valve that controls the flow of air in a carburettor.

chokebore /'tʃoːkˌbɔr/ n a shotgun with a bore narrowing towards the muzzle.

chokedamp /-ˌdæmp/ n carbonic acid gas generated in mines.

choker /-ər/ n a necklace worn tight round the neck; a high collar.

choler /'kɒlər/ n bile; irascibility, anger.

cholera /'kɒlərə/ n a severe, infectious intestinal disease.

choleric /'kɒlərɪk/ adj irascible; tending to anger; angry.

cholesterol /kə'lestəˌrɒl/ **cholesterin** n a substance found in animal tissues, blood and animal fats, thought to be a cause of hardening of the arteries.

chomp /tʃɒmp/ vt to chew noisily and with relish, champ.

chondr-, chondri-, chondro- /'kɒndrə/ prefix cartilage.

chondrify /-faɪ/ vti (**chondrifying, chondrified**) to change into cartilage.—**chondrification** n.

choose /tʃuːz/ vb (**choosing, chose,** *pp* **chosen**) vt to select (one thing) rather than another. • vi to decide, to think fit.—**chooser** n.

choosy /'tʃuːzi/ adj (**choosier, choosiest**) (*inf*) cautious; fussy; particular.—**choosily** adv.—**choosiness** n.

chop[1] /tʃɒp/ vt (**chopping, chopped**) to cut by striking; to cut into pieces. • n a cut of meat and bone from the rib, loin, or shoulder; a downward blow or motion; **get the chop** (*sl*) to be dismissed from one's employment; to be killed.

chop[2] n a mark or brand denoting quality.

chopfallen /'tʃɒpˌfɔlən/ *see* **chapfallen.**

chopper /'tʃɒpər/ n a tool for chopping; a cleaver; a small hand axe; (*sl*) a helicopter.

choppy /-i/ adj (**choppier, choppiest**) (*sea*) running in rough, irregular waves; jerky.—**choppily** adv.—**choppiness** n.

chops /tʃɒps/ npl the jaws or cheeks.

chopsticks /'tʃɒpstɪks/ n a pair of wooden or plastic sticks used in Asian countries to eat with.

chop suey /tʃɒp'suːi/ n a Chinese-American dish consisting of stir-fried vegetables and meat or seafood served with rice.

choral[1] /'kɔrəl/ adj relating to, sung by, or written for, a choir or chorus.—**chorally** adv.

choral[2], **chorale** /kər'æl/ n a slow hymn or psalm sung to a traditional or composed melody, *esp* by a choir.

chord[1] /kɔrd/ n (*mus*) three or more notes played simultaneously.—**chordal** adj.

chord[2] n a straight line joining the ends of an arc; a feeling of sympathy, recognition or remembering (**strike a chord**).

chore /tʃɔr/ n a piece of housework; a regular or tedious task.

chorea /kə'riə/ n a neurological disorder characterized by jerky involuntary movements, *esp* of the arms, legs and face.—**choreal, choreic** adj.

choreograph /'kɔriəˌgræf/ vt to devise the steps for a ballet, dance, etc.

choreography /ˌkɔriˈɒgrəfi/ n the art of devising ballets or dances.—**choreographer** n.—**choreographic** adj.—**choreographically** adv.

choric /'kɔrɪk/ adj of or for a Greek chorus.

chorion /'kɔriən/ n the exterior membrane of a seed or foetus.—**chorionic, chorial** adj.

chorister /'kɔrɪstər/ n a member of a choir.

chorizo /tʃə'riːzoː/ n (*pl* **chorizos**) a spicy pork sausage.

chorography /kɔː'rɒgrəfi/ or /kə-/ n the geographical description of a region.—**chorographer** n.—**chorographic, chorographical** adj.

choroid /'kɔrɔɪd/ n the vascular membrane of the retina.

chorology /kɔː'rɒlədʒi/ n the study of the geographical distribution of plants and animals.

chortle /'tʃɔrtəl/ vi to chuckle exultantly.—*also* n.

chorus /'kɔrəs/ n (*pl* **choruses**) a group of singers and dancers in the background to a play, musical, etc; a group of singers, a choir; music sung by a chorus; a refrain; an utterance by many at once. • vt (**chorusing, chorused**) to sing, speak or shout in chorus.

chorus girl n one who sings and dances in the chorus of a musical.—**chorus boy** nm.

chose /tʃoːz/, **chosen** /'tʃoːzən/ *see* **choose.**

chough /tʃʌf/ n a red-legged crow.

chow /tʃaʊ/ n a breed of thick-coated dog, originally from China.—*also* **chow chow**; (*sl*) food.

chowder /'tʃaʊdər/ n a thick clam and potato soup.

chow mein /ˌtʃaʊ'meɪn/ n a Chinese-American dish of fried, crispy noodles with meat and vegetables.

chrestomathy /kres'tɒməθi/ n (*pl* **chrestomathies**) a collection of extracts for learning a foreign language; a phrasebook; an anthology.

chrism /'krɪzəm/ n consecrated oil.—**chrismal** adj.

chrisom /'krɪzəm/ n an infant's baptismal robe.

Christ /kraɪst/ n Jesus of Nazareth, regarded by Christians as the Messiah.

christen /'krɪsən/ vt to enter the Christian Church by baptism; to give a name to; (inf) to use for the first time.—**christener** n.—**christening** n.

Christendom /'krɪsəndəm/ n all Christians, or Christian countries regarded as a whole.

Christian /'krɪstʃən/ n a person who believes in Christianity. • adj relating to, believing in, or based on the doctrines of Christianity; kind, gentle, humane.

Christian Era n the present era reckoned from the birth of Christ.

Christianity /ˌkrɪstʃi'ænəti/ or /-ti'æn-/ n the religion based on the teachings of Christ.

Christianize /'krɪstʃə,naɪz/ vt to convert to Christianity.—**Christianization** n.—**Christianizer** n.

Christianly adj like or befitting a Christian.

Christian name n a name given when one is christened; (loosely) any forename.

Christian Science n a system of religion founded by Mary Baker Eddy, 1866, in which sin and disease are regarded as mental errors to be overcome by faith.—**Christian Scientist** n.

Christlike /'kraɪst,laɪk/ adj resembling Christ.

Christmas /'krɪsməs/ n (pl **Christmases**) an annual festival (25 December) in memory of the birth of Christ.

Christmas card n a greeting card, usu decorative, sent at Christmas.

Christmas Eve n the day and esp the night before Christmas Day.

Christmas rose n the black hellebore.

Christmastide n Christmas Eve (24 December) to Epiphany (6 January).

Christmas tree n an evergreen tree decorated at Christmas; an imitation tree.

Christology /krɪs'tɒlədʒi/ n the branch of theology that studies Christ's nature.—**Christological** adj.—**Christologist** n.

chrom-, chromo- /kro:m/ prefix colour.

chromate /'kro:,meɪt/ n a salt or ester of chromic acid.

chromatic /kro:'mætɪk/ adj of or in colour; (mus) using tones outside the key in which the passage is written.—**chromatically** adv.—**chromaticism** n.

chromatics n sing the science of colour.

chromatic scale n a twelve-note musical scale that proceeds by semitones.

chromatin /'kro:mətɪn/ n a protoplasmic substance in a cell nucleus forming chromosomes.—**chromatinic** adj.

chromatography /ˌkro:mə'tɒɡrəfi/ n the separation of the components of a substance by passing it over or through a substance that absorbs selectively.—**chromatograph** n.—**chromatographer** n.—**chromatographic** adj.—**chromatographically** adv.

chrome /kro:m/ n chromium; a chromium pigment; something plated with an alloy of chromium.

-chrome /kro:m/ adj suffix coloured. • n suffix colour, pigment.

chrome green n a green pigment made from a compound of chromium.

chrome red n a red pigment made from a compound of chromium.

chrome yellow n a yellow pigment made from a compound of chromium.

chromic /'kro:mɪk/ adj of chromium.

chromium /'kro:mi:əm/ n a hard metallic element used in making steel alloys and electroplating to give a tough surface.

chromo-, chrom- /'kro:mo:/ prefix colour.

chromogen /'kro:mədʒən/ n the colouring matter of plants.—**chromogenic** adj.

chromolithography /ˌkro:mo:lɪ'θɒɡrəfi/ n the art of printing in colours from stone.—**chromolithograph** n.—**chromolithographer** n.—**chromolithographic** adj.

chromosome /'kro:mə,so:m/ n any of the microscopic rod-shaped bodies bearing genes.

chromosphere /-,sfi:r/ n the rose-coloured outer gaseous envelope of the sun above the photosphere.—**chromospheric** adj.

chron- /krɒn/, **chrono-** /-ə/ prefix time.

chronic /'krɒnɪk/ adj (disease) long-lasting; regular; habitual.—**chronically** adv.—**chronicity** n.

chronicle /'krɒnɪkəl/ n a record of events in chronological order; an account; a history. • vt to record in a chronicle.—**chronicler** n.

chronogram /'krɒnə,ɡræm/ n an inscription which includes in it the date of some event.—**chronogrammatic, chronogrammatical** adj.

chronograph /'krɒnə,ɡræf/ or /'kro:nə-/ n an instrument for recording minute intervals of time; a stopwatch.—**chronographer** n.—**chronographic** adj.

chronologic /ˌkrɒnə,lɒdʒɪk/, **chronological** /ˌkrɒnə'lɒdʒɪkəl/ adj arranged in order of occurrence.—**chronologically** adv.

chronology /'krɒnɒ,lədʒi/ n (pl **chronologies**) the determination of the order of events, eg in history; the arrangement of events in order of occurrence; a table of events listed in order of occurrence.—**chronologist** n.

chronometer /-,nɒmətər/ n a very accurate instrument for measuring time exactly.

chronometry /-,nɒmətri/ n the scientific measurement of time.—**chronometric, chronometrical** adj.—**chronometrically** adv.

chronoscope /'krɒnə,sko:p/ n an instrument for measuring by electricity the velocity of a projectile.—**chronoscopic** adj.

chrys- /kraɪs/, **chryso-** /-ə/ prefix gold.

chrysalis /'krɪsəlɪs/ n (pl **chrysalises, chrysalides**) the pupa of a moth or butterfly, enclosed in a cocoon.

chrysanthemum /krɪ'sænθəməm/ n a plant with a brightly coloured flower head.

chryselephantine /ˌkrɪsɛlə'fæntaɪn/ adj composed (or overlaid) partly with gold and partly with ivory.

chrysoberyl /'krɪsə,berəl/ n a yellowish-green gem.

chrysolite /'krɪsə,laɪt/ n a green-coloured and sometimes transparent gem.—**chrysolitic** adj.

chrysoprase /-,preɪz/ n a variety of chalcedony of an apple-green colour.

chthonian /'kθo:ni:ən/ or /'θɒ:-/ **chthonic** /'kθɒnɪk/ or /'θɒnɪk/ adj (Greek gods) of the underworld, as opposed to Olympian.

chub /tʃʌb/ n (pl **chub, chubs**) a small freshwater fish of the carp family.

chubby /'tʃʌbi/ adj (**chubbier, chubbiest**) plump.—**chubbiness** n.

chuck¹ /tʃʌk/ vt to throw, to toss; (inf) to stop, to give up. • n (usu with **the**) a giving up; dismissal.

chuck² n a device on a lathe, etc, that holds the work or drill; a cut of beef from the neck to the ribs.

chuck³ vt to make a noise like a hen calling to her chickens. • n a hen's call.

chuck⁴ n (dial) darling.

chuckle /'tʃʌkəl/ vt to laugh softly; to gloat. • n a quiet laugh.—**chuckler** n.

chuck wagon n a provision cart.

chuff¹ /tʃʌf/ n a surly fellow, a boor.

chuff² vi to make a puffing sound, as a steam engine. • n such a sound.

chug /tʃʌɡ/ n the explosive sound of a car exhaust, etc. • vi (**chugging, chugged**) to make such a sound.

chukker /'tʃʌkər/, **chukka** /'tʃʌkə/ n each period of play in a game of polo.

chum¹ /tʃʌm/ n (inf) a close friend, esp of the same sex. • vi (**chumming, chummed**) to be friendly (with); to room together.

chum² n a salmon of the Pacific Northwest coast of North America.

chummy /'tʃʌmi/ adj (**chummier, chummiest**) friendly, close to.—**chummily** adv.—**chumminess** n.

chump /tʃʌmp/ n (inf) a stupid person; a fool.

chunk /tʃʌŋk/ n a short, thick piece or lump, as wood, bread, etc.—**chunky** adj.

chunky /'tʃʌŋki/ adj (**chunkier, chunkiest**) short and thick; (clothing) of heavy material.—**chunkily** adv.—**chunkiness** n.

Chunnel /'tʃʌnəl/ n (inf) the Channel Tunnel linking England and France.

church /tʃɜːrtʃ/ n a building for public worship, esp Christian worship; the clerical profession; a religious service; (with cap) all Christians; (with **the**) a particular Christian denomination.

churchgoer /-,ɡo:ər/ n one who goes to church regularly.—**churchgoing** adj, n.

churchman /-mən/ n (pl **churchmen**) a member of the Church; a clergyman.—**churchwoman** n (pl **churchwomen**).

churchwarden /-'wɔːrdən/ n in the Anglican church, an elected lay representative who administers the secular matters of a parish church.

churchyard /-jard/ *n* the yard around a church often used as a burial ground.

churl /tʃərl/ *n* formerly one of the lowest orders of freemen; a peasant; a surly ill-bred person.

churlish /'tʃərlɪʃ/ *adj* surly, ill-mannered.—**churlishly** *adv.*—**churlishness** *n*.

churn /tʃərn/ *n* a large metal container for milk; a device that can be vigorously turned to make milk or cream into butter. • *vt* to agitate in a churn; to make (butter) this way; to stir violently; (*with* **out**) (*inf*) to produce quickly or one after the other or without much effort.

churr /tʃər/ *see* **chirr**.

chute /ʃuːt/ *n* an inclined trough or a passage for sending down water, logs, rubbish, etc; a fall of water, a rapid; an inclined slide for children; a slide into a swimming pool.

chutney /'tʃətni/ *n* a relish of fruits, spices, and herbs.

chutzpah, chutzpa /'hʊtzpə/ or /hets-/, /xuːts-/, /-pɒ/ *n* shameless audacity, presumption, or gall.

chyle /kaɪl/ *n* a milk-like fluid separated from digested matter in the stomach, absorbed by the lacteal vessels and assimilated into the blood.—**chylaceous, chylous** *adj*.

chyme /kaɪm/ *n* the pulpy mass of digested food prior to the separation of the chyle.

Ci (*symbol*) curie.

CIA /'siːaɪ'eɪ/ *abbr* = Central Intelligence Agency.

ciao *It.* /tʃaʊ/ *interj* used to express greeting or farewell.

ciborium /sə'bɔrɪəm/ *n* (*pl* **ciboria**) a covered chalice for holding the sacrament; a canopy over an altar.

cicada /sɪ'keɪdə/ or /-'kɒdə/, **cicala** /-lə/ *n* (*pl* **cicadas, cicadae** *or* **cicalas, cicale**) a large fly-like insect with transparent wings, the male producing a loud chirp or drone.

cicatrix /'sɪkətrɪks/ *n* (*pl* **cicatrices**) the scar remaining after a wound has healed; a scarlike mark.—**cicatricial** *adj.*—**cicatricose** *adj*.

cicatrize /'sɪkə,traɪz/ *vt* to heal a wound by inducing the skin to form a cicatrix; to mark with scars.—**cicatrization** *n.*—**cicatrizer** *n*.

cicely /'sɪsəli/ *n* (*pl* **cicelies**) a species of umbelliferous plants allied to chervil.

cicerone /'sɪsə,ro:ni/ *n* (*pl* **cicerones, ciceroni**) a guide who explains the antiquities and chief features of a place.

CID /'siː'aɪ'diː/ *abbr* = Criminal Investigation Department.

-cide /saɪd/ *n suffix* killing, or killer of, as in *regicide*.

cider /saɪdər/ *n* fermented apple juice as a drink.

cigar /sɪ'gɑr/ *n* a compact roll of tobacco leaf for smoking.

cigarette /,sɪgə'ret/ or /'sɪgəret/ *n* shredded tobacco rolled in fine paper for smoking.

cilia /'sɪlɪə/ *npl* (*sing* **cilium**) the hair of the eyelids; long minute hair-like appendages on the margins of vegetable bodies; the minute vibrating filaments lining or covering certain organs.—**ciliated** *adj*.

cilice /'sɪlɪs/ *n* haircloth.

Cimmerian /sɪ'mɪrɪən/ *adj* intensely dark; gloomy; pertaining to the Cimmerii, a legendary people mentioned by Homer as living in perpetual darkness.

C in C *abbr* = Commander in Chief.

cinch /sɪntʃ/ *n* (*sl*) a firm hold, an easy job; a saddle band or girth.

cinchona /sɪŋ'kəʊnə/ *n* a South American tree that yields quinine and other drugs.

cinchonism /'sɪŋkə,nɪzəm/ *n* a medical condition characterized by buzzing in the ears, deafness, etc, caused by the excessive use of quinine.

cincture /'sɪŋktʃər/ *n* a belt or girdle worn round the waist; a raised or carved ring at the bottom and top of a pillar.

cinder /'sɪndər/ *n* a tiny piece of partly burned wood, etc; (*pl*) ashes from wood or coal.—**cindery** *adj*.

cine- /'sɪneɪ/ or /'sɪni/ *prefix* motion picture or cinema, as in *cinecamera, cinefilm*.

cineast, cineaste /'sɪneɪ,æst/ or /'sɪni-/, *Fr.* /siːnɒ'æst/ *n* a film enthusiast.

cinema /'sɪnəmə/ *n* a place where motion pictures are shown; film as an industry or art form.—**cinematic** *adj.*—**cinematically** *adv*.

cinematography /,sɪnəmə'tɒgrəfi/ *n* the art or science of motion-picture photography.—**cinematographic** *adj.*—**cinematographer** *n*.

cinéma vérité /,sɪne,məveri'teɪ/ *n* cinema photography of real-life scenes and situations, etc, to create realism.

cineraria /,sɪnə'reriə/ *n* a genus of garden plants of the aster family with bright flowers.

cinerarium /-ɪəm/ *n* (*pl* **cineraria**) a place for keeping a person's ashes after cremation.

cinerary /,sɪnə'reri/ *adj* of, pertaining to, or containing, ashes.

cinereous /sɪ'niːrɪəs/ *adj* ash-grey.

cingulum /'sɪŋgjʊləm/ *n* (*pl* **cingula**) belt.

cinnabar /'sɪnə,bɑr/ *n* red sulphide of mercury. • *adj* vermilion.

cinnamon /'sɪnəmən/ *n* a tree of the laurel family; its aromatic edible bark; a spice made from this; a yellowish-brown colour. • *adj* yellowish brown.—**cinnamonic, cinamic** *adj*.

cinnamon stone *n* a variety of the garnet.

cinque /sɪŋk/ *n* a five at dice or cards.

cinquecento /,tʃɪŋkwi'tʃentoː/ *n* the 16th century and Italian fine art of that period. • *adj* designed or executed in such Italian style.

cinquefoil /'sɪŋkfɔɪl/ *n* a plant with leaves divided into five lobes; (*archit*) ornamentation resembling five leaves.

cipher /'saɪfər/ *n* the numeral 0, zero; any single Arabic numeral; a thing or person of no importance, a nonentity; a method of secret writing. • *vt* to convert (a message) into cipher.—*also* **cypher**.

circa /'sərkə/ *prep* about.

circadian /sər'keɪdɪən/ *adj* of or pertaining to biological processes that occur in 24-hour cycles.

circinate /'sərsɪ,neɪt/ *adj* (*leaf*) rolled up with the tip inwards.

circle /'sərkəl/ *n* a perfectly round plane figure; the line enclosing it; anything (built) in the form of a circle; the curved seating area above the stalls in a theatre; a group, set or class (of people); extent, scope, as of influence. • *vti* to encompass; to move in a circle; to revolve (round); to draw a circle round.—**circler** *n*.

circlet /'sərklət/ *n* a small circle; a circular band or hoop.

circuit /'sərkɪt/ *n* a distance round; a route or course; an area so enclosed; the path of an electric current; a visit to a particular area by a judge to hold courts; the area itself; a chain or association, eg of cinemas controlled by one management; sporting events attended regularly by the same competitors and at the same venues; a motor-racing track.—**circuital** *adj*.

circuit breaker *n* a switch that interrupts an electric circuit under certain abnormal conditions.

circuitous /sər'kjuːɪtəs/ *adj* roundabout, indirect.—**circuitously** *adv*.

circuitry /'sərkətri/ *n* (*pl* **circuitries**) the plan of an electric circuit; the components of a circuit.

circular /'sərkjʊlər/ *adj* shaped like a circle, round; (*argument*) using as evidence the conclusion which it is seeking to prove; moving round a circle. • *n* an advertisement, etc addressed to a number of people.—**circularity, circularness** *n*.

circularize /-jʊlə,raɪz/ *vt* to make circular; to send circulars to; to canvass.—**circularization** *n.*—**circularizer** *n*.

circular saw *n* a power-driven saw with a circular blade.

circulate /'sərkjʊ,leɪt/ *vti* to pass from hand to hand or place to place; to spread or be spread about; to move round, finishing at the starting point.—**circulative** *adj.*—**circulator** *n.*—**circulatory** *adj*.

circulating decimal *n* the recurring decimal.

circulating library *n* a lending library.

circulation /,sərkjʊ'leɪʃən/ *n* the act of circulating; a movement to and fro; the regular cycle of blood flow in the body; the number of copies sold of a newspaper, etc; currency.

circum- /'sərkəm/ or /sər'kəm/ *prefix* round, about.

circumambient /,sərkəm'æmbɪənt/ *adj* enclosing, or being surrounded, on all sides.—**cicumambience, cicumabiency** *n*.

circumcise /'sərkəm,saɪz/ *vt* to cut off the foreskin of a male in a religious rite or for medical reasons; to cut off the clitoris and/or labia minora of a female for socio-cultural reasons.—*see* **clitoridectomy**.

circumcision /'sərkəm,sɪʒən/ *n* the act of circumcising; spiritual purification.

circumference /sər'kəmfərəns/ *n* the line bounding a circle, a ball, etc; the length of this line.—**circumferential** *adj*.

circumflex /'sərkəm,fleks/ *n* an accent (^) placed over a vowel to indicate contraction, length, etc.—**circumflexion** *n*.

circumfuse /,sərkəm'fjuːz/ *vt* to pour or spread around; to bathe (with).—**circumfusion** *n*.

circumlocution /-lə'kjuːʃən/ *n* the use of more words than are necessary; a roundabout or evasive expression.—**circumlocutory** *adj*.

circumnavigate /-'nævɪˌgeɪt/ *vt* to sail or fly completely round (the world).—**circumnavigable** *adj*.—**circumnavigation** *n*.—**circumnavigator** *n*.

circumnutate /-njuː'teɪt/ *vi* (*bot*) to turn successively to all points of the compass.—**circumnutation** *n*.

circumpolar /-'pəʊlər/ *adj* near the north or south pole; (*astron*) always above the horizon.

circumscribe /'sɜːkəmˌskraɪb/ *vt* to draw a line around; to enclose; to limit or restrict.—**circumscription** *n*.

circumspect /-ˌspekt/ *adj* prudent, cautious; careful; discreet.—**circumspection** *n*.—**circumspective** *adj*.

circumstance /-ˌstæns/ *n* an occurrence, an incident; a detail; ceremony; (*pl*) a state of affairs; condition in life.

circumstantial /ˌsɜːkəm'stænʃəl/ *adj* detailed; incidental; (*law*) strongly inferred from direct evidence.—**circumstantially** *adv*.

circumstantiality /-ˌstænʃɪ'ælɪtɪ/ *n* (*pl* **circumstantialities**) the state of being circumstantial; fullness of detail.

circumstantiate /-'stænʃɪˌeɪt/ *vt* to describe or verify in detail.—**circumstantiation** *n*.

circumvallate /-'vælˌeɪt/ *vt* to surround with a rampart.—**circumvallation** *n*.

circumvent /ˌsɜːkəm'vent/ *vt* to evade, bypass; to outwit.—**circumventer, circumventor** *n*.—**circumvention** *n*.

circumvolution /-və'luːʃən/ *n* the act of rolling round; the state of being rolled round; a coil.—**circumvolutory** *adj*.

circus /'sɜːkəs/ *n* (*pl* **circuses**) a large arena for the exhibition of games, feats of horsemanship, etc; a travelling show of acrobats, clowns, etc; a company of people travelling round giving displays; houses built in a circle; an open space in a town where streets meet; (*inf*) noise, disturbance; loud, extravagant behaviour.

cirque /sɜːk/ *n* a natural amphitheatre or ring.

cirrhosis /sɪ'rəʊsɪs/ *n* a hardened condition of the tissues of an organ, *esp* the liver.—**cirrhosed** *adj*.—**cirrhotic** *adj*.

cirriped /'sɪrɪˌped/, **cirripede** /'sɪrɪˌpiːd/ *adj* having feet resembling cirri; pertaining to the Cirripedia, a subclass of parasitic crustaceans, as the barnacles and acorn shells.

cirrocumulus /ˌsɪrəʊ'kjuːmjʊləs/ *n* (*pl* **cirrocumuli**) a cloud broken up into small fleecy masses.

cirrostratus /-'strætəs/ *n* (*pl* **cirrostrati**) a horizontal or slightly inclined light fleecy cloud.

cirrouse, cirrous /'sɪrəs/ *adj* terminating in a curl, tuft, or tendril.

cirrus /'sɪrəs/ *n* (*pl* **cirri**) thin, wispy clouds.

CIS /'siːˌaɪ'es/ *abbr* = Commonwealth of Independent States: a federation of former Soviet republics, such as Russia, Ukraine, who wish to retain voluntary links with one another.

cis- /sɪs/ *prefix* on this side of.

cisalpine /sɪs'ælˌpaɪn/ *adj* this side of the Alps with regard to Rome, south of the Alps.

cisco /'sɪskəʊ/ *n* (*pl* **ciscoes, ciscos**) a North American freshwater whitefish.

cismontane /sɪs'mɒnˌteɪn/ *adj* on this (northern) side of the Alps.

cist /sɪst/ or /kɪst/ *n* a prehistoric stone tomb consisting of two rows of stone and covered with a flat stone slab; a box or chest.

Cistercian /sɪs'tɜːʃən/ *n* one of a Benedictine order of monks, founded 1098 at Citeaux, France. • *adj* pertaining to the Cistercians.

cistern /'sɪstərn/ *n* a tank or reservoir for storing water, *esp* in a toilet.

citadel /'sɪtədel/ or /-dəl/ *n* a fortress in or near a city.

citation /saɪ'teɪʃən/ *n* a quotation; a source or authority cited; a commendation, *esp* for bravery; (*law*) a summons to appear.

cite /saɪt/ *vt* to summon officially to appear in court; to quote; to give as an example or authority.—**citable, citeable** *adj*.

cithara /'sɪθərə/ *n* an ancient lyre.—*also* **kithara**.

citify /'sɪtɪˌfaɪ/ *vt* (**citifying, citifed**) to assume city ways, habits, dress.

citizen *n* a member of a city, state or nation.—**citizenship** *n*.

citizenry /'sɪtɪzənrɪ/ *n* (*pl* **citizenries**) citizens collectively.

citizen's band *n* a shortwave band reserved for private radio communication.

citrate /'sɪtreɪt/ *n* a salt or ester of citric acid.

citric /'sɪtrɪk/ *adj* of or obtained from citrus fruits or citric acid.

citric acid *n* a sour acid found in fruits and used as a flavouring.

citrine /-trɪn/ or /-ˌtriːn/ *adj* lemon-coloured.

citron /-trən/ *n* a large fruit-like a lemon; the tree bearing it; a yellow-green colour.

citronella /ˌsɪtrə'nelə/ *n* a fragrant Asian grass which yields an aromatic oil used in soap, perfumes, and in insect repellents.

citrus /'sɪtrəs/ *n* (*pl* **citruses**) a genus of trees including the lemon, orange, etc; the fruit of these trees. • *adj* of or relating to citrus trees or shrubs or their fruit.

cittern /'sɪtərn/ *n* a medieval stringed instrument.

city /'sɪtɪ/ *n* (*pl* **cities**) an important or cathedral town; a town created a city by charter; the people of a city; business circles, *esp* financial services.—*also adj*.

city editor *n* the editor in charge of local news.

city fathers *npl* the people who take part in running a city.

city hall *n* the townhall; the government of a city or its officers; (*inf*) bureaucracy.

city slicker *n* (*inf*) one who adopts city ways; a suave, unreliable person.

city-state /-ˌsteɪt/ *n* (*hist*) a sovereign state comprising a city and its surrounding territory.

civet /'sɪvət/ *n* a cat-like animal of central Africa and South Asia; the pungent substance secreted by this animal used in perfumery.

civic /'sɪvɪk/ *adj* of a city, citizen or citizenship. • *npl* the principles of good citizenship; the study of citizenship.—**civically** *adv*.

civil /'sɪvəl/ *adj* of citizens or the state; not military or ecclesiastical; polite, obliging; (*law*) relating to crimes other than criminal ones or to private rights.—**civilly** *adv*.

civil defence *n* the organization of civilians against enemy attack.

civil disobedience *n* refusal to pay taxes, etc, as part of a political campaign; nonviolent protest to achieve an end.

civil engineer *n* an engineer who designs and constructs roads, bridges, etc.

civilian /sɪ'vɪljən/ *n* a person who is not a member of the armed forces.

civility /sɪ'vɪlɪtɪ/ *n* (*pl* **civilities**) good manners, politeness.

civil rights *npl* the personal rights of a citizen.

civil service *n* those employed in the service of a state apart from the military.—**civil servant** *n*.

civil war *n* a war between citizens of the same state or country.

civilization /ˌsɪvɪlaɪ'zeɪʃən/ *n* the state of being civilized; the process of civilizing; an advanced stage of social culture; moral and cultural refinement.

civilize /'sɪvɪˌlaɪz/ *vt* to bring out from barbarism; to educate in arts and refinements.—**civilizer** *n*.

civilized /'sɪvɪˌlaɪzd/ *adj* no longer in a savage or uncultured state.

civvy /'sɪvɪ/ *adj* (*sl*) civilian. • *n* (*pl* **civvies**) (*sl*) civilian clothes.

Cl (*chem symbol*) = chlorine.

cl *abbr* = centilitre(s).

clack /klæk/ *vt* to make a sudden, sharp sound; to chatter rapidly and continuously. • *n* a sudden, sharp sound as of wood striking wood.

clad[1] /klæd/ *see* **clothe**.

clad[2] *vt* (**cladding, clad**) to bond one material to another for protection (*iron cladding*).—**cladding** *n*.

claim /kleɪm/ *vt* to demand as a right; to call for; to require; to profess (to have); to assert; to declare to be true. • *n* the act of claiming; a title, right to something; a thing claimed, *esp* a piece of land for mining.—**claimable** *adj*.—**claimer** *n*.

claimant /-mənt/ *n* a person who makes a claim.

clairvoyance /klɛr'vɔɪəns/ *n* the power of seeing things not present to the senses, second sight.

clairvoyant /klɛr'vɔɪənt/ *n* a person with the gift of clairvoyance. • *adj* possessing clairvoyance; having remarkable insight.

clam /klæm/ *n* edible marine bivalve mollusc. • *vb* (**clamming, clammed**) *vt* to gather clams. • *vi* (*with* **up**) (*inf*) to remain silent, refuse to talk.

clamant /'kleɪmənt/ *adj* insistent, crying; clamorous.

clambake /'klæmbeɪk/ *n* clams baked with seaweed; a picnic at which baked clams form the chief dish.

clamber /'klæmbər/ or /'klæmər/ *vi* to climb with difficulty, using the hands as well as the feet. • *n* a climb performed in this way.—**clamberer** *n*.

clammy /'klæmɪ/ *adj* (**clammier, clammiest**) damp and sticky.—**clammily** *adv*.—**clamminess** *n*.

clamour, clamor /'klæmər/ *n* a loud confused noise; an uproar; an insistent demand. • *vi* to demand loudly; to make an uproar.—**clamorous** *adj*.

clamp /klæmp/ *n* a device for gripping objects tightly together. • *vt* to grip with a clamp; to attach firmly. • *vi* (*with* **down**) to put a stop to forcefully. • *vt* to attach a wheelclamp to a wheel to immobilize an illegally parked car.

clan /klæn/ *n* a group of people with a common ancestor, under a single chief; people with the same surname; a party or clique.

clandestine /klæn'destɪn/ or /-taɪn/ *adj* done secretly; surreptitious; sly.—**clandestinely** *adv*.

clang /klæŋ/ *n* a loud metallic sound. • *vti* to make or cause to make a clang.

clangour, clangor /klæŋər/ *n* a sharp clang; repeated clanging.—**clangourous, clangorous** *adj*.—**clangourously, clangorously** *adv*.

clank /klæŋk/ *n* a short, harsh metallic sound. • *vt* to make or cause to make a clank.

clannish /klænɪʃ/ *adj* closely united and excluding others.—**clannishly** *adv*.

clansman /klænzmən/ *n* (*pl* **clansmen**) a member of a clan.—**clanswoman** *nf* (*pl* **clanswomen**).

clap /klæp/ *vti* (**clapping, clapped**) to strike (the hands) together sharply; to applaud in this way; to slap; to flap (wings) loudly; to put or place suddenly or vigorously. • *n* the sound of hands clapping; a sudden sharp noise; a sudden sharp slap.

clapboard /klæpbord/ or /klæbərd/ *n* a narrow, thin board used for building by overlapping each piece.

clapper /klæpər/ *n* the tongue of a bell.

claptrap /klæptræp/ *n* flashy display, empty words.

claque /klæk/ *n* an organized body of people paid to applaud or express disapproval at theatres; interested admirers.

clarence /klærəns/ or /klerəns/ *n* a closed four-wheeled carriage with a curved front.

claret /klærət/ or /kle-/ *n* a dry red wine of Bordeaux in France; its purple-red colour.

claret cup *n* a summer drink composed of iced claret, lemon, brandy, etc.

clarify /klærɪ̩faɪ/ or /kle-/ *vti* (**clarifying, clarified**) to make or become clear or intelligible; to free or become free from impurities.—**clarification** *n*.—**clarifier** *n*.

clarinet /̩klærɪ'net/ or /kle-/ *n* an orchestral woodwind instrument.—**clarinettist** *n*.

clarion /klærɪən/ or /kle-/ *n* a shrill trumpet formerly used in war; a rousing sound. • *adj* ringing.

clarity /klærɪtɪ/ or /kle-/ *n* clearness.

clarkia /klɑrkɪə/ *n* a bright-flowered garden plant.

clary /kleri/ *n* (*pl* **claries**) meadow and wild sage.

clash /klæʃ/ *n* a loud noise of striking weapons, cymbals, etc; a contradiction, disagreement; a collision. • *vti* to make or cause to make a clash by striking together; to conflict; to collide; to be at variance (with); (*colours*) to be unsuitable or not pleasing when put together.—**clasher** *n*.

clasp /klæsp/ *n* a hold, an embrace; a catch or buckle. • *vt* to grasp firmly, to embrace; to fasten with a clasp.—**clasper** *n*.

clasp knife *n* a knife with a blade or blades that shut into the handle.

class /klæs/ *n* a division, a group; a kind; a set of pupils who are taught together; a grade of merit or quality; standing in society, rank; (*inf*) high quality, excellence; style. • *vt* to put into a class.

class-conscious *adj* aware of and taking part in the conflict between labouring and other classes.—**class-consciousness** *n*.

classic /klæsɪk/ *adj* of the highest class or rank, *esp* in literature; of the best Greek and Roman writers; of music conforming to certain standards of form, complexity, etc; traditional; authoritative. • *n* a work of literature, art, cinema, etc of the highest excellence; a definitive work of art.

classical /klæsɪkəl/ *adj* influenced by, of or relating to ancient Roman and Greek art, literature and culture; traditional; serious; refined.—**classicality** *n*.—**classically** *adv*.

classicism /klæsɪ̩sɪzəm/, **classicalism** /klæsɪkə̩lɪzəm/ *n* the use of ancient Roman and Greek style.

classicist /klæsɪ̩sɪst/, **classicalist** /klæsɪkə̩lɪst/ *n* a scholar of the classics.—**classicistic** *adj*.

classics /klæsɪks/ *n* (*with* **the**) the study of ancient Greek and Roman literature; any literature considered to be a model of its type.

classification /̩klæsɪfɪ'keɪʃən/ *n* the organization of knowledge into categories; a category or a division of a category into which knowledge or information has been put.—**classificational** *adj*.—**classificatory** *adj*.

classified /klæsɪ̩faɪd/ *adj* arranged by a system of classification; (*information*) secret and restricted to a select few; (*advertisements*) grouped according to type.

classify /klæsɪ̩faɪ/ *vt* (**classifying, classified**) to arrange in classes, to categorize; to restrict for security reasons.—**classifiable** *adj*.—**classifier** *n*.

classless /klæsləs/ *adj* not divided into classes; not belonging to a particular class.—**classlessness** *n*.

classmate /-meɪt/ *n* a member of the same class in a school, college, etc.

classroom /-ruːm/ *n* a room where pupils or students are taught.

classy /klæsɪ/ *adj* (**classier, classiest**) (*sl*) stylish; elegant.—**classily** *adv*.—**classiness** *n*.

clastic /klæstɪk/ *adj* (*geol*) composed of fragments.

clatter /klætər/ *n* a rattling noise; noisy talk. • *vti* to make or cause a clatter.—**clattery** *adj*.

clause /klɔz/ *n* a single article or stipulation in a treaty, law, contract, etc; (*gram*) a short sentence; a division of a sentence.—**clausal** *adj*.

claustral /klɔstrəl/ *adj* of or pertaining to a cloister, cloistral.

claustrophobia /̩klɔstrə'foːbɪə/ *n* a morbid fear of confined spaces.—**claustrophobe** *n*.—**claustrophobic** *adj*.—**claustrophobically** *adv*.

clavate /kleɪveɪt/, **claviform** /-fɔrm/ *adj* club-shaped.

clavichord /klævɪ̩kɔrd/ *n* a medieval keyboard instrument, the predecessor of the piano.—**clavichordist** *n*.

clavicle /klævɪkəl/ *n* one of the two bones that connect the shoulder blades with the breast bone, the collarbone.—**clavicular** *adj*.

clavier /klævɪər/ *n* a musical instrument with a keyboard; the keyboard.

claw /klɔ/ *n* the sharp hooked nail of an animal or bird; the pointed end or pincer of a crab, etc; a claw-like thing. • *vti* to seize or tear with claws or nails; to clutch or scratch (at); (*with* **back**) to recover (something) with difficulty; to get back money by taxing; to take back part of what was handed out, *esp* by taxation.—**clawer** *n*.

claw hammer *n* a hammer with a claw for drawing out nails.

clay /kleɪ/ *n* a sticky ductile earthy material.—**clayey** *adj*.

claymore /kleɪmɔr/ *n* a large two-edged sword formerly used in Scotland.

clay pigeon *n* a brittle clay disc or other object propelled into the air as a shooting target; someone in a vulnerable position.

clean /kliːn/ *adj* free from dirt or impurities; unsoiled; morally or ceremonially pure; complete, decisive; free of errors; free of suggestive language; not carrying firearms or drugs. • *adv* entirely; outright; neatly. • *vti* to remove dirt from; (*with* **out**) to remove dirt out of; (*sl*) to take away everything from someone, *esp* money; (*with* **up**) to leave clean; (*sl*) to get rid of corrupt people, a system, etc; to gain a large profit.—**cleanable** *adj*.—**cleanness** *n*.

clean-cut /kliːn̩kʌt/ *adj* sharply defined, clear-cut; well-shaped.

cleaner /-ər/ *n* a substance or device used for cleaning; a person employed to clean; (*pl*) a dry cleaner.

clean-limbed *adj* having well-proportioned or shapely limbs.

cleanly /-lɪ/ *adj* (**cleanlier, cleanliest**) clean in habits or person; pure; neat. • *adv* in a clean manner.—**cleanliness** *n*.

cleanse /klenz/ *vt* to make clean or pure.—**cleansable** *adj*.

cleanser /-ər/ *n* something that cleanses, *esp* a detergent, face cream, etc.

clear /klɪr/ *adj* bright, not dim; transparent; without blemish; easily seen or heard; unimpeded, open; free from clouds; quit (of); plain, distinct, obvious; keen, discerning; positive, sure; without debt. • *adv* plainly; completely; apart from. • *vti* to make or become clear; to rid (of), remove; to free from suspicion, vindicate; to disentangle; to pass by or over without touching; to make as a profit; (*with* **off**) (*inf*) to depart; (*with* **up**) to explain; to tidy up; (*weather*) to become fair.—**clearness** *n*.

clearance /klɪrəns/ *n* the act of clearing; permission, authority to proceed; the space between two objects in motion.

clear-cut /klɪr̩kʌt/ *adj* having a sharp, clearly defined outline, as if chiselled; straightforward and open.

clear-headed /-̩hedɪd/ *adj* showing sense, alertness, judgment.—**clear-headedly** *adv*.—**clear-headedness** *n*.

clearing /-ɪŋ/ *n* a tract of land cleared of trees, etc for cultivation.

clearing bank *n* a bank that uses a clearing house to exchange cheques and credits with other banks.

clearing house /-ˌhɐʊs/ *n* an office where cheques are sorted and exchanged by the clearing banks; a central agency for the collection, classification and distribution of information.

clearly /-li/ *adv* in a clear manner; evidently.

clear-sighted /-ˌsəitəd/ *adj* discerning, objective.

clearstory /-ˌstoːri/ *see* **clerestory**.

cleat /kliːt/ *n* a wedge; a strip of wood nailed crossways to a footing, etc; a projection for making ropes fast to.

cleavage /ˈkliːvidʒ/ *n* the way a thing splits; divergence; the hollow between the breasts.

cleave[1] /kliːv/ *vti* (**cleaving, cleft, cleaved** *or* **clove,** *pp* **cleft, cleaved** *or* **cloven**) to divide by a blow; split; to sever.—**cleavable** *adj*.

cleave[2] *vi* (**cleaved, clave**) to be faithful to; to stick.

cleaver /ˈkliːvər/ *n* a butcher's heavy chopper.

cleavers /ˈkliːvərz/ *n* goose-grass.

cleek /kliːk/ *n* an iron-headed golf club with a narrow straight face; (*Scot*) a large hook or crook.

clef /klɛf/ *n* a sign on a music stave that indicates the pitch of the notes.

cleft /klɛft/ *n* a fissure or crack.

cleft palate *n* a congenital fissure of the hard palate in the roof of the mouth.

cleistogamy /kləiˈstəgæmi/ *n* (*bot*) self-fertilization without opening of the flower.—**cleistogamous, cleistogamic** *adj*.

clematis /ˈklɛmətɪs/ *or* /kləˈmætɪs/ *n* a climbing plant with large colourful flowers.

clemency /ˈklɛmənsi/ *n* (*pl* **clemencies**) mercy, leniency; mildness, *esp* of weather.

clement /ˈklɛmənt/ *adj* merciful, gentle; (*weather*) mild.

clench /klɛntʃ/ *vt* (*teeth, fist*) to close tightly; to grasp. • *n* a firm grip.

clerestory /ˈkliːrˌstəri/ *or* /-stəri/ *n* (*pl* **clerestories**) the upper story, with windows, of the nave of a church.—*also* **clearstory.**—**clerestoried, clearstoried** *adj*.

clergy /ˈklərdʒi/ *n* (*pl* **clergies**) ministers of the Christian church collectively.

clergyman /-ˌmən/ *n* (*pl* **clergymen**) a member of the clergy.

cleric /ˈklɛrɪk/ *n* a member of the clergy.

clerical /ˈklɛrɪkəl/ *adj* of or relating to the clergy or a clergyman; of or relating to a clerk or a clerk's work.—**clerically** *adv*.

clerical collar *n* a narrow stiff white collar buttoned at the back and worn by the clergy.—*also* **dog collar.**

clericalism /-ˌlɪzəm/ *n* clerical influence, *esp* of an undue kind.

clerihew /ˈklɛrɪˌhjuː/ *n* a short nonsensical or satirical poem, *usu* in four lines of varying length, eg Sir Christopher Wren / Said, "I'm going to dine with some men. / If anyone calls, / Say I'm designing St Paul's."

clerk /klərk/ *n* an office worker who types, keeps files, etc; a layman with minor duties in a church; a public official who keeps the records of a court, town, etc.—**clerkdom** *n*.—**clerkship** *n*.

clerkly /-li/ *adj* (**clerklier, clerkliest**) pertaining to a clerk, or to penmanship. • *adv* in a scholarly manner.

clever /ˈklɛvər/ *adj* able; intelligent; ingenious; skilful, adroit.—**cleverly** *adv*.—**cleverness** *n*.

clew /kluː/ *n* a ball of thread; the corner of a sail to which a sheet is attached. • *vt* to truss up (sails) to the yard of a ship.

cliché /kliːˈʃeɪ/ *or* /ˈkliː-/ *n* a hackneyed phrase; something that has become commonplace.—**cliché'd, clichéd** *adj*.

click /klɪk/ *n* a slight, sharp sound. • *vi* to make such a sound; (*inf*) to establish immediate friendly relations with; to succeed; (*inf*) to become plain or evident; to fall into place.—**clicker** *n*.

client /ˈklaɪənt/ *n* a person who employs another professionally; a customer.—**cliental** *adj*.

clientele /ˌklaɪənˈtɛl/ *or* /ˌkliːɒnˈtɛl/ *n* clients, customers.

cliff /klɪf/ *n* a high steep rock face.

cliffhanger /-ˌhæŋər/ *n* the perilous situation at the climax of each episode of a serialized film or book; any dramatic or suspenseful situation.—**cliffhanging** *adj*.

climacteric /klaɪˈmæktərɪk/ *or* /ˌklaɪmækˈtɛrɪk/ *n* a critical period, a turning point, *esp* in the life of an individual; the male menopause. • *adj* forming a crisis.—*also* **climacterical.**

climate /ˈklaɪmət/ *n* the weather characteristics of an area; the prevailing attitude, feeling, atmosphere.—**climatic, climatical, climatal** *adj*.

climatology /ˌklaɪməˈtɒlədʒi/ *n* the science of climates.—**climatologic, climatological** *adj*.—**climatologist** *n*.

climax /ˈklaɪmæks/ *n* the highest point; a culmination; sexual orgasm; the highlight or most interesting part of a story, drama or music. • *vti* to reach, or bring to a climax.—**climactic, climactical** *adj*.

climb /klaɪm/ *vti* to mount with an effort; to ascend; to rise; (*plants*) to grow upwards by clinging onto walls, fences or other plants; (*with* **down**) to descend from a higher level; to retreat from a position previously held, eg in a debate or argument; to yield. • *n* an ascent.

climber /ˈklaɪmər/ *n* a mountaineer or rock climber; a climbing plant; a socially ambitious person.

clime /klaɪm/ *n* (*poet*) a country, region, or tract.

clinch /klɪntʃ/ *vt* (*argument, etc*) to confirm or drive home. • *vi* (*boxing*) to grip the opponent with the arms to hinder his punching. • *n* the act of clinching; (*inf*) an embrace.

clincher /ˈklɪntʃər/ *n* a decisive point in an argument.

cling /klɪŋ/ *vi* (**clinging, clung**) to adhere, to be attached (to); to keep hold by embracing or entwining.—**clinger** *n*.

clingstone /ˈklɪŋstoːn/ *n* a fruit, eg the peach, with pulp adhering to the stone.—*also adj*.

clinic /ˈklɪnɪk/ *n* a place where outpatients are given medical care or advice; a place where medical specialists practise as a group; a private or specialized hospital; the teaching of medicine by treating patients in the presence of students.

clinical /ˈklɪnɪkəl/ *adj* of or relating to a clinic; based on medical observation; plain, simple; detached, cool, objective.—**clinically** *adv*.

clink[1] /klɪŋk/ *n* a slight metallic ringing sound. • *vti* to make or cause to make such a sound.

clink[2] *n* (*sl*) prison.

clinker /ˈklɪŋkər/ *n* very hard-burnt brick; a mass of partly vitrified brick; slag; a fine specimen.

clinker-built /-ˌbɪlt/ *adj* built so that the planks of a boat overlap each other like weather-boarding.

clinkstone /-ˌstoːn/ *n* an igneous rock that emits a clinking sound when struck.

clinometer /klaɪˈnɒmɪtər/ *n* an instrument for measuring the angles of slopes or the dip of rock strata; a kind of plumb level.—**clinometric, clinometrical** *adj*.—**clinometry** *n*.

clinquant /ˈklɪŋkənt/ *adj* glittering. • *n* tinsel.

clip[1] /klɪp/ *vt* (**clipping, clipped**) to cut or trim with scissors or shears; to punch a small hole in, *esp* a ticket; (*words*) to shorten or slur; (*inf*) to hit sharply. • *n* the piece clipped off; a yield of wool from sheep; an extract from a film; (*inf*) a smart blow; speed.

clip[2] *vt* (**clipping, clipped**) to hold firmly; to secure with a clip. • *n* any device that grips, clasps or hooks; a magazine for a gun; a piece of jewellery held in place by a clip.

clipboard /ˈklɪpbord/ *n* a writing board with a spring clip for holding paper.

clip joint /-ˌdʒɔɪnt/ *n* (*sl*) a place, such as nightclub or restaurant, that overcharges or defrauds its customers.

clipper /ˈklɪpər/ *n* a fast sailing ship.

clippers /-s/ *n* a hand tool, sometimes electric, for cutting hair; nail clippers.

clipping /ˈklɪpɪŋ/ *n* an item cut from a publication, film, etc, a cutting.

clique /kliːk/ *n* a small exclusive group, a set.—**cliquey, cliquish** *adj*.

clitoridectomy /ˌklɪtərɪˈdɛktəmi/ *n* (*pl* **clitoridectomies**) the excision of the clitoris, performed for cultural reasons, and often referred to as female circumcision or female genital mutilation.

clitoris /ˈklɪtərɪs/ *n* a small sensitive erectile organ of the vulva.—**clitoral** *adj*.

cloaca /kloːˈeɪkə/ *n* (*pl* **cloacae**) a sewer; the cavity receiving the alimentary canal and urinary duct in birds, reptiles, many fishes, and the lower mammals.—**cloacal** *adj*.

cloak /kloːk/ *n* a loose sleeveless outer garment; a covering; something that conceals, a pretext. • *vt* to cover as with a cloak; to conceal.

cloak-and-dagger /ˈkloːkənˈdægər/ *adj* involving intrigue or espionage; undercover.

cloakroom /ˈkloːkruːm/ *n* a room where overcoats, luggage, etc, may be left.

clobber /ˈklɒbər/ *vt* (*sl*) to hit hard and repeatedly; to defeat; to criticize severely.

cloche /kloːʃ/ *or* /klɒʃ/ *n* a bell-shaped glass or plastic cover for food or outdoor plants; a woman's bell-shaped hat.

clock[1] /klɒk/ *n* a device for measuring time; any timing device with a dial and displayed figures; a dandelion head after flowering. • *vt* to time (a race, etc) using a stopwatch or other device; (*inf*) to register a certain speed; (*sl*) to hit; (*with* **off, out**) to stop work, *esp* by registering the time of one's departure on a card; (*with* **on, in**) to start work, *esp* by registering the time of one's arrival on a card.

clock[2] *n* a woven or embroidered ornament on a sock or stocking.

clockwise /'klɒkwaɪz/ *adv* moving in the direction of a clock's hands.—*also adj.*

clockwork /-wɜrk/ *n* the mechanism of a clock or any similar mechanism with springs and gears. • *adj* mechanically regular.

clod /klɒd/ *n* a lump of earth or clay; a stupid person.

cloddish /'klɒdɪʃ/ *adj* stupid; phlegmatic.

clodhopper /'klɒd,hɒpər/ *n* (*inf*) a clumsy person; (*usu pl*) a large heavy shoe.

clog /klɒg/ *n* a wooden-soled shoe. • *vt* (**clogging, clogged**) to cause a blockage in; to impede, obstruct.

cloggy /'klɒgi/ *adj* (**cloggier, cloggiest**) lumpy, clogging; adhesive, sticky.—**clogginess** *n*.

cloisonné /,klwɒzɒ'neɪ, *Fr.* /klwazɔ'neɪ/ *n* enamel decoration with the colours of the pattern set in spaces partitioned off by wires. • *adj* inlaid with partitions; decorated in outline with bands of metal.

cloister /'klɔɪstər/ *n* a roofed pillared walk, *usu* with one side open, in a convent, college, etc; a religious retreat. • *vt* to confine or keep apart as if in a convent.

cloistered /'klɔɪstərd/ *adj* solitary, secluded.

cloistral /'klɔɪstrəl/ *adj* pertaining to or confined in a cloister; secluded; claustral.

clone /kloʊn/ *n* a group of organisms or cells derived asexually from a single ancestor; an individual grown from a single cell of its parent and genetically identical to it; (*inf*) a person or thing that resembles another. • *vt* to propagate a clone from; to make a copy of.—**clonal** *adj*.

clonus /'kloʊnəs/ *n* (*pl* **clonuses**) (*med*) a series of convulsive spasms.—**clonic** *adj.*—**clonicity** *n.*

close[1] /kloʊz/ *adj* near; reticent, secret; nearly alike; nearly even or equal; dense, compact; cut short; sultry, airless; narrow; careful; restricted. • *adv* closely; near by. • *n* a courtyard; the entrance to a courtyard; the precincts of a cathedral.—**closely** *adv.*—**closeness** *n.*

close[2] *vt* to make closed; to stop up (an opening); to draw together; to conclude; to shut; (*with* **down**) to wind up, eg a business. • *vi* to come together; to complete; to finish. • *n* a completion, end.

close call *n* a close shave, a narrow escape.

close(d) corporation *n* a corporation in which vacancies are filled up by its members.

closed /kloʊzd/ *adj* shut up; with no opening; restricted; not open to question or debate; not open to the public, exclusive.

closed book *n* something too difficult to understand; something put aside for ever.

closed circuit *n* the transmission of TV signals by cable to receivers connected in a particular circuit.

closed shop *n* a firm employing only members of a trade union.

close-fisted /'kloʊz,fɪstɪd/ *adj* mean with money.

close-hauled /-,hɔld/ *adj* with sails trimmed to keep as near to the wind as possible.

close(d) season *n* certain months in the year in which it is illegal to kill certain game, protected wild birds, fish, etc.

close shave, close thing *n* a close call, a narrow escape.

closet /'klɒzət/ *n* a small room or a cupboard for clothes, supplies, etc; a small private room. • *vt* to enclose in a private room for a confidential talk.

close-up /'kloʊz,ʌp/ *n* a film or television shot taken from very close range; a close examination.

closure /'kloʊʒər/ *n* closing; the condition of being closed; something that closes; (*parliament, etc*) a decision to end further debate and move to an immediate vote.

clot /klɒt/ *n* a thickened mass, *esp* of blood; (*sl*) an idiot.• *vti* (**clotting, clotted**) to form into clots, to curdle, coagulate.

cloth /klɒθ/ *n* (*pl* **cloths**) woven, knitted or pressed fabric from which garments, etc are made; a piece of this; a tablecloth; clerical dress; (*with* **the**) the clergy.

cloth binding *n* a book binding of linen over cardboard.

clothe /kloʊð/ *vt* (**clothing, clothed** *or* **clad**) to cover with garments; to dress; to surround, endow (with).

clothes /kloʊz/ *or* /kloʊðz/ *npl* garments, apparel.

clotheshorse /-,hɔrs/ *n* a wooden or metal frame for drying linen, etc; a dressy person.

clothesline /-laɪn/ *n* a rope on which washing is hung to dry.

clothespin /-pɪn/ *n* a plastic, wooden or metal clip for attaching washing to a line.

clothier /'kloʊðiər/ *n* one who manufactures or sells cloth and clothes.

clothing /'kloʊðɪŋ/ *n* clothes.

cloud /klaʊd/ *n* a visible mass of water vapour floating in the sky; a mass of smoke, etc; a threatening thing, a gloomy look; a multitude; **on cloud nine** (*inf*) blissfully happy; **under a cloud** suspected of wrongdoing, disgraced. • *vt* to darken or obscure; to confuse; to depress.—**cloudless** *adj.*

cloudberry /'klaʊd,beri/ *n* a low-growing Eurasian plant of the raspberry family with amber-coloured fruit.

cloudburst /-bɜrst/ *n* a sudden rainstorm.

cloud chamber *n* (*physics*) a chamber filled with vapour used for detecting the tracks of high-energy particles.

cloud-cuckoo-land /klaʊd'kuku:,lænd/ *n* a realm of fantasy, imagination and impossible dreams.

cloudlet /'klaʊdlɪt/ *n* a small cloud.

cloudy /'klaʊdi/ *adj* (**cloudier, cloudiest**) of or full of clouds; not clear; gloomy.—**cloudily** *adv.*—**cloudiness** *n.*

clout /klaʊt/ *n* a blow; (*sl*) power, influence.

clove[1] /kloʊv/ *see* **cleave.**

clove[2] *n* a segment of a bulb, as garlic.

clove[3] *n* the dried flower bud of a tropical tree, used as a spice.

clove hitch *n* a knot used to secure a rope around a spar or pole.

cloven /'kloʊvən/ *adj* divided; split.—*see also* **cleave.**

cloven hoof *n* the split hoof of oxen, sheep, etc; the mark of the Devil; an evil influence.

clove pink *n* the carnation.

clover /'kloʊvər/ *n* a low-growing plant with three leaves used as fodder; a trefoil; **in clover** (*inf*) luxury.

cloverleaf /'kloʊvər,li:f/ *n* connecting roads built in the shape of a clover leaf.

clown /klaʊn/ *n* a person who entertains with jokes, antics, etc, *esp* in a circus; a clumsy or boorish person. • *vi* to act the clown, behave comically or clumsily.—**clownish** *adj.*

cloy /klɔɪ/ *vt* to sicken with too much sweetness or pleasure.—**cloyingly** *adv.*

club /klʌb/ *n* a heavy stick used as a weapon; a stick with a head for playing golf, etc; an association of people for athletic, social, or common purposes; its premises; a suit of playing cards with black clover-like markings. • *vb* (**clubbing, clubbed**) *vt* to beat with or use as a club. • *vi* to form into a club for a common purpose.

clubbable, clubable /'klʌbəbəl/ *adj* suitable for a club, sociable.

clubfoot /'klʌb,fʊt/ *n* a congenital malformation of the foot.

clubhaul /-,hɔl/ *vt* (*naut*) to tack by dropping the lee anchor as soon as the wind is out of the sails, bringing the ship's head to the wind.

clubhouse /-haʊs/ *n* premises used by a club.

club moss /-mɒs/ *n* the lycopodium.

club sandwich *n* a three-layered sandwich.

cluck /klʌk/ *n* the call of a hen. • *vi* to make such a noise.

clue /klu:/ *n* a guide to the solution of a mystery or problem. • *vt* (**cluing, clued**) (*with* **in, up**) to provide with helpful information.

clueless /'klu:ləs/ *adj* (*inf*) stupid, incompetent.

clumber /'klʌmbər/ *n* a breed of spaniel, a field spaniel.

clump /klʌmp/ *n* a cluster of trees; a cluster of bacteria; a lump; (*of hair*) a handful; the sound of heavy footsteps.

clumsy /'klʌmzi/ *adj* (**clumsier, clumsiest**) unwieldy; awkward; lacking tact, skill or grace.—**clumsily** *adv.*—**clumsiness** *n.*

clung /klʌŋ/ *see* **cling.**

clunk /klʌŋk/ *n* a dull metallic sound. • *vi* to make this sound.

clupeid /'klu:pi,ɪd/ *n* one of the genus of fishes to which the herring belongs.—*also adj.*

cluster /'klʌstər/ *n* a bunch, *esp* of things growing or tied together; a swarm; a group. • *vti* to form or arrange in a cluster.—**clustery** *adj.*

clutch[1] /klʌtʃ/ *vt* to seize, to grasp tightly; to snatch at. • *n* a tight grip; a device for throwing parts of a machine into or out of action; the pedal operating this device; (*pl*) power.

clutch[2] *n* a nest of eggs; a brood of chicks.

clutter /ˈklʌtər/ n a disordered mess; confusion. • vti to litter; to put into disorder.

Clydesdale /ˈklaɪdzdeɪl/ n a heavy breed of carthorse.

clypeal, clypeate /ˈklɪpiˌeɪt/ adj shield-shaped.

clypeus /ˈklɪpiəs/ n (pl **clypei**) a shield-like part of an insect's head.

clyster /ˈklɪstər/ n a liquid injected into the lower intestines by a syringe, an enema.

Cm (chem symbol) curium.

cm abbr = centimetre.

CNN /ˈsiːˌɛnɛn/ abbr = Cable News Network.

CO abbr = Colorado; Commanding Officer.

Co (chem symbol) = cobalt.

Co. abbr = Company; County.

co- /koʊ/ prefix together with, jointly.

c/o abbr = care of.

coach /koʊtʃ/ n a long-distance bus; a railway carriage; a large, covered four-wheeled horse-drawn carriage; a sports instructor; a tutor in a specialized subject. • vti to teach or train.

coach dog n a Dalmatian dog.

coachman /ˈkoʊtʃmən/ n (pl **coachmen**) the driver of a horse carriage.

coaction /koʊˈækʃən/ or /ˈkoʊˌækʃən/ n compulsion; an acting together.—**coactive** adj.—**coactivity** n.

coadjutor /koʊˈædjʊtər/ n a helper; an assistant to a bishop.—**coadjutrix** nf.

coadunate /-nɪt/ or /-ˌneɪt/ adj (bot) united, growing together.—**coadunation** n.—**coadunative** adj.

coagulant /koʊˈægjʊlənt/ n a substance that causes coagulation.

coagulate /-ˌleɪt/ vti to change from a liquid to partially solid state, to clot, curdle.—**coagulation** n.—**coagulative** adj.—**coagulator** n.

coagulum /-ləm/ n (pl **coagula**) a clot (of blood); a curdled mass.

coal /koʊl/ n a black mineral used for fuel; a piece of this; an ember.

coalesce /ˌkoʊəˈles/ vi to come together and form one, to merge.—**coalescence** n.—**coalescent** adj.

coalfield /ˈkoʊlfiːld/ n a region yielding coal.

coalfish /-fɪʃ/ n (pl **coalfish, coalfishes**) the pollack.

coal gas n gas obtained from coal and formerly used for lighting and heating.

coalition /ˌkoʊəˈlɪʃən/ n a temporary union of parties or states.—**coalitional** adj.—**coalitionist, coalitioner** n.

Coal Measure n that part of the Carboniferous series in which coal is found.

coal oil /ˈkoʊlˌɔɪl/ n petroleum; kerosene.

coal tar /-ˌtɑr/ n a thick opaque liquid distilled from bituminous coal and from which many rich dye colours are obtained.

coaming /ˈkoʊmɪŋ/ n the raised wood or iron border round the outside of a ship's hatch.

coaptation /ˌkoʊæpˈteɪʃən/ n the adjustment or adaptation of parts to one another.

coarse /kɔrs/ adj rough; large in texture, rude, crude; inferior.—**coarsely** adv.—**coarseness** n.

coarse-grained /ˈkɔrsˌɡreɪnd/ adj having a coarse grain; ill-tempered; gross.

coarsen /ˈkɔrsən/ vti to make or become coarse.

coast /koʊst/ n an area of land bordering the sea; the seashore. • vi to sail along a coast; to travel down a slope without power; to proceed with ease.—**coastal** adj.

coaster /ˈkoʊstər/ n a ship engaged in coastal trade; a tray for a decanter; a small mat for drinks; a roller coaster.

coastguard n an organization which monitors the coastline and provides help for ships in difficulties, prevents smuggling, etc.

coastline /ˈkoʊstlaɪn/ n the outline of the shore.

coat /koʊt/ n a sleeved outer garment; the natural covering of an animal; a layer. • vt to cover with a layer or coating.

coat hanger n a piece of wood, wire or plastic curved to fit the shoulders for hanging a garment from a hook.

coati /koʊˈɒti/, **coatimundi** /ˌkoʊtəˈmʌndi/ n a raccoon-like South American animal.

coating /ˈkoʊtɪŋ/ n a surface coat or layer; material for coats.

coat of arms n the heraldic bearings of a family, city, institution, etc.

coat of mail n chain mail.

coax /koʊks/ vt to persuade gently; to obtain by coaxing; to make something work by patient effort.—**coaxer** n.—**coaxingly** adv.

coaxial /koʊˈæksiəl/ adj having a common axis.

coaxial cable n a transmission cable having a double conductor separated by insulating material, as for a television.

cob¹ /kɒb/ n a sturdy riding horse; a corn cob; a round lump of coal; a male swan.

cob² n a composition of clay and straw used for building.

cobalt /ˈkoʊbɒlt/ n a metallic element; a deep blue pigment made from it.

cobalt-60 n a radioisotope used in radiotherapy.

cobalt-blue n a greenish-blue pigment derived from cobalt.

cobalt bomb n a radioisotope (cobalt-60) used in radiotherapy; a nuclear weapon made from a hydrogen bomb encased in cobalt.

cobber /ˈkɒbər/ n (Austral) (sl) a chum, a pal.

cobble¹ /ˈkɒbəl/ n a cobblestone, a rounded stone used for paving. • vt to pave with cobblestones.

cobble² vt to repair, to make (shoes); to put together roughly or hastily.

cobbler¹ /ˈkɒblər/ n a person who mends shoes; a clumsy workman.

cobbler² n an iced drink of wine or spirits, fruit and sugar; fruit covered with a rich crust as a pudding.

cobelligerent /ˌkoʊbəˈlɪdʒərənt/ n a power cooperating with another in carrying on a war.

cobnut /ˈkoʊbnʌt/ n a large hazelnut.

Cobol /ˈkoʊbɒl/ n (comput) a high-level programming language for general business use (Common Business Orientated Language).

cobra /ˈkoʊbrə/ n a venomous hooded snake of Africa and India.

cobweb /ˈkɒbwɛb/ n a spider's web; a flimsy thing; an entanglement.—**cobwebbed** adj.—**cobwebby** adj.

coca /ˈkoʊkə/ n either of two South American shrubs; their leaves, chewed as a stimulant.

Coca-Cola n (trademark) a brown-coloured carbonated soft drink flavoured with coca leaves, etc.

cocaine, cocain /koʊˈkeɪn/ n an intoxicating addictive drug obtained from coca leaves, used in anaesthesia.

cocainism /koʊˈkeɪˌnɪzəm/ n a morbid state resulting from excess of cocaine.

cocainize /koʊˈkeɪnˌaɪz/ vt to subject to, or render insensible by, cocaine; to treat with cocaine.—**cocainization** n.

cocci /ˈkɒki/ see **coccus.**

coccus /ˈkɒkəs/ n (pl **cocci**) a spherical bacterium; one of the separable carpels of a dry fruit.—**coccal, coccoid** adj.

coccyx /ˈkɒksɪks/ n (pl **coccyges**) a small triangular bone at the base of the spine.—**coccygeal** adj.

cochineal /ˈkoʊtʃəˌniːl/ or /-ˈniːl/ n a scarlet dye obtained from dried insects.

cochlea /ˈkɒkliə/ n (pl **cochleae**) the spiral-shaped cavity of the inner ear.

cochleate /liˌeɪt/ or /-ɪt/, **cochleated** /-əd/ adj shell-shaped, screw-like.

cock¹ /kɒk/ n the adult male of the domestic fowl; the male of other birds; a tap or valve; the hammer of a gun; a cocked position. • vt to set erect, to stick up; to set at an angle; to bring the hammer (of a gun) to firing position; (with **up**) to make a complete mess of.—**cockup** n.

cock² n a small pile of hay.

cockade /kɒˈkeɪd/ n a rosette worn on the hat as a badge.

cock-a-hoop /ˌkɒkəˈhuːp/ adj elated, exultant.

Cockaigne /kɒkˈeɪn/ n an imaginary land of plenty.—also **Cockayne.**

cock-a-leekie /ˌkɒkəˈliːki/ n soup made of chicken boiled with leeks, etc.

cockalorum /ˌkɒkəˈlɔrəm/ n a young cock; a perky or self-important person.

cock-and-bull story /ˈkɒkənˈbʊl/ n an incredible story.

cockatoo /ˌkɒkəˈtuː/ n (pl **cockatoos**) a large crested parrot.

cockatrice /ˈkɒkətrɪs/ or /-ˌtrɪs/ n a fabulous serpent possessing the power of killing by a glance of its eye, a basilisk.

Cockayne see **Cockaigne.**

cockchafer /ˈkɒkˌtʃeɪfər/ n a large winged beetle.

cockcrow /ˈkɒkˌkroʊ/ n the time of dawn, early morning.

cocked hat n a hat with turned-up brims pointed in front and behind; **to knock into a cocked hat** to beat easily.

cockerel /ˈkɒkərəl/ n a young cock, rooster.

cocker spaniel /ˈkɒkər/ n a small breed of spaniel.

cockeyed /ˈkɒkaɪd/ adj (inf) having a squint; slanting; daft, absurd.

cockfight /ˈkɒkˌfaɪt/ n an organized fight between gamecocks.

cockhorse /ˈkɒkˌhɔrs/ n a rocking horse.

cockle¹ /ˈkɒkəl/ n an edible shellfish with a rounded shell.

cockle² *vti* to curl up, to pucker. • *n* a wrinkle, a bulge.

cockle³ *n* a purple-flowered weed, the plant corncockle or darnel.

cockleshell /ˈkɒkəlʃel/ *n* the shell of a cockle; a frail boat.

cockloft /ˈkɒkˌlɒft/ *n* a small upper loft; a garret.

cockney /ˈkɒkni/ *n* (*pl* **cockneys**) a person born in the East End of London; the dialect of this area.

cockpit /ˈkɒkpit/ *n* the compartment of a small aircraft for the pilot and crew, the flight deck; an arena for cock fighting; the driver's seat in a racing car.

cockroach /ˈkɒkrəʊtʃ/ *n* a nocturnal beetle-like insect.

cockscomb /ˈkɒkskəʊm/ *n* a cock's crest; a jester's cap resembling a cock's comb; a decorative plant with red or yellow flowers; a vain young fop.—*also* **coxcomb**.

cockshy /ˈkɒkʃaɪ/ *n* (*pl* **cockshies**) a thing set up to be thrown at; a throw at a cockshy.

cocksure /ˈkɒkʃʊər/ or /-ˈʃər/ *adj* quite certain; over-confident.

cocktail /ˈkɒkteɪl/ *n* an alcoholic drink containing a mixture of spirits or other liqueurs; an appetizer, *usu* containing shellfish, served as the first course of a meal.

cocky /ˈkɒki/ *adj* (**cockier, cockiest**) cheeky; conceited; arrogant.—**cockily** *adv*.—**cockiness** *n*.

coco /ˈkəʊkəʊ/ *n* (*pl* **cocos**) the coconut palm.

cocoa /ˈkəʊkəʊ/ *n* a powder of ground cacao seeds; a drink made from this.

cocoa bean *n* the seed of the cacao plant.

cocoa butter *n* a waxy substance derived from cocoa beans and used in perfumery, confectionery, etc.

coconut /ˈkəʊkəˌnʌt/ *n* the fruit of the coconut palm.

coconut matting *n* rough matting made from the fibrous outer husks of coconuts.

coconut palm *n* a tall palm tree that is grown widely in the tropics for its fruit, the coconut.

coconut shy *n* a fairground stall where coconuts are set up as targets.

cocoon /kəˈkuːn/ *n* a silky case spun by some insect larvae for protection in the chrysalis stage; a cosy covering. • *vt* to wrap in or as in a cocoon; to protect oneself by cutting oneself off from one's surroundings.

cocotte¹ /kəˈkɒt/ *n* a small fireproof dish for cooking and individual serving of food.

cocotte² *n* a promiscuous woman.

COD *abbr* = cash on delivery; collect on delivery.

cod /kɒd/ *n* (*pl* **cod, cods**) a large edible fish of the North Atlantic.

coda /ˈkəʊdə/ *n* (*mus*) a passage at the end of a composition or section to give a greater sense of finality; a supplementary section at the end of a novel.

coddle /ˈkɒdəl/ *vt* to treat as an invalid, to pamper; to cook (eggs) in lightly boiling water.—**coddler** *n*.

code /kəʊd/ *n* a system of letters, numbers or symbols used to transmit secret messages, or to simplify communication; a systematic body of laws; a set of rules or conventions; (*comput*) a set of program instructions. • *vt* to put into code.

codeine /ˈkəʊdiːn/ *n* an analgesic substance.

codeword, codename *n* a word used in planning and when referring to a secret operation.

codex /ˈkəʊdeks/ *n* (*pl* **codices**) a volume of ancient manuscripts of an ancient text.

codger /ˈkɒdʒər/ *n* (*sl*) a buffer, an old man.

codicil /ˈkəʊdəsɪl/ or /ˈkɒd-/ *n* an addition to a will modifying, adjusting, or supplementing its contents.—**codicillary** *adj*.

codify /ˈkəʊdəˌfaɪ/ or /ˈkɒd-/ *vt* (**codifying, codified**) to collect or arrange (laws, rules, regulations, etc) into a system.—**codifier** *n*.—**codification** *n*.

codlin /ˈkɒdlɪn/ *n* a kind of stewing apple.

codling *n* a young cod.

cod-liver oil /ˈkɒdˌlɪvər/ *n* oil derived from the livers of cod and related fish which is rich in vitamins A and D.

codpiece /ˈkɒdpiːs/ *n* a baggy appendage once worn in front of men's breeches.

codswallop /ˈkɒdzˌwɒləp/ *n* (*sl*) nonsense.

co-ed /ˈkəʊed/ or /kəʊˈed/ *adj* (*inf*) coeducational. • *n* (*inf*) a girl attending a coeducational school or college.

coeducation /ˌkəʊedʒʊˈkeɪʃən/ *n* the teaching of students of both sexes in the same institution.—**coeducational** *adj*.—**coeducationally** *adv*.

coefficient /ˌkəʊɪˈfɪʃənt/ *n* (*math*) a numerical or constant factor in an algebraic term.

coelacanth /ˈsiːləˌkænθ/ *n* a type of primitive fish that is extinct except for one species.

coelenterate /siːˈlentəˌreɪt/ *n* any of a group of aquatic creatures with a bulbous or tube-shaped body and a mouth surrounded by tentacles, such as sea anemones, jellyfish and corals.—*also adj*.

coeliac /ˈsiːliˌæk/ *adj* of or pertaining to the abdomen. • *n* a person with celiac disease.—*also* **celiac**.

coeliac disease *n* a chronic digestive disease of young children, causing malnutrition and diarrhoea.

coenobite /ˈsenəˌbaɪt/ or /ˈsiːnə-/ *n* one of a religious order living in a convent or in community.—*also* **cenobite**.

coequal /kəʊˈiːkwəl/ *adj* having complete equality.—**coequality** *n*.—**coequally** *adv*.

coerce /kəʊˈɜːs/ *vt* to compel; to force by threats.—**coercible** *adj*.—**coercion** *n*.

coercion /kəʊˈɜːʃən/ *n* the act of coercing; forcible compulsion; government by force.—**coercionary** *adj*.—**coercionist** *n*.

coercive /kəʊˈɜːsɪv/ *adj* having the power to force; compelling.—**coerciveness** *n*.

coessential /ˌkəʊɪˈsenʃəl/ *adj* of the same substance.—**coessentiality, coessentialness** *n*.

coeternal /ˌkəʊɪˈtɜːnəl/ *adj* equally eternal.—**coeternally** *adv*.

coeval /kəʊˈiːvəl/ *adj* contemporaneous. • *n* a person of the same age, a contemporary.—**coevality** *n*.—**coevally** *adv*.

coexist /ˌkəʊɪɡˈzɪst/ *vi* to exist together at the same time; to live in peace together.—**coexistence** *n*.—**coexistent** *adj*.

coextensive /ˌkəʊɪkˈstensɪv/ *adj* extending over the same space or time; equally extensive.

C of E *abbr* = Church of England.

coffee /ˈkɒfi/ *n* a drink made from the seeds of the coffee tree; the seeds, or the shrub; a light-brown colour.

coffee bean *n* the seed of the coffee plant.

coffee house /-ˌhaʊs/, **coffee bar** /-ˌbɑːr/, **coffee shop** /-ˌʃɒp/ *n* a refreshment house where coffee is served.

coffee mill /-ˌmɪl/ *n* a machine for grinding coffee beans.

coffeepot /-ˌpɒt/ *n* a pot for making coffee in.

coffee table /-ˌteɪbəl/ *n* a low table for holding drinks, books, etc.

coffee table book *n* a large book for display, not reading.

coffer /ˈkɒfər/ *n* a strong chest for holding money or valuables.

cofferdam /ˈkɒfərˌdæm/ *n* a watertight structure enclosing a submerged area which can be pumped dry to allow construction or essential repair work.

coffin /ˈkɒfɪn/ *n* a box for a dead body to be buried or cremated in.

coffin bone *n* a bone inside a horse's hoof.

coffle /ˈkɒfəl/ *n* a gang of slaves, animals, etc chained together.

cog¹ /kɒɡ/ *n* a tooth-like projection on the rim of a wheel.

cog² *vti* (**cogging, cogged**) to load dice in order to cheat. • *n* a trick.

cogent /ˈkəʊdʒənt/ *adj* persuasive, convincing.—**cogently** *adv*.—**cogency** *n*.

cogitate /ˈkɒdʒəˌteɪt/ *vi* to think deeply, to ponder.—**cogitation** *n*.—**cogitator** *n*.

cognac /ˈkɒnjæk/ *n* a superior grape brandy distilled in France.

cognate /ˈkɒɡneɪt/ *adj* having a common source or origin; kindred, related.—**cognation** *n*.

cognition /kɒɡˈnɪʃən/ *n* the mental act of perceiving; knowledge.—**cognitive** *adj*.

cognizable /ˈkɒɡnɪzəbəl/ or /ˌkɒɡˈnaɪzəbəl/, /ˈkɒn-/ *adj* knowable; (*law*) within the cognizance of a court.

cognizance /ˈkɒɡnɪzəns/ or /ˈkɒn-/ *n* judicial knowledge or notice; extent of knowledge; awareness, perception; (*her*) a distinctive crest or badge.

cognizant /ˈkɒɡnɪzənt/ or /ˈkɒn-/ *adj* aware, informed (of).

cognize /ˈkɒɡnaɪz/ or /kɒɡˈnaɪz/ *vt* to have cognition of.

cognomen /kɒɡˈnəʊmen/ *n* (*pl* **cognomens, cognomina**) a surname; a nickname.

cognoscente /ˌkɒɡnəˈʃenti/ or /-ˈsenti/ *n* (*pl* **cognoscenti**) (*usu pl*) a connoisseur.

cogwheel /ˈkɒɡwiːl/ *n* a wheel with a toothed rim for gearing.

cohabit /kəʊˈhæbɪt/ *vi* to live together as husband or wife.—**cohabitant, cohabiter** *n*.—**cohabitation** *n*.

cohere /kəʊˈhɪr/ *vi* to stick together; to remain united; to be consistent.

coherent /kəʊˈhɪrənt/ *adj* cohering; capable of intelligible speech; consistent.—**coherently** *adv*.—**coherence** *n*.

cohesion /kəʊˈhiːʒən/ *n* the act of cohering or sticking together; the force that causes this; interdependence.—**cohesive** *adj*.

cohort /'kɔːhɔrt/ *n* a tenth part of a Roman legion; any group of persons banded together; a follower, a comrade.

coif /kɔɪf/ *n* a close-fitting cap.

coiffeur /kwɒ'fər/ *n* a hairdresser.—**coiffeuse** *nf*.

coiffure /kwɒ'fjʊr/ *n* a hairstyle.

coil[1] /kɔɪl/ *vti* to wind in rings or folds; to twist into a circular or spiral shape. • *n* a coiled length of rope; a single ring of this; (*elect*) a spiral wire for the passage of current; an intrauterine contraceptive device.—**coiler** *n*.

coil[2] *n* (*arch*) tumult, disturbance.

coin /kɔɪn/ *n* a piece of legally stamped metal used as money. • *vt* to invent (a word, phrase); to make into money, to mint; to make a lot of money quickly.

coinage /'kɔɪnɪdʒ/ *n* the act of coining; the issue of coins, currency; a coined word.

coincide /ˌkoʊɪn'saɪd/ *vi* to occupy the same portion of space; to happen at the same time; to agree exactly, to correspond.

coincidence /koʊ'ɪnsɪdəns/ *n* the act of coinciding; the occurrence of an event at the same time as another without apparent connection.

coincident /-dənt/ *adj* coinciding.

coincidental /koʊˌɪnsɪ'dentəl/ *adj* happening by coincidence.—**coincidentally** *adv*.

coin-op /'kɔɪnɒp/ *n* a self-service launderette, etc where the machines are operated by coins.

Cointreau /'kwɒntroʊ/ (*trademark*) *n* a clear liqueur with orange flavouring.

coir /kɔɪər/ *n* the prepared fibre of the husks of coconuts.

coitus /'kɔɪtəs/ or /'koʊɪt-/, **coition** /'kɔɪʃən/ *n* sexual intercourse.—**coital** *adj*.

coitus interruptus /'kɔɪtəsˌɪntə'rʌptəs/ *n* the interruption of coitus by withdrawal of the penis before ejaculation.

Coke /koʊk/ *n* (*trademark*) short for Coca-Cola.

coke[1] /koʊk/ *n* coal from which gas has been expelled. • *vt* to convert (coal) into coke.

coke[2] *n* (*sl*) cocaine.

col /kɒl/ *n* a pass between mountain peaks; an atmospheric depression between two anticyclones.

col- *prefix* the form of *com-* before *l*.

Col. *abbr* = Colonel.

cola[1] /'koʊlə/ *see* **colon**[1].

cola[2] *n* a carbonated drink flavoured with extracts from the kola nut and coca leaves.—*also* **kola**.

colander /'kɒləndər/ or /'kʌl-/ *n* a bowl with holes in the bottom for straining cooked vegetables, pasta, etc.

cola nut *see* **kola nut**.

colcannon /kɒl'kænən/ *n* an Irish dish of boiled cabbage and potatoes mashed together and seasoned with salt, pepper, etc.

colchicum /'kɒltʃɪkəm/ or /'kɒlkɪ-/ *n* meadow saffron; a narcotic made from its seeds.

colcothar /'kɒlkɔːθər/ *n* red peroxide of iron used as a pigment.

cold /koʊld/ *adj* lacking heat or warmth; lacking emotion, passion or courage; unfriendly; dead; (*scent*) faint; (*sl*) unconscious. • *adv* (*inf*) without prior knowledge or preparation; completely. • *n* absence of heat; the sensation caused by this; cold weather; a virus infection of the respiratory tract.—**coldish** *adj*.—**coldly** *adv*.—**coldness** *n*.

cold-blooded /'koʊldˌblʌdɪd/ *adj* having a body temperature that varies with the surrounding air or water, as reptiles and fish; without feeling; callous; ruthless; in cold blood.—**cold-bloodedness** *n*.

cold chisel *n* a tempered chisel for cutting cold iron.

cold cream *n* a creamy preparation for cleansing and softening the skin.

cold feet *n* (*inf*) fear.

cold frame *n* an unheated plant frame with a glass top for protecting seedlings, etc.

cold front *n* the forward edge of a cold air mass approaching a warmer mass.

cold-shoulder *vt* (*inf*) to treat with indifference or hostility.—**cold shoulder** *n*.

cold sore *n* one or more blisters appearing near the mouth, caused by the virus herpes simplex.

cold storage *n* storage in refrigerated areas; (*with* **in**) (*inf*) abeyance, being set aside for future use.

cold sweat *n* a cooling and moistening of the skin usually associated with fear or shock.

cold turkey *n* (*sl*) sudden withdrawal of narcotic drugs from an addict as a cure; the symptoms (*eg* nausea, vomiting, cramps) resulting from this withdrawal.

cold war *n* enmity between two nations characterized by military tension and political hostility.

cole /koʊl/ *n* cabbage plants in general.

coleopteran /ˌkɒli'ɒptəˌrɑn/ or /ˌkɒli-/ *n* (*pl* **coleopterans**, **coleoptera**) any of the beetles, an order of insects having the outer pair of wings formed into hard sheathes for the inner pair.—**coleopterous** *adj*.

coleslaw /'koʊlˌslɔ/ *n* raw shredded cabbage, carrots, onions in a dressing, used as a salad.

coleus /'koʊliəs/ *n* (*pl* **coleuses**) a plant cultivated for its variegated foliage.

colic /'kɒlɪk/ *n* acute spasmodic pain in the abdomen.—**colicky** *adj*.

coliseum /ˌkɒlə'siːəm/ *n* a large building, such as a stadium, used for sports events and other public entertainments; (*with cap*) the Colosseum.

colitis /kə'laɪtɪs/ *n* inflammation of the colon.—**colitic** *adj*.

collaborate /kə'læbəˌreɪt/ *vi* to work jointly or together, *esp* on a literary project; to side with the invaders of one's country.—**collaboration** *n*.—**collaborator** *n*.—**collaborative** *adj*.

collage /kə'lɒʒ/ *n* art made up from scraps of paper, material and other odds and ends pasted onto a hard surface.

collagen /'kɒlədʒən/ *n* a protein present in connective tissue and bones which yields gelatin when boiled.

collapse /kə'læps/ *vi* to fall down; to come to ruin, to fail; to break down physically or mentally. • *n* the act of collapsing; a breakdown, prostration.

collapsible, collapsable /-ɪbəl/ *adj* designed to fold compactly.—**collapsibility** *n*.

collar /'kɒlər/ *n* the band of a garment round the neck; a decoration round the neck, a choker; a band of leather or chain put round an animal's neck. • *vt* to put a collar on; (*inf*) to seize; to arrest.

collarbone /-ˌboːn/ *n* one of the two bones that connect the shoulder blades with the breast bone, the clavicle.

collate /'kɒleɪt/ or /'kɒ-/, /kə'leɪt/ *vt* to examine and compare (manuscripts, etc); to put (pages) together in sequence; (*bishop*) to appoint to a benefice.—**collation** *n*.—**collator** *n*.

collateral /kə'lætərəl/ *n* security pledged for the repayment of a loan. • *adj* side by side; accompanying but secondary; descended from the same ancestor but not directly.—**collaterally** *adv*.

collation /kɒ'leɪʃən/ or /'kɒ-/, /kə-/ *n* the act of collating, a comparison; a light meal; the presentation to a benefice by a bishop, who is the patron.

colleague /'kɒliːg/ *n* an associate in the same profession or office; a fellow worker.

collect[1] /kə'lekt/ *vti* to bring together, gather or assemble; to regain command of (oneself); to concentrate (thoughts, etc); to ask for or receive money or payment. • *adj* (*telephone call*) paid for by the person called.

collect[2] /'kɒlekt/ *n* a short comprehensive prayer for a particular occasion.

collectible, collectable /kə'lektəbəl/ *adj* (*antiques, etc*) of interest to a collector. • *n* an object worth collecting.

collectanea *npl* passages selected from various authors; a miscellany.

collected /kə'lektəd/ *adj* self-possessed, cool.—**collectedly** *adv*.

collection /kə'lekʃən/ *n* act of collecting; an accumulation; money collected at a meeting, etc; a group of things collected for beauty, interest, rarity or value; the periodic showing of a designer's fashions; a regular gathering of post from a postbox.

collective /kə'lektɪv/ *adj* viewed as a whole, taken as one; combined, common; (*gram*) used in the singular to express a multitude. • *n* a collective enterprise, as a farm.—**collectively** *adv*.

collective bargaining *n* negotiations on working conditions between representatives of employees and management.

collective farm *n* a farm or number of smallholdings run on a cooperative basis, usually under state supervision.

collective noun *n* a singular noun covering a number of person or things (*eg family, flock*).

collectivism /kə'lektəˌvɪzəm/ *n* the political or economic theory of collective ownership of the means of production and distribution by the state or people.—**collectivist** *n*.—**collectivistic** *adj*.

collectivize /kə'lɛktə,vaɪz/ *vt* to bring into public ownership in accordance with the principle of collectivism.—**collectivization** *n*.

collector /kə'lɛktər/ *n* a person who collects things, eg stamps, butterflies, as a hobby or so as to inspect them, as tickets.

colleen /kɒ'li:n/ *n* (*Irish*) a girl.

college /'kɒlɪdʒ/ *n* an institution of higher learning; a school offering specialized knowledge; the buildings housing a college; an organized body of professionals.

collegian /kə'li:dʒən/ *n* a student or recent graduate of a college.

collegiate /kə'li:dʒi:ɪt/, **collegial** *adj* of or belonging to a college; containing, connected with or having the status of a college.

collet /'kɒlɪt/ *n* the part of a ring in which the stone is set.

collide /kə'laɪd/ *vi* to come into violent contact (with); to dash together; to conflict; to disagree.

collie /'kɒli/ or /'kɔ:li/ *n* a breed of dog with a pointed muzzle and long hair, used as a sheepdog.

colligate /'kɒlə,geɪt/ *vt* to bind together; to bring (isolated facts) under a general principle.—**colligation** *n*.—**colligative** *adj*.

collimate /'kɒlə,meɪt/ *vt* to bring into the same line; to make parallel.—**collimation** *n*.

collinear /kə'lɪniər/ or /kɔ:-/ *adj* in the same straight line.—**collinearity** *n*.

collision /kə'lɪʒən/ *n* state of colliding together; a violent impact of moving bodies, a crash; a clash of interests, etc.

collision course *n* one that, if continued on, will end in disaster.

collocate /'kɒlə,keɪt/ *vt* to place together; to arrange.

collocation /,kɒlə'keɪʃən/ *n* a placing in a particular order; an arrangement, relative situation.

collodion /kə'lo:dɪən/ *n* a preparation of soluble pyroxylin with ether, used in photography.

colloid /'kɒlɔɪd/ *adj* like glue or jelly; (*chem*) of a gummy noncrystalline kind. • *n* a viscid inorganic transparent substance.—**colloidal** *adj*.—**colloidality** *n*.

collop /'kɒləp/ *n* a slice of meat.

colloquial /kə'lo:kwiəl/ *adj* used in familiar but not formal talk, not literary.—**colloquially** *adv*.

colloquialism /-,lɪzəm/ *n* a colloquial word or phrase.

colloquium /kə'lo:kwiəm/ *n* (*pl* **colloquiums, colloquia**) a conference, seminar.

colloquy /'kɒləkwi/ *n* (*pl* **colloquies**) a conversation; a written dialogue.

collotype /'kɒlə,taɪp/ *n* a gelatine photographic plate used for printing from in ink.—**collotypic** *adj*.

collude /kə'lu:d/ *vi* to act together; to conspire, *esp* to defraud.

collusion /kə'lu:ʒən/ *n* the act of colluding; an agreement to commit fraud or deception.—**collusive** *adj*.

collyrium /kə'lɪriəm/ *n* (*pl* **collyria, collyriums**) an eye salve.

collywobbles /'kɒli,wɒbəlz/ *npl* (*sl*) abdominal pain or discomfort; nervousness.

colobus /'kɒləbəs/ *n* any of a genus of long-tailed African monkeys with shortened or absent thumbs.

colocynth /'kɒləsɪnθ/ *n* a kind of cucumber; the pulp it yields dried and powdered and used as a purgative.

cologne /kə'lo:n/ *n* eau-de-Cologne, a scented liquid.

colon[1] /'ko:lən/ *n* (*pl* **colons, cola**) the part of the large intestine from the caecum to the rectum.—**colonic** *adj*.

colon[2] *n* (*pl* **colons**) a punctuation mark (:) between the semicolon and the full stop, *usu* written before an explanation or a list.

colonel /'kɜ:nəl/ *n* a commissioned officer junior to a brigadier but senior to a lieutenant colonel.—**colonelcy, colonelship** *n*.

colonial /kə'lo:niəl/ *adj* of or pertaining to a colony or colonies; (*with cap*) pertaining to the thirteen British colonies that became the US. • *n* a person who takes part in founding a colony, a settler.—**colonially** *adv*.

colonialism /-,lɪzəm/ *n* the policy of acquiring and governing colonies.—**colonialist** *adj, n*.

colonist /'kɒlənɪst/ *n* a person who settles in a colony.

colonize /-,naɪz/ *vt* to establish a colony in; to settle in a colony.—**colonization** *n*.—**colonizer** *n*.

colonnade /-'neɪd/ *n* a range of columns placed at regular intervals; a similar row, as of trees.

colony /'kɒləni/ *n* (*pl* **colonies**) an area of land acquired and settled by a distant state and subject to its control; a community of settlers; a group of people of the same nationality or interests living in a particular area; a collection of organisms in close association.

colophon /'kɒlə,fɒn/ or /-fən/ *n* a publisher's imprint or decorative device on a book; (*formerly*) an inscription at the end of a book giving the printer's or writer's name.

color /'kʌlər/ *see* **colour**.

colorable /'kʌlərəbəl/ *see* **colourable**.

colored /'kʌlərd/ *see* **coloured**.

colorfast /'kʌlər,fæst/ *see* **colourfast**.

colorful /-,fʊl/ *see* **colourful**.

coloring /-ɪŋ/ *see* **colouring**.

colorist /-ɪst/ *see* **colourist**.

colorize /-,aɪz/ *see* **colourize**.

colorless /-ləs/ *see* **colourless**.

Colorado beetle /,kɒlə'rædo:/ or /,kælə'rædo:/ *n* a yellowish beetle with ten longitudinal black stripes on its back, destructive to potatoes.

colorant /'kʌlərənt/ *n* a colouring matter.

coloration /,kʌlə'reɪʃən/ *n* colouring.

coloratura, colorature /,kʌlərə'tʊrə/ or /-'tjʊrə/, /kɒl-/ *adj* (*mus*) highly ornamented or florid. • *n* a vocal passage sung in this way.

colorific /,kʌlə'rɪfɪk/ *adj* producing colour.

colorimeter /,kʌlə'rɪmətər/ *n* an instrument for measuring the intensity of colour, strength of dyes, etc.—**colorimetric, colorimetrical** *adj*.—**colorimetry** *n*.

Colosseum /,kɒlə'si:əm/ *n* a large amphitheatre in Rome built in the 1st century.

colossal /kə'lɒsəl/ *adj* gigantic, immense; (*inf*) amazing, wonderful.—**colossally** *adv*.

colossus /kə'lɒsəs/ *n* (*pl* **colossi, colossuses**) a gigantic statue; something immense.

colostomy /kə'lɒstəmi/ *n* (*pl* **colostomies**) a surgical opening into the bowl forming an artificial anus.

colostrum /kə'lɒstrəm/ *n* the first milk secreted after parturition; biestings.—**colostral** *adj*.

colotomy /kə'lɒtəmi/ *n* (*pl* **colotomies**) an incision in the colon.

colour /'kʌlər/ *n* the eye's perception of wavelengths of light with different colours corresponding to different wavelengths; the attribute of objects to appear different according to their differing ability to absorb, emit, or reflect light of different wavelengths; colour of the face or skin; pigment; dye; paint; (*literature*) use of imagery, vividness; (*mus*) depth of sound; (*pl*) a flag; a symbol of a club, team, etc. • *vt* to give colour to, paint; to misrepresent; to influence. • *vi* to emit colour; (*face*) to redden in anger or embarrassment; to blush; to change colour, to ripen.—*also* **color**.

colourable /'kʌlərəbəl/ *adj* capable of being coloured; specious, plausible.—*also* **colorable**.

colour bar *n* discrimination based on race, *esp* by White races against other races.

colour-blind *adj* unable to distinguish colours, *esp* red and green.—**colour blindness** *n*.

colour code *n* a system of identifying by colours, eg of electrical wires.

coloured /'kʌlərd/ *adj* possessing colour; biased, not objective; of a darker skinned race. • *n* a person of a darker skinned race.—*also* **colored**.

colourfast /'kʌlər,fæst/ *adj* of a material made with non-running or non-fading colours after washing.—*also* **colorfast**.

colour filter *n* (*photog*) a thin plate or layer for adjusting depth and brightness of required colours.

colourful /-,fʊl/ *adj* full of colour; vivid.—*also* **colorful**.—**colourfully** *adv*.

colouring /-ɪŋ/ *n* appearance in term of colour; disposition or use of colour; a substance for giving colour.—*also* **coloring**.

colourist /-ɪst/ *n* an artist whose works are characterized by beauty of colour.—*also* **colorist**.—**colouristic** *adj*.

colourize /-,aɪz/ *vt* to add colour to a black-and-white film using a special device.—*also* **colorize**.

colourless *adj* lacking colour; dull, uninteresting, characterless.—*also* **colorless**.—**colourlessly** *adv*.—**colourlessness** *n*.

colporteur /'kɒl,pɔrtər/ *n* a person who hawks books, *esp* bibles.

colt /ko:lt/ *n* a young male horse; a young, inexperienced person; an inexperienced player of a sport.

colter /'ko:ltər/ *see* **coulter**.

coltish /-ɪʃ/ *adj* like a colt; frisky; inexperienced.

coltsfoot /'ko:ltsfʊt/ *n* (*pl* **coltsfoots**) a yellow-flowered weed.

colubrine /'kɒlju,braɪn/ *adj* of, like or pertaining to snakes.

columbarium /kɒləmˈbɛriəm/ n (pl **columbaria**) a dovecote; a place with niches for cinerary urns.

Columbian /kəˈlɛmbiən/ adj pertaining to the US.

Columbine /ˈkɒləmˌbaɪn/ n a female character or dancer in a pantomime, sweetheart of Harlequin.

columbine[1] /ˈkɒləmˌbaɪn/ adj pertaining to or like a dove or pigeon.

columbine[2] n a garden plant, aquilegia.

columbium /kəˈlɛmbiəm/ n a metallic element now called niobium.

columella /ˌkɒljuːˈmɛlə/ or /-jə-/ n (pl **columellae**) (biol) a central axis or column.—**columellar** adj.

column /ˈkɒləm/ n a round pillar for supporting or decorating a building; something shaped like this; a vertical division of a page; a narrow-fronted deep formation of troops; a long line of people; a feature article appearing regularly in a newspaper, etc.—**columnar** adj.—**columned, columnated** adj.

columnist /-nɪst/ or /-mɪst/ n a journalist who contributes a regular newspaper or magazine column.

colza /ˈkɒlzə/ n rape seed.

colza oil n an oil made from rape seed.

coma[1] /ˈkoːmə/ n (pl **comas**) deep prolonged unconsciousness.

coma[2] n (pl **comae**) (astron) the nebulous hair-like envelope around the nucleus of a comet; (bot) the silky hairs at the end of a seed; the branches forming the leafy head of a tree.—**comal** adj.

comate /ˈkoːˌmeɪt/ adj (bot) hairy.

comatose /ˈkoːməˌtoːs/ adj in a coma; lethargic, sleepy.

comb /koːm/ n a toothed instrument for separating hair, wool, etc; a part of a machine like this; the crest of a cock; a honeycomb. • vt to arrange (hair) or dress (wool) with a comb; to seek for thoroughly.

combat /ˈkɒmbæt/ vti to strive against, oppose; to do battle. • n a contest; a fight; struggle.—**combatable** adj.—**combater** n.

combatant /ˈkɒmbætənt/ or /kəm-/, /ˈkɒmbætənt/, /ˈkɛm-/ adj fighting. • n a person engaged in a fight or contest.

combative /ˌkɒmˈbætɪv/ or /ˌkɛm-/ adj aggressive, keen to fight.

comber /ˈkoːmər/ n a wool-combing machine; a long curling wave, a breaker.

combination /ˌkɒmbɪˈneɪʃən/ n the act of combining; a union of separate parts; persons allied for a purpose; a sequence of numbers which opens a combination lock; a motorcycle and sidecar.

combination lock /-lɒk/ n a lock which can only be opened by moving a set of dials to show a specific sequence of numbers.

combinations npl an all-in-one undergarment also covering the arms and legs.

combine /kəmˈbaɪn/ vti to join together; to unite intimately; to possess together; to cooperate; (chem) to form a compound with. • n an association formed for commercial or political purposes; a machine for harvesting and threshing grain.—**combinable** adj.—**combiner** n.

combo /ˈkɒmboː/ n (pl **combos**) a small jazz band; (inf) any small group.

combust /kəmˈbʌst/ vt to burn.

combustible /kəmˈbʌstəbəl/ adj capable of burning; easily set alight; excitable. • n a combustible thing.—**combustibility, combustibleness** n.

combustion /kəmˈbʌtʃən/ n the process of burning; the process in which substances react with oxygen in air to produce heat.

combustion chamber n the space in the cylinder of an engine in which the gas compressed by the piston is exploded.

come /kʌm/ vi (**coming, came**, pp **come**) to approach; to arrive; to reach; to happen (to); to originate; to turn out (to be); to occur in a certain order; to be derived or descended; to be caused; to result; to be available; (sl) to experience a sexual orgasm; (with **about**) to happen; (naut) to change to a new tack; (with **across**) to meet with unexpectedly; to communicate the intended information or impression; to provide what is expected; (sl) to pay up; (with **along**) to make progress; (with **at**) to find out; to attack; (with **away**) to get detached; to leave with; (with **between**) to cause the estrangement of (two people); (with **by**) to obtain, esp by chance; to pass; (with **down**) to descend; to fall; to suffer an illness; to leave university; (with **down on**) to reprimand; (with **forward**) to offer oneself for some duty, volunteer; (with **from**) (inf) to have an awareness of the circumstances causing one's attitudes or actions; to understand what someone means; (with **in**) to enter, arrive; (race) to finish in a certain position; to perform a certain function; to become popular or fashionable; (money) to be received as

income; to turn out to be; (with **into**) to enter; to receive as an inheritance; (with **of**) to result from; (with **off**) to become detached; to fall from; to emerge from or finish something in a specified way; to succeed; to be reduced in price, etc; (inf) to happen; (inf) to have the intended effect; (with **on**) to advance, make progress; (electricity, etc) to begin functioning; to enter on to the stage or set; (with **out**) to become public or be published; to go on strike; to declare oneself in public; to present oneself openly as homosexual; to transpire; to make one's debut; (with **over**) to change sides; to communicate effectively; to make an impression; (inf) to become affected with a certain feeling; (with **round, around**) to recover one's normal state; to look in as a visitor; to regain consciousness; to change one's opinion, accede to something; (with **to**) to regain consciousness, revive; (total) to amount to; (with **through**) to overcome; to survive; (with **under**) to be subjected to; to be classed among; (with **up**) to approach; to grow; to come to a higher place or rank; (sun) to rise; to occur; to arise for discussion, etc; (with **upon**) to discover or meet unexpectedly; (with **up with**) to overtake; to put forward for discussion.

comeback /ˈkʌmbæk/ n (inf) a return to a career or to popularity; (inf) a witty answer.

comedian /kəˈmiːdiən/ n an actor of comic parts; an entertainer who tells jokes; a person who behaves in a humorous manner.

comedienne /kəˌmiːdiˈɛn/ nf a female comedian.

comedown /ˈkʌmdaʊn/ n a downfall; a disappointment.

comedy /ˈkɒmədi/ n (pl **comedies**) an amusing play or film; drama consisting of amusing plays; an amusing occurrence; humour.—**comedic** adj.

comehither /ˈkʌmˌhɪðər/ adj (sl) flirtatious; charmingly seductive.

comely /ˈkʌmli/ or /ˈkɒmli/ adj (**comelier, comeliest**) pleasing to the eye, good-looking.—**comeliness** n.

come-on /ˈkʌmˌɒn/ n (inf) an enticement, lure.

comer /ˈkʌmər/ n (inf) a person or thing showing promise of success.

comestible /kəˈmɛstɪbəl/ n (usu pl) anything to eat.

comet /ˈkɒmət/ n a celestial body that travels round the sun, with a visible nucleus and a luminous tail.—**cometary, cometic** adj.

comeuppance /kʌmˈʌpəns/ n (inf) a deserved retribution.

comfit /ˈkʌmfɪt/ n a candy; a sugared almond.

comfort /ˈkʌmfərt/ vti to bring consolation to; to soothe; to cheer. • n consolation; relief; bodily ease; (pl) things between necessities and luxuries.—**comforting** adj.

comfortable /ˈkʌmftərbəl/ or /-fərtəbəl/, /-frtəbəl/ adj promoting comfort; at ease; adequate; (inf) financially well off.—**comfortably** adv.

comforter /ˈkʌmfərtər/ n one who comforts; a woollen scarf; a baby's dummy teat; a quilted bedcover.

comfort station n (inf) a public lavatory.

comfrey /ˈkʌmfri/ n a tall bell-flowered hairy plant.

comfy /ˈkʌmfi/ adj (**comfier, comfiest**) (inf) comfortable.

comic /ˈkɒmɪk/ adj of comedy; causing amusement. • n a comedian; an entertaining person; a paper or book with strip cartoons.

comical /ˈkɒmɪkəl/ adj funny, laughable; droll, ludicrous.—**comically** adv.

comic book /ˈkɒmɪkˌbʊk/ n a book or magazine containing stories told in strip cartoons.

comic opera n a musical play with a comic theme.

comic relief n a humorous scene or character in a tragedy that alleviates tension.

comic strip n a series of drawings that depict a story in stages.

coming /ˈkʌmɪŋ/ adj approaching next; of future importance or promise.

comitia /koːˈmɪʃiə/ or /-ˈmɪʃə/ n (pl **comitia**) one of the three Roman public assemblies for passing laws, declaring war, etc.

comity /ˈkɒmɪti/ n (pl **comities**) civility, politeness; acts of international courtesy.

comma /ˈkɒmə/ n a punctuation mark (,) that indicates a slight pause or break in a sentence or separates items in a list.

command /kəˈmænd/ vti to order; to bid; to control; to have at disposal; to evoke, compel; to possess knowledge or understanding of; to look down over; to be in authority (over), to govern. • n an order; control; knowledge; disposal; position of authority; something or someone commanded; an instruction to a computer.

commandant /ˌkɒmənˈdænt/ or /-ˈdɒnt/, /ˈkɒm-/ n an officer in command of troops or a military establishment, esp a fortress.

commandeer /ˌkɒmənˈdiːr/ vt to seize for military purposes; to appropriate for one's own use.

commander /kə'mændər/ *n* a person who commands, a leader; a naval officer ranking next below a captain.—**commandership** *n*.

commander in chief *n* the commander of a state's entire forces.

commanding /-ɪŋ/ *adj* in command; dominating; impressive.

commandment /kə'mændmənt/ *n* a command; a divine law, *esp* one of the Ten Commandments in the Bible.

command module *n* the operational part of a spacecraft.

commando /kə'mændoː/ *n* (*pl* **commandos, commandoes**) a member of an elite military force trained to raid enemy territory.

comme il faut /ˌkɒmiːlˈfoː/, *Fr.* /kɒmiːlˈfoː/ as it should be; correct; well bred.

commemorate /kə'memə,reɪt/ *vt* to keep in the memory by ceremony or writing; to be a memorial of.—**commemoration** *n*.—**commemorative, commemoratory** *adj*.—**commemorator** *n*.

commence /kə'mens/ *vti* to begin.

commencement /-mənt/ *n* a start; a ceremony of conferring degrees; the day of this.

commend /kə'mend/ *vt* to speak favourably of, to praise; to recommend; to entrust.—**commendable** *adj*.—**commendably** *adv*.—**commendatory** *adj*.

commendation /ˌkɒmen'deɪʃən/ *n* the act of commending, praise; an award.

commensal /kə'mensəl/ *adj* (*biol*) living together, but not at the expense of another; (*person, organization*) living and feeding with another. • *n* one of two commensal plants or animals; a dinner companion.—**commensalism, commensality** *n*.

commensurable /kə'mensərəbəl/ or /-sjərəbəl/ *adj* measurable by the same standard; divisible without a remainder by the same quantity; proportionate (to).—**commensurability** *n*.

commensurate /kə'mensəret/ or /-ʃərət/, /-sjərət/ *adj* having the same extent or measure; proportionate.—**commensuration** *n*.

comment /'kɒment/ *n* a remark, observation, criticism; an explanatory note; talk, gossip. • *vi* to make a comment (upon); to annotate.—**commenter** *n*.

commentary /'kɒmən,teri/ *n* (*pl* **commentaries**) a series of explanatory notes or remarks; a verbal description on TV or radio of an event as it happens, *esp* sport.—*also* **running commentary**.—**commentarial** *adj*.

commentate /'kɒmən,teɪt/ *vt* to act as a commentator.

commentator /'kɒmən,teɪtər/ *n* one who reports and analyses events, trends, etc, as on television.

commerce /'kɒmərs/ *n* trade in goods and services on a large scale between nations or individuals.

commercial /kə'mərʃəl/ *adj* of or engaged in commerce; sponsored by an advertiser; intended to make a profit. • *n* a broadcast advertisement.—**commerciality** *n*.—**commercially** *adv*.

commercial art *n* art designed for use in all aspects of advertising and packaging.—**commercial artist** *n*.

commercialism /kə'mərʃe,lɪzəm/ *n* commercial methods or principle.—**commercialist** *n*.—**commercialistic** *adj*.

commercialize /-,laɪz/ *vt* to put on a business basis; to exploit for profit.—**commercialization** *n*.

commercial traveller *n* a sales representative or travelling salesman.

commie /'kɒmi/ *n* (*pl* **commies**) (*derog*) a communist.

commination /ˌkɒmɪ'neɪʃən/ *n* a threatening of divine punishment and vengeance, denunciation, cursing.—**comminatory** *adj*.

commingle /kə'mɪŋgəl/ *vti* to mix together, to mingle.

comminute /'kɒmɪ,njuːt/ *vt* to reduce to minute particles or powder.—**comminution** *n*.

commiserate /kə'mɪzə,reɪt/ *vti* to sympathize (with); to feel pity for.—**commiseration** *n*.—**commiserator** *n*.

commissar /'kɒmɪ,sɑr/ *n* (*formerly*) a head of a government department in the USSR.

commissariat /ˌkɒmɪ'serɪət/ *n* a supply of provisions; the department in charge of this, as for an army.

commissary /'kɒmɪseri/ or /kə'mɪs-/ *n* (*pl* **commissaries**) a store, as in an army camp, where food and supplies are sold; a restaurant in a film studio, factory, etc.—**commissarial** *adj*.

commission /kə,mɪʃən/ *n* authority to act; a document bestowing this; appointment as a military officer of the rank of lieutenant or above; a body of people appointed (by government) for specified duties; a task or duty or business committed to someone; a special order for something, *esp* a picture or other art object; a percentage on sales paid to a salesman or agent; brokerage. • *vt* to empower or appoint by commission; to employ the service of; to authorize.—**commissional, commissionary** *adj*.

commissioner /kə'mɪʃənər/ *n* a person empowered by a commission; various types of civil servant; a member of a commission.

commissure /'kɒmɪ,sjur/ *n* (*anat*) a line of junction, a seam; the point of union between two bodies.—**commissural** *adj*.

commit /kə'mɪt/ *vti* (**committing, committed**) to entrust; to consign (to prison); to do, to perpetrate a crime, etc; to pledge, to involve.—**committer** *n*.

commitment /-mənt/ *n* the act of committing; an engagement that restricts freedom; an obligation; an order for imprisonment or confinement in a mental institution.—*also* **committal**.

committed /-əd/ *adj* dedicated; pledged by a commitment.

committee /kə'mɪti/ *n* a body of people appointed from a larger body to consider or manage some matter.

commode /kə,moːd/ *n* a chamber pot enclosed in a stool; a chest of drawers.

commodious /kə'moːdiəs/ *adj* roomy; (*arch*) useful.

commodity /kə'mɒdəti/ *n* (*pl* **commodities**) an article of trade; a useful thing; (*pl*) goods.

commodore /'kɒmə,dor/ *n* a naval officer ranking below a rear admiral and above a captain; the senior commander of a fleet; the president of a yacht club.

common /'kɒmən/ *adj* belonging equally to more than one; public; usual, ordinary; widespread; familiar; frequent; easily obtained, not rare; low, vulgar; (*noun*) applying to any of a class. • *n* a tract of open public land; (*pl*) the common people; the House of Commons.—**commonality** *n*.—**commonly** *adv*.—**commonness** *n*.

commonage /'kɒmənədʒ/ *n* the right of pasturing on common land.

commonalty /'kɒmənəlti/, **commonality** /ˌkɒmə'næləti/ *n* (*pl* **commonalties, commonalities**) the common people.

common chord *n* a note accompanied by its third and fifth.

common denominator *n* a common multiple of the denominators of two or more fractions; a characteristic in common.

commoner /'kɒmənər/ *n* an ordinary person, not a member of the nobility.

common law *n* the body of law developed in England based on custom and judicial precedents, as distinct from statute law. • *adj* denoting a marriage recognized in law not by an official ceremony, but after a man and woman have cohabited for a number of years.

common market *n* a grouping of nations formed to facilitate trade by removing tariff barriers; (*with caps*) the European Union.

common measure *n* a number that will divide two or more numbers without a remainder.

commonplace /'kɒmən,pleɪs/ *adj* ordinary, unremarkable. • *n* a platitude; an ordinary thing.

Commons /'kɒmənz/ *n* (*with* **the**) the House of Commons, the lower House of the British Parliament.

common sense *n* ordinary, practical good sense.—**commonsense** *adj*.

common time *n* (*mus*) two or four beats in a bar.

commonweal /'kɒmən,wiːl/ *n* the public good.

commonwealth /-,welθ/ *n* a political community; a sovereign state, republic; a federation of states; (*with cap*) an association of sovereign states and dependencies ruled or formerly ruled by Britain.

commotion /kə'moːʃən/ *n* a violent disturbance; agitation; upheaval.—**commotional** *adj*.

communal /kə'mjuːnəl/ or /'kɒm-/ *adj* of a commune or community; shared in common.—**communality** *n*.—**communally** *adv*.

communalism /-,lɪzəm/ *n* a political system based on local self-government.—**communalist** *n*.—**communalistic** *adj*.

communalize /-,laɪz/ *vt* to make over to a community.—**communalization** *n*.

communard /'kɒmju,nard/ *n* one who advocates government by communes.

commune[1] /'kɒmjuːn/ *n* a group of people living together and sharing possessions; the smallest administrative division in several European countries.

commune[2] /kə'mjuːn/ *vi* to converse intimately; to communicate spiritually.

communicable /kə'mju:nɪkəbəl/ *adj* able to be communicated; (*disease*) easily passed on.—**communicability, communicableness** *n*.

communicant /kə'mju:nɪkənt/ *n* a person who receives Holy Communion.

communicate /kə'mju:nə,keɪt/ *vti* to impart, to share; to succeed in conveying information; to pass on; to transmit, *esp* a disease; to be connected.—**communicator** *n*.—**communicatory** *adj*.

communication /kə,mju:nə'keɪʃən/ *n* the act of communicating; information; a connecting passage or channel; (*pl*) connections of transport; (*pl*) means of imparting information, as in newspapers, radio, television.

communications satellite *n* an artificial satellite orbiting the earth used to relay telephone, radio and TV signals.

communicative /kə'mju:nɪkətɪv/ or /-,keɪtɪv/ *adj* inclined to talk and give information.

communion /kə'mju:nɪən/ *n* common possession, sharing; fellowship; an emotional bond with; union in a religious body; (*with cap*) Holy Communion, the Christian sacrament of the Eucharist when bread and wine are consecrated and consumed.—**communional** *adj*.

communiqué /kə,mju:nə'keɪ/ or /kə'mju:nə,keɪ/ *n* an official communication, *esp* to the press or public.

communism /'kɒmju,nɪzəm/ *n* a social system under which private property is abolished and the means of production are owned by the people; (*with cap*) a political movement seeking the overthrow of capitalism based on the writings of Karl Marx; the system as instituted in the former USSR and elsewhere.—**communistic** *adj*.

communist /-nɪst/ *n* a supporter of communism; (*with cap*) a member of a Communist party.

community /kə'mju:nɪti/ *n* (*pl* **communities**) an organized political or social body; a body of people in the same locality; the general public, society; any group having work, interests, etc in common; joint ownership; common character; a group of plants and animals of a region, dependent on each other for life and survival.

community centre *n* a place providing social and recreational facilities for a local community.

commutative /kə'mju:tətɪv/ *n* relating to or involving substitution; (*math*) having a result that is independent of the order in which the elements are combined; (*addition, etc*) showing this property.

commutator /'kɒmju:,teɪtər/ *n* a device for reversing the direction of electric current.

commute /kə'mju:t/ *vti* to travel a distance daily from home to work; to exchange (for); to change (to); to reduce (a punishment) to one less severe.—**commutable** *adj*.—**commutation** *n*.

commuter /-ər/ *n* a person who commutes to and from work.

comose /'ko:mo:s/ *adj* hairy; tufted.

compact¹ /'kɒmpækt/ *n* an agreement; a contract, a treaty.

compact² *adj* closely packed; condensed; terse; firm; taking up space neatly. • *vt* to press or pack closely; to compose (of). • *n* a small cosmetic case, *usu* containing face powder and a mirror.—**compacter** *n*.—**compactly** *adv*.—**compactness** *n*.

compact disc /'kɒmpækt/ *n* a small mirrored disc containing music (or audio-visual material) encoded digitally in metallic pits which are read optically by a laser beam.

compact video disc *n* a laser disc, similar to an audio compact disc, which plays sound and pictures.

companion¹ /kəm'pænjən/ *n* an associate in an activity; a partner; a friend; one of a pair of matched things; a low-ranking member of an order of knighthood.—**companionship** *n*.

companion² *n* a wooden shelter over a companionway.

companionable /-əbəl/ *adj* friendly, sociable.—**companionability** *n*.—**companionably** *adv*.

companionway /-,weɪ/ *n* a ladder or staircase on a ship.

company /'kʌmpəni/ *n* (*pl* **companies**) any assembly of people; an association of people for carrying on a business, etc; a society; a military unit; the crew of a ship; companionship, fellowship; a guest, visitor(s).

comparable /'kɒmpərəbəl/ or /kəm'perəbəl/ *adj* able or suitable to be compared (*with* **with**); similar.—**comparably** *adv*.—**comparability** *n*.

comparative /kəm'perətɪv/ or /-'pærətɪv/ *adj* estimated by comparison; relative, not absolute; (*gram*) expressing more.—**comparatively** *adv*.

compare /kəm'per/ *vt* to make one thing the measure of another; to observe similarity between, to liken; to bear comparison; (*gram*) to give comparative and superlative forms of (an adjective). • *vi* to make comparisons; to be equal or alike.—**comparer** *n*.

comparison /kəm'perɪsən/ *n* the act of comparing; an illustration; a likeness; (*gram*) the use of *more* or *er* with an adjective.

compartment /kəm'pɑrtmənt/ *n* a space partitioned off; a division of a railway carriage; a separate section or category.—**compartmental** *adj*.—**compartmented** *adj*.

compartmentalize /,kɒmpɑrt'mentə,laɪz/ *vt* to divide into categories, *esp* excessively.—**compartmentalization** *n*.

compass /'kʌmpəs/ *n* a circuit, circumference; an extent, area; the range of a voice; an instrument with a magnetic needle indicating north, south, east, west; (*often pl*) a two-legged instrument for drawing circles, etc.—**compassable** *adj*.

compassion /kəm'pæʃən/ *n* sorrow for another's sufferings; pity.

compassionate /-ət/ *adj* showing compassion; merciful.—**compassionately** *adv*.

compass points *n* north, south, east, west, etc.

compatible /kəm'pætəbəl/ *adj* agreeing or fitting in (with); of like mind; consistent; (*body organ*) able to be transplanted successfully.—**compatibly** *adv*.—**compatibility** *n*.

compatriot /kəm'peɪtrɪət/ *n* a fellow countryman.—*also adj*.—**compatriotic** *adj*.

compeer /'kɒmpiːr/ or /-'piːr/ *n* an equal; a companion.

compel /kəm'pel/ *vt* (**compelling, compelled**) to force, constrain; to oblige; to obtain by force.—**compeller** *n*.

compelling /-ɪŋ/ *adj* evoking powerful feelings, eg interest, admiration.

compendious /kəm'pendɪəs/ *adj* containing much in a small space, succinct.

compendium /kəm'pendɪəm/ *n* (*pl* **compendiums, compendia**) an abridgement; a summary; a collection; an assortment of things in one box.

compensate /'kɒmpən,seɪt/ *vti* to counterbalance; to make up for; to recompense.—**compensator** *n*.—**compensatory, compensative** *adj*.

compensation /,kɒmpən'seɪʃən/ *n* the act of compensating; a sum given to compensate, *esp* for loss or injury; an exaggerated display of ability in one area as a cover-up for a lack in another.

compete /kəm'piːt/ *vi* to strive; to contend; to take part in a competition, *esp* sporting.

competence /'kɒmpətəns/ *n* the quality of being capable; sufficiency; capacity; an adequate income to live on.

competency /-si/ *n* (*pl* **competencies**) competence; (*law*) the capacity to testify in court.

competent /-tənt/ *adj* fit, capable; adequate; with enough skill for; legally qualified.—**competently** *adv*.

competition /,kɒmpə'tɪʃən/ *n* act of competing; rivalry; a contest in skill or knowledge; a match.

competitive /kəm'petɪtɪv/ *adj* of, or involving, competition; of sufficient value in terms of price or quality to ensure success against rivals.—**competitively** *adv*.—**competitiveness** *n*.

competitor /kəm'petɪtər/ *n* a person who competes; an opponent; a rival.

compile /kəm'paɪl/ *vt* to collect or make up from various sources; to amass; to gather data, etc for a book; (*comput*) to translate high-level program instructions into machine code using a compiler.—**compilation** *n*.

compiler /-'paɪlər/ *n* a person who compiles a book, etc; (*comput*) a program that translates high-level program instructions into machine code.

complacence /kəm'pleɪsəns/ **complacency** /-,siː/ *n* (*pl* **complacencies, complacences**) self-satisfaction; gratification.

complacent /kəm'pleɪsənt/ *adj* self-satisfied.—**complacently** *adv*.—**complacency, complacence** *n*.

complain /kəm'pleɪn/ *vi* to find fault, to grumble; to be ill; (*poet*) to express grief, to make a mourning sound.—**complainer** *n*.

complainant /kəm'pleɪnənt/ *n* (*law*) a plaintiff.

complaint /kəm'pleɪnt/ *n* a statement of some grievance; a cause of distress or dissatisfaction; an illness.

complaisant /kəm'pleɪzənt/ *adj* disposed to please, obliging; compliant.—**complaisance** *n*.

complement /'kɒmpləmənt/ *n* something making up a whole; a full allowance (of equipment or number); the entire crew of a ship, including officers. • *vt* to make complete.

complementary /ˌkɒmplɪ'mentəri/ *adj* completing; together forming a balanced whole.

complete /kəm'pliːt/ *adj* entire; free from deficiency; finished; thorough. • *vt* to make complete; to finish.—**completeness** *n*.—**completer** *n*.—**completive** *adj*.

completely /-li/ *adv* entirely, utterly.

completion /kəm'pliːʃən/ *n* the act of completing; accomplishment; fulfilment.

complex /'kɒmpleks/ *adj* having more than one part; intricate, not simple; difficult. • *n* a complex whole; a collection of interconnected parts, buildings or units; a group of mostly unconscious impulses, etc strongly influencing behaviour; (*inf*) an undue preoccupation; a phobia.—**complexity** *n* (*pl* complexities).

complex fraction *n* (*math*) a fraction with fractions for the numerator or denominator or both.

complexion /kəm'plekʃən/ *n* a colour, texture and look of the skin; aspect, character.

complexity /kəm'pleksəti/ *n* (*pl* complexities) the state of being complex, complexness.

complex number *n* (*math*) a number having both real and imaginary parts.

complex sentence *n* a sentence with one principal clause and one or more subordinate clauses.

compliance, compliancy /kəm'plaɪəns/ *n* the act of complying with another's wishes; acquiescence.

compliant /-ənt/ *adj* yielding, submissive.—**compliantly** *adv*.

complicate /'kɒmpləˌkeɪt/ *vt* to make intricate or involved; to mix up.

complicated /-əd/ *adj* intricately involved; difficult to understand.

complication /ˌkɒmplɪ'keɪʃən/ *n* a complex or intricate situation; a circumstance that makes (a situation) more complex; (*med*) a condition or disease following an original illness.

complicity /kəm'plɪsɪti/ *n* (*pl* complicites) partnership in wrongdoing.

compliment /'kɒmpləmənt/ *n* a polite expression of praise, a flattering tribute; (*pl*) a formal greeting or expression of regard. • *vt* to pay a compliment to, to flatter; to congratulate (on).

complimentary /ˌkɒmplə'mentəri/ *adj* conveying or expressing a compliment; given free of charge.

complin, compline /'kɒmplɪn/ or /-plaɪn/ *n* (*RC Church*) the last service of the day following vespers.

comply /kəm'plaɪ/ *vi* (**complying, complied**) to act in accordance (with); to yield, to agree.—**complier** *n*.

compo /'kɒmpoʊ/ *n* (*pl* compos) a mixture of plaster, stucco, etc; (*sl*) compensation.

component /kəm'poʊnənt/ *adj* going to the making of a whole, constituent. • *n* a component part.—**componential** *adj*.

comport /kəm'pɔrt/ *vti* to conduct (oneself); to be compatible, to accord (with).—**comportment** *n*.

compose /kəm'poʊz/ *vt* to make up, to form; to construct in one's mind, to write; to arrange, to put in order; to settle; to adjust; to tranquillize; (*print*) to set up type. • *vi* to create musical works, etc.

composed /-'poʊzd/ *adj* calm, self-controlled.—**composedly** *adv*.

composer /-'poʊzər/ *n* a person who composes, *esp* music.

composite /'kɒmpəzɪt/ *adj* made up of distinct parts or elements; (*archit*) blending Ionic and Corinthian orders; (*bot*) having many flowers in the guise of one, as the daisy. • *n* a composite thing or flower.

composition /ˌkɒmpə'zɪʃən/ *n* the act or process of composing; a work of literature or music, a painting; a short written essay; the general make-up of something; a chemical compound.—**compositional** *adj*.

compositor /kəm'pɒzɪtər/ *n* a person who puts together, or sets up, type for printing.

compos mentis /ˌkɒmpəs'mentɪs/ *adj* of sound mind, sane.

compost /'kɒmpoʊst/ *n* a mixture of decomposed organic matter for fertilizing soil.

composure /kəm'poʊʒər/ *n* the state of being composed, calmness.

compote /'kɒmpoʊt/ or /-pɒt/ *n* fruit preserved in syrup.

compound[1] /'kɒmpaʊnd/ *n* a substance or thing made up of a number of parts or ingredients, a mixture; a compound word made up of two or more words. • *vt* to combine (parts, elements, ingredients) into a whole, to mix; to intensify by adding new elements; to settle (debt) by partial payment. • *vi* to become joined in a compound; to come to terms of agreement. • *adj* compounded or made up of several parts; not simple.—**compounder** *n*.

compound[2] *n* an enclosure in which a building stands.

compound eye *n* the eye in insects consisting of numerous separate visual units.

compound fracture *n* a fracture in which the shattered bone protrudes through the skin.

compound interest *n* interest paid on the principal sum of capital and the interest that it has accrued.

compound sentence *n* a sentence with more than one principal clause.

comprador /ˌkɒmprə'dɔr/ *n* a native agent for a foreign company in China or Japan.

comprehend /ˌkɒmprɪ'hend/ *vt* to grasp with the mind, to understand; to include, to embrace.—**comprehendible** *adj*.—**comprehension** *n*.

comprehensible /-'hensɪbəl/ *adj* capable of being understood.—**comprehensibly** *adv*.—**comprehensibility** *n*.

comprehensive /-'hensɪv/ *adj* wide in scope or content, including a great deal; (*car insurance policy*) covering most risks including third party, fire, theft. • *n* a comprehensive school.—**comprehensively** *adv*.—**comprehensiveness** *n*.

compress /kəm'pres/ *vt* to press or squeeze together; to bring into a smaller bulk; to condense. • *n* a soft pad for compressing an artery, etc; a wet or dry bandage or pad for relieving inflammation or discomfort.—**compressed** *adj*.—**compressible** *adj*.—**compressive** *adj*.

compression /kəm'preʃən/ *n* the act of compressing; the increase in pressure in an engine to compress the gases so that they explode.—**compressional** *adj*.

compressor /-'presər/ *n* a machine for compressing air or other gases.

comprise /kəm'praɪz/ *vt* to consist of, to include.—**comprisable** *adj*.—**comprisal** *n*.

compromise /'kɒmprəˌmaɪz/ *n* a settlement of a dispute by mutual concession; a middle course or view between two opposed ones. • *vti* to adjust by compromise; to lay open to suspicion, disrepute, etc.—**compromiser** *n*.

compromised /'kɒmprəmaɪzd/ *adj* (*reputation*) open to disrepute, tarnished.

comptroller /kən'troʊlər/ or /kɒmp-/ *n* the form of controller used in some titles.

compulsion /kəm'pʌlʃən/ *n* the act of compelling; something that compels; an irresistible urge.

compulsive /-sɪv/ *adj* compelling; acting as if compelled.—**compulsively** *adv*.

compulsory /-səri/ *adj* enforced, obligatory, required by law, etc; involving compulsion; essential.—**compulsorily** *adv*.

compunction /kəm'pʌŋkʃən/ *n* pricking of the conscience; remorse; scruple.—**compunctious** *adj*.

computation /ˌkɒmpjuː'teɪʃən/ *n* the act or process of computing; a reckoning, an estimate.—**computational** *adj*.

compute /kəm'pjuːt/ *vt* to determine mathematically; to calculate by means of a computer. • *vi* to reckon; to use a computer.—**computability** *n*.—**computable** *adj*.—**computation** *n*.

computer /kəm'pjuːtər/ *n* an electronic device that processes data in accordance with programmed instructions.

computer-aided tomography, computer-assisted tomography *see* **CAT**.

computer game *n* a game on cassette or disk to play on a home computer by means of operating the keys according to the images appearing on the screen.

computer graphics *n* the production and manipulation of pictorial images on a computer screen.

computerize /kəm'pjuːtəˌraɪz/ *vt* to equip with computers; to control or perform (a process) using computers; to store or process data using a computer.—**computerization** *n*.

computerized axial tomography *see* **CAT**.

computer language *n* a code used to provide instructions and data to a computer.

computer literate *adj* capable of or proficient in using computers.

computer virus *n* a program introduced into a computer system with the intention of sabotaging or destroying data.

comrade /'kɒmræd/ *n* a companion; a fellow member of a Communist party.—**comradely** *adv*.—**comradeship** *n*.

comsat /'kɒmˌsæt/ *n* communications satellite.

con[1] /kɒn/ vt (**conning, conned**) (*inf*) to swindle, trick. • *n* (*inf*) a confidence trick.

con[2] *n* against, as in **pro and con**.

con[3] *prep* with.

con[4] *vt* (**conning, conned**) to direct the course of (a ship).

con[5] *vt* (**conning, conned**) to study; to learn by heart.

con[6] *n* (*sl*) a convict.

con- /kɒn/ or /kən/ *prefix* com-.

con amore *It.* /ˌkɒnæ'mɔreɪ/ *adj, adv* (*mus*) with love.

conation /koː'neɪʃən/ *n* (*psychol*) the faculty of voluntary agency, including volition and desire.

conative /'kɒnətɪv/ or /'koːn-/ *adj* (*verb*) expressing endeavour or effort; pertaining to the faculty of conation.

con brio *It.* /kɒn'brioː/ *adj, adv* (*mus*) with spirit.

concatenate /kən'kætɪˌneɪt/ *vt* to link together. • *adj* linked.

concatenation /-'neɪʃən/ *n* a string of connected ideas or events.

concave /kɒnkeɪv/ or /kɒn'keɪv/ *adj* curving inwards, hollow. • *n* a concave line or surface.—**concavity** *n* (*pl* **concavities**).

concavo-concave /kɒn'keɪvoːkɒn'keɪv/ *adj* hollow on both surfaces, as a lens.

concavo-convex /-kɒn'veks/ *adj* concave on one side, convex on the other.

conceal /kən'siːl/ *vt* to hide, to keep from sight; to keep secret.—**concealment** *n*.

concede /ken'siːd/ *vt* to grant; to admit to be true, to allow; to agree to be certain in outcome.—**conceder** *n*.

conceit /kən'siːt/ *n* an over-high opinion of oneself; vanity; a farfetched comparison, a quaint fancy.

conceited /-əd/ *adj* full of conceit, vain.—**conceitedly** *adv*.

conceivable /kən'siːvəbəl/ *adj* capable of being imagined or believed; possible.—**conceivably** *adv*.

conceive /kən'siːv/ *vti* to become pregnant (with); to form in the mind; to think out, to imagine; to understand; to express.

concenter /kən'sentər/ *see* **concentre**.

concentrate /'kɒnsənˌtreɪt/ *vt* to bring or converge together to one point; to direct to a single object or purpose; to collect one's thoughts or efforts; (*chem*) to increase the strength of by diminishing bulk, to condense. • *n* a concentrated product, *esp* a food reduced in bulk by eliminating fluid; a foodstuff relatively high in nutrients.—**concentrator** *n*.

concentration /ˌkɒnsən'treɪʃən/ *n* the act or process of concentrating; the direction of attention to a single object; a drawing together of forces; the simultaneous firing of many weapons.—**concentrative** *adj*.

concentration camp *n* a camp where persons (as prisoners of war, political prisoners, and refugees) are detained or confined.

concentre /kən'sentər/ *vti* to bring or come to a common centre.—*also* **concenter**.

concentric /kən'sentrɪk/, **concentrical** /-əl/ *adj* having a common centre.—**concentrically** *adv*.—**concentricity** *n*.

concept /'kɒnsept/ *n* a general idea, *esp* an abstract one.

conceptacle /kən'septəkəl/ *n* (*bot*) that which holds anything; a follicle.

conception /kən'sepʃən/ *n* the act of conceiving; the fertilizing of an ovum by a sperm; a thing conceived; an idea, a notion.—**conceptional** *adj*.

conceptual /kən'septʃuəl/ *adj* relating to mental conception or concepts.

conceptualism /-ˌlɪzəm/ *n* (*philos*) the theory that universal truths exist in the mind apart from any concrete embodiment.—**conceptualist** *n*.—**conceptualistic** *adj*.

conceptualize /-ˌlaɪz/ *vt* to form a concept of in the mind based on evidence, experience, etc.—**conceptualization** *n*.

concern /kən'sərn/ *vt* to relate or apply to; to fill with anxiety; to interest (oneself) in; to take part, to be mixed up (in). • *n* a thing that concerns one; anxiety, misgiving; interest in or regard for a person or thing; a business or firm.

concerned /kən'sərnd/ *adj* troubled, worried; interested.—**concernedly** *adv*.

concerning /-ɪŋ/ *prep* about; regarding.

concert /'kɒnsərt/ *n* a musical entertainment; harmony; agreement or union; **in concert** working together; (*musicians*) playing together.

concerted /kən'sərtəd/ *adj* planned or arranged by mutual agreement; combined; (*mus*) arranged in separate parts for musicians or singers.

concertina /ˌkɒnsər'tiːnə/ *n* a hexagonal musical instrument, similar to an accordion, which produces sound by squeezing bellows which pass air over metal reeds.

concertino /ˌkɒntʃər'tiːnoː/ *n* (*pl* **concertini**) a short concerto.

concerto /kən'tʃertoː/ *n* (*pl* **concertos, concerti**) a musical composition for a solo instrument and orchestra.

concert pitch *n* a pitch slightly above normal; a state of exceptional efficiency.

concession /kə'nseʃən/ *n* the act of conceding; something conceded; a grant of rights, land, etc by a government, corporation, or individual; the sole right to sell a product within an area; a reduction in price (of admission, travel, etc) for certain people.—**concessionary** *adj*.—**concessible** *adj*.

concessionaire, concessioner /kənˌseʃə'nɛr/ *n* a person holding a concession.

concessive /kən'sesɪv/ *adj* of or expressing concession.

conch /kɒntʃ/ or /kɒŋk/ *n* (*pl* **conchs, conches**) a tropical marine spiral shell, sometimes used as a trumpet.

concha /'kɒŋkə/ *n* (*pl* **conchae**) the external ear or its cavity; (*archit*) the dome of a semicircular apse.—**conchal** *adj*.

conchiferous /kɒŋ'kɪfərəs/ *adj* producing shells.

conchology /-'kɒlədʒi/ *n* the branch of zoology that studies molluscs and their shells.—**conchological** *adj*.—**conchologist** *n*.

concierge /ˌkɒsi'ɛrʒ/ or /kɒn-/ *n* a resident doorkeeper or janitor, *esp* in France.

conciliar /kən'sɪliər/ *adj* of or pertaining to ecclesiastical councils.

conciliate /kən'sɪlieɪt/ *vt* to win over from hostility; to make friendly; to appease; to reconcile.—**conciliation** *n*.—**conciliator** *n*.—**conciliatory** *adj*.

concinnity /kən'sɪnəti/ *n* (*pl* **concinnities**) neatness, elegance, *esp* in speech or writing.—**concinnous** *adj*.

concise /kən'saɪs/ *adj* brief, condensed, terse.—**concisely** *adv*.—**conciseness** *n*.

concision /kən'sɪʒən/ *n* conciseness; (*arch*) mutilation.

conclave /'kɒnkleɪv/ *n* a private or secret meeting; a meeting of cardinals in seclusion to choose a pope; the meeting place.—**conclavist** *n*.

conclude /kən'kluːd/ *vti* to bring or come to an end, to finish; to effect, to settle; to infer; to resolve.

conclusion /kən'kluːʒən/ *n* concluding; the end or close; an inference; a final opinion; (*logic*) a proposition deduced from premises.

conclusive /-sɪv/ *adj* decisive; convincing, removing all doubt.—**conclusively** *adv*.

concoct /kən'kɒkt/ *vt* to make by combining ingredients; to devise, to plan; to invent (a story).—**concocter, concoctor** *n*.—**concoctive** *adj*.

concoction /-'kɒkʃən/ *n* the act of concocting; something concocted; a mixture; a lie.

concomitance /kən'kɒmɪtəns/ *n* the state of being concomitant; coexistence.

concomitant /-'kɒmɪtənt/ *n* an accompanying thing or circumstance.—*also adj*.

concord /'kɒnkɔrd/ or /'kɒŋ-/ *n* agreement, harmony; a treaty; grammatical agreement.—**concordant** *adj*.

concordance /kən'kɔrdəns/ or /kəŋ-/ *n* agreement; an alphabetical index of words in a book or in the works of an author with their contexts.

concordant /-kɔrdənt/ *adj* agreeing, harmonious.

concordat /kən'kɔrdæt/ *n* a compact or agreement, *esp* between church and state.

concourse /'kɒnkɔrs/ or /'kɒŋ-/ *n* a crowd; a gathering of people or things, eg events; an open space or hall where crowds gather, eg a railway or airport terminal.

concrescence /kən'krɛsəns/ *n* (*biol*) a growing together, coalescence.—**concrescent** *adj*.

concrete /'kɒnkriːt/ or /'kɒŋ-/ *adj* having a material existence; (*gram*) denoting a thing, not a quality, not abstract; actual, specific (*a concrete example*); made of concrete. • *n* anything concrete; a mixture of sand, cement, etc with water, used in building. • *vti* to form into a mass, to solidify; to build or cover with concrete.

concretion /kən'kriːʃən/ *n* a solidified mass; a stone-like mass found in some parts of the body, calculus.—**concretionary** *adj*.

concubinage /kɒn'kjuːbɪnədʒ/ or /kɒŋ-/ *n* the act of living with a woman without being legally married.

concubine /'kɒŋkjuˌbaɪn/ or /'kɒn-/ *n* a secondary wife (in polygamous societies); (*formerly*) a mistress of a king or nobleman.—**concubinage** *n*.

concupiscence /kən'kju:pɪsəns/ *n* sexual desire, lust.—**concupiscent** *adj*.

concur /kən'kə:r/ or /kən-/ *vi* (**concurring, concurred**) to happen together, to coincide; to cooperate; to be of the same opinion, to agree.—**concurrence** *n*.

concurrence /-əns/ *n* the act of concurring; agreement; consent.

concurrent /-ənt/ *adj* existing, acting or occurring at the same time; coinciding.—**concurrently** *adv*.

concuss /kən'kʌs/ *vt* to shake violently, to agitate; to cause concussion of the brain to.

concussion /kən'kʌʃən/ *n* the violent shock of an impact or explosion; loss of consciousness caused by a violent blow to the head.—**concussive** *adj*.

condemn /kən'dɛm/ *vt* to express strong disapproval of; to find guilty; to blame or censure; to declare unfit for use; to force into unwillingly.—**condemnable** *adj*.—**condemnation** *n*.—**condemnatory** *adj*.—**condemner** *n*.

condense /kən'dɛns/ *vt* to reduce to a smaller compass, to compress; to change from a gas into a liquid; to concentrate; to express in fewer words. • *vi* to become condensed.—**condensable, condensible** *adj*.—**condenser** *n*.—**condensation** *n*.

condensed milk *n* milk that has been sweetened and reduced by evaporation.

condenser /kən'dɛnsər/ *n* an apparatus for reducing gases or vapour to a liquid or solid form; a device for storing electricity; a lens for concentrating light.

condescend /ˌkɒndə'sɛnd/ *vi* to waive one's superiority; to deign, to stoop; to act patronizingly.—**condescension** *n*.

condescending /-ɪŋ/ *adj* kindly in a lordly fashion to inferiors; patronizing.

condescension /-'sɛnʃən/ *n* a condescending act or manner.

condign /kən'daɪn/ *adj* deserved, merited; suitable.

condiment /'kɒndəmənt/ *n* a seasoning or relish.

condition /kən'dɪʃən/ *n* the state or nature of things; anything required for the performance, completion or existence of something else; physical state of health; an abnormality, illness; a prerequisite; (*pl*) attendant circumstances. • *vt* to be essential to the happening or existence of; to stipulate; to agree upon; to make fit; to make accustomed (to); to bring about a required effect by subjecting to certain stimuli.

conditional /-əl/ *adj* depending on conditions; not absolute; (*gram*) expressing condition. • *n* a conditional clause or conjunction.—**conditionality** *n*.—**conditionally** *adv*.

conditioner /-ər/ *n* a person or thing that conditions; a creamy substance for bringing the hair into a glossy condition.

conditioning /-ɪŋ/ *n* a bringing into a required state or state of fitness for an objective.

condo /'kɒndo:/ *n* (*pl* **condos, condoes**) (*inf*) a condominium.

condole /kən'do:l/ *vt* (*with* **with**) to express sympathy for another.—**condolatory** *adj*.—**condoler** *n*.

condolence /kən'do:ləns/, **condolement** /-mənt/ *n* sympathy.

con dolore *It. adv* (*mus*) mournfully.

condom /'kɒndəm/ *n* a sheath for the penis, used as a contraceptive and to prevent infection.

condominium /ˌkɒndə'mɪniəm/ *n* (*pl* **condominiums**) a block of apartments, each apartment being individually owned; joint rule; a country ruled by more than one other country.

condone /kən'do:n/ *vt* to overlook, to treat as nonexistent; to pardon an offence.—**condonation** *n*.—**condoner** *n*.

condor /'kɒndər/ *n* a large South American vulture.

condottiere /ˌkɒndɒt'jɛri/ *n* (*pl* **condottieri**) a military adventurer, a captain of mercenaries.

conduce /kən'du:s/ or /-dju:s/ *vi* to tend to bring about, to contribute (to).—**conducer** *n*.

conducive /-'du:sɪv/ or /-dju:sɪv/ *adj* leading to or helping to cause or produce a result.

conduct /'kɒndʌkt/ *vti* to lead; to guide; to convey; to direct (an orchestra); to carry on or manage (a business); to transmit (electricity, heat); to behave (oneself). • *n* management, direction; behaviour.—**conductible** *adj*.—**conductibility** *n*.

conductance /kən'dʌktəns/ *n* the ability of a specified system to conduct electricity.

conduction /kən'dʌkʃən/ *n* the conducting or transmission of heat or electricity through a medium; the transmission of nerve impulses.

conductive /-tɪv/ *adj* having the power to transmit heat or electricity.—**conductivity** *n* (*pl* **conductivities**).

conductor /kən'dʌktər/ *n* a person who conducts an orchestra; one in charge of passengers on a train, or who collects fares on a bus; a substance that conducts heat or electricity.—**conductress** *nf*.

conduit /'kɒnduɪt/ or /-djuɪt/ *n* a channel or pipe that carries water, etc.

conduplicate /kɒn'du:plɪkɪt/ or /-'dju:-/ *adj* (*bot*) folded lengthwise along the middle.—**conduplication** *n*.

condyle /'kɒndɪl/ or /-daɪl/ *n* the rounded head at the end of a bone fitting into another bone.—**condylar** *adj*.

condyloid /-də,lɔɪd/ *adj* shaped like, resembling or connected with a condyle.

cone /ko:n/ *n* a solid pointed figure with a circular or elliptical base; any cone-shaped object (*an ice-cream cone*); a warning ballard on roads, etc; the scaly fruit of the pine, fir, etc.

coney /'ko:ni/ *see* **cony**.

confab /'kɒnfæb/ *n* (*inf*) an informal talk, chat.

confabulate /kən'fæbju,leɪt/ *vi* to talk familiarly together.—**confabulation** *n*.—**confabulator** *n*.—**confabulatory** *adj*.

confection /kən'fɛkʃən/ *n* sweets, ice cream, preserves, etc; anything overfussy, fanciful or ornate.

confectionary /-,ɛri/ *n* (*pl* **confectionaries**) a place where confectionery is made or sold. • *adj* of or pertaining to confectionery.

confectioner /-ər/ *n* a person who makes or sells confectionery.

confectionery /-,ɛri/ *n* (*pl* **confectioneries**) candies.

confederacy /kən'fɛdərəsi/ *n* (*pl* **confederacies**) a union of states, an alliance; a combination of persons for illegal purposes; (*with cap*) the Confederate States of America.

confederate /kən'fɛdərət/ *adj* banded together by treaty, united in confederation. • *vti* to bring or come into alliance or confederacy. • *n* a member of a confederacy; a partner in design, an accomplice; an ally.

Confederate States *npl* in US history, the eleven Southern States that seceded from the Union in 1861, leading to the Civil War in which they were defeated in 1865.

confederation /kən,fɛdə'reɪʃən/ *n* the act or state of confederating; an alliance of individuals, organizations, states or cantons (as in Switzerland).—**confederationism** *n*.—**confederationist** *n*.

confer /kən'fər/ *vt* (**conferring, conferred**) to grant or bestow; to compare views or take counsel; to consult.—**conferment, conferral** *n*.—**conferrable** *adj*.—**conferrer** *n*.

conferee, conferree /ˌkɒnfə'ri:/ *n* one on whom something is conferred; a member of a conference.

conference /'kɒnfərəns/ *n* a meeting for discussion or consultation.—**conferential** *adj*.

conferva /kən'fərvə/ *n* (*pl* **confervae, confervas**) a genus containing green freshwater algae.—**conferval** *adj*.—**confervoid** *adj*.

confess /kən'fɛs/ *vt* to acknowledge or admit; to disclose (sins) to a confessor; (*priest*) to hear confession of. • *vi* to make or hear a confession.

confessedly /-ədli/ *adv* avowedly.

confession /kən'fɛʃən/ *n* admission or acknowledgement of a fault or sin, *esp* to a confessor; a thing confessed; a statement of one's religious beliefs, creed.—**confessionary** *adj*.

confessional /-əl/ *n* an enclosure in a church where a priest hears confessions.

confessor /-sər/ *n* a priest who hears confessions and grants absolution; one who confesses.

confetti /kən'fɛti/ *npl* small bits of coloured paper thrown at weddings.

confidant /ˌkɒnfɪ'dɒnt/ or /'kɒnfɪ,dɒnt/, /-dænt/ *n* a person trusted with one's secrets.—**confidante** *nf*.

confide /kən'faɪd/ *vti* to put confidence (in); to entrust; to impart a confidence or secret.—**confider** *n*.

confidence /'kɒnfɪdəns/ *n* firm trust, faith; belief in one's own abilities; boldness; something revealed confidentially.

confidence trick *n* the persuading of a victim to hand over valuables as proof of confidence.

confident /'kɒnfɪdənt/ *adj* full of confidence; positive, assured.—**confidently** *adv*.

confidential /ˌkɒnfɪ'dɛnʃəl/ *adj* spoken or written in confidence, secret; entrusted with secrets.—**confidentiality, confidentialness** *n*.—**confidentially** *adv*.

confiding /kən'faɪdɪŋ/ *adj* unsuspicious.—**confidingly** *adv*.

configuration /kən‚fɪgjʊ'reɪʃən/ or /-gə'reɪʃən/ n arrangement of parts; external shape, general outline; aspect; (astrol) the relative position of the planets; the make-up of a computer system.—**configurational, configurative** adj.

confine /'kɒnfaɪn/ n; /kən'faɪn/ vt to restrict, to keep within limits; to keep shut up, as in prison, a sickbed, etc; to imprison. • n (pl) borderland, edge, limit.—**confinable, confineable** adj.

confined /-nd/ adj narrow, enclosed, of limited space.

confinement /kən'faɪnmənt/ n a being confined; the period of childbirth.

confirm /kən'fɜːrm/ vt to make stronger; to establish firmly; to make valid, to ratify; to corroborate; to administer rite of confirmation to.

confirmation /‚kɒnfər'meɪʃən/ n the act of confirming; convincing proof; the rite by which people are admitted to full communion in Christian churches.

confirmatory /kən'fɜːrmə‚tɔːri/, **confirmative** /-meɪtɪv/ adj giving extra proof; corroborative.

confirmed /kən'fɜːrmd/ adj habitual; settled in belief, mode of life, etc; having undergone the rite of confirmation.

confiscate /'kɒnfɪ‚skeɪt/ vt to appropriate to the state as a penalty; to seize by authority.—**confiscable** adj.—**confiscation** n.—**confiscator** n.—**confiscatory** adj.

conflagration /‚kɒnflə'greɪʃən/ n a massively destructive fire.—**conflagrative** adj.

conflation /kən'fleɪʃən/ n a fusing together; a combining of two variant readings of a text into one.—**conflate** vt.

conflict /'kɒnflɪkt/ n a fight; a contest; strife, quarrel; emotional disturbance. • vi to be at variance; to clash (with); to struggle.—**confliction** n.—**conflictive, conflictory** adj.

conflicting /-ɪŋ/ adj contradictory.

confluence /'kɒnfluəns/, **conflux** /'kɒn‚flæks/ n the point where two rivers meet; a coming together.

confluent /-ənt/ adj flowing or running together. • n a tributary river or stream.

confocal /kɒn'fəʊkəl/ adj having a common focus.

conform /kən'fɔːrm/ vi to comply, to be obedient (to); to act in accordance with. • vt to adapt; to make like.—**conformer** n.

conformable /-əbəl/ adj compliant; corresponding, adapted (to); in parallel order.—**conformability, conformableness** n.—**conformably** adv.

conformation /‚kɒnfər'meɪʃən/ n arrangement of parts, structure; adaptation.

conformist /kən'fɔːrmɪst/ n one who conforms to established rules, standards, etc; compliance with the rites and doctrines of an established church. —**conformism** n.

conformity /kən'fɔːrmɪti/, **conformance** /-məns/ n (pl **conformities, conformances**) correspondence; agreement; conventional behaviour; compliance.

confound /kən'faʊnd/ vt to mix up, to obscure; to perplex, to astound; to overthrow; to mistake one thing for another.—**confounder** n.

confounded /-ɪd/ adj astonished; confused; annoying; (inf) damned.—**confoundedly** adv.

confraternity /‚kɒnfrə'tɜːrnəti/ n (pl **confraternities**) a brotherhood or society of men associated for a common purpose.—**confraternal** adj.

confrère /'kɒn‚freɪ/ n an associate, a colleague.

confront /kən'frʌnt/ vt to stand in front of, to face; to bring face to face (with); to encounter; to oppose.—**confronter** n.

confrontation /'kɒnfrən'teɪʃən/ n the coming face to face with; hostility without actual warfare, esp between nations.

Confucian /kən'fjuːʃən/ adj pertaining to Confucius, the Chinese philosopher. • n a follower of the teachings of Confucius.

confuse /kən'fjuːz/ vt to throw into disorder; to mix up; to mistake one thing for another; to perplex, to disconcert; to embarrass; to make unclear.—**confusable** adj.—**confusing** adj.—**confusingly** adv.

confused /-d/ adj perplexed; disordered; mentally unbalanced.—**confusedly** adv.

confusion /kən'fjuːʒən/ n the act or state of being confused; disorder; embarrassment, discomfiture; lack of clarity.

confute /kən'fjuːt/ vt (argument, etc) to prove wrong; to convict of error; to overcome in argument.—**confutation** n.—**confutative** adj.—**confuter** n.

conga /'kɒŋgə/ n a Cuban dance in which the dancers move along in a long line; music for this. • vi (**congaing, congaed**) to do this dance.

congé /'kɒ̃ʒeɪ/ n dismissal; (arch) a formal bow, esp at parting.

congeal /kən'dʒiːl/ vti to change from a liquid to a solid by cooling, to jell.—**congealment** n.

congelation /‚kɒndʒə'leɪʃən/ n the act of congealing; a congealed state or substance.

congener /'kɒndʒənər/ n a person or thing of the same kind as another.

congeneric /‚kɒndʒə'nerɪk/ adj of the same genus or origin.

congenial /kən'dʒiːniəl/ adj of a similar disposition or with similar tastes, kindred; suited, agreeable (to).—**congenially** adv.—**congeniality, congenialness** n.

congenital /kən'dʒenɪtəl/ adj existing or dating since birth, as in certain defects.—**congenitally** adv.

conger eel /'kɒŋgər/ n a large marine eel.

congeries /'kɒndʒə‚riːz/ or /kɒn'dʒiːriːz/ n (used as sing or pl) a gathered mass, a heap; a conglomeration.

congest /kən'dʒest/ vt to overcrowd. • vi (med) to affect with congestion.—**congested** adj.—**congestible** adj.

congestion /kən'dʒestʃən/ n an overcrowding; (med) an excessive accumulation of blood in any organ; an accumulation of traffic causing obstruction.—**congestive** adj.

conglobate /kən'gləʊbeɪt/ or /'kɒngləʊ‚beɪt/ vti to form into a mass.—**conglobation** n.

conglomerate /kən'glɒmə‚rət/ adj stuck together in a mass. • vt to gather into a ball. • n a coarse-grained rock of embedded pebbles; a large corporation consisting of companies with varied and often unrelated interests.—**conglomeratic, conglomeritic** adj.

conglomeration /kən‚glɒmə'reɪʃən/ n the act of conglomerating; a mass stuck together; a miscellaneous collection.

conglutinate /kən'gluːtɪn‚eɪt/ vt to glue together. • adj glued together; united by an adhesive substance.—**conglutination** n.—**conglutinative** adj.

congou /'kɒŋguː/ n a kind of black Chinese tea.

congratulate /kən'grætʃə‚leɪt/ or /-'grædʒ-/ vt to express sympathetic pleasure at success or good fortune of, to compliment; to feel satisfied or pleased with oneself.—**congratulation** n.—**congratulator** n.—**congratulatory** adj.

congratulations /kən‚grætʃə'leɪʃəns/ npl an expression of joy or pleasure.

congregate /'kɒŋgrə‚geɪt/ vti to flock together, to assemble; to gather into a crowd or mass.—**congregator** n.

congregation /‚kɒŋgrə'geɪʃən/ n a gathering, an assembly; a body of people assembled for worship.

congregational /-əl/ adj of a congregation; (with cap) of or pertaining to Congregationalism.

Congregationalism /-‚lɪzəm/ n a form of church government in which each congregation has management of its own affairs.—**Congregationalist** adj, n.

congress /'kɒŋgres/ n an association or society; an assembly or conference, esp for discussion and action on some question; (with cap) the legislature of the US, comprising the Senate and the House of Representatives.

congressional /kən'greʃənəl/ adj of, or relating to, a congress.—**congressionalist** n.

Congressman /'kɒŋgresmən/ n (pl **Congressmen**) a member of Congress.—**Congresswoman** nf (pl **Congresswomen**).

congruent /-wənt/ or /-ənt/ adj in agreement; harmonious; (geom) having identical shape and size so that all parts correspond.—**congruence, congruency** n.

congruous /'kɒŋgruəs/ adj accordant; fit.—**congruity** n.

conic /'kɒnɪk/, **conical** /-əl/ adj of a cone; cone-shaped.

conics /-ɪks/ n (used as sing) the branch of geometry that deals with conic sections.

conic section n a curve formed from a cone—an ellipse, a parabola, or a hyperbola.

conidium /kə'nɪdiəm/ (pl **conidia**) a reproductive cell formed of certain fungi.—**conidial** adj.

conifer /'kɒnɪfə/ or /'kəʊ:-/ n any evergreen trees and shrubs with true cones (as pines) and others (as yews).—**coniferous** adj.

coniferous /'kənɪfərəs/ adj bearing fruit cones.

conine, conin /'kəʊnɪ‚ɪːn/ or /'kəʊni:n/ n a very poisonous alkaloid existing in the hemlock.

conium /'kɔːniəm/ or /kɔːˈnaiəm/ n a genus of biennial poisonous plants including the hemlock.

conjectural /kənˈdʒɛktʃərəl/ adj depending on conjecture, doubtful.—**conjecturally** adv.

conjecture /kənˈdʒɛktʃər/ n a guess, guesswork. • vt to make a conjecture, to guess, surmise.—**conjecturer** n.—**conjecturable** adj.—**conjectural** adj.

conjoin /kənˈdʒɔin/ vt to join together; to connect or associate. • vi to be joined.—**conjoinedly** adv.—**conjoiner** n.

conjoint /kənˈdʒɔint/ adj united, combined; cooperating.—**conjointly** adv.

conjugal /'kɔndʒʊgəl/ adj of or relating to marriage.—**conjugality** n.—**conjugally** adv.

conjugate /'kɔndʒʊˌgeit/ vt to give the parts of (a verb); to unite.—**conjugable** adj.—**conjugation** n.—**conjugator** n.—**conjugative** adj.

conjugation /ˌkɔndʒʊˈgeiʃən/ n the act of conjugating; a group of verbs with the same inflections; the union of cells in reproduction.—**conjugational** adj.

conjunct /kɔnˈdʒɛŋkt/ adj, n joined together; associated.

conjunction /kənˈdʒɛŋkʃən/ n (gram) a word connecting words, clauses or sentences; a union; a simultaneous occurrence of events; the apparent proximity of two or more planets.—**conjunctional** adj.

conjunctiva /ˌkɔndʒɛŋkˈtivə/ or /kɒnˈdʒɛŋktivə/ n (pl **conjunctivas**, **conjunctivae**) the mucous membrane that lines the inner surface of the eyelids and the exposed area of the eyeball.—**conjunctival** adj.

conjunctive /kənˈdʒɛŋktiv/ adj serving to unite; closely connected; (gram) of or pertaining to conjunctions. • n a conjunction.—**conjunctively** adv.

conjunctivitis /kənˌdʒɛŋktiˈvaitis/ n inflammation of the conjunctiva.

conjuncture /kənˈdʒɛŋktʃər/ n a combination of many circumstances or causes; a critical time.—**conjunctural** adj.

conjuration /ˌkɔndʒʊˈreiʃən/ n the act of conjuring or invoking; an incantation; an enchantment; a solemn entreaty.

conjure /'kɔndʒər/ or /'kɛn-/ vti to practise magical tricks; to call up (spirits) by invocation.

conjurer, conjuror /'kɔndʒərər/ or /'kɛn-/ n one who conjures or is skilled in sleight of hand.

conk /kɒŋk/ n (sl) the nose or head. • n a blow to the nose or head. • vt to hit, esp on the head. • vi (with **out**) (sl) (machine) to break down entirely; to collapse suddenly from exhaustion.

conker /'kɔŋkər/ n (inf) the horse chestnut; (pl) a children's game using conkers on a string.

con man n (inf) a swindler, one who defrauds by means of a confidence trick.

con moto /kɒnˈmoːtoː/, It. /kɒnˈmɒtɒ/ adj (mus) spirited.

connate /kɒˈneit/ adj inborn, congenital; (leaves) united at the base.

connatural /ˌkɒnˈnætʃərəl/ adj congenital; having the same nature.

connect /kəˈnɛkt/ vti to fasten together, to join; to relate together, to link up; (trains, buses, etc) to be timed to arrive as another leaves so that passengers can continue their journey; to establish a link by telephone; (sl) to punch or kick; to uncover (a source of drugs).—**connectible, connectable** adj.—**connector, connecter** n.

connection /kəˈnɛkʃən/ n the act of connecting; the state of being connected; a thing that connects; a relationship, bond; a train, bus, etc timed to connect with another; an opportunity to transfer between trains, buses, etc; context; a link between components in an electric circuit; a relative; (sl) a supply or the supplier of illicit drugs; (pl) clients, customers.—**connectional** adj.

connective /kəˈnɛktiv/ adj serving to connect.—**connectively** adv.

connectivity /kəˈnɛktiviti/ n the ability of computers of different kinds to communicate.

conning tower n the armoured pilot house of a submarine.

conniption /kəˈnipʃən/ n (sl) a fit of hysteria or rage.

connivance /kəˈnaivəns/ n the act of conniving; pretence of ignorance; passive cooperation in a crime or fault; collusion.

connive /kəˈnaiv/ vi to permit tacitly; to wink (at); to plot.—**conniver** n.

connivent /-ənt/ adj converging.

connoisseur /ˌkɒnəˈsər/ or /-ˈsʊr/ n a trained discriminating judge, esp of the fine arts.

connotation /ˌkɒnəˈteiʃən/ n a consequential meaning, an implication.—**connotative, connotive** adj.

connote /kəˈnoːt/ vt to imply; to indicate; to mean.

connubial /kəˈnuːbiəl/ or /-njuː-/ adv of or relating to marriage.—**connubiality** n.—**connubially** adv.

conoid /'kɔːnɔid/ n (geom) a solid formed by revolution of a conic section about its axis. • adj somewhat conical.—also **conoidal**.

conquer /'kɔŋkər/ vt to gain victory (over), to defeat; to acquire by conquest; to overcome, to master. • vi to be victor.—**conqueror** n.

conquest /'kɔn,kwɛst/ or /'kɔŋ-/ n conquering; the winning of a person's affection; a person or thing conquered.

conquistador /kɒnˈkwistə,dɔr/ n (pl **conquistadors, conquistadores**) a member of the Spanish forces that conquered Mexico and Peru in the 16th century.

Cons. abbr = Conservative.

consanguineous /kɒnsæŋˈgwiniəs/ or /-sæn-/, **consanguine** /-ˈsæŋgwin/ adj related by blood or birth.—**consanguinity** n.

conscience /'kɒnʃəns/ n the knowledge of right and wrong that affects a person's action and behaviour; the sense of guilt or virtue induced by actions, behaviour, etc; an inmost thought; conscientiousness.

conscience clause n a clause in an act giving relief to persons having religious scruples to some requirement in it.

conscience investment n the investment in companies whose activities do not offend the investor's moral principles.—also **ethical investment**.

conscience money n money paid, usu anonymously, to atone for some dishonest act or illegal monetary gain.

conscience-stricken adj feeling extreme guilt or remorse.

conscientious /ˌkɒnʃiˈɛnʃəs/ adj following the dictates of the conscience; scrupulous; careful, thorough.—**conscientiously** adv.—**conscientiousness** n.

conscientious objector n a person who refuses to serve in the military forces on moral or religious grounds.

conscionable /'kɒnʃənəbəl/ adj governed by conscience, just.—**conscionably** adv.

conscious /'kɒnʃəs/ adj aware (of); awake to one's surroundings; (action) realized by the person who does it, deliberate.—**consciously** adv.

consciousness /-nəs/ n the state of being conscious; perception; the whole body of a person's thoughts and feelings.

conscript /'kɒn,skript/ for n, adj, for vb enrolled into service by compulsion; drafted. • n a conscripted person (as a military recruit). • /kənˈskript/ vt to enlist compulsorily.

conscription /kənˈskripʃən/ n compulsory military or naval service; the persons enrolled.—**conscriptional** adj.

consecrate /'kɒnsə,kreit/ vt to set apart as sacred, to sanctify; to devote (to).—**consecration** n.—**consecrator** n.—**consecratory, consecrative** adj.

consecration /ˌkɒnsəˈkreiʃən/ n the act of consecrating; a setting apart or devoting to a sacred use or office; (with cap) (RC Church) the part of Mass when the bread and wine are blessed.

consecution /ˌkɒnsəˈkjuːʃən/ n a following on; a logical sequence.

consecutive /kənˈsɛkjʊtiv/ adj following in regular order without a break; successive; (gram) expressing consequence.—**consecutively** adv.

consensual /kənˈsɛnsʊəl/ adj caused by sympathetic action.

consensus /kənˈsɛnsəs/ n an opinion held by all or most; general agreement, esp in opinion.

consent /kənˈsɛnt/ vi to agree (to); to comply; to acquiesce. • n agreement, permission; concurrence.—**consenter** n.

consequence /'kɒnsəkwəns/ n a result, an outcome; importance; (pl) an unpleasant result of an action; a game in which each player writes part of a story without knowing what has gone before.

consequent /-kwənt/ adj occurring as a result.

consequential /ˌkɒnsəˈkwɛnʃəl/ adj pompous, self-important; resultant.—**consequentiality, consequentialness** n.—**consequentially** adv.

consequently /-ˌkwɛntli/ adv as a result, therefore.

conservancy /kənˈsərvənsi/ n (pl **conservancies**) in UK, an authority controlling a river or port; conservation.

conservation /ˌkɒnsərˈveiʃən/ n the act of conserving; preservation of the environment and natural resources.—**conservational** adj.—**conservationist** n.

conservation of energy *n* the fact that the amount of energy in a closed system remains the same although its form changes.

conservatism /kən'sɜrvə,tɪzəm/ *n* opposition to change; a political ideology favouring preservation and defence of tradition.

conservative /-tɪv/ *adj* traditional, conventional; cautious; moderate. • *n* a conservative person; (*with cap*) a member of the Conservative Party in Britain and other countries.—**conservatively** *adv*.

conservatoire /kən'sɜrvə,twar/ *n* an institution for instruction in music.

conservator /kən'sɜrvə,tər/ or /'kɒnsɜr,veɪtər/ *n* a custodian, a keeper; a preserver; a member of a conservancy.

conservatory /kən'sɜrvə,tɔri/ or /-tri:/ *n* (*pl* **conservatories**) a greenhouse attached to a house; a conservatoire.

conserve /kən'sɜrv/ *vt* to keep from loss or injury; to preserve (a foodstuff) with sugar. • *n* a type of jam using whole fruit.—**conservable** *adj*.—**conserver** *n*.

consider /kən'sɪdər/ *vti* to reflect (upon), to contemplate; to examine, to weigh the merits of; to take into account; to regard as; to be of the opinion; to act with respect; to allow for.—**considerer** *n*.

considerable /kən'sɪdərəbəl/ *adj* a fairly large amount; worthy of respect.—**considerably** *adv*.

considerate /kən'sɪdərət/ *adj* careful of the feelings of others.—**considerately** *adv*.

consideration /kən,sɪdə'reɪʃən/ *n* the act of considering; deliberation; a point of importance; an inducement; thoughtfulness; deference; a payent.

considered /kən'sɪdərd/ *adj* well thought out.

considering /kən'sɪdərɪŋ/ *prep* in view of. • *adv* all in all. • *conj* seeing that.

consign /kə'saɪn/ *vt* to hand over, to commit; to send goods addressed (to).—**consignable** *adj*.—**consignation** *n*.

consignee /,kɒn'saɪni:/ or /kən,saɪ'ni:/ *n* the person to whom goods are consigned.

consignment /kən'saɪnmənt/ *n* consigning; goods, etc consigned.

consignor /kən'saɪnər/ or /kən,saɪn,ɔr/, /-ər/ *n* the person by whom goods are consigned.

consist /kən'sɪst/ *vi* to be made up (of); to be comprised (of).

consistency /kən'sɪstənsi/ *n* (*pl* **consistencies**) degree of density, *esp* of thick liquids; the state of being consistent.

consistent /kən'sɪstənt/ *adj* compatible, not contradictory; uniform in thought or action.—**consistently** *adv*.

consistory /kən'sɪstəri/ *n* a solemn assembly or the place where it meets; the ecclesiastical court of the pope and cardinals, of an Anglican bishop, or of Presbyterian presbyters.—**consistorial, consistorian** *adj*.

consolation /,kɒnsə'leɪʃən/ *n* someone or something that offers comfort in distress.—**consolatory** *adj*.

consolation prize *n* a prize for the runner up or loser in a competition.

console¹ /kən'soːl/ *vt* to bring consolation to, to cheer in distress.—**consolable** *adj*.—**consoler** *n*.

console² /'kɒnsoːl/ *n* a desk containing the controls of an electronic system; the part of an organ containing the pedals, stops, etc; an ornamental bracket supporting a shelf or table.

consolidate /kə'sɒlɪ,deɪt/ *vti* to solidify; to establish firmly, to strengthen; to combine into a single whole.—**consolidator** *n*.

consolidation /kən,sɒlɪ'deɪʃən/ *n* the act of consolidating; solidification.

consols /'kɒn,sɒlz/ or /kən'sɒlz/ *npl* British government securities consolidated into a single stock.

consommé /'kɒnsə,meɪ/ or /,kɒnsə'meɪ/ *n* a clear soup made from meat stock.

consonance /'kɒnsənəns/, **consonancy** /-i/ *n* (*pl* **consonance, consonancies**) agreement of sounds; harmony; concord.

consonant /-nənt/ *n* a letter of the alphabet that is not a vowel; the sound representing such a letter. • *adj* consistent, in keeping (with).—**consonantal** *adj*.

consort /'kɒn,sɔrt/ *n*, a husband or wife, *esp* of a reigning queen or king; a ship sailing with another. • *vti* to associate, to keep company with (often dubious companions).—**consorter** *n*.

consortium /kən'sɔrtiəm/ or /-'sɔrʃəm/ *n* (*pl* **consortia**) an international banking or financial combination.—**consortial** *adj*.

conspectus /kən'spɛktəs/ *n* a general sketch or digest of some subject, a synopsis.

conspicuous /kən'spɪkjuəs/ *adj* easily seen, prominent; outstanding, eminent.—**conspicuousness** *n*.—**conspicuously** *adv*.

conspiracy /kən'spɪrəsi/ *n* (*pl* **conspiracies**) a secret plan for an illegal act; the act of conspiring.

conspirator /kən'spɪrətər/ *n* one who conspires.—**conspiratorial, conspiratory** *adj*.—**conspiratorially** *adv*.

conspire /kən'spaɪr/ *vti* to combine secretly for an evil purpose; to plot, to devise.

con spirito *It.* /kɒn'spɪrɪtoː/ *adj, adv* (*mus*) with spirit.

constable /'kɒnstəbəl/ *n* in UK, a policeman or policewoman of the lowest rank; a governor of a royal castle.

constabulary /kən'stæbju:,lɛri/ *n* (*pl* **constabularies**) in UK, a police force.—*also adj*.

constancy /'kɒnstənsi/ *n* being constant; steadfastness; fidelity.

constant /'kɒnstənt/ *adj* fixed; unchangeable; unchanging; faithful; firm and steadfast; continual. • *n* (*math, physics*) a quantity that does not vary.

constantly /-li/ *adv* continually, continuously, often.

constellate /'kɒnstə,leɪt/ *vti* to form into a constellation.

constellation /,kɒnstə'leɪʃən/ *n* a group of fixed stars; an assembly of the famous.—**constellatory** *adj*.

consternate /'kɒnstər,neɪt/ *vt* to dismay.

consternation /,kɒnstər'neɪʃən/ *n* surprise and alarm; shock; dismay.

constipate /'kɒnstɪ,peɪt/ *vt* to cause constipation in.—**constipated** *adj*.

constipation /'kɒnstɪ'peɪʃən/ *n* infrequent and difficult movement of the bowels.

constituency /kən'stɪtʃuənsi/ *n* (*pl* **constituencies**) a body of electors; the voters in a particular district or area.

constituent /kən'stɪtʃuənt/ *adj* forming part of a whole, component; having the power to revise the constitution. • *n* a component part; a member of an elective body; a voter in a district.

constitute /'kɒnstɪ,tuːt/ or /-,tjuːt/ *vt* to set up by authority, to establish; to frame, to form; to appoint; to compose, to make up.—**constituter, constitutor** *n*.

constitution /,kɒnstɪ'tuːʃən/ or /-,tjuːʃən/ *n* fundamental physical condition; disposition; temperament; structure, composition; the system of basic laws and principles of a government, society, etc; a document stating these specifically.

constitutional /-əl/ *adj* of or pertaining to a constitution; authorized or limited by a constitution, legal; inherent, natural. • *a* walk for the sake of one's health.—**constitutionally** *adv*.—**constitutionality** *n*.

constitutionalism /-nə,lɪzəm/ *n* constitutional government; adherence to constitutional principles.—**constitutionalist** *n*.

constitutive /'kɒnstɪ,tuːtɪv/ or /-,tjuːtɪv/ *adj* having the power to enact, constituent; elemental; essential; productive.

constrain /kən'streɪn/ *vt* to compel, to force; to hinder by force; to confine, to imprison.—**constrainer** *n*.

constrained /kənstreɪnd/ *adj* enforced; embarrassed, inhibited; showing constraint.

constraint /kən'streɪnt/ *n* compulsion; forcible confinement; repression of feeling; embarrassment; a condition that restricts freedom.

constrict /kən'strɪkt/ *vt* to draw together, to squeeze, to compress.

constricted /-ɪd/ *adj* narrowed, cramped.

constriction /-ʃən/ *n* compression; tightness.—**constrictive** *adj*.

constrictor /-ər/ *n* a constrictive muscle; a snake that crushes its prey.

construct /kən'strʌkt/ *n & vt* to make, to build, to fit together; to compose. • *n* a structure; an interpretation; an arrangement, *esp* of words in a sentence.—**constructible** *adj*.—**constructor, constructer** *n*.

construction /kən'strʌkʃən/ *n* a constructing; anything constructed; a structure, building; interpretation, meaning; (*gram*) two or more words grouped together to form a phrase, clause or sentence.—**constructional** *adj*.

constructive /kən'strʌktɪv/ *adj* helping to improve, promoting development.—**constructively** *adv*.

constructivism /-,ɪzəm/ *n* nonrepresentational art, *esp* sculpture based on movement and using machine-made materials.

construe /kən'struː/ *vti* (**construing, construed**) to translate word for word; to analyse grammatically; to take in a particular sense, to interpret.—**construer** *n*.

consubstantiation /ˌkɒnsəbˌstænʃiˈeɪʃən/ n the doctrine that the body and blood of Christ are in a mysterious manner substantially present in the Eucharistic elements after Consecration.

consuetude /ˈkɒnswɪˌtuːd/ n an established custom.—**consuetudinary** adj.

consul /ˈkɒnsəl/ n a government official appointed to live in a foreign city to attend to the interests of his country's citizens and business there.—**consular** adj.

consulate /-ət/ or /-sjəl-/ n the official residence of a consul; the office of a Roman consul.

consult /kənˈsʌlt/ vti to seek advice from, esp a doctor or lawyer; to seek information from, eg a work of reference; to deliberate, to confer.—**consulter, consultor** n.

consultant /kənˈsʌltənt/ n a specialist who gives professional or technical advice; a senior physician or surgeon in a hospital; a person who consults another.—**consultancy** n (pl **consultancies**).

consultation /ˌkɒnsəlˈteɪʃən/ n the act of consulting; a conference, esp with a professional adviser.—**consultative, consultatory, consultive** adj.

consultative /kənˈsʌltətɪv/ or /-ˌteɪtɪv/, **consultatory** /-ˌtɔːrɪ/ adj advisory; deliberative.

consumable /kənˈsuːməbəl/ adj able to be consumed. • n (usu pl) something bought to be used.

consume /kənˈsuːm/ or /-ˈsjuːm/ vti to destroy; to use up; to eat or drink up; to waste away; to utilize economic goods.

consumer /kənˈsuːmər/ or /-ˈsjuː-/ n a person who uses goods and services, the end user.

consumer goods npl commodities for domestic consumption which are not used for the production of other goods and services.

consumerism /-ˌɪzəm/ n protection of the interests of consumers; encouragement to buy consumer goods.

consumer price index n an index of the prices of the food, clothing and housing necessary for life.

consummate[1] /ˈkɒnsəˌmeɪt/ or /-sjə-/ adj, vt to bring to perfection, to be the crown of; (marriage) to complete by sexual intercourse.—**consummation** n.—**consummative, consummatory** adj.—**consummator** n.

consummate[2] adj complete, perfect, highly skilled.

consumption /kənˈsʌmpʃən/ n the act of consuming; the state of being consumed or used up; (econ) expenditure on goods and services by consumers; tuberculosis.

consumptive /kənˈsʌmptɪv/ adj tending to consume; affected with consumption. • n a person with tuberculosis.

contact /ˈkɒnˌtækt/ n touch, touching; connection; an acquaintance, esp one willing to provide help or introductions in business, etc; a connection allowing the passage of electricity; (med) a person who has been in contact with a contagious disease. • vti to establish contact with.—**contactual** adj.

contact lens n a thin correctional lens placed over the cornea of the eye.

contagion /kənˈteɪdʒən/ n the communicating of a disease by contact; a disease spread in this way; a corrupting influence.

contagious /-dʒəs/ adj (disease) spread by contact; capable of spreading disease by contact; (influence) catching, infectious.—**contagiousness** n.

contain /kənˈteɪn/ vt to hold, to enclose; to comprise, to include; to hold back or restrain within fixed limits.

container /kənˈteɪnə/ n a receptacle, etc designed to contain goods or substances; a standardized receptacle used to transport commodities.

containerize /-ˌaɪz/ vt to put or convey (cargo) in large standardized containers.

containment /kənˈteɪnmənt/ n the prevention of the expansion of a hostile power; the prevention of the release of dangerous quantities of radioactive material from a nuclear reactor.

containment building n a building enclosing a nuclear reactor to limit the spread of radiation, esp in the event of an accident.

contaminate /kənˈtæmɪneɪt/ vt to render impure by touch or mixing, to pollute, esp by radioactive contact.—**contaminant** n.—**contaminator** n.

contamination /kəntæmɪˈneɪʃən/ n the act of contaminating; the state of being contaminated; a thing that contaminates.

conte /kɔ̃t/ n a short story.

contemn /kənˈtem/ vt to despise; to disregard scornfully.—**contemner, contemnor** n.—**contemnible** adj.

contemplate /ˈkɒntəmˌpleɪt/ vti to look at steadily; to reflect upon, to meditate; to have in view, to intend.—**contemplator** n.

contemplation /ˌkɒntɛmˈpleɪʃən/ n the act of contemplating; pious meditation; intention.

contemplative /kənˈtempləˌtɪv/ adj thoughtful, meditative, of or given to contemplation; dedicated to religious contemplation.—**contemplatively** adv.—**contemplativeness** n.

contemporaneous /kəmˌtempəˈreɪniəs/ adj existing or occurring at the same time; of the same period.—**contemporaneously** adv.—**contemporaneity** n.

contemporary /kənˈtempəˌreri/ adj living or happening at the same time; of about the same age; present day; of or following present-day trends in style, art, fashion, etc. • n (pl **contemporaries**) a person living at the same time; a person of the same age.—**contemporarily** adv.

contempt /kənˈtempt/ n the feeling one has towards someone or something considered low, worthless etc; the condition of being despised; disregard.

contemptible /-ɪbəl/ adj deserving contempt.—**contemptibly** adv.—**contemptibility** n.

contemptuous /kənˈtemptʃuəs/ adj showing or feeling contempt; disdainful.—**contemptuously** adv.—**contemptuousness** n.

contend /kənˈtend/ vti to take part in a contest, to strive (for); to quarrel; to maintain (that), to assert or argue strongly for.—**contender** n.

content[1] /ˈkɒntent/ n (usu pl) what is in a container; (usu pl) what is in a book; substance or meaning.

content[2] /kənˈtent/ adj satisfied (with), not desiring more; willing (to); happy; pleased. • n quiet satisfaction. • vt to make content; to satisfy.—**contentment** n.

contented /kənˈtentəd/ adj content; gratified, satisfied.—**contentedly** adv.

contention /kənˈtenʃən/ n contending, struggling, arguing; a point in dispute; an assertion in an argument.—**contentional** adj.

contentious /kənˈtenʃəs/ adj tending to argue; likely to cause dispute, controversial.—**contentiously** adv.

conterminous /kɒnˈtɜːmɪnəs/ adj having a common boundary (with), contiguous.—also **coterminous**.

contest /kɒnˈtest/ vti, n to call in question, to dispute; to fight to gain, to compete for; to strive. • n a struggle, an encounter; a competition; a debate; a dispute.—**contestable** adj.—**contestation** n.—**contester** n.

contestant /kənˈtestənt/ n a competitor in a contest; a person who contests.

context /ˈkɒnˌtekst/ n the parts of a written work or speech that precede and follow a word or passage, contributing to its full meaning; associated surroundings, setting.—**contextual** adj.—**contextually** adv.

contextualize /kənˈtekstʃuəˌlaɪz/ vt to place in or treat as part of a context.

contexture /kənˈtekstʃər/ n a structure; a fabric; a style of composition.—**contextural** adj.

contiguous /kənˈtɪɡjuəs/ adj touching, adjoining; near; adjacent.—**contiguity** n.

continent[1] /ˈkɒntɪnənt/ n one of the six or seven main divisions of the earth's land; (with cap) the mainland of Europe, excluding the British Isles; a large extent of land.

continent[2] adj able to control urination and defecation; practising self-restraint; chaste.—**continence, continency** n.

continental /ˌkɒntɪˈnentəl/ adj of a continent; (with cap) of or relating to Europe, excluding the British Isles; of or relating to the former thirteen British colonies later forming the USA. • n an inhabitant of the Continent.—**continentalism** n.—**continentalist** n.—**continentally** adv.

continental breakfast n a light morning meal of coffee and rolls.

continental drift n (geol) the (theoretical) gradual process of separation of the continents from their original solid land mass.

continental shelf n the sea bed, under relatively shallow seas, bordering a continent.

contingency /kənˈtɪndʒənsi/ n (pl **contingencies**) a possibility of a future event or condition; something dependent on a future event.

contingent /kənˈtɪndʒənt/ adj possible, that may happen; chance; dependent (on); incidental (to). • n a possibility; a quota of troops.—**contingently** adv.

continual /kənˈtɪnjuəl/ adj frequently repeated, going on all the time.—**continuality** n.—**continually** adv.

continuance /kenˈtɪnjuəns/ n uninterrupted succession; duration.

continuant /kə'tɪnjʊənt/ *n* a consonant whose sound can be prolonged, as *f*, *v*.

continuation /kən,tɪnju'eɪʃən/ *n* a continuing; prolongation; resumption; a thing that continues something else, a sequel, a further instalment.

continue /kən'tɪnju:/ *vt* to go on (with); to prolong; to extend; to resume, to carry further. • *vi* to remain, to stay; to last; to preserve.—**continuable** *adj.*—**continuer** *n.*—**continuingly** *adv.*

continuity /,kɒntə'nu:ɪti/ or /-'nju:-/ *n* (*pl* **continuities**) continuousness; uninterrupted succession; the complete script or scenario in a film or broadcast.

continuous /kən'tɪnjuːəs/ *adj* continuing; occurring without interruption.—**continuously** *adv.*—**continuousness** *n.*

continuum /kən'tɪnuːəm/ *n* (*pl* **continua, continuums**) a continuous and homogeneous whole.

contort /kən'tɔrt/ *vti* to twist out of a normal shape, to pull awry.—**contorted** *adj.*—**contortion** *n.*—**contortional** *adj.*

contortionist /kən'tɔrʃənɪst/ *n* a person who can twist his or her body into unusual postures, *esp* as entertainment.—**contortionistic** *adj.*

contour /'kɒn,tur/ *n* the outline of a figure, land, etc; the line representing this outline; a contour line. • *adj* made according to a shape or form (*contour chair*).

contour line *n* a line on a map that passes through all points at the same altitude.

contra /'kɒntrə/ *n* a thing that may be argued against.

contra- /'kɒntrə/ *prefix* against.

contraband /'kɒntrə,bænd/ *n* smuggled goods; smuggling. • *adj* illegal to import or export.—**contrabandist** *n.*

contraband of war *n* certain commodities used in warfare; the traffic in them with belligerent states; goods supplied to one belligerent and seizable by another.

contrabass /'kɒntrə,beɪs/ *n* an instrument sounding an octave lower than another instrument of the same class; the largest instrument of the violin class, the double bass.—**contrabassist** *n.*

contrabassoon /,kɒntrəbə'su:n/ *n* the largest instrument of the oboe class.—**contrabassoonist** *n.*

contraception /,kɒntrə'sepʃən/ *n* the deliberate prevention of conception, birth control.

contraceptive /,kɒntrə'septɪv/ *n* a contraceptive drug or device.—*also adj.*

contract /'kɒntrækt/ *vt, n* to draw closer together; to confine; to undertake by contract; (*debt*) to incur; (*disease*) to become infected by; (*word*) to shorten by omitting letters. • *vi* to shrink; to become smaller or narrower; to make a contract; (*with* **out**) to decide not to take part in or join, eg a pension scheme. • *n* a bargain; an agreement to supply goods or perform work at a stated price; a written agreement enforceable by law.—**contractibility** *n.*—**contractible** *adj.*

contract bridge *n* a form of bridge in which the players contract to take a certain number of tricks.

contractile /kən'træktɪl/ *adj* able or causing to grow smaller.—**contractility** *n.*

contraction /kən'trækʃən/ *n* the act of contracting; the state of being contracted; a contracted word; a labour pain in childbirth.—**contractional** *adj.*—**contractive** *adj.*

contractor /'kɒn,træktər/ *n* a person who makes a business contract, *esp* a builder; something that draws together, eg a muscle.

contractual /kən'træktʃuːəl/ *adj* of a contract.—**contractually** *adv.*

contradance /'kɒntrə,dɒns/ *see* **contredanse**.

contradict /,kɒntrə'dɪkt/ *vti* to assert the contrary or opposite of; to deny; to be at variance (with); to lack consistency.—**contradictable** *adj.*—**contradicter, contradictor** *n.*

contradiction /,kɒntrə'dɪkʃən/ *n* the act of contradicting; a denial.—**contradictory** *adj.*

contradistinction /,kɒntrədɪ'stɪŋkʃən/ *n* a distinction by opposite qualities.—**contradistinctive** *adj.*

contradistinguish /-dɪ'stɪŋgwɪʃ/ *vt* to mark the difference between two things by contrasting their opposite qualities.

contralto /kən'trɒltəʊ/ or /-'træltəʊ/ *n* (*pl* **contraltos**) a singing voice having a range between tenor and mezzo-soprano; a person having this voice.

contraposition /,kɒntrəpə'zɪʃən/ *n* opposition, antithesis.

contraption /kən'træpʃən/ *n* (*inf*) a device, a gadget.

contrapuntal /,kɒntrə'pʌntəl/ *adj* of or according to counterpoint.—**contrapuntally** *adv.*

contrapuntist /-ɪst/ *n* one skilled in the rules of counterpoint.

contrariety /,kɒntrə'raɪəti/ *n* (*pl* **contrarieties**) opposition; inconsistency, discrepancy.

contrariwise /'kɒntreriwaɪz/ *adv* on the other hand; conversely.

contrary /'kɒn,treri/ *adj* opposed; opposite in nature; wayward, perverse. • *n* (*pl* **contraries**) the opposite. • *adv* in opposition to; in conflict with.—**contrarily** *adv.*—**contrariness** *n.*

contrast /kɒn'træst/ *vi* to show marked differences. • *vt* to compare so as to point out the differences. • *n* the exhibition of differences; difference of qualities shown by comparison; the degree of difference between colours or tones when put together.

contravene /,kɒntrə'vi:n/ *vt* to infringe (a law), to transgress; to conflict with, to contradict.—**contravener** *n.*—**contravention** *n.*

contredanse /'kɒntrə,dɒns/ *n* a dance in which the partners are arranged in opposite lines; the music for this.—*also* **contradance**.

contretemps /'kɒntrə,tɑ̃/ *n* (*pl* **contretemps**) a confusing, embarrassing or awkward occurrence.

contribute /kən'trɪbju:t/ *vti* to give to a common stock or fund; to write (an article) for a magazine or newspaper; to furnish ideas, etc.—**contributive** *adj.*

contribution /,kɒntrɪ'bju:ʃən/ *n* the act of contributing; something contributed; a literary article; a payment into a collection.

contributor /-ər/ *n* a person who contributes, *esp* the writer of an article for a newspaper, etc; a factor, a contributory cause.—**contributorial** *adj.*

contributory /kən'trɪbjutəri/ or /kən'trɪbu,tɔri/ *adj* giving, donating; partly responsible, sharing in.

con trick *n* (*inf*) confidence trick.

contrite /'kɒntraɪt/ or /kən'traɪt/ *adj* deeply repentant, feeling guilt.—**contritely** *adv.*—**contrition** *n.*

contrivance /kən'traɪvəns/ *n* something contrived, *esp* a mechanical device, invention; inventive ability; an artificial construct; a stratagem.

contrive /kən'traɪv/ *vt* to plan ingeniously; to devise, to design, to manage; to achieve, *esp* by some ploy or trick; to scheme.—**contriver** *n.*

contrived /-'traɪvd/ *adj* skilful but overdone; (*writing*) not spontaneous or natural or flowing.

control /kən'trɒ:l/ *v, n* restraint; command, authority; a check; a means of controlling; a standard of comparison for checking an experiment; (*pl*) mechanical parts by which a car, aeroplane, etc is operated. • *vt* (**controlling, controlled**) to check; to restrain; to regulate; to govern; (*experiment*) to verify by comparison.

controllable /-əbəl/ *adj* able to be controlled.—**controllably** *adv.*

controller /kən'trɒ:lər/ *n* a person who controls, *esp* one in charge of expenditure or finances.

control tower *n* a tower at an airport from which flight directions are given.

controversial /,kɒntrə'vɜrʃəl/ *adj* causing controversy, open to argument.—**controversialism** *n.*—**controversialist** *n.*—**controversially** *adv.*

controversy /'kɒntrə,vɜrsi/ or /kən'trɒvərsi/ *n* (*pl* **controversies**) a discussion of contrary opinions; dispute, argument.

controvert /'kɒntrə,vɜrt/ or /-'vɜrt/ *vt* to contend against; to refute; to disprove.—**controverter** *n.*—**controvertible** *adj.*

contumacious /,kɒntju:'meɪʃəs/ *adj* resisting authority, insubordinate; obstinate.

contumacy /kɒn'tju:məsi/ or /'kɒntjuməsi/ *n* (*pl* **contumacies**) stubborn resistance to authority, *esp* contempt of court.—**contumacious** *adj.*

contumelious /,kɒntju:'mi:liəs/ *adj* haughtily contemptuous or offensive; supercilious.

contumely /kɒn'tju:mli/ or /'kɒntju:mli/ *n* (*pl* **contumelies**) haughty and contemptuous rudeness; scornful and insolent abuse; reproach, disgrace.

contuse /kən'tju:z/ or /-,tu:z/ *vt* to wound or bruise without breaking the skin.—**contusive** *adj.*

contusion /kən'tu:ʃən/ or /-tju:-/ *n* a wound that does not break the skin, a bruise.—**contusioned** *adj.*

conundrum /kə'nʌndrəm/ *n* a riddle involving a pun; a puzzling question.

conurbation /ˌkɒnərˈbeɪʃən/ n a vast urban area around and including a large city.

convalesce /ˌkɒnvəˈles/ vi to recover health and strength after an illness; to get better.—**convalescence** n.

convalescent /-ˈlesənt/ adj recovering health; aiding the recovery of full health. • n a patient recovering after an illness.

convection /kənˈvekʃən/ n the transmission of heat through a liquid by currents; the process whereby warmer air rises while cooler air drops.—**convectional** adj.—**convective** adj.

convector /kənˈvektər/ n a heater that circulates warm air.

convene /kənˈviːn/ vti to call together for a meeting.—**convenable** adj.—**convener** n.

convenience /kənˈviːniəns/ n what suits one; a useful appliance.

convenience food n food that is easily and quickly prepared.

convenience store n a small store open for extended hours that sells packaged, canned, or bottled foods and drinks as well as common household items.

convenient /-iənt/ adj handy; suitable; causing little or no trouble.—**conveniently** adv.

convent /ˈkɒnvənt/ or /-vent/ n a house of a religious order, esp an establishment of nuns.

conventicle /kənˈventikəl/ n a meeting house; a secret meeting; an assembly for worship, usu by a schism; (formerly) a prohibited meeting of Nonconformists or Covenanters.

convention /kənˈvenʃən/ n a political or ecclesiastical assembly or meeting; an agreement between nations, a treaty; established usage, social custom.

conventional /-əl/ adj of or based on convention or social custom; not spontaneous; lacking imagination or originality; following accepted rules; (weapons) non-nuclear.—**conventionality** n (pl **conventionalities**).—**conventionally** adj.

conventionalism /-ˌɪzəm/ n that which is received as established by usage, etc; adherence to established usage.—**conventionalist** n.

conventionalize /-ˌaɪz/ vt to make conventional.—**conventionalization** n.

conventual /kənˈventʃuəl/ adj belonging to a convent. • n a member or inmate of a convent.

converge /kənˈvərdʒ/ vti to come or bring together.—**convergence, convergency** n.—**convergent** adj.

conversable /kənˈvərsəbəl/ adj disposed to converse, sociable.

conversant /kənˈvərsənt/ adj well acquainted; proficient; familiar (with).—**conversance, conversancy** n.

conversation /ˌkɒnvərˈseɪʃən/ n informal talk or exchange of ideas, opinions, etc between people.—**conversational** adj.—**conversationally** adv.

conversationalist /-ʃənəlɪst/, **conversationist** /-ɪst/ n a person who is good at conversation.

conversation piece n originally an 18th-century picture showing a group in an outdoor or indoor setting; something unusual or novel that provokes conversation; a play that focuses interest on dialogue as much as on action.

conversazione It. /ˌkɒnvərsɒˈtsjɑne/ n (pl **conversazioni, conversaziones**) a meeting for conversation, esp on literary or scientific topics.

converse[1] /ˈkɒnˌvərs/ n; /kənˈvərs/ vi to engage in conversation (with). • n familiar talk, conversation.—**converser** n.

converse[2] /kənˈvərs/ n; /ˈkɒnvərs/ adj opposite, contrary. • n something that is opposite or contrary.—**conversely** adv.

conversion /kənˈvərʒən/ n change from one state, or from one religion, to another; something converted from one use to another; an alteration to a building undergoing a change in function; (rugby) a score after a try by kicking the ball over the crossbar.—**conversional, conversionary** adj.

convert /kənˈvərt/ vt to change from one thing, condition or religion to another; to alter; to apply to a different use; (rugby) to make a conversion after a try. • n a converted person, esp one who has changed religion.

converter, convertor /kənˈvərtər/ n one who converts; an iron retort used for converting pig iron into steel in the Bessemer process; a kind of electrical induction coil.

converter reactor n a nuclear reactor that changes fertile material to fissile material.

convertible /kənˈvərtibəl/ adj able to be converted. • n an automobile with a folding or detachable roof.—**convertibility** n.

convex /kɒnˈveks/ adj curving outward like the surface of a sphere.—**convexly** adv.—**convexity** n.

convexo-concave /kɒnˈveksoːkɒnˈkeɪv/ or /kən-/ adj convex on one side, concave on the other.

convexo-convex /-kɒnˈveks/ adj curving outwards on both sides, as a lens.

convey /kənˈveɪ/ vt to transport; to conduct, to transmit; to make known, to communicate; (law) to make over (property).—**conveyable** adj.—**conveyor, conveyer** n.

conveyance /kənˈveɪəns/ n the act of conveying; a means of transporting, a vehicle; (law) the act of transferring property.—**conveyancer** n.

conveyancing /-ənsɪŋ/ n the business of drawing up deeds, leases, etc, and investigating titles to property.

conveyor belt n a continuous moving belt or linked plates for moving objects in a factory.

convict /kənˈvikt/ vt to prove or pronounce guilty. •/ˈkɒnˌvikt/ n a convicted person serving a prison sentence.

conviction /kənˈvikʃən/ n act of convicting; a settled opinion; a firm belief.

convince /kənˈvins/ vt to persuade by argument or evidence; to satisfy by proof.—**convincer** n.—**convincible** adj.

convincing /-ɪŋ/ adj compelling belief.—**convincingly** adv.

convivial /kenˈviviəl/ adj sociable, jovial.—**conviviality** n.—**convivially** adv.

convocation /ˌkɒnvəˈkeɪʃən/ n the act of convoking an assembly, esp of bishops, clergy or heads of a university; an assembly of clergy.—**convocational** adj.—**convocator** n.

convoke /kənˈvoːk/ to call or summon together; to convene.—**convoker** n.

convolute /ˈkɒnvəˌluːt/ vt to form into a rolled or coiled shape. • adj (bot) rolled upon itself; coiled.

convoluted /-əd/ adj twisted; coiled; complicated, difficult to understand.

convolution /ˌkɒnvəˈluːʃən/ n a rolling together, a coiling; a fold, a twist; a complicated or confused matter.

convolve /kənˈvɒlv/ vt to roll together.

convolvulus /kənˈvɒlvjuləs/ n (pl **convolvuluses, convolvuli**) a twining plant with bell-shaped flowers.

convoy /ˈkɒnvɔɪ/ n a group of ships or vehicles travelling together for protection. • vt to travel thus.

convulse /kənˈvels/ vt to agitate violently; to shake with irregular spasms. • vi (inf) to cause to shake with uncontrollable laughter.—**convulsive** adj.—**convulsively** adv.

convulsion /kenˈvelʃən/ n a violent involuntary contraction of a muscle or muscles; an agitation, tumult; (pl) a violent fit of laughter.

cony, coney /ˈkoːni/ n (pl **conies, coneys**) rabbit, or the skin or fur of a rabbit used in making clothes.

coo /kuː/ n the note of the pigeon; a soft murmuring sound. • vt (**cooing, cooed**) to utter the cry of a dove or pigeon; to speak softly; to act or murmur in a loving manner.

cook /kʊk/ vt to prepare (food) by heat; (inf) to fake (accounts, etc); to subject to great heat. • vi to be a cook; to undergo cooking; (with **up**) to plot; to make up a story. • n a person who cooks; one whose job is to cook.—**cookable** adj.

cookbook /ˈkʊkˌbʊk/, **cookery book** n a book of recipes and other information for preparing food.

cook-chill n (catering) a method in which meals are pre-cooked, chilled rapidly and then reheated as required.

cooker /ˈkʊkər/ n an electric or gas appliance for cooking.

cookery /ˈkʊkəri/ n the art or practice of cooking.

cookhouse /ˈkʊkhɒʊs/ n a kitchen, esp outdoors.

cookie[1], **cooky** /ˈkʊki/ n (pl **cookies**) a small flat sweet cake; (sl) a person.

cookie[2] n (comput) a small file which is transmitted to, and stored on, the hard disk of a computer, which acts as a sort of identification.

cool /kuːl/ adj moderately cold; calm; indifferent; unenthusiastic; cheeky. • vti to make or become cool. • n coolness; composure.—**coolly** adv.—**coolness** n.

coolant /ˈkuːlənt/ n a fluid or other substance for cooling machinery.

cooler /ˈkuːlə/ n that which cools; a vessel for cooling liquids, etc; a drink of spirits; (sl) prison.

cool-headed /ˈkuːlhedəd/ adj not easily excited.

coolie, cooly /ˈkuːli/ n (pl **coolies**) an Indian or Chinese hired labourer.

cooling tower n a tall hollow construction used in some industries, in which water is cooled and reused.

coon /kuːn/ *n* (*US*) *short for* raccoon.

cooncan /kuːnˈkæn/ *n* a card game for two.

coop /kuːp/ *n* a small pen for poultry. • *vt* to confine as in a coop.

co-op /ˈkoʊɒp/ *n* a cooperative.

cooper /ˈkuːpər/ *n* one who makes and repairs barrels, etc.

cooperage /-ədʒ/ *n* the business or workshop of a cooper; the price for a cooper's work.

cooperate /koʊˈɒpəˌreɪt/ *vi* to work together, to act jointly.—**cooperation** *n*.—**cooperator** *n*.

cooperative /koʊˈɒpərtɪv/ or /-rətɪv/ *adj* willing to cooperate; helpful. • *n* an organization or enterprise owned by, and operated for the benefit of, those using its services.—**cooperatively** *adv*.

co-opt /koʊˈɒpt/ *vt* to elect or choose as a member by the agreement of the existing members.—**co-optation, co-option** *n*.—**co-optative, co-optive** *adj*.

coordinate /koʊˈɔːrdɪˌneɪt/ *vt* to integrate (different elements, etc) into an efficient relationship; to adjust to; to function harmoniously. • *n* an equal person or thing; any of a series of numbers that, in a given frame of reference, locate a point in space; (*pl*) separate items of clothing intended to be worn together. • *adj* equal in degree or status.—**coordinately** *adv*.—**coordinator** *n*.

coordination /koʊˌɔːrdɪˈneɪʃən/ *n* the act of coordinating; the state of being coordinated; balanced and harmonious movement of the body.

coot /kuːt/ *n* a European water-bird with dark plumage and a white spot on the forehead; a silly person.

cootie /ˈkuːti/ *n* (*sl*) a louse.

cop[1] /kɒp/ *vb* (**copping, copped**) *vt* (*sl*) to arrest, catch. • *vi* (*with* **out**) (*sl*) to fail to perform, to renege. • *n* (*sl*) capture; a policeman.

cop[2] *n* a conical ball of thread on a spindle.

copaiba /koʊˈpeɪbə/ or /-ˈpaɪ-/ *n* an aromatic resinous balsam from various South American and West Indian trees.

copal /ˈkoʊpəl/ *n* a gum resin used in varnishes.

coparcenary /koʊˈpɑːrsəˌnɛreɪ/ *n* joint heirship.

coparcener /-sənər/ *n* a coheir.

copartner /koʊˈpɑːrtnər/ *n* a joint partner.—**copartnership** *n*.

cope[1] /koʊp/ *vi* to deal successfully with; to contend on even terms (with).

cope[2] *n* a large semicircular ecclesiastical vestment worn by bishops and priests over the surplice; a canopy, *esp* of heaven.

Copernican /kəˈpɜːrnɪkən/ *adj* of or relating to Copernicus and his teaching that the earth and planets revolve around the sun.

copestone /ˈkoʊpˌstoʊn/ *n* the top stone of a structure; a crowning touch.

copier /ˈkɒpiər/ *n* a copying machine, a photocopier.

copilot /ˈkoʊˌpaɪlət/ *n* a second pilot in an aircraft.

coping /ˈkoʊpɪŋ/ *n* the top masonry of a wall.

coping saw *n* a saw with a U-shaped frame and narrow blade used for cutting outlines in wood.

copious /ˈkoʊpiəs/ *adj* plentiful, abundant.—**copiously** *adv*.—**copiousness** *n*.

cop-out /ˈkɒpˌaʊt/ *n* (*sl*) an evasion; a means of avoiding responsibility.

copper[1] /ˈkɒpər/ *n* a reddish ductile metallic element; a bronze coin. • *adj* made of, or of the colour of, copper. • *vt* to cover with copper.—**coppery** *adj*.

copper[2] *n* (*sl*) a police officer.

copper-bottomed *adj* to be trusted; financially sound.

copperhead /ˈkɒpərˌhɛd/ *n* a South American snake.

copperplate /ˈkɒpərˌpleɪt/ *n* a polished plate of copper for engraving or printing; a print from this; copybook writing.

coppersmith /ˈkɒpərˌsmɪθ/ *n* a worker in copper.

copra /ˈkɒprə/ *n* the dried kernel of the coconut after the oil has been removed.

copro- /ˈkɒproʊ/ *prefix* dung.

coprolite /ˈkɒproʊˌlaɪt/ *n* fossil dung.—**coprolitic** *adj*.

coprophagous /kɒˈprɒfəgəs/ *adj* feeding on dung, as certain beetles.—**coprophagy** *n*.

coprophilia /ˌkɒproʊˈfiliə/ *n* an abnormal interest in faeces; love of obscenity.

coprophilous /-ˈfiləs/ *adj* growing in dung.

copse /kɒps/ *n* a thicket of small trees and shrubs.

Copt /kɒpt/ *n* a native Egyptian Christian.

copter /ˈkɒptər/ *n* *short for* a helicopter.

Coptic /ˈkɒptɪk/ *adj* pertaining to the Copts, their church or their language. • *n* the language spoken by Copts.

copula /ˈkɒpjʊlə/ *n* (*pl* **copulas, copulae**) a link, a connecting part; (*gram*) a word that joins the subject and predicate in a sentence or proposition.—**copular** *adj*.

copulate /ˈkɒpjʊˌleɪt/ *vi* to have sexual intercourse.—**copulation** *n*.—**copulatory** *adj*.

copulative /-tɪv/ *adj* joining, uniting; (*gram*) serving as a copula; uniting ideas as well as words. • *n* a copulative conjunction.

copy /ˈkɒpi/ *n* (*pl* **copies**) a reproduction; a transcript; a single specimen of a book; a model to be copied; a manuscript for printing; newspaper text; text for an advertisement; subject matter for a writer. • *vt* (**copying, copied**) to make a copy of, to reproduce; to take as a model, to imitate.

copybook /-bʊk/ *n* a book of handwriting exercises.

copy-edit *vt* to correct and prepare text for printing.

copyhold /-ˌhoʊld/ *n* (*English law*) a tenure of estate by copy of the court roll or custom of the manor.

copyholder /-ər/ *n* a tenant by copyhold; (*print*) a reader's assistant.

copyist /ˈkɒpiɪst/ *n* one who copies.

copyright /ˈkɒpiˌraɪt/ *n* the exclusive legal right to the publication and sale of a literary, dramatic, musical, or artistic work in any form. • *adj* protected by copyright.

copywriter /-ˌraɪtər/ *n* a writer of advertising or publicity copy.—**copywriting** *n*.

coq au vin /ˌkoʊkoʊˈvæ̃/ *n* a dish of chicken cooked in wine.

coquet /koʊˈkɛt/ *vi* (**coquetting, coquetted**) to flirt with; to seek to attract attention or admiration; to trifle.

coquetry /ˈkoʊkɪtri/ *n* (*pl* **coquetries**) the act of coquetting; flirtatious behaviour.

coquette /koʊˈkɛt/ *n* a woman who trifles with men's affections.—**coquettish** *adj*.

coquito /koʊˈkiːtoʊ/ *n* (*pl* **coquitos**) a tall Chilean palm producing edible nuts and palm honey.

coracle /ˈkɒrəkəl/ or /ˈkɒ-/ *n* a boat with a wicker frame covered with leather.

coracoid /ˈkɒrəˌkɔɪd/ or /ˈkɒ-/ *n* a hook-like process of the scapula or bladebone.

coral /ˈkɒrəl/ or /ˈkɒ-/ *n* the hard skeleton secreted by certain marine polyps. • *adj* made of coral, *esp* jewellery; of the colour of coral, deepish pink.

coralline /ˈkɒrəˌlaɪn/ or /ˈkɒ-/, **coralloid** /-lɔɪd/ or /ˈkɒ-/ *adj* consisting of, or like, coral; of a colour like coral. • *n* a coral-like seaweed or animal.

coral reef *n* a formation or bank of coral.

coral tree *n* an American tree with blood-red flowers.

corban *n* an offering to God in fulfilment of a vow.

corbeil /ˈkɔːrbəl/ or /-ˌbɛl/ *n* (*archit*) a sculptured basket of flowers, fruit, etc.

corbel /ˈkɔːrbəl/ *n* a stone or timber projection from a wall to support something. • *vt* (**corbelling, corbelled** or **corbeling, corbeled**) to furnish with or support by corbel.

corbicula *n* (*pl* **corbiculae**) the receptacle for pollen in the honey bee.

cord /kɔːrd/ *n* a thick string or thin rope; something that binds; a slender electric cable; a ribbed fabric, *esp* corduroy; (*pl*) corduroy trousers; any part of the body resembling string or rope (*spinal cord*).

cordage /-ɪdʒ/ *n* a quantity of cords or ropes; ropes and rigging collectively.

cordate /ˈkɔːrdeɪt/ *adj* heart-shaped.

cordial /ˈkɔːrdʒəl/ or /-diəl/ *adj* hearty, warm; friendly; affectionate. • *n* a fruit-flavoured drink.—**cordially** *adv*.—**cordialness** *n*.

cordiality /kɔːrdiˈæliti/ *n* (*pl* **cordialities**) sincere sympathethic geniality; sincerity; heartiness.

cordiform /ˈkɔːrdəˌfɔːrm/ *adj* heart-shaped.

cordillera /kɔːrˈdɪlərə/ or /-ˌkɔːrdɪˈljɛrə/ *n* a continuous ridge or chain of mountains, *esp* of the Andes mountains.

cordite /ˈkɔːrˌdaɪt/ *n* an explosive used in bullets and shells.

cordless /ˈkɔːrdləs/ *adj* (*electrical device*) operated by a battery.

cordon /ˈkɔːrdən/ *n* a chain of police or soldiers preventing access to an area; a piece of ornamental cord or ribbon given as an award. • *vt* (*with* **off**) (*area*) to prevent access to.

cordon bleu *Fr.* /ˌkɔːrdɔ̃ˈbluː/ or /ˌkɔːrdɔ̃-/ *n* the highest distinction in any profession; a first-class cook.—*also adj*.

cordon sanitaire /ˌkɔrdɒnˌsaniˈter/ n a barrier around an infected area; a buffer zone.

cordovan /ˈkɔrdəvən/ n a Spanish leather made of goatskin or split horsehide, tanned and dressed.—also **cordwain**.

cords /ˈkɔrdz/ npl (inf) corduroy trousers.

corduroy /ˈkɔrdəˌrɔɪ/ or /-dju-/ n a strong cotton fabric with a velvety ribbed surface; (pl) trousers of this.

corduroy road n a roadway formed of logs laid crosswise across swampy ground, etc.

cordwain /ˈkɔrdˌweɪn/ see **cordovan**.

cordwainer /-ər/ n (arch) a worker in leather; a shoemaker.

core /kɔr/ n the innermost part, the heart; the inner part of an apple, etc containing seeds; the region of a nuclear reactor containing the fissile material; (comput) a form of magnetic memory used to store one bit of information. • vt to remove the core from.—**corer** n.

coreopsis /ˌkɔriˈɒpsɪs/ or /ˌkɒri-/ n a kind of plant with rayed flowers and seeds with two small horns at the end.

corespondent /ˌkoːrɪˈspɒndənt/ n (law) a person named as having committed adultery with the husband or wife from whom a divorce is sought.—**corespondency** n.

corgi /ˈkɔrgi/ n (pl **corgis**) a Welsh breed of dog with short legs and a sturdy body.

coriaceous /ˌkɔriˈeɪʃəs/ adj of leather; leathery.

coriander /ˈkɔriˌændər/ n a plant with aromatic seeds used for flavouring food.

Corinthian /kəˈrɪnθiən/ adj of or pertaining to Corinth, a Greek city noted for its luxury and licentiousness; luxurious; conducted by amateurs; (archit) denoting the Corinthian order. • n a man about town; a gentleman yachtsman or sportsman.

Corinthian order n the lightest and most ornate of the classic orders of architecture, with a bell-shaped capital and ornamented with acanthus leaves.

corium /ˈkɔriəm/ n (pl **coria**) the innermost layer of skin of the cuticle.

cork /kɔrk/ n the outer bark of the cork oak used esp for stoppers and insulation; a stopper for a bottle, esp made of cork. • adj made of cork. • vt to stop up with a cork; to give a taste of cork to (wine).

corkage /ˈkɔrkɪdʒ/ n a charge made by a restaurant for serving wine, esp when brought in by the customer from outside.

corked /-d/ adj (wine) contaminated by a decayed cork.

corker /ˈkɔrkər/ n (sl) something conclusive or superlatively good; a flagrant lie.

corkscrew /ˈkɔrkskruː/ n a tool for drawing corks from wine bottles. • adj spiral-shaped, resembling a corkscrew.

corky /ˈkɔrki/ adj made of, or like, cork.

corm /kɔrm/ n the bulb-like underground stem of the crocus, etc; a solid bulb.—**cormous** adj.

cormel /ˈkɔrməl/ n a new corm developing from a mature one.

cormorant /ˈkɔrmərənt/ n a large voracious sea bird with dark plumage and webbed feet.

corn[1] /kɔrn/ n a grain or seed of a cereal plant; plants that yield grain; maize; (sl) something corny.

corn[2] n a small hard painful growth on the foot.

corn[3] vt to preserve or cure, as with salt.

corn(ed) beef n cooked salted beef.

corn circle see **crop circle**.

corncob /-ˈkɒb/ n the central part of an ear of maize to which the corn kernels are attached; a corncob pipe.

corncockle n a plant with purplish flowers that grows among corn.

corncrake /-ˌkreɪk/ n a bird with a harsh cry, the landrail.

corncrib /-ˌkrɪb/ n a storehouse for corn.

cornea /ˈkɔrniə/ n (pl **corneas, corneae**) the transparent membrane in front of the eyeball.—**corneal** adj.

cornel /ˈkɔrnəl/ n the cornelian cherry or dogwood, yielding an acrid edible red berry.

cornelian /kɔrˈniːliən/ n a dull-red semi-transparent form of chalcedony.—also **carnelian**.

corneous /ˈkɔrniəs/ adj horny.

corner /ˈkɔrnər/ n the point where sides or streets meet; an angle; a secret or confined place; a difficult or dangerous situation; (football, hockey) a free kick from the corner of the pitch; a monopoly over the supply of a good or service giving control over the market price; one of the opposite angles in a boxing ring. • vt to force into a corner; to monopolize supplies of (a commodity). • vi to turn round a corner; to meet at a corner or angle.

cornerstone /-ˌstoːn/ n the principal stone, esp one at the corner of a foundation; an indispensable part; the most important thing or person.

cornet /ˈkɔrnət/ n a tapering valved brass musical instrument; a cone-shaped wafer for ice cream.

cornetist, cornettist /kɔrˈnetɪst/ n a performer on the cornet.

cornfield /-ˌfiːld/ n a field planted with corn or other cereal plants.

cornflakes /-ˌfleɪks/ npl a breakfast cereal made from split and toasted maize.

cornflour /-ˈflaʊr/ n a type of corn or maize flour used for thickening sauces.—also **cornstarch**.

cornflower /-ˌflaʊr/ n a blue-flowered wild plant growing in cornfields.

cornice /ˈkɔrnɪs/ n a plaster moulding round a ceiling or on the outside of a building.

corniche /ˈkɔrnɪʃ/ or /kɔrˈniːʃ/ n a coastal road, esp one along a cliff offering spectacular views.

corniculate /kɔrˈnɪkjuːlɪt/ or /-ˌleɪt/ adj horned; spurred.

Corn Laws npl British laws (1436–1834) for regulating the import and export of corn, repealed 1846–9.

corn pone n a type of Indian cornbread made with milk and eggs.

cornstalk /-ˌstɒk/ n a stem of corn; (sl) a youth or girl of Australian birth.

cornstarch /-ˌstɑrtʃ/ see **cornflour**.

cornucopia /ˌkɔrnjuˈkoːpiə/ n a horn-shaped container overflowing with fruits, flowers, etc; great abundance, an inexhaustible store.

cornute /kɔrˈnjuːt/ or /-ˈnuːt/, **cornuted** /-əd/ adj (biol) horned; horn-like.

corny /ˈkɔrni/ adj (**cornier, corniest**) (inf) hackneyed; banal; trite; overly sentimental.—**cornily** adv.—**corniness** n.

corolla /kəˈrɒlə/ or /-ˈroːlə/ n the inner envelope of a flower composed of two or more petals.

corollary /kəˈrɒləri/ n (pl **corollaries**) an additional inference from a proposition already proved; a result.

corona /kəˈroːnə/ n (pl **coronas, coronae**) a top; a crown; a luminous halo or envelope round the sun or moon; the flat projecting part of a cornice.

coronal /kəˈroːnəl/ adj pertaining to the corona. • n a crown or garland.

coronary /ˈkɔrəˌneri/ or /ˈkɑrə-/ adj pertaining to the arteries supplying blood to the heart. • n (pl **coronaries**) a coronary artery; coronary thrombosis.

coronary thrombosis n blockage of one of the coronary arteries by a blood clot.

coronation /ˌkɔrəˈneɪʃən/ or /ˌkɑrə-/ n the act or ceremony of crowning a sovereign.

coroner /ˈkɔrənər/ or /ˈkɑr-/ n a public official who inquires into the causes of sudden or accidental deaths.—**coronership** n.

coronet /ˈkɔrəˌnet/ or /ˈkɑr-/, /-net/ n a small crown; an ornamental headdress.

corpora /ˈkɔrpərə/ see **corpus**.

corporal[1] /ˈkɔrpərəl/ or /-prəl/ n a noncommissioned officer below the rank of sergeant.—**corporalship** n.

corporal[2] adj of or relating to the body; physical, not spiritual.—**corporality, corporally** adv.

corporal[3] n a communion cloth.

corporate /ˈkɔrpərət/ or /-prət/ adj legally united into a body; of or having a corporation; united.—**corporately** adv.

corporation /ˌkɔrpəˈreɪʃən/ n a group of people authorized by law to act as one individual; a city or town council.—**corporative** n.

corporator /-ˈreɪtər/ n a member of a corporation.

corporeal /kɔrˈpɔriəl/ adj having a body or substance, material.—**corporeality, corporealness** n.—**corporeally** adv.

corposant /ˈkɔrpəˌsænt/ or /-ˌzænt/ n a flame-like electric discharge from a ship's mast and rigging in thundery weather, St. Elmo's fire.

corps /kɔr/ n (pl **corps**) an organized subdivision of the military establishment; a group or organization with a special function (medical corps).

corps de ballet /ˌkɔrdəbæˈleɪ/ n all the dancers in a ballet company.

corps diplomatique /ˌkɔrdɪpləməˈtiːk/ n all the ambassadors at a particular capital, the diplomatic corps.

corpse /kɔrps/ n a dead body. • vi (theat sl) to laugh or create laughter mischievously on stage.

corpulent /ˈkɔrpjulənt/ adj fleshy, fat.—**corpulence, corpulency** n.

corpus /'kɔrpəs/ *n* (*pl* **corpora**) a body or collection, *esp* of written works; the chief part of an organ.

Corpus Christi /ˌkrɪsti/ *n* (*RC Church*) a festival in honour of the Eucharist, held on the Thursday after Trinity Sunday.

corpuscle /'kɔrpəsəl/ *n* a red or white blood cell.—**corpuscular** *adj*.

corpus delicti /-dɪ'lɪk,taɪ/ *n* (*law*) the essence of a crime charged.

corral /'kɔræl/ *n* a pen for livestock; an enclosure with wagons; a strong stockade. • *vt* (**corralling, corralled**) to form a corral; to put or keep in a corral.

correct /kə'rekt/ *vt* to set right, to remove errors from; to reprove, to punish; to counteract; to neutralize; to adjust. • *adj* free from error; right, true, accurate; conforming to a fixed standard; proper.—**correctable, correctible** *adj*.—**correctly** *adv*.—**correctness** *n*.—**corrector** *n*.

correction /kə'rekʃən/ *n* the act of correcting; punishment.—**correctional** *adj*.

correctitude /kə'rektɪ,tuːd/ or /-,tjuːd/ *n* correctness, *esp* of conduct.

corrective /kə'rektɪv/ *adj* serving to correct or counteract. • *n* that which corrects.—**correctively** *adv*.

correlate /'kɔrə'leɪt/ *vti* to have or to bring into mutual relation; to correspond to one another. • *n* either of two things so related that one implies the other.—**correlation** *n*.—**correlative** *adj*.

correlation /ˌkɔrə'leɪʃən/ or /ˌkɑ-/ *n* reciprocal relation; similarity or parallelism of relation or law; the interdependence of functions, organs, natural forces, or phenomena.—**correlational** *adj*.

correlative /kə'relətɪv/ *adj* having or expressing reciprocal or mutual relation. • *n* the antecedent to a pronoun.—**correlativeness, correlativity** *n*.

correspond /ˌkɔrə'spɒnd/ or /ˌkɑ-/ *vi* to answer, to agree; to be similar (to); to tally; to communicate by letter.

correspondence /ˌkɔrə'spɒndəns/ or /ˌkɑ-/ *n* communication by writing letters; the letters themselves; agreement.

correspondence school *n* an institution offering tuition (**correspondence courses**) by post.

correspondent /ˌkɔrə'spɒndənt/ *n* a person who writes letters; a journalist who gathers news for newspapers, radio or television from a foreign country. • *adj* similar, analogous.

corridor /'kɔrɪdɔr/ or /'kɑr-/, /-dər/ *n* a long passage into which compartments in a train or rooms in a building open; a strip of land giving a country without a coastline access to the sea.

corrie /'kɔri/ or /'kɑri/ *n* (*Scot*) a round hollow on a hillside.

corrigendum /ˌkɔrɪ'dʒɛndəm/ or /ˌkɑr-/ *n* (*pl* **corrigenda**) an error in a book, etc, for which a correction slip is printed.

corrigible /'kɔrədʒəbəl/ or /'kɑr-/ *adj* capable of being amended, correct, or reformed.—**corrigibility** *n*.

corroborant /kə'rɒbərənt/ *adj* corroborating. • *n* a corroborating fact.

corroborate /kə'rɒbə,reɪt/ *vt* to confirm; to make more certain; to verify.—**corroboration** *n*.—**corroborative** *adj*.—**corroborator** *n*.

corroboree /kə'rɒbəri/ *n* an Australian festivity and dance.

corrode /kə'roːd/ *vti* to eat into or wear away gradually, to rust; to disintegrate.—**corrodant, corrodent** *n*.—**corroder** *n*.—**corrodible** *adj*.—**corrosion** *n*.

corrosion /kə'roːʒən/ *n* the act of corroding; a corroded condition.

corrosive /kə'roːzɪv/ *adj* causing corrosion. • *n* a corrosive substance, as acid.—**corrosively** *adv*.—**corrosiveness** *n*.

corrosive sublimate *n* a poisonous compound of mercury.

corrugate /'kɔrʊ,geɪt/ or /'kɑr-/ *vt* to form into parallel ridges and grooves.—**corrugated** *adj*.—**corrugation** *n*.

corrugated iron *n* sheet iron pressed in alternate parallel ridges and grooves and galvanized.

corrugated paper *n* paper used for packaging with one surface in parallel ridges.

corrupt /kə'rʌpt/ *adj* dishonest; taking bribes; depraved; rotten, putrid. • *vti* to make or become corrupt; to infect; to taint.—**corrupter, corruptor** *n*.—**corruptive** *adj*.—**corruptly** *adv*.—**corruptness** *n*.

corruptible /kə'rʌptəbəl/ *adj* open to corruption.—**corruptibility** *n*.

corruption /kə'rʌpʃən/ *n* the act of corrupting; the state of being corrupted; physical dissolution.—**corruptionist** *n*.

corsage /kɔr'sɒʒ/ *n* a small bunch of flowers for pinning to a dress; the part of a woman's dress covering the bust.

corsair /'kɔrser/ or /kɑr,ser/ *n* a pirate; a pirate ship.

corse /kɔrs/ *n* (*poet*) a corpse.

corselet, corslet /'kɔrslɪt/ or /'kɔrsə,let/ *n* light body armour, *esp* for the breast.

corset /'kɔrsət/ *n* a close-fitting undergarment, worn to support the torso.

corsetière /ˌkɔrsə'tɪr/ or /-'tjɛr/ *n* a woman who makes and fits corsets.—**corsetier** *nm*.

cortege, cortège /'kɔr,teʒ/ *n* a train of attendants; a retinue; a funeral procession.

Cortes /'kɔrtez/, *Sp*. /'kɔrtes/ *n* the national and legislative assembly of Spain and (formerly) Portugal.

cortex /'kɔr,teks/ *n* (*pl* **cortices**) an outer layer of tissue of any organ, eg the outer grey matter of the brain; the outer tissue of a plant stem; bark of a tree.—**cortical** *adj*.

corticate /'kɔrtə,kət/ or /-,keɪt/, **corticated** *adj* covered with bark or a bark-like substance.—**cortication** *n*.

cortisone /'kɔrtə,zoːn/ *n* a hormone produced by the adrenal glands, the synthetic version of which is used to treat arthritis, allergies and skin disorders, etc.

corundum /kə'rʌndəm/ *n* a hard mineral of many colours used as an abrasive and as gemstones.

coruscate /'kɔrə,skeɪt/ or /'kɑr-/ *vi* to sparkle, to flash.—**coruscation** *n*.

corvée /kɔr'veɪ/ *n* the exacting of unpaid labour in the feudal system.

corves /kɔrvz/ *see* **corf**.

corvette /'kɔr,vet/ *n* a fast escort warship.

corvine /'kɔr,vaɪn/ *adj* of or pertaining to a crow or raven.

corymb /'kɔrɪmb/, or /'kɑr-/, /-ɪm/ *n* an inflorescence with the flowers all nearly at the same level and the lower stalks are the longest.—**corymbose, corybous** *adj*.

coryphaeus /ˌkɔrə'fiːəs/ *n* (*pl* **coryphaei**) the leader of the chorus in ancient Greek drama.

coryphée /ˌkɔrɪ'feɪ/ or /ˌkɔr-/ *n* a ballet dancer.

coryza /kə'raɪzə/ *n* a severe cold in the head with inflammation of the mucous membrane of the nose.

cos /kɒs/ *abbr* = cosine.

cosec /'kɔːsek/ *abbr* = cosecant.

cosecant /kɔː'siːkənt/ *n* (*geom*) the secant of the complement of the given angle or arc of 90°.

coseismal /kɔː'saɪsməl/ or /-'saɪz-/, **coseismic** /-mɪk/ *adj* showing simultaneous shocks of an earthquake.

cosh /kɒʃ/ *vt* (*sl*) to bludgeon.

cosher /'kɒʃər/ *vt* to pamper, to coddle.

cosignatory /kɔː'sɪgnə,tɔːri/ *n* a person signing along with another.

cosine /kɔː'saɪn/ *n* a trigonometrical function of an angle that in a right-angled triangle is equal to the ratio of the length of the adjacent side to the hypotenuse.

cosmetic /kɒz'metɪk/ *n* a preparation for improving the beauty, *esp* of the face. • *adj* beautifying or correcting faults in the appearance.—**cosmetically** *adv*.

cosmetic surgery *n* surgery carried out to improve the appearance.

cosmic /ˌkɒzmɪk/, **cosmical** /-əl/ *adj* of or pertaining to the universe and the laws that govern it; vast in extent, intensity, or comprehensiveness.—**cosmically** *adv*.

cosmo- /'kɒzmoː/ or /-mə/ *prefix* universe.

cosmogony /kɒz'mɒgəni/ *n* (*pl* **cosmogonies**) the origin of the universe; a theory or treatise on this.—**cosmogonal** *adj*.—**cosmogonic, cosmogonical** *adj*.—**cosmogonist** *n*.

cosmography /kɒz'mɒgrəfi/ *n* the description and mapping of the universe or the earth as a whole.—**cosmographer, cosmographist** *n*.—**cosmographic, cosmographical** *adj*.

cosmology /kɒz'mɒlədʒi/ *n* the science of the nature, origins, and development of the universe.—**cosmological, cosmologic** *adj*.—**cosmologist** *n*.

cosmonaut /'kɒzmə,nɒt/ *n* a Russian astronaut.

cosmopolitan /ˌkɒzmə'pɒlɪtən/ *adj* of all parts of the world; free from national prejudice; at home in any part of the world. • *n* a well-travelled person; a person without national prejudices.—**cosmopolitanism** *n*.

cosmopolite /kɒz'mɒpə,laɪt/ *n* a citizen of the world, a person without patriotism; an animal or plant found worldwide.—**cosmopolitism** *n*.

cosmos /kɒz'moːs/ or /-məs/ *n* the universe as an ordered whole; any orderly system.

Cossack /'kɒsæk/ *n* a member of a Russian people skilled as horsemen. • *adj* pertaining to Cossacks.

cosset /'kɒsɛt/ *vt* to make a pet of; to pamper.

cost /kɒst/ *vt* (**costing, cost**) to involve the payment, loss, or sacrifice of; to have as a price; to estimate and fix the price of. • *n* a price; an expense; expenditure of time, labour, etc; a loss, a penalty; (*pl*) the expenses of a lawsuit.

costa /'kɒstə/ *n* (*pl* **costae**) a rib.—**costal** *adj*.

costard /'kɒstərd/ *n* a large kind of English apple; (*arch*) a head.

costate /'kɒsˌteɪd/ or /'kɒs-/ *adj* ribbed.

cost-effective /ˌkɒstə'fɛktɪv/ *adj* giving a satisfactory return for the amount spent on outlay.

costive /'kɒstɪv/ *adj* constipated.

costly /'kɒstli/ *adj* (**costlier, costliest**) expensive; involving great sacrifice.—**costliness** *n*.

costmary /'kɒstˌmɛri/ *n* (*pl* **costmaries**) a perennial plant with fragrant leaves, formerly used for flavouring ale.

cost-of-living index *n* consumer price index.

costume /'kɒˌstjuːm/ or /-ˌtuːm/ *n* a style of dress, *esp* belonging to a particular period, fashion, etc; clothes of an unusual or historical nature, as worn by actors in a play, etc; fancy dress.

costume jewellery *n* imitation gems or cheap jewellery worn for decorative effect.

costumer /-ər/, **costumier** /-ɪər/ *n* a dealer in fancy dress for the theatre, etc.

cosy /'koʊzi/ *adj* (**cosier, cosiest**) warm and comfortable; snug; friendly for an ulterior motive. • *n* a cover to keep a thing warm.—*also* **cozy**.—**cosily** *adv*.—**cosiness** *n*.

cot[1] /'kɒt/ *n* a child's box-like bed; a narrow collapsible bed.

cot[2] *abbr* = cotangent.

cotangent /'koʊˌtændʒənt/ *n* a trigonometrical function of an angle that in a right-angled triangle is equal to the ratio of the length of the adjacent side to the opposite side.

cot death *n* the sudden death of a baby during sleep from an unexplained cause.—*also* **crib death**.

cote /koʊt/ *n* a shed or shelter for animals or birds, *esp* doves.

cotenant /koʊ'tɛnənt/ or /'koʊˌtɛn-/ *n* a joint tenant.—**cotenancy** *n*.

coterie /'koʊtəri/ *n* a small circle of people with common interests; a social clique.

coterminous /koʊ'tərmənəs/ *see* **conterminous**.

cotidal /koʊ'taɪdəl/ *adj* (*chart lines*) joining those places where high tide occurs at the same time.

cotillion /kə'tɪljən/ or /koʊ-/ *n* a brisk, lively dance for eight or more people; music for such a dance; a formal ball.

cotoneaster /kəˌtoʊni'æstər/ *n* an ornamental shrub of the rose family with red or orange berries.

cotta /'kɒtə/ *n* (*pl* **cottae, cottas**) a short surplice.

cottage /'kɒtədʒ/ *n* a small house, *esp* in the country.

cottage cheese *n* a soft cheese made from loose milk curds.

cottage industry *n* manufacture carried out in the home, eg weaving, basketry.

cottager /-ər/ *n* a person who lives or holidays in a cottage.

cotter[1], **cottar** /'kɒtər/ *n* a farm labourer who has the use of a cottage for which he works in lieu of rent.

cotter[2] /'kɒtər/ *n* a bolt, wedge, etc used to secure parts of machinery to prevent movement.

cotter pin *n* a split pin that secures (a cotter, etc) by spreading the ends after insertion.

cotton /'kɒtən/ *n* soft white fibre of the cotton plant; fabric or thread made of this; thread. • *adj* made of cotton. • *vi* (*with* **on**) (*inf*) to realize the meaning of, to understand; to take a liking to.—**cottony** *adj*.

cotton candy *see* **candyfloss**.

cotton grass *n* a plant with long silky hairs.

cottontail *n* an American rabbit.

cotton wool *n* raw cotton that has been bleached and sterilized for use as a dressing, etc; absorbent cotton; a state of being protected.

cotyledon /ˌkɒtə'leɪdən/ *n* a seed lobe or rudimentary leaf or leaves of an embryo; kinds of plant, chiefly evergreens.—**cotyledonal** *adj*.—**cotyledonary** *adj*.—**cotyledonous, cotyledonoid** *adj*.

cotyloid /ˌkɒtə'lɔɪd/, **cotyloidal** /-əl/ *adj* cup-shaped.

couch /kaʊtʃ/ *n* a piece of furniture, with a back and armrests, for seating several persons; a bed, *esp* as used by psychiatrists for patients. • *vt* to express in words in a particular way; to lie down; to deposit in a bed or layer; (*arch*) to crouch ready for springing; to depress or remove (a cataract in the eye).—**coucher** *n*.

couchant /'kaʊtʃənt/ *adj* (*her*) lying down with the head up.

couch grass *n* a kind of coarse grass that spreads rapidly.

couching /'kaʊtʃɪŋ/ *n* the operation of removing a cataract from the eye by depressing or removing the crystalline lens; a style of embroidery.

couch potato *n* (*sl*) a person who would rather watch television in leisure time than participate in sports, etc.

cougar /'kuːgər/ *n* a puma.

cough /kɒf/ *vi* to expel air from the lungs with a sudden effort and noise; (*with* **up**) (*inf*) to hand over or tell unwillingly. • *n* the act of coughing; a disease causing a cough.

cough drop *n* a lozenge that when sucked relieves a cough.

cough syrup *n* a medicinal liquid to relieve coughing.

could /kʊd/ or /kəd/ *see* **can**[1].

couldn't /kʊdnt/ = could not.

coulee /'kuːli/ *n* a dry ravine with sloping sides; a flow of lava.

coulisse /kuː'liːs/ *n* a piece of grooved timber in which anything slides; one of the side scenes of a stage; (*pl*) the space between the side scenes.

couloir /kuːlwɑr/ *n* a steeply ascending gorge in a mountainside.

coulomb /'kuːlɒm/ *n* an SI unit of electric charge; the quantity of electricity conveyed by a current of one ampere in one second.

coulter /'koʊltər/ *n* a vertical blade at the front of a ploughshare.—*also* **colter**.

coumarin /'kuːmərɪn/ *n* an aromatic crystalline substance obtained from the tonka bean and used in perfumes and medicines.—**coumaric** *adj*.

council /'kaʊnsəl/ *n* an elected or appointed legislative or advisory body; a central body uniting a group of organizations; an executive body whose members are equal in power and authority.—**councillor, councilor** *n*.—**councillorship, councilorship** *n*.

councillor, councilor /-ər/ *n* a member of a council.—**councillorship, councilorship** *n*.

councilman /-mən/ *n* (*pl* **councilmen**) a member of a council, a councillor.

counsel /'kaʊnsəl/ *n* advice; consultation, deliberate purpose or design; a person who gives counsel, a lawyer or a group of lawyers; a consultant. • *vb* (**counselling** *or* **counseling, counselled** *or* **counseled**) *vt* to advise; to recommend. • *vi* to give or take advice.

counselling, counseling /-ɪŋ/ *n* professional guidance for an individual or a couple from a qualified person.

counsellor, counselor /-ər/ *n* one who gives advice, *esp* legal advice, an adviser a lawyer.

count[1] /kaʊnt/ *n* a European noble.

count[2] *vt* to number, to add up; to reckon; to consider to be; to call aloud (beats or time units); to include or exclude by counting; (*with* **against**) to have an adverse effect. • *vi* to name numbers or add up items in order; to mark time; to be of importance or value; to rely (upon); (*with* **on**) to rely on; (*with* **out**) (*inf*) to exclude, leave out; to pronounce after a count a floored boxer to be the loser. • *n* an act of numbering or reckoning; the total counted; a separate and distinct charge in an indictment; rhythm.

countdown /'kaʊntdaʊn/ *n* the descending count backwards to zero, eg to the moment a rocket lifts off.

countenance /'kaʊntənəns/ *n* the whole form of the face; appearance; support. • *vt* to favour, give approval to.

counter[1] /'kaʊntər/ *n* one who or that which counts; a disc used for scoring, a token; a table in a bank or shop across which money or goods are passed.

counter[2] *adv* contrary; adverse; in an opposite direction; in the wrong way. • *adj* opposed; opposite. • *n* a return blow or parry; an answering move. • *vti* to oppose; to retort; to give a return blow; to retaliate.

counter- /'kaʊntər/ *prefix* rival; opposed; reversed; matched.

counteract /ˌkaʊntər'ækt/ *vt* to act in opposition to so as to defeat or hinder; to neutralize.—**counteraction** *n*.—**counteractive** *adj*.

counterattack /'kaʊntərəˌtæk/ or *n* an attack in response to an attack. • *vt* to make a counterattack.

counterattraction /'kaʊntərəˌtrækʃən/ *n* a rival attraction; attraction in an opposite direction.

counterbalance /'kaʊntərˌbæləns/ *n* a weight balancing another. • *vt* to act as a counterbalance; to act against with equal power.

counterchange /ˌkaʊntər'tʃeɪndʒ/ *vti* to interchange; to chequer.

countercharge /'kaʊntərˌtʃɑrdʒ/ *n* an opposing charge, *esp* by an accused person against his or her accuser. • *vt* to charge in opposition to another.

countercheck /-ˌtʃɛk/ *n* a check on a check; an opposing check; (*arch*) a retort.

counterclaim /ˈkaʊntərˌkleɪm/ *n* an opposing claim, *esp* by a defendant in a lawsuit.—**counterclaimant** *n*.

counterclockwise /ˌkaʊntərˈklɒkˌwaɪz/ *adj* moving in a direction contrary to the hands of a clock as viewed from the front.—*also adv*.—*also* **anticlockwise**.

counterespionage /ˌkaʊntərˈɛspiəˌnɒʒ/ *n* spying on or exposing enemy spies.

counterfeit /ˈkaʊntərˌfɪt/ *vt* to imitate; to forge; to feign, simulate. • *adj* made in imitation, forged; feigned, sham. • *n* an imitation, a forgery.—**counterfeiter** *n*.

counterfoil /-ˌfɔɪl/ *n* a detachable section of a cheque or ticket, kept as a receipt or record; a stub.

counterintelligence /ˌkaʊntərɪnˈtɛlɪdʒəns/ *n* activities intended to frustrate enemy espionage and intelligence-gathering operations.

counterirritant /ˌkaʊntərˈɪrɪtənt/ *n* an application or action irritating the body surface to relieve internal inflammation.—**counterirritation** *n*.

countermand /-ˈmænd/ *vt* to revoke or annul, as an order or command; to cancel the orders of another. • *n* a command cancelling another.

countermarch /ˈkaʊntərˌmɑrtʃ/ *vti* to march in the reverse direction. • *n* such a march.

countermeasure /-ˌmɛʒər/ *n* an action taken to neutralize or retaliate against some threat or danger, etc.

countermine /-ˌmaɪn/ *n* a mine made to intercept that of an enemy. • *vi* to make a countermine; to counterplot.

counteroffensive /-əˌfɛnsɪv/ *n* a counterattack, *esp* by defenders of a position.

counterpane /-ˌpeɪn/ *n* a bedspread.

counterpart /-ˌpɑrt/ *n* a thing exactly like another, a duplicate; a corresponding or complementary part or thing.

counterplot /-ˌplɒt/ *n* a plot to defeat another plot. • *vi* (**counterplotting, counterplotted**) to plot in retaliation.

counterpoint /-ˌpɔɪnt/ *n* (*mus*) a melody added as an accompaniment to another. • *vt* to set in contrast.

counterpoise /-ˌpɔɪz/ *n* a weight, force or influence that balances another; equilibrium. • *vt* to counterbalance.

counterproductive /-prəˈdʌktəv/ *adj* producing a contrary effect on productivity or usefulness; hindering the desired end.

Counter-Reformation /ˌkaʊntərˌrɛfərˈmeɪʃən/ *n* the reforming movement in the Roman Catholic Church following the Protestant Reformation.

counter-revolution /-ˌrɛvəˈluːʃən/ *n* a revolution undoing the work of a previous one.—**counter-revolutionary** *adj, n*.

countersign /ˈkaʊntərˌsaɪn/ *vt* to authenticate a document by an additional signature. • *n* an additional signature to a document to attest it; a word to be given in answer to a sentry's challenge; an additional mark.—**countersignature** *n*.

countersink /-ˌsɪŋk/ *vt* (**countersinking, countersunk**) to enlarge the upper part of a hole so that the screw head will sit flush with, or below, the surface; to drive (a screw) into such a hole. • *n* a tool for countersinking.

countertenor /-ˌtɛnər/ *n* a high tenor voice with an alto range; a person who sings countertenor.

counterterrorism /ˌkaʊntərˈtɛrərɪzəm/ *n* terrorist act(s) perpetrated in revenge for former terrorist act(s).

countervail /ˌkaʊntərˈveɪl/ *or* /ˈkaʊntər-/ *vt* to counterbalance, compensate for.

counterweight /ˈkaʊntərˌweɪt/ *n* a counterbalancing weight or power.

countess /ˈkaʊntəs/ *n* a woman with the rank of count or earl; the wife or widow of a count.

counting house *n* a book-keeping office or department.

countless /ˈkaʊntləs/ *adj* innumerable.

countrified, countryfied /ˈkʌntrɪˌfaɪd/ *adj* in the manner of the country; rural.

country /ˈkʌntri/ *n* (*pl* **countries**) a region or district; the territory of a nation; a state; the land of one's birth or residence; rural parts; country-and-western. • *adj* rural.

country-and-western *n* a style of white folk music of the southeastern US.—*also* **country music**.

country club *n* a social and sporting facility in a rural setting.

country dance *n* a dance with the couples face to face in two lines.

country house *n* a gentleman's country residence.

countryman /-mən/ *n* (*pl* **countrymen**) a person who lives in the country; a person from the same country as another.—**countrywoman** *nf* (*pl* **countrywomen**).

countryside /-ˌsaɪd/ *n* a rural district.

county /ˈkaʊnti/ *n* (*pl* **counties**) in UK, an administrative subdivision for local government; in US, an administrative subdivision of a state.—*also adj*.

county palatine *n* a county having royal powers in the administration of justice.

county town, county seat *n* the capital of a county.

coup /kuː/ *n* a sudden telling blow; a masterstroke; a coup d'état.

coup de grâce /ˌkuːdəˈɡrɒs/ *n* (*pl* **coups de grâce**) a finishing or fatal blow.

coup d'état /ˌkuːdeɪˈtɒ/ *n* (*pl* **coups d'état**) a sudden and unexpected bold stroke of policy; the sudden overthrow of a government.

coup de théâtre /ˌkuːdeɪˈtætrə/, *Fr.* /ˌkuːtteɪˈɑːtr/ *n* (*pl* **coups de théâtre**) a sudden dramatic or sensational action.

coupé /ˈkuːp/, *Fr.* /kuːˈpeɪ/ *n* a closed, four-seater, two-door automobile with a sloping back.

couple /ˈkʌpəl/ *n* two of the same kind connected together; a pair; a husband and wife; a pair of equal and parallel forces. • *vt* to link or join together. • *vi* to copulate.

couplet /ˈkʌplət/ *n* two consecutive lines of verse that rhyme with each other.

coupling /ˈkʌplɪŋ/ *n* a device for joining parts of a machine or two railway carriages.

coupon /ˈkuːpɒn/ *or* /ˈkjuː-/ *n* a detachable certificate on a bond, presented for payment of interest; a certificate entitling one to a discount, gift, etc.

courage /ˈkɛrɪdʒ/ *n* bravery; fortitude; spirit.—**courageous** *adj*.—**courageously** *adv*.—**courageousness** *n*.

courgette /kʊrˈʒɛt/ *n* a zucchini.

courier /ˈkʊriːər/ *n* a messenger, *esp* diplomatic; a tourist guide; a carrier of illegal goods between countries.

course /kɔrs/ *n* a race; a path or track; a career; a direction or line of motion; a regular sequence; the portion of a meal served at one time; conduct; behaviour; the direction a ship is steered; a continuous level range of brick or masonry of the same height; the chase of a hare by greyhounds; a length of time; an area set aside for a sport or a race; a series of studies; any of the studies. • *vt* to hunt. • *vi* to move swiftly along an indicated path; to chase with greyhounds.

courser /ˈkɔrsər/ *n* one who courses; a dog trained for coursing; (*poet*) a swift and spirited horse.

coursing /ˈkɔrsɪŋ/ *n* the sport of pursuing game with hunting dogs.

court /kɔrt/ *n* an uncovered space surrounded by buildings or walls; a short street; a playing space, as for tennis, etc; a royal palace; the retinue of a sovereign; (*law*) a hall of justice; the judges, etc engaged there; address; civility; flattery. • *vt* to seek the friendship of; to woo; to flatter; to solicit; to risk. • *vi* to carry on a courtship.

courteous /ˈkɔrtiːəs/ *adj* polite; obliging.—**courteously** *adv*.—**courteousness** *n*.

courtesan /ˌkɔrtiˈzæn/ *or* /ˈkɔrt-/ *n* (*formerly*) a prostitute, or mistress of a courtier.

courtesy /ˈkɔrtisi/ *n* (*pl* **courtesies**) politeness and kindness; civility; a courteous manner or action.

courthouse /ˈkɔrtˌhʊs/ *n* a public building that houses law courts.

courtier /ˈkɔrtiːər/ *n* one in attendance at a royal court.

courtly /ˈkɔrtli/ *adj* (**courtlier, courtliest**) well-mannered, polite; of a court.—**courtliness** *n*.

court martial /ˈkɔrtˌmɑrʃəl/ *n* (*pl* **courts martial, court martials**) a court of justice composed of naval or military officers for the trial of disciplinary offences.

court-martial *vt* (**court-martialling, court-martialled** *or* **court-martialing, court-martialed**) to try by court martial.

court plaster *n* a superior kind of sticking plaster, originally used by ladies at court for ornamental patches on the face.

courtship /-ˌʃɪp/ *n* the act of wooing.

courtyard /-ˌjɑrd/ *n* an enclosed space adjoining or in a large building.

couscous /ˈkuːskuːs/ *n* a North African dish of cracked wheat steamed and served with a meat and vegetable stew.

cousin /'kʌzən/ *n* the son or daughter of an uncle or aunt.—**cousinly** *adj.*—**cousinship** *n.*

couture /ku:'tʃuːr/ or /-'tur/, /-tjuːr/, *Fr.* /ku'tyʀ/ *n* the design and manufacture of expensive fashion clothes.

couturier /ku:'turi,ei/, *Fr.* /kytyˌʀjei/ *n* a designer of expensive fashion clothes.—**couturière** *nf.*

couvade /ku:'vɒd/ *n* a primitive custom by which when a child is born the father takes to his bed, where he receives the attentions *usu* given to the mother.

cove /koːv/ *n* a small sheltered bay or inlet in a body of water; a curved moulding at the juncture of a wall and ceiling.—*also* **coving**.

coven /'kʌvən/ *n* an assembly of witches.

covenant /'kʌvənənt/ *n* a written agreement; a solemn agreement of fellowship and faith between members of a church; an agreement to pay annually a sum to a charity. • *vt* to promise by a covenant. • *vi* to enter into a formal agreement.—**covenantal** *adj.*—**covenanted** *adj.*

covenantee /ˌkʌvənən'ti:/ *n* one in whose favour a covenant is made.

covenantor /'kʌvənəntər/ *n* one who enters into a covenant.

cover /'kʌvər/ *vt* to overspread the top of anything with something else; to hide; to save from punishment; to shelter; to clothe; to understudy; to insure against damage, loss, etc; to report for a newspaper; to include; to make a journey over; (*male animal*) to copulate. • *vi* to spread over, as a liquid does; to provide an excuse or alibi (for); to work, eg as a salesman, in a certain area; to have within firing range. • *n* that which is laid on something else; a bedcover; a shelter; a covert; an understudy; something used to hide one's real actions, etc; insurance against loss or damage; a place laid at a table for a meal.—**coverer** *n.*

coverage /'kʌvərɪdʒ/ *n* the amount, extent, etc covered by something; the amount of reporting of an event for newspaper, television, etc.

coverall /-ˌɔːl/ *n* (*usu pl*) a one-piece garment that completely covers and protects one's clothing.

cover charge *n* a charge made by a restaurant over and above the cost of the food and service.

cover girl *n* an attractive girl whose picture is used on magazine covers.

covering /'kʌvərɪŋ/ *n* that which covers or protects; dress.

covering letter *n* a letter containing an explanation of an accompanying item.

coverlet /'kʌvərlət/ *n* a bedspread.

coversine /'koːvərs/ *n* the versed sine of the complement of an angle or arc.

covert /'koːvərt/ or /koː'vərt/, /kʌ-/ *adj* covered; secret, concealed. • *n* a place that protects or shelters; a thicket; shelter for game.—**covertly** *adv.*

coverture /'koːvərtʃər/ *n* a cover; shelter; (*law*) the status of a married woman.

cover-up /'kʌvərˌʌp/ *n* something used to hide one's real activities, etc; a concerted effort to keep an act or situation from being made public.

covet /'kʌvət/ *vt* to desire earnestly; to lust after; to long to possess (what belongs to another).—**coveter** *n.*—**covetous** *adj.*—**covetousness** *n.*

covetous /'kʌvətəs/ *adj* avaricious, grasping, acquisitive.—**covetousness** *n.*

covey /'kʌvi/ *n* a hatch or brood of birds, *esp* partridges.

coving /'koːvɪŋ/ *n* a curved moulding at the juncture of a wall and ceiling.—*also* **cove**.

cow[1] /kau/ *n* the mature female of domestic cattle; the mature female of various other animals, as the whale, elephant, etc; (*sl*) a disagreeable woman.

cow[2] *vt* to take the spirit out of, to intimidate.

coward /'kauərd/ *n* a person lacking courage; one who is afraid.

cowardice /'kauərdɪs/ *n* lack of courage.

cowardly /'kauərdli/ *adj* of, or like, a coward.—**cowardliness** *n.*

cowbane /'kauˌbein/ *n* water hemlock.

cowbird /-ˌbərd/ *n* an American blackbird so called from its accompanying cattle.

cowboy /-ˌbɔi/ *n* a person who tends cattle or horses.—*also* **cowhand**; (*inf*) one who is engaged in dubious business activities.

cowcatcher /-ˌkætʃər/ *n* a wedge-shaped iron frame on the front of a locomotive to push aside obstacles.

cower /'kauər/ *vi* to crouch or sink down through fear, etc; to tremble.

cowfish /'kaufɪʃ/ *n* (*pl* **cowfish, cowfishes**) a name given to various fishes and other marine animals, as the dolphin.

cowgirl /-ˌgərl/ *n* a woman who works as a cowhand.

cowherd /-ˌhərd/ *n* a person employed to tend cattle.

cowhide /-ˌhaid/ *n* the tanned and dressed skins of cows; a stout flexible whip made of rawhide.

cowl /kaul/ *n* a hood; the hooded habit of a monk; the draped neckline of a woman's dress or sweater; a chimney corner.

cowlick /'kauˌlɪk/ *n* a tuft of hair turned up or brushed over the forehead.

cowling /'kaulɪŋ/ *n* the metal covering of an aeroplane engine.

coworker /'koːwərkər/ *n* a fellow worker.

cowpat /'kauˌpæt/ *n* a piece of cow dung.

cow pony /-ˌpoːni/ *n* a mustang used by cowboys.

cowpox /-ˌpɒks/ *n* a disease of cows that produces vesicles from which the vaccine for inoculation against smallpox is obtained.

cowpuncher /-ˌpʌntʃər/, **cowpoke** /-ˌpoːk/ *n* (*US inf*) a cowboy.

cowry, cowrie /'kauri/ *n* (*pl* **cowries**) a marine mollusc with a glossy, brightly speckled shell.

cowslip /'kauˌslɪp/ *n* a common wild plant with small fragrant yellow flowers.

cox /kɒks/ *n* a coxswain. • *vt* to act as a coxswain.

coxa /'kɒksə/ *n* (*pl* **coxae**) the hip joint.—**coxal** *adj.*

coxalgia /kɒks'ældʒiə/ or /-dʒə/ *n* a pain in, or disease of, the hip joint.—**coxalgic** *adj.*

coxcomb /'kɒkskoːm/ *n* a cockscomb; a vain conceited person, a fop.

coxcombry /'kɒkskəmri/ *n* (*pl* **coxcombries**) affected airs, foppishness.

coxswain /'kɒksən/ or /-swein/ *n* a person who steers a boat, *esp* a lifeboat or racing boat.—*also* **cockswain**.

coy /kɔi/ *adj* playfully or provocatively demure; bashful.—**coyly** *adv.*—**coyness** *n.*

coyote /kai'oːti/ or /'kaio:t/ *n* (*pl* **coyotes, coyote**) a small prairie wolf of North America.

coypu /'kɔipu:/ *n* (*pl* **coypus, coypu**) an aquatic beaver-like animal, originally from South America.

coz /kʌz/ *n* (*arch*) cousin.

cozen /'kʌzən/ *vt* to cheat, to beguile; to act deceitfully.—**cozenage** *n.*—**cozener** *n.*

cozy /'koːzi/ *see* **cosy**.

cp. *abbr* = compare.

CP *abbr* = Communist Party; Canadian Press.

Cpl *abbr* = Corporal.

CPU *abbr* = central processing unit.

Cr (*chem symbol*) chromium.

cr. *abbr* = credit; creditor.

crab /kræb/ *n* any of numerous chiefly marine broadly built crustaceans. • *vi* (**crabbing, crabbed**) to fish for crabs; to complain.

crab-apple *n* a wild apple.

crabbed /kræbd/ *adj* bad-tempered, morose; (*writing*) cramped; hard to decipher.

crabby /'kræbi/ *adj* bad-tempered.—**crabbily** *adv.*—**crabbiness** *n.*

crab louse *n* a species of body louse.

crabstick /'kræbstɪk/ *n* a cudgel; a surly person.

crack /kræk/ *vt* to burst, break or sever; to utter a sharp, abrupt cry; to injure; to damage mentally; to open a bottle; (*sl*) to make (a joke); (*inf*) to break open (a safe); to decipher (a code). • *vi* to make a sharp explosive sound; (*inf*) to lose control under pressure; to shift erratically in vocal tone; (*with* **up**) (*inf*) to be unable to cope; (*sl*) to take the drug crack. • *n* a chink or fissure; a narrow fracture; a sharp sound; a sharp resonant blow; an altered tone of voice; a chat, gossip; a wisecrack; (*inf*) an attempt; an expert; (*sl*) the drug cocaine packaged in the form of pellets.

crackbrained /'krækˌbreind/ *adj* crazy.

crackdown /-ˌdaun/ *n* repressive action to quell disorder, etc.

cracked /krækt/ *adj* split, broken; blemished; insane; legally imperfect.

cracker /'krækər/ *n* a firework that explodes with a loud crack; a paper tube that when pulled explodes harmlessly and releases a paper hat and plastic toy; a thin, crisp biscuit; (*sl*) a person or thing of great ability or excellence.

crackerjack /'krækərˌdʒæk/ *n* (*sl*) a fine specimen.

crackers /'krækərz/ *adj* (*sl*) crazy.

crackhead /'krækhɛd/ *n* (*sl*) a person who is addicted to the drug crack.

crack house /-ˌhɒʊs/ *n* (*sl*) a place where the drug crack is made available by dealers.

cracking /-ɪŋ/ *adj* (*inf*) fast-moving; excellent. • *n* the act of hacking into computer games; **to get cracking** to start to do something with vim and vigour.

crackle /'krækəl/ *vi* to make a slight, sharp explosive noise. • *vt* to cover with a delicate network of minute cracks. • *n* a noise of frequent and slight cracks and reports; a surface glaze on glass or porcelain.—**crackly** *adj*.

crackling /'kræklɪŋ/ *n* (*usu pl*) the browned crisp rind of roast pork.

cracknel /'kræknəl/ *n* a thick puffy fancy biscuit.

crackpot /'krækpɒt/ *n* (*inf*) an eccentric, a crazy person. • *adj* (*inf*) crazy, unpractical.

cracksman /'kræksmən/ *n* (*pl* **cracksmen**) a burglar.

-cracy /krəsi/ *n suffix* government by, as in *democracy*.

cradle /'kreɪdəl/ *n* a baby's crib or a small bed, often on rockers; infancy; birthplace or origin; a case for a broken limb; a framework of timbers, *esp* for supporting a boat; the rest for a telephone handset. • *vt* to rock or place in a cradle; to nurse or train in infancy.

cradlesong /-ˌsɒŋ/ *n* a lullaby.

cradling /'kreɪdlɪŋ/ *n* the open timbers or ribs of a vaulted ceiling.

craft /kræft/ *n* manual skill; a skilled trade; the members of a skilled trade; cunning; (*pl* **craft**) a boat, ship, or aircraft.

craftsman /'kræftsmən/ *n* (*pl* **craftsmen**) a person skilled in a particular craft.—**craftsmanship** *n*.—**craftswoman** *nf* (*pl* **craftswomen**).

crafty /'kræfti/ *adj* (**craftier, craftiest**) cunning, wily.—**craftily** *adv*.—**craftiness** *n*.

crag /kræg/ *n* a rough steep rock or cliff.

craggy /'krægi/ *adj*, **cragged** /-d/ *adj* (**craggier, craggiest**) full of crags; rugged.—**cragginess** *n*.

crake /kreɪk/ *n* the corncrake.

cram /kræm/ *vb* (**cramming crammed**) *vt* to pack tightly, to stuff; to fill to overflowing; (*inf*) to prepare quickly for an examination. • *vi* to eat greedily.

crambo /'kræmbo:/ *n* (*pl* **cramboes**) a game in which rhymes have to be found for a given word.

cramp /kræmp/ *n* a spasmodic muscular contraction of the limbs; (*pl*) abdominal spasms and pain; a clamp. • *vt* to affect with muscular spasms; to confine narrowly; to hamper; to secure with a cramp. • *vi* to suffer from cramps.

cramped /kræmpd/ *adj* restricted, narrow; (*handwriting*) small and irregular.

crampon /'kræmpɒn/, **crampoon** /'kræmpu:n/ *n* a metal frame with spikes attached to boots for walking or climbing on ice.

cranberry /'kræn.bɛri/ or /-bəri/ *n* (*pl* **cranberries**) a small red sour berry; the shrub it grows on.

crane /kreɪn/ *n* a large wading bird with very long legs and neck, and a long straight bill; a machine for raising, shifting, and lowering heavy weights. • *vti* to stretch out (the neck).

crane fly *n* the daddy-longlegs.

cranesbill *n* a kind of wild geranium.

craniology /ˌkreɪniˈɒlədʒi/ *n* the scientific study of skulls and their characteristics.—**craniological** *adj*.—**craniologist** *n*.

craniometer /-ˈɒmətər/ *n* an instrument for measuring the skull.

craniometry /-ˈɒmətri/ *n* the measurement and study of skulls.—**craniometric, craniometrical** *adj*.

craniotomy /-ˈɒtəmi/ *n* (*pl* **craniotomies**) the operation of crushing the head of a dead fetus for facilitating delivery; the operation of opening the skull for neurosurgery.

cranium /'kreɪniəm/ *n* (*pl* **craniums, crania**) the skull, *esp* the part enclosing the brain.—**cranial** *adj*.

crank /kræŋk/ *n* a right-angled arm attached to a shaft for turning it; (*inf*) an eccentric person, *usu* one with strange or unorthodox opinions; an irritable or rude person. • *vt* to provide with a crank; to turn or wind; (*with* **up**) (*engine*) to start with a crank handle; (*inf*) to speed up; (*sl*) to inject a narcotic drug.

crankcase /'kræŋkkeɪs/ *n* the housing for a crankshaft in an internal combustion engine, etc.

crankpin /'kræŋk.pɪn/ *n* a cylindrical pin parallel with the shaft axis of a crank upon which the connecting rod acts to turn the crank.

crankshaft /'kræŋk.ʃæft/ *n* a shaft with one or more cranks for transmitting motion.

cranky /'kræŋki/ *adj* (**crankier, crankiest**) (*inf*) eccentric; shaky; cross.—**crankily** *adv*.—**crankiness** *n*.

cranny /'kræni/ *n* (*pl* **crannies**) a fissure, crack, crevice.

crap /kræp/ *n* (*sl*) nonsense; (*vulg*) faeces. • *vi* (**crapping, crapped**) (*vulg*) to defecate.—**crappy** *adj*.

crape /kreɪp/ *n* crepe; a black gauze-like crimped silk material used for mourning.

craps /kræps/ *n* (*sing or pl*) a gambling game played with two dice.

crapshooter /'kræpʃu:tər/ *n* a player of craps.

crapulence /'kræpjuːləns/ *n* sickness from drinking to excess.—**crapulent, crapulous** *adj*.

craquelure /'krækə.luːr/ *n* a network of tiny cracks found on old paintings caused by cracking of the varnish.

crash /kræʃ/ *n* a loud, sudden confused noise; a violent fall or impact; a sudden failure, as of a business or a computer; a collapse, as of the financial market. • *adj* done with great speed, suddenness or effort. • *vti* to clash together with violence; to make a loud clattering noise; (*aircraft*) to land with a crash; to involve a car in a collision with one or more other vehicles or with a hard object; to collapse, to ruin; (*inf*) to intrude into (a party); (*with* **out**) *vi* (*sl*) to fall asleep; to pass out; to stay the night somewhere other than home.

crash dive *n* an emergency dive by a submarine.

crash helmet *n* a cushioned helmet worn by airmen, motorcyclists, etc for protection.

crash-land /'kræʃ.lænd/ *vti* (*aircraft*) to make an emergency landing without lowering the undercarriage, or to be landed in this way.—**crash-landing** *n*.

crass /kræs/ *adj* gross; dense; very stupid.—**crassly** *adv*.—**crassness, crassitude** *n*.

-crat /kræt/ *n suffix* a supporter or member of a particular form of government or class.

cratch /krætʃ/ *n* a rack for fodder.

crate /kreɪt/ *n* an open box of wooden slats, for shipping; (*sl*) an old vehicle or aircraft. • *vt* to pack in a crate.

crater /'kreɪtər/ *n* the mouth of a volcano; a cavity caused by the landing of a meteorite, the explosion of a bomb, shell, etc; an ancient Greek goblet.—**craterous** *adj*.

cravat /krə'væt/ *n* a neckcloth.

crave /kreɪv/ *vt* to have a strong desire (for); to ask humbly, to beg.—**craving** *n*.

craven /'kreɪvən/ *adj* spiritless, cowardly. • *n* a coward.

craw /krɒ/ *n* a bird's crop.

crawfish /'krɒfɪʃ/ *n* (*pl* **crawfish**) a crayfish; the spiny lobster.

crawl /krɒl/ *vi* to move along the ground on hands and knees; to move slowly and with difficulty; to creep; (*inf*) to seek favour by servile behaviour; to swarm (with). • *n* the act of crawling; a slow motion; a racing stroke in swimming.—**crawler** *n*.

crayfish /'kreɪfɪʃ/ *n* (*pl* **crayfish**) any of numerous freshwater crustaceans; the spiny lobster.

crayon /'kreɪɒn/ or /-ən/ *n* a stick or pencil of coloured chalk; a drawing done with crayons. • *vt* to draw with a crayon.—**crayonist** *n*.

craze /kreɪz/ *n* a passing infatuation; excessive enthusiasm; a crack in pottery glaze. • *vt* to produce cracks; to render insane.—**crazed** *adj*.

crazy /'kreɪzi/ *adj* (**crazier, craziest**) (*inf*) mad, insane; foolish; ridiculous; unsound; madly in love with; (*paving*) composed of irregular pieces.—**crazily** *adv*.—**craziness** *n*.

crazy paving *n* a form of paving in which stones of different shapes and sizes are pieced together.

creak /kri:k/ *vi* to make a shrill grating sound. • *n* such a sound.

creaky /'kri:ki/ *adj* (**creakier, creakiest**) apt to creak.—**creakiness** *n*.

cream /kri:m/ *n* the rich, fatty part of milk; the choicest part of anything; a yellowish white colour; a type of face or skin preparation; any preparation of the consistency of cream (eg *shoe cream*). • *vt* to add or apply cream to; to beat into a soft, smooth consistency; to skim cream from; to remove the best part of. • *vi* to form cream or scum; to break into a creamy froth.

cream cheese *n* soft cheese made from soured milk or cream.

creamer /'kri:mər/ *n* a machine or dish for separating cream from milk; a jug for cream or milk; a powder used as a substitute for cream in drinks.

creamery /'kri:məri/ *n* (*pl* **creameries**) a place where dairy products are made or sold.

cream of tartar *n* purified tartar or argol, potassium bitartrate.

creamy *adj* (**creamier, creamiest**) like cream.—**creaminess** *n*.

crease /kri:s/ *n* a line made by folding; a wrinkle; (*cricket*) a line made by a batsman or bowler marking the limits of their position. • *vti* to make or form creases; to become creased; (*sl*) to find something very funny.

create /kri'eɪt/ *vt* to cause to come into existence; to form out of nothing. • *vi* to make something new, to originate; (*sl*) to make a fuss.

creatine, creatin /'kriə,ti:n/ *n* a white crystalline substance in muscular tissue.

creation /kri'eɪʃən/ *n* the act of creating; the thing created; the whole world or universe; a production of the human mind; (*with cap*) the universe as created by God.—**creational** *adj*.

creationism /-,nɪzəm/ *n* the belief in special creation, not evolution; the belief that God creates a soul for every human being at birth.—**creationist** *adj*, *n*.

creative /kri'eɪtɪv/ *adj* of creation; having the power to create; imaginative, original, constructive.—**creatively** *adv*.—**creativeness** *n*.—**creativity** *n*.

creator /kri'eɪtər/ *n* one who creates, *esp* God.

creature /'kri:tʃər/ *n* a living being; a created thing; one dependent on the influence of another.—**creatural, creaturely** *adj*.

crèche /kreʃ/ or /kreɪʃ/ *n* a day nursery for very young children.

credence /'kredəns/ *n* belief or trust, *esp* in the reports or testimony of another.

credentials /krə'denʃəls/ *npl* documents proving the identity, honesty or authority of a person.

credibility gap *n* a gap between what is claimed in official statements and the true facts of a situation.

credible /'kredɪbəl/ *adj* believable; trustworthy.—**credibility, credibleness** *n*.—**credibly** *adv*.

credit /'kredɪt/ *n* belief; trust; honour; good reputation; approval; trust in a person's ability to pay; time allowed for payment; a sum at a person's disposal in a bank; the entry in an account of a sum received; the side of the account on which this is entered; (*educ*) a distinction awarded for good marks in an examination; (*pl*) a list of those responsible for a film, television programme, etc. • *vt* to believe; to trust; to have confidence in; to attribute to; to enter on the credit side of an account.

creditable /'kredɪtəbəl/ *adj* worthy of praise.—**creditableness, creditability** *n*.—**creditably** *adv*.

credit card *n* a card issued by a bank, department store, etc authorizing the purchase of goods and services on credit.

creditor /'kredɪtər/ *n* a person to whom money is owed.

credit rating *n* an appraisal of a person's or a business's creditworthiness.

credits *npl* a list of those involved in the production of a film or television show.

creditworthy /'kredɪt,wɜːði/ *adj* worthy of being given credit as judged by the capacity to earn, repay debts promptly, etc.—**creditworthiness** *n*.

credo /'kri:doː/ or /'kreɪ-/ *n* (*pl* **credos**) a creed.

credulous /'kredjuləs/ *adj* over-ready to believe; easily imposed on.—**credulously** *adv*.—**credulity** *n*.

creed /kri:d/ *n* a system of religious belief or faith; a summary of Christian doctrine; any set of principles or beliefs.—**creedal, credal** *adj*.

creek /kri:k/ *n* a natural stream of water smaller than a river.

creel /kri:l/ *n* a wicker fishing basket; a wickerwork cage.

creep /kri:p/ *vi* (**creeping, crept**) to move slowly along the ground, as a worm or reptile; (*plant*) to grow along the ground or up a wall; to move stealthily or slowly; to fawn; to cringe; (*flesh*) to feel as if things were creeping over it. • *n* (*inf*) a dislikable or servile person; (*pl: inf*) shrinking horror.

creeper /'kri:pər/ *n* a creeping or climbing plant.

creepy /'kri:pi/ *adj* (**creepier, creepiest**) making one's flesh crawl; causing fear or disgust.—**creepily** *adv*.—**creepiness** *n*.

creepy-crawly /'kri:pi,krɒli/ *n* (*pl* **creepy-crawlies**) (*inf*) a small crawling insect.

cremate /'kri:meɪt/ or /krɪ'meɪt/, /krə-/ *vt* to burn (a corpse) to ashes.—**cremation** *n*.—**cremationism** *n*.—**cremationist** *n*.

crematorium /'kri:mə,tɔːriəm/ *n* (*pl* **crematoriums, crematoria**) a place where bodies are cremated.

crematory /'kri:mə,tɔːri/ *adj* pertaining to cremation. • *n* (*pl* **crematories**) a place for burning the dead, a crematorium.

crème, creme /kri:m/, *Fr.* /krɛm/ *n* cream.

crème de la crème /,kremdəlɒ'krem/ *n* the cream of the cream, the very best.

crème de menthe /,kremdə'mɒnθ/ or /-'menθ/, /-'mint/ *n* a green-coloured peppermint liqueur.

crenate /'kri:,neɪt/, **crenated** *adj* (*leaves*) scalloped.—**crenation, crenature** *n*.

crenellated, crenelated /'krenə,leɪtɪd/ *adj* having battlements.—**crenellation, crenelation** *n*.

crenulate, crenulated /'krenju:,leɪt/ *adj* (*leaves*) finely notched, indented.—**crenulation** *n*.

Creole /'kri:oːl/ *n* a descendant of European settlers in the West Indies or South America; a white descendant of French settlers in the southern US; a person of mixed European and Negro ancestry; the language of any of these groups.

creole /'kri:oːl/ *n* a language combining two or more original languages, one of which is European.

creosol /'kri:ə,sɒl/ *n* an oily liquid resembling phenol, a constituent of creosote.

creosote /'kri:ə,soːt/ *n* an oily substance derived from tar used as a wood preservative. • *vt* to treat with creosote.—**creosotic** *adj*.

crepe /kreɪp/, **crêpe** /krep/ *n* a thin, crinkled cloth of silk, rayon, wool, etc.—*also* **crape**; thin paper like crepe; a thin pancake.

crepe de Chine /,kreɪpdə'ʃi:n/ *n* a silk crepe.

crepe paper, crêpe paper *n* a thin soft coloured paper that resembles crepe.

crepe rubber *n* a type of ribbed rubber used for the soles of shoes.

crêpe suzette /,kreɪsu:'zet/, *Fr.* /kreɪp'syzet/ *n* (*pl* **crêpes suzettes**) a thin orange-flavoured pancake with a hot liqueur sauce.

crepitate /'krepɪ,teɪt/ *vi* to make a slight, sharp crackling noise.—**crepitation** *n*.

crept /krept/ *see* **creep**.

crepuscular /krə'pʌskju:lər/ *adj* pertaining to or resembling twilight; active at twilight, as certain animals.

crescendo /krə'ʃendo:/ *adv* (*mus*) gradually increasing in loudness or intensity; moving to a climax. • *n* (*pl* **crescendos, crescendi**) a crescendo passage or effect.

crescent /'kresənt/ *n* the figure of the moon in its first or last quarter; a narrow, tapering curve; a curving street. • *adj* crescent-shaped; (*arch*) increasing.—**crescentic** *adj*.

cresol /'kri:,sɒl/ *n* a phenol obtained from coal and wood tar.

cress /kres/ *n* any of various plants with pungent leaves, used in salads.

cresset /'kresɪt/ *n* a light set on a beacon; an open frame of iron containing fire, used as a torch.

crest /krest/ *n* a plume of feathers on the head of a bird; the ridge of a wave; the summit of a hill; a distinctive device above the shield on a coat of arms. • *vti* to mount to the top of; to take the form of a crest; to provide or adorn with a crest, to crown.—**crested** *adj*.

crestfallen /'krest,fɒlən/ *adj* dejected.

cresting /'krestɪŋ/ *n* an ornamental finish, *esp* along a rooftop; ornamentation on top of furniture, a mirror, etc.

Cretaceous /krɪ'teɪʃəs/ *n* a geological group between the Jurassic and Tertiary formations. • *adj* of the last Mesozoic era.

cretaceous /krɪ'teɪʃəs/ *adj* composed of or like chalk; chalky.

Cretan /'kri:tən/ *adj* of or pertaining to Crete or its inhabitants.

cretin /'kretɪn/ *n* a person suffering from mental and physical retardation due to a thyroid disorder; (*inf*) an idiot.—**cretinism** *n*.—**cretinoid, cretinous** *adj*.

cretonne /kri'tɒn/ *n* an unglazed cotton fabric printed with coloured patterns on one side.

crevasse /krə'væs/ *n* a deep cleft in a glacier; a deep crack.

crevice /'krevɪs/ *n* a crack, a fissure.

crew /kru:/ *n* the people operating a ship or aircraft; a group of people working together. • *vi* to act as a member of the crew of a ship, etc.

crewcut *n* a very short hairstyle for men.

crewel /'kru:əl/ *n* a fine twisted or worsted yarn used in embroidery.—**crewelist** *n*.

crew neck *n* a plain closely-fitting neckline in sweaters.

crib /krɪb/ *n* a rack for fodder, a manger; a child's cot with high sides; a model of the manger scene representing the birth of Jesus; (*inf*) something copied from someone else; (*inf*) a literal translation of foreign texts used (*usu* illicitly) by students in examinations, etc. • *vti* (**cribbing, cribbed**) (*inf*) to copy illegally, plagiarize.

cribbage /ˈkrɪbɪdʒ/ *n* a card game for two to four players.

crib death *see* **cot death.**

cribellum /krɪˈbɛləm/ *n* (*pl* **cribella**) a spinning organ in front of the spinnerets of certain spiders.

cribriform /ˈkrɪbrɪˌfɔrm/ *adj* with small holes like a sieve.

crick /krɪk/ *n* a painful stiffness of the muscles of the neck. • *vt* to produce a crick in.

cricket[1] /ˈkrɪkɪt/ *n* a leaping grasshopper-like insect with the ability, in the male of the species, to produce a chirping sound by rubbing together the leathery forewings.

cricket[2] *n* a game played with wickets, bats, and a ball, by eleven players on each side.—**cricketer** *n.*

cried /kraɪd/ *see* **cry.**

crier /ˈkraɪər/ *n* one who cries; an officer who makes public proclamations.

crime /kraɪm/ *n* a violation of the law; an offence against morality or the public welfare; wrong-doing; (*inf*) a shame, disappointment.

criminal /ˈkrɪmɪnəl/ *adj* of the nature of, or guilty of, a crime. • *n* a person who has committed a crime.—**criminality** *adv.*—**criminally** *adv.*

criminal conversation *n* (*formerly*) a legal action for damages for illegal sexual intercourse; adultery.

criminology /ˌkrɪməˈnɒlədzi/ *n* the scientific study of crime.—**criminological, criminologic** *adj.*—**criminologist** *n.*

crimp[1] /krɪmp/ *vt* to press into small folds; to frill; to corrugate; (*hair*) to curl.—**crimper** *n.*

crimp[2] *n* a person luring or pressganging sailors aboard a vessel. • *vt* to decoy thus.

crimson /ˈkrɪmzən/ *n* a deep-red colour inclining to purple. • *adj* crimson-coloured. • *vti* to dye with crimson; to blush.

cringe /krɪndʒ/ *vi* to shrink in fear or embarrassment; to cower; to behave with servility; to fawn.

cringle /ˈkrɪŋgəl/ *n* a loop of rope containing a metal ring for another rope to pass through.

crinite /ˈkraɪˌnaɪt/ *adj* hairy.

crinkle /ˈkrɪŋkəl/ *vt* to wrinkle; to corrugate; to crimp; to rustle. • *vi* to curl; to be corrugated or crimped. • *n* a wrinkle.—**crinkly** *adj.*

crinoid /ˈkrɪˌnɔɪd/ *adj* lily-shaped. • *n* a stone lily, a kind of sea urchin.

crinoline /ˈkrɪnəˌlɪn/ *n* a hooped skirt made to project all round; a stiff fabric for stiffening a garment.

crinum /ˈkrɪnəm/ *n* any of several handsome tropical plants.

cripple /ˈkrɪpəl/ *vt* to deprive of the use of a limb; to disable. • *n* a lame or otherwise disabled person. • *adj* lame.

crippling /ˈkrɪplɪŋ/ *adj* harmful; unbearable.

crisis /ˈkraɪsɪs/ *n* (*pl* **crises**) a turning point; a critical point in a disease; an emergency; a time of serious difficulties or danger.

crisp /krɪsp/ *adj* dry and brittle; bracing; brisk; sharp and incisive; decided; very clean and tidy. • *n* a potato snack; in US, a potato chip. • *vt* to make crisp.—**crisply** *adv.*—**crispness** *n.*

crispate /ˈkrɪspeɪt/, **crispated** *adj* curled; (*bot*) with a wavy margin.—**crispation** *n.*

crispy /ˈkrɪspi/ *adj* (**crispier, crispiest**) crisp.—**crispily** *adv.*—**crispiness** *n.*

crisscross /ˈkrɪsˌkrɒs/ *vti* to mark with cross lines. • *n* an intersecting; a mark of a cross; a game of noughts and crosses. • *adj* crossing; in cross lines. • *adv* crosswise.

cristate /ˈkrɪsteɪt/, **cristated** /-ɪd/ *adj* crested; tufted.

criterion /kraɪˈtɪrɪən/ *n* (*pl* **criteria**) a standard, law or rule by which a correct judgment can be made.

critic /ˈkrɪtɪk/ *n* a person skilled in judging the merits of literary or artistic works; one who passes judgment; a fault-finder.

critical /ˈkrɪtɪkəl/ *adj* skilled in criticism; censorious; relating to the turning point of a disease; crucial.—**critically** *adv.*

criticism /ˈkrɪtɪsɪzəm/ *n* being critical; an adverse comment; a review or analysis of a book, play, work of art, etc by a critic.

criticize /ˈkrɪtɪˌsaɪz/ *vt* to pass judgment on; to find fault with; to examine critically.—**criticizer** *n.*

critique /ˌkrɪˈtiːk/ *n* a critical article or review.

critter /ˈkrɪtər/ *n* (*dial*) a creature.

croak /kroːk/ *n* a deep hoarse discordant cry. • *vti* to utter a croak; (*inf*) to die, to kill.—**croakily** *adv.*—**croakiness** *n.*—**croaky** *adj.*

Croatian, Croat /kroˈæt/ *adj* of or pertaining to Croatia, its people or language. • *n* an inhabitant of Croatia; the language of Croatia, a dialect of Serbo-Croatian.

crochet /kroˈʃeɪ/ or /ˈkroˈ-/ *n* a kind of knitting done with a hooked needle. • *vti* (**crocheting, crocheted**) to do this; to make crochet articles.—**crocheter** *n.*

crocidolite /kroˈsɪdəˌlaɪt/ *n* blue asbestos.

crock[1] /krɒk/ *n* an earthenware pot.

crock[2] *n* a broken-down horse; (*sl*) a worn-out or unfit person. • *vti* to become or make unfit.

crock[3] *n* soot on a kettle, etc. • *vt* to blacken with soot.

crockery /ˈkrɒkəri/ *n* china dishes, earthenware vessels, etc.

crocket /ˈkrɒkət/ *n* a small curved ornament on the angles of spires, canopies, etc.

crocodile /ˈkrɒkəˌdaɪl/ *n* a large amphibious reptile, similar to an alligator; its skin, used to make handbags, shoes, etc; a line of schoolchildren walking in pairs.

crocodile tears *npl* insincere grief.

crocodilian /ˌkrɒkəˈdɪlɪən/ *adj* pertaining to crocodiles. • *n* any of the order of reptiles that includes alligators and crocodiles.

crocus /ˈkroˈkəs/ *n* (*pl* **crocuses**) a bulbous plant with yellow, purple, or white flowers.

croft /krɒft/ *n* a small plot of land with a rented farmhouse, *esp* in Scotland.—**crofter** *n.*

croissant /krəˈsɒ̃/, *Fr.* /krwaˈsɒ̃/ *n* a rich bread roll.

Cro-Magnon man /kroˈmægnɒn/ or /-ˈmægnən/ *n* a race of man living in late Palaeolithic times.

cromlech /ˈkrɒmˌlɛk/ *n* a prehistoric monument of rough stones in a circle and *usu* surrounding a lofty pillar of stone.

crone /kroːn/ *n* a withered old woman.

crony /ˈkroːni/ *n* (*pl* **cronies**) an intimate friend.

crook /kruk/ *n* a shepherd's hooked staff; a bend, a curve; a swindler, a dishonest person. • *adj* (*sl*) unwell. • *vti* to bend or to be bent into the shape of a hook.

crooked /ˈkrukəd/ *adj* bent, twisted; dishonest.—**crookedly** *adv.*—**crookedness** *n.*

croon /kruːn/ *vi* to hum in a low gentle voice. • *vt* to sing songs in a soft gentle manner.—**crooner** *n.*

crop /krɒp/ *n* a year's or a season's produce of any cultivated plant; harvest; any collection of things appearing at the same time; a pouch in a bird's gullet; a hunting whip; hair cut close or short. • *vti* (**cropping, cropped**) to clip short; to bite off or eat down (grass); (*land*) to yield; to sow, to plant; (*geol*) to come to the surface; to sprout; (*with* **up**) (*inf*) to occur or appear by chance or unexpectedly.

crop circle *n* a circular patch of corn in a cornfield that has been flattened by an as yet unexplained whirling movement.

crop-eared /-ˌɪrd/ *adj* with clipped ears; short-haired.

cropper /-ər/ *n* a thing that crops; a cloth-facing machine; a pouter pigeon; (*sl*) a heavy fall.

croquet /kroˈkeɪ/ or /ˈkroˈkeɪ/ *n* a game played with mallets, balls and hoops. • *vt* (**croqueting, croqueted**) to drive away an opponent's ball by striking one's own placed in contact with it.

croquette /kroˈkɛt/ *n* a ball of minced meat, fish or potato seasoned and fried brown.

crosier /ˈkroˈʒər/ or /-ziər/ *n* the pastoral staff of a bishop.—*also* **crozier.**

cross /krɒs/ *n* a figure formed by two intersecting lines; a wooden structure, consisting of two beams placed across each other, used in ancient times for crucifixion; the emblem of the Christian faith; a symbol or mark (X); a focal point in a town; a burden, or affliction; a device resembling a cross; a cross-shaped medal; a hybrid. • *vti* to pass across; to intersect; to meet and pass; to place crosswise; to mark with a cross; to make the sign of the cross over; to thwart, to oppose; to modify (a breed) by intermixture (with). • *adj* transverse; reaching from side to side; intersecting; out of temper, peevish.—**crosser** *n.*—**crossly** *adv.*—**crossness** *n.*

crossbar /-bar/ *n* a horizontal bar, as that across goal posts or a bicycle frame.

crossbill /-bɪl/ *n* a bird whose mandibles cross when the bill is closed.

crossbow /-boː/ *n* a bow set crosswise on the stock from which bolts are shot along a groove.

crossbreed /-briːd/ *vt* (**crossbreeding, crossbred**) to breed animals by mating different varieties. • *n* an animal produced in this way.

crosscheck /-tʃɛk/ vt to verify by checking different opinions or sources.

cross-country /krɒs'kʌntri/ adj across fields; denoting cross-country racing or skiing.—also n.

crosscurrent /'krɒs,kʌrənt/ n a current that flows across another in water or air; ideas running counter to those generally held.

crosse /krɒs/ n a long-handled racket in which the ball is caught and carried in lacrosse.

cross-examine /,krɒsɪg'zæmɪn/ vt to question closely; (law) to question (a witness) who has already been questioned by counsel on the other side.—**cross-examiner** n.—**cross-examination** n.

cross-eyed /'krɒs,aɪd/ adj squinting.—**cross-eye** n.

cross-fertilization /krɒs,fɜrtɪlaɪ'zeɪʃən/ n fertilization of the ovules of a flower by the pollen of another.

cross-fertilize /krɒs'fɜrtɪ,laɪz/ vt to fertilize (a plant) with pollen from another.

crossfire /'krɒs,faɪr/ n converging gunfire from two or more positions; animated debate or argument.

cross-grained /greɪnd/ adj contrary or awkward; with an irregular grain or fibre.

crosshatch /-hætʃ/ vt to shade with crossed lines.

crossing /-ɪŋ/ n an intersection of roads or railway lines; a place for crossing a street; the crossbreeding of animals and plants.

cross-legged /-lɛgɪd/ or /-lɛgd/ adj seated with one leg crossed over the other.

crosspatch /-pætʃ/ n (inf) a bad-tempered person.

crosspiece /-piːs/ n a transverse piece.

cross-platform adj (comput) applies to the use of software and files on computer with a different hardware system.

cross-purpose /-pɜrpəs/ n a contrary purpose; **be at cross-purposes** to talk without either party realizing that the other is talking about a different thing.

cross-question /krɒs'kwɛstʃən/ vt to question to elicit details or test the accuracy of an account already given.—**cross-questioning** n.

cross-refer /,krɒsrɪ'fɜr/ vt to mark (text, a book, etc) in such a way as to direct the reader to another page, etc with more information.

cross-reference /'krɒs,rɛfərəns/ n a note directing the reader to a different section of a book or document.

crossroad /-roːd/ n a road crossing another; (pl) where two roads cross; (fig) the time when a decisive action has to be made.

cross section /-,sɛkʃən/ n a cutting at right angles to length; the surface then shown; a random selection of the public.—**cross-sectional** adj.

cross-stitch /-stɪtʃ/ n a stitch formed of two stitches of the same length, one crossing the other.

crosstalk /-stɒk/ n interference in lines of communication, esp telephone lines; a quick-witted flow of conversation; repartee.

crosstie /-taɪ/ n a railway sleeper.

crosstree /-triː/ n (naut) one of several pieces of timber across the head of a lower mast to support the mast above.

crosswalk /-wɒk/ n a street crossing for pedestrians.

crosswind /-wɪnd/ n a side or unfavourable wind.

crosswise /-waɪz/, **crossways** /-weɪz/ adv in the manner of a cross.

crossword (puzzle) /-wɜrd/ n a puzzle in which interlocking words to be inserted vertically and horizontally in a squared diagram are indicated by clues.

crotch /krɒtʃ/ n the region of the body where the legs fork, the genital area; any forked region.

crotchet /'krɒtʃət/ n (mus) a note equal to the duration of a half-minim.—also **quarter note**.

crotchety /'krɒtʃəti/ adj peevish, ill-tempered.—**crotchetiness** n.

crouch /kraʊtʃ/ vi to squat or lie close to the ground; to cringe, to fawn.

croup[1] /kruːp/ n inflammation of the windpipe causing coughing and breathing problems, esp in children.—**croupous, croupy** adj.

croup[2], **croupe** n the rump or buttocks of certain animals; the place behind the saddle of a horse.

croupier /'kruːpɪər/ or /-pi,eɪ/ n a person who presides at a gaming table and collects or pays out the money won or lost.

crouton /'kruː,tɒn/ n a small piece of fried or toasted bread sprinkled onto soups.

crow /kroː/ n any of various usu large, glossy, black birds; a cawing cry, the shrill sound of a cock. • vi (**crowing, crowed** or **crew**) to make a sound like a cock; to boast in triumph; to utter a cry of pleasure.—**crower** n.

crowbar /-bɑr/ n an iron bar for use as a lever.

crowberry /'kroː,bɛri/ n an evergreen shrub with black berries; the edible berry of this shrub.

crowd /kraʊd/ n a number of people or things collected closely together; a dense multitude, a throng; (inf) a set; a clique. • vti to press closely together; to fill to excess; to push, to thrust; to importune.—**crowded** adj.

crowfoot /'kroː,fʊt/ n (pl **crowfoots**) any of several kinds of buttercup with yellow or white flowers and leaves like a crow's foot.

crown /kraʊn/ n a wreath worn on the head; the head covering of a monarch; regal power; the sovereign; the top of the head; the top of a tree; a summit; a reward; the part of a tooth above the gum. • vt to invest with a crown; to adorn or dignify; to complete; to reward; to put an artificial crown on a tooth; (sl) to strike on the head; (cap) the sovereign or realm of the monarch.

crown colony n a British colony subject to the control of the home government.

crown glass n a fine, thick kind of glass.

crown land n in the UK land or real property belonging to the sovereign.

crown prince n the heir apparent to a throne.

crown princess n the heiress apparent to a throne; the wife of a crown prince.

crown saw n a kind of circular saw.

crownwork n the covering or replacement of the crown of a tooth; the making of crowns; a fortified outwork.

crow's-foot /'kroːz,fʊt/ n (pl **crow's-feet**) a wrinkle at the corner of the eye; an arrangement of cords to suspend an awning; a decorative embroidery stitch.

crow's-nest /-,nɛst/ n a lookout or watchtower on the main topmast of a sailing vessel.

crozier see **crosier**.

CRT /,siː'ɑr'tiː/ abbr = cathode-ray tube.

cruces /'kruːsiːz/ see **crux**.

crucial /'kruːʃəl/ adj decisive; severe; critical.—**crucially** adv.

cruciate /'kruːʃət/ adj (bot) cross-shaped.

crucible /'kruːsəbəl/ n a heat-resistant container for melting ores, etc.

crucifer /'kruːsəfər/ n any of many plants with four petals arranged like a cross, as the mustard, etc; the bearer of a large cross in a religious procession.

crucifier /'kruːsəfaɪr/ n one who crucifies.

crucifix /'kruːsəfɪks/ n a cross with the sculptured figure of Christ.

crucifixion /,kruːsə'fɪkʃən/ n a form of execution by being nailed or bound to a cross by the hands and feet; (with cap) the death of Christ in this manner.

cruciform /'kruːsə,fɔrm/ adj cross-shaped.

crucify /'kruːsə,faɪ/ vt (**crucifying, crucified**) to put to death on a cross; to cause extreme pain to; to defeat utterly in an argument; to ridicule mercilessly.

crud /krʌd/ n (sl) a deposit of encrusted filth; nuclear waste; a contemptible person.

crude /kruːd/ adj in a natural state; unripe; raw; immature; harsh in colour; unfinished, rough; lacking polish; blunt; vulgar. • n crude oil.—**crudely** adv.—**crudeness** n.

crude oil n unrefined petroleum.

crudités /,kruːdɪ'teɪ/ or /-diː-/, Fr. /kʀydi'teɪ/ npl coarsely chopped raw vegetables eaten with a dip.

crudity /'kruːditi/ n (pl **crudities**) crudeness; a crude act or expression.

cruel /'kruːəl/ adj (**crueller, cruellest**) disposed to give pain to others; merciless; hard-hearted; fierce; painful; unrelenting.—**cruelly** adv.—**cruelty** n.

cruelty /-ti/ n (pl **cruelties**) inhumanity; savageness; a cruel act.

cruet /'kruːət/ n a small glass bottle for vinegar and oil, used at the table; a set of containers holding salt, pepper, vinegar.

cruise /kruːz/ vi to sail to and fro; to wander about; to move at the most efficient speed for sustained travel. • vt to cruise over or about. • n a voyage from place to place for military purposes or in a liner for pleasure.

cruise missile n a subsonic low-flying guided missile.

cruiser /-ər/ n fast warship smaller than a battleship; a pleasure yacht or motorboat.

crumb /krʌm/ n a fragment of bread; the soft part of bread; a little piece of anything; (sl) a despicable person. • vi to cover food with breadcrumbs before cooking.

crumble /'krʌmbəl/ vt to break into crumbs; to cause to fall into pieces. • vi to disappear gradually, to disintegrate.—**crumbly** adj.

crumby /'krʌmi/ adj (**crumbier, crumbiest**) in crumbs; soft.—**crumbiness** n.

crummy /'krʌmi/ adj (**crummier, crummiest**) (sl) dirty, squalid, worthless; slightly ill.—**crumminess** n.

crump /krʌmp/ n a bursting shell; the crunching or exploding sound of this. • vi to explode. • vt to shell; to hit (a ball) hard.

crumpet /'krʌmpɪt/ n a soft cake with holes on one side, often eaten toasted; (sl) a sexually attractive woman.

crumple /'krʌmpəl/ vti to twist or crush into wrinkles; to crease; to collapse. • n a wrinkle or crease made by crumpling.—**crumply** adj.

crunch /krʌntʃ/ vti to crush with the teeth; to tread underfoot with force and noise; to make a sound like this; to chew audibly. • n the sound or act of crunching; (with **the**) (inf) the crucial moment, the time of vital decision.

crunchy /'krʌntʃi/ adj (**crunchier, crunchiest**) crisp; able to be crunched.—**crunchily** adv.—**crunchiness** n.

crupper /'krʌpər/ n a looped leather band attached to the back of a saddle and passing under the horse's tail; the hindquarters of a horse.

crural /'krʊrəl/ adj of the leg or thigh; leg-shaped.

crus /krʌs/ or /kruːs/ n (pl **crura**) the leg proper; a part resembling a leg.

crusade /kruːˈseɪd/ n a medieval Christian military expedition to recover the Holy Land; a vigorous concerted action for the defence of a cause or the advancement of an idea. • vi to engage in a crusade.—**crusader** n.

cruse /kruːz/ n a small earthenware pot or dish for holding liquids.

crush /krʌʃ/ vt to press between two opposite bodies; to squeeze; to break by pressure; to bruise; to ruin; to quell; to defeat; to mortify. • vi to be pressed out of shape or into a smaller compass. • n a violent compression or collision; a dense crowd; (inf) a large party; a drink made from crushed fruit; (sl) an infatuation.—**crushable** adj.—**crusher** n.

crust /krʌst/ n any hard external coating or rind; the exterior solid part of the earth's surface; a shell or hard covering; (sl) a means of livelihood. • vti to cover or become covered with a crust.—**crusty** adj (**crustier, crustiest**).—**crustily** adv.—**crustiness** n.

crustacean /krʌsˈteɪʃən/ n any aquatic animal with a hard shell, including crabs, lobsters, shrimps, and barnacles.—also adj.—**crustaceous** adj.

crutch /krʌtʃ/ n a staff with a crosswise head to support the weight of a lame person; something that supports; a prop; the crotch.

crux /krʌks/ n (pl **cruxes, cruces**) a difficult problem; the essential or deciding point.

cry /kraɪ/ vb (**crying, cried**) vi to call aloud; to proclaim; to exclaim vehemently; to implore; to shed tears; (with **off**) (inf) to cancel (an agreement, arrangement, etc), to renege; (with **out**) to shout due to fear or pain. • vt to utter loudly and publicly; (with **out for**) to be in dire need of. • n (pl **cries**) an inarticulate sound; an exclamation of wonder or triumph; an outcry; clamour; an urgent appeal; a spell of weeping; a battle cry; a catchword; the particular sound made by an animal or bird.

crybaby /-ˌbeɪbi/ n (pl **crybabies**) a child who weeps easily; a person who cries or complains often.

cryo- /kraɪoː/ or /-ə/ prefix frost; freezing.

cryoextraction /ˌkraɪoːkˈstrækʃən/ n the extraction of juice from grapes that have been frozen before pressing to obtain a higher level of sugar and fruitier taste.

cryogen /'kraɪoːdʒən/ n a substance for producing freezing temperatures.

cryogenics /ˌkraɪoːˈdʒɛnɪks/ n sing the science of very low temperatures and their effects.

cryolite /'kraɪoːˌlaɪt/ n a mineral from which aluminium is produced.

cryometer /kraɪˈɒmətər/ n an instrument for measuring very low temperatures.—**cryometry** n.

cryonic suspension /kraɪˈɒnɪk/ n the process of freezing a corpse in the hope that it may be restored to life in the future.

cryonics /kraɪˈɒnɪks/ n (sing) the use of extreme cold to preserve living tissue (eg organs) for future use.

cryosurgery /ˌkraɪoːˈsɜːrdʒəri/ n surgery involving freezing to destroy or remove diseased tissue.

crypt /krɪpt/ n an underground chamber or vault, esp under a church, used as a chapel or for burial.

crypt- /krɪpt/, **crypto-** /ˈkrɪptoː/ prefix hidden.

cryptaesthesia, cryptesthesia /ˌkrɪptəsˈθiːsiə/ n clairvoyance; extrasensory perception.

cryptic /'krɪptɪk/, **cryptical** /-əl/ adj hidden, secret; mysterious; obscure in meaning.

cryptogam /'krɪptəˌgæm/ n a plant without stamens or pistil, a non-flowering plant, as mosses, ferns, etc.—**cryptogamic, cryptogamous** adj.

cryptogram /-ˌgræm/ n a coded message, cipher.

cryptograph /-ˌgræf/ n a piece of writing in cipher.

cryptography /krɪpˈtɒgrəfi/ n the art of code writing and breaking.—**cryptographer** n.—**cryptographic** adj.

cryptozoology /ˌkrɪptəzuˈɒlədʒi/ n the study of creatures whose existence has yet to be proved, eg the yeti, the Loch Ness monster.

crystal /'krɪstəl/ n a solid piece, eg of quartz, geometrically shaped owing to regular arrangement of its atoms; very clear, brilliant glass; articles of such glass, as goblets; (sl) the drug methamphetamine packaged and sold as a stimulant in powdered form.—also **crystal meth**. • adj made of crystal.—**crystalline** adj.

crystal gazing n the act of peering into a ball of crystal supposedly to see what is going to happen in the future.

crystalline /'krɪstəˌlaɪn/ or /-ˌiːn/ adj pertaining to or having the form of a crystal; clear; transparent.—**crystallinity** n.

crystalline lens n a transparent biconvex solid body enclosed in a capsule between the vitreous and acqueous humours of the eye.

crystallize /'krɪstəˌlaɪz/ vti to form crystals; to give definite form; to express clearly the theme and content of an argument, proposition, etc.—**crystallization** n.

crystallography /ˌkrɪstəˈlɒgrəfi/ n the science of the forms and structure of crystals.—**crystallographer** n.—**crystallographic** adj.

crystalloid /'krɪstəˌlɔɪd/ adj resembling a crystal; of a crystalline structure, opposite to colloid. • n a crystalloid substance; one of certain bodies that in solution diffuse readily through animal membranes.

Cs (chem symbol) = caesium.

c/s abbr = cycles per second.

CS gas n an irritant gas used in quelling riots and disturbances.

CST abbr = Central Standard Time.

ct abbr = carat; cent; court.

ctenidium /təˈniːdiəm/ n pl **ctenidia**) one of the respiratory organs of molluscs.

ctenoid /'tiːnɔɪd/ adj having a comb-like margin.

Cu (chem symbol) = copper.

cu. abbr = cubic.

cub /kʌb/ n a young carnivorous mammal; a young, inexperienced person; (with cap) a Cub Scout. • vi (**cubbing, cubbed**) to bring forth cubs.

cubage /'kjuːˌbədʒ/, **cubature** /-ˌbətʃər/ n the act of determining the contents of a solid; the contents so measured.

cubbyhole /'kʌbiˌhoːl/ n a small or snug place; a pigeonhole.

cube /kjuːb/ n a solid body with six equal square sides or faces; a cube-shaped block; the product of a number multiplied by itself twice. • vt to raise (number) to the third power, or cube; to cut into cube-shaped pieces.

cubeb /'kjuːbeb/ n a species of pepper of Asia; its small spicy berry dried and used as a stimulant.

cube root n the number that gives the stated number when cubed.

cubic /'kjuːbɪk/ adj having the form or properties of a cube; three-dimensional.

cubical /-əl/ adj of or pertaining to volume; cube-shaped.

cubicle /-əl/ n a small separate sleeping compartment in a dormitory, etc.

cubiculum /kjuːˈbɪkjuːləm/ n (pl **cubicula**) a burial chamber in a catacomb.

cubism /'kjuːˌbɪzəm/ n a style of painting in which objects are depicted as fragmented and reorganized geometrical forms.—**cubist** n.—**cubistic** adj.—**cubistically** adv.

cubit /'kju:bɪt/ n an ancient measure of about 18 inches; the forearm from the elbow to the wrist.

cubital /-əl/ adj of the forearm.

cuboid /'kju:bɔɪd/ adj like a cube. • n a regular solid contained by parallelograms.

Cub Scout n a junior branch of the Scout Association.

cuckold /'kʌkəʊld/ n a man whose wife has committed adultery.—**cuckoldry** n.

cuckoo /'kʊku:/ or /'kuku:/ n a bird with a dark plumage, a curved bill and a characteristic call that lays its eggs in the nests of other birds. • adj (inf) crazy, silly.

cuckoo clock n a clock that strikes the hours with a cuckoo call.

cuckoopint /-ˌpɪnt/ n a European plant with large leaves, purple flowers and bearing red berries.

cuckoo spit n a white froth exuded by froghopper larvae on the leaves of plants.

cucullate /kju:'kʌlˌeɪt/ or /-ɪt/, /'kju:kəˌleɪt/, /-lɪt/, **cucullated** /-təd/ adj hooded; hood-shaped.

cucumber /'kju:ˌkʌmbər/ n a long juicy fruit used in salads and as a pickle; the creeping plant that bears it.

cucurbit /kju:'kɜːrbɪt/ n any of an order of succulent, climbing, tendril-bearing plants with a fleshy fruit, including cucumbers, pumpkins, melons, etc.

cud /kʌd/ n the food that a ruminating animal brings back into the mouth to chew again; **chew the cud** to consider and mull over.

cudbear /'kʌdˌbər/ n a purple dye made from lichens.

cuddle /'kʌdəl/ vt to embrace or hug closely. • vt to nestle together. • n a close embrace.

cuddlesome /-səm/ adj tempting to cuddle.

cuddly /'kʌdli/ adj (**cuddlier, cuddliest**) given to cuddling; tempting to cuddle.

cuddy /'kʌdi/ n (**cuddies**) (naut) the cabin of a half-decked boat; a small cabin, a galley.

cudgel /'kʌdʒəl/ n a short thick stick for beating. • vt (**cudgelling, cudgelled** or **cudgeling, cudgeled**) to beat with a cudgel.—**cudgeller, cudgeler** n.

cudweed /'kʌdwi:d/ n a plant with a fine down, belonging to the aster family.

cue[1] /kju:/ n the last word of a speech in a play, serving as a signal for the next actor to enter or begin to speak; any signal to do something; a hint. • vt (**cueing** or **cuing, cued**) to give a cue to.

cue[2] n a tapering rod used in snooker, billiards, and pool to strike the cue ball.

cue ball n (snooker, etc) the ball that a player strikes in order to hit other balls.

cuff[1] /kʌf/ n a blow with the fist or the open hand. • vt to strike such a blow.

cuff[2] n the end of a sleeve; a covering round the wrist; the turn-up on a trouser leg.

cufflink /'kʌflɪŋk/ n a decorative clip for fastening the edges of a shirt cuff.

cuirass /kwɪ'ræs/ n defensive armour for the breast and back, a breastplate.

cuirassier /ˌkwɪrə'si:r/ n a cavalry soldier armed with a cuirass.

cuisine /kwɪ'zi:n/ n a style of cooking or preparing food; the food prepared.

cuisse /kwɪs/ n defensive armour for the thighs.

culch /kʌltʃ/ n materials forming a spawning bed for oysters; oyster spawn.

cul-de-sac /'kʌldəˌsæk/ or /'kʊl-/ n (pl **culs-de-sac, cul-de-sacs**) a street blocked off at one end; a blind alley; a position, job leading nowhere.

-cule /kju:l/ n suffix forming diminutives, as animalcule.

culinary /'kʌlɪˌneri/ or /'kju:-/, /'kʊ-/ adj of or relating to cooking.

cull /kʌl/ vt to select; to pick out, gather. • n the selection of certain animals with the intention of killing them.—**culler** n.

cullet /'kʌlət/ n broken or refuse glass for recycling.

culm[1] /kʌlm/ n the stem of grasses.

culm[2] n inferior anthracite coal.

culminate /'kʌlmɪˌneɪt/ vti to reach the highest point of altitude, rank, power, etc; (astron) to reach the meridian; to bring to a head or the highest point.—**culminant** adj.—**culmination** n.

culottes /ku:'lɒts/ or /'ku:-/ npl a women's flared trousers that resemble a skirt.

culpable /'kʌlpəbəl/ adj deserving censure; criminal; blameworthy.—**culpably** adv.—**culpability** n.

culprit /'kʌlprɪt/ n a person accused, or found guilty, of an offence.

cult /kʌlt/ n a system of worship; devoted attachment to a person, principle, etc; a religion regarded as unorthodox or spurious; its body of adherents; a current fashion.—**cultic** adj.—**cultism** n.—**cultist** n.

cultivate /'kʌltɪˌveɪt/ vt to till and plant; to improve by care, labour, or study; to seek the society of; to civilize or refine.—**cultivated** adj.

cultivation /'kʌltə'veɪʃən/ n the act of cultivating; the state of being cultivated; tillage; culture.

cultivator /'kʌltɪˌveɪtər/ n a machine for breaking up soil for cultivation; someone who cultivates.

cultrate /'kʌlˌtreɪt/, **cultrated** /-ɪd/ adj (bot) shaped like a pruning knife; pointed and sharp-edged.

cultural /'kʌltʃərəl/ adj pertaining to culture.—**culturally** adv.

culture /'kʌltʃər/ n appreciation and understanding of the arts; the skills, arts, etc of a given people in a given period; the entire range of customs, beliefs, social forms, and material traits of a religious, social, or racial group; the scientific cultivation of plants to improve them and find new species; improvement of the mind, manner, etc; a growth of bacteria, etc in a prepared substance. • vt to cultivate bacteria for study or use.

cultured /'kʌltʃərd/ adj educated to appreciate the arts; having good taste; artificially grown, as cultured pearls.

cultured pearl n a pearl induced to grow artificially by the injection of a foreign body into the closed shell.

culture shock n loss of bearings and distress caused by an uprooting from a familiar environment or culture.

culverin /'kʌlvərɪn/ n a 16th-century long cannon with serpent-shaped handles.

culvert /'kʌlvərt/ n a drain or conduit under a road.

cum /kʌm/ prep with.

cumarin see **coumarin**.

cumber /'kʌmbər/ vt to hamper, to burden. • n a hindrance.

cumbersome /-səm/ adj inconveniently heavy or large, unwieldy.

cumin, cummin /'kʌmɪn/ or /kju:-/ n a plant cultivated for its seeds which are used as a spice.

cummerbund /'kʌmərˌbʌnd/ n a sash worn as a waistband, esp with a man's tuxedo.

cumshaw /'kʌmˌʃɔ/ n in China, a present or bonus.

cumulate /'kju:mjʊˌleɪt/ vt to accumulate; to combine into one; to build up by adding new material.—**cumulation** n.

cumulative /'kju:mjʊlətɪv/ adj augmenting or giving force; growing by successive additions; gathering strength as it grows.—**cumulatively** adv.

cumulative voting n a system of voting in which each voter has as many votes as there are candidates, and may give all to one candidate.

cumulus /'kju:mjʊləs/ n (pl **cumuli**) a cloud form having a flat base and rounded outlines.

cuneate /'kju:niət/ adj wedge-shaped.

cuneiform /kju:'neɪəˌfɔrm/ or /-'ni:ə-/, /'kju:nɪ-/ adj wedge-shaped.—also **cuneal**. • n the wedge-shaped characters of ancient Assyrian and Persian writing.

cunnilingus /ˌkʌnɪ'lɪŋgəs/ n sexual stimulation of the female genitals by the tongue.

cunning /'kʌnɪŋ/ adj ingenious; sly; designing; subtle. • n slyness, craftiness.

cup /kʌp/ n a small, bowl-shaped container for liquids, usu with a handle; the amount held in a cup; a drink made from a mixture of drinks with one main ingredient (eg claret cup); one of two shaped supporting parts of a brassiere; an ornamental cup used as a trophy. • vt (**cupping, cupped**) to take or put as in a cup; to curve (the hands) into the shape of a cup.

cupbearer /'kʌpˌbɛrər/ n one who serves wine at a banquet, esp an officer of a royal household.

cupboard /'kʌbərd/ n a closet or cabinet with shelves for cups, plates, utensils, food etc.

cupel /'kju:pəl/ n a small flat vessel used to assay precious metals. • vt (**cupelling, cupelled** or **cupeling, cupeled**) to refine precious metals from lead in a cupel.

cupful /'kʌpˌfʊl/ n (pl **cupfuls**) as much as a cup will contain.

Cupid /'kju:pɪd/ n the god of love in Roman mythology.

cupidity /kju:'pɪdɪti/ n greed of gain; covetousness.

cupola /'kju:pələ/ n a dome, esp of a pointed or bulbous shape; a furnace for melting metals.—**cupolated** adj.

cupreous /'kju:priəs/ or /'ku:-/ adj of or like copper; coppery.

cupric /'kju:prɪk/ or /'ku:-/, **cuprous** /-prəs/ adj containing copper.

cupriferous /kju:'prɪfərəs/ or /ku:-/ adj yielding copper.

cuprite /'kju:praɪt/ n red oxide of copper.

cupule /'kju:pju:l/ n (biol) a cup-shaped part, as of the acorn.

cur /kɜr/ n a mongrel dog; a despicable person.

curable /'kjɜrəbəl/ or /'kjur-/ adj able to be cured, remediable.—**curability** n.—**curably** adv.

curaçao /ˌkjɜrə'soː/ or /ˌkjɜrə'soː/ n an orange-flavoured liqueur.

curacy /'kjɜrəʃi/ or /'kjurə-/ n (pl **curacies**) the office or district of a curate.

curare, curari /kju'rɑri/ or /ku-/ n a substance extracted from vines and used by South American Indians to poison arrows.

curarine /-rɪn/ n an alkaloid extract of curare used as a muscle relaxant.

curarize /-raɪz/ vt to poison with curare.—**curarization** n.

curassow /'kjɜrə,soː/ or /'kjurə-/ n a large turkey-like bird of South America.

curate /'kjurət/ or /'kjɜrət/ n an assistant of a vicar or rector.

curative /'kjɜrətɪv/ or /'kjɜrə-/ adj tending to cure. • n a curative agent or drug.

curator /'kjɜreɪtər/ or /'kjʊ-, /kjʊ'reɪtər/ n a superintendent of a museum, art gallery, etc.—**curatorial** adj.

curb /kɜrb/ vt to restrain; to check; to keep in subjection. • n that which checks, restrains, or subdues; a line of raised stone forming the edge of a pavement.—also **kerb**.

curbing /-ɪŋ/ n curbstones collectively; material for curbstones.—also **kerbing**.

curb roof n a roof with a double slope, the lower being steeper.

curbstone /'kɜrbstoːn/ n the stone edge of a path.—also **kerbstone**.

curcuma /'kɜrkjuːmə/ n one of several kinds of plant including turmeric.

curd /kɜrd/ n the coagulated part of soured milk, used to make cheese.—**curdy** adj.—**curdiness** n.

curdle /'kɜrdəl/ vti to turn into curds; to coagulate; (with the blood) to cause terror.—**curdler** n.

cure /'kjɜr/ or /'kjur/ n the act or art of healing; a remedy; restoration to health. • vt to heal; to rid of; to preserve meat or fish by drying, salting, etc.

curé /kju'reɪ/, Fr. /ky'ʀeɪ/ n a French parish priest.

curettage /kju'rɛtɪdʒ/ or /-rɪ'tɒdʒ/ n surgical scraping to remove growths or dead tissue, etc.

curette, curet /kju'rɛt/ n a surgical instrument for scraping a body cavity. •vt (**curetting, curetted**) to scrape with this.

curfew /'kɜrfjuː/ n a signal, as a bell, at a fixed evening hour as a sign that everyone must be indoors; the signal or hour.

curia /'kjuriə/ or /'kjɜ-/ n (pl **curiae**) the papal court; a senate house of ancient Rome; one of the divisions of the Roman people; a medieval court of justice.

curie /'kjuri/ or /kju'riː/ n a unit of radioactivity.

curio /'kjuriːo/ n (pl **curios**) an item valued as rare or unusual.

curiosity /ˌkjuri'ɒsɪti/ n (pl **curiosities**) the quality of being curious; inquisitiveness; a strange, rare or interesting object.

curious /'kjuriəs/ adj anxious to know; prying, inquisitive; strange, remarkable, odd.—**curiously** adv.—**curiousness** n.

curium /'kjuriəm/ n an artificially made radioactive metallic element derived from plutonium.

curl /kɜrl/ vti to form into a curved shape, to coil; to twist into ringlets; to proceed in a curve, to bend; to play at curling; (with **up**) to rest with the body in a curved shape and the legs drawn up; to relax in a comfortable place; (inf) to give up; to be embarrassed and sickened by. • n a ringlet of hair; a spiral form, a twist; a bend or undulation.

curler /'kɜrlər/ n a small pin or roller used for curling the hair; a person who plays curling.

curlew /'kɜrluː/ n a bird with a long curved bill and long legs.

curlicue /'kɜrlɪˌkjuː/ n an exaggerated ornamental curl.

curling /'kɜrlɪŋ/ n a Scottish game in which two teams slide large smooth stones on ice into a target circle.

curling stone n a heavy round flat stone with a handle used in curling.

curling tongs n a pair of tongs heated to curl hair.

curly /'kɜrli/ adj (**curlier, curliest**) full of curls.—**curliness** n.

curmudgeon /kɜr'mʌdʒən/ n an ill-natured churlish person; a miser.—**curmudgeonly** adj.

currant /'kɜrənt/ n a small variety of dried grape; a shrub that yields a red or black fruit.

currency /'kɜrənsi/ n (pl **currencies**) the time during which a thing is current; the state of being in use; the money current in a country.

current /'kɜrənt/ adj generally accepted; happening now; presently in circulation. • n a body of water or air in motion, a flow; the transmission of electricity through a conductor; a general tendency.

current account n a bank account, usu with no interest, from which money is withdrawn by cheques or cash cards; a checking account.

currently /-li/ adv at the present time.

curricle /'kɜrɪkəl/ n a two-wheeled open carriage drawn by two horses abreast.

curriculum /kə'rɪkjuləm/ n (pl **curricula, curriculums**) a prescribed course of study.—**curricular** adj.

curriculum vitae /-'viːtaɪ/ n (pl **curricula vitae**) a brief survey of one's career.

currier /'kɜriər/ n a leather dresser.—**curriery** n.

currish /'kɜrɪʃ/ adj snappy; quarrelsome; rude.

curry[1] /'kɜri/ n (pl **curries**) a spicy dish with a hot sauce; curry seasoning. • vt (pl **currying, curried**) to flavour with curry.

curry[2] vt (**currying, curried**) to rub down and groom (a horse); to dress leather after tanning; to beat; (with **favour**) to use flattery to ingratiate.

currycomb /'kɜri,koːm/ n a metal comb for grooming horses.

curse /kɜrs/ n a calling down of destruction or evil; a profane oath; a swear word; a violent exclamation of anger; a scourge. • vti to invoke a curse on; to swear, to blaspheme; to afflict, to torment.

cursed /'kɜrsəd/ or /kɜrst/ adj damnable.

cursive /'kɜrsɪv/ adj running; flowing. • n a script with the letters joined, as in handwriting.

cursor /'kɜrsər/ n a flashing indicator on a computer screen indicating position; the transparent slide on a slide rule.

cursorial /kər'sɔriəl/ adj (bird) with limbs adapted for running or walking.

cursory /'kɜrsəri/ adj hasty, passing; superficial, careless.—**cursorily** adv.

curt /kɜrt/ adj short; abrupt; concise; rudely brief.—**curtly** adv.—**curtness** n.

curtail /kər'teɪl/ vt to cut short; to reduce; to deprive of part (of).—**curtailment** n.

curtain /'kɜrtən/ n a cloth hung as a screen at a window, etc; the movable screen separating the stage from the auditorium; (pl: sl) the end, death. • vt to enclose in, or as with, curtains.

curtain call n (theat) a call from the audience for performers to appear at the end to receive applause.

curtain lecture n a private reprimand from a wife to her husband.

curtain-raiser n a short play preceding the main one; an introductory item.

curtilage /'kɜrtəlɪdʒ/ n (law) a yard, garden or enclosure of a house, included in the same fence.

curtsy, curtsey /'kɜrtsi/ n (pl **curtsies, curtseys**) a formal gesture of greeting or respect, involving bending the knees, made by women. • vi (**curtsying, curtsied** or **curtseying, curtseyed**) to make a curtsy.

curvaceous /kər'veɪʃəs/ adj (inf) having an attractive body with shapely curves.

curvature /'kɜrvətʃər/ n a bending; a curved form.

curve /kɜrv/ n a bending without angles; a bent form or thing; (geom) a line of which no part is straight. • vti to form into a curve, to bend.—**curvy** adj (**curvier, curviest**).

curvet /kər'vɛt/ n a particular leap of a horse; a frisk or bound. •vi (**curvetting, curvetted** or **curveting, curveted**) to leap as a horse; to frisk or bound.

curvilinear /ˌkɜrvɪ'lɪniər/, **curvilineal** /-əl/ adj consisting of or bounded by curved lines.—**curvilinearity** n.

cusec /'kjuːsɛk/ n a unit of flow of one cubic foot of water per second.

cushion /'kʊʃən/ n a case stuffed with soft material for resting on; the elastic border around a snooker table; the air mass supporting a hovercraft. • vt to furnish with cushions; to protect by padding; to give protection against difficulties, etc; to soften the effect of.—**cushiony** adj.

cushy /'kʊʃi/ adj (**cushier, cushiest**) (inf) easy, comfortable.

cusp /kʌsp/ n an apex or point; the point at each end of a crescent moon; (astrol) the transitional point of a house; (archit) the pointed intersection between two arcs; a cone-shaped point on a tooth; a fold or flap of a heart valve.

cuspid /'kʌspɪd/ n a canine tooth.

cuspidate /'kʌspɪ,deɪt/ or /-dɪt/, **cuspidal** /-pɪ,dəl/ adj of, like or having a cusp; (leaves, etc) ending in a point.

cuspidor /'kʌspɪ,dɔr/ n a spittoon.

cuss /kʌs/ n (sl) an annoying person; a curse. • vt (sl) to curse.

cussed /'kʌsɪd/ adj (sl) cursed; stubborn, perverse.

cussedness /-nəs/ n (sl) contrariness.

custard /'kʌstərd/ n a sauce mixture of milk, eggs and sugar.

custard apple /'kʌstərd'æpəl/ n a West Indian tree; its dark fruit with a soft edible pulp.

custodian /kə'stoːdiən/ n one who has the care of anything; a keeper; a caretaker.

custody /'kʌstədi/ n (pl **custodies**) guardianship; imprisonment; security.—**custodial** adj.

custom /'kʌstəm/ n a regular practice; usage; traditions of a people or a society; frequent repetition of the same act; business patronage; (pl) duties on imports.

customary /-əri/ adj habitual; conventional; common.—**customarily** adv.

custom-built /-'bɪlt/ adj made to a customer's specifications.

customer /-mər/ n a person who buys from a shop or business, esp regularly; (inf) a person.

custom house /'kʌstəm,haʊs/ n an office or building where duties are paid on exported or imported goods and vessels are entered and cleared.

cut /kʌt/ vb (**cutting, cut**) vt to cleave or separate with a sharp instrument; to make an incision in; to wound with a sharp instrument; to divide; to trim; to intersect; to abridge; to diminish; to pass deliberately without recognition; to wound the feelings deeply; to reduce or curtail; to grow a new tooth through the gum; to divide (a pack of cards) at random; to switch off (a light, an engine); (inf) to stay away from class, school, etc; (with **back**) to prune vegetation; to economize; (with **down**) to fell a tree; to reduce expenditure, consumption, etc; to make a smaller garment from an old one; to kill; (with **off**) to take away by cutting or slicing; to stop abruptly, esp a telephone conversation; to sever relations; to be so placed as to foil something, eg an escape; (with **out**) to delete; to cut into shapes; (inf) to force out a rival; to give up an indulgence or habit; (with **up**) to cut into pieces; to wound with a knife; (inf) to affect deeply. • vi to make an incision; to perform the work of an edged instrument; to grow through the gums; (cinema) to change to another scene, to stop photographing; (with **in**) to butt in; to interpose oneself; to interrupt with comments; to drive between two vehicles, leaving insufficient space; (with **out**) (engine) to stop working. • n an incision or wound made by a sharp instrument; a gash; a sharp stroke; a sarcastic remark; a passage or channel cut out; a slice; a block on which an engraving is cut; the fashion or shape of a garment; the deliberate ignoring of an acquaintance; the division of a pack of cards; a diminution in price below another merchant; (sl) a share, as of profits. • adj divided or separated; gashed; having the surface ornamented or fashioned; not wrought or hand-made; reduced in price.

cutaneous /kju:'teɪniəs/ adj pertaining to the skin.

cutaway /'kʌtə,weɪ/ n a drawing (of a machine) with part of the exterior covering cut away to show the internal mechanism; (film) a scene shot separately from but relevant to the main action.

cutback /'kʌtbæk/ n a reduction, esp in expenditure; a flashback.

cutch /kʌtʃ/ see **catechu**.

cute /kju:t/ adj (inf) acute, shrewd; pretty or attractive, esp in a dainty way.—**cutely** adv.—**cuteness** n.

cut glass n flint glass cut into facets or figures.

cuticle /'kju:tɪkəl/ n the skin at the base of the fingernail or toe nail; epidermis.—**cuticular** adj.

cutie /'kju:ti/ n (sl) a bright smart girl.

cutis /'kju:tɪs/ n (pl **cutes, cutises**) the vascular layer of the skin, below the epidermis.

cutlass /'kʌtləs/ n a sailor's short heavy sword.

cutler /'kʌtlər/ n a maker of or dealer in knives.

cutlery /'kʌtləri/ n knives, forks, etc for eating and serving food.

cutlet /'kʌtlət/ n a neck chop of lamb, etc; a small slice cut off from the ribs or leg; minced meat in the form of a cutlet.

cutoff /'kʌt,ɔf/ n a short or straight road; a new shorter channel cut by a river across a bend; a device for stopping steam from entering a cylinder.

cutout /-,aʊt/ n a switch to cut off an electric light from a circuit.

cutpurse /-pərs/ n a pickpocket.

cutter /'kʌtər/ n someone or something that cuts; a small, swift sailing vessel; a light boat carried by larger ships.

cutthroat /'kʌtθroːt/ n a murderer. • adj merciless; (razor) having a long blade in a handle.

cutthroat trout /-trəʊt/ n a North American trout with a red or orange marking under its jaw.

cutting /'kʌtɪŋ/ n a piece cut off or from; an incision; a newspaper clipping; a slip from a plant for propagation; a passage or channel cut out; the process of editing a film or recording; a recording. • adj (wind) sharp, biting; (remarks) hurtful.

cuttlebone /'kʌtəlboːn/ n the internal bone of the cuttlefish, used for polishing, etc.

cuttlefish /-fɪʃ/ n (pl **cuttlefish, cuttlefishes**) a marine creature with a flattened body that squirts ink when threatened.

cutwater /'kʌt,wɔtər/ n the fore part of a ship's prow.

cutwork /-,wərk/ n appliqué work.

CV abbr = curriculum vitae.

cwt. abbr = hundredweight.

cyan /'saɪæn/ n a blue colour, one of the primary colours.

cyanamide, cyanamid /saɪ'ænə,maɪd/ n a chemical compound of calcium carbide and nitrogen, used as a fertilizer.

cyanate /'saɪ,neɪt/ n a compound of cyanic acid with a base.

cyanic acid /saɪ'ænɪk/ n a strong acid composed of cyanogen and oxygen.

cyanide /'saɪə,naɪd/ n a poison.

cyanogen /saɪ'ænədʒən/ n a colourless poisonous gas burning with a purple flame and with the odour of peach blossom.

cyanosis /,saɪə'noːsɪs/ n a condition of the body in which its surface becomes blue due to insufficient aeration of the blood.—**cyanotic** adj.

cyanotype /,saɪnoː'təɪp/ n a photographic process in which the picture is taken in Prussian blue; a blueprint.

cyber café /'saɪbər'kæfeɪ/ n a café for use by the customers to enable them to browse the Internet.

cybernetics /-'netɪks/ n (sing) the study of communication and control functions in living organisms, and in mechanical and electronic systems.—**cybernetic** adj.

cyberphobia /-'foːbɪə/ n a morbid fear or intense dislike of computers.—**cyberphobic** adj.

cyberspace /-'speɪs/ n all of the data stored on a large computer or network through which a virtual reality user can move.

cyclamen /'sɪkləmən/ n a plant of the primrose family, with pink, purple or white flowers.

cycle /'saɪkəl/ n a recurring series of events or phenomena; the period of this; a body of epics or romances with a common theme; a group of songs; a bicycle, motorcycle, or tricycle. • vi to go in cycles; to ride a bicycle or tricycle.

cyclic /'saɪklɪk/ or /'sɪk-/, **cyclical** /'saɪklɪkəl/ or /'sɪk-/ adj moving or recurring in cycles.—**cyclically** adv.

cyclist /'saɪklɪst/ n a person who rides a bicycle.

cycloid /'saɪklɔɪd/ n a curve traced by a point on a circle as it rolls along a straight line.—**cycloidal** adj.

cyclometer /saɪ'klɒmɪtər/ n an instrument for registering the revolutions of a wheel.—**cyclometry** n.

cyclone /'saɪkloːn/ n a violent circular storm; an atmospheric movement in which the wind blows spirally round towards a centre of low barometric pressure.—**cyclonic** adj.

Cyclopean /,saɪklə'piːən/ or /-'kloːpiən/ adj pertaining to the Cyclops, the legendary one-eyed giant; one-eyed; huge and rough; vast, massive; (archit) built of huge stones without mortar.

cyclopedia, cyclopaedia /,saɪklə'piːdiə/ n an encyclopedia.—**cyclopedic, cyclopaedic** adj.

cyclorama /,saɪklo:'rɑːmə/ n a series of moving pictures extended circularly so as to appear in natural perspective to the viewer standing in the centre.—**cycloramic** adj.

cyclotron /'saɪklə,trɒn/ n an apparatus for accelerating charged particles in a magnetic field.

cygnet /'sɪgnət/ n a young swan.

cylinder /'sɪlɪndər/ n a hollow figure or object with parallel sides and circular ends; an object shaped like a cylinder; any machine part of this shape; the piston chamber in an engine.—**cylindrical** adj.—**cylindrically** adv.

cylindroid /'sɪlɪnˌdrɔɪd/ *adj* like a cylinder. • *n* a solid body resembling a cylinder but with the ends elliptical.

cyma /'saɪmə/ *n* (*pl* **cymae, cymas**) (*archit*) ogee moulding of a cornice.

cymbal /'sɪmbəl/ *n* (*mus*) one of a pair of two brass plates struck together to produce a ringing or clashing sound.—**cymbalist** *n*.

cyme /saɪm/ *n* a flower cluster in which the main stem ends in a flower, while from each side of the main stem secondary stems branch off to end a flower, and tertiary stems from those, etc.—**cymose** *adj*.

Cymric /'kɪmrɪk/ *adj* pertaining to the Cymry, or the Welsh. • *n* the Welsh language.

cynic /'sɪnɪk/ *n* a morose, surly, or sarcastic person; a sceptic about people, motives and actions; one of a sect of ancient Greek philosophers.—**cynicism** *n*.

cynical /'sɪnɪkəl/ *adj* sceptical of or sneering at goodness; shameless in admitting unworthy motives.—**cynically** *adv*.

cynosure /'sɪnəˌʃʊr/ or /'saɪnə-/ *n* a centre of attraction or admiration.

cypher /'saɪfər/ *see* **cipher**.

cypress /'saɪprəs/ *n* an evergreen tree with hard wood.

Cyprian /'sɪpriən/ *adj* of Cyprus; of Aphrodite, the Greek goddess of love; wanton, lascivious. • *n* a native of Cyprus; a prostitute.

cyprinid /'sɪprɪˌnɪd/ *n* any of a family of freshwater fishes, including the carp.

cyprinoid /'sɪprɪˌnɔɪd/ *adj* of or resembling a cyprinid; carp-like.

Cypriot /'sɪpriɒt/ *adj* pertaining to Cyprus, or to its inhabitants. • *n* a native of Cyprus.

Cyrillic /sɪ'rɪlɪk/ *adj* of or pertaining to St Cyril, or to the Slavonic alphabet. • *n* the alphabet of the Slavonic languages.

cyst /sɪst/ *n* a closed sac developing abnormally in the structure of plants or animals.—**cystic** *adj*.

cystic fibrosis /'sɪstɪk/ *n* a congenital disorder in young children characterized by chronic respiratory and digestive problems.

cystitis /sɪ'staɪtɪs/ *n* inflammation of the urinary bladder.

cystocele /'sɪstoˌsiːl/ *n* a hernia caused by protrusion of the bladder.

cystoid /'sɪsˌtɔɪd/ *adj* cyst-like. • *n* a growth resembling a cyst.

cystolith /'sɪstoːˌlɪθ/ or /-tə-/ *n* a stone in the bladder.

cystoscope /'sɪstəˌskoːp/ *n* an instrument for examining the urinary bladder.—**cystoscopic** *adj*.—**cystoscopy** *n*.

cystotomy /sɪs'tɒtəmi/ *n* (*pl* **cystotomies**) the opening of the human bladder for the removal of a stone, etc.

cyt-, cyto- /'saɪtoː/ or /-ə/ *prefix* cell.

cytogenesis, cytogeny *n* cell formation in plants and animals.

cytology /saɪ'tɒlədʒi/ *n* the scientific study of cells; cell structure.—**cytological** *adj*.—**cytologist** *n*.

cytoplasm /'saɪtoːˌplæzəm/ *n* the substance of a cell as opposed to its nucleus.—**cytoplasmic** *adj*.

cytoscreening *n* the examination of smear tests for indications of cervical cancer.

czar /zɑr/ *see* **tsar**.

czardas /'tʃɑrdæʃ/ *n* a Hungarian national dance with varying tempos; the music for it.

czarevitch /'zɑrəvɪtʃ/ *see* **tsarevitch**.

czarina, czaritsa /zɑr'iːnə/ *see* **tsarina, tsaritsa**.

Czech /tʃɛk/ *n* a native, or the language, of the Czech Republic.

D

D (*symbol*) (*mus*) the second note of the C major scale; (*chem*) deuterium ; five hundred.

d. *abbr* = penny or pennies (*UK currency before 1971*).

dab¹ /dæb/ *vt* (**dabbing, dabbed**) to touch lightly with something moist or soft. • *n* a quick light tap; a small lump of anything moist or soft.—**dabber** *n*.

dab² *n* a species of European flounder.

dab³ *n* (*inf*) a dab hand.

dabble /'dæbəl/ *vi* to move hands, feet, etc gently in water or another liquid; (*usu with* **at, in, with**) to do anything in a superficial or dilettante way. • *vt* to splash.—**dabbler** *n*.

dabchick /'dæb,tʃɪk/ *n* a water bird, the little grebe.

dab hand *n* (*inf*) an adept person, an expert.

da capo /dæ'kæpoː/ *adj, adv* (*mus*) from the beginning.

dace /deɪs/ *n* (*pl* **dace**) a small freshwater fish of the carp family.

dacha /'dætʃə/ *n* in Russia, a house in the country used as a holiday and summer residence.

dachshund /'dækshənd/ or /dɒk-/ *n* a breed of short-legged, long-bodied hound.

dacoit /də'kɔɪt/ *n* one of a group of robbers in India and Burma, who plunder in bands.—*also* **dakoit**.

dactyl /'dæktɪl/ *n* a poetic foot of three syllables, one long and two short.—**dactylic** *adj, n*.

dactylogram /dæk'tɪlə,græm/ *n* a fingerprint.

dactylography /,dæktə'lɒgrəfɪ/ *n* the science of fingerprints.—**dactylographer** *n*.—**dactylographic** *adj*.

dactylology /-'lɒlədʒɪ/ *n* the art of communicating ideas with the fingers; sign language.

dad /dæd/ *n* (*inf*) father.

Dada /'dɑːdɒ/ *n* a school of art and literature that aims at suppressing all relations between thought and expression.—**Dadaism** *n*.— **Dadaist** *n*—**Dadaistic** *adj*.

daddy /'dædɪ/ *n* (*pl* **daddies**) (*inf*) father.

daddy longlegs /-'lɒŋ,legz/ *n* (*inf*) any of various spiders or insects with long, slender legs, *esp* a crane fly.

dado /'deɪdoː/ *n* (*pl* **dadoes**) the lower part of a room wall when separately panelled or decorated.

daff /dæf/ *vi* (*Scot*) to sport, to play.

daffodil /'dæfədɪl/ *n* a yellow spring flower, a narcissus; its pale yellow colour.

daft /dæft/ *adj* (*inf*) silly, weak-minded; giddy; mad.—**daftly** *adv*.—**daftness** *n*.

dagger /'dægər/ *n* a short weapon for stabbing; a reference mark used in printing (†).—*also* **obelisk**.

dago /'deɪgoː/ *n* (*pl* **dagos, dagoes**) (*offensive*) a foreigner, *esp* from Spain or Portugal.

daguerreotype /də'gɛroː,taɪp/ *n* an early photographic process using a copper plate; a picture taken by this process.—**daguerreotypy** *n*.

dahlia /'deɪlɪə/ *n* a half-hardy tuberous perennial of the aster family grown for its colourful blooms.

daily /'deɪlɪ/ *adj, adv* (happening) every day; constantly, progressively. • *n* (*pl* **dailies**) a newspaper published every weekday; (*inf*) a charwoman.

dainty /'deɪntɪ/ *adj* (**daintier, daintiest**) delicate; choice; nice, fastidious. • *n* (*pl* **dainties**) a titbit, a delicacy.—**daintily** *adv*.—**daintiness** *n*.

daiquiri /'dækərɪ/ *n* (*pl* **daiquiris**) a cocktail of rum, sugar and lime juice.

dairy /'dɛrɪ/ *n* (*pl* **dairies**) a building or room where milk is stored and dairy products made; a shop selling these; a company supplying them.

dairy cattle *npl* cows reared for milk production.

dairying /-ɪŋ/ *n* the business or occupation of a dairy farmer.

dairyman /-mən/ *n* (*pl* **dairymen**) a person who works in a dairy or deals in dairy products.

dairy products *npl* milk and products made from it, *eg* butter, cheese, yogurt.

dais /'daɪəs/ or /'deɪɪs/ *n* a low platform at one end of a hall or room.

daisy /'deɪzɪ/ *n* (*pl* **daisies**) any of various plants with a yellow centre and white petals.

daisywheel /'deɪzɪ,wiːl/ *n* (*comput*) a flat, wheel-shaped, printing device with characters at the ends of spokes.

dal /dɒl/ *n* a split-grain pulse commonly used in Indian cooking.—*also* **dhal**.

Dalai Lama /,dɒlaɪ'lɒmə/ *n* the chief lama of Tibet.

dale /deɪl/ *n* a valley.

dalliance /'dælɪəns/ *n* idle or frivolous time-wasting; trifling; flirtation.

dally /'dælɪ/ *vi* (**dallying, dallied**) to lose time by idleness or trifling; to play or trifle (with); to flirt.—**dallier** *n*.

dallymoney *n* (*sl*) alimony paid by one partner in a former sexual relationship to the other.

Dalmatian /dæl'meɪʃən/ *n* a large short-haired dog with black spot-like markings on a white body.

dalmatic /dæl'mætɪk/ *n* a loose vestment with open sides worn *esp* by a bishop.

dam¹ /dæm/ *n* an artificial embankment to retain water; water so contained. • *vt* (**damming, dammed**) to retain (water) with such a barrier; to stem, obstruct, restrict.

dam² *n* the mother of a four-footed animal.

damage /'dæmədʒ/ *n* injury, harm; loss; (*inf*) price, cost; (*pl*) (*law*) payment in compensation for loss or injury. • *vt* to do harm to, to injure.—**damageable** *adj*.—**damager** *n*.—**damaging** *adj*.

damask /'dæməsk/ *n* a reversible, figured, woven fabric, *esp* linen or silk. • *adj* made of this; having a pinkish colour like a damask rose.

damask rose *n* a rose with greyish-pink blooms and a sweet fragrance used in perfume making.

dame /deɪm/ *n* the comic, female role in a pantomime *usu* played by a man; (*sl*) a woman; (*with cap*) the title of a woman who has been awarded an order of chivalry equivalent to the title of a Knight; the wife of a knight or baronet.

dammar, damar /'dæmər/ *n* a resin used for varnish.

damn /dæm/ *vt* to condemn, censure; to ruin; to curse; to consign to eternal punishment. • *vti* to prove guilty. • *interj* (*sl*) expressing irritation or annoyance. • *n* (*sl*) something having no value. • *adj, adv* damned.

damnable /'dæmnəbəl/ *adj* deserving damnation; despicable; hateful; offensive; wicked; (*inf*) annoying.—**damnably** *adv*.

damnation /dæm'neɪʃən/ *n* the state of being condemned to hell; the act of damning. • *interj* expressing annoyance, irritation, etc.

damnatory /'dæmnətɔrɪ/ *adj* assigning to, or containing a threat of, damnation.

damned /dæmd/ *adj* (*inf*) damnable; extremely.—*also adv*.

damnify /'dæmnɪ,faɪ/ *vt* (**damnifying, damnified**) (*law*) to cause loss or damage to.

damp /dæmp/ *n* humidity, moisture; in mines, poisonous or foul gas. • *adj* slightly wet, moist. • *vt* to moisten; (*with* **down**) to stifle, reduce.—**damply** *adv*.—**dampness** *n*.

dampen /'dæmpən/ *vti* to make or become damp. • *vt* to stifle.—**dampener** *n*.

damper /-ər/ *n* a depressive influence; a metal plate in a flue for controlling combustion; (*mus*) a device for stopping vibration in stringed instruments; (*Austral*) unleavened bread.

damsel /'dæmzəl/ *n* (*formerly*) a girl.

damselfly /'dæmzəl,flaɪ/ *n* (*pl* **damselflies**) an insect resembling the dragonfly but having wings that fold when at rest.

damson /'dæmzən/ *n* a small, dark-purple variety of plum; the colour of this; the tree on which this fruit grows.

dance /dæns/ *vti* to move rhythmically, *esp* to music; to skip or leap lightly; to execute (steps); to cause to dance or to move up and down. • *n* a piece of dancing; a dance performance of an artistic nature; a party with music for dancing; music for accompanying dancing.—**dancer** *n*.—**dancing** *adj, n*.

D and C *n* (*med*) dilation (of the cervix) and curettage (of the womb).

dandelion /'dændɪˌlaɪən/ *n* a common wild plant with ragged leaves, a yellow flower and a fluffy seed head.

dander[1] /'dændər/ *n* scurf from various animals, *eg* cats, dogs, that may be allergenic; temper; fighting spirit.

dander[2] *vi* (*Scot*) to saunter. • *n* a sauntering stroll.

Dandie Dinmont /'dændɪˈdɪnˌmɒnt/ or /-mənt/ *n* a breed of terrier.

dandify /'dændəˌfaɪ/ *vt* to give the character or style of a dandy to; to make trim or smart like a dandy.—**dandification** *n*.

dandle /'dændəl/ *vt* to play with (a baby) on the knee, to fondle.—**dandler** *n*.

dandruff /'dændrəf/ *n* scales of skin on the scalp, under the hair, scurf.—**dandruffy** *adj*.

dandy /'dændɪ/ *n* (*pl* **dandies**) a man who likes to dress too fashionably. • *adj* (**dandier, dandiest**) (*inf*) excellent, fine.—**dandyish** *adj*.—**dandyism** *n*.

dandy-brush *n* a stiff brush for grooming horses.

Dane /deɪn/ *n* a native or citizen of Denmark.

Danegeld /'deɪngeld/ *n* an annual tax imposed in England in the reign of Ethelred II to maintain forces against the Danes.

Danelaw, Danelagh /'deɪnlɔː/ *n* the code of laws established by the Danes on their settlement in England; that part of the country where these laws were in force.

dang /dæŋ/ *adj, adv, interj, n* a euphemistic form of **damn**.

danger /'deɪndʒər/ *n* exposure to injury or risk; a source of harm or risk.

dangerous /'deɪndʒərəs/ *adj* involving danger; unsafe; perilous.—**dangerously** *adv*.—**dangerousness** *n*.

dangle /'dæŋgəl/ *vi* to hang and swing loosely. • *vt* to carry something so that it hangs loosely; to display temptingly.—**dangler** *n*.

Danish /'deɪnɪʃ/ *adj* of the people or language of Denmark. • *n* the language of Denmark.

Danish pastry *n* a sweet pastry topped with fruity icing and nuts.

dank /dæŋk/ *adj* disagreeably damp.—**dankly** *adv*.—**dankness** *n*.

danseur /dɒ̃ˈsɜːr/ *n* a professional dancer, a ballet dancer.—**danseuse** *nf*.

dap /dæp/ *vb* (**dapping, dapped**) *vi* to drop bait gently into water. • *vt* to dip lightly; to bounce (a ball). • *n* a bounce.

daphne /'dæfnɪ/ *n* a genus of small evergreen shrubs with fragrant flowers, allied to the laurel.

dapper /'dæpər/ *adj* nimble; neat in appearance, spruce.

dapple /'dæpəl/ *vti* to mark with or show patches of a different colour; to variegate. • *adj* marked in such a way. • *n* something so marked.

dapple-grey /-'greɪ/ *adj* mottled with darker grey. • *n* a horse of this colour.

Dardanian /dɑːrˈdeɪnɪən/, **Dardan** /dɑːrdən/ *adj* pertaining to Dardania, an ancient city of Troy, in Asia Minor, or its people. • *n* a Trojan.

dare /dɛr/ *vti* (**daring, dared** *or* **durst**) to be bold enough; to venture, to risk; to defy, to challenge. • *n* a challenge.—**darer** *n*.

daredevil /'dɛrˌdevəl/ *n* a rash, reckless person. • *adj* daring, bold; courageous.—**daredevilry, daredeviltry** *n*.

daring /'dɛrɪŋ/ *adj* fearless; courageous; unconventional. • *n* adventurous courage.—**daringly** *adv*.

dark /dɑːrk/ *adj* having little or no light; of a shade of colour closer to black than white; (*person*) having brown or black skin or hair; gloomy; (*inf*) secret, unknown; mysterious. • *n* a dark state or colour; ignorance; secrecy.—**darkly** *adv*.—**darkness** *n*.

darken /'dɑːrkən/ *vti* to make or become dark or darker.—**darkener** *n*.

dark horse *n* a competitor about whom little is known; a person of reserved character; a surprise political candidate.

darkish /dɑːrˈkɪʃ/ *adj* quite dark.

darkroom /'dɑːrkruːm/ *n* a room for processing photographs in darkness or safe light.

darksome /-səm/ *adj* gloomy.

darling /'dɑːrlɪŋ/ *n* a dearly loved person; a favourite. • *adj* lovable; much admired.

darn[1] /dɑːrn/ *vt* to mend a hole in fabric or a garment with stitches. • *n* an area that has been darned.—**darner** *n*.

darn[2] *interj* a form of **damn** as a mild oath.—*also adj*.

darnel /'dɑːrnəl/ *n* a kind of rye grass.

darning /'dɑːrnɪŋ/ *n* a patch made by darning; material, garments, etc to be darned.

dart /dɑːrt/ *n* a small pointed missile; a sudden movement; a fold sewn into a garment for shaping it; (*pl*) an indoor game in which darts are thrown at a target. • *vti* to move rapidly; to send out rapidly.

dartboard /'dɑːrtbɔːrd/ *n* a circular cork or wooden target used in the game of darts.

darter /'dɑːrtər/ *n* one of several kinds of bird or fish.

Darwinian /dɑːrˈwɪnɪən/ *adj* pertaining to Charles Darwin, the naturalist (1809–82) or Darwinism. • *n* an evolutionist.

Darwinism /'dɑːrwɪˌnɪzəm/ *n* the theory of natural selection advocated by Darwin.—**Darwinist** *n*.

dash /dæʃ/ *vti* to fling violently; to rush quickly; (*hopes*) to shatter; (*one's spirits, etc*) to depress, confound; to write quickly. • *n* a short race; a rush; a small amount of something added to food; a tinge; a punctuation mark (—); a dashboard; vigour, verve; display.

dashboard /'dæʃbɔːrd/ *n* an instrument panel in a car.

dasher /'dæʃər/ *n* one who or that which dashes; a dashing person; the part of a churn that agitates cream.

dashing /'dæʃɪŋ/ *adj* debonair; spirited, stylish, dapper.—**dashingly** *adv*.

dastard /'dæstərd/ *n* a malicious coward.

dastardly /'dæstərdlɪ/ *adj* mean, cowardly; base.—**dastardliness** *n*.

dasyure /'dæsɪʊr/ *n* a small carnivorous Australian marsupial.

DAT *abbr* = digital audio tape.

data /'dætə/ or /'deɪtə/ *npl* (*sing* **datum**) (*often used as sing*) facts, statistics, or information either historical or derived by calculation or experimentation.

data bank, database /'dætəˌbeɪs/ or /'deɪtə-/ *n* a large store of information for analysis, *esp* one held in a computer.

data capture *n* the process of translating information into computer-readable form.

data processing *n* the analysis of information stored in a computer for various uses, *eg* stock control, statistical research, mathematical modelling, etc.

data warehouse *n* a system which collects data from a wide range of sources, and is processed as a management tool regarding trends, marketing etc.

date[1] /deɪt/ *n* a day or time of occurrence; a statement of this in a letter, etc; a period to which something belongs; a duration; an appointment, *esp* with a member of the opposite sex. • *vt* to affix a date to; to note the date of; to reckon the time of; (*inf*) to make a date with; (*inf*) to see frequently a member of the opposite sex. • *vi* to reckon from a point in time; to show signs of belonging to a particular period.—**datable, dateable** *adj*.—**dater** *n*.

date[2] *n* the sweet fruit of the date palm, a palm tree of tropical regions.

dated /'deɪtəd/ *adj* old-fashioned; out of style; bearing a date.—**datedness** *n*.

dateless /'deɪtləs/ *adj* without a date; timeless; classic.

dateline /-laɪn/ *n* a line on a newspaper story giving the date and place of writing. • *vt* to provide with a dateline.

date line *n* the line running north to south along the 180-degree meridian, east of which is one day earlier than west of it.—*also* **International Date Line**.

dative /'deɪtɪv/ *adj* (*gram*) denoting an indirect object. • *n* the dative case.—**datival** *adj*.—**datively** *adv*.

datum /'dætəm/ or /'deɪtəm/ *n* (*pl* **data**) a single unit of information; a thing given or taken for granted; something known or assumed as fact and made the basis of reasoning or calculation; an assumption or premise from which inferences are drawn; (*pl* **datums**) (*geol*) a level, line or point used as a reference in surveying.

datura /dəˈtjʊrə/ *n* any of several kinds of strongly scented narcotic plant.

daub /dɔːb/ *vt* to smear or overlay (with clay, etc); to paint incompetently. • *n* a smear; a poor painting.—**dauber** *n*.

daughter /'dɔːtər/ *n* a female child or descendant; a female member of a family, race, etc; a woman in relation to her native country or place; (*physics*) a nucleus, particle, etc, produced from another by radioactive decay; (*biol*) a cell produced by the division of another.

daughter-in-law /-ɪnˌlɔː/ *n* (*pl* **daughters-in-law**) the wife of one's son.

daughterly /-lɪ/ *adj* of or befitting a daughter.—**daughterliness** *n*.

daunt /dɒnt/ *vt* to intimidate; to discourage.—**daunter** *n*.—**dauntingly** *adv*.

dauntless /ˈdɒntləs/ *adj* incapable of being discouraged; intrepid, fearless.—**dauntlessly** *adv*.—**dauntlessness** *n*.

dauphin /ˈdɒfɪn/ or /doːˈfæ/ *n* the title of the eldest son of the king of France, 1349–1830.

dauphine, dauphiness /ˈdoːfiˌneɪ/ *n* the wife of the dauphin.

davenport /ˈdævənˌpɔrt/ *n* a large sofa, often able to be converted into a bed; a small ornamental writing desk.

davit /ˈdævət/ or /ˈdeɪvət/ *n* a small crane with tackle for raising or lowering a lifeboat, etc over a ship's side.

Davy Jones /ˌdeɪviˈdʒoːnz/ *n* the spirit of the sea.

Davy Jones's locker *n* the seabed, the deep, *esp* as the grave of those who die at sea.

daw /dɒ/ *n* a bird of the crow family; a jackdaw.

dawdle /ˈdɒdəl/ *vi* to move slowly and waste time, to loiter.—**dawdler** *n*.

dawn /dɒn/ *vi* (*day*) to begin to grow light; to begin to appear. • *n* daybreak; a first sign.

day /deɪ/ *n* the time when the sun is above the horizon; the twenty-four hours from midnight to midnight; daylight; a particular period of success or influence; (*usu pl*) a period, an epoch.

daybook /ˈdeɪbʊk/ *n* a diary; an account book for recording the day's transactions.

daybreak /ˈdeɪbreɪk/ *n* the first appearance of daylight, dawn.

daydream /ˈdeɪdriːm/ *n* a reverie. • *vi* to have one's mind on other things; to fantasize.—**daydreamer** *n*.

daylight /ˈdeɪlaɪt/ *n* the light of the sun; dawn; publicity; a visible gap; the dawning of sudden realization or understanding.

day release *n* a system whereby workers are released for part-time education without any loss of pay.

days /deɪz/ *adv* during the day regularly.

daytime /ˈdeɪtaɪm/ *n* the time of daylight.

day-to-day /ˈdeɪtəˈdeɪ/ *adj* daily; routine.

daze /deɪz/ *vt* to stun, to bewilder. • *n* confusion, bewilderment.—**dazedly** *adv*.—**dazedness** *n*.

dazzle /ˈdæzəl/ *vt* to confuse the sight of or be partially blinded by strong light; to overwhelm with brilliance. • *n* the act of dazzling; a thing that dazzles; an overpoweringly strong light; bewilderment.—**dazzlement** *n*.—**dazzler** *n*.—**dazzlingly** *adv*.

dB, db *abbr* = decibels.

DBS *abbr* = direct broadcasting by satellite.

DC *abbr* = District of Columbia.

dc, DC *abbr* = direct current.

DD *abbr* = Doctor of Divinity.

D-day /ˈdiːdeɪ/ *n* the date (June 6, 1944) of the Allied cross-channel invasion of France during World War II; any date set aside for an important event.

DDT *abbr* = dichlorodiphenyltrichloroethane, a chemical used as an insecticide.

de *prep* from, concerning; of.

de- /dɪ/ or /diː/ *prefix* down; off; completely; un-.

de-accessioning /ˌdiːækˈseʃənɪŋ/ *n* the disposal, *usu* by selling, of an artefact or painting in a public collection.

deacon /ˈdiːkən/ *n* (*Anglican, RC churches*) an ordained member of the clergy ranking below a priest; (*Presbyterian churches*) a lay church officer who assists the minister.—**deaconship** *n*.

deaconess /ˌdiːkəˈnɛs/ or /ˈdiːkənəs/ *n* a churchwoman appointed to do work in a parish; a member of an institution or order trained to carry on systematic charitable work; in a convent, the nun who attends to the altar.

deactivate /diːˈæktɪˌveɪt/ *vt* (*bomb*) to make inactive or harmless.—**deactivation** *n*.—**deactivator** *n*.

dead /dɛd/ *adj* without life; inanimate, inert; no longer used; lacking vegetation; emotionally or spiritually insensitive; without motion; (*fire, etc*) extinguished; (*limb, etc*) numb; (*colour, sound etc*) dull; (*a ball*) out of play; complete, exact; unerring. • *adv* in a dead manner; completely; utterly. • *n* a dead person; the quietest time.—**deadness** *n*.

deadbeat /ˈdɛdbiːt/ *n* (*inf*) a lazy or socially inept person; a vagrant.

dead duck *n* (*sl*) a person or thing destined to fail.

deaden /ˈdɛdən/ *vt* to render numb or insensible; to deprive of vitality; to muffle.—**deadener** *n*.—**deadeningly** *adv*.

dead end *n* a cul-de-sac; a hopeless situation.

dead-end /ˈdɛdˌɛnd/ *adj* (*job*) holding no chance of advancement; having no hope of success in the future (*dead-end kids*).

deadening /ˈdɛdənɪŋ/ *n* material for soundproofing a room.

deadeye /ˈdɛdaɪ/ *n* an expert marksman; (*naut*) a round, laterally flattened wooden block pierced with three holes through which the lanyards are passed, used for extending the shrouds.

deadfall /ˈdɛdfɒl/ *n* a trap with a falling weight, which can kill or disable; a tangled mass of fallen trees.

deadhead /ˈdɛdhɛd/ *n* a person who has a free pass on trains or to places of amusement, etc; a transport vehicle travelling empty. • *vt* to remove dead flower heads from (a plant); to provide free admission to. • *vi* to travel or gain admission without payment; to drive an empty transport vehicle.

dead heat *n* a race in which two or more finish equal, a tie.

dead letter *n* a law or rule that is no longer enforced; a letter that cannot be delivered and is returned to the sender.

deadlight /ˈdɛdlaɪt/ *n* (*naut*) a storm shutter for a cabin window; a skylight not made to open.

deadline /ˈdɛdlaɪn/ *n* the time by which something must be done.

deadlock /ˈdɛdlɒk/ *n* (*inf*) a clash of interests making progress impossible; a standstill.—*also vt*.

deadly /ˈdɛdli/ *adj* (**deadlier, deadliest**) fatal; implacable; (*inf*) tedious. • *adv* death-like; intensely.—**deadliness** *n*.

deadly nightshade *n* a poisonous plant with purple flowers and black berries.—*also* **belladonna**.

deadpan /ˈdɛdpæn/ *adj* (*inf*) deliberately expressionless or emotionless.—*also adv*.

dead reckoning *n* the taking of a ship's position by log and compass, not astronomical observations.

dead set *adv* with determination.

dead weight *n* a very heavy load; an oppressive burden.

dead wood /ˈdɛdwʊd/ *n* (*inf*) a useless person or thing.

deaf /dɛf/ *adj* unable to hear; hearing badly; not wishing to hear.—**deafly** *adv*.—**deafness** *n*.

deafen /ˈdɛfən/ *vt* to deprive of hearing.—**deafeningly** *adv*.

deaf-mute *n* a deaf and dumb person.

deal[1] /diːl/ *vb* (**dealing, dealt**) *vt* (*a blow*) to deliver, inflict; (*cards, etc*) to distribute; (*with* **with**) to do business with; (*problem, task*) to solve. • *vi* to do business (with); to trade (in). • *n* a portion, quantity; (*inf*) a large amount; a dealing of cards; a business transaction.

deal[2] *n* fir or pinc wood.—*also adj*.

dealer /ˈdiːlər/ *n* a trader; a person who deals cards; (*sl*) a seller of illegal drugs.

dealings /ˈdiːlɪŋz/ *npl* personal or business transactions.

dealt /dɛlt/ *see* **deal**.

dean /diːn/ *n* the head of a cathedral chapter; a college fellow in charge of discipline; the head of a university or college faculty.—**deanship** *n*.

deanery /ˈdiːnəri/ *n* (*pl* **deaneries**) the office or residence of a dean.

dear /diːr/ *adj* loved, precious; charming; expensive; a form of address in letters. • *n* a person who is loved. • *adv* at a high price.—**dearness** *n*.

dearie, deary /ˈdiːri/ *n* (*pl* **dearies**) (*inf*) a darling, a dear.

dearly /ˈdiːrli/ *adv* with great affection; at a high price or rate.

dearth /dɜrθ/ *n* scarcity, lack.

death /dɛθ/ *n* the end of life, dying; the state of being dead; the destruction of something.

deathbed /ˈdɛθbɛd/ *n* the bed in which a person dies or is about to die.

deathblow /-ˌbloː/ *n* a blow causing death.

death duty *n* a tax paid on an inheritance after a death.—*also* **death tax**.

deathless /-lɪs/ *adj* immortal.—**deathlessly** *adv*.—**deathlessness** *n*.

deathly /ˈdɛθli/ *adj* like death, pale, still; deadly. • *adv* in a manner causing or tending to death; to a degree resembling death; (*inf*) extremely (*deathly quiet*).—**deathliness** *n*.

death mask *n* a plaster cast of a face taken immediately after death.

death rate *n* the yearly proportion of deaths to population.—*also* **mortality rate**.

death rattle *n* a deep gurgling noise sometimes made by a dying person.

death row *n* the section of a prison housing inmates sentenced to death.

death's head /ˈdɛθsˌhɛd/ *n* a skull or representation of a skull, emblematic of death.

death's-head moth *n* a large moth with skull-like markings.

death tax *see* **death duty**.

deathtrap *n* an unsafe place, thing or structure.

death warrant *n* official authorization for the execution of a person condemned to death; anything that guarantees the destruction of hope or expectation.

deathwatch beetle *n* a small beetle that makes a ticking sound, superstitiously supposed to forebode death.

deathwatch /'dɛθˌwɒtʃ/ *n* a vigil beside a dying person; a guard over a criminal prior to execution.

death wish *n* a *usu* unconscious wish for one's own death or that of another.

deb /dɛb/ *n* (*inf*) a debutante.

debacle /deɪ'bɒkəl/ or /-'bækəl/, /də-/ *n* a sudden disastrous break-up or collapse; a break-up of river ice.

debar /di:'bɑr/ *vt* (**debarring, debarred**) to exclude, to bar.— **debarment** *n*.

debark /di:'bɑrk/ or /dɪ-/ *vti* to land from a ship, to disembark.— **debarkation** *n*.

debase /di:'beɪs/ *vt* to lower in character or value; (*coinage*) to degrade.—**debasement** *n*.—**debaser** *n*.

debatable /dɪ'beɪtəbəl/ *adj* open to question, disputed.—**debatably** *adv*.

debate /də'beɪt/ *n* a formal argument; a discussion, *esp* in parliament. • *vt* to consider, contest. • *vi* to discuss thoroughly; to join in debate.—**debater** *n*.

debauch /də'bɔtʃ/ *vti* to corrupt, dissipate; to lead astray, to seduce.—**debaucher** *n*.

debauchee /ˌdɛbɒ'tʃi:/ or /-'ʃi:/ *n* a dissolute person, a libertine.

debauchery /də'bɒtʃəri/ *n* (*pl* **debaucheries**) depraved over-indulgence; corruption; profligacy.

debenture /də'bɛntʃər/ *n* a bond with guaranteed interest and forming a first charge on assets; a certificate acknowledging a debt; a certificate entitling a refund of customs duty.

debilitate /də'bɪlɪˌteɪt/ *vt* to weaken, to enervate.—**debilitation** *n*.—**debilitative** *adj*.

debility /də'bɪlɪti/ *n* (*pl* **debilities**) weakness, infirmity.

debit /'dɛbɪt/ *n* the entry of a sum owed, opposite to the credit; the left side of a ledger used for this. • *vt* to charge to the debit side of a ledger.

debonair, debonnaire /ˌdɛbə'nɛr/ *adj* having a carefree manner; courteous, gracious, charming.—**debonairly** *adv*.

debouch /də'bəʊtʃ/ or /-'bu:ʃ/ *vi* to march or to flow out from a narrow space to open ground.—**debouchment** *n*.

debrief /di:'bri:f/ *vt* (*diplomat, etc*) to make a report following a mission; to obtain such information.—**debriefing** *n*.

debris /'də'bri:/ or /dɛ-/ *n* (*pl* **debris**) broken and scattered remains, wreckage.

debt /dɛt/ *n* a sum owed; a state of owing; an obligation.

debtor /'dɛtər/ *n* a person, company, etc who owes money to another.

debug /di:'bʌg/ *vt* (**debugging, debugged**) (*inf*) (*room, etc*) to clear of hidden microphones; (*machine, program, plan, etc*) to locate and remove errors from; to remove insects from.

debunk /di:'bʌŋk/ *vt* (*inf*) (*claim, theory*) to expose as false.—**debunker** *n*.

debut /deɪ'bju:/ or /'deɪ-/ *n* a first appearance as a public performer or in society. • *vi* to make one's debut.

debutant /'dɛbju:ˌtɒnt/ or /'deɪ-/ *n* one making a debut, *esp* a sportsman.

debutante /'dɛbju:ˌtɒnt/ or /'deɪ-/ *n* a young woman making her first appearance in upper-class society; a young woman regarded as wealthy, aristocratic and indolent.

Dec. *abbr* = December.

decade /'dɛkeɪd/ or /dɛ'keɪd/ *n* a period of ten years; a group of ten.—**decadal** *adj*.

decadence /'dɛkədəns/, **decadency** /-si/ *n* a state of deterioration in standards, *esp* of morality.

decadent /'-dənt/ *adj* deteriorating; self-indulgent.—**decadently** *adv*.

decaffeinated /di:'kæfɪˌneɪtəd/ *adj* (*coffee, tea, carbonated drinks, etc*) with caffeine reduced or removed.

decagon /'dɛkəˌgɒn/ *n* a ten-sided plane figure.—**decagonal** *adj*.

decahedron /ˌdɛkə'hi:drən/ *n* a solid with ten faces.—**decahedral** *adj*.

decalcify /di:'kælsɪˌfaɪ/ *vt* (**decalcifying, decalcified**) to deprive (bone etc) of its lime.

decalitre, decaliter /'dɛkəˌli:tər/ *n* a unit of ten litres.

Decalogue /'dɛkəˌlɒg/ *n* the Ten Commandments.

decametre, decameter /'dɛkəˌmi:tər/ *n* a unit of ten metres.

decamp /dɪ'kæmp/ *vi* to leave suddenly or secretly.—**decampment** *n*.

decanal /'dɪkeɪnəl/ or /'dɛkə-/ *adj* of a dean or his office; of the south side of the choir of a church, etc.

decant /dɪ'kænt/ *vt* (*wine, etc*) to pour from one vessel to another, leaving sediment behind.—**decantation** *n*.

decanter /dɪ'kæntər/ *n* an ornamental bottle (*usu* glass) for holding wines, etc.

decapitate /dɪ'kæpɪˌteɪt/ *vt* to behead.—**decapitation** *n*.—**decapitator** *n*.

decapod /'dɛkəˌpɒd/ *adj* having ten feet or ten arms. • *n* a ten-footed crustacean, or ten-armed cephalopod.—**decapodal, decapodan, decapodous** *adj*.

decarbonate /di:'kɑrbəˌneɪt/ *vt* to deprive of carbon dioxide.— **decarbonation** *n*.

decarbonize /-ˌnaɪz/ *vt* take carbon or carbon deposit from.— **decarbonization** *n*.

decare /dɪ'ker/ *n* a measure of 1,000 square metres.

decasyllable /'dɛkəˌsɪləbəl/ *n* a ten-syllabled line or word.— **decasyllabic** *adj, n*.

decathlon /də'kæθlɒn/ *n* a track-and-field contest consisting of ten events.—**decathlete** *n*.

decay /dɪ'keɪ/ *vti* to rot, to decompose; to deteriorate, to wither. • *n* the act or state of decaying; a decline, collapse.

decease /dɪ'si:s/ *n* death. • *vi* to die.

deceased /dɪ'si:st/ *adj* dead. • *n* the dead person.

deceit /dɪ'si:t/ *n* the act of deceiving; cunning; treachery; fraud.

deceitful /-fʊl/ *adj* treacherous; insincere; misleading.—**deceitfully** *adv*.—**deceitfulness** *n*.

deceive /dɪ'si:v/ *vt* to cheat; to mislead; to delude; to impose upon.—**deceivable** *adj*.—**deceiver** *n*.—**deceivingly** *adv*.

decelerate /di:'sɛləˌreɪt/ *vt, vi* to reduce speed.—**deceleration** *n*.—**decelerator** *n*.

December /dɪ'sɛmbər/ *n* the twelfth and last month of the year with 31 days.

Decembrist /-brɪst/ *n* one of the conspirators who took part in the insurrection against Tsar Nicholas I of Russia, on his accession, December 1825.

decency /'di:sənsi/ *n* (*pl* **decencies**) being decent; conforming to accepted standards of proper behaviour.

decennial /dɪ'sɛnɪəl/ *adj* lasting for, or occurring, every ten years.—**decennially** *adv*.

decennium /-ɪəm/ *n* (*pl* **decenniums, decennia**) a ten-year period, a decade.

decent /'di:sənt/ *adj* respectable, proper; moderate; not obscene; (*inf*) quite good; (*inf*) kind, generous.—**decently** *adv*.

decentralize /di:'sɛntrəˌlaɪz/ *vt* (*government, organization*) to divide among local centres.—**decentralist** *adj, n*.—**decentralization** *n*.

deception /də'sɛpʃən/ or /di-/ *n* the act of deceiving or the state of being deceived; illusion; fraud.

deceptive /də'sɛptɪv/ or /di-/ *adj* apt to mislead; ambiguous; unreliable.—**deceptively** *adv*.—**deceptiveness** *n*.

deci- /'dɛsɪ/ *prefix* one tenth.

decibel /'dɛsɪbəl/, /-ˌbɛl/ *n* a unit for measuring sound level.

decide /dɪ'saɪd/ *vti* to determine, to settle; to give a judgment on; to resolve.—**decidable** *adj*.

decided /-ɪd/ *adj* unhesitating; clearly marked.

decidedly /-ɪdli/ *adv* definitely, certainly.

decider /-ər/ *n* a deciding round, a final heat.

deciduous /dɪ'sɪdʒuəs/ or /-djuəs/ *adj* (*trees, shrubs*) shedding all leaves annually, at the end of the growing season.—**deciduousness** *n*.

decilitre, deciliter /'dɛsɪˌli:tər/ *n* a unit equal to one-tenth of a litre.

decillion /dɪ'sɪljən/ *n* in UK, the tenth power of a million, a unit followed by 60 zeros; in US, the eleventh power of a thousand, a unit followed by 33 zeros.—**decillionth** *adj*.

decimal /'dɛsɪməl/ *adj* of tenths, of numbers written to the base 10. • *n* a tenth part; a decimal fraction.—**decimally** *adv*.

decimal classification *see* **Dewey Decimal System**.

decimal currency *n* currency in which units are divisible by ten.

decimal fraction *n* a fraction whose denominator is ten or a power of ten, indicated by figures after a decimal point.

decimalize /-ˌlaɪz/ *vt* to express as a decimal or to convert to a decimal system.—**decimalization** *n*.

decimal point *n* a dot written before the numerator in a decimal fraction (*eg* $0.5 = \frac{1}{2}$).

decimal system *n* a system of weights and measures in which units are related in multiples or submultiples of ten.

decimate /'dɛsɪˌmeɪt/ *vt* to kill every tenth person; to reduce by one tenth; to kill a great number.—**decimation** *n.*—**decimator** *n.*

decimetre, decimeter /'dɛsɪˌmiːtər/ *n* a measure of length, one tenth of a metre.

decipher /dɪ'saɪfər/ *vt* to decode; to make out (indistinct writing, meaning, etc).—**decipherable** *adj.*—**decipherer** *n.*—**decipherment** *n.*

decision /dɪ'sɪʒən/ *n* a settlement; a ruling; a judgment; determination, firmness; (*boxing*) a win on points.—**decisional** *adj.*

decisive /-'saɪsɪv/ *adj* determining the issue, positive; conclusive, final.—**decisively** *adv.*—**decisiveness** *n.*

deck /dɛk/ *n* the floor on a ship, aircraft, bus or bridge; a pack of playing cards; the turntable of a record-player; the playing mechanism of a tape recorder; (*sl*) the ground, the floor. • *vt* to cover; to adorn.

deck chair *n* a folding chair made of canvas suspended in a frame.

deck hand /'dɛkˌhænd/ *n* a seaman who performs manual tasks.

deckle edge *n* the ragged edge, as on handmade paper.—**deckle-edged** *adj.*

deckle /'dɛkəl/ *n* a gauge on a papermaking machine for determining the width.

declaim /dɪ'kleɪm/ *vti* to state dramatically; to recite.—**declaimer** *n.*

declamation /ˌdɛkləˈmeɪʃən/ *n* the art of declaiming according to rhetorical rules; impassioned oratory; distinct and correct enunciation of words in vocal music.

declamatory /dɪ'klæməˌtɔri/ *adj* pertaining to, or characterized by, declamation; noisy in style; appealing to the passions.—**declamatorily** *adv.*

declaration /ˌdɛkləˈreɪʃən/ *n* the act of declaring or proclaiming; that which is declared; an assertion; publication; a statement reduced to writing.

declarative /dɪ'klɛrətɪv/ *or* /dɪ-/ *adj* making a declaration.—**declaratively** *adv.*

declaratory /-əˌtɔri/ *adj* declarative; explanatory, affirmative.—**declaratorily** *adv.*

declare /dɪ'klɛr/ *vt* to affirm, to proclaim; to admit possession of (dutiable goods). • *vi* (*law*) to make a statement; (*with* **against, for**) to announce one's support.—**declarable** *n.*

déclassé /ˌdeɪˈklæseɪ/ *adj* fallen in the social scale.

declassify /diːˈklæsɪˌfaɪ/ *vt* (**declassifying, declassified**) to remove a document, etc from the list of official secrets.—**declassification** *n.*

declension /dɪ'klɛnʃən/ *n* (*gram*) variation in the form of a noun and its modifiers to show case and number; a complete set of such variations of a noun, etc.—**declensional** *adj.*

declination /ˌdɛklɪˈneɪʃən/ *n* a downward bend; (*astron*) the angular distance of a star and the celestial equator; (*compass*) the angle between true north and the magnetic north.—**declinational** *adj.*

decline /dɪ'klaɪn/ *vi* to refuse; to move down; to deteriorate, fall away; to fail; to diminish; to draw to an end; to deviate. • *vt* to reject, to refuse; (*gram*) to give the cases of a declension. • *n* a diminution; a downward slope; a gradual loss of physical and mental faculties.—**declinable** *adj.*—**decliner** *n.*

declivity /dɪ'klɪvɪti/ *n* (*pl* **declivities**) a downward slope.—**declivitous** *adj.*

decoct /dɪ'kɒkt/ *vt* to boil anything to extract its essence.

decoction /dɪ'kɒkʃən/ *n* an extract obtained by boiling or digesting in hot water; the act of decocting.

decode /diːˈkoːd/ *vt* to translate a code into plain language.

decoder /-ər/ *n* one who decodes; (*comput*) a device for converting data from one form to another, *eg* binary to decimal.

decollate /dɪ'kɒlˌeɪt/ *vt* to separate (collated papers); (*arch*) to behead.—**decollator** *n.*

decollation /ˌdiːkɒ'leɪʃən/ *n* the act of decollating; (*art*) a representation of a beheading, *esp* of St John the Baptist.

décolletage /ˌdeɪkɒl'tɒʒ/ *n* a low-cut dress or neckline.

décolleté /deɪ'kɒlteɪ/ *adj* having a low neckline.

decolonize /diːˈkɒləˌnaɪz/ *vt* to allow a colony to become independent.

decolour, decolorize /diːˈkʌləˌraɪz/ *vt* to remove colour from, to bleach.—**decoloration** *n.*—**decolorization** *n.*

decompose /ˌdiːkəm'poːz/ *vti* to separate or break up into constituent parts, *esp* as part of a chemical process; to resolve into its elements. • *vi* to decay.—**decomposable** *adj.*—**decomposition** *n.*

decompress /ˌdiːkəm'prɛs/ *vt* to decrease the pressure on, *esp* gradually; to return (a diver, etc) to a condition of normal atmospheric pressure.—**decompression** *n.*—**decompressive** *adj.*—**decompressor** *n.*

decompression sickness *n* a condition affecting divers, astronauts, etc, resulting from too rapid a return from high pressure to atmosphere and characterized by cramps and paralysis.

decongestant /ˌdiːkən'dʒɛstənt/ *n* a medical preparation that relieves congestion, *eg* catarrh.

deconsecrate /diːˈkɒnsɪˌkreɪt/ *vt* to transfer (a church) from ecclesiastical use.—**deconsecration** *n.*

decontaminate /-'tæməˌneɪt/ *vt* to free from (radioactive, etc) contamination.—**decontamination** *n.*—**decontaminator** *n.*

decontrol /ˌdiːkən'troːl/ *vt* (**decontrolling, decontrolled**) to release from control, *esp* government control.

décor, decor /'deɪkɔr/ *or* /də'kɔr/ *n* general decorative effect, *eg* of a room; scenery and stage design.

decorate /'dɛkəˌreɪt/ *vt* to ornament; to paint or wallpaper; to honour with a badge or medal.

decoration /ˌdɛkə'reɪʃən/ *n* decorating; an ornament; a badge or an honour.

decorative /'dɛkrətɪv/ *adj* ornamental, pretty to look at.—**decoratively** *adv.*—**decorativeness** *n.*

decorator /'dɛkəˌreɪtər/ *n* a person who decorates, *esp* houses.

decorous /'dɛkərəs/ *adj* proper, decent; showing propriety and dignity.—**decorously** *adv.*—**decorousness** *n.*

decorticate /diːˈkɔrtɪˌkeɪt/ *vt* to remove the bark, rind, or husk from; to remove the cortex of an organ by surgery. • *vi* to peel or come off, as bark, skin.—**decortication** *n.*—**decorticator** *n.*

decorum /dɪ'kɔrəm/ *n* what is correct in outward appearance, propriety of conduct, decency.

decoy /'diːkɔɪ/ *vt* to lure into a trap. • *n* anything intended to lure into a snare.—**decoyer** *n.*

decrease /'diːˌkriːs/ *n*, /dɪ'kriːs/ *vti* to make or become less. • *n* a decreasing; the amount of diminution.—**decreasingly** *adv.*

decree /dɪ'kriː/ *n* an order, edict or law; a judicial decision. • *vt* (**decreeing, decreed**) to decide by sentence in law; to appoint.—**decreeable** *adj.*—**decreer** *n.*

decrement /'dɛkrɪmənt/ *n* a decrease; the amount of this; (*math*) a negative increment of a variable.—**decremental** *adj.*

decrepit /dɪ'krɛpɪt/ *adj* worn out by the infirmities of old age; in the last stage of decay.—**decrepitly** *adv.*

decrepitate /dɪ'krɛpɪˌteɪt/ *vti* to heat (a salt, mineral) until it crackles; to crackle under extreme heat.—**decrepitation** *n.*

decrepitude /-ˌtjuːd/ *or* /ˌtjuːd/ *n* the state or condition of being decrepit; feebleness and decay, *esp* that due to old age.

decrescendo /ˌdiːkre'ʃɛndoː/ *or* /ˌdeɪkrɪ-/ *n* (*pl* **decrescendos**) (*mus*) a sign (>) that the volume of sound is to be gradually reduced; a gradual decrease in force of tone or a passage where this occurs. • *adj* gradually diminishing in loudness.—*also* **diminuendo.**

decrescent /dɪ'krɛsənt/ *adj* growing less; (*moon*) waning.—**decrescence** *n.*

decretal /dɪ'kriːtəl/ *n* (*RC Church*) a papal decree; a book of edicts. • *adj* of a decree or decretal.

decry /dɪ'kraɪ/ *vt* (**decrying, decried**) to disparage, to censure as worthless.—**decrial** *n.*—**decrier** *n.*

dectet /dɛk'tɛt/ *n* a group of eight musicians or voices.

decumbent /dɪ'kʌmbənt/ *adj* lying down, prostrate, reclining; (*bot*) resting on the ground, trailing.—**decumbence, decumbency** *n.*

decuple /'dɛkjuˌpəl/ *adj* tenfold. • *n* a number repeated ten times. • *vt* to increase tenfold.

decurion /dɪ'kjuːriən/ *n* a Roman officer commanding ten men.

decurrent /dɪ'kʌrənt/ *adj* (*plant*) running or extending downward.

decussate /dɪ'kʌsɪt/ *adj*, /dɪ'kʌseɪt/ *vti* to intersect in the form of an X. • *adj* X-shaped; (*leaves*) in pairs, at right angles to those above and below.—**decussation** *n.*

dedicate /'dɛdɪˌkeɪt/ *vt* to consecrate (to some sacred purpose); to devote wholly or chiefly; to inscribe (to someone).—**dedicatee** *n.*—**dedicator** *n.*—**dedicatory, dedicative** *adj.*

dedicated /'dɛdɪˌkeɪtəd/ *adj* devoted to a particular cause, profession, etc; single-minded; assigned to a particular function.

dedication /ˌdɛdɪ'keɪʃən/ *n* the act of dedicating; a dedicatory inscription in a book, etc; devotion to a cause, ideal, etc.

deduce /dɪ'duːs/ or /-'djuːs/ *vt* to derive (knowledge, a conclusion) from reasoning; infer.—**deducible** *adj*.

deduct /dɪ'dʌkt/ *vt* to take (from); to subtract.

deductible /-ɪbəl/ *adj* capable of being deducted; allowable as a deduction against income tax.—**deductibility** *n*.

deduction /dɪ'dʌkʃən/ *n* deducting; the amount deducted; deducing; a conclusion that something is true because it necessarily follows from a set of general premises known to be valid.—**deductive** *adj*.—**deductively** *adv*.

deed /diːd/ *n* an act; an exploit; a legal document recording a transaction.

deem /diːm/ *vti* to judge; to think, to believe.

deep /diːp/ *adj* extending or placed far down or far from the outside; fully involved; engrossed; profound, intense; heartfelt; penetrating; difficult to understand; secret; cunning; sunk low; low in pitch; (*colour*) of high saturation and low brilliance. • *adv* in a deep manner; far in, into. • *n* that which is deep; the sea.—**deeply** *adv*.—**deepness** *n*.

deepen /'diːpən/ *vt* to make deeper in any sense; to increase. • *vi* to become deeper.—**deepener** *n*.

deepfreeze /'diːpˌfriːz/ *n* a refrigerator in which food is frozen and stored.

deep-freeze *vt* (**deep-freezing, deep-froze** or **deep-freezed,** *pp* **deep-frozen, deep-freezed**) to freeze (food) so that it keeps for a long period of time; to store in a freezer. • *n* a freezer.

deep-fry *vt* (**deep-frying, deep-fried**) to fry food in deep fat in order to cook or brown it without turning.—**deep-fryer** *n*.

deep-laid *adj* (*plans, etc*) secret and elaborate.

deep-rooted *adj* (*feelings, opinions, etc*) firmly established; ingrained; deep-seated.

deep-seated *adj* having its seat far beneath the surface; deep-rooted.

Deep South *n* the southeastern states of the USA.

deep space *n* the region of outer space beyond our solar system.

deer /diːr/ *n* (*pl* **deer, deers**) a four-footed animal with antlers, *esp* on the males, including stag, reindeer, etc.

deerhound /'diːrˌhaʊnd/ *n* a large rough-haired greyhound.—*also* **Scottish deerhound**.

deerstalker /-ˌstɔːkər/ *n* a person who hunts deer; a soft hat peaked at the front and back.

de-escalate /diː'ɛskəˌleɪt/ *vti* to reduce the intensity of.—**de-escalation** *n*.

deface /dɪ'feɪs/ *vt* to disfigure; to obliterate.—**defaceable** *adj*.—**defacement** *n*.—**defacer** *n*.

de facto /diː'fæktɔː/ or /deɪ-/ *adv* in fact; in reality.—*also adj*.

defalcate /diː'fælkeɪt/ or /-'fɔl-/, /dɪ-/ *vi* to embezzle money held in trust.—**defalcation** *n*.—**defalcator** *n*.

defamation /ˌdɛfə'meɪʃən/ or /diːf-/ *n* the act of injuring someone's good name or reputation without justification, either orally or in writing; the condition of being defamed.

defamatory /dɪ'fæmətɔri/ *adj* containing that which is injurious to the character or reputation of someone.—**defamatorily** *adv*.

defame /dɪ'feɪm/ *vt* to destroy the good reputation of; to speak evil of.—**defamer** *n*.

default /dɪ'fɔlt/ or /dɪ'-/ *n* neglect to do what duty or law requires; failure to fulfil a financial obligation; (*comput*) a basic setting or instruction to which a program reverts. • *vi* to fail in one's duty (as honouring a financial obligation, appearing in court).

defaulter /-ər/ *n* one who defaults; one who fails to appear in court when required, or to make a proper account of money or property entrusted to his charge; on the Stock Exchange, one who fails to meet his engagements.

defeasance /dɪ'fiːzəns/ *n* (*law*) annulment; a condition annexed to a deed, which being performed renders the deed void.

defeasible /dɪ'fiːzɪbəl/ *adj* able to be annulled.—**defeasibility** *n*.

defeat /dɪ'fiːt/ or /diː-/ *vt* to frustrate; to win a victory over; to baffle. • *n* a frustration of plans; overthrow, as of an army in battle; loss of a game, race, etc.—**defeater** *n*.

defeatism /-ɪzəm/ *n* disposition to accept defeat.—**defeatist** *n, adj*.

defecate /'dɛfəˌkeɪt/ *vi* to empty the bowels. • *vt* (*chem*) to free from impurities, to refine.—**defecation** *n*.—**defecator** *n*.

defect /dɪ'fɛkt/ *vi,* /'diːfɛkt/ *n* a deficiency; a blemish, fault. • *vi* to desert one's country or a cause, transferring one's allegiance (to another).—**defector** *n*.

defection /də'fɛkʃən/ *n* desertion of duty or allegiance.

defective /-tɪv/ *adj* having a defect; faulty; incomplete. • *n* a person defective in physical or mental powers.—**defectively** *adv*.—**defectiveness** *n*.

defence, defense /də'fɛns/ *n* resistance or protection against attack; a means of resisting an attack; protection; vindication; (*law*) a defendant's plea; the defending party in legal proceedings; (*sport*) defending (the goal, etc) against the attacks of the opposing side; the defending players in a team.—**defenceless, defenseless** *adj*.—**defencelessness, defenselessness** *n*.

defend /də'fɛnd/ or /dɪ-/ *vt* to guard or protect; to maintain against attack; (*law*) to resist, as a claim; to contest (a suit).—**defendable** *adj*.—**defender** *n*.

defendant /də'fɛndənt/ or /dɪ-/ *n* a person accused or sued in a lawsuit.

defensible /də'fɛnsɪbəl/ or /dɪ-/ *adj* able to be defended or justified.—**defensibly** *adv*.—**defensibility** *n*.

defensive /də'fɛnsɪv/ or /dɪ-/ *adj* serving to defend; in a state or posture of defence.—**defensively** *adv*.—**defensiveness** *n*.

defer[1] /də'fər/ *vt* (**deferring, deferred**) to put off to another time; to delay.—**deferrable, deferable** *adj*.—**deferrer** *n*.

defer[2] *vi* (**deferring, deferred**) to yield to another person's wishes, judgment or authority.

deference /'dɛfərəns/ *n* a deferring or yielding in judgment or opinion; polite respect.

deferent /'dɛfərənt/ *adj* deferential (*anat*) conveying (a fluid, etc) away.

deferential /ˌdɛfə'rɛnʃəl/ *adj* expressing deference or respect.—**deferentially** *adv*.

deferment /diː'fɜrmənt/ or /dɪ-/ *n* a delay; postponement.

deferral /də'fərəl/ *n* a deferment.

deferred /diː'fɜrd/ or /dɪ-/ *adj* postponed; (*stock, shares*) having its dividend payable after other shares.

defiance /də'faɪəns/ *n* the act of defying; wilful disobedience; a challenge.

defiant /-ənt/ *adj* characterized by defiance; challenging.—**defiantly** *adv*.

deficiency /də'fɪʃənsi/ or /dɪ-/ *n* (*pl* **deficiencies**) being deficient; lack, shortage; deficit.

deficient /də'fɪʃənt/ or /dɪ-/ *adj* insufficient, lacking.—**deficiently** *adv*.

deficit /'dɛfɪsɪt/ *n* the amount by which an amount falls short of what is required; excess of expenditure over income, or liabilities over assets.

defilade /ˌdɛfɪ'leɪd/ *vt* to raise (a rampart) to protect defensive lines from guns placed in a high position. • *n* protection provided in this way.

defile[1] /də'faɪl/ or /diː-/ *vt* to pollute or corrupt.—**defilement** *n*.—**defiler** *n*.

defile[2] *n* a long, narrow pass or way, through which troops can pass only in single file. • *vt* to march in single file.

define /də'faɪn/ *vt* to fix the bounds or limits of; to mark the limits or outline of clearly; to describe accurately; to fix the meaning of.—**definable** *adj*.—**definer** *n*.

definite /'dɛfɪnɪt/ *adj* defined; having distinct limits; fixed; exact; clear.—**definiteness** *n*.

definitely /-li/ *adv* certainly; distinctly. • *interj* used to agree emphatically.

definition /ˌdɛfɪ'nɪʃən/ *n* a description of a thing by its properties; an explanation of the exact meaning of a word, term, or phrase; sharpness of outline.—**definitional** *adj*.

definitive /-ɪv/ *adj* defining or limiting; decisive, final.—**definitively** *adv*.—**definitiveness** *n*.

definitude /dɪ'fɪnəˌtud/ or /-ˌtjuːd/ *n* the quality of being definite; definiteness, precision.

deflagrate /'dɛfləˌgreɪt/ or /'diː-/ *vt* to set fire to. • *vi* to cause to burn with sudden and sparkling combustion.—**deflagration** *n*.

deflate /də'fleɪt/ or /diː-/ *vt* to release gas or air from; to reduce in size or importance; to reduce the money supply, restrict credit, etc to reduce inflation in the economy.—**deflator** *n*.

deflation /də'fleɪʃən/ or /diː-/ *n* deflating; a reduction in the supply of money, causing a fall in prices.—**deflationary** *adj*.—**deflationist** *adj, n*.

deflect /dəˈflɛkt/ or /di-/ *vti* to turn or cause to turn aside from a line or proper course.—**deflective** *adj*.—**deflector** *n*.

deflection /dɪˈflɛkʃən/ or /di-/ *n* the action of deflecting or the state of being deflected from a straight line or regular path; deviation; the turning of a magnetic needle away from its zero; the amount of this.

defloration /ˌdiːflɔrˈeɪʃən/ *n* a deflowering.

deflower /diːˈflaʊr/ *vt* to deprive of virginity; to corrupt the beauty, innocence of.—**deflowerer** *n*.

defoliant /diːˈfoːliənt/ *n* a chemical that kills foliage.

defoliate /-ˌeɪt/ *vt* to strip (a plant or tree) of its leaves.—**defoliation** *n*.—**defoliator** *n*.

deforce /diːˈfɔrs/ *vt* (*law*) to keep (property) out of the legal owner's possession by force; (*Scots law*) to resist (an officer of law in execution of his duty).—**deforcement** *n*.

deforest /diːˈfɔrəst/ or /-fɒrəst/ *vt* to clear of trees.—**deforestation** *n*.—**deforester** *n*.

deform /dəˈfɔrm/ or /di-/ *vt* to spoil the natural form of; to put out of shape.—**deformer** *n*.

deformation /ˌdɛfɔrˈmeɪʃən/ or /ˌdi-/ *n* the act of deforming; a change for the worse; a perverted form of word.

deformed /dəˈfɔrmd/ or /di-/ *adj* misshapen; warped.

deformity /dɪˈfɔrmɪti/ *n* (*pl* **deformities**) the condition of being deformed; a deformed part of the body; a defect.

defraud /dɪˈfrɒd/ *vt* to remove (money, rights, etc) from a person by cheating or deceiving.—**defraudation** *n*.—**defrauder** *n*.

defray /dɪˈfreɪ/ *vt* to provide money (to pay expenses, etc).—**defrayable** *adj*.—**defrayal** *n*.—**defrayer** *n*.

defrock /diːˈfrɒk/ *vt* to expel from the priesthood, to unfrock.

defrost /diːˈfrɒst/ *vt* to unfreeze; to free from frost or ice. • *vi* to become unfrozen.

deft /dɛft/ *adj* skilful, adept; nimble.—**deftly** *adv*.—**deftness** *n*.

defunct /dɪˈfʌŋkt/ *adj* no longer being in existence or function or in use.—**defunctive** *adj*.

defuse /diːˈfjuːz/ *vt* to disarm an explosive (bomb or mine) by removing its fuse; to decrease tension in a (crisis) situation.

defy /dɪˈfaɪ/ *vt* (**defying, defied**) to resist openly and without fear; to challenge (a person) to attempt something considered dangerous or impossible; to resist attempts at; to elude.—**defier** *n*.

dégagé /deɪˈgæʒeɪ/ *adj* unconstrained, at ease.

degauss /diːˈgaʊs/ *vt* to neutralize or remove a magnetic field.—**degausser** *n*.

degeneracy /dɪˈdʒɛnərəsiː/ *n* (*pl* **degeneracies**) the condition or quality of being degenerate; an instance of degeneracy; something that is degenerate.

degenerate /-eɪt/ *vi*, /dɪˈdʒɛnərət/ *adj* having declined in physical or moral qualities; sexually deviant. • *vi* to become or grow worse. • *n* a degenerate person.—**degenerately** *adv*.

degeneration /dɪˌdʒɛnəˈreɪʃən/ *n* the act, state, or process of growing worse; degeneracy; decline; the morbid impairment of any structural tissue or organ.

degenerative /-tɪv/ *adj* of the nature of, or tending to, degenerate.—**degeneratively** *adv*.

deglutinate /diːˈgluːtnˌeɪt/ *vt* to extract gluten from; to unglue.—**deglutination** *n*.

deglutition /diːˌgluːˈtɪʃən/ *n* the power to swallow, a swallowing.

degradable /diːˈgreɪdəbəl/ or /dɪ-/ *adj* capable of being broken down by biological or chemical action.

degradation /ˌdɛgrəˈdeɪʃən/ *n* a degrading or being degraded in quality, rank or status; a degraded state; (*geol*) a lowering of land by erosion; (*RC Church*) the unfrocking of a priest.

degrade /dɪˈgreɪd/ *vt* to reduce in rank or status; to disgrace; to decompose; to be lowered by erosion.—**degrader** *n*.

degrading /-ɪŋ/ *adj* humiliating; (*geol*) eroding.—**degradingly** *adv*.

degree /dəˈgriː/ *n* a step in an ascending or descending series; a stage in intensity; the relative quantity in intensity; a unit of measurement in a scale; an academic title awarded as of right or as an honour.

degression /dɪˈgrɛʃən/ *n* a going down; a decrease, *esp* in taxation rate.—**degressive** *adj*.

dehisce /diːˈhɪs/ *vi* (*fruits, seed pods, etc*) to burst open.

dehiscent /-ənt/ *adj* (*fruits*) opening to release seeds.—**dehiscence** *n*.

dehorn /diːˈhɔrn/ *vt* to cut back, or deprive of, horns.—**dehorner** *n*.

dehumanize /diːˈhjuːməˌnaɪz/ *vt* to remove human qualities from; to deprive of personality or emotion, to render mechanical.—**dehumanization** *n*.

dehydrate /diːˈhaɪˌdreɪt/ *vt* to remove water from. • *vi* to lose water, *esp* from the bodily tissues.—**dehydration** *n*.—**dehydrator** *n*.

dehypnotize /diːˈhɪpnəˌtaɪz/ *vt* to rouse from a hypnotic state.

de-ice /diːˈaɪs/ *vt* to prevent the formation of or to remove ice from a surface.—**de-icer** *n*.

deicide /ˈdiːəˌsaɪd/ *n* the killing of a god; the killer of a god.—**deicidal** *adj*.

deictic /ˈdaɪktɪk/ *adj* (*gram*) demonstrative; (*logic*) proving directly.—**deictically** *adv*.

deific /diˈɪfɪk/ *adj* making, or tending to make, divine.

deify /ˈdiːəˌfaɪ/ *vt* (**deifying, deified**) to make into a god; to worship as a god, glorify.—**deification** *n*.—**deifier** *n*.

deign /deɪn/ *vi* to condescend; to think it worthy to do (something).

deil /diːl/ *n* (*Scot*) the devil.

deism /ˈdiːˌɪzəm/ *n* belief in the existence of God, but not religious revelation.—**deist** *n*.—**deistic, deistical** *adj*.

deity /ˈdiːɪti/ or /ˈdeɪɪ-/ *n* (*pl* **deities**) a god or goddess; the rank or essence of a god; (*with cap and* **the**) God.

déjà vu /ˌdeɪʒəˈvuː/ or /-ʒɒ-/ *n* the illusion that you have already experienced the present situation.

deject /dəˈdʒɛkt/ *vt* to have a depressing effect on.

dejecta /diˈjɛktə/ *npl* excrement, droppings.

dejected /diˈjɛktɪd/ or /dɪ-/ *adj* morose, depressed.—**dejectedly** *adv*.—**dejectedness** *n*.

dejection /dəˈdʒɛkʃən/ *n* depression; lowness of spirits.

de jure /dɪˈdʒuri/ or /deɪˈjureɪ/ *adv* according to the law, by right.

delaine /dəˈkleɪn/ *n* a light fabric of wool and cotton.

delate /dəˈleɪt/ *vt* (*formerly*) to inform against (a person); to report (an offence).—**delation** *n*.—**delator** *n*.

delay /dəˈleɪ/ *vt* to postpone; to detain, obstruct. • *vi* to linger. • *n* a delaying or being delayed; the time period during which something is delayed.—**delayer** *n*.

dele /ˈdiːli/ *vt* (**deleing, deled**) (*print*) to take out a letter, etc, in proofreading. • *n* a mark that a letter, etc, is to be deleted.

delectable /dəˈlɛktəbəl/ *adj* delightful, delicious.—**delectability** *n*.—**delectably** *adv*.

delectation /ˌdiːlɛkˈteɪʃən/ *n* delight, enjoyment.

delegate /ˈdɛləgeɪt/ *vt* to appoint as a representative; to give powers or responsibilities to (an agent or assembly). • *n* a deputy or an elected representative.—**delegable** *adj*.

delegation /ˌdɛləˈgeɪʃən/ *n* the act of delegating; a group of people empowered to represent others.

delete /dəˈliːt/ *vt* to strike out (something written or printed); to erase.

deleterious /ˌdɛləˈtiːriəs/ *adj* harmful or destructive.

deletion /dəˈliːʃən/ *n* the act of deleting; a word, passage, etc, deleted from a text; the absence of a normal part of a chromosome.

delft, delftware /ˈdɛlftwɛr/ *n* a type of blue-glazed earthenware, originally from Delft in Holland.

deli /ˈdɛli/ *n* (*pl* **delis**) (*inf*) a delicatessen.

deliberate /dəˈlɪbərət/ *vt* to consider carefully. • *vi* to discuss or debate thoroughly; to consider. • *adj* well thought out; intentional; cautious.—**deliberately** *adv*.—**deliberateness** *n*.—**deliberator** *n*.

deliberation /ˌdəlɪbəˈreɪʃən/ *n* careful consideration; thorough discussion; caution.

deliberative /dəˈlɪbəˌrətɪv/ *adj* of or appointed for deliberation; as a result of deliberation.—**deliberatively** *adv*.

delicacy /ˈdɛləkəsi/ *n* (*pl* **delicacies**) delicateness; sensibility; a luxurious food.

delicate /ˈdɛləkət/ *adj* fine in texture; fragile, not robust; requiring tactful handling; of exquisite workmanship; requiring skill in techniques.—**delicately** *adv*.—**delicateness** *n*.

delicatessen /ˌdɛləkəˈtɛsən/ *n* a store selling prepared foods, *esp* imported delicacies.

delicious /dəˈlɪʃəs/ *adj* having a pleasurable effect on the senses, *esp* taste; delightful.—**deliciously** *adv*.—**deliciousness** *n*.

delict /dəˈlɪkt/ or /ˈdi-/ *n* a legal offence.

delight /dəˈlaɪt/ *vt* to please greatly. • *vi* to have or take great pleasure (in). • *n* great pleasure; something that causes this.—**delighter** *n*.

delighted /-ɪd/ *adj* very pleased; filled with delight.—**delight-edly** *adv*.—**delightedness** *n*.

delightful /-fʊl/ *adj* giving great pleasure.—**delightfully** *adv*.—**delightfulness** *n*.

delimit /diːˈlɪmɪt/ **delimitate** *vt* to fix or mark the boundaries of.—**delimitation** *n*.—**delimitative** *adj*.

delineate /dəˈlɪnɪˌeɪt/ *vt* to describe in great detail; to represent by drawing.—**delineation** *n*.—**delineative** *adj*.

delineator /-ər/ *n* one who delineates; an adjustable tailor's pattern.

delinquency /dəˈlɪŋkwənsi/ *n* (*pl* **delinquencies**) neglect of or failure in duty; a misdeed; a fault; antisocial or illegal behaviour, *esp* by young people.—*also* **juvenile delinquency**.

delinquent /-kwənt/ *adj* negligent; guilty of an offence. • *n* a person guilty of a misdeed, *esp* a young person who breaks the law.

deliquesce /ˌdɛləˈkwɛs/ *vi* to melt and become liquid by absorbing moisture from the atmosphere.—**deliquescence** *n*.—**deliquescent** *adj*.

delirious /dəˈlɪːrɪəs/ *adj* mentally confused, light-headed; wildly excited.—**deliriously** *adv*.—**deliriousness** *n*.

delirium /dəˈlɪːrɪəm/ *n* (*pl* **deliriums, deliria**) a state of mental disorder, *esp* caused by a feverish illness; wild enthusiasm.

delirium tremens /ˈtrɛmɛnz/ *n* a disorder of the brain, causing delusions and violent trembling, as the result of excessive drinking.

deliver /dəˈlɪvər/ *vt* (*goods, letters, etc*) to transport to a destination; to distribute regularly; to liberate, to rescue; to give birth; to assist at a birth; (*blow*) to launch; (*baseball*) to pitch; (*speech*) to utter.—**deliverable** *adj*.—**deliverer** *n*.

deliverance /dəˈlɪvərəns/ *n* the act of rescuing or liberating.

delivery /dəˈlɪvəri/ *n* (*pl* **deliveries**) the act of delivering; anything delivered or communicated; the manner of delivering (a speech, etc); the manner of bowling in cricket, etc; the act of giving birth.

dell /dɛl/ *n* a small hollow, *usu* with trees.

delocalize /diːˈloːkəˌlaɪz/ *vt* to deprive of local character; to remove from a locality.—**delocalization** *n*.

delouse /diːˈlaʊs/ *vt* to rid the lice from.

Delphic /ˈdɛlfɪk/, **Delphian** /-fɪən/ *adj* relating to the ancient Greek city or its famous oracle which imparted enigmatic prophecies; obscure or ambiguous in meaning.

delphinium /dɛlˈfɪnɪəm/ *n* a garden plant with spikes of, *usu* blue, flowers.

delta /ˈdɛltə/ *n* the fourth letter of the Greek alphabet; an alluvial deposit at the mouth of a river.—**deltaic** *adj*.

delta wing *n* a triangular-shaped aircraft wing.

deltoid /ˈdɛltɔɪd/ *adj* of the shape of the letter delta; triangular. • *n* (*anat*) a muscle that lifts the upper arm.

delude /dəˈluːd/ *vt* to mislead, to deceive.—**deluder** *n*.

deluge /ˈdɛljuːʒ/ or /-juːdʒ/ *n* a flood; anything happening in a heavy rush. • *vt* to inundate.

delusion /dəˈluːʒən/ *n* a false belief; a persistent false belief that is a symptom of mental illness.—**delusional** *adj*.

delusive /dəˈluːsɪv/ *adj* deluding or tending to delude; deceptive; false.—**delusively** *adv*.

delusory /dəˈluːsəri/ *adj* delusive.

deluxe /dəˈlɛks/ *adj* luxurious, of superior quality.

delve /dɛlv/ *vti* to search deeply; to dig.—**delver** *n*.

demagnetize /diːˈmægnəˌtaɪz/ *vt* to remove the magnetic properties of.—**demagnetization** *n*.—**demagnetizer** *n*.

demagogic /ˌdɛməˈɡɒdʒɪk/, /-ˈɡɒɡɪk/, /-ˈɡoʊdʒɪk/, **demagogical** *adj* of, pertaining to, or characteristic of a demagogue.—**demagogically** *adv*.

demagogue, demagog /ˈdɛməˌɡɒɡ/ *n* a political orator who derives power from appealing to popular prejudices.

demagoguery /-ˈɡɒɡəri/ *n* demagogy; the rhetoric of a demagogue.

demagogy /-ˈɡɒdʒi/ or /-ˈɡɒɡi/ *n* the principles or practice of a demagogue; rule by a demagogue.

demand /dəˈmænd/ *vt* to ask for in an authoritative manner. • *n* a request or claim made with authority for what is due; an urgent claim; desire for goods and services shown by consumers.—**demandable** *adj*.—**demander** *n*.

demandant /-dənt/ *n* a plaintiff.

demanding /-ɪŋ/ *adj* constantly making demands; requiring great skill, concentration or effort.—**demandingly** *adv*.

demantoid /dɪˈmæntɔɪd/ *n* an emerald green garnet used as a gem.

demarcate /ˈdiːmɑrˌkeɪt/ *vt* to delimit; to define or mark the bounds of.—**demarcator** *n*.

demarcation, demarkation /ˌdiːmɑrˈkeɪʃən/ *n* the act of marking off a boundary or setting a limit to; a limit; the strict separation of the type of work done by members of different trade unions.

démarche /deɪˈmɑrʃ/ *n* a diplomatic announcement of policy or plan.

demark /diːˈmɑrk/ *vt* to demarcate.

dematerialize /ˌdiːməˈtɪːrɪəˌlaɪz/ *vti* to deprive of or give up material form.—**dematerialization** *n*.

deme /diːm/ *n* a territorial subdivision or township of ancient Greece; (*biol*) a group within a species with similar cell structure, etc.

demean /dəˈmiːn/ *vt* to lower in dignity.—**demeaning** *adj*.

demeanour, demeanor /dəˈmiːnər/ *n* behaviour; bearing.

dement /dəˈmɛnt/ *vt* to make insane, to drive mad.

demented /-əd/ *adj* crazy, insane.—**dementedly** *adv*.

dementia /dɪˈmɛnʃə/ or /-ʃɪə/ *n* the failure or loss of mental powers.

demerge /diːˈmɜrdʒ/ *vt* to separate a previously merged business corporation into several companies.—**demerger** *n*.

demerit /diːˈmɛrɪt/ *n* a fault, a defect; a mark recording poor work by a student, etc.

demersal /dəˈmɜrsəl/ *adj* (*zool*) found in deep water or on the sea bottom.

demesne /dəˈmiːn/ or /-ˈmeɪn/ *n* (*law*) one's own land; (*hist*) a landed estate attached to a manor; a domain.

demi- /ˈdɛmi/ *prefix* half.

demigod /ˈdɛmiˌɡɒd/ *n* a being that is part mortal part god; a god-like individual.—**demigoddess** *nf*.

demijohn /-ˌdʒɒn/ *n* a large bottle, often in a wicker case.

demilitarize /diːˈmɪlətəˌraɪz/ *vt* to remove armed forces, weapons systems, etc from.—**demilitarization** *n*.

demimondaine /ˈdɛmimɒnˌdeɪn/ or /-mɔ̃ˌdeɪn/ *n* a member of the demimonde, a courtesan.

demimonde /ˈdɛmiˌmɒnd/ or /-ˈmɔ̃d/ *n* a class of women not recognized by society, *esp* in 19th-century France, because of promiscuity; any socially disreputable group.

demise /dəˈmaɪz/ *n* (*formal*) death; termination, end. • *vt* to give or grant by will. • *vi* to pass by bequest or inheritance.—**demisable** *adj*.

demisemiquaver /ˌdɛmiˈsɛmiˌkweɪvər/ *n* (*mus*) a note with a time value of half a semiquaver.—*also* **thirty-second note**.

demitasse /ˈdɛmiˌtæs/ *n* a small cup (of black coffee).

demiurge /ˈdɛmiˌɜrdʒ/ *n* in Platonic philosophy, the creator of the world; in Gnostic philosophy, an agent of the Supreme Being in the creation of man and the material universe; in ancient Greece, the chief magistrate of some states.—**demiurgic** *adj*.

demo /ˈdɛmoː/ *n* (*pl* **demos**) (*inf*) a demonstration.

demob /diːˈmɒb/ *vt* (**demobbing, demobbed**) (*inf*) to demobilize. • *n* (*inf*) demobilization.

demobilize /diːˈmoːbəˌlaɪz/ *vt* to discharge from the armed forces.—**demobilization** *n*.

democracy /dəˈmɒkrəsi/ *n* (*pl* **democracies**) a form of government by the people through elected representatives; a country governed by its people; political, social or legal equality.

democrat /ˈdɛməˌkræt/ *n* a person who believes in or promotes democracy; (*with cap*) a member of the Democratic Party in the US.

democratic /ˌdɛməˈkrætɪk/ *adj* of, relating to, or supporting the principles of democracy; favouring or upholding equal rights; (*with cap*) of or pertaining to the Democratic Party in the US.—**democratically** *adv*.

democratize /dəˈmɒkrəˌtaɪz/ *vt* to make democratic. • *vi* to become democratic.—**democratization** *n*.

démodé /deɪmoːˈdeɪ/ *adj* out of fashion.

demodulate /diːˈmɒdjʊˌleɪt/ *vt* to extract a modulating (radio, video, etc) wave or signal from a modulated carrier wave.—**demodulator** *n*.—**demodulation** *n*.

demography /dəˈmɒɡrəfi/ *n* the study of population statistics concerning birth, marriage, death and disease.—**demographer, demographist** *n*.—**demographic** *adj*.—**demographically** *adv*.

demoiselle /ˌdɛmwæˈzɛl/ *n* a damsel; a small crane of North Africa, southeast Europe and central Asia.

demolish /dəˈmɒlɪʃ/ *vt* (*a building*) to pull down or knock down; (*an argument*) to defeat; (*inf*) to eat up.—**demolisher** *n*.—**demolishment** *n*.

demolition /ˌdɛməˈlɪʃən/ *n* a demolishing or being demolished, *esp* by explosives.—**demolitionist** *adj, n*.

demon /'di:mən/ *n* an evil spirit; a cruel person; someone who is very skilled, energetic, hard-working, etc.—**demonic** *adj.*—**demonically** *adv.*

demonetize /di:'mɒnɪˌtaɪz/ *vt* to withdraw (coin) from circulation; to abandon (gold etc) as a currency.—**demonetization** *n.*

demoniac, demoniacal /də'mo:niˌæk/ or /'di:məˌnaɪæk/ *adj* of or like a demon; possessed by evil; frenzied, energetic. • *n* a person possessed by a demon.—**demoniacally** *adv.*

demonism /'di:məˌnɪzəm/ *n* belief in demons; the nature of a demon.—**demonist** *n.*

demonize /-aɪz/ *vt* to make into or represent as a demon.

demonolater /-ələtər/ *n* a demon worshipper.—**demonolatry** *n.*

demonology /-'nɒlədʒi/ *n* the study of demons and superstitions about them.—**demonologist** *n.*

demonstrable /də'mɒnstrəbəl/ *adj* able to be demonstrated or proved.—**demonstrability** *n.*—**demonstrably** *adv.*

demonstrate /'demənˌstreɪt/ *vt* to indicate or represent clearly; to provide certain evidence of, prove; to show how something (a machine, etc) works. • *vi* to show one's support for a cause, etc by public parades and protests; to act as a demonstrator of machinery, etc.—**demonstrational** *adj.*

demonstration /ˌdemən'streɪʃən/ *n* proof by evidence; a display or exhibition; a display of feeling; a public manifestation of opinion, as by a mass meeting, march, etc; a display of armed force.

demonstrative /də'mɒnstrətɪv/ *adj* displaying one's feelings openly and unreservedly; indicative; conclusive; (*gram*) describing an adjective or pronoun indicating the person or thing referred to.—**demonstratively** *adv.*—**demonstrativeness** *n.*

demonstrator /'demənˌstreɪtər/ *n* a person who shows consumer goods to the public; one who or that which shows how a machine, etc works; a person who takes part in a public protest.

demoralize /dɪ'mɒrəˌlaɪz/ *vt* to lower the morale of, discourage.—**demoralization** *n.*—**demoralizer** *n.*

demos /'di:ˌmɒs/ *n* in ancient Greece, the common people of a state; the population personified.

demote /di:'mo:t/ or /də-/ *vt* to reduce in rank or position.—**demotion** *n.*

demotic /də'mɒtɪk/ *adj* pertaining to the people; in the simplified style of ancient Egyptian writing.

demulcent /də'mʌlsənt/ *adj* softening; soothing. • *n* a medicine that allays irritation.

demur /də'mər/ *vi* (**demurring, demurred**) to raise objections.—**demurral** *n.*

demure /də'mjʊr/ *adj* modest, reserved; affectedly quiet and proper; coy.—**demurely** *adv.*—**demureness** *n.*

demurrage /də'mərɪdʒ/ *n* a charge for keeping a ship, truck, etc beyond the time agreed for unloading.

demurrer /də'mərər/ *n* (*law*) a plea that an opponent's facts are irrelevant; exception taken.

demy /di'maɪ/ *n* (*pl* **demies**) a size of paper for printing (22½ x 17½ ins) or writing (20 x 15½ ins).

demystify /di:'mɪstəˌfaɪ/ *vt* (**demystifying, demystified**) to remove the mystery from; clarify.—**demystification** *n.*

den /den/ *n* a cave or lair of a wild beast; a place where people gather for illegal activities; a room in a house for relaxation or study.

denarius /də'neriəs/ *n* (*pl* **denarii**) in ancient Rome, a silver coin; a gold coin worth 25 silver denarii.

denary /'di:nəri/ *adj* of ten; decimal.

denationalize /di:'næʃənəˌlaɪz/ *vt* to transfer (industry, etc) from state control to private ownership.—**denationalization** *n.*

denaturalize /di:'nætʃərəˌlaɪz/ *vt* to make unnatural; to deprive of acquired citizenship.—**denaturalization** *n.*

denature /di:'neɪtʃər/ *vt* to modify the nature of; to change the properties of (a protein) by the action of an acid or heat; to render (alcohol) unfit for consumption.—**denaturant** *n.*—**denaturation** *n.*

dendriform /'dendrɪˌfɔrm/ or /-drə-/ *adj* branching, like a tree.

dendrite /'dendraɪt/ *n* a stone or mineral with tree-like markings; a fine branch of one of the nerve cells that conduct impulses.—**dendritic** *adj.*

dendrochronology /ˌdendro:krə'nɒlədʒi/ *n* the dating of past events by studying the annual growth rings in trees.—**dendrochronological** *adj.*

dendroid /'dendrɔɪd/ *adj* resembling a tree in appearance.

dendrology /den'drɒlədʒi/ *n* the scientific study of trees.—**dendrologic, dendrological** *adj.*—**dendrologist** *n.*

dene /ˌdi:n/ *n* a low sandy tract near sea, a dune.

denegation /ˌdenə'geɪʃən/ *n* a denial.

dengue /'deŋgi/ *n* a tropical disease transmitted by the mosquito, causing fever and pain in the joints.

deniable /dɪ'naɪəbəl/ *adj* able to be denied; questionable.—**deniably** *adv.*

denial /dɪ'naɪəl/ *n* the act of denying; a refusal of a request, etc; a refusal or reluctance to admit the truth of something.

denier[1] /'denjər/ *n* a unit of weight used to measure the fineness of silk, nylon or rayon fibre, *esp* as used in women's tights, etc.

denier[2] /dɪ'naɪr/ *one* who denies.

denigrate /'denɪˌgreɪt/ *vt* to disparage the character of; to belittle.—**denigration** *n.*—**denigrator** *n.*

denim /'denəm/ *n* a hard-wearing cotton cloth, *esp* used for jeans; (*pl*) denim trousers or jeans.

denizen /'denɪzən/ *n* an inhabitant, resident; an animal or plant established in a region where it is not native.

denominate /də'nɒmɪˌneɪt/ *vt* to give a name to; to designate.

denomination /dəˌnɒmɪ'neɪʃən/ *n* a name or title; a religious group comprising many local churches, larger than a sect; one of a series of related units, *esp* monetary.

denominational /dɪˌnɒmɪ'neɪʃənəl/ *adj* of, belonging to or controlled by a religious denomination.—**denominationally** *adv.*

denominationalism /-ɪzəm/ *n* denominational spirit, policy or principles; adherence to these.—**denominationalist**.

denominative /di:'nɒmɪnətɪv/ *adj* giving a name; (*gram*) formed from a substantive or adjectival stem; connotative. • *n* a verb formed from a substantive or adjectival stem.

denominator /di:'nɒmɪˌneɪtər/ *n* the part of a fractional expression written below the fraction line.

denotation /ˌdi:no:'teɪʃən/ *n* the action of denoting; expression by marks, signs or symbols; a sign, indication; a mark by which a thing is made known; designation, meaning.

denotative /ˌdi:no:'teɪtɪv/ *adj* having the power to denote or point out; significant.—**denotatively** *adv.*

denote /di:'no:t/ *vt* to indicate, be the sign of; to mean.—**denotement** *n.*

denouement, dénouement /ˌdeɪnu:'mũ/ *n* the resolution of a plot or story; the solution, the outcome.

denounce /di:'naʊns/ *vt* to condemn or censure publicly; to inform against; to declare formally the ending of (treaties, etc).—**denouncement** *n.*—**denouncer** *n.*

dense /dens/ *adj* difficult to see through; massed closely together; dull-witted, stupid.—**densely** *adv.*—**denseness** *n.*

density /'densɪti/ *n* (*pl* **densities**) the degree of denseness or concentration; stupidity; the ratio of mass to volume.

dent /dent/ *n* a depression made by pressure or a blow. • *vti* to make a dent or become dented.

dental /'dentəl/ *adj* of or for the teeth.—**dentally** *adv.*

dental floss *n* waxed thread for cleaning between the teeth.

dental hygienist *n* a professionally trained and qualified person who checks and cleans teeth.—*also* **hygienist**.

dentate /'denteɪt/ *adj* toothed, notched.

denticle /'dentɪkəl/ *n* a small tooth or tooth-like projection.

denticulate /den'tɪkjʊlət/ or /-ˌleɪt/ *adj* (*leaf*) having small teeth.

dentiform /'dentəˌfɔrm/ *adj* tooth-shaped.

dentifrice /'dentəfrɪs/ *n* toothpowder or toothpaste.

dentil /'dentɪl/ *n* (*arch*) a small, square, projecting block on a moulding.

dentin, dentine /'denti:n/ *n* the hard, bone-like substance forming the main part of teeth.

dentist /'dentɪst/ *n* a person qualified to treat tooth decay, gum disease, etc.

dentistry /-ɪstri/ *n* the area of medicine dealing with the care of teeth and the treatment of diseases of the teeth and gums; the practice of this as a profession.

dentition /den'tɪʃən/ *n* the process or period of cutting the teeth; the arrangement of teeth.

dentoid /'denˌtɔɪd/ *adj* tooth-shaped.

denture /'dentʃər/ *n* (*usu pl*) a set of artificial teeth.

denude /dɪ'nu:d/ or /-'nju:d/ *vt* to make naked; to deprive, strip.—**denudation** *n.*—**denuder** *n.*

denunciate /di'nʌnsiˌeɪt/ *vt* (*rare*) to denounce.—**denunciator** *n.*

denunciation /dɪˌnʌnsi'eɪʃən/ *n* the act of denouncing; a threat.—**denunciator** *n.*—**denunciatory** *adj.*

deny /dɪˈnaɪ/ or /də-/ *vt* (**denying, denied**) to declare to be untrue; to repudiate; to refuse to acknowledge; to refuse to assent to a request, etc.

deodand /ˈdiːoʊˌdænd/ *n* (*law*) (*hist*) a chattel that, having caused death, was forfeited to the crown.

deodar /ˈdiːəˌdɑr/ *n* a tall Himalayan cedar tree yielding a valuable timber.

deodorant /diːˈoʊdərənt/ *n* a substance that removes or masks unpleasant odours.

deodorize /diːˈoʊdəˌraɪz/ *vt* to remove the odour or smell from.—**deodorization** *n.*—**deodorizer** *n.*

deoxidize /diːˈɒksəˌdaɪz/ *vt* to deprive of oxygen.

depart /dəˈpɑrt/ *vi* to go away, leave; to deviate (from).

departed /-əd/ *adj* (*time, etc*) long past; (*person*) recently dead.

department /dəˈpɑrtmənt/ *n* a unit of specialized functions into which an organization or business is divided; a province; a realm of activity.

departmental /ˌdiːpɑrtˈmɛntəl/ *adj* of, having, or organized into departments.—**departmentally** *adv.*

departmentalism /-ɪzəm/ *n* departmental structure, *esp* a bureaucratic one.

departmentalize /-aɪz/ *vt* to split into departments; to subdivide.—**departmentalization** *n.*

department store *n* a large store divided into various departments selling different types of goods.

departure /dəˈpɑrtʃər/ *n* a departing; a deviating from normal practice; a new venture, course of action, etc.

depend /dəˈpɛnd/ or /dɪ-/ *vi* to be determined by or connected with anything; to rely (on), put trust (in); to be reliant on for support, *esp* financially.

dependable /-əbəl/ *adj* able to be relied on.—**dependably** *adv.*—**dependability** *n.*

dependant, dependent /-dənt/ or /dɪ-/ *n* a person who is dependent on another, *esp* financially.

dependence, dependance /-dəns/ *n* the state of being dependent; reliance, trust; a physical or mental reliance on a drug, person, etc.

dependency /-si/ *n* (*pl* **dependencies**) dependence; a territory controlled by another country.

dependent, dependant *adj* relying on another person, thing, etc for support, money, etc; contingent; subordinate.

depersonalize /diːˈpərsənəˌlaɪz/ *vt* to eliminate the individual character from a person, organization, etc; to make impersonal.—**depersonalization** *n.*

depict /dəˈpɪkt/ or /dɪ-/ *vt* to represent pictorially; to describe.—**depicter, depictor** *n.*—**depiction** *n.*

depilate /ˈdɛpɪˌleɪt/ *vt* to remove hair from.—**depilation** *n.*—**depilator** *n.*

depilatory /dəˈpɪləˌtəri/ *n* (*pl* **depilatories**) a substance for removing superfluous hair. • *adj* removing hair.

deplane /diːˈpleɪn/ *vti* to alight or unload from an aircraft.

deplete /diːˈpliːt/ *vt* to use up a large quantity of.—**depletion** *n.*—**depletive** *adj.*

deplorable /diːˈplɔrəbəl/ *adj* shocking; extremely bad.—**deplorably** *adv.*

deplore /diːˈplɔr/ *vt* to regret deeply; to complain of; to deprecate.—**deplorer** *n.*—**deploringly** *adv.*

deploy /diːˈplɔɪ/ *vt* (*military forces*) to distribute and position strategically. • *vi* to adopt strategic positions within an area.—**deployment** *n.*

deplume /diːˈpluːm/ *vt* to strip of feathers, to pluck; to strip of position, honour, etc.—**deplumation** *n.*

depolarize /diːˈpoʊləˌraɪz/ *vt* to deprive of or counteract the polarity of.—**depolarization** *n.*

depone /diːˈpoʊn/ *vti* (*Scot*) to testify upon oath, to depose.

deponent /diːˈpoʊnənt/ *adj* (*gram*) (*verb*) passive in form but active in meaning. • *n* (*gram*) a deponent verb; (*law*) one who makes a deposition.

depopulate /diːˈpɒpjʊˌleɪt/ *vt* to reduce the population of.—**depopulation** *n.*—**depopulator** *n.*

deport /diːˈpɔrt/ *vt* to expel (an undesirable person) from a country; to behave (in a certain manner).—**deportable** *adj.*

deportation /ˌdiːpɔrˈteɪʃən/ *n* forcible removal from a country, *esp* of an undesirable person.

deportee /ˌdiːpɔrˈtiː/ *n* a deported person.

deportment /diːˈpɔrtmənt/ *n* manners; bearing; behaviour.

depose /diːˈpoʊz/ *vt* to remove from power; to testify, *esp* in court.—**deposable** *adj.*—**deposer** *n.*

deposit /diːˈpɒzət/ or /də-/ *vt* to place or lay down; to pay money into a bank or other institution for safekeeping, to earn interest, etc; to pay as a first instalment; to let fall, leave. • *n* something deposited for safekeeping; money put in a bank; money given in part payment or security; material left in a layer, *eg* sediment.

depositary /diːˈpɒzɪteri/ *n* (*pl* **depositaries**) the person to whom something is entrusted; a depository.

deposition /ˌdɛpəˈzɪʃən/ or /ˌdiːp-/ *n* the act of depositing or deposing; a being removed from office or power; a sworn testimony, *esp* in writing.

depositor /diːˈpɒzɪtər/ *n* a person who deposits money in a bank, etc.

depository /-ˌtɔri/ *n* (*pl* **depositories**) a place where anything is deposited; a depositary.

depot /ˈdɛpoʊ/ or /ˈdiːpoʊ/ *n* a warehouse, storehouse; a place for storing military supplies; a military training centre; a bus or railway station.

deprave /diːˈpreɪv/ *vt* to pervert; to corrupt morally.—**depravation** *n.*—**depraver** *n.*

depraved /-ˈpreɪvd/ *adj* morally debased; corrupt; made bad or worse.—**depravedly** *adv.*

depravity /diːˈprævɪti/ *n* (*pl* **depravities**) moral corruption; extreme wickedness.

deprecate /ˈdɛprɪˌkeɪt/ *vt* to criticize, *esp* mildly or politely; to belittle.—**deprecation** *n.*—**deprecative** *adj.*—**deprecator** *n.*

deprecative /ˈdɛprɪkətɪv/ *adj* deprecatory.

deprecatory /-ˈkətəri/ *adj* apologetic; disapproving, belittling.

depreciate /diːˈpriːʃiˌeɪt/ *vti* to make or become lower in value.—**depreciator** *n.*—**depreciatory, depreciative** *adj.*

depreciation /dɪˌpriːʃiˈeɪʃən/ or /-siˈeɪʃən/ *n* a fall in value, *esp* of an asset through wear and tear; an allowance for this deducted from gross profit; disparagement.

depredate /ˈdɛprəˌdeɪt/ *vt* to pillage; to rob; to lay waste; to prey upon.—**depredator** *n.*

depredation /ˌdɛprəˈdeɪʃən/ *n* plundering; pillage.

depress /diːˈprɛs/ *vt* to push down; to sadden, dispirit; to lessen the activity of.—**depressing** *adj.*—**depressingly** *adv.*

depressant /-ənt/ *adj* causing depression. • *n* a substance that reduces the activity of the nervous system; a drug that acts as a depressant.

depressed /diːˈprɛst/ or /dɪ-/ *adj* cast down in spirits; lowered in position; flattened from above, or vertically.

depression /diːˈprɛʃən/ *n* excessive gloom and despondency; an abnormal state of physiological inactivity; a phase of the business cycle characterized by stagnation, widespread unemployment, etc; a falling in or sinking; a lowering of atmospheric pressure, often signalling rain.

depressive /-sɪv/ *adj* depressing; tending to suffer from mental depression.—**depressively** *adv.*

depressor /-sər/ *n* one who or that which depresses; a muscle that draws down an organ or part.

deprive /diːˈpraɪv/ or /də-/ *vt* to take a thing away from; to prevent from using or enjoying.—**deprivation** *n.*

deprived /-ˈpraɪvd/ *adj* lacking the essentials of life, such as adequate food, shelter, education, etc.

dept. *abbr* = department.

depth /dɛpθ/ *n* deepness; the distance downwards or inwards; the intensity of emotion or feeling; the profundity of thought; intensity of colour; the mid point of the night or winter; the lowness of sound or pitch; the quality of being deep.

depth charge *n* a bomb designed to explode under water, used against submarines.

depurate /ˈdɛpjʊˌreɪt/ *vti* to free or become free from impurities.—**depuration** *n.*—**depurative** *adj.*—**depurator** *n.*

deputation /ˌdɛpjuːˈteɪʃən/ *n* a person or group appointed to represent others.

depute /dɪˈpjuːt/ *vt* to appoint as one's representative; to delegate.

deputize /ˈdɛpjuːˌtaɪz/ *vi* to act as deputy.—**deputization** *n.*

deputy /ˈdɛpjuːti/ *n* (*pl* **deputies**) a delegate, representative, or substitute.

deracinate /diːˈræsɪˌneɪt/ *vt* to tear up by the roots.—**deracination** *n.*

derail /diːˈreɪl/ *vti* (*train*) to cause to leave the rails.—**derailment** *n.*

derailleur /diːˈreɪlər/ *n* a system of gearing on a bicycle.

derange /diːˈreɪndʒ/ *vt* to throw into confusion; to disturb; to make insane.—**deranged** *adj.*—**derangement** *n.*

derby /'dɜrbi/ *n* (*pl* **derbies**) a bowler hat.

deregulate /di:'regjʊˌleɪt/ *vt* to remove (*eg* government) regulations or controls from (an industry, etc).—**deregulation** *n*.

derelict /'derəˌlɪkt/ *adj* abandoned, deserted and left to decay; negligent. • *n* a person abandoned by society; a wrecked ship or vehicle.

dereliction /ˌderɪ'lɪkʃən/ *n* neglect (of duty); abandonment.

deride /də'raɪd/ *vt* to scorn, mock.

de rigueur /ˌdərɪ'gɜr/ *adj* required by fashion or etiquette.

derisible /dɪ'rɪzɪbəl/ *adj* open to derision.

derision /də'rɪʒən/ *n* ridicule.

derisive /də'raɪsɪv/ *adj* full of derision; mocking, scornful.—**derisively** *adv*.—**derisiveness** *n*.

derisory /-səri/ *adj* showing or deserving of derision.

derivation /ˌderɪ'veɪʃən/ *n* the tracing of a word to its root; origin; descent.—**derivational** *adj*.

derivative /də'rɪvətɪv/ *adj* derived from something else; not original. • *n* something that is derived; a word formed by derivation; (*math*) the rate of change of one quantity with respect to another.—**derivatively** *adv*.

derive /də'raɪv/ *vt* to take or receive from a source; to infer, deduce (from). • *vi* to issue as a derivative (from).—**derivable** *adj*.—**deriver** *n*.

dermal /'dɜrməl/ *adj* of the skin; consisting of skin.

dermatitis /ˌdɜrmə'taɪtɪs/ *n* inflammation of the skin.

dermatology /ˌdɜrmə'tɒlədʒi/ *n* the science of the skin and its diseases.—**dermatologic, dermatological** *adj*.—**dermatologist** *n*.

dermic /'dɜrmɪk/ *adj* dermal.

dermis /'dɜrmɪs/ *n* the fine skin below the epidermis containing blood vessels.

derogate /'derəˌgeɪt/ *vti* to detract (from); to lose face; to degenerate; to take a part (from).—**derogation** *n*.

derogatory /də'rɒgətəri/ *adj* disparaging; deliberately offensive.—**derogatorily** *adv*.

derrick /'derɪk/ *n* any crane-like apparatus; a tower over an oil well, etc, holding the drilling machinery.

derring-do /ˌderɪŋ'du:/ *n* bravery, reckless valour.

derringer /'derɪndʒər/ *n* a pocket pistol with a short barrel of very large calibre.

dervish /'dɜrvɪʃ/ *n* a member of a Muslim religious order vowing chastity and poverty, noted for frenzied, whirling dancing.

desalinate /di:'sælɪˌneɪt/ *vt* to remove the salt from (seawater, etc).—**desalination** *n*.—**desalinator** *n*.

descant /'desˌkænt/ *n* a musical accompaniment sung or played in counterpoint to the main melody.—*also vi*.

descend /də'send/ *vi* to come or climb down; to pass from a higher to a lower place or condition; (*with* **on, upon**) to make a sudden attack upon, or visit unexpectedly; to sink in morals or dignity; to be derived. • *vt* to go, pass, or extend down.

descendant /də'sendənt/ *n* a person who is descended from an ancestor; something derived from an earlier form.

descendent *adj* descending; sinking.

descendible /-əbəl/ *adj* (*law*) that may be inherited; transmissible.

descent /də'sent/ *n* a descending; a downward motion or step; a way down; a slope; a raid or invasion; lineage, ancestry.

describe /də'skraɪb/ *vt* to give a verbal account of; to trace out.—**describable** *adj*.—**describer** *n*.

description /də'skrɪpʃən/ *n* a verbal or pictorial account; a sort, a kind.

descriptive /də'skrɪptɪv/ *adj* tending to or serving to describe.—**descriptively** *adv*.—**descriptiveness** *n*.

descry /də'skraɪ/ *vt* (**descrying, descried**) to catch sight of.

desecrate /'desəˌkreɪt/ *vt* to violate a sacred place by destructive or blasphemous behaviour.—**desecration** *n*.—**desecrator, desecrater** *n*.

desegregate /di:'segrəˌgeɪt/ *vt* to abolish (racial or sexual) segregation in.—**desegregation** *n*.

desert[1] /də'zɜrt/ *n* (*often pl*) a deserved reward or punishment.

desert[2] *vt* to leave, abandon, with no intention of returning; to abscond from the armed forces without permission.—**deserter** *n*.—**desertion** *n*.

desert[3] /'dezərt/ *n* a dry, barren region, able to support little or no life; a place lacking in some essential quality.

desertification /dəˌzɜrtɪfɪ'keɪʃən/ *n* the transformation of fertile land into arid waste or desert through soil erosion, overcultivation, etc.

desertion /dɪ'zɜrʃən/ *n* deserting; being forsaken.

deserve /də'zɜrv/ *vt* to merit or be suitable for (some reward, punishment, etc).

deserved /-vəd/ *adj* justly earned, merited.—**deservedly** *adv*.—**deservedness** *n*.

deserving /-ɪŋ/ *adj* worthy of support, *esp* financially.

deshabille /ˌdezæ'bi:el/ or /ˌdeɪzæ'bi:l/ *see* **dishabille**.

desiccate /'desɪˌkeɪt/ *vti* to dry or become dried up; to preserve (food) by drying.—**desiccation** *n*.—**desiccative** *adj*.

desiccator /-ər/ *n* an apparatus for drying foods and other substances.

desiderate /də'zɪdərˌeɪt/ *vt* to feel the lack of, to desire earnestly.—**desideration** *n*.—**desiderative** *adj*.

desideratum /dəˌzɪdə'rætəm/ or /-ˌsɪd-/ *n* (*pl* **desiderata**) anything desired; a want or desire generally felt and recognized.

design /də'zaɪn/ *vt* to plan; to create; to devise; to make working drawings for; to intend. • *n* a working drawing; a mental plan or scheme; the particular form or disposition of something; a decorative pattern; purpose; (*pl*) dishonest intent.

designate /'dezɪgˌneɪt/ *vt* to indicate, specify; to name; to appoint to or nominate for a position, office. • *adj* (*after noun*) appointed to office but not yet installed.—**designator** *n*.

designation /ˌdezɪg'neɪʃən/ *n* the act of designating; nomination; a distinguishing name or title.

designedly /də'zaɪnədli/ *adv* intentionally.

designer /də'zaɪnər/ *n* a person who designs things; a person who is renowned for creating high-class fashion clothes. • *adj* (*inf*) trendy, of the latest, *esp* expensive, fashion.

designer drug *n* a synthetic narcotic or hallucinogenic substance which mimics the chemical structure and effects of banned drugs but is not yet covered by anti-drug laws.

designing /-ɪŋ/ *adj* crafty, scheming. • *n* the art or practice of making designs.

desirable /də'zaɪrəbəl/ *adj* arousing (sexual) desire; advisable or beneficial; worth doing.—**desirability** *n*.—**desirably** *adv*.

desire /də'zaɪr/ *vt* to long or wish for; to request, ask for. • *n* a longing for something regarded as pleasurable or satisfying; a request; something desired; sexual craving.

desirous /-əs/ *adj* desiring; craving.

desist /də'sɪst/ *vi* to stop (doing something).—**desistance** *n*.

desk /desk/ *n* a piece of furniture with a writing surface and *usu* drawers; a counter behind which a cashier, etc sits; the section of a newspaper responsible for a particular topic.

desktop *n* the surface of a desk; (*comput*) the backdrop on a computer screen on which icons and windows appear.

desktop publishing *n* the use of a computer with sophisticated page-layout programs and a laser printer to produce professional-looking printed matter.

desman /'desmən/ *n* (*pl* **desmans**) a small amphibious animal similar to a mole.

desmoid /-ˌmɔɪd/ *adj* having the characteristics of, or resembling, a ligament; (*tumour*) fibrous.

desolate /'desələt/ *adj* solitary, lonely; devoid of inhabitants; laid waste; forlorn, disconsolate; overwhelmed with grief. • *vt* to depopulate; to devastate, lay waste; to make barren or unfit for habitation; to leave alone, forsake, abandon; to overwhelm with grief.—**desolately** *adv*.—**desolateness** *n*.—**desolator, desolater** *n*.

desolated /'desəˌleɪtəd/ *adj* wretched, lonely, miserable.

desolation /ˌdesə'leɪʃən/ *n* destruction, ruin; a barren state; loneliness; wretchedness.

despair /də'sper/ *vi* to have no hope. • *n* utter loss of hope; something that causes despair.

despatch /də'spætʃ/ *see* **dispatch**.

desperado /ˌdespə'rɒdoʊ/ *n* (*pl* **desperadoes, desperados**) a violent criminal.

desperate /'despərət/ *adj* (almost) hopeless; reckless through lack of hope; urgently requiring (money, etc); (*remedy*) extreme, dangerous.—**desperately** *adv*.—**desperateness** *n*.

desperation /ˌdespə'reɪʃən/ *n* loss of hope; recklessness from despair.

despicable /də'spɪkəbəl/ or /'despɪk-/ *adj* contemptible, worthless.—**despicableness** *n*.—**despicably** *adv*.

despise /də'spaɪz/ *vt* to regard with contempt or scorn; to consider as worthless, inferior.

despite /də'spaɪt/ *prep* in spite of.

despoil /də'spɔɪl/ *vt* to plunder, rob.—**despoiler** *n*.—**despoilment** *n*.

despoliation /dəˌspoʊli'eɪʃən/ *n* despoilment; pillage.

despond /dəˈspɒnd/ *vi* to lose hope, to be dejected. • *n* despondency.

despondency /-densi/, **despondence** /-ɒns/ *n* a being despondent; depression or dejection of spirits through loss of resolution or hope.

despondent /dəˈspɒndənt/ *adj* dejected, depressed.—**despondently** *adv*.

despot /ˈdespɒt/ *n* a ruler possessing absolute power; a tyrant.

despotic /-ˈspɒtɪk/, **despotical** /-kəl/ *adj* of, pertaining to, or of the nature of a despot or of despotism; arbitrary, tyrannical.—**despotically** *adv*.

despotism /-zəm/ *n* absolute power, tyranny; a state governed by a despot.

desquamate /ˈdeskwəˌmeɪt/ *vti* to peel or scale off.—**desquamation** *n*.

dessert /dəˈzərt/ *n* the sweet course at the end of a meal.

dessertspoon /-ˌspuːn/ *n* a spoon in between a teaspoon and a tablespoon in size, used for eating desserts.

destination /ˌdestɪˈneɪʃən/ *n* the place to which a person or thing is going.

destine /ˈdestɪn/ *vt* to set aside for some specific purpose; to predetermine; intend.

destiny /ˈdestɪni/ *n* (*pl* **destinies**) the power supposedly determining the course of events; the future to which any person or thing is destined; a predetermined course of events.

destitute /ˈdestɪˌtuːt/ or /-tjuːt/ *adj* (*with* **of**) lacking some quality; lacking the basic necessities of life, very poor.

destitution /ˌdestɪˈtuːʃən/ or /-ˈtjuːʃən/ *n* extreme poverty.

destroy /dəˈstrɔɪ/ *vt* to demolish, ruin, to put an end to; to kill.

destroyer /-ər/ *n* one who or that which destroys; a fast small warship.

destruct /dəˈstrʌkt/ *vt* to destroy deliberately (a missile, etc). • *n* the act of destructing (a missile, etc).

destructible /-ɪbəl/ *adj* subject to destruction; able to be destroyed.—**destructibility** *n*.

destruction /dəˈstrʌkʃən/ *n* the act or process of destroying or being destroyed; ruin.

destructionist /-ɪst/ *n* an anarchist.

destructive /-tɪv/ *adj* causing destruction; (*with* **of** *or* **to**) ruinous; (*criticism*) intended to discredit, negative.—**destructively** *adv*.—**destructivity** *n*.

destructor /-ər/ *n* a furnace for burning up rubbish, etc; an explosive device for blowing up a malfunctioning rocket, etc.

desuetude /dəˈsuːɪˌtuːd/ or /-tjuːd/ *n* disuse, discontinuance.

desultory /ˈdesəlˌtɔri/ *adj* going aimlessly from one activity or subject to another, not methodical.—**desultorily** *adv*.—**desultoriness** *n*.

detach /dəˈtætʃ/ *vt* to release; to separate from a larger group; (*mil*) to send off on special assignment.

detachable /-əbəl/ *adj* able to be detached.—**detachability** *n*.—**detachably** *adv*.

detached /dəˈtætʃd/ *adj* separate; free from bias or emotion; (*house*) not joined to another; aloof.

detachment /-mənt/ *n* indifference; freedom from emotional involvement or bias; the act of detaching; a thing detached; a body of troops detached from the main body and sent on special service.

detail /dəˈteɪl/ or /ˈdiːteɪl/ *vt* to describe fully; (*mil*) to set apart for a particular duty. • *n* an item; a particular or minute account; (*art*) treatment of smaller parts; a reproduction of a smaller part of a picture, statue, etc; a small detachment for special service.

detailed /ˈdiːteɪld/ or /diːˈteɪld/, /dəˈteɪld/ *adj* giving full details; thorough.

detain /diˈteɪn/ *vt* to place in custody or confinement; to delay.—**detainment** *n*.

detainee /ˌdiːteɪˈniː/ or /dəˈteɪˌniː/ *n* a person who is held in custody.

detainer /-ər/ *n* the (wrongful) detaining of person or goods; a writ for holding on another charge a person already arrested.

detect /dəˈtekt/ *vt* to discover the existence or presence of; to notice.

detectable /-əbəl/ *adj* able to be detected.—**detectability** *n*.

detection /dəˈtekʃən/ *n* a discovery or a being discovered; the job or process of detecting.

detective /dəˈtektɪv/ *n* a person or a police officer employed to find evidence of crimes.

detector /-ər/ *n* a device for detecting the presence of something.

detent /ˈdəˌtent/ *n* a catch for locking machinery or regulating the striking of a clock.

détente, detente /deɪˈtɑːt/ *n* relaxation of tension between countries.

detention /dəˈtenʃən/ *n* the act of detaining or withholding; a being detained; confinement; the act of being kept in (school after hours) as a punishment.

deter /dəˌtər/ *vt* (**deterring, deterred**) to discourage or prevent (from acting).—**determent** *n*.

deterge /dəˈtərdʒ/ or /diː-/ *vt* to cleanse, as a wound.

detergent /dəˈtərdʒənt/ *n* a cleaning agent, *esp* one made from a chemical compound rather than fats, as soap. • *adj* having cleaning power.

deteriorate /dɪˈtiːriəˌreɪt/ *vt* to make or become worse.—**deterioration** *n*.—**deteriorative** *adj*.

determinable /diːˈtərmɪnəbəl/ or /dɪ-/ *adj* capable of being definitely ascertained; defined with clearness; terminable.—**determinability** *n*.—**determinably** *adv*.

determinant /dəˈtərmɪnənt/ *adj* determining. • *n* something that determines, a decisive factor; (*math*) an algebraic term expressing the sum of certain products arranged in a square or matrix.

determinate /dəˈtərmɪnət/ *adj* definitely bounded in time, space, position, etc; fixed; clearly defined; distinct; resolute, decisive; (*bot*) having the terminal flower bud opening first, followed by those on lateral branches.—**determinately** *adv*.—**determinateness** *n*.

determination /dəˌtərmɪˈneɪʃən/ *n* the act or process of making a decision; a decision resolving a dispute; firm intention; resoluteness.

determinative /dəˈtərmɪnətɪv/ *adj* determining, limiting, or defining; tending to define the genus or species. • *n* that which serves to determine the quality or character of something else; a demonstrative pronoun; an ideograph.—**determinatively** *adv*.

determine /dəˈtərmɪn/ *vt* to fix or settle officially; to find out; to regulate; to impel. • *vi* to come to a decision.

determined /-mɪnd/ *adj* full of determination, resolute.—**determinedly** *adv*.—**determinedness** *n*.

determiner /-mɪnər/ *n* one who or that which determines; (*gram*) a word that limits the meaning of a noun, *esp* an article or possessive pronoun.

determinism /-ɪzəm/ *n* the theory that all events, including human actions, are determined by preceding causes, thereby precluding free will.—**determinist** *n*.—**deterministic** *adj*.—**deterministically** *adv*.

deterrent /-ənt/ *n* something that deters; a nuclear weapon that deters attack through fear of retaliation. • *adj* deterring.—**deterrence** *n*.

detest /dɪˈtest/ *vt* to dislike intensely.—**detester** *n*.

detestable /-əbəl/ *adj* intensely disliked, abhorrent.—**detestably** *adv*.

detestation /ˌdiːteˈsteɪʃən/ *n* extreme dislike; a detestable person or thing.

dethrone /diːˈθroːn/ *vt* to remove from a throne, to depose.—**dethronement** *n*.—**dethroner** *n*.

detinue /ˈdetɪˌnjuː/ or /-ˌnuː/ *n* (*law*) a writ for recovery of property wrongfully detained.

detonate /ˈdetəˌneɪt/ *vti* to explode or cause to explode rapidly and violently.

detonation /-ˈneɪʃən/ *n* a sudden explosion with a loud report.

detonator /ˈdetəˌneɪtər/ *n* a device that sets off an explosion.

detour /ˈdiːtʊər/ *n* a deviation from an intended course, *esp* one serving as an alternative to a more direct route. • *vti* to make or send by a detour.

detoxification centre *n* an institution that treats alcoholism or drug addiction.

detoxify /diːˈtɒksɪˌfaɪ/ *vt* (**detoxifying, detoxified**) to extract poison or toxins from.—**detoxification** *n*.

detract /diːˈtrækt/ *vt* to take away. • *vi* to take away (from).—**detractor** *n*.

detraction /diːˈtrækʃən/ *n* defamation; slander; depreciation.—**detractive** *adj*.—**detractively** *adv*.

detrain /diːˈtreɪn/ *vt*, *vi* to set down or alight from a train.—**detrainment** *n*.

detriment /ˈdetrɪmənt/ *n* (a cause of) damage or injury.

detrimental /ˌdetrɪˈmentəl/ *adj* harmful.—**detrimentally** *adv*.

detrition /diːˈtrɪʃən/ *n* a wearing down by rubbing or friction.

detritus /dəˈtraɪtəs/ *n* debris; loose matter, *esp* formed by rubbing away or erosion of a larger mass (*eg* a rock).—**detrital** *adj*.

de trop /dəˈtroː/ *adj* too much; out of place; (*person*) not wanted.

detumescence /ˌdiːtuːˈmesəns/ or /-tjuː-/ *n* the diminution of a swelling, *esp* of an erect penis.—**detumescent** *adj*.

deuce[1] /duːs/ or /djuːs/ n a playing card or dice with two spots; (tennis) the score of forty-all.

deuce[2] interj (inf) the devil!—an exclamation of surprise or annoyance.

deuced /'djuːsd/ or /'djuːst/ adj (inf) confounded.

deus ex machina /ˌdeɪʊseks'mækɪnə/ or /ˌdiːəs-/ n divine intervention; an artificial solution of difficulties, esp in a play.

deuter(o)- /'duːtərɒ/ or /ˌdjuː-/ prefix second.

deuteragonist /ˌduːtə'rægənɪst/ or /ˌdjuː-/ n (Greek drama) the second principal actor.

deuterium /duː'tiːrɪəm/ or /djuː-/ n heavy hydrogen, used as a moderator in nuclear reactors to slow the rate of fission.

deuterocanonical /ˌduːtərɒkæ'nɒnɪkəl/ or /ˌdjuː-/ adj of or belonging to a second canon or to the Apocrypha.

deuterogamy /ˌduːtər'ɒgəmɪ/ or /ˌdjuː-t-/ n a second marriage.

deuteron /'duːtəˌrɒn/ or /ˌdjuː-/ n the nucleus of a heavy hydrogen atom.

deutoplasm /-ˌplæzəm/ n the albuminous part of the yolk that provides food for the embryo in an egg.—**deutoplasmic** adj.

Deutschmark, Deutsche Mark /'dɔɪtʃmɑːrk/ n the former monetary unit of Germany (now the euro).

deutzia /'djuːtsɪə/ or /'dɔɪt-/ n a small shrub of the saxifrage family with clusters of white flowers.

deva /'deɪvə/ n (Hinduism) a god.

devaluate /diː'væljuːeɪt/ vt to devalue.

devalue /diː'vælju:/ vt (**devaluing, devalued**) to reduce the exchange value of (a currency).—**devaluation** n.

devastate /'devəˌsteɪt/ vt to lay waste; to destroy; to overwhelm.—**devastatingly** adv.—**devastation** n.—**devastator** n.

develop /də'veləp/ vt to evolve; to bring to maturity; to show the symptoms of (eg a habit, a disease); to treat a photographic film or plate to reveal an image; to improve the value of. • vi to grow (into); to become apparent.

developer /-ər/ n a person who develops; a person or organization that develops property; a reagent for developing photographs.

developing country n a poor country that is attempting to improve its social conditions and encourage industrial growth.

development /-mənt/ n the process of growing or developing; a new situation that emerges; a piece of land or property that has been developed.—**developmental** adj.

deviant /'diːviənt/ adj that which deviates from an accepted norm. • n a person whose behaviour deviates from the accepted standards of society.—**deviance, deviancy** n.

deviate /'diːviˌeɪt/ vi to diverge from a course, topic, principle, etc.—**deviator** n.

deviation /ˌdiːvi'eɪʃən/ n a deviating from normal behaviour, official ideology, etc; deflection of a compass needle by magnetic disturbance; (statistics) difference from a mean.

device /də'vaɪs/ n a machine, implement, etc for a particular purpose; an invention; a scheme, a plot.

devil /'devəl/ n (with cap) in Christian and Jewish theology, the supreme spirit of evil, Satan; any evil spirit; an extremely wicked person; (inf) a reckless, high-spirited person; (inf) someone or something difficult to deal with; (inf) a person. • vb (**devilling, devilled** or **deviling, deviled**) vt to cook food with a hot seasoning. • vi to act as a drudge to someone; to do research for an author or barrister.

devilfish /-fɪʃ/ n (**devilfish, devilfishes**) the manta, a very large ray; a large species of octopus.

devilish /-ɪʃ/ adj fiendish; mischievous. • adv (inf) very.—**devilishly** adv.—**devilishness** n.

devil-may-care /ˌdevəlmeɪ'kɛr/ adj audacious, contemptuous of authority.

devilment /-mənt/ n mischievous behaviour.

devilry /'devəlrɪ/ n (pl **devilries**) wickedness; malicious mischief.

devil's advocate n a person who advocates an opposing cause, esp for the sake of argument.

devious /'diːviəs/ adj indirect; not straightforward; underhand, deceitful.—**deviously** adv.—**deviousness** n.

devisable /-əbəl/ adj capable of being imagined; (law) (real estate) capable of being bequeathed.—**devisability** n.

devise /də'vaɪz/ vt to invent, contrive; to plan; (law) to leave (real estate) by will. • n (law) a bequest (of real estate); property so bequeathed.—**deviser** n.

devisee /ˌdevə'ziː/ or /dɪ'vaɪziː/ n (law) a person to whom (real estate) has been bequeathed.

devisor /-ər/ n (law) a person who bequeathes, esp real estate.

devitalize /diː'vaɪtəˌlaɪz/ vt to deprive of vitality or vigour.—**devitalization** n.

devitrify /diː'vɪtrəˌfaɪ/ vt (**devitrifying, devitrified**) to deprive of glassy quality, to make opaque.—**devitrification** n.

devoid /də'vɔɪd/ adj (with **of**) lacking; free from.

devoirs /də'vwɑːz/ npl civilities; one's best.

devolution /ˌdevə'luːʃən/ or /ˌdiː-/ n a transfer of authority, esp from a central government to regional governments; a passing on from one person to another.

devolve /də'vɒlv/ vti to hand on or be handed on to a successor or deputy.—**devolvement** n.

devote /də'vəʊt/ vt to give or use for a particular activity or purpose.

devoted /-ɪd/ adj zealous; loyal; loving.—**devotedly** adv.—**devotedness** n.

devotee /ˌdevə'tiː/ or /ˌdiː-/ n (with **of** or **to**) a person who is enthusiastically or fanatically devoted to something; a religious zealot.

devotion /də'vəʊʃən/ n given to religious worship; piety; strong affection or attachment (to); ardour; (pl) prayers.

devotional /-əl/ adj of devotions; devout. • n a brief religious service.

devour /də'vaʊr/ vt to eat up greedily; to consume; to absorb eagerly by the senses or mind.

devout /də'vaʊt/ adj very religious, pious; sincere, dedicated.—**devoutly** adv.—**devoutness** n.

dew /duː/ or /djuː/ n air moisture, deposited on a cool surface, esp at night.

dew point n the air temperature at which dew forms.

dewberry /'duːbərɪ/ or /'djuː-/ n (pl **dewberries**) a kind of trailing blackberry plant; its dark blue fruit.

dewclaw /'duːklɒ/ or /'djuː-/ n a rudimentary toe above a dog's paw or above the hoof of a deer, etc.

Dewey Decimal System /'duːi/ or /'djuː-/ n a method of classifying library books into ten main subject areas.—**also decimal classification.**

dewlap /-læp/ n a flap of skin hanging under the throat of some animals, eg cows; loose skin on the throat of an elderly person.

dewy /'duːi/ or /'djuː-/ adj (**dewier, dewiest**) wet with dew.—**dewily** adv.—**dewiness** n.

dewy-eyed /-ˌaɪd/ adj sentimental, naive.

dexter /'dekstər/ adj right; (her) to the viewer's left and the wearer's right.

dexterity /deks'terəti/ n manual skill, adroitness.

dexterous /'dekstrəs/ adj possessing manual skill; quick, mentally or physically; adroit; clever.—**dexterously** adv.—**dexterousness** n.

dextral /'dekstrəl/ adj on the right-hand side; right-handed; (shell) with whorls going to the right.—**dextrality** n.—**dextrally** adv.

dextrin, dextrine /'dekstrɪn/ n a white gummy substance found in plant sap, etc, and used as gum and a thickening agent.

dextrorotation /ˌdekstrɒrɒ'teɪʃən/ n right-handed or clockwise rotation.—**dextrorotary, dextrorotatory** adj.

dextrorse /'dekstrɔːs/ adj (bot) twining spirally from left to right.—**dextrorsely** adv.

dextrose /'dekstrəʊs/ n a form of glucose found in fruit, honey and animal tissues.

dextrous /'dekstrəs/ adj dexterous.

DFC abbr = Distinguished Flying Cross.

dhak /dæk/ n an Indian tree with brilliant red flowers.

dhal /dɒl/ see **dal.**

dharma /'dɑːmə/ n (Hinduism, Buddhism) the law requiring virtue and righteousness; its practice in daily life.

dhobi /'dəʊbi/ n (pl **dhobis**) in India, a laundryman.

dhole /dəʊl/ n (pl **dholes, dhole**) an Asian wild dog that hunts in packs.

dhoti /'dəʊti/ n (pl **dhotis**) a loincloth worn by men in India.

dhow /daʊ/ n an Arab coastal vessel with a triangular sail.

di- /daɪ/ prefix two; twice; double.

diabase /'daɪəbeɪs/ n dolerite, a dark coloured igneous rock.

diabetes /ˌdaɪə'biːtiːz/ n a medical disorder marked by the persistent and excessive discharge of urine.

diabetes mellitus /-mə'lɪtəs/ n a breakdown in the body's ability to absorb carbohydrates caused by a deficiency of insulin, which results in abnormally high levels of sugar in the blood and urine.

diabetic /ˌdaɪə'betɪk/ adj of or suffering from diabetes. • n a person with diabetes.

diablerie /diːˈæbləri/ or /daɪ-/ *n* a devil's work, sorcery; devil-lore; mischief.

diabolic /ˌdaɪəˈbɒlɪk/ *adj* devilish; cruel, wicked.—**diabolically** *adv*.—**diabolicalness** *n*.

diabolical /ˌdaɪəˈbɒlɪkəl/ *adj* diabolic; (*inf*) extremely bad or annoying.

diabolism /daɪˈæbəˌlɪzəm/ *n* devil worship; witchcraft.—**diabolist** *n*.

diabolize /-ˌlaɪz/ *vt* to make into or represent as a devil.

diaconal /daɪˈækənəl/ or /diː-/ *adj* of or pertaining to a deacon.

diaconate /daɪˈækəˌneɪt/ or /diːˌ, /-nət/ *n* the office or dignity of a deacon; deacons collectively.

diacritic /ˌdaɪəˈkrɪtɪk/ *adj* diacritical. • *n* a diacritical mark.

diacritical /ˌdaɪəˈkrɪtɪkəl/ *adj* distinguishing, distinctive, *esp* of accents, etc attached to letters to indicate pronunciation.—**diacritically** *adv*.

diacritical mark *n* a mark, such as an accent, used above or below a letter to indicate differences in sound.

diactinic /ˌdaɪækˈtɪnɪk/ *adj* transparent to actinic rays.—**diactinism** *n*.

diadelphous /ˌdaɪəˈdɛlfəs/ *adj* (*flowers*) with stamens in two bundles.

diadem /ˌdaɪəˈdɛm/ *n* a crown or jewelled headband worn by royalty.

diaeresis /daɪˈərəsɪs/ *see* **dieresis**.

diagnose /ˌdaɪəɡˈnoːs/ or /-ˈnoːz/, /ˈdaɪəɡˌnoːs/, /-ˌnoːz/ *vt* to ascertain by diagnosis.—**diagnosable, diagnoseable** *adj*.

diagnosis /ˌdaɪəɡˈnoːsɪs/ *n* (*pl* **diagnoses**) the identification of a disease from its symptoms; the analysis of the nature or cause of a problem.—**diagnostician** *n*.

diagnostic /ˌdaɪəɡˈnɒstɪk/ *adj* of or aiding diagnosis; characteristic. • *n* a symptom distinguishing a disease; a characteristic; (*pl: used as sing*) the art of diagnosing.—**diagnostically** *adv*.

diagonal /daɪˈæɡənəl/ *adj* slanting from one corner to an opposite corner of a polygon. • *n* a straight line connecting opposite corners.—**diagonally** *adv*.

diagram /ˈdaɪəˌɡræm/ *n* a figure or plan drawn in outline to illustrate the form or workings of something. • *vt* (**diagramming, diagrammed** *or* **diagraming, diagramed**) to demonstrate in diagram form.

diagrammatic, diagrammatical *adj* having the form or nature of a diagram; of or pertaining to diagrams.—**diagrammatically** *adv*.

diagraph /ˈdaɪəˌɡræf/ *n* an instrument for enlarging maps, etc mechanically.

dial /ˈdaɪəl/ *n* the face of a watch or clock; a graduated disk with a pointer used in various instruments; the control on a radio or television set indicating wavelength or station; the numbered disk on a telephone used to enter digits to connect calls; an instrument for telling the time by the sun's shadow. • *vt* (**dialling, dialled** *or* **dialing, dialed**) to measure or indicate by a dial; to make a telephone connection by using a dial or numbered keypad.

dialect /ˈdaɪəˌlɛkt/ *n* the form of language spoken in a particular region or social class.—**dialectal** *adj*.—**dialectally** *adv*.

dialectic /ˈdaɪəˌlɛktɪk/ *n* the pursuit of truths in philosophy through logical debate.—**dialectical** *adj*.—**dialectically** *adv*.

dialectology /-ˌtɒlədʒi/ *n* the study of dialects.—**dialectological** *adj*.—**dialectologist** *n*.

dialogue, dialog /ˈdaɪəˌlɒɡ/ *n* a conversation, *esp* in a play or novel; an exchange of opinions, negotiation.

dial tone *n* a sound heard over the telephone indicating that the line is clear.

dialyse, dialyze /ˈdaɪəˌlaɪz/ *vt* to separate crystalline from colloid parts of a mixture by filtration.—**dialysation, dialyzation** *n*.

dialyser, dialyzer /-ˌlaɪzer/ *n* a machine for dialysing, *esp* one that act as a kidney.

dialysis /daɪˈæləsɪs/ *n* (*pl* **dialyses**) the removal of impurities from the blood by filtering it through a membrane.—**dialytic** *adj*.—**dialytically** *adv*.

diamagnetic /ˌdaɪəmæɡˈnɛtɪk/ *adj* cross-magnetic, tending to point east and west.—**diamagnetically** *adv*.

diamagnetism /-ˈmæɡnətˌɪzəm/ *n* the property of certain bodies when under the influence of magnetism and freely suspended of taking a position at right angles to the magnetic meridian.

diamanté /ˌdiːəˈmɒnteɪ/ *adj* glittering with rhinestones, sequins or imitation jewels. • *n* a material ornamented in this way.

diameter /daɪˈæmətər/ *n* a straight line bisecting a circle; the length of this line.

diametric /ˌdaɪəˈmɛtrɪk/, **diametrical** /-əl/ *adj* of or along a diameter; completely opposed.—**diametrically** *adv*.

diamond /ˈdaɪmənd/ or /ˈdaɪə-/ *n* a valuable gem, a crystallized form of pure carbon; (*baseball*) the playing field, *esp* the infield; a suit of playing cards denoted by a red lozenge. • *adj* composed of, or set with diamonds; shaped like a diamond; denoting the 60th (or 75th) anniversary of an event.

diamondback /-ˌbæk/ *n* a large rattlesnack with diamond-shaped markings.

dianthus /daɪˈænθəs/ *n* (*pl* **dianthuses**) any of a large genus of ornamental plants, including carnations and pinks.

diapason /ˌdaɪəˈpeɪzən/ or /-sən/ *n* the entire compass of a voice or instrument; a recognized musical standard of pitch; the foundation stops of an organ.

diaper /ˈdaɪpər/ *n see* **nappy**.

diaphanous /daɪˈæfənəs/ *adj* (*fabrics*) delicate, transparent.—**diaphanously** *adv*.—**diaphanousness** *n*.

diaphoretic /ˌdaɪəfəˈrɛtɪk/ *adj* causing profuse perspiration. • *n* a diaphoretic drug.

diaphragm /ˈdaɪəˌfræm/ *n* the midriff, a muscular structure separating the chest from the abdomen; any thin dividing membrane; a device for regulating the aperture of a camera lens; a contraceptive cap covering the cervix; a thin vibrating disk used in a telephone receiver, microphone, etc.—**diaphragmatic** *adj*.—**diaphragmatically** *adv*.

diarchy /ˈdaɪɑrki/ *n* (*pl* **diarchies**) government by two independent authorities.—*also* **dyarchy**.

diarist /ˈdaɪərɪst/ *n* one who keeps a diary; the author of a diary.

diarrhoea, diarrhea /ˌdaɪəˈriːə/ *n* excessive looseness of the bowels.—**diarrhoeal, diarrheal, diarrhoeic, diarrheic** *adj*.

diary /ˈdaɪəri/ *n* (*pl* **diaries**) a daily record of personal thoughts, events, or business appointments; a book for keeping a daily record.

Diaspora /daɪˈæspərə/ *n* the dispersion of the Jews after the Babylonian captivity; the Jewish communities outside Israel; (*without cap*) the dispersion of any peoples outside their native area.

diastase /ˈdaɪəˌsteɪz/ *n* any enzyme that converts starch into sugar.—**diastatic, diastasic** *adj*.

diastole /daɪˈæstəliː/ *n* the dilation of the chambers of the heart during which they fill with blood.—**diastolic** *adj*.

diatessaron /ˌdaɪəˈtɛsəˌrɒn/ *n* the combination of the four Gospels into a single narrative.

diathermancy /ˌdaɪəˈθərmənsi/ *n* the property of transmitting radiant heat.—**diathermanous** *adj*.

diathermic /-mɪk/ *adj* having diathermancy; allowing heat rays to pass freely.

diathermy /ˈdaɪəˌθərmi/ *n* the use of electric current to warm or destroy body tissues as part of medical treatment.

diathesis /daɪˈæθəsɪs/ *n* (*pl* **diatheses**) a constitutional tendency, *esp* to disease; a predisposing factor.

diatom /ˈdaɪəˌtɒm/ *n* a microscopic alga found in fresh and seawater and in soil.—**diatomaceous** *adj*.

diatomite /daɪˈætəˌmaɪt/ *n* soft earth formed from the shells of diatoms and used as a filter, etc.

diatonic /ˈdaɪəˌtɒnɪk/ *adj* (*mus*) using only the major and minor scales, as opposed to the chromatic scale.—**diatonically** *adv*.—**diatonicism** *n*.

diatribe /ˈdaɪəˌtraɪb/ *n* a lengthy and abusive verbal attack.

dib /dɪb/ *vti* (**dibbing, dibbed**) to dibble; (*fishing*) to drop bait gently into water; to dip lightly.

dibasic /daɪˈbeɪsɪk/ *adj* containing two atoms of hydrogen replaceable by a basic radical.—**dibasicity** *n*.

dibber /ˈdɪbər/ *n* a dibble.

dibble /-əl/ *n* a pointed tool used to make holes in the ground for seedlings. • *vt* to make a hole in the ground with a dibber.

dicast /ˈdaɪkæst/ *n* in ancient Athens, a juryman.

dice /daɪs/ *n* (*the pl of* **die**[2] *but used as sing*) a small cube with numbered sides used in games of chance. • *vt* to gamble using dice; to cut (food) into small cubes.

dicentra /daɪˈsɛntrə/ *n* a member of a genus of perennial plants with heart-shaped flowers.

dicephalous /daɪˈsɛfələs/ *adj* two-headed.

dicey /ˈdaɪsi/ *adj* (**dicier, diciest**) (*inf*) risky.

dichloride /daɪˈklɔraɪd/ *see* **bichloride**.

dichogamous /ˌdaɪkɒˈgæməs/, **dichogamic** /-mɪk/ *adj* (*bot*) with stamens and pistils maturing at different times, preventing self-fertilization.—**dichogamy** *n*.

dichotomy /daɪˈkɒtəmɪ/ *n* (*pl* **dichotomies**) a division into two parts.—**dichotomous, dichotomic** *adj*.

dichroic /daɪˈkroːɪk/, **dichroitic** /ˌdaɪkroːˈɪtɪk/ *adj* (*crystal*) showing two colours; dichromatic.

dichroism /ˈdaɪkroːɪzəm/ *n* the property by which a crystallized body exhibits different colours according to the direction of light transmitted through it.

dichromatic /ˌdaɪkroːˈmætɪk/ *adj* two-coloured.—*also* **dichroic**; being able to see only two of the three primary colours, colour-blind; (*biol*) having one of two varieties of seasonal coloration.—**dichromatism** *n*.

dichromic /ˌdaɪˈkroːmɪk/ *adj* seeing only two of the three primary colours, dichromatic.

dick /dɪk/ *n* (*sl*) a detective; (*sl*) a person.

dickens /ˈdɪkɪnz/ *interj* (*inf*) the devil.

dicker /ˈdɪkər/ *vi* to barter or trade on a small scale; to haggle.• *n* a barter; a deal; haggling.

dicky, dickey[1] /ˈdɪki/ *n* (*pl* **dickies, dickeys**) a false shirt-front; a seat at the back of a sports car.

dicky, dickey[2] *adj* (**dickier, dickiest**) (*sl*) shaky, unsound.

dicrotic /daɪˈkrɒtɪk/ *adj* having a double or secondary pulse beat.—**dicrotism** *n*.

dicta /ˈdɪktə/ *see* **dictum**.

Dictaphone /ˈdɪktəˌfoːn/ *n* (*trademark*) a machine that records dictation and later reproduces it for typing.

dictate /ˈdɪkteɪt/ *or* /dɪkˈteɪt/ *vt* to say or read for another person to write or for a machine to record; to pronounce, order with authority. • *vi* to give dictation; to give orders (to). • *n* an order, rule, or command; (*usu pl*) an impulse, ruling principle.

dictation /dɪkˈteɪʃən/ *n* the act of dictating words to be written down by another; the thing dictated; an authoritative utterance.

dictator /dɪkˈteɪtər/ *n* a ruler with absolute authority, *usu* acquired by force.

dictatorial /dɪktəˈtɔːrɪəl/ *adj* like a dictator; tyrannical; domineering.—**dictatorially** *adv*.

dictatorship /dɪkˈteɪtəˌʃɪp/ *n* the office or government of a dictator; a country governed by a dictator; absolute power.

diction /ˈdɪkʃən/ *n* a way of speaking, enunciation; a person's choice of words.

dictionary /ˈdɪkʃəˌneri/ *n* (*pl* **dictionaries**) a reference book containing the words of a language or branch of knowledge alphabetically arranged, with their meanings, pronunciation, origin, etc.

Dictograph /ˈdɪktəˌgræf/ *n* (*trademark*) a sound recording instrument used for recording or monitoring telephone conversations.

dictum /ˈdɪktəm/ *n* (*pl* **dictums, dicta**) an authoritative pronouncement.

did /dɪd/ *see* **do**.

Didache /ˈdɪdəˌkiː/ *n* the title of a 2nd-century AD treatise on Christian doctrine and order, discovered 1883.

didactic /daɪˈdæktɪk/ *or* /də-/ *adj* intended to teach; instructive; in a lecturing manner.—**didactically** *adv*.—**didacticism** *n*.

didactics /-tɪks/ *n* (*used as sing*) the art of teaching.

diddle /ˈdɪdəl/ *vi* (*sl*) to cheat.—**diddler** *n*.

didn't /ˈdɪdənt/ = did not.

didymium /dɪˈdɪmɪəm/ *n* a mixture of rare earths, formerly thought to be an element, used for colouring glass.

didymous /ˈdɪdəməs/ *adj* (*biol*) growing in pairs; paired or double.

die[1] /daɪ/ *vb* (**dying, died**) *vi* to cease existence; to become dead; to stop functioning; to feel a deep longing; (*with* **out**) to become extinct. • *vi* to experience a particular form of death.

die[2] *n* a dice.

die[3] *n* (*pl* **dies**) an engraved stamp for pressing coins; a casting mould; a tool used in cutting the threads of screws or bolts, etc.

diecious /daɪˈiːʃəs/ *see* **dioecious**.

diehard /ˈdaɪhɑːrd/ *n* a person who prolongs futile resistance, *usu* an extreme conservative.

dielectric /ˌdaɪəˈlektrɪk/ *adj* nonconducting. • *n* any medium, as glass, that transmits electric force by induction.

dieresis /daɪˈerəsɪs/ *n* (*pl* **diereses**) a sign (¨) placed over the second of two separate vowels to show that each has a separate sound in pronunciation, as *Zoë*; a division in a line of verse.—*also* **diaeresis**.—**dieretic, diaeretic** *adj*.

diesel /ˈdiːzəl/ *n* a vehicle driven by a diesel engine.

diesel engine *n* an internal combustion engine in which ignition is produced by the heat of highly compressed air alone.

diesel oil *n* a form of petroleum for diesel engines, ignited by the heat of compression.

diesis /ˈdaɪəsɪs/ (*pl* **dieses**) *n* the double dagger used in printing (‡); (*mus*) the difference between a greater and lesser semitone.

diet[1] /ˈdaɪət/ *n* food selected to adjust weight, to control illness, etc; the food and drink usually consumed by a person or animal. • *vt* to put on a diet. • *vi* to eat according to a special diet.—**dieter** *n*.

diet[2] *n* a legislative assembly in some countries.

dietary /ˈdaɪəˌteri/ *adj* pertaining to a diet.

dietetic /-ˈtetɪk/, **dietetical** /-əl/ *adj* regulating food or diet.—**dietetically** *adv*.

dietetics /-ɪks/ *n* (*used as sing*) the scientific study of diet and nutrition.

differ /ˈdɪfər/ *vi* to be unlike, distinct (from); to disagree.

difference /ˈdɪfrəns/ *n* the act or state of being unlike; disparity; a distinguishing feature; the amount or manner of being different; the result of the subtraction of one quantity from another; a disagreement or argument.

different /-ənt/ *adj* distinct, separate; unlike, not the same; unusual.—**differently** *adv*.

differentia /ˌdɪfərˈenʃɪə/ *n* (*pl* **differentiae**) (*logic*) what distinguishes a thing from others, *esp* one subclass from another of the same class.

differential /-ʃəl/ *adj* of or showing a difference; (*math*) relating to increments in given functions. • *n* something that marks the difference between comparable things; the difference in wage rates for different types of labour, *esp* within an industry.—**differentially** *adv*.

differential calculus *n* the branch of calculus dealing with the rate of change of given functions with respect to their variables.

differential gear *n* a type of gear that allows powered wheels in a motor vehicle to turn at different speeds (*eg* when cornering).

differentiate /ˌdɪfəˈrenʃɪˌeɪt/ *vt* to make different; to become specialized; to note differences; (*math*) to calculate the derivative of.

differentiation /-ənʃɪˈeɪʃən/ *n* the act of differentiating; (*biol*) specialization; (*math*) the calculation of a differential.

difficult /ˈdɪfɪˌkəlt/ *adj* hard to understand; hard to make, do, or carry out; not easy to please.

difficulty /-ˌkəlti/ *n* (*pl* **difficulties**) the state of being difficult; a problem, etc that is hard to deal with; an obstacle; a troublesome situation; a disagreement.

diffidence /ˈdɪfədəns/ *n* lack of confidence in one's own ability; shyness, modesty.

diffident /-dənt/ *adj* shy, lacking self-confidence, not assertive.—**diffidently** *adv*.

diffract /dɪˈfrækt/ *vti* to cause, or cause to undergo, diffraction.—**diffractive** *adj*.

diffraction /-ʃən/ *n* the breaking up of a ray of light into coloured bands of the spectrum, or into a series of light and dark bands.

diffuse /dɪˈfjuːz/ *vt* to spread widely in all directions. • *vti* (*gases, fluids, small particles*) to intermingle. • *adj* spread widely, not concentrated; wordy, not concise.—**diffusely** *adv*.

diffusion /-ən/ *n* the act of diffusing; a spreading abroad; the passing by osmosis through animal membranes.

diffusive /-sɪv/ *adj* extending; spreading widely.—**diffusively** *adv*.—**diffusiveness** *n*.

dig /dɪg/ *vt* (**digging, dug**) to use a tool or hands, claws, etc in making a hole in the ground; to unearth by digging; to excavate; to investigate; to thrust (into); to nudge; (*sl*) to understand, approve. • *n* (*sl*) a thrust; an archaeological excavation; a cutting remark.

digamist /ˈdɪgəmɪst/ *n* one who marries for a second time.—**digamous** *adj*.—**digamy** *n*.

digamma /daɪˈgæmə/ *n* a letter of the ancient Greek alphabet, in sound approaching that of V or W.

digastric /daɪˈgæstrɪk/ *adj* (*muscle*) with two swollen ends. • *n* a neck muscle that helps lower the jaw.

digenesis /daɪˈdʒenəsɪs/ *n* (*biol*) an alternating process of reproduction, sexual in one generation, asexual in the following.—**digenetic** *adj*.

digest[1] /daɪˈdʒest/ *or* /də-/ *vt* to convert (food) into assimilable form; to reduce (facts, laws, etc) to convenient form by classifying or summarizing; to form a clear view of (a situation) by reflection. • *vi* to become digested.

digest[2] *n* an abridgment of any written matter; a periodical synopsis of published or broadcast material.

digester /-tər/ *n* one who makes a digest; a thing that digests; an apparatus for extracting the essence of a substance by heat.

digestible /-təbəl/ *adj* capable of being digested.—**digestibility, digestibly** *adv.*

digestion /-ʃən/ *n* the act or process of digesting.—**digestional** *adj.*

digestive /-tɪv/ *adj* pertaining to, performing or aiding digestion. • *n* a thing that aids digestion; a sweet wholemeal biscuit.

digger /ˈdɪgər/ *n* an implement or machine for digging; (*inf*) an Australian or New Zealander (used as a form of address).

digispeak /ˌdɪdʒɪˈpiːk/ *n* (*comput*) the use of acronyms in online communication in which frequently-used terms or phrases are abbreviated.

digit /ˈdɪdʒɪt/ *n* any of the basic counting units of a number system, including zero; a human finger or toe.

digital /ˈdɪdʒətəl/ *adj* of, having or using digits; using numbers rather than a dial to display measurements; of or pertaining to a digital computer or digital recording.—**digitally** *adv.*

digital audio tape *n* a magnetic tape capable of being used in digital recording, giving high-quality audio reproduction.

digital clock *n* a clock that displays the time in figures.

digital computer *n* a computer that processes information in the form of characters and digits in electronic binary code.

digitalin /ˌdɪdʒɪˈtælɪn/ *n* a poison extracted from foxglove leaves.

digitalis /-lɪs/ *n* a drug derived from foxglove leaves, used as a heart stimulant.

digital recording *n* the conversion of sound into discrete electronic pulses (representing binary digits) for recording.

digital watch *n* a watch that displays the time in figures.

digitate /ˈdɪdʒɪˌteɪt/, **digitated** /-ɪd/ *adj* having separate fingers or toes.—**digitation** *n.*

digitigrade /ˈdɪdʒɪtɪˌgreɪd/ *adj* (cats, dogs, etc) walking on the toes. • *n* an animal that walks in this way.

digitize /ˈdɪdʒɪˌtaɪz/ *vt* (*data, images*) to translate into digital form for input into a computer.—**digitization** *n.*

diglot /ˈdaɪˌglɒt/ *adj* bilingual. • *n* a book with the text in two languages.

dignified /ˌdɪgnəˈfaɪd/ *adj* possessing dignity; noble; serious.—**dignifiedly** *adv.*

dignify /ˌdɪgnəˈfaɪ/ *vt* (**dignifying, dignified**) to confer dignity; to exalt; to add the appearance of distinction (to something).

dignitary /ˈdɪgnəˌteri/ *n* (*pl* **dignitaries**) a person in a high position or rank.

dignity /ˈdɪgnɪti/ *n* (*pl* **dignities**) noble, serious, formal in manner and appearance; sense of self-respect, worthiness; a high rank, *eg* in the government.

digraph /ˈdaɪgræf/ *n* a combination of two sounds or characters to represent one simple sound, as *ph* in *phone*.—**digraphic** *adj.*—**digraphically** *adv.*

digress /daɪˈgres/ *vi* to stray from the main subject in speaking or writing.—**digression** *n.*

digressive /-ɪv/ *adj* tending to digress; deviating from the subject.—**digressively** *adv.*—**digressiveness** *n.*

dihedral /daɪˈhiːdrəl/ *adj* (*angle*) having two intersecting plane faces or sides. • *n* a dihedral angle; the angle between aircraft wings for improving stability.

dik-dik /ˈdɪkdɪk/ *n* a small East African antelope.

dike[1] /daɪk/ *see* **dyke**[2].

dike[2] *n* an embankment to prevent flooding or form a barrier to the sea; a ditch; a causeway.—*also* **dyke**.

dilapidate /dɪˈlæpɪˌdeɪt/ *vt* to bring into partial ruin by neglect or misuse. • *vi* to become dilapidated.

dilapidated /-əd/ *adj* in a state of disrepair; shabby.

dilapidation /dɪˌlæpɪˈdeɪʃən/ *n* a state of damage or disrepair.

dilatation /ˌdaɪləˈteɪʃən/ *n* a dilating, *esp* as part of a medical procedure; an abnormal enlargement of an organ, etc.—**dilatational** *adj.*

dilatation and curettage *n* a surgical procedure for opening the cervix and scraping the uterus.

dilate /ˈdaɪˌleɪt/ *vti* to make wider or larger; to increase the width of; to expand, amplify, enlarge; to extend in time, protract, prolong, lengthen. • *vi* to become wider or larger; to spread out, widen, enlarge, expand; to discourse or write at large; to enlarge.—**dilatable** *adj.*—**dilatabilty** *n.*

dilation /daɪˈleɪʃən/ *n* the action or process of dilating; something dilated.

dilator /daɪˈleɪtər/ *n* that which dilates; a surgical instrument for opening or expanding an orifice; a muscle that dilates the parts on which it acts.

dilatory /ˈdɪləˌtori/ *adj* tardy; causing or meant to cause delay.—**dilatorily** *adv.*—**dilatoriness** *n.*

dilemma /dɪˈlemə/ *n* a situation where each of two alternative courses is undesirable; any difficult problem or choice.—**dilemmatic** *adj.*

dilettante /ˌdɪləˈtɒnt/ or /ˈdɪlə-/, /-ˌtænti/ *n* (*pl* **dilettantes, dilettanti**) a person who dabbles in a subject for amusement only.

diligence[1] /ˈdɪlɪdʒəns/ *n* careful attention; assiduity; industry.

diligence[2] /ˈdɪlɪdʒəns/, *Fr* /diːliːˈʒɑ̃s/ *n* (*formerly*) a French stagecoach.

diligent /ˈdɪlɪdʒənt/ *adj* industrious; done with proper care and effort.—**diligently** *adv.*

dill /dɪl/ *n* a yellow-flowered herb whose leaves and seeds are used for flavouring and in medicines.

dillydally /ˈdɪliˌdæli/ *vi* (**dillydallying, dillydallied**) (*inf*) to dawdle, loiter.

dilute /daɪˈluːt/ or /dɪ-/ *vt* to thin down, *esp* by mixing with water; to weaken the strength of. • *adj* diluted.—**diluter, dilutor** *n.*—**diluteness** *n.*

dilution /-ˈluːʃən/ *n* the act of diluting; a weak liquid.

diluvial /daɪˈluːviəl/ or /də-/, **diluvian** /-ən/ *adj* pertaining to, produced by, or resulting from, a deluge or flood, *esp* the Flood of the Bible.

diluvium /-viəm/ (*pl* **diluviums, diluvia**) *n* (*formerly*) geological deposits caused by water action, drift.

dim /dɪm/ *adj* (**dimmer, dimmest**) faintly lit; not seen, heard, understood, etc clearly; gloomy; unfavourable; (*inf*) stupid. • *vti* (**dimming, dimmed**) to make or cause to become dark.—**dimly** *adv.*—**dimness** *n.*

dime /daɪm/ *n* a US or Canadian coin worth ten cents.

dimension /dəˈmenʃən/ or /daɪ-/ *n* any linear measurement of width, length, or thickness; extent; size.

dimensional /-əl/ *adj* of or pertaining to dimension or magnitude; (*geom*) of or pertaining to (a specified number of) dimensions.—**dimensionality** *n.*—**dimensionally** *adv.*

dimerous /ˈdaɪmərəs/ *adj* (*flowers*) having two members in each whorl; (*insects*) having a foot composed of two parts.

dimeter /ˈdɪmɪtər/ *n* (a line of) verse of two measures, a measure being one or two feet, according to the metre.

diminish /dɪˈmɪnɪʃ/ *vti* to make or become smaller in size, amount, or importance.—**diminishable** *adj.*—**diminishment** *n.*

diminuendo /dəˌmɪnjuːˈendo/ *see* **decrescendo**.

diminution /ˌdɪmɪˈnjuːʃən/ or /-njuː-/ *n* act or process of being made smaller.

diminutive /dɪˈmɪnjutɪv/ or /-njə-/ *adj* very small. • *n* a word formed by a suffix to mean small (*eg duckling*) or to convey affection (*eg Freddie*).

dimity /ˈdɪməti/ (*pl* **dimities**) *n* a light, strong striped or figured cotton cloth used for curtains, etc.

dimmer /ˈdɪmər/ *n* a switch for reducing the brightness of an electric light.

dimorphism /daɪˈmɔrfɪzəm/ *n* the quality of assuming, crystallizing or existing in two forms.—**dimorphic, dimorphous** *adj.*

dimple /ˈdɪmpəl/ *n* a small hollow, *usu* on the cheek or chin. • *vti* to make or become dimpled; to reveal dimples.—**dimply** *adj.*

dimwit /ˈdɪmwɪt/ *n* (*inf*) an idiotic person, a fool.—**dimwitted** *adj.*—**dimwittedly** *adv.*—**dimwittedness** *n.*

din /dɪn/ *n* a loud persistent noise. • *vt* (**dinning, dinned**) to make a din; (*with* **into**) to instil by continual repetition.

dinar /ˈdɪnɑr/ *n* the monetary unit of Yugoslavia and various North African countries.

dine /daɪn/ *vi* to eat dinner. • *vt* to entertain to dinner.

diner /ˈdaɪnər/ *n* a person who dines; a dining car on a train; a small, cheap eating place.

dinette /daɪˈnet/ *n* a small area in a house for eating in.

ding /dɪŋ/ *vi* to sound, as a bell, with a continuous monotonous tone. • *vt* to impress by noisy repetition. • *n* the ringing sound of a bell.

ding-dong /ˈdɪŋˌdɒŋ/ *n* the sound of a metallic body produced by blows, as a bell; (*inf*) a violent argument. • *adj* characterized by a rapid succession of blows; (*insults, etc*) vigorously maintained. • *vi* to ring as or like a bell. • *vt* to assail with constant repetition; to repeat with mechanical regularity.

dinghy /'dɪŋi/ or /'dɪŋgi/ *n* (*pl* **dinghies**) a small open boat propelled by oars or sails; a small inflatable boat.

dingle /'dɪŋgəl/ *n* a small wooded hollow.

dingo /'dɪŋgo:/ *n* (*pl* **dingoes**) an Australian wild dog.

dingy /'dɪndʒi/ *adj* (**dingier, dingiest**) dirty-looking, shabby.— **dingily** *adv*.—**dinginess** *n*.

dining car *n* a restaurant car on a train.

dining room *n* a room used for eating meals.

dinkum /'dɪŋkəm/ *adj* genuine, honest.

dinky /'dɪŋki/ *adj* (**dinkier, dinkiest**) (*inf*) small; of no consequence, unimportant; (*Scot*) neat and attractive, smart.

dinner /'dɪnər/ *n* the principal meal of the day; a formal meal in honour of a person or occasion.

dinner jacket *n* a tuxedo.

dinosaur /'daɪnə,sɔr/ *n* any of an order of extinct reptiles, typically enormous in size; (*inf*) a person or thing regarded as outdated.

dinothere /'daɪnə,θiːr/ *n* a huge, extinct animal like an elephant.

dint /dɪnt/ *n* (*arch*) a mark left by a blow, a dent; **by dint of** by force of. • *vt* make a dint in.

diocesan /daɪ'ɒsɪsən/ or /-zən/ *adj* of or pertaining to a diocese; the bishop of a diocese.

diocese /'daɪəsiːs/ *n* the district over which a bishop has authority.

diode /'daɪ,o:d/ *n* a semiconductor device for converting alternating to direct current; a basic thermionic valve with two electrodes.

dioecious /daɪ'iːʃəs/ *adj* (*bot, zool*) having male and female organs respectively in separate individuals.—*also* **diecious**.

dioptase /daɪ'ɒp,teɪs/ *n* a vitreous emerald green ore of copper.

dioptre, diopter /daɪ'ɒptər/ *n* a unit for measuring the refractive power of a lens.

dioptric /daɪ'ɒptrɪk/, **dioptrical** /-əl/ *adj* assisting vision by means of the refraction of light in viewing distant objects.

dioptrics /daɪ'ɒp,trɪks/ *n* (*used as sing*) the area of optics dealing with the refraction of light.

diorama /,daɪə'ræmə/ *n* a miniature three-dimensional scene, *esp* in a museum; any small-scale model with figures; a device for producing changing effects using special lighting on a translucent picture.—**dioramic** *adj*.

diorite /'daɪə,rɔɪt/ *n* a granite-like rock consisting of felspar and hornblende.

dioxide /daɪ'ɒks,aɪd/ *n* an oxide with two molecules of oxygen to one molecule of the other constituents.

dip /dɪp/ *vt* (**dipping, dipped**) to put (something) under the surface (as of a liquid) and lift quickly out again; to immerse (as a sheep in an antiseptic solution). • *vi* to go into water and come out quickly; to suddenly drop down or sink out of sight; to read superficially; to slope downwards. • *n* a dipping of any kind; a sudden drop; a mixture in which to dip something.

dip., Dip. *abbr* = diploma.

diphtheria /dɪf'θɪːrɪə/ or /dɪp-/ *n* an acute infectious disease causing inflammation of the throat and breathing difficulties.—**diphtherial** *adj*.

diphtheritic /,dɪfθə'rɪtɪk/, **diphtheric** /-'θerɪk/ *adj* of or like diphtheria; affected by diphtheria.

diphthong /'dɪfθɒŋ/ or /'dɪp-/ *n* the union of two vowel sounds pronounced in one syllable; a ligature.—**diphthongal** *adj*.

diphyllous /daɪ'fɪləs/ *adj* (*bot*) having two leaves.

diploblastic /,dɪplə'blæstɪk/ *adj* (*zool*) with two germ layers.

diplodocus /dɪp'lɒdəkəs/ or /-'lo:də-/ (*pl* **diplodocuses**) *n* an extinct reptile with a very long tail and neck and a small head.

diploe /'dɪplo:,iː/ *n* the soft spongy tissue between the two layers of the skull.—**diploic** *adj*.

diploma /dɪ'plo:mə/ *n* (*pl* **diplomas**) a certificate given by a college or university to its graduating students; the course of study leading to a diploma; (*pl often* **diplomata**) an official document, a charter.

diplomacy /dɪ'plo:məsi/ *n* (*pl* **diplomacies**) the management of relations between nations; skill in handling affairs without arousing hostility.

diplomat /'dɪplə,mæt/ *n* a person employed or skilled in diplomacy.

diplomatic /,dɪplə'mætɪk/, **diplomatical** /-kə/ *adj* of diplomacy; employing tact and conciliation; tactful.—**diplomatically** *adv*.

diplomatic corps *n* all the ambassadors at a particular capital, the corps diplomatique.

diplomatic immunity *n* the exemption from local laws and taxes accorded to foreign diplomats in the country where they are stationed.

diplomatist *n* a diplomat.

dipole /'daɪ,po:l/ *n* two equal and opposite electric charges or magnetic poles a small distance apart; a molecule in which the centres of negative and positive charge do not coincide; a directional aerial consisting of two metal rods.—**dipolar** *adj*.

dipper /'dɪpər/ *n* a ladle; any of various diving birds.

dippy /'dɪpi/ *adj* (**dippier, dippiest**) (*sl*) eccentric; crazy.

dipso /'dɪpso:/ *n* (*pl* **dipsos**) (*inf*) a dipsomaniac.

dipsomania /,dɪpsə'meɪnɪə/ *n* a compulsive craving for alcohol.

dipsomaniac /-'meɪnɪ,æk/ *n* a person with an uncontrollable craving for alcohol. • *adj* of or having dipsomania.—**dipsomaniacal** *adj*.

dipstick /'dɪpstɪk/ *n* a rod with graduated markings to measure fluid level.

dipteral /'dɪptərəl/ *adj* (*archit*) having a double row of columns, as a temple, etc.

dipteran /'dɪptərən/ *n* any of a large order of insects including flies, mosquitoes, midges, having one pair of true wings and piercing or sucking mouthparts.

dipterous /'dɪptərəs/ *adj* (*insects*) two-winged; (*seeds*) with appendages resembling wings.

diptych /'dɪptɪk/ *n* a pair of paintings or carvings on two panels hinged together.

dire /daɪr/ *adj* dreadful; ominous; desperately urgent.—**direly** *adv*.—**direness** *n*.

direct /dɪ'rekt/ or /daɪ-/ *adj* straight; in an unbroken line, with nothing in between; frank; truthful. • *vt* to manage, to control; to tell or show the way; to point to, to aim at; (*a letter or parcel*) to address; to carry out the organizing and supervision of; to train and lead performances; to command. • *vi* to determine a course; to act as a director.—**directness** *n*.

direct current *n* an electric current that flows in one direction only.

direct debit *n* a pre-arranged regular debit of a bank account, *usu* to make a recurring payment.

direction /dɪ'rekʃən/ or /daɪ-/ *n* management, control; order, command; a knowing or telling what to do, where to go, etc; any way in which one may face or point; (*pl*) instructions.

directional /-ʃənəl/ *adj* relating to direction in space; (*aerial*) transmitting in one direction only.—**directionality** *n*.—**directionally** *adv*.

direction finder *n* a device used to locate the direction of incoming radio signals, used in navigation.

directive /dɪ'rektɪv/ or /daɪ-/ *adj* directing; authoritatively guiding or ruling. • *n* an order, instruction.

directly /dɪ'rektli/ or /daɪ-/ *adv* in a direct manner; immediately; in a short while.

Directoire /,dɪrek'twar/ *adj* of or imitating the low-necked high-waisted dress or curving oriental furniture of the Directoire or Directory period in France (1795–99).

director /dɪ'rektər/ or /daɪ-/ *n* person who directs, *esp* the production of a show for stage or screen; one of the persons directing the affairs of a company or an institution.—**directorial** *adj*.—**directorship** *n*.

directorate /-ət/ *n* a board of directors; the position of a director.— *also* **directorship**.

directory /-təri/ or /daɪ-/ *n* (*pl* **directories**) an alphabetical or classified list, as of telephone numbers, members of an organization, charities, etc.

direct tax *n* a tax paid by the actual person or organization on which it is levied.

direful /'daɪr,fʊl/ *adj* dreadful, dire.—**direfully** *adv*.

dirge /'dərdʒ/ *n* a song or hymn played or sung at a funeral; a slow, mournful piece of music.

dirigible /'dɪrɪdʒəbəl/ or /dɪ'rɪdʒ-/ *adj* able to be steered. • *n* an airship.

dirk /dərk/ *n* a small dagger, *esp* as formerly worn by Scottish Highlanders.

dirndl /'dərndəl/ *n* a woman's full skirt with a tight waistband.

dirt /dərt/ *n* filth; loose earth; obscenity; scandal. • *adj* made of dirt.

dirt-cheap /-,tʃiːp/ *adj* (*inf*) very cheap.

dirty /'dərti/ *adj* (**dirtier, dirtiest**) filthy; unclean; dishonest; mean; (*weather*) stormy; obscene. • *vti* (**dirtying, dirtied**) to make or become dirty.—**dirtily** *adv*.—**dirtiness** *n*.

dis- /dɪs/ *prefix* not, the reverse of; away from, apart; deprive of.

disability /ˌdɪsəˈbɪləti/ or /ˈdɪs-/ *n* (*pl* **disabilities**) a lack of physical, mental or social fitness; something that disables, a handicap.

disable /dɪsˈeɪbəl/ *vt* to make useless; to cripple; (*law*) to disqualify.—**disablement** *n*.

disabled /dɪsˈeɪbəld/ *adj* having a physical handicap.

disabuse /ˌdɪsəˈbjuːz/ *vt* to free from a mistaken impression.

disaccord /ˌdɪsəˈkɔːd/ *vi* to disagree, to be at variance. • *n* disagreement, incongruity.

disadvantage /ˌdɪsədˈvæntɪdʒ/ *n* an unfavourable condition or situation; loss, damage. • *vt* to put at a disadvantage.

disadvantaged /-tɪdʒd/ *adj* deprived or discriminated against in social and economic terms.

disadvantageous /ˌdɪsˌædvənˈteɪdʒəs/ *adj* causing disadvantage; unfavourable.—**disadvantageously** *adv*.

disaffected /ˌdɪsəˈfɛktɪd/ *adj* discontented, no longer loyal.—**disaffectedly** *adv*.—**disaffection** *n*.

disaffirm /ˌdɪsəˈfɪrm/ *vt* (*law*) to set aside, to reverse.—**disaffirmation** *n*.

disafforest /ˌdɪsəˈfɒrəst/ or /ˈdɪsəˌfɔːr-/ *vt* to change from the legal state of forest to that of ordinary land; to remove forest from.—**disafforestation** *n*.

disagree /ˌdɪsəˈɡriː/ *vi* (**disagreeing, disagreed**) to differ in opinion; to quarrel; (*with* **with**) to have a bad effect on.—**disagreement** *n*.

disagreeable /-əbəl/ *adj* nasty, bad tempered.—**disagreeableness** *n*.—**disagreeably** *adv*.

disagreement /-mənt/ *n* refusal to agree; a difference; a quarrel or dispute.

disallow /ˌdɪsəˈlaʊ/ *vt* to refuse to allow or to accept the truth or value of.—**disallowance** *n*.

disannul /ˌdɪsəˈnɛl/ *vt* (**disannulling, disannulled**) to annul completely; to make void.

disappear /ˌdɪsəˈpɪːr/ *vi* to pass from sight completely; to fade into nothing.—**disappearance** *n*.

disappoint /ˌdɪsəˈpɔɪnt/ *vt* to fail to fulfil the hopes of (a person).—**disappointed** *adj*.—**disappointing** *adj*.—**disappointingly** *adv*.

disappointment /-mənt/ *n* the frustration of one's hopes; annoyance due to failure; a person or thing that disappoints.

disapprobation /ˌdɪsˌæprəˈbeɪʃən/ *n* disapproval, condemnation.

disapproval /ˌdɪsəˈpruːvəl/ *n* the action or fact of disapproving; condemnation of what is wrong.

disapprove /ˌdɪsəˈpruːv/ *vti* to express or have an unfavourable opinion (of).—**disapprovingly** *adv*.

disarm /dɪsˈɑːrm/ *vt* to deprive of weapons or means of defence; to defuse (a bomb); to conciliate. • *vi* to abolish or reduce national armaments.

disarmament /-ˈɑːrməmənt/ *n* the reduction or abolition of a country's armed forces and weaponry.

disarming /-ˈɑːrmɪŋ/ *adj* allaying opposition, conciliating; ingratiating, endearing.—**disarmingly** *adv*.

disarrange /ˌdɪsəˈreɪndʒ/ *vt* to make untidy; to disorganize.—**disarrangement** *n*.

disarray /ˌdɪsəˈreɪ/ *n* disorder, confusion; undress. • *vt* to put into disorder.

disarticulate /ˌdɪsɑːrˈtɪkjʊˌleɪt/ *vt* to separate, to take to pieces.—**disarticulation** *n*.—**disarticulator** *n*.

disaster¹ /dɪˈzæstər/ *n* a devastating and sudden misfortune; utter failure.—**disastrous** *adj*.—**disastrously** *adv*.

disavow /ˌdɪsəˈvaʊ/ *vt* to deny, disclaim; to repudiate.—**disavowal** *n*.—**disavower** *n*.

disband /dɪsˈbænd/ *vt* to disperse; to break up and separate.—**disbandment** *n*.

disbar /dɪsˈbɑːr/ *vt* (**disbarring, disbarred**) to deprive (a barrister) of the right to practice.—**disbarment** *n*.

disbelief /ˌdɪsbəˈliːf/ *n* a disbelieving; mental rejection of a statement or assertion; positive unbelief.

disbelieve /-ˈliːv/ *vt* to believe to be a lie. *vi* to have no faith (in).—**disbeliever** *n*.

disburden /dɪsˈbɜːrdən/ *vt* to throw off a burden; to relieve of anything annoying or oppressive. • *vi* to ease one's mind.—**disburdenment** *n*.

disburse /dɪsˈbɜːrs/ *vt* to pay out.—**disburser** *n*.

disbursement /-mənt/ *n* a paying out (of money); expenditure.

discalced /dɪsˈkælst/ *adj* (*friars, etc*) barefoot, wearing sandals.

discard /dɪsˈkɑːrd/ *vti* to cast off, get rid of; (*cards*) to throw away a card from one's hand. • *n* something discarded; (*cards*) a discarded card.

disc brake, disk brake *n* a brake in which two flat discs press against a central plate on the wheel hub.

discern /dɪˈsɜːrn/ *vt* to perceive; to see clearly.—**discernible** *adj*.—**discernibly** *adv*.

discerning /-ɪŋ/ *adj* discriminating; perceptive.—**discerningly** *adv*.—**discernment** *n*.

discharge /dɪsˈtʃɑːrdʒ/ *vt* to unload; to send out, emit; to release, acquit; to dismiss from employment; to shoot a gun; to fulfil, as duties. • *vi* to unload; (*gun*) to be fired; (*fluid*) to pour out. • *n* the act or process of discharging; something that is discharged; an authorization for release, acquittal, dismissal, etc.

disciple /dɪˈsaɪpəl/ *n* a person who believes in and helps to spread another's teachings, a follower; (*with cap*) one of the twelve apostles of Christ.—**discipleship** *n*.

disciplinarian /ˌdɪsɪplɪˈnɛriən/ *n* a person who insists on strict discipline.

disciplinary /ˈdɪsɪplɪˌnɛri/ *adj* of or for discipline.

discipline /ˈdɪsɪplɪn/ *n* a field of learning; training and conditioning to produce obedience and self-control; punishment; the maintenance of order and obedience as a result of punishment; a system of rules of behaviour. • *vt* to punish to enforce discipline; to train by instruction; to bring under control.—**disciplinable** *adj*.—**disciplinal** *adj*.

disc jockey *n* (*inf*) a person who announces records on a programme of broadcast music, or in discotheques.

disclaim /dɪsˈkleɪm/ *vi* to deny connection with; to renounce all legal claim to.

disclaimer /-ər/ *n* a denial of legal responsibility; a written statement embodying this.

disclose /dɪsˈkloːz/ *vt* to bring into the open, to reveal.—**disclosure** *n*.

disclosure /-ˈkloːʒər/ *n* the act of revealing anything secret; discovery; an uncovering.

disco /ˈdɪskoː/ *n* (*pl* **discos**) (*inf*) a discotheque.

discography /dɪsˈkɒɡrəfi/ *n* (*pl* **discographies**) a classified list or survey of gramophone records or CDs.—**discographer** *n*.

discoid /ˈdɪskɔɪd/ *adj* round and flat like a disc.—*also* **discoidal**. • *n* anything with the shape of a disc.

discolour, discolor /dɪsˈkʌlər/ *vti* to ruin the colour of; to fade, stain.—**discolouration** *n*.

discomfit /dɪsˈkʌmfɪt/ *vt* to defeat; to rout; to frustrate; to thwart; to disconcert.

discomfiture /-fɪtʃər/ *n* defeat; disappointment; confusion.

discomfort /dɪsˈkʌmfərt/ or /ˈdɪs-/ *n* uneasiness; something causing this. • *vt* to make uncomfortable; to make apprehensive or uneasy.

discommode /ˌdɪskəˈmoːd/ *vt* to put to inconvenience.

discompose /ˌdɪskəmˈpoːz/ *vt* to disturb the calmness of; to ruffle.—**discomposure** *n*.

disconcert /ˌdɪskənˈsɜːrt/ *vt* to confuse; to upset; to embarrass.—**disconcerting** *adj*.—**disconcertingly** *adv*.

disconnect /ˌdɪskəˈnɛkt/ *vt* to separate or break the connection of.—**disconnection** *n*.

disconnected /-əd/ *adj* not connected, detached; disjointed; incoherent.—**disconnectedly** *adv*.—**disconnectedness** *n*.

disconsolate /dɪsˈkɒnsələt/ *adj* miserable; dejected.—**disconsolately** *adv*.—**disconsolation** *n*.

discontent /ˌdɪskənˈtɛnt/ *n* lack of contentment, dissatisfaction.—*also* **discontentment**. • *adj* not content; dissatisfied; discontented. • *vt* to deprive of contentment; to dissatisfy.

discontented /-əd/ *adj* feeling discontent; unhappy, unsatisfied.—**discontentedly** *adv*.

discontinuance /ˌdɪskənˈtɪnjuːəns/ *n* a discontinuing or breaking off; interruption; (*law*) the termination of a suit by the plaintiff.

discontinuation /-ˈtɪnjuːˈeɪʃən/ *n* a discontinuing; discontinuance; a breach or interruption of continuity.

discontinue /-ˈtɪnjuː/ *vti* to stop or come to a stop; to give up, *esp* the production of something; (*law*) to terminate (a suit).

discontinuity /ˌdɪskɒntɪˈnjuːiti/ *n* (*pl* **discontinuities**) a being discontinuous; lack or failure of continuity or sequence; a break or gap in a structure; (*geol*) a point at which the character of the earth alters abruptly; (*math*) a function that is discontinuous.

discontinuous /ˌdɪskən'tɪnjuːəs/ *adj* not continuous, incoherent, intermittent; (*math*) of a function that varies discontinuously and whose differential coefficient may therefore become infinite.—**discontinuously** *adv*.

discord /'dɪskɔrd/ *n* lack of agreement, strife; (*mus*) a lack of harmony; harsh clashing sounds.

discordant /-dənt/ *adj* at variance; inharmonious; jarring; incongruous.—**discordance, discordancy** *n*.—**discordantly** *adv*.

discotheque, discothèque /'dɪskə,tɛk/ *n* an occasion when people gather to dance to recorded pop music; a club or party, etc where this takes place; equipment for playing such music.

discount /'dɪskaunt/ *n* a reduction in the amount or cost; the percentage charged for doing this. • *vt* to deduct from the amount, cost; to allow for exaggeration; to disregard; to make less effective by anticipation. • *vi* to make and give discounts.—**discountable** *adj*.—**discounter** *n*.

discountenance /dɪs'kauntənəns/ *vt* to refuse moral support to; to discourage, frown upon.

discourage /dɪs'kərɪdʒ/ *vt* to deprive of the will or courage (to do something); to try to prevent; to hinder.—**discouragingly** *adv*.

discouragement /-mənt/ *n* the action or fact of discouraging; the state or feeling of being discouraged; something that discourages; a disheartening or deterring influence.

discourse /'dɪskɔrs/ *n* a formal speech or writing; conversation. • *vi* to talk or write about.

discourteous /dɪs'kɔrtɪəs/ *adj* lacking in courtesy, rude.—**discourteously** *adv*.—**discourteousness** *n*.

discourtesy /dɪs'kɔrtəsi/ *n* (*pl* **discourtesies**) lack of courtesy or consideration; rudeness; an inconsiderate or rude act.

discover /dɪs'kəvər/ *vt* to see, find or learn of for the first time.—**discoverable** *adj*.—**discoverer** *n*.

discovert /dɪs'kəvərt/ *adj* (*law*) (*single woman, divorcée, widow*) without a husband.—**discoverture** *n*.

discovery /dɪs'kəvəri/ *n* (*pl* **discoveries**) the act of discovering or state of being discovered; something discovered; (*law*) a process obliging on the parties to an action to disclose relevant facts or documents.

discredit /dɪs'krɛdɪt/ *n* damage to a reputation; doubt; disgrace; lack of credibility. • *vt* to damage the reputation of; to cast doubt on the authority or credibility of.

discreditable /dɪs'krɛdɪtəbəl/ *adj* bringing discredit or disgrace.—**discreditably** *adv*.

discreet /dɪs'kriːt/ *adj* wisely cautious, prudent; unobtrusive.—**discreetly** *adv*.—**discreetness** *n*.

discrepancy /dɪs'krɛpənsi/ *n* (*pl* **discrepancies**) difference; a disagreement, as between figures in a total.

discrepant /-pənt/ *adj* inconsistent; not tallying.—**discrepantly** *adv*.

discrete /dɪs'kriːt/ *adj* individually distinct; discontinuous.—**discretely** *adv*.—**discreteness** *n*.

discretion /dɪs'krɛʃən/ *n* the freedom to judge or to choose; prudence; wise judgment; skill.

discretionary /-ˌɛri/ *adj* left to or done at one's own discretion.

discriminate /dɪ'skrɪmɪ,neɪt/ *vi* to be discerning in matters of taste or judgment; to make a distinction; to treat differently, *esp* unfavourably due to prejudice.

discriminating /-ˌneɪtɪŋ/ *adj* judicious; discerning; discriminatory.—**discriminatingly** *adv*.

discrimination /dɪˌskrɪmɪ'neɪʃən/ *n* prejudicial treatment of a person, minority group, etc, based on sex, religion, race, etc; penetration, discernment.

discriminative /dɪs'krɪmɪ,nətɪv/ *adj* serving to discriminate or distinguish; discerning; discriminatory.—**discriminatively** *adv*.

discriminator /dɪs,krɪmɪ'neɪtər/ *n* one who or that which discriminates; (*electronics*) a circuit that converts a property of a signal into an amplitude variation.

discriminatory /-nə'tɔri/ *adj* discriminating; showing prejudice or favouritism; biased.—**discriminatorily** *adv*.

discursive /dɪ'skərsɪv/ *adj* wandering from one subject to another; digressive.—**discursively** *adv*.—**discursiveness** *n*.

discus /'dɪskəs/ *n* (*pl* **discuses, disci**) a heavy disk with a thickened middle, thrown by athletes.

discuss /dɪs'kʌs/ *vt* to talk over; to investigate by reasoning or argument.—**discussible, discussable** *adj*.

discussion /-ʃən/ *n* an argument; a debate; the airing of a question.

disdain /dɪs'deɪn/ *vt* to scorn, treat with contempt. • *n* scorn; a feeling of contemptuous superiority.—**disdainful** *adj*.—**disdainfully** *adv*.

disdainful /dɪs'deɪnful/ *adj* showing or feeling disdain; contemptuous; haughty.—**disdainfully** *adv*.—**disdainfulness** *n*.

disease /dɪ'ziːz/ *n* an unhealthy condition in an organism caused by infection, poisoning, etc; sickness; a harmful condition or situation.—**diseased** *adj*.

disembark /dɪs'ɪmbɑrk/ *vti* to land from a ship, debark.—**disembarkation** *n*.

disembarrass /ˌdɪsɪm'bærəs/ *vt* to free from embarrassment; to relieve (of); to disentangle.—**disembarrassment** *n*.

disembody /ˌdɪsɪm'bɒdi/ *vi* (**disembodying, disembodied**) to free (a soul, spirit, etc) from the body.—**disembodiment** *n*.

disembogue /ˌdɪsɪm'boːg/ *vti* (**disemboguing, disembogued**) (*river etc*) to discharge, pour forth (its water).

disembowel /ˌdɪsɪm'bauəl/ *vt* (**disembowelling, disembowelled** *or* **disemboweling, disemboweled**) to remove the entrails of; to remove the substance of.—**disembowelment** *n*.

disenchant /ˌdɪsɪn'tʃænt/ *vt* to disillusion.—**disenchantment** *n*.

disencumber /ˌdɪsɪn'kɛmbər/ *vt* to free from burden or hindrance.

disendow /ˌdɪsɪn'dau/ *vt* to deprive (a church) of endowments.—**disendowment** *n*.

disenfranchise /ˌdɪsɪn'fræntʃaɪz/ *see* **disfranchise**.

disengage /ˌdɪsɪn'geɪdʒ/ *vt* to separate or free from engagement or obligation; to detach, to release.—**disengaged** *adj*.—**disengagement** *n*.

disentail /ˌdɪsɪn'teɪl/ *vt* to release from entail.—*also n*.

disentangle /ˌdɪsɪn'tæŋgəl/ *vt* to untangle; to free from complications.—**disentanglement** *n*.

disenthrall, disenthral /ˌdɪsɪn'θrɒl/ *vt* (**disenthralling, disenthralled**) to free from bondage, to emancipate.

disestablish /ˌdɪsɪ'stæblɪʃ/ *vt* to displace from a settled position; to sever (church) from connection with the state.—**disestablishment** *n*.

disesteem /ˌdɪsɪ'stiːm/ *vt* to regard with disfavour, to dislike. • *n* lack of favour or regard.

diseur *Fr.* /di:'zør/ *n* a reciter of monologues for entertainment.—**diseuse** *nf*.

disfavour, disfavor /dɪs'feɪvər/ *n* dislike; disapproval. • *vt* to treat with disfavour.

disfeature /dɪs'fiːtʃər/ *vt* to disfigure.

disfigure /dɪs'fɪgər/ *vt* to spoil the beauty or appearance of.—**disfigurer** *n*.

disfigurement /-mənt/, **disfiguration** /-ˌeɪʃən/ *n* the act of disfiguring; a disfigured state; a thing that disfigures; a blemish, a defect.

disfranchise /dɪs'fræntʃaɪz/ *vt* to deprive of the right to vote.—*also* **disenfranchise**.—**disfranchisement, disenfranchisement** *n*.

disgorge /dɪs'gɔrdʒ/ *vt* to emit violently from the throat, to vomit; to empty; to surrender (*eg* stolen property).—**disgorgement** *n*.

disgrace /dɪs'greɪs/ *n* a loss of trust, favour, or honour; something that disgraces. • *vt* to bring disgrace or shame upon.—**disgracer** *n*.

disgraceful /-ful/ *adj* causing or deserving disgrace, shameful.—**disgracefully** *adv*.—**disgracefulness** *n*.

disgruntled /dɪs'grɛntəld/ *adj* dissatisfied, resentful.—**disgruntlement** *n*.

disguise /dɪs'gaɪz/ *vt* to hide what one is by appearing as something else; to hide what (a thing) really is. • *n* the use of a changed appearance to conceal identity; a false appearance.—**disguisedly** *adv*.—**disguiser** *n*.

disgust /dɪs'gʌst/ *n* sickening dislike; repugnance; aversion. • *vt* to cause disgust in.—**disgustedly** *adv*.

dish *n* /dɪʃ/ any of various shallow concave vessels to serve food in; the amount of food served in a dish; the food served; a shallow concave object, as a dish aerial; (*inf*) an attractive person. • *vt* (*with* **out**) (*inf*) to distribute freely; (*with* **up**) to serve food at mealtimes; (*inf*) to present (*eg* facts).

dishabille *Fr.* /ˌdɪsæ'biːl/ *n* a partly clad state, undress.—*also* **deshabille**.

dish aerial, dish antenna *n* a microwave antenna used in radar, telescopes, telecommunications, etc having a concave reflector.

disharmonize /dɪs'hɑrmə,naɪz/ *vt* to put out of harmony; to set at variance.

disharmony /dɪsˈhɑːmənɪ/ n (pl **disharmonies**) a lack of harmony between sounds; discord; a discordant situation, etc.—**disharmonious** adj.

dishcloth /ˈdɪʃklɒθ/ n a cloth for washing dishes.

dishearten /dɪsˈhɑːtən/ vt to discourage.—**dishearteningly** adv.—**disheartenment** n.

dishevelled, disheveled /dɪˈʃevəld/ adj rumpled, untidy.—**dishevelment** n.

dishonest /dɪsˈɒnəst/ adj not honest.—**dishonestly** adv.—**dishonesty** n.

dishonour, dishonor /dɪsˈɒnər/ n loss of honour; disgrace, shame. • vt to bring shame on, to disgrace; to refuse to pay, as a cheque.

dishonourable, dishonorable /-əbəl/ adj lacking honour, disgraceful.—**dishonourably, dishonorably** adv.

dishtowel /ˈdɪʃˌtaʊəl/ n a towel for drying dishes.

dishwasher /-ˌwɒʃər/ n an appliance for washing dishes; a person employed to wash dishes.

dishwater /-ˌwɒtər/ n water used for washing dishes; something that looks like or tastes like this.

dishy /ˈdɪʃɪ/ adj (**dishier, dishiest**) (inf) physically attractive, good-looking.

disillusion /ˌdɪsɪˈluːʒən/ vt to free from (mistaken) ideals or illusions. • n the state of being disillusioned.—**disillusionment** n.

disincentive /ˌdɪsɪnˈsentɪv/ n a discouragement to action or effort.

disinclination /ˌdɪsˌɪnkləˈneɪʃən/ n reluctance, unwillingness.

disinclined /ˌdɪsɪnˈklaɪnd/ adj unwilling.

disinfect /dɪsɪnˈfekt/ vt to destroy germs.—**disinfection** n.

disinfectant /ˌdɪsɪnˈfektənt/ n any chemical agent that inhibits the growth of or destroys germs.

disinformation /ˌdɪsˌɪnfərˈmeɪʃən/ n false information given out by intelligence agencies to mislead foreign spies.

disingenuous /ˌdɪsɪnˈdʒenjuːəs/ adj insincere, not candid or straightforward.—**disingenuously** adv.—**disingenuousness** n.

disinherit /ˌdɪsɪnˈherɪt/ vt to deprive of the right to an inheritance.—**disinheritance** n.

disintegrate /dɪsˈɪntəˌgreɪt/ vti to break or cause to break into separate pieces.—**disintegration** n.—**disintegrator** n.

disinter /dɪsˈɪntər/ vt (**disinterring, disinterred**) to take out of a grave; to bring out from obscurity, to unearth.—**disinterment** n.

disinterest /dɪsˈɪntərest/ n lack of partiality or bias. • vt to cease to concern (oneself).

disinterested /dɪsˈɪntrestəd/ adj impartial; objective.—**disinterestedly** adv.—**disinterestedness** n.

disjoin /ˈdɪsˌdʒɔɪn/ or /-ˈdʒɔɪn/ vt to separate. • vi to become detached.

disjoint /dɪsˈdʒɔɪnt/ vt to dislocate; to take to pieces. • adj (math) having no elements in common; (obs) disjointed.

disjointed /-ˈdʒɔɪntəd/ adj incoherent, muddled, esp of speech or writing.—**disjointedly** adv.—**disjointedness** n.

disjunction /dɪsˈdʒʌŋkʃən/ n severance, disconnection.—also **disjuncture**; (logic) a compound proposition presenting alternative terms only one of which is true.

disjunctive /dɪsˈdʒʌŋktɪv/ adj disjoining; alternative; (gram) marking an adverse or oppositional sense; syntactically independent; (logic) presenting alternative terms.—**disjunctively** adv.

disk[1] /dɪsk/ n a disc; a cylindrical pad of cartilage between the vertebrae; a gramophone record.

disk[2] n any flat, thin circular body; something resembling this, as the sun; (comput) a storage device in a computer, either floppy or hard.

disk brake see **disc brake.**

disk drive n (comput) a mechanism that allows a computer to read data from, and write data to, a disk.

dislike /dɪsˈlaɪk/ vt to consider unpleasant. • n aversion, distaste.—**dislikable, dislikeable** adj.

dislocate /ˈdɪsloˌkeɪt/ vt to put (a joint) out of place, to displace; to upset the working of.

dislocation /ˌdɪsloˈkeɪʃən/ n the act of dislocating; a joint put out of its socket; an imperfection in a crystalline structure; (geol) a displacement of stratified rocks, a fault.

dislodge /dɪsˈlɒdʒ/ vt to force or move out of a hiding place, established position, etc.—**dislodgment, dislodgement** n.

disloyal /dɪsˈlɔɪəl/ adj unfaithful; false to allegiance, disaffected.—**disloyally** adv.

disloyalty /-tɪ/ (pl **disloyalties**) n the state of being unfaithful; a disloyal act.

dismal /ˈdɪsməl/ adj gloomy, miserable, sad; (inf) feeble, worthless. —**dismally** adv.

dismantle /dɪsˈmæntəl/ vt to pull down; to take apart.—**dismantlement** n.

dismast /dɪsˈmæst/ vt to deprive (a ship) of a mast or masts.

dismay /dɪsˈmeɪ/ n apprehension, discouragement. • vt to fill with dismay.

dismember /dɪsˈmembər/ vt to cut or tear off the limbs from; to cut or divide into pieces.—**dismemberment** n.

dismiss /dɪsˈmɪs/ vt to send away; to remove from an office or employment; to stop thinking about; (law) to reject a further hearing (in court); (cricket) to bowl a batsman or side out.—**dismissible** adj.

dismissal /-əl/ n the act of dismissing; a removal from office, etc.

dismissive /-ˈmɪsɪv/ adj rejecting; offhand.—**dismissively** adv.

dismount /dɪsˈmaʊnt/ vti to alight from a horse or bicycle; to remove from a mount or setting.

disobedience /ˌdɪsoˈbiːdɪəns/ or /-əˈbiː-/ n the withholding of obedience; a refusal to obey; violation of a command by omitting to conform to it, or of a prohibition by acting in defiance of it; an instance of this.

disobedient /-ənt/ adj failing or refusing to obey.—**disobediently** adv.

disobey /ˌdɪsoˈbeɪ/ or /-əˈbeɪ/ vt (**disobeying, disobeyed**) to refuse to follow orders.

disoblige /ˌdɪsəˈblaɪdʒ/ vt to ignore the wishes of; to inconvenience.—**disobligingly** adv.

disorder /dɪsˈɔːdər/ n lack of order; untidiness; a riot; an illness or interruption of the normal functioning of the body or mind. • vt to throw into confusion; to upset.

disorderly /-lɪ/ adj untidy; unruly, riotous.—**disorderliness** n.

disorganize /dɪsˈɔːgəˌnaɪz/ vt to confuse or disrupt an orderly arrangement.—**disorganization** n.

disorient /dɪsˈɔːrɪənt/, **disorientate** /-ɪd/ vt to cause the loss of sense of time, place or identity; to confuse.—**disorientation** n.

disown /dɪsˈoːn/ vt to refuse to acknowledge as one's own.

disparage /dɪsˈpærɪdʒ/ vt to belittle.—**disparagingly** adv.—**disparagement** n.

disparate /ˈdɪspərət/ adj unequal, completely different.—**disparately** adv.—**disparateness** n.

disparity /dɪsˈperətɪ/ n (pl **disparities**) essential difference; inequality.

dispassionate /dɪsˈpæʃənət/ adj unemotional; impartial.—**dispassionately** adv.—**dispassionateness** n.

dispatch /dɪsˈpætʃ/ vt to send off somewhere; to perform speedily; to kill. • n a sending off (of a letter, a messenger etc); promptness; haste; a written message, esp of news.—also **despatch.—dispatcher** n.

dispel /dɪsˈpel/ vt (**dispelling, dispelled**) to drive away and scatter.

dispensable /dɪˈspensəbəl/ adj able to be done without; unimportant.—**dispensability** n.

dispensary /dɪˈspensərɪ/ n (pl **dispensaries**) a place in a hospital, a chemist shop, etc where medicines are made up and dispensed; a place where medical treatment is available.

dispensation /ˌdɪspenˈseɪʃən/ or /-pən-/ n the act of distributing or dealing out; exemption from a rule, penalty, etc.

dispense /dɪˈspens/ vt to deal out, distribute; to prepare and distribute medicines; to administer.

dispenser /dɪˈspensər/ n a person who dispenses medicines; a machine, etc, that dispenses measured quanitites or units of something.

dispermous /daɪˈspɜːməs/ adj (bot) two-seeded.

dispersal /dɪˈspɜːsəl/ n the act of dispersing; dispersion.

disperse /dɪˈspɜːs/ vt to scatter in different directions; to cause to evaporate; to spread (knowledge); to separate (light, etc) into different wavelengths. • vi to separate, become dispersed.—**dispersedly** adv.

dispersion /dɪˈspɜːʒən/ n a dispersing, or state of being dispersed; (physics) the separation of light into colours by diffraction or refraction; (statistics) the scattering of data about a mean.

dispersive /dɪˈspɜːsɪv/ adj tending to disperse; producing dispersion.—**dispersively** adv.

dispirit /dɪˈspɪrɪt/ vt to depress the spirits of; to dishearten; to render cheerless.

dispirited /-əd/ *adj* depressed, discouraged.—**dispiritedly** *adv*.

displace /dɪs'pleɪs/ *vt* to take the place of, to oust; to remove from a position of authority.

displaced person *n* a person who has become a refugee from their own country, *eg* due to war or famine.

displacement /-mənt/ *n* the act of displacing; substitution; apparent change of position; the weight of water displaced by a solid body immersed in it.

display /dɪs'pleɪ/ *vt* to show, expose to view; to exhibit ostentatiously. • *n* a displaying; an eye-catching arrangement, exhibition; a computer monitor for presenting visual information.

displease /dɪs'pliːz/ *vt* to cause offence or annoyance to.

displeasure /-'plɛʒər/ *n* a feeling of being displeased; dissatisfaction.

disport /dɪs'pɔːt/ *vt* to amuse or divert (oneself). • *vi* to display gaily.

disposable /dɪ'spoːzəbəl/ *adj* designed to be discarded after use; available for use. • *n* something disposable, *eg* a baby's nappy.

disposal /dɪ'spoːzəl/ *n* a disposing of something; order, arrangement.

dispose /dɪ'spoːz/ *vt* to place in order, arrange; to influence. • *vi* to deal with or settle; to give, sell or transfer to another; to throw away.

disposed /dɪ'spoːzd/ *adj* inclined (towards something).

disposition /ˌdɪspə'zɪʃən/ *n* a natural way of behaving towards others; tendency; arrangement.—**dispositional** *adj*.

dispossess /ˌdɪspə'zes/ *vt* to deprive, rid (of); to eject.—**dispossession** *n*.— **dispossessor** *n*.

dispraise /dɪs'preɪz/ *vt* to disparage; to censure. • *n* depreciation; a reproach.—**dispraisingly** *adv*.

disproof /dɪs'pruːf/ *n* a disproving or refuting; evidence that refutes.

disproportion /ˌdɪsprə'pɔːʃən/ *n* a lack of symmetry, a being out of proportion. • *vt* to render or make out of due proportion.—**disproportional** *adj*.—**disproportionally** *adv*.

disproportionate /ˌdɪsprə'pɔːʃənət/ *adj* out of proportion.—**disproportionately** *adv*.

disprove /dɪs'pruːv/ *vt* to prove (a claim, etc) to be incorrect.—**disprovable** *adj*.

disputable /dɪs'pjuːtəbəl/ or /'dɪspjətəbəl/ *adj* likely to cause dispute, arguable.—**disputability** *n*.—**disputably** *adv*.

disputant /'dɪspjuːtənt/ *n* a person involved in a dispute.

disputation /ˌdɪspjuː'teɪʃən/ *n* an argument; an exercise in debate.

disputatious /ˌdɪspjuː'teɪʃəs/ *adj* fond of argument, contentious.—**disputatiously** *adv*.—**disputatiousness** *n*.

dispute /dɪs'pjuːt/ *vt* to make the subject of an argument or debate; to query the validity of. • *vi* to argue. • *n* an argument; a quarrel.

disqualify /dɪs'kwɒlɪˌfaɪ/ *vt* (**disqualifying, disqualified**) to make ineligible because of a violation of rules; to make unfit or unsuitable, to disable.—**disqualifier** *n*.—**disqualification** *n*.

disquiet /dɪs'kwaɪət/ *vt* to trouble, disturb; to make uneasy or restless. • *n* disturbance; uneasiness, anxiety, worry; restlessness. • *adj* restless; uneasy; disturbed.—**disquieting** *adj*.

disquietude /dɪs'kwaɪəˌtuːd/ or /-ˌtjuːd/ *n* restlessness; disturbance; a feeling, occasion or cause of disquiet.

disquisition /ˌdɪskwɪ'zɪʃən/ *n* a careful examination of a subject.

disregard /ˌdɪsrɪ'gɑːd/ *vt* to pay no attention to; to consider as of little or no importance. • *n* lack of attention, neglect.

disrelish /dɪs'relɪʃ/ *vt* to dislike.—*also n*.

disrepair /ˌdɪsrɪ'peər/ or /-ri-/ *n* a worn-out condition through neglect of repair.

disreputable /dɪsre'pjuːtəbəl/ *adj* of bad reputation; not respectable; discreditable.—**disreputably** *adv*.

disrepute /ˌdɪsrɪ'pjuːt/ or /'dɪsrɪˌpjuːt/ *n* disgrace, discredit.

disrespect /ˌdɪsrə'spekt/ *n* lack of respect, rudeness.—**disrespectful** *adj*.—**disrespectfully** *adv*.

disrobe /dɪs'roːb/ *vti* to undress; to uncover.

disrupt /dɪs'rʌpt/ *vti* to break up; to create disorder or confusion; to interrupt.—**disruption** *n*.

disruptive /dɪs'rʌptɪv/ *adj* causing disruption.—**disruptively** *adv*.

dissatisfaction /ˌdɪsætɪs'fækʃən/ *n* disapproval; discontent; something that dissatisfies.

dissatisfactory /-'fæktəri/ *adj* unsatisfactory.

dissatisfy /dɪ'sætɪsˌfaɪ/ *vt* (**dissatisfying, dissatisfied**) to fail to please, to make discontented.

dissect /'daɪsekt/ *vt* to cut apart (a plant, an animal, etc) for scientific examination; to analyse and interpret in fine detail.—**dissection** *n*.—**dissector** *n*.

disseise, disseize /dɪs'siːz/ *vt* to deprive of possession; to dispossess unlawfully.—**disseisor, disseizor** *n*.

disseisin, disseizin /-zɪn/ *n* the act of unlawfully dispossessing a person or an estate.

dissemble /dɪ'sembəl/ *vti* to pretend or to conceal (*eg* true feelings) by pretence.—**dissemblance** *n*.—**dissembler** *n*.

disseminate /dɪ'semɪˌneɪt/ *vt* to spread or scatter (ideas, information, etc) widely.—**dissemination** *n*.—**disseminator** *n*.

dissension /dɪ'senʃən/ *n* disagreement, *esp* when resulting in conflict.

dissent /dɪ'sent/ *vi* to hold a different opinion; to withhold assent. • *n* a difference of opinion.—**dissenter** *n*.

dissentient /dɪ'senʃənt/ *adj* disagreeing with the majority. • *n* a person who dissents.

dissepiment /dɪ'sepɪmənt/ *n* (*biol*) a calcareous or membraneous partition, a septum.

dissertate /ˌdɪsər'teɪt/ *vi* to hold forth, to discourse.—**dissertator** *n*.

dissertation /-ʃən/ *n* a written thesis, *esp* as required for a university degree, etc.

disservice /dɪs'ɜːvɪs/ *n* an ill turn, a harmful action.

dissever /-vər/ *vti* to cut apart, to disunite.—**disseverance, disseverment** *n*.

dissident /'dɪsɪdənt/ *adj* disagreeing. • *n* a person who disagrees strongly with government policies, *esp* one who suffers harassment or imprisonment as a result.—**dissidence** *n*.

dissimilar /dɪ'sɪmɪlər/ *adj* unlike, different.—**dissimilarly** *adv*.

dissimilarity /'dɪsɪmɪ'lerɪti/ *n* (*pl* **dissimilarities**) lack of similarity; a difference, distinction.

dissimulate /dɪ'sɪmjʊˌleɪt/ *vt* to dissemble.—**dissimulation** *n*.—**dissimulator** *n*.

dissipate /'dɪsɪˌpeɪt/ *vt* to scatter, dispel; to waste, squander (money, etc). • *vi* to separate and vanish.—**dissipater, dissipator** *n*.

dissipated /-əd/ *adj* dissolute, indulging in excessive pleasure; scattered, wasted.—**dissipatedly** *adv*.—**dissipatedness** *n*.

dissipation /ˌdɪsɪ'peɪʃən/ *n* dispersion; wastefulness; frivolous or dissolute living.

dissociate /dɪ'soːsiˌeɪt/ or /-ʃiˌeɪt/ *vti* to separate or cause to separate the association of (people, things, etc) in consciousness; to repudiate a connection with.—**dissociation** *n*.

dissociation /dɪˌsoːsi'eɪʃən/ or /-ˌʃi'eɪʃən/ *n* a dissociating or being dissociated; (*chem*) decomposition of a molecule into single atoms, etc; (*psychol*) the separation of an attitude, belief, etc, from the rest of the personality.

dissoluble /dɪ'sɒljuːbəl/ *adj* soluble.—**dissolubility** *n*.

dissolute /dɪsə'luːt/ *adj* lacking moral discipline, debauched.—**dissolutely** *adv*.—**dissoluteness** *n*.

dissolution /dɪsə'luːʃən/ *n* separation into component parts; the dissolving of a meeting or assembly (*eg* parliament); the termination of a business or personal relationship; death; the process of dissolving.

dissolve /dɪ'sɒlv/ *vt* to cause to pass into solution; to disperse (a legislative assembly); to melt; (*partnership, marriage*) to break up legally, annul. • *vi* to become liquid; to fade away; to be overcome by emotion.—**dissolvable** *adj*.—**dissolver** *n*.

dissolvent /-vənt/ *adj* able to dissolve. • *n* a substance that dissolves.

dissonance /'dɪsənəns/ *n* a harsh or inharmonious sound; discord; lack of agreement; (*mus*) an incomplete or unfulfilled chord requiring resolution into harmony.

dissonant /-nənt/ *adj* inharmonious; discordant; disagreeing; (*mus*) producing dissonance.—**dissonantly** *adv*.

dissuade /dɪ'sweɪd/ *vt* to prevent or discourage by persuasion.—**dissuasion** *n*.—**dissuasive** *adj*.

dissyllable /daɪ'sɪləbəl/ or /'daɪ-/ *n* a word of two syllables.—*also* **disyllable**.—**dissyllabic, disyllabic** *adj*.

dissymmetry /dɪ'sɪmɪtri/ *n* (*pl* **dissymmetries**) an absence or lack of symmetry; symmetry in opposite directions, like right and left hands.—**dissymmetrical, dissymmetric** *adj*.

distaff /dɪ'stæf/ *n* the stick on which wool for flax is wound for spinning; (*arch*) a woman, women.

distaff line *n* the female line of a family.

distal /'dɪstəl/ *adj* (*anat*) relatively distant from the centre of the body or point of attachment.—**distally** *adv*.

distance /-təns/ *n* the amount of space between two points or things; a distant place or point; remoteness, coldness of manner. • *vt* to place at a distance, physically or emotionally; to outdistance in a race, etc.

distant /-ənt/ *adj* separated by a specific distance; far-off in space, time, place, relation, etc; not friendly, aloof.—**distantly** *adv.*

distaste /dɪs'teɪst/ *n* aversion; dislike.

distasteful /-fʊl/ *adj* unpleasant, offensive.—**distastefully** *adv.*—**distastefulness** *n.*

distemper /dɪs'tempər/ *n* an infectious and often fatal disease of dogs and other animals; a type of paint made by mixing colour with egg or glue instead of oil; a painting made with this.

distend /dɪs'tend/ *vti* to swell or cause to swell, *esp* from internal pressure.

distensible /dɪs'tensəbəl/ *adj* able to be distended.

distension, distention /-ʃən/ *n* a distending or being distended; a swelling.

distich /'dɪstɪk/ *n* (*pl* **distichs**) (*poetry*) a couplet.

distichous /-əs/ *adj* (*bot*) arranged in two rows on opposite sides of an axis.—**distichously** *adv.*

distil, distill /'dɪstɪl/ *vti* (**distils** *or* **distills, distilling, distilled**) to treat by, or cause to undergo, distillation; to purify; to extract the essence of; to let or cause to fall in drops.

distillate /'dɪstɪlət/ *or* /-leɪt/, /-stɪl-/ *n* a product of distillation.

distillation /ˌdɪstɪ'leɪʃən/ *n* the conversion of a liquid into vapour by heat and then cooling the vapour so it condenses again, separating out the liquid's constituents or purifying it in the process; a distillate.—**distillatory** *adj.*

distiller /dɪ'stɪlər/ *n* an individual or organization that distils, *eg* a brewery.

distillery /-əri/ *n* (*pl* **distilleries**) a place where distilling, *esp* of alcoholic spirits, is carried on.

distinct /dɪ'stɪŋkt/ *adj* different, separate (from); easy to perceive by the mind or senses.—**distinctly** *adv.*—**distinctness** *n.*

distinction /dɪ'stɪŋkʃən/ *n* discrimination, separation; a difference seen or made; a distinguishing mark or characteristic; excellence, superiority; a mark of honour.

distinctive /dɪ'stɪŋktɪv/ *adj* clearly marking a person or thing as different from another; characteristic.—**distinctively** *adv.*—**distinctiveness** *n.*

distingué *Fr.* /diːstæŋ'geɪ/ *adj* of superior manner, distinguished, striking.

distinguish /dɪ'stɪŋgwɪʃ/ *vt* to see or recognize as different; to mark as different, characterize; to see or hear clearly; to confer distinction on; to make eminent or known. • *vi* to perceive a difference.—**distinguishable** *adj.*

distinguished /dɪ'stɪŋgwɪʃt/ *adj* eminent, famous; dignified in appearance or manners.

distort /dɪ'stɔrt/ *vt* to pull or twist out of shape; to alter the true meaning of, misrepresent.

distortion /-ʃən/ *n* a distorting or being distorted; a distorted feature; (*optics*) a faulty image; (*electronics*) an unwanted change in a signal, etc.—**distortional** *adj.*

distract /dɪ'strækt/ *vt* to draw (*eg* the mind or attention) to something else; to confuse.—**distractingly** *adv.*

distracted /-əd/ *adj* bewildered, confused.—**distractedly** *adv.*

distraction /-ʃən/ *n* something that distracts the attention; an amusement; perplexity; extreme agitation.—**distractive** *adj.*—**distractively** *adv.*

distrain /dɪ'streɪn/ *vt* to seize and hold goods or chattels as security for payment of a debt.—**distrainer, distrainor** *n.*—**distrainment** *n.*

distrainee /-'niː/ *n* a person who is distrained upon.

distraint /dɪ'streɪnt/ *n* the act of distraining for debt; seizure.

distrait /dɪ'streɪt/ *adj* absent-minded, preoccupied.

distraught /dɪ'strɔt/ *adj* extremely distressed.

distress /dɪ'stres/ *n* physical or emotional suffering, as from pain, illness, lack of money, etc; a state of danger, desperation. • *vt* to cause distress to.—**distressingly** *adv.*

distressful /-fʊl/ *adj* suffering or causing distress.—**distressfully** *adv.*—**distressfulness** *n.*

distributary /dɪ'strɪbjuˌteri/ *n* (*pl* **distributaries**) a river branch that does not return to the main stream.

distribute /dɪ'strɪbjuːt/ *or* /'dɪ-/ *vt* to divide and share out; to spread, disperse throughout an area.—**distributable** *adj.*

distribution /-ʃən/ *n* a distributing or a being distributed; allotment; a thing distributed; diffusion; the geographical range or occurence of an organism; classification; (*law*) the

apportioning of an estate among the heirs; (*commerce*) the marketing of goods to customers, their handling and transport; (*statistics*) the way numbers denoting characteristics in a statistical population are distributed.—**distributional** *adj.*

distributor /-tər/ *n* an agent who sells goods, *esp* wholesale; a device for distributing current to the spark plugs in an engine.

district /'dɪstrɪkt/ *n* a territorial division defined for administrative purposes; a region or area with a distinguishing character.

district attorney *n* in the US, a lawyer who is the state's prosecutor in a judicial district.

District of Columbia *n* a federal area whose boundary is that of Washington, the capital.

distrust /dɪs'trʌst/ *n* suspicion, lack of trust. • *vt* to withhold trust or confidence from; to suspect.—**distrustful** *adj.*—**distrustfully** *adv.*—**distrustfulness** *n.*

disturb /dɪ'stɜrb/ *vt* to interrupt; to cause to move from the normal position or arrangement; to destroy the quiet or composure of.

disturbance /-əns/ *n* a disturbing or being disturbed; an interruption; an outbreak of disorder and confusion.

disturbed /dɪ'stɜrbd/ *adj* showing symptoms of emotional illness.

disulphate, disulfate /daɪ'sʌlfeɪt/ *n* a sulphate containing one atom of hydrogen, replaceable by a basic element.

disulphide, disulfide /-faɪd/ *n* a sulphide in which two atoms of sulphur are contained.

disunite /dɪsˈjuːnəɪt/ *vt* to divide, disrupt. • *vi* to separate.

disuse /dɪs'juːz/ *n* the state of being neglected or unused.—**disused** *adj.*

disyllable /daɪ'sɪləbəl/ *see* **dissyllable**.

ditch /dɪtʃ/ *n* any long narrow trench dug in the ground. • *vt* to make a ditch in; (*sl*) to drive (a car) into a ditch; (*sl*) to make a forced landing of (an aircraft); (*sl*) to get rid of.

dither /'dɪðər/ *vi* to hesitate, vacillate. • *n* a state of confusion; uncertainty.—**ditherer** *n.*

dithyramb /'dɪθɪˌræm/ *or* /-'ræmb/ *n* a hymn sung in honour of Dionysus, the Greek god of wine; an impassioned speech or writing.—**dithyrambic** *adj, n.*—**dithyrambically** *adv.*

dittany /'dɪtəni/ *n* (*pl* **dittanies**) *n* an aromatic pink-flowered plant of the mint family formerly considered to have magical properties.

ditto /'dɪtoː/ *n* (*pl* **dittos**) the same again, as above—used in written lists and tables to avoid repetition. • *vt* (**dittoing, dittoed**) to repeat.

ditto marks *npl* two small marks (ᴵᴵ) placed under an item repeated.

ditty /'dɪti/ *n* (*pl* **ditties**) a simple song.

diuretic /ˌdaɪjʊ'retɪk/ *n* a substance or drug that acts to increase the discharge of urine.—*also adj.*

diurnal /daɪ'ɜrnəl/ *adj* occurring daily; of the daytime; having a daily cycle.—**diurnally** *adv.*

diva /'diːvə/ *n* (*pl* **divas, dive**) an accomplished female opera singer; a prima donna.

divalent /daɪ'veɪlənt/ *adj* (*chem*) having a valence of two.

divan /dɪ'væn/ *n* a long couch without back or sides; a bed of similar design.

dive /daɪv/ *vi* (**diving, dived** *or* **dove, dived**) to plunge headfirst into water; (*aircraft*) to descend or fall steeply; (*diver, submarine*) to submerge; to plunge (*eg* the hand) suddenly into anything; to dash headlong, lunge. • *n* a headlong plunge; a submerging of a submarine, etc; a sharp descent; a steep decline; (*sl*) a disreputable public place.

dive bomber *n* an aircraft designed to release its bombs during a steep dive for superior accuracy.—**dive-bomb** *vt.*

diver /-ər/ *n* a person who dives; a person who works or explores underwater from a diving bell or in a diving suit; any of various aquatic birds.

diverge /daɪ'vɜrdʒ/ *vi* to branch off in different directions from a common point; to differ in character, form, etc; to deviate from a path or course.—**divergence** *n.*—**divergent** *adj.*

divers /'daɪvərz/ *adj* (*arch*) various; sundry.

diverse /'daɪvərs/ *adj* different; assorted, various.—**diversely** *adv.*—**diverseness** *n.*

diversify /daɪ'vɜrsɪˌfaɪ/ *vb* (**diversifying, diversified**) *vt* to vary; to invest in a broad range of securities to lessen risk of loss. • *vi* to engage in a variety of commercial operations to reduce risk.—**diversification** *n.*

diversion /daɪ'vərʒən/ or /dɪ-/ *n* turning aside from a course; a recreation, amusement; a drawing of attention away from the principal activity; a detour when a road is temporarily closed to traffic.—**diversionary** *adj*.

diversity /'daɪvərsɪti/ or /dɪ-/ *n* (*pl* **diversities**) the condition or quality of being diverse; unlikeness; a difference, distinction; variety.

divert /daɪ'vərt/ *vt* to turn aside from one course onto another; to entertain, amuse.

diverticulitis /,daɪvər,tɪkjʊ'laɪtɪs/ *n* inflammation of a diverticulum.

diverticulum /,daɪvərtɪ'kjʊləm/ *n* (*pl* **diverticula**) a pocket or side branch off a passage or cavity in the body, *esp* the intestine.

divertimento /dɪ,vərtɪ'mento/ or /dɪ,ver-/ *n* (*pl* **divertimenti, divertimentos**) a light, pleasant vocal or instrumental composition.

divertissement /diː'vertɪsmənt/, *Fr.* /diːvertiːs'mɑ̃/ *n* an amusement; a recreation, a light entertainment, a ballet, etc, as an interlude between the acts of a play; an entr'acte; (*mus*) a divertimento.

divest /daɪ'vest/ *vt* to strip of clothing, equipment, etc; to deprive of rights, property, power, etc.—**divestiture, divestment** *n*.

divide /dɪ'vaɪd/ *vt* to break up into parts; to distribute, share out; to sort into categories; to cause to separate from something else; to separate into opposing sides; (*parliament*) to vote or cause to vote by division; (*math*) to ascertain how many times one quantity contains another. • *vi* to become separated; to diverge; to vote by separating into two sides. • *n* a watershed; a split.—**dividable** *adj*.

divided highway *see* **dual carriageway**.

dividend /'dɪvɪ,dend/ *n* a number which is to be divided; the money earned by a company and divided among the shareholders; a bonus derived from some action.

divider /dɪ'vaɪdər/ *n* something that divides; a screen, furniture or plants, etc used to divide up a room; (*pl*) measuring-compasses.

divi-divi /'dɪvɪ,dɪvɪ/ (*pl* **divi-divis**) *n* a South American tropical plant; its astringent husks used for dyeing and tanning.

divination /,dɪvɪ'neɪʃən/ *n* the art of foretelling the future or discovering hidden knowledge by supernatural means; intuitive perception.—**divinatory** *adj*.

divine /dɪ'vaɪn/ *adj* of, from, or like God or a god; (*inf*) excellent. • *n* a clergyman; a theologian. • *vt* to foretell the future by supernatural means; to discover intuitively; to dowse. • *vi* to practise divination.—**divinely** *adv*.—**diviner** *n*.

diving bell *n* an open-bottomed chamber for working under water, supplied with compressed air.

diving board *n* a platform or springboard for diving from.

diving suit *n* a watertight suit with a helmet and air supply, used by divers.

divining rod *n* a forked twig used for dowsing.

divinity /'dɪvɪnɪti/ *n* (*pl* **divinities**) any god; theology; the quality of being God or a god.

divisible /dɪ'vɪsɪbəl/ *adj* able to be divided.—**divisibility** *n*.

division /dɪ'vɪʒən/ *n* a dividing or being divided; a partition, a barrier; a portion or section; a military unit; separation; (*Parliament*) a separation into two opposing sides to vote; a disagreement; (*math*) the process of dividing one number by another.—**divisional** *adj*.

divisive /dɪ'vɪsɪv/ or /dɪ'vaɪsɪv/, /-zɪv/ *adj* creating disagreement or disunity.—**divisively** *adv*.—**divisiveness** *n*.

divisor /dɪ'vaɪzər/ *n* a number that is to be divided into another number (the dividend).

divorce /dɪ'vors/ *n* the legal dissolution of marriage; separation. • *vt* to terminate a marriage by divorce; to separate.

divorcé, divorcee /,dɪvor'siː/ *n* a divorced person.—**divorcée** *nf*.

divorcement /dɪ'vorsmənt/ *n* the act or process of divorcing.

divot /'dɪvət/ *n* a lump of turf dug from the ground while making a golf swing, etc.

divulge /daɪ'vʌldʒ/ or /dɪ/ *vt* to tell or reveal.—**divulgence** *n*.

divvy /'dɪvɪ/ *n* (*pl* **divvies**) in the UK, a dividend; in the US, a portion. • *vt* (**divvying, divvied**) (*usu with* **up**) to share out.

Dixie /'dɪksi/ *n* the southern States of the US.

Dixieland /-,lænd/ *n* Dixie; a New Orleans jazz style.

dizzy /'dɪzi/ *adj* (**dizzier, dizziest**) confused; causing giddiness or confusion; (*sl*) silly; foolish. • *vt* to make dizzy; to confuse.—**dizzily** *adv*.—**dizziness** *n*.

DJ *abbr* = disc jockey; dinner jacket.

dl *abbr* = decilitre.

DM *abbr* = Deutschmark.

dm *abbr* = decimetre.

DMus *abbr* = Doctor of Music.

DMZ *abbr* = demilitarized zone.

DNA *abbr* = deoxyribonucleic acid, the main component of chromosomes that stores genetic information.

do /duː/ *vt* (*pres t* **does, doing, did,** *pp* **done**) to perform; to work; to end, to complete; to make; to provide; to arrange, to tidy; to perform; to cover a distance; to visit; (*sl*) to serve time in prison; (*sl*) to cheat, to rob; (*sl*) to assault; (*with* **in**) (*inf*) to kill; to tire out. • *vi* to act or behave; to be satisfactory; to manage. • *n* (*pl* **dos, do's**) (*inf*) a party; (*inf*) a hoax. *Do* has special uses where it has no definite meaning, as in asking questions (*Do you like milk?*), emphasizing a verb (*I do want to go*), and standing for a verb already used (*My dog goes where I do*).

DOA *abbr* = dead on arrival.

Doberman (pinscher) /'doːbərmən('pɪnʃər)/ *n* a breed of dog with a smooth glossy black-and-tan coat and docked tail.

doc /dɒk/ *n* (*inf*) doctor.

docent /'doːsənt/ *n* a person licensed to teach in a university, but of lower grade and authority than a professor.

docile /'dɒsaɪl/ or /'doː-/ *adj* easily led; submissive.—**docilely** *adv*.—**docility** *n*.

dock¹ /dɒk/ *vt* (*an animal's tail*) to cut short; (*wages, etc*) to deduct a portion of.

dock² *n* a wharf; an artificial enclosed area of water for ships to be loaded, repaired, etc; (*pl*) a dockyard. • *vt* to come or bring into dock; to join (spacecraft) together in space.

dock³ *n* an enclosed area in a court of law reserved for the accused.

dockage /'dɒkɪdʒ/ *n* the provision of accommodation for the docking of vessels; money paid for the use of a dock.

docker /-ər/ *n* a labourer who works at the docks.—*also* **longshoreman** *n*.

docket /'dɒkət/ *n* a label or document recording the contents of a package, delivery instructions, payment advice, or details of payment of customs duties; in US, a list of lawsuits to be tried by a court. • *vt* (*goods*) to put a docket on; (*lawsuit*) to enter on a docket.

dockyard /-jard/ *n* an area with docks and facilities for repairing and refitting ships.

doctor /'dɒktər/ *n* a person qualified to treat diseases or physical disorders; the highest academic degree; the holder of such a degree. • *vt* to treat medically; (*machinery, etc*) to patch up; to tamper with, falsify; (*inf*) to castrate or spay.—**doctoral** *adj*.

doctorate /-tərət/ *n* the highest degree in any discipline given by a university, conferring the title of doctor.

doctrinaire /,dɒktrɪ'ner/ *adj* obsessed by theory rather than by experience. • *n* a person so obsessed.—**doctrinairism** *n*.

doctrine /-trɪer/ *n* a principle of belief.—**doctrinal** *adj*.—**doctrinally** *adv*.

document /'dɒkjʊmənt/ *n* a paper containing information or proof of anything. • *vt* to provide or prove with documents.—**documental** *adj*.—**documentation** *n*.

documentary /-'mentəri/ *adj* consisting of documents; presenting a factual account of an event or activity. • *n* (*pl* **documentaries**) a nonfiction film.

dodder /'dɒdər/ *vt* to tremble or shake through old age or weakness; to walk slowly and shakily.—**dodderer** *n*.—**doddery** *adj*.

dodecagon /doː'dekəgɒn/ *n* a geometric figure with twelve angles and sides.

dodecahedron /,doːdekə'hiːdrən/ *n* a solid figure with twelve faces.—**dodecahedral** *adj*.

dodge /dɒdʒ/ *vi* to move quickly in an irregular course. • *vt* to evade (a duty) by cunning; to avoid by a sudden movement or shift of position; to trick. • *n* a sudden movement; (*inf*) a clever trick.—**dodger** *n*.

dodgy /'dɒdʒi/ *adj* (**dodgier, dodgiest**) (*inf*) cunning; risky.

dodo /'doːdoː/ *n* (*pl* **dodos, dodoes**) a large, clumsy bird, now extinct.

doe /doː/ *n* (*pl* **does, doe**) a female deer, rabbit, or hare.

doer /'duːər/ *n* a person who acts, as opposed to thinking or talking; an active energetic person.

does /dʌs/ *see* **do**.

doeskin /'doːskɪn/ *n* the skin of a doe; a fine woollen cloth with a smooth finish.

doesn't /'dʌzənt/ = does not.

doff /dɒf/ vt to take off (esp one's hat) in greeting or as a sign of respect.

dog /dɒg/ n a canine mammal of numerous breeds, commonly kept as a domestic pet; the male of the wolf or fox; a despicable person; a device for gripping things. • vt (**dogging, dogged**) to pursue relentlessly.—**dog-like** adj.

dogcart n a light, two-wheeled carriage with cross seats back to back.

dog collar n a collar for a dog; (inf) a clerical collar.

dog days npl the warmest days of the year.

doge /dəʊdʒ/ n (formerly) the chief magistrate in republican Venice and Genoa.

dog-eared adj worn, shabby; (book) having the corners of the pages turned down.—**dog-ear** vt.

dogfight /ˈdɒgfaɪt/ n (loosely) a fiercely disputed contest; combat between two fighter planes, esp at close quarters.

dogfish /-fɪʃ/ n (pl **dogfish, dogfishes**) any of various small shark-like fish.

dogged /ˈdɒgəd/ adj tenacious.—**doggedly** adv.—**doggedness** n.

doggerel /ˈdɒgərəl/ n trivial or worthless verse.

doggish adj like a dog, surly; (sl) showily stylish.—**doggishly** adv.—**doggishness** n.

doggo /ˈdɒgəʊ/ adv (sl) silent and still; **lie doggo** to lie low, stay hidden.

doggone /ˈdɒgɒn/ interj (sl) darn, damn. • adj (sl) cursed, confounded. • vt (sl) to damn.

doggy /ˈdɒgi/ adj (**doggier, doggiest**) of or like a dog; fond of dogs; (sl) showily stylish. • n (pl **doggies**) a pet name for a dog; a little dog.—also **doggie**.

doghouse /ˈdɒghaʊs/ n a dog kennel; **in the doghouse** (inf) in disgrace.

dogleg /-leg/ n something having a sharp angle or a sharp bend, as a road or fairway on a golf course. • adj crooked like a dog's hind leg.—also **doglegged**.

dogma /ˈdɒgmə/ n (pl **dogmas, dogmata**) a belief taught or held as true, esp by a church; a doctrine; a belief.

dogmatic /dɒgˈmætɪk/, **dogmatical** /-əl/ adj pertaining to a dogma; forcibly asserted as if true; overbearing.—**dogmatically** adv.

dogmatics /-ɪks/ n (used as sing) the study of religious dogmas; doctrinal theology.

dogmatize /-ˌtaɪz/ vt to assert in a dogmatic manner.—**dogmatism** n.—**dogmatist** n.

do-gooder /duːˈgʊdər/ n a well-meaning person, esp if naive or ineffectual.—**do-gooding** n.

dog paddle n an elementary form of swimming in which the arms and legs paddle rapidly in the water.—**dog-paddle** vi.

dog rose n a prickly wild rose.

dogsbody /ˈdɒgzˌbɒdi/ n (pl **dogsbodies**) (inf) a drudge.

dogtooth /-ˌtuːθ/ (pl **dogteeth**) n a canine tooth; (archit) a small conical ornament resembling a petal in Early English architecture.

dogtrot /ˈdɒgtrɒt/ n a gentle trot; a covered passageway.

dogwatch /-wɒtʃ/ n (naut) one of two watches on board ship of two hours each, between 4 and 8 pm.

dogwood /-wʊd/ n any of several shrubs with clusters of small flowers.

doily /ˈdɔɪli/ n (pl **doilies**) a small ornamented mat, laid under food on dishes, eg cakes.—also **doyley**.

doing /ˈduːɪŋ/ n an action or its result; (pl) things done; actions.

doit /dɔɪt/ n a small old Dutch copper coin; a thing of little value.

do-it-yourself /ˈduːɪtjʊrˈsɛlf/ n domestic repairs, woodwork, etc undertaken as a hobby or to save money.—also adj.—**do-it-yourselfer** n.

dolabriform /dəʊˈlæbrɪˌfɔrm/, **dolabrirate** adj (bot) hatchet-shaped.

Dolby /ˈdɒlbi/ n (trademark) an electronic noise-reduction system used in sound-recording and playback systems.

dolce /ˈdɒltʃeɪ/ /-reɪʃ/ adj soft. • adv (mus) gently.

doldrums /ˈdɒldrəmz/ or /ˈdɒl-/ npl inactivity; depression; boredom; the regions of the ocean about the equator where there is little wind.

dole /dəʊl/ n (inf) money received from the state while unemployed; a small portion. • vt to give (out) in small portions.

doleful /ˈdəʊlfʊl/ adj sad, gloomy.—**dolefully** adv.—**dolefulness** n.

dolerite /ˈdɒləˌraɪt/ n a dark-coloured basic igneous rock composed of augite, felspar and iron; basaltic greenstone.

dolichocephalic /ˌdɒlɪˌkɒsɪˈfælɪk/ adj with a skull long in proportion to its breadth, long-headed.—**dolichocephaly** n.

doll /dɒl/ n a toy in the form of a human figure; a ventriloquist's dummy; (sl) a woman.

dollar /ˈdɒlər/ n the unit of money in the US, Canada, Australia and many other countries.

dollop /ˈdɒləp/ n (inf) a soft mass or lump; a portion, serving.

dolly /ˈdɒli/ n (pl **dollies**) (inf) a child's word for a doll; a wheeled platform for a camera. • vi (**dollying, dollied**) to manoeuvre a camera dolly.

Dolly Varden /ˌdɒliˈvardən/ n a brightly spotted trout of western North America; a large lop-sided hat worn by women.

dolman /ˈdɒlmən/ n (pl **dolmans**) a loose robe; a short cloak.

dolman sleeve n a full, wide sleeve narrowing to a wristband.

dolmen /ˈdɒlmən/ n a prehistoric structure of two or more erect stones supporting a horizontal slab.

dolomite /ˈdɒləˌmaɪt/ n a white mineral obtained from sedimentary rock; a sedimentary rock similar to limestone.—**dolomitic** adj.

doloroso /ˌdoːləˈroːsoː/, Fr. /ˌdɔləˈrɔsə/ adv (mus) sadly.

dolorous /ˈdɒlərəs/ adj mournful, doleful.—**dolorously** adv.—**dolorousness** n.

dolour, dolor /ˈdɒlər/ n grief, sorrow, distress.

dolphin /ˈdɒlfɪn/ n a marine mammal with a beak-like snout, larger than a porpoise but smaller than a whale.

dolphinarium /ˌdɒlfɪˈnɛriəm/ n (pl **dolphinariums, dolphinaria**) a large pool or aquarium for keeping and displaying dolphins.

dolt /dəʊlt/ n a dull or stupid person.—**doltish** adj.—**doltishly** adv.—**doltishness** n.

Dom /dɒm/ n (RC Church) the title of certain dignitaries; a former Portuguese title of rank, as Don.

domain /dəˈmeɪn/ n an area under the control of a ruler or government; a field of thought, activity, etc.

domain name n (comput) an Internet site, service or computer main representing a business or an organization.

dome /dəʊm/ n a large, rounded roof; something high and rounded.—also vt.

domed /ˈdəʊmd/ adj having, or shaped like, a dome.

domesday /ˈduːmzdeɪ/ n the day of God's Last Judgment of mankind.—also **doomsday**.

Domesday Book n the record of William I's survey of England in 1086.

domestic /dəˈmɛstɪk/ adj belonging to the home or family; not foreign; (animals) tame. • n a servant in the home. —**domestically** adv.

domestic science n the study of household skills; home economics.

domesticate /dəˈmɛstɪˌkeɪt/ vt to tame; to make home-loving and fond of household duties.—**domestication** n.

domesticity /ˌdoːməˈstɪsɪti/ or /ˌdɒm-/ n (pl **domesticities**) home life; being domestic.

domicile /ˈdɒməˌsaɪl/ or /-sɪl/ n a house; a person's place of residence. • vt to establish, to settle permanently.—**domiciliary** adj.

domiciliate /ˌdɒməˈsɪliˌeɪt/ or /ˌdoːmə-/ vt to domicile.—**domiciliation** n.

dominant /ˈdɒmənənt/ adj commanding, prevailing over others; overlooking from a superior height. • n (mus) the fifth note of a diatonic scale.—**dominance** n.—**dominantly** n.

dominate /ˈdɒməˌneɪt/ vt to control or rule by strength; to hold a commanding position over; to overlook from a superior height.—**domination** n.—**dominator** n.

domineer /ˌdɒməˈniːr/ vti to act in an arrogant or tyrannical manner.—**domineeringly** adv.

dominical /dəˈmɪnɪkəl/ adj pertaining to Christ as Lord, or to Sunday.

dominie /ˈdɒmɪni/ n (Scot) a schoolteacher; (inf) a clergyman.

dominion /dəˈmɪnjən/ n a territory with one ruler or government; the power to rule; authority.

domino /ˈdɒməˌnoː/ n (pl **dominoes, dominos**) a flat oblong tile marked with up to six dots; (pl) a popular game usu using a set of 28 dominoes; a loose cloak, usu worn with an eye mask, at masquerades.

Don /dɒn/ n a Spanish title for a gentleman or nobleman.—**Doña** nf.

don¹ vt (**donning, donned**) to put on; to invest with; to assume.

don² n a head, fellow or tutor at Oxford or Cambridge universities; (loosely) any university teacher; a Mafia leader.

donate /ˈdoːneɪt/ or /doːˈneɪt/ vt to give as a gift or donation, esp to a charity.—**donator** n.

donation /doːˈneɪʃən/ *n* a donating; a contribution or gift, *esp* to a charity.

donative /ˈdɒnətɪv/ *n* a gift; largess, a donation. • *adj* given by donation.

done[1] /dʌn/ *see* **do**.

done[2] *adj* completed; cooked sufficiently; socially acceptable; (*with* **for**) (*sl*) doomed; dead; exhausted; discarded.

donee /doːˈniː/ *n* a person to whom a gift is made.

donjon /ˈdʌndʒən/ *or* /ˈdɒn-/ *n* the central tower of a castle, a keep.

donkey /ˈdɒŋki/ *n* (*pl* **donkeys**) a small animal resembling a horse.

donkey engine *n* a portable auxiliary engine.

donkey jacket *n* a thick waterproof jacket, *esp* worn by labourers.

donkey's years *npl* (*inf*) a very long time.

donkey-work /ˈdɑŋki‚wɜrk/ *n* the groundwork; drudgery.

Donna /ˈdɒnə/ *n* a term of respect to a lady in Italy.

donnish /ˈdɒnɪʃ/ *adj* (*inf*) resembling a university don.—**donnishly** *adv*.—**donnishness** *n*.

donor /ˈdoːnər/ *n* a person who donates something, a donator; a person who gives their blood, organs, etc for medical use.

don't /doːnt/ = do not.

donut /ˈdoː‚nʌt/ *n* (*sl*) a doughnut.

doodad /ˈduːdæd/ *n* (*inf*) a small item whose name is lost or forgotten.

doodle /ˈduːdəl/ *vi* to scribble aimlessly. • *vt* to draw (something) absentmindedly. • *n* a meaningless drawing or scribble.—**doodler** *n*.

doom[1] /duːm/ *n* a grim destiny; ruin. • *vt* condemn to failure, destruction, etc.

doom[2] *see* **doum**.

doomsday /ˈduːmzdeɪ/ *n* the day of God's Last Judgment of mankind.—*also* **domesday**.

door /doːr/ *n* a movable barrier to close an opening in a wall; a doorway; a means of entry or approach.

doorjamb /ˈdoːr‚dʒæm/ *n* one of the two vertical sides of a door frame; a doorpost.

doorkeeper /-kiː‚pər/ *n* a person guarding a door.

doorman /-mæn/ *or* /-mən/ *n* (*pl* **doormen**) a uniformed attendant stationed at the entrance to large hotels, offices, etc.

doormat /-mæt/ *n* a mat placed at the entrance to a doorway for wiping one's feet; (*inf*) a submissive or easily bullied person.

doornail /-neɪl/ *n* (*formerly*) a large nail with which doors were studded; **dead as a doornail** most certainly dead.

doorplate /-pleɪt/ *n* a plate with the name of the occupant of a building.

doorpost /-poːst/ *n* the straight vertical side-post of a door, jamb.

doorstop /-stɒp/ *n* a device for preventing a door from moving or fixed to the bottom of a door to prevent it hitting a wall when opening, etc.

doorway /-weɪ/ *n* an opening in a wall, etc filled by a door.

dope /doːp/ *n* a thick pasty substance used for lubrication; (*inf*) any illegal drug, such as cannabis or narcotics; (*sl*) a stupid person; (*sl*) information. • *vt* to treat with dope. • *vi* to take addictive drugs.

dopey, dopy /ˈdoːpi/ *adj* (**dopier, dopiest**) (*sl*) stupid; (*inf*) half asleep.—**dopiness** *n*.

doppelgänger, doppelganger /ˈdɒpəl‚gɛŋər/ *n* a ghostly double of a living person.

Dorian /ˈdoːriən/ *adj* of or relating to an early Greek race that overthrew the Mycenaean civilization. • *n* a member of that race.

Doric /ˈdɒrɪk/ *adj* of the Dorians or their dialect; of or belonging to the oldest and simplest style of Greek architecture. • *n* the dialect of the Dorians; any broad dialect.

dormant /ˈdɔrmənt/ *adj* sleeping; quiet, as if asleep; inactive.—**dormancy** *n*.

dormer /ˈdɔrmər/ *n* an upright window that projects from a sloping roof.

dormitory /ˈdɔrmɪtɔri/ *n* (*pl* **dormitories**) a large room with many beds, as in a boarding school.

dormouse /ˈdɔrmeʊs/ *n* (*pl* **dormice**) a small mouse-like creature that hibernates in winter.

dorp /dɔrp/ *n* (*S Africa*) a small town.

dorsal /ˈdɔrsəl/ *adj* of, on, or near the back.—**dorsally** *adv*.

dorsiventral /‚dɔrsɪˈventrəl/ *adj* (*leaves*) having a differentiated back and front.

dory[1] /ˈdoːri/ *n* (*pl* **dories**) a light flat-bottomed boat with a sharp bow and high sides.

dory[2] *n* (*pl* **dories**) an edible yellow seafish.—*also* **John Dory**.

dosage /ˈdoːsɪdʒ/ *n* the administration of a medicine in doses; the size of a dose; the operation of dosing.

dose /doːs/ *n* the amount of medicine, radiation, etc administered at one time; a part of an experience; (*sl*) a venereal disease. • *vt* to administer a dose (of medicine) to.

doss /dɒs/ *vi* (*sl*) to sleep, *esp* in a dosshouse.

dossal, dossel /ˈdɒsəl/ *n* a hanging of silk or damask at the back and sides of an altar.

dosshouse /ˈdɒs‚heʊs/ *n* (*sl*) a cheap lodging house.

dossier /ˈdɒsi‚eɪ/ *n* a collection of documents about a subject or person, a file.

dot /dɒt/ *n* a small round speck, a point; the short signal in Morse code. • *vt* (**dotting, dotted**) to mark with a dot; to scatter (about).—**dotter** *n*.

dotage /ˈdoːtɪdʒ/ *n* weakness and infirmity caused by old age.

dotard /ˈdoːtərd/ *n* a person in their dotage.

dote /doːt/ *vi* (*with* **on** *or* **upon**) to show excessive affection.—**doter** *n*.

dot matrix printer /ˈdɒtˈmeɪtrɪks/ *n* (*comput*) a printer in which each printed character is formed by pins selected from a rectangular array.

dotted /ˈdɒtɪd/ *see* **dot**.

dotterel, dottrel /ˈdɒtərəl/ *n* a small plover of Europe and Asia, now rare; a similar Australian bird.

dottle /ˈdɒtəl/ *n* a remnant of tobacco left in a smoked pipe.

dotty /ˈdɒti/ *adj* (**dottier, dottiest**) (*inf*) eccentric, slightly mad.—**dottily** *adv*.—**dottiness** *n*.

double /ˈdʌbəl/ *adj* twice as large, as strong, etc; designed or intended for two; made of two similar parts; having two meanings, characters, etc; (*flowers*) having more than one circle of petals. • *adv* twice; in twos. • *n* a number or amount that is twice as much; a person or thing identical to another; (*film*) a person closely resembling an actor and who takes their place to perform stunts, etc; (*pl*) a game between two pairs of players. • *vti* to make or become twice as much or as many; to fold, to bend; to bend sharply backwards; to sail around; to have an additional purpose.—**doubly** *adv*.

double agent *n* a spy secretly acting for two governments at the same time.

double-barrelled, double-barreled /-ˈbærəld/ *adj* (*gun*) having two barrels; (*surname*) having two parts; (*question*) serving a double purpose.

double bass /-beɪs/ *n* the largest instrument of the violin family.—**double bassist** *n*.

double boiler *n* two saucepans fitting into each other so that the contents of the upper are cooked while boiling in the lower.

double-breasted /-brestɪd/ *adj* (*suit*) having one half of the front overlap the other.

double cream *n* cream with a high fat content.

double-cross /-‚krɒs/ *vt* to betray an associate, to cheat. • **double cross** *n*.—**double-crosser** *n*.

double-dealing /ˈdʌbəl‚diːlɪŋ/ *n* treachery, deceit.—**double-dealer** *n*.

double-edged /-‚edʒd/ *adj* acting in two ways; (*remarks*) having two possible meanings (*eg* well-meaning or malicious).

double entendre /‚dʌbəlɒnˈtɒndrə/ *n* a word or phrase with two meanings, one of which is *usu* indecent.

double entry *n* (*bookkeeping*) a system where each transaction is entered as a debit in one account and a credit in another.—**double-entry** *adj*.

double-faced /ˈdʌbəl‚feɪst/ *adj* having two faces; hypocritical.

double-jointed /-‚dʒɔɪntɪd/ *adj* having joints which allow the limbs, figures, etc an unusual degree of flexibility.

double-park /-‚pɑrk/ *vt* to park alongside a car which is already parked beside the kerb.

double-quick /-ˈkwɪk/ *adj, adv* very quick. • *vti* to march quickly.

double standard *n* a principle that is applied more strictly to one person or group than to another.

doublet /ˈdʌblət/ *n* (*formerly*) a man's close-fitting jacket; one of a pair of similar things.

doublethink /ˈdʌbəlθɪŋk/ *n* a belief in two conflicting ideas, principles, etc.

doubleton /-tən/ *n* two cards only of a suit (in a player's hand).

doubloon /dʌˈbluːn/ *n* an old Spanish gold coin.

doubt /deʊt/ *vi* to be uncertain or undecided. • *vt* to hold in doubt; to distrust; to be suspicious of. • *n* uncertainty; (*often pl*) lack of confidence in something, distrust.—**doubter** *n*.

doubtful /'dɐutful/ *adj* feeling doubt; uncertain; suspicious.—**doubtfully** *adv*.—**doubtfulness** *adv*.

doubtless /-ləs/ *adv* no doubt; probably. • *adj* assured; certain.—**doubtlessly** *adv*.—**doubtlessness** *n*.

douce /du:s/ *adj* (*Scot*) sober; sedate; prudent; modest.

douceur *Fr.* /du:'sœr/ *n* a gift for services rendered, or to secure favour; a bribe.

douche /du:ʃ/ *n* a jet of water directed on or into a part of the body; a device for applying this. • *vt* to cleanse or treat with a douche.

dough /do:/ *n* a mixture of flour and water, milk, etc used to make bread, pastry, or cake; (*inf*) money.

doughboy /-bɔɪ/ *n* a boiled dumpling; (*sl*) a soldier.

doughnut /-nʌt/ *n* a small, fried, *usu* ring-shaped, cake.—*also* **donut**.

doughty /'dɐuti/ *adj* (**doughtier, doughtiest**) valiant; strong.—**doughtily** *adv*.—**doughtiness** *n*.

doughy /'do:i/ *adj* (**doughier, doughiest**) soft, like dough.—**doughiness** *n*.

doum, doom /du:m/ or /dɐum/ *n* an Egyptian palm tree.

dour /dur/ or /dɐur/ *adj* stern; sullen; grim.—**dourly** *adv*.—**dourness** *n*.

douse /dɐus/ *vt* to plunge into or soak with water; to put out, extinguish.

dove[1] /dʌv/ *see* **dive**.

dove[2] *n* a small bird of the pigeon family; (*politics, diplomacy*) an advocate of peace or a peaceful policy.

dovecote, dovecot /'dʌvko:t/ *n* a shelter and breeding place for domesticated pigeons.

dovetail /-teɪl/ *n* a wedge-shaped joint used in woodwork. • *vt* to fit or combine together.

dowager /'dɐuədʒər/ *n* a widow possessing property or title from her husband; (*inf*) a dignified elderly woman.

dowdy /'dɐudi/ *adj* (**dowdier, dowdiest**) poorly dressed, not stylish.—**dowdily** *adv*.—**dowdiness** *n*.

dowel /'dɐuəl/ *n* a headless wooden or metal pin used for fastening wood or stone. • *vt* (**doweling, doweled** *or* **dowelling, dowelled**) to fasten with dowels.

dower /'dɐuər/ *n* a widow's share of her husband's estate.

down[1] *adv* towards or in a lower physical position; to a lying or sitting position; toward or to the ground, floor, or bottom; to a source or hiding place; to or in a lower status or in a worse condition; from an earlier time; in cash; to or in a state of less activity. • *adj* occupying a low position, *esp* lying on the ground; depressed, dejected. • *prep* in a descending direction in, on, along, or through. • *n* a low period (as in activity, emotional life, or fortunes); (*inf*) a dislike, prejudice. • *vti* to go or cause to go or come down; to defeat; to swallow.

down[2] /dɐun/ *n* soft fluffy feathers or fine hairs.

down[3] /dɐun/ *n* (*usu pl*) a tract of bare hilly land used for pasturing sheep; banks or rounded hillocks of sand.

downbeat /'dɐunbi:t/ *adj* (*mus*) the first beat in the bar, the downward gesture of a conductor's baton; (*inf*) dismal; relaxed.

downcast /-kæst/ *adj* dejected; (*eyes*) directed downwards.

downer /-ər/ *n* (*sl*) a depressant drug, *esp* a barbiturate; a depressing experience or situation.

downfall /-fɒl/ *n* a sudden fall (from power, etc); a sudden or heavy fall of rain or snow.

downgrade /-greɪd/ *n* a descending slope. • *vt* to reduce or lower in rank or position; to disparage.

download /-lo:d/ *vt* copy or transfers software or data from one storage device or computer to another. • *n* a transfer of software or data.

down payment *n* a deposit.

downpour /-pɔr/ *n* a heavy fall of rain.

downright /-raɪt/ *adj* frank; absolute. • *adv* thoroughly.

downscale, down-market /-skeɪl/ or /-mɑrkɪt/ *adj* (*goods, services*) of inferior quality.

downside /-saɪd/ *n* the less appealing or advantageous aspect of something.

downsize /-saɪz/ *vt* to produce a smaller version of (*eg* a car); to reduce the numbers in a workforce by means of redundancy.

Down's syndrome *n* a chromosomal abnormality resulting in a flat face, slanting eyes and mental retardation.

downstage /dɐun'steɪdʒ/ or /'dɐun-/ *adv* to the front of the stage.

downstairs /-'stɑrz/ *adv* to or on a lower floor. • *adj* on the ground floor or a lower floor. • *n* (*used as sing or pl*) the lower part of a house, the ground floor.

down-to-earth /-tə'ərθ/ *adj* practical, sensible.

downtown /dɐun'tɐun/ *n* the main business district of a town or city.—*also adj*.

downtrodden /-ˌtrɒdən/ *adj* oppressed, trampled underfoot.

downturn /-tərn/ *n* a decline in (economic) activity or prosperity.

down under *n* (*inf*) Australia or New Zealand.

downward /-wərd/ *adj* moving from a higher to a lower level, position or condition. • *adv* towards a lower place, position, etc; from an earlier time to a later.—*also* **downwards**.

downwind /-wɪnd/ *adv* in the direction the wind is blowing.—*also adj*.

downy /'dɐuni/ *adj* (**downier, downiest**) like, covered with, or made of, down.

dowry /'dɐuəri/ *n* (*pl* **dowries**) the money or possessions that a woman brings to her husband at marriage.

dowse /dɐuz/ *vi* to search for water, treasure, etc with a divining rod.—**dowser** *n*.

doxology /dɒk'sɒlədʒi/ *n* (*pl* **doxologies**) a hymn of praise to God.

doxy /'dɒksi/ *n* (*pl* **doxies**) (*arch*) a sweetheart, a prostitute.

doyen /'dɔɪən/ or /-'ɛn/, /'dwɒjã/ *n* a senior member of a group; an expert in a field; the oldest example of a category.—**doyenne** *nf*.

doyley /'dɔɪli/ *see* **doily**.

doze /do:z/ *vi* to sleep lightly. • *n* a light sleep, a nap.—**dozer** *n*.

dozen /'dʌzən/ *n* a group of twelve.—**dozenth** *adj*.

dozy /'do:zi/ *adj* (**dozier, doziest**) drowsy; (*inf*) stupid.—**dozily** *adv*.—**doziness** *n*.

DPhil, D.Phil *abbr* = Doctor of Philosophy.

Dr *abbr* = Doctor; debtor.

drab /dræb/ *adj* (**drabber, drabbest**) dull, uninteresting; of a dull brown colour. • *n* a dull yellowy brown colour; cloth of this colour.—**drably** *adv*.—**drabness** *n*.

drabble /'dræbəl/ *vt* to make wet or dirty by dragging through mud or water.

dracaena /drə'si:nə/ *n* any of a genus of tropical liliaceous palmlike plants.

drachm /dræm/ *n* in UK, a unit of capacity ($^1/_8$th fluid ounce); in US, a dram; a drachma.

drachma /'drækmə/ *n* (*pl* **drachmas, drachmae**) the monetary unit of Greece.

draconian /drə'ko:niən/ or /dreɪ-/ *adj* (*laws, etc*) very cruel, severe; (*with cap*) of the 7th-century Athenian statesman Draco or his extremely harsh laws.

draft /dræft/ *n* a rough plan, preliminary sketch; an order for the payment of money by a bank; a smaller group selected from a larger for a specific task; in the US, conscription. • *vt* to draw a rough sketch or outline of; to select for a special purpose; in the US, to conscript.—*also US* **draught**.

draftboard, draftsboard *see* **draughtboard**.

draftee /dræf'ti/ *n* a conscript.

draftsman /'dræftsmən/ *see* **draughtsman**.

drafty /'dræfti/ *see* **draughty**.

drag /dræg/ *vb* (**dragging, dragged**) *vt* to pull along by force; to draw slowly and heavily; to search (in water) with a dragnet or hook. • *vi* to trail on the ground; to move slowly and heavily; (*sl*) to draw on a cigarette. • *n* something used for dragging, a dragnet, a heavy harrow; something that retards progress; a braking device; (*sl*) something boring or tedious; (*sl*) women's clothes worn by a man; (*sl*) a draw at a cigarette.

dragée /'dræʒeɪ/ *n* a coated nut or ball of sugar; a silver-coated ball used as a cake decoration; a pill coated with sugar.

draggle /'drægəl/ *vt* to wet or soil by dragging in the mud or along the ground. • *vi* to become dirty or wet by dragging in the mud, etc.

dragnet /'drægnet/ *n* a net for scouring a riverbed, pond, etc to search for anything; a coordinated hunt for an escaped criminal, etc.

dragon /'drægon/ *n* a mythical winged reptile; an authoritarian or grim person, *esp* a woman.

dragonfly /-ˌflaɪ/ *n* (*pl* **dragonflies**) an insect with a long slender abdomen, large eyes and iridescent wings.

dragoon /drə'gu:n/ *n* a soldier on horseback, a cavalryman. • *vt* to force into submission by bullying commands.

drail /dreɪl/ *n* a weighted fishhook for dragging through water.

drain /dreɪn/ *vt* to draw off liquid gradually; to make dry by removing liquid gradually; to exhaust physically or mentally; to drink the entire contents of a glass. • *vi* to flow away gradually; to become dry as liquid trickles away. • *n* a sewer, pipe, etc by which water is drained away; something that causes exhaustion or depletion.—**drainer** *n*.

drainage /'dreɪnɪdʒ/ *n* a draining; a system of drains; something drained off.

draining board, drainboard /-bɔrd/ *n* a sloping, *usu* grooved, surface beside a sink for draining washed dishes.

drainpipe /-pəɪp/ *n* a pipe that carries waste liquid, sewage, etc out of a building.

drake /dreɪk/ *n* a male duck.

dram /dræm/ *n* a small drink of spirits; a small amount; a unit of capacity ($^1/_8$th fluid ounce); a unit of weight (avoirdupois 27.243 grains or 0.00265 ounce/apothecaries' weight 3 scruples or 60 grains).

drama /'drɑmə/ or /'dræmə/ *n* a play for the stage, radio or television; dramatic literature as a genre; a dramatic situation or a set of events.

dramatic /drə'mætɪk/ *adj* of or resembling drama; exciting, vivid.—**dramatically** *adv*.

dramatics /drə'mætɪks/ *n* (*used as sing or pl*) the producing or performing of plays; (*used as sing*) exaggerated behaviour, histrionics.

dramatis personae /ˌdræmətɪspər'sɔːnaɪ/ or /-ni/ *n* the characters in a play.

dramatist /'dræmətɪst/ *n* a person who writes plays.

dramatization /ˌdræmətɪ'zeɪʃən/ *n* the action or process of dramatizing; an event or novel, etc, adapted to the form of a play.

dramatize /'dræmə'taɪz/ *vt* to write or adapt in the form of a play; to express in an exaggerated or dramatic form.—**dramatizer** *n*.

dramaturge, dramaturg /-ˌtɜrdʒ/ *n* a playwright; a literary adviser; an expert in dramaturgy.

dramaturgy /-ˌtɜrdʒi/ *n* the art of dramatic composition; representation and stage effect.—**dramaturgic, dramaturgical** *adj*.

drank /dræŋk/ *see* **drink**.

drape /dreɪp/ *vt* to cover or hang with cloth; to arrange in loose folds; to place loosely or untidily. • *n* a hanging cloth or curtain; (*pl*) curtains.

draper /'dreɪpər/ *n* a seller of cloth.

drapery /'dreɪpəri/ *n* (*pl* **draperies**) fabrics or curtains, *esp* as arranged in loose folds; the trade of a draper.

drastic /'dræstɪk/ *adj* acting with force and violence.—**drastically** *adv*.

drat /dræt/ *interj* (*sl*) a euphemism for damn.

dratted /'drætəd/ *adj* (*sl*) confounded; annoying.

draught /drɑft/ *n* a current of air, *esp* in an enclosed space; the pulling of a load using an animal, etc; something drawn; a dose of medicine or liquid; an act of swallowing; the depth of water required to float a ship; beer, wine, etc stored in bulk in casks; a flat counter used in the game of draughts; (*pl*) (*used as sing*) a game for two players using 24 round pieces on a draughtboard.

draughtboard *n* a square board identical to a chessboard used for playing draughts.—*also* **draftboard, draftsboard**.

draughtsman[1] /'dræftsmən/ *n* (*pl* **draughtsmen**) a person who makes detailed drawings or plans.—*also US* **draftsman**.—**draughtsmanship, draftsmanship** *n*.

draughtsman[2] *n* (*pl* **draughtsmen**) *n* a flat counter used in the game of draughts.—*also US* **checker, draftsman**.

draughty /'drɑfti/ *adj* (**draughtier, draughtiest**) letting in or exposed to drafts of air.—*also US* **drafty**.—**draughtiness, draftiness** *n*.

Dravidian /drə'vɪdiːən/ *adj* pertaining to an ancient race and their languages, spoken in southern India and Sri Lanka. • *n* a member of this race; a family of languages spoken by the Dravidians.

draw /drɔ/ *vti* (**drawing, drew**, *pp* **drawn**) to haul, to drag; to cause to go in a certain direction; to pull out; to attract; to delineate, to sketch; to receive (as a salary); to bend (a bow) by pulling back the string; to leave (a contest) undecided; to write up, to draft (a will); to produce or allow a current of air; to draw lots; to get information from; (*ship*) to require a certain depth to float; (*with* on) to approach; to use (a resource); to withdraw (money) from (an account, etc); to put on (clothes); (*with* out) to extract; to prolong, extend; to cause (someone) to speak freely; to take (money) from an account; (*with* up) to bring or come to a standstill; to draft (a document); to straighten oneself; to form

soldiers into an array. • *n* the act of drawing; (*inf*) an event that attracts customers, people; the drawing of lots; a drawn game.

drawback /'drɔbæk/ *n* a hindrance, handicap.

drawbridge /-brɪdʒ/ *n* a bridge (*eg* over a moat) designed to be drawn up.

drawee /ˌdrɔ'iː/ *n* one on whom an order, bill of exchange, or a draft is drawn.

drawer /'drɔər/ or /drɔr/ *n* a person who draws; a person who draws a cheque; a sliding box-like compartment (as in a table, chest, or desk); (*pl*) knickers, underpants.

drawing /'drɔɪŋ/ *n* a figure, plan, or sketch drawn by using lines.

drawing pin *n* a thumbtack.

drawing room *n* a room where visitors are entertained, a living room.

drawl /drɔl/ *vt* to speak slowly and with elongated vowel sounds. • *n* drawling speech.—**drawler** *n*.—**drawlingly** *adv*.

drawn[1] /drɔn/ *see* **draw**.

drawn[2] *adj* looking strained because of tiredness or worry.

drawstring /'drɔstrɪŋ/ *n* a string or tape threaded through fabric which when pulled gathers it up or closes an opening (*eg* in a purse).

dray /dreɪ/ *n* a low, stoutly built cart used for heavy loads.

dread /dred/ *n* great fear or apprehension. • *vt* to fear greatly.

dreadful /'dredful/ *adj* full of dread; causing dread; extreme (*dreadful tiredness*); (*sl*) bad, disagreeable.—**dreadfully** *adv*.—**dreadfulness** *n*.

dreadlocks /-lɒks/ *npl* hair worn in long matted strands by male Rastafarians.

dreadnought, dreadnaught /-nɒt/ *n* a battleship with main armament entirely of big guns; a heavy cloth; an overcoat of this cloth.

dream /driːm/ *n* a stream of thoughts and images experienced during sleep; a day-dreaming state, a reverie; an ambition; an ideal. • *vb* (**dreaming, dreamt** *or* **dreamed**) *vi* to have a dream during sleep; to fantasize. • *vt* to dream of; to imagine as a reality; (*with* up) to devise, invent.—**dreamer** *n*.

dreamy /'driːmi/ *adj* (**dreamier, dreamiest**) given to dreaming, unpractical; (*inf*) attractive, wonderful.—**dreamily** *adv*.—**dreaminess** *n*.

dreary /-ri/ *adj* (**drearier, dreariest**) dull; cheerless.—**drearily** *adv*.—**dreariness** *n*.

dredge[1] /dredʒ/ *n* a device for scooping up material from the bottom of a river, harbour, etc. • *vt* to widen, deepen, or clean with a dredge; to scoop up with a dredge; (*with* up) (*inf*) to discover, reveal, *esp* through effort.

dredge[2] *vt* to coat (food) by sprinkling.

dredger[1] /'dredʒər/ *n* a vessel fitted with dredging equipment.

dredger[2] *n* a container with a perforated lid for sprinkling.

dreggy /'dregi/ *adj* (**dreggier, dreggiest**) full of dregs; like dregs.

dregs /dregz/ *npl* solid impurities that settle on the bottom of a liquid; residue; (*inf*) a worthless person or thing.

drench /drentʃ/ *vt* to soak, saturate.

dress /dres/ *n* clothing; a one-piece garment worn by women and girls comprising a top and skirt; a style or manner of clothing. • *vt* to put on or provide with clothing; to decorate; (*wound*) to wash and bandage; (*animal*) to groom; to arrange the hair; to prepare food (*eg* poultry, fish) for eating by cleaning, gutting, etc; (*with* up) to attire in best clothes; to improve the appearance of. • *vi* to put on clothes; to put on formal wear for an occasion; (*with* up) to put on fancy dress, etc.

dressage /drə'sɒʒ/ *n* the training of a horse in deportment and obedience.

dress circle *n* the first tier of seats in a theatre above the stalls.

dresser /'dresər/ *n* a person who assists an actor to dress; a type of kitchen sideboard.

dressing /-ɪŋ/ *n* a sauce or stuffing for food; manure spread over the soil; dress or clothes; the bandage, ointment, etc applied to a wound.

dressing-down /'dresɪŋ'daʊn/ *n* a severe scolding.

dressing gown *n* a loose garment worn when one is partially clothed.

dressmaker /'dresˌmeɪkər/ *n* a person who makes clothes.—**dressmaking** *n*.

dress rehearsal *n* rehearsal in full costume.

dressy /'dresi/ *adj* (**dressier, dressiest**) stylish; elaborate; showy.—**dressily** *adv*.—**dressiness** *n*.

drew /'druː/ *see* **draw**.

dribble /'drɪbəl/ vi to flow in a thin stream or small drips; to let saliva trickle from the mouth. • vt (soccer, basketball, hockey) to move (the ball) along little by little with the foot, hand, stick, etc. • n the act of dribbling; a thin stream of liquid.—**dribbler** n.

driblet /'drɪblət/ n a small amount; a drop, trickle.

dried /draɪd/ see **dry**.

drier /'draɪər/ see **dry, dryer**.

drift /drɪft/ n a heap of snow, sand, etc deposited by the wind; natural course, tendency; the general meaning or intention (of what is said); the extent of deviation (of an aircraft, etc) from a course; an aimless course; the action or motion of drifting. • vt to cause to drift. • vi to be driven or carried along by water or air currents; to move along aimlessly; to be piled into heaps by the wind.

driftage /'drɪftədʒ/ n matter that drifts ashore; deviation from a course caused by air or sea currents.

drifter /-ər/ n a person who wanders aimlessly.

driftwood /'drɪftwʊd/ n wood cast ashore by tides.

drill[1] /drɪl/ n an implement with a pointed end that bores holes; the training of soldiers, etc; repetitious exercises or training as a teaching method; (inf) correct procedure or routine. • vt to make a hole with a drill; to instruct or be instructed by drilling.

drill[2] n a machine for planting seeds in rows; a furrow in which seeds are planted; a row of seeds planted in this way.—also vt.

drilling platform n the fixed or mobile structure supporting the equipment and accommodation facilities, etc for drilling an offshore oil well.

drilling rig n the machinery required to drill an oil well.

drily /'draɪlɪ/ see **dry**.

drink /drɪŋk/ vb (**drinking, drank,** pp **drunk**) vt to swallow (a liquid); to take in, absorb; to join in a toast. • vi to consume alcoholic liquor, esp to excess. • n liquid to be drunk; alcoholic liquor; (sl) the sea.—**drinker** n.

drip /drɪp/ vti (**dripping, dripped**) to fall or let fall in drops. • n a liquid that falls in drops; the sound of falling drops; (med) a device for administering a fluid slowly and continuously into a vein; (inf) a weak or ineffectual person.—**dripper** n.

drip-dry /'drɪp,draɪ/ adj (clothing) drying easily and needing relatively little ironing.—also vti.

dripping /'drɪpɪŋ/ n fat that drips from meat during roasting.

drive /draɪv/ vb (**driving, drove,** pp **driven**) vt to urge, push or force onward; to direct the movement or course of; to convey in a vehicle; to carry through strongly; to impress forcefully; to propel (a ball) with a hard blow. • vi to be forced along; to be conveyed in a vehicle; to work, to strive (at). • n a trip in a vehicle; a stroke to drive a ball (in golf, etc); a driveway; a military attack; an intensive campaign; dynamic ability; the transmission of power to machinery.

drive-in /'draɪv,ɪn/ n a cinema, restaurant, etc, where customers are served in their cars.—also adj.

drivel /'drɪvəl/ n nonsense. • vi (**drivelling, drivelled** or **driveling, driveled**) to talk nonsense.—**driveller, driveler** n.

driven /-ən/ see **drive**.

driver /'draɪvər/ n one who or that which drives; a chauffeur; (golf) a wooden club used from the tee.

driveway /-,weɪ/ n a road for vehicles, often on private property.

drizzle /'drɪzəl/ n fine light rain.—also vi.—**drizzly** adj.

drogue /droːg/ n a sea anchor; a small parachute that slows down or stabilizes something (as a jet aircraft); a funnel-shaped device that enables an aeroplane to be refuelled from a tanker plane while in flight; a buoy at the end of a harpoon line; a windsock.

droit /drɔɪt/ Fr. /drwa/ n equity; a right of ownership, esp in land; custom; duty.

droll /droːl/ adj oddly amusing; whimsical.—**drollness** n.—**drolly** adv.

drollery /'droːlərɪ/ n (pl **drolleries**) the quality of being droll; buffoonery; a droll act.

dromedary /'drɒmə,dɛrɪ/ n (pl **dromedaries**) a one-humped camel.

drone /droːn/ n a male honey-bee; a lazy person; a deep humming sound; a monotonous speaker or speech; an aircraft piloted by remote control. • vi to make a monotonous humming sound; to speak in a monotonous manner.

drool /druːl/ vi to slaver, dribble; to show excessive enthusiasm for.

droop /druːp/ vi to bend or hang down; to become weak or faint. • n the act or an instance of drooping.

droopy /'druːpɪ/ adj (**droopier, droopiest**) drooping; tending to droop; (sl) tired, depressed.—**droopily** adv.—**droopiness** n.

drop /drɒp/ n a small amount of liquid in a roundish shape; something shaped like this, as a sweet; a tiny quantity; a sudden fall; the distance down; (pl) liquid medicine, etc dispensed in small drops. • vb (**dropping, dropped**) vi to fall in drops; to fall suddenly; to go lower, to sink; to come (in); (with in) to visit (with) informally; (with out) to abandon or reject (a course, society, etc). • vt to let fall, to cause to fall; to lower or cause to descend; to set down from a vehicle; to mention casually; to cause (the voice) to be less loud; to give up (as an idea).—**dropper** n.

drop-dead adv slang reference to a very attractive individual; drop-dead gorgeous.

drop kick n a kick made by dropping the ball onto the ground and kicking as it bounces.—**drop-kick** vt.

droplet /'drɒplət/ n a tiny drop (as of liquid).

dropout /-aʊt/ n a student who abandons a course of study; a person who rejects normal society.

droppings /-ɪŋz/ npl animal dung.

dropsy /-sɪ/ n an unnatural accumulation of serious fluid in any cavity of the body or its tissues.—**dropsical** adj.

droshky, drosky /'drɒʃkɪ/ n (pl **droshkies, droskies**) a light four-wheeled open Russian carriage.

dross /drɒs/ n a surface scum on molten metal; rubbish, waste matter.

drought /draʊt/ n a long period of dry weather.—**droughty** adj.

drove[1] /droːv/ see **drive**.

drove[2] n a group of animals driven in a herd or flock, etc; a large moving crowd of people.

drover /'droːvər/ n a person whose occupation is to drive cattle.

drown /draʊn/ vti to die or kill by suffocation in water or other liquid. • vt to flood; to drench; to become deeply immersed in some activity; to blot out (a sound) with a louder noise; to remove (sorrow, etc) with drink.

drowse /draʊz/ vi to be nearly asleep.

drowsy /'draʊzɪ/ adj (**drowsier, drowsiest**) sleepy; soporific; lethargic; inactive.—**drowsily** adv.—**drowsiness** n.

drub /drʌb/ vt (**drubbing, drubbed**) to thrash; to defeat convincingly.

drudge /drʌdʒ/ vi to do boring or very menial work. • n a person who drudges, esp a servant.—**drudger** n.—**drudgingly** adv.

drudgery /'drʌdʒərɪ/ n (pl **drudgeries**) dull, boring work.

drug /drʌg/ n any substance used in medicine; a narcotic. • vt (**drugging, drugged**) to administer drugs to; to stupefy.

drugget /'drʌgɪt/ n a coarse woollen or cotton fabric; a rug made of this.

druggist /'drʌgɪst/ n a pharmacist.

drugstore /-stɔr/ n a retail store selling medicines and other miscellaneous articles such as cosmetics, film, etc.

druid /'druːɪd/ n (often with cap) a priest of the ancient inhabitants (probably Celtic) of Britain, Gaul and Germany; a member of a modern society reviving druidism.—**druidic, druidical** adj.

druidism /'druːɪ,dɪzəm/ n the beliefs, manners, rites and customs of the druids.

drum /drʌm/ n a round percussion instrument, played by striking a membrane stretched across a hollow cylindrical frame; the sound of a drum; anything shaped like a drum, as a container for liquids. • vb (**drumming, drummed**) vi to play a drum; to beat or tap rhythmically. • vt (with in) to instil (knowledge) into a person by constant repetition; (with up) to summon as by drum; to create (business, etc) by concerted effort; to originate.

drumhead /'drʌmhɛd/ n the membrane stretched across the end of a drum.

drummer /'drʌmər/ n a person who plays a drum; (inf) a travelling salesman.

drumstick /-stɪk/ n a stick for beating a drum; the lower part of a cooked leg of poultry.

drunk[1] /drʌŋk/ see **drink**.

drunk[2] adj intoxicated with alcohol. • n a drunk person.

drunkard /'drʌŋkərd/ n an habitual drunk.

drunken /-kən/ adj intoxicated; caused by excessive drinking.—**drunkenly** adv.—**drunkenness** n.

drupe /druːp/ n a fleshy fruit with a stone, as a plum.—**drupaceous** adj.

drupelet /-lət/ n a small drupe in a compound fruit, eg raspberry.

druse /druːz/ n a crust of crystals; a rock cavity lined with this.

Druse, Druze *n* a member of a fanatical politico-religious sect in Syria and Lebanon.

dry /draɪ/ *adj* (**drier, driest**) free from water or liquid; thirsty; marked by a matter-of-fact, ironic or terse manner of expression; uninteresting, wearisome; (*bread*) eaten without butter, etc; (*wine*) not sweet; not selling alcohol. • *vti* (**drying, dried**) to make or become dry; (*with* **out**) to be treated for alcoholism or drug addiction.—**drily, dryly** *adv*.—**dryness** *n*.

dryad /ˈdraɪˌæd/ or /-əd/ *n* (*pl* **dryads, dryades**) (*Greek myth*) a wood nymph.

dry-clean /ˈdraɪˌkliːn/ *vt* to clean with solvents as opposed to water.—**dry-cleaner** *n*.—**dry-cleaning** *n*.

dry dock *n* a dock that can be drained of water to make ship repairs easier.

dryer /ˈdraɪr/ *n* a device for drying, as a tumble-drier; a clothes horse.—*also* **drier**.

dry ice *n* solid carbon dioxide.

dry rot *n* decay of timber caused by a fungus; any form of moral decay or corruption.

dry run *n* (*inf*) a rehearsal.

dry-salt /ˈdraɪˌsɔlt/ *vt* to cure (meat, etc) by salting and drying.

drysalter /-ˌsɔltər/ *n* (*formerly*) a dealer in dyes, oils, etc.—**drysaltery** *n*.

DSC *abbr* = Distinguished Service Cross.

DSM *abbr* = Distinguished Service Medal.

DSO *abbr* = Distinguished Service Order.

dt, DT *abbr* = delirium tremens.

DTP *abbr* = desktop publishing.

dual /ˈduːəl/ or /ˈdjuː-/ *adj* double; consisting of two.

dual carriageway *n* a road with traffic travelling in opposite directions separated by a central reservation.—*also* **divided highway**.

dualism /-ˌlɪzəm/ *n* a twofold division; (*philos*) the doctrine that the universe is based on two principles, *eg* good and evil, mind and matter.—**dualist** *n*.—**dualistic** *adj*.—**dualistically** *adv*.

duality /-ˌlɪti/ *n* (*pl* **dualities**) the condition or quality of being two or in two parts, dualism; dichotomy.

dub[1] /dʌb/ *vt* (**dubbing, dubbed**) to confer knighthood on; to nickname.

dub[2] *vt* (**dubbing, dubbed**) to replace the soundtrack of (a film), *eg* with one in a different language; to add sound effects or music to (a film, broadcast, etc); to transfer (a recording) to a new tape.

dubbin, dubbing /ˈdʌbɪn/ or /ˈdʌbɪŋ/ *n* a grease for softening and waterproofing leather.

dubiety /duːˈbaɪəti/ or /djuː-/ *n* (*pl* **dubieties**) doubtfulness, uncertainty; a matter of doubt.

dubious /ˈduːbiəs/ or /ˈdjuː-/ *adj* doubtful (about, of); uncertain as to the result; untrustworthy.—**dubiously** *adv*.—**dubiousness** *n*.

ducal /ˈduːkəl/ or /ˈdjuː-/ *adj* of or pertaining to a duke, a dukedom or a duchy.—**ducally** *adv*.

ducat /ˈdʌkət/ *n* a gold or silver coin formerly in use in Europe; (*pl*) (*sl*) money.

duce /ˈduːtʃeɪ/ *n* a chief, a leader; (*with cap*) the title used by the Italian Fascist dictator, Benito Mussolini (1922–43).

duchess /ˈdʌtʃəs/ *n* the wife or widow of a duke; a woman having the same rank as a duke in her own right.

duchy /ˈdʌtʃi/ *n* (*pl* **duchies**) the territory of a duke, a dukedom.

duck[1] /dʌk/ *vt* to dip briefly in water; to lower the head suddenly, *esp* to avoid some object; to avoid, dodge. • *vi* to dip or dive; to move the head or body suddenly; to evade a duty, etc. • *n* a ducking movement.

duck[2] *n* (*pl* **ducks, duck**) a water bird related to geese and swans; the female of this bird; its flesh used as food.

duck[3] *n* a plain cotton cloth; (*pl*) trousers or light clothes made from this and worn in hot climates.

duckbill, duck-billed platypus /ˈdʌkbɪl/ *n* an Australian egg-laying furred mammal with webbed feet and a broad bill.—*also* **platypus**.

duckboard /-bɔrd/ *n* a path of wooden slats laid over muddy or wet ground.

duckling /-lɪŋ/ *n* a young duck.

duckweed /-wiːd/ *n* a common floating freshwater plant.

ducky, duckie /ˈdʌki/ *adj* (**duckier, duckiest**) (*inf*) fine; satisfactory; cute. • *n* (*pl* **duckies**) (*inf*) a term of endearment, darling.

duct /ˈdʌkt/ *n* a channel or pipe for fluids, electric cable, etc; a tube in the body for fluids to pass through.

ductile /ˈdʌktaɪl/ *adj* malleable; yielding.

dud /dʌd/ *adj* (*sl*) worthless. • *n* (*sl*) anything worthless; an ineffectual person.

dude /duːd/ *n* a dandy; a city person on holiday in a ranch.

dudeen /duːˈdiːn/ or /θuː-/ *n* a short clay tobacco pipe.

dudgeon /ˈdʌdʒən/ *n* resentment, indignation; (*arch*) the hilt of a dagger.

due /duː/ or /djuː/ *adj* owed as a debt; immediately payable; fitting, appropriate; appointed or expected to do or arrive. • *adv* directly, exactly. • *n* something due or owed; (*pl*) fees.

duel /ˈduːəl/ or /ˈdjuː-/ *n* combat with weapons between two persons over a matter of honour, etc; conflict of any kind between two people, sides, ideas, etc. • *vi* (**duelling, duelled** or **dueling, dueled**) to fight in a duel.—**duellist, duelist** *n*.

duello /duːˈɛloː/ or /djuː-/ *n* (*pl* **duellos**) the duelists' code.

duenna /duːˈɛnə/ or /djuː-/ *n* an older woman acting as a chaperone of young women in Spanish or Portuguese families.

duet /duːˈɛt/ or /djuː-/ *n* a musical composition for two performers.—**duettist** *n*.

duffel, duffle /ˈdʌfəl/ *n* a coarse, heavy woollen cloth.

duffel bag, duffle bag *n* a large circular drawstring bag for personal belongings.

duffel coat, duffle coat *n* a heavy, hooded overcoat, fastened with toggles.

duffer /ˈdʌfər/ *n* an incompetent person, *esp* an elderly one.

dug /dʌg/ *see* **dig**.

dugong /ˈduːgɒŋ/ *n* an aquatic herbivorous mammal resembling the seal and walrus; the sea cow.

dugout /ˈdʌgaʊt/ *n* a boat made from the hollowed out tree trunk; a rough underground shelter.

duiker /ˈdɔɪkər/ *n* (*pl* **duikers, duiker**) a small South African antelope.

duke /duːk/ or /djuːk/ *n* the highest order of British nobility; the title of a ruler of a European duchy.

dukedom /ˈduːkdəm/ or /ˈdjuːk-/ *n* a duchy; the rank, position or title of a duke.

dulcet /ˈdʌlsət/ *adj* sweet-sounding, melodious.—**dulcetly** *adv*.

dulcimer /ˈdʌlsɪmər/ *n* a musical instrument with wire strings that are struck with a hammer; a folk-music instrument with *usu* three strings that are played by plucking.—*also* **dulcimore**.

dulia /duːˈlaɪə/ or /djuː-/ *n* the veneration paid to saints and angels as the servants of God.

dull /dʌl/ *adj* not sharp or pointed; not bright or clear; stupid; boring; not active. • *vti* to make or become dull.—**dully** *adv*.—**dullness** *n*.

dullard /ˈdʌlərd/ *n* a slow-witted person.

dulse /dʌls/ *n* a red edible seaweed found on rocks.

duly /ˈduːli/ or /ˈdjuː-/ *adv* properly; suitably.

dumb /dʌm/ *adj* not able to speak; silent; (*inf*) stupid.—**dumbly** *adv*.—**dumbness** *n*.

dumbbell /ˈdʌmˌbel/ *n* one of a pair of heavy weights used for muscular exercise; (*sl*) a fool.

dumbfound, dumfound /ˈdʌmfaʊnd/ or /dʌmˈfaʊnd/ *vti* to astonish, surprise.

dumbwaiter /ˈdʌmˌweɪtər/ *n* a stand with revolving shelves for holding food; a revolving tray for holding food; a small elevator or lift for carrying food, etc, between floors.

dum-dum /ˈdʌmdʌm/ *n* (*sl*) a foolish person.

dumdum (bullet) *n* a soft-nosed, expanding bullet.

dumdum *n* (*sl*) a stupid person; a dummy.

dummy /ˈdʌmi/ *n* (*pl* **dummies**) a figure of a person used to display clothes; (*sl*) a soother or pacifier for a baby; a stupid person; an imitation; (*bridge*) the exposed cards of the dealer's partner.

dump /dʌmp/ *vt* to drop or put down carelessly in a heap; to deposit as rubbish; to abandon or get rid of; to sell goods abroad at a price lower than the market price abroad; (*with* **on**) (*sl*) to censure strongly the words or actions of others. • *n* a place for refuse; a temporary store; (*inf*) a dirty, dilapidated place; (*pl*) (*inf*) despondency, low spirits.—**dumper** *n*.

dumpling /ˈdʌmplɪŋ/ *n* a rounded piece of dough cooked by boiling or steaming; a short, fat person.

dumpster /ˈdʌmpstər/ *n* a large garbage can.

dumpy /ˈdʌmpi/ *adj* (**dumpier, dumpiest**) short and thick.—**dumpily** *adv*.—**dumpiness** *n*.

dun[1] /dʌn/ *adj* (**dunner, dunnest**) greyish-brown.—**dunness** *n*.

dun[2] *vt* (**dunning, dunned**) to press persistently for payment of a debt.

dunce /dʌns/ *n* a person who is stupid or slow to learn.

dunderhead /ˈdʌndərˌhɛd/ *n* a stupid person, a dunce.—**dunderheaded** *adj*.

dune /djuːn/ or /duːn/ *n* a hill of sand piled up by the wind.

dung /dʌŋ/ *n* excrement; manure; filth. • *vt* to spread with manure.—**dungy** *adj*.

dungaree /ˌdʌŋɡəˈriː/ *n* a coarse cotton cloth; (*pl*) overalls or trousers made from this.

dungeon /ˈdʌndʒən/ *n* an underground cell for prisoners.

dunghill /ˈdʌŋhɪl/ *n* a heap of dung.

dunk /dʌŋk/ *vti* to dip (cake, etc) into liquid, *eg* coffee.

dunlin /ˈdʌnlɪn/ *n* a small red-backed sandpiper of northern regions.

dunnage /ˈdʌnɪdʒ/ *n* loose wood, etc, used to pack cargo or keep it out of bilge water in a ship's hold; baggage.

dunnite /ˈdʌnɔɪt/ *n* a powerful explosive used *esp* in shells.

duo /ˈduːoː/ or /ˈdjuːoː/ *n* (*pl* **duos, dui**) a pair of performers; (*inf*) two persons connected in some way.

duodecimal /ˌdjuːoːˈdɛsɪməl/ *adj* of twelve; proceeding by twelves. • *n* a twelfth; a system of computing by twelves.

duodecimo /-ˌmoː/ *n* (*pl* **duodecimos**) a book of sheets folded into twelve leaves; this book size.—*also* **twelvemo**.

duodenary /-ˈdɛnəri/ *adj* duodecimal.

duodenum /ˌduːoːˈdiːnəm/ or /ˌdjuː-/, /duːˈɒdənəm/ *n* (*pl* **duodena, duodenums**) the first part of the small intestine.—**duodenal** *adj*.

duologue /ˈduːəˌlɒɡ/ or /ˈdjuː-/ *n* a play with two actors; a conversation between two people.

dup *vt* (**dupping, dupped**) (*arch*) to open.

dupe /duːp/ or /djuːp/ *n* a person who is cheated. • *vt* to deceive; to trick.—**dupable** *adj*.—**duper** *n*.—**dupery** *n*.

duple /ˈduːpəl/ or /ˈdjuː-/ *adj* double; (*mus*) of two beats to the bar.

duplex /ˈduːˌplɛks/ or /ˈdjuː-/ *adj* having two parts, double. • *n* a flat or apartment on two floors.—**duplexity** *n*.

duplicate /ˈduːplɪkət/ or /ˈdjuː-/ *adj* in pairs, double; identical; copied exactly from an original. • *n* one of a pair of identical things; a copy. • *vt* to make double; to make an exact copy of; to repeat.—**duplicable** *adj*.

duplication /ˌduːplɪˈkeɪʃən/ or /ˌdjuː-/ *n* the act of duplicating; a copy; multiplication by two.—**duplicative** *adj*.

duplicator /ˈduːplɪˌkeɪtər/ or /ˈdjuː-/ *n* a machine for making copies, *esp* of a document.

duplicity /duːˈplɪsɪti/ or /djuː-/ *n* (*pl* **duplicities**) treachery; deception.—**duplicitous** *adj*.

durable /ˈdʊrəbəl/ or /ˈdjʊ-/ *adj* enduring, resisting wear, etc.—**durability** *n*.—**durably** *adv*.

duralumin /duːˈræljuːmɪn/ or /djuː-/ *n* a strong alloy of aluminium with copper, magnesium, manganese and silicon.

dura mater /ˌdʊrəˈmeɪtər/ or /ˌdjʊr-/ *n* the tough outer membrane that envelops the brain and spinal cord.

duramen /duːˈreɪmən/ or /djuː-/ *n* the inner heartwood of a tree.

durance /ˈdʊrəns/ or /ˈdjʊr-/ *n* imprisonment.

duration /dʊˈreɪʃən/ or /djʊ-/ *n* the time in which an event continues.

durbar /ˈdɜrbɑr/ *n* (*formerly*) a state levee or reception in India and Africa.

duress /dʊˈrɛs/ or /djʊ-/, /ˈdʊ-/, /ˈdjʊ-/ *n* compulsion by use of force or threat; unlawful constraint; imprisonment.

durian, durion /ˈdʊriən/ *n* an oval fruit with a foul smell and a pleasant taste; the Asian tree that bears it.

during /ˈdjʊrɪŋ/ *prep* throughout the duration of; at a point in the course of.

durmast /ˈdɜrmæst/ *n* a dark European oak yielding a tough wood.

durst /dɜrst/ *see* **dare**.

dusk /dʌsk/ *n* (the darker part of) twilight.

dusky /ˈdʌski/ *adj* (**duskier, duskiest**) having a dark colour.—**duskily** *adv*.—**duskiness** *n*.

dust /dʌst/ *n* fine particles of solid matter. • *vt* to free from dust; to sprinkle with flour, sugar, etc.

dustbin /ˈdʌstbɪn/ or /ˈdʌsbɪn/ *n* a container for household refuse.—*also* **garbage can, trash can**.

dust bowl *n* a drought area subject to dust storms.

dust cover *n* a dust jacket.

duster (coat), dustcoat *n* a coat for keeping off dust, worn *esp* by early motorists.

duster /ˈdʌstər/ *n* a cloth for dusting; a device for dusting; a duster coat; a light housecoat.

dustman /ˈdʌstmən/ or /ˈdʌsmən/ *n* (*pl* **dustmen**) a garbageman.

dust jacket *n* a paper cover for a book.

dust wrapper *n* a dust jacket.

dusty /ˈdʌsti/ *adj* (**dustier, dustiest**) covered with dust.—**dustily** *adv*.—**dustiness** *n*.

Dutch /dʌtʃ/ *adj* pertaining to Holland, its people, or language. • *n* the Dutch language.

Dutch courage *n* courage obtained from alcohol; alcoholic drink.

Dutch elm disease *n* a fungal disease which withers the foliage of elm trees and eventually kills them.

Dutch oven *n* a metal box for cooking before an open fire.

Dutch treat *n* a meal, etc, where each pays for himself or herself.

Dutch uncle *n* a person with stern kindness.

duteous /ˈduːtiːəs/ or /ˈdjuːt-/ *adj* (*poet*) dutiful.—**duteously** *adv*.—**duteousness** *n*.

dutiable /ˈduːtiːəbəl/ or /ˈdjuːt-/ *adj* (*goods, etc*) subject to duty.—**dutiability** *n*.

dutiful /ˈduːtɪfʊl/ or /ˈdjuːt-/ *adj* performing one's duty; obedient.—**dutifully** *adv*.—**dutifulness** *n*.

duty /ˈduːti/ or /ˈdjuːti/ *n* (*pl* **duties**) an obligation that must be performed for moral or legal reasons; respect for one's elders or superiors; actions and responsibilities arising from one's business, occupation, etc; a tax on goods or imports, etc.

duty-free /-ˈfriː/ *adj* free from tax or duty.

duumvir /duːˈʌmvər/ or /ˈduːəm-/ /djuː-/ *n* (*pl* **duumvirs, duumviri**) in ancient Rome, either of two officers of high rank acting together in one capacity or public function; either member of a duumvirate.

duumvirate /duːˈʌmvɪrət/ or /djuː-/ *n* a governing body of two; two such people.

duvet /ˈduːveɪ/ *n* a thick, soft quilt used instead of bedclothes.—*also* **continental quilt**.

DVD /ˈdiːˈviːˈdiː/ *abbr* = digital video disc.

dwarf /dwɔrf/ *n* (*pl* **dwarfs, dwarves**) a person, animal or plant of abnormally small size. • *vt* to stunt; to cause to appear small.

dwarfish /ˈdwɔrfɪʃ/ *adj* like a dwarf; very small.—**dwarfishness** *n*.

dweeb /dwiːb/ *n* (*sl*) a bore or person perhaps considered unfashionable, a dull person.—*adj* **dweeby, dweebish**.

dwell /dwɛl/ *vi* (**dwelling, dwelt** *or* **dwelled**) to live (in a place); (*with* **on**) to focus the attention on; to think, talk, or write at length about.—**dweller** *n*.

dwelling /ˈdwɛlɪŋ/ *n* the house, etc where one lives, habitation.

dwindle /ˈdwɪndəl/ *vi* to shrink, diminish; to become feeble.

Dy (*chem symbol*) dysprosium.

dyad /ˈdaɪæd/ *n* a pair; (*chem*) a bivalent atom, element, or radical.—**dyadic** *adj*.

dyarchy /ˈdaɪˌɑrki/ *see* **diarchy**.

dye /daɪ/ *vt* (**dyeing, dyed**) to give a new colour to. • *n* a colouring substance, *esp* in solution; a colour or tint produced by dyeing.—**dyer** *n*.

dyeing /ˈdaɪɪŋ/ *n* the process or work of giving colour to fabrics using dyes.

dyed-in-the-wool /ˌdaɪdɪnðəˈwʊl/ *adj* uncompromising in attitude or opinion.

dyestuff /ˈdaɪˌstʌf/ *n* material yielding a dye.

dying[1] /ˈdaɪɪŋ/ *see* **die**[1].

dying[2] *adj* passing away from life; decaying physically; drawing to a close; expiring. • *n* death.

dyke[1] /daɪk/ *see* **dike**[2].

dyke[2] *n* (*derog*) a lesbian.

dynamic /daɪˈnæmɪk/ *adj* relating to force that produces motion; (*person*) forceful, energetic.—**dynamically** *adv*.

dynamics /-s/ *n* (*used as sing*) the branch of science that deals with forces and their effect on the motion of bodies.

dynamism /ˈdaɪnəˌmɪzəm/ *n* dynamic influence or power; (*philos*) the theory that the universe is constituted of forces.—**dynamist** *n*.—**dynamistic** *adj*.

dynamite /ˈdaɪnəˌmaɪt/ *n* a powerful explosive; a potentially dangerous situation; (*inf*) an energetic person or thing. • *vt* to blow up with dynamite.—**dynamiter** *n*.

dynamo /ˈdaɪnəˌmoː/ *n* (*pl* **dynamos**) a device that generates electric current.

dynamoelectric /ˌdaɪnəˌmoːɪˈlɛktrɪk/, **dynamoelectrical** /-moːˈɪlɛktrɪkəl/ *adj* of or denoting the production of electricity from mechanical energy or of mechanical energy from electricity.

dynamometer /ˌdaɪnəˈmɒmɪtər/ *n* an instrument for measuring energy expended.

dynast /ˈdaɪˌnæst/ *n* a ruler, *usu* a hereditary one.

dynasty /ˈdaɪnəsti/ *n* (*pl* **dynasties**) a line of hereditary rulers or leaders of any powerful family or similar group.—**dynastic** *adj*.—**dynastically** *adv*.

dyne /daɪn/ *n* a unit of force, causing in one gram an acceleration per second of one centimetre per second; the unit of force in the cgs system.

dys- /dɪs/ *prefix* bad, unfavourable.

dysentery /ˈdɪsənˌteri/ or /-tri/ *n* painful inflammation of the large intestine with associated diarrhoea.—**dysenteric** *adj*.

dysergy /ˈdɪsərdʒi/ *n* (*business*) the possibility that the merger of two companies will produce a combined operation of less productivity and efficiency, the opposite of synergy.

dysfunction /dɪsˈfʌŋkʃən/ *n* a failure in normal functioning.—**dysfunctional** *adj*.

dysgenic /dɪsˈdʒenɪk/ *adj* having a bad effect on the hereditary qualities of a race.

dysgenics /dɪsˈdʒenɪks/ *n* (*used as sing*) the study of the causes of reduction in quality of a race.

dyslexia /dɪsˈlɛksiə/ *n* impaired ability in reading or spelling.—**dyslexic** *adj*, *n*.

dysmenorrhoea, dysmenorrhea /ˌdɪsmɛnəˈriːə/ *n* painful menstruation.—**dysmenorrhoeal, dysmenorrheal** *adj*.

dyspepsia /dɪsˈpɛpsiə/ *n* indigestion, *esp* chronic.

dyspeptic /dɪsˈpɛptɪk/ *adj* of or afflicted with indigestion. • *n* a dyspeptic sufferer.

dysphagia /dɪsˈfeɪdʒə/ or /-dʒiə/ *n* difficulty in swallowing.—**dysphagic** *adj*.

dysphasia /ˌdɪsˈfeɪʒə/ or /-ziə/ *n* a deficiency in the use or understanding of language.—**dysphasic** *adj*.

dysphoria /dɪsˈfɔriə/ *n* morbid restlessness, fidgets.—**dysphoric** *adj*.

dyspnoea, dyspnea /dɪspˈniːə/ *n* shortness of breath, difficulty in breathing.—**dyspnoeal, dyspneal, dyspneic, dyspnoeic** *adj*.

dysprosium /dɪsˈproːziəm/ *n* a soft metallic element used in lasers and magnetic alloys.

dystrophy /ˈdɪstrəfi/ *n* various hereditary disorders causing progressive weakening of the muscles (*muscular dystrophy*).—**dystrophic** *adj*.

dysuria /dɪsˈjʊriə/ *n* difficulty in passing urine.—**dysuric** *adj*.

E

E. *abbr* = east; eastern.

E- /iː/ *prefix* used to indicate a standard system (for packaging, weight, content, etc) within the European Community.

each /iːtʃ/ *adj* every one of two or more.

eager /'iːɡər/ *adj* enthusiastically desirous (of); keen (for); marked by impatient desire or interest.—**eagerly** *adv*.—**eagerness** *n*.

eager beaver *n* (*inf*) an exceptionally diligent person.

eagle /'iːɡəl/ *n* a bird of prey with keen eyes and powerful wings; (*golf*) a score of two strokes under par.

eagle-eyed /-ˌaɪd/ *adj* having very sharp eyesight.

eagle owl *n* a type of large owl, also known as the great horned owl.

eaglet /'iːɡlət/ *n* a young eagle.

ear[1] /iːr/ *n* (the external part of) the organ of hearing; the sense or act of hearing; attention; something shaped like an ear.

ear[2] *n* the part of a cereal plant (*eg* corn, maize) that contains the seeds.

earache /'iːrˌeɪk/ *n* a pain in the ear.

eardrum /-ˌdrʌm/ *n* the membrane within the ear that vibrates in response to sound waves.

eared /'iːrd/ *adj* having ears.

earing /'iːrɪŋ/ *n* (*naut*) a rope attaching the upper corner of a sail to a yard or stanchion.

earl /ɜːrl/ *n* a member of the British nobility ranking between a marquis and a viscount.—**countess** *nf*.

earldom /ɜːrldəm/ *n* the position or estate of an earl.

early /'ɜːrli/ *adj* (**earlier, earliest**) before the expected or normal time; of or occurring in the first part of a period or series; of or occurring in the distant past or near future.—*also adv*.—**earliness** *n*.

earmark /'iːrmɑːrk/ *vt* to set aside for a specific use; to put an identification mark on. • *n* a distinguishing mark.

earn /ɜːrn/ *vt* to gain (money, etc) by work or service; to acquire; to deserve; to earn interest (on money invested, etc).

earnest /'ɜːrnɪst/ *adj* sincere in attitude or intention.—**earnestly** *adv*.—**earnestness** *n*.

earnings /'ɜːrnɪŋz/ *npl* wages or profits; something earned.

earphone /'iːrˌfoːn/ *n* a device held to or worn over the ear, through which sound is transmitted; a headphone.

earpiece /'iːrpiːs/ *n* a telephone earphone.

earplug /-plʌɡ/ *n* a piece of wadding or wax inserted in the ear to prevent noise or water penetration.

earring /'iːrɪŋ/ *n* an ornament worn on the ear lobe.

earshot /'iːrʃɒt/ *n* hearing distance.

ear-splitting /-ˌsplɪtɪŋ/ *adj* very loud.

earth /ɜːrθ/ *n* the world that we inhabit; solid ground, as opposed to sea; soil; the burrow of a badger, fox, etc; a connection between an electric device or circuit with the earth; (*inf*) a large amount of money. • *vt* to cover with or bury in the earth; to connect an electrical circuit or device to earth.

earthborn /'ɜːrθbɔːrn/ *adj* mortal.

earthbound /-ˌbaʊnd/ *adj* confined to the earth; heading towards the earth.

earthen /'ɜːrθən/ *adj* composed of earth; made of baked clay.

earthenware /-ˌwer/ *n* pottery, etc made from baked clay.

earthly /-li/ *adj* (**earthlier, earthliest**) of the earth; material, worldly.—**earthliness** *n*.

earthquake /-ˌkweɪk/ *n* a violent tremor of the earth's crust.

earth science *n* any of the sciences (*eg* geology) concerned with the nature and composition of the earth.

earthward /-wərd/, **earthwards** *adv* towards the earth.

earthwork /-ˌwɜːrk/ *n* an excavation of earth; a fortification.

earthworm /-ˌwɜːrm/ *n* any of various common worms that live in the soil.

earthy /'ɜːrθi/ *adj* (**earthier, earthiest**) of or resembling earth; crude.—**earthiness** *n*.

earwax /'iːrˌwæks/ *n* cerumen, the brown wax found in the ear.

earwig /'iːrwɪɡ/ *n* a small insect with a pincer-like appendage at the end of its body.

ease /iːz/ *n* freedom from pain, discomfort or disturbance; rest from effort or work; effortlessness; lack of inhibition or restraint, naturalness. • *vt* to relieve from pain, trouble, or anxiety; to relax, make less tight, release; to move carefully and gradually. • *vi* (*often with* **off**) to become less active, intense, or severe.

easeful /-fəl/ *adj* restful.

easel /'iːzəl/ *n* a supporting frame, *esp* one used by artists to support their canvases while painting.

easement /'iːzmənt/ *n* relief; something that gives ease or relief; (*law*) right of way over someone else's land.

easily /'iːzɪli/ *adv* with ease; by far; probably.

east /'iːst/ *n* the direction of the sunrise; the compass point opposite west; (*with cap preceded by* **the**) the area of the world east of Europe. • *adj, adv* in, towards, or from the east.

Easter /'iːstər/ *n* the Christian festival observed on a Sunday in March or April in commemoration of the resurrection of Christ.

easterly /'iːstərli/ *adj* situated towards or belonging to the east, coming from the east. • *n* (*pl* **easterlies**) a wind from the east.

eastern /'iːstərn/ *adj* of or in the east.

easterner /'iːstərnər/ *n* someone from the east.

easternmost /-ˌmoːst/ *adj* farthest to the east.

easting /'iːstɪŋ/ *n* the distance travelled by a vessel eastwards from a given meridian.

eastward /'iːstwərd/ *adj* towards the east.—**eastwards** *adv*.

easy /'iːzi/ *adj* (**easier, easiest**) free from pain, trouble, anxiety; not difficult or requiring much effort; (*manner*) relaxed; lenient; compliant; unhurried; (*inf*) open to all alternatives. • *adv* with ease.—**easiness** *n*.

easy chair *n* a comfortable chair.

easygoing /-ˌɡoːɪŋ/ *adj* placid, tolerant, relaxed.

eat /iːt/ *vt* (**eating, ate,** *pp* **eaten**) to take into the mouth, chew and swallow as food; to have a meal; to consume, to destroy bit by bit; (*also with* **into**) to corrode; (*inf*) to bother, cause anxiety to; (*with* **up**) to consume completely; (*inf*) to listen or absorb avidly; (*with* **out**) to preoccupy. • *vi* (*with* **out**) to eat away from home, *esp* in a restaurant. • *n* (*pl: inf*) food.—**eater** *n*.

eatable /'iːtəbəl/ *adj* suitable for eating; fit to be eaten. • *n* (*pl*) food.

eating disorder *n* a psychological disorder identified by unusual or abnormal eating patterns.

eau de Cologne /ˌoːdəkəˈloːn/ *n* (*pl* **eaux de Cologne**) a perfume originally from Cologne.

eau de vie /-ˌoːdəˈviː/ *n* brandy.

eaves /iːvz/ *npl* the overhanging edge of a roof.

eavesdrop /'iːvzdrɒp/ *vi* (**eavesdropping, eavesdropped**) to listen secretly to a private conversation.—**eavesdropper** *n*.

ebb /ɛb/ *n* the flow of the tide out to sea; a decline. • *vi* (*tide water*) to flow back; to become lower, to decline.

ebon /'ɛbən/ *n* (*poet*) ebony.

ebonite /'ɛbəˌnaɪt/ *n* a hard black rubber substance.

ebonize /'ɛbənaɪz/ *vt* to make black by staining like ebony.

ebony /'ɛbəni/ *n* (*pl* **ebonies**) a hard heavy wood. • *adj* black as ebony.

ebracteate /iːˈbræktiət/ *adj* without bracts.

ebullient /ɪˈbɛliənt/ or /-bʊl-/ *adj* exuberant, enthusiastic; boiling.—**ebullience, ebulliency** *n*.—**ebulliently** *adv*.

ebullition /ˌɛbəˈlɪʃən/ or /ˌɛbjuː-/ *n* boiling; an outburst (of passion, feeling, etc).

EC *abbr* = European Community.

eccentric /ɪkˈsɛntrɪk/ or /ɛk-/ *adj* deviating from a usual or accepted pattern; unconventional in manner or appearance, odd; (*circles*) not concentric; off centre; not precisely circular. • *n* an eccentric person.—**eccentrically** *adv*.

eccentricity /-ˈtrɪsɪti/ *n* (*pl* **eccentricities**) strangeness of behaviour; an eccentric or unusual habit.

ecclesiastic[1] /ɪˌkliːziˈæstɪk/ *n* a member of the clergy.

ecclesiastic[2], **ecclesiastical** /-əl/ *adj* of or relating to the Christian Church or clergy.—**ecclesiastically** *adv*.

ecclesiasticism /-tɪˌsɪzəm/ *n* excessive attachment to the forms, usages, organization and privileges of the Christian Church.

ecclesiology /ɪˌkliːziˈɒlədʒi/ or /ɪ-/ *n* the study of the Christian Church and its development; the study of church architecture and decoration.—**ecclesiological** *adj.*—**ecclesiologist** *n*.

ecdysis /ˈɛkdaɪsɪs/ (*pl* **ecdyses**) *n* sloughing of skin, moulting.

ECG /ˈiːˈsiːˈdʒiː/ *abbr* = electrocardiogram.

echelon /ˈɛʃəˌlɒn/ or /ˈeɪʃəˌlɔ̃/ *n* a stepped formation of troops, ships, or aircraft; a level (of authority) in a hierarchy.

echidna /ɪˈkɪdnə/ *n* (*pl* **echidnas, echidnae**) an Australian nocturnal, toothless, spiny, egg-laying animal.

echinoderm /ɪˈkaɪnəˌdɜrm/ *n* one of a class of animals which includes starfish and sea urchins.

echinus /ɪˈkaɪnəs/ *n* (*pl* **echini**) a sea urchin.

echo /ˈɛkoː/ *n* (*pl* **echoes**) a repetition of sound caused by the reflection of sound waves; imitation; the reflection of a radar signal by an object. • *vb* (**echoing, echoed**) *vi* to resound; to produce an echo. • *vt* to repeat; to imitate; to send back (a sound) by an echo.

echo chamber *n* a room with walls that reflect sound, used for making acoustic measurements and creating special sound effects.

echoic /ɛˈkoːɪk/ *adj* like an echo; imitative.

echolocation /ˈɛkoːloːˌkeɪʃən/ *n* finding unseen objects by means of reflected sound waves.

echo sounder *n* an instrument for determining the depth beneath a ship using sound waves.—**echo sounding** *n*.

éclair /eɪˈklɛr/ or /ɪ-/ *n* a small oblong shell of choux pastry covered with chocolate and filled with cream.

eclampsia /ɛkˈlæmpsiə/ *n* (*med*) a serious condition occurring in the last three months of pregnancy, caused by toxins in the blood and causing convulsions.

éclat /eɪˈklɒ/ *n* success; applause; striking effect; social distinction.

eclectic /ɪkˈlɛktɪk/ *adj* selecting from or using various styles, ideas, methods, etc; composed of elements from a variety of sources. • *n* a person who adopts an eclectic method.—**eclectically** *adv.*—**eclecticism** *n*.

eclipse /ɪˈklɪps/ *n* the obscuring of the light of the sun or moon by the intervention of the other; a decline into obscurity, as from overshadowing by others. • *vt* to cause an eclipse of; to overshadow, darken; to surpass.—**eclipser** *n*.

ecliptic /ɪˈklɪptɪk/ *n* the apparent path of the sun's motion relative to the stars.—**ecliptically** *adv*.

eclogue /ˈɛkˌlɒg/ *n* a short, *esp* pastoral poem.

eco- /ˈiːkoː/ *prefix* ecology; ecological.

ecology /ɪˈkɒlədʒi/ *n* (the study of) the relationships between living things and their environments.—**ecological** *adj.*—**ecologist** *n*.

e-commerce /ˌiˈkɒmərs/ *n* electronic commerce; undertaking business transactions online.

econometrics /ɪˌkɒnəˈmetriks/ *n sing* the application of mathematical and statistical methods in economics.

economic /ˌɛkəˈnɒmɪk/ or /ˌiːk-/ *adj* pertaining to economics or the economy; (*business, etc*) capable of producing a profit.

economical /-əl/ *adj* thrifty.—**economically** *adv*.

economics /ˌiːkəˈnɒmiks/ *n sing* the social science concerned with the production, consumption and distribution of goods and services; (*pl*) financial aspects.

economist /ɪˈkɒnəmɪst/ *n* an expert in economics.

economize /ɪˈkɒnəˌmaɪz/ *vti* to spend money carefully; to save; to use prudently.—**economization** *n*.

economy /ɪˈkɒnəmi/ *n* (*pl* **economies**) careful use of money and resources to minimize waste; an instance of this; the management of the finances and resources, etc of a business, industry or organization; the economic system of a country.

ecosphere /ˈiːkoːˌsfɪːr/ *n* the parts of the universe where life can exist.

ecosystem /-ˌsɪstəm/ *n* (*ecology*) a system comprising a community of living organisms and its surroundings.

ecru /ˈeɪkruː/ *n* beige.

ecstasy /ˈɛkstəsi/ *n* (*pl* **ecstasies**) intense joy; (*sl: often with cap*) the synthetic amphetamine-based drug MDMA, which reduces social and sexual inhibitions.—**ecstatic** *adj.*—**ecstatically** *adv*.

ECT /ˈiːˈsiːˈtiː/ *abbr* = electroconvulsive therapy.

ecto-, ect- /ˈɛktoː/ *prefix* outside.

ectoderm /ˈɛktoːˌdɜrm/ *n* the outer layer of an embryo or skin.

ectomorph /-ˌmɔrf/ *n* a person with a lightly built physique.—**ectomorphic** *adj.*—**ectomorphy** *n*.

-ectomy /ˈɛktəmi/ *n suffix* denoting surgical removal of a part.

ectopic /ɛkˈtɒpɪk/ *adj* (*anat*) in an abnormal position; (*fertilized egg*) developing abnormally outside the uterus.

ectoplasm /ˈɛktoːˌplæzəm/ *n* the outer layer of the cytoplasm of a cell; a substance supposedly exuded from the body of spiritualist mediums during trances.—**ectoplasmic** *adj*.

ectype /ˈɛkˌtaɪp/ *n* a reproduction or imitation of an original design.

ECU *abbr* = European Currency Unit; *see* **euro**.

ecumenical /ˌɛkjuːˈmenɪkəl/ or /ˌiːk-/ *adj* of the whole Christian Church; seeking Christian unity worldwide.—**ecumenicalism, ecumenicism** *n.*—**ecumenically** *adv*.

eczema /ˈɛksɪmə/ or /ɛkˈziːmə/ *n* inflammation of the skin causing itching and the formation of scaly red patches.—**eczematous** *adj*.

edacious /ɪˈdeɪʃəs/ *adj* gluttonous, greedy.—**edacity** *n*.

Edam /ˈiːdæm/ *n* a mild-flavoured round Dutch cheese, *usu* with a red waxy rind.

eddy /ˈɛdi/ *n* (*pl* **eddies**) a swiftly revolving current of air, water, fog, etc. • *vi* (**eddying, eddied**) to move round and round.

edelweiss /ˈeɪdəlˌvaɪs/ *n* a small white-flowered alpine herb.

edema /ɪˈdiːmə/ *see* **oedema**.

Eden /ˈiːdən/ *n* (*Bible*) the garden where Adam and Eve lived after the creation; a paradise.

edentate /ɪˈdenˌteɪt/ or /ɪ-/ *adj* (*zool*) toothless.

edge /ɛdʒ/ *n* the border, brink, verge, margin; the sharp cutting side of a blade; sharpness, keenness; force, effectiveness. • *vt* to supply an edge or border to; to move gradually.—**edger** *n*.

edgeways /ˈɛdʒˌweɪz/, **edgewise** /-ˌwaɪz/ *adv* with the edge forwards; sideways.

edging /ˈɛdʒɪŋ/ *n* any border for decoration or strengthening.

edgy /ˈɛdʒi/ *adj* (**edgier, edgiest**) irritable.—**edgily** *adv.*—**edginess** *n*.

edible /ˈɛdɪbəl/ *adj* fit or safe to eat.—**edibility, edibleness** *n*.

edict /ˈiːdɪkt/ *n* a decree; a proclamation.—**edictal** *adj*.

edifice /ˈɛdɪfɪs/ *n* a substantial building; any large or complex organization or institution.—**edificial** *adj*.

edify /ˈɛdɪˌfaɪ/ *vt* (**edifying, edified**) to improve the moral character or mind of (a person).—**edification** *n.*—**edifier** *n.*—**edifyingly** *adv*.

edile /ˈiːdaɪl/ *see* **aedile**.

edit /ˈɛdɪt/ *vt* to prepare (text) for publication by checking facts, grammar, style, etc; to be in charge of a publication; (*cinema*) to prepare a final version of a film by selection and arrangement of photographed sequences.

edition /ɪˈdɪʃən/ *n* a whole number of copies of a book, etc printed at a time; the form of a particular publication.

editio princeps /ɪˌdɪʃiˈprɪnseps/ (*pl* **editiones principes**) *n* the first printed edition of a book.

editor /ˈɛdɪtər/ *n* a person in charge of a newspaper or other publication; a person who edits written material for publication; one who prepares the final version of a film; a person in overall charge of the form and content of a radio or television programme.—**editorship** *n*.

editorial /ˌɛdɪˈtoːriəl/ *adj* of or produced by an editor. • *n* an article expressing the opinions of the editor or publishers of a newspaper or magazine.—**editorialist** *n.*—**editorially** *adv*.

EDP *abbr* = Electronic Data Processing.

educable, educatable /ˈɛdʒʊkəbəl/ or /-dʒʊ-/ *adj* able to be educated.

educate /ˈɛdʒʊˌkeɪt/ or /-dʒʊ-/ *vt* to train the mind, to teach; to provide schooling for.—**educator** *n*.

education /ˌɛdʒʊˈkeɪʃən/ or /-dʒʊ-/ *n* the process of learning and training; instruction as imparted in schools, colleges and universities; a course or type of instruction; the theory and practice of teaching.—**educational** *adj.*—**educationally** *adv*.

educationalist /-əlɪst/, **educationist** /-ɪst/ *n* an expert in education.

educative /ˈɛdʒʊˌkətɪv/ or /-dʒʊ-/ *adj* educating.

educe /ɛˈdjuːs/ *vt* to elicit (information, etc); to infer.—**educible** *adj*.

edulcorate /əˈdʌlkəˌreɪt/ *vt* to free from acids and other impurities by washing.—**edulcoration** *n*.

edutainment /ˌɛdʒʊˈteɪnmənt/ or /-dʒʊ-/ *n* programmes or classes aimed at combining information with material of an entertaining nature.

EEC /ˈiːˈiːˈsi/ *abbr* = European Economic Community (now European Union).

EEG /ˈiːˈiːˈdʒi/ *abbr* = electroencephalogram.

eel /iːl/ *n* a snake-like fish.

eelpout /-ˌpɐʊt/ *n* a type of freshwater fish, found in Europe, North America and Asia; another name for the burbot.

e'en /iːn/ *n* (*poet*) evening.

e'er /ɛr/ *adv* (*poet*) ever.

eerie /ˈiːri/ *adj* (**eerier, eeriest**) causing fear; weird.—**eerily** *adv*.—**eeriness** *n*.

efface /ɪˈfeɪs/ *vt* to rub out, obliterate; to make (oneself) humble or inconspicuous.—**effaceable** *adj*.—**effacement** *n*.—**effacer** *n*.

effect /ɪˈfɛkt/ *n* the result of a cause or action by some agent; the power to produce some result; the fundamental meaning; an impression on the senses; an operative condition; (*pl*) personal belongings; (*pl: theatre, cinema*) sounds, lighting, etc to accompany a production. • *vt* to bring about, accomplish.—**effecter** *n*.—**effectible** *adj*.

effective /-tɪv/ *adj* producing a specified effect; forceful, striking in impression; actual, real; operative.—**effectively** *adv*.—**effectiveness** *n*.

effectual /ɪˈfɛktʃuːəl/ *adj* able to produce the desired effect.—**effectuality, effectualness** *n*.—**effectually** *adv*.

effectuate /-ˌeɪt/ *vt* to make happen.—**effectuation** *n*.

effeminate /ɪˈfɛmənət/ *adj* (*man*) displaying what are regarded as feminine qualities.—**effeminacy, effeminateness** *n*.

effendi /eˈfɛndi/ (*pl* **effendis**) *n* a Turkish title of respect, equivalent to sir or Mr.

efferent /ˈɛfərənt/ *adj* (*anat*) conveying or discharging outwards.

effervesce /ˌɛfərˈvɛs/ *vt* (*liquid*) to froth and hiss as bubbles of gas escape; to be exhilarated.—**effervescence** *n*.—**effervescent** *adj*.—**effervescible** *adj*.

effete /ɪˈfiːt/ *adj* decadent, weak.—**effeteness** *n*.

efficacious /ˌɛfɪˈkeɪʃəs/ *adj* achieving the desired result.—**efficacy, efficaciousness** *n*.

efficient /ɪˈfɪʃənt/ or /ɪ-/ *adj* achieving results without waste of time or effort; competent.—**efficiently** *adv*.—**efficiency** *n* (*pl* **efficiencies**).

effigy /ˈɛfɪdʒi/ *n* (*pl* **effigies**) a sculpture or portrait; a crude figure of a person, *esp* for exposure to public contempt and ridicule.

effloresce /ˌɛflɔˈrɛs/ *vi* to blossom; (*chem*) to turn to powder when exposed to air, to crystallize; to become encrusted with crystals as a result of loss of water.—**efflorescence** *n*.—**efflorescent** *adj*.

effluence /ˈɛfluːəns/, **efflux** /ˈɛfˌlʌks/ *n* something that flows out.

effluent /ˈɛfluːənt/ *adj* flowing out. • *n* that which flows out, *esp* sewage.

effluvium /ɪˈfluːvɪəm/ *n* (*pl* **effluvia, effluviums**) an offensive vapour or smell.—**effluvial** *adj*.

effort /ˈɛfərt/ *n* exertion; an attempt, try; a product of great exertion.—**effortful** *adj*.

effortless /-ləs/ *adj* done with little effort, or seemingly so.—**effortlessly** *adv*.—**effortlessness** *n*.

effrontery /ɪˈfrʌntəri/ *n* (*pl* **effronteries**) impudent boldness, insolence.

effulgent /ɪˈfʌldʒənt/ *adj* radiant, brilliant.—**effulgence** *n*.

effuse /ɪˈfjuːz/ *vt* (*liquid, words*) to flow or pour out.

effusion /ɪˈfjuːʒən/ *n* a pouring out; an unrestrained outpouring, as of emotion; something poured out.

effusive /ɪˈfjuːsɪv/ *adj* gushing, emotionally unrestrained; demonstrative.—**effusiveness** *n*.

eft /ɛft/ *n* a newt.

e.g., eg, eg. *abbr* = for example (*Latin exempli gratia*).

egad /iːˈɡæd/ *interj* (*arch*) an exclamation of surprise, pleasure or admiration.

egalitarian /ɪˌɡælɪˈtɛrɪən/ *adj* upholding the principle of equal rights for all.—*also n*.—**egalitarianism** *n*.

egest /ɪˈdʒɛst/ *vt* to excrete.—**egestion** *n*.

egesta /ɪˈdʒɛstə/ *npl* excrement.

egg[1] /ɛɡ/ *n* the oval hard-shelled reproductive cell laid by birds, reptiles and fish; the egg of the domestic poultry used as food; ovum.—**eggy** *adj*.

egg[2] *vt* (*with* **on**) to incite (someone to do something).

egger /ɛɡər/ *n* a type of large moth.

egghead /ˈɛɡˌhɛd/ *n* (*inf*) an intellectual.

eggnog /ˈɛɡnɒɡ/ *n* a drink made from egg, beaten up with hot milk, sugar and brandy.

eggplant /-plænt/ *see* **aubergine**.

eggshell /ˈɛɡʃɛl/ *n* the hard outer covering of an egg. • *adj* fragile; (*paint*) having a slight sheen.

egis /ˈiːdʒɪs/ *see* **aegis**.

eglantine /ˈɛɡlənˌtaɪn/ *n* the sweetbrier; the wild rose.

ego /ˈiːɡoː/ *n* (*pl* **egos**) the self; self-image, conceit.

egocentric /ˌiːɡoːˈsɛntrɪk/ *adj* self-centred.—**egocentricity** *n*.

egoism /ˈiːɡoːˌɪzəm/ *n* self-concern; self-centredness.—**egoist** *n*.—**egoistic, egoistical** *adj*.—**egoistically** *adv*.

egotism /-tɪzəm/ *n* excessive reference to oneself; conceit.—**egotist** *n*.—**egotistic, egotistical** *adj*.—**egotistically** *adv*.

ego trip *n* (*inf*) an activity undertaken to boost one's own self-esteem or importance in the eyes of others.—**ego-trip** *vi*.

egregious /ɪˈɡriːdʒəs/ *adj* outstandingly bad.—**egregiousness** *n*.

egress /ˈiːˌɡrɛs/ *n* the way out, exit.

egression /ɪˈɡrɛʃən/ *n* the act of going out or emerging; egress.

egret /ˈiːɡrɛt/ *n* a type of heron.

Egyptology /ˌiːdʒɪpˈtɒlədʒi/ *n* the study of Egyptian antiquities and hieroglyphics.—**Egyptologist** *n*.

eh /eɪ/ *interj* an exclamation of inquiry or surprise.

eider /ˈaɪdər/ *n* a large marine duck, the down of which has commercial value as a filling for quilts etc.

eiderdown /-ˌdaʊn/ *n* the down of the eider duck used for stuffing quilts, etc; a thick quilt with a soft filling.

eidolon /aɪˈdoːlɒn/ *n* (*pl* **eidolons, eidola**) *n* an apparition or phantom.

eight /eɪt/ *n, adj* one more than seven; the symbol for this (8, VIII, viii); (the crew of) an eight-oared rowing boat.

eighteen /eɪˈtiːn/ *n, adj* one more than seventeen; the symbol for this (18, XVIII, xviii).—**eighteenth** *adj*.

eighteenmo /eɪˈtinmoː/ (*pl* **eighteenmos**) *n* a book whose sheets are folded into eighteen leaves.

eightfold /ˈeɪtfoːld/ *adj, adv* consisting of eight units; being eight times as great or many.

eighth /eɪtθ/ *adj, n* one after seventh; one of eight equal parts.

eighty /ˈeɪti/ *n* (*pl* **eighties**) eight times ten; the symbol for this (80, LXXX, lxxx); (*pl*) the numbers from 80 to 89.—**eightieth** *adj, n*.

einsteinium /aɪnˈstaɪnɪəm/ *n* an artificial radioactive element.

eisteddfod /aɪsˈtɛðˌvɒd/ or /-fəd/ *n* (*pl* **eisteddfods, eisteddfodau**) a Welsh competitive festival of the arts, *esp* singing.—**eisteddodic** *adj*.

either /ˈaɪðər/ or /ˈiːðər/ *adj, n* the one or the other of two; each of two. • *conj* correlative to *or*.

ejaculate /ɪˈdʒækjuːˌleɪt/ *vti* to emit a fluid (as semen); to exclaim.—**ejaculation** *n*.—**ejaculator** *n*.—**ejaculatory** *adj*.

eject /ɪˈdʒɛkt/ *vt* to turn out, to expel by force. • *vi* to escape from an aircraft or spacecraft using an ejector seat.—**ejection** *n*.—**ejector** *n*.

ejecta /ɪˈdʒɛktə/ *npl* matter discharged by an erupting volcano.

ejector seat *n* an escape seat, *esp* in combat aircraft, that can be ejected with its occupant in an emergency by means of explosive bolts.

e-journal /ˌiːˈdʒɜːrnəl/ *n* an online publication that can be accessed on the Web, commonly used in the academic world.

eke /iːk/ *vt* (*with* **out**) to supplement; to use (a supply) frugally; to make (a living) with difficulty.

elaborate /ɪˈlæbəˌreɪt/ *vt*, /ɪˈlæbərət/ *adj* highly detailed; planned with care and exactness. • *vt* to work out or explain in detail.—**elaborateness** *n*.—**elaboration** *n*.—**elaborative** *adj*.—**elaborator** *n*.

élan /eɪˈlɑ̃/ *n* verve, spirit.

eland /ˈiːlənd/ *n* an African antelope with spirally twisted horns.

elapse /ɪˈlæps/ *vi* (*time*) to pass by.

elasmobranch /ɪˈlæzməˌbræŋk/ *n* (*pl* **elasmobranchs**) a member of a class of fish that includes sharks and skates.

elastic /ɪˈlæstɪk/ or /i-/ *adj* returning to the original size and shape if stretched or squeezed; springy; adaptable. • *n* fabric, tape, etc incorporating elastic thread.—**elastically** *adv*.—**elasticity** *n*.

elasticated /-keɪtəd/ *adj* made elastic by the use of elastic thread.

elate /ɪˈleɪt/ or /i-/ *vt* to fill with happiness or pride.—**elated** *adj*.—**elatedness** *n*.—**elation** *n*.

elbow /ˈɛlboː/ *n* the joint between the forearm and upper arm; the part of a piece of clothing covering this; any sharp turn or bend, as in a pipe. • *vt* to shove away rudely with the elbow; to jostle.

elbow grease *n* (*inf*) effort, hard work.

elbowroom /ˈɛlboːruːm/ *n* space to move, scope.

elder[1] /ˈɛldər/ *n* a tree or shrub with flat clusters of white or pink flowers.

elder[2] *n* an older person; an office bearer in certain churches.—**eldership** *n*.

elderberry /-ˌbɛri/ n (pl **elderberries**) (the fruit of) an elder.

elderly /-li/ adj quite old.—**elderliness** n.

eldest /ˈɛldəst/ n oldest, first born.

El Dorado, eldorado /ˌɛldɔːˈrɑːdoː/ n an imaginary land of vast wealth.

eldritch, eldrich /ˈɛldrɪtʃ/ adj (Scot) weird; hideous.

elecampane /ˌɛləkæmˈpeɪn/ n a plant of the aster family, from the roots of which a tonic medicine is made.

elect /ɪˈlɛkt/ or /iː-/ vti to choose by voting; to make a selection (of); to make a decision on. • adj chosen for an office but not installed.

election /ɪˈlɛkʃən/ or /iː-/ n the public choice of a person for office, esp a politician.

electioneer /ɪˌlɛkʃəˈnɪːr/ or /iː-/ vi to work on behalf of a candidate for election.—**electioneering** n.

elective /ɪˈlɛktɪv/ or /iː-/ adj pertaining to, dependant on, or exerting the power of, choice.—**electivity, electiveness** n.

elector /ɪˈlɛktər/ or /iː-/ n a person who has a vote at an election.—**electorship** n.

electoral /ɪˈlɛktərəl/ or /iː-/, /-ˈtɔːrəl/ adj of elections or electors.

electorate /ɪˈlɛktərɪt/ or /iː-/ n the whole body of qualified electors.

electric /ɪˈlɛktrɪk/ or /iː-/ adj of, producing or worked by electricity; exciting, thrilling. • npl electric fittings.

electrical /-kəl/ adj of or relating to electricity.—**electrically** adv.

electric chair n a chair used in executing condemned criminals by electrocution.

electric eel n an eel-like fish capable of giving an electric shock.

electric eye n a photoelectric cell.

electric guitar n a guitar that is electronically amplified.

electrician /ˌiːlɛkˈtrɪʃən/ or /ˌɛl-/, /ˌɪˌlɛk-/ n a person who installs and repairs electrical devices.

electricity /ˌiːlɛkˈtrɪsɪti/ or /ˌɛl-/, /ˌɪˌlɛk-/ n a form of energy comprising certain charged particles, such as electrons and protons; an electric current.

electrify /ɪˈlɛktrəˌfaɪ/ or /iː-/ vt (**electrifying, electrified**) to charge with electricity; to modify or equip for the use of electric power; to astonish or excite.—**electrifiable** adj.—**electrification** n.—**electrifier** n.

electro-, electr- /ɪˈlɛktro:/ or /iː-/ prefix of or by electricity.

electrocardiogram /-ˈkɑrdiəˌɡræm/ or /iː-/ n the tracing made by an electrocardiograph.

electrocardiograph /-ˈkɑrdiəˌɡræf/ n a device for recording the electrical activity of the heart.—**electrocardiographic, electrocardiographical** adj.—**electrocardiography** n.

electrochemistry /-ˈkɛmɪstri/ or /iː-/ n the area of chemistry dealing with chemical changes caused by electricity.—**electrochemical** adj.—**electrochemist** n.

electroconvulsive therapy /-kənˈvʌlsɪv/ n treatment of certain types of mental illness by passing an electric current through the brain.

electrocute /ɪˈlɛktrəˌkjuːt/ or /iː-/ vt to kill or execute by electricity.—**electrocution** n.

electrode /ɪˈlɛkˌtroːd/ or /iː-/ n a conductor through which an electric current enters or leaves an electrolyte, gas discharge tube or thermionic valve.

electrodynamics /-daɪˈnæmɪks/ n sing the area of physics dealing with electric currents.—**electrodynamic, electrodynamical** adj.

electroencephalogram /-ɛnˈsɛfələˌɡræm/ n the tracing produced by an electroencephalograph.

electroencephalograph /-ˌɡræf/ n a device for recording the electrical activity of the brain.—**electro-encephalographic** adj.—**electroencephalographically** adv.—**electroencephalography** n.

electrokinetics /ɪˌlɛktroːkɪˈnɛtɪks/ or /iː-/, /-trə-/ n sing the area of physics dealing with electricity in motion.—**electrokinetic** adj.

electrolysis /ˌɪlɛkˈtrɒləsɪs/ or /ˌiː-/, /ˌɛl-/ n the passage of an electric current through an electrolyte to effect chemical change; the destruction of living tissue, esp hair roots, by the use of an electric current

electrolyte /ɪˈlɛktrəˌlaɪt/ or /iː-/ n a solution that conducts electricity.

electrolyze /-ˌlaɪz/ vt to cause to undergo electrolysis.—**electrolyzation** n.—**electrolyzer** n.

electromagnet /ɪˌlɛktroːˈmæɡnət/ or /iː-/ n a metal core rendered magnetic by the passage of an electric current through a surrounding coil.

electromagnetic /-tɪk/ adj pertaining to, or produced by, electromagnetism.—**electromagnetically** adv.

electromagnetism /-tɪˌzəm/ n magnetism produced by an electric current; the area of science dealing with the relations between electricity and magnetism.

electrometallurgy /-ˈmɛtəˌlɔːrdʒi/ n metallurgy using a slow electric current to precipitate certain metals from their solutions, or to separate metals from their ores.—**electrometallurgical** adj.—**electrometallurgist** n.

electrometer /ˌɪlɛkˈtrɒmətər/ or /iː-/ n an instrument for measuring electricity.—**electrometric, electrometrical** adj.—**electrometry** n.

electromotive /ɪˌlɛktrəˈmoːtɪv/ or /iː-/ adj producing an electric current.

electromotive force n a source of energy producing an electric current; the amount of energy drawn from such a source per unit current of electricity passing through it, measured in volts.

electron /ɪˈlɛktrɒn/ or /iː-/ n a negatively charged elementary particle that forms the part of the atom outside the nucleus.

electronegative /ɪˌlɛktroːˈnɛɡətɪv/ or /iː-/ adj with a negative electrical charge.

electronic /ˌɪlɛkˈtrɒnɪk/ or /iː-/, /ɪ-/, /ˌɛl-/ adj of or worked by streams of electrons flowing through semiconductor devices, vacuum or gas; of or concerned with electrons or electronics.—**electronically** adv.

electronic mail n messages, etc, sent and received via computer terminals, email, e-mail.

electronic publishing n the use of the Internet to publish and distribute material, whether text, databases or other types of information.

electronics /-ɪks/ n sing the study, development and application of electronic devices; (pl) electronic circuits.

electron microscope n a powerful microscope that uses a stream of electrons instead of light to produce magnified images.

electronvolt n a unit of energy equivalent to the energy gained by an electron that has been accelerated through a potential difference of one volt.

electrophorus /ˌɪlɛkˈtrɒfərəs/ or /iː-/ n (pl **electrophori**) an instrument for generating static electricity by induction.

electroplate /ɪˈlɛktrəˌpleɪt/ or /iː-/, /-troː-/ vt to plate or cover with metal (eg silver) by electrolysis. • n electroplated objects.—**electroplater** n.

electropositive /ɪˌlɛktroːˈpɒzɪtɪv/ or /iː-/ adj with a positive electrical charge.

electroscope /ɪˈlɛktrəˌskoːp/ or /iː-/ n an instrument for showing the presence or quality of electricity.—**electroscopic** adj.

electrostatics /-ˈstætɪks/ or /-troː-/ n sing the branch of physics concerned with static electric charges.—**electrostatic** adj.—**electrostatically** adv.

electrotherapeutics /-ˈθɛrəpjuːtɪks/ n sing the area of medicine dealing with the use of electrotherapy.

electrotherapy /-ˈθɛrəpi/ n the treatment of disease using electricity.—**electrotherapist** n.

electrotype /ɪˈlɛktrəˌtəɪp/ or /iː-/ n (print) a facsimile made by covering a mould or plate of the original with a coating of copper or nickel. • vt to make a copy in this way.—**electrotyper** n.

electrum /ɪˈlɛktrəm/ or /iː-/ n an alloy of gold and silver.

electuary /ɪˈlɛktʃuːɛri/ or /iː-/ n (pl **electuaries**) a medicinal drug mixed with honey or syrup.

eleemosynary /ˌɛləˈmɒsənɛri/ or /ɛliə-/, /-ˈmɒz-/ adj dependent on charity; (money) given as charity.

elegant /ˈɛləɡənt/ adj graceful; refined; dignified and tasteful in manner and appearance.—**elegance, elegancy** n.—**elegantly** adv.

elegiac /ɛˈlədʒaɪˌək/ adj characteristic of elegy; mournful.

elegize /ˈɛləˌdʒaɪz/ vt to write an elegy about.—**elegist** n.

elegy /ˈɛlədʒi/ n (pl **elegies**) a slow mournful song or poem.

element /ˈɛləmənt/ n a constituent part; any of the 105 known substances composed of atoms with the same number of protons in their nuclei; a favourable environment for a plant or animal; a wire that produces heat in an electric cooker, kettle, etc; any of the four substances (earth, air, fire, water) that in ancient and medieval thought were believed to constitute the universe; (pl) atmospheric conditions (wind, rain, etc); (pl) the basic principles, rudiments.

elemental /ˌɛləˈməntəl/ *adj* of elements or primitive natural forces.—**elementally** *adv*.

elementary /ˌɛləˈmɛntəri/ or /-tri/ *adj* concerned with the basic principles of a subject.—**elementariness** *n*.

elementary particle *n* any of the subatomic particles, such as electrons, protons and neutrons, not made up of other particles.

elemi /ˈɛləmi/ *n* (*pl* **elemis**) a resin used in medicines and varnishes.

elenchus /ɪˈlɛŋkəs/ *n* (*pl* **elenchi**) (*logic*) refutation of an argument.—**elenctic** *adj*.

elephant /ˈɛləfənt/ *n* (*pl* **elephants, elephant**) a large heavy mammal with a long trunk, thick skin, and ivory tusks.—**elephantoid** *adj*.

elephantiasis /ˌɛləfənˈtaɪəsɪs/ *n* (*pl* **elephantiases**) a disease in which the limbs or scrotum become enormously enlarged.—**elephantiasic** *adj*.

elephantine /ˈɛləfænˌtaɪn/ or /-ˌtiːn/, /ˌɛləˈfænˌtaɪn/, /-ˌtiːn/ *adj* of or like elephants; very big or clumsy.

elevate /ˈɛləveɪt/ *vt* to lift up; to raise in rank; to improve in intellectual or moral stature.

elevated /-ˌveɪtəd/ *adj* raised; (*fig*) inflated; (*inf*) tipsy.

elevation /ˌɛləˈveɪʃən/ *n* a raised place; the height above the earth's surface or above sea level; the angle to which a gun is aimed above the horizon; a drawing that shows the front, rear, or side view of something.

elevator /ˈɛləˌveɪtər/ *n* a cage or platform for moving something from one level to another; a moveable surface on the tailplane of an aircraft to produce motion up and down; a lift; a building for storing grain.

eleven /ɪˈlɛvən/ *adj, n* one more than ten; the symbol for this (11, XI, xi); (*soccer, etc*) a team of eleven players.—**eleventh** *adj, n*.

elf /ɛlf/ *n* (*pl* **elves**) a mischievous fairy.—**elfin** *adj*.—**elfish, elvish** *adj*.

elflock /ˈɛlfˌlɒk/ *n* an intricately twisted lock of hair.

elicit /ɪˈlɪsɪt/ or /i-/ *vt* to draw out (information, etc).—**elicitable** *adj*.—**elicitation** *n*.—**elicitor** *n*.

elide /ɪˈlaɪd/ or /i-/ *vt* (*linguistics*) to cut off a syllable or vowel.

eligible /ˈɛlɪdʒəbəl/ *adj* suitable to be chosen, legally qualified; desirable, *esp* as a marriage partner.—**eligibility** *n*.—**eligibly** *adv*.

eliminate /ɪˈlɪməˌneɪt/ or /i-/ *vt* to expel, get rid of; to eradicate completely; (*sl*) to kill; to exclude (*eg* a competitor) from a competition, *usu* by defeat.—**eliminable** *adj*.—**elimination** *n*.—**eliminative, eliminatory** *adj*.—**eliminator** *n*.

elision /ɪˈlɪʒən/ or /i-/ *n* (*linguistics*) the cutting off of a syllable or vowel.

elite, élite /ɪˈliːt/ or /eɪ-/ *n* a superior group; (*typewriting*) a letter size having twelve characters to the inch.

elitism /-ˌɪzəm/ *n* leadership or rule by an elite; advocacy of such a system.—**elitist** *n*.

elixir /ɪˈlɪksər/ or /i-/ *n* (*alchemy*) a substance thought to have the power of transmuting base metals into gold, or of conferring everlasting life; any medicine claimed as a cure-all; a sweet syrup containing a medicine.

Elizabethan /ɪˌlɪzəˈbiːθən/ or /i-/ *adj* pertaining to Queen Elizabeth I of England and her reign (1558–1603), *esp* its architecture and literature; pertaining to Queen Elizabeth II of Great Britain and her reign (1952–). • *n* a person alive in the reign of Elizabeth I.

elk /ɛlk/ *n* (*pl* **elks, elk**) the largest existing deer of Europe and Asia.

ell /ɛl/ *n* an old measure of length used for cloth, based on the length of a man's arm, approximately equal to 45 inches (1.15 metres).

ellipse /ɪˈlɪps/ or /i-/ *n* (*geom*) a closed plane figure formed by the plane section of a right-angled cone; a flattened circle.

ellipsis /ɪˈlɪpsɪs/ or /i-/ *n* (*pl* **ellipses**) the omission of words needed to complete the grammatical construction of a sentence; the mark (...) used to indicate such omission.

ellipsoid /ɪˈlɪpˌsɔɪd/ or /i-/ *n* (*geom*) an elliptical spheroid; an oval.—**ellipsoidal** *adj*.

elliptic /ɪˈlɪptɪk/ or /i-/, **elliptical** /-əl/ *adj* of or like an ellipse; having a part understood.—**elliptically** *adv*.

ellipticity /ɪlˌɪpˈtɪsəti/ *n* (*geom*) the extent of deviation of an oval from a circle or sphere.

elm /ɛlm/ *n* a tall deciduous shade tree with spreading branches and broad top; its hard heavy wood.

elocution /ˌɛləˈkjuːʃən/ *n* skill in public speaking.—**elocutionary** *adj*.—**elocutionist** *n*.

elongate /iːˈlɒŋˌgeɪt/ or /ˈiːlɒŋˌgeɪt/ *vti* to make or become longer.—**elongation** *n*.

elope /ɪˈloːp/ or /i-/ *vi* to run away secretly with a lover, *esp* to get married.—**elopement** *n*.—**eloper** *n*.

eloquence /ˈɛləkwəns/ *n* skill in the use of words; speaking with fluency, power or persuasiveness.

eloquent /ˈɛləkwənt/ *adj* (*speaking, writing, etc*) fluent and powerful.

else /ɛls/ *adv* besides; otherwise.

elsewhere /ˈɛlsˌwɛr/ *adv* in another place.

elucidate /ɪˈluːsɪˌdeɪt/ or /i-/ *vt* to make clear, to explain.—**elucidation** *n*.—**elucidative, elucidatory** *adj*.—**elucidator** *n*.

elude /ɪˈluːd/ or /i-/ *vt* to avoid stealthily; to escape the understanding or memory of a person.—**eluder** *n*.—**elusion** *n*.

elusive /ɪˈluːsɪv/ or /i-/ *adj* escaping; baffling; solitary, difficult to contact.—**elusiveness** *n*.

elver /ˈɛlvər/ *n* a young eel.

elves, elvish /ˈɛlvɪʃ/ *see* **elf**.

Elysian /ɪˈlɪziən/ or /ɪˈlɪʒ-/, /ɪˈliː-/ *adj* of or resembling Elysium; paradisiacal, blissful.

Elysium /ɪˈlɪziəm/ or /ɪˈlɪʒ-/, /ɪˈliː-/ *n* the ancient Greek paradise; a condition of perfect happiness.

elytron /ˈɛləˌtrɒn/, **elytrum** /-trəm/ *n* (*pl* **elytra**) one of the hard wing cases of a beetle.—**elytroid, elytrous** *adj*.

em /ɛm/ *n* (*print*) a measure of width, equal to one sixth of an inch (approx 4 mm).

emaciate /ɪˈmeɪsiˌeɪt/ or /i-/ *vti* to make or become very thin and weak.—**emaciated** *adj*.—**emaciation** *n*.

email, e-mail /ˌiːˈmeɪl/ *n* short for electronic mail.

emanate /ˈɛməˌneɪt/ *vi* to issue from a source.—**emanative** *adj*.—**emanator** *n*.—**emanatory** *adj*.

emanation /ˌɛməˈneɪʃən/ *n* something coming from or caused by something else.—**emanational** *adj*.

emancipate /ɪˈmænsəˌpeɪt/ or /i-/ *vt* to liberate, *esp* from bondage or slavery.—**emancipative** *adj*.—**emancipator** *n*.—**emancipatory** *adj*.

emancipation /ɪˌmænsəˈpeɪʃən/ or /i-/ *n* the act of freeing; freedom, liberation.—**emancipationist** *n*.

emarginate /iˈmɑrdʒɪnɪt/ or /-ˌneɪt/, /ɪ-/, **emarginated** *adj* (*leaf*) notched at the edges or tip.—**emargination** *n*.

emasculate /ɪˈmæskjʊlɪt/ or /i-/ *vt* to castrate; to deprive of vigour, strength, etc.—**emasculation** *n*.—**emasculative, emasculatory** *adj*.—**emasculator** *n*.

embalm /ɛmˈbɒm/ or /ɪm-/ *vt* to preserve (a dead body) with drugs, chemicals, etc.—**embalmer** *n*.—**embalmment** *n*.

embank /ɛmˈbæŋk/ or /ɪm-/ *vt* to enclose or protect with an embankment.

embankment /-mənt/ *n* an earth or stone mound made to hold back water or to carry a roadway.

embargo /ɛmˈbɑrgoː/ or /ɪm-/ *n* (*pl* **embargoes**) an order of a government forbidding ships to enter or leave its ports; any ban or restriction on commerce by law; a prohibition, ban. • *vt* (**embargoing, embargoed**) to lay an embargo on; to requisition.

embark /ɛmˈbɑrk/ or /ɪm-/ *vti* to put or go on board a ship or aircraft to begin a journey; to make a start in any activity or enterprise.—**embarkation** *n*.—**embarkment** *n*.

embarrass /ɛmˈbɛrəs/ or /ɪm-/ *vt* to make (a person) feel confused, uncomfortable or disconcerted.—**embarrassing** *adj*.—**embarrassment** *n*.

embassy /ˈɛmbəsi/ *n* (*pl* **embassies**) a person or group sent to a foreign government as ambassadors; the official residence of an ambassador.

embattle /ɛmˈbætl/ or /ɪm-/ *vt* to arrange troops for battle; to prepare for battle.—**embattled** *adj*.

embay /ɛmˈbeɪ/ or /ɪm-/ *vt* to bring or drive a ship into a bay.

embed /ɛmˈbɛd/ or /ɪm-/ *vt* (**embedding, embedded**) to fix firmly in surrounding matter.—**embedment** *n*.

embellish /ɛmˈbɛlɪʃ/ or /ɪm-/ *vt* to decorate, to adorn.—**embellisher** *n*.—**embellishment** *n*.

ember /ˈɛmbər/ *n* a piece of glowing coal or wood in a fire; (*pl*) the smouldering remains of a fire.

embezzle /ɛmˈbɛzəl/ or /ɪm-/ *vt* to steal (money, securities, etc entrusted to one's care).—**embezzlement** *n*.—**embezzler** *n*.

embitter /ɛmˈbɪtər/ or /ɪm-/ *vt* to cause to feel bitter.—**embitterment** *n*.

emblazon /ɛmˈbleɪzən/ or /ɪm-/ *vt* to make bright with colour; to ornament with heraldic devices.—**emblazonment** *n*.

emblazonry /-ri/ *n* heraldic decoration, blazonry.

emblem /ˈembləm/ *n* a symbol; a figure adopted and used as an identifying mark.

emblematic /ˌembləˈmætɪk/, **emblematical** /-əl/ *adj* of emblems; symbolic.—**emblematically** *adv*.

emblements /ˈembləmənts/ *npl* (*law*) the annual crops produced by the labour of the cultivator; the profit from these crops.

embody /emˈbɒdi/ or /ɪm-/ *vt* (**embodying, embodied**) to express in definite form; to incorporate or include in a single book, law, system, etc.—**embodiment** *n*.

embolden /emˈboːldən/ or /ɪm-/ *vt* to inspire with courage; to make bold.

embolism /ˈembəˌlɪzəm/ *n* the obstruction of a blood vessel by a blood clot, air bubble, etc.—**embolismic** *adj*.

embolus /ˈembələs/ *n* (*pl* **emboli**) material obstructing a blood vessel, *eg* a blood clot or air bubble.

embonpoint /ˌɑ̃bɔ̃ˈpwɑ̃/ *n* plumpness.

emboss /emˈbɒs/ or /ɪm-/ *vt* to ornament with a raised design.—**embosser** *n*.—**embossment** *n*.

embouchure /ˈɒmbuˌʃʊr/ *n* the mouth of a river; (*mus*) the mouthpiece of a wind instrument; the correct positioning of the mouth when playing a wind instrument.

embowel /emˈbaʊəl/ or /ɪm-/ *vt* (**embowelling, embowelled** *or* **emboweling, emboweled**) (*arch*) to remove the intestines from, disembowel; to embed, to bury.

embower /emˈbaʊər/ or /ɪm-/ *vt* (*arch*) to cover with, or as with, a bower.

embrace /emˈbreɪs/ or /ɪm-/ *vt* to take and hold tightly in the arms as a sign of affection; to accept eagerly (*eg* an opportunity); to adopt (*eg* a religious faith); to include. • *n* the act of embracing, a hug.—**embraceable** *adj*.—**embracement** *n*.

embracer /-ər/ *n* one who embraces; (*law*) one who attempts to influence a jury corruptly.

embracery /emˈbreɪsəri/ *n* (*law*) the act of attempting to corrupt or influence a jury.

embranchment /emˈbræntʃmənt/ *n* the act of branching out.

embrasure /emˈbreɪʒər/ or /ɪm-/ *n* an opening in a wall or parapet from which to fire guns; a window or door having its sides slanted on the inside.

embrocate /ˈembroːkeɪt/ *vt* to rub a diseased or injured part of the body with a lotion.

embrocation /ˌembroːˈkeɪʃən/ *n* a liniment for applying to, or rubbing, an injured part of the body.

embroider /emˈbrɔɪdər/ or /ɪm-/ *vt* to ornament with decorative stitches; to embellish (*eg* a story).—**embroiderer** *n*.

embroidery /-dri/ *n* (*pl* **embroideries**) decorative needlework; elaboration or exaggeration (of a story, etc).

embroil /emˈbrɔɪl/ or /ɪm-/ *vt* to involve (a person) in a conflict, argument, or problem.—**embroiler** *n*.—**embroilment** *n*.

embryo /ˈembrioː/ *n* (*pl* **embryos**) an animal during the period of its growth from a fertilized egg up to the third month; a human product of conception up to about the second month of growth; a thing in a rudimentary state.—**embryoid** *adj*.

embryology /ˌembriˈɒlədʒi/ *n* the scientific study of embryos.—**embryological, embryologic** *adj*.—**embryologist** *n*.

embryonic /ˌembriˈɒnɪk/, **embryonal** /-ˈɒnəl/ *adj* immature, existing at an early stage.—**embryonically** *adv*.

emend /iˈmend/ or /ɪ-/ *vt* to correct mistakes in written material.—**emendable** *adj*.—**emendation** *n*.

emerald /ˈemərəld/ *n* a rich green gemstone; its colour.

emerge /iˈmɜːrdʒ/ or /ɪ-/ *vi* to appear up out of, to come into view; to be revealed as the result of investigation.—**emergence** *n*.—**emergent** *adj*.

emergency /iˈmɜːrʒənsi/ or /ɪ-/ *n* (*pl* **emergencies**) an unforeseen situation demanding immediate action; a serious medical condition requiring instant treatment.

emeritus /iˈmerɪtəs/ *adj* retired but still holding one's title or rank.—*also n*.

emersed /iˈmɜːrst/ *adj* (*bot*) rising out of water.

emersion /iˈmɜːrʃən/ *n* the act of emerging.

emery /ˈeməri/ *n* a hard granular mineral used for grinding and polishing; a hard abrasive powder.

emery board *n* a nailfile made from cardboard covered with powdered emery.

emery paper *n* a stiff paper covered with powdered emery.

emetic /iˈmetɪk/ *n* a medicine that induces vomiting.—*also adj*.—**emetically** *adv*.

emf, EMF *abbr* = electromotive force.

emigrant /ˈemɪgrənt/ *n* a person who emigrates.

emigrate /ˈemɪˌgreɪt/ *vi* to leave one's country for residence in another.—**emigration** *n*.

émigré /ˈemɪˌgreɪ/ *n* an emigrant, usually someone forced to emigrate.

eminence /ˈemɪnəns/, **eminency** /-i/ *n* (*pl* **eminences, eminencies**) high rank or position; a person of high rank or attainments; (*with cap*) the title for a cardinal of the RC Church; a raised piece of ground, a high place.

eminent /ˈemɪnənt/ *adj* famous; conspicuous; distinguished.—**eminently** *adv*.

emir /ɛˈmɪr/ *n* a ruler in parts of Africa and Asia.

emirate /ˈemərət/ or /-ˌreɪt/ *n* the territory governed by an emir.

emissary /ˈemɪˌseri/ *n* (*pl* **emissaries**) a person sent on a mission on behalf of another, *esp* a government.

emit /iˈmɪt/ or /i-/ *vt* (**emitting, emitted**) to send out (light, heat, etc); to put into circulation; to express, to utter.—**emission** *n*.—**emissive** *adj*.—**emitter** *n*.

Emmenthal(er), Emmental /ˈemənˌtɒl/ *n* a hard Swiss cheese with lots of holes.

emmet /ˈemɪt/ *n* (*dial*) an ant.

emollient /iˈmɒliənt/ or /i-/ *adj* softening and soothing, *esp* the skin. • *n* a preparation used for skin care.—**emollience** *n*.

emolument /iˈmɒljumənt/ or /ɛ-/ *n* a fee received, salary.

emote /iˈmoːt/ or /i-/ *vi* to display emotion theatrically.

emoticon *n* (*comput*) an icon representing emotion made up of standard keyboard characters.

emotion /iˈmoːʃən/ or /i-/ *n* a strong feeling of any kind.

emotional /-əl/ *adj* of emotion; inclined to express excessive emotion.—**emotionality** *n*.—**emotionally** *adv*.—**emotionalism** *n*.

emotive /iˈmoːtɪv/ *adj* characterized by or arousing emotion.—**emotiveness, emotivity** *n*.

empale /emˈpeɪl/ *see* **impale**.

empanel /emˈpænəl/ or /ɪm-/ *vt* (**empanelling, empanelled** *or* **empaneling, empaneled**) (*law*) to enrol (for a jury); to enter on a jury list.—*also* **impanel**.

empathize /ˈempəˌθaɪz/ *vi* to treat with or feel empathy.

empathy /ˈempəθi/ *n* the capacity for participating in and understanding the feelings or ideas of another.—**empathic, empathetic** *adj*.

emperor /ˈempərər/ *n* the sovereign ruler over an empire.—**emperorship** *n*.

emperor penguin *n* an Antarctic penguin, the largest species known.

empery /ˈempəri/ *n* (*pl* **emperies**) (*arch*) power, dominion.

emphasis /ˈemfəsɪs/ *n* (*pl* **emphases**) particular stress or prominence given to something; force or vigour of expression; clarity of form or outline.

emphasize /ˈemfəˌsaɪz/ *vt* to place stress on.

emphatic /emˈfætɪk/ or /ɪm-/ *adj* spoken, done or marked with emphasis; forceful, decisive.—**emphatically** *adv*.—**emphaticalness** *n*.

emphysema /ˌemfɪˈziːmə/ or /-ˈsiː-/ *n* a medical condition marked by the distension of the air sacs in the lungs, causing breathlessness.—**emphysematous** *adj*.

empire /ˈempaɪr/ *n* a large state or group of states under a single sovereign, *usu* an emperor; nations governed by a single sovereign state; a large and complex business organization.

empiric /emˈpɪrɪk/ or /ɪm-/ *adj* empirical. • *n* an empirical worker; a quack.

empirical /-əl/ *adj* based on observation, experiment or experience only, not theoretical.—**empirically** *adv*.—**empiricalness** *n*.

empiricism /emˈpɪrɪˌsɪzəm/ or /ɪm-/ *n* (*philos*) the theory that experience is the only source of knowledge; the use of empirical methods.—**empiricist** *n*.

emplacement /emˈpleɪsmənt/ or /ɪm-/ *n* a position prepared for a gun or artillery.

emplane /emˈpleɪn/ *vti* to put on board a plane; to board a plane.

employ /emˈplɔɪ/ or /ɪm-/ *vt* to give work and pay to; to make use of.—**employable** *adj*.

employee /-i/ *n* a person who is hired by another person for wages.

employer /-ər/ *n* a person, business, etc that employs people.

employment /-mənt/ n an employing; a being employed; occupation or profession.

empoison /ɛmˈpɔɪzən/ vt to taint, corrupt.

emporium /ɛmˈpɔriəm/ or /ɪm-/ n (pl **emporiums, emporia**) a large shop carrying many different items.

empower /ɛmˈpauər/ or /ɪm-/ vt to give official authority to.—**empowerment** n.

empress /ˈɛmprəs/ n the female ruler of an empire; the wife or widow of an emperor.

empty /ˈɛmpti/ or /ˈɛmti/ adj (**emptier, emptiest**) containing nothing; not occupied; lacking reality, substance, or value; hungry. • vb (**emptying, emptied**) vt to make empty; to transfer or discharge (the contents of something) by emptying. • vi to become empty; to discharge contents. • n (pl **empties**) empty containers or bottles.—**emptily** adv.—**emptiness** n.

empty-handed /-ˌhændəd/ adj with nothing in one's hands; without gain.

empty-headed /-ˌhɛdəd/ adj scatterbrained.

empyema /ˌɛmpaɪˈiːmə/ or /ˌɛmpi-/ n (pl **empyemata**) a collection of pus, esp in the chest.—**empyemic** adj.

empyrean /ɛmˈpaɪˈriːən/ or /ˌɛmpi-/, /ˌɛmpiˈriːən/ n (arch) the highest heaven. • adj pertaining to the highest heaven; celestial.

EMS abbr = European Monetary System.

EMU abbr = European Monetary Union.

emu /ˈiːmjuː/ n a fast-running Australian bird, related to the ostrich.

emulate /ˈɛmjuˌleɪt/ vt to try to equal or do better than; to imitate; to rival or compete.—**emulation** n.—**emulative** adj.—**emulator** n.

emulous /ˈɛmjuləs/ adj wanting to excel; competitive.

emulsify /ɪˈmʌlsəˌfaɪ/ vti (**emulsifying, emulsified**) to make or become an emulsion.—**emulsification** n.—**emusifier** n.

emulsion /ɪˌmʌlʃən/ n a mixture of mutually insoluble liquids in which one is dispersed in droplets throughout the other; a light-sensitive substance on photographic paper or film.—**emulsive** adj.

emunctory /ɪˈmʌŋktəri/ n (pl **emunctories**) (anat) an excretory duct or canal. • adj excretory.

en /ɛn/ or /ɪn/ n (print) a measure of width, equal to half an em.

enable /ɪˈneɪbəl/ or /ɛ-/ vt to give the authority or means to do something; to make easy or possible.—**enabler** n.

enact /ɪˈnækt/ or /ɛ-/ vt to make into law; to act (a play, etc).—**enactive** adj.—**enactment** n.—**enactor** n.—**enactory** adj.

enamel /ɪˈnæməl/ n a glass-like substance used to coat the surface of metal or pottery; the hard outer layer of a tooth; a usu glossy paint that forms a hard coat. • vt (**enamelling, enamelled** or **enameling, enameled**) to cover or decorate with enamel.—**enameller, enameler, enamellist, enamelist** n.—**enamelwork** n.

enamour, enamor /ɪˈnæmər/ or /ɛ-/ vt to inspire with love.—**enamoured, enamored** adj.

enarthrosis /ˌɛnɑrˈθroːsɪs/ n (pl **enarthroses**) (anat) a ball-and-socket joint.

en bloc /ãˈblɒk/ adv in a mass.

encage /ɛnˈkeɪdʒ/ vt to shut up in, or as in, a cage.

encamp /ɛnˈkæmp/ vt to place or stay in a camp.—**encampment** n.

encapsulate /ɛnˈkæpsuˌleɪt/ or /-sjuː-/ vt to enclose or be enclosed in, as a capsule; to summarize.—**encapsulation** n.

encase /ɛnˈkeɪs/ vt to enclose (as if) in a case.—**encasement** n.

encaustic /ɛnˈkɒstɪk/ adj (ceramics) with colours burned in. • n the art of painting in melted wax; a piece of work done by this method.

enceinte /ɛnˈsænt/, Fr. /ɑ̃ˈsæt/ adj pregnant.

encephalic /ˌɛnsəˈfælɪk/ or /ˌɛnk-/ adj of the brain.

encephalitis /ɛnˌsɛfəˈlaɪtɪs/ or /ˌɛnkɛf-/ n inflammation of the brain.—**encephalitic** adj.

encephalogram /ɛnˈsɛfələˌgræm/ or /ɛnˈkɛf-/ n an electroencephalogram.—**encephalograph** n.

enchain /ɛnˈtʃeɪn/ vt to hold fast with, or as with, a chain.—**enchainment** n.

enchant /ɛnˈtʃænt/ vt to bewitch, to delight.—**enchanter** n.—**enchantment** n.—**enchantress** nf.

enchase /ɛnˈtʃeɪs/ vt to engrave, to emboss.

encircle /ɛnˈsɜrkəl/ vt to surround; to move or pass completely round.—**encirclement** n.

enclasp /ɪnˈklæsp/ or /ɛn-/ vt to clasp.

enclave /ˈɒnkleɪv/ or /ˈɛn-/ n an area of a country's territory entirely surrounded by foreign territory.

enclitic /ɛnˈklɪtɪk/ adj (linguistics) attached to the preceding word and treated as a suffix, eg "thee" in "prithee". • n an enclitic word.—**enclitically** adv.

enclose /ɪnˈkloːz/ or /ɛn-/ vt to shut up or in; to put in a wrapper or parcel, usu together with a letter.—**enclosable** adj.—**encloser** n.

enclosure /ɪnˈkloːʒər/ or /ɛn-/ n an enclosing; an enclosed area; something enclosed with a letter, in a parcel, etc.

encomiast /ɛnˈkoːmiˌæst/ n a composer of an encomium.—**encomiastic** adj.

encomium /ɛnˈkoːmiəm/ n (pl **encomiums, encomia**) a usu formal expression of high praise in speech or writing.

encompass /ɛnˈkʌmpəs/ or /ɪn-/ vt to encircle or enclose; to include.—**encompassment** n.

encore /ˈɒŋkɔr/ or /ˈɒn-/ interj once more! • n a call for the repetition of a performance.—also vt.

encounter /ɛnˈkauntər/ vt to meet, esp unexpectedly; to fight, engage in battle with; to be faced with (problems, etc). • n a meeting; a conflict, battle.

encourage /ɪnˈkʌrədʒ/ or /ɛn-/ vt to inspire with confidence or hope; to urge, incite; to promote the development of.—**encouragement** n.—**encourager** n.—**encouragingly** adv.

encroach /ɪnˈkroːtʃ/ or /ɛn-/ vi to infringe another's territory, rights, etc; to advance beyond an established limit.—**encroacher** n.—**encroachingly** adv.—**encroachment** n.

encrust /ɛnˈkrʌst/ vt to cover with a hard crust; to form a crust on the surface of; to decorate a surface with jewels.—**encrustation** n.

encumber /ɛnˈkʌmbər/ or /ɪn-/ vt to weigh down; to hinder the function or activity of.—**encumberingly** adv.

encumbrance /ɛnˈkʌmbrəns/ or /ɪn-/ n something that is a hindrance or burden.

encumbrancer /-ər/ n a person who has a legal claim on an estate.

encyclical /ɛnˈsɪklɪkəl/ adj circulated widely.—also **encyclic**. • n a letter addressed by the pope to all Roman Catholic bishops.

encyclopedia, encyclopaedia /ɛnˌsaɪkləˈpiːdiə/ or /ɪn-/, /ən-/ n a book or series of books containing information on all branches of knowledge, or treating comprehensively a particular branch of knowledge, usu in alphabetical order.

encyclopedic, encyclopaedic /-ˈpiːdɪk/ adj comprehensive.—**encyclopedically, encyclopaedically** adv.

encyclopedist, encyclopaedist /-ɪst/ n a compiler of an encyclopedia.

encyst /ɪnˈsɪst/ or /ɛn-/, /ən-/ vti (biol) to enclose, or become enclosed in, a cyst or vesicle.—**encystment** n.

end /ɛnd/ n the last part; the place where a thing stops; purpose; result, outcome. • vt to bring to an end; to destroy. • vi to come to an end; to result (in). • adj final; ultimate.

end-, endo- /ɛndo:/ or /-də/ prefix within.

endanger /ɪnˈdeɪndʒər/ or /ɛn-/, /ən-/ vt to put in danger.—**endangerment** n.

endear /ɪnˈdiːr/ or /ɛn-/, /ən-/ vt to make loved or more loved.—**endearing** adj.—**endearingly** adv.

endearment /-mənt/ n something that endears; a word or words of affection.

endeavour, endeavor /ɪnˈdɛvər/ or /ɛn-/, /ən-/ vi to try or attempt (to). • n an attempt.

endemic /ɛnˈdɛmɪk/ adj (disease) locally prevalent; (plant) peculiar to a locality. • n an endemic disease; an endemic plant.—**endemicity** n.—**endemically** adv.

ending /-ɪŋ/ n reaching or coming to an end; the final part.

endive /ˈɛndaɪv/ n an annual or biennial herb widely cultivated as a salad plant; a variety of chicory used in salads.

endless /ˈɛndləs/ adj unending; uninterrupted; extremely numerous.—**endlessly** adv.—**endlessness** n.

endo-, end- /ˈɛndo:/ prefix within.

endocarditis /ˌɛndo:kɑrˈdaɪtɪs/ n inflammation of the endocardium.—**endocarditic** adj.

endocardium /ˌɛndo:ˈkɑrdiəm/ n (pl **endocardia**) the membrane lining the heart cavities.

endocarp /ˈɛndo:ˌkɑrp/ n the inner coat or shell of a fruit.—**endocarpal, endocarpic** adj.

endocrine /ˈɛndo:ˌkraɪn/ or /-ˌkrɪn/ adj secreting internally, specifically producing secretions that are distributed in the body by the bloodstream.—also **endocrinal**. • n an endocrine gland.

endocrine gland *n* a gland that secretes hormones directly into the bloodstream, *eg* the pituitary and thyroid.

endocrinology /ˌɛndoʊkrɪˈnɒlədʒɪ/ *n* the scientific study of endocrine glands and hormones.—**endocrinologic, endocrinological** *adj.*—**endocrinologist** *n*.

endoderm /ˈɛndoʊˌdɜrm/ *n* the inner layer of embryonic cells in an egg from which an organism is formed.—*also* **entoblast, entoderm.**—**endodermal, endodermic, entodermal, entodermic** *adj*.

endogamy /ɛnˈdɒgəmi/ *n* the practice of marrying only within the same tribe.—**endogamous** *adj*.

endogenous /ɛnˈdɒdʒɪnəs/ *adj* growing from or on the inside.—**endogeny** *n*.

endomorph /ˈɛndoʊˌmɔrf/ *n* a mineral enclosed within another mineral; a person with a heavily built physique.—**endomorphic** *adj.*—**endomorphy** *n*.

endomorphism /-ˈmɔrfɪzəm/ *n* (*geol*) metamorphosis of molten rock within older rock.

endoparasite /ˌɛndoʊˈpærəˌsaɪt/ *n* an internal parasite.—**endoparasitic** *adj*.

endoplasm /ˈɛndoʊˌplæzəm/ *n* (*biol*) the inner layer of protoplasm.

endorse /ɪnˈdɔrs/ or /ɛn-/, /ən-/ *vt* to write one's name, comment, etc on the back of to approve; to record an offence on a driving licence; to support.—**endorsable** *adj.*—**endorsee** *n.*—**endorsement** *n.*—**endorser** *n*.

endoscope /ˈɛndoʊˌskoʊp/ *n* a medical instrument for examining the interior of the body.—**endoscopic** *adj.*—**endoscopist** *n.*—**endoscopy** *n*.

endosmosis /ˌɛndɒsˈmoʊsɪs/ *n* (*biol*) osmosis inwards through the porous membrane of a cell, etc, by a surrounding liquid.

endosperm /ˈɛndoʊˌspɜrm/ *n* the albumen of a seed.—**endospermic** *adj*.

endothelium /ˌɛndoʊˈθiːliəm/ *n* (*pl* **endothelia**) (*anat*) a tissue which lines blood vessels.

endow /ɪnˈdaʊ/ or /ɛn-/, /ən-/ *vt* to give money or property to provide an income for; to provide with a special power or attribute.—**endower** *n*.

endowment /-mənt/ *n* an endowing; an income, etc settled on an individual or organization; a natural quality or gift.

endpaper /ˈɛndˌpeɪpər/ *n* either of two folded sheets of paper pasted against the inside covers of a book and attached to the first and last pages.

end product *n* the final result of a manufacturing or other process.

endue /ɪnˈdjuː/ or /ɛn-/, /ən-/ *vt* (**enduing, endued**) to provide with a quality or power.—*also* **indue**.

endurance /ɪnˈdʊrəns/ or /ɛn-/, /ən-/ *n* the ability to withstand pain, hardship, strain, etc.

endure /ɪnˈdjʊr/ or /ɛn-/, /ən-/, /-ˈdjər/, /-dər/ *vt* to undergo, tolerate (hardship, etc) *esp* with patience. • *vi* to continue in existence, to last out.—**endurable** *adj.*—**endurability** *n.*—**endurably** *adv*.

enduring /-ɪŋ/ *adj* lasting, permanent.—**enduringly** *adv*.

endways /ˈɛndˌweɪz/ *adv* on end, with the end foremost.

enema /ˈɛnɪmə/ *n* (*pl* **enemas, enemata**) the injection of a liquid into the rectum to void the bowels; the liquid injected.

enemy /ˈɛnəmi/ *n* (*pl* **enemies**) a person who hates or dislikes and wishes to harm another; a military opponent; something harmful or deadly.

energetic /ˌɛnərˈdʒɛtɪk/ *adj* lively, active; done with energy.—**energetically** *adv*.

energetics /-ɪks/ *n sing* the science of energy.

energize /ˈɛnərdʒaɪz/ *vt* to fill with energy; to invigorate; to apply an electric current to.—**energizer** *n*.

energy /ˈɛnərdʒi/ *n* (*pl* **energies**) capacity of acting or being active; vigour, power; (*physics*) capacity to do work.

enervate /ˈɛnərˌveɪt/ *vt* to lessen the strength or vigour of; to enfeeble in mind and body.—**enervation** *n.*—**enervative** *adj.*—**enervator** *n*.

enface /ɛnˈfeɪs/ or /ɪn-/ *vt* to write or stamp on the face of a document.

enfant terrible /ˌɑ̃fɑ̃tɛˈriːbl/ *n* (*pl* **enfants terribles**) a person who makes awkward remarks.

enfeeble /ɪnˈfiːbəl/ or /ɛn-/, /ən-/ *vt* to make feeble.—**enfeeblement** *n.*—**enfeebler** *n*.

enfeoff /ɛnˈfɛf/ or /-ˈfiːf/ *vt* (*law*) to give a freehold property to; to convey.—**enfeoffment** *n*.

enfilade /ˌɛnfɪˈleɪd/ *n* gunfire directed (at troops, etc) in a line from end to end.—*also vt*.

enfold /ɪnˈfoʊld/ or /ɛn-/, /ən-/ *vt* to wrap up; to hug in the arms.—**enfolder** *n.*—**enfoldment** *n*.

enforce /ɛnˈfɔrs/ or /ɪn-/, /ən-/ *vt* to compel obedience by threat; to execute with vigour.—**enforceable** *adj.*—**enforcement** *n.*—**enforcer** *n*.

enfranchise /ɛnˈfrænˌtʃaɪs/ or /ɪn-/ *vt* to admit to citizenship; to grant the vote to.—**enfranchisement** *n.*—**enfranchiser** *n*.

engage /ɪnˈgeɪdʒ/ or /ɛn-/, /ən-/ *vt* to pledge as security; to promise to marry; to keep busy; to hire; to attract and hold, *esp* attention or sympathy; to cause to participate; to bring or enter into conflict; to begin or take part in a venture; to connect or interlock, to mesh.—**engager** *n*.

engaged /ɪnˈgeɪdʒd/ or /ɛn-/, /ən-/ *adj* entered into a promise to marry; reserved, occupied or busy.

engagement /ɪnˈgeɪdʒmənt/ or /ɛn-/, /ən-/ *n* the act or state of being engaged; a pledge; an appointment agreed with another person; employment; a battle.

engaging /-ɪŋ/ *adj* pleasing, attractive.—**engagingly** *adv.*—**engagingness** *n*.

engender /ɪnˈdʒɛndər/ or /ɛn-/, /ən-/ *vt* to bring into existence.—**engenderment** *n*.

engine /ˈɛndʒɪn/ *n* a machine by which physical power is applied to produce a physical effect; a locomotive; (*formerly*) a mechanical device, such as a large catapult, used in war.

engineer /ˌɛndʒɪˈnɪːr/ *n* a person trained in engineering; a person who operates an engine, etc; a member of a military group devoted to engineering work; a designer or builder of engines. • *vt* to contrive, plan, *esp* deviously.

engineering /-ɪŋ/ *n* the art or practice of constructing and using machinery; the art and science by which natural forces and materials are utilized in structures or machines.

English /ˈɪŋglɪʃ/ *adj* of, relating to, or characteristic of England, the English people, or the English language. • *n* the language of the English people, the US and many areas formerly under British control; English language and literature as a subject of study.

engorge /ɪnˈgɔrdʒ/ or /ɛn-/, /ən-/ *vt* to congest with blood; to consume (food) greedily.—**engorgement** *n*.

engrained /ɪnˈgreɪnd/ or /ɛn-/, /ən-/ *see* **ingrained**.

engrave /ɪnˈgreɪv/ or /ɛn-/, /ən-/ *vt* to produce by cutting or carving a surface; to cut to produce a representation that may be printed from; to lodge deeply (in the mind, etc).—**engraver** *n*.

engraving /-ɪŋ/ *n* a print made from an engraved surface.

engross /ɪnˈgroʊs/ or /ɛn-/, /ən-/ *vt* to occupy (the attention) fully; to copy in large handwriting; to prepare the final text of.—**engrossing** *adj.*—**engrossment** *n*.

engulf /ɪnˈgʌlf/ or /ɛn-/, /ən-/ *vt* to flow over and enclose; to overwhelm.—**engulfment** *n*.

enhance /ɪnˈhæns/ or /ɛn-/, /ən-/ *vt* to increase in value, importance, attractiveness, etc; to heighten.—**enhancement** *n.*—**enhancer** *n*.

enigma /ɪˈnɪgmə/ or /ɛ-/, /ə-/ *n* someone or something that is puzzling or mysterious.—**enigmatic, enigmatical** *adj.*—**enigmatically** *adv*.

enjoin /ɪnˈdʒɔɪn/ or /ɛn-/, /ən-/ *vt* to command, order someone with authority; to forbid, to prohibit.—**enjoiner** *n.*—**enjoinment** *n*.

enjoy /ɪnˈdʒɔɪ/ or /ɛn-/, /ən-/ *vt* to get pleasure from, take joy in; to use or have the advantage of; to experience.—**enjoyment** *n*.

enjoyable /-əbəl/ *adj* giving enjoyment.—**enjoyably** *adv*.

enkindle /ɪnˈkɪndəl/ or /ɛn-/, /ən-/ *vt* to set on fire; (*fig*) to inflame.

enlace /ɪnˈleɪs/ or /ɛn-/, /ən-/ *vt* to entwine; to enfold.—**enlacement** *n*.

enlarge /ɪnˈlɑrdʒ/ or /ɛn-/, /ən-/ *vti* to make or grow larger; to reproduce (a photograph) in a larger form; to speak or write at length (on).

enlargement /-mənt/ *n* an act, instance, or state of enlarging; a photograph, etc that has been enlarged.

enlarger /-ər/ *n* a device for making photographic enlargements.

enlighten /ɪnˈlaɪtən/ or /ɛn-/, /ən-/ *vt* to instruct; to inform.—**enlightening** *adj.*—**enlightenment** *n*.

enlightened /-ˈlaɪtənd/ *adj* well-informed, tolerant, unprejudiced.

enlist /ɪnˈlɪst/ or /ɛn-/, /ən-/ *vt* to engage for service in the armed forces; to secure the aid or support of. • *vi* to register oneself for the armed services.—**enlistee** *n.*—**enlistment** *n*.

enliven /ɪnˈlaɪvən/ or /ɛn-/, /ən-/ vt to make more lively or cheerful.—**enlivening** adj.—**enlivenment** n.

en masse /ɑ̃ˈmæs/ adv all together; in a large group.

enmesh /ɪnˈmɛʃ/ or /ɛn-/, /ən-/ vt to catch in a net; to entangle.—also **inmesh, immesh**.

enmity /ˈɛnmɪti/ n (pl **enmities**) hostility, esp mutual hatred.

ennage /ɛˈneɪdʒ/ n (print) the number of ens in a text.

ennea- /ˈɛnɪə/ prefix nine.

ennead /ˈɛniˌæd/ n a set of nine.—**enneadic** adj.

enneagon /ˈɛnɪəˌɡɒn/ n a plane figure with nine sides and nine angles.

ennoble /ɪˈnoːbəl/ or /ɛn-/, /ən-/ vt to make noble, dignify; to raise (a person) to a rank of nobility.—**ennoblement** n.—**ennobler** n.

ennui /ˈɒnwiː/ n boredom, apathy.

enology /ɪˈnɒlədʒi/ see **oenology**.

enormity /ɪˈnɔrmɪti/ n (pl **enormities**) great wickedness; a serious crime; huge size, magnitude.

enormous /ɪˈnɔrməs/ adj extremely large.—**enormously** adv.

enough /ɪˈnʌf/ or /iː-/, /ɛ-/, /ə-/ adj adequate, sufficient. • adv so as to be sufficient; very; quite. • n a sufficiency. • interj stop!

enounce /ɪˈnaʊns/ vt to proclaim, to enunciate.

en passant /ˌɑ̃pæˈsɑ̃/ adv in passing.

enquire, enquirer see **inquire**.

enquiry see **inquiry**.

enrage /ɪnˈreɪdʒ/ or /ɛn-/, /ən-/ vt to fill with anger.—**enraged** adj.—**enragement** n.

enrapture /ɪnˈræptʃər/ or /ɛn-/, /ən-/ vt to fill with pleasure or delight.

enrich /ɪnˈrɪtʃ/ or /ɛn-/, /ən-/ vt to make rich or richer; to ornament; to improve in quality by adding to.—**enricher** n.—**enrichment** n.

enrol, enroll /ɪnˈroːl/ or /ɛn-/, /ən-/ vti (**enrols** or **enrolls, enrolling, enrolled**) to enter or register on a roll or list; to become a member of a society, club, etc; to admit as a member.—**enrollee** n.—**enroller** n.—**enrolment, enrollment** n.

en route /ɑ̃ˈruːt/ adv along or on the way.

ensanguine /ɛnˈsæŋɡwɪn/ vt to smear or cover with blood.

ensconce /ɪnˈskɒns/ or /ɛn-/, /ən-/ vt to establish in a safe, secure or comfortable place.

ensemble /ɒnˈsɒmbəl/ n something regarded as a whole; the general effect; the performance of the full number of musicians, dancers, etc; a complete harmonious costume.

enshrine /ɪnˈʃraɪn/ or /ɛn-/, /ən-/ vt to enclose (as if) in a shrine; to cherish as sacred.—also **inshrine**.—**enshrinement** n.

enshroud /ɪnˈʃraʊd/ or /ɛn-/, /ən-/ vt to cover with, or as with, a shroud.

ensiform /ˈɛnsɪˌfɔrm/ adj sword-shaped.

ensign /ˈɛnsaɪn/ or /-sən/ n a flag; the lowest commissioned officer in the US Navy.

ensilage /ˈɛnsɪlɪdʒ/ or /ˈɪn-/ n storage in a pit or silo; silage.

ensile /ɪnˈsaɪl/ or /ɛn-/ vt to store in a silo.—**ensilability** n.

enslave /ɪnˈsleɪv/ or /ɛn-/ vt to make into a slave; to subjugate.—**enslavement** n.—**enslaver** n.

ensnare /ɪnˈsnɛr/ or /ɛn-/, /ən-/ vt to trap in, or as in, a snare.—**ensnarement** n.

ensue /ɪnˈsuː/ or /ɪnˈsjuː/, /ɛn-/, /ən-/ vi (**ensuing, ensued**) to occur as a consequence or in time.—**ensuing** adj.

en suite /ɑ̃ˈswiːt/ adv, adj in a single unit.

ensure /ɪnˈʃʊr/ or /ɛn-/, /ən-/ vt to make certain, sure, or safe.—**ensurer** n.

enswathe /ɪnˈswɒθ/, or /ɛn-/, /ən-/ vt to wrap, swathe.

ENT /ˈiːˈɛnˈtiː/ abbr = ear, nose, and throat.

entablature /ɪnˈtæblətʃər/ or /ɛn-/ n the part of a building resting on top of columns.

entablement /ɪnˈteɪbəlmənt/ or /ɛn-/ n a platform for a statue, above the dado and base.

entail /ɪnˈteɪl/ or /ɛn-/, /ən-/ vt to involve, necessitate as a result; to restrict the inheritance of property to a designated line of heirs. • n the act of entailing or the estate entailed.—**entailer** n.—**entailment** n.

entangle /ɪnˈtæŋɡəl/ or /ɛn-/, /ən-/ vt to tangle, complicate; to involve in a tangle or complications.—**entanglement** n.—**entangler** n.

entelechy /ɛnˈtɛləki/ or /ɪn-/ n (pl **entelechies**) (philos) actuality.

entente (cordiale) Fr. /ɑ̃ˌtɑ̃tkɔrdiˈæl/ n a friendly understanding or relationship between two or more countries.

enter /ˈɛntər/ vi to go or come in or into; to come on stage; to begin, start; (with **for**) to register as an entrant. • vt to come or go into; to pierce, penetrate; (an organization) to join; to insert; (proposal, etc) to submit; to record (an item) in a diary, etc.—**enterable** adj.—**enterer** n.

enteric /ɛnˈtɛrɪk/, **enteral** /-rəl/ adj intestinal.—**enterally** adv.

enteritis /ˌɛntəˈraɪtɪs/ n inflammation of the intestines, usu causing diarrhoea.

enteron /ˌɛntəˈrɒn/ (pl **entera**) the alimentary canal.

enterotomy /ˌɛntəˈrɒtəmi/ n (pl **enterotomies**) dissection of, or an incision into, the bowels.

enterprise /ˈɛntərˌpraɪz/ n a difficult or challenging undertaking; a business project; readiness to engage in new ventures.—**enterpriser** n.

enterprising /-ɪŋ/ adj adventurous, energetic and progressive.—**enterprisingly** adv.

entertain /ˌɛntərˈteɪn/ vt to show hospitality to; to amuse, please (a person or audience); to have in mind; to consider.

entertainer /-ər/ n a person who entertains in public, esp professionally.

entertaining /-ɪŋ/ adj amusing; diverting.—**entertainingly** adv.

entertainment /-mənt/ n entertaining; amusement; an act or show intended to amuse and interest an audience, etc.

enthral, enthrall /ɪnˈθrɒl/ or /ɛn-/, /ən-/ vt (**enthrals** or **enthralls, enthralling, enthralled**) to captivate.—**enthralment, enthrallment** n.

enthrone /ɪnˈθroːn/ or /ɛn-/, /ən-/ vt to install ceremonially, as a monarch or bishop.—**enthronement** n.

enthuse /ɪnˈθuːz/ or /-ˈθjuːz/, /ɛn-/, /ən-/ vti to fill with or express enthusiasm.

enthusiasm /ɪnˈθuːziˌæzəm/ or /-ˈθjuːz-/, /ɛn-/, /ən-/ n intense interest or liking; something that arouses keen interest.

enthusiast /ɪnˈθuːziˌæst/ or /-ˈθjuːz-/, /ɛn-/, /ən-/, /-ɪəst/ n a person filled with enthusiasm for something.

enthusiastic /-ɪk/ adj filled with enthusiasm.—**enthusiastically** adv.

enthymeme /ˈɛnθɪˌmiːm/ n (logic) a syllogism in which one premise is suppressed.

entice /ɪnˈtaɪs/ or /ɛn-/, /ən-/ vt to attract by offering some pleasure or reward.—**enticement** n.—**enticer** n.—**enticing** adj.

entire /ɪnˈtaɪr/ or /ɛn-/, /ən-/ adj whole; complete.—**entireness** n.

entirely /-li/ adv fully; completely.

entirety /-əti/ or /-ti/ n (pl **entireties**) completeness; the total.

entitle /ɪnˈtaɪtəl/ or /ɛn-/, /ən-/ vt to give a title to; to give a right (to).—**entitlement** n.

entity /ˈɛntɪti/ n (pl **entities**) existence, being; something that has a separate existence.

entoblast /ˈɛntoːˈblæst/, **entoderm** /-dɛrm/ see **endoderm**.

entomb /ɪnˈtuːm/ or /ɛn-/, /ən-/ vt to place in, or as in, a tomb.—**entombment** n.

entomic /ɛnˈtɒmɪk/ adj of insects.

entomo-, entom- /ˈɛntəmoː/ prefix insect.

entomology /ˌɛntəˈmɒlədʒi/ n the branch of zoology that deals with insects.—**entomological, entomologic** adj.—**entomologist** n.

entomophagous /ˌɛntəˈmɒfəɡəs/ adj insect-eating.

entomophilous /-fələs/ adj fertilized by insects.

entopic /ɛnˈtɒpɪk/ adj (anat) in a normal position.

entourage /ˌɒntuˈrɒʒ/ n a retinue, group of attendants.

entozoic /ˌɛntəˈzoːɪk/ adj living within an animal.

entozoan /ˌɛntəˈzoːən/ n (pl **entozoa**) a parasite which lives inside an animal.

entr'acte /ˈɒntrækt/ n a light entertainment, a ballet, etc, as an interlude between the acts of a play or opera.

entrails /ˈɛntreɪlz/ npl the insides of the body, the intestines.

entrain /ɪnˈtreɪn/ or /ɛn-/, /ən-/ vti to put or get onto a train.

entrance[1] /ˈɛntrəns/ n the act of entering; the power or authority to enter; a means of entering; an admission fee.

entrance[2] /ɪnˈtræns/ vt to put into a trance; to fill with great delight.—**entrancement** n.—**entrancing** adj.

entrant /ˈɛntrənt/ n a person who enters (eg a competition, profession).

entrap /ɪnˈtræp/ or /ɛn-/, /ən-/ vt (**entrapping, entrapped**) to catch, as if in a trap; to lure into a compromising or incriminatory situation.—**entrapment** n.—**entrapper** n.

entreat /ɪnˈtriːt/ or /ɛn-/, /ən-/ vt to request earnestly; to implore, beg.—**entreaty** n (pl **entreaties**).

entrecôte /ˈɒntrəˌkoːt/ n a boned cut of beef from between the ribs.

entrée, entree /'ɒntreɪ/ or /'ɑ̃treɪ/ *n* a dish served before the main meal; in US, the principal dish of a meal; the right or power of admission.

entremets *Fr.* /ˌɒntrə'meɪ/ *n* (*pl* **entremets**) a dessert.

entrench /ɪn'trɛntʃ/ or /ɛn-/, /ən-/ *vt* to dig a trench as a defensive perimeter; to establish (oneself) in a strong defensive position.—**entrencher** *n*.—**entrenchment** *n*.

entrepôt /'ɒntrəˌpoː/ *n* an intermediate centre of trade and transhipment.

entrepreneur /ˌɒntrəprə'nər/ *n* a person who takes the commercial risk of starting up and running a business enterprise.—**entrepreneurial** *adj*.—**entrepreneurship** *n*.

entresol /'ɒntrəˌsɒl/ *n* a floor between the ground and first floor, a mezzanine.

entropy /'entrəpi/ *n* (*pl* **entropies**) a measure of the unavailable energy in a closed thermodynamic system; disorder, disorganization.

entrust /ɪn'trɛst/ or /ɛn-/, /ən-/ *vt* (*usu with* **with**) to confer as a responsibility, duty, etc; (*usu with* **to**) to place something in another's care.—**entrustment** *n*.

entry /'entri/ *n* (*pl* **entries**) the act of entering; a place of entrance; an item recorded in a diary, journal, etc; a person or thing taking part in a contest.

entwine /ɪn'twaɪn/ or /ɛn-/, /ən-/ *vt* to twine together or around.—**entwinement** *n*.

enucleate /ɪ'njuːkliˌeɪt/ or /ɪ'nuːk-/ *vt* to remove the nucleus from.

E number *n* a series of numbers with the prefix E used to identify food additives within the European Union.

enumerate /ɪ'njuːməˌreɪt/ or /ɪ'nuː-/ *vt* to count; to list.—**enumeration** *n*.—**enumerator** *n*.

enunciate /ɪ'nʌnsiˌeɪt/ *vt* to state definitely; to pronounce clearly.—**enunciation** *n*.—**enunciator** *n*.—**enunciative** *adj*.

enure /ɪ'njʊr/ *see* **inure**.

enuresis /ˌenjʊ'riːsɪs/ *n* urinary incontinence; bedwetting.—**enuretic** *adj*.

envelop /ɪn'vɛləp/ *vt* to enclose completely (as if) with a covering.—**envelopment** *n*.

envelope /'envəˌloːp/ or /'ɒn-/ *n* something used to wrap or cover, *esp* a gummed paper container for a letter; the bag containing the gas in a balloon or airship.

envenom /ɪn'vɛnəm/ or /ɛn-/, /ən-/ *vt* to put poison into; (*fig*) to embitter.

enviable /'enviəbəl/ *adj* causing envy; fortunate.—**enviably** *adv*.

envious /'enviəs/ *adj* filled with envy.—**enviously** *adv*.

environ /ɪn'vaɪrən/ or /ɛn-/, /ən-/ *vt* to surround or enclose.

environment /-mənt/ *n* external conditions and surroundings, *esp* those that affect the quality of life of plants, animals and human beings.—**environmental** *adj*.—**environmentally** *adv*.

environmentalist /-ˌmentəlɪst/ *n* a person who is concerned with improving the quality of the environment.—**environmentalism** *n*.

environs /ɪn'vaɪrənz/ or /'envɪrənz/ *npl* the surrounding area or outskirts of a district or town.

envisage /ɪn'vɪzədʒ/ or /ɛn-/, /ən-/ *vt* to have a mental picture of.—**envisagement** *n*.

envoy /'ɒnvɔɪ/ or /'ɛn-/ *n* a diplomatic agent; a representative.

envy /'ɛnvi/ *n* (*pl* **envies**) resentment or discontent at another's achievements, possessions, etc; an object of envy. • *vt* (**envying, envied**) to feel envy of.—**envier** *n*.

enwrap /ɪn'ræp/ or /ɛn-/, /ən-/ *vt* to wrap up.

enzootic /ˌenzoː'tɪk/ *adj* (*disease*) affecting animals in a particular district.

enzyme /'enzaɪm/ *n* a complex protein, produced by living cells, that induces or speeds chemical reactions in plants and animals.

eon /'iːɒn/ *see* **aeon**.

eonian /'iːɒniən/ *see* **aeonian**.

eonism *n* (*psychiatry*) a tendency in a male to adopt female clothing and mannerisms, transvestitism.

eosin, eosine /'iːoˌsɪn/ *n* a pink coal tar dye.—**eosinic** *adj*.

EP *abbr* = Extended Play (gramophone record).

epact /'iːpækt/ *n* (*astron*) the difference between the solar and the lunar month, about eleven days in the year.

eparch /'ɛpark/ *n* (*Greek Orthodox Church*) a metropolitan or other bishop; a governor of an eparchy.

eparchy /'ɛparki/, **eparchate** /-keɪt/ *n* (*pl* **eparchies, eparchates**) a Greek province; the diocese of an eparch.—**eparchial** *adj*.

epaulette, epaulet /ˌɛpə'lɒt/ or /'ɛpəˌlɒt/ *n* a piece of ornamental fabric or metal worn on the shoulder, *esp* on a uniform.

épée /eɪ'peɪ/ *n* a sword used in fencing.—**épéeist** *n*.

epenthesis /ɛ'pɛnθɪsɪs/ or /ɪ-/ *n* (*pl* **epentheses**) (*linguistics*) the insertion of a letter or syllable in the middle of a word.

epergne /ɪ'pərn/ *n* a branched centrepiece or ornamental stand for a dinner table.

epexegesis /ɛˌpɛksi'dʒiːsɪs/ *n* (*pl* **epexegeses**) (*linguistics*) the use of additional words to clarify a meaning.—**epexegetic, epexegetical** *adj*.

ephah /'iːfə/ *n* a Hebrew dry measure, equal to about one bushel (33 litres).

ephebe /'ɛfiːb/ *n* a young citizen (aged 18 to 20) of ancient Greece.

ephedrine /'ɛfədrɪn/ *n* an alkaloid used to treat asthma and hay fever.

ephemeral /ɪ'fɛmərəl/ or /ɪ'fiːm-/ *adj* existing only for a very short time. • *n* an ephemeral thing or organism.—**ephemerality, empheralness** *n*.

ephemeris /ɪ'fɛmərɪs/ or /ɪ'fiːm-/ *n* (*pl* **ephemerides**) an astronomical almanac showing the daily positions of the sun, moon and planets.

ephod /'iːfɒd/ or /'ɛfɒd/ *n* a vestment worn by a Jewish priest.

ephor /'ɛfɔr/ *n* (*pl* **ephors, ephori**) a magistrate in ancient Greece.

epi-, ep- /'ɛpɪ/ *prefix* upon, at, in addition.

epiblast /'ɛpɪˌblæst/ *n* the outer layer of the embryonic cells in an egg from which an organism is formed.—**epiblastic** *adj*.

epic /'ɛpɪk/ *n* a long poem narrating the deeds of a hero; any literary work, film, etc in the same style. • *adj* relating to or resembling an epic.

epicarp /'ɛpɪkarp/ *n* the outer skin of a fruit.

epicene /'ɛpɪˌsiːn/ *adj* having characteristics of both sexes; lacking characteristics of either sex, sexless.

epicentre, epicenter /'ɛpɪˌsentər/ *n* the area of the earth's surface directly above the focus of an earthquake.—**epicentral** *adj*.

epicure /'ɛpɪˌkjʊr/ *n* a person who has cultivated a refined taste in food, wine, literature, etc.—**epicurism, epicureanism** *n*.

epicurean /ˌɛpɪkjʊ'riːən/ *adj* given to sensuous enjoyment.

epicycle /'ɛpɪˌsaɪkəl/ *n* (*geom*) a small circle, the centre of which is situated on the circumference of a larger circle.—**epicyclic** *adj*.

epicycloid /ˌɛpɪ'saɪklɔɪd/ *n* (*geom*) a curve described by a point in the circumference of one circle which rolls round the circumference of another circle.

epidemic /ˌɛpɪ'dɛmɪk/ *adj, n* (*a disease*) attacking many people at the same time in a community or region.—**epidemical** *adj*.

epidemiology /ˌɛpɪdiː'ɒlədʒi/ *n* the area of medicine dealing with epidemic diseases.—**epidemiological** *adj*.—**epidemiologist** *n*.

epidermis /ˌɛpɪ'dərmɪs/ *n* an outer layer, *esp* of skin.—**epidermal, epidermic, epidermoid** *adj*.

epidiascope /ˌɛpɪ'daɪˌskoːp/ *n* a projector for magnifying opaque as well as transparent pictures.

epidural /ˌɛpɪ'dərəl/ or /-'dʊrəl/, /-'dj-/ *n* a spinal anaesthetic used for the relief of pain during childbirth.

epigastrium /ˌɛpɪ'gæstriəm/ *n* (*pl* **epigastria**) the upper part of the abdomen.

epigenesis /ˌɛpɪdʒə'nɛsɪs/ *n* the theory that an organism is created by the division or segmentation of a fertilized egg cell; a form of geological metamorphism of rock brought about by outside forces; the depositing of ore in already formed rock.—**epigenesist, epigenist** *n*.—**epigenetic** *adj*.—**epigentically** *adv*.

epiglottis /ˌɛpɪ'glɒtəs/ *n* (**epiglottises, epiglottides**) a thin flap of cartilaginous tissue over the entrance to the larynx.—**epiglottal, epiglottic** *adj*.

epigram /'ɛpɪˌgræm/ *n* a short witty poem or saying.—**epigrammatic** *adj*.—**epigrammatically** *adv*.

epigrammatize /-'græməˌtaɪz/ *vti* to compose an epigram (about).—**epigrammatist** *n*.

epigraph /'ɛpɪˌgræf/ *n* a quotation at the beginning of a book or chapter; an inscription on a building or monument.—**epigraphic, epigraphical** *adj*.

epigraphy /ɛ'pɪgrəfi/ *n* the study of inscriptions.—**epigraphist, epigrapher** *n*.

epilepsy /'ɛpɪˌlɛpsi/ *n* a disorder of the nervous system marked typically by convulsive attacks and loss of consciousness.

epileptic /ˌɛpɪ'lɛptɪk/ *adj* of or affected with epilepsy. • *n* a person affected with epilepsy.—**epileptically** *adv*.

epilogue /'epə,lɒg/ *n* the concluding section of a book or other literary work; a short speech addressed by an actor to the audience at the end of a play.—**epilogist** *n*.

epiphany /ɛ'pɪfəni/ or /ɪ-/ *n* (*pl* **epiphanies**) a moment of sudden revelation or insight; (*with cap*) a festival of the Christian Church in commemoration of the coming of the Magi to Christ.

epiphenomenon /,epɪfɪ'nɒmɪnən/ *n* (*pl* **epiphenomena**) a by-product; (*med*) an attendant symptom.

epiphyte /'epɪ,faɪt/ *n* (*bot*) a plant which grows on another plant but is not fed by it.—**epiphytic** *adj*.

episcopacy /ɪ'pɪskəpəsi/ *n* (*pl* **episcopacies**) the system of church government by bishops.

episcopal /ɪ'pɪskəpəl/ *adj* of bishops; governed by bishops.—**episcopally** *adv*.

episcopalian /ɪ,pɪskə'peɪliən/ *adj* pertaining to episcopacy. • *n* a member or supporter of an episcopal church.—**episcopalianism** *n*.

episcopate /ɪ'pɪskəpət/ *n* the office of a bishop.

episiotomy /ɛ,piːzi'ɒtəmi/ or /ɛ,pɪz-/ *n* (*pl* **episiotomies**) a cut made in the perineum during childbirth to prevent tearing.

episode /'epɪ,so:d/ *n* a piece of action in a dramatic or literary work; an incident in a sequence of events.

episodic /-ɪk/, **episodical** /-ɪkəl/ *adj* happening at irregular intervals; digressive.—**episodically** *adv*.

epispastic /,epɪ'spæstɪk/ *adj* producing a blister.

epistaxis /,epɪ'stæksɪs/ *n* (*med*) nosebleed.

epistemology /ɪ,pɪstɪ'mɒlədʒi/ *n* the science of the processes and grounds of knowledge.

epistle /ɪ'pɪsəl/ *n* (*formal*) a letter; (*with cap*) a letter written by one of Christ's Apostles to various churches and individuals.

epistler /-ər/ *n* someone who reads the Epistle in the communion service; one who writes an epistle.

epistolary /ɪ'pɪstə,leri/ *adj* pertaining to, contained in, or conducted by letters.

epistrophe /ɪ'pɪstrəfi/ *n* (*rhetoric*) the practice of ending several successive clauses or sentences with the same word.

epistyle /'epɪ,staɪl/ *n* an architrave.

epitaph /'epɪ,tæf/ *n* an inscription in memory of a dead person, *usu* on a tombstone.—**epitaphic** *adj*.—**epitaphist** *n*.

epithalamium /,epɪθə'leɪmiəm/ *n* (*pl* **epithalamia**) a nuptial song or poem.—**epithalamic** *adj*.

epithelioma /,epɪθiːli'ɒmə/ *n* (*pl* **epitheliomas**, **epitheliomata**) a cancer of the epithelium.—**epitheliomatous** *adj*.

epithelium /,epɪ'θiːliəm/ *n* (*pl* **epithelia**) any of the cells that line the surface of the membranes of the body.—**epithelial** *adj*.

epithet /'epɪ,θet/ *n* a descriptive word or phrase added to or substituted for a person's name (*Vlad the Impaler*).—**epithetic**, **epithetical** *adj*.

epitome /ɪ'pɪtəmi/ *n* a typical example; a paradigm; personification; a condensed account of a written work.—**epitomic**, **epitomical** *adj*.—**epitomist** *n*.

epitomize /ɪ'pɪtə,maɪz/ *vt* to be or make an epitome of.—**epitomization** *n*.—**epitomizer** *n*.

epoch /'epɒk/ or /'iːpɒk/, /'epək/ *n* a date in time used as a point of reference; an age in history associated with certain characteristics; a unit of geological time.—**epochal** *adj*.

epode /'ep,oːd/ *n* a kind of lyric poem; the last part of a lyric ode.

eponym /'epə,nɪm/ *n* a person after whom something is named; a name so derived.—**eponymous, eponymic** *adj*.—**eponymy** *n*.

epopee /'epə,pi/ or /,epə'pi/ *n* an epic poem; epic poetry.

EPOS /'iːpɒs/ *abbr* = Electronic Point Of Sale.

epos /'ep,ɒs/ *n* early unwritten epic poetry; an epic poem; the subject of an epic poem.

epoxy /ɪ'pɒksi/ *adj* (*chem*) of or containing an oxygen atom and two other groups, usually carbon, which are themselves linked with other groups.

epoxy resin *n* a strong synthetic resin containing epoxy groups, used in laminates and adhesives.

epsilon /'epsɪ,lɒn/ *n* the 5th letter of the Greek alphabet.

equable /'ekwəbəl/ *adj* level, uniform; (*climate*) free from extremes of hot and cold; even-tempered.—**equability**, **equableness** *n*.—**equably** *adv*.

equal /'iːkwəl/ *adj* the same in amount, size, number, or value; impartial, regarding or affecting all objects in the same way; capable of meeting a task or situation. • *n* a person that is equal.

• *vt* (**equalling, equalled** *or* **equaling, equaled**) to be equal to, *esp* to be identical in value; to make or do something equal to.—**equally** *adv*.

equality /iː'kwɒlɪti/ *n* (*pl* **equalities**) being equal.

equalize /'iːkwə,laɪz/ *vti* to make or become equal; (*games*) to even the score.—**equalization** *n*.—**equalizer** *n*.

equanimity /,ekwə'nɪmɪti/ *n* (*pl* **equanimities**) evenness of temper; composure.—**equanimous** *adj*.

equate /i'kweɪt/ *vt* to make, treat, or regard as comparable. • *vi* to correspond as equal.

equation /i'kweɪʒən/ *n* an act of equalling; the state of being equal; a *usu* formal statement of equivalence (as in logical and mathematical expressions) with the relations denoted by the sign (=); an expression representing a chemical reaction by means of chemical symbols.—**equational** *adj*.

equator /i'kweɪtər/ *n* an imaginary circle passing round the globe that is equidistant from the North and South poles.—**equatorial** *n*.

equerry /'ekwəri/ or /i'kweri/ *n* (*pl* **equerries**) an officer in the British royal household.

equestrian /i'kwestriən/ *adj* pertaining to horses and riding; on horseback. • *n* a skilled rider.—**equestrienne** *nf*.—**equestrianism** *n*.

equi- /'ekwɪ/ or /'iːkwɪ/ *prefix* equal.

equiangular /,ekwɪ'æŋgjuːlər/ or /'iːkwɪ-/ *adj* having equal angles.

equidistant /,ekwɪ'dɪstənt/ or /'iːkwɪ-/ *adj* at equal distances.—**equidistance** *n*.

equilateral /,ekwɪ'lætərəl/ or /'iːkwɪ-/ *adj* having all sides equal.

equilibrate /i'kwɪlɪ,breɪt/ or /,iːkwɪ'laɪbreɪt/ *vti* to balance.—**equilibration** *n*.

equilibrist /i'kwɪləbrɪst/ *n* a tightrope walker; an acrobat.—**equilibristic** *adj*.

equilibrium /,iːkwɪ'lɪbriəm/ or /'ekwɪ-/ *n* (*pl* **equilibriums**, **equilibria**) a state of balance of weight, power, force, etc.

equine /'ekwaɪn/ or /'iːk-/ *adj* of or resembling a horse.

equinox /'ekwɪ,nɒks/ or /'iːk-/ *n* the two times of the year when night and day are equal in length (around 21 March and 23 September).—**equinoctial** *adj*.

equip /i'kwɪp/ *vt* (**equipping, equipped**) to provide with all the necessary tools or supplies.—**equipper** *n*.

equipage /'ekwɪpɪdʒ/ *n* a carriage with horses and liveried attendants.

equipment /i'kwɪpmənt/ *n* the tools, supplies and other items needed for a particular task, expedition, etc.

equipoise /'ekwɪ,pɔɪz/ or /'iːkwɪ-/ *n* balance, equilibrium.

equipollent /,ikwɪ'pɒlənt/ *adj* equal in power.—**equipollence** *n*.

equiponderant /,ikwɪ'pɒndərənt/ *vti* to make or be equal in weight.—**equiponderant** *adj*.

equisetum /,ekwɪ'siːtəm/ *n* (*pl* **equisetums**, **equiseta**) a plant of the group that includes horsetails.

equitable /'ekwɪtəbəl/ *adj* just and fair; (*law*) pertaining to equity as opposed to common or statute law.—**equitableness** *n*.—**equitably** *adv*.

equitation /,ekwɪ'teɪʃən/ *n* horsemanship.

equity /'ekwɪti/ *n* (*pl* **equities**) fairness; (*law*) a legal system based on natural justice developed into a body of rules supplementing the common law; (*pl*) ordinary shares in a company.

equivalence /i'kwɪvələns/ or /-ɪ-/, **equivalency** /-i/ *n* (*pl* **equivalences, equivalencies**) equality of value or power; (*chem*) the property of having equal valency.

equivalent /i'kwɪvələnt/ *adj* equal in amount, force, meaning, etc; virtually identical, *esp* in effect or function. • *n* an equivalent thing.

equivocal /i'kwɪvəkəl/ *adj* ambiguous; uncertain; questionable; arousing suspicion.—**equivocality, equivocacy** *n*.—**equivocally** *adv*.

equivocate /i'kwɪvə,keɪt/ *vi* to use ambiguous language, *esp* in order to confuse or deceive.—**equivocation** *n*.—**equivocator** *n*.—**equivocatory** *adj*.

equivoque, equivoke /'ekwɪ,voːk/ or /i'kwɪ-/ *n* a pun; an ambiguous expression.

Er (*chem symbol*) erbium.

era /'erə/ or /'iːrə/ *n* an historical period typified by some special feature; a chronological order or system of notation reckoned from a given date as a basis.

eradiate /i'reɪdi,eɪt/ *vti* to emit rays, to radiate.—**eradiation** *n*.

eradicate /i'rædɪ,keɪt/ *vt* to obliterate.—**eradicable** *adj*.—**eradication** *n*.—**eradicator** *n*.

erase /ɪˈreɪs/ *vt* to rub out, obliterate; to remove a recording from magnetic tape; to remove data from a computer memory or storage medium.—**erasable** *adj*.—**erasion** *n*.

eraser /-ər/ *n* a piece of rubber, etc for rubbing out marks or writing.

erasure /ɪˈreɪʃər/ *n* an erasing; something rubbed out.

erbium /ˈɜːbiəm/ *n* a soft metallic element of the rare earth group.

ere /ɛr/ *prep, conj* (*poet*) before.

erect /ɪˈrɛkt/ *adj* upright; not leaning or lying down; (*sexual organs*) rigid and swollen with blood from sexual stimulation. • *vt* to construct, set up.—**erectable** *adj*.—**erecter, erector** *n*.—**erectness** *n*.

erectile /ɪˈrɛktaɪl/ *adj* (*penis, clitoris, etc*) able to become enlarged and rigid through sexual stimulation.—**erectility** *n*.

erection /ɪˈrɛkʃən/ *n* construction; something erected, as a building; swelling; of the penis, due to sexual excitement.

erector /ɪˈrɛktər/ *n* a person who, or a thing that, erects; a muscle that erects.

eremite /ˈɛrˌmaɪt/ *n* a hermit.—**eremitic, eremitical** *adj*.—**eremitism** *n*.

erethism /ˈɛrɪˌθɪzəm/ *n* (*med*) an abnormal degree of excitement in an organ or tissue of the body.

erg /ɜrg/ *n* the unit for measuring work or energy.

ergo /ˈɛrgoː/ or /ˈɜr-/ *adv* therefore.

ergometer /ərˈgɒmɪtər/ *n* an instrument for measuring work performed or force produced.

ergonomics /ˌɜrgəˈnɒmɪks/ *n sing* the study of the interaction between people and their working environment with the aim of improving efficiency.—**ergonomic** *adj*.—**ergonomically** *adv*.—**ergonomist** *n*.

ergot /ˈɜrgət/ *n* a disease of rye and other cereals caused by a fungus; this fungus; a medicine derived from an ergot fungus.

ergotism /ˈɜrgətˌɪzəm/ *n* a toxic condition in humans caused by ergot fungus or chronic excessive use of an ergot drug.

erica /ˈɛrɪkə/ *n* a genus of flowering plants, including the heaths.

ericaceous /ˌɛrɪˈkeɪʃəs/ *adj* of the heath family.

eristic /ɛrˈɪstɪk/, **eristical** /-əl/ *adj* (*logic*) seeking to win an argument rather than find the truth.

ermine /ˈɜrmɪn/ *n* (*pl* **ermines, ermine**) the weasel in its winter coat; the white fur of the winter coat; a rank or office whose official robe is edged with ermine.

erne, ern /ɜrn/ *n* the sea eagle.

erode /ɪˈroːd/ *vt* to eat or wear away gradually.

erogenous /ɪˈrɒdʒɪnəs/ *adj* sexually arousing; sensitive to sexual stimulation.

erosion /ɪˈroːʒən/ *n* the act of eroding; gradual destruction or eating away; an eroded part.—**erosive, erosional** *adj*.

erotic /ɪˈrɒtɪk/, **erotical** /-əl/ *adj* of sexual love; sexually stimulating.—**erotically** *adv*.

erotica /ɪˈrɒtɪkə/ *n* sexually explicit literature or art.

eroticism /ɪˈrɒtɪˌsɪzəm/, **erotism** /-tɪzəm/ *n* erotic nature; sexually arousing themes in literature and art; sexual desire.

erotomania /ɪˌroːtəˈmeɪniə/ *n* excessive sexual desire.—**erotomaniac** *n*.

err /ɜr/ or /ɛr/ *vi* to be or do wrong.

errand /ˈɛrənd/ *n* a short journey to perform some task, *usu* on behalf of another; the purpose of this journey.

errant /ˈɛrənt/ *adj* going astray, *esp* doing wrong; moving aimlessly.

errantry /ˈɛrəntri/ *n* (*pl* **errantries**) the state or conduct of a knight errant.

erratic /ɪˈrætɪk/ *adj* capricious; irregular; eccentric, odd.—**erratically** *adv*.

erratum /ɛˈrætəm/ *n* (*pl* **errata**) a written or printed error; a page bearing a list of corrigenda.—*also* **corrigendum**.

erroneous /ɪˈroːniəs/ *adj* incorrect; mistaken.—**erroneously** *adv*.

error /ˈɛrər/ *n* a mistake, an inaccuracy; a mistaken belief or action; (*statistics*) the difference between an approximation of a value and the actual value, *usu* expressed as a percentage.

ersatz /ˈɛrˌzæts/ or /ˈɜrˌzæts/ *adj* made in imitation; synthetic.

Erse /ɜrs/ *n* Scottish Gaelic; Irish Gaelic.—*also adj*.

erstwhile /ˈɜrstˌwaɪl/ *adv* formerly. • *adj* former.

eructation /ˌiːrʌkˈteɪʃən/ *n* the act of belching.

erudite /ˈɛruːˌdɔɪt/ or /ˈɛrjuː-/ *adj* scholarly, having great knowledge.—**eruditely** *adv*.—**erudition** *n*.

erupt /ɪˈrʌpt/ *vi* to burst forth; to break out into a rash; (*volcano*) to explode, ejecting ash and lava into the air.—**eruptible** *adj*.

eruption /ɪˈrʌpʃən/ *n* the ejection of lava from a volcano; an outbreak; a rash, pimples.—**eruptional** *adj*.—**eruptive** *adj*.

eryngo, eringo /ɪˈrɪŋgoː/ or /ɪ-/ *n* (*pl* **eryngoes, eryngos, eringoes, eringos**) one of a genus of plants including the sea holly.

erysipelas /ˌɛrɪˈsɪpɪləs/ *n* an acute bacterial disease, characterized by a fever and skin inflammation.—**erysipelatous** *adj*.

erythema /ˌɛrɪˈθiːmə/ *n* (*med*) a superficial patchy redness of the skin.—**erythematic, erythematous, erythemic** *adj*.

erythrocyte /ɪˈrɪθroːˌsaɪt/ *n* a red blood corpuscle.—**erythrocytic** *adj*.

Es (*chem symbol*) einsteinium.

escalade /ˌɛskəˈleɪd/ *n* the act of scaling the walls of a fortified place by ladders.

escalate /ˈɛskəˌleɪt/ *vi* to increase rapidly in magnitude or intensity.—**escalation** *n*.

escalator /ˈɛskəˌleɪtər/ *n* a motorized set of stairs arranged to ascend or descend continuously.

escallop /ɛˈskæləp/ *n* a scallop.

escalope /ˈɛskəˌlɒp/ *n* a thin cut of meat, *esp* veal.

escapade /ˈɛskəˌpeɪd/ *n* a wild or mischievous adventure.

escape /ɪˈskeɪp/ *vt* to free oneself from confinement, etc; to avoid, remain unnoticed; to be forgotten. • *vi* to achieve freedom; (*gas, liquid*) to leak. • *n* an act or instance of escaping; a means of escape; a leakage of liquid or gas; a temporary respite from reality.—**escapable** *adj*.—**escaper** *n*.

escapee /ɪˈskeɪpi/ or /ɪskeɪˈpi/ *n* a person who has escaped, *esp* a prisoner.

escapement /ɪˈskeɪpmənt/ *n* a device in a watch or clock by which the motions of the pendulum or balance are regulated.

escape velocity *n* the minimum velocity required for a rocket, etc to escape the gravitational pull of the earth or other celestial body.

escapism /ɪˈskeɪpɪzəm/ *n* the tendency to avoid or retreat from reality into fantasy.—**escapist** *n, adj*.

escapologist /ˌɛskeɪˈpɒlədʒɪst/ *n* a performer who escapes from handcuffs, locked boxes, etc.—**escapology** *n*.

escargot /ˌɛskarˈgoː/ or /ɛsˈkargoː/ *n* a snail prepared as food.

escarp /ɪˈskarp/ *n* a steep bank in front of a rampart.

escarpment /-mənt/ *n* a steep side of a ridge or plateau.

eschatology /ˌɛskəˈtɒlədʒi/ *n* (*pl* **eschatologies**) the study of death, judgment, heaven and hell, and how humanity relates to them.

escheat /ɪsˈtʃiːt/ *n* (*law*) (*formerly*) the lapsing of property to the state in the absence of an heir or by forfeiture; property that passes to the state in this way. • *vt* to confiscate property by escheat. • *vi* to revert to the state by escheat.

eschew /ɛsˈtʃuː/ *vt* to avoid as habit, *esp* on moral grounds.—**eschewal** *n*.—**eschewer** *n*.

escort /ˈɛskɔrt/ *n* a person, group, ship, aircraft, etc accompanying a person or thing to give protection, guidance, or as a matter of courtesy; a person who accompanies another on a social occasion. • *vt* to attend as escort.

escritoire /ˌɛskriˈtwɒr/ *n* a writing desk.

escrow /ˈɛskroː/ *n* (*law*) a contract kept by a third party until the fulfilment of a condition.

escudo /ɛsˈkuːdoː/, *Sp.* /ɛsˈkuːðo/, *Port.* /ɪʃˈkuːduː/ *n* (*pl* **escudos**) formerly the monetary unit of Portugal, now the euro.

esculent /ˈɛskjulənt/ *adj* edible.

escutcheon /ɪsˈkʌtʃən/ *n* a shield bearing a coat of arms.

esker, eskar /ˈɛskər/ *n* (*geol*) a ridge of gravel, glacially deposited.

Eskimo /ˈɛskɪˌmoː/ *n* (*pl* **Eskimos, Eskimo**) the Inuit people; a group of peoples of eastern Siberia; a member of these peoples; their language.—*also adj*.

Eskimo dog *n* a powerful type of dog with a thick coat bred to pull sledges.

esophagus /iːˈsɒfəgəs/ *see* **oesophagus**.

esoteric /ˌɛsoˈtɛrɪk/ *adj* intended for or understood by a select few; secret; private.—**esoterically** *adv*.—**esotericism** *n*.

ESP /ˌiˌɛsˈpi/ *abbr* = extrasensory perception.

esp. *abbr* = especially.

espadrille /ˈɛspəˌdrɪl/ *n* a flat shoe *usu* having a fabric upper and rope soles.

espalier /ɛˈspæljər/ *n* a plant (as a fruit tree) trained to grow flat against a support; the trellis on which such plants are trained.

esparto /ɛˈspɑːtoː/ *n* (*pl* **espartos**) either of two Spanish and Algerian grasses used *esp* in paper-making.

especial /ɪˈspɛʃəl/ *adj* notably special, unusual; particular to one person or thing.—**especially** *adv*.

Esperanto /ˌɛspəˈræntoː/ *n* an artificial international language.

espionage /ˈɛspɪəˌnɒʒ/ *n* spying or the use of spies to obtain information.

esplanade /ˌɛspləˈneɪd/ or /-ˈnɒd/, /ˈɛsp-/ *n* a level open space for walking or driving, *esp* along a shore.

espouse /ɪˈspaʊz/ *vt* to adopt or support a cause.—**espousal** /ɛˈspaʊzəl/ *n*.—**espouser** *n*.

espresso /ɛˈsprɛsoː/ *n* (*pl* **espressos**) coffee brewed by forcing steam through finely ground darkly roasted coffee beans; an apparatus for making espresso.

esprit /ɛˈspriː/ or /ˈɛspriː/ *n* wit; liveliness.

esprit de corps /-dəˈkɔːr/ *n* a sense of loyalty and attachment to a group to which one belongs.

espy /ɛˈspaɪ/ or /ɪ-/ *vt* (**espying, espied**) to catch sight of.—**espial** *n*.—**espier** *n*.

Esq *abbr* = esquire.

esquire /ɪˈskwaɪr/ or /ɛˈskwaɪr/ *n* a general courtesy title used instead of Mr in addressing letters.

essay /ˈɛseɪ/ *n* a short prose work *usu* dealing with a subject from a limited or personal point of view; an attempt. • *vt* (**essaying, essayed**) to try, to attempt.

essayist /ˈɛseɪɪst/ *n* an essay writer.

essence /ˈɛsəns/ *n* that which makes a thing what it is; a substance distilled or extracted from another substance and having the special qualities of the original substance; a perfume.

essential /ɪˈsɛnʃəl/ or /iː-/ *adj* of or containing the essence of something; indispensable, of the greatest importance. • *n* (*often pl*) indispensable elements or qualities.—**essentiality, essentialness** *n*.—**essentially** *adv*.

essential oil *n* any of various plant oils used in perfumery.

establish /ɪˈstæblɪʃ/ *vt* to set up (*eg* a business) permanently; to settle (a person) in a place or position; to get generally accepted; to place beyond dispute, prove as a fact.—**establisher** *n*.

established *adj* (*church, religion*) officially recognized as the national church or religion of a country.

establishment /-mənt/ *n* the act of establishing; a commercial organization or other large institution; the staff and resources of an organization; a household; (*with cap*) those people in institutions such as the government, civil service and commerce who use their power to preserve the social, economic and political status quo.

establishmentarian /ɪˌstæblɪʃmənˈtɛrɪən/ *adj*, of an established church; supporting the established church system. • *n* a person who advocates official recognition of a church or religion.—**establishmentarianism** *n*.

estaminet *Fr.* /ɛsˈtæmiˈneɪ/ *n* a café.

estancia /ɛsˈtɒnsiːə/ *n* a cattle ranch in Latin America.

estate /əˈsteɪt/ *n* landed property; a large area of residential or industrial development; a person's total possessions, *esp* at their death; a social or political class.

estate agent *see* realtor.

estate car *n* a car with extra carrying space reached through a rear door.—*also* **station wagon**.

esteem /ɪˈstiːm/ *vt* to value or regard highly; to consider or think. • *n* high regard, a favourable opinion.

ester /ˈɛstər/ *n* (*chem*) a compound of acid and alcohol.

esthete /ˈɛsˌθiːt/, **esthetics** /ɛsˈθɛtɪks/ *see* **aesthete, aesthetics**.

estheticism /ɛsˈθɛtɪˌsɪzəm/ *see* **aestheticism**.

estimable /ˈɛstɪməbəl/ *adj* worthy of esteem; calculable.

estimate /ˈɛstəmət/ *vt* to judge the value, amount, significance of; to calculate approximately. • *n* an approximate calculation; a judgment or opinion; a preliminary calculation of the cost of a particular job.—**estimative** *adj*.

estimation /ˌɛstəˈmeɪʃən/ *n* estimating; an opinion, judgment; esteem.

estimator /ˈɛstəˌmeɪtər/ *n* someone or something that estimates.

estival /ˈɛstəvəl/ or /ɛsˈtaɪvəl/ *see* **aestival**.

estivation /ˌɛstəˈveɪʃən/ *see* **aestivation**.

estop /ɛˈstɒp/ *vt* (**estopping, estopped**) (*law*) to prohibit by estoppel.

estoppel /ɛˈstɒpəl/ *n* (*law*) a legal impediment arising as a result of one's previous action.

estrange /ɪˈstreɪndʒ/ *vt* to alienate the affections or confidence of.—**estranged** *adj*.—**estrangement** *n*.

estrogen /ˈɛstrədʒən/ *see* **oestrogen**.

estrus /ˈɛstrəs/, *Brit.* /ˈiːstrəs/ *see* **oestrus**.

estuarine /ˈɛstʃuːərɑɪn/ *adj* pertaining to, or formed in, an estuary.

estuary /ˈɛstʃuːˌɛri/ *n* (*pl* **estuaries**) an arm of the sea at the mouth of a river.

esurient /iˈsuːrɪənt/ *adj* voracious, greedy.—**esurience** *n*.

ETA *abbr* = Estimated Time of Arrival.

eta /ˈeɪtə/ or /ˈiːtə/ *n* the 7th letter of the Greek alphabet.

étagère /ˌeɪtæˈjɛr/ *n* an ornamental stand.

et al *abbr* = *et alii*, and others.

etc, etc. *abbr* = et cetera.

et cetera, etcetera /ɛtˈsɛtərə/ or /-ˈsɛtrə/ *n* and so forth.

etceteras /ɛtˈsɛtərəz/ or /-ˈsɛtrəz/ *npl* the usual extra things or persons.

etch /ɛtʃ/ *vti* to make lines on (metal, glass) *usu* by the action of acid; to produce (as a design) by etching; to delineate clearly.—**etcher** *n*.

etching /ˈɛtʃɪŋ/ *n* the art or process of producing designs on and printing from etched plates; an impression made from an etched plate.

ETD *abbr* = Estimated Time of Departure.

eternal /ɪˈtɜːnəl/ or /iː-/ *adj* continuing forever without beginning or end, everlasting; unchangeable; (*inf*) seemingly endless.—**eternality, eternalness** *n*.—**eternally** *adv*.

eternalize /-aɪz/ *vt* to make eternal.—**eternalization** *n*.

eternity /ɪˈtɜːnɪti/ or /iː-/ *n* (*pl* **eternities**) infinite time; the timelessness thought to constitute life after death; (*inf*) a very long time.

etesian /ɪˈtiːʒən/ *adj* (*winds*) blowing from the northwest in the Mediterranean for about forty days each summer.

ethane /ˈɛθeɪn/ or /ˈiːθ-/ *n* a colourless gaseous hydrocarbon found in natural gas and used *esp* as fuel.

ethene /ˈɛθiːn/ *see* **ethylene**.

ether /ˈiːθər/ *n* (*chem*) a light flammable liquid used as an anaesthetic or solvent; the upper regions of space, the invisible elastic substance formerly believed to be distributed evenly through all space.—**etheric** *adj*.

ethereal /ɪˈθɪərɪəl/ *adj* delicate; spiritual; celestial.—**ethereality, etherealness** *n*.—**ethereally** *adv*.

etherealize /-ˌaɪz/ *vt* to make ethereal; to regard as ethereal.—**etherealization** *n*.

etherize /ˈiːθəraɪz/ *vt* (*patient*) to anaesthetize, using ether.—**etherization** *n*.

ethic /ˈɛθɪk/ *n* a moral principle or set of principles. • *adj* ethical.

ethical /ˈɛθɪkəl/ *adj* of or pertaining to ethics; conforming to the principles of proper conduct, as established by society, a profession, etc; (*med*) legally available only on prescription.—**ethically** *adv*.—**ethicalness, ethicality** *n*.

ethical investment *n* the investment in companies whose activities do not offend the investor's moral principles.—*also* **conscience investment**.

ethics /ˈɛθɪks/ *n sing* the philosophical analysis of human morality and conduct; system of conduct or behaviour, moral principles.—**ethicist** *n*.

Ethiopian /ˌiːθiˈoːpɪən/ *adj* of or pertaining to Ethiopia, its languages or people.—*also n*.

ethmoid /ˈɛθmɔɪd/ *adj* (*anat*) denoting a light, spongy bone that forms the roof of the nose.—*also* **ethmoidal**. • *n* the ethmoid bone.

ethnic, ethnical /ˈɛθnɪk/ *adj* of races or large groups of people classed according to common traits and customs.—**ethnically** *adv*.

ethnic cleansing *n* the planned expulsion, extermination or removal of people from a religious or ethnic minority within an area, region or country.

ethno- /ˈɛθnoː/ *prefix* indicating race; people; culture.

ethnography /ɛθˈnɒɡrəfi/ *n* the area of anthropology dealing with the scientific description of human races.—**ethnographer** *n*.—**ethnographic, ethnographical** *adj*.

ethnology /ɛθˈnɒlədʒi/ *n* the scientific study of the origins and culture, etc of different races and peoples.—**ethnologic, ethnological** *adj*.—**ethnologist** *n*.

ethology /iːˈθɒlədʒi/ *n* the scientific study of animal behaviour.—**ethologic, ethological** *adj*.—**ethologist** *n*.

ethos /ˈiːˌθɒs/ *n* the distinguishing character, sentiment, moral nature, or guiding beliefs of a person, group, or institution.

ethyl /'εθɪl/ *n* the radical from which common alcohol and ether are derived.

ethylene /'εθə‚li:n/ *n* a colourless sweet-smelling gaseous hydrocarbon obtained from petroleum and used to manufacture chemicals including polythene.—*also* **ethene**.

etiolate /'i:tɪə‚leɪt/ *vti* (*green plants*) to bleach by depriving of light; to make or become pale and sickly.—**etiolation** *n*.

etiology /‚i:tɪ'ɒlədʒɪ/ *n* (*pl* **etiologies**) the study of causation, *esp* causes of diseases.—*also* **aetiology**.—**etiological** *adj*.—**etiologist** *n*.

etiquette /'ɛtɪkət/ or /-kɛt/ *n* the form of conduct or behaviour prescribed by custom or authority to be observed in social, official or professional life.

Etruscan /ɪ'trʌskən/ *n* an inhabitant of ancient Etruria (now Tuscany); the language of ancient Etruscans.—*also adj*.

étude /eɪ'tu:d/ or /-'tju:d/, /'eɪ-/ *n* (*mus*) a short study or exercise for a solo instrument.

étui /'ε‚twi:/ *n* (*pl* **étuis**) a pocket case for sewing implements and other small articles.

etymology /‚ɛtɪ'mɒlədʒɪ/ *n* (*pl* **etymologies**) the study of the source and meaning of words; an account of the source and history of a word.—**etymological, etymologic** *adj*.—**etymologist** *n*.

etymon /'ɛtɪ‚mɒn/ *n* (*pl* **etymons, etyma**) the root of a word, or its original meaning.

EU *abbr* = European Union.

Eu (*chem symbol*) europium.

eucalyptol /‚ju:kə'lɪptɒl/ or /-to:l/ *n* a liquid contained in eucalyptus oil.

eucalyptus, eucalypt /‚ju:kə'lɪptəs/ *n* (*pl* **eucalyptuses, eucalypti** or **eucalypts**) any of a genus of mostly Australian evergreen trees cultivated for their resin, oil, and wood; a type of oil obtained from its leaves.

Eucharist /'ju:kərɪst/ *n* the Christian sacrament of communion in which bread and wine are consecrated; the consecrated elements in communion.—**Eucharistic, Eucharistical** *adj*.

euchre /'ju:kər/ *n* a card game for two, three or four players.

Euclidean /ju:'klɪdɪən/ *adj* pertaining to or accordant with the geometrical principles of Euclid, the Greek mathematician (*fl* 3rd century BC).

eudemonism, eudaemonism /ju:'di:mən‚ɪzəm/ *n* the ethical doctrine that regards happiness as the chief end in moral conduct.

eudiometer /‚ju:di'ɒmətər/ *n* an instrument for measuring the amount of oxygen in the air.

eugenics /ju:'dʒɛnɪks/ *n sing* the science of improving the human race by selective breeding.—**eugenic** *adj*.—**eugenically** *adv*.—**eugenicist** *n*.

euhemerism /ju:'hi:mər‚ɪzəm/ or /-'hɛmər-/ *n* the theory that the classical deities are deified heroes and that the myths connected with them are based on real history.—**euhemerist** *n*.—**euhemeristic** *adj*.—**euhemeristically** *adv*.

eulogize /'ju:lə‚dʒaɪz/ *vt* to extol in speech or writing.—**eulogist, eulogizer** *n*.—**eulogistic, eulogistical** *adj*.—**eulogistically** *adv*.

eulogy /'ju:lədʒɪ/ *n* (*pl* **eulogies**) a speech or piece of writing in praise or celebration of someone or something.

eunuch /'ju:nək/ *n* a castrated man.

euonymus /ju:'ɒnɪməs/ *n* a genus of small trees, containing the spindle tree.

euphemism /'ju:fə‚mɪzəm/ *n* a mild or inoffensive word substituted for a more unpleasant or offensive term; the use of such inoffensive words.—**euphemistic** *adj*.—**euphemistically** *adv*.

euphonic /ju:'fɒnɪk/, **euphonical** /-əl/ *adj* sounding pleasant to the ear.—**euphonically** *adv*.

euphonium /ju:'fo:nɪəm/ *n* a brass musical instrument with its oval bell pointed backwards.

euphony /'ju:fənɪ/ *n* (*pl* **euphonies**) a pleasing sound, *esp* words.—**euphonious** *adj*.

euphorbia /ju:'fɔrbɪə/ *n* a member of the large genus of plants of the spurge family.

euphoria /ju:'fɔrɪə/ *n* a feeling of elation.—**euphoric** *adj*.—**euphorically** *adv*.

euphuism /'ju:fju:‚ɪzəm/ *n* an affected style of prose using elaborate antithesis, alliteration, and conceits; the pedantic or affected use of words or language.—**euphuist** *n*.—**euphuistic, euphuistical** *adj*.

Eurasian /jʊr'eɪʒən/ or /jə-/ *adj* of Europe and Asia (Eurasia) taken as one continent; of mixed European and Asian descent.—*also n*.

eureka /jʊ'ri:kə/ or /jə-/ *interj* used to express triumph on a discovery.

eurhythmics /jʊ'rɪðmɪks/ *see* **eurythmics**.

euro /'jʊro:/ or /'jər/ *n* the name for the European unit of currency.

Euro- /'jʊro:/ or /'jər-/ *prefix* Europe; European.

Eurocrat /'jʊro:‚kræt/ or /'jər-/ *n* a member of the administration of the European Community.

Europe /'jʊrəp/ or /'jər-/ *n* a continent extending from Asia in the east to the Atlantic Ocean in the west.

European /‚jʊrə'pɪən/ or /'jər-/ *adj* relating to or native to Europe. • *n* a native or inhabitant of Europe; a person of European descent.

European Economic Community *or* **European Community** *n* the official name of the European Common Market, whose members aimed to eliminate all obstacles to the free movement of goods, services, capital and labour between the member countries and to set up common external commercial, agricultural, and transport policies.

europium /jʊ'ro:pɪəm/ *n* a soft metallic element of the rare earth group.

eurythmics /ju:'rɪðmɪks/ *npl* the art of representing musical harmony by physical gestures.—*also* **eurhythmics**.

Eustachian tube /ju:'steɪʃən/ or /-ʃɪən/ *n* a tube that leads from the middle ear to the pharynx.

euthanasia /‚ju:θə'neɪʒə/ *n* the act or practice of killing painlessly, *esp* to relieve incurable suffering.

eV *abbr* = electronvolt.

evacuate /ɪ'vækju:‚eɪt/ or /i-/ *vti* to move (people, etc) from an area of danger to one of safety; to leave or make empty; to discharge wastes from the body.—**evacuation** *n*.—**evacuative** *adj*.—**evacuator** *n*.

evacuee /ɪ‚vækju:'i/ or /i-/ *n* an evacuated person.

evade /ɪ'veɪd/ or /i-/ *vt* to manage to avoid, *esp* by dexterity or slyness.—**evadable** *adj*.—**evader** *n*.

evaluate /ɪ'vælju:‚eɪt/ or /i-/ *vt* to determine the value of; to assess.—**evaluation** *n*.—**evaluator** *n*.

evanescent /‚ɛvə'nɛsənt/ *adj* fading away, vanishing; ephemeral.—**evanescence** *n*.

evangel /ɪ'vændʒəl/ or /i-/ *n* the Christian gospel.

evangelical /‚i:væn'dʒɛlɪkəl/ or /‚ɛvən-/ *adj* of or agreeing with Christian teachings, *esp* as presented in the four Gospels; pertaining to various Christian sects that believe in salvation through personal conversion and faith in Christ.—**evangelicalism** *n*.

evangelism /ɪ'vændʒə‚lɪzəm/ or /i-/ *n* preaching the Christian gospel; missionary zeal.

evangelist /-lɪst/ *n* a person who preaches the gospel; one of the writers of the four Gospels.—**evangelistic** *adj*.—**evangelistically** *adv*.

evangelize /ɪ'vændʒə‚laɪz/ or /i-/ *vt* to preach or spread the gospel; to seek converts to a particular cause.—**evangelization** *n*.—**evangelizer** *n*.

evaporate /ɪ'væpə‚reɪt/ or /i-/ *vti* to change into a vapour; to remove water from; to give off moisture; to vanish; to disappear.—**evaporable** *adj*.—**evaporation** *n*.—**evaporative** *adj*.—**evaporator** *n*.

evaporated milk *n* tinned unsweetened milk thickened by evaporation.

evasion /ɪ'veɪʒən/ or /i-/ *n* the act of evading; a means of evading, *esp* an equivocal reply or excuse.—**evasive** *adj*.—**evasively** *adv*.—**evasiveness** *n*.

eve /i:v/ *n* the evening or the whole day, before a festival; the period immediately before an event; (*formerly*) evening.

evection /ɪ'vɛkʃən/ or /i-/ *n* (*astron*) a periodical irregularity of the moon's motion.

even /'i:vən/ *adj* level, flat; smooth; regular, equal; balanced; exact; divisible by two. • *vti* to make or become even; (*with* up) to balance (debts, etc). • *adv* exactly; precisely; fully; quite; at the very time; used as an intensive to emphasize the identity of something (*he looked content, even happy*), to indicate something unexpected (*she refused even to look at him*), or to stress the comparative degree (*she did even better*).—**evenly** *adv*.—**evenness** *n*.

even-handed /-‚hændəd/ *adj* impartial, fair.—**even-handedness** *n*.

evening /'i:vnɪŋ/ *n* the latter part of the day and early part of the night.

evening primrose *n* a plant with yellow flowers that open in the evening.

evens /'iːvənz/ *npl* (*bet*) winning the same as the stake if successful; offered at such odds, as a horse.—*also* **even money**.

evensong /'iːvənˌsɒŋ/ *n* vespers; evening prayers.

event /ɪ'vɛnt/ or /-i-/ *n* something that happens; a social occasion; contingency; a contest in a sports programme.

even-tempered /ˌiːvən'tɛmpərd/ *adj* calm.

eventful /ɪ'vɛntfəl/ or /-i-/ *adj* full of incidents; momentous.

eventide /'iːvənˌtaɪd/ *n* (*formerly*) evening.

eventual /ɪ'vɛntʃuəl/ *adj* happening at some future unspecified time; ultimate.—**eventually** *adv*.

eventuality /ɪˌvɛntʃu'ælɪti/ *n* (*pl* **eventualities**) a possible occurrence.

eventuate /ɪ'vɛntʃuˌeɪt/ *vi* to result.—**eventuation** *n*.

ever /'ɛvər/ *adv* always, at all times; at any time; in any case.

evergreen /'ɛvərˌgriːn/ *adj* (*plants, trees*) having foliage that remains green all year.—*also n*.

everlasting /ˌɛvər'læstɪŋ/ *adj* enduring forever; (*plants*) having flowers that may be dried without loss of form or colour.—**everlastingly** *adv*.

evermore /ˌɛvər'mɔr/ *adv* forever.

evert /ɪ'vɜrt/ *vt* to turn inside out.—**eversible** *adj*.—**eversion** *n*.

every /'ɛvri/ *adj* being one of the total.

everybody /'ɛvriˌbɒdi/ or /-ˌbɛdi/, **everyone** /-ˌwɛn/ *pron* every person.

everyday /-ˌdeɪ/ or /-'deɪ/ *adj* happening daily; commonplace; worn or used on ordinary days.

everything /-θɪŋ/ *pron* all things, all; something of the utmost importance.

everywhere /-ˌwɛr/ *adv* in every place.

evict /ɪ'vɪkt/ *vt* to expel from land or from a building by legal process; to expel.—**eviction** *n*.—**evictor** *n*.

evidence /'ɛvɪdəns/ *n* an outward sign; proof, testimony, *esp* matter submitted in court to determine the truth of alleged facts. • *vt* to demonstrate clearly; to give proof or evidence for.

evident /'ɛvɪdənt/ *adj* easy to see or understand.—**evidently** *adv*.

evidential /ˌɛvɪ'dɛnʃəl/ *adj* relating to, providing, or based on evidence.—**evidentially** *adv*.

evil /'iːvəl/ or /-ɪl/ *adj* wicked; causing or threatening distress or harm. • *n* a sin; a source of harm or distress.—**evilly** *adv*.—**evilness** *n*.

evildoer /-ˌduːər/ *n* a wicked person.—**evildoing** *n*.

evil eye *n* a stare superstitiously believed to inflict harm; the power to cause harm in this manner.

evince /ɪ'vɪns/ *vt* to indicate that one has (*eg* a quality); to demonstrate.—**evincible** *adj*.—**evincive** *adj*.

eviscerate /ɪ'vɪsəˌreɪt/ *vt* to take out the intestines of, disembowel.—**evisceration** *n*.—**eviscerator** *n*.

evocative /i'vɒkətɪv/ or /ɪ-/ *adj* serving to evoke.—**evocatively** *n*.

evoke /ɪ'voːk/ or /ɪ-/ *vt* to call forth or up.—**evocable** *adj*.—**evocation** *n*.—**evoker** *n*.

evolution /ˌɛvə'luːʃən/ or /ˌiːvə-/, /-'ljuːʃən/ *n* a process of change in a particular direction; the process by which something attains its distinctive characteristics; a theory that existing types of plants and animals have developed from earlier forms.—**evolutionary, evolutional** *adj*.

evolutionist /-ɪst/ *adj* pertaining to evolution. • *n* someone who believes in the theory of evolution.

evolve /i'vɒlv/ or /ɪ-/ *vi* to develop by or as if by evolution.—**evolvable** *adj*.—**evolvement** *n*.

ewe /juː/ *n* a female sheep.

ewer /'juːər/ *n* a large pitcher or jug with a wide spout.

ex[1] /ɛks/ *n* (*inf*) a former husband, wife, etc.

ex[2] *prep* out of, from.

ex- *prefix* out, forth; quite, entirely; formerly.

exacerbate /ɛk'sæsərˌbeɪt/ or /ɪg-/ *vt* to make more violent, bitter, or severe.—**exacerbatingly** *adv*.—**exacerbation** *n*.

exact /ɪg'zækt/ *adj* without error, absolutely accurate; detailed. • *vt* to compel by force, to extort; to require.—**exactable** *adj*.—**exactness** *n*.—**exactor, exacter** *n*.

exacting /ɪg'zæktɪŋ/ *adj* greatly demanding; requiring close attention and precision.—**exactingness** *n*.

exaction /ɪg'zækʃən/ *n* the extortion of money, etc; an outrageous demand; something exacted.

exactitude /ɪg'zæktɪˌtuːd/ or /-ˌtjuːd/ *n* (the state of) being exact.

exactly /ɪg'zæktli/ *adv* in an exact manner; precisely. • *interj* quite so!

exaggerate /ɪg'zædʒəˌreɪt/ *vt* to enlarge (a statement, etc) beyond what is really so or believable.—**exaggeration** *n*.—**exaggerative** *adj*.—**exaggerator** *n*.

exalt /ɪg'zɒlt/ *vt* to raise up, *esp* in rank, power, or dignity.—**exalted** *adj*.—**exalter** *n*.

exaltation /ˌɛgzɒl'teɪʃən/ *n* elevation; rapture; a flock of larks.

exam /ɪg'zæm/ *n* (*inf*) an examination.

examination /ɪgˌzæmɪ'neɪʃən/ *n* an examining, close scrutiny; a set of written or oral questions designed as a test of knowledge; the formal questioning of a witness on oath.—**examinational** *adj*.

examine /ɪg'zæmɪn/ *vt* to look at closely and carefully, to investigate; to test, *esp* by questioning.—**examinable** *adj*.—**examiner** *n*.

examinee /ɪgˌzæmɪ'niː/ *n* a person who is being tested in an examination.

example /ɪg'zæmpəl/ *n* a representative sample; a model to be followed or avoided; a problem to be solved in order to show the application of some rule; a warning to others.

exanimate /ɛks'ænɪmət/ *adj* dead, defunct, lifeless.—**exanimation** *n*.

exarch /'ɛksɑrk/ *n* a bishop of the Eastern Orthodox Church; the governor of a province under the Byzantine Empire.

exarchate, exarchy /ɛk'sɑrkɪt/ or /-ˌkeɪt/, /'ɛksˌɑr-/ *n* the area of jurisdiction of an exarch.

exasperate /ɪg'zæspəˌreɪt/ *vt* to annoy intensely.—**exasperatedly** *adv*.—**exasperating** *adj*.—**exasperation** *n*.

Excalibur /ɛks'kælɪbər/ *n* in legend, King Arthur's sword.

ex cathedra /ˌɛkskə'θiːdrə/ *adj* with authority.

excavate /'ɛkskəˌveɪt/ *vt* to form a hole or tunnel by digging; to unearth; to expose to view (historical remains, etc) by digging away a covering.—**excavation** *n*.—**excavator** *n*.

exceed /ɛk'siːd/ or /ɪk-/ *vt* to be greater than or superior to; to go beyond the limit of.—**exceedable** *adj*.—**exceeder** *n*.

exceedingly /-ɪŋli/ *adv* very, extremely.

excel /ɛk'sɛl/ or /ɪk-/ *vb* (**excelling, excelled**) *vt* to outdo, to be superior to. • *vi* (*with* **in, at**) to do better than others.

excellence /'ɛksələns/ *n* that in which one excels; superior merit or quality; (*with cap*) a title of honour given to certain high officials.—*also* **Excellency**.

excellent /'ɛksələnt/ *adj* very good, outstanding.—**excellently** *adv*.

excelsior /ɛk'sɛlsiˌɔr/ or /ɪk-/ *interj* higher. • *n* soft wood shavings for stuffing.

except /ɛk'sɛpt/ or /ɪk-/ *vt* to exclude, to take or leave out. • *prep* not including; other than.—**exceptable** *adj*.

excepting /-'sɛptɪŋ/ *prep* except, not including.

exception /ɛk'sɛpʃən/ or /ɪk-/ *n* the act of excepting; something excepted; an objection.

exceptionable /-əbəl/ *adj* open to objection.—**exceptionably** *adv*.

exceptional /ɛk'sɛpʃənəl/ or /ɪk-/ *adj* unusual, forming an exception; superior.—**exceptionally** *adv*.

excerpt /'ɛksɜrpt/ or /'ɛgz-/ *n* an extract from a book, film, etc. • *vt* to select or quote (a passage from a book).—**exerptible** *adj*.—**excerption** *n*.

excess /'ɛksɛs/ or /ɪk'-/ *n*, *adj* the exceeding of proper established limits; the amount by which one thing or quantity exceeds another; (*pl*) overindulgence in eating or drinking; unacceptable conduct.

excessive /ɛk'sɛsəv/ *adj* greater than what is acceptable, too much.—**excessively** *adv*.—**excessiveness** *n*.

exchange /ɛks'tʃeɪndʒ/ *vt* to give and take (one thing in return for another); to give to and receive from another person. • *n* the exchanging of one thing for another; the thing exchanged; the conversion of money in one currency into a sum of equivalent value in another currency; the system of settling commercial debts between foreign governments, *eg* by bills of exchange; a place where things and services are exchanged, *esp* a marketplace for securities; a centre or device in which telephone lines are interconnected.—**exchangeable** *adj*.—**exchangeability** *n*.—**exchanger** *n*.

exchange rate *n* the rate at which one foreign currency may be exchanged for another.

exchequer /ɛks'tʃɛkər/ *n* (*with cap*) the British governmental department in charge of finances; (*inf*) personal finances.

excise[1] /ˈɛksaɪz/ *n* a tax on the manufacture, sale, or use of certain articles within a country.—**excisable** *adj*.

excise[2] /ɛkˈsaɪz/ *vt* to remove by cutting out.—**excision** *n*.

exciseman /ˈɛksaɪzˌmæn/ *n* (*pl* **excisemen**) (*formerly*) an officer employed to collect and enforce excise.

excitable /ɛkˈsaɪtəbəl/ *adj* easily excited.—**excitability, excitableness** *n*.

excitant /ˈɛksɪtənt/ or /ɪkˈsaɪtənt/ *n* a stimulant. • *adj* stimulating.

excitation /ˌɛksaɪˈteɪʃən/ or /-sɪ-/ *n* the act of exciting; the state of excitement.—**excitative, excitatory** *adj*.

excite /ɛkˈsaɪt/ or /ɪk-/ *vt* to arouse the feelings of, *esp* to generate feelings of pleasurable anticipation; to cause to experience strong emotion; to stir up, agitate; to rouse to activity; to stimulate a physiological response, eg in a bodily organ.

excited /-əd/ *adj* experiencing or expressing excitement.—**excitedly** *adv*.—**excitedness** *n*.

excitement /ɛkˈsaɪtmənt/ or /ɪk-/ *n* a feeling of strong, *esp* pleasurable, emotion; something that excites.

exciting /ɪkˈsaɪtɪŋ/ *adj* causing excitement; stimulating.—**excitingly** *adv*.

exclaim /ɪkˈskleɪm/ *vti* to shout out or utter suddenly and with strong emotion.—**exclaimer** *n*.

exclamation /ˌɛkskləˈmeɪʃən/ *n* a sudden crying out; a word or utterance exclaimed.—**exclamational** *adj*.

exclamation point, exclamation mark *n* the punctuation mark (!) placed after an exclamation.

exclamatory /ɪkˈsklæməˌtɔri/ *adj* of or expressing exclamation.—**exclamatorily** *adv*.

exclave /ˈɛkskleɪv/ *n* a small part of a country lying within the territory of another country.

exclude /ɛkˈskluːd/ *vt* to shut out, to keep out; to reject or omit; to eject.—**excluder** *n*.—**exclusion** *n*.

exclusive /ɛkˈskluːsɪv/ or /ɪks-/ *adj* excluding all else; reserved for particular persons; snobbishly aloof; fashionable, high-class, expensive; unobtainable or unpublished elsewhere; sole, undivided.—**exclusively** *adv*.—**exclusiveness** *n*.—**exclusivity** *n*.

excogitate /ɛksˈkɒdʒɪˌteɪt/ *vt* to devise, to invent; to discover by thinking.—**excogitation** *n*.—**excogitative** *adj*.

excommunicate /ˌɛkskəˈmjuːnɪˌkeɪt/ *vt* to bar from association with a church; to exclude from fellowship.—**excommunication** *n*.—**excommunicative** *adj*.—**excommunicator** *n*.

excoriate /ɛksˈkɔriˌeɪt/ *vt* to strip of the skin; to flay.—**excoriation** *n*.

excrement /ˈɛkskrəmənt/ *n* waste matter discharged from the bowels.—**excremental, excrementitious** *adj*.

excrescence /ɛkˈskrɛsəns/ *n* an outgrowth, *esp* abnormal, from a plant or animal; a disfigurement.

excrescent /ɛkˈskrɛsənt/ *adj* pertaining to excrescence; superfluous.

excreta /ɛkˈskriːtə/ or /ɪk-/ *npl* waste matter discharged from the body, faeces, urine.

excrete /ɪkˈskriːt/ *vt* to eliminate or discharge wastes from the body.—**excreter** *n*.—**excretion** *n*.—**excretive, excretory** *adj*.

excruciate /ɪkˈskruːʃiˌeɪt/ *vt* to inflict severe pain upon; to torture.—**excruciation** *n*.

excruciating /-ˌeɪtɪŋ/ *adj* intensely painful or distressful; (*inf*) very bad.—**excruciatingly** *adv*.

exculpate /ˈɛkskʌlˌpeɪt/ *vt* to free (a person) from alleged fault or guilt.—**exculpable** *adj*.—**exculpation** *n*.

exculpatory /-ˈkʌlpəˌtɔri/ *adj* tending or serving to exculpate.

excurrent /ɛksˈkɜrənt/ *adj* (*bot*) (*leaf*) having a midrib running beyond the edge; (*tree*) having a projecting stem; (*zool*) having a duct, etc, whose contents flow out.

excursion /ɪkˈskɜrʃən/ *n* a pleasure trip; a short journey.

excursionist /-ɪst/ *n* someone going on an excursion.

excursive /ɛksˈkɜrsɪv/ *adj* digressing, rambling.—**excursively** *adv*.

excursus /ɛkˈskɜrsəs/ or /ɪks-/ *n* (*pl* **excursuses, excursus**) a dissertation added as a supplement to a work, giving additional information on certain points; a digression from the main subject of a work.

excusable /ɪkˈskjuːzəbəl/ *adj* able to be excused.—**excusably** *adv*.

excuse /ɪkˈskjuːz/ *vt* to pardon; to forgive; to give a reason or apology for; to be a reason or explanation of; to let off. • *n* an apology, a plea in extenuation.

ex-directory /ˌɛksdaɪˈrɛktəri/ *adj* (*telephone number*) not listed in the telephone directory by request.

execrable /ˈɛksɪkrəbəl/ *adj* appalling.—**execrableness** *n*.

execrate /ˈɛksɪˌkreɪt/ *vt* to denounce as evil; to abhor.—**execration** *n*.—**execrative, execratory** *adj*.

executant /ɪgˈzɛkjutənt/ *n* a person who executes or performs, *esp* an artist, musician, etc.

execute /ˈɛksɪˌkjuːt/ *vt* to carry out, put into effect; to perform; to produce (*eg* a work of art); to make legally valid; to put to death by law.—**executable** *adj*.—**executer** *n*.

execution /ˌɛksɪˈkjuːʃən/ *n* the act or process of executing; the carrying out or suffering of a death sentence; the style or technique of performing, *eg* music.

executioner /-ər/ *n* a person who executes a death sentence upon a condemned prisoner.

executive /ɪgˈzɛkjutɪv/ *n* a person or group concerned with administration or management of a business or organization; the branch of government with the power to put laws, etc into effect. • *adj* having the power to execute decisions, laws, decrees, etc.

executor /-ər/ *n* a person appointed by a testator to see the terms of a will implemented.—**executorial** *adj*.—**executorship** *n*.

executory /ɪgˈzɛkjuˌtɔri/ *adj* (*law*) pertaining to the execution of laws; to be carried out at a future date.

executrix /ɪgˈzɛkjutrɪks/ *n* (*pl* **executrices, executrixes**) a female executor.

exegesis /ˌɛksɪˈdʒiːsɪs/ *n* (*pl* **exegeses**) an explanation or interpretation of a text or passage, *esp* of the Bible.

exegetic, exegetical /ˌɛksəˈdʒɛtɪk/ *adj* expository; interpretative.

exegetics /ˌɛksəˈdʒɛtɪks/ *n sing* the study of exegesis.

exemplar /ɪgˈzɛmplər/ or /-ˌplɑr/ *n* a model; a typical instance or example.

exemplary /ɪgˈzɛmpləri/ *adj* deserving imitation; serving as a warning.—**exemplarily** *adv*.—**exemplariness** *n*.

exemplify /ɪgˈzɛmplɪˌfaɪ/ *vt* (**exemplifying, exemplified**) to illustrate by example; to be an instance or example of.—**exemplification** *n*.—**exemplifier** *n*.

exempt /ɪgˈzɛmpt/ *adj* not liable, free from the obligations required of others. • *vt* to grant immunity (from).—**exemptible** *adj*.—**exemption** *n*.

exercise /ˈɛksərˌsaɪz/ *n* the use or application of a power or right; regular physical or mental exertion for health, amusement or acquisition of some skill; something performed to develop or test a specific ability or skill; (*often pl*) manoeuvres carried out for military training and discipline. • *vt* to use, exert, employ; to engage in regular physical activity to strengthen the body, etc; to train (troops) by means of drills and manoeuvres; to engage the attention of; to perplex.—**exercisable** *adj*.

exergue /ɛgˈzɜrg/ or /ˈɛk-/ *n* the space below the principal design on a coin or medal for the insertion of a date, etc.—**exergual** *adj*.

exert /ɪgˈzɜrt/ *vt* to bring (*eg* strength, influence) into use.

exertion /ɪgˈzɜrʃən/ *n* an exerting; a strenuous effort.—**exertive** *adj*.

exeunt /ˈɛksiˌʌnt/ (*Latin*) they go off, a stage direction.

exfoliate /ɛksˈfoːliˌeɪt/ *vi* to flake off; (*tree*) to shed bark.—**exfoliation** *n*.

ex gratia /ɛksˈgreɪʃə/ *adj* given as a favour or where no legal obligation exists.

exhalant /ɛksˈheɪlənt/ or /ɪgz-/ *adj* exhaling. • *n* a duct, organ, etc used for exhaling.

exhale /ɛksˈheɪl/ or /ɪgz-/ *vt* to breathe out.—**exhalation** *n*.

exhaust /ɛgˈzɒst/ or /ɪg-/ *vt* to use up completely; to make empty; to use up, tire out; (*subject*) to deal with or develop completely. • *n* the escape of waste gas or steam from an engine; the device through which these escape.—**exhausted** *adj*.—**exhauster** *n*.—**exhaustible** *adj*.—**exhausting** *adj*.

exhaustion /ɛgˈzɒstʃən/ or /ɪg-/ *n* the act of exhausting or being exhausted; extreme weariness.

exhaustive /ɛgˈzɒstɪv/ or /ɪg-/ *adj* comprehensive, thorough.—**exhaustively** *adv*.

exhibit /ɛgˈzɪbɪt/ or /ɪg-/ *vt* to display, *esp* in public; to present to a court in legal form. • *n* an act or instance of exhibiting, something exhibited; something produced and identified in court for use as evidence.—**exhibitor** *n*.—**exhibitory** *adj*.

exhibition /ˌɛgzɪˈbɪʃən/ *n* a showing, a display; a public show; an allowance made to a student.

exhibitioner /-ər/ *n* a student who holds an exhibition.

exhibitionism /-ˌnɪzəm/ *n* an excessive tendency to show off one's abilities; a compulsion to expose oneself indecently in public.—**exhibitionist** *n*.—**exhibitionistic** *adj*.

exhilarant /ɛgˈzɪlərənt/ or /ɪg-/ *adj* exhilarating. • *n* something that exhilarates.

exhilarate /ɛgˈzɪləˌreɪt/ or /ɪg-/ *vt* to make very happy; to invigorate.—**exhilarating** *adj*.—**exhilaration** *n*.—**exhilarator** *n*.

exhort /ɛgˈzɔrt/ or /ɪg-/ *vt* to urge or advise strongly.—**exhortation** *n*.—**exhortative, exhortatory** *adj*.—**exhorter** *n*.

exhume /ɛksˈuːm/ or /ɪgz-/, /ɛgz-/, /-hjuːm/ *vt* to dig up (a dead person) for detailed examination.—**exhumation** *n*.—**exhumer** *n*.

exigency, exigence /ˈɛksɪdʒənsi/ or /ɛgˈzɪdʒən-/, /ɪg-/ *n* (*pl* **exigencies, exigences**) a pressing need; emergency.

exigent /ˈɛksɪdʒənt/ or /ɛgz-/ *adj* urgent; exacting.—**exigently** *adv*.

exigible /ˈɛksɪdʒəbəl/ *adj* (*debt etc*) liable to be exacted.

exiguous /ɛgˈzɪgjʊəs/ or /ɪg-/ *adj* very small in amount, meagre.—**exiguity, exiguousness** *n*.

exile /ˈɛksaɪl/ or /ˈɛgzaɪl/ *n* prolonged absence from one's own country, either through choice or as a punishment; an exiled person. • *vt* to banish, to expel from one's native land.—**exilic, exilian** *adj*.

exist /ɛgˈzɪst/ or /ɪg-/ *vi* to have being; to just manage a living; to occur in a specific place under specific conditions.

existence /ɛgˈzɪstəns/ or /ɪg-/ *n* the state or fact of existing; continuance of life; lifestyle; everything that exists.

existent /ɛgˈzɪstənt/ or /ɪg-/ *adj* real, actual; existing; current.

existential /ˌɛgzɪˈstenʃəl/ or /ˌɛksɪs-/ *adj* of or pertaining to existence; existentialist.

existentialism /-ˌlɪzəm/ *n* (*philos*) a movement stressing personal freedom and responsibility in relation to existence.—**existentialist** *n, adj*.

exit /ˈɛksɪt/ or /ˈɛgzɪt/ *n* a way out of an enclosed space; death; a departure from a stage. • *vi* to leave, withdraw; to go offstage.

ex libris /ɛksˈliːbriːs/ *adj* from the library of. • *n* (*pl* **ex libris**) a book plate.

exocrine /ˈɛksoˌkraɪn/ *adj* secreting though a duct; of or relating to exocrine glands or their secretions.

exocrine gland *n* a gland that releases secretions through a duct, *eg* a sweat gland.

exoderm *see* **ectoderm**.

exodus /ˈɛksədəs/ *n* the departure of many people; (*with cap*) the departure of the Israelites from Egypt led by Moses; (*Bible*) the second book of the Old Testament.

ex officio /ˌɛksəˈfɪʃioː/ or /-ˈfɪs-/ *adv, adj* by virtue of an official position.

exogamy /ɛkˈsɒgəmi/ *n* the practice of marrying only outside one's own tribe.—**exogamous** *adj*.

exogenous /ɛkˈsɒdʒənəs/ *adj* (*biol*) produced by external growth; a used or influenced by external factors.—**exogenously** *adv*.

exonerate /ɪgˈzɒnəˌreɪt/ *vt* to absolve from blame; to relieve from a responsibility, obligation.—**exoneration** *n*.—**exonerative** *adj*.—**exonerator** *n*.

exophthalmos, exophthalmus /ˌɛksɒfˈθælməs/ *n* protrusion of the eyeball.—**exophthalmic** *adj*.

exorbitant /ɪgˈzɔrbɪtənt/ *adj* (*prices, demands, etc*) unreasonable, excessive.—**exorbitance** *n*.

exorcise, exorcize /ˈɛksɔrˌsaɪz/ or /-ər-/ *vt* to expel an evil spirit (from a person or place) by ritual and prayer.—**exorciser, exorcizer** *n*.—**exorcism** *n*.—**exorcist** *n*.

exordium /ɛkˈsɔrdiəm/ *n* (*pl* **exordiums, exordia**) the opening part of a speech or composition.—**exordial** *adj*.

exoteric /ˌɛksoˈterɪk/ *adj* accessible to ordinary people; external.—**exoterically** *adv*.—**exotericism** *n*.

exotic /ɛgˈzɒtɪk/ or /ɪg-/ *adj* foreign; strange; excitingly different or unusual.—**exotically** *adv*.—**exoticism** *n*.—**exoticness** *n*.

exotica /-ɪkə/ *npl* exotic items, *esp* as a collection.

expand /ɛkˈspænd/ or /ɪk-/ *vt* to increase in size, bulk, extent, importance; to describe in fuller detail. • *vi* to become larger; to become more genial and responsive.—**expandable, expandible** *adj*.—**expander** *n*.

expanse /ɛkˈspæns/ or /ɪk-/ *n* a wide area of land, etc; the extent of a spread-out area.

expansible /ɛkˈspænsəbəl/ or /ɪk-/ *adj* capable of expansion, or of being expanded.—**expansibility** *n*.

expansile /-saɪl/ *adj* capable of expansion, or of causing expansion.

expansion /-ʃən/ *n* the act of expanding or being expanded; something expanded; the amount by which something expands; the fuller development of a theme, etc.—**expansionary** *adj*.

expansive /-sɪv/ *adj* able to or having the capacity to expand or cause expansion; comprehensive; (*person*) genial, communicative.—**expansively** *adv*.—**expansiveness** *n*.

ex parte /ɛksˈpɑrti/ *adj* (*law*) on behalf of one side only; partisan.

expatiate /ɛkˈspeɪʃiˌeɪt/ or /ɪk-/ *vi* to speak or write at length; to enlarge.—**expatiation** *n*.—**expatiator** *n*.

expatriate /ɛksˈpeɪtrɪət/ or /-ˈpætrɪət/ *adj* living in another country; self-exiled or banished. • *n* an expatriate person. • *vti* to exile (oneself) or banish (another person). —**expatriation** *n*.

expect /ɛkˈspɛkt/ or /ɪk-/ *vt* to anticipate; to regard as likely to arrive or happen; to consider necessary, reasonable or due; to think, suppose.

expectant /ɛkˈspɛktənt/ or /ɪk-/ *adj* expecting, hopeful; filled with anticipation; pregnant.—**expectantly** *adv*.—**expectancy, expectance** *n*.

expectation /ˌɛkspɛkˈteɪʃən/ *n* the act or state of expecting; something that is expected to happen; (*pl*) prospects for the future, *esp* of inheritance.—**expectative** *adj*.

expectorant /ɛkˈspɛktərənt/ *n* a medicine that promotes expectoration.

expectorate /ɛkˈspɛktəˌreɪt/ *vti* to bring up (mucus) from the respiratory tract by coughing; to spit.—**expectoration** *n*.—**expectorator** *n*.

expedience, expediency /ɛkˈspiːdiənsi/ or /ɪk-/ *n* (*pl* **expediencies, expediences**) fitness, suitability; an inclination towards expedient methods.—**expediential** *adj*.

expedient /ɛkˈspiːdiənt/ or /ɪk-/ *adj* suitable or desirable under the circumstances. • *n* a means to an end; a means devised or used for want of something better.—**expediently** *adv*.

expedite /ˈɛkspəˌdaɪt/ *vt* to carry out promptly; to facilitate.—**expediter, expeditor** *n*.

expedition /ˌɛkspəˈdɪʃən/ *n* a journey to achieve some purpose, as exploration, etc; the party making this journey; speedy efficiency, promptness.

expeditionary /ˌɛkspəˈdɪʃəˌneri/ *adj* of or constituting an expedition.

expeditious /ˌɛkspəˈdɪʃəs/ *adj* speedy; efficient.—**expeditiously** *adv*.

expel /ɛkˈspɛl/ or /ɪk-/ *vt* (**expelling, expelled**) to drive out, to eject; to banish.—**expellable** *adj*.—**expellee** *n*.—**expeller** *n*.

expend /ɛkˈspɛnd/ or /ɪk-/ *vt* to spend (money, time, energy, etc); to use up, consume.—**expender** *n*.

expendable /ɛkˈspɛndəbəl/ or /ɪk-/ *adj* able to be consumed, not worth keeping; available for sacrifice to achieve some objective.—**expendability** *n*.

expenditure /ɛkˈspɛndɪtʃər/ or /ɪk-/ *n* the act or process of expending money, etc; the amount expended.

expense /ɛkˈspɛns/ or /ɪk-/ *n* a payment of money for something, expenditure; a cause of expenditure; (*pl*) money spent on some activity (*eg* travelling on business); reimbursement for this.

expense account *n* an account of expenses to be reimbursed to an employee.

expensive /ɛkˈspɛnsɪv/ or /ɪk-/ *adj* causing or involving great expense; costly.—**expensively** *adv*.—**expensiveness** *n*.

experience /ɛkˈspiːriəns/ or /ɪk-/ *n* observation or practice resulting in or tending towards knowledge; knowledge gained by seeing and doing; a state of being affected from without (as by events); an affecting event. • *vt* to have experience of.

experienced /-ənst/ *adj* wise or skilled through experience.

experiential /ɛkˌspiːriˈɛnʃəl/ or /ɪk-/ *adj* of or based on experience.

experiment /ɛkˈspɛrɪmənt/ or /ɪk-/, /-ˌmɛnt/ *n* any test or trial to find out something; a controlled procedure carried out to discover, test, or demonstrate something. • *vi* to carry out experiments.—**experimentation** *n*.—**experimenter** *n*.

experimental /ɛkˌspɛrɪˈmɛntəl/ or /ɪk-/ *adj* of, derived from, or proceeding by experiment; empirical; provisional.—**experimentalism** *n*.—**experimentally** *adv*.

expert /ˈɛkspɔrt/ *adj* thoroughly skilled; knowledgeable through training and experience. • *n* a person with special skills or training in any art or science.—**expertly** *adv*.—**expertness** *n*.

expertise /ˌɛkspərˈtiːz/ *n* expert knowledge or skill.

expiate /'ɛkspi‚eɪt/ *vt* to pay the penalty for; to make amends for.—**expiation** *n.*—**expiator** *n.*—**expiatory** *adj.*

expire /ɛk'spaɪr/ or /ɪk-/ *vti* to come to an end; to lapse or become void; to breathe out; to die.—**expiration** *n.*—**expirer** *n.*

expiry /ɛk'spaɪərɪ/ or /ɪk-/ *n* (*pl* **expiries**) the ending of a period of validity, *eg* of a passport.

explain /ɛk'spleɪn/ or /ɪk-/ *vt* to make plain or clear; to give a reason for, account for.—**explainable** *adj.*—**explainer** *n.*

explanation /‚ɛksplə'neɪʃən/ *n* an act or process of explaining; something that explains, *esp* a statement.

explanative, explanatory /ɛk'splænə‚tɔrɪ/ or /ɪk-/ *adj* serving as an explanation.—**explanatorily** *adv.*

expletive /'ɛksplətɪv/ or /ɪk'spliːtəv/ *n* a violent exclamation or swearword.

explicable /'ɛksplɪkəbəl/ or /ɪk'splɪkəbəl/ *adj* able to be explained.

explicate /'ɛksplɪ‚keɪt/ *vt* to analyse the implications of; to explain in great detail.—**explication** *n.*—**explicative, explicatory** *adj.*—**explicator** *n.*

explicit /ɛk'splɪsɪt/ or /ɪk-/ *adj* clearly stated, not merely implied; outspoken, frank; graphically detailed.—**explicitly** *adv.*—**explicitness** *n.*

explode /ɛk'sploːd/ or /ɪk-/ *vti* to burst or cause to blow up with a loud noise, as in the detonation of a bomb; (*emotions*) to burst out; (*population*) to increase rapidly; to expose (a theory, etc) as false.—**exploder** *n.*

exploit /'ɛksplɔɪt/ or /ɪk-/ *n* a bold achievement. • *vt* to utilize, develop (raw materials, etc); to take unfair advantage of, *esp* for financial gain.—**exploitable** *adj.*—**exploitation** *n.*—**exploitative** *adj.*

exploratory, explorative /ɛk'splɔrə‚tɔrɪ/ or /ɪk-/ *adj* for the purpose of exploring or investigating.

explore /ɛk'splɔr/ or /ɪk-/ *vti* to examine or inquire into; to travel through (a country) for the purpose of (geographical) discovery; to examine minutely.—**exploration** *n.*—**explorer** *n.*

explosion /ɛk'sploːʒən/ or /ɪk-/ *n* an act or instance of exploding; a sudden loud noise caused by this; an outburst of emotion; a rapid increase or expansion.

explosive /ɛk'sploːsɪv/ or /ɪk-/ *adj* liable to or able to explode; liable or threatening to burst out with violence and noise. • *n* an explosive substance.—**explosively** *adv.*

exponent /ɛk'spoːnənt/ or /ɪk-/ *n* a person who explains or interprets something; a person who champions, advocates, or exemplifies; (*math*) an index of the power to which an expression is raised.

exponential /‚ɛkspə'nɛnʃəl/ or /-tʃəl/ *adj* of, relating to or having an exponent; (*math*) having a variable in an exponent; able to be expressed by an exponential function. • *n* an exponential function.—**exponentially** *adv.*

exponential function *n* a mathematical function in which the constant quantity of the expression is raised to the power of a variable quantity, i.e. the exponent.

export /'ɛks‚pɔrt/ *vt* to send out (goods) of one country for sale in another. • *n* the act of exporting; the article exported.—**exportable** *adj.*—**exportation** *n.*—**exporter** *n.*

exposé /‚ɛkspoː'zeɪ/ *n* a revelation of crime, dishonesty, etc.

expose /ɛk'spoːz/ or /ɪk-/ *vt* to deprive of protection or shelter; to subject to an influence (as light, weather); to display, reveal; to uncover or disclose.—**exposable** *adj.*—**exposal** *n.*—**exposer** *n.*

exposed /ɪk'spoːzd/ or /ɛk-/ *adj* open to view; not shielded or protected.—**exposedness** *n.*

exposition /‚ɛkspə'zɪʃən/ *n* a public show or exhibition; a detailed explanation; a speech or writing explaining a process, thing, or idea.—**expositional** *adj.*

expositive, expository /ɛk'spɒzɪ‚tɔrɪ/ or /ɪk-/ *adj* of, pertaining to or conveying exposition; explanatory.—**expositively, expositorily** *adv.*

ex post facto /‚ɛkspoːst'fæktoː/ *adj* (*law*) enacted retrospectively. • *adv* after the fact.

expostulate /ɛk'spɒstʃə‚leɪt/ or /ɪk-/ *vi* to argue with, *esp* to dissuade.—**expostulation** *n.*—**expostulator** *n.*—**expostulatory, expostulative** *adj.*

exposure /ɛk'spoː‚ʒər/ or /ɪk-/ *n* an exposing or state of being exposed; time during which light reaches and acts on a photographic film, paper or plate; publicity.

expound /ɛk'spaʊnd/ or /ɪk-/ *vt* to explain or set forth in detail.—**expounder** *n.*

express /ɛk'sprɛs/ or /ɪk-/ *vt* to represent in words; to make known one's thoughts, feelings, etc; to represent by signs, symbols, etc; to squeeze out. • *adj* firmly stated, explicit; (*train, bus, etc*) travelling at high speed with few or no stops. • *adv* at high speed, by express service. • *n* an express train, coach, etc; a system or company for sending freight, etc at rates higher than standard.—**expresser** *n.*—**expressible** *adj.*

expression /ɛk'sprɛʃən/ or /ɪk-/ *n* an act of expressing, *esp* by words; a word or phrase; a look; intonation; a manner of showing feeling in communicating or performing (*eg* music); (*math*) a collection of symbols serving to express something.—**expressional** *adj.*—**expressionless** *adj.*

expressionism /-‚nɪzəm/ *n* a style of art, literature, music, etc that seeks to depict the subjective emotions aroused in the artist by objects and events, not objective reality.—**expressionist** *n.*—**expressionistic** *adj.*

expressive /ɛk'sprɛsɪv/ or /ɪk-/ *adj* serving to express; full of expression.—**expressively** *adv.*—**expressiveness** *n.*

expressly /ɛk'sprɛslɪ/ or /-ɪk/ *adv* explicitly; for a specific purpose.

expressway /ɛk'sprɛsweɪ/ or /ɪk-/ *n* a motorway.

expropriate /ɛks'proː‚prɪ‚eɪt/ *vt* to remove (property) from its owner, to dispossess.—**expropriable** *adj.*—**expropriation** *n.*—**expropriator** *n.*

expulsion /ɛk'spʌlʃən/ or /ɪk-/ *n* the act of expelling or being expelled.—**expulsive** *adj.*

expunge /ɛk'spʌndʒ/ or /ɪk-/ *vt* to obliterate, to erase.—**expunction** *n.*—**expunger** *n.*

expurgate /'ɛkspər‚geɪt/ *vt* to cut from a book, play, etc any parts supposed to be offensive or erroneous.—**expurgation** *n.*—**expurgator** *n.*—**expurgatory, expurgatorial** *adj.*

exquisite /'ɛkskwɪzɪt/ or /ɛk'skwɪzɪt/ *adj* very beautiful, refined; sensitive, showing discrimination; acutely felt, as pain or pleasure.—**exquisitely** *adv.*

exsanguinate /ɛk'sæŋwɪ‚neɪt/ *vt* to drain of blood.—**exsanguination** *n.*

exsanguine /ɛk'sæŋgwɪn/ *adj* bloodless.

exscind /ɛk'sɪnd/ *vt* to cut off; to cut out, excise.

exsert /ɛk'sɜrt/ or /ɪk-/ *vt* to thrust outwards.—**exsertile** *adj.*—**exsertion** *n.*

exsiccate /'ɛksɪ‚keɪt/ *vt* to dry up.—**exsiccation** *n.*

extant /'ɛkstənt/ or /ɛk'stænt/, /ɪk-/ *adj* still existing.

extemporaneous /ɛk‚stɛmpə'reɪnɪəs/ or /ɪk‚stɛm-/, **extemporary** /ɛk'stɛmpə‚rɛrɪ/ or /ɪk-/ *adj* spoken, acted, etc without preparation.—**extemporaneously, extemporarily** *adv.*

extempore /ɛk'stɛmpərɪ/ or /ɪk-/ *adv, adj* without preparation, impromptu.

extemporize /-‚raɪz/ *vi* to do something extemporaneously.—**extemporization** *n.*

extend /ɛk'stɛnd/ or /ɪk-/ *vt* to stretch or spread out; to stretch fully; to prolong in time; to cause to reach in distance, etc; to enlarge, increase the scope of; to hold out (*eg* the hand); to accord, grant; to give, offer, (*eg* sympathy). • *vi* to prolong in distance or time; to reach in scope.

extended family /ɛk'stɛndəd/ *n* a family with three or more generations of blood relations living as a unit.

extendible, extendable /-dəbəl/ *adj* able to be extended.—**extendibility, extendability** *n.*

extensible /ɛk'stɛnsɪbəl/ or /ɪk-/, **extensile** *adj* extendible.—**extensibility, extensibleness** *n.*

extension /-ʃən/ *n* the act of extending or state of being extended; extent, scope; an added part, *eg* to a building; an extra period; a programme of extramural teaching provided by a college, etc; an additional telephone connected to the principal line.

extensive /ɛk'stɛnsɪv/ or /ɪk-/ *adj* large; having a wide scope or extent.—**extensively** *adv.*—**extensiveness** *n.*

extensometer /‚ɛkstɛn'sɒmɪtər/ *n* a type of micrometer for measuring the expansion of a body.

extensor /ɛk'stɛnsər/ or /ɪk-/ *n* a muscle that extends or straightens a limb.

extent /ɛk'stɛnt/ or /ɪk-/ *n* the distance over which a thing is extended; the range or scope of something; the limit to which something extends.

extenuate /ɛk'stɛnju‚eɪt/ or /ɪk-/ *vt* to make (guilt, a fault, or offence) seem less.—**extenuating** *adj.*—**extenuator** *n.*—**extenuatory** *adj.*

extenuation /ɛkˌstɛnjʊˈeɪʃən/ or /ɪk-/ n an extenuating or being extenuated, partial justification; something that extenuates, an excuse.

exterior /ɛkˈstiːriər/ or /ɪk-/ adj of, on, or coming from the outside; external; (paint, etc) suitable for use on the outside. • n the external part or surface; outward manner or appearance.

exteriorize /ɛkˈstiːriəraɪz/ or /ɪk-/ vt to externalize; (med) to move (an organ, etc) out of the body, usu to facilitate surgery.

exterminate /ɛkˈstɜːmɪˌneɪt/ or /ɪk-/ vt to destroy completely.—**exterminable** adj.—**extermination** n.—**exterminatory** adj.

exterminator /ɛkˈstɜːmɪˌneɪtər/ or /ɪk-/ n one who or that which exterminates; a person who is employed to destroy pests, etc.

extern, externe /ˈɛkstɜːn/ n a non-resident doctor.

external /ɛkˈstɜːnəl/ or /ɪk-/ adj outwardly perceivable; of, relating to, or located on the outside or outer part. • n an external feature.—**externally** adv.

externality /ˌɛkstɜːˈnælɪtiː/ or /ɪk-/ n (pl **externalities**) a being external or externalized; something external; (philos) a being external to the perceiving mind.

externalize /ɛkˈstɜːnəˌlaɪz/ or /ɪk-/ vt to make external; to attribute an external existence to; to express (feelings, etc) esp in words; (psychol) to project (opinions, feelings) onto others or one's surroundings.—**externalization** n.

exterritorial /ˌɛkstɛrɪˈtɔːriəl/ adj extraterritorial.—**exterritoriality** n.

extinct /ɛkˈstɪŋkt/ or /ɪk-/ adj (animals) not alive, no longer existing; (fire) not burning, out; (volcano) no longer active.—**extinction** n.

extine n (bot) the outer coat of the pollen grain.

extinguish /ɪkˈstɪŋgwɪʃ/ vt to put out (a fire, light, etc); to bring to an end.—**extinguishable** adj.—**extinguishment** n.

extinguisher /-ər/ n a device for putting out a fire.

extirpate /ˈɛkstərˌpeɪt/ vt to destroy totally, as by uprooting.—**extirpation** n.—**extirpative** adj.—**extirpator** n.

extol, extoll /ɪkˈstoːl/ vt (**extols** or **extolls, extolling, extolled**) to praise highly.—**extoller** n.—**extollment, extolment** n.

extort /ɪkˈstɔːt/ vt to obtain (money, promises, etc) by force or improper pressure.—**extorter** n.—**extortive** adj.

extortion /ɛkˈstɔːʃən/ or /ɪk-/ n the act or practice of extorting; the criminal instance of this; oppressive or unjust exaction.—**extortionary** adj.—**extortioner, extortionist** n.

extortionate /-ʃənət/ adj exorbitant; excessively high in price.—**extortionately** adv.

extra /ˈɛkstrə/ adj additional. • adv unusually; in addition. • n something extra or additional, esp a charge; a special edition of a newspaper; a person who plays a non-speaking role in a film.

extra- /ˈɛkstrə/ prefix outside, beyond.

extract /ɪkˈstrækt/ vt to take or pull out by force; to withdraw by chemical or physical means; to abstract, excerpt. • n the essence of a substance obtained by extraction; a passage taken from a book, play, film, etc.—**extractable, extractible** adj.—**extractability, extractibility** n.

extraction /ɪkˈstrækʃən/ n the act of extracting; lineage; something extracted.

extractive /ɪkˈstræktɪv/ adj tending or serving to extract.

extractor /ɛkˈstræktər/ n one who extracts; a thing that extracts, esp a device for removing teeth or delivering a baby; a device for extracting stale air or fumes from a room.—also **extractor fan**.

extracurricular /ˌɛkstrəkəˈrɪkjʊlər/ adj not part of the regular school timetable; beyond one's normal duties or activities.

extradite /ˈɛkstrəˌdaɪt/ vt to surrender (an alleged criminal) to the country where the offence was committed.—**extraditable** adj.—**extradition** n.

extrados /ɛkˈstreɪdɒs/ n (pl **extrados, extradoses**) (archit) the upper or outer curve of an arch.

extragalactic /ˌɛkstrəgəˈlæktɪk/ adj outside the Galaxy.

extrajudicial /-dʒuːˈdɪʃəl/ adj out of the ordinary course of legal proceedings.

extramarital /-ˈmɛrɪtəl/ adj occurring outside marriage, esp sexual relationships.

extramundane /-ˈmʌndeɪn/ adj beyond the material world.

extramural /-ˈmjʊrəl/ adj (course, studies) outside the usual courses run by a university, etc; outside a city's walls or boundaries.—**extramurally** adv.

extraneous /ɪkˈstreɪnɪəs/ adj coming from outside; not essential.—**extraneously** adv.

extraordinary /ɛkˈstrɔːdɪnɛri/ or /ˌɛkstrəˈɔːdɪnɛri/ adj not usual or regular; remarkable, exceptional.—**extraordinarily** adv.—**extraordinariness** n.

extrapolate /ɛkˈstræpəˌleɪt/ vti to infer (unknown data) from known data.—**extrapolation** n.—**extrapolator** n.

extrasensory perception /ˌɛkstrəˈsɛnsəri/ n the claimed ability to obtain information by means other than the ordinary physical senses.

extraterritorial /-ˌtɛrɪˈtɔːriəl/ adj outside territorial boundaries; (embassy etc) outside the jurisdiction of the country in which it is.—also **exterritorial**.

extraterritoriality /-ˌtɛrɪˌtɔːriˈælɪti/ n exemption granted to foreign diplomats from the legal jurisdiction of the country to which they are posted; a country's jurisdiction over its nationals abroad.

extravagant /ɪkˈstrævəgənt/ adj lavish in spending; (prices) excessively high; wasteful; (behaviour, praise, etc) lacking in restraint, flamboyant, profuse.—**extravagantly** adv.—**extravagance** n.

extravaganza /ɪkˌstrævəˈgænzə/ n an elaborate musical production; a spectacular show, play, film, etc.

extravagate /ɛkˈstrævəˌgeɪt/ vi (arch) to wander; to be extravagant.—**extravagation** n.

extravasate /ɛkˈstrævəˌseɪt/ vt (anat) to force blood, etc out of its proper vessel; to exude. • vi to flow out.—**extravasation** n.

extraversion /ˌɛkstrəˈvɜːʒən/ see **extroversion**.

extravert /-ˌvɜːt/ see **extrovert**.

extreme /ɪkˈstriːm/ adj of the highest degree or intensity; excessive, immoderate, unwarranted; very severe, stringent; outermost. • n the highest or furthest limit or degree; (often pl) either of the two points marking the ends of a scale or range.—**extremely** adv.—**extremeness** n.

extremist /ɪkˈstriːmɪst/ n a person of extreme views, esp political.—**extremism** n.

extremity /ɪkˈstrɛmɪti/ n (pl **extremities**) the utmost point or degree; the most remote part; the utmost violence, vigour, or necessity; the end; (pl) the hands or feet.

extricable /ˈɛkstrɪkəbəl/ adj able to be extricated.

extricate /-ˌkeɪt/ vt to release from difficulties; to disentangle.—**extrication** n.

extrinsic /ɛkˈstrɪnsɪk/ adj external; not inherent or essential.—**extrinsically** adv.

extrorse /ɛkˈstrɔːs/ adj (bot) turned outwards.

extroversion /ˌɛkstrəˈvɜːʒən/ n the state of having thoughts and activities directed towards things other than oneself.—also **extraversion**.

extrovert /ˈɛkstrəˌvɜːt/ n a person more interested in the external world than his own thoughts and feelings.—also **extravert**.—**extroverted, extraverted** adj.

extrude /ɪkˈstruːd/ vt to force or push out; to mould (metal or plastic) by forcing through a shaped die.—**extrusion** n.—**extrusive** adj.

exuberant /ɪɡˈzuːbərənt/ or /-ˈzjuː/ adj lively, effusive, high-spirited; profuse.—**exuberance** n.—**exuberantly** adv.

exuberate /-ˌreɪt/ vi to be exuberant; (arch) to abound.

exudate /ˈɛɡzjuˌdeɪt/ n exuded matter, eg sweat.

exudation /-ˈdeɪʃən/ n an exuding or being exuded; exuded matter, eg sweat.—**exudative** adj.

exude /ɪɡˈzjuːd/ or /-ˈzuːd/ vt to cause or allow to ooze through pores or incisions, as sweat, pus; to display (confidence, emotion) freely.

exult /ɪɡˈzʌlt/ vi to rejoice greatly.—**exultation** n.

exultant /ɪɡˈzʌltənt/ adj exulting, joyful; triumphant.—**exultantly** adv.

exuviae /ɪɡˈzuːviː/ or /-iː/ npl the cast-off skins, shells, etc, of animals.—**exuvial** adj.

exuviate /-viˌeɪt/ vt (skin) to shed, slough.—**exuviation** n.

eyas /ˈaɪəs/ n a young hawk.

eye /aɪ/ n the organ of sight; the iris; the faculty of seeing; the external part of the eye; something resembling an eye, as the hole in a needle, the leaf-bud on a potato, etc. • vt (**eyeing** or **eying, eyed**) to look at; to observe closely.

eyeball /ˈaɪbɒl/ n the ball of the eye. • vt (sl) to stare at.

eyebright /-braɪt/ n a plant with small white and purplish flowers, formerly used as a lotion to treat disorders of the eye.

eyebrow /-braʊ/ n the hairy ridge above the eye.

eye-catching /-kætʃɪŋ/ *adj* attractive or striking in appearance.— **eye-catcher** *n*.

eyeful /-fʊl/ *adj* (*inf*) a close look, gaze; an attractive vision, *esp* a woman.

eyeglass /-glæs/ *n* a lens for correcting defective vision, a monocle.

eyeglasses *npl* spectacles.

eyelash /-læʃ/ *n* the fringe of fine hairs along the edge of each eyelid.

eyeless /-ləs/ *adj* without eyes; blind.

eyelet /-lət/ *n* a small hole for a rope or cord to pass through, as in sails, garments, etc.

eyelid /-lɪd/ *n* the lid of skin and muscle that moves to cover the eye.

eye-liner /-ˌlaɪnər/ *n* a cosmetic used to apply a line round the eye.

eye-opener /-ˌoːpənər/ *n* something that comes as a shock or surprise.

eyephone /-foːn/ *n* a device in the style of a headset which provides the user with stereoscopic images and stereo sound used in virtual reality simulation.

eyepiece /-piːs/ *n* the lens or lenses at the end nearest the eye of an optical instrument, *eg* a telescope.

eyeprint /-prɪnt/ *n* the pattern of veins in the retina, which is unique to an individual and used as a means of identification.

eye-shadow /-ʃædoː/ *n* a coloured powder applied to accentuate or decorate the eyelids.

eyeshot /-ʃɒt/ *n* seeing distance.

eyesight /-saɪt/ *n* the faculty of seeing.

eyesore /-sɔr/ *n* anything offensive to the sight.

eyespot /-spɒt/ *n* a rudimentary visual organ; (*on butterflies, etc*) a marking resembling an eye.

eyetooth /-tuːθ/ *n* (*pl* **eyeteeth**) a canine tooth in the upper jaw.

eyewash /-wɒʃ/ *n* (*inf*) nonsense, drivel.

eye-witness /-ˌwɪtnəs/ *n* a person who sees an event, such as an accident or a crime, and can describe what happened.

eyrie /ˈɛri/ or /ˈiːri/ *n* the nest of an eagle or other bird of prey; any high inaccessible place or position.—*also* **aerie**.

F

F *abbr* = Fahrenheit; (*chem symbol*) fluorine.

f, F /ɛf/ *n* the 6th letter of the English alphabet.

fa /fɑ/ *n* (*music*) the fourth note in the sol-fa musical notation.—*also* **fah**.

fabaceous /ˈfæbeɪʃɪən/ *adj* (*bot*) bean-like.

Fabian /ˈfeɪbɪən/ *adj* pertaining to the tactics of the Roman general, Fabius Maximus; cautiously persistent; watchful. • *n* a member of the Fabian Society.

Fabian Society *n* a society seeking socialism by moral persuasion.

fable /ˈfeɪbəl/ *n* a story, often with animal characters, intended to convey a moral; a lie, fabrication; a story involving mythical, legendary or supernatural characters or events.

fabled /ˈfeɪbəld/ *adj* related in fables; fictitious.

fabric /ˈfæbrɪk/ *n* cloth made by knitting, weaving, etc; framework, structure.

fabricate /ˈfæbrɪˌkeɪt/ *vt* to construct, manufacture; to concoct (*eg* a lie); to forge.—**fabrication** *n*.—**fabricator** *n*.

fabulist /ˈfæbjʊlɪst/ *n* a writer of fables; a liar.

fabulous /ˈfæbjʊləs/ *adj* told in fables; incredible, astonishing; (*inf*) very good.—**fabulously** *adv*.

façade, facade /fəˈsɒd/ *n* the main front or face of a building; an outward appearance, *esp* concealing something hidden.

face /feɪs/ *n* the front part of the head containing the eyes, nose, mouth, chin, etc; facial expression; the front or outer surface of anything; external show or appearance; dignity, self respect; impudence, effrontery; a coal face. • *vt* to be confronted by (a problem, etc); to deal with (an opponent, problem, etc) resolutely; to be opposite to; to turn (a playing card) face upwards; to cover with a new surface. • *vi* to turn the face in a certain direction; to be situated in or have a specific direction.

face card *n* the king, queen or jack in a pack of cards.

faceless /-ləs/ *adj* lacking a face; anonymous.

face-lift /-lɪft/ *n* plastic surgery to smooth and firm the face; an improvement or renovation, *esp* to the outside of a building.

faceoff /ˈfeɪsɒf/ *n* the act of starting or restarting play in ice hockey by dropping the puck between two opposing players' sticks; a direct confrontation.

facer /-ər/ *n* someone who, or something which, faces; (*inf*) an unexpected setback.

face-saving *adj* allowing the preservation of dignity and prevention of humiliation.

facet /ˈfæsət/ *n* a small plane surface (as on a cut gem); an aspect of character, a problem, issue, etc.

facetiae /fəˈsiːʃɪˌiː/ *npl* witty sayings; books characterized by coarse wit.

facetious /fəˈsiːʃəs/ *adj* joking, *esp* in an inappropriate manner.—**facetiously** *adv*.—**facetiousness** *n*.

face value *n* the value indicated on the face of (*eg* a coin or share certificate); apparent worth or significance.

facia /ˈfeɪʃə/ *or* /ˈfæʃə/, /-ɪə/ *see* **fascia**.

facial /ˈfeɪʃəl/ *adj* of or pertaining to the face. • *n* a beauty treatment for the face.—**facially** *adv*.

facies /ˈfeɪʃiːz/ *n* (*pl* **facies**) the general appearance of a person or a group of plants, animals or rocks; the face.

facile /ˈfæsaɪl/ *or* /ˈfæsɪl/ *adj* easy to do; superficial.

facilitate /fəˈsɪlɪˌteɪt/ *vt* to make easier; to help forward.—**facilitator** *n*.—**facilitation** *n*.

facility /ˈfəsɪlɪti/ *n* (*pl* **facilities**) the quality of being easily done; aptitude, dexterity; something, *eg* a service or equipment, that makes it easy to do something.

facing /ˈfeɪsɪŋ/ *n* a lining at the edge of a garment; a covering on a surface for decoration or protection.

facsimile /fækˈsɪmɪli/ *n* an exact copy of a book, document, etc; a method of transmitting printed matter (text and graphics) through the telephone system.—*also* **fax**.

fact /fækt/ *n* a thing known to have happened or to exist; reality; a piece of verifiable information; (*law*) an event, occurrence, etc as distinguished from its legal consequences.

faction¹ /ˈfækʃən/ *n* a small group of people in an organization working together in a common cause against the main body; dissension within a group or organization.—**factional** *adj*.—**factionally** *adv*.—**factious** *adj*.

faction² *n* a book, film, etc based on facts but presented as a blend of fact and fiction.

factitious /fækˈtɪʃəs/ *adj* contrived, artificial.—**factitiously** *adv*.

factitive /ˈfæktɪtɪv/ *adj* (*gram*) causative.

factor /ˈfæktər/ *n* any circumstance that contributes towards a result; (*math*) any of two or more numbers that, when multiplied together, form a product; a person who acts for another.

factor8 /-eɪt/ *n* a blood-clotting agent used in the treatment of haemophilia.

factorage /ˈfæktərɪdʒ/ *n* a factor's commission.

factorial /fækˈtɔrɪəl/ *n* (*math*) an integer multiplied by all lower integers, *eg* 4 x 3 x 2 x 1.

factorize /ˈfæktəˌraɪz/ *vt* to reduce to factors.—**factorization** *n*.

factory /ˈfæktəri/ *n* (*pl* **factories**) a building or buildings where things are manufactured.

factory farm *n* a farm, which rears livestock intensively ,using modern manufacturing processes.—**factory farming** *n*.

factory ship *n* a ship that processes the catch of a fishing fleet.

factotum /fækˈtoːtəm/ *n* a person employed to do all kinds of work.

facts of life *npl* knowledge of human sexual reproduction.

factual /ˈfæktʃʊəl/ˌ*adj* based on, or containing, facts; actual.—**factually** *adv*.

facula /ˈfækjʊlə/ *n* (*pl* **faculae**) a bright spot or streak on the surface of the sun.

facultative /ˈfækəlteɪtɪv/ *adj* enabling; optional; contingent.

faculty /ˈfækəlti/ *n* (*pl* **faculties**) any natural power of a living organism; special aptitude; a teaching department of a college or university, or the staff of such a department.

fad /fæd/ *n* a personal habit or idiosyncrasy; a craze.—**faddish, faddy** *adj*.—**faddism** *n*.—**faddist** *n*.

fade /feɪd/ *vi* to lose vigour or brightness of colour gradually; to vanish gradually. • *vt* to cause (an image or a sound) to increase or decrease in brightness or intensity gradually.—*also n*.

fadeless /-ləs/ *adj* unfading.

fading /-ɪŋ/ *n* decay; loss of colour; (*radio*) a deterioration in quality of reception.

faeces /ˈfiːsiːz/ *npl* excrement.—*also* **feces**.—**faecal, fecal** *adj*.

faerie, faery /ˈfeɪəri/ *n* (*pl* **faeries**) (*arch*) the fairy world; enchantment.

Faeroese /ˌfeɪroˈiːz/ *n* (*pl* **Faeroese**) an inhabitant of the Faeroes in the North Atlantic; the language of the Faeroes.—*also adj*.—*also* **Faroese**.

fag /fæg/ *vti* (**fagging, fagged**) to become or cause to be tired by hard work. • *n* (*formerly*) a British public schoolboy who performs chores for senior pupils; (*inf*) drudgery; (*sl*) a cigarette.

fag-end *n* the useless remains of anything; (*sl*) a cigarette-end.

faggot, fagot /ˈfæɡət/ *n* a bundle of sticks for fuel; (*sl*) a nasty old woman.

faggoting, fagoting /-ɪŋ/ *n* a method of decorating textile fabrics.

fah /fɑ/ *see* **fa**.

Fahrenheit /ˈfærənˌhaɪt/ *adj* of, using, or being a temperature scale with the freezing point of water marked at 32° and the boiling point at 212°.

faïence, faience /ˈfaɪɑs/, *Fr.* /fajˈɑs/ *n* a type of decorated earthenware.

fail /feɪl/ *vi* to weaken, to fade or die away; to stop operating; to fall short; to be insufficient; to be negligent in duty, expectation, etc; (*exam, etc*) to be unsuccessful; to become bankrupt. • *vt* to disappoint the expectations or hopes of; to be unsuccessful in an exam, etc; to leave, to abandon; to grade (a candidate) as not passing a test, etc. • *n* failure in an examination.

failing /-ɪŋ/ *n* a fault, weakness. • *prep* in default or absence of.

faille /faɪl/ *or* /feɪl/ *n* a soft silk, used for dresses and hat trimmings.

fail-safe *adj* designed to operate safely even if a fault develops; foolproof.

failure /ˈfeɪljər/ *n* failing, non-performance, lack of success; the ceasing of normal operation of something; a deficiency; bankruptcy; an unsuccessful person or thing.

fain /feɪn/ *adv* (*arch*) willingly; gladly. • *adj* willing; glad.

fainéant, faineant /ˈfeɪˌneɪɑ̃/, *Fr.* /fɛneɪˈɑ̃/ *adj* indolent.

faint /feɪnt/ *adj* dim, indistinct; weak, feeble; timid; on the verge of losing consciousness. • *vi* to lose consciousness temporarily from a decrease in the supply of blood to the brain, as from shock. • *n* an act or condition of fainting.—**faintly** *adv*.—**faintness** *n*.

faint-hearted *adj* lacking courage and resolution.

fainting /-ɪŋ/ *n* a sudden and temporary loss of consciousness.

fair[1] /fɛr/ *adj* pleasing to the eye; clean, unblemished; (*hair*) light-coloured; (*weather*) clear and sunny; (*handwriting*) easy to read; just and honest; according to the rules; moderately large; average. • *adv* in a fair manner; squarely.—**fairness** *n*.

fair[2] /fɛr/ *n* a gathering for the sale of goods, *esp* for charity; a competitive exhibition of farm, household, or manufactured goods; a fun-fair.

fair game *n* a legitimate target for attack or ridicule.

fairground /ˈfɛrɡraʊnd/ *n* an open area where fairs are held.

fairing /feɪrɪŋ/ *n* a structure attached to the exterior of an aircraft, ship, motor vehicle, etc to reduce drag.

fairly /ˈfɛrli/ *adv* in a fair manner; justly; moderately.

fair play *n* justice, honesty; impartiality.

fairway /ˈfɛrweɪ/ *n* a navigable channel; the mowed part of a golf course between the tee and the green.

fair-weather *adj* (*friend*) unreliable in troubled times.

fairy /ˈfɛri/ *n* (*pl* **fairies**) an imaginary supernatural being, *usu* in human form.

fairyland /ˈfɛriˌlænd/ *n* the country of fairies; a beautiful, enchanting place.

fairy ring *n* a dark or bare ring in grass caused by fungi.

fairy story, fairy tale *n* a story about fairies; an incredible story; a fabrication.

fait accompli /ˌfeɪtəˈkɒmpli/ or /-əˈkõpli/, *Fr.* /fɛtakõˈpliː/ *n* (*pl* **faits accomplis**) something already done; an irreversible act.

faith /feɪθ/ *n* trust or confidence in a person or thing; a strong conviction, *esp* a belief in a religion; any system of religious belief; fidelity to one's promises, sincerity.

faithful /ˈfeɪθfʊl/ *adj* loyal; true; true to the original, accurate.—**faithfully** *adv*.—**faithfulness** *n*.

faithless /ˈfeɪθləs/ *adj* treacherous, disloyal; untrustworthy.—**faithlessly** *adv*.—**faithlessness** *n*.

fake /feɪk/ *vt* to make (an object) appear more real or valuable in order to deceive; to pretend, simulate. • *n* a faked article, a forgery; an impostor, not genuine.—**faker** *n*.

fakir /ˈfeɪkiːr/ or /fəˈkiːr/ *n* a Muslim or Hindu religious mendicant or ascetic.

Falangist /fəˈlændʒɪst/ *n* a supporter of the Spanish Falange, a fascist party founded in 1933.

falbala /ˈfɒlˌbɒlə/ or /fælˈbælə/ *n* a flounce on a dress.

falcate /ˈfælkeɪt/, **falciform** /ˈfælsɪˌfɔrm/ *adj* sickle-shaped.

falchion /ˈfɒltʃiən/ *n* a broad, curved sword.

falcon /ˈfɒlkən/ or /ˈfæl-/ *n* a type of hawk trained for use in falconry.

falconer /-ər/ *n* a person who hunts with, or who breeds and trains hawks for hunting.—**falconry** *n*.

falconet /-ət/ *n* a small falcon.

falderal /ˈfɒldəˌrɒl/ *n* a trifling ornament.

faldstool /ˈfɒldstuːl/ *n* an armless chair, used by a bishop.

fall /fɒl/ *vi* (**falling, fell,** *pp* **fallen**) to descend by force of gravity; to come as if by falling; to collapse; to drop to the ground; to become lower, weaker, less; to lose power, status, etc; to lose office; to slope in a downward direction; to be wounded or killed in a battle; to pass into a certain state; to become pregnant; to take place, happen; to be directed by chance; to come by inheritance; (*with* **about**) to laugh uncontrollably; (*with* **back**) to retreat; (*with* **behind**) to fail to keep up with; to become in arrears with; (*with* **for**) to fall in love with; to be fooled by (a lie, trick, etc); (*with* **out**) to quarrel; to leave one's place in a military formation; (*with* **through**) to fail to happen. • *n* act or instance of falling; something which falls; the amount by which something falls; a decline in status, position; overthrow; a downward slope; a decrease in size, quantity, value; (*US*) autumn; (*wrestling*) a scoring move by pinning both shoulders of an opponent to the floor at once.

fallacious /fəˈleɪʃəs/ *adj* misleading.—**fallaciously** *adv*.—**fallaciousness** *n*.

fallacy /ˈfæləsi/ *n* (*pl* **fallacies**) a false idea; a mistake in reasoning.

fallal /fəˈlɒl/ *n* a piece of finery, an ornament.

fallen /ˈfɒlən/ *adj* sunk to a lower state or condition; overthrown.

fall guy *n* (*inf*) a person who is easily cheated; a scapegoat.

fallible /ˈfælɪbəl/ *adj* liable to make mistakes.—**fallibly** *adv*.—**fallibility** *n*.

Fallopian tube /fəˈloːpiən/ *n* either of the two tubes through which the egg cells pass from the ovary to the uterus.

fall-out /ˈfɒlaʊt/ *n* a deposit of radioactive dust from a nuclear explosion; a by-product.

fallow[1] /ˈfæloː/ *adj* (*land*) ploughed and left unplanted for a season or more.

fallow[2] *adj* yellowish-brown.

fallow deer *n* a small European deer with a brownish-yellow coat which becomes spotted with white in summer.

false /dɒls/ *adj* wrong, incorrect; deceitful; artificial; disloyal, treacherous; misleading, fallacious.—**falsely** *adv*.—**falseness** *n*.

falsehood /ˈfɒlshʊd/ *n* being untrue; the act of deceiving; a lie.

falsetto /ˈfælseːtoː/ *n* (*pl* **falsettos**) an artificial tone higher in key than the natural compass of the voice.

falsify /ˈfælsɪˌfaɪ/ *vt* (**falsifying, falsified**) to misrepresent; to alter (a document, etc) fraudulently; to prove false.—**falsification** *n*.

falsity /ˈfælsɪti/ *n* (*pl* **falsities**) the quality of being false; an error, a lie.

falter /ˈfæltər/ *vi* to move or walk unsteadily, to stumble; to hesitate or stammer in speech; to be weak or unsure, to waver.—**falteringly** *adv*.

fame /feɪm/ *n* the state of being well known; good reputation.—**famed** *adj*.

familiar /fəˈmɪljər/ *adj* well-acquainted; friendly; common; well-known; too informal, presumptuous. • *n* a spirit or demon supposed to aid a witch, etc; an intimate.—**familiarly** *adv*.—**familiarity** *n*.

familiarize /-ˌraɪz/ *vt* to make well known or acquainted; to make (something) well known.—**familiarization** *n*.

family /ˈfæmɪli/ or /ˈfæmli/ *n* (*pl* **families**) parents and their children; a person's children; a set of relatives; the descendants of a common ancestor; any group of persons or things related in some way; a group of related plants or animals; a unit of a crime syndicate (as the Mafia).

family allowance *n* formerly, the name for child benefit.

family circle *n* close relatives.

family name *n* a surname.

family planning *n* birth control.

family tree *n* a genealogical diagram.

famine /ˈfæmɪn/ *n* an acute scarcity of food in a particular area; an extreme scarcity of anything.

famish /ˈfæmɪʃ/ *vti* to make or be very hungry.

famous /ˈfeɪməs/ *adj* renowned; (*inf*) excellent.—**famously** *adv*.

famulus /ˈfæmjuləs/ *n* (*pl* **famuli**) a magician's assistant.

fan[1] /fæn/ *n* a handheld or mechanical device used to set up a current of air. • *vt* (**fanning, fanned**) to cool, as with a fan; to ventilate; to stir up, to excite; to spread out like a fan.

fan[2] *n* an enthusiastic follower of some sport, hobby, person, etc.

fanatic /ˈfænətɪk/ *n* a person who is excessively enthusiastic about something.—**fanatical** *adj*.—**fanatically** *adv*.

fanaticism /ˈfænətɪˌsɪzəm/ *n* excessive enthusiasm.

fanaticize /ˈfænətɪˌsaɪz/ *vti* to make or become fanatical.

fan belt *n* the belt that drives the cooling fan in a car engine.

fancied /ˈfænsiːd/ *adj* imaginary.

fancier /ˈfænsiər/ *n* a person with a special interest in something, *esp* plant or animal breeding.

fanciful /ˈfænsɪfʊl/ *adj* not factual, imaginary; indulging in fancy; elaborate or intricate in design.—**fancifully** *adv*.

fan club *n* an organized group of followers of a celebrity.

fancy /ˈfænsi/ *n* (*pl* **fancies**) imagination; a mental image; a whim; fondness. • *adj* (**fancier, fanciest**) not based on fact, imaginary; elegant or ornamental. • *vt* (**fancying, fancied**) to imagine; to have a fancy or liking for; (*inf*) to be sexually attracted to.

fancy dress *n* a costume worn at masquerades or parties, *usu* representing an animal, historical character, etc.

fancy-free *adj* uncommitted, carefree.

fancy man *n* (*sl*) a woman's lover; a pimp.

fancy woman *n* (*sl*) a mistress, prostitute.

fancywork *n* ornamental needlework.

fandango /fænˈdæŋgoː/ *n* (*pl* **fandangos**) a Spanish dance, music for this dance, tomfoolery.

fanfare /ˈfænfer/ *n* a flourish of trumpets.

fang /fæŋ/ *n* a long sharp tooth, as in a canine; the long hollow tooth through which venomous snakes inject poison.

fanlight /ˈfænləit/ *n* a semicircular window with radiating bars like the ribs of a fan.

fanny /ˈfæni/ *n* (*pl* **fannies**) (*vulg*) female genitals; (*US sl*) the buttocks.

fantail /ˈfænteil/ *n* a pigeon with a tail that opens out like a fan.

fantan /ˈfæntæn/ *n* a Chinese gambling game in which players make guesses about hidden counters.

fantasia /fænˈteizə/ or /-ziə/ *n* an improvised musical or prose composition.

fantasize /ˈfæntəˌsaiz/ *vt* to imagine in an extravagant way. • *vi* to daydream.

fantast /ˈfæntæst/ *n* a visionary or dreamer.

fantastic /fænˈtæstik/ *adj* unrealistic, fanciful; unbelievable; imaginative; (*inf*) wonderful.—**fantastically** *adv*.

fantasy /ˈfæntəsi/ *n* (*pl* **fantasies**) imagination; a product of the imagination, *esp* an extravagant or bizarre notion or creation; an imaginative poem, play or novel.

fanzine /ˈfænziːn/ *n* a magazine produced by and for the fans of a celebrity, football club, etc.

FAO *abbr* = Food and Agricultural Organization of the United Nations.

far /far/ *adj* (**farther, farthest** *or* **further, furthest**) remote in space or time; long; (*political views, etc*) extreme. • *adv* very distant in space, time, or degree; to or from a distance in time or position, very much.—**farness** *n*.

farad /ˈferəd/ *n* a unit of electrical capacitance.

faradic /fəˈrædik/ *adj* pertaining to the phenomenon of induced electricity or to faradization.

faradize /ˈfærəˌdaiz/ *vt* to treat by use of a faradic current.—**faradization** *n*.—**faradizer** *n*.

farandole /ˌferənˈdɒl/ *n* a lively dance, originating in Provence.

faraway /ˈfarəwei/ *adj* distant, remote; dreamy.

farce /fars/ *n* a style of light comedy; a drama using such comedy; a ludicrous situation.—**farcical** *adj*.—**farcically** *adv*.

farceur /ˈfarsər/, **farceuse** /-juːz/ *n* a writer of or actor in a farce; a wit.

farcy /ˈfarsi/ *n* (*pl* **farcies**) a disease of horses, closely allied to glanders.

fardel /ˈfardəl/ *n* (*arch*) a bundle or burden.

fare /fer/ *n* money paid for transportation; a passenger in public transport; food. • *vi* to be in a specified condition.

Far East *n* the countries of East and Southeast Asia including China, Japan, North and South Korea, Indochina, eastern Siberia and adjacent islands.

farewell /ferˈwel/ *interj* goodbye.—*also n*.

far-fetched *adj* unlikely.

far-flung *adj* spread over a wide area; remote.

farina /fəˈriːnə/ *n* flour or meal obtained by grinding the seeds of cereals and leguminous plants; starch.

farinaceous /ˌfærɪˈneiʃəs/ *adj* consisting of, or made from, farina; mealy.

farinose /ˈfærɪˌnoːz/ *adj* producing farina; resembling farina.

farm /farm/ *n* an area of land (with buildings) on which crops and animals are raised. • *vt* to grow crops or breed livestock; to cultivate, as land; to breed fish commercially; (*with* **out**) to put out (work, etc) to be done by others, to subcontract.

farmer /-ər/ *n* a person who manages or operates a farm.

farm hand /-hænd/ *n* a worker on a farm.

farmhouse /-həus/ *n* a house on a farm.

farming /-iŋ/ *adj* pertaining to, or engaged in, agriculture. • *n* the business or practice of agriculture.

farmstead /-sted/ *n* a farm with the buildings belonging to it.

farmyard /-jard/ *n* a yard close to or surrounded by farm buildings.

faro /ˈfaroː/ *n* a gambling card game.

farouche /fəˈruːʃ/ *adj* sullen; unsociable.

far-out *adj* (*sl*) weird, bizarre; fantastic, wonderful. • *interj* used to express delight.

farrago /fəˈrɑːgoː/ *n* (*pl* **farragoes**) a confused collection.—**farraginous** *adj*.

far-reaching *adj* having serious or widespread consequences.

farrier /ˈfæriər/ *n* a person who shoes horses.

farrow /ˈfæroː/ *n* a litter of pigs. • *vti* to give birth to (pigs).

far-seeing *adj* having foresight.

fart /fart/ *vi* (*vulg*) to expel wind from the anus.—*also n*.

farther /ˈfarðər/ *adj* at or to a greater distance. • *adv* to a greater degree.

farthest /-ðist/ *adj* at or to the greatest distance. • *adv* to the greatest degree.

farthing /ˈfarðiŋ/ *n* a former British monetary unit.

farthingale /ˈfarðiŋˌgeil/ *n* a hooped support worn beneath a skirt to expand it at the hip line.

fasces /ˈfæsiːz/ *npl* a bundle of rods with an axe used in ancient Rome as a symbol of authority.

fascia /ˈfeiʃə/ or /ˈfæʃə/, /-iə/ *n* (*pl* **fasciae**) the instrument panel of a motor vehicle, the dashboard; the flat surface above a shop front, with the owner's name, etc.—*also* **facia**.

fascicle /ˈfæsikəl/ *n* one part of a book published by instalments.—*also* **fascicule**; a small collection, group or bundle; (*bot*) a cluster of leaves, roots, etc.

fascicular /fæˈsikjulər/, **fasciculate** /-lət/ *adj* (*bot*) arranged in fascicles.

fascicule /ˈfæsikjul/ *n* a fascicle.

fasciculus /fæˈsikjuləs/ *n* (*pl* **fasciculi**) (*anat*) a bundle of nerve fibres; a fascicle.

fascinate /ˈfæsiˌneit/ *vt* to hold the attention of, to attract irresistibly.—**fascination** *n*.

fascinating /-iŋ/ *adj* having great interest or charm.

fascine /fæˈsiːn/ or /fə-/ *n* a long bundle of sticks bound together, used for fortifying ditches, building earthworks, etc.

Fascism /ˈfæʃizəm/ *n* a system of government characterized by dictatorship, belligerent nationalism, racism, and militarism.—**Fascist** *n, adj*.

fash /fæʃ/ *vti* (*Scot*) to bother, worry. • *n* worry; trouble.

fashion /ˈfæʃən/ *n* the current style of dress, conduct, speech, etc; the manner or form of appearance or action. • *vt* to make in a particular form; to suit or adapt.—**fashioner** *n*.

fashionable /-əbəl/ *adj* conforming to the current fashion; attracting or frequented by people of fashion.—**fashionably** *adv*.

fast[1] /fæst/ *adj* swift, quick; (*clock*) ahead of time; firmly attached, fixed; (*colour, dye*) non-fading; wild, promiscuous. • *adv* firmly, thoroughly, rapidly, quickly.

fast[2] *vi* to go without all or certain foods. • *n* a period of fasting.

fastback /ˈfæstbæk/ *n* a car with a roof that forms one continuous slope from roof to rear.

fast breeder reactor *n* a nuclear reactor that produces more fissile material than it uses.

fasten /ˈfæsən/ *vti* to secure firmly; to attach; to fix or direct (the eyes, attention) steadily.

fastener /-ər/, **fastening** /-iŋ/ *n* a clip, catch, etc for fastening.

fast food *n* food, such as hamburgers, kebabs, pizzas, etc prepared and served quickly.

fast-forward *vt* to move (video or music tape, etc) on at high speed.

fastidious /fæˈstidiəs/ *adj* hard to please; daintily refined; oversensitive.—**fastidiously** *adv*.—**fastidiousness** *n*.

fastigiate /fæˈstidʒiət/ or /-ieit/ *adj* (*biol*) narrowing at the apex.

fastness /ˈfæstnəs/ *n* swiftness; colourfast quality; a stronghold.

fast track *n* a hectic and competitive lifestyle or career.—**fast-track** *adj*.

fat /fæt/ *adj* (**fatter, fattest**) plump; thick; fertile; profitable. • *n* an oily or greasy material found in animal tissue and plant seeds; the richest or best part of anything; a superfluous part.—**fatness** *n*.

fatal *adj* causing death; disastrous (to); fateful.—**fatally** *adv*.

fatalism /ˈfeitəˌlizəm/ *n* belief that all events are predetermined by fate and therefore inevitable; acceptance of this doctrine.—**fatalist** *n*.—**fatalistic** *adj*.

fatality /fəˈtæliti/ *n* (*pl* **fatalities**) a death caused by a disaster or accident; a person killed in such a way; a fatal power or influence.

fat cat *n* (*sl*) a rich person.

fate /feit/ *n* the ultimate power that predetermines events, destiny; the ultimate end, outcome; misfortune, doom, death.

fated /ˈfeitəd/ *adj* doomed; destined by fate.

fateful /-ful/ *adj* having important, *usu* unpleasant, consequences.—**fatefully** *adv*.

Fates /feits/ *npl* (*Greek myth*) the three goddesses of destiny, Atropos, Clotho and Lachesis.

fathead /ˈfæthed/ *n* (*inf*) an idiot.

father /ˈfɒðər/ n a male parent; an ancestor; a founder or originator; (*with cap*) God; a title of respect applied to monks, priests, etc. • *vt* to be the father of; to found, originate.—**fatherhood** n.

father-in-law n (*pl* **fathers-in-law**) the father of one's husband or wife.

fatherland /-ˌlænd/ n one's native country.

fatherless *adj* without a living father.

fatherly /-li/ *adj* pertaining to a father; kind, affectionate, as a father. • *adv* like a father.

fathom /ˈfæðəm/ n a nautical measure of 6 feet (1.83 m). • *vt* to measure the depth of; to understand.

fatidic /ˈfeɪtɪdɪk/, **fatidical** *adj* having the gift of prophecy.

fatigue /fəˈtiːg/ n tiredness from physical or mental effort; the tendency of a material to break under repeated stress; any of the menial or manual tasks performed by military personnel; (*pl*) the clothing worn on fatigue or in the field. • *vti* (**fatiguing, fatigued**) to make or become tired.

fatling /ˈfætlɪŋ/ n a young animal fattened for slaughter.

fatten /ˈfætən/ *vt* to make fat or fleshy; to make abundant.—**fattening** *adj*.

fat transfer n a cosmetic surgery procedure to take fat from parts of the body, *eg* hips, and insert it in the face to reduce wrinkling.

fatty /ˈfæti/ *adj* (**fattier, fattiest**) resembling or containing fat. • n (*pl* **fatties**) (*inf*) a fat person.

fatty acid n any of various organic carboxylic acids (*eg* palmitic, stearic and oleic) present in fats and oils.

fatuous /ˈfætʃʊəs/ *adj* foolish, idiotic.—**fatuously** *adv*.—**fatuousness** n.—**fatuity** n.

fatwa, fatwah /ˈfætwə/ n a decision by a mufti or Muslim judge.

faubourg /ˈfoːbʊr/ or /-bərg/, *Fr.* /foːˈbʊr/ n a suburb, *esp* of Paris in France.

faucal /ˈfɔːʃəl/ *adj* (*anat*) of the fauces; (*sound*) deeply guttural.

fauces /ˈfɔːsiːz/ n (*pl* **fauces**) (*anat*) the upper part of the throat.

faucet /ˈfɔːsət/ n a fixture for draining off liquid (as from a pipe or cask); a device controlling the flow of liquid through a pipe or from a container.—*also* **tap**.

faugh /foː/ (*conventionalized pronunciation; sound produced by expulsion of air, often with vibration of lips*) *interj* an expression of disgust or abhorrence.

fault /fɒlt/ n a failing, defect; a minor offence; (*tennis, etc*) an incorrect serve or other error; a fracture in the earth's crust causing displacement of strata. • *vt* to find fault with, blame. • *vi* to commit a fault.

fault-finding *adj* censorious, critical.—**fault-finder** n.

faultless /-ləs/ *adj* without fault; perfect; blameless.—**faultlessly** *adv*.—**faultlessness** n.

faulty /-ti/ *adj* (**faultier, faultiest**) imperfect; defective; wrong.—**faultily** *adv*.—**faultiness** n.

faun /fɒn/ n (*Roman myth*) a woodland deity, half man, half beast.

fauna /ˈfɒnə/ n (*pl* **faunas, faunae**) the animals of a region, period, or specific environment.

faute de mieux *Fr.* /ˌfoːtdəˈmjuː/ in the absence of anything better.

fauteuil /foːˈtɔɪ/, *Fr.* /foːˈtœj/ n an armchair; a stall in a theatre.

faux pas /foːˈpɒ/ n (*pl* **faux pas**) an embarrassing social blunder.

faveolate /fəˈviːəˌleɪt/ *adj* honeycombed.

favonian /fəˈvoːnɪən/ *adj* of or pertaining to the west wind; (*poet*) favourable.

favour, favor /ˈfeɪvər/ n goodwill; approval; a kind or helpful act; partiality; a small gift given out at a party; (*usu pl*) a privilege granted or conceded, *esp* sexual. • *vt* to regard or treat with favour; to show support for; to oblige (with); to afford advantage to, facilitate.

favourable, favorable /ˈfeɪvərəbəl/ or /ˈfeɪvr-/ *adj* expressing approval; pleasing; propitious; conducive (to).—**favourably, favorably** *adv*.

favourite, favorite /ˈfeɪvərɪt/ or /ˈfeɪvr-/ n a favoured person or thing; a competitor expected to win. • *adj* most preferred.

favouritism, favoritism /ˈfeɪvərɪˌtɪzəm/ or /ˈfeɪvr-/ n the showing of unfair favour.

fawn[1] /fɒn/ n a young deer; a yellowish-brown colour. • *adj* fawn-coloured.

fawn[2] *vi* (*dogs, etc*) to crouch, etc in a show of affection; to flatter in an obsequious manner.—**fawner** n.—**fawning** n.

fax /fæks/ n a document sent by facsimile transmission; a device for sending faxes. • *vt* to send (a document) by facsimile transmission.

fay /feɪ/ n a fairy.

faze /feɪz/ *vt* (*inf*) to disturb; to discompose, to disconcert; to daunt.

FBI /ˈɛfˌbiːˈaɪ/ *abbr* = Federal Bureau of Investigation.

FC *abbr* = Football Club.

Fe (*chem symbol*) iron.

fealty /ˈfiːəlti/ n (*pl* **fealties**) (*feudal society*) the loyalty due from a vassal to his feudal lord.

fear /fiːr/ n an unpleasant emotion excited by danger, pain, etc; a cause of fear; anxiety; deep reverence. • *vt* to feel fear, be afraid of; to be apprehensive, anxious; to be sorry. • *vi* to be afraid or apprehensive.—**fearless** *adj*.—**fearlessly** *adv*.—**fearlessness** n.

fearful /-fʊl/ *adj* causing intense fear; timorous; apprehensive (of); (*inf*) very great, very bad.—**fearfully** *adv*.

fearless /-ləs/ *adj* brave, intrepid.—**fearlessly** *adv*.—**fearlessness** n.

fearnought, fearnaught /ˈfiːrnɒt/ n a strong woollen cloth.

fearsome /ˈfiːrsəm/ *adj* causing fear, frightful.

feasible /ˈfiːzəbəl/ *adj* able to be done or implemented, possible.—**feasibly** *adv*.—**feasibility** n.

feast /fiːst/ n an elaborate meal prepared for some special occasion; something that gives abundant pleasure; a periodic religious celebration. • *vi* to have or take part in a feast. • *vt* to entertain with a feast.—**feaster** n.

feat /fiːt/ n an action of remarkable strength, skill, or courage.

feather /ˈfɛðər/ n any of the light outgrowths that form the covering of a bird, consisting of a hollow central shaft with a vane of fine barbs on each side; a plume; something resembling a feather; the water thrown up by the turn of the blade of an oar. • *vt* to ornament with feathers; to turn (an oar or propeller blade) so that the edge is foremost.—**feathering** n.—**feathery** *adj*.

feather bed n a mattress stuffed with feathers.

featherbrain /-breɪn/, **featherhead** /-hɛd/ n (*inf*) a silly, forgetful person.

featherbrained /-breɪnd/ *adj* frivolous, giddy.

featheredge /-ɛdʒ/ n a thin piece of board with one wedge-shaped side.

featherstitch /-stɪt/ n a zigzag stitch with a featherlike appearance.

featherweight /-ˌweɪt/ n a lightweight thing or person; an insignificant thing or person; a boxer weighing from 118–126 lbs (53.5–57 kg); a wrestler weighing from 127–137 lbs (58–62 kg).

feathery /ˈfɛðəri/ *adj* like or covered with feathers.—**featheriness** n.

feature /ˈfiːtʃər/ n any of the parts of the face; a characteristic trait of something; a special attraction or distinctive quality of something; a prominent newspaper article, etc; the main film in a cinema programme. • *vti* to make or be a feature of (something).

featureless /-ləs/ *adj* lacking prominent or distinctive features.

Feb. *abbr* = February.

febrifuge /ˈfɛbrɪˌfjʊdʒ/ n a drug that reduces fever.—**febrifugal** *adj*.

febrile /ˈfiːbraɪl/ or /ˈfɛb-/ *adj* of fever; feverish.

February /ˈfɛbrʊəri/ or /ˈfɛbjʊəri/, /-uːəri/ n (*pl* **Februaries**) the second month of the year, having 28 days (or 29 days in leap years).

feces /ˈfiːsiːz/ *see* **faeces**.

feckless /ˈfɛklɪs/ *adj* incompetent, untrustworthy.—**fecklessly** *adv*.—**fecklessness** n.

feculent /ˈfɛkjʊlənt/ *adj* muddy, turbid; full of dregs or sediment.—**feculence** *adj*.

fecund /ˈfiːkənd/ or /ˈfɛk-/ *adj* fertile, prolific.—**fecundity** n.

fecundate /-ˌdeɪt/ *vt* to impregnate.—**fecundation** n.

fed /fɛd/ *see* **feed**.

fedayee /ˌfɛdaːˈjiː/ n (*pl* **fedayeen**) an Arab commando or guerrilla.

federal /ˈfɛdərəl/ or /ˈfɛdr-/ *adj* designating, or of a union of states, etc, in which each member surrenders some of its power to a central authority; of a central government of this type.—**federalism** n.—**federalist** n.—**federally** *adv*.

federalize /-ˌlaɪz/ *vt* to unite (states, etc) in a federal union; to put under federal authority.—**federalization** n.

federate /ˈfɛdəˌreɪt/ *vti* to unite in a federation. • *adj* united in a league; on a federal basis.—**federative** *adj*.

federation /ˌfɛdəˈreɪʃən/ n a union of states, groups, etc, in which each subordinates its power to a central authority; a federated organization.

fedora /fə'dɔːrə/ *n* a soft felt hat with a curled brim and a crown .creased lengthways.

fee /fiː/ *n* the price paid for the advice or service of a professional; a charge for some privilege, as membership of a club; (*law*) an inheritance in land.

feeble /'fiːbəl/ *adj* weak, ineffective.—**feebly** *adv.*—**feebleness** *n*.

feeble-minded /-ˌmaɪndəd/ *adj* mentally defective; of low intelligence.

feed /fiːd/ *vb* (**feeding, fed**) *vt* to give food to; to give as food to; to supply with necessary material; to gratify. • *vi* to consume food. • *n* food for animals; material fed into a machine; the part of a machine supplying this material.

feedback /'fiːdbæk/ *n* a return to the input of part of the output of a system; information about a product, service, etc returned to the supplier for purposes of evaluation.

feeder /'fiːdər/ *n* a person or thing that feeds; a baby's feeding-bottle; a device for supplying material to a machine; a subsidiary road, railway, etc acting as a link with the central transport network.

feel /fiːl/ *vb* (**feeling, felt**) *vt* to perceive or explore by the touch; to find one's way by cautious trial; to be conscious of, experience; to have a vague or instinctual impression of; to believe, consider. • *vi* to be able to experience the sensation of touch; to be affected by; to convey a certain sensation when touched. • *n* the sense of touch; feeling; a quality as revealed by touch.

feeler /'fiːlər/ *n* a tactile organ (as a tentacle or antenna) of an animal; a tentative approach or suggestion to test another person's reactions.

feel-good *adj* that which generates the feeling of well-being; feel-good factor.

feeling /-ɪŋ/ *n* the sense of touch; mental or physical awareness; a physical or mental impression; a state of mind; sympathy; emotional sensitivity; a belief or opinion arising from emotion; (*pl*) emotions, sensibilities.

feet /fiːt/ *see* **foot**.

feign /feɪn/ *vt* to invent; to pretend.

feint /feɪnt/ *n* a pretended attack, intended to take the opponent off his guard, as in boxing.—*also vi.*

feldspar /'feldspɑːr/ *n* any member of the group of hard rock-forming minerals.—*also* **felspar**.—**feldspathic, felspathic** *adj*.

felicitate /fɪ'lɪsɪˌteɪt/ *vt* to congratulate.—**felicitation** *n*.

felicitous /fɪ'lɪsɪtəs/ *adj* (*words, etc*) apt, well-chosen; agreeable in manner; happy.—**felicitously** *adv*.

felicity /fɪ'lɪsɪtɪ/ *n* (*pl* **felicities**) happiness; apt and pleasing style in writing, speech, etc.

feline /'fiːlaɪn/ *adj* of cats; cat-like.—**felinity** *n*.

fell[1] /fel/ *see* **fall**.

fell[2] *vt* to cut, beat, or knock down; to kill, to sew (a seam) by folding one raw edge under the other.

fell[3] *n* a skin, hide, pelt.

fell[4] *adj* (*poet*) cruel, fierce, bloody, deadly.

fellah /'felə/ *n* (*pl* **fellahs, fellahin, fellaheen**) an Arab peasant.

fellatio /fə'leɪʃɪəʊ/ *n* sexual stimulation of the penis with the mouth.

felloe /'feləʊ/, **felly** /'felɪ/ *n* (*pl* **felloes, fellies**) one of the curved pieces of wood which form the outer section of a wheel; the outer section of a wheel, the circumference.

fellow /'feləʊ/ *n* an associate; a comrade; an equal in power, rank, or position; the other of a pair, a mate; a member of the governing body in some colleges and universities; a member of a learned society; (*inf*) a man or boy. • *adj* belonging to the same group or class.

fellowship /'feləʊʃɪp/ *n* companionship; a mutual sharing; a group of people with the same interests; the position held by a college fellow.

felo de se /'feləʊdəˌseɪ/ *n* (*pl* **felones de se, felos de se**) the act of suicide; a person who commits suicide.

felon /'felən/ *n* a person guilty of a felony.

felonious /fə'ləʊnɪəs/ *adj* done with the intention of committing a crime; criminal; malignant.—**feloniously** *adv.*—**feloniousness** *n*.

felony /'felənɪ/ *n* (*pl* **felonies**) (*formerly*) a grave crime.

felspar /'felspɑːr/ *see* **feldspar**.

felt[1] /felt/ *see* **feel**.

felt[2] *n* a fabric made from woollen fibres, often mixed with fur or hair, pressed together. • *vti* to make into or become like felt.

felting /-ɪŋ/ *n* the material from which felt is made; the process of manufacturing felt.

felucca /fɪ'lʌkə/ *n* a small boat with oars and lateen sails, used in the Mediterranean.

female /'fiːmeɪl/ *adj* of the sex that produces young; of a woman or women; (*pipe, plug, etc*) designed with a hollow part for receiving an inserted piece. • *n* a female animal or plant.

feminine /'femɪnɪn/ *adj* of, resembling, or appropriate to women; (*gram*) of that gender to which words denoting females belong.—**femininity** *n*.

feminism /'femɪˌnɪzəm/ *n* the movement to win political, economic and social equality for women.—**feminist** *adj, n*.

feminize /'femɪˌnaɪz/ *vti* to make or become feminine.—**feminization** *n*.

femme de chambre *Fr.* /famdə'ʃãbr/ *n* (*pl* **femmes de chambre**) a chambermaid.

femme fatale /ˌfæmfæ'tæl/, *Fr.* /famfə'tal/ *n* (*pl* **femmes fatales**) a dangerously seductive woman.

femur /'fiːmər/ *n* (*pl* **femurs, femora**) the thighbone.—**femoral** *adj*.

fen /fen/ *n* an area of low-lying marshy or flooded land.

fence /fens/ *n* a barrier put round land to mark a boundary, or prevent animals, etc from escaping; a receiver of stolen goods. • *vt* to surround with a fence; to keep (out) as by a fence. • *vi* to practise fencing; to make evasive answers; to act as a fence for stolen goods.—**fencer** *n*.

fencing /'fensɪŋ/ *n* fences; material for making fences; the art of fighting with foils or other types of sword.

fend /fend/ *vi* (*with* **for**) to provide a livelihood for.

fender /'fendər/ *n* anything that protects or fends off something else, as old tyres along the side of a vessel, or the part of a car body over the wheel.

fenestrated /'fenəstreɪtəd/ or /fə'nes-/, **fenestrate** /'fenəstreɪt/ or /fə'nes-/ *adj* having windows.

fenestration /ˌfenə'streɪʃən/ *n* the design and arrangement of windows in a building.

feng shui /'feŋʃuːi/ *n* a form of geomancy with its base in Chinese mythology concerning the positioning of buildings and household items and their relationship to their surroundings as they affect people.

fennec /'fenɪk/ *n* a type of small fox, found in Africa.

fennel /'fenəl/ *n* a European herb of the carrot family grown for its foliage and aromatic seeds; a herb grown for its edible bulbous stem tasting of aniseed.

fennelflower *n* one of a variety of Mediterranean plants, with white, blue or yellow flowers.—*also* **love-in-a-mist**.

fenny /'fenɪ/ *adj* marshy.

fenugreek /'fenjuːˌgriːk/ *n* a Mediterranean plant with white flowers and pungent seeds.

feoff /fiːf/ or /fef/ *see* **fief**.

feral /'fiːrəl/ or /'ferəl/, **ferine** /'fiːraɪn/ or /'feraɪn/ *adj* wild, untamed; like a wild beast.

fer-de-lance /ˌferdə'lɒns/ *n* a yellowish, highly poisonous snake of tropical America.

feretory /'ferəˌtɔːrɪ/ *n* (*pl* **feretories**) a shrine for the relics of a saint; a chapel for keeping this.

ferial /'ferɪəl/ *adj* (*RC: Church*) (*a day*) ordinary, not a festival or a fast.

ferment /'fɜːment/ *n* an agent causing fermentation, as yeast; excitement, agitation. • *vti* to (cause to) undergo fermentation; to (cause to) be excited or agitated.—**fermentable** *adj*.—**fermenter** *n*.

fermentation /ˌfɜːment'eɪʃən/ *n* the breakdown of complex molecules in organic components caused by the influence of yeast or other substances.

fermentative /ˌfɜːmen'teɪtɪv/ *adj* of or pertaining to fermentation; capable of or causing fermentation.

fermion /'fɜːmiˌɒn/ *n* a type of subatomic particle.

fermium /'fɜːmiəm/ *n* an artificially-produced radioactive metallic element.

fern /fɜːn/ *n* any of a large class of nonflowering plants having roots, stems, and fronds, and reproducing by spores.—**ferny** *adj*.

fernery /'fɜːnərɪ/ *n* (*pl* **ferneries**) a place for growing ferns.

ferny /'fɜːnɪ/ *adj* (**fernier, ferniest**) full of ferns; of or characteristic of ferns.

ferocious /fə'rəʊʃəs/ *adj* savage, fierce.—**ferociously** *adv.*—**ferocity, ferociousness** *n*.

ferrate /'fereɪt/ *n* a salt of ferric acid.

ferret /'fɛrɛt/ n a variety of the polecat, used in unearthing rabbits. • vt to drive out of a hiding-place; (with out) to reveal by persistent investigation. • vi to hunt with ferrets.—**ferreter** n.—**ferrety** adj.

ferriage /'fɛrɪɪdʒ/ n the act of conveying by ferry; the fare paid for this.

ferric /'fɛrɪk/ adj of or containing iron.

ferriferous /'fɛrɪfərəs/ adj yielding iron.

Ferris wheel /'fɛrɪs/ n a large upright revolving wheel with suspended seats, popular in amusement parks.

ferroconcrete /,fɛro:'kɒŋkri:t/ n reinforced concrete.

ferrocyanic acid /,fɛrə'saɪænɪk-/ n an acid formed by the union of iron and cyanogen.

ferromagnetism /,fɛro:'mægnə,tɪzɒm/ n magnetism possessed by iron, and some other metals, which is retained even after the removal of the magnetizing field.—**ferromagnetic** adj.

ferromanganese /,fɛro:'mæŋgə,ni:z/ or /-ni:s/ n an alloy of iron and manganese.

ferrotype /'fɛro:təɪp/ n a photograph taken on a sensitized iron plate.

ferrous /'fɛrəs/ adj containing iron.

ferruginous /fə'ru:dʒɪnəs/ adj containing, or impregnated with, iron; rust-coloured, reddish brown.

ferrule /'fɛru:l/ n a metal ring or cap on a cane, umbrella, etc, to keep it from splitting.—also **ferule**.

ferry /'fɛri/ vt (**ferrying, ferried**) to convey (passengers, etc) over a stretch of water; to transport from one place to another, esp along a regular route. • n (pl **ferries**) a boat used for ferrying; a ferrying service; the location of a ferry.—**ferryman** n (pl **ferrymen**).

fertile /'fərtaɪl/ or /-təl/ adj able to bear offspring; (land) easily supporting plants and vegetation; (animals) capable of breeding; (eggs) able to grow and develop; prolific; (mind, brain) inventive.—**fertility, fertileness** n.

fertility /'fərtɪlɪti/ n the state or quality of being fertile.

fertilize /'fərtɪ,laɪz/ vt to make (soil) fertile by adding nutrients; to impregnate; to pollinate.—**fertilization** n.

fertilizer /'fərtɪ,laɪzər/ n natural organic or artificial substances used to enrich the soil.

ferula /'fərʊlə/ n (pl **ferulas, ferulae**) a genus of plants of the parsley family, from one of which asafoetida is produced.

ferule /'fəru:l/ see **ferrule**.

fervency /'fərvənsi/ n earnestness; ardour.

fervent /'fərvənt/, **fervid** /'fərvɪd/ adj passionate; zealous.—**fervently, fervidly** adv.—**fervency** n.

fervour, fervor /'fərvər/ n intensity of feeling; zeal; warmth.

fescue /'fɛskju:/ n a kind of grass, often grown for pasture and fodder.

fesse /fɛs/ n (her) a broad horizontal band across the middle of a shield.

festal /'fɛstəl/ adj of a feast or holiday; festive.—**festally** adv.

fester /'fɛstər/ vti to become or cause to become infected; to suppurate; to rankle.

festival /'fɛstɪvəl/ n a time of celebration; performances of music, plays, etc given periodically.

festive /'fɛstɪv/ adj merry, joyous.—**festively** adv.—**festiveness** n.

festivity /'fɛstɪvɪti/ n (pl **festivities**) a festive celebration.

festoon /fɛ'stu:n/ n a decorative garland of flowers, etc hung between two points. • vt to adorn as with festoons.—**festoonery** n.

feta /'fɛtə/ n a type of white goat's milk cheese, esp popular in Greece.

fetal /'fi:təl/ adj pertaining to the fetus.—also **foetal**.

fetch[1] /fɛtʃ/ vt to go for and bring back; to cause to come; (goods) to sell for (a certain price); (inf) to deal (a blow, slap, etc); (with up) to come to stand, arrive at; **fetch and carry** to run errands for another.—**fetcher** n.

fetch[2] n an apparition of a living person, a wraith; a person's double.

fetching /'fɛtʃɪŋ/ adj attractive.—**fetchingly** adv.

fête, fete /feɪt/ n a festival; a usu outdoor sale, bazaar or entertainment in aid of charity. • vt to honour or entertain (as if) with a fête.

fetial /'fi:ʃəl/ n (pl **fetiales**) a priestly herald in ancient Rome who performed rites accompanying a declaration of war or peace.

feticide /'fi:tɪ,saɪd/ n the destruction of a fetus in the womb.—also **foeticide**.

fetid /'fɛtɪd/ or /'fi:tɪd/ adj stinking.—also **foetid**.

fetish, fetich /'fɛtɪʃ/ n an object believed by primitive peoples to have magical properties; any object or activity regarded with excessive devotion.

fetishism, fetichism /'fɛtɪ,ʃɪzəm/ n the transfer of sexual desire to an inanimate object, or to some part of the body other than the sexual organs; worship of, or belief in, fetishes—**fetishist, fetichist** n.

fetlock /'fɛtlɒk/, **fetterlock** /-ər-/ n the joint on a horse's leg behind and above the hoof.

fetter /'fɛtər/ n (usu pl) a shackle for the feet; anything that restrains. • vt to put into fetters; to impede, restrain.—**fetterer** n.

fettle /'fɛtəl/ n good condition or repair.

fettucine, fettuccine, fettucini /fɛtu'tʃi:ni:/ n a kind of pasta cut in strips.

feud /fju:d/ n a state of hostilities, esp between individuals, families, or clans; a dispute.—also vi.

feudal /'fju:dəl/ adj pertaining to feudalism; (inf) old-fashioned, redundant.

feudalism /-,lɪzəm/ n the economic and social system in medieval Europe, in which land, worked by serfs, was held by vassals in exchange for military and other services to overlords.—**feudalist** n.—**feudalistic** adj.

feudality /-lɪti/ n (pl **feudalities**) the state of being feudal; a feudal estate.

feudalize /-,laɪz/ vt to make feudal.—**feudalization** n.

feudatory /'fju:də,tori/ adj pertaining to, or held by, feudal tenure.

feudist /fju:dɪst/ n someone taking part in a feud or argument.

feuilleton /,fəjə'tõ/, Fr. /fœjtõ/ n in France, etc, the section of a newspaper containing reviews, fiction, etc; an article in this; serialization in a newspaper.—**feuilletonist** n—**feuilletonistic** adj.

fever /'fi:vər/ n an abnormally increased body temperature; any disease marked by a high fever; a state of restless excitement.—**fevered** adj.

feverfew /'fi:vər,fju:/ n a perennial European herb, formerly used to reduce fevers.

feverish /'fi:vərɪʃ/, **feverous** /'fi:vərəs/ adj having a fever; indicating a fever; restlessly excited. **feverishly** adv. **feverishness** n.

few /fju:/ adj, n a small number, not many.—**fewness** n.

fey /feɪ/ adj strange and unusual.—**feyness** n.

fez /fɛz/ n (pl **fezzes**) a red brimless high cap, usu with black tassel, worn esp by men in eastern Mediterranean countries.

ff abbr = and the following pages; (mus) fortissimo—very loud.

fiacre /fɪ'ækr/ n a type of horse-drawn carriage.

fiancé /,fɪɒn'seɪ/ or /,fɪ'ɒnseɪ/, /-õ-/ n a person engaged to be married.—**fiancée** nf.

fiasco /fɪ'æsko:/ n (pl **fiascos, fiascoes**) a complete and humiliating failure.

fiat /fɪ'æt/ or /faɪ'æt/ n an order by authority; a decree.

fib /fɪb/ n a lie about something unimportant. • vi (**fibbing, fibbed**) to tell a gib.—**fibber** n.

fibre, fiber /'faɪbər/ n a natural or synthetic thread, eg from cotton or nylon, which is spun into yarn; a material composed of such yarn; texture; strength of character; a fibrous substance, roughage.—**fibred, fibered** adj.

fibreglass, fiberglass /-,glæs/ n glass in fibrous form, often bonded with plastic, used in making various products.

fibre optics, fiber optics /-,ɒptɪks/ n sing the transmission of information in the form of light signals along thin transparent fibres of glass.—**fibre-optic, fiber-optic** adj.

fibril /'faɪbrɪl/, **fibrilla** /-lə/ n (pl **fibrils, fibrillae**) a small fibre.—**fibrilar, fibrillar, fibrillose** adj.

fibrillation /,faɪbrɪ'leɪʃən/ n the rapid and irregular twitching of muscle fibres, esp in the heart.

fibrin /'faɪbrɪn/ n a white protein in the blood, which causes coagulation.

fibrinous /'faɪbrɪnəs/ adj composed of, or resembling, fibrin.

fibroid /'faɪbrɔɪd/ adj (anat) containing or resembling fibre. • n a benign tumour in the uterus.

fibroin /,faɪ'bro:ɪn/ n a protein that is the main constituent of silk and cobwebs.

fibroma /,faɪ'bro:mə/ n (pl **fibromata, fibromas**) a benign fibrous tumour.

fibrosis /,faɪ'bro:sɪs/ n the abnormal growth of fibrous tissue in an organ or part of the body.

fibrositis /ˌfaɪbrəˈsaɪtɪs/ *n* inflammation of fibrous tissues, *esp* muscles.

fibrous /ˈfaɪbrəs/ *adj* composed of fibres.—**fibrousness** *n*.

fibula /ˈfɪbjulə/ *n* (*pl* **fibulae, fibulas**) the outer of the two bones of the lower leg.—**fibular** *adj*.

fiche /fiːʃ/ *n* (*pl* **fiche**) a microfiche.

fichu /ˈfiːʃuː/ or /fiːˈʃuː/ *n* a woman's light three-cornered scarf worn over the neck and shoulders.

fickle /ˈfɪkəl/ *adj* inconstant; capricious.—**fickleness** *n*.

fictile /ˈfɪktaɪl/ *adj* moulded from clay; able to be moulded from clay.

fiction /ˈfɪkʃən/ *n* an invented story; any literary work with imaginary characters and events, as a novel, play, etc; such works collectively.—**fictional** *adj*.—**fictionally** *adv*.

fictitious /ˈfɪktɪʃəs/ *adj* imaginary, not real; feigned.—**fictitiously** *adv*.

fictive /ˈfɪktɪv/ *adj* pertaining to fiction; creating or created by the imagination.—**fictively** *adv*.

fid /ˈfɪd/ *n* (*naut*) an iron or wooden bar used to support a topmast; a pin used to open the strands of a rope.

fid. *abbr* = fidelity.

fiddle /ˈfɪdəl/ *n* (*inf*) a violin; (*sl*) a swindle. • *vt* (*inf*) to play on a violin; (*sl*) to swindle; to falsify. • *vi* to handle restlessly, to fidget.—**fiddler** *n*.

fiddle-de-dee /ˌfɪdəldiˈdiː/ *interj* an expression of incredulity or impatience.

fiddle-faddle /ˈfɪdəlˌfædəl/ *n* nonsense; trifles. • *vi* to fuss over unimportant matters.

fiddlehead /ˈfɪdəlˌhed/ *n* an ornament at the prow of a ship.

fiddler /ˈfɪdlər/ *n* one who fiddles; (*inf*) a violinist.

fiddlestick[1] /ˈfɪdəlstɪks/ *n* a bow for playing the violin.

fiddlesticks[2] *interj* nonsense!

fiddling /ˈfɪdlɪŋ/ *adj* trifling, petty.

fidelity /fɪˈdɛlɪti/ *n* (*pl* **fidelities**) faithfulness, loyalty; truthfulness; accuracy in reproducing sound.

fidget /ˈfɪdʒɪt/ *vi* to (cause to) move restlessly. • *n* nervous restlessness; a fussy person.—**fidgetingly** *adv*.—**fidgety** *adj*.

fiducial /ˈfɪduːʃəl/ or /fɪˈdjuː-/ *adj* (*physics*) taken as a standard of reference; based on trust or faith.—**fiducially** *adv*.

fiduciary /fɪˈduːʃəri/ or /fɪˈdjuː-/ *adj* of, held or given in trust; (*paper currency*) depending on public confidence for value. • *n* a trustee.

fie /faɪ/ *interj* for shame; an expression of disgust or dismay.

fief /fiːf/ *n* (*feudalism*) heritable land held by a vassal; an area in which one has control or influence.—*also* **feoff**.

field[1] /fiːld/ *n* an area of land cleared of trees and buildings, used for pasture or crops; an area rich in a natural product (*eg* gold, coal); a battlefield; a sports ground; an area affected by electrical, magnetic or gravitational influence, etc; the area visible through an optical lens; a division of activity, knowledge, etc; all competitors in a contest; (*comput*) a section of a record in a database. • *vt* (*cricket, baseball, etc*) to catch or stop and return the ball as a fielder; to put (*eg*. a team) into the field to play; (*inf*) to handle (*eg* questions) successfully.

field[2] *see* **fjeld**.

field day *n* a day of sports and athletic competition; (*inf*) any day of unusual happenings or success.

fielder /ˈfiːldər/ *n* (*cricket, baseball, etc*) a person who is not in the batting side, a person who fields.—*also* **fieldsman** (*pl* **fieldsmen**).

field event *n* (*usu pl*) an athletic competition involving jumping or throwing, as opposed to running.

fieldfare *n* a European thrush, which migrates to Britain for winter.

field glasses *npl* small, portable binoculars for use outdoors.

field hockey *n* an outdoor game played by two teams of 11 players with a ball and clubs curved at one end.—*also* **hockey**.

fieldmouse *n* a small, noctural mouse that lives in woods and fields.

fieldwork *n* research done outside the laboratory or place of work by scientists, archaeologists, social workers, etc.—**fieldworker** *n*.

fiend /fiːnd/ *n* an evil spirit; an inhumanly wicked person; (*inf*) an avid fan.—**fiendish** *adj*.—**fiendishly** *adv*.

fierce /fiːrs/ *adj* ferociously hostile; angry, violent; intense; strong, extreme.—**fiercely** *adv*.—**fierceness** *n*.

fiery /ˈfiːri/ *adj* (**fierier, fieriest**) like or consisting of fire; the colour of fire; intensely hot; spicy; passionate, ardent; impetuous; irascible.—**fierily** *adv*.—**fieriness** *n*.

fiesta /fiˈɛstə/ *n* a religious celebration, a festival, *esp* in Spain and Latin America.

fife /faɪf/ *n* a type of small flute with a shrill sound used *esp* in military music to accompany drums.—**fifer** *n*.

fife rail /ˈfaɪfreɪl/ *n* (*naut*) a rail round the mast holding belaying pins.

fifteen /fɪfˈtiːn/ or /ˈfɪf-/ *adj, n* one more than fourteen; the symbol for this (15, XV, xv); the first point scored by a side in a game of tennis; a rugby football team.—**fifteenth** *adj, n*.

fifth /fɪfθ/ *adj, n* last of five; (being) one of five equal parts; (*mus*) an interval of three tones and a semitone; a gear in a motor vehicle used when driving at speed.—**fifthly** *adv*.

fifth column *n* a subversive organization within a country, which is ready to give help to an enemy.—**fifth columnist** *n*.

fifty /ˈfɪfti/ *adj, n* (*pl* **fifties**) five times ten; the symbol for this (50, L, l).—**fiftieth** *adj*.

fifty-fifty /ˈfɪftiˈfɪfti/ *adj, adv* (*inf*) evenly, equally; (*chance*) an equal possibility of winning.

fig /fɪg/ *n* a tree yielding a soft, pear-shaped fruit; a thing of little or no importance.

fig. *abbr* = figure; figuratively.

fight /faɪt/ *vb* (**fighting, fought**) *vi* to engage in battle in war or in single combat; to strive, struggle (for). • *vt* to engage in or carry on a conflict with; to achieve (one's way) by fighting; to strive to overcome; (*with* **off**) to repel; to ward off or repress through effort. • *n* fighting; a struggle or conflict of any kind; a boxing match.—**fighting** *n*.

fighter /ˈfaɪtər/ *n* a person who fights; a person who does not yield easily; an aircraft designed to destroy enemy aircraft.

fighting chance *n* a small chance of success given supreme effort.

figment /ˈfɪgmənt/ *n* something imagined or invented.

figurant /ˈfɪgjurənt/ *n* a ballet dancer who performs as one of a group.—**figurante** *nf*.

figuration /ˌfɪgjuˈreɪʃən/ *n* the giving of form; representation; a figure, a shape; (*mus*) the use of florid counterpoint.

figurative /ˈfɪgjurətɪv/ or /-gər-/ *adj* metaphorical, not literal; using or full of figures of speech; emblematic; pictorial.—**figuratively** *adv*.

figure /ˈfɪgjuər/ or /ˈfɪgər/ *n* a character representing a number; a number; value or price; bodily shape or form; a graphic representation of a thing, person or animal; a design; a geometrical form; a statue; appearance; a personage; (*dancing, skating*) a set of steps or movements; (*pl*) arithmetic. • *vt* to represent in a diagram or outline; to imagine; (*inf*) to consider; (*inf*) to believe; (*with* **out**) (*inf*) to solve. • *vi* to take a part (in), be conspicuous (in); to calculate.—**figurer** *n*.

figured /-ərd/ *adj* depicted as a figure; adorned with figures.

figurehead /ˈfɪgjurˌhed/ or /ˈfɪgər-/ *n* a carved figure on the bow of a ship; a nominal head or leader.

figure of speech *n* an expression not intended to be taken literally, as a metaphor or simile.

figure skating *n* ice skating in which prescribed figures are outlined.

figurine /ˌfɪgjuˈriːn/ or /ˈfɪg-/ *n* a statuette.

filagree /ˈfɪləˌgriː/ *see* **filigree**.

filament /ˈfɪləmənt/ *n* a slender thread or strand; a fibre; the fine wire in an electric light bulb that is made incandescent by current; (*bot*) the anther-bearing stalk of a stamen.—**filamentary, filamentous** *adj*.

filar /ˈfaɪlər/ *adj* of or pertaining to thread; (*microscope, etc*) having fine threads in the eyepiece for measuring tiny distances.

filature /ˈfɪlətʃər/ *n* the reeling of silk from cocoons; a place where this is done.

filbert /ˈfɪlbərt/ *n* the edible nut of the cultivated hazel.

filch /fɪltʃ/ *vt* to steal (something of little value), to pilfer.—**filcher** *n*.

file[1] /faɪl/ *n* a container for keeping papers, etc, in order; an orderly arrangement of papers; a line of persons or things; (*comput*) a collection of related data under a specific name. • *vt* to dispatch or register; to put on public record. • *vi* to move in a line; to apply.—**filer** *n*.

file[2] *n* a tool, *usu* steel, with a rough surface for smoothing or grinding. • *vt* to cut or smooth with, or as with, a file; to polish, improve.—**filer** *n*.

filefish /ˈfaɪlˌfɪʃ/ *n* (*pl* **filefish, filefishes**) a tropical fish, of the family of triggerfish, with a narrow body and rough skin.

filester *see* **fillister**.

filet /fɪ'leɪ/ or /'fɪlət/ n a net with a square mesh.

filial /'fɪlɪəl/ adj of, or expected from, a son or daughter.—**filially** adv.—**filialness** n.

filiation /ˌfɪlɪ'eɪʃən/ n the relation of child to father; lineage, line of descent; the formation of branches of a society, etc; a branch so formed.

filibeg /'fɪlɪˌbeg/ n a kilt.—also **philabeg**.

filibuster /'fɪlɪˌbʌstər/ n a member of a legislature who obstructs a bill by making long speeches. • vti to obstruct (a bill) by such methods.—**filibusterer** n.

filiform /'fɪlɪˌfɔrm/ adj threadlike.

filigree /'fɪlɪˌgriː/ n a kind of lace-like ornamental work in precious metal. • vt (**filigreeing, filigreed**) to decorate with filigree.—also **filagree**.

filing /'faɪlɪŋ/ n a particle rubbed off with a file.

Filipino /ˌfɪlɪ'piːnoː/ n (pl **Filipinos**) a native or inhabitant of the Philippines.—also adj.

fill /fɪl/ vt to put as much as possible into; to occupy wholly; to put a person into (a position or job, etc); (US) to supply the things called for (in an order, etc); to close or plug (holes, etc); (with **in**) to complete (a form, design, etc) by writing or drawing; (inf) to provide with the latest news or facts; (with **out**) to make fuller or heavier; to fill in (a form, etc). • vi to become full; (with **in**) to act as a substitute for; (with **out**) to become fuller or heavier. • n enough to make full or to satisfy; anything that fills.

filler /'fɪlər/ n one who or that which fills; a substance used to plug a hole or increase the bulk of something.

fillet /'fɪlət/ or /fɪ'leɪ/ n a thin boneless strip of meat or fish; a ribbon, etc worn as a headband; (archit) a narrow band used between mouldings. • vt to bone and slice (fish or meat).

filling /'fɪlɪŋ/ n a substance used to fill a tooth cavity; the contents of a sandwich, pie, etc. • adj (meal, etc) substantial.

filling station n a place where petrol is sold to motorists, a service station.

fillip /'fɪlɪp/ n a blow with the nail of the finger; a stimulus.

fillister, filister /'fɪlɪstər/ n a plane used to cut grooves, rabbets, etc.—also **filester**.

filly /'fɪli/ n (pl **fillies**) a young female horse, usu less than four years.

film /fɪlm/ n a fine, thin skin, coating, etc; a flexible cellulose material covered with a light-sensitive substance used in photography; a haze or blur; a motion picture. • vti to cover or be covered as with a film; to photograph or make a film (of).—**filmic** adj.

film card see **microfiche**.

film star n a leading cinema actor or actress.

filmy /'fɪlmi/ adj (**filmier, filmiest**) gauzy, transparent; blurred, hazy.—**filmily** adv.—**filminess** n.

filose /'faɪloːs/ adj threadlike.

filter /'fɪltər/ n a device or substance straining out solid particles, impurities, etc, from a liquid or gas; a device for removing or minimizing electrical oscillations, or sound or light waves, of certain frequencies; a traffic signal at certain road junctions that allows vehicles to turn left or right while the main lights are red. • vti to pass through or as through a filter; to remove with a filter.—**filterable, filtrable** adj.

filter tip n the porous tip of a cigarette designed to reduce the intake of tar during smoking.—**filter-tipped** adj.

filth /fɪlθ/ n dirt; obscenity.

filthy /'fɪlθi/ adj (**filthier, filthiest**) dirty, disgusting; obscene; (inf) extremely unpleasant.—**filthily** adv.—**filthiness** n.

filtrate /'fɪltreɪt/ vt to filter. • n a liquid that has been filtered.—**filtration** n.

fimbriate /'fɪmbrɪˌeɪt/ **fimbriated** /-ɪd/ adj (bot) fringed.

fin /fɪn/ n an organ by which a fish, etc steers itself and swims; a rubber flipper used for underwater swimming; any fin-shaped object used as a stabilizer, as on an aircraft or rocket. • vb (**finning, finned**) vi (fish, whale. etc) to agitate the fins. • vt to furnish with fins.

finable, fineable /'faɪnˌæbəl/ adj liable to a fine.

finagle /fɪ'neɪgəl/ vt (inf) to obtain or achieve through cunning or deceit; to use trickery or deceit on someone.

final /'faɪnəl/ adj of or coming at the end; conclusive. • n (often pl) the last of a series of contests; a final examination.—**finally** adv.

finale /fɪ'næli/ n the concluding part of any public performance; the last section in a musical composition.

finalist /'faɪnəlɪst/ n a contestant in a final.

finality /faɪ'næliti/ or /fə-/ n (pl **finalities**) the state or quality of being final; completeness, conclusiveness.

finalize /'faɪnəˌlaɪz/ vt to make complete, to bring to an end.—**finalization** n.

finally /'faɪnəli/ or /'faɪnli/ adv at last; lastly; completely.

finance /'faɪˌnæns/ or /fɪ'næns/ n the management of money; (pl) money resources. • vt to supply or raise money for.

financial /faɪ'nænʃəl/ or /fɪ-/ adj of finance.—**financially** adv.

financier /faɪnæn'sɪːr/ or /ˌfɪ-/ n a person skilled in finance.

finback /'fɪnbæk/ n a whale with a prominent dorsal fin; the rorqual.

finch /fɪntʃ/ n any of numerous songbirds of the Fringillidae family.

find /faɪnd/ vb (**finding, found**) vt to discover by chance; to come upon by searching; to perceive; to recover (something lost); to reach, attain; to decide and declare to be; (with about) to discover; to solve; to detect in an offence. • vi to reach a decision (as by a jury). • n a discovery, something found.—**findable** adj.

finder /'faɪndər/ n one who or that which finds; a discoverer; a device for sighting the field of view of a camera, telescope, etc.

fin de siècle /ˌfædə'sjekl/ adj of or typical of the end of a century, esp the 19th century. • n the end of a century.

finding /'faɪndɪŋ/ n a discovery; the conclusion reached by a judicial enquiry.

fine[1] /faɪn/ adj very good; with no impurities, refined; (weather) clear and bright; not heavy or coarse; very thin or small; sharp; subtle; elegant. • adv in a fine manner; (inf) very well.—**finely** adv.—**fineness** n.

fine[2] n a sum of money imposed as a punishment. • vt to punish by a fine.—**finable, fineable** adj.

fine arts npl painting, sculpture, engraving, etc valued for their aesthetic qualities.

fine-draw /-drɔ/ vt (**fine-drawing, fine-drew**, pp **fine-drawn**) to sew up (a darn) so neatly that the join cannot be noticed; to draw out (wire) to an extreme fineness.—**fine-drawn** adj.

finely /'faɪnli/ adv in a fine manner; discriminatingly; subtly; in tiny pieces.

fineness /'faɪnnɪs/ n the state or quality of being fine; the quantity of pure metal contained in an alloy.

finery /'faɪnəri/ n (pl **fineries**) elaborate clothes, jewellery, etc.

finespun /'faɪnˌspʌn/ adj delicate, fine; over-subtle.

finesse /fɪ'nes/ n delicacy or subtlety of performance; skilfulness, diplomacy in handling a situation; (bridge) an attempt to take a trick with a card lower than a higher card held by an opponent. • vt to achieve by finesse; to play (a card) as a finesse.

fine-tooth(ed) comb /'faɪn'tuːθt/ n a comb with closely set fine teeth for trapping nits, etc.

fine-tune /-'tuːn/ or /-'tjuːn/ vt to make fine adjustments to something in order to improve its effectiveness.

finger /'fɪŋgər/ n one of the digits of the hand, usu excluding the thumb; anything shaped like a finger; (inf) the breadth of a finger. • vt to touch with fingers; (mus) to use the fingers in a certain way when playing; to mark this way on music; (sl) to inform against.—**fingerer** n.

fingerboard /-ˌbɔrd/ n the part of a violin, guitar, etc against which the strings are pressed by the fingers.

finger bowl n a small bowl containing water for rinsing the fingers at the table.

fingered /'fɪŋgərd/ adj marked by handling; having a finger or fingers; (mus) marked to show how the fingers are used.

fingering /'fɪŋgərɪŋ/ n the manner of using the fingers in playing a musical instrument; the indication of this in a musical score.

fingering[2] n a fine knitting yarn.

fingerling /'fɪŋgərlɪŋ/ n a young fish, esp a trout.

fingernail /-ˌneɪl/ n the nail on a finger.

fingerpost n a direction post in the shape of a pointing finger.

fingerprint /-prɪnt/ n the impression of the ridges on a fingertip, esp as used for purposes of identification.—also vt.

fingerstall /-ˌstɔl/ n a protective covering for a finger.

finial /'fɪnɪəl/ n (archit) a pointed ornament at the top of a spire, gable, etc.—**finialed** adj.

finical /'fɪnɪkəl/ adj fastidious, over-particular, fussy; affectedly fine.—**finicality** n.—**finically** adv.

finicky /'fɪnɪki/ **finicking** adj too particular, fussy.

fining /'faɪnɪŋ/ n the act or process of clarifying or refining; a liquid used to clarify wine, beer, etc.

finis /fɪ'niː/ or /'fɪnɪs/ n the end, used at the conclusion of books, films, etc.

finish /'fɪnɪʃ/ *vt* to bring to an end, to come to the end of; to consume entirely; to perfect; to give a desired surface effect to. • *vi* to come to an end. • *n* the last part, the end; anything used to finish a surface; the finished effect; means or manner of completing or perfecting; polished manners, speech, etc.—**finisher** *n*.

finishing school *n* a private school for girls which teaches social etiquette.

finite /'faɪnaɪt/ *adj* having definable limits; (*verb form*) having a distinct grammatical person and number.—**finitely** *adv*—**finiteness** *n*.

Finn /fɪn/ *n* a native of Finland.

finnan haddock, Finnan haddie /ˌfɪnən'hædi/ *n* a kind of smoked haddock, named after *Findon*, a Scottish fishing village.

finned /fɪnd/ *adj* having a fin or fins.

Finnish /'fɪnɪʃ/ *adj* of or relating to Finland or its language. • *n* the language of Finland.

finny /'fɪni/ *adj* (**finnier, finniest**) pertaining to, or abounding in, fish; having a fin or fins.

fino /'fiːnoː/ *n* (*pl* **finos**) a dry sherry.

fiord /fjɔrd/ *n see* **fjord**.

fir /fər/ *n* a kind of evergreen, cone-bearing tree; its timber.

fire /'faɪr/ *n* the flame, heat and light of combustion; something burning; burning fuel in a grate to heat a room; an electric or gas fire; a destructive burning; a strong feeling; a discharge of firearms. • *vti* to ignite; to supply with fuel; to bake (bricks, etc) in a kiln; to excite or become excited; to shoot (a gun, etc); to hurl or direct with force; to dismiss from a position.—**fireable** *adj*.—**firer** *n*.

fire alarm *n* a device that uses a bell, hooter, etc to warn of a fire.

firearm /'faɪrˌɑrm/ *n* a handgun.

fireball /-ˌbɒl/ *n* a ball of fire; a meteor; the hot gas cloud created by a nuclear explosion.

firebox /-ˌbɒks/ *n* the furnace in a steam locomotive.

firebrand /-ˌbrænd/ *n* a piece of burning wood; a person who starts trouble.

firebreak /'faɪrbreɪk/ *n* a strip of land cleared of vegetation to halt the spread of a fire.

firebrick /-brɪk/ *n* a brick made of fireclay to withstand the action of fire.

fire brigade *n* an organized body specially trained and equipped for fighting fires.

firebug /-ˌbʌg/ *n* (*inf*) an arsonist.

fireclay /-ˌkleɪ/ *n* a fire-resisting clay.

firecracker /-ˌkrækər/ *n* a small explosive firework.

firedamp /-ˌdæmp/ *n* a combustible mine gas, chiefly methane.

firedog /-ˌdɒg/ *n* a metal standard used for open fires to support the logs; andirons.

fire-eater /-ˌitɔr/ *n* a performer who pretends to eat fire; a quarrelsome person.—**fire-eating** *adj*, *n*.

fire engine *n* a vehicle equipped for fire-fighting.

fire escape *n* a means of exit from a building, *esp* a stairway, for use in case of fire.

fire extinguisher *n* a container with a spray nozzle, holding water or chemicals for putting out a fire

firefighter /-ˌfaɪtər/ *n* a person who fights fires, *esp* a member of a fire department; fireman.

firefly /-ˌflaɪ/ *n* (*pl* **fireflies**) a winged nocturnal beetle whose abdomen glows with a soft intermittent light.

fireguard /-ˌgɑrd/ *n* a protective grating placed in frontof a fire.

fire insurance *n* insurance against loss by fire.

fire irons *npl* tools for tending a domestic fire, *esp* a poker, tongs, and shovel.

firelighter /-ˌlaɪtər/ *n* a prepared block of ignitable material used for lighting a fire.

firelock /-ˌlɒk/ *n* a flintlock.

fireman /-mən/ *n* (*pl* **firemen**) a member of a fire brigade; firefighter; a person employed to tend furnaces.

fireplace /'faɪrˌpleɪs/ *n* a place for a fire, *esp* a recess in a wall; the area surrounding this.

fireplug /-ˌplʌg/ *n* a connection in a water main for a hose; a hydrant.

fire power /-ˈpaʊər/ *n* the amount of fire that a military unit can deliver on a target.

fireproof /-ˌpruːf/ *adj* not easily destroyed by fire. • *vt* to make fireproof.

fire raiser *n* an arsonist.—**fire raising** *n*.

firescreen /-skriːn/ *n* a movable ornamental screen for keeping the heat of a fire off the face; a screen for decorating an empty fireplace.

fireship /-ʃɪp/ *n* a ship filled with explosives to set an enemy's ships on fire.

fireside /-ˌsaɪd/ *n* the area in a room nearest the fireplace; home.

fire station *n* a building where firemen and fire-fighting equipment are based.—*also* **firehouse, station house**.

firetrap /-ˌtræp/ *n* a building easily set on fire or hard to get out of if on fire.

firewarden /-wɔrdən/ *n* an officer responsible for protecting forests against fire.

firewater /-wɒtər/ *n* (*inf*) strong alcoholic drink.

firewood /-ˌwʊd/ *n* wood for fuel.

firework /-ˌwɔrk/ *n* a device packed with explosive and combustible material used to produce noisy and colourful displays; (*pl*) such a display; (*pl*) a fit of temper, an outburst of emotions.

firing /'faɪrɪŋ/ *n* baking in intense heat, *esp* of clay; fuel; the act of discharging a firearm; the act of adding fuel to a fire.

firing line *n* the front line of a military position; the forefront of any activity.

firing squad *n* a detachment with the task of firing a salute at a military funeral or carrying out an execution.

firkin /'fɔrkɪn/ *n* a small wooden barrel containing butter, etc; (*Brit*) a measure of one quarter of a barrel (41 litres/9 gallons).

firm[1] /fɔrm/ *adj* securely fixed; solid, compact; steady; resolute; definite. • *vti* to make or become firm.—**firmly** *adv*.—**firmness** *n*.

firm[2] *n* a business partnership; a commercial company.

firmament /'fɔrməmənt/ *n* the sky, viewed poetically as a solid arch or vault.—**firmamental** *adj*.

first /fɔrst/ *adj* before all others in a series; 1st; earliest; foremost, as in rank, quality, etc. • *adv* before anyone or anything else; for the first time; sooner. • *n* any person or thing that is first; the beginning; the winning place, as in a race; low gear; the highest award in a university degree.

first aid /-ˈeɪd/ *n* emergency treatment for an injury, etc, before regular medical aid is available.

first-born /'fɔrstˌbɔrn/ *or* /-ˈbɔrn/ *adj* eldest. • *n* the eldest child in a family.

first-class /-ˈklæs/ *adj* of the highest quality, as in accommodation, travel. • *n* the best accommodation on a plane, train, etc; the highest class in an examination, etc.

first-degree burn /'fɔrstdɪ'gri/ *n* (*med*) a mild burn causing a painful reddening of the skin but no blistering or charring.

first fruits *npl* fruit which is the first to ripen; the earliest returns or results from an enterprise.

firsthand /'fɔrst'hænd/ *adj* obtained directly from a source.

First Lady *n* the wife of the US president.

firstling /'fɔrstlɪŋ/ *n* the first offspring.

firstly /'fɔrstli/ *adv* in the first place.

First Minister *n* the chief minister of the Northern Ireland Assembly; the chief minister of the Scottish Assembly.

first night *n* the opening performance of a play.

first person *n* (*gram*) pronouns and verbs referring to the person speaking.

first-rate /'fɔrst'reɪt/ *adj, adv* of the best quality; (*inf*) excellent.

firth /fɔrθ/ *n* an arm of the sea, *esp* a river mouth.—*also* **frith**.

fiscal /'fɪskəl/ *adj* of or relating to public revenue; financial. • *n* a prosecuting official in some countries.

fish[1] /fɪʃ/ *n* (*pl* **fish, fishes**) any of a large group of cold-blooded animals living in water, having backbones, gills for breathing and fins; the flesh of fish used as food. • *vi* to catch or try to catch fish; (*with* **for**) to try to obtain by roundabout methods. • *vt* (*often with* **out**) to grope for, find, and bring to view.—**fishable** *adj*.

fish[2] *n* a rigid strip of wood or metal used to strengthen a mast, joint, etc. • *vt* to strengthen or join with a fish.

fish-eye lens /'fɪʃˌaɪ/ *n* a wide-angled lens with a curved protruding front.

fisher /'fɪʃər/ *n* a person who fishes; (*zool*) another name for the pekan, a marten found in North America.

fisherman /'fɪʃərmən/ *n* (*pl* **fishermen**) a person who fishes for sport or for a living; a ship used in fishing.

fishery /'fɪʃəri/ *n* (*pl* **fisheries**) the fishing industry; an area where fish are caught.

fishfinger *n* a small oblong piece of fish covered in breadcrumbs.—*also* **fish stick**.

fishing /'fɪʃɪŋ/ n the art, sport or business of catching fish.

fishing rod n a wooden, metal or fibreglass rod used with a line to catch fish.

fish meal n granules of dried fish used as fertilizer and food for livestock.

fishmonger /'fɪʃˌmʌŋɡər/ or /-mɛŋ-/ n a shop that sells fish.

fishnet /'fɪʃnɛt/ n a coarse open-mesh fabric.—*also adj.*

fishplate /'fɪʃˌpleɪt/ n an iron plate, one of a pair used to join railway rails.

fishpond /'fɪʃˌpɒnd/ n a pond in which fish are kept.

fish stick *see* **fishfinger.**

fishwife /'fɪʃwaɪf/ n (pl **fishwives**) a woman who guts or sells fish; a coarse, scolding woman.

fishy /'fɪʃi/ adj (**fishier, fishiest**) like a fish in odour, taste, etc; (*inf*) creating doubt or suspicion.—**fishily** adv.—**fishiness** n.

fissile /'fɪsaɪl/ adj capable of undergoing nuclear fission; easily split.—**fissility** n.

fission /'fɪʃən/ n a split or cleavage; the reproductive division of biological cells; the splitting of the atomic nucleus resulting in the release of energy, nuclear fission.—**fissionable** adj.

fissiparous /fɪ'sɪpərəs/ adj reproducing, multiplying or propagating by fission.

fissiped /'fɪsɪˌped/, **fissipedal** adj (*zool*) having the toes separated, *eg* dogs, cats, etc.

fissirostral /ˌfɪsɪ'rɒstrəl/ adj (*birds*) with a deeply cleft beak, *eg* swallows.

fissure /'fɪʃər/ n a narrow opening or cleft, esp in a rock. • *vti* to crack or split apart.

fist /fɪst/ n the hand when tightly closed or clenched.

fistic /'fɪstɪk/ adj (*joc*) of or pertaining to boxing.

fisticuffs /'fɪstɪˌkʌfs/ npl a fight with the fists.

fistula /'fɪstjʊlə/ n (pl **fistulas, fistulae**) an abnormal passage, as from an abscess to the skin.

fistulous /-ləs/ adj resembling a fistula; hollow, like a pipe.

fit[1] /fɪt/ adj (**fitter, fittest**) suited to some purpose, function, etc; proper, right; healthy; (*sl*) inclined, ready. • *n* the manner of fitting. • *vb* (**fitting, fitted**) *vt* to be suitable to; to be the proper size, shape, etc, for; to adjust so as to fit; (*with* **out**) to equip, to outfit. • *vi* to be suitable or proper; to have the proper size or shape.—**fittable** adj.—**fitly** adv.—**fitness** n.

fit[2] n any sudden, uncontrollable attack, as of coughing; an outburst, as of anger; a short period of impulsive activity; a seizure involving convulsions or loss of consciousness.

fitch /fɪtʃ/ n the polecat; the hair of a polecat; a brush made of this.

fitful /'fɪtful/ adj marked by intermittent activity; spasmodic.—**fitfully** adv.—**fitfulness** n.

fitment /'fɪtmənt/ n a piece of equipment, *esp* fixed furniture.

fitter /'fɪtər/ n a person who specializes in fitting clothes; a person skilled in the assembly and operation of a particular piece of machinery.

fitting /'fɪtɪŋ/ adj appropriate; suitable, right. • *n* an act of one that fits, *esp* a trying on of altered clothes; a small often standardized electrical part.—**fittingly** adv.—**fittingness** n.

five /faɪv/ adj, n one more than four; the symbol for this (5, V, v).

fivefold /'faɪvfoːld/ adj, adv having five units or members; being five times as great or as many.

fiver /'faɪvər/ n (*inf*) in UK, a £5 note; in US, a $5 bill.

fives /faɪvz/ n sing a ball game similar to squash, played in a walled court.

fix /fɪks/ vt to fasten firmly; to set firmly in the mind; to direct (one's eyes) steadily at something; to make rigid; to make permanent; to establish (a date, etc) definitely; to set in order; to repair; to prepare (food or meals); (*inf*) to influence the result or action of (a race, jury, etc) by bribery; (*inf*) to punish. • *vi* to become fixed; (*inf*) to prepare or intend. • *n* the position of a ship, etc, determined from the bearings of two known positions; (*inf*) a predicament; (*inf*) a situation that has been fixed; (*inf*) something whose supply becomes continually necessary or greatly desired, as a drug, entertainment, activity, etc.—**fixable** adj.

fixated /fɪk'seɪtɪd/ adj having a fixation.

fixation /fɪk'seɪʃən/ n a fixing; (*psychol*) an unhealthy obsession, *esp* one leading to arrested emotional development.

fixative /'fɪksətɪv/ n a substance used to fix things in position; a substance that prevents (colours, perfumes, etc) fading or evaporating.

fixed /fɪkst/ adj firm; not moving; lasting; intent.—**fixedly** adv.—**fixedness** n.

fixer /'fɪksər/ n a chemical that fixes photographs, making the image permanent; (*sl*) a person who fixes something, *esp* by illegal means.

fixings /'fɪksɪŋz/ npl trimmings.

fixity /'fɪksɪti/ n (pl **fixities**) the state of being fixed; stability; permanence.

fixture /'fɪkstʃər/ n what is fixed to anything, as to land or to a house; a fixed article of furniture; a firmly established person or thing; a fixed or appointed time or event.

fizz /fɪz/ vi to make a hissing or sputtering sound. • *n* this sound; any effervescent drink.—**fizzy** adj.—**fizziness** n.

fizzle /'fɪzəl/ vi to make a weak fizzing sound; (*with* **out**) (*inf*) to end feebly, die out, *esp* after a promising start.

fjeld /fjɛld/ or /fjɛl/ n in Scandinavia, a high, barren plateau.—*also* **field.**

fjord /fiːˈɔːrd/ or /fjɔːrd/ or /'fiːɔːrd/ n a long, narrow inlet of the sea between high cliffs, *esp* in Norway.—*also* **fiord.**

FL abbr = Flight Lieutenant.

fl. abbr = fluid; floor; *floruit* (flourished).

flab /flæb/ n (*inf*) fat.

flabbergast /'flæbərˌɡæst/ vt (*inf*) to astonish, startle.

flabby /'flæbi/ adj (**flabbier, flabbiest**) fat and soft; weak and ineffective.—**flabbily** adv.—**flabbiness** n.

flabellate /fləˈbɛlˌeɪt/ or /-ɪt/, **flabelliform** /-ɪˌfɔrm/ adj (*bot*) fan-shaped.

flabellum /fləˈbɛləm/ n (pl **flabella**) (*RC*) a large fan.

flaccid /'flæsɪd/ or /'flæksɪd/ adj not firm or stiff; limp, weak.—**flaccidity** n.

flack /flæk/ *see* **flak.**

flacon /'flækən/, *Fr.* /flaˈkõː/ n a small bottle or flask.

flag[1] /flæɡ/ vi (**flagging, flagged**) to grow limp; to become weak, listless.

flag[2] n a piece of cloth, *usu* with a design, used to show nationality, party, a particular branch of the armed forces, etc, or as a signal. • *vt* (**flagging, flagged**) to decorate with flags; to signal to (as if) with a flag; (*usu with* **down**) to signal to stop.

flag[3] n a hard, flat stone used for paving, a flagstone. • *vt* (**flagging, flagged**) to pave with flagstones.

flag[4] n a plant with a sword-shaped leaf, the iris; a long thin plant blade.

flag day n a day on which charitable donations are solicited in exchange for small flags; (*with caps*) in US, 14 June, the anniversary of the adoption of the stars and stripes, 1777.

flagellant /'flædʒələnt/ or /fləˈdʒɛlənt/ n a person who scourges himself or herself or others as a sign of religious penance or for sexual gratification.—**flagellantism** n.

flagellate /'flædʒəˌleɪt/ vt to scourge, to whip.—**flagellation** n.—**flagellator** n..

flagelliform /fləˈdʒɛlɪˌfɔrm/ adj long, tapering and flexible; shaped like the thong of a whip.

flagellum /fləˈdʒɛləm/ n (pl **flagella, flagellums**) (*biol, zool*) a whiplike appendage; (*bot*) a runner.

flageolet[1] /ˌflædʒəˈlɛt/ or /'flædʒ-/ or /ˌflædʒəˈleɪ/ n a small flute resembling the treble recorder.

flageolet[2] n a type of edible bean.

flagging /'flæɡɪŋ/ n a pavement of flagstones.

flagitious /fləˈdʒɪʃəs/ adj atrocious, abominably wicked.—**flagitiously** adv.—**flagitiousness** n.

flag of convenience n a flag of a country flown by a ship registered there by the owners to benefit from less rigorous taxes or safety regulations.

flagon /'flæɡən/ n a pottery or metal container for liquids with a handle and spout and often a lid.

flagrant /'fleɪɡrənt/ adj conspicuous, notorious.—**flagrancy, flagrance** n.—**flagrantly** adv.

flagrante delicto /fləˈɡræntidiˈlɪkˌtoː/ adv in the very act, red-handed.

flagrante delicto *see* **in flagrante delicto.**

flagship /'flæɡʃɪp/ n the ship that carries the admiral and his flag; the most important vessel of a shipping line; the chief or leading item of a group or collection.

flagstaff /'flægstæf/, **flagpole** /'flægpoːl/ *n* a pole on which a flag is displayed.

flagstone /'flægstoːn/ *n* hard, evenly stratified rock easily split into slabs for paving.

flag-waver /'flæg,weɪvər/ *n* an excessively patriotic person, a jingoist.

flail /fleɪl/ *n* a tool for threshing by hand. • *vt* to beat with a flail. • *vi* (*usu with* **about**) to wave (the arms, etc) wildly.

flair /fleɪr/ *n* natural ability, aptitude; discernment; (*inf*) stylishness, sophistication.

flak /flæk/ *n* shells fired by anti-aircraft guns; criticism, opposition.—*also* **flack**.

flake /fleɪk/ *n* a small piece of snow; a small thin layer chipped from a larger mass of something. • *vt* to form into flakes. • *vi* (*with* **out**) (*inf*) to collapse or fall asleep from exhaustion.—**flaker** *n*.

flaky /'fleɪki/ *adj* (**flakier, flakiest**) of or resembling flakes; liable to flake; (*sl*) nervous; (*sl*) odd, eccentric.—**flakily** *adv*.—**flakiness** *n*.

flam /flæm/ *vt* (**flamming, flammed**) (*dial*) to deceive.

flambé, flambée /'flɒmbeɪ/ *or* /flɒm'beɪ/, /flæm-/ *adj* (*food*) covered with flaming brandy or other spirit.—*also vt*.

flambeau /'flæmboː/ *n* (*pl* **flambeaux, flambeaus**) a lighted, flaming torch; a large ornamental candlestick.

flamboyant /flæm'bɔɪənt/ *adj* brilliantly coloured; ornate; strikingly elaborate; dashing, exuberant.—**flamboyance, flamboyancy** *n*.—**flamboyantly** *adv*.

flame /fleɪm/ *n* the burning gas of a fire, appearing as a tongue of light; the state of burning with a blaze; a thing like a flame; an intense emotion; (*inf*) a sweetheart. • *vi* to burst into flame; to become bright red with emotion.

flamen /'fleɪmən/ *n* (*pl* **flamens, flamines**) in ancient Rome, a priest devoted to the service of a special deity.

flamenco /flə'mɛnkoː/ *n* (*pl* **flamencos**) a type of vigorous Spanish dance and music of gipsy origin.

flame-thrower /-,θroːər/ *n* a weapon that shoots a jet of flaming liquid.

flaming /'fleɪmɪŋ/ *adj* emitting flames; very hot; gaudy; exaggerated; intense.—**flamingly** *adv*.

flamingo /flə'mɪŋ,goː/ *n* (*pl* **flamingos, flamingoes**) any of several wading birds with rosy-pink plumage and long legs and neck.

flammable /'flæməbəl/ *adj* liable to catch fire; easily set on fire.—**flammability** *n*.

flamy /-i/ *adj* (**flamier, flamiest**) resembling flame; flame-coloured.

flan /flæn/ *n* an open case of pastry or sponge cake with a sweet or savoury filling.

flânerie *Fr.* /flɑn'ʀi/ *or* /flɑnə-/ *n* idleness.

flâneur *Fr.* /flɑ'nœr/ *n* an idle person, a lounger.

flange /flændʒ/ *n* a raised edge, as on a wheel rim to keep it on a rail; a projecting rib. • *vt* to provide with a flange.—**flanged** *adj*.

flank /flæŋk/ *n* the fleshy part of the side from the ribs to the hip; the side of anything; the right or left side of a formation of troops. • *vt* to attack the flank of; to skirt the side of; to be situated at the side of.

flanker /'flæŋkər/ *n* (*mil*) a soldier or fortification used to protect a flank.

flannel /'flænəl/ *n* a soft light cotton or woollen cloth; a small cloth for washing the face and hands; (*sl*) nonsense, equivocation; (*pl*) trousers of such cloth. • *vt* (**flannelling, flannelled** *or* **flanneling, flanneled**) to wash with a flannel; (*inf*) to flatter.—**flannelly** *adj*.

flannelette /,flænə'lɛt/ *n* a soft cotton fabric.

flap /flæp/ *vi* (**flapping, flapped**) to move up and down, as wings; to sway loosely and noisily, as curtains in the wind, etc; to move or hang like a flap; (*inf*) to get into a panic or fluster. • *n* the motion or noise of a flap; anything broad and flexible, either hinged or hanging loose; a light blow with a flat object; (*inf*) agitation, panic.

flapdoodle /'flæp'duːdəl/ *n* (*inf*) nonsense.

flapjack /'flæpdʒæk/ *n* a chewy cake made with oats and syrup; a kind of pancake.

flapper /'flæpər/ *n* someone who, or something which, flaps; (*inf*) a fashionable young woman of the 1920s often of unconventional dress and behaviour.

flare /fleɪr/ *vi* to burn with a sudden, bright, unsteady flame; to burst into emotion, *esp* anger; to widen out gradually. • *n* an unsteady flame; a sudden flash; a bright light used as a signal or illumination; a widened part or shape.

flare-up /-,ʌp/ *n* a sudden burst of fire; (*inf*) a sudden burst of emotion.

flash /flæʃ/ *n* a sudden, brief light; a brief moment; a sudden brief display; (*TV, radio*) a sudden brief news item about an important event; (*photog*) a device for producing a brief intense light; a sudden onrush of water; **flash in the pan** a misfire; a showy start not followed up. • *vi* to send out a sudden, brief light; to sparkle; to come or pass suddenly; (*sl*) to expose the genitals indecently. • *vt* to cause to flash; to send (news, etc) swiftly; (*inf*) to show off. • *adj* (*inf*) flashy.—**flasher** *n*.

flashback /'flæʃbæk/ *n* an interruption in the continuity of a story, etc, by telling or showing an earlier episode.

flashboard /-,bɔrd/ *n* a board placed on a dam to increase its height and hence the depth of the water contained.

flashbulb /-,bʌlb/ *n* a small bulb giving an intense light used in photography.

flash flood *n* a sudden brief flood caused by a heavy rainfall.

flash gun *n* (*photog*) a device for holding and operating a flashbulb.

flashing /'flæʃɪŋ/ *n* a piece of lead or other metal, used to keep a roof watertight.

flashlight /'flæʃlaɪt/ *n* an electric torch; a flash of electric light used to take photographs in dark conditions.

flashpoint /'flæʃpɔɪnt/ *n* the lowest temperature at which vapour, as from oil, will ignite with a flash; the point where a situation will erupt into violence.

flashy /'flæʃi/ *adj* (**flashier, flashiest**) pretentious; showy, gaudy.—**flashily** *adv*.—**flashiness** *n*.

flask /flæsk/ *n* a slim-necked bottle; a vacuum flask.

flasket /'flæskɪt/ *n* a small flask; a long, shallow basket.

flat /flæt/ *adj* (**flatter, flattest**) having a smooth level surface; lying spread out; broad, even, and thin; not fluctuating; (*tyre*) deflated; dull, tedious; (*drink*) not fizzy; (*battery*) drained of electric current. • *adv* in a flat manner or position; exactly; (*mus*) below true pitch. • *n* anything flat, *esp* a surface, part, or expanse; a flat tyre; a set of rooms on one floor of a building.—*also* **apartment**.—**flatly** *adv*.—**flatness** *n*.

flatcar /-,kɑr/ *n* an open, sideless rail truck.

flatfish /-,fɪʃ/ *n* (*pl* **flatfish, flatfishes**) any of an order of marine fishes that as adults have both eyes on one side.

flatfoot /-,fʊt/ *n* (*pl* **flatfeet, flatfoots**) a condition in which the arch of the instep is flattened; (*sl*) a policeman.

flat-footed /-,fʊtɪd/ *adj* having flatfoot; (*inf*) awkward; (*inf*) unprepared; (*inf*) determined, blunt.—**flat-footedly** *adv*.—**flat-footedness** *n*.

flatiron /'flæt,aɪrn/ *n* an iron used for clothes, linen, etc, heated by being placed upon a hot stove, etc.

flat spin *n* a spin or manoeuvre in which an aircraft is more horizontal than vertical; (*inf*) a confused or agitated state.

flatten /'flætən/ *vti* to make or become flat.—**flattener** *n*.

flatter /'flætər/ *vt* to praise excessively or insincerely, *esp* out of self-interest or to win favour; to display to advantage; to represent as more attractive, etc than reality; to gratify the vanity of; to encourage falsely.—**flatterer** *n*.—**flattering** *adj*.—**flatteringly** *adv*.

flattery /'flætəri/ *n* (*pl* **flatteries**) compliments; insincere praise.

flattie /'flæti/ *n* (*inf*) a woman's shoe with a flat heel.

flatting /-ɪŋ/ *n* (*metallurgy*) the process of rolling metal into flat sheets.

flatulence, flatulency /'flætjʊləns/ *n* wind in the stomach; windiness, verbosity; pomposity.

flatulent /'flætjʊlənt/ *adj* causing or affected with intestinal gas; pretentious, vain.—**flatulently** *adv*.

flatways, flatwise /-,waɪz/ *adv* flat side downwards.

flatworm /-,wɜrm/ *n* any of various parasitic worms having a flattened body.

flaunt /flɒnt/ *vi* to move or behave ostentatiously; (*flag*) to wave in the wind. • *vt* to display.—**flaunter** *n*.—**flauntingly** *adv*.

flaunty /'flɒnti/ *adj* (**flauntier, flauntiest**) inclined to flaunting.

flautist /'flɒtɪst/ *or* /'flaʊ-/ *n* a flute player.—*also* **flutist**.

flavescent /flə'vesənt/ *adj* turning yellow; yellowish.

flavin, flavine /'fleɪvɪn/ *n* a yellow dye and antiseptic.

flavorous /'fleɪvərəs/ *adj* tasty.

flavour, flavor /'fleɪvər/ n the taste of something in the mouth; a characteristic quality. • vt to give flavour to.—**flavourer, flavorer** n.—**flavoursome, flavorsome** adj.

flavouring, flavoring /-ɪŋ/ n any substance used to give flavour to food.

flaw /flɔː/ n a defect; a crack. • vti to make or become flawed.

flaw[2] n a gust of wind, a squall.

flawless adj perfect.—**flawlessly** adv.—**flawlessness** n.

flax /flæks/ n a blue-flowered plant cultivated for its fibre and seed; the fibre of this plant.

flaxen /'flæksən/, **flaxy** /-si/ adj made of flax; pale yellow.

flaxseed /'flæksiːd/ n the seed of the flax plant, from which linseed oil is obtained.

flay /fleɪ/ vt to strip off the skin; to berate, criticize severely.—**flayer** n.

flea /fliː/ n a small wingless jumping bloodsucking insect.

fleabane /-beɪn/ n a plant of the aster family.

fleabite /-baɪt/ n the bite of a flea; a minor inconvenience.

fleabitten /-bɪtn/ adj marked with fleabites; (inf) shabby, wretched; (horses) flecked with red spots on a light ground.

fleam /fliːm/ n a lancet used for bleeding cattle.

flea market n an open-air street market, usu selling second-hand articles.

fleapit /'fliːpɪt/ n (inf) a shabby cinema or theatre.

flèche /fleʃ/ or /fleɪʃ/ n (archit) a slender spire, esp at the intersection of the nave and transept.

fleck /flek/ n a spot or speckle of colour; a tiny particle. • vt to mark with flecks.

flection /'flekʃən/ see **flexion**.

fled /fled/ see **flee**.

fledge /fledʒ/ vt (birds) to rear until ready to fly; to cover or provide with feathers, esp an arrow.

fledgling, fledgeling /'fledʒlɪŋ/ n a young bird just fledged; an inexperienced person, a trainee.

flee /fliː/ vti (**fleeing, fled**) to run away from danger, etc; to pass away quickly, to disappear.—**fleer** n.

fleece /fliːs/ n the woollen coat of sheep or similar animal. • vt to remove wool from; to defraud.

fleecy /'fliːsi/ adj (**fleecier, fleeciest**) like a fleece, woolly.—**fleecily** adv.—**fleeciness** n.

fleer /'fliːr/ n a derisive look, sneer. • vti to sneer (at), to mock.

fleet[1] /fliːt/ n a number of warships under one command; (often with cap) a country's navy; any group of cars, ships, buses, etc, under one control.

fleet[2] adj swift moving; nimble.—**fleetly** adv.—**fleetness** n.

fleeting /'fliːtɪŋ/ adj brief, transient.—**fleetingly** adv.

Fleming /'flemɪŋ/ n a native or inhabitant of Flanders.

Flemish /'flemɪʃ/ adj of the people of Flanders, or their language.

flense /flens/, **flench** /flentʃ/ vt (whale, seal) to strip blubber from.

flesh /fleʃ/ n the soft substance of the body, esp the muscular tissue; the pulpy part of fruits and vegetables; meat; the body as distinct from the soul; all mankind; a yellowish-pink colour. • vt (usu with out) to give substance to.

fleshings /'fleʃɪŋz/ npl flesh-coloured tights.

fleshly /'fleʃli/ adj (**fleshlier, fleshliest**) having to do with the body and its desires, material, sensual.—**fleshliness** n.

flesh wound n a superficial wound.

fleshy /'fleʃi/ adj (**fleshier, fleshiest**) of or resembling flesh; plump; succulent; sensual.—**fleshiness** n.

fleur-de-lis /ˌflɜːrdə'liː/, **fleur-de-lys** /-'liːs/ n (pl **fleurs-de-lis, fleurs-de-lys**) a heraldic lily, the emblem of France.

fleury /'flɜːri/ adj (her) decorated with a fleur-de-lis.—also **flory**.

flew /fluː/ see **fly**.

flews /fluːz/ npl the pendulous lips of a bloodhound, etc.

flex /fleks/ vti to bend (a limb or joint, etc); to contract (a muscle). • n an insulated cable used to connect electric appliances to the mains.—also **cord**.

flexible /'fleksɪbəl/ adj easily bent, pliable; adaptable; versatile; docile.—**flexibility** n.—**flexibly** adv.

flexile /'fleksɪl/ adj supple; docile; flexible.—**flexility** n.

flexion /'flekʃən/ n the act or process of bending; a curve; (gram) an inflection.—also **flection**.

flexitime, flextime /'fleksˌtaɪm/ n the staggering of working hours to enable each employee to work the full quota of time but at periods most convenient for the individual.

flexor /'fleksər/ n a muscle that acts to bend a joint or limb.

flexuous, flexose /'fleksjuəs/ adj winding, sinuous; unsteady.—**flexuosity** n.

flexure /'flekʃər/ n the act of bending; the state of being bent; (math) the curving of a line or surface.—**flexural** adj.

flibbertigibbet /'flɪbərtiˌdʒɪbət/ n an impish, flighty or gossipy person.

flick /flɪk/ n a light stroke or blow; (inf) a cinema film. • vt to strike or propel with a flick; a flicking movement.

flicker /'flɪkər/ vi to burn unsteadily, as a flame; to move quickly to and fro. • n a flickering moment of light or flame; a flickering movement.—**flickeringly** adv.—**flickery** adj.

flick knife /-naɪf/ n a knife with a retractable blade released by pressing a button.

flier /'flaɪər/ see **flyer**.

flies see **fly**.

flight[1] /flaɪt/ n the act, manner, or power of flying; distance flown; a group of creatures or things flying together; an aircraft scheduled to fly a certain trip; a trip by aircraft; a set of stairs, as between landings; a mental act of soaring beyond the ordinary; a set of feathers on a dart or arrow.

flight[2] n an act or instance of fleeing.

flight-deck n the cockpit of an aircraft.

flightless /'flaɪtləs/ adj (birds, insects) incapable of flying.

flight recorder n a device that records information about the flight performance of an aircraft.

flighty /'flaɪti/ adj (**flightier, flightiest**) irresponsible, capricious, frivolous.—**flightily** adv.—**flightiness** n.

flimflam /'flɪmflæm/ vt (**flimflamming, flimflammed**) to deceive. • n nonsense; a trick.

flimsy /'flɪmzi/ adj (**flimsier, flimsiest**) weak, insubstantial; light and thin; (excuse etc) unconvincing. • n (pl **flimsies**) thin paper; copy written on this.—**flimsily** adv.—**flimsiness** n.

flinch /flɪntʃ/ vi to draw back, as from pain or fear; to wince.—**flincher** n.—**flinchingly** adv.

flinders /'flɪndərz/ npl fragments.

fling /flɪŋ/ vb (**flinging, flung**) vt to cast, throw aside, esp with force; to put or send suddenly or without warning. • vi to kick out violently; to move or rush quickly or impetuously. • n the act of flinging; a lively dance; a period of pleasurable indulgence.—**flinger** n.

flint /flɪnt/ n a very hard rock that produces sparks when struck with steel; an alloy used for producing a spark in lighters.

flint glass n a lustrous kind of glass; lead glass.

flintlock /'flɪntlɒk/ n a type of old-fashioned gun fired by sparks from a flint.

flinty /'flɪnti/ adj (**flintier, flintiest**) like flint, hard; cruel.—**flintily** adv.—**flintiness** n.

flip[1] /flɪp/ n a drink made from any alcoholic beverage sweetened and mixed with beaten egg.

flip[2] vb (**flipping, flipped**) vt to toss with a quick jerk, to flick; to snap (a coin) in the air with the thumb; to turn or turn over. • vi to move jerkily; (inf) to burst into anger.

flip-flop /'flɪpflɒp/ n a backward handspring; an electronic circuit that can assume either of two states when activated; a rubber-soled sandal with a strap that fits between the toes .—also **thong**.

flippant /'flɪpənt/ adj impertinent; frivolous.—**flippancy** n.—**flippantly** adv.

flipper /'flɪpər/ n a limb adapted for swimming; a flat rubber shoe expanded into a paddle, used in underwater swimming.

flip side n the reverse side of a gramophone record; the less attractive or well-known aspect of a person or thing.

flirt /flɜːrt/ vi to make insincere amorous approaches; to trifle or toy (eg with an idea). • n a person who toys amorously with the opposite sex.—**flirtation** n.—**flirter** n.—**flirtingly** adv.

flirtatious /flɜːr'teɪʃəs/ adj fond of flirting, coquettish.—**flirtatiously** adv.

flit /flɪt/ vi (**flitting, flitted**) to move lightly and rapidly; to vacate (a premises) stealthily. • the act of flitting, a removal.

flitch /flɪtʃ/ n a side of bacon, salted and cured; a plank cut from a tree.

flitter /'flɪtər/ vi to flit about; to flicker, flutter.

flivver /'flɪvər/ n (sl) an old or cheap car.

float /fləʊt/ vi to rest on the surface of or be suspended in a liquid; to move lightly; to wander aimlessly. • vt to cause to float; to put into circulation; to start up a business, esp by offering shares for sale. • *n* anything that floats; a cork or other device used on a fishing line to signal that the bait has been taken; a low flat vehicle decorated for exhibit in a parade; a small sum of money available for cash expenditures.—**floatable** *adj*.

floatage /ˈfloːtɪdʒ/ *see* **flotage**.

floatation /floˈteɪʃən/ *see* **flotation**.

floater /ˈfloːtər/ *n* something that floats; a person lacking strong political convictions; (*inf*) a blunder.

floating /ˈfloːtɪŋ/ *adj* swimming, or buoyed up, on the surface of a liquid; (*anat*) displaced; (*vote, etc*) not settled; (*capital*) in circulation, available for use.

floccose /ˈflɒkˌoːs/ *adj* tufted.

floccule /ˈflɒkjuːl/ *n* a mass of fleecy material; a small tuft or flake.

flocculent /ˈflɒkjʊlənt/ *adj* woolly or flaky.—**flocculence, flocculency** *n*.

flocculus /ˈflɒkjʊləs/ *n* (*pl* **flocculi**) a tufted mass; (*astron*) a mass of gas appearing as a mark on the sun.—*also* **plage**.

floccus /ˈflɒkəs/ *n* (*pl* **flocci**) down, such as that found on young birds; a tuft of hair.

flock[1] /flɒk/ *n* a group of certain animals as birds, sheep, etc, living and feeding together; a group of people or things. • *vi* to assemble or travel in a flock or crowd.

flock[2] *n* a tuft of wool or cotton fibre; woollen or cotton waste used for stuffing furniture.—**flocky** *adj*.

floe /floː/ *n* a sheet of floating ice.

flog /flɒg/ *vt* (**flogging, flogged**) to beat harshly with a rod, stick or whip; (*sl*) to sell.—**flogger** *n*.—**flogging** *n*.

flong /flɒŋ/ *n* (*printing*) paper used for stereotyping.

flood /flʌd/ *n* an overflowing of water on an area normally dry; the rising of the tide; a great outpouring, as of words. • *vt* to cover or fill, as with a flood; to put too much water, fuel, etc on or in. • *vi* to gush out in a flood; to become flooded.—**floodable** *adj*.—**flooder** *n*.

floodgate /ˈflʌdgeɪt/ *n* a gate for controlling the flow of water, a sluice.

floodlight /-laɪt/ *n* a strong beam of light used to illuminate a stage, sports field, stadium, building exterior, etc. • *vt* (**flood-lighting, floodlit**) to illuminate with floodlights.

flood tide *n* the rising or inflowing tide.

floor /flɔr/ *n* the inside bottom surface of a room, flooring; the bottom surface of anything, as the ocean; a storey in a building; the area in a legislative assembly where the members sit and debate; the lower limit, the base. • *vt* to provide with a floor; to knock down (a person) in a fight; (*inf*) to defeat; (*inf*) to shock, to confuse.

floorage /ˈflɔrɪdʒ/ *n* the area of a floor.

floorboard /ˈflɔrbɔrd/ *n* one of the boards making up a floor.

flooring /-ɪŋ/ *n* material for making or covering a floor; a floor.

floor plan *n* a scale drawing of the layout of a floor of a building.

floor show *n* entertainment with singers and dancers, etc in a nightclub.

floozy, floozie, floosie /ˈfluːzi/ *n* (*pl* **floozies, floosies**) (*sl*) a disreputable woman.

flop /flɒp/ *vi* (**flopping, flopped**) to sway or bounce loosely; to move in a heavy, clumsy or relaxed manner; (*inf*) to fail. • *n* a flopping movement; a collapse; (*inf*) a complete failure.

floppy /ˈflɒpi/ *adj* (**floppier, floppiest**) limp, hanging loosely. • *n* (*pl* **floppies**) a floppy disk.—**floppily** *adv*.—**floppiness** *n*.

floppy disk *n* (*comput*) a flexible magnetic disk in a protective casing used for data storage and retrieval.

flora /ˈflɔrə/ *n* (*pl* **floras, florae**) the plants of a region or a period.

floral /ˈflɔrəl/ *or* /ˈflɒ-/ *adj* pertaining to flowers.—**florally** *adv*.

Florentine /ˈflɒrənˌtiːn/ *or* /-taɪn/ *or* /ˈflɑr-/ *n* a native or inhabitant of Florence.—*also adj*.

florescence /flɔˈresəns/ *or* /flɑ-/ *n* the process, state or time of flowering.

floret /ˈflɔrɪt/ *n* one of the small flowers forming the head of a plant.

floriated, floreated /ˈflɔriˌeɪtəd/ *adj* ornamented with floral decorations; flowery.

floribunda /ˌflɒrɪˈbɛndə/ *or* /ˌflɑr-/ *n* any of several varieties of hybrid roses with large clusters of flowers.

floriculture /ˈflɒrɪˌkʌltʃər/ *or* /ˈflɔr-/ *n* the cultivation of flowers.—**floricultural** *adj*.—**floriculturist** *n*

florid /ˈflɒrɪd/ *or* /ˈflɑ-/ *adj* flowery; elaborate; (*complexion*) ruddy.—**floridity** *n*.—**floridly** *adv*.

florist /ˈflɒrɪst/ *n* a person who sells or grows flowers and ornamental plants.

flory /ˈflɔri/ *see* **fleury**.

floss /flɒs/ *n* a mass of short silky fibres, as from the rough outside of the silkworm's cocoon; fine silk used in embroidery; dental floss.

flossy /-i/ *adj* (**flossier, flossiest**) like floss, silky, downy; (*sl*) flashy.

flotage /ˈfloːtɪdʒ/ *n* flotation; a craft afloat; flotsam.—*also* **floatage**.

flotation /floˈteɪʃən/ *n* the act or process of floating; the launching of a business venture.—*also* **floatation**.

flotilla /fləˈtɪlə/ *n* a small fleet of ships.

flotsam /ˈflɒtsəm/ *n* wreckage or debris found floating in the sea.

flounce[1] /flaʊns/ *vi* to move in an emphatic or impatient manner. • *n* the act of flouncing, a plunge.

flounce[2] *n* a frill of material sewn to the skirt of a dress. • *vt* to add flounces to.

flouncing /-ɪŋ/ *n* a material used for making flounces.

flounder[1] /ˈflaʊndər/ *vi* to move awkwardly and with difficulty; to be clumsy in thinking or speaking.

flounder[2] *n* (*pl* **flounder, flounders**) a small flatfish used as food.

flour /flaʊr/ *n* the finely ground powder of wheat or other grain. • *vt* to sprinkle with flour.—**floury** *adj*.

flourish /ˈflɒrɪʃ/ *or* /ˈflʌrɪʃ/ *vi* (*plants*) to grow luxuriantly; to thrive, prosper; to live and work at a specified time. • *vt* to brandish dramatically. • *n* embellishment; a curve made by a bold stroke of the pen; a sweeping gesture; a musical fanfare.—**flourisher** *n*.

flout /flaʊt/ *vt* to treat with contempt, to disobey openly. • *n* an insult.—**flouter** *n*.—**floutingly** *adv*.

flow /floː/ *vi* (*liquids*) to move (as if) in a stream; (*tide*) to rise; to glide smoothly; (*conversation, etc*) to continue effortlessly; to be characterized by smooth and easy movement; to hang free or loosely; to be plentiful. • *n* a flowing; the rate of flow; anything that flows; the rising of the tide.

flow chart /-ˌtʃɑrt/ *n* a diagram representing the sequence of and relationships between different steps or procedures in a complex process, *eg* manufacturing.

flower /ˈflaʊr/ *n* the seed-producing structure of a flowering plant, blossom; a plant cultivated for its blossoms; the best or finest part. • *vt* to cause to bear flowers. • *vi* to produce blossoms; to reach the best stage.

floweret /ˈflaʊrət/ *or* /ˈflaʊrˈet/ *n* a little flower.

flowerpot /-ˌpɒt/ *n* a pot used to contain a growing plant.

flowery /ˈflaʊri/ *adj* full of or decorated with flowers; (*language*) full of elaborate expressions.—**floweriness** *n*.

flown /floːn/ *see* **fly**.

fl. oz. *abbr* = fluid ounce.

flu /fluː/ *n* (*inf*) influenza.

fluctuate /ˈflʌktʃuˌeɪt/ *vi* (*prices, etc*) to be continually varying in an irregular way.—**fluctuation** *n*.

flue[1] /fluː/ *n* a shaft for the passage of smoke, hot air, etc, as in a chimney.

flue[2] *n* soft downy matter; fluff.

flue[3] *n* a type of fishing net.

fluent /ˈfluːənt/ *adj* able to write and speak a foreign language with ease; articulate, speaking and writing easily and smoothly; graceful.—**fluency** *n*.—**fluently** *adv*.

fluff /flʌf/ *n* soft, light down; a loose, soft mass, as of hair; (*inf*) a mistake, bungle. • *vt* to pat or shake until fluffy; (*inf*) to forget, to bungle.

fluffy /ˈflʌfi/ *adj* (**fluffier, fluffiest**) like fluff; soft and downy; feathery.—**fluffily** *adv*.—**fluffiness** *n*.

fluid /ˈfluːɪd/ *n* a substance able to flow freely, as a liquid or gas does. • *adj* able to flow freely; able to change rapidly or easily.—**fluidal** *adj*.—**fluidity** *n*.—**fluidly** *adv*.

fluid ounce *n* a US unit of capacity equal to one sixteenth of a US pint; a UK unit of capacity equal to one twentieth of an imperial pint

fluke[1] /fluːk/ *n* a flatfish; a flattened parasitic worm.

fluke[2] *n* the part of an anchor that fastens in the sea bed, river bottom, etc; the barbed end of a harpoon; one of the lobes of a whale's tail.

fluke[3] *n* a stroke of luck. • *vti* to make or score by a fluke.

fluky, flukey /'flu:ki/ *adj* (**flukier, flukiest**) obtained by luck; uncertain.—**flukiness** *n*.

flume /flu:m/ *n* a channel for water; a ravine with a stream; a chute with a flow of water into a swimming pool. • *vt* to transport or divert by a flume.

flummery /'fləməri/ *n* (*pl* **flummeries**) (*inf*) an empty compliment; a pudding, a kind of custard or blancmange.

flummox /'fləməks/ *vt* (*inf*) to bewilder, perplex.

flung /flʌŋ/ *see* **fling**.

flunk /flʌŋk/ *vti* (*sl*) to fail, as in school work; to shirk.

flunky, flunkey /'flʌŋki/ *n* (*pl* **flunkies, flunkeys**) a servile person, toady; a person who does menial work; a liveried servant.

fluor /'flu:ɔr/ *see* **fluorspar**.

fluoresce /flə'res/ *vi* to display fluorescence.

fluorescence /flə'resəns/ *n* the property of producing light when acted upon by radiant energy; light so produced.—**fluorescent** *adj*.

fluorescent lamp /flə'resənt/ *n* a glass tube coated with a fluorescent substance that emits light when acted upon by ultraviolet radiation.

fluoridate /'flɔrɪˌdeɪt/ *vt* to add fluoride to drinking water to reduce tooth decay.—**fluoridation** *n*.

fluoride /'flɔraɪd/ *n* any of various compounds of fluorine.

fluorinate /'flɔrɪˌneɪt/ *vt* to treat or mix with fluorine.—**fluorination** *n*.

fluorine, fluorin /'flɔri:n/ *n* a chemical element, a pale greenish-yellow corrosive gas.

fluoroscope /'flɔrəˌskoːp/ *n* an instrument with a fluorescent screen, used for studying X-ray images.—**fluoroscopy** *n*.

fluorspar /'flu:ɔrspɑr/ *n* a transparent, or semi-transparent, material, composed of calcium fluoride.—*also* **fluor**.

flurry /'fləri/ *n* (*pl* **flurries**) a sudden gust of wind, rain, or snow; a sudden commotion. • *vti* (**flurrying, flurried**) to (cause to) become flustered.

flush¹ /flʌʃ/ *n* a rapid flow, as of water; sudden, vigorous growth; a sudden excitement; a blush; a sudden feeling of heat, as in a fever. • *vi* to flow rapidly; to blush or glow; to be washed out by a sudden flow of water. • *vt* to wash out with a sudden flow of water; to cause to blush; to excite. • *adj* level or in one plane with another surface; (*inf*) abundant, well-supplied, *esp* with money.—**flusher** *n*.

flush² *vt* to make game birds fly away suddenly.—**flusher** *n*.

flush³ *n* (*poker, etc*) a hand of cards all of the same suit.

fluster /'flʌstər/ *vti* to make or become confused. • *n* agitation or confusion.

flute /flu:t/ *n* an orchestral woodwind instrument in the form of a straight pipe (with finger holes and keys) held horizontally and played through a hole located near one end; a decorative groove. • *vi* to play or make sounds like a flute; to cut grooves in.—**fluty** *adj*.

fluter /'flu:tər/ *n* a person who makes flutes; a tool used in making flutes; a flute player.

fluting /'flu:tɪŋ/ *n* decorative channels or grooves in pillars, etc; pleats like this in a skirt, etc.

flutist /'fli:tɪst/ *n* a flute player, flautist.

flutter /'flʌtər/ *vi* (*birds*) to flap the wings; to wave about rapidly; (*heart*) to beat irregularly or spasmodically. • *vt* to cause to flutter. • *n* rapid, irregular motion; nervous excitement; commotion, confusion; (*inf*) a small bet.—**flutterer** *n*.—**fluttery** *adj*.

fluty /'flu:ti/ *adj* (**flutier, flutiest**) soft and clear like the sound of a flute.—**flutily** *adv*.—**flutiness** *n*.

fluvial /'flu:vɪəl/, **fluviatile** /'flu:vɪəˌtaɪl/ *adj* of or found in streams and rivers.

flux /flʌks/ *n* a continual flowing or changing; a substance used to help metals fuse together, as in soldering.

fluxion /'flʌkʃən/ *n* a flowing; an excessive flow; (*math*) differential calculus.—**fluxional, fluxionary** *adj*.

fly¹ /flaɪ/ *n* (*pl* **flies**) a two-winged insect; a natural or imitation fly attached to a fish-hook as bait.

fly² *vb* (**flying, flew**, *pp* **flown**) *vi* to move through the air, *esp* on wings; to travel in an aircraft; to control an aircraft; to take flight, flee; to pass quickly; (*inf*) to depart quickly. • *vt* to cause to fly, as a kite; to escape, flee from; to transport by aircraft. • *n* a flap that conceals buttons, a zip, etc on trousers; material forming the outer roof of a tent; a device for regulating machinery, a flywheel.—**flyable** *adj*.

fly³ *adj* (*inf*) sly, astute.

flyaway /'flaɪəweɪ/ *adj* (*hair etc*) loose; (*person*) flighty.

flyblow /'flaɪˌbloː/ *n* the egg or larva of a fly. • *vt* (**flyblowing, flyblew**, *pp* **flyblown**) to contaminate (meat, etc) by laying eggs (*esp* of a blowfly) in it.

flyby /'flaɪˌbaɪ/ *n* (*pl* **flybys**) a flight past a target, *esp* by a spacecraft past a celestial body to collect scientific data.

fly-by-night /-naɪt/ *adj* (*inf*) unreliable, untrustworthy; transitory. • *n* an untrustworthy person, *esp* one who evades responsibilities or debts by flight.

flycatcher /'flaɪˌkætʃər/ *n* a bird that catches insects on the wing.

flyer /flaɪr/ *n* something that flies or moves very fast; a pilot.—*also* **flier**.

fly fishing /'flaɪˌfɪʃɪŋ/ *n* fishing using artificial flies as lures.—**fly-fish** *vi*.

flying /'flaɪɪŋ/ *adj* capable of flight; fleeing; fast-moving. • *n* the act of flying an aircraft, etc.

flying boat *n* a sea plane in which the boat forms the fuselage and float.

flying buttress *n* a buttress connected to a wall by an arch, serving to resist outward pressure.

flying colours *npl* great success; triumph.

flying doctor *n* a doctor who visits patients (*eg* in isolated communities) by aircraft.

flying fish /'flaɪɪŋ'fɪʃ/ *n* any of numerous fishes of warm seas with winglike fins used in gliding through the air.

flying fox *n* a large fruit bat of Africa and Asia.

flying saucer *n* an unidentified flying disc-shaped object, purportedly from outer space.

flying squad *n* a small detachment of police officers mobilized for swift action.

flying squirrel *n* a nocturnal squirrel with folds of skin joining its legs, enabling it to glide.

flying start *n* a start in a race when the competitor is already moving when passing the starting line; a promising start in anything.

flyleaf /'flaɪli:f/ *n* (*pl* **flyleaves**) the blank leaf at the beginning or end of a book.

flyover /'flaɪˌoːvər/ *n* a bridge that carries a road or railway over another; a fly-past.

flypaper /'flaɪˌpeɪpər/ *n* paper with a sticky poisonous coating that is hung up to trap and kill flies.

fly-past /'flaɪpæst/ *n* a processional flight of aircraft.

flyte /flaɪt/ *see* **flite**.

flytrap /'flaɪtræp/ *n* any of various insect-eating plants; a device for catching flies.

flyweight /'flaɪweɪt/ *n* a boxer weighing not more than 112 pounds (51 kg).

flywheel /'flaɪwi:l/ *n* a heavy wheel which stores energy by inertia, used to regulate machinery.

FM *abbr* = Field Marshal; frequency modulation.

Fm (*chem symbol*) fermium.

f-number /'ɛfˌnʌmbər/ *n* (*photog*) a number used to calculate the ratio of light passing through a lens.

FO *abbr* (*Brit*) = Foreign Office.

foal /foːl/ *n* the young of the horse or a related animal. • *vti* to give birth to a foal.

foam /foːm/ *n* froth or fine bubbles on the surface of liquid; something like foam, as frothy saliva; a rigid or springy cellular mass made from liquid rubber, plastic, etc. • *vi* to cause or emit foam.

foamy /-i/ *adj* (**foamier, foamiest**) of, like, or covered with foam.—**foamily** *adv*.—**foaminess** *n*.

f.o.b. *abbr* = free on board.

fob¹ /fob/ *n* the chain or ribbon for attaching a watch to a waistcoat; any object attached to a watch chain; a small pocket in a waistcoat for a watch.

fob² *vt* (**fobbing, fobbed**) (*with* **off**) to cheat; to put off; to palm off (upon).

focal /'foːkəl/ *adj* of or pertaining to a focus.—**focally** *adv*.

focalize /'foːkəˌlaɪz/ *vti* to (cause to) focus.—**focalization** *n*.

focal length *n* the distance between the focal point and optical centre of a lens or mirror.

fo'c's'le, fo'c's'le /'foːksəl/ *see* **forecastle**.

focus /'foːkəs/ *n* (*pl* **focuses, foci**) a point where rays of light, heat, etc meet after being bent by a lens, curved mirror, etc; correct adjustment of the eye or lens to form a clear image; a centre of activity or interest. • *vt* (**focusing, focused** *or* **focussing, focussed**) to adjust the focus of; to bring into focus; to concentrate.—**focusable** *adj.*—**focuser** *n*.

fodder /'fɒdər/ *n* dried food for cattle, horses, etc.

FOE *abbr* = Friends of the Earth.

foe /fəʊ/ *n* an enemy, an adversary.

foehn /feɪn/ *Gr.* /fœn/ *see* **föhn**.

foeman *n* (*arch*) an adversary in war.

foetal /'fiːtəl/ *see* **fetal**.

foeticide /'fiːtɪˌsaɪd/ *see* **feticide**.

foetid /'fetɪd/ *or* /'fiːt-/ *see* **fetid**.

foetus /'fiːtəs/ *n* (*pl* **foetuses**) the unborn young of an animal, *esp* in its later stages; in humans, the offspring in the womb from the fourth month until birth.—*also* **fetus** (*pl* **fetuses**).—**fetal, foetal** *adj*.

fog[1] /fɒg/ *n* (a state of poor visibility caused by) a large mass of water vapour condensed to fine particles just above the earth's surface; a state of mental confusion; (*photog*) cloudiness on a developed photograph. • *vti* (**fogging, fogged**) to make or become foggy.

fog[2] *n* a second growth of grass in autumn; winter pasture; (*Scot*) moss.

fogbound /'fɒgbaʊnd/ *n* unable to function due to fog; obscured by or enveloped in a fog.

fogey, fogy /'fəʊgɪ/ *n* (*pl* **fogeys, fogies**) a person of old-fashioned or eccentric habits.—**fogeyish, fogyish** *adj*.

foggy /'fɒgɪ/ *adj* (**foggier, foggiest**) thick with fog; mentally confused; indistinct, opaque.—**foggily** *adv*.—**fogginess** *n*.

foghorn /'fɒghɔːn/ *n* a horn (in a ship, etc) sounded in a fog as a warning.

fogy *see* **fogey**.

föhn /fən/ *n* a warm, dry, Alpine wind.—*also* **foehn**.

foible /'fɔɪbəl/ *n* a slight weakness or failing; an idiosyncrasy; the weakest part of the blade of a sword.

foil[1] /fɔɪl/ *vt* to defeat; to frustrate; to trample a trail to spoil scent. • *n* (*arch*) the trail of hunted game.—**foilable** *adj*.

foil[2] *n* a very thin sheet of metal; a backing for a mirror or gem; anything that sets off or enhances another by contrast; (*archit*)a small arc or space in the tracery of a window. • *vt* to cover, back or adorn with foil; to set off.

foil[3] *n* a long, thin blunted sword used for fencing.

foison /'fɔɪzən/ *n* (*arch*) an abundance.

foist /fɔɪst/ *vt* (*with* **in** *or* **into**) to introduce stealthily or without permission; (*with* **off** *or* **on**) to pass off as genuine.

folacin /'fɒləsɪn/ *or* /'fɒl-/ *see* **folic acid**.

fold[1] /fəʊld/ *vt* to cover by bending or doubling over so that one part covers another; to wrap up, envelop; to interlace (one's arms); to clasp (one's hands); to embrace; to incorporate (an ingredient) into a food mixture by gentle overturnings. • *vi* to become folded; to fail completely; to collapse, *esp* to go out of business. • *n* something folded, as a piece of cloth; a crease or hollow made by folding.—**foldable** *adj*.

fold[2] *n* a pen for sheep; a group of people or institutions having a common belief, activity, etc. • *vt* to pen in a fold.

-fold *suffix* times repeated, *eg* tenfold.

foldaway /'fəʊldəˌweɪ/ *adj* (*bed, etc*) collapsible.

folder /'fəʊldər/ *n* a folded cover or large envelope for holding loose papers.

folderol /'fɒldəˌrɒl/ *see* **falderal**.

folding /-ɪŋ/ *n* the act or process of folding. • *adj* which folds or can be folded.

foliaceous /ˌfəʊlɪˈeɪʃəs/ *adj* resembling or having leaves; (*rock*) having thin layers.

foliage /'fəʊlɪədʒ/ *n* leaves, as of a plant or tree.

foliar /'fəʊlɪər/ *adj* of or pertaining to leaves.

foliate /'fəʊlɪət/ *adj* resembling or having leaves. • *vti* to beat (metal) into foil; to divide into thin layers; to produce leaves; (*archit*) to decorate with foils; to number the leaves of a book.

foliation /ˌfəʊlɪˈeɪʃən/ *n* (*bot*) the act of producing leaves or the state of having leaves; the act or process of beating a metal into thin plates.

folic acid /'fɒlɪk/ *or* /'fəʊlɪk/ *n* a B-complex vitamin used in treating anaemia.—*also* **folacin**.

folio /'fəʊlɪəʊ/ *n* (*pl* **folios**) a large sheet of paper folded once to make two leaves of a book; a book of sheets in this size, the largest commonly used; the number of a page in a book. • *vt* (**folioing, folioed**) to number the pages of.

foliose /'fəʊlɪˌəʊs/ *adj* (*bot*) having many leaves; of or resembling leaves.

folk /fəʊk/ *n* (*pl* **folk, folks**) a people of a country or tribe; people in general, *esp* those of a particular area; relatives; folk music. • *adj* of or originating among the ordinary people.—**folkish** *adj*.

folk etymology *n* the perversion of a word in an attempt to explain it, as "sparrow grass" for "asparagus."

folklore /'fəʊklɔːr/ *n* the traditional beliefs, customs, legends, etc of a people; the study of these.—**folkloric, folkloristic** *adj*.—**folklorist** *n*.

folk music *n* traditional music.

folk song *n* a traditional song.

folksy /'fəʊksɪ/ *adj* (**folksier, folksiest**) (*inf*) simple, plain; friendly.—**folksiness** *n*.

folktale *n* an anonymous, timeless, and placeless tale circulated orally among a people.

follicle /'fɒlɪkəl/ *n* any small sac, cavity, or gland.—**follicular, folliculate, folliculated** *adj*.

follow /'fɒləʊ/ *vt* to go or come after; to pursue; to go along (a path, road, etc); to copy; to obey; to adopt, as an opinion; to watch fixedly; to focus the mind on; to understand the meaning of; to monitor the progress of; to come or occur after in time; to result from; (*with* **through**) to pursue (an aim) to a conclusion; (*with* **up**) to pursue a question, inquiry, etc, that has been started. • *vi* to go or come after another; to result; (*with* **on**) (*cricket*) to take a second innings immediately after a first; (*with* **suit**) to play a card of the same suit; to do the same thing; (*with* **through**) (*sport*) to continue a stroke or motion of a bat, club, etc after the ball has been struck; (*with* **up**) to pursue steadily; to supplement.—**followable** *adj*.

follower /-wər/ *n* a disciple or adherent; a person who imitates another.

following /-wɪŋ/ *n* a body of adherents or believers. • *adj* next after; now to be stated.

follow-on /-ˌɒn/ *n* (*cricket*) an immediate return to bat by a side which has scored a certain number of runs fewer than its opponents in the first innings.

follow-through /-ˌθruː/ *n* (*golf, tennis, etc*) the continuation of a swing after hitting the ball.

follow-up /-ˌʌp/ *n* the continuing after a beginning; a steady pursuit.

folly /'fɒlɪ/ *n* (*pl* **follies**) a lack of sense; a foolish act or idea; an extravagant and fanciful building which serves no practical purpose.

foment /fəʊ'mɛnt/ *vt* to stir up (trouble); to bathe with warm water or lotions.—**fomenter** *n*.

fomentation /ˌfəʊmɛn'teɪʃən/ *n* the act of formenting; instigation; the application of a warm lotion to ease pain or swelling.

fond /fɒnd/ *adj* loving, affectionate; doting, indulgent; (*arch*) overcredulous, simple; (*with* **of**) having a liking for.—**fondly** *adv*.— **fondness** *n*.

fondant /'fɒndənt/ *n* a soft sugar mixture for sweets and icings; a sweet made from this.

fondle /'fɒndəl/ *vt* to caress.—**fondler** *n*.—**fondlingly** *adv*.

fondue /fɒn'duː/ *n* melted cheese used as a dip with small pieces of bread.

font[1] /fɒnt/ *n* a receptacle for baptismal water; a receptacle for holy water.—**fontal** *adj*.

font[2] *see* **fount**[1].

fontanameter /fɒn'tænəˌmətər/ *n* a device for measuring the pressure within the skull of a foetus in the womb.

fontanelle, fontanel /ˌfɒntə'nɛl/ *n* one of the open spaces in between the bones of an infant's skull.

food /fuːd/ *n* any substance, *esp* a solid, taken in by a plant or animal to enable it to live and grow; anything that nourishes.

foodie /'fuːdɪ/ *n* (*sl*) a person whose main focus is food whether reading about it, preparing it or eating it.

food poisoning *n* an acute illness caused by harmful bacteria or toxins in food.

food processor *n* an electric appliance used to perform various functions when preparing food, as chopping, mixing and grating.

foodstuff /'fuːdstʌf/ *n* a substance used as food.

fool /fuːl/ *n* a person lacking wisdom or common sense; (*Middle Ages*) a jester; a dupe; a cold dessert made from whipped cream mixed with fruit purée. • *vt* to deceive, make a fool of. • *vi* to act jokingly; to spend time idly; to tease or meddle with.

foolery /'fuːlərɪ/ *n* (*pl* **fooleries**) foolish behaviour, buffoonery.

foolhardy /'fu:l,hɑrdi/ *adj* (**foolhardier, foolhardiest**) foolishly bold; rash.—**foolhardiness** *n.*

foolish /'fu:lɪʃ/ *adj* unwise; ridiculous; ill-judged.—**foolishly** *adv.*—**foolishness** *n.*

foolproof /'fu:lpru:f/ *adj* proof against failure; easy to understand; easy to use.

foolscap /'fulskæp/ or /'fu:l-/ *n* a large size of writing paper.

fool's errand *n* a pointless undertaking.

fool's paradise *n* illusory happiness.

foot /fut/ *n* (*pl* **feet**) the end part of the leg, on which one stands; anything a resembling foot, as the lower part of a chair, table, etc; the lower part or edge of something, bottom; a measure of length equal to 12 inches (30.48 cm); the part of a garment that covers the foot; an attachment on a sewing machine that grips the fabric; a group of syllables serving as a unit of metre in verse. • *vi* to dance. • *vt* to walk, dance over or on; to pay the entire cost of (a bill).

footage /'futədʒ/ *n* measurement in feet, *esp* film exposed.

foot-and-mouth disease /'fu:tn'mauθ/ *n* a contagious disease of cattle.

football /'futbɒl/ *n* a field game played with an inflated leather ball by two teams; the ball used.—**footballer** *n.*

footboard /'futbɔrd/ *n* a treadle on a machine; a step on a carriage.

footbridge /'futbridʒ/ *n* a narrow bridge for pedestrians.

footer /'futər/ *n* (*sl*) football.

footfall /'futfɒl/ *n* the sound of a footstep.

foot-fault *n* (*tennis*) overstepping the base line when serving. • *vi* to commit a foot-fault.

footgear /'futgi:r/ *n* shoes and socks, etc.

foothill /'futhɪl/ *n* a hill at the foot of higher hills.

foothold /'futho:ld/ *n* a ledge, etc for placing the foot when climbing, etc; a place from which further progress may be made.

footie /'fu:ti/ *see* **footy**.

footing /'futɪŋ/ *n* the basis upon which something rests; status, relationship; a foothold; (*archit*) a projecting course at the base of a wall.

footle /'futəl/ *vi* to potter.

footlights /'futlaɪts/ *npl* a row of lights in front of a stage floor.

footling /'fu:tlɪŋ/ *adj* trifling.

footloose /'futlu:s/ *adj* free, untramelled.

footman /'futmən/ *n* (*pl* **footmen**) a liveried servant or attendant.

footmark /'futmɑrk/ *n* a footprint.

footnote /'futno:t/ *n* a note or comment at the foot of a page.

footpad /'futpæd/ *n* (*arch*) a highwayman on foot.

footpath /'futpæθ/ *n* a narrow path for pedestrians.

foot-pound /'fu:t,paund/ *n* a unit of energy, equal to the work required to raise a one pound weight through one foot; equivalent to 0.042 joule.

footprint /'futprɪnt/ *n* the impression left by a foot.

foot-rot *n* an inflammation of the feet of sheep and cattle; a plant disease affecting stalks and trunks; (*sl*) athlete's foot.

foots /'futs/ *npl* the sediment of oil or sugar.

footsie /'futsi/ *n* (*inf*) amorous touching together of feet; (*inf*) clandestine dealings.

footslog /'futslɒg/ *vt* (**footslogging, footslogged**) (*inf*) to march.

footsore /'futsɔr/ *adj* having sore or tired feet from excessive walking.

footstalk /'futstɔk/ *n* (*bot*) the supporting stem of a plant or flower; (*zool*) the attachment of a barnacle.

footstall /'futstɔl/ *n* a woman's stirrup (used on a sidesaddle).

footstool /'futstu:l/ *n* a stool for the feet of a seated person.

footwear /'futwɛr/ *n* shoes and socks, etc.

footwork /'futwɜrk/ *n* skilful use of the feet in boxing, football, dancing, etc.

footy /'fu:ti/ or /'futi/ *n* (*sl*) football.—*also* **footie**.

foozle /'fu:zəl/ *n* (*golf*) a bungled shot. • *vi* to bungle (a shot).

fop /fɒp/ *n* someone obsessed with fashion and appearance.

foppery /'fɒpəri/ *n* (*pl* **fopperies**) the appearance, manner or dress of a fop.

foppish /'fɒpɪʃ/ *adj* affected in dress and manners.—**foppishly** *adv.*—**foppishness** *n.*

for /fər/ or /fɔr/ *prep* because of, as a result of; as the price of, or recompense of; in order to be, to serve as; appropriate to, or adapted to; in quest of; in the direction of; on behalf of; in place of; in favour of; with respect to; notwithstanding, in spite of; to the extent of; throughout the space of; during. • *conj* because.

for- *prefix* expressing prohibition or neglect; bad effect; intensity.

forage /'fɒrədʒ/ or /'fɑr-/ *n* food for domestic animals, *esp* when taken by browsing or grazing; a search for provisions. • *vi* to search for food.—**forager** *n.*

foramen /fɒ'reɪmən/ *n* (*pl* **foraminia, foramens**) a short passage or opening, *esp* in a bone.

foraminifer /,fɔrə'mɪnɪfər/ *n* a member of a group of protozoa having a shell with very minute apertures, through which parts of its body pass.

forasmuch as /,fɔrəz'mʌtʃ/ *conj* seeing that, since.

foray /'fɔreɪ/ *n* a sudden raid. • *vti* to plunder.—**forayer** *n.*

forbad, forbade /fər'bæd/ or /fər-/ *see* **forbid**.

forbear /fɔr'bɛr/ *vb* (**forbearing, forbore,** *pp* **forborne**) *vi* to endure, to avoid. • *vt* to hold oneself back from.—**forbearer** *n.*—**forbearingly** *adv.*

forbearance /fɔr'bɛrəns/ *n* patience; self-control.

forbid /fɔr'bɪd/ *vt* (**forbidding, forbad** *or* **forbade,** *pp* **forbidden** *or* **forbid**) to command (a person) not to do something; to render impossible, prevent.—**forbiddance** *n.*—**forbidder** *n.*

forbidding /-ɪŋ/ *adj* unfriendly, solemn, strict.—**forbiddingly** *adv.*

forbore /fɔr'bɔr/, **forborne** /-'bɔrn/ *see* **forbear**.

force /fɔrs/ *n* strength, power, effort; (*physics*) (the intensity of) an influence that causes movement of a body or other effects; a body of soldiers, police, etc prepared for action; effectiveness; violence, compulsion; legal or logical validity. • *vt* to compel or oblige by physical effort, superior strength, etc; to achieve by force; to press or drive against resistance; to produce with effort; to break open, penetrate; to impose, inflict; to cause (plants, animals) to grow at a greater rate than normal.—**forceable** *adj.*—**forcer** *n.*

forced /fɔrst/ *adj* compulsory; strained.—**forcedly** *adv.*—**forcedness** *n.*

force-feed *vt* (**force-feeding, force-fed**) to compel a person to swallow food.

forceful /'fɔrsful/ *adj* powerful, effective.—**forcefully** *adv.*—**forcefulness** *n.*

force majeure /,fɔrs mæ'ʒɜr/ *n* compelling force, unavoidable circumstances.

forcemeat /'fɔrsmi:t/ *n* finely chopped meat, seasoned and used as a stuffing.

force pump *n* a pump that forces water beyond the range of atmospheric pressure.

forceps /'fɔrseps/ *n* (*pl* **forceps, forcipes**) an instrument for grasping and holding firmly, or exerting traction upon objects, *esp* by jewellers and surgeons.

forcible /'fɔrsəbəl/ *adj* powerful; done by force.—**forcibleness** *n.*—**forcibly** *adv.*

ford /fɔrd/ *n* a shallow crossing place in a river, stream, etc. • *vt* to wade across.—**fordable** *adj.*

fore /fɔr/ *adj* in front. • *n* the front. • *adv* in, at or towards the front. • *interj* (*golf*) a warning cry to anybody who may be hit by the ball.

fore- *prefix* in front; beforehand.

fore-and-aft /'fɔrən'æft/ *adj* (*naut*) (situated) at both bow and stern.

forearm[1] /'fɔrɑrm/ *n* the arm between the elbow and the wrist.

forearm[2] /fɔ'ɑrm/ *vt* to arm in advance.

forebear /'fɔrbɛr/ *n* (*usu pl*) an ancestor.

forebode /fɔr'bo:d/ *vt* to be a sign or warning (of trouble, etc) in advance; to have a premonition of (an event).—**foreboder** *n.*

foreboding /fɔr'bo:dɪŋ/ *n* a feeling that evil is going to happen, a presentiment.

forecast /'fɔrkæst/ *vt* (**forecasting, forecast** *or* **forecasted**) to predict (an event, the weather, etc) through rational analysis; to serve as a forecast of. • *n* a prediction, *esp* of weather; foresight.—**forecaster** *n.*

forecastle /'fo:ksəl/ *n* the forward part of a ship containing the crew's quarters.—*also* **fo'c's'le, fo'c'sle**.

foreclose /fɔr'klo:z/ *vt* to remove the right of redeeming (a mortgage); to bar, exclude; to hinder.—**foreclosable** *adj.*—**foreclosure** *n.*

forecourt /'fɔrkɔrt/ *n* an enclosed space in front of a building, as in a filling station.

forefather /'fɔr,fɒðər/ *n* (*usu pl*) an ancestor.

forefinger /'fɔːˌfɪŋgər/ *n* the finger next to the thumb.
forefoot /'fɔːfut/ *n* (*pl* **forefeet**) a front foot of an animal; (*naut*) the foremost piece of the keel.
forefront /'fɔːfrʌnt/ *n* the very front, vanguard.
foregather /fɔːˈgæðər/ *see* **forgather**.
forego[1] /fɔːˈgoː/ *see* **forgo**.
forego[2] *vt* (**foregoing, forewent**, *pp* **foregone**) to precede.—**foregoer** *n*.
foregoing /fɔːˈgoːɪŋ/ or /'fɔː-/ *adj* going before, preceding.
foregone conclusion /fɔːˈgɒn-/ or /'fɔːˌgɒn-/ *n* an inevitable result, easily predictable.
foreground /'fɔːgraund/ *n* the part of a picture or view nearest the spectator's vision.
forehand /'fɔːhænd/ *n* (*tennis, etc*) a stroke made with the hand facing forwards; the part of a horse in front of the rider. • *adj* (*tennis stroke*) made with the palm leading.
forehanded /-əd/ *adj* thrifty; well-off.—**forehandedness** *n*.
forehead /'fɔːhɛd/ *n* the part of the face above the eyes.
foreign /'fɒrən/ or /fɒrən/ *adj* of, in, or belonging to another country; involving other countries; alien in character; introduced from outside.
foreigner /-ər/ *n* a person from another country; a stranger.
foreignism /'fɒrɪnˌɪzəm/ or /'fɑr-/ *n* a foreign mannerism, custom or saying, or an imitation of any of these.
foreign office *n* the government department which handles foreign affairs.—*also* **state department**.
forejudge /fɔːˈdʒʌdʒ/ *vti* to judge before hearing evidence.
foreknow /fɔːˈnoː/ *vt* (**foreknowing, foreknew**, *pl* **foreknown**) to know beforehand.—**foreknowledge** *n*.
foreland /'fɔːlænd/ *n* a promontory, a headland.
foreleg /'fɔːlɛg/ *n* a front leg of an animal.
forelock /'fɔːlɒk/ *n* the lock of hair growing above the forehead.
foreman /'fɔːmən/ *n* (*pl* **foremen**) a person who supervises workers in a factory, etc; the spokesperson of a jury.—**forewoman** *nf* (*pl* **forewomen**).
foremast /'fɔːmæst/ or /-məst/ *n* the mast nearest the bow of a sailing vessel.
foremost /'fɔːmoːst/ *adj* first in importance; most advanced in rank or position. • *adv* in the first place.
forenoon /'fɔːnuːn/ *n* time before midday; morning.
forensic /fəˈrɛnsɪk/ *adj* of, belonging to or used in courts of law.—**forensicality** *n*.—**forensically** *adv*.
forensic medicine *n* the application of medical expertise to legal and criminal investigations.
foreordain /ˌfɔːrɔːˈdeɪn/ *vt* to arrange in advance; to predestine.—**foreordainment, foreordination** *n*.
forepeak /'fɔːpiːk/ *n* (*naut*) the end of a ship's hold in the angle of the bow.
foreplay /'fɔːpleɪ/ *n* mutual sexual stimulation before intercourse.
forerun /fɔːˈrʌn/ *vt* (**forerunning, foreran**, *pp* **forerun**) to precede, to foreshadow.
forerunner /'fɔːˌrʌnər/ *n* a person or thing that comes in advance of another; a portent.
foresail /'fɔːseɪl/ or /-səl/ *n* (*naut*) the largest sail on the foremast of a sailing vessel.
foresee /fɔːˈsiː/ *vt* (**foreseeing, foresaw**, *pp* **foreseen**) to be aware of beforehand.—**foreseeable** *adj*.—**foreseer** *n*.
foreshadow /fɔːˈʃædoː/ *vt* to represent or indicate beforehand.—**foreshadower** *n*.
foresheet /'fɔːʃiːt/ *n* a rope for controlling a foresail; (*pl*) the inner part of a boat's bows.
foreshore /'fɔːʃɔːr/ *n* a strip of land next to the shore; the shore between the high and low water marks.
foreshorten /fɔːˈʃɔːtən/ *vt* in drawing, etc, to shorten some lines of (an object) to give the illusion of proper relative size.
foresight /'fɔːsaɪt/ *n* foreseeing; the power to foresee; prudent provision for the future.—**foresighted** *adj*.—**foresightedness** *n*.
foreskin /'fɔːskɪn/ *n* the loose skin that covers the end of the penis.
forest /'fɒrəst/ or /'fɑrəst/ *n* a thick growth of trees, etc covering a large tract of land; something resembling a forest. • *vt* to plant with trees; to make into forest.—**forestal, forestial** *adj*.
forestall /fɔːˈstɔːl/ *vt* to prevent by taking action beforehand; to anticipate.—**forestaller** *n*.—**forestalment, forestallment** *n*.
forestation /fɒrəˈsteɪʃən/ or /fɑrə-/ *n* the planting of trees over a large area.

forestay /'fɔːsteɪ/ *n* (*naut*) a strong rope reaching from the top of the foremast to the bow of a vessel.
forester /'fɒrəstər/ or /'fɑrə-/ *n* a person trained in forestry.
forestry /'fɒrəstri/ or /'fɑrə-/ *n* the science of planting and cultivating forests.
foretaste /'fɔːteɪst/ *n* partial experience in advance; anticipation. • *vt* to taste before possession; to have a foretaste of.
foretell /fɔːˈtɛl/ *vt* (**foretelling, foretold**) to forecast, to predict.—**foreteller** *n*.
forethought /'fɔːθɒt/ *n* thought for the future; provident care.—**forethoughtful** *adj*.
foretime /'fɔːtaɪm/ *n* the past, old times.
foretoken /'fɔːˌtoːkən/ *vt* to portend, foreshadow. • *n* an omen.
foretop /'fɔːtɒp/ or /-təp/ *n* (*naut*) a platform at the head of the foremast.
fore-topgallant mast /'fɔːˌtɒpˌgælˌəntˌmæst/ or /-təˌgæl-/, /-məst/ *n* the mast above the fore-topmast, carrying the fore-topgallant sail.
fore-topmast /fɔːˈtɒpmæst/ or /-məst/ *n* (*naut*) the mast immediately above the foremast, carrying the fore-topsail.
for ever, forever /fərˈɛvər/ or /fɔːˈɛvər/ *adv* for all future time; continually.
for evermore, forevermore /fərˌɛvərˈmɔːr/ or /fɔː-/ *adv* for ever.
forewarn /fɔːˈwɔːn/ *vt* to warn beforehand.—**forewarner** *n*.—**forewarningly** *adv*.
forewent /-ˈwɛnt/ *see* **forego**[2].
forewind /'fɔːwɪnd/ *n* (*naut*) a favourable wind.
forewoman /'fɔːˌwumən/ *n* (*pl* **forewomen**) a person who supervises workers in a factory, etc; the spokesperson of a jury.
foreword /'fɔːwərd/ *n* an introduction to a book to explain its purpose, often by someone other than the author.
forfeit /'fɔːfət/ *n* something confiscated or given up as a penalty for a fault; (*pl*) a game in which a player redeems a forfeit by performing a ludicrous task. • *vt* to lose or be penalized by forfeiture.—**forfeiter** *n*.—**forfeiture** *n*.
forfend /fɔːˈfɛnd/ *vt* to protect; (*arch*) to avert, ward off.
forficate /'fɔːfɪkɪt/ or /-ˌkeɪt/ *adj* (*zool*) scissor-shaped, forked.
forgather /fɔːˈgæðər/ *vi* to assemble, meet.—*also* **foregather**.
forgave /fərˈgeɪv/ or /fɔː-/ *see* **forgive**.
forge[1] /fɔːdʒ/ *n* (a workshop with) a furnace in which metals are heated and shaped.• *vt* to shape (metal) by heating and hammering; to counterfeit (*eg* a signature). • *vi* to commit forgery.—**forgeable** *adj*.—**forger** *n*.
forge[2] *vt* to move steadily forward with effort.
forgery /'fɔːdʒəri/ *n* (*pl* **forgeries**) fraudulently copying; a forged copy; a spurious thing.
forget /fərˈgɛt/ *vti* (**forgetting, forgot**, *pp* **forgotten**) to be unable to remember; to overlook or neglect; **forget oneself** to lose self-control; to act unbecomingly.—**forgettable** *adj*.—**forgetter** *n*.
forgetful /fərˈgɛtfʊl/ *adj* apt to forget, inattentive.—**forgetfully** *adv*.—**forgetfulness** *n*.
forget-me-not /fərˈgɛtmɪˌnɒt/ *n* a plant with bright-blue or white flowers.
forgive /fərˈgɪv/ *vt* (**forgiving, forgave**, *pp* **forgiven**) to cease to feel resentment against (a person); to pardon. • *vi* to be merciful or forgiving.—**forgivable** *adj*.—**forgiveness** *n*.—**forgiver** *n*.
forgiving /-ɪŋ/ *adj* willing to forgive; merciful, kind.—**forgivingly** *adv*.
forgo /fɔːˈgoː/ *vt* (**forgoing, forwent**, *pp* **forgone**) to give up, abstain from.—*also* **forego**.—**forgoer** *n*.
forgot /fɔːˈgɒt/, **forgotten** *see* **forget**.
fork /fɔːk/ *n* a small, *usu* metal, instrument with two or more thin prongs set in a handle, used in eating and cooking; a pronged agricultural or gardening tool for digging, etc; anything that divides into prongs or branches; one of the branches into which a road or river divides; the point of separation. • *vi* to divide into branches; to follow a branch of a fork in a road, etc. • *vt* to form as a fork; to dig, lift, etc with a fork; (*with* **out**) (*sl*) to pay or hand over (money, goods, etc).
forked /fɔːkt/ *adj* shaped like a fork; branching, opening into two or more parts; zigzag, *eg* lightning.
fork-lift truck /'fɔːkˌlɪft/ *n* a vehicle with power-operated prongs for raising and lowering loads.
forlorn /fɔːˈlɔːn/ *adj* alone; wretched.—**forlornly** *adv*.
forlorn hope *n* a faint hope; a desperate enterprise.

form /fɔrm/ *n* general structure; the figure of a person or animal; a mould; a particular mode, kind, type, etc; arrangement; a way of doing something requiring skill; a conventional procedure; a printed document with blanks to be filled in; a class in school; condition of mind or body; a chart giving information about racehorses; changed appearance of a word to show inflection; (*sl*) a criminal record. • *vt* to shape; to train; to develop (habits); to constitute. • *vi* to be formed.—**formable** *adj*.

form[2] *see* **forme**.

formal /'fɔrməl/ *adj* in conformity with established rules or habits; regular; relating to the outward appearance only; ceremonial; punctilious; stiff.—**formally** *adv*.

formaldehyde /fɔr'mældə,haid/ or /fər-/ *n* a colourless pungent gas used in solution as a disinfectant and preservative.

formalin /'fɔrməlɪn/ *n* an aqueous solution of formaldehyde used as an antiseptic or preservative.—*also* **formol**.

formalism /'fɔrmə,lɪzəm/ *n* strict observance of outward form or conventional usage.—**formalist** *n*.—**formalistic** *adj*.

formality /fɔr'mælɪti/ *n* (*pl* **formalities**) strict observance of established rules or customs; an act or procedure required by law or convention.

formalize /'fɔrmə,laɪz/ *vt* to make formal; to clothe with legal formality.—**formalization** *n*.

format /'fɔrmæt/ *n* the size, form, shape in which books, etc are issued; the general style or presentation of something, *eg* a television programme; (*comput*) the arrangement of data on magnetic disk, etc for access and storage. • *vt* (**formatting, formatted**) to arrange in a particular form, *esp* for a computer.

formate /'fɔrmeɪt/ *n* a salt of formic acid.

formation /fɔr'meɪʃən/ *n* the act or process of making or producing; that which is formed; structure; regular array or prearranged order; (*geol*) a group of strata with common characteristics.—**formational** *adj*.

formative /'fɔrmətɪv/ *adj* pertaining to formation and development; shaping; (*gram*) used in forming words.—**formatively** *adv*.—**formativeness** *n*.

forme /fɔrm/ *n* a frame with type assembled in it for printing.—*also* **form**.

former /'fɔrmər/ *adj* of or occurring in a previous time; the first mentioned (of two).—**formerly** *adv*.

formerly /'fɔrmərli/ *adv* previously; heretofore.

formic /'fɔrmɪk/ *adj* of or pertaining to ants or formic acid.

Formica /fɔr'məɪkə/ *n* (*trademark*) a heat-resistant laminated sheeting.

formic acid /'fɔrmɪk/ *n* a colourless pungent liquid found *esp* in ants and many plants.

formicary /'fɔrmɪ,keri/, **formicarium** *n* (*pl* **formicaries, formicaria**) an anthill.

formication /,fɔrmɪ'keɪʃən/ *n* an irritation of the skin, resembling the sensation made by insects crawling over it.

formidable /fɔr'mɪdəbəl/ or /'fɔrmɪd-/ *adj* causing fear or awe; difficult to defeat or overcome; difficult to handle.—**formidability** *n*.—**formidably** *adv*.

formless /'fɔrmləs/ *adj* without distinct form, shapeless.—**formlessness** *n*.

formol *see* **formalin**.

formula /'fɔrmjulə/ *n* (*pl* **formulas, formulae**) a set of symbols expressing the composition of a substance; a general expression in algebraic form for solving a problem; a prescribed form; a formal statement of doctrines; a list of ingredients, as for a prescription or recipe; a fixed method according to which something is to be done; a prescribed recipe for baby food.—**formulaic** *adj*.

formularize /'fɔrmju:lər,aɪz/ or /-mjə-/ *vt* to formulate.—**formularization** *n*.—**formularizer** *n*.

formulary /'fɔrmju,leri/ *n* (*pl* **formularies**) a book of prescribed forms, or of prayers, ritual, etc; (*med*) a book giving details of the formulas and preparation of pharmaceutical products. • *adj* of formulas or ritual.

formulate /'fɔrmju,leɪt/ *vt* to express in a formula; to devise.—**formulation** *n*.—**formulator** *n*.

formulism /'fɔrmju,lɪzəm/ *n* adherence to formulas.—**formulist** *adj*, *n*.

fornicate[1] /'fɔrnɪ,keɪt/ *vi* to have sexual intercourse without being married.—**fornication** *n*.—**fornicator** *n*.

fornicate[2], **fornicated** *adj* (*archit*) vaulted, arched.

fornix /'fɔr,nɪks/ *n* (*pl* **fornices**) (*anat*) an arch-shaped part.

forsake /for'seɪk/ *vt* (**forsaking, forsook**, *pp* **forsaken**) to desert; to give up, renounce.—**forsaker** *n*.

forsooth /for'su:θ/ *adv* (*arch*) in truth.

forswear /fɔr'swer/ *vb* (**forswearing, forswore**, *pp* **forsworn**) *vt* to reject, renounce; to deny; to perjure (oneself).

forsythia /fɔr'sɪθɪə/ *n* a widely cultivated, yellow-flowered shrub.

fort /fɔrt/ *n* a fortified place for military defence.

forte[1] /'fɔrteɪ/ *n* something at which a person excels.

forte[2] *adv* (*mus*) loudly.

forte-piano /,fɔrtəpi'æno:/ or /-'pjæno:/ *adj*, *adv* (*music*) loud, then soft.

forth /fɔrθ/ *adv* forwards; onwards; out; into view; **and so forth** and the like.

forthcoming /fɔrθ'kʌmɪŋ/ or /'fɔrθ-/ *adj* about to appear; readily available; responsive.—**forthcomingness** *n*.

forthright /'fɔrθraɪt/ or /fɔr'raɪt/ *adj* frank, direct, outspoken; decisive.—**forthrightly** *adv*.—**forthrightness** *n*.

forthwith /fɔrθ'wɪθ/ or /-'wɪð/ *adv* immediately, without delay.

fortification /,fɔrtəfɪ'keɪʃən/ *n* the act or process of fortifying; a wall, barricade, etc built to defend a position.

fortify /'fɔrtə,faɪ/ *vt* (**fortifying, fortified**) to strengthen physically, emotionally, etc; to strengthen against attack, as with forts; to support; (*wine, etc*) to add alcohol to; (*milk*) to add vitamins to.—**fortifiable** *adj*.—**fortifier** *n*.

fortissimo /fɔr'tɪsə,mo:/ *adv* (*mus*) very loud. • *n* (*pl* **fortissimos, fortissimi**) (*mus*) a passage played very loudly.

fortitude /'fɔrtɪ,tu:d/ or /-,tju:d/ *n* courage in adversity; patient endurance, firmness.—**fortitudinous** *adj*.

fortnight /'fɔrtnaɪt/ *n* a period of two weeks or fourteen consecutive days.

fortnightly /'fɔrt,naɪtli/ *adj*, *adv* once a fortnight.

Fortran /'fɔrtræn/ *n* (*comput*) a high-level programming language used for scientific and mathematical problem-solving.

fortress /'fɔrtrəs/ *n* a strong fort or fortified town.

fortuitous /fɔr'tu:ɪtəs/ or /-'tju:-/ *adj* happening by chance.—**fortuitously** *adv*.—**fortuitousness** *n*.

fortuity /fɔr'tu:ɪti/ or /-'tju:-/ *n* (*pl* **fortuities**) fortuitousness; accident, chance.

fortunate /'fɔrtʃənət/ *adj* having or occurring by good luck.—**fortunately** *adv*.

fortune /'fɔrtʃən/ *n* the supposed arbitrary power that determines events; luck; destiny; prosperity, success; vast wealth.

fortune hunter *n* someone who seeks to become rich, *esp* by marrying for money.

fortune-teller /'fɔrtʃən,telər/ *n* a person who claims to foretell a person's future.—**fortune-telling** *n*.

forty /'fɔrti/ *n* (*pl* **forties**) four times ten, the symbol for this (40, XL, xl).—*also adj*.—**fortieth** *adj*.

forty-five /,fɔrti'faɪv/ *n* a gramophone record played at 45 revolutions per minute; (*with cap*) the Jacobite rebellion of 1745 in Scotland.

forty-niner /,fɔrti'naɪnər/ *n* a pioneer who went to California in 1849 to look for gold.

forty-ninth parallel *n* the parallel of 49° north of the equator, *esp* as forming the border between Canada and the US.

forty winks *n* (*sing or pl*) a nap.

forum /'fɔrəm/ *n* (*pl* **forums, fora**) an assembly or meeting to discuss topics of public concern; a medium for public debate, as a magazine; the marketplace and centre of public affairs in ancient Rome.

forward /'fɔrwərd/ *adj* at, toward, or of the front; advanced; onward; prompt; bold; presumptuous; of or for the future. • *vt* to promote; to send on. • *n* (*sport*) an attacking player in various games. • *adv* toward the front; ahead.—**forwardness** *n*.

forwardly /-li/ *adv* pertly; promptly; forwards.

forwards /-s/ *adv* towards the front, in an onward direction.

forwent /fɔr'went/ *see* **forgo**.

forzando /fɔr'tsando:/ *adv* (*music*) with sudden emphasis.

fossa /'fɒsə/ *n* (*pl* **fossae**) (*anat*) a groove, pit or cavity.

Fosse, foss /fɒs/ *n* a ditch or moat, *esp* in a fortification.

fossick /'fɒsɪk/ *vt* to search for by picking over, to rummage.—**fossicker** *n*.

fossil /'fɒsəl/ *n* the petrified remains of an animal or vegetable preserved in rock; (*inf*) a thing or person regarded as outmoded or redundant. • *adj* of or like a fossil; dug from the earth.

fossiliferous /,fɒsɪ'lɪfərəs/ *adj* containing fossils.

fossilize /-aɪz/ *vti* to change or become changed into a fossil.—**fossilization** *n*.

fossorial /fɒˈsɔːriəl/ *adj* (*zool*) used for digging.

foster /ˈfɒstər/ *vt* to encourage; to bring up (a child that is not one's own). • *adj* affording, giving, sharing or receiving parental care although not related.—**fosterer** *n*.

fosterage /ˈfɒstərˌɪdʒ/ *n* the act of fostering.

fosterling /ˈfɒstərlɪŋ/ *n* a foster child.

foudroyant /fuːˈdrɔɪənt/, Fr /fuːdʀwaˈjɑ̃/ *adj* sudden and overwhelming; dazzling, like lightning.

fought /fɔt/ *see* **fight**.

foul /faʊl/ *adj* stinking, loathsome; extremely dirty; indecent; wicked; (*language*) obscene; (*weather*) stormy; (*sports*) against the rules. • *adv* unfairly. • *vt* to make filthy; to dishonour; to obstruct; to entangle (a rope, etc); to make a foul against, as in a game; (*with* **up**) to contaminate; to ruin, bungle; to cause to become blocked or entangled. • *vi* to be or become fouled; (*with* **up**) to become blocked or entangled. • *n* (*sports*) a hit, blow, move, etc that is foul.—**foully** *adv*.—**foulness** *n*.

foulard /fuːˈlɑːrd/ *n* a light silk, or silk-cotton, fabric; a scarf made of this fabric.

foul-mouthed /ˈfaʊlˈmaʊθd/ or /-maʊθt/ *adj* using abusive or obscene language.

foul play *n* fouls in sport; violent crime, murder.

found[1] /faʊnd/ *see* **find**.

found[2] *vt* to bring into being; to establish (as an institution) often with provision for future maintenance.

found[3] *vt* to melt and pour (metal) into a mould to produce castings.

foundation /faʊnˈdeɪʃən/ *n* an endowment for an institution; such an institution; the base of a house, wall, etc; a first layer of cosmetic applied to the skin; an underlying principle, etc; a supporting undergarment, as a corset.—**foundational** *adj*.—**foundationary** *adj*.

founder[1] /ˈfaʊndər/ *n* one who founds an institution, a benefactor.

founder[2] *n* a person who casts metal.

founder[3] *vi* (*ship*) to fill with water and sink; to collapse; to fail.

foundling /ˈfaʊndlɪŋ/ *n* a deserted child whose parents are unknown.

foundry /ˈfaʊndri/ *n* (*pl* **foundries**) a workshop or factory where metal castings are produced.

fount[1] /faʊnt/ *n* a set of printing type or characters of one style and size.—*also* **font**.

fount[2] *n* a source.

fountain /ˈfaʊntən/ *n* a natural spring of water; a source; an artificial jet or flow of water; the basin where this flows; a reservoir, as for ink. • *vti* to (cause to) flow or spurt like a fountain.

fountainhead *n* a spring from which a stream flows; a first source.

fountain pen *n* a pen with an internal reservoir or cartridge of ink which supplies the nib.

four /fɔr/ *n* one more than three; the symbol for this (4, IV, iv); the fourth in a series or set; something having four units as members (as a four-cylinder engine); a four-oared boat or its crew.—*also adj*.

fourchette /furˈʃɛt/ *n* (*anat*) a fold of skin situated at the rear of the vulva.

four flush /ˈforˌflʌʃ/ *n* a poker hand with four cards of one suit.

four-flusher /-ər/ *n* a bluffer.

fourfold /ˈforfold/ *adj* having four units or members; being four times as great or as many.—*also adv*.

fourhanded /ˈforˌhændɪd/ *adj* for four players; (*mus*) for two players.

four-letter word *n* any of various words regarded as offensive or obscene typically containing four letters.

four-poster /ˈforˈpostər/ *n* a bed with four posts and a canopy.

fourscore /ˈforˈskor/ *n* eighty.

foursome /ˈforsəm/ *n* a group or set of four; (*golf*) a game between two pairs in which each pair has one ball.

foursquare /ˈforˈskwɛr/ *adj* square; firm. • *adv* squarely; firmly.

four-stroke /ˈforˈstrok/ *adj* (*internal-combustion engine*) having a piston that operates a cycle of four strokes for every explosion.

fourteen /ˈforˈtiːn/ *n, adj* four and ten; the symbol for this (14, XIV, xiv).—**fourteenth** *adj*.

fourth /forθ/ *adj* next after third. • *n* one of four equal parts of something.—**fourthly** *adv*.

fourth dimension *n* time as added to the three spatial dimensions (length, breadth, depth).

fourth estate *n* journalists or the press in general.

Fourth of July *n* Independence Day of USA.

fowl /faʊl/ *n* any of the domestic birds used as food, as the chicken, duck, etc; the flesh of these birds. • *vi* to hunt or snare wildfowl.—**fowler** *n*.—**fowling** *n*.

fox /fɒks/ *n* (*pl* **foxes, fox**) any of various small, alert wild mammals of the dog family; the fur of the fox; a sly, crafty person. • *vt* to deceive by cunning. • *vi* (*inf*) to bemuse, puzzle.

foxglove /ˈfɒksglʌv/ *n* a tall plant with spikes of purple or white flowers.

foxhole /ˈfɒkshoːl/ *n* a pit dug in the ground as a protection against enemy fire.

foxhound /ˈfɒkshaʊnd/ *n* any of various large swift powerful hounds of great endurance used in hunting foxes.

foxtail /ˈfɒksteɪl/ *n* a type of grass found in Europe, Asia and South America.

fox-terrier *n* any of a breed of small lively terriers formerly used to dig out foxes.

foxtrot /ˈfɒkstrɒt/ *n* a dance for couples in 4/4 time. • *vi* (**foxtrotting, foxtrotted**) to dance the foxtrot.

foxy /ˈfɒksi/ *adj* (**foxier, foxiest**) reddish-brown; crafty; resembling a fox; physically attractive.—**foxily** *adv*.—**foxiness** *n*.

foyer /ˈfɔɪeɪ/ *n* an anteroom; an entrance hallway, as in a hotel or theatre.

FP *abbr* = former pupil.

Fr (*chem symbol*) francium.

fr *abbr* = franc.

Fra /frɒ/ *n* (*title*) a friar.

fracas /ˈfrækɑs/ or /ˈfrækɒ/, /ˈfreɪkəs/ *n* (*pl* **fracas, fracases**) uproar; a noisy quarrel.

fraction /ˈfrækʃən/ *n* a small part, amount, etc; (*math*) a quantity less than a whole, expressed as a decimal or with a numerator and denominator.—**fractionary** *adj*.—**fractionally** *adv*.

fractional /ˈfrækʃənəl/ *adj* of or pertaining to fractions; inconsiderable, very small.

fractional distillation *n* the process used for separating a mixture of liquids into component parts by distillation.

fractionate /ˈfrækʃəˌneɪt/ *vt* to separate (elements of a mixture) by distillation.—**fractionation** *n*.

fractionize /-aɪz/ *vt* to divide into fractions.—**fractionization** *n*.

fractious /ˈfrækʃəs/ *adj* quarrelsome; peevish.—**fractiously** *adv*.—**fractiousness** *n*.

fracture /ˈfræktʃər/ *n* the breaking of any hard material, *esp* a bone. • *vti* to break; to cause or suffer a fracture.—**fracturable** *adj*.—**fractural** *adj*.

fragile /ˈfrædʒaɪl/ or /-dʒəl/ *adj* easily broken; frail; delicate.—**fragilely** *adv*.—**fragility, fragileness** *n*.

fragment /ˈfrægmənt/ *n* a piece broken off or detached; an incomplete portion. • *vti* to break or cause to break into fragments.—**fragmentation** *n*.

fragmentary /ˈfrægmənˌteri/ *adj* consisting of fragments; incomplete.—**fragmentarily** *adv*.—**fragmentariness** *n*.

fragrance /ˈfreɪgrəns/, **fragrancy** /-si/ *n* (*pl* **fragrances, fragrancies**) a pleasant scent, a perfume.

fragrant /ˈfreɪgrənt/ *adj* sweet-scented.—**fragrantly** *adv*.

frail[1] /freɪl/ *adj* physically or morally weak; fragile.—**frailly** *adv*.—**frailness** *n*.

frail[2] *n* a rush basket; the quantity of fruit held in a frail.

frailty /ˈfreɪlti/ *n* (*pl* **frailties**) physical or moral weakness; infirmity; a failing.

fraise /freɪz/ *n* a palisade of pointed sticks, used in a rampart; a type of neck ruff; a tool used to enlarge a drill hole.

framboesia, frambesia /fræmˈbiːziə/ *n* an infectious tropical disease, causing red skin eruptions and joint pain.—*also* **yaws**.

frame /freɪm/ *vt* to form according to a pattern; to construct; to put into words; to enclose (a picture) in a border; (*sl*) to falsify evidence against (an innocent person). • *n* something composed of parts fitted together and united; the physical make-up of an animal, *esp* a human body; the framework of a house; the structural case enclosing a window, door, etc; an ornamental border, as around a picture; (*snooker*) a triangular mould for setting up balls before play; (*snooker*) a single game.—**framable, frameable** *adj*.—**framer** *n*.

frame of reference *n* an arbitrary system of axes for describing the position or motion of something or from which physical laws are derived; a set or system (as of facts and ideas) serving to orient; a viewpoint, a theory.

frame-up /-ˌʌp/ n (sl) a conspiracy to have someone falsely accused of a crime.

framework /-ˌwɜrk/ n a structural frame; a basic structure (as of ideas); frame of reference.

franc /fræŋk/ n a unit of money in Switzerland and formerly of Belgium and France (now the euro).

franchise /ˈfræntʃaɪz/ n the right to vote in public elections; authorization to sell the goods of a manufacturer in a particular area. • vt to grant a franchise.—**franchisement** n.

Franciscan /fræn'sɪskən/ n a member of the Order of Friars Minor founded by St Francis of Assisi in 1209.

francium /ˈfrænsɪəm/ n a radioactive metallic element.

Franco- /ˈfræŋko:/ prefix France; French.

francolin /ˈfræŋko:lɪn/ n a kind of partridge, found in Africa and Asia.

Francophile /ˈfræŋkəˌfaɪl/ n a lover of France or its customs, etc.

francophone /ˈfræŋkəˌfoːn/ adj French-speaking. • n a person whose first language is French.

frangible /ˈfrændʒɪbəl/ adj fragile, easily broken.—**frangibility** n.

frangipane /ˈfrændʒɪˌpeɪn/ n a paste or cake made with almonds and cream.

frangipani /ˌfrændʒɪˈpæni/ n (pl **frangipanis, frangipani**) a tropical American shrub, the flowers of which are used to make a perfume.

Frank /fræŋk/ n a member of a West Germanic people who conquered Gaul in the 4th century AD.—**Frankish** adj.

frank adj free and direct in expressing oneself; honest, open. • vt to mark letters, etc with a mark denoting free postage. • n a mark indicating free postage.—**frankly** adv.—**frankness** n.

Frankenstein /ˈfræŋkənˌstaɪn/ n a work that ruins its originator.

frankfurter /ˈfræŋkˌfɜrtər/ n a type of smoked sausage.

frankincense /ˈfræŋkɪnˌsens/ n a fragrant gum resin.

franklin /ˈfræŋklɪn/ n a middle-class landowner in 14th and 15th century England.

frantic /ˈfræntɪk/ adj violently agitated; furious, wild.—**frantically, franticly** adv.

frap /fræp/ vt (**frapping, frapped**) (naut) to bind tightly.

frappé /ˈfræpeɪ/ adj iced; chilled.

frater[1] /ˈfreɪtər/ n a friar.

frater[2] n (arch) a refectory.

fraternal /frə'tɜrnəl/ adj of or belonging to a brother or fraternity; friendly, brotherly.—**fraternalism** n.—**fraternally** adv.

fraternity /frə'tɜrnɪti/ n (pl **fraternities**) brotherly feeling; a society of people with common interests.

fraternize /ˈfrætərnaɪz/ vt to associate in a friendly manner.—**fraternization** n.

fratricide /ˈfætrɪˌsaɪd/ n the murder of a brother; a person guilty of this.—**fratricidal** adj.

Frau /frau/ n (pl **Frauen, Fraus**) (a title of) a married German woman.

fraud /frɔd/ n deliberate deceit; an act of deception; (inf) a deceitful person; an impostor.

fraudulent /ˈfrɔdjʊlənt/ adj deceiving or intending to deceive; obtained by deceit.—**fraudulence, fraudulency** n.—**fraudulently** adv.

fraught /frɔt/ adj filled or loaded (with); (inf) anxious; difficult.

Fräulein /ˈfrɔɪlaɪn/ n (pl **Fräulein, Fräuleins**) (a title of) an unmarried German woman.

fraxinella /ˌfræksɪˈnelə/ n a white-flowered Eurasian plant.

fray[1] /freɪ/ n a fight, a brawl.

fray[2] vti (fabric, etc) to (cause to) wear away into threads, esp at the edge of; (nerves, temper) to make or become irritated or strained.

frazil /ˈfræzəl/ n the ice that forms in a stream.

frazzle /ˈfræzəl/ vt to exhaust; to fray, tatter. • n (inf) a state of exhaustion.

freak[1] /friːk/ n an unusual happening; any abnormal animal, person, or plant; (inf) a person who dresses or acts in a notably unconventional manner; an ardent enthusiast. • vi (with out) (inf) to hallucinate under the influence of drugs; to experience intense emotional excitement.—**freakish** adj.

freak[2] vt to variegate; to spot or streak.

freakish /ˈfriːkɪʃ/ adj very unusual; changing suddenly.—**freakishly** adv.—**freakishness** n.

freckle /ˈfrekəl/ n a small, brownish spot on the skin. • vti to make or become spotted with freckles.—**freckled, freckly** adj.

free /friː/ adj (**freer, freest**) not under the control or power of another; having social and political liberty; independent; able to move in any direction; not burdened by obligations; not confined to the usual rules; not exact; generous; frank; with no cost or charge; exempt from taxes, duties, etc; clear of obstruction; not fastened. • adv without cost; in a free manner. • vt (**freeing, freed**) to set free; to clear of obstruction, etc.—**freely** adv.

freebie /ˈfriːbi/ n (sl) something provided free of charge.

freeboard /ˈfriːbɔrd/ n the part of the side of a ship between the upper side of the deck and the water-line.

freebooter /ˈfriːˌbuːtər/ n a pirate; a plunderer.

freeborn /ˈfriːbɔrn/ adj born of free parents, as opposed to in slavery.

freedman /ˈfriːdmən/ n (pl **freedmen**) an emancipated slave.

freedom fighter /ˈfriːdəm/ n a person violently resisting an oppressive political regime.

freedom /ˈfriːdəm/ n being free; exemption from obligation; unrestricted use; a right or privilege.

free enterprise n the freedom of business from government intervention or control.

free fall n the descent of a body under the force of gravity alone, as a parachutist before the parachute opens.

free fight n an indiscriminate contest, a melée.

free-for-all /ˈfriːfərˌɔl/ n (inf) a disorganized fight or brawl involving as many participants as are willing.

free hand /ˈfriːˌhænd/ n freedom to act as desired.

freehand adj (drawing, etc) drawn by the hand without the aid of instruments.

freehanded /-hænˌdɪd/ adj generous; liberal.—**freehandedly** adv.—**freehandedness** n.

freehold /ˈfriːˌhoːld/ n tenure without rent; absolute ownership; an estate so held.—**freeholder** n.

free house n in the UK, a public house which is allowed to sell drinks from more than one brewer.

free kick n (soccer, rugby) a place kick awarded because of a foul or infringement by an opponent.

freelance /ˈfriːlæns/ n a person who pursues a profession without long-term commitment to any employer.—also **freelancer**. • vt to work as a freelance.

free-living /ˈfriːlɪvɪŋ/ n (organisms) not parasitic.—**free-liver** n.

freeload /ˈfriːˌloːd/ vi to impose upon another's hospitality.—**freeloader** n.

free love n sexual intercourse without the restraints of marriage.

freeman /ˈfriːmən/ n (pl **freemen**) someone who is not a slave; someone with civic rights.

freemartin /ˈfriːˌmɑrtən/ n a sexually imperfect and sterile cow calf, born as the twin of a bull calf.

Freemason /ˈfriːˌmeɪsən/ n a member of the widespread secret order dedicated to brotherly love, faith and charity.

freemasonry /ˈfriːˌmeɪsənri/ n mutual help between persons of similar interests.

free port n a port where goods are received and shipped free of customs duty.

free-range /ˈfriːˌreɪndʒ/ adj (hens) allowed to roam freely, not confined in a battery; (eggs) produced by hens raised in this way.

freesheet n a newspaper distributed free of charge.

freesia /ˈfriːʒə/ or /ˈfriːziə/ n a sweet-scented African plant of the iris family.

freespoken /ˈfriːˈspoːkən/ adj outspoken, blunt.—**freespokenness** n.

freestanding /ˈfriːˌstændɪŋ/ adj (furniture) standing on its own; not attached.

freestone /ˈfriːstoːn/ n a type of limestone or sandstone that is suitable for working.

freestyle /ˈfriːstaɪl/ n a swimming competition in which the competitor chooses the stroke.

freethinker /friːˈθɪŋkər/ n a person who rejects authority in religion, etc; a sceptic.

free trade n trade based on the unrestricted international exchange of goods with tariffs used only as a source of revenue.—**free-trader** n.

free verse n verse without a fixed metrical pattern.

freeway /ˈfriːweɪ/ n in North America, a fast road, a motorway.

freewheel /friːˈwiːl/ n a device for temporarily disconnecting and setting free the back wheel of a bicycle from the driving gear. • vi to ride a bicycle with the gear disconnected; to drive a car with the gear in neutral.—**freewheeler** n.

free will /ˈfriːˈwɪl/ *n* voluntary choice or decision; freedom of human beings to make choices that are not determined by prior causes or by divine intervention.

freeze /friːz/ *vb* (**freezing, froze,** *pp* **frozen**) *vi* to be formed into, or become covered by ice; to become very cold; to be damaged or killed by cold; to become motionless; to be made speechless by strong emotion; to become formal and unfriendly. • *vt* to harden into ice; to convert from a liquid to a solid with cold; to make extremely cold; to act towards in a stiff and formal way; to act on *usu* destructively by frost; to anaesthetize by cold; to fix (prices, etc) at a given level by authority; to make (funds, etc) unavailable to the owners by authority.—**freezable** *adj*.

freeze-dry /ˈfriːzˌdraɪ/ *vt* (**freeze-drying, freeze-dried**) to preserve (food) by rapid freezing and then drying in a vacuum.

freeze-frame *n* a frame of a motion picture or television film that is repeated to give the illusion of a static picture.

freezer /ˈfriːzər/ *n* a compartment or container that freezes and preserves food for long periods.

freezing /-ɪŋ/ *adj* very cold.

freezing point *n* the temperature at which a liquid solidifies.

freight /freɪt/ *n* the transport of goods by water, land, or air; the cost for this; the goods transported. • *vt* to load with freight; to send by freight.

freightage /ˈfreɪtɪdʒ/ *n* the conveyance of cargo; the cargo conveyed; a charge made for transporting cargo.

freight car *n* a rail truck for carrying freight.

freighter /ˈfreɪtər/ *n* one who freights; a ship or aircraft carrying freight.

French /frentʃ/ *adj* of France, its people, culture, etc. • *n* the language of France.

French bread *n* bread in a long, slender loaf.

French Canada *n* Quebec and other parts of Canada where mainly French is spoken.

French Canadian *n* a Canadian whose first language is French. • *adj* **French-Canadian** pertaining to French-speaking Canadians.

French chalk *n* a soapstone used as a dry lubricant and to mark cloth, etc.

French doors *see* **French windows**.

French dressing *n* a salad dressing made from vinegar, oil and seasonings.

French fries, french fries *npl* thin strips of potato fried in oil, etc, chips.

French horn *n* an orchestral brass instrument with a narrow conical tube wound twice in a circle, a funnel shaped mouthpiece, and a flaring bell.

Frenchify /ˈfrentʃɪˌfaɪ/ *vti* (**Frenchifies, Frenchifying, Frenchified**) (*inf*) to make or become French.

French leave *n* leave taken without permission; a hasty or secret departure.

French letter *n* a condom.

French polish *n* a shellac varnish for furniture.

French roof *n* a mansard roof.

French toast *n* toast with one side buttered and the other toasted; bread soaked in milk and batter and fried lightly.

French windows *npl* a pair of casement windows extending to the floor that are placed in an outside wall and open on to a patio, garden, etc.—*also* **French doors**.

frenetic /frəˈnetɪk/ *adj* frantic, frenzied.—**frenetically** *adv*.

frenzy /ˈfrenzi/ *n* (*pl* **frenzies**) wild excitement; violent mental derangement. • *vt* (**frenzying, frenzied**) to infuriate, to madden.—**frenzied** *adj*.—**frenziedly** *adv*.

frequency /ˈfriːkwənsi/ *n* (*pl* **frequencies**) repeated occurrence; the number of occurrences, cycles, etc in a given period.

frequency modulation *n* the transmission of signals by radio waves whose frequency varies according to the amplitude of the signal.

frequent /ˈfriːkwənt/ *adj* coming or happening often. • *vi* to visit often; to resort to.—**frequenter** *n*.—**frequently** *adv*.

frequentative /frɪˈkwentətɪv/ *adj* (*gram*) expressing repetition and intensity (of a verb). • *n* a frequentative verb.

fresco /ˈfreskoː/ *n* (*pl* **frescos, frescoes**) a picture painted on walls covered with damp freshly laid plaster. • *vt* (**frescoing, frescoed**) to paint in fresco.

fresh /freʃ/ *adj* recently made, grown, etc; not salted, pickled, etc; not spoiled; lively, not tired; not worn, soiled, faded, etc; new, recent; inexperienced; cool and refreshing; (*wind*) brisk;

(*water*) not salt; (*inf*) presumptuous, impertinent. • *adv* newly.—**freshly** *adv*.—**freshness** *n*.

freshen /ˈfreʃən/ *vi* to make or become fresh.—**freshener** *n*.

fresher /ˈfreʃər/ *n* (*pl* **freshers**) a freshman.

freshet /ˈfreʃət/ *n* a flood caused by melting snow or heavy rain; a stream of fresh water.

freshman /ˈfreʃmən/ *n* (*pl* **freshmen**) a first year student at university, college or high school.

freshwater /ˈfreʃˌwɒtər/ *adj* of a river; not sea-going.

fret[1] /fret/ *vti* (**fretting, fretted**) to make or become worried or anxious; to wear away or roughen by rubbing.

fret[2] *n* a running design of interlacing small bars. • *vt* (**fretting, fretted**) to furnish with frets.

fret[3] *n* any of a series of metal ridges along the finger-board of a guitar, banjo, etc used as a guide for depressing the strings.

fretful /ˈfretful/ *adj* troubled; peevish; irritable; impatient.—**fretfully** *adv*.—**fretfulness** *n*.

fretsaw /ˈfretsɒ/ *n* a narrow saw held under tension in a frame used for cutting intricate designs in wood or metal.

fretwork /ˈfretwɜrk/ *n* decorative carving consisting of frets.

Freudian /ˈfrɔɪdiən/ *adj* of or pertaining to the psychoanalytic theories of Sigmund Freud. • *n* a psychoanalyst who follows the theories of Freud.—**Freudianism** *n*.

Freudian slip *n* a slip of the tongue said to betray an unconscious feeling.

Fri. *abbr* = Friday.

friable /ˈfraɪəbəl/ *adj* easily crumbled.—**friability** *n*.

friar /ˈfraɪər/ *n* a member of certain Roman Catholic religious orders.

friarbird /-ˌbɜrd/ *n* an Australasian songbird with a tongue specially adapted to extract nectar.

friary /ˈfraɪri/ *n* (*pl* **friaries**) a monastery of friars.

fribble /ˈfrɪbəl/ *vt* to fritter away. • *vi* to trifle.—**fribbler** *n*.

fricandeau, fricando /ˌfrɪkənˈdoː/ or /ˈfrɪkənˌdoː/ *n* (*pl* **fricandeaus, fricandeaux, fricandoes**) a dish made from spiced, stewed veal.

fricassee /ˈfrɪkəˌsiː/ or /-ˈsiː/ *n* a dish made of stewed poultry, rabbit, etc in a white sauce. • *vt* (**fricasseeing, fricasseed**) to cook in this way.

fricative /ˈfrɪkeɪtɪv/ *n* (*phonetics*) a sound, *eg* "f" produced by the friction of breath in a narrow opening. • *adj* pertaining to a fricative.

friction /ˈfrɪkʃən/ *n* a rubbing of one object against another; conflict between differing opinions, ideas, etc; the resistance to motion of things that touch.—**frictional** *adj*.

friction clutch *n* a clutch that transmits motion by friction.

Friday /ˈfraɪdeɪ/ or /-di/ *n* the sixth day of the week.

fridge /frɪdʒ/ *n* (*inf*) a refrigerator.

fried /fraɪd/ *see* **fry**[1].

friend /frend/ *n* a person whom one knows well and is fond of; an ally, supporter, or sympathizer. • *vt* (*arch*) to befriend.—**friendless** *adj*.—**friendship** *n*.

friendly /ˈfrendli/ *adj* (**friendlier, friendliest**) like a friend; kindly; favourable. • *n* a sporting game played for fun, not in competition.—**friendlily** *adv*.—**friendliness** *n*.

friendly society *n* an association for mutual insurance against sickness, etc.

friendship /ˈfrendʃɪp/ *n* the state of being friends; intimacy united with affection or esteem; mutual attachment; goodwill.

frier /ˈfraɪər/ *see* **fry**[1].

frieze[1] /friːz/ *n* a decorative band along the top of the wall of a room; (*archit*) the part of an entablature between the architrave and cornice, often filled with sculpture.

frieze[2] *n* a coarse woollen cloth with a rough shaggy nap on one side.

frigate /ˈfrɪgət/ *n* a warship smaller than a destroyer used for escort, anti-submarine, and patrol duties.

frigate bird *n* a swift-flying tropical sea bird.

fright /fraɪt/ *n* sudden fear; a shock; (*inf*) something unsightly or ridiculous in appearance.

frighten /ˈfraɪtən/ *vt* to terrify, to scare; to force by frightening.—**frightener** *n*.—**frighteningly** *adv*.

frightful /ˈfraɪtful/ *adj* terrible, shocking; (*inf*) extreme, very bad.—**frightfully** *adv*.—**frightfulness** *n*.

frigid /ˈfrɪdʒɪd/ *adj* extremely cold; not warm or friendly; unresponsive sexually.—**frigidity** *n*.—**frigidly** *adv*.

Frigid Zone *n* either of the cold areas within the Arctic or Antarctic circles where the sun's rays are very oblique.

frigorific /ˌfrɪgəˈrɪfɪk/ *adj* (*arch*) causing cold.

frijol /ˈfriːˌhoːl/ or /friːˈhoːl/ *n* (*pl* **frijoles**) a type of bean, widely cultivated for eating in Mexico.

frill /frɪl/ *n* a piece of pleated or gathered fabric used for edging; something superfluous, an affectation. • *vt* to decorate with a frill or frills.—**frilled** *adj.*—**frilly** *adj.*

fringe /frɪndʒ/ *n* a decorative border of hanging threads; hair hanging over the forehead; an outer edge; a marginal or minor part. • *vt* to be or make a fringe for. • *adj* at the outer edge; additional; minor; unconventional.

fringe benefit *n* a benefit given by an employer to supplement an employee's wages; any additional advantage.

frippery /ˈfrɪpəri/ *n* (*pl* **fripperies**) cheap, gaudy clothes or ornaments; trivia.

Frisbee /ˈfrɪzbi/ *n* (*trademark*) a plastic disc that is spun through the air for recreation or sport.

frisette /frɪˈset/ *n* a curly fringe, *esp* of false hair.—*also* **frizette**.

frisk /frɪsk/ *vi* to leap playfully. • *vt* (*inf*) to search (a person) by feeling for concealed weapons, etc. • *n* a gambol, dance, or frolic.—**frisker** *n.*

frisky /ˈfrɪski/ *adj* (**friskier, friskiest**) lively, playful.—**friskily** *adv.*—**friskiness** *n.*

frisson /ˈfriːsɒn/ or /-sɔ̃/ *n* an emotional thrill, a shiver of excitement.

frit, fritt /frɪt/ *n* the mixture of sand and fluxes from which glass is made. • *vt* (**fritting, fritted**) to make into frit.

frith /frɪθ/ *see* **firth**.

frit fly *n* a small fly destructive to grain.

fritillary /frɪˈtɪləri/ or /ˈfrɪtɪlˌeri/ *n* (*pl* **fritillaries**) a flowering plant of the lily kind, the petals of which are variegated with purple, dice-shaped marks; a butterfly with brownish wings spotted with black or silver.

fritt *see* **frit**.

fritter[1] /ˈfrɪtər/ *n* a slice of fruit or meat fried in batter.

fritter[2] *vt* (*with* **away**) to waste; to break into tiny pieces.—**fritterer** *n.*

frivol /ˈfrɪvəl/ *vb* (**frivolling, frivolled** *or* **frivoling, frivoled**) *vi* to behave in a frivolous way; to trifle. • *vt* to squander.

frivolity /frɪˈvɒliti/ *n* (*pl* **frivolities**) a trifling act, thought, or action.

frivolous /ˈfrɪvələs/ *adj* irresponsible; trifling; silly.—**frivolously** *adv.*—**frivolousness** *n.*

frizette /frɪˈzet/ *n see* **frisette**.

frizz /frɪz/ *vti* (*hair*) to (cause to) form into small tight curls. • *n* hair that is frizzed.—**frizzer** *n.*

frizzle[1] /ˈfrɪzəl/ *vt* to frizz. • *n* a small tight curl.—**frizzler** *n.*

frizzle[2] *vti* to sizzle, as in frying; to scorch by frying.

frizzy /ˈfrɪzi/, **frizzly** /ˈfrɪzli/ *adj* (**frizzier, frizziest** *or* **frizzlier, frizzliest**) (*hair*) in tight wiry curls.—**frizziness, frizzliness** *n.*

fro /frоː/ *adv* away from; backward; **to and fro** back and forward.

frock /frɒk/ *n* a dress; a smock; a loose wide-sleeved gown worn by a monk. • *vt* to put on a frock; to invest with the office of priest.

frock coat *n* a double-breasted skirted coat for men.

frog[1] /frɒg/ *n* a small tailless web-footed jumping amphibian.

frog[2] *n* a decorative loop used to fasten clothing; an attachment on a belt for carrying a sword.—**frogged** *adj.*

frog[3] *n* a section of rail where two lines cross.

frog[4] *n* a tender horny substance growing in the middle of the sole of a horse's foot.

frogfish /ˈfrɒgfɪʃ/ *n* (*pl* **frogfish, frogfishes**) a variety of angler fish.

froggy /ˈfrɒgi/ *adj* (**froggier, froggiest**) resembling or containing a frog or frogs.

froghopper /ˈfrɒgˌhɒpər/ *n* a small jumping insect whose larvae secrete a spittle-like protective covering.

frogman /ˈfrɒgmən/ *n* (*pl* **frogmen**) a person who wears rubber suit, flippers, oxygen supply, etc and is trained in working underwater.

frogmarch /ˈfrɒgmɑrtʃ/ *vt* to carry an unwilling person by the legs and arms face down; to move (a person) by force.—*also n.*

frolic /ˈfrɒlɪk/ *n* a lively party or game; merriment, fun. • *vi* (**frolicking, frolicked**) to play happily.—**frolicker** *n.*

frolicsome /ˈfrɒlɪksəm/, **frolicky** *adj* fond of frolicking; playful.

from /frɒm/ or /frəm/ *prep* beginning at, starting with; out of; originating with; out of the possibility or use of.

---

fromage frais /frɒmɒʒ ˈfrei/ *n* a smooth white curd cheese eaten plain or with added fruit as a dessert.

fromenty /ˈfrɒmənti/ *see* **frumenty**.

frond /frɒnd/ *n* a large leaf with many divisions, *esp* of a palm or fern.

frondescence /frɒnˈdesəns/ *n* (*bot*) the act of producing leaves; foliage.—**frondescent** *adj.*

frons /frɒnz/ *n* (*pl* **frontes**) a plate found on the head of an insect.

front /frʌnt/ *n* outward behaviour; (*inf*) an appearance of social standing; etc; the part facing forward; the first part; a forward or leading position; the promenade of a seaside resort; the advanced battle area in warfare; a person or group used to hide another's activity; an advancing mass of cold or warm air. • *adj* at, to, in, on, or of the front. • *vti* to face; to stand or be situated opposite to or over against; to serve as a front (for); to have the front turned in a particular direction.

frontage /ˈfrʌntɪdʒ/ *n* the front part of a building or plot of land; the width or extent of the front of a shop, building, piece of land, etc.

frontal /ˈfrʌntəl/ *adj* of or belonging to the front; of or pertaining to the forehead. • *n* a decorative covering for the front of an altar; a small pediment over a window or door.—**frontally** *adv.*

front bench *n* in the British House of Commons, either of the two rows of benches occupied by the leading figures (**front benchers**) in the Government or Opposition.

front door *n* a main entrance to a building.

frontier /frʌnˈtiːr/ or /ˈfrɒn-/, /ˈfrʌn-/, /ˈfrɒn-/ *n* the border between two countries; the limit of existing knowledge of a subject.

frontispiece /ˈfrʌntɪsˌpiːs/ *n* an illustration opposite the title page of a book; (*archit*) the main face of a building.

frontlet /ˈfrʌntlət/ *n* a band worn on the forehead; an animal's forehead.

frontrunner /ˈfrʌntˌrʌnər/ *n* the favourite to win a race, election, etc.

frontward /ˈfrʌntwərd/ **frontwards** *adj, adv* towards the front.

frost /frɒst/ *n* temperature at or below freezing point; a coating of powdery ice particles; coldness of manner. • *vt* to cover (as if) with frost or frosting; to give a frost-like opaque surface to (glass).

frostbite /ˈfrɒstbaɪt/ *n* injury to a part of the body by exposure to cold.—**frostbitten** *adj.*

frosting /ˈfrɒstɪŋ/ *n* icing for a cake.

frosty /ˈfrɒsti/ *adj* (**frostier, frostiest**) cold with frost; cold or reserved in manner, chilly, distant.—**frostily** *adv.*—**frostiness** *n.*

froth /frɒθ/ *n* foam; foaming saliva; frivolity. • *vi* to emit or gather foam.

frothy /-i/ *adj* (**frothier, frothiest**) full of or composed of froth; frivolous; insubstantial.—**frothily** *adv.*—**frothiness** *n.*

froufrou /ˈfruːfruː/ *n* the rustling sound made by the material, *esp* silk, of a dress etc, when in motion.

froward /ˈfrоːwərd/ *adj* (*arch*) obstinate; wayward.

frown /fraʊn/ *vi* to contract the brow as in anger or thought; (*with* **upon**) to regard with displeasure or disapproval. • *n* a wrinkled brow; a stern look.—**frowner** *n.*—**frowningly** *adv.*

frowst /fraʊst/ *n* (*inf*) a close, stuffy atmosphere.

frowsty /-i/ *adj* stuffy; musty.

frowzy, frowsy /ˈfrauzi/ *adj* (**frowzier, frowziest** *or* **frowsier, frowsiest**) dirty and untidy; unkempt.

froze /frоːz/ *see* **freeze**.

frozen[1] /ˈfrоːzən/ *see* **freeze**.

frozen[2] *adj* formed into or covered by ice; damaged or killed by cold; (*food, etc*) preserved by freezing; motionless; made speechless by strong emotion; formal and unfriendly; extremely cold; (prices, wages, etc) fixed at a given level; (funds, etc) unrealizable.

FRS *abbr* = Fellow of the Royal Society.

fructiferous /frʌkˈtɪfərəs/ *adj* (*plant etc*) bearing fruit.

fructify /ˈfrʌktɪˌfaɪ/ *vb* (**fructifies, fructifying, fructified**) *vt* to make fruitful, fertilize. • *vi* to bear fruit; to become fruitful.—**fructification** *n.*

fructose /ˈfrʌktiːs/ or /-оːz-/, /ˈfrʌk-/ *n* a type of sugar found in ripe fruit and honey.

fructuous /ˈfrʌktjʊəs/ *adj* fruitful.

frugal /ˈfruːgəl/ *adj* economical, thrifty; inexpensive, meagre.—**frugality** *n.*—**frugally** *adv.*

frugivorous /fruːˈdʒɪvərəs/ *adj* fruit-eating.

fruit /fruːt/ *n* the seed-bearing part of any plant; the fleshy part of this used as food; the result or product of any action. • *vti* to bear or cause to bear fruit.

fruitage /ˈfruːtɪdʒ/ *n* the process of bearing fruit; a collective term for all fruits.

fruiter /ˈfruːtər/ *n* a fruit grower; a fruit tree.

fruiterer /ˈfruːtərər/ *n* a dealer in fruit.

fruitful /ˈfruːtfʊl/ *adj* producing lots of fruit; productive.—**fruitfully** *adv*.—**fruitfulness** *n*.

fruition /fruːˈɪʃən/ *n* a coming to fulfilment, realization.

fruitless /ˈfruːtləs/ *adj* unproductive; pointless; useless.—**fruitlessly** *adv*.—**fruitlessness** *n*.

fruit machine *n* a coin-operated gambling machine, using symbols of fruit to indicate a winning combination.

fruit salad *n* a dish of various fruits sliced and mixed.

fruity /ˈfruːti/ *adj* (**fruitier, fruitiest**) like, or tasting like, fruit; (*inf*) (*voice*) mellow; (*inf*) salacious.—**fruitiness** *n*.

frumenty /ˈfruːmənti/ *n* a sort of porridge, made from hulled wheat and boiled milk.—*also* **fromenty, furmenty**.

frump /frʌmp/ *n* a drab and dowdy woman.—**frumpish, frumpy** *adj*.

frustrate /ˈfrʌstreɪt/ *vt* to prevent from achieving a goal or gratifying a desire; to discourage, irritate, tire; to disappoint.—**frustrater** *n*.—**frustratingly** *adv*.—**frustration** *n*.

frustule /ˈfrʌstjuːl/ *n* the shell of a diatom.

frustum /ˈfrʌstəm/ *n* (*pl* **frustums, frusta**) (*geom*) the part of a cone, pyramid, etc, left after the top is cut off.

frutescent /fruːˈtesənt/ *adj* pertaining to, having the form of, or resembling a shrub.

fruticose /ˈfruːtɪˌkoːs/ or /-ˌkoːz/ *adj* resembling a shrub.

fry[1] /fraɪ/ *vti* (**frying, fried**) to cook over direct heat in hot fat. • *n* (*pl* **fries**) a dish of things fried.

fry[2] *n* (*pl* **fries**) recently hatched fishes; the young of a frog, etc.

fryer /ˈfraɪər/ *n* a person who fries; a pan, etc, for frying in; a piece of meat for frying.—*also* **frier**.

f-stop *n* any of the standard settings of the aperture in a camera lens.

ft. *abbr* = foot or feet.

FTA *abbr* = Free Trade Agreement.

FTP /ˌeftiːˈpiː/ *abbr* = File Transfer Protocol, a protocol used for moving files over a network such as the Internet.

fuchsia /ˈfjuːʃə/ *n* any of a genus of decorative shrubs with purplish-red flowers.

fuchsine, fuchsin /ˈfuːksɪn/ *n* a crystalline substance, made into a dark red dye.

fucus /ˈfjuːkəs/ *n* (*pl* **fuci, fucuses**) a kind of large brown flat seaweed.—**fucoid, fucoidal** *adj*.

fuddle /ˈfʌdəl/ *vt* to make drunk; to make confused.

fuddy-duddy /ˈfʌdiˌdʌdi/ *n* (*pl* **fuddy-duddies**) a person with old-fashioned or staid views.

fudge[1] /fʌdʒ/ *n* a soft sweet made of butter, milk, sugar, flavouring, etc; (*print*) a piece of late matter inserted in the stop-press column of a newspaper; a made-up story. • *vi* to refuse to commit oneself; to cheat; to contrive by imperfect or improvised means. • *vt* to fake; to fail to come to grips with; to make or do anything in a bungling, careless manner.

fudge[2] *n* nonsense. • *interj* expressing annoyance or disbelief.

fuehrer *see* **führer**.

fuel /ˈfjuːəl/ *n* material burned to supply heat and power, or as a source of nuclear energy; anything that serves to intensify strong feelings. • *vti* (**fuelling, fuelled** *or* **fueling, fueled**) to supply with or obtain fuel.—**fueller, fueler** *n*.

fug /fʌɡ/ *n* (*inf*) a hot, stale atmosphere.

fugacious /fjuːˈɡeɪʃəs/ *adj* fleeting; elusive; volatile; (*bot*) (*petals, etc*) falling off very early.—**fugaciously** *adv*.—**fugaciousness** *n*.

fugacity /-ˈɡæsɪti/ *n* fugaciousness; the property of a gas to escape or expand.

fugitive /ˈfjuːdʒɪtɪv/ *n* a person who flees from danger, pursuit, or duty. • *adj* fleeing, as from danger or justice; fleeting, transient; not permanent.—**fugitively** *adv*.

fugleman /ˈfjuːɡəlmən/ *n* (*pl* **fuglemen**) (*formerly*) a soldier who stands in front of others to demonstrate drill; a ringleader.

fugue /fjuːɡ/ *n* a polyphonic musical composition with its theme taken up successively by different voices.—**fugal** *adj*.—**fugally** *adv*.

fuguist /ˈfjuːɡɪst/ *n* a composer of fugues.

führer /ˈfjʊrər/ *n* (*German*) a leader, *esp* a dictator; (*with cap*) the title of Adolf Hitler (1889-1945), leader of the German Nazi party.

-ful /fʊl/ *adj suffix* full of, *eg doleful*. • *n suffix* the amount needed to fill, *eg cupful*.

fulcrum /ˈfʊlkrəm/ or /ˈfel-/ *n* (*pl* **fulcrums, fulcra**) the fixed point on which a lever turns; a critical factor determining an outcome.

fulfil, fulfill /fʊlˈfɪl/ *vt* (**fulfils** *or* **fulfills, fulfilling, fulfilled**) to carry out (a promise, etc); to achieve the completion of; to satisfy; to bring to an end, complete.—**fulfiller** *n*.—**fulfilment, fulfillment** *n*.

fulgent /ˈfeldʒənt/ *adj* (*poet*) shining, radiant.—**fulgency** *n*.—**fulgently** *adv*.

fulgurate /ˌfelɡjʊˈreɪt/ *vi* to flash (like lightning).—**fulgurant** *adj*.

fulgurite /ˈfelɡjʊˌraɪt/ *n* rock or sand that has been vitrified by lightning.

fuliginous /fjuːˈlɪdʒɪnəs/ *adj* sooty, smoky.—**fuliginously** *adv*.

full[1] /fʊl/ *adj* having or holding all that can be contained; having eaten all one wants; having a great number (of); complete; having reached to greatest size, extent, etc. • *n* the greatest amount, extent etc. • *adv* completely, directly, exactly.

full[2] *vt* to clean and thicken (cloth) by beating.

fullback *n* (*football, rugby, hockey, etc*) one of the defensive players at the back; the position held by this player.

full-blooded *adj* vigorous, hearty.—**full-bloodedly** *adv*.

full-blown *adj* in full bloom; matured, fully developed.

full-bodied *adj* (*flavour*) characterized by richness and fullness.

full dress *n* dress worn for formal or ceremonial occasions.—**full-dress** *adj*.

fuller[1] /ˈfʊlər/ *n* someone who fulls cloth.

fuller[2] *n* a tool used for grooving and shaping iron; a groove made by this.

fuller's earth *n* a type of clay used for fulling.

full face *adj, adv* seen from in front.

full-frontal *adj* (*inf*) (*nude person or photograph*) with the genitals clearly visible; unrestrained.—**full frontal** *n*.

full house *n* (*poker*) a hand with three cards of the same value and a pair.—*also* **full hand**; (*theatre, etc*) a performance for which all seats are sold; (*bingo*) a complete set of winning numbers.

full moon *n* the moon at its phase when the whole disc is illuminated; the period of this.

fullness /ˈfʊlnəs/ *n* the state of being full; **fullness of time** the proper or destined time.—*also* **fulness**.

full-scale *adj* actual size.

full-stop *n* the punctuation mark (.) at the end of a sentence.—*also* **period**.

full time *n* the finish of a match.

full-time *adj* working or lasting the whole time.—**full-timer** *n*.

fully /ˈfʊli/ *adv* thoroughly, completely; at least.

fully-fledged *adj* (*bird*) mature; having full status.—*also* **full-fledged**.

fulmar /ˈfʊlmər/ *n* an Arctic sea bird.

fulminant /ˈfelmɪnənt/ or /ˈfʊl-/ *adj* fulminating; sudden; (*pain*) sharp, piercing.

fulminate /ˈfelmɪˌneɪt/ or /ˈfʊl-/ *vi* to issue protests with violence or threats; to inveigh (against). • *vt* to utter or exclaim, as a denunciation. • *n* an explosive compound of fulminic acid.—**fulmination** *n*.—**fulminator** *n*.—**fulminatory** *adj*.

fulminic acid /fel'mɪnɪk/ or /fʊl-/ *n* an unstable acid composed of cyanogen and oxygen.

fulness *see* **fullness**.

fulsome /ˈfʊlsəm/ *adj* excessively praising, obsequious.—**fulsomely** *adv*.—**fulsomeness** *n*.

fulvous /ˈfelvəs/ *adj* tawny.

fumarole /ˈfjuːməˌroːl/ *n* a small hole in a volcano from which gases issue.

fumatorium *n* (*pl* **fumatoriums, fumatoria**) an airtight room where insects, plants, etc, are fumigated.

fumble /ˈfembəl/ *vi* to grope about. • *vt* to handle clumsily; to say or act awkwardly; to fail to catch (a ball) cleanly. • *n* an awkward attempt.—**fumbler** *n*.—**fumblingly** *adv*.

fume /fjuːm/ *n* (*usu pl*) smoke, gas or vapour, *esp* if offensive or suffocating. • *vi* to give off fumes; to express anger. • *vt* to subject to fumes.—**fumingly** *adv*.

fumigate /ˈfjuːmɪˌɡeɪt/ *vt* to disinfect or exterminate (pests, etc) using fumes.—**fumigation** *n*.—**fumigator** *n*.

fumitory /ˈfjuːmɪtəri/ n (pl **fumitories**) a plant, found mainly in Europe, the leaves of which were formerly used as a treatment for skin diseases.

fun /fʌn/ n (what provides) amusement and enjoyment. • vi (**funning, funned**) to joke.

funambulist /fjuːˈnæmbjulɪst/ n a tightrope walker.

function /ˈfʌŋkʃən/ n the activity characteristic of a person or thing; the specific purpose of a certain person or thing; an official ceremony or social entertainment; (math) a quantity whose value depends on the varying value of another. • vi to perform a function; to act, operate.

functional /-əl/ adj of a function or functions; practical, not ornamental; (disease) affecting the functions only, not organic.— **functionally** adv.

functionalism /-ə‚lɪzəm/ n the theory and practice of design for practical application.—**functionalist** adj, n.

functionary /-ɛri/ n (pl **functionaries**) a person in an official capacity.

fund /fʌnd/ n a supply that can be drawn upon; a sum of money set aside for a purpose; (pl) ready money. • vt to provide funds for; to convert (a debt) into stock; to place in a fund.

fundament /ˈfʌndəmənt/ n foundation, basis; (euphemism) the buttocks; the anus.

fundamental /‚fʌndəˈmentəl/ adj basic; essential. • n that which serves as a groundwork; an essential.—**fundamentality, fundamentalness** n.—**fundamentally** adv.

fundamentalism /-‚lɪzəm/ n belief in the literal truth of the Bible, Koran etc.—**fundamentalist** adj, n.—**fundamentalistic** adj.

fundus /ˈfʌndəs/ n (pl **fundi**) (anat) the base or deepest part of an organ.

funeral /ˈfjuːnərəl/ n the ceremony associated with the burial or cremation of the dead; a procession accompanying a coffin to a burial.

funeral director n a person who manages funerals.

funereal /fjuːˈniːriəl/ adj suiting a funeral, dismal, mournful.— **funereally** adv.

fungal /ˈfʌŋgəl/ adj of or pertaining to a fungus; caused by a fungus.

fungible /ˈfʌndʒəbəl/ adj (law) replaceable by another, similar specimen. • n a fungible thing, eg a coin.

fungicide /ˈfʌŋgɪ‚saɪd/ n a substance that destroys fungi.—**fungicidal** adj.

fungiform /ˈfʌndʒə‚fɔːm/ adj resembling a mushroom.

fungoid /ˈfʌŋgɔɪd/ adj resembling a fungus.

fungous /ˈfʌŋgəs/ adj of, pertaining to or like fungi; fungal; developing suddenly.

fungus /ˈfʌŋgəs/ n (pl **fungi, funguses**) any of a major group of lower plants, as mildews, mushrooms, yeasts, etc, that lack chlorophyll and reproduce by spores.—**fungic** adj.

funicular /fəˈnɪkjulər/ adj of rope or its tension. • n a cable railway ascending a mountain.

funiculus /fjuːˈnɪkjuːləs/ n (pl **funiculi**) (anat) a small cord, ligature or fibre.

funk /fʌŋk/ n (inf) panic, fear; a coward; funky music. • vti (inf) to show fear; to shirk.—**funker** n.

funky[1] /ˈfʌŋki/ adj (**funkier, funkiest**) panicky; fearful.

funky[2] adj (**funkier, funkiest**) (inf) (pop, jazz music, etc) soulful, bluesy; fashionable.—**funkiness** n.

funnel /ˈfʌnəl/ n an implement, usually a cone with a wide top and tapering to a narrow tube, for pouring fluids, powders, into bottles, etc; a metal chimney for the escape of smoke, steam, etc. • vti (**funnelling, funnelled** or **funneling, funneled**) to pour or cause to pour through a funnel.

funny /ˈfʌni/ adj (**funnier, funniest**) causing laughter; puzzling, odd; (inf) unwell, queasy. • n (pl **funnies**) a joke; (pl) comic strips, esp in a newspaper.—**funnily** adv.—**funniness** n.

funny bone n the part of the elbow where a sensitive nerve rests close to the bone, producing a tingling sensation if struck.

fur /fɜr/ n the short, soft, fine hair on the bodies of certain animals; their skins with the fur attached; a garment made of fur; a fabric made in imitation of fur; a fur-like coating, as on the tongue. • vti (**furring, furred**) to cover or become covered with fur.

furbelow /ˈfɜrbə‚loː/ n a flounce or other trimming on clothing.

furbish /ˈfɜrbɪʃ/ vt to polish, to burnish; to renovate.—**furbisher** n.

furcate /ˈfɜr‚keɪt/ vi to fork, divide. • adj forked, branching.— **furcation** n.

furfur /ˈfɜrfər/ n (pl **furfures**) scurf, dandruff.

furfuraceous /‚fɜrfəˈreɪʃəs/ adj resembling bran; resembling dandruff.

Furies /ˈfjuːriːz/ see **fury**.

furioso /ˈfjuːriːoːsoː/ adv (mus) wildly.

furious /ˈfjuːriəs/ or /ˈfjuːr-/ adj full of anger; intense; violent, impetuous.—**furiously** adv.—**furiousness** n.

furl /fɜrl/ vt to roll up (a sail, flag, etc) tightly and make secure; to fold up, close.—**furlable** adj.—**furler** n.

furlong /ˈfɜrlɒŋ/ n 220 yards, one-eighth of a mile (201 metres).

furlough /ˈfɜrloː/ n leave of absence from duty, esp for military personnel. • vt to grant a furlough to.

furmenty /ˈfɜrmənti/ see **frumenty**.

furnace /ˈfɜrnəs/ n an enclosed chamber in which heat is produced to burn refuse, smelt ore, etc.

furnish /ˈfɜrnɪʃ/ vt to provide (a room, etc) with furniture; to equip with what is necessary; to supply.—**furnisher** n.

furnishings /-ɪŋz/ npl furniture, carpets, etc.

furniture /ˈfɜrnɪtʃər/ n the things in a room, etc that equip it for living, as chairs, beds, etc; equipment.

furore, furor /ˈfjuːrɔr/ or /ˈfjɜr-/, /-ər/ n fury, indignation; widespread enthusiasm.

furrier /ˈfɜriər/ n a dealer in furs.

furriery /-i/ n (pl **furrieries**) the fur trade; a collective name for furs.

furrow /ˈfɜroː/ n the groove in the earth made by a plough; a groove or track resembling this; a wrinkle. • vti to make furrows in; to wrinkle.—**furrower** n.—**furrowy** adj.

furry /ˈfɜri/ adj (**furrier, furriest**) like, made of, or covered with, fur.—**furrily** adv.—**furriness** n.

further /ˈfɜrðər/ adv at or to a greater distance or degree; in addition. • adj more distant, remote; additional. • vt to help forward, promote.—**furtherer** n.

furtherance /ˈfɜrðərəns/ n a helping forward.

furthermore /‚fɜrðərˈmɔr/ adv moreover, besides.

furthermost /-ˈmoːst/ adj most remote.

furthest /ˈfɜrðəst/ adj at or to the greatest distance.

furtive /ˈfɜrtɪv/ adj stealthy; sly and secretive.—**furtively** adv.— **furtiveness** n.

furuncle /ˈfjurenkəl/ n (med) a boil.—**furuncular** adj.

fury /ˈfjɜri/ or /ˈfjuri/ n (pl **furies**) intense rage; a frenzy; a violently angry person; (with cap) (Greek, Roman myth) one of the three winged goddesses of vengeance with serpents for hair, Alecto, Megaera, and Tisiphone.

furze /fɜrz/ n gorse.

fuscous /ˈfʌskəs/ adj dark-coloured, esp brownish-black.

fuse /fjuːz/ vti to join or become joined by melting; to (cause to) melt by the application of heat; to equip a plug, circuit, etc with a fuse; to (cause to) fail by blowing a fuse. • n a tube or wick filled with combustible material for setting off an explosive charge; a piece of thin wire that melts and breaks when an electric current exceeds a certain level.—also **fuze**.

fusee /fjuːˈziː/ n a large-headed match; a conical spindle in a clock, around which the chain is wound.—also **fuzee**.

fuselage /ˈfjuːzə‚lɒʒ/ or /ˈfjuːs-/, /-lɒdʒ/, /-lɪdʒ/ n the body of an aircraft.

fusel oil /ˈfjuːzəl/ or /-səl/ n a poisonous liquid mixture of various alcohols, formed as a byproduct of distillation.

fusible /ˈfjuːzəbəl/ adj able to be fused; (metal, alloy) having a melting point below 148.9 °C (300 °F) and used in fuses, etc.— **fusibility** n.—**fusibly** adv.

fusiform /ˈfjuːzə‚fɔrm/ adj spindle-shaped.

fusil /ˈfjuːzəl/ or /-sɪl/ n a light flintlock musket.

fusilier, fusileer /‚fjuːzəˈliːr/ n (formerly) a British soldier armed with a flintlock musket; a soldier in certain infantry regiments.

fusillade /‚fjuːzəˈleɪd/ or /-‚lɒd/, /-sə-/ n a firing of shots in continuous or rapid succession; an outburst, as of criticism. • vt to attack or shoot down by fusillade.

fusion /ˈfjuːʒən/ n the act of melting, blending or fusing; a product of fusion; union, partnership; nuclear fusion.

fuss /fʌs/ n excited activity, bustle; a nervous state; (inf) a quarrel; (inf) a showy display of approval. • vi to worry over trifles; to whine, as a baby.—**fusser** n.

fussy /ˈfʌsi/ adj (**fussier, fussiest**) worrying over details; hard to please; fastidious; over-elaborate.—**fussily** adv.—**fussiness** n.

fustian /'fʌstiən/ or /-tʃən/ *n* a kind of coarse twilled cotton cloth, *eg* corduroy; ranting language, bombast. • *adj* made of fustian; turgid.

fustic /'fʌstik/ *n* a large tropical American tree; its wood; the yellow obtained from it.

fusty /'fʌsti/ *adj* (**fustier, fustiest**) smelling of mould or damp; outmoded in ideas or opinions.—**fustily** *adv.*—**fustiness** *n.*

futhark, futharc, futhork, futhorc /'fuːθɔrk/ *n* a phonetic alphabet made up of runes.

futile /'fjuːtaɪl/ or /-təl/ *adj* useless; ineffective.—**futilely** *adv.*—**futility** *n.*

futon /'fuːtɒn/ *n* a light cotton mattress.

futtock /'fʌtək/ *n* (*naut*) one of the upright curved ribs of a ship, springing from the keel.

future /'fjuːtʃər/ *adj* that is to be; of or referring to time yet to come. • *n* the time to come; future events; likelihood of eventual success; (*gram*) the future tense; (*pl*) commodities purchased at a prescribed price for delivery at some future date.

futurism /'fjuːtʃə,rizəm/ *n* a movement in art, music, and literature begun in Italy about 1909 marked by an effort to give formal expression to the energy of mechanical processes; a point of view that finds meaning or fulfillment in the future.—**futurist** *adj*, *n.*

futuristic /,fjuːtʃə'rɪstɪk/ *adj* forward-looking in design, appearance, intention, etc.—**futuristically** *adv.*

futurity /fjuː'tʃɔriti/ or /-'tʃʊr/ *n* (*pl* **futurities**) time or events yet to come.

futurology /,fjuːtʃə'rɒlədʒi/ *n* the forecasting of future trends in human affairs.—**futurologist** *n.*

fuze /fjuːz/ *see* **fuse**.

fuzee /fjuː'ziː/ or /'fjuːˌzi/ *see* **fusee**.

fuzz /fʌz/ *n* fine light particles of fibre (as of down or fluff); a blurred effect; fluff; (*sl*) police. • *vi* to fly off in minute particles; to become blurred.

fuzzword /'fʌzwərd/ *see* **buzzword**.

fuzzy /'fʌzi/ *adj* (**fuzzier, fuzziest**) like fuzz; fluffy; blurred.—**fuzzily** *adv.*—**fuzziness** *n.*

-fy /faɪ/ *vb suffix* to make, *eg solidify*.

G

G /dʒiː/ (symbol) (mus) the 5th note of the scale of C; gravitational constant; (physcs) conductance; giga; (sl) grand ($1000 or £1000).

g abbr = gallons(s); gram(s); gravity; acceleration due to gravity.

Ga (chem symbol) gallium.

GA abbr = General Assembly (of the United Nations); Georgia.

Ga. abbr = Georgia.

gab /gæb/ vi (**gabbing, gabbed**) (inf) to talk in a rapid or thoughtless manner, chatter. • n (inf) idle talk.—**gabber** n.

gabardine, gaberdine /ˈgæbərˌdiːn/ or /-ˈdiːn/ n a firm cloth of wool, rayon, or cotton; (formerly) a long, loose upper garment worn by men, esp Jews, in the Middle Ages; a raincoat; any of various other garments made of gabardine.

gabble /ˈgæbəl/ vti to talk or utter rapidly or incoherently; to utter inarticulate or animal sounds.—**gabbler** n.

gabbro /ˈgæbroː/ n (pl **gabbros**) a dark igneous rock like granite.—**gabbroic** adj.

gabby /ˈgæbɪ/ adj (**gabbier, gabbiest**) (inf) talkative.

gabelle /gəˈbel/ n (formerly) a tax on salt in France.

gabion /ˈgeɪbɪən/ n (formerly) a large cylindrical basket filled with earth or stones, used in military defence; a similar metal container used in engineering and underwater construction.

gable /ˈgeɪbəl/ n the triangular upper part of a wall enclosed by the sloping ends of a pitched roof.—**gabled** adj.

gablet /ˈgeɪblət/ n a small ornamental gable used for the summit of niches etc.

gad /gæd/ vi (**gadding, gadded**) (usu with **about**) to wander restlessly or idly in search of pleasure.—**gadder** n.

gadabout /ˈgædəˌbaʊt/ n (inf) a person that wanders restlessly in search of pleasure or amusement.

gadfly /ˈgædflaɪ/ n (pl **gadflies**) any of various flies that bite or annoy livestock; an irritating person.

gadget /ˈgædʒɪt/ n a small, often ingenious, mechanical or electronic tool or device.—**gadgety** adj.

gadgetry /ˈgædʒɪtrɪ/ n gadgets; the use of gadgets.

gadoid /ˈgeɪdɔɪd/ adj, n (a fish) of the cod family.

gadolinite /ˈgædəlɪˌnaɪt/ n a silicate of yttrium.

gadolinium /ˌgædəˈlɪnɪəm/ n a magnetic metallic element of the rare earth group.—**gadolinic** adj.

gadroon /gəˈdruːn/ n an ornamental edge of inverted fluting; a decorative border, esp on silver.

gadwall /ˈgædwɒl/ n (pl **gadwalls, gadwall**) a large freshwater duck, prized as game.

Gael /geɪl/ n a person who speaks Gaelic, esp a Scottish Highlander or Irishman.

Gaelic /ˈgeɪlɪk/ n the Celtic language of Ireland, the Scottish Highlands, and the Isle of Man.—also adj.

gaff /gæf/ n a pole with a sharp hook for landing large fish; (naut) a high boom or yard for hoisting a sail aft of a mast; (Brit sl) one's home. • vt to land (a fish) with a gaff.

gaffe /gæf/ n a social blunder.

gaffer /ˈgæfər/ n an old man, often a countryman; an overseer or foreman; the senior electrician of a film crew.

gaff-topsail /ˈgæfˌtɒpˌseɪl/ n (naut) a light sail set above a gaff.

gag /gæg/ n something put over or into the mouth to prevent talking; any restraint of free speech; a joke. • vb (**gagging, gagged**) vt to cause to retch; to keep from speaking, as by stopping the mouth of. • vi to retch; to tell jokes.

gaga /ˈgɒgɒ/ adj (inf) senile; slightly crazy.

gage /geɪdʒ/ see **gauge**.

gaggle /ˈgægəl/ n a flock of geese when not in flight; (inf) a disorderly collection of people.

gahnite /ˈgɒnˌaɪt/ n a greenish and dark-brown mineral.

gaiety /ˈgeɪətɪ/ n (pl **gaieties**) happiness, liveliness; colourful appearance.

gaige /geɪdʒ/ n the Chinese word for "radical reform" or peristroika.

gaily /ˈgeɪlɪ/ adv in a cheerful manner; with bright colours.

gain /geɪn/ vt to obtain, earn, esp by effort; to win in a contest; to attract; to get as an addition (esp profit or advantage); to make an increase in; to reach. • vi to make progress; to increase in weight. • n an increase esp in profit or advantage; an acquisition.

gainful /ˈgeɪnful/ adj profitable.—**gainfully** adv.—**gainfulness** n.

gainsay /geɪnˈseɪ/ or /ˈgeɪnseɪ/ vt (**gainsaying, gainsaid**) (formal) to dispute; to deny.—**gainsayer** n.

gait /geɪt/ n a manner of walking or running; the sequence of footsteps made by a moving horse.

gaiter /ˈgeɪtər/ n a cloth or leather covering for the lower leg.

gal¹ /gæl/ n (sl) a girl.

gal², gall. abbr = gallon.

gala /ˈgɑːlə/ or /ˈgeɪlə/ n a celebration, festival.

galactic /gəˈlæktɪk/ adj of a galaxy; huge.

galago /gəˈleɪgoː/ n (pl **galagos**) an African genus of lemurs; a bushbaby.

galantine /ˈgælənˌtiːn/ n a dish composed of chicken, veal or other white meat, boned, seasoned, tied up, boiled, shaped and served cold in its own jelly.

galatea /ˌgæləˈtiːə/ n a cotton fabric, often with blue and white stripes.

Galatians /gəˈleɪʃənz/ n sing (New Testament) the epistles of St Paul addressed to the Galatians.

galavant /ˈgæləˌvænt/ see **gallivant**.

galaxy /ˈgæləksɪ/ n (pl **galaxies**) any of the systems of stars in the universe; any splendid assemblage; (with cap) the galaxy containing the Earth's solar system; the Milky Way.

galbanum /ˈgælbənəm/ n an odorous and bitter gum resin used in medicine.

gale /geɪl/ n a strong wind, specifically one between 32 to 63 mph; an outburst.

galea /ˈgeɪlɪə/ n (pl **galeae**) (bot, zool) a helmet-like structure.—**galeate, galeated** adj.

galena /gəˈliːnə/ n a sulphide of lead.

Galenic /gəˈlenɪk/ adj of Galen (c.AD130c.200), the Greek physician and philosopher, or his works.

Galilean¹ /ˌgælɪˈliːən/ adj of Galilee or its inhabitants • n a native of Galilee; (often pl) a Christian; (with the) Jesus Christ.

Galilean² /ˌgælɪˈliːən/ adj of or pertaining to Galileo (1564-1642), the Italian astronomer and mathematician.

galilee /ˈgælɪˌliː/ n a small chapel or porch at the western entrance to a church.

galingale, galangal /ˈgælɪŋˌgeɪl/ n a kind of sedge; the aromatic root of an Asian plant.

galiot, galliot /ˈgælɪət/ n a heavily built two-masted Dutch trading vessel; (formerly) a small light galley used in the Mediterranean.

galipot /ˈgælɪˌpɒt/ n a white resinous juice that exudes from pine trees.

galivant /ˈgælɪˌvænt/ see **gallivant**.

gall¹ /gɒl/ n bile; bitter feeling; (inf) impudence.

gall² n a diseased growth on plant tissue produced by fungi, insect parasites, or bacteria.

gall³ n a skin sore caused by rubbing. • vt to chafe or hurt by rubbing; to irritate.

gallant /ˈgælənt/ adj dignified, stately; brave; noble; (man) polite and chivalrous to women.—**gallantly** adv.—**gallantness** n.—**gallantry** n (pl **gallantries**).

gallantry /ˈgæləntrɪ/ n (pl **gallantries**) (an act of) bravery, dashing courage; courtliness, a polite act.

gall bladder /ˈgɒlˌblædər/ n a membranous sac attached to the liver in which bile is stored.

galleass /ˈgælɪˌæs/ n a large low-built three-masted vessel propelled by sails and oars, and carrying twenty or more guns.

galleon /ˈgælɪən/ n a large sailing ship of the 15th–18th centuries.

gallery /ˈgælərɪ/ n (pl **galleries**) a covered passage for walking; a long narrow outside balcony; a balcony running along the inside wall of a building; (the occupants of) an upper area of seating in a theatre; a long narrow room used for a special purpose, eg shooting practice; a room or building designed for the exhibition of works of art; the spectators at a golf tournament, tennis match, etc.—**galleried** adj.

galley /'gælɪ/ n a long, usu low, ship of ancient or medieval times, propelled by oars; the kitchen of a ship, aircraft; (print) a shallow tray for holding type; proofs printed from such type.—also **galley proof.**

galliard /'gælɪ,ɑrd/ n a lively dance in triple time.

Gallic /'gælɪk/ adj of or pertaining to France; of ancient Gaul or its people.

gallic /'gælɪk/ adj of or made of gallnuts; (chem) of or containing gallium in the trivalent state.

Gallican /'gælɪkən/ adj of the Roman Catholic Church in France.

Gallicanism /-,nɪzəm/ n the doctrine of the national party in the French Roman Catholic Church, tending to restrict papal control, opposed to Ultramontanism.

Gallice /'gælɪs/ adv in French.

Gallicism /'gælɪ,sɪzəm/ n a French expression or idiom.

Gallicize, Gallicise /'gælɪ,saɪz/ vt to make French in manners, idiom etc.

galligaskins /,gælɪ'gæskɪnz/ npl trousers, leggings worn in the 16th and 17th centuries.

gallimaufry /,gælɪ'mɔfri/ n (pl **gallimaufries**) a medley, a hotch-potch.

gallinaceous /,gælɪ'neɪʃəs/ adj of or relating to a group of heavy-bodied largely land-loving birds including pheasants and domestic fowl.

galling /'gælɪŋ/ adj irritating, exasperating.

gallipot /'gælɪ,pɒt/ n a small glazed pot, esp for medicine.

gallium /'gælɪəm/ n a metallic element that is liquid at room temperature and is used in thermometers, semiconductor devices, etc.

gallivant /'gælɪ,vænt/ vi (inf) to go about in search of amusement.—also **galivant, galavant.**

galliwasp /'gælɪ,wɒsp/ n a West Indian lizard.

gallnut /'gɔl,nʌt/ n a round excrescence produced on the oak by the puncturing of the leaf buds by an insect, the gall beetle.

gallon /'gælən/ n a unit of liquid measure comprising 4 quarts or 3.78 litres (in UK, 4.54 litres); (pl) (inf) a large amount.

galloon /gə'luːn/ n a narrow braid or trimming of silk, gold lace, embroidery etc.

gallop /'gæləp/ n the fastest gait of a horse, etc; a succession of leaping strides; a fast pace. • vti to go or cause to go at a gallop; to move swiftly.—**galloper** n.

gallowglass /'gælo,glæs/ n a heavily armed footsoldier; a chief's retainer in Ireland in the 13th-16th centuries.

gallows /'gælo:z/ n (pl **gallowses, gallows**) a wooden frame used for hanging criminals.

gallstone /'gɔlsto:n/ n a small solid mass in the gall bladder.

Gallup Poll /'gæləp/ n a sampling of public opinion, esp to help forecast an election.

galop /'gæləp/ n a dance.

galore /gə'lɔr/ adv in great quantity; in plentiful supply.

galosh /gə'lɒʃ/ n a waterproof overshoe.

galumph /gə'lʌmf/ vi (inf) to prance triumphantly, or clumsily.

galvanic /gæl'vænɪk/ adj producing electricity by chemical action; stimulating (people) into action.—**galvanically** adv.

galvanism /'gælvə,nɪzəm/ n (arch) electricity produced by the chemical action of certain bodies or an acid on a metal; the medical use of this.

galvanize /'gælvə,naɪz/ vt to apply an electric current to; to startle; to excite; to plate (metal) with zinc.—**galvanization** n.—**galvanizer** n.

galvanometer /,gælvə'nɒmətər/ n an instrument for detecting or measuring small electric currents.—**galvanometric, galvanometrical** adj.—**galvanometry** n.

galvanoscope /-skɒp/ n an instrument for measuring the direction and presence of electricity by movements of a magnetic needle.

gam¹ /gæm/ n a school of whales; a visit by one captain of a whaler to another; • vb (**gams, gammed, gamming**) vt to call upon the captain of a whaler. • vi (whales) to gather together in schools.

gam² n (sl) a well-shaped leg.

gambado /gæm'bɒdo:/ n (pl **gambados, gambadoes**) n a kind of leather legging used by horsemen; a flourish or curvet.

gambier, gambir /'gæmbiər/ or /'gæmbi:r/ n a vegetable extract used medicinally as an astringent, and also for tanning and dyeing.

gambit /'gæmbɪt/ n (chess) an opening in which a piece is sacrificed to gain an advantage; any action to gain an advantage.

gamble /'gæmbəl/ vi to play games of chance for money; to take a risk for some advantage. • vt to risk in gambling, to bet. • n a risky venture; a bet.—**gambler** n.—**gambling** n.

gamboge /gæm'bo:dʒ/ or /-'bu:ʒ/ n a yellow gum resin from SE Asia, used as a pigment and as a purgative.—also **cambogia**; bright yellow colour.

gambol /'gæmbəl/ vi (**gambolling, gambolled** or **gamboling, gamboled**) to jump and skip about in play; to frisk. • n a caper, a playful leap.

gambrel /'gæmbrəl/ n the hock of a horse; a bent stick of wood or metal resembling a horse's leg, used by butchers; a gambrel roof.

gambrel roof n a curved roof with a small gable at each end; a roof with a double slope on each side so that each side is shaped like a horse's leg.

game¹ /geɪm/ n any form of play, amusement; activity or sport involving competition; a scheme, a plan; wild birds or animals hunted for sport or food, the flesh of such animals. • vi to play for a stake. • adj (inf) brave, resolute; (inf) willing.—**gamely** adv.—**gameness** n.

game² adj (limbs) injured, crippled, lame.

gamecock /'geɪmkɒk/ n (formerly) a cock bred and trained for fighting.

gamekeeper /'geɪm,ki:pər/ n a person who breeds and takes care of game birds and animals, as on an estate.—**gamekeeping** n.

game point n (tennis) the situation when the next point scored wins the game for one side or player.

gamesmanship /'geɪmzmənʃɪp/ n (inf) the art of winning games by questionable acts just short of cheating.

gamesome /'geɪmsəm/ adj sportive.

gamester /'geɪmstər/ n a gambler.

gamete /'gæmi:t/ or /gə'mi:t/ n a reproductive cell that unites with another to form the cell that develops into a new individual.—**gametal, gametic** adj.

gamic /'gæmɪk/ adj (zool) having a sexual character.

gamin /'gæmɪn/ n a mischievous urchin.

gamine /'gæmi:n/ or /gæ'mi:n/ n a boyish girl or woman with impish appeal.

gaming /'geɪmɪŋ/ n the act of playing games for stakes; gambling.—also adj.

gamma /'gæmə/ n the third letter of the Greek alphabet.

gamma radiation, gamma rays n shortwave electromagnetic radiation from a radioactive substance.

gammer /'gæmər/ n (rare) (usu humorous) an old woman.

gammon /'gæmən/ n cured or smoked ham; meat from the hindquarters of a side of bacon.

gamogenesis /,gæmo:'dʒɛnəsɪs/ n (bot) sexual reproduction.

gamopetalous /-'pɛtələs/ adj with petals united at the base.

gamophyllous /-'fɪləs/ adj (flowers) with leaves cohering at the edges.

gamosepalous /-'sɛpələs/ adj (flowers) with sepals united at the edges to form a calyx.

gamut /'gæmət/ n a complete range or series; (mus) the whole range of notes of a voice or instrument.

gamy, gamey /'geɪmi/ adj (**gamier, gamiest**) having the strong smell or flavour of cooked game; (inf) spirited, lively.—**gaminess** n.

-gamy /gəmi/ n suffix marriage; sexual union.

gander /'gændər/ n an adult goose; (inf) a quick look.

gang /gæŋ/ n a group of persons, esp labourers, working together; a group of persons acting or associating together, esp for illegal purposes. • vti to form into or act as a gang.—**ganged** adj.

gangland /-lænd/ n the criminal fraternity.

gangling /-glɪŋ/, **gangly** /'gæŋgli/ adj tall, thin and awkward in appearance and movement.

ganglion /-glɪən/ n (pl **ganglia, ganglions**) a mass of nerve cells from which nerve impulses are transmitted.—**ganglionic** adj.

gangplank /-plæŋk/ n a moveable ramp by which to board or leave a ship.

gangrene /-gri:n/ n death of body tissue when the blood supply is obstructed.—**gangrenous** adj.

gangsta /-stə/ n a variant of rap music with its source the US West Coast with lyrics focused on gang culture; ~ **rapper** a performer of this style of music. • adj belonging to gangsta music.

gangster /'gæŋstər/ n a member of a criminal gang.

gangue, gang /gæŋ/ *n* the earth or matrix in which ore is found.

gangway /'gæŋweɪ/ *n* a passageway, *esp* an opening in a ship's side for loading, etc; a gangplank.

ganister, gannister /'gænɪstər/ *n* a kind of silicious clay rock or hard sandstone; a refractory material used for lining furnaces.

ganja /'gændʒə/ or /'gɒn-/ *n* marijuana.

gannet /'gænət/ *n* any of various large voracious fish-eating sea birds.

ganoid /'gænɔɪd/ *adj* (*fish*) having enamelled bony scales, like the sturgeon. • *n* a ganoid fish.

gantlet /'gɒntlɪt/ or /'gɒnt-/, /'gænt-/ *see* **gauntlet**.

gantry /'gæntri/ *n* (*pl* **gantries**) a metal framework, often on wheels, for a travelling crane; a wheeled framework with a crane, platforms etc for servicing a rocket to be launched.

gaol /dʒeɪl/, **gaolbird, gaoler** *see* **jail, jailbird, jailer**.

gap /gæp/ *n* a break or opening in something, as a wall or fence; an interruption in continuity, an interval; a mountain pass; a divergence, disparity. • *vt* (**gapping, gapped**) to make a gap in.—**gappy** *adj*.

gape /geɪp/ *vi* to open the mouth wide; to stare in astonishment, *esp* with the mouth open; to open widely. • *n* the act of gaping; a wide opening.—**gaping** *adj*.—**gapingly** *adv*.

gaper /'geɪpər/ *n* a person who gapes; one of various types of shellfish that have a space between the valves.

gap year *n* a break of one year between school and college or university planned for the student to access work or experience seen as valuable in terms of personal development.

gar /gɑr/ *n* (*pl* **gar, gars**) a garfish.

garage (strake) /gə'rɒʒ/ or /-'rɒdʒ/, /-'rædʒ/, /-'ræʒ/ *n* an enclosed shelter for motor vehicles; a place where motor vehicles are repaired and serviced, and fuel sold. • *vt* to put or keep in a garage.

garage sale *n* a sale of unwanted household goods, held in a garage or other part of the house.

garb /gɑrb/ *n* clothing, style of dress. • *vt* to clothe.

garbage /'gɑrbɪdʒ/ *n* food waste; unwanted or useless material; rubbish; (*comput*) useless data; another word, *esp* in the US, for rubbish.

garble /'gɑrbəl/ *vt* to distort (a message, story, etc) so as to mislead.—**garbler** *n*.

garboard (strake) /'gɑrbɔrd/ *n* (*naut*) the plank or plate on a ship's bottom next to the keel.

garbology /gɑr'bɒlədʒi/ *n* the study of the disposal of waste material.—**garbologist** *n*.

garçon /gɑr'sɔ̃/ *n* a waiter.

garden /'gɑrdən/ *n* an area of ground for growing herbs, fruits, flowers, or vegetables; a yard; a fertile, well-cultivated region; a public park or recreation area, *usu* laid-out with plants and trees. • *vi* to make, or work in, a garden.—**gardener** *n*.—**gardening** *n*.

gardenia /gɑr'diːniə/ *n* a tree or shrub with beautiful fragrant white or yellow flowers.

garfish /'gɑrfɪʃ/ *n* (*pl* **garfish, garfishes**) a long, slender freshwater fish with a spearlike snout and a thick-scaled body.

gargantuan /gɑr'gæntʃʊən/ *adj* colossal, prodigious.

garget /'gɑrgət/ *n* a disease in cattle.

gargle /'gɑrgəl/ *vti* to rinse the throat by breathing air from the lungs through liquid held in the mouth. • *n* a liquid for this purpose; the sound made by gargling.—**gargler** *n*.

gargoyle /'gɑrgɔɪl/ *n* a grotesquely carved face or figure, *usu* acting as a spout to drain water from a gutter; a person with an ugly face.—**gargoyled** *adj*.

garibaldi /ˌgɛrɪ'bɒldi/ or /ˌgær-/ *n* a type of loose blouse, orig red.

garish /'gɛrɪʃ/ or /'gæ-/ *adj* crudely bright, gaudy.—**garishly** *adv*.—**garishness** *n*.

garland /'gɑrlənd/ *n* a wreath of flowers or leaves worn or hung as decoration. • *vt* to decorate with a garland.

garlic /'gɑrlɪk/ *n* a bulbous herb cultivated for its compound bulbs used in cookery; its bulb.—**garlicky** *adj*.

garment /'gɑrmənt/ *n* an item of clothing.

garner /'gɑrnər/ *vt* to gather, store.

garnet /'gɑrnət/ *n* a semiprecious stone, red, yellow or green in colour.

garnish /'gɑrnɪʃ/ *vt* to decorate; to decorate (food) with something that adds colour or flavour. • *n* something used to garnish food.—**garnisher** *n*.—**garniture** *n*.

garnishee /ˌgɑrnɪ'ʃiː/ *vt* (**garnisheeing, garnisheed**) (*law*) to warn by garnishment. • *n* (*law*) the person into whose hands

the property of another is attached pending the satisfaction of the claims of a third party.

garnishment /'gɑrnɪʃmənt/ *n* embellishment; (*law*) notice to holder of another's attached property not to give it to him but to account for it in court; a summons; (*arch*) notice to third party to appear in suit.

garniture /'gɑrnɪtʃər/ *n* embellishment, trimmings (*esp* on a dish of food).

garpike /'gɑrpaɪk/ *n* the garfish.

garret /'gɛrət/ or /'gær-/ *n* an attic.

garrison /'gɛrɪsən/ or /'gær-/ *n* troops stationed at a fort; a fortified place with troops. • *vt* to station (troops) in (a fortified place) for its defence.

garrotte, garrote, garotte /gə'rɒt/ *n* a method of execution by strangling with an iron collar; the iron collar used. • *vt* to execute by garrotte; to half-throttle and rob.—**garrotter, garroter, garotter** *n*.

garrulous /'gɛrʊləs/ or /'gær-/ *adj* excessively talkative.—**garrulously** *adv*.—**garrulousness, garrulity** *n*.

garter /'gɑrtər/ *n* an elasticated band used to support a stocking or sock.

garth /gɑrθ/ *n* a courtyard surrounded by a cloister; (*arch*) a yard, garden or paddock.

gas /gæs/ *n* (*pl* **gases, gasses**) an air-like substance with the capacity to expand indefinitely and not liquefy or solidify at ordinary temperatures; any mixture of flammable gases used for lighting or heating; any gas used as an anaesthetic; any poisonous substance dispersed in the air, as in war; (*inf*) empty talk; gasoline. • *vt* (**gases** *or* **gasses, gassing, gassed**) to poison or disable with gas; (*inf*) to talk idly and at length.

gasbag /'gæsbæg/ *n* (*inf*) an idle talker.

gas chamber *n* an airtight room where animals or people are killed by poisonous gas.

gasconade /ˌgæskə'neɪd/ *n* (*rare*) boastful or blustering talk. • *vi* to bluster, to boast.

gaseous /'gæsiəs/ or /'gæʃəs/ *adj* having the form of or being gas; of or being related to gases; lacking substance or solidity.—**gaseousness** *n*.

gash /gæʃ/ *n* a long, deep, open cut. • *vt* to cut deep.

gasholder *n* a circular hollow tank, open at the bottom and closed at the top, for storing gas prior to distribution.

gasify /'gæsɪfaɪ/ *vti* (**gasifying, gasified**) to turn into gas.—**gasification** *n*.

gasket /'gæskət/ *n* a piece or ring of rubber, metal, etc sandwiched between metal surfaces to act as a seal.

gaslight /'gæslaɪt/ *n* a type of lamp using a jet of gas to provide illumination.

gasman /-mæn/ *n* (*pl* **gasmen**) an employee of a gas company who reads meters, etc.

gasolier, gaselier /ˌgæsə'lɪr/ *n* a branched hanging support for gas lights.

gasoline, gasolene /'gæsəˌliːn/ *n* (*US*) a liquid fuel or solvent distilled from petroleum.—*also* **petrol**.—**gasolinic** *adj*.

gasometer /gæ'sɒmɪtər/ *n* an instrument for measuring gas; a gasholder.

gasometry /gæ'sɒmɪtri/ *n* the science or process of measuring gas.

gasp /gæsp/ *vi* to draw in the breath suddenly and audibly, as from shock; to struggle to catch the breath. • *vt* to utter breathlessly. • *n* the act of gasping.—**gaspingly** *adv*.

gassy /'gæsi/ *adj* (**gassier, gassiest**) impregnated with or like a gas; given to pretentious talk; inflated.

gastr-, gastro- /'gæstrɒ/ *prefix* stomach.

gastric /'gæstrɪk/ *adj* of, in, or near the stomach.

gastric juice *n* digestive fluid secreted by glands in the stomach lining.

gastric ulcer *n* an ulcer of the lining of the stomach.

gastritis /gæ'straɪtɪs/ *n* inflammation of the stomach.—**gastritic** *adj*.

gastroenteric /ˌgæstrɒɛn'tɛrɪk/ *adj* of or pertaining to the stomach or intestinal tract.

gastroenteritis /-ɛntə'raɪtɪs/ *n* inflammation of the mucous membrane of the stomach and intestines.—**gastroenteritic** *adj*.

gastrointestinal /-ɪn'tɛstɪnəl/ or /-ɪntɛs'taɪnəl/ *adj* of or pertaining to the stomach or intestines.

gastrology /gæs'trɒlədʒi/, **gastroenterology** /-ɛntə'rɒlədʒi/ *n* the study of diseases of the stomach and intestinal tract.

gastronome /'gæstrə,no:m/, **gastronomer** /-ər/, **gastronomist** /-ıst/ *n* a connoisseur of food.

gastronomy /gæ'strɒnəmi/ *n* the art and science of good eating.—**gastronomic, gastronomical** *adj*.—**gastronomically** *adj*.

gastropod /'gæstrə,pɒd/ *n* any of a large class of molluscs (as snails) with a flattened foot for moving and *usu* with stalk-like sense organs.—**gastropodan** *adj, n*.—**gastropodous** *adj*.

gastrula /'gæstrulə/ *n* (*pl* **gastrulas, gastrulae**) the fertilized ovum at a certain period in its development.

gasworks /'gæswərks/ *n sing* a place where gas is manufactured.

gate /geıt/ *n* a movable structure controlling passage through an opening in a fence or wall; a gateway; a movable barrier; a structure controlling the flow of water, as in a canal; a device (as in a computer) that outputs a signal when specified input conditions are met; the total amount or number of paid admissions to a football match, etc. • *vt* to supply with a gate; to keep within the gates (of a university) as a punishment.

gâteau, gateau /gæ'to:/ *n* (*pl* **gâteaux, gateaux**) a large cream cake.

gate-crasher /'geıt,kræʃər/ *n* a person who attends a party, etc without being invited.—**gatecrash** *vi*.

gatefold /'geıtfo:ld/ *n* an oversize page in a book or magazine that is folded in.

gatehouse /-hʊs/ *n* a house built over or beside a gate.

gatekeeper /-,ki:pər/ *n* a person who controls entrance to a gate.

gate-leg(ged) table /'geıtleg/ *n* a table with drop leaves supported by movable legs.

gatepost /'geıtpo:st/ *n* a post on which a gate is hung, or to which it is attached when closed.

gateway /'geıtweı/ *n* an opening for a gate; a means of entrance or exit.

gather /'gæðər/ *vt* to bring together in one place or group; to get gradually; to collect (as taxes); to harvest; to draw (parts) together; to pucker fabric by pulling a thread or stitching; to understand, infer. • *vi* to come together in a body; to cluster around a focus of attention; (*sore*) to swell and fill with pus.—**gatherable** *adj*.—**gatherer** *n*.

gathering /-ıŋ/ *n* the act of gathering or assembling together; an assembly; folds made in a garment by gathering.

Gatling gun /'gætlıŋ/ *n* a machine gun with clustered barrels, which are discharged in succession by turning a handle.

gauche /go:ʃ/ *adj* socially inept; graceless, tactless.—**gauchely** *adv*.—**gaucheness** *n*.

gaucherie /,go:ʃə'ri:/ or /'go:ʃə,ri:/ *n* awkwardness, tactlessness; a tactless or awkward act.

gaucho /'gaʊtʃo:/ *n* (*pl* **gauchos**) a cowboy of the pampas of South America.

gaud /gɒd/ *n* a piece of finery, a trinket or ornament.

gaudery /'gɒdi/ *n* (*pl* **gauderies**) cheap, showy finery.

gaudy /'gɒdi/ *adj* (**gaudier, gaudiest**) excessively ornamented; tastelessly bright.—**gaudily** *adv*.—**gaudiness** *n*.

gauffer /'gɒfər/ or /'gɒf-/ *see* **goffer**.

gauge /geıdʒ/ *n* measurement according to some standard or system; any device for measuring; the distance between rails of a railway; the size of the bore of a shotgun; the thickness of sheet metal, wire, etc. • *vt* to measure the size, amount, etc of.—*also* **gage**.—**gaugeable, gagable** *adj*.—**gauger, gager** *n*.

Gaul /gɒl/ *n* an ancient region of Western Europe corresponding roughly to modern France and Belgium; a native of Gaul.

Gaullism /'go:lızəm/ *n* the policies pertaining to General de Gaulle, first president of the Fifth Republic in France (1959–69); the political movement based on de Gaulle's policies and principles.—**Gaullist** *n, adj*.

gaunt /gɒnt/ *adj* excessively thin as from hunger or age; looking grim or forbidding.—**gauntness** *n*.

gauntlet[1] /'gɒntlət/ *n* a knight's armoured glove; a long glove, often with a flaring cuff.—*also* **gantlet** *n*.

gauntlet[2] *n* (*formerly*) a type of military punishment in which a victim was forced to run between two lines of men who struck him as he passed.

gaur /'gaʊər/ *n* a large fierce, dark-coloured ox found in SE Asia and India.

gauss /gaʊs/ *n* (*pl* **gauss, gausses**) the unit of measurement for magnetic flux density.

gauze /gɒz/ *n* any very thin, loosely woven fabric, as of cotton or silk; a firm woven material of metal or plastic filaments; a surgical dressing.

gauzy /'gɒzi/ *adj* (**gauzier, gauziest**) like gauze, thin, transparent.—**gauzily** *adv*.—**gauziness** *n*.

gave /geıv/ *see* **give**.

gavel /'gævəl/ *n* a hammer used by a chairman, auctioneer, judge, etc to command proceedings.

gavial /'geıviəl/ *n* an Indian crocodile with a long narrow snout.

gavotte /gə'vɒt/ *n* a lively dance of French peasant origin.

gawk /gɒk/ *vi* to stare at stupidly.

gawky /'gɒki/ *adj* (**gawkier, gawkiest**) clumsy, awkward, ungainly.—**gawkily** *adv*.—**gawkiness** *n*.

gay /geı/ *adj* homosexual ; joyous and lively; colourful. • *n* a homosexual.—**gayness** *n*.

gaze /geız/ *vi* to look steadily. • *n* a steady look.—**gazer** *n*.

gazebo /gə'zi:bo:/ *n* (*pl* **gazebos, gazeboes**) a summerhouse or belvedere, elevated to command a wide view.

gazelle /gə'zɛl/ *n* (*pl* **gazelles, gazelle**) any of numerous small swift Asian or African antelopes.

gazette /gə'zɛt/ *n* a newspaper, now mainly in newspaper titles; an official publication listing government appointments, legal notices, etc.

gazetteer /,gæzə'ti:r/ *n* a book or section of a book that lists and describes places; an index of geographical place names.

gazpacho /gə'spætʃo:/ *n* a Spanish soup of tomatoes and other vegetables, served cold.

GB *abbr* = Great Britain.

Gd (*chem symbol*) gadolinium.

GDP /'dʒi:,di:,pi:/ *abbr* = Gross Domestic Product.

Ge /geı/ (*chem symbol*) germanium.

gear /gi:r/ *n* clothing; equipment, *esp* for some task or activity; a toothed wheel designed to mesh with another; (*often pl*) a system of such gears meshed together to transmit motion; a specific adjustment of such a system; a part of a mechanism with a specific function. • *vt* to connect by or furnish with gears; to adapt (one thing) to conform with another.

gearbox /'gi:rbɒks/ *n* a metal case enclosing a system of gears.

gearing /'gi:rıŋ/ *n* a particular arrangement of gears.

gearshift /'gi:rʃıft/ *n* a lever used to engage or change gear, *esp* in a motor vehicle.

gearwheel /-wi:l/ *n* a cogwheel.

gecko /'gɛko:/ *n* (*pl* **geckos, geckoes**) a small lizard of warm regions that feeds on insects.

gee /dʒi:/ *vi* (**geeing geed**) (*often with* **up**) to make a horse go faster. • *interj* a mild oath.

geese /gi:s/ *see* **goose**.

geezer /'gi:zər/ *n* (*sl*) an old man.

Geiger counter /'gaıgər/ *n* an electronic device for detecting and measuring radioactive emissions.

geisha /'geıʃə/ *n* (*pl* **geisha, geishas**) a Japanese girl trained as an entertainer to serve as a hired companion to men.

gel /dʒɛl/ *n* a jelly-like substance, as that applied to style and sculpt hair before drying it. • *vti* (**gelling, gelled**) to become or cause to become a gel.—*also* **jell**.

gelatin, gelatine /'dʒɛlətın/ *n* a tasteless, odourless substance extracted by boiling bones, hoofs, etc and used in food, photographic film, medicines, etc.

gelatinize /dʒı'lætı,naız/ *vt* to make or become gelatinous; to coat with gelatin.—**gelatinization** *n*.—**gelatinizer** *n*.

gelatinous /dʒə'lætınəs/ *adj* of or like gelatin; jelly-like in consistency.

gelation /dʒə'leıʃən/ *n* solidification (of liquids) by cold.

geld /gɛld/ *vt* (**gelding, gelded** *or* **gelt**) to castrate, *esp* a horse.

gelding /'gɛldıŋ/ *n* a castrated horse.

gelid /'dʒɛlıd/ *adj* intensely cold; icy.—**gelidity** *n*.

gelignite /'dʒɛlıg,naıt/ *n* an explosive consisting of nitroglycerin absorbed in a base of wood pulp mixed with sodium or potassium nitrate.

gem /dʒɛm/ *n* a precious stone, *esp* when cut and polished for use as a jewel; a person or thing regarded as extremely valuable or beloved. • *vt* (**gemming, gemmed**) to decorate or set with gems.

geminate /'dʒɛmınət/, **geminated** /-ıd/ *adj* growing or occurring in pairs.

gemination /-'neıʃən/ *n* duplication; (*rhetoric*) the repetition of a word, etc, for effect.

Gemini /'dʒɛmı,naı/ or /-,ni:/ *n* the third sign of the zodiac, represented by the twins Castor and Pollux, operative 21 May–20 June.—**Geminian** *adj*.

gemma /'dʒɛmə/ n (pl **gemmae**) a growth on an animal or plant budding off as a separate individual.

gemmate /'dʒɛm,eɪt/ vi to have buds; to propagate by gemmae.— **gemmation** n.—**gemmiparous** adj.

gemmule /'dʒɛmjuːl/ n a small bud or gemma; an ovule; a cell produced by certain moulds.

gemot, gemote /gə'moːt/ n an assembly or local court in pre-Norman England.

gemsbok /'gɛmzbɒk/ n (pl **gemsbok, gemsboks**) a large, straight-horned South African antelope with a broad black stripe along its length.

gemstone /'dʒɛmstoːn/ n a mineral or substance used as a gem.

gendarme /'ʒɒndɑːm/ n an armed policeman in France and Belgium.

gendarmerie, gendarmery /ʒɒn'dɑːməri/ n a force of gendarmes.

gender /'dʒɛndər/ n the classification by which words are grouped as feminine, masculine, or neuter; (inf) the sex of a person.

gene /dʒiːn/ n any of the complex chemical units in the chromosomes by which hereditary characteristics are transmitted.

genealogy /,dʒiːni'ɒlədʒi/ or /-ælədʒi/ n (pl **genealogies**) a recorded history of one's ancestry; the study of family descent; lineage.—**genealogical** adj.—**genealogist** n.

genera /'dʒɛnərə/ see **genus**.

generable /-əbəl/ adj capable of being generated.

general /'dʒɛnərəl/ adj not local, special, or specialized; of or for a whole genus, relating to or covering all instances or individuals of a class or group; widespread, common to many; not specific or precise; holding superior rank, chief. • n something that involves or is applicable to the whole; a commissioned officer above a lieutenant general; a leader, commander; the title of the head of some religious orders.—**generalness** n.

general anaesthetic n an anaesthetic effecting the whole body and producing unconsciousness.

general delivery n the department of a post office that will hold mail until it is called for.—also **poste restante**.

general election n a national election to choose representatives in every constituency.

generalissimo /,dʒɛnərə'liːsɪmoː/ n (pl **generalissimos**) a military commander of combined air, naval and ground forces.

generality /,dʒɛnə'ræliti/ n (pl **generalities**) the quality or state of being general; a vague or inadequate statement.

generalization /,dʒɛnərəlaɪ'zeɪʃən/ or /-lɪ-/ n general inference; induction; a general notion formed by attributing the characteristic(s) of a particular part or member (of a class, community etc) to the whole.

generalize /'dʒɛnərə,laɪz/ vti to form general conclusions from specific instances; to talk (about something) in general terms.—**generalization** n.—**generalizer** n.

generally /'dʒɛnərəli/ adv widely; popularly; usually; not specifically.

general practitioner n a non-specialist doctor who treats all types of illnesses in the community.

general-purpose /'dʒɛnərəl'pɜːpəs/ adj having all kinds of uses.

generalship /'dʒɛnərəlʃɪp/ n the office of general; military skill; management skill.

general staff n officers who advice and assist a military commander.

general strike n a strike of all workers in a city, region or country.

generate /'dʒɛnə,reɪt/ vt to bring into existence; to produce.

generation /,dʒɛnə'reɪʃən/ n the act or process of generating; a single succession in natural descent; people of the same period; production, as of electric current.

generation gap n the difference in attitudes and understanding between one generation and another.

generative /'dʒɛnərətɪv/ adj pertaining to generation; having the power to generate.

generator /'dʒɛnə,reɪtər/ n one who or that which generates; a machine that changes mechanical energy to electrical energy.

generic /dʒə'nɛrɪk/ adj of a whole class, kind, or group.—**generically** adv.

generosity /-'rɒsɪti/ n (pl **generosities**) the quality of being generous; liberality; munificence; a generous act.

generous /'dʒɛnərəs/ adj magnanimous; of a noble nature; willing to give or share; large, ample.—**generously** adv.—**generousness** n.

genesis /'dʒɛnəsɪs/ n (pl **geneses**) the beginning, origin; (with cap) the first book of the Old Testament.

genet /'dʒɛnɪt/ n an animal of southern Europe, western Asia and Africa, related to the civet and valued for its fur; any fur made in imitation of genet.

genetic /dʒə'nɛtɪk/, **genetical** /-əl/ adj of or relating to the origin, development or causes of something; of or relating to genes or genetics.—**genetically** adv.

genetic code n the order of genetic information in a cell, which determines hereditary characteristics.

genetic engineering n the modification of genetic information in the cell of a plant or animal to improve yield, performance, etc.

genetic fingerprinting n the analysis of bodily tissue or fluids to identify the unique genetic character of an individual, as used in criminal investigations, the determination of paternity, etc.

genetics /dʒə'nɛtɪks/ n sing the branch of biology dealing with heredity and variation in plants and animals.—**geneticist** n.

genial[1] /'dʒiːnɪəl/ adj kindly, sympathetic and cheerful in manner; mild, pleasantly warm.—**geniality, genialness** n.—**genially** adv.

genial[2] adj of the chin.

geniculate /dʒə'nɪkjuːlɪt/ or /-,leɪt/, **geniculated** /-td/ adj having knee-like joints; bent at a sharp angle.

genie /'dʒiːni/ n (pl **genies, genii**) (fairy tales) a spirit with supernatural powers which can fulfil your wishes.—also **jinni**.

genital /'dʒɛnɪtəl/ adj of reproduction or the sexual organs.

genitals, genitalia /,dʒɛnɪ'teɪliə/ npl the (external) sexual organs.—**genitalic** adj.

genitive /'dʒɛnɪtɪv/ adj (gram) of or belonging to the case of nouns, pronouns and adjectives expressing ownership or relation. • n the genitive case.—**genitival** adj.

genius /'dʒiːnjəs/ n (pl **geniuses**) a person possessing extraordinary intellectual power; (with for) natural ability, strong inclination.

genocide /'dʒɛnə,saɪd/ n the systematic killing of a whole race of people.—**genocidal** adj.

genre /'ʒɑ̃rə/ or /'ʒɒnrə/ n a distinctive type or category, esp of literary composition; a style of painting in which everyday objects are treated realistically.

gens /dʒɛnz/ n (pl **gentes**) in ancient Rome, a clan or house; one of a number of related families claiming a common ancestor or having a name or religious rites etc in common.

gent /dʒɛnt/ n (inf) a gentleman.

genteel /dʒɛn'tiːl/ adj polite or well-bred; affectedly refined.—**genteelly** adv.—**genteelness** n.

gentes see **gens**.

gentian /'dʒɛnʃən/ or /-ʃiən/ n an alpine plant, usu with blue flowers.

gentian violet n a crystalline substance used as an antiseptic.

gentile /'dʒɛntaɪl/ n a person who is not a Jew.—also adj.

gentility /dʒɛn'tɪlɪti/ n (pl **gentilities**) refinement, good manners.

gentle /'dʒɛntəl/ adj belonging to a family of high social station; refined, courteous; generous; kind; kindly; patient; not harsh or rough.—**gentleness** n.—**gently** adv.

gentleman /-mən/ n (pl **gentlemen**) a man of good family and social standing; a courteous, gracious and honourable man; a polite term of address.—**gentlemanly** adj.

gentleman-at-arms /-æt'ɑːmz/ n (pl **gentlemen-at-arms**) one of the bodyguard of the UK sovereign on state occasions.

gentlewoman /-,wʊmən/ n (pl **gentlewomen**) a woman of noble or gentle birth; a lady.

gentrify /'dʒɛntrɪfaɪ/ vt (**gentrifying, gentrified**) to convert a working-class house or district to more expensive middle-class tastes.—**gentrification** n.

gentry /'dʒɛntri/ n people of high social standing; (formerly) landed proprietors not belonging to the nobility.

genuflect /'dʒɛnjʊ,flɛkt/ vi to act in a servile way; to bend the knee in worship or respect.—**genuflection** n.—**genuflector** n.

genuine /'dʒɛnjʊɪn/ or /-aɪn/ adj not fake or artificial, real; sincere.—**genuinely** adv.—**genuineness** n.

genus /'dʒiːnəs/ or /'dʒɛnəs/ n (pl **genera**) (biol) a taxonomic division of plants and animals below a family and above a species; a class of objects divided into several subordinate species.

geo- /'dʒiːoː/ prefix earth.

geocentric /,dʒiːoː'sɛntrɪk/ adj viewed as from the centre of the earth; having the earth as a centre.—**geocentrically** adv.

geod abbr = geodesic; geodesy; geodetic.

geode /'dʒiːoːd/ n a cavity lined with crystals, usu within a rock.

geodesic /,dʒiːoː'diːsɪk/ or /-'dɛsɪk/ adj geodetic.—also **geodesical**.

• *n* (*math*) the shortest distance between two points on a curved surface, determined by triangulation.

geodesic dome *n* a lightweight domed structure made of interlocking polygons.

geodesy /dʒiː'ɒdɪsi/ *n* the mathematical determination of the exact positions of geographical points and the shape and size of the earth.—**geodesic** *adj*.—**geodic** *adj*.

geodetic /dʒiːoʊ'dɛtɪk/, **geodetical** /-əl/ *adj* of, pertaining to, determined by, or carried out by geodesy.

geography /ˌdʒiːə'ɡræfi/ *n* (*pl* **geographies**) the science of the physical nature of the earth, such as land and sea masses, climate, vegetation, etc, and their interaction with the human population; the physical features of a region.—**geographer** *n*.—**geographical**, **geographic** *adj*.—**geographically** *adv*.

geologize /dʒi'ɒlədʒaɪz/ *vti* to study geology or the geology of.

geology /dʒi'ɒlədʒi/ *n* the science relating to the history and structure of the earth's crust, its rocks and fossils.—**geological**, **geologic** *adj*.—**geologically** *adv*.—**geologist**, **geologer** *n*.

geomancy /'dʒiːoʊˌmænsi/ *n* divination by figures or lines.—**geomancer** *n*.—**geomantic** *adj*.

geometer /dʒi'ɒmɪtər/, **geometrician** /-mətvɪsɪən/ *n* one who studies or is skilled in geometry.

geometric /ˌdʒiə'mɛtrɪk/, **geometrical** /-əl/ *adj* pertaining to, or done by, geometry; (*design, etc*) consisting of simple geometric shapes.—**geometrically** *adv*.

geometric progression *n* a sequence in which the terms differ by a constant ratio (e.g. 1, 2, 4, 8, 16 ...).

geometrize /dʒi'ɒmətraɪz/ *vti* to work or make by geometrical methods; to study geometry.

geometry /dʒi'ɒmətri/ *n* the branch of mathematics dealing with the properties, measurement, and relationships of points, lines, planes, and solids.—**geometric**, **geometrical** *adj*.—**geometrically** *adv*.

geophagy /dʒi'ɒfədʒi/, **geophagia**, **geophagism** *n* the practice of eating certain kinds of clay, earth or chalk.—**geophagist** *n*.—**geophagous** *adj*.

geophysics /ˌdʒiːoʊ'fɪzɪks/ *n sing* the physics of the earth.—**geophysical**.—*adj*.—**geophysicist** *n*.

geopolitics /ˌdʒiːoʊ'pɒlɪtɪks/ *n sing* the study of the relationship between the geographical situation of a nation and its politics; the study of the effect of a nation's geography on its politics, *esp* in relation to that nation's relationship with other nations.

geoponic /ˌdʒiːoʊ'pɒnɪk/ *adj* agricultural.

geoponics /-s/ *n sing* the scientific study of agriculture.

georgette /dʒɔːr'dʒɛt/ *n* a thin silk fabric.

Georgian /'dʒɔːrdʒən/ *adj* of the times or reigns of the four Georges (1714–1830) or of George V (1910–36) who ruled Britain; pertaining to Georgia in the US; pertaining to Georgia in the Caucasus. • *n* a person from Georgia; a person who lived in Georgian times; one who lives as if he or she belonged to Georgian times.

georgic /'dʒɔːrdʒɪk/, **georgical** /-əl/ *adj* of or pertaining to husbandry; rural. • *n* a poem on agriculture; (*with cap: pl*) a poem on agriculture by Virgil.

geothermal /ˌdʒiːoʊ'θɜːrməl/, **geothermic** /-mɪk/ *adj* of, relating to, or using the heat of the earth's interior.

geotropism /dʒi'ɒtrəˌpɪzəm/ *n* (*bot*) a tendency in the roots of certain plants to turn in the direction of the earth.—**geotropic** *adj*.—**geotropically** *adv*.

geranium /dʒə'reɪniəm/ *n* a garden plant with red, pink or white flowers.

gerbil, gerbille /'dʒɜːrbɪl/ *n* a type of burrowing desert rodent of Asia and Africa.—*also* **jerbil**.

gerent /'dʒɪrənt/ *n* (*rare*) a ruler, a manager.

gerfalcon /'dʒɜːrˌfɔːlkən/ or /-ˌfɒkən/, /-ˌfæl-/ *see* **gyrfalcon**.

geriatric /ˌdʒɛri'ætrɪk/ *adj* relating to geriatrics or old people; (*inf*) old, decrepit. • *n* an aged person.

geriatrics /-s/ *n sing* a branch of medicine dealing with the diseases and care of old people.—**geriatrician, geriatrist** *n*.

germ /dʒɜːrm/ *n* a simple form of living matter capable of growth and development into an organism; any microscopic, disease-causing organism; an origin or foundation capable of growing and developing.

German /'dʒɜːrmən/ *adj* of or relating to Germany, its people or their language. • *n* a native of Germany.

german *adj* of the same stock or parentage; germane.

germander /dʒɜːr'mændər/ *n* a plant of the mint family.

germane /dʒɜːr'meɪn/ *adj* relevant.—**germanely** *adv*.—**germaneness** *n*.

Germanic /dʒɜːr'mænɪk/ *adj* of Germans or Germany or of a German-speaking nation. • *n* the family of languages derived from Indo-European that comprises the English, Dutch, German, Scandinavian and Gothic languages.

Germanism /'dʒɜːrmənˌɪzəm/ *n* a German idiom, custom, or characteristic.

germanium /dʒɜːr'meɪniəm/ *n* a rare metallic element used in transistors.

Germanize /'dʒɜːrməˌnaɪz/ *vti* to make or become German in language, custom, manners etc.—**Germanization** *n*.

German measles *n sing* a mild contagious disease similar to measles.—*also* **rubella**.

Germanophile /dʒɜːr'mænəˌfaɪl/ *n* a lover of Germany or its customs, etc.

Germanophobe /-ˌfoʊb/ *n* a person who has an irrational fear of Germany.—**Germanophobia** *n*.

German shepherd *n* any of a breed of large smooth-haired dogs often used by the police and for guarding property.—*also* **Alsatian**.

German silver *n* an alloy of nickel, copper and zinc.—*also* **nickel silver**.

germ cell *n* a reproductive cell.

germicide /'dʒɜːrmɪˌsaɪd/ *n* a substance used to destroy germs.—**germicidal** *adj*.

germinal /'dʒɜːrmɪnəl/ *adj* incipient; of or pertaining to a germ or germs or seed buds; in the French revolutionary calendar, the seventh month (March 22-April 20).

germinate /'dʒɜːrmɪˌneɪt/ *vti* to start developing; to sprout, as from a seed.—**germinable, germinative** *adj*.—**germination** *germinator* *n*.

germ warfare *n* the use of disease-causing bacteria against enemy forces.

gerontocracy /ˌdʒɛrɒn'tɒkrəsi/ *n* (*pl* **gerontocracies**) government by old men.—**gerontocratic** *adj*.

gerontology /ˌdʒɛrən'tɒlədʒi/ *n* the study of aging and its effects and problems.—**gerontological** *adj*.—**gerontologist** *n*.

gerrymander /ˌdʒɛri'mændər/ *vt* to rearrange the boundaries of (voting districts) to favour a particular party or candidate.

gerund /'dʒɛrənd/ *n* the participle of a verb used as a noun.—**gerundial** *adj*.

gerundive /dʒɛ'rɛndɪv/ *adj* of or like a gerund. • *n* a passive verbal adjective.

gesso /'dʒɛsoʊ/ *n* (*pl* **gessoes**) a prepared ground of plaster for painting on; plaster of Paris.

gestalt /ɡə'ʃtɒlt/ *n* (*pl* **gestalts, gestalten**) an integral pattern or system of phenomena forming a functional unit in which the whole is more than the sum of its parts.

Gestapo /ɡə'stɒpoʊ/ *n* the secret police of Nazi Germany.

gestate /'dʒɛsteɪt/ *vt* to carry (young) in the womb during pregnancy; to develop (a plan, etc) gradually in the mind.—**gestational, gestative** *adj*.—**gestatory** *adj*.

gestation /dʒɛ'steɪʃən/ *n* the act or period of carrying young in the womb; pregnancy.

gesticulate /dʒɛ'stɪkjʊˌleɪt/ *vi* to make expressive gestures, *esp* when speaking.—**gesticulation** *n*.—**gesticulative** *adj*.—**gesticulator** *n*.

gesture /'dʒɛstʃər/ *n* movement of part of the body to express or emphasize ideas, emotions, etc. • *vi* to make a gesture.—**gestural** *adj*.—**gesturer** *n*.

get /ɡɛt/ *vb* (**getting, got,** *pp* **got, gotten**) *vt* to obtain, gain, win; to receive; to acquire; to go and bring; to catch; to persuade; to cause to be; to prepare; (*inf*) (*with vb aux* **have** *or* **has**) to be obliged to; to possess; (*inf*) to strike, kill, baffle; defeat, etc; (*inf*) to understand; (*with* **across**) to cause to be understood; (*with* **in**) to bring in; (*crops, etc*) to gather; to insert; (*with* **off**) to acquit, to secure favourable treatment of; (*letters*) to post; (*with* **out**) to cause to leave or escape; to cause to become known or published; (*with* **out of**) to avoid doing; (*with* **over**) to communicate effectively. • *vi* to come; to go; to arrive; to come to be; to manage or contrive; (*with* **about, around**) to be up and on one's feet, *esp* after being unwell; to be socially active; (*news, gossip*) to become circulated; (*with*) **across**) to be understood; (*with* **at**) to reach; (*inf*) to mean, imply; to irritate, pester relentlessly; (*inf*) to criticize; (*inf*) to corrupt, bribe, influence illegally; (*with* **away**) to escape; (*with* **by**) (*inf*) to manage, to survive; (*with* **in**) (*vehicle*, *etc*) to enter; to arrive; (*university, college, etc*) to be offered a place; (*with* **off**) to come off, down, or out of; to be acquitted; to escape the consequences of; to begin, depart; (*with* **on**) to go on or into; to put on; to proceed; to grow older; to become late; to manage; to succeed; (*with* **on with**) to establish a friendly relationship; (*with* **out**) to go out or away; to leave or escape; to take out; to become known or published; (*with* **over**) to overcome; to recover from; to forget; (*with* **round, around**) to evade, circumvent; to coax, cajole; (*with* **through**) to use up, spend, consume; to finish; to manage to survive; (*examination, test*) to succeed or pass; to contact by telephone; (*with* **up**) to rise to one's feet; to get out of bed; (*inf*) to organize; (*inf*) to dress in a certain style; (*inf*) to be involved in (mischief, etc).—**getable, gettable** *adj*.

get-at-able /gɛtˈætəbəl/ *adj* accessible.

getaway /ˈgɛtəweɪ/ *n* the act of escaping; a start in a race, etc.

get-together /ˈgɛtəˌgɛðər/ *n* (*inf*) an informal social gathering or meeting.

get-up /ˈgɛtʌp/ *n* (*inf*) dress, costume.

get-up-and-go /-ənˈgoʊ/ *n* (*inf*) energy, enthusiasm.

getter /ˈgɛtər/ *n* one who gets or acquires.

geum /ˈdʒiːəm/ *n* a genus of the rose family, with yellow, orange, red or white flowers.

gewgaw /ˈguːgɔː/ or /ˈgjuː-/ *n* a showy ornament; a trinket.

geyser /ˈgaɪzər/ *n* a natural spring from which columns of boiling water and steam gush into the air at intervals; a water heater.

gharry, gharri /ˈgæri/ *n* (*pl* **gharries**) a cart or carriage in India that is available for hire.

ghastly /ˈgæstli/ *adj* (**ghastlier, ghastliest**) terrifying, horrible; (*inf*) intensely disagreeable; pale, unwell looking.—**ghastliness** *n*.

ghat, ghaut /gɒt/ *n* in India, a mountain pass or a chain of mountains; a landing-place with steps; a flight of steps to a river or a temple.

ghazi /ˈgɒzi/ *n* (*pl* **ghazies**) a Muslim slayer of infidels; a Turkish title bestowed on distinguished commanders; a warrior champion.

ghee /giː/ *n* clarified butter.

gherkin /ˈgərkɪn/ *n* a small cucumber used for pickling.

ghetto /ˈgɛtoʊ/ *n* (*pl* **ghettos, ghettoes**) a section of a city in which members of a minority group live, *esp* because of social, legal or economic pressure.

ghetto blaster *n* (*inf*) a large portable stereo cassette player and radio with built-in speakers.

ghillie /ˈgɪli/ *n* (*pl* **ghillies**) a gillie.

ghost /goʊst/ *n* the supposed disembodied spirit of a dead person, appearing as a shadowy apparition; a faint trace or suggestion; a false image in a photographic negative. • *vt* to ghostwrite.

ghostly /ˈgoʊstli/ *adj* (**ghostlier, ghostliest**) of or like a ghost.—**ghostliness** *n*.

ghost town *n* a town abandoned by most or all of its inhabitants.

ghostwrite /ˈgoʊstˌraɪt/ *vt* (**ghostwriting, ghostwrote,** *pp* **ghostwritten**) to write books, speeches, articles, etc for another who professes to be the author.—**ghostwriter** *n*.

ghoul /guːl/ *n* (*Muslim folklore*) an evil spirit that robs graves and feeds on the dead; a person with macabre tastes or interests.—**ghoulish** *adj*.—**ghoulishly** *adv*.

GHQ *abbr* = General Headquarters.

GI /dʒiːˈaɪ/ *n* (*pl* **GI's, GIs**) (*inf*) a private soldier in the US Army.

giant /ˈdʒaɪənt/ *n* a huge legendary being of great strength; a person or thing of great size, strength, intellect, etc. • *adj* incredibly large.—**giantess** *nf*.

giant panda *n* a large black and white bear-like herbivore.—*also* **panda**.

giaour /ˈdʒaʊr/ *n* (*derog*) a Muslim term for an unbeliever, *esp* a Christian.

gibber /ˈdʒɪbər/ *vi* to utter meaningless or inarticulate sounds.

gibberish /-ɪʃ/ *n* unintelligible talk, nonsense.

gibbet /ˈdʒɪbət/ *n* a gallows; a structure from which bodies of executed criminals were hung and exposed to public scorn.

gibbon /ˈgɪbən/ *n* a small tailless ape of southeastern Asia and the East Indies.

gibbous /ˈgɪbəs/ *adj* protuberant; humped; irregularly rounded; (*moon*) between full and half.

gibe *n* a taunt, sneer. • *vti* to jeer, scoff (at).—*also* **jibe.—giber, jiber** *n*.—**gibingly, jibingly** *adv*.

giblets /ˈdʒɪbləts/ *npl* the edible internal organs of a bird.

gid *n* a disease in sheep, marked by staggering.

giddy /ˈgɪdi/ *adj* (**giddier, giddiest**) frivolous, flighty; having a feeling of whirling around as if about to lose balance and fall; causing giddiness. • *vti* (**giddying, giddied**) to make giddy, to become giddy.—**giddily** *adv*.—**giddiness** *n*.

gie /giː/ *vt* (*Scot*) to give.

GIFT /gɪft/ *abbr* = Gamete Intra-Fallopian Transfer; a technique that helps infertile couples to have children.

gift *n* something given; the act of giving; a natural ability. • *vt* to present with or as a gift.—**giftedness** *n*.

gifted /ˈgɪftəd/ *adj* having great natural ability.

gig[1] /gɪg/ *n* a light two-wheeled horse-drawn carriage; a long, light boat.

gig[2] *n* (*inf*) a single booking for a jazz or pop band, etc; a single night's performance. • *vi* (**gigging, gigged**) to perform a gig.

giga- /ˈgɪgə/ or /ˈdʒɪgə/, /ˈgaɪgə/ *prefix* one billion (109); (*comput*) 230.

gigantesque /dʒaɪˌgænˈtɛsk/ *adj* as if by or for a giant.

gigantic /dʒaɪˈgæntɪk/ *adj* exceedingly large.—**gigantically** *adv*.—**giganticness** *n*.

giggle /ˈgɪgəl/ *vi* to laugh in a nervous or silly manner. • *n* a laugh in this manner; (*inf*) a prank, a joke.—**giggler** *n*.—**giggly** *adj*.

gigolo /ˈdʒɪgəˌloʊ/ or /ˈʒɪg-/ *n* (*pl* **gigolos**) a man paid to be a woman's escort.

gigot /ˈʒiːˈgoʊ/ or /ˈdʒɪgət/ *n* a leg of mutton.

gigue /ʒiːg/ *n* a lively tune; a dance similar to a jig.

gild[1] /gɪld/ *see* **guild**.

gild[2] *vt* (**gilding, gilded** *or* **gilt**) to coat with gold leaf; to give a deceptively attractive appearance to.—**gilder** *n*

gilder /ˈgɪldər/ *see* **guilder**.

gilding /-ɪŋ/ *n* the art or proceess of overlaying or covering with gold leaf; gold leaf applied to a surface; a superficial covering.

gill[1] /gɪl/ *n* an organ, *esp* in fish, for breathing in water.

gill[2] *n* in US, a liquid measure equal to 4 fluid ounces (0.25 pint) or 23.6 millimetres; in UK, 5 fluid ounces (0.25 pint) or 28.4 millimetres.

gillie, gilly /ˈgɪli/ *n* (*pl* **gillies**) (*Scot*) a Highland attendant, *esp* one who accompanies a shooting or fishing party.—*also* **ghillie**.

gills /gɪls/ *npl* the wattle below the beak of a bird, as in certain domestic fowl; one of the radiating plates under the cap of a mushroom; a person's cheeks or jowls.

gillyflower /ˈdʒɪliˌflaʊr/ *n* one of various scented plants of the mustard family, *eg* wallflower, stock, etc.

gilt[1] /gɪlt/ *see* **gild**.

gilt[2] *n* gilding; a substance used for this.

gilt-edged /ˈgɪltˌɛdʒd/ *adj* (*securities*) considered a secure investment.

gimbal /ˈdʒɪmbəl/ or /ˈgɪmbəl/ *n* (*usu pl*) one of two rings moving within each other at right angles, used to suspend a ship's compass, etc.

gimcrack /ˈdʒɪmkræk/ *adj* showy, cheap and useless.

gimlet /ˈgɪmlət/ *n* a small tool with a screw point for boring holes.

gimmick /ˈgɪmɪk/ *n* a trick or device for attracting notice, advertising or promoting a person, product or service.—**gimmickry** *n*.—**gimmicky** *adj*.

gimp /gɪmp/ *n* an interlaced silk twist or trimming interwoven with wire or cord, used for furniture, dresses etc.—*also* **guimpe**.

gin[1] /dʒɪn/ *n* an alcoholic spirit distilled from grain and flavoured with juniper berries.

gin[2] *n* a trap for catching small animals; a type of crane; a machine for separating the seeds from raw cotton. • *vt* (**ginning, ginned**) to trap with a gin; to separate seeds from cotton.

ginger /ˈdʒɪndʒər/ *n* a tropical plant with fleshy roots used as a flavouring; the spice prepared by drying and grinding; (*inf*) vigour; a reddish-brown.—**gingery** *adj*.

ginger ale, ginger beer *n* a carbonated soft drink flavoured with ginger.

gingerbread /ˈdʒɪndʒərˌbrɛd/ *n* a cake flavoured with ginger.

gingerly /ˈdʒɪndʒərli/ *adv* with care or caution. • *adj* cautious.—**gingerliness** *n*.

ginger snap /ˈdʒɪndʒərˌsnæp/ *n* a ginger-flavoured biscuit.

gingham /ˈgɪŋəm/ *n* a cotton fabric with stripes or checks.

gingival /dʒɪnˈdʒaɪvəl/ *adj* of the gums.

gingivitis /ˌdʒɪndʒɪˈvaɪtɪs/ *n* inflammation of the gums.

ginglymus /ˈdʒɪndʒlɪˌməs/ *n* (*pl* **ginglymi**) (*anat*) a joint like a hinge.

gink /gɪŋk/ *n* (*sl*) a boy or man, *esp* an eccentric one.

ginkgo /'gɪŋkgo:/ *n* (*pl* **ginkgoes**) a Japanese tree with handsome fan-shaped foliage; the maidenhair tree.

ginseng /'dʒɪnsɛŋ/ *n* a plant found in China and North America; its root, said to have an invigorating effect on the mind and body.

gip /dʒɪp/ *see* **gyp**.

Gipsy /'dʒɪpsi/ *see* **Gypsy**.

giraffe /dʒɪ'ræf/ *n* (*pl* **giraffes, giraffe**) a large cud-chewing mammal of Africa, with very long legs and neck.

girandole /'dʒɪrən‚do:l/, **girandola** *n* a branched chandelier; a revolving firework or water jet; a pendant or earring with small stones around a larger one; one of several mines connected in a group.

girasol /'dʒɪrə‚sɒl/, **girosol, girasole** /-‚so:l/ *n* a variety of opal; the fire opal.

gird /gərd/ *vt* (**girding, girded** *or* **girt**) to encircle or fasten with a belt; to surround; to prepare (oneself) for action.

girder /'gərdər/ *n* a large steel beam for supporting joists, the framework of a building, etc.

girdle /'gərdəl/ *n* a belt for the waist.

girl /gərl/ *n* a female child; a young woman; (*inf*) a woman of any age.—**girlhood** *n*.—**girlish** *adj*.

girlfriend /'gərlfrɛnd/ *n* a female friend, *esp* with whom one is romantically involved.

Girl Guide *n* a member of the Girl Guides, a scouting organization founded in Britain in 1910.

girlie /'gərli/ *n* a little girl; a young woman; (*inf*) a woman.

girlie magazine *n* a magazine that contains photographs of nude or semi-nude females.

girlish /'gərlɪʃ/ *adj* of or like a girl.—**girlishly** *adv*.—**girlishness** *n*.

Girl Scout *n* a member of the Girl Scouts, a youth organization founded in the US in 1912.

giro /'dʒaɪro:/ *n* (*pl* **giros**) a credit-transfer system between financial organizations; a payment so made.

Girondist /ʒi'rɒndɪst/ *n* a member of the Gironde, the moderate Republican party during the Revolution in France (179193).

girt[1] /gərt/ *see* **gird**.

girt[2] *adj* (*naut*) moored so taut by two cables as not to swing to the wind or tide.

girth /gərθ/ *n* the thickness round something; a band put around the belly of a horse, etc to hold a saddle or pack.

gist /dʒɪst/ *n* the principal point or essence of anything.

gîte /ʒi:t/ *n* self-catering holiday accommodation in France.

give /gɪv/ *vb* (**giving, gave**, *pp* **given**) *vt* to hand over as a present; to deliver; to hand over in or for payment; to pass (regards etc) along; to act as host or sponsor of; to supply; to yield; (*advice*) to offer; (*punishment, etc*) to inflict; to sacrifice; to perform; (*with* **away**) to make a gift of; to give (the bride) to the bridegroom; to sell cheaply; to reveal, betray; (*with* **in**) to deliver, hand in (a document, etc); (*with* **off**) to emit (fumes, etc); (*with* **out**) to discharge; to make public, to announce; to emit; to distribute; (*with* **over**) to devote time to a specific activity; to cease (an activity); to transfer to another; to set aside for a particular purpose; (*with* **up**) to hand over; to stop, renounce; to cease; to resign (a position); to stop trying; to despair of; to surrender; to devote oneself completely (to). • *vi* to bend, move, etc from force or pressure; (*inf*) to be happening; (*with* **in**) to concede, admit defeat; (*with* **out**) to become used up or exhausted; to fail; (*with* **over**) (*inf*) to stop (an activity). • *n* capacity or tendency to yield to force or strain; the quality or state of being springy; (*with* **in**) to submit; (*with* **out**) to become worn out; (*with* **up**) to accept defeat or failure to do something, to surrender.—**givable, giveable** *adj*.

give-and-take /'gɪvən'teɪk/ *n* mutual concessions; free-flowing exchange of ideas and conversation.

giveaway /'gɪvəweɪ/ *n* (*inf*) an unintentional revelation; a free gift to encourage sales; a freesheet.

given[1] /'gɪvən/ *see* **give**.

given[2] *adj* accustomed (to) by habit, etc; specified; assumed; granted.

giver /'gɪvər/ *n* a person who gives.

gizzard /'gɪzərd/ *n* the second stomach of a bird, used for grinding food.

glabrous /'gleɪbrəs/ *adj* without hair, smooth-skinned.

glacé /'glæseɪ/ *or* /glæ'seɪ/ *adj* candied, covered in icing, as fruit. • *vt* (**glacéing, glacéed**) to cover with icing; to candy.

glacial /'gleɪʃəl/ *or* /-sɪəl/ *adj* extremely cold; of or relating to glaciers or a glacial epoch.—**glacially** *adv*.

glaciate /'gleɪsi‚eɪt/ *vti* to subject to glacial action; to cover or become covered with glaciers.—**glaciation** *n*.

glacier /'gleɪʃər/ *or* /-ʃiər/, /-siər/ *n* a large mass of snow and ice moving slowly down a mountain.

glacis /'glæsi/ *or* /-sɪs/, /'gleɪ-/ *n* (*pl* **glacis**) a sloping bank of earth in front of a fortification for its defence; a slope (on a tank) to throw off hostile shot.

glad /glæd/ *adj* (**gladder, gladdest**) happy; causing joy; very willing; bright.—**gladly** *adv*.—**gladness** *n*.

gladden /'glædən/ *vti* to make or become glad.—**gladdener** *n*.

glade /gleɪd/ *n* an open space in a wood or forest.

gladiate /'glædi‚eɪt/ *adj* sword-shaped.

gladiator /'glædi‚eɪtər/ *n* (*ancient Rome*) a person trained to fight with men or beasts in a public arena.—**gladiatorial** *adj*.

gladiolus /‚glædi:'o:ləs/ *n* (*pl* **gladiolus, gladioli**) any of a genus of the iris family with sword-like leaves and tall spikes of funnel-shaped flowers.

gladsome /'glædsəm/ *adj* joyous.

glair /glɛr/ *n* white of egg; size made from this; a sticky substance; any sticky or glairy matter. • *vt* to smear with glair.—**glaireous** *adj*.

glairy /'glɛri/ *adj* (**glairier, glairiest**) like or smeared with glair.—**glairiness** *n*.

glamorize, glamourize /'glæmə‚raɪz/ *vt* to make glamorous.—**glamorization, glamourization** *n*.—**glamorizer, glamourizer** *n*.

glamour, glamor /'glæmər/ *n* charm, allure; attractiveness, beauty.—**glamorous, glamourous** *adj*.—**glamorousness, glamourousness** *n*.

glance /glæns/ *vi* to strike obliquely and go off at an angle; to flash; to look quickly. • *n* a glancing off; a flash; a quick look.—**glancingly** *adv*.

gland /glænd/ *n* an organ that separates substances from the blood and synthesizes them for further use in, or for elimination from, the body.

glanders /'glændərz/ *n* (*sing or pl*) a contagious bacterial disease *esp* of horses, often fatal.—**glandered** *adj*.—**glanderous** *adj*.

glandular /'glændjulər/ *adj* of, having or resembling glands; (*plants*) covered with hair tipped with glands.

glare /glɛr/ *n* a harsh, uncomfortably bright light, *esp* painfully bright sunlight; an angry or fierce stare. • *vi* to shine with a steady, dazzling light; to stare fiercely.

glaring /'glɛrɪŋ/ *adj* dazzling; obvious, conspicuous.—**glaringly** *adv*.—**glaringness** *n*.

glasnost /'glæznɒst/ *or* /'glæs-/ *n* the Russian word for "openness," applied to the policy, initiated by President Gorbachev of the former USSR, of greater frankness and openness in Soviet affairs.—**glasnostian** *adj*.

glass /glæs/ *n* a hard brittle substance, *usu* transparent; glassware; a glass article, as a drinking vessel; (*pl*) spectacles or binoculars; the amount held by a drinking glass. • *adj* of or made of glass. • *vt* to equip, enclose, or cover with glass.

glass-blowing *n* the art, skill or process of blowing air into molten glass and shaping it.—**glass-blower** *n*.

glassware /'glæswɛr/ *n* objects made of glass, *esp* drinking vessels.

glasswort /'glæswərt/ *n* a fleshy plant of marshy areas, from which soda was formerly obtained for use in making glass.

glassy /'glæsi/ *adj* (**glassier, glassiest**) resembling glass; smooth; expressionless, lifeless.—**glassily** *adv*.—**glassiness** *n*.

glaucoma /glɔ'ko:mə/ *n* a disease of the eye caused by pressure.—**glaucomatous** *adj*.

glaucous /'glɔkəs/ *adj* sea-green; covered with bloom of a blueish-white colour, green with a bluish-grey tinge.

glaze /gleɪz/ *vt* to provide (windows etc) with glass; to give a hard glossy finish to (pottery, etc); to cover (foods, etc) with a glossy surface. • *vi* to become glassy or glossy. • *n* a glassy finish or coating.—**glazer** *n*.

glazier /'gleɪziər/ *or* /-ʒər/ *n* a person who fits glass in windows.—**glaziery** *n*.

glazing /'gleɪzɪŋ/ *n* a glaze; the operation of setting glass or applying a glaze; windowpanes; glass; semi-transparent colours passed thinly over other colours to tone down their effect.

gleam /gli:m/ *n* a subdued or moderate beam of light; a brief show of some quality or emotion, *esp* hope. • *vi* to emit or reflect a beam of light.—**gleamingly** *adv*.

glean /gli:n/ *vti* to collect (grain left by reapers); to gather (facts, etc) gradually.—**gleanable** *adj*.—**gleaner** *n*.

gleaning /'gliːnɪŋ/ n the act of collecting after reapers; (often pl) that which is collected laboriously from various sources.

glee /gliː/ n joy and gaiety; delight; (mus) a song in parts for three or more male voices.—**gleeful** adj.—**gleefully** adv.—**gleefulness** n.

gleeful /'gliːfʊl/ adj merry, joyous; triumphant.—**gleefully** adv.—**gleefulness** n.

gleet /gliːt/ n a thin mucous discharge, esp from the urethra, resulting from gonorrhoeal disease.

glen /glen/ n a narrow valley.

glengarry /glen'gærɪ/ n (pl **glengarries**) (often cap) a boat-shaped cap originating in Scotland.

glib /glɪb/ adj (**glibber, glibbest**) speaking or spoken smoothly, to the point of insincerity; lacking depth and substance.—**glibly** adv.—**glibness** n.

glide /glaɪd/ vti to move smoothly and effortlessly; to descend in an aircraft or glider with little or no engine power. • n a gliding movement.—**glidingly** adv.

glider /'glaɪdər/ n an engineless aircraft carried along by air currents.

gliding /-ɪŋ/ n the sport of flying gliders.

glim /glɪm/ n (sl) a light, a candle.

glimmer /'glɪmər/ vi to give a faint, flickering light; to appear faintly. • n a faint gleam; a glimpse, an inkling.

glimmering /-ɪŋ/ n a faint gleam; a glimpse, an inkling.

glimpse /glɪmps/ n a brief, momentary view. • vt to catch a glimpse of.—**glimpser** n.

glint /glɪnt/ n a brief flash of light; a brief indication. • vti to (cause to) gleam brightly.

glioma /glaɪ'oːmə/ n (pl **gliomata, gliomas**) a tumour of rapid growth on the brain, spinal cord, or auditory nerve.

glissade /glɪ'sɒd/ or /-'seɪd/ vi to slide down a snow-covered slope without the aid of skis. • n a sliding ballet step.—**glissader** n.

glissando /glɪ'sændoː/ or /-'sɒndoː/ n (pl **glissandi, glissandos**) (mus) a run by sliding the fingers over the keys of a piano; a quick slur on a violin.

glisten /'glɪsən/ vi to shine, as light reflected from a wet surface.—**glisteningly** adv.

glister /'glɪstər/ vi (poet) to sparkle, to glitter.—also n.

glitch /glɪtʃ/ n a malfunction in a, usu electronic, system.

glitter /'glɪtər/ vi to sparkle; (usu with **with**) to be brilliantly attractive. • n a sparkle; showiness, glamour; tiny pieces of sparkling material used for decoration.—**glittering** adj.—**glittery** adj.

glitz /glɪts/ n (sl) gaudiness; ostentatious glamour.—**glitzy** adj (**glitzier, glitziest**).

gloaming /'gloːmɪŋ/ n twilight.

gloat /gloːt/ vi to gaze or contemplate with wicked or malicious satisfaction.—**gloater** n.—**gloatingly** adv.

global /'gloːbəl/ adj worldwide; comprehensive.—**globally** adv.

global village n the world considered as a single community because of instantaneous communications.

global warming n the process caused by a blanket of 'greenhouse gases' building up around the earth trapping heat from the sun. Carbon dioxide, released by burning fossil fuels is one of the main causes.—see **greenhouse effect**.

globate /'gloːˌbeɪt/, **globated** /-ɪd/ adj globe-shaped.

globe /gloːb/ n anything spherical or almost spherical; the earth, or a model of the earth.

globeflower /'gloːbˌflaʊər/ n a plant with round yellow flowers.

globetrotter /'gloːbˌtrɒtər/ n a person who travels widely.—**globetrotting** n, adj.

globin /'gloːbɪn/ n a constituent of red blood corpuscles.

globoid /'gloːbɔɪd/ adj nearly globular. • n a globoid figure.

globose /'gloːkəˌboːs/, **globous** /-bəs/ adj globe-like, spherical.

globosity /-'bɒsɪtɪ/, **globoseness** n

globular /'glɒbjʊlər/ adj spherical.

globule /'glɒbjuːl/ n a small spherical particle; a drop, pellet; a blood corpuscle.

globulin /'glɒbjʊlɪn/ n an albuminous protein forming one of the constituents of blood, muscle, and the cellular tissue of plants.

glockenspiel /'glɒkənˌspiːl/ or /-ˌʃpiːl/ n an orchestral percussion instrument with tuned metal bars, played with hammers.

glomerate /'glɒmərɪt/ adj gathered into a roundish head or mass; compactly clustered.

glomerule /glɒˌmerjʊl/ n a clustered flowerhead.

gloom /gluːm/ n near darkness; deep sadness. • vti to look sullen or dejected; to make or become cloudy or murky.

gloomy /'gluːmɪ/ adj (**gloomier, gloomiest**) almost dark, obscure; depressed, dejected.—**gloomily** adv.—**gloominess** n.

gloria /'glɔːrɪə/ n a halo or aureole; a light fabric of silk, etc; (with cap) a prayer of praise, esp the Gloria in excelsis and Gloria patri; a musical setting of these.

glorify /'glɔːrɪˌfaɪ/ vt (**glorifying, glorified**) to worship; to praise, to honour; to cause to appear more worthy, important, or splendid than in reality.—**glorifiable** adj.—**glorification** n.—**glorifier** n.

glorious /'glɔːrɪəs/ adj having or deserving glory; conferring glory or renown; beautiful; delightful.—**gloriously** adv.—**gloriousness** n.

glory /'glɔːrɪ/ n (pl **glories**) great honour or fame, or its source; adoration; great splendour or beauty; heavenly bliss. • vi (**glorying, gloried**) (with **in**) to exult, rejoice proudly.

gloss[1] /glɒs/ n the lustre of a polished surface; a superficially attractive appearance. • vt to give a shiny surface to; (with **over**) to hide (an error, etc) or make seem right or inconsequential.—**glosser** n.

gloss[2] n an explanation of an unusual word (in the margin or between the lines of a text); a misleading explanation; a glossary. • vt to provide with glosses; to give a misleading sense of.—**glosser** n.

glossa /'glɒsə/ n (pl **glossae, glossas**) the tongue, esp of insects.—**glossal** adj.

glossary /'glɒsərɪ/ n (pl **glossaries**) a list of specialized or technical words and their definitions.—**glossarial** adj.—**glossarist** n.

glossitis /glɒ'saɪtɪs/ n inflammation of the tongue.

glossography /glə'sɒgrəfɪ/ n the making of glossaries or glosses.—**glossographer** n.

glossy /'glɒsɪ/ adj (**glossier, glossiest**) having a shiny or highly polished surface; superficial; (magazines) lavishly produced. • n (pl **glossies**) a magazine with many colour pictures, printed on coated paper, esp a fashion magazine.—**glossily** adv.—**glossiness** n.

glottal /'glɒtəl/ adj of, pertaining to, or produced by the glottis.

glottis /'glɒtɪs/ n (**glottises, glottides**) the opening between the vocal cords in the larynx.—**glottidean** adj.

glove /glʌv/ n a covering for the hand; a baseball player's mitt; a boxing glove. • vt to cover (as if) with a glove.

glover /'glʌvər/ n a maker or seller of gloves.

glow /gloː/ vi to shine (as if) with an intense heat; to emit a steady light without flames; to be full of life and enthusiasm; to flush or redden with emotion. • n a light emitted due to intense heat; a steady, even light without flames; a reddening of the complexion; warmth of emotion or feeling.

glower /'glaʊər/ vi to scowl; to stare sullenly or angrily. • n a scowl, a glare.—**gloweringly** adv.

glow-worm n a beetle that emits light from the abdomen.

gloxinia /glɒk'sɪnɪə/ n a tropical plant with showy bell-shaped flowers, cultivated as a houseplant.

glucose /'gluːkoːs/ or /-oːz/ n a crystalline sugar occurring naturally in fruits, honey, etc.

glue /gluː/ n a sticky, viscous substance used as an adhesive. • vt (**gluing, glued**) to join with glue.—**gluer** n.

gluey /'gluːɪ/ adj (**gluier, glueist**) like glue, sticky.

glum /glʌm/ adj (**glummer, glummest**) sullen; gloomy.—**glumly** adv.—**glumness** n.

glumaceous /gluː'meɪʃəs/ adj bearing or resembling glumes.

glume /gluːm/ n the husk of corn or grasses.

glut /glʌt/ vt (**glutting, glutted**) to over-supply (the market). • n a surfeit, an excess of supply.

gluteal /'gluːtɪəl/ adj pertaining to the buttocks.

gluten /'gluːtən/ n a sticky elastic protein substance, esp of wheat flour, that gives cohesiveness to dough.—**glutenous** adj.

gluteus /'gluːtɪəs/ n (pl **glutei**) any of the three muscles that form the buttocks.

glutinous /'gluːtɪnəs/ adj resembling glue, sticky.—**glutinousness, glutinosity** n.

glutton /'glʌtən/ n a person who eats and drinks to excess; a person who has a tremendous capacity for something (eg for work); a wolverine.—**gluttonous** adj.

gluttony /'glʌtənɪ/ n the act or habit of eating and drinking to excess.

glyceride /'glɪsəˌraɪd/ n an ester of glycerol.

glycerin, glycerine /'glɪsəˌrɪn/ n the popular and commercial name for glycerol.

glycerol /'glɪsəˌrɒl/ n a colourless, syrupy liquid made from fats and oils, used in making skin lotions, explosives, etc.—**glyceric** adj.

glycogen /'glaɪkədʒən/ *n* a polysaccharide consisting of glucose units; the form in which carbohydrate is stored in the liver and muscles in man and animals.

glycol /'glaɪkɒl/ *n* a viscid liquid intermediate between glycerine and alcohol; antifreeze.

glycosuria /ˌglaɪkəˈsjʊrɪə/ *n* a disease marked by excess sugar in the urine.—**glycosuric** *adj*.

glyph /glɪf/ *n* (*arch*) a perpendicular fluting.—**glyphic** *adj*.

glyptic /'glɪptɪk/ *adj* pertaining to engraving on gems; figured. • *n* the art of engraving designs on precious stones, ivory, etc.

glyptography /glɪpˈtɒgrəfɪ/ *n* the art of cutting designs or engraving on a gem.

gm *abbr* = gram(s).

GM *abbr* = genetically modified.

GMT /ˌdʒiːemˈtiː/ *abbr* = Greenwich Mean Time.

gnarl /narl/ *n* a knot on the trunk or branch of a tree.

gnarled /narld/ *adj* (*tree trunks*) full of knots; (*hands*) rough, knobbly; crabby in disposition.

gnash /næʃ/ *vti* to grind (the teeth) in anger or pain. • *n* a grinding of the teeth.—**gnashingly** *adv*.

gnat /næt/ *n* any of various small, two-winged insects that bite or sting.

gnathic /'næθɪk/, **gnathial**, /'næθɪəl/ *adj* of or pertaining to jaws.

gnaw /nɒ/ *vti* (**gnawing**, **gnawed**, *pp* **gnawed** *or* **gnawn**) to bite away bit by bit; to torment, as by constant pain.—**gnawable** *adj*.—**gnawer** *n*.

gneiss /naɪs/ *n* a granite-like rock formed by layers of quartz, mica, etc.—**gneissic, gneissoid, gneissose** *adj*.

gnocchi /'njɒki/ *npl* small dumplings made from flour, semolina or potatoes.

gnome /noːm/ *n* (*folklore*) a dwarf who dwells in the earth and guards its treasure; a small statue of a gnome used as a garden decoration; a small and ugly person; (*sl*) an international banker or financier.—**gnomish** *adj*.

gnomic /'noːmɪk/ *adj* dealing in or containing pithy or sententious sayings; didactic.—**gnomically** *adv*.

gnomon /'noːmɒn/ *n* the indicator on a sundial that casts a shadow to indicate the time of day.—**gnomonic** *adj*.—**gnomonically** *adv*.

gnosis /'noːsɪs/ *n* (*pl* **gnoses**) higher knowledge, mysticism or insight.

gnostic /'nɒstɪk/ *adj* of, pertaining to, or having knowledge; (*with cap*) pertaining to the Gnostics or Gnosticism.—*also* **gnostical**. • *n* (*with cap*) a member of an early Christian sect seeking salvation by knowledge, not faith.

Gnosticism /'nɒstɪˌsɪzəm/ *n* the doctrine of the Gnostics.

GNP /'dʒiːenˌpiː/ *abbr* = Gross National Product.

gnu /nuː/ *or* /njuː/ *n* (*pl* **gnus, gnu**) either of two large African antelopes with an ox-like head.—*also* **wildebeest**.

go[1] /goː/ *vb* (**going, went**, *pp* **gone**) *vi* to move on a course; to proceed; to work properly; to act, sound, as specified; to result; to become; to be accepted or valid; to leave, to depart; to die; to be allotted or sold; to be able to pass (through); to fit (into); to be capable of being divided (into); to belong; (*with* **about**) to handle (a task, etc) efficiently; to undertake (duties, etc); (*sailing*) to change tack; (*with* **into**) to enter; to become a member of; to examine or investigate; to discuss; (*with* **off**) to explode; to depart; (*food, etc*) to become stale or rotten; to fall asleep; to proceed, occur in a certain manner; to take place as planned; to stop liking (something or someone); (*with* **on**) to continue; to happen; to talk effusively; to nag; to enter on stage; (*with* **out**) to depart; (*light, fire, etc*) to become extinguished; to cease to be fashionable; to socialize; (*radio or TV show*) to be broadcast; to spend time with, *esp* a person of the opposite sex; (*with* **over**) to change one's loyalties (to); to be received or regarded in a certain way; to examine and repair (something); (*with* **round**) to circulate; to be sufficient for everyone; (*with* **slow**) to work at a slow rate as part of an industrial dispute; (*with* **through**) to continue to the end (with); to be approved; to use up completely; to experience (an illness, etc); to search thoroughly; (*with* **together**) to match, to be mutually suited; (*inf*) to associate frequently, *esp* as lovers; (*with* **up**) in the UK, to enter or return to college or university; (*with* **with**) to match; to accompany; to associate frequently, *esp* as lovers; (*with* **without**) to be deprived of or endure the lack of (something). • *vt* to travel along; (*inf*) to put up with. • *n* (*pl* **goes**) a success; (*inf*) a try; (*inf*) energy.

go[2] *n* a Japanese board game.

goa /goːə/ *n* an Asian gazelle, the male of which has horns that curve backwards.

goad /goːd/ *n* a sharp-pointed stick for driving cattle, etc; any stimulus to action. • *vt* to drive (as if) with a goad; to irritate, nag persistently.

go-ahead *n* (*inf*) permission to proceed. • *adj* (*inf*) enterprising, ambitious.

goal /goːl/ *n* the place at which a race, trip, etc is ended; an objective; the place over or into which the ball or puck must go to score in some games; the score made; the position of goalkeeper.

goalie /'goːli/ *n* (*inf*) a goalkeeper.

goalkeeper /'goːlˌkiːpər/ *n* a player who defends the goal.—**goalkeeping** *n*.

goat /goːt/ *n* a mammal related to the sheep that has backward curving horns, a short tail, and *usu* straight hair; a lecherous man.

goatee /goːˈtiː/ *n* a small pointed beard.

goatherd /'goːthɜrd/ *n* a person who looks after goats.

goatish /-ɪʃ/ *adj* pertaining to or like a goat; (*arch*) lustful; rank-smelling.—**goatishly** *adv*.—**goatishness** *n*.

goatsbeard, goat's-beard *n* a European grass-like plant with yellow flowers; an American plant with compound leaves and small white flowers.

goatskin /'goːtskɪn/ *n* the skin of a goat; a bottle or garment made of this.

goatsucker /'goːtˌsʌkər/ *n* a nocturnal bird with dull mottled plumage.—*also* **nightjar**.

gob[1] /gɒb/ *n* (*sl*) the mouth.

gob[2] *n* a lump or clot of something; (*inf*) spittle. • *vi* (**gobbing, gobbed**) (*inf*) to spit.

gobbet /'gɒbət/ *n* a lump of something.

gobble /'gɒbəl/ *vt* to eat greedily; (*often with* **up**) to take, accept or read eagerly. • *vi* to make a throaty gurgling noise, as a male turkey.

gobbledygook, gobbledegook /'gɒbəldiˌgʊk/ *or* /-ˌguːk/ *n* (*sl*) nonsense, pretentious jargon.

gobbler /'gɒblər/ *n* (*inf*) a turkey cock.

go-between *n* a messenger, an intermediary.

goblet /'gɒblət/ *n* a large drinking vessel with a base and stem but without a handle.

goblin /'gɒblɪn/ *n* an evil or mischievous elf.

goby /'goːbi/ *n* (*pl* **goby, gobies**) a sea fish with a large head and a long thin body.

go-cart *n* a small cart for children to play in or pull; a stroller; a handcart.

god /gɒd/ *n* any of various beings conceived of as supernatural and immortal, *esp* a male deity; an idol; a person or thing deified; (*with cap*) in monotheistic religions, the creator and ruler of the universe.

godchild /'gɒdtʃaɪld/ *n* (*pl* **godchildren**) the child a godparent sponsors.

goddaughter /'gɒdˌdɒtər/ *n* a female godchild.

goddess /'gɒdəs/ *n* a female deity; a woman of superior charms or excellence.

godfather /'gɒdˌfɑːðər/ *n* a male godparent; the head of a Mafia crime family or other criminal organization.

god-fearing *adj* religious.

godforsaken /'gɒdfərˌseɪkən/ *or* /ˌgɒdfərˈseɪkən/ *adj* desolate, wretched.

godhead /'gɒdhɛd/ *n* the divine nature, deity; God.

godhood /'gɒdhʊd/ *n* the quality or condition of being a god; divinity.

godless /'gɒdləs/ *adj* irreligious; wicked.—**godlessly** *adv*.—**godlessness** *n*.

godlike /'gɒdlaɪk/ *adj* like a god, divine.

godly /'gɒdli/ *adj* (**godlier, godliest**) religious; holy; devout; devoted to God.—**godliness** *n*.

godmother /'gɒdˌmʌðər/ *n* a female godparent.

godown /goːˈdaʊn/ *n* in India and China, a warehouse or storeroom.

godparent /'gɒdˌpɛrənt/ *n* a person who sponsors a child, as at baptism or confirmation, taking responsibility for its faith.

godsend /'gɒdsɛnd/ *n* anything that comes unexpectedly and when needed or desired.

godson /'gɒdsʌn/ *n* a male godchild.

Godspeed /'gɒdspiːd/ *n* success, good luck.

godwit /'gɒdwɪt/ *n* any of a genus of wading birds with a long bill, related to the snipes but resembling curlews.

goer /'goːər/ *n* a regular attender; something, as a car, that goes fast; an enthusiastic person.

gofer /ˈgoːfər/ n (inf) a person who runs errands, as in an office.

goffer /ˈgoːfər/ or /ˈgɒ-/ vt to make wavy or frilly with a hot iron, to crimp.—also **gauffer**.

go-getter n (inf) an ambitious person.

goggle /ˈgɒgəl/ vi to stare with bulging eyes. • npl large spectacles, sometimes fitting snugly against the face, to protect the eyes.

goggle-eyed adj with wide staring eyes.

go-go dancer n a scantily-clad dancer employed in a disco or nightclub.

going /ˈgoːɪŋ/ n an act or instance of going, a departure; the state of the ground, eg for walking, horse-racing; rate of progress. • adj that goes; commonly accepted; thriving; existing.

going-over n (pl goings-over) (inf) a thorough inspection; (sl) a beating.

goings-on /ˌgoːɪnzˈɒn/ npl events or actions, esp when disapproved of.

goitre, goiter /ˈgoːɪtər/ n an abnormal enlargement of the thyroid gland.—**goitrous** adj.

gold /goːld/ n a malleable yellow metallic element used esp for coins and jewellery; a precious metal; money, wealth; a yellow colour. • adj of, or like, gold.

goldbeater's skin n a membrane prepared from the large intestine of an ox used to separate layers of gold in goldbeating.

goldbeating n the process of beating gold until it is very thin.—**goldbeater** n.

gold card n a credit card that entitles the cardholder to extra benefits.

gold-digger n a person who mines gold; (inf) a woman who uses feminine charms to extract money or gifts from men.—**gold-digging** adj.

golden /ˈgoːldən/ adj made of or relating to gold; bright yellow; priceless; flourishing.—**goldenly** adv.—**goldenness** n.

golden age n the fabled early age of innocence and perfect human happiness; the flowering of a nation's civilization or art.

golden calf n (Bible) a golden calf made by Aaron and worshipped by the Israelites; wealth worshipped as a god.

golden eagle n a large eagle of the northern hemisphere.

golden fleece n (Greek myth) the ram's fleece in search of which Jason sailed with the Argonauts; an order of knighthood in Austria and Spain.

golden handcuffs npl financial incentives to induce an employee to remain in a particular job for an agreed period.

golden handshake n (inf) financial compensation awarded an employee for loss of employment.

golden mean n neither too much nor too little; moderation.

goldenrod /ˈgoːldənrɒd/ n a tall plant of the aster family with yellow flowers.

golden rule n a guiding principle.

goldeye /ˈgoːldaɪ/ n a silvery freshwater of central North America, often smoked for food.

goldfield /ˈgoːldfiːld/ n a district containing gold deposits and diggings.

gold-filled adj coated with gold.

goldfinch /ˈgoːldfɪntʃ/ n a common European finch with yellow and black wings.

goldfish /ˈgoːldfɪʃ/ n (pl goldfish, goldfishes) a small gold-coloured fish of the carp family, kept in ponds and aquariums.

goldilocks /ˈgoːldilɒks/ n any of various plants with yellow flowers, eg the buttercup; (with cap) a name for someone, usu female, with golden hair.

gold leaf n gold beaten into very thin sheets, used for gilding.

gold mine n a mine where gold is extracted; (inf) a source of wealth.

gold plate n vessels of gold; a thin covering of gold.—**gold-plated** adj.

gold rush n a rush to a new gold field, as to the Yukon in 1897.

goldsmith /ˈgoːldsmiθ/ n a worker in gold; a dealer in gold plate.

gold standard n a monetary standard in which the basic currency unit equals a specified quantity of gold.

golf /gɒlf/ n an outdoor game in which the player attempts to hit a small ball with clubs around a turfed course into a succession of holes in the smallest number of strokes.—**golfer** n.

golf ball n a hard dimpled ball used in golf; the spherical printing head in some typewriters.

golf club n a club with a wooden or metal head used in golf; a golf association or its premises.

golf course, golf links n a tract of land laid out for playing golf.

golliard /ˈgoːliərd/ n a medieval wandering jester or scholar.

golliwog, golliwogg /ˈgɒliˌwɒg/ n a cloth doll with a black face.

golly[1] /ˈgɒli/ n (inf) a golliwog.

golly[2] interj expressing surprise.

gonad /ˈgoːnæd/ n a primary sex gland that produces reproductive cells, such as an ovary or testis.—**gonadal, gonadic** adj.

gondola /ˈgɒndələ/ n a long, narrow, black boat used on the canals of Venice; a cabin suspended under an airship or balloon; an enclosed car suspended from a cable used to transport passengers, esp skiers up a mountain; a display structure in a supermarket, etc.

gondolier /ˌgɒndəˈliːr/ n a person who propels a gondola with a pole.

gone[1] /gɒn/ see **go[1]**.

gone[2] adj departed; dead; lost; (inf) in an excited state; (inf) pregnant for a specified period.

goner n (sl) a person or thing that is ruined, dead, or about to die.

gonfalon /ˈgɒnfələn/ n a banner, usu with streamers, hung from a crossbar, used in ecclesiastical processions; a military flag or standard with a pointed edge.

gong /gɒŋ/ n a disk-shaped percussion instrument struck with a usu padded hammer; (sl) a medal. • vi to sound a gong.

Gongorism /ˈgɒŋgəˌrizəm/ n (a passage of) a florid pedantic Spanish literary style resembling euphuism.

goniometer /ˌgoːniˈɒmitər/ n an instrument for measuring solid angles; an instrument used to determine the location of a distant radio station.—**goniometry** n.

gonorrhoea, gonorrhea /ˌgɒnəˈriːə/ n a venereal disease causing a discharge of mucous and pus from the genitals.—**gonorrhoeal, gonorrheal, gonorrhoeic, gonorrheic** adj.

goo /guː/ n (sl) sticky matter; sickly sentimentality.

good /gud/ adj (**better, best**) having the right or proper qualities; beneficial; valid; healthy or sound; virtuous, honourable; enjoyable, pleasant, etc; skilled; considerable. • n something good; benefit; something that has economic utility; (with **the**) good persons; (pl) personal property; commodities; (pl) the desired or required articles. • adv (inf) well; fully.—**goodish** adj.

goodbye /gudˈbaɪ/ interj a concluding remark at parting; farewell.—also n.

good-for-nothing adj useless, worthless. • a worthless person.

Good Friday n the Friday before Easter, commemorating the Crucifixion of Christ.

good-humoured adj genial, cheerful.—**good-humouredly** adv.—**good-humouredness** n.

good-looking adj handsome.

goodly /ˈgudli/ adj (**goodlier, goodliest**) considerable; ample.—**goodliness** n.

goodman /ˈgudmən/ n (pl goodmen) (formerly) the master of a house, a husband; a man not born into the aristocracy.

good-natured adj amiable, easy-going.—**good-naturedly** adv.—**good-naturedness** n.

goodness /ˈgudnəs/ n the state of being good; the good element in something; kindness; virtue. • interj an exclamation of surprise.

Good Samaritan n a person who helps those in distress (after the compassionate figure mentioned in the Bible.—Luke 10:33).

good-tempered adj having a pleasant and kindly nature.

good turn n a favour; an act of kindness.

goodwill /gudˈwɪl/ or /ˈgudwɪl/ n benevolence; willingness; the established custom and reputation of a business.

goodwoman n (pl goodwomen) (formerly) the mistress of a house, a wife; a woman not born into the aristocracy.

goody /ˈgudi/ n (pl goodies) something pleasant or sweet; a goddy-goody. • interj an expression (usu used by a child) signifying pleasure.

goody-goody /ˈgudiˌgudi/ adj insufferably virtuous. • n (pl goody-goodies) a goody-goody person.

gooey /ˈguːi/ adj (**gooier, gooiest**) (inf) soft and sticky; sweet; sentimental.

goof /guːf/ n (sl) a stupid person; a blunder. • vi (sl) to bungle.

goofy /ˈguːfi/ adj (**goofier, goofiest**) (sl) silly, stupid.—**goofily** adv.—**goofiness** n.

goon /guːn/ n (sl) a thug; a stupid person.

goop /guːp/ n (sl) any sticky, semi-liquid substance; (sl) a rude person.

goosander /guːˈsændər/ n a web-footed migratory waterfowl.

goose[1] /guːs/ n (pl geese) a large, long-necked, web-footed bird related to swans and ducks; its flesh as food; a female goose as distinguished from a gander; (inf) a foolish person.

goose[2] vt (sl) to poke (a person) between the buttocks.

gooseberry /'gu:s͵beri/ or /-bəri/, /'gu:z-/ n (pl **gooseberries**) the acid berry of a shrub related to the currant and used *esp* in jams and pies.

goose bumps, goose pimples, goose flesh /'gu:sbʌmps/ n a bumpy condition of the skin caused *usu* by cold or fear and so called because of its resemblance to the flesh of a plucked goose.

goosegrass n a species of creeping plant on which geese feed.

gooseneck /'gu:snɛk/ n (*naut*) a bent iron fitted to the extremity of a boom or yard.

goose step n a stiff-legged marching step used by some armies when passing in review.

goose-step vi (**goose-stepping, goose-stepped**) to march in a stiff-legged manner using the goose step.

gopher /'go:fər/ n a North American burrowing, rat-like rodent; a ground squirrel; a burrowing tortoise.

gopherwood n the wood Noah's Ark is reputed to have been made from, possibly cypress; the yellowwood.

gore[1] /gor/ n (clotted) blood from a wound.

gore[2] n a tapering section of material used to shape a garment, sail, etc.

gore[3] vt to pierce or wound as with a tusk or horns.

gorge /gɔrdʒ/ n a ravine. • vt to swallow greedily; to glut. • vi to feed gluttonously.—**gorgeable** adj.—**gorger** n.

gorgeous /'gɔrdʒəs/ adj strikingly attractive; brilliantly coloured; (*inf*) magnificent.—**gorgeously** adv.—**gorgeousness** n.

Gorgon /'gɔrgən/ n (*Greek myth*) one of three female monsters with live snakes for hair whose looks turned the beholder to stone; (*without cap*) any ugly or formidable woman.

gorgonian /gɔr'go:niən/ n any of a genus of flexible branching coral.

Gorgonzola /͵gɔrgən'zo:lə/ n a semi-hard blue-veined cheese with a rich flavour, originating in Italy.

gorilla /gə'rilə/ n an anthropoid ape of western equatorial Africa related to the chimpanzee but much larger.

gormand /gurmɔnd/ *see* **gourmand**.

gormandize /'gur͵mɔndaɪz/ vti to eat like a glutton.—**gormandizer** n.

gorse /gors/ n a spiny yellow-flowered European shrub.

gory /'gɔri/ adj (**gorier, goriest**) bloodthirsty; causing bloodshed; covered in blood.—**gorily** adv.—**goriness** n.

gosh /gɒʃ/ *interj* an exclamation of surprise.

goshawk /'gɒshɔk/ n any of several long-tailed hawks with short rounded wings.

gosling /'gɒzlɪŋ/ n a young goose.

go-slow n a deliberate slowing of the work rate by employees as a form of industrial action.

gospel /'gɒspəl/ n the life and teachings of Christ contained in the first four books of the New Testament; (*with cap*) one of these four books; anything proclaimed or accepted as the absolute truth.

gospeller, gospeler /'gɒspələr/ n the reader of the gospel in a communion service; an evangelist.

gossamer /'gɒsəmər/ n very fine cobwebs; any very light and flimsy material. • adj light as gossamer.

gossip /'gɒsɪp/ n one who chatters idly about others; such talk. • vi to take part in or spread gossip.—**gossiper** n.—**gossipingly** adv.—**gossipy** adj.

gossipmonger /'gɒsɪp͵mʌŋgər/ or /-mɒŋgər/ n a gossip.

got *see* **get**.

Goth /gɒθ/ n any member of a Germanic people that conquered most of the Roman Empire in the 3rd–5th centuries AD.

Gothic /'gɒθɪk/ adj of a style of architecture with pointed arches, steep roofs, elaborate stonework, etc. • n German black letter type; a bold type style without serifs.—**Gothically** adv.

gotten *see* **get**.

gouache /gu:'ɒʃ/ or /gwɒʃ/ n a method of painting with opaque watercolours.

Gouda /'gu:də/ n a type of large flat round Dutch cheese.

gouge /gaudʒ/ n a chisel with a concave blade used for cutting grooves. • vt to scoop or force out (as if) with a gouge.

gouger /-ər/ n one who or that which gouges; a swindler.

goujons /'gu:ʒɒs/ *npl* narrow fried strips of fish or chicken in breadcrumbs.

goulash /'gu:læʃ/ n a rich stew made with beef or veal seasoned with paprika.

gourami /'gu:rəmi/ or /-'rɒmi/ n (pl **gourami, gouramis**) an oriental fish cultivated for food.

gourd /gord/ n any trailing or climbing plant of a family that includes the squash, melon, pumpkin, etc; the fruit of one species or its dried, hollowed-out shell, used as a cup, bowl, etc or ornament.

gourmand /gur'mɒnd/ n a person who likes good food and drink, often to excess.—*also* **gormand**.—**gourmandism** n.

gourmandise, gormandise /'gurmən͵daɪz/ n the (sometimes excessive) love of good food.

gourmet /gur'meɪ/ or /-'gur-/, /'gɔr-/ n a person who likes and is an excellent judge of fine food and drink.

gout /gaut/ n a disease causing painful inflammation of the joints; *esp* of the great toe.—**gouty** adj.—**goutiness** n.

Gov., gov *abbr* = government; governor.

govern /'gʌvərn/ vti to exercise authority over; to rule, to control; to influence the action of; to determine.—**governable** adj.—**governability, governableness** n.

governance /'gʌvərnəns/ n the action, function, or power of government.

governess /'gʌvərnəs/ n a woman employed in a private home to teach and train the children.

government /'gʌvərnmənt/ or /'gʌvərmənt/ n the exercise of authority over a state, organization, etc; a system of ruling, political administration, etc; those who direct the affairs of a state, etc.—**governmental** adj.

governor /'gʌvərnər/ or /'gʌvənər/ n a person appointed to govern a province, etc; the elected head of any state of the US; the director or head of a governing body of an organization or institution; (*sl*) an employer; a mechanical device for automatically controlling the speed of an engine.—**governorship** n.

governor general n (pl **governors-general**) the representative of the Crown as head of state in a country in the Commonwealth.

Govt, govt *abbr* = government.

gowan /'gauən/ n (*Scot*) the daisy.

gown /gaun/ n a loose outer garment, specifically a woman's formal dress, a nightgown, a long, flowing robe worn by clergymen, judges, university teachers, etc; a type of overall worn in the operating room. • vt to dress in a gown, to supply with the gown.

goy /gɔɪ/ n (pl **goyim, goys**) (*sl*) Jewish for Gentile.

GP *abbr* = general practitioner.

GPO *abbr* = general post office.

Gr. *abbr* = Grecian; Greece; Greek.

grab /græb/ vt (**grabbing, grabbed**) to take or grasp suddenly; to obtain unscrupulously; (*inf*) to catch the interest or attention of. • n a sudden clutch or attempt to grasp; a mechanical device for grasping and lifting objects.—**grabber** n.

grabble /'græbəl/ vi to feel about, to grope.—**grabbler** n.

grace /greɪs/ n beauty or charm of form, movement, or expression; good will; favour; a delay granted for payment of an obligation; a short prayer of thanks for a meal. • vt to decorate; to dignify.

graceful /-ful/ adj having beauty of form, movement, or expression.—**gracefully** adv.—**gracefulness** n.

graceless /-ləs/ adj unattractive; lacking sense of what is proper; clumsy.—**gracelessly** adv.—**gracelessness** n.

grace note n (*mus*) an ornamental note.

Graces *npl* (*Greek myth*) the three sister goddesses who are the givers of charm and beauty.

gracile /'græsaɪl/ or /-sɪl/ adj slender.—**gracility** n.

gracious /'greɪʃəs/ adj having or showing kindness, courtesy, etc; compassionate; polite to supposed inferiors; marked by luxury, ease, etc; *interj* an expression of surprise.—**graciously** adv.—**graciousness** n.

grackle /'grækəl/ n an Asian bird like a starling; an American bird with shiny black plumage; the crow blackbird.

grad /græd/ n (*sl*) a graduate.

gradate /'greɪdeɪt/ vti to change or cause to change gradually from one stage, degree, colour, etc to another; to arrange by grade or degree.

gradation /greɪ'deɪʃən/ or /grə-/ n a series of systematic steps in rank, degree, intensity, etc; arranging in such stages; a single stage in a gradual progression; progressive change.—**gradational** adj.

grade /greɪd/ n a stage or step in a progression; a degree in a scale of quality, rank, etc; a group of people of the same rank, merit, etc; the degree of slope; a sloping part; a mark or rating in an examination, etc. • vt to arrange in grades; to give a grade to; to make level or evenly sloping.

grade crossing n US and Canadian name for a level crossing.

gradient /ˈgreɪdiənt/ n a sloping road or railway; the degree of slope in a road, railway, etc.

gradin, gradine /greɪˈdiːn/ n one of a tier of seats; a ledge at the back of an altar.

gradual /ˈgrædʒʊəl/ adj taking place by degrees.—**gradually** adv.—**gradualness** n.

graduate /ˈgrædʒʊət/ n a person who has completed a course of study at a school, college, or university; a receptacle marked with figures for measuring contents. • adj holding an academic degree or diploma; of or relating to studies beyond the first or bachelor's degree.—**graduator** n.

graduation /grædʒʊˈeɪʃən/ n graduating or being graduated; the ceremony at which degrees are conferred by a college or university; an arranging or marking in grades or stages.

Graeco- see **Greco-**.

graffiti /grəˈfiːti/ npl (sing **graffito**) inscriptions or drawings, often indecent, on a wall or other public surface.

graft /ɡræft/ n a shoot or bud of one plant inserted into another, where it grows permanently; the transplanting of skin, bone, etc; the getting of money or advantage dishonestly.—**grafter** n.—**grafting** n.

grail /greɪl/ n in medieval legend, the dish or chalice that was used by Christ at the Last Supper, and the object of many knights' quests.—also **Holy Grail**.

grain /greɪn/ n the seed of any cereal plant, as wheat, corn, etc; cereal plants; a tiny, solid particle, as of salt or sand; a unit of weight, 0.0648 gram; the arrangement of fibres, layers, etc of wood, leather, etc; the markings or texture due to this; natural disposition. • vt to form into grains; to paint in imitation of the grain of wood, etc. • vi to become granular.—**grainer** n.

grainy /ˈgreɪni/ adj (**grainier, grainiest**) resembling grains in form or texture.—**graininess** n.

gram¹ /græm/ n the basic unit of weight in the metric system, equal to one thousandth of a kilogram (one twenty-eighth of an ounce).

gram² n any of various leguminous plants grown for their edible seeds.

gram. abbr = grammar; grammatical.

grama (grass) /ˈgræmə/ n a low pasture grass of western and southwestern USA and South America.

gramarye, gramary /ˈgræməri/ n (arch) magic, necromancy.

gramercy /ˈgræmərsi/ interj (arch) an expression of great thanks; expressing great surprise.

gramineous /grəˈmɪniəs/ adj of or like grass; grassy.

graminivorous /græmɪˈnɪvərəs/ adj feeding on grasses.

grammar /ˈgræmər/ n the study of the forms of words and their arrangement in sentences; a system of rules for speaking and writing a language; a grammar textbook; the use of language in speech or writing judged with regard to correctness of spelling, syntax, etc.

grammarian /grəˈmɛriən/ n one who studies grammar; the author of a grammar.

grammatical /grəˈmætɪkəl/ adj conforming to the rules of grammar.—**grammatically** adv.

gramophone /ˈgræməfoːn/ n a record player, esp an old mechanical model with an acoustic horn.—also **phonograph**.

grampus /ˈgræmpəs/ n (pl **grampuses**) a marine mammal, as the blackfish or killer whale.

granadilla /grænəˈdɪlə/ n a passion-fruit.

granary /ˈgrænəri/ or /ˈgreɪn-/ n (pl **granaries**) a building for storing grain.

grand /grænd/ adj higher in rank than others; most important; imposing in size, beauty, extent, etc; distinguished; illustrious; comprehensive; (inf) very good; delightful. • n a grand piano; (inf) a thousand pounds or dollars.—**grandly** adv.—**grandness** n.

grand-aunt n a father's or mother's aunt.—also **great-aunt**.

grandchild /ˈgræntʃaɪld/ n (pl **grandchildren**) the child of a person's son or daughter.

granddad /ˈgrændæd/ n (inf) grandfather; an old man.

granddaughter /ˈgrænˌdɒtər/ n the daughter of a person's son or daughter.

grand duke n the ruler of a state or principality.

grandee /grænˈdiː/ n a high-ranking person.

grandeur /ˈgrændər/ or /-djər/, /-dʒər/ n splendour; magnificence; nobility; dignity.

grandfather /ˈgrænˌfɒðər/ or /ˈgrænd-/ n the father of a person's father or mother.

grandfather clock n a large clock with a pendulum in a tall, upright case.

grandiloquent /grænˈdɪləkwənt/ adj using pompous words.—**grandiloquence** n.

grandiose /ˈgrændiˈoːs/ or /ˈgræn-/ adj having grandeur; imposing; pompous and showy.—**grandiosely** adv.—**grandiosity** n.

grand jury n a jury in the US that examines evidence in a case to determine whether an indictment should be made.

grandma /ˈgrændmə/ or /ˈgrænmə/, /-mʊ/, **grandmama** n (inf) grandmother.

grand mal /grɑːˈmæl/ n severe epilepsy.

grandmaster /grændˈmæstər/ n an expert player (as of chess) who has scored consistently well in international competition.

grandmother /ˈgrænˌmʊðər/ or /ˈgrænd-/ n the mother of a person's father or mother.

grandnephew /ˈgrændˌnefjuː/ or /ˈgræn-/ n a nephew's or niece's son.—also **great-nephew**.

grandniece /ˈgrændniːs/ or /ˈgræn-/ n a nephew's or niece's daughter.—also **great-niece**.

grand opera n opera in which the whole text is set to music.

grandpa /ˈgrændpə/ or /ˈgræn-/, /-pʊ/, **grandpapa** n (inf) grandfather.

grandparent /ˈgrænˌperənt/ or /ˈgrænd-/ n a grandfather or grandmother.

grand piano n a large piano with a horizontal harp-shaped case.

Grand Prix /grɑːˈpriː/ n (pl **Grand Prix**) any of a series of formula motor races held in different countries throughout the season; an important contest in other sports, including horse racing, tennis, and athletics.

grand slam n (tennis, golf) a winning of all the major international championships in a season; (bridge) a bidding for and winning all the tricks in a deal; (baseball) a home run hit when there is a runner on each base.

grandson /ˈgrænsən/ or /ˈgrænd-/ n the son of a person's son or daughter.

grandstand /ˈgrændstænd/ or /ˈgræn-/ n the main structure for seating spectators at a sporting event.

grand tour n (formerly) a trip round Europe taken by the sons of wealthy Englishmen to complete their education; (inf) a sightseeing or educational tour.

grand-uncle n a father's or mother's uncle.—also **great-uncle**.

grange /greɪndʒ/ n a country house with outbuildings etc; a local lodge of a powerful agricultural association; (with **the**) this association; (formerly) an outlying farm building where a monastery or local lord stored crops or tithes; (arch) a granary.

grangerize /ˈgrændʒəˌraɪz/ vt interleave (a book) with illustrations taken from other books; to remove illustrations, etc, from books for this purpose.—**grangerism** n.—**grangerization** n.

granite /ˈgrænɪt/ n a hard, igneous rock consisting chiefly of feldspar and quartz; unyielding firmness of endurance.—**granitic, granitoid** adj.

granivorous /grəˈnɪvərəs/ adj grain-eating; living on seeds.—**granivore** n.

granny, grannie /ˈgræni/ n (pl **grannies**) (inf) a grandmother; (inf) an old woman.

granny knot n a wrongly tied reef knot, which is insecure.

grant /grænt/ vt to consent to; to give or transfer by legal procedure; to admit as true. • n the act of granting; something granted, esp a gift for a particular purpose; a transfer of property by deed; the instrument by which such a transfer is made.

grantee /grænˈtiː/ n the person to whom property is transferred by deed, etc.

granter /ˈgræntər/ n one who grants.

grantor /ˈgræntər/ n one who transfers property by deed, etc.

granular /ˈgrænjʊlər/ adj consisting of granules; having a grainy texture.—**granularity** n.

granulate /ˈgrænjʊˌleɪt/ vt to form or crystallize into grains or granules. • vi to collect into grains or granules; to become roughened and grainy in surface texture.—**granulation** n.—**granulative** adj.—**granulator, granulater** n.

granule /ˈgrænjuːl/ n a small grain or particle.

grape /greɪp/ n a small round, juicy berry, growing in clusters on a vine; a dark purplish red.—**grapey, grapy** adj.

grape fern n a fern with crescent-shaped fronds, moonwort.

grapefruit /ˈgreɪpfruːt/ n (pl **grapefruit, grapefruits**) a large, round, sour citrus fruit with a yellow rind.

grape hyacinth n any of various small plants of the lily family bearing tight clusters of blue grape-like flowers.

grapeshot /'greɪpʃɒt/ *n* cannon shot packed in layers, scattering when fired.

grapevine /-vaɪn/ *n* a type of woody vine on which grapes grow; an informal means of communicating news or gossip.

graph /græf/ *n* a diagram representing the successive changes in the value of a variable quantity or quantities. • *vt* to illustrate by graphs.

-graph *n suffix* a writing or recording device; something written, drawn or recorded.

-grapher /-ər/ *n suffix* denoting a person with specified skills; denoting a person who writes or draws in a certain way.

graphic /'græfɪk/, **graphical** /'græfɪkəl/ *adj* described in realistic detail; pertaining to a graph, lettering, drawing, painting, etc.—**graphically** *adv.*—**graphicalness, graphicness** *n*.

graphic arts *npl* the fine and applied arts involving design, illustration and printing.

graphics /'græfɪks/ *n sing or pl* the use of drawings and lettering; the drawings, illustrations, etc used in a newspaper, magazine, television programme, etc; information displayed in the form of diagrams, illustrations and animation on a computer monitor.

graphite /'græfaɪt/ *n* a soft, black form of carbon used in pencils, for lubricants, etc.—**graphitic** *adj*.

graphology /grə'fɒlədʒi/ *n* the study of handwriting, *esp* as a clue to character.—**graphological** *adj.*—**graphologist** *n*.

graph paper *n* ruled paper for drawing graphs and diagrams.

-graphy /grəfi/ *n suffix* denoting a form of writing, representation or description.

grapnel /'græpnəl/ *n* a small anchor with multiple claws.

grapple /'græpəl/ *vt* to seize or grip firmly. • *vi* to struggle hand-to-hand with; to deal or contend with. • *n* a grapnel; an act of grappling, a wrestle; a grip.—**grappler** *n*.

grappling iron, grappling hook *n* an iron bar with claws at one end for anchoring a boat, securing a ship alongside or raising sunken objects.

grasp /græsp/ *vt* to grip, as with the hand; to seize; to understand. • *vi* to try to clutch, seize; (*with* **at**) to take eagerly. • *n* a firm grip; power of seizing and holding; comprehension.—**graspable** *adj.*—**grasper** *n*.

grasping /'græspɪŋ/ *adj* greedy, avaricious.—**graspingly** *adv.*—**graspingness** *n*.

grass /græs/ *n* any of a large family of plants with jointed stems and long narrow leaves including cereals, bamboo, etc; such plants grown as lawn; pasture; (*sl*) marijuana; (*sl*) an informer. • *vi* to cover with grass; (*sl*) to inform, betray.

grasshopper /'græs,hɒpər/ *n* any of a group of plant-eating, winged insects with powerful hind legs for jumping.

grassland /'græslænd/ *n* land reserved for pasture; land, such as prairie, where grass dominates.

grass roots /'græsruːts/ *npl* (*inf*) the common people, the ordinary members of a political or other organization; the basic level, the essentials.

grass snake *n* a small nonpoisonous European snake with a greenish body and yellow markings.

grass widow, grass widower *n* (*inf*) a person whose spouse is frequently absent.

grassy /'græsi/ *adj* (**grassier, grassiest**) abounding in, covered with, or like, grass.—**grassiness** *n*.

grate[1] /greɪt/ *n* a frame of metal bars for holding fuel in a fireplace; a fireplace; a grating.

grate[2] *vt* to grind into particles by scraping; to rub against (an object) or grind (the teeth) together with a harsh sound; to irritate. • *vi* to rub or rasp noisily; to cause irritation.

grateful /'greɪtful/ *adj* appreciative; welcome.—**gratefully** *adv.*—**gratefulness** *n*.

grater /'greɪtər/ *n* a metal implement with a jagged surface for grating food.

gratification /,grætɪfɪ'keɪʃən/ *n* the act of gratifying; satisfaction; pleasure; (*arch*) a reward or recompense.

gratify /'grætɪ,faɪ/ *vt* (**gratifying, gratified**) to please; to indulge.—**gratification** *n.*—**gratifier** *n.*—**gratifyingly** *adv*.

grating[1] /'greɪtɪŋ/ *n* a open framework or lattice of bars placed across an opening.

grating[2] *adj* harsh; irritating.—**gratingly** *adv*.

gratis /'grætɪs/ or /'greɪ-/ *adj, adv* free of charge.

gratitude /'grætɪ,tuːd/ or /-,tjuːd/ *n* a being thankful for favours received.

gratuitous /grə'tuːətəs/ or /-'tjuːətəs/ *adj* given free of charge;

done without cause, unwarranted.—**gratuitously** *adv.*—**gratuitousness** *n*.

gratuity /grə'tuːɪti/ or /-'tjuːɪti/ *n* (*pl* **gratuities**) money given for a service, a tip.

grav /græv/ *n* a unit of acceleration equal to standard free fall (1 grav = 9.8 metres (32 feet) per second).

gravamen /grə'veɪmɛn/ *n* (*pl* **gravamens, gravamina**) the principal part of a legal complaint or accusation.

grave[1] /greɪv/ *n* a hole dug in the ground for burying the dead; any place of burial, a tomb.

grave[2] *adj* serious, important; harmful; solemn, sombre; (*sound*) low in pitch. • *n* an accent (`) over a vowel.—**gravely** *adv.*—**graveness** *n*.

gravel /'grævəl/ *n* coarse sand with small rounded stones. • *vt* (**gravelling, gravelled** *or* **graveling, graveled**) to cover or spread with gravel.—**gravelish** *adj*.

gravelly /'grævəli/ *adj* like gravel; (*voice*) deep and rough-sounding.

graven /'greɪvən/ *adj* engraved; fixed indelibly.

graven image *n* an idol.

graver /'greɪvər/ *n* an engraving tool.

gravestone /'greɪvstoːn/ *n* a stone marking a grave, *usu* inscribed with the name and details of the deceased.

graveyard /'greɪvjɑrd/ *n* a burial-ground, cemetery.

gravid /'grævɪd/ *adj* pregnant.—**gravidity, gravidness** *n.*—**gravidly** *adv*.

gravimeter /grə'vɪmɪtər/ *n* an instrument for measuring the specific gravity of liquid or solid bodies; an instrument for measuring gravity at particular geographical locations.—**gravimetry** *n*.

gravimetric /,grævɪ'mɛtrɪk/, **gravimetrical** /-kəl/ *adj* of or relating to measurement by weight; determined by weight.—**gravimetrically** *adv*.

gravitate /'grævə,teɪt/ *vi* to move or tend to move under the force of gravitation.—**gravitater** *n*.

gravitation /,grævə'teɪʃən/ *n* a natural force of attraction that tends to draw bodies together.—**gravitational** *adj.*—**gravitationally** *adv*.

gravitative /-tɪv/ *adj* pertaining to or determined by gravitation; likely to gravitate, causing something to gravitate.

gravity /'grævɪti/ *n* (*pl* **gravities**) importance, *esp* seriousness; weight; the attraction of bodies toward the centre of the earth, the moon, or a planet.

gravy /'greɪvi/ *n* (*pl* **gravies**) the juice given off by meat during cooking; the sauce made from this juice; (*sl*) money easily obtained.

gravy boat *n* a small boat-shaped dish for holding and serving gravy or sauces.

gravy train *n* (*sl*) a source of easy money.

gray /greɪ/ *see* **grey**.

graybeard *see* **greybeard**.

grayling /'greɪlɪŋ/ *n* (*pl* **grayling, graylings**) a freshwater fish.

gray matter *see* **grey matter**.

gray squirrel *see* **grey squirrel**

graywacke *see* **greywacke**.

graze[1] /greɪz/ *vi* to feed on growing grass or pasture. • *vt* to put (animals) to feed on growing grass or pasture.—**grazer** *n*.

graze[2] *vt* to touch lightly in passing; to scrape, scratch. • *n* an abrasion, *esp* on the skin, caused by scraping on a surface.—**grazingly** *adv*.

grazier /'greɪzər/ *n* a person who grazes cattle and prepares them for the market.

grazing /-ɪŋ/ *n* pasture; the crops, plants, etc, growing on this for animals to feed from.

grease /griːs/ *n* melted animal fat; any thick, oily substance or lubricant. • *vt* to smear or lubricate with grease.

greasepaint /'griːspeɪnt/ *n* make-up used by actors.

greaser /'griːsər/ *n* (*sl*) a mechanic; a motorcyclist, often a member of a gang; a member of the engine room crew on a commercial ship; (*derog*) an unpleasant, fawning person.

greasy /'griːsi/ *adj* (**greasier, greasiest**) covered with grease; full of grease; slippery; oily in manner.—**greasily** *adv.*—**greasiness** *n*.

great /greɪt/ *adj* of much more than ordinary size, extent, etc; much above the average; intense; eminent; most important; more distant in a family relationship by one generation; (*often with* **at**) (*inf*) skilful; (*inf*) excellent; fine. • *n* (*inf*) a distinguished person.—**greatly** *adv.*—**greatness** *n*.

great-aunt *n* a parent's aunt.—*also* **grand-aunt**.

greatcoat /'greɪtkoːt/ *n* a large heavy coat.

Great Dane *n* a breed of very large smooth-haired dogs.

great divide *n* a watershed between major drainage systems; a significant point of division, *esp* death.

great-nephew *n* a nephew's or niece's son.—*also* **grandnephew**.

great-niece *n* a nephew's or niece's daughter.—*also* **grandniece**.

great-uncle *n* a parent's uncle.—*also* **grand-uncle**.

great tit *n* a common yellow, black and white Eurasian tit.

Great War *n* the First World War 1914–18.

greave /griːv/ *n* armour for the lower leg.

greaves /-z/ *npl* the sediment of melted tallow; (*often sing*) armour to protect the legs from the ankle to the knee.

grebe /griːb/ *n* any of a family of swimming and diving birds.

Grecian /'griːʃən/ *adj* pertaining to Greece; in the Greek style; Greek. • *n* a native or inhabitant of Greece; a Greek scholar.

Grecism *n* a Greek idiom, phrase, spirit or style; a reverent imitation of these, *eg* in architecture or literature.

Grecize *vti* to give a Greek form to; to imitate Greek.

Greco- /'griːkoː/ or /'grɛkoː/ *prefix* Greek.

Greco-Roman *adj* of or relating to the ancient Greek and Romans.

greed /griːd/ *n* excessive desire, *esp* for food or wealth.

greedy /'griːdi/ *adj* (**greedier**, **greediest**) wanting more than one needs or deserves; having too strong a desire for food and drink.—**greedily** *adv*.—**greediness** *n*.

Greek /griːk/ *adj* of Greece, its people, or its language. • *n* a native of Greece; the language used by Greeks; (*inf*) something unintelligible.

Greek cross *n* a cross with four equal arms.

Greek fire *n* (*ancient history*) a weapon used in sea battles consisting of an unidentified substance that ignited on contact with water.

green /griːn/ *adj* of the colour green; covered with plants or foliage; having a sickly appearance; unripe; inexperienced, naive; not fully processed or treated; concerned with the conservation of natural resources; (*inf*) jealous. • *n* a colour between blue and yellow in the spectrum; the colour of growing grass; something of a green colour; (*pl*) green leafy vegetables, as spinach, etc; (*often with cap*) a person concerned with the future of the earth's environment; a grassy plot, *esp* the end of a golf fairway.—**greenish** *adj*.—**greenly** *adv*.—**greenness** *n*.—**greeny** *adj*.

greenback /'griːnbæk/ *n* a legal-tender note of US currency.

green bean *n* any of various beans with narrow edible pods.

green belt /'griːnbelt/ *n* a belt of parkland, farms, etc surrounding a community, designed to prevent urban sprawl.

greenery /'griːnəri/ *n* (*pl* **greeneries**) green vegetation.

green-eyed /-aɪd/ *adj* jealous.

green-eyed monster *n* jealousy.

greenfinch /'griːnfɪntʃ/ *n* a European and Asian bird with yellow and green plumage.

green fingers *n* gardening expertise. US equivalent—**green thumb**.

greenfly /'griːnflaɪ/ *n* (*pl* **greenflies**) an insect pest that infests garden plants and crops.

greengage /'griːngeɪdʒ/ *n* a small greenish sweet variety of plum.

greenheart /'griːnhɑːt/ *n* a tropical American tree that yields a dark durable timber; the timber.

greenhorn /'griːnhɔːn/ *n* an inexperienced person; a person easily duped.

greenhouse /'griːnhʊs/ *n* a heated building, mainly of glass, for growing plants.

greenhouse effect *n* action of radiant heat from the sun passing through the glass of greenhouses etc., warming the contents inside, where such heat is thus trapped; application of the same effect to a planet's atmosphere.—*see* **global warming**.

greening[1] /'griːnɪŋ/ *n* a type of cooking apple that is green when ripe.

greening[2] *n* growing awareness of the environment.

green light *n* permission to proceed with a plan, etc.

green pepper *n* the unripe fruit of the sweet pepper eaten raw or cooked.

greenroom *n* the actors' rest room in a theatre, the room where they can receive visitors.

greensand /'griːnsænd/ *n* a green sandstone.

greenshank *n* a large European wading bird with greenish legs and feet.

greenstone /-stoːn/ *n* New Zealand jade; any green igneous rock that contains chlorite or epidote.

green thumb *see* **green fingers**.

greensward /-swɔːd/ *n* (*arch*) (a stretch of) turf.

green tea *n* a drink made from dried unfermented tea leaves.

Greenwich Mean Time *n* the time of the meridian of Greenwich, England, used as the basis of worldwide standard time.

greenwood /'griːnwʊd/ *n* leafy woodland.

greet /griːt/ *vt* to address with friendliness; to meet (a person, event, etc) in a specified way; to present itself to.—**greeter** *n*.

greeting /-ɪŋ/ *n* the act of welcoming with words or gestures; an expression of good wishes; (*pl*) a message of regards.

gregarious /grɪˈgɛərɪəs/ *adj* (*animals*) living in flocks and herds; (*people*) sociable, fond of company.—**gregariously** *adv*.—**gregariousness** *n*.

Gregorian /grəˈgɔːrɪən/ *adj* pertaining to or established by Gregory, the name of various popes.

Gregorian calendar *n* the reformed calendar introduced in 1582 by Pope Gregory XIII and currently in use.

gremlin /'gremlɪn/ *n* an imaginary creature blamed for disruption of any procedure or of malfunction of equipment, *esp* in an aircraft.

grenade /grəˈneɪd/ *n* a small bomb thrown manually or projected (as by a rifle or special launcher).

grenadier[1] /ˌgrɛnəˈdiːr/ *n* a soldier of the British Grenadier Guards, the first regiment of the household infantry; (*formerly*) a foot soldier who threw grenades; (*formerly*) a company made up of the tallest and strongest soldiers in the regiment.

grenadier[2] *n* a sea fish with a large head and a long, narrow tail.

grenadine[1] /'grɛnəˌdiːn/ *n* a gauze-like dress fabric.

grenadine[2] *n* a syrup made from pomegranates; a red-orange colour.

gressorial /grɛˈsɔːrɪəl/ *adj* adapted for walking; (*birds*) having three toes of the feet forward, two of them connected, and one behind.

grew /gruː/ *see* **grow**.

grey /greɪ/ *n* any of a series of neutral colours ranging between black and white; something (as an animal, garment, cloth, or spot) of a grey colour. • *adj* grey in colour; having grey-coloured hair; darkish; dreary; vague, indeterminate.—*also* **gray**.—**greyish** *adj*.—**greyness** *n*.

greybeard /'greɪbɪrd/ *n* an old man, *esp* one considered to be wise; an earthenware jug.—*also* **graybeard**.

grey economy *n* the term used to describe unofficial trading which is not accounted for in a country's official economic statistics.

greyhound /'greɪhaʊnd/ *n* any of a breed of tall and slender dogs noted for its great speed and keen sight.

grey jay *n* a North American jay with grey, black and white plumage.—*also* **Canada jay**.

greylag (goose) /'greɪˌlæg/ *n* the common wild goose of Europe and Asia.

grey matter *n* grey-coloured nerve tissue of the brain and spinal cord; (*inf*) brains, intelligence.

grey squirrel *n* a common squirrel with grey fur originally from North America.

greywacke /'greɪˌwækə/ or /-wækə/ *n* a hard conglomerate rock of pebbles and sand.—*also* **graywacke**.

grid /grɪd/ *n* a gridiron, a grating; an electrode for controlling the flow of electrons in an electron tube; a network of squares on a map used for easy reference; a national network of transmission lines, pipes, etc for electricity, water, gas, etc.

griddle /'grɪdəl/ *n* a flat metal surface for cooking.

griddlecake *n* a pancake.

gridiron /'grɪdaɪrn/ *n* a framework of iron bars for cooking; anything resembling this, as a field used for American football.

gridlock /'grɪdlɒk/ *n* a traffic jam that halts all traffic at a street crossing; the breakdown of an organization or a system.

grief /griːf/ *n* extreme sorrow caused as by a loss; deep distress.

grief-stricken *adj* full of sorrow.

grievance /'griːvəns/ *n* a circumstance thought to be unjust and cause for complaint.

grieve /griːv/ *vti* to feel or cause to feel grief.—**griever** *n*.—**grieving** *adj*, *n*.

grievous /'griːvəs/ *adj* causing or characterized by grief; deplorable; severe.—**grievously** *adv*.—**grievousness** *n*.

griffin /'grɪfɪn/, **griffon**[1] /'grɪfən/ *n* a mythical animal with the body and tail of a lion and an eagle's beak and wings.—*also* **gryphon**.

griffon[2] /'grɪfən/ *n* a small dog with a wire-haired coat; a large hawk with a pale body and black wings, found in Africa, Asia and warm parts of Europe.

grig /grɪg/ *n* an extravagantly vivacious person; the sand eel; a young eel; a hen with short legs; heather.

grill /grɪl/ *vt* to broil by direct heat using a grill or gridiron; (*inf*) to question relentlessly. • *n* a device on a cooker that radiates heat downward for broiling or grilling; a gridiron; broiled or grilled food; a grille; a grillroom.—**griller** *n*.

grillage /ˈgrɪlɪdʒ/ *n* an arrangement of planks and crossbeams forming a foundation in loose or marshy soil.

grille, grill /grɪl/ *n* an open grating forming a screen.

grillroom *n* a restaurant that specializes in grilled food.

grilse /grɪls/ *n* (*pl* **grilses, grilse**) a young salmon returning from the sea to spawn for the first time.

grim /grɪm/ *adj* (**grimmer, grimmest**) hard and unyielding, stern; appearing harsh, forbidding; repellent, ghastly in character.—**grimly** *adv*.—**grimness** *n*.

grimace /ˈgrɪməs/ *n* a contortion of the face expressing pain, anguish, humour, etc. • *vi* to contort the face in pain, etc.—**grimacer** *n*.—**grimacingly** *adv*.

grimalkin /grɪˈmælkɪn/ or /-ˈmɒlkɪn/ *n* an old she-cat; a spiteful, bad-tempered old woman.

grime /graɪm/ *n* soot or dirt, rubbed into a surface, as the skin. • *vt* to dirty, soil with grime.

grimy /ˈgraɪmi/ *adj* (**grimier, grimiest**) dirty, soiled.—**griminess** *n*.

grin /grɪn/ *vi* (**grinning, grinned**) to smile broadly as in amusement; to show the teeth in pain, scorn, etc. • *n* a broad smile.—**grinner** *n*.

grind /graɪnd/ *vb* (**grinding, ground**) *vt* to reduce to powder or fragments by crushing; to wear down, sharpen, or smooth by friction; to rub (the teeth) harshly together; to oppress, tyrannize; to move or operate by a crank. • *vi* to be crushed, smoothed, or sharpened by grinding; to jar or grate; to work monotonously; to rotate the hips in an erotic manner. • *n* the act or sound of grinding; hard monotonous work.

grinder /graɪndər/ *n* someone or something that grinds; a molar tooth.

grindstone /ˈgraɪndstoːn/ *n* a circular revolving stone for grinding or sharpening tools.

gringo /ˈgrɪŋgoː/ *n* (*pl* **gringos**) (*offensive*) among Hispanics, a foreigner, *esp* North Americans.

grip /grɪp/ *n* a secure grasp; the manner of holding a bat, club, racket, etc; the power of grasping firmly; mental grasp; mastery; a handle; a small travelling bag. • *vt* (**gripping, gripped**) to take firmly and hold fast.

gripe /graɪp/ *vt* to cause sharp pain in the bowels of; (*sl*) to annoy. • *vi* (*sl*) to complain.—**griper** *n*.—**gripingly** *adv*.

grippe /grɪp/ *n* (*formerly*) influenza.

gripper /-ər/ *n* one who or that which grips; a mechanical device for seizing and holding.

grisaille /grɪˈzeɪl/ or /-ˈzaɪl/ *n* a method of painting in grey tints so as to represent a solid body in relief; a decorative painting in grey monochrome, *esp* on glass.

griseous /ˈgrɪʃəs/ *adj* bluish-grey.

grisette *n* a lively young French working girl, *esp* a flirtatious one; an edible toadstool.

griskin *n* the lean part of a loin of pork.

grisly /ˈgrɪzli/ *adj* (**grislier, grisliest**) terrifying; ghastly; arousing horror.—**grisliness** *n*.

grison *n* a carnivorous mammal of Central and South America, which resembles a weasel.

grist /grɪst/ *n* grain that is to be or has been ground; matter forming the basis of a story or analysis.

gristle /ˈgrɪsəl/ *n* cartilage, *esp* in meat.—**gristly** *adj*.—**gristliness** *n*.

grit /grɪt/ *n* rough particles, as of sand; firmness of spirit; stubborn courage. • *vt* (**gritting, gritted**) to clench or grind together (*eg* the teeth); to spread grit on (*eg* an icy road).

grits /grɪts/ *npl* oats, hulled and coarsely ground; coarsely ground maize, boiled in water or milk as a food.—*also* (*US*) **hominy grits**.

gritty /-ti/ *adj* (**grittier, grittiest**) composed of, containing, or resembling, grit; courageous.—**grittily** *adv*.—**grittiness** *n*.

grivet /grɪvət/ *n* an Ethiopian monkey with a long tail and tufts of white hair on either side of the face.

grizzle /ˈgrɪzəl/ *vt* (*inf*) to fret; to complain. • *vti* to (cause to) become grey. • *n* a grey colour; hair that is, or is becoming, grey; a wig of grey hair.—**grizzled** *adj*.

grizzled /ˈgrɪzəld/ *adj* streaked with grey; grey-haired.

grizzly /ˈgrɪzli/ *adj* (**grizzlier, grizzliest**) greyish; grizzled. • *n* (*pl* **grizzlies**) the grizzly bear.

grizzly bear *n* a large powerful bear of North America.

groan /groːn/ *vi* to utter a deep moan; to make a harsh sound (as of creaking) under sudden or prolonged strain. • *n* a deep moan; a creaking sound.—**groaner** *n*.—**groaningly** *adv*.

groat /groːt/ *n* (*formerly*) a British silver coin worth fourpence; a trifling sum.

groats /groːts/ *npl* hulled grain broken into fragments, *esp* oats.

grocer /ˈgroːsər/ or /-ʃər/ *n* a dealer in food and household supplies.

grocery /ˈgroːsəri/ or /-ʃəri/, /-ʃri/ *n* (*pl* **groceries**) a grocer's shop; (*pl*) goods, *esp* from a grocer.

grog /grɒg/ *n* rum diluted with water, often spiced and served hot.

groggy /ˈgrɒgi/ *adj* (**groggier, groggiest**) (*inf*) weak and unsteady, *usu* through illness, exhaustion or alcohol.—**groggily** *adv*.—**grogginess** *n*.

grogram /ˈgrɒgrəm/ *n* a coarse cloth of silk or silk and mohair or wool.

groin /grɔɪn/ *n* the fold marking the junction of the lower abdomen and the thighs; the location of the genitals.

grommet /ˈgrɒmət/ *n* a plastic or rubber ring used to protect wire, a cable, etc passing through a hole; a ring formed of a strand of rope laid round, used in pipe joints or sails.—*also* **grummet**; (*formerly*) a cannon-wad made of rope, and rammed between the powder and the ball.

gromwell /ˈgrɒm,wɛl/ or /-wəl/ *n* a herb of the borage family.

groom /gruːm/ *n* a person employed to care for horses; a bridegroom. • *vt* to clean and care for (animals); to make neat and tidy; to train (a person) for a particular purpose.—**groomer** *n*.—**grooming** *n*.

groomsman /ˈgruːmzmən/ *n* (*pl* **groomsmen**) one who attends a bridegroom; a best man.

groove /gruːv/ *n* a long, narrow channel; a spiral track in a gramophone record for the stylus; a settled routine. • *vt* to make a groove in.

groovy /ˈgruːvi/ *adj* (**groovier, grooviest**) (*sl*) excellent.

grope /groːp/ *vi* to search about blindly as in the dark; to search uncertainly for a solution to a problem. • *vt* to find by feeling; (*sl*) to fondle sexually. • *n* the act of groping.—**groper** *n*.—**gropingly** *adv*.

grosbeak /ˈgroːsbiːk/ *n* any finch-like bird of Europe or America with a large stout conical bill.

groschen /ˈgroːʃən/ *n* (*pl* **groschen**) (*formerly*) a 10-pfennig coin used in Germany; (*formerly*) a silver coin current in Germany; (*formerly*) in Austria, a coin with a value of one hundredth of a schilling.

grosgrain /ˈgroːgreɪn/ *n* a stout double-corded silk; a fabric or ribbon of this.

gros point /ˈgroːpɔɪnt/ *n* a large needlepoint stitch covering two vertical and two horizontal threads; a piece of needlework done in this.

gross /groːs/ *adj* fat and coarse-looking; flagrant, dense, thick; lacking in refinement; earthy; obscene; total, with no deductions. • *n* (*pl* **grosses**) an overall total; (*pl* **gross**) twelve dozen. • *vt* to earn as total revenue.—**grossly** *adv*.—**grossness** *n*.

gross domestic product *n* the total value of goods and services produced by a country in one year.

gross national product *n* the gross domestic product plus income earned from abroad.

grot[1] /grɒt/ *n* (*poet*) a grotto.

grot[2] /grɒt/ *n* (*Brit sl*) unpleasant mess.—**grotty** *adj* (**grottier, grottiest**) nasty, unattractive; in bad condition; unsatisfactory.

grotesque /groːˈtɛsk/ *adj* distorted or fantastic in appearance, shape, etc; ridiculous; absurdly incongruous. • *n* a grotesque person or thing; a decorative device combining distorted plant, animal and human forms.—**grotesquely** *adv*.—**grotesqueness** *n*.

grotesquery, grotesquerie /-ˈtɛskəri/ *n* (*pl* **grotesqueries**) *n* something that is fantastic or distorted in shape, etc.

grotto /ˈgrɒtoː/ *n* (*pl* **grottoes, grottos**) a cave, *esp* one with attractive features.

grotty /ˈgrɒti/ *see* **grot**.

grouch /graʊtʃ/ *vi* (*inf*) to grumble or complain. • *n* (*inf*) a grumble; a person who grumbles.—**groucher** *n*.

grouchy /ˈgraʊtʃi/ *adj* (**grouchier, grouchiest**) bad-tempered.—**grouchily** *adv*.—**grouchiness** *n*.

ground /graʊnd/ *n* the solid surface of the earth; soil; the background, as in design; the connection of an electrical conductor with the earth; (*pl*) a basis for belief, action, or argument; the area about and relating to a building; a tract of land; sediment. • *vti* to set on the ground; to run aground or cause to run aground; to base, found, or establish; to instruct in the first principles of; to prevent (aircraft) from flying.

ground control *n* the communications and tracking equipment and staff that monitor aircraft and spacecraft in flight and during takeoff and landing.

ground cover *n* low-growing shrubs, plants and other foliage on the ground.

ground floor *n* the floor of a building on a level with the ground.

ground hog /ˈgraʊndhɒg/ *n* a woodchuck.

grounding /-ɪŋ/ *n* basic general knowledge of a subject.

ground ivy *n* a trailing Eurasian plant with bluish-purple flowers.

groundless /-ləs/ *adj* without reason.—**groundlessly** *adv*.

groundnut /-nʌt/ *n* a climbing plant of North America with an underground nut; another name for a peanut.

ground rule *n* a fundamental rule or principle.

groundsel /ˈgraʊnsəl/ *n* a weed of the aster family with yellow flowers.

groundsheet /ˈgraʊndʃiːt/ *n* a waterproof sheet placed on the ground in, or as part of, a tent.

groundsman /ˈgraʊndzmən/ *n* (*pl* **groundsmen**) a man who looks after a cricket pitch, football pitch, park, etc.

groundswell /ˈgraʊndswel/ *n* a large rolling wave; a wave of popular feeling.

groundwork /ˈgraʊndwɜːk/ *n* foundation, basis.

group /gruːp/ *n* a number of persons or things considered as a collective unit; a small musical band of players or singers; a number of companies under single ownership; two or more figures forming one artistic design. • *vti* to form into a group or groups.

grouper /ˈgruːpər/ *n* (*pl* **grouper, groupers**) an edible sea fish.

groupie /ˈgruːpi/ *n* a devoted fan.

group therapy *n* (*psychol*) the simultaneous treatment of patients with similar problems through mutual discussion and exchange of experiences.

grouse[1] /graʊs/ *n* (*pl* **grouse, grouses**) a game bird; its flesh as food.

grouse[2] *vi* (*inf*) to complain.—**grouser** *n*.

grout /graʊt/ *n* a thin mortar used as between tiles. • *vt* to fill with grout.—**grouter** *n*.

grove /groːv/ *n* a small wood, generally without undergrowth.

grovel /ˈgrɒvəl/ *vi* (**grovelling, grovelled** *or* **groveling, groveled**) to lie and crawl in a prostrate position as a sign of respect, fear or humility.—**groveller, groveler** *n*.—**grovellingly, grovelingly** *adv*.

grow /groː/ *vb* (**growing, grew,** *pp* **grown**) *vi* to come into being; to be produced naturally; to develop, as a living thing; to increase in size, quantity, etc; (*with* **on**) to become more accustomed or acceptable to; (*with* **up**) to mature; to arise, develop. • *vt* to cause or let grow; to raise, to cultivate.—**growable** *adj*.—**grower** *n*.

growing pains *npl* muscular discomfort sometimes experienced by growing children; difficulties experienced in the early stages of a project.

growl /graʊl/ *vi* to make a rumbling, menacing sound such as an angry dog makes. • *vt* to express in a growling manner. • *n* a growling noise; a grumble.—**growler** *n*.

growler /ˈgraʊlər/ *n* one who growls; (*arch*) a four-wheeled cab; a small iceberg; a beer jug or beer can.

grown-up *n* a fully grown person, an adult. • *adj* mature, adult; fit for an adult.

growth /groːθ/ *n* the act or process of growing; progressive increase, development; something that grows or has grown; an abnormal formation of tissue, as a tumour.

groyne /grɔɪn/ *n* a timber structure to stop the shifting of sand on a beach.

grub /grʌb/ *vb* (**grubbing, grubbed**) *vi* to dig in the ground; to work hard. • *vt* to clear (ground) of roots; to uproot. • *n* the worm-like larva of a beetle; (*sl*) food.

grubber /ˈgrʌbər/ *n* one who or that which grubs; a grub hoe.

grubby /ˈgrʌbi/ *adj* (**grubbier, grubbiest**) dirty.—**grubbily** *adv*.—**grubbiness** *n*.

grudge /grʌdʒ/ *n* a deep feeling of resentment or ill will. • *vt* to be reluctant to give or admit something.—**grudger** *n*.—**grudging** *adj*.—**grudgingly** *adv*.

gruel /ˈgruːəl/ *n* a thin porridge cooked in water or milk.

gruelling, grueling /ˈgruːəlɪŋ/ *adj* severely testing, exhausting.

gruesome /ˈgruːsəm/ *adj* causing horror or loathing.

gruff /grʌf/ *adj* rough or surly; hoarse.—**gruffly** *adv*.—**gruffness** *n*.

grugru /ˈgruːˌgruː/ *n* the larva of a South American weevil, cooked for food as a delicacy; the palm tree on which this lives.

grumble /ˈgrʌmbəl/ *vti* to mutter in discontent; to make a rumbling sound. • *n* a complaint; a grumbling sound.—**grumbler** *n*.—**grumblingly** *adv*.

grump /grʌmp/ *n* (*inf*) a bad-tempered person.

grumpy /ˈgrʌmpi/ *adj* (**grumpier, grumpiest**) bad-tempered, peevish.—**grumpily** *adv*.—**grumpiness** *n*.

grunt /grʌnt/ *vi* to make a gruff guttural sound like a pig; to say or speak in such a manner. • *n* a low gruff sound; (*sl*) a US infantry man.

grunter /ˈgrʌntər/ *n* one who or that which grunts; an edible marine American fish; a pig.

Gruyère /ˈgruːjɛr/ *n* a hard, pale yellow Swiss cheese *usu* with holes.

gryphon *see* **griffin**.

G-string /ˈdʒiːstrɪŋ/ *n* a string on an instrument tuned to the note G; a string or strip worn round the waist and between the legs.

G-suit /ˈdʒiːsuːt/ *n* a (gravity) suit designed to counteract the physiological effects of acceleration on airmen and astronauts.

GT /ˈdʒiːtiː/ *abbr* = *gran turismo*, a luxury sports car.

guaco /ˈgwɒkoː/ *n* (*pl* **guacos**) a tropical American plant, used as an antidote to snakebites.

guaiacum /ˈgwaɪəkəm/ *n* any of various tropical and West Indian shrubs or trees; the wood from these; a gum obtained from them, used medicinally and in the manufacture of varnishes.

guan /gwɒn/ *n* an American bird similar to a turkey.

guanaco /gwəˈnɒkoː/ *n* (*pl* **guanacos, guanaco**) the wild llama of South America.

guanine /ˈgwɒniːn/ *n* a nitrogenous base component of the nucleic acids, DNA and RNA, also found in guano.

guano /ˈgwɒnoː/ *n* (*pl* **guanos**) dung of sea birds used as manure; a similar artificially produced fertilizer.

guarantee /ˌgɛrənˈtiː/ *or* /ˌgærənˈtiː/ *n* a pledge or security for another's debt or obligation; a pledge to replace something if it is substandard, etc; an assurance that something will be done as specified; something offered as a pledge or security; a guarantor. • *vt* (**guaranteeing, guaranteed**) to give a guarantee for; to promise.

guarantor /ˈgɛrəntɔːr/ *or* /ˈgɛrəntər/, /ˈgæ-/ *n* a person who gives a guaranty or guarantee.

guaranty /ˈgɛrənti/ *or* /ˈgær-/ *n* (*pl* **guaranties**) (*law*) a guarantee.

guard /gɑːd/ *vt* to watch over and protect; to defend; to keep from escape or trouble; to restrain. • *vi* to keep watch (against); to act as a guard. • *n* defence; protection; posture of readiness for defence; any device to protect against injury or loss; a person or group that guards; (*boxing, fencing, cricket*) a defensive attitude; a railway official in charge of a train; (*with cap: pl*) a regiment of British or European household troops.—**guardable** *adj*.—**guarder** *n*.

guarded /ˈgɑːdəd/ *adj* discreet; cautious.—**guardedly** *adv*.—**guardedness** *n*.

guardhouse /ˈgɑːdhaʊs/ *n* a building used by a military guard when not walking a post; a military jail for temporary confinement.

guardian /ˈgɑːdiən/ *n* a custodian; a person legally in charge of a minor or someone incapable of taking care of their own affairs.—**guardianship** *n*.

guardrail /ˈgɑːdreɪl/ *n* a railing, *eg* at the side of a road, to prevent falling; a short metal rod placed inside the rails to keep a train's wheels on the track.

guardsman /ˈgɑːdzmən/ *n* (*pl* **guardsmen**) in the UK an officer or soldier of a Guards battalion or regiment; in the US an officer or soldier of the National Guard.

guard's van *n* the railway carriage where the guard travels, *usu* at the back of a train.—*also US* **caboose**.

guava /ˈgwɒvə/ *n* a tropical shrubby tree widely cultivated for its sweet acid yellow fruit.

gubernatorial /ˌguːbərnəˈtɔːriəl/ *adj* pertaining to a governor or to his office.

gudgeon /ˈgʌdʒən/ *n* a small edible freshwater fish; a fish used as bait in fishing; a person who is easily imposed upon; an iron pin or shaft on which a wheel revolves; (*naut*) one of the sockets into which a rudder is fixed.

guelder-rose /'gɛldər/ n a cultivated variety of cranberry bush with large heads of sterile flowers.

Guelph, Guelf /gwɛlf/ n a member of a powerful Italian political party in the Middle Ages, which supported the pope and sought the independence of Italy; a member of a secret society in 19th-century Italy, supporting Italian independence.

guerdon /'gərdən/ n (poet) reward. • vt to reward, to recompense.

guernsey /'gərnzi/ n a particular breed of dairy cattle originally from the island of Guernsey; a close-fitting knitted woollen jersey; (Austral) a woollen top worn by a football player.

guerrilla, guerilla /gə'rɪlə/ n a member of a small force of irregular soldiers, making surprise raids.—also adj.

guess /gɛs/ vt to form an opinion of or state with little or no factual knowledge; to judge correctly by doing this; to think or suppose. • n an estimate based on guessing.—**guessable** adj.—**guesser** n.

guesstimate /'gɛstɪmət/ n (inf) an estimate based mainly on guesswork.

guesswork /'gɛswərk/ n the process or result of guessing.

guest /gɛst/ n a person entertained at the home, club, etc of another; any paying customer of a hotel, restaurant, etc; a performer appearing by special invitation.

guesthouse n a private home or boarding-house offering accommodation.

guestroom n a room kept for guests.

guffaw /gə'fɔ/ n a crude noisy laugh. • vi to laugh boisterously.

guidance /'gaɪdəns/ n leadership; advice or counsel.

guide /gaɪd/ vt to point out the way for; to lead; to direct the course of; to control. • n a person who leads or directs others; a person who exhibits and explains points of interest; something that provides a person with guiding information; a device for controlling the motion of something; a book of basic instruction; a Girl Guide.—**guidable** adj.—**guider** n.—**guiding** adj, n.

guidebook /'gaɪdbʊk/ n a book containing directions and information for tourists.

guided missile n a military missile whose course is controlled by radar or internal instruments, etc.

guideline /'gaɪdlaɪn/ n a principle or instruction which determines conduct or policy.

guidepost /'gaɪdpoʊst/ n a direction post; a guiding principle.

guidon /'gaɪdən/ n a forked or pointed military flag, used esp by troops of light cavalry.

guild /gɪld/ n a club, society; an association of people with common interests formed for mutual aid and protection, as craftsmen in the Middle Ages.—also **gild**.

guilder /'gɪldər/ n (formerly) a coin of the Netherlands; a coin of Netherlands Antilles and Surinam; a gold or silver coin formerly in circulation in Germany, Austria and the Netherlands.—also **gilder, gulden**.

guildhall /gɪld'hɒl/ or /'gɪld-/ n the meeting place of a guild or corporation.

guile /gaɪl/ n craftiness, deceit.—**guileful** adj.—**guilefully** adv.—**guilefulness** n.

guileless /-ləs/ adj without guile; ingenuous.—**guilelessly** adv.—**guilelessness** n.

guillemot /'gɪlɪˌmɒt/ n a small sea bird of the auk family.

guilloche /gɪ'lɒʃ/ n (archit) an ornament resembling braided ribbons.

guillotine /'gɪləˌtin/ or /'giːə-/ n an instrument for beheading by a heavy blade descending between grooved posts; a device or machine for cutting paper; a rule for limiting time for discussion in a legislature. • vt to execute (someone) by guillotine.—**guillotiner** n.

guilt /gɪlt/ n the fact of having done a wrong or committed an offence; a feeling of self-reproach from believing one has done a wrong.

guiltless /-ləs/ adj innocent.

guilty /'gɪlti/ adj (**guiltier, guiltiest**) having guilt; feeling or showing guilt.—**guiltily** adv.—**guiltiness** n.

guimpe /gæmp/ or /gɪmp/ n a short blouse worn under a pinafore dress; a piece of cloth used to disguise a low-cut neckline; the starched cloth that covers the shoulders and front of a nun's habit; gimp.

guinea /'gɪni/ n a former English gold coin equal to 21 shillings (£1.05).

guinea fowl n a domestic African bird of the pheasant family.

guinea pig n a rodent-like animal commonly kept as a pet, and often used in scientific experiments; a person or thing subject to an experiment.

guipure (lace) /giː'pyuːr/ n a coarse lace in which the pattern is supported by bars connecting the motifs rather than founded on a net base; a kind of gimp.

guise /gaɪz/ n an external appearance, aspect; an assumed appearance or pretence.

guitar /gɪ'tɑr/ n a stringed musical instrument with a long, fretted neck, and a flat body, which is plucked with a plectrum or the fingers.—**guitarist** n.

gular /'gjuːlər/ adj of, in or pertaining to the gullet or throat.

gulch /gʌltʃ/ n a deep, narrow ravine.

gulden /'gʊldən/ see **guilder**.

gules /gjuːlz/ n (her) the colour red, also indicated by vertical parallel lines.

gulf /gʌlf/ n a large area of ocean reaching into land; a wide, deep chasm; a vast separation.

Gulf Stream n a warm ocean current flowing from the Gulf of Mexico northward towards Europe.

gulfweed /'gʌlfwiːd/ n brown seaweed with air bladders which floats in dense masses in warm Atlantic waters.—also **sargasso, sargasso weed**.

gull /gʌl/ n any of numerous long-winged web-footed sea birds.

gullet /'gʌlət/ n the esophagus; the throat.

gullible /'gʌləbəl/ adj easily deceived.—**gullibility** n.—**gullibly** adv.

gully /'gʌli/ n (pl **gullies**) a narrow trench cut by running water after rain; (cricket) a fielding position between the slips and point. • vt (**gullying, gullied**) to make gullies in.

gulp /gʌlp/ vt to swallow hastily or greedily; to choke back as if swallowing. • n a gulping or swallowing; a mouthful.—**gulper** n.—**gulpingly** adv.

gum¹ /gʌm/ n the firm tissue that surrounds the teeth.

gum² n a sticky substance found in certain trees and plants; an adhesive; chewing gum. • vb (**gumming, gummed**) vt to coat or unite with gum. • vi to become sticky or clogged; (with **up**) (inf) to mess up, prevent from working properly.

gum ammoniac n a gum resin.—also **ammoniac**.

gum arabic n the gum obtained from certain species of acacia trees and used in the manufacture of adhesives and in pharmacy.

gumbo /'gʌmboː/ n (pl **gumbos**) a rich soup thickened with okra.

gumboil /'gʌmbɔɪl/ n an abscess in the gum.

gumboot /'gʌmbuːt/ n a rubber, waterproof boot, a wellington.

gumma /'gʌmə/ n (pl **gummas, gummata**) a syphilitic tumour.—**gummatous** adj.

gummy /'gʌmi/ adj (**gummier, gummiest**) sticky; revealing the gums, toothless.—**gummily** adv.—**gumminess** n.

gumption /'gʌmpʃən/ n (inf) shrewd practical common sense; initiative.

gum resin n a mixture of gum and resin exuded from certain plants and trees.

gumtree n a eucalyptus, or one of various other trees that yield gum.

gun /gʌn/ n a weapon with a metal tube from which a projectile is discharged by an explosive; the shooting of a gun as a signal or salute; anything like a gun. • vb (**gunning, gunned**) vi to shoot or hunt with a gun; (with **for**) to search out in order to hurt or kill. • vt (inf) to shoot (a person); (sl) to advance the throttle of an engine.

gunboat /'gʌnboːt/ n a small armed ship.

gunboat diplomacy n the threat of force used to back diplomatic activity.

guncotton n a highly explosive substance formed by the action of nitric and sulphuric acid upon cotton, or some other vegetable fibre.

gun dog n a dog trained to flush out or retrieve game shot by hunters.

gunfire /'gʌnˌfaɪr/ n repeated and consecutive gunshots; the use of guns, etc, rather than other military options.

gunk /gʌŋk/ n (inf) dirty, greasy, matter; gunge.

gunman /'gʌnmən/ n (pl **gunmen**) an armed gangster; a hired killer.

gunmetal /'gʌnmetəl/ n bronze with a dark tarnish; its dark-grey colour.

gunnel /'gʌnəl/ see **gunwale**.

gunner /'gʌnər/ n a soldier, etc who helps fire artillery; a naval warrant officer in charge of a ship's guns.

gunnery /'gʌnəri/ n the science of the design and operation of large guns.

gunny /'gʌni/ *n* (*pl* **gunnies**) a strong coarse fabric made from jute used for sacking.

gunpoint /'gʌnpɔɪnt/ *n* the muzzle of a gun; the threat of being shot.

gunpowder /'gʌnˌpaʊdər/ *n* an explosive powder used in guns, for blasting, etc.

gunrunning /'gʌnˌrʌnɪŋ/ *n* the smuggling of firearms into a country.—**gunrunner** *n*.

gunshot /'gʌnʃɒt/ *n* the range of a gun; the instance of shooting a gun or the shot fired from it.

gun-shy *adj* afraid of a loud noise; markedly distrustful.

gunslinger /'gʌnˌslɪŋər/ *n* (*sl*) a gunman or gunfighter.

gunstock /'gʌnstɒk/ *n* the wooden or metal mounting of a gun barrel.

gunwale /'gʌnəl/ *n* the upper edge of a ship's or boat's side.—*also* **gunnel**.

guppy /'gʌpi/ *n* (*pl* **guppies**) a small vividly-coloured fish of South America and the West Indies popular for aquariums.

gurgitation /ˌɡɜrdʒəˈteɪʃən/ *n* a whirling motion, a surging.

gurgle /'ɡɜrɡəl/ *vi* (*liquid*) to make a low bubbling sound; to utter with this sound. • *n* a bubbling sound.—**gurglingly** *adv*.

gurnard /'ɡɜrnərd/ *n* (*pl* **gurnard**, **gurnards**) a spiny sea fish with an armoured head.

guru /'ɡuːruː/ or /'ɡuru:/ *n* (*pl* **gurus**) a Hindu or Sikh spiritual teacher; an influential leader or teacher, *esp* of a religious cult.

gush /ɡʌʃ/ *vi* to issue plentifully; to have a sudden flow; to talk or write effusively. • *vt* to cause to gush. • *n* a sudden outpouring.—**gushingly** *adv*.

gusher /'ɡʌʃər/ *n* an effusive person; an oil well from which oil spouts forth.

gushy /'ɡʌʃi/ *adj* (**gushier, gushiest**) expressing excessive admiration.—**gushily** *adv*.—**gushiness** *n*.

gusset /'ɡʌsət/ *n* a small triangular piece of cloth inserted in a garment to strengthen or enlarge a part.

gust /ɡʌst/ *n* a sudden brief rush of wind; a sudden outburst. • *vi* to blow in gusts.

gustation /ɡəˈsteɪʃən/ *n* the act of tasting; the ability to taste; taste.—**gustatory** *adj*.

gusto /'ɡʌsto:/ *n* great enjoyment, zest.

gusty /'ɡʌsti/ *adj* (**gustier, gustiest**) windy; irritable.—**gustily** *adv*.—**gustiness** *n*.

gut /ɡʌt/ *n* (*often pl*) the bowels or the stomach; the intestine; tough cord made from animal intestines; (*pl*) (*sl*) daring; courage. • *vt* (**gutting, gutted**) to remove the intestines from; to destroy the interior of.

gutless /-ləs/ *adj* (*inf*) cowardly, lacking determination.—**gutlessness** *n*.

gutsy /'ɡʌtsi/ *adj* (**gutsier, gutsiest**) (*sl*) brave, courageous; passionate; greedy.

gutta /'ɡʌtə/ *n* (*pl* **guttae**) (*archit*) a small loop-like ornament, *esp* in a Doric entablature; (*med*) (*formerly*) a drop.

gutta-percha /ˌɡʌtəˈpɜrtʃə/ *n* the flexible hardened juice of a tropical tree; one of several trees yielding this.

guttate /'ɡʌteɪt/ **guttated** *adj* (*plants*) spotted; drop-like.

gutter /'ɡʌtər/ *n* a channel for carrying off water, *esp* at a roadside or under the eaves of a roof; a channel or groove to direct something (as of a bowling alley); the lowest condition of human life. • *adj* marked by extreme vulgarity or indecency. • *vt* to provide with a gutter. • *vi* to flow in rivulets; (*candle*) to melt unevenly; (*candle flame*) to flutter.—**guttering** *n*.

guttering /'ɡʌtərɪŋ/ *n* the system of gutters, pipes, etc, on exterior walls for carrying off rainwater; material for making gutters.

guttersnipe /'ɡʌtərˌsnaɪp/ *n* a dirty child who plays in the streets, *esp* slum areas.

guttural /'ɡʌtərəl/ *adj* formed or pronounced in the throat; harsh-sounding.—**gutturally** *adv*.—**gutturalness, gutturality, gutturalism** *n*.

gutturalize /-ˌlaɪz/ *vt* to form (a sound) in the throat; to speak in a harsh manner.—**gutturalization** *n*.

guy[1] /ɡaɪ/ *n* a rope, chain, etc, for fixing or steadying anything. • *vt* to fix or steady with a guy.

guy[2] *n* (*Brit*) an effigy of Guy Fawkes made from old clothes stuffed with newspapers, etc burnt on the anniversary of the Gunpowder Plot (5 November); (*inf*) a man or boy; (*pl*) (*inf*) men or women; a shabby person. • *vt* to tease.

guzzle /'ɡʌzəl/ *vti* to gulp down food or drink greedily.—**guzzler** *n*.

gybe /dʒaɪb/ *vti* (*sail, boom*) to swing over from one side to the other; (*yacht*) to alter course in this way.—*also* **jibe**.

gym /dʒɪm/ *n* (*inf*) a gymnasium.

gymkhana /dʒɪmˈkɒnə/ *n* a meeting featuring sports contests or athletic skills, *esp* horse-riding.

gymnasium /dʒɪmˈneɪziəm/ *n* (*pl* **gymnasiums, gymnasia**) a room or building equipped for physical training and sports.

gymnast /'dʒɪmnæst/ or /-nəst/ *n* a person skilled in gymnastics.

gymnastic /dʒɪmˈnæstɪk/ *adj* pertaining to gymnastics.—**gymnastically** *adv*.

gymnastics /-ˈnæstɪks/ *n sing* training in exercises devised to strengthen the body; (*pl*) gymnastic exercises; (*pl*) feats of dexterity or agility.

gymnosophist /dʒɪmˈnɒsəfɪst/ *n* one of a class of ancient Hindu philosophers who lived bare-footed and lightly clothed or naked.

gymnosperm /'dʒɪmnoˌspɜrm/ *n* a plant whose seeds are not enclosed in a covering; a conifer or a conifer-like plant.—**gymnospermous** *adj*.

gynaecocracy, gynecocracy /ˌɡaɪnəˈkɒkrəsiː/ *n* (*pl* **gynaecocracies, gynecocracies**) female rule or supremacy.—**gynaecocratic, gynecocratic** *adj*.

gynaecology, gynecology /ˌɡaɪnəˈkɒlədʒiː/ *n* the branch of medicine that deals with the diseases and disorders of the female reproductive system.—**gynaecological, gynecological, gynaecologic, gynecologic** *adj*.—**gynaecologist, gynecologist** *n*.

gynarchy *n* (*pl* **gynarchies**) gynaecocracy.

gynoecium /ɡaɪˈniːsiəm/ or /dʒ-/ *n* (*pl* **gynoecia**) (*bot*) the female organs of a flower.

gynopathy /ɡaɪnəˈpæθiː/ *n* the condition of feeling threatened by women.—**gynopathic** *adj*.

gynophore *n* the long stalk on which the pistil is situated, as in the passion flower.—**gynophoric** *adj*.

gyp /dʒɪp/ *vt* (**gypping, gypped**) (*sl*) to cheat (someone). • *n* a swindle; a swindler; a college servant at Cambridge University; (*sl*) acute pain.—*also* **gip**.

gypsum /'dʒɪpsəm/ *n* a chalk-like mineral used to make plaster of Paris and fertilizer.—**gypseous, gypsiferous** *adj*.

Gypsy /'dʒɪpsi/ *n* (*pl* **Gypsies**) a member of a travelling people, *orig* from India, now spread throughout Europe and North America; (*without cap*) a person who looks or lives like a Gypsy.—*also* **Gipsy** (*pl* **Gipsies**).

gyral /'dʒaɪrəl/ *adj* rotatory, whirling; pertaining to a gyrus.

gyrate /'dʒaɪreɪt/ *vi* to revolve; to whirl or spiral.—**gyration** *n*.—**gyratory** *adj*.

gyre /'dʒaɪr/ *vt* (*poet*) to gyrate. • (*poet*) a gyration.

gyrfalcon /'dʒɜrˌfɒlkən/ *n* a large northern falcon, often used for hunting.—*also* **gerfalcon**.

gyro /'dʒaɪro:/ *n* (*pl* **gyros**) (*inf*) a gyroscope; a gyrocompass.

gyrocompass /'dʒaɪro:ˌkʌmpəs/ *n* a compass mounted on a gyroscope to keep it stable.

gyroscope /'dʒaɪrəˌsko:p/ *n* a wheel mounted in a ring so that its axis is free to turn in any direction, so that when spinning rapidly it keeps its original plane of rotation.—**gyroscopic** *adj*.

gyrose /'dʒaɪro:s/ *adj* (*bot*) turned round like a crook.

gyrostabilizer /'dʒaɪro:ˌsteɪbɪˌlaɪzər/ *n* a device of two or more gyroscopes to prevent rolling of a ship or aircraft.

gyrostat /'dʒaɪro:stæt/ *n* a gyrostabilizer.

gyrus /'dʒaɪrəs/ *n* (*pl* **gyri**) a convolution (of the brain).

gyve /'dʒaɪv/ *vt* to fetter. • *n* (*usu pl*) shackles.

H

H /eɪtʃ/ (chem symbol) hydrogen.

ha /hɒ/ *interj* used to express surprise, triumph, etc.—*also* **hah**.

ha. *abbr* = hectare(s).

Habakkuk /ˈhæbəkək/ or /hɔˈbæk-/ *n* (*Bible*) one of the minor Old Testament book of prophets.

habeas corpus /ˌheɪbɪəsˈkɔrpəs/ *n* a writ requiring that a prisoner be brought before a court, *esp* to ascertain the legality of his or her detention.

haberdasher /ˈhæbərˌdæʃər/ *n* a dealer in sewing accessories; a dealer in men's clothing.—**haberdashery** *n*.

habergeon /ˈhæbərdʒən/ *n* a sleeveless coat of chain mail covering the neck and breast.

habile /ˈhæbɪl/ *adj* skilful.

habiliment /hɔˈbɪlɪmənt/ *n* (*often pl*) clothing, attire.

habilitate /hɔˈbɪlɪˌteɪt/ *vi* to qualify for a post. • *vt* to provide working capital for a mine.—**habilitation** *n*.—**habilitator** *n*.

habit /ˈhæbɪt/ *n* a distinctive costume, as of a nun, etc; a thing done often and hence easily; a usual way of doing things; an addiction, *esp* to narcotics. • *vt* to clothe.

habitable /-əbəl/ *adj* capable of being lived in.—**habitability** *n*.—**habitably** *adv*.

habitat /ˈhæbɪˌtæt/ *n* the normal environment of an animal or plant.

habitation /ˌhæbɪˈteɪʃən/ *n* the act of inhabiting; a dwelling or residence.—**habitational** *adj*.

habited /ˈhæbɪtəd/ *adj* wearing a habit or a dress.

habit-forming /-ˌfɔrmɪŋ/ *adj* addictive.

habitual /hɔˈbɪtʃʊəl/ *adj* having the nature of a habit; regular.—**habitually** *adv*.—**habitualness** *n*.

habituate /hɔˈbɪtʃʊˌeɪt/ *vt* to accustom.—**habituation** *n*.

habitude /ˈhæbɪˈtjud/ or /-ˈtud/ *n* a custom or tendency; familiarity.—**habitudinal** *adj*.

habitué /hɔˈbɪtʃʊˌeɪ/ *n* a frequent visitor to a place.

hacienda /ˌhæsiˈendə/ *n* (in Spanish-speaking countries) a large estate or ranch; the main house on such an estate.

hack¹ /hæk/ *vt* to cut or chop (at) violently; to clear (vegetation) by chopping; (*comput*) to gain illegal access to confidential data. • *n* a gash or notch; a harsh, dry cough.

hack² *n* a riding horse for hire; an old worn-out horse; a mediocre or unexceptional writer; a coach for hire; (*inf*) a taxicab. • *vti* to ride a horse cross-country. • *adj* banal, hackneyed.

hackbut /ˈhæk͵bʌt/ *n* a type of arquebus.—*also* **hagbut**.

hacker /ˈhækər/ *n* a person who hacks; (*inf*) (*comput*) a person who uses computers as a hobby, *esp* one who uses a personal computer to gain illegal access to the computer systems of government departments or large corporations.

hacking /ˈhækɪŋ/ *adj* (*cough*) short, dry, spasmodic.

hackles /ˈhækəlz/ *npl* the hairs on the back of a dog, cat, etc, which stick out when the animal is angry or afraid.

hackney /ˈhækni/ *n* a horse for driving or riding; any of an English breed of high-stepping horses; a carriage or vehicle for hire.

hackneyed /ˈhæknid/ *adj* made trite or banal through overuse.

hacksaw /ˈhæksɒ/ *n* a fine-toothed saw for cutting metal.

had /hæd/ *see* **have**.

haddock /ˈhædək/ *n* (*pl* **haddocks, haddock**) an important Atlantic food fish related to the cod.

Hades /ˈheɪdiːz/ *n* (*Greek myth*) the home of the dead; (*inf*) hell.—**Hadean** *adj*.

Hadith /ˈhædɪθ/ or /hæˈdiːθ/ *n* (*pl* **Hadith, Hadiths**) the traditions surrounding Muhammed and his sayings; an appendix to the Koran.

hadj /hædʒ/ *n* (*pl* **hadjes**) a pilgrimage to Mecca, required of all Muslims.—*also* **hajj** (*pl* **hajjes**).

hadji /ˈhædʒi/ *n* (*pl* **hadjis**) a Muslim who has made the pilgrimage to Mecca.—*also* **haji, hajji** (*pl* **hajjis, hajis**).

hadn't /ˈhædənt/ = had not.

haema-, haemo- /ˈhɛmoː/ or /-mə/, /hɛmˈoː/, /-ə/ *prefix* blood.

haemal /-məl/ *adj* of or relating to the blood, blood vessels or the part of the body that contains the heart.

haematic /hiːˈmætɪk/ *adj* of, containing, acting on, or relating to blood. • *n* a drug that increases the level of haemoglobin in blood.

haematite /ˈhɛmətaɪt/ *n* native ferric oxide, an important iron ore.

haematoid /ˈhiːmətɔɪd/ *adj* relating to blood; blood-like.

haemoptysis /ˈhiːmoʊtaɪsɪs/ or /ˈhiːmə-/ *n* the spitting or coughing up of blood or mucus containing blood.

hafiz /ˈhɒfɪz/ *n* a Muslim who knows the Koran by heart; a title of respect; the guardian of the Mosque.

hafnium /ˈhæfnɪəm/ *n* a silvery metallic element found in zirconium.

haft /hæft/ *n* the handle of a weapon or tool.

hag /hæg/ *n* an ugly or unpleasant old woman; a witch.—**haggish** *adj*.—**haggishness** *n*.

Haggadah /hɔˈgædɔ/ or /hægæˈdæ/ *n* (*pl* **Haggadoth**) (*Judaism*) a parable or illustration of a commentary on Scripture; a book containing the order for the traditional Passover feast; a narrative of the flight from Egypt that is the main part of the Passover feast.

haggard /ˈhægərd/ *n adj* having an exhausted, untidy look.—**haggardly** *adv*.—**haggardness** *n*.

haggis /ˈhægɪs/ *n* (*pl* **haggises, haggis**) a traditional Scottish dish made of minced offal with suet, onions, oatmeal, seasonings, etc.

haggle /ˈhægəl/ *vi* to bargain; barter; to dispute over terms; to cavil. • *n* the act of haggling.—**haggler** *n*.

hagiography /ˌhægiˈɒgrəfi/ *n* (*pl* **hagiographies**) the history or legends of the saints; an uncritical biography.—**hagiographer, hagiographist** *n*.—**hagriographic, hagiographical** *adj*.

hah *see* **ha**.

ha-ha¹ /hɒˈhɒ/ *interj* an exclamation of mockery; an outburst of laughter.—*also* **haw-haw**.

ha-ha² *n* a fence sunk in the ground as a boundary of a park or garden.

haiku /ˈhaɪkuː/ *n* (*pl* **haiku**) a Japanese verse form of three lines.

hail¹ /heɪl/ *vt* to greet; to summon by shouting or signalling, as a taxi; to welcome with approval, to acclaim. • *vi* (*with* **from**) to come from. • *interj* an exclamation of tribute, greeting, etc. • *n* a shout to gain attention; a distance within which one can be heard calling.—**hailer** *n*.

hail² *n* frozen raindrops; something, as abuse, bullets, etc, sent forcefully in rapid succession. • *vti* to pour down like hail.

Hail Mary *n* (*RC Church*) a prayer to the Virgin Mary beginning with these words.

hailstone /ˈheɪlstoːn/ *n* a pellet of hail.

hailstorm /-stɔrm/ *n* a sudden storm of hail.

hair /hɛr/ *n* a threadlike growth from the skin of mammals; a mass of hairs, *esp* on the human head; a threadlike growth on a plant.

haircut /ˈheɪrkʌt/ *n* a shortening and styling of hair by cutting it; the style of cutting.

hairdo /-duː/ *n* (*pl* **hairdos**) a particular style of hair after cutting, etc.

hairdresser /-ˌdrɛsər/ *n* a person who cuts, styles, colours, etc, hair.—**hairdressing** *n*.

hairgrip /-grɪp/ *n* a clip for holding hair in position; a bobby pin.

hairless /-lɛs/ *adj* without hair; having little hair.

hairline /-laɪn/ *n* a very thin line; the outline of the hair on the head.

hairnet /-nɛt/ *n* a net used to keep the hair in place.

hairpiece /-piːs/ *n* a wig or toupee; an additional piece of hair attached to a person's real hair.

hairpin /-pɪn/ *n* U-shaped pin used to hold hair in place.

hairpin bend *n* a sharply curving bend in a road, etc.

hair-raising /-ˌreɪzɪŋ/ *adj* terrifying, shocking.

hair's-breadth *n* a very small space or amount.

hairsplitting /-splɪtɪŋ/ *adj* making petty distinctions; quibbling. • *n* the act of making petty distinctions.—**hairsplitter** *n*.

hairspring /-sprɪŋ/ *n* a slender, hair-like coil spring, as in a watch.

hairstyle /-staɪl/ *n* the way in which hair is arranged.—**hairstylist** *n*.

hairweaving /-wiːvɪŋ/ *n* the technique of attaching strands of false hair to the follicles of the head.

hairy /'heri/ *adj* (**hairier, hairiest**) covered with hair; (*inf*) difficult, dangerous.—**hairiness** *n*.

haji, hajji *see* **hadji**.

hajj *see* **hadj**.

hake /heɪk/ *n* (*pl* **hake, hakes**) a marine food fish related to the cod.

hakim /'hɒkɪm/ *n* a judge, administrator or governor of an Islamic country; a Muslim physician.

Halakah, Halacha /hɑ'lɒxɑ/ *n* (*pl* **Halakoth, Halachoth**) (*Judaism*) traditional law containing minor precepts in addition to the Mosaic law; legal literature in general.

halal /hæ'læl/ *n* meat from animals butchered according to Muslim law. • *adj* of or pertaining to such meat.—*also* **hallal**.

halation /hɒ'leɪʃən/ *n* (*photog, TV*) a halo-like appearance round an object, caused by light reflection.

halberd, halbert /'hælbərd/ *n* a medieval weapon consisting of a long staff to which an axe with a spear-like point was affixed.

halberdier /ˌhælbər'diːr/ *n* a soldier armed with a halberd.

halcyon /'hælsɪən/ *adj* calm, gentle, peaceful. • *n* a fabled bird (probably the kingfisher) that nested at sea and calmed it.

hale /heɪl/ *adj* healthy and strong.

half /hæf/ *n* (*pl* **halves**) either of two equal parts of something; (*inf*) a half-price ticket for a bus, etc; (*inf*) half a pint. • *adj* being a half; incomplete; partial. • *adv* to the extent of a half; (*inf*) partly.

half-and-half *n* something half one thing and half another, *esp* a mixture of mild and bitter beer. • *adj* partly one thing and partly another. • *adv* in two equal parts.

halfback /'hæfbæk/ *n* (*football, hockey*) a player occupying a position between the forwards and the fullbacks; a player in this position in other sports.

half-baked *adj* (*inf*) poorly planned or thought-out; (*inf*) stupid.

half-brother *n* a brother through one parent only.

half-caste *n* a person whose parents are of different races.

half cock *n* the middle position of a gun's hammer; **at half cock** not prepared.—**half-cocked** *adj*.

half-hearted /hæf'hɑrtəd/ *adj* with little interest, enthusiasm, etc.—**half-heartedly** *adv*.—**half-heartedness** *n*.

half-hour *n* 30 minutes; the point 30 minutes after the beginning of an hour.

half-life *n* the time taken for half the atoms in a radioactive substance to decay.

half-mast *n* the position to which a flag is lowered as a sign of mourning.

half-measure *n* (*often pl*) an inadequate action; a compromise.

half-moon *n* the moon at its phase when half the disc is illuminated; something shaped like this. • *adj* in the shape of a half-moon.

half-nelson *n* a wrestling hold, pinning the arm of an opponent behind the back from behind.

half note *n* (*mus*) a note with the time value of half of a semibreve.—*also* **minim**.

halfpenny /'heɪpəni/ or /'heɪpni/ (*pl* **halfpence**) *n* a bronze coin worth two farthings in pre-decimal British currency.

half-sister *n* a sister through one parent only.

half title *n* a short title on the page before the title page of a book, a bastard title.

half-term *n* a short holiday in the middle of a school term.

half-time /hæf'taɪm/ *n* (*sport*) an interval between two halves of a game.

halftone /hæf'tɔːn/ *n* an illustration printed from a relief plate, showing light and shadow by means of minute dots.

half-track *n* a (military) vehicle with wheels in front but driven by caterpillar tracks at the rear.

half-truth *n* a statement that is only partly true.

half volley *n* (*tennis, etc*) the striking of the ball the instant it bounces.

halfway /'hæfweɪ/ or /hæf'weɪ/ *adj* midway between two points, etc.

halfwit /'hæfwɪt/ *n* a stupid or silly person; a mentally retarded person.—**halfwitted** *adj*.—**halfwittedly** *adv*.—**halfwittedness** *n*.

halibut /'hælɪbət/ *n* (*pl* **halibut, halibuts**) a large marine flatfish used as food.

halide /'hælaɪd/ or /'heɪl-/ *n* a compound containing halogen; a haloid.

halitosis /ˌhælɪ'tɔːsɪs/ *n* bad-smelling breath.

hall /hɒl/ *n* a public building with offices, etc; a large room for exhibits, gatherings, etc; the main house on a landed estate; a

college building, *esp* a dining room; a vestibule at the entrance of a building; a hallway.

hallal *see* **halal**.

Hallel /hæ'leɪl/ or /'hælɛl/ *n* (*Judaism*) Psalms 113-118 chanted as part of morning services during Passover and other festivals.

hallelujah, halleluiah /ˌhælə'luːjə/ or /ˌhæleɪ-/ *interj* an exclamation of praise to God. • *n* a praising of God; a musical composition having this as its theme.—*also* **alleluia**.

halliard *see* **halyard**.

hallmark /'hɒlmɑrk/ *n* a mark used on gold, silver or platinum articles to signify a standard of purity, weight, date of manufacture; a mark or symbol of high quality; a characteristic feature. • *vt* to stamp with a hallmark.

hallo *see* **hello**.

hallow /'hæloʊ/ *vt* to make or regard as holy.—**hallowed** *adj*.—**hallowedness** *n*.—**hallower** *n*.

Hallowe'en, Halloween /ˌhælə'wiːn/ or /ˌhɒlə-/ *n* the eve of All Saints' Day, October 31.

Hallowmas /'hæloʊməs/ or /-ˌmæs/ *n* (*formerly*) All Saints' Day, November 1.

Hallstatt, Hallstadt /'hɒlstæt/ *adj* of or denoting the final period of the Bronze Age and the first period of the Iron Age (9th – 4th centuries BC).

hallucinate /hɒ'luːsə'neɪt/ *vti* to have or cause to have hallucinations.—**hallucinator** *n*.

hallucination /hɒˌluːsə'neɪʃən/ *n* the apparent perception of sights, sounds, etc, that are not actually present; something perceived in this manner.—**hallucinational, hallucinative** *adj*.—**hallucinatory** *adj*.

hallucinogen /hɒ'luːsənədʒən/ *n* a drug that produces hallucinations.—**hallucinogenic** *adj*.

hallux /'hæloʊks/ *n* (*pl* **halluces**) the big toe; the first digit on the back foot of an amphibian, bird, mammal, or reptile.

halm *see* **haulm**.

halo /'heɪloʊ/ *n* (*pl* **haloes, halos**) a circle of light, as around the sun; a symbolic ring of light around the head of a saint in pictures; the aura of glory surrounding an idealized person or thing. • *vt* (**haloing, haloed**) to surround with a halo.

halogen /'hælədʒən/ or /'heɪ-/ *n* any of the five chemical elements fluorine, chlorine, bromine, iodine and astatine.—**halogenous** *adj*.

halt[1] /hɒlt/ *n* a temporary interruption or cessation of progress; a minor station on a rail line. • *vti* to stop or come to a stop.

halt[2] *vi* to falter; to hesitate.—**halting** *adj*.

halter /'hɒltər/ *n* a rope or strap for tying or leading an animal; a style of women's dress top tied behind the neck and waist leaving the back and arms bare. • *vt* to put a halter on (a horse, etc).

halve /hæv/ *vt* to divide equally into two; to reduce by half; (*golf*) to play one hole in the same number of strokes as one's opponent.

halves /hævz/ *see* **half**.

halyard /'hæljərd/ *n* a line for hoisting or lowering a sail, yard, or flag.—*also* **halliard**.

ham /hæm/ *n* the upper part of a pig's hind leg, salted, smoked, etc; the meat from this area; (*inf*) the back of the upper thigh; (*inf*) an actor who overacts; (*inf*) a licensed amateur radio operator. • *vti* (**hamming, hammed**) to speak or move in an exaggerated way; to overact.

hamadryad /ˌhæmə'draɪæd/ *n* (*pl* **hamadryads, hamadryades**) (*Greek myth*) a wood nymph; a giant cobra, the king cobra.

hamadryas /ˌhæmə'draɪəs/ *n* a North African baboon, the male of which has a heavy mane of silvery hair.

hamal /hɒ'mɒl/ or /-'mɒl/ *n* a porter in several Muslim countries.—*also* **hammal, hammaul**.

Hamburg /'hæmbɜrg/ *n* a rich, black grape; a breed of black domestic fowl.

hamburger /'hæmˌbɜrgər/ *n* a cooked patty of ground beef, often in a bread roll with pickle, etc.

hame[1] /heɪm/ *n* either of two curved bars for the traces on the collar of a draught horse.

hame[2] *n* (*Scot*) home.

ham-handed /hæm'hændəd/, **ham-fisted** /hæm'fɪstəd/ *adj* (*inf*) clumsy.

Hamite /'hæmaɪt/ *n* a descendant of Ham, son of Noah; a member of the Hamitic race.

Hamitic /hɒ'mɪtɪk/ *adj* relating to Ham, the races descended from him, or the languages they speak. • *n* any of a group of languages spoken in North Africa.

hamlet /'hæmlət/ *n* a very small village.

hammal, hammaul *see* **hamal**.

hammer /'hæmər/ *n* a tool for pounding, driving nails, etc, having a heavy head and a handle; a thing like this in shape or use, as the part of the gun that strikes the firing pin; a bone of the middle ear; a heavy metal ball attached to a wire thrown in athletic contests; **hammer and tongs** with great force. • *vti* to strike repeatedly, as with a hammer; to drive, force, or shape, as with hammer blows; (*inf*) to defeat utterly.—**hammerer** *n*.

hammerhead /'hæmər,hed/ *n* a shark with a mallet-shaped head.

hammock /'hæmək/ *n* a length of strong cloth or netting suspended by the ends and used as a bed.

hammy /'hæmi/ *adj* (**hammier, hammiest**) (*inf*) overacting; exaggerated.

hamper[1] /'hæmpər/ *vt* to hinder; to interfere with; to encumber.—**hamperer** *n*.

hamper[2] *n* a large, *usu* covered, basket for storing or transporting food and crockery, etc.

hamster /'hæmstər/ *n* a small short-tailed rodent with cheek pouches.

hamstring /'hæmstriŋ/ *n* any of the tendons at the back of the thigh that flex and rotate the leg. • *vt* (**hamstringing, hamstrung**) to cripple by severing the hamstring of; to render useless, to thwart.

hamulus /'hæmjuləs/ *n* (*pl* **hamuli**) a small hook-like projection at the end of the bones or between the fore and hind wings of a bee or bee-like insect.—**hamular** *adj*.

hand /hænd/ *n* the part of the arm below the wrist, used for grasping; a side or direction; possession or care; control; an active part; a promise to marry; skill; one having a special skill; handwriting; applause; help; a hired worker; a source; one of a ship's crew; anything like a hand, as a pointer on a clock; the breadth of a hand, four inches when measuring the height of a horse; the cards held by a player at one time; a round of card play ; (*inf*) applause. • *adj* of, for, or controlled by the hand. • *vt* to give as with the hand; to help or conduct with the hand. • *vi* (*with* **on**) to pass to the next.

handbag /'hændbæg/ *n* a woman's small bag for carrying personal items.—*also* **bag, pocket book, purse**.

handbill /'hændbɪl/ *n* a small printed notice to be passed out by hand.

handbook /'hændbuk/ *n* a book containing useful instructions.

handcart /'hændkɑrt/ *n* a small cart pulled or pushed by hand.

handcuff /'hændkəf/ *n* (*usu pl*) either of a pair of connected steel rings for shackling the wrists of a prisoner. • *vt* to manacle.

handed /'hændəd/ *adj* having or involving (a specified kind or number of) hands.

handfast /'hændfæst/ *vt* (*formerly*) to pledge or betroth; to grip with the hand. • *n* a contract of betrothal.

handful /'hændful/ *n* as much as will fill the hand; a few; (*inf*) a person who is difficult to handle or control.

handicap /'hændɪˌkæp/ *n* a mental or physical impairment; a contest in which difficulties are imposed on, or advantages given to, contestants to equalize their chances; such a difficulty or advantage; any hindrance. • *vt* (**handicapping, handicapped**) to give a handicap to; to hinder.—**handicapper** *n*.

handicapped /-kæpt/ *adj* mentally or physically disabled.

handicraft /'hændɪˌkræft/ *n* a skill involving the hands, such as basketwork, pottery, etc; an item of pottery, etc made by hand.

handiwork /'hændɪwərk/ *n* handmade work; something done by a person or thing.

handkerchief /'hæŋkərtʃɪf/ or /-ˌtʃiːf/ *n* a small cloth for blowing the nose, etc.

handle /'hændəl/ *vt* to touch, hold, or move with the hand; to manage or operate with the hands; to manage, deal with; to buy and sell (goods). • *vi* to react in a specified way. • *n* a part of anything designed to be held or grasped by the hand.—**handleable** *adj*.—**handling** *n*.

handlebar /'hændəlˌbɑr/ *n* (*often pl*) the curved metal bar with a grip at each end used to steer a bicycle, etc; a bushy moustache with curved ends.

handler /'hændlər/ *n* a person who trains or controls animals, such as a police dog.

handless /'hændləs/ *adj* awkward, clumsy.

handmade /-meɪd/ *adj* made by hand, carefully crafted.

handmaid(en) /'hændmeɪd/ or /-ˌmeɪdən/ *n* a female servant.

hand-out /'hændeut/ *n* an item of food, clothing, etc, given free to the needy; a statement given to the press to replace or supplement an oral presentation.

hand-picked *adj* carefully selected.

handrail /'hændreɪl/ *n* a narrow rail for gripping as a support.

hands-on *adj* involving active participation and operating experience.

handsaw /'hændˌsɒ/ *n* any saw that is used in one hand only.

handsel /'hænsəl/ *n* (*formerly*) a good-luck gift on beginning something; a housewarming present; a New Year gift. • *vt* to give a handsel to; to inaugurate; to be first to use something.

handset /'hændset/ *n* a telephone earpiece and mouthpiece as a single unit.

handshake /'hændʃeɪk/ *n* a grasping and shaking of a person's hand as a greeting or when concluding an agreement.

handsome /'hænsəm/ *adj* good-looking; dignified; generous; ample.—**handsomely** *adv*.—**handsomeness** *n*.

handspike /'hændspaɪk/ *n* an iron-shod bar or pipe used as a lever.

handspring /'hændspriŋ/ *n* (*gymnastics*) a leaping forwards or backwards from a standing position into a handstand then back onto the feet.

handstand /'hændstænd/ *n* the act of supporting the body on the hands with the feet in the air.

hand-to-hand *adj* (*fighting*) at close quarters.

hand-to-mouth *adj* having barely enough food or money to survive.—*also adv*.

handwriting /'hændˌraɪtɪŋ/ *n* writing done by hand; a style of such writing.—**handwritten** *adj*.

handy /'hændi/ *adj* (**handier, handiest**) convenient, near; easy to use; skilled with the hands.—**handily** *adv*.—**handiness** *n*.

handyman /'hændɪˌmæn/ *n* (*pl* **handymen**) a person who does odd jobs.

hang /hæŋ/ *vb* (**hanging, hung**) *vt* to support from above, *esp* by a rope, chain, etc, to suspend; (*door, etc*) to attach by hinges to allow to swing freely; to decorate with pictures, or other suspended objects; (*wallpaper*) to stick to a wall; to exhibit (works of art); to prevent (a jury) from coming to a decision; (*pt, pp* **hanged**) to put to execute or kill by suspending by the neck. • *vi* to be suspended, so as to dangle loosely; (*clothing, etc*) to fall or flow in a certain direction; to lean, incline, or protrude; to depend; to remain in the air; to be in suspense; to fall or droop; (*pt, pp* **hanged**) to die by hanging; (*with* **about, around**) to loiter; (*with* **back**) to hesitate, be reluctant; (*with* **out**) to meet regularly at a particular place. • *n* the way in which anything hangs; (*sl*) a damn.

hangar /'hæŋər/ *n* a large shelter where aircraft are built, stored or repaired.—*also vt*.

hangbird /'hæŋbərd/ *n* the Baltimore oriole; any North American bird that builds a hanging nest.

hangdog /'hæŋdɒg/ *adj* abject or ashamed in appearance or manner.

hanger /'hæŋər/ *n* a device on which something is hung; one who hangs things.

hanger-on *n* (*pl* **hangers-on**) a sycophantic follower.

hang-glider /'hæŋˌglaɪdər/ *n* an unpowered aircraft consisting of a metal frame over which a lightweight material is stretched, with a harness for the pilot suspended below.—**hang gliding** *n*.

hanging /'hæŋɪŋ/ *n* the act of executing a person by suspending them by the neck; something hung, as a picture; (*pl*) decorative draperies hung on walls. • *adj* suspended in the air; undecided; overhanging; situated on a steep slope.

hangman /'hæŋmæn/ or /-mən/ *n* (*pl* **hangmen**) a person who executes prisoners by hanging them.

hangnail /'hæŋneɪl/ *n* a thin strip of torn skin at the root of a fingernail.

hangout /'hæŋeut/ *n* a favourite meeting place.

hangover /'hæŋˌoːvər/ *n* the unpleasant after-effects of excessive consumption of alcohol; something surviving from an earlier time.

hang-up /'hæŋəp/ *n* an emotional preoccupation with something.

hank /hæŋk/ *n* a coiled or looped bundle of wool, rope, etc.

hanker /'hæŋkər/ *vi* (*with* **after, for**) to desire longingly.—**hankerer** *n*.—**hankering** *n*.

hanky, hankie /'hæŋki/ *n* (*pl* **hankies**) (*inf*) a handkerchief.

hanky-panky /'hæŋkiˈpæŋki/ *n* (*inf*) foolish behaviour; dishonesty; illicit sexual relations.

Hansard /'hænsərd/ *n* the official, printed verbatim reports of British parliamentary proceedings.

hanse /'hænsə/ n a medieval guild of merchants; a fee paid by new members of such a guild; (with cap) a town of the Hanseatic League; the Hanseatic League.—**hanseatic** adj.

Hanseatic League /ˌhænsiˈætɪk/ n a confederacy of merchants or commercial towns in northern Germany and elsewhere, which lasted from the 14th–19th centuries.

hansom (cab) /'hænsəm/ n a light two-wheeled covered horse-drawn carriage, with the driver's seat raised behind.

hap /hæp/ vb (**happing, happed**) vi (arch) to happen or befall. • vt to cover up; to wrap up warmly. • n (arch) chance; luck; a fortunate accident; a covering of any kind.

haphazard /hæp'hæzərd/ adj not planned; random. • adv by chance.—**haphazardly** adv.—**haphazardness** n.

hapless /'hæpləs/ adj unfortunate, unlucky.—**haplessness** n.

haploid /'hæplɔɪd/ adj (cell nucleus, organism) possessing only half the normal number of chromosomes. • n a single set of unpaired chromosomes.

haply /'hæpli/ adv (formerly) by chance.

happen /'hæpən/ vi to take place; to be, occur, or come by chance.

happening /-ɪŋ/ n an occurrence; an improvization.

happy /'hæpi/ adj (**happier, happiest**) fortunate; having, expressing, or enjoying pleasure or contentment; pleased; appropriate, felicitous.—**happily** adv.—**happiness** n.

happy-go-lucky adj irresponsible; carefree.

happy hour n a particular time of day when a bar, hotel, etc, sells drinks at reduced prices

happy medium n a middle course between extremes.

hapteron /'hæptərən/ n (pl **haptera**) the tissue in seaweed and related plants that enables them to attach themselves to a host object.

haptic /'hæptɪk/ adj of or relating to the sense of touch.

harakiri /ˌhærəˌkɪri/ n ritual suicide by disembowelment.—also **harikari**.

harangue /həˈræŋ/ n a tirade; a lengthy, forceful speech. • vti to make a harangue, to address vehemently.—**haranguer** n.

harass /həˈræs/ or /ˈhɛrəs/, /ˈhærəs/ vt to annoy, to irritate; to trouble (an enemy) by constant raids and attacks.—**harasser** n.—**harassment** n.

harbinger /'hɑːrbɪndʒər/ n a person or thing that announces or presages the arrival of another, a forerunner.

harbour, harbor /'hɑːrbər/ n a protected inlet for anchoring ships; any place of refuge. • vt to shelter or house; (grudge, etc) to keep in the mind secretly. • vi to take shelter.—**harbourer, harborer** n.

harbourage, harborage /'hɑːrbərɪdʒ/ n a port or anchorage for ships.

hard /hɑːrd/ adj firm, solid, not easily cut or punctured; difficult to comprehend; difficult to accomplish; difficult to bear, painful; severe, unfeeling, ungenerous; indisputable, intractable; (drugs) addictive and damaging to health; (weather) severe; (currency) stable in value; (news) definite, not speculative; (drink) very alcoholic; (water) having a high mineral content that prevents lathering with soap; (colour, sound) harsh. • adv with great effort or intensity; earnestly, with concentration; so as to cause hardness; with difficulty; with bitterness or grief; close, near by.—**hardness** n.

hardback /'hɑːrdbæk/ n a book bound with a stiff cover.—also adj.

hard-bitten /'hɑːrd,bɪtən/ adj (inf) tough, seasoned.

hardboard /'hɑːrd,bɔːrd/ n a stiff board made of compressed wood chips.

hard-boiled adj (eggs) boiled until solid; (inf) unfeeling.

hard cash n payment in coins and notes as opposed to cheque, credit card, etc.

hard copy n output (as from microfilm or a computer) on paper.

hard core n the stubborn inner group in an organization that is resistant to change; the heavy foundation material for a road.

hard-core adj of a hard core; utterly entrenched; (pornography) showing sexual acts in explicit detail.

hard disk n (comput) a rigid magnetic disk in a sealed unit capable of much greater storage capacity than a floppy disk.

harden /'hɑːrdən/ vti to make or become hard.—**hardener** n.

hard-headed /'hɑːrd,hɛdəd/ adj shrewd and unsentimental; practical.—**hard-headedly** adv.—**hard-headedness** n.

hardhearted /'hɑːrd,hɑːrtəd/ adj unfeeling; cruel.—**hardheartedly** adv.—**hardheartedness** n.

hard-hitting adj forcefully effective.

hard line n an aggressive, unyielding policy.—**hard-line** adj.—**hardliner** n.

hardly /'hɑːrdli/ adv scarcely; barely; with difficulty; not to be expected.

hardpan /'hɑːrdpæn/ n a hard, impervious layer of clay below the soil; a solid foundation.

hard sell n an aggressive selling technique.

hardship /'hɑːrdʃɪp/ n something that causes suffering or privation.

hard shoulder n in UK, a surfaced strip of land alongside a motorway for vehicles to make emergency stops.

hardtack /'hɑːrdtæk/ n a hard, saltless biscuit formerly eaten by seamen.

hard-up adj (inf) short of money.

hardware /'hɑːrdwɛr/ n articles made of metal as tools, nails, etc; (comput) the mechanical and electronic components that make up a computer system.

hardwood /'hɑːrdwʊd/ n the close-grained wood of deciduous trees.

hardy /'hɑːrdi/ adj (**hardier, hardiest**) bold, resolute; robust; vigorous; able to withstand exposure to physical or emotional hardship.—**hardily** adv.—**hardiness** n.

hare /hɛr/ n (pl **hare, hares**) any of various timid, swift, long-eared mammals, resembling but larger than the rabbit.

harebell /'hɛrbel/ n the bluebell; the wild hyacinth.

harebrained /'hɛrbreɪnd/ adj flighty; foolish.

harelip /'hɛrlɪp/ n a congenital deformity of the upper lip in the form of a vertical fissure.—**harelipped** adj.

harem /'hɛrəm/ n the usu secluded part of a Muslim household where the women live; the women in a harem.

haricot /'hɛrɪˌkoʊ/ n a type of French bean with an edible light-coloured seed.

harikari see **harakiri**.

hark /hɑːrk/ vi to listen; (with **back**) to retrace a course; to revert (to).

harken /'hɑːrkən/ see **hearken**.

harlequin /'hɑːrləkwɪn/ n the performer in a pantomime who wears parti-coloured garments and carries a wand. • adj fantastic or full of trickery; colourful.

harlequinade /ˌhɑːrləkwɪˈneɪd/ n a play or the part of a pantomime in which Harlequin plays a leading role; buffoonery.

harlot /'hɑːrlət/ n (formerly) a prostitute.—**harlotry** n.

harm /hɑːrm/ n hurt; damage; injury. • vt to inflict hurt, damage, or injury upon.—**harmer** n.

harmattan /hɑːrˈmætən/ n a hot dust-laden wind that blows from the interior to the west coast of Africa.

harmful /'hɑːrmfʊl/ adj hurtful.—**harmfully** adv.—**harmfulness** n.

harmless /'hɑːrmləs/ adj not likely to cause harm.—**harmlessly** adv.—**harmlessness** n.

harmonic /hɑːrˈmɒnɪk/ adj (mus) of or in harmony. • n an overtone; (pl) the science of musical sounds.—**harmonically** adv.

harmonica /hɑːrˈmɒnɪkə/ n a small wind instrument that produces tones when air is blown or sucked across a series of metal reeds; a mouth-organ.

harmonious /hɑːrˈmoʊniəs/ adj fitting together in an orderly and pleasing manner; agreeing in ideas, interests, etc; melodious.—**harmoniously** adv.

harmonium /hɑːrˈmoʊniəm/ n a keyboard musical instrument whose tones are produced by thin metal reeds operated by foot bellows.

harmonize /'hɑːrməˌnaɪz/ vi to be in harmony; to sing in harmony. • vt to make harmonious.—**harmonization** n.

harmony /'hɑːrməni/ n (pl **harmonies**) a pleasing agreement of parts in colour, size, etc; agreement in action, ideas, etc; the pleasing combination of musical tones in a chord; a collation of parallel narratives, esp of the Gospels, with a commentary.

harness /'hɑːrnəs/ n the leather straps and metal pieces by which a horse is fastened to a vehicle, plough, etc; any similar fastening or attachment, eg for a parachute, hang-glider. • vt to put a harness on; to control so as to use the power of.—**harnesser** n.

harp /hɑːrp/ n a stringed musical instrument played by plucking. • vi (with **on** or **upon**) to talk persistently (on some subject).—**harpist, harper** n.

harpoon /hɑːrˈpuːn/ n a barbed spear with an attached line, for spearing whales, etc. • vt to strike with a harpoon.—**harpooner** n.

harpsichord /'hɑːrpsɪˌkɔːrd/ n a musical instrument resembling a grand piano whose strings are plucked by a mechanism rather than struck.—**harpsichordist** n.

harpy /'hɑrpi/ *n* (*pl* **harpies**) a grasping, vicious person.

harquebus *see* **arquebus**.

harridan /'herɪdən/ *n* a disreputable, shrewish old woman.

harrier /'hærɪər/ *n* a small breed of hound used for hunting hares; a cross-country runner.

harrow /'hero:/ *n* a heavy frame with spikes, spring teeth, or disks for breaking up and levelling ploughed ground. • *vt* to draw a harrow over (land); to cause mental distress to.—**harrower** *n.*—**harrowing** *adj*, *n.*—**harrowment** *n.*

harry /'heri/ *vt* (**harrying, harried**) to torment or harass.

harsh /hɑrʃ/ *adj* unpleasantly rough; jarring on the senses or feelings; rigorous; cruel.—**harshly** *adv.*—**harshness** *n.*

hart /hɑrt/ *n* (*pl* **hart, harts**) a male deer, especially the red deer, aged five years or more.

hartal /'hɑrtəl/ *n* (*Hinduism*) the closing of shops as a sign of mourning or as a political gesture.

hartebeest, hartbeest /'hɑrtəˌbiːst/ *n* a South African antelope.

hartshorn /'hɑrtʃɔrn/ *n* the antler of a hart; sal volatile.

harum-scarum /ˌherəm'skerəm/ *adj* (*inf*) rash, reckless. • *n* a giddy rash person.

haruspex /hə'ruːspeks/ *n* (*pl* **haruspices**) in ancient Rome, a soothsayer who foretold events by inspecting the entrails of sacrificial animals.

harvest /'hɑrvəst/ *n* (the season of) gathering in the ripened crops; the yield of a particular crop; the reward or product of any exertion or action. • *vti* to gather in (a crop). • *vt* to win by achievement.—**harvester** *n.*—**harvesting** *n.*

harvester /-ər/ *n* a person who harvests; a harvesting machine *esp* a combine harvester.

harvest moon *n* the full moon nearest the time of the September equinox.

has /hæz/ *see* **have**.

has-been *n* (*inf*) a person or thing that has lost its former popularity or celebrity status.

hash[1] /hæʃ/ *n* a chopped mixture of reheated cooked meat and vegetables. • *vt* to chop up (meat or vegetables) for hash; to mix or mess up.

hash[2] *n* (*inf*) hashish.

hashish /hæ'ʃiːʃ/ or /'hæ-/ *n* resin derived from the leaves and shoots of the hemp plant, smoked or chewed as an intoxicant.

hasn't /'hæzənt/ = has not.

hasp /hæsp/ *n* a hinged fastening for a door, etc, *esp* a metal piece fitted over a staple and fastened as by a bolt or padlock.

hassock /'hæsək/ *n* a firm cushion used as a footstool or seat.

hast /hæst/ (*arch*) the second person sing of **have**, used with **thou**.

hastate /'hæsteɪt/ *adj* spear-shaped (of a leaf).

haste /heɪst/ *n* quickness of motion; urgency. • *vi* (*poet*) to hasten.

hasten /'heɪsən/ *vt* to accelerate; to cause to hurry. • *vi* to move or act with speed.—**hastener** *n.*

hasty /'heɪsti/ *adj* (**hastier, hastiest**) done in a hurry; rash, precipitate.—**hastily** *adv.*—**hastiness** *n.*

hat /hæt/ *n* a covering for the head. • *vt* (**hatting, hatted**) to cover with a hat.

hatband /'hætbænd/ *n* a band or ribbon around the base of a hat; a black cloth band worn as a token of mourning.

hatbox /'hætbɒks/ *n* a box or case for a hat or hats.

hatch[1] /hætʃ/ *n* a small door or opening (as on an aircraft or spaceship); an opening in the deck of a ship or in the floor or roof of a building; a lid for such an opening; a hatchway.

hatch[2] *vt* to produce (young) from the egg, *esp* by incubating; to devise (*eg* a plot). • *vi* to emerge from the egg; to incubate.—**hatchable** *adj.*—**hatcher** *n.*

hatch[3] *vt* (*drawing, engraving*) to shade using closely spaced parallel lines or incisions.—**hatching** *n.*

hatchback /'hætʃbæk/ *n* a sloping rear end on a car with a door; a car of this design.

hatchery /'hætʃəri/ *n* (*pl* **hatcheries**) a place for hatching eggs, *esp* of fish.

hatchet /'hætʃət/ *n* a small axe with a short handle.

hatchet job *n* (*inf*) devastating or malicious verbal or written criticism.

hatchet man *n* a person hired to perform unpleasant tasks; a critic specializing in invective.

hatchment /'hætʃmənt/ *n* (*her*) a diamond-shaped tablet bearing a dead person's armorial bearings, placed on a house or tomb.

hatchway /'hætʃweɪ/ *n* an opening in a ship's deck or in a floor or roof; a passage giving access to an enclosed space (as a cellar).

hate /heɪt/ *vt* to feel intense dislike for. • *vi* to feel hatred; to wish to avoid. • *n* a strong feeling of dislike or contempt; the person or thing hated.—**hater** *n.*

hateful /'heɪtful/ *adj* deserving or arousing hate.—**hatefully** *adv.*—**hatefulness** *n.*

hath /hæθ/ (*arch*) the third person sing of **have**.

hatred /'heɪtrəd/ *n* intense dislike or enmity.

hatter /'hætər/ *n* a person who makes or sells hats.

hat trick *n* (*cricket*) the taking of three wickets with three successive bowls; the scoring of three successive goals, points, etc in any game.

hauberk /'hɒbərk/ *n* a coat of armour, often sleeveless, formed of chain mail, which reached below the knees.

haugh /hɒ/ *n* (*Scot*) a small, low-lying riverside meadow.

haughty /'hɒti/ *adj* (**haughtier, haughtiest**) having or expressing arrogance.—**haughtily** *adv.*—**haughtiness** *n.*

haul /hɒl/ *vti* to move by pulling; to transport by truck, etc. • *n* the act of hauling; the amount gained, caught, etc, at one time; the distance over which something is transported.

haulage /'hɒlɪdʒ/ *n* the transport of commodities; the charge for this.

haulier /-ər/ *n* a person or business that transports goods by road.

haulm /hɒm/ *n* the stalk of potatoes, peas, etc, *esp* after the crop has been gathered.—*also* **halm**.

haunch /hɒntʃ/ *n* the part of the body around the hips; the leg and loin of a deer, sheep, etc.—**haunched** *adj*.

haunt /hɒnt/ *vt* to visit often or continually; to recur repeatedly to. • *vi* to linger; to appear habitually as a ghost. • *n* a place often visited.—**haunter** *n.*

haunted /'hɒntəd/ *adj* supposedly visited by ghosts; obsessed; anxious, worried.

haunting /'hɒntɪŋ/ *adj* constantly recurring in the mind; unforgettable.—**hauntingly** *adv.*

Hausa /'haʊsə/ or /-zə/ *n* a member of the negroid people of West Africa living chiefly in Nigeria; the language of these people.

haustellum /'hɒstɛləm/ *n* (*pl* **haustella**) the tip of the proboscis of the housefly or similar insects used for sucking foods.

hautbois, hautboy /'hoːbɔɪ/ *n* (*pl* **hautbois, hautboy**) (*arch*) the oboe.

haute couture /ˌoːtkuː'tʃʊr/ or /-'tuːr/, /ˌhoːt-/ *n* high fashion.

haute cuisine /ˌoːtkwɪ'ziːn/ *n* high-class cooking.

hauteur /oː'tər/ *n* arrogance, haughtiness.

Havana (cigar) *n* a cigar rolled from Cuban tobacco.

have /hæv/ *vt* (**has, having,** *pp* **had**) to have in one's possession; to possess as an attribute; to hold in the mind; to experience; to give birth to; to allow, or tolerate; to arrange or hold; to engage in; to cause, compel, or require to be; to be obliged; (*sl*) to have sexual intercourse with; to be pregnant with; (*inf*) to hold at a disadvantage; (*inf*) to deceive; to accept or receive; to consume food, drink, etc; to show some quality; to perplex.

haven /'heɪvən/ *n* a place where ships can safely anchor; a refuge.

haven't /'hævənt/ = have not.

haver /'heɪvər/ *vi* (*Scot*) to talk foolishly or in consequently; to dither. • *n* (*pl*) nonsense.

haversack /'hævərˌsæk/ *n* a canvas bag similar to a knapsack but worn over one shoulder.

havoc /'hævək/ *n* widespread destruction or disorder. • *vt* (**havocking, havocked**) to lay waste.

haw /hɒ/ *n* (the berry of) the hawthorn.

Hawaiian /hə'waɪən/ *adj* pertaining to Hawaii, its inhabitants or its language. • *n* an inhabitant of Hawaii; a Polynesian language spoken in Hawaii.

hawfinch /'hɒfɪntʃ/ *n* a rare European finch with a stout bill, brown plumage and black-and-white wings.

haw-haw *see* **ha-ha**[1].

hawk[1] /hɒk/ *n* any of numerous birds of prey; a person who advocates aggressive or intimidatory action. • *vti* to hunt with a hawk; to strike like a hawk.—**hawkish** *adj.*—**hawkishly** *adv.*

hawk[2] *vti* to clear the throat (of) audibly. • *n* the sound of this.

hawk[3] *vt* to offer goods for sale, as in the street; to spread gossip. • *vi* to peddle.

hawker /'hɒkər/ *n* a person who goes about offering goods for sale; a person who hunts with a trained hawk.

hawk-eyed *adj* keen-sighted; vigilant.

hawkweed /'hɒkwiːd/ *n* a yellow-flowered plant of the aster family.

hawse /hɒz/ n (naut) the part of a ship's bows where the hawse-holes are situated; the distance from the bow of an anchored ship to the anchor. • vi (naut) to pitch violently when at anchor.

hawsehole /'hɒzhoʊl/ n (naut) one of the two holes in the upper part of a ship's bows through which the anchor cables pass when the vessel is moored.

hawser /'hɒzər/ n (naut) a heavy rope for towing, mooring, etc.

hawthorn /'hɒθɔrn/ n any of a genus of spring-flowering spiny shrubs or trees with white or pink flowers and red fruit.

hay /heɪ/ n grass cut and dried for fodder.

haybox /'heɪbɒks/ n an airtight box packed with hay or any other natural insulating material used to keep partially cooked food warm and allow to cook by retained heat.

haycock /-kɒk/ n a conical pile of hay left in the fields to dry out.

hay fever n an allergic reaction to pollen, causing irritation of the nose and eyes.

haymaker /-meɪkər/ n one who lifts and spreads hay; either of two machines used in haymaking; a wild punch.

haystack /-stæk/, **hayrick** /-rɪk/ n a pile of stacked hay ready for storing.

haywire /-waɪr/ adj (inf) out of order; disorganized.

hazard /'hæzərd/ n a risk; a danger; an obstacle on a golf course. • vt to risk; to venture.—**hazardable** adj.

hazardous /-əs/ adj dangerous; risky.—**hazardously** adv.—**hazardousness** n.

haze /heɪz/ n a thin vapour of fog, smoke, etc. in the air; slight vagueness of mind. • vti to make or become hazy.

hazel /'heɪzəl/ n a tree with edible nuts; a light-brown colour. • adj light-brown.

hazelnut /-ˌnʌt/ n the edible nut of the hazel.

hazy /'heɪzi/ adj (**hazier, haziest**) misty; vague.—**hazily** adv.—**haziness** n.

H-bomb n a hydrogen bomb.

HC abbr = Holy Communion; House of Commons.

HCF abbr = highest common factor.

HDTV abbr = high-definition television.

HE abbr = high explosive; His Eminence; His (or Her) Excellency.

He (chem symbol) helium.

he /hi/ pron the male person or animal named before; a person (male or female). • n a male person or animal.

head /hed/ n the part of an animal or human body containing the brain, eyes, ears, nose and mouth; the top part of anything; the foremost part; the chief person; (pl) a unit of counting; the striking part of a tool; mind; understanding; the topic of a chapter, etc; crisis, conclusion; pressure of water, steam, etc; the source of a river, etc; froth, as on beer. • adj at the head, top or front; coming from in front; chief, leading. • vt to command; to lead; to cause to go in a specified direction; to set out; to travel (in a particular direction); to strike (a football) with the head.—**headless** adj.

headache /'hedeɪk/ n a continuous pain in the head; (inf) a cause of worry or trouble.—**headachy** adj.

headband /-bænd/ n a ribbon or band worn around the head; a narrow strip of cloth stitched to the top of the spine of a book for protection or decoration.

headboard /-bɔrd/ n a board that forms the head of a bed, etc.

headdress /-dres/ n a decorative covering for the head.

headed /-əd/ adj having (a specified kind of) head; having a heading.

header /-ər/ n a dive with the head first; (soccer) the action of striking the ball with the head.

headfirst /hed'fɜrst/ adj with the head in front; recklessly.—also adv.

headgear /'hedgiːr/ n a covering for the head, a hat, cap, etc.

head-hunt /-hʌnt/ vt to cut off and preserve the heads of enemies as trophies; a person who recruits executive personnel.—**head-hunter** n.—**head-hunting** n.

heading /-ɪŋ/ n something forming the head, top, or front; the title, topic, etc of a chapter, etc; the direction in which a vehicle is moving.

headland /-lænd/ n a promontory; unploughed land at the ends of a furrow.

headless /-ləs/ adj being without a head; leaderless.

headlamp /-læmp/, **headlight** /-laɪt/ n a light at the front of a vehicle.

headline /-laɪn/ n printed lines at the top of a newspaper article giving the topic; a brief news summary. • vt to give featured billing or publicity to.

headlong /-lɒŋ/ adj, adv with the head first; with uncontrolled speed or force; rashly.

headman /-mən/ n (pl **headmen**) the chieftain or leader of a tribe; a foreman or overseer.

headmaster /-ˌmæstər/, **headmistress** /-ˌmɪstrəs/ n the principal of a school.—**headmastership, headmistress-ship** n.

headmost /-moʊst/ adj foremost.

head-on adj, adv with the head or front foremost; without compromise.

head over heels adv as if somersaulting; completely, utterly, deeply.

headphone /-foʊn/ n one of two radio receivers held to the head by a band.

headquarters /-ˌkwɔrtərz/ n the centre of operations of one in command, as in an army; the main office in any organization.

headrest /-rest/ n a support for the head.

headroom /-ruːm/ n space overhead, as in a doorway or tunnel.

heads-up adj self-assured and excellent.

headset /-set/ n a set of headphones, usu with a microphone.

headshrinker /-ˌʃrɪŋkər/ n (sl) a psychiatrist.

headstall /-ˌstɔl/ n the part of a bridle that fits round a horse's head.

head start n an early start; any other competitive advantage.

headstone /-stoʊn/ n a marker placed at the head of a grave.

headstrong /-strɒŋ/ adj determined to do as one pleases; obstinate.

head waiter n the head of the dining-room staff in a restaurant.

headwaters /-ˌwɔtərz/ npl the small streams that are the source of a river.

headway /-weɪ/ n forward motion; progress.

headwind /-wɪnd/ n a wind blowing against the direction of a ship or aircraft.

headword /-wɜrd/ n a term placed at the beginning (as of an entry in a dictionary).

headwork /-wɜrk/ n mental work; the decoration on the keystone of an arch.

heady /'hedi/ adj (**headier, headiest**) (alcoholic drinks) intoxicating; invigorating, exciting; impetuous.—**headily** adv.—**headiness** n.

heal /hiːl/ vti to make or become healthy; to cure; (wound, etc) to repair by natural processes.—**healable** adj.—**healer** n.—**healingly** adv.

health /helθ/ n physical and mental well-being; freedom from disease, etc; the condition of body or mind; a wish for one's health and happiness, as in a toast.

health farm n a residential establishment for improving health through a strict regime of diet and exercise.

health foods npl foods that are organically grown, unprocessed and additive-free.

healthful /-fʊl/ adj healthy.—**healthfully** adv.—**healthfulness** n.

health maintenance organization n a health care organization which meets medical needs in return for a fee.

healthy /'helθi/ adj (**healthier, healthiest**) having or producing good health; beneficial; sound.—**healthily** adv.—**healthiness** n.

heap /hiːp/ n a mass or pile of jumbled things; (pl) (inf) a large amount. • vt to throw in a heap; to pile high; to fill (a plate, etc) full or to overflowing.—**heaper** n.

hear /hiːr/ vb (**hearing, heard**) vt to perceive by the ear; to listen to; to conduct a hearing of (a law case, etc); to be informed of; to learn. • vi to be able to hear sounds; (with **of** or **about**) to be told.—**hearable** adj.—**hearer** n.

hearing /'hiːrɪŋ/ n the sense by which sound is perceived by the ear; an opportunity to be heard; the distance over which something can be heard, earshot.

hearing aid n a small electronic amplifier worn behind the ear to improve hearing.

hearken /'hɑrkən/ vi to listen to.—also **harken**.—**hearkener** n.

hearsay /'hiːrseɪ/ n rumour, gossip.

hearse /hɜrs/ n a vehicle for transporting a coffin to a funeral.

heart /hɑrt/ n the hollow, muscular organ that circulates the blood; the central, vital, or main part; the human heart as the centre of emotions, esp sympathy, courage, etc; a conventional design representing a heart; one of a suit of playing cards marked with such a symbol in red.

heartache /'hɑrteɪk/ n sorrow or grief.

heart attack n a sudden instance of abnormal heart functioning, esp coronary thrombosis.

heartbeat /'hɑrtbiːt/ n the rhythmic contraction and dilation of the heart.

heartbreak /'hɑrtbreɪk/ *n* overwhelming sorrow or grief.—**heartbreaker** *n*.

heartbreaking /-ɪŋ/ *adj* causing heartbreak; pitiful.—**heartbreakingly** *adv*.

heartbroken /'hɑrt,bro:kən/ *adj* overcome by sorrow or grief.—**heartbrokenly** *adv*.—**heartbrokenness** *n*.

heartburn /'hɑrtbərn/ *n* a burning sensation in the lower chest.

hearten /'hɑrtən/ *vt* to encourage; to cheer up.—**hearteningly** *adv*.

heart failure *n* the inability of the heart to supply enough blood to the body; a cessation of heart activity leading to death.

heartfelt /'hɑrtfɛlt/ *adj* deeply felt; sincere.

hearth /hɑrθ/ *n* the floor of a fireplace and surrounding area; this as symbolic of house and home.

hearthstone /'hɑrθsto:n/ *n* a stone forming a hearth; soft stone used to whiten hearths, floors, steps, etc.

heartily /'hɑrtɪli/ *adv* in a vigorous or enthusiastic way; sincerely.

heartland /'hɑrtlænd/ *n* the central or most vital part of an area, region, etc.

heartless /-ləs/ *adj* lacking compassion; unfeeling.—**heartlessly** *adv*.—**heartlessness** *n*.

heart-rending *adj* causing much mental anguish.

heartsease /-si:z/ *n* the wild pansy.

heartsick /-sɪk/ *adj* extremely unhappy, despondent.—**heartsickness** *n*.

heartstrings /-strɪŋz/ *npl* deepest feelings.

heart-throb /-θrɒb/ *n* (*inf*) the object of a person's infatuation; a heartbeat.

heart-to-heart *n* an intimate conversation. • *adj* intimate; candid.

heartwood /-wʊd/ *n* the central older wood of a tree, *usu* harder and darker than the outer rings.—*also* **duramen**.

hearty /'hɑrti/ *adj* (**heartier, heartiest**) warm and friendly; (*laughter, etc*) unrestrained; strong and healthy; nourishing and plentiful.—**heartiness** *n*.

heat /hi:t/ *n* energy produced by molecular agitation; the quality of being hot; the perception of hotness; hot weather or climate; strong feeling, *esp* ardour, anger, etc; a single bout, round, or trial in sports; the period of sexual excitement and readiness for mating in female animals; (*sl*) coercion. • *vti* to make or become warm or hot; to make or become excited.

heated /'hi:təd/ *adj* made hot; excited, impassioned.—**heatedly** *adv*.—**heatedness** *n*.

heater /-ər/ *n* a device that provides heat; (*sl*) a pistol.

heath /hi:θ/ *n* an area of uncultivated land with scrubby vegetation; any of various shrubby plants that thrive on sandy soil, *eg* heather.

heathen /'hi:ðən/ *n* (*pl* **heathens, heathen**) anyone not acknowledging the God of Christian, Jew, or Muslim belief; a person regarded as irreligious, uncivilized, etc. • *adj* of or denothing a heathen; irreligious; pagan.—**heathendom** *n*.

heathenish /-ɪʃ/ *adj* relating to or resembling a heathen or heathenish culture; rude, ignorant or uncultured.—**heathenishly** *adv*.—**heathenishness** *n*.

heathenism /-,nɪzəm/ *n* ignorance of God; paganism; idolatry.

heather /'hi:ðər/ *n* a common evergreen shrub of northern and alpine regions with small sessile leaves and tiny *usu* purplish pink flowers.—**heathery** *adj*.

heating /'hi:tɪŋ/ *n* a system of providing heat, as central heating; the warmth provided.

heat wave *n* a prolonged period of unusually hot weather.

heave /hi:v/ *vb* (**heaving, heaved**) *vt* to lift or move, *esp* with great effort; to utter (a sigh, etc) with effort; (*inf*) to throw. • *vi* to rise and fall rhythmically; to vomit; to pant; to gasp; to haul; (**heaving, hove**) (*with* **to**) (*ship*) to come to a stop. • *n* the act or effort of heaving.—**heaver** *n*.

heaven /'hɛvən/ *n* (*usu pl*) the visible sky; (*sometimes cap*) the dwelling place of God and his angels where the blessed go after death; any place or state of great happiness; (*pl*) *interj* an exclamation of surprise.

heavenly /-li/ *adj* of or relating to heaven or heavens; divine; (*inf*) excellent, delightful.—**heavenliness** *n*.

heavy /'hɛvi/ *adj* (**heavier, heaviest**) hard to lift or carry; of more than the usual, expected, or defined weight; to an unusual extent; hard to do; stodgy, hard to digest; cloudy; (*industry*) using massive machinery to produce basic materials, as chemicals and steel; (*ground*) difficult to make fast progress on; clumsy; dull, serious. • *n* (*pl* **heavies**) (*theatre*) a villain; (*sl*) a person hired to threaten violence, a thug.—**heavily** *adv*.—**heaviness** *n*.

heavy duty *adj* made to withstand heavy strain or rough usage.

heavy-handed *adj* clumsy; tactless; oppressive.—**heavy-handedly** *adv*.—**heavy-handedness** *n*.

heavy metal *n* a type of rock music characterized by a heavy beat and reliance on loudly amplified instruments.

heavy spar *see* **barium sulphate**.

heavy water *n* deuterium oxide, water in which the normal hydrogen content has been replaced by deuterium.

heavyweight /'hɛvi,weɪt/ *n* a professional boxer weighing more than 175 pounds (79 kg) or wrestler weighing over 209 pounds (95 kg); (*inf*) a very influential or important individual.

hebdomad /hɛb'dɒməd/ *n* (*formerly*) seven; a group of seven; a week.

hebdomadal /-əl/ *adj* weekly.—**hebdomadally** *adv*.

Hebe /'hi:bi/ *n* (*Greek myth*) the goddess of youth.

hebetate /'hɛbəteɪt/ *vti* to make or become dull. • *adj* (*plant*) having a blunt or soft point.—**hebetation** *n*.

hebetude /'hɛbətju:d/ *n* mental dullness or lethargy.—**hebetudinous** *adj*.

Hebraic /hɪ'breɪ,ɪk/, **Hebraical** /-əl/ *adj* of or pertaining to the Hebrews, Jewish language or literature.—**Hebraically** *adv*.

Hebraism /hɪ'breɪzəm/ *n* a linguistic usage, custom or idiom borrowed from and characteristic of the Hebrew language, or to the Jewish people or culture.

Hebraist /hɪ'breɪɪst/ *n* one who studies or is learned in the Hebrew language and culture.—**Hebraistic, Hebraistical** *adj*.—**Hebraistically** *adv*.

Hebrew /hɪ'bru:/ *n* a member of an ancient Semitic people; an Israelite; a Jew; the ancient Semitic language of the Hebrews; its modern form. • *adj* pertaining to the Hebrew people; Jewish.

Hecate /'hɛkəti/ *n* (*Greek myth*) a goddess of the underworld.

hecatomb /'hɛkə,tu:m/ *n* in ancient Greece, the ritual sacrifice of 100 oxen; any large sacrifice or slaughter.

heck /hɛk/ *interj* an expression of surprise or grief.

heckle /'hɛkəl/ *vti* to harass (a speaker) with questions or taunts.—**heckler** *n*.

hect- /hɛkt/, **hecto-** /hɛkto:/ *prefix* hundred.

hectare /'hɛktər/ *n* a metric measure of area, equivalent to 10,000 square metres (2.47 acres).

hectic /'hɛktɪk/ *adj* involving intense excitement or activity.—**hectically** *adv*.

hectogram /'hɛktə,græm/ *n* a metric unit of mass equivalent to 100 grams (3.527 ounces).

hectograph /-,græf/ *n* a process for copying a manuscript by transferring it onto a layer of gelatin coated with glycerin; the machine that uses this process. • *vt* to copy in this way.—**hectographic** *adj*.—**hectographically** *adv*.

hector /'hɛktər/ *vt* to bully; to annoy. • *n* a bully.

he'd = /'hi:d/ he had, he would.

hedge /hɛdʒ/ *n* a fence consisting of a dense line of bushes or small trees; a barrier or means of protection against something, *esp* financial loss; an evasive or noncommittal answer or statement. • *vt* to surround or enclose with a hedge; to place secondary bets as a precaution. • *vi* to avoid giving a direct answer in an argument or debate.—**hedger** *n*.—**hedgy** *adj*.

hedgehog /'hɛdʒhɒg/ *n* a small insectivorous mammal with sharp spines on the back.

hedgerow /'hɛdʒ,ro:/ *n* a line of shrubs or trees separating or enclosing fields.

hedonism /'hɛdə,nɪzəm/ *n* the doctrine that personal pleasure is the chief good.—**hedonistic** *adj*.—**hedonist** *n*.

heebie-jeebies /,hi:bɪi'dʒi:biz/ *npl* (*sl*) nervousness, jitters.

heed /hi:d/ *vt* to pay close attention (to). • *n* careful attention.—**heeder** *n*.

heedful /'h:dfʊl/ *adj* paying attention; mindful.—**heedfully** *adv*.—**heedfulness** *n*.

heedless /-ləs/ *adj* inattentive; thoughtless.—**heedlessly** *adv*.—**heedlessness** *n*.

heehaw /'hi:hɒ/ *n* (an imitation of) the bray of a donkey, a crude laugh. • *vi* to bray like a donkey.

heel[1] /hi:l/ *n* the back part of the foot, under the ankle; the part covering or supporting the heel in stockings, socks, etc, or shoes; a solid attachment forming the back of the sole of a shoe; (*inf*) a despicable person. • *vt* to furnish with a heel; to follow closely; (*inf*) to provide with money, etc. • *vi* to follow along at the heels of someone.—**heelless** *adj*.

heel[2] *vti* to tilt or become tilted to one side, as a ship.

heelball /'hiːlbɒl/ *n* a black, waxy substance used to blacken the heels and soles of shoes; a waxy substance used in brass rubbing.

heeler /'hiːlər/ *n* a person who works for a local political organization, *esp* a ward heeler; (*Austral*) a dog that herds cattle by snapping at their heels.

heeltap /'hiːltæp/ *n* a small layer of leather in the heel of a shoe; the dregs of an alcoholic drink left at the bottom of a glass.

heft /heft/ *vt* to asses the weight of an object by holding it in the hand; to lift; to become used to. • *n* weight; the main part.

hefty /'hefti/ *adj* (**heftier, heftiest**) (*inf*) heavy; large and strong; big.—**heftily** *adv*.—**heftiness** *n*.

Hegelian /he'geɪlɪən/ *adj* relating to or pertaining to the German philosopher Georg Hegel (1770-1831) or his theories.—**Hegelianism** *n*.

hegemony /hə'dʒeməni/ *n* (*pl* **hegemonies**) leadership, domination, *esp* of one nation over others.—**hegemonic** *adj*.

Hegira /'hedʒɪrə/ or /hɪ'gɪːrə/ *n* the flight of Mohammed from Mecca in AD 622, marking the start of the Muslim era.—*also* **Hejira**.

heifer /'hefər/ *n* a young cow that has not calved.

height /haɪt/ *n* the topmost point; the highest limit; the distance from the bottom to the top; altitude; a relatively great distance above a given level; an eminence; a hill.

heighten /'haɪtən/ *vti* to make or come higher or more intense.—**heightener** *n*.

heinous /'heɪnəs/ *adj* outrageously evil; wicked.—**heinously** *adj*.—**heinousness** *n*.

heir /-ɛr/ *n* a person who inherits or is entitled to inherit another's property, title, etc.—**heirless** *adj*.

heirdom /-'ɛrdəm/ *n* succession by right of blood; inheritance.

heiress /-'ɛrəs/ *n* a woman or girl who is an heir, *esp* to great wealth.

heirloom /-'ɛrluːm/ *n* any possession handed down from generation to generation.

heist /haɪst/ *n* (*sl*) a robbery. • *vt* (*sl*) to steal.—**heister** *n*.

Hejira /'hedʒɪrə/ or /hɪ'gɪːrə/ *see* **Hegira**.

held /held/ *see* **hold**[1].

heliacal /hɪ'laɪəkəl/ *adj* emerging from or passing into the light of the sun.

helianthus /ˌhiːliˈænθəs/ *n* any of a genus of plants with large yellow flowers, including the sunflower and Jerusalem artichoke.

helical /'helɪkəl/ *adj* like a helix, spiral.—**helically** *adv*.

helicoid /'helɪkɔɪd/ *adj* resembling a flattened spiral. • *n*. a spirally curved geometrical figure.

helicopter /'helɪˌkɒptər/ *n* a kind of aircraft lifted and moved, or kept hovering, by large rotary blades mounted horizontally.

heliculture /'helɪˌkʌltʃər/ *n* the rearing of snails for food.

helio- /'hiːlio/ *prefix* sun.

heliocentric /ˌhiːlɪəˈsentrɪk/ *adj* having the sun as the centre; measured or viewed from the sun's centre.—**heliocentrically** *adv*.—**heliocentricity, heliocentricism** *n*.

heliochrome /-'kroːm/ *n* a photograph in natural colours.

heliograph /-'græf/ *n* a signalling device using the sun's rays reflected by a mirror.—**heliographer** *n*.—**heliographic** *adj*.—**heliography** *n*.

heliogravure /-grə'vjuːr/ *n* photogravure, the process of photoengraving or etching.

heliolatry /-'lætri/ *n* sun worship.

heliometer /ˌhiːli'ɒmətər/ *n* a refracting telescope used to measure small angular distances between celestial bodies.

heli-skiing *n* the use of helicopters to take skiers to high, uncrowded off-piste slopes.

heliostat /'hiːliəˌstæt/ *n* an instrument that sends signals by reflecting the light of the sun in a constant direction.

heliotrope /-ˌtroːp/ *n* a genus of plants whose flowers follow the course of the sun; a green-hued variety of chalcedony with small red spots; a bloodstone; the bluish-pink colour of the flower heliotrope; an instrument used in geodetic surveying.—**heliotropic** *adj*

heliotropism /ˌhiːli'ɒtrəˌpɪzəm/ *n* the movement of flowers or leaves towards the sun.—**heliotropic** *adj*.

heliport /'helɪˌpɔrt/, **helipad** /-ˌpæd/ *n* a landing and takeoff place for a helicopter.

helium /'hiːliəm/ *n* a light nonflammable gaseous element.

helix /'hiːlɪks/ *n* (*pl* **helices, helixes**) a spiral line, as a line coiled round; (*zool*) a snail or its shell; (*anat*) the folded rim of the external ear ; (*archit*) a small volute on a capital.

hell /hel/ *n* (*Christianity*) the place of punishment of the wicked after death; the home of devils and demons; any place or state of supreme misery or discomfort; (*inf*) a cause of this. • *interj* (*inf*) an exclamation of anger, surprise, etc.

he'll /'hiːl/ = he will.

hellbent /'hel,bent/ *adj* (*inf*) rashly determined.

hellebore /'heliˌbor/ *n* any of a genus of mostly poisonous plants, including the Christmas rose.

Hellene /'helən/, **Hellenian** /'heliːn/ *n* a Greek.

Hellenic /'helənɪk/ or /-liːnɪk/ *adj* of or relating to classical Greece and the Greeks; relating to classical and modern Greeks and their language. • *n* a branch of the Indo-European family of languages made up of Greek and its dialects.

Hellenism /-ˌnɪzəm/ *n* the national character of the Greeks; the ideals and principles of classical Greece; the love of Greek culture and art.

Hellenist /-ˌnɪst/ *n* a non-Greek, especially a Jew, who spoke Greek in classical times; a student of Greek culture and language.

Hellenistic /-ˌnɪstɪk/ *adj* relating to or characteristic of classical Greece; relating to Greeks or to Hellenism.

Hellenize /-ˌnaɪz/ *vt* to adopt classical Greek culture or customs; to use or study the Greek language.—**Hellenization** *n*.—**Hellenizer** *n*.

hellish /'helɪʃ/ *adj* of, pertaining to, or resembling hell; very wicked; (*inf*) very unpleasant.—**hellishly** *adv*.—**hellishness** *n*.

hello /hə'loː/ *interj* an expression of greeting. • *n* (*pl* **hellos**) the act of saying "hello."—*also* **hallo, hullo** (*pl* **hallos, hullos**).

helm[1] /helm/ *n* (*naut*) the tiller or wheel used to steer a ship; any position of control or direction, authority. • *vt* to steer; to control.

helm[2] /helm/ *n* (*arch*) a helmet. • *vt* to provide or cover with a helmet.

helmet /'helmət/ *n* protective headgear worn by soldiers, policemen, divers, etc.—**helmeted** *adj*.

helminth /'helmɪnθ/ *n* a worm, *esp* an intestinal one, a fluke.

helminthic /hel'mɪnθɪk/ *adj* pertaining to worms. • *n* a drug used to treat intestinal worms.

helminthoid /hel'mɪnθɔɪd/ *adj* worm-shaped.

helminthology /ˌhelmɪnθ'ɒlədʒi/ *n* the study of parasitic worms.

helmsman /'helmsmən/ *n* (*pl* **helmsmen**) a person who steers.—**helmswoman** *nf* (*pl* **helmswomen**).

helot /'helət/ *n* a serf or slave; (*with cap*) in ancient Sparta, a state-owned slave.

helotry /'helətri/ *n* slavery or serfdom; the class of slaves or serfs.

help /help/ *vt* to make things better or easier for; to aid; to assist; to remedy; to keep from; to serve or wait on. • *vi* to give aid; to be useful.—*interj* used to ask for assistance. • *n* the action of helping; aid; assistance; a remedy; a person that helps, *esp* a hired person.—**helper** *n*.

helpful /'helpful/ *adj* giving help; useful.—**helpfully** *adv*.—**helpfulness** *n*.

helping /-ɪŋ/ *n* a single portion of food.

helpless /-ləs/ *adj* unable to manage alone, dependent on others; weak and defenceless.—**helplessly** *adv*.—**helplessness** *n*.

helpmate /-meɪt/, **helpmeet** /-miːt/ *n* a helpful companion, *esp* a wife or husband.

helter-skelter /'heltər'skeltər/ *adv* in confused haste. • *adj* disorderly. • *n* a tall spiral slide *usu* found in an amusement park.

helve /helv/ *n* the handle of a tool.

Helvetia /hel'viːʃə/ or /-ʃiə/ *n* the Latin name for Switzerland.

Helvetian /hel'viːʃən/ *adj* of or relating to Helvetia; Swiss. • *n* a native or citizen of Switzerland.

hem /hem/ *n* the edge of a garment, etc, turned back and stitched or fixed. • *vt* (**hemming, hemmed**) to finish (a garment) with a hem; (*with in*) to enclose, confine.—**hemmer** *n*.

he-man *n* (*pl* **he-men**) (*inf*) an excessively masculine or strongly built male.

hematite /'hiːməˌtaɪt/ *n* native ferric oxide, an important iron ore.—*also* **haematite**.

hematology /ˌhiːmə'tɒlədʒi/ *n* the branch of medicine dealing with blood and its diseases.—**hematologic, hematological** *adj*.—**hematologist** *n*.

hemi- /'hemi/ *prefix* half; partial.

hemicycle /'hemiˌsaɪkəl/ *n* a half-circle, semicircle.—**hemicyclic** *adj*.

hemidemisemiquaver /-demiˌsemikweɪvər/ *n* (*mus*) a sixty-fourth note.

hemihedral /hemi'hedrəl/ *adj* (*crystal*) having only half the normal number of faces.

hemiplegia /-'pli:dʒɪə/ *n* paralysis of one side.—**hemiplegic** *adj, n.*

hemisphere /-'sfɪːr/ *n* half of a sphere or globe; any of the halves (northern, southern, eastern, or western) of the earth.—**hemispheric, hemispherical** *adj.*—**hemispherically** *adv.*

hemistitch /'hemɪstɪk/ *n* half of a line of verse.

hemline /'hemlaɪn/ *n* the bottom edge of a skirt or dress.

hemlock /'hemlɒk/ *n* a poisonous plant with small white flowers; a poison made from this plant.

hemmer /'hemər/ *n* one who stitches hems; a machine for hemming.

hemoglobin /ˌhiːmə'gloːbɪn/ *n* the oxygen-carrying red colouring matter of the red blood corpuscles.

hemophilia /-'fiːlɪə/ *n* a hereditary condition in which the blood fails to clot normally.—**hemophiliac, hemophile** *n.*—**hemophilic** *adj.*

hemorrhage /'hemərɪdʒ/ *n* the escape of blood from a blood vessel; heavy bleeding. • *vi* to bleed heavily.—**hemorrhagic** *adj.*

hemorrhoids /'hemə.rɔɪd/ *npl* swollen or bleeding veins around the anus.—*also* **piles.**—**hemorrhoidal** *adj.*

hemp /'hemp/ *n* a widely cultivated Asian herb of the mulberry family; its fibre, used to make rope, sailcloth, etc; a narcotic drug obtained from different varieties of this plant.—*also* **cannabis, marijuana.**—**hempen** *adj.*

hemstitch /'hemstɪtʃ/ *n* an ornamental stitch.—**hemstitcher** *n.*

hen /hen/ *n* the female of many birds, *esp* the chicken.

henbane /'henbeɪn/ *n* a poisonous, sticky, hairy plant of the nightshade family.

hence /hens/ *adv* from here; from this time; from this reason.

henceforth /hens'fɔrθ/, **henceforward** /-'fɔrwərd/ *adv* from now on.

henchman /'hentʃmən/ *n* (*pl* **henchmen**) a trusted helper or follower.

hendecagon /hen'dekə.gɒn/ *n* an eleven-sided plane figure.—**hendecagonal** *adj.*

hendecasyllable /-'sɪləbəl/ *n* a verse of eleven syllables.—**hendecasyllabic** *adj.*

hendiadys /hen'daɪədɪs/ *n* the use of two connected words to express one idea, as "with might and main."

henna /'henə/ *n* a tropical plant; a reddish-brown dye extracted from its leaves used to tint the hair or skin. • *vt* to dye with henna.

hennery /'henəri/ *n* (*pl* **henneries**) a poultry farm.

henotheism /'henə.θiːɪzəm/ *n* the worship of one god while recognizing the existence of others.—**henotheist** *n, adj.*—**henotheistic** *adj.*

henpeck /'henpek/ *vt* to nag and domineer over (one's husband).—**henpecked** *adj.*

henry /'henri/ *n* (*pl* **henries, henrys**) a unit of electrical inductance.

hent /hent/ *vt* (*arch*) to seize; to grasp. • *n* (*arch*) a clutching; intention; anything that has been gasped by the mind.

hepat- /'hepæt/, **hepato-** /'hepæto:/ *prefix* liver.

hepatic /hɪ'pætɪk/ *adj* of, like, or pertaining to the liver. • *n* a drug for treating the liver.

hepatitis /ˌhepə'təɪtɪs/ *n* inflammation of the liver.

heptad /'heptæd/ *n* a group of seven; the number seven; an atom or element with the valency of seven.

heptagon /'heptəgɒn/ *n* a polygon of seven angles and seven sides.—**heptagonal** *adj.*

heptahedron /ˌheptə'hiːdrən/ *n* (*pl* **heptahedrons, heptahedra**) a solid figure with seven plane faces.—**heptahedral** *adj.*

heptameter /hep'tɒmətər/ *n* a verse line of seven metrical feet.

heptarchy /'hep'tɑrki/ *n* (*pl* **heptarchies**) government by seven rulers; a state divided into seven regions each with its own ruler; the seven kingdoms of Anglo-Saxon England.

Heptateuch /'heptə.tjuːk/ *n* (*Bible*) the first seven books of the Old Testament.

her /hər/ *pron* the objective and possessive case of the personal pronoun **she.** • *adj* of or belonging to a female.

herald /'herəld/ *n* a person who conveys news or messages; a forerunner, harbinger; (*Middle Ages*) an official at a tournament. • *vt* to usher in; to proclaim.

heraldic /-ɪk/ *adj* of a herald or heraldry.—**heraldically** *adv.*

heraldry /-ri/ *n* (*pl* **heraldries**) the study of genealogies and coats of arms; ceremony; pomp.—**heraldist** *n.*

herb /hərb/ or /'ɜrb/ *n* any seed plant whose stem withers away annually; any plant used as a medicine, seasoning, etc.

herbaceous /hər'beɪʃəs/ or /'ɜrb-/ *adj* of or like herbs; green and leafy.

herbage /'hɔrbɪdʒ/ or /'ɜrb-/ *n* pasturage; the succulent parts of herbs.

herbal /'hɔrbəl/ or /'ɜrb-/ *adj* of herbs. • *n* a book listing and describing plants with medicinal properties.

herbalist /-ɪst/ *n* a person who practises healing by using herbs; a person who grows or deals in herbs.

herbarium /hər'beriəm/ or /'ɜrb-/ *n* (*pl* **herbariums, herbaria**) a (place or container for a) systematic collection of dried plants.—**herbarial** *adj.*

herb Christopher *see* **baneberry.**

herbicide /'hɔrbɪ.saɪd/ or /'ɜrb-/ *n* a substance for destroying plants.—**herbicidal** *adj.*

herbivore /'hɔrbɪ.vɔːr/ or /'ɜrb-/ *n* a plant-eating animal.

herbivorous /-əs/ *adj* herb-eating; (*animals*) plant-eating.—**herbivorousness** *n.*

herby /'hɔrbɪ/ or /'ɜrb-/ *adj* (**herbier, herbiest**) herb-like; rich in herbs.

herculean /ˌhɔrkjuː'liən/ or /-kjuː-/ *adj* of extraordinary strength, size, or difficulty; (*with cap*) of or like the Roman god Hercules.

herd /hərd/ *n* a large number of animals, *esp* cattle, living and feeding together. • *vi* to assemble or move animals together. • *vt* to gather together and move as if a herd; to tend, as a herdsman.—**herder** *n.*

herdsman /'hɔrdsmən/ *n* (*pl* **herdsmen**) a person who tends a herd of animals.

here /hiːr/ *adv* at or in this place; to or into this place; now; on earth.

hereabout /ˌhiːrə'baʊt/, **hereabouts** /-ə'baʊts/ *adv* in this area.

hereafter /hiːr'æftər/ *adv* after this, in some future time or state. • *n* (*with* **the**) the future, life after death.

hereat /-'æt/ *adv* (*arch*) because of this.

hereby /-baɪ/ *adv* by this means.

hereditable /hɪ'redɪtəbəl/ *adj* that may be inherited, heritable.—**hereditability** *n.*—**hereditably** *adv.*

hereditament /'herɪdɪtəmənt/ or /hɪ'redɪ-/ *n* (*law*) property capable of being inherited.

hereditary /hɪ'redɪtəri/ *adj* descending by inheritance; transmitted to offspring.—**hereditarily** *adv.*—**hereditariness** *n.*

heredity /hɪ'redɪti/ *n* (*pl* **heredities**) the transmission of genetic material that determines physical and mental characteristics from one generation to another.

herein /hiːr'ɪn/ *adv* (*formal*) in this place, document, etc.

hereinafter /ˌhiːr'ɪn'æftər/ *adv* (*formerly*) afterwards of this.

hereof /hiːr'ɒf/ *adv* of this.

heresiarch /he'riːzi.ɑrk/ *n* the leader or fonder of a heretical movement or sect.

heresy /'herəsi/ *n* (*pl* **heresies**) a religious belief regarded as contrary to the orthodox doctrine of a church; any belief or opinion contrary to established or accepted theory.

heretic /'herətɪk/ *n* a dissenter from an established belief or doctrine.—**heretical** *adj.*—**heretically** *adv.*

hereto /hiːr'tuː/ *adv* (*formal*) to this matter, document, etc.

heretofore /ˌhiːr'tuː'fɔr/ *adv* (*formal*) until now.

hereunder /hiːr'ɜndər/ *adv* (*formal*) below.

hereupon /ˌhiːrə'pɒn/ *adv* (*formal*) on this matter, issue, etc; immediately after this.

herewith /hiːr'wɪð/ or /-'wɪθ/ *adv* (*formal*) with this.

heriot /'heriət/ *n* a tribute, *usu* cattle, paid to a feudal lord on the death of a tenant by his heir.

heritable /'herɪtəbəl/ *adj* able to be inherited, hereditable.—**heritably** *adv.*

heritage /'herɪtɪdʒ/ *n* something inherited at birth; anything deriving from the past or tradition; historical sites, traditions, practices, etc regarded as the valuable inheritance of contemporary society.

heritor /'herɪtər/ *n* (*law*) one who inherits; a proprietor.

hermaphrodite /hər'mæfrə.daɪt/ *n* an animal or organism with both male and female reproductive organs; a plant with stamens and pistils in the same floral envelope.—**hermaphroditic** *adj.*—**hermaphroditically** *adv.*

hermaphrodite brig *n* a brig square-rigged forward and schooner-rigged aft.

hermaphroditism /-dɪ.tɪzəm/, **hermaphrodism** /-.dɪzəm/ *n* the state of being an hermaphrodite.

hermeneutics /ˌhɔrmɪ'nuːtɪks/ or /-'njuː-/ *n sing* the science of - interpretation, *esp* of the Bible.—**hermeneutic, hermeneutical** *adj.*—**hermeneutically** *adv.*

hermetic /hər'metɪk/, **hermetical** /-əl/ adj perfectly closed and airtight; of alchemy, magical.—**hermetically** adv.

hermit /'hɜrmɪt/ n a person who lives in complete solitude, esp for religious reasons; a recluse.—**hermitic, hermitical** adj.—**hermitically** adv.

hermitage /'hɜrmɪtɪdʒ/ n the dwelling place of a hermit; a secluded retreat.

hern /hɜrn/ n (arch) the heron.

hernia /'hɜrnɪə/ n (pl **hernias, herniae**) the protrusion of an organ, esp part of the intestine, through an opening in the wall of the cavity in which it sits; a rupture.—**hernial** adj.—**herniated** adj.

hero /hi'roː/ n (pl **heroes**) a person of exceptional bravery; a person admired for superior qualities and achievements; the central male character in a novel, play, etc.

heroic /'hi'rɔɪk/ adj of, worthy of, or like a hero; having the qualities of a hero; daring, risky; (poetry) of or about heroes and their deeds, epic; (language) grand, high-flown. • n heroic verse; (pl) melodramatic talk or behaviour.—**heroically** adv.

heroic age n the age in which the legendary heroes of a nation, esp ancient Greece and Rome, are fabled to have lived in.

heroic couplet n a rhyming couplet in iambic pentameter, used in English heroic verse.

heroic verse n a verse form used in epic poetry, ie the hexameter in Greek and Latin poetry, the iambic pentameter in English, and the Alexandrine in French.

heroin /'hero:ɪn/ n a powerfully addictive drug derived from morphine.

heroine /'hero:ɪn/ n a woman with the attributes of a hero; the leading female character in a novel, film or play.

heroism /'hero:ɪzəm/ n the qualities or conduct of a hero; bravery.

heron /'herən/ n a slim wading bird with long legs and neck.

heronry /'herənri/ n (pl **heronries**) a heron rookery; a breeding place for herons.

herpes /'hɜrpiːz/ n any of several virus diseases marked by small blisters on the skin or mucous membranes.—**herpetic** adj.

herpetology /ˌhɜrpɪ'tɒlədʒi/ n the study of snakes and amphibians.—**herpetologist** n.

Herr /her/, Ger. /hɛr/ n (pl **Herren**) a title, the German equivalent of Mister or Sir.

herring /'herɪŋ/ n (pl **herrings, herring**) a small food fish of commercial importance.

herringbone /'herɪŋˌboːn/ n a kind of cross-stitch; a zigzag pattern used in brickwork; (skiing) a method of walking uphill with the skis pointing outwards. • vt to work in cross-stitch; to decorate with a herringbone pattern. • vi to ascend a ski slope in herringbone fashion.

hers /hɜrz/ pron something or someone belonging to her.

herself /hər'self/ pron the reflexive form of **she** or **her**.

hertz /hɜrts/ n (pl **hertz**) the unit of frequency equal to one cycle per second.

he's /'hiːz/ = he is; he has.

Hesiodic /'hiːsiɒdɪk/ adj pertaining to or in the style of Hesiod, a Greek didactic poet of the 8th century BC.

hesitancy /'hezɪtənsi/ n (pl **hesitancies**) an act of hesitating; the state of being hesitant; indecision.

hesitant /'hezɪtənt/ adj hesitating; indecisive; reluctant; shy.—**hesitantly** adv.

hesitate /ˌhezɪ'teɪt/ vi to be slow in acting due to uncertainty or indecision; to be reluctant (to); to falter or stammer when speaking.—**hesitater** n.—**hesitatingly** adv.

hesitation /ˌhezɪ'teɪʃən/ n the act of hesitating; a pause in speech.

Hesperian /'hespiːrɪən/ adj of or relating to the Hesperides; western. • n a native or inhabitant of a western land.

Hesperides /'hesperədiːz/ n (Greek myth) (pl) the nymphs who guarded the golden apples given by Gaia to Hera on her marriage to Zeus; (sing) the garden containing the golden apples.

Hesperus /'hespərəs/ n the evening star, esp Venus.

Hessian /'heʃən/ adj pertaining to the German state of Hesse. • n a native or inhabitant of Hesse; a mercenary soldier.

hessian /'heʃən/ n a coarse cloth made of jute.

hest /'hest/ n (arch) a behest; a command.

hetaera, hetaira /hɪ'tiːrə/ n (pl **hetaerae, hetaeras, hetairai**) a female prostitute or courtesan, esp in ancient Greece.—**hetaeric, hetairic** adj.

heter- /'hetər/, **hetero-** /'hetəro:/ prefix another; abnormal; different, other; unequal.

heterocercal /ˌhetəro:'siːrəl/ adj (fish) having the upper lobe of the tail longer than the lower lobe.

heterochromatic /-krə'mætɪk/ adj of different colours.

heteroclite /-'klɔɪt/ n an irregularly inflected or unusual word; an unusual person or thing. • adj irregular; deviating from the ordinary.—also **heteroclitic**.

heterodox /'hetəroˌdɒks/ adj contrary to established beliefs or opinions; unorthodox; heterical.

heterodoxy /-ˌdɒksi/ n (pl **heterodoxies**) the state of being heterodox; an unorthodox doctrine or opinion; heresy.

heterodyne /-ˌdaɪn/ vt to impose (a radio frequency wave) on a transmitting wave to produce pulsations of audible frequency. • adj having or produced by combining waves of different lengths.

heterogamous /ˌhetə'rɒgəməs/ adj (bot) bearing two kinds of flowers that differ sexually.

heterogeneous /ˌhetəro:'dʒiːnəs/ adj opposite or dissimilar in character, quality structure, etc; not homogeneous; disparate.—**heterogeneity** n.—**heterogeneously** adv.

heterogenesis /ˌhetəro:'dʒenəsɪs/ n the production by certain organisms of offspring differing in structure and habit from the parent, but reverting in subsequent generations to the original type.—**heterogenetic** adj.

heterogenous /ˌhetə'rɒdʒənəs/ adj (biol) originating outside the body; foreign.—**heterogeny** n.

heterologous /ˌhetə'rɒləgəs/ adj (biol) abnormal in type or structure; derived from a different species; consisting of the same elements in varying proportions.—**heterology** n.

heteromorphism /ˌhetəro:'mɔːrfɪzəm/ n (biol) deviation from the natural form or structure.—**heteromorphic** adj.

heteronomous /ˌhetə'rɒnəməs/ adj differing from the normal type; subject to external law, rule or authority.—**heteronomously** adv.

heteronym /'hetərəˌnɪm/ n a word spelled in the same way as another or others but having a different meaning, as brake (in a vehicle) and brake (fern).—**heteronymous** adj.

heterophyllous /ˌhetəro:'fɪləs/ adj (plants) having leaves of different forms on the same stem.—**heterophylly** n.

heterosexual /ˌhetəro:'sekʃʊəl/ adj sexually attracted to the opposite sex. • n a heterosexual person.—**heterosexuality** n.—**heterosexually** adv.

hetman /'hetmən/ n (pl **hetmen**) (formerly) a Cossack prince or general.

het-up /het'ʊp/ adj (inf) agitated, annoyed.

heulandite /'hjuːlənˌdaɪt/ n a vitreous transparent brittle mineral.

heuristic /hjʊ'rɪstɪk/ adj assisting or leading to discovery or invention.—**heuristically** adv.

hew /hjuː/ vb (**hewing, hewed**, pp **hewed, hewn**) vt to strike or cut with blows using an axe, etc; to shape with such blows. • vi to conform (to a rule, principle, etc).—**hewer** n.

hex /heks/ vt to bewitch; to bring bad luck. • n a magic spell; a curse; a witch.

hex-/heks/, **hexa-** /heksə/ prefix six.

hexachord /'heksəˌkɔrd/ n (mus) a diatonic series of six notes with a semitone between third and fourth.

hexad /'heksæd/ n a group or series of six; the number or sum of six; a chemical element, atom, or radical that can be combined with, or replaced by, six atoms of hydrogen.—**hexadic** adj.

hexagon /'heksəgɒn/ n a polygon having six sides and six angles.—**hexagonal** adj.—**hexagonally** adv.

hexagram /'heksəˌgræm/ n a plane figure having six angles and six sides; a six-pointed star formed by two intersecting triangles; a group of six lines which may be combined into 64 different patterns in I Ching.

hexahedron /ˌheksə'hiːdrən/ n a solid bounded by six plane faces.—**hexahedral** adj.

hexameter /hek'sæmɪtər/ n a line of Greek or Latin verse consisting of six feet the last usually being a spondee; a verse line consisting of six metric feet.—**hexametric, hexametrical** adj.

hexapod /'heksəˌpɒd/ n any of a large class of anthropods; an animal with six legs; an insect. • adj having six legs.—also **hexapodous**.

Hexateuch /'heksəˌtuːk/ or /-ˌtjuːk/ n (Bible) the first six books of the Old Testament.

hey /heɪ/ interj an expression of joy, surprise or to call attention.

heyday /'heɪdeɪ/ n a period of greatest success, happiness, etc.

244

HF *abbr* = high frequency.

Hf (*chem symbol*) = hafnium.

Hg (*chem symbol*) = mercury.

HGV *abbr* = heavy goods vehicle.

hi /haɪ/ *interj* an exclamation of greeting.

hiatus /haɪˈeɪtəs/ *n* (*pl* **hiatuses, hiatus**) a break in continuity; a lacuna; (*med*) an aperture; (*phonetics*) the concurrence of two vowels in two successive syllables.—**hiatal** *adj*.

hibernaculum /haɪbərˈnækjuːləm/ *n* (*pl* **hibernacula**) the winter quarters of a hibernating animal; the bud-scales of a winter bud.

hibernal *adj* /ˈhaɪbərnəl/ of or happening in winter; wintry.

hibernate /ˈhaɪbərneɪt/ *vi* to spend the winter in a dormant condition like deep sleep; to be inactive.—**hibernation** *n*.—**hibernator** *n*.

Hibernian /haɪˈbɜːrniən/ *adj* relating to Ireland. • *n* a native or inhabitant of Ireland.

hibiscus /hɪˈbɪskəs/ or /haɪ-/ *n* any plant of a tropical or subtropical genus of plants with large showy flowers.

hiccup, hiccough /ˈhɪkʌp/ *n* a sudden involuntary spasm of the diaphragm followed by inhalation and closure of the glottis producing a characteristic sound; (*inf*) a minor setback. • *vt* (**hiccuping, hiccuped** *or* **hiccupping, hiccupped**) to have hiccups.

hic jacet /hɪk ˈdʒeɪsɛt/ or /hɪk ˈdʒækɛt/ *n* (*Latin* here lies) an inscription on tombstones.

hick /hɪk/ *n* (*inf*) an unsophisticated person, *esp* from a rural area.

hickory /ˈhɪkəri/ *n* (*pl* **hickories**) a North American tree of the walnut family; its wood; its smooth-shelled edible nut.

hid /hɪd/ *see* **hide**[1].

hidalgo /hɪˈdælɡo/ *n* (*pl* **hidalgoes**) a low-ranking Spanish nobleman.

hidden /ˈhɪdən/ *adj* concealed or obscured.

hide[1] /haɪd/ *vb* (**hiding, hid**, *pp* **hidden, hid**) *vt* to conceal, put out of sight; to keep secret; to screen or obscure from view. • *vi* to conceal oneself. • *n* a camouflaged place of concealment used by hunters, bird-watchers, etc.—**hider** *n*.

hide[2] *n* the raw or dressed skin of an animal; (*inf*) the human skin.

hide[3] *n* an ancient English measure of land.

hide-and-seek *n* a children's game in which one player must find the others, who have hidden themselves.

hidebound /ˈhaɪdbaʊnd/ *adj* obstinately conservative and narrow-minded; (*animals*) having a tight or contracted hide that impedes movement; (*trees*) having a tight bark that restricts growth.

hideous /ˈhɪdiəs/ *adj* visually repulsive; horrifying.—**hideously** *adv*.—**hideousness** *n*.

hiding[1] /ˈhaɪdɪŋ/ *n* (*inf*) a thrashing, a beating.

hiding[2] *n* concealment.

hiding place *n* a place of concealment.

hidrosis /hɪdroˈsɪs/ or /haɪ-/ *n* perspiration; any skin disease affecting the sweat glands.

hidrotic /hɪdroˈtɪk/ or /haɪ-/ *adj* of or promoting perspiration. • *n* a drug that stimulates sweating.

hie /haɪ/ *vti* (**hieing** *or* **hying, hied**) (*poet*) to speed; to hasten.

hier- /haɪr/, **hiero-** /haɪro/ *prefix* sacred.

hierarch /ˈhaɪərˌɑːrk/ *n* the chief ruler of an ecclesiastical body; a person at a high level of hierarchy.

hierarchism /ˈhaɪərˌɑːrkɪzəm/ *n* hierarchical principles; government by a hierarchy.—**hierarchist** *n*.

hierarchy /ˈhaɪərˌɑːrki/ *n* (*pl* **hierarchies**) a group of persons or things arranged in order of rank, grade, etc.—**hierarchical, hierarchic** *adj*.—**hierarchically** *adv*.

hieratic /haɪərˈætɪk/ *adj* of or relating to priests; sacred; consecrated; of or relating to a cursive form of hieroglyphics used by priests in ancient Egypt. • *n* the Egyptian hieratic script.—**hieratically** *adv*.

hierocracy /haɪərˈoːkrəsi/ *n* (*pl* **hierocrocies**) government by priests or ecclesiastics.

hieroglyph /ˈhaɪrˌəɡlɪf/ *n* a character used in a system of hieroglyphic writing.

hieroglyphic /haɪrˌəɡlɪfɪk/ *n* a sacred character or symbol; (*pl*) the picture writings of the ancient Egyptians and others. • *adj* pertaining to hieroglyphs; emblematic.—**hieroglyphically** *adv*.

hierology /ˌhaɪˈrɒlədʒi/ *n* (*pl* **hierologies**) the sacred literature of people; a biography of a saint.

hierophant /ˈhaɪrəˌfænt/ *n* in ancient Greece, a priest who initiated novices into the sacred mysteries; a person who explains arcane mysteries.

hifalutin /ˌhaɪfəˈluːtɪn/ *see* **highfalutin**.

hi-fi *n* /ˈhaɪfaɪ/ (*inf*) high fidelity; equipment for reproducing high quality musical sound.

higgle /ˈhɪɡəl/ *vi* to dispute over trifling matters; to haggle.

higgledy-piggledy /ˌhɪɡəldɪˈpɪɡəldi/ *adj, adv* (*inf*) in confusion; jumbled up.

high /haɪ/ *adj* lofty, tall; extending upward a (specified) distance; situated at or done from a height; above others in rank, position, etc; greater in size, amount, cost, etc than usual; raised or acute in pitch; (*meat*) slightly bad; (*inf*) intoxicated; (*inf*) under the influence of drugs. • *adv* in or to a high degree, rank, etc. • *n* a high level, place, etc; an area of high barometric pressure; (*inf*) a euphoric condition induced by alcohol or drugs.

high and dry *adj* helpless; stranded; (*ship*) out of the water.

high and mighty *adj* (*inf*) arrogant.

High Arctic *n* the regions of Canada, *esp* the northern islands, within the Arctic Circle.—*also* **High North**.

highball /ˈhaɪbɒl/ *n* a cool drink with spirits, soda, etc, served in a tall glass.

highborn *adj* of noble birth.

highboy /-bɔɪ/ *n* (*US*) a chest of drawers on legs; a tallboy.

highbrow /-braʊ/ *n* (*inf*) an intellectual. • *adj* (*inf*) interested in things requiring learning.

High Church *n* the part of the Anglican Church that attaches great importance to the authority of the Church, its sacraments and priesthood.—**High-Church** *adj*.

high-class *adj* of good quality; of or appropriate to the upper social classes.

high commissioner *n* the senior diplomatic representative sent by one Commonwealth country to another instead of an ambassador; the chief officer in a colony or other dependency.

higher /ˈhaɪər/ *adj* more high. • *adv* in or to a higher position.

higher education *n* education at college or university level.

higher-up *n* (*inf*) a person of higher rank.

high explosive *n* a very powerful chemical explosive, such as gelignite.

highfalutin /ˌhaɪfəˈluːtɪn/, **highfaluting** /-tɪŋ/ *adj* (*inf*) pretentious; pompous.—*also* **hifalutin**.

high fidelity *n* the high quality reproduction of sound.

high-five *n* an action or gesture as a greeting, acclamation or celebration where two people slap their open right hands together at head height or above.

high-flown *adj* extravagantly ambitious; bombastic.

high-flyer, high-flier *n* an ambitious person; a person of great ability in any profession.—**high-flying** *adj*.

high frequency *n* any radio frequency between 3 and 30 megahertz.

high-handed *adj* overbearing, arbitrary.—**high-handedly** *adv*.—**high-handedness** *n*.

high-hat *vti* (**high-hatting, high-hatted**) to affect superiority; to treat patronizingly. • *n* a person who behaves in this way.

highjack, highjacker *see* **hijack**.

high jinks *npl* (*inf*) mischievous sport or tricks.

high jump *n* an athletic event in which a competitor jumps over a high bar; (*inf*) (*with* **the**) a severe reprimand.

highland /ˌhaɪlənd/ *adj* of or in mountains. • *n* a region with many hills or mountains; (*pl*) mountainous country; (*with cap*) the mountainous region occupying most of northern Scotland.

highlander *n* a person who lives in a highland area; (*with cap*) an inhabitant of the Scottish Highlands.

Highland fling *n* a lively Scottish dance by one person.

highlife /ˈhaɪlaɪf/ *n* (*W Africa*) a style of jazz music combining American and African elements.

high life *n* fashionable society; its manner of living.—**high-life** *adj*.

highlight /ˈhaɪlaɪt/ *n* the lightest area of a painting, etc; the most interesting or important feature; (*pl*) a lightening of areas of the hair using a bleaching agent. • *vt* to bring to special attention; to give highlights to.

highly /ˈhaɪli/ *adv* highly, very much; favourably; at a high level, wage, rank, etc.

highly strung *adj* nervous and tense; excitable; high-strung.

High Mass *n* (*RC Church*) a ceremonial mass, *usu* at the high altar, at which a deacon or subdeacon assist the celebrant.

high-minded /haɪˈmaɪndəd/ *adj* having high ideals, etc.—**high-mindedness** *n*.

highness /ˈhaɪnəs/ *n* the state or quality of being high; (*with cap and poss pron*) a title used in speaking to or of royalty.

high-pitched *adj* (*sound*) shrill; (*roof*) steep.

high-powered, high-power *adj* (*lens, etc*) producing great magnification; energetic; powerful; highly competent.

high priest *n* a chief priest, *esp* the principal priest of the Jewish hierarchy; an unofficial leader of fashion, etc.

high-rise *adj* (*building*) having multiple storeys.• *n* a building of this kind.

highroad *n* a chief road, a highway; an easy course or method.

high roller *n* a gambler; an extravagant person; a leader of fashion.—**high rolling** *adj, n*.

high school *n* a secondary school.

high seas *npl* open ocean waters outside the territorial limits of any nation.

high season *n* the busiest time of the year for a holiday resort, etc.

high-sounding *adj* imposing, pompous.

high-spirited *adj* courageous; lively.—**high-spiritedness** *n*.

high-strung *adj* strung to a high pitch; extremely sensitive; highly strung.

hightail /'haɪteɪl/ *vi* to leave in a great rush.

high tide *n* the tide at its highest level; the time of this; an acme.

high time *adv* (*inf*) fully time.• *n* an especially good or enjoyable time.

high treason *n* treason against the ruler or state.

high-up *n* (*inf*) a person of high status or position.

high water *n* high tide.—**highwater** *adj*.

highwater mark *n* the highest point reached by a high tide; any maximum.

highway /'haɪweɪ/ *n* a public road; a main thoroughfare.

highwayman /'haɪweɪmən/ *n* (*pl* **highwaymen**) one who robs travellers on a highway.

high wire *n* a high tightrope.

hijack /'haɪdʒæk/ *vt* to steal (goods in transit) by force; to force (an aircraft) to make an unscheduled flight.• *n* an act of hijacking.—*also* **highjack**.—**hijacker, highjacker** *n*.

hike /haɪk/ *vi* to take a long walk.• *vt* (*inf*) to pull up, to increase.• *n* a long walk; a tramp.—**hiker** *n*.

hilarious /hɪ'leriəs/ *adj* highly amusing.—**hilariously** *adv*.—**hilariousness** *n*.—**hilarity** *n*.

hilarity /hɪ'leriti/ *n* mirth; merriment; cheerfulness.

hill /hɪl/ *n* a natural rise of land lower than a mountain; a heap or mound; an slope in a road, etc. *vt* to bank up; to draw earth around (plants) in mounds.

hillbilly /'hɪlbɪli/ *n* (*pl* **hillbillies**) (*inf*) a person from the mountainous areas of southeastern US; country music.—*also adj*.

hillock /'hɪlək/ *n* a small hill.—**hillocked, hillocky** *adj*.

hilly /'hɪli/ *adj* (**hillier, hilliest**) abounding with or characterized by hills; rugged.—**hilliness** *n*.

hilt /hɪlt/ *n* the handle of a sword, dagger, tool, etc.

hilum /'haɪləm/ *n* (*pl* **hila**) a scar on the surface of a seed indicating where it was attached to the seed grain; the nucleus of a starch grain.

him /hɪm/ *pron* the objective case of **he**.

himation /hɪ'mæʃən/ *n* (*pl* **himatia**) in ancient Greece, a square-shaped cloak draped around the body.

himself /hɪm'self/ *pron the reflexive* (he killed himself) *or emphatic* (he himself was lucky) *form of* **he, him**.

Himyaritic /'hɪmjə,rɪt/ *n* an extinct language of the Semitic family of the Afro-Asian family; an Arabian dialect.• *adj* of or relating to the Hymarite people of Arabia or their language.

hind[1] /haɪnd/ *adj* (**hinder, hindmost** *or* **hindermost**) situated at the back; rear.

hind[2] *n* (*pl* **hinds, hind**) a female deer.

hinder /'hɪndər/ *vt* to obstruct, delay or impede.• *vi* to impose instructions or impediments.• *adj* belonging to or constituting the back or rear of anything.—**hinderer** *n*.

Hindi /'hɪndi/ *n* the official language of India ; a group of dialects of northern India.

hindmost /'haɪndmoːst/, **hindermost** /'hɪndərmoːst/ *adj* farthest behind.

hindquarters /'haɪnd,kwɑrtərz/ *npl* the hind legs and accompanying parts of a quadruped.

hindrance /'hɪndrəns/ *n* the act of hindering; an obstacle, impediment.

hindsight /'haɪndsaɪt/ *n* understanding an event after it has occurred.

Hindu /'hɪnduː/ *n* (*pl* **Hindus**) any of several peoples of India; a follower of Hinduism.

Hinduism /'hɪnduːˌɪzəm/ *n* the dominant religion of India, characterized by an emphasis on religious law, a caste system and belief in reincarnation.

hinge /hɪndʒ/ *n* a joint or flexible part on which a door, lid, etc turns; a natural joint, as of a clam; a small piece of gummed paper for sticking stamps in an album.• *vti* to attach or hang by a hinge; to depend.

hinny /'hɪni/ *n* (*pl* **hinnies**) the sterile offspring of a male horse and a female donkey or ass.• *vi* to neigh.

hint /hɪnt/ *n* an indirect or subtle suggestion; a slight mention; a little piece of practical or helpful advice.• *vt* to suggest or indicate indirectly.• *vi* to give a hint.—**hinter** *n*.

hinterland /'hɪntərˌlænd/ *n* the land behind that bordering a coast or river; a remote area.

hip[1] /hɪp/ *n* either side of the body below the waist and above the thigh.

hip[2] *n* the fruit of the wild rose.

hip[3] *interj* used as part of a cheer (*hip, hip, hurrah*).

hip[4] *adj* (*sl*) stylish, up-to-date.

hippie, hippy /'hɪpi/ *n* (*pl* **hippies**) (*sl*) a person who adopts an alternative lifestyle, *eg* involving mysticism, psychedelic drugs, or communal living, to express alienation from conventional society.

hippo /'hɪpoː/ *n* (*pl* **hippos**) (*inf*) a hippopotamus.

hippocras /'hɪpə,kræs/ *n* an old English cordial of spiced wine.

Hippocratic oath /'hɪpə,krætɪk/ *n* an oath taken by a doctor to observe the code of medical ethics derived from Hippocrates, a Greek physician of the 5th century BC.

hippodrome /'hɪpə,droːm/ *n* a dance hall, music hall, etc; in ancient Greece, a stadium for horse and chariot races.

hippogriff /'hɪpə,grɪf/ *n* (*Greek myth*) a monster with a griffin's head, wings and claws, and the body of a horse.

hippopotamus /'hɪpə,pɒtəməs/ *n* (*pl* **hippopotamuses, hippopotami**) a large African water-loving mammal with thick dark skin, short legs, and a very large head and muzzle.

hircine /'hɜr,saɪn/ *or* /-sɪn/ *adj* of or resembling a goat; smelling like a goat.

hire /haɪr/ *vt* to pay for the services of (a person) or the use of (a thing).• *n* the payment for the temporary use of anything; the fact or state of being hired.—**hirable, hireable** *adj*.—**hirer** *n*.

hireling /'haɪrlɪŋ/ *n* a person who works only for money, *esp* for doing something unpleasant.

hire-purchase *n* a system by which a person takes possession of an article after paying a deposit and then becomes the owner only after payment of a series of instalments is completed.

hirsute /'hɜr'suːt/ *or* /'hɜrsuːt/, /-sjuːt/ *adj* covered in hair; of or pertaining to hair.—**hirsuteness** *n*.

his /hɪz/ *poss pron* of or belonging to *him*.—*also adj*.

Hispanic /hɪ'spænɪk/ *adj* of or derived from Spain, Spanish or Spanish-speaking countries.• *n* a person of Hispanic descent, *esp* in the US.

Hispanicism /hɪ'spænɪˌsɪzəm/ *n* a word or expression borrowed from Spanish.

hispid /'hɪspɪd/ *adj* bristly; covered with stiff hairs.—**hispidity** *n*.

hiss /hɪs/ *vi* to make a sound resembling a prolonged *s*; to show disapproval by hissing.• *vt* to say or indicate by hissing.• *n* the act or sound of hissing.—**hisser** *n*.

hist. *abbr* = history; historian; historical.

hist- /'hɪst/, **histo-** /'hɪsto:/ *prefix* tissue.

histamine /'hɪstəmɪn/ *or* /'hɪstəmiːn/ *n* a substance released by the tissues in allergic reactions, acting as an irritant.—**histaminic** *adj*.

histogenesis /ˌhɪstə'dʒenəsɪs/ *n* the formation of organic tissue.—**histogenetic** *adj*.—**histogenetically** *adv*.

histogram /ˌhɪstə'græm/ *n* a statistical diagram representing frequency distribution in terms of columns.

histology /hɪs'tɒlədʒi/ *n* the study of the microscopic structure of animal and plant tissues.—**histologic, histological** *adj*.—**histologically** *adv*.—**histologist** *n*.

historian /hɪ'stɔriən/ *n* a person who writes or studies history.

historic /hɪ'stɒrɪk/ *adj* (potentially) important or famous in history.

historical /hɪ'stɒrɪkəl/ *adj* belonging to or involving history or historical methods; concerning actual events as opposed to myth or legend; based on history.—**historically** *adv*.—**historicalness** *n*.

historicity /hɪ'stɒrɪsɪti/ *n* historical authenticity; genuineness.

historiography /hɪˌstɔrɪˈɒɡrəfi/ *n* the principles of historical writing, *esp* that based on the use of primary sources and techniques of research; the study of methods of historical research and writing.—**historiographic, historiographical** *adj*.—**historiographically** *adv*.

historiographer /hɪˌstɔrɪˈɒɡrəfər/ *n* a writer of history, *esp* an official historian.

history /ˈhɪstɔri/ *or* /ˈhɪstrɪ/ *n* (*pl* **histories**) a record or account of past events; the study and analysis of past events; past events in total; the past events or experiences of a specific person or thing; an unusual or significant past.

histrionic /ˌhɪstrɪˈɒnɪk/, **histrionical** /-əl/ *adj* of actors or the theatre; melodramatic.—**histrionically** *adv*.

histrionics /ˌhɪstrɪˈɒnɪks/ *n* (*used as sing or pl*) the art of theatrical representation; melodramatic behaviour or tantrums to attract attention.

hit /hɪt/ *vti* (**hitting, hit**) to come against (something) with force; to give a blow (to), to strike; to strike with a missile; to affect strongly; to arrive at; (*with* **on**) to discover by accident or unexpectedly. • *n* a blow that strikes its mark; a collision; a successful and popular song, book, etc; (*inf*) an underworld killing; (*sl*) a dose of a drug.

hit-and-run *n* a motor vehicle accident in which the driver leaves the scene without stopping or informing the authorities.

hitch /hɪtʃ/ *vt* to move, pull, etc with jerks; to fasten with a hook, knot, etc; to obtain a ride by hitchhiking. • *vi* to hitchhike. • *n* a tug; a hindrance, obstruction; a kind of knot used for temporary fastening; (*inf*) a ride obtained from hitchhiking.—**hitcher** *n*.

hitchhike /ˈhɪtʃhaɪk/ *vt* to travel by asking for free lifts from motorists along the way.—**hitchhiker** *n*.

hither /ˈhɪðər/ *adv* (*formal*) to or towards this place.

hitherto /ˈhɪðərtu/ *adv* (*formal*) until this time.

hit list *n* (*sl*) a list of people to be eliminated, etc.

hit man *n* a hired assassin.

Hittite /ˈhɪtˌaɪt/ *n* a member of an ancient people of Asia Minor; the language of these people. • *adj* of or pertaining to the Hittite people or their language or inscriptions.

HIV /ˈeɪtʃˈaɪˈviː/ *abbr* = human immunodeficiency virus, the virus that causes **AIDS**.

hive /haɪv/ *n* a shelter for a colony of bees; a beehive; the bees of a hive; a crowd of busy people; a place of great activity. • *vt* to gather (bees) into a hive. • *vi* to enter a hive; (*with* **off**) to separate from a group.

hives /haɪvz/ *n* (*used as sing or pl*) a rash on the skin often caused by an allergy; nettle rash.

hiya /ˈhaɪjə/ *interj* an exclamation of greeting.

HM *abbr* = Her (or His) Majesty ('s).

HMS /ˈeɪtʃˈemˈes/ *abbr* = Her (or His) Majesty's Ship.

Ho (*chem symbol*) = holmium.

ho /hoː/ *interj* an exclamation used to attract attention.

hoard /hɔrd/ *n* an accumulation of food, money, etc, stored away for future use. • *vti* to accumulate and store away.—**hoarder** *n*.

hoarding /ˈhɔrdɪŋ/ *n* a temporary screen of boards erected around a construction site; a billboard.

hoarfrost /hɔrˈfrɒst/ *n* a covering of minute ice crystals.—*also* **white frost**.

hoarse /hɔrs/ *adj* (*voice*) rough, as from a cold; (*person*) having a hoarse voice.—**hoarsely** *adv*.—**hoarseness** *n*.

hoary /ˈhɔri/ *adj* (**hoarier, hoariest**) white or grey with age; having whitish or greyish hairs; (*joke, etc*) ancient, hackneyed.—**hoarily** *adv*.

hoax /hoːks/ *n* a deception; a practical joke. • *vt* to deceive by a hoax.—**hoaxer** *n*.

hob /hɒb/ *n* a ledge near a fireplace for keeping kettles, etc hot; a flat surface on a cooker incorporating hot plates or burners.

hobble /ˈhɒbəl/ *vi* to walk unsteadily, to limp. • *vt* to fasten the legs of (horses, etc) loosely together to prevent straying. • *n* a limp; a rope, etc, used to hobble a horse.—**hobbler** *n*.

hobbledehoy /ˈhɒbəldɪˌhɔɪ/ *n* (*arch*) (*pl* **hobbledehoys**) an inexperienced and awkward young person.

hobby /ˈhɒbi/ *n* (*pl* **hobbies**) a spare-time activity carried out for personal amusement; (*arch*) a hobbyhorse.—**hobbyist** *n*.

hobbyhorse *n* a child's toy comprising a stick with a horse's head; a rocking horse; a favourite topic for discussion.

hobgoblin /ˈhɒbˌɡɒblɪn/ *n* a mischievous goblin.

hobnail /ˈhɒbnɪl/ *n* a short nail with a wide head, used on the soles of heavy shoes.—**hobnailed** *adj*.

hobnob /ˈhɒbnɒb/ *vi* (**hobnobbing, hobnobbed**) to spend time with in a friendly manner.

hobo /ˈhoːboː/ *n* (*pl* **hoboes, hobos**) a migrant labourer; a tramp.—**hoboism** *n*.

hock[1] /hɒk/ *vt* (*sl*) to give something in security for a loan.—**hocker** *n*.

hock[2] *n* the joint bending backward on the hind leg of a horse, etc.

hock[3] *n* a variety of German white wine.

hockey /ˈhɒki/ *n* an outdoor game played by two teams of 11 players with a ball and clubs curved at one end.—*also* **field hockey**; ice hockey.

hockshop /ˈhɒkˌʃɒp/ *n* (*inf*) a pawnshop.

hocus /ˈhoːkəs/ *vt* (**hocusses, hocussing, hocussed** *or* **hocuses, hocusing, hocused**) to cheat or trick; to dupe; to doctor alcohol in order to stupefy a person so as to cheat him or her; to stupefy with a drug. • *n* a trick; drugged alcohol.

hocus-pocus /ˌhoːkəsˈpoːkəs/ *n* meaningless words used by a conjurer; sleight of hand; deception. • *vti* (**hocus-pocuses, hocus-pocusing, hocus-pocused** *or* **hocus-pocusses, hocus-pocussing, hocus-pocussed**) to play tricks (on).

hod /hɒd/ *n* a trough on a pole for carrying bricks or mortar on the shoulder; a coal scuttle.

hodgepodge /ˈhɒdʒpɒdʒ/ *n* a jumble.

hoe /hoː/ *n* a long-handled tool for weeding, loosening the earth, etc. • *vti* (**hoeing, hoed**) to dig, weed, till, etc, with a hoe.

hog /hɒɡ/ *n* a domesticated male pig raised for its meat; (*inf*) a selfish, greedy, or filthy person. • *vt* (**hogging, hogged**) to take more than one's due; to hoard greedily.

hogfish /-fɪ/ *n* (*pl* **hogfish, hogfishes**) a fish with a bristled head of warm Atlantic waters; the wrasse.

Hogmanay /ˌhɒɡməˈneɪ/ *n* (*Scot*) New Year's Eve.

hogshead /ˈhɒɡzhed/ *n* a large cask or barrel; one of several measures of liquid capacity, *esp* one of 63 gallons (238.5 litres).

hogwash /ˈhɒɡwɒʃ/ *n* swill fed to pigs; rubbishy or nonsensensical writing or speech.

hoi polloi /ˌhɔɪpəˈlɔɪ/ *n* (*often derog*) the common people; the masses.

hoist /hɔɪst/ *vt* to raise aloft, *esp* with a pulley, crane, etc. • *n* a hoisting; an apparatus for lifting to a higher flower; a lift, elevator.—**hoister** *n*.

hoity-toity /ˌhɔɪtɪˈtɔɪti/ *adj* arrogant or haughty. • *interj* an exclamation of surprise.

hokey-pokey /ˌhoːkiˈpoːki/ *n* another word for hocus-pocus.

hol- /hɒl/, **holo-** /ˈhɒloː/ *prefix* whole.

hold[1] /hoːld/ *vb* (**holding, held**) *vt* to take and keep in one's possession; to grasp; to maintain in a certain position or condition; to retain; to contain; to own, to occupy; to support, sustain; to remain firm; to carry on, as a meeting; to regard; to believe, to consider; to bear or carry oneself; (*with* **back**) to withhold; to restrain; (*with* **down**) to restrain; (*inf*) to manage to retain one's job, etc; (*with* **forth**) to offer (*eg* an inducement); (*with* **off**) to keep apart; (*with* **up**) to delay; to hinder; to commit an armed robbery. • *vi* to go on being firm, loyal, etc; to remain unbroken or unyielding; to be true or valid; to continue; (*with* **back**) to refrain; (*with* **forth**) to speak at length; (*with* **off**) to wait, to refrain; (*with* **on**) to maintain a grip on; to persist; (*inf*) to keep a telephone line open. • *n* the act or manner of holding; grip; a dominating force on a person.—**holdable** *adj*.—**holder** *n*.

hold[2] *n* the storage space in a ship or aircraft used for cargo.

holdall /ˈhoːldɒl/ *n* a portable container for miscellaneous articles.—*also* **carryall**.

holder /ˈhoːldər/ *n* one who holds; a device for holding things; a person who has control of something; one who is in possession of a financial document.

holdfast /ˈhoːldfæst/ *n* a hook or clamp; the act of gripping strongly; the organ by which seaweed and related plants attach themselves to a host object.

holding /ˈhoːldɪŋ/ *n* (*often pl*) legally held property, *esp* land, stocks, and bonds.

hold-up /ˈhoːldʌp/ *n* a delay; an armed robbery.

hole /hoːl/ *n* a hollow place; a cavity; a pit; an animal's burrow; an aperture; a perforation; a small, squalid, dingy place; (*inf*) a difficult situation; (*golf*) a small cavity into which the ball is hit; the tee, the fairway, etc leading to this. • *vti* to make a hole in (something); to drive into a hole; (*with* **up**) to hibernate; (*inf*) to hide oneself.

holey /'həʊli/ *adj* full of holes.

holiday /'hɒlə,deɪ/ *n* a period away from work, school, etc for travel, rest or recreation; a day of freedom from work, etc, *esp* one set aside by law. • *vi* to spend a holiday.—*also* **vacation**.

holiday-maker /'hɒlədeɪ,meɪkər/ *n* a vacationer.

holily /'həʊlɪli/ *adv* in a holy manner.

holiness /'həʊlɪnəs/ *n* sanctity; (*with cap and poss pron*) the title of the Pope.

holism /'həʊlɪzəm/ *n* (*philos*) the creation by creative evolution of wholes that are greater than the sum of the parts; (*med*) consideration of the whole body in the treatment of disease.—**holistic** *adj*.—**holistically** *adv*.

holland /'hɒlənd/ *n* an unbleached linen either glazed or unglazed used for furnishing.

hollandaise sauce /'hɒlən,deɪz/ *n* a rich sauce of egg yolks, lemon juice, butter, etc.

Hollands /'hɒləndz/ *n* a kind of Dutch gin sold in stone bottles.

hollow /'hɒlo:/ *adj* having a cavity within or below; recessed, concave; empty or worthless. • *n* a hole, cavity; a depression, a valley.• *vti* to make or become hollow.—**hollowly** *adv*.—**hollowness** *n*.

hollow-eyed *adj* with the eyes deep-set or sunken from tiredness, etc.

holly /'hɒli/ *n* (*pl* **hollies**) an evergreen shrub with prickly leaves and red berries.

hollyhock /'hɒli,hɒk/ *n* a tall-stemmed plant with spikes of large flowers.

holmium /'həʊlmiəm/ *n* a malleable white metallic element.

holoblastic /,hɒlo:'blæstɪk/ or /,hɒlo:-/ *adj* wholly germinal.

holocaust /'hɒlə,kɒst/ *n* a great destruction of life, *esp* by fire; (*with cap and* **the**) the mass extermination of European Jews by the Nazis 1939–45.—**holocaustal, holocaustic** *adj*.

hologram /'hɒlə,græm/ *n* an image made without the use of a lens on photographic film by means of interference between two parts of a laser beam, the result appearing as a meaningless pattern until suitably illuminated, when it shows as a three-dimensional image.

holograph /-,grɑːf/ *n* a document wholly in the handwriting of the author.

holography /hə'lɒgrəfi/ *n* the technique of making or using holograms.—**holographic** *adj*.—**holographically** *adv*.

holohedral /,hɒlə'hiːdrəl/ *adj* showing all the planes necessary for the perfect symmetry of the crystal system.

holophrastic /-'fræstɪk/ *adj* (*linguistics*) describing the stage in language development where most utterances are single words; having the force of a whole phrase; polysynthetic.

holothurian /-'θʊəriən/ *n* any echinoderm of the class that contains the sea cucumber. • *adj* of, related or belonging to the holothurians.

holpen /'həʊlpən/ or /'hɒ:-/ *vb* (*arch*) a past participle of *help*.

holster /'həʊlstər/ *n* a leather case attached to a belt for a pistol.—**holstered** *adj*.

holt /həʊlt/ *n* an otter's den; the burrowed lair of any animal; (*poet*) a wood; a wooded hill.

holus-bolus /'həʊləs,bəʊləs/ *adv* (*inf*) at a gulp, all at once.

holy /'həʊli/ *adj* (**holier, holiest**) dedicated to religious use; without sin; deserving reverence. • *n* (*pl* **holies**) a holy place, innermost shrine.

Holy Communion *n* the celebration of the Eucharist.

Holy Ghost *n* (*Christianity*) the third person of the Trinity.

Holy Grail *n* in medieval legend, the dish or chalice that was used by Christ at the Last Supper, and the object of many knights' quests.

Holy Land *n* Palestine.

Holy Spirit *n* the Holy Spirit.

holystone /'həʊli,stoːn/ *n* sandstone used by sailors to scour ships' decks. • *vt* to scrub a ship's deck with holystone.

Holy Thursday *see* **Ascension Day**.

Holy Week *n* the week before Easter Sunday.

hom- /'həʊm/, **homo-** /'həʊmoː/ *prefix* same; like.

homage /'hɒmɪdʒ/ or /'ɒm/ *n* a public demonstration of respect or honour towards someone or something.

hombre /'ɒmbreɪ/ or /'hɒm-/ *n* (*sl*) a man.

homburg /'hɒmbərg/ *n* a man's soft felt hat with a narrow curled brim and a lengthwise dent in the crown.

home /həʊm/ *n* the place where one lives; the city, etc where one was born or reared; a place thought of as home; a household and its affairs; an institution for the aged, orphans, etc. • *adj* of one's home or country; domestic. • *adv* at, to, or in the direction of home; to the point aimed at. • *vi* (*birds*) to return home; to be guided onto a target; to head for a destination; to send or go home.

home economics *n* (*sing or pl*) the art and science of household management, nutrition, care.

home-grown /həʊm'groːn/ *adj* grown or produced at home or nearby; characteristic of a particular locale.

homeland /'həʊm,lænd/ *n* the country where a person was born.

homely /'həʊmli/ *adj* (**homelier, homeliest**) simple, everyday; crude; not good-looking.—**homeliness** *n*.

home-made /'həʊm,meɪd/ *adj* made, or as if made, at home.

homeopathy, homoeopathy /,həʊmi'ɒpəθi/ *n* the system of treating disease by small quantities of drugs that cause symptoms similar to those of the disease.—**homeopath, homeopathist** *n*.—**homeopathic** *adj*.—**homeopathically** *adv*.

homer /'həʊmər/ *n* (*baseball*) a home run; a homing pigeon; (*inf*) work done on an informal basis, without declaring the earnings.

Homeric /həʊ'merɪk/ or /hə-/ *adj* pertaining to the poet Homer, or his works; heroic.—**Homerically** *adv*.

home run *n* (*baseball*) a hit that allows the batter to touch all bases and score a run.

homesick /'həʊm,sɪk/ *adj* longing for home.—**homesickness** *n*.

homespun /-spʌn/ *adj* cloth made of yarn spun at home; coarse cloth like this.

homestead /-sted/ *n* a farmhouse with land and buildings.—**homesteader** *n*

home stretch, home straight *n* the part of a race track between the last turn and the finish line; the final part.

home truth *n* an unpleasant fact that a person has to face about himself or herself.

homeward /'həʊm,wərd/ *adj* going towards home. • *adv* homewards.

homewards /-wərdz/ *adv* towards home.

homework /-wərk/ *n* work, *esp* piecework, done at home; schoolwork to be done outside the classroom; preliminary study for a project.

homey /'həʊmi/ *adj*, **homeyness** *n see* **homy**.

homicidal /hɒmɪ'saɪdəl/ *adj* characterized by homicide; likely to commit suicide.

homicide /'hɒmɪ,saɪd/ *n* the killing of a person by another; a person who kills another.—**homicidal** *adj*.—**homicidally** *adv*.

homiletic /,hɒmɪ'letɪk/, **homiletical** /-əl/ *adj* of or relating to a homily or sermon; of or relating to homiletics.—**homiletically** *adv*.

homiletics /'letɪks/ *n sing* the art of writing or preaching sermons.

homily /'hɒmɪli/ *n* (*pl* **homilies**) a sermon; moralizing talk or writing.—**homilist** *n*.

homing /'həʊmɪŋ/ *adj* (*pigeon*) trained to fly home after being transported long distances; (*missile, etc*) designed to guide itself onto a target.

hominid /'hɒmɪnɪd/ *adj* of or relating to the zoological species that includes present-day man and his ancestors. • *n* a member of this species.

hominoid /'hɒmɪ,nɔɪd/ *adj* resembling man; of or belonging to primates.

hominy (grits) /'hɒmɪni/ *n* in the US, ground maize boiled in water to make a thin porridge.

homo[1] /'həʊmoː/ *n* any member of the genus *Homo* that includes modern man.

homo[2] *n* (*pl* **homos**) (*inf*) a male homosexual.

homocentric /,həʊmoː'sentrɪk/ or /,hɒmoː-/ *adj* concentric; having the same centre.

homogeneous /,hɒmə'dʒiːniəs/ or /,hɒmə-/ *adj* composed of parts that are of identical or a similar kind or nature; of uniform structure.—**homogeneity, homogeneousness** *n*.

homogenize /hə'mɒdʒə,naɪz/ *vt* to break up the fat particles (in milk or cream) so they do not separate; to make or become homogeneous.—**homogenization** *n*.—**homogenizer** *n*.

homograph /'hɒmə,græf/ *n* a word spelled the same as another word but with a different meaning and derived from a different root.

homologous /hə'mɒləgəs/ *adj* corresponding in relative position, structure, and descent.

homologue, homolog /ˈhɒməˌlɒg/ *n* something that exhibits homology.

homology /həˈmɒlədʒi/ *n* (*pl* **homologies**) a similarity often attributed to a common origin; affinity of structure.—**homological** *adj.*—**homologically** *adv.*

homonym /ˈhɒmənɪm/ *n* a word with the same spelling or pronunciation as another, but a different meaning.—**homonymic** *adj.*—**homonymy** *n.*

Homoousian /ˌhɒmoːˈuːsiən/ *n* a Christian who believes that Jesus is of the same essence as God.

homophobia /ˌhɒməˈfoːbiə/ *n* fear and hatred of homosexuals; persecution of homosexuals.—**homophobe** *n.*—**homophobic** *adj.*

homophone /ˈhɒməˈfoːn/ *n* a letter or group of letters having the same sound as another letter or group of letters; one of a group of words with identical pronunciations but with different meanings or spellings or both.—**homophony** *n.*

homophonous /həˈmɒfənəs/ *adj* alike in sound but different in meaning; relating to or denoting a homophone.

homoplastic /ˌhɒməˈplæstɪk/ *adj* similar in structure; derived from a donating individual of a tissue graft of the same species as the recipient.

Homo sapiens /ˌhoːmoːˈseɪpiənz/ *n* the species designating mankind.

homosexual /ˌhoːmoːˈsɛkʃuəl/ *adj* sexually attracted towards a person of the same sex. • *n* a homosexual person.—**homosexuality** *n.*—**homosexually** *adv.*

homunculus /həˈmʌŋkjuləs/ *n* (*pl* **homunculi**) a dwarf; a miniature man.

homy /ˈhoːmi/ *adj* (**homier, homiest**) cosy, home-like.—*also* **homey.**—**hominess, homeyness** *n.*

Hon. *abbr* = Honourable.

hon *abbr* = honorary; honourable.

hone /hoːn/ *n* a stone for sharpening cutting tools. • *vt* to sharpen (as if) on a hone.

honest /ˈɒnəst/ *adj* truthful; trustworthy; sincere or genuine; gained by fair means; frank, open.—**honestness** *n.*

honestly /ˈɒnəstli/ *adv* in an honest manner; really.

honesty /ˈɒnəsti/ *n* (*pl* **honesties**) the quality of being honest; a European plant with purple flowers that forms transparent seed pods.

honey /ˈhʌni/ *n* (*pl* **honeys**) a sweet sticky yellowish substance that bees make as food from the nectar of flowers; sweetness; its colour; (*inf*) darling. • *adj* of, resembling honey; much loved.

honeybee /ˈhʌniˌbiː/ *n* the common bee of the genus that produces honey.

honeycomb /-ˌkoːm/ *n* the structure of six-sided wax cells made by bees to hold their honey, eggs, etc; anything arranged like this. • *vt* to fill with holes like a honeycomb.

honeydew /-ˌdjuː/ *n* a sugary deposit on leaves secreted by aphids; a variety of melon with yellowish skin and pale green flesh.—**honeydewed** *adj.*

honeyed, honied /ˈhʌniːd/ *adj* flattering; of, containing, or resembling honey.—**honeyedly, honiedly** *adv.*

honeymoon /ˈhʌniˌmuːn/ *n* the vacation spent together by a newly married couple.—*also vi.*—**honeymooner** *n.*

honeysuckle /-ˌsɛkəl/ *n* a climbing shrub with small fragrant flowers.

hong /hɒŋ/ *n* (*formerly*) in China, a factory or warehouse, or a commercial establishment owned by a foreigner.

honk /hɒŋk/ *n* (a sound resembling) the call of the wild goose; the sound made by an old-fashioned motor horn. • *vti* to cry like a goose; to sound (a motor horn); (*sl*) to be sick.

honky-tonk /ˈhɒŋkiˌtɒnk/ *n* a style of ragtime piano playing.

honorarium /ˈɒnəˌreriəm/ *n* (*pl* **honorariums, honoraria**) a voluntary payment for professional services for which no fees are nominally due.

honorary /ˈɒnəreri/ *adj* given as an honour; (*office*) voluntary, unpaid.

honorific /ˈɒnərɪfɪk/ *adj* conferring honour.—**honorifically** *adv.*

honour, honor /ˈɒnər/ *n* high regard or respect; glory; fame; good reputation; integrity; chastity; high rank; distinction; (*with cap*) the title of certain officials, as judges; cards of the highest value in certain card games. • *vt* to respect greatly; to do or give something in honour of; to accept and pay (a cheque when due, etc).—**honourer, honorer** *n.*

honourable, honorable /ˈɒnəˌrəbəl/ *adj* worthy of being honoured; honest; upright; bringing honour; (*with cap*) a title of respect for certain officials, as Members of Parliament, when addressing each other.—**honourably, honorably** *adv.*

hooch /huːtʃ/ *n* (*US sl*) alcoholic liquor, *esp* when illicitly distilled or obtained.

hood[1] /hʊd/ *n* a loose covering to protect the head and back of the neck; any hood-like thing as the (folding) top of a car, etc; (*US*) the hinged metal covering over an automobile engine—*see* **bonnet.**

hood[2] *n* (*inf*) a hoodlum.

hoodlum /ˈhʊdləm/ *n* a gangster; a young hooligan.—**hoodlumism** *n.*

hoodoo /ˈhuːduː/ *n* (*pl* **hoodoos**) voodoo; a person or thing thought to bring bad luck. • *vt* (**hoodooing, hoodooed**) to bring ill luck to.—**hoodooism** *n.*

hoodwink /ˈhʊdwɪŋk/ *vt* to mislead by trickery.—**hoodwinker** *n.*

hooey /ˈhuːi/ *n* nonsense; humbug. • *interj* conveying disbelief.

hoof /huːf/ *n* (*pl* **hoofs, hooves**) the horny covering on the ends of the feet of certain animals, as horses, cows, etc.

hook /hʊk/ *n* a piece of bent or curved metal to catch or hold anything; a fishhook; something shaped like a hook; a strike, blow, etc, in which a curving motion is involved. • *vt* to seize, fasten, hold, as with a hook; (*rugby*) to pass the ball backwards from a scrum.

hookah /ˈhʊkə/ *n* an oriental tobacco-pipe with a long tube connected to a container of water, which cools the smoke as it is drawn through.

hooked /hʊkd/ *adj* shaped like a hook; (*sl*) addicted.—**hookedness** *n.*

hooker /ˈhʊkər/ *n* (*sl*) a prostitute; (*rugby football*) a player in the scrum whose task is to hook the ball.

hookworm /ˈhʊkwərm/ *n* a parasitic worm with hooked mouthparts that can bore through the skin and cause disease.

hooky /ˈhʊki/ *n* truancy from school.

hooligan /ˈhuːlɪgən/ *n* a lawless young person.—**hooliganism** *n.*

hoop /huːp/ *n* a circular band of metal or wood; an iron band for holding together the staves of barrels; anything like this, as a child's toy or ring in a hoop skirt. • *vt* to bind (as if) with hoops.—**hooped** *adj.*

hooper /ˈhuːpər/ *n* a cooper; the wild swan.

hoopla /ˈhuːplə/ *n* a fairground game in which a player tries to throw a hoop over an object; (*US inf*) noise; bustle; ballyhoo.

hoopoe /ˈhuːpuː/ *n* a bird with a fanlike crest and pinky brown plumage.

hooray, hoorah /hʊˈreɪ/ *see* **hurrah.**

hoosegow /ˈhuːsgaʊ/ *n* (*US sl*) jail.

hoot /huːt/ *n* the sound that an owl makes; a similar sound, as made by a train whistle; a shout of scorn; (*inf*) laughter; (*inf*) an amusing person or thing. • *vi* to utter a hoot; to blow a whistle, etc. • *vt* to express (scorn) of (someone) by hooting.—**hooter** *n.*

hooves /huːvz/ *see* **hoof.**

hop[1] /hɒp/ *vi* (**hopping, hopped**) to jump up on one leg; to leap with all feet at once, as a frog, etc; (*inf*) to make a quick trip. • *n* a hopping movement; (*inf*) an informal dance; a trip, *esp* in an aircraft.

hop[2] *n* a climbing plant with small cone-shaped flowers; (*pl*) the dried ripe cones, used for flavouring beer.

hope /hoːp/ *n* a feeling that what is wanted will happen; the object of this; a person or thing on which one may base some hope. • *vt* to want and expect. • *vi* to have hope (for).—**hoper** *n.*

hopeful /ˈhoːpful/ *adj* filled with hope; inspiring hope or promise of success. • *n* a person who hopes to or looks likely to be a success.—**hopefulness** *n.*

hopefully /-li/ *adv* in a hopeful manner; it is hoped.

hopeless /ˈhoːpləs/ *adj* without hope; offering no grounds for hope or promise of success; impossible to solve; (*inf*) incompetent.—**hopelessly** *adv.*—**hopelessness** *n.*

hoplite /ˈhɒplaɪt/ *n* in ancient Greece, a heavily armed foot soldier.

hopper /ˈhɒpər/ *n* a hopping insect; a funnel-shaped container with an opening at the bottom from which its contents can be discharged into a receptacle.

hopscotch /ˈhɒpskɒtʃ/ *n* a children's game in which the players hop through a sequence of squares drawn on the ground.

horary /ˈhɒrəri/ *adj* of or pertaining to or lasting an hour; noting the hours; hourly.

Horatian /hə'reɪʃən/ *adj* of or pertaining to the Roman poet Horace (658 BC) or his works.

horde /hɔrd/ *n* a crowd or throng; a swarm.

horizon /hə'raɪzən/ *n* the apparent line along which the earth and sky meet; the limit of a person's knowledge, interest, etc.

horizontal /ˌhɔrə'zɒntəl/ *adj* level; parallel to the plane of the horizon.—**horizontally** *adv*.—**horizontalness** *n*.

hormone /'hɔrmoːn/ *n* a product of living cells formed in one part of the organism and carried to another part, where it takes effect; a synthetic compound having the same purpose.—**hormonal** *adj*.

horn /hɔrn/ *n* a bony outgrowth on the head of certain animals; the hard substance of which this is made; any projection like a horn; a wind instrument, *esp* the French horn or trumpet; a device to sound a warning. • *vt* to wound with a horn; (*with* in) to intrude.

hornbeam /'hɔrnbiːm/ *n* a tree of the birch family.

hornbill /-bɪl/ *n* a tropical bird with a horny protuberance on its large beak.

hornblende /-blɛnd/ *n* a dark mineral of silica with magnesium, lime or iron.

hornbook /-buk/ *n* a framed child's primer made of a thin slab of wood or paper on which numbers, the alphabet and the Lord's Prayer were printed and protected with a covering of transparent horn; any elementary primer.

horned /hɔrnd/ *adj* having horns.

hornet /'hɔrnət/ *n* a large wasp with a severe sting.

hornpipe /'hɔrnpaɪp/ *n* a lively dance, formerly associated with British sailors; the music for such a dance; an obsolete wind instrument.

hornswoggle /-ˌswɒgəl/ *vt* to deceive; to swindle.

horny /'hɔrni/ *adj* (**hornier, horniest**) like horn; hard; callous; (*sl*) sexually aroused.—**hornily** *adv*.—**horniness** *n*.

horologe /'hɔrəˌlɒdʒ/ or /-ˌloːdʒ/ *n* any instrument that tells the time; a timepiece.

horology /hə'rɒlədʒi/ *n* the science of measuring time; the art of making clocks, watches, etc.— **horologic, horological** *adj*.— **horologist, horologer** *n*.

horoscope /'hɔrəˌskoːp/ *n* a chart of the zodiacal signs and positions of planets, etc, by which astrologers profess to predict future events, *esp* in the life of an individual.

horrendous /hə'rɛndəs/ *adj* horrific; (*inf*) disagreeable.—**horrendously** *adv*.

horrible /'hɔrəbəl/ *adj* arousing horror; (*inf*) very bad, unpleasant, etc.—**horribleness** *n*.—**horribly** *adv*.

horrid /'hɔrɪd/ *adj* terrible; horrible.—**horridly** *adv*.—**horridness** *n*.

horrific /hə'rɪfɪk/ *adj* arousing horror; horrible.—**horrifically** *adv*.

horrify /'hɔrəˌfaɪ/ *vt* (**horrifying, horrified**) to fill with horror; to shock.—**horrification** *n*.—**horrifyingly** *adv*.

horripilation /ˌhɔrɪpə'leɪʃən/ *n* gooseflesh; the bristling of the skin caused by chill or fright.

horror /'hɔrər/ *n* the strong feeling caused by something frightful or shocking; strong dislike; a person or thing inspiring horror. • *adj* (*film, story, etc*) designed to frighten.

hors de combat *Fr.* /ˌɔrdəkɔ̃'ba/ *adj* excluded from competition; unrivalled; unequalled; disabled.

hors d'oeuvre /ˌɔr'dɜrv/, *Fr.* /ɔr'dœvr/ *n* (*pl* **hors d'oeuvre, hors d'oeuvres**) an appetizer served at the beginning of a meal.

horse /hɔrs/ *n* a four-legged, solid-hoofed herbivorous mammal with a flowing mane and a tail, domesticated for carrying loads or riders, etc; cavalry; a vaulting horse; a frame with legs to support something.

horsebox /'hɔrsbɒks/ *n* a trailer used for transporting a horse.

horse brass *n* a decorative brass ornament attached to a horse's harness.

horse chestnut *n* a large tree with large palmate leaves and erect clusters of flowers.

horseflesh /-flɛʃ/ *n* horses; the flesh of a horse, *esp* for eating.

horsehair /-hɛr/ *n* hair from the mane or the tail of a horse, used for padding, etc.

horse latitude *n* either of two oceanic regions between 30 degrees north and 30 degrees south latitude, marked by calms.

horse laugh *n* a boisterous, *usu* derisive laugh.

horseleech /-liːtʃ/ *n* a large carnivorous leech; an insatiable person.

horseman /-mən/ *n* (*pl* **horsemen**) a person skilled in the riding or care of horses.—**horsemanship** *n*.

horseplay /-pleɪ/ *n* rough, boisterous fun.

horsepower /-ˌpaʊər/ *n* (*pl* **horsepower**) a unit for measuring the power of engines, etc, equal to 746 watts or 33,000 foot-pounds per minute.

horseradish /-ˌrædɪʃ/ *n* a tall herb of the mustard family; a sauce or relish made with its pungent root.

horse sense *n* common sense.

horseshoe /-ʃuː/ *n* a flat U-shaped, protective metal plate nailed to a horse's hoof; anything shaped like this.

horsetail /-teɪl/ *n* a plant with jointed stems and whorls of small dark toothlike leaves; the tail of a horse, *esp* when used as a symbol of rank or as a standard.

horse-trade /-treɪd/ *n* a negotiation marked by shrewd bargaining and mutual concessions.—*also vi*.

horsewhip /-wɪp/ *n* a whip with a long thong used on horses. • *vt* (**horsewhipping, horsewhipped**) to flog with a horsewhip.

horsewoman /-ˌwumən/ *n* (*pl* **horsewomen**) a woman skilled at riding.

horsy, horsey /'hɔrsi/ *adj* (**horsier, horsiest**) of or resembling a horse; preoccupied with horses, horse racing, etc.—**horsily** *adv*.—**horsiness** *n*.

hortatory /'hɔrtətɔri/, **hortative** /'hɔrtətɪv/ *adj* exhorting; encouraging.—**hortatorily** *adv*.

horticulture /'hɔrtɪˌkʌltʃər/ *n* the art or science of growing flowers, fruits, and vegetables.—**horticultural** *adj*.—**horticulturally** *adv*.—**horticulturist** *n*.

hosanna, hosannah /hoː'zænə/ *interj* an exclamation of praise to God. • *n* the cry of hosanna; a shout of praise.

hose[1] /hoːz/ *n* a flexible tube used to convey fluids. • *vt* to spray with a hose.

hose[2] *n* (*pl* **hose, hosen**) stockings, socks, tights collectively.

Hosea /hoː'zeɪə/ *n* (*Bible*) an Old Testament book containing the oracles of Hosea, a Hebrew prophet of the 8th century BC.

hosier /'hoːziər/ or /'hoːʒər/ *n* a person who sells stockings, socks, etc.

hospice /'hɒspɪs/ *n* a home for the care of the terminally ill; a place of rest and shelter for travellers.

hospitable /hɒ'spɪtəbəl/ or /'hɒsp-/ *adj* offering a generous welcome to guests or strangers; sociable.—**hospitableness** *n*.—**hospitably** *adv*.

hospital /'hɒspɪtəl/ *n* an institution where the sick or injured are given medical treatment.

hospitality /ˌhɒspɪ'tælɪti/ *n* (*pl* **hospitalities**) the act, practice, or quality of being hospitable.

hospitalize /'hɒspɪtəˌlaɪz/ *vt* to place in a hospital.—**hospitalization** *n*.

hospitaler, hospitaller /'hɒspɪtələr/ *n* (*often cap*) a member of a medieval charitable religious order, *esp* one who worked in a hospital.

host[1] /hoːst/ *n* a person who receives or entertains a stranger or guest at his house; an animal or plant on or in which another lives; a compere on a television or radio programme. • *vti* to act as a host (to a party, television programme, etc).

host[2] *n* a very large number of people or things.

host[3] *n* the wafer of bread used in the Eucharist or Holy Communion.

hostage /'hɒstɪdʒ/ *n* a person given or kept as security until certain conditions are met.

hostel /'hɒstəl/ *n* a lodging place for the homeless, travellers, or other groups.—**hosteler, hosteller** *n*.—**hosteling, hostelling** *n*.

hostelry /'hɒstəlri/ *n* (*pl* **hostelries**) (*formerly*) an inn.

hostess /'hoːstəs/ *n* a woman acting as a host; a woman who entertains guests at a nightclub, etc.

hostile /'hɒstaɪl/ or /'hɒstəl/ *adj* of or being an enemy; unfriendly.—**hostilely** *adv*.

hostility /hɒ'stɪlɪti/ *n* (*pl* **hostilities**) enmity, antagonism; (*pl*) deliberate acts of warfare.

hostler /'hɒslər/ or /'ɒslər/ *see* **ostler**.

hot /hɒt/ *adj* (**hotter, hottest**) of high temperature; very warm; giving or feeling heat; causing a burning sensation on the tongue; full of intense feeling; following closely; electrically charged; (*inf*) recent, new; (*inf*) radioactive; (*inf*) stolen. • *adv* in a hot manner.—**hotly** *adv*.—**hotness** *n*.

hot air *n* (*sl*) empty talk.

hotbed /'hɒtbed/ *n* a bed of heated earth enclosed by low walls and covered by glass for forcing plants; ideal conditions for the growth of something, *esp* evil.

hot-blooded *adj* easily excited.—**hot-bloodedness** *n*.

hotchpotch /'hɒtʃpɒtʃ/ *n* a thick meat and vegetable stew; a hodgepodge.

hot dog *n* a sausage, *esp* a frankfurter, served in a long soft roll.

hotel /hoˈtel/ *n* a commercial establishment providing lodging and meals for travellers, etc.

hotelier /hoˈtelɪər/ *n* the owner or manager of a hotel.

hotfoot /'hɒtfʊt/ *adv* with all speed; quickly.

hothead /'hɒthed/ *n* an impetuous person.—**hot-headed** *adj*.—**hot-headedly** *adv*.—**hot-headedness** *n*.

hothouse /'hɒthʊs/ *n* a heated greenhouse for raising plants; an environment that encourages rapid growth.

hot line /'hɒtlaɪn/ *n* a direct telephone link between heads of government for emergency use.

hotplate *n* a heated surface for cooking or keeping food warm ; a small portable heating device.

hotpot /'hɒtpɒt/ *n* a dish of meat cooked with potatoes in a tight-lidded pot.

hot seat *n* (*inf*) a dangerous position; (*sl*) the electric chair.

Hottentot /'hɒtən̩tɒt/ *n* (*pl* **Hottentots, Hottentot**) (*hist*) a member of a people of the Cape of Good Hope region of South Africa, with pale brown skin; any of the languages spoken by these people.

hot water *n* (*inf*) trouble.

houmous, houmus /'hʊməs/ *see* **hummus**.

hound /haʊnd/ *n* a dog used in hunting; a contemptible person. • *vt* to hunt or chase as with hounds; to urge on by harassment.—**hounder** *n*.

hour /aʊr/ *n* a period of 60 minutes, a 24th part of a day; the time for a specific activity; the time; a special point in time; the distance covered in an hour; (*pl*) the customary period for work, etc.

hourglass /'aʊrglæs/ *n* an instrument for measuring time by trickling sand in a specified period.

houri /'hʊri/ *n* (*pl* **houris**) a beautiful woman of the Muslim paradise; a voluptuous young woman.

hourly /'aʊrli/ *adj* occurring every hour; done during an hour; frequent. • *adv* at every hour; frequently.

house /haʊs/ *n* a building to live in, *esp* by one person or family; a household; a family or dynasty including relatives, ancestors and descendants; the audience in a theatre; a business firm; a legislative assembly; house music. • *vt* to provide accommodation or storage for; to cover, encase.

house arrest *n* detention in one's own house, as opposed to prison.

houseboat /'haʊsbɒt/ *n* a boat furnished and used as a home.

housebound /'haʊsbaʊnd/ *adj* confined to the house through illness, injury, etc.

housebreaker /'haʊsˌbreɪkər/ *n* a burglar; a person employed to demolish buildings.—**housebreaking** *n*.

house-broken /'haʊsˌbroʊkən/ *adj* (*dogs, cats, etc*) trained not to mess in the house; (*inf*) well-mannered.

housefly /'haʊsflaɪ/ *n* (*pl* **houseflies**) a common fly found in houses, which is attracted by food and can spread disease.

household /'haʊsoʊld/ *n* all those people living together in the same house. • *adj* pertaining to running a house and family; domestic; familiar.

householder /'haʊsˌhoʊldər/ *n* the person who owns or rents a house.

housekeeper /'haʊsˌkiːpər/ *n* a person who runs a home, *esp* one hired to do so.

housekeeping /'haʊsˌkiːpɪŋ/ *n* the daily running of a household; (*inf*) money used for domestic expenses; routine maintenance of equipment, records, etc in an organization.

housel /'haʊzəl/ *n* (*formerly*) the Eucharist.

houseleek /'haʊsliːk/ *n* a plant with a rosette of succulent leaves and pink flowers that grows on walls.

housemaid /'haʊsmeɪd/ *n* a female servant employed to do housework.

houseman /'haʊsmən/ *n* (*pl* **housemen**) an intern.

housemaster /'haʊsˌmæstər/ *n* a male teacher at a boarding school responsible for the pupils in his house.

house martin *n* a type of swallow with a forked tail.

house music *n* a pop music style, using electronic bass and synthesizers, a fast hypnotic beat and sporadic vocals, that originated in Chicago.

house party *n* a party, *usu* in a large house, where the guests stay over for several days; the guests themselves.

house plant /'haʊsplænt/ *n* an indoor plant.

houseproud /'haʊsˌpraʊd/ *adj* concerned with tidiness and cleanliness, often to excess.

house warming /'haʊsˌwɔːrmɪŋ/ *n* a party given to celebrate moving into a new house.

housewife /'haʊswaɪf/ *n* (*pl* **housewives**) the woman who keeps house.—**housewifely** *adj*.—**housewifeliness** *n*.—**housewifery** *n*.

housework /'haʊswɜːrk/ *n* the cooking, cleaning, etc, involved in running a home.—**houseworker** *n*.

housing /'haʊzɪŋ/ *n* houses collectively; the provision of accommodation; a casing enclosing a piece of machinery, etc; a slot or groove in a piece of wood, etc, to receive an insertion.

hove /hoʊv/ *see* **heave**.

hovel /'hʌvəl/ or /'hɒv-/ *n* a small miserable dwelling. • *vt* (**hoveling, hoveled** *or* **hovelling, hovelled**) to shelter in a hovel.

hover /'hʌvər/ *vi* (*bird, etc*) to hang in the air stationary; to hang about, to linger.—**hoverer** *n*.—**hoveringly** *adv*.

hovercraft /'hʌvərˌkræft/ *n* a land or water vehicle that travels supported on a cushion of air.

how /haʊ/ *adv* in what way or manner; by what means; to what extent; in what condition.

howbeit /haʊˈbiːɪt/ *conj* (*arch*) though; although.

howdah /'haʊdə/ *n* a seat fixed on the back of an elephant or camel.

how do you do *interj* a formal greeting, *esp* when meeting for the first time.

how-do-you-do, how-d'ye-do *n* (*inf*) a difficult situation, mess.

howdy /'haʊdi/ *n* (*inf*) how do you do; hello.

however /haʊˈevər/ *adv* in whatever way or degree; still, nevertheless.

howitzer /'haʊɪtsər/ *n* a short cannon that fires shells at a steep trajectory.

howl /haʊl/ *vi* to utter the long, wailing cry of wolves, dogs, etc; to utter a similar cry of anger, pain, etc; to shout or laugh in pain, amusement, etc. • *vt* to utter with a howl; to drive by howling. • *n* the wailing cry of a wolf, dog, etc; any similar sound.

howler /'haʊlər/ *n* (*inf*) a stupid mistake.

howsoever /ˌhaʊsoʊˈevər/ *conj* still; nevertheless. • *adv* by whatever means; in whatever manner.

hoy /hɔɪ/ *n* a coastal vessel; a freight barge. • *interj* a cry used to call attention.

hoya /'hɔɪə/ *n* a plant with pink, yellow or white flowers.

hoyden /'hɔɪdən/ *n* a tomboy; a wild girl.—**hoydenish** *adj*.

HP *abbr* = hire purchase; horsepower; high pressure; Houses of Parliament.

HQ *abbr* = headquarters.

hr *abbr* = hour.

HRH *abbr* = His or Her Royal Highness.

HT *abbr* = high tension.

HTML /'eɪtʃtiːɛmɛl/ *abbr* = HyperText Markup Language, the basic language in which pages on the Internet are written.

HTTP /'eɪtʃtiːtiːpiː/ *abbr* = HyperText Transport Protocol, the structure used to connect the many servers on the Web.

hub /hʌb/ *n* the centre part of a wheel; a centre of activity.

hubba-hubba /'hʌbəˌhʌbə/ *interj* an exclamation of delight.

hubble-bubble /'hʌbəlˌbʌbəl/ *n* a bubbling noise; confused talk; a hookah.

hubbub /'hʌbʌb/ *n* a confused noise of many voices; an uproar.

hubby /'hʌbi/ *n* (*pl* **hubbies**) (*inf*) a husband.

hubcap /'hʌbkæp/ *n* a metal cap that fits over the hub of a car wheel.

hubris /'hjuːbrɪs/ *n* arrogance, presumption.—**hubristic** *adj*.

huckaback /'hʌkəˌbæk/ *n* an absorbent linen or cotton fabric used for towels, etc.

huckleberry /'hʌkəlberi/ *n* (*pl* **huckleberries**) a North American shrub with dark-blue berries; the fruit of this plant.

huckster /'hʌkstər/ *n* a person using aggressive or questionable methods of selling.—**hucksterism** *n*.

huddle /'hʌdəl/ *vti* to crowd together in a confined space; to curl (oneself) up. • *n* a confused crowd or heap.—**huddler** *n*.

Hudibrastic /ˌhjuːdɪˈbræstɪk/ *adj* mock-heroic, in the style of *Hudibras*, a poem by Samuel Butler (161280).

hue /hjuː/ *n* colour; a particular shade or tint of a colour.

hued /hjuːd/ *adj* having a colour or hue as specified.

huff /hʌf/ *n* a state of smouldering resentment. • *vi* to blow; to puff.

huffish /'hʌfɪʃ/ *adj* prone to fits of anger or petulance.

huffy /'hʌfi/ *adj* (**huffier, huffiest**) disgruntled, moody.—**huffily** *adv*.—**huffiness** *n*.

hug /hʌg/ vb (**hugging, hugged**) vt to hold or squeeze tightly with the arms; to cling to; to keep close to. • vi to embrace one another. • n a strong embrace.—**huggable** adj.—**hugger** n.

huge /hjuːdʒ/ or /juːdʒ/ adj very large, enormous.—**hugely** adv.—**hugeness** n.

huggermugger /ˈhʌgərˌmʌgər/ n secrecy, concealment; confusion. • adj secret, clandestine; confused, jumbled. • adv in confusion. • vt to conceal, to hush up. • vi to muddle.

hula /ˈhuːlə/, **hula-hula** n a Polynesian dance performed by men or women; the music for this.

hulk /hʌlk/ n the body of a ship, esp if old and dismantled; a large, clumsy person or thing.

hulking /ˈhʌlkɪŋ/, **hulky** /-i/ adj unwieldy, bulky.

hull /hʌl/ n the outer covering of a fruit or seed; the framework of a ship. • vt to remove the hulls of; to pierce the hull of (a ship, etc).—**huller** n.—**hull-less** adj.

hullabaloo, hullaballoo /ˌhʌləbəˈluː/ n (pl **hullabaloos, hullaballoos**) a loud commotion, uproar.

hullo /həˈloː/ see **hello**.

hum /hʌm/ vb (**humming, hummed**) vi to make a low continuous vibrating sound; to hesitate in speaking and utter an inarticulate sound; (inf) to be lively, busy; (sl) to stink. • vt to sing with closed lips. • n a humming sound; a murmur; (sl) a stink.

human /ˈhjuːmən/ or /ˈjuː-/ adj of or relating to human beings; having the qualities of humans as opposed to animals; kind, considerate. • n a human being.—**humanness** n.

human being n a member of the races of Homo sapiens; a man, woman or child.

humane /hjuːˈmeɪn/ or /juː-/ adj kind, compassionate, merciful.—**humanely** adv.—**humaneness** n.

human immunodeficiency virus n either of two strains of a virus, also know as HIV, that inhibits the body from developing resistance to diseases and leads to the development of AIDS.

human interest adj (newspaper story, etc) appealing to the emotions.

humanism /ˈhjuːməˌnɪzəm/ or /ˈjuː-/ n belief in the promotion of human interests, intellect and welfare.

humanist /ˈhjuːmənɪst/ or /ˈjuː-/ n one versed in the knowledge of human nature; a student of the humanities.—**humanistic** adj.

humanitarian /hjuːˌmænɪˈterɪən/ or /juː-/ adj concerned with promoting human welfare. • n a humanitarian person.—**humanitarianism** n.—**humanitarianist** n.

humanity /hjuːˈmænɪti/ or /juː-/ n (pl **humanities**) the human race; the state or quality of being human or humane; philanthropy; kindness; (pl) the study of literature and the arts, as opposed to the sciences.

humanize /ˈhjuːməˌnaɪz/ or /ˈjuː-/ vti to make or become human.—**humanization** n.—**humanizer** n.

humankind /ˈhjuːmənˌkaɪnd/ or /ˈjuː-/ n the human species; humanity.

humanly /ˈhjuːmənli/ or /juː-/ adv in a way characteristic of humans; within the limits of human capabilities.

humanoid /ˈhjuːmənɔɪd/ or /ˈjuː-/ adj resembling a human being in appearance or character. • n a humanoid thing.

humble /ˈhʌmbəl/ adj having a low estimation of one's abilities; modest, unpretentious; servile. • vt to lower in condition or rank; to humiliate.—**humbleness** n.—**humbly** adv.

humblebee /ˈhʌmbəlˌbiː/ n another name for the bumblebee.

humble pie n apology, usu under pressure.

humbug /ˈhʌmbʌg/ n fraud, sham, hoax; an insincere person; a peppermint-flavoured sweet. • vt (**humbugging, humbugged**) to cheat or impose upon; to hoax.—**humbugger** n.—**humbuggery** n.

humdinger /ˈhʌmˌdɪŋər/ n (inf) a remarkable person or thing.

humdrum /ˈhʌmdrʌm/ adj dull, ordinary, boring.—**humdrumness** n.

humerus /ˈhjuːmərəs/ n (pl **humeri**) the bone extending from the shoulder to the elbow in humans.—**humeral** adj.

humid /ˈhjuːmɪd/ adj (air) moist, damp.—**humidly** adv.—**humidness** n.

humidifier /hjuːˈmɪdɪˌfaɪr/ n a device employed to increase the amount of water vapour in a room.

humidify /hjuːˈmɪdɪˌfaɪ/ vt (**humidifying, humidified**) to make humid.—**humidification** n.—**humidifier** n.

humidity /hjuːˈmɪdɪti/ n (a measure of the amount of) dampness in the air.

humidor /ˈhjuːmɪˌdɔr/ n a humid cabinet or room where cigars are kept moist.

humiliate /hjuːˈmɪliˌeɪt/ vt to cause to feel humble; to lower the pride or dignity of.—**humiliatingly** adv.—**humiliator** n.—**humiliatory** adj.

humiliation /ˌhjuːmɪliˈeɪʃən/ n the act of humiliation; the state of being humiliated; mortification; abasement.

humility /hjuːˈmɪlɪti/ n (pl **humilities**) the state of being humble; modesty.

hummingbird /ˈhʌmɪŋˌbərd/ n a tiny brightly coloured tropical bird with wings that vibrate rapidly, making a humming sound.

hummock /ˈhʌmək/ n a hillock.—**hummocky** adj.

hummus /ˈhʌməs/ n a dip or appetizer of puréed chick peas, sesame seeds and garlic.—also **houmous, houmus**.

humoresque /ˌhjuːməˈresk/ n a light musical piece.

humorist /ˈhjuːmərɪst/ or /juː-/ n a person who writes or speaks in a humorous manner.—**humoristic** adj.

humorous /ˈhjuːmərəs/ or /juː-/ adj funny, amusing; causing laughter.—**humorously** adv.—**humorousness** n.

humour, humor /ˈhjuːmər/ or /ˈjuːmər/ n the ability to appreciate or express what is funny, amusing, etc; the expression of this; temperament, disposition; state of mind; (formerly) any of the four fluids of the body (blood, phlegm, yellow and black bile) that were thought to determine temperament. • vt to indulge; to gratify by conforming to the wishes of.—**humourful, humorful** adj.

humourless, humorless /-ləs/ adj done or said without humour; lacking a sense of humour.—**humourlessness, humorlessness** n.

humourology, humorology /hjuːməˈrɒlədʒi/ n the study of humour.

hump /hʌmp/ n a rounded protuberance; a fleshy lump on the back of an animal (as a camel or whale); a deformity causing curvature of the spine. • vt to hunch; to arch.

humpback /ˈhʌmpbæk/ n a hunchback.—**humpbacked** adj.

humph /həmf/ interj expressing annoyance.

humus /ˈhjuːməs/ n dark brown or black organic matter in the soil formed from partially decomposed leaves, plants, etc.

Hun /hʌn/ n one of the ancient Tartar races that overran Europe in the 4th and 5th centuries; a vandal; (Hist derog) a German.

hunch /hʌntʃ/ n a hump; (inf) an intuitive feeling. • vt to arch into a hump. • vi to move forward jerkily.

hunchback /ˈhʌntʃbæk/ n a person with curvature of the spine.

hunchbacked /-bækt/ adj having an abnormal convex curvature of the thoracic spine.

hundred /ˈhʌndrəd/ adj, n (pl **hundreds, hundred**) ten times ten; the symbol for this (100, C, c); the hundredth in a series or set.

hundredfold /-ˌfoːld/ adj, adv one hundred times as great or many.

hundredth /ˈhʌndrədθ/ adj the last of a hundred.

hundredweight /ˈhʌndrədˌweɪt/ n (pl **hundredweight, hundredweights**) a unit of weight, equal to 110 pounds in US and 112 pounds in the UK.

hung /hʌŋ/ see **hang**.

Hungarian /hʌŋˈgerɪən/ adj pertaining to Hungary, its inhabitants, or language. • n an inhabitant of Hungary; the language spoken in Hungary.

hunger /ˈhʌŋgər/ n (a feeling of weakness or emptiness from) a need for food; a strong desire. • vi to feel hunger; to have a strong desire (for).

hunger strike n refusal to take food as a protest.

hung-over /hʌŋˈoːvər/ adj (sl) suffering from a hangover.

hungry /ˈhʌŋgri/ adj (**hungrier, hungriest**) desiring food; craving for something; greedy.—**hungrily** adv.—**hungriness** n.

hunk /hʌŋk/ n (inf) a large piece, lump, etc; (sl) a sexually attractive man.—**hunky** adj.

hunker /ˈhʌŋkər/ vi to squat, crouch down. • npl the haunches or buttocks.

hunkydory /ˌhʌŋkiˈdɔri/ adj first-rate.

hunt /hʌnt/ vti to seek out to kill or capture (game) for food or sport; to search (for); to chase. • n a chase; a search; a party organized for hunting.

hunter /ˈhʌntər/ n a person who hunts; a horse used in hunting.—**huntress** nf.

hunting /ˈhʌntɪŋ/ n the art or practice of one who hunts; a pursuit; a search.

huntsman /'hʌntsmən/ *n* (*pl* **huntsmen**) a person who manages a hunt and looks after the hounds.

hurdle /'hɜːdəl/ *n* a portable frame of bars for temporary fences or for jumping over by horses or runners; an obstacle. (*pl*) a race over hurdles.—**hurdler** *n*.

hurdy-gurdy /'hɜːdɪ,gɜːdi/ *n* (*pl* **hurdy-gurdies**) a mechanical instrument such as a barrel organ.

hurl /hɜːl/ *vt* to throw violently; to utter vehemently. • *n* a violent throw; a ride in a car.—**hurler** *n*.

hurling /'hɜːlɪŋ/, **hurley** /'hɜːli/ *n* an Irish form of field hockey.

hurly-burly /'hɜːlɪ,bɜːli/ *n* (*pl* **hurly-burlies**) uproar; confusion.

hurrah /hə'rɑː/ *interj* an exclamation of approval or joy.—*also* **hooray, hoorah**.

hurricane /'hʌrɪ,keɪn/ *n* a violent tropical cyclone with winds of at least 74 miles (119 kilometres) per hour.

hurried /'hʌriːd/ *adj* performed with great haste.—**hurriedly** *adv*.—**hurriedness** *n*.

hurry /'hʌri/ *n* (*pl* **hurries**) rush; urgency; eagerness to do, go, etc. • *vb* (**hurrying, hurried**) *vt* to cause to move or happen more quickly. • *vi* to move or act with haste.—**hurryingly** *adv*.

hurt /hɜːt/ *vb* (**hurting, hurt**) *vt* to cause physical pain to; to injure, damage; to offend. • *vi* to feel pain; to cause pain.—**hurter** *n*.

hurtful /'hɜːtfʊl/ *adj* causing hurt, mischievous.—**hurtfully** *adv*.—**hurtfulness** *n*.

hurtle /'hɜːtəl/ *vti* to move or throw with great speed and force.

husband /'hʌzbənd/ *n* a man to whom a woman is married. • *vt* to conserve; to manage economically.—**husbander** *n*.

husbandman /-mən/ *n* (*pl* **husbandmen**) a farmer.

husbandry /'hʌzbəndri/ *n* management of resources; farming.

hush /hʌʃ/ *vti* to make or become silent. • *n* a silence or calm.

hush-hush /hʌʃ'hʌʃ/ *adj* (*inf*) secret.

hush money *n* (*sl*) money paid to a person to keep a discreditable fact secret.

husk /hʌsk/ *n* the dry covering of certain fruits and seeds; any dry, rough, or useless covering. • *vt* to strip the husk from.—**husker** *n*.

husky[1] /'hʌski/ *adj* (**huskier, huskiest**) (*voice*) hoarse; rough-sounding; hefty, strong.—**huskily** *adv*.—**huskiness** *n*.

husky[2] *n* (*pl* **huskies**) an Arctic sled dog.

hussar /hʊ'zɑː/ *n* a member of any of various European light cavalry regiments, *usu* with an elegant dress uniform.

hussy /'hʌsi/ *n* (*pl* **hussies**) a cheeky woman; a promiscuous woman.

hustings /'hʌstɪŋz/ *n* (*pl or sing*) the process of, or a place for, political campaigning.

hustle /'hʌsəl/ *vt* to jostle or push roughly or hurriedly; to force hurriedly; (*sl*) to obtain by rough or illegal means. • *vi* to move hurriedly. • *n* an instance of hustling.—**hustler** *n*.

hut /hʌt/ *n* a very plain or crude little house or cabin.

hutch /hʌtʃ/ *n* a pen or coop for small animals; a hut.

huzzah /'hʌzə/ *interj* (*formerly*) hurrah.

hyacinth /'haɪəsɪnθ/ *n* a plant of the lily family with spikes of bell-shaped flowers; the orange gemstone jacinth; a light violet to moderate purple.—**hyacinthine** *adj*.

Hyades /'haɪə,diːz/ *n* (*Greek myth*) five nymphs, the daughters of Atlas; the five stars in the constellation Taurus.

hyaline /'haɪəlɪn/ or /-,laɪn/, /-,liːn/ *adj* glassy; transparent.

hybrid /'haɪbrɪd/ *n* the offspring of two plants or animals of different species; a mongrel. • *adj* crossbred.—**hybridism** *n*.—**hybridity** *n*.

hybridize /'haɪbrɪ,daɪz/ *vti* to produce hybrids; to interbreed.—**hybridizable** *adj*.—**hybridization** *n*.—**hybridizer** *n*.

hydatid /'haɪdətɪd/ *n* a watery cyst in animal tissue; a large bladder containing the larvae of the tapeworm.—*also adj*.

hydr- /haɪdr/, **hydro-** /haɪdrəʊ/ *prefix* water, fluids.

hydra /'haɪdrə/ *n* (*pl* **hydras, hydrae**) (*usu with cap*) a legendary many-headed water serpent; any of numerous freshwater polyps having a mouth surrounded by tentacles.

hydrangea /haɪ'dreɪndʒə/ or /-dʒiə/ *n* a shrub with large heads of white, pink, or blue flowers.

hydrant /'haɪdrənt/ *n* a large pipe with a valve for drawing water from a water main; a fireplug.

hydrate /'haɪdreɪt/ *n* a chemical compound of water with some other substance. • *vt* to (cause to) combine with or absorb water.—**hydration** *n*.—**hydrator** *n*.

hydraulic /haɪ'drɒlɪk/ *adj* operated by water or other liquid, *esp* by moving through pipes under pressure; of hydraulics.—**hydraulically** *adv*.

hydraulics /haɪ'drɒlɪks/ *n sing* the science dealing with the mechanical properties of liquids, as water, and their application in engineering.

hydric /'haɪdrɪk/ *adj* of or containing hydrogen; of or containing water.

hydride /'haɪdraɪd/ *n* any compound of hydrogen and another element.

hydriodic /,haɪdrɪ'ɒdɪk/ or /-draɪ-/ *adj* composed of hydrogen and iodine.

hydro[1] /'haɪdrəʊ/ *n* (*pl* **hydros**) a hotel or resort offering hydropathic treatment.

hydro[2] *adj* short for hydroelectric.

hydro- *prefix* indicating or denoting water, liquid or fluid; indicating the presence of hydrogen in a chemical compound; indicating a hydroid.

hydrocarbon /,haɪdrə'kɑːbən/ *n* any organic compound containing only hydrogen and carbon.

hydrocele /'haɪdrə,siːl/ *n* an accumulation of fluid in a body cavity, *esp* in the scrotum.

hydrocephalus /,haɪdrə'sefələs/, **hydrocephaly** /-i/ *n* an accumulation of fluid in the brain.—**hydrocephalic** *adj*.

hydrochloric acid *n* a strong, highly corrosive acid that is a solution of the gas hydrogen chloride in water.

hydrochloric /,haɪdrə'klɒrɪk/ *adj* composed of hydrogen and chlorine.

hydrocyanic /,haɪdrəsaɪ'ænɪk/ *adj* composed of hydrogen and cyanic.

hydrodynamics /,haɪdrəʊdaɪ'næmɪks/ *n sing* the science of the mechanical properties of fluids.—**hydrodynamic** *adj*.—**hydrodynamically** *adv*.

hydroelectricity /,haɪdrəʊɪlek'trɪsɪti/ *n* electricity generated by water power.—**hydroelectric** *adj*.

hydrofluoric /,haɪdrəʊ'flʊrɪk/ *adj* composed of hydrogen and fluorine.

hydrofoil /'haɪdrə,fɔɪl/ *n* a vessel equipped with vanes that lift the hull out of the water to allow fast cruising speeds.

hydrogen /'haɪdrədʒən/ *n* a flammable, colourless, odourless, tasteless, gaseous chemical element, the lightest substance known.

hydrogenate /haɪ'drɒdʒɪ,neɪt/ or /'haɪdrədʒə,neɪt/ *vt* to combine with or treat with hydrogen.—**hydrogenation** *n*.—**hydrogenator** *n*.

hydrogen bomb *n* a powerful bomb that produces explosive energy through the fusion of hydrogen nuclei.

hydrography /haɪ'drɒgrəfi/ *n* the study, surveying and mapping of the oceans, seas, lakes, and rivers as on a chart.—**hydrographer** *n*.—**hydrographic, hydrographical** *adj*.

hydrokinetics /,haɪdrəʊkɪ'netɪks/ *n sing* the branch of physics concerned with the study of fluids in motion.

hydrology /haɪ'drɒlədʒi/ *n* the science of the properties of water and its distribution on the earth and in the atmosphere.—**hydrologic, hydrological** *adj*.—**hydrologist** *n*.

hydrolysis /haɪ'drɒlɪsɪs/ *n* the chemical breakdown of organic compounds by interaction with water.

hydrolyze /'haɪdrə,laɪz/ *vti* to decompose by hydrolysis.—**hydrolyzation** *n*.—**hydrolyzer** *n*.

hydromechanics /,haɪdrəʊmɪ'kænɪks/ *n sing* the science of the use of fluids as motive- power also called hydrodynamics.

hydromel /'haɪdrə,mel/ *n* a mixture of honey and water that is fermented to make mead.

hydrometer /haɪ'drɒmɪtər/ *n* a device for measuring the densities of liquids.—**hydrometric, hydrometrical** *adj*.—**hydrometry** *n*.

hydropathy /haɪ'drɒpəθi/ *n* the use of water to treat diseases.—**hydropathic, hydropathical** *adj*.—**hydropathist, hydropath** *n*.

hydrophane /'haɪdrə,feɪn/ *n* a partially opaque, white type of opal that becomes translucent in water.

hydrophobia /,haɪdrə'fəʊbiə/ *n* a morbid fear of water; rabies.—**hydrophobic** *adj*.

hydrophone /'haɪdrə,fəʊn/ *n* an instrument that detects sound through water.

hydrophyte /'haɪdrə,faɪt/ *n* a plant that will grow only in water or sodden soil.—**hydrophitic** *adj*.

hydroplane /'haɪdrə,pleɪn/ *n* a light motor boat that skims through the water at high speed with its hull raised out of the water; a fin that directs the vertical movement of a submarine;

an attachment to an aircraft that enables it to glide along the surface of water. • *vi* (of a boat) to rise out of the water in the manner of a hydroplane.

hydroponics /ˌhaɪdrə'pɒnɪks/ *n sing* a way of growing of plants in gravel, etc, through which water containing dissolved inorganic nutrient salts is passed.—**hydroponically** *adv*.

hydroscope /'haɪdrə,skoːp/ *n* any instrument that makes observations of underwater objects.

hydrosphere /'haɪdrə,sfiːr/ *n* the moisture-bearing envelope that surrounds the earth.

hydrostatics /ˌhaɪdrə'stætɪks/ *n sing* the branch of physics concerned with the study of fluids at rest.—**hydrostatic** *adj*.

hydrotherapy /ˌhaɪdrə'θɛrəpi/ *n* (*pl* **hydrotherapies**) the treatment of certain diseases and physical conditions by the external application of water.—**hydrotherapist** *n*.

hydrous /'haɪdrəs/ *adj* containing water.

hyena /haɪ'iːnə/ *n* a nocturnal, carnivorous, scavenging mammal like a wolf.—*also* **hyaena**.

Hygeia /haɪ'dʒiːə/ *n* (*Greek myth*) the goddess of health.

hygiene /'haɪdʒiːn/ *n* the principles and practice of health and cleanliness.—**hygienic** *adj*.—**hygienically** *adv*.

hygienist /haɪ'dʒɛnɪst/ or /haɪ'dʒiːnɪst/ *n* a person skilled in the practice of hygiene.

hygrometer /haɪ'grɒmɪtər/ *n* an instrument for measuring the humidity of the atmosphere.—**hygrometric** *adj*.—**hygrometrically** *adv*.—**hygrometry** *n*.

hygroscope /'haɪgrə,skoːp/ *n* an instrument that shows changes in the humidity of the atmosphere.

hygroscopic /ˌhaɪgrə'skɒpɪk/ *adj* readily absorbing and retaining moisture from the air.—**hygroscopically** *adv*.

hylozoism /ˌhaɪlə'zoːɪzəm/ *n* (*philos*) the doctrine that life is a property of matter; materialism.—**hylozoic** *adj*.—**hylozoist** *n*.

Hymen /'haɪmɛn/ *n* (*Greek myth*) the god of marriage.

hymen *n* the mucous membrane partly closing the vaginal orifice.—**hymenal** *adj*.

hymeneal /ˌhaɪmɪ'niːəl/ *adj* of marriage, nuptial.

hymenopteran /ˌhaɪmə'nɒptərən/ *n* (*pl* **hymenopterans, hymenopterana**) any of a large order of insects that have two pairs of membranous wings.—**hymenopterous** *adj*.

hymn /hɪm/ *n* a song of praise to God or other object of worship.

hymnal /'hɪmnəl/ *n* a hymn book.

hymn book *n* a book of hymns.

hymnology /hɪm'nɒlədʒi/ *n* the study of the composition of hymns.—**hymnologist** *n*.

hyoid /'haɪɔɪd/ *adj* U-shaped; of or relating to the hyoid bone at the base of the tongue.

hyoscine /'haɪə,siːn/ *see* **scopolamine**.

hyp- /hɪp/ or /haɪp/ **hypo-** *prefix* below; slightly.

hype[1] /haɪp/ *n* (*sl*) a hypodermic needle. • *vi* (*sl*) to inject a narcotic drug with a needle.

hype[2] *n* (*sl*) deception; aggressive or extravagant publicity. • *vt* to publicize or promote a product, etc in this manner.

hyped-up *adj* aggressively publicized; (*sl*) stimulated as if by injection of a drug.

hyper- /'haɪpər/ *prefix* above; too; exceeding.

hyperactive /ˌhaɪpər'æktɪv/ *adj* abnormally active.—**hyperactivity** *n*.

hyperesthesia, hyperaesthesia /ˌhaɪpərəs'θiːzɪə/ *n* increased sensitivity of any of the sense organs.—**hyperaesthetic** *adj*.

hyperbola /haɪ'pərbələ/ *n* (*pl* **hyperbolas, hyperbolae**) (*geom*) a curve formed by a plane intersecting a cone at a greater angle to its base than its side.

hyperbole /haɪ'pərbəli/ *n* a figure of speech using absurd exaggeration.

hyperbolic /ˌhaɪpər'bɒlɪk/, **hyperbolical** /-əl/ *adj* pertaining to or containing hyperbole, exaggerated; pertaining to or of the nature of a hyperbola.

hyperborean /ˌhaɪpərbɔ'riːən/ *adj* of or relating to the extreme north. • *n* an inhabitant of the extreme north; (*Greek myth*) (*with cap*) one of the people who lived in the sunny land beyond the north wind.

hypercritical /ˌhaɪpər'krɪtɪkəl/ *adj* excessively critical.—**hypercritically** *adv*.—**hypercriticism** *n*.

hypermetric /ˌhaɪpər'mɛtrɪk/ *adj* beyond the normal metre of a line; having one syllable too many.

hypersensitive /ˌhaɪpər'sɛnsɪtɪv/ *adj* extremely vulnerable; abnormally sensitive to a drug, pollen, etc.—**hypersensitivity** *n*.

hypersonic /ˌhaɪpər'sɒnɪk/ *adj* travelling at speeds at least five times faster than sound; of sound frequencies above 1,000 megahertz.—**hypersonics** *n*.

hypertension /ˌhaɪpər'tɛnʃən/ *n* abnormally high blood pressure.—**hypertensive** *adj*.

hypertext /'haɪpərtɛkst/ *n* computer software/hardware that allows the user to pick up on one word in a document as a route to another area of the document or a different document.

hyperthyroidism /ˌhaɪpər'θaɪrɔɪˌdɪzəm/ *n* the overproduction of the thyroid hormone by the thyroid gland.—**hyperthyroid** *adj, n*.

hypertrophy /haɪ'pərtrəfi/ *n* (*pl* **hypertrophies**) abnormal enlargement of an organ or part.—**hypertrophic** *adj*.

hypervitaminosis /ˌhaɪpər,vaɪtəmɪ'noːsɪs/ *n* the pathological condition that results from the excessive intake of vitamins.

hyphen /'haɪfən/ *n* a punctuation mark (-) used to join two syllables or words, or to divide words into parts. • *vt* to hyphenate.

hyphenate /'haɪfə,neɪt/ *vt* to join words by a hyphen.—**hyphenation** *n*.

hypnosis /hɪp'noːsɪs/ *n* (*pl* **hypnoses**) a relaxed state resembling sleep in which the mind responds to external suggestion.

hypnotherapy /ˌhɪpno:'θɛrəpi/ *n* the use of hypnosis in treatment of emotional and psychological disorders.

hypnotic /hɪp'nɒtɪk/ *adj* of or producing hypnosis; (*person*) susceptible to hypnosis. • *n* a drug causing sleep; a person susceptible to hypnosis.—**hypnotically** *adv*.

hypnotism /'hɪpnə,tɪzəm/ *n* the act of inducing hypnosis; the study and use of hypnosis.—**hypnotist** *n*.

hypnotize /'hɪpnə,taɪz/ *vt* to put in a state of hypnosis; to fascinate.—**hypnotizer** *n*.

hypo- /'haɪpo/ *prefix* below; slightly.

hypocaust /'haɪpə,kɒst/ *n* the hot-air chamber under a Roman bath.

hypochondria /ˌhaɪpə'kɒndriə/ *n* chronic anxiety about health, often with imaginary illnesses.

hypochondriac /ˌhaɪpə'kɒndrɪˌæk/ *n* a person suffering from hypochondria. • *adj* pertaining to or affected with hypochondria.—**hypochondriacally** *adv*.

hypocorism /haɪ'pɒkə,rɪzəm/ *n* a diminutive pet name; a euphemism.—**hypocoristic, hypocoristical** *adj*.

hypocrisy /hɪ'pɒkrəsi/ *n* (*pl* **hypocrisies**) a falsely pretending to possess virtues, beliefs, etc; an example of this.—**hypocritical** *adj*.—**hypocritically** *adv*.

hypocrite /'hɪpəkrɪt/ *n* a person who pretends to be what he or she is not.

hypocycloid /ˌhaɪpə'saɪklɔɪd/ *n* (*geom*) a curve traced by the point on the circumference of a circle, which rolls on to the inside of another circle.

hypodermic /ˌhaɪpə'dɜrmɪk/ *adj* injected under the skin. • *n* a hypodermic needle, syringe or injection.

hypodermic syringe *n* a syringe with a hollow (hypodermic) needle through which blood samples can be drawn.

hypogastrium /ˌhaɪpə'gæstrɪəm/ *n* (*pl* **hypogastria**) the middle part of the lower region of the abdomen.

hypogeal /ˌhaɪpə'dʒiːəl/, **hypogean** /-ən/, **hypogeous** /-əs/ *adj* (*bot*) underground; occuring or living underground.

hypogene /'haɪpə,dʒiːn/ *adj* (*rocks*) formed under the surface of the ground.

hypostasis /haɪ'pɒstəsɪs/ *n* (*pl* **hypostates**) the essential personality of a substance; (*Christianity*) any of the three persons of the Godhead which together make up the Holy Trinity; (*med*) an excess of blood in the organs as the result of poor circulation.—**hypostatic** *adj*.

hypostatize /haɪ'pɒstətaɪz/ *vt* to regard as real; to embody or personify.—**hypostatization** *n*.

hypostyle /'haɪpə,staɪl/ *n* a roof supported by columns; a covered colonnade; a pillared hall or court.

hypotenuse /haɪ'pɒtə,nuːs/ or /-,njuːz/, /-,nuːz/ *n* the side opposite to the right angle in a right-angled triangle.

hypothecate /haɪ'pɒθɪ,keɪt/ or /hɪ-/ *vt* to pledge (a property) without delivery of title or possession.—**hypothecation** *n*.—**hypothecator** *n*.

hypothermia /ˌhaɪpo:'θɜrmɪə/ *n* an abnormally low body temperature.

hypothesis /haɪˈpɒθɪsɪs/ *n* (*pl* **hypotheses**) something assumed for the purpose of argument; a theory to explain some fact that may or may not prove to be true; supposition; conjecture.

hypothesize /haɪˈpɒθɪˌsaɪz/ *vti* to form or assume as a hypothesis.

hypothetical /ˌhəɪpəˈθetɪkəl/ *adj* based on hypothesis, conjectural.—**hypothetically** *adv*.

hypothyroidism /ˌhəɪpoːˈθaɪrɔɪˌdɪzəm/ *n* deficient activity of the thyroid glands.

hypsometry /hɪpˈsɒmətri/ *n* the science of measuring altitude.—**hypsometric** *adj*

hyrax /ˈhaɪræks/ *n* (*pl* **hyraxes, hyraces**) a small African hamster-like mammal related to the elephant.

hyson /ˈhaɪsən/ *n* Chinese green tea.

hyssop /ˈhɪsəp/ *n* an aromatic plant with blue flowers formerly used in medicine.

hysterectomy /ˌhɪstəˈrektəmi/ *n* (*pl* **hysterectomies**) surgical removal of the womb.

hysteresis /ˌhɪstəˈriːsɪs/ *n*. (*pl* **hystereses**) magnetic inertia.—**hysteretic** *adj*.

hysteria /hɪˈstɪəriə/ or /-ˈstiːriə/ *n* a mental disorder marked by excitability, anxiety, imaginary organic disorders, etc; frenzied emotion or excitement.

hysteric /hɪˈsterɪk/ *n* a hysterical person; (*pl*) fits of hysteria; (*inf*) uncontrollable laughter.

hysterical /hɪˈsterɪkəl/ *adj* caused by hysteria; suffering from hysteria; (*inf*) extremely funny.—**hysterically** *adv*.

hysterotomy /ˌhɪstərˈɒtəmi/ *n* (*pl* **hysterotomies**) a surgical incision into the womb.

Hz *abbr* = hertz.

I

I¹ /aɪ/ *pron* the person who is speaking or writing, used in referring to himself or herself.

I² (*chem symbol*) iodine.

I. *abbr* = island(s); isle(s).

IAEA *abbr* = International Atomic Energy Authority.

iamb /ˈaɪæmb/, **iambus** /aɪˈæmbəs/ *n* (*pl* **iambi, iambs, iambuses**) a metrical foot consisting of two syllables, the first short or unstressed and the second long or stressed.—**iambic** *adj*.

-iana, -ana *n suffix* sayings of, publications about, as *Shakespeariana*, etc.

-iatric, -iatrical *adj* pertaining to doctors and medicine.

Iberian /aɪˈbiːriən/ *adj* pertaining to Spain and Portugal; pertaining to Iberia, the ancient name of the southwest European peninsula now comprising Spain and Portugal.

ibex /ˈaɪbeks/ *n* (*pl* **ibexes, ibices, ibex**) any of various wild mountain goats with large horns.

ibid *abbr* = *ibidem*, in, in the same book, page, etc.

ibis /ˈaɪbɪs/ *n* (*pl* **ibises, ibis**) a wading bird with a curved bill.

Ibo /ˈiːboː/ *n* (*pl* **Ibo, Ibos**) a member of a Black people of southern Nigeria; their language.

ICBM *abbr* = intercontinental ballistic missile.

ice /aɪs/ *n* water frozen solid; a sheet of this; a portion of ice cream or water ice. • *vti* (*often with* **up** *or* **over**) to freeze; to cool with ice; to cover with icing.

ice age *n* a period when much of the earth's surface was covered in glaciers; (*with caps*) the Pleistocene glacial epoch.

iceberg /ˈaɪsbɜrg/ *n* a great mass of mostly submerged ice floating in the sea.

iceblink /ˈaɪsblɪŋk/ *n* a streak of whiteness on the horizon, caused by the reflection of light from masses of ice in the distance.

icebound /ˈaɪsbaund/ *adj* (*ship, etc*) surrounded, and immobilized, by ice.

icebox /ˈaɪsbɒks/ *n* a compartment in a refrigerator for making ice.

icebreaker, iceboat /ˈaɪsboːt/ *n* a powerful and reinforced vessel for breaking a channel through ice.

icecap *n* a mass of slowly spreading glacial ice.

ice cream *adj* a sweet frozen food, made from flavoured milk or cream.

ice dance *n* a type of ballroom dancing by skaters on ice.

icefall /ˈaɪsfɒl/ *n* a steep part of a glacier, resembling a frozen waterfall.

ice field /ˈaɪsfiːld/ *n* an extensive field of floating ice.

ice floe *n* a sheet of floating ice.

ice hockey *n* an indoor or outdoor hockey game played on ice by two teams of six skaters with curved sticks and a flat disk called a puck.

Icelander /ˈaɪslændər/ *n* a native or inhabitant of Iceland.

Icelandic /aɪsˈlændɪk/ *adj* of or pertaining to Iceland or its language, literature and people. • *n* the language of Iceland.

ice pack *n* a field of broken and drifting ice, consisting of great masses packed together; a cloth or small bag filled with crushed ice for soothing sores and swellings on the body.

ice pick *n* a pointed awl with a handle for chipping or breaking up ice.

ice plant *n* a type of plant with leaves that glisten as if covered with ice.

ice skate *n* a boot with a steel blade fixed to the sole for skating on ice.—*also vi*.—**ice skater** *n*.

ichneumon /ɪkˈnjuːmən/ *n* a North African mongoose.

ichneumon fly *n* an insect that lays its eggs in the bodies of other insects.

ichnite /ˈɪknaɪt/, **ichnolite** /-nəlaɪt/ *n* a fossil footprint.

Ichor /ˈaɪkɔr/ *n* (*Greek myth*) the ethereal fluid believed to run, instead of blood, in the veins of the classical gods.—**ichorous** *adj*.

ichthy- /ˈɪkθini/, **icthyo-** /ˈɪkθioː/ *prefix* fish.

ichthyic /ˈɪkθɪk/ *adj* pertaining to fishes.

ichthyoid /ˈɪkθɔɪd/, **ichthyoidal** /-əl/ *adj* resembling a fish.

ichthyology /ˌɪkθiˈɒlədʒi/ *n* the study of fish.—**ichthyologic, ichthyological** *adj*.—**ichthyologist** *n*.

ichthyophagous /ɪkθiˈɒfəgəs/ *adj* fish-eating.—**ichthyophagy** *n*.

ichthyornis /ˌɪkθiˈɔrnɪs/ *n* an extinct species of toothed fish-eating bird.

ichthyosaur /ˈɪkθiəˌsɔr/ **ichthyosaurus** /-rəs/ *n* (*pl* **ichthyosaurs, ichthosauri**) a gigantic, extinct, marine reptile.

ichthyosis /ˌɪkθiˈoːsɪs/ *n* a disease in which the skin becomes dry and scaly.

icicle /ˈaɪsɪkəl/ *n* a hanging tapering length of ice formed when dripping water freezes.—**icicled** *adj*.

icily /ˈaɪsɪli/ *adv* in an icy manner, coldly.

iciness /-nəs/ *n* the state of being icy, coldness.

icing /ˈaɪsɪŋ/ *n* a semi-solid sugary mixture used to cover cakes, etc.—*also* **frosting**.

icon /ˈaɪkɒn/ *n* an image; (*Eastern Church*) a sacred image, *usu* on a wooden panel; a symbol on a computer screen that represents something or some process or function in the computer.—*also* **ikon**.—**iconic, iconical** *adj*.

iconoclast /aɪˈkɒnəˌklæst/ *n* a person who attacks revered or traditional beliefs, opinions, etc.—**iconoclasm** *n*.—**iconoclastic** *adj*.—**iconoclastically** *adv*.

iconography /ˌaɪkəˈnɒgrəfi/ *n* (*pl* **iconographies**) the art of representation by means of images (statues), pictures, or engravings; the study of this art.—**iconographer** *n*.—**iconographic, iconographical** *adj*.

iconolatry /ˌaɪkəˈnɒlətri/ *n* the worship of images.

iconology /ˌaɪkəˈnɒlədʒi/ *n* the study of icons.

icosahedron /ˌaɪkəsəˈhiːdrən/ *n* (*pl* **icosahedrons, icosahedra**) (*geom*) a solid bounded by 20 plane faces.

icterus /ˈɪktərəs/ *n* jaundice.—**icteric** *adj*.

ictus /ˈɪktəs/ *n* (*pl* **ictuses, ictus**) a stress in verse.

icy /ˈaɪsi/ *adj* (**icier, iciest**) full of, made of, or covered with ice; slippery or very cold; cold in manner.

ID *abbr* = identification.

ID card *n* an identity card.

I'd /aɪd/ = I had; I should; I would.

id /ɪd/ *n* (*psychoanal*) the primitive psychological instincts in the unconscious which are the source of psychic activity.

ide /aɪd/ *n* a small European fish.

idea /aɪˈdiːə/ *n* a mental impression of anything; a vague impression, notion; an opinion or belief; a scheme; a supposition; a person's conception of something; a significance or purpose.

ideal /aɪˈdiːəl/ *or* /-diːl/ *adj* existing in the mind or as an idea; satisfying an ideal, perfect. • *n* the most perfect conception of anything; a person or thing regarded as perfect; a standard for attainment or imitation; an aim or principle.—**ideally** *adv*.—**idealness** *n*.

idealism /aɪˈdiːəˌlɪzəm/ *n* the pursuit of high ideals; the conception or representation of things in their ideal form as against their reality.—**idealist** *n*.—**idealistic** *adj*.—**idealistically** *adv*.

ideality /ˌaɪdiˈæliti/ *n* (*pl* **idealities**) the quality of being ideal; the faculty to form ideals.

idealize /aɪˈdiːəˌlaɪz/ *vt* to consider or represent as ideal.—**idealization** *n*.—**idealizer** *n*.

ideate /ˈaɪdiˌeɪt/ *vti* to imagine.

idée fixe /ˌiːdeɪˈfiːks/ *n* (*pl* **idées fixes**) a fixed idea; an obsession.

identical /aɪˈdentɪkəl/ *adj* exactly the same; having the same origin.—**identically** *adv*.—**identicalness** *n*.

identifiable /aɪˈdentɪˌfaɪəbəl/ *adj* able to be identified.—**identifiableness** *n*.

identification /aɪˌdentɪfɪˈkeɪʃən/ *n* the act of identifying; the state of being identified; that which identifies.

identify /aɪˈdentɪˌfaɪ/ *vt* (**identifying, identified**) to consider to be the same, equate; to establish the identity of; to associate closely; to regard (oneself) as similar to another.—**identifier** *n*.

identity /aɪˈdɛntɪti/ n (pl **identities**) the state of being exactly alike; the distinguishing characteristics of a person, personality; the state of being the same as a specified person or thing.

identity card n a card carrying personal details, a photograph, etc of an individual as carried by staff of an organization, journalists, etc.

ideogram, ideograph /ˈɪdɪəˌgræm/ or /ˈɪdɪəˌgræf/ n a symbol, as in Chinese writing, used instead of a word to represent an idea or thing; a graphic sign.

ideography /ˌɪdiˈɒgræfi/ n the direct representation of ideas by symbols.—**ideographic, ideographical** adj.

ideologist /ˌaɪdiˈɒlədʒɪst/, **ideologue** /ˈaɪdɪəˌlɒg/ or /ˈɪd-/, /-ˈdiː-/ n one occupied with ideals or ideals; a theorist.

ideology /ˌaɪdiˈɒlədʒi/ or /ˌɪd-/ n (pl **ideologies**) the doctrines, beliefs or opinions of an individual, social class, political party, etc.—**ideological, ideologic** adj.

ides /aɪdz/ n the 15th day of March, May, July, or October and the 13th day of any other month in the ancient Roman calender.

idiocy /ˈɪdiəsi/ n (pl **idiocies**) mental deficiency; stupidity, imbecility; something stupid or foolish.

idiom /ˈɪdiəm/ n an accepted phrase or expression with a different meaning from the literal; the usual way in which the words of a language are used to express thought; the dialect of a people, region, etc; the characteristic style of a school of art, literature, etc.—**idiomatic, idiomatical** adj.—**idiomatically** adv.

idiopathy /ˌɪdiˈɒpəθi/ n a disease whose cause is unknown.—**idiopathic** adj.

idiosyncrasy /ˌɪdioˈsɪŋkrəsi/ n (pl **idiosyncrasies**) a type of behaviour or characteristic peculiar to a person or group; a quirk, eccentricity.—**idiosyncratic** adj.—**idiosyncratically** adv.

idiot /ˈɪdiət/ n a severely mentally retarded adult; (inf) a foolish or stupid person.

idiot board n an autocue.

idiotic /-ˈɒtɪk/ adj stupid; senseless.—**idiotically** adv.

idle /ˈaɪdəl/ adj not employed, unoccupied; not in use; averse to work; useless; worthless. • vt to waste or spend (time) in idleness. • vi to move slowly or aimlessly; (engine) to operate without transmitting power.—**idleness** n.—**idler** n.—**idly** adv.

idler /ˈaɪdlər/ n someone who idles; a lazy person.

idol /ˈaɪdəl/ n an image or object worshipped as a god; a person who is intensely loved, admired or honoured.

idolatry /aɪˈdɒlətri/ n the worship of idols; excessive admiration or devotion.—**idolatrous** adj.—**idolater** n.

idolize /ˈaɪdəˌlaɪz/ vt to make an idol of, for worship; to love to excess.—**idolization** n.—**idolizer** n.

idyll, idyl /ˈɪdɪl/ n a short simple poem, usu evoking the romance and beauty of rural life; a romantic or picturesque event or scene; a romantic or pastoral musical composition.—**idyllist** n.

idyllic /ɪˈdɪlɪk/ adj pertaining to or of the nature of an idyll, pastoral; romantic, picturesque.—**idyllically** adv.

i.e. abbr = id est, that is.

if /ɪf/ conj on condition that; in the event that; supposing that; even though; whenever; whether.

iffy /ˈɪfi/ adj (inf) uncertain, unreliable.

igloo /ˈɪgluː/ n (pl **igloos**) an Eskimo house built of blocks of snow and ice.

igneous /ˈɪgniəs/ adj of fire; (rocks) produced by volcanic action or intense heat beneath the earth's surface.

ignite /ɪgˈnaɪt/ vti to set fire to; to catch fire; to burn or cause to burn.—**ignitable** adj.

ignition /ɪgˈnɪʃən/ n an act or instance of igniting; the starting of an internal combustion engine; the mechanism that ignites an internal combustion engine.

ignoble /ɪgˈnoːbəl/ adj dishonourable, despicable; base, of low birth.—**ignobly** adv.

ignominious /ˌɪgnəˈmɪniəs/ adj bringing disgrace or shame; humiliating, degrading.—**ignominiously** adv.

ignominy /ɪgˌnɒmɪni/ or /-məni/ n (pl **ignominies**) disgrace, dishonour; a cause of ignominy, a disgraceful act.

ignoramus /ˌɪgnəˈreɪməs/ or /-ˈræməs/ n (pl **ignoramuses**) an ignorant person.

ignorance /ˈɪgnərəns/ n the state of being ignorant; a lack of knowledge.

ignorant /ˈɪgnərənt/ adj lacking knowledge; uninformed, uneducated; resulting from or showing lack of knowledge.—**ignorance** n.—**ignorantly** adv.

ignore /ɪgˈnɔr/ vt to disregard; to deliberately refuse to notice someone.—**ignorable** adj.—**ignorer** n.

iguana /ɪgˈwɒnə/ n any of a family of large lizards of tropical America.—**iguanian** adj, n.

iguanodon /ɪˈgwɒnəˌdɒn/ n a gigantic, extinct, herbivorous lizard.

ihram /ɪˈræm/ or /-ˈrɒm/ n the distinctive white robes worn by Muslims on pilgrimage to Mecca.

ikebana /ˌɪkəˈbænə/ n the Japanese art of flower arranging.

ikon see **icon**.

ileac /ˈɪliːækl/, **ileal** /-æl/ adj (anat) pertaining to the ileum.

ileum /ˈɪliəm/ n (anat) the lower part of the small intestine.

ilk /ɪlk/ n a type or sort.

ill /ɪl/ adj (**worse, worst**) not in good health; harmful; bad; hostile; faulty; unfavourable. • adv badly, wrongly; hardly, with difficulty. • n trouble; harm; evil.

ill. abbr = illustrated; illustration.

I'll /aɪl/ = I shall; I will.

ill-advised adj unwise.

ill at ease adj uneasy, embarrassed.

ill-bred adj bad-mannered.—**ill-breeding** n.

ill-considered adj lacking consideration; not thought out properly.

ill-disposed adj unfavourably inclined (towards).

illegal /ɪˈliːgəl/ adj against the law.—**illegally** adv.—**illegality** n.

illegible /ɪˈlɛdʒɪbəl/ adj impossible to read.—**illegibility, illegibleness** n.—**illegibly** adv.

illegitimate /ˌɪləˈdʒɪtəmət/ adj born of parents not married to each other; contrary to law, rules, or logic.—**illegitimacy, illegitimateness** n.—**illegitimately** adv.

ill-fated adj unlucky.

ill-favoured, ill-favored adj unattractive; unpleasant.

ill-founded adj not based on reliable facts; unsubstantiated.

ill-gotten adj illegally or dishonestly acquired.

ill-humoured, ill-humored adj bad tempered; sullen.—**ill-humour, ill-humor** n.

illiberal /ɪˈlɪbərəl/ adj narrow-minded; mean.—**illiberality, illiberalness** n.—**illiberally** adv.

illicit /ɪˈlɪsɪt/ adj improper; unlawful.—**illicitly** adv.

illimitable /ɪˈlɪmɪtəbəl/ adj limitless, infinite.—**illimitability** n.

illiterate /ɪˈlɪtərət/ adj uneducated, esp not knowing how to read or write. • n an illiterate person.—**illiteracy** n.—**illiterately** adv.

ill-mannered adj rude.

ill-natured adj spiteful.

illness /ˈɪlnəs/ n a state of ill-health; sickness.

illogical /ɪˈlɒdʒɪkəl/ adj not logical or reasonable.—**illogicality, illogicalness** n.—**illogically** adv.

ill-starred adj unlucky.

ill-timed adj occurring or done at an unsuitable time.

ill-treat vt to treat unkindly, unfairly, etc.—**ill-treatment** n.

illume /ɪˈluːm/ vt (poet) to light up, illuminate.

illuminant /ɪˈluːmɪnənt/ n a substance or device that illuminates.

illuminate /ɪˈluːmɪˌneɪt/ vt to give light to; to light up; to make clear; to inform; to decorate as with gold or lights.—**illumination** n.—**illuminative** adj.—**illuminator** n.

illuminati /ɪˌluːmɪˈnæti/ or /-ˈnɒti/ npl (sing **illuminato**) a name given to persons professing special spiritual or intellectual enlightenment.

illumination /ɪˌluːmɪˈneɪʃən/ n a supply of light; the act of illuminating; the state of being illuminated; (Brit, esp pl) decorative coloured lights used in public places.

illumine /ɪˈluːmɪn/ vt (poet) to illuminate.

illuminism /-ɪzəm/ n the belief in and profession of special spiritual and intellectual enlightenment.

ill-usage n ill-use, abuse.

ill-use vt to treat badly, etc. • n abuse.

illusion /ɪˈluːʒən/ n a false idea or conception; an unreal or misleading image or appearance.—**illusional, illusionary** adj.

illusionism /-ˌnɪzəm/ n (philos) a disbelief in objective existence.

illusionist /ɪˈluːʒənɪst/ n a magician or conjuror.—**illusionism** n.

illusory /ɪˈluːsəri/ or /-zəri/, **illusive** /ɪˈluːsɪv/ adj deceptive; based on illusion.—**illusorily** adv.—**illusoriness** n.

illustrate /ˈɪləˌstreɪt/ vt to explain, as by examples; to provide (books, etc) with explanatory pictures, charts, etc; to serve as an example.—**illustratable** adj.—**illustrative** adj.—**illustrator** n.

illustration /ˌɪləˈstreɪʃən/ n the act of illustrating; the state of being illustrated; an example that explains or corroborates; a picture or diagram in a book, etc.—**illustrational** adj.

illustrious /ɪˈlʌstriəs/ adj distinguished, famous.—**illustriousness** n.

ill-will n antagonism, hostility.

I'm /aɪm/ = I am.

image /'ɪmɪdʒ/ n a representation of a person or thing; the visual impression of something in a lens, mirror, etc; a copy; a likeness; a mental picture; the concept of a person, product, etc held by the public at large. • vt to make a representation of; to reflect; to imagine.

imagery /'ɪmɪdʒrɪ/ n (pl **imageries**) the work of the imagination; mental pictures; figures of speech; images in general or collectively.

imaginable /ɪ'mædʒɪnəbəl/ adj able to be imagined.—**imaginably** adv.

imaginal /ɪ'mædʒɪnəl/ adj pertaining to an image; pertaining to an imago.

imaginary /ɪ'mædʒɪnerɪ/ adj existing only in the imagination.—**imaginarily** adv.

imagination /ɪˌmædʒɪ'neɪsən/ n the image-forming power of the mind, or the power of the mind that modifies the conceptions, esp the higher form of this power exercised in art and poetry; creative ability; resourcefulness in overcoming practical difficulties, etc.

imaginative /ɪ'mædʒɪnətɪv/ adj having or showing imagination; produced by imagination.—**imaginatively** adv.

imagine /ɪ'mædʒɪn/ vt to form a mental image of; to believe falsely; (inf) to suppose; to guess. • vi to employ the imagination.—**imaginer** n.

imagist /-ɪst/ n a member of a group of poets, active between 1912 and 1917, who sought clarity of expression through use of precise images.

imago /ɪ'meɪgoː/ n (pl **imagoes, imagines**) an insect in its fully developed state; an idealized mental image of oneself or another.

imam /ɪ'mæm/ or /-mɒm/ n a leader of prayer in a mosque; a title given to various Muslim religious leaders.

imamate /ɪ'mæmeɪt/ n a region controlled by an imam; the rank or term of office of an imam.

imaret /ˌɪmə'ret/ n a hostel in Turkey giving accommodation to pilgrims or travellers.

IMAX /'aɪmæks/ n (trademark) a form of cinematography in which extra-large film is shot and then projected on a giant screen.

imbalance /ɪm'bæləns/ n a lack of balance, as in proportion, emphasis, etc.

imbecile /'ɪmbəsəl/ or /-sɪl/, /-saɪl/ n an adult with a mental age of a three- to eight-year-old child; an idiotic person. • adj stupid or foolish.

imbecility /-sɪlɪtɪ/ n (pl **imbecilities**) mental or physical weakness.

imbed vt (**imbedding, imbedded**) to embed.

imbibe /ɪm'baɪb/ vti to drink, esp alcoholic liquor; to absorb mentally.—**imbiber** n.

imbibition /ˌɪmbɪ'bɪsən/ n (chem) the process of a gel or solid absorbing a liquid; (photog) the process, used in colour printing, of using gelatine to absorb dyes.

imbricate /'ɪmbrɪˌkeɪt/, **imbricated** /-əd/ adj (tiles, leaves) overlapping.—**imbrication** n.

imbroglio /ɪm'broːlioː/ n (pl **imbroglios**) a complicated, confusing situation; a confused misunderstanding.

imbrue /ɪm'bruː/ vt (**imbruing, imbrued**) to wet or moisten; to soak; to drench, esp in blood.—also **embrue**.

IMF abbr = International Monetary Fund.

imitable /'ɪmɪtəbəl/ adj able to be imitated.—**imitability, imitableness** n.

imitate /'ɪmɪˌteɪt/ vt to try to follow as a pattern or model; to mimic humorously, impersonate; to copy, reproduce.—**imitator** n.

imitation /ˌɪmɪ'teɪsən/ n an act or instance of imitating; a copy; an act of mimicking or impersonation.—**imitational** adj.

imitative /'ɪmɪˌteɪtɪv/ adj imitating or inclined to imitate; characterized by imitation; copying an original, esp something superior.

immaculate /ɪ'mækjʊlət/ adj spotless; flawless; pure, morally unblemished.—**immaculacy, immaculateness** n.—**immaculately** adv.

Immaculate Conception n (RC Church) the doctrine that the Virgin Mary was conceived without original sin.

immanent /'ɪmənənt/ adj (qualities) inherent; (God) pervading the universe.—**immanence, immanency** n.

immaterial /ˌɪmə'tiːrɪəl/ adj spiritual as opposed to physical; unimportant.—**immateriality, immaterialness** n.

immaterialism /ˌɪmə'tiːriəˌlɪzəm/ n (philos) the doctrine that matter has no existence independent of the mind.—**immaterialist** n.

immaterialize /-ˌlaɪz/ vt to make immaterial.

immature /ˌɪmə'tʃʊr/ or /-'tʃər/ adj not mature.—**immaturity, immatureness** n.

immeasurable /ɪ'meʒərəbəl/ adj not able to be measured; immense, limitless.—**immeasurably** adv.

immediate /ɪ'miːdɪət/ adj acting or occurring without delay; next, nearest, without intervening agency; next in relationship; in close proximity, near to; directly concerning or touching a person or thing.—**immediacy, immediateness** n.

immediately /-lɪ/ adv without delay; directly; near, close by. • conj as soon as.

immemorial /ˌɪmə'mɔːrɪəl/ adj existing in the distant past, beyond the reach of memory.—**immemorially** adv.

immense /ɪ'mens/ adj very large in size or extent; limitless; (inf) excellent.—**immensely** adv.

immensity /-sɪtɪ/ n (pl **immensities**) the character of being immense; immeasurableness; infinite space; vastness in extent or bulk.

immensurable /ɪ'mensərəbəl/ adj immeasurable.

immerse /ɪ'mɜrs/ vt to plunge into a liquid; to absorb or engross; to baptize by total submergence.—**immersible** adj.

immersion /ɪ'mɜrʒən/ n the act of immersing; the state of being immersed; baptism by dipping the whole person into water.

immesh /ɪ'me/ see **enmesh**.

immethodical /ˌɪmə'θɒdɪkəl/ adj without method or order.

immigrant /'ɪmɪgrənt/ n a person who immigrates; a person recently settled in a country but not born there.

immigrate /'ɪmɪˌgreɪt/ vi to come into a new country, esp to settle permanently.—**immigration** n.—**immigrator** n.—**immigratory** adj.

imminent /'ɪmɪnənt/ adj about to happen; impending.—**imminence** n.—**imminently** adv.

immiscible /ɪ'mɪsɪbəl/ adj incapable of being mixed.—**immiscibility** n.

immobile /ɪ'moːbaɪl/ or /-bəl/ adj not able to be moved; motionless.—**immobility** n.

immobilize /ɪ'moːbəˌlaɪz/ vt to make immobile.—**immobilization** n.

immoderate /ɪ'mɒdərət/ adj excessive, unrestrained.—**immoderately** adv.—**immoderation, immoderateness** n.

immodest /ɪ'mɒdəst/ adj lacking in modesty or decency.—**immodestly** adv.—**immodesty** n.

immolate /'ɪməˌleɪt/ vt to kill as a sacrifice.—**immolation** n.—**immolator** n.

immoral /ɪ'mɒrəl/ adj against accepted standards of proper behaviour; sexually degenerate; corrupt; wicked.—**immorally** adv.

immorality /ˌɪmə'rælɪtɪ/ n (pl **immoralities**) the quality of being immoral; an immoral act or practice.

immortal /ɪ'mɔːrtəl/ adj living for ever; enduring; having lasting fame. • n an immortal being or person; (pl) the gods of classical mythology.—**immortality** n.—**immortally** adv.

immortalize /-ˌlaɪz/ vt to render immortal; to bestow lasting fame upon.—**immortalization** n.

immortelle /ˌɪmɔr'tel/ n a type of flower that retains its colour when dried.

immovable /ɪ'muːvəbəl/ adj firmly fixed; impassive, unyielding; (property) land, buildings, etc.—**immovability, immovableness** n.—**immovably** adv.

immune /ɪ'mjuːn/ adj not susceptible to a specified disease through inoculation or natural resistance; conferring immunity; exempt from a certain obligation, tax, duty, etc.

immunity /ɪ'mjuːnɪtɪ/ n (pl **immunities**) the state of being immune.

immunize /'ɪmjʊˌnaɪz/ vt to make immune, esp against infection.—**immunization** n.

immuno- /'ɪmjuːnoː/ or /ɪ'mjuːnoː/ prefix immunity.

immunology /'ɪmjuːnɒlədʒi/ n the branch of medical science dealing with immunity to disease.—**immunologic, immunological** adj.—**immunologist** n.

immure /ɪ'mjʊr/ vt to enclose within walls; to shut up (in prison), confine.

immutable /ɪ'mjuːtəbəl/ adj not capable of change; unalterable.—**immutability, immutableness** n.—**immutably** adv.

imp /ɪmp/ n a mischievous child; a little devil.

impact /'ɪmpækt/ *n* violent contact; a shocking effect; the force of a body colliding with another. • *vt* to force tightly together. • *vi* to hit with force.—**impaction** *n*.

impacted /ɪm'pæktəd/ *adj* (*tooth*) unable to emerge through the gum because of an obstruction, *esp* proximity to another tooth.

impair /ɪm'peɪr/ *vt* to make worse, less, etc.—**impairer** *n*.—**impairment** *n*.

impala /ɪm'pælə/ *n* (*pl* **impalas, impala**) a type of African antelope.

impale /ɪm'peɪl/ *vt* to fix on, or pierce through, with something pointed.—**impalement** *n*.—**impaler** *n*.

impalpable /ɪm'pælpəbəl/ *adj* not able to be sensed by touch; difficult to apprehend or grasp with the mind.—**impalpability** *n*.—**impalpably** *adv*.

impanel *see* **empanel**.

imparity /ɪm'pærɪti/ *n* (*pl* **imparities**) inequality; disproportion; disparity.

impart /ɪm'pɑrt/ *vt* to give, convey; to reveal, disclose.—**imparter** *n*.

impartial /ɪm'pɑrʃəl/ *adj* not favouring one side more than another, unbiased.—**impartiality, impartialness** *n*.—**impartially** *adv*.

impartible /ɪm'pɑrtəbəl/ *adj* (*law*) which cannot be partitioned.

impassable /ɪm'pæsəbəl/ *adj* (*roads, etc*) incapable of being travelled through or over.—**impassability, impassableness** *n*.—**impassably** *adv*.

impasse /'ɪmpæs/ *n* a situation from which there is no escape; a deadlock.

impassioned /ɪm'pæʃənd/ *adj* passionate; ardent.—**impassionedly** *adv*.

impassive /ɪm'pæsɪv/ *adj* not feeling or showing emotion; imperturbable.—**impassively** *adv*.—**impassiveness, impassivity** *n*.

impaste /ɪm'peɪst/ *vt* (*art*) to paint (onto canvas) in thick layers.—**impastation** *n*.

impasto /ɪm'pæstoʊ/ *n* (*art*) the effect produced by applying thick layers of paint to a canvas; the technique of applying paint in thick layers.

impatiens /ɪm'peɪʃəns/ *or* /-ənz/ *n* (*pl* **impatiens**) one of a genus of plants of this name, including balsam and touch-me-not.

impatient /ɪm'peɪʃənt/ *adj* lacking patience; intolerant of delay, etc; restless.—**impatience** *n*.—**impatiently** *adv*.

impeach /ɪm'piːtʃ/ *vt* to question a person's honesty; to try (a public official) on a charge of wrongdoing.—**impeachable** *adj*.—**impeacher** *n*.—**impeachment** *n*.

impearl /ɪm'pɜrl/ *vt* (*arch*) to adorn with pearls; to make like pearls.

impeccable /ɪm'pekəbəl/ *adj* without defect or error; faultless.—**impeccability** *n*.—**impeccably** *adv*.

impecunious /ˌɪmpɪ'kjuːniəs/ *adj* having little or no money.—**impecuniousness, impecuniosity** *n*.

impedance /ɪm'piːdəns/ *n* the total resistance in an electric circuit to the flow of alternating current.

impede /ɪm'piːd/ *vt* to obstruct or hinder the progress of.—**impeder** *n*.—**impedingly** *adv*.

impediment /ɪm'pedəmənt/ *n* something that impedes; an obstruction; a physical defect, as a stammer that prevents fluency of speech.—**impedimental** *adj*.

impedimenta /ɪmˌpedə'mentə/ *npl* heavy items of baggage, *esp* military equipment.

impel /ɪm'pel/ *vt* (**impelling, impelled**) to urge or force into doing something; to propel.—**impeller** *n*.

impend /ɪm'pend/ *vi* to be imminent; to threaten.—**impending** *adj*.

impenetrable /ɪm'penətrəbəl/ *adj* unable to be pierced or penetrated; incomprehensible; unable to be seen through.—**impenetrability** *n*.—**impenetrably** *adv*.

impenitent /ɪm'penɪtənt/ *adj* not sorry or feeling guilty; unrepentant.—**impenitence, impenitency** *n*.

imperative /ɪm'perətɪv/ *adj* urgent, pressing; authoritative; obligatory; designating or of the mood of a verb that expresses a command, entreaty, etc. • *n* a command; (*gram*) the imperative mood of a verb.

imperator /ˌɪmpə'rætər/ *or* /-tɔr/, /-'reɪ-/ *n* (*ancient Rome*) a commander-in-chief; a title given to a victorious general; a title given to the head of state.

imperceptible /ˌɪmpər'septəbəl/ *adj* not able to be detected by the mind or senses; slight, minute, gradual.—**imperceptibility** *n*.—**imperceptibly** *adv*.

impercipient /ˌɪmpər'sɪpiənt/ *adj* lacking perception.

imperfect /ɪm'pɜrfɪkt/ *adj* having faults, flaws, mistakes, etc; defective; incomplete; (*gram*) designating a verb tense that indicates a past action or state as incomplete or continuous. • (*gram*) an imperfect tense.

imperfection /ˌɪmpər'fekʃən/ *n* the state or quality of being imperfect; a defect, fault.

imperforate /ɪm'pɜrfərət/ *adj* not perforated; (*anat*) without the normal opening.

imperial /ɪm'piːriəl/ *adj* of an empire, emperor, or empress; majestic; of great size or superior quality; of the British non-metric system of weights and measures.—**imperially** *adv*.

imperialism /ɪm'piːriəˌlɪzəm/ *n* the policy of forming and maintaining an empire, as by subjugating territories, establishing colonies, etc.—**imperialist** *n*.—**imperialistic** *adj*.—**imperialistically** *adv*.

imperil /ɪm'perɪl/ *vt* (**imperiling, imperiled** *or* **imperilling, imperilled**) to put in peril, to endanger.

imperious /ɪm'piːriəs/ *adj* tyrannical; arrogant.—**imperiously** *adv*.

imperishable /ɪm'perɪʃəbəl/ *adj* indestructible, not subject to decay; permanently enduring.—**imperishability** *n*.

imperium /ɪm'piːriəm/ *n* (*pl* **imperia**) supreme power; an empire.

impermanent /ɪm'pɜrmənənt/ *adj* not permanent.—**impermanence, impermanency** *n*.

impermeable /ɪm'pɜrmiəbəl/ *adj* not allowing fluids to pass through; impervious.—**impermeability** *n*.

impermissible /ˌɪmpər'mɪsəbəl/ *adj* not permissible.

impersonal /ɪm'pɜrsənəl/ *adj* not referring to any particular person; cold, unfeeling; not existing as a person; (*verb*) occurring only in the third person singular, *usu* with "it" as subject.—**impersonality** *n*.—**impersonally** *adv*.

impersonate /ɪm'pɜrsəˌneɪt/ *vt* to assume the role of another person as entertainment or for fraud.—**impersonation** *n*.—**impersonator** *n*.

impertinent /ɪm'pɜrtɪnənt/ *adj* impudent; insolent; irrelevant.—**impertinence** *n*.—**impertinently** *adv*.

imperturbable /ˌɪmpər'tɜrbəbəl/ *adj* not easily disturbed; calm; impassive.—**imperturbability** *n*.—**imperturbably** *adv*.—**imperturbation** *n*.

impervious /ɪm'pɜrviəs/ *adj* incapable of being penetrated, as by water; not readily receptive (to) or affected (by).

impetigo /ˌɪmpə'taɪɡoʊ/ *n* (*pl* **impetigos**) a contagious bacterial skin disease.—**impetiginous** *adj*.

impetrate /'ɪmpəˌtreɪt/ *vt* to obtain by supplication, *esp* by prayer.—**impetration** *n*.

impetuous /'ɪmpetʃʊəs/ *adj* acting or done suddenly with impulsive energy.—**impetuosity** *n*.—**impetuously** *adv*.

impetus /'ɪmpɪtəs/ *n* (*pl* **impetuses**) the force with which a body moves against resistance; driving force or motive.

impiety /ɪm'paɪəti/ *n* (*pl* **impieties**) want of piety; ungodliness; an act of irreverence or wickedness.

impinge /ɪm'pɪndʒ/ *vi* (*with* **on, upon**) to have an impact; to encroach.—**impingement** *n*.—**impinger** *n*.

impious /'ɪmpiəs/ *adj* showing lack of reverence; wicked.—**impiously** *adv*.

impish /'ɪmpɪʃ/ *adj* of or like an imp.—**impishly** *adv*.—**impishness** *n*.

implacable /ɪm'plækəbəl/ *adj* not able to be appeased or pacified; inflexible, inexorable.—**implacability** *n*.—**implacably** *adv*.

implant /ɪm'plænt/ *vt* to plant firmly; to fix (ideas, etc) firmly in the mind. • *n* something implanted in tissue surgically.—**implantation** *n*.—**implanter** *n*.

implausible /ɪm'plɔzəbəl/ *adj* not plausible.—**implausibility** *n*.—**implausibly** *adv*.

implead /ɪm'pliːd/ *vt* to sue, prosecute.

implement /'ɪmpləmənt/ *n* something used in a given activity. • *vt* to carry out, put into effect.—**implemental** *adj*.—**implementation** *n*.—**implementer, implementor** *n*.

implicate /'ɪmplɪˌkeɪt/ *vt* to show to have a part, *esp* in a crime; to imply.—**implicative** *adj*.

implication /ˌɪmplɪ'keɪʃən/ *n* an implicating or being implicated; that which is implied; an inference not expressed but understood; deduction.

implicit /ɪm'plɪsɪt/ *adj* implied rather than stated explicitly; unquestioning, absolute.—**implicitly** *adv*.—**implicitness, implicity** *n*.

implode /ɪm'ploʊd/ *vi* to collapse inwards.

implore /ɪmˈplɔr/ vt to request earnestly; to plead, entreat.—imploration n.—implorer n.—imploringly adv.

imply /ɪmˈplaɪ/ vt (implying, implied) to hint, suggest indirectly; to indicate or involve as a consequence.

impolite /ˌɪmpəˈlaɪt/ adj not polite, rude.—impolitely adv.—impoliteness n.

impolitic /ɪmˈpɒlɪtɪk/ adj contrary to good policy; unwise; injudicious; indiscreet.—impoliticly adv.

imponderable /ɪmˈpɒndərəbəl/ adj not able to be weighed or measured. • n something difficult to measure or assess.—imponderability n.—imponderably adv.

import /ɪmˈpɔrt/ or /ˈɪmpɔrt/ vt to bring (goods) in from a foreign country for sale or use; to mean; to signify. • vi to be of importance, to matter. • n something imported; meaning; importance.—importable adj.—importer n.

importance /ɪmˈpɔrtəns/ n the quality of being important; a high place in public estimation; high self-esteem.

important /ɪmˈpɔrtənt/ adj having great significance or consequence; (person) having power, authority, etc.—importantly adv.

importation /-ˈteɪʃən/ n the act or business of importing; imported goods.

importunate /ɪmˈpɔrtʃənət/ adj persistent in asking or demanding.

importune /ɪmˈpɔrtˈuːn/ or /-ˈtjuːn/ vt to ask urgently and repeatedly.—importuner n.—importuning n.

importunity /ˌɪmpɔrˈtuːnɪtɪ/ or /-ˈtjuː-/ n (pl importunities) persistent solicitation or demand; incessant insistence; urgency.

impose /ɪmˈpoːz/ vt to put (a burden, tax, punishment) on or upon; to force (oneself) on others; to lay pages of type or film and secure them. • vi (with on or upon) to take advantage of; to cheat or defraud.—imposable adj.—imposer n.

imposing /-ɪŋ/ adj impressive because of size, appearance, dignity, etc.—imposingly adv.

imposition /ˌɪmpəˈzɪʃən/ n the act of imposing; something imposed, as a tax; an unfair burden; (print) the arrangement of pages of type or film in the correct order.

impossibility /ɪmˌpɒsəˈbɪlɪtɪ/ n (pl impossibilites) the character of being impossible; that which cannot be, or be supposed to be, done.

impossible /ɪmˈpɒsəbəl/ adj not capable of existing, being done, or happening; (inf) unendurable, outrageous.—impossibly adv.

impost /ˈɪmpoːst/ n a tax or duty, esp imposed by customs.

impostor, imposter /ɪmˈpɒstər/ n a person who acts fraudulently by impersonating another.

imposture /ɪmˈpɒstʃər/ n a fraud, deception.

impotent /ˈɪmpətənt/ adj lacking in necessary strength, powerless; (man) unable to engage in sexual intercourse.—impotence, impotency n.—impotently adv.

impound /ɪmˈpaʊnd/ vt to take legal possession of; to shut up (an animal) in a pound.—impoundage, impoundment n.—impounder n.

impoverish /ɪmˈpɒvərɪʃ/ vt to make poor; to deprive of strength.—impoverishment n.

impracticable /ɪmˈpræktɪkəbəl/ adj not able to be carried out, not feasible.—impracticability n.—impracticably adv.

impractical /ɪmˈpræktɪkəl/ adj not practical; not competent in practical skills.—impracticality n.—impractically adv.

imprecate /ˈɪmprəˌkeɪt/ vti to invoke evil (on); to curse or utter curses.—imprecatory adv.

imprecation /ˌɪmprəˈkeɪʃən/ n a curse.

imprecise /ˌɪmprəˈsaɪs/ adj not precise; ill-defined.—imprecisely adv.—imprecision n.

impregnable /ɪmˈpregnəbəl/, impregnatable adj secure against attack, unyielding.—impregnability n.—impregnably adv.

impregnate /ɪmˈpregˌneɪt/ vt to cause to become pregnant, to fertilize; to saturate, soak (with); to imbue, pervade.—impregnation n.—impregnator n.

impresario /ˌɪmprəˈsɑrioː/ or /-ˈserioː/ n (pl impresarios) the manager of an opera, a concert series, etc.

impress[1] /ɪmˈpres/ vt to make a strong, usu favourable, impression on; to fix deeply in the mind; to stamp with a mark; to imprint. • n an imprint.—impresser n.—impressible adj.

impress[2] vt to coerce into military service.—impressment n.

impression /ɪmˈpreʃən/ n the effect produced in the mind by an experience; a mark produced by imprinting; a vague idea, notion; the act of impressing or being impressed; a notable or strong influence on the mind or senses; the number of copies of a book printed at one go.—also printing; an impersonation or act of mimicry.—impressional adj.

impressionable ɪmˈpreʃənəbəl/ or /-ˈpreʃnəbəl/ n easily impressed or influenced.—impressionability n.—impressionably adv.

impressionism /ɪmˈpreʃəˌnɪzəm/ n painting, writing, etc in which objects are painted or described so as to reproduce only their general effect or impression without selection or elaboration of details.—impressionist adj, n.—impressionistic adj.

impressive /ɪmˈpresɪv/ adj tending to impress the mind or emotions; arousing wonder or admiration.—impressiveness n.

impressment /-mənt/ n the act of seizing (things) for public use or conscripting (people) into public service.

imprest /ˈɪmprest/ n a sum of money advanced.

imprimatur /ˌɪmprɪˈmætər/ or /-ˈmeɪtər/, /-tʊr/ n permission or licence to publish a book, etc; an authoritative mark of approval; sanction.

imprint /ɪmˈprɪnt/ vt to stamp or impress a mark on, etc; to fix firmly in the mind. • n a mark made by imprinting; a lasting effect; a note in a book giving the facts of publication.—imprinter n.

imprison /ɪmˈprɪzən/ vt to put in a prison; to confine, as in a prison.—imprisoner n.—imprisonment n.

improbable /ɪmˈprɒbəbəl/ adj unlikely to be true or to happen.—improbability n.—improbably adv.

improbity /ɪmˈproːbɪtɪ/ n (pl improbities) wickedness, dishonesty.

impromptu /ɪmˈprɒmptuː/ or /-tjuː/ adj, adv unrehearsed, unprepared. • n something impromptu, as a speech.

improper /ɪmˈprɒpər/ adj lacking propriety, indecent; incorrect; not suitable or appropriate.—improperly adv.

improper fraction n a fraction in which the numerator is greater than or equal to the denominator, as $^4/_3$.

impropriety /ˌɪmprəˈpraɪətɪ/ n (pl improprieties) the quality of being improper; indecency; an improper act, etc.

improve /ɪmˌpruːv/ vt to make or become better.—improvable adj.—improver n.—improvingly adj.

improvement /ɪmˈpruːvmənt/ n the act of improving or being improved; an alteration that improves or adds to the value of something.

improvident /ɪmˈprɒvɪdənt/ adj lacking foresight or thrift; wanting care to provide for the future; careless.—improvidence n.

improvisation /ɪmprəvaɪˈzeɪʃən/ n the act of improvising; the act of composing poetry, music, etc, extemporaneously; an impromptu.—improvisational adj.

improvise /ˈɪmprəˌvaɪz/ vti to compose, perform, recite, etc without preparation; to make or do with whatever is at hand.—improviser n.

imprudent /ɪmˈpruːdənt/ adj rash, lacking discretion; unwise.—imprudence n.—imprudently adv.

impudent /ˈɪmpjʊdənt/ adj disrespectfully bold; impertinent.—impudence n.—impudently adv.

impugn /ɪmˈpjuːn/ vt to oppose or challenge as false; to discredit.—impugnation, impugnment n.—impugner n.

impuissant Fr. /ɛ̃pɥiˈsã/ adj powerless, weak.—impuissance n.

impulse /ˈɪmpʌls/ n a sudden push or thrust; a stimulus transmitted through a nerve or a muscle; a sudden instinctive urge to act.

impulsion /ɪmˈpʌlʃən/ n the act of impelling; the state of being impelled; impetus; an irrational urge, compulsion.

impulsive /ɪmˈpʌlsɪv/ adj tending to act on impulse; forceful, impelling; acting momentarily.—impulsively adv.—impulsiveness n.

impunity /ɪmˈpjuːnɪtɪ/ n (pl impunities) exemption or freedom from punishment or harm.

impure /ɪmˈpjʊr/ or /-pjər/ adj unclean; adulterated.

impurity /ɪmˈpjʊrɪtɪ/ or /-pjər-/ n (pl impurities) a being impure; an impure substance or constituent.

impute /ɪmˈpjuːt/ vt to attribute (esp a fault or misbehaviour) to another.—imputable adj.—imputation n.—imputative adj.—imputer n.

In (chem symbol) indium.

in. abbr = inch(es).

in /ɪn/ prep inside; within; at; as contained by; during; at the end of; not beyond; affected by; being a member of; wearing; using; because of; into. • adv to or at a certain place; so as to be contained by a certain space, condition, etc; (games) batting, in play. • adj that is in power; inner; inside; gathered, counted, etc; (inf) currently smart, fashionable, etc.

inability /ˌɪnəˈbɪlɪtɪ/ n (pl inabilities) lack of ability.

in absentia /ˌɪnæbˈsenʃə/ or /-ʃɪə/, /-tɪə/ adv in the absence of.

inaccessible /ˌɪnækˈsɛsɪbəl/ *adj* not accessible, unapproachable.—**inaccessibility** *n*.—**inaccessibly** *adv*.

inaccurate /ɪnˈækjʊrət/ *adj* not accurate, imprecise.—**inaccuracy** *n*.—**inaccurately** *adv*.

inaction /ɪnˈækʃən/ *n* idleness, inertia.

inactive /ɪnˈæktɪv/ *adj* not active.—**inactively** *adv*.—**inactivity** *n*.

inadequate /ɪnˈædəkwət/ *adj* not adequate; not capable.—**inadequacy** *n*.—**inadequately** *adv*.

inadmissible /ˌɪnədˈmɪsəbəl/ *adj* not admissible, *esp* as evidence.—**inadmissibility** *n*.—**inadmissibly** *adv*.

inadvertent /ˌɪnədˈvɜːtənt/ *adj* not attentive or observant, careless; due to oversight.—**inadvertence, inadvertency** *n*.—**inadvertently** *adv*.

inadvisable /ˌɪnədˈvaɪzəbəl/ *adj* not advisable; inexpedient.—**inadvisability** *n*.—**inadvisably** *adv*.

inalienable /ɪnˈeɪlɪənəbəl/ *adj* that cannot or should not be surrendered or transferred to another.—**inalienability** *n*.—**inalienably** *adv*.

inalterable /ɪnˈɒltərəbəl/ *adj* unalterable.—**inalterability** *n*.

inamorata /ɪnˌæməˈrɑːtə/ *n* (*pl* **inamoratas**) a woman with whom one is in love; a sweetheart.

inamorato /ɪnˌæməˈrɑːtoː/ *n* (*pl* **inamoratos**) a man who is in love, a lover.

inane /ɪˈneɪn/ *adj* lacking sense, silly.—**inanely** *adv*.

inanimate /ɪnˈænəmət/ *adj* not animate; showing no signs of life; dull.—**inanimately** *adv*.—**inanimateness, inanimation** *n*.

inanition /ˌɪnəˈnɪʃən/ *n* emptiness; exhaustion from lack of nourishment.

inanity /ɪnˈænɪti/ *n* (*pl* **inanities**) (*arch*) emptiness; silliness; frivolity; a silly action or remark.

inapplicable /ˌɪnəˈplɪkəbəl/ or /ɪnˈæplɪk-/ *adj* not applicable.—**inapplicability** *n*.

inapposite /ɪnˈæpəzɪt/ *adj* not apposite, unsuitable.—**inappositely** *adv*.

inappreciable /ˌɪnəˈpriːʃəbəl/ *adj* not to be appreciated or estimated; of no consequence.

inappreciative /ˌɪnəˈpriːʃətɪv/ *adj* unappreciative.

inapproachable /ˌɪnəˈprəʊtʃəbəl/ *adj* not approachable, inaccessible.

inappropriate /ˌɪnəˈprəʊprɪət/ *adj* unsuitable.—**inappropriately** *adv*.—**inappropriateness** *n*.

inapt /ɪnˈæpt/ *adj* inappropriate; unfit, unskilful.—**inaptitude** *n*.

inarticulate /ˌɪnɑːˈtɪkjʊlət/ *adj* not expressed in words; incapable of being expressed in words; incapable of coherent or effective expression of ideas, feelings, etc.—**inarticulately** *adv*.

inartistic /ˌɪnɑːˈtɪstɪk/ *adj* not artistic; not appreciative of art.—**inartistically** *adv*.

inasmuch /ˌɪnəzˈmʌtʃ/ *adv* in like degree; (*with* **as**) seeing that; because.

inattentive /ˌɪnəˈtɛntɪv/ *adj* not attending; neglectful.—**inattention** *n*.

inaudible /ɪnˈɔːdəbəl/ *adj* unable to be heard.—**inaudibility** *n*.—**inaudibly** *adv*.

inaugural /ɪˈnɒɡjʊrəl/ or /-ɡər-/ *n* of or pertaining to an inauguration; a speech made at an inauguration.

inaugurate /ɪˈnɒɡjʊˌreɪt/ or /-ɡər-/ *vt* to admit ceremonially into office; to open (a building, etc) formally to the public; to cause to begin, initiate.—**inauguration** *n*.—**inaugurator** *n*.

inauspicious /ˌɪnɔːˈspɪʃəs/ *adj* ill-starred; unlucky; unfavourable; unfortunate.

inboard /ˈɪnbɔːd/ *adv, adj* towards the centre or within an aircraft, ship, etc.

inborn /ˈɪnbɔːn/ *adj* present from birth; hereditary.

inbred /ɪnˈbrɛd/ or /ˈɪn-/ *adj* innate; produced by inbreeding.

inbreed /ɪnˈbriːd/ *vti* (**inbreeding, inbred**) to breed by continual mating of individuals of the same or closely related stocks.

in-built /ˈɪnbɪlt/ *adj* built in.

Inc. *abbr* = Incorporated.

incalculable /ɪnˈkælkjʊləbəl/ *adj* beyond calculation; unpredictable.—**incalculability** *n*.—**incalculably** *adv*.

incalescent /ˌɪnkəˈlɛsənt/ *adj* (*chem*) increasing in heat.—**incalescence** *n*.

in camera /ɪnˈkæmərə/ *adv* in private; in a judge's chamber as opposed to open court.

incandesce /ˌɪnkænˈdɛs/ *vi* to glow with heat.

incandescent /ˌɪnkænˈdɛsənt/ *adj* glowing or luminous with intense heat.—**incandescence** *n*.

incantation /ˌɪnkænˈteɪʃən/ *n* words chanted in magic spells or rites.—**incantational, incantatory** *adj*.

incapable /ɪnˈkeɪpəbəl/ *adj* lacking capability; not able or fit to perform an activity.—**incapability** *n*.—**incapably** *adv*.

incapacitate /ˌɪnkəˈpæsɪˌteɪt/ *vt* to weaken, to disable; to make ineligible.—**incapacitation** *n*.

incapacity /ˌɪnkəˈpæsɪti/ *n* (*pl* **incapacities**) lack of power or strength, inability; ineligibility.

incarcerate /ɪnˈkɑːsəˌreɪt/ *vt* to put in prison, to confine.—**incarceration** *n*.—**incarcerator** *n*.

incarnate /ɪnˈkɑːnət/ *adj* endowed with a human body; personified. • *vt* to give bodily form to; to be the type or embodiment of.—**incarnation** *n*.

incautious /ɪnˈkɔːʃəs/ *adj* not cautious, reckless.—**incautiously** *adv*.—**incautiousness, incaution** *n*.

incendiarism /ɪnˈsɛndɪəˌrɪzəm/ *n* the act of burning illegally; arson.

incendiary /ɪnˈsɛndɪəri/ *adj* pertaining to arson; (*bomb*) designed to start fires; tending to stir up or inflame. • *n* (*pl* **incendiaries**) a person that sets fire to a building, etc maliciously, an arsonist; an incendiary substance (as in a bomb); a person who stirs up violence, etc.

incense[1] /ɪnˈsɛns/ *vt* to make extremely angry.

incense[2] *n* a substance that gives off a fragrant odour when burned; the fumes so produced; any pleasant odour.

incentive /ɪnˈsɛntɪv/ *n* a stimulus; a motive. • *adj* serving as a stimulus to action.

incept /ɪnˈsɛpt/ *vt* (*biol*) to ingest.

inception /ɪnˈsɛpʃən/ *n* the beginning of something.

inceptive /ɪnˈsɛptɪv/ *adj* noting a beginning, initial.

incertitude /ɪnˈsɜːtɪˌtjuːd/ or /-ˌtjuːd/ *n* doubt, uncertainty.

incessant /ɪnˈsɛsənt/ *adj* never ceasing; continual, constant.—**incessancy** *n*.—**incessantly** *adv*.

incest /ˈɪnsɛst/ *n* sexual intercourse between persons too closely related to marry legally.

incestuous /ɪnˈsɛstʃʊəs/ *adj* involving incest; guilty of incest.

inch /ɪntʃ/ *n* a measure of length equal to $\frac{1}{12}$ foot (2.54 cm); a very small distance or amount. • *vti* to move very slowly, or by degrees.

inchmeal /ˈɪntʃˌmiːl/ *adv* inch by inch, gradually.

inchoate /ɪnˈkoːət/ or /-eɪt/, /ˈɪn-/ *adj* just begun; at a very early stage.—**inchoation** *n*.—**inchoative** *adj*.

incidence /ˈɪnsɪdəns/ *n* the degree or range of occurrence or effect.

incident /ˈɪnsɪdənt/ *adj* likely to happen as a result; falling upon or affecting. • *n* something that happens; an event, *esp* a minor one; a minor conflict.

incidental /ˌɪnsɪˈdɛntəl/ *adj* happening in connection with something more important; happening by chance. • *npl* miscellaneous items, minor expenses.

incidental music *n* background music for a film, play, etc.

incidentally /ˌɪnsɪˈdɛntəli/ *adv* in passing, as an aside.

incinerate /ɪnˈsɪnəˌreɪt/ *vt* to reduce to ashes.—**incineration** *n*.

incinerator /-ər/ *n* a furnace for burning rubbish.

incipient /ɪnˈsɪpiənt/ *adj* beginning to be or appear; initial.—**incipience, incipiency** *n*.

incise /ɪnˈsaɪz/ *vt* to cut or carve into a surface; to engrave.—**incised** *adj*.

incision /ɪnˈsɪʒən/ *n* incising; a cut made into something, *esp* by a surgeon into a body.

incisive /ɪnˈsaɪsɪv/ *adj* keen, penetrating, decisive; biting.—**incisively** *adv*.—**incisiveness** *n*.

incisor /ɪnˈsaɪzər/ *n* any of the front cutting teeth in the mouth.

incite /ɪnˈsaɪt/ *vt* to urge to action; to rouse.—**incitement** *n*.—**inciter** *n*.—**incitingly** *adv*.

incivility /ˌɪnsɪˈvɪlɪti/ *n* (*pl* **incivilities**) lack of civility or courtesy; impoliteness.

incl. *abbr* = including; inclusive.

inclement /ɪnˈklɛmənt/ *adj* (*weather*) rough, stormy; lacking mercy; harsh.—**inclemency** *n*.

inclination /ˌɪnklɪˈneɪʃən/ *n* a propensity or disposition, *esp* a liking; a deviation from the horizontal or vertical; a slope; inclining or being inclined; a bending movement, a bow.—**inclinational** *adj*.

incline /ɪnˈklaɪn/ *vi* to lean, to slope; to be disposed towards an opinion or action. • *vt* to cause to bend (the head or body) forwards; to cause to deviate, *esp* from the horizontal or vertical. • *n* a slope.—**inclinable** *adj*.—**incliner** *n*.

inclinometer /ˌɪnklɪ'nɒmətər/ *n* an instrument used to measure the angle made by an aircraft with the horizontal.

include /ɪn'kluːd/ *vt* to enclose, contain; to comprise as part or a larger group, amount, etc.—**includable, includible** *adj*.—**inclusion** *n*.

inclusive /ɪn'kluːsɪv/ *adj* comprehensive; including the limits specified.—**inclusively** *adv*.

incognito /ˌɪnkɒg'niːtoː/ *adj, adv* under an assumed name or identity. • *n* (*pl* **incognitos**) a person appearing or living incognito; the name assumed by such a person.—**incognita** *nf* (*pl* **incognitas**).

incognizant /ɪn'kɒgnɪzənt/ *adj* (*usu with* **of**) unaware.—**incognizance** *n*.

incoherent /ˌɪnkoː'hiːrənt/ *adj* lacking organization or clarity; inarticulate in speech or thought.—**incoherence, incoherency** *n*.—**incoherently** *adv*.

incombustible /ˌɪnkəm'bʌstɪbəl/ *adj* not able to be burned or ignited. • *n* an incombustible substance.—**incombustibility** *n*.—**incombustibly** *adv*.

income /'ɪnkʌm/ or /'ɪŋkəm/ *n* the money etc received for labour or services, or from property, investments, etc.

incomer /'ɪnˌkʌmər/ *n* one who comes in; one who succeeds, as a tenant.

income tax *n* a tax levied on the net income of a person or business.

incoming /'ɪnˌkʌmɪŋ/ *adj* coming; accruing. • *n* the act of coming in; that which comes in; income.

incommensurable /ˌɪnkə'menʃərəbəl/ *adj* not able to be measured or judged comparatively.—**incommensurability** *n*.—**incommensurably** *adv*.

incommensurate /ˌɪnkə'menʃərət/ *adj* not commensurate; disproportionate; inadequate; incommensurable.

incommode /ˌɪnkə'moːd/ *vt* to give inconvenience or trouble to; to disturb.—**incommodious** *adj*.

incommunicable /ˌɪnkə'mjuːnɪkəbəl/ *adj* not capable of being communicated.—**incommunicability** *n*.—**incommunicably** *adv*.

incommunicado /ˌɪnkəˌmjuːnɪ'kædoː/ *adj* not allowed to communicate with others.

incommunicative /ˌɪnkə'mjuːnɪkətɪv/ *adj* not disposed to give information, reserved.

incommutable /ˌɪnkə'mjuːtəbəl/ *adj* which cannot be exchanged or commuted.

incomparable /ɪn'kɒmpərəbəl/ or /-prəbəl/ *adj* beyond comparison, matchless; not amenable to comparison.—**incomparability** *n*.—**incomparably** *adv*.

incompatible /ˌɪnkəm'pætɪbəl/ *adj* not able to exist together in harmony; antagonistic; inconsistent.—**incompatibility** *n*.—**incompatibly** *adv*.

incompetent /ɪn'kɒmpətənt/ *adj* lacking the necessary ability, skill, etc. • *n* an incompetent person.—**incompetence, incompetency** *n*.—**incompetently** *adv*.

incomplete /ˌɪnkəm'pliːt/ *adj* unfinished; lacking a part or parts.—**incompletely** *adv*.—**incompleteness, incompletion** *n*.

incomprehensible /ɪnˌkɒmprə'hensɪbəl/ *adj* not to be understood or grasped by the mind; inconceivable.—**incomprehensibility** *n*.—**incomprehensibly** *adv*.

incomprehension /ɪnˌkɒmprə'henʃən/ *n* inability or failure to understand.

incompressible /ˌɪnkəm'presɪbəl/ *adj* incapable of being reduced in volume by pressure; resisting pressure.—**incompressibility** *n*.—**incompressibly** *adv*.

incomputable /ˌɪnkəm'pjuːtəbəl/ *adj* incalculable, which cannot be reckoned.

inconceivable /ˌɪnkən'siːvəbəl/ *adj* impossible to comprehend; (*inf*) unbelievable.—**inconceivably** *adv*.

inconclusive /ˌɪnkən'kluːsɪv/ *adj* leading to no definite result; ineffective; inefficient.—**inconclusively** *adv*.—**inconclusiveness** *n*.

incondensable, incondensible /ˌɪnkən'densəbəl/ *adj* which cannot be condensed or compressed.

inconformity /ˌɪnkən'fɔːrməti/ *n* lack of conformity.

incongruity /ɪnkɒŋ'gruːɪti/ *n* (*pl* **incongruities**) unsuitableness of one thing to another, inconsistency; absurdity.

incongruous /ɪn'kɒŋgruəs/ *adj* lacking harmony or agreement of parts; unsuitable; inappropriate.—**incongruously** *adv*.—**incongruousness, incongruence** *n*.

inconsequential /ɪnˌkɒnsə'kwenʃəl/, **inconsequent** /ɪn'kɒnsəkwənt/ *adj* not following logically; irrelevant.—**inconsequence** *n*.—**inconsequentiality** *n*.—**inconsequentially, inconsequently** *adv*.

inconsiderable /ˌɪnkən'sɪdərəbəl/ *adj* trivial.—**inconsiderably** *adv*.

inconsiderate /ˌɪnkən'sɪdərət/ *adj* uncaring about others; thoughtless.—**inconsiderately** *adv*.—**inconsideration** *n*.

inconsistency /ˌɪnkən'sɪstənsi/ *n* (*pl* **inconsistencies**) the quality of being inconsistent; incongruity.—**inconsistently** *adv*.

inconsistent /ˌɪnkən'sɪstənt/ *adj* not compatible with other facts; contradictory; irregular, fickle.

inconsolable /ˌɪnkən'soːləbəl/ *adj* not able to be comforted.—**inconsolability** *n*.—**inconsolably** *adv*.

inconsonant /ɪn'kɒnsənənt/ *adj* not in harmony or agreement.—**inconsonance** *n*.

inconspicuous /ˌɪnkən'spɪkjuəs/ *adj* not conspicuous.—**inconspicuously** *adv*.—**inconspicuousness** *n*.

inconstant /ɪn'kɒnstənt/ *adj* subject to change; unstable; variable; fickle; capricious.—**inconstancy** *n*.

inconsumable /ˌɪnkən'suːməbəl/ or /-'sjuː-/ *adj* which cannot be consumed or used up.

incontestable /ˌɪnkən'testəbəl/ *adj* not admitting of question or doubt; incontrovertible.—**incontestability** *n*.—**incontestably** *adv*.

incontinent /ɪn'kɒntɪnənt/ *adj* unable to control the excretion of bodily wastes; lacking self-restraint.—**incontinence** *n*.

incontrovertible /ˌɪnkɒntrə'vɜːtɪbəl/ *adj* not admitting of controversy; indisputable.—**incontrovertibility** *n*.—**incontrovertibly** *adv*.

inconvenience /ˌɪnkən'viːnɪəns/ *n* want of convenience; unfitness; that which incommodes; disadvantage. • *vt* to put to inconvenience; to annoy.—**inconvenient** *adj*.

inconvertible /ˌɪnkən'vɜːtɪbəl/ *adj* incapable of being converted into or exchanged for something else.—**inconvertibility** *n*.—**inconvertibly** *adv*.

inconvincible /ˌɪnkən'vɪnsəbəl/ *adj* unable or unwilling to be convinced.

incoordination /ˌɪnkoːˌɔːdɪ'neɪʃən/ *n* lack of coordination.

incorporate /ɪn'kɔːpəˌreɪt/ *vt* to combine; to include; to embody; to merge; to form into a corporation. • *vi* to unite into one group or substance; to form a corporation. • *adj* united; formed into a corporation.—**incorporation** *n*.—**incorporative** *adj*.—**incorporator** *n*.

incorporeal /ˌɪnkɔːr'pɔːrɪəl/ *adj* not corporeal, without substance; spiritual; (*law*) intangible, and existing only in contemplation of the law.—**incorporeally** *adv*.—**incorporeity, incorporeality** *n*.

incorrect /ˌɪnkə'rekt/ *adj* faulty; inaccurate; improper.—**incorrectly** *adv*.—**incorrectness** *n*.

incorrigible /ɪn'kɒrɪdʒɪbəl/ *adj* not able to be corrected, reformed or altered.—**incorrigibility** *n*.—**incorrigibly** *adv*.

incorrupt /ˌɪnkə'rʌpt/, **incorrupted** /-ɪd/ *adj* free from physical or moral taint; unimpaired; upright, *esp* above the influence of corruption or bribery; honest.

incorruptible /ˌɪnkə'rʌptɪbəl/ *adj* incapable of physical corruption, decay or dissolution; incapable of being bribed; not liable to moral perversion or contamination.—**incorruptibility** *n*.—**incorruptibly** *adv*.

increase /ɪn'kriːs/ *vti* to make or become greater in size, quality, amount, etc. • *n* increasing or becoming increased; the result or amount by which something increases.—**increasable** *adj*.—**increaser** *n*.—**increasingly** *adv*.

incredible /ɪn'kredɪbəl/ *adj* unbelievable; (*inf*) wonderful.—**incredibility** *n*.—**incredibly** *adv*.

incredulity /ˌɪnkrə'djuːlɪti/ *n* scepticism; disbelief.

incredulous /ɪn'kredjuləs/ *adj* not able or willing to accept as true; unbelieving.—**incredulously** *adv*.—**incredulousness** *n*.

increment /'ɪnkrəmənt/ *n* (the amount of) an increase; an addition.—**incremental** *adj*.

increscent /ɪn'kresənt/ *adj* (*moon*) waxing, growing.

incriminate /ɪn'krɪmɪˌneɪt/ *vt* to involve in or indicate as involved in a crime or fault.—**incrimination** *n*.—**incriminator** *n*.—**incriminatory** *adj*.

incubate /'ɪŋkjubeɪt/ *vti* to sit on and hatch (eggs); to keep (eggs, embryos, etc) in a favourable environment for hatching or developing; to develop, as by planning.—**incubation** n.—**incubative, incubatory** adj.

incubator /'ɪnkjuˌbeɪtər/ n an apparatus in which eggs are hatched by artificial heat; an apparatus for nurturing premature babies until they can survive unaided.

incubus /'ɪnkjʊbəs/ n (pl **incubi, incubuses**) an evil spirit believed in folklore to have intercourse with women as they sleep; something oppressive or disturbing, as a nightmare.

inculcate /'ɪnkəlˌkeɪt/ vt to teach by frequent repetition or urging.—**inculcation** n.—**inculcator** n.

inculpate /ɪn'kəlpeɪt/ or /'ɪn-/ vt to blame, censure; to incriminate.—**inculpation** n.—**inculpative, inculpatory** adj.

incumbency /ɪn'kəmbənsi/ n (pl **incumbencies**) a duty or obligation; a term of office.

incumbent /ɪn'kəmbənt/ adj resting (on or upon) one as a duty or obligation; currently in office. • n the holder of an office, etc.

incunabulum /ˌɪnkjuː'næbjʊləm/ n (pl **incunabula**) any book printed before 1500; the early stages of anything.—**incunabular** adj.

incur /ɪn'kər/ vt (**incurring, incurred**) to bring upon oneself (something undesirable).—**incurrable** adj.

incurable /ɪn'kjʊrəbəl/ adj incapable of being cured; beyond the power of skill or medicine; lacking remedy; incorrigible. • n a person diseased beyond cure.—**incurability** n.—**incurably** adv.

incurious /ɪn'kjʊriəs/ adj indifferent, heedless.—**incuriosity** n.

incursion /ɪn'kərʒən/ n an invasion or raid into another's territory, etc.—**incursive** adj.

incurvate /ɪn'kərvɪt/ or /-ˌveɪt/, /'ɪnkər-/ vti to curve inwards. • adj curved or bent inwards.—**incurvation** n.

incus /'ɪnkəs/ n (pl **incudes**) a bone found in the middle ear.

incuse /ɪn'kjuːz/ n a design stamped onto a coin.

indebted /ɪn'dɛtəd/ adj in debt; obliged; owing gratitude.—**indebtedness** n.

indecency /ɪn'diːsənsi/ n (pl **indecencies**) lack of decency, modesty, or good manners; something indecent, vulgar, or obscene.

indecent /ɪn'diːsənt/ adj offending against accepted standards of decent behaviour.—**indecently** adv.

indecent assault n a sexual assault not involving rape.

indecent exposure n the offence of deliberately exposing one's genitals in public.

indeciduous /ˌɪndɪ'sɪdʒuːəs/ adj (bot) not deciduous; evergreen.

indecipherable /ˌɪndə'saɪfərəbəl/ adj which cannot be deciphered; illegible.

indecision /ˌɪndɪ'sɪʒən/ n not being able to make a decision; hesitation.

indecisive /ˌɪndɪ'saɪsɪv/ adj inconclusive; irresolute.—**indecisively** adv.—**indecisiveness** n.

indeclinable /ˌɪndɪ'klaɪnəbəl/ adj (gram) which cannot be declined, having no inflected forms.

indecorous /ɪn'dɛkərəs/ adj violating decorum, or any accepted rule of conduct.—**indecorum** n.

indeed /ɪn'diːd/ adv truly, certainly. • interj expressing irony, surprise, disbelief, etc.

indefatigable /ˌɪndɪ'fætɪgəbəl/ adj tireless.—**indefatigability** n.—**indefatigably** adv.

indefeasible /ˌɪndɪ'fiːzəbəl/ adj not to be defeated or made void, as a title.—**indefeasibility** n.—**indefeasibly** adv.

indefensible /ˌɪndɪ'fɛnsəbəl/ adj unable to be defended or justified.—**indefensibility** n.—**indefensibly** adv.

indefinable /ˌɪndɪ'faɪnəbəl/ adj that cannot be defined.—**indefinably** adv.

indefinite /ɪn'dɛfənɪt/ adj not certain, undecided; imprecise, vague; having no fixed limits.—**indefinitely** adv.—**indefiniteness** n.

indefinite article n the word "a" or "an."

indehiscent /ˌɪndɪ'hɪsənt/ adj (bot) not opening when mature.—**indehiscence** n.

indelible /ɪn'dɛləbəl/ adj not able to be removed or erased; (pen, ink, etc) making an indelible mark.—**indelibility** adv.—**indelibly** adv.

indelicacy /ɪn'dɛlɪkəsi/ n (pl **indelicacies**) lack of delicacy; something offensive to modesty or refined taste.

indelicate /ɪn'dɛlɪkət/ adj improper; rough, crude; tactless.—**indelicately** adv.

indemnify /ɪn'dɛmnəˌfaɪ/ vt (**indemnifying, indemnified**) to insure against loss, damage, etc; to repay (for damage, loss, etc).—**indemnification** n.—**indemnifier** n.

indemnity /ɪn'dɛmnɪti/ n (pl **indemnities**) compensation for damage or loss; insurance against future loss or injury.

indemonstrable /ˌɪndɪ'mɒnstrəbəl/ or /ɪn'dɛmən-/ adj which cannot be demonstrated or proved.

indent /ɪn'dɛnt/ vt to make notches in; to begin (a line of text) farther in from the margin than the rest. • vi to form an indentation. • n a dent or notch.—**indentor** n.

indentation /ˌɪndɛn'teɪʃən/ n a being indented; a notch, cut, inlet, etc; a dent; a spacing in from the margin—also **indention, indent**.

indenture /ɪn'dɛntʃər/ n a written agreement, a contract binding one person to work for another. • vt to bind by indentures.

independence /ˌɪndɪ'pɛndəns/ n the state of being independent.

Independence Day n the anniversary of the adoption of the American Declaration of Independence on 4 July 1776.

independency /ˌɪndɪ'pɛndənsi/ n (pl **independencies**) a self-governing political unit.

independent /ˌɪndɪ'pɛndənt/ adj freedom from the influence or control of others; self-governing; self-determined; not adhering to any political party; not connected with others; not depending on another for financial support. • n a person who is independent in thinking, action etc.—**independently** adv.

in-depth /'ɪnˌdɛpθ/ adj detailed, thorough.

indescribable /ˌɪndɪ'skraɪbəbəl/ adj unable to be described; too beautiful, horrible, intense, etc for words.—**indescribability** n.—**indescribably** adv.

indestructible /ˌɪndɪ'strʌktəbəl/ adj not able to be destroyed.—**indestructibility** n.—**indestructibly** adv.

indeterminable /ˌɪndɪ'tɜːrmɪnəbəl/ adj which cannot be ascertained, settled or classified.

indeterminate /ˌɪndɪ'tɜːrmɪnət/ adj vague, uncertain; not defined or fixed in value.—**indeterminacy, indetermination** adv.—**indeterminately** adv.

indeterminism /ˌɪndɪ'tɜːrmɪˌnɪzəm/ n (philos) the doctrine that the will has a certain freedom, independent of motives.

index /'ɪndɛks/ n (pl **indexes, indices**) an alphabetical list of names, subjects, items, etc mentioned in a printed book, usu listed alphabetically at the end of the text; a figure showing ratio or relative change, as of prices or wages; any indication or sign; a pointer or dial on an instrument; the exponent of a number. • vt to make an index of or for.—**indexer** n.

index arbitrage see **arbitrage**.

index finger n the forefinger.

Indiaman /'ɪndiəmən/ n (pl **Indiamen**) (formerly) a commercial sailing vessel involved in trade with India.

Indian /'ɪndiən/ n a native of India; an American Indian, the original inhabitants of the continent of America; the language of the people of India; a member of the aboriginal peoples of North and South America. • adj of or pertaining to a native of India; of or pertaining to the aboriginal peoples of North and South America.

Indian corn n maize.

Indian file n single file.

Indian ink n a solid black pigment; a black ink made from this.—also **India ink**.

Indian summer n a period of unusually warm weather in the autumn.

indiarubber n an elastic gummy substance obtained from the milky juice of several tropical trees and used for rubbing out pencil marks.

Indic /'ɪndɪk/ adj a term sometimes applied to the Indo-European languages of India, eg Sanskrit, Hindi, Bengali, etc.

indicant /'ɪndɪkənt/ n something which indicates.

indicate /'ɪndɪˌkeɪt/ vt to point out; to show or demonstrate; to be a sign or symptom of; to state briefly, suggest.—**indicatable** adj.—**indication** n.—**indicatory** adj.

indicative /ɪn'dɪkətɪv/ adj serving as a sign (of); (gram) denoting the mood of the verb that affirms or denies.

indicator /'ɪndɪˌkeɪtər/ n a thing that indicates or points; a measuring device with a pointer, etc; an instrument showing the operating condition of a piece of machinery, etc; a device giving updated information, such as a departure board in a railway station or airport; a flashing light used to warn of a change in direction of a vehicle.

indices /'ɪndɪˌsɛz/ *see* **index**.

indicia /ɪn'dɪʃiə/ *npl* (*sing* **indicium**) distinguishing markings.

indict /ɪn'daɪt/ *vt* to charge with a crime; to accuse.

indictable /ɪn'daɪtəbəl/ *adj* subject to being indicted; making one liable to indictment.

indictment /ɪn'daɪtmənt/ *n* a formal written statement framed by a prosecuting authority charging a person of a crime.

indifferent /ɪn'dɪfrənt/ or /-fərənt/ *adj* showing no concern, uninterested; unimportant; impartial; average; mediocre.—**indifference** *n*.—**indifferently** *adv*.

indifferentism /ɪn'dɪfrənˌtɪzəm/ *n* systematic indifference, *esp* with regard to religion.—**indifferentist** *n*.

indigen, indigene /'ɪndɪdʒiːn/ *n* a native (person, animal, etc).

indigenous /ɪn'dɪdʒənəs/ *adj* existing naturally in a particular country, region, or environment; native.

indigent /'ɪndɪdʒənt/ *adj* poor, needy.—**indigence** *n*.

indigestible /ˌɪndɪ'dʒɛstəbəl/ *adj* difficult or impossible to digest.—**indigestibility** *n*.

indigestion /ˌɪndɪ'dʒɛstʃən/ *n* a pain caused by difficulty in digesting food.

indigestive /ˌɪndɪ'dʒɛstɪv/ *adj* pertaining to, or having, indigestion.

indign /ɪn'daɪn/ *adj* (*arch*) unworthy; disgraceful.

indignant /ɪn'dɪgnənt/ *adj* expressing anger, *esp* at mean or unjust action.—**indignantly** *adv*.

indignation /ˌɪndɪg'neɪʃən/ *n* anger at something regarded as unfair, wicked, etc.

indignity /ɪn'dɪgnɪti/ *n* (*pl* **indignities**) humiliation; treatment making one feel degraded, undignified.

indigo /'ɪndɪˌgoʊ/ *n* (*pl* **indigos, indigoes**) a deep blue dye or colour.

indirect /ˌɪndɪ'rɛkt/ or /-daɪ-/ *adj* not straight; roundabout; secondary; dishonest.—**indirectly** *adv*.—**indirectness** *n*.

indirect evidence *n* circumstantial or inferential evidence.

indirection /ˌɪndə'rɛkʃən/ or /-daɪ-/ *n* indirect means or procedure; lack of direction; deceit.

indirect object *n* (*gram*) a person or thing affected by a verb but less directly than the object.

indirect speech *n* reported speech.

indirect tax *n* a tax levied on goods and services (which increases prices) rather than directly on individuals or companies.

indiscernible /ˌɪndɪ'sɜːnəbəl/ *adj* not discernible.—**indiscernibly** *adv*.

indiscipline /ɪn'dɪsɪplɪn/ *n* lack of discipline.

indiscreet /ˌɪndɪ'skriːt/ *adj* not discreet; tactless.—**indiscreetly** *adv*.

indiscrete /ˌɪndɪ'skriːt/ *adj* not separated into distinct parts.

indiscretion /ˌɪndɪ'skrɛʃən/ *n* an indiscreet act; rashness.—**indiscretionary** *adj*.

indiscriminate /ˌɪndɪ'skrɪmɪnət/ *adj* not making a careful choice; confused; random; making no distinctions.—**indiscriminately** *adv*.—**indiscrimination** *n*.—**indiscriminative** *adj*.

indispensable /ˌɪndɪ'spɛnsəbəl/ *adj* absolutely essential.—**indispensability** *n*.—**indispensably** *adv*.

indispose /ˌɪndɪ'spoʊz/ *vt* to make unfit or unwell; to disincline.

indisposed /ˌɪndɪ'spoʊzd/ *adj* ill or sick; reluctant; disinclined.

indisposition /ˌɪndɪspə'zɪʃən/ *n* disinclination; a slight illness.

indisputable /ˌɪndɪ'spjuːtəbəl/ *adj* unquestionable; certain.—**indisputability** *n*.—**indisputably** *adv*.

indissoluble /ˌɪndɪ'sɒljubəl/ *adj* permanent; not able to be dissolved or destroyed.—**indissolubility** *n*.—**indissolubly** *adv*.

indistinct /ˌɪndɪ'stɪŋkt/ *adj* not clearly marked; dim; not distinct.—**indistinctly** *adv*.—**indistinctness** *n*.

indistinctive /ˌɪndɪ'stɪŋktɪv/ *adj* not capable of making distinctions; lacking distinctive characteristics.—**indistinctiveness** *n*.

indistinguishable /ˌɪndɪ'stɪŋgwɪʃəbəl/ *adj* not distinguishable; lacking identifying characteristics.—**indistinguishability** *n*.—**indistinguishably** *adv*.

indite /ɪn'daɪt/ *vt* (*arch*) to write.

indium /'ɪndiəm/ *n* a soft metallic element used in alloys and electronic circuitry.

individual /ˌɪndɪ'vɪdʒʊəl/ *adj* existing as a separate thing or being; of, by, for, or relating to a single person or thing. • *n* a single thing or being; a person.

individualist /-ɪst/ *n* a person who thinks or behaves with marked independence.—**individualism** *n*.—**individualistic** *adj*.—**individualistically** *adv*.

individuality /ˌɪndɪvɪdʒʊ'ælɪti/ *n* (*pl* **individualities**) the condition of being individual; separate or distinct existence; distinctive character.

individualize /ˌɪndɪ'vɪdʒʊəˌlaɪz/ *vt* to mark as distinct, particularize; to distinguish individually.—**individualization** *n*.

individually /ˌɪndɪ'vɪdʒʊəli/ *adv* in a distinctive manner; one by one; separately; personally.

individuate /ˌɪndɪ'vɪdʒʊˌeɪt/ *vt* to individualize.—**individuation** *n*.

indivisible /ˌɪndɪ'vɪzɪbəl/ *adj* not divisible.—**indivisibility** *n*.—**indivisibly** *adv*.

indocile /ɪn'dɒsaɪl/ or /-'doː-/ *adj* unteachable; intractable.—**indocility** *n*.

indoctrinate /ɪn'dɒktrɪˌneɪt/ *vt* to systematically instruct in doctrines, ideas, beliefs, etc.—**indoctrination** *n*.—**indoctrinator** *n*.

Indo-European /ˌɪndoːˌjʊərə'piən/ or /-ˌjər-/ *adj* of a family of languages (including English) spoken in most of Europe and Asia as far east as northern India. —*also n*.

indolent /'ɪndələnt/ *adj* idle; lazy.—**indolence** *n*.—**indolently** *adv*.

indomitable /ɪn'dɒmɪtəbəl/ *adj* not easily discouraged or defeated.—**indomitability** *n*.—**indomitably** *adv*.

indoor /'ɪndɔr/ *adj* done, used, or situated within a building.

indoors /ɪn'dɔrz/ *adv* in or into a building.

indorse /ɪn'dɔrs/ *see* **endorse**.

indraft /'ɪndræft/ *n* an inlet or inward current.

indubitable /ɪn'duːbɪtəbəl/ or /-'djuː-/ *adj* not capable of being doubted.—**indubitability** *n*.—**indubitably** *adv*.

induce /ɪn'duːs/ or /-'djuːs/ *vt* to persuade; to bring on; to draw (a conclusion) from particular facts; to bring about (an electric or magnetic effect) in a body by placing it within a field of force.—**inducer** *n*.—**inducible** *adj*.

inducement /-mənt/ *n* something that induces; a stimulus; a motive.

induct /ɪn'dʌkt/ *vt* to place formally in an office, a society, etc; to enrol (*esp* a draftee) in the armed forces.

inductance /-əns/ *n* the property of an electric circuit by which an electromotive force is produced by a variation in the current in the same or a neighbouring circuit; the measure of inductance in an electric circuit.

inductile /ɪn'dʌktɪl/ *adj* not ductile, not pliant.

induction /ɪn'dʌkʃən/ *n* the act or an instance of inducting, *eg* into office; reasoning from particular premises to general conclusions; the inducing of an electric or magnetic effect by a field of force.—**inductional** *adj*.

inductive /ɪn'dʌktɪv/ *adj* proceeding by or producing induction; operating by induction; susceptible to being acted on by induction.

inductor /ɪn'dʌktər/ *n* one who inducts; (*elect*) that part of an apparatus that acts inductively.

indue /ɪn'duː/ or /-'djuː/ *see* **endue**.

indulge /ɪn'dʌldʒ/ *vt* to satisfy (a desire); to gratify the wishes of; to humour. • *vi* to give way to one's desire.—**indulger** *n*.

indulgence /-əns/ *n* indulging or being indulged; a thing indulged in; a favour or privilege; (*RC Church*) a remission of punishment still due for a sin after the guilt has been forgiven.

indulgent /ɪn'dʌldʒənt/ *adj* indulging or characterized by indulgence; lenient.—**indulgently** *adv*.

induline, indulin /'ɪnduˌliːn/ or /-lɪn/, /-djuː-/ *n* a dark blue dye.

indult /'ɪnˌdʌlt/ *n* (*RC Church*) a licence from the Pope authorizing something not sanctioned by Church law.

induplicate /ɪn'duːplɪkɪt/ or /-'djuː-/, **induplicated** /-ɪd/ *adj* (*bot*) bent inwards.

indurate /'ɪndjʊˌreɪt/ *vt* to make hard or callous. • *vi* to grow hard or callous.—**induration** *n*.—**indurative** *adj*.

indusium /ɪn'duːziəm/ or /-'djuː-/ *n* (*pl* **indusia**) (*bot*) the covering of the growing spores in many ferns.—**indusial** *adj*.

industrial /ɪn'dʌstriəl/ *adj* relating to or engaged in industry; used in industry; having many highly developed industries.—**industrially** *adv*.

industrialism /ɪn'dʌstriəˌlɪzəm/ *n* social and economic organization characterized by large industries, machine production, urban workers, etc.

industrialist /ɪn'dʌstriəlɪst/ *n* a person who owns or manages an industrial enterprise.

industrialize /ɪn'dʌstriəˌlaɪz/ *vti* to make or become industrial.—**industrialization** *n*.

industrial relations *n* the relations between employees and employers.

industrious /ɪnˈdʌstrɪəs/ *adj* hard-working.—**industriously** *adv.*—**industriousness** *n.*

industry /ˈɪndəstrɪ/ *n* (*pl* **industries**) organized production or manufacture of goods; manufacturing enterprises collectively; a branch of commercial enterprise producing a particular product; any large-scale business activity; the owners and managers of industry; diligence.

indwelling /ɪnˈdwɛlɪŋ/ *vti* (**indwelling, indwelt**) to dwell (in).

inebriate /ɪˈniːbrɪˌeɪt/ *vt* to intoxicate, *esp* with alcoholic drink. • *n* a drunkard. • *adj* inebriated.—**inebriation** *n.*

inebriated /-ɪd/ *adj* drunken.

inedible /ɪnˈɛdɪbəl/ *adj* not fit to be eaten.—**inedibility** *n.*

inedited /ɪnˈɛdɪtɪd/ *adj* unpublished; not edited.

ineducable /ɪnˈɛdʒʊkəbəl/ or /-djʊ-/ *adj* impossible to educate, *esp* due to mental deficiency.

ineffable /ɪnˈɛfəbəl/ *adj* too intense or great to be spoken; unutterable; too sacred to be spoken.—**ineffability** *n.*—**ineffably** *adv.*

ineffaceable /ˌɪnɪˈfeɪsəbəl/ *adj* which cannot be effaced.—**ineffaceability** *n.*

ineffective /ˌɪnɪˈfɛktɪv/ *adj* not effective.—**ineffectively** *adv.*—**ineffectiveness** *n.*

ineffectual /ˌɪnɪˈfɛktʃʊəl/ *adj* not effectual; futile.—**ineffectuality** *n.*—**ineffectually** *adv.*

inefficacious /ˌɪnɛfɪˈkeɪʃəs/ *adj* not having the power to produce a desired effect.—**inefficacy** *n.*

inefficiency /ˌɪnɪˈfɪʃənsɪ/ *n* (*pl* **inefficiences**) the quality or condition of being inefficient; an instance of inefficiency or incompetence.

inefficient /ˌɪnɪˈfɪʃənt/ *adj* not efficient.—**inefficiently** *adv.*

inelastic /ˌɪnɪˈlæstɪk/ *adj* not elastic; inflexible, unyielding.—**inelastically** *adv.*—**inelasticity** *n.*

inelegant /ɪnˈɛləgənt/ *adj* ungraceful; lacking refinement or polish.—**inelegance** *n.*

ineligible /ɪnˈɛlɪdʒəbəl/ *adj* not eligible.—**ineligibility** *n.*

ineluctable /ˌɪnɪˈlɛktəbəl/ *adj* not possible to escape from or avoid.—**ineluctably** *adv.*

inept /ɪnˈɛpt/ or /ɪˈnɛpt/ *adj* unsuitable; unfit; foolish; awkward; clumsy.—**ineptitude** *n.*—**ineptly** *adv.*

inequality /ˌɪnɪˈkwɒlɪtɪ/ *n* (*pl* **inequalities**) lack of equality in size, status, etc; unevenness.

inequitable /ɪnˈɛkwɪtəbəl/ *adj* unjust, unfair.—**inequitably** *adv.*

inequity /ɪnˈɛkwɪtɪ/ *n* (*pl* **inequities**) lack of equity; injustice.

ineradicable /ˌɪnɪˈrædɪkəbəl/ *adj* which cannot be eradicated.

inert /ɪˈnɜːt/ *adj* without power to move or to resist; inactive; dull; slow; with few or no active properties.—**inertly** *adv.*—**inertness** *n.*

inertia /ɪˈnɜːʃə/ *n* (*physics*) the tendency of matter to remain at rest (or continue in a fixed direction) unless acted on by an outside force; disinclination to act.

inertial /ɪnˈɜːʃɪəl/ *adj* of, or pertaining to, inertia.

inescapable /ˌɪnɪˈskeɪpəbəl/ *adj* which cannot be escaped, inevitable.

inessential /ˌɪnɪˈsɛnʃəl/ *adj* not essential.

inestimable /ɪnˈɛstɪməbəl/ *adj* not to be estimated; beyond measure or price; incalculable; invaluable.—**inestimably** *adv.*

inevitable /ɪnˈɛvɪtəbəl/ *adj* sure to happen; unavoidable. • *n* something that is inevitable.—**inevitability** *n.*—**inevitably** *adv.*

inexact /ˌɪnɪgˈzækt/ *adj* not strictly true or correct.—**inexactitude** *n.*—**inexactly** *adv.*

inexcusable /ˌɪnɪkˈskjuːzəbəl/ *adj* without excuse; unpardonable.—**inexcusably** *adv.*

inexhaustible /ˌɪnɪgˈzɔːstɪbəl/ *adj* not to be exhausted or spent; unfailing; unwearied.—**inexhaustibility** *n.*—**inexhaustibly** *adv.*

inexorable /ɪnˈɛksərəbəl/ *adj* unable to be persuaded by persuasion or entreaty, relentless.—**inexorability** *n.*—**inexorably** *adv.*

inexpedient /ˌɪnɪkˈspiːdɪənt/ *adj* unsuitable to circumstances; inadvisable.—**inexpedience, inexpediency** *n.*

inexpensive /ˌɪnɪkˈspɛnsɪv/ *adj* cheap.—**inexpensively** *adv.*

inexperience /ˌɪnɪkˈspiːrɪəns/ *n* want of experience or of the knowledge that comes by experience.

inexperienced /-d/ *adj* lacking experience; unpractised; unskilled; unversed.

inexpert /ɪnˈɛkspɜːt/ *adj* unskilled; lacking the knowledge or dexterity derived from practice.

inexpiable /ɪnˈɛkspɪəbəl/ *adj* which cannot be expiated.

inexplicable /ˌɪnɪkˈsplɪkəbəl/ or /ɪnˈɛks-/ *adj* not to be explained, made plain, or intelligible; not to be interpreted or accounted for.—**inexplicability** *n.*—**inexplicably** *adv.*

inexplicit /ˌɪnɪkˈsplɪsɪt/ *adj* not clear.

inexpressible /ˌɪnɪkˈsprɛsɪbəl/ *adj* incapable of being expressed, uttered, or described.—**inexpressibly** *adv.*

inexpressive /ˌɪnɪkˈsprɛsɪv/ *adj* lacking expression or distinct significance.

inextensible /ˌɪnɛkˈstɛnsəbəl/ or /-ɪk-/ *adj* which cannot be extended.—**inextensibility** *n.*

inextinguishable /ˌɪnɪkˈstɪŋgwɪʃəbəl/ *adj* which cannot be extinguished, unquenchable.

in extremis /ˌɪnɛkˈstreɪmɪs/ or /-triːmɪs/, /-trɛmɪs/ *adv* close to death; in a very difficult situation.

inextricable /ɪnˈɛkstrɪkəbəl/ or /ˌɪnɪkˈstrɪk-/ *adj* that cannot be disentangled, solved, or escaped from.—**inextricably** *adv.*

infallible /ɪnˈfælɪbəl/ *adj* incapable of being wrong; dependable; reliable.—**infallibility** *n.*—**infallibly** *adv.*

infamous /ˈɪnfəməs/ *adj* having a bad reputation; notorious; causing a bad reputation; scandalous.

infamy /ˈɪnfəmɪ/ *n* (*pl* **infamies**) ill fame; public disgrace; ignominy.

infancy /ˈɪnfənsɪ/ *n* (*pl* **infancies**) early childhood; the beginning or early existence of anything.

infant /ˈɪnfənt/ *n* a very young child; a baby.

infanta /ɪnˈfæntə/ *n* a title for a Spanish princess, not the heir apparent.

infante /ɪnˈfæntɪ/ *n* a title for a Spanish prince, not the heir apparent.

infanticide /ɪnˈfæntɪˌsaɪd/ *n* the killing of an infant; a person who does this.—**infanticidal** *adj.*

infantile /ˈɪnfənˌtaɪl/ *adj* of infants; like an infant, babyish.

infantile paralysis *n* poliomyelitis.

infantry /ˈɪnfəntrɪ/ *n* (*pl* **infantries**) soldiers trained to fight on foot.

infatuate /ɪnˈfætʃuːˌeɪt/ or /-tjuː-/ *vt* to inspire with intense, foolish, or short-lived passion.—**infatuated** *adj.*—**infatuatedly** *adv.*

infatuation /-ˈeɪʃən/ *n* an extravagant passion.

infect /ɪnˈfɛkt/ *vt* to contaminate with disease-causing microorganisms; to taint; to affect, *esp* so as to harm.—**infective** *adj.*

infection /ɪnˈfɛkʃən/ *n* an infecting or being infected; an infectious disease; a diseased condition.

infectious /ɪnˈfɛkʃəs/ *adj* (*disease*) able to be transmitted; causing or transmitted by infection; tending to spread to others.—**infectiousness** *n.*

infectious hepatitis *n* an infectious disease which causes inflammation of the liver.

infectious mononucleosis *n* an infectious disease characterized by inflammation of the lymph glands.—*also* **glandular fever**.

infelicitous /ˌɪnfəˈlɪsɪtəs/ *adj* unfortunate; unhappy; inappropriate; ill-timed.

infelicity /ˌɪnfɪˈlɪsɪtɪ/ *n* (*pl* **infelicities**) misfortune; unhappiness; inappropriateness; an infelicitous act or expression.

infer /ɪnˈfɜː/ *vt* (**inferring, inferred**) to conclude by reasoning from facts or premises; to accept as a fact or consequence.—**inferable** *adj.*—**inferrer** *n.*

inference /ˈɪnfərəns/ *n* an inferring; something inferred or deduced; a reasoning from premises to a conclusion.—**inferential** *adj.*

inferior /ɪnˈfiːrɪər/ *adj* lower in position, rank, degree, or quality. • *n* an inferior person.—**inferiority** *n.*

inferiority complex *n* (*psychol*) an acute sense of inferiority expressed by a lack of confidence or in exaggerated aggression.

infernal /ɪnˈfɜːnəl/ *adj* of hell; hellish; fiendish; (*inf*) irritating, detestable.—**infernally** *adv.*

inferno /ɪnˈfɜːnəʊ/ *n* (*pl* **infernos**) hell; intense heat; a devastating fire.

infertile /ɪnˈfɜːtaɪl/ *adj* not fertile.—**infertility** *n.*

infest /ɪnˈfɛst/ *vt* to overrun in large numbers, *usu* so as to be harmful; to be parasitic in or on.—**infestation** *n.*—**infester** *n.*

infidel /ˈɪnfɪdəl/ *n* a person who does not believe in a certain religion; a person who has no religion.

infidelity /ˌɪnfɪˈdɛlɪti/ n (pl **infidelities**) unfaithfulness, esp in marriage.

infield /ˈɪnfiːld/ n (cricket) the area of the ground near the wicket; (baseball) the area of the field enclosed by the baselines.

infielder /ˈɪnfiːldər/ n (baseball, cricket) a player in an infield position.

infighting /ˈɪnˌfaɪtɪŋ/ n (boxing) exchanging punches at close quarters; intense competition within an organization.—**infighter** n.

infiltrate /ˈɪnfɪlˌtreɪt/ vti to filter or pass gradually through or into; to permeate; to penetrate (enemy lines, etc) gradually or stealthily, eg as spies.—**infiltration** n.—**infiltrator** n.

infinite /ˈɪnfɪnɪt/ adj endless, limitless; very great; vast.—**infinitely** adv.

infinitesimal /ˌɪnfɪnɪˈtɛsɪməl/ adj immeasurably small.—**infinitesimally** adv.

infinitive /ɪnˈfɪnɪtɪv/ n (gram) the form of a verb without reference to person, number or tense.—**infinitival** adj.

infinitude /ɪnˈfɪnɪˌtuːd/ or /-ˈtjuːd/ n the condition or quality of being infinite; infinity.

infinity /ɪnˈfɪnɪti/ n (pl **infinities**) the condition or quality of being infinite; an unlimited number, quantity, or time period.

infirm /ɪnˈfɜːm/ adj physically weak, esp from old age or illness; irresolute.

infirmary /ɪnˈfɜːməri/ n (pl **infirmaries**) a hospital or place for the treatment of the sick.

infirmity /ɪnˈfɜːməti/ n (pl **infirmities**) being infirm; a physical weakness.

infix /ɪnˈfɪks/ vt to fix or insert in.

in flagrante delicto /ˌɪn fləˈɡrænti dɪˈlɪktoː/ adv in the very act of commiting the crime, red-handed.—also **flagrante delicto**.

inflame /ɪnˈfleɪm/ vti to arouse, excite, etc, or to become aroused, excited, etc; to undergo or cause to undergo inflammation.—**inflamingly** adv.

inflammable /ɪnˈflæməbəl/ adj able to catch fire, flammable; easily excited.—**inflammability** n.

inflammation /ˌɪnfləˈmeɪʃən/ n an inflaming or being inflamed; redness, pain, heat, and swelling in the body, due to injury or disease.

inflammatory /ɪnˈflæmətɔri/ or /-tri/ adj rousing excitement, anger, etc; of or caused by inflammation.—**inflammatorily** adv.

inflatable /ɪnˈfleɪtəbəl/ adj able to be inflated.

inflate /ɪnˈfleɪt/ vti to fill or become filled with air or gas; to puff up with pride; to increase beyond what is normal, esp the supply of money or credit.—**inflatedly** adv.—**inflater, inflator** n.

inflation /ɪnˈfleɪʃən/ n an inflating or being inflated; an increase in the currency in circulation or a marked expansion of credit, resulting in a fall in currency value and a sharp rise in prices.

inflationary /-ˌneri/ adj pertaining to or causing inflation.

inflationist /-ist/ n, adj (someone) in favour of a policy of an increased issue of money and availability of credit, with inflation as a consequence.

inflect /ɪnˈflɛkt/ vt to change the form (of a word) by inflection; to vary the tone of (the voice).—**inflective** adj.—**inflector** n.

inflection /ɪnˈflɛkʃən/ n a bend; the change in the form of a word to indicate number, case, tense, etc; a change in the tone of the voice.—**inflectional** adj.

inflexible /ɪnˈflɛksɪbəl/ adj not flexible; stiff, rigid; fixed; unyielding.—**inflexibility** n.—**inflexibly** adv.

inflict /ɪnˈflɪkt/ vt to impose (pain, a penalty, etc) on a person or thing.—**inflicter, inflictor** n.—**infliction** n.

inflorescence /ˌɪnfləˈrɛsəns/ n the producing of blossoms; the arrangement of flowers on a stem; a flower cluster; flowers collectively.—**inflorescent** adj.

inflow /ˈɪnfloː/ n something which flows in.

influence /ˈɪnfluːəns/ n the power to affect others; the power to produce effects by having wealth, position, ability, etc; a person with influence. • vt to have influence on.—**influenceable** adj.

influent /ˈɪnfluːənt/ adj flowing in.

influential /ˌɪnfluːˈɛnʃəl/ adj having or exerting great influence.—**influentially** adv.

influenza /ˌɪnfluːˈɛnzə/ n a contagious feverish virus disease marked by muscular pain and inflammation of the respiratory system.—**influenzal** adj.

influx /ˈɪnflɛks/ n a sudden inflow of people or things to a place.

info /ˈɪnfoː/ n (sl) information.

inform /ɪnˈfɔːm/ vt to provide knowledge of something to. • vi to give information to the police, etc, esp in accusing another.

informal /ɪnˈfɔːməl/ adj not formal; not according to fixed rules or ceremony, etc; casual.—**informally** adv.

informality /-ˈmælɪti/ n (pl **informalities**) the lack of regular, customary, or legal form; an informal act.

informant /ɪnˈfɔːmənt/ n a person who gives information.

information /ˌɪnfərˈmeɪʃən/ n something told or facts learned; news; knowledge; data stored in or retrieved from a computer.—**informational** adj.

information technology n (the study of) the collection, retrieval, use, storage and communication of information using computers and microelectronic systems.

information theory n mathematical and statistical analysis of information communication systems.

informative /ɪnˈfɔːmətɪv/, **informatory** /-tɔri/ adj conveying information, instructive.—**informatively** adv.

informer /ɪnˈfɔːmər/ n a person who informs on another, esp to the police for a reward.

infra- /ˈɪnfrə/ prefix below; within; beneath; after.

infraction /ɪnˈfrækʃən/ n a violation of a law, pact, etc.

infra dig /ˌɪnfrə ˈdɪɡ/ adj (inf) beneath one's dignity.

infrangible /ɪnˈfrændʒɪbəl/ adj unbreakable; inviolable.—**infrangibility** n.

infrared /ˌɪnfrəˈrɛd/ n (radiation) having a wavelength longer than light but shorter than radio waves; of, pertaining to, or using such radiation.

infrasonic /ˌɪnfrəˈsɒnɪk/ adj (soundwaves) having a frequency below the audible range.—**infrasound** n.

infrastructure /ˈɪnfrəˌstrʌktʃər/ n the basic structure of any system or organization; the basic installations, such as roads, railways, factories, etc that determine the economic power of a country.

infrequent /ɪnˈfriːkwənt/ adj seldom occurring; rare.—**infrequence, infrequency** n.—**infrequently** adv.

infringe /ɪnˈfrɪndʒ/ vt to break or violate, esp an agreement or a law.—**infringement** n.

infundibular /ˌɪnfɛnˈdɪbjʊlər/, **infundibulate** /-leɪt/ adj funnel-shaped.

infuriate /ɪnˈfjʊriˌeɪt/ vt to enrage; to make furious.—**infuriating** adj.—**infuriatingly** adv.

infuse /ɪnˈfjuːz/ vt to instil or impart (qualities, etc); to inspire; to steep (tea leaves, etc) to extract the essence.—**infuser** n.

infusible[1] /ɪnˈfjuːzɪbəl/ adj incapable of being fused or melted.—**infusibility** n.

infusible[2] adj capable of being infused.—**infusibility** n.

infusion /ɪnˈfjuːʒən/ n the act of infusing; something obtained by infusing.

infusorial earth /ˌɪnfjuːˈsɔːriəl/ n a silicious deposit composed chiefly of the shells of microscopic vegetable organisms called diatoms, used as a polishing powder and in the manufacture of dynamite.

ingenious /ɪnˈdʒiːniəs/ adj clever, resourceful, etc; made or done in an original or clever way.—**ingeniously** adv.—**ingeniousness** n.

ingénue /ˌæʒəˈnjuː/ or /-nuː/ n a naive young woman.

ingenuity /ˌɪndʒɪˈnjuːɪti/ n (pl **ingenuities**) skill in contriving or inventing; resourcefulness.

ingenuous /ɪnˈdʒɛnjuəs/ adj naive, innocent; candid.—**ingenuously** adv.—**ingenuousness** n.

ingest /ɪnˈdʒɛst/ vt to take (as food) into the body.—**ingestion** n.—**ingestive** adj.

ingle /ˈɪŋɡəl/ n (arch) a fireplace.

inglenook /ˈɪŋɡəlˌnʊk/ n (a seat in) a recess by a large open fireplace.

inglorious /ɪnˈɡlɔːriəs/ adj disgraceful, shameful; obscure.

ingot /ˈɪŋɡət/ n a brick-shaped mass of cast metal, esp gold or silver.

ingrain /ˈɪŋɡreɪn/ vt to make a deep impression upon; (arch) to dye.—also **engrain**.

ingrained /ɪnˈɡreɪnd/ or /ˈɪn-/ adj (habits, feelings, etc) firmly established; (dirt) deeply embedded.—also **engrained**.

ingrate /ˈɪŋɡreɪt/ adj (arch) ungrateful. • n an ungrateful person.

ingratiate /ɪnˈɡreɪʃiˌeɪt/ vt to bring oneself into another's favour.—**ingratiating, ingratiatory** adj.—**ingratiation** n.

ingratitude /ɪnˈɡrætɪˌtuːd/ or /-ˌtjuːd/ n absence of gratitude; insensibility to kindness.

ingredient /ɪnˈɡriːdiənt/ n something included in a mixture; a component.

ingress /ˈɪŋgrɛs/ *n* entrance.

in-group /ˈɪngruːp/ *n* a group favouring its own members at the expense of members of other groups.

ingrowing /ˈɪnˌgroʊɪŋ/ *adj* (*toe nail, etc*) growing abnormally into the flesh.

ingrowth /ˈɪnˌgroʊθ/ *n* the process of growing inwards; something which grows inwards.

inguinal /ˈɪngwɪnəl/ *adj* of the groin or its vicinity.

ingurgitate /ɪnˈgɔrdʒɪˌteɪt/ *vt* to swallow greedily.—**ingurgitation** *n*.

inhabit /ɪnˈhæbɪt/ *vt* to live in; to occupy; to reside.

inhabitable /ɪnˈhæbɪtəbəl/ *adj* fit for habitation.—**inhabitability** *n*.—**inhabitation** *n*.

inhabitant /-tənt/ *n* a person or animal inhabiting a specified place.—**inhabitancy, inhabitance** *n*.

inhalant /ɪnˈheɪlənt/ *n* a medicine, etc that is inhaled.

inhalation /-həˈleɪʃən/ *n* the act of inhaling.

inhale /ɪnˈheɪl/ *vti* to breathe in.

inhaler /ɪnˈheɪlər/ *n* a device that dispenses medicines in a fine spray for inhalation.

inharmonic /ˌɪnhɑrˈmɒnɪk/, **inharmonious** /ˌɪnhɑrˈmoːniəs/ *adj* lacking harmony; discordant.

inhere /ɪnˈhiːr/ *vi* to be inherent.

inherent /ɪnˈhɛrənt/ or /ɪnˈhiːr-/ *adj* existing as an inseparable part of something.—**inherence, inherency** *n*.—**inherently** *adv*.

inherit /ɪnˈhɛrɪt/ *vt* to receive (property, a title, etc) under a will or by right of legal succession; to possess by genetic transmission. • *vi* to receive by inheritance; to succeed as heir.—**inheritor** *n*.

inheritable /-əbəl/ *adj* capable of being inherited.

inheritance /-əns/ *n* the action of inheriting; something inherited.

inhibit /ɪnˈhɪbɪt/ *vt* to restrain; to prohibit.—**inhibitor, inhibiter** *n*.

inhibition /ˌɪnhɪˈbɪʃən/ *n* an inhibiting or being inhibited; a mental process that restrains or represses an action, emotion, or thought.

inhospitable /ˌɪnhɒˈspɪtəbəl/ or /ɪnˈhɒsp-/ *adj* not hospitable; affording no shelter; barren; cheerless.—**inhospitably** *adv*.—**inhospitality** *n*.

in-house /ˈɪnhəʊs/ or /-ˈhəʊs/ *adj* within an organization.

inhuman /ɪnˈhjuːmən/ or /ɪnˈjuːmən/ *adj* lacking in the human qualities of kindness, pity, etc; cruel, brutal, unfeeling; not human.

inhumane /ˌɪnhjuːˈmeɪn/ *adj* not humane; inhuman.

inhumanity /ˌɪnhjuːˈmænɪti/ *n* (*pl* **inhumanites**) the quality of being inhuman; cruelty.

inhume /ɪnˈhjuːm/ *vt* to bury, inter.—**inhumation** *n*.—**injumer** *n*.

inimical /ɪˈnɪmɪkəl/ *adj* hostile; adverse, unfavourable.—**inimically** *adv*.

inimitable /ɪˈnɪmɪtəbəl/ *adj* impossible to imitate; matchless.—**inimitably** *adv*.

iniquitous /ɪˈnɪkwɪtəs/ *adj* marked by iniquity.

iniquity /ɪˈnɪkwɪti/ *n* (*pl* **iniquities**) wickedness; great injustice.

initial /ɪˈnɪʃəl/ *adj* of or at the beginning. • *n* the first letter of each word in a name; a large letter at the beginning of a chapter, etc. • *vt* (**initialing, initialed** *or* **initialling, initialled**) to sign with initials.—**initialer, initialler** *n*.—**initially** *adv*.

initialize /ɪˈnɪʃəˌlaɪz/ *vt* (*comput*) to format (a disk) to suit a particular processor.—**initialization** *n*.

initiate /ɪˈnɪʃiˌeɪt/ *vt* to bring (something) into practice or use; to teach the fundamentals of a subject to; to admit as a member into a club, etc, *esp* with a secret ceremony. • *n* an initiated person.—**initiator** *n*.—**initiatory** *adj*.

initiation /-ˈeɪʃən/ *n* the act of initiating; a formal, often secret, ceremony of admission.

initiative /ɪˈnɪʃətɪv/ or /ɪˈnɪʃiətɪv/ *n* the action of taking the first step; ability to originate new ideas or methods.

inject /ɪnˈdʒɛkt/ *vt* to force (a fluid) into a vein, tissue, etc, *esp* with a syringe; to introduce (a remark, quality, etc), to interject.—**injectable** *adj*.

injection /ɪnˈdʒɛkʃən/ *n* an injecting; a substance that is injected.—**injective** *adj*.

injector /-ər/ *n* someone who, or something which, injects; a device for injecting fuel into an internal combustion engine; a device for filling the boiler of a steam engine with water.

injudicious /ˌɪndʒuːˈdɪʃəs/ *adj* not judicious; indiscreet; unwise.

injunction /ɪnˈdʒʌŋkʃən/ *n* a command; an order; a court order prohibiting or ordering a given action.—**injunctive** *adj*.

injure /ˈɪndʒər/ *vt* to harm physically or mentally; to hurt, do wrong to.—**injurer** *n*.

injurious /ɪnˈdʒʊriəs/ *adj* causing injury.

injury /ˈɪndʒəri/ *n* (*pl* **injuries**) physical damage; harm.

injury time *n* (*sport*) time added to compensate for stoppages through injuries to players.

injustice /ɪnˈdʒʌstɪs/ *n* the state or practice of being unfair; an unjust act.

ink /ɪŋk/ *n* a coloured liquid used for writing, printing, etc; the dark protective secretion of an octopus, etc. • *vt* to cover, mark, or colour with ink.

inkhorn /ˈɪŋkhɔrn/ *n* (*formerly*) a container for ink.

inkling /ˈɪŋklɪŋ/ *n* a hint; a vague notion.

inkstand /ˈɪŋkstænd/ *n* a stand for an ink bottle.

inkwell /ˈɪŋkˌwɛl/ *n* a container for ink.

inky /ˈɪŋki/ *adj* (**inkier, inkiest**) like very dark ink in colour; black; covered with ink.—**inkiness** *n*.

inlaid /ˈɪnleɪd/ *see* **inlay**.

inland /ˈɪnlænd/ or /-lənd/ *adj* of or in the interior of a country. • *n* an inland region. • *adv* into or toward this region.—**inlander** *n*.

in-law *n* a relative by marriage.

inlay /ˈɪnleɪ/ or /ɪnˈleɪ/ *vt* (**inlaying, inlaid**) to decorate a surface by inserting pieces of metal, wood, etc. • *n* inlaid work; material inlaid.—**inlaid** *adj*.

inlet /ˈɪnlɛt/ or /-lət/ *n* a narrow strip of water extending into a body of land; an opening; a passage, pipe, etc for liquid to enter a machine, etc. • *vt* (**inletting, inletted**) to inlay; to insert.

in loco parentis /ɪn ˌloːkoː pəˈrɛntɪs/ (*Latin*) in the place of a parent.

inmate /ˈɪnmeɪt/ *n* a person confined with others in a prison or institution.

in memoriam /ɪn məˈmoriəm/ (*Latin*) in memory of.

inmost /ˈɪnmoːst/ *adj* farthest within; most secret.

inn /ɪn/ *n* a small hotel; a restaurant or tavern, *esp* in the countryside.

innards /ˈɪnərdz/ *npl* (*inf*) the stomach and intestines, internal organs.

innate /ɪˈneɪt/ or /ˈɪ-/ *adj* existing from birth; inherent; instinctive.—**innately** *adv*.

inner /ˈɪnər/ *adj* further within; inside, internal; private, exclusive. • *n* (*archery*) the innermost ring on a target.

inner city *n* the central area of a city, *esp* as affected by overcrowding and poverty.

innermost /ˈɪnərˌmoːst/ *adj* furthest within.

inner tube *n* the separate inflatable tube within a pneumatic tire.

innervation /ˌɪnərˈveɪʃən/ *n* the arrangement of nerve filaments in the body; special activity or stimulus in any part of the nervous system.

inning /ˈɪnɪŋ/ *n* (*baseball*) a team's turn at bat.

innings /-z/ *n* (*pl* **innings**) (*cricket*) a turn at bat for a batsman or side; the number of runs scored at this time; an opportunity to demonstrate one's abilities.

innkeeper /ˈɪnˌkiːpər/ *n* a person who owns or manages an inn.

innocence /ˈɪnəsəns/ *n* the condition or quality of being innocent.

innocent /ˈɪnəsənt/ *adj* not guilty of a particular crime; free from sin; blameless; harmless; inoffensive; simple, credulous, naive. • *n* an innocent person, as a child.—**innocence** *n*.—**innocently** *adv*.

innocuous /ɪˈnɒkjuəs/ *adj* harmless.—**innocuously** *adv*.—**innocuousness** *n*.

innominate /ɪˈnɒmɪnət/ *adj* without a name.

innovate /ˈɪnəˌveɪt/ *vi* to introduce new methods, ideas, etc; to make changes.—**innovation** *n*.—**innovative, innovatory** *adv*.

innovator /-ər/ *n* one who introduces, or seeks to introduce, new things.

innoxious /ɪˈnɒkʃəs/ *adj* harmless.

innuendo /ˌɪnjuˈɛndoː/ *n* (*pl* **innuendos, innuendoes**) a hint or sly remark, *usu* derogatory; an insinuation.

Innuit /ˈɪnjuːɪt/ or /ˈɪnuɪt/ *see* **Inuit**.

innumerable /ɪˈnuːmərəbəl/ or /-ˈnjuː-/, **innumerous** /-əs/ *adj* too many to be counted; very numerous.—**innumerability** *n*.—**innumerably** *adv*.

innumerate /ɪˈnuːmərət/ or /-ˈnjuː-/ *adj* lacking knowledge or understanding of mathematics and science; not numerate.—*also n*.

inobservance /ˌɪnəbˈzərvəns/ *n* inattention; failure to observe (law, etc).—**inobservant** *adj*.

inoculate /ɪ'nɒkjuˌleɪt/ *vt* to inject a serum or a vaccine into, *esp* in order to create immunity; to protect as if by inoculation.—**inoculation** *n*.—**inoculative** *adj*.

inodorous /ɪn'oːdərəs/ *adj* without odour.

inoffensive /ˌɪnə'fensɪv/ *adj* harmless, not offensive.

inofficious /ˌɪnə'fɪʃəs/ *adj* contrary to moral duty.

inoperable /ɪn'ɒprəbəl/ or /-'ɒpərəbəl/ *adj* not suitable for surgery.—**inoperability** *n*.

inoperative /ɪn'ɒprətɪv/ or /-'ɒpərətɪv/ *adj* not working; producing no effect.

inopportune /ɪn'ɒpərˌtuːn/ or /-ˌtjuːn/ *adj* unseasonable; untimely.—**inopportuneness, inopportunity** *n*.

inordinate /ɪn'ɔrdɪnət/ *adj* excessive.—**inordinately** *adv*.

inorganic /ˌɪnɔr'gænɪk/ *adj* not having the structure or characteristics of living organisms; denoting a chemical compound not containing carbon.—**inorganically** *adv*.

inorganic chemistry *n* the chemistry of all substances except those containing carbon.

inosculate /ɪn'ɒskjuˌleɪt/ *vti* (*anat, of blood vessels, fibres, etc*) to join closely, be closely joined.—**inosculation** *n*.

inpatient /'ɪnˌpeɪʃənt/ *n* a patient being treated while remaining in hospital.

in perpetuum /ˌɪn pər'petuːˌʊm/ *adv* perpetually, forever.

in posse /ɪn 'pɒsi/ *adj, adv* having a possible but not an actual existence, potential.

input /'ɪnpʊt/ *n* what is put in, as power into a machine, data into a computer, etc. • *vt* (**inputting, input** *or* **inputted**) to put in; to enter (data) into a computer.

inquest /'ɪnkwest/ *n* a judicial inquiry held by a coroner, *esp* into a case of violent or unexplained death; (*inf*) any detailed inquiry or investigation.

inquietude /ɪn'kwaɪəˌtuːd/ or /-ˌtjuːd/ *n* unease, disquiet.

inquiline /'ɪnkwɪˌlaɪn/ *n* (*zool*) an animal which lives in the abode of another but does not harm it, *eg* a hermit crab.—**inquilinous** *adj*.

inquire /ɪn'kwaɪr/ *vi* to request information about; (*usu with* **into**) to investigate. • *vt* to ask about.—*also* **enquire.**—**inquirer, enquirer** *n*.

inquiry /ɪn'kwaɪri/ *n* (*pl* **inquiries**) the act of inquiring; a search by questioning; an investigation; a question; research.—*also* **enquiry.**

inquisition /ˌɪnkwə'zɪʃən/ *n* a detailed examination or investigation; (*with cap and* **the**) (*RC Church*) formerly the tribunal for suppressing heresy.—**inquisitional** *adj*.

inquisitive /ɪn'kwɪzɪtɪv/ *adj* eager for knowledge; unnecessarily curious; prying.—**inquisitively** *adv*.—**inquisitiveness** *n*.

inquisitor /ɪn'kwɪzɪtər/ *n* a person who questions searchingly or forcefully; (*often cap*) a member of the Inquisition.

inquisitorial /ɪn'kwɪzɪ'tɔrɪəl/ *adj* of or resembling an inquisitor; prying.—**inquisitorially** *adv*.

in re /ɪn 'riː/ or /-'reɪ/ *prep* in the matter of.

inroad /'ɪnroːd/ *n* a raid into enemy territory; an encroachment or advance.

inrush /'ɪnrʌʃ/ *n* a sudden inward flow or influx.

insalivate /ɪn'sælɪˌveɪt/ *vt* to mix (food) with saliva while chewing.—**insalivation** *n*.

insalubrious /ˌɪnsə'luːbrɪəs/ *adj* (*climate, place*) unhealthy.—**insalubrity** *n*.

insane /ɪn'seɪn/ *adj* not sane, mentally ill; of or for insane people; very foolish.—**insanely** *adv*.

insanitary /ɪn'sænɪteri/ *adj* unclean, likely to cause infection or ill-health.—**insanitariness, insanitation** *n*.

insanity /ɪn'sænɪti/ *n* (*pl* **insanities**) derangement of the mind or intellect; lunacy; madness.

insatiable /ɪn'seɪʃəbəl/ *adj* not easily satisfied; greedy.—**insatiability** *n*.—**insatiability** *adv*.—**insatiably** *adv*.

insatiate /ɪn'seɪʃɪət/ *adj* insatiable.

inscribe /ɪn'skraɪb/ *vt* to mark or engrave (words, etc) on (a surface); to add (a person's name) to a list; to dedicate (a book) to someone; to autograph; to fix in the mind.—**inscribable** *adj*.

inscription /ɪn'skrɪpʃən/ *n* an inscribing; words, etc inscribed on a tomb, coin, stone, etc.—**inscriptional** *adj*.

inscrutable /ɪn'skruːtəbəl/ *adj* hard to understand, incomprehensible; enigmatic.—**inscrutability** *n*.—**inscrutably** *adv*.

insect /'ɪnsekt/ *n* any of a class of small arthropods with three pairs of legs, a head, thorax, and abdomen and two or four wings.

insectary /ɪn'sektəri/ or /'ɪnˌsek-/, /'ɪnsekˌteri/ *n* (*pl* **insectaries**) a place for keeping insects.

insecticide /ɪn'sektəˌsaɪd/ *n* a substance for killing insects.—**insecticidal** *adj*.

insectivore /ɪn'sektɪˌvɔr/ *n* an order of mammals that are small, nocturnal, and feed on insects or other invertebrates; any insect-eating plant or animal.—**insectivorous** *adj*.

insecure /ˌɪnsɪ'kjʊr/ *adj* not safe; feeling anxiety; not dependable.—**insecurely** *adv*.

insecurity /-'kjʊrɪti/ *n* (*pl* **insecurities**) the condition of being insecure; lack of confidence or sureness; instability; something insecure.

inseminate /ɪn'seməˌneɪt/ *vt* to fertilize; to impregnate.—**insemination** *n*.—**inseminator** *n*.

insensate /ɪn'senseɪt/ *adj* not feeling sensation; stupid; without regard or feeling; cold.

insensible /ɪn'sensəbəl/ *adj* unconscious; unaware; indifferent; imperceptible.—**insensibility** *n*.—**insensibly** *adv*.

insensitive /ɪn'sensɪtɪv/ *adj* not sensitive, unfeeling.

insentient /ɪn'senʃənt/ *adj* inert; inanimate.

inseparable /ɪn'sepərəbəl/ or /-'sepərəbəl/ *adj* not able to be separated; closely attached, as romantically.—**inseparability** *n*.—**inseparably** *adv*.

insert /ɪn'sərt/ *vt* to put or fit (something) into something else. • *n* something inserted.—**insertion** *n*.

insertion /ɪn'sərʃən/ *n* the act of inserting; something which is inserted.

in-service /'ɪnˌsərvɪs/ *adj* (*training*) given during employment.

insessorial /ˌɪnse'sɔrɪəl/ *adj* (*ornithology*) adapted for perching.

inset /'ɪnset/ *n* something inserted within something larger; an insert. • *vt* (**insetting, inset**) to set in, insert.—**insetter** *n*.

inshore /'ɪnʃɔr/ *adj, adv* near or towards the shore.

inshrine *see* enshrine.

inside /ɪn'saɪd/ or /'ɪn-/ *n* the inner side, surface, or part; (*pl: inf*) the internal organs, stomach, bowels. • *adj* internal; known only to insiders; secret. • *adv* on or in the inside; within; indoors; (*sl*) in prison. • *prep* in or within.

inside job *n* (*inf*) a crime committed with the help of someone connected with the victim or premises involved.

inside out *adj* reversed; with the inner surface facing the outside.

insider /ɪn'saɪdər/ *n* a person within a place or group; a person with access to confidential information.

insidious /ɪn'sɪdɪəs/ *adj* marked by slyness or treachery; more dangerous than seems evident.—**insidiously** *adv*.—**insidiousness** *n*.

insight /'ɪnsaɪt/ *n* the ability to see and understand clearly the inner nature of things, *esp* by intuition; an instance of such understanding.—**insightful** *adj*.

insignia /ɪn'sɪgnɪə/ *n* (*pl* **insignias, insignia**) a mark or badge of authority; a distinguishing characteristic.

insignificant /ˌɪnsɪg'nɪfɪkənt/ *adj* having little or no importance; trivial; worthless; small, inadequate.—**insignificance, insignificancy** *n*.—**insignificantly** *adv*.

insincere /ˌɪnsɪn'sɪr/ *adj* not sincere; hypocritical.—**insincerely** *adv*.—**insincerity** *n*.

insinuate /ɪn'sɪnjuˌeɪt/ *vt* to introduce or work in slowly, indirectly, etc; to hint.—**insinuator** *n*.

insinuation /-'eɪʃən/ *n* the act of insinuating; an indirect or sly hint.

insipid /ɪn'sɪpɪd/ *adj* lacking any distinctive flavour; uninteresting, dull.—**insipidity, insipidness** *n*.—**insipidly** *adv*.

insist /ɪn'sɪst/ *vi* (*often with* **on** *or* **upon**) to take and maintain a stand. • *vt* to demand strongly; to declare firmly.—**insister** *n*.

insistent /ɪn'sɪstənt/ *adj* insisting or demanding.—**insistence, insistency** *n*.—**insistently** *adv*.

in situ /ɪn 'sɪtjuː/ or /-sɪtuː/ or /'siː-/ *adj* in the original or natural place or position.

insobriety /ˌɪnsə'braɪəti/ *n* drunkenness.

in so far, insofar /ˌɪnsoː'fɑr/ *adv* to such a degree or extent.

insole /'ɪnsoːl/ *n* the innser sole of a shoe, etc; a thickness of material used as a inner sole.

insolent /'ɪnsələnt/ *adj* disrespectful; impudent, arrogant; rude.—**insolence** *n*.—**insolently** *adv*.

insoluble /ɪn'sɒljubəl/ *adj* incapable of being dissolved; impossible to solve or explain.—**insolubility** *n*.—**insolubly** *adv*.

insolvent /ɪn'sɒlvənt/ *adj* unable to pay one's debts; bankrupt.—**insolvency** *n*.

insomnia /ɪnˈsɒmnɪə/ *n* abnormal inability to sleep.

insomniac /-ɪˌæk/ *n* a person who suffers from insomnia.

insomuch /ˌɪnsoˈmʌtʃ/ *adv* (*with* **as** *or* **that**) to such an extent; (*with* **as**) inasmuch.

insouciant /ɪnˈsuːsɪənt/ *adj* calm and unconcerned, carefree.—**insouciance** *n*.

inspect /ɪnˈspɛkt/ *vt* to look at carefully; to examine or review officially.—**inspection** *n*.—**inspectional** *adj*.—**inspective** *adj*.

inspector /-ər/ *n* an official who inspects in order to ensure compliance with regulations, etc; a police officer ranking below a superintendent.—**inspectorate** *n*.—**inspectoral, inspectorial** *adj*.—**inspectorship** *n*.

inspectorate /-rət/ *n* the office, district or rank of an inspector; a body of inspectors.

inspiration /ˌɪnspɪˈreɪʃən/ *n* an inspiring; any stimulus to creative thought; an inspired idea, action, etc.—**inspirational** *adj*.

inspiratory /ɪnˈspɪrətɔrɪ/ *adj* pertaining to inhalation.

inspire /ɪnˈspaɪr/ *vt* to stimulate, as to some creative effort; to motivate by divine influence; to arouse (a thought or feeling) in (someone); to cause.—**inspiring** *adj*.—**inspiringly** *adv*.

inspirit /ɪnˈspɪrɪt/ *vt* to put life into, invigorate; to animate, cheer.

inst. *abbr* = instant (this month).

instability /ˌɪnstəˈbɪlɪtɪ/ *n* (*pl* **instabilities**) lack of stability; inconstancy.

install, instal /ɪnˈstɔl/ *vt* (**installs** *or* **instals, installing, installed**) to formally place in an office, rank, etc; to establish in a place; to settle in a position or state.—**installer** *n*.

installation /ˌɪnstəˈleɪʃən/ *n* the act of installing or being installed; machinery, equipment, etc that has been installed.

instalment, installment /ɪnˈstɔlmənt/ *n* a sum of money to be paid at regular specified times; any of several parts, as of a magazine story or television serial.

instance /ˈɪnstəns/ *n* an example; a step in proceeding; an occasion. • *vt* to give as an example.

instant /ˈɪnstənt/ *adj* immediate; (*food*) concentrated or precooked for quick preparation. • *n* a moment; a particular moment.

instantaneous /ˌɪnstənˈteɪnɪəs/ *adj* happening or done very quickly.—**instantaneously** *adv*.—**instantaneousness, instantaneity** *n*.

instanter /ɪnˈstæntər/ *adv* (*law*) immediately.

instantly /ˈɪnstəntlɪ/ *adv* immediately.

instate /ɪnˈsteɪt/ *vt* to install in an office or rank.

instead /ɪnˈstɛd/ *adv* in place of the one mentioned.

instep /ˈɪnstɛp/ *n* the upper part of the arch of the foot, between the ankle and the toes.

instigate /ˈɪnstɪˌɡeɪt/ *vt* to urge on, goad; to initiate.—**instigation** *n*.—**instigator** *n*.

instil, instill /ɪnˈstɪl/ *vt* (**instils** *or* **instills, instilling, instilled**) to put (an idea, etc) in or into (the mind) gradually.—**instillation** *n*.—**instiller** *n*.

instinct /ˈɪnstɪŋkt/ *n* the inborn tendency to behave in a way characteristic of a species; a natural or acquired tendency; a knack.

instinctive /ɪnˈstɪŋktɪv/, **instinctual** /-tʊəl/ *adj* of, relating to, or prompted by instinct.—**instinctively, instinctually** *adv*.

institute /ˈɪnstɪˌtuːt/ *or* /-ˌtjuːt/ *vt* to organize, establish; to start, initiate. • *n* an organization for the promotion of science, art, etc; a school, college, or department of a university specializing in some field.—**institutor, instituter** *n*.

institution /ˌɪnstɪˈtuːʃən/ *or* /-ˈtjuː-/ *n* an established law, custom, etc; an organization having a social, educational, or religious purpose; the building housing it; (*inf*) a long-established person or thing.

institutional /-əl/ *adj* of or resembling an institution; dull, routine.

institutionalize /ˌɪnstɪˈtuːʃənəˌlaɪz/ *or* /-ˈtjuː-/ *vt* to make or become an institution; to place in an institution; to make a person dependent on an institutional routine and unable to cope on their own.—**institutionalization** *n*.

instruct /ɪnˈstrʌkt/ *vt* to provide with information; to teach; to give instructions to; to authorize.—**instructible** *adj*.—**instructor** *n*.—**instructress** *nf*.

instruction /ɪnˈstrʌkʃən/ *n* an order, direction; the act or process of teaching or training; knowledge imparted; (*comput*) a command in a program to perform a particular operation; (*pl*) orders, directions; detailed guidance.—**instructional** *adj*.

instructive /ɪnˈstrʌktɪv/ *adj* issuing or containing instructions; giving information, educational.—**instructively** *adv*.

instructor /-ər/ *n* someone who instructs; a teacher.

instrument /ˈɪnstrəmənt/ *n* a thing by means of which something is done; a tool or implement; any of various devices for indicating, measuring, controlling, etc; any of various devices producing musical sound; a formal document. • *vt* to orchestrate.

instrument panel *n* a panel in a vehicle or machine in which instruments monitoring speed, engine status, etc are mounted.

instrumental /ˌɪnstrəˈmɛntəl/ *adj* serving as a means of doing something; helpful; of, performed on, or written for a musical instrument or instruments.—**instrumentality** *n*.—**instrumentally** *adv*.

instrumentalist /-ˈmɛntəlɪst/ *n* a person who plays a musical instrument.

instrumentation /ˌɪnstrəmɛnˈteɪʃən/ *n* the arrangement of a musical composition for different instruments; the use or provision of tools or instruments.

insubordinate /ˌɪnsəˈbɔrdɪnət/ *adj* not submitting to authority; rebellious.—**insubordination** *n*.

insubstantial /ˌɪnsəbˈstænʃəl/ *adj* unreal, imaginary; weak or flimsy.—**insubstantiality** *n*.—**insubstantially** *adv*.

insufferable /ɪnˈsʌfərəbəl/ *adj* intolerable; unbearable.—**insufferably** *adv*.

insufficient /ˌɪnsəˈfɪʃənt/ *adj* not sufficient.—**insufficiency, insufficience** *n*.—**insufficiently** *adv*.

insufflate /ˈɪnsəˌfleɪt/ *vt* to blow (air, powder) into or onto.—**insufflation** *n*.—**insufflator** *n*.

insular /ˈɪnsʊlər/ *or* /ˈɪnsjʊ-/ *adj* of or like an island or islanders; narrow-minded; illiberal.—**insularity, insularism** *n*.

insulate /ˈɪnsəˌleɪt/ *or* /ˈɪnsjə-/ *vt* to set apart; to isolate; to cover with a non-conducting material in order to prevent the escape of electricity, heat, sound, etc.—**insulation** *n*.—**insulator** *n*.

insulation /ˌɪnsəˈleɪʃən/ *or* /-sjə-/ *n* the act of insulating; the material used for insulating.

insulator /ˈɪnsəˌleɪtər/ *or* /ˈɪnsjə-/ *n* something which insulates; a non-conductor of electricity, heat or sound.

insulin /ˈɪnsəlɪn/ *or* /ˈɪnsjə-/ *n* a hormone that controls absorption of sugar by the body, secreted by islets of tissue in the pancreas.

insult /ɪnˈsʌlt/ *vt* to treat with indignity or contempt; to offend. • *n* an insulting remark or act.—**insulter** *n*.

insuperable /ɪnˈsuːpərəbəl/ *or* /ɪnˈsjuː-/, /-ˈprəbəl/ *adj* unable to be overcome.—**insuperability** *n*.—**insuperably** *adv*.

insupportable /ˌɪnsəˈpɔrtəbəl/ *adj* unbearable, intolerable.

insurable /ɪnˈʃʊrəbəl/ *adj* able to be insured.

insurance /ɪnˈʃʊrəns/ *or* /-ˈʃərəns/ *n* insuring or being insured; a contract purchased to guarantee compensation for a specified loss by fire, death, etc; the amount for which something is insured; the business of insuring against loss.

insure /ɪnˈʃʊr/ *or* /-ˈʃər/ *vt* to take out or issue insurance on; to ensure. • *vi* to contract to give or take insurance.

insurer /ɪnˈʃʊrər/ *or* /-ˈʃərər/ *n* someone who insures, an underwriter; a company which sells insurance.

insurgent /ɪnˈsɜrdʒənt/ *adj* rebellious, rising in revolt. • *n* a person who fights against established authority, a rebel.—**insurgence** *n*.—**insurgency** *n*.

insurmountable /ˌɪnsərˈmaʊntəbəl/ *adj* which cannot be overcome, insuperable.

insurrection /ˌɪnsəˈrɛkʃən/ *adj* a rising or revolt against established authority.—**insurrectional** *adj*.—**insurrectionary** *n*, *adj*.—**insurrectionism** *n*.—**insurrectionist** *n*.

intact /ɪnˈtækt/ *adj* unimpaired; whole.

intaglio /ɪnˈtælɪoː/ *n* (*pl* **intaglios**) a design carved or engraved below the surface; a printing technique using engraved surfaces.—**intagliated** *adj*.

intake /ˈɪnteɪk/ *n* the place in a pipe, etc where a liquid or gas is taken in; a thing or quantity taken in, as students, etc; the process of taking in.

intangible /ɪnˈtændʒəbəl/ *adj* that cannot be touched, incorporeal; representing value but without material being, as good will; indefinable. • *n* something that is intangible.—**intangibility** *n*.—**intangibly** *adv*.

integer /ˈɪntɪdʒər/ *n* any member of the set consisting of the positive and negative whole numbers and zero, such as -5, 0, 5.

integral /ˈɪntəɡrəl/ *or* /ɪnˈtɛɡrəl/ *adj* necessary for completeness; whole or complete; made up of parts forming a whole. • *n* the result of a mathematical integration.—**integrally** *adv*.

integral calculus *n* (*maths*) the determination of definite and indefinite integrals and their use in the solution of differential equations.

integrant /ˈɪntəgrənt/ *adj* component, making part of a whole.

integrate /ˈɪntəˌgreɪt/ *vti* to make whole or become complete; to bring (parts) together into a whole; to remove barriers imposing segregation upon (racial groups); to abolish segregation; (*math*) to find the integral of.—**integration** *n*.—**integrative** *adj*.

integrated circuit *n* a small electronic circuit assembled from microcomponents mounted on chips of semiconducting material.

integrator /ˈɪntəˌgreɪtər/ *n* someone who, or something which, integrates.

integrity /ɪnˈtɛgrɪti/ *n* honesty, sincerity; completeness, wholeness; an unimpaired condition.

integument /ɪnˈtɛgjʊmənt/ *n* a natural covering as skin, a rind, a husk, etc.—**integumental, integumentary** *adj*.

intellect /ˈɪntəˌlɛkt/ *n* the ability to reason or understand; high intelligence; a very intelligent person.—**intellective** *adj*.

intellection /ˌɪntəˈlɛkʃən/ *n* thought.

intellectual /ˌɪntəˈlɛktʃʊəl/ *adj* of, involving, or appealing to the intellect; requiring intelligence. • *n* an intellectual person.—**intellectuality** *n*.—**intellectually** *adv*.

intellectualism /ˌɪntəˈlɛktʃʊəˌlɪzəm/ *n* the use of the intellect; (*philos*) the theory that all knowledge is derived from the intellect; (*derog*) excessive emphasis on the value of the intellect.—**intellectualist** *n*.

intellectualize /ˌɪntəˈlɛktʃʊəˌlaɪz/ *vt* to make intellectual; to use the intellect on. • *vi* to become intellectual; to use the intellect.—**intellectualization** *n*.

intelligence /ɪnˈtɛlɪdʒəns/ *n* the ability to learn or understand; the ability to cope with a new situation; news or information; those engaged in gathering secret, *esp* military, information.

intelligence quotient *n* a measure of a person's intelligence, calculated by dividing mental age by actual age and multiplying by 100.

intelligent /ɪnˈtɛlɪdʒənt/ *adj* having or showing intelligence; clever, wise, etc.—**intelligently** *adv*.

intelligentsia /ɪnˌtɛlɪˈdʒɛntsɪə/ *n* intellectuals collectively.

intelligible /ɪnˈtɛlɪdʒəbəl/ *adj* able to be understood; clear.—**intelligibility** *n*.—**intelligibly** *adv*.

intemperate /ɪnˈtɛmpərət/ or /-prət/ *adj* indulging excessively in alcoholic drink; unrestrained; (*climate*) extreme.—**intemperance** *n*.—**intemperately** *adv*.

intend /ɪnˈtɛnd/ *vt* to mean, to signify; to propose, have in mind as an aim or purpose.—**intender** *n*.

intendancy /-dənsɪ/ *n* (*pl* **intendancies**) the rank or office of an intendant.

intendant /-dənt/ *n* a superintendent or manager (*esp* under a monarch in France, Spain and Portugal).

intended /-dɪd/ *adj* planned. • *n* (*inf*) a fiancé or fiancée.

intendment /-mənt/ *n* the true meaning of something, as fixed by law.

intense /ɪnˈtɛns/ *adj* very strong, concentrated; passionate, emotional.—**intensely** *adv*.

intensify /ɪnˈtɛnsəˌfaɪ/ *vti* (**intensifying, intensified**) to make or become more intense.—**intensification** *n*.

intensity /ɪnˈtɛnsɪti/ *n* (*pl* **intensities**) the state or quality of being intense; density, as of a negative plate; the force or energy of any physical agent.

intensive /ɪnˈtɛnsɪv/ *adj* of or characterized by intensity; thorough; denoting careful attention given to patients right after surgery, etc.—**intensively** *adv*.

intensive care *n* 24-hour monitoring and treatment of acutely ill patients in hospital; the specialized unit administering this.

intent /ɪnˈtɛnt/ *adj* firmly directed; having one's attention or purpose firmly fixed. • *n* intention; something intended; purpose or meaning.—**intently** *adv*.—**intentness** *n*.

intention /ɪnˈtɛnʃən/ *n* a determination to act in a specified way; anything intended.

intentional /ɪnˈtɛnʃənəl/ *adj* done purposely.—**intentionality** *n*.—**intentionally** *adv*.

inter /ɪnˈtɜr/ *vt* (**interring, interred**) to bury.

inter- /ˈɪntər/ *prefix* between, among.

interact /ˌɪntərˈækt/ *vi* to act upon each other.—**interaction** *n*.—**interactional** *adj*.

interactive /ˌɪntərˈæktɪv/ *adj* interacting; (*comput*) allowing two-way communication between a device, such as a computer or compact video disc, and its user.—**interactivity** *n*.

inter alia /ˌɪntər ˈeɪlɪə/ or /ˈælɪə/ *adv* among other things.

interbreed /ˌɪntərˈbriːd/ *vti* (**interbreeding, interbred**) to breed within the same breed or family; to breed by crossing one species with another.

intercalary /ɪnˈtɜrkələri/ or /-ˈkæləri/ *adj* inserted into the calendar to harmonize it with the solar year, *eg* February 29 as inserted in the leap year.

intercalate /ɪnˈtɜrkəˌleɪt/ *vt* to insert (an intercalary day) into the calendar.—**intercalation** *n*.

intercede /ˌɪntərˈsiːd/ *vi* to intervene on another's behalf; to mediate.—**interceder** *n*.

intercellular /ˌɪntərˈsɛljʊlər/ *adj* lying between cells.

intercept /ˌɪntərˈsɛpt/ *vt* to stop or catch in its course. • *n* a point of intersection of two geometric figures; interception by an interceptor.—**interception** *n*.—**interceptive** *adj*.

interceptor intercepter /ˌɪntərˈsɛptər/, *n* a high-speed fighter aircraft used to intercept and destroy enemy aircraft.

intercession /ˌɪntərˈsɛʃən/ *n* the act of interceding, *esp* by prayer; mediation.—**intercessional, intercessory** *adj*.—**intercessor** *n*.—**intercessorial** *adj*.

interchange /ˌɪntərˈtʃeɪndʒ/ *vt* to give and receive one thing for another; to exchange, to put (each of two things) in the place of the other; to alternate. • *n* an interchanging; a junction on a motorway designed to prevent traffic intersecting.

interchangeable /-əbəl/ *adj* able to be interchanged.—**interchangeability** *n*.—**interchangeably** *adv*.

intercollegiate /ˌɪntərkəˈliːdʒət/ *adj* between or among colleges or universities.

intercolumniation /-kəˌlʌmniˈeɪʃən/ *n* the distance between pillars; the spacing between pillars.—**intercolumniar** *adj*.

intercom /ˈɪntərˌkɒm/ *n* (*inf*) a system of intercommunicating, as in an aircraft.

intercommunicate /ˌɪntərkəˈmjuːnɪˌkeɪt/ *vi* to have mutual communication; to have passage to each other.—**intercommunicable** *adj*.—**intercommunication** *n*.

interconnect /ˌɪntərkəˈnɛkt/ *vti* to connect by reciprocal links.—**interconnection** *n*.

intercontinental /ˌɪntərˌkɒntɪˈnɛntəl/ *adj* between continents.

intercostal /ˌɪntərˈkɒstəl/ *adj* (*anat*) lying between the ribs.

intercourse /ˈɪntərˌkɔrs/ *n* a connection by dealings or communication between individuals or groups; sexual intercourse, copulation.

intercross /ˌɪntərˈkrɒs/ *vti* to crossbreed.

intercurrent /ˌɪntərˈkɜrənt/ *adj* occurring at the same time; (*disease*) occurring during the course of another.—**intercurrence** *n*.

interdependence /ˌɪntərdɪˈpɛndəns/ or /-dɪ-/, **interdependency** *n* dependence on each other.—**interdependent** *adj*.

interdict /ˈɪntərdɪkt/ *vt* to prohibit (an action); to restrain from doing or using something. • *n* an official prohibition.—**interdiction** *n*.—**interdictory** *adj*.

interdisciplinary /ˌɪntərˈdɪsəplɪnˌɛri/ *adj* involving two or more different branches of knowledge.

interest /ˈɪntrəst/ or /-tərəst/ *n* a feeling of curiosity about something; the power of causing this feeling; a share in, or a right to, something; anything in which one has a share; benefit; money paid for the use of money; the rate of such payment. • *vt* to excite the attention of; to cause to have a share in; to concern oneself with.

interested /-ɪd/ or /-təˌrɛstɪd/ *adj* having or expressing an interest; affected by personal interest, not impartial.—**interestedly** *adv*.

interesting /ˈɪntrəstɪŋ/ or /ˈɪntəˌrɛstɪŋ/ *n* engaging the attention.

interface /ˈɪntərˌfeɪs/ *n* a surface that forms the common boundary between two things; an electrical connection between one device and another, *esp* a computer. • *vt* (*elect*) to modify the input and output configurations of (devices) so that they may connect and communicate with each other; to connect using an interface; to be interactive (with).—**interfacial** *adj*.—**interfacially** *adv*.

interfacing /ˈɪntərˌfeɪsɪŋ/ *n* a layer of fabric between the neck, etc of a garment and its facing to give body.

interfere /ˌɪntərˈfiːr/ *vi* to clash; to come between; to intervene; to meddle; to obstruct.—**interfering** *adj*.

interference /ˌɪntərˈfiːrəns/ *n* an interfering; (*radio, TV*) the interruption of reception by atmospherics or by unwanted signals.

interferometer /ˌɪntərfəˈrɒmɪtər/ *n* (*physics*) an instrument used to measure the length of light waves by interference phenomena.

interferon /ˌɪntərˈfɪəˌrɒn/ *n* a protein, produced by cells in response to a virus, which then prevents the virus from growing.

interfuse /ˌɪntərˈfjuːz/ *vti* to mix, blend.—**interfusion** *n*.

intergalactic /ˌɪntərɡəˈlæktɪk/ *adj* occurring or existing between galaxies.

interglacial /ˌɪntərˈɡleɪʃəl/ or /-siəl/ *adj* occurring between two glacial periods.

intergrade /ˈɪntərˌɡreɪd/ *vi* (*usu biol*) to change form gradually.—**intergradation** *n*.

interim /ˈɪntərɪm/ *n* an intervening period of time. • *adj* provisional, temporary. • *adv* meanwhile.

interior /ɪnˈtiːriːər/ *adj* situated within; inner; inland; private. • *n* the interior part, as of a room, country, etc.

interior angle *n* the angle between two adjacent sides of a polygon.

interior design *n* the art or business of an interior designer—*also* **interior decoration**.

interior designer *n* a person whose profession is the planning of the decor and furnishings of the interiors of houses, offices, etc.—*also* **interior decorator**.

interj. *abbr* = interjection.

interject /ˌɪntərˈdʒɛkt/ *vt* to throw in between; to interrupt with.—**interjector** *n*.—**interjectory** *adj*.

interjection /ˌɪntərˈdʒɛkʃən/ *n* an interjecting; an interruption; an exclamation.—**interjectional** *adj*.—**interjectionally** *adv*.

interlace /ˌɪntərˈleɪs/ *vti* to combine (as if) by lacing or weaving together.—**interlacement** *n*.

interlard /ˌɪntərˈlɑrd/ *vt* to insert something foreign into.

interleaf /ˈɪntərˌliːf/ *n* (*pl* **interleaves**) an additional, blank leaf inserted into a book.

interleave /ˌɪntərˈliːv/ *vti* to insert an extra page (*usu* blank) in a book.

interline /ˌɪntərˈlaɪn/ *vt* to write between lines.—**interlinear** *adj*.—**interlineation** *n*.

interlining /ˈɪntərˌlaɪnɪŋ/ *n* an extra lining between the lining and the outer fabric of a garment, etc; the material for this.

interlink /ˌɪntərˈlɪŋk/ *vt* to link together.

interlock /ˌɪntərˈlɒk/ *vti* to lock or become locked together; to join with one another.

interlocution /ˌɪntərləˈkjuːʃən/ *n* dialogue, discussion.

interlocutor /ˌɪntərˈlɒkjʊtər/ *n* a person who takes part in a conversation.—**interlocutress, interlocutrix** *nf*.

interlocutory /ˌɪntərˈlɒkjʊtəri/ *adj* conversational; (*law*) pronounced during legal proceedings.

interlope /ˈɪntərˌloːp/ *vi* to intrude in a matter in which one has no real concern.

interloper /-ər/ *n* a person who meddles; an intruder.

interlude /ˈɪntərˌluːd/ *n* anything that fills time between two events, as music between acts of a play.

interlunar /ˌɪntərˈluːnər/ *adj* coming between the old and the new moon.

intermarry /ˌɪntərˈmɛri/ or /-mæri/ *vi* (**intermarrying, intermarried**) (*different races, religions, etc*) to become connected by marriage; to marry within one's close family.—**intermarriage** *n*.

intermediary /ˌɪntərˈmiːdiːəri/ *n* (*pl* **intermediaries**) a mediator. • *adj* acting as a mediator; intermediate.

intermediate /ˌɪntərˈmiːdiət/ *adj* in the middle; in between.

interment /ɪnˈtərmənt/ *n* burial.

intermezzo /ˌɪntərˈmɛtsoː/ *n* (*pl* **intermezzos, intermezzi**) a short musical composition between parts of an opera, play, etc; a movement between sections of an extended instrumental work; a similar composition intended as an independent work.

interminable /ɪnˈtərmɪnəbəl/ *adj* lasting or seeming to last forever; endless.—**interminably** *adv*.

intermingle /ˌɪntərˈmɪŋɡəl/ *vti* to mingle or mix together.

intermission /ˌɪntərˈmɪʃən/ *n* an interval of time between parts of a performance.

intermit /ˌɪntərˈmɪt/ *vb* (**intermitting, intermitted**) *vt* to cause to cease for a time; to suspend. • *vi* to cease for a time; to be suspended.

intermittent /ˌɪntərˈmɪtənt/ *adj* stopping and starting again at intervals; periodic.—**intermittence, intermittency** *n*.—**intermittently** *adv*.

intermix /ˌɪntərˈmɪks/ *vti* to mix together.

intermixture /ˌɪntərˈmɪkstʃər/ *n* the act of mixing together; a mixture.

intern[1] /ˈɪntərn/ *vt* to detain and confine within an area, *esp* during wartime.—**internment** *n*.

intern[2] *n* a doctor serving in a hospital, *usu* just after graduation from medical school, a houseman.

intern[3], **interne** *n* an apprentice journalist, teacher, etc.

internal /ɪnˈtərnəl/ *adj* of or on the inside; of or inside the body; intrinsic; domestic.—**internality** *n*.—**internally** *adv*.

internal combustion engine *n* an engine producing power by the explosion of a fuel-and-air mixture within the cylinders.

international /ˌɪntərˈnæʃənəl/ *adj* between or among nations; concerned with the relations between nations; for the use of all nations; of or for people in various nations. • *n* a sporting competition between teams from different countries; a member of an international team of players.—**internationality** *n*.—**internationally** *adv*.

International Date Line *n* the line running north to south along the 180-degree meridian, east of which is one day earlier than west of it.

internationalism /ˌɪntərˈnæʃənəˌlɪzəm/ *n* an attitude, belief, or policy favouring the promotion of cooperation and understanding between nations.—**internationalist** *n*.

interne /ˈɪnˌtərn/ *see* **intern**[3].

internecine /ˌɪntərˈnɛsiːn/ or /-aɪn/, /-niːs-/ *adj* extremely destructive to both sides.

internee /ˌɪntərˈniː/ *n* a person who is interned.

Internet /ˈɪntərnɛt/ *n* the worldwide system of linked computer networks.

internist /ɪnˈtərnɪst/ *n* a physician who specializes in internal diseases.

internode /ˈɪntərˌnoːd/ *n* (*bot*) the space on a plant stem between two nodes or leaf joints.—**internodal** *adj*.

internuncial /ˌɪntərˈnɛnʃəl/ *adj* pertaining to an internuncio; (*anat*) transmitting nervous signals.

internuncio /ˌɪntərˈnɛnˌʃoː/ or /-ʃiˌoː/, /-siˌoː/, /-ˈnʊntsiˌoː/ *n* a representative of the Pope.

interpellate /ɪnˈtərpəˌleɪt/ *vt* to question (an official) about government policy or about personal conduct.—**interpellation** *n*.—**interpellator** *n*.

interpenetrate /ˌɪntərˈpɛnəˌtreɪt/ *vt* to penetrate thoroughly. • *vi* to penetrate each other.—**interpenetration** *n*.—**interpenetrative** *adj*.

interplanetary /ˌɪntərˈplænətəri/ *adj* between or among planets.

interplay /ˈɪntərˌpleɪ/ *n* the action of two things on each other, interaction.

interplead /ˌɪntərˈpliːd/ *vi* (**interpleading, interpleaded, interplead, interpled**) (*law*) to discuss a point incidentally arising, or concerning a third party.

interpleader /-ər/ *n* (*law*) the discussion of a point incidentally arising or concerning a third party.

Interpol /ˈɪntərˌpɒl/ (*acronym*) International Criminal Police Organization.

interpolate /ɪnˈtərpəˌleɪt/ *vt* to change (a text) by inserting new material; to insert between or among others; (*math*) to estimate a value between two known values.—**interpolator** *n*.—**interpolation** *n*.

interpose /ˌɪntərˈpoːz/ *vti* to place or come between; to intervene (with); to interrupt (with).—**interposer** *n*.—**interposition** *n*.

interpret /ɪnˈtərprət/ *vt* to explain; to translate; to construe; to give one's own conception of, as in a play or musical composition. • *vi* to translate between speakers of different languages.—**interpretational** *adj*.

interpretation /-ˈteɪʃən/ *n* an act or instance of interpreting; an explanation; a rendering (of a piece of music, theatre, etc).

interpreter /ɪnˈtərprətər/ *n* a person who translates orally for persons speaking in different languages; (*comput*) a program that translates an instruction into machine code.

interracial /ˌɪntərˈreɪʃəl/ *adj* between or among races.

interregnum /ˌɪntərˈrɛɡnəm/ *n* (*pl* **interregnums, interregna**) the period between two reigns, governments, etc; a suspension of normal government; a pause in a continuous series.

interrelate /ˌɪntərəˈleɪt/ *vti* to be or place in a mutually dependant or reciprocal relationship.—**interrelation** *n*.—**interrelationship** *n*.

interrogate /ɪnˈtɛrəˌɡeɪt/ *vti* to question, *esp* formally.—**interrogation** *n*.—**interrogational** *adj*.—**interrogator** *n*.

interrogative /ˌɪntəˈrɒgətɪv/ *adj* asking a question. • *n* a word used in asking a question.—**interrogatively** *adv*.

interrogatory /ˌɪntəˈrɒgətɔri/ *adj* questioning. • *n* (*pl* **interrogatories**) examination by questions.—**interrogatorily** *adv*.

interrupt /ˌɪntəˈrʌpt/ *vt* to break into (a discussion, etc) or break in upon (a speaker, worker, etc); to make a break in the continuity of. • *vi* to interrupt an action, talk, etc.—**interrupter** *n*.—**interruptive** *adj*.

interruption /-ˈʌpʃən/ *n* the act of interrupting; a hindrance; a remark interposed in a conversation, etc.

intersect /ˌɪntərˈsekt/ *vti* to cut or divide by passing through or crossing; (*lines, roads, etc*) to meet and cross each other.

intersection /ˈɪntərˌsekʃən/ *n* an intersecting; the place where two lines, roads, etc meet or cross.—**intersectional** *adj*.

interspace /ˈɪntərˌspeɪs/ *n* a space between things.

intersperse /ˌɪntərˈspərs/ *vt* to scatter or insert among other things; to diversify with other things scattered here and there.—**interspersion** *n*.

interstate /ˈɪntərˌsteɪt/ *adj* between or among different states of a federation.

interstellar /ˌɪntərˈstelər/ *adj* between or among stars.

interstice /ɪnˈtərstɪs/ *n* a crack; a crevice; a minute space.

interstitial /ˌɪntərˈstɪʃəl/ *adj* occurring in interstices.

intertexture /ˌɪntərˈtekstʃər/ *n* the act or product of interweaving.

intertribal /ˌɪntərˈtraɪbəl/ *adj* between or among tribes.

intertwine /ˌɪntərˈtwaɪn/ *vti* to twine or twist closely together.

interval /ˈɪntərvəl/ *n* a space between things; the time between events; (*mus*) the difference of pitch between two notes.

intervene /ˌɪntərˈviːn/ *vi* to occur or come between; to occur between two events, etc; to come in to modify, settle, or hinder some action, etc.—**intervener, intervenor** *n*.—**intervention** *n*.—**interventional** *adj*.

interventionist /ˌɪntərˈvenʃənɪst/ *n* a person who favours intervention. • *adj* of or in favour of intervention.—**interventionism** *n*.

interview /ˈɪntərˌvjuː/ *n* a meeting in which a person is asked about his or her views, etc, as by a newspaper or television reporter; a published account of this; a formal meeting at which a candidate for a job is questioned and assessed by a prospective employer. • *vt* to have an interview with.—**interviewer** *n*.

interviewee /-vjuːˈiː/ *n* a person who is interviewed.

interweave /ˌɪntərˈwiːv/ *vti* (**interweaving, interwove** *or* **interweaved,** *pp* **interwoven** *or* **interweaved**) to weave together, interlace; to intermingle.

interwind /ˈɪntərwɪnd/ *vt* (**interwinding, interwound**) to wind together.

intestate /ɪnˈtesteɪt/ *adj* having made no will. • *n* a person who dies intestate.—**intestacy** *n*.

intestine /ɪnˈtestaɪn/ *or* /-ɪŋ/ *n* the lower part of the alimentary canal between the stomach and the anus.—**intestinal** *adj*.

intifada /ˌɪntɪˈfɑːdə/ *n* the Arabic word for "uprising," *esp* the uprising in Israel of Palestinian inhabitants.

intimacy /ˈɪntɪməsi/ *n* (*pl* **intimacies**) close or confidential friendship; familiarity; sexual relations.

intimate /ˈɪntɪmət/ *adj* most private or personal; very close or familiar, *esp* sexually; deep and thorough. • *n* an intimate friend. • *vt* to indicate; to make known; to hint or imply.—**intimately** *adv*.

intimation /-ˈmeɪʃən/ *n* the act of intimating; a notice, announcement.

intimidate /ɪnˈtɪmɪˌdeɪt/ *vt* to frighten; to discourage, silence, etc *esp* by threats.—**intimidation** *n*.—**intimidator** *n*.

intinction /ɪnˈtɪŋʃən/ *n* (*Eastern Church*) the practice of administering both parts of Holy Communion at the same time by dipping the bread into the wine.

into /ˈɪntuː/ *or* /ˈɪntə/ *prep* to the interior or inner parts of; to the middle; to a particular condition; (*inf*) deeply interested or involved in.

intolerable /ɪnˈtɒlərəbəl/ *adj* unbearable.—**intolerably** *adv*.

intolerance /ɪnˈtɒlərəns/ *n* lack of toleration of the opinions or practices of others; inability to bear or endure.—**intolerant** *adj*.

intonate /ˈɪntəˌneɪt/ *vti* to recite in a singing voice, chant.

intonation /ˌɪntəˈneɪʃən/ *n* intoning; variations in pitch of the speaking voice; an accent.—**intonational** *adj*.

intone /ɪnˈtoːn/ *vti* to speak or recite in a singing tone; to chant.—**intoner** *n*.

in toto /ɪn ˈtoːtoː/ *adv* completely; as a whole; entirely.

intoxicant /ɪnˈtɒksɪkənt/ *n* something that intoxicates, *esp* a drug or an alcoholic drink.—*also adj*.

intoxicate /ɪnˈtɒksɪˌkeɪt/ *vt* to make drunken; to elate; to poison.—**intoxicatingly** *adv*.

intoxication /-ˈkeɪʃən/ *n* drunkenness; great excitement; poisoning.

intra- /ˈɪntrə/ *prefix* within.

intracranial /ˌɪntrəˈkreɪniəl/ *adj* within the skull.

intractable /ɪnˈtræktəbəl/ *adj* unmanageable, uncontrollable; (*problem, illness, etc*) difficult to solve, alleviate, or cure.—**intractability** *n*.—**intractably** *adv*.

intrados /ɪnˈtreɪdɒs/ *n* (*pl* **intrados, intradoses**) the inner and lower curve of an arch.

intramural /ˌɪntrəˈmjʊrəl/ *adj* (*education*) within an institution or organization.

intranet /ˈɪntrənet/ *n* a system that works in a similar way to the Internet, but which has limited access and may work, for example, in an office.

intransigent /ɪnˈtrænzɪdʒənt/ *or* /-sɪdʒənt/ *adj* unwilling to compromise, irreconcilable.—**intransigence** *n*.—**intransigently** *adv*.

intransitive /ɪnˈtrænzɪtɪv/ *or* /-sɪtɪv/ *adj* (*gram*) denoting a verb that does not take a direct object.—**intransitively** *adv*.

intrauterine /ˌɪntrəˈjuːtəˌrɪn/ *or* /-ˌraɪn/ *adj* inside the uterus.

intrauterine device *n* a small loop or coil inserted into the uterus as a contraceptive.

intravenous /ˌɪntrəˈviːnəs/ *adj* into a vein.—**intravenously** *adv*.

in-tray /ˈɪntreɪ/ *n* a tray holding documents, etc, awaiting attention.

intrench /ɪnˈtrentʃ/ *see* **entrench**.

intrepid /ɪnˈtrepɪd/ *adj* bold; fearless; brave.—**intrepidity** *n*.—**intrepidly** *adv*.

intricate /ˈɪntrɪkət/ *adj* difficult to understand; complex, complicated; involved, detailed.—**intricacy** *n*.—**intricately** *adv*.

intrigue /ɪnˈtriːg/ *n* a secret or underhand plotting; a secret or underhanded plot or scheme; a secret love affair. • *vb* (**intriguing, intrigued**) *vi* to carry on an intrigue. • *vt* to excite the interest or curiosity of.—**intriguer** *n*.

intrinsic /ɪnˈtrɪnzɪk/ *adj* belonging to the real nature of a person or thing; inherent.—**intrinsically** *adv*.

intro- /ˈɪntroː/ *prefix* within, into.

intro *n* (*pl* **intros**) (*inf*) introduction.

introduce /ˌɪntrəˈdjuːs/ *vt* to make (a person) acquainted by name (with other persons); to bring into use or establish; to present (legislation, etc) for consideration or approval; to present a radio or television programme; to bring into or insert.—**introducer** *n*.

introduction /ˌɪntrəˈdʌkʃən/ *n* an introducing or being introduced; the presentation of one person to another; preliminary text in a book; a preliminary passage in a musical composition.

introductory /ˌɪntrəˈdʌktəri/ *adj* serving as an introduction; preliminary.—**introductorily** *adv*.

introit /ˈɪntrɔɪt/ *n* (*RC Church, Church of England*) a psalm or passage of scripture sung by the choir as the priest approaches the altar before Mass or Holy Communion.

intromission /ˌɪntrəˈmɪʃən/ *n* insertion; introduction.

intromit /ˌɪntrəˌmɪt/ *vt* to insert.—**intromittent** *adj*.

introspect /ˌɪntrəˈspekt/ *vi* to examine one's own thoughts and feelings.

introspection /-ˈspekʃən/ *n* examination of one's own mind and feelings, etc.—**introspectional, introspective** *adj*.

introversion /ˌɪntrəˈvərʒən/ *n* the act of introverting; the state of being introverted; the direction of, or tendancy to direct, one's thoughts and concerns inward.

introvert /ˈɪntrəˌvərt/ *vt* to turn or direct inward. • *vi* to produce introversion in. • *n* a person who is more interested in his or her own thoughts, feelings, etc than in external objects or events. • *adj* characterized by introversion.—**introversive** *adj*.

intrude /ɪnˈtruːd/ *vti* to force (oneself) upon others unasked.—**intruder** *n*.—**intrudingly** *adj*.

intrusion /ɪnˈtruːʒən/ *n* the act or an instance of intruding; the forcible entry of molten rock into and between existing rocks.—**intrusional** *adj*.

intrusive /ɪnˈtruːsɪv/ *adj* intruding; tending to intrude; (*rocks*) formed by intrusion.—**intrusively** *adv*.

intrust /ɪnˈtrʌst/ *see* **entrust**.

intubate /ˈɪntuˌbeɪt/ *or* /-tjuː-/ *vt* (*med*) to insert a tube into (the larynx, etc).—**intubation** *n*.

intuit /ɪnˈtuːɪt/ *or* /-tjuː-/ *vt* to know by intuition.

intuition /ˌɪntuːˈtʃən/ *or* /-tjuː-/ *n* a perceiving of the truth of something immediately without reasoning or analysis; a hunch, an insight.—**intuitional** *adj*.—**intutionally** *adv*.

intuitive /ɪn'tuːɪtɪv/ or /-tjuː-/ *adj* perceiving or perceived by intuition.—**intuitively** *adv*.

intuitivism /-vɪzəm/ *n* the doctrine that ethical principles are matters of intuition.—**intuitivist** *n*.

intuitonism /-nˌɪzəm/, **intuitionalism** /-nəlɪm/ *n* the doctrine that the immediate perception of truth is by intuition.—**intuitionist, intuitionalist** *n*.

intumescence /ˌɪntuːmɛs'əns/, **intumescency** /-si/ *n* a swelling up; a tumid state.—**intumescent** *adj*.

intussusception /ˌɪntəssə'sɛpʃən/ *n* (*med*) the protrusion of the upper part of the intestinal canal into the lower part; (*biol*) the expansion of a cell.

intwine /ɪn'twaɪn/ *see* **entwine**.

Inuit /'ɪnjuːɪt/ or /'ɪnʊɪt/ *n* (*pl* **Inuit, Inuits**) an Eskimo from Greenland or North America.—*also* **Innuit**.

Inuktitut /ɪn'ʊktɪtʊt/ *n* the language of the Inuit.

inulin /'ɪnuːlɪn/ *n* a starchy constituent of many plants.

inunction /ɪn'ʌŋkʃən/ *n* the act of applying ointment; the act of anointing or smearing with oil.

inundate /'ɪnənˌdeɪt/ *vt* to cover as with a flood; to deluge.—**inundation** *n*.—**inundator** *n*.

inure /ɪ'njʊr/ *vt* to accustom to, *esp* to something unpleasant.—*also* **enure**.—**inurement, enurement** *n*.

inurn /ɪn'ɜrn/ *vt* to put (ashes) in an urn.

inutile /ɪn'juːˈl/ *adj* useless.

invade /ɪn'veɪd/ *vt* to enter (a country) with hostile intentions; to encroach upon; to penetrate; to crowd into as if invading.—**invader** *n*.

in vacuo /ɪn 'vækjuːɒ/ *adv* in a vacuum.

invaginate /ɪn'vædʒɪˌneɪt/ *vt* (*anat*) to fold back a part of a tubular organ on itself so that it is sheathed.

invagination /-'neɪʃən/ *n* the process of invaginating; the state of being invaginated.

invalid[1] /ɪn'vælɪd/ *adj* not valid.

invalid[2] /'ɪnvəˌlɪd/ *n* a person who is ill or disabled. • *vt* to cause to become an invalid; to disable; to cause to retire from the armed forces because of ill-health or injury.

invalidate /ɪn'vælɪˌdeɪt/ *vt* to render not valid; to deprive of legal force.—**invalidation** *n*.

invalidity /ˌɪnvə'lɪdɪti/ *n* (*pl* **invalidities**) a lack of validity; a state of illness or disability.

invaluable /ɪn'væljʊbəl/ or /-juːəbəl/ *adj* too valuable to be measured in money.—**invaluably** *adv*.

Invar /'ɪnˌvɑr/ *n* (*trademark*) an alloy of nickel and steel, used in scientific instruments because of its invariability.

invariable /ɪn'veriəbəl/ *adj* never changing; constant.—**invariability** *n*.—**invariably** *adv*.

invasion /ɪn'veɪʒən/ *n* the act of invading with military forces; an encroachment, intrusion.

invasive /ɪn'veɪsɪv/ *adj* marked by military aggression; tending to spread; tending to infringe.

invective /ɪn'vɛktɪv/ *n* the use of violent or abusive language or writing.

inveigh /ɪn'veɪ/ *vi* to speak violently or bitterly (against).—**inveigher** *n*.

inveigle /ɪn'veɪgəl/ or /-'viːgəl/ *vt* to entice or trick into doing something.—**inveiglement** *n*.—**inveigler** *n*.

invent /ɪn'vɛnt/ *vt* to think up; to think out or produce (a new device, process, etc); to originate; to fabricate (a lie, etc).—**inventible, inventable** *adj*.—**inventor** *n*.

invention /ɪn'vɛnʃən/ *n* something invented; inventiveness.—**inventional** *adj*.

inventive /ɪn'vɛntɪv/ *adj* pertaining to invention; skilled in inventing.—**inventiveness** *n*.

inventory /'ɪnvənˌtɔri/ *n* (*pl* **inventories**) an itemized list of goods, property, etc, as of a business; the store of such goods for such a listing; a list of the property of an individual or an estate. • *vt* (**inventorying, inventoried**) to make an inventory of; to enter in an inventory.—**inventoriable** *adj*.—**inventorial** *adj*.

inveracity /ˌɪnvə'ræsəti/ *n* (*pl* **inveracities**) untruthfulness.

inverse /'ɪnvɜrs/ or /-'vɜrs/ *adj* reversed in order or position; opposite, contrary. • *n* an inverse state or thing.—**inversely** *adv*.

inversion /ɪn'vɜrʒən/ *n* an inverting or being inverted; something inverted.—**inversive** *adj*.

invert /ɪn'vɜrt/ *vt* to turn upside down or inside out; to reverse in order, position or relationship.—**invertible** *adj*.

invertebrate /ɪn'vɜrtəbreɪt/ *adj* without a backbone.—*also* **invertebral.** • *n* an animal without a backbone.

inverted comma *n* a quotation mark.

invest /ɪn'vɛst/ *vt* to commit (money) to property, stocks and shares, etc for profit; to devote effort, time, etc on a particular activity; to install in office with ceremony; to furnish with power, authority, etc. • *vi* to invest money.

investigate /ɪn'vɛstɪˌgeɪt/ *vti* to search (into); to inquire, examine.—**investigative, investigatory** *adj*.

investigation /ɪnˌvɛstɪ'geɪʃən/ *n* the act of investigating; an inquiry; a search to uncover facts, etc.—**investigational** *adj*.

investigator /-ər/ *n* one who investigates, *esp* a private detective.

investiture /ɪn'vɛstɪˌtʃər/ *n* the act or right of giving legal possession; the ceremony of investing a person with an office, robes, title, etc.

investment /ɪn'vɛstmənt/ *n* the act of investing money productively; the amount invested; an activity in which time, effort or money has been invested.

investor /ɪn'vɛstər/ *n* a person who invests money.

inveterate /ɪn'vɛtərət/ *adj* firmly established, ingrained; habitual.—**inveteracy** *n*.—**inveterately** *adv*.

invidious /ɪn'vɪdiəs/ *adj* tending to provoke ill-will, resentment or envy; (*decisions, etc*) unfairly discriminating.—**invidiously** *adv*.—**invidiousness** *n*.

invigorate /ɪn'vɪgəˌreɪt/ *vt* to fill with vigour and energy; to refresh.—**invigorating** *adj*.—**invigoration** *n*.—**invigorative** *adj*.—**invigorator** *n*.

invincible /ɪn'vɪnsɪbəl/ *adj* unconquerable.—**invincibility** *n*.—**invincibly** *adv*.

inviolable /ɪn'vaɪələbəl/ *adj* not to be broken or harmed.—**inviolability** *n*.—**inviolably** *adv*.

inviolate /ɪn'vaɪələt/ *adj* not violated; unbroken, unharmed.—**inviolacy** *n*.

invisible /ɪn'vɪzɪbəl/ *adj* unable to be seen; hidden.—**invisibility** *n*.—**invisibly** *adv*.

invitation /ˌɪnvɪ'teɪʃən/ *n* a message used in inviting.

invite /ɪn'vaɪt/ *vt* to ask to come somewhere or do something; to ask for; to give occasion for; to tempt; to entice. • *n* (*inf*) an invitation.

inviting /ɪn'vaɪtɪŋ/ *adj* attractive, enticing.—**invitingly** *adv*.

in vitro /ɪn 'viːtrəʊ/ *adv, adj* (*biological experiments, etc*) occurring outside the living body and in an artificial environment.

in vivo /ɪn 'viːvəʊ/ *adv, adj* (*biological processes, etc*) occurring inside the living body.

invocation /ˌɪnvə'keɪʃən/ *n* the act of invoking; a formula used in invoking.—**invocatory** *adj*.

invoice /'ɪnvɔɪs/ *n* a document listing goods dispatched, *usu* with particulars of their price and quantity; to demand due settlement. • *vt* to submit an invoice for or to.

invoke /ɪn'vəʊk/ *vt* to call on (God, etc) for help, blessing, etc; to resort to (a law, etc) as pertinent; to implore.

involucel /ɪn'vɒljuːˌsɛl/ *n* (*bot*) a bract around part of a flower head.

involucre /'ɪnvəˌluːkər/ *n* (*bot*) a ring of bracts around the base of a flower cluster.

involuntary /ɪn'vɒlənteri/ *adj* not done by choice; not consciously controlled.—**involuntarily** *adv*.—**involuntariness** *n*.

involute /'ɪnvəˌluːt/, **involuted** *adj* intricate; (*bot*) folded or rolled inwards (*eg* leaves, flowers); curled spirally.

involution /ˌɪnvə'luːʃən/ *n* something which is involute; the act of involving; involvement, complication; (*anat*) the return of an organ or tissue to its normal size after distension; (*math*) the process of raising an arithmetical or algebraic quantity to a given power.

involve /ɪn'vɒlv/ *vt* to affect or include; to require; to occupy, to make busy; to complicate; to implicate.—**involvement** *n*.

invulnerable /ɪn'vɛlnərəbəl/ *adj* not capable of being wounded or hurt in any way.—**invulnerability** *n*.—**invulnerable** *adj*.

inward /'ɪnwərd/ *adj* situated within or directed to the inside; relating to or in the mind or spirit. • *adv* inwards.

inwardly /'ɪnwərdli/ *adv* within; in the mind or spirit; towards the inside or centre.

inwards /'ɪnwərdz/ *adv* towards the inside or interior; in the mind or spirit.

inweave /ɪn'wiːv/ *vt* (**inweaving, inwove** or **inweaved,** *pp* **inwoven** or **inweaved**) to weave in.

inwrought /ɪn'rɒt/ or /'ɪnrɒt/ *adj* worked into or onto (fabric, etc); adorned with figures or patterns.

Io /ˈaɪoː/ (*chem symbol*) ionium.

iodic /aɪˈɒdɪk/ *adj* pertaining to, or containing, iodine.

iodide /ˈaɪəˌdaɪd/ *n* a compound of iodine.

iodine /ˈaɪəˌdaɪn/ or /-ˌdiːn/ *n* a nonmetallic element, found in seawater and seaweed, whose compounds are used in medicine and photography.

iodism /ˈaɪəˌdɪzəm/ *n* poisoning caused by overdoses of iodine.

iodize /ˈaɪəˌdaɪz/ *vt* to treat or combine with iodine.

iodoform /aɪˈoːdəˌfɔrm/ *n* a compound of iodine, used as an antiseptic.

ion /ˈaɪɒn/ or /ˈaɪən/ *n* an electrically charged atom or group of atoms formed through the gain or loss of one or more electrons.

Ionic /aɪˈɒnɪk/ *adj* of a Greek style of architecture that is characterized by ornamental scrolls on the tops of columns.

ionic *adj* of or occurring in the form of ions.

ionize /ˈaɪəˌnaɪz/ *vti* to change or become changed into ions.—**ionization** *n*.

ionosphere /aɪˈɒnəˌsfiːr/ *n* the series of ionized layers high in the stratosphere from which radio waves are reflected.—**ionospheric** *adj*.

iota /aɪˈoːtə/ *n* the ninth letter of the Greek alphabet; a very small quantity; a jot.

IOU /ˌaɪoːˈjuː/ *n* (*pl* **IOUs**) a written note promising to pay a sum of money to the holder.

IPA *abbr* = International Phonetic Alphabet.

ipecac /ˈɪpɪˌkæk/, **ipecacuanha** /ˌɪpɪˌkækjuːˈænə/ *n* a South American plant, the root of which is made into a medicine used as an emetic and purgative.

ipso facto /ˌɪpsoːˈfæktoː/ *adv* by the fact or act itself.

IQ *abbr* = Intelligence Quotient.

Ir (*chem symbol*) iridium.

IRA *abbr* = Irish Republican Army.

Iranian /ɪˈreɪnɪən/ or /-ˈrɒnɪən/ *n* a native or inhabitant of Iran; a branch of the Indo-European group of languages including Persian; modern Persian.—*also adj*.

irascible /ɪˈræsɪbəl/ *adj* easily angered; hot-tempered.—**irascibility** *n*.—**irascibly** *adv*.

irate /aɪˈreɪt/ *adj* enraged, furious.—**irately** *adv*.

IRC *abbr* = Internet Relay Chat, a type of "meeting to chat" facility on the Internet which takes place in a chatroom.

ire /aɪr/ *n* anger; wrath.

irenic /aɪˈriːnɪk/, **irenical** /-əl/ *adj* aiming at peace.

iridaceous /ˌɪrɪˈdeɪʃəs/ *adj* (*bot*) of, or pertaining to, the iris family.

iridescent /ˌɪrɪˈdesənt/ *adj* exhibiting a spectrum of shimmering colours, which change as the position is altered.—**iridescence** *n*.

iridium /ɪˈrɪdɪəm/ *n* a metallic element that is extraordinarily resistant to corrosion.

iris[1] /ˈaɪrɪs/ *n* (*pl* **irises**, **irides**) the round, pigmented membrane surrounding the pupil of the eye.

iris[2] *n* (*pl* **irises**) a perennial herbaceous plant with sword-shaped leaves and brightly coloured flowers.

Irish /ˈaɪrɪʃ/ *adj* of Ireland or its people. • *n* the Celtic language of Ireland.

Irish bull *see* **bull**[3].

Irish coffee *n* coffee mixed with Irish whiskey and topped with fresh cream.

Irish moss *see* **carrageen**.

Irish stew *n* a stew of mutton, onions and potatoes.

iritis /ˌaɪˈraɪtɪs/ *n* (*med*) inflammation of the iris.

irk /ərk/ *vt* to annoy, irritate.

irksome /ˈirˈkʊtsk/ *adj* tedious; tiresome.

iron /ˈaɪrn/ *n* a metallic element, the most common of all metals; a tool, etc of this metal; a heavy implement with a heated flat underface for pressing cloth; (*pl*) shackles of iron; firm strength; power; any of certain golf clubs with angled metal heads. • *adj* of iron; like iron, strong and firm. • *vti* to press with a hot iron; (*with* **out**) to correct or settle a problem through negotiation or similar means.—**ironer** *n*.

Iron Age *n* the period when most tools and weapons were made of iron, following the Bronze Age in around 1100 BC.

ironbark /ˈaɪrnbark/ *n* a type of eucalyptus tree.

ironbound /-baʊnd/ *adj* bound with iron; unyielding.

ironclad /ˌaɪrnˈklæd/ *adj* covered in iron; difficult to change or break.

iron curtain *n* the name of the physical and ideological barrier which once separated the former Soviet Union and Communist Eastern Europe from the rest of Europe.

iron grey *adj* a slightly greenish dark grey.

ironic /aɪˈrɒnɪk/, **ironical** /-əl/ *adj* of or using irony.—**ironically** *adv*.

ironing /ˈaɪrnɪŋ/ *n* the act of ironing; items of clothing, etc, for ironing.

ironing-board *n* a narrow flat surface to iron clothes on.

iron lung *n* a large respirator that encloses all of the body but the head.

iron maiden *n* a medieval instrument of torture consisting of a hinged coffin-like box fitted with spikes which was closed around the victim.

ironmonger /ˈaɪrnˌmʌŋgər/ *n* a dealer in metal utensils, tools, etc; a hardware shop.—**ironmongery** *n*.

iron rations *npl* emergency food rations for military use.

ironstone /ˈaɪrnˌstoːn/ *n* a type of iron ore; a type of hardwearing earthenware.

ironwood /ˈaɪrnwʊd/ *n* a name given to the timber of certain trees, which is of exceptional hardness and durability.

ironwork /ˈaɪrnˌwərk/ *n* articles made of iron, *esp* decorative railings, etc.

ironworks /-s/ *n* (*pl* or *sing*) a factory where iron is smelted, cast, or wrought.

irony /ˈaɪrəni/ or /ˈaɪrni/ *n* (*pl* **ironies**) an expression in which the intended meaning of the words is the opposite of their usual sense; an event or result that is the opposite of what is expected.

irradiance /ɪˈreɪdiːənʃ/ *n* the act of emitting rays of light; lustre.

irradiant /ɪˈreɪdiənt/ *adj* emitting rays of light; shining brightly.

irradiate /ɪˈreɪdiˌeɪt/ *vt* to shine upon; to light up; to enlighten; to radiate; to expose to X-rays or other radiation. • *vi* to emit rays; to shine.—**irradiative** *adj*.—**irradiator** *n*.

irradiation /ɪˌreɪdiˈeɪʃən/ *n* the act of irradiating; the condition of being irradiated; the apparent extension of the edges of an illuminated object seen against a dark background; the use of radiation in medicine.

irrational /ɪˈræʃənəl/ *adj* not rational, lacking the power of reason; senseless; unreasonable; absurd.—**irrationality** *n*.—**irrationally** *adv*.

irrational number *n* a real number (*eg* π) that cannot be expressed as the result of dividing one integer by another.

irreclaimable /ˌɪrɪˈkleɪməbəl/ *adj* which cannot be reclaimed.

irreconcilable /ɪˈrekənˌsaɪləbəl/ *adj* not able to be brought into agreement; incompatible.—**irreconcilability** *n*.—**irreconcilably** *adv*.

irrecoverable /ˌɪrɪˈkʌvərəbəl/ *adj* beyond recovery.—**irrecoverably** *adv*.

irrecusable /ˌɪrɪˈkjuːzəbəl/ *adj* which must be accepted.

irredeemable /ˌɪrɪˈdiːməbəl/ *adj* not able to be redeemed.—**irredeemably** *adv*.

irredentist /ˌɪrɪˈdentɪst/ *n* an advocate of the return of a country of neighbouring regions claimed by another on language and other grounds.—**irredentism** *n*.

irreducible /ˌɪrɪˈduːsɪbəl/ *adj* unable to be reduced from one form, state, degree, etc to another.—**irreducibility** *n*.—**irreducibly** *adv*.

irrefragable /ɪˈrefrəgəbəl/ *adj* irrefutable, unanswerable.

irrefrangible /ˌɪrɪˈfrændʒɪbəl/ *adj* inviolable; (*physics*) which cannot be refracted.

irrefutable /ˌɪrɪˈfjuːtəbəl/ or /ɪˈrefjutəbəl/ *adj* unable to deny or disprove; indisputable.—**irrefutability** *adv*.—**irrefutably** *adv*.

irregular /ɪˈregjulər/ *adj* not regular, straight or even; not conforming to the rules; imperfect; (*troops*) not part of the regular armed forces.—**irregularly** *adv*.

irregularity /-ˈlerɪti/ *n* (*pl* **irregularities**) departure from a rule, order or method; crookedness.

irrelative /ɪˈrelətɪv/ *adj* unconnected, unrelated.

irrelevant /ɪˈreləvənt/ *adj* not pertinent; not to the point.—**irrelevance, irrelevancy** *n*.—**irrelevantly** *adv*.

irreligion /ˌɪrəˈlɪdʒən/ *n* lack of religious belief; disregard for, or hostility towards, religion.

irreligious /ˌɪrɪˈlɪdʒəs/ *adj* impious, irreverent.

irremediable /ˌɪrəˈmiːdiəbəl/ *adj* which cannot be remedied.

irremissible /ˌɪrəˈmɪsɪbəl/ *adj* unpardonable; (*obligation*) binding.

irremovable /ˌɪrɪˈmuːvəbəl/ *adj* not removable.—**irremovability** *adv*.—**irremovably** *adv*.

irreparable /ɪˈrepərəbəl/ *adj* that cannot be repaired, rectified or made good.—**irreparably** *adv*.

irreplaceable /ˌɪrə'pleɪsəbəl/ *adj* unable to be replaced.—**irreplaceability** *n*.

irrepressible /ˌɪrə'presɪbəl/ *adj* unable to be controlled or restrained.—**irrepressibly** *adv*.

irreproachable /ˌɪrə'prɔːtʃəbəl/ *adj* blameless; faultless.—**irreproachability** *n*.—**irreproachably** *adv*.

irresistible /ˌɪrə'zɪstɪbəl/ *adj* not able to be resisted; overpowering; fascinating; very charming, alluring.—**irresistibility** *adv*.—**irresistibly** *adv*.

irresolute /ɪ'rezə,luːt/ *adj* lacking resolution, uncertain, hesitating.—**irresolutely** *adv*.—**irresoluteness, irresolution** *n*.

irresolvable /ˌɪrə'zɒlvəbəl/ *adj* which cannot be resolved or solved.

irrespective /ˌɪrə'spektɪv/ *adj* (*with* **of**) regardless.—**irrespectively** *adv*.

irresponsible /ˌɪrə'spɒnsɪbəl/ *adj* not showing a proper sense of the consequences of one's actions; unable to bear responsibility.—**irresponsibility** *n*.—**irresponsibly** *adv*.

irresponsive /ˌɪrə'spɒnsɪv/ *adj* not responsive.

irretentive /ˌɪrɪ'tentɪv/ *adj* not retentive.

irretrievable /ˌɪrə'triːvəbəl/ *adj* that cannot be recovered; irreparable.—**irretrievability** *n*.—**irretrievably** *adj*.

irreverent /ɪ'revərənt/, **irreverential** /-ʃəl/ *adj* not reverent, disrespectful.—**irreverence** *n*.—**irreverently** *adv*.

irreversible /ˌɪrə'vɜːsɪbəl/ *adj* not able to be reversed; unable to be revoked or altered.—**irreversibility** *n*.—**irreversibly** *adv*.

irrevocable /ɪ'revəkəbəl/ or /ɪrə'voːk-/ *adj* unable to be revoked, unalterable.—**irrevocability** *n*.—**irrevocably** *adv*.

irrigate /'ɪrə,ɡeɪt/ *vt* to supply (land) with water as by means of artificial ditches, pipes, etc; (*med*) to wash out (a cavity, wound, etc).—**irrigable** *adj*.—**irrigation** *n*.—**irrigative** *adj*.—**irrigator** *n*.

irritable /'ɪrɪtəbəl/ *adj* easily annoyed, irritated, or provoked; (*med*) excessively sensitive to a stimulus.—**irritability** *n*.—**irritably** *adv*.

irritant /'ɪrɪtənt/ *adj* irritating; causing irritation. • *n* something that causes irritation.

irritate /'ɪrɪ,teɪt/ *vt* to provoke to anger; to annoy; to make inflamed or sore.—**irritative** *adj*.—**irritator** *n*.

irritation /-'teɪʃən/ *n* the act of irritating; the state of being irritated; someone who, or something which, irritates.

irrupt /ɪ'rʌpt/ *vi* to enter forcibly or suddenly.—**irruption** *n*.

is *see* **be**.

ISBN /'aɪesbiːen/ *abbr* = International Standard Book Number.

ISDN /'aɪesbiːen/ *abbr* = Integrated Services Digital Network. A means of transmitting data, voice and video digitally over a telecommunications line.

isinglass /'aɪzɪŋ,ɡlæs/ *n* a gelatin prepared from fish bladders; mica, *esp* in thin sheets.

Islam /'ɪzlæm/ or /-lɒm/, /-'læm/ *n* the Muslim religion, a monotheistic religion founded by Mohammed; the Muslim world.—**Islamic** *adj*.

island /'aɪlənd/ *n* a land mass smaller than a continent and surrounded by water; anything like this in position or isolation.

islander /-ər/ *n* a native or inhabitant of an island.

isle /aɪl/ *n* an island, *esp* a small one.

islet /'aɪlət/ *n* a small island.

-ism /'ɪzəm/ *n suffix* indicating a system or doctrine, as *Protestantism*; a state or condition, as *barbarism*; action, as *criticism*; a peculiarity or idiom, as *archaism*, *gallicism*; a morbid condition caused by abuse of drugs, as *alcoholism*.

isn't /'ɪzənt/ = is not.

isobar /'aɪso,bɑr/ *n* a line on a map connecting places of equal atmospheric pressure at a given time or period.—**isobaric** *adj*.—**isobarism** *n*.

isochromatic /ˌaɪso:kro'mætɪk/ *adj* of the same colour; (*photog*) giving equal intensity to different colours.

isochronal /aɪ'so:kro:nəl/, **isochronous** /-əs/ *adj*

isoclinal /ˌaɪso'klaɪnəl/, **isoclinic** /-'klɪnɪk/ *adj* having the same dip or inclination.

isodynamic /ˌaɪso:daɪ'næmɪk/ *adj* having equal force.

isogon /'aɪso:'ɡɒn/ *n* (*geom*) a figure with equal angles.

isohel /'aɪso:,hel/ *n* a line on a map, linking places with the same hours of sunshine.

isohyet /ˌaɪso:'haɪɪt/ *n* a line on a map, linking places with the same rainfall.

isolate /'aɪsə,leɪt/ *vt* to set apart from others; to place alone; to quarantine a person or animal with a contagious disease; to separate a constituent substance from a compound.—**isolator** *n*.

isolation /ˌaɪsə'leɪʃən/ *n* the state of being isolated; the act of isolating.

isolationism /ˌaɪsə'leɪʃə,nɪzəm/ *n* a policy of refraining from involvement in international affairs.—**isolationist** *adj, n*.

isomer /'aɪsəmər/ *n* any of two or more chemical compounds whose molecules contain the same atoms but in different arrangements.—**isomeric** *adj*.—**isomerism** *n*.

isometric /ˌaɪso:'metrɪk/, **isometrical** /-əl/ *adj* having equality of measure; relating to muscular contraction involving little shortening of the muscle; (*drawing*) projecting an image to scale in three dimensions with the axis equally inclined.—**isometrically** *adv*.

isometrics /-s/ *n* (*sing or pl*) physical exercises in which muscles are contracted against each other or in opposition to fixed objects.

isomorphism /ˌaɪso:'mɔrfɪsm/ *n* (*biol*) similarity in form; (*chem*) the quality of having the same crystalline form despite being formed of different elements.—**isomorphic, isomorphous** *adj*.

isopod /'aɪso:,pɒd/ *n* a type of crustacean with seven pairs of equal legs, *eg* the woodlouse.

isosceles /aɪ'sɒsɪ,liːz/ *adj* denoting a triangle with two equal sides.

isoseismic /ˌaɪso:'sazmɪk/, **isoseismal** /-məl/ *adj* pertaining to points at which earthquake shock is of the same intensity. • *n* a line on a map, linking these points.

isotherm /'aɪso:,θɜrm/ *n* a line on a map connecting points of the same temperature.—**isothermal** *adj*.

isotope /'aɪsə,to:p/ *n* any of two or more forms of an element having the same atomic number but different atomic weights.—**isotopic** *adj*.—**isotopically** *adv*.

Israelite /'ɪzriə,laɪt/ or /-rə,laɪt/ *n* (*Bible*) a descendant of the Hebrew patriarch Jacob.

issuable /'ɪsuːəbəl/ *adj* which can be issued.

issuance /'ɪʃuːəns/ *n* the act of issuing.

issue /'ɪsuː/ *n* an outgoing; an outlet; a result; offspring; a point under dispute; a sending or giving out; all that is put forth at one time (an issue of bonds, a periodical, etc). • *vb* (**issuing, issued**) *vi* to go or flow out; to result (from) or end (in); to be published. • *vt* to let out; to discharge; to give or deal out, as supplies; to publish.

isthmian /'ɪsmiən/ or /'ɪsθ-/ *adj* of or pertaining to an isthmus.

isthmus /'ɪsməs/ or /'ɪsθ-/ *n* (*pl* **isthmuses, isthmi**) a narrow strip of land having water at each side and connecting two larger bodies of land.—**isthmoid** *adj*.

istle /'ɪstli/ *n* a tough fibre made from a species of Mexican agave, used to make cord.—*also* **ixtle**.

it /ɪt/ *pron* the thing mentioned; the subject of an impersonal verb; a subject or object of indefinite sense in various constructions. • *n* the player, as in tag, who must catch another.

it'll /'ɪtəl/ = it will; it shall.

it's /ɪts/ = it is; it has.

Italian /ɪ'tæljən/ *adj* of Italy or its people. • *a* native of Italy; the Italian language.

Italianate /ɪ'tæljə,neɪt/ *adj* Italian in style or character.

Italic /aɪ'tælɪk/ or /ɪ-/ *adj* (*language*) of ancient Italy.

italic /aɪ'tælɪk/ or /ɪ-/ *adj* denoting a type in which the letters slant upward to the right (*this is italic type*). • *n* (*usu pl*) italic type or handwriting.

italicize /ɪ'tælɪ,saɪz/ *vi* to write in italics. • *vt* to underline a word to indicate italics.—**italicization** *n*.

itch /ɪtʃ/ *n* an irritating sensation on the surface of the skin causing a need to scratch; an insistent desire. • *vi* to have or feel an irritating sensation in the skin; to feel a restless desire.

itchy /'ɪtʃi/ *adj* (**itchier, itchiest**) pertaining to or affected with an itch.—**itchiness** *n*.

item /'aɪtəm/ *n* an article; a unit; a separate thing; a bit of news or information.

itemize /'aɪtə,maɪz/ *vt* to specify the items of; to set down by items.—**itemization** *n*.

iterate /'ɪtə,reɪt/ *vt* to say or do again or repetitively.—**iteration** *n*.—**iterative** *adj*.

ithyphallic /ˌɪθɪ'fælɪk/ *adj* (*poet*) in the manner of the rites or hymns to Bacchus.

itinerancy /aɪˈtɪnərənsi/ or /ɪ-/, **itineracy** /-rəsi/ *n* (*pl* **itineran-cies, itineracies**) the act of travelling from place to place, *esp* to carry out an official duty.

itinerant /aɪˈtɪnərənt/ *adj* travelling from place to place. • *n* a traveller.

itinerary /aɪˈtɪnərɛri/ or /ɪ-/ *n* (*pl* **itineraries**) a route; a record of a journey; a detailed plan of a journey.

its /ɪts/ *poss pron* relating to or belonging to **it**.

itself /ɪtˈself/ *pron* the reflexive and emphatic form of **it**.

IUD *abbr* = intrauterine device.

I've /aɪv/ = I have.

IVF *abbr* = in vitro fertilization: a technique for helping infertile couples to have children, in which a woman's eggs are fertilized by the father's sperm in a laboratory and then re-implanted in the womb.

ivory /ˈaɪvəri/ *n* (*pl* **ivories**) the hard, creamy-white substance forming the tusks of elephants, etc; any substance like ivory; creamy white. • *adj* of or like ivory; creamy white.

ivory tower *n* a place or situation which excludes the realities of everyday life.—**ivory towered** *adj*.

ivy /ˈaɪvi/ *n* (*pl* **ivies**) a climbing or creeping vine with a woody stem and evergreen leaves.—**ivied** *adj*.

ixtle /ˈɪkstli/ or /ˈɪst-/ *see* **istle**.

J

J *abbr* = joule(s).

jab /dʒæb/ *vti* (**jabbing, jabbed**) to poke or thrust roughly; to punch with short, straight blows. • *n* a sudden thrust or stab; (*inf*) an injection with a hypodermic needle.

jabber /'dʒæbər/ *vti* to speak or say rapidly, incoherently, or foolishly. • *n* such talk.—**jabberer** *n*.

jabiru /'dʒæbɪˌruː/ *n* a stork-like bird of tropical America; an Australian stork.

jaborandi /ˌdʒæbəˈrændi/ *n* a tropical American plant that yields an alkaloid used to stimulate perspiration and as a diuretic.

jabot /'ʒæbɔː/ *n* an ornamental frill worn down the front of a blouse or shirt.

jacamar /'dʒækəmɑr/ *n* a South American bird similar to a kingfisher.

jacana, jaçana /'dʒækənə/ or /-sənə/ *n* a small tropical wading bird.

jacaranda /ˌdʒækəˈrændə/ *n* a South American tree with hard, heavy wood and purple flowers; any one of several similar trees; the fragrant wood from such trees.

jacinth /'dʒæsɪnθ/ or /'dʒeɪ-/ *n* a reddish-orange gem, a variety of zircon.

jack /dʒæk/ *n* any of various mechanical or hydraulic devices used to lift something heavy; a playing card with a knave's picture on it, ranking below the queen; a small flag flown on a ship's bow as a signal or to show nationality; (*bowls*) a small white ball used as a target. • *vt* (*with* **in**) (*sl*) to abandon (an attempt at something); (*with* **up**) to raise (a vehicle) by means of a jack; to increase (prices, etc).

jackal /'dʒækəl/ *n* (*pl* **jackals, jackal**) any of various wild dogs of Africa and Asia.

jackanapes /'dʒækəˌneɪps/ *n* a conceited or upstart person; a pert child; (*arch*) a monkey.

jackass /'dʒækæs/ *n* a male donkey; a fool.

jackboot /'dʒækbuːt/ *n* a leather military boot extending above the knee; authoritarian rule, oppression.

jackdaw /'dʒækdɔː/ *n* a black bird like the crow but smaller.

jackeroo, jackaroo /ˌdʒækəˈruː/ *n* (*pl* **jackeroos, jackaroos**) (*Austral sl*) a young person training to be a manager on a sheep or cattle station.

jacket /'dʒækət/ *n* a short coat; an outer covering, as the removable paper cover of a book. • *vt* to cover with a jacket or cover.—**jacketed** *adj*.

jackfruit /'dʒækfruːt/ *n* an East Indian tree or its fruit, which is similar to breadfruit.

jack-in-the-box *n* a toy consisting of a box from which a figure on a spring pops out when the lid is lifted.

jackknife /'dʒæknaɪf/ *n* (*pl* **jackknives**) a pocket-knife; a dive in which the diver touches his feet with knees straight and then straightens out. • *vi* to dive in this way; (*articulated truck*) to lose control so that the trailer and cab swing against each other.

jack-of-all-trades *n* (*pl* **jacks-of-all-trades**) a person who does many different types of work.

jack-o'-lantern *n* a lantern made from a hollowed-out pumpkin with holes cut in it to resemble a face; a will-o'-the-wisp.

jackpot /'dʒækpɒt/ *n* the accumulated stakes in certain games, as poker; **hit the jackpot** (*sl*) to win; to gain an enormous amount.

jack rabbit /'dʒækˌræbət/ *n* a large hare with long ears, common in North America.

jacksnipe /'dʒæksnaɪp/ *n* (*pl* **jacksnipes, jacksnipe**) a kind of small snipe; a sandpiper.

jack-tar *n* (*inf*) a sailor.

Jacobean /ˌdʒækəˈbiːən/ *adj* pertaining to the time or reign of James I of England and VI of Scotland. • *n* a person of this period, *esp* a poet.

Jacobin /'dʒækəbɪn/ *n* a French Dominican friar; a member of a violent democratic faction that exercised a powerful influence in the French Revolution; an extreme revolutionary.—**Jacobinic, Jacobinical** *adj*.—**Jacobinism** *n*.

Jacobite /'dʒækəˌbaɪt/ *n* a supporter of James II of England and VII of Scotland after his abdication or of his descendants.—*also adj*.—**Jacobitism** *n*.

jaconet /'dʒækənət/ *n* a fine soft white cotton material resembling cambric.

jacquard /'dʒækɑrd/ *n* a loom for weaving patterns; a pattern woven on a jacquard loom.

jactitation /ˌdʒæktɪˈteɪʃən/ *n* boasting; (*med*) a restless, feverish tossing of the body in illness; (*law*) a false pretence of being married to another, or likely to harm another person.

jacuzzi /dʒəˈkuːzi/ *n* (*trademark*) a device that swirls water in a bath; a bath containing such a device.

jade /dʒeɪd/ *n* a hard, ornamental semiprecious stone; its light green colour.

jaded /'dʒeɪdəd/ *adj* tired, exhausted; satiated.—**jadedly** *adv*.—**jadedness** *n*.

jadeite /'dʒeɪdaɪt/ *n* a form of jade found in Burma.

jag¹ /dʒæg/ *n* a sharp, tooth-like notch or projection. • *vt* (**jagging, jagged**) to cut into notches; to prick.

jag² *n* (*sl*) intoxication from drugs or alcohol; (*sl*) a drinking spree.

jagged /'dʒægəd/ *adj* having sharp notches or projecting points; notched or ragged.—**jaggedly** *adv*.—**jaggedness** *n*.

jaggery, jaggary, jagghery /'dʒægəri/ *n* a coarse East Indian sugar made from palm sap.

jaggy /'dʒægi/ *adj* (**jaggier, jaggiest**) jagged.

jaguar /'dʒægwɑr/ or /-jʊɑr/ *n* (*pl* **jaguars, jaguar**) a large American black-spotted yellow wild cat similar to the leopard.

jail /dʒeɪl/ *n* a prison; imprisonment. • *vt* to send to or confine in prison.

jailbird /'dʒeɪlbərd/ *n* a person who is or has been confined in jail.

jailer, jailor /'dʒeɪlər/ *n* a person in charge of prisoners in a jail.

Jain /dʒaɪn/ *n* an adherent of Jainism. • *adj* pertaining to the Jains or their religious system.—*also* **Jaina, Jainist**.

Jainism /-ˌnɪzəm/ *n* a Hindu religion of India similar to Buddhism.

jalap, jalop /'dʒæləp/ *n* the root of a Mexican plant used formerly as a purgative; the plant itself or similar plants; the resin from the plant.—**jalapic** *adj*.

jalopy /dʒəˈlɒpi/ *n* (*pl* **jalopies**) an old battered vehicle.

jalousie /'ʒæləˌziː/ *n* a blind with slats like a Venetian blind or a louvred shutter; a louvre window.

jam¹ /dʒæm/ *n* a preserve made from fruit boiled with sugar until thickened; (*inf*) something easy or desirable.

jam² *vb* (**jamming, jammed**) *vt* to press or squeeze into a confined space; to crowd full with people or things; to cause (machinery) to become wedged and inoperable; to cause interference to a radio signal rendering it unintelligible. • *vi* to become stuck or blocked; (*sl*) to play in a jam session. • *n* a crowded mass or congestion in a confined space; a blockage caused by jamming; (*inf*) a difficult situation.—**jammer** *n*.

jamb /dʒæm/ *n* the straight vertical side-post of a door, fireplace, etc.

jamboree /ˌdʒæmbəˈriː/ *n* a large party or spree; a large, *usu* international, gathering of Scouts.

jam-packed *adj* filled to capacity.

jam session *n* (*sl*) an unrehearsed performance by jazz, rock or other musicians, *usu* for their own enjoyment.

Jan. *abbr* = January.

jangle /ˌdʒæŋɡəl/ *vi* to make a harsh or discordant sound, as bells. • *vt* to cause to jangle; to irritate.—*also n*.

janitor /'dʒænɪtər/ *n* a person who looks after a building, doing routine maintenance, etc.—**janitorial** *adj*.

janizary, janissary /'dʒænɪˌzeri/ *n* (*pl* **janizaries, janissaries**) (*formerly*) a foot-guard of the Turkish sultans; a Turkish infantryman.

Jansenism /'dʒænsəˌnɪzəm/ *n* the doctrine of sovereign and irresistible grace, promulgated in the 17th century in opposition to the Jesuits; the religion based on these doctrines.—**Jansenist** *n, adj*.—**Jansenistic** *adj*.

January /'dʒænjuˌeri/ *n* (*pl* **Januaries**) the first month of the year, having 31 days.

japan /dʒə'pæn/ *vt* (**japanning, japanned**) to cover with a hard black glossy lacquer.

Japanese /ˌdʒæpə'niːz/ *adj* of Japan, its people or language. • *n* the language of Japan; an inhabitant of Japan.

jape /dʒeɪp/ *n* a joke, jest.—**japer** *n*.—**japery** *n*.

japonica /dʒə'pɒnɪkə/ *n* any of various species of Japanese plants, Japanese quince, pear, etc; the camellia.

jar[1] /dʒɑr/ *vb* (**jarring, jarred**) *vi* to make a harsh, discordant noise; to have an irritating effect (on one); to vibrate from an impact; to clash. • *vt* to jolt. • *n* a grating sound; a vibration due to impact; a jolt.

jar[2] *n* a short cylindrical glass vessel with a wide mouth; (*inf*) a pint of beer.

jardiniere /ˌʒɑrdɪ'njɛr/ *n* an ornamental flower-stand of porcelain or metal; mixed diced vegetables stewed in a sauce and served around a meat dish.

jargon[1] /'dʒɑrgən/ *n* the specialized or technical vocabulary of a science, profession, etc; obscure and *usu* pretentious language. • *vi* to talk in jargon.—**jargonistic** *adj*.

jargon[2], **jargoon** *n* a translucent, colourless, yellowish, or smoky kind of zircon.

jargonize /-ˌnaɪz/ *vti* to put into or talk in jargon.—**jargonization** *n*.

jarl /dʒɑrl/ *n* an Old Norse chief, a noble.

jasmine, jasmin /'dʒæzmɪn/ *n* any of a genus of climbing shrubs with fragrant white or yellow flowers.

jasper /'dʒæspər/ *n* an opaque, many-shaded variety of quartz that, when polished, is made into a variety of ornamental articles and jewellery; a style of porcelain with a dull surface of green or blue.

jaundice /'dʒɒndɪs/ *n* a condition characterized by yellowing of the skin, caused by excess of bile in the bloodstream; bitterness; resentment; prejudice.

jaundiced /'dʒɒndɪst/ *adj* affected with jaundice; jealous, envious, disillusioned.

jaunt /dʒɒnt/ *n* a short journey, *usu* for pleasure. • *vi* to make such a journey.

jaunty /'dʒɒnti/ *adj* (**jauntier, jauntiest**) sprightly or self-confident in manner.—**jauntily** *adv*.—**jauntiness** *n*.

Javanese /ˌdʒævə'niːz/ *n* (*pl* **Javanese**) a native or inhabitant of Java; the language of Java.—*also adj*.

javelin /'dʒævəlɪn/ or /-vlɪn/ *n* a light spear, *esp* one thrown some distance in a contest.

jaw /dʒɔ/ *n* one of the bones in which teeth are set; either of two movable parts that grasp or crush something, as in a vice; (*sl*) a friendly chat, gossip; argument. • *vi* (*sl*) to talk boringly and at length.

jawbone /'dʒɔbəʊn/ *n* a bone of the jaw, *esp* of the lower jaw.

jawbreaker *n* a machine for crushing rocks, etc; (*inf*) a word that is difficult to pronounce.

jay /dʒeɪ/ *n* any of several birds of the crow family with raucous voices, roving habits, and destructive behaviour to other birds.

jaycee /dʒeɪ'siː/ *n* a young member of a Junior Chamber of Commerce.

jaywalk /'dʒeɪwɒk/ *vi* to walk across a street carelessly without obeying traffic rules or signals.—**jaywalker** *n*.

jazz /dʒæz/ *n* a general term for American popular music, characterized by syncopated rhythms and embracing ragtime, blues, swing, jive, and bebop; (*sl*) pretentious or nonsensical talk or actions. • *vt* (*with* **up**) (*inf*) to play (a piece of music) in a jazz style; to enliven, add colour to.

jazzerati /'dʒæzəˌrɒti/ *npl* famous or accomplished jazz musicians.

jazzy /'dʒæzi/ *adj* (**jazzier, jazziest**) of or like jazz; (*sl*) lively.—**jazzily** *adj*.—**jazziness** *n*.

jealous /'dʒɛləs/ *adj* apprehensive of or hostile toward someone thought of as a rival; envious of, resentful; anxiously vigilant or protective.—**jealously** *adv*.—**jealousness** *n*.

jealousy /'dʒɛləsi/ *n* (*pl* **jealousies**) suspicious fear or watchfulness, *esp* the fear of being supplanted by a rival.

jean /dʒiːn/ *n* a hardwearing twilled cotton cloth; (*pl*) trousers made from this or denim.

jeep /dʒiːp/ *n* a small robust vehicle with heavy duty tires and four-wheel drive for use on rough terrain, *esp* by the military.

jeer /dʒiːr/ *vt* to laugh derisively. • *vi* to scoff (at). • *n* a jeering remark.—**jeerer** *n*.—**jeeringly** *adv*.

jehad *see* jihad.

Jehovah /dʒə'həʊvə/ *n* (*Bible*) Hebrew name of God in the OT.

jejune /dʒɪ'dʒuːn/ *adj* lacking significance, dull; naive; lacking in nourishment.—**jejunely** *adv*.—**jejuneness** *n*.

jell /dʒɛl/ *vti* to become or make into jelly; to crystallize, as a plan.—*also* **gel**.

jelly /'dʒɛli/ *n* (*pl* **jellies**) a jam made with fruit juice; a gelatinous food made from fruit syrup or meat juice; any substance like this. • *vt* (**jellying, jellied**) to turn into jelly, to congeal.—**jellied** *adj*.

jellyfish /'dʒɛlɪfɪʃ/ *n* (*pl* **jellyfish, jellyfishes**) a sea creature with a nearly transparent body and long tentacles.

jennet /'dʒɛnˌɛt/ *n* a small Spanish horse; a female donkey.

jenny /'dʒɛni/ *n* (*pl* **jennies**) a machine for spinning; a female of some animals, as a wren or donkey.

jeopardize /'dʒɛpərˌdaɪz/ *vt* to endanger, put at risk.

jeopardy /'dʒɛpərdi/ *n* (*pl* **jeopardies**) great danger or risk.

jequirity /dʒɪ'kwɪrəti/ *n* (*pl* **jequirities**) an Indian shrub with parti-coloured seeds.

jerbil /'dʒɜrbɪ/ *see* gerbil.

jerboa /dʒɜr'bəʊ/ *n* a small desert rodent with long hind legs and a long tail.

jeremiad /ˌdʒɛrə'maɪəd/ or /-æd/ *n* a long mournful lament or complaint.

jerk[1] /dʒɜrk/ *n* a sudden sharp pull or twist; a sudden muscular contraction or reflex; (*inf*) a stupid person. • *vti* to move with a jerk; to pull sharply; to twitch.

jerk[2] *vt* to preserve (meat) by cutting it into long strips and drying it in the sun. • *n* jerked meat (—*also* **jerky**).

jerkin /'dʒɜrkɪn/ *n* a close-fitting sleeveless jacket. **jerkiness** *n*.

jerky[1] /'dʒɜrki/ *see* **jerk**[2].

jerky[2] *adj* (**jerkier, jerkiest**) moving with jerks.—**jerkily** *adv*.—**jerkiness** *n*.

jeroboam /ˌdʒɛrə'bəʊəm/ *n* a huge bottle four times ordinary size, *esp* for champagne.

jerry-built *adj* cheaply and flimsily constructed.—**jerry-builder** *n*.—**jerry-building** *n*.

jerry can *n* a flat-sided container for liquids, *esp* fuel or water, with a capacity of about five gallons (25 litres).

jersey /'dʒɜrzi/ *n* (*pl* **jerseys**) any plain machine-knitted fabric of natural or artificial fibres; a knitted sweater.

Jerusalem artichoke *n* (the edible tuber of) the North American sunflower.

jess, jesse /dʒɛs/ *n* a short leather strap fixed to the leg of a hawk or falcon.

jest /dʒɛst/ *n* a joke; a thing to be laughed at. • *vi* to jeer; to joke.

jester /'dʒɛstər/ *n* a person who makes jokes, *esp* an entertainer employed in a royal household in the Middle Ages.

Jesuit /'dʒɛzjuɪt/ or /'dʒɛz- /, /-juɪt/ *n* a member of the Catholic Society of Jesus, founded by Ignatius Loyola in 1534; an insidious, crafty intriguer.—**Jesuitic, Jesuitical** *adj*.

Jesuitism /-ˌtɪzəm /, **Jesuitry** /-tri/ *n* (a following of) the principles, system, or practices of the Jesuits; subtle duplicity; disingenuousness.

Jesus (Christ) /'dʒiːzəs/ *n* the Jewish religious teacher and founder of Christianity.

Jesus freak *n* (*sl*) a fervent Christian, *esp* a young member of an evangelical group.

jet[1] /dʒɛt/ *n* a hard black compact mineral that can be polished and is used in jewellery; a lustrous black.—**jet-black** *adj*.

jet[2] *n* a stream of liquid or gas suddenly emitted; a spout for emitting a jet; a jet-propelled aircraft. • *vti* (**jetting, jetted**) to gush out in a stream; (*inf*) to travel or convey by jet.

jet engine *n* an engine, such as a gas turbine, producing jet propulsion.

jet lag /-læg/ *n* fatigue caused by disruption of the daily bodily rhythms, associated with crossing time zones at high speed.—**jet-lagged** *adj*.

jet propulsion *n* propulsion of aircraft, boats, etc, by the discharge of gases from a rear vent.—**jet-propelled** *adj*.

jetsam /'dʒɛtsəm/ *n* cargo thrown overboard from a ship in distress to lighten it, *esp* such cargo when washed up on the shore.

jet set *n* the wealthy and fashionable social elite who travel widely for pleasure.—**jetsetter** *n*.

jet stream *n* the jet of exhaust gases from a jet engine; high-altitude winds.

jettison /'dʒɛtɪsən/ or /-zən/ *vt* to abandon, to throw overboard.

jetty /'dʒɛti/ *n* (*pl* **jetties**) a wharf; a small pier.

Jew /dʒuː/ *n* a person descended, or regarded as descended, from the ancient Israelites; a person whose religion is Judaism.

jewel /'dʒuːəl/ *n* a precious stone; a gem; a piece of jewellery; someone or something highly esteemed; a small gem used as a bearing in a watch. • *vt* (**jewelling, jewelled** *or* **jeweling, jeweled**) to adorn or provide with jewels.

jeweller, jeweler /'dʒuːələr/ *n* a person who makes, repairs or deals in jewellery, watches, etc.

jewellery, jewelry /'dʒuːləri/ *or* /'dʒuːəlri /, /'dʒuːlri/ *n* jewels such as rings, brooches, etc, worn for decoration.

Jewish /'dʒuːɪʃ/ *adj* of or like Jews.

Jewry /'dʒuri/ *n* (*pl* **Jewries**) the Jewish people.

jew's harp *n* a small metal musical instrument that makes a twanging sound when held between the lips and plucked.

Jezebel /'dʒɛzəˌbɛl/ *n* a woman of abandoned or licentious demeanour.

jib[1] /dʒɪb/ *n* a triangular sail extending from the foremast in a ship. • *vti* (jibbing, jibbed) to pull (a sail) round to the other side; (*sail*) to swing round.—**jibber** *n*.

jib[2] *n* the projecting arm of a crane.

jib[3] *vi* to refuse to go on; to balk.

jibe /dʒaɪb/ *see* **gybe**.

jiffy, jiff /dʒɪfi/ *n* (*pl* **jiffies, jiffs**) (*inf*) a very short time.

jig /dʒɪg/ *n* a lively springing dance; the music for this; a device used to guide a tool. • *vt* (**jigging, jigged**) to dance in lively manner, as in a jig; to jerk up and down rapidly.

jigger[1] /'dʒɪgər/ *see* **chigoe.**

jigger[2] *n* any of various mechanical devices that operate with a jigging motion; a small glass for spirits; a person or thing that jigs; (*naut*) small tackle, a small sail.

jiggermast /-ˌmæst/ *n* the stern mast in a two-masted sailing vessel; a small aftermost mast in a four-master.

jiggery-pokery /ˌdʒɪgəri'pokəri/ *n* (*inf*) underhand work; trickery.

jiggle /'dʒɪgəl/ *vt* to jerk; to move (something) up and down lightly. • *n* a jerky movement.

jigsaw /'dʒɪgsɔ/ *n* a saw with a narrow fine-toothed blade for cutting irregular shapes. • *vt* to cut with a jigsaw.

jigsaw (puzzle) *n* a picture mounted on wood or stiff cardboard and then cut up into irregular pieces, which are then assembled for amusement.

jihad /dʒɪ'hæd/ *n* a holy war waged by Muslims against nonbelievers; a crusade for or against a cause.—*also* **jehad.**

jilt /dʒɪlt/ *vt* to discard (a lover) unfeelingly, *esp* without warning.—**jilter** *n*.

jimjams /'dʒɪmdʒæmz/ *npl* (*sl*) delirium tremens; nervous jitters.

jingle /'dʒɪŋgəl/ *n* a metallic tinkling sound like a bunch of keys being shaken together; a catchy verse or song with easy rhythm, simple rhymes, etc. • *vti* (to cause) to make a light tinkling sound.—**jingler** *n*.

jingly /-li/ *adj* (**jinglier, jingliest**) tinkling.

jingo /'dʒɪŋgo:/ *n* (*pl* **jingoes**) a blustering patriot, a warmonger.

jingoism /-ˌɪzəm/ *n* advocacy of an aggressive foreign policy.—**jingoist** *adj, n.*—**jingoistic** *adj.*—**jingoistically** *adv.*

jink /dʒɪŋk/ *n* a rapid swerve from side to side in order to dodge; (*pl*) high spirits. • *vti* to move nimbly; to dodge.

jinni /dʒɪ'niː/ *n* (*pl* **jinn**) (*fairy tales*) a spirit with supernatural powers that can fulfil your wishes.—*also* **genie.**

jinx /dʒɪŋks/ *n* (*inf*) someone or something thought to bring bad luck.

JIT *abbr* = just-in-time.

jitter /'dʒɪtər/ *vi* (*inf*) to feel nervous or to act nervously. • *npl* (*inf*) (*with* **the**) an uneasy nervous feeling; fidgets.

jitterbug /'dʒɪtərˌbʌg/ *n* a fast acrobatic dance for couples, *esp* popular in the 1940s. • *vi* (**jitterbugging, jitterbugged**) to dance the jitterbug.

jittery /'dʒɪtəri/ *adj* (*inf*) nervous.—**jitteriness** *n*.

jive /dʒaɪv/ *n* improvised jazz played at a fast tempo; dancing to this music; (*sl*) foolish, exaggerated, or insincere talk. • *vti* to dance the jive.

Jnr, jnr *abbr* = Junior.

job /'dʒɒb/ *n* a piece of work done for pay; a task; a duty; the thing or material being worked on; work; employment; (*sl*) a criminal enterprise; (*inf*) a difficult task. • *adj* hired or done by the job. • *vti* (**jobbing, jobbed**) to deal in (goods) as a jobber; to sublet (work, etc).

jobber /'dʒɒbər/ *n* a person who jobs; a person who buys and sells goods as a middleman; in UK, a broker.

jobbery /'dʒɒbəri/ *n* profiting personally from a public office.

jobless /'dʒɒbləs/ *adj* unemployed. • *n* unemployed people collectively.—**joblessness** *n*.

job lot *n* a miscellaneous collection of items sold as one lot; any miscellaneous collection of cheap items.

jock /dʒɒk/ *n* (*inf*) a jockey; a jockstrap; a male athlete; a disc jockey.

jockey /'dʒɒki/ *n* (*pl* **jockeys**) a person whose job is riding horses in races. • *vti* (**jockeying, jockeyed**) to act as a jockey; to manœuvre for a more advantageous position; to swindle or cheat.

jockstrap /'dʒɒkstræp/ *n* a support for the genitals worn by men participating in sport, an athletic supporter.

jocose /dʒə'ko:s/ *adj* playful, humorous.—**jocosely** *adv.*—**jocoseness** *n*.

jocosity /-'kɒsɪti/ *n* (*pl* **jocosities**) a being jocose; a playful action; a humorous remark.

jocular /'dʒɒkjulər/ *adj* joking; full of jokes.—**jocularity** *n.*—**jocularly** *adv.*

jocund /'dʒɒkənd/ *adj* merry, cheerful; jovial.—**jocundity** *n.*—**jocundly** *adv.*

jodhpurs /'dʒɒdpərz/ *npl* riding breeches cut loose at the hips but close-fitting from knee to ankle.

joey /'dʒo:i/ *n* (*pl* **joeys**) (*Austral inf*) a young kangaroo; any young animal or a small child.

jog /dʒɒg/ *vb* (**jogging, jogged**) *vt* to give a slight shake or nudge to; to rouse, as the memory. • *vi* to move up and down with an unsteady motion; to run at a relaxed trot for exercise; (*horse*) to run at a jogtrot. • *n* a slight shake or push; a nudge; a slow walk or trot.—**jogger** *n*.

joggle /'dʒɒgəl/ *vti* to move or shake slightly. • *n* a slight jolt.

jogtrot /'dʒɒgtrɒt/ *n* a slow even-paced trot. • *vi* (**jogtrotting, jogtrotted**) to move at a slow even-paced trot.

john /dʒɒn/ *n* (*US sl*) a toilet; an easy prey.

John Barleycorn *n* a personification of malt liquor.

John Dory /dʒɒn'dɔri/ *n* an edible yellow seafish, the dory.

joie de vivre /ˈʒwɒdə'viːvrə/ *n* great enjoyment of life.

join /dʒɔɪn/ *vti* to bring and come together (with); to connect; to unite; to become a part or member of (a club, etc); to participate (in a conversation, etc); (*with* **up**) to enlist in the armed forces; to unite, connect. • *n* a joining; a place of joining.

joinder /'dʒɔɪndər/ *n* the act of joining; (*law*) the coupling of two or more causes of action into the same declaration; the coupling of two issues or two parties.

joiner /'dʒɔɪnər/ *n* a carpenter, *esp* one who finishes interior woodwork; (*inf*) a person who is involved in many clubs and activities, etc.

joinery /'dʒɔɪnəri/ *n* the trade of a joiner; the work of a joiner.

joint /dʒɔɪnt/ *n* a place where, or way in which, two things are joined; any of the parts of a jointed whole; the parts where two bones move on one another in an animal; a division of an animal carcass made by a butcher; (*sl*) a cheap bar or restaurant; (*sl*) a gambling or drinking den; (*sl*) a cannabis cigarette. • *adj* common to two or more; sharing with another. • *vt* to connect by a joint or joints; to divide (an animal carcass) into parts for cooking.

joint account *n* a bank account accessible to two or more people, for deposting or withdrawing funds.

jointer /'dʒɔɪntər/ *n* a tool for pointing; a kind of plane; someone or something that forms joints.

jointly /-li/ *adv* in common; together.

joint stock *n* capital held in common and distributed as shares among the owners.

joint-stock company *n* a company whose capital is owned jointly by stockholders who may sell their individual shares.

jointure /'dʒɔɪntʃər/ *n* landed estate or other property settled on a woman in consideration of her marriage, to be enjoyed by her after the death of her husband; the provision made to enable this; (*arch*) a joining or being joined.

joint venture *n* the sharing of expertise or commercial risk by two or more businesses, etc.

joist /dʒɔɪst/ *n* any of the parallel beams supporting floorboards or the laths of a ceiling.

jojoba /ho:'ho:bə/ *n* a broad-leaved evergreen shrub with edible seeds yielding a valuable oil.

joke /dʒo:k/ *n* something said or done to cause laughter; a thing done or said merely in fun; a person or thing to be laughed at. • *vi* to make jokes.—**jokingly** *adv.*

joker /'dʒo:kər/ *n* a person who jokes; (*sl*) a person; an extra playing card made use of in certain games.

jokey, joky /-kɪ/ *adj* (**jokier, jokiest**) full, or fond, of jokes.
jollify /'dʒɒlɪˌfaɪ/ *vti* (**jollifying, jollified**) to make merry, *esp* with drink; to make jolly.—**jollification** *n*.
jollity /'dʒɒlɪtɪ/ *n* (*pl* **jollities**) the state of being jolly.
jolly /'dʒɒlɪ/ *adj* (**jollier, jolliest**) full of fun; delightful; (*inf*) enjoyable. • *vti* (**jollying, jollied**) (*inf*) to try to make (a person) feel good; to make fun of (someone).
Jolly Roger *n* a pirate's flag with a white skull and crossbones on a black background.
jolt /dʒɒːlt/ *vt* to give a sudden shake or knock to; to move along jerkily; to surprise or shock suddenly. • *n* a sudden jar or knock; an emotional shock.—**joltingly** *adv*.—**jolty** *adj*.
jonquil /'dʒɒnkwɪl/ *n* a species of narcissus.
jooal *see* **joual**.
jorum /'dʒɔːrəm/ *n* a large drinking vessel; its contents, *esp* punch.
josh /dʒɒʃ/ *vi* (*sl*) to tease gently. • *n* (*sl*) friendly teasing; a teasing joke.—**josher** *n*.—**joshingly** *adv*.
joss /dʒɒs/ *n* a Chinese god or idol.
joss stick *n* a stick of incense.
jostle /ˌdʒɒsəl/ *vti* to shake or knock roughly; to collide or come into contact (with); to elbow for position. • *n* a jostling; a push.
jot /dʒɒt/ *n* a very small amount. • *vt* (**jotting, jotted**) to note (down) briefly.—**jotter** *n*.
jotting /'dʒɒtɪŋ/ *n* something noted down, *esp* a memorandum.
joual *n* in Canada, a form of urban, working-class French in Quebec that has non-standard syntax and many borrowings from English.
joule /dʒuːl/ *n* (*physics*) a unit of energy equal to work done when a force of one newton acts over a distance of one metre.
jounce /dʒaʊns/ *vti* to bump; to jolt (someone or something). • *n* a bump, a jolt.
journal /'dʒɜːnəl/ *n* a daily record of happenings, as a diary; a newspaper or periodical; (*bookkeeping*) a book of original entry for recording transactions; that part of a shaft or axle that turns in a bearing.
journalese /ˌdʒɜːnəˈliːz/ *n* a facile style of writing found in many magazines, newspapers, etc.
journalism /'dʒɜːnəˌlɪzəm/ *n* the work of gathering news for or producing a newspaper, magazine or news broadcast.
journalist /-ɪst/ *n* a person who writes for or edits a newspaper, etc; one who keeps a diary.—**journalistic** *adj*.—**journalistically** *adv*.
journalize /'dʒɜːnəˌlaɪz/ *vt* to enter in a journal; to keep a daily record.—**journalization** *n*.—**journalizer** *n*.
journey /'dʒɜːnɪ/ *n* (*pl* **journeys**) a travelling or going from one place to another; the distance covered when travelling. • *vi* (**journeying, journeyed**) to make a journey.—**journeyer** *n*.
journeyman /'dʒɜːnɪmən/ *n* (*pl* **journeymen**) a person whose apprenticeship is completed and who is employed by another; a reliable workman.
joust /dʒaʊst/ *n* a fight on horseback between two knights with lances. • *vi* to engage in a joust, to run at the tilt.—**jouster** *n*.
Jove /dʒɒːv/ *n* the Roman god Jupiter; **by Jove** a mild oth; an exclamation of surprise.
jovial /'dʒɒːvɪəl/ *adj* full of cheerful good humour.—**joviality** *n*.—**jovially** *adv*.
Jovian /'dʒɒːvɪən/ *adj* (*Roman myth*) of or like Jove or Jupiter.
jowl[1] /dʒaʊl/ *n* the lower jaw; (*usu pl*) the cheek.
jowl[2] *n* the loose flesh around the throat; the similar flesh in an animal, as a dewlap.
jowly /'dʒaʊlɪ/ *adj* (**jowlier, jowliest**) having heavy jowls.—**jowliness** *n*
joy /dʒɔɪ/ *n* intense happiness; something that causes this; its expression.
joyful /'dʒɔɪfʊl/ *adj* filled with, expressing, or causing joy, glad.—**joyfully** *adv*.—**joyfulness** *n*.
joyless /'dʒɔɪləs/ *adj* not occasioning joy, unhappy; bleak.—**joylessly** *adv*.—**joylessness** *n*.
joyous /'dʒɔɪəs/ *adj* joyful, very happy.—**joyously** *adv*.—**joyousness** *n*.
joyride /'dʒɔɪraɪd/ *n* (*inf*) a car ride, often in a stolen vehicle and at reckless speed, just for pleasure.—**joy-rider** *n*.—**joyriding** *n*.
joystick /'dʒɔɪstɪk/ *n* (*inf*) the control lever of an aircraft; (*comput*) a device for controlling cursor movement on a monitor *usu* for computer games.
JP *abbr* = Justice of the Peace.

Jr., jr *abbr* = Junior.
jt *abbr* = joint.
jubilant /'dʒuːbɪlənt/ *adj* triumphant; expressing joy; rejoicing.—**jubilance** *n*.—**jubilantly** *adv*.
Jubilate /ˌdʒuːbɪˈlæteɪ/ or /juːbɪ-/ *n* (*Bible*) the 100th psalm, *esp* as a canticle in morning service; (*mus*) a setting of the 100th psalm.
jubilate /'dʒuːbɪˌleɪt/ *vi* to exult, to show joy.—**jubilation** *n*.
jubilee /dʒuːbɪˈliː/ or /'dʒuː-/ *n* a 50th or 25th anniversary; a time of rejoicing.
Judaic /dʒuːˈdeɪɪk/, **Judaical** /-kəl/ *adj* of the Jews or Judaism.—**Judaically** *adv*.
Judaism /'dʒuːdeɪˌɪzəm/ *n* the religion of the Jews, based on the Old Testament and the Talmud.—**Judaist** *n*.—**Judaistic** *adj*.
Judaize /'dʒuːdeɪˌaɪz/ *vi, vt* to make or become Judaistic in belief, customs, precepts, etc.—**Judaization** *n*.
Judas /'dʒuːdəs/ *n* a traitor who pretends to be a friend; (*without cap*) a peephole, as in a cell door.
judder /'dʒʌdər/ *vi* to vibrate violently. • *n* a spasmodic or rapid shaking.
Judean /dʒuːˈdiːən/ *adj* of, pertaining to, or from, the ancient region of Judaea.
judge /dʒʌdʒ/ *n* a public official with authority to hear and decide cases in a court of law; a person chosen to settle a dispute or decide who wins; a person qualified to decide on the relative worth of anything. • *vti* to hear and pass judgment (on) in a court of law; to determine the winner of (a contest) or settle (a dispute); to form an opinion about; to criticize or censure; to suppose, think.—**judgeable** *adj*.—**judgingly** *adv*.
judgeship /-ʃɪp/ *n* the office of a judge; his or her jurisdiction.
judgment, judgement /'dʒʌdʒmənt/ *n* a judging; a deciding; a legal decision; an opinion; the ability to come to a wise decision; censure.
judgmental, judgemental /dʒʌdʒˈmentəl/ *adj* of or depending on judgment; tending to make moral or personal judgments.—**judgmentally, judgementally** *adv*.
Judgment Day *n* (*Christianity*) the time of God's final judgment of mankind; (*without cap*) a final judgment; a day of reckoning.
judicable /'dʒuːdɪkəbəl/ *adj* that may be judged; liable to be judged.
judicator /'dʒuːdɪˌkeɪtər/ *n* one who judges.
judicatory /'dʒuːdɪkəˌtɔːrɪ/ *n* (*pl* **judicatories**) a system of courts, a judiciary. • *adj* of or pertaining to the administration of justice.
judicature /'dʒuːdɪkətʃər/ or /-ˈdɪkətʃər/ *n* a court or courts of justice; the power of dispensing justice by legal trial and judgment; jurisdiction; a body of judges; a tribunal.
judicial /dʒuːˈdɪʃəl/ *adj* of judges, courts, or their functions.—**judicially** *adv*.
judiciary /dʒuːˈdɪʃɪrɪ/ *adj* of judges or courts. • *n* (*pl* **judiciaries**) the part of government that administers justice; a system of courts in a country; judges collectively.
judicious /dʒuːˈdɪʃəs/ *adj* possessing or characterized by sound judgment.—**judiciously** *adv*.—**judiciousness** *n*.
judo /'dʒuːdoː/ *n* a Japanese system of unarmed combat, adapted as a competitive sport from jujitsu.—**judoist** *n*.
jug /dʒʌg/ *n* a vessel for holding and pouring liquids, with a handle and curved lip; a pitcher; (*sl*) prison. • *vt* (**jugging, jugged**) to stew meat (*esp* hare) in an earthenware pot; (*sl*) to put into prison.—**jugful** *n*.
jugate /dʒuːˈgeɪt/ *adj* coupled together; (*bot*) having leaflets in pairs.
juggernaut /'dʒʌgərˌnɒt/ *n* a terrible, irresistible force; a large heavy truck; (*with cap*) a Hindu god; his idol, dragged annually in processional car, under whose wheels devotees formerly threw themselves.
juggle /'dʒʌgəl/ *vi* to toss up balls, etc and keep them in the air. • *vt* to manipulate skilfully; to manipulate so as to deceive. • *n* the act of juggling; manipulation.—**jugglery** *n*.
juggler /'dʒʌglər/ *n* one who juggles, a conjurer; a manipulator, a cheat.
jugular /'dʒʌgjʊlər/ *adj* (*anat*) of the neck or throat. • *n* a jugular vein.
jugular vein *n* (*anat*) any of the large veins in the neck carrying blood from the head.
juice /dʒuːs/ *n* the liquid part of fruit, vegetables or meat; liquid secreted by a bodily organ; (*inf*) vitality; (*inf*) electric current; (*inf*) engine fuel.
juicer /'dʒuːsər/ *n* a mechanical or electrical device for extracting juice from fruit and vegetables; (*sl*) a person who drinks to excess.

juicy /'dʒu:si/ *adj* (**juicier, juiciest**) full of juice; (*inf*) very interesting; (*inf*) highly profitable.—**juicily** *adv.*—**juiciness** *n*.

jujitsu /dʒu:'dʒɪtsu:/ *n* a traditional Japanese system of unarmed defence in which an opponent's strength is used against him.

juju /'dʒu:dʒu:/ *n* an object of superstitious worship in West Africa used as a fetish or charm; the magic attributed to this.—**jujuism** *n*.

jujube /'dʒu:dʒu:b/ *n* a gelatinous, fruit-flavoured lozenge; the fruit of any of several small trees of the buckthorn family; the trees themselves.

jukebox /'dʒu:kbɒks/ *n* a coin-operated automatic record or CD player.

Jul. *abbr* = July.

julep /'dʒu:lɛp/ *n* a tall drink of bourbon or brandy and sugar over crushed ice, garnished with mint.

Julian /'dʒu:liən/ *adj* of or pertaining to Julius Caesar or to the Julian calendar.

Julian calendar *n* a calendar introduced in 46BC by Julius Caesar, in which the year was made to consist of 365 days with a leap year of 366 days every fourth year.

julienne /ˌdʒu:li'ɛn/ *adj* (*vegetables*) cut into very thin strips. • *n* a clear soup containing such vegetable.

July /dʒu:'laɪ/ *n* (*pl* **Julies**) the seventh month of the year, having 31 days.

jumble /'dʒɛmbəl/ *vt* (*often with* **up**) to mix together in a disordered mass. • *n* items mixed together in a confused mass; articles for a jumble sale.—**jumbly** *adj*.

jumbo /'dʒɛmbo:/ *n* (*pl* **jumbos**) something very large of its kind. • *adj* very large.

jumbo jet *n* a very large jet airliner.

jumbuck /'dʒɛmbək/ *n* (*Austral*) a sheep.

jump /dʒɛmp/ *vi* to spring or leap from the ground, a height, etc; to jerk; to pass suddenly, as to a new topic; to rise suddenly, as prices; (*sl*) to be lively; (*often with* **at**) to act swiftly and eagerly; (*with* **at**) to accept or agree too eagerly; (*with* **on**) (*inf*) to reprimand or criticize harshly. • *vt* to leap or pass over (something); to leap upon; to cause (prices, etc) to rise; to fail to turn up (for trial when out on bail); (*inf*) to attack suddenly; (*inf*) to react to prematurely; (*sl*) to leave suddenly. • *n* a jumping; a distance jumped; a sudden transition; an obstacle; a nervous start.

jumper /'dʒɛmpər/ *n* a knitted garment for the upper body; a sleeveless dress for wearing over a blouse, etc.

jumper cable, jump lead *n* one of two cables for transferring electric charge from one battery to another, used to start a car with a flat battery by using the battery of another vehicle.

jump jet *n* (*inf*) a jet aircraft that can take off and land vertically.

jump-start *vt* to start a motor vehicle by pushing it in low gear so the engine turns over or by using jump leads; (*inf*) to set a (sluggish system, etc) in motion.

jumpsuit /'dʒɛmpsu:t/ *n* a one-piece garment, as worn by paratroopers.

jumpy /'dʒɛmpi/ *adj* (**jumpier, jumpiest**) moving in jerks, etc; apprehensive; easily startled.—**jumpily** *adv.*—**jumpiness** *n*.

Jun. *abbr* = June.

jun., Jun. *abbr* = junior.

junction /'dʒɛŋkʃən/ *n* a place or point where things join; a place where roads or railway lines, etc meet, link or cross each other.—**junctional** *adj*.

juncture /'dʒɛŋktʃər/ *n* a junction; a point of time; a crisis.

June /dʒu:n/ *n* the sixth month of the year, having 30 days.

jungle /'dʒɛŋgəl/ *n* an area overgrown with dense tropical trees and other vegetation, etc; any scene of wild confusion, disorder, or of ruthless competition for survival.

jungly /-li/ *adj* (**junglier, jungliest**) pertaining to or covered with jungle.

junior /'dʒu:njər/ *adj* younger in age; of more recent or lower status; of or relating to youth or childhood. • *n* a person who is younger, of lower rank, etc; a young person employed in minor capacity in an office; in the US, a student in the third year of college or school.

Junior *adj* being the younger, often used after the name of the son if the same as the father's.

juniper /'dʒu:nɪpər/ *n* an evergreen shrub that yields purple berries.

junk[1] /dʒɛŋk/ *n* a flat-bottomed sailing vessel prevalent in the China Seas.

junk[2] *n* discarded useless objects; (*inf*) rubbish, trash; (*sl*) any narcotic drug, such as heroin. • *vt* (*inf*) to scrap. • *adj* cheap, worthless; showy but without substance.

junk bond *n* a security that offers a high yield but often involves a high risk of default.

Junker /'dʒɛŋkər/ *n* (*formerly*) a member of the Prussian aristocracy known for its political conservatism and militarism.

junker /'dʒɛŋkər/ *n* (*sl*) a jalopy.

junket /'dʒɛŋkɛt/ *n* curdled milk, sweetened and flavoured; a picnic; an excursion, *esp* one by an official at public expense. • *vi* to go on a junket.

junketeer /dʒɛŋkə'ti:r/ *n* to make a practice of going on free trips. • *vi* someone who does this.

junk food *n* a snack or fast food with little nutritional value.

junkie, junky /'dʒɛŋki/ *n* (*pl* **junkies**) (*sl*) an addict of a particular activity, food, etc; a drug addict.

junk mail *n* unsolicited mail, *eg* advertising leaflets.

Juno /'dʒu:no:/ *n* (*Roman myth*) the queen of the gods, sister and wife of Jupiter; a queenly woman.—**Junoesque** *adj*.

junta /'hʊntə/ *or* /'hɛn-/, /'dʒɛn-/ *n* a group of people, *esp* military, who assume responsibility for the government of a country following a coup d'état or revolution.

Jupiter /'dʒu:pɪtər/ *n* (*Roman myth*) the king of the gods, Jove; (*astron*) the largest planet in the solar system.

jural /'dʒʊrəl/ *adj* of law; of moral rights and obligations.—**jurally** *adv*.

Jurassic /dʒʊ'ræsɪk/ *adj* (geol) of or pertaining to the middle system of the Mesozoic Era marked by the existence of dinosaurs and the appearance of birds and mammals. • *n* the Jurassic period.

jurat /'dʒʊræt/ *n* (law) a record of the time, place, etc, of an affidavit.

juridical, juridic /dʒʊ'rɪdɪkəl/ *adj* of judicial proceedings or law.—**juridically** *adv*.

jurisconsult /ˌdʒʊrɪskən'sɛlt/ *n* one learned in law, a jurist.

jurisdiction /ˌdʒʊrɪs'dɪkʃən/ *n* the right or authority to apply the law; the exercise of such authority; the limits of territory over which such authority extends.—**jurisdictional** *adj.*—**jurisdictionally** *adv*.

jurisprudence /ˌdʒʊrɪs'pru:dəns/ *n* the science or philosophy of law; a division of law.—**jurisprudential** *adj.*—**jurisprudentially** *adv*.

jurisprudent /ˌdʒʊrɪs'pru:dənt/ *adj, n* (a person) skilled in law.

jurist /'dʒʊrɪst/ *n* an expert on law; a judge.—**juristic** *adj.*—**juristically** *adv*.

juror /'dʒʊrər/ *n* a member of a jury; a person who takes an oath.

jury[1] /'dʒʊri/ *or* /'dʒɜri/ *n* (*pl* **juries**) a body of *usu* 12 people sworn to hear evidence and to deliver a verdict on a case; a committee or panel that decides winners in a contest.

jury[2] *adj* (*naut*) makeshift, temporary.

juryman /'dʒʊrimæn/ *n* (*pl* **jurymen**) a male juror.

jury-rigged *adj* (*yacht, etc*) rigged in a temporary or makeshift way.

jurywoman /'dʒʊriˌwʊmən/ *n* (*pl* **jurywomen**) a female juror.

jussive /'dʒɛsɪv/ *adj* (*gram*) imperative, expressing command. • *n* (*gram*) a jussive word, mood or form.

just /dʒɛst/ *adj* fair, impartial; deserved, merited; proper, exact; conforming strictly with the facts. • *adv* exactly; nearly; only; barely; a very short time ago; immediately; (*inf*) really; justly, equitably; by right.—**justly** *adv.*—**justness** *n*.

justice /'dʒɛstəs/ *n* justness, fairness; the use of authority to maintain what is just; the administration of law; a judge.

justice of the peace *n* a magistrate who summarily tries minor cases within his or her jurisdiction.

justiciable /dʒɛ'stɪʃəbəl/ *adj* subject to trial; able to be settled by law.—**justiciability** *n*.

justiciar /dʒɛ'stɪʃi:r/ *n* (*formerly*) in England, the administrator of justice, chief justice.

justiciary /dʒɛ'stɪʃieri/ *n* (*pl* **justiciaries**) an officer who administers justice; a justiciar. • *adj* of or pertaining to the administration of justice.

justifiable /'dʒɛstɪˌfaɪəbəl/ *adj* capable of being justified or defended.—**justifiability** *n.*—**justifiably** *adv*.

justification /ˌdʒɛstɪfɪ'keɪʃən/ *n* the act of justifying; vindication or defence; a showing adequate reason; absolution; (*print*) the spacing out of type to the full length of a line.

justify /'dʒɛstɪˌfaɪ/ *vt* (**justifying, justified**) to prove or show to be just or right; to vindicate; to space out (a line of type) so that it fills the required length.

jut /dʒɛt/ *vti* (**jutting, jutted**) to project; to stick out. • *n* a part that projects.

jute /dʒuːt/ *n* the fibre of either of two tropical plants used for making sacking, etc.

juvenescent /ˌdʒuːvɪˈnəsənt/ *adj* becoming young.—**juvenescence** *n*.

juvenile /ˈdʒuːvəˌnaɪl/ *adj* young; immature; of or for young persons. • *n* a young person.

juvenile delinquency *n* (*pl* **delinquencies**) antisocial or illegal behaviour by young people *usu* under 18.—**juvenile delinquent** *n*.

juvenilia /ˌdʒuːvəˈnɪliə/ or /-ˈnaɪljə/ *npl* works produced in an artist's or author's youth.

juvenility /-lɪti/ *n* (*pl* **juvenilities**) the state of being juvenile; youthfulness; a childish act.

juxtapose /ˌdʒʌkstəˈpoːz/ *vt* to place side by side, *esp* for comparison.—**juxtaposition** *n*.

K

K *abbr* = **kelvin**(s); one thousand; (*comput*) 1024 words, bits or bytes; (*chem symbol*) potassium.

kabbala, kabala /kə'bɒlə/ or /'kæbələ/ *see* **cabbala**.

kabuki /kə'buːki/ *n* classical Japanese theatre.

Kabyle /kə'baɪl/ or /-'biːl/ *n* (*pl* **Kabyles, Kabyle**) an Algerian Berber, or his dialect.

Kaddish /'kædɪʃ/ *n* (*pl* **Kaddishim**) a Jewish daily prayer, used by mourners for the year following, and on the anniversary of, someone's death.

kaftan /'kæftən/ or /-ˌtæn/, /kɒf'tɒn/ *see* **caftan**.

kaiak /'kaɪæk/ *see* **kayak**.

kainite /'kaɪnɔɪt/ *n* a mineral fertilizer.

Kaiser /'kaɪzər/ *n* (*formerly*) the title of the emperors of Germany and Austria.

kaka /'kɒkɒ/ *n* a New Zealand parrot with a long beak.

kakapo /'kɒkəˌpoː/ *n* an owl-like parrot, a flightless nocturnal bird nesting in burrows in New Zealand.

kakemono /ˌkækə'moːnoː/ *n* a Japanese hanging picture of paper or silk, mounted on rollers.

kaki /'kɒki/ *n* (*pl* **kakis**) the Japanese persimmon.

kale, kail /keɪl/ *n* a variety of cabbage with crinkled leaves.

kaleidoscope /kə'laɪdəˌskoːp/ *n* a small tube containing bits of coloured glass reflected by mirrors to form symmetrical patterns as the tube is rotated; anything that constantly changes.—**kaleidoscopic** *adj.*—**kaleidoscopically** *adv.*

kalends /'kælendz/ *see* **calends**.

kaleyard, kailyard /'keɪlˌjɑrd/ *n* (*Scot*) a kitchen garden.

Kali /'kɒli/ *n* (*Hindu myth*) the goddess of destruction.

kalif, khalif /'kɒlɪf/ or /'kælɪf/ *see* **caliph**.

kalmia /'kælmɪə/ *n* the American mountain laurel.

Kalmuck, Kalmyk /'kælmʌk/ *n* (*pl* **Kalmucks, Kalmuck, Kalmyks, Kalmyk**) *n* a member of a Mongolian Buddhist people; the variety of the Mongolian language. • *adj* of or pertaining to the Kalmuck or their language.

kalong /'kɒlɒŋ/ *n* a large Indonesian or tropical fruitbat; a flying fox.

kalpak /'kælˌpæk/ *see* **calpac**.

kalsomine /'kɒlsəˌmaɪn/ or /-mɪn/ *see* **calcimine**.

Kamasutra /ˌkɒmə'suːtrə/ *n* an ancient Hindu manual on erotic love.

kame /keɪm/ *n* (*Scot*) an elongated gravel or sand mound or hill of glacial origin; a comb.

kami /'kɒmi/ *n* (*pl* **kami**) a divinity or demigod in the Shinto religion of Japan, from whom the Japanese emperors were supposed to have been descended.

kamikaze /ˌkæmɪ'kɒzi/ *n* (*World War II*) a Japanese aircraft packed with explosives for making a suicidal crashing attack; the pilot of such an aircraft.

kamseen /kæm'siːn/, **kamsin** /'kæmsɪn/ *see* **khamsin**.

kangaroo /ˌkæŋgə'ruː/ *n* (*pl* **kangaroos**) an Australian marsupial with short forelegs and strong, large hind legs for jumping.

kangaroo court *n* an illegal court operated by an unauthorized body, which perverts the proper course of justice.

Kantian /'kæntiən/ *adj* of the German philosopher Immanuel Kant (1724–1804) or his philosophy.

kaolin /'keɪəlɪn/ *n* a white clay used in porcelain, etc.

kapellmeister /kə'pɛlˌmaɪstər/ *n* (*pl* **kapellmeister**) the musical director of an orchestra etc, *esp* in an 18th-century aristocratic household.

kapok /'keɪpɒk/ *n* the silky fibres around the seeds of a tropical tree, used for stuffing cushions, etc.

kappa /'kæpə/ *n* the tenth letter of the Greek alphabet.

kaput /kæ'put/ *adj* (*sl*) broken, ruined.

karabiner /ˌkærə'biːnər/ or /'kærə-/ *n* (*mountaineering*) a spring-loaded hook for securing ropes.

karakul /'kærəˌkul/ *n* (the black fur of) a breed of sheep from the Bukhara region of central Asia.

karaoke /ˌkɛri:'oːkiː/ *n* a CD music system that plays recordings of popular songs with the vocal part removed to allow amateurs to sing along.

karat /'kɛrət/ *n* a measure of weight for precious stones; a measure of the purity of gold.—*also* **carat**.

karate /kə'rɒti/ *n* a Japanese system of unarmed combat using sharp blows of the feet and hands.

Karen /kə'rɛn/ *n* (*pl* **Karens, Karen**) *n* a member of a Thai people in Burma, or their language.

karma /'kɒrmə/ *n* (*Buddhism, Hinduism*) the sum of a person's actions during one of their existences, held to determine their destiny in the next; (*inf*) a certain aura that a person or place is felt to possess.—**karmic** *adj.*

karoo, karroo /kə'ruː/ *n* (*pl* **karoos, karroos**) (*S Africa*) (*sometimes with a cap*) a series of clayey tablelands, *usu* barren except in the wet season; a system of rocks in, or a period; of this period.

kart /kɑrt/ *n* a small motorized vehicle used in racing.—*also* **go-kart**.

karting /-ɪŋ/ *n* kart racing.

karyo- /'kærioː/ *prefix* = nucleus.

katydid /'keɪtɪdɪd/ *n* a large green North American insect like a grasshopper.

kauri /kauˈri/ *n* (*pl* **kauris**) a New Zealand pine with oval leaves from which a resinous gum is extracted; the wood or gum from this tree.

kava /'kɒvə/ *n* a Polynesian shrub; an intoxicating and narcotic drink made from it.

kayak /'kaɪæk/ *n* an Eskimo canoe made of skins on a wooden frame.—*also* **kaiak**.

kazoo /kə'zuː/ *n* (*pl* **kazoos**) a small tube-shaped musical instrument through which one hums to vibrate a membrane-covered hole at the end or side

KB *abbr* = kilobyte.

KBE *abbr* = Knight Commander of the Order of the British Empire.

kc *abbr* = kilocycle.

kcal *abbr* = kilocalorie.

KCB *abbr* = Knight Commander of the Order of the Bath.

KE *abbr* = kinetic energy.

kebab /kə'bɒb/ or /-bæb/ *n* small cubes of grilled meat and vegetables, *usu* served on a skewer.

keck /kɛk/ *vi* to make a sound as if about to vomit; to feel or express loathing.

keddah /'kɛdə/ *n* in India and Burma, an enclosure for catching wild elephants.

kedge /kɛdʒ/ *n* a small anchor for kedging a ship. • *vt* to move (a ship) by hauling on a cable attached to a kedge.

kedgeree /'kɛdʒəri/ or /-'riː/ *n* a dish containing fish, rice and hard-boiled eggs.

keef /kiːf/ *see* **kif**.

keek /kiːk/ *vt* (*Scot*) to peep cheekily.

keel /kiːl/ *n* one of the main structural members of a ship extending along the bottom from stem to stern to which the frame is attached; any structure resembling this. • *vti* (to cause) to turn over.

keelhaul /'kiːlhɒl/ *vt* (*formerly*) to drag under water beneath the bottom of a ship from one side to the other; to reprimand sternly.

keelson /'kiːlsən/ *n* a beam of timber laid on the middle of the floor timbers over the keel of a vessel to strengthen it.—*also* **kelson**.

keen[1] /kiːn/ *adj* eager, enthusiastic; intellectually acute, shrewd; having a sharp point or fine edge; (*senses*) perceptive, penetrating; extremely cold and piercing; intense; (*prices*) very low so as to be competitive.—**keenly** *adv.*—**keenness** *n.*

keen[2] *n* a dirge or lament for the dead. • *vi* to lament the dead.

keep /kiːp/ *vb* (**keeping, kept**) *vt* to celebrate, observe; to fulfil; to protect, guard; to take care of; to preserve; to provide for; to make regular entries in; to maintain in a specified state; to hold for the future; to hold and not let go; (*with* **at**) to harass (a person) into continuing (some task, etc); (*with* **back**) to refuse to disclose; to restrain; (*with* **down**) to repress; to subdue; (*with* **from**) to abstain or restrain from; to preserve as a secret (from someone); (*with* **to**) to cause to adhere strictly to; (*with* **up**) to persist in; to continue; to maintain in good condition. • *vi* to stay in a specified condition; to continue, go on; to refrain or restrain oneself; to stay fresh, not spoil; (*with* **at**) to persist; (*with* **away**) to prevent from approaching; (*with* **down**) to stay hidden; (*with* **on**) to talk or nag continuously; (*with* **to**) (cause to) adhere strictly to; (*with* **up**) to maintain the same pace, level of knowledge, etc as another; to stay informed; to continue relentlessly. • *n* food and shelter; care and custody; the inner stronghold of a castle.

keeper /'ki:pər/ *n* one who guards, watches, or takes care of persons or things.

keeping /-ɪŋ/ *n* care, charge; observance; agreement, conformity.

keepsake /-seik/ *n* something kept in memory of the giver.

kef /kɛf/ *see* **kif**.

keg /kɛg/ *n* a small barrel.

kelp /kɛlp/ *n* a large brown seaweed.

kelpie /'kɛlpi/ *n* (*pl* **kelpies**) in Scottish folklore, a malevolent water sprite, supposed to take the form of a horse.

Keltic /'kɛltik/ *see* **Celtic**.

kelvin /'kɛlvin/ *n* a unit of temperature of the Kelvin scale.

Kelvin scale *n* temperature on a scale where absolute zero (-273.15° Celsius) is taken as zero degrees.

ken /kɛn/ *n* understanding; view; sight. • *vt* (**kenning, kenned** *or* **kent**) to know; to recognize at sight.

kendo /'kɛndo:/ *n* a Japanese style of fencing with bamboo staves.

kennel /'kɛnəl/ *n* a small shelter for a dog, a doghouse; (*often pl*) a place where dogs are bred or kept. • *vt* (**kennelling, kennelled** *or* **kenneling, kenneled**) to keep in a kennel.

keno /ki:no/ *n* a game of chance, similar to bingo, played with numbered balls and cards.

kenosis /kɪ'no:sɪs/ *n* (*theology*) the self-limitation of Christ in laying aside his divinity and becoming man.—**kenotic** *adj*.

kentledge /'kɛntlədʒ/ *n* (*naut*) ballast of scrap metal.

kepi /'kepi/ *or* /'keipi/ *n* (*pl* **kepis**) a French military peaked cap.

kept /kept/ *see* **keep**.

keratin /'keratin/ *n* a tough, fibrous protein, the substance of hair, nails, feathers, etc.

keratitis /kɛrə'taɪtɪs/ *n* inflammation of the cornea.

keratose /'kɛrə,to:s/ *adj* (*sponges*) having a horn-like skeleton.

kerb /kərb/ *n* a line of raised stone forming the edge of a pavement; a curb.

kerbing /'kərbɪŋ/ *n* kerbstones collectively; material for kerbstones, curbing.

kerbstone /'kərbsto:n/ *n* the stone edge of a path, curbstone.

kerchief /'kərtʃɪf/ *or* /-tʃi:f/ *n* a piece of square cloth worn on the head.

kerf /kərf/ *n* a cut or slit made by a saw, etc.

kermes /'kərmi:z/ *n* the dried bodies of female scale insects from which a dye of a deep cherry red colour is obtained; an oak tree found in Europe and Asia, on which these insects live.

kermis /'kərmis/ *n* an open-air festival or fair.

kern[1], **kerne** /kərn/ *n* (*formerly*) a lightly armed Irish or Scottish medieval foot-soldier; a troop of these; (*arch*) a peasant.

kern[2] *n* (*print*) the part of a type or character that overhangs the following piece of type or character.

kernel /'kərnəl/ *n* the inner edible part of a fruit or nut; the essential part of anything.

kerosene, kerosine /'kɛrə,si:n/ *n* a fuel oil distilled from petroleum, paraffin.

kersey /'kərzi/ *n* a coarse smooth-faced woollen cloth.

kerseymere /'kərzɪmi:r/ *n* a twilled cloth of fine wool.

kestrel /'kestrəl/ *n* a type of small falcon.

ketch /kɛtʃ/ *n* a small two-masted sailing vessel.

ketchup /'kɛtʃəp/ *n* any of various thick sauces, *esp* one made from puréed tomato, for meat, fish, etc.—*also* **catchup, catsup**.

ketone /'ki:to:n/ *n* a class of chemical compounds, the simplest being acetone.

kettle /'kɛtəl/ *n* a container with a handle and spout for boiling water.

kettledrum /'kɛtəl,drʌm/ *n* a musical instrument consisting of a hollow metal body with a parchment head, the tension of which controls the pitch and is adjusted by screws.

kevel /'kɛvəl/ *n* (*naut*) a cleat for belaying ropes.

key[1] /ki:/ *n* a device for locking and unlocking something; a thing that explains or solves, as the legend of a map, a code, etc; a

controlling position, person, or thing; one of a set of parts or levers pressed in a keyboard or typewriter, etc; (*mus*) a system of related tones based on a keynote and forming a given scale; style or mood of expression; a roughened surface for improved adhesion of plaster, etc; an electric circuit breaker. • *vt* to furnish with a key; to bring into harmony. • *adj* controlling; important.

key[2] *n* a low island or reef.

keyboard /'ki:bɔrd/ *n* a set of keys in a piano, organ, microcomputer, etc.

keyhole /'ki:ho:l/ *n* an opening (in a lock) into which a key is inserted.

keyhole surgery *n* surgery performed through small incisions in the body using fibre-optic tubes both for internal examination and as conduits for tiny surgical instruments.

Keynesianism /'keɪnziə,nɪzəm/ *n* the economic theories based on the works of the English economist John Maynard Keynes (1883–1946).—**Keynesian** *adj*.

keynote /'ki:no:t/ *n* the basic note of a musical scale; the basic idea or ruling principle. • *vt* to give the keynote of; to give the keynote speech at.

keypad /'ki:pæd/ *n* a small *usu* hand-held keyboard of numbered buttons used to tap in a telephone number, operate a calculator, etc.

key signature *n* the sharps or flats at the beginning of a musical stave to indicate the key.

keystone /'ki:sto:n/ *n* the middle stone at the top of an arch, holding the stones or other pieces in place.

keystroke /'ki:stro:k/ *n* the depressing of a key on a typewriter, computer keyboard, etc.

kg /'keidʒi:/ *abbr* = kilogram(s).

KGB /,keidʒi:'bi:/ *abbr* = (*formerly*) the secret police of the USSR.

khaddar, khadi /'kɒdi/ *n* an Indian homespun cotton cloth.

khaki /'kæki/ *or* /'kɒki/, /'kɑrki/ *adj* dull yellowish-brown. • *n* (*pl* **khakis**) strong, twilled cloth of this colour; (*often pl*) a khaki uniform or trousers.

khamsin /'kæmsɪn/ *n* a hot southerly wind, *esp* in Egypt, that blows for about 50 days in spring.—**kamseen, kamsin**.

khan /kɒn/ *or* /kæn/ *n* the title of a ruler, prince, or governor in Asia.

khanate /'kɒn,eɪt/ *or* /'kæn-/ *n* the rule or jurisdiction of a khan.

khedive /kɪ'di:v/ *n* the title of the viceroy of Egypt (1867–1914).

khoraschot /'xo:rəfɒt/ *n* the policy in the former USSR, initiated by President Gorbachev, of the decentralized economic accountability of managers in industrial production and other enterprises.

kHz *abbr* = kilohertz.

kiang /ki'æŋ/ *n* a wild ass of Tibet.

kibble /'kɪbəl/ *vt* to grind coarsely. • *n* a raiseable bucket used in wells, mines etc.

kibbutz /kɪ'buts/ *n* (*pl* **kibbutzim**) an agricultural commune in Israel.

kibbutznik /kɪ'butsnɪk/ *n* a person who lives in a kibbutz.

kibe /kaɪb/ *n* ulcerated chilblain, *esp* one on the heel.

kiblah, kibla /'kɪblɒ/ *n* the point to which Muslims turn at prayer, Mecca.

kibosh /'kaɪbɒʃ/ *n* (*sl*) nonsense.

kick /kɪk/ *vt* to strike with the foot; to drive, force, etc as by kicking; to score (a goal, etc) by kicking; (*with* **about, around**) (*inf*) to abuse physically or mentally; to discuss or analyse (a problem, etc) in a relaxed unsystematic manner; (*with* **out**) (*inf*) to eject, dismiss; (*with* **up**) (*inf*) to cause (trouble, etc). • *vi* to strike out with the foot; to recoil, as a gun; (*inf*) to complain; (*with* **about, around**) (*inf*) to wander idly; to be unused or forgotten; (*with* **off**) (*football*) to give the ball the first kick to start play; (*inf*) to start. • *n* an act or method of kicking; a sudden recoil; (*inf*) a thrill; (*inf*) an intoxicating effect.—**kicker** *n*.

kickback /'kɪkbæk/ *n* a recoil; (*inf*) a returning of part of a sum of money received in payment.

kickoff /'kɪkɒf/ *n* (*football*) a kick putting the ball into play; the beginning or start of proceedings, *eg* a discussion.

kickshaw /'kɪkʃɒ/ *n* a trifle, trinket; (*arch*) a small, light, fancy dish, a delicacy.

kickstand /'kɪkstænd/ *n* a retractable stand for parking a bicycle or motorbike.

kid /kɪd/ *n* a young goat; soft leather made from its skin; (*inf*) a child. • *vti* (**kidding, kidded**) (*inf*) to tease or fool playfully; (*goat*) to bring forth young.—**kidder** *n*.

kiddy, kiddie /'kɪdi/ *n* (*pl* **kiddies**) (*inf*) a child.

kidnap /'kɪdnæp/ *vt* (**kidnapping, kidnapped** *or* **kidnaping, kidnaped**) to seize and hold to ransom, as of a person.—**kidnapper, kidnaper** *n*.

kidney /'kɪdni/ *n* (*pl* **kidneys**) either of a pair of glandular organs excreting waste products from the blood as urine; an animal's kidney used as food.

kidney bean *n* any of various cultivated beans, *esp* a large dark red bean seed.

kidney stone *n* a hard mineral deposit in the kidney.

kidskin /'kɪdskɪn/ *n* a soft leather made from the skin of a young goat.

kief /kiːf/ *see* **kif**.

kier /kiːr/ *n* a vat in which cloth is boiled for bleaching.

kieselguhr /'kiːzəl,gʊr/ *n* mineral remains of algae, used for filtering and insulation purposes etc.

kif /kɪf/ *n* a drowsy state of well-being produced by marijuana; marijuana itself; any drug producing a similar state.—*also* **keef, kef, kief**.

kill /kɪl/ *vt* to cause the death of; to destroy; to neutralize (a colour); to spend (time) on trivial matters; to turn off (an engine, etc); (*inf*) to cause severe discomfort or pain to. • *n* the act of killing; an animal or animals killed.—**killer** *n*.

killdeer /'kɪldiːr/ *n* a large North American plover with a mournful call.

killer whale /'kɪlər/ *n* a carnivorous black-and-white toothed whale.

killick /'kɪlɪk/, **killock** *n* (*naut*) a heavy stone used as an anchor; a small anchor.

killing /'kɪlɪŋ/ *adj* (*inf*) tiring; very amusing; causing death, deadly. • *n* the act of killing, murder; (*inf*) a sudden (financial) success.—**killingly** *adv*.

killjoy /'kɪldʒɔɪ/ *n* a person who spoils other people's enjoyment.

kiln /kɪln/ *n* a furnace or large oven for baking or drying (lime, bricks, etc).

kilo /'kiːloʊ/ *n* (*pl* **kilos**) kilogram; kilometre.

kilo- /'kiːloʊ/ *prefix* one thousand.

kilobyte /'kɪləbaɪt/ *n* 1024 bytes.

kilocalorie /'kɪlə,kæləri/ *n* a Calorie.

kilocycle /'kɪlə,saɪkəl/ *n* a kilohertz.

kilogram /'kɪləgræm/ *n* a unit of weight and mass, equal to 1000 grams or 2.2046 pounds.

kilohertz /'kɪlə,hɜːrts/ *n* one thousand cycles per second, 1000 hertz.

kilolitre, kiloliter /'kɪlə,liːtər/ *n* one thousand litres.

kilometre, kilometer /kɪ'lɒmɪtər/ *or* /'kɪlə,miːtər/ *n* a unit of length equal to 1000 metres or 0.62 mile.—**kilometric** *adj*.

kiloton /'kɪlə,tɒn/ *n* a unit of explosive force equal to 1000 tons of TNT.

kilowatt /'kɪlə,wɒt/ *n* a unit of electrical power, equal to 1000 watts.

kilowatt-hour *n* a unit of energy equal to work done by one kilowatt in one hour.

kilt /kɪlt/ *n* a knee-length pleated skirt made from tartan material, worn *usu* by men as part of the Scottish Highland dress.

kilter /'kɪltər/ *n* good working order; good condition (*out of kilter*).

kimono /kɪ'moʊnoʊ/ *or* /-nə/ *n* (*pl* **kimonos**) a loose Japanese robe.

kin /kɪn/ *n* relatives; family.—*see* **kith**.

kind[1] /kaɪnd/ *n* sort; variety; class; a natural group or division; essential character.

kind[2] *adj* sympathetic; friendly; gentle; benevolent.—**kindness** *n*.

kindergarten /'kɪndər,gɑrtən/ *n* a class or school for very young children.

kind-hearted /'kaɪnd,hɑrtɪd/ *adj* benevolent; kind, warm.—**kind-heartedly** *adv*.

kindle /'kɪndəl/ *vt* to set on fire; to excite (feelings, interest, etc). • *vi* to catch fire; to become aroused or excited.

kindling /'kɪndlɪŋ/ *n* material, such as bits of dry wood, for starting a fire.

kindly /'kaɪndli/ *adj* (**kindlier, kindliest**) kind; gracious; agreeable; pleasant. • *adv* in a kindly manner; favourably.—**kindliness** *n*.

kindred /'kɪndrəd/ *n* a person's family or relatives; family relationship; resemblance. • *adj* related; like, similar.

kine /kaɪn/ *n* (*pl*) (*arch*) cattle.

kinematic /,kɪnə'mætɪk/ *or* /,kaɪ-/ *adj* of pure motion, without reference to force etc.

kinematics /-s/ *n sing* the science of pure motion.

kinetic /kɪ'nɛtɪk/ *or* /kaɪ-/ *adj* of or produced by movement.—**kinetically** *adv*.

kinetic art *n* sculpture, etc that moves or has moving parts.

kinetic energy *n* energy derived from motion.

kinetics /kɪ'nɛtɪks/ *or* /kaɪ-/ *n* (*used as sing*) the science of the effects of forces in producing or changing motion; the study of the mechanisms and rates of chemical reactions.

king /kɪŋ/ *n* the man who rules a country and its people; a man with the title of ruler, but with limited power to rule; man supreme in a certain sphere; something best in its class; the chief piece in chess; a playing card with a picture of a king on it, ranking above a queen; (*draughts*) a piece that has been crowned.

King Charles spaniel *n* a small breed of spaniel with black and brown markings.

kingcup /'kɪŋkʌp/ *n* the marsh marigold; any of various yellow-flowered, five-petalled plants, such as the buttercup or clematis.

kingdom /'kɪŋdəm/ *n* a country headed by a king or queen; a realm, domain; any of the three divisions of the natural world: animal: vegetable, mineral.

kingfisher /'kɪŋ,fɪʃər/ *n* a short-tailed diving bird that feeds chiefly on fish.

King James Bible, King James Version *n* the version of the Bible published by the sanction of James I of England and VI of Scotland in 1611 and appointed to be read in churches.—*also* **Authorized Version**.

kinglet /'kɪŋlət/ *n* a minor king; a small bird with a yellow crown found throughout North America.

kingly /'kɪŋli/ *adj* (**kinglier, kingliest**) of, resembling, or fit for a king.—**kingliness** *n*.

king-of-arms /'kɪŋəv'ɑrmz/ *n* (*pl* **kings-of-arms**) chief officer of the Heralds' College.

kingpin /'kɪŋpɪn/ *n* (*sl*) the chief person in a company, group, etc; the pin in a car, etc that attaches the stub axle to the axle beam and allows limited movement to the stub axle; the foremost pin in tenpin bowling; the central pin in ninepins; the crux of an argument.

kingship /'kɪŋʃɪp/ *n* the office or authority of a king; the art of ruling as king.

king-size /'kɪŋ,saɪz/, **king-sized** *adj* larger than standard size.

kink /kɪŋk/ *n* a tight twist or curl in a piece of string, rope, hair, etc; a painful cramp in the neck, back, etc; a minor problem in some course of action; a personality quirk; (*Brit sl*) a sexual deviation; (*pl*) (*Scot*) a convulsive fit of laughter; (*US*) a bright, original idea. • *vt* to form kinks.

kinkajou /'kɪŋkə,dʒuː/ *n* nocturnal long-tailed quadruped of Central and Southern America similar to a racoon.—*also* **honeybear**; a short-tailed primate with spiny protrusions from the neck.—*also* **potto**.

kinky /'kɪŋki/ *adj* (**kinkier, kinkiest**) full of kinks; (*inf*) eccentric; (*inf*) sexually bizarre.—**kinkiness** *n*.

kino (gum) /'kiːnoʊ/ *n* an astringent vegetable gum of a dark red colour, used in medicine, tanning etc.

kinsfolk /'kɪnzfoʊk/ *n* blood relations.

kinship /'kɪnʃɪp/ *n* blood relationship; close connection.

kinsman /'kɪnzmən/, **kinswoman** /-,wʊmən/ *n* (*pl* **kinsmen, kinswomen**) a relative, *esp* by blood.

kiosk /'kiːɒsk/ *n* a small open structure used for selling newspapers, confectionery, etc; a public telephone booth.

kip /kɪp/ *vi* (**kipping, kipped**) (*sl*) to sleep. • *n* (*sl*) sleep, a lodging.

kipper /'kɪpər/ *n* a kippered herring, etc. • *vt* to cure (fish) by salting and drying or smoking.

kirk /kɜrk/ *n* (*Scot*) a church.

kirsch /kiːrʃ/, **kirschwasser** /'kɪrʃ,vɒsər/ *n* a type of brandy made from cherries.

kismet /'kɪzmɛt/ *or* /'kɪs-/ *n* fate, destiny.

kiss /kɪs/ *vti* to touch with the lips as an expression of love, affection or in greeting; to touch the lips with those of another person as a sign of love or desire; to touch lightly. • *n* an act of kissing; a light, gentle touch.—**kissable** *adj*.

kissagram /'kɪsə,græm/ *n* a celebratory telegram or message delivered with a kiss.

kiss-and-tell /'kɪsən,tɛl/ *adj* (*inf*) pertaining to the publication of memoirs that reveal hitherto secret details.

kisser /'kɪsər/ *n* one who kisses; (*Brit sl*) the mouth or face.

kiss of life *n* mouth-to-mouth resuscitation.

kist /kɪst/ n (Scot) a chest or box; (arch) a cist; (S Africa) a large chest or box used for storing linen, esp for a trousseau.

kit /kɪt/ n clothing and personal equipment, etc; tools and equipment for a specific purpose; a set of parts with instructions ready to be assembled. • vt (**kitting, kitted**) (usu with out or up) to provide with kit.

kitchen /'kɪtʃən/ n a place where food is prepared and cooked.

kitchenette /ˌkɪtʃɪ'nɛt/ n a small kitchen.

kitchen garden n a garden where vegetables are grown for domestic use.

kite /kaɪt/ n a bird of prey with long narrow wings and a forked tail; a light frame covered with a thin covering for flying in the wind.

kith /kɪθ/ n friends and relations, now only in **kith and kin**.

kithara /'kɪθərə/ see **cithara**.

kitsch /kɪtʃ/ n art, literature, etc regarded as pretentious, inferior, or in poor taste.—also adj.—**kitschy** adj.

kitten /'kɪtən/ n a young cat; the young of other small mammals. • vti to give birth to kittens.

kittenish /'kɪtənɪʃ/ adj like a kitten, playful; (woman) flirtatious.

kittiwake /'kɪtiˌweɪk/ n either of two types of gull with black-tipped wings.

kittle /'kɪtəl/ adj (Scot) difficult to manage, capricious. • vt (Scot) to tickle; to cause (someone) to be puzzled or to bother someone.

kitty /'kɪti/ n (pl **kitties**) the stakes in a game of poker or other gambling game; a shared fund of money; affectionate name for a cat or kitten.

kiwi /'kiːwi/ n (pl **kiwis**) a flightless bird of New Zealand; (inf) a New Zealander.

kiwi fruit n a fruit of an Asian vine.—also **Chinese gooseberry**.

KKK abbr = Ku Klux Klan.

kl abbr = kilolitre.

klaxon /'klæksən/ n a type of old-fashioned motor horn.

kleptomania /ˌklɛptoˈmeɪniə/ n an uncontrollable impulse to steal.—**kleptomaniac** n.

klipspringer /'klɪpˌsprɪŋər/ n a small antelope of South Africa.

kloof /kluːf/ n a ravine, a deep narrow valley, in South Africa.

klystron /'klaɪstron/ n an electronic device that generates and amplifies microwaves.

km abbr = kilometre(s).

knack /næk/ n an ability to do something easily; a trick; a habit.

knacker /'nækər/ n one who buys worn-out horses or old houses, ships, etc, for destruction.

knackwurst /'nækwərst/ n a type of spicy German sausage.

knap /næp/ (**knapping, knapped**) vt to break, snap or hit something.

knapsack /'næpsæk/ n a bag for carrying equipment or supplies on the back.

knapweed /'næpwiːd/ n a purple-flowered weed.

knar /nɑr/ see **knur**.

knave /neɪv/ n (formerly) a tricky or dishonest man; the jack in a pack of playing cards.—**knavish** adj.—**knavishly** adv.

knavery /'neɪvəri/ n (pl **knaveries**) dishonesty; fraud; deceit.

knead /niːd/ vt to squeeze and press together (dough, clay, etc) into a uniform lump with the hands; to make (bread, etc) by kneading; to squeeze and press with the hands.—**kneader** n.

knee /niː/ n the joint between the thigh and the lower part of the human leg; anything shaped like a bent knee. • vt (**kneeing, kneed**) to hit or touch with the knee.

kneecap /'niːkæp/ n the small bone covering and protecting the front part of the knee-joint. • vt (**kneecapping, kneecapped**) to maim by shooting into the kneecap.

knee-deep /-'diːp/ adj deep enough to cover the knees; deeply involved.

knee jerk /-ˌjərk/ n an involuntary jerk when the tendon below the knee is tapped.

kneejerk adj responding automatically.

kneel /niːl/ vi (**kneeling, kneeled** or **knelt**) to go down on one's knee or knees; to remain in this position.—**kneeler** n.

knell /nɛl/ n the sound of a bell rung slowly and solemnly at a death or funeral; a warning of death, failure, etc. • vi (bell) to ring a knell; to summon, announce, etc (as if) by a knell.

knelt /nɛlt/ see **kneel**.

knew /nuː/ or /njuː/ see **know**.

Knickerbocker /'nɪkərˌbokər/ n a New Yorker; a descendant of the founders of the original city.

knickerbockers /-s/ npl baggy breeches fastened by a band at the knee.

knickers /'nɪkərz/ npl an undergarment covering the lower body and having separate leg holes, worn by women and girls.

knickknack /'nɪknæk/ n a small ornament or trinket.—also **nicknack**.

knife /naɪf/ n (pl **knives**) a flat piece of steel, etc with a sharp edge set in a handle, used to cut or as a weapon; a sharp blade forming part of a tool or machine. • vt to cut or stab with a knife.

knife edge /'naɪfˌedʒ/ n the sharp edge of a knife; anything resembling this, such as the blade of an ice skate; a sharp wedge used as a pivot for a balance; a critical or precarious situation.

knight /naɪt/ n (Middle Ages) a medieval mounted soldier; a man who for some achievement is given honorary rank entitling him to use "Sir" before his given name; a chessman shaped like a horse's head. • vt to make (a man) a knight.—**knightly** adj.—**knightliness** n.

knight-errant /'naɪtˈɛrənt/ n (pl **knights-errant**) a quixotic person; (Middle Ages) a knight who went in quest of adventure, to show his prowess, chivalry etc.

knight-errantry /-i/ n the practices or customs of knights-errant; quixotic behaviour.

knighthood /'naɪtˌhud/ n the character, rank, or dignity of a knight; the order of knights.

knit /nɪt/ vb (**knitting, knitted** or **knit**) vt to form (fabric or a garment) by interlooping yarn using knitting needles or a machine; to cause (eg broken bones) to grow together; to link or join together closely; to draw (the brows) together. • vi to make knitted fabric from yarn by means of needles; to grow together; to become joined or united. • n a knitted garment or fabric.—**knitter** n.

knitting /'nɪtɪŋ/ n work being knitted.

knitting needle n a long thin eyeless needle, usu made of plastic or steel, used in knitting.

knitwear /'nɪtwɛr/ n knitted clothing.

knives /naɪvz/ see **knife**.

knob /nob/ n a rounded lump or protuberance; a handle, usu round, of a door, drawer, etc.

knobby /'nobi/ adj (**knobbier, knobbiest**) full of knobs.

knobkerrie /'nobˌkɛri/ n a round-headed stick used as a weapon in South Africa.

knock /nok/ vi to strike with a sharp blow; to rap on a door; to bump, collide; (engine) to make a thumping noise; (with **off**) (inf) to finish work; (with **up**) (tennis, etc) to practise before a match. • vt to strike; (inf) to criticize; (with **about, around**) to wander around aimlessly; to treat roughly; (with **back**) (inf) to drink, swallow quickly; to reject, refuse; (with **down**) to indicate a sale at an auction; (with **down** or **off**) to hit so as to cause to fall; (with **off**) (inf) to do or make hastily and without effort; to reduce in price; to discontinue, esp work; (sl) to kill; (sl) to steal; (with **out**) to make unconscious or exhausted; to eliminate in a knockout competition; (inf) to amaze; (with **up**) (inf) to make or arrange hastily; (cricket) to score a certain number of runs; to rouse; (sl) to make pregnant. • n a knocking, a hit, a rap.

knockabout /'nokəˌbʌut/ adj rough, boisterous.

knockdown adj cheap; (furniture) easy to dismantle.

knocker /'nokər/ n a device hinged against a door for use in knocking; (Brit sl: usu pl) a woman's breasts.

knock-kneed adj having inward-curving legs.

knockout /'nokˌaut/ n a punch or blow that produces unconsciousness; a contest in which competitors are eliminated at each round; (inf) an attractive or extremely impressive person or thing.

knoll /noːl/ n a small round hill.

knot /not/ n a lump in a thread, etc formed by a tightened loop or tangling; a fastening made by tying lengths of rope, etc; an ornamental bow; a small group, cluster; a hard mass of wood where a branch grows out from a tree, which shows as a roundish, cross-grained piece in a board; a unit of speed of one nautical mile per hour; something that ties closely, esp the bond of marriage. • vti (**knotting, knotted**) to make or form a knot (in); to entangle or become entangled.—**knotter** n.

knotgrass /'notgræs/ n a weed with a jointed stem and green flowers; any of various similar plants.

knothole /'nothoːl/ n a hole in wood once filled by a knot.

knotting /'notɪŋ/ n a kind of lace work made with knots; a sealer applied to knots before priming wood as protection from sap.

knotty /'noti/ adj (**knottier, knottiest**) full of knots; hard to solve; puzzling.—**knottiness** n.

know /noː/ *vt* (**knowing, knew**, *pp* **known**) to be well informed about; to be aware of; to be acquainted with; to recognize or distinguish.—**knowable** *adj*.

know-all /ˈnoːˌɔl/ *n* a know-it-all.

know-how /-ˌhaʊ/ *n* practical skill, experience.

knowing /-ɪŋ/ *adj* having knowledge; shrewd; clever; implying a secret understanding.—**knowingly** *adv*.—**knowingness** *n*.

know-it-all /-ɪtˌɔl/ *n* a person who acts as if they know about everything.

knowledge /ˈnɒlɪdʒ/ *n* what one knows; the body of facts, etc accumulated over time; fact of knowing; range of information or understanding; the act of knowing.

knowledgeable /ˈnɒlɪdʒəbəl/ *adj* having knowledge or intelligence; well-informed.—**knowledgeably** *adv*.

known /noːn/ *see* **know**.

knuckle /ˈnʌkəl/ *n* a joint of the finger, *esp* at the roots of the fingers; the knee of an animal used as food. • *vi* (*with* **down**) (*inf*) to apply oneself in earnest (to some task, duty, etc); (*with* **under**) to submit, to give in.

knuckle-duster /-ˌdʌstər/ *n* a metal device that fits over the knuckles, used for inflicting severe injury by punching.

knur, knurr /nər/ *n* a *k*not either in a tree trunk or in wood; a hard lump.—*also* **knar**.

knurl /nərl/ *n* a small ridge, *esp* one of a series on a metal surface to prevent slippage.

KO /ˈkeɪoː/ *abbr* = knockout.

koa /ˈkoːə/ *n* a Hawaiian tree; the hard wood it produces used in making furniture.

koala /koːˈɒlə/ *n* an Australian tree-dwelling marsupial with thick, grey fur.

koan /ˈkoːæn/ *n* an insoluble riddle used as a meditation exercise in Zen Buddhism.

kob /kɒb/ *n* a South African water antelope.

kobold /ˈkoːbəld/ *n* a household goblin or elf; a spirit of mines and other underground places.

Kohinoor, Koh-i-nor /ˈkoːɪˌnʊr/ *n* a famous, very large Indian diamond, which has belonged to the British Crown since 1849.

kohl /koːl/ *n* a fine powder, as of antimony, used for darkening the eyelids.

kohlrabi /koːlˈræbi/ *n* (*pl* **kohlrabies**) a variety of cabbage with a thick stem, used as a vegetable.

kola nut /ˈkoːlə/ *n* the seed of either of two tropical trees which has stimulant properties and is chewed or used in making sweet drinks.—*also* **cola nut**.

kolinsky /kəˈlɪnski/ *n* (*pl* **kolinskies**) an Asian mink; its fur.

kolkhoz /ˈkɒlkɒz/ or /kɛlkˈhɒz/ *n* a collective farm in Russia.

koodoo /ˈkuːduː/ *n* an African striped antelope with long spiral horns.—*also* **kudu**.

kook /kuːk/ *n* (*inf*) a person regarded as silly, eccentric, etc.

kookaburra /ˈkʊkəˌbərə/ *n* an Australian kingfisher with a harsh cry like loud laughter.

kooky, kookie /ˈkuːki/ *adj* (**kookier, kookiest**) (*inf*) crazy; eccentric.

kop /kɒp/ *n* (*S Africa*) an isolated hill.

kopeck, kopek /ˈkoːpɛk/ *n* a Russian coin, one hundred of which comprise one ruble.

kopje /ˈkɒpi/ *n* (*S Africa*) a hillock or small hill.

Koran /kɔrˈæn/ or /kə-/ *n* the sacred book of the Muslims.—**Koranic** *adj*.

Korean /kəˈriːən/ *n* a native or inhabitant of Korea; the language spoken in North and South Korea.• *adj* of or pertaining to Korea, its language or people.

kosher /ˈkoːʃər/ *adj* (*Judaism*) clean or fit to eat according to dietary laws; (*inf*) acceptable, genuine. • *n* kosher food.

koto /ˈkoːtoː/ *n* (*pl* **kotos**) a Japanese musical instrument with silk strings, similar to a zither.

kowtow /ˈkaʊtaʊ/ *vi* to show exaggerated respect (to) by bowing.

kph *abbr* = kilometres per hour.

Kr (*chem symbol*) krypton.

kraal /kræl/ *n* an African village consisting of a group of huts surrounded by a pallisade; a sheepfold, or cattle pen. • to pen sheep or cattle in a kraal.

krait /kraɪt/ *n* a deadly Asian rock snake.

kraken /ˈkrækən/ *n* a gigantic fabled sea monster supposed to live in the sea off Norway.

kremlin /ˈkrɛmlɪn/ *n* a Russian citadel; (*with cap and* **the**) the citadel in Moscow, housing the former palace, cathedrals, and the Russian government; (*with cap*) the central government of Russia.

kriegspiel /ˈkriːɡspiːl/ *n* (*sometimes with cap*) (*mil*) a game with blocks or models representing the various sections of an army as if in actual warfare, used in training; a chess game for two players, each playing on their own board with their own pieces, unseen by the other, with the moves regulated by a third person also with a board unseen by either player.

krill /krɪl/ *n* (*pl* **krill**) the tiny shrimp-like plankton eaten by many whales.

kris /kriːs/ *n* a Malaysian or Indonesian knife or dagger with a wavy blade.—*also* **crease, creese**.

Krishna /ˈkrɪʃnə/ *n* a great deity of later Hinduism.—**Krishnaism** *n*.

krona /ˈkroːnə/ *n* (*pl* **kronor**) the monetary unit of Sweden.

króna /ˈkroːnə/ *n* (*pl* **krónur**) the monetary unit of Iceland.

krone /ˈkroːnə/ *n* (*pl* **kroner**) the monetary unit of Denmark and Norway.

krypton /ˈkrɪptɒn/ *n* a colourless, odourless gas used in fluorescent lights and lasers.

Kt *abbr* = Knight.

kudos /ˈkuːdɒz/ or /-doːs/, /-dɛs/ *n* (*used as sing*) (*inf*) fame, glory, prestige.

kudu /ˈkuːduː/ *see* **koodoo**.

Kufic /ˈkuːfɪk/ *see* **Cufic**.

Ku Klux Klan /ˌkuːklʌksˈklæn/ *n* an American secret society hostile to Blacks, Jews, Catholics, etc.

kulak /ˈkuːlæk/ *n* an independent well-to-do peasant in Russia.

kumiss /ˈkuːmɪs/ *n* a spirit made in central Asia from fermented mare's milk and sometimes used as a medicine.

kümmel /ˈkʊməl/ *n* a liqueur flavoured with caraway seeds.

kumquat /ˈkʌmkwɒt/ *n* a small fruit like an orange with a sweet rind.

kung fu /kʊŋˈfuː/ *n* a Chinese system of unarmed combat.

Kurd /kərd/ *n* a native of Kurdistan, an area of plateaus and mountains covering eastern Turkey, northern Iraq, western Iran, and Armenia.

Kurdish /ˈkərdɪʃ/ *adj* pertaining to the Kurds or to their language. • *n* the language of the Kurds.

kvass, kvas /kvæs/ *n* a Russian rye beer that has stale bread as one of its ingredients.—*also* **quass**.

kw. *abbr* = kilowatt(s).

kwashiorkor /ˌkwɒʃiˈɔrkɔr/ *n* a disease, *esp* of children, caused by protein deficiency and characterized by a distended stomach and changes in skin pigmentation.

kwh *abbr* = kilowatt-hour(s).

kyanize /ˈkaɪəˌnaɪz/ *vt* to preserve wood from dry rot by injecting corrosive sublimate.—**kyanization** *n*.

kymograph /ˈkaɪməˌɡræf/ *n* an instrument for recording pressure, oscillations, sound waves, etc, *eg* an apparatus for determining the pressure of blood, by means of a stylus on a continually rotating drum of paper; (*phonetics*) an instrument to measure muscular strength in the tongue, lips, etc; an instrument that records the angular oscillations of an aircraft in the air.—*also* **cymograph**.

Kyrie (eleison) /ˈkiːriˌeɪ/ *n* a prayer, part of a mass; a musical setting of this; the response in an Anglican communion service.

L

L, l /ɛl/ *n* the 12th letter of the English alphabet; something shaped like an L.

l *abbr* = litre(s).

La (*chem symbol*) lanthanum.

la /lɒ/ *n* the name given to the sixth note of the diatonic scale in solmization.

laager /ˈlɒgər/ *n* (*S Africa*) a camp in a circle of wagons.—*also* **lager**.

lab /læb/ *n* (*inf*) laboratory.

labarum /ˈlæbərəm/ *n* (*pl* **labara**) a banner used in Christian processions.

label /ˈleɪbəl/ *n* a slip of paper, cloth, metal, etc attached to anything to provide information about its nature, contents, ownership, etc; a term of generalized classification. • *vt* (**labelling, labelled** *or* **labeling, labeled**) to attach a label to; to designate or classify (as).—**labeller, labeler** *n*.

labellum /ləˈbeləm/ *n* (*pl* **labella**) the lower petal of an orchid.

labia /ˈleɪbiə/ *npl* (*sing* **labium**) the lips of the female genitals, comprising the outer pair (*labia majora*) and the inner pair (*labia minora*).

labial /ˈleɪbiəl/ *adj* of the lips or labia.

labialize /-aɪz/ *vt* (*phonetics*) to pronounce (a sound) by rounding one's lips.—**labialization** *n*.

labiate /-eɪt/ *adj, n* (*bot*) (a plant) with the corolla or calyx divided into two parts, resembling lips.

labile /ˈleɪbaɪl/ *or* /-bɪl/ *adj* (*chem*) unstable.

labiodental /ˌleɪbioʊˈdɛntəl/ *adj* (*phonetics*) (*sound*) formed by the lips and teeth.

labionasal /-ˈneɪsəl/ *adj* (*phonetics*) formed by the lips and nose.

labium /ˈleɪbiəm/ *see* **labia**.

labor *see* **labour**.

Labor Day *n* a public holiday to honour workers, held in Canada and the United States on the first Monday in September.

laboratory /ˈlæbrəˌtɔri/ *or* /ləˈbɒrə-, /ləˈbɒrətri/ *n* (*pl* **laboratories**) a room or building where scientific work and research is carried out.

laborious /ləˈbɔriəs/ *adj* requiring much work; hard-working; laboured.—**laboriously** *adv*.—**laboriousness** *n*.

labour, labor /ˈleɪbər/ *n* work, physical or mental exertion; a specific task; all wage-earning workers; workers collectively; the process of childbirth. • *vi* to work; to work hard; to move with difficulty; to suffer (delusions, etc); to be in childbirth. • *vt* to develop in unnecessary detail.

Labour Day *n* a public holiday in many countries in honour of labour, usually held on 1 May.

laboured, labored /-bərd/ *adj* done with effort; strained.—**labouredly, laboredly** *adv*.

labourer, laborer /-bərər/ *n* a person who labours, *esp* a person whose work requires strength rather than skill.

labour *or* **labor union** *n* in the US, an organized association of employees of any trade or industry for the protection of their income and working conditions.

Labrador retriever *n* a breed of large, smooth-coated sporting dog.

labradorite /ˈlæbrəˈdɔraɪt/ *n* a type of feldspar.

labret /ˈlæbrɪt/ *n* a shell, etc, worn as an ornament in the lip.

labrum /ˈleɪbrəm/ *n* (*pl* **labra** /-brə/) the liplike shield of an insect's mouth.

laburnum /ləˈbɜrnəm/ *n* a small tree or shrub with hanging yellow flowers.

labyrinth /ˈlæbərɪnθ/ *n* a structure containing winding passages through which it is hard to find one's way; a maze.—**labyrinthine** *adj*.

lac[1] /læk/ *n* a resinous substance secreted by certain insects.

lac[2] *see* **lakh**.

lace /leɪs/ *n* a cord, etc used to draw together and fasten parts of a shoe, a corset, etc; a delicate ornamental fabric of openwork design using fine cotton, silk, etc. • *vt* to fasten with a lace or laces; to intertwine, weave; to fortify (a drink, etc) with a dash of spirits.

lacerate /ˈlæsəˌreɪt/ *vt* to tear jaggedly; to wound (feelings, etc).—**laceration** *n*.

laches /ˈlætʃɪz/ *or* /ˈleɪ-/ *n* (*law*) undue delay in claiming one's rights, etc.

lachrimatory /ˈlækrɪmətəri/ *n* (*pl* **lachrimatories**) a vessel used to hold tears, found in ancient Roman tombs.

lachrymal /ˈlækrɪməl/ *adj* of tears; relating to the glands that secrete tears.—*also* **lacrimal**.

lachrymose /ˈlækrɪˌmoʊs/ *adj* tending to shed tears; sad.—**lachrymosity** *n*.

laciniate /ləˈsɪniət/, **laciniated** /-əd/ *adj* (*biol*) cut into narrow lobes, fringed.

lack /læk/ *n* the fact or state of not having any or not having enough; the thing that is needed. • *vti* to be deficient in or entirely without.

lackadaisical /ˌlækəˈdeɪzɪkəl/ *adj* showing lack of energy or interest; listless.—**lackadaisically** *adv*.

lackey /ˈlæki/ *n* a male servant of low rank; a servile hanger-on.

lacklustre, lackluster /ˈlækˌlʌstər/ *adj* lacking in brightness or vigour; dull.

laconic /ləˈkɒnɪk/ *adj* using few words; concise.—**laconically** *adv*.—**laconicism** *n*.

lacquer /ˈlækər/ *n* a glossy varnish. • *vt* to coat with lacquer, to make glossy.

lacrimal *see* **lachrymal**.

lacrosse /ləˈkrɒs/ *n* a game played by two teams of 10 players with the aim of throwing a ball through the opponents' goal using a long stick topped with a netted pouch for catching and carrying the ball.

lact-, lacto- /ˈlæktoʊ/ *prefix* milk.

lactate /lækˈteɪt/ *vi* (*mammals*) to secrete milk.

lactation /-ˈteɪʃən/ *n* the secretion of milk.—**lactational** *adj*.

lacteal /ˈlæktɪəl/ *adj* pertaining to, or resembling, milk; (*anat*) conveying chyle.

lactescent /lækˈtesənt/ *adj* milky; (*plant, insect*) yielding a milky juice.—**lactescence** *n*.

lactic /ˈlæktɪk/ *adj* of or relating to milk; obtained from sour milk or whey; involving the production of lactic acid.

lactic acid *n* an organic acid normally present in sour milk.

lactiferous /lækˈtɪfərəs/ *adj* producing milk, or a milky juice.

lacto-, lact- /ˈlæktoʊ/ *prefix* milk.

lactometer /lækˈtɒmɪtər/ *n* an instrument used for determining the quality of milk.

lactose /ˈlæktoʊs/ *or* /-toʊz/ *n* a sugar present in milk.

lacuna /ləˈkjuːnə/ *n* (*pl* **lacunas, lacunae**) a gap, *esp* a missing portion in a text.—**lacunary** *adj*.

lacustrine /ləˈkʌstraɪn/ *adj* pertaining to lakes; growing by lakesides.

lacy /ˈleɪsi/ *adj* (**lacier, laciest**) resembling lace.—**lacily** *adv*.—**laciness** *n*.

lad /læd/ *n* a boy; a young man; a fellow, chap.

ladder /ˈlædər/ *n* a portable metal or wooden framework with rungs between two vertical supports for climbing up and down; something that resembles a ladder in form or use.

ladder back chair *n* a type of chair with a tall slatted back.

laddie /ˈlædi/ *n* a boy; a young lad.

lade /leɪd/ *vt* (**lading, laded**, *pp* **laden** *or* **laded**) (*ship*) to load (with cargo); (*with* **with**) to burden; to spoon up (liquid), *eg* with a ladle.

laden /ˈleɪdən/ *adj* loaded with cargo; burdened.

la-di-da, la-de-da /ˌlɑːdiːˈdɑː/ *adj* (*inf*) affected; foppish. • *n* an affected or foppish person.

ladies' room *n* a public lavatory for women.

lading /ˈleɪdɪŋ/ *n* the act of loading; that which is loaded; cargo; freight.

ladle /ˈleɪdəl/ *n* a long-handled, cup-like spoon for scooping liquids; a device like a ladle in shape or use. • (*with* **out**) (*inf*) to give (money, etc) generously.—**ladleful** *n*.

lady /ˈleɪdi/ *n* (*pl* **ladies**) a polite term for any woman; (*with cap*) a title of honour given to various ranks of women in the British peerage.

Lady Day *n* 25 March, the feast of the Annunciation.

ladybird /-ˌbəːd/, **ladybug** /ˈleɪdɪˌbʌg/ n a small, *usu* brightly coloured beetle.

lady-in-waiting n (*pl* **ladies-in-waiting**) a female member of a royal household, who attends upon a queen or princess.

lady-killer n (*inf*) a man who is or thinks he is particularly attractive to women.

ladylike /ˈleɪdɪˌlaɪk/ adj like or suitable for a lady; refined, polite.

ladylove /ˈleɪdɪlʌv/ n (*arch*) a sweetheart.

ladyship /ˈleɪdɪʃɪp/ n a title used in speaking to or of a woman with the rank of Lady.

lady-slipper n an orchid with flowers resembling slippers.

lady's-smock n a flowering plant that is also known as the cuckooflower.

laevorotation see **levorotation**.

laevulose see **levulose**.

lag[1] /læg/ vi (**lagging, lagged**) to fall behind, hang back; to fail to keep pace in movement or development; to weaken in strength or intensity. • n a falling behind; a delay.

lag[2] vt (**lagging, lagged**) to insulate (pipes, etc) with lagging.

lag[3] n (*sl*) a convict; a term of imprisonment.

lagan /ˈlægən/ n goods, or wreckage, lying on the seabed.—*also* **ligan.**

lager[1] /ˈlɒgər/ n a light beer that has been aged for a certain period.

lager[2] see **laager**.

laggard /ˈlægərd/ n a person who lags behind; a loiterer. • adj backward, slow.—**laggardly** adv.

lagging /ˈlægɪŋ/ n insulating material used to lag pipes, boilers, etc.

lagoon /ləˈguːn/ n a shallow lake or pond, *esp* one connected with a larger body of water; the water enclosed by a circular coral reef.

laic /ˈleɪɪk/, **laical** /-əl/ adj non-clerical, lay; secular.

laicize /ˈleɪɪˌsaɪz/ vt to make non-clerical or lay; to open to lay persons.—**laicization** n.

laid /ˈleɪd/ see **lay**[2].

laid-back /ˈleɪdˌbæk/ adj relaxed, easy-going.

laid paper n paper impressed with fine lines from the wires on which the pulp is laid.

lain /leɪn/ see **lie**[2].

lair /lɛr/ n the dwelling or resting place of a wild animal; (*inf*) a secluded place, a retreat.

laird /lɛrd/ n (*Scot*) a landowner.

laissez-faire, laisser-faire /ˌlɛseɪˈfɛr/ n the policy of non-interference with individual freedom, *esp* in economic affairs.— **laissez-faireism, laisser-faireism** n.

laity /ˈleɪtɪ/ n laymen, as opposed to clergymen.

lake[1] /leɪk/ n a large inland body of water.

lake[2] n a purplish-red pigment, originally made from lac.

lakh /læk/ or /lɒk/ n (*India*) 100,000, *esp* rupees.

lam[1] /læm/ vt (**lamming, lammed**) (*inf*) to beat or thrash.

lam[2] n a sudden flight, *esp* to evade capture by the authorities.

lama /ˈlɒmə/ n a monk or priest of Lamaism.

Lamaism /-ˌɪzəm/ n a form of Buddhism in Tibet and Mongolia.—**lamaist** n.—**Lamaistic** adj.

lamasery /-ˌsɛri/ n (*pl* **lamaseries**) a monastery of lamas.

lamb /læm/ n a young sheep; its flesh as food; (*inf*) an innocent or gentle person. • vi to give birth to a lamb; to tend (ewes) at lambing time.

lambada /ləmˈbɒdə/ n (the music for) a lively erotic dance of Brazilian origin, in which couples dance with their stomachs touching.

lambast, lambaste /læmˈbeɪst/ vt (*inf*) to beat or censure severely.

lambda /ˈlæmdə/ n the Greek letter L.

lambdoid /ˈlæmˈdɔɪd/ adj shaped like lambda.

lambent /ˈlæmbənt/ adj (*flame*) playing lightly over a surface; marked by radiance; brilliant.—**lambency** n.

lambert /ˈlæmbərt/ n a measure of brightness, the brightness of a surface radiating one lumen per square centimetre.

lambkin /ˈlæmkɪn/ n a little lamb.

lambrequin /ˈlæmbrɪkɪn/ or /ˈlæmbər-/ n a short hanging over a door, mantelpiece, etc.

lambrusco /lɒmˈbruskoː/ or /læm-/, /-ˈbruːs-/ n a sparkling red Italian wine.

lambskin /ˈlæmskɪn/ n the skin of a lamb with the wool on or as leather, for making clothes, etc.

lame /leɪm/ adj disabled or crippled, *esp* in the feet or legs; stiff and painful; weak, ineffectual. • vt to make lame.—**lamely** adv.—**lameness** n.

lamé /ˈlæˈmeɪ/ or /ˈlæmeɪ/ n a fabric interwoven with metallic threads.

lame duck n a weak, ineffectual person; an elected official serving between the end of his or her term and the inauguration of a successor.

lamella /ləˈmɛlə/ n (*pl* **lamellae, lamellas**) a thin plate, scale, or film.—**lamellar, lamellate, lamellose** adj.

lamelliform /ləˈmɛlɪˌfɔrm/ adj lamella-shaped.

lament /ləˈmɛnt/ vti to feel or express deep sorrow (for); to mourn. • n a lamenting; an elegy, dirge, etc mourning some loss or death.—**lamenter** n.

lamentable /ləˈmɛntəbəl/ or /ˈlæmɛntəbəl/ adj distressing, deplorable.—**lamentably** adv.

lamentation /ˌlæmɛnˈteɪʃən/ n a lamenting; a lament, expression of grief.

lamented /ləˈmɛntəd/ adj grieved for.

lamia /ˈleɪmɪə/ n (*pl* **lamias, lamiae**) (*myth*) a monster, half snake, half woman.

lamina /ˈlæmɪnə/ n (*pl* **laminae, laminas**) a thin plate, scale or layer; the expanded part of a foliage leaf.—**laminose** adj.

laminate /ˈlæmɪneɪt/ vt to cover with one or more thin layers; to make by building up in layers. • n a product made by laminating. • adj laminated.—**laminator** n.

laminated /-əd/ adj built in thin sheets or layers; covered by a thin film of plastic, etc.

lamination /ˌlæmɪˈneɪʃən/ n divisibility, or division, into thin plates.

Lammas /ˈlæməs/ n (*RC Church*) a feast held on August 1; (*formerly*) a harvest festival celebrated on August 1.

lammergeier, lammergeyer /ˈlæmərgaɪər/ n a vulture found in southern Europe, Africa and Asia, the bearded vulture.

lamp /læmp/ n any device producing light, either by electricity, gas, or by burning oil, etc; a holder or base for such a device; any device for producing therapeutic rays.

lampas /ˈlæmpəs/ n a disease of horses, which causes swelling in the roof of the mouth; a type of flowered silk.

lampblack /ˈlæmpblæk/ n fine charcoal or soot.

lampion /ˈlæmpiən/ n a small lamp.

lamplighter /ˈlæmpˌlaɪtər/ n (*formerly*) someone who lit street lamps.

lampoon /læmˈpuːn/ n a piece of satirical writing attacking someone. • vt to ridicule maliciously in a lampoon.—**lampooner** n.—**lampoonery** n.

lamppost /ˈlæmppoːst/ n a post supporting a street lamp.

lamprey /ˈlæmpri/ n (*pl* **lamprey, lampreys**) an animal resembling an eel but having a jawless, round sucking mouth.

LAN /læn/ (*abbr*) local area network: a number of computers in close proximity linked together in order to transfer information and share peripherals such as printers.

lanate /ˈleɪneɪt/ adj woolly.

lance /læns/ n a long wooden spear with a sharp iron or steel head. • vt to pierce (as if) with a lance; to open a boil, etc with a lancet.

lance corporal n a noncommissioned officer of the lowest rank in the British army.

lanceolate /ˈlænsiələt/ adj (*bot*) tapering to a point at either end.

lancer /ˈlænsər/ n a cavalry soldier formerly armed with a lance; (*pl*) a kind of dance, a quadrille.

lancet /ˈlænsət/ n a small, *usu* two-edged, pointed surgical knife.

lancet arch n a sharply pointed arch.

lanceted /-əd/ adj (*archit*) with one or more lancet arches or windows.

lancet window n a tall narrow window with a lancet arch.

lancewood /ˈlænswʊd/ n a tough, elastic wood.

land /lænd/ n the solid part of the earth's surface; ground, soil; a country and its people; property in land. • vt to set (an aircraft) down on land or water; to put on shore from a ship; to bring to a particular place; to catch (a fish); to get or secure (a job, prize, etc); to deliver (a blow). • vi to go ashore from a ship; to come to port; to arrive at a specified place; to come to rest.

landamman /ˈlændəmæn/ n (*Switzerland*) the chief official in some cantons.

landau /ˈlændau/ n a four-wheeled horse-drawn carriage with a roof that folds down.

landaulet, landaulette /ˌlændəˈlɛt/ n a small landau.

landed /ˈlændəd/ adj consisting of land; owning land.

landfall /-fɔl/ n a sighting of land, *esp* from a ship at sea; the land sighted.

landfill /-fɪl/ *n* a large pit in which refuse is buried between layers of soil.—*also adj.*

landgrave /-greɪv/ *n* (*formerly*) a title given to certain counts in Germany.

landgravine /-grə‚vaɪn/ *n* the wife of a landgrave; the title given to a woman landgrave.

landing /'lændɪŋ/ *n* the act of coming to shore or to the ground; the place where persons or goods are loaded or unloaded from a ship; a platform at the end of a flight of stairs.

landing craft *n* a small military vessel designed for landing troops and equipment ashore.

landing gear *n* the undercarriage of an aircraft.

landing stage *n* a platform for landing goods or people from a ship.

landing strip *n* an airstrip.

landlady /'lænd‚leɪdi/ *n* (*pl* **landladies**) a woman who owns and rents property; a woman who owns and runs a boarding house, pub, etc.

landlocked /'lændlɒkt/ *adj* surrounded by land.

landlord /-lɔrd/ *n* a man who owns and rents property; a man who owns and runs a boarding house, pub, etc.

landlubber /'lænd‚lʌbər/ *n* a person who has had little experience of the sea.

landmark /'lændmɑrk/ *n* any prominent feature of the landscape distinguishing a locality; an important event or turning point.

landmass /-‚mæs/ *n* a large expanse of land.

land mine *n* an explosive charge shallowly buried in the ground, *usu* detonated by stepping or driving on it.

Land of the Midnight Sun *n* (*inf*) the Arctic.

landowner /-o:nər/ *n* a person who owns land.—**landowning** *adj, n.*

landscape /-skeɪp/ *n* an expanse of natural scenery seen in one view; a picture of natural, inland scenery. • *vt* to make (a plot of ground) more attractive, as by adding lawns, bushes, trees, etc.

landscape gardening *n* the decorative design and planting of gardens and grounds in imitation of natural scenery.—**landscape gardener** *n.*

landscapist /'lændskeɪpɪst/ *n* an artist who paints landscapes.

landslide /'lændslaɪd/ *n* the sliding of a mass of soil or rocks down a slope; an overwhelming victory, *esp* in an election.

landsman /'lændzməns/ *n* (*pl* **landsmen**) a person who resides and works on land, as opposed to the sea.

Landtag /'lændtæk/ *n* the legislative assembly of each state in present-day Germany and Austria.

landward /'lændwərd/ *adv, adj* towards the land.—**landwards** *adv.*

lane /leɪn/ *n* a narrow road, path, etc; a path or strip specifically designated for ships, aircraft, cars, etc; one of the narrow strips dividing a running track, swimming pool, etc for athletes and swimmers; one of the narrow passages along which balls are bowled in a bowling alley.

langlauf /'læŋ‚lʊf/ *n* cross-country skiing.—**langläufer** *n.*

langouste *Fr.* /lɑ̃'gu:st/ or /'lɒŋgu:st/ *n* the spiny lobster.

langoustine *Fr.* /‚lɑ̃gu:'sti:n/ or /'lɒŋgus‚ti:n/ *n* a large prawn or small lobster.

langsyne /læŋ'zaɪn/ *adv* (*Scot*) long ago.

language /'læŋgwɪdʒ/ *n* human speech or the written symbols for speech; any means of communicating; a special set of symbols used for programming a computer; the speech of a particular nation, etc; the particular style of verbal expression characteristic of a person, group, profession, etc.

langue d'oc *Fr.* /lɑ̃g'dɒk/ *n* a form of medieval French spoken in the South of France.

languid /'læŋgwɪd/ *adj* lacking energy or vitality; apathetic; drooping, sluggish.—**languidly** *adv.*—**languidness** *n.*

languish /'læŋgwɪʃ/ *vi* to lose strength and vitality; to pine; to suffer neglect or hardship; to assume a pleading or melancholic expression.—**languisher** *n.*—**languishment** *n.*

languor /'læŋgər/ *n* physical or mental fatigue or apathy; dreaminess; oppressive stillness.—**languorous** *adj.*

langur /lʌŋ'gu:r/ *n* a long-tailed monkey, found in South Asia.

laniard *n see* **lanyard**.

laniary /læni'eri/ *n* (*pl* **laniaries**) a canine tooth.

laniferous /læni'fərəs/, **lanigerous** /-nɪdʒ-/ *adj* wool-bearing.

lank /læŋk/ *adj* tall and thin; long and limp.—**lankly** *adv.*—**lankness** *n.*

lanky /'læŋki/ *adj* (**lankier, lankiest**) lean, tall, and ungainly.—**lankily** *adv.*—**lankiness** *n.*

lanner /'lænər/ *n* a falcon found in Mediterranean countries, North Africa and South Asia; the female of this species.

lanneret /-ət/ *n* the male lanner falcon.

lanolin, lanoline /'lænəlɪn/ *n* wool grease used in cosmetics, ointments, etc.

lantern /'læntərn/ *n* a portable transparent case for holding a light; a structure with windows on top of a door or roof to provide light and ventilation; the light-chamber of a lighthouse.

lantern jaw *n* a long thin jaw.

lanthanide /'lænθə‚naɪd/ *n* any of a series of related chemical elements with atomic numbers from 57 (lanthanum) to 71 (lutetium).

lanthanum /'lænθənəm/ *n* a metallic element.

lanyard /'lænjərd/ or /-jɑrd/ *n* a rope used for fastening things on board a ship; a cord worn round the neck to hold a knife, whistle, etc.

laodicean /‚leɪo:dɪ'si:ən/ *adj* indifferent, *esp* towards religion.

lap[1] /læp/ *vti* (**lapping, lapped**) to take in (liquid) with the tongue; (*waves*) to flow gently with a splashing sound.

lap[2] *n* the flat area from waist to knees formed by a person sitting; the part of the clothing covering this.

lap[3] *n* an overlapping; a part that overlaps; one complete circuit of a race track. • *vb* (**lapping, lapped**) *vt* to fold (over or on); to wrap. • *vi* to overlap; to extend over something in space or time.

laparotomy /‚læpər'ɒtəmi/ *n* (*pl* **laparotomies**) (*med*) the operation of cutting the abdominal wall.

lapdog /'læpdɒg/ *n* a dog small and docile enough to be held on the lap.

lapel /lə'pɛl/ *n* a part of a suit, coat, jacket, etc folded back and continuous with the collar.—**lapelled** *adj.*

lapidary /'læpɪ‚deri/ *adj* of or relating to stones; inscribed on stone; concise, like an inscription. • *n* (*pl* **lapidaries**) a cutter or engraver of gems.—**lapidarian** *adj.*

lapidate /'læpɪdeɪt/ *vt* to stone (to death).—**lapidation** *n.*

lapidify *vti* (**lapidifying, lapidified**) to turn to stone.

lapis lazuli /‚læpɪs'læzʊlaɪ/ or /-li/, /-jʊ-/ *n* an azure, opaque, semi-precious stone.

lap of honour *n* a ceremonial circuit of the field by a winning person or team.

lappet /'læpɪt/ *n* a small, loose flap.

lapse /læps/ *n* a small error; a decline or drop to a lower condition, degree, or state; a moral decline; a period of time elapsed; the termination of a legal right or privilege through disuse. • *vi* to depart from the usual or accepted standard, *esp* in morals; to pass out of existence or use; to become void or discontinued; (*time*) to slip away.—**lapsable, lapsible** *adj.*—**lapser** *n.*

lapsus /-əs/ *n* (*pl* **lapsus**) a slip or error.

laptop /'læptɒp/ *n* a small portable computer that can comfortably be used on the lap.

lapwing /'læpwɪŋ/ *n* a crested plover.

larboard /'lɑrbərd/ *n* (*naut*) (*formerly*) the port or left side of a ship.

larceny /'lɑrsəni/ *n* (*pl* **larcenies**) the theft of someone else's property.—**larcenist, larcener** *n.*—**larcenous** *adj.*

larch /lɑrtʃ/ *n* a cone-bearing tree of the pine family.

lard /lɑrd/ *n* melted and clarified pig fat. • *vt* to insert strips of bacon or pork fat (in meat) before cooking; to embellish.

larder /'lɑrdər/ *n* a room or cupboard where food is stored.

lares /'lɛri:z/ *npl* (*Roman myth*) the household gods.

large /lɑrdʒ/ *adj* great in size, amount, or number; bulky; big; spacious; bigger than others of its kind; operating on a big scale.—**largeness** *n.*

large intestine *n* the section of the digestive system comprising the caecum, colon and rectum.

largely /'lɑrdʒli/ *adv* much, in great amounts; mainly, for the most part.

largen /-ən/ *vt* to make larger, to enlarge.

large-scale /-skeɪl/ *adj* drawn on a big scale to reveal much detail; extensive.

largess, largesse /lɑr'dʒɛs/ or /-'ʒɛs/ *n* the generous distribution of money, gifts, favours, etc; generosity.

larghetto /lɑr'gɛto/ *adv* (*mus*) slowly. • *n* (*pl* **larghettos**) a passage of music played in this way.

largish /'lɑrdʒɪʃ/ *adj* quite large.

largo /'lɑrgo:/ *adv* (*mus*) slow and dignified. • *n* (*pl* **largos**) a passage of music played in this way.

lariat /'leriət/ or /'læriət/ *n* a rope for tethering grazing horses; a lasso.

lark[1] /lark/ *n* any of a family of songbirds.

lark[2] *n* a playful or amusing adventure; a harmless prank. • *vi* (*usu with* **about**) to have fun, frolic.—**larky** *adj*.

larkspur /'larkspər/ *n* an annual delphinium.

larrigan /'lærigən/ *n* a knee-high leather boot worn by trappers.

larrikin /'lærikin/ *n* (*Austral sl*) a hooligan.

larrup /'lærəp/ *vt* (*dial*) to thrash, flog.

larva /'larvə/ *n* (*pl* **larvae**) the immature form of many animals after emerging from an egg before transformation into the adult state, *eg* a caterpillar.—**larval** *adj*.

laryngeal /lə'rindʒiəl/ *adj* pertaining to, or situated near, the larynx.

laryngitis /,lerin'dʒɔitis/ *n* inflammation of the larynx.—**laryngitic** *adj*.

laryngo-, laryng- /'leriŋgo:/ *prefix* larynx.

laryngology /,lerin'golədʒi/ *n* the medical study of the larynx.—**laryngologist** *n*.

laryngoscope /,loriŋgə'sko:p/ *n* a medical instrument for examining the larynx.—**laryngoscopy** *n*.

laryngotomy /,lerin'gotəmi/ *n* (*pl* **laryngotomies**) (*med*) the operation of cutting into the larynx.

larynx /'leriŋks/ *n* (*pl* **larynxes, larynges**) the structure at the upper end of the windpipe, containing the vocal cords.

lasagna, lasagne /lə'zɒnjə/ *n* pasta formed in thin wide strips; a dish of lasagne baked in layers with cheese, minced meat and tomato sauce.

lascar /'læskər/ *n* an East Indian sailor.—*also* **lashkar**.

lascivious /lə'siviəs/ *adj* lecherous, lustful; arousing sexual desire.—**lasciviously** *adv*.—**lasciviousness** *n*.

lase /leiz/ *vi* (*gem, gas*) able to act as a laser.

laser /'leizər/ *n* a device that produces an intense monochromatic beam of coherent light or other electromagnetic radiation.

laser printer *n* a computer printer that uses a laser beam and photoconductive drum to produce high quality text output.

lasertripsy /-,tripsi/ *n* a medical procedure for removing kidney stones, etc, by the use of laser beams.

lash /læʃ/ *vt* to strike forcefully (as if) with a lash; to fasten or secure with a cord, etc; to attack with criticism or ridicule. • *vi* to move quickly and violently; (*rain, waves, etc*) to beat violently against; (*with* **out**) to attack suddenly either physically or verbally; (*inf*) to spend extravagantly (on). • *n* the flexible part of a whip; an eyelash; a stroke (as if) with a whip.—**lasher** *n*.

lashkar *see* **lascar**.

lass /læs/, **lassie** /'læsi/ *n* a young woman or girl.

Lassa fever *n* an infectious viral disease of Africa.

lassitude /'læsi,tu:d/ or /-,tju:d/ *n* weariness.

lasso /lə'su:/ or /'læso:/ *n* (*pl* **lassos, lassoes**) a long rope or leather thong with a running noose for catching horses, cattle, etc. • *vt* (**lassoes** or **lassos, lassoing, lassoed**) to catch (as if) with a lasso.—**lassoer** *n*.

last[1] /læst/ *n* a shoemaker's model of the foot on which boots and shoes are made or repaired. • *vt* to shape with a last.

last[2] *vi* to remain in existence, use, etc; to endure. • *vt* to continue during; to be enough for.

last[3] *adj* being or coming after all the others in time or place; only remaining; the most recent; least likely; conclusive. • *adv* after all the others; most recently; finally. • *n* the one coming last.

last-ditch *adj* being a final effort to avoid disaster.

last hurrah *n* a final appearance; a swan song.

lasting /-iŋ/ *adj* enduring.—**lastingly** *adv*.

lastly /-li/ *adv* at the end, in the last place, finally.

last-minute *adj* at the last possible time when something can be done.

last rites *npl* the sacraments prescribed for a person near death.

last straw *n* a final addition to one's burdens that results in collapse or defeat.

last word *n* the final remark in an argument; a definitive statement; the latest fashion.

Lat. *abbr* = Latin.

lat. *abbr* = latitude.

latch /lætʃ/ *n* a fastening for a door, gate, or window, *esp* a bar, etc that fits into a notch. • *vti* to fasten with a latch.

latchet /'lætʃət/ *n* (*arch*) a strap or lace for fastening a shoe.

latchkey /'lætʃki:/ *n* the key of an outer door.

late /leit/ *adj, adv* after the usual or expected time; at an advanced stage or age; near the end; far on in the day or evening; just prior to the present; deceased; not long past; until lately; out of office.—**lateness** *n*.

latecomer /'leit,kʌmər/ *n* a person or thing that arrives late.

lateen /lə'ti:n/ *n* a triangular sail used on boats in the Mediterranean.—**lateenrigged** *adj*.

lately /'leitli/ *adv* recently, in recent times.

latent /'leitənt/ *adj* existing but not yet visible or developed.—**latency** *n*.—**latently** *adv*.

later /'leitər/ *adv* subsequently; afterwards.—*also compar of* **late**.

lateral /'lætərəl/ *adj* of, at, from, towards the side.—**laterally** *adv*.

lateral thinking *n* a solving of problems by employing unorthodox thought processes.

latest /'leitest/ *adj* most recent or fashionable. • *n* (*inf: with* **the**) the most up-to-date fashion, news, etc.—*also superl of* **late**.

latex /'leiteks/ *n* (*pl* **latexes, latices**) the milky juice produced by certain plants, used in the manufacture of rubber.

lath /læθ/ *n* (*pl* **laths**) a thin narrow strip of wood used in constructing a framework for plaster, etc.

lathe /leið/ *n* a machine that rotates wood, metal, etc for shaping.

lather /'læðər/ *n* a foam made by soap or detergent mixed with water; frothy sweat; a state of excitement or agitation. • *vti* to cover with or form lather.—**lathery** *adj*.

lathi /'læti/ *n* a long, heavy stick, carried by policemen in India.

Latin /'lætin/ *adj* of ancient Rome, its people, their language, etc; denoting or of the languages derived from Latin (Italian, Spanish, etc), the peoples who speak them, their countries, etc. • *n* a native or inhabitant of ancient Rome; the language of ancient Rome; a person, as a Spaniard or Italian, whose language is derived from Latin.

Latinate /'læti,neit/ *adj* of, resembling or derived from Latin.

Latinist /-,nist/ *n* a Latin scholar.

Latinity /-,niti/ *n* Latin style.

Latinize /-,naiz/ *vt* to translate into Latin; to give Latin characteristics to.—**Latinization** *n*.—**Latinizer** *n*.

Latino /lə'ti:no:/ *n* a person of Latin American origin living in the US.

latish /'leitiʃ/ *adj* somewhat late.

latitude /'læti,tu:d/ or /-,tju:d-/ *n* the distance from north or south of the equator, measured in degrees; a region with reference to this distance; extent; scope; freedom from restrictions on actions or opinions.—**latitudinal** *adj*.—**latitudinally** *adv*.

latitudinarian /,læti,tu:di'neriən/ *adj* claiming or showing freedom of thought, *esp* regarding religion. • *n* a person with such an outlook.—**latitudinarianism** *n*.

latria /'lætriə/ *n* (*RC Church*) supreme worship, offered to God alone.

latrine /lə'tri:n/ *n* a lavatory, as in a military camp.

-latry /lətri/ *n suffix* worship, *esp* excessively.

latter /'lætər/ *adj* later; more recent; nearer the end; being the last mentioned of two.

latter-day *adj* present-day; modern.

latterly /'lætərli/ *adv* recently.

lattice /'lætis/ *n* a network of crossed laths or bars.—**latticed** *adj*.

laud /lɒd/ *vt* to praise; to extol.

laudable /'lɒdəbəl/ *adj* praiseworthy.—**laudability** *n*.—**laudably** *adv*.

laudanum /'lɒdənəm/ *n* (*formerly*) any of various opium preparations; a solution of opium in alcohol.

laudation /lɒ'deiʃən/ *n* praise.

laudatory /'lɒdətəri/, **laudative** /-tiv/ *adj* expressing praise.

laugh /læf/ *vi* to emit explosive inarticulate vocal sounds expressive of amusement, joy or derision. • *vt* to utter or express with laughter; (*with* **off**) to dismiss as of little importance, make a joke of. • *n* the act or sound of laughing; (*inf*) an amusing person or thing.—**laugher** *n*.—**laughing** *adj*, *n*.—**laughingly** *adv*.

laughable /'læfəbəl/ *adj* causing laughter; ridiculous.—**laughably** *adv*.

laughing gas *n* nitrous oxide.

laughing stock *n* an object of ridicule.

laughter /'læftər/ *n* the act or sound of laughing.

launch[1] /lɒntʃ/ *vt* to throw, hurl or propel forward; to cause (a vessel) to slide into the water; (*rocket, missile*) to set off; to put into action; to put a new product onto the market. • *vi* to involve oneself enthusiastically. • *n* the act or occasion of launching.

launch[2] *n* an open, or partly enclosed, motor boat.

launch pad, launching pad *n* a platform from which a spacecraft is launched.

launder /'lɒndər/ *vti* to wash and iron clothes. • *vt* to legitimize (money) obtained from criminal activity by passing it through foreign banks, or investing in legitimate businesses, etc.—**launderer** *n*.

Launderette /lɒn'drɛt/ *n* (*trademark*) an establishment equipped with coin-operated washing machines and driers for public use.

laundress /'lɒndrɛs/ *n* a woman who earns her living by doing laundry.

Laundromat /'lɒndrəmæt/ *n* (*trademark*) the US name for a Launderette (*trademark*).

laundry /'lɒndri/ *n* (*pl* **laundries**) a place where clothes are washed and ironed; clothes sent to be washed and ironed.

laureate /'lɒriət/ *adj* crowned with laurel leaves as a mark of honour. • *n* the recipient of an honour or distinction; a poet laureate.—**laureateship** *n*.

laurel /'lɒrəl/ *n* an evergreen shrub with large, glossy leaves; the leaves used by the ancient Greeks as a symbol of achievement.

lava /'lævə/ *n* molten rock flowing from a volcano; the solid substance formed as this cools.

lavabo /lə'veɪbəʊ/ or /-'væbəʊ/ *n* (*pl* **lavaboes, lavabos**) (*RC Church*) the ritual washing of the celebrant's hands at the Eucharist; a washbasin.

lavation /lə'veɪʃən/ *n* the act of washing.

lavatory /'lævətɒri/ *n* (*pl* **lavatories**) a sanitary device for the disposal or faeces and urine; a room equipped with this.—*also* **bathroom, toilet**.

lavender /'lævəndər/ *n* the fragrant flowers of a perennial shrub dried and used in sachets; a pale purple.

laver /'leɪvər/ or /'lævər/ *n* an edible seaweed.

lavish /'lævɪʃ/ *vt* to give or spend freely. • *adj* abundant, profuse; generous; extravagant.—**lavishly** *adv*.—**lavishness** *n*.

law /lɔː/ *n* all the rules of conduct in an organized community as upheld by authority; any one of such rules; obedience to such rules; the study of such rules, jurisprudence; the seeking of justice in courts under such rules; the profession of lawyers, judges, etc; (*inf*) the police; a sequence of events occurring with unvarying uniformity under the same conditions; any rule expected to be observed.

law-abiding *adj* obeying the law.

lawbreaker /lɔː'breɪkər/ *n* a person who violates the law.—**lawbreaking** *adj*, *n*.

lawful /'lɔːful/ *adj* in conformity with the law; recognized by law.—**lawfully** *adv*.—**lawfulness** *n*.

lawgiver /'lɔːgɪvər/ *n* a maker of a code of laws.

lawless /'lɔːləs/ *adj* not regulated by law; not in conformity with law, illegal.—**lawlessly** *adv*.—**lawlessness** *n*.

lawmaker /'lɔːmeɪkər/ *n* a maker of laws, a legislator.

lawn[1] /lɔːn/ *n* a fine sheer cloth of linen or cotton.—**lawny** *adj*.

lawn[2] *n* land covered with closely cut grass, *esp* around a house.

lawn darts *n* an outdoor game of darts using a lawn as a board, at which are fired foot-long metal darts.

lawn mower *n* a hand-propelled or power-driven machine to cut lawn grass.

lawn tennis *n* tennis played on a grass court.

lawrencium /lɒ'rensiəm/ *n* a radioactive metallic element.

lawsuit /'lɔːsuːt/ *n* a suit between private parties in a law court.

lawyer /'lɔːjər/ *n* a person whose profession is advising others in matters of law or representing them in a court of law.

lax /læks/ *adj* slack, loose; not tight; not strict or exact.—**laxly** *adv*.—**laxness** *n*.

laxative /'læksətɪv/ *n* a substance that promotes emptying of the bowels.—*also adj*.

laxity /'læksɪti/ *n* the state or quality of being lax, laxness.

lay[1] /leɪ/ *see* **lie**[2].

lay[2] *vt* (**laying, laid**) to put down; to allay or suppress; to place in a resting position; to place or set; to place in a correct position; to produce (an egg); to devise; to present or assert; to stake a bet; (*with* **down**) to put down; to surrender, relinquish; to begin to build; to establish (guidelines, rules, etc); to store, *esp* wine; to record tracks in a music studio; (*with* **in**) to store, to stockpile; (*with* **off**) to suspend from work temporarily or permanently; (*with* **on**) to supply, provide; to install (electricity, etc); (*with* **out**) to plan in detail; to arrange for display; to prepare (a corpse) for

viewing; (*inf*) to spend money, *esp* lavishly; (*with* **up**) to store for future use; to disable or confine through illness. • *vi* (*inf*) to leave (a person or thing) alone; (*with* **into**) to attack physically or verbally. • *n* a way or position in which something is situated.

lay[3] *n* a simple narrative poem, *esp* as intended to be sung; a ballad.

lay[4] *adj* of or pertaining to those who are not members of the clergy; not belonging to a profession.

layabout /'leɪəˌbaʊt/ *n* a loafer, lazy person.

lay-by /'leɪbaɪ/ *n* (*Austral*) a deposit payment system that reserves an article for a purchaser until full settlement; (*Brit*) a pull-in place for motorists to stop at the side of a main road.—**lay by** *vt* to set aside or save for future needs.

layer /'leɪər/ *n* a single thickness, fold, etc; the runner of a plant fastened down to take root; a hen that lays. • *vti* to separate into layers; to form by superimposing layers; to (cause to) take root by propagating a plant shoot still attached to its parent.

layette /leɪ'ɛt/ *n* a complete set of clothes, equipment and accessories for a newborn baby.

lay figure *n* a jointed model of the human body used by artists for hanging drapery on; a person regarded as a puppet or nonentity.

laying /'leɪɪŋ/ *n* a sitting of eggs; the first coat of plaster.

layman /'leɪmən/ *n* (*pl* **laymen**) a person who is not a member of the clergy; a non-specialist, someone who does not possess professional knowledge.—**laywoman** *nf* (*pl* **laywomen**).

layoff /'leɪɒf/ *n* a period of involuntary unemployment.

layout /'leɪaʊt/ *n* the manner in which anything is laid out, *esp* arrangement of text and pictures on the pages of a newspaper or magazine, etc; the thing laid out.

layover /'leɪˌoʊvər/ *n* in the US, a stop on a journey, *esp* waiting for a connection.

lazar /'læzər/ *n* (*arch*) a leper.

lazaret, lazarette /ˌlæzə'rɛt/ (*also* **lazaretto** /-'rɛtəʊ/) *n* (*pl* **lazarettos, lazarets, lazarettes**) (*naut*) a part of a ship's hold; (*formerly*) a hospital for people suffering from infectious diseases.

laze /leɪz/ *vti* to idle or loaf.

lazulite /'læzəlaɪt/ *n* an azure blue mineral.

lazy /'leɪzi/ *adj* (**lazier, laziest**) disinclined to work or exertion; encouraging or causing indolence; sluggishly moving.—**lazily** *adv*.—**laziness** *n*.

lazybones /'leɪziˌbəʊnz/ *n* a lazy person.

lb *abbr* = pound(s) weight.

lbw /ˌɛlbiː'dʌbəˌljuː/ *abbr* = (*cricket*) leg before wicket.

LCD /ˌɛlsiː'diː/ *abbr* = liquid-crystal display; (*also without cap*) lowest common denominator.

L/Cpl *abbr* = lance corporal.

lea[1] /liː/ *n* (*poet*) a meadow, grassland.

lea[2] *n* a measure of yarn, varying from 80 yards (approx 73 metres) for wool to 300 yards (approx 274 metres) for linen.

leach /liːtʃ/ *vt* to wash (soil, ore, etc) with a filtering liquid; to extract (a soluble substance) from some material. • *vi* to lose soluble matter through a filtering liquid.—**leacher** *n*.

lead[1] /liːd/ *vb* (**leading, led**) *vt* to show the way, *esp* by going first; to direct or guide on a course; to direct by influence; to be head of (an expedition, orchestra, etc); to be ahead of in a contest; to live, spend (one's life); (*with* **on**) to lure or entice, *esp* into mischief. • *vi* to show the way, as by going first; (*with* **to**) to tend in a certain direction; to be or go first. • *n* the role of a leader; first place; the amount or distance ahead; anything that leads, as a clue; the leading role in a play, etc; the right of playing first in cards or the card played.

lead[2] /lɛd/ *n* a heavy, soft, bluish-grey, metallic element; a weight for sounding depths at sea, etc; bullets; a stick of graphite, used in pencils; (*print*) a thin strip of metal used to space lines of type. • *adj* of or containing lead. • *vt* (**leading, leaded**) to cover, weight, or space out with lead.

leaden /'lɛdən/ *adj* made of lead; very heavy; dull grey; gloomy.—**leadenly** *adv*.

leader /'liːdər/ *n* the person who goes first; the principle first violin-player in an orchestra; the director of an orchestra; the inspiration or head of a movement, such as a political party; a person whose example is followed; the leading editorial in a newspaper; the leading article.

leadership /'liːdərʃɪp/ *n* the act of leading; the ability to be a leader; the leaders of an organization or movement collectively.

lead glass *n* flint glass.

lead-in /ˈliːdɪn/ n introductory material; the connection between a radio transmitter or receiver with an aerial or transmission cable.

leading[1] /ˈliːdɪŋ/ adj capable of guiding or influencing; principal; in first position.

leading[2] /ˈlɛdɪŋ/ n a covering of lead; (print) the body of a type, larger than the size, giving space.

leading article /ˈliːdɪŋ-/ n an article in a newspaper stating editorial opinion on a given subject; the leader.

leading light n the most important member of a group or organization.

leading question n a question worded so as to suggest the desired answer.

leadsman /ˈliːdsmən/ n (pl **leadsmen**) a sailor who heaves the lead.

lead time /ˈliːd-/ n the period between the design of a product and its manufacture.

leaf /liːf/ n (pl **leaves**) any of the flat, thin (usu green) parts growing from the stem of a plant; a sheet of paper; a very thin sheet of metal; a hinged or removable part of a table top. • vi to bear leaves; (with **through**) to turn the pages of.

leafage /ˈliːfɪdʒ/ n foliage.

leafless /-ləs/ adj without leaves.

leaflet /ˈliːflət/ n a small or young leaf; a sheet of printed information (often folded), esp advertising matter distributed free. • vi to distribute leaflets (to).

leaf mould n compost or soil composed of decaying leaves and other vegetable matter; any of various fungal diseases of plants.

leafy /ˈliːfɪ/ adj (**leafier, leafiest**) having many or broad leaves; resembling leaves.—**leafiness** n.

league[1] /liːg/ n an association of nations, groups, etc for promoting common interests; an association of sports clubs that organizes matches between members; any class or category. • vti (**leaguing, leagued**) to form into a league.

league[2] n (formerly) a varying measure of distance, averaging about three miles (5km).

leak /liːk/ n a crack or hole through which liquid or gas may accidentally pass; the liquid or gas passing through such an opening; confidential information made public deliberately or accidentally. • vi to (let) escape though an opening; to disclose information surreptitiously.—**leaker** n.

leakage /ˈliːkədʒ/ n the act of leaking; that which enters or escapes by leaking.

leaky /ˈliːkɪ/ adj (**leakier, leakiest**) leaking or likely to leak.—**leakiness** n.

leal /liːl/ adj (Scot) loyal.

lean[1] /liːn/ adj thin, with little flesh or fat; spare; meagre. • n meat with little or no fat.—**leanness** n.

lean[2] vb (**leaning, leaned** or **leant**) vi to bend or slant from an upright position; to rest supported (on or against); to rely or depend for help (on). • vt to cause to lean.

leaning /ˈliːnɪŋ/ n inclination, tendency.

leant /lɛnt/ see **lean**[1].

lean-to /ˈliːnˌtuː/ n (pl **lean-tos**) a building whose rafters rest on another building.

leap /liːp/ vb (**leaping, leaped** or **leapt**) vi to jump; (with **at**) to accept something offered eagerly. • vt to pass over by a jump; to cause to leap. • n an act of leaping; bound; space passed by leaping; an abrupt transition.—**leaper** n.

leapfrog /ˈliːpˌfrɒg/ n a game in which one player vaults over another's bent back. • vi (**leapfrogging, leapfrogged**) to vault in this manner; to advance in alternate jumps.

leap year n a year with an extra day (29 February) occurring every fourth year.

learn /lɜːn/ vti (**learning, learned** or **learnt**) to gain knowledge of or skill in; to memorize; to become aware of, realize.—**learner** n.

learned /ˈlɜːnəd/ adj having learning; erudite; acquired by study, experience, etc.—**learnedly** adv.

learning /ˈlɜːnɪŋ/ n a gaining of knowledge; the acquiring of knowledge or skill through study.

lease /liːs/ n a contract by which an owner lets land, property, etc to another person for a specified period. • vt to grant by or hold under lease.—**leaseable** adj.—**leaser** n.

leaseback /ˈliːsbæk/ n the process of selling an asset, esp a building, and then renting it.

leasehold /ˈliːshoʊld/ n the act of holding by lease; the land, buildings, etc held by lease.—**leaseholder** n.

leash /liːʃ/ n a cord, strap, etc by which a dog or animal is held in check. • vt to hold or restrain on a leash.

least /liːst/ adj smallest in size, degree, etc; slightest. • adv to the smallest degree. • n the smallest in amount.

leastways /ˈliːstweɪz/ adv at least.

leather /ˈlɛðər/ n material made from the skin of an animal prepared by removing the hair and tanning; something made of leather. • vt to cover with leather; to thrash.

leatherback /ˈlɛðərbæk/ n the largest existing sea turtle, having a flexible shell.

Leatherette /ˌlɛðəˈrɛt/ n (trademark) an imitation leather.

leatherjacket /ˈlɛðərdʒækɪt/ n a tropical fish with a leathery skin; the larva of the cranefly.

leathern /ˈlɛðərn/ adj (arch) made of, or resembling, leather.

leatherneck /ˈlɛðərnɛk/ n (sl) a member of the US Marine Corps.

leathery /ˈlɛðərɪ/ adj like leather; tough and flexible.

leave[1] /liːv/ n permission to do something; official authorization to be absent; the period covered by this.

leave[2] vb (**leaving, left**) vt to depart from; to cause or allow to remain in a specified state; to cause to remain behind; to refrain from consuming or dealing with; to have remaining at death, to bequeath; to have as a remainder; to allow to stay or to continue doing without interference; to entrust or commit to another; to abandon. • vi to depart; (with **off**) to stop, desist.—**leaver** n.

leaved /liːvd/ adj having leaves.

leaven /ˈlɛvən/ n a substance to make dough rise, esp yeast; something that changes or enlivens. • vt to raise with leaven; to modify, to enliven.—**leavening** n.

leaves /liːvz/ see **leaf**.

leave-taking n a departure, farewell.

leavings /ˈliːvɪŋz/ npl leftovers; remnants; refuse.

leben /ˈleɪbən/ n a food made from soured milk, eaten in North Africa and the Levant.

Lebensraum /ˈleɪbənsˌraʊm/ n a piece of territory claimed by another country on the basis that it is needed to accommodate the country's expanding population.

lech /lɛtʃ/ vt (sl) to lust after.

lecher /ˈlɛtʃər/ n a lecherous man.

lecherous /-əs/ adj characterized by or encouraging lechery.

lechery /-əri/ n (pl **lecheries**) unrestrained sexuality; debauchery.

lecithin /ˈlɛsɪθɪn/ n any of a group of fatty compounds found in plant and animal tissues, used as an emulsifier and antioxidant.

lectern /ˈlɛktərn/ n a reading stand in a church; any similar reading support.

lection /ˈlɛkʃən/ n a reading from scripture for a particular day; a variant reading of a text.

lectionary /-əri/ n (pl **lectionaries**) a book listing lessons from scripture to be read at religious services on particular days.

lector /ˈlɛktər/ n a lecturer or reader at a university.

lecture /ˈlɛktʃər/ n an informative talk to a class, etc; a lengthy reprimand. • vti to give a lecture (to); to reprimand.—**lecturer** n.

lectureship /-ʃɪp/ n the position of lecturer.

LED /lɛd/ or /ˌɛliːˈdiː/ abbr = light-emitting diode.

led /lɛd/ see **lead**[1].

lederhosen /ˈleɪdərˌhoʊzən/ npl leather shorts with braces worn by men in Austria and Bavaria.

ledge /lɛdʒ/ n a narrow horizontal surface resembling a shelf projecting from a wall, rock face, etc; an underwater ridge of rocks; a rock layer containing ore.—**ledgy** adj.

ledger /ˈlɛdʒər/ n a book in which a record of debits, credits, etc is kept.

ledger line n a short line added above or below a musical staff to extend its range.—also **leger line**.

lee /liː/ n a shelter; the side or part away from the wind.

leech /liːtʃ/ n a blood-sucking worm; a person who clings to or exploits another.

leek /liːk/ n a vegetable that resembles a greatly elongated green onion.

leer /lɪər/ n a sly, oblique or lascivious look. • vi to look with a leer.—**leeringly** adv.

leery /ˈliːrɪ/ adj (**leerier, leeriest**) (with **of**) suspicious, wary.

lees /liːz/ npl sediment in the bottom of a wine bottle, etc.

leeward /ˈliːwərd/ adj, n (naut) (in) the quarter towards which the wind blows.

leeway /ˈliːweɪ/ n the distance a ship or aircraft has strayed sideways of its course; freedom of action as regards expenditure of time, money, etc.

left[1] /lɛft/ *see* **leave**[2].

left[2] *adj* of or on the side that is towards the west when one faces north; worn on the left hand, foot, etc. • *n* the left side; (*often cap*) of or relating to the left in politics; the left hand; (*boxing*) a blow with the left hand.

left-hand *adj* of or towards the left side of a person or thing; for use by the left hand.

left-handed /lɛft'hændəd/ *adj* using the left hand in preference to the right; done or made for use with the left hand; ambiguous, backhanded. • *adv* with the left hand.—**left-handedly** *adv*.—**left-handedness** *n*.

left-hander /-'hændər/ *n* a left-handed person; a blow delivered with the left fist.

left-luggage office *n* (*Brit*) a place at an airport, railway station, etc., where luggage may be left for a small charge with an attendant for safekeeping; a checkroom in the US.

leftist /'lɛftɪst/ *adj* tending to the left in politics. • *n* a person tending towards the political left.—**leftism** *n*.

leftovers /'lɛft,oːvərz/ *npl* unused portions of something, *esp* uneaten food.

leftward /'lɛftwərd/ *adj, adv* on or toward the left.—**leftwards** *adv*.

left-wing /'lɛftwɪŋ/ *adj* of or relating to the liberal faction of a political party, organization, etc.—**left-winger** *n*.

lefty /'lɛfti/ *n* (*pl* **lefties**) (*inf*) a left-winger; (*US sl*) a left-handed person.

leg /lɛg/ *n* one of the limbs on which humans and animals support themselves and walk; the part of a garment covering the leg; anything shaped or used like a leg; a branch or limb of a forked object; a section, as of a trip; any of a series of games or matches in a competition.

legacy /'lɛgəsi/ *n* (*pl* **legacies**) money, property, etc left to someone in a will; something passed on by an ancestor or remaining from the past.

legal /'liːgəl/ *adj* of or based on law; permitted by law; of or for lawyers.—**legally** *adv*.

legalese /liːgə'liːz/ *n* legal language as used in documents.

legalism /'liːgə,lɪzəm/ *n* observance of the letter rather than the spirit of the law, red tape.—**legalist** *n*.—**legalistic** *adj*.—**legalistically** *adv*.

legality /lɪ'gælɪti/ or /liː-/ *n* (*pl* **legalities**) conformity with the law.

legalize /'liːgə,laɪz/ *vt* to make lawful.—**legalization** *n*.

legal tender *n* a currency which a creditor is legally bound to accept in payment of a debt.

legate /'lɛgət/ *n* an envoy, *esp* from the Pope; an official emissary.—**legatine** *adj*.

legatee /,lɛgə'tiː/ *n* a person to whom a legacy is bequeathed.

legation /lɪ'geɪʃən/ *n* a diplomatic minister and staff; the headquarters of a diplomatic minister.—**legationary** *adj*.

legato /lɛ'gɒtoː/ *adj, adv* (*mus*) smoothly and evenly.

leg before wicket *n* (*cricket*) the dismissal of a batsman for illegally preventing the ball from hitting the wicket by obstructing it with his or her leg.

leg bye *n* (*cricket*) a run made when the ball touches any part of the batsman except the hand.

legend /'lɛdʒənd/ *n* a story handed down from the past; a notable person or the stories of his or her exploits; an inscription on a coin, etc; a caption; an explanation of the symbols used on a map.—**legendry** *n*.

legendary /'lɛdʒənd,ɛri/ *adj* of, based on, or presented in legends; famous, notorious.

legerdemain /,lɛdʒərdə'meɪn/ *n* trickery, sleight of hand.

leger line *see* **ledger line**.

legged /'lɛgd/ *adj* having legs.

leggings /'lɛgɪŋz/ *npl* protective outer coverings for the lower legs; a leg-hugging fashion garment for women.

leggy /'lɛgi/ *adj* (**leggier, leggiest**) having long and shapely legs.—**legginess** *n*.

leghorn /'lɛghɔrn/ *n* fine plaited straw; a hat made of this; (*with cap*) a breed of domestic fowl.

legible /'lɛdʒɪbəl/ *adj* able to be read.—**legibility** *n*.—**legibly** *adv*.

legion /'liːdʒən/ *n* an infantry unit of the ancient Roman army; a large body of soldiers; a large number, a multitude.

legionary /-əri/ *adj* of a legion. • *n* (*pl* **legionaries**) a member of a legion; a soldier in a legion of the ancient Roman army.

legionnaire /,liːdʒə'nɛr/ *n* a member of certain military forces or associations.

Legionnaire's disease *n* a serious and sometimes fatal bacterial infection which causes symptoms like pneumonia (first identified after an outbreak at an American Legion convention in 1976).

legislate /'lɛdʒɪs,leɪt/ *vi* to make or pass laws. • *vt* to bring about by legislation.

legislation /,lɛdʒɪs'leɪʃən/ *n* the act or process of law-making; the laws themselves.

legislative /'lɛdʒɪs,leɪtɪv/ *adj* of legislation or a legislature; having the power to make laws.

legislator /'lɛdʒɪs,leɪtər/ *n* a member of a legislative body.

legislature /'lɛdʒɪs,leɪtʃər/ *n* the body of people who have the power of making laws.

legist /'lɛdʒɪst/ *n* someone versed in the law.

legit /lɪ'dʒɪt/ *adj* (*sl*) legitimate.

legitimate /lɪ'dʒɪtɪmət/ *adj* lawful; reasonable, justifiable; conforming to accepted rules, standards, etc; (*child*) born of parents married to each other.—**legitimacy** *n*.—**legitimately** *adv*.

legitimatize /lɪ'dʒɪtɪmə,taɪz/ *vt* to legitimize.

legitimist /'lɪdʒɪtɪmɪst/ *n* a supporter of a hereditary title to a monarchy.—**legitimism** *n*.

legitimize /lɪ'dʒɪtɪ,maɪz/ *vt* to make or declare legitimate.—**legitimization** *n*.

legume /'lɛgjuːm/ *n* any of a large family of plants having seeds growing in pods, including beans, peas, etc; the pod or seed of such a plant used as food.

leguminous /lɪ'gjuːmɪnəs/ *adj* (*bot*) belonging to a family of flowering and pod-bearing plants.

legwork /'lɛgwərk/ *n* (*inf*) work that involves a lot of walking.

lei /'leɪi/ or /leɪ/ *n* a garland of flowers worn around the neck, given as a token of affection in Hawaii.

leister /'liːstər/ *n* a pronged spear used for catching salmon.

leisure /'liːʒər/ or /'lɛ-/ *n* ease, relaxation, *esp* freedom from employment or duties. • *adj* free and unoccupied.—**leisured** *adj*.

leisurely /-li/ *adj* relaxed, without hurry.

leitmotif, leitmotiv /'laɪtmoː,tiːf/ *n* a dominant theme.

lemma /'lɛmə/ *n* (*pl* **lemmas, lemmata**) (*logic*) a premise believed to be true.

lemming /'lɛmɪŋ/ *n* a small arctic rodent; one of a group wilfully heading on a course for destruction.

lemon /'lɛmən/ *n* (a tree bearing) a small yellow oval fruit with an acid pulp; pale yellow; (*sl*) a person or thing considered disappointing or useless.—**lemony** *adj*.

lemonade /,lɛmə'neɪd/ *n* a lemon-flavoured drink.

lemon grass *n* a tropical grass with lemon-scented leaves used in cooking and which yields an aromatic oil.

lemur /'liːmər/ *n* a Madagascan arboreal primate related to the monkey.

lemuroid /-ɔɪd/, **lemurine** /-,raɪn/ or /-,riːn/ *adj* pertaining to, or resembling, a lemur.

lend /lɛnd/ *vb* (**lending, lent**) *vt* to give the use of something temporarily in expectation of its return; to provide (money) at interest; to give, impart. • *vi* to make loans.—**lender** *n*.

length /lɛŋkθ/ or /lɛŋθ/ *n* the extent of something from end to end, *usu* the longest dimension; a specified distance or period of time; something of a certain length taken from a larger piece; a long expanse; (*often pl*) the degree of effort put into some action.

lengthen /'lɛŋkθən/ or /'lɛŋ-/ *vti* to make or become longer.

lengthwise /'lɛŋkθwaɪz/ or /lɛŋθ-/, **lengthways** /-weɪz/ *adv* in the direction of the length.

lengthy /'lɛŋkθi/ or /'lɛŋθi/ *adj* (**lengthier, lengthiest**) long, *esp* too long.—**lengthily** *adv*.—**lengthiness** *n*.

lenient /'liːnɪənt/ *adj* not harsh or severe; merciful.—**leniency, lenience** *n*.—**leniently** *adv*.

lenitive /'lɛnɪtɪv/ *adj* easing pain.

lenity /'lɛnɪti/ *n* (*pl* **lenities**) clemency, mercy; leniency.

leno /'liːnoː/ *n* (*pl* **lenos**) a way of weaving fabric; a fabric woven in this way.

lens /lɛnz/ *n* a curved piece of transparent glass, plastic, etc used in optical instruments to form an image; any device used to focus electromagnetic rays, sound waves, etc; a similar transparent part of the eye that focuses light rays on the retina.

Lent /lɛnt/ *n* the forty weekdays from Ash Wednesday to Easter, observed by Christians as a period of fasting and penitence.—**Lenten** *adj*.

lent /lɛnt/ *see* **lend**.

lentamente /ˌlɛntəˈmɛnteɪ/ *adv* (*mus*) slowly.

lenticular /lɛnˈtɪkjʊlər/ *adj* doubly convex.

lentigo /ˈlɛntɪɡo/ *n* (*pl* **lentigines**) a freckle.

lentil /ˈlɛntɪl/ *n* any of several leguminous plants with edible seeds; their seed used for food.

lento /ˈlɛnto/ *adj, adv* (*mus*) slow, slowly. • *n* (*pl* **lentos**) a piece of music played in this way.

Leo /ˈliːo/ *n* (*astrol*) the fifth sign of the zodiac, in astrology operative July 22–August 21; (*astron*) the Lion, a constellation in the northern hemisphere.

Leonid /ˈliːənɪd/ *n* (*pl* **Leonids, Leonides**) (*astron*) one of the meteors that fall in showers during the November of certain years, their chief point being in the constellation of Leo.

leonine /ˈliːəˌnaɪn/ *adj* of or like a lion.

leopard /ˈlɛpərd/ *n* a large tawny feline with black spots found in Africa and Asia.—*also* **panther.—leopardess** *nf*.

leotard /ˈliːətɑːd/ *n* a skintight one-piece garment worn by dancers and others engaged in strenuous exercise.

leper /ˈlɛpər/ *n* a person with leprosy.

lepidopteran /lɛpɪˈdɒtərən/ or /ˌlɛpɪdɒˈtɛrən/ *n* (*pl* **lepidopterans, lepidoptera**) any of a large order of insects, such as moths or butterflies, that as adults have four wings covered with minute, often coloured, scales and that as larvae are caterpillars.—**lepidopterous** *adj*.

lepidopterist /lɛpɪˈdɒtərɪst/ *n* an expert on moths and butterflies.

lepidosiren /ˌlɛpɪdoˈsaɪrən/ *n* an eel-like mudfish found in South America

leporine /lɛpəˈriːn/ or /-ˈraɪn/ *adj* pertaining to hares; hare-like.

leprechaun /ˈlɛprəˌkɒn/ *n* (*Irish folklore*) a fairy.

leprosy /ˈlɛprəsi/ *n* a chronic infectious bacterial disease of the skin, often resulting in disfigurement.—**leprous** *adj*.

lepton /ˈlɛptɒn/ *n* (*phys*) any of various elementary particles, such as electrons and muons, that participate in weak interactions with other elementary particles.

lesbian /ˈlɛzbɪən/ *n* a female homosexual. • *adj* of or characteristic of lesbians.—**lesbianism** *n*.

lèse-majesté, lese-majesty /liːzˈmædʒəsti/ *n* high treason; a crime against royalty.

lesion /ˈliːʒən/ *n* any change in an organ or tissue caused by injury or disease; an injury.

less /lɛs/ *adj* not so much, not so great, etc; fewer; smaller. • *adv* to a smaller extent. • *n* a smaller amount. • *prep* minus.

lessee /ˈlɛsiː/ *n* a person who holds property under a lease.

lessen /ˈlɛsən/ *vti* to make or become less.

lesser /-ər/ *adj* less in size, quality or importance.

lesson /ˈlɛsən/ *n* something to be learned or studied; something that has been learned or studied; a unit of learning or teaching; (*pl*) a course of instruction; a selection from the Bible, read as a part of a church service.

lessor /lɛˈsɔr/ *n* a person who lets property on a lease.

lest /lɛst/ *conj* in order, or for fear, that not; that.

let[1] /ˈlɛt/ *n* a stoppage; (*tennis*) a minor obstruction of the ball that requires a point to be replayed.

let[2] *vb* (**letting, let**) *vt* to allow, permit; to rent; to assign (a contract); to cause to run out, as blood; as an auxiliary in giving suggestions or commands (*let us go*); (*with* **down**) to lower; to deflate; to disappoint; to untie; to lengthen; (*with* **off**) to allow to leave (a ship, etc); to cause to explode or fire; to release, excuse from (work, etc); to deal leniently with, refrain from punishing; to allow (gas, etc) to escape; (*with* **out**) to release; to reveal; to rent out; to make a garment larger; (*with* **up**) to relax; to cease. • *vi* to be rented; (*with* **on**) (*inf*) to pretend; (*inf*) to reveal (a secret, etc); to pretend. • *n* the letting of property or accommodation.

let-down /ˈlɛtdaʊn/ *n* a disappointment.

lethal /ˈliːθəl/ *adj* deadly.—**lethality** *n*.—**lethally** *adv*.

lethargy /ˈlɛθɑːdʒi/ *n* (*pl* **lethargies**) an abnormal drowsiness; sluggishness; apathy.—**lethargic** *adj*.—**lethargically** *adv*.

let's /lɛts/ = let us.

letter /ˈlɛtər/ *n* a symbol representing a phonetic value in a written language; a character of the alphabet; a written or printed message; (*pl*) literature; learning; knowledge; literal meaning. • *vt* to mark with letters.

letter bomb *n* an explosive device concealed in an envelope and sent through the post.

letter box *n* a slit in the doorway of a house or building through which letters are delivered; a postbox.

lettered /ˈlɛtərd/ *adj* literate; highly educated; marked with letters.

letterhead /ˈlɛtərˌhɛd/ *n* a name, address, etc printed as a heading on stationery; stationery printed with a heading.

lettering /ˈlɛtərɪŋ/ *n* the act or process of inscribing with letters; letters collectively; a title; an inscription.

letterpress /ˈlɛtərˌprɛs/ *n* a method of printing; the printed matter of a book, as opposed to the illustrations.

lettuce /ˈlɛtəs/ *n* a plant with succulent leaves used in salads.

letup *n* a relaxation of effort.

leukemia, leukaemia /luːˈkiːmɪə/ *n* a chronic disease characterized by an abnormal increase in the number of white blood cells in body tissues and the blood.

leukocyte /ˈluːkəˌsaɪt/ *n* a white blood cell.

leukoma /luːˈkoːmə/ *n* a white, opaque scar on the cornea of the eye.

leukorrhea *n* a mucous discharge from the vagina.

leukotomy /luːˈkɒtəmi/ *n* (*pl* **leukotomies**) the severing of nerve fibres in the frontal lobes of the brain formerly used to relieve certain severe mental disorders.

lev /lɛv/ *n* (*pl* **leva**) the monetary unit of Bulgaria.

levanter /lɪˈvæntər/ *n* an easterly wind in the Mediterranean.

levantine /lɪˈvæntaɪn/ or /ˈlɛvən-/ *n* a kind of reversible silk cloth.

levator /lɪˈveɪtər/ *n* (*anat*) a muscle that serves to raise a part of the body.

levee[1] /ˈlɛvi/ *n* a reception of visitors formerly held by a sovereign or other important person on rising from bed; a reception *usu* in honour of a particular person.

levee[2] *n* an embankment beside a river.

level /ˈlɛvəl/ *n* a horizontal line or plane; a position in a scale of values; a flat area or surface; an instrument for determining the horizontal. • *adj* horizontal; having a flat surface; at the same height, rank, position, etc; steady. • *vti* (**leveling, leveled** *or* **levelling, levelled**) to make or become level; to demolish; to raise and aim (a gun, criticism, etc).—**levelly** *adv*.

level crossing *n* (*Brit*) a place where a road crosses a railway line on the same level *esp* where gates or barriers close the road to allow trains to pass; a grade crossing in the US.

leveler, leveller /ˈlɛvələr/ *n* one who levels; an advocate of social equality.

level-headed /ˌlɛvəlˈhɛdəd/ *adj* having an even temper and sound judgment.—**level-headedly** *adv*.

lever /ˈliːvər/ *n* a bar used for prising or moving something; a means to an end; a device consisting of a bar turning about a fixed point; any device used in the same way, *eg* to operate machinery. • *vt* to raise or move (as with) a lever.

leverage /ˈlɛvərɪdʒ/ or /ˈliːvər-/ *n* the action of a lever; the mechanical advantage gained by the use of a lever; power, influence.

leveret /ˈlɛvərət/ *n* a hare less than a year old.

leviable /ˈlɛvɪəbəl/ *adj* subject to a levy; (*goods*) which may be levied upon or seized.

leviathan /ləˈvaɪəθən/ *n* something huge.

levigate /ˈlɛvɪˌɡeɪt/ *vt* to grind to a fine powder.

Levi's /ˈliːˌvaɪz/ *n* (*trademark*) jeans made from (blue or black) denim.

levitate /ˈlɛvɪˌteɪt/ *vti* to rise or cause to rise into the air and float without support.—**levitation** *n*.

levity /ˈlɛvɪti/ *n* (*pl* **levities**) excessive frivolity; lack of necessary seriousness.

levorotation /ˌliːvoːroːˈteɪʃən/ *n* left-handed or counterclockwise rotation.—*also* **laevorotation. levorotatory** *adj*.

levulose /ˈliːvjʊˌloːs/ or /-ˌloːz/ *n* a fruit found in sugar.—*also* **laevulose.**

levy /ˈlɛvi/ *vt* (**levying, levied**) to collect by force or authority, as a tax, fine, etc; an amount levied; to enrol or conscript troops; to prepare for or wage war. • *n* (*pl* **levies**) a levying; the amount levied.—**levier** *n*.

lewd /ljuːd/ *adj* indecent; lustful; obscene.—**lewdly** *adv*.—**lewdness** *n*.

lewis /ˈluːɪs/ *n* an appliance for lifting heavy blocks of stone.

lewisite /ˈluːɪˌsaɪt/ *n* a blistering liquid obtained from arsenic and acetylene, used in gas form in chemical warfare.

lexical /ˈlɛksɪkəl/ *adj* of or pertaining to words in a language; of a lexicon or dictionary.—**lexically** *adv*.

lexicographer /ˌlɛksɪˈkɒɡrəfər/ *n* a person skilled in lexicography.

lexicography /-ˈɡrəfi/ *n* the process of writing or compiling a dictionary; the principles and practices of dictionary making.—**lexicographic, lexicographical** *adj*.—**lexicographically** *adv*.

lexicology /ˌlɛksɪˈkɒlədʒi/ n the branch of linguistics dealing with the meaning and use of words.—**lexicological** adj.—**lexicologist** n.

lexicon /ˈlɛksɪkən/ n a dictionary; a special vocabulary, as of a specific language, branch of knowledge, etc.

lexis /ˈlɛksɪs/ n the total of words or vocabulary in a language.

ley /leɪ/, **ley-line** n a straight line joining two landmarks, supposedly of prehistoric origin.

LF abbr = low frequency.

Li (chem symbol) lithium.

li /liː/ n the Chinese equivalent of a mile, equivalent to approximately 590 yards.

liability /ˌlaɪəˈbɪlɪti/ n (pl **liabilities**) a being liable; something for which one is liable; (inf) a handicap, disadvantage; (pl) debts, obligations, disadvantages.

liable /ˈlaɪəbəl/ adj legally bound or responsible; subject to; likely (to).

liaise /liˈeɪz/ vi to form a connection and retain contact with.

liaison /liˈeɪzɒn/ or /ˌliːeɪˈzɒn/ n intercommunication as between units of a military force; an illicit love affair; a thickening for sauces, soups, etc, as egg yolks or cream.

liana, liane /liˈænə/ n a climbing plant found in tropical forests.

liar /ˈlaɪər/ n a person who tells lies.

Lias /ˈlaɪəs/ n (geol) the lowest division of rocks of the Jurassic system.—**Liassic** adj.

lib /lɪb/ n (inf) liberation.

libation /lɪˈbeɪʃən/ n the act of pouring wine or oil on the ground, as a sacrifice; the liquid so poured out; a drink.

libel /ˈlaɪbəl/ n any written or printed matter tending to injure a person's reputation unjustly; (inf) any defamatory or damaging assertion about a person. • vt (**libeling, libeled** or **libelling, libelled**) to utter or publish a libel against.— **libeler, libeller** n.—**libelous, libellous** adj.

liberal /ˈlɪbərəl/ adj ample, abundant; not literal or strict; tolerant; (education) contributing to a general broadening of the mind, non-specialist; favouring reform or progress. • n a person who favours reform or progress.—**liberally** adv.

liberalism /ˈlɪbərəˌlɪzəm/ n liberal opinions, principles or politics.

liberality /ˌlɪbəˈrælɪti/ n (pl **liberalities**) generosity; breadth of mind.

liberalize /ˈlɪbərəˌlaɪz/ vti to make or become less strict.—**liberalization** n.

liberate /ˈlɪbəˌreɪt/ vt to set free from foreign occupation, slavery, etc.—**liberator** n.

liberation /ˌlɪbəˈreɪʃən/ n the act of liberating; the state of being liberated; the pursuit of social, political or economic equality by or on behalf of those being discriminated against.

liberation priest n a priest who is active in working for social and political justice.

liberation theology n the belief that Christianity requires commitment to social and political change, as well as faith, esp in South America.

libertarian /ˌlɪbərˈtɛriən/ n a person who advocates liberty, esp in conduct or thought; a believer in free will.—**libertarianism** n.

liberticide /lɪˈbɜːtɪsaɪd/ n a destroyer of liberty; the destruction of liberty.

libertine /ˈlɪbərˌtiːn/ or /-ˌtaɪn/ n a dissolute person; a freethinker. • adj unrestrained, morally or socially; licentious.—**libertinism, libertinage** n.

liberty /ˈlɪbərti/ n (pl **liberties**) freedom from slavery, captivity, etc; the right to do as one pleases, freedom; a particular right, freedom, etc granted by authority; an impertinent attitude; authorized leave granted to a sailor.

libidinous /lɪˈbɪdɪnəs/ adj lustful, lascivious.

libido /lɪˈbɪˌdoː/ n (pl **libidos**) the sexual urge.—**libidinal** adj.

Libra /ˈliːbrə/ n (astrol) the 7th sign of the zodiac, operative 24 September–23 October; a constellation represented as a pair of scales.—**Libran** n, adj.

librarian /laɪˈbrɛriən/ n a person in charge of a library or trained in librarianship.

librarianship, library science n the profession of organizing collections of books, etc for reference by others.

library /ˈlaɪˌbreri/ n (pl **libraries**) a collection of books, tapes, records, photographs, etc for reference or borrowing; a room, building or institution containing such a collection; (comput) a set, usu general purpose, programs or subroutines for use in programming.

librate /laɪˈbreɪt/ vi to waver; to balance.—**libratory** adj.

libration /laɪˈbreɪʃən/ n the act of oscillating; the act of balancing; an apparent irregularity in the motion of the moon or a satellite.

librettist /lɪˈbrɛtɪst/ n a writer of a libretto.

libretto /lɪˈbrɛtoː/ n (pl **libretti, librettos**) the text to which an opera, oratorio, etc is set.—**librettist** n.

Libyan /ˈlɪbiən/ n a native or inhabitant of Libya.—also adj.

lice /laɪs/ see **louse**.

licence /ˈlaɪsəns/ n a formal or legal permission to do something specified; a document granting such permission; freedom to deviate from rule, practice, etc; excessive freedom, an abuse of liberty.—also **license**. • vt to grant a license to or for; to permit.—**licenser, licensor** n.

license plate n (US) a plate on the front or rear of a motor vehicle that displays its registration number.—also UK **number-plate**.

licensee /ˌlaɪsənˈsiː/ n a person who is granted a licence.

licentiate /laɪˈsɛnʃiət/ or /-ʃət/ n a person holding a certificate of competence in a profession; a degree between that of bachelor and doctor in some universities; one licensed to preach.—**licentiateship** n.

licentious /laɪˈsɛnʃəs/ adj morally unrestrained; lascivious.—**licentiousness** n.

lichee /ˈliːtʃi/ see **litchi**.

lichen /ˈlaɪkən/ n any of various small plants consisting of an alga and a fungus living in symbiotic association, growing on stones, trees, etc.

lichenology /ˌlaɪkəˈnɒlədʒi/ n the study of lichens.

lich gate /ˈlɪtʃgeɪt/ n (Brit) a roofed gate of a churchyard, under which a coffin can be rested.—also **lych gate**.

lichi /ˈliːtʃi/ see **litchi**.

licit /ˈlɪsɪt/ adj lawful.—**licitly** adv.

lick /lɪk/ vt to draw the tongue over, esp to taste or clean; (flames, etc) to flicker around or touch lightly; (inf) to thrash; (inf) to defeat. • n a licking with the tongue; (inf) a sharp blow; (inf) a short, rapid burst of activity.

lickerish /ˈlɪkərɪʃ/ adj (arch) lustful; greedy.

lickety-split /ˌlɪkətiˈsplɪt/ adv (US inf) very fast.

licking /ˈlɪkɪŋ/ n (inf) a severe beating; a defeat.

lickspittle /ˈlɪkˌspɪtəl/ n a servile flatterer.

liquorice /ˈlɪkərɪʃ/ or /-rɪs/ n a black extract made from the root of a European plant, used in medicine and confectionery; a licorice-flavoured sweet.—also US **licorice**.

lictor /ˈlɪktər/ n an official serving a magistrate in ancient Rome.

lid /lɪd/ n a removable cover as for a box, etc; an eyelid.—**lidded** adj.

lido /ˈliːˌdoː/ or /ˈlaɪ-/ n (pl **lidos**) an open air swimming pool and recreational complex for public use.

lie[1] /laɪ/ n an untrue statement made with intent to deceive; something that deceives or misleads. • vi (**lying, lied**) to speak untruthfully with an intention to deceive; to create a false impression.

lie[2] vi (**lying, lay**, pp **lain**) to be or put oneself in a reclining or horizontal position; to rest on a support in a horizontal position; to be in a specified condition; to be situated; to exist. • n the way in which something is situated.

lied /liːd/ or /liːt/ n (pl **lieder**) a German song or ballad.

lie detector n a polygraph device used by police and security services that monitors sharp fluctuations in involuntary physiological responses as evidence of stress, guilt, etc when deliberately lying.

lief /liːf/ adv (arch) willingly.

liege /liːdʒ/ or /liːʒ/ n (feudalism) a lord or sovereign.—also **liege lord**; a subject or vassal.

lien /liːn/ or /ˈliːən/ n (law) a right to keep another's property pending payment of a debt due to the holder.

lierne /liˈɜːrn/ n (archit) a cross-rib or branch rib in vaulting.

lieu /luː/ or /ljuː/ n place; stead (esp in lieu of, in place of, instead of).

lieutenant /ˈlɛftənənt/ or /ˈluː-/ n a commissioned army officer ranking below a captain; a naval officer next below a lieutenant commander; a deputy, a chief assistant to a superior.—**lieutenancy** n.

lieutenant-governor (pl **lieutenant-governors**) n a deputy governor.

life /laɪf/ n (pl **lives**) that property of plants and animals (ending at death) that enables them to use food, grow, reproduce, etc;

the state of having this property; living things collectively; the time a person or thing exists; one's manner of living; one's animate existence; vigour, liveliness; (*inf*) a life sentence; a biography. • *adj* of animate being; lifelong; using a living model; of or relating to or provided by life insurance.

life-belt /'laɪfbelt/ *n* an inflatable ring to support a person in the water; a safety belt.

lifeblood /-blʌd/ *n* the blood necessary to life; a vital element.

lifeboat /-bo:t/ *n* a small rescue boat carried by a ship; a specially designed and equipped rescue vessel that helps those in distress along the coastline.

life buoy /-bɔɪ/ *n* a ring-shaped buoyant device to keep a person afloat.

life cycle *n* a sequence of stages through which a living being passes during its lifetime.

lifeguard /-gɑrd/ *n* an expert swimmer employed to prevent drownings.

life jacket *n* a sleeveless jacket or vest of buoyant material to keep a person afloat.

lifeless /-ləs/ *adj* dead; unconscious; dull.—**lifelessly** *adv.*—**lifelessness** *n*.

lifelike /-laɪk/ *adj* resembling a real life person or thing.

lifeline /-laɪn/ *n* a rope for raising or lowering a diver; a rope for rescuing a person, *eg* as attached to a lifebelt; a vitally important channel of communication or transport.

lifelong /-lɒŋ/ *adj* lasting one's whole life.

life peer *n* a British peer whose title lapses with death.

life preserver *n* a club used as a weapon of self-defence; a lifebelt or life jacket.

lifer /laɪfər/ *n* (*sl*) a person sentenced to prison for life.

life raft *n* a raft kept on board ship for use in emergencies.

lifesaving /'laɪfseɪvɪŋ/ *adj* something (as drugs) designed to save lives. • *n* the skill or practice of saving lives, *esp* from drowning.—**lifesaver** *n*.

life science *n* a science dealing with living organisms and life processes, such as biology, zoology, etc.

life sentence *n* imprisonment for life, or a long period, as punishment for a grave offence.

life-size, life-sized *adj* of the size of the original.

lifestyle /'laɪfstaɪl/ *n* the particular attitudes, living habits, etc of a person.

lifetime /-taɪm/ *n* the length of time that a person lives or something lasts.

lift /lɪft/ *vt* to bring to a higher position, raise; to raise in rank, condition, etc; (*sl*) to steal; to revoke. • *vi* to exert oneself in raising something; to rise; to go up; (*fog, etc*) to disperse; (*with* **off**) (*rocket, etc*) to take off. • *n* act or fact of lifting; distance through which a thing is lifted; elevation of mood, etc; elevated position or carriage; a ride in the direction in which one is going; help of any kind; (*Brit*) a cage or platform for moving something from one level to another.—*also US* **elevator**; upward air pressure maintaining an aircraft in flight.—**lifter** *n*.

liftoff /'lɪftɒf/ *n* the vertical thrust of a spacecraft, etc at launching; the time of this.

ligament /'lɪgəmənt/ *n* a band of tissue connecting bones; a unifying bond.

ligan /'laɪgən/ *see* **lagan**.

ligate /lɪ'geɪt/ *vt* to tie up (with a ligature).—**ligation** *n*.

ligature /'lɪgətʃər/ *n* a tying or binding together; a tie, bond, etc; two or more printed letters joined together, as *œ*; a thread used to suture a blood vessel, etc in surgery.

light[1] /laɪt/ *n* the agent of illumination that stimulates the sense of sight; electromagnetic radiation such as ultraviolet, infrared or X-rays; brightness, illumination; a source of light, as the sun, a lamp, etc; daylight; a thing used to ignite something; a window; knowledge, enlightenment; aspect or appearance. • *adj* having light; bright; pale in colour. • *adv* palely. • *vt* (**lighting, lit** *or* **lighted**) to ignite; to cause to give off light; to furnish with light; to brighten, animate.

light[2] *adj* having little weight; not heavy; less than usual in weight, amount, force, etc; of little importance; easy to bear; easy to digest; happy; dizzy, giddy; not serious; moderate; moving with ease; producing small products. • *adv* lightly. • *vi* (**lighting, lit** *or* **lighted**) to come to rest after travelling through the air; to dismount, to alight; to come or happen on or upon; to strike suddenly, as a blow.—**lightly** *adv.*—**lightness** *n*.

lighten[1] /'laɪtən/ *vti* to make or become light or lighter; to shine, flash.—**lightener** *n*.

lighten[2] *vti* to make or become lighter in weight; to make or become more cheerful; to mitigate.—**lightener** *n*.

lighter[1] /'laɪtər/ *n* a small device that produces a naked flame to light cigarettes.

lighter[2] *n* a large barge used in loading or unloading larger ships.

lighterage /'laɪtərɪdʒ/ *n* the transport of goods by lighter; the price paid for the service; lighters collectively.

light-fingered *adj* thievish.

light-headed *adj* dizzy; delirious.—**light-headedly** *adv*.

light-hearted /'laɪt,hɑrtəd/ *adj* carefree.—**light-heartedly** *adv*.

lighthouse /'laɪthəʊs/ *n* a tower with a bright light to guide ships.

lighting /'laɪtɪŋ/ *n* the process of giving light; equipment for illuminating a stage, television set, etc; the distribution of light on an object, as in a work of art.

lightning /'laɪtnɪŋ/ *n* a discharge or flash of electricity in the sky. • *adv* fast, sudden.

lightning conductor *or* **rod** *n* a metal rod placed high on a building and grounded to divert lightning from the structure.

light opera *n* an operetta.

light pen *n* a pen-shaped photoelectric device used to communicate with a computer by pointing at the monitor; a similar device used for reading bar codes.

lightship /'laɪt,ʃɪp/ *n* a ship equipped with a warning beacon and moored at a place dangerous to navigation.

lightsome /'laɪtsəm/ *adj* (*arch, poet*) carefree; graceful, nimble.

lights out *n* (a signal indicating) the time prescribed for retiring to bed, as in a military barracks.

lightweight /'laɪtweɪt/ *adj* of less than average weight; trivial, unimportant. • *n* a person or thing of less than average weight; a professional boxer weighing 130-135 pounds (59-61 kg); a person of little importance or influence.

light-year *n* the distance light travels in one year.

lignaloes *see* **eaglewood**.

ligneous /'lɪgnɪəs/ *adj* of or like wood.

ligniform /'lɪgnɪ,fɔrm/ *adj* resembling wood.

lignify /'lɪgnɪ,faɪ/ *vti* (**lignifies, lignifying, lignified**) (*bot*) to make or become wood, or woody.—**lignification** *n*.

lignin /'lɪgnɪn/ *n* a woody fibre.

lignite /'lɪgnaɪt/ *n* a soft brownish-black coal with the texture of the original wood.—**lignitic** *adj*.

lignum vitae /,lɪgnəm'vaɪti/ *or* /-'vi:taɪ/ *n* the heavy hard wood of the South American guaiacum tree.

ligroin /lɪ'groːɪn/ *n* a solvent distilled from petroleum.

ligulate /'lɪgjʊlət/ *adj* (*bot*) strap-shaped.

ligule /'lɪgju:l/ *n* (*bot*) a membranous appendage at the top of a sheathing petiole in grasses; one of the rays of a composite plant.

likable, likeable /'laɪkəbəl/ *adj* attractive, pleasant, genial, etc.—**likably, likeably** *adv*.

like[1] /laɪk/ *adj* having the same characteristics; similar; equal. • *adv* (*inf*) likely. • *prep* similar to; characteristic of; in the mood for; indicative of; as for example. • *conj* (*inf*) as; as if. • *n* an equal; counterpart.

like[2] *vt* to be pleased with; to wish. • *vi* to be so inclined.

likelihood /'laɪklɪhʊd/ *n* probability.

likely /'laɪkli/ *adj* (**likelier, likeliest**) reasonably to be expected; suitable; showing promise of success. • *adv* probably.—**likeliness** *n*.

like-minded *adj* sharing the same tastes, ideas, etc.—**likemindedness** *n*.

liken /'laɪkən/ *vt* to compare.

likeness /'laɪknəs/ *n* a being like; something that is like, as a copy, portrait, etc; appearance, semblance.

likewise /'laɪkwaɪz/ *adv* the same; also.

liking /'laɪkɪŋ/ *n* fondness; affection; preference.

lilac /'laɪlək/ *or* /-lɒk/, /-læk/ *n* a shrub with large clusters of tiny, fragrant flowers; a pale purple. • *adj* lilac coloured.

Lilliputian /,lɪlɪ'pju:ʃən/ *adj* tiny; petty. • *n* a tiny person, a midget.

Li-Lo /'laɪloʊ/ *n* (*pl* **Li-Los**) (*trademark*) an inflatable rubber or plastic mattress.

lilt /lɪlt/ *n* a light rhythmic song or tune; a springy motion. • *vi* (*music, song*) to have a lilt; to move buoyantly.—**lilting** *adj*.

lily /'lɪli/ *n* (*pl* **lilies**) a bulbous plant having typically trumpet-shaped flowers; its flower.

lily-livered *adj* cowardly.

lily of the valley *n* a small plant of the lily family with white bell-shaped flowers and fragrant scent.

lily-white *adj* pure white; (*inf*) pure, incorruptible.

lima bean *n* a kind of bean that produces flat, edible pale green seeds; its edible seed.

limb /lɪm/ *n* a projecting appendage of an animal body, as an arm, leg, or wing; a large branch of a tree; a participating member, agent; an arm of a cross.—**limbless** *adj*.

limbate /'lɪmˌbeɪt/ *adj* (*bot*) with a border of a different colour.

limber[1] /'lɪmbər/ *adj* flexible, able to bend the body easily. • *vt* to make limber. • *vi* to become limber; (*with* **up**) to stretch and warm the muscles in readiness for physical exercise.

limber[2] *n* the detachable wheeled section of a gun carriage.

limbo[1] /'lɪmbo:/ *n* (*pl* **limbos**) (*Christianity*) the abode after death assigned to unbaptized souls; a place for lost, unwanted, or neglected persons or things; an intermediate stage or condition between extremes.

limbo[2] *n* (*pl* **limbos**) a West Indian dance that involves bending over backwards and passing under a horizontal bar that is progressively lowered.

lime[1] /laɪm/ *n* a white calcium compound used for making cement and in agriculture. • *vt* to treat or cover with lime.

lime[2] *n* a small yellowish-green fruit with a juicy, sour pulp; the tree that bears it; its colour.

lime[3] *n* the linden tree.

limekiln /'laɪmkɪln/ *n* a furnace for making lime.

limelight /'laɪmlaɪt/ *n* intense publicity; a type of lamp, formerly used in stage lighting, in which lime was heated to produce a brilliant flame.

limen /'laɪmən/ *n* (*pl* **limens, limina**) (*psychol*) the point at which the effect of a stimulus is just discernible.

limerick /'lɪmərɪk/ *n* a type of humorous verse consisting of five lines.

limestone /'laɪmstoːn/ *n* a type of rock composed mainly of calcium carbonate.

limey /laɪmi/ *n* (*pl* **limeys**) (*US sl*) a British person.

limit /'lɪmɪt/ *n* a boundary; the greatest amount allowed; (*inf*) as much as one can tolerate. • *vt* to set a limit to; to restrict.—**limitable** *adj*.

limitary /'lɪmɪˌtəri/ *adj* restrictive; restricted.

limitation /ˌlɪmɪ'teɪʃən/ *n* the act of limiting or being limited; a hindrance to ability or achievement.

limited /'lɪmɪtəd/ *adj* confined within bounds; lacking imagination or originality.

limited liability *n* responsibility for the debts of a company only to the extent of the amount of capital stock held.

limitless /'lɪmɪtləs/ *adj* boundless, immense.—**limitlessly** *adv*.—**limitlessness** *n*.

limn /lɪm/ *vt* to paint or draw.—**limner** *n*.

limnology /lɪm'nɒlədʒi/ *n* the scientific study of freshwater bodies (*eg*. lakes and ponds) in terms of their support for plant and animal life, physical geography, chemical composition, etc.

limo /'lɪmoː/ *n* (*inf*) limousine.

limousine /ˌlɪmə'ziːn/ or /'lɪməˌziːn/ *n* (*sl*) a large luxury car.

limp[1] /lɪmp/ *vi* to walk with or as with a lame leg. • *n* a lameness in walking.—**limper** *n*.—**limpingly** *adv*.

limp[2] *adj* not firm; lethargic; wilted; flexible.—**limply** *adv*.—**limpness** *n*.

limpet /'lɪmpət/ *n* a mollusc with a low conical shell that clings to rocks.

limpid /'lɪmpɪd/ *adj* perfectly clear; transparent.—**limpidity** *n*.

limpkin /'lɪmpkɪn/ *n* a kind of American wading bird.

limy /'laɪmi/ *adj* (**limier, limiest**) containing, or resembling, lime.

linage /'laɪnɪdʒ/ *n* the number of written or printed lines on a page.

linchpin /'lɪntʃpɪn/ *n* a pin passed through an axle to keep a wheel in position; a person or thing regarded as vital to an organization, project, etc.

linden /'lɪndən/ *n* a tree with deciduous heart-shaped leaves and small fragrant yellow flowers.

line[1] /laɪn/ *vt* (**lining, lined**) to put, or serve as, a lining in.

line[2] *n* a length of cord, rope, or wire; a cord for measuring, making level; a system of conducting fluid, electricity, etc; a thin threadlike mark; anything resembling such a mark, as a wrinkle; edge, limit, boundary; border, outline, contour; a row of persons or things, as printed letters across a page; a succession of persons, lineage; a connected series of things; the course a moving thing takes; a course of conduct, actions, etc; a whole

system of transportation; a person's trade or occupation; a field of experience or interest; (*inf*) glib, persuasive talk; a verse; the forward combat position in warfare; fortifications, trenches or other defences used in war; a stock of goods; a piece of information; a short letter, note; (*pl*) all the speeches of a character in a play; • *vb* (**lining, lined**) *vt* to mark with lines; to form a line along; to cover with lines; to arrange in a line. • *vi* to align.

lineage /'lɪniɪdʒ/ *n* direct descent from an ancestor; ancestry.

lineal /'lɪniəl/ *adj* hereditary; direct; linear.—**lineally** *adv*.

lineament /'lɪniəmənt/ *n* (*usu pl*) a facial feature.

linear /'lɪniər/ *adj* of, made of, or using a line or lines; narrow and long; in relation to length only.—**linearity** *n*.—**linearly** *adv*.

linear accelerator *n* a device for accelerating elementary particles in a straight line by successively activating electric fields at regular intervals along their path.

lineate /'lɪniˌeɪt/ *adj* marked with lines.

lineation /ˌlɪni'eɪʃən/ *n* the drawing, or arrangement, of lines.

line drawing *n* a drawing made with solid lines.

line-engraving *n* an engraving with fine lines; the art of this type of engraving.

linen /'lɪnən/ *n* thread or cloth made of flax; household articles (sheets, cloths, etc) made of linen or cotton cloth.

line-out *n* (*Rugby Union*) the method of restarting a game after the ball has been put into touch, the forwards forming two opposing parallel lines at right angles to the touch-line and jumping for the ball that is thrown in.

line printer *n* a high-speed computer printer that prints each line as a single unit instead of character by character.

liner /'laɪnər/ *n* a large passenger ship or aircraft travelling a regular route.

linesman /'laɪnzmən/ *n* (*pl* **linesmen**) an official in certain games who assists the referee in deciding when the ball is out of play, etc.

lineup /'laɪnʌp/ *n* an arrangement of persons or things in a line, *eg* for inspection.

ling. *abbr* = linguistics.

ling[1] /lɪŋ/ *n* a type of heather.

ling[2] *n* (*pl* **ling, lings**) a sea fish of northern waters used as food.

linger /'lɪŋgər/ *vi* to stay a long time; to delay departure; to dawdle or loiter; to dwell on in the mind; to remain alive though on the point of death.—**lingerer** *n*.—**lingering** *adj*.—**lingeringly** *adv*.

lingerie /lɔːʒə'reɪ/ or /'lɒ̃-/, /-'riː/ *n* women's underwear and nightclothes.

lingo /'lɪŋgoː/ *n* (*pl* **lingoes**) (*inf*) a dialect, jargon, etc.

lingua franca /ˌlɪŋgwə'fræŋkə/ *n* (*pl* **lingua francas, linguae francae**) a language used for communication between speakers of different languages.

lingual /'lɪŋgwəl/ *adj* of, or pronounced with, the tongue.—**lingually** *adv*.

linguiform /'lɪŋgwɪˌfɔrm/ *adj* tongue-shaped.

linguist /'lɪŋgwɪst/ *n* a person who is skilled in speaking foreign languages.

linguistic /lɪŋ'gwɪstɪk/ *adj* of or pertaining to language or linguistics.—**linguistically** *adv*.

linguistics /lɪŋ'gwɪstɪks/ *n* (*used as sing*) the science of language.

lingulate /'lɪŋgjʊˌleɪt/ *adj* tongue-shaped.

liniment /'lɪnɪmənt/ *n* a soothing medication, *usu* applied to the skin.

lining /'laɪnɪŋ/ *n* a material used to cover the inner surface of a garment, etc; any material covering an inner surface.

link /lɪŋk/ *n* a single loop or ring of a chain; something resembling a loop or ring or connecting piece; a person or thing acting as a connection, as in a communication system, machine or organization. • *vti* to connect or become connected.

linkage /'lɪŋkɪdʒ/ *n* a linking; a series or system of links.

linkboy /'lɪŋkbɔɪ/ *n* (*formerly*) someone who guided others through dark streets with a torch.

linkman /'lɪŋkmən/ *n* (*pl* **linkmen**) (*radio, TV*) a presenter who links items, reports, etc, *esp* on a sports programme.

links /lɪŋks/ *npl* (*also used as sing*) flat sandy soil; a golf course, *esp* by the sea.

linkup *n* a linking together.

linn /lɪn/ *n* (*Scot*) a waterfall; the pool beneath a waterfall; a ravine.

Linnaean, Linnean /lɪ'neɪəs/ or /lɪ'niːəs/ *adj* pertaining to the Swedish naturalist Linnaeus or to his system of classification.

linnet /'lɪnət/ *n* a small brown or grey songbird.

lino /'laɪnoː/ *n* (*inf*) (*pl* **linos**) linoleum.

linocut /'laɪnoʊ;kɛt/ *n* a design cut in relief on a piece of linoleum; a print made from this.

linoleum /lɪ'noʊliəm/ *n* a floor covering of coarse fabric backing with a smooth, hard decorative coating.

Linotype /'laɪnoʊtaɪp/ *n* (*trademark*) a typesetting machine that casts lines in one piece.

linsang /'lɪnsæŋ/ *n* a type of civet, found in Indonesia and Borneo.

linseed /'lɪnsiːd/ *n* the seed of flax, from which linseed oil is made.

linseed oil *n* oil made from flax seeds, used in paint and varnish.

linsey-woolsey /ˌlɪnzi'wʊlzi/ *n* a sturdy coarse fabric of linen or cotton and wool mixed.

linstock /'lɪnstɒk/ *n* (*formerly*) a staff holding a match, used to light a cannon.

lint /lɪnt/ *n* scraped and softened linen used to dress wounds; fluff.

lintel /'lɪntəl/ *n* the horizontal crosspiece spanning a doorway or window.

lintwhite /'lɪntˌwəɪt/ *n* (*Scot, arch*) a linnet.

lion /'laɪən/ *n* a large, flesh-eating feline mammal with a shaggy mane in the adult male; a person of great courage or strength.—**lioness** *nf*.

lion-hearted *adj* extremely brave.

lionize /'laɪənaɪz/ *vt* to treat as or make famous.—**lionization** *n*.—**lionizer** *n*.

lip /lɪps/ *n* either of the two fleshy flaps that surround the mouth; anything like a lip, as the rim of a jug; (*sl*) insolent talk. • *vt* (**lipping, lipped**) to touch with the lips; to kiss; to utter.

lipid /'lɪpɪd/ *n* an organic compound in fats, which is soluble in solvents but insoluble in water.

lipo- /'lɪpoʊ;/, **lip-** /lɪp/ *prefix* fat, fatty.

lipoid /'lɪpɔɪd/, **lipoidal** /-əl/ *adj* fatty, resembling fat. • *n* a fatlike substance.

liposuction /'lɪpoʊsʌkʃən/ or /'lɑɪ-/ *n* cosmetic surgery involving the removal of fat from under the skin of the thighs, stomach, etc using a suction device inserted through an incision.

lipped /lɪpt/ *adj* having lips or rounded edges.

lip-read *vt* (**lip-reading, lip-read**) to understand another's speech by watching their lip movements.

lip service *n* support expressed but not acted upon.

lipstick /'lɪpstɪk/ *n* a small stick of cosmetic for colouring the lips; the cosmetic itself.

lip-sync, lip-synch *vt* to move the lips in time with a prerecorded soundtrack (of dialogue or music) on film or television.

liquate /lɪ'kweɪt/ *vt* to melt (metals) to separate or purify them.—**liquation** *n*.

liquefacient /ˌlɪkwə'feɪʃənt/ *adj* serving to liquefy. • *n* something that liquefies.

liquefy /'lɪkwəfaɪ/ *vti* (**liquefying, liquefied**) to change to a liquid.—**liquefaction** *n*.—**liquefier** *n*.

liquescent /lɪ'kwesənt/ *adj* becoming liquid.

liqueur /lɪ'kjər/ or /-kjʊr/ *n* a sweet and variously flavoured alcoholic drink.

liquid /'lɪkwɪd/ *n* a substance that, unlike a gas, does not expand indefinitely and, unlike a solid, flows readily. • *adj* in liquid form; clear; limpid; flowing smoothly and musically, as verse; (*assets*) readily convertible into cash.—**liquidity** *n*.

liquidate /'lɪkwɪˌdeɪt/ *vt* to settle the accounts of; to close a (bankrupt) business and distribute its assets among its creditors; to convert into cash; to eliminate, kill.

liquidation /ˌlɪkwɪ'deɪʃən/ *n* the act of liquidating or paying off; the settlement of the affairs of a bankrupt person or business.

liquidator /'lɪkwɪˌdeɪtər/ *n* an official who winds up a business.

liquidize /'lɪkwɪˌdaɪz/ *vt* to make liquid.

liquidizer /'lɪkwɪˌdaɪzər/ *n* a domestic appliance for liquidizing and blending foods.

liquid paraffin *n* an oily distillate of petroleum used as a laxative.—*also* **mineral oil**.

liquor /'lɪkər/ *n* an alcoholic drink; any liquid, *esp* that in which food has been cooked.

liquor store *n* a place where alcohol is sold for consumption off the premises.—*also* **off-licence, package store**.

lira /'liːrə/ *n* (*pl* **lire, liras**) the monetary unit of Turkey and former monetary unit of Italy, replaced by the euro.

lisle /lail/ *n* a fine tightly-twisted cotton thread.

lisp /lɪsp/ *vi* to substitute the sounds *th* (as in *thin*) for *s* or *th* (as in *then*) for *z*; a speech defect or habit involving such pronun-

ciation; to utter imperfectly. • *vt* to speak or utter with a lisp.—*also n*.—**lisper** *n*.

lissom /'lɪsəm/ *adj* lithe; supple; agile, etc.—**lissomeness** *n*.

list[1] /lɪst/ *n* a series of names, numbers, words, etc written or printed in order. • *vt* to make a list of; to enter in a directory, etc.

list[2] *vti* to tilt to one side, as a ship. • *n* such a tilting.

listed /lɪstəd/ *adj* (*company, etc*) having its shares quoted on a stock exchange; (*building*) of architectural interest and protected from demolition or alteration without permission.

listed building *n* a building officially designated as of historic or architectural interest and protected from alteration or demolition.

listen /'lɪsən/ *vi* to try to hear; to pay attention, take heed; (*with in*) to intercept radio or telephone communications; to tune into a radio broadcast; to eavesdrop.

listener /'lɪsənər/ *n* a person who listens; a person listening to a radio broadcast.

listeriosis /lɪˌstiːri'oʊsɪs/ *n* chronic food poisoning caused by the bacteria *Listeria*.

listing /'lɪstɪŋ/ *n* a list, or an individual entry therein; the act of making a list; (*pl*) a guide giving details of events, *eg* music, theatre, taking place in a particular area, published in a newspaper or magazine.

listless /lɪstləs/ *adj* lacking energy or enthusiasm because of illness, dejection, etc; languid.—**listlessly** *adv*.—**listlessness** *n*.

lit /lɪt/ *see* **light**[1], **light**[2].

lit. *abbr* = literal; literary; literature; litre.

litany /'lɪtəni/ *n* (*pl* **litanies**) a type of prayer in which petitions to God are recited by a priest and elicit set responses from the congregation; any tedious or automatic recital.

litchi /'liːtʃi/ *n* a fruit consisting of a soft, sweet white pulp in a thin brown shell; the tree that bears this fruit.—*also* **lichee, lichi**.

-lite /laɪt/ *n suffix* stone; mineral; fossil.

liter /'liːtər/ *see* **litre**.

literacy /'lɪtərəsi/ *n* the ability to read and write.

literal /'lɪtərəl/ *adj* in accordance with the exact meaning of a word or text; in a basic or strict sense; prosaic, unimaginative; real.—**literalness, literality** *n*.—**literally** *adv*.

literalism /'lɪtərəˌlɪzəm/ *n* adherence to the literal sense of a word or saying.—**literalist** *n*.

literary /'lɪtərˌɛri/ *adj* of or dealing with literature; knowing much about literature.—**literarily** *adv*.—**literariness** *n*.

literate /'lɪtərət/ *adj* able to read and write; educated.—*also n*.

literati /ˌlɪtə'rɒti/ *npl* educated people.

literatim /ˌlɪtə'rætɪm/ *adv* letter for letter.

literature /'lɪtərətʃər/ or /'lɪtrə-/ *n* the writings of a period or of a country, *esp* those valued for their excellence; of style or form; all the books and articles on a subject; (*inf*) any printed matter.

-lith /lɪθ/ *n suffix* stone or rock.

litharge /'lɪθɑrdʒ/ *n* an oxide of lead.

lithe /laɪð/ *adj* supple, flexible.—**litheness** *n*.

lithesome /'laɪðsəm/ *adj* lithe, supple.

lithia /'lɪθiə/ *n* an oxide of lithium.

lithic /'lɪθɪk/ *adj* of or pertaining to stone.

lithium /'lɪθiəm/ *n* the lightest metallic element.

litho /'lɪθoʊ/ *n* (*pl* **lithos**) a lithograph; lithography.

lithograph /ˌlɪθə'græf/ *n* a print, etc made by lithography.—**lithographic** *adj*.—**lithographically** *adv*.

lithography /lɪ'θɒgrəfi/ *n* printing from a flat stone or metal plate, parts of which have been treated to repel ink.—**lithographer** *n*.

lithoid /'lɪθɔɪd/, **lithoidal** /-əl/ *adj* stonelike.

lithology /lɪ'θɒlədʒi/ *n* the study of rocks and their physical characteristics.—**lithologic, lithological** *adj*.

lithophyte /'lɪθəˌfaɪt/ *n* a stony polyp; a plant which grows on a rocky surface.

lithosphere /'lɪθəˌsfiːr/ *n* the solid outer part of the earth.

lithotomy /lɪ'θɒtəmi/ *n* (*pl* **lithotomies**) (*med*) the operation of cutting into the bladder to remove a stone.—**lithotomic** *adj*.

lithotripter, lithotriptor /ˌlɪθə'trɪptər/ *n* an instrument that fragments kidney or bladder stones, etc by ultrasound without the need for invasive surgery.

lithotrity /lɪ'θɒtrəti/ *n* (*pl* **lithotrities**) (*med*) the operation of crushing a stone in the bladder.

litigant /'lɪtɪgənt/ *n* a person engaged in a lawsuit.

litigate /'lɪtɪˌgeɪtʃən/ *vti* to bring or contest in a lawsuit.—**litigator** *n*.

litigation /ˌlɪtɪˈgeɪʃən/ *n* the act or processs of carrying on a lawsuit; a judicial contest.

litigious /lɪˈtɪdʒəs/ *adj* of or causing lawsuits; fond of engaging in lawsuits; contentious.—**litigiousness** *n*.

litmus /ˈlɪtməs/ *n* a colouring material obtained from certain lichens that turns red in acid solutions and blue in alkaline solutions.

litotes /laɪˈtəʊtiːz/ *n* (*pl* **litotes**) (*rhetoric*) understatement for effect.

litre, liter /ˈliːtər/ *n* a measure of liquid capacity in the metric system, equivalent to 1.76 pints.—*also* **litre**.

Litt.D, Lit.D *abbr* = Doctor of Letters; Doctor of Literature.

litter /ˈlɪtər/ *n* rubbish scattered about; young animals produced at one time; straw, hay, etc used as bedding for animals; a stretcher for carrying a sick or wounded person. • *vt* to make untidy; to scatter about carelessly.

littérateur /ˌlɪtəræˈtər/ *n* a writer.

litterbug /ˈlɪtərˌbʌg/ *n* a person who drops refuse in public places.

little /ˈlɪtəl/ *adj* not great or big, small in size, amount, degree, etc; short in duration; small in importance or power; narrow-minded. • *n* small in amount, degree, etc. • *adv* less, least, slightly; not much; not in the least.

little people *npl* (*folklore*) supernatural beings such as fairies, elves and leprechauns.

littoral /ˈlɪtərəl/ *adj* of or along the seashore.

liturgics /lɪˈtɜːdʒɪks/ *n sing* the study of liturgies.

liturgist /ˈlɪtədʒɪst/ *n* someone who studies or composes liturgies.

liturgy /ˈlɪtədʒi/ *n* (*pl* **liturgies**) the prescribed form of service of a church.—**liturgical** *adj*.—**liturgically** *adv*.

livable /ˈlɪvəbəl/ *adj* worth living; suitable for living in.

live[1] /lɪv/ *vi* to have life; to remain alive; to endure; to pass life in a specified manner; to enjoy a full life; to reside; (*with* **in, out**) (*employee*) to reside at (or away from) one's place of work; (*with* **together**) (*unmarried couple*) to cohabit. • *vt* to carry out in one's life; to spend; pass; (*with* **down**) to survive or efface the effects of (a crime or mistake) by waiting until it is forgotten or forgiven.

live[2] *adj* having life; of the living state or living beings; of present interest; still burning; unexploded; carrying electric current; broadcast during the actual performance.

liveable /ˈlɪvəbəl/ *see* **livable**.

livelihood /ˈlaɪvliˌhʊd/ *n* employment; a means of living.

livelong /ˈlaɪvlɒŋ/ *adj* of the whole length of (the day).

lively /ˈlaɪvli/ *adj* (**livelier, liveliest**) full of life; spirited; exciting; vivid; keen. • *adv* in a lively manner.—**liveliness** *n*.

liven /ˈlaɪvən/ *vti* to make or become lively.—**livener** *n*.

liver /ˈlɪvər/ *n* the largest glandular organ in vertebrate animals, which secretes bile, etc and is important in metabolism; the liver of an animal used as food; a reddish-brown colour.

liveried /ˈlɪvəˌriːd/ *adj* wearing a livery.

liverish /ˈlɪvərɪʃ/ *adj* suffering from liver disorder; peevish.

liverwort /ˈlɪvərˌwɜːt/ *n* a cryptogamous plant, found in wet places.

liverwurst /ˈlɪvərˌwɜːst/ *n* sausage made with liver.

livery /ˈlɪvəri/ *n* (*pl* **liveries**) an identifying uniform, as that worn by a servant.

liveryman /ˈlɪvərimən/ *n* (*pl* **liverymen**) a keeper of a livery stable; a member of a livery company.

lives /laɪvz/ *see* **life**.

livestock /ˈlaɪvstɒks/ *n* (*farm*) animals raised for use or sale.

live wire *n* (*inf*) a lively, energetic person.

livid /ˈlɪvɪd/ *adj* (*skin*) discoloured, as from bruising; greyish in colour; (*inf*) extremely angry.—**lividly** *adv*.—**lividness, lividity** *n*.

living /ˈlɪvɪŋ/ *adj* having life; still in use; true to life, vivid; of life, for living in. • *n* a being alive; livelihood; manner of existence.

living room *n* a room in a house used for general entertainment and relaxation.

living wage *n* a wage sufficient to maintain a reasonable standard of comfort.

lixiviate /ˈlɪksɪviˌeɪt/ *vt* to wash (soil, ore, etc) with a filtering liquid; to extract (a soluble substance) from some material.—**lixiviation** *n*.

lizard /ˈlɪzərd/ *n* a reptile with a slender body, four legs, and a tapering tail.

llama /ˈlæmə/ *n* a South American animal, related to the camel, used for carrying loads and as a source of wool.

llano /ˈlænəʊ/ or /ˈljæ-/ *n* (*pl* **llanos**) one of the vast, level plains of South America.

LLB /ˈɛlˈɛlˈbiː/ *abbr* = Bachelor of Laws.

LLD /ˈɛlˈɛlˈdiː/ *abbr* = Doctor of Laws.

LLM /ˈɛlˈɛlˈɛm/ *abbr* = Master of Laws.

lm *abbr* = lumen.

LNG /ˈɛlˈɛnˈdʒiː/ *abbr* = liquefied natural gas.

lo /ləʊ/ *interj* behold!, see!

loach /ləʊtʃ/ *n* an edible freshwater fish.

load /ləʊd/ *n* an amount carried at one time; something borne with difficulty; a burden; (*often pl*) (*inf*) a great amount. • *vt* to put into or upon; to burden; to oppress; to supply in large quantities; to alter, as by adding a weight to dice or an adulterant to alcoholic drink; to put a charge of ammunition into (a firearm); to put film into (a camera); (*comput*) to install a program in memory. • *vi* to take on a load.—**loader** *n*.

loaded /ˈləʊdəd/ *adj* (*sl*) having plenty of money; drunk; under the influence of drugs.

loadstar /ˈləʊdstɑr/ *see* **lodestar**.

loadstone /ˈləʊdstəʊn/ *see* **lodestone**.

loaf[1] /ˈləʊf/ *n* (*pl* **loaves**) a mass of bread of regular shape and standard weight; food shaped like this; (*sl*) the head.

loaf[2] *vi* to pass time in idleness.—**loafer** *n*.

loam /ˈləʊm/ *n* rich and fertile soil.

loamy /ˈləʊmi/ *adj* (**loamier, loamiest**) consisting of or full of loam.—**loaminess** *n*.

loan /ˈləʊn/ *n* the act of lending; something lent, *esp* money. • *vti* to lend.—**loanable** *adj*.—**loaner** *n*.

loath /ˈləʊθ/ *adj* unwilling.—*also* **loth**.—**loathly** *adv*.

loathe /ˈləʊð/ *vt* to dislike intensely; to detest.—**loather** *n*.—**loathing** *n*.

loathsome /ˈləʊðsəm/ *adj* giving rise to loathing; detestable.—**loathsomeness** *n*.

loaves /ˈləʊvz/ *see* **loaf**[1].

lob /ˈlɒb/ *vti* (**lobbing, lobbed**) to toss or hit (a ball) in a high curve. • *n* a high-arching throw or kick.

lobar /ˈləʊbər/ *adj* of or relating to a lobe.

lobate /ˈləʊbeɪt/ *adj* having lobes; lobelike.

lobby /ˈlɒbi/ *n* (*pl* **lobbies**) an entrance hall of a public building; a person or group that tries to influence legislators. • *vti* (**lobbying, lobbied**) to try to influence (legislators) to support a particular cause or take certain action.

lobbyist /ˈlɒbiˌɪst/ *n* someone employed to lobby.

lobe /ləʊb/ *n* a rounded projection, as the lower end of the ear; any of the divisions of the lungs or brain.

lobelia /ləˈbiːliə/ *n* a genus of garden plants, usually with blue flowers.

loblolly /ˈlɒblɒli/ *n* (*pl* **loblollies**) a type of American pine tree; (*naut*) gruel.

lobotomy /ləˈbɒtəmi/ *n* (*pl* **lobotomies**) surgical incision into the lobe of an organ; a leukotomy.

lobscouse /ˈlɒbskʌʊs/ *n* a sailor's dish of meat, vegetables and ship's biscuit.

lobster /ˈlɒbstər/ *n* (*pl* **lobsters, lobster**) any of a family of edible sea crustaceans with four pairs of legs and a pair of large pincers.

lobule /ˈlɒbjuːl/ *n* a small lobe.—**lobular, lobulate** *adj*.

local /ˈləʊkəl/ *adj* of or belonging to a particular place; serving the needs of a specific district; of or for a particular part of the body. • *n* an inhabitant of a specific place; (*inf*) a pub serving a particular district.—**locally** *adv*.—**localness** *n*.

locale /ləʊˈkæl/ *n* a place or area, *esp* in regard to the position or scene of some event.

localism /ˈləʊkəˌlɪzəm/ *n* a word, idiom or custom restricted to a particular locality; narrowness of outlook.

locality /ləʊˈkælɪti/ *n* (*pl* **localities**) a neighbourhood or a district; a particular scene, position, or place; the fact or condition of having a location in space and time.

localize /ˈləʊkəˌlaɪz/ *vt* to limit, confine, or trace to a particular place.—**localization** *n*.

locate /ləʊˈkeɪt/ or /ˈləʊ-/ *vt* to determine or indicate the position of something; to set in or assign to a particular position.

location /ləʊˈkeɪʃən/ *n* a specific position or place; a locating or being located; a place outside a studio where a film is (partly) shot; (*comput*) an area in memory where a single item of data is stored.

locative /ˈlɒkətɪv/ *adj, n* (a grammatical case) indicating place.

loc. cit. *abbr* = loco citato (Latin *in the place cited*).

loch /lɒk/, *Scot.* /lɒx/ *n* (*Scot*) a lake.

loci /ˈləʊkaɪ/ *see* **locus**.

lock[1] /lɒk/ *n* a fastening device on doors, etc, operated by a key or combination; part of a canal, dock, etc in which the level of the water can be changed by the operation of gates; the part of a gun by which the charge is fired; a controlling hold, as used in wrestling. • *vt* to fasten with a lock; to shut; to fit, link; to jam together so as to make immovable. • *vi* to become locked; to interlock.—**lockable** *adj*.

lock[2] *n* a curl of hair; a tuft of wool, etc.

lockage /'lɒkɪdʒ/ *n* a system of canal locks; the act of going through a lock; the fee paid for so doing.

locker /'lɒkər/ *n* a small cupboard, chest, etc that can be locked, *esp* one for storing possessions in a public place.

locker room *n* room equipped with lockers for storing possessions in a public place.

locket /'lɒkət/ *n* a small ornamental case, *usu* holding a lock of hair, photograph or other memento, hung from the neck.

lockjaw /'lɒkɔ/ *n* tetanus.

lockout /'lɒkʊt/ *n* the exclusion of employees from a workplace by an employer, as a means of coercion during an industrial dispute.

locksmith /'lɒksmɪθ/ *n* a person who makes and repairs locks and keys.

lockup /'lɒkʌp/ *n* a jail; a garage or storage room.

loco /'lo:ko:/ *adj* (*sl*) crazy.

locomotion /,lo:kə'mo:ʃən/ *n* motion, or the power of moving, from one place to another.

locomotive /-'mo:tɪv/ *n* an electric, steam, or diesel engine on wheels, designed to move a railway train. • *adj* of locomotion.

locomotor /-'mo:tər/ *adj* of or pertaining to locomotion. locomotive.

locular /'lɒkjʊlər/, **loculate** /-,leɪt/ *adj* (*biol*) split into compartments.

loculus /'lɒkjʊləs/, **locule** *n* (*pl* **loculi, locules**) (*biol*) a small cavity or cell.

locum /'lo:kəm/ *n* (*inf*) a locum tenens.

locum tenens /'lo:kəm'ti:nɒnz/ *n* (*pl* **locum tenentes**) a person who stands in for a professional colleague, *esp* for a doctor, chemist or clergyman.

locus /'lo:kəs/ *n* (*pl* **loci**) a place; (*math*) the path of a point or curve, moving according to some specific rule; the aggregate of all possible positions of a moving or generating element.

locust /'lo:kəst/ *n* a type of large grasshopper often travelling in swarms and destroying crops; a type of hard-wooded leguminous tree.

locution /lə'kju:ʃən/ *n* a word, phrase or expression; an act or mode of speaking.

lode /lo:d/ *n* an ore deposit.

lodestar /'lo:dstɑr/ *n* a star, *usu* the North Star, used to guide navigation.—*also* **loadstar**.

lodestone /'lo:dsto:n/ *n* a magnetic oxide of iron; a piece of this oxide, used as a magnet or a crude compass.—*also* **loadstone**.

lodge /lɒdʒ/ *n* a small house at the entrance to a park or stately home; a country house for seasonal leisure activities; a resort hotel or motel; the local chapter or hall of a fraternal society; a beaver's lair. • *vt* to house temporarily; to shoot, thrust, etc firmly (in); to bring before legal authorities; to confer upon. • *vi* to live in a place for a time; to live as a paying guest; to come to rest and stick firmly (in).

lodger /'lɒdʒər/ *n* a person who lives in a rented room in another's home.

lodging /'lɒdʒɪŋ/ *n* a temporary residence; (*pl*) accommodation rented in another's house.

lodgment, lodgement /'lɒdʒmənt/ *n* the act of lodging; the state of being lodged; an accumulation of something deposited; (*mil*) a foothold in enemy territory.

loess /'lo:es/ *n* a light brown deposit of fine silt and clay found in Asia, Europe and America.—**loessial, loessal** *adj*.

loft /lɒft/ *n* a space under a roof; a storage area under the roof of a barn or stable; a gallery in a church or hall. • *vt* to send into a high curve.

lofty /'lɒfti/ *adj* (**loftier, loftiest**) (*objects*) of a great height, elevated; (*person*) noble, haughty, superior in manner.—**loftily** *adv*.—**loftiness** *n*.

log[1] /lɒg/ *n* a section of a felled tree; a device for ascertaining the speed of a ship; a record of speed, progress, etc, *esp* one kept on a ship's voyage or aircraft's flight. • *vb* (**logging, logged**) *vt* to record in a log; to sail or fly (a specified distance). • *vi* (*with* **on, off**) (*comput*) to establish or disestablish communication

with a mainframe computer from a remote terminal in a multi-user system.—**logger** *n*.

log[2] *n* a logarithm.

loganberry /'lo:gən,beri/ *n* (*pl* **loganberries**) a hybrid developed from the blackberry and the red raspberry.

logarithm /'lo:gə,rɪðəm/ *n* the exponent of the power to which a fixed number (the base) is to be raised to produce a given number, used to avoid multiplying and dividing when solving mathematical problems.—**logarithmic** *adj*.—**logarithmically** *adv*.

logbook /'lɒgbʊk/ *n* an official record of a ship's or aircraft's voyage or flight; an official document containing details of a vehicle's registration.

loge /lo:dʒ/ *n* a box in a theatre.

loggerhead /'lɒgər,hed/ *n* (*arch*) a blockhead; (*pl*) a dispute, confrontation (*to be at loggerheads with someone*); (*zool*) a type of turtle.

loggia /'lo:dʒə/ or /'lɒ-/ *n* (*pl* **loggias, loggie**) a covered open gallery or balcony on the side of a building.

logging /'lo:gɪŋ/ *n* the business of cutting down timber.

logic /'lɒdʒɪk/ *n* correct reasoning, or the science of this; way of reasoning; what is expected by the working of cause and effect.—**logician** *n*.

logical /'lɒdʒɪkəl/ *adj* conforming to the rules of logic; capable of reasoning according to logic.—**logically** *adv*.—**logicality** *n*.

logician /lə'dʒɪʃən/ *n* someone versed in logic.

logistics /lə'dʒɪstɪks/ *n* (*used as sing*) the science of the organization, transport and supply of military forces; the planning and organization of any complex activity.—**logistic** *adj*.—**logistically** *adv*.

log jam *n* a blockage of logs floating in a watercourse; a deadlock, standstill.

logo /'lo:go:/ *n* (*pl* **logos**) (*inf*) a logotype.

logo- /'lɒgo:/ or /-ə/ *prefix* word, speech.

logogram /'lɒgə,græm/, **logograph** /-,græf/ *n* a sign or letter representing a word or phrase.

logographer /lə'gɒgrəfər/ *n* an annalist or writer of speeches in ancient Greece.

logography /lə'gɒgrəfi/ *n* a method of printing in which a type represents a word instead of a letter.

logogriph /'lɒgə,grif/ *n* a word puzzle based on an anagram.

logomachy /lə'gɒməki/ *n* (*pl* **logomachies**) a dispute over words.

loggorhea /,lɒgə'ri:ə/ *n* excessive or incoherent talkativeness.

Logos /'lɒgɒs/ *n* (*Christianity*) the Divine Word; the second person of the Trinity, Jesus Christ.

logotype /'lɒgə,tɔɪp/ *n* a printed symbol representing a corporation, product, etc; a trademark, emblem.

logrolling /'lɒg,ro:lɪŋ/ *n* in US, the undemocratic trading of votes between politicians to ensure the passage of legislation of mutual interest.

-logue, -log /lɒg/ *n suffix* indicating a particular type of speech or writing, as in monologue, travelogue.

logwood /'lɒgwʊd/ *n* a wood of a deep-red colour, used in dyeing.

-logy /lədʒi/ *n suffix* science, theory or doctrine of, *eg astrology*; type of writing or discourse, *eg phraseology*.

logy /'lo:gi/ *adj* (**logier, logiest**) dull, sluggish.

loin /lɔɪn/ *n* (*usu pl*) the lower part of the back between the hipbones and the ribs; the front part of the hindquarters of an animal used for food.

loincloth /'lɔɪnklɒθ/ *n* a cloth worn around the loins.

loiter /'lɔɪtər/ *vi* to linger or stand about aimlessly.—**loiterer** *n*.

loll /lɒl/ *vi* to lean or recline in a lazy manner, to lounge; (*tongue*) to hang loosely.—**loller** *n*.

lollapalooza, lollapaloosa /lɒləpə'lu:zə/ *n* (*sl*) something or someone exceptional.

Lollard /'lɒlərd/ *n* (*hist*) a follower of the 14th-century English religious reformer, John Wycliff.

lollipop /'lɒli,pɒp/ *n* a flat boiled sweet at the end of a stick.

lollop /'lɒləp/ *vi* to run or walk with an ungainly, bouncing rhythm.

lolly /'lɒli/ *n* (*pl* **lollies**) (*inf*) a lollipop; (*sl*) money.

loment /'lo:mənt/ *n* a plant pod that breaks at maturity into single-seeded joints.

London Pride *n* a type of saxifrage plant with pink flowers.

lone /lo:n/ *adj* by oneself; isolated; without companions, solitary.—**loneness** *n*.

lonely /'lo:nli/ *adj* (**lonelier, loneliest**) isolated; unhappy at being alone; (*places*) remote, rarely visited.—**loneliness** *n*.

loner /ˈloːnər/ n a person who avoids the company of others.

lonesome /ˈloːnsəm/ adj having or causing a lonely feeling.—**lonesomely** adv.

long. abbr = longitude.

long[1] /lɒŋ/ adj measuring much in space or time; having a greater than usual length, quantity, etc; tedious, slow; far-reaching; well-supplied. • adv for a long time; from start to finish; at a remote time.

long[2] vi to desire earnestly, esp for something not likely to be attained.

longanimity /ˌlɒŋɡəˈnɪmɪti/ n long-suffering, forbearance.

longboat /ˈlɒŋboːt/ n the largest boat carried aboard a ship.

longbow /ˈlɒŋboː/ n a large hand-drawn bow.

longcloth /-klɒθ/ n a fine cotton fabric.

long-distance adj travelling or communicating over long distances.

longe /lʌndʒ/ see **lunge**[2].

longeron /ˈlɒndʒərən/ n the principal longitudinal spar of an aircraft's fuselage.

longevity /lɒnˈdʒɛvɪti/ n long life.

longhand /ˈlɒŋhænd/ n ordinary handwriting, as opposed to shorthand.

long-headed adj shrewd.

longhorn /ˈlɒŋhɔrn/ n a breed of long-horned cattle.

longicorn /ˈlɒndʒɪkɔrn/ n a type of beetle with long antennae.

longing /ˈlɒŋɪŋ/ n an intense desire.—**longingly** adv.

longitude /ˈlɒŋɡɪˌtuːd/ or /ˈlɒndʒ-/, /-tjuːd/ n distance east or west of the prime meridian, expressed in degrees or time.

longitudinal /ˈlɒŋɡɪˌtuːdɪnəl/ or /ˈlɒndʒ-/, /-tjuːd-/ adj of or in length; running or placed lengthways; of longitude.—**longitudinally** adv.

long johns npl (inf) warm underpants with long legs.

long jump n an athletic event consisting of a horizontal running jump.

long-lived adj having or tending to live a long time.

long-playing adj of or relating to an LP record.

long-range adj reaching over a long distance or period of time.

longshore /ˈlɒŋʃɔr/ adj found on, or pertaining to, the shore.

longshoreman /ˈlɒŋʃɔrmən/ n (pl **longshoremen**) a person who loads and unloads ships at a port.

long shot n a wild guess; a competitor, etc who is unlikely to win; a project that has little chance of success.

long-sighted adj only seeing distant objects clearly.—**long-sightedly** adv.

long-standing adj having continued for a long time.

long-suffering adj enduring pain, provocation, etc patiently

long-term adj of or extending over a long time.

longueur /lɒŋˈɡər/, Fr. /loːnˈɡœr/ n a tedious period of time.

long wave n a radio wave of a frequency less than 300 kHz.

longways /ˈlɒŋweɪz/, **longwise** /ˈlɒŋwaɪz/ adv in the direction of the length (of something), lengthways.

long-winded /ˈlɒŋwaɪndəd/ adj speaking or writing at great length; tiresome.—**long-windedly** adv.—**long-windedness** n.

loo /luː/ n (pl **loos**) (Brit inf) a lavatory, a toilet.

looby /ˈluːbi/ n (pl **loobies**) a clumsy, stupid person.

loofah /ˈluːfə/ n the fibrous skeleton of a type of gourd used as a sponge for scrubbing.—also **luffa**.

look /lʊk/ vi to try to see; to see; to search; to appear, seem; to be facing in a specified direction; (with **in**) to pay a brief visit; (with **up**) to improve in prospects. • vt to direct one's eyes on; to have an appearance befitting. • n the act of looking; a gaze, glance; appearance; aspect; (with **after**) to take care of; (with **over**) to examine; (with **up**) to research (for information, etc) in book; to visit.

look-alike n a person that looks like another.

looker /ˈlʊkər/ n (inf) an attractive woman.

looker-on n (pl **lookers-on**) a spectator.

look-in n a brief visit.

looking glass n a mirror.

lookout /ˈlʊkbʊt/ n a place for keeping watch; a person assigned to watch.

look-see n (inf) a brief inspection.

loom[1] /luːm/ n a machine or frame for weaving yarn or thread. • vt to weave on a loom.

loom[2] vi to come into view indistinctly and often threateningly; to come ominously close, as an impending event.

loon[1] /luːn/ n a large fish-eating diving bird.

loon[2] n (sl) a clumsy or stupid person; a crazy person.

loony, looney /ˈluːni/ n (pl **loonies**) a lunatic. • adj (**loonier, looniest**) (sl) crazy, demented.—**looniness** n.

loop /luːp/ n a figure made by a curved line crossing itself; a similar rounded shape in cord, rope, etc crossed on itself; anything forming this figure; (comput) a set of instructions in a program that are executed repeatedly; an intrauterine contraceptive device; a segment of film or magnetic tape. • vt to make a loop of; to fasten with a loop. • vi to form a loop or loops.

looper /ˈluːpər/ n a caterpillar that crawls by arching itself into loops.

loophole /ˈluːphoːl/ n a means of evading an obligation, etc; a slit in a wall for looking or shooting through.

loopy /ˈluːpi/ adj (**loopier, loopiest**) (inf) slightly mad, cracked.

loose /luːz/ adj free from confinement or restraint; not firmly fastened; not tight or compact; not precise; inexact; (inf) relaxed. • vt to release; to unfasten; to untie; to detach; (bullet) to discharge. • vi to become loose.—**loosely** adv.—**looseness** n.

loose cannon n a person who acts independently and often obstreperously.

loose-leaf adj having pages or sheets that can easily be replaced or removed.

loosen /ˈluːzən/ vti to make or become loose or looser.—**loosener** n.

loosestrife /ˈluːsstraɪf/ n a kind of plant with golden or purple flowers.

loot /luːt/ n goods taken during warfare, civil unrest, etc; (sl) money. • vti to plunder, pillage.—**looter** n.

lop /lɒp/ vt (**lopping, lopped**) to sever the branches or twigs from a tree; to cut off or out as superfluous.

lope /loːp/ vi to move or run with a long bounding stride.—also n.—**loper** n.

lop-eared adj having drooping ears.

lophobranchiate /ˈlɒfəˌbrænkiːɪt/ adj (fish) with gills arranged in tufts.

lopsided /lɒpˈsaɪdəd/ adj having one side larger in weight, height, or size than the other; badly balanced.—**lopsidedly** adv.—**lopsidedness** n.

loquacious /loːˈkweɪʃəs/ adj talkative.—**loquaciously** adv.—**loquacity** n.

loquat /ˈloːkwɒt/ n an evergreen tree found in China and Japan; its edible fruit.

loquitur /ˈlɒkwɪtər/ (theatre) (formerly) he or she speaks (as a stage direction).

lord /lɔrd/ n a ruler, master or monarch; a male member of the nobility; (with cap and **the**) God; a form of address used to certain peers, bishops and judges.

lordling /ˈlɔrdlɪŋ/ n a young or minor lord.

lordly /-li/ adj (**lordlier, lordliest**) noble; haughty; arrogant.—**lordliness** n.

Lord Mayor n the mayor of the City of London and certain other UK boroughs and towns—also **Lord Provost** in Scotland.

lordosis /lɔrˈdoːsɪs/ n forward curvature of the spine.

Lord Privy Seal n a British cabinet minister without specific responsibilities.

Lord Provost see **Lord Mayor**.

Lord's Day n (with **the**) Sunday.

lordship /ˈlɔrdʃɪp/ n the rank or authority of a lord; rule, dominion; (with **his** or **your**) a title used in speaking of or to a lord.

Lord's Prayer n (with **the**) the prayer taught by Jesus to His disciples beginning 'Our Father'.

lords spiritual npl the bishops and archbishops who are members of the British House of Lords.

lords temporal npl the peers other than bishops and archbishops in the British House of Lords.

lore /lɔr/ n knowledge; learning, esp of a traditional nature; a particular body of tradition.

lorgnette /lɔrˈnjɛt/ n a long-handled opera glass; a pair of spectacles fixed to a long handle, into which they fold.

lorica /loːˈraɪkə/ n (pl **loricae**) the hard outer shell of certain animals.—**loricate, loricated** adj.

lorikeet /ˈlɒriˌkiːt/ or /ˈlɒri-/ n a small, brightly coloured parrot.

loris /ˈlɒrɪs/ n (pl **loris**) a small, nocturnal, climbing primate, found in South and South-East Asia.

lorn /lɔrn/ adj (poet) forsaken; forlorn.

lorry /ˈlɒri/ n (pl **lorries**) a large motor vehicle for transporting heavy loads.—also US **truck**.

lory /'lɔːrɪ/ n (pl **lories**) a small parrot with brilliant plumage.

lose /luːz/ vb (**losing, lost**) vt to have taken from one by death, accident, removal, etc; to be unable to find; to fail to keep, as one's temper; to fail to see, hear, or understand; to fail to have, get, etc; to fail to win; to cause the loss of; to wander from (one's way, etc); to squander. • vi to suffer (a) loss.—**losable** adj.—**loser** n.

losel /'luːzəl/ n (dial) a worthless person.

loss /lɒs/ n a losing or being lost; the damage, trouble caused by losing; the person, thing, or amount lost.

loss leader n an item sold at a price below its value in order to attract customers.

lost /lɒst/ adj no longer possessed; missing; not won; destroyed or ruined; having wandered astray; wasted.

lot /lɒt/ n an object, such as a straw, slip of paper, etc drawn from others at random to reach a decision by chance; the decision thus arrived at; one's share by lot; fortune; a plot of ground; a group of persons or things; an item or set of items put up for auction; (often pl) (inf) a great amount; much; (inf) sort. • vt (**lotting, lotted**) to divide into lots.

lota, lotah /'ləʊtə/ n a brass or copper water pot.

loth see **loath**.

Lothario /lə'θɑːrɪəʊ/ or /-'θɛːrɪəʊ/ n (pl **Lotharios**) a libertine.

lotion /'ləʊʃən/ n a liquid for cosmetic or external medical use.

lottery /'lɒtərɪ/ n (pl **lotteries**) a system of raising money by selling numbered tickets that offer the chance of winning a prize; an enterprise, etc which may or may not succeed.

lotto /'lɒtəʊ/ n a game of chance based on the drawing of prize numbers.

lotus /'ləʊtəs/ n a type of waterlily; (Greek legend) a plant whose fruit induced contented forgetfulness.

lotus-eater n a person dedicated to a life of idle pleasure.

lotus position n an erect sitting position in yoga with the legs crossed close to the body.

louche /luːʃ/ adj untrustworthy, shady.

loud /laʊd/ adj characterized by or producing great noise; emphatic; (inf) obtrusive or flashy.—**loudly** adv.—**loudness** n.

louden /-ən/ vi to grow louder. • vt to make louder.

loudspeaker /'laʊdˌspiːkər/ n a device for converting electrical energy into sound.

lough /lɒk/, Ir. /lɒx/ n a lake; an arm of the sea.

louis, louis d'or /'luːiː/ n (pl **louis, louis d'or**) (formerly) a French gold coin, with a value of 20 francs.

lounge /laʊndʒ/ vi to move, sit, lie, etc in a relaxed way; to spend time idly. • n a room with comfortable furniture for sitting, as a waiting room at an airport, etc; a comfortable sitting room in a hotel or private house.

lounger /'laʊndʒər/ n a comfortable couch or chair for relaxing on; a person who lounges.

lour /laʊr/ vi to look sullen; to become dark, gloomy, threatening.—also **lower**.—**louringly, loweringly** adv.

louse /laʊs/ n (pl **lice**) any of various small wingless insects that are parasitic on humans and animals; any similar but unrelated insects that are parasitic on plants; (inf) (pl **louses**) a mean, contemptible person.

lousy /'laʊzɪ/ adj (**lousier, lousiest**) infested with lice; (sl) disgusting, of poor quality, or inferior; (sl) well supplied (with).—**lousily** adv.—**lousiness** n.

lout /laʊt/ n a clumsy, rude person.—**loutish** adj.

louvre, louver, /'luːvər/ n one of a set of slats in a door or window set parallel and slanted to admit air but not rain.—**louvred, louvered,** adj.

lovable /'lʌvəbəl/ adj easy to love or feel affection for.—**lovability** n.—**lovably** adv.

lovage /'lʌvɪdʒ/ n a European herb used as a seasoning in food.

love /lʌv/ n a strong liking for someone or something; a passionate affection for another person; the object of such affection; (tennis) a score of zero. • vti to feel love (for).

love affair n a romantic or sexual relationship between two people.

lovebird /'lʌvbərd/ n any of various small parrots.

love child n an illegitimate child.

love-in-a-mist n a flowering garden plant, fennelflower.

loveless /'lʌvləs/ adj without love; not feeling or receiving love.—**lovelessly** adv.

lovelock /'lʌvlɒk/ n a curl worn on the forehead.

lovelorn /'lʌvlɔːrn/ adj pining from love.

lovely /'lʌvlɪ/ adj (**lovelier, loveliest**) beautiful; (inf) highly enjoyable. • n (pl **lovelies**) a lovely person.—**loveliness** n.

lovemaking /'lʌvˌmeɪkɪŋ/ n sexual activity, esp intercourse, between lovers.

lover /'lʌvər/ n a person in love with another person; a person, esp a man, having an extramarital sexual relationship; (pl) a couple in love with each other; someone who loves a specific person or thing.

lovesick /'lʌvsɪk/ adj languishing through love.—**lovesickness** n.

lovey-dovey /'lʌvɪˌdʌvɪ/ adj (sl) displaying affection in an excessive or exaggerated manner.

loving /'lʌvɪŋ/ adj affectionate.—**lovingly** adv.—**lovingness** n.

loving cup n a large cup with two or more handles passed round a group for all to drink from.

low¹ /ləʊ/ n the sound a cow makes, a moo. • vi to make this sound.

low² adj not high or tall; below the normal level; less in size, degree, amount, etc than usual; deep in pitch; depressed in spirits; humble, of low rank; vulgar, coarse; not loud. • adv in or to a low degree, level, etc. • n a low level, degree, etc; a region of low barometric pressure.

Low Arctic n the Arctic south of the Arctic Circle.

lowborn /'ləʊbɔːrn/, **lowbred** /'ləʊbrɛd/ adj of humble birth.

lowboy /'ləʊbɔɪ/ n a table with drawers.

lowbrow /'ləʊbraʊ/ n (inf) a person regarded as uncultivated and lacking in taste.—also adj.

low comedy n comedy reliant on farce or physical slapstick.

lowdown /'ləʊdaʊn/ n (sl: with **the**) the true, pertinent facts

low-down adj (inf) mean, contemptible.

lower case n small letters (not capitals) used for printing.

lower class n the class of people having the lowest status in society.

lower house, lower chamber n one of the two chambers in a bicameral legislature, such as the British House of Commons or the US House of Representatives.

lower¹ /'ləʊər/ adj below in place, rank, etc; less in amount, degree, etc. • vt to let or put down; to reduce in height, amount, etc; to bring down in respect, etc. • vi to become lower.—**lowerable** adj.

lower² /laʊr/ or /'ləʊər/ see **lour**.

lowermost adj lowest.

low frequency n a radio frequency between 300 and 30 kilohertz.

low-key, low-keyed adj of low intensity, subdued.

lowland /'ləʊlənd/ n low-lying land; (pl) a flat region. • adj of or pertaining to lowlands.—**lowlander** n.

low-level language n (comput) a programming language that corresponds more to machine language than human language.

lowlife n (pl **lowlifes**) (sl) a criminal.

lowly /'ləʊlɪ/ adj (**lowlier, lowliest**) humble, of low status; meek.—**lowliness** n.

Low Mass n a Mass without music or elaborate ritual.

low-rise adj (building) having only one or two storeys.—also n.

low spirited adj unhappy, depressed.

low-tech adj of or involving low technology.

low technology n unsophisticated technology limited to the provision of basic human needs.

low tension adj using, conveying, or operating at a low voltage.

low tide n (the time of) the tide when it is at its lowest level; a low point.

low water n low tide.

lox¹ /lɒks/ n a type of smoked salmon.

lox² n liquid oxygen.

loyal /'lɔɪəl/ adj firm in allegiance to a person, cause, country, etc, faithful; demonstrating unswerving allegiance.—**loyally** adv.—**loyalty** n.

loyalist /-ɪst/ n a person who supports the established government, esp during a revolt.—**loyalism** n.

lozenge /'lɒzɪndʒ/ n a four-sided diamond-shaped figure; a cough drop, sweet, etc, originally diamond-shaped.

LP n a long-playing record, usu 12 inches (30.5 cm) in diameter and played at a speed of 33 ¹/₃ revolutions per minute.

LPG abbr = liquefied petroleum gas.

Lr (chem symbol) lawrencium.

LSD n a powerful hallucinatory drug (lysergic acid diethylamide).

Lt abbr = lieutenant.

Ltd abbr = limited liability (used by private companies only).

LU (chem symbol) lutetium.

luau /'luːaʊ/ n a sumptuous feast in Hawaii; a warm welcome; an unexpected source of wealth; a bonanza.

lubber /'lʌbər/ n a clumsy person.

lubricant /'luːbrɪkənt/ n a substance that lubricates.

lubricate /ˈluːbrɪˌkeɪt/ *vt* to coat or treat (machinery, etc) with oil or grease to lessen friction; to make smooth, slippery, or greasy. • *vi* to act as a lubricant.—**lubrication** *n*.

lubricator /-ər/ *n* person who or thing that lubricates; a device used for oiling machines.

lubricity /-sɪti/ *n* slipperiness; evasiveness; lewdness.

lucarne /luːˈkɑːrn/ *n* a dormer window, *esp* in a spire.

lucent /ˈluːsənt/ *adj* bright, shining.—**lucency** *n*.

lucerne /luːˈsɜːrn/ *see* **alfalfa**.

lucid /ˈluːsɪd/ *adj* easily understood; sane.—**lucidly** *adv*.—**lucidity** *n*.

Lucifer /ˈluːsɪfər/ *n* Satan.

luck /lʌk/ *n* chance; good fortune.

luckless /ˈlʌkləs/ *n* unfortunate, unlucky.—**lucklessly** *adv*.—**lucklessness** *n*.

lucky /ˈlʌki/ *adj* (**luckier, luckiest**) having or bringing good luck.—**luckily** *adv*.—**luckiness** *n*.

lucrative /ˈluːkrətɪv/ *adj* producing wealth or profit; profitable.—**lucratively** *adv*.—**lucrativeness** *n*.

lucre /ˈluːkər/ *n* (*derog*) riches, money.

lucubrate /ˈluːkjuˌbreɪt/ *vi* to study, *esp* by night.—**lucubrator** *n*.

lucubration /ˌluːkjʊˈbreɪʃən/ *n* study, *esp* nocturnal; (*often pl*) a literary compositon produced as the result of protracted study.

ludicrous /ˈluːdɪkrəs/ *adj* absurd, laughable.—**ludicrously** *adv*.

luff /lʌf/ *n* (*naut*) the part of ship towards the wind. • *vti* (*naut*) to turn (a ship) into the wind.

luffa *see* **loofah**.

Luftwaffe /ˈluftˌvɒfə/ *n* the German Air Force.

lug[1] /lʌg/ *vt* (**lugging, lugged**) to pull or drag along with effort.

lug[2] *n* an ear-like projection by which a thing is held or supported.

luge /luːʒ/ *n* a small one-person toboggan.

luggage /ˈlʌgɪdʒ/ *n* the suitcases and other baggage containing the possessions of a traveller.

lugger /ˈlʌgər/ *n* a small vessel rigged with one or more lugsails.

lugsail /ˈlʌgseɪl/ or /-səl/ *n* a square sail, with no boom or lower yard, which hangs nearly at right angles to the mast.

lugubrious /luːˈguːbriəs/ or /lʊ-/ *adj* mournful, dismal.—**lugubriously** *adv*.

lugworm /ˈlʌgwɜːrm/ *n* a marine worm used as bait.

lukewarm /ˈluːkwɔːrm/ *adj* barely warm, tepid; lacking enthusiasm.

lull /lʌl/ *vt* to soothe, to calm; to calm the suspicions of, *esp* by deception. • *n* a short period of calm.

lullaby /ˈlʌləˌbaɪ/ *n* (*pl* **lullabies**) a song to lull children to sleep.

lulu /ˈluːluː/ *n* (*inf*) a wonderful or remarkable person or thing.

lumbago /lʌmˈbeɪgoʊ/ *n* rheumatic pain in the lower back.

lumbar /ˈlʌmbər/ *adj* of or in the loins.

lumber[1] /ˈlʌmbər/ *n* timber, logs, beams, boards, etc, roughly cut and prepared for use (mainly in the US); articles of unused household furniture that are stored away; any useless articles. • *vi* to cut down timber and saw it into lumber (mainly in the US). • *vt* to clutter with lumber; to heap in disorder.

lumber[2] *vi* to move heavily or clumsily.—**lumberer** *n*.

lumbering[1] /ˈlʌmbərɪŋ/ *adj* moving clumsily and heavily.—**lumberingly** *adv*.

lumbering[2] *n* the cutting down and sawing of trees into timber as a business.

lumberjack /ˈlʌmbərˌdʒæk/ *n* a person employed to fell trees and transport and prepare timber.

lumbrical /ˈluːmbrɪkəl/ or /-brək-/ *adj* wormlike.

lumen /ˈluːmən/ *n* (*pl* **lumina, lumens**) the SI unit of light flux; (*anat*) a duct within a tubular organ.

luminary /ˈluːmɪnəri/ *n* (*pl* **luminaries**) a body that gives off light, such as the sun; a famous or notable person.

luminescent /ˌluːmɪˈnesənt/ *adj* emitting light but not heat.—**luminescence** *n*.

luminosity /ˌluːmɪˈnɒsiti/ *n* (*pl* **luminosities**) the quality of being luminous; something luminous; (*astron*) the degree of light emitted by a star when compared with the sun.

luminous /ˈluːmɪnəs/ *adj* emitting light; glowing in the dark; clear, easily understood.—**luminously** *adv*.

lump /lʌmp/ *n* a small, compact mass of something, *usu* without definite shape; an abnormal swelling; a dull or stupid person. • *adj* in a lump or lumps. • *vt* to treat or deal with in a mass. • *vi* to become lumpy.

lumper /ˈlʌmpər/ *n* a docker.

lumpfish /ˈlʌmpfɪʃ/ *n* (*pl* **lumpfish, lumpfishes**) a sea fish found in the North Atlantic, with horny spines and a sucker with which it clings to objects.

lumpish /ˈlʌmpɪʃ/ *adj* like a lump; heavy; dull, stupid.

lump sum *n* a sum of money (*esp* cash) paid as a whole and not in instalments.

lumpy /ˈlʌmpi/ *adj* (**lumpier, lumpiest**) filled or covered with lumps.—**lumpily** *adv*.—**lumpiness** *n*.

lunacy /ˈluːnəsi/ *n* (*pl* **lunacies**) insanity; utter folly.

lunar /ˈluːnər/ *adj* of or like the moon.

lunar eclipse *n* an eclipse when the earth passes between the sun and the moon.

lunar month *n* a month measured by the complete revolution of the moon, 29.5 days.

lunar year *n* a year of twelve lunar months, 354.33 days.

lunate /ˈluːneɪt/, **lunated** *adj* crescent-shaped.

lunatic /ˈluːnətɪk/ *adj* insane; utterly foolish. • *n* an insane person.

lunatic fringe *n* the members of an organization regarded as being fanatical or extreme.

lunation /luːˈneɪʃən/ *n* a lunar month, the time taken for the moon to revolve once around the earth.

lunch /lʌntʃ/ *n* a light meal, *esp* between breakfast and dinner; **out to lunch** (*sl*) crazy; eccentric. • *vi* to eat lunch.—**luncher** *n*.

luncheon /ˈlʌntʃən/ *n* lunch, *esp* a formal lunch.

luncheon meat *n* processed meat in tins ready to eat.

lune /luːn/ *n* (*geom*) a figure formed on a plane or sphere by two intersecting arcs of circles.

lunette /luːˈnet/ *n* anything shaped like a crescent; an arched opening in a vaulted roof to admit light.

lung /lʌŋ/ *n* either of the two sponge-like breathing organs in the chest of vertebrates.

lunge[1] /lʌndʒ/ *n* a sudden forceful thrust, as with a sword; a sudden plunge forward. • *vti* to move, or cause to move, with a lunge.—**lunger** *n*.

lunge[2] *n* a long halter for training a horse; the use of this in training horses. • *vt* to train with a lunge.—*also* **longe**.

lungfish /ˈlʌŋfɪʃ/ *n* (*pl* **lungfish, lungfishes**) a freshwater fish with lungs as well as gills.

lungi /ˈlʊŋgiː/ *n* a long piece of cloth worn as a skirt or loincloth by Indian men.

lungwort /ˈlʌŋwɔːrt/ *n* a Eurasian plant with dark-coloured leaves spotted with white.

lunisolar /ˌluːnɪˈsoʊlər/ *adj* pertaining to the sun and moon; produced by the sun and moon in unison.

lunula, lunule /ˈluːnjʊlə/ *n* (*pl* **lunulae, lunules**) the white crescent-shaped part near the root of the fingernail.

lupine[1] /ˈluːpɪn/ *n* a garden plant of the pea family.

lupine[2] /ˈluːpaɪn/ *adj* of or resembling a wolf.

lupulin /ˈluːpʊlɪn/ or /-lə-/, /-ˈpjuː-/ *n* a powder, obtained from hops, used as a sedative.

lupus /ˈluːpəs/ *n* any of several autoimmune diseases marked by lesions of the skin.

lurch /lɜːrtʃ/ *vi* to lean or pitch suddenly to the side. • *n* a sudden roll to one side.—**lurchingly** *adv*.

lurdan /ˈlɜːrdən/ *adj* (*arch*) stupid. • *n* a stupid person.

lure /lʊr/ or /lɜːr/ *n* something that attracts, tempts or entices; a brightly coloured fishing bait; a device used to recall a trained hawk; a decoy for wild animals. • *vt* to entice, attract, or tempt.—**luringly** *adv*.

lurid /ˈlʊrɪd/ or /ˈlɜːr-/ *adj* vivid, glaring; shocking; sensational.—**luridly** *adv*.—**luridness** *n*.

lurk /lɜːrk/ *vi* to lie hidden in wait; to loiter furtively.—**lurker** *n*.

luscious /ˈlʌʃəs/ *adj* delicious; richly sweet; delighting any of the senses.—**lusciously** *adv*.—**lusciousness** *n*.

lush[1] /lʌʃ/ *adj* tender and juicy; of or showing abundant growth.—**lushly** *adv*.—**lushness** *n*.

lush[2] *n* (*sl*) an alcoholic.

lust /lʌst/ *n* strong sexual desire (for); an intense longing for something. • *vi* to feel lust.—**lustful** *adj*.—**lustfully** *adv*.

lustral /ˈlʌstrəl/ *adj* of or relating to ceremonial purification; of or relating to a lustrum.

lustrate /ˈlʌstreɪt/ *vt* to purify by sacrifice or ceremonial washing.—**lustration** *n*.

lustre, luster /ˈlʌstər/ *n* gloss; sheen; brightness; radiance; brilliant beauty or fame; glory; a chandelier with pendants of cut glass; a fabric with a lustrous surface; a substance used to give lustre to an object; a metallic glaze on pottery; the quality and intensity of light reflected from the surface of minerals.—**lustrous** *adj*.—**lusterless** *adj*.

lustreware, lusterware /ˈlʊstərˌwɛr/ *n* earthenware decorated with luster.

lustrum /ˈlʊstrəm/ *n* (*pl* **lustrums, lustra**) a period of five years.

lusty /ˈlʊsti/ *adj* (**lustier, lustiest**) strong; vigorous; healthy.— **lustily** *adv*.—**lustiness** *n*.

lute¹ /luːt/ *n* an old, round-backed stringed musical instrument plucked with the fingers.

lute² *n* clay or cement used to make joints airtight, etc.

lutenist /ˈluːtənɪst/, **lutist** /ˈluːtɪst/ *n* a lute player.

luteous /ˈluːtiəs/ *adj* greenish-yellow.

lutetium /luːˈtiːʃiəm/ *n* a metallic element.

Lutheran /ˈluːθərən/ *adj* pertaining to Martin Luther (1483-1546), the German religious reformer, or to the Lutheran Church and its doctrines. • *n* a follower of Martin Luther; a member of the Lutheran Church.—**Lutheranism** *n*.

Lutheran Church *n* the Protestant church founded by Martin Luther in Germany in the 16th century.

lux /lʊks/ *n* (*pl* **lux**) a unit of illumination.

luxate /ˈlʊksˌeɪt/ *vt* to put out of joint.—**luxation** *n*.

luxuriant /lʌɡˈʒʊriənt/ or /lʌkˈʃʊr-/ *adj* profuse, abundant; ornate; fertile.—**luxuriance** *n*.

luxuriate /lʌɡˈʒʊrɪˌeɪt/ or /lʌkˈʃʊr-/ *vi* to enjoy immensely, to revel (in).—**luxuriation** *n*.

luxurious /lʌɡˈʒʊriəs/ or /lʌkˈʃʊr-/ *adj* constituting luxury; indulging in luxury; rich, comfortable.—**luxuriously** *adv*.— **luxuriousness** *n*.

luxury /ˈlʌkʃəri/ or /ˈlʌɡʒəri/ *n* (*pl* **luxuries**) indulgence and pleasure in sumptuous and expensive food, accommodation, clothes, etc; (*often pl*) something that is costly and enjoyable but not indispensable. • *adj* relating to or supplying luxury.

lx *abbr* = lux.

lycanthrope /ˈlaɪkənˌθroːp/ *n* a werewolf; (*med*) a sufferer from lycanthropy.

lycanthropy /-i/ *n* the supposed power of changing from a human being into a werewolf; (*med*) a form of mental illness in which the sufferer believes himself or herself to be a wolf.

lycée /liːˈseɪ/ *n* (*pl* **lycées**) a state secondary school in France.

lyceum /laɪˈsiːəm/ *n* a public lecture hall.

lychee /ˈliːtʃi/ *see* **lichee**.

lych gate /ˈlɪtʃɡeɪt/ *see* **lich gate**.

lychnis /ˈlɪknɪs/ *n* a genus of flowering plants, including the ragged robin and campion.

lycopod /ˈlaɪkəˌpɒd/ *n* a kind of moss, also known as the club moss.

lycopodium /ˌlaɪkəˈpoːdiəm/ *n* any of a genus of perennial plants, the club mosses; an inflammable yellow powder in the spore cases of certain species, used in fireworks.

Lycra /ˈlaɪkrə/ *n* (*trademark*) an elastic synthetic material used for tight-fitting garments, such as bicycle shorts and swimwear.

lyddite /ˈlɪdaɪt/ *n* a powerful explosive, composed chiefly of picric acid.

lye /laɪ/ *n* an alkaline solution.

lying /ˈlaɪŋ/ *see* **lie¹, lie²**.

lying-in *n* (*pl* **lyings-in, lying-ins**) childbirth.

Lyme disease /laɪm/ *n* an infectious disease, carried by ticks, that produces fever, pains in the joints and a rash, and can result in paralysis or chronic fatigue, and, rarely, death.

lymph /lɪmf/ *n* a clear, yellowish body fluid, found in intercellular spaces and the lymphatic vessels.

lymphatic /lɪmˈfætɪk/ *adj* of, relating to, or containing lymph; sluggish. • *n* a vessel that contains or conveys lymph.

lymph node *n* any of numerous nodules of tissue distributed along the course of lymphatic vessels that produce lymphocytes.

lympho- /ˈlɪmfə-/ *prefix* lymph; lymph tissue; lymphatic system.

lymphocyte /ˈlɪmfəˌsaɪt/ *n* a white blood cell formed in the lymph nodes, which helps to protect against infection.—**lymphocytic** *adj*.

lymphoid /ˈlɪmfɔɪd/ *adj* relating to lymph glands; resembling lymph.

lymphoma /lɪmˈfoːmə/ *n* (*pl* **lymphomata**) a tumour of the lymphoid tissue.

lyncean /ˈlɪnˌsiən/ *adj* pertaining to or resembling the lynx; sharp-eyed.

lynch /lɪntʃ/ *vt* to murder (an accused person) by mob action, without lawful trial, as by hanging.—**lyncher** *n*.—**lynching** *n*.

lynx /lɪŋks/ *n* (*pl* **lynxes, lynx**) a wild feline of Europe and North America with spotted fur.

lynx-eyed /-aɪd/ *adj* keen-sighted.

lyonnaise /ˌliːəˈnɒz/, *Fr.* /ljɔˈnɛz/ *adj* (*cooking*) with onions.

lyrate /ˈlaɪrət/ **lyrated** *adj* lyre-shaped.

lyre /laɪr/ *n* an ancient musical instrument of the harp family.

lyrebird /ˈlaɪrbərd/ *n* an Australian bird with a tail shaped like a lyre.

lyric /ˈlɪrɪk/ *adj* denoting or of poetry expressing the writer's emotion; of, or having a high voice with a light, flexible quality. • *n* a lyric poem; (*pl*) the words of a popular song.

lyrical /ˈlɪrɪkəl/ *adj* lyric; (*inf*) expressing rapture or enthusiasm.—**lyrically** *adv*.

lyricism /ˈlɪrɪˌsɪzəm/ *n* lyrical quality or expression.

lyricist /ˈlɪrɪsɪst/ *n* a person who writes lyrics, *esp* for popular songs.

lyrist /ˈlaɪrɪst/ *n* a lyric poet; a lyre player.

lysergic acid /laɪˈsɜrdʒɪk/ *see* **LSD**.

lysin /ˈlaɪsɪn/ *n* a specific antibody in blood that can destroy cells.

lysine /ˈlaɪsiːn/ *n* an amino acid formed by the digestion of dietary protein.

-lysis /lɪsɪs/ *n suffix* disintegration; decomposition.

lysis /ˈlaɪsɪs/ *n* (*pl* **lyses**) (*biol*) the process of destroying cells with a lysin; (*med*) the gradual abatement of an acute disease.

-lyte /ˈlaɪt/ *n suffix* denoting a substance able to be disintegrated or decomposed.

-lytic /ˈlɪtɪk/ *adj suffix* indicating a disintegration or decomposition.

M

M *abbr* = mega-; medium; motorway.

M. *abbr* = Master; Monsieur

m *abbr* = metre(s); mile(s); million(s).

MA *abbr* = Master of Arts.

ma /mɒ/ *n* (*inf*) mother.

ma'am /mæm/ or /mɑm/ *n* madam (used as a title of respect, *esp* when addressing royalty).

macabre /mə'kɒbrə/ or /-'kæbrə/, /-'kɒb/ *adj* gruesome; grim; of death.

macaco /mə'kɒkɔ:/ *n* (*pl* **macacos**) one of various lemurs, *esp* the ruffled lemur and the ring-tailed lemur.

macadam /mə'kædəm/ *n* a road surface composed of successive layers of small stones compacted into a solid mass.

macadamia /ˌmækə'deɪmɪə/ *n* an Australian tree bearing white flowers and an edible seed (the macadamia nut).

macadamize /mə'kædəˌmaɪz/ *vt* to surface (a road) with macadam.—**macadamization** *n*.

macaque /mə'kæk/ *n* a short-tailed monkey of Asia and Africa.

macaroni /ˌmækə'rɔ:ni/ *n* (*pl* **macaronis, macaronies**) a pasta made chiefly of fine wheat flour and made into tubes; an 18th-century dandy who copied continental mannerisms etc.

macaronic /ˌmækə'rɒnɪk/ *adj* (*verse*) using words from more than one language, or a mixture of everyday words and Latin words or words with Latin endings. • *n* (*often pl*) macaronic verse.

macaroon /ˌmækə'ru:n/ *n* a small cake or biscuit made with sugar, egg whites and ground almonds or coconut.

macaw /mə'kɒ/ *n* a large parrot with brightly coloured plumage.

Maccabean /ˌmækə'bi:ən/ *adj* pertaining to the Maccabees, a family of Jewish patriots who led a successful revolt against the Syrians, or to its most famous member, Judas Maccabaeus.

maccaboy /'mækəˌbɔɪ/ *n* a kind of snuff, *usu* rose-scented.

mace[1] /meɪs/ *n* a staff used as a symbol of authority by certain institutions.

mace[2] *n* an aromatic spice made from the external covering of the nutmeg.

macédoine /'mæsɪˌdwɒn/, *Fr.* /mɑseɪ'dwɑn/ *n* a dish of mixed fruits, served hot or cold; a dish of diced vegetables, *usu* in jelly or syrup; any mixture.

macerate /'mæsəˌreɪt/ *vti* to soften or become soft or separated through soaking; to make or become thin.—**maceration** *n*.—**macerator** *n*.

Mach /mɒk/ or /mæk/ *see* **Mach number**.

machete /mə'ʃeti/ or /mə'tʃeti/ *n* a large knife used for cutting, or as a weapon.

Machiavellian /ˌmækɪə'velɪən/ *adj* cunning; deceitful.

machicolation /məˌtʃɪkə'leɪʃən/ *n* (*arch*) a projecting parapet, *usu* found on medieval castles, with openings for dropping stones, etc, on assailants; such an opening.—**machicolated** *adj*.

machinate /'mækɪˌneɪt/ or /'mæʃ-/ *vti* to scheme, plan, *esp* to do harm.—**machinator** *n*.

machination /ˌmæʃɪ'neɪʃən/ or /ˌmækɪ-/ *n* (*usu pl*) an artifice; an intrigue; a plot; the act of plotting or intriguing.

machine /mə'ʃi:n/ *n* a structure of fixed and moving parts, for doing useful work; an organization functioning like a machine; the controlling group in a political party; a device, as the lever, etc that transmits, or changes the application of energy. • *vt* to shape or finish by machine-operated tools. • *adj* of machines; done by machinery.

machine code, machine language *n* (*comput*) programming instructions in binary or hexadecimal code.

machine gun *n* an automatic gun, firing a rapid stream of bullets.—*also vt*.

machine-readable /mə'ʃi:n'ri:dəbəl/ *adj* directly usable by a computer.

machinery /mə'ʃi:nəri/ *n* machines collectively; the parts of a machine; the framework for keeping something going.

machine tool *n* a mechanized tool for cutting or shaping metals, wood, etc.

machinist /mə'ʃi:nɪst/ *n* one who makes, repairs, or operates machinery.

machismo /mə'tʃɪzmɔ:/ or /-'kɪzmɔ:/ *n* strong or assertive masculinity; virility.—**macho** *adj*.

Mach number /mɒk/ *n* the ratio of the speed of a body in a particular medium to the speed of sound in the same medium. Mach 1 is equal to the speed of sound.

mackerel /'mækrəl/ *n* (*pl* **mackerel, mackerels**) a common oily food fish.

Mackinaw (coat) /'mækɪnɔ:/ *n* a short, double-breasted coat made of a heavy woollen plaid material.

mackintosh /'mækɪnˌtɒʃ/ *n* a waterproof raincoat.

mackle /'mækəl/ *n* (*printing*) a blurred or imprecise impression, which produces the effect of a double printing.—*also* **macule**.

macle /'mækəl/ *n* a type of crystal in two parts, containing carbon impurities, sometimes used as a gemstone.

macramé /'mækrəmeɪ/ *n* (the art of) knotting or weaving coarse thread to produce ornamental work.

macro- /'mækrɔ:/ *prefix* = long, large.

macrobiotic /ˌmækrɔ:baɪ'ɒtɪk/ *adj* (*diet*) composed of an extremely restricted range of foods, *usu* vegetables and whole grains.

macrocephalic /ˌmækrɔ:sə'fælɪk/ *adj* having an unusually large skull.—*also* **megacephalic** *adj*.—**macrocephaly** *n*.

macrocosm /'mækrɔ:ˌkɒzəm/ *n* the universe; any complex system.—**macrocosmic** *adj*.

macroeconomics /ˌmækrɔ:ˌi:kə'nɒmɪks/ *n* (*used as sing*) the study of the economy in terms of total national income, production and investment.—**macroeconomic** *adj*.

macron /'mækrɒn/ *n* a mark placed over a letter to indicate a stressed or long vowel (-).

macropterous /mæ'krɒptərəs/ *adj* (*zool*) large-winged.

macroscopic /ˌmækrɔ:'skɒpɪk/ *adj* visible to the naked eye; regarded in terms of large elements.

macrospore /'mækrɔ:ˌspɔr/ *see* **megaspore**.

macula /'mækjʊlə/ *n* (*pl* **maculae**) a spot or mark on the skin; a coloured area near the retina, where vision is *esp* sharp.—**macular** *adj*.—**maculation** *n*.

macule' /'mækju:l/ *see* **mackle**.

mad /mæd/ *adj* (**madder, maddest**) insane; frantic; foolish and rash; infatuated; (*inf*) angry.

madam /'mædəm/ *n* a polite term of address to a woman; a woman in charge of a brothel; (*inf*) a precocious little girl.

madame /mə'dæm/ or /'mædəm/ *n* (*pl* **mesdames**) the title of a married French woman; used as a title equivalent to Mrs.

madcap /'mædkæp/ *adj* reckless, impulsive.—*also n*.

madden /'mædən/ *vti* to make or become insane, angry, or wildly excited.—**maddening** *adj*.—**maddeningly** *adv*.

madder[1] /'mædər/ *see* **mad**.

madder[2] *n* a plant of the genus from whose root a red dye and pigment are extracted; the red dye so obtained; a synthetic pigment used in paints and inks.

madding /'mædɪŋ/ *adj* (*arch*) raging; furious; causing (someone or something) to be raging.

made /meɪd/ *see* **make**.

Madeira /mə'dɪrə/ *n* a rich, strong, white wine made in the North Atlantic island of Madeira.

madeleine /'mædəˌleɪn/ *n* a small sponge cake with a coating of red jam covered with coconut.

mademoiselle /ˌmædmwɑ'zel/ *n* (*pl* **mesdemoiselles**) the title of an unmarried French girl or woman; used as a title equivalent to Miss; a French teacher or governess.

made-to-order /'meɪdtə'ɔrdər/ *adj* produced to a customer's specifications; being ideally suited for a particular purpose.

madhouse /'mædhəʊs/ *n* (*inf*) as mental institution; a state of uproar or confusion.

madly /'mædli/ *adv* in an insane manner; at great speed, force; (*inf*) excessively.

madman /'mædmæn/ *n* (*pl* **madmen**) an insane person.

madness /'mædnəs/ *n* insanity; foolishness; excitability.

Madonna /mə'dɒnə/ *n* the Virgin Mary, *esp* as seen in pictures or statues.

madras /mə'dræs/ *n* a strong cotton or silk material, *usu* striped.

madrepore /'mædrə,pɔr/ *n* any of several corals, often forming tropical coral reefs.—**madreporic** *adj*.

madrigal /'mædrɪgəl/ *n* a 16th-century love song or pastoral poem in the form of an unaccompanied part-song; 14th-century Italian song derived from a pastoral poem.—**madrigalist** *n*.

maduro /mə'dʊrɔ:/ *adj* (*cigar*) dark and full-flavoured. • *n* (*pl* **maduros**) such a cigar.

madwoman /'mæd,wʊmən/ *n* (*pl* **madwomen**) an insane person.

madwort /-,wɔrt/ *n* a small herb with yellow or white flowers, formerly reputed to cure madness; a type of small, low-growing, flowering plant with hairy leaves and blue flowers.

maelstrom /'meɪlstrəm/ *n* a whirlpool; a state of turbulence or confusion.

maenad /'mi:næd/ *n* (**maenads, maenades**) (*Greek myth*) a female adherent of Dionysus; a frantic, agitated woman.—*also* **menad**.

maestoso /maɪ'stɔːzɔ:/ *adj*, *adv* (*mus*) in a majestic manner.

maestro /'maɪstrɔ:/ *n* (*pl* **maestros**) a master of an art, *esp* a musical composer, conductor, or teacher.

mae west /meɪ'wɛst/ *n* (*inf*) an inflatable life jacket.

Mafia /'mɒfiə/ or /'mæ-/ *n* a secret society composed chiefly of criminal elements, originating in Sicily.

mafioso /,mæfi'ɔːsɔ:/ or /,mɒ-/ *n* (*pl* **mafiosos, mafiosi**) a member of the Mafia.

mag. *abbr* = magazine.

magazine /,mægə'zi:n/ *n* a military store; a space where explosives are stored, as in a fort; a supply chamber, as in a camera, a rifle, etc; a periodical publication containing articles, fiction, photographs, etc.

magdalen, magdalene /'mægdələn/ *n* a reformed prostitute; (*rare*) an institution for housing and reforming prostitutes.

magenta /mə'dʒɛntə/ *n* a purplish-red dye; purplish red.—*also adj*.

maggot /'mægət/ *n* a wormlike larva, as of the housefly.—**maggoty** *adj*.—**maggotiness** *n*.

magi /'meɪdʒaɪ /, **magian** /'meɪdʒiən/ *see* **magus**.

magic /'mædʒɪk/ *n* the use of charms, spells, etc to supposedly influence events by supernatural means; any mysterious power; the art of producing illusions by sleight of hand, etc. • *adj* of or relating to magic; possessing supposedly supernatural powers; (*inf*) wonderful. • *vt* (**magicking, magicked**) to influence, produce or take (away) by or as if by magic.—**magical** *adj*.—**magically** *adv*.

magician /mə'dʒɪʃən/ *n* one skilled in magic; a conjurer.

magisterial /,mædʒɪ'stiːriəl/ *adj* of, or suitable for a magistrate; authoritative.—**magisterially** *adv*.

magistracy /'mædʒɪstrəsi/ *n* (*pl* **magistracies**) the office, jurisdiction or dignity of a magistrate; magistrates collectively.

magistral /-əl/ *adj* or or pertaining to a master or teacher, magisterial; (*med*) specially prescribed; (*fortification*) in a strategic position.

magistrate /'mædʒɪstreɪt/ or /-,strət/ *n* a public officer empowered to administer the law.—**magistrateship, magistrature** *n*.

magma /'mægmə/ *n* (*pl* **magmas, magmata**) a stratum of hot molten rock within the earth's crust, which solidifies on the surface as lava.

Magna Carta, Magna Charta /,mægnə'kɔrtə/ *n* in England, the Great Charter, forming the basis of civil liberty, granted by King John to the barons, church and freemen in 1215.

magnanimity /,mægnə'nɪmɪti/ *n* (*pl* **magnanimities**) generosity.

magnanimous /mæg'nænɪməs/ *adj* noble and generous in conduct or spirit, not petty.—**magnanimously** *adv*.

magnate /'mægneɪt/ or /-nət/ *n* a very wealthy or influential person.

magnesia /mæg'ni:ʒə/ or /-ʃə/, /-ʒə/ *n* a magnesium compound used as a mild laxative.

magnesium /mæg'ni:ziəm/ *n* a white metallic element that burns very brightly.

magnet /'mægnət/ *n* any piece of iron or steel that has the property of attracting iron; anything that attracts.

magnetic /mæg'nɛtɪk/ *adj* of magnetism or a magnet; producing or acting by magnetism; having the ability to attract or charm people.—**magnetically** *adv*.

magnetic declination *n* deviation of the magnetic needle from true north; the measure of this.

magnetic equator *n* the imaginary point near the equator where the magnetic needle has no dip, the aclinic line.

magnetic field *n* any space in which there is an appreciable magnetic force.

magnetic needle *n* a thin piece of magnetized iron, steel, etc, used in a compass and other instruments, that indicates the direction of a magnetic field.

magnetic north *n* the northerly direction of the earth's magnetic field, as pointed to by a compass needle.

magnetic pole *n* either of the two variable points in the regions of the earth's northern and southern poles to which a magnetic needle points.

magnetic resonance imaging *n* a method of viewing the body's internal organs by the use of radio waves.

magnetics /mæg'nɛtɪks/ *n sing* the science of magnetism.

magnetic tape *n* a thin plastic ribbon with a magnetized coating for recording sound, video signals, computer data, etc.

magnetism /'mægnə,tɪzəm/ *n* the property, quality, or condition of being magnetic; the force to which this is due; personal charm.

magnetize /'mægnɪ,taɪz/ *vt* to make magnetic; to attract strongly.—**magnetization** *n*.—**magnetizer** *n*.

magneto /mæg'ni:tɔ:/ *n* (*pl* **magnetos**) a small generator with permanent magnets for generating high voltages, *esp* the ignition spark in an internal combustion engine.

magnetoelectricity /mæg,ni:tɔ:ɪlɛk'trɪsɪti/ *n* electric phenomena produced by magnetism.

magnetometer /,mægnə'tɒmɪtər/ *n* an instrument for measuring and comparing magnetic fields.

magneton /'mægnɪ,tɒn/ *n* one of two units of magnetic moment.

magnet school *n* a school in which resources are devoted to developing excellence in one particular field, *eg* science.

Magnificat /mæg'nɪfɪ,kæt/ *n* the hymn of the Virgin Mary (Luke 1:46-55); a musical setting of this; (*without cap*) any hymn of praise.

magnification /,mægnɪfɪ'keɪʃən/ *n* magnifying or being magnified; the degree of enlargement of something by a lens, microscope, etc.

magnificence /mæg'nɪfɪsəns/ *n* grandeur of appearance; splendour; pomp.

magnificent /mæg'nɪfɪsənt/ *adj* splendid, stately or sumptuous in appearance; superb, of very high quality.—**magnificently** *adv*.

magnifico /mæg'nɪfɪ,kɔ:/ *n* (*pl* **magnificoes**) a person of importance or high rank; (*formerly*) a title of a Venetian nobleman.

magnify /'mægnɪ,faɪ/ *vt* (**magnifying, magnified**) to exaggerate; to increase the apparent size of (an object) as (with) a lens.—**magnifiable** *adj*.—**magnifier** *n*.

magniloquent /mæg'nɪləkwənt/ *adj* pompous in style or speech, bombastic.—**magniloquence** *n*.—**magniloquently** *adv*.

magnitude /'mægnɪ,tu:d/ or /-tju:d/ *n* greatness of size, extent, etc; importance; (*astron*) the apparent brightness of a star.

magnolia /mæg'nɔ:liə/ *n* a spring-flowering shrub or tree with evergreen or deciduous leaves and showy flowers.

magnum /'mægnəm/ *n* (*pl* **magnums**) a wine bottle that holds twice the normal quantity.

magnum opus /,mægnəm'ɔ:pəs/ *n* (*pl* **magna opera**) the great or chief work of an artist or author.

magpie /'mægpaɪ/ *n* a black and white bird of the crow family; a person who chatters; an acquisitive person.

maguey /'mægweɪ/ *n* any of several species of a tropical American plant, *esp* one from which fibre is obtained or that is used in the production of alcoholic drinks; the fibre from such a plant.

magus /'meɪgəs/ *n* (*pl* **magi**) a Zoroastrian priest; (*with cap*) any of the three wise men who paid homage to Christ at His birth; a magician, sorcerer.—**magian** *adj*, *n*.

Magyar /'mægjɑr/ *adj* pertaining to the Hungarian or Magyar race or language; (*sleeve*) cut as part of the bodice, with no armhole seam.

Mahabharata /mə'hɒ,bɑrətə/ *n* a great Hindu epic that narrates the dynastic wars of ancient India.

maharajah, maharaja /,mɒhə'rɒdʒə/ *n* the former title of an Indian prince.

maharani, maharanee /,mɒhə'rɒni/ *n* the wife of a maharajah.

mahatma /mə'hætmə/ *n* (*Hinduism, Buddhism*) a wise man, a sage; (*with cap*) (*Hinduism*) a title or respect for a man of great spirituality.

mahi-mahi /'mɒhi:,mɒhi/ *n* either of two dolphin fish (genus *Coryphaena*) of the Pacific Ocean, a food fish.

mahjong, mah-jongg /mɒ'dʒɒŋ/ n an orig Chinese game for four people played with decorative tiles.

mahlstick /'mɔl,stɪk/ or /'mɔl-/ see **maulstick**.

mahogany /mə'hɒgəni/ n (pl **mahoganies**) the hard, reddish-brown wood of a tropical tree; a reddish-brown colour.

Mahometan /mə'hɒmɪtən/ see **Muhammedan**.

mahout /mə'hʊt/ n (India) an elephant driver.

maid /meɪd/ n a maiden; a woman servant.

maiden /'meɪdən/ n a girl or young unmarried woman. • adj unmarried or virgin; untried; first.—**maidenhood** n.

maidenhair (fern) /'meɪdən,heɪ/ n a delicate-leafed fern with small light green leaflets.

maidenhead /'meɪdən,hed/ n the hymen.

maidenly /'meɪdənli/ adj like or suitable to a maiden; modest; gentle.—**maidenliness** n.

maiden name n the surname of a woman before marriage.

maiden over n (cricket) an over during which no runs are scored.

maid of honour n the principal unmarried attendant of a bride; a small almond-flavoured tart.

maidservant /'meɪd,sɜrvənt/ n a female servant.

maieutic /meɪ'uːtɪk/ adj of the Socratic method of teaching by means of questions.

mail[1] /meɪl/ n a body armour made of small metal rings or links.

mail[2] n letters, packages, etc transported and delivered by the post office; a postal system. • vt to send by mail.—**mailable** adj.

mailbox /'meɪlbɒks/ n a receptacle into which mail is delivered; (comput) within the electronic mail system, a disk file or memory area in which messages for a particular destination (or person) are placed.

mailman /'meɪlmən/ or /-mæn/ n (pl **mailmen**) in the US, the person who collects or delivers mail.

mail order n an order for goods to be sent by post.

maim /meɪm/ vt to cripple; to mutilate.

main /meɪn/ adj chief in size, importance, etc; principal. • n (often pl but used a sing) a principal pipe in a distribution system for water, gas, etc; the essential point.

mainframe /'meɪnfreɪm/ n a large computer that can handle multiple tasks concurrently.

mainland /-lənd/ n the principal land mass of a continent, as distinguished from nearby islands.

mainline /-laɪn/ n the principal road, course, etc.

mainly /-li/ adv chiefly, principally.

mainmast /-mæst/ n (naut) the principal mast of a sailing ship with more than one mast.

mainsail /-seɪl/ or /-səl/ n (naut) the principal lowermost sail on the mainmast.

mainsheet /-ʃiːt/ n (naut) one of the ropes by which the mainsail is extended and fastened, controlling its angle.

mainspring /-sprɪŋ/ n the principal spring in a clock, watch, etc; the chief incentive, motive, etc.

mainstay /-steɪ/ n a chief support.

mainstream /-striːm/ n a major trend, line of thought, etc.—also adj.

maintain /meɪn'teɪn/ vt to preserve; to support, to sustain; to keep in good condition; to affirm.—**maintainable** adj.—**maintainer** n.

maintenance /'meɪntənəns/ n upkeep; (financial) support, esp of a spouse after a divorce.

maintop /'meɪntɒp/ n (naut) the platform on top of the mainmast.

maisonette /,meɪzə'net/ n a small house; self-contained living quarters, usu on two floors with its own entrance, as part of a larger house.

maître d'hôtel /,meɪtrədo:'tel/ or /,met-/ n (pl **maîtres d'hôtel**) n a head waiter; a hotel manager or owner; a house steward.

maize /meɪz/ n corn; a light yellow colour.

Maj abbr (mil) = major.

majestic /mə'dʒestɪk/ adj dignified; imposing.—**majestically** adv.

majesty /'mædʒəsti/ n (pl **majesties**) grandeur; (with cap) a title used in speaking to or of a sovereign.

majolica /mə'dʒɒlɪkə/ or /mə'jɒl-/ n a fine, soft, enamelled kind of pottery of Italian origin, with a glaze of bright metallic oxides.

major /'meɪdʒər/ adj greater in size, importance, amount, etc; (surgery) very serious, life-threatening; (mus) higher than the corresponding minor by half a tone. • vi to specialize (in a field of study). • n in the UK, a lieutenant-colonel and in the US, an officer ranking just above a captain; (mus) a major key, chord or scale.

major-domo /,meɪdʒər'do:mo:/ n (pl **major-domos**) a head steward; a butler.

majority /mə'dʒɒrɪti/ n (pl **majorities**) the greater number or part of; the excess of the larger number of votes cast for a candidate in an election; full legal age; the military rank of a major.

majuscule /'mædʒə,skjuːl/ n a capital letter used in printing or in writing. • adj of, pertaining to or written in such letters.—**majuscular** adj.

make /meɪk/ vb (**making, made**) vt to cause to exist, occur, or appear; to build, create, produce, manufacture, etc; to prepare for use; to amount to; to have the qualities of; to acquire, earn; to understand; to do, execute; to cause or force; to arrive at, reach; (with **believe**) to imagine, pretend; (with **good**) to make up for, pay compensation; (with **out**) to write out; to complete (a form, etc) in writing; to attempt to understand; to discern, identify; (with **up**) to invent, fabricate, esp to deceive; to prepare; to make complete; to put together; to settle differences between. • vi (with **do**) to manage with what is available; (with **for**) to go in the direction of; to bring about; (with **good**) to become successful or wealthy; (with **off**) to leave in haste; (with **out**) to pretend; to fare, manage; (with **up**) to become reconciled; to compensate for; to put on make-up for the stage. • n style, brand, or origin; manner of production.—**maker** n.

make-believe /'meɪkbə'liːv/ adj imagined, pretended.—also n.

makeshift /'meɪkʃɪft/ adj being a temporary substitute.—also n.

make-up /'meɪkʌp/ n the cosmetics, etc used by an actor; cosmetics generally; the way something is put together, composition; nature, disposition.

makeweight /-weɪt/ n something added to make up the required weight; anything of little value added to fill a lack.

making /-ɪŋ/ n the act or process of making, creation; (pl) earnings; (pl) potential; (pl) (sl) the materials for rolling a cigarette.

Makkah /'məkə/ see **mecca**.

mal- /mæl/ prefix = bad or badly, wrong, ill.

malacca /mə'lækə/ n the tough stem of a species of climbing palm, rattan; a brown walking stick made of this.—also **malacca cane**.

malachite /'mælə,kɔɪt/ n copper carbonate occurring as a green mineral, used as an ore and for making ornaments.

malacology /,mælə'kɒlədʒi/ n the science of molluscs.—**malacological** adj.—**malacologist** n.

malacostracan /,mælə'kɒstrəkən/ adj (crustacean) soft-shelled.

maladjusted /,mælə'dʒʌstəd/ adj poorly adjusted, esp to the social environment.—**maladjustment** n.

maladministration /,mælədmɪnɪ'streɪʃən/ n corrupt or incompetent management of public affairs.—**maladminister** vb.

maladroit /,mælə'drɔɪt/ adj clumsy.—**maladroitness** n.

malady /'mælədi/ n (pl **maladies**) a disease, illness.

Malaga /'mæləgə/ n a sweet, white dessert wine from the Spanish port of Malaga.

Malagasy /,mælə'gæsi/ n (pl **Malagasy, Malagasies**) a native of Madagascar; the language of Madagascar. • adj pertaining to Madagascar, its language or people.

malaise /mə'leɪz/ n a feeling of discomfort or of uneasiness.

malamute /'mælə,mjuːt/ n a powerful Alaskan dog with a dense grey coat used to pull sledges.—also **malemute**.

malanders /'mæləndərz/ n sing a disease in horses, the main symptom of which is an eczema-like patch on the horse's leg.

malapert /'mælə,pɜrt/ adj (arch) impudent; pert; saucy.

malapropism /'mæləprɒ,pizəm/ n a ludicrous misuse of words.—**malapropian** adj.

malapropos /,mælæprə'po:/ adj out of place, ill-timed. • adv in an inapproriate way; unseasonably.

malar /'meɪlər/ adj of or relating to the cheek or cheekbone. • n the cheekbone.

malaria /mə'leriə/ n an infectious disease caused by mosquito bites, and characterized by recurring attacks of fevers and chills.—**malarial** adj.

malcontent /'mælkən,tent/ adj discontented and potentially rebellious.—also n.

mal de mer /,mældə'mer/ n seasickness.

male /meɪl/ adj denoting or of the sex that fertilizes the ovum; of, like, or suitable for men and boys; masculine. • n a male person, animal or plant.—**maleness** n.

malediction /,mælə'dɪkʃən/ n a curse, an imprecation; a denunciation of evil; a slander.—**maledictory** adj.

malefactor /'mælə,fæktər/ n a criminal, an evildoer.—**malefaction** n.

maleficent /mə'lɛfɪsənt/ *adj* harmful, causing evil; mischief-making.—**maleficently** *adv*.—**maleficence** *n*.

malemute /'mælə'mjuːt/ *see* **malamute**.

malevolent /mə'lɛvələnt/ *adj* ill-disposed toward others; spiteful, malicious.—**malevolence** *n*.—**malevolently** *adv*.

malfeasance /mæl'fiːzəns/ *n* (*law*) an illegal action, official misconduct.—**malfeasant** *adj*, *n*.

malformation /ˌmælfɔr'meɪʃən/ *n* faulty or abnormal formation of a body or part.—**malformed** *adj*.

malfunction /mæl'fʌŋkʃən/ *n* faulty functioning. • *vi* to function wrongly.

malgré lui *Fr.* /'mɑlgreɪˌluːiː/ *adv* against one's wishes, despite oneself.

malic acid /'mælɪk/ *adj* a colourless crystalline acid derived from fruit, *esp* apples.

malice /'mælɪs/ *n* active ill will, intention to inflict injury upon another.—**malicious** *adj*.—**maliciously** *adv*.—**maliciousness** *n*.

malign /mə'laɪn/ *adj* harmful; evil. • *vt* to slander; to defame.—**malignity** *n*.—**malignly** *adv*.

malignant /mə'lɪgnənt/ *adj* having a wish to harm others; injurious; (*disease*) rapidly spreading, resistant to treatment, *esp* of a tumour.—**malignancy** *n*.—**malignantly** *adv*.

malignity /-nəti/ *n* (*pl* **malignities**) the state of being malignant or deadly; (*often pl*) (an act of) malice; virulence.

malinger /mə'lɪŋgər/ *vi* to feign illness in order to evade work, duty.—**malingerer** *n*.

malison /'mælizən/ or /-sən/ *n* (*arch*) a curse, execration.

mall /mɒl/ *n* a shaded avenue, open to the public; (*also US*) short for shopping mall; a shopping street for pedestrians only; an enclosed shopping centre.

mallard /'mælərd/ or /-ɒrd/ *n* (*pl* **mallard, mallards**) a common wild duck, the ancestor of domestic breeds of duck.

malleable /'mæliəbəl/ *adj* pliable; capable of being shaped.—**malleability** *n*.

mallee /'mæli/ *n* a dwarf eucalyptus found in Australia; (*with the*) a sparsely populated area in Australia, the bush.

mallemuck /'mælə,mʌk/ *n* any of various sea birds, incl the fulmar and petrel.

malleolar /mə'liːələr/ *adj* pertaining to the ankle.

mallet /'mælət/ *n* a small, *usu* wooden-headed, short-handled hammer; a long-handled version for striking the ball in the games of polo and croquet.

mallow /'mæloː/ *n* any of a widely found genus of plants with pink flowers and palm-shaped leaves; a similar plant, *eg* marshmallow.

malm /mɒm/ *n* soft friable limestone rock; a loamy soil derived from this; a clay and chalk mixture used as an ingredient in brickmaking.

malmsey /'mɒmzi/ *n* (*pl* **malmseys**) a strong, full-flavoured sweet wine orig from Greece but now also made in Madeira, Spain, etc.

malnutrition /ˌmælnju:'trɪʃən/ or /ˌmælnjuː-/ *n* lack of nutrition.

malodorous /mæl'oːdərəs/ *adj* having a foul smell, bad-smelling.—**malodorously** *adv*.—**malodorousness** *n*.

Malpighian /mæl'pɪgiən/ *adj* (*anat*) pertaining to various structures, such as the capillary system, discovered by the Italian anatomist Marcello Malpighi (1628-94).

malpractice /mæl'præktəs/ *n* professional misconduct, *esp* by a medical practitioner.

malt /mɒlt/ *n* a cereal grain, such as barley, which is soaked and dried and used in brewing; (*inf*) malt liquor, malt whisky.—**malty** *adj*.

maltha /'mɒlθə/ *n* a natural black bitumen; a mineral wax.

Malthusian /mæl'θuːziən/ *adj* of or pertaining to the British political economist Thomas Malthus (1766-1834) or his theory, which maintains that population tends to outgrow its means of subsistence and should be checked by means of birth control. • *n* an advocate of this theory.—**Malthusianism** *n*.

maltose /'mɒltoːz/ *n* a sugar obtained from starch by the action of diatase or malt and used in bacteriological cultures and baby foods.

maltreat /mæl'triːt/ *vt* to treat roughly or badly.—**maltreatment** *n*.

maltster /'mɒltstər/ *n* a maker of or dealer in malt.

malvoisie /'mælvwəzi/ *n* a French dessert wine similar to malmsey.

mama /'mɒmə/ *n* (*inf*) mother.—*also* **mamma**.

mamba /'mæmbə/ *n* a partly tree-living green or black poisonous snake of tropical and southern Africa.

Mameluke /'mæmə,luːk/ *n* (*formerly*) a member of the ruling class in Egypt.

mamma[1] /'mɒmə/ *see* **mama**.

mamma[2] /'mæmə/ *n* (*pl* **mammae**) the milk-secreting organ of female mammals, such as the udder of a cow, or breast of a woman.—**mammary** *adj*.

mammal /'mæməl/ *n* any member of a class of warm-blooded vertebrates that suckle their young with milk.—**mammalian** *adj*.

mammalogy /mæ'mɒlədʒi/ *n* the branch of zoology involving the study of mammals.—**mammalogical** *adj*.—**mammalogist** *n*.

mammee /mæ'miː/ *n* a tropical American tree with edible fruit; the large red-skinned fruit from this tree.—*also* **mamee apple**.

mammiferous /mæ'mɪfərəs/ or /mə-/ *adj* having breasts.

mammilla /mæ'mɪlə/ or /mə-/ *n* (*pl* **mamillae**) a nipple; a nipple-shaped thing.

mammillary /'mæmə,lɛri/ *adj* of or like the breast or a nipple.

mammock /'mæmək/ *vt* (*inf*) to break in pieces; to shred. • *n* a small piece.

mammon /'mæmən/ *n* riches regarded as an object of worship and greedy pursuit; (*with cap*) (*Bible*) the pursuit of wealth personified as a false god.—**mammonism** *n*.—**mammonist** *n*.

mammoth /'mæməθ/ *n* an extinct elephant with long, curved tusks. • *adj* enormous.

mammy /'mæmi/ *n* (*pl* **mammies**) (*inf*) mother, as used by a child.

man /mæn/ *n* (*pl* **men**) a human being, *esp* an adult male; the human race; an adult male with manly qualities, *eg* courage, virility; a male servant; an individual person; a person with specific qualities for a task, etc; an ordinary soldier, as opposed to an officer; a member of a team, etc; a piece in games such as chess, draughts, etc; a husband. • *vt* (**manning, manned**) to provide with men for work, defence, etc.

manacle /'mænəkəl/ *n* (*usu pl*) a handcuff. • *vt* to handcuff; to restrain.

manage /'mænɪdʒ/ *vt* to control the movement or behaviour of; to have charge of; to direct; to succeed in accomplishing. • *vi* to carry on business; to contrive to get along.—**manageable** *adj*.

management /'mænɪdʒmənt/ *n* those carrying out the administration of a business; the managers collectively; the technique of managing or controlling.

manager /'mænɪdʒər/ *n* a person who manages a company, organization, etc; an agent who looks after the business affairs of an actor, writer, etc; a person who organizes the training of a sports team; a person who manages efficiently.

manageress /ˌmænɪdʒə'rɛs/ *n* a woman who manages a business, shop, etc.

managerial /ˌmænɪ'dʒiːriəl/ *adj* of or pertaining to a manager or management.—**managerially** *adv*.

manakin /'mænəkɪn/ *n* any of a genus of small South American birds with bright plumage and short beaks; a manikin.

mañana /mæn'jɒnə/ *adv* tomorrow; by and by. • *n* an unspecified time in the future.

man-at-arms /'mænæt'ɑrmz/ *n* (*pl* **men-at-arms**) an armed soldier, *esp* of medieval times.

manatee /ˌmænə'tiː/ *n* a large aquatic animal resembling a whale found in tropical seas, the sea cow.

manchineel /ˌmæntʃɪ'niːl/ *n* a poisonous tropical American tree.

manciple /'mænsɪpəl/ *n* a catering official or steward, *esp* in a monastery, college, or Inn of Court.

Mancunian /mæŋ'kjuːniən/ *adj* of Manchester. • *n* a citizen of Manchester.

mandamus /mæn'deɪməs/ *n* (*pl* **mandamuses**) (*law*) (*formerly*) a writ issued by a superior court directing the person or inferior court to whom it is issued to perform some specified act or public duty.

mandarin /'mændərɪn/ *n* (*formerly*) a high-ranking bureaucrat of the Chinese empire; any high-ranking official, *esp* one given to pedantic sometimes obscure public pronouncements; (*with cap*) the Beijing dialect that is the official pronunciation of the Chinese language; the fruit of a small spiny Chinese tree that has been developed in cultivation.—*also* **tangerine**.

mandarin collar *n* a narrow, stand-up collar, open in front.

mandatary /'mændə,tɛri/ *n* (*pl* **mandataries**) a person or nation to whom a mandate is given.

mandate /ˈmændeɪt/ *n* an order or command; the authority to act on the behalf of another, *esp* the will of constituents expressed to their representatives in legislatures. • *vt* to entrust by mandate.

mandatory /ˈmændəˌtɔri/ *adj* of, containing, or having the nature of a mandate; required by mandate; compulsory; (*nation*) holding a mandate. • *n* a mandatary.—**mandatorily** *adv*.

mandible /ˈmændɪbəl/ *n* the lower jaw of a vertebrate; the mouth parts of an insect; either jaw of a beaked animal.—**mandibular** *adj*.

mandolin /ˌmændəˈlɪn/ or /ˈmæn-/, /-dɒ:-/ *n* a stringed instrument similar to a lute, with four or five pairs of strings.

mandragora /mænˈdrægərə/ *n* (*poet*) mandrake; a narcotic obtained from it.

mandrake /ˈmændreɪk/ *n* a plant of the nightshade family with narcotic properties that, in folklore, shrieked when uprooted; the May apple.

mandrel, mandril /ˈmændrəl/ *n* the shank of a lathe, to which work is fixed while turned; the revolving arbor of a circular saw or other machine tool; the spindle that drives the headstock of a lathe.

mandrill /ˈmændrɪl/ *n* a large baboon of West Africa, the male having a red and blue backside.

manducate /ˈmændjʊˌkeɪt/ *vt* (*poet*) to chew, eat.

mane /meɪn/ *n* long hair that grows on the back of the neck of the horse, lion, etc.

man-eater /ˈmæniːtər/ *n* an animal that eats human flesh.

manège, manege /mæˈneɪʒ/ *n* a school for training horses and teaching horsemanship; the movements of a trained horse.

manes /ˈmɒneɪz/ or /ˈmeɪniːz/ *n* (*pl: often cap*) in Ancient Rome, ancestral spirits, shades; gods of the lower world; *sing* the spirit of a dead person.

maneuver /məˈnuːvər/ or /-ˈnjuː-/ *see* **manoeuvre**.

manful /ˈmænfʊl/ *adj* showing courage and resolution.—**manfully** *adv*.

mangabey /ˈmæŋɡəˌbeɪ/ *n* (*pl* **mangabeys**) a large, slender, arboreal, African monkey.

manganate /ˈmæŋɡəˌneɪt/ *n* a salt of manganic acid.

manganese /ˈmæŋɡəˌniːz/ *n* a hard brittle metallic element; its oxide.

manganic /mænˈɡænɪk/ *adj* pertaining to, resembling, or containing manganese in the trivalent state.

mange /meɪndʒ/ *n* a skin disease affecting mainly domestic animals, which causes itching.

mangel-wurzel /ˈmæŋɡəlˌwɜrzəl/ *n* a variety of beet used as cattle-fodder.

manger /ˈmeɪndʒər/ *n* a trough in a barn or stable for livestock fodder.

mangle[1] /ˈmæŋɡəl/ *vt* to crush, mutilate; to spoil, ruin.

mangle[2] *n* a machine for drying and pressing sheets, etc between rollers. • *vt* to smooth through a mangle.

mango /ˈmæŋɡoː/ *n* (*pl* **mangoes**) a yellow-red fleshy tropical fruit with a firm central stone.

mangonel /ˈmæŋɡənəl/ *n* an ancient military engine for hurling stones.

mangosteen /ˈmæŋɡəˌstiːn/ *n* a tropical Indian tree; its red-brown, sweet, juicy fruit about the size of an orange.

mangrove /ˈmæŋɡroːv/ *n* a tropical tree or shrub with root-forming branches.

mangy /ˈmeɪndʒi/ *adj* (**mangier, mangiest**) having mange; scruffy, shabby.—**manginess** *n*.

manhandle /ˈmænˌhændəl/ *vt* to handle roughly; to move by human force.

manhole /ˈmænhoːl/ *n* a hole through which one can enter a sewer, drain, etc.

manhood /ˈmænhʊd/ *n* the state or time of being a man; virility; courage, etc.

man-hour /-aʊr/ *n* the time unit equal to one hour of work done by one person.

manhunt /ˈmænhʌnt/ *n* a hunt for a fugitive.—**manhunter** *n*.

mania /ˈmeɪniə/ *n* a mental disorder displaying sometimes violent behaviour and great excitement; great excitement or enthusiasm; a craze.

maniac /ˈmeɪniˌæk/ *n* a madman; a person with wild behaviour; a person with great enthusiasm for something.—**maniacal** *adj*.

manic /ˈmænɪk/ *adj* affected with, characterized by, or relating to mania.

manic-depressive /-dɪˈpresɪv/ *adj* of a mental disorder characterized by alternating periods of mania and deep depression. • *n* a person suffering from this.

Manichaeism, Manicheism /ˈmænɪˈkiːɪzəm/ *n* the doctrine of the Manicheans, who held the dualistic theory of two eternal equal beings or principles, light (God), the author of all good, and darkness (Evil or Satan), the author of all evil, locked in a constant struggle for ascendancy; any similar doctrine.—**Manichaean, Manichean** *n, adj*.

Manichee /ˈmænɪˈki/ *n* one of the sect of Manicheans.

manicure /ˈmænɪˌkjʊr/ *n* trimming, polishing etc of fingernails.—*also vt*.—**manicurist** *n*.

manifest /ˈmænɪˌfest/ *adj* obvious, clearly evident. • *vt* to make clear; to display, to reveal. • *n* a list of a ship's or aircraft's cargo; a list of passengers on an aircraft.—**manifestation** *n*.—**manifestly** *adv*.

manifestation /-ˈsteɪʃən/ *n* the act of manifesting; the state of being manifested; the demonstration of the reality or existence of a quality, person, etc; the form of revelation of an idea, divine being, etc.

manifesto /ˌmænɪˈfestoː/ *n* (*pl* **manifestoes, manifestos**) a public printed declaration of intent and policy issued by a government or political party.

manifold /ˈmænɪˌfoːld/ *adj* having many forms, parts, etc; of many sorts. • *n* a pipe (*eg* in an engine) with many inlets and outlets. • *vt* to make copies of.—**manifolder** *n*.

manikin /ˈmænɪkɪn/ *n* a little man, a dwarf; an anatomical model of the body; a mannequin.—*also* **mannikin**.

manila, manilla /məˈnɪlə/ *n* a strong, buff-coloured paper originally made from hemp from the Philippines.

manioc /ˈmænɪˌɒk/ *n* cassava, a tropical plant from the roots of which tapioca and cassava are prepared.

maniple /ˈmænɪpəl/ *n* (*formerly*) a band worn on the left arm by a priest at mass; a company of a Roman legion.

manipulate /məˈnɪpjʊˌleɪt/ *vt* to work or handle skilfully; to manage shrewdly or artfully, often in an unfair way.—**manipulation** *n*.—**manipulative** *adj*.—**manipulator** *n*.

manipulation /-ˈleɪʃən/ *n* the act or process of manipulating; the state of being manipulated; the movement of bones, etc, by a physiotherapist; shrewd or knowing management of others for one's own ends.—**manipulatory** *adj*.

manitou /ˌmænɪˈtuː/ *n* among some Indian peoples of northeast North America, a good or evil spirit.

mankind /mænˈkaɪnd/ *n* the human race.

manly /ˈmænli/ *adj* (**manlier, manliest**) appropriate in character to a man; strong; virile.—**manliness** *n*.

man-made /-ˈmeɪd/ *adj* manufactured or created by man; artificial, synthetic.

manna /ˈmænə/ *n* (*Bible*) the food miraculously given to the ancient Israelites in the wilderness; any help that comes unexpectedly.

manned /mænd/ *adj* performed by a person; (*spacecraft, etc*) having a human crew.

mannequin /ˈmænəkɪn/ *n* a model in a fashion show; a life-size model of the human body, used to fit or display clothes.

manner /ˈmænər/ *n* a method of way of doing something; behaviour; type or kind; habit; (*pl*) polite social behaviour.

mannered /ˈmænərd/ *adj* full of mannerisms; artificial, stylized, etc.

mannerism /ˈmænəˌrɪzəm/ *n* an idiosyncracy; an affected habit or style in dress, behaviour or gesture; (*with cap*) a post-Reformation movement in art that held that beauty should be represented as an ideal and used exaggeration and distortion of naturalistic forms to attain this.—**mannerist** *adj, n*.

mannerless /-ləs/ *n* rude, bad-mannered.

mannerly /ˈmænərli/ *adj* polite; respectful. • *adv* politely; respectfully.—**mannerliness** *n*.

mannikin /ˈmænəkɪn/ *see* **manikin**.

mannish /ˈmænɪʃ/ *adj* like or pertaining to a man; (*woman*) masculine, aping men.—**mannishly** *adv*.—**mannishness** *n*.

manoeuvre /məˈnuːvər/ *n* a planned and controlled movement of troops, warships, etc; a skilful or shrewd move; a stratagem. • *vti* to perform or cause to perform manoeuvres; to manage or plan skilfully; to move, get, make, etc by some scheme.—*also US* **maneuver**.—**maneuverable, manoeuvrable** *adj*.—**maneuverer, manoeuvrer** *n*.

man-of-war /ˌmænəvˈwɔr/ or /-əˈwɔr/ *n* (*pl* **men-of-war**) a (sailing) warship.

manometer /mə'nɒmɪtər/ *n* an instrument for measuring the pressure of gases and liquids.—**manometric, manometrical** *adj*.

manor /'mænər/ *n* a landed estate; the main house on such an estate; (*sl*) a police district.—**manorial** *adj*.

manpower /'mænpaʊr/ *n* power furnished by human strength; the collective availability for work of people in a given area.

manqué /'mɒŋkeɪ/ *adj* potential; unsuccessful, failed.

mansard (roof) /'mænsard/ *n* a roof with a break in its slope, the lower part being steeper than the upper.

manse /mæns/ *n* a nonconformist clergyman's house; (*Scot*) the house of a minister, *esp* a Church of Scotland parish minister; (*arch*) a large house.

manservant /'mæn,sərvənt/ *n* (*pl* **menservants**) a male servant, *esp* a valet.

mansion /'mænʃən/ *n* a large, imposing house.

manslaughter /'mæn,slɒtər/ *n* the killing of a human being by another, *esp* when unlawful but without malice.

mansuetude /'mænswɪ,tjuːd/ *n* (*arch*) gentleness, mildness.

manta (ray) /'mæntə/ *n* a very large fish with a flattened body and wing-like fins.

mantel /'mæntəl/ *n* the facing above a fireplace; the shelf above a fireplace.—*also* **mantelpiece**.

mantelet /'mæntəlɪt/ *n* a woman's short cape of the mid-19th century; a movable, protective screen, formerly used by besiegers, gunners, pioneers, etc.—*also* **mantlet**.

mantic /'mæntɪk/ *adj* of, having the power of, or pertaining to divination.

manticore /'mæntɪkər/ *n* a fabulous beast with a human head, the body of a lion, and the tail of a scorpion.

mantilla /mæn'tɪlə/ *n* a scarf, *usu* of lace, worn as a headdress in Spain and South America; a woman's light cloak or hood.

mantis /'mæntɪs/ *n* (*pl* **mantises, mantes**) an insect that preys on other insects.—*also* **praying mantis**.

mantissa /mæn'tɪsə/ *n* (*math*) the decimal part of a logarithm.

mantle /'mæntəl/ *n* a loose cloak; anything that envelops or conceals; a fine mesh cover on a gas or oil lamp that emits light by incandescence. • *vt* to cover as with a mantle. • *vi* to be or become covered.

mantlet /'mæntəlɪt/ *see* **mantelet**.

mantra /'mæntrə/ *n* (*Hinduism, Buddhism*) a devotional incantation used in prayer, meditation and in certain forms of yoga.

mantua /'mæntjʊə/ *n* a woman's loose gown of the 17th and 18th centuries, worn with the front of the skirt caught up or back to show an underskirt.

manual /'mænjʊəl/ *adj* of the hands; operated, done, or used by the hand; involving physical skill or hard work rather than the mind. • *n* a handy book for use as a guide, reference, etc; a book of instructions.—**manually** *adv*.

manufactory /,mænjʊ'fæktəri/ *n* (*pl* **manufactories**) (*obs*) a factory, workshop.

manufacture /,mænjʊ'fæktʃər/ *vt* to make, *esp* on a large scale, using machinery; to invent, fabricate. • *n* the production of goods by manufacturing.—**manufacturer** *n*.

manumit /,mænjʊ'mɪt/ *vt* (**manumitting, manumitted**) to release from slavery; to free.—**manumission** *n*.—**manumitter** *n*.

manure /mə'nʊr/ *or* /-'njʊr/ *n* animal dung used to fertilize soil. • *vt* to spread manure on.

manus /'meɪnəs/ *n* (*pl* **manus**) (*zool*) the hand or that part of the anatomy corresponding to the hand; in ancient Roman law, the fact of a woman's legal subjugation to her husband.

manuscript /'mænjʊskrɪpt/ *n* a book or document that is handwritten or typewritten as opposed to printed; an author's original handwritten or typewritten copy as submitted to a publisher before typesetting and printing.

many /'mɛni/ *adj* (**more, most**) numerous. • *n* a large number of persons or things.

manyplies /'mɛni,plaɪz/ *n sing* a ruminant's third stomach, the omasum.

many-sided /-,saɪdɪd/ *adj* with many aspects; versatile.—**many-sidedness** *n*.

Maori /'maʊri/ *n* (*pl* **Maoris, Maori**) a member of the indigenous peoples of New Zealand; their language.—*also adj*.

map /mæp/ *n* a representation of all or part of the earth's surface, showing either natural features as continents and seas, etc or man-made features as roads, railways etc. • *vt* (**mapping, mapped**) to make a map of.

maple /'meɪpəl/ *n* a tree with two-winged fruits, grown for shade, wood, or sap; its hard light-coloured wood; the flavour of the syrup or sugar made from the sap of the sugar maple.

maple leaf *n* the leaf of the maple tree, considered as an emblem of Canada.

Mar. *abbr* = March.

mar /mɒr/ *vt* (**marring, marred**) to blemish, to spoil, to impair.

marabout[1], **marabou** /'mærə,buː/ *n* a large African stork with handsome feathers and a short neck; its down, used as trimming, etc; a material produced from a fine raw silk.

marabout[2], 'mærə,buːt/ *n* in North Africa, a Muslim hermit or saint; the shrine or burial place of a marabout.

maraca /mə'rɒkə/ *or* /-'rækə/ *n* a dried gourd or plastic shell filled with beans, pebbles, etc and shaken as a rhythm instrument.

maraschino /,mærə'ʃiːnoː/ *or* /-'skiːnoː/, /,mɛrə-/ *n* a strong sweet liqueur made from a type of wild cherry.

maraschino cherry *n* a cherry preserved in maraschino.

marasmus /mə'ræzməs/ *n* emaciation or atrophy, *esp* in babies.—**marasmic** *adj*.

marathon /'mɛrəθɒn/ *n* a foot race of 26 miles, 385 yards (42.195 km); any endurance contest.

maraud /mə'rɒd/ *vi* to roam in search of plunder.—**marauder** *n*.—**marauding** *adj*.

marble /'marbəl/ *n* a hard limestone rock that takes a high polish; a block or work of art made of marble; a little ball of stone, glass, etc; (*pl*) a children's game played with such balls; (*pl*) (*sl*) wits. • *adj* of or like marble.—**marbly** *adj*.

marbled /'marbəld/ *adj* veined or mottled like marble; (*meat*) streaked with fat.

marc /mark/ *n* (*winemaking*) the refuse from pressed fruit; a brandy derived from this.

marcasite /'markə,saɪt/ *n* white iron pyrites; a white metal, *esp* steel, cut and polished for use in jewellery.

marcel (wave) /mar'sɛl/ *n* a style of artificially waving the hair, popular in the 1920s and 1930s. • *vt* (**marcelling, marcelled**) to style in regular waves.

marcescent /mar'sɛsənt/ *adj* (*bot*) withering without falling off.—**marcescence** *n*.

March /martʃ/ *n* the third month of the year having 31 days.

march *vi* to walk with regular steps, as in military formation; to advance steadily. • *vt* to make a person or group march. • *n* a steady advance; a regular, steady step; the distance covered in marching; a piece of music for marching.—**marcher** *n*.

marching orders *npl* official orders for infantry to move to a particular destination; (*inf*) a notice of dismissal.

marchioness /,marʃə'nes/ *or* /'mar-/ *n* the wife or widow of a marquess; a woman of the rank of marquess.

Mardi gras /'mardi,grɒ/ *n* the last day before Lent, Shrove Tuesday, a day of carnival in some cities, *esp* New Orleans.

mare /mɛr/ *n* a mature female horse, mule, donkey.

mare clausum /'mɒreɪ'klaʊsum/ *or* /-ri-/ *n* (*law*) a body of water under one country's jurisdiction and closed to foreign ships.

mare liberum /-'lɪbərəm/ *n* (*law*) a body of water open to ships of all countries.

maremma /mə'rɛmə/ *n* (*pl* **maremme**) an unhealthy marshy coastal district, *esp* in Italy.

mare's-tail /'mɛrz,teɪl/ *n* an aquatic plant with tiny flowers and tapering leaves; a wisp of trailing alto-cirrus cloud indicating strong winds at high altitude.

margaric /mar'gærɪk/ *or* /-'gar-/, /'margərɪk/ *adj* pertaining to, or like, a pearl.

margarine /'mardʒərɪn/ *n* a butter substitute made from vegetable and animal fats, etc.

margarite /'margə,raɪt/ *n* a pearly translucent mineral related to mica; a bead-like rock formation.

margay /'margeɪ/ *n* a South American tiger cat.

margin /'mardʒɪn/ *n* a border, edge; the blank border of a printed or written page; an amount beyond what is needed; provision for increase, error, etc; (*commerce*) the difference between cost and selling price.

marginal /-əl/ *adj* written in the margin; situated at the margin or border; close to the lower limit of acceptability; very slight, insignificant; (*Brit politics*) denoting a constituency where the sitting MP has only a small majority. • *n* a marginal constituency.—**marginally** *adv*.

marginalia /,mardʒɪ'neɪliə/ *npl* notes written in the margin of a book, etc.

marginalize /'mɑrdʒɪnəˌlaɪz/ vt to transfer someone away from the centre of affairs in order to render them powerless.

marginate /'mɑrdʒɪˌneɪt/ adj (biol) having a margin. • vt to border something with a margin.—**margination** n.

margrave /'mɑrgreɪv/ n (formerly) a German nobleman, one rank above a count.

margraviate, margravate /'mɑrgrəvət/ n the domain or jurisdiction of a margrave.

margravine /'mɑrgrəˌviːn/ n a female margrave; a margrave's wife or widow.

marguerite /ˌmɑrgrə'riːt/ n a large daisy with white or yellow flowers.

Marian /'meriən/ adj pertaining to the Virgin Mary, or to Mary, Queen of England, or to Mary, Queen of Scots. • n one who worships the Virgin Mary; a partisan of Mary, Queen of England or Mary, Queen of Scots.

marigold /'merɪˌgoːld/ n a plant with a yellow or orange flower.

marijuana, marihuana /ˌmerɪ'wɒnə/ n a narcotic obtained by smoking the dried flowers and leaves of the hemp plant.—also **cannabis, pot.**

marimba /mə'rɪmbə/ n a South American xylophone.

marina /mə'riːnə/ n a small harbour with pontoons, docks, services, etc for yachts and pleasure craft.

marinade /'merɪneɪd/ or /-'neɪd/ n a seasoning liquid in which meat, fish, etc is soaked to enhance flavour or to tenderize it before cooking. • vt to soak in a marinade.—also **marinate.**

marine /mə'riːn/ adj of, in, near, or relating to the sea; maritime; nautical; naval. • n a soldier trained for service on land or sea; naval or merchant ships.

mariner /'mærɪnər/ n a seaman, sailor.

Mariolatry /ˌmeri'ɒlətri/ n the exaggerated worship of the Virgin Mary.

marionette /ˌmeriə'net/ n a little jointed doll or puppet moved by strings or wires.

marital /'merɪtəl/ adj of marriage, matrimonial.

maritime /'merɪˌtaɪm/ adj on, near, or living near the sea; of navigation, shipping, etc.

marjoram /'mɑrdʒərəm/ n a fragrant herb used in cooking and salads.

mark[1] /mɑrk/ n a spot, scratch, etc on a surface; a distinguishing sign or characteristic; a cross made instead of a signature; a printed or written symbol, as a punctuation mark; a brand or label on an article showing the maker, etc; an indication of some quality, character, etc; a grade for academic work; a standard of quality; impression, influence, etc; a target; (sl) a potential victim for a swindle. • vt to make a mark or marks on; to identify as by a mark; to show plainly; to heed; to grade, rate; (Brit football) to stay close to an opponent so as to hinder his play.

mark[2] n the former monetary unit of Germany, now replaced by the euro.

marked /mɑrkt/ adj having a mark or marks; noticeable; obvious.—**markedly** adv.

marker /'mɑrkər/ n one that marks; something used for marking.

market /'mɑrkət/ n a meeting of people for buying and selling merchandise; a space or building in which a market is held; the chance to sell or buy; demand for (goods, etc); a region where goods can be sold; a section of the community offering demand for goods. • vti to offer for sale; to sell, buy domestic provisions.—**marketability** n.—**marketable** adj.

marketing /'mɑrkətɪŋ/ n act of buying or selling; all the processes involved in moving goods from the producer to the consumer.

market-making n the activity of buying and selling stocks, shares, bonds, securities, etc.—**market-maker** n.

marketplace /'mɑrkətˌpleɪs/ n a market in a public square; the world of economic trade and activity; a sphere in which ideas, opinions, etc compete for acceptance.

market research n the gathering of factual information from consumers concerning their preferences for goods and services.

marking /'mɑrkɪŋ/ n the conferring of a mark or marks; the characteristic arrangement of marks, as on fur or feathers.

marksman /'mɑrksmən/ n (pl **marksmen**) one who is skilled at shooting.—**marksmanship** n.

markup /'mɑrkʌp/ n a selling at an increased price; the amount of increase.—also vt.

marl[1] /mɑrl/ n a mixture of clay and carbonate of lime, used as a manure. • vt to manure with marl.—**marly** adj.

marl[2] vt (naut) to wind with marlines, securing with a hitch at each turn.

marline, marlin, marling /'mɑrlɪn/ n (naut) a two-stranded cord, often tarred, used for winding round ropes, splicing, etc.

marlinespike, marlinspike, marlingspike /'mɑrlɪnˌspaɪk/ n a pointed piece of iron used for opening the strands of a rope in splicing, etc.

marmalade /'mɑrməˌleɪd/ n a jam-like preserve made from oranges, sugar and water.

marmoreal /mɑr'mɔriəl/, **marmorean** /-ən/ adj of or like marble.

marmoset /'mɑrməˌzet/ n a small monkey of South and Central America.

marmot /'mɑrmət/ n a widely distributed rodent with rough fur, a bushy tail and short legs.

maroon[1] /mə'ruːn/ n a dark brownish red.—also adj; a type of distress rocket.

maroon[2] vt to abandon alone, esp on a desolate island; to leave helpless and alone.

marque /mɑrk/ n a brand of a product, esp a car.

marquee /mɑr'kiː/ n a large tent used for entertainment; a canopy over an entrance, as to a theatre.

marquess /'mɑrkwɪs/ n in the UK, a title of nobility ranking between a duke and an earl.

marquetry, marqueterie /'mɑrkɪtri/ n (pl **marquetries, marqueteries**) decorative inlaid veneers of wood, ivory, etc used esp in furniture.

marquis /mɑr'kiː/ n (pl **marquises, marquis**) (Europe) a nobleman equivalent in rank to a British marquess.

marquisate /-sət/ n the estate, dignity, or lordship of a marquis.

marquise /mɑr'kiːz/ n a marchioness; a gemstone or ring setting cut in an oval pointed form.

marriage /'merɪdʒ/ or /'mæ-/ n the legal contract by which a woman and man become wife and husband; a wedding, either religious or civil; a close union.

marriageable /'merɪdʒəbəl/ or /'mæ-/ adj of an age to marry.—**marriageability** n.

marron glacé /ˌmæˌrõglæ'seɪ/ n (pl **marrons glacés**) a cooked chestnut coated with sugar.

marrow /'meroː/ or /'mæ-/ n the fatty tissue in the cavities of bones; the best part or essence of anything; a widely grown green fruit eaten as a vegetable.

marrowbone /-ˌboːn/ n a bone containing marrow used in cooking.

marrowfat /-ˌfæt /, **marrow pea** n a late variety of pea that has large seeds; the seed of one of these.

marry[1] /'meri/ or /'mæri/ vb (**marrying, married**) vt to join as wife and husband; to take in marriage; to unite. • vi to get married.

marry[2] interj (arch) indeed, forsooth.

Mars /mɑrz/ n the Roman god of war; the planet next to Earth, further away from the sun; (alchemy) iron.

Marsala /mɑr'sælə/ or /-'sɒlə/ n a sweet fortified wine from Sicily.

Marseillaise /ˌmɑrseɪ'jez/ adj pertaining to the city of Marseilles in France or to its inhabitants. • n the French national anthem, orig a well-known song of the French Revolution, composed in 1792.

marsh /'mɑrʃ/ n an area of boggy, poorly drained land.—**marshiness** n.—**marshy** adj.

marshal /'mɑrʃəl/ n in some armies, a general officer of the highest rank; an official in charge of ceremonies, parades, etc. • vt (**marshalling, marshalled** or **marshaling, marshaled**) (ideas, troops) to arrange in order; to guide.—**marshaller** n.

marsh mallow /'mɑrʃˌmeloː/ or /-ˌmæloː/ n a perennial plant with a pink flower and a mucilaginous root used in confectionery and medicine.

marshmallow n a soft spongy confection made of sugar, gelatin, etc; (formerly) a sweet paste made from the root of the marsh mallow.

marsupial /mɑr'suːpiəl/ adj of an order of mammals that carry their young in a pouch. • n an animal of this kind, as a kangaroo, opossum.

marsupium /-əm/ n (pl **marsupia**) in female marsupials, an external pouch for carrying and nurturing young.

mart /mɑrt/ n a market.

martagon /'mɑrtəgən/ n a variety of lily with purple-red flowers found in Europe and Asia; a Turk's-cap lily.

Martello tower /mɑr'teloː/ n (formerly) a small round fort used for coastal defence.

marten /'mɑrtən/ n (pl **martens, marten**) a carnivorous tree-dwelling weasel-like mammal.

martial /'mɑrʃəl/ adj warlike; military.—**martially** adv.

martial arts *npl* systems of self-defence, *usu* from the Orient, practised as sports, as karate or judo.

martial law *n* rule by military authorities over civilians, as during a war or political emergency.

Martian /'marʃən/ *adj* of or relating to the planet Mars. • *n* an inhabitant of Mars.

martin /'martɪn/ *n* one of various types of bird similar to the swallow, with a characteristic shape of tail; the house martin.

martinet /ˌmartɪ'nɛt/ *n* one who exerts strong discipline.— **martinetish, martinettish** *adj*.

martingale, martingal /'martɪŋˌgeɪl/ *n* a broad strap passing from the noseband to the girth of a horse between its forelegs to keep its head down and prevent it from rearing; a gambling system of doubling successive stakes; (*naut*) a short spar under the bowsprit used as a lower stay for the jib boom or flying jib boom.

martini /mar'tiːni/ *n* (*trademark*) (*often with cap*) Italian vermouth; a cocktail of gin and vermouth.

Martinmas /'martɪnməs/ *n* St Martin's Day, November 11, a Christian festival; one of the Scottish quarter days.

martlet /'martlət/ *n* (*arch*) a martin; (*her*) a bird without legs or beak.

martyr /'martər/ *n* a person tortured for a belief or cause; a person who suffers from an illness. • *vt* to kill as a martyr; to make a martyr of.—**martyrdom** *n*.

martyrize /-ˌraɪz/ *vt* to martyr.

martyrology /ˌmartə'rɒlədʒi/ *n* (*pl* **martyrologies**) a register or history of martyrs; the study of the lives of the martyrs.— **martyrological, martyrologic** *adj*.—**martyrologist** *n*.

martyry /'martəri/ *n* (*pl* **martyries**) a shrine in honour of a martyr.

marvel /'marvəl/ *n* anything wonderful; a miracle. • *vti* (**marvelling, marvelled** *or* **marveling, marveled**) to become filled with wonder, surprise, etc.—**marvellous, marvelous** *adj*.

Marxian /'marksɪən/ *n* a student or advocate of Marxism.—*also adj*.

Marxism /'marksɪzəm/ *n* the theory and practice developed by Karl Marx and Friedrich Engels advocating public ownership of the means of production and the dictatorship of the proletariat until the establishment of a classless society.—**Marxist** *adj, n*.

marzipan /'marzɪˌpæn/ *or* /-'pæn/ *n* a paste made from ground almonds, sugar and egg white, used to coat cakes or make confectionery.

mascara /mæ'skerə/ *n* a cosmetic for darkening the eyelashes.

mascle /'mæsəl/ *n* (*her*) a lozenge perforated with a lozenge shape; a voided lozenge.

mascot /'mæskɒt/ *n* a person, animal or thing thought to bring good luck.

masculine /'mæskjʊlɪn/ *adj* having characteristics of or appropriate to the male sex; (*gram*) of the male gender.—**masculinity** *n*.

MASH *abbr* = mobile army surgical hospital.

mash /mæʃ/ *n* any soft, pulpy mass; crushed malt and hot water for brewing; (*inf*) mashed potatoes. • *vt* to crush into a mash.

mashie /'mæʃi/ *n* (*formerly*) an iron golf club with a deep, short blade, more or less lofted.

mask[1] /mask/ *n* a covering to conceal or protect the face; a moulded likeness of the face; anything that conceals or disguises; a respirator placed over the nose and mouth to aid or prevent inhalation of a gas; (*surgery*) a protective gauze placed over the nose and mouth to prevent the spread of germs; (*photog*) a screen used to cover part of a sensitive surface to prevent exposure by light. • *vt* to cover or conceal as with a mask; to disguise one's intentions or character.—**masked** *adj*.

mask[2] *see* **masque**.

masker /'mæskər/ *n* a masked person; a participant in a masque or masquerade.—*also* **masquer**.

masochism /'mæsəˌkɪzəm/ *n* abnormal pleasure, *esp* sexual, obtained from having physical or mental pain inflicted on one by another person.—**masochist** *n*.—**masochistic** *adj*.

mason /'meɪsən/ *n* a person skilled in working or building with stone; (*with cap*) a Freemason.

masonic /mə'sɒnɪk/ *adj* (*often cap*) relating to Freemasonry.

masonry /'meɪsənri/ *n* (*pl* **masonries**) stonework.

Masora, Masorah /mə'sɔrə/ *or* /mæsə'rɒ/ *n* a critical work in Hebrew by the rabbis of the 6-10th cents., indicating how the verbal text of the Bible is to be written in accordance with ancient rules; the critical notes and commentaries of this.—**Masoretic** *adj*.

masque /mæsk/ *n* a poetic drama with pageantry, pantomime, dance, song, etc, popular in 16th and 17th-century England; the words and music for one of these; a masquerade.—*also* **mask**.

masquer /'mæskər/ *see* **masker**.

masquerade /ˌmæskə'reɪd/ *n* a ball or party at which fancy dress and masks are worn; a pretence, false show. • *vi* to take part in a masquerade; to pretend to be what one is not.—**masquerader** *n*.

Mass /mæs/ *n* (*RC Church*) the celebration of the Eucharist.

mass /mæs/ *n* (*pl* **masses**) a quantity of matter of indefinite shape and size; a large quantity or number; bulk; size; the main part; (*physics*) the property of a body expressed as a measure of the amount of material contained in it; (*pl*) the common people, *esp* the lower social classes. • *adj* of or for the masses or for a large number. • *vti* to gather or form into a mass.

massacre /'mæsəkər/ *n* the cruel and indiscriminate killing of many people or animals. • *vt* to kill in large numbers.

massage /mə'sɒʒ/ *or* /-'sɒdʒ/ *n* a kneading and rubbing of the muscles to stimulate the circulation of the blood. • *vt* to give a massage to.

massé shot /mæ'seɪ/ *n* in billiards, a stroke with the cue held upright, *usu* to cause the ball to curve round another ball before it hits the intended ball.

masseur /mə'sər/ *n* a man who gives a massage professionally.— **masseuse** *nf*.

massif /mæ'siːf/ *or* /'mæsɪf/ *n* a central mountain mass; a large plateau with distinct edges.

massive /'mæsɪv/ *adj* big, solid, or heavy; large and imposing; relatively large in comparison to normal; extensive.—**massively** *adv*.—**massiveness** *n*.

mass media *npl* newspapers, radio, television, and other means of communication with large numbers of people.

mass production *n* quantity production of goods, *esp* by machinery and division of labour.

massy /'mæsi/ *adj* (**massier massiest**) (*arch*) massive.

mast /mæst/ *n* a tall vertical pole used to support the sails on a ship; a vertical pole from which a flag is flown; a tall structure supporting a television or radio aerial.

mastaba, mastabah /'mæstəbə/ *n* an early Egyptian tomb with a flat roof, the prototype of the pyramids.

mast cell *n* a large blood-borne cell that has a fast-acting role in the body's immune system in fighting inflammation.

mastectomy /mæs'tɛktəmi/ *n* the removal of a breast by surgery.

master /'mæstər/ *n* a man who rules others or has control over something, *esp* the head of a household; an employer; an owner of an animal or slave; the captain of a merchant ship; a male teacher in a private school; an expert craftsman; a writer or painter regarded as great; an original from which a copy can be made, *esp* a phonograph record or magnetic tape; (*with cap*) a title for a boy; one holding an advanced academic degree. • *adj* being a master; chief; main; controlling. • *vt* to be or become master of; (*in art, etc*) to become expert.—**mastership** *n*.

master-at-arms /-ət'armz/ *n* (*pl* **masters-at-arms**) a ship's chief petty officer with responsibility for policing, administration, etc.

masterful /'mæstərˌfʊl/ *adj* acting the part of a master; domineering; expert; skilful.—**masterfully** *adv*.—**masterfulness** *n*.

masterly /-li/ *adj* expert; skilful.—**masterliness** *n*.

mastermind /-ˌmaɪnd/ *n* a very clever person, *esp* one who plans or directs a project. • *vt* to be the mastermind of.

masterpiece /-ˌpiːs/ *n* a work done with extraordinary skill; the greatest work of a person or group.

masterstroke /-ˌstroːk/ *n* brilliant stroke of policy, skill, etc.

masterwork /-ˌwərk/ *n* a masterpiece.

mastery /'mæstəri/ *or* /-tri/ *n* control as by a master; victory; expertise.

masthead /'mæsthɛd/ *n* the top of a mast; the title and ownership details, etc of a newspaper or periodical printed on the front page.

mastic /'mæstɪk/ *n* an aromatic resin from mastic trees used chiefly in varnishes; a type of putty used for sealing wood, plaster, etc.

masticate /'mæstɪˌkeɪt/ *vt* to chew food before swallowing; to reduce to a pulp.—**mastication** *n*.—**masticator** *n*.

masticatory /-kəˌtɔri/ *adj* adapted for, or pertaining to, chewing. • *n* (*pl* **masticatories**) (*med*) something chewed in order to promote the flow of saliva.

mastiff /'mæstɪf/ *n* a breed of large, thickset dogs used chiefly as watchdogs.

mastitis /mæˈstaɪtɪs/ *n* an inflammation of a female breast or an udder.

mastodon /ˈmæstəˌdɒn/ *n* any of an extinct genus of mammals allied to the elephant.—**mastodonic** *adj*.

mastoid /ˈmæstɔɪd/ *n* the bony prominence behind the ear.

masturbate /ˈmæstərˌbeɪt/ *vi* to manually stimulate one's sexual organs to achieve orgasm without sexual intercourse.—**masturbation** *n*.

mat¹ /mæt/ *n* a piece of material of woven fibres, etc, used for protection, as under a vase, etc, or on the floor; a thick pad used in wrestling, gymnastics, etc; anything interwoven or tangled into a thick mass. • *vti* (**matting, matted**) to cover as with a mat; to interweave or tangle into a thick mass.

mat² *adj* without lustre, dull.—*also* **matt**.

matador /ˈmætəˌdɔr/ *n* the bullfighter who kills the bull with a sword.

match¹ /mætʃ/ *n* a thin strip of wood or cardboard tipped with a chemical that ignites under friction.

match² *n* any person or thing equal or similar to another; two persons or things that go well together; a contest or game; a mating or marriage. • *vt* to join in marriage; to put in opposition (with, against); to be equal or similar to; (*one thing*) to suit to another. • *vi* to be equal, similar, suitable, etc.

matchboard /ˈmætʃbɔrd/ *n* one of a number of thin planks tongued and grooved to fit together, used for panelling, etc.

matchbox /-bɒks/ *n* a small box for holding matches.

matchless /-ləs/ *adj* unequalled.—**matchlessly** *adv*.

matchmaker /-ˌmeɪkər/ *n* a person who arranges marriages for people; one who schemes to bring about the marriage of two others; a maker of matches.

match play *n* (*golf*) scoring by the number of holes won as opposed to strokes played.

match point *n* (*tennis, badminton, etc*) the situation where the winner of the next point wins the match.

matchwood /ˈmætʃwʊd/ *n* wood suitable for making matches; wood splinters or fragments.

maté /ˈmæteɪ/ *n* an evergreen South American shrub, related to holly; an infusion of its dried leaves which makes a mildly stimulating tea,.—*also* **Paraguay tea**.

mate¹ /meɪt/ *n* an associate or colleague; (*inf*) a friend; one of a matched pair; a marriage partner; the male or female of paired animals; an officer of a merchant ship, ranking below the master. • *vti* to join as a pair; to couple in marriage or sexual union.

mate² *vt* to checkmate.

matelote /ˈmætloː/ *n* a stew of fish cooked with wine, etc.

mater /ˈmeɪtər/ *n* (*sl*) mother.

materfamilias /ˌmeɪtərfəˈmɪliˌæs/ *n* (*pl* **matresfamilias**) the mother of a family or mistress of a household.

material /məˈtiːriəl/ *adj* of, derived from, or composed of matter, physical; of the body or bodily needs, comfort, etc, not spiritual; important, essential, etc. • *n* what a thing is, or may be made of; elements or parts; cloth, fabric; (*pl*) tools, etc needed to make or do something; a person regarded as fit for a particular task, position, etc.

materialism /məˈtiːriəˌlɪzəm/ *n* concern with money and possessions rather than spiritual values; the doctrine that everything in the world, including thought, can be explained only in terms of matter.—**materialist** *n*.—**materialistic** *adj*.

materiality /məˌtiriˈæləti/ *n* (*pl* **materialities**) the quality or state of being material; material existence; substance.

materialize /məˈtiːriəˌlaɪz/ *vt* to give material form to. • *vi* to become fact; to make an unexpected appearance.—**materialization** *n*.

materially /məˈtiːriəli/ *adv* physically; to a great extent; substantially.

materia medica /məˌtiːriəˈmedɪkə/ *n* the science of substances used in medicine including pharmacology, pharmacy, etc; a substance employed as a medicine or in making drugs.

materiel, matériel /məˌtiriˈel/ *n* the baggage, munitions, and provisions of an army or of any other organization.

maternal /məˈtərnəl/ *adj* of, like, or from a mother; related through the mother's side of the family.—**maternally** *adv*.

maternity /məˈtərnɪti/ *n* motherhood; motherliness. • *adj* relating to pregnancy.

matey /ˈmeɪti/ *n* a crony or companion (often used when directly addressing such). • *adj* (**matier, matiest**) (*inf*) friendly, sociable.—**mateyness, matiness** *n*.—**matily** *adv*.

math /mæθ/ *n* (*inf*) mathematics.

mathematical /ˌmæθəˈmætɪkəl/, **mathematic** /ˌmæθəˈmætɪk/ *adj* of, like or concerned with mathematics; exact and precise.—**mathematically** *adv*.

mathematics /ˌmæθəˈmætɪks/ *n* (*used as sing*) the science dealing with quantities, forms, space, etc and their relationships by the use of numbers and symbols; (*sing or pl*) the mathematical operations or processes used in a particular problem, discipline, etc.—**mathematician** *n*.

maths /mæθs/ *n* (*inf*) mathematics.

matin /ˈmæt'n/, **matinal** /-nəl/ *adj* of or pertaining to the morning or to matins.

matinée /ˈmætɪˌneɪ/ *n* a daytime, *esp* an afternoon performance of a play, etc.

matins /ˈmætɪnz/ *n* (*sing or pl*) (*Anglican Church*) a morning prayer; (*RC Church*) one of the canonical hours of prayer; (*poet*) a bird's morning song.

matriarch /ˈmeɪtriˌɑrk/ *n* a woman who heads or rules her family or tribe.—**matriarchal, matriarchic** *adj*.

matriarchy /ˈmeɪtriˌɑrki/ *n* (*pl* **matriarchies**) form of social organization in which the mother is the ruler of the family or tribe and in which descent is traced through the mother.

matrices /ˈmeɪtrɪˌsiz/ or /ˈmæ-/ *see* **matrix**.

matricide /ˈmætrɪˌsaɪd/ or /ˈmeɪt-/ *n* a person who kills his (her) mother; the killing of one's mother.—**matricidal** *adj*.

matriculate /məˈtrɪkjuˌleɪt/ *vti* to enrol, *esp* as a student.—**matriculation** *n*.

matrimony /ˈmætrɪˌmoːni/ *n* (*pl* **matrimonies**) the act or rite of marriage; the married state.—**matrimonial** *adj*.—**matrimonially** *adv*.

matrix /ˈmeɪtrɪks/ *n* (*pl* **matrices, matrixes**) the place, substance, etc from which something originates; a mould; the connective intercellular substance in bone, cartilage, or other tissue; (*math*) a rectangular grid of quantities in rows and columns used in solving certain problems.

matron /ˈmeɪtrən/ *n* a wife or widow, *esp* one of mature appearance and manner; a woman in charge of domestic and nursing arrangements in a school, hospital or other institution.—**matronal** *adj*.

matronly /ˈmeɪtrənli/ *adj* pertaining to or suitable for a matron; sedate, dignified; (*figure*) plump.—**matronliness** *n*.

matronymic /ˌmætrəˈnɪmɪk/ *see* **metronymic**.

matt /mæt/ *see* **mat**².

matter /ˈmætər/ *n* what a thing is made of; material; whatever occupies space and is perceptible to the senses; any specified substance; content of thought or expression; a quantity; a thing or affair; significance; trouble, difficulty; pus. • *vi* to be of importance.

matter-of-fact *adj* unimaginative or emotionless; relating to facts, not opinions, imagination, etc.

matting /ˈmætɪŋ/ *n* a coarse material, such as woven straw or hemp, used for making mats.

mattock /ˈmætək/ *n* a pick with one head like an axe, the other like an adze.

mattress /ˈmætrɪs/ *n* a casing of strong cloth filled with cotton, foam rubber, coiled springs, etc, used on a bed.

maturate /ˈmætʃəˌreɪt/ *vti* (*med*) a less common word for suppurate, that is to discharge pus, to fester; (*arch*) to bring or come to maturity.—**maturative** *adj*.

maturation /ˌmætʃəˈreɪʃən/ *n* the process of ripening or coming to maturity; (*biol*) the progressive generation of cells already present in the ovary and testis, mitosis; (*rare*) the act of discharging pus, suppuration.

mature /məˈtʃʊr/ or /-ˈtʃər/ *adj* mentally and physically well-developed, grown-up; (*fruit, cheese, etc*) ripe; (*bill*) due; (*plan*) completely worked out. • *vti* to make or become mature; to become due.—**maturely** *adv*.—**matureness** *n*.

maturity /-əti/ *n* the state of being mature; full development; the date a loan becomes due.

matutinal /ˌmætjuːˈtaɪnəl/ *adj* of, happening during, or pertaining to the morning; early.—**matutinally** *adv*.

maud /mɒd/ *n* (*Scot*) a grey-striped woollen plaid worn by shepherds.

maudlin /ˈmɒdlɪn/ *adj* foolishly sentimental; tearfully drunk.

maul /mɒl/ *vt* to bruise or lacerate; to paw.

maulstick /ˈmɒlˌstɪk/ *n* a long stick used by painters as a rest for the hand while painting.—*also* **mahlstick**.

maund /mɒnd/ *n* any of various Asian units of weight, varying from 25 pounds (11 kilograms) to 82 pounds (37 kilograms), according to locality.

maunder /'mɒndər/ *vi* to speak, act or move listlessly or purposelessly.—**maunderer** *n*.

Maundy Thursday the Thursday before Good Friday, in remembrance of the Last Supper.

mausoleum /ˌmɔːzə'liːəm/ or /ˌmɒsə-/ *n* (*pl* **mausoleums, mausolea**) a large tomb.

mauve /moːv/ *n* any of several shades of pale purple. • *adj* of this colour.

maverick /'mævrɪk/ *n* an independent-minded or unorthodox individual; an unbranded animal, *eg* a stray calf.

mavis /'meɪvɪs/ *n* the song thrush.

mavourneen, mavournin /mə'voːrnɪn/ *n* (*Irish*) my darling.

maw /mɒ/ *n* the stomach, crop or throat of animals, *esp* those who require large quantities of food; (*inf*) the throat and stomach of a person who eats food indiscriminately and in large quantities.

mawkish /'mɒkɪʃ/ *adj* maudlin; insipid.—**mawkishly** *adv*.—**mawkishness** *n*.

max. /mæks/ *abbr* = maximum.

maxilla /mæk'sɪlə/ *n* (*pl* **maxillae, maxillas**) the upper jawbone; in some insects, any of several parts of the mouth used as a secondary jaw.—**maxillar, maxillary** *adj*.

maxim /'mæksɪm/ *n* a concise rule of conduct; a precept.

maxima /'mæksɪmə/ *see* **maximum**.

maximal /'mæksɪməl/ *adj* of, consisting of, or pertaining to a maximum; (*math*) last in order. • *n* (*math*) in an ordered set, the member last in order.—**maximally** *adv*.

maximalist /'mæksɪməlɪst/ *n* one who insists on maximum demands without compromise; (*often with cap*) one who advocates direct action as a means of accomplishing something, *esp* social and political ends.

maximize /'mæksɪˌmaɪz/ *vt* to increase to a maximum.—**maximization** *n*.

maximum /'mæksɪməm/ *n* (*pl* **maxima, maximums**) the greatest quantity, number, etc. • *adj* highest; greatest possible reached.

maxixe /mə'ʃiʃə/ *n* a Brazilian round dance similar to the tango, and like the two-step in rhythm.

maxwell /'mækswel/ *n* a unit of magnetic flux in the cgs system.

May /meɪ/ *n* the fifth month of the year having 31 days.

may /meɪ/ *vb aux* (*past* **might**) expressing possibility; permission; wish or hope.

maya /'maɪjə/ *n* (*Hinduism*) illusion, *esp* that of the world as experienced by the senses as non-material.

May apple /'meɪæpəl/ *n* an American plant with an egg-shaped edible fruit; its fruit.

maybe /'meɪbi/ *adv* perhaps.

May Day *n* the first day of May, celebrated as a traditional spring festival; observed in many countries as a labour holiday.

Mayday /'meɪdeɪ/ *n* the international radio-telephone signal indicating a ship or aircraft in distress.

mayhem /'meɪhem/ *n* violent destruction, confusion.

mayn't /'meɪənt/ = may not.

mayonnaise /ˌmeɪə'neɪz/ *n* a salad dressing made from egg yolks whisked with oil and lemon juice or vinegar.

mayor /'meɪər/ or /mer/ *n* the chief administrative officer of a municipality.—**mayoral** *adj*.—**mayorship** *n*.

mayoralty /'meɪərəlti/ or /'mer-/ *n* (*pl* **mayoralties**) the office or term of office of a mayor.

mayoress /'meɪəres/ *n* the wife of a mayor; a female mayor.

maypole /'meɪpoːl/ *n* a flower-decked pole hung with ribbons around which May Day festivities are held.

Mazdaism /'mæzdəˌɪzəm/ *n* Zoroastrianism.

maze /meɪz/ *n* a confusing, intricate network of pathways, *esp* one with high hedges in a garden; a labyrinth; a confused state.—*adj* **maze** like.

mazer /'meɪzər/ *n* (*arch*) a large drinking cup of hard wood or metal.

mazuma /mə'zuːmə/ *n* (*sl*) money.

mazurka, mazourka /mə'zɜːrkə/ *n* a Polish folk dance in triple time; a musical composition for or imitating this.

mazy /'meɪzi/, **mazier** /-ər/, **maziest** /-əst/ *adj* intricate, winding; perplexing.—**mazily** *adv*.—**maziness** *n*.

MB *abbr* = Bachelor of Medicine; megabyte.

MBA *abbr* = Master of Business Administration.

MD *abbr* = Doctor of Medicine; Managing Director.

Md (*chem symbol*) mendelevium.

MDMA *abbr* = methylene dioxymethamphetamine, a synthetic drug used as the stimulant Ecstasy.

me /miː/ *pers pron* the objective case of I.

ME[1] *abbr* = myalgic encephalomyelitis.

mead /miːd/ *n* a wine made from a fermented solution of honey and spices.

meadow /'medoː/ *n* a piece of land where grass is grown for hay; low, level, moist grassland.

meadowlark /'medoːlɑːrk/ *n* one of two North American yellow-breasted songbirds related to the Baltimore oriole; any of several birds of South, Central and North America.

meadowsweet /'medoːˌswiːt/ *n* a fragrant white-flowered plant of Europe and Asia.

meagre, meager /'miːgər/ *adj* thin, emaciated; lacking in quality or quantity.—**meagrely, meagerly** *adv*.—**meagreness, meagerness** *n*.

meal[1] /miːl/ *n* any of the times for eating, as lunch, dinner, etc; the food served at such a time.

meal[2] *n* any coarsely ground edible grain; any substance similarly ground.—**mealiness** *n*.—**mealy** *adj*.

mealy-mouthed /'miːli'mauðd/ *adj* not outspoken and blunt; euphemistic; devious in speech.

mean[1] /miːn/ *adj* selfish, ungenerous; despicable; shabby; bad-tempered; (*sl*) difficult; (*sl*) expert.—**meanly** *adv*.—**meanness** *n*.

mean[2] *adj* halfway between extremes; average. • *n* what is between extremes.

mean[3] *vb* (**meaning, meant**) *vt* to have in mind; to intend; to intend to express; to signify. • *vi* to have a (specified) degree of importance, effect, etc.

meander /miː'ændər/ *n* a winding path *esp* a labyrinth; a winding of a stream or river. • *vi* (*river*) to wind; to wander aimlessly.—**meandering** *adj*.

meanie /'miːni/ *n* (*inf*) one who is mean, selfish, etc.—*also* **meanie** (*pl* **meanies**).

meaning /'miːnɪŋ/ *n* sense; significance; import. • *adj* significant.—**meaningful** *adj*.—**meaningless** *adj*.

means /miːnz/ *npl* that by which something is done; resources; wealth.

meant /ment/ *see* **mean**[3].

meantime /'miːntaɪm/, **meanwhile** /'miːnwaɪl/ *adv* in or during the intervening time; at the same time. • *n* the intervening time.

meany /'miːni/ *see* **meanie**.

measles /'miːzəlz/ *n* (*used as sing*) an acute, contagious viral disease, characterized by small red spots on the skin.

measly /'miːzli/ *adj* (**measlier, measliest**) (*inf*) slight, worthless; having measles.

measure /'meʒər/ *n* the extent, dimension, capacity, etc of anything; a determining of this, measurement; a unit of measurement; any standard of valuation; an instrument for measuring; a definite quantity measured out; a course of action; a statute, law; a rhythmical unit. • *vt* to find out the extent, dimensions etc of, *esp* by a standard; to mark off by measuring; to be a measure of. • *vi* to be of specified measurements.—**measurable** *adj*.—**measurably** *adv*.

measured /'meʒərd/ *adj* set or marked off by a standard; rhythmical, regular; carefully planned or considered.

measureless /'meʒərləs/ *adj* infinite, without limit.—**measurelessly** *adv*.

measurement /'meʒərmənt/ *n* a measuring or being measured; an extent or quantity determined by measuring; a system of measuring or of measures.

meat /miːt/ *n* animal flesh; food as opposed to drink; the essence of something.

meatball /'miːtbɒl/ *n* a small ball of ground meat *usu* mixed with breadcrumbs and spices; (*inf*) a stupid or foolish person.

meatus /miː'eɪtəs/ *n* (*pl* **meatuses, meatus**) any passage in the body, *eg* the ear canal.

meaty /'miːti/ *adj* (**meatier, meatiest**) full of meat; full of substance.

mecca /'mekə/ *n* a place of pilgrimage or a goal of aspiration; a resort or attraction that is visited by a large number of people; (*with cap*) Islam's holiest city, the birthplace of Muhammed (*c*. AD 570).—*also* **Makkah**.

mechanic /mə'kænɪk/ *n* a person skilled in maintaining or operating machines, cars, etc.

mechanical /mə'kænɪkəl/ *adj* of or using machinery or tools; produced or operated by machinery; done as if by a machine, lacking thought or emotion; of the science of mechanics.— **mechanically** *adv*.

mechanician /ˌmɛkə'nɪʃən/ *n* a person skilled in mechanics or machinery; a technician; a mechanist.

mechanics /mə'kænɪks/ *n* (*used as sing*) the science of motion and the action of forces on bodies; knowledge of machinery; (*pl*) the technical aspects of something.

mechanism /'mɛkənɪzəm/ *n* the working parts of a machine; any system of interrelated parts; any physical or mental process by which a result is produced.

mechanist /'mɛkənɪst/ *n* an expert in mechanics, a mechanician; an advocate of mechanistic philosophy.

mechanistic /-'nɪstɪk/ *adj* of or pertaining to mechanics; of or relating to mechanism; attributing phenomena to physical or biological causes.— **mechanistically** *adv*.

mechanize /'mɛkə,naɪz/ *vt* to make mechanical; to equip with machinery or motor vehicles.— **mechanization** *n*.— **mechanized** *adj*.

meconium /mɪ'koːnɪəm/ *n* the first faeces of a baby; the juice of the poppy; opium.

MEd *abbr* = Master of Education.

medal /'mɛdəl/ *n* a small, flat piece of inscribed metal, commemorating some event or person or awarded for some distinction.— **medallic** *adj*.

medallion /mə'dæljən/ *n* a large medal; a design, portrait, etc shaped like a medal; a medal worn on a chain around the neck.

medallist, medalist /'mɛdəlɪst/ *n* one awarded a medal.

meddle /'mɛdəl/ *vi* to interfere in another's affairs.— **meddler** *n*.— **meddlesome** *adj*.

Mede /miːd/ *n* an inhabitant of Media, an ancient country in southwest Asia to the south of the Caspian Sea.— **Median** *n, adj*.

media /'miːdɪə/ *see* **medium**.

mediaeval /ˌmiːdɪ'iːvəl/ or /mɛd-/, /ˌmɛdɪ-/ *see* **medieval**.

mediaevalism /-ˌlɪzəm/, **mediaevalist** /-lɪst/ *see* **medievalism**.

medial /'miːdɪəl/ *adj* of or in the middle; mean, average; (*math*) pertaining to or denoting an average; median; (*phonetics*) denoting a sound made by using an average amount of muscular tension, neither strongly vocalized nor gently pronounced.

median /'miːdɪən/ *adj* middle; intermediate. • *n* a median number, point, line, etc.

mediant /'miːdɪənt/ *n* (*mus*) the third of any scale.—*also adj*.

mediastinum /ˌmiːdɪə'staɪnəm/ *n* (*pl* **mediastina**) (*anat*) a membranous partition, *esp* that between the lungs; the part of the body between the lungs containing the heart and associated valves, etc.— **mediastinal** *adj*.

mediate /'miːdɪ,eɪt/ *vt* to intervene (in a dispute); to bring about agreement. • *vi* to be in an intermediate position; to be an intermediary. • *adj* involving an intermediary, not direct or immediate.— **mediately** *adv*.— **mediative** *adj*.

mediation /ˌmiːdɪ'eɪʃən/ *n* the act of mediating; reconciliation; intervention, *esp* by a neutral nation seeking a settlement between warring nations.

mediatize /'miːdɪə,taɪz/ *vt* to annex (a state) while leaving its ruler his title.— **mediatization** *n*.

mediator /'miːdɪ,eɪtər/ *n* one who or that which mediates; a person who acts as an intermediary; an intercessor.— **mediatory** *adj*.

medic /'mɛdɪk/ *n* (*inf*) a medical student; (*inf*) a physician or surgeon.

medicable /'mɛdɪkəbəl/ *adj* potentially curable.

medical /'mɛdɪkəl/ *adj* relating to the practice or study of medicine. • *n* (*inf*) a medical examination.— **medically** *adv*.

medicament /mə'dɪkəmənt/ or /'mɛdɪ-/ *n* a medicine or healing application.

medicate /'mɛdɪ,keɪt/ *vt* to treat with medicine; to impregnate (soap, shampoo, etc) with medication.— **medicative** *adj*.

medication /ˌmɛdɪ'keɪʃən/ *n* treatment with drugs, medicines, etc; a drug, medicine, or remedy.

medicine /'mɛdɪsɪn/ *n* any substance used to treat or prevent disease; the science of preventing, treating or curing disease.— **medicinal** *adj*.— **medicinally** *adv*.

medico /'mɛdɪ,koː/ *n* (*inf*) a doctor or medical student.

medieval /mɪd'iːvəl/ or /mɛd-/, /ˌmɛdɪ-/ *adj* of or like the Middle Ages.—*also* **mediaeval**.

medievalism /-ˌlɪzəm/ *n* the spirit, *esp* in religion and art, customs, etc, characteristic of the Middle Ages; a study of these; any one of

these extant since the Middle Ages, or a contemporary imitation of it.—*also* **mediaevalism**.— **medievalist, mediaevalist** *n*.

mediocre /ˌmiːdi'oːkər/ *adj* average; ordinary; inferior.— **mediocrity** *n*.

meditate /'mɛdɪ,teɪt/ *vi* to think deeply; to reflect; to empty the mind in order to concentrate on nothing or on one thing, *esp* as a religious exercise.— **meditator** *n*.

meditation /-'teɪʃən/ *n* the act of meditating; contemplation of spiritual or religious matters.

meditative /'mɛdɪtətɪv/ or /-ˌteɪtɪv/ *adj* expressing or characterized by meditation; thoughtful.— **meditatively** *adv*.— **meditativeness** *n*.

Mediterranean /ˌmɛdɪtə'reɪnɪən/ *n* the Mediterranean Sea. • *adj* of, or relating to (the area around) the Mediterranean Sea; denoting a subdivision of the Caucasian race characterized by a slender build and dark complexion; (*climate*) characterized by hot, dry summers and warm, wet winters.

medium /'miːdɪəm/ *n* (*pl* **media, mediums**) the middle state or condition; a substance for transmitting an effect; any intervening means, instrument, or agency; (*pl* **media**) a means of communicating information (*eg* newspapers, television, radio); (*pl* **mediums**) a person claiming to act as an intermediary between the living and the dead. • *adj* midway; average.

medlar /'mɛdlər/ *n* a small fruit tree of Europe and Asia; its apple-like fruit; any one of several trees similar to this; the fruit from one of these.

medley /'mɛdlɪ/ *n* (*pl* **medleys**) a miscellany; a musical piece made up of various tunes or passages.

Médoc /meɪ'dɒk/ or /'mɛdɒk/ *n* a red wine from the Bordeaux region of France.

medulla /mə'dɛlə/ *n* (*pl* **medullas, medullae**) (*anat*) the marrow of bones; inner tissue; (*bot*) the pith of plants.— **medular, medullary** *adj*.

medulla oblongata /ˌɒblɒŋ'gætə/ *n* (*pl* **medulla oblongatas, medullae oblongatae**) the nervous tissue of the lower part of the cranium, which governs respiration, the action of the heart, etc.

medusa /mə'djuːsə/ or /-'djuː-/ *n* (*pl* **medusas, medusae**) a jellyfish; one of two coelenterate life cycles, when it has a sac-like, umbrella-shaped body that is capable of moving freely in water. —*also* **medusan, medusoid**.— **medusan** *adj*.

meed /miːd/ *n* (*poet*) recompense, reward.

meek /miːk/ *adj* patient, long-suffering; submissive.— **meekly** *adv*.— **meekness** *n*.

meerschaum /'miːrʃəm/ or /-ʃɒm/ *n* a creamy claylike silicate of magnesium from which pipe bowls and building stones are made; a tobacco pipe with a bowl made of this.

meet[1] /miːt/ *vb* (**meeting, met**) *vt* to encounter, to come together; to make the acquaintance of; to contend with, deal with; to experience; to be perceived by (the eye, etc); (*demand, etc*) to satisfy; (*bill, etc*) to pay. • *vi* to come into contact with; to be introduced. • *n* a meeting to hunt or for an athletics competition.

meet[2] *adj* (*arch*) fit, suitable.

meeting /'miːtɪŋ/ *n* a coming together; a gathering.

mega- /'mɛgə/ *prefix* great, large; a million of; (*inf*) greatest.

megabyte /'mɛgəbaɪt/ *n* (*comput*) a unit of information, approximately equal to one million bytes.

megacephalic /ˌmɛgəsə'fælɪk/ *see* **macrocephalic**.

megacycle /'mɛgə,saɪkəl/ *n* a megahertz.

megahertz /'mɛgəhɜːrts/ *n* a unit of frequency equal to one million hertz.

megalith /'mɛgəlɪθ/ *n* a huge stone, *esp* part of a prehistoric monument.— **megalithic** *adj*.

megalomania /ˌmɛgələ'meɪnɪə/ *n* a mental illness characterized by delusions of grandeur; (*inf*) a lust for power.— **megalomaniac** *n, adj*.— **megalomaniacal** *adj*.

megaphone /'mɛgə,foːn/ *n* a device to amplify and direct the voice.

megapode /'mɛgə,poːd/ *n* any of a family of birds of Australia and the South Pacific that builds mounds of sand, etc, to incubate its eggs.

megaspore /'mɛgə,spɔːr/ *n* the protective covering containing the embryo in flowering plants.—*also* **macrospore**; the larger spore of certain mosses, ferns and fungi, which forms the female gametophyte.

megass, megasse /mə'gæs/ or /-'gɒs/ *n* a type of paper produced from the residue left after the extraction of sugar from cane.

megathere /ˌmɛgəˈθiːr/ *n* a huge extinct animal allied to the sloth.—**megatherian** *adj*.

megaton /ˈmɛgəˌtʌn/ *n* a unit of explosive force equivalent to one million tons of TNT.

megavolt /ˈmɛgəvoːlt/ *n* a million volts.

megawatt /ˈmɛgəwɒt/ *n* one million watts.

megilp /məˈgɪlp/ *n* a mixture of linseed oil and mastic varnish or turpentine, used as a base in oil colours.

megohm /ˈmɛgoːm/ *n* a million ohms.

megrim /ˈmiːgrɪm/ *n* (*arch*) a sick or neuralgic headache, *usu* of one side of the head, a migraine; a whim, caprice; (*pl*) a disease of horses or cattle, characterized by vertigo, the staggers.

meiosis /maɪˈoːsɪs/ *n* (*pl* **meioses**) (*biol*) the process of cell division where a nucleus splits into four, each new nucleus having half the number of chromosomes that the orig one had; a rhetorical understatement, *esp* one where a negative is used instead of its opposite, *eg* "a not inconsiderable amount" instead of "a large amount"; litotes; (*rare*) any division or separation.—**meiotic** *adj*.—**meiotically** *adv*.

Meistersinger /ˈmaɪstərˌsɪŋər/ *n* (*pl* **Meistersinger, Meistersingers**) a member of one of the various guilds in German cities of the 14th-16th cents., which instituted the development of poetry and music by establishing competitive standards.

melamine /ˈmɛləˌmiːn/ *n* a resinous material used for adhesives, coatings, and laminated products.

melancholy /ˈmɛlənkɒli/ *n* gloominess or depression; sadness.
• *adj* sad; depressed.—**melancholia** *n*.—**melancholic** *adj*.

mélange /meɪˈlɒ̃ʒ/ *n* a (confused) mixture; a medley; (*geol*) a hotchpotch of variously shaped rocks of different periods and sizes.

melanin /ˈmɛlənɪn/ *n* a dark brown pigment in the skin, hair, and eyes of humans and animals.

melanism /ˈmɛlənɪzəm/, **melanosis** /-noːsɪs/ *n* dark coloration of the skin in pale-skinned people or dark-coloured feathers, etc, in birds and animals, caused by abnormal deposits of black or dark pigment in skin tissue, the opposite of albinism.—**melanistic, melanotic** *adj*.

melanoma /ˌmɛləˈnoːmə/ *n* (*pl* **melanomas, melanomata**) a skin tumour composed of darkly pigmented cells.

melee, mêlée /ˈmeɪleɪ/ *or* /ˈmɛleɪ/, /ˈmeˈleɪ/ *n* a confused, noisy struggle.

melic /ˈmɛlɪk/ *adj* (*poem*) meant to be sung, often used of ancient Greek lyric poetry.

melilot /ˈmɛlɪlɒt/ *n* a species of sweet-scented trefoil or clover, with clusters of small yellow or white flowers.—*also* **sweet clover**.

melinite /ˈmɛlɪˌnaɪt/ *n* a high explosive similar to lyddite.

meliorate /ˈmiːliəˌreɪt/ *vti* to improve; to grow better; to make (something) better.—**meliorable** *adj*.—**meliorative** *adj, n*.—**meliorator** *n*.

melioration /-ˈreɪʃən/ *n* the process of improving; the state of being improved; an improvement.

meliorism /ˈmiːliəˌrɪzəm/ *n* the doctrine that in nature there is a tendency to gradual improvement and this may be accelerated by human effort.

melliferous /mɛˈlɪfərəs/ *adj* forming or yielding honey.

mellifluous /mɛˈlɪfluːəs/, **mellifluent** /-uːənt/ *adj* (*voice, sounds*) sweetly flowing, smooth.—**mellifluously** *adv*.—**mellifluousness** *n*.

mellow /ˈmɛloː/ *adj* (*fruit*) sweet and ripe; (*wine*) matured; (*colour, light, sound*) soft, not harsh; kind-hearted and understanding.
• *vti* to soften through age; to mature.—**mellowness** *n*.

melodeon /məˈloːdiən/ *n* a kind of accordion; a small reed organ.

melodic /məˈlɒdɪk/ *adj* pertaining to or having melody.—**melodically** *adv*.

melodious /məˈloːdiəs/ *adj* full of melody, tuneful, musical; sweet-sounding.—**melodiously** *adv*.—**melodiousness** *n*.

melodist /ˈmɛlədɪst/ *n* a singer; a composer of melodies.

melodize /ˈmɛləˌdaɪz/ *vti* to make (something) melodious; to compose a melody (for something); to sing a melody.

melodrama /ˈmɛləˌdræmə/ *or* /-drɒmə/ *n* a play, film, etc filled with overdramatic emotion and action; drama of this genre; sensational events or emotions.—**melodramatic** *adj*.—**melodramatically** *adv*.—**melodramatist** *n*.

melody /ˈmɛlədi/ *n* (*pl* **melodies**) a tune; a pleasing series of sounds.—**melodic** *adj*.—**melodious** *adj*.

melon /ˈmɛlən/ *n* the large juicy many-seeded fruit of trailing plants, as the watermelon, cantaloupe.

melt /mɛlt/ *vti* (**melting, melted,** *pp* **molten**) to make or become liquid; to dissolve; to fade or disappear; to soften or be softened emotionally.—**melting** *adj*.—**meltingly** *adv*.

meltdown /ˈmɛltdaun/ *n* the melting of the fuel core of a nuclear reactor; the drastic collapse of almost anything.

melting point /ˈmɛltɪŋ/ *n* the temperature at which a solid melts.

melting pot *n* a place, situation, or product of mixing many different races, traditions, cultures, etc.

melton /ˈmɛltən/ *n* a kind of thick woollen cloth, with a surface nap, often used for overcoats.

meltwater /ˈmɛltwɒtər/ *n* water derived from the melting of snow or ice.

member /ˈmɛmbər/ *n* a person belonging to a society or club; a part of a body, such as a limb; a representative in a legislative body; a distinct part of a complex whole.

membership /ˈmɛmbərʃɪp/ *n* the state of being a member; the number of members of a body; the members collectively.

membrane /ˈmɛmbreɪn/ *n* a thin pliable sheet or film; the fibrous tissue that covers or lines animal organs.—**membranous, membranaceous** *adj*.

memento /məˈmɛntoː/ *n* (*pl* **mementos, mementoes**) a reminder, *esp* a souvenir.

memento mori /-ˈmɔːri/ *or* /-raɪ/ *n* (*pl* **memente mori**) (an object that serves as) a reminder of death.

memo /ˈmɛmoː/ *n* (*pl* **memos**) a memorandum.

memoir /ˈmɛmwɑr/ *n* an historical account based on personal experience; (*pl*) an autobiographical record.

memorabilia /ˌmɛmərəˈbiːliə/ *or* /-biːljə/ *npl* (*sing* **memorabile**) things worthy of remembrance or record; clothing, letters, manuscripts, notes, etc, once belonging to or written by famous people or connected with famous events and thought worthy of collection.

memorable /ˈmɛmərəbəl/ *adj* worth remembering; easy to remember.—**memorably** *adv*.

memorandum /ˌmɛməˈrændəm/ *n* (*pl* **memorandums**) an informal written communication as within an office; (*pl* **memoranda**) a note to help the memory.

memorial /məˈmɔːriəl/ *adj* serving to preserve the memory of the dead. • *n* a remembrance; a monument.

memorialist /-ɪst/ *n* one who prepares, signs or presents a memorial; one who writes memoirs.

memorialize /mɪˈmɔːriəˌlaɪz/ *vt* to commemorate; to honour by means of a memorial.—**memorialization** *n*.—**memorializer** *n*.

memorize /ˈmɛməˌraɪz/ *vt* to learn by heart, to commit to memory.—**memorization** *n*.

memory /ˈmɛməri/ *or* /ˈmɛmri/ *n* (*pl* **memories**) the process of retaining and reproducing past thoughts and sensations; the sum of things remembered; an individual recollection; commemoration; remembrance; the part of a computer that stores information.—*also* **store**.

memsahib /ˈmɛmˌsæɪb/ *or* /-sɒɪb/ *n* (*formerly*) a form of address for a European married woman in India.

men /mɛn/ *see* man.

menace /ˈmɛnəs/ *n* a threat; (*inf*) a nuisance. • *vt* to threaten.—**menacing** *adj*.—**menacingly** *adv*.

menad /ˈmiˌnæd/ *see* maenad.

ménage /meɪˈnæʒ/ *or* /-nɒʒ/ *n* a household.

ménage à trois *Fr.* /meɪˌnɑʒɑˈtrwɑ/ *n* (*pl* **ménages à trois**) a relationship in which a married couple and a lover of one of them live together.

menagerie /məˈnæʒəri/ *or* /-ˈnædʒ-/, /-ˈnɒʒ-/ *n* a place where wild animals are kept for exhibition; a collection of wild animals.

mend /mɛnd/ *vt* to repair; (manners, etc) to reform, improve. • *vi* to become better. • *n* the act of mending; a repaired area in a garment, etc.

mendacity /mɛnˈdæsɪti/ *n* (*pl* **mendacities**) telling lies; a falsehood.—**mendacious** *adj*.—**mendaciously** *adv*.

mendelevium /ˌmɛndəˈliːviəm/ *n* an artificially produced radioactive metallic element.

Mendelism /ˈmɛndəˌlɪzəm/ *n* the theories of the Austrian monk and geneticist Gregor Mendel (1822–84) respecting heredity, as set out in Mendel's laws with later modifications.—**Mendelian** *adj*.

mendicant /ˈmɛndɪkənt/ *adj* begging; (*religious orders*) reliant on alms. • *n* a mendicant friar.—**mendicancy, mendicity** *n*.

mending /ˈmɛndɪŋ/ *n* garments requiring to be repaired.

menhaden /mɛnˈheɪdən/ *n* (*pl* **menhadens, menhaden**) an inedible American fish, yielding a valuable oil.

menhir /ˈmɛnhiːr/ *n* a tall, monolithic obelisk, sometimes crudely carved, dating from the Bronze Age in the UK or the Neolithic Age in Europe.

menial /ˈmiːniəl/ *adj* consisting of work of little skill; servile. • *n* a domestic servant; a servile person.

meninges /mɪˈnɪndʒiːz/ *npl* (*sing* **meninx**) the three membranes covering and protecting the brain and the spinal cord.—**meningeal** *adj*.

meningitis /ˌmɛnɪnˈdʒaɪtɪs/ *n* inflammation of the membranes enveloping the brain or spinal cord.

meniscus /məˈnɪskəs/ *n* (*pl* **menisci, meniscuses**) a crescent; the crescent-shaped surface of a liquid contained in a tube; a lens convex on one side and concave on the other; (*anat*) the cartilage between the bones of joints, *esp* at the knee.

menology /mɪˈnɒlədʒi/ *n* (*pl* **menologies**) an ecclesiastical calendar; a calendar of saints, *esp* in the Orthodox Church.

menopause /ˈmɛnəˌpɒz/ *n* the time of life during which a woman's menstrual cycle ceases permanently.—**menopausal** *adj*.

menorrhagia /ˈmɛnəˈreɪdʒiə/ *n* an excessive menstrual flow.

menses /ˈmɛnsiːz/ *n* (*pl* **menses**) menstruation; the monthly discharge of blood, etc, from the uterus; the days during which this occurs.

Menshevik /ˈmɛnʃəˌvɪk/ *n* (*pl* **Mensheviks, Mensheviki**) (*hist*) a member of the more moderate Russian socialist party (1903-17) or of a liberal opposition party set up after the Revolution.—**Menshevism** *n*.—**Menshevist** *adj, n*.

menstruation /ˌmɛnˈstreɪʃən/ *n* the monthly discharge of blood from the uterus.—**menstrual** *adj*.—**menstruate** *vi*.

menstruum /ˈmɛnstrʊm/ *n* (*pl* **menstruums, menstrua**) a solvent, *esp* if used in making drugs.

mensurable /ˈmɛnʃərəbəl/ *adj* measurable; (*mus*) of a fixed rhythm.—**mensurability** *n*.

mensuration /ˌmɛnʃʊˈreɪʃən/ *n* the science of measurement; the act or process of measuring or taking the dimensions of anything; measurement.

mental /ˈmɛntəl/ *adj* of, or relating to the mind; occurring or performed in the mind; having a psychiatric disorder; (*inf*) crazy, stupid.—**mentally** *adv*.

mentality /mɛnˈtæliti/ *n* (*pl* **mentalities**) intellectual power; disposition, character.

menthol /ˈmɛnθɒl/ *n* peppermint oil.—**mentholated** *adj*.

mention /ˈmɛnʃən/ *n* a brief reference to something in speech or writing; an official recognition or citation. • *vt* to refer to briefly; to remark; to honour officially.—**mentionable** *adj*.

mentor /ˈmɛntɔr/ *n* a wise and trusted adviser.

menu /ˈmɛnjuː/ *n* the list of dishes served in a restaurant; a list of options on a computer display.

meow /miːˈaʊ/ *n* the cry of a cat; a spiteful remark.—*also vi*.

Mephistophelean, Mephistophelian /ˌmɛfɪstəˈfiːliən/ *adj* pertaining to or like Mephistopheles, the devil of the Faust legend; fiendish, cynical; diabolic.

mephitis /mɪˈfaɪtɪs/ *n* a noxious gas emitted from the ground; a foul stench.—**mephitic, mephitical** *adj*.

mercantile /ˈmɔrkənˌtaɪl/ *adj* of merchants or trade.

mercantilism /ˈmɔrkəntɪˌlɪzəm/ *n* a theory popular in 17th and 18th century Europe suggesting that the wealth of a nation increases in proportion to the level of the foreign trade surplus, therefore trade and commerce with other countries, the founding of colonies, a merchant navy etc should be encouraged; (*rare*) commercialism—**mercantilist** *n, adj*.

mercenary /ˈmɔrsəˌnɛri/ *adj* working or done for money only. • *n* (*pl* **mercenaries**) a soldier hired to fight for a foreign army.—**mercenarily** *adv*.—**mercenariness** *n*.

mercer /ˈmɔrsər/ *n* a dealer in textiles, *esp* silk and velvet.

mercerize /ˈmɔrsəˌraɪz/ *vt* to treat cotton thread so as to strengthen it and make it resemble silk.—**mercerization** *n*.

merchandise /ˈmɔrtʃənˌdaɪs/ or /-daɪz/ *n* commercial goods. • *vti* to sell, to trade; to promote sales by display or advertising.—**merchandiser** *n*.

merchandising /-ɪŋ/ *n* the display of goods in a store, etc; the exploitation of a fictional character, pop group, etc, by the production of goods with their image, name, etc.

merchant /ˈmɔrtʃənt/ *n* a trader; a retailer; (*sl*) a person fond of a particular activity.

merchantable /ˈmɔrtʃəntəbəl/ *adj* marketable.

merchantman /ˈmɔrtʃəntmən/ *n* (*pl* **merchantmen**) a trading ship.

merchant marine, merchant navy *n* commercial shipping.

merciful /ˈmɔrsɪˌfʊl/ *adj* compassionate, humane.—**mercifulness** *n*.

mercifully /ˈmɔrsɪˌfʊli/ *adv* in a merciful way; (*inf*) thank goodness.

merciless /ˈmɔrsɪləs/ *adj* cruel, pitiless; without mercy.—**mercilessly** *adv*.—**mercilessness** *n*.

mercurial /mərˈkjʊriəl/ *adj* of, containing, or caused by mercury; lively, sprightly; volatile.—**mercurially** *adv*.

mercuric /mərˈkjʊrɪk/ *adj* (*chem*) of or containing bivalent mercury.

mercurous /mərˈkjuːrəs/ or /ˈmɔrkjʊrəs/ *adj* (*chem*) of or containing monovalent mercury.

Mercury /ˈmɔrkjʊri/ *n* the innermost planet, and the smallest; the Roman god of thieves, traders etc; in ancient Rome, the messenger of the gods.

mercury *n* a heavy silvery liquid metallic element used in thermometers etc.

mercy /ˈmɔrsi/ *n* clemency; compassion; kindness; pity.

mere /miːr/ *adj* nothing more than; simple, unmixed.

merely /ˈmiːrli/ *adv* simply; solely.

meretricious /ˌmɛrəˈtrɪʃəs/ *adj* tawdry, superficially attractive; insincere.

merganser /mərˈgænsər/ *n* (*pl* **mergansers, merganser**) a large, diving fish-eating duck with a long narrow bill with serrated edges; a sawbill.

merge /mɔrdʒ/ *vti* to blend or cause to fuse together gradually; to (cause to) combine, unite.

merger /ˈmɔrdʒər/ *n* a combining together, *esp* of two or more commercial organizations.

meridian /məˈrɪdiən/ *n* the imaginary circle on the surface of the earth passing through the north and south poles.

meridional /məˈrɪdiənəl/ *adj* of a meridian; of the south.—**meridionally** *adv*.

meringue /məˈræŋ/ *n* a mixture of egg whites beaten with sugar and baked; a small cake or shell made from this, *usu* filled with cream.

merino /məˈriːnoː/ *n* (*pl* **merinos**) a breed of sheep with fine silky wool; the wool or the cloth made from it.

merit /ˈmɛrɪt/ *n* excellence; worth; (*pl*) (*of a case*) rights and wrongs; a deserving act. • *vt* to be worthy of, to deserve.

meritocracy /ˌmɛrɪˈtɒkrəsi/ *n* (*pl* **meritocracies**) rule by those most skilled or talented; a social system or government based on this; the most talented group in a society.

meritorious /ˌmɛrɪˈtɔriəs/ *adj* deserving of merit or honour.—**meritoriously** *adv*.—**meritoriousness** *n*.

merle /mɔrl/ *n* (*Scot*) a blackbird. • *adj* (*dog, esp a collie*) having blue-grey fur with black tinges or streaks.

merlin /ˈmɔrlɪn/ *n* a small dark-coloured falcon, often used in falconry.

merlon /ˈmɔrlɒn/ *n* the part of a parapet or battlement between two embrasures.

mermaid /ˈmɔrmeɪd/ *n* (*legend*) a woman with a fish's tail.—**merman** *nm* (*pl* **mermen**).

meroblastic /ˌmɛroːˈblæstɪk/ *adj* (*biol*) (*fertilized egg*) of or pertaining to the splitting of cells in the white only and not the entire ovum.

Merovingian /ˌmɛroːˈvɪndʒiən/ *adj* pertaining to the first Frankish dynasty of French kings (*c*.500-751). • *n* a member or adherent of this dynasty.

merry /ˈmɛri/ *adj* (**merrier, merriest**) cheerful; causing laughter; lively; (*inf*) slightly drunk.—**merrily** *adv*.—**merriment** *n*.

merry-go-round /ˈmɛriɡoːˌraʊnd/ *n* a revolving platform of hobbyhorses, etc, a carousel.

merrymaking /ˈmɛriˌmeɪkɪŋ/ *n* festivity, fun.—**merrymaker** *n*.

merrythought /ˈmɛriˌθɒt/ *n* (*rare*) the forked bone of a chicken's breast, the wishbone.

mes-, meso- /ˈmɛsoː/ or /ˈmɛz-/ *prefix* middle.

mesa /ˈmeɪsə/ *n* a rocky plateau with steep sides *usu* found in arid regions.

mésalliance /meɪˈzæliˌõs/, *Fr.* /meɪzaliˈõs/ *n* a misalliance; a marriage with one of lower social position.

mescaline /ˈmɛskəˌliːn/ *n* a hallucinogenic drug derived from the mescal cactus.

mesdames /meɪˈdɒm/, *Fr.* /meɪˈdam/ *see* **madame**.

mesdemoiselles *Fr.* /meɪdmwaˈzɛl/ *see* **mademoiselle**.

mesembryanthemum /mɪˌzɛmbriˈænθɪməm/ *n* one of a genus of flowering, succulent plants with thick and fleshy leaves and showy flowers.

mesentery /ˈmesənˌteri/ n (pl **mesenteries**) the membrane attaching the small intestines to the abdominal wall.—**mesenteric** adj.

mesh /meʃ/ n an opening between cords of a net, wires of a screen, etc; a net; a network; a snare; (geared wheels, etc) engagement. • vt to entangle, ensnare. • vi to become entangled or interlocked.

mesial /ˈmiːziəl/ adj (anat) in or toward the middle line of the body.—**mesially** adv.

mesmerism /ˈmezməˌrizəm/ n hypnotism.—**mesmerist** n.

mesmerize /ˈmezməˌraɪz/ vt to hypnotize; to fascinate.—**mesmeric** adj.—**mesmerizer** n.

mesne /miːn/ adj (law) intervening, intermediate.

meso-, mes- /ˈmesoː/ or /ˈmez-/ prefix middle.

mesoblast /ˈmesoːˌblæst/ n (biol) the middle germinal layer of an ovum, the basis of muscles, bones, blood etc.—also **mesoderm**.

mesocarp /ˈmesoːˌkɑrp/ n the middle layer of the seed vessel of a fruit.

mesocephalic /ˌmesoːsəˈfælɪk/ or /ˌmez-/ adj, n (person) with a head or skull of medium proportions.

mesoderm /ˈmesoːˌdərm/ see **mesoblast**.

mesogastrium /ˌmesoːˈɡæstriəm/ or /ˌmez-/ n the membrane that supports the embryonic stomach.—**mesogastric** adj.

Mesolithic /ˌmezoːˈlɪθɪk/ n, adj of or pertaining to the archaeological era between the Palaeolithic and Neolithic (c.12000-3000BC).

meson /ˈmezɒn/ or /ˈmiːzɒn/ n an unstable elementary particle having a mass between that of proton and an electron.

mesophyll /ˈmesoːfɪl/ n the internal tissues of a leaf that are between the upper and lower epidermal layers and contain chlorophyll.—**mesophyllic, mesophyllous** adj.

mesophyte /ˈmesoːˌfaɪt/ n a plant requiring an average water supply.—**mesophytic** adj.

mesothorax /-ˈθɔræks/ n (pl **mesothoraxes, mesothoraces**) the middle ring of an insect's thorax, with the second pair of walking legs and the front pair of wings.

Mesozoic /ˌmesoːˈzoːɪk/ or /ˌmez-/ adj pertaining to the era of geological time lasting from about 248 to 65 million years ago. • n this era.

mesquite, mesquit /ˈmeskiːt/ n a small pod-bearing tree of the southwest US whose pods are used as fodder.

mess /mes/ n a state of disorder or untidiness, esp if dirty; a muddle; an unsightly or disagreeable mixture; a portion of soft and pulpy or semi-liquid food; a building where service personnel dine; a communal meal. • vti to make a mess (of), bungle; to eat in company; to potter (about).

message /ˈmesɪdʒ/ n any spoken, written, or other form of communication; the chief idea that the writer, artist, etc seeks to communicate in a work.

messenger /ˈmesɪndʒər/ n a person who carries a message.

Messiah /məˈsaɪə/ n the promised saviour of the Jews; Jesus Christ.—**Messianic** adj.

messieurs /ˈmesərz/, Fr. /meɪˈsjø/ see **monsieur**.

Messrs /ˈmesərz/ pl of Mr.

messuage /ˈmeswɪdʒ/ n (law) a dwelling house with its adjacent buildings and land for the use of the household.

messy /ˈmesi/ adj (**messier, messiest**) dirty; confused; untidy.—**messily** adv.—**messiness** n.

mestizo /meˈstiːzoː/ n (pl **mestizos, mestizoes**) a person of mixed parentage, esp the child of a Spanish American and an American Indian.

met /met/ see **meet**.

meta- /ˈmetə/, **met-** /met/ prefix after, with, or implying change.

metabolism /məˈtæbəˌlizəm/ n the total processes in living organisms by which tissue is formed, energy produced and waste products eliminated.—**metabolic** adj.

metabolize /məˈtæbəˌlaɪz/ vt to process by metabolism; to assimilate.

metacarpal /ˌmetəˈkɑrpəl/ adj pertaining to the metacarpus. • n a bone of the metacarpus.

metacarpus /ˌmetəˈkɑrpəs/ n (pl **metacarpi**) the bones of that part of the hand that is between the wrist and the fingers, or the corresponding part in other animals.

metacentre, metacenter /ˈmetəˌsentər/ n the point in a floating body where the verticals intersect when the body is tilted and on the position of which its equilibrium or stability depends.—**metacentric** adj.

metage /ˈmitɪdʒ/ n the official weighing or measuring of the contents of something; the fee paid for this.

metagenesis /ˌmetəˈdʒenəsɪs/ n the alternation of sexual and asexual generations.—**metagenetic** adj.—**metagenetically** adv.

metal /ˈmetəl/ n any of a class of chemical elements which are often lustrous, ductile solids, and are good conductors of heat, electricity, etc, such as gold, iron, copper, etc; any alloy of such elements as brass, bronze, etc; anything consisting of metal.—**metalled** adj.

metallic /məˈtælɪk/ adj of, relating to, or made of metal; similar to metal.

metalliferous /ˌmetəˈlɪfərəs/ adj yielding metal or metallic ores.

metalline /ˈmetəlɪn/ or /-ˌlaɪn/ adj metallic; impregnated with or yielding metal.

metallize, metalize /ˈmetəˌlaɪz/ vt to give metallic qualities to; to coat or treat with metal.

metallography /ˌmetəˈlɒɡrəfi/ n the science or description of the structure of metals and alloys; (print) lithography using metal plates to print an image.

metalloid /ˈmetəˌlɔɪd/ n a nonmetallic element that possesses some of the chemical properties associated with metals. • adj of or having the properties of a metalloid; resembling a metal.—also **metalloidal**.

metallurgy /ˈmetəˌlərdʒi/ or /məˈtælərdʒi/ n the science of separating metals from their ores and preparing them for use by smelting, refining, etc.—**metallurgical** adj.—**metallurgist** n.

metamere /ˈmetəˌmiːr/ n a segment of a body, as in earthworms, crayfish, etc.

metameric /ˌmetəˈmerɪk/ adj (zool) of or having metameres; (chem) having the same elements and molecular weight but different properties.—**metamerism** n.

metamorphism /ˌmetəˈmɔrˌfizəm/ n the change in the structure of rocks through heat, pressure, etc.

metamorphosis /ˌmetəˈmɔrfəsɪs/ n (pl **metamorphoses**) a complete change of form, structure, substance, character, appearance, etc; transformation; the marked change in some animals at a stage in their growth, eg chrysalis to butterfly.—**metamorphic** adj.—**metamorphose** vi.

metaphor /ˈmetəfər/ n a figure of speech in which a word or phrase is used for another of which it is an image.—**metaphoric, metaphorical** adj.—**metaphorically** adv.

metaphrase /ˈmetəˌfreɪz/ n a word-for-word translation, the opposite of paraphrase. • vt to alter the wording of something, esp to alter the meaning; to translate literally.

metaphrast /ˈmetəˌfræstɪk/ n one who alters text, esp one who changes the form, as from verse to prose.—**metaphrastic, metaphrastical** adj.

metaphysical /ˌmetəˈfɪzɪkəl/ adj of or pertaining to metaphysics; abstruse, abstract; supernatural; (poetry) fantastic or oversubtle in style.—**metaphysically** adv.

metaphysics /ˌmetəˈfɪzɪks/ n sing the branch of philosophy that seeks to explain the nature of being and reality; speculative philosophy in general.—**metaphysician** n.

metaplasm /ˈmetəˌplæzəm/ n (biol) that part of the contents of a cell consisting of inert matter; (gram) a change in a word by the adding or dropping of a letter.—**metaplasmic** adj.

metastasis /məˈtæstəsɪs/ n (pl **metastases**) a change or shift in the location of a disease, often used of the spreading of cancer cells; a transformation or change; (rare) metabolism.—**metastatic** adj.

metatarsal /ˌmetəˈtɑrsəl/ adj pertaining to the metatarsus. • n one of the bones of the metatarsus.

metatarsus /ˌmetəˈtɑrsəs/ n (pl **metatarsi**) (anat) in humans, the instep, the middle part of the foot between the tarsus and the toes; in other animals, the part corresponding to this.

metathesis /məˈtæθəsɪs/ n (pl **metatheses**) the transposition of the letters or syllables of a word; (chem) a reaction between two compounds in which the first and second parts of one unite with the second and first parts of the other.—**metathetic, metathetical** adj.

metathorax /ˌmetəˈθɔræks/ n (pl **metathoraxes, metathoraces**) the hindmost segment of an insect's thorax, with the third pair of walking legs and the second pair of wings.

metazoan /ˌmetəˈzoːən/ n an animal belonging to a division of the animal kingdom in which the body is made up of a large number of cells, ie all animals except sponges and protozoans.

mete /miːt/ *vt* to allot; to portion (out).

metempsychosis /ˌmetəmsaɪˈkoːsɪs/ *n* (*pl* **metempsychoses**) the transmigration of the soul after the death of the body to another body or form.

meteor /ˈmiːtiər/ or /-ɔːr/ *n* a small particle of matter which travels at great speed through space and becomes luminous through friction as it enters the earth's atmosphere; a shooting star.

meteoric /ˌmiːtiˈɔrɪk/ *adj* of or relating to a meteor; dazzling, transitory.

meteorite /ˈmiːtiəˌraɪt/ *n* a meteor that has fallen to earth without being completely vaporized.—**meteoritic** *adj*.

meteorograph /ˈmiːtiərəgræf/ or /ˌmiːtiˈɔrəgræf/ *n* an instrument for recording various meteorological conditions simultaneously.

meteoroid /ˈmiːtiəˌrɔɪd/ *n* a small body moving through space, often orbiting the sun which can be seen as a meteor if it enters the earth's atmosphere.

meteorology /ˌmiːtiəˈrɒlədʒi/ *n* a study of the earth's atmosphere, particularly weather and climate.—**meteorological** *adj*.—**meteorologist** *n*.

-meter /mɪtər/ or /miːtər/ *suffix* denoting a device for measuring; metre(s) in length.

meter[1] /ˈmiːtər/ *n* a device for measuring and recording a quantity of gas, water, time, etc supplied; a parking meter. • *vt* to measure using a meter.

meter[2] *see* **metre**[1], **metre**[2].

methane /ˈmeθeɪn/ *n* a colourless, odourless, flammable gas formed by the decomposition of vegetable matter, as in marshes.

methinks /mɪˈθɪŋks/ *vb* (*pt* **methought**) (*arch*) it appears or seems to me.

method /ˈmeθəd/ *n* the mode or procedure of accomplishing something; orderliness of thought; an orderly arrangement or system.

methodical /məˈθedɪkəl/ *adj* orderly, systematic.—**methodically** *adv*.

Methodist /ˈmeθədɪst/ *n* a member of a Christian denomination founded by John Wesley.—**Methodism** *n*.

methodize /ˈmeθəˌdaɪz/ *vt* to reduce to method; systematize.

methodology /ˌmeθəˈdɒlədʒi/ *n* (*pl* **methodologies**) the methods and procedures used by a science or discipline; the philosophical analysis of method and procedure.

methought /mɪˈθɔt/ *see* **methinks**.

meths /meθs/ *n* (*inf*) methylated spirit.

Methuselah /məˈθuːzələ/ or /-ˈθjuːzələ/ *n* a wine bottle eight times the size of an ordinary bottle; (*Old Testament*) a patriarch reputed to have been 969 years old when he died; a very old person.

methyl /ˈmeθəl/ *n* a compound composed of organic material and metals in which metal groups are bound directly to a metal atom.

methylated spirit *n* a form of alcohol, adulterated to render it undrinkable, used as a solvent.

methylene /ˈmeθəˌliːn/ *n* a bivalent organic radical found in unsaturated hydrocarbons; an inflammable liquid obtained from the distillation of wood.

meticulous /məˈtɪkjuləs/ *adj* very precise about small details.—**meticulously** *adv*.—**meticulousness** *n*.

métier /meɪˈtjeɪ/ or /ˈmeɪ-/ *n* a person's calling or trade, *esp* if that person has a natural leaning toward it; a strong point, forte.

Metol /ˈmiːˌtɒl/ or /-ˌtoːl/ *n* (*trademark*) a colourless, soluble organic substance used as a photographic developer.

metonymy /mɪˈtɒnəmi/ *n* (**metonymies**) a figure of speech in which a thing is replaced by its attribute, *eg* "the pen is mightier than the sword."—**metonym** *n*.—**metonymical, metonymic** *adj*.

metope /ˈmetəpi/ or /ˈmetoːp/ *n* (*archit*) the space between two triglyphs of a Doric frieze.

metre[1] /ˈmiːtər/ *n* rhythmic pattern in verse, the measured arrangement of syllables according to stress; rhythmic pattern in music.—*also* **meter**.

metre[2] *n* the basic unit of length in the metric system, consisting of 100 centimetres and equal to 39.37 inches.—*also* **meter**.

metric /ˈmetrɪk/ *adj* based on the metre as a standard of measurement; of, relating to, or using the metric system.

metrical /ˈmetrɪkəl/ *adj* of, relating to, or composed in rhythmic metre.—**metrically** *adv*.

metrication /ˌmetrɪˈkeɪʃən/ *n* conversion of an existent system of units into the metric system.

metrics /ˈmetrɪks/ *n sing* the study of verse form; the art of composing verse.

metric system *n* a decimal system of weights and measures based on the metre, litre and the kilogram.

metro /ˈmetroː/ *n* (*pl* **metros**) an urban underground railway system, such as in Paris and other cities.

metrology /mɪˈtrɒlədʒi/ *n* (*pl* **metrologies**) the science of weights and measures or units of measurement; any of the various systems of units.

metronome /ˈmetrəˌnoːm/ *n* an instrument that beats musical tempo.—**metronomic** *adj*.

metronymic /ˌmetrəˈnɪmɪk/ *adj* (*name*) derived from one's mother or a female ancestor. • *n* such a name.—*also* **matronymic**.

metropolis /məˈtrɒpəlɪs/ *n* the main city, often a capital of a country, state, etc; any large and important city.—**metropolitan** *adj*.

mettle /ˈmetəl/ *n* courage, spirit.

mettled /-əd/ *adj* mettlesome.

mettlesome /ˈmetlsəm/ *adj* high-spirited, full of courage.

meunière /munˈjer/ *adj* (*fish*) coated with flour, cooked in butter and served with parsley and lemon juice.

mew[1] /mjuː/ *vi* (*cat*) to emit a high-pitched cry. • *n* the cry of a cat.

mew[2] *n* a gull found in northern areas.

mew[3] *n* a cage for hawks. • *vti* (*hawk*) to shed (feathers), to moult; to put in a mew, to confine.

mewl /mjuːl/ *vi* (*baby*) to cry feebly, to whimper; to mew. • *n* a whimper.

mews /mjuːz/ *nsing* or *pl* a yard or road lined with buildings formerly used stables and later converted into living accommodation.

mezzanine /ˈmezəniːn/ or /ˈmezəˈniːn/ *n* an intermediate storey between others; a theatre balcony.

mezzo /ˈmetsoː/ *adv* (*mus*) moderately; quite. • *n* (*pl* **mezzos**) a mezzo-soprano.

mezzo-relievo /ˈmetsoːrɪˈliːvoː/ or /ˈmezoː-/ *n* (*pl* **mezzo-relievos**) a carving in half-relief, where the figures project in neither high relief nor low relief from the background.

mezzo-soprano /-səˈprænoː/ or /-ˈprɒnoː/ *n* (*pl* **mezzo-sopranos**) (*mus*) a singer, or a part, between soprano and contralto.

mezzotint /ˈmetsoːtɪnt/ or /ˈmezoː-/ *n* a method of engraving on copper in which lights are made by scraping a roughened surface; a print so made. • *vt* to engrave a copper plate using this method.

mfr *abbr* = manufacture; manufacturer.

Mg (*chem symbol*) magnesium.

mg *abbr* = milligram.

Mgr *abbr* = manager.

MHz *abbr* = megahertz.

MI *abbr* = military intelligence; myocardial infarction.

mi. *abbr* = mile; mill.

MIA *abbr* = missing in action.

miasma /miːˈæzmə/ or /maɪ-/ *n* (*pl* **miasmas, miasmata**) an unwholesome, foreboding atmosphere; an unpleasant vapour, as from decaying swamp matter.—**miasmal, miasmatic, miasmic** *adj*.

mica /ˈmaɪkə/ *n* a mineral that crystallizes in thin, flexible layers, resistant to heat.—**micaceous** *adj*.

mice /maɪs/ *see* **mouse**.

Michaelmas /ˈmaɪkəlməs/ *n* a church festival commemorating the archangel Michael, celebrated on September 29.

micra /ˈmaɪkrə/ *see* **micron**.

micro /ˈmaɪkroː/ *n* (*pl* **micros**) a microwave oven; (*comput*) a microcomputer, a microprocessor.

micro- /ˈmaɪkroː/, **micr-** /ˈmaɪkr/ *prefix* small.

microbe /ˈmaɪkroːb/ *n* a microscopic organism, *esp* a disease-causing bacterium.—**microbial, microbic** *adj*.

microbiology /ˌmaɪkroːbaɪˈɒlədʒi/ *n* the biology of bacteria and other microorganisms and their effects.—**microbiological, microbiologic** *adj*.—**microbiologically** *adv*.—**microbiologist** *n*.

microbus /-ˈbʌs/ *n* (*pl* **microbuses, microbusses**) a station wagon that resembles a small bus.

microcephalic /-ˈsefælɪk/, **microcephalous** /-ləs/ *adj* having an unusually small head.—**microcephaly** *n*.

microchip /ˈmaɪkroːtʃɪp/ *n* a small wafer of silicon, etc, containing electronic circuits.—*also* **chip**.

microcircuit /-ˌsɜːrkɪt/ *n* a miniature electronic circuit, *esp* an integrated circuit.—**microcircuitry** *n*.

microclimate /-ˌklaɪmət/ n the climate of a restricted specific place within an area as opposed to the climate of the area.—**microclimatic** adj.

micrococcus /ˌmaɪkroʊˈkɒkəs/ n (**micrococci**) a round bacterium, a source of fermentation and of zymotic disease.—**micrococcal** adj.

microcomputer /ˈmaɪkroʊkəmˌpjuːtər/ n a computer in which the central processing unit is contained in one or more microprocessors.

microcosm /ˌmaɪkroʊˈkɒzəm/ n a miniature universe or world.—**microcosmic, microcosmical** adj.—**microcosmically** adv.

microcyte /ˈmaɪkroʊˌsaɪt/ n an unusually small red blood corpuscle, often present in disease.—**microcytic** adj.

microdot /-ˌdɒt/ n a photographic reproduction of a document, plan, etc reduced to a tiny dot, esp for reasons of espionage.

microeconomics /-iːkəˈnɒmɪks/ n sing the branch of economics concerned with the activities of consumers, firms, and commodities.—**microeconomic** adj.

microfiche /-ˌfiːtʃ/ n (pl **microfiche, microfiches**) a sheet of microfilm containing pages of printed matter.—also **film card**.

microfilm /-fɪlm/ n film on which documents, etc, are recorded in reduced scale. • vt to record on microfilm.

microfloppy /-ˌflɒpi/ n (pl **microfloppies**) a floppy disk of 3.5 inches diameter contained in a hard covering.

micrograph /-ˌɡræf/ n a photograph of something as seen through a microscope; a device for executing minute engraving or writing.

micrography /maɪˈkrɒɡrəfi/ n the description, study or representation of microscopic objects; the process of writing in miniature.—**micrographic** adj.

micrometer /maɪˈkrɒmɪtər/ n any of various instruments for measuring minute distances, angles, thicknesses, or apparent diameters, sometimes used with a microscope.

micrometre, micrometer /ˈmaɪkroʊˌmiːtər/ n a unit of length of one thousandth of a millimetre, a micron.

micrometry n the measurement of tiny objects, distances, etc, by a micrometer.—**micrometric, micrometrical** adj.—**micrometrically** adv.

micron /ˈmaɪkrɒn/ n (pl **microns, micra**) one millionth of a metre, a micrometer.

microorganism /ˌmaɪkroʊˈɔːrɡəˌnɪzəm/ n an organism visible only through a microscope.

microphone /ˈmaɪkrəˌfoʊn/ n an instrument for transforming sound waves into electric signals, esp for transmission, or recording.—**microphonic** adj.

microphotograph /ˌmaɪkroʊˈfoʊtəˌɡræf/ n a photograph taken through a microscope or of microscopic size, in which the details cannot be distinguished by the naked eye; a photomicrograph.—**microphotographic** adj.—**microphotography** n.

microphyte /ˈmaɪkroʊˌfaɪt/ n a microscopic vegetable growth, esp a parasitic one.—**microphytic** adj.

microprocessor /ˌmaɪkroʊˈproʊˌsesər/ n a computer processor contained on one or more integrated circuits.

microscope /ˈmaɪkrəˌskoʊp/ n an optical instrument for making magnified images of minute objects by means of a lens or lenses.

microscopic /ˈmaɪkrəˌskɒpɪk/ adj of, with, like, a microscope; visible only through a microscope; very small.—**microscopically** adv.

microscopy /maɪˈkrɒskəpi/ n (pl **microscopies**) the use of microscopes; microscopic investigation.—**microscopist** n.

microseism /ˈmaɪkroʊˌsiːzəm/ n a faint earth tremor, probably not related to earthquakes.—**microseismic** adj.

microtome /ˈmaɪkroʊˌtoʊm/ n an instrument for cutting thin sections for microscopic examination, used particularly in biology.

microwave /ˈmaɪkroʊˌweɪv/ n an electromagnetic wave between 1 and 100 centimetres in length; (inf) a microwave oven. • vt to cook (food) in a microwave oven.—**microwavable, microwaveable** adj.

microwave oven n a cooker in which food is cooked or heated by microwaves.

micturate /ˈmɪktʃʊreɪt/ vi to urinate.—**micturition** n.

mid /mɪd/ adj middle. • prep amid.

mid. /mɪd/ abbr = middle.

mid- /mɪd/ prefix middle.

midday /ˈmɪddeɪ/ n the middle of the day, noon.

midden /ˈmɪdən/ n a dunghill, a refuse heap.

middle /ˈmɪdəl/ adj halfway between two given points, times, etc; intermediate; central. • n the point halfway between two extremes; something intermediate; the waist. • vt to put in the middle; (naut) to fold (a sail) in the middle.

middle age n the time between youth and old age, c.40-60.—**middle-aged** adj.

Middle Ages npl the period of European history between about AD 500 and 1500.

middle class n the class between the lower and upper classes, mostly composed of professional and business people.—**middle-class** adj.

Middle East n a general term applied currently to an area extending from the eastern Mediterranean to the Gulf of Arabia; (formerly) that part of Southern Asia from the Tigris and Euphrates to Burma.

middleman /ˈmɪdəlmən/ n (pl **middlemen**) a dealer between producer and consumer; an intermediary.

middle-of-the-road adj avoiding extremes, esp political extremes.—**middle-of-the-roader** n.

middleweight /ˈmɪdəlˌweɪt/ n a professional boxer weighing 154-160 pounds (70-72.5 kilograms); a wrestler weighing usu 172-192 pounds (78-87 kilograms).

middling /ˈmɪdəlɪŋ/ adj of medium quality, size, etc; second-rate. • adv moderately.—**middlingly** adv.

middy /ˈmɪdi/ n (pl **middies**) (inf) a midshipman; a middy blouse; (Austral) a glass of beer, usu containing half a pint.

middy blouse n a loose blouse with a sailor collar.

midge /mɪdʒ/ n a small gnat-like insect with a painful bite.

midget /ˈmɪdʒət/ n a very small person, a dwarf; something small of its kind.—also adj.

midi /ˈmɪdi/ n a coat or skirt that reaches to mid calf.

midland /ˈmɪdlənd/ n the middle part of a country; (pl) (with cap) central England; the industrial and manufacturing area of that part of England. • adj of or in midland; inland.

midlife /ˈmɪdəlˌlaɪf/ n (pl **midlives**) middle age.—also adj.

midmost adj in or nearest the middle. • adv in the middle.

midnight /ˈmɪdnaɪt/ n twelve o'clock at night.

Midrash /ˈmɪdræʃ/ n (pl **Midrashim**) a critical exposition of or a sermon on the Jewish scriptural law or some portion of it; one of the various collections of these originating between AD 400 and 1200.

midrib /ˈmɪdrɪb/ n the principal central vein of a leaf.

midriff /-rɪf/ n the middle part of the torso between the abdomen and the chest.—also adj.

midship /-ʃɪp/ adj (naut) of or pertaining to the middle part of a ship.

midshipman /-ʃɪpmən/ n (pl **midshipmen**) in some navies, a noncommissioned officer ranking immediately below a sublieutenant; this naval rank; (formerly) a naval cadet officer; an American fish with light-producing organs.

midships /-ʃɪps/ adv (naut) at, near or toward the middle of a ship, amidships.

midst /mɪdst/ n middle. • prep amidst, among.

midsummer /mɪdˈsʌmər/ or /ˈmɪd-/ n the middle of summer.—also adj.

Midsummer Day n June 24, celebrated as the summer solstice or in commemoration of the birth of St John the Baptist.

Midsummer Eve n the day before Midsummer Day, June 23.

midway /ˈmɪdweɪ/ adv halfway. • n a middle course of action; the area of a carnival where the sideshows are.

midwife /-waɪf/ n (pl **midwives**) a person trained to assist women before, during, and after childbirth.—**midwifery** n.

mien /miːn/ n the expression of the face; demeanour.

miff /mɪf/ n (inf) a petty quarrel, a tiff; a sulky mood. • vti to take offence; to offend.

miffy /mɪfi/ adj (**miffier, miffiest**) (inf) touchy, huffy; over-sensitive.—**miffiness** n.

might[1] /maɪt/ see **may**.

might[2] n power, bodily strength.

mightn't /ˈmaɪtənt/ = might not.

mighty /maɪti/ adj (**mightier, mightiest**) powerful, strong; massive; (inf) very.—**mightily** adv.—**mightiness** n.

mignonette /ˌmɪnjəˈnet/ n a sweet-scented plant with spikes of small green-white flowers; a greyish-green colour; a delicate bobbin lace.

migraine /ˈmaɪɡreɪn/ n an intense, periodic headache, usu limited to one side of the head.

migrant /'maɪgrənt/ n a person or animal that moves from one region or country to another; an itinerant agricultural labourer. • adj migrating.

migrate /'maɪgreɪt/ vi to settle in another country or region; (birds, animals) to move to another region with the change in season.—**migration** n.—**migratory** adj.

mikado /mɪ'kɑːdoː/ n (sl **mikados**) (arch) (often with cap) the Japanese emperor.

mike /maɪk/ n (inf) a microphone. • vt to provide with a microphone; to transmit by microphone.

mil /mɪl/ n a unit of length of one thousandth of an inch; (gunnery) an angle of one sixty-four-hundredth of a circumference; a millilitre.

mil. abbr = military; militia.

milady /mɪ'leɪdi/ n (pl **miladies**) (formerly) a word used in Europe for an aristocratic Englishwoman.

milage /'maɪlɪdʒ/ see **mileage**.

milch /mɪltʃ/ adj yielding milk, used esp of cattle.

milch cow n a cow from which milk is obtained for human consumption; a ready source of gain.

mild /maɪld/ adj (temper) gentle; (weather) temperate; bland; feeble.—**mildly** adv.—**mildness** n.

mildew /'mɪlduː/ or /-djuː/ n a fungus that attacks some plants or appears on damp cloth, etc as a whitish coating. • vti to affect or be affected with mildew.—**mildewy** adj.

mile /maɪl/ n a unit of linear measure equal to 5,280 feet (1.61 km); the nautical mile is 6,075 feet (1.85 km).

mileage /'maɪlɪdʒ/ n total miles travelled; an allowance per mile for travelling expenses; the average number of miles that can be travelled, as per litre of fuel.—also **milage**.

milestone /'maɪlstoːn/ n a stone marking the number of miles to a place; an important event in life, history, etc.

milfoil /'mɪlfɔɪl/ n a yarrow plant; one of various pond plants with feather-like leaves and small flowers.

miliaria /ˌmɪli'erɪə/ n a skin disease resulting from blocked sweat glands and characterized by an acute itchiness, heat rash.—**miliarial** adj.

miliary /'mɪliˌeri/ or /-əri/ adj (growth, lesion) very small; (skin disease) marked by small lesions resembling millet seeds.

milieu /mɪl'juː/ or /-'juʊ/ n (pl **milieus, milieux**) environment, esp social setting.

militant /'mɪlɪtənt/ adj agressive and ready to fight, esp for some cause; combative, engaged in warfare.—also n.—**militance, militancy** n.—**militantly** adv.

militarism /'mɪlɪtəˌrɪzəm/ n military spirit; a policy of aggressive military preparedness.

militarist /'mɪlɪtərɪst/ n a believer in militarism; a student of military science.—**militaristic** adj.—**militaristically** adv.

militarize /-ˌraɪz/ vt to equip and prepare for war.—**militarization** n.

military /'mɪlɪteri/ adj relating to soldiers or to war; warlike. • n (pl **militaries**) the armed forces.

militate /'mɪlɪˌteɪt/ vt to have influence or force; to produce an effect or change.

militia /mɪ'lɪʃə/ n an army composed of civilians called out in time of emergency.—**militiaman** n (pl **militiamen**).

milk /mɪlk/ n a white nutritious liquid secreted by female mammals for feeding their young. • vt to draw milk from; to extract money, etc, from; to exploit.—**milker** n.

milkmaid /'mɪlkmeɪd/ n a girl or woman who milks cows or works in a dairy.

milkman /-mæn/ n (pl **milkmen**) a person who sells or delivers milk to homes.

milk run n (sl) a routine journey.

milksop /'mɪlksɒp/ n a weak cowardly man or boy.—**milksoppy** adj.

milk toast n toasted bread soaked in warm milk, often eaten by babies and invalids.

milk tooth n any of the first teeth of a mammal.

milkweed /'mɪlkwiːd/ n a plant found mainly in North America yielding a milky sap and with pointed pods containing tufted seeds; any plant with a milky sap.—also **silkweed**.

milkwort /-wərt/ n a kind of plant with small blue, pink or white flowers.

milky /'mɪlki/ adj (**milkier, milkiest**) of, filled with, consisting of, yielding, or resembling milk; timid.—**milkily** adv.—**milkiness** n.

Milky Way n (with **the**) the galaxy to which the Earth belongs; the system of stars, nebulae, etc, that can be seen in the night sky as a trailing ribbon of light and forms part of the Galaxy.

mill[1] /mɪl/ n an apparatus for grinding by crushing between rough surfaces; a building where grain is ground into flour; a factory. • vt to produce or grind in a mill; (coins) to put a raised edge on. • vi to move around confusedly.—**miller** n.

mill[2] n a unit of money equal to one tenth of a cent.

millboard /'mɪlbɔrd/ n a thick pasteboard, often black or grey, that forms the front and back covers and spine of a book, usu covered by the book binding.

millenarian /ˌmɪli'nerɪən/ adj consisting of or pertaining to a thousand years; pertaining to the millennium or to millenarianism. • n a believer in the millennium; an advocate of millenarianism.

millenarianism n (Christianity) the belief that the Second Coming of Christ will be preceded or followed by a thousand years of holiness.

millenary /'mɪlənˌeri/ or /mɪ'lɛnəri/ adj of or pertaining to a thousand; millenarian. • n (pl **millenaries**) a thousandth anniversary; one thousand as a total, esp one thousand years; a millenarian.

millennium /mɪ'lɛnɪəm/ n (pl **millennia, milleniums**) a period of a thousand years; (Christianity) a period of a thousand years of holiness preceding or following the Second Coming of Christ; a coming time of happiness.—**millennial** adj.—**millennially** adv.

millepede /'mɪlɪpiːd/ see **millipede**.

millepore /-pɔr/ n a tropical coelenterate resembling a coral, with a smooth surface perforated with very small pores.

miller /'mɪlər/ n one who or that which mills; an owner of a mill; a moth with a floury appearance.

millesimal /mɪ'lɛsɪməl/ adj pertaining to a thousandth. • n a thousandth.

millet /'mɪlət/ n a cereal grass used for grain and fodder.

milli- /'mɪli/ prefix a thousandth part.

milligram /'mɪliˌgræm/ n a thousandth of a gramme.

millilitre, milliliter /'mɪliˌliːtər/ n a thousandth (.001) of a litre.

millimetre, millimeter /'mɪliˌmiːtər/ n a thousandth (.001) of a metre.

milliner /'mɪlɪnər/ n a designer or seller of women's hats.—**millinery** n.

milling /'mɪlɪŋ/ n the act of grinding in or passing through a dressing mill; the process of making a serrated edge on a coin, etc; the serrated edge of such a coin; a stratagem to stop cattle stampeding.

million /'mɪljən/ n (pl **million, millions**) a thousand thousands, the number one followed by six zeros: 1,000,000; (inf) a very large number.—**millionth** adj.

millionaire /'mɪljəˌner/ or /ˌmɪljə'nɛr/ n a person who owns at least a million of money; one who is extremely rich.

millipede /'mɪlɪpiːd/ n a wormlike arthropod with many legs and a segmented body.—also **millepede**.

millpond /'mɪlpɒnd/ n a reservoir of water for driving a mill; any stretch of calm water.

millrace /'mɪlreɪs/ n a current of water that drives a mill; the channel in which this flows.

millstone /'mɪlstoːn/ n a stone used for grinding corn; a heavy burden.

millwright /'mɪlraɪt/ n a person who designs, builds, and repairs mills or mill parts.

milord /mɪ'lɔrd/ n (formerly) a word used in Europe for an aristocratic or rich Englishman.

milt /mɪlt/ n the sperm of a male fish; its reproductive glands when filled with this; the spleen of some animals. • vt to fertilize (the roe of female fish), esp artificially.

milter /'mɪltər/ n a male fish in the breeding season.

Miltonic /mɪl'tɒnɪk/, **Miltonian** /mɪl'toːnɪən/ adj pertaining to, characteristic of, or resembling the writings of the English poet John Milton (1608–74).

mime /maɪm/ n a theatrical technique using action without words; a mimic. • vi to act or express using gestures alone; (singers, musicians) to perform as if singing or playing live to what is actually a prerecorded piece of music.—**mimer** n.

mimeograph /'mɪmɪəˌgræf/ n a machine for making multiple copies of a letter, drawing, etc, by means of a stencil fixed to an inked drum, and masking the non-printing areas; a copy produced from this machine. • *vti* to produce copies (of something) by using this machine.

mimesis /mɪˈmiːsɪs/ or /maɪ-/ *n* (*art, literature, etc*) the realistic representation of objects, people, everyday life, etc; (*biol*) mimicry; (*med*) a condition characterized by symptoms that occur in other diseases but that cannot be found by objective medical testing; a disease that mimics the symptoms of another disease.

mimetic /maɪˈmetɪk/ *adj* of or given to imitation or mimicry; (*biol*) pertaining to or having the ability to mimic.—**mimetically** *adv*.

mimic /ˈmɪmɪk/ *n* a person who imitates, *esp* an actor skilled in mimicry. • *adj* related to mimicry; make-believe; sham. • *vt* (**mimicking, mimicked**) to imitate or ridicule.—**mimicker** *n*.

mimicry /ˈmɪmɪkri/ *n* (*pl* **mimicries**) practice, art, or way of mimicking; (*biol*) the resemblance of an animal to its environment, another animal, etc, to provide protection from predators, mimesis.

mimosa /mɪˈmoːzə/ *n* any of a genus of leguminous plants, *usu* with clustered yellow flowers, whose leaves and stems fold when touched or when exposed to light; the sensitive plant; any of several related or similar plants.

Min. *abbr* = Minister; Ministry.

min. *abbr* = minimum; minute(s).

mina[1] /ˈmaɪnə/ *n* (*pl* **minas, minae**) a weight and coin, current in ancient Anatolia, equal to one sixtieth of a talent.

mina[2] *see* **myna.**

minaret /ˌmɪnəˈret/ or /ˈmɪnəˌret/ *n* a high, slender tower on a mosque from which the call to prayer is made.

minatory /ˈmɪnətɒri/, **minatorial** /-riəl/ *adj* threatening.—**minatorily** *adv*.

mince /mɪns/ *vt* to chop or cut up into small pieces; to diminish or moderate one's words. • *vi* to speak or walk with affected daintiness.—**mincer** *n*.—**mincing** *adj*.—**mincingly** *adv*.

mincemeat /ˈmɪnsmiːt/ *n* a mixture of chopped apples, raisins, etc, used as a pie filling; finely chopped meat.

mind /maɪnd/ *n* the faculty responsible for intellect, thought, feelings, speech; memory; intellect; reason; opinion; sanity. • *vt* to object to, take offence to; to pay attention to; to obey; to take care of; to be careful about; to care about. • *vi* to pay attention; to be obedient; to be careful; to object.

mind-bending *adj* (*inf*) (*drugs, etc*) unbalancing the mind; (*inf*) stretching credibility to the limits.—**mind-bender** *n*.—**mind-bendingly** *adv*.

mind-blowing *adj* (*inf*) (*drugs*) hallucinatory.

mind-boggling *adj* (*inf*) astonishing, bewildering.—**mind-boggler** *n*.

minded /ˈmaɪndəd/ *adj* disposed, inclined; (in compounds) having a mind as described, *eg* small-minded.—**mindedness** *n*.

minder /ˈmaɪndər/ *n* a person who looks after or protects another.

mind-expanding *adj* producing awareness; psychedelic, distorting.

mindful /ˈmaɪndfʊl/ *adj* heedful, not forgetful.—**mindfully** *adv*.—**mindfulness** *n*.

mindless /-ləs/ *adj* unthinking, stupid; requiring little intellectual effort.—**mindlessly** *adv*.—**mindlessness** *n*.

mindset /-set/ *n* attitude, *esp* when fixed or rigid; a habit.

mind's eye *n* the visual memory or imagination.

mine[1] /maɪn/ *poss pron* belonging to me.

mine[2] *n* an excavation from which minerals are dug; an explosive device concealed in the water or ground to destroy enemy ships, personnel, or vehicles that pass over or near them; a rich supply or source. • *vt* to excavate; to lay explosive mines in an area. • *vi* to dig or work a mine.

mine detector *n* a device for indicating the whereabouts of explosive mines.—**mine detection** *n*.

minefield /ˈmaɪnfiːld/ *n* an area sown with explosive mines; a situation containing hidden problems.

minelayer /ˈmaɪnˌleɪər/ *n* a ship or aircraft for laying mines.

miner /ˈmaɪnər/ *n* a person who works in a mine.

mineral /ˈmɪnərəl/ *n* an inorganic substance, found naturally in the earth; any substance neither vegetable nor animal. • *adj* relating to or containing minerals.

mineralize /ˈmɪnərəˌlaɪz/ *vt* to convert (something) into a mineral; to impregnate (something) with mineral matter; to change something into a fossil-like object. • *vi* (*gases, etc, in molten rock*) to transform a metal into an ore.—**mineralization** *n*.

mineral kingdom *n* the group of natural substances that consist of only inorganic matter.

mineralogy /ˌmɪnəˈrɒlədʒi/ *n* the science of minerals.—**mineralogical** *adj*.—**mineralogically** *adv*.—**mineralogist** *n*.

mineral water *n* water containing mineral salts or gases, often with medicinal properties.

minestrone /ˌmɪnəˈstroːni/ *n* a soup of vegetables with pieces of pasta.

minesweeper /ˈmaɪnˌswiːpər/ *n* a ship for clearing away explosive mines.—**minesweeping** *n*.

mingle /ˈmɪŋgəl/ *vti* to mix; to combine.—**mingler** *n*.

mingy /ˈmɪndʒi/ *adj* (**mingier, mingiest**) (*inf*) meagre in quantity; miserly, mean.

mini /ˈmɪni/ *n* (*pl* **minis**) something smaller than others of its type; a miniskirt.

mini- /ˈmɪni/ *prefix* small.

miniature /ˈmɪnɪtʃər/ or /-nɪətʃ-/ *adj* minute, on a small scale. • *n* a painting or reproduction on a very small scale.—**miniaturist** *n*.

miniaturize /ˈmɪnɪtʃəˌraɪz/ or /-nɪətʃ-/ *vt* to greatly reduce the size of.—**miniaturization** *n*.

minibar /ˈmɪnɪbɑr/ *n* a small refrigerator in a hotel bedroom, stocked with alcoholic drinks.

minibus /-ˌbʌs/ *n* (*pl* **minibuses, minibusses**) a small bus for carrying up to twelve passengers.

minicab /-ˌkæb/ *n* a saloon car used as a taxi, which can be booked by telephone but not hailed.

minicar /-ˌkɑr/ *n* a very small car.

minicomputer /-kəmˌpjuːtər/ *n* a computer intermediate in size and processing power between a mainframe and a microcomputer.

minim /ˈmɪnɪm/ *n* a unit of fluid measure of one sixtieth of a fluid dram (0.0616ml) in the US and one twentieth of a scruple (0.592ml) in the UK; (*mus*) a half note.

minima /ˈmɪnɪmə/ *see* **minimum.**

minimal /ˈmɪnɪməl/ *adj* very minute; least possible.—**minimality** *n*.—**minimally** *adv*.

minimalism /ˌmɪnɪməˈlɪzəm/ *n* a style in the creation of art, music, etc, that uses the fewest possible elements to achieve the greatest effect.—**minimalist** *n, adj*.

minimize /ˈmɪnɪmaɪz/ *vt* to reduce to or estimate at a minimum.—**minimization** *n*.

minimum /ˈmɪnɪməm/ *n* (*pl* **minimums, minima**) the least possible amount; the lowest degree or point reached.

mining /ˈmaɪnɪŋ/ *n* the act, process, or industry of excavating from the earth; (*mil*) the laying of explosive mines.

minion /ˈmɪnɪən/ *n* a servile flatterer or dependant; an obsequious person acting on behalf of or carrying out the wishes of another. • *adj* dainty, graceful.

miniseries /ˈmɪnɪˌsɪriːz/ *n* (*pl* **miniseries**) (*TV*) the dramatization of a novel, etc, shown in several episodes; (*sport*) a short series.

miniskirt /ˈmɪnɪˌskɜrt/ *n* a very short skirt.

minister /ˈmɪnɪstər/ *n* a clergyman serving a church; an official heading a government department; a diplomat. • *vi* to serve as a minister in a church; to give help (to).—**ministerial** *adj*.—**ministerially** *adv*.

ministrant /ˈmɪnɪstrənt/ *adj* serving as a minister. • *n* a person who ministers.

ministration /ˌmɪnɪˈstreɪʃən/ *n* the act or process of giving aid; the act of ministering religiously.

ministry /ˈmɪnɪstri/ *n* (*pl* **ministries**) the act of ministering; the clergy; the profession of a clergyman; a government department headed by a minister; the building housing a government department.

minium /ˈmɪnɪəm/ *n* red oxide of lead, used as a pigment in paints; red lead.

miniver /ˈmɪnɪvər/ *n* a white fur, orig from the Siberian squirrel, used as a trimming on ceremonial robes, etc.

mink /mɪŋk/ *n* (*pl* **mink, minks**) any of several carnivorous weasel-like mammals valued for its durable soft fur.

minnesinger /ˈmɪnɪˌsɪŋgər/ *n* any of the German lyric poets and musicians of the 12th-14th centuries who sang about love and beauty.

minnow /ˈmɪnoː/ *n* (*pl* **minnow, minnows**) a small, slender freshwater fish.

minor /ˈmaɪnər/ *adj* lesser in size, importance, degree, extent, etc; (*mus*) lower than the corresponding major by a half step. • *n* (*law*) a person under full legal age; (*education*) a secondary area of study requiring fewer credits; (*mus*) a minor key, interval, or scale; (*sport*) a minor league, *esp* in baseball. • *vi* (*with* **in**) to take a subject requiring fewer credits.

Minorite /ˈmaɪnəˌraɪt/, **Minorist** /-rɪst/ *n* a Franciscan friar, *esp* one of the order of Friars Minor.

minority /maɪˈnɒrɪti/ or /mɪ-/ *n* (*pl* **minorities**) the smaller part or number; a political or racial group smaller than the majority group; the state of being under age.

Minotaur /ˈmɪnətər/ or /ˈmaɪ-/ *n* (*Greek myth*) a monster with the head of a bull and the body of a man, which ate human flesh.

minster /ˈmɪnɪstər/ *n* a large and important church, often with cathedral status.

minstrel /ˈmɪnɪstrəl/ *n* a travelling entertainer and musician in the Middle Ages; a performer in a minstrel show.

minstrel show *n* a variety show with performers singing and dancing wearing black face make-up.

minstrelsy /-trəlsi/ *n* (*pl* **minstrelsies**) the art or occupation of minstrels; minstrels collectively; a collection of ballad poetry.

mint[1] /mɪnt/ *n* the place where money is coined; a large amount of money; a source of supply. • *adj* unused, in perfect condition. • *vt* (*coins*) to imprint; to invent.—**minter** *n*.

mint[2] *n* an aromatic plant whose leaves are used for flavouring.—**minty** *adj*.

mintage /ˈmɪntɪdʒ/ *n* a coin, etc, produced in a mint; the process of producing coins, etc, in a mint; the fee paid to a mint for coining gold or silver; an official mark on a coin.

mint julep *n* a tall drink of bourbon or brandy and sugar over crushed ice, garnished with mint.

minuend /ˈmɪnjuˌend/ *n* (*math*) the number from which another number is to be subtracted.

minuet /ˌmɪnjuˈet/ *n* (the music for) a slow, graceful dance in triple time.

minus /ˈmaɪnəs/ *prep* less; (*inf*) without. • *adj* involving subtraction; negative; less than. • *n* a sign (-), indicating subtraction or negative quantity.

minute[1] /ˈmɪnɪt/ *n* the sixtieth part of an hour or a degree; a moment; (*pl*) an official record of a meeting. • *vt* to record or summarize the proceedings (of).

minute[2] /maɪˈnjuːt/ *adj* tiny; detailed; exact.—**minuteness** *n*.

minutely[1] /ˈmɪnɪtli/ *adj* occurring every minute. • *adv* every minute.

minutely[2] /maɪˈnjuːtli/ *adv* in a minute manner; precisely.

minuteman /ˈmɪnɪtmæn/ *n* (*pl* **minutemen**) (*sometimes cap*) a member of the militia in the War of American Independence, ready to fight at a minute's notice.

minutiae /mɪˈnuːʃɪaɪ/ or /-ˈnjuː-/, /maɪ-/, /-ʃɪə/, /-ʃə/ *npl* (*sing* **minutia**) small or unimportant details.

minx /mɪŋks/ *n* a pert, forward girl; (*arch*) a prostitute.—**minxish** *adj*.

Miocene /ˈmaɪəˌsiːn/ *adj* pertaining to the middle division of the Tertiary formation after the Olicene and before the Pliocene eras, marked by the appearance of grasses and grazing mammals. • *n* this division or rock formation.

miosis /maɪˈoʊsɪs/ *n* abnormal contraction of the pupil of the eye.—*also* **myosis**.—**miotic** *adj, n*.

miracle /ˈmɪrəkəl/ *n* an extraordinary event attributed to the supernatural; an unusual or astounding event; a remarkable example of something.

miraculous /mɪˈrækjuləs/ *adj* supernatural; wonderful; able to work miracles.—**miraculously** *adv*.—**miraculousness** *n*.

mirage /mɪˈrɑːʒ/ *n* an optical illusion in which a distant object or expanse of water seems to be nearby, caused by light reflection from hot air; anything illusory or fanciful.

mire /maɪr/ *n* an area of wet, soggy, or muddy ground. • *vt* to sink in mire; to dirty; to embroil in difficulties.

mirk /mɜːrk/ *see* **murk**.

mirky /ˈmɜːrki/ *see* **murky**.

mirror /ˈmɪrər/ *n* a smooth surface that reflects images; a faithful depiction. • *vt* (**mirroring, mirrored**) to reflect or depict faithfully.

mirth /mɜːrθ/ *n* merriment, *esp* with laughter.

mirthful /ˈmɜːrfʊl/ *adj* full of merriment.—**mirthfully** *adv*.—**mirthfulness** *n*.

mirthless /-ləs/ *adj* lacking laughter; miserable.—**mirthlessly** *adv*.—**mirthlessness** *n*.

mis-[1] /mɪs/ *prefix* wrong(ly); bad(ly); no, not.

mis-[2] *see* **miso-**.

misadventure /ˌmɪsədˈventʃər/ *n* an unlucky accident; bad luck.

misalliance /ˌmɪsəˈlaɪəns/ *n* an unsuitable alliance, *usu* by marriage with a person of lower social status; a mésalliance.

misanthrope /ˈmɪsənˌθroʊp/ or /ˌmɪz-/, **misanthropist** /mɪˈsænθrəpɪst/ or /-ˈzæn-/ *n* a person who hates or distrusts mankind.

misanthropic /ˌmɪsənˈθrɒpɪk/ or /ˌmɪz-/ *adj* of or characterized by hatred of his or her fellow human beings.—**misanthropically** *adv*.—**misanthropy** *n*.

misapprehend /ˌmɪsæprɪˈhend/ *vt* to misunderstand; to misconceive.—**misapprehension** *n*.

misappropriate /ˌmɪsəˈproʊpriˌeɪt/ *vt* to appropriate wrongly or dishonestly; to use illegally; to embezzle.—**misappropriation** *n*.

misbehave /ˌmɪsbɪˈheɪv/ *vi* to behave badly. • *vt* to behave (oneself) badly.—**misbehavior, misbehaviour** *n*.

misc. *abbr* = miscellaneous.

miscalculate /ˌmɪsˈkælkjuˌleɪt/ *vti* to calculate wrongly.—**miscalculation** *n*.

miscarriage /ˈmɪsˌkærɪdʒ/ *n* the spontaneous expulsion of a foetus prematurely; mismanagement or failure.

miscarry /ˈmɪsˌkæri/ *vi* (**miscarrying, miscarried**) to spontaneously expel a foetus from the uterus; to be unsuccessful; to fail.

miscellaneous /ˌmɪsəˈleɪniəs/ *adj* consisting of various kinds; mixed.—**miscellaneously** *adv*.—**miscellaneousness** *n*.

miscellany /ˈmɪsələni/ *n* (*pl* **miscellanies**) a mixed collection; a book comprising miscellaneous writings, etc.

mischance /ˈmɪstʃæns/ *n* bad luck; an unlucky event.

mischief /ˈmɪstʃɪf/ *n* wayward behaviour; damage.

mischievous /ˈmɪstʃɪvəs/ *adj* harmful, prankish.—**mischievously** *adv*.—**mischievousness** *n*.

miscible /ˈmɪsɪbəl/ *adj* (*chem*) (*liquids*) capable of being mixed.—**miscibility** *n*.

misconceive /ˌmɪskənˈsiːv/ *vt* to conceive wrongly; to misjudge; to misapprehend; to misunderstand.—**misconceiver** *n*.

misconception /ˌmɪskənˈsepʃən/ *n* a mistaken idea; misunderstanding.

misconduct /mɪsˈkɒndʌkt/ *n* dishonest management; improper behaviour. • *vt* to conduct (oneself) badly; to manage dishonestly.

misconstrue /ˌmɪskənˈstruː/ *vt* (**misconstruing, misconstrued**) to misinterpret.—**misconstruction** *n*.

miscreant /ˈmɪskrɪənt/ *n* an unscrupulous villain; (*arch*) a heretic. • *adj* unscrupulous; (*arch*) heretical.

misdeed /mɪsˈdiːd/ *n* a wrong or wicked act; crime; sin, etc.

misdemeanour, misdemeanor /ˌmɪsdəˈmiːnər/ *n* (*law*) a minor offence, a misdeed.

miser /ˈmaɪzər/ *n* a greedy, stingy person who hoards money for its own sake.

miserable /ˈmɪzrəbəl/ or /ˈmɪzər-/ *adj* wretched; unhappy; causing misery; bad, inadequate; pitiable.—**miserableness** *n*.—**miserably** *adv*.

Miserere /ˌmiːzeˈreɪreɪ/ *n* the 51st Psalm, appointed for penitential acts; a musical setting of this psalm; (*without cap*) a misericord in a choir stall.

misericord, misericorde /ˈmɪzərɪˌkɔrd/ *n* a small ledge, often carved, on the underside of a folding seat in the stall of a church against which a worshipper can lean when standing; in the Middle Ages, a small dagger for giving a death thrust to a seriously wounded person, *esp* a knight; (*Christianity*) the relaxation of monastic rules for elderly or infirm monks or nuns; a room in a monastery for those with such a dispensation.

miserly /ˈmaɪzərli/ *adj* like a miser; tending to hoard; very mean.—**miserliness** *n*.

misery /ˈmɪzəri/ *n* (*pl* **miseries**) extreme pain, unhappiness, or poverty; a cause of such suffering.

misfeasance /mɪsˈfiːzəns/ *n* (*law*) the wrong performance of something that is itself legal.—**misfeasor** *n*.

misfire /mɪsˈfaɪr/ *vi* (*engine, etc*) to fail to ignite, start; to fail to succeed.—*also n*.

misfit /ˈmɪsfɪt/ *n* something that fits badly; a maladjusted person.

misfortune /mɪsˈfɔrtʃən/ *n* ill luck; trouble; a mishap; bad luck.

misgiving /mɪsˈɡɪvɪŋ/ *n* a feeling of misapprehension, mistrust.

misguided /mɪsˈɡaɪdəd/ *adj* foolish; mistaken.—**misguidedly** *adv*.

mishap /ˈmɪshæp/ *n* an unfortunate accident.

mishmash /ˈmɪʃmæʃ/ *n* a confused mixture, hotchpotch.

Mishnah, Mishna /ˈmɪʃnə/ *n* (*Judaism*) the oral law; the written form of this, which was collected in the 2nd century and forms the text of the earlier part of the Talmud.

misinform /ˌmɪsɪnˈfɔrm/ *vt* to supply with wrong information.—**misinformant, misinformer** *n*.—**misinformation** *n*.

misjudge /mɪsˈdʒʌdʒ/ *vt* to judge wrongly, to form a wrong opinion.—**misjudgment** *n*.

mislay /mɪsˈleɪ/ *vt* (**mislaying, mislaid**) to lose something temporarily; to put down or install improperly.—**mislayer** *n*.

mislead /mɪsˈliːd/ *vt* (**misleading, misled**) to deceive; to give wrong information to; to lead into wrongdoing.—**misleader** *n*.

misleading /mɪsˈliːdɪŋ/ *adj* deceptive; confusing.—**misleadingly** *adv*.

misnomer /mɪsˈnoːmər/ *n* an incorrect or unsuitable name or description.—**misnomered** *adj*.

miso- /ˈmɪsoː/, **mis-** /mɪs/ *prefix* hatred of.

misogamy /mɪˈsɒgəmi/ *n* hatred of marriage.—**misogamic** *adj*.—**misogamist** *n*.

misogynist /ˌmɪsəˈdʒɪnɪst/ *n* a hater or distruster of women. •—**misogynistic** *adj*.

misogyny /mɪˈsɒdʒɪni/ *n* hatred of women.—**misogynic** *adj*.

misplace /mɪsˈpleɪs/ *vt* to put in a wrong place; (*trust, etc*) to place unwisely.—**misplacement** *n*.

misprint /mɪsˈprɪnt/ *vt* to print incorrectly. • *n* an error in printing.

misprision /mɪsˈprɪʒən/ *n* (*law*) the concealment of a seriously criminal act; the knowledge of the commission of treason and the failure to report this; (*arch*) contempt; the disparagement or undervaluing of something.

mispronounce /ˌmɪsprəˈnaʊns/ *vt* to pronounce wrongly.—**mispronunciation** *n*.

misquote /mɪsˈkwoːt/ *vt* to quote wrongly.—**misquotation** *n*.

misread /mɪsˈriːd/ *vt* (**misreading, misread**) to read or to interpret wrongly.

misrepresent /ˌmɪsrɛprɪˈzɛnt/ *vt* to represent falsely; to give an untrue idea of.—**misrepresentation** *n*.—**misrepresentative** *adj*.

misrule *n* bad government. • *vt* to govern badly; to govern in an inhumane manner or with injustice.

miss[1] /mɪs/ *n* (*pl* **misses**) a girl; (*with cap*) a title used before the surname of an unmarried woman or girl.

miss[2] *vt* to fail to reach, hit, find, meet, hear; to omit; to fail to take advantage of; to regret or discover the absence or loss of. • *vi* to fail to hit; to fail to be successful; to misfire, as an engine. • *n* a failure to hit, reach, obtain, etc.

missal /ˈmɪsəl/ *n* a book containing the prayers for Mass.

misshapen /mɪˈʃeɪpən/ *adj* badly shaped; deformed.

missile /ˈmɪsəl/ or /-saɪl/ *n* an object, as a rock, spear, rocket, etc, to be thrown, fired, or launched.

missing /ˈmɪsɪŋ/ *adj* absent; lost; lacking.

missing link *n* something required to complete a series; a hypothetical animal supposedly intermediate between the anthropoid apes and man.

mission /ˈmɪʃən/ *n* a group of people sent by a church, government, etc to carry out a special duty or task; the sending of an aircraft or spacecraft on a special assignment; a vocation. • *adj* of a mission; (*archit*) of a style of church building established by Spanish missioners in the southwest USA.

missionary /ˈmɪʃəˌnɛri/ *n* (*pl* **missionaries**) a person who tries to convert unbelievers to his or her religious faith, *esp* abroad; one sent on a mission. • *adj* of a religious mission; tending to propagandize.

missionary position *n* (*inf*) a position for sexual intercourse with the partners face to face and the man on top.

mission control *n* a command centre that controls space flights from the ground.

missioner *n* a missionary; a person in charge of a parochial mission.

missis /ˈmɪsɪz/ *n* (*inf*) (*usu with* **the**) one's wife; (*inf*) a name used when directly addressing a woman.—*also* **missus**.

missive /ˈmɪsɪv/ *n* (*formal*) a letter or message, often official. • *adj* (*rare*) sent specially, or intended to be sent.

misspent /mɪsˈspɛnt/ *adj* wasted, frittered away.

missus /ˈmɪsəz/ *see* **missis**.

mist /mɪst/ *n* a large mass of water vapour, less dense than a fog; something that dims or obscures. • *vti* to cover or be covered, as with mist.

mistake /mɪˈsteɪk/ *vb* (**mistaking, mistook**, *pp* **mistaken**). • *vt* to misunderstand; to misinterpret. • *vi* to make a mistake. • *n* a wrong idea, answer, etc; an error of judgment; a blunder; a misunderstanding.—**mistakable** *adj*.—**mistakably** *adv*.

mistaken /mɪˈsteɪkən/ *adj* erroneous, ill-judged.—**mistakenly** *adv*.

mister /ˈmɪstər/ *n* (*inf*) sir; (*with cap*) the title used before a man's surname.

mistime /mɪsˈtaɪm/ *vt* to do or say at the wrong time; to time wrongly.

mistletoe /ˈmɪsəlˌtoː/ *n* an evergreen parasitic plant with white berries used as a Christmas decoration.

mistreat /mɪsˈtriːt/ *vt* to treat wrongly or badly.—**mistreatment** *n*.

mistress /ˈmɪstrəs/ *n* a woman who is head of a household; a woman with whom a man is having a prolonged affair; a female schoolteacher; (*with cap*) the title used before a married woman's surname.

mistrust /mɪsˈtrʌst/ *n* lack of trust. • *vt* to doubt; to suspect.—**mistrustful** *adj*. —**mistrustfully** *adv*

misty /ˈmɪsti/ *adj* (**mistier, mistiest**) full of mist; dim, obscure.—**mistily** *adv*.—**mistiness** *n*.

misunderstand /ˌmɪsʌndərˈstænd/ *vt* (**misunderstanding, misunderstood**) to fail to understand correctly.

misunderstanding /ˌmɪsʌndərˈstændɪŋ/ *n* a mistake as to sense; a quarrel or disagreement.

misunderstood /ˌmɪsʌndərˈstʊd/ *adj* not fully understood; not appreciated properly.

misuse /mɪsˈjuːz/ *vt* to use for the wrong purpose or in the wrong way; to ill-treat, abuse. • *n* improper or incorrect use.

mite /maɪt/ *n* any of numerous very small parasitic or free-living insects; (*money, etc*) a very small amount.

miter /ˈmaɪtər/ *see* **mitre**.

mitigate /ˈmɪtɪˌgeɪt/ *vti* to become or make less severe.—**mitigable** *adj*.—**mitigation** *n*.—**mitigator** *n*.

mitosis /mɪˈtoːsɪs/ or /maɪ-/ *n* (*pl* **mitoses**) *n* a process by which plant or animal cells divide, in which the nucleus of a somatic cell splits into nuclei, each with the same number of chromosomes as there were in the orig cell.—**mitotic** *adj*, *adv*.

mitral /ˈmaɪtrəl/ *adj* of or like a mitre; (*anat*) pertaining to the mitral valve.

mitral valve *n* a valve of the heart between the left atrium and the left ventricle.

mitre, miter /ˈmaɪtər/ *n* the headdress of a bishop; a diagonal joint between two pieces of wood to form a corner. • *vt* to join with a mitre corner.—**miterer** *n*.

mitt /mɪt/ *n* a glove covering the hand but only the base of the fingers; (*sl*) a hand; a boxing glove; a baseball glove.

mitten /ˈmɪtən/ *n* a glove with a thumb but no separate fingers.

mix /ˈmɪks/ *vt* to blend together in a single mass; to make by blending ingredients, as a cake; to combine; (*with* **up**) to make into a mixture; to make disordered; to confuse or mistake. • *vi* to be mixed or blended; to get along together. • *n* a mixture.—**mixable** *adj*.

mixed /mɪkst/ *adj* blended; made up of different parts, classes, races, etc; confused.

mixed bag *n* (*inf*) a collection of diverse things or people.

mixed economy *n* an economic system containing both state-owned industries and private enterprise.

mixed-up *adj* (*inf*) perplexed, mentally confused.

mixer /ˈmɪksər/ *n* a device that blends or mixes; a person considered in terms of their ability (good or bad) to get on with others; a soft drink added to an alcoholic beverage.

mixture /ˈmɪkstʃər/ *n* the process of mixing; a blend made by mixing.

mix-up *n* a mistake; confusion, muddle; (*inf*) a fight.

mizzen, mizen /ˈmɪzən/ *n* (*naut*) the lowest sail on the mizzenmast of a vessel; the mizzenmast. • *adj* pertaining to something used with the mizzenmast.

mizzenmast, mizenmast *n* (*naut*) the aftermost mast when there are three masts on a ship; the aftermast on other ships.

mizzle /ˈmɪzəl/ *vi* to rain in very minute drops, to drizzle. • *n* a very fine rain.

mkt *abbr* = market.

ml *abbr* = mile; millilitre.

Mlle(s) *abbr* = mademoiselle, mesdemoiselles.

MM *abbr* = Messieurs.

mm *abbr* = millimetre.

MN *abbr* = Minnesota.

Mn (*chem symbol*) manganese.

mnemonic /nɪˈmɒnɪk/ *adj* of or aiding memory.—*n* a device to aid the memory.—**mnemonically** *adv*.

mnemonics /nɪˈmɒnɪks/ *n sing* a technique of assisting the memory by using formulae to remember things.

Mnemosyne /niːˈmɒzɪniː/ *n* (*Greek myth*) the goddess of memory.

Mo (*chem symbol*) molybdenum.

moa /ˈmoːə/ *n* any one of several extinct species of large, wingless birds of New Zealand.

Moabite /ˈmoːəˌbaɪt/ *adj* pertaining to the ancient kingdom of Moab, now part of Jordan. • *n* an inhabitant of Moab.

moan /moːn/ *n* a low mournful sound as of sorrow or pain. • *vti* to utter a moan; to complain.—**moaner** *n*.—**moaningly** *adv*.

moat /moːt/ *n* a deep ditch surrounding a fortification or castle, *usu* filled with water.

mob /mɒb/ *n* a disorderly or riotous crowd; a contemptuous term for the masses; (*sl*) a gang of criminals. • *vt* (**mobbing, mobbed**) to attack in a disorderly group; to surround.—**mobbish** *adj*.

mobcap /ˈmɒbkæp/ *n* a plain cap, *usu* surrounded with a frill, worn indoors by women in the 18th century.

mobile /ˈmoːbaɪl/ or /ˈmoːbəl/ *adj* movable, not fixed; easily changing; characterized by ease in change of social status; capable of moving freely and quickly; (*inf*) having transport. • *n* a suspended structure of wood, metal, etc with parts that move in air currents.—**mobility** *n*.

mobilize /ˈmoːbɪˌlaɪz/ *vt* to prepare for action, *esp* war by readying troops for active service; to organize for a particular reason; to put to use.—**mobilization** *n*.

mobocracy /mɒˈbɒkrəsi/ *n* (*pl* **mobocracies**) political rule or ascendancy of the mob; a ruling mob.—**mobocrat** *n*.—**mobocratic** *adj*.—**mobocratically** *adv*.

mobster /ˈmɒbstər/ *n* (*sl*) a gangster.

moccasin /ˈmɒkəsɪn/ *n* a flat shoe based on Amerindian footwear; any soft, flexible shoe resembling this.

mocha /ˈmoːkə/ *n* a type of coffee, orig from Arabia; a flavouring made from coffee and chocolate.—*also adj*.

mock /mɒk/ *vt* to imitate or ridicule; to behave with scorn; to defy; (*with* **up**) to make a model of. • *n* ridicule; an object of scorn. • *adj* false, sham, counterfeit.—**mocker** *n*.—**mockingly** *adv*.

mockery /ˈmɒkəri/ *n* (*pl* **mockeries**) derision, ridicule, or contempt; imitation, *esp* derisive; someone or something that is mocked; an inadequate person, thing, or action.

mock-heroic *adj* parodying the heroic style of literature or, particularly, poetry, *esp* when the subject matter is unheroic. • *n* a burlesque imitation of an epic poem or of the heroic style in general.—**mock-heroically** *adv*.

mockingbird /ˈmɒkɪŋˌbərd/ *n* a grey American bird with the ability to imitate with exactness the call of other birds.

mockup, mock-up *n* a full-scale working model of a machine, etc.

mod /mɒd/ *n* (*often with cap*) a member of a British youth group of the mid-1960s who wore highly fashionable clothes and opposed the rockers, another youth group; a member of a revival of this group, in the late 1970s and early 1980s, whose opposition was to skinheads.

mod. *abbr* = moderate, moderato, modern.

modal /ˈmoːdəl/ *adj* of mode or form, not substance; (*gram*) expressing mood; (*philos*) asserting with qualification; (*mus*) of or composed in a mode.—**modality** *n*.—**modally** *adv*.

mode /moːd/ *n* a way of acting, doing or existing; a style or fashion; form; (*mus*) any of the scales used in composition; (*statistics*) the predominant item in a series of items; (*gram*) mood.

model /ˈmɒdəl/ *n* a pattern; an ideal; a standard worth imitating; a representation on a smaller scale, *usu* three-dimensional; a person who sits for an artist or photographer; a person who displays clothes by wearing them. • *adj* serving as a model; representative of others of the same style. • *vb* (**modelling, modelled** *or* **modeling, modeled**) *vt* (*with* **after, on**) to create by following a model; to display clothes by wearing. • *vi* to serve as a model for an artist, etc.—**modeler, modeller** *n*.

modem /ˈmoːdəm/ *n* a device that links two computers via the telephone network for transmitting data.

moderate /ˈmɒdərət/ *vti* to make or become moderate; to preside over. • *adj* having reasonable limits; avoiding extremes; mild, calm; of medium quality, amount, etc. • *n* a person who holds moderate views.—**moderately** *adv*.—**moderateness** *n*.

moderation /ˌmɒdəˈreɪʃən/ *n* moderateness; freedom from excess; equanimity.

moderato /ˌmɒdəˈrɒtoː/ *adv* (*mus*) moderately.

moderator /ˈmɒdəˌreɪtər/ *n* a mediator; (*physics*) a substance that slows the speed of neutrons in a nuclear reactor; (*Presbyterian Church*) a minister who presides at a court, assembly, synod, etc.

modern /ˈmɒdərn/ *adj* of the present or recent times; up-to-date.—**modernity** *n*.—**modernly** *adv*.

modernism /ˈmɒdərˌnɪzəm/ *n* modern view, methods or usage; the theory or practice of modern art, literature, etc; (*Christianity*) rationalistic theology.—**modernist** *adj*, *n*.—**modernistic** *adj*.—**modernistically** *adv*.

modernize /ˈmɒdərˌnaɪz/ *vti* to make or become modern.—**modernization** *n*.

modest /ˈmɒdəst/ *adj* moderate; having a humble opinion of oneself; unpretentious.—**modestly** *adv*.

modesty /ˈmɒdəsti/ *n* (*pl* **modesties**) the quality or state of being modest; propriety of behaviour or manner; diffidence.

modicum /ˈmɒdɪkəm/ *n* (*pl* **modicums, modica**) a small quantity.

modification /ˌmɒdɪfɪˈkeɪʃən/ *n* a modifying or being modified; the result of this; a modified form; an adjustment, alteration; (*biol*) a change in an organism caused by environmental factors but not passed on.—**modificator** *n*.—**modificatory, modificative** *adj*.

modifier /ˈmɒdɪˌfaɪr/ *n* one who or that which modifies; (*gram*) a word, clause or phrase that qualifies or limits the meaning of another word, etc, a qualifier.

modify /ˈmɒdɪˌfaɪ/ *vt* (**modifying, modified**) to lessen the severity of; to change or alter slightly; (*gram*) to limit in meaning, to qualify.—**modifiable** *adj*.—**modifiability** *n*.

modillion /məˈdɪljən/ *n* (*archit*) an ornamental bracket under a cornice in the Corinthian order.

modiolus /məˈdaɪələs/ (*pl* **modioli**) *n* (*anat*) the pillar of the cochlea of the internal ear.

modish /ˈmoːdɪʃ/ *adj* fashionable, stylish.—**modishly** *adv*.—**modishness** *n*.

modiste /mɒˈdiːst/ *n* a person who makes fashionable dresses or hats.

modulate /ˈmɒdjuˌleɪt/ or /-dʒəleɪt/ *vti* to adjust; to regulate; to vary the pitch, intensity, frequency, etc, of.—**modulator** *n*.—**modulatory** *adj*.

modulation /-ˈleɪʃən/ *n* a modulating or being modulated; a change in pitch or intensity of the voice; (*gram*) inflection, *esp* to change meaning; (*mus*) a transition from one key to another by progression; (*electronics*) the variation of amplitude, frequency or phase of a signal or wave in response to another signal or wave, *esp* in the transfer to carrier waves.

module /ˈmɒdjuːl/ *n* a unit of measurement; a self-contained unit, *esp* in a spacecraft; (*archit*) a semi-diameter of a shaft, etc, used as a standard for regulating other proportions; (*education*) one of a set of learning units making up a course of study.—**modular** *adj*.

modulus /ˈmɒdjuləs/ *n* (*pl* **moduli**) a quantity expressing the measure of some function or property, *eg* elasticity.

modus operandi /ˈmoːdəsˌppəˈrændi/ *n* (*pl* **modi operandi**) a method of operating, procedure.

modus vivendi /ˈmoːdəsvɪˈvɪˈendi/ *n* (*pl* **modi vivendi**) a compromise, as between two parties in dispute; a way of living.

mofette, moffette /məˈfet/ *n* a fissure in an almost extinct volcano from which carbon dioxide and other gases issue; the gases.

mogul, moghul /ˈmoːgəl/ *n* (*inf*) an important person, a magnate; (*with cap*) a ruler of the former Moghul Empire in India.

mohair /ˈmoːhɛr/ *n* the long, fine hair of the Angora goat; the silk cloth made from it.

Mohammedan *n*, *adj* a word for Muslim, formerly common but never used among Muslims.

Mohave /moːˈhɒvi/ *n* (*pl* **Mohaves, Mohave**) one of a North American Indian people who occupied the land along the Colorado river.—*also* **Mojave**.

Mohawk /ˈmoːhɒk/ *n* (*pl* **Mohawks, Mohawk**) one of a North American Indian people who occupied the area from the St Lawrence to the Mohawk river. • *n* the language of the Mohawk people.

Mohican /moːˈhiːkən/ *see* **Mahican**.

mohican /moːˈhiːkən/ *n* a hairstyle in which the sides of the head are shaved, leaving a central band of hair, often dyed or in spikes, from the forehead to the nape of the neck.

moidore /ˈmɔɪdɔr/ *n* an ancient Portuguese gold coin.

moiety /ˈmɔɪəti/ *n* (*pl* **moieties**) one of two parts or shares; a half.

moiré /ˈmɔːˈeɪ/ or /ˈmwɔː/ *n* a fabric, *usu* silk, that has a surface pattern suggesting rippling water; such a pattern impressed on a fabric.

moiré effect *n* a pattern created when the same pattern is superimposed on another version of itself.

moist /mɔɪst/ *adj* damp; slightly wet.—**moistly** *adv.*—**moistness** *n.*

moisten /ˈmɔɪsən/ *vti* to make or become moist.—**moistener** *n.*

moisture /ˈmɔɪstʃər/ *n* liquid in a diffused, absorbed, or condensed state.

moisturize /ˈmɔɪstʃəˌraɪz/ *vt* (*skin, air, etc*) to add moisture to.—**moisturizer** *n.*

Mojave /moˈhɒvi/ *see* **Mohave**.

moke *n* /moːk/ (*sl*) a boring person; (*Brit*) a donkey; (*Austral*) a horse out of the top class.

molar[1] /ˈmoːlər/ *n* a back tooth, used for grinding food.

molar[2] *adj* of or in the whole mass of matter as distinguished from the properties or motions of atoms or molecules.

molasses /məˈlæsɪs/ or /-sɪz/ *n* (*pl* **molasses**) the thick brown sugar that is produced during the refining of sugar; treacle.

mold /ˈmoːld/ *see* **mould**.

mole[1] /moːl/ *n* a spot on the skin, *usu* dark-coloured and raised.

mole[2] *n* a small burrowing insectivore with soft dark fur; a spy within an organization.

mole[3] *n* a large breakwater.

mole[4] *n* the basic SI unit of substance.

molecular /məˈlɛkjʊlər/ *adj* of or inherent in molecules.

molecular biology *n* the branch of biology dealing with the molecular basis of heredity and of protein synthesis.

molecular formula *n* the chemical formula that indicates both the number and type of any atom present in a molecular substance.

molecular weight *n* the total of the atomic weights of all the atoms present in a molecule; the average mass per molecule of any substance relative to one-twelfth the mass of an atom of carbon-12.

molecule /ˈmɒləˌkjuːl/ *n* the simplest unit of a substance, retaining the chemical properties of that substance; a small particle.

molehill /ˈmoːlhɪl/ *n* a mound of earth thrown up by a burrowing mole.

moleskin /-skɪn/ *n* the fur of a mole; a twilled cotton cloth with a soft surface resembling a mole's fur, used for work clothes; (*pl*) trousers made of moleskin.

molest /ˈmɒləst/ *vt* to annoy; to attack or assault, *esp* sexually.—**molestation** *n.*—**molester** *n.*

moll /mɒl/ *adj* (*sl*) a female partner of a thief or other criminal; a prostitute.

mollify /ˈmɒləˌfaɪ/ *vt* (**mollifying, mollified**) to make less severe or violent; to soften.—**mollification** *n.*—**mollifier** *n.*—**mollifyingly** *adv.*

mollusk, mollusc /ˈmɒləsk/ *n* an invertebrate animal *usu* enclosed in a shell, as oysters, etc.—**molluscan, molluskan** *adj, n.*

mollycoddle /ˈmɒliˌkɒdəl/ *vti* to care for someone in an indulgent way; to coddle, pamper. • *n* someone so treated.—**mollycoddler** *n.*

moloch /ˈmoːlɒk/ or /ˈmɒlək/ *n* a spiny Australian lizard with a horned head, found in desert areas; (*with cap*) (*Old Testament*) an ancient Semitic fire god to whom children were offered as a sacrifice.

molt /moːlt/ *vi* to shed hair, skin, horns, etc prior to replacement of new growth. • *n* a moulting.—*also* **moult.**—**molter** *n.*

molten /ˈmoːltən/ *adj* melted by heat.

molto /ˈmoːltoː/ *adj* (*mus*) very (modifying another musical direction).

moly /ˈmoːli/ *n* (*pl* **molies**) (*Greek myth*) a herb with a black root and a white flower with the power of counteracting the spells of Circe.

molybdenum /məˈlɪbdənəm/ *n* a metallic element used in alloys, *esp* strengthening steel.—**molybdous, molybdic** *adj.*

mom /mɒm/ *n* (*US inf*) mother.

moment /ˈmoːmənt/ *n* an indefinitely brief period of time; a definite point in time; a brief time of importance.

momenta /moːˈmɛntə/ *see* **momentum**.

momentarily /ˌmoːmənˈtɛrɪli/ *adv* for a short time; in an instant; at any moment.

momentary /ˈmoːmənˌtɛri/ *adj* lasting only for a moment.—**momentariness** *n.*

momentous /moːˈmɛntəs/ *adj* very important.—**momentously** *adv.*—**momentousness** *n.*

momentum /moːˈmɛntəm/ *n* (*pl* **momenta, momentums**) the impetus of a moving object, equal to the product of its mass and its velocity.

mommy /ˈmɛmi/ or /ˈmɒmi/ *n* (*pl* **mommies**) (*US inf*) mother.

Mon. *abbr* = Monday.

monachism /ˈmɒnəˌkɪzəm/ *n* monasticism; the monastic life or system.—**monachal** *adj.*

monad /ˈmɒnæd/ or /ˈmoː-/ *n* a unit, number one; (*philos*) the ultimate unit of being or evolution in Leibniz's theory; (*chem*) a radical or atom with a valency of one; (*biol*) a single-celled organism.—**monadic, monadical** *adj.*—**monadically** *adv.*

monadelphous /ˌmɒnəˈdɛlfəs/ *adj* (*bot*) having stamens in one bundle of filaments wrapped around the style.

monadism /ˈmɒnæˌdɪzəm/ or /ˈmoː-/ *n* (*philos*) the theory, *esp* as propounded by Leibniz, that the real universe is composed of monads.

monandrous /məˈnædrəs/ *adj* having only one husband or male partner at a time; (*flowers*) having one stamen only; (*plants*) having flowers with only one stamen.

monandry /məˈnædri/ *n* the custom of having only one husband at a time; (*bot*) a being monandrous.

monarch /ˈmɒnərk/ *n* a sovereign who rules by hereditary right; a powerful or dominant thing or person.—**monarchal, monarchic, monarchical** *adj.*—**monarchically** *adv.*

monarchism /ˈmɒnərˌkɪzəm/ *n* the principles of, or devotion to, monarchy.—**monarchist** *n, adj.*—**monarchistic** *adj.*

monarchy /ˈmɒnərki/ *n* (*pl* **monarchies**) a government headed by a monarch; a kingdom.

monastery /ˈmɒnəstəri/ *n* (*pl* **monasteries**) the residence of a group of monks, or nuns.—**monasterial** *adj.*

monastic /məˈnæstɪk/, **monastical** /-əl/ *adj* of monks or monasteries. • *n* a monk; a recluse.—**monastically** *adv.*—**monasticism** *n.*

Monday /ˈmɛndeɪ/ or /di/ *n* the second day of the week.

monecious /məˈniːʃəs/ *see* **monoecious**.

monetarism /ˈmɒnətəˌrɪzəm/ *n* (*economics*) the theory that control of the money supply is the key to achieving low inflation and economic growth.—**monetarist** *n, adj.*

monetary *adj* of the coinage or currency of a country; of or relating to money.—**monetarily** *adv.*

monetize /ˈmɒnətəri/ *vt* to convert into money; to give a standard of current value to.—**monetization** *n.*

money /ˈmɛni/ *n* (*pl* **moneys, monies**) coins or paper notes authorized by a government as a medium of exchange; property; wealth.

moneychanger *n* one who changes money into other coinage at fixed rate; a machine that dispenses coins.

moneyed /ˈmɛniːd/ *adj* rich.—*also* **monied**.

moneylender *n* a person who lends money for interest, *esp* as a business.—**moneylending** *n.*

monger /ˈmɒŋgər/ *n* a dealer.

mongoose /ˈmɒŋguːs/ *n* (*pl* **mongooses**) a small predatory mammal of Africa and Asia.

mongrel /ˈmɒŋgrəl/ *n* an animal or plant of mixed or unknown breed, *esp* a dog. • *adj* of mixed breed or origin.—**mongrelism** *n.*—**mongrelly** *adj.*

mongrelize /ˈmɒŋgrəˌlaɪz/ *vt* to render mongrel.—**mongrelization** *n.*

monied /ˈmɛniːd/ *see* **moneyed**.

monies /ˈmɛniːz/ *see* **money**.

moniker, monicker /ˈmɒnɪkər/ *n* (*sl*) a name; a nickname.

moniliform /məˈnɪlɪˌfɔrm/ *adj* (*biol*) shaped like a necklace.

monism /ˈmɒnɪzəm/ or /ˈmoːn-/ *n* (*philos*) the theory that there is only one kind of being and that matter and mind are ultimately identical.—**monist** *n, adj.*—**monistic** *adj.*—**monistically** *adv.*

monition /məˈnɪʃən/ *n* an admonition; a formal notice from an ecclesiastical court to an offender; a summons; a warning.

monitor /ˈmɒnɪtər/ *n* a student chosen to help the teacher; any device for regulating the performance of a machine, aircraft, etc; a screen for viewing the image being produced by a television camera; a display screen connected to a computer. • *vti* (*TV or radio transmissions, etc*) to observe or listen to for political or technical reasons; to watch or check on; to regulate or control, a machine, etc.—**monitorial** *adj.*

monitory /ˈmɒnɪtəri/ *adj* conveying a warning. • *n* (*pl* **monitories**) a letter containing an admonition or warning, *esp* a papal letter.

monk /mʌŋk/ *n* a male member of a religious order living in a monastery.

monkey /'mʌŋki/ *n* any of the primates except man and the lemurs, *esp* the smaller, long-tailed primates; a mischievous child; (*sl*) £500 or $500. • *vi* (**monkeying, monkeyed**) (*inf*) to play, trifle, or meddle.

monkey business *n* (*inf*) mischief; underhand dealings.

monkey wrench *n* a large wrench with an adjustable jaw.

monkfish /'mʌŋkfiʃ/ *n* (*pl* **monkfish, monkfishes**) an angelfish.

monkhood /'mʌŋkhʊd/ *n* the character or condition of a monk; monks collectively.

monkish /'mʌŋkiʃ/ *adj* pertaining to or resembling a monk; monastic.—**monkishly** *adv*.—**monkishness** *n*.

monkshood, monk's-hood /'mʌŋkshʊd/ *n* a poisonous plant, aconite.

mono /'mɒnɒ:/ *adj* (*inf*) monophonic. • *n* (*pl* **monos**) (*inf*) monophonic sound.

mono- /'mɒnɒ:/, **mon-** /'mɒn/ *prefix* alone, sole, single.

monobasic /ˌmɒnə'beisik/ *adj* (*chem*) having one base or atom of a base.

monocarp /ˌmɒnə'karp/ *n* a monocarpic plant.

monocarpic /ˌmɒnə'karpik/, **monocarpous** /-'karpəs/ *adj* (*bot*) bearing fruit only once.

monochord /'mɒnə,kɔrd/ *n* a one-stringed musical instrument with a sound box for determining musical intervals.

monochromatic /ˌmɒnəkrə'mætik/ *adj* consisting of one colour.—**monochromatically** *adv*.

monochrome /ˌmɒnə'krɔ:m/ *n* a painting, drawing, or print in a single colour. • *adj* in one colour or shades of one colour; black and white—**monochromic** *adj*.

monocle /'mɒnəkəl/ *n* a single eyeglass held in place by the face muscles.—**monocled** *adj*.

monocline /'mɒnəklain/ *n* a geological formation in which the strata are tilted one way only.—**monoclinal** *adj*.

monocotyledon /ˌmɒnə,kɒti'liːdən/ *n* any plant with one seed leaf and three-part flowers, incl grasses, lilies and orchids.—**monocotyledonous** *adj*.

monocrat /ˌmɒnə'kræt/ *n* one who governs alone; an advocate of autocracy or monarchy.—**monocracy** *n*.

monocular /mə'nɒkjulər/ *adj* pertaining to, for, or with one eye only; adapted for use with one eye.

monodrama /'mɒnə,dræmə/ or /-drɒmə/ *n* a dramatic piece for one actor.—**monodramatic** *adj*.

monody /'mɒnədi/ *n* (*pl* **monodies**) in Greek tragedy, a lyrical poem sung by one actor alone; a plaintive poem or song for one voice, a dirge, an elegy; (*mus*) a composition for one voice, *usu* accompanied.—**monodic, monodical** *adj*.—**monodist** *n*.

monoecious /mə'niːʃəs/ *adj* (*bot*) having stamens and pistils on the same plant but on different flowers; (*zool*) hermaphroditic.—*also* **monecious**.—**monoeciously** *adv*.

monogamy /mə'nɒgəmi/ *n* the practice of being married to only one person at a time.—**monogamist** *n*.—**monogamous** *adj*.

monogenesis /ˌmɒnə'dʒenəsis/ *n* derivation from a single cell, resulting in an organism like the adult of the species; asexual reproduction from a single cell; the supposed descent of all organisms from one orig cell; the supposed descent of all human beings from one orig pair.—**monogenous** *adj*.

monogenetic /-'dʒenətik/ *adj* pertaining to or having the property of monogenesis; (*animals*) born, living and dying on a single host; (*rocks*) originating from a single source or by a single process.

monogram /'mɒnə,græm/ *n* the embroidered or printed initials of one's name on clothing, stationery, etc.—**monogrammed** *adj*.—**monogrammatic** *adj*.

monograph /-,græf/ *n* a learned paper written on one particular subject. • *vt* to write such a paper on.—**monographer** *n*.—**monographic** *adj*.—**monographically** *adv*.

monolith /-,liθ/ *n* a single large block of stone; any massive, unyielding structure.—**monolithic** *adj*.—**monolithically** *adv*.

monologue, monolog /-,lɒg/ *n* a long speech; a soliloquy, a skit, etc for one actor only.—**monologuist, monologist** *n*.

monomania /ˌmɒnə'meiniə/ *n* an irrational obsession with a single subject, object, idea, etc.—**monomaniac** *n*.—**monomaniacal** *adj*.

monometallic *adj* containing only one metal; of monometallism.

monometallism /ˌmɒnə'metlizəm/ *n* the use of a single metal, often gold or silver, as a standard of currency; the economic

system underpinning such a standard.—**monometallist** *n*.

monomial /mə'nɒːmiəl/ *n* (*math*) an expression consisting of one term; (*biol*) a taxonomic classification consisting of one term.—*also* adj.

monomorphic /ˌmɒnə'mɔrfik/, **monomorphous** /-'mɔrfəs/ *adj* (*species*) of one type or structure or with parts that have only one type or structure; (*individual organism*) unchanging in shape throughout its life cycle; (*chem*) denoting a chemical compound with a single crystalline form.

monopetalous *adj* (*bot*) (*flowers*) having the corolla in one piece; possessing a single petal.

monophobia /ˌmɒnə'fɔːbiə/ *n* an overwhelming fear of being alone.—**monophobic** *adj*.

monophonic /ˌmɒnə'fɒnik/ *adj* (*sound reproduction*) using one channel only for transmission.—**monophonically** *adv*.

monophthong /'mɒnəf,θɒŋ/ *n* a simple single vowel sound; two different written vowels pronounced as a single sound.—**monophthongal** *adj*.

monoplane /'mɒnə,plein/ *n* an aeroplane with a single pair of wings.

monoplegia /ˌmɒnə'pliːdʒə/ or /-dʒiə/ *n* paralysis affecting one limb or one group of muscles only.—**monoplegic** *adj*, *n*.

monopolize /mə'nɒpə,laiz/ *vt* to get, have, or exploit a monopoly of; to get full control of.—**monopolization** *n*.—**monopolizer** *n*.

monopoly /mə'nɒpəli/ *n* (*pl* **monopolies**) exclusive control in dealing in a particular commodity or supplying a service; exclusive use or possession; that which is exclusively controlled; such control granted by a government.—**monopolism** *n*.—**monopolist** *n*.—**monopolistic** *adj*.—**monopolistically** *adv*.

monorail /'mɒːnə,reil/ *n* a single track railway, often with suspended carriages.

monosepalous /ˌmɒːnə'sepələs/ *adj* (*bot*) (*flowers*) having the calyx undivided; possessing a single sepal.

monosodium glutamate /ˌmɒnə'soːdiəm'gluːtə,meit/ *n* a chemical additive used to give food a meaty taste.

monospermous /ˌmɒnə'spɜrməs/, **monospermal** /-'spɜrməl/ *adj* (*plants*) one-seeded.

monostich /ˌmɒnə'stik/ *n* a poem in one line.—**monostichic** *adj*.

monosyllabic /ˌmɒnəsi'læbik/ *adj* (*word*) having one syllable; characterized by or made up of one syllable; terse; curt.—**monosyllabically** *adv*.

monosyllable /'mɒnə,siləbəl/ *n* a word of one syllable.

monotheism /'mɒnə,θiːizəm/ *n* the doctrine of or belief in the existence of only one God.—**monotheist** *n*.—**monotheistic** *adj*.—**monotheistically** *adv*.

monotone /'mɒnə,toːn/ *n* an utterance or musical tone without a change in pitch; a tiresome sameness of style, colour, etc.—**monotonic** *adj*.—**monotonically** *adv*.

monotonous /mə'nɒtənəs/ *adj* unvarying in tone; with dull uniformity, wearisome.—**monotonously** *adv*.—**monotonousness** *n*.

monotony /mə'nɒtəni/ *n* (*pl* **monotonies**) lack of variety; irksome sameness.

monotreme *n* one of a primitive order of Australian egg-laying mammals, with a single vent for digestive, urinary and genital organs.—**monotrematous** *adj*.

Monotype *n* (*trademark*) a hot-metal typesetting machine that casts each character separately; type so cast.

monotype /'mɒnə,taip/ *n* (*print*) one print from a metal or glass plate with a painted image; (*biol*) a genus or species that has only a single type.—**monotypic** *adj*.

monovalent /ˌmɒnə'veilənt/ *adj* (*chem*) with a valency of one; univalent.—**monovalence, monovalency** *n*.

monoxide /mə'nɒksaid/ *n* an oxide with one oxygen atom in each molecule.

Monseigneur /mɔ̃sen'jər/, *Fr.* /mɔ̃se'njœr/ *n* (*pl* **Messeigneurs**) a French title given to princes, prelates and bishops.

monsieur /mə'sjuː/, *Fr.* /mə'sjø/ *n* (*pl* **messieurs**) the French equivalent of sir in address and of Mr with a name.

Monsignor /mʌn'siːnjər/ or /mɒn-/ *n* (*pl* **Monsignors, Monsignore**) (*RC Church*) a title given, *usu* by the Pope, to some prelates or priests.

monsoon /mɒn'suːn/ *n* a seasonal wind of southern Asia; the rainy season.

monster /'mɒnstər/ *n* any greatly malformed plant or animal; an imaginary beast; a very wicked person; a very large animal or thing. • *adj* very large, huge.

monstrance /'mɒnstrəns/ n (*RC Church*) a transparent vessel, *usu* set in a gold or silver frame, in which the consecrated Host is carried in procession or exhibited.

monstrosity /mɒn'strɒsiti/ n (*pl* **monstrosities**) the state or quality of being monstrous; an ugly, unnatural or monstrous thing or person.

monstrous /'mɒnstrəs/ *adj* abnormally developed; enormous; horrible.—**monstrously** *adv.*—**monstrousness** n.

montage /'mɒntɪdʒ/ n a rapid sequence of film shots, often superimposed; the art or technique of assembling various elements, *esp* pictures or photographs; such an assemblage.

montane /'mɒnteɪn/ *adj* of or inhabiting mountains or mountainous terrain.

monte /'mɒnti/ n a gambling card game orig played with dice or cards in Spain.

Montessori method /ˌmɒntə'sɔri/ n a system of educating very young children, through play, based on free discipline, with each child developing at his own pace.

month /mɛnθ/ n any of the twelve divisions of the year; a calendar month.

monthly /'mɛnθli/ *adj* continuing for a month; done, happening, payable, etc every month. • n a monthly periodical. • *adv* once a month; every month.

monticule /'mɒntiˌkjuːl/ n a hillock; a small mound resulting from a volcanic eruption.

monument /'mɒnjumənt/ n an obelisk, statue or building that commemorates a person or an event; an exceptional example.

monumental /ˌmɒnju'mɛntəl/ *adj* of, like, or serving as a monument; colossal; lasting.—**monumentality** n.—**monumentally** *adv.*

moo /muː/ n the long deep sound made by a cow. • *vi* (*cattle*) to low; to make a deep long noise like a cow.

mooch /muːtʃ/ *vt* (*sl*) to wander around aimlessly; (*sl*) to cadge, steal.—**moocher** n.

mood /muːd/ n a temporary state of mind or temper; a gloomy feeling; a predominant feeling or spirit; (*gram*) that form of a verb indicating mode of action; (*mus*) mode.

moody /'muːdi/ *adj* (**moodier, moodiest**) gloomy; temperamental.—**moodily** *adv.*—**moodiness** n.

moon /muːn/ n the natural satellite that revolves around the earth and shines by reflected sunlight; any natural satellite of another planet; something shaped like the moon. • *vi* to behave in an idle or abstracted way.

moonbeam /'muːnbiːm/ n a ray of moonlight.

mooncalf /-kæf/ n (*pl* **mooncalves**) a born fool; an idler; (*arch*) a monster.

moonflower /-flaʊr/ n any of a family of climbing or creeping plants with trumpet-shaped flowers that bloom at night; a tropical plant, orig found in Mexico, with white flowers that bloom at night.

moonlight /-laɪt/ n the light of the moon. • *vi* (*inf*) to have a secondary (*usu* night-time) job.—**moonlighter** n.

moonlit /-lɪt/ *adj* lit by the moon.

moonraker, moonsail n (*naut*) a small sail carried above a skysail.

moonshine /-ʃaɪn/ n moonlight; (*inf*) nonsense, foolish talk; (*sl*) illegally distilled spirits.

moonshiner /-ˌʃaɪnər/ n (*sl*) a distiller of illicit whiskey; a whiskey smuggler.

moonstone /-stoːn/ n a translucent yellowish or yellowish-white stone that exhibits pearly blue-tinged reflections, used as a gemstone.

moonstruck /-strʊk/, **moonstricken** /-ˌstrɪkən/ *adj* besotted with love or sentiment; demented.

moonwort /-wɜrt/ n a fern with crescent-shaped fronds, grape fern; honesty.

moony /'muːni/ *adj* (**moonier, mooniest**) of or like the moon; crescent-shaped; round; listless, dreamy; absent-minded.

Moor /mʊr/ or /mɔr/ (*hist*) a North African Muslim of mixed Arab and Berber ancestry.

moor[1] /mʊr/ or /mɔr/ n a tract of open wasteland, *usu* covered with heather and often marshy.

moor[2] *vti* (*a ship*) to secure or be secured by cable or anchor.

moorage /'mʊrɪdʒ/ n the act of mooring a vessel; a place or charge for mooring.

moorcock /'mʊrkɒk/ or /'mɔr-/ n the male red grouse.

moorfowl /-faʊl/ n (*arch*) red grouse collectively.

moorhen /-hɛn/ n an aquatic dark-coloured bird with a red bill and a characteristic red mark above the bill, found in ponds and lakes; the female red grouse.

mooring /'mʊrɪŋ/ or /'mɔr-/ n the act of mooring; the place where a ship is moored; (*pl*) the lines, cables, etc by which a ship is moored.

Moorish /'mʊrɪʃ/ or /'mɔr/ *adj* pertaining to the Moors; denoting a Spanish architectural style of the 13th-16th centuries, one of the distinguishing features of which is the horseshoe arch.

moorland /'mʊrlænd/ or /'mɔr/ n a stretch of moors.

moose /muːs/ n (*pl* **moose**) the largest member of the deer family, native to North America.

moot /muːt/ *adj* debatable; hypothetical. • *vt* (**mooting, mooted**) to propose for discussion.

mop /mɒp/ n a rag, sponge, etc fixed to a handle for washing floors or dishes; a thick or tangled head of hair. • *vt* (**mopping, mopped**) to wash with a mop.

mope /moːp/ *vi* to be gloomy and apathetic. • n a person who mopes, a moper.—**moper** n.—**mopey** *adj.*—**mopingly** *adv.*

moped /'moːpɛd/ n a light, motor-assisted bicycle.

moppet /'mɒpət/ n a pet name for a small child, *esp* a girl; (*arch*) a rag doll.

moquette /'mɒkət/ n a material with short velvety pile used for carpets and upholstery.

MOR *abbr* = middle-of-the-road.

moraine /mə'reɪn/ n a mass of earth, stones, etc, deposited by a glacier.—**morainal, morainic** *adj.*

moral /'mɒrəl/ *adj* of or relating to character and human behaviour, particularly as regards right and wrong; virtuous, *esp* in sexual conduct; capable of distinguishing right from wrong; probable, although not certain; psychological, emotional. • n a moral lesson taught by a fable, event, etc; (*pl*) principles; ethics.

morale /mə'ræl/ n moral or mental condition with respect to courage, discipline, confidence, etc.

moralism /'mɒrəˌlɪzəm/ n moralizing; a moral attitude or maxim; the practice of or belief in a system of morals independent of religion.

moralist /'mɒrəlɪst/ n a teacher or student of morals; one for whom morality needs no religious sanction; one concerned with the morals of others.—**moralistic** *adj.*—**moralistically** *adv.*

morality /mə'ræliti/ n (*pl* **moralities**) virtue; moral principles; a particular system of moral principles.

morality play n a medieval allegorical play.

moralize, moralise /'mɒrəˌlaɪz/ *vt* to explain or interpret morally; to give a moral direction to. • *vi* to make moral pronouncements.—**moralization, moralisation** n.—**moralizer, moraliser** n.

morally /'mɒrəli/ *adv* in a moral manner, ethically; virtually, practically.

moral philosophy n ethics.

Moral Rearmament n an international evangelical movement, founded in the US by Frank Buchman (1938), that seeks moral and spiritual revival following conservative Christian principles.—*also* **Buchmanism.**

morass /mə'ræs/ n a bog, marsh.

moratorium /ˌmɒrə'tɔriəm/ n (*pl* **moratoria, moratoriums**) a legally authorized delay in the payment of money due; an authorized delay or suspension of any activity.—**moratory** *adj.*

morbid /'mɔrbɪd/ *adj* diseased, resulting as from a diseased state of mind; gruesome.—**morbidly** *adv.*—**morbidness** n.

morbidity /'mɔrbɪdɪti/ n the state of being morbid; the relative incidence of disease.

morbific /'mɔrbɪfɪk/ *adj* causing or producing disease.

morceau *Fr.* /mɑr'soː/ n (*pl* **morceaux**) a small piece, a morsel; a short work, *usu* a musical one.

mordacious /mɔr'deɪʃəs/ *adj* biting; sarcastic; cutting.—**mordaciously** *adv.*—**mordacity** n.

mordant /'mɔrdənt/ *adj* biting, caustic; corrosive. • n a chemical fixative; a corrosive substance.—**mordancy** n.—**mordantly** *adv.*

mordent /'mɔrdənt/ n (*mus*) a trill created by one note rapidly alternating with another one degree below it, used as an ornament.

more /mɔr/ *adj* (*superl* **most**) greater; further; additional.—*also comparof* **many, much.** • *adv* to a greater extent or degree; again; further.

moreen /mɔ'ri:n/ or /mə-/ n a stout woollen fabric used *esp* for furnishings, often embossed or figured with a watered pattern.

morel[1] /mɔ'rel/ n an edible mushroom with a brownish cap.

morel[2] n a nightshade, *esp* the black nightshade.

morello /mə'relo:/ n (*pl* **morellos**) a small dark-red cherry with a tart flavour.

moreover /mɔr'o:vər/ adv in addition to what has been said before; besides.

mores /'mɔrz/ npl customs so fundamentally established that they have the force of law.

Moresque /mo:'resk/ adj (*archit*) Moorish style. • n an example of such decoration or architecture; a design in this style.

morganatic /,mɔrgə'nætik/ adj (*marriage*) between a royal person and one of lower rank the children of which are legitimate but neither they nor the morganatic wife or husband share royal rank or property.—**morganatically** adv.

morgue /mɔrg/ n a place where the bodies of unknown dead or those dead of unknown causes are temporarily kept prior to burial; a collection of reference materials, *eg* newspaper clippings.

moribund /'mɔribʌnd/ adj in a dying state; near death.—**moribundity** n.

morion /'mɔri,ɒn/ or n a 16th-century hat-shaped helmet without beaver or visor.

Mormon /'mɔrmən/ n a member of the Church of Latter-Day Saints whose authority is the Bible and the Book of Mormon, revelations to Joseph Smith in 1827.—**Mormonism** n.

morn /mɔrn/ n (*poet*) dawn, morning; (*Scot*) tomorrow.

mornay /'mɔrneɪ/ n a white sauce flavoured with cheese. • adj (*eggs, etc*) cooked with this sauce.

morning /'mɔrniŋ/ n the part of the day from midnight or dawn until noon; the early part of anything. • adj of or in the morning.

morning coat n a tailcoat, *usu* grey, with a cutaway front.

morning-glory n (*pl* **morning-glories**) any of various twining plants with showy blue bell-shaped flowers.

morning sickness n a period of nausea and vomiting in the early stages of pregnancy.

morning star n a planet, *esp* Venus, rising before the sun.

morning suit n a man's formal suit of a morning coat and striped trousers.

morning watch n (*naut*) a watch on board ship from 4 am to 8 am.

morocco /mə'rɒko:/ n (*pl* **moroccos**) a fine kind of grained leather of goatskin or sheepskin, used in bookbinding and for shoes.

moron /'mɔrɒn/ n an adult mentally equal to a 8 to 12-year-old child; (*inf*) a very stupid person.—**moronic** adj.—**moronically** adv.—**moronism, moronity** n.

morose /'mɔro:s/ adj sullen, surly; gloomy.—**morosely** adv.—**moroseness** n.

morpheme /'mɔrfi:m/ n the smallest meaningful unit of language as a base, prefix or suffix.—**morphemic** adj.—**morphemically** adv.

Morpheus /'mɔrfiəs/ n (*Greek myth*) the god of dreams and of sleep.

morphine /'mɔrfi:n/, **morphia** /'mɔrfiə/ n an alkaloid derived from opium, used as an anaesthetic and sedative.—**morphinic** adj.

morphinism /'mɔrfi,nizəm/ n addiction to morphine; poisoning caused by the excessive use of morphine.

morphogen /'mɔrfə,dʒen/ n that substance in an embryo that determines what the structure will become.

morphology /mɔr'fɒlədʒi/ n a branch of biology dealing with the form and structure of organisms; the study of word formation in a language.—**morphological** adj.—**morphologist** n.

morris (dance) /'mɒris/ n a traditional English dance accompanied by tambourines, bells, castanets, violin, concertina, etc, and *usu* performed by men in costumes representing the Robin Hood legend or other characters from English folklore.

morrow /'mɒro:/ n (*arch, poet*) morning; the following day.

morse /mɔrs/ n a jewelled clasp on a cope.

Morse code /mɔrs/ n a code in which letters are represented by dots and dashes or long and short sounds, and are transmitted by visual or audible signals.

morsel /'mɔrsəl/ n a small quantity or a small piece of anything.

mort[1] /'mɔrt/ n a note or notes sounded on a hunting horn to notify a kill.

mort[2] n (*dial*) a great amount or number (of).

mort[3] n a salmon in its third year.

mortal /'mɔrtəl/ adj subject to death; causing death, fatal; hostile; very intense. • n a human being.—**mortally** adv.

mortality /mɔr'tæliti/ n (*pl* **mortalities**) state of being mortal; death on a large scale, as from war; number or frequency of deaths in a given period relative to population.

mortality rate n the yearly proportion of deaths to population.—*also* **death rate**.

mortar /'mɔrtər/ n a mixture of cement or lime with sand and water used in building; an artillery piece that fires shells at low velocities and high trajectories; a bowl in which substances are pounded with a pestle.

mortarboard /'mɔrtər,bɔrd/ n a small square board for holding mortar; a square black college or university cap with a tassel.

mortgage /'mɔrgidʒ/ n a transfer of rights to a piece of property *usu* as security for the payment of a loan or debt that becomes void when the debt is paid. • vt to make over as a security or pledge; to put an advance claim on.

mortgagee /,mɔrgi'dʒi:/ n one to whom a mortgage is made or given.

mortgagor /'mɔrgidʒɔr/, **mortgager** /-dʒər/ n one who grants a mortgage.

mortician /mɔr'tiʃən/ n in the US, a person who manages funerals; the US word for an **undertaker**.

mortification /,mɔrtifi'keiʃən/ n the act of mortifying; gangrene; (*Christianity*) subjugation of passions and appetite by abstinence; humiliation; vexation, chagrin caused by something that injures one's pride; (*Scots law*) a charitable bequest of lands.

mortify /'mɔrti,fai/ vti (**mortifying, mortified**) to subdue by repression or penance; to humiliate or shame; to become gangrenous.—**mortifier** n.—**mortifyingly** adv.

mortise, mortice /'mɔrtis/ n a hole in a piece of wood to receive a projection of another piece made to fit.

mortise lock n a lock fitted into a mortise in the frame of a door.

mortmain /'mɔrtmein/ n (*law*) a tenure of land held by a corporation, ecclesiastical or other, which cannot transfer ownership.

mortuary /'mɔrtʃu:,eri/ n (*pl* **mortuaries**) a place of temporary storage for dead bodies.

morula /'mɔrulə/ n (*pl* **morulas, morulae**) the spherical mass of cells produced by the splitting of the ovum in its primary stage.—**morular** adj.

Mosaic /'mo:zeik/, **Mosaical** /-kəl/ adj pertaining to Moses, the lawgiver of the Bible, or to the law, institutions, etc, given through him, or to his writings.

mosaic /'mo:zeik/ n a surface decoration made by inlaying small pieces (of glass, stone, etc) to form figures or patterns; a design made in mosaic. • adj of or made of mosaic. • vt (**mosaicking, mosaicked**) to adorn with or make into mosaic.—**mosaicist** n.

moschatel /'mɒskətel/ n a plant with a pale-green flower and a musky smell.

Moselle, Mosel /'mozəl/ n a German dry white wine from the Moselle valley.

mosey /'mo:zi/ vi (*inf*) (*often with* **along, on down**) to go, to saunter, to amble.

Moslem /'mɒzləm/ or /'mɒs-/ see **Muslim**.

mosque /mɒsk/ n a place of worship for Muslims.

mosquito /mɒs'ki:to:/ n (*pl* **mosquitoes, mosquitos**) a small two-winged bloodsucking insect.

moss /mɒs/ n a very small green plant that grows in clusters on rocks, moist ground, etc.

mossback /'mɒsbæk/ n (*sl*) a turtle or a crab, lobster, oyster, etc, that is so old that it has moss growing on its back; (*inf*) an out-of-date or provincial person.

mosstrooper n one of a gang of marauders that ravaged the borderland of England and Scotland in the mid-17th century.

mossy /'mɒsi/ adj (**mossier, mossiest**) overgrown with, or like, moss.—**mossiness** n.

most /mo:st/ adj (*compar* **more**) greatest in number; greatest in amount or degree; in the greatest number of instances.—*also* **superl** of **many, much**. • adv in or to the greatest degree or extent. • n the greatest amount or degree; (*with pl*) the greatest number (of).

-most /mo:st/ adj *suffix* forming a superlative, *eg* hindmost.

mostly /'mo:stli/ adv for the most part; mainly, usually.

mot juste /'mo:,ʒust/ n (*pl* **mots justes**) exactly the right word.

mote[1] /mo:t/ n a very small particle, a speck (of dust); a mite.

mote[2] *vi* (*arch*) might, must.

motel /mo:'tel/ *n* an hotel for motorists with adjacent parking.

motet /mo:'tet/ *n* (*mus*) (*RC Church*) a short sacred vocal composition, an anthem, *usu* unaccompanied.

moth /mɒθ/ *n* a four-winged chiefly night-flying insect related to the butterfly.

mothball /'mɒθbɒl/ *n* a small ball of camphor or naphthalene used to protect stored clothes from moths.

moth-eaten *adj* eaten into by moths; dilapidated; outmoded.

mother /'mʌðər/ *n* a female who has given birth to offspring; an origin or source. • *adj* of or like a mother; native. • *vt* to be the mother of or a mother to.

motherhood /'mʌðərhʊd/ *n* the state of being a mother; the qualities of feelings of being a mother; mothers collectively.

mother-in-law *n* (*pl* **mothers-in-law**) the mother of one's spouse.

motherland /'mʌðərlænd/ *n* a person's native land or the country of a person's forebears.

motherly /'mʌðərli/ *adj* of, proper to a mother; like a mother.—**motherliness** *n*.

mother-of-pearl *n* the iridescent lining of the shell of the pearl oyster.

motif /mo:'ti:f/ *n* a recurrent theme in a musical composition — *also* **motive**.

motile /'mo:taɪl/ *adj* (*biol*) able to move without outside aid; exhibiting movement. • *n* (*psychol*) a person whose perception of the material world comprises, to a very strong degree, the imagery of movement, *esp* his own.—**motility** *n*.

motion /'mo:ʃən/ *n* activity, movement; a formal suggestion made in a meeting, law court, or legislative assembly; evacuation of the bowels. • *vti* to signal or direct by a gesture.

motionless /mo:ʃənləs/ *adj* not moving, still.—**motionlessness** *n*.

motion picture *n* a film, movie.

motivate /'mo:tɪ,veɪt/ *vt* to supply a motive to; to instigate.—**motivator** *n*.

motivation /,mo:tɪ'veɪʃən/ *n* a motivating or being motivated; incentive; (*psychol*) the mental function or instinct that produces, sustains and regulates behaviour in humans and animals.—**motivational** *adj*.

motive /'mo:tɪv/ *n* something (as a need or desire) that causes a person to act; a motif in music. • *adj* moving to action; of or relating to motion.—**motiveless** *adj*.—**motivity** *n*.

motley /'mɒtli/ *adj* multicoloured; composed of diverse elements.

motmot /'mɒtmɒt/ *n* any of various tropical American blue and brownish-green, long-tailed birds similar to the jay, of the same family as the kingfisher.

motor /'mo:tər/ *n* anything that produces motion; a machine for converting electrical energy into mechanical energy; a motor car. • *adj* producing motion; of or powered by a motor; of, by or for motor vehicles; of or involving muscular movements. • *vi* to travel by car.

motorbike /'mo:tər,baɪk/ *n* a motorcycle.

motorboat /'mo:tər,bo:t/ *n* a boat propelled by an engine or motor.

motorbus /'mo:tər,bʌs/ *n* (*pl* **motorbuses, motorbusses**) a bus driven by a motor engine.

motorcade /'mo:tər,keɪd/ *n* a procession of motor vehicles.

motorcar *n* a *usu* four-wheeled vehicle powered by an internal combustion engine.—*also* **automobile**.

motorcycle /'mo:tərsaɪkəl/ *n* a two-wheeled motor vehicle.—**motorcyclist** *n*.

motorist /'mo:tərɪst/ *n* a person who drives a car.

motorize /'mo:təraɪz/ *vt* to equip with a motor; to equip with motor vehicles.—**motorization** *n*.

motorman /'mo:tər,mæn/ *n* (*pl* **motormen**) the driver of a tram or an underground train, or other vehicle powered by electricity; a person who operates a motor.

motor scooter *n* a small-wheeled motorcycle with an enclosed engine.

motorway /'mo:tər,weɪ/ *n* a road with controlled access for fast-moving traffic.—*also* **freeway**.

mottle /'mɒtəl/ *vt* to mark with coloured blotches or spots; to variegate. • *n* a pattern of coloured blotches of spots, as on marble; one of the coloured blotches in such a pattern.

mottled /'mɒtəld/ *adj* marked with blotches of various colours.

motto /'mɒto:/ *n* (*pl* **mottoes, mottos**) a short saying adopted as a maxim or ideal; a slogan on a heraldic crest; a quotation prefixed to a book, etc; verses, etc, in a Christmas cracker.

mouflon, moufflon /'mu:flɒn/ *n* (*pl* **mouflons, mouflon, moufflons, moufflon**) a wild large-horned sheep with a short fleece, found in Corsica and Sardinia.

Mouillé /mu:'jeɪ/ *adj* softened in sound, palatalized, *eg gl* in *seraglio*.

moujik *see* **muzhik**.

mould[1] /mo:ld/ *n* a fungus producing a furry growth on the surface of organic matter. • *vi* to become mouldy.—*also US* **mold**.

mould[2] *n* a hollow form in which something is cast; a pattern; something made in a mould; distinctive character. • *vt* to make in or on a mould; to form, shape, guide.—*also US* **mold**.—**mouldable** *adj*.—**moulder** *n*.

moulder /'mo:ldər/ *vi* to decay to rot, to crumble to dust.

moulding /'mo:ldɪŋ/ *n* anything made in a mould; a shaped strip of wood or plaster, as around the upper walls of a room.—*also* **moulding**.

mouldy /'mo:ldi/ *adj* (**mouldier, mouldiest**) containing or covered with mould; musty, stale; antiquated; (*sl*) dull, boring.—*also US* **moldy**.—**mouldiness** *n*.

moulin /mo:lin/ *n* a deep crack in a glacier through which water and debris drain.

moult /mo:lt/ *see* **molt**.

mound /maʊnd/ *n* an artificial bank of earth or stones; a heap or bank of earth. • *vt* to form into a mound.

mount[1] /maʊnt/ *n* a high hill.

mount[2] *vi* to increase. • *vt* to climb, ascend; to get up on (a horse, platform, etc); to provide with horses; (*a jewel*) to fix on a support; (*a picture*) to frame. • *n* a horse for riding; (*for a picture*) a backing.—**mountable** *adj*.—**mounter** *n*.

mountain /'maʊntən/ *n* a land mass higher than a hill; a vast number or quantity. • *adj* of or in mountains.

mountaineer /,maʊntə'ni:r/ *n* one who climbs mountains.

mountaineering /-ɪŋ/ *n* the technique of climbing mountains.

mountainous /'maʊntənəs/ *adj* having many mountains; very high; huge.—**mountainously** *adv*.—**mountainousness** *n*.

mountebank /'maʊntə,bæŋk/ *n* (*formerly*) an itinerant quack doctor; a boastful pretender, a charlatan, an impostor.

mounted /'maʊntəd/ *adj* seated on horseback or on a bicycle, etc; serving on horseback, as a policeman; placed on a suitable support.

Mountie /'maʊnti/ *n* (*inf*) a member of the Royal Canadian Mounted Police.

mourn /mɔrn/ *vti* (*someone dead*) to grieve for; (*something regrettable*) to feel or express sorrow for.—**mourner** *n*.

mournful /'mɔrnfʊl/ *adj* expressing grief or sorrow; causing sorrow.—**mournfully** *adv*.—**mournfulness** *n*.

mourning /'mɔrnɪŋ/ *adj* grieving. • *n* the expression of grief; dark clothes worn by mourners.

mousaka *see* **moussaka**.

mouse /maʊs/ *n* (*pl* **mice**) a small rodent with a pointed snout, long body and slender tail; a timid person; a hand-held device used to position the cursor and control software on a computer screen.

mouser /-ər/ *n* an animal that is skilled at catching mice, *esp* a cat.

moussaka, mousaka /mu'sɒkə/ *n* a Greek dish comprising aubergines, minced lamb and tomatoes topped with a cheese or white sauce.

mousse /mu:s/ *n* a chilled dessert made of fruit, eggs, and whipped cream; a similar savoury dish made with meat or fish; a foamy substance applied to the hair to help it keep its style.

mousseline /'mu:sli:n/ or /mu:'sli:n/ *n* a sheer fabric resembling muslin, made of rayon or silk; mousseline sauce.

mousseline sauce *n* a white sauce to which whipped cream or the white of an egg has been added.

moustache /'mʊstæʃ/ or /mə'stæʃ/ *n* the hair on the upper lip.

mousy, mousey /'maʊsi/ *adj* (**mousier, mousiest**) mouse-like; grey-brown in colour; quiet, stealthy; timid, retiring.—**mousily** *adv*.—**mousiness** *n*.

mouth /maʊθ/ *n* (*pl* **mouths**) the opening in the head through which food is eaten, sound uttered or words spoken; the lips; opening, entrance, as of a bottle, etc. • *vt* to say, *esp* insincerely; to form words with the mouth without uttering sound. • *vi* to utter pompously; to grimace.—**mouther** *n*.

mouthful /'maʊθfʊl/ *n* (*pl* **mouthfuls**) as much (food) as fills the mouth; a word or phrase that is difficult to say correctly; (*sl*) a pertinent remark.

mouth organ *n* a harmonica.

mouthpiece /-piːs/ *n* the part of a musical instrument placed in the mouth; a person, periodical, etc that expresses the views of others.

mouth-to-mouth resuscitation *n* a method of artificial respiration in which air is forced into the victim's lungs by blowing into the mouth.

mouthwash /-wɒʃ/ *n* a flavoured, often antiseptic liquid for rinsing the mouth.

mouthwatering *adj* appetizing; tasty.

movable, moveable /ˈmuːvəbəl/ *adj* that may be moved. • *npl* personal property.—**movably** *adv.*—**movability** *n.*

move /muːv/ *vt* (**moving, moved**) to shift or change place; to set in motion; to rouse the emotions; to put (a motion) formally. • *vi* to go from one place to another; to walk, to carry oneself; to change place; to evacuate the bowels; to propose a motion as in a meeting; to change residence; (*chess, draughts, etc*) to change the position of a piece on the board. • *n* the act of moving; a movement, *esp* in board games; one's turn to move; a premeditated action.

movement /ˈmuːvmənt/ *n* act of moving; the moving part of a machine, *esp* a clock; the policy and activities of a group; a trend, *eg* in prices; a division of a musical work; tempo.

mover /ˈmuːvər/ *n* one who moves; (*inf*) a driving force, an innovator; a proposer of a motion.

movie /ˈmuːvi/ *n* a cinema film, motion picture; (*pl*) the showing of a motion picture; the motion-picture medium or industry.

moving /ˈmuːvɪŋ/ *adj* arousing the emotions; changing position; causing motion.—**movingly** *adv.*

mow /moʊ/ *vti* (**mowing, mowed**, *pp* **mowed** *or* **mown**) (*grass, etc*) to cut from with a sickle or lawn mower; (*with* **down**) to cause to fall like cut grass.—**mower** *n.*

moxa /ˈmɒksə/ *n* down obtained from plants, used in Oriental medicine as a counterirritant or for cauterizing by burning on the skin; any plant that yields such down.

mozzarella /ˌmɒtsəˈrelə/ *or* /ˌmɛt-/ *n* a white moist Italian curd cheese made originally from buffalo milk.

MP *abbr* = Member of Parliament.

mpg *abbr* = miles per gallon.

mph *abbr* = miles per hour.

MPV *abbr* = multipurpose vehicle.

Mr /ˈmɪstər/ *n* (*pl* **Messrs**) used as a title before a man's name or an office he holds.

MRI *abbr* = magnetic resonance imaging.

Mrs /ˈmɪsɪz/ *n* (*pl* **Mrs** *or* **Mesdames**) used as a title before a married woman's name.

MS *abbr* = (*pl* **MSS**) manuscript; multiple sclerosis.

Ms /mɪz/ *or* /məz/ *n* the title used before a woman's name instead of Miss or Mrs.

MSc *abbr* = Master of Science.

MSG *abbr* = monosodium glutamate.

Mt *abbr* = mount.

much /mʌtʃ/ *adj* (*compar* **more**, *superl* **most**) plenty. • *adv* considerably; to a great extent.

muchness /ˈmʌtʃnəs/ *n* (*arch*) bulk, greatness; **much of a muchness** just about the same.

mucilage /ˈmjuːsɪlɪdʒ/ *n* a adhesive prepared for use; a sticky substance obtained from some plants.—**mucilaginous** *adj.*

muck /mʌk/ *n* moist manure; black earth with decaying matter; mud, dirt, filth. • *vt* to spread manure; to make dirty; (*with* **out**) to clear of muck. • *vi* to move or load muck; (*with* **about, around**) to engage in useless activity.

mucker /ˈmʌkər/ *n* (*mining*) a person who clears broken rocks or other waste; (*Brit sl*) a friend; (*US sl*) a coarse person.

muckworm *n* a grub or larva bred in manure or mud; (*inf*) a skinflint, a hoarder.

mucky /ˈmʌki/ *adj* (**muckier, muckiest**) of or like muck; muddy; filthy.—**muckily** *adv.*—**muckiness** *n.*

mucous /ˈmjuːkəs/ *adj* slimy, sticky; like mucus.—**mucosity** *n.*

mucous membrane *n* the mucus-secreting lining of body cavities.

mucus /ˈmjuːkəs/ *n* the slimy secretion that keeps mucous membranes moist.

mud /mʌd/ *n* soft, wet earth. • *vt* (**muds, mudding, mudded**) to muddy; to throw mud at; to vilify.

muddle /ˈmʌdəl/ *vt* to confuse; to mix up. • *n* confusion, mess.

muddleheaded *adj* silly; confused; absent-minded.—**muddleheadedness** *n.*

muddy /ˈmʌdi/ *adj* (**muddier, muddiest**) like or covered with mud; not bright or clear; confused. • *vti* (**muddying, muddied**) to make or become dirty or unclear.—**muddily** *adv.*—**muddiness** *n.*

mudguard /ˈmʌdɡɑːd/ *n* a screen on a wheel to catch mud splashes.

mudlark *n* (*formerly*) a person who worked or dabbled in mud, *esp* a scavenger on the banks of tidal rivers; (*arch sl*) a mischievous, poorly dressed child who frequented city streets. (*Austral sl*) a horse that performs well on wet, muddy ground.

muesli /ˈmjuːzli/ *n* a mixture of rolled oats, dried fruit, nuts, etc eaten with milk.

muezzin /muːˈezɪn/ *n* a Muslim official who proclaims from the minaret of a mosque the hour of prayer, and summons the faithful to worship.

muff[1] /mʌf/ *n* a warm soft fur cover for warming the hands.

muff[2] *n* a bungling performance; failure to hold a ball when trying to catch it. • *vti* to bungle.

muffin /ˈmʌfɪn/ *n* baked yeast roll.

muffle /ˈmʌfəl/ *vt* to wrap up for warmth or to hide; (*sound*) to deaden by wrapping up.

muffler /ˈmʌflər/ *n* a long scarf; any means of deadening sound; a device for reducing the noise of a vehicle exhaust.

Mufti /ˈmʌfti/ *n* (*pl* **Muftis**) an official expounder of Muslim law.

mufti /ˈmʌfti/ *n* civilian dress worn by a naval or military officer when off duty.

mug /mʌɡ/ *n* a cylindrical drinking cup, *usu* of metal or earthenware; its contents; (*sl*) the face; (*sl*) a fool. • *vb* (**mugging, mugged**) *vt* to assault, *usu* with intent to rob.

mugger[1] /ˈmʌɡər/ *n* a person who assaults with intent to rob.

mugger[2], **muggar, muggur** /ˈmʌɡər/ *n* a broad-snouted Asian crocodile that lives in marshes and pools.

muggins /ˈmʌɡɪnz/ *n* (*sl*) an idiot. • *pron* oneself (used deprecatingly).

muggy /ˈmʌɡi/ *adj* (**muggier, muggiest**) (*weather*) warm, damp and close.—**mugginess** *n.*

mugwump /ˈmʌɡwʌmp/ *n* an independent in politics; (*formerly*) a chief, a bigwig.

mujik *see* **muzhik.**

mukluk /ˈmʌklɛk/ *n* a laced winter boot with a heavy rubber sole and a fabric upper portion, modelled after a traditional Inuit boot.

mulatto /məˈlætoʊ/ *or* /-ˈlɒtoʊ/, /mjuː-/ *n* (*pl* **mulattos, mulattoes**) a person with one black parent and one white parent.

mulberry /ˈmʌlˌberi/ *or* /ˈmʌlbəri/ *n* (*pl* **mulberries**) a tree on whose leaves silkworms feed; its berry.

mulch /mʌltʃ/ *n* loose, organic, strawy dung providing a protective covering around the roots of plants. • *vt* to spread mulch.

mulct /mʌlkt/ *vt* to punish with a fine; to acquire money, etc, by fraud or deception. • *n* a fine, *esp* for some misdemeanour.

mule[1] /mjuːl/ *n* the offspring of a male donkey and a female horse; a machine for spinning cotton; an obstinate person; (*sl*) a person used to smuggle drugs.

mule[2] *n* a slipper without a heel.

muleteer /ˌmjuːləˈtɪːr/ *n* a mule driver.

muliebrity /ˌmjuːliˈebrəti/ *n* (*formal*) womanhood; the qualities of womanhood.

mulish /ˈmjuːlɪʃ/ *adj* like a mule; stubborn, intractable, wilful.—**mulishly** *adv.*—**mulishness** *n.*

mull[1] /mʌl/ *vti* (*inf*) to ponder (over).

mull[2] *vt* (*wine, etc*) to heat, sweeten and spice.—**mulled** *adj.*

mullah, mulla /ˈmʌlə/ *or* /ˈmʊlə/ (*formerly*) a Muslim theologian or teacher; a Muslim title of respect.

muller /ˈmʌlər/ *n* a flat-bottomed pestle for grinding (drugs, paints) on a slab.

mullet /ˈmʌlət/ *n* (*pl* **mullets, mullet**) any of various types of food fish.

mulligatawny /ˌmʌlɪɡəˈtɔːni/ *n* a curry-flavoured meat soup.

mullion /ˈmʌljən/ *n* an upright bar or division between the panes of a window or the panels of a screen, etc, *esp* in a Gothic arch; a projecting ridge on a rock face. • *vt* to provide with or divide by mullions.

mullock *n* (*Austral*) a rock containing no gold or from which gold has been extracted, rubbish; (*dial*) disorder.

mult-, multi- /ˈmʌlti/ *prefix* much, many.

multangular, multiangular *adj* many-angled.

multeity /mɛl'teɪəti/ n multiplicity.

multicoloured, multicolored /'mʌltɪˌkʌlərd/ adj many-coloured.

multifarious /ˌmʌltɪ'fɛrɪəs/ adj multiform; diversified, of great variety; manifold.—**multifariously** adv.—**multifariousness** n.

multifid /'mʌltɪfɪd/, **multifidous** /-fɪdəs/ adj (bot) cleft into many parts or lobe-like elements.

multifoil /-fɔɪl/ n (archit) an ornament with over five leaf-like divisions.—also adj.

multiform /-ˌfɔrm/ adj having many shapes; of many kinds.—**multiformity** n.

multilateral /ˌmʌltɪ'lætərəl/ adj having many sides; with several nations or participants.—**multilaterally** adv.

multilingual /-'lɪŋgwəl/ or /-'lɪŋgjʊəl/ adj speaking or in more than two languages.—**multilingually** adv.

multimedia n, adj the process of combining computer data, sound and video images to create an environment similar to television.

multimillionaire n a person with two or more millions of money.

multinational /ˌmʌltɪ'næʃənəl/ n a business operating in several countries.—also adj.

multinomial /ˌmʌltɪ'noʊmɪəl/ n (math) an expression that consists of the sum of several terms, a polynomial.—also adj.

multiplane /ˌmʌltɪ'pleɪn/ n an aeroplane with two or more pairs of wings.

multiple /'mʌltɪpəl/ adj of many parts; manifold; various; complex. • n (math) a number exactly divisible by another.

multiple sclerosis n a disease of the nervous system with loss of muscular coordination, etc.

multiplex /'mʌltɪˌplɛks/ adj (radio, telecommunications) the use of a single channel of communication to transmit more than one signal; in map-making, the use of three or more cameras so that the end product appears to be rendered in three dimensions; manifold, multiple. • vi to transmit messages or send signals in a multiplex system. • vt to send (several signals) simultaneously on one frequency.

multipliable /'mʌltɪˌplaɪəbəl/, **multiplicable** /-ˌplɪkəbəl/ adj able to be multiplied.

multiplicand /ˌmʌltɪplɪ'kænd/ n a number to be multiplied by another.

multiplicate /'mʌltɪplɪˌkeɪt/ adj (rare) consisting of many.

multiplication /ˌmʌltɪplɪ'keɪʃən/ n the act of multiplying; the process of repeatedly adding a quantity to itself a certain number of times, or any other process which has the same result.—**multiplicational** adj.

multiplicative /'mʌltɪplɪˌkeɪtɪv/ adj relating to the mathematical operation of mutiplication; tending to multiply; able to multiply.

multiplicity /ˌmʌltɪ'plɪsɪti/ n (pl **multiplicities**) a great number or variety (of).

multiplier /'mʌltɪˌplaɪər/ n a thing or person that multiplies; the number by which another is to be multiplied.

multiply /'mʌltɪˌplaɪ/ vti (**multiplying, multiplied**) to increase in number, degree, etc; to find the product (of) by multiplication.

multitude /'mʌltɪˌtuːd/ or /-ˌtjuːd/ n a large number (of people).

multitudinous /ˌmʌltɪ'tuːdɪnəs/ or /-'tjuːdɪnəs/ adj of a multitude; very many; having innumerable elements.—**multitudinously** adv.—**multitudinousness** n.

mum[1] /mʌm/ n (inf) mother.

mum[2] adj silent, not speaking. • n silence. • vi (**mumming, mummed**) to act as a mummer.—also **mumm**.

mumble /'mʌmbəl/ vti to speak indistinctly, mutter. • n a mumbled utterance.—**mumbler** n.—**mumblingly** adv.

mumbo jumbo /ˌmʌmboʊ'dʒʌmboʊ/ n (pl **mumbo jumbos**) meaningless ritual, talk, etc.

mumchance /'mʌmˌtʃæns/ adj (arch) silent; tongue-tied.

mumm see **mum**[2].

mummer /'mʌmər/ n a person who acts in a play without words; an actor.

mummery /'mʌməri/ n (pl **mummeries**) performance by mummers; ridiculous ceremonial, pretentious display.

mummify /'mʌmɪˌfaɪ/ vt (**mummifying, mummified**) to embalm (a body) as a mummy; to shrivel, to desiccate.—**mummification** n.

mummy[1] /'mʌmi/ n (pl **mummies**) (inf) mother.

mummy[2] n (pl **mummies**) a carefully preserved dead body, esp an embalmed corpse of ancient Egypt.

mumps /mʌmps/ n sing or pl an acute contagious virus disease characterized by swelling of the salivary glands, fever and pain beneath the ear.

munch /mʌntʃ/ vti to chew steadily.—**muncher** n.

mundane /mʌn'deɪn/ adj routine, everyday; banal; worldly.—**mundanely** adv.

mungo /'mʌŋgoʊ/ n (pl **mungos**) a cheap woollen material made from cloth waste.

municipal /mjuː'nɪsɪpəl/ or /ˌmjuːnɪ'sɪpəl/ adj of or concerning a city, town, etc or its local government.—**municipally** adv.

municipality /mjuːˌnɪsɪ'pælɪti/ n (pl **municipalities**) a city or town having corporate status and powers of self-government; the governing body of a municipality.

municipalize /mjuː'nɪsɪpəˌlaɪz/ vt to bring under municipal control; to constitute a place as a municipality.—**municipalization** n.

munificent /mjuː'nɪfɪsənt/ adj extremely generous, bountiful.—**munificence** n.—**munificently** adv.

muniment /'mjuːnɪmənt/ n (rare) a defence, a fortification; (pl) (law) deeds, charters, and other papers for proving title to land.

munition /mjuː'nɪʃən/ vt to equip with arms. • n (pl) war supplies, esp weapons and ammunition.

muntjac, muntjak /'mʌntdʒæk/ n any of various small, brown Asian deer with small antlers and a cry similar to that of a dog.

mural /'mjʊrəl/ adj relating to a wall. • n a picture or design painted directly onto a wall.—**muralist** n.

murder /'mɜrdər/ n the intentional and unlawful killing of one person by another; (inf) something unusually difficult or dangerous to do or deal with. • vti to commit murder (upon), to kill; to mangle, to mar.—**murderer** n.—**murderess** nf.

murderous /'mɜrdərəs/ adj capable of or bent on murder; deadly.—**murderously** adv.—**murderousness** n.

murex /'mjʊrəks/ n (pl **murices, murexes**) any of a genus of marine gasteropods, one species of which yields a purple dye used in ancient Greece and Rome.

murine /'mjuːˌraɪn/ adj pertaining to or resembling a mouse or rat; affected, caused or transmitted by rats or mice. • n any animal belonging to the same family as rats and mice.

murk /mɜrk/ n indistinct gloom, darkness. • adj (arch) dark, obscured by fog or mist.—also **mirk**.

murky /'mɜrki/ adj (**murkier, murkiest**) dark, gloomy; darkly vague or obscure.—also **mirky**.—**murkily** adv.—**murkiness** n.

murmur /'mɜrmər/ n a continuous low, indistinct sound; a mumbled complaint; (med) an abnormal sound made by the heart. • vti to make a murmur; to say in a murmur.—**murmurer** n.—**murmurous** adj.

murphy /'mɜrfi/ n (pl **murphies**) (inf) a potato.

murrain /'mɜrɪn/ n any infectious disease of cattle, such as foot-and-mouth disease; (arch) a plague.

murrhine, murrine /'mɜˌraɪn/ n of or pertaining to an unknown substance (possibly jade or porcelain) used to make delicate pottery in ancient Rome. • n this substance.—also **murra**.

murther /'mɜrðər/ n (arch) murder.—**murtherer** n.

muscadine /'mʌskədɪn/ or /-ˌdaɪn/ n a type of woody plant that produces a grape used to make wine.

muscat /'mʌskæt/ n any of various types of sweet white grapes used to make wine; muscatel.

muscatel, muscadel /ˌmʌskə'tɛl/ n a sweet wine made from muscat grapes.

muscle /'mʌsəl/ n fibrous tissue that contracts and relaxes, producing bodily movement; strength; brawn; power. • vi (inf) to force one's way (in).

muscle-bound adj having some of the muscles abnormally enlarged and lacking in elasticity as from too much exercise; inflexible, rigid.

muscovado, muscavado /ˌmʌskə'vɑːdoʊ/ n raw sugar left after the molasses has evaporated from sugar cane.

Muscovite /'mʌskəˌvaɪt/ n a person who lives in, or originates from, Moscow; (arch) a Russian. • adj (arch) Russian.

muscovite /'mʌskəˌvaɪt/ n a type of mica often found in granite and sedimentary rocks.

Muscovy (duck) /'mʌskəvi/ n a green-brown duck with white markings and a characteristic red fleshy growth on its beak.—also **musk duck**.

muscular /'mʌskjʊlər/ adj of or done by a muscle; having well-developed muscles; strong.—**muscularity** n.—**muscularly** adv.

musculature /'mʌskjʊlətʃər/ n the entire system of muscles in a living thing; the system of muscles in an organ or a part of this system.

muse /mju:z/ *vti* to ponder, meditate; to be lost in thought. • *n* a fit of abstraction.—**muser** *n.*

museum /mju:'ziəm/ *n* a building for exhibiting objects of artistic, historic or scientific interest.

mush /mʌʃ/ *n* a thick porridge of boiled meal; any thick, soft mass; (*inf*) sentimentality.

mushroom /'mʌʃru:m/ *n* a fleshy fungus with a capped stalk, some varieties of which are edible. • *vi* to gather mushrooms; to spread rapidly, to increase.

mushy /'mʌʃi/ *adj* (**mushier, mushiest**) soft, pulpy; (*sl*) sentimental, soppy.—**mushily** *adv.*—**mushiness** *n.*

music /'mju:zɪk/ *n* the art of combining tones into a composition having structure and continuity; vocal or instrumental sounds having rhythm, melody or harmony; an agreeable sound.

musical /'mju:zɪkəl/ *adj* of or relating to music or musicians; having the pleasant tonal qualities of music; having an interest in or talent for music. • *n* a play or film incorporating dialogue, singing and dancing.—**musicality** *n.*—**musically** *adv.*

musicale /mju:zɪ'kæl/ *n* a musical party.

musician /mju:'zɪʃən/ *n* one skilled in music, *esp* a performer.—**musicianly** *adj.*—**musicianship** *n.*

musicology /mju:zɪ'kɒlədʒi/ *n* the study of the history, forms, etc of music.—**musicological** *adj.*—**musicologist** *n.*

musing /'mju:sɪŋ/ *adj* meditative; lost in thought.—**musingly** *adv.*

musk /mʌsk/ *n* an animal secretion with a strong odour, used in perfumes; the odour of musk; a plant with a similar odour.

musk duck *see* Muscovy.

muskellunge /'mʌskə,lʌndʒ/ *n* (*pl* **muskellunges, muskellunge**) a large North American game fish similar to the pike.

musket /'mʌskət/ *n* a long-barrelled, smoothbore shoulder gun formerly used by infantrymen.

musketeer /mʌskə'tiːr/ *n* (*formerly*) a soldier armed with a musket.

musketry /'mʌskətri/ *n* small-arm fire; practice in this; muskets or musketeers collectively.

muskmelon /'mʌskmɛlən/ *n* any of several varieties of widely cultivated melon with a netted or ribbed skin and sweet light-coloured or green flesh and a musky smell; any one of several types of melon related to the honeydew and cantaloupe.

muskrat /'mʌskræt/ *n* (*pl* **muskrats, muskrat**) a large North American aquatic rodent, related to the vole, that emits a musky secretion; the fur from this.—*also* **musquash.**

musky /'mʌski/ *adj* (**muskier, muskiest**) like or smelling of musk; sweet-smelling.—**muskiness** *n.*

Muslim /'mɛzlɪm/ or /-ləm/ *n* an adherent of Islam. • *adj* of Islam, its adherents and culture.—*also* **Moslem.**

muslin /'mɛzlɪn/ *n* a fine cotton cloth.

musquash /'mʌskwɒʃ/ *n* the fur of the muskrat; the muskrat.

muss /mʌs/ *vt* (*often with* up) (*inf*) to disarrange, to rumple. • *n* a state of disorder.

mussel /'mʌsəl/ *n* an edible marine bivalve shellfish.

must[1] /mʌst/ *aux vb expressing*: necessity; probability; certainty. • *n* (*inf*) something that must be done, had, etc.

must[2] *n* newly pressed grape juice, unfermented or partially fermented wine; the pulp and skin of crushed grapes.

must[3] *see* musth.

must[4] *see* musty.

mustachio /mə'stætʃio:/ *n* (*pl* **mustachios**) (*often pl*) a moustache, *usu* bushy or shaped.

mustang /'mʌstæŋ/ *n* a small hardy semi-wild horse of the American prairies.

mustard /'mʌstərd/ *n* the powdered seeds of the mustard plant used as a condiment; a brownish-yellow colour; (*sl*) zest.

muster /'mʌstər/ *vt* to assemble or call together, as troops for inspection or duty; to gather. • *vi* to be assembled, as troops. • *n* gathering; review; assembly.

musth, must /mʌst/ *n* a state of sexual frenzy in the males of elephants and certain other large mammals. • *adj* denoting an animal in musth.

musty /'mʌsti/ *adj* (**mustier, mustiest**) mouldy, damp; stale.—**mustily** *adv.*—**mustiness, must** *n.*

mutable /'mju:təbəl/ *adj* able or tending to change or be changed; fickle, inconstant.—**mutability** *n.*—**mutably** *adv.*

mutant /'mju:tənt/ *n* a mutation; an organism whose structure has undergone mutation. • *adj* mutating.

mutate /mju:'teɪt/ *vti* to experience or cause to experience change or alteration.

mutation /mju:'teɪʃən/ *n* the act or process of mutating; alteration; (*biol*) a sudden change in some inheritable characteristic of a species; (*linguistics*) a change in a vowel sound when assimilated with another, *esp* an umlaut.—**mutational** *adj.*

mutatis /mju:,tætɪs/, **mutandis** /mju:'tændɪs/ (*Latin*) with the necessary changes.

mute /mju:t/ *adj* silent; dumb; (*colour*) subdued. • *n* a person who is unable to speak; a device that softens the sound of a musical instrument. • *vt* to lessen the sound of a musical instrument.—**mutely** *adv.*—**muteness** *n.*

mutilate /'mju:tɪ,leɪt/ *vt* to maim; to damage by removing an essential part of.—**mutilation** *n.*—**mutilative** *adj.*—**mutilator** *n.*

mutineer /mju:tɪ'niːr/ *n* a person who takes part in a mutiny.

mutinous /'mju:tɪnəs/ *adj* threatening mutiny, rebellious; taking part in a mutiny.—**mutinously** *adv.*

mutiny /'mju:tɪni/ *vi* (**mutinying, mutinied**) to revolt against authority, *esp* in military service. • *n* (*pl* **mutines**) a rebellion against authority, *esp* by soldiers and sailors against officers.

mutism /'mju:tɪzəm/ *n* the inability to speak; dumbness; silence; (*psychiatry*) a state in which a person remains silent although there is no physical cause for this.

mutt /mʌt/ *n* (*sl*) a fool; a mongrel dog.

mutter /'mʌtər/ *vti* to utter in a low tone or indistinctly; to grumble.—**mutterer** *n.*—**mutteringly** *adv.*

mutton /'mʌtən/ *n* the edible flesh of sheep.

muttonchops *n* whiskers on the side of the face, narrow at the top, broad at the bottom.

mutual /'mju:tʃuəl/ *adj* given and received in equal amount; having the same feelings one for the other; shared in common.—**mutuality** *n.*—**mutually** *adv.*

mutule /'mju:tʃu:l/ *n* (*archit*) a projecting block under the corona of the Doric cornice.

muzhik /'mu:ʒɪk/ *n* a peasant in pre-Revolutionary Russia.—*also* **mujik, moujik.**

muzz /mʌz/ *vt* (*inf*) to make (anything) muzzy.

muzzle /'mʌzəl/ *n* the projecting nose or mouth of an animal; a strap fitted over the jaws to prevent biting; the open end of a gun barrel. • *vt* to put a muzzle on; to silence or gag.—**muzzler** *n.*

muzzy /'mʌzi/ *adj* (**muzzier, muzziest**) confused, dazed; dizzy; blurred; dull.—**muzzily** *adv.*—**muzziness** *n.*

MW *abbr* = medium wave; megawatt.

Mx *abbr* = maxwell.

my /maɪ/ *poss adj* of or belonging to me.

myalgia /maɪ'ældʒə/ or /-dʒiə/ *n* pain, stiffness or cramp in the voluntary muscles or in one muscle.

myalgic encephalomyelitis *n* a viral condition affecting the nervous system, characterized by fatigue and muscle pains.—*also* **post-viral syndrome.**

mycelium /maɪ'si:liəm/ *n* (*pl* **mycelia**) a cellular spawn of fungi.

mycetoma /'maɪsə,to:mə/ *n* (*pl* **mycetomas, mycetomata**) a fungoid disease, *usu* of feet, often caused by a wound.

mycology /maɪ'kɒlədʒi/ *n* the science of fungi or mushrooms; the fungi found in a particular area.—**mycologist** *n.*

mycosis /maɪ'ko:sɪs/ *n* (*pl* **mycoses**) the presence of, or a disease caused by, a parasitic fungus.

mydriasis /mɪ'draɪəsɪs/ *n* excessive dilatation of the pupil of the eye.

mydriatic /-tɪk/ *adj* causing mydriasis. • *n* a drug that induces mydriasis.

myelitis /maɪə'laɪtɪs/ *n* inflammation of the spinal cord or of bone marrow.

myna (bird) /'maɪnə/ *n* any of several Asian birds resembling the starling, some species of which can imitate speech.—*also* **mina (bird).**

Mynheer /'maɪ,niːr/ *n* a Dutch title used before a name, as "Mister" as a term of respect.

myocarditis /,maɪo:kɑr'daɪtɪs/ *n* an inflammation of the myocardium.

myocardium /,maɪo:'kɑrdiəm/ *n* (*pl* **myocardia**) the muscular parts of the heart.—**myocardial** *adj.*

myology /maɪ'ɒlədʒi/ *n* a branch of medicine concerned with studying the muscles or the diseases affecting them.

myope /'maɪo:p/ *n* a short-sighted person.

myopia /maɪ'o:piə/ *n* short-sightedness.—**myopic** *adj.*—**myopically** *adv.*

myosis *see* **miosis.**

myosotis, myosote /ˌmaɪəˈsoːtɪs/ *n* any of various small plants with blue, pink, or white flowers, incl the forget-me-not.

myriad /ˈmɪrɪəd/ *n* a great number of persons or things. • *adj* innumerable.

myriapod /ˈmɪrɪəˌpɒd/ *n* an arthropod with many legs and a segmented body, incl millipedes and centipedes.—**myriapodan** *adj, n.*—**myriapodous** *adj.*

myrica /ˈmaɪrɪkə/ *n* the root bark of the candleberry or wax myrtle.

myrmecology /ˈmaɪrmɛˌkɒlədʒi/ or /ˈmɪr-/ *n* the scientific study of ants.—**myrmecological** *adj.*—**myrmecologist** *n.*

myrmecophagous /ˈmaɪrmɛˌkɒfəgəs/ *adj* feeding on ants; (*jaws, etc*) adapted for eating ants.

Myrmidon /ˈmɜːrmɪdən/ *n* (*pl* **Myrmidons, Myrmidones**) (*Greek myth*) one of a tribe of Thracian warriors formed by Zeus from an anthill who accompanied Achilles to the Trojan war; a brutal, unprincipled or unquestioning follower or subordinate.—*also adj.*

myrobalan /maɪˈrɒbələn/ *n* any of several tropical trees containing tannin and bearing a fruit that when dried was used medicinally and in dyeing and tanning; the dye from such a fruit.

myrrh /mɜːr/ *n* a fragrant gum resin used in perfume, incense, etc.

myrtaceous /mɜːrˌteɪʃəs/ *adj* of the myrtle family, incl eucalyptus, clove and guava, with leaves that secrete oil.

myrtle /ˈmɜːrtəl/ *n* an evergreen shrub with fragrant leaves; a trailing periwinkle.

myself /maɪˈsɛlf/ *pron* emphatic and reflexive form of I; in my normal state.

mystagogue /ˈmɪstəˌgɒg/ *n* an initiator into or interpreter of mysteries—**mystagogic** *adj.*—**mystagogy** *n.*

mysterious /mɪˈstɪːrɪəs/ *adj* difficult to understand or explain, obscure; delighting in mystery.—**mysteriously** *adv.*—**mysteriousness** *n.*

mystery /ˈmɪstəri/ *n* (*pl* **mysteries**) something unexplained and secret; a story about a secret crime, etc; secrecy.

mystic /ˈmɪstɪk/ *n* one who seeks direct knowledge of God or spiritual truths by self-surrender. • *adj* mystical.

mystical /-kəl/ *adj* having a meaning beyond normal human understanding; magical.—**mystically** *adv.*

mysticism /-ˌsɪzəm/ *n* the beliefs or practices of a mystic; belief in a reality accessible by intuition, not the intellect; obscurity of thought or doctrine.

mystify /ˈmɪstɪˌfaɪ/ *vt* (**mystifying, mystified**) to puzzle, bewilder, to confuse.—**mystification** *n.*—**mistifier** *n.*—**mistifyingly** *adv.*

myth /mɪθ/ *n* a fable; a fictitious event; a traditional story of gods and heroes, taken to be true.—**mythic** *adj.*

mythical /ˈmɪθɪkəl/ *adj* imaginary, unreal, untrue; having to do with myths, mythic.—**mythically** *adv.*

mythicize /ˈmɪθɪˌsaɪz/ *vt* to treat as myth; to interpret mythically; to turn (something) into myth.

mythologist /mɪˈθɒlədʒɪst/ *n* a student of myths; a writer of myths.

mythology /mɪˈθɒlədʒi/ *n* (*pl* **mythologies**) myths collectively; the study of myths.—**mythological** *adj.*

mythopoeic /ˌmɪθəpɔːˈiːɪk/ *adj* producing or creating myths.—**mythopoeia, mythopoeisis** *n.*

myxoedema, myxedema /ˌmɪksəˈdiːmə/ *n* an illness leading to physical and mental degeneration due to underactivity of the thyroid gland and thus severe thyroxine deficiency

myxomycete /ˌmɪksoːmaɪˈsiːt/ *n* any of various organisms forming a network of creamy filaments on decaying wood, leaves, etc, and displaying characteristics of both plants and animals.

N

N (*chem symbol*) nitrogen. • *abbr* = North.

N, n /ɛn/ *n* the 14th letter of the English alphabet; an indefinite number.

n/a *abbr* (*in commerce*) = no account.

NA *abbr* = North America.

Na (*chem symbol*) sodium.

nab /næb/ *vt* (**nabbing, nabbed**) (*sl*) to catch, arrest.

nabob /ˈneɪbɒb/ *n* in India, a deputy or administrator under the Mogul Empire; one who has amassed wealth in India; a very wealthy man.

nacelle /nəˈsɛl/ *n* the car of an aircraft.

nacho /ˈnɒtʃoː/ or /ˈnætʃoː/ *n* a Mexican snack consisting of a tortilla chip often served grilled with melted cheese, chilli, etc.

nacre /ˈneɪkər/ *n* mother-of-pearl; the shellfish that yields it.

nacreous /ˈneɪkrɪəs/ *adj* having an iridescent lustre; resembling mother of pearl.

nadir /ˈneɪdiːr/ or /-dər/, /ˈnæd-/ *n* the point opposite the zenith; the lowest point; the depths of despair.

naevus /ˈniːvəs/ *see* **nevus**.

nag[1] /næg/ *vti* (**nagging, nagged**) to scold constantly; to harass; to be felt persistently. • *n* a person who nags.

nag[2] *n* (*inf*) a horse.

Naga /ˈnɒgə/ *n* (*pl* **Nagas, Naga**) (*Hindu myth*) a deified serpent, *esp* the cobra; a member of the Naga tribes; a class of mendicant Hindus. • *adj* pertaining to an ancient race who invaded India about the 6th century BC, or to certain Burmese border tribes.

nagana /nəˈgɒnɑ/ *n* a disease caused by the tsetse-fly.

Nagari /ˈnɒgəri/ *n* the name of the Sanskrit alphabet.

nagelflue /ˈnægəlˌfluː/ *n* a peculiar alpine conglomerate rock, interspersed with nail-like pebbles.

nagor /ˈnægər/ *n* a Senegal antelope.

Nahum /ˈneɪhəm/ *n* one of the prophetical books of the Old Testament.

naiad /ˈnaɪæd/ *n* (*pl* **naiads, naiades**) a water nymph; (*pl*) an order of aquatic plants; a family of freshwater bivalves.

naiant /ˈneɪənt/ *adj* (*her*) representing fishes swimming in a horizontal position.

naif, naïf /nɒˈiːf/ *adj* naive.

nail /neɪl/ *n* a horny plate covering the end of a human finger or toe; a thin pointed metal spike for driving into wood as a fastening or hanging device. • *vt* to fasten with nails; to fix, secure; (*inf*) to catch or hit; (*inf*) to arrest.

nailfile *n* a small metal file or strip of cardboard coated with emery used for trimming and shaping the nails.

nail polish *n* a lacquer for giving a clear or coloured shiny surface to nails.

nainsook /ˈneɪnsʊk/ *n* a kind of closely woven muslin originally Indian.

naissant /ˈneɪzənt/ *adj* (*her*) issuing forth or rising from some ordinary, and showing only the foreparts of the body.

naive, naïve /naɪˈiːv/ *adj* inexperienced; unsophisticated; (*argument*) simple.—**naively, naïvely** *adv*.

naiveté, naïveté /naɪˌiːvəˈteɪ/ or /naɪˈiːvəti/, **naivety** *n* natural, unaffected simplicity or ingenuousness.

naked /ˈneɪkəd/ *adj* bare, without clothes; without a covering; without addition or ornament; (*eye*) without optical aid.—**nakedness** *n*.

namby-pamby /ˌnæmbɪˈpæmbi/ *adj* weakly sentimental or affectedly pretty or fine. • *n* (*pl* **namby-pambies**) an affected person.

name /neɪm/ *n* a word or term by which a person or thing is called; a title; reputation; authority. • *vt* to give a name to; to call by name; to designate; to appoint to an office; (*a date, price, etc*) to specify.

name-calling /-ˌkɔːlɪŋ/ *n* verbal abuse, *esp* in place of reasoned debate.

name-dropping /-ˌdrɒpɪŋ/ *n* the practice of mentioning the names of famous or important people as if they were friends, in order to impress others.—**name-dropper** *n*.

nameless /ˈneɪmləs/ *adj* without a name; obscure; anonymous; unnamed; indefinable; too distressing or horrifying to be described.

namely /ˈneɪmli/ *adv* that is to say.

nameplate /ˈneɪmpleɪt/ *n* a small plate on a door of a room, house, etc displaying the name of the occupant.

namesake /ˈneɪmseɪk/ *n* a person or thing with the same name as another.

nan bread, naan bread *n* a type of slightly leavened Indian bread in a flattened oval shape.

nankeen, nankin /næŋˈkiːn/ or /næn-/ *n* a buff-coloured cotton cloth, originally from China.

nanny /ˈnæni/ *n* (*pl* **nannies**) a child's nurse.

nanny goat *n* a female domestic goat.

nano- /ˈnænoː/ or /ˈneɪnoː/ *prefix* one thousand millionth (10-9) part of, *eg* **nanosecond**.

nanosecond (ns) *n* one billionth of a second.

nap[1] /næp/ *n* a short sleep, doze. • *vi* (**napping, napped**) to take a nap.

nap[2] *n* a hairy surface on cloth or leather; such a surface.

napalm /ˈneɪpɒm/ *n* a substance added to petrol to form a jelly-like compound used in firebombs and flame-throwers. • *vt* to attack or burn with napalm.

nape /neɪp/ *n* the back of the neck.

napery /ˈneɪpəri/ *n* household linen, *esp* for the table.

naphtha /ˈnæpθə/ or /ˈnæf-/ *n* a clear, volatile, inflammable bituminous liquid hydrocarbon exuding from the earth or distilled from coal tar, etc; rock oil.

naphthalene /ˈnæfθəˌliːn/ *n* a white crystalline hydrocarbon distilled from coal tar, used in making dyes, explosives and in mothballs.

napiform /ˈneɪpəˌfɔːm/ *adj* turnip-shaped.

napkin /ˈnæpkɪn/ *n* a square of cloth or paper for wiping fingers or mouth or protecting clothes at table, a serviette; a nappy.

napoleon /nəˈpoːliən/ *n* a gold coin formerly current in France, value 20 francs.

Napoleonic /nəˌpoːliˈɒnɪk/ *adj* of or like Emperor Napoleon I.

nappy[1] /ˈnæpi/ *adj* (**nappier, nappiest**) covered with nap or pile.

nappy[2] *n* (*pl* **nappies**) a piece of soft material, *esp* towelling or a disposable material, wrapped round a baby's bottom to absorb its excrement.—*also US* **diaper**.

narceine /ˈnɑːsiːn/ or /-ɪn/ *n* an alkaloid obtained from opium and used as a sedative.

narcissism /ˈnɑːsɪˌsɪzəm/ *n* excessive interest in one's own body or self.—**narcissistic** *adj*.

narcissus /nɑːˈsɪsəs/ *n* (*pl* **narcissi, narcissuses**) a spring-flowering bulb plant, *esp* the daffodil.

narco- /ˈnɑːkoː/ *prefix* indicating torpor or narcotics.

narcosis /nɑːˈkoːsɪs/ *n* (*pl* **narcoses**) a state of unconsciousness or drowsiness produced by narcotics.

narcotic /nɑːˈkɒtɪk/ *adj* inducing sleep. • *n* a drug, often addictive, used to relieve pain and induce sleep.

narcotism /-ɪzəm/ *n* a morbid dependence on narcotics.

narcotize /ˈnɑːkəˌtaɪz/ *vt* to use a narcotic upon.—**narcotization** *n*.

nard /nɑːd/ *n* spikenard, an aromatic plant; an aromatic unguent prepared from it.

nardoo /nɑːˈduː/ *n* a genus of Australian acotyledonous aquatic plants, Australian pillwort, the spore cases of which are used as bread.

narghile /ˈnɑːgəli/ *n* a small hookah pipe.

narrate /nəˈreɪt/ or /nɒˈreɪt/ *vt* (*a story*) to tell, relate; to give an account of; (*film, TV*) to provide a spoken commentary for.

narration /nəˈreɪʃən/ *n* the act of narrating; a statement, written or verbal.

narrative /ˈnɒrətɪv/ *n* a spoken or written account of a sequence of events, experiences, etc; the art or process of narration.—*also adj*.

narrator /ˈnɛrˌeɪtər/ or /nəˈreɪt-/ *n* one who narrates.

narrow /'nɛroː/ or /'nær-/ adj small in width; limited; with little margin; (views) prejudiced or bigoted. • n (usu pl) the narrow part of a pass, street, or channel. • vti to make or grow narrow; to decrease; to contract.—**narrowly** adv.—**narrowness** n.

narrow gauge adj denoting the distance of less than standard gauge (4 feet, 8.5 inches/1.44 metres) between rail metals.

narrow-minded /'nɛroː'maɪndɪd/ or /'nær-/ adj prejudiced, bigoted; illiberal.—**narrow-mindedness** n.

narthex /'nɑrθɛks/ n in Early Christian churches the western portico, railed off for catechumens and penitents.

narwhal /'nɑrwəl/ n an Arctic whale, the male of which has a long spiral tusk.

nary /'nɛri/ = never a, ne'er a.

NASA /'næsə/ or /'næsə/ abbr = National Aeronautics and Space Administration.

nasal /'neɪzəl/ adj of the nose; sounded through the nose. • n a sound made through the nose.—**nasally** adv.

nascent /'neɪsənt/ or /'næs-/ adj just starting to grow or develop.

naseberry /'neɪzbɛri/ n (pl **naseberries**) sapodilla plum tree.

naso- /'neɪzoː/ prefix nose.

nasturtium /nə'stɜrʃəm/ n an ornamental garden plant with bright flowers, a pungent odour, and edible leaves.

nasty /'næsti/ adj (**nastier, nastiest**) unpleasant; offensive; ill-natured; disagreeable; (problem) hard to deal with; (illness) serious or dangerous.—**nastily** adv.—**nastiness** n.

Nat. abbr = national; native; natural.

natal /'neɪtəl/ adj pertaining to one's birth or birthday; indigenous.—**natality** n.

natant /'neɪtənt/ adj swimming; (her) (fish) floating on the surface.

natation /nə'teɪʃən/ n the act or art of swimming.—**natational** adj.

natatorial /ˌneɪtə'tɔriəl/, **natatory** adj swimming or adapted for swimming.

nates /'neɪtiːz/ npl (sing **natis**) the buttocks.

nation /'neɪʃən/ n people of common territory, descent, culture, language, or history; people united under a single government.

national /'næʃnəl/ adj of a nation; common to a whole nation, general. • n a citizen or subject of a specific country.—**nationally** adv.

national anthem n a patriotic song or hymn adopted officially by a nation for ceremonial and public occasions.

national debt n the total money currently on loan to the government of a nation.

National Guard n in US, state militia that can be called into federal service.

nationalism /'næʃnəˌlɪzəm/ n patriotic sentiments, principles, etc; a policy of national independence or self-government; fanatical patriotism, chauvinism.—**nationalist** n.—**nationalistic** adj.

nationality /ˌnæʃə'næliti/ n (pl **nationalities**) the status of belonging to a nation by birth or naturalization; a nation or national group.

nationalize /'næʃnəˌlaɪz/ vt to make national; to convert into public or government property.—**nationalization** n.

national park n an area designated by a government as of important scenic, historical, or environmental value.

native /'neɪtɪv/ adj inborn; natural to a person; innate; (language, etc) of one's place of birth; relating to the indigenous inhabitants of a country or area; occurring naturally. • n a person born in the place indicated; a local inhabitant; an indigenous plant or animal; an indigenous inhabitant, esp a non-White under colonial rule.

Native American n a member of an Indian people in the United States. • adj of or pertaining to such a people or community.

nativism /'neɪtɪˌvɪzəm/ n (philos) the doctrine of innate ideas; in US, the advocacy of the claim of native as opposed to that of naturalized Americans.—**nativist** adj, n.—**nativistic** adj.

nativity /nə'tɪvɪti/ n (pl **nativities**) birth; a horoscope at the time of one's birth; (with cap) the birth of Christ.

NATO /'neɪtoː/ abbr = North Atlantic Treaty Organization.

natrolite /'nætrəˌlaɪt/ or /'neɪtrə-/ n a hydrated silicate of aluminium and soda.

natron /'neɪtrɒn/ or /-trən/ n a native carbonate of soda.

natter /'nætər/ vi (inf) to chat, talk aimlessly.—also n.

natty /'næti/ adj (**nattier, nattiest**) tidy, neat, smart.—**nattily** adv.—**nattiness** n.

natural /'nætʃərəl/ adj of or produced by nature; not artificial; innate, not acquired; true to nature; lifelike; normal; at ease; (mus) not flat or sharp. • n (inf) a person or thing considered to have a natural aptitude (for) or to be an obvious choice (for); (inf) a certainty; (mus) a natural note or a sign indicating one.—**naturalness** n.

natural childbirth n giving birth using techniques of relaxation, controlled breathing, etc rather than with anaesthetics.

natural gas n gas trapped in the earth's crust, a combustible mixture of methane and hydrocarbons extracted for fuel.

natural history n the study of nature, esp the animal, mineral, and vegetable world.

naturalism /'nætʃərəˌlɪzəm/ or /'nætʃrə-/ n (art, literature) the theory or practice of describing nature, character, etc in realistic detail; (philos) a theory of the world based on scientific as opposed to spiritual or supernatural explanations.—**naturalistic** adj.

naturalist /'nætʃərəlɪst/ or /'nætʃrə-/ n a person who studies natural history; a person who advocates or practises naturalism.

naturalization /ˌnætʃərəlaɪ'zeɪʃən/ n the act of investing a foreigner with the rights and privileges of a natural-born citizen.

naturalize /'nætʃərəˌlaɪz/ or /'nætʃrə-/ vt to confer citizenship upon (a person of foreign birth); (plants) to become established in a different climate. • vi to become established as if native.

natural law n law based on innate moral sense.

naturally /'nætʃərəli/ or /'nætʃrə-/ adv in a natural manner, by nature; of course.

natural number n any of the whole numbers starting with 1.

natural philosophy n physics.

natural resource n a naturally occurring source of wealth as in land, oil, coal, water power, etc.

natural science n the study of material things.

natural selection n the principle that evolution is determined by the survival of the fittest.

nature /'neɪtʃər/ n the phenomena of physical life not dominated by man; the entire material world as a whole, or forces observable in it; the essential character of anything; the innate character of a person, temperament; kind, class; vital force or functions; natural scenery.

nature worship n the worship of the deified forces of nature.

naught /nɒt/ see **nought**.

naughty /'nɒti/ adj (**naughtier, naughtiest**) mischievous or disobedient; titillating.—**naughtily** adv.—**naughtiness** n.

naumachia /nɔ'meɪkiə/, **naumachy** /'nɔməki/ n (pl **naumachiae, naumachiae, naumachies**) a sea fight; a show representing a sea fight.

nausea /'nɒziə/ n a desire to vomit; disgust.

nauseate /'nɒziˌeɪt/ vti to arouse feelings of disgust; to feel nausea or revulsion.—**nauseating** adj.

nauseous /'nɒʃəs/ or /'nɒziəs/ adj causing nausea; disgusting.—**nauseously** adv.—**nauseousness** n.

nautch /nɒtʃ/ n in India, a dance performed by girls; a dancing exhibition.

nautical /'nɒtɪkəl/ adj of ships, sailors, or navigation.

nautically /-li/ adv in a nautical manner.

nautical mile n an international unit of measure for air and sea navigation equal to 6,075 feet (1.85 km).

nautilus /'nɒtɪləs/ n (pl **nautiluses, nautili**) a genus of cephalopods, including those furnished with a chambered spinal univalve shell; a shellfish with webbed arms once supposed to sail upon the sea; a kind of diving bell.

naval /'neɪvəl/ adj of the navy; of ships.

nave[1] /neɪv/ n the central space of a church, distinct from the chancel and aisles.

nave[2] n the central block of a wheel, the hub.

navel /'neɪvəl/ n the small scar in the abdomen caused by severance of the umbilical cord; a central point.

navigability /ˌnævɪgə'bɪlɪti/ n the quality or state of being navigable.

navigable /'nævɪgəbəl/ adj (rivers, seas) that can be sailed upon or steered through.—**navigably** adv.

navigate /'nævɪgeɪt/ vti to steer or direct a ship, aircraft, etc; to travel through or over (water, air, etc) in a ship or aircraft; to find a way through, over, etc, and to keep to a course.

navigation /ˌnævɪ'geɪʃən/ n the act, art or science of navigating; the method of calculating the position of a ship, aircraft, etc.—**navigational** adj.

navigator /'nævɪˌgeɪtər/ n one who navigates; one skilled in the science of navigation.

navvy /'nævi/ *n* (*pl* **navvies**) a labourer, *esp* one who works on roads or railways.

navy /'neivi/ *n* (*pl* **navies**) (*often with cap*) the warships of a nation; a nation's entire sea force, including ships, men, stores, etc; navy blue.

navy blue *n* an almost black blue.

nawab /nə'wæb/ or /-'wɒb/ *n* an Indian viceroy; a nabob.

nay /nei/ *adv* (*arch*) no; not only so; yet more; or rather, and even. • *n* a refusal or denial.

Nazarene /næzə'riːn/ *n* a native of Nazareth, applied to Jesus Christ, his followers, and the early Christians as a term of contempt; in the early Church, one of a sect of Judaising Christians.

Nazarite, Nazirite /'næzə,rait/ *n* a native of Nazareth; a Jew devoted by vow to God to a life of abstinence and purity (Numbers 6).

Nazi /'nɒtsi/ or /'nætsi/ *n* (*pl* **Nazis**) a member of the German National Socialist party (1930s).—*also adj.*

NB *abbr* = nota bene (note well).

Nb (*chem symbol*) niobium.

NBC *abbr* = National Broadcasting Company.

NCO *abbr* = noncommissioned officer.

Nd (*chem symbol*) neodymium.

NE *abbr* = northeast, northeastern.

Ne (*chem symbol*) neon.

Neanderthal /ni'ændər,θɒl/ or /-,tɒl/ *adj* denoting or characteristic of Neanderthal man; primitive.

Neanderthal man *n* a type of primitive human inhabiting Europe in Palaeolithic times.

neap /niːp/ *adj* of either of the lowest high tides in the month. • *n* a neap tide.

Neapolitan /niə'pɒlitən/ *adj* pertaining to Naples or to its inhabitants.

Neapolitan ice cream *n* brick ice cream in layers of different colours and flavours.

near /niːr/ *adj* (**nearer, nearest**) close, not distant in space or time; closely related, intimate; approximate; (*escape, etc*) narrow. • *adv* to or at a little distance; close by; almost. • *prep* close to. • *vti* to approach; to draw close to.—**nearness** *n*.

nearby /niːr'bai/ *adj* neighbouring; close by in position.

Near East *n* another name for the Middle East; formerly included Turkey, the Balkans and the area of the Ottoman Empire.

nearly /'niːrli/ *adv* almost, closely.

near miss *n* a bomb, mortar, etc that just fails to hit the target; any type of shot that misses its target; a situation in which two aircraft narrowly avoid a midair collision.

near-sighted /'niːr,saitəd/ *adj* short-sighted, myopic.—**near-sightedness** *n*.

neat[1] /niːt/ *adj* clean and tidy; skilful; efficiently done; well made; (*alcoholic drink*) undiluted; (*US sl*) nice, pleasing, etc.—**neatly** *adv.*—**neatness** *n*.

neat[2] *n* cattle of the bovine genus. • *adj* pertaining to bovine animals.

neaten /'niːtən/ *vt* to make tidy and neat.

neath /niːθ/ *prep* (*poet*) beneath.

neb /neb/ *n* (*Scot*) a bird's beak; a mouth; a nose or snout; a projecting part, a point.

nebula /'nebjulə/ *n* (*pl* **nebulae, nebulas**) a gaseous mass or star cluster in the sky appearing as a hazy patch of light.—**nebular** *adj*.

nebular hypothesis *n* the theory that the solar system in its primal condition existed in the form of a nebula, from which the sun, planets, and satellites were produced by condensation.

nebulosity /,nebju'lɒsiti/ *n* (*pl* **nebulosities**) the state or quality of being nebulous.

nebulous /'nebjuləs/ *adj* indistinct; formless.

necessarily /,nesə'serili/ *adv* as a natural consequence.

necessary /'nesə,seri/ *adj* indispensable; required; inevitable. • *n* (*pl* **necessaries**) something necessary; (*pl*) essential needs.

necessitarianism /nə,sesi'teriə,nizəm/ *n* (*philos*) the doctrine of necessity, or that man cannot control his actions by his own free will; fatalism.—**necessitarian** *n*.

necessitate /nə'sesi,teit/ *vt* to make necessary; to compel.

necessitous /nə'sesitəs/ *adj* urgent; pressing; needy.

necessity /nə'sesiti/ *n* (*pl* **necessities**) a prerequisite; something that cannot be done without; compulsion; need.

neck /nek/ *n* the part of the body that connects the head and shoulders; that part of a garment nearest the neck; a neck-like part, *esp* a narrow strip of land; the narrowest part of a bottle; a strait. • *vti* (*sl*) to kiss and caress.

neckerchief /'nekərtʃif/ or /-tʃiːf/ *n* a cloth square worn around the neck.

necklace /'nekləs/ *n* a string or band, often of precious stones, beads, or pearls, worn around the neck.

neckline /'neklain/ *n* the line traced by the upper edge of a garment below the neck.

necktie /'nektai/ *n* a man's tie.

necro-, necr- /'nekrɒ/ *prefix* corpse.

necrobiosis /,nekrobai'osis/ *n* the decay of living tissue.—**necrobiotic** *adj*.

necrology /nə'krɒlədʒi/ *n* (*pl* **necrologies**) a register or account of the dead.—**necrological** *adj*.

necromancer /'nekrə,mænsər/ *n* one who practises necromancy; a conjurer; a wizard.

necromancy /'nekrə,mænsi/ *n* predicting the future by alleged communication with the dead; sorcery.—**necromantic** *adj*.

necrophagous /ne'krɒfəgəs/ *adj* (*animal*) feeding on carrion.

necrophilia /nekrə'filiə/ *n* erotic interest in or copulation with corpses.—*also* **necromania.**—**necrophile** *n.*—**necrophiliac** *n*.

necropolis /nə'krɒpəlis/ *n* (*pl* **necropolises, necropoleis**) a cemetery.

necropsy /'nekrɒpsi/ *n* (*pl* **necropsies**) a post-mortem examination.

necrosis /nə'krosis/ *n* mortification and death of a bone; gangrene; a disease in plants, characterized by small black spots.—**necrotic** *adj*.

nectar /'nektər/ *n* a sweetish liquid in many flowers, used by bees to make honey; any delicious drink.

nectareous, nectarous /-'teriəs/ *adj* producing, or sweet, like nectar.

nectarine /nektə'riːn/ or /'nek-/ *n* a smooth-skinned peach.

nectary /'nektəri/ *n* (*pl* **nectaries**) that part of a flower which secretes a saccharine fluid.

nee, née /nei/ *adj* (*literally*) born: indicating the maiden name of a married woman.

need /niːd/ *n* necessity; a lack of something; a requirement; poverty. • *vt* to have a need for; to require; to be obliged.

needful /'niːdful/ *adj* necessary, required, vital. • *n* (*inf*) what is required, *esp* money.—**needfulness** *n*.

needle /'niːdəl/ *n* a small pointed piece of steel for sewing; a larger pointed rod for knitting or crocheting; a stylus; the pointer of a compass, gauge, etc; the thin, short leaf of the pine, spruce, etc; the sharp, slender metal tube at the end of a hypodermic syringe. • *vt* to goad, prod, or tease.

needlepoint /'niːdəlpoint/ *n* a type of embroidery worked on canvas; point lace.

needless /'niːdləs/ *adj* not needed, unnecessary; uncalled for, pointless.—**needlessly** *adv.*—**needlessness** *n*.

needlework /'niːdəl,wərk/ *n* sewing, embroidery.

needn't /'niːdənt/ = need not.

needs /niːdz/ *adv* necessarily; indispensably.

needy /'niːdi/ *adj* (**needier, neediest**) in need, very poor.

neep /niːp/ *n* (*Scot*) a turnip.

ne'er /ner/ *adv* (*poet*) never.

ne'er-do-well /'nerduː,wel/ *adj* good-for-nothing; improvident; lazy. • *n* an irresponsible person.

nefarious /nə'feriəs/ *adj* wicked, evil.

neg. *abbr* = negative(ly).

negate /nə'geit/ *vt* to nullify; to deny.

negation /nə'geiʃən/ *n* a negative statement, denial; the opposite or absence of something; a contradiction.

negative /'negətiv/ *adj* expressing or meaning denial or refusal; lacking positive attributes; (*math*) denoting a quantity less than zero, or one to be subtracted; (*photog*) reversing the light and shade of the original subject, or having the colours replaced by complementary ones; (*elect*) of the charge carried by electrons; producing such a charge. • *n* a negative word, reply, etc; refusal; something that is the opposite or negation of something else; (*in debate, etc*) the side that votes or argues for the opposition; (*photog*) a negative image on transparent film or a plate. • *vt* to refuse assent, contradict; to veto.—**negatively** *adv*.

neglect /nə'glekt/ or /ni-/ *vt* to pay little or no attention to; to disregard; to leave uncared for; to fail to do something. • *n* disregard; lack of attention or care.

neglectful /-ful/ *adj* careless; heedless; slighting.—**neglectfully** *adv*.

negligee /'nɛglɪ,ʒeɪ/ *n* a woman's loosely fitting dressing gown.

negligence /'nɛglɪdʒəns/ *n* lack of attention or care; an act of carelessness; a carelessly easy manner.

negligent /'nɛglɪdʒənt/ *adj* careless, heedless.—**negligently** *adv*.

negligible /'nɛglɪdʒɪbəl/ *adj* that need not be regarded; unimportant; trifling.

negotiable /nə'goʊʃəbəl/ *adj* able to be legally negotiated; (*bills, drafts, etc*) transferable.—**negotiability** *n*.

negotiate /nə'goʊʃɪ,eɪt/ *vti* to discuss, bargain in order to reach an agreement or settlement; to settle by agreement; (*fin*) to obtain or give money value for (a bill); (*obstacle, etc*) to overcome.

negotiation /nə,goʊʃɪ'eɪʃən/ or /-sɪ'eɪʃən/ *n* the act of negotiating or transacting business; a treaty.

negotiator /-tər/ *n* one who negotiates.

Negrillo /nə'grɪloʊ/ *n* (*pl* **Negrillos, Negrilloes**) one of a pigmy Negroid race found in Africa.

Negrito /nə'griːtoʊ/ *n* (*pl* **Negritos, Negritoes**) one of a diminutive Negroid race of the Philippines and Polynesia.

Negro /'niːgroʊ/ *n* (*pl* **Negroes**) (*old fashioned*) a member of the dark-skinned, indigenous peoples of Africa; a member of the Negroid group; a person with some Negro ancestors.—*also adj*.—**Negress** *nf*.

Negroid /'niːgrɔɪd/ *adj* denoting, or of, one of the major groups of humankind, including most of the peoples of Africa south of the Sahara.

Negus /'niːgəs/ *n* (*pl* **Neguses**) a title of the ruler of Ethiopia.

negus *n* (*pl* **neguses**) a beverage of hot water and wine, sweetened and spiced.

neigh /neɪ/ *vi* (**neighing, neighed**) to whinny; to make a sound like the cry of a horse. • *n* the cry of a horse; a whinny.

neighbour, neighbor /'neɪbər/ *n* a person who lives near another; a person or thing situated next to another; a fellow human being. • *vt* to be near, to adjoin.

neighbourhood, neighborhood /-,hʊd/ *n* a particular community, area, or district; the people in an area.

neighbouring, neighboring /-ɪŋ/ *adj* adjoining, nearby.

neighbourly, neighborly /-lɪ/ *adj* characteristic of a neighbour, friendly. • *adv* in a neighbourly or social manner.—**neighbourliness, neighborliness** *n*.

neither /'naɪðər/ or /'niː-ð-/ *adj, pron* not one or the other (of two); not either. • *conj* not either; also not.

nek /nɛk/ *n* (*S Africa*) a depression or pass in a mountain range.

nekton /'nɛktən/ *n* a collective term for minute forms of organic life found at various depths in seas and lakes.—**nektonic** *adj*.

nelson /'nɛlsən/ *n* (*wrestling*) a type of hold in which the arms are placed under an opponent's arms from behind so that pressure can be exerted by the palms on the back of the opponent's neck.

nemato-, nemat- /'nɛmətoʊ/ or /-tə/ *prefix* thread, fibre.

nematode /'nɛmə,toʊd/ *adj* thread-like. • *n* a threadworm.

nem. con. *adv* no one contradicting.

nem. diss. *adv* no one dissenting.

Nemean /nɪ'miːən/ or /'niː.mi-/ *adj* pertaining to the Nemea valley of ancient Greece or to the games held there.

nemesis /'nɛməsɪs/ *n* (*pl* **nemeses**) retribution; just punishment; an agent of defeat.

neo- /'niːoʊ/ *prefix* new, newly.

neodymium /,niːoʊ'dɪmiəm/ *n* a silvery-white metallic element used in alloys, etc.

Neolithic /,niːə'lɪθɪk/ *adj* of the later Stone Age, marked by the use of polished stone implements.

neologism /niː'ɒlədʒ,ɪzəm/ *n* a new word; the coining of new words, neology; the introduction of new doctrines.—**neologistic, neologistical** *adj*.

neologist /-,dʒɪst/ *n* an innovator in language or religion, *esp* one who holds doctrinal views opposed to the orthodox interpretation of revealed religion.

neologize /-,dʒaɪz/ *vt* to introduce new words, phrases, or religious doctrines.

neology /-dʒi/ *n* neologism; doctrines or rationalistic theological interpretation at variance with orthodox belief.

neon /'niːɒn/ *n* an inert gaseous element that gives off a bright orange glow, used in lighting and advertisements.

neophyte /'niːə,faɪt/ *n* a novice; one recently baptised; a convert. • *adj* recently entered.

neoplasm /'niːə,plæzəm/ *n* tissue growth more or less distinct from that in which it occurs.

neoplastic /,niːə'plæstɪk/ *adj* newly formed.

neoplasty /'niːə,plæsti/ *n* the restoration of tissue by plastic surgery.

NeoPlatonism /,niːoʊ'pleɪtə,nɪzəm/ *n* a system of eclectic philosophy combining the doctrines of Plato with Oriental mysticism in the 3rd century AD.—**NeoPlatonist** *n*.

neoteric /,niːoʊ'tɛrɪk/ *adj* recent in origin; newfangled, modern.—**neoterically** *adv*.

neotropical /,niːoʊ'trɒpɪkəl/ *adj* of tropical or South America.

Neozoic /,niːoʊ'zoʊɪk/ *adj* noting rocks from the Trias to the present time.

Nepalese /,nɛpə'liːz/ *n, adj* (a) Nepali.

Nepali /nə'pɒli/ *n* (*pl* **Nepali, Nepalis**) a native or inhabitant of Nepal; the language of Nepal.—*also adj*.

nepenthe /nɪ'pɛnθi/ or /nɪ-/ *n* a drug supposed by the ancient Greeks to have the power of causing forgetfulness of sorrow.—**nepenthean** *adj*.

nephew /'nɛfjuː/ *n* the son of a brother or sister.

nephology /ni:'fɒlədʒi/ or /nɪ-/ *n* the study of clouds.—**nephological** *adj*.—**nephologist** *n*.

nephralgia /nə'fræ1dʒiə/ or /-'fræ1dʒə/ *n* pain or disease in the kidneys.—**nephralgic** *adj*.

nephrite /'nɛfraɪt/ *n* jade.

nephritic /nɪ'frɪtɪk/ *adj* of or pertaining to the kidneys or kidney disease; affected with disease of the kidneys.

nephritis /nɪ'fraɪtɪs/ *n* inflammation of the kidneys.

nephro- or **nephr-** /'nɛfroʊ/ *prefix* kidney; kidneys.

nephrology /nə'frɒlədʒi/ *n* study of the kidneys.

nephrotomy /nə'frɒtəmi/ *n* (*pl* **nephrotomies**) incision into the kidney.

ne plus ultra /,neɪplʊs'ʊltrɒ/ *n* (*Latin*) the farthest attainable point; the acme, the perfect state.—*also* **non plus ultra**.

nepotism /'nɛpə,tɪzəm/ *n* undue favouritism shown to relatives, *esp* in securing jobs.

Neptune /'nɛptuːn/ or /-tjuːn/ *n* the Roman god of the sea; the sea personified; the 8th planet from the sun.

Neptunian /nɛp'tjuːniən/ or /-'tuː-/ *adj* pertaining to the classical deity Neptune, god of the sea, or to the sea; deposited by the agency of the sea.

neptunium /nɛp'tjuːniəm/ *n* a radioactive metallic element.

nerd /nɜrd/ *n* (*sl*) a boring, straight-laced person; a creep.

Nereid /'niːriːd/ *n* (*pl* **Nereides**) (*Greek myth*) a sea nymph.

nereis /'niːriːɪs/ *n* (*zool*) a sea worm.

neroli /'niːrəli/ *n* the essential oil of orange flowers.

nervate /'nɜr,veɪt/ *adj* (*bot*) ribbed.

nervation /nɜr'veɪʃən/ *n* (*bot*) the arrangement of veins, venation.

nerve /nɜrv/ *n* any of the fibres or bundles of fibres that transmit impulses of sensation or of movement between the brain and spinal cord and all parts of the body; courage, coolness in danger; (*inf*) audacity, boldness; (*pl*) nervousness, anxiety. • *vt* to give strength, courage, or vigour to.

nerve cell *n* a cell transmitting impulses in nerve tissue.—*also* **neuron, neurone.**

nerve centre, nerve center *n* a group of closely connected cells; (*mil, etc*) a centre of control from which instructions are sent out.

nerve gas *n* a poison gas that affects the nervous system.

nerveless /'nɜrvləs/ *adj* calm, cool; weak, feeble.—**nervelessly** *adv*.

nerve-racking, nerve-wracking /-,rækɪŋ/ *adj* straining the nerves, stressful.

nervous /'nɜrvəs/ *adj* excitable, highly strung; anxious, apprehensive; affecting or acting on the nerves or nervous system.

nervous breakdown *n* (*inf*) a (*usu* temporary) period of mental illness resulting from severe emotional strain or anxiety.

nervous system *n* the brain, spinal cord, and nerves collectively.

nervure /'nɜrvjʊr/ *n* the veins of leaves; the horny ribs supporting the membranous wings of an insect.

nervy /'nɜrvi/ *adj* (**nervier, nerviest**) (*inf*) anxious, agitated; (*inf*) impudent, cheeky.

nescience /'neɪʃens/ *n* ignorance; agnosticism.—**nescient** *adj*.

ness /nɛs/ *n* a headland or cape, a promontory.

-ness /nəs/ *suffix* state, quality of being.

nest /nɛst/ *n* a structure or place where birds, fish, mice, etc, lay eggs or give birth to young; a place where young are nurtured; a swarm or brood; a lair; a cosy place; a set of boxes, tables, etc of different sizes, designed to fit together. • *vi* to make or occupy a nest.

nest egg *n* money put aside as a reserve or to establish a fund.

nestle /'nɛsəl/ *vti* to rest snugly; to lie snugly, as in a nest; to lie sheltered or half-hidden.

nestling /'nɛslɪŋ/ or /'nɛst-/ *n* a young bird that has not left the nest.

Nestor /'nɛstər/ *n* (*Greek myth*) a Greek sage of the Trojan war; a wise old man.

Nestorianism /nɛsˈtɔːriən‚ɪzəm/ *n* the 5th-century doctrine of Nestorius, Bishop of Constantinople, who taught that there were two natures in Christ, one human and one divine, which did not unit and form one person; also that the Virgin Mary was not the Mother of God.—**Nestorian** *n, adj.*

net[1] /nɛt/ *n* an openwork material of string, rope, or twine knotted into meshes; a piece of this used to catch fish, to divide a tennis court, etc; a snare. • *vti* (**netting, netted**) to snare or enclose as with a net; to hit (a ball) into a net or goal.

net[2], **nett** *adj* clear of deductions, allowances or charges. • *n* a net amount, price, weight, profit, etc. • *vt* (**netting, netted**) to clear as a profit.

nether /'nɛðər/ *adj* lower or under.

nether world /'nɛðərwərld/ *n* the underworld, hell.

nethermost /-‚mo:st/ *adj* lowest.

netizen *n* literally 'net citizen', someone who uses the Internet.

netsuke /'netsuki/ *n* a Japanese ornamental toggle for fastening the front of a garment.

netting /'nɛtɪŋ/ *n* netted fabric.

nettle /'nɛtəl/ *n* a wild plant with stinging hairs. • *vt* to irritate, annoy.

nettle rash *n* a cutaneous skin eruption resembling the effects of a nettle sting.

network /'nɛtwərk/ *n* an arrangement of intersecting lines; a group of people who co-operate with each other; a chain of interconnected operations, computers, etc; (*radio, TV*) a group of broadcasting stations connected to transmit the same programme simultaneously. • *vt* to broadcast on a network; (*comput*) to interconnect systems so that information, software, and peripheral devices, such as printers, can be shared.

networking /-ɪŋ/ *n* the making of contacts and trading information as for career advancement; the interconnection of computer systems.

neural /'njurəl/ or /'nərəl/ *adj* of or pertaining to the nerves.

neuralgia /njuˈrældʒə/ or /nəˈræl-/ *n* pain along a nerve.—**neuralgic** *adj.*

neuralgic /-ɪk/ *adj* pertaining to neuralgia.

neurasthenia /‚njurəsˈθiːniə/ or /‚nərəs-/ *n* brain and nerve exhaustion, as from influenza, etc.

neurectomy /nuˈrɛktəmi/ or /nju-/ *n* (*pl* **neurectomies**) excision of a nerve.

neuritis /njuˈraɪtɪs/ or /nəˈraɪt-/ *n* inflammation of a nerve.

neuro-, neur- /'njuro:/ or /'nɛro:/ *prefix* nerve.

neuroglia /njuˈroɡliə/ or /nəˈro-/ *n* the delicate connective tissue between the nerve fibres of the brain and spinal cord.

neurology /njuˈrɒlədʒi/ or /nəˈro-/ *n* the branch of medicine studying the nervous system and its diseases.—**neurological** *adj.*—**neurologist** *n.*

neuroma /njuˈroːmə/ or /nəˈroː-/ *n* (*pl* **neuromas, neuromata**) a fibrous tumour occuring in nerve tissue.

neuron, neurone /'njurɒn/ or /'nərɒn/ *see* **nerve cell.**

neuropathic /‚nuroːˈpæθɪk/ or /‚njur-/ *adj* pertaining to, or suffering from, nervous disease; affecting the nerves.—**neuropath** *n.*—**neuropathically** *adv.*

neuropathology /‚njuro:pəˈθɒlədʒi/ or /‚nɛro:-/ *n* the study of diseases of the nervous system.—**neuropathologist** *adj.*

neuropathy /njuˈrɒpəθi/ or /nəˈro-/ *n* disease of the nervous system.

neuropteran /njuˈrɒptərən/ or /nəˈro-/ *n* (*pl* **neuropterans**) any of an order of insects characterized by four transparent, finely reticulated, membranous wings. • *adj* with four wings marked with a network of nerves.—*also* **neuropterous.**

neurosis /njuˈroːsɪs/ or /nəˈroː-/ *n* (*pl* **neuroses**) a mental disorder with symptoms such as anxiety and phobia.

neurosurgery /‚njuro:ˈsərdʒəri/ or /‚nər-/ *n* the branch of surgery dealing with the nervous system.—**neurosurgical** *adj.*

neurotic /njuˈrɒtɪk/ or /nəˈro-/ *adj* suffering from neurosis; highly strung; of or acting upon the nerves. • *n* someone with neurosis.

neurotomy /njuˈrɒtəmi/ or /nəˈro-/ *n* (*pl* **neurotomies**) dissection of the nerves.

neurotransmitter /'njuro:træns‚mɪtər/ or /'nər-/ *n* a chemical by which nerves cells communicate with each other or with muscles.

neuter /'nu:tər/ or /'nju:-/ *adj* (*gram*) of gender, neither masculine nor feminine; (*biol*) having no sex organs; having undeveloped sex organs in the adult. • *n* a neuter person, word, plant, or animal. • *vt* to castrate or spay.

neutral /'nu:trəl/ or /'nju:-/ *adj* nonaligned; not taking sides with either party in a dispute or war; having no distinctive characteristics; (*colour*) dull; (*chem*) neither acid nor alkaline; (*physics*) having zero charge. • *n* a neutral state, person, or colour; a position of a gear mechanism in which power is not transmitted.

neutrality /nu:ˈtrælɪti/ or /nju:-/ *n* the state of being neutral.

neutralize /'nu:trə‚laɪz/ or /'nju:-/ *vt* to render ineffective; to counterbalance; to declare neutral.—**neutralization** *n.*—**neutralizer** *n.*

neutrally /'nu:trəli/ or /'nju:-/ *adv* in a neutral manner.

neutrino /nu:ˈtriːno:/ or /nju:-/ *n* (*pl* **neutrinos**) (*phsyics*) a stable elementary particle with almost zero mass and spin 1/2.

neutron /'nu:trɒn/ or /'nju:-/ *n* an elementary particle with no electric charge and the same mass approximately as a proton.

neutron bomb *n* a nuclear bomb with a small blast that releases neutrons, destroying life but leaving property undamaged.

neutron number *n* the number of neutrons in the nucleus of an atom.

neutron star *n* a star composed solely of densely packed neutrons that has collapsed under its own gravity.

névé /'neɪveɪ/ *n* the granular compressed snow that forms glacier ice.

never /'nɛvər/ *adv* at no time, not ever; not at all; in no case; (*inf*) surely not.

nevermore /‚nɛvərˈmɔr/ *adv* never again.

never-never /‚nɛvərˈnɛvər/ *adj* imaginary, ideal.

nevertheless /‚nɛvərðəˈlɛs/ *adv* all the same, notwithstanding; in spite of, however.

nevus /'ni:vəs/ *n* (*pl* **nevi**) a birthmark, a mole.—*also* **naevus.**—**nevoid** *adj.*

new /nu:/ or /nju:/ *adj* recently made, discovered, or invented; seen, known, or used for the first time; different, changed; recently grown, fresh; unused; unaccustomed; unfamiliar; recently begun. • *adv* again; newly; recently.

new blood *n* a recent arrival in an organization expected to bring new ideas and revitalize the system.

newborn /'nu:bɔrn/ or /'nju:-/ *adj* newly born; reborn.

newcomer /'nu:‚kəmər/ or /'nju:-/ *n* a recent arrival.

New Deal *n* the economic and social measures introduced into the USA by President Roosevelt in 1933 to combat the great economic crisis that began in 1929.

newel /'nu:əl/ or /'nju:əl/ *n* the central pillar of a spiral staircase; the end post of a banister.

New England *n* six northeastern states of the USA.

newfangled /'nu:‚fæŋɡəld/ or /'nju:-/, /-'fæŋɡəld/ *adj* (*contemptuous*) new; novel, very modern.

Newfoundland /‚nu:fənd'lænd/ or /'nu:fəndlənd/ *n* a large variety of dog, originally from Newfoundland.

newly /'nu:li/ or /'nju:-/ *adv* recently, lately.

newlywed /'nu:liwɛd/ or /nju:-/ *n* a recently married person.

new moon *n* the moon when first visible as a crescent.

news /nu:z/ or /nju:z/ *npl* current events; recent happenings; the mass media's coverage of such events; a programme of news on television or radio; information not known before.

newscast /'nu:zkæst/ or /'nju:z-/ *n* radio or television news broadcast.—**newscaster** *n.*

newsagent /-‚eɪdʒənt/ or /'nju:-/, **newsdealer** /-di:l‚ər/ *n* a retailer of newspapers, magazines, etc.

newsflash /-‚flæʃ/ *n* an important news item broadcast separately and often interrupting other programmes.

newsgroup *n* on the Internet, a group of people who use an online service to discuss a particular topic.

newsletter /-‚lɛtər/ or /'nju:z-/ *n* a bulletin regularly distributed among the members of a group, society, etc, containing information and news of activities, etc.

newspaper /-‚peɪpər/ or /'nu:s-/, /nju:-/ *n* a printed periodical containing news published daily or weekly.

newsprint /-prɪnt/ or /'nu:z-/ *n* an inexpensive paper on which newspapers are printed.

newsreel /-ri:l/ or /'nju:z-/ *n* a short film presenting news of current events with a commentary.

newsroom /-ru:m/ or /-'nju:z-/ *n* the department of a newspaper or broadcasting system that prepares news for publication or broadcasting; a room, etc, where newspapers, magazines, etc, may be read.

New Style calendar *n* the Gregorian or present style of computing the calendar, which replaced the Julian calendar.

newsworthy /'nju:z,wɜrði/ or /'nu:z-/ *adj* timely and important or interesting.

newt /nu:t/ or /'nju:t/ *n* any of various small amphibious lizard-like creatures.

New Testament *n* the second part of the Bible including the story of the life and teachings of Christ.

newton /'nu:tən/ or /'nju:-/ *n* the SI unit of force that when acting for 1 second on a mass of 1 kilogram imparts an acceleration of 1 metre per second.

Newtonian /nu:'to:niən/ *adj* pertaining to, discovered by, or invented by, Sir Isaac Newton, the philosopher, or to his system.

new town *n* any of various towns built in the UK since 1946 as planned units sponsored by government to house overspill population from nearby cities, aid urban redevelopment, etc.

New World *n* the Americas.

New Year's (Day) *n* the first day of a new year; 1 January, a legal holiday in many countries.

New Year's Eve *n* the evening of the last day of the year; 31 December.—*also* **Hogmanay**.

next /nekst/ *adj* nearest; immediately preceding or following; adjacent. • *adv* in the nearest time, place, rank, etc; on the first subsequent occasion.

next of kin *n* the nearest relative of a person.

nexus /'neksəs/ *n* (*pl* **nexus, nexuses**) a connecting principle or link.

NI *abbr* = Northern Ireland.

Ni (*chem symbol*) nickel.

nib /nɪb/ *n* a pen point. • *vt* (**nibbing, nibbed**) to furnished with a nib; to cut or insert a pen nib.

nibble /'nɪbəl/ *vti* to take small bites at (food, etc); to bite (at) lightly and intermittently.—**nibbler** *n*.

Nibelungenlied /'ni:bə,luŋənli:d/ *n* a medieval German epic poem.

niblick /'nɪblɪk/ *n* a golf club with a heavy head, used for lofting.

nice /naɪs/ *adj* pleasant, attractive, kind, good, etc; particular, fastidious; delicately sensitive.—**nicely** *adv*.

nice-looking *adj* pretty, handsome.

Nicene Creed /'naɪsi:n/ or /'naɪ-/, /-'si:n/ *n* the creed, one of the three held by the Anglican Church, drawn up by the Ecumenical Council of the Early Christian Church at the Council of Nicaea in Asia Minor in 325AD, with additions made at the Council of Constantinople in 381.

niceness /'naɪsnəs/ *n* the state or quality of being nice; delicacy of perception or touch.

nicety /'naɪsəti/ *n* (*pl* **niceties**) a subtle point of distinction; refinement.

niche /ni:ʃ/ or /nɪtʃ/ *n* a shallow recess in a wall for a statue, etc; a place, use, or work for which a person or thing is best suited.

nick /nɪk/ *n* a small cut, chip, etc, made on a surface; (*sl*) a police station, prison. • *vt* to make a nick in; to wound superficially; (*sl*) to steal; (*sl*) to arrest.

nickel /'nɪkəl/ *n* a silvery-white metallic element used in alloys and plating; a US or Canadian coin worth five cents.

nickelodeon /nɪkə'lo:diən/ *n* (*US*) an early type of jukebox.

nickel silver *n* an alloy of nickel, copper and zinc.—*also* **German silver**.

nicker /'nɪkər/ *vi* to neigh, to snigger.—*also n*.

nicknack /'nɪk,næk/ *see* **knickknack**.

nickname /'nɪkneɪm/ *n* a substitute name, often descriptive, given in fun; a familiar form of a proper name. • *vt* to give as a nickname.

nicotiana /nɪkə:ti'ænə/ or /-ʃi'ænə/ *n* any of the *Nicotiana* genus of plants of Australia and America, *eg* tobacco.

nicotine /'nɪkə,ti:n/ or /,nɪkə'ti:n/ *n* a poisonous alkaloid present in tobacco.

nictitate /'nɪktɪ,teɪt/, **nictate** /'nɪk,teɪt/ *vi* to wink.—**nictitation, nictation** *n*.

nictitating membrane *n* a membrane that can be drawn over the eye beneath the eyelid present in many birds, reptiles, fish and some mammals.

nidificate /'nɪdɪfɪ,keɪt/ *vi* to build a nest.

nidification /,nɪdɪfɪ'keɪʃən/ *n* the act of building a nest, rearing young, etc.

nidify /'nɪdɪ,faɪ/ *vi* (**nidifying, nidified**) to nidificate.

nidus /'naɪdəs/ *n* (*pl* **nidi, niduses**) the developing place of spores, seeds, germs, insects' eggs, etc; an accumulation of eggs, tubercles, etc; a nest or hatching place.

niece /ni:s/ *n* the daughter of a brother or sister.

niello /ni'ɛlo:/ *n* (*pl* **nielli, niellos**) an ornamental engraving in black on silver, gold, brass, etc; a black alloy used in this. • *vt* (**nielloing, nielloed**) to engrave or decorate with niello.

Niflheim /'nɪvəlheɪm/ or /-haɪm/ *n* (*Scandinavian myth*) the region of eternal mist and cold.

nifty /'nɪfti/ *adj* (**niftier, niftiest**) (*sl*) neat, stylish.—**niftily** *adv*.—**niftiness** *n*.

niggard /'nɪgərd/ *adj* meanly covetous; parsimonious; miserly; niggardly. • *n* one who is meanly covetous; a stingy person, a miser.

niggardliness /'nɪgərdlinəs/ *n* the state of being niggardly; stinginess.

niggardly /'nɪgərdli/ *adj* giving grudgingly, ungenerous. • *adv* like a niggard.

niggle /'nɪgəl/ *vi* to waste time on petty details; to be finicky.

niggler /-ər/ *n* one who trifles at handiwork.

niggling /-ɪŋ/ *adj* finicky, fussy; petty; gnawing, irritating.—**nigglingly** *adv*.

nigh /naɪ/ *adj, adv, prep* near.

night /naɪt/ *n* the period of darkness from sunset to sunrise; nightfall; a specified or appointed evening.

night blindness *n* poor vision in near darkness.

nightcap /'naɪtkæp/ *n* a cap worn in bed; (*inf*) an alcoholic drink taken just before going to bed.

nightclothes /-klo:ðz/ *npl* clothes for wearing in bed, as a nightgown, pyjamas, etc.

nightclub /-klʊb/ *n* a place of entertainment for drinking, dancing, etc, at night.

nightdress /-drɛs/ *n* a loose garment worn in bed by women and girls.

nightfall /-fɔl/ *n* the close of the day.

nightflower /-flaʊr/ *n* a flower that opens at night.

nightglass /-glæs/ *n* a short telescope for night use.

nightgown /-gaʊn/ *n* a nightdress.

nightie /'naɪti/ *n* (*inf*) a nightdress, nightgown.—*also* **nighty**.

nightingale /'naɪtɪŋ,geɪl/ *n* a songbird celebrated for its musical song at night.

nightjar /'naɪtdʒɑr/ *n* a nocturnal bird with dull mottled plumage.

night life /'naɪtlaɪf/ *n* social entertainment at night, *esp* in towns.

night-light /-laɪt/ *n* a dim light kept burning at night.

nightlong /-lɒŋ/ *adj* lasting through the night.

nightly /'naɪtli/ *adj, adv* done or happening by night or every night.

nightmare /'naɪtmɛr/ *n* a frightening dream; any horrible experience.—**nightmarish** *adj*.

night owl *n* (*inf*) a person who stays up late at night.

night school *n* an educational institution where classes are held in the evening.

nightshade /'naɪtʃeɪd/ *n* a flowering plant related to the potato and tomato, *esp* deadly nightshade (belladonna).

nightshirt /-ʃərt/ *n* a long shirt for sleeping in.

nightspot /-spɒt/ *n* (*inf*) a nightclub.

nightstick /-stɪk/ *n* US word for a truncheon.

nighttime /-taɪm/ *n* night.

night watch *n* a watch by night or the person keeping it; (*pl*) night-time.

night watchman *n* the person who guards a building at night.

nighty /'naɪti/ *n* (*pl* **nighties**) (*inf*) a nightie.

nigrescent /nɪ'grɛsənt/ *adj* blackish, growing black.—**nigrescence** *n*.

nihil /'naɪhɪl/ or /'ni:-/ *n* (*Latin*) nothing, nil.

nihil ad rem /ni:lɔdrɛm/ *adj* (*Latin*) irrelevant.

nihilism /'naɪɪlɪzəm/ or /'naɪhɪlɪzəm/, /'ni:-/ *n* the belief that nothing has real existence, scepticism; the rejection of customary beliefs in morality, religion, etc.

nihilist /'naɪhɪlɪst/ *n* a supporter of nihilism.—**nihilisitic** *adj*.

nihility /naɪ'hɪləti/ *n* nonexistence.

nil /nɪl/ *n* nothing.

nilgai /'ni:lgaɪ/, **nilgau** /-gə/ *n* (*pl* **nilgai, nilgais, nilgau, nilgaus**) a large short-horned Indian antelope.

Nilometer /naɪlˈɒmətər/ n a graduated pillar for measuring the rise of water in the River Nile during its floods; a river gauge.

Nilotic /naɪˈlɒtɪk/ adj pertaining to the River Nile.

nimble /ˈnɪmbəl/ adj agile; quick.—**nimbly** adv.

nimbus /ˈnɪmbəs/ n (pl **nimbi, nimbuses**) (art) the halo or cloud of light surrounding the heads of divinities, saints, and sovereigns; a rain cloud.

NIMBY /ˈnɪmbi/ abbr = not in my back yard.

niminy-piminy /ˌnɪmɪnɪˈpɪmɪnɪ/ adj mincing, prim.

Nimrod /ˈnɪmrɒd/ n a distinguished hunter, from Nimrod, "the mighty hunter" (Genesis 10.9).

nincompoop /ˈnɪnkəmˌpuːp/ or /ˈnɪŋ-/ n a stupid, silly person.

nine /naɪn/ adj, n one more than eight. • n the symbol for this (9, IX, ix); the ninth in a series or set; something having nine units as members.

ninefold /ˈnaɪnfoːld/ adj having nine units or members; being nine times as great or as many.

ninepins /ˈnaɪnpɪnz/ see **skittles**.

nineteen /naɪnˈtiːn/ or /ˈnaɪn-/ adj, n one more than eighteen. • n the symbol for this (19, XIX, xix).—**nineteenth** adj.

nineteenth /-ˈtiːnθ/ adj being one of 19 equal parts. • n a nineteenth part.

nineteenth hole n (golf) (sl) the bar in the clubhouse.

ninetieth /ˈnaɪntɪɪθ/ adj next after 89. • n a ninetieth part.

ninety /ˈnaɪntɪ/ adj, n nine times ten. • n the symbol for this (90, XC, xc); (in pl) **nineties**; the numbers from 90 to 99; the same numbers in a life or century.

ninja /ˈnɪndʒə/ n a Japanese warrior trained in ninjutsu.—also adj.

ninjutsu /nɪnˈdʒʊtsuː/ n an ancient Japanese martial art which practises techniques of stealth or invisibility, orig for the purpose of espionage and political assassination.

ninny /ˈnɪnɪ/ n (pl **ninnies**) a person of weak character or mind, a simpleton.

ninon /niˈnɒn/, Fr. /niˈnõː/ n a light silk material.

ninth /naɪnθ/ adj, n next after eighth; one of nine equal parts of a thing.

Niobe /ˈnaɪəbi/ n an inconsolable bereaved woman; (Greek myth) a heroine who was turned to stone while weeping for her slain children.—**Niobean** adj.

niobic /naɪˈoːbɪk/ adj of or containing pentavalent niobium.

niobium /naɪˈoːbiəm/ n a metallic element used in alloys.

nip[1] /nɪp/ vt (**nipping, nipped**) to pinch, pinch off; to squeeze between two surfaces; (dog) to give a small bite; to prevent the growth of; (plants) to have a harmful effect on because of cold. • n a pinch; a sharp squeeze; a bite; severe frost or biting coldness.

nip[2] n a small drink of spirits. • vti (**nipping, nipped**) to drink in nips.

nipa /ˈniːpə/ n an East Indian palm.

nipper /ˈnɪpər/ n a person or thing that nips; the pincer of a crab or lobster; (pl) pliers, pincers, etc; (Brit inf) a small child.

nipple /ˈnɪpəl/ n the small protuberance on a breast or udder through which the milk passes; a teat-like rubber part on the cap of a baby's bottle; a projection resembling a nipple.

nippy /ˈnɪpɪ/ adj (**nippier, nippiest**) (weather) frosty; (inf) quick, nimble.

nirvana /nərˈvɒnə/ or /-ˈvænə/ n (Buddhism) the highest religious state, when all desire of existence and worldly good is extinguished, and the soul is absorbed into the Deity.

nisi /ˈnaɪsaɪ/ adj (decree, order, rule, etc) valid unless cause is shown be the contrary by a fixed date, at which it is made absolute.

nisi prius /-ˈpraɪəs/ n (law) a writ, beginning with these words, directing a sheriff to empanel a jury; the name of certain courts for the trial of civil actions in the counties. / a trial of civil causes by judges of assize.

nit /nɪt/ n the egg of a louse or other parasitic insect.

niter /ˈnaɪtər/ see **nitre**.

niton /ˈnaɪtɒn/ n a gaseous radioactive element, radon.

nit-picking /ˈnɪtˌpɪkɪŋ/ n (inf) concern with petty details in order to find fault.—also adj.

nitrate /ˈnaɪtreɪt/ n a salt of nitric acid; a fertilizer made of this.—**nitration** n.

nitre /ˈnaɪtər/ n potassium nitrate, saltpetre.—also **niter**.

nitric /ˈnaɪtrɪk/ adj containing nitrogen.

nitric acid n a corrosive, caustic liquid used to make explosives, fertilizers, etc.

nitride /ˈnaɪtraɪd/ n a compound of nitrogen with a metal, also with phosphorus, silicon or boron.

nitrification /ˌnaɪtrɪfɪˈkeɪʃən/ n the process of converting into nitre.

nitrify /ˈnaɪtrɪˌfaɪ/ vti (**nitrifying, nitrified**) to make or become nitrous.

nitrite /ˈnaɪtraɪt/ n a salt of nitrous acid.

nitro-, nitr- /ˈnaɪtro:/ prefix containing nitrogen; made with nitric acid.

nitrogen /ˈnaɪtrədʒən/ n a gaseous element forming nearly 78 per cent of air.

nitrogenize /naɪˈtrɒdʒəˌnaɪz/ or /ˈnaɪtrədʒəˌnaɪz/ vt to impregnate with nitrogen.—**nitrogenization** n.

nitrogenous /ˌnaɪˈtrɒdʒɪnəs/ adj pertaining to, or containing, nitrogen.

nitroglycerin, nitroglycerine /ˌnaɪtro:ˈglɪsərɪn/ n a powerful explosive made by adding glycerine to a mixture of nitric and sulphuric acids.

nitrous /ˈnaɪtrəs/ adj resembling, obtained from, or impregnated with, nitre.

nitrous acid n a compound of four volumes of nitrogen and one of oxygen.

nitrous oxide n a compound of one volume of oxygen and two volumes of nitrogen; laughing gas.

nitty-gritty /ˌnɪtɪˈgrɪtɪ/ n (sl) basic elements; harsh realities; practical details.

nitwit /ˈnɪtwɪt/ n (inf) a stupid person.

nival /ˈnaɪvəl/ adj of or pertaining to snow.

niveous /ˈnɪviəs/ adj resembling snow, snow-like.

nix[1] /nɪks/ n (German myth) a water sprite; (Scot) a kelpie.—**nixie** nf.

nix[2] n (sl) nothing. • interj (sl) look out! be careful!

nizam /nɪˈzɒm/ or /naɪˈzæm/ n (with cap) a title of the ruler of Hyderabad, India; a Turkish army soldier.

No[1] (chem symbol) nobelium.

No[2] abbr = number.

No[3], **Noh** /no:/ n (pl **No, Noh**) Japanese classic drama-drama.

no adv (used to express denial or disagreement) not so, not at all, by no amount. • adj not any; not a; not one, none; not at all; by no means. • n (pl **noes, nos**) a denial; a refusal; a negative vote or voter.

Noachian /no:ˈeɪkiən/, **Noachic** /-ˈækɪk/ adj pertaining to the patriarch Noah, the deluge, or his times.

nob[1] /nɒb/ n a knob; (sl) the head.

nob[2] n (at cribbage) knave of suit of turn-up card.

nob[3] n (sl) a member of the upper classes; a wealthy person.

nobble /ˈnɒbəl/ vt (sl) to tamper with (a racehorse) to prevent its winning; to obtain (money) by dishonest means; to suborn (a juror, etc) by bribes or threats; to defeat by underhand methods; to steal; to kidnap.

nobelium /no:ˈbiːliəm/ n a radioactive metallic element.

Nobel prize /ˈno:bel/ n an international prize, usually given annually, for distinction in one of six areas: physics, chemistry, physiology and medicine, economics, literature, and promoting peace.

nobility /no:ˈbɪlɪtɪ/ n (pl **nobilities**) nobleness of character, mind, birth, or rank; the class of people of noble birth.

noble /ˈno:bəl/ adj famous or renowned; excellent in quality or character; of high rank or birth. • n a person of high rank in society.

nobleman /-mən/ n (pl **noblemen**) a peer.—**noblewoman** nf (pl **noblewomen**).

nobleness /-nəs/ n the state of quality of being noble.

noblesse oblige /no:ˈblesɒˈbliːʒ/ n rank has its obligations.

nobly /ˈno:bli/ adv in a noble manner; of noble rank.

nobody /ˈno:bədi/ or /-bədi/, /-bɒdi/ n (pl **nobodies**) a person of no importance. • pron no person.

nock /nɒk/ n a notch in a bow or arrow for the string; (naut) the forward upper corner of some sails. • vt to fit (an arrow) to string.

nocti-, noct- /ˈnɒkti/ or /-tə/ prefix night.

noctiluca /ˌnɒktəˈluːkə/ n (pl **noctilucae**) a phosphorescent animalcule.

noctule /ˈnɒktjuːl/ n the largest British kind of bat.

nocturn /ˈnɒktərn/ n (RC Church) a part of matins.

nocturnal /nɒkˈtərnəl/ adj of, relating to, night; active by night.—**nocturnally** adv.

nocturne /ˈnɒktərn/ n a picture of a night scene; a musical composition appropriate to the night; a lullaby.

nocuous /ˈnɒkjuːəs/ adj hurtful.

nod /nɒd/ *vti* (**nodding, nodded**) to incline the head quickly, *esp* in agreement or greeting; to let the head drop, be drowsy; to indicate by a nod; (*with* **off**) (*inf*) to fall asleep. • *n* a quick bob of the head; a sign of assent or command.

nodal /'nəʊdəl/ *adj* pertaining to nodes.

noddy /'nɒdi/ *n* (*pl* **noddies**) a simpleton; a tropical sea bird; a four-wheeled carriage with a door at the back.

node /nəʊd/ *n* a knob; a knot; a point of intersection; (*med*) a swelling; (*bot*) the joint of a stem and leaf or leaves; (*astron*) two points at which the orbit of a planet intersects the ecliptic; (*math*) the point at which a curve crosses itself; the point of rest in a vibrating body.

nodical /'nɒdɪkəl/ or /'nəʊdɪ-/ *adj* (*astron*) pertaining to nodes.

nodose /nə'dəʊs/ *adj* having knots or nodes, knotty, knobbed.—**nodosity** *n*.

nodular /'nɒdʒʊlər/, **nodulose** /-ˌləʊs/, **nodulous** /-dʒələs/ *adj* pertaining to, or like, a nodule.

nodule /'nɒdjuːl/ *n* a small lump or tumour.—**nodular** *adj*.

nodus /'nəʊdəs/ *n* (*pl* **nodi**) a knotty point, a complication in the plot of a story, etc.

noel, noël /nəʊ'ɛl/ *n* Christmas, *esp* in carols.

noetic /nəʊ'ɛtɪk/ or /nəʊ'iːtɪk/ *adj* pertaining to, performed by, or originating in, the mind or intellect, intellectual, abstract. • *n* the science of the intellect.—*also* **noemics**.

no-fault /nəʊ'fɔːlt/ *adj* (*insurance*) providing damages without blame being fixed; (*divorce*) concluded without blame being charged.

nog[1] /nɒg/ *n* a wooden peg or block; a stump. • *vt* (**nogging, nogged**) to secure with nogs.

nog[2] *n* an East Anglian strong beer.

nog[3] *n* (an) eggnog.

noggin /'nɒgɪn/ *n* a small quantity of alcoholic drink; (*inf*) the head.

nogging /'nɒgɪŋ/ *n* a partition formed of timber scantlings filled up with bricks.

no-go area /'nəʊ'gəʊ/ *n* an area that certain individuals or groups are forbidden to enter.

nohow /'nəʊhaʊ/ *adv* in no way, by no means.

noil /nɔɪl/ *n* a short wool-combing.

noise /nɔɪz/ *n* a sound, *esp* a loud, disturbing or unpleasant one; a din; unwanted fluctuations in a transmitted signal; (*pl*) conventional sounds, words, etc made in reaction, such as sympathy. • *vt* to make public.

noiseless /'nɔɪzləs/ *adj* making no sound, silent.—**noiselessly** *adv*.—**noiselessness** *n*.

noisette /nwɒ'zɛt/ *n* a small round piece of meat.

noisome /'nɔɪsəm/ *adj* harmful, noxious; foul-smelling.

noisy /nɔɪzi/ *adj* (**noisier, noisiest**) making much noise; turbulent, clamorous.—**noisily** *adv*.—**noisiness** *n*.

nolens volens /ˌnəʊ'lɛnz'vəʊlenz/ *adv* (*Latin*) willingly or unwillingly, willy-nilly.

noli me tangere /ˌnəʊˌlaɪmiˈtændʒəri/ *n* (*Latin*) a warning not to meddle; an erosive ulcer, lupus; a wild cucumber; a picture of Christ as he appeared to Mary Magdalen at the sepulchre.

nolle prosequi /ˌnɒliˈprɒsɪˌkwaɪ/ *n* an English legal term indicating the plaintiff's abandonment of his suit.

nolo episcopari /ˌnəʊlɔːˈɛpəskɔːˌpɑri/ *n* (*Latin*) unwillingness to accept office.

nomad /'nəʊmæd/ *n* one of a people or tribe who move in search of pasture; a wanderer.—**nomadic** *adj*.

nomadic /nəʊ'mædɪk/ *adj* wandering; leading a wandering life; pastoral.—**nomadically** *adv*.

no-man's-land *n* an unclaimed piece of land; a strip of land, *esp* between armies, borders; an ambiguous area, subject, etc.

nombril /'nɒmbrɪl/ *n* (*her*) the centre of an escutcheon.

nom de guerre /ˌnɒmdə'gɛr/ or /nɔ̃-/ *n* (*pl* **noms de guerre**) a pseudonym, an assumed name.

nom de plume /ˌnɒmdə'pluːm/ or /nɔ̃-/ *n* (*pl* **noms de plume**) a pseudonym.

nome /nəʊm/ *n* a province of modern Greece; a territorial division in ancient Egypt.

nomenclator /'nəʊmənˌkleɪtər/ *n* an ancient Roman slave who named persons met; one who gives names to things, an inventor of names.

nomenclature /'nəʊmənˌkleɪtʃər/ or /'nɒm-/, /nəʊ'mɛnklətʃər/ *n* a system of names, terminology, used in a science, etc, or for parts of a device, etc.

nominal /'nɒmɪnəl/ *adj* of or like a name; existing in name only; having minimal real worth, token.

nominalism /'nɒmɪnəˌlɪzəm/ *n* (*philos*) the doctrine that general notions exist only in the mind or in name, opposite to realism.

nominalist /ˌnɒmɪnə'lɪst/ *n* one who holds the doctrine of nominalism.—**nominalistic** *adj*.

nominally /'nɒmɪnəli/ *adv* in name only.

nominate /'nɒmɪˌneɪt/ *vt* to appoint to an office or position; (*candidate*) to propose for election.—**nominator** *n*.

nomination /ˌnɒmɪ'neɪʃən/ *n* the act or right of nominating; the state of being nominated.

nominative /'nɒmɪnətɪv/ *adj* (*gram*) denoting the case of the subject of a verb; appointed, not elected. • *n* (*gram*) the nominative case or a word in it.

nominee /ˌnɒmɪ'niː/ *n* a person who is nominated.

nomo-, nom- /'nəʊmɔː/ or /-məl/, /'nɒmɔː/, /-ə/ *prefix* law.

nomography /nə'mɒgrəfi/ *n* (*pl* **nomographies**) the art of drawing up laws.—**nomographic, nomographical** *adj*.

nomology /nəʊ'mɒlədʒi/ *n* the science of the laws of the mind.—**nomological** *adj*.—**nomologist** *n*.

nomothetic /ˌnɒmə'θɛtɪk/ or /ˌnəʊm-/, **nomothetical** /-əl/ *adj* legislative, founded on a system of laws.

non- /nɒn/ *prefix* not, reversing the meaning of a word.

nonage /'nəʊnɪdʒ/ or /'nɒn-/ *n* minority, legal infancy; an early stage.

nonagenarian /ˌnəʊnədʒə'nɛriən/ or /ˌnɒn-/ *n* a person who is in his or her nineties.

nonagon /'nɒnəgɒn/ *n* a plane figure with 9 sides and 9 angles.—**nonagonal** *adj*.

nonalcoholic /ˌnɒnælkə'hɒlɪk/ *adj* (*drinks, etc*) containing little or no alcohol.

nonaligned /ˌnɒnə'laɪnd/ *adj* not in alliance with any side, *esp* in power politics.

nonce /nɒns/ *n* **for the nonce** for this time only.

nonce word *n* a word coined for one occasion.

nonchalance /ˌnɒnʃə'lɒns/ or /'nɒnʃəˌlɒns/, /-ləns/ *n* coolness; indifference.

nonchalant /ˌnɒnʃə'lɒnt/ or /'nɒnʃəˌlɒnt/, /lənt-/ *adj* calm; cool, unconcerned, indifferent.—**nonchalantly** *adv*.

noncombatant /nɒnkɒm'bætənt/ or /nɒnkəm-/, /-'kɒmbætənt/, /-'kʌm-/ *n* a member of the armed forces whose duties do not include fighting, as a doctor or chaplain; a civilian during wartime.

noncommissioned officer /ˌnɒnkə'mɪʃənd/ *n* (*mil*) a subordinate officer, as a corporal, sergeant, etc, appointed from the ranks.

noncommittal /ˌnɒnkə'mɪtəl/ *adj* not revealing one's opinion.—**noncommittally** *adv*.

non compos mentis /ˌnɒnkɒmpəs'mɛntɪs/ *adj* (*Latin*) of unsound mind, not responsible.

nonconductor /ˌnɒnkən'dʌktər/ *n* a substance that will not conduct electricity or heat.

nonconformist /ˌnɒnkən'fɔrmɪst/ *n* a person who does not conform to prevailing attitudes, behaviour, etc; (*with cap*) in Britain, a Protestant who does not belong to the established church.—*also adj*.

nonconformity /ˌnɒnkən'fɔrmɪti/ *n* (*with cap*) refusal to conform to the established church; a want of conformity, irregularity.

noncooperation /ˌnɒnkəʊˌɒpər'eɪʃən/ *n* refusal to cooperate, *esp* with government decree, etc.—**noncooperative** *adj*.

nondescript /'nɒndɪskrɪpt/ *adj* hard to classify, indeterminate; lacking individual characteristics. • *n* a nondescript person or thing.

none /nʌn/ *pron* no one; not anyone; (*pl verb*) not any; no one. • *adv* not at all.

noneffective /ˌnɒnə'fɛctɪv/ *adj* not effective; (*soldier, sailor*) not qualified for active service.—*also n*.

nonentity /nɒn'ɛntɪti/ *n* (*pl* **nonentities**) a person or thing of no significance.

nones /nəʊnz/ *npl* in the ancient Roman calendar the ninth day before the Ides, reckoned inclusively, ie 7th of March, May, July, October, and the 5th of the other months; (*RC Church*) the devotional office for the ninth hour or 3 p.m.

nonesuch /'nʌnˌsʌtʃ/ *n* an unrivalled person or thing, a nonpareil; a plant like clover used for fodder.—*also* **nonsuch**.

nonet /nɒ'nɛt/ *n* a group of nine connected objects or people; (*mus*) a piece for nine players.

nonetheless /ˌnʌnðə'lɛs/ or /'nʌnðəlɛs/ *conj* nevertheless.

nonevent /ˌnɒnɪˈvent/ *n* an event or experience that is unexpectedly disappointing.

nonfeasance /nɒnˈfiːzəns/ *n* (*law*) the omission of an obligatory act.

nonferrous /nɒnˈferəs/ *adj* containing no iron.

nonflammable /nɒnˈflæməbəl/ *adj* not easily set on fire.

nonillion /noːˈnɪljən/ *n* in the US and France, tenth power of a thousand (1 followed by 30 ciphers); in Britain, the ninth power of one million (1 followed by 54 ciphers).—**nonillionth** *adj*.

nonintervention /ˌnɒnɪntərˈvenʃən/ *n* the policy of refusing to interfere in the affairs of others, *esp* nations.—**noninterventionist** *adj*.

nonjuror /nɒnˈdʒʊərər/ *n* one who refused to take the oath of allegiance to William and Mary in 1689.

non-lethal /nɒnˈliːθəl/ *adj* (*international affairs*) pertaining to foreign aid given to provide medicine, clothing or food rather than weapons.

nonmetal /nɒnˈmetəl/ *n* a chemical element (*eg* carbon) that is not a metal.

nonmoral /nɒnˈmɒrəl/ *adj* unconcerned with morality; without moral standards.

nonpareil /ˈnɒnpərəl/ or /ˌnɒnpəˈreɪl/ *adj* without an equal; (*person or thing*) unrivalled, matchless, unsurpassed. • *n* unequalled excellence; (*print*) a 6-point type; a variety of apple; a kindof bird, moth, wheat, etc.

nonpartisan /ˌnɒnˈpɑːrtizən/ or /ˌnɒnpɑːrtɪˈzæn/ *adj* not aligned to one particular political party.

nonparty /nɒnˈpɑːrti/ *adj* free from party obligations.

nonplus /nɒnˈplʌs/ *vt* (**nonplusses, nonplussing, nonplussed** *or* **nonpluses, nonplusing, nonplused**) to cause to be so perplexed that one cannot, go, speak, act further. • *n* (*pl* **nonpluses**) a state of perplexity, a standstill.

non plus ultra *see* **ne plus ultra**.

non-profit /nɒnˈprɒfɪt/ *adj* (*organization*) not conducted for the purpose of making money.

nonproliferation /ˌnɒnprəˌlɪfəˈreɪʃən/ *n*, *adj* (placing) restriction on the acquisition or production of, *esp* nuclear weapons.

nonrepresentational /ˌnɒnˌreprizənˈteɪʃənəl/ *adj* (*art*) abstract.

nonsense /ˈnɒnsens/ *or* /-səns/ *n* words, actions, etc, that are absurd and have no meaning.—*also adj*. • *interj* absurd!

nonsensical /ˌnɒnˈsensɪkəl/ *adj* absurd; unmeaning.—**nonsensically** *adv*.

non sequitur /nɒnˈsekwɪtər/ *n* a statement that has no relevance to what has preceded it.

nonstarter /nɒnˈstɑːrtər/ *n* a person who is unlikely to succeed; (*horse, racing car, etc*) withdrawn at the last moment.

nonstick /nɒnˈstɪk/ *adj* (*saucepans*) coated with a surface that prevents food from sticking.

nonstop /nɒnˈstɒp/ *adj* (*train, plane, etc*) not making any intermediate stops; not ceasing. • *adv* without stopping or pausing.

nonsuch /ˈnʌnsʌtʃ/ *see* **nonesuch**.

nonsuit /nɒnˈsuːt/ *or* /-ˈsjuːt/ *n* the withdrawal of a suit during trial either voluntarily or by judgment of the court on the discovery of error or defect in the pleadings. • *vt* to pronounce a nonsuit against.

nonunion /nɒnˈjuːniən/ *adj* not belonging to a trade union.

nonviolence /nɒnˈvaɪələns/ *n* the abstaining from physical force to achieve civil rights.—**nonviolent** *adj*.

noodle[1] /ˈnuːdəl/ *n* (often *pl*) pasta formed into a strip.

noodle[2] *n* (*inf*) a foolish person; (*sl*) the head.

nook /nʊk/ *n* a secluded corner, a retreat; a recess.

noon /nuːn/ *n* midday; twelve o'clock in the day. • *adj* pertaining to noon.

noonday /ˈnuːndeɪ/, **noontide** /ˈnuːntaɪd/, **noontime** /ˈnuːntaɪm/ *adj* pertaining to noon, or midday. • *n* noon.

no one /ˈnoːwen/ *pron* nobody.

noose /nuːs/ *n* a loop of rope with a slipknot, used for hanging, snaring, etc. • *vt* to tie in a noose; to make a noose in or of.

nopal /ˈnoːpəl/ *n* an American cactus, the food of the cochineal insect.

nope /noːp/ *adv* (*sl*) no.

nor /nɔːr/ *or* /nər/ *conj* and not; not either.

Nor *abbr* = Norman; north; Norway; Norwegian.

Nordic /ˈnɔːrdɪk/ *adj* (*physical type*) characterized by tall stature, long head, light skin and hair, and blue eyes; (skiing) including cross-country runs and jumping.

Norfolk jacket /ˈnɔːrfək/ *n* a man's loose jacket with a belt.

noria /ˈnɔːriə/ *n* a water-raising apparatus in Spain, etc, a waterwheel.

norm /nɔːrm/ *n* a standard or model, *esp* the standard of achievement of a large group.—**normative** *adj*.

normal /ˈnɔːrməl/ *adj* regular; usual; stable mentally. • *n* anything normal; the usual state, amount, etc.—**normalcy** *n*.—**normality** *n*.—**normally** *adv*.

normalize /ˈnɔːrməˌlaɪz/ *vti* to make or become normal.—**normalization** *n*.

Norman /ˈnɔːrmən/ *n* any of the people of Normandy who conquered England in 1066; a native or inhabitant of Normandy in France. • *adj* pertaining to the Normans or Normandy; (*archit*) of a style introduced into England by the Normans, characterized by rounded arches and massive square towers.—*also* **Normanesque**.

Norn /nɔːrn/ *n* (*Scand myth*) one of the three fates, Urd, Verdande and Skuld, representing the past, the present and the future.

Norse /nɔːrs/ *adj* of ancient Scandinavia or its inhabitants; of Norway. • *n* the language of Norway.

Norseman /ˈnɔːrsmən/ *n* (*pl* **Norsemen**) any of the ancient Scandinavian people, the Vikings.

north /nɔːrθ/ *n* one of the four points of the compass, opposite the sun at noon, to the right of a person facing the sunset; the direction in which a compass needle points; (*often with cap*) the northern part of one's country or the earth. • *adj* in, of, or towards the north; from the north. • *adv* in or towards the north.

northeast /nɔːrθˈiːst/ *adj*, *n* (of) the direction midway between north and east.

northeaster /-ər/ *n* a northeast wind.

northeasterly /-ərli/ *adj* towards or coming from the northeast. • *n* (*pl* **northeasterlies**) a northeast wind or storm.

northeastern /-ərn/ *adj* belonging to the northeast, or in that direction.

northeastward /nɔːrθˈiːstwərd/ *adj* towards or in the northeast.—*also adv*.—**northeastwards** *adv*.

norther /ˈnɔːrðər/ *n* a wind or storm from the north, *esp* a strong gale that prevails in the Gulf of Mexico from September to March.

northerly /ˈnɔːrðərli/ *adj* in, from, or towards the north. • *n* (*pl* **northerlies**) a northerly wind.

northern /ˈnɔːrðərn/ *adj* of or in the north.

northerner /-ər/ *n* a native or inhabitant of the north.

northern hemisphere *n* the half of the earth north of the Equator.

northern lights *npl* the aurora borealis.

northernmost /ˈnɔːrðərnˌmoːst/ *adj* farthest north.

northing /ˈnɔːrθɪŋ/ *n* distance northward.

North Pole *n* the northern end of the axis of the earth at a latitude of 90 degrees north.

north star *n* the polar star.

northward /ˈnɔːrθwərd/ *adj* towards or in the north.—*also adv*.—**northwards** *adv*.

northwest /nɔːrθˈwest/ *adj*, *n* (of) the direction midway between north and west.

northwester /-ər/ *n* a northwest wind.

northwesterly /-ərli/ *adj* towards or coming from the northwest. • *n* (*pl* **northwesterlies**) a northwest wind or storm.

northwestern /-ərn/ *adj* belonging to the northwest, or in that direction.

northwestward /nɔːrθˈwestwərd/ *adj* towards or in the northwest.—*also adv*.—**northwestwards** *adv*.

Norwegian /nɔːrˈwiːdʒən/ *adj*, *n* (of or relating to) the language, people, etc, of Norway.

nose /noːz/ *n* the part of the face above the mouth, used for breathing and smelling, having two nostrils; the sense of smell; anything like a nose in shape or position. • *vt* to discover as by smell; to nuzzle; to push (away, etc) with the front forward. • *vi* to sniff for; to inch forwards; to pry.

nosebag /ˈnoːzbæg/ *n* a bag containing fodder hung from a horse's head.

noseband /-bænd/ *n* the part of a bridle that covers the horse's nose.

nosebleed /-bliːd/ *n* a bleeding from the nose.

nose dive *n* a swift downward plunge of an aircraft, nose first; any sudden sharp drop, as in prices.—**nose-dive** *vi*.

nosegay /ˈnoːzgeɪ/ *n* a bouquet.

nose job *n* (*sl*) cosmetic plastic surgery to reshape the nose.

nosey /ˈnoːzi/ *see* **nosy**.

nosh /nɒʃ/ *n* (*sl*) food, a meal. • *vt* to chew. • *vi* to eat.

nosing /'no:zɪŋ/ *n* the rounded edge of a step, etc, or the metal shield for it.

noso- /'no:so:/ or /'no:sə/ *prefix* disease.

nosography /nə'spgrəfɪ/ *n* the systematic description of diseases.

nosology /nə'splədʒɪ/ *n* the classification of the diseases of animals and plants.—**nosological** *adj*.—**nosologically** *adv*.—**nosologist** *n*.

nostalgia /nɒ'stældʒə/ or /-dʒɪə/, /nə-/ *n* yearning for past times or places.

nostalgic /nɒ'stældʒɪk/ *adj* feeling or expressing nostalgia; longing for one's youth.—**nostalgically** *adv*.

nostology /nɒ'stɒlədʒɪ/ *n* the study of senility or ageing, gerontology.—**nostologic** *adj*.

nostril /'nɒstrəl/ *n* one of the two external openings of the nose for breathing and smelling.

nostrum /'nɒstrəm/ *n* a quack remedy, patent medicine.

nosy /'no:zɪ/ *adj* (**nosier, nosiest**) (*inf*) inquisitive, snooping.—**nosily** *adv*.—**nosiness** *n*.—*also* **nosey**.

nosy parker /-'pɑrkər/ *n* (*inf*) a prying person, busybody.

not /nɒt/ *adv expressing* denial, refusal, or negation.

nota bene /ˌno:tə'benei/ note this.—*abbr* = **NB**.

notabilia /ˌno:tə'bɪlɪə/ *npl* things worthy of note.

notability /ˌno:tə'bɪlɪtɪ/ *n* (*pl* **notabilities**) the quality of being notable; a notable person or thing.

notable /'no:təbəl/ *adj* worthy of being noted or remembered; remarkable, eminent. • *n* an eminent or famous person.—**notably** *adv*.

notandum /no:'tændəm/ *n* (*pl* **notanda**) a thing to be noted.

notarial /no:'terɪəl/ *adj* pertaining to, or done by, a notary.

notary /'no:tərɪ/ *n* (*pl* **notaries**) a notary public.

notary public *n* (*pl* **notaries public**) a public official authorized to certify deeds, contracts, etc.

notation /no:'teɪʃən/ *n* a system of symbols or signs to represent quantities, etc, *esp* in mathematics, music, etc.

notch /nɒtʃ/ *n* a V-shaped cut in an edge or surface; (*inf*) a step, degree; a narrow pass with steep sides. • *vt* to cut notches in.

note /no:t/ *n* a brief summary or record, written down for future reference; a memorandum; a short letter; notice, attention; an explanation or comment on the text of a book; a musical sound of a particular pitch; a sign representing such a sound; a piano or organ key; the vocal sound of a bird. • *vt* to notice, observe; to write down; to annotate.

notebook /'no:tbʊk/ *n* a book with blank pages for writing in.

noted /-ɪd/ *adj* celebrated, well-known.

note paper /-ˌpeɪpər/ *n* paper for writing letters.

noteworthy /-ˌwɜrðɪ/ *adj* outstanding; remarkable.

nothing /'nʌθɪŋ/ *n* no thing; not anything; nothingness; a zero; a trifle; a person or thing of no importance or value. • *adv* in no way, not at all.

nothingness /-nəs/ *n* the state of being nothing; unconsciousness; worthlessness.

notice /'no:tɪs/ *n* an announcement; a warning; a placard giving information; a short article about a book, play, etc; attention, heed; a formal warning of intention to end an agreement at a certain time. • *vt* to observe; to remark upon. • *vi* to be aware of.

noticeable /-əbəl/ *adj* easily noticed or seen.—**noticeably** *adv*.

notice board *n* a board on which notices are posted.

notifiable /'no:tɪˌfaɪəbəl/ *adj* (*infectious diseases*) that must be reported to health authorities.

notification /ˌno:tɪfɪ'keɪʃən/ *n* the act of notifying; a notice or paper bearing it.

notify /'no:tɪˌfaɪ/ *vt* (**notifying, notified**) to inform; to report, give notice of.

notion /'no:ʃən/ *n* a general idea; an opinion; a whim.

notional /-əl/ *adj* hypothetical, abstract; imaginary.

notions /'no:ʃənz/ *npl* small useful articles, as thread, needles, etc; haberdashery.

noto- /'no:to:/ or /'no:tə/ *prefix* back.

notochord /'no:təˌkɔrd/ *n* the rudimentary form of the vertebral column; a band forming the basis of the spinal column.—**notochordal** *adj*.

notoriety /no:tə'raɪtɪ/ *n* the state of being notorious; disrepute, infamy; public exposure.

notorious /no:'tɔrɪəs/ or /nə-/ *adj* widely known, *esp* unfavourably.—**notoriously** *adv*.

notornis /no:'tɔrnɪs/ *n* the gigantic short-winged coot of New Zealand.

nototherium /ˌno:to:'θɪrɪəm/ *n* (*pl* **nototheria**) an extinct gigantic marsupial of Australia.

notwithstanding /ˌnɒtwɪθ'stændɪŋ/ or /-wɪð-/ *prep* in spite of. • *adv* nevertheless. • *conj* although.

nougat /'nu:gət/ *n* a chewy sweet consisting of sugar paste with nuts.

nought /nɒt/ *n* nothing; a zero. • *adv* in no degree.—*also* **naught**.

noughts and crosses *n sing* a game in which two players place noughts and crosses into squares on a grid with nine spaces, the winner being the first to form a row of three noughts or crosses.

noumenon /'nu:məˌnɒn/ or /'nau-/ *n* (*pl* **noumena**) an object of purely intellectual intuition; (*philos*) the substance or real existing under the phenomenal.—**noumenal** *adj*.

noun /naun/ *n* (*gram*) a word that names a person, a living being, an object, action etc; a substantive.

nourish /'nʌrɪʃ/ *vt* to feed; to encourage the growth of; to raise, bring up.

nourishing /-ɪŋ/ *adj* containing nourishment; health-giving; beneficial.

nourishment /-mənt/ *n* food; the act of nourishing.

nous /naʊs/ *n* pure intellect; common sense.

nouveau riche /ˌnu:vo:'ri:ʃ/ *n* (*pl* **nouveaux riches**) the new rich, a parvenu.—*also adj*.

Nov *abbr* = November.

nova /'no:və/ *n* (*pl* **novas, novae**) a new star that explodes into bright luminosity before subsiding.

novel /'nɒvəl/ *n* a relatively long prose narrative that is usually fictitious and in the form of a story. • *adj* new and unusual; of a kind not seen before.

novelette /ˌnɒvə'let/ *n* a short novel.—**novelettish** *adj*.

novelist /'nɒvəlɪst/ *n* a writer of novels.

novelize /'nɒvəˌlaɪz/ *vt* to turn (a play, film, etc) into a novel.—**novelization** *n*.

novella /nə'velə/ *n* (*pl* **novellas, novelle**) a short novel.

novelty /'nɒvəltɪ/ *n* (*pl* **novelties**) a novel thing or occurrence; a new or unusual thing; (*pl*) cheap, small objects for sale.

November /no:'vembər/ *n* the eleventh month, having 30 days.

novena /no:'vi:nə/ *n* (*pl* **novenae**) (*RC Church*) a prayer made for nine days to obtain a request through intercession of the Virgin or saint.

novice /'nɒvɪs/ *n* a person on probation in a religious order before taking final vows; a beginner.

novitiate, noviciate /no:'vɪʃɪət/ or /-ieɪt/ *n* a probationary period, initiation; a novice; a place where novices live.

now /nau/ *adv* at the present time; by this time; at once; nowadays. • *conj* since; seeing that. • *n* the present time. • *adj* of the present time.

nowadays /'nauəˌdeɪz/ *adv* in these days; at the present time.

noway /'no:weɪ/ *adv* not at all. • *interj* (**no way**) used to express emphatic denial or refusal.

nowhere /'no:wer/ *adv* not in, at, or to anywhere.

nowise /'no:waɪz/ *adv* not in any manner or degree.

noxious /'nɒkʃəs/ *adj* harmful, unhealthy.—**noxiously** *adv*.—**noxiousness** *n*.

noyade /nwɒ'jɒd/ *n* execution by drowning, *esp* that system of capital punishment for political offenders employed by the French revolutionists of 1789.

noyau /'nɒjo:/ *n* (*pl* **noyaux**) a liqueur flavoured with bruised bitter almonds.

nozzle /'nɒzəl/ *n* the spout at the end of a hose, pipe, etc.

Np (*chem symbol*) neptunium.

NT *abbr* = New Testament.

-n't /ənt/ = not.

nth /enəθ/ *adj* (*maths*) of or having an unspecified number; (*inf*) utmost, extreme.

nu /nju:/ *n* the 13th letter of the Greek alphabet.

nuance /'nu:ɒns/ or /'nju:-/ *n* a subtle difference in meaning, colour, etc.

nub /nʌb/ *n* a lump or small piece; (*inf*) the central point or gist of a matter.

nubbin /'nʌbɪn/ *n* a small or imperfect ear of maize; undeveloped fruit.

nubecula /nju'bekjulə/ *n* (*pl* **nubeculae**) the Magellanic clouds, a small galaxy; cloudy appearance; a light film on the eye.

nubile /'nu:baɪl/ or /'nju:-/ adj (girl) marriageable; attractive.

nuclear /'nu:klɪər/ or /'nju:-/ adj of or relating to a nucleus; using nuclear energy; having nuclear weapons.

nuclear bomb n a bomb whose explosive power derives from uncontrolled nuclear fusion or fission.

nuclear energy n energy released as a result of nuclear fission or fusion.

nuclear family n father, mother and children.

nuclear fission n the splitting of a nucleus of an atom either spontaneously or by bombarding it with particles.

nuclear fusion n the combining of two nuclei into a heavier nucleus, releasing energy in the process.

nuclear power n electrical or motive power produced by a nuclear reactor.

nuclear reactor n a device in which nuclear fission is maintained and harnessed to produce energy.

nuclear waste n radioactive waste.

nucleate /'nu:klɪət/ or /'nju:-/ adj having a nucleus.

nucleic acid /nu:'kleɪk/ or /-'kli:k/, /nju:-/ n DNA, RNA or similar complex acid present in all living cells.

nucleo-, nucle- /'nu:klɪo:/ or /'nju:-/ prefix nucleus; nucleic acid.

nucleolus /ˌnu:kli'o:ləs/ or /ˌnju:-/ n (pl nucleoli) a minute body inside a nucleus.

nucleonics /ˌnu:kli'ɒnɪks/ or /ˌnju:-/ n (used as sing) the physics and technology of the applications of nuclear energy.

nucleus /'nu:klɪəs/ or /'nju:-/ n (pl nuclei, nucleuses) the central part or the core around which something may develop, or be grouped or concentrated; the centrally positively charged portion of an atom; the part of an animal or plant cell that contains genetic material.

nude /nu:d/ or /nju:d/ adj naked; bare; undressed. • n a naked human figure, esp in a work of art; the state of being nude.—**nudity** n.

nudge /nʌdʒ/ vt to touch gently with the elbow to attract attention or urge into action; to push slightly. • n a gentle touch, as with the elbow.

nudibranch /'nu:dɪbræŋk/ or /'nju:-/ n any of the order Nudibranchia of shell-less molluscs with naked gills.

nudism /'nu:dɪzəm/ or /'nju:-/ n the practice of going nude, esp in groups at designated places and times.

nudist /'nu:dɪst/ or /'nju:-/ n one who believes in going nude.—also adj.

nudity /'nu:dɪti/ or /'nju:-/ n (pl nudities) nakedness.

nugatory /'nu:gəˌtɒri/ or /'nju:-/ adj trifling, worthless; inoperative, not valid; useless.

nugget /'nʌgət/ n a small lump, esp of gold in its natural state.

nuisance /'nu:səns/ or /'nju:-/ n a person or thing that annoys or causes trouble.

nuke /nu:k/ or /nju:k/ vt (sl) to attack and destroy with a nuclear weapon; (sl) to cook or heat (food) in microwave oven. • n a nuclear weapon.

null /nʌl/ adj without legal force; invalid.

nullah /'nʌlə/ n in the East Indies, a watercourse or canal; a ravine.

nulla-nulla /ˌnʌlə'nʌlə/ n (Austral) a hard wooden club.

nullifier /'nʌlɪˌfaɪər/ n one who nullifies.

nullify /'nʌlɪˌfaɪ/ vt (nullifying, nullified) to make null, to cancel out.—**nullification** n.

nullipara /nʌ'lɪpərə/ n (pl nulliparae) a woman who has never given birth to a child, esp if not a virgin.

nullipore /'nʌlɪˌpɔr/ n a marine coral-like plant with calcareous fronds.

nullity /'nʌlti/ n (pl nullities) the state of being null; a legally invalid document or act; something ineffectual, worthless, etc.

num abbr = number; numeral.

numb /nʌm/ adj deadened; having no feeling (due to cold, shock, etc). • vt to make numb.—**numbness** n.

number /'nʌmbər/ n a symbol or word indicating how many; a numeral identifying a person or thing by its position in a series; a single issue of a magazine; a song or piece of music, esp as an item in a performance; (inf) an object singled out; a total of persons or things; (gram) the form of a word indicating singular or plural; a telephone number; (pl) arithmetic; (pl) numerical superiority. • vti to count; to give a number to; to include or be included as one of a group; to limit the number of; to total.

numberless /-ləs/ adj too many to count.

number one n the first in a list, series, etc; (inf) oneself or one's own interests; (inf) the most important person or thing; (inf) a best-selling pop record. • adj most important, urgent, etc.

numberplate n a plate at the front and the back of a motor vehicle showing the registration number.—also US **license plate**.

Number Ten n 10 Downing Street, the London residence of the British prime minister.

numbles /'nʌmblz/ npl humbles, entrails, esp of a deer.

numbskull /'nʌmskəl/ see numskull.

numerable /'nu:mərəbəl/ or /'nju:-/ adj countable.—**numerably** adv.

numeral /'nu:mərəl/ or /'nju:-/ n a symbol or group of symbols used to express a number (eg two = 2 or II, etc).

numerate /'nu:mərət/ or /'nju:-/ adj having a basic understanding of arithmetic. • vt to reckon or enumerate; to point or read, as figures.

numerati /ˌnju:mə'ræti/ or /-'rɒti/ npl people, esp financiers, who are proficient at arithmetic.

numeration /ˌnu:mə'reɪʃən/ or /ˌnju:-/ n the act of numbering; the art of reading in words numbers expressed by symbols.

numerator /'nu:məˌreɪtər/ or /'nju:-/ n the number above the line in a fraction.

numeric, numerical /nu:'merɪkəl/ or /nju:-/, adj of or relating to numbers; expressed in numbers.

numerology /ˌnu:mə'rɒlədʒi/ or /ˌnju:-/ n the study of the supposed occult meaning of numbers.

numerous /'nu:mərəs/ or /'nju:-/ adj many, consisting of many items.

numismatics /ˌnu:mɪz'mætɪks/ or /ˌnju:-/ n (used as sing) the study of coins, medals, etc.—also **numismatology**.—**numismatic** adj.

numismatist /-'mɪzmətɪst/ n one skilled in numismatics; a student of coins.

nummular /'nʌmju:lər/ adj pertaining to, or like, coins.

nummulite /'nʌmju:ˌlɔɪt/ n a many-chambered fossil foraminifer resembling a coin.—**nummulitic** adj.

numskull /'nʌmskəl/ n a dolt, a blockhead.—also **numbskull**.

nun /nʌn/ n a woman belonging to a religious order.

Nunc Dimittis /ˌnʌŋkdɪ'mɪtɪs/ n a canticle.

nunciature /'nʌnsiəˌtʃər/ n the office of a nuncio; the tenure of it.

nuncio /'nʌnsio:/ or /nʌn-/ n (pl nuncios) the pope's ambassador at a foreign court.

nuncupate /'nʌŋkju:ˌpeɪt/ vt to declare, to make a will verbally, not in writing.

nuncupative /'nʌŋkju:ˌpeɪtɪv/ adj (law) verbal, not written; nominal.

nunnery /'nʌnəri/ n (pl nunneries) a convent of nuns.

nuptial /'nʌpʃəl/ adj relating to marriage. • npl a wedding ceremony; marriage.

nurse /nɜrs/ n a person trained to care for the sick, injured or aged; a person who looks after another person's child or children. • vt to tend, to care for; (baby) to feed at the breast; (hatred) to foster; to tend with an eye to the future.

nursemaid /'nɜrsmeɪd/ n a woman in charge of children, a nanny.

nursery /'nɜrsri/ or /-əri/ n (pl nurseries) a room set aside for children; a place where children may be left in temporary care; a place where young trees and plants are raised for transplanting.

nurseryman /'nɜrsərimən/ n (pl nurserymen) a person who owns or works in a plant nursery.

nursery rhyme n a short traditional poem or song for young children.

nursery school n a school for young children, usu between three and five years old.

nursery slope n a gently inclined slope for novice skiers.

nursing /'nɜrsɪŋ/ n the profession of a nurse.

nursing home n an establishment providing care for convalescent, chronically ill, or disabled people.

nursling, nurseling /'nɜrslɪŋ/ n an infant; one who is nursed.

nurture /'nɜrtʃər/ vt to feed; to bring up, educate. • n the act of bringing up a child; nourishment.

nut /nʌt/ n a kernel (sometimes edible) enclosed in a hard shell; a usu metallic threaded block screwed on the end of a bolt; (sl) a mad person; (sl) a devotee, fan. • vt (nutting, nutted) to gather nuts.

nutant /'nu:tənt/ or /'nju:-/ adj (bot) having the top bent downward.

nutation /nuːˈteɪʃən/ or /njuː-/ *n* nodding; the periodic vibratory movement of the axis of the earth; (*bot*) the turning of flowers towards the sun.—**nutational** *adj*.

nut-brown *adj* coloured like a ripe hazelnut.

nut case /ˈnʌtkeɪs/ *n* (*sl*) a crazy or foolish person.

nutcracker /ˈnʌtˌkrækər/ *n* (*usu pl*) a tool for cracking nuts; a bird with speckled plumage.

nuthatch /ˈnʌthætʃ/ *n* a small climbing bird feeding on nuts.

nutmeg /ˈnʌtmeg/ *n* the aromatic kernel produced by a tree, grated and used as a spice.

nutria /ˈnuːtriə/ or /ˈnjuː-/ *n* the fur or skin of the coypu, a South American beaver.

nutrient /ˈnuːtriənt/ or /ˈnjuː-/ *n* a substance that nourishes. • *adj* promoting growth.

nutriment /ˈnuːtrɪmənt/ or /ˈnjuː-/ *n* nourishing food, nourishment.

nutrition /nuːˈtrɪʃən/ or /njuː-/ *n* the act or process by which plants and animals take in and assimilate food in their systems; the study of the human diet.—**nutritional** *adj*.

nutritionist /nuːˈtrɪʃənɪst/ or /njuː-/ *n* a specialist who studies and advises on the human diet.

nutritious /nuːˈtrɪʃəs/ or /njuː-/ *adj* efficient as food; health-giving, nourishing.

nutritive /ˈnuːtrɪtɪv/ or /ˈnjuː-/ *adj* serving as good. • *n* an article of food.—**nutritively** *adv*.

nuts /nʌts/ *adj* (*inf*) very keen (on); (*inf*) crazy.

nuts and bolts *npl* (*inf*) the basic facts or details.

nutshell /ˈnʌtʃel/ *n* the hard covering of a nut; a tiny receptacle; a compact way of expression.

nutting /ˈnʌtɪŋ/ *n* nut-gathering.

nutty /ˈnʌti/ *adj* (**nuttier, nuttiest**) tasting of or containing nuts; (*sl*) very enthusiastic; (*sl*) crazy, mad, etc.

nux vomica /nʌksˈvɒmɪkə/ *n* the fruit of an East Indian plant (*Strychnos Nux vomica*), which yields the deadly poison strychnine.

nuzzle /ˈnʌzəl/ *vti* to push (against) or rub with the nose or snout; to nestle, snuggle.

NW *abbr* = northwest, northwestern.

NY *abbr* = New York (city or state).

nyctalopia /ˌnɪktəˈloːpiə/ *n* night blindness; the inability to see clearly except at night.

nyctitropism /ˌnɪktɪˈtroːpɪzəm/ *n* (*bot*) the so-called sleep of plants, turning in certain direction at night.—**nyctitropic** *adj*.

nylon /ˈnaɪlɒn/ *n* any of numerous strong, tough, elastic, synthetic materials used *esp* in plastics and textiles; (*pl*) stockings made of nylon.

nymph /nɪmf/ *n* (*myth*) a spirit of nature envisaged as a maiden; (*poet*) a lovely young maiden; the chrysalis of an insect.—**nymphean** *adj*.

nymphet /nɪmˈfet/ or /ˈnɪmfət/ *n* a sexually desirable pre-adolescent girl.

nympho /ˈnɪmfoː/ *n* (*pl* **nymphos**) (*inf*) a nymphomaniac.

nympholepsy /ˈnɪmfəˌlepsi/ *n* (*pl* **nympholepsies**) frenzy caused by desire of the unattainable.

nympholept /ˈnɪmfəˌlept/ *n* one inspired by violent enthusiasm for an ideal.—**nympholeptic** *adj*.

nymphomania /ˌnɪmfəˈmeɪniə/ *n* uncontrollable sexual desire in women.—**nymphomaniac** *adj, n.*—**nymphomaniacal** *adj*.

nystagmus /nɪˈstægməs/ *n* a condition of the eye, with spasmodic movement of the eyeballs.—**nystagmic** *adj*.

NZ *abbr* = New Zealand.

O

O, o /oː/ *n* the 15th letter of the English alphabet; something shaped like the letter O; nought, nothing, zero.

O., o. *abbr* = octavo; old; only.

O (*chem symbol*) oxygen. • *interj* an exclamation of wonder, pain, etc.

O' *prefix* (in *Irish urnames*) descendant of.

o' *prep* (*inf, arch*) short for *of* or *on*.

-o /oː/ *n, adj suffix* (*inf*) indicating a diminutive, *cheapo*; (*inf*) forming an interjection, *cheerio*.

oaf /oːf/ *n* (*pl* **oafs**) a loutish or stupid person.—**oafish** *adj*.—**oafishly** *adv*.

oak /oːk/ *n* a tree with a hard durable wood, having acorns as fruits.

oak apple *n* a spongy excrescence growing on the leaves or young branches of the oak, caused by the gallfly.

oaken /-ən/ *adj* made of or consisting of oak.

oakum /ˈoːkəm/ *n* a loose fibre obtained by unpicking old rope and used for caulking.

O & M *abbr* = organization and method(s).

OAP *abbr* = old age pensioner, senior citizen.

OAPEC *abbr* = Organization of Arab Petroleum Exporting Countries.

oar /ɔːr/ *n* a pole with a flat blade for rowing a boat; an oarsman.

oarlock /ˈɔːlɒk/ *n see* **rowlock**.

oarsman /ˈɔːzmən/ *n* (*pl* **oarsmen**) a person who rows a boat.—**oarsmanship** *n*.

OAS *abbr* = Organization of American States.

oasis /oːˈeɪsɪs/ *n* (*pl* **oases**) a fertile place in a desert; a refuge.

oast /oːst/ *n* a kiln for drying hops or barley.

oatcake /ˈoːtkeɪk/ *n* a thin broad cake of oatmeal.

oaten /-ən/ *adj* made of oats.

oath /oːθ/ *n* (*pl* **oaths**) a solemn declaration to a god or a higher authority that one will speak the truth or keep a promise; a swear word; a blasphemous expression.

oatmeal /ˈoːtmiːl/ *n* ground oats; a porridge of this; a pale greyish-brown colour.

oats /oːts/ *npl* a cereal grass widely cultivated for its edible grain; the seeds.

OAU *abbr* = Organization of African Unity.

ob. *abbr* = (*Latin*) *obiit*, died.

ob- /ɒb/ *prefix* before, against, toward, in front of, reversed.

obbligato /ˌɒblɪˈɡɑːtoː/ *adj* (*mus*) forming an integral part of a musical composition. • *n* (*pl* **obbligatos, obbligati**) an indispensable instrumental part or accompaniment written especially for the instrument named.—*also* **obligato** (*pl* **obligatos, obligati**).

obcordate /ɒbˈkɔːdeɪt/ *adj* (*bot*) inversely cordate.

obdurate /ˈɒbdʒʊrət/ or /-dʊr-/ *adj* hard-hearted; unyielding, stubborn.—**obduracy** *n*.—**obdurately** *adv*.

OBE *abbr* = Order of the British Empire.

obeah /ˈoːbiə/ *see* **obi**.

obedience /oːˈbiːdɪəns/ *n* the condition of being obedient; observance of orders, instructions, etc; respect for authority.

obedient /oːˈbiːdɪənt/ *adj* obeying; compliant; submissive to authority, dutiful.—**obediently** *adv*.

obeisance /oːˈbeɪsəns/ or /-biː-/ *n* a bow or curtsey; an act of reverence or homage.

obelisk /ˈɒbəlɪsk/ *n* a four-sided tapering pillar *usu* with a pyramidal top; a reference mark used in printing (†).—*also* **dagger**.

obelize /ˈɒbəˌlaɪz/ *vt* to mark with an obelus.

obelus /ˈɒbələs/ *n* (*pl* **obeli**) a mark (— *or* ÷ *or* †) used in old MSS to indicate a doubtful or spurious reading; in modern writing, a break (—).

obese /oːˈbiːs/ *adj* very fat.—**obesity** *n*.

obey /oːˈbeɪ/ *vti* (**obeying, obeyed**) to carry out (orders, instructions); to comply (with); to submit (to).

obfuscate /ˈɒbfʊˌskeɪt/ *vt* to bewilder or confuse; to darken.—**obfuscation** *n*.

obi¹ /ˈoːbi/ *n* (*pl* **obis, obi**) a Japanese woman's sash.

obi² *n* (*pl* **obis**) in the West Indes and Africa, a system of secret sorcery or magical rites.—*also* **obeah**.

obit /ˈoːbɪt/ *n* (*inf*) an obituary.

obiter dictum /ˌɒbɪtər ˈdɪktəm/ *n* (*pl* **obiter dicta**) (*Latin*) a casual remark or opinion expressed incidentally, as by a judge or writer.

obituary /oːˈbɪtʃuːəri/ or /əˈbɪtʃ-/ *n* (*pl* **obituaries**) an announcement of a person's death, often with a short biography.—**obituarist** *n*.

object /ˈɒbdʒɛkt/ or /-dʒɪkt/ *n* something that can be recognized by the senses; a person or thing toward which action, feeling, etc, is directed; a purpose or aim; (*gram*) a noun or part of a sentence governed by a transitive verb or a preposition. • *vti* to state or raise an objection; to oppose; to disapprove.—**objector** *n*.

object ball *n* (*billiards*) the ball meant to be hit by the cue ball.

object glass *n* the lens of a microscope or telescope nearest to the object to be observed and forming the image.

objectify /ɒbˈdʒɛktɪˌfaɪ/ *vt* (**objectifying, objectified**) to render objective; to embody; to materialize.—**objectification** *adj*.

objection /əbˈdʒɛkʃən/ *n* the act of objecting; a ground for, or expression of, disapproval.

objectionable /əbˈdʒɛkʃənəbəl/ *adj* causing an objection; disagreeable.—**objectionably** *adv*.

objective /əbˈdʒɛktɪv/ *adj* relating to an object; not influenced by opinions or feelings; impartial; having an independent existence of its own, real; (*gram*) of, or appropriate to an object governed by a verb or a preposition. • *n* the thing or placed aimed at; (*gram*) the objective case.—**objectively** *adv*.

objectivism /əbˈdʒɛktɪˌvɪzəm/ *n* (*philos*) the doctrine that the knowledge of the non-ego is anterior to that of the ego; (*art, literature*) the representation of persons and incidents as they really appear.—**objectivist** *adj, n*.—**objectivistic** *adj*.

objectivity /ˌɒbdʒɛkˈtɪvɪti/ *n* the state or quality of being objective.

object lesson *n* a convincing practical illustration of some principle.

object program *n* (*comput*) a computer program derived from the conversion of a source program into machine code by a compiler or assembler.

objet d'art /ɒbʒeɪˈdɑːr/ *n* (*pl* **objets d'art**) a small decorative object.

objurgate /ˈɒbdʒərˌɡeɪt/ *vt* to chide or reprove, to scold.—**objurgation** *n*.

objurgatory /ɒbˈdʒɜːɡəˌtɔːri/ *adj* containing reproof or censure.

oblanceolate /ɒbˈlænsiələt/ *adj* (*bot*) lanceolate in the reversed order.

oblate¹ /ˈɒbleɪt/ or /ɒ:-/ *n* (*RC Church*) a secular priest who has devoted himself and his property to the monastery he has entered. *adj* dedicated to a monastic or religious life.

oblate² *adj* (*spheroid*) depressed or flattened at the poles; orange-shaped.

oblation /oːˈbleɪʃən/ *n* an offering or sacrifice; anything presented in religious worship, *esp* the Eucharist.—**oblatory, oblational** *adj*.

obligate /ˈɒblɪˌɡeɪt/ *vt* to bind by a contract, promise, sense of duty, etc.

obligation /ˌɒblɪˈɡeɪʃən/ *n* the act of obligating; a moral or legal requirement; a debt; a favour; a commitment to pay a certain amount of money; the amount owed under such an obligation.

obligato *see* **obbligato**.

obligatory /əˈblɪɡətəri/ *adj* binding, not optional; compulsory.

oblige /əˈblaɪdʒ/ *vt* to compel by moral, legal, or physical force; (*person*) to make grateful for some favour; to do a favour for.

obligee /ˌɒblɪˈdʒiː/ *n* (*law*) a person in whose favour a bond is made; a creditor.

obliging /əˈblaɪdʒɪŋ/ *adj* ready to do favours.—**obligingly** *adv*.

obligor /ˌɒblɪˈɡɔːr/ *n* (*law*) a person who is bound by a bond; a debtor.

oblique /əˈbliːk/ or /oː-/ *adj* slanting, at an angle; diverging from the straight; indirect, allusive. • *n* an oblique line.—**obliquely** *adv*.

oblique angle *n* an angle greater or less than a right angle.

oblique case *n* (*gram*) any case except the nominative and vocative.

obliquity /əˈblɪkwɪti/ *n* (*pl* **obliquities**) obliqueness; a slanting direction; deviation from a moral code.

obliterate /əˈblɪtəˌreɪt/ *vt* to wipe out, to erase, to destroy.— **obliteration** *n*.

oblivion /əˈblɪviən/ *n* a state of forgetting or being forgotten; a state of mental withdrawal.

oblivious /əˈblɪviəs/ *adj* forgetful, unheeding; unaware (of).

oblong /ˈɒblɒŋ/ *adj* rectangular. • *n* any oblong figure.

obloquy /ˈɒbləkwi/ *n* (*pl* **obloquies**) reproachful language, detraction; calumny; slander, disgrace.

obnoxious /ɒbˈnɒkʃəs/ or /əb-/ *adj* objectionable; highly offensive.—**obnoxiously** *adv*.—**obnoxiousness** *n*.

oboe /ˈoːbəʊ/ *n* an orchestral woodwind instrument having a mouthpiece with a double reed.—**oboist** *n*.

obolus /ˈɒbələs/, **obol** *n* (*pl* **oboli, obols**) an ancient Greek silver coin; a modern Greek weight = 1/10th of a gram.

obovate /ɒbˈoːveɪt/ *adj* (*bot*) inversely ovate.

obs *abbr* = observation; obsolete.

obscene /ɒbˈsiːn/ or /əb-/ *adj* indecent, lewd; offensive to a moral or social standard.—**obscenely** *adv*.

obscenity /ɒbˈsɛnɪti/ or /əb-/ *n* (*pl* **obscenities**) the state or quality of being obscene; an obscene act, word, etc.

obscurant /əbˈskjʊrənt/ *adj, n* (a person) opposed to enlightenment, reactionary.—**obscurantism** *n*.—**obscurantist** *adj, n*.

obscure /ɒbˈskjʊr/ or /əb-/ *adj* not clear; dim; indistinct; remote, secret; not easily understood; inconspicuous; unimportant, humble. • *vt* to make unclear, to confuse; to hide.—**obscurely** *adv*.

obscurity /ɒbˈskjʊrɪti/ or /əb-/ *n* (*pl* **obscurities**) the state or quality of being obscure; an obscure thing or person.

obsequies /ˈɒbsɪkwiːz/ *npl* (*sing* **obsequy**) funeral rites, a funeral.

obsequious /ɒbˈsiːkwiəs/ or /əb-/ *adj* subservient; fawning.— **obsequiously** *adv*.

observable /ɒbˈzɜːvəbəl/ or /əb-/ *adj* worthy of observation; remarkable.—**observably** *adv*.

observance /ɒbˈzɜːvəns/ or /əb-/ *n* the observing of a rule, duty, law, etc; a ceremony or religious rite.

observant /ɒbˈzɜːvənt/ or /əb-/ *adj* watchful; attentive, mindful.—**observantly** *adv*.

observation /ɒbzərˈveɪʃən/ *n* the act or faculty of observing; a comment or remark; careful noting of the symptoms of a patient, movements of a suspect, etc prior to diagnosis, analysis or interpretation.—**observational** *adj*.—**observationally** *adv*.

observatory /ɒbˈzɜːrvəˌtɔːri/ or /əb-/ *n* (*pl* **observatories**) a building for astronomical observation; an institution whose primary purpose is making such observations.

observe /ɒbˈzɜːv/ or /əb-/ *vt* to notice; to perceive; (*a law, etc*) to keep to or adhere to; to arrive at as a conclusion; to examine scientifically. • *vi* to take notice; to make a comment (on).— **observable** *adj*.

observer /-ər/ *n* a person who observes; a delegate who attends a formal meeting but may not take part; an expert analyst and commentator in a particular field.

obsess /ɒbˈsɛs/ or /əb-/ *vt* to possess or haunt the mind of; to preoccupy.—**obsessive** *adj, n*.—**obsessively** *adv*.

obsession /ɒbˈsɛʃən/ or /əb-/ *n* a fixed idea, often associated with mental illness; a persistent idea or preoccupation; the condition of obsessing or being obsessed.

obsidian /ɒbˈsɪdiən/ or /əb-/ *n* a hard glassy dark-coloured volcanic lava.

obsolescent /ˌɒbsəˈlɛsənt/ *adj* becoming obsolete, going out of date.—**obsolescence** *n*.

obsolete /ˈɒbsəˌliːt/ or /ˌɒbsəˌliːt/ *adj* disused, out of date.

obstacle /ˈɒbstəkəl/ *n* anything that hinders something; an obstruction.

obstetrics /ɒbˈstɛtrɪks/ or /əb-/ *n sing* the branch of medicine concerned with the care and treatment of women during pregnancy and childbirth.—**obstetric, obstetrical** *adj*.— **obstetrician** *n*.

obstinate /ˈɒbstənət/ *adj* stubborn, self-willed; intractable; persistent.—**obstinacy** *n*.—**obstinately** *adv*.

obstreperous /ɒbˈstrɛpərəs/ or /əb-/ *adj* unruly, turbulent, noisy.

obstruct /ɒbˈstrʌkt/ or /əb-/ *vt* to block with an obstacle; to impede; to prevent, hinder; to keep (light, etc) from.

obstruction /ɒbˈstrʌkʃən/ or /əb-/ *n* that which obstructs; the act or an example of obstructing; a hindrance, obstacle.

obstructionism /-ˌnɪzəm/ *n* the systematic hindering of political business, etc.—**obstructionist** *adj, n*.

obstructive /ɒbˈstrʌktɪv/ or /əb-/ *adj* tending to obstruct; preventing, hindering.—**obstructively** *adv*.—**obstructiveness** *n*.

obtain /ɒbˈteɪn/ or /əb-/ *vt* to get, to acquire, to gain. • *vi* to be prevalent, hold good.—**obtainable** *adj*.—**obtainment** *n*.

obtect /ɒbˈtɛkt/ *adj* (*pupa*) protected by a hard outer case.

obtrude /ɒbˈtruːd/ or /əb-/ *vti* to push (an opinion, oneself) on others uninvited; to intrude.—**obtruding** *adj*.

obtrusion /ɒbˈtruːʒən/ *n* the act of obtruding; an unwelcome intrusion.

obtrusive /ɒbˈtruːsɪv/ *adj* apt to obtrude, pushy; protruding, sticking out.—**obtrusively** *adv*.—**obtrusiveness** *n*.

obtund /ɒbˈtɛnd/ or /əb-/ *vt* (*med*) to blunt, to deaden.

obturate /ˈɒbtʃʊrət/ *vt* to stop, to block or seal up; (*gun breech*) to close.—**obturation** *n*.—**obturator** *n*.

obtuse /ɒbˈtuːs/ or /əb-/, /-tjuːs/ *adj* mentally slow; not pointed; dull, stupid; (*geom*) greater than a right angle.—**obtusely** *adv*.—**obtuseness** *n*.

obverse /ˈɒbvɜːrs/ or /ɒbˈvɜːrs/ *n* the front or top side; (*coin*) the head; a counterpart. • *adj* facing the viewer; with the top wider than the base.—**obversely** *adv*.

obversion /ɒbˈvɜːrʃən/ *n* (*logic*) the immediate inference by which we deny the opposite of anything affirmed.

obvert /ɒbˈvɜːrt/ or /əb-/ *vt* (*logic*) to infer by obversion; to turn toward, to face.

obviate /ˈɒbviˌeɪt/ *vt* to make unnecessary; (*danger, difficulty*) to prevent, clear away.—**obviation** *n*.

obvious /ˈɒbviəs/ *adj* easily seen or understood; evident.—**obviously** *adv*.—**obviousness** *n*.

obvolute /ˈɒbvəˌluːt/ *adj* arranged so as to overlap, as the margins of an organ or part of a plant.

oc- /ɒk/ *prefix* the form of *ob-* before *c*.

ocarina /ˌɒkəˈriːnə/ *n* an egg-shaped wind instrument played like a flute.

occasion /əˈkeɪʒən/ *n* a special occurrence or event; a time when something happens; an opportunity; reason or grounds; a subsidiary cause. • *vt* to cause; to bring about.

occasional /əˈkeɪʒənəl/ *adj* infrequent, not continuous; intermittent; produced for an occasion; (*a cause*) incidental.

occasionalism /-ˌnɪzəm/ *n* (*philos*) the Cartesian theory of occasional causes, that bodily actions are caused and controlled by divine agency and not by the human will / the Cartesian doctrine that apparent action of mind on matter is due to the invervention of God.

occasionally /-li/ *adv* intermittently; now and then; infrequently.

occident /ˈɒksɪdənt/ *n* the west; (*with cap*) specifically Europe and America; the countries west of Asia and Turkey in Europe.—**Occidental, occidental** *adj*.

occipital /ɒkˈsɪpɪtəl/ *adj* of or pertaining to the occiput.

occiput /ˈɒksɪˌpʊt/ *n* (*pl* **occipita, occiputs**) (*anat*) the back part of the skull or head.

occlude /əˈkluːd/ *vti* to shut out or in; to stop up, close; (*chem*) to absorb and retain.

occluded front *n* (*meteorol*) the phenomenon formed by a cold front overtaking a warm front and lifting the warm air above the earth's surface.

occlusion /əˈkluːʒən/ *n* the act of occluding; (*dentistry*) the position of the teeth when the jaws are closed; an occluded front.

occult /ɒˈkʌlt/ *adj* supernatural, magical; secret.—*also n*.

occultation /-ˈteɪʃən/ *n* (*astron*) a temporary disappearance or obscuration, as the eclipse of a star or planet by the moon, etc.

occulted /ɒˈkʌltəd/ *adj* (*astron*) hidden from the vision, as a star, etc.

occultism /-ˌtɪzəm/ *n* mysticism, spiritualism, theosophy, etc.— **occultist** *n*.

occult sciences *npl* magic, alchemy and astrology.

occupancy /ˈɒkjʊpənsi/ *n* (*pl* **occupancies**) the act of taking and holding in possession; the time of possession.

occupant /ˈɒkjʊpənt/ *n* a person who occupies, resides in, holds a position or place, etc.

occupation /ˌɒkjʊˈpeɪʃən/ *n* the act of occupying; the state of being occupied; employment or profession; a pursuit.—**occupational** *adj*.

occupational therapy *n* therapy by means of work in the arts and crafts, to aid recovery from disease or injury.—**occupational therapist** *n*.

occupier /'ɒkjʊˌpaɪər/ *n* an occupant.

occupy /'ɒkjʊˌpaɪ/ *vt* (**occupying, occupied**) to live in; (*room, office*) to take up or fill; (*a position*) to hold; to engross (one's mind); (*city, etc*) to take possession of.

occur /ə'kər/ or /ɒ:-/ *vi* (**occurring, occurred**) to happen; to exist; to come into the mind of.

occurrence /ə'kərəns/ *n* a happening, an incident, an event; the act or fact of occurring.

ocean /'oːʃən/ *n* a large stretch of sea, *esp* one of the earth's five oceans; a huge quantity or expanse.

oceangoing *adj* (*vessel*) designed and equipped for travelling on the open ocean.

oceanarium /ˌoːʃə'neriəm/ *n* (*pl* **oceanariums, oceanaria**) a large seawater aquarium for displays of marine life.

Oceania /ˌoːʃɪ'æniə/ or /ˌoːsi-/ *n* the Pacific islands.—**Oceanic** *adj*.

oceanic /ˌoːʃɪ'ænɪk/ or /ˌoːsi-/ *adj* of or relating to the ocean; formed or found in the ocean.

Oceanid /oː'siːənɪd/ *n* (*pl* **Oceanids, Oceanides**) (*Greek myth*) a sea nymph.

oceanography /ˌoːʃə'nɒɡrəfi/ *n* the study of the oceans including their physical and chemical make-up, marine biology, and their exploitation.—**oceanographer** *n*.

ocellate, ocellated /'ɒsɪlət/ *adj* marked with small spots or eyes.

ocellus /ɒ'seləs/ *n* (*pl* **ocelli**) the facet of a compound eye; an eye-like spot, as on a peacock's tail, etc.

ocelot /'ɒsəˌlɒt/ or /'oː-/ *n* a medium-sized spotted wildcat of North and South America.

och /ɒx/ *interj* (*Scot, Irish*) expressing of surprise, contempt, disagreement, disappointment, etc.

ochre, ocher /'oːkər/ *n* a yellow to orange-coloured clay used as a pigment.

ochlo-, ochl- /ɒklɒ/ *prefix* mob.

ochlocracy /ɒk'lɒkrəsi/ *n* (*pl* **ochlocracies**) mob rule.—**ochlocrat** *n*.—**ochlocratic** *adj*.

o'clock /ə'klɒk/ *adv* indicating the hour; indicating a relative direction or position, twelve o'clock being directly ahead or above.

OCR /oːsi'ɑr/ *abbr* = optical character reader; optical character recognition.

Oct *abbr* = October.

octa- /'ɒktə/ *prefix* eight.

octachord /'ɒktəˌkɔrd/ *n* an eight-stringed musical instrument; a series of eight notes, diatonic scale.—**octachordal** *adj*.

octad /'ɒktæd/ *n* a group of eight; the number eight; (*chem*) an element or radical with a valency of eight.—**octadic** *adj*.

octagon /'ɒktəɡɒn/ *n* a plane figure having eight equal sides.—**octagonal** *adj*.

octahedral /ˌɒktə'hiːdrəl/ *adj* having eight equal sides.

octahedron /ˌɒktə'hiːdrən/ *n* (*pl* **octahedrons, octahedra**) a solid figure contained by eight equal equilateral triangles.

octal /'ɒktəl/ *n* (*comput*) a number system with 8 as its base, one digit being equivalent to three bits.

octameter /ɒk'tæmɪtər/ *n* an eight-foot verse.

octane /'ɒkteɪn/ *n* a hydrocarbon found in petrol.

octane number, octane rating *n* a measure of the anti-knock quality of a liquid motor fuel expressed as a percentage.

octant /'ɒktənt/ *n* the eighth part of a circle; an instrument for measuring angles; (*astron*) an aspect of two planets, etc, when 45 degrees apart.

octave /'ɒktɪv/ *n* (*mus*) the eighth full tone above or below a given tone, the interval of eight degrees between a tone and either of its octaves, or the series of tones within this interval.

octavo /ɒk'tɪvoː/ or /ɒk'teɪvoː/ *n* (*pl* **octavos**) a sheet of printing paper folded in eight leaves or 16 pages (8vo); this size, average $9^1/_2$ x 6ins). • *adj* having eight leaves or 16 pages to the sheet.

octennial /ɒk'teniəl/ *adj* recurring every eighth year; continuing eight years.—**octennially** *adv*.

octet, octette /ɒk'tet/ *n* a group of eight (performers, lines of a sonnet); a composition for eight instruments or voices.

octillion /ɒk'tɪljən/ *n* the eighth power of a million (1 with 48 ciphers) in US and France, the ninth power of a thousand (1 with 27 ciphers).—**octillionth** *adj*.

octo- /'ɒktoː/ *prefix* eight.

October /ɒk'toːbər/ *n* the tenth month of the year, having 31 days.

octodecimo /ˌɒktoː'desɪˌmoː/ *adj* consiting of 18 leaves or 36 pages to a sheet. • *n* (*pl* **octodecimos**) a book of such size (18mo).

octogenarian /ˌɒktədʒə'neriən/ *n* a person who is in his or her eighties.

octopod /'ɒktəˌpɒd/ *n* an animal with eight feet; an eight-armed mollusc.—*also adj*.

octopus /'ɒktəpəs/ *n* (*pl* **octopuses, octopi**) a mollusc having a soft body and eight tentacles covered with suckers.

octoroon /ˌɒktə'ruːn/ *n* the offspring of a white person and a quadroon.

octosyllable /ˌɒktə'sɪləbəl/ *n* a word or verse of eight syllables.—**octosyllabic** *adj*.

octroi /'ɒktrwɒ/ *n* in France and Belgium, a tax levied upon articles brought into the gates of a city; duty on goods.

octuple /ɒk'tʌpəl/ *adj* eight-fold.

ocular /'ɒkjulər/ *adj* of, by, or relating to the eye; resembling an eye in form or function.

oculist /'ɒkjulɪst/ *n* (*formerly*) an opththalmologist.

OD /oː'diː/ *n* (*inf*) an overdose of a drug, *esp* a narcotic. • *vi* (**OD'ing, OD'd**) to take an overdose.

od /ɒd/ *n* a hypothetical natural force once used to explain magnetism, mesmerism, etc.

odalisque, odalisk /'oːdəlɪsk/ *n* a female slave or concubine in the harem of a sultan; (*art*) the depiction of a woman in eastern garments reclining.

odd /ɒd/ *adj* eccentric; peculiar; occasional; not divisible by two; with the other of the pair missing; extra or left over. • *npl* probability; balance of advantage in favour of one against another; excess of one number over another, *esp* in betting; likelihood; disagreement; strife; miscellaneous articles, scraps.—**oddly** *adv*.—**oddness** *n*.

oddball /'ɒdbɒl/ *n* (*sl*) an eccentric person. • *adj* bizarre.

Oddfellow /'ɒdfeloː/ *n* a member of the order of the benevolent society of the Oddfellows, a friendly society similar to Freemasons.

oddity /'ɒdɪti/ *n* (*pl* **oddities**) the state of being odd; an odd thing or person; peculiarity.

odd man out *n* a person left when others pair off.

oddment /'ɒdmənt/ *n* an odd piece left over, *esp* of fabric.

odds and ends *npl* miscellaneous articles, scraps.

odds-on *adj* (*horse, etc*) (judged to be) having a better than even chance of winning; likely to happen, succeed, win, etc.

ode /oːd/ *n* a lyric poem marked by lofty feeling and dignified style.

odeum /'oːdiəm/ or /-'diːəm/ *n* (*pl* **odeums, odea**) a hall for musical performances.

odious /'oːdiəs/ *adj* causing hatred or offence; disgusting.—**odiously** *adv*.—**odiousness** *n*.

odium /'oːdiəm/ *n* general dislike.

odometer /oː'dɒmətər/ *n* an instrument attached to the axle of a vehicle to measure the distance it travels.

odonto-, odont- /oː'dɒntoː/ *prefix* tooth.

odontoglossum /oːdɒntə'ɡlɒsəm/ *n* a tropical orchid.

odontoid /oː'dɒntɔɪd/ *adj* tooth-shaped, tooth-like.

odontology /ˌoːdɒn'tɒlədʒi/ *n* dental science.—**odontological** *adj*.—**odontologist** *n*.

odor *n see* **odour**.

odoriferous /ˌoːdə'rɪfərəs/ *adj* diffusing fragrance; (*sl*) smelly.

odorless /-ləs/ *adj* without odour.

odorous /'oːdərəs/ *adj* having or emitting a scent; smelly; fragrant.

odour /'oːdər/ *n* smell; scent; aroma; a characteristic or predominant quality.— *also* **odor**.

odyssey /'ɒdɪsi/ *n* (*pl* **odysseys**) a long adventurous journey; an intellectual or spiritual quest.

Oe (*symbol*) oersted.

OECD *abbr* = Organization for Economic Cooperation and Development.

oecumenical /ˌekjuː'menɪkəl/ *adj* a rare spelling of **ecumenical**.

OED *abbr* = Oxford English Dictionary.

oedema /ɪ'diːmə/ *n* (*pl* **oedemata**) a swelling in a body or plant caused by excess fluid.—*also* **edema**.—**oedematous** *adj*.

Oedipus complex /'iːdɪpəs/ *n* (*psychoanal*) a complex arising from the relationship of a son to his parents.

oeil de boeuf *Fr.* /ʏldi'bøf/ *n* a small round or oval window in the roof or frieze of a large building.

oeillade *Fr.* /ʏ'leɪd/ *n* a suggestive glance or ogle.

oeno- /'iːnoː/, **oen-** *prefix* wine.

oenology /iː'nɒlədʒi/ *n* the science of wines.—*also* **enology**.—**oenological, enological** *adj*.—**oenologist, enologist** *n*.

o'er /'oːər/ *prep, adv* (*poet*) over.

oersted /'ərsted/ *n* the cgs unit of magnetic field strength.

oesophagus *n* (*pl* **oesophagi**) that part of the alimentary canal that takes food, etc, from the pharynx to the stomach.—*also* **esophagus**.

oestrogen *n* a hormone that develops and maintains female characteristics of the body.—*also* **estrogen**.

oestrus, oestrum *n* violent desire, frenzy; the period of ovulation of mammals, heat.—**oestrous** *adj.*—*also* **estrus, estrum**.

oeuvre /'ɔːvrə/ *n* (*pl* **oeuvres**) a work of art, literature, music, etc; the life's work of an artist, writer or composer.

of /əv/ or /ɒv/ *prep* from; belonging or relating to; concerning; among; by; during; owing to.

of- /ɒf/ *prefix* the form of *ob-* before *f*.

off /ɒf/ *adv* away, from; detached, gone; unavailable; disconnected; out of condition; entirely. • *prep* away from; not on. • *adj* distant; no longer operating; cancelled; (*food or drink*) having gone bad; on the right-hand side; (*runners, etc*) having started a race.

offal /'ɒfəl/ *n* the entrails of an animal eaten as food.

offbeat *adj* unconventional, eccentric.

off-Broadway *adj* denoting a type of small scale, experimental and generally noncommercial theatre situated outside theatrical Broadway in New York.

off-colour *adj* unwell; risqué.

offend /ə'fend/ *vt* to affront, displease; to insult. • *vi* to break a law.—**offender** *n*.

offence, offense /ə'fens/ *n* an illegal action, crime; a sin; an affront, insult; a cause of displeasure or anger.

offensive /ə'fensɪv/ *adj* causing offence; repulsive, disagreeable; insulting; aggressive. • *n* an attack; a forceful campaign for a cause, etc.—**offensively** *adv.*—**offensiveness** *n*.

offer /'ɒfər/ *vt* to present for acceptance or rejection; to show willingness (to do something); to present for consideration; to bid; (*a prayer*) to say. • *vi* to present itself; to declare oneself willing. • *n* something offered; a bid or proposal.

offering /'ɒfərɪŋ/ *n* a gift, present; a sacrifice.

offertory /'ɒfər,tɔːri/ or /'ɒfrə-/ *n* (*pl* **offertories**) (*Anglican Church*) the sentences read in the Communion service during the collection of the alms; the alms collecting; (*RC Church*) an anthem chanted during Mass while the priest prepares the elements a church collection; the part of the service when it is taken.

offhand /ɒf'hænd/ or /'ɒfhænd/ *adv* impromptu; without thinking. • *adj* inconsiderate; curt, brusque; unceremonious.

office /'ɒfɪs/ *n* a room or building where business is carried out; the people there; (*with cap*) the location, staff, of authority of a Government department, etc; a task or function; a position of authority; a duty; a religious ceremony, rite.

officer /'ɒfɪsər/ *n* an official; a person holding a position of authority in a government, business, club, military services, etc; a policeman.

official /ə'fɪʃəl/ *adj* of an office or its tenure; properly authorized; formal. • *n* a person who holds a public office.—**officially** *adv*.

officialdom /-dəm/ *n* a body of officials.

officialese /ə'fɪʃə'liːz/ *n* the jargon of official documents or as expressed by officials.

officiant /ə'fɪʃiənt/ *n* an officiating clergyman.

officiate /ə'fɪʃi,eɪt/ *vi* to conduct a ceremony; to act in an official capacity; to perform the functions of a priest, minister, rabbi, etc.

officious /ə'fɪʃəs/ *adj* interfering, meddlesome; offering unwanted advice.—**officiously** *adv.*—**officiousness** *n*.

offing /'ɒfɪŋ/ *n* the near or foreseeable future.

offish /'ɒfɪʃ/ *adj* (*inf*) distant, stiff.

off-key *adj* sung or played in the wrong key; out of tune; out of step.

off-licence *n* a licence to sell alcohol for consumption off the premises; a place so licensed.—*also US* **liquor store, package store**.

off-line *adj* (*comput*) not connected to the central processor; disconnected.

off-load *vt* to unload; to get rid off.

off-piste *adj* pertaining to skiing in areas away from the normal runs.

offprint /'ɒfprɪnt/ *n* a separately printed copy or part of a publication.

off-putting *adj* discouraging, daunting.

off-roading *n* the sport or hobby of driving on dirt tracks or other rugged terrain.—**off-roader** *n*.

offscourings *npl* refuse, dregs.

offset /'ɒfset/ *vt* (**offsetting, offset**) to compensate for, counterbalance. • *n* compensation; a method of printing in which an image is transferred from a plate to a rubber surface and then to paper; a sloping ledge on the face of a wall.

offset printing *n* printing in which the impression is transferred from a plate to a rubber surface and then to paper.

offshoot /'ɒfʃuːt/ *n* a branch or shoot growing from the main stem; something derivative.

offshore /'ɒfʃɔr/ *adv* at sea some distance from the shore.

offside /ɒf'saɪd/ *adj, adv* illegally in advance of the ball.

offspring /'ɒfsprɪŋ/ *n* a child, progeny; a result.

offstage /ɒf'steɪdʒ/ or /'ɒf-/ *adj, adv* out of sight of the audience; behind the scenes.

off-the-peg *adj* (*clothes*) produced ready to wear in standard sizes.

off-the-wall *adj* (*sl*) innovative, unusual, unexpected.

off-white *n, adj* (a) white tinged with yellow or grey.

oft /ɒft/ *adv* (*poet*) often.

often /'ɒfən/ or /'ɒftən/ *adv* many times, frequently.

ogdoad /,ɒgdoː'æd/ *n* eight, a set of eight.

ogee /'ɔːdʒiː/ or /-'dʒiː/ *n* an architectural wave-like moulding shaped like an S.

ogen melon *n* a type of small melon similar to a cantaloupe with sweel orange flesh.

ogham, ogam /'ɒgəm/ *n* an ancient British alphabet, the letters formed by notches; a character in it.

ogive /'ɔːdʒaɪv/ or /-'dʒaɪv/ *n* a diagonal groin of a vault; a pointed arch.—**ogival** *adj*.

ogle /'ɔːgəl/ *vti* (**ogling, ogled**) to gape at; to make eyes at; to look at lustfully.—**ogler** *n*.

Ogpu /'ugpuː/ *n* the secret police of Soviet Russia (1923–34).

ogre /'ɔːgər/ *n* a man-eating giant; a hideous person.

oh /oː/ *interj* expressing surprise, delight, pain, etc.

ohm /oːm/ *n* a unit of electrical resistance.

ohmmeter /'oːm,miːtər/ *n* an instrument for measuring electrical resistance.

oho /oː'hoː/ *interj* an exclamation of surprise.

-oid /ɔɪd/ *suffix* like, as in *spheroid*.

oil /ɔɪl/ *n* any of various greasy, combustible liquid substances obtained from animal, vegetable, and mineral matter; petroleum; an oil painting; (*pl*) paint mixed by grinding a pigment in oil • *vt* to smear with oil, lubricate.—**oiled** *adj*.

oilcake /'ɔɪlkeɪk/ *n* a cattle food of linseed.

oilcan *n* a container with a long spout for releasing oil for lubricating in individual drops.

oilcloth /'ɔɪlklɒθ/ *n* a waterproof fabric impregnated with oil or synthetic resin.

oil colour *n* a colour in which oil is used as a vehicle for pigment.

oiler /'ɔɪlər/ *n* an oilcan; a greaser.

oil field *n* an area on land or under the sea that produces petroleum.

oilman /'ɔɪlmən/ *n* (*pl* **oilmen**) a dealer in oils.

oil painting *n* a painting in oils; the art of painting in oils.

oil palm *n* an African palm whose fruit yields an edible oil.

oil rig *n* a drilling rig for extracting oil or natural gas.

oilskin /'ɔɪlskɪn/ *n* fabric made waterproof by treatment with oil; a waterproof garment of oilskin or a plastic-coated fabric.

oil slick *n* a mass of oil floating on the surface of water.

oil well *n* a well from which petroleum is extracted.

oily /'ɔɪli/ *adj* (**oilier, oiliest**) like or covered with oil; greasy; too suave or smooth, unctuous.—**oiliness** *n*.

oink /ɔɪŋk/ *n* (*inf*) the grunt of a pig.—*also vi*.

ointment /'ɔɪntmənt/ *n* a fatty substance used on the skin for healing or cosmetic purposes; a salve.

Oireachtas /'ɔrəktəs/ *n* the legislature of Ireland, consisting of the president, the Dáil Eireann (the Chamber of Deputies) and the Seanad Eireann (the Senate).

OK, okay /oː'keɪ/ *adj, adv* (*inf*) all right; correct(ly). • *n* (*pl* **OK's, okays**) approval. • *vt* (**OK'ing, OK'ed** *or* **okaying, okayed**) to approve, sanction as OK.

okapi /oː'kæpi/ *n* (*pl* **okapis, okapi**) an African animal allied to the giraffe but smaller and with a shorter neck.

okay *see* **OK**.

okra /'ɔːkrə/ *n* a tall annual plant yielding long seed-pods used as a vegetable.

old /oːld/ *adj* aged; elderly, not young; having lived or existed for a long time; long used, not new; former; of the past, not modern; experienced; worn out; of long standing.

Old Bailey *n* the central criminal court of England.

old boy *n* a former pupil of a school; (*inf*) a friendly form of address; an old person.—**old girl** *nf*.

old boy network *n* (*inf*) the monopoly of power by a privileged elite who attended the best public schools and universities.

Old Catholic *n* one of a body of Roman Catholics who refused to accept the dogma of papal infallibility (1870).

old country *n* the birthplace of an immigrant or an immigrant's ancestors.

olden /'o:ldən/ *adj* relating to a bygone era.

Old English *n* the English language during the 7th to the 11th centuries.—*also* Anglo-Saxon.

Old English sheepdog *n* a breed of sheepdog with an extremely long shaggy coat.

old-fashioned *adj* out of date; in a fashion of an older time.

Old French *n* the French language from the 7th to the early 14th centuries.

Old Glory *n* a nickname for the Stars and Stripes, the US flag.

old gold *adj* of the colour of tarnished gold.

old guard *n* the (original) conservative elements within a political party or other organization.

old hat *adj* old-fashioned, clichéd.

old lady *n* (*inf*) one's wife or mother.

old maid *n* (*derog*) a woman, *esp* an older woman who has never married; a prim, prudish, fussy person.

old man *n* (*inf*) father, husband; (*inf*) someone in charge, *esp* the captain of a ship.

old master *n* a painting by one of the best painters working in Europe in ther 16th and 17th centuries; one of these painters.

Old Nick *n* (*inf*) the Devil.

old school *n* supporters of traditional or conservative values and practices.

old school tie *n* a distinctive tie which indicates which school one attended; the elitism and solidarity use associated with British public schools and their products.

Old Style *n* the old mode of reckoning time acording to the Julian year of 365 and a quarter days.

Old Testament *n* the Christian designation for the Holy Scriptures of Judaism, the first of the two general divisions of the Christian Bible.

old-time *adj* of an earlier period; old-fashioned.

old-timer *n* an old man; a veteran; a person who has been in the same job, position, etc, for many years.

old wives' tale *n* a belief sustained by tradition, not accuracy.

Old World *n* Europe, Asia, and Africa.

old-world *adj* traditional, quaint; antiquated.

oleaginous /ˌo:li'ædʒənəs/ *adj* oily; unctuous.

oleander /ˌo:li'ændər/ *n* a poisonous evergreen shrub with handsome fragrant flowers.

oleaster /ˌo:li'æstər/ *n* the wild olive; a yellow-flowered shrub like it.

oleate /'o:li:ˌeɪt/ *n* a salt of oleic acid.

olefin, olefine /'o:ləfɪn/ *n* a hydrocarbon containing two atoms of hydrogen and one atom of carbon.—**olefinic** *adj*.

oleic /o:'li:ɪk/ *adj* obtained from oil.

oleic acid *n* an oily acid obtained from the saponiication of linseed and other oils, or in the making of soap.

olein /'o:li:ɪn/ *n* the pure liquid part of oil or fat.

oleo- /'o:lio/ *prefix* oil.

oleograph /'o:lioˌgræf/ *n* a lithograph in oil colours.

olfactory /o:l'fæktəri/ or /-ɒl-/ *adj* relating to the sense of smell. • *n* (*pl* **olfactories**) (*usu pl*) an organ of smell.

olibanum /o:'lɪbənəm/ *n* a gum resin used in incense; the frankincense of the ancients.

oligarch /'ɒlɪˌgɑrk/ *n* a member of an oligarchy.

oligarchy /'ɒlɪˌgɑrki/ *n* (*pl* **oligarchies**) government by a small group of people; the members of such a government; a state ruled in this way.—**oligarchic, oligarchical** *adj*.

oligo-, olig- /'ɒlɪgo:/ *prefix* few, small.

Oligocene /'ɒlɪgəˌsi:n/ *n* (*geol*) a term used to denote certain strata intermediate between the Eocene and Miocene.

olio /'o:lio:/ *n* (*pl* **olios**) a hotchpotch, a stew; a miscellany.

olivaceous /ˌɒlɪ'veɪʃəs/ *adj* olive-green.

olivary /'ɒlɪvəri/ *adj* olive-shaped, oval.

olive /'ɒlɪv/ *n* an evergreen tree cultivated for its edible hardstoned fruit and oil; its fruit; a yellow-green colour. • *adj* of a yellow-green colour.

olive branch *n* a gesture of reconciliation of desire to make peace.

olive drab *n a* a dull greyish-olive colour; cloth or clothes in this colour, *esp* the US Army uniform.

olive oil *n* an edible yellow oil obtained from the fruit of the olive by pressing.

olivine /'ɒlɪˌvi:n/ *n* a variety of chrysolite.

olla podrida /ˌɒləpə'dri:də/ *n* a mixed stew or hash of meat and vegetables, a favourite Spanish dish; any incongruous mixture.

ology /'ɒlədʒi/ *n* (*pl* **ologies**) (*sl*) a branch of knowledge, a science.

Olympiad /ə'lɪmpiˌæd/ *n* in ancient Greece, the interval (four years) between the celebration of the Olympic games; a system of chronology reckoning from the first Olympiad, 776 BC.

Olympian /ə'lɪmpiən/ *adj* of Olympus, home of the Greek gods; Olympic; stately; condescending. • *n* a great person.

Olympic /ə'lɪmpɪk/ *adj* pertaining to Olympia in Elis, where the Olympic games were celebrated.

Olympic Games *n sing or pl* an ancient athletic contest revived in 1896 as an international meeting held every four years in a different country.—*also* **Olympics**.

OM *abbr* = Order of Merit.

om /o:m/ *n* (*Hinduism*) the mystic name of the supreme being uttered when invoking Brahma; (*modern occultism*) spiritual essence, supreme truth and virtue.

-oma /'o:mə/ *n suffix* indicating a tumour.

omasum /o:'meɪsəm/ *n* (*pl* **omasa**) the third stomach of ruminant animals.

ombre, omber /'ɒmbər/ *n* an old card game for three players.

ombudsman /'ɒmbədzmən/ or /-bʊdz-/, /-'bɛdz-/ *n* (*pl* **ombudsmen**) an official appointed to investigate citizens' or consumers' complaints.

omega /o:'meɪgə/ or /-'mɛgə/ *n* the last letter of the Greek alphabet.

omelette, omelet /'ɒmlət/ or /-'əlɛt/ *n* eggs beaten and cooked flat in a pan.

omen /'o:mən/ *n* a sign or warning of impending happiness or disaster.

omentum /o:'mɛntəm/ *n* (*pl* **omenta, omentums**) (*anat*) the caul or adipose membrane attached to the stomach.

omerta /o:'mɜrtə/ *n* a conspiracy of silence, *esp* as practised by the Mafia.

omicron /'ɒmɪkrɒn/ or /'o:-/ *n* the 15th letter of the Greek alphabet.

ominous /'ɒmənəs/ *adj* relating to an omen; foreboding evil; threatening.—**ominously** *adv*.

omission /o:'mɪʃən/ *n* something that has been left out or neglected; the act of omitting.

omit /o:'mɪt/ *vt* (**omitting, omitted**) to leave out; to neglect to do, leave undone.

omni- /'ɒmni/ *prefix* all; universally.

omnibus /'ɒmnɪbəs/ *n* (*pl* **omnibuses**) (*formal*) a bus; a book containing several works *usu* by one author.

omnifarious /ˌɒmnɪ'fɛriəs/ *adj* of all kinds.

omnipotent /ɒm'nɪpətənt/ *adj* all-powerful, almighty; having very great power.—**omnipotence** *n*.

omnipresent /ˌɒmnɪ'prɛzənt/ *adj* present everywhere, uniquitous.—**omnipresence** *n*.

omniscient /ɒm'nɪsiənt/ or /-ʃənt/ *adj* knowing all things.—**omnisciently** *adv*.—**omniscience** *n*.

omnium-gatherum /ˌɒmniəm'gæθərəm/ *n* a miscellaneous collection of persons or things.

omnivore /'ɒmnɪˌvɔr/ *n* an omnivorous animal or person.

omnivorous /ɒm'nɪvərəs/ *adj* eating any sort of food; taking in everything indiscriminately.

omophagic /omo'fægɪk/, **omophagous** /-gəs/ *adj* eating raw flesh.—**omophagia** *n*.

omphalos /'ɒmfəˌlɒs/ *n* centre, hub; (*ancient Greece*) a boss on a shield.

on /ɒn/ *prep* in contact with the upper surface of; supported by, attached to, or covering; directed toward; at the time of; concerning, about; using as a basis, condition or principle; immediately after; (*sl*) using; addicted to. • *adv* (so as to be) covering or in contact with something; forward; (*device*) switched on; continuously in progress; due to take place; (*actor*) on stage; on duty. • *adj* (*cricket*) designating the part of the field on the batsman's side in front of the wicket. • *n* (*cricket*) the on side.

onager /'ɒnəgər/ *n* (*pl* **onagri, onagers**) the wild ass.

onanism /'o:nəˌnɪzəm/ *n* masturbation; coitus interruptus.—**onanist** *n, adj*.

once /wʌns/ *adv* on one occasion only; formerly; at some time. • *conj* as soon as. • *n* one time.

once-over *n* a preliminary survey.

onco- /ˈɒnkoː/ *prefix* swelling, tumour.

oncology /ɒnˈkɒlədʒi/ *n* the branch of medicine dealing with tumours.—**oncologist** *n*.

oncoming /ˈɒnˌkʌmɪŋ/ *adj* approaching.

one /wʌn/ *adj* single; undivided, united; the same; a certain unspecified (time, etc). • *n* the first and lowest cardinal number; an individual thing or person; (*inf*) a drink; (*inf*) a joke. • *pron* an indefinite person, used to apply to many people; someone.

one-armed bandit *n* (*inf*) a slot machine for gambling, operated by pulling down a lever on its side.

one-horse *adj* (*sl*) paltry.

oneiro- /əˈnaɪroː/ *prefix* dream.

one-liner *n* (*inf*) a brief joke or witty comment.

oneness /ˈwʌnnəs/ *n* unity, singleness, concord.

one-night stand *n* a performance given for one night only in a certain place; (*inf*) (a partner in) a sexual liaison that lasts one night only.

one-off *n, adj* (something) performed or made only once.

onerous /ˈɒnərəs/ or /ˈoːn-/ *adj* oppressive, burdensome; troublesome.

oneself /wʌnˈsɛlf/ *pron reflex form of* one.

one-sided *adj* favouring one side; unequal.

one-time *adj* sometime, former.

one-track *adj* with a single line of rails; with room for only one idea at a time.

one-upmanship /wʌnˈʌpmənʃɪp/ *n* the skill of being one jump ahead of or going one better than someone or something else.

one-way *adj* (*traffic*) restricted to one direction; requiring no reciprocal action or obligation.

ongoing /ˈɒnˌɡoːɪŋ/ *adj* progressing, continuing.

onion /ˈʌnjən/ *n* an edible bulb with a pungent taste and odour.

on-line *adj* referring to equipment that is connected to and controlled by the central processor of a computer.

onlooker /ˈɒnˌlʊkər/ *n* a spectator.

only /ˈoːnli/ *adj* alone of its kind; single, sole. • *adv* solely, merely; just; not more than. • *conj* except that, but.

onoma- /ˈɒnoːmə/ *prefix* name.

onomastic /ˌɒnəˈmæstɪk/ *adj* of or pertaining to a name or names.

onomastics /ˌɒnəˈmæstɪks/ *n sing* the study of proper names.

onomatopoeia /ˌɒnəˌmætəˈpiːə/ *n* the formation of a word to imitate a sound.—**onomatopoeic** *adj*.

onrush /ˈɒnrʌʃ/ *n* a powerful rushing forwards.

onset /ˈɒnsɛt/ *n* a beginning; an assault, attack.

onshore /ˈɒnʃɔr/ *adj, adv* towards the land; on land, not the sea.

onslaught /ˈɒnslɒt/ *n* a fierce attack.

onto /ˈɒntuː/ *prep* to a position on.

onto- /ɒntə-/ *prefix* being.

ontogeny, ontogenesis /ɒnˈtɒdʒəni/ *n* (*biol*) the history of the evolution of individual organisms.—**ontogenic, ontogenetic** *adj*.

ontology /ɒnˈtɒlədʒi/ *n* (*philos*) the logic of pure being or reality; metaphysics.—**ontological** *adj*.—**ontologically** *adv*.

onus /ˈoːnəs/ *n* (*pl* **onuses**) responsibility, duty; burden.

onward /ˈɒnwərd/ *adj* advancing, forward. • *adv* to the front, ahead, forward.

onwards /ˈɒnwərdz/ *adv* onward.

onyx /ˈɒnɪks/ *n* a limestone similar to marble with layers of colour.

oo- /oːə/ *prefix* egg.

oodles /ˈuːdəlz/ *npl* (*sl*) an abundance.

oogamous /oːˈɒɡəməs/ *adj* heterogamous.

oogenesis /ˌoːəˈdʒɛnɪsɪs/ *n* the formation of an ovum.—**oogenetic** *adj*.

ooh /uː/ *interj* expressing surprise, delight, pain, etc.

oolite /ˈoːəˌlaɪt/ *n* a limestone composed of grains like the roe of a fish.—**oolitic** *adj*.

oology /oːˈɒlədʒi/ *n* the scientific study of birds' eggs; a treatise on birds' eggs.—**oological** *adj*.—**oologist** *n*.

oolong /ˈuːlɒŋ/ *n* a Chinese black tea the flavour of which resembles green tea.

oomiak *see* **umiak**.

oompah /ˈuːmpɒ/ *n* an imitation of the deep sound of a brass instrument such as the tuba.

oomph /ˈuːmf/ *n* (*inf*) energy, verve; sex appeal.

oops /uːps/ or /ʊps/ *interj* expressing surprise or apology, *esp* when making a mistake.

oosperm /ˈuːspɔrm/ *n* a fertilized ovum.

ootheca /uːˈθiːkə/ *n* (*pl* **oothecae**) the egg case of certain molluscs and insects containing the eggs.—**oothecal** *adj*.

ooze /uːz/ *vti* to flow or leak out slowly; to seep; to exude. • *n* soft mud or slime.

op. *abbr* = opera; operation; operator; optical; opposite; opus.

op- /ɒp/ *prefix* form of *ob-* before *p*.

opacity /oːˈpæsɪti/ *n* (*pl* **opacities**) the state of being opaque; obscurity.

opah /ˈoːpə/ *n* a bright-coloured sea fish like the mackerel, the kingfish.

opal /ˈoːpəl/ *n* a white or bluish stone with a play of iridescent colours.

opalescent /ˌoːpəˈlɛsənt/ *adj* resembling opal in its reflection of light, iridescent.—**opalescence** *n*.

opaline /ˈoːpəˌlaɪn/ *adj* pertaining to or resembling the opal.

opaque /oːˈpeɪk/ *adj* not letting light through; neither transparent nor translucent.—**opaquely** *adv*.—**opaqueness** *n*.

op. cit. *abbr* = (*Latin*) in the work cited.

OPEC /ˈoːpɛk/ *abbr* = Organization of Petroleum Exporting Countries.

open /ˈoːpən/ *adj* not closed; accessible; uncovered, unprotected; not fenced; free from trees; spread out, unfolded; public; lacking reserve; (*a person*) forthcoming; generous; readily understood; liable (to); unrestricted; (*syllable*) ending with a vowel; (*consonant*) made without stopping the stream of breath. • *vti* to make or become accessible; to unfasten; to begin; to expand, unfold; to come into view. • *n* a wide space; (*sport*) a competition that any player can enter.—**openness** *n*.

open air *n* outdoors.

open-and-shut *adj* easily solved; straightforward.

opencast mining *see* **strip mining**.

open-ended *adj* with no fixed limit of time or amount.

open-eyed *adj* vigilant.

opener /ˈoːpənər/ or /ˈoːpnər/ *n* a device for opening cans or bottles.

openhanded *adj* generous.—**openhandedness** *n*.

openhearted *adj* responsive to emotional appeal, frank.—**openheartedness** *n*.

open-heart surgery *n* surgery on the heart whilst its function is performed temporarily by a heart-lung machine.

opening /ˈoːpənɪŋ/ or /ˈoːpnɪŋ/ *n* a gap, aperture; a beginning; a chance; a job opportunity. • *adj* initial.

open letter *n* a letter addressed to an individual but published in a newspaper for all to see.

openly /ˈoːpənli/ *adv* frankly; publicly.

open-minded *adj* unprejudiced.—**open-mindedness** *n*.

open-mouthed *adj* having the mouth open in surprise; gaping, expectant.

open secret *n* a supposed secret which is actually widely known.

open sesame *n* a way of getting into something usually inaccessible.

openwork /ˈoːpənˌwɜrk/ *n* a pattern with interstices.

opera /ˈɒpərə/ or /ˈɒprə/ *n* a dramatic work represented through music and song; plural form of **opus**.

operable /ˈɒpərəbəl/ *adj* capable of being put into action, practicable; (*med*) capable of being operated upon.

opera bouffe /ˌɒpərəˈbuːf/ *n* a comic or farcical opera.

opera glasses *n* a small binocular telescope used in theatres, etc.

opera hat *n* a man's collapsible top hat.

opera house *n* a theatre for opera.

operate /ˈɒpəˌreɪt/ *vi* to work, to function; to produce a desired effect; to carry out a surgical operation. • *vt* (*a machine*) to work or control; to carry on, run.

operatic /ˌɒpəˈrætɪk/ *adj* of or relating to opera; exaggerated, overacting.

operating system *n* the software in a computer which controls basic operations such as accepting keyboard input, printing, file handling and displaying error messages.

operation /ˌɒpəˈreɪʃən/ *n* a method of operating; a procedure; a military action; a surgical procedure.

operational /ˌɒpəˈreɪʃənəl/ *adj* of or relating to an operation; functioning; ready for use; involved in military activity.—**operationally** *adv*.

operations research, operational research *n* the application of mathematical techniques to the analysis of business methods.

operative /ˈɒpərətɪv/ or /ˈɒprətɪv/ *adj* functioning; in force, effective; of, by surgery. • *n* a mechanic; a secret agent; a private detective.

operator /'ɒpəˌreɪtər/ n a person who operates or works a machine, esp a telephone switchboard; a person who owns or runs a business; a person who manipulates.

operculum /ə'pɔrkjuləm/ or /ɔː'p–/ n (pl **opercula, operculums**) (biol) a cap, lid, or cover; the plate closing the orifice of a univalve; a shell; the gill cover of a fish.—**opercular, operculate** adj.

operetta /ˌɒpə'rɛtə/ n a light opera.

ophidian /ɒ'fɪdɪən/ n any of the Ophidia, an order of reptiles including the snakes.—also adj.

ophiology /ˌɒfɪ'ɒlədʒɪ/ n that branch of natural history which treats of snakes.—**ophiological** adj.—**ophiologist** n.

ophite /ɒ'faɪt/ n serpentine marble.

ophthalmia /ɒf'θælmɪə/ or /ɒp–/ n inflammation of the eye.

ophthalmic /ɒf'θælmɪk/ or /ɒp–/ adj of, relating to, or situated near, the eye.

ophthalmo-, ophthalm- /ɒf'θælmə/ or /ɒp–/ prefix eye or eyeball.

ophthalmology /ˌɒpθæl'mɒlədʒɪ/ or /ɒf–/ n the branch of medicine dealing with diseases of the eye.—**ophthalmologist** n.

ophthalmoscope /ɒf'θælməˌskəʊp/ or /ɒp–/ n an instrument for examining the interior of the eye.

ophthalmoscopy /–i/ n examination of the eye.—**ophthalmoscopic** adj.

-opia /'əʊpɪə/ n suffix indicating a visual defect.

opiate /'əʊpɪət/ n a narcotic drug that contains opium; something that induces sleep or calms feelings.

opine /əʊ'paɪn/ vt to hold or express the opinion (that).

opinicus /əʊ'pɪnɪkəs/ n (her) a fabulous winged animal with the head and wings of a griffin, the body of a lion, and the tail of a camel.

opinion /ə'pɪnjən/ n a belief that is not based on proof; judgment; estimation, evaluation; a formal expert judgment; professional advice.

opinionated /ə'pɪnjəˌneɪtəd/ adj unduly confident in one's opinions, dogmatic.

opinionative /–tɪv/ adj fond of preconceived ideas; self-conceited.—**opinionatively** adv.

opium /'əʊpɪəm/ n a narcotic drug produced from an annual Eurasian poppy.

opossum /ə'pɒsəm/ n (pl **opossums, opossum**) a small nocturnal and arboreal marsupial.

oppidan /'ɒpɪˌdæn/ adj urban, town-dwelling.

oppilate /'ɒpəˌleɪt/ vt (med) to block up, to obstruct.—**oppilation** n.

opponent /ə'pəʊnənt/ n a person who opposes another; an adversary, antagonist. • adj opposing.

opportune /ˌɒpər'tuːn/ or /–tjuːn/ adj well-timed; convenient.—**opportunely** adv.

opportuneness /–nəs/ n seasonableness.

opportunist /–ɪst/ n a person who forms or adapts his or her views or principles to benefit from opportunities; to seize opportunities as they may arise.—**opportunism** n.

opportunity /ˌɒpər'tuːnəti/ or /–'tjuːn–/ n (pl **opportunities**) chance; a favourable combination of circumstances.

opposable /ə'pəʊzəbəl/ adj that may be opposed.—**opposability** n.—**opposably** adv.

oppose /ə'pəʊz/ vt to put in front of or in the way of; to place in opposition; to resist; to fight against; to balance against.—**opposer** n.

opposite /'ɒpəzɪt/ adj placed on opposed sides of; face to face; diametrically different; contrary. • n a person or thing that is opposite; an antithesis. • prep, adv across from.

opposite number n a person in a corresponding position on the other side; a counterpart.

opposition /ˌɒpə'zɪʃən/ n the act of opposing or the condition of being opposed; resistance; antithesis; hostility; a political party opposing the government; (astron) the diametrically opposite position of two heavenly bodies, when 180 degrees apart.

oppress /ə'prɛs/ vt to treat unjustly; to subjugate; to weigh down in the mind.—**oppressor** n.

oppression /ə'prɛʃən/ n the act of oppressing; the state of being oppressed; persecution; physical or mental distress.

oppressive /ə'prɛsɪv/ adj tyrannical; burdensome; (weather) sultry, close.—**oppressively** adv.—**oppressiveness** n.

opprobrious /ə'prəʊbrɪəs/ adj abusive; infamous.

opprobrium /ə'prəʊbrɪəm/ n a reproach with disdain or contempt; disgrace, ignominy.

oppugn /ə'pjuːn/ vt to reason against, to controvert; to resist.—**oppugnant** adj, n.—**oppugner** n.

opsonin /'ɒpsənɪn/ n a chemical agent in blood serum, which makes bacteria vulnerable to phagocytic activity.—**opsonic** adj.

opt /ɒpt/ vi to choose, to exercise an option; (with **in**) to choose to participate in something; (with **out**) to choose not to participate in something.

optative /'ɒptətɪv/ or /ɒp'teɪtɪv/ adj (gram) expressing a desire or wish. • n an optative mood or form of a verb.

optic /'ɒptɪk/ adj relating to the eye or sight. • n (inf) the eye; a device for dispensing a standard measure of spirits, etc.

optical /'ɒptɪkəl/ adj of or relating to the eye or light; optic; aiding or correcting vision; visual.—**optically** adv.

optical character reader n a device that allows printed characters, figures, etc to be scanned and input to a computer, by a process of optical character recognition, the identification of printed text by photoelectric means.

optical disc n a compact disc used as a high-capacity storage medium for computers.

optical fibre n thin glass fibre through which light can be transmitted.

optician /ɒp'tɪʃən/ n a person who makes or sells optical aids.

optics /'ɒptɪks/ n sing the branch of physics dealing with light and vision.

optimal /'ɒptɪməl/ adj optimum.—**optimally** adv.

optimism /'ɒptɪˌmɪzəm/ n a tendency to take the most cheerful view of things; hopefulness; the belief that good must ultimately prevail.—**optimist** n.—**optimistic** adj.—**optimistically** adv.

optimum /'ɒptɪməm/ n (pl **optima, optimums**) the best, most favourable condition.—also adj.

option /'ɒpʃən/ n the act of choosing; the power to choose; a choice; the right to buy, sell or lease at a fixed price within a specified time.

optional /'ɒpʃənəl/ adj left to choice; not compulsory.—**optionally** adv.

optometer /'ɒptəˌmɪtər/ n an instrument for measuring the limits of distinct vision.

opulent /'ɒpjʊlənt/ adj wealthy; luxuriant.—**opulence** n.

opuntia /ɒ'pʊnʃɪə/ n any of a genus of cacti; the Indian fig.

opus /'əʊpəs/ n (pl **opuses, opera**) an artistic or literary work; a musical composition, esp any of the numbered works of a composer.

or[1] /ɔːr/ or /ər/ conj denoting an alternative; the last in a series of choices.

or[2] n (her) gold, denoted by small engraved dots.

ora see **os**[1].

orach, orache /'ɒrɪtʃ/ n mountain spinach.

oracle /'ɒrəkəl/ or /'ɒ–/ n a place in ancient Greece where a deity was consulted; the response given (often ambiguous); a wise adviser; sage advice.—**oracular** adj.

oral /'ɔːrəl/ adj of the mouth; spoken, not written; (drugs) taken by mouth. • n a spoken examination.—**orally** adv.

oral history n the history of past events as recorded from interviews with people living at the time.

orange /'ɒrɪndʒ/ or /'ɒ–/ n a round, reddish-yellow, juicy, edible citrus fruit; the tree bearing it; its colour. • adj orange-coloured.

orangeade /ˌɒrɪndʒ'eɪd/ or /'ɒ–/ n a drink made with the juice of oranges.

Orangeman /'ɒrɪndʒmən/ n (pl **Orangemen**) a member of an Irish protestant society, named after William of Orange.

orangery /'ɒrɪndʒəri/ or /–dʒri/, /'ɒ–/ n (pl **orangeries**) a hothouse for the cultivation of oranges; an orange garden.

orange stick n a small thin pointed stick, orig orangewood, used in manicuring the nails.

orang-utan, orangoutang /ɔːˌræŋuː'tæn/ n a large, long-armed, herbivorous anthropoid ape.

orate /ɒ'reɪt/ or /'ɔːr–/ vi to make an oration; (inf) to hold forth.

oration /ɒ'reɪʃən/ or /ər–/ n a formal or public speech.

orator /'ɒrətər/ or /'ɒ–/ n an eloquent public speaker.—**oratorical** adj.

oratorio /ˌɒrə'tɔːrɪəʊ/ or /ˌɒ–/ n (pl **oratorios**) a sacred story set to music for voices and instruments.

oratory /'ɒrəˌtɔːri/ or /'ɒ–/ n (pl **oratories**) the art of public speaking; eloquence; a place for prayer.

orb /ɔːrb/ n a sphere or globe; an ornamental sphere surmounted by a cross, esp as carried by a sovereign at a coronation.

orbicular, orbiculate, orbiculated /ɔr'bɪkjʊlər/ *adj* orb-shaped, spherical.—**orbicularity** *n*.

orbit /'ɔrbɪt/ *n* (*astron*) a curved path along which a planet or satellite moves; a field of action or influence; the eye socket; (*physics*) the path of an electron around the nucleus of an atom. • *vti* to put (a satellite, etc) into orbit; to circle round.—**orbital** *adj*.

orca /'ɔrkə/ *n* a grampus; the killer whale; a sea monster.

orchard /'ɔrtʃərd/ *n* an area of land planted with fruit trees.

orchestra /'ɔrkəstrə/ *n* a group of musicians playing together under a conductor; their instruments; the space (or pit) in a theatre where they sit; the stalls of a theatre.—**orchestral** *adj*.

orchestrate /'ɔrkə,streit/ *vt* to arrange music for performance by an orchestra; to arrange, organize to best effect.—**orchestration** *n*.—**orchestrator** *n*.

orchestrion /ɔr'kɛsfriən/ *n* a large automatic barrel organ.

orchid /'ɔrkɪd/ *n* a plant with unusually shaped flowers in brilliant colours comprising three petals of uneven size.

orchil /'ɔrtʃɪl/ *n* a red or violet dye obtained from lichen; the lichen.—*also* **archil**.

orchis /'ɔrtʃɪs/ *n* a genus of wild orchid with curiously shaped roots and flowers.

orcinol, orcin /'ɔrsɪn/ *n* a substance obtained from lichens yielding dye.

ordain /ɔr'deɪn/ *vti* to confer holy orders upon; to appoint; to decree; to order, to command.—**ordainer** *n*.—**ordainment** *n*.

ordeal /ɔr'diːl/ *n* a severe trial or test; an exacting experience.

order /'ɔrdər/ *n* arrangement; method; relative position; sequence; an undistinguished condition; tidiness; rules of procedure; an efficient state; a class, group, or sort; a religious fraternity; a style of architecture; an honour or decoration; an instruction or command; a rule or regulation; a state or condition, *esp* with regard to functioning; a request to supply something; the goods supplied; (*zool*) divisions between class and family or genus. • *vti* to put or keep (things) in order; to arrange; to command; to request (something) to be supplied.

ordered /'ɔrdərd/ *adj* marked by regularity and discipline; being arranged or identifiable according to a rule; being labelled by ordinal numbers.

orderly /'ɔrdərli/ *adj* in good order; well-behaved; methodical. • *n* (*pl* **orderlies**) a hospital attendant; a soldier attending an officer.—**orderliness** *n*.

ordinal /'ɔrdɪnəl/ *adj* showing position in a series. • *n* an ordinal number.

ordinal number *n* a number denoting its order in a sequence, as first, second, etc.

ordinance /'ɔrdɪnəns/ *n* a decree, a law; a rite.

ordinary /'ɔrdɪneri/ *adj* normal, usual; common; plain, unexceptional.• *n* (*pl* **ordinaries**) a meal for all comers at fixed charges and a fixed time, an inn providing this; archbishop in province, bishop in diocese; prescribed form of service; an ecclesiastical judge; a prison chaplain; (*her*) that part of the escutcheon contained between straight and other lines one of the simple charges.—**ordinarily** *adv*.

ordinary seaman *n* a seaman of the lowest rank, below able-bodied seaman

ordinate /'ɔrdɪnət/ *n* (*geom*) one of the co-ordinates of a point; a straight line in a curve terminated on both sides by the curve and bisected by the diameter.

ordination /,ɔrdɪ'neɪʃən/ *n* the act of ordaining or being ordained; admission to the ministry.

ordnance /'ɔrdnəns/ *n* military stores; artillery.

Ordovician /,ɔrdə'vɪsɪən/ or /,ɔrdoː'vɪʃiən/ *adj* (*geol*) of the period between the Cambrian and Silurian.

ordure /'ɔrdjʊr/ *n* excrement; dung.

ore /ɔr/ *n* a substance from which minerals can be extracted.

öre /'ʊrə/ or /'ərə/ *n* (*pl* **öre**) a monetary unit in Sweden, (Øre) Denmark and Norway.

oread /'ɔri,æd/ *n* a mountain nymph (Greek).

oregano /ɔ'rɛgənoː/ *n* an aromatic herb whose leaves, either fresh of dried, are used to flavour food.

organ /'ɔrgən/ *n* a *usu* large and complex musical wind instrument with pipes, stops, and a keyboard; a part of an animal or plant that performs a vital or natural function; the means by which anything is done; a medium of information or opinion, a periodical.

organdy, organdie /'ɔrgəndi/ *n* (*pl* **organdies**) a light transparent, *usu* stiffened cotton fabric.

organ grinder *n* the player of a barrel organ.

organic /ɔr'gænɪk/ *adj* of or relating to bodily organs; (disease) affecting a bodily organ; of, or derived from, living organisms; systematically arranged; structural; (*chem*) of the class of compounds that are formed from carbon; (vegetables, etc) grown without the use of artificial fertilizers or pesticides.—**organically** *adv*.

organism /'ɔrgə,nɪzəm/ *n* an animal or plant, any living thing; an organized body.

organist /'ɔrgənɪst/ *n* a person who plays an organ.

organization /,ɔrgənaɪ'zeɪʃən/ or /-nɪ-/, /-nə-/ *n* the act or process of organizing; the state of being organized; arrangement, structure; an organized body or association.

organize /'ɔrgə,naɪz/ *vt* to arrange in an orderly way; to establish; to institute; to persuade to join a cause, group, etc; to arrange for.—**organizer** *n*.

organogenesis /,ɔrgəno:'dʒɛnɪsɪs/ or /ɔr'gæno:-/ *n* organic development.—**organogenetic** *adj*.—**organogenetically** *adv*.

organography /,ɔrgə'nɛgrəfi/ *n* a scientific description of the organs of animals or plants.—**organographic** *adj*.

organology /,ɔrgə'nɒlədʒi/ *n* that branch of physiology which treats of animal organs.—**organological** *adj*.—**organologist** *n*.

organon /'ɔrgə,nɒn/ *n* (*pl* **organa, organons**) a body of rules for regulating scientific or philosophical investigation; a method of thought, a logical system.

organotherapy /,ɔrgəno:θɛrəpi/ *n* the treatment of disease with organic extracts.

organzine /'ɔrgən,zaɪn/ *n* a strong silk thread of a very fine texture; a fabric made from it.

orgasm /'ɔrgæzəm/ *n* the climax of sexual excitement.—**orgasmic** *adj*.

orgeat /'ɔrdʒiət/ or /-ʒæt/ *n* a drink made of barley water flavoured with almonds.

orgy /'ɔrgi/ *n* (*pl* **orgies**) a wild party or gathering of people, with excessive drinking and indiscriminate sexual activity; overindulgence in any activity.—**orgiastic** *adj*.

oriel /'ɔriəl/ *n* a projecting angular recess with a window; the window.

orient /'ɔri,ɛnt/ or /'ɒr-/, /-ənt/ *n* the East, or Asia, *esp* the Far East.

orient, orientate /'ɔri,ɛnt/ or /'ɒr-/, /'ɔriɛn,teɪt/ *vti* to adjust (oneself) to a particular situation; to arrange in a direction, *esp* in relation to the points of the compass; to face or turn in a particular direction.

oriental /,ɔri'ɛntəl/ or /,ɒr-/ *adj* (*often cap*) of the Orient, its people or languages.

Orientalism /ɔri:'ɛntəlɪzəm/ or /ɒr-/ *n* an idiom or custom characteristic of the East.

Orientalist /-ɪst/ *n* an expert in Oriental languages, history, etc.

orientation /,ɔri:ɛn'teɪʃən/ or /,ɒr-/ *n* arrangement; alignment; position relative to a compass direction; one's way of thinking or direction of interest.

orienteering /,ɔriɛn'tiːrɪŋ/ or /,ɒr-/ *n* the sport of racing on foot over difficult country using a map and compass.

orifice /'ɔrɪfɪs/ or /'ɒr-/ *n* an opening or mouth of a cavity.

oriflamme /'ɔri,flæm/ or /'ɒr-/ *n* the ancient royal standard of France, a red flag split at one end and forming flame-shaped streamers; a party symbol; a blaze of colour.

orig. *abbr* = origin; original(ly).

origami /,ɔri'gæmi/ or /,ɒr/ *n* the Japanese art of paper folding to make complicated shapes.

origin /'ɔridʒɪn/ or /'ɒr-/ *n* the source or beginning of anything; ancestry or parentage.

original /ə'rɪdʒɪnəl/ *adj* relating to the origin or beginning; earliest, primitive; novel; unusual; inventive, creative. • *n* an original work, as of art or literature; something from which copies are made; a creative person; an eccentric.—**originality** *n*.—**originally** *adv*.

original sin *n* the inherent tendency of mankind to sin, derived from Adam and imputed to his descendants.

originate /ə'rɪdʒɪ,neɪt/ *vti* to initiate or begin; to bring or come into being.—**origination** *n*.—**originator** *n*.

orinasal /,ɔri'neɪzəl/ *adj* (*vowel*) sounded with both the mouth and nose.—*also n*.

oriole /'ɔriəl/ or /-oːl/ *n* kinds of yellow, black-winged bird.

orison /'ɔrɪzən/ or /'ɒr-/ *n* (*arch*) a prayer.

orle /ɔrl/ *n* (*her*) an ordinary in the form of a fillet round a shield; (*archit*) a fillet under the capital of a column.

Orlon /'ɔrlɒn/ *n* (*trademark*) an acrylic fibre.

orlop /'ɔrlɒp/ *n* the lowest deck of a ship with three or more decks.

ormer /'ɔrmər/ *n* a mollusc, sea ear.

ormolu /'ɔrmǝluː/ *n* an imitation gold made of copper and tin alloy, used for decoration.

ornament /'ɔrnǝmǝnt/ *n* anything that enhances the appearance of a person or thing; a small decorative object. • *vt* to adorn, to decorate with ornaments.

ornamental /ˌɔrnǝ'mɛntǝl/ *adj* serving as an ornament; decorative, not useful.—**ornamentally** *adv.*

ornamentation /-'teɪʃǝn/ *n* the act or process of ornamenting; something that decorates.

ornate /ɔr'neɪt/ *adj* richly adorned; (*style*) highly elaborate.—**ornately** *adv.*—**ornateness** *n.*

ornery /'ɔrnǝri/ *adj* (*sl*) of a bad disposition, hard to manage.

ornitho- /'ɔrnɪθoː/, **ornith-** /'ɔrnɪθ/ *prefix* bird.

ornithology /ˌɔrnɪ'θɒlǝdʒi/ *n* the study of birds.—**ornithological** *adj.*—**ornithologically** *adv.*—**ornithologist** *n.*

ornithopter /'ɔrnɪθɒptǝr/ *n* an aircraft with flapping wings.

ornithorhynchus /ˌɔrnɪθǝ'ræŋkǝs/ *n* an Australian genus of monotremes, including the platypus.

oro- /'ɔroː/ *prefix* mountain.

orogeny /oː'rɒdʒɪni/, **orogenesis** /ˌɔroː'dʒɛnɪsɪs/ *n* the formation of mountains.—**orogenic, orogenetic** *adj.*

orography, orology /oː'rɒgrǝfi/ *n* the geography of mountains and mountain systems, their mapping, etc.—**orographic, orological** *adj.*

oroide /oː'rɔɪd/ *n* a gold-coloured alloy of tin and copper.

orotund /'ɒrǝˌtʌnd/ or /'ɔr-/ *adj* (*voice*) full, resonant; (*style*) pompous, high-flown.

orphan /'ɔrfǝn/ *n* a child whose parents are dead. • *vt* to cause to become an orphan.—*also adj.*

orphanage /'ɔrfǝnɪdʒ/ *n* a residential institution for the care of orphans.

Orphean /'ɔrfijǝn/ *adj* of or pertaining to Orpheus, the celebrated bard of Classic mythology, or his music; melodious, enchanting.

Orphic /'ɔrfɪk/ *adj* of Orpheus or his cult; mystical.

orphrey /'ɔrfri/ *n* an embroidered band or bands of gold or silver on the front of an ecclesiastical vestment from the neck downward, *esp* on a cope.

orpiment /'ɔrpɪmǝnt/ *n* a yellow compound of arsenic, used as a pigment.

orpine /'ɔrpɪn/ *n* a succulent plant with fleshy leaves and purple flowers.

orrery /'ɒrǝri/ *n* (*pl* **orreries**) a moving model of the solar system, which illustrates by balls mounted on rods the motions, magnitudes, and positions of the planets.

orris /'ɒrɪs/ or /'ɒr-/ *n* a kind of iris.

orrisroot /'ɒrɪsˌruːt/ or /'ɒr-/ *n* the dried roots of the Florentine orris, used in perfumery and medicine.

ortho- /'ɔrθoː/ *prefix* straight, right, true.

orthocephalic /ˌɔrθoːsɛ'fælɪk/, **orthocephalous** /-fælǝs/ *adj* (*anat*) with a skull of medium proportions, between brachycephalic and dolichocephalic.

orthochromatic /ˌɔrθoːkroː'mætɪk/ *adj* (*photog*) giving the correct relative tones to colours, isochromatic.

orthoclase /'ɔrθoːˌkleɪs/ *n* potash feldspar.

orthodontics /ˌɔrθǝ'dɒntɪks/ *n sing* the branch of dentistry dealing with the correction of irregularities in the teeth.—**orthodontic** *adj.*—**orthodontist** *n.*

orthodox /'ɔrθǝˌdɒks/ *adj* conforming with established behaviour or opinions; not heretical; generally accepted, conventional; (*with cap*) of or relating to a conservative political or religious group.

orthodoxy /'ɔrθǝˌdɒksi/ *n* (*pl* **orthodoxies**) the state or quality of being orthodox; an orthodox practice or belief.

orthoepy /'ɔrθoːˌɛpi/ or /ɔr'θoːɪpi/ *n* the science of correct pronunciation.—**orthoepic** *adj.*—**orthepist** *n.*

orthogenesis /ˌɔrθoː'dʒɛnɪsɪs/ *n* evolution following a definite line, determinate variation.—**orthogenetic** *adj.*

orthognathous /ˌɔr'θɒˌnǝθǝs/ *adj* having an upright jaw, neither receding nor protruding.—**orthognathism** *n.*

orthogonal /ɔr'θɒgǝnǝl/ *adj* rectangular.—**orthogonally** *adv.*

orthography /ɔr'θɒgrǝfi/ *n* (*pl* **orthographies**) the art of spelling and writing words with grammatical correctness; a map projection with a point of sight supposedly infinitely distant.—**orthographer** *n.*—**orthographic, orthographical** *adj.*

orthopaedics, orthopedics /ˌɔrθǝ'piːdɪks/ *n* the study and surgical treatment of bone and joint disorders.—**orthopaedic** *adj.*—**orthopaedist** *n.*

orthopteran /ɔr'θɒptǝrǝn/ *n* (*pl* **orthopterans, orthoptera**) any of the Orthoptera order of insects, having their two outer wings overlapping at the top when shut, as in grasshoppers.—**orthopterous** *adj.*

orthoptic /ɔr'θɒptɪk/ *adj* of correct seeing. • *n* the peep-sight of a rifle.

orthotropism /ˌɔrθoː'trɒpɪzǝm/ *n* vertical growth in plants.—**orthotropic** *adj.*—**orthotropous** *adj.*

ortolan /'ɔrtǝlǝn/ *n* a small bird, allied to the bunting, much esteemed for its flesh.

oryx /'ɒrɪks/ *n* (*pl* **oryxes, oryx**) a straight-horned African antelope.

OS *abbr* = ordinary seaman; Ordnance Survey (national mapping agency in the UK).

Os (*chem symbol*) osmium.

os[1] *n* (*pl* **ossa**) (*anat*) bone.

os[2] *n* (*pl* **ora**) (*anat*) the mouth.

Oscar /'ɒskǝr/ *n* any of several small gold statuettes awarded annually by the US Academy of Motion Picture Arts and Sciences for outstanding achievements.

oscillate /'ɒsɪˌleɪt/ *vi* to swing back and forth as a pendulum; to waver, vacillate between extremes of opinion, etc.—**oscillation** *n.*

oscillator /-tǝr/ *n* a device for producing alternating current.

oscillatory /ɒ'sɪlǝtǝri/ or /'ɒsɪˌleɪtǝri/ *adj* swinging; vibrating.

oscilloscope /ǝ'sɪlǝˌskoːp/ *n* a device for viewing oscillations on a display screen of a cathode-ray tube.

osculate /'ɒskjuˌleɪt/ *vti* (*species*) to have features in common; (*geom*) to make contact (with); (*humorous*) to kiss, to touch.—**osculation** *n.*

osculatory /'ɒskjulǝtǝri/ *adj* pertaining to kissing. • *n* a tablet or board on which the picture of Christ or the Virgin Mary are painted for worshippers to kiss.

-ose /oːs/ or /oːz/ *suffix* full of.

osier /'oːziǝr/ *n* a willow, the twigs of which are used in basketmaking.

Osiris /oː'saɪrɪs/ *n* the best loved of the Egyptian gods, husband of Iris and father of Horus.

-osis /'oːsɪs/ *n suffix* indicating a particular state, *esp* a diseased condition, *thrombosis*; increase, development of, *fibrosis*.

Osmanli /ɒz'mænli/ or /ɒs-/ *adj* of or pertaining to the Ottoman Empire.—*also n.*

osmium /'ɒzmiǝm/ *n* a hard bluish-white metallic element used in alloys.

osmometry /ɒs'mɒmǝtri/ *n* the measurement of smells.

osmosis /ɒz'moːsɪs/ or /ɒs-/ *n* (*pl* **osmoses**) the percolation and intermixture of fluids separated by a porous membrane.—**osmotic** *adj.*—**osmotically** *adv.*

osmunda, osmund /ɒz'mʌndǝ/ *n* the flowering fern of the genus Osmunda.

osnaburg /'ɒznǝbɜrg/ *n* a coarse linen cloth.

osprey /ˌ ɒspreɪ/ or /-pri/ *n* (*pl* **ospreys**) a large fish-eating bird of prey.

ossa *see* **os**[2].

ossein /'ɒsiɪn/ *n* gelatinous tissue in bone.

osseous /'ɒsiǝs/ *adj* pertaining to, consisting of, or like, bone.

ossicle /'ɒsɪkǝl/ *n* a little bone, *esp* of the ear; (*pl*) hard structures of small size, as the calcareous plates of the starfish.—**ossicular** *adj.*

ossiferous /'ɒsɪfǝrǝs/ *adj* producing or containing bone.

ossification /ˌɒsɪfɪ'keɪʃǝn/ *n* conversion of soft animal tissue into bone.

ossifrage /ˌɒsɪfreɪdʒ/ *n* an old name for the osprey or lammergeier.

ossify /'ɒsɪˌfaɪ/ *vb* (**ossifying, ossified**) *vt* to convert into bone or into a bone-like substance; to harden. • *vi* to become bone; to grow rigid and unprogressive.

ossuary /'ɒsjuri/ *n* (*pl* **ossuaries**) an urn for bones.

osteal /ɒ'stiːl/ *adj* osseous.

osteitis /ˌɒsti'aɪtɪs/ *n* inflammation of the bone.

ostensible /ɒ'stɛnsɪbǝl/ *adj* apparent; seeming; pretended.—**ostensibly** *adv.*

ostensive /-sɪv/ *adj* showing, exhibiting.

ostentation /ˌɒstɛn'teɪʃǝn/ *n* a showy, pretentious display.—**ostentatious** *adj.*—**ostentatiously** *adv.*

osteo-, oste- /'ɒstioː/ *prefix* bone.

osteoarthritis /ˌɒstio:ɑːˈθrəɪtɪs/ *n* painful inflammation of the joints, *esp* the hips, knees and others that bear weight.—**osteoarthritic** *adj*.

osteology /ˌɒstiˈɒlədʒi/ *n* that part of anatomy treating of bones, their structure, etc; a bony structure.—**osteological** *adj*.—**osteologist** *n*.

osteoma /ˌɒstiˈoːmə/ *n* (*pl* **osteomas, osteomata**) a bone tumour.

osteomalacia /ˌɒstio:məˈleɪʃə/ *n* softening of the bones.

osteomyelitis /ˌɒstio:maɪˈlaɪtɪs/ *n* an infectious disease causing inflammation of the bone marrow.

osteopathy /ˌɒstiˈɒpəθi/ *n* the treatment of disease by manipulation of the bones and muscles, often as an adjunct to medical and surgical measures.—**osteopath** *n*.

osteophyte /ˌɒstiəˈfəɪt/ *n* an abnormal growth from a bone.—**osteophytic** *adj*.

osteoplasty /ˌɒstio:ˈplæsti/ *n* (*pl* **osteoplasties**) surgery involving bone replacement and grafting.—**osteoplastic** *adj*.

osteoporosis /ˌɒstio:pəˈroːsɪs/ *n* the development of brittle bones due to a calcium deficiency in the bone matrix.—**osteoporotic** *adj*.

osteotome /ˌɒstio:ˈtoːm/ *n* an instrument used in dissecting bones.—**osteotomy** *n*.

ostiary /ˈɒstʃəri/ *n* (*pl* **ostiaries**) (*RC Church*) a church doorkeeper.

ostler /ˈɒslər/ *n* (*formerly*) a man who attended to horses at an inn, a hostler.

ostracize /ˈɒstrəˌsaɪz/ *vt* to exclude, banish from a group, society, etc.—**ostracism** *n*.

ostrich /ˈɒstrɪtʃ/ *n* (*pl* **ostriches, ostrich**) a large, flightless, swift-running African bird.

Ostrogoth /ˈɒstrəˌɡɒθ/ *n* an eastern Goth.

OT *abbr* = Old Testament.

otalgia /əˈtældʒiə/ *n* earache.

other /ˈʌðər/ *adj* second; remaining; different; additional. • *pron* the other one; some other one.

other-directed *adj* guided primarily by the influence or example of others.

otherness /-nəs/ *n* diversity.

otherwhere /-wer/ *adv* (*arch*) elsewhere.

otherwhile /-ˌhwaɪl/ or /-ˌwaɪl/ *adv* (*arch*) at another time.

otherwise /-ˌwaɪz/ *adv* if not, or else; differently.

otherworldly /ˌʌðərˈwɜːldli/ *adj* spiritual; unworldly.—**otherworldliness** *n*.

otic /ˈɒtɪk/ or /ˈoː-/ *adj* of the ear.

otiose /ˈoːtioːs/ or /ˈoːʃ-/, /-oːz/ *adj* superfluous, serving no practical purpose; futile; at leisure.—**otiosity** *n*.

otitis /oːˈtəɪtɪs/ *n* inflammation of the ear.

oto- /ˈoːtoː/ *prefix* ear.

otolith /ˈoːtəlɪθ/ *n* a chalky concretion in the ear.—**otolithic** *adj*.

otology /oːˈtɒlədʒi/ *n* that part of anatomy which treats of the ear, its structure, etc.—**otological** *adj*.—**otologist** *n*.

otoscope /-ˌskoːp/ *n* an instrument for examining the interior of the ear.

OTT *abbr* = over the top.

ottava rima /ɒˌtævəˈriːmə/ *n* (*poet*) an Italian stanza of eight lines of five accents each with three rhymes, the seventh and eighth forming a couplet; a stanza of eight five-foot lines rhyming abababcc.

otter /ˈɒtər/ *n* (*pl* **otters, otter**) a fish-eating mammal with smooth fur and a flat tail.

ottoman /ˈɒtəmən/ *n* an upholstered, backless chair or couch. • *adj* (*with cap*) of or relating to a former Turkish dynasty and empire; Turkish.

ouananiche /ˈwɒnɪʃ/ *n* a landlocked form of Atlantic salmon found in lakes in Eastern Canada.

oubliette /ˌuːbliˈet/ *n* an underground dungeon with its entrance in the roof in which prisoners condemned to perpetual imprisonment or secret death were confined.

ouch[1] /aʊtʃ/ *interj* an exclamation of pain or annoyance.

ouch[2] *n* a clasp, a jewel; the setting of a gem.

ought[1] /ɒt/ *aux vb* expressing obligation or duty; to be bound, to be obliged (to); a variant spelling of **aught**.

ought[2] *see* **aught**.

Ouija board /ˈwiːdʒiː oː/ /-dʒə/ *n* (*trademark*) a board with letters and symbols used to obtain messages at seances.

ounce[1] /aʊns/ *n* a unit of weight, equal to one sixteenth of a pound or 28.34 grams; one sixteenth of a pint, one fluid ounce.

ounce[2] *n* the snow leopard; (*poet*) the lynx or an animal like it.

our /aʊr/ or /ɑr/ *poss adj*, *pron* relating or belonging to us.

ours /ˈaʊrz/ or /ɑrz/ *pron* belonging to us.

ourselves /aʊrˈselvz/ or /ɑr-/ *pron* emphatic and reflexive form of we.

-ous /əs/ *suffix* full of, as in *joyous*; (*chem*) containing in lower proportion, as in *ferrous* as opposed to *ferric*.

ousel *see* **ouzel**.

oust /aʊst/ *vt* to eject, expel, *esp* by underhand means; to remove forcibly.

out /aʊt/ *adv* not in; outside; in the open air; to the full extent; beyond bounds; no longer holding office; ruled out, no longer considered; loudly and clearly; no longer included (in a game, fashion, etc); in error; on strike; at an end; extinguished; into the open; published; revealed; (*radio conversation*) transmission ends. • *prep* out of; out through; outside. • *adj* external; outward. • *n* an exit; means of escape.

out- *prefix* out, outside, away from; external; separate; more, longer.

out-and-out *adj* thoroughgoing; absolute; complete.

outback /ˈaʊtbæk/ *n* a remote area inland, *esp* in Australia.

outbalance *vt* to exceed in weight.

outbid /aʊtˈbɪd/ *vt* (**outbidding, outbid**, *pp* **outbidden** *or* **outbid**) to bid higher than.

outboard /ˈaʊtbɔːrd/ *adj* (*engine*) outside a ship, etc. • *n* an engine attached to the outside of a boat.

outbrave /ˌaʊtˈbreɪv/ *vt* to excel in bravery; to defy.

outbreak /ˈaʊtbreɪk/ *n* a sudden eruption (of disease, strife, etc).

outbuilding /ˈaʊtˌbɪldɪŋ/ *n* a detached subsidiary building.

outburst /ˈaʊtbɜːrst/ *n* a bursting out; a spurt; an explosion of anger, etc.

outcast /ˈaʊtkæst/ *n* a person who is rejected by society.

outcaste /ˈaʊtkæst/ *n* one who has lost caste, a pariah. • *vt* to expel from a caste.

outclass /aʊtˈklæs/ *vt* to surpass or excel greatly.

outcome /ˈaʊtkʌm/ *n* the result, consequence.

outcrop /ˈaʊtkrɒp/ *n* an exposed rock surface. • *vi* (**outcropping, outcropped**) to crop out at the surface.

outcry /ˈaʊtkraɪ/ *n* (*pl* **outcries**) protest; uproar.

outdated /aʊtˈdeɪtəd/ *n* obsolete, old-fashioned.

outdistance /aʊtˈdɪstəns/ *vt* to get well ahead of.

outdo /aʊtˈduː/ *vt* (**outdoing, outdid**, *pp* **outdone**) to surpass, to do more than, to excel.

outdoor /ˈaʊtdɔːr/ *adj* existing, taking place, or used in the open air.

outdoors /aʊtˈdɔːrz/ *adv* in or into the open air; out of doors. • *n* the open air, outside world.

outer /ˈaʊtər/ *adj* further out or away.

outermost /ˈaʊtərˌmoːst/ *adj* furthest out; most distant.

outer space *n* any region of space beyond the earth's atmosphere.

outface /aʊtˈfeɪs/ *vt* to stare down or out of countenance; to defy.

outfall /ˈaʊtfɔl/ *n* the lower end of a watercourse; a point of discharge.

outfield /ˈaʊtfiːld/ *n* the outer part of a cricket or baseball field.

outfit /ˈaʊtfɪt/ *n* the equipment used in an activity; clothes worn together, an ensemble; a group of people associated in an activity. • *vt* (**outfitting, outfitted**) to provide with an outfit or equipment.

outfitter /ˈaʊtˌfɪtər/ *n* a supplier of equipment or clothes.

outflank /aʊtˈflæŋk/ *vt* to get round the side of (an enemy); to circumvent.

outflow /ˈaʊtfloː/ *n* a flowing out; something that flows out.

outfox /aʊtˈfɒks/ *vt* to outwit by superior cunning.

outgeneral /aʊtˈdʒenərəl/ *vt* to outdo in strategy.

outgo /aʊtˈɡoː/ *vt* (**outgoing, outwent**, *pp* **outgone**) to go beyond; to surpass.

outgoing /ˈaʊtˌɡoːɪŋ/ *adj* departing; retiring; sociable, forthcoming. • *n* an outlay; (*pl*) expenditure.

outgrow /aʊtˈɡroː/ *vt* (**outgrowing, outgrew**, *pp* **outgrown**) to become too big for; to grow taller than; to grow out of.

outgrowth /ˈaʊtɡroːθ/ *n* an offshoot.

outgun /aʊtˈɡʌn/ *vt* (**outgunning, outgunned**) to defeat by greater firepower; (*inf*) to surpass.

outhouse /ˈaʊthaʊs/ *n* a shed, etc, adjoining a main house.

outing /ˈaʊtɪŋ/ *n* a pleasure trip; an excursion.

outlandish /aʊtˈlændɪʃ/ *adj* unconventional; strange; fantastic.

outlast /aʊtˈlæst/ *vt* to endure longer than.

outlaw /ˈaʊtlɔ/ *vt* to declare illegal. • *n* an outlawed person; a habitual or notorious criminal.

outlay /ˈaʊtleɪ/ *n* a spending (of money); expenditure.

outlet /ˈaʊtlet/ or /-lət/ *n* an opening or release; a means of expression; a market for goods or services.

outlier /'ʊtˌlaɪr/ *n* a part of a rock or stratum detached at some distance from the principal mass.

outline /'ʊtlaɪn/ *n* a profile; a general indication; a rough sketch or draft.—*also vt.*

outlive /ʊt'lɪv/ *vt* to live longer than, outlast; to live through; to survive.

outlook /'ʊtlʊk/ *n* mental attitude; view; prospect.

outlying /'ʊtˌlaɪŋ/ *adj* detached; remote, distant.

outmanoeuvre, outmaneuver /ˌʊtməˈnuːvər/ *vt* to outwit in tactics.

outmatch /ʊt'mætʃ/ *vt* to be more than a match for.

outmoded /ʊt'moʊdəd/ *adj* old-fashioned.

outmost /'ʊtmoʊst/ *adj* outermost.

outnumber /ʊt'nʌmbər/ *vt* to exceed in number.

out-of-date *adj* no longer valid, unfashionable; outmoded.

out-of-pocket *adj* (*expenses*) paid for in cash; having lost money.

outpoint *vt* to accumulate more points than.

out-of-the-way *adj* uncommon; secluded.

outpatient /'ʊtˌpeɪʃənt/ *n* a person treated at, but not resident in, a hospital.

outpoint /ʊt'pɔɪnt/ *vt* to accumulate more points than.

outpost /'ʊtpoʊst/ *n* (*mil*) a post or detachment at a distance from a main force.

outpouring /'ʊtˌpɔːrɪŋ/ *n* an effusion, an emotional speech.

output /'ʊtpʊt/ *n* the quantity (of goods, etc) produced, *esp* over a given period; information delivered by a computer, *esp* to a printer; (*elect*) the useful voltage, current, or power delivered.—*also vt.*

outrage /'ʊtreɪdʒ/ *n* an extremely vicious or violent act; a grave insult or offence; great anger, etc, aroused by this.—*also vt.*—**outrageous** *adj*.

outrageous /ʊt'reɪdʒəs/ *adj* flagrant; atrocious; violent; excessive.—**outrageously** *adv*.—**outrageousness** *n*.

outrank /ʊt'ræŋk/ *vt* to be of a higher rank than; to be of a higher priority.

outré /'uːtreɪ/ *adj* outraging decorum; eccentric, unconventional; extravagant.

outride /ʊt'raɪd/ *vt* (**outriding, outrode,** *pp* **outridden**) to ride faster or farther than; to keep afloat through (a storm).

outrider /'ʊtˌraɪdər/ *n* a mounted escort who goes in advance of a carriage, car, etc.

outrigger /'ʊtˌrɪgər/ *n* a projecting spar for a sail, etc; a projection with a float extending from a canoe to prevent capsizing; a canoe of this type; a projecting frame to support the elevator or tail of an aircraft or the rotor of a helicopter.

outright /'ʊtraɪt/ or /ʊt'raɪt/ *adj* complete, downright, direct. • *adv* at once; without restrictions.

outrun /ʊt'rʌn/ *vt* (**outrunning, outran,** *pp* **outran**) to run faster than; to exceed; to go beyond; to escape by running.

outset /'ʊtset/ *n* the start, beginning.

outshine /ʊt'ʃaɪn/ *vt* (**outshining, outshone**) to outdo in brilliance, ability; to shine longer and brighter than.

outside /ʊt'saɪd/ or /'ʊtsaɪd/ *n* the outer part or surface, the exterior. • *adj* outer; outdoor; (*chance, etc*) slight. • *adv* on or to the outside. • *prep* on or to the exterior of; beyond.

outsider /ʊt'saɪdər/ *n* a person or thing not included in a set, group, etc, a non-member; a contestant, *esp* a horse, not thought to have a chance in a race.

outsize /'ʊtsaɪz/ *adj* of a larger than usual size.

outskirts /'ʊtskɜːrts/ *npl* districts remote from the centre, as of a city.

outsmart /ʊt'smɑːrt/ *vt* to outwit.

outspan /ʊt'spæn/ *vt* (**outspanning, outspanned**) (*S Africa*) to unyoke ox teams from a wagon; to encamp. • *n* a halting place.

outspoken /ʊt'spoʊkən/ *adj* candid in speech, frank, blunt.

outstanding /ʊt'stændɪŋ/ *adj* excellent; distinguished, prominent; unpaid; unresolved, still to be done.

outstation /'ʊtˌsteɪʃən/ *n* a distant post or station.

outstay /ʊt'steɪ/ *vt* to stay longer than or too long.

outstrip /ʊt'strɪp/ *vt* (**outstripping, outstripped**) to surpass; to go faster than.

outtalk /ʊt'tɔːk/ *vt* to talk down.

outvote /ʊt'voʊt/ *vt* to defeat by a higher number of votes.

outward /'ʊtwərd/ *adj* directed toward the outside; external; clearly apparent. • *adv* toward the outside.

Outward Bound movement *n* an educational scheme to promote youth adventure training.

outwardly /-li/ *adv* externally.

outwards /-z/ *adv* outward.

outwear /ʊt'wer/ *vt* (**outwearing, outwore,** *pp* **outworn**) to outlast; to wear out.

outweigh /ʊt'weɪ/ *vt* to count for more than, to exceed in value, weight, or importance.

outwent *see* **outgo**.

outwit /ʊt'wɪt/ *vt* (**outwitting, outwitted**) to get the better of, defeat, by wit or cunning.

outwork /'ʊtwərk/ *n* a defence constructed beyond the main body of a fort, etc; work done outside a factory.

ouzel /'uːzəl/ *n* kinds of small bird; a blackbird.—*also* **ousel**.

ouzo /'uːzoʊ/ *n* a Greek aniseed-flavoured spirit.

ova *see* **ovum**.

oval /'oʊvəl/ *adj* egg-shaped; elliptical. • *n* anything oval.

ovariotomy /ˌoʊværiˈɒtəmi/ *n* (*pl* **ovariotomies**) the surgical operation of removing a tumour from the ovary.

ovaritis /'oʊvəˈraɪtɪs/ *n* inflammation of the ovary.

ovary /'oʊvəri/ *n* (*pl* **ovaries**) one of the two female reproductive organs producing eggs.—**ovarian** *adj*.

ovate /'oʊveɪt/ *adj* (*bot*) oval, egg-shaped.

ovation /oʊ'veɪʃən/ *n* enthusiastic applause or public welcome.

oven /'ʌvən/ *n* an enclosed, heated compartment for baking or drying.

ovenbird /'ʌvənˌbərd/ *n* a kind of bird with a dome-shaped nest.

oven-ready *adj* (*food*) prepared for immediate cooking in the oven.

ovenware /'ʌvənˌwer/ *n* attractive heat-resistant dishes in which food can be cooked and served.

over /'oʊvər/ *prep* higher than; on top of; across; to the other side of; above; more than; concerning. • *adv* above; across; in every part; completed; from beginning to end; up and down; in addition; too. • *adj* upper; excessive; surplus; finished; remaining. • *n* (*cricket*) the number of balls bowled before changing ends.

over- *prefix* in excess, too much; above.

overact /ˌoʊvərˈækt/ *vti* to act in an exaggerated manner, to overdo a part.

overactive /ˌoʊvərˈæktɪv/ *adj* abnormally or excessively active.—**overactivity** *n*.

overall /'oʊvərˌɒl/ *adj* including everything. • *adv* as a whole; generally. • *n* a loose protective garment; (*pl*) a one-piece protective garment covering body and legs.

overarch /ˌoʊvərˈɑːrtʃ/ *vti* to form an arch (over).

overarm /'oʊvərˌɑːrm/ *adj, adv* (*sport*) bowled, thrown, performed, etc with the arm raised above the shoulder.

overawe /ˌoʊvərˈɒ/ *vt* to restrain by awe, daunt.

overbalance /ˌoʊvərˈbæləns/ *vti* to fall over; to upset; to outweigh. • *n* a surplus.

overbear /ˌoʊvərˈber/ *vt* (**overbearing, overbore,** *pp* **overborne**) to dominate, to repress, to bear down.

overbearing /-ɪŋ/ *adj* domineering; overriding.—**overbearingly** *adv*.

overblown /ˌoʊvərˈbloʊn/ *adj* excessive, pretentious.

overboard /'oʊvərˌbɔːrd/ *adv* over the side of a ship, etc; (*inf*) to extremes of enthusiasm.

overbook /ˌoʊvərˈbʊk/ *vti* to sell tickets (for) in excess of the available seats or space.

overburden /ˌoʊvərˈbərdən/ *vt* to load too heavily.

overcall /ˌoʊvərˈkɒl/ *vti* (*bridge*) to bid more on (a hand) than it is worth; to take a bid away from (a partner).

overcame *see* **overcome**.

overcapitalize /ˌoʊvərˈkæpɪtəˌlaɪz/ *vt* to float (a company) with too great a capital.—**overcapitalization** *n*.

overcast /'oʊvərˌkæst/ *adj* clouded over.

overcharge /ˌoʊvərˈtʃɑːrdʒ/ *vt* (*battery*) to overload; to fill to excess; to demand too high a price (from). • *n* an excessive or exorbitant charge or load.

overcloud /ˌoʊvərˈklaʊd/ *vti* to cover or become covered with clouds; to make or become dark or depressed.

overcoat /'oʊvərˌkoʊt/ *n* a warm, heavy topcoat.

overcome /ˌoʊvərˈkʌm/ *vti* (**overcoming, overcame,** *pp* **overcome**) to get the better of; to prevail; to render helpless or powerless, as by tears, laughter, emotion, etc; to be victorious; to surmount obstacles, etc.

overcompensation /'oʊvərˌkɒmpənˈseɪʃən/ *n* (*psychoanal*) an excess of compensation, often resulting in an overbearing manner.—**overcompensatory** *adj*.

overcrop /ˌoʊvərˈkrɒp/ *vt* (**overcropping, overcropped**) to exhaust (land) by excessive cultivation.

overcrowd /ˌoːvərˈkraʊd/ *vti* to make or become too crowded.

overdo /ˌoːvərˈduː/ *vt* (**overdoing, overdid,** *pp* **overdone**) to do to excess; to overact; to cook (food) too much.— **overdone** *adj*.

overdose /ˈoːvərˌdoːs/ *n* an excessive dose —*also vti*.

overdraft /ˈoːvərˌdræft/ *n* an overdrawing, an amount overdrawn, at a bank.

overdraw /ˌoːvərˈdrɒː/ *vti* (**overdrawing, overdrew,** *pp* **overdrawn**) to draw in excess of a credit balance; to exaggerate in describing; to make an overdraft.

overdress /ˌoːvərˈdres/ *vti* to dress too warmly, too showily, or too formally.

overdrive /ˈoːvərˌdraɪv/ *n* a high gear in a motor vehicle to reduce wear for travelling at high speed. • *vt* (**overdriving, overdrove,** *pp* **overdriven**) to drive too hard, overtax.

overdue /ˌoːvərˈduː/ or /-ˈdjuː/ *adj* past the time for payment, return, performance, etc; in arrears; delayed.

overeat /ˌoːvərˈiːt/ *vi* (**overeating, overate,** *pp* **overeaten**) to eat too much.

overestimate /ˌoːvərˈestɪˌmeɪt/ *vt* to set too high an estimate on or for. • *n* an excessive estimate.—**overestimation** *n*.

overexpose /ˌoːvərɪkˈspoːz/ or /ˌoːvərek-/ *vt* (*phot*) to expose (a film) to light for too long.—**overexposure** *n*.

overflow /ˌoːvərˈfloː/ *vti* (**overflowing, overflowed,** *pp* **overflown**) to flow over, flood; to exceed the bounds (of); to abound (with emotion, etc). • *n* that which overflows; surplus, excess; an outlet for surplus water, etc.

overgrow /ˌoːvərˈgroː/ *vti* (**overgrowing, overgrew,** *pp* **overgrown**) to cover with growth; to grow too big or fast (for); to outgrow.—**overgrowth** *n*.

overgrown /ˌoːvərˈgroːn/ *adj* grown beyond the normal size; rank; ungainly.

overhand /ˈoːvərˌhænd/ *adj, adv* (*sport*) bowled, thrown, performed, etc with the hand above the shoulder.

overhang /ˌoːvərˈhæŋ/ *vti* (**overhanging, overhung**) to hang or project over. • *n* a projecting part.

overhaul /ˌoːvərˈhɒl/ *vt* to examine for, or make, repairs; to overtake.—*also n*.

overhead /ˌoːvərˈhed/ *adj, adv* above the head; in the sky. • *n* (often *pl*) the general, continuing costs of a business, as of rent, light, etc.

overhear /ˌoːvərˈhiːr/ *vt* (**overhearing, overheard**) to hear without the knowledge of the speaker.

overheat /ˌoːvərˈhiːt/ *vti* to make or become excessively hot; to stimulate unduly.

overjoyed /ˌoːvərˈdʒɔɪd/ *adj* highly delighted.

overkill /ˈoːvərkɪl/ *n* the capability to employ more weapons, etc than are necessary to destroy an enemy; excess capacity for a task.

overland /ˈoːvərˌlænd/ or /ˌoːvərˈlænd/ *adj, adv* by, on, or across land.

overlap /ˌoːvərˈlæp/ *vt* (**overlapping, overlapped**) to extend over (a thing or each other) so as to coincide in part.—*also n*.

overlay /ˌoːvərˈleɪ/ *vt* (**overlaying, overlaid**) to cover with a coating, to spread over. • *n* a coating.

overleaf /ˌoːvərˈliːf/ *adv* on the other side of the leaf of a book.

overlie /ˌoːvərˈlaɪ/ *vt* (**overlying, overlay,** *pp* **overlain**) to lie on top of; to stifle thus.

overload /ˌoːvərˈloːd/ *vt* to put too great a burden on; (*elect*) to charge with too much current.

overlong /ˌoːvərˈlɒŋ/ *adj, adv* too long.

overlook /ˌoːvərˈlʊk/ *vt* to fail to notice; to look at from above; to excuse.

overlord /ˈoːvərˌlɔrd/ *n* a lord ranking above other lords; an absolute or supreme ruler.

overman /ˌoːvərˈmæn/ *vt* (**overmanning, overmanned**) to supply with too many workers.

overmaster /ˌoːvərˈmæstər/ *vt* to dominate wholly, to overpower.

overmuch /ˌoːvərˈmʌtʃ/ *adj, adv* too much.

overnice /ˈoːvərˌnɔɪs/ *adj* too particular.

overnight /ˌoːvərˈnɔɪt/ *adv* for the night; in the course of the night; suddenly. • *adj* done in the night; lasting the night.

overpass /ˈoːvərˌpæs/ *n* a flyover; a road crossing another road, path, etc, at a higher level. • *vt* (**overpassing, overpassed,** *pp* **overpast**) to pass beyond, to overstep; to surpass.

overplay /ˌoːvərˈpleɪ/ *vt* to place too much emphasis on; to behave in an exaggerated or affected manner.

overplus /ˈoːvərˌplʌs/ *n* a surplus, an excess.

overpower /ˌoːvərˈpaʊər/ *vt* to overcome by superior force, to subdue; to overwhelm.

overpowering /-ɪŋ/ *adj* overwhelming; compelling; unbearable.

overproduction /ˌoːvərprəˈdʌkʃən/ *n* supply in excess of the demand.

overqualified /ˌoːvərˈkwɒlɪˌfaɪd/ *adj* having more qualifications or experience that required for a particular job.

overrate /ˌoːvərˈreɪt/ *vt* to value or assess too highly.

overreach /ˌoːvərˈriːtʃ/ *vt* to extend beyond; to circumvent, outwit; to fail by trying too much or being too subtle.

overreact /ˌoːvərriˈækt/ *vi* to show an excessive reaction to something.

override /ˌoːvərˈraɪd/ *vt* (**overriding, overrode,** *pp* **overridden**) to ride over; to nullify; to prevail.

overrule /ˌoːvərˈruːl/ *vt* to set aside by higher authority; to prevail over.

overrun /ˌoːvərˈrʌn/ *vt* (**overrunning, overran,** *pp* **overrun**) to attack and defeat; to swarm over; to exceed (a time limit, etc).

overseas /ˌoːvərˈsiːz/ *adj, adv* across or beyond the sea; abroad.

oversee /ˌoːvərˈsiː/ *vt* (**overseeing, oversaw,** *pp* **overseen**) to supervise; to superintend. • *n* **overseer** *n*.

oversell /ˌoːvərˈsel/ *vt* (**overselling, oversold**) to sell more than can be delivered, *esp* stocks.

overset /ˌoːvərˈset/ *vti* (**oversetting, overset**) to upset, to disturb; to overthrow.

oversew /ˈoːvərˌsoː/ *vt* (**oversewing, oversewed,** *pp* **oversewn**) to stitch over again to reinforce; to stitch over an edge to prevent fraying.

overshadow /ˌoːvərˈʃædoː/ *vt* to throw a shadow over; to appear more prominent or important than.

overshoe /ˈoːvərˌʃuː/ *n* a galosh.

overshoot /ˌoːvərˈʃuːt/ *vt* (**overshooting, overshot**) to shoot or send beyond (a target, etc); (*aircraft*) to fly or taxi beyond the end of a runway when landing or taking off.—*also n*.

oversight /ˈoːvərˌsɔɪt/ *n* a careless mistake or omission; supervision.

oversize /ˈoːvərˌsaɪz/, **oversized** /-ˌsaɪzd/ *adj* of larger than average size.

overslaugh /ˈoːvərˌslɒ/ *n* (*mil*) the passing over of an ordinary duty because of a special one.

oversleep /ˌoːvərˈsliːp/ *vi* (**oversleeping, overslept**) to sleep beyond the intended time.

overspend /ˌoːvərˈspend/ *vt* (**overspending, overspent**) to spend more than necessary; to wear out, tire. • *vi* to spend more than one can afford.

overstate /ˌoːvərˈsteɪt/ *vt* to state too strongly, to exaggerate.— **overstatement** *n*.

overstay /ˌoːvərˈsteɪ/ *vt* to remain longer than or beyond the limits of.

overstep /ˌoːvərˈstep/ *vt* (**overstepping, overstepped**) to exceed; (*a limit*) to step beyond.

overstock /ˌoːvərˈstɒk/ *vt* to lay in too large a stock of or for, to glut.—*also n*.

overstrung /ˌoːvərˈstrʌŋ/ *adj* too highly strung; too sensitive.

oversubscribe /ˌoːvərsəbˈskraɪb/ *vt* to apply for more shares in (an issue) than can be allotted.

overt /oˈvɜrt/ or /ˈoːvɜrt/ *adj* openly done, unconcealed; (*law*) done with evident intent, deliberate.—**overtly** *adv*.

overtake /ˌoːvərˈteɪk/ *vt* (**overtaking, overtook,** *pp* **overtaken**) to catch up with and pass; to come upon suddenly.

overtax /ˌoːvərˈtæks/ *vt* to make too great demands on; to tax too heavily.

overthrow /ˌoːvərˈθroː/ *vt* (**overthrowing, overthrew,** *pp* **overthrown**) to throw over, overturn; (*government, etc*) to bring down by force.—*also n*.

overtime /ˈoːvərˌtaɪm/ *adv* beyond regular working hours. • *n* extra time worked; payment for this.

overtone /ˈoːvərˌtoːn/ *n* an additional subtle meaning; an implicit quality; (*mus*) a harmonic; the colour of light reflected (as by a paint).

overtook *see* **overtake**.

overtop /ˌoːvərˈtɒp/ *vt* (**overtopping, overtopped**) to be higher than, to tower above.

overtrain /ˌoːvərˈtreɪn/ *vti* to train too hard.

overtrump /ˌoːvərˈtrʌmp/ *vt* to play a higher trump than (the card that has trumped another).

overture /ˈoːvərˌtʃər/ n an initiating of negotiations; a formal offer, proposal; (mus) an instrumental introduction to an opera, etc.

overturn /ˌoːvərˈtɜrn/ vti to upset, turn over; to overthrow.

overview /ˈoːvərˌvjuː/ n a general survey.

overweening /ˌoːvərˈwiːnɪŋ/ adj arrogant, presumptuous, conceited.

overweight /ˌoːvərˈweit/ adj weighing more than the proper amount. • n excess weight.

overwhelm /ˌoːvərˈwɛlm/ vt to overcome totally; to submerge; to crush; to overpower with emotion.

overwhelming /-ɪŋ/ adj irresistible; uncontrollable; vast; vastly superior; extreme.

overwork /ˌoːvərˈwɜrk/ vti to work or use too hard or too long.

overwrite /ˌoːvərˈrait/ vt (**overwriting, overwrote, overwritten**) to write in an overly elaborate style; to write too much; to write data to a computer disk thereby erasing the existing contents.

overwrought /ˌoːvərˈrɒt/ adj over-excited; too elaborate.

ovi- /ˈoːvi/ prefix egg.

oviduct /ˈoːviˌdʌkt/ n the tube which conducts the ovum from the ovary to the uterus.

oviferous /ˈoːviˌfərəs/ adj egg-carrying.

oviform /ˈoːviˌfɔrm/ adj egg-shaped.

ovine /ˈoːvain/ adj pertaining to sheep.

oviparous /oːˈvipərəs/ adj producing young by eggs.—**oviparity** n.

oviposit /ˌoːviˈpozit/ vi to lay or deposit eggs.—**oviposition** n.

ovipositor /ˌoːviˈpozitər/ n the organ in certain insects by which its eggs are deposited.

ovisac /ˈoːviˌsæk/ n the cavity in the ovary which contains the ovum.

ovoid /ˈoːvoid/ adj egg-shaped.

ovolo /ˈoːvəˌloː/ n (pl **ovoli**) (archit) a round or convex egg-shaped moulding.

ovoviviparous /ˌoːvoˈviːvipərəs/ adj producing eggs containing the young in a living state, as certain animals.—**ovoviviparity** n.

ovulate /ˈovjuˌleit/ vi to discharge or produce eggs from an ovary.—**ovulation** n.

ovule /ˈoːvjuːl/ n the germ borne by the placenta of a plant and subsequently developing into a seed.—**ovular** adj.

ovum /ˈoːvəm/ n (pl **ova**) an unfertilized female egg cell.

owe /oː/ vti to be in debt; to be obliged to pay; to feel the need to give, do, etc, as because of gratitude.

owing /ˈoːɪŋ/ adj due, to be paid; owed; (with **to**) because of, on account of.

owl /aul/ n a nocturnal bird of prey with a large head and eyes; a person of nocturnal habits, solemn appearance, etc.—**owlish** adj.

owlet /ˈaulət/ n a young owl.

own[1] /oːn/ vti to possess; to acknowledge, admit; to confess to.

own[2] adj belonging to oneself or itself, often used reflexively (my own, their own).

owner /ˈoːnər/ n one who owns, a possessor, a proprietor.—**ownership** n.

ox /ɒks/ n (pl **oxen**) a cud-chewing mammal of the cattle family; a castrated bull.

oxalate /ˈɒksəˌleit/ n a salt of oxalic acid.

oxalic acid /ɒkˈsælɪk/ n a poisonous acid obtained from oxalis.

oxalis /ˈɒksəlɪs/ n wood sorrel.

oxbow /ˈɒksboː/ n a horseshoe loop in a stream; the U-shaped collar of a yoke.

Oxbridge /ˈɒksbrɪdʒ/ n, adj (of) the British universities of Oxford and Cambridge.

oxen see **ox**.

ox-eye /ˈɒksai/ n a kind of flower; a large eye.

Oxfam (abbr) the Oxford Committee for Famine Relief.

Oxford Group n a former name of Moral Rearmament.

Oxford movement n an Anglican high-church movement begun in Oxford in 1833.

oxidation /ɒksiˈdeiʃən/ n the operation of converting into an oxide.

oxide /ˈɒksaid/ n a compound of oxygen with another element.

oxidize /ˈɒksidaiz/ vti to cause to undergo a chemical reaction with oxygen; to rust.—**oxidization** n.

oxlip /ˈɒkslɪp/ n a variety of primula; a hybrid between primrose and cowslip.

Oxon. /ˈɒksən/ abbr = (degrees, etc) of Oxford.

Oxonian /ɒkˈsoːniən/ adj pertaining to Oxford. • n a graduate or member of Oxford University.

oxtail /ˈɒksteil/ n the tail of an ox, esp skinned and used for stews, soups, etc.

oxy- /ˈɒksi/ prefix sharp; oxygen.

oxyacetylene /ˌɒksiəˈsetiˌliːn/ n a mixture of oxygen with acetylene used in a blowlamp to cut or weld metal.—also adj.

oxygen /ˈɒksidʒən/ n a colourless, odourless, tasteless, highly reactive gaseous element forming part of air, water, etc, and essential to life and combustion.—**oxygenic, oxygenous** adj.

oxygenate /ˈɒksidʒəˌneit/ or /ɒkˈsi-/ vt to combine or supply with oxygen.—**oxygenation** n.

oxygenize /ˈɒksidʒəˌnaiz/ vt to oxygenate.—**oxygenizer** n.

oxygen tent n a canopy over a hospital bed, etc, within which a supply of oxygen is maintained.

oxyhemoglobin, oxyhaemoglobin /ˌɒksiˌhiːməˈgloːbin/ n a loose compound of oxygen and haemoglobin.

oxyhydrogen /ˌɒksiˈhaidrədʒən/ n a mixture of oxygen with acetylene and hydrogen, as in a blowlamp, by which an intense heat is produced by the combination of gases.

oxymoron /ˌɒksiˈmɔrɒn/ n (pl **oxymora**) a figure of speech combining contradictory words, "faith unfaithful kept him falsely true."

oxytone /ˈɒksiˌtoːn/ adj (linguistics) having an acute sound; having the last syllable accented. • n an acute sound; a word with the acute accent on the last syllable.

oyez, oyes /oːˈjes/ or /-ˈjez/ interj the introductory cry of an official or public crier demanding attention or silence.

oyster /ˈoistər/ n an edible marine bivalve shellfish.

oystercatcher /ˈoistərˌkætʃər/ n a wading sea bird.

oz abbr = ounce(s).

Oz /ɒz/ n (Austral sl) Australia.

ozokerite, ozocerite /oːˈzoːkəˌrait/ or /-ˈsərait/, /ˌoːzoːˈsiːˌrait/ n a waxy fossil resin used for candles.

ozone /ˈoːzoːn/ n a condensed form of oxygen; (inf) bracing seaside air.—**ozonic, ozonous** adj.

ozone layer n a layer of ozone in the stratosphere that absorbs ultraviolet rays from the sun.

ozonize /-ˌnaiz/ vt to charge with ozone.—**ozonization** n.—**ozonizer** n.

P

P¹ /piː/ *abbr* = parking; *(chess)* pawn.

P² *(chem symbol)* phosphorus.

p *abbr* = page; penny, pence.

PA *abbr* = Panama; personal assistant; public address (system).

Pa *(chem symbol)* protactinium.

pa /pɒ/ or /pɑ/ *n (inf)* father, papa.

p.a. *abbr* = per annum.

paca /ˈpækə/ *n* a burrowing rodent found in Central and South America.

pace¹ /peɪs/ *n* a single step; the measure of a single stride; speed of movement. • *vti* to measure by paces; to walk up and down; to determine the pace in a race; to walk with regular steps.—**pacer** *n*.

pace² *prep* with the permission of; with due respect to.

pacemaker /ˈpeɪsmeɪkər/ *n* a person who sets the pace in a race; an electronic device inserted in the heart, used to regulate heartbeat.

pacer /ˈpeɪsər/ *n* a horse trained to pace; a pacemaker.

pacha /ˈpæʃə/ *see* **pasha**.

pachinko /pəˈtʃɪŋkoː/ *n* a Japanese variation on pinball.

pachisi /pəˈtʃiːzi/ *n* an Indian game, similar to backgammon.

pachouli /pəˈtʃuːli/ *see* **patchouli**.

pachyderm /ˈpækɪˌdərm/ *n* any large thick-skinned mammal, *esp* an elephant.—**pachydermatous** *adj*.

pacific /pəˈsɪfɪk/ *adj* promoting peace; mild, conciliatory.—**pacifically** *adv*.

Pacific salmon *n* a salmon of the coastal North Pacific Ocean and its tributaries.

pacifier /ˈpæsəˌfaɪr/ *n* a person or thing that pacifies; the US word for a baby's dummy.

pacifism /ˈpæsəˌfɪzəm/ *n* opposition to the use of force under any circumstances, specifically the refusal to participate in war.—**pacifist** *n*.

pacify /ˈpæsəˌfaɪ/ *vt* (**pacifying, pacified**) to soothe; to calm; to restore peace to.—**pacification** *n*.

pack /pæk/ *n* a load or bundle (*esp* one carried on the back); a set of playing cards; a group or mass; a number of wild animals living together; an organized troop (as of Cub Scouts); a compact mass (as of snow); a small package used as a container for goods for sale. • *vt* to put together in a bundle or pack; (*suitcase*) to fill; to crowd; to press tightly so as to prevent leakage; to carry in a pack; to send (off); (*sl: gun, etc*) to carry; (*sl: punch*) to deliver with force. • *vi* (*snow, ice*) to form into a hard mass; to assemble one's belongings in suitcases or boxes. • *adj* used for carrying packs, loads, etc.—**packer** *n*.

package /ˈpækɪdʒ/ *n* a parcel, a wrapped bundle; several items, arrangements, etc offered as a unit. • *vt* to make a parcel of; to group together several items, etc.—**packager** *n*.

package holiday, package tour *n* a holiday or tour with all the fares, accommodation, food, etc, arranged for an all-inclusive price.

package store *n* (*US*) a place where alcohol is sold for consumption off the premises.—*also US* **liquor store**, *UK* **off-licence**.

packaging /ˈpækɪdʒɪŋ/ *n* the wrapping round a product offered for sale; the presentation of a product.

pack animal *n* an animal, such as a mule or camel, used for carrying loads.

packed out *adj* (*inf*) crowded.

packet /ˈpækət/ *n* a small box or package; (*sl*) a considerable sum; a vessel carrying mail, etc, between one port and another.

packhorse *n* a horse used for carrying goods.

pack ice *n* sea ice formed into a mass by the crushing together of floes, etc.

packing /ˈpækɪŋ/ *n* material for protecting packed goods or for making airtight or watertight; the act of filling a suitcase, box, etc.

packsaddle /ˈpæksædəl/ *n* a saddle for carrying goods.

pact /pækt/ *n* an agreement or treaty.

pad¹ /pæd/ *n* the dull sound of a footstep. • *vi* (**padding, padded**) to walk, *esp* with a soft step.

pad² *n* a piece of a soft material or stuffing; several sheets of paper glued together at one edge; the cushioned thickening of an animal's sole; a piece of folded absorbent material used as a surgical dressing; a flat concrete surface; (*sl*) one's own home or room. • *vt* (**padding, padded**) to stuff with soft material; to fill with irrelevant information.

padding /ˈpædɪŋ/ *n* stuffing; anything unimportant or false added to achieve length or amount.

paddle¹ /ˈpædəl/ *vi* to wade about or play in shallow water.

paddle² *n* a short oar with a wide blade at one or both ends; a implement shaped like this, used to hit, beat or stir. • *vti* (*canoe, etc*) to propel by a paddle; to beat as with a paddle; to spank.—**paddler** *n*.

paddock /ˈpædək/ *n* an enclosed field in which horses are exercised or grazed.

paddy¹ /ˈpædi/ *n* (*pl* **paddies**) threshed unmilled rice; a rice field.

paddy² *n* (*pl* **paddies**) (*sl*) rage, a fit of temper.

pademelon, paddymelon /ˈpædəˌmɛlən/ *n* (*Austral*) a small wallaby.

padlock /ˈpædlɒk/ *n* a detachable lock used to fasten doors etc. • *vt* to secure with a padlock.

padre /ˈpɒdreɪ/ or /ˈpæd-/ *n* a military chaplain.

padrone /pəˈdroːni/ or /-neɪ/ *n* an innkeeper, *esp* in Italy.

paduasoy /ˈpædjuːəˌsɔɪ/ or /ˈpædʒuː-/ *n* a silk fabric.

paean /ˈpiːən/ *n* a song of triumph or thanks; praise.—*also* **pean**.

paediatrics /ˌpiːdiˈætrɪks/ *n sing* the branch of medicine dealing with children and their diseases.—*also* **pediatrics**.—**paediatric** *adj*.—**paediatrician** *n*.

paedo- /ˈpiːdoː/ *prefix* child.—*also* **pedo-**.

paedology /piːˈdɒlədʒi/ *n* the study of children.—*also* **pedology**.—**paedologic, paedological** *adj*.—**paedologically** *adv*.—**paedologist** *n*.

paedophilia /ˌpiːdəˈfiːliə/ or /ˌpedə-/ *n* sexual attraction towards children.—*also* **pedophilia**.—**paedophiliac, paedophilic** *adj*.—**paedophile** *n*.

paeon /ˈpiːən/ *n* a four-syllabled metrical foot, comprising, in any order, three short and one long syllable.

pagan /ˈpeɪɡən/ *n* a heathen; a person who has no religion. • *adj* irreligious; heathen, non-Christian.—**paganism** *n*.—**paganist** *adj, n*.

paganize /ˈpeɪɡəˌnaɪz/ *vt* to make pagan. • *vi* to become pagan.

page¹ /peɪdʒ/ *n* a boy attendant at a formal function (as a wedding); a uniformed boy employed to run errands. • *vt* to summon by messenger, loudspeaker, etc.

page² *n* a sheet of paper in a book, newspaper etc. • *vt* (*a book*) to number the pages of.—*also* **paginate**.

pageant /ˈpædʒənt/ *n* a spectacular procession or parade; representation in costume of historical events; a mere show.

pageantry /ˈpædʒəntri/ *n* (*pl* **pageantries**) grand or formal display; pomp.

pageboy /ˈpeɪdʒbɔɪ/ *n* a page; a medium-length hairstyle with the ends of the hair turned under.

pager /ˈpeɪdʒər/ *n* a device carried on a person so he or she can be summoned.—*also* **bleeper**.

paginal /ˈpædʒənəl/ *adj* consisting of pages; page for page.

paginate /ˈpædʒəˌneɪt/ *see* **page²**.

pagination /-ˈneɪʃən/ *n* the act of numbering the pages of a book; the arrangement and number of pages.

pagoda /pəˈɡoːdə/ *n* an oriental temple in the form of a tower.

Pahlavi /ˈpɒlɑvi/ *n* the Persian dialect in which Zoroastrian scriptures were written.

paid /peɪd/ *see* **pay**.

pail /peɪl/ *n* a bucket.

pain /peɪn/ *n* physical or mental suffering; hurting; (*pl*) trouble, exertion. • *vt* to cause distress to.

pained /peɪnd/ *adj* hurt, offended.

painful /ˈpeɪnful/ *adj* giving pain, distressing.—**painfully** *adv*.—**painfulness** *n*.

painkiller /ˈpeɪnˌkɪlər/ *n* a drug that relieves pain.

painless /ˈpeɪnləs/ *adj* without pain.—**painlessly** *adv*.

painstaking /ˈpeɪnˌsteɪkɪŋ/ or /ˈpeɪnzˌteɪkɪŋ/ *adj* very careful, laborious.—**painstakingly** *adv*.

paint /peɪnt/ *vt* (*a picture*) to make using oil pigments, etc; to depict with paints; to cover or decorate with paint; to describe. • *vi* to make a picture. • *n* a colouring pigment; a dried coat of paint.

painter[1] /ˈpeɪntər/ *n* a person who paints, *esp* an artist.

painter[2] *n* a bow rope for tying up a boat.

painting /ˈpeɪntɪŋ/ *n* the act or art of applying paint; a painted picture.

pair /per/ *n* a set of two things that are equal, suited, or used together; any two persons or animals regarded as a unit. • *vti* to form a pair (of); to mate.

paisley /ˈpeɪzli/ *n* an intricate pattern of curved shapes; a soft woollen fabric with this design; a shawl made of this material. • *adj* of this pattern or material.

pajamas /pəˈdʒɑməz/ or /-ˈdʒæməz/ *see* **pyjamas**.

pakeha /ˈpækɪhə/ *n* (*New Zealand*) a non-Maori, *esp* a white person.

pal /pæl/ *n* a close friend. • *vi* (**palling, palled**) (*with* **up**) (*inf*) to make friends (with).

palace /ˈpælɪs/ *n* the official residence of a sovereign, president or bishop; a large stately house or public building.

paladin /ˈpælədɪn/ *n* a knight-errant, *esp* of the court of Charlemagne.

palatable /ˈpælətəbəl/ *adj* (*taste*) pleasant; (*fig*) pleasant or acceptable.—**palatability** *n*.—**palatably** *adv*.

palate /ˈpælət/ *n* the roof of the mouth; taste; mental relish.

palatial /pəˈleɪʃəl/ *adj* of or like a palace.—**palatially** *adv*.—**palatialness** *n*.

palaver /pəˈlævər/ *n* idle chatter; flattery; cajolery. • *vt* to flatter, cajole. • *vi* to talk idly.

palaeo- /ˈpeɪlɪoː/ or /-ə/, *Brit.* /ˈpælioː/ or /-ə/ *prefix* old; ancient; prehistoric.

palaeobotany /ˌpeɪlioːˈbɒtəni/ or /ˌpælioː-/ *n* the study of fossil plants.—*also US* **paleobotany**.

palaeography /ˌpeɪlioˈɒɡrəfi/ *n* the study of ancient writing and manuscripts.—*also US* **paleography**.—**palaeographic, palaeographical** *adj*.—**palaeographer** *n*.

Palaeolithic /ˌpeɪlioˈlɪθɪk/ *adj* pertaining to the early Stone Age.—*also US* **Paleolithic**.

palaeontology /ˌpeɪlioɒnˈtɒlədʒi/ or /-lɪɑn-/ *n* the study of fossils.—*also US* **paleontology**.—**palaeontological** *adj*.—**palaeontologist** *n*.

Palaeozoic /ˌpeɪlioˈzoːɪk/ *adj* pertaining to the geological period in which fossils of the earliest forms of life appear which began 600 million years ago and ended 225 million years ago.—*also US* **Paleozoic**.

palaeozoology /ˌpeɪlioɒzuːˈɒlədʒi/ *n* the study of fossil animals.—*also US* **paleozoology**.—**palaeozoological** *adj*.—**palaeozoologist** *n*.

pale[1] /peɪl/ *n* a fence stake; a boundary; (*her*) a vertical stripe in the middle of a shield.

pale[2] *adj* (*complexion*) with less colour than usual; (*colour, light*) faint, wan, dim. • *vti* to make or become pale.—**palely** *adv*.—**paleness** *n*.

paleface /ˈpeɪlfeɪs/ *n* (*derog*) a term for a white person, supposedly used by Native Americans.

paleo- /ˈpeɪlioː/ or /ˈpælioː/ *see* **palaeo-**.

paleobotany /ˌpeɪlioːˈbɒtəni/ or /ˌpælioː-/ *see* **palaeobotany**.

paleography /ˌpeɪlioˈɒɡrəfi/ *see* **palaeography**.

Paleolithic /ˌpeɪlioˈlɪθɪk/ *see* **Palaeolithic**.

Paleozoic /ˌpeɪlioˈzoːɪk/ *see* **Palaeozoic**.

paleozoology /ˌpeɪlioɒzuːˈɒlədʒi/ *see* **palaeozoology**.

palette /ˈpælət/ *n* a small, wooden board on which coloured paints are mixed.

palette knife *n* (*pl* **palette knives**) a thin knife used for mixing colours; a round-ended, flexible knife used in cookery.

palfrey /ˈpɒlfri/ *n* (*arch*) a saddle horse, *esp* for a woman.

palimony /ˈpælɪmoːni/ *n* (*inf*) the payment of alimony from one partner in a formal long-term sexual relationship to the other.

palimpsest /ˈpælɪmpˌsest/ *n* a manuscript which has been written on more than once, the former writing being still discernible in spite of erasure.

palindrome /ˈpælɪnˌdroːm/ *n* a word or sentence reading the same forwards as backwards, *eg* "Able was I ere I saw Elba".—**palindromic** *adj*.

paling /ˈpeɪlɪŋ/ *n* a row of stakes in a fence; a railing.

palingenesis /ˌpælɪnˈdʒenɪsɪs/ *n* (*pl* **palingeneses**) (*theology*) spiritual rebirth through baptism.—**palingenetic** *adj*.

palinode /ˈpælɪˌnoːd/ *n* a poem retracting a former poem.

palisade /ˌpælɪˈseɪd/ *n* a fence made of pointed stakes driven into the ground; a pointed stake used in a fence of this kind.

palish /ˈpeɪlɪʃ/ *adj* somewhat pale.

pall[1] /pɒl/ *n* a heavy cloth over a coffin; (*of smoke*) a mantle.

pall[2] *vi* to become boring; to become satiated.

Palladian /pəˈleɪdiən/ *adj* in the pseudo-classical style of the architect Andrea Palladio (1518–80).

palladium /pəˈleɪdiəm/ *n* a rare greyish-white metal found with platinum.

pallbearer /ˈpɒlˌberər/ *n* someone who carries the coffin at a funeral.

pallet[1] /ˈpælət/ *n* a portable platform for lifting and stacking goods.

pallet[2] *n* a straw bed.

palletize, palletise /ˈpæləˌtaɪz/ *vt* to stack, transport or store on pallets.—**palletization, palletisation** *n*.

palliasse /ˈpæliˌæs/ *n* a straw mattress.—*also* **paillasse**.

palliate /ˈpæliˌeɪt/ *vt* to extenuate, to excuse; to alleviate without curing.—**palliation** *n*.—**palliator** *n*.

palliative /ˈpæliətɪv/ *adj* alleviating without curing; excusing, extenuating. • *n* a thing that palliates.

pallid /ˈpælɪd/ *adj* wan, pale.—**pallidness** *n*.

pallium /ˈpæliəm/ *n* (*pl* **pallia, palliums**) a white woollen scarf worn by an archbishop; (*anat*) the cerebral cortex and surrounding matter; (*zool*) a mollusc's outer fold of skin.

pallor /ˈpælər/ *n* paleness, *esp* of the face.

pally /ˈpæli/ *adj* (**pallier, palliest**) friendly with; intimate.

palm[1] /pɒm/ or /pɒlm/ *n* the underside of the hand between fingers and wrist. • *vt* to conceal in or touch with the palm; (*with* **off**) to pass off by fraud, foist.

palm[2] *n* a tropical branchless tree with fan-shaped leaves; a symbol of victory.

palmaceous /pælˈmeɪʃəs/ *adj* of the palm family.

palmar /ˈpælmər/ *adj* of or in the palm of the hand.

palmate /ˈpælmeɪt/, **palmated** *adj* like an open hand; (*bot*) having leaves with lobes radiating from a common point; (*zool*) web-footed.—**palmation** *n*.

palmer /ˈpɒmər/ *n* (*formerly*) a pilgrim returning from the Holy Land, carrying a palm branch as a token of the pilgrimage.

palmetto /pælˈmetoː/ or /pɒl-/ *n* (*pl* **palmettos, palmettoes**) a species of small palm tree.

palmistry /ˈpɒmɪstri/ or /ˈpɒlm-/ *n* foretelling the future from lines of the hand.—**palmist** *n*.

Palm Sunday *n* the Sunday before Easter.

palm-top /ˈpɒmtɒp/ or /ˈpɒlm-/ *n* a portable computer small enough to fit in the palm of the hand.

palmy /ˈpɒmi/ or /ˈpɒlmi/ *adj* (**palmier, palmiest**) abounding in palm trees; (*fig*) flourishing, prosperous.

palmyra /pælˈmaɪrə/ *n* a palm found in Asia, the leaves of which are used for matting and thatching.

palomino /ˌpæləˈmiːnoː/ *n* (*pl* **palominos**) a horse with a golden or cream-coloured coat and a white mane and tail.

palp /pælp/, **palpus** /ˈpælpəs/ *n* (*pl* **palps, palpi**) a jointed feeler attached to the mouth parts of an insect.

palpable /ˈpælpəbəl/ *adj* tangible; easily perceived, obvious.—**palpability** *n*.—**palpably** *adj*.

palpate /ˈpælpeɪt/ *vt* to examine by touch, *esp* medically.—**palpation** *n*.

palpebral /pælˈpiːbrəl/ *adj* of the eyelids.

palpitate /ˈpælpɪˌteɪt/ *vi* (*heart*) to beat abnormally fast; to tremble, flutter.—**palpitation** *n*.

palsy /ˈpɒlzi/ *n* (*pl* **palsies**) paralysis; a condition marked by an uncontrollable tremor of a part of the body. • *vt* (**palsying, palsied**) to paralyse; to make helpless.

palter /ˈpɒltər/ *vi* to be insincere.

paltry /ˈpɒltri/ *adj* (**paltrier, paltriest**) almost worthless; trifling.—**paltrily** *adv*.—**paltriness** *n*.

pampas /ˈpæmpəs/ *npl* the treeless, grassy plains of South America.

pampas grass *n* a tall-stemmed South American grass growing in thick tussocks.

pamper /ˈpæmpər/ *vt* to overindulge; to coddle, spoil.—**pamperer** *n*.

pampero /pæm'peɪroː/ or /-'peroː/ n (pl **pamperos**) a cold south or south west wind which blows across the pampas.

pamphlet /'pæmflət/ n a thin, unbound booklet, esp one attacking or advocating a cause, etc; a brochure.—**pamphleteer** n.

Pan /'pæn/ n (Greek myth) the god of woods and fields.—**Pandean** adj.

pan[1] /pæn/ n a wide metal container, a saucepan; (of scales) a tray; a depression in the earth filled with water; severe criticism; the bowl of a lavatory. • vb (**panning, panned**) •vi (with **out**) (inf) to turn out, esp to turn out well; to succeed. • vt to wash gold-bearing gravel in a pan; (inf) to disparage, find fault with.

pan[2] n a betel leaf; a mixture of betel nuts and lime wrapped in a betel leaf used for chewing.

pan[3] vti (**panning, panned**) (film camera) to move horizontally to follow an object or provide a panoramic view.—also n.

pan- /pæn/ prefix all; general.

panacea /,pænə'siːə/ n a cure-all, universal remedy.—**panacean** adj.

panache /pə'næʃ/ n flair; sense of style.

panada /pə'nɒdə/ or /-'neɪ-/ n (cooking) bread boiled to a pulp and flavoured, used as a sauce base or as stuffing.

panama /'pænə,mɒ/ n a hat of a fine, straw-like material.

Pan-American /,pænə'merɪkən/ adj of or pertaining to North, South and Central America collectively; advocating unity among American countries.

panatella /,pænə'telə/ n a long, slim cigar.

pancake /'pænkeɪk/ or /'pæŋ-/ n a round, thin cake made from batter and cooked on a griddle; a thing shaped thus. • vi (aircraft) to descend vertically in a level position.

panchromatic /,pænkro'mætɪk/ adj (photog) sensitive to light of all colours.

pancreas /'pæŋkrɪəs/ n a large gland secreting a digestive juice into the intestine and also producing insulin.—**pancreatic** adj.

pancreatin /'pæŋkrɪətɪn/ n a clear fluid secreted by the pancreas, often extracted from animals and used in medicine.

panda /'pændə/ n a large black and white bear-like herbivore (also **giant panda**); a related reddish-brown raccoon-like animal with a ringed tail —also **lesser panda**.

Pandean /pæn'dɪən/ adj pertaining to the god Pan.

pandemic /pæn'demɪk/ adj epidemic over a large region, universal.

pandemonium /,pændə'moːnɪəm/ n (pl **pandemoniums**) uproar; chaos.

pander /'pændər/ n a go-between in sexual liaisons; a pimp. • vi (usu with **to**) to gratify or exploit a person's desires or weaknesses, etc.—**panderer** n.

pandit /'pʌndɪt/ see **pundit**.

P & L abbr = profit and loss.

pane /peɪn/ n a sheet of glass in a frame of a window, door, etc.—**paned** adj.

panegyric /,pænɪ'dʒaɪrɪk/ n an ovation or eulogy in praise of a person or event.—**panegyrical** adj.—**panegyrist** n.

panegyrize /'pænɪdʒɪ,raɪz/ vti to compose a panegyric (about); to praise highly.

panel /'pænəl/ n a usu rectangular section or division forming part of a wall, door, etc; a board for instruments or controls; a lengthwise strip in a skirt, etc; a group of selected persons for judging, discussing, etc. • vt (**panelling, panelled** or **paneling, paneled**) to decorate with panels.

panelling, paneling /'pænəlɪŋ/ n panels collectively; sheets of wood, plastic, etc used for panels.

panellist, panelist /'pænəlɪst/ n a member of a panel.

panelology /'pænə,lədʒɪ/ n the collection of comic books as a hobby.

pang /pæŋ/ n a sudden sharp pain or feeling.

pangenesis /pæn'dʒenəsɪs/ n (formerly) the theory that reproductive cells contain particles from all parts of the parents.—**pangenetic** adj.

pangolin /pæŋ'goːlɪn/ n an insectivorous mammal, also known as the spiny anteater, found in Africa and Asia.

panhandle[1] /'pæn,hændəl/ n a narrow, projecting tongue of land.

panhandle[2] vi (inf) to beg, esp from passers-by. • vt (inf) to obtain by begging.

panic /'pænɪk/ n a sudden overpowering fright or terror.—also adj. • vti (**panicking, panicked**) to affect or be affected with panic.—**panicky** adj.

panic button n a switch for setting off an alarm; (sl) a frenzied response.

panicle /'pænɪkəl/ n (bot) an irregularly bunched flower cluster.

panic-stricken, panic-struck adj affected by panic.

paniculate /'pænɪkjʊlət/, **paniculated** /-əd/ adj (bot) arranged in panicles.

panjandrum /pæn'dʒændrəm/ n a pompous official.

panne /pæn/ n a soft, velvet-like fabric.

pannier /'pænjər/ n a large basket for carrying loads on the back of an animal or the shoulders of a person; a bag or case slung over the rear wheel of a bicycle or motorcycle.

pannikin /'pænɪkɪn/ n a small metal drinking-cup.

panoply /'pænəplɪ/ n (pl **panoplies**) a complete array; a full suit of armour.—**panoplied** adj.

panorama /,pænə'ræmə/ n a complete view in all directions; a comprehensive presentation of a subject; a constantly changing scene.—**panoramic** adj.—**panoramically** adv.

panpipes /'pæn,paɪp/ npl a wind instrument consisting of short hollow tubes of different lengths, originally of reed, bound together.

pansy /'pænzɪ/ n (pl **pansies**) a garden flower of the violet family, with velvety petals; (sl) an effeminate boy or man.

pant /pænt/ vi to breathe noisily, gasp; to yearn (for or after something). • vt to speak while gasping.

pantalets, pantalettes /,pæntə'lets/ npl a woman's long ruffled drawers.

pantaloon /,pæntə'luːn/ n (pantomine) a foolish old man on whom the clown plays tricks.

pantaloons /,pæntə'luːn/ npl (hist) a man's tight breeches fastened at the calf or the foot; (inf) baggy trousers.

pantheism /'pænθɪ,zəm/ n the doctrine that the universe in its totality is God; willingness to worship all, or several gods.—**pantheist** n.—**pantheistic, pantheistical** adj.

pantheon /'pænθɪɒn/ n a temple to all the gods; a building in which the famous dead of a nation are buried or remembered; a group of famous persons.

panther /'pænθər/ n (pl **panther, panthers**) a leopard, esp one with a black unspotted coat; a puma.

pantihose /'pæntɪ,hoːz/ n women's tights.—also **panty hose**.

panties /'pæntɪz/ npl (inf) short underpants.

pantile /'pæntaɪl/ n a roof tile with an S-shaped cross-section.

panto /'pæntoː/ n (pl **pantos**) (Brit inf) a pantomime.

pantograph /'pæntə,græf/ n an instrument for copying drawings, maps, etc, to scale.

pantomime /'pæntə,maɪm/ n (Brit) a Christmas theatrical entertainment with music and jokes; a drama without words, using only actions and gestures; mime. • vti to mime.—**pantomimic** adj.

pantomimist /'pæntə,maɪmɪst/ n a person who performs in a pantomime; one who composes a pantomime.

pantoum /pæntaʊm/ n a verse form of four-lined rhyming stanzas.

pantry /'pæntrɪ/ n (pl **pantries**) a small room or cupboard for storing cooking ingredients and utensils, etc.

pants /pænts/ npl trousers; underpants.

panty hose /'pæntihoːz/ see **pantihose**.

panzer /'pænzər/ adj (division) armoured. • n a tank, or other armoured vehicle, from a panzer division; (pl) armoured troops.

pap /pæp/ n soft, bland food for infants, invalids, etc; any oversimplified or insipid writing, ideas, etc.

papa /'pɒpə/ or /pə'pɒ/ n (inf) father.

papacy /'peɪpəsɪ/ n (pl **papacies**) the office or authority of the pope; papal system of government.

papal /'peɪpəl/ adj of the pope or the papacy.—**papally** adv.

paparazzo /,pæpə'rætsoː/ n (pl **paparazzi** /-tsɪ/) a freelance photographer who pursues celebrities for sensational or candid shots for publication in newspapers and magazines.

papaveraceous /,pæpəvə'reɪʃəs/ adj (bot) pertaining or belonging to the poppy family.

papaw /pə'pɔː/ or /'pɔ,pɔː/ n (the small edible fruit of) a North American tree of the custard-apple family; another name for papaya.—also **pawpaw**.

papaya /pə'paɪjə/ n (a West Indian tree bearing) an elongated melon-like fruit with edible yellow flesh and small black seeds.

paper /'peɪpər/ n the thin, flexible material made from pulped rags, wood, etc which is used to write on, wrap in, or cover walls; a single sheet of this; an official document; a newspaper; an essay or lecture; a set of examination questions; (pl) personal documents. • adj like or made of paper. • vt to cover with wallpaper.

paperback /'peɪpər,bæk/ n a book bound in a flexible paper cover. • adj pertaining to such a book or the publication of such books.

papering /'peɪpərɪŋ/ n the process of covering with paper; paper so used.

paperknife n (pl **paperknives**) a blunt knife for opening letters or cutting folded paper.

paper money n banknotes; paper currency authorized by a government as representing value.

paperweight /'peɪpər,weɪt/ n a small heavy object for keeping papers in place.

paperwork /'peɪpər,wɜrk/ n clerical work of any kind.

papery /'peɪpəri/ adj like paper in appearance or consistency.—**paperiness** n.

papeterie /'pæpətri/ n a case containing paper and writing materials.

papier-mâché /'peɪpər mə'ʃeɪ/ n a substance made of paper pulp mixed with size, glue, etc and moulded into various objects when moist.

papilla /pə'pɪlə/ n (pl **papillae**) a small, nipple-like protuberance.—**papillary, papillate, papillose** adj.

papoose /pə'puːs/ n an American Indian young child.

pappus /'pæpəs/ n (pl **pappi**) (bot) the feathery substance on the seeds of some plants, eg dandelion, thistle.

pappy /'pæpi/ adj (**pappier, pappiest**) semi-liquid, like pap.

paprika /'pæprɪkə/ or /pə'priːkə/ n a mild red condiment ground from the fruit of certain peppers.

Pap test, Pap smear /pæp-/ n a technique for the early detection of cancer by examining specially stained cells from the cervix, etc.

papule /'pæpjuːl/, **papula** /-jʊlə/ n (pl **papules, papulae** /-jʊliː/) a small, solid elevation of the skin.—**papular** adj.

papyrology /,pæpɪ'rɒlədʒi/ n the study of papyri.—**papyrologist** n.

papyrus /pə'paɪrəs/ n (pl **papyri, papyruses**) an aquatic plant; paper made from this plant, as used in ancient times.

par /pɑr/ n the standard or normal level; the established value of a currency in foreign-exchange rates; the face value of stocks, shares, etc; (golf) the score for a hole required by an expert player; equality.

par- /pɑr/ or /pɜr/, **para-** prefix beside; against; irregular; abnormal; associated in a subsidiary or accessory capacity.

para /'pærə/ n (pl **paras**) (inf) a paragraph; a paratrooper.

parabasis /'pærəbəsɪs/ n (pl **parabases**) (classical Greek comedy) an address to the audience by the chorus.

parable /'pærəbəl/ or /'pæ-/ n a short story used to illustrate a religious or moral point.—**parabolist** n.

parabola /pə'ræbələ/ n (pl **parabolas**) (maths) the curve formed by the cutting of a cone by a plane parallel to its side.

parabolic[1] /,pærə'bɒlɪk/ or /,pæ-/ adj of or like a parabola; parabolical.

parabolic[2], **parabolical** adj of or expressed in a parable.—**parabolically** adv.

paraboloid /pə'ræbə,lɔɪd/ n (geom) a solid formed by the revolution of a parabola on its axis.

parachronism /pəræ'krɒnɪzəm/ n an error in chronology, esp in postdating an event.

parachute /'pærə,ʃuːt/ or /'pæ-/ n a fabric umbrella-like canopy used to retard speed of fall from an aircraft. • vti to drop, descend by parachute.—**parachutist** n.

paraclete /'pærə,kliːt/ or /'pæ-/ n a mediator.

parade /pə'reɪd/ n a ceremonial procession; an assembly of troops for review; ostentatious display; public walk, promenade. • vti to march or walk through, as for display; to show off; to assemble in military order.

paradigm /'pærə,daɪm/ n a pattern or model; a list of grammatical inflexions of a word.—**paradigmatic** adj.—**paradigmatically** adv.

paradise /'pærə,daɪs/ n heaven; (Bible) the Garden of Eden; any place of perfection.

paradisiacal /-'dɪsɪkəl/, **paradisiac** adj like, or pertaining to, paradise.

paradox /'pærə,dɒks/ n a self-contradictory statement that may be true; an opinion that conflicts with common beliefs; something with seemingly contradictory qualities or phases.—**paradoxical** adj.—**paradoxically** adv.

paraesthesia /pɛ,rəs'θiːsɪə/ n (med) an abnormal tickling sensation on the skin.—also US **paresthesia**.—**paraesthetic** adj.

paraffin /'pærəfɪn/ n a white waxy tasteless substance obtained from shale, wood, etc; a distilled oil used as fuel, kerosene.—**paraffinic** adj.

paragenesis /,pærə'dʒenəsɪs/, **paragenesia** n (geol) the sequence of formation of the various minerals in a mass of rock—**paragenetic** adj.

paragoge /,pærə'goʊdʒi/, **paragogue** n (linguistics) the addition of a letter or a syllable to a word.

paragon /'pærəgɒn/ n a model of excellence or perfection.

paragraph /'pærə,græf/ n a subdivision in a piece of writing used to separate ideas, marked by the beginning of a new line; a brief mention in a newspaper. • vt to divide into paragraphs.—**paragraphic** adj.—**paragraphically** adv.

Paraguay tea /'pærə,gweɪ/ or /-waɪ/ n an infusion of the dried leaves of maté, which makes a mildly stimulating tea.—also **yerba maté**.

parakeet /'pærə,kiːt/ n a small parrot.

paraldehyde /pə'rældə,haɪd/ n a colourless liquid used as a sedative.

paraleipsis /,pærə'laɪpsɪs/, **paralipsis** /,pærə'lɪpsɪs/ n (pl **paraleipses, paralipses**) (rhetoric) drawing attention to something by deliberately understating it.

parallax /'pærə,læks/ n the apparent angular shifting of an object caused by a change in position of the observer; (astron) the difference in the apparent position of a heavenly body and its true place.

parallel /'pærə,lɛl/ adj equidistant at every point and extended in the same direction; side by side; never intersecting; similar, corresponding. • n a parallel line, surface, etc; a likeness, counterpart; comparison; a line of latitude. • vt (**paralleling, paralleled**) to make or be parallel; to compare.

parallelepiped /,pærəlɛl'ɛpɪ,ped/ or /-lə'pəɪpɪd/ n a regular solid figure bounded by six parallelograms, of which the opposite pairs are equal and parallel.

parallelism /'pærəlɛlɪzəm/ n the state or quality of being parallel.

parallelogram /,pærə'lɛlə,græm/ n a four-sided plane figure whose opposite sides are parallel.

paralogism /pə'rælə,dʒɪzəm/ n (logic) a fallacy in reasoning made unconsciously by the reasoner.

paralyze, paralyse /'pærə,laɪz/ vt to affect with paralysis; to bring to a stop.—**paralysation** n.

paralysis /pə'rælɪsɪs/ n (pl **paralyses** /-,siːz/) a partial or complete loss of voluntary muscle function or sensation in any part of the body; a condition of helpless inactivity.—**paralytic** adj, n.

paramatta /,pærə'mætə/ n a light fabric of cotton and wool.—also **parramatta**.

paramedic /,pærə'mɛdɪk/ n a a person trained to provide emergency medical treatment and to support professional medical staff.

paramedical /,pærə'mɛdɪkəl/ adj (services) supplementing and assisting the work of professional medical staff.

parameter /pə'ræmətər/ n (math) an arbitrary constant, the value of which influences the content but not the structure of an expression; (inf) a limit or condition affecting action, decision, etc.—**parametric** adj.—**parametrically** adv.

paramilitary /,pærə'mɪlɪteri/ or /-tri/ adj (forces) organized on a military pattern and ancillary to military forces.

paramo /'pærə,moʊ/ n (pl **paramos**) a high bleak plateau in the Andes.

paramount /'pærə,maʊnt/ adj of great importance.

paramour /'pærə,mʊr/ n an illicit lover.

parang /'pæræŋ/ n a heavy Malay sheath knife.

paranoia /,pærə'nɔɪə/ n a mental illness characterized by delusions of grandeur and persecution; (inf) unfounded fear, suspicion.—**paranoiac** adj, n.

paranoid /'pærə,nɔɪd/ adj of or like paranoia; (inf) highly suspicious or fearful.—also n.

paranormal /,pærə'nɔrməl/ adj beyond the scope of normal experience or scientific explanation.—**paranormally** adv.

parapet /'pærəpət/ n a low, protective wall along the edge of a roof, balcony, or bridge, etc.—**parapeted** adj.

paraph /'pæræf/ n a mark or flourish after a signature.

paraphernalia /,pærəfə'neɪljə/ npl personal belongings; accessories; (law) what a wife possesses in her own right.

paraphrase /'pærə,freɪz/ n expression of a passage in other words in order to clarify meaning. • vt to restate.—**paraphrastic** adj.

paraplegia /,pærə'pliːdʒə/ n paralysis of the lower half of the body.—**paraplegic** adj.

parasailing /ˈpærəseɪlɪŋ/ *n* the sport of gliding through the air attached to an open parachute and towed by a speedboat.—**parasailer, parasailor** *n*.

parascending /ˌpærəˈsəndɪŋ/ *n* a form of parachuting in which participants wearing open parachutes are towed into the air by a vehicle or speedboat and then released to glide to the ground.—**parascender** *n*.

paraselene /ˌperəsiˈliːni/ *n* (*pl* **paraselenae** /-niː/) (*astron*) a bright spot on a lunar halo.

parasite /ˈperəˌsaɪt/ *n* an organism that lives on and feeds off another without rendering any service in return; a person who sponges off another.—**parasitic** *adj*.—**parasitically** *adv*.

parasiticide /-ˈsɪtɪˌsaɪd/ *n* a substance which kills parasites.

parasitism /ˈperəsaɪˌtɪzəm/ *n* the parasite-host relationship; the state or behaviour of a parasite.

parasitize /ˈperəsɪˌtaɪz/ *n* to infest with parasites.

parasitology /-ˈtɒlədʒi/ *n* the study of parasites.—**parasitologist** *n*.

parasol /ˈpærəˌsɒl/ *n* a lightweight umbrella used as a sunshade.

parasynthesis /ˌperəˈsɪnθəsɪs/ *n* (*gram*) derivation from a compound plus affix, *eg* faint-hearted, which is made up from faint + heart + -ed.

parataxis /ˌperəˈtæksɪs/ *n* (*gram*) use of successive clauses without connecting words.

parathyroid /ˌperəˈθaɪrɔɪd/ *adj* (*anat*) lying near the thyroid gland. • *n* a gland near the thyroid that secretes a hormone that regulates the body's calcium levels.

paratroops /ˈpærətruːps/ *npl* troops dropped by parachute into the enemy area.—**paratrooper** *n*.

paravane /ˈperəˌveɪn/ *n* a device shaped like a torpedo, with serrated teeth for destroying the moorings of sea mines.

parboil /ˈparˌbɔɪl/ *vt* to boil briefly as a preliminary cooking procedure.

parbuckle /ˈparˌbʌkəl/ *n* a rope sling for raising or lowering casks.

parcel /ˈparsəl/ *n* a tract or plot of land; a wrapped bundle; a package; a collection or group of persons, animals, or things. • *vt* (**parcelling, parcelled** *or* **parceling, parceled**) to wrap up into a parcel; (*with* **out**) to apportion.

parcenary /ˈparsəˌneri/ *n* joint heirship.

parcener /ˈparsənər/ *n* a coheir.

parch /partʃ/ *vti* to make or become hot and dry, thirsty; to scorch, roast.—**parched** *adj*.

parchment /ˈpartʃmənt/ *n* the skin of a sheep, etc prepared as a writing material; paper like parchment.

pard /pard/ *n* (*arch*) a leopard.

pardon /ˈpardən/ *vt* to forgive; to excuse; to release from penalty. • *n* forgiveness; remission of penalty.—**pardonable** *adj*.—**pardonably** *adv*.

pardoner /ˈpardənər/ *n* one who pardons; (*hist*) a person licensed to sell papal indulgences.

pare /per/ *vt* to cut or shave; to peel; to diminish.

paregoric /ˌperɪˈgɒrɪk/ *n* (*formerly*) an opium-based drug used to treat diarrhoea and coughs.

parenchyma /pəˈreŋkɪmə/ *n* (*bot*) the soft cellular tissue or pith of plants; (*anat*) the soft tissue of the glandular organs of the body.—**parenchymatous, parenchymal** *adj*.

parent /ˈperənt/ *n* a father or a mother; an organism producing another; a source.—**parental** *adj*.—**parentally** *adv*.—**parenthood** *n*.

parentage /ˈperəntɪdʒ/ *n* descent, extraction from parents.

parenthesis /pəˈrenθəsɪs/ *n* (*pl* **parentheses**) an explanatory comment in a sentence contained within brackets and set in a sentence, independently of grammatical sequence; the brackets themselves ().—**parenthetic, parenthetical** *adj*.—**parenthetically** *adv*.

parenthesize, parenthesise /pəˈrenθəˌsaɪz/ *vt* to insert as a parenthesis; to enclose in parentheses.

parenting /ˈperəntɪŋ/ *n* the act of being a parent; the role of a parent in relation to a child; that role in relation to someone who is not the child of a parent.

paresis /pəˈriːsɪs/ *or* /ˈperɪsɪs/ *n* partial or slight paralysis.—**paretic** *adj*.

par excellence /ˌpar eksəˈlɑːs/ *or* /par ˈeksəˌlɑːs/ *adv* pre-eminently; to the highest degree.

parfait /parˈfeɪ/ *n* a rich iced dessert of whipped cream, eggs, etc served in a tall glass; layers of ice cream served in a tall glass.

parget /ˈpardʒət/ *n* a type of plaster. • *vt* to cover with parget.

parhelion /parˈhiːlɪən/ *n* (*pl* **parhelia**) a bright spot on a solar halo.

pariah /pəˈraɪə/ *n* a social outcast; a member of a low caste in southern India and Burma.

parietal /pəˈraɪətəl/ *adj* (*anat*) pertaining to the wall of a cavity of the body; pertaining to the large lateral bones of the skull.

paring /ˈperɪŋ/ *n* the act of paring; what is pared off, rind.

pari-mutuel /ˌpæriːˈmjuːtʃuːˌel/ *n* (*pl* **pari-mutuels, pari-mutuels**) a mechanical betting system in which the losers' stakes, less a deduction for the management, are divided among the winners.

pari passu /ˌparɪ ˈpæsuː/ *or* /ˌperi/ *adv* (*law*) with equal pace, together; in equal degree.

parish /ˈperɪʃ/ *n* an ecclesiastical area with its own church and clergy; the inhabitants of a parish.

parishioner /pəˈrɪʃənər/ *n* an inhabitant of a parish.

parisyllabic /ˌpærɪsɪˈlæbɪk/ *adj* (*inflected noun or verb*) having an equal number of syllables in all or most inflected forms.

parity /ˈperɪti/ *n* (*pl* **parities**) equality; equality of value at a given ratio between different kinds of money, etc; being at par.

park /park/ *n* land kept as a game preserve or recreation area; a piece of ground in an urban area kept for ornament or recreation; an enclosed stadium, *esp* for ball games; a large enclosed piece of ground attached to a country house. • *vti* (*vehicle*) to leave in a certain place temporarily; to manoeuvre into a parking space.

parka /ˈparkə/ *n* a warm hooded garment, often of fur, for wear in arctic conditions.

parking lot /ˈparkɪŋ/ *n* a car park.

parking meter *n* a coin-operated machine that registers the purchase of parking time for a motor vehicle.

Parkinsonism /ˈparkɪnsəˌnɪzəm/ *n* Parkinson's disease.

Parkinson's disease *n* a progressive nervous disease resulting in tremor, muscular rigidity, partial paralysis and weakness.

Parkinson's Law *n* any of various humorous observations on human behaviour framed as economic laws, *esp* the notion that work expands to fill the time available for its completion (named after the English writer C N Parkinson b.1909).

parlance /ˈparləns/ *n* a manner of speech, idiom.

parkland /ˈparklənd/ *n* open grassland with widely scattered groves of trees.

parley /ˈparleɪ/ *or* /ˈparleɪ/, /ˈparli/ *n* a conference, *esp* with an enemy. • *vi* to discuss, *esp* with an enemy with a view to bringing about a peace.

parliament /ˈparləmənt/ *n* a legislative assembly made up of representatives of a nation or part of a nation; (*with cap*) the supreme governing and legislative body of various countries, *esp* the UK.

parliamentarian /ˌparləmənˈterɪən/ *n* a skilled parliamentary debater; an expert on parliamentary rules; (*with cap*) (*hist*) a supporter of the English Parliament against Charles I.

parliamentary /ˌparləˈmentri/ *or* /-ˈmentəri/ *adj* of, used in, or enacted by a parliament; conforming to the rules of a parliament; having a parliament.

parlour /ˈparlər/ *n* a room in a house used primarily for conversation or receiving guests; a room or a shop used for business.

parlour game *n* a game usually played indoors.

parlous /ˈparləs/ *adj* (*arch*) dangerous; shrewd.—**parlously** *adv*.—**parlousness** *n*.

parmales /parˈmæləs/ *n* any of the order Parmales of single-celled algae found in the polar regions.

Parmesan /ˈparmɪˌzɒn/ *or* /-zən/, /-zæn/, /-ʒɒn/, /-ʒæn/, /-ˈzɒn/, /-ˈʒɒn/ *n* a hard cheese with a sharp flavour used, *esp* grated, as a garnish.

parochial /pəˈroːkiəl/ *adj* of or relating to a parish; narrow; provincial in outlook.—**parochially** *adv*.

parochialism /pəˈroːkiəlɪzəm/ *n* narrow-mindedness.

parody /ˈperədi/ *or* /ˈpæ-/ *n* (*pl* **parodies**) a satirical or humorous imitation of a literary or musical work or style. • *vt* (**parodying, parodied**) to make a parody of.—**parodic** *adj*.—**parodist** *n*.

paroicous /pəˈrɔɪʃəs/, **paroecious** /ˌperəˈiːʃəs/ *adj* (*bot*) with the two sexes developing in close proximity.

parole /pəˈroːl/ *n* word of honour; the release of a prisoner before his sentence has expired, on condition of future good behaviour. • *vt* to release on parole.

parolee /ˈpæˈliː/ *n* a person on parole.

paronomasia /ˌperənəˈmeɪziə/ *n* a pun or play on words.

paronym /ˈperənɪm/ *n* (*gram*) a paronymic word.

paronymic, paronymous /pə'rɒnıməs/ *adj* (*gram*) with the same derivation; with the same sound but different spelling and meaning.

parotid /pə'rɒtɪd/ *adj* (*anat*) situated near the ear. • *n* a parotid gland.

parotitis /ˌperə'taıtıs/, **parotiditis** *n* mumps.

paroxysm /'perək,sızəm/ *n* a sudden attack of a disease; a violent convulsion of pain or emotion; an outburst of laughter.— **paroxysmal** *adj*.

parquet /par'keı/ or /'par-/ *n* an inlaid hard wood flooring; the stalls of a theatre below the balcony. • *vt* to furnish (a room) with a parquet floor.

parquetry /'parkıtri/ *n* mosaic woodwork used to cover floors.

parr /par/ *n* (*pl* **parrs, parr**) a young salmon.

parramatta /ˌperə'mætə/ *see* **paramatta**.

parrot /'perət/ *n* a tropical or subtropical bird with brilliant plumage and the ability to mimic human speech; one who repeats another's words without understanding. • *vt* to repeat mechanically.

parrotfish /'perət,fıʃ/ *n* (*pl* **parrotfish, parrotfishes**) a brightly coloured tropical fish, with mouth parts resembling a parrot's beak.

parry /'peri/ *vt* (**parrying, parried**) to ward off, turn aside. • *n* (*pl* **parries**) a defensive movement in fencing.

parse /pars/ or /parz/ *vti* (*words*) to classify; (*sentences*) to analyse in terms of grammar; to give a grammatical description of a word or group of words.

parsec /'parsek/ *n* (*astron*) a unit of measure for stellar distances equal to 3.26 light years, approx 19 million miles.

Parsee /par'si:/ *n* an Indian adherent of the Zoroastrian religion.—**Parseeism** *n*.

parsimony /'parsı,mo:ni/ *n* extreme frugality; meanness, stinginess.—**parsimonious** *adj*.

parsley /'parsli/ *n* a bright green herb used to flavour or garnish some foods.

parsnip /'parsnıp/ *n* a biennial plant cultivated for its long tapered root used as a vegetable.

parson /'parsən/ *n* an Anglican clergyman in charge of a parish; (*inf*) any, *esp* Protestant, clergyman.

parsonage /'parsənıdʒ/ *n* the house provided for a parson by his church.

part /part/ *n* a section; a portion (of a whole); an essential, separable component of a piece of equipment or a machine; the role of an actor in a play; a written copy of his/her words; (*mus*) one of the melodies of a harmony; the music for it; duty, share; one of the sides in a conflict; a parting of the hair; (*pl*) qualities, talent; the genitals; a region, land or territory. • *vt* to separate; to comb the hair so as to leave a parting. • *vi* to become separated; to go different ways.

partake /par'teık/ *vi* (**partaking, partook**; *pp* **partaken**) to participate (in); (*food or drink*) to have a portion of.

partan /'partən/ *n* (*Scot*) a crab.

parterre /par'ter/ *n* an ornamental flower garden; the area of a ground floor of a theatre that lies underneath the balconies.

parthenocarpy /'parθəno:ˌkarpi/ *n* (*bot*) the formation of fruit without seeds having been formed or fertilized.

parthenogenesis /ˌparθəno:'dʒenəsıs/ *n* reproduction without sexual union; virgin birth.—**parthenogenetic** *adj*.

partial /'parʃəl/ *adj* incomplete; biased, prejudiced; (*with* **to**) having a liking or preference for.—**partially** *adv*.

partiality /ˌparʃi'ælıti/ *n* (*pl* **partialities**) biased judgment; (*with* **for**) liking, fondness.

partible /'partəbəl/ *adj* able to be divided or separated.

participant /par'tısəpənt/ *n* one who participates; a sharer.

participate /par'tısəpeıt/ *vi* to join in or take part with others (in some activity).—**participator** *n*.—**participatory** *adj*.

participation /-'peıʃən/ *n* the act of participating; the state of being related to a political body.

participle /'partı,sıpəl/ or /par'tısəpəl/ *n* (*gram*) a verb form used in compound forms or as an adjective.—**participial** *adj*.—**participially** *adv*.

particle /'partıkəl/ *n* a tiny portion of matter; a speck; a very small part; (*gram*) a word that cannot be used alone, a prefix, a suffix.

parti-coloured *adj* differently coloured in different parts, variegated.

particular /par'tıkjulər/ or /pər-/, /pə-/ *adj* referring or belonging to a specific person or thing; distinct; exceptional; careful; fastidious. • *n* a detail, single item; (*pl*) detailed information.

particularism /par'tıkjulə,rızəm/ or /pər-/, /pə-/ *n* exclusive devotion to one party or sect; the principle of political freedom for each state in a federation; the theological doctrine that salvation is only for the elect.—**particularist** *n*.

particularity /par,tıkju'lerıti/ or /pər-/, /pə-/ *n* (*pl* **particularities**) the quality of being particular, as distinguished from universal; exactness; fastidiousness.

particularize /par'tıkjulə,raız/ or /pər-/, /pə-/ *vt* to describe in detail; to mention one by one.—**particularization** *n*.

particularly /par'tıkjulerli/ or /pər-/, /pə-/ *adv* very; especially; in detail.

parting /'partıŋ/ *n* a departure; a breaking or separating; a dividing line in combing hair. • *adj* departing, *esp* dying; separating; dividing.

partisan, partizan /'partı,zæn/ or /-təz-/, /-ən/, /-'zæn/ *n* a strong supporter of a person, party, or cause.—*also adj*.—**partisanship, partizanship** *n*.

partite /'partaıt/ *adj* (*bot*) divided almost to the base.

partition /par'tıʃən/ *n* division into parts; that which divides into separate parts; a dividing wall between rooms. • *vt* to divide.

partitive /'partıtıv/ *adj* (*gram*) denoting a part or partition. • *n* a partitive word.

partizan /'partı,zæn/ *see* **partisan**.

partly /'partli/ *adv* in part; to some extent.

partner /'partnər/ *n* one of two or more persons jointly owning a business who share the risks and profits; one of a pair who dance or play a game together; either member of a married or non-married couple. • *vt* to be a partner (in or of); to associate as partners.

partnership /'partnərʃıp/ *n* a contract between two or more people involved in a joint business venture; the state of being a partner.

part of speech *n* each of the categories (*eg* verb, noun, adjective) into which words are divided according to their grammatical and semantic functions.

partook /par'tuk/ *see* **partake**.

partridge /'partrıdʒ/ *n* (*pl* **partridge, partridges**) a stout-bodied game bird of the grouse family.

part song *n* a song with two or more voice parts.

part-time *adj* working fewer than the full number of hours.— **part-timer** *n*.—**part time** *adv*.

parturient /par'turiənt/ or /-'tjur-/ *adj* pertaining to childbirth; about to give birth, in labour.

parturition /ˌpartu'rıʃən/ or /-tjur-/, /-tʃur/ *n* the act of childbirth.

party /'parti/ *n* (*pl* **parties**) a group of people united for political or other purpose; a social gathering; a person involved in a contract or lawsuit; a small company, detachment; a person consenting, accessory; (*inf*) an individual. • *vb* (**partying, partied**) *vi* to attend social parties. • *vt* to give a party for. • *adj* of or for a party.

party line *n* a telephone line shared by two or more subscribers; the policies of a political body.

parvenu /'parvən,u:/ *n* someone regarded as vulgar or an upstart, following a rise in his social or economic status.—**parvenue** *nf*.

pas /pɒ/ *n* (*pl* **pas**) (*ballet*) a step or series of steps; a dance sequence.

PASCAL /'pæskəl/ *n* a high-level computer programming language used *esp* for teaching.

pascal /'pæskəl/ *n* the SI unit of pressure.

pas de deux /pɑ də 'də/ *n* (*pl* **pas de deux**) a ballet sequence for two dancers.

pasha /'pæʃə/ *n* a Turkish title given to a high official; (*formerly*) a provincial governor in the Ottoman Empire.—*also* **pacha**.

pasque-flower /'pæsk,flauər/ *n* a type of anemone which flowers around Easter.

pasquinade /ˌpæskwı'neıd/ *n* a lampoon or rude satire.

pass /pæs/ *vb* (**passing, passed**) *vi* to go past; to go beyond or exceed; to move from one place or state to another; (*time*) to elapse; to go; to die; to happen; (*with* **for**) to be considered as; (*in exam*) to be successful; (*cards*) to decline to make a bid; (*law*) to be approved by a legislative assembly. • *vt* to go past, through, over, etc; (*time*) to spend; to omit; (*law*) to enact; (*judgment*) to pronounce; to excrete; (*in test, etc*) to gain the required marks; to approve. • *n* a narrow passage or road; a permit; (*in a test, etc*) success; transfer of (a ball) to another player; a gesture of the hand; (*inf*) an uninvited sexual approach.

passable /'pæsəbəl/ *adj* fairly good, tolerable; (*a river, etc*) that can be crossed.—**passably** *adv.*

passage /'pæsɪdʒ/ *n* act or right of passing; transit; transition; a corridor; a channel; a route or crossing; a lapse of time; a piece of text or music.

passageway /-ˌweɪ/ *n* a narrow way, *esp* flanked by walls, that allows passage; a corridor.

passbook /'pæsbʊk/ *n* a bankbook.

passé /pæ'seɪ/ *adj* past its best; outdated.

passementerie /pæs'mɛntri/ *n* a decorative trimming of gold or silver lace, braid, beads, etc.

passenger /'pæsəndʒər/ *n* a traveller in a public or private conveyance; one who does not pull his/her weight.

passe-partout /ˌpæspɑr'tuː/ *n* a frame for a picture in which the picture, glass and backing are held together by gummed paper; a master key.

passer-by /ˌpæsər'baɪ/ *n* (*pl* **passers-by**) one who happens to pass or go by.

passerine /'pæsəˌriːn/ *adj* pertaining to the order of birds which perch.—*also n.*

passim /'pæsɪm/ *adv* here and there; throughout.

passing /'pæsɪŋ/ *adj* transient; casual. • *n* departure, death.

passion /'pæʃən/ *n* compelling emotion, such as love, hate, envy; ardent love, *esp* sexual desire; (*with cap*) the suffering of Christ on the cross; the object of any strong desire.—**passionless** *adj.*

passional /-əl/ *adj* pertaining to passion; due to passion.

passionate /-ət/ *adj* moved by, showing, strong emotion or desire; intense; sensual.—**passionately** *adv.*

passion flower *n* a chiefly tropical climbing vine.

passion fruit *n* the edible fruit of a passion flower.

Passion play *n* a play representing Christ's Passion.

Passion Sunday *n* the second Sunday before Easter.

passive /'pæsɪv/ *adj* acted upon, not acting; submissive; (*gram*) denoting the voice of a verb whose subject receives the action.—**passively** *adv.*—**passivity** *n.*

passive resistance *n* nonviolent noncooperation with the authorities.

passive smoking *n* the involuntary inhalation of smoke from others' cigarettes.

Passover /'pæsˌoʊvər/ *n* (*Judaism*) a spring holiday, celebrating the liberation of the Israelites from slavery in Egypt.

passport /'pæspɔrt/ *n* an official document giving the owner the right to travel abroad; something that secures admission or acceptance.

password /'pæswɔrd/ *n* a secret term by which a person is recognized and allowed to pass; any means of admission; a sequence of characters required to access a computer system.

past /pæst/ *adj* completed; ended; in time already elapsed. • *adv* by. • *prep* beyond (in time, place, or amount). • *n* time that has gone by; the history of a person, group, etc; a personal background that is hidden or questionable.

pasta /'pæstə/ or /'pɒstə/ *n* the flour paste from which spaghetti, noodles, etc is made; any dish of cooked pasta.

paste /peɪst/ *n* a soft plastic mixture; flour and water forming dough or adhesive; a fine glass used for artificial gems. • *vt* to attach with paste; (*sl*) to beat, thrash.

pasteboard /'peɪstbɔrd/ *n* a stiff board made from sheets of paper pasted together. • *adj* flimsy.

pastel /pæ'stɛl/ *n* a dried mixture of chalk, pigments and gum used for drawing; a drawing made with such; a soft, pale colour. • *adj* delicately coloured.

pastelist /-ɪst/ *n* an artist who uses pastels.

pastern /'pæstərn/ *n* the part of a horse's foot between the fetlock and the hoof.

Pasteur treatment *n* (*med*) a method of inoculation against rabies by successive injections of vaccine.

pasteurize /'pæstʃəˌraɪz/ or /-təˌraɪz/ *vt* (*milk, etc*) to sterilize by heat or radiation to destroy harmful organisms.—**pasteurization** *n.*

pastiche /pæ'stiːʃ/ *n* (*pl* **pastiches**) a literary, musical, or artistic work in imitation of another's style, or consisting of pieces from other sources.—*also* **pasticcio** (*pl* **pasticci**).

pastille /pæ'stiːl/, **pastil** /pæ'stɪl/ *n* an aromatic or medicated lozenge.

pastime /'pæstaɪm/ *n* a hobby; recreation, diversion.

pastor /'pæstər/ *n* a clergyman in charge of a congregation.

pastoral /'pæstərəl/ *adj* of shepherds or rural life; pertaining to spiritual care, *esp* of a congregation.—**pastorally** *adv.*

pastorale /ˌpæstə'ræl/ or /'pæstəˌræli/ *n* a musical composition with a pastoral subject.

pastorate /'pæstərət/ *n* the office or jurisdiction of a pastor; a collective term for pastors.

pastrami /pə'strɑmi/ *n* highly seasoned smoked beef.

pastry /'peɪstri/ *n* (*pl* **pastries**) dough made of flour, water, and fat used for making pies, tarts, etc; (*pl*) baked foods made with pastry.

pasturage /'pæstərɪdʒ/ *n* the right to graze animals; pasture.

pasture /'pæstʃər/ *n* land covered with grass for grazing livestock; the grass growing on it. • *vt* (*cattle, etc*) to put out to graze in a pasture.

pasty[1] /'peɪsti/ *n* (*pl* **pasties**) meat, etc enclosed in pastry and baked.

pasty[2] *adj* (**pastier, pastiest**) like paste; pallid and unhealthy in appearance.—**pastily** *adv.*—**pastiness** *n.*

pat[1] /pæt/ *vti* (**patting, patted**) to strike gently with the palm of the hand or a flat object; to shape or apply by patting. • *n* a light tap, *usu* with the palm of the hand; a light sound; a small lump of shaped butter.

pat[2] *adj* apt; exact; glib.—*also adv.*

patagium /pə'teɪdʒɪəm/ *n* (*pl* **patagia**) (*zool*) the wing membrane of a bat.

patch /pætʃ/ *n* a piece of cloth used for mending; a scrap of material; a shield for an injured eye; a black spot of silk, etc worn on the face; an irregular spot on a surface; a plot of ground; a bandage; an area or spot. • *vt* to repair with a patch; to piece together; to mend in a makeshift way.—**patchable** *adj.*—**patcher** *n.*

patchouli, patchouly /pə'tʃuːli/ *n* an Asian plant which yields an essential oil from which a perfume is made.

patchwork /'pætʃwərk/ *n* needlework made of pieces sewn together; something made of various bits.

patchy /'pætʃi/ *adj* (**patchier, patchiest**) irregular; uneven; covered with patches.—**patchily** *adv.*—**patchiness** *n.*

pate /peɪt/ *n* the head.

pâté /pæ'teɪ/ or /'pæteɪ/ *n* a rich spread made of meat, fish, herbs, etc.

pâté de foie gras /ˌpæteɪdəfwɒ'grɒ/ *n* (*pl* **pâtés de foie gras**) a rich paste made from goose liver.

patella /pə'tɛlə/ *n* (*pl* **patellae**) (*anat*) the kneecap.—**patellar** *adj.*

paten /'pætən/ *n* (*Christian Church*) a plate used for the bread at the Eucharist.

patent /'pætənt/ or /'peɪt-/ *adj* plain; apparent; open to public inspection; protected by a patent. • *n* a government document, granting the exclusive right to produce and sell an invention, etc for a certain time; the right so granted; the thing protected by such a right. • *vt* to secure a patent for.—**patentable** *adj.*

patentee /ˌpætən'tiː/ or /ˌpeɪt-/ *n* a holder of a patent.

patent leather *n* leather with a hard, glossy finish.

patent medicine *n* a medicine made and sold under patent and available without a prescription.

patent office *n* an office which issues patents.

patently /'peɪtəntli/ *adv* obviously, openly.

patentor /'pætəntər/ or /'peɪt-/ *n* the grantor of a patent.

paterfamilias *n* (*pl* **patresfamilias**) the (male) head of a family.

paternal /pə'tərnəl/ *adj* fatherly in disposition; related through the father.—**paternally** *adv.*

paternalism /pə'tərnəˌlɪzəm/ *n* a system that provides for human needs but allows no individual responsibility.—**paternalist** *adj, n.*—**paternalistic** *adj.*—**paternalistically** *adv.*

paternity /pə'tərnɪti/ *n* fatherhood; origin or descent from a father.

paternity suit *n* a lawsuit to determine whether a particular man is the father of a particular child.

paternity test *n* a blood test to establish whether a man is or is not the father of a particular child.

paternoster /ˌpætər'nɒstər/ *n* the Lord's Prayer in Latin; every eleventh bead in a rosary; a fishing line with hooks at intervals; an elevator consisting of a continuously revolving belt of linked compartments.

path /pæθ/ *n* (*pl* **paths**) a way worn by footsteps; a track for people on foot; a direction; a course of conduct.

-path *n suffix* denoting an expert in a specific area of medicine; denoting a person suffering from a specified disorder.

pathetic /pə'θɛtɪk/ *adj* inspiring pity; (*sl*) uninteresting, inadequate.—**pathetically** *adv.*

pathetic fallacy *n* the attribution of human emotions to inanimate objects.

pathfinder /'pæθ₁faɪndər/ *n* a person who discovers a way; a person who explores untraversed regions to mark out a new route; a person or thing that marks a spot; a radar device for homing on to a target or navigating.—**pathfinding** *n*.

patho- /'pæθə:/ *prefix* disease.

pathogen /'pæθədʒən/ *n* an agent, such as a microorganism, that causes disease.—**pathogenic** *adj*.

pathogenesis /₁pæθə'dʒenəsɪs/, **pathogeny** /pə'θɒdʒəni/ *n* the origin and development of a disease.—**pathogenetic** *adj*.

pathognomonic /₁pæθənɒ'mɒnɪk/ *adj* characteristic of a particular disease.

pathological /₁pæθə'lɒdʒɪkəl/, **pathologic** /'pæθə₁lɒdʒɪk/ *adj* of pathology; of the nature of, caused or altered by disease; (*inf*) compulsive.—**pathologically** *adv*.

pathologist /'pæθə₁lɒdʒɪst/ or /₁pəθɒlə'dʒɪst/ *n* a medical specialist who diagnoses by interpreting the changes in tissue and body fluid caused by a disease.

pathology /pə'θɒlədʒi/ *n* (*pl* **pathologies**) the branch of medicine that deals with the nature of disease, *esp* its functional and structural effects; any abnormal variation from a sound condition.

pathos /'peɪθɒs/ *n* a quality that excites pity or sadness; an expression of deep feeling.

pathway /'pæθweɪ/ *n* a path; (*chem*) a sequence of enzyme-catalyzed reactions.

-pathy /'pæθi/ or /'pəθi/ *n suffix* feeling; disease; medical treatment.

patience /'peɪʃəns/ *n* the capacity to endure or wait calmly; a card game for one —*also* **solitaire**.

patient /'peɪʃənt/ *adj* even-tempered; able to wait or endure calmly; persevering. • *n* a person receiving medical, dental, etc treatment.—**patiently** *adv*.

patina /pə'ti:nə/ or /'pætɪnə/ *n* a green incrustation on old bronze; a surface appearance of something grown beautiful by age or use; a superficial covering or exterior.

patio /'pætɪo:/ *n* (*pl* **patios**) an inner, *usu* roofless, courtyard; a paved area adjoining a house, for outdoor lounging, dining, etc.

patisserie /pə'ti:səri/ *n* a pastry shop; pastries.

patois /'pætwɒ/ or /'pætwɒ/ *n* (*pl* **patois**) a dialect.

patriarch /'peɪtri₁ɑrk/ *n* the father and head of a family or tribe; a man of great age and dignity.—**patriarchal** *adj*.

patriarchate /-ət/ *n* the office, rank or jurisdiction of a patriarch; people ruled by a patriarch.

patriarchy /-i/ *n* (*pl* **patriarchies**) government by the head of a family, tribe, etc; a community ruled in this way.

patrician /pə'trɪʃən/ *n* (*ancient Rome*) a member of the nobility. • *adj* aristocratic; oligarchic.

patricide /'pætrɪsaɪd/ *n* the unlawful killing of one's father; a person who kills his or her father.—**patricidal** *adj*.

patrimony /'pætrɪ₁moːni/ *n* (*pl* **patrimonies**) an estate or right inherited from a father or one's ancestors; an ecclesiastical endowment or estate.—**patrimonial** *adj*.

patriot /'peɪtriət/ *n* one who strongly supports and serves his or her country.—**patriotic** *adj*.—**patriotically** *adv*.

patriotism /₁peɪtri'ɒtɪzəm/ *n* love for or loyalty to one's country.

patristic /pə'trɪstɪk/, **patristical** /-əl/ *adj* pertaining to the theology and writings of the fathers of the early Christian church.

patrol /pə'troːl/ *vti* (**patrolling, patrolled**) to walk around a building or area in order to watch, guard, inspect. • *n* the act of going the rounds; a unit of persons or vehicles employed for reconnaissance, security, or combat; a subdivision of a Scout or Guide group.—**patroller** *n*.

patrolman /-mən/ *n* (*pl* **patrolmen**) (*chiefly US*) a policeman who patrols a particular area.

patron /'peɪtrən/ *n* a regular client or customer; a person who sponsors and supports the arts, charities, etc; a protector.—**patronal** *adj*.

patronage /'peɪtrənɪdʒ/ or /'pæt-/ *n* the support given or custom brought by a patron; clientele; business; trade; the power to grant political favours; such favours.

patronize, patronise /'peɪtrənaɪz/ or /'pæt-/ *vt* to treat with condescension; to sponsor or support; to be a regular customer of.—**patronization** *n*.

patronizing /-ɪŋ/ *adj* condescending.—**patronizingly** *adv*.

patronymic /₁pætrə'nɪmɪk/ *adj* derived from the name of an ancestor. • *n* a name derived from an ancestor.

patsy /'pætsi/ *n* (*pl* **patsies**) (*sl*) a gullible person; a sucker.

patten /'pætən/ *n* a wooden shoe on a metal ring, worn as a protection from the damp.

patter[1] /'pætər/ *vi* to make quick tapping sounds, as if by striking something; to run with light steps. • *n* the sound of tapping or quick steps.

patter[2] *vi* to talk rapidly and glibly; to mumble (prayers, etc) mechanically. • *vt* to repeat speech mechanically, to gabble. • *n* rapid speech, *esp* that of a salesman, comedian, etc; glib speech; chatter; jargon.

pattern /'pætərn/ *n* a decorative arrangement; a model to be copied; instructions to be followed to make something; a regular way of acting or doing; a predictable route, movement, etc. • *vt* to make or do in imitation of a pattern.—**patterned** *adj*.

patty /'pæti/ *n* (*pl* **patties**) a small pie; a flat cake of ground meat, fish, etc, *usu* fried.

patulous /'pætjʊləs/ *adj* (*bot*) spreading, extended.

paucity /'pɔsɪti/ *n* fewness; lack of; scarcity.

paulownia /pɒ'loːniə/ *n* a member of a Japanese genus of trees, with heart-shaped leaves and purple flowers.

paunch /pɒntʃ/ *n* the belly, *esp* a potbelly.

paunchy /'pɒntʃi/ *adj* (**paunchier, paunchiest**) having a big belly.—**paunchiness** *n*.

pauper /'pɔpər/ *n* a very poor person; (*formerly*) a person dependent on charity.—**pauperism** *n*.

pauperize, pauperise /'pɔpəraɪz/ *vt* to reduce to pauperism.

pause /pɔz/ *n* a temporary stop, *esp* in speech, action or music. • *vi* to cease in action temporarily, wait; to hesitate.

pavage /'peɪvɪdʒ/ *n* a tax paid for paving streets.

pavane, pavan /pəvɒn/ *n* (the music for) an old stately dance.

pave /peɪv/ *vt* (*a road, etc*) to cover with concrete to provide a hard level surface; **pave the way** to prepare a smooth easy way; to facilitate development.—**paving** *n*.

pavement /'peɪvmənt/ *n* flat slabs, tiles, etc forming a surface, *esp* on a public thoroughfare.

pavilion /pə'vɪljən/ *n* an annexe; a temporary building for exhibitions; a large ornate tent.

pavonine /'pævə₁naɪn/ *adj* pertaining to peacocks; resembling a peacock.

paw /pɒ/ *n* a foot of a mammal with claws; (*sl*) a hand. • *vti* to touch, dig, hit, etc with paws; to maul; to handle clumsily or roughly.

pawky /'pɒki/ *adj* (**pawkier, pawkiest**) (*Scot*) having a dry sense of humour.

pawn[1] /pɒn/ *n* the piece of lowest value in chess; a person used to advance another's purpose.

pawn[2] *vt* to deposit an article as security for a loan; to wager or risk. • *n* a thing pawned; the state of being given as a pawn.—**pawner** *n*.

pawnbroker /'pɒn₁broːkər/ *n* a person licensed to lend money at interest on personal property left with him as security.—**pawnbroking** *n*.

pawnshop /'pɒnʃɒp/ *n* a pawnbroker's shop.

pawpaw /'pɒpɒ/ *see* **papaw**.

paxwax /'pækswæks/ *n* a strong tendon in an animal's neck.

pay /peɪ/ *vti* (**paying, paid**) to give (money) to in payment for a debt, goods or services; to give in compensation; to yield a profit; to bear a cost; to suffer a penalty; (*homage, attention*) to give. • *n* payment for services or goods; salary, wages.—**paying** *adj*.—**payer** *n*.

payable /'peɪəbəl/ *adj* that must be paid, due; to be paid on a specified date.

pay dirt *n* soil, gravel, etc worth mining for minerals; (*inf*) a source of wealth.

PAYE *abbr* = pay-as-you-earn; the deduction of income tax from wages or salaries at source.

payee /'peɪ₁i/ *n* one to whom money is paid.

payload /'peɪloːd/ *n* cargo that earns revenue; the total load of an aircraft, spacecraft, satellite, etc.

paymaster /'peɪmæstər/ *n* a person in charge of paying wages and salaries.

payment /'peɪmənt/ *n* the act of paying; amount paid; reward.

paynim /'peɪnɪm/ *n* (*arch*) a heathen; a Muslim.

payola /peɪ'oːlə/ *n* a bribe paid for the clandestine promotion of a product, *esp* one paid to a disc jockey to play a particular record; a system of such bribes.

payphone /'peɪfoːn/ *n* a coin-operated telephone.

payroll /'peɪrəʊl/ n a list of employees and their wages; the actual money for paying wages.

Pb (chem symbol) lead.

PBX abbr = private branch exchange.

PC /ˌpiːˈsiː/ abbr = personal computer; police constable; political correctness, politically correct.

pc, p.c. abbr = per cent; postcard.

PCB abbr = polychlorinated biphenyl; printed circuit board.

Pd (chem symbol) palladium.

pd abbr = paid.

PDF /'piːdiːˈɛf/ abbr = (comput) Portable Document Format, a file transfer system that renders a document viewable even without the software program which was initially used to create it.

p.d.q. abbr = pretty damn quick.

PE abbr = physical education.

pea /piː/ n the edible, round, green seed of a climbing leguminous annual plant.

peace /piːs/ n tranquillity, stillness; freedom from contention, violence or war; a treaty that ends a war.

peaceable /'piːsəbəl/ adj inclined to peace.—**peaceably** adv.—**peaceableness** n.

Peace Corps n a US government organization that sends volunteers to work on social, educational, agricultural, etc projects in developing countries.

peace dividend n a benefit to a nation generated from the reduction in defence spending when a conflict is ended, to be used for purposes other than armaments etc.

peaceful /'piːsfʊl/ adj having peace; tranquil; quiet.—**peacefully** adv.—**peacefulness** n.

peacemaker /'piːsˌmeɪkər/ n one who makes or restores peace; one who reconciles enemies.—**peacemaking** adj, n.

peace offering n a conciliatory gift.

peace pipe n a tobacco pipe smoked by American Indians as a sign of peace.

peace process n the sequence or progress of negotiations towards the settlement of conflict.

peach /piːtʃ/ n a round, sweet, juicy, downy-skinned stone-fruit; the tree bearing it; a yellowish pink colour; (sl) a well-liked person or thing.

peachy /'piːtʃi/ adj (**peachier, peachiest**) of or resembling a peach; (inf) great, excellent.—**peachily** adv.—**peachiness** n.

peacock /'piːkɒk/ n (**peacocks, peacock**) a male peafowl with a large brilliantly coloured fan-like tail; a person who is a show-off.

peafowl /'piːfaʊl/ n (**peafowls, peafowl**) a peacock or a peahen.

pea-green adj bright green.

peahen /'piːhen/ n a female peafowl.

peak /piːk/ n the summit of a mountain; the highest point; the pointed end of anything; maximum value; the eyeshade of a cap, visor. • vti (politician, actor, etc) to reach or cause to reach the height of power, popularity; (prices) to reach and stay at the highest level.

peaked /piːkd/ adj pointed; having a peak; peaky.

peaky /'piːki/ adj (**peakier, peakiest**) drawn, emaciated; sickly; peaked.

peal /piːl/ n a reverberating sound as of thunder, laughter, bells, etc; a set of bells, the changes rung on them. • vti to sound in peals, ring out.

pean /'piːən/ see **paean**.

peanut /'piːnʌt/ n a leguminous plant with underground pods containing edible seeds; the pod or any of its seeds; (pl) (sl) a trifling thing or amount.

peanut butter n a food paste made by grinding roasted peanuts.

pear /peər/ n a common juicy fruit of tapering oval shape; the tree bearing it.

pearl /pɜːl/ n the lustrous white round gem produced by oysters; mother-of-pearl; anything resembling a pearl intrinsically or physically; one that is choice and precious; a bluish medium grey. • vti to fish for pearls; to form drops (on), to bespangle.—**pearler** n.—**pearliness** n.

pearl button n a button covered with mother-of-pearl.

pearl diver n a person who dives for pearl oysters.

pearl oyster n any of various marine bivalve molluscs that yield pearls.

pearly /'pɜːli/ adj (**pearlier, pearliest**) clear, lustrous, like a pearl; covered with pearls; bluish grey. • n (pl **pearlies**) (pl) a London costermonger's dress covered with pearl buttons.

Pearly Gates npl (inf) the gates of Heaven.

pearmain /'pɛəmeɪn/ n a variety of apple.

peasant /'pezənt/ n (inf) a countryman or countrywoman; an agricultural labourer; (derog) a lout.

peasantry /-ri/ n peasants as a class.

pease /piːz/ n (arch) a pea.

peashooter /'piːˌʃuːtər/ n a toy blowpipe through which peas, etc, are blown.

peasouper /'piːˌsuːpər/ n (sl) a thick yellow fog.

peat /piːt/ n decayed vegetable matter from bogs, which is dried and cut into blocks for fuel or used as a fertilizer.—**peaty** adj.

pebble /'pebəl/ n a small rounded stone; an irregular, grainy surface.—**pebbled** adj.—**pebbly** adj.

pecan /'piːkæn/ or /'piːkæn, piːˈkɒn/ n a hickory tree widely grown in the US and Mexico for its edible nuts; its wood; its thin-shelled nut.

peccable /'pekəbəl/ adj liable to sin.—**peccability** n.

peccadillo /ˌpekəˈdɪləʊ/ n (pl **peccadilloes, peccadillos**) a trifling misdeed, indiscretion.

peccary /'pekəri/ n (pl **peccaries, peccary**) an American wild piglike mammal.

peccavi /pekˈɑːvi/ n (pl **peccavis**) a confession of guilt.

peck /pek/ vt to strike with the beak or a pointed object; to pick at one's food; (inf) to kiss lightly; to nag.—also n.

pecker /'pekər/ n something, esp a bird, that pecks; (sl) penis.

pecking order n a social hierarchy in groups of some birds (eg hens), characterized by the pecking of those lower in the scale and submitting to being pecked by those higher; any social hierarchy.

peckish /'pekɪʃ/ adj (inf) hungry; irritable.—**peckishly** adv.—**peckishness** n.

pecten /'pektɪn/ n (pl **pectens, pectines**) (zool) a comblike membrane on the eyes of birds and some reptiles.

pectin /'pektɪn/ n a carbohydrate found in fruits and vegetables, yielding a gel that is used to set jellies.—**pectic** adj.

pectoral /'pektərəl/ adj of or relating to the breast, chest. • n the muscle in the chest; something worn on the breast.

peculate /'pekjʊˌleɪt/ vt to appropriate money entrusted to one's care, to embezzle.—**peculation** n.—**peculator** n.

peculiar /pəˈkjuːliːər/ adj belonging exclusively (to); special; distinct; characteristic; strange.—**peculiarly** adv.

peculiarity /pəˌkjuːliˈerɪti/ n (pl **peculiarities**) an idiosyncrasy; a characteristic; an oddity.

pecuniary /pəˈkjuːnɪeri/ adj of or consisting of money.—**pecuniarily** adv.

pedagogue /'pedəˌgɒg/ n a schoolteacher.—**pedagogic, pedagogical** adj.

pedagogy /'pedəˌgɒdʒi/ n the art or science of teaching.

pedal[1] /'pedəl/ n a lever operated by the foot. • vt (**pedalling, pedalled** or **pedaling, pedaled**) to operate or propel by pressing pedals with the foot.—**pedaller, pedaler** n.

pedal[2] adj (zool) pertaining to the foot or feet.

pedalo /'pedəˌləʊ/ n (pl **pedalos**) a small pedal-operated pleasure boat.

pedant /'pedənt/ n a person who attaches too much importance to insignificant details.

pedantic /pəˈdæntɪk/ adj of, relating to, or being a pedant; narrowly learned.—**pedantically** adv.

pedantry /'pedəntri/ n (pl **pedantries**) an ostentatious display of learning; the state of being a pedant.

pedate /'pedeɪt/ adj (bot) having lateral sections divided into lobes; (zool) having, or resembling, feet.

peddle /'pedəl/ vt to go from place to place selling small items; to sell (drugs, etc) illegally.

peddler /'pedlər/ n a person who peddles goods; a person who sells drugs illegally.

pederast /'pedəˌræst/ n a person who practises pederasty.

pederasty /-i/ n sex between a man and a boy.

pedestal /'pedəstəl/ n the base that supports a column, statue, etc. • vt to set on a pedestal; to serve as a pedestal for.

pedestrian /pəˈdestriən/ adj on foot; dull, commonplace. • n a person who walks.

pedestrianism /-ɪzəm/ n walking, or a fondness for walking; the quality of being dull or commonplace.

pedestrianize, pedestrianise /-aɪz/ vti to convert (an area) for use by pedestrians only.—**pedestrianization** n.

pedicab /'pediˌkæb/ n a pedal-driven rickshaw.

pedicular /pə'dıkjʊlər/, **pediculous** /-ləs/ *adj* pertaining to lice; infested with lice.—**pediculosis** *n*.

pedicure /'pedı,kjʊr/ *n* cosmetic care of the feet, toes, and nails; a person trained to care for feet in this way.

pediform /'pedı,fɔrm/ *adj* foot-shaped.

pedigree /'pedı,griː/ *n* a line of descent of an animal; a recorded purity of breed of an individual; a genealogy; lineage; derivation. • *adj* having a known ancestry.—**pedigreed** *adj*.

pediment /'pedımənt/ *n* a triangular ornament crowning the front of a classical building, *esp* a Greek temple.—**pedimental, pedimented** *adj*.

pedometer /pə'dɒmıtər/ *n* an instrument for measuring the distance walked by recording the number of steps taken.

peduncle /pə'dʌŋkəl/ *n* a flower stalk.—**peduncular** *adj*.

pedunculate /pə'dʌŋkjʊlət/, **pedunculated** /-leıtəd/ *adj* having, or growing upon, a peduncle.

pee /piː/ *vi* (*sl*) to urinate. • *n* urination; urine.

peek /piːk/ *vi* to look quickly or furtively.—*also n.*.

peekaboo /'piːkə,buː/ *n* a child's game in which one person hides behind his or her hands then peeps out suddenly, shouting, "peekaboo!".

peel /piːl/ *vt* to remove skin or rind from; to bare. • *vi* to flake off, as skin or paint. • *n* rind, *esp* that of fruit and vegetables.—**peeling** *n*.

peeler /'piːlər/ *n* a device for peeling; (*sl*) a stripteaser.

peen /piːn/ *n* the pointed or thin end of a hammer-head.

peep[1] /piːp/ *vi* to make shrill noises as a young bird. • *n* a peeping sound.

peep[2] *vi* to look hastily or furtively; to look through a slit or narrow opening; to be just showing. • *n* a furtive or hurried glance, a glimpse; (*of day*) the first appearance.

peeper /'piːpər/ *n* one who peeps; (*sl*) the eye; (*sl*) a private detective.

peephole /'piːphoːl/ *n* a small hole, *esp* in a door, to spy through.

peeping Tom *n* a person who peeps furtively, a voyeur.

peepshow /'piːpʃoː/ *n* a small show, *esp* of erotic pictures, viewed through a hole with a lens; a live show with a nude model, viewed from a booth.

peepul /'piːpəl/ *n* an Indian fig tree, sacred to Buddhists.—*also* **pipal**.

peer[1] /piːr/ *vi* to look closely; to look with difficulty; to peep out.

peer[2] *n* an equal in rank, ability, etc; a nobleman.—**peeress** *nf*.

peerage /'piːrıdʒ/ *n* the rank or title of a peer; peers collectively; a book with a list of peers.

peer group *n* a group of people of the same age, background, education, interests, etc.

peerless /'piːrləs/ *adj* having no equal, matchless.

peeve /piːv/ *vt* (*inf*) to annoy.

peeved /'piːvd/ *adj* annoyed, resentful.

peevish /'piːvıʃ/ *adj* fretful, irritable.—**peevishly** *adv*.—**peevishness** *n*.

peg /peg/ *n* a tapered piece (of wood) for securing or hanging things on, for marking position; a predetermined level at which (a price) is fixed; (*mus*) one of the movable parts for tuning the string of an instrument. • *vti* (**pegging, pegged**) to fasten or mark with a peg; (*a price*) to keep steady; (*with* **away at**) to work steadily, persevere.

Pegasus /'pegəsəs/ *n* (*Greek myth*) the winged horse ridden by Bellerophon.

peignoir /'peınwɑr/ *n* a woman's dressing gown.

pejorative /pı'dʒɒrətıv/ *adj* (*word, etc*) disparaging, derogatory. • *n* a disparaging word.—**pejoratively** *adv*.

peke /piːk/ *n* (*sl*) a Pekingese dog.

Pekingese, Pekinese /,piːkıŋ'iːz/ *n* (*pl* **Pekingese, Pekinese**) a breed of small dog with long, silky hair, short legs, and a pug nose.

pekoe /'piːkoː/ *n* a scented black Chinese tea.

pelage /'pelıdʒ/ *n* the hair, wool or fur of an animal.

pelagian /pə'leıdʒıən/ *adj* (*marine life*) of or inhabiting the open sea.—*also n*.—**pelagic** *adj*.

pelargonium /,pelər'goːnıəm/ *n* a member of a widely cultivated genus of flowering plants, including geraniums.

pelf /pelf/ *n* (*derog*) money, wealth.

pelican /'pelıkən/ *n* a large fish-eating waterbird with an expandable pouched bill.

pelisse /pe'liːs/ *n* a woman's long cloak, *usu* trimmed with fur.

pellagra /pə'lægrə/ or /-leıgrə/, /-lɒgrə/ *n* a disease affecting the skin and nervous system caused by a deficiency of nicotinic acid.—**pellagrous** *adj*.

pellet /'pelət/ *n* a small ball of paper, bread, etc; a pill; a small ball of hair, bones, etc regurgitated by a bird of prey; a piece of shot. • *vt* to form into pellets.

pellicle /'pelıkəl/ *n* a thin skin or film.—**pellicular** *adj*.

pellitory /'pelı,tɔri/ *n* (*pl* **pellitories**) a European flowering plant, growing in walls.

pell-mell /pel'mel/ *adv, adj* in a disorderly rush; confusedly; headlong.

pellucid /pə'luːsıd/ or /-'ljuː-/ *adj* (*water, etc*) transparent; (*speech, writing, etc*) clear, lucid.—**pellucidity, pellucidness** *n*.

pelmet /'pelmət/ *n* a canopy for a window frame to hide a curtain rail, etc; a valance.

pelota /pə'lɒtə/ or /-'loːtə/ *n* a Basque ball game similar to tennis, played with basket-shaped rackets against a wall.

pelt[1] /pelt/ *vt* to throw missiles, or words, at. • *vi* (*rain*) to fall heavily; to hurry, rush. • *n* a rush.—**pelter** *n*.

pelt[2] *n* a *usu* undressed skin of an animal with its hair, wool, or fur.

peltry /'peltri/ *n* (*pl* **peltries**) a collective term for the pelts of animals.

pelvis /'pelvıs/ *n* (*pl* **pelvises, pelves**) the bony cavity that joins the lower limbs to the body; the bones forming this.—**pelvic** *adj*.

pemmican, pemican /'pemıkən/ *n* a cake of dried lean meat formerly used by North American Indians; a mixture of beef and suet used as emergency rations.

pemphigus /'pemfıgəs/ *n* a rare skin disease, characterized by watery blisters.—**pemphigoid, pemphigous** *adj*.

pen[1] /pen/ *n* an implement used with ink for writing or drawing. • *vt* (**penning, penned**) to write, compose.

pen[2] *n* a small enclosure for cattle, poultry, etc; a small place of confinement. • *vt* (**penning, penned**) to enclose in a pen, shut up.

pen[3] *n* a female swan.

pen[4] *n* (*sl*) a penitentiary.

penal /'piːnəl/ *adj* relating to, liable to, or prescribing punishment; punitive.—**penally** *adv*.

penal code *n* a code of laws concerning crimes and offences and their punishment.

penalize /-aız/ *vt* to impose a penalty; to put under a disadvantage.—**penalization** *n*.

penalty /'penəlti/ *n* (*pl* **penalties**) a punishment attached to an offence; suffering or loss as a result of one's own mistake; a disadvantage imposed for breaking a rule as in sports; a fine.

penalty area *n* (*soccer*) the area in front of goal in which a foul by a defending player results in the award of a penalty kick.

penalty box *n* (*ice hockey*) an area of the ice where players are sent as a penalty.

penance /'penəns/ *n* voluntary suffering to atone for a sin; a sacramental rite consisting of confession, absolution, and penance. • *vt* to impose a penance on.

pence /pens/ *see* **penny**.

penchant /'penʃənt/ or /'pɑ̃ʃɑ̃/ *n* inclination, strong liking (for).

pencil /'pensəl/ *n* a pointed rod-shaped instrument with a core of graphite or crayon for writing, drawing, etc; a set of convergent light rays or straight lines; a fine paintbrush. • *vt* (**pencilling, pencilled** *or* **penciling, penciled**) to write, draw, or colour with a pencil; (*with* **in**) to commit tentatively.—**penciller, penciler** *n*.

pendant, pendent /'pendənt/ *n* a hanging ornament, *esp* a jewel on a necklace, bracelet, etc; a light-fitting suspended from a ceiling. • *adj* (*usu* **pendent**) hanging; projecting; undecided.—**pendency** *n*.

pendentive /pen'dentıv/ *n* (*archit*) a portion of a dome supported by a single pillar.

pending /'pendıŋ/ *adj* undecided; unfinished; imminent. • *prep* during; until, awaiting.

pendragon /pen'drægən/ *n* (*hist*) a chief of the ancient Britons or Welsh.

pendulous /'pendjʊləs/ *adj* hanging downwards and swinging freely.—**pendulously** *adv*.

pendulum /'pendjʊləm/ *n* a weight suspended from a fixed point so as to swing freely; such a device used to regulate the movement of a clock; something that swings to and fro.

peneplain, peneplane /'piːnə,pleın/ *n* (*geol*) a tract of land which is almost a plain.

penetrable /'penətrəbəl/ *adj* able to be penetrated.—**penetrability** *n*.

penetralia /ˌpɛnəˈtreɪlɪə/ *npl* the inner parts of a temple, etc; mysteries.

penetrant /ˈpɛnətrənt/ *adj* penetrating. • *n* something which, or someone who, penetrates.

penetrate /ˈpɛnəˌtreɪt/ *vti* to thrust, force a way into or through something; to pierce; to permeate; to understand.—**penetrator** *n*.—**penetrative** *adj*.

penetrating /-ɪŋ/ *adj* acute, discerning; (*voice*) easily heard through other sounds.—**penetratingly** *adv*.

penetration /-treɪʃən/ *n* the capability, act, or action of penetrating; acute insight.

penguin /ˈpɛŋgwɪn/ *n* a flightless, marine bird with black and white plumage, *usu* found in the Antarctic.

penicillate /ˈpɛnɪsɪlət/ or /pɛnɪˈsɪlət/ *adj* (*biol*) having, or forming, small tufts.

penicillin /ˌpɛnɪˈsɪlən/ *n* an antibiotic produced naturally and synthetically from moulds.

penile /ˈpiːnaɪl/ *adj* of, like, or affecting the penis.

peninsula /pəˈnɪnsjələ/ or /-sə-/ *n* a piece of land almost surrounded by sea.—**peninsular** *adj*.

penis /ˈpiːnəs/ *n* (*pl* **penises, penes**) the male copulative and urinary organ in mammals.

penitence /ˈpɛnɪtəns/ *n* sorrow for committing a sin, repentance.

penitent /ˈpɛnɪtənt/ *adj* feeling regret for sin, repentant, contrite. • *n* a person who atones for sin.—**penitently** *adv*.

penitential /ˌpɛnɪˈtɛnʃəl/ *adj* of or expressing penance; being penitent.—**penitentially** *adv*.

penitentiary /ˌpɛnɪˈtɛnʃərɪ/ *n* (*pl* **penitentiaries**) (*US*) a state or federal prison. • *adj* pertaining to penance; pertaining to the reformatory treatment of prisoners.

penknife /ˈpɛnnaɪf/ *n* (*pl* **penknives**) a small knife, *usu* with one or more folding blades, that fits into the pocket.

penman /ˈpɛnmən/ *n* (*pl* **penmen**) a writer.

penmanship /ˈpɛnmənʃɪp/ *n* the art, or style, of writing.

pen name *n* a literary pseudonym.—*also* **nom de plume**.

pennant /ˈpɛnənt/ *n* a long tapering flag used for identifying vessels and for signalling; such a flag symbolizing a championship.

penniless /ˈpɛnɪləs/ *adj* having no money; poor.—**pennilessly** *adv*.—**pennilessness** *n*.

pennon /ˈpɛnən/ *n* a small, pointed or swallow-tailed flag of a medieval knight; a long tapering streamer on a ship.

penny /ˈpɛnɪ/ *n* (*pl* **pence** *denoting sum*, **pennies** *denoting separate coins*) a bronze coin of the UK worth one hundredth of a pound; (*formerly*) a bronze coin of the UK worth one twelfth of a shilling, or one two hundred and fortieth of a pound; (*US*) a one cent coin.

pennyroyal /ˌpɛnɪˈrɔɪəl/ *n* an aromatic plant of the mint family.

pennyweight /ˈpɛnɪˌweɪt/ *n* a weight, equivalent to 24 grains or $^1/_{20}$ of an ounce (troy).

pennywort /ˈpɛnɪˌwɜrt/ *n* a kind of round-leafed plant, growing variously in walls or in marshes.

pennyworth /ˈpɛnɪˌwɜrθ/ *n* a penny's worth (of a purchase); a small amount.

penology /piːˈnɒlədʒɪ/ *n* the study of the punishment and prevention of crime.—*also* **poenology**.—**penological** *adj*.—**penologist** *n*.

pen pal *n* a friend with whom one is in contact only through correspondence.

pensile /ˈpɛnsaɪl/ *adj* suspended; pendulous.

pension /ˈpɛnʃən/ *n* a periodic payment to a person beyond retirement age, or widowed, or disabled; a periodic payment in consideration of past services. • *vt* to grant a pension to; (*with* **off**) to dismiss or retire from service with a pension.—**pensionable** *adj*.

pensionary /-ɛrɪ/ *adj* by way of pension. • *n* (*pl* **pensionaries**) a pensioner.

pensioner /-ər/ *n* a person who receives a pension; a senior citizen.

pensive /ˈpɛnsɪv/ *adj* thoughtful, musing; wistful, melancholic.—**pensively** *adv*.—**pensiveness** *n*.

pentacle /ˈpɛntəkəl/ *see* **pentagram**.

pentad /ˈpɛntæd/ *n* a group of five; the number five.

pentadactyl /ˌpɛntəˈdæktəl/ *adj* (*zool*) having five fingers or toes.

pentagon /ˈpɛntəgɒn/ *n* (*geom*) a polygon with five sides; (*with cap*) the pentagonal headquarters of the US defence establishment; the US military leadership collectively.—**pentagonal** *adj*.

pentagram /ˈpɛntəˌgræm/ *n* a five-pointed star, often used as a magic symbol.—*also* **pentacle**.

pentahedron /ˌpɛntəˈhiːdrən/ *n* (*pl* **pentahedrons, pentahedra**) a solid figure with five faces.

pentamerous /pɛnˈtæmərəs/ *adj* (*bot, zool*) with five parts.

pentameter /pɛnˈtæmətər/ *n* a verse of five metrical feet.

pentangle /ˈpɛnˌtæŋgəl/ *n* a pentagram.

Pentateuch /ˈpɛntəˌtuːk/ or /-tjuːk/ *n* the collective name for the first five books of the Old Testament.

pentathlon /pɛnˈtæθlɒn/ *n* an athletic contest involving participation by each contestant in five different events.—**pentathlete** *n*.

pentatonic /ˌpɛntəˈtɒnɪk/ *adj* (*mus*) of five notes.

pentavalent /ˌpɛntəˈveɪlənt/ *adj* (*chem*) with a valency of five.

Pentecost /ˈpɛntəˌkɒst/ *n* a Christian festival on the seventh Sunday after Easter; Whit Sunday.

Pentecostal /ˌpɛntəˈkɒstəl/ *adj* denoting a mainly Protestant Christian movement, now with various organized forms, emphasizing the immediate presence of God in the Holy Spirit; of Pentecost or the influence of the Holy Spirit. • *n* a member of a Pentecostal church.—**Pentecostalist** *adj, n*.

penthouse /ˈpɛnthaʊs/ *n* an apartment on the roof or in the top floor of a building.

pentstemon /pɛntˈstiːmən/ *n* a flowering garden plant of the family including the beard-tongues.—*also* (*chiefly US*) **penstemon**.

pent-up *adj* (*emotion*) repressed, confined.

penult /pəˈnʌlt/ or /piːˈnʌlt/ *n* the penultimate syllable of a word. • *adj* last but one.

penultimate /pəˈnʌltɪmət/ *adj* last but one.—*also adj*.

penumbra /pəˈnʌmbrə/ *n* (*pl* **penumbrae, penumbras**) a shaded region around the shadow of an opaque object, *esp* the shadow of the moon or earth in an eclipse; the lighter outer part of a sunspot; (*art*) the boundary of light and shade in a picture.—**penumbral** *adj*.

penurious /pəˈnjʊərɪəs/ *adj* grudging with money, stingy; poor; scanty.—**penuriously** *adv*.—**penuriousness** *n*.

penury /ˈpɛnjʊrɪ/ *n* (*pl* **penuries**) extreme poverty; want.

peon /ˈpiːɒn/ *n* a Spanish American labourer; (*formerly*) a Spanish American labourer compelled to work to pay off debts.

peonage /ˈpiːɒnɪdʒ/, **peonism** /ˈpiːɒnɪzəm/ *n* the condition of being a peon; the system of compelling someone to work for a creditor to pay off debts.

peony /ˈpiːənɪ/ *n* (*pl* **peonies**) a plant with large, showy, red, pink or white flowers.

people /ˈpiːpəl/ *n* the body of enfranchised citizens of a state; a person's family, relatives; the persons of a certain place, group, or class; persons considered indefinitely; human beings; (*pl*) all the persons of a racial or ethnic group, typically having a common language, institutions, homes, and culture. • *vt* to populate with people.

pep /pɛp/ *n* (*inf*) energy, vigour; bounce. • *vt* (**pepping, pepped**) (*usu with* **up**) to enliven by injecting with pep.

pepper /ˈpɛpər/ *n* a sharp, hot condiment made from the fruit of various plants; the fruit of the pepper plant, which can be red, yellow, or green, sweet or hot, and is eaten as a vegetable. • *vt* to sprinkle or flavour with pepper; to hit with small shot; to pelt; to beat.

peppercorn /ˈpɛpərˌkɔrn/ *n* a dried pepper berry.

pepper mill *n* hand mill for grinding peppercorns.

peppermint /ˈpɛpərˌmɪnt/ *n* a pungent and aromatic mint plant; its oil used for flavouring; a sweet flavoured with peppermint.

pepperoni /ˌpɛpəˈroːnɪ/ *n* a spicy beef and pork sausage.

pepperwort /ˈpɛpərwɜrt/ *n* a form of aquatic or marsh fern; a type of cress.

peppery /ˈpɛpərɪ/ *adj* of, like, full of, pepper; fiery; hot-tempered.—**pepperiness** *n*.

peppy /ˈpɛpɪ/ *adj* (**peppier, peppiest**) full of bounce; lively.—**peppiness** *n*.

pepsin, pepsine /ˈpɛpsɪn/ *n* a digestive enzyme contained in gastric juice.

pep talk *n* (*inf*) a vigorous talk made with the intention of arousing enthusiasm, increasing confidence, etc.

peptic /ˈpɛptɪk/ *adj* of or promoting digestion; of, producing, or caused by the action of the digestive juices.

peptic ulcer *n* an ulcer of the stomach lining or duodenum.

peptone /ˈpɛptoːn/ *n* a product of the action of pepsin on proteins.

peptonize /ˈpɛptəˈnaɪz/ *vt* to convert into peptone.

per /pər/ *prep* for or in each; through, by, by means of; (*inf*) according to.

peradventure /ˌpərədˈvɛntʃər/ or /ˌpɛr-/ *adv* (*arch*) by chance; perhaps.

perambulate /pəˈræmbjuˌleɪt/ *vti* to walk around.—**perambulation** *n*.—**perambulatory** *adj*.

perambulator /-ər/ *n* one who or that which perambulates; (*Brit formal*) a pram.

per annum *adv* yearly; each year.

percale /pərˈkeɪl/ *n* a cotton fabric, often used for sheets.

per capita *adj, adv* of or for each person.

perceive /pərˈsiːv/ *vt* to become aware of, apprehend, through the senses; to recognize.—**perceivable** *adj*.—**perceivably** *adv*.

per cent, percent /pərˈsɛnt/ *adv* in, for each hundred. • *n* a percentage.

percentage /pərˈsɛntədʒ/ *n* rate per hundred parts; a proportion; (*inf*) profit, gain.

percept /ˈpərsɛpt/ *n* something which is perceived.

perceptible /pərˈsɛptɪbəl/ *adj* able to be perceived; discernible.—**perceptibility** *n*.—**perceptibly** *adv*.

perception /pərˈsɛpʃən/ *n* the act or faculty of perceiving; discernment; insight; a way of perceiving, view.—**perceptional** *adj*.

perceptive /pərˈsɛptɪv/ *adj* able to perceive; observant.—**perceptively** *adv*.—**perceptivity, perceptiveness** *n*.

perch[1] /pərtʃ/ *n* (*pl* **perch, perches**) a spiny-finned chiefly freshwater edible fish.

perch[2] *n* a pole on which birds roost or alight; an elevated seat or position. • *vti* to alight, rest, on a perch; to balance (oneself) on; to set in a high position.

perchance /pərˈtʃæns/ *adv* (*arch*) by chance; perhaps.

Percheron /ˈpərtʃəˌrɒn/ *n* a sturdy breed of draughthorse.

percipient /pərˈsɪpiənt/ *adj* perceiving; perceptive. • *n* a person who perceives.—**percipience** *n*.

percolate /ˈpərkəˌleɪt/ *vt* (*liquid*) to pass through a filter or pores; to brew coffee. • *vi* to ooze through; to spread gradually.—**percolation** *n*.

percolator /-ər/ *n* a coffeepot in which boiling water is forced through ground coffee beans.

percuss /pərˈkʌs/ *vt* to tap sharply; (*med*) to tap (the patient's body) gently to find out the condition of an internal organ by sound.

percussion /pərˈkʌʃən/ *n* impact, collision; musical instruments played by striking with sticks or hammers, *eg* cymbals, drums, etc; such instruments regarded as a section of an orchestra; (*med*) tapping the body to discover the condition of an organ by the sounds.—**percussive** *adj*.

percussionist /-ɪst/ *n* a person who plays a percussion instrument.

percutaneous /ˌpərkjuˈteɪniəs/ *adj* (*med*) done through the skin.

per diem /pərˈdiːem/ *adv, adj* every day. • *n* a daily allowance, as for expenses.

perdition /pərˈdɪʃən/ *n* utter loss of the soul; eternal damnation; (*arch*) total destruction, ruin.

peregrinate /ˈpɛrəɡrɪˌneɪt/ *vti* to travel, roam about.—**peregrinator** *n*.—**peregrination** *n*.

peregrine /ˈpɛrəɡrən/ *n* a type of falcon common to most areas of the world.

peremptory /pəˈrɛmptəri/ *adj* urgent; absolute; dogmatic; dictatorial.—**peremptorily** *adv*.—**peremptoriness** *n*.

perennial /pəˈrɛniəl/ *adj* perpetual; lasting throughout the year. • *n* (*bot*) a plant lasting more than two years.—**perennially** *adv*.

perestroika /ˌpɛrɛsˈtrɔɪkə/ *n* the Russian word for reform and reconstruction, applied to the policy initiated by President Gorbachev of the former USSR of dismantling the monolithic state institutions and replacing them with democratic forms of legislation and administration.—**perestroikan** *adj*.

perfect /ˈpərfɛkt/ *adj* faultless; exact; excellent; complete. • *n* (*gram*) a verb form expressing completed action or designating a present state that is the result of an action in the past. • *vt* to improve; to finish; to make fully accomplished in anything.—**perfecter** *n*.—**perfectness** *n*.

perfectible /pərˈfɛktɪbəl/ *adj* capable of being made perfect.—**perfectibility** *n*.

perfection /pərˈfɛkʃən/ *n* the act of perfecting; the quality or condition of being perfect; great excellence; faultlessness; the highest degree; a perfect person or thing.

perfectionist /-ɪst/ *n* one who demands the highest standard.—**perfectionism** *n*.

perfectly /-li/ *adv* thoroughly, completely; quite well; in a perfect manner.

perfecto /pərˈfɛktoː/ *n* (*pl* **perfectos**) a large cigar, tapered at both ends.

perfervid /pərˈfərvɪd/ *adj* (*arch*) very fervid, ardent.

perfidious /pərˈfɪdiəs/ *adj* treacherous, faithless; deceitful.—**perfidiously** *adv*.—**perfidiousness** *n*.

perfidy /ˈpərfɪdi/ *n* (*pl* **perfidies**) breach of faith; treachery.

perfoliate /pərˈfoːliət/ *adj* (*bot*) with a stalk which apparently passes through the leaf.

perforate /ˈpərfəˌreɪt/ *vt* to pierce; to make a hole or row of holes, by boring through. • *adj* perforated.—**perforatory** *adj*.—**perforator** *n*.

perforation /ˌpərfəˈreɪʃən/ *n* the act of perforating; the condition of being perforated; a hole; a row of holes to facilitate tearing.

perforce /pərˈfɔrs/ *adv* (*arch*) by necessity.

perform /pərˈfɔrm/ *vti* to carry out, do; to put into effect; to act; to execute; to act before an audience; to play a musical instrument.—**performable** *adj*.—**performing** *adj*.

performance /-əns/ *n* the act of performing; a dramatic or musical production; an act or action; (*inf*) a fuss; the capabilities of a vehicle, aircraft, etc. • *adj* high-performance.

performer /-ər/ *n* a person who performs, *esp* one who entertains an audience.

perfume /ˈpərfjuːm/ or /pərˈfjuːm/ *n* a pleasing odour; fragrance; a mixture containing fragrant essential oils and a fixative. • *vt* to scent; to put perfume on.—**perfumer** *n*.

perfumery /pərˈfjuːməri/ *n* (*pl* **perfumeries**) a place where perfume is sold; perfume in general.

perfunctory /pərˈfɛŋktəri/ *adj* superficial, hasty; done merely as a matter of form, half-hearted; performed carelessly; indifferent.—**perfunctorily** *adv*.—**perfunctoriness** *n*.

perfuse /pərˈfjuːz/ *vt* (*with* **with**) to suffuse, permeate.—**perfusion** *n*.—**perfusive** *adj*.

pergola /ˈpərɡələ/ *n* an arbour or walk arched by a latticework structure supporting climbing plants.

perhaps /pərˈhæps/ *adv* possibly, maybe.

peri- /ˈpɛri/ *prefix* around; near.

perianth /ˈpɛriˌænθ/ *n* the outer part of a flower, comprising the calyx and corolla together.

periapt /ˈpɛriˌæpt/ *n* an amulet.

pericarditis /ˌpɛrikɑrˈdaɪtɪs/ *n* inflammation of the pericardium.

pericardium /ˌpɛriˈkɑrdiəm/ *n* (*pl* **pericardia**) the membrane enclosing the heart.—**pericardiac, pericardial** *adj*.

pericarp /ˈpɛriˌkɑrp/ *n* the part of a fruit developed from the wall of the ovary.—**pericarpial** *adj*.

perichondrium /ˌpɛriˈkɒndriəm/ *n* (*pl* **perichondria**) the membrane covering a cartilage.

periclase /ˈpɛriˌkleɪs/ *n* magnesium oxide as a mineral in crystal or grain form.

pericranium /ˌpɛriˈkreɪniəm/ *n* (*pl* **pericrania**) the membrane surrounding the cranium.

peridot /ˈpɛriˌdɒt/ *n* a pale green semi-precious form of olivine.

perigee /ˈpɛriˌdʒiː/ *n* the point of the moon's, or a planet's, orbit, when it is nearest the earth.—**perigean** *adj*.

perihelion /ˌpɛriˈhiːliən/ *n* (*pl* **perihelia**) the point of a planet's or comet's orbit when it is nearest the sun.

peril /ˈpɛrɪl/ *n* danger, jeopardy; risk, hazard.

perilous /-əs/ *adj* dangerous.—**perilously** *adv*.

perimeter /pəˈrɪmɪtər/ *n* a boundary around an area; (*math*) the curve or line bounding a closed figure; the length of this.—**perimetric** *adj*.—**perimetry** *n*.

perineum /ˌpɛriˈniːəm/ *n* the area between the genitals and the anus.—**perineal** *adj*.

period /ˈpiːriəd/ *n* a portion of time; menstruation; an interval of time as in an academic day, playing time in a game, etc; an age or era in history, epoch; a stage in life; (*gram*) a full stop (.); (*astron*) a planet's time of revolution. • *interj* an exclamation used for emphasis.

periodic /ˌpiːriˈɒdɪk/ *adj* relating to a period; recurring at regular intervals, cyclic; intermittent.—**periodically** *adv*.—**periodicity** *n*.

periodical /-əl/ *adj* periodic. • *n* a magazine, etc issued at regular intervals.

periodic table *n* a list of chemical elements tabulated by their atomic number.

periodontics /ˌpɛriəˈdɒntɪks/ *n sing* the branch of dentistry dealing with disorders of the gums and tissues around the teeth.—**periodontal** *adj*.—**periodontist** *n*.

periosteum /ˌpɛriˈɒstiəm/ *n* (*pl* **periostea**) the membrane covering the bones.

periostitis /ˌpɛrɪɒsˈtaɪtɪs/ *n* inflammation of the periosteum.

peripatetic /ˌpɛrɪpəˈtɛtɪk/ *adj* itinerant; (*teacher/coach*) travelling from one school to another.—*also n*.

peripheral /pəˈrɪfərəl/ *adj* incidental, superficial; relating to a periphery; (*equipment*) for connection to a computer. • *n* a device such as a printer, scanner, etc used with a computer.—**peripherally** *adv*.

periphery /pəˈrɪfəri/ *n* (*pl* **peripheries**) the outer surface or boundary of an area; the outside surface of anything.

periphrasis /pəˈrɪfrəsɪs/ *n* (*pl* **periphrases**) a roundabout way of speech; circumlocution.

periphrastic /ˌpɛrɪˈfræstɪk/ *adj* using periphrasis; circumlocutory.—**periphrastically** *adv*.

peripteral /pəˈrɪptərəl/ *adj* (*archit*) with a row of columns on every side.

periscope /ˈpɛrəˌskoʊp/ *n* a device with mirrors that enables the viewer to see objects above or around an obstacle or above water, as from a submarine.

periscopic /ˌpɛrəˈskɒpɪk/ *adj* (*lens*) with a view around; of a periscope.—**periscopically** *adv*.

perish /ˈpɛrɪʃ/ *vi* to be destroyed or ruined; to die, *esp* violently; (*rubber, etc*) to deteriorate, rot. • *vt* to cause to rot or perish.

perishable /-əbəl/ *adj* liable to spoil or decay. • *n* something perishable, *esp* food.—**perishability** *n*.

peritoneum /ˌpɛrɪtəˈniəm/ *n* (*pl* **peritoneums, peritonea**) a membrane that lines the walls of the abdomen.—**peritoneal** *adj*.

peritonitis /ˌpɛrɪtəˈnaɪtɪs/ *n* inflammation of the peritoneum.—**peritonitic** *adj*.

periwinkle[1] /ˈpɛrɪˌwɪŋkəl/ *n* any of various edible small marine gastropods with spiralled shells.

periwinkle[2] *n* any of various evergreen trailing plants with blue or white flowers.

perjure /ˈpɜːrdʒər/ *vt* to commit perjury, swear falsely.—**perjurer** *n*.

perjury /ˈpɜːrdʒəri/ *n* (*pl* **perjuries**) (*law*) the crime of giving false witness under oath, swearing to what is untrue.

perk[1] /pɜːrk/ *n* (*usu pl*) (*inf*) a perquisite.

perk[2] *vti* (*usu with* **up**) to recover self-confidence; to become lively or cheerful; to prick up, as of a dog's ears; to smarten up.

perky /ˈpɜːrki/ *adj* (**perkier, perkiest**) pert, cheeky; lively, jaunty.—**perkily** *adv*.—**perkiness** *n*.

perm /pɜːrm/ *n* a straightening or curling of hair by use of chemicals or heat lasting through many washings. •*vt* (*hair*) to give a perm to.—*also* **permanent wave**.

permafrost /ˈpɜːrməˌfrɒst/ *n* subsoil that is permanently frozen.

permanence /ˈpɜːrmənəns/ *n* the condition or quality of being permanent.

permanency /-i/ *n* (*pl* **permanencies**) permanence; a person or thing that is permanent.—**permanently** *adv*.

permanent /ˈpɜːrmənənt/ *adj* lasting, or intended to last, indefinitely.

permanent wave *n* a perm.

permanganate /pərˈmæŋɡəneɪt/ or /-nət/ *n* a salt of an acid of manganese, *esp* permanganate of potash.

permeable /ˈpɜːrmiəbəl/ *adj* admitting the passage of a fluid.—**permeability** *n*.—**permeably** *adv*.

permeate /ˈpɜːrmiˌeɪt/ *vti* to fill every part of, saturate; to pervade, be diffused (through); to pass through by osmosis.—**permeation** *n*.

permissible /pərˈmɪsɪbəl/ *adj* allowable.—**permissibility** *n*.

permission /pərˈmɪʃən/ *n* authorization; consent.

permissive /pərˈmɪsɪv/ *adj* allowing permission; lenient; sexually indulgent.—**permissively** *adv*.—**permissiveness** *n*.

permit /pərˈmɪt/ *vti* (**permitting, permitted**) to allow to be done; to authorize; to give opportunity. • *n* a licence.—**permitter** *n*.

permutation /ˌpɜːrmjuˈteɪʃən/ *n* any radical alteration; a change in the order of a series; any of the total number of groupings within a group; an ordered arrangement of a set of objects.—**permutational** *adj*.

permute /pərˈmjuːt/ *vt* to put into a different order.

pernicious /pərˈnɪʃəs/ *adj* destructive; very harmful.—**perniciously** *adv*.—**perniciousness** *n*.

pernickety /pərˈnɪkɪti/ *adj* (*inf*) fussy, fastidious; over-attentive to detail.

perorate /ˈpɛrəˌreɪt/ *vi* to speak at length.

peroration /ˌpɛrəˈreɪʃən/ *n* the final part of a speech or discourse.

peroxide /pəˈrɒksaɪd/ *n* hydrogen peroxide; a colourless liquid used as an antiseptic and as a bleach.

perpendicular /ˌpɜːrpənˈdɪkjʊlər/ *adj* upright, vertical; (*geom*) at right angles (to). • *n* a perpendicular line, position or style.—**perpendicularity** *n*.—**perpendicularly** *adv*.

perpetrate /ˈpɜːrpəˌtreɪt/ *vt* (*something evil, criminal, etc*) to do; (*a blunder, etc*) to commit.—**perpetration** *n*.—**perpetrator** *n*.

perpetual /pərˈpɛtʃʊəl/ *adj* continuous; everlasting; (*plant*) blooming continuously throughout the season.—**perpetually** *adv*.

perpetuate /pərˈpɛtʃʊeɪt/ *vt* to cause to continue; to make perpetual.—**perpetuation** *n*.—**perpetuator** *n*.

perpetuity /ˌpɜːrpəˈtʃuːɪti/ or /-ˈtjuː-/, /-ˈtuː-/ *n* (*pl* **perpetuities**) endless duration, eternity; perpetual continuance; an annuity payable forever.

perplex /pərˈplɛks/ *vt* to puzzle, bewilder, confuse; to complicate.

perplexity /-ɪti/ *n* (*pl* **perplexities**) bewilderment, a being at a loss; a perplexing thing, a dilemma.

perquisite /ˈpɜːrkwəzɪt/ *n* an expected or promised privilege, gain, or profit incidental to regular wages or salary; a tip, gratuity; something claimed as an exclusive right.—*also* **perk**.

perron /ˈpɛrən/ *n* a flight of steps outside a building, leading to the first floor.

perry /ˈpɛri/ *n* (*pl* **perries**) a cider-like drink made from pears.

per se /pərˈseɪ/ *adv* by itself; by its very nature, intrinsically.

persecute /ˈpɜːrsəˌkjuːt/ *vt* to harass, oppress, *esp* for reasons of race, religion, etc; to worry persistently.—**persecutor** *n*.

persecution /ˌpɜːrsəˈkjuːʃən/ *n* a persecuting or being persecuted; unfair or cruel treatment for reasons of race, religion, etc; a time of persecution.

perseverance /ˌpɜːrsəvəˈrɒns/ *n* persisting efforts of belief, *esp* in the face of opposition; steadfastness; (*Christianity*) continuance in grace.—**perseverant** *adj*.

persevere /ˌpɜːrsəˈviːr/ *vi* to persist, maintain effort, steadfastly, *esp* in face of difficulties.—**perseveringly** *adv*.

persiennes /ˌpɜːrsiˈɛnz/, *Fr*. /pɛrˈsjɛn/ *npl* outside window shutters with horizontal louvres.

persiflage /ˈpɜːrsəˌflɒʒ/ *n* frivolous talk, banter.

persimmon /pərˈsɪmən/ *n* one of a species of tropical American trees; the fruit of such a tree.

persist /pərˈsɪst/ *vi* to continue in spite of obstacles or opposition; to persevere; to last.—**persister** *n*.

persistence /pərˈsɪstəns/, **persistency** /-tənsi/ *n* a persisting; tenacity of purpose.

persistent /pərˈsɪstənt/ *adj* persevering; stubborn.—**persistently** *adv*.

persnickety /pərˈsnɪkɪti/ *adj* the US word for **pernickety**.

person /ˈpɜːrsən/ *n* (*pl* **persons**) a human being, individual; the body (including clothing) of a human being; (*in a play*) a character; one who is recognized by law as the subject of rights and duties; (*gram*) one of the three classes of personal pronouns and verb forms, referring to the person(s) speaking, spoken to, or spoken of.

persona /pərˈsoʊnə/ *n* (*pl* **personae**) a person; a character in a play, etc; (*pl*) public role or image.

personable /ˈpɜːrsənəbəl/ *adj* pleasing in personality and appearance.—**personableness** *n*.—**personably** *adv*.

personage /ˈpɜːrsənɪdʒ/ *n* a distinguished person.

persona grata /pərˈsoʊnəˌɡrɑːtə/ *n* (*pl* **personae gratae**) a person who is acceptable or welcome, *esp* a diplomat to a foreign government.

personal /ˈpɜːrsənəl/ *adj* concerning a person's private affairs, or his or her character, habits, body, etc; done in person; (*law*) of property that is movable; (*gram*) denoting person.

personality /ˌpɜːrsəˈnælɪti/ *n* (*pl* **personalities**) one's individual characteristics; excellence or distinction of social and personal traits; a person with such qualities; a celebrity.

personalize /ˈpɜːrsənəˌlaɪz/ *vt* to mark with name, initials, etc; to endow with personal characteristics; to take personally; to personify.—**personalization** *n*.

personally /ˈpɜːrsənəli/ *adv* in person; in one's own opinion; as though directed to oneself.

personalty /ˈpɜːrsənəlti/ *n* (*pl* **personalties**) (*law*) personal property.

persona non grata /ˈpɜːrsoʊnəˌnɒnˈɡrɑːtə/ *n* (*pl* **personae non gratae**) a person who is not acceptable or welcome, *esp* to a foreign government.

personate /ˈpɜːrsəˌneɪt/ *vt* to play the part of (in a play etc); (*law*) to pretend to be (someone else) for fraudulent purposes.—**personation** *n*.—**personator** *n*.

personification /pər,sɒnəfɪ'keɪʃən/ *n* representation of an abstract idea or a thing as a person; an embodiment, a type; a perfect example.

personify /pər'sɒnə,faɪ/ *vt* (**personifying, personified**) to think of, represent, as a person; to typify.—**personifier** *n*.

personnel /pərsə'nɛl/ *n* the employees of an organization or company; the department that hires them.

perspective /pərs'pɛktɪv/ *n* objectivity; the art of drawing so as to give an impression of relative distance or solidity; a picture so drawn; relation, proportion, between parts of a subject; vista, prospect. • *adj* of or in perspective.

perspicacious /,pərspɪ'keɪʃəs/ *adj* of clear understanding; shrewd; discerning.—**perspicaciously** *adv*.—**perspicacity** *n*.

perspicuous /pər'spɪkjuːəs/ *adj* clearly expressed, lucid.—**perspicuity** *n*.

perspiration /,pərspə'reɪʃən/ *n* the salty fluid excreted on to the surface of the skin, sweat; the act of perspiring.

perspire /pər'spaɪr/ *vti* to excrete (moisture) through the pores of the skin to cool the body, to sweat.—**perspiringly** *adv*.

persuadable /pər'sweɪdəbəl/, **persuasible** /pər'sweɪsɪbəl/ *adj* able to be persuaded.—**persuadability, persuasibility** *n*.

persuade /pər'sweɪd/ *vt* to convince; to induce by argument, reasoning, advice, etc.—**persuader** *n*.

persuasion /pər'sweɪʒən/ *n* the act of persuading; a conviction or opinion; a system of religious beliefs; a group adhering to such a system.

persuasive /pər'sweɪsɪv/ *adj* able to persuade; influencing the mind or emotions.—**persuasively** *adv*.—**persuasiveness** *n*.

pert /pərt/ *adj* impudent, cheeky; sprightly.—**pertly** *adv*.—**pertness** *n*.

pertain /pər'teɪn/ *vi* to belong to; to be appropriate to; to have reference to.

pertinacious /,pərtɪ'neɪʃəs/ *adj* persistent; unyielding; obstinate.—**pertinacity, pertinaciousness** *n*.

pertinent /'pərtɪnənt/ *adj* relevant, apposite; to the point.—**pertinence** *n*.—**pertinently** *adv*.

perturb /pər'tərb/ *vt* to trouble; to agitate; to throw into confusion; (*astron*) to cause to undergo perturbation.—**perturbable** *adj*.—**perturbably** *adv*.—**perturbingly** *adv*.

perturbation /,pərtər'beɪʃən/ *n* the state of being troubled, mental agitation; (*astron*) an irregularity or deviation in a regular orbit produced by some additional force.

peruse /pə'ruːz/ *vt* to read carefully, to examine.—**perusal** *n*.

pervade /pər'veɪd/ *vt* to permeate or spread through; to be rife among.—**pervasion** *n*.

pervasive /pər'veɪsɪv/ *adj* able or tending to pervade.—**pervasively** *adv*.—**pervasiveness** *n*.

perverse /pər'vərs/ *adj* deviating from right or truth; persisting in error; wayward; contrary.—**perversely** *adv*.—**perverseness** *n*.

perversion /pər'vərʒən/ *n* an abnormal way of obtaining sexual gratification, *eg* sadism; a perverted form or usage of something.

perversity /pər'vərsɪti/ *n* (*pl* **perversities**) a being perverse; a disposition to thwart or annoy; a perverse act.

pervert /pər'vərt/ *vt* to corrupt; to misuse; to distort. • *n* a person who is sexually perverted.—**perverter** *n*.—**pervertible** *adj*.

perverted /-əd/ *adj* wrong; harmful; unnatural; sexually deviant.—**pervertedly** *adv*.

pervious /'pərvɪəs/ *adj* giving passage, permeable; open to new ideas.

pesade /pə'seɪd/ or /-'zɒd/ *n* (*dressage*) a position in which the horse is standing on its hind legs and raises its forelegs.

peseta /pə'seɪtə/ *n* the former unit of currency in Spain, now replaced by the euro.

pesky /'pɛski/ *adj* (**peskier, peskiest**) (*inf*) troublesome, annoying.

peso /'peɪsoː/ *n* (*pl* **pesos**) a unit of currency in several Latin American countries and the Philippines.

pessary /'pɛsəri/ *n* (*pl* **pessaries**) (*med*) a surgical appliance or suppository inserted into the vagina.

pessimism /'pɛsə,mɪzəm/ *n* a tendency to see in the world what is bad rather than good; a negative outlook that always expects the worst.—**pessimist** *n*.—**pessimistic** *adj*.—**pessimistically** *adv*.

pest /pɛst/ *n* anything destructive, *esp* a plant or animal detrimental to man such as rats, flies, weeds, etc; a person who pesters or annoys.

pester /'pɛstər/ *vt* to annoy or irritate persistently.—**pesterer** *n*.

pesticide /'pɛstɪsaɪd/ *n* any chemical for killing pests.—**pesticidal** *adj*.

pestiferous /pɛ'stɪfərəs/ *adj* spreading infection; (*fig*) physically or morally noxious.

pestilence /'pɛstɪləns/ *n* an outbreak of a fatal epidemic disease; anything regarded as harmful.

pestilent /'pɛstɪlənt/ *adj* irritating; likely to cause a fatal epidemic.—**pestilently** *adv*.

pestilential /'pɛstɪlɛnʃəl/ *adj* of the nature of or conveying pestilence; harmful; annoying.—**pestilentially** *adv*.

pestle /'pɛsəl/ *n* a *usu* club-shaped tool for pounding or grinding substances in a mortar. • *vt* to beat, pound, or pulverize with a pestle.

pet /pɛt/ *n* a domesticated animal kept as a companion; a person treated as a favourite. • *adj* kept as a pet; spoiled, indulged; favourite; particular. • *vti* (**petting, petted**) to stroke or pat gently; to caress; (*inf*) to kiss, embrace, etc in making love.

petal /'pɛtəl/ *n* any of the leaf-like parts of a flower's corolla.—**petaline** *adj*.—**petalled** *adj*.

petard /pɪ'tɑrd/ *n* (*formerly*) a small bomb used to blow in a door, etc.

peter /'piːtər/ *vi* (*with* **out**) to come to an end; to dwindle to nothing.

petersham /'piːtərʃəm/ *n* a thick corded ribbon used in dressmaking as a stiffening; a thick woollen fabric used for overcoats, etc.

Peter's Pence *n* (*RC Church*) voluntary contributions to the papal treasury; (*formerly*) in England, an annual tax, until its abolishment by Henry VIII, of one penny levied on every house and paid to the Pope.

petiolate /'pɛti,oːlət/ *adj* (*bot*) growing on a petiole.

petiole /'pɛti,oːl/ *n* (*bot*) a leaf stalk.

petit /'pɛti/ *adj* (*esp law*) of lesser importance.

petite /pə'tiːt/ *adj* (*woman*) small and trim in figure.

petition /pə'tɪʃən/ *n* a formal application or entreaty to an authority; a written demand for action by a government, etc, signed by a number of people. • *vti* to present a petition to; to ask humbly.—**petitionary** *adj*.—**petitioner** *n*.

petit mal /,pɛti'mæl/ or /,pɒti-/ *n* a mild form of epilepsy.

petit point /'pɛtipɔɪnt/ *n* a fine stitch used in needlepoint.

petrel /'pɛtrəl/ *n* a dark-coloured sea bird capable of flying far from land.

petrifaction /,pɛtrɪ'fækʃən/, **petrification** /,pɛtrɪ'fɪkeɪʃən/ *n* the process of changing animal or vegetable material into stone.

petrify /'pɛtrɪfaɪ/ *vti* (**petrifying, petrified**) to turn or be turned into stone; to stun or be stunned with fear, horror, etc.

petro- /'pɛtroː/ *prefix* rock, stone; petroleum.

petrochemical /,pɛtroː'kɛmɪkəl/ *n* any chemical obtained from natural gas or petroleum.

petrodollar /'pɛtroː,dɒlər/ *n* a notional unit of money earned by the export of petroleum.

petroglyph /'pɛtroː,glɪf/ *n* a rock carving or drawing.

petrography /pɛ'trɒgrəfi/ *n* the scientific description and classification of rocks.—**petrographer** *n*.—**petrographic, petrographical** *adj*.

petrol /'pɛtrəl/ *n* fuel obtained from petroleum; (*US*) gasoline.

petrolatum /,pɛtrə'lɒtəm/ *n* a greasy, jelly-like substance obtained from petroleum and used for ointments, etc.

petroleum /pə'troːlɪəm/ *n* a crude oil consisting of hydrocarbons occurring naturally in certain rock strata and distilled to yield petrol, paraffin, etc.

petrology /pɪ'trɒlədʒi/ *n* (*pl* **petrologies**) the study of rocks and their structure.

petrous /'pɛtrəs/ *adj* of, or like, rock.

petticoat /'pɛti,koːt/ *n* an underskirt; a slip; (*inf*) woman.

pettifog /'pɛtifɒg/ *vi* to be, or behave like, a pettifogger.

pettifogger /-ər/ *n* an inferior or crooked lawyer; someone who quibbles over details.

pettish /'pɛtɪʃ/ *adj* peevish, sulky.

pettitoes /'pɛtitoːz/ or /'pɛti-/ *npl* pig's trotters, *esp* as food.

petty /'pɛti/ *adj* (**pettier, pettiest**) trivial; small-minded; minor.—**pettily** *adv*.—**pettiness** *n*.

petty officer *n* a noncommissioned officer in the navy.

petulant /'pɛtjʊlənt/ or /-tʊ-/ *adj* showing impatience or irritation; bad-humoured.—**petulance** *n*.—**petulantly** *adv*.

petunia /pə'tuːnɪə/ or /-tju:-/ *n* a plant with funnel-shaped purple or white flowers.

petuntse /pə'tʌntseɪ/ or /-'tʊnseɪ/ *n* a fine white clay used with kaolin in the manufacture of porcelain.

pew /pju:/ *n* a wooden, bench-like seat in a church, often enclosed; (*sl*) a chair.

pewit /'pi:wɪt/ *n* the lapwing.—*also* **peewit**.

pewter /'pju:tər/ *n* an alloy of tin and lead with a silvery-grey colour; dishes, etc, made of pewter.—**pewterer** *n*.

pfennig /'fenɪg/, *Ger.* /pfɛnɪʃ/ *n* (*pl* **pfennigs, pfennige**) a former unit of currency in Germany worth one hundredth of a Deutschmark.

PG *abbr* = parental guidance: denoting a motion-picture suitable for all ages, but advising parental guidance.

PGA *abbr* = Professional Golfers' Association.

phaeton /'feɪtən/ or /'feɪə-/ *n* a light, open, four-wheeled horse-drawn carriage.

phagocyte /'fægə,saɪt/ *n* a white corpuscle which devours harmful micro-organisms and other foreign bodies.

phagocytosis /,fægə'saɪtɒsɪs/ *n* the process by which a phagocyte devours foreign bodies.

phalange /'fælændʒ/ or /fə'lændʒ/ *see* **phalanx**.

phalangeal /fə'lændʒɪəl/ *adj* (*anat*) of or pertaining to a phalanx.

phalanger /fə'lændʒər/ *n* a small tree-living marsupial of Australasia, with a long tail and bushy fur.

phalanx /'fælæŋks/ or /'feɪ-/ *n* (*pl* **phalanxes, phalanges**) a massed body or rank of people; (*pl* **phalanges**) a bone of a finger or toe.

phalarope /'fælə,ro:p/ *n* a small wading bird, with a straight bill and webbed feet.

phallic /'fælɪk/ *adj* pertaining to, or resembling, a phallus.

phallicism /'fælɪsɪzəm/, **phallism** /'fælɪzəm/ *n* the worship of the phallus as the emblem of the generative power in nature.

phallus /'fæləs/ *n* (*pl* **phalli, phalluses**) the male reproductive organ.

phanerogam /'fænərə,gæm/ *n* (*bot*) a flowering plant.—**phanerogamic, phanerogamous** *adj*.

phantasm /'fæn,tæzəm/ *n* a phantom; a vision of an absent person.

phantasmagoria /fæn,tæzmə'gɔrɪə/, **phantasmagory** /fæn,tæzmə'gɔrɪ/ *n* a series of shifting images, like those seen in a dream.—**phantasmagoric, phantasmagorical** *adj*.

phantom /'fæntəm/ *n* a spectre or apparition. • *adj* illusionary.

pharaoh /'feɪro:/ *n* (*also with cap*) the title of the kings of ancient Egypt.—**pharaonic** *adj*.

Pharisaic /,ferɪ'seɪɪk/, **Pharisaical** /-əl/ *adj* pertaining to, or characteristic of, the Pharisees; (*fig*) hypocritical.

Pharisee /'ferɪsi:/ *n* a member of a Jewish religious sect, characterized by its strict observance of the letter of the law; (*fig*) a self-righteous person, a hypocrite.

pharmaceutical /,fɑrmə'su:tɪkəl/ or /-'sju:-/ *adj* of, relating to pharmacy or drugs. • *n* a medicinal drug.

pharmaceutics /,fɑrmə'su:tɪks/ or /-'sju:-/ *n sing* the science of pharmacy.

pharmacist /'fɑrməsɪst/ *n* one licensed to practise pharmacy.

pharmacology /,fɑrmə'kɒlədʒɪ/ *n* the science dealing with the effects of drugs on living organisms.—**pharmacological** *adj*.—**pharmacologist** *n*.

pharmacopoeia /,fɑrməkə'pi:ə/ *n* a book containing a list of drugs with directions for their use.—**pharmacopoeial** *adj*.

pharmacy /'fɑrməsɪ/ *n* (*pl* **pharmacies**) the preparation and dispensing of drugs and medicines; a drugstore.

pharyngeal /fə'rɪndʒɪəl/, **pharyngal** /fə'rɪŋgəl/ *adj* pertaining to, or situated near, the pharynx.

pharyngitis /,ferɪn'dʒaɪtɪs/ *n* inflammation of the pharynx.

pharyngology /,ferɪn'gɒlədʒɪ/ *n* the medical study of the pharynx.

pharyngoscope /,ferɪŋgə'sko:p/ *n* an instrument used for looking at the pharynx.

pharyngotomy /,ferɪŋ'gɒtəmɪ/ *n* (*pl* **pharynotomies**) the surgical operation of making an incision into the pharynx.

pharynx /'ferɪŋks/ *n* (*pl* **pharynges, pharynxes**) the cavity leading from the mouth and nasal passages to the larynx and oesophagus.

phase *n* (*pl* **phases**) an amount of the moon's or a planet's surface illuminated at a given time; a characteristic period in a regularly recurring sequence of events or stage in a development. • *vt* to do by stages or gradually; (*with* **out**) (*making, using, etc*) to stop gradually.—**phasic** *adj*.

PhD /,pi:eɪtʃ'di:/ *abbr* = Doctor of Philosophy.

pheasant /'fezənt/ *n* a richly coloured game bird.

phellem /'felem/ or /'feləm/ *n* (*bot*) cork.

phenacetin /fɪ'næsətɪn/ *n* a drug used for the relief of pain and fever.

Phenobarbital /,fi:no:'bɑrbɪ,tɒl/ *n* (*trademark*) a crystalline barbiturate used as a hypnotic and sedative.

phenol /'fi:nɒl/ *n* carbolic acid.

phenology /fɪnɒ'lədʒɪ/ *n* the study of the influence of climate on certain recurrent phenomena of animal and plant life.

phenomenal /fə'nɒmənəl/ *adj* perceptible through the senses; remarkable; outstanding.—**phenomenally** *adv*.

phenomenalism /-ɪzəm/ *n* (*philos*) the doctrine that all knowledge is derived from sense impressions.—**phenomenalist** *n*.

phenomenon /fə'nɒmənɒn/ or /-nən/ *n* (*pl* **phenomena, phenomenons**) anything perceived by the senses as a fact; a fact or event that can be scientifically described; a remarkable thing or person.

phenyl /'fenəl/ or /'fi:-/ *n* the hydrocarbon radical of phenol.

pheromone /'ferə,mo:n/ *n* a molecule that functions as a chemical communication signal between individuals of the same species.

phew /fju:/ *interj* an exclamation of relief, surprise, etc.

phi /faɪ/ *n* the 21st letter of the Greek alphabet.

phial /'faɪəl/ *n* a small glass bottle; a vial.

Phi Beta Kappa /,faɪbeɪtə'kæpə/ *n* (*US*) (a member of) the oldest college fraternity.

phil- /fɪl/, **philo-** /fɪlə/ or /fɪlɒ/ *prefix* loving.

philander /fɪ'lændər/ *vi* (*man*) to flirt with women for amusement.—**philanderer** *n*.

philanthropist /fɪ'lænθrəpɪst/ *n* a person who tries to benefit others.

philanthropy /fɪ'lænθrəpɪ/ *n* (*pl* **philanthropies**) love of mankind, *esp* as demonstrated by benevolent or charitable actions.—**philanthropic, philanthropical** *adj*.—**philanthropically** *adv*.

philatelist /fɪ'lætəlɪst/ *n* a person who collects or studies stamps.

philately /fɪ'lætəlɪ/ *n* the study and collecting of postage and imprinted stamps; stamp collecting.—**philatelic** *adj*.—**philatelically** *adv*.

philharmonic /,fɪlhɑr'mɒnɪk/ or /,fɪlər-/ *adj* loving music.

philhellene /fɪlhe'li:n/ *n* a lover or supporter of Greece.

philippic /fɪ'lɪpɪk/ *n* a bitter denunciation, an invective.

philistine /'fɪlɪ,sti:n/ or /-staɪn/ *n* a person with no feeling for culture; an uncultured, conventional person; (*with cap*) a member of a warlike race hostile to ancient Israel. • *adj* uncultured.—**philistinism** *n*.

philogyny /fɪ'lɒdʒənɪ/ *n* fondness for women.—**phylogynous** *adj*.—**phylogynist** *n*.

philology /fɪ'lɒlədʒɪ/ *n* the study, *esp* comparative, of languages and their history and structure.—**philological** *adj*.—**philologist, philologer** *n*.

philomel /'fɪlə,mel/ *n* (*poet*) a nightingale.

philosopher /fɪ'lɒsəfər/ *n* a person who studies philosophy; a person who acts calmly and rationally.

philosophic /,fɪlə'sɒfɪk/, **philosophical** /,fɪlə'sɒfɪkəl/ *adj* of, relating to, or according to philosophy; serene; temperate; resigned.—**philosophically** *adv*.

philosophize /fɪ'lɒsəfaɪz/ *vi* to reason like a philosopher; to speculate, moralize.—**philosophizer** *n*.

philosophy /fɪ'lɒsəfɪ/ *n* (*pl* **philosophies**) the study of the principles underlying conduct, thought, and the nature of the universe; general principles of a field of knowledge; a particular system of ethics; composure; calmness.

philtre, philter /'fɪltər/ *n* a love potion.

phlebitis /flə'baɪtɪs/ *n* (*med*) an inflammation of a vein.—**phlebitic** *adj*.

phlebotomize /flə'bɒtə,maɪz/ *vti* (*med*) to practise phlebotomy (on).

phlebotomy /flə'bɒtəmɪ/ *n* (*pl* **phlebotomies**) a surgical incision into a vein to let blood.—**phlebotomist** *n*.

phlegm /flem/ *n* a thick mucus discharged from the throat, as during a cold; sluggishness; apathy.

phlegmatic /fleg'mætɪk/, **phlegmatical** /-əl/ *adj* unemotional, composed; sluggish.—**phlegmatically** *adv*.

phloem /'flo:em/ *n* (*bot*) the tissue which carries food around a plant.

phlogiston /flo:'dʒɪstən/ or /-stɒn/ *n* (*chem*) an inflammable element once believed to exist in all combustible bodies.

phlox /flɒks/ *n* (*pl* **phlox, phloxes**) a North American flowering plant.

phobia /'fəːbiə/ *n* an irrational, excessive, and persistent fear of some thing or situation.—**phobic** *adj*, *n*.

phoenix /'fiːnɪks/ *n* a mythical bird that set fire to itself and rose from its ashes every 500 years; a symbol of immortality.

phon /fɒn/ *n* a unit of loudness.

phonate /'fəːneɪt/ *vi* to utter vocal sounds.—**phonation** *n*.

phone /fəːn/ *n*, *vti* (*inf*) (to) telephone.

phone book *n* (*inf*) telephone book.

phone-in *n* a radio programme in which questions or comments by listeners are broadcast.

phonetic /fə'netɪk/ *adj* relating to, or representing, speech sounds.—**phonetically** *adv*.

phonetician /ˌfɒnə'tiːʃən/ *n* a student of, or expert in, phonetics.

phonetics /fə'netɪks/ *n sing* the science concerned with pronunciation and the representation of speech sounds.

phonetist /fə'netɪst/ *n* a phonetician; an advocate of phonetic spelling.

phoney, phony /'fəːni/ *adj* (**phonier, phoniest**) (*inf*) not genuine. • *n* (*pl* **phoneys, phonies**) a fake; an insincere person.—**phoneyness, phoniness** *n*.

phonics /'fɒnɪks/ *n sing* a phonetics-based method of teaching reading.—**phonic** *adj*.

phonogram /'fəːnəˌɡræm/ *n* (*phonetics*) a written character representing a particular sound.

phonograph /'fəːnəˌɡrɑːf/ *n* a device for reproducing sounds from a vinyl disc.

phonography /fə'nɒɡrəfi/ *n* spelling based on pronunciation; a system of shorthand writing based on sound.

phonology /fə'nɒlədʒi/ *n* (*pl* **phonologies**) the study of speech sounds and their development, and of the sound systems of language.—**phonological** *adj*.—**phonologist** *n*.

phony *see* **phoney**.

phosgene /'fɒzdʒiːn/ *n* a poisonous gas used in chemical warfare and in industry.

phosphate /'fɒsfeɪt/ *n* a compound of phosphorus.—**phosphatic** *adj*.

phosphene /'fɒsfiːn/ *n* the sensation of luminous rings seen when a closed eye is pressed.

phosphide /'fɒsfaɪd/ *n* a compound of phosphorus with another element.

phosphite /'fɒsfaɪt/ *n* a salt of phosphorous acid.

phosphorescence /ˌfɒsfə'resəns/ *n* the property of giving off light without noticeable heat, as phosphorus does; such light.—**phosphorescent** *adj*.

phosphorous /'fɒsfərəs/ *adj* containing phosphorus in lower or higher proportions.

phosphorus /'fɒsfərəs/ *n* a highly reactive, poisonous nonmetallic element; a phosphorescent substance or body, *esp* one that glows in the dark.

photic /'fəːtɪk/ *adj* of, or pertaining to, light.

photo /'fəːtəː/ *n* (*pl* **photos**) a photograph.

photo- *prefix* light; a photographic process.

photocell /'fəːtəːˌsel/ *n* a photoelectric cell.

photochemical /fəːtəː'kemɪkəl/ *adj* of or relating to the effect of radiant energy, *esp* light.

photochemistry /ˌfəːtəː'kemɪstri/ *n* the branch of chemistry concerned with the effect of radiant energy in producing chemical changes; photochemical properties or processes.

photocopy /'fəːtəːˌkɒpi/ *n* (*pl* **photocopies**) a photographic reproduction of written or printed work. • *vt* (**photocopying, photocopied**) to copy in this way.—**photocopier** *n*.

photoelectric cell /ˌfəːtəːə'lektrɪk-/ *n* a cell whose electrical properties are affected by light; any device in which light controls an electric circuit that operates a mechanical device, as for opening doors.—*also* **photocell**.

photoengraving /ˌfəːtəː'ɪnɡreɪvɪŋ/ or /-'ɒnɡreɪv-/ *n* any photomechanical process of making printing plates.

photo finish *n* the finish of a race where the decision on the winner has to be determined by a photograph as the contestants are so close; any race where the winning margin is small.

photogenic /ˌfəːtəː'dʒenɪk/ or /-'dʒiːnɪk/ *adj* likely to look attractive in photographs; (*biol*) generating light.—**photogenically** *adv*.

photograph /'fəːtəˌɡrɑːf/ *n* an image produced by photography.—*also* **photo**.

photographic *adj* of or like a photograph; minutely accurate like a photograph; (*memory*) capable of retaining facts, etc, after reading for only a brief time.—**photographically** *adv*.

photography /fə'tɒɡrəfi/ *n* the art or process of recording images permanently and visibly by the chemical action of light on sensitive material, producing prints, slides or film.—**photographer** *n*.

photogravure /ˌfəːtəːɡrə'vjʊr/ *n* a printing process using an intaglio plate photographically produced; printed matter so produced.

photojournalism /ˌfəːtəː'dʒɜːnəˌlɪzəm/ *n* a form of news reporting in which the story is presented mainly through photographs.—**photojournalist** *n*.

photolithograph /ˌfəːtəː'lɪθəˌɡrɑːf/ *n* a picture produced by photolithography.

photolithography /ˌfəːtəːlɪ'θɒɡrəfi/ *n* (*print*) lithography using plates made from photographs.

photomechanical /ˌfəːtəːmə'kænɪkəl/ *adj* of or relating to a printing process that utilizes photography in plate-making.—**photomechanically** *adv*.

photometer /fəː'tɒmɪtər/ *n* an instrument for measuring the intensity of light.

photometry /fəː'tɒmɪtri/ *n* the area of physics concerned with the measurement of light; the use of a photometer.

photomicrograph /ˌfəːtəː'maɪkrəˌɡrɑːf/ *n* a photograph taken through a microscope.—**photomicrography** *n*.

photophobia /ˌfəːtəː'fəːbiə/ *n* (*med*) oversensivity (of the eyes) to light; (*psychol*) fear or, or aversion to, sunlight.

photosphere /'fəːtəːˌsfɪːr/ *n* the surface of a star, *esp* the sun.

Photostat /'fəːtəːˌstæt/ *n* (*trademark*) a device for making photographic copies of documents, etc; a copy made in this way. • *vt* (*often without cap*) to copy in this way.—**Photostatic** *adj*.

photosynthesis /ˌfəːtəː'sɪnθəsɪs/ *n* (*bot*) the process by which a green plant manufactures sugar from carbon dioxide and water in the presence of light.—**photosynthetic** *adj*.—**photosynthetically** *adv*.

photosynthesize /ˌfəːtəː'sɪnθəsaɪz/ *vti* (*plants, etc*) to produce by or carry on photosynthesis.

phototelegraphy /ˌfəːtəː'telɪɡrəfi/ *n* the telegraphic transmission of photographs and drawings.

phrasal /'freɪzəl/ *adj* of or consisting of a phrase or phrases.—**phrasally** *adv*.

phrasal verb *n* (*gram*) a *usu* simple verb that combines with a preposition or adverb, or both, to convey a meaning more than the sum of its parts, *eg come out*.

phrase /'freɪz/ *n* a group of words that does not contain a finite verb but which expresses a single idea by itself; a pointed saying; a high-flown expression; (*mus*) a short, distinct musical passage. • *vt* to express orally, put in words; (*mus*) to divide into melodic phrases.

phrase book *n* a book containing idiomatic expressions of a foreign language and their translations.

phraseogram /'freɪziəˌɡræm/ *n* a shorthand symbol representing a phrase.

phraseology /ˌfreɪzi'ɒlədʒi/ *n* (*pl* **phraseologies**) mode of expression, wording; phrases used by a particular group.—**phraseological** *adj*.

phrasing /'freɪzɪŋ/ *n* the wording of a speech or a piece of writing; (*mus*) the division of a melodic line, etc, into musical phrases.

phrenetic *see* **frenetic**.

phrenic /'frenɪk/ *adj* (*anat*) of, or pertaining to, the diaphragm.

phrenology /frə'nɒlədʒi/ *n* the belief that intelligence and ability may be judged from the shape of a person's skull; study of the shape of the skull based on this belief.—**phrenological** *adj*.—**phrenologist** *n*.

phthisis /'fθaɪsɪs/ or /'θaɪsɪs/ *n* a wasting disease, *esp* tuberculosis of the lungs.

phycology /faɪ'kɒlədʒi/ *n* the study of algae.

phylactery /fɪ'læktəri/ *n* (*pl* **phylacteries**) (*Judaism*) a small case containing Hebrew texts, worn by Jewish men during prayers.

phyletic /faɪ'letɪk/ *adj* relating to the racial development of an animal or plant type.

phyllode /'fɪləːd/ *n* (*bot*) a flattened petiole with the functions of a leaf.

phyllotaxy /ˌfɪlə'tæksi/, **phyllotaxis** /-'tæksɪs/ *n* (*pl* **phyllotaxies, phyllotaxes**) (*bot*) the arrangement of leaves on a stem.

phylloxera /ˌfɪlɒk'sɪːrə/ or /fɪ'lɒksərə/ *n* (*pl* **phylloxeras, phylloxerae**) an insect which attacks vines.

phylogeny /faɪ'lɒdʒəni/, **phylogenesis** /ˌfaɪlo'dʒenəsɪs/ *n* (*pl* **phylogenies, phylogeneses**) (*biol*) the racial evolution of an animal or plant type.—**phylogenic, phylogenetic** *adj*.

phylum /'faɪləm/ *n* (*pl* **phyla**) a major division of the animal or plant kingdom.

physic /'fɪzɪk/ *vt* (**physicking, physicked**) (*arch*) to administer medicine to.

physical /'fɪzɪkəl/ *adj* relating to the world of matter and energy, the human body, or natural science. • *n* a general medical examination.—**physically** *adv*.

physical chemistry *n* the branch of chemistry concerned with the effect of chemical structure on physical properties and of physical changes brought about by chemical reactions.

physical education *n* education in fitness and cure of the body, stressing athletics and hygiene.

physical therapy *n* the treatment of disorders and disease by physical and mechanical means (as massage, exercise, water, heat, etc).—*also* **physiotherapy**.

physician /fɪ'zɪʃən/ *n* a doctor of medicine.

physicist /'fɪzɪsɪst/ *n* a specialist in physics.

physics /'fɪzɪks/ *n* the branch of science concerned with matter and energy and their interactions in the fields of mechanics, acoustics, optics, heat, electricity, magnetism, radiation, atomic structure and nuclear phenomena; the physical processes and phenomena of a particular system.

physio- /'fɪzɪo/ *prefix* nature.

physiocrat /'fɪzɪoːˌkræt/ *n* a supporter of the doctrine of government according to a natural order based on land as the sole form of wealth.

physiognomy /ˌfɪzɪ'ɒnəmi/ *n* (*pl* **physiognomies**) the art of judging character from facial features; facial expression, face; physical features generally.—**physiognomic, physiognomical** *adj*.—**physiognomist** *n*.

physiography /ˌfɪzɪ'ɒɡrəfi/ *n* the study of the earth's natural features, physical geography.—**physiographer** *n*.

physiology /ˌfɪzɪ'ɒlədʒi/ *n* the science of the functioning and processes of living organisms.—**physiological** *adj*.—**physiologist** *n*.

physiotherapy /ˌfɪzɪoː'θerəpi/ *n* physical therapy.—**physiotherapist** *n*.

physique /fɪ'ziːk/ *n* bodily structure and appearance; build.

phytogenesis /ˌfaɪto'dʒenəsɪs/, **phytogeny** /-'tɒdʒɪni/ *n* the study of plant evolution.

phyton /'faɪtən/ or /-tɒn/ *n* (*bot*) the smallest unit of a plant capable of growing into a new plant.

pi[1] /paɪ/ *n* the 16th letter of the Greek alphabet; (*math*) the Greek letter (π) used as a symbol for the ratio of the circumference to the diameter of a circle, approx. 3.14159.

pi[2] *n* (*pl* **pis**) (*print*) a jumble of type; any disorder. • *vt* to mix, disarrange (type). • *vi* to become mixed up.—*also* **pie**.

piacular /paɪ'ækjʊlər/ *adj* expiatory; sinful.

piaffe /piː'æf/ *n* (*dressage*) a slow trot.

pia mater /ˌpaɪə'meɪtər/ or /ˌpiːə-/ *n* (*anat*) the inner membrane enclosing the brain.

pianissimo /ˌpiə'nɪsɪˌmoː/ *adv* (*mus*) very softly.

pianist /'piənɪst/ or /pi'ænɪst/, /'pjænɪst/ *n* a person who plays the piano.

piano /pi'ænoː/ or /'pjænoː/ *n* (*pl* **pianos**) a large stringed keyboard instrument in which each key operates a felt-covered hammer that strikes a corresponding steel wire or wires.

pianoforte /ˌpiænoː'fɔːteɪ/ *n* (*pl* **pianofortes**) a piano.

piastre, piaster /pi'æstər/ *n* a unit of currency in Egypt, Lebanon, Sudan, Syria and South Vietnam.

piazza /pi'ætsə/ or /pi'ɒtsə/ *n* in Italy, a public square; a covered walkway or gallery; a veranda.

pibroch /'piːbrɒx/ or /-brɒk/ *n* a kind of music composed for Scottish bagpipes.

pica /'paɪkə/ *n* (*print*) a standard measurement, equal to 12 points.

picaresque /ˌpɪkə'resk/ *adj* pertaining to a genre of fiction describing the exploits of rogues.

picaroon /ˌpɪkə'ruːn/ *n* (*arch*) a robber, pirate or marauder.

picayune /ˌpɪkə'juːn/ *adj* (*inf*) of little value.

piccalilli /ˌpɪkə'lɪli/ *n* a kind of pickle made with cauliflower, onions, etc.

piccolo /'pɪkəˌloː/ *n* (*pl* **piccolos**) a small shrill flute.

pick /pɪk/ *n* a heavy tool with a shaft and pointed crossbar for breaking ground; a tool for picking, such as a toothpick or

icepick; a plectrum; right of selection; choice; best (of). • *vti* to break up or remove with a pick; to pluck at; to nibble (at), eat fussily; to contrive; to choose; (*fruit, etc*) to gather; to steal from a pocket; (*lock*) to force open; (*with* **up**) to lift; to acquire; to call for; to recover; (*inf*) to make the acquaintance of casually; to learn gradually; to resume; to give a lift to; to increase speed.

pickaback /'pɪkəˌbæk/ *see* **piggyback**.

pickaxe, pickax /'pɪkæks/ *n* (*pl* **pickaxes**) a pick with a long pointed head for breaking up hard ground, etc.

pickerel /'pɪkərəl/ or /'pɪkrəl/ *n* (*pl* **pickerel, pickerels**) a North American freshwater fish of the pike family.

picket /'pɪkət/ *n* a pointed stake; a patrol or group of men selected for a special duty; a person posted by strikes outside a place of work to persuade others not to enter. • *vt* (**picketing, picketed**) to tether to a picket; to post as a military picket; to place pickets, or serve as a picket (at a factory, etc).

pickings /'pɪkɪŋz/ *npl* gleanings, perquisites.

pickle /'pɪkəl/ *n* vegetables preserved in vinegar; (*inf*) a plight, mess. • *vt* to preserve in vinegar.

pickled /-d/ *adj* preserved in pickle; (*sl*) drunk.

picklock /'pɪklɒk/ *n* an instrument for picking locks; someone, *esp* a thief, who picks locks.

pick-me-up *n* a tonic.

pickpocket /'pɪkˌpɒkət/ *n* a person who steals from pockets.

pick-up /'pɪkəp/ *n* the act of picking up; a person or thing picked up; (*elect*) a device for picking up current; the power to accelerate rapidly; the balanced arm of a record player; a pickup truck.

pickup truck *n* a light truck with an enclosed cab and open body.

picnic /'pɪknɪk/ *n* a *usu* informal meal taken on an excursion and eaten outdoors; an outdoor snack; the food so eaten; an easy or agreeable task. • *vi* (**picnicking, picnicked**) to have a picnic.—**picnicker** *n*.

picot /'piːkoː/ *n* a small loop of thread used as an edging to lace.

picotee /ˌpɪkəˌtiː/ or /ˌpɪkə'tiː/ *n* a type of small carnation.

picric acid *n* a toxic acid used as a dye and an explosive.

pictograph /'pɪktəˌɡræf/ *n* a picture representing a word or idea.

pictorial /pɪk'tɔːriəl/ *adj* relating to pictures, painting, or drawing; containing pictures; expressed in pictures; graphic.—**pictorially** *adv*.

picture /'pɪktʃər/ *n* drawing, painting, photography, or other visual representation; a scene; an impression or mental image; a vivid description; a cinema film. • *vt* to portray, describe in a picture; to visualize.

picturesque /ˌpɪktʃə'resk/ *adj* striking, vivid, usually pleasing; making an effective picture.—**picturesquely** *adv*.—**picturesqueness** *n*.

piddle /'pɪdəl/ *vt* to squander. • *vi* (*inf*) to idle; to urinate.

piddling /'pɪdlɪŋ/ *adj* (*inf*) trifling, insignificant.

piddock /'pɪdək/ *n* a bivalve, boring, shellfish.

pidgin /'pɪdʒɪn/ *n* a jargon for trade purposes, using words and grammar from two or more different languages.

pie[1] /paɪ/ *n* a baked dish of fruit, meat, etc, with an under or upper crust of pastry, or both.

pie[2] *see* **pi**[2].

piebald /'paɪbɒld/ *adj* covered with patches of two colours. • *n* a piebald horse, etc.

piece /piːs/ *n* a distinct part of anything; a single object; a literary, dramatic, artistic, or musical composition; (*sl*) a firearm; a man in chess or draughts; an opinion, view; a short distance. • *vt* to fit together, join.—**piecer** *n*.

pièce de résistance /ˌpjesdəreɪ'ziːstãs/ *n* (*pl* **pièces de résistance**) the most important item or dish.

piecemeal /'piːsmiːl/ *adv* gradually; bit by bit.

piecework /'piːswərk/ *n* work paid for according to the quantity produced.

pied /paɪd/ *adj* of mixed colours, mottled.

pied-à-terre /ˌpjeɪdə'ter/ *n* (*pl* **pieds-à-terre**) a flat for occasional use; a second home.

pier /piːr/ *n* a structure supporting the spans of a bridge; a structure built out over water and supported by pillars, used as a landing place, promenade, etc; a heavy column used to support weight.

pierce /piːrs/ *vt* to cut or make a hole through; to force a way into; (*fig*) to touch or move. • *vi* to penetrate.

piercing /'piːrsɪŋ/ *adj* penetrating; keen; (*cold, pain*) acute.—**piercingly** *adv*.

Pierrot /'pjɛrɔː/ *n* (*pantomime*) a male character, *usu* in a loose white costume with a whitened face; a clown in such a costume.

Pietà /ˌpiːɛ'tɒ/ *n* a picture or sculpture of the Virgin mourning over the dead Christ.

piety /'paɪəti/ *n* (*pl* **pieties**) religious devoutness; the characteristic of being pious.

piezoelectricity /paɪˌiːzo'ɪlɛk'trɪsɪti/ *n* the production of electricity in certain types of crystal through the application of mechanical stress.—**piezoeletric, piezoelectrical** *adj.*—**piezoelectrically** *adv*.

piffle /'pɪfəl/ *n* (*inf*) silly stuff, nonsense. • *vi* to talk nonsense.

pig /pɪg/ *n* a domesticated animal with a broad snout and fat body raised for food; a hog; a greedy or filthy person; an oblong casting of metal poured from the smelting furnace; (*sl*) a policeman. • *vi* (**pigging, pigged**) (*sow*) to give birth; (*inf*) to live in squalor.

pigeon /'pɪdʒən/ *n* a bird with a small head and a heavy body; (*inf*) a person who is easily conned.

pigeonhole /'pɪdʒənˌhoːl/ *n* a small compartment for filing papers, etc; a category *usu* failing to reflect actual complexities. • *vt* to file, classify; to put aside for consideration, shelve.

pigeon-toed *adj* having the toes turned inward.

piggery /'pɪgəri/ *n* (*pl* **piggeries**) a place where pigs are reared; a pigsty.

piggish /'pɪgɪʃ/ *adj* greedy, dirty, selfish, like a pig.—**piggishly** *adv.*—**piggishness** *n*.

piggy /'pɪgi/ *n* (*pl* **piggies**) a child's name for a young or little pig. • *adj* (**piggier, piggiest**) piggish.

piggyback /'pɪgɪˌbæk/ *n* a ride on the shoulders or back of a person. • *adv* carried on the shoulders or back; transported on top of a larger object.—*also* **pickaback**.

piggy bank *n* a container for coins, often shaped like a pig.

pigheaded /pɪg'hɛdəd/ *adj* stupidly stubborn.—**pigheadedly** *adv.*—**pigheadedness** *n*.

piglet /'pɪglət/ *n* a young pig.

pigment /'pɪgmənt/ *n* paint; a naturally occurring substance used for colouring.—**pigmentary** *adj*.

pigmentation /ˌpɪgmən'teɪʃən/ *n* (*biol*) coloration of the tissues of plants and animals caused by pigment; the depositing of pigments by cells.

pigmy /'pɪgmi/ *see* **pygmy**.

pignut /'pɪgnʌt/ *n* an earthnut.

pigskin /'pɪgskɪn/ *n* leather made from the skin of a pig.

pigsticker /'pɪgˌstɪkər/ *n* a person who goes pigsticking.

pigsticking /'pɪgˌstɪkɪŋ/ *n* the hunting of wild boar with a spear, *usu* on horseback.

pigsty /'pɪgstaɪ/ *n* (*pl* **pigsties**) a pen for pigs; a dirty hovel.

pigtail /'pɪgteɪl/ *n* a tight braid of hair.—**pigtailed** *adj*.

pika /'paɪkə/ *n* a small rodent of mountains and deserts of western North America and Asia that has small ears and no tail.

pike[1] /paɪk/ *n* a sharp point or spike; the top of a spear. • *vt* to pierce or kill with a pike.

pike[2] *n* (*pl* **pike, pikes**) a long-snouted fish, important as a food and game fish.

pike perch *n* (**pike perch, pike perches**) any of various fishes of the perch family resembling the pike.

pikestaff /'paɪkstæf/ *n* the shaft of a pike.

pilaf, pilaff /'piːlæf/ or /pɪ'læf/ *n* a dish of spiced rice cooked in stock with, optionally, meat or fish.—*also* **pilau**.

pilaster /pɪ'læstər/ *n* a rectangular pillar, *usu* set in a wall.

pilch /pɪltʃ/ *n* (*arch*) a triangular flannel wrap for a baby.

pilchard /'pɪltʃərd/ *n* a fish of the herring family.

pile[1] /paɪl/ *n* a heap or mound of objects; a large amount; a lofty building; a pyre; (*sl*) a fortune. • *vt* (*with* **up, on**) to heap or stack; to load; to accumulate. • *vi* to become heaped up; (*with* **up, out, on**) to move confusedly in a mass.

pile[2] *n* a vertical beam driven into (the ground) as a foundation for a building, etc. • *vt* to support with piles; to drive piles into.

pile[3] *n* the nap of a fabric or carpet; soft, fine fur or wool.

pileate /'pɪliˌeɪt/, **pileated** /'pɪliˌeɪtəd/ *adj* (*biol*) crested.

piledriver /'paɪlˌdraɪvər/ *n* a machine for driving in piles.

piles /paɪlz/ *npl* haemorrhoids.

pile-up /'paɪlʌp/ *n* an accumulation of tasks, etc; (*inf*) a collision of several vehicles.

pilfer /'pɪlfər/ *vti* to steal in small quantities.—**pilferage** *n.*—**pilferer** *n*.

pilgrim /'pɪlgrɪm/ *n* a person who makes a pilgrimage.

pilgrimage /-ɪdʒ/ *n* a journey to a holy place as an act of devotion; any long journey; a life's journey.

piliferous /pɪ'lɪfərəs/ *adj* (*esp bot*) hairy.

piliform /'pɪlɪfɔːm/ *adj* (*bot*) in the form of or like a hair.

pill /pɪl/ *n* medicine in round balls or tablet form; (*with cap*) an oral contraceptive.

pillage /'pɪlɪdʒ/ *n* looting, plunder. • *vti* to plunder, *esp* during war.—**pillager** *n*.

pillar /'pɪlər/ *n* a slender, vertical structure used as a support or ornament; a column; a strong supporter of a cause.

pillar box *n* a red public letter box in the shape of a pillar that stands on the pavement.

pillbox /'pɪlbɒks/ *n* a box for pills, *esp* a decorative one; a small round hat without a brim; (*mil*) a small, fortified, concrete shelter.

pillion /'pɪljən/ *n* a seat behind the driver for a passenger on a motorcycle, etc.

pillory /'pɪləri/ *n* (*pl* **pillories**) (*formerly*) stocks in which criminals were put as punishment. • *vt* (**pillorying, pilloried**) to expose to public scorn and ridicule.

pillow /'pɪloː/ *n* a cushion that supports the head during sleep; something that supports to equalize or distribute pressure. • *vti* to rest on, serve as, a pillow.

pillowcase /-ˌkeɪs/, **pillowslip** /-ˌslɪp/ *n* a removable cover for a pillow.

pilose /'paɪloːz/ *adj* (*biol*) hairy.

pilot /'paɪlət/ *n* a person who operates an aircraft; one who directs ships in and out of harbour; a guide; a television show produced as a sample of a proposed series. • *vt* to direct the course of, act as pilot; to lead or guide.

pilotage /-ɪdʒ/ *n* the work or fee of a pilot.

pilot light *n* a burning gas flame used to light a larger jet; an electric indicator light.

pilule /'pɪljuːl/ *n* a small pill.—**pilular** *adj*.

pimento /pɪ'mɛntoː/ *n* (*pl* **pimentos**) allspice; a pimiento.

pimiento /ˌpɪmɪ'ɛntoː/ or /pɪm'jɛntoː/ *n* a sweet red pepper (capiscum) used in salads and cooked dishes.

pimp /pɪmp/ *n* a prostitute's agent.—*also vt*.

pimpernel /'pɪmpərˌnɛl/ *n* a primulaceous plant with small scarlet, blue or white flowers.

pimple /'pɪmpəl/ *n* a small, raised, inflamed swelling of the skin.—**pimpled** *adj*.

pimply /'pɪmpli/ *adj* (**pimplier, pimpliest**) covered with pimples.

PIN /pɪn/ *abbr* = Personal Identification Number (issued by a bank to a customer to validate electronic transactions).

pin /pɪn/ *n* a piece of metal or wood used to fasten things together; a small piece of pointed wire with a head; an ornament or badge with a pin or clasp for fastening to clothing; (*bowling*) one of the clubs at which the ball is rolled. • *vt* (**pinning, pinned**) to fasten with a pin; to hold, fix; (*with* **down**) to get (someone) to commit himself or herself as to plans, etc; (*a fact, etc*) to establish.

pinafore /'pɪnəˌfɔr/ *n* a sleeveless garment worn over a dress, blouse, etc.

pinaster /'pɪnæstər/ *n* a Southern European pine tree.

pince-nez /'pænsneɪ/ or /pæ̃s'neɪ/ *n* (*pl* **pince-nez**) eyeglasses clipped to the nose by a spring.

pincers /'pɪnsərz/ *npl* a tool with two handles and jaws used for gripping and drawing out nails, etc; a grasping claw, as of a crab.

pinch /pɪntʃ/ *vti* to squeeze or compress painfully; to press between the fingers; to nip; (*sl*) to steal; (*sl*) to arrest. • *n* a squeeze or nip; what can be taken up between the finger and thumb, a small amount; a time of stress; an emergency.

pinchbeck /'pɪntʃbɛk/ *n* a copper and zinc alloy, used as imitation gold.

pinched /pɪntʃt/ *adj* appearing to be squeezed; drawn by cold or stress.

pincushion /'pɪnˌkʊʃən/ *n* a pad for holding pins.

Pindaric /pɪn'dærɪk/ *adj* (*ode*) associated with the poet Pindar.

pine[1] /paɪn/ *n* an evergreen coniferous tree with long needles and well-formed cones; a tree of the pine family; its wood.

pine[2] *vi* to languish, waste away through longing or mental stress; (*with* **for**) to long.

pineal gland /'pɪnɪəl/ or /'paɪnɪəl/ *n* a pea-sized gland in the brain.

pineapple /'pain‚æpəl/ *n* a tropical plant; its juicy, fleshy, yellow fruit.

pinfold /'pinfo:ld/ *n* a pound for stray cattle. • *vt* to shut into, or as if into, such a pound.

ping /piŋ/ *n* a high-pitched ringing sound. • *vti* to strike with a ping, emit a ping.—**pinger** *n*.

ping-pong /'piŋpɒŋ/ *n* a name for table tennis; (*with caps*) (*trademark*) table tennis equipment.

pinion[1] /'pinjən/ *n* the outer joint of a bird's wing; a wing feather. • *vt* to cut off a pinion; to bind arms to sides, restrain.

pinion[2] *n* a cogwheel.

pink[1] /piŋk/ *n* any of various garden plants with a fragrant flower, including carnations; a pale red colour; a huntsman's red coat; the highest type. • *adj* pink-coloured; (*inf*) radical in political views.

pink[2] *vt* to stab, pierce; (*cloth, etc*) to cut a zigzag edge on; to perforate with pinking shears.

pinkeye /'piŋkai/ *n* an inflammation of the conjunctiva, affecting animals and humans.

pinkie, pinky /'piŋki/ *n* (*pl* **pinkies**) the little finger on the human hand.

pinking shears *npl* shears with notched edges for pinking edges of cloth.

pin money *n* money given to a woman by her husband for personal expenses.

pinna /'pinə/ *n* (*pl* **pinnae, pinnas**) (*biol*) the fin of a fish; the feather or wing of a bird; the leaflet of a pinnate leaf.

pinnace /'pinəs/ *n* (*naut*) a small light schooner-rigged vessel with oars; an eight-oared small boat belonging to a warship.

pinnacle /'pinəkəl/ *n* a slender tower crowning a roof, etc; a rocky peak of a mountain; the highest point, climax.

pinnate /'pineit/, **pinnated** /-əd/ *adj* shaped like a feather; (*leaf*) divided into leaflets.

pinniped /'pini‚ped/ *adj* (*zool*) with fin-like feet or flippers.

pinny /'pini/ *n* (*pl* **pinnies**) (*sl*) a pinafore.

pinochle, pinocle /'pi:‚nɒkəl/ *n* a card game.—*also* **pinuchle**.

pinpoint /'pinpoint/ *vt* to locate or identify very exactly.

pinprick /'pinprik/ *n* a small puncture as made by a pin; a trivial annoyance.

pins and needles *npl* a tingling feeling in the fingers, toes, etc, caused by impeded blood circulation returning to normal; (*with* on) in an anxious or expectant state.

pinstripe /'pinstraip/ *n* a very narrow stripe in suit fabrics, etc.

pint /paint/ *n* a liquid measure equal to half a quart or one eighth of a gallon (0.47 litres); (*inf*) a drink of beer.

pintail /'pinteil/ *n* (*pl* **pintails, pintail**) a type of duck.

pintle /'pintəl/ *n* a bolt or pin *esp* comprising a pivot.

pinto /'pinto:/ *n* (*pl* **pintos**) a piebald horse.

pinuchle *see* **pinochle**.

pin-up *n* (*sl*) a photograph of a naked or partially naked person; a person who has been so photographed; a photograph of a famous person.

pioneer /‚paiə'ni:r/ *n* a person who initiates or explores new areas of enterprise, research, etc; an explorer; an early settler; (*mil*) one who prepares roads, sinks mines, etc. • *vti* to initiate or take part in the development of; to act as a pioneer (to); to explore (a region).

pious /'paiəs/ *adj* devout; religious; sanctimonious.—**piously** *adv*.—**piousness** *n*.

pip[1] /pip/ *n* the seed in a fleshy fruit, *eg* apple, orange.

pip[2] *n* a spot with a numerical value on a playing card, dice, etc; (*inf*) insignia on a uniform showing an officer's rank; a signal on a radar screen.

pip[3] *vi* (**pipping, pipped**) (*bird*) to chirp, to peep; (*hatching bird*) to pierce (its shell).

pipal *see* **peepul**.

pipe /paip/ *n* a tube of wood, metal etc for making musical sounds; (*pl*) the bagpipes; a stem with a bowl for smoking tobacco; a long tube or hollow body for conveying water, gas, etc. • *vt* to play on a pipe; (*gas, water, etc*) to convey by pipe; to lead, summon with the sound of a pipe(s); to trim with piping. • *vi* (*sl*) to take the drug crack.

pipeclay /'paipklei/ *n* a white clay, used to make tobacco pipes and to whiten leather, etc. • *vt* to whiten using pipeclay.

pipeline /'paiplain/ *n* a pipe (often underground) used to convey oil, gas, etc; a direct channel for information; the processes through which supplies pass from source to user.

piper /'paipər/ *n* a person who plays a pipe, *esp* bagpipes.

pipette, pipet /pai'pet/ or /pi-/ *n* a hollow glass tube into which liquids are sucked for measurement.

piping /'paipiŋ/ *n* a length of pipe, pipes collectively; a tube-like fold of material used to trim seams; a strip of icing, cream, for decorating cakes, etc; the art of playing a pipe or bagpipes; a high-pitched sound. • *adj* making a high-pitched sound.

piping hot *adj* very hot.

pipistrelle, pipistrel /‚pipi'strel/ *n* a small brown bat.

pipit /'pipit/ *n* a type of songbird.

pipkin /'pipkin/ *n* a small earthenware pot.

pippin /'pipin/ *n* one of several types of eating apple.

pipsqueak /'pipskwi:k/ *n* (*inf*) a contemptible or insignificant person.

piquant /'pi:‚kænt/ or /-'kɒnt/, /'pi:kænt/ *adj* strong-tasting; pungent, sharp; stimulating.—**piquancy** *n*.—**piquantly** *adv*.

pique /pi:k/ *n* resentment, ill-feeling. • *vt* (**piquing, piqued**) to cause resentment in; to offend.

piqué /pi:'kei/ *n* a corded cotton fabric.

piquet /pi'ket/ *n* a card game for two.

piracy /'pairəsi/ *n* (*pl* **piracies**) robbery at sea; the hijacking of a ship or aircraft; infringement of copyright; unauthorized use of patented work.

piragua /pi'rɒgwə/ or /-'rægwə/ *see* **pirogue**.

piranha /pi'rɒnə/ or /-'rænə/ *n* a small voracious freshwater fish of tropical America with sharp teeth and a strong jaw.

pirate /'pairət/ *n* a person who commits robbery at sea; a hijacker; one who infringes copyright. • *vti* to take by piracy; to publish or reproduce in violation of a copyright.—**piratical, piratic** *adj*.

pirogue /pi'ro:g/ *n* a dugout canoe.—*also* **piragua**.

pirouette /‚piru:'et/ *n* a spin on the toes in ballet.—*also vi*.

piscatorial /‚piskə'tɔriəl/, **piscatory** /'piskətɔri/ *adj* of, or pertaining to, fish or fishing.

Pisces /'pəisi:z/ *n* the Fishes, in astrology the twelfth sign of the zodiac, operative from 19 February–20 March.—**Piscean** *adj, n*.

pisciculture /'pisi‚kʌltʃər/ *n* the controlled rearing and breeding of fish.—**piscicultural** *adj*.—**pisciculturist** *n*.

piscina /pi'si:nə/ or /-'sainə/ *n* (*pl* **piscinae, piscinas**) (*RC Church*) a basin with a drain in a church wall, used for rinsing sacred vessels after Mass.

piscine /'pisain/ *adj* pertaining to fish.

piscivorous /pi'sivərəs/ *adj* fish-eating.

pisiform /'pisi‚fɔrm/ *adj* pea-shaped.

pismire /'pis‚mair/ *n* an ant.

piss /pis/ *vi* (*vulg sl*) to urinate. • *n* urine.

pistachio /pi'stæʃio:/ *n* (*pl* **pistachios**) a tree found in Mediterranean countries and West Asia; the edible nut of this tree.

piste /pi:st/ *n* a ski trail of packed snow; (*fencing*) the rectangular area where a bout takes place.

pistil /'pistil/ *n* the seed-bearing part of a flower.

pistillate /'pistilət/ *adj* (*bot*) having a pistil; with a pistil but no stamens.

pistol /'pistəl/ *n* a small, short-barrelled handgun. • *vt* (**pistolling, pistolled** *or* **pistoling, pistoled**) to shoot with a pistol.

pistole /pi'sto:l/ *n* (*formerly*) a gold coin used in Europe.

piston /'pistən/ *n* a disc that slides to and fro in a close-fitting cylinder, as in engines, pumps.

pit /pit/ *n* a deep hole in the earth; a (coal) mine; a scooped-out place for burning something; a sunken or depressed area below the adjacent floor area; a space at the front of the stage for the orchestra; the area in a securities or commodities exchange in which members do the trading; the scar left by smallpox, etc; the stone of a fruit; a place where racing cars refuel. • *vti* (**pitting, pitted**) to set in competition; to mark or become marked with pits; to make a pit stop.

pit-a-pat /'pitə‚pæt/ *adv* with quick, light steps or beats. • *n* quick, light steps or beats. • *vi* (**pit-a-patting, pit-a-patted**) to make quick, light steps or beats.

pitch[1] /pitʃ/ *vti* (*tent, etc*) to erect by driving pegs, stakes, etc, into the ground; to set the level of; (*mus*) to set in key; to express in a style; to throw, hurl; to fall heavily, plunge, *esp* forward. • *n* a throw; height, intensity; a musical tone; a place where a street trader or performer works; distance between threads (of a screw); amount of slope; a sound wave frequency; a sports field; (*cricket*) the area between the wickets; sales talk.

pitch[2] *n* the black, sticky substance from distillation of tar, etc; any of various bituminous substances. • *vt* to smear with pitch.

pitch-black /'pɪtʃ'blæk/ *adj* black, or extremely dark.

pitchblende /'pɪtʃblend/ *n* a black mineral, composed largely of uranium oxide, that also yields radium.

pitch-dark /'pits'dɑrk/ *adj* completely dark.

pitcher /'pɪtʃər/ *n* a large water jug; (*baseball*) the player who pitches the ball.

pitchfork /'pɪtʃfɔrk/ *n* a long-handled fork for tossing hay, etc. • *vt* to lift with this; to thrust suddenly or willy-nilly into.

pitchy /'pɪtʃi/ *adj* (**pitchier, pitchiest**) resembling, or smeared with, pitch.

piteous /'pɪtiəs/ *adj* arousing pity; heart-rending.—**piteously** *adv*.—**piteousness** *n*.

pitfall /'pɪtfɒl/ *n* concealed danger; unexpected difficulty.

pith /pɪθ/ *n* the soft tissue inside the rind of citrus fruits; the gist, essence; importance.

pithy /'pɪθi/ *adj* (**pithier, pithiest**) like or full of pith; concise and full of meaning.—**pithily** *adv*.—**pithiness** *n*.

pitiable /'pɪtiəbəl/ *adj* deserving pity, lamentable, wretched.—**pitiableness** *n*.—**pitiably** *adv*.

pitiful /'pɪtɪfʊl/ *adj* causing pity, touching; contemptible, paltry.—**pitifully** *adv*.—**pitifulness** *n*.

pitiless /'pɪtɪləs/ or /'pɪti-/ *adj* without pity, ruthless.—**pitilessly** *adv*.—**pitilessness** *n*.

pitman /'pɪtmən/ *n* (*pl* **pitmen**) a miner.

pittance /'pɪtəns/ *n* a very small quantity or allowance of money.

pituitary /pɪ'tuːɪteri/ or /-'tjuː-/ *adj* of or pertaining to the pituitary gland; (*arch*) of or secreting mucus. • *n* (*pl* **pituitaries**) the pituitary gland.

pituitary gland *n* a ductless gland at the base of the brain that affects growth and sexual development.

pity /'pɪti/ *n* (*pl* **pities**) sympathy with the distress of others; a cause of grief; a regrettable fact. • *vt* (**pitying, pitied**) to feel pity for.—**pityingly** *adv*.

pityriasis /ˌpɪtə'raɪəsɪs/ *n* (*pl* **pityriases**) a skin disease characterized by scaly, pink eruptions.

pivot /'pɪvət/ *n* a pin on which a part turns, fulcrum; a key person upon whom progress depends; a cardinal point or factor. • *vt* to turn or hinge (on) a pivot; to attach by a pivot. • *vi* to run on, or as if on, a pivot.—**pivotal** *adj*.

pixel /'pɪksəl/ *n* any of the tiny units that form an image (as on a television screen, computer monitor).

pixie, pixy /'pɪksi/ *n* (*pl* **pixies**) a fairy or elf.

pixilated /'pɪksəˌleɪtɪd/ *adj* acting as if influenced by pixies; unconventional, eccentric, whimsical; (*sl*) drunk.

pizza /'piːtsə/ *n* a baked dough crust covered with cheese, tomatoes, etc.

pizzeria /ˌpiːtsə'riːə/ *n* a pizza restaurant.

pizzicato /ˌpɪtsɪ'kætoː/ or /-'kɒtoː/ *n* (*pl* **pizzicati, pizzicatos**) (*mus*) a note or passage played by plucking the string of a violin or other bowed instrument.—*also adj*.

placable /'plækəbəl/ *adj* easily to placate.—**placability** *n*.

placard /'plækɑrd/ or /-kɑrd/ *n* a poster or notice for public display.

placate /plə'keɪt/ or /'plæ-/, /'pleɪ-/ *vt* to appease; to pacify.—**placation** *n*.—**placatory** *adj*.

place /pleɪs/ *n* a locality, spot; a town or village; a building, residence; a short street, a square; space, room; a particular point, part, position, etc; the part of space occupied by a person or thing; a position or job; a seat; rank, precedence; a finishing position in a race. • *vt* to put; to put in a particular place; to find a place or seat for; to identify; to estimate; to rank; (*order*) to request material from a supplier. • *vi* to finish second or among the first three in a race.

placebo /plə'siːboː/ *n* (*pl* **placebos, placeboes**) something harmless given by a doctor to fool a patient into thinking he is undergoing treatment.

place mat /'pleɪsmæt/ *n* a small mat serving as an individual table cover for a person at a meal.

placement /'pleɪsmənt/ *n* a placing or being placed; location or arrangement.

place name *n* the name of a geographical locality.

placenta /plə'sentə/ *n* (*pl* **placentas, placentae**) the organ in the uterus of a female mammal that nourishes the foetus.—**placental** *adj*.

placer /'plæsər/ *n* a deposit containing a valuable mineral found in a river, etc.

placid /'plæsɪd/ *adj* calm, tranquil.—**placidity** *n*.—**placidly** *adv*.

placket /'plækət/ *n* a slit at the waist of a dress or skirt to make it easy to put on or take off.

placoid /'plækɔɪd/ *adj* platelike.

plafond *Fr.* /pla'fɔ̃ː/ *n* a ceiling, *esp* one of elaborate design; a card game.

plagal /'pleɪgəl/ *adj* (*musical composition*) having its principal notes between the fifth of the key and its octave.

plagiarism /'pleɪdʒəˌrɪzəm/ *n* the act of stealing from another author's work, literary theft; that which is plagiarized.—**plagiarist** *n*.—**plagiaristic** *adj*.

plagiarize /'pleɪdʒəˌraɪz/ *vt* to appropriate writings from another author.—**plagiarizer** *n*.

plague /pleɪg/ *n* a highly contagious and deadly disease; (*inf*) a person who is a nuisance. • *vt* (**plaguing, plagued**) to afflict with a plague; (*inf*) to annoy, harass.

plaguey, plaguy /'pleɪgi/ *adj* (*arch*) (*inf*) troublesome, vexatious.

plaice /pleɪs/ *n* (*pl* **plaice, plaices**) any of various flatfishes, *esp* a flounder.

plaid /plæd/ *n* a long wide piece of woollen cloth used as a cloak in Highland dress; cloth with a tartan or chequered pattern.

plain /pleɪn/ *adj* level, flat; understandable; straightforward; manifest, obvious; blunt; unadorned; not elaborate; not coloured or patterned; not beautiful; ugly; pure; unmixed. • *n* a large tract of level country.—**plainness** *n*.

plain clothes *npl* ordinary clothes, not uniform, as worn by a policeman on duty.—*also adj*.

plainly /-li/ *adv* clearly, intelligibly.

plain sailing *n* easy progress over an unobstructed course.

plainsman /'pleɪnzmən/ *n* (*pl* **plainsmen**) an inhabitant of a plain.

plainsong /'pleɪnsɒŋ/ *n* an old, plain kind of church music chanted in unison.

plain-spoken /'pleɪn'spoːkən/ *adj* frank, outspoken.

plaint /pleɪnt/ *n* (*poet*) lamentation, sad song; (*law*) formal statement of grievance.

plaintiff /'pleɪntɪf/ *n* (*law*) a person who brings a civil action against another.

plaintive /'pleɪntɪv/ *adj* sad, mournful.—**plaintively** *adv*.—**plaintiveness** *n*.

plait /pleɪt/ *n* intertwined strands of hair, straw, etc; a pigtail. • *vti* (**plaiting, plaited**) to twist strands (of hair) together into a plait.

plan /plæn/ *n* a scheme or idea; a drawing to scale of a building; a diagram, map; any outline or sketch. • *vti* (**planning, planned**) to make a plan of; to design; to arrange beforehand, intend; to make plans.

planar /'pleɪnər/ *adj* of or located in a plane; flat.

planarian /plə'nerɪən/ *n* a type of flatworm.

planchet /'plænʃət/ *n* a plain metal disc from which a coin is made.

planchette /plæn'ʃet/ *n* a heart-shaped board on wheels, holding a pencil which is supposed to write automatically, giving messages from spirits, when a hand is rested upon it.

plane¹ /pleɪn/ *n* a tall tree with large broad leaves.

plane² *n* a tool with a steel blade for smoothing level wooden surfaces. • *vt* to smooth with a plane.

plane³ *n* any level or flat surface; a level of attainment; one of the main supporting surfaces of an aeroplane; an aeroplane. • *adj* flat or level. • *vi* to fly while keeping the wings motionless; to skim across the surface of water; to travel by aeroplane.

planet /'plænət/ *n* a celestial body that orbits the sun or other star.

planetarium /ˌplænə'terɪəm/ *n* (*pl* **planetariums, planetaria**) a machine used to exhibit the planets, their motions around the sun and their relative distances and magnitudes; a building for housing this instrument; a model of the solar system.

planetary /'plænəˌteri/ *adj* (*astrol*) under the influence of one of the planets; terrestrial; wandering, erratic.

planetoid /'plænəˌtɔɪd/ *n* an asteroid.

plangent /'plændʒənt/ *adj* (*sound*) loud and deep; resounding.—**plangency** *n*.

planimeter /plə'nɪmɪtər/ *n* an instrument for measuring the area of an irregular plane figure.

planimetry /-tri/ *n* the measurement of plane figures.

planish /'plænɪʃ/ *vt* (*metal*) to smooth and flatten with a hammer or between rollers.

planisphere /'plænɪˌsfiːr/ *n* a sphere projected on a plane or a map of the heavens.

plank /plæŋk/ *n* a long, broad, thick board; one of the policies forming the platform of a political party. • *vt* to cover with planks.

planking /'plæŋkɪŋ/ *n* planks collectively; the act of laying boards.

plankton /'plæŋktən/ *n* the microscopic organisms that float on seas, lakes, etc.

planner /'plænər/ *n* a person who plans; an official who plans architectural development and land use.—**planning** *n*.

planoconcave /ˌpleɪnoˈkɒnkeɪv/ or /-ˈkeɪv/ *adj* (*lens*) with one side flat and the other concave.

planoconvex /ˌpleɪnoˈkɒnvɛks/ or /-ˈvɛks/ *adj* (*lens*) with one side flat and the other convex.

plant /plænt/ *n* a living organism with cellulose cell walls, which synthesizes its food from carbon dioxide, water and light; a soft-stemmed organism of this kind, as distinguished from a tree or shrub; the machinery, buildings, etc of a factory, etc; (*sl*) an act of planting; (*sl*) something or someone planted. • *vt* (*seeds, cuttings*) to put into the ground to grow; to place firmly in position; to found or establish; (*sl*) to conceal something in another's possession in order to implicate.

plantain[1] /'plæn'teɪn/ or /'plæn-/ *n* a low-growing weed with tough leaves.

plantain[2] *n* a tropical broad-leaved tree yielding an edible fruit similar to the banana.

plantar /'plæntər/ *adj* (*anat*) pertaining to the sole of the foot.

plantation /plænˈteɪʃən/ *n* a large cultivated planting of trees; an estate where tea, rubber, cotton, etc, is grown, cultivated by local labour.

planter /'plæntər/ *n* a person who owns or runs a plantation; a machine that plants; a decorative container for plants.

plantigrade /'plæntɪˌɡreɪd/ *adj* (*zool*) walking on the sole of the foot. • *n* a plantigrade animal.

plaque /plæk/ *n* an ornamental tablet or disc attached to or inserted in a surface; a film of mucus on the teeth that harbours bacteria.

plash /plæʃ/ *n* a splash; a marshy pool or puddle.—**plashy** *adj* (**plashier, plashiest**).

plasm /'plæzəm/ *n* a kind of protoplasm; plasma.

plasma /'plæzmə/ *n* the colourless liquid part of blood, milk, or lymph; a collection of charged particles resembling gas but conducting electricity and affected by a magnetic field.

plasmodium /plæzˈmoːdiəm/ *n* (*pl* **plasmodia**) (*biol*) a mass of protoplasm formed by the union of single-cell organisms; (*med*) any of a genus of parasitic protozoa which cause malaria.

plasmolysis /plæzˈmɒlɪsɪs/ *n* (*biol*) the shrinkage of the protoplasm of a plant cell occurring as a result of loss of water.

plasmolyze /'plæzmoːˌlaɪz/ *vt* to subject to plasmolysis.

plaster /'plæstər/ *n* an adhesive dressing for cuts; a mixture of sand, lime and water that sets hard and is used for covering walls and ceilings. • *vt* to cover as with plaster; to apply like a plaster; to make lie smooth and flat; to load to excess.—**plasterer** *n*.

plasterboard /'plæstərˌbɔrd/ *n* a thin board formed by layers of plaster and paper, used in wide sheets for walls, etc.

plaster cast *n* a rigid dressing of gauze impregnated with plaster of Paris; a sculptor's model in plaster of Paris.

plastered /'plæstərd/ *adj* (*sl*) intoxicated.

plaster of Paris *n* gypsum and water made into a quick-setting paste.

plastic[1] /'plæstɪk/ *adj* able to be moulded; pliant; made of plastic; (*art*) relating to modelling or moulding. • *n* any of various non-metallic compounds, synthetically produced, that can be moulded, cast, squeezed, drawn, or laminated into objects, films, or filaments.—**plastically** *adv*.

plastic[2] *n* colloquial term for charge cards, store cards, credit cards etc. used to pay for goods and services instead of cash.

plasticity /-ˈstɪsɪti/ *n* the ability to be moulded or altered; the ability to retain a shape attained by pressure deformation.

plastic surgery *n* surgery to repair deformed or destroyed parts of the body.

plastron /'plæstrən/ *n* a breastplate; a trimming on a dress front; a shirt front; a bony plate on the underside of a tortoise or turtle.

plat /plæt/ *n* a small plot of ground.

platan /'plætən/ *n* a plane tree.

plate /pleɪt/ *n* a flat sheet of metal on which an engraving is cut; an illustration printed from it; a full-page illustration separate from text; a sheet of metal photographically prepared with text, etc, for printing from; a sheet of glass with sensitized film used as a photographic negative; a trophy as prize at a race; a coating of metal on another metal; utensils plated in silver or gold; plated ware; a flat shallow dish from which food is eaten; a helping of food; the part of a denture that fits the palate; (*inf*) a

denture. • *vt* (*a metal*) to coat with a thin film of another metal; to cover with metal plates.

plateau /plæ'toː/ *n* (*pl* **plateaus, plateaux**) a flat, elevated area of land; a stable period; a graphic representation showing this.

plated /'pleɪtɪd/ *adj* coated with metal, *esp* silver or gold.

plate glass *n* rolled, ground, and polished sheet glass.

platelet /'pleɪtlət/ *n* a small disc-shaped cell in the blood involved in the process of blood clotting.

platen /'plætən/ *n* the roller on a typewriter; (*print*) a plate which presses the paper against the type.

plater /'pleɪtər/ *n* someone who, or something which, plates; a mediocre racehorse.

platform /'plætfɔrm/ *n* a raised floor for speakers, musicians, etc; a stage; a place or opportunity for public discussion; the raised area next to a railway line where passengers board trains; a statement of political aims.

plating /'pleɪtɪŋ/ *n* the act or process of plating; a thin coating of metal; a coating of metal plates.

platinize /'plætɪˌnaɪz/ *vt* to coat with platinum.

platinum /'plætɪnəm/ *n* a valuable, silvery-white metal used for jewellery, etc.

platinum-blond *adj* (*hair*) silvery blond. • *n* someone with hair of this colour.—**platinum-blonde** *nf*.

platitude /'plætɪtuːd/ or /-tjuːd/ *n* a dull truism; a commonplace remark.—**platitudinous** *adj*.

platitudinize /-ˈtuːdɪˌnaɪz/ or /-ˈtjuːdɪ-/ *vi* to utter platitudes.

platonic /pləˈtɒnɪk/ *adj* (*love*) spiritual and free from physical desire; (*with cap*) relating to Plato, the Greek philosopher, or his teachings.—**platonically** *adv*.

platoon /pləˈtuːn/ *n* a military unit divided into squads or sections.

platter /'plætər/ *n* an oval flat serving dish.

platy /'pleɪti/ - *prefix* flat.

platyhelminth /ˌplætiˈhɛlmɪnθ/ *n* a type of flatworm.

platypus /'plætɪpəs/ or /-pʊs/ *n* (*pl* **platypuses**) a small aquatic egg-laying mammal of Australia and Tasmania, with webbed feet, a bill like a duck's, dense fur, and a broad flat tail.—*also* **duck-billed platypus**.

platyrrhine /'plætiˌraɪn/ **platyrrhinian** *adj* (*zool*) broad-nosed.

plaudit /'plɔdɪt/ *n* (*usu pl*) a commendation; a round of applause.

plausible /'plɔzɪbəl/ *adj* apparently truthful or reasonable.—**plausibility** *n*.—**plausibly** *adv*.

play /pleɪ/ *vi* to amuse oneself (with toys, games, etc); to act carelessly or trifle (with somebody's feelings); to gamble; to act on the stage or perform on a musical instrument; (*light*) to flicker, shimmer; (*water*) to discharge or direct on. • *vt* to participate in a sport; to be somebody's opponent in a game; to perform a dramatic production; (*instrument*) to produce music on; (*hose*) to direct; (*fish*) to give line to; to bet on. • *n* fun, amusement; the playing of, or manner of playing, a game; the duration of a game; a literary work for performance by actors; gambling; scope, freedom to move.—**playable** *adj*.

playact /'pleɪˌækt/ *vi* to behave affectedly or overdramatically; to make believe, pretend; to act in a play.—**playacting** *n*.—**playactor** *n*.

playback /'pleɪbæk/ *n* the act of reproducing recorded sound or pictures, *esp* soon after they are made; a mechanism in an audio or video recorder for doing this.—*also vt*.

playbill /'pleɪbɪl/ *n* a poster advertising a theatrical performance.

playboy /'pleɪbɔɪ/ *n* a person who lives for pleasure.

player /'pleɪər/ *n* a person who plays a specified game or instrument; an actor.

playfellow /'pleɪˌfɛloː/ *see* **playmate**.

playful /'pleɪfəl/ *adj* full of fun; humorous; sportive; fond of sport or amusement.—**playfully** *adv*.—**playfulness** *n*.

playgoer /'pleɪˌɡoːər/ *n* a person who goes to the theatre, *esp* one who attends frequently or regularly.—**playgoing** *adj*, *n*.

playground /'pleɪɡraʊnd/ *n* an area outdoors for children's recreation.

playhouse /'pleɪhʊs/ *n* a theatre.

playing card *n* one of a set of 52 cards used for playing games, each card having an identical pattern on one side and its own symbol on the reverse.

playing field *n* a place for playing sport.

playlet /'pleɪlət/ *n* a short play.

playmate /'pleɪmeɪt/ *n* a friend in play.—*also* **playfellow**.

playpen /'pleɪpən/ *n* a portable *usu* collapsible enclosure in which a young child may be left to play safely.

plaything /'pleɪθɪŋ/ n a toy; a thing or person treated as a toy.

playtime /'pleɪtaɪm/ n a time for recreation, esp at a school.

playwright /'pleɪraɪt/ n a writer of plays.

plaza /'plɑːzə/ n a public square in a town or city; (US) an area for the parking and servicing of cars.

plea /pliː/ n (law) an answer to a charge, made by the accused person; a request; an entreaty.

plead /pliːd/ vti (**pleading, pleaded, plead** or **pled**) to beg, implore; to give as an excuse; to answer (guilty or not guilty) to a charge; to argue (a law case).—**pleadable** adj.—**pleader** n.

pleading /'pliːdɪŋ/ n advocacy of a cause in a court of law; one of the allegations and counter allegations made alternately, usu in writing, by the parties in a legal action; the act or instance of making a plea; a sincere entreaty. • adj begging, imploring.—**pleadingly** adv.

pleasant /'plɛzənt/ adj agreeable; pleasing.—**pleasantly** adv.—**pleasantness** n.

pleasantry /'plɛzəntri/ n (pl **pleasantries**) a polite or amusing remark.

please /pliːz/ vti to satisfy; to give pleasure to; to be willing; to have the wish. • adv as a word to express politeness or emphasis in a request; an expression of polite affirmation.

pleased /pliːzd/ adj gratified.

pleasing /'pliːzɪŋ/ adj giving pleasure; agreeable.—**pleasingly** adv.

pleasurable /'plɛʒərəbəl/ adj gratifying, delightful.—**pleasurably** adv.

pleasure /'plɛʒər/ n enjoyment, recreation; gratification of the senses; preference.

pleat /pliːt/ n a double fold of cloth, etc pressed or stitched in place. • vt to gather into pleats.

pleb /plɛb/ n a plebeian; (sl) a common person.

plebeian /plɪ'biːən/ adj relating to the common people; base, vulgar. • n a commoner of ancient Rome; a vulgar, coarse person.—**plebeianism** n.

plebiscite /'plɛbɪ‚saɪt/ n a direct vote of the electorate on a political issue such as annexation, independent nationhood, etc.

plectrum /'plɛktrəm/ n (pl **plectra, plectrums**) a thin piece of metal, etc for plucking the strings of a guitar, etc.

pledge /plɛdʒ/ n a solemn promise; security for payment of a debt; a token or sign; a toast. • vt to give as security; to pawn; to bind by solemn promise; to drink a toast to.

pledgee /ple'dʒiː/ n someone to whom a pledge is given.

pledget /'plɛdʒɪt/ n a small pad of lint, etc, used to apply pressure to wounds.

pleiad /'plaɪəd/ n a brilliant group (of people).

Pleiades /'plaɪə‚diːz/ npl a cluster of seven stars in the constellation Taurus.

plein-air /pleɪn'ɛr/ adj (art) depicting the effects of light and atmosphere outdoors.

Pleistocene /'pleɪstə‚siːn/ adj (geol) pertaining to the earliest division of the Quaternary Period.

plenary /'plɛnəri/ or /pliːn-/ adj full, complete; (assembly, etc) attended by all the members.—**plenarily** adv.

plenipotentiary /‚plɛnɪpə'tɛnʃəri/ adj possessing full powers. • n (pl **plenipotentiaries**) an envoy with authority to act at his own discretion.

plenitude /'plɛnɪ‚tuːd/ or /-tjuːd/ n abundance.

plenteous /'plɛntɪəs/ adj abundant.

plentiful /'plɛntɪ‚ful/ adj abundant, copious.—**plentifully** adv.—**plentifulness** n.

plenty /'plɛnti/ n an abundance; more than enough; a great number. • adv (sl) quite.

plenum /'pliːnəm/ n (pl **plenums, plena**) a full assembly; a space filled with matter.

pleonasm /'pliːə‚næzəm/ n (rhetoric) the use of unnecessary words, eg "he is blind and cannot see".—**pleonastic** adj.

plesiosaurus, plesiosaur /'pliːsiəsɔr/ n a large, extinct, long-necked swimming reptile.

plessor /'plɛsər/ see **plexor**.

plethora /'plɛθərə/ n overabundance, glut; (med) an excess of red corpuscles in the blood.—**plethoric** adj.

pleura /'plʊərə/ or /'plʊrə/ n (pl **pleurae**) the membrane enclosing the lungs.—**pleural** adj.

pleurisy /'plʊərɪsi/ or /'plʊrɪsi/ n inflammation of the membranes enclosing the lungs.—**pleuritic** adj.

pleuropneumonia /‚plʊərə:njuː'moːniə/ or /‚plʊr-/, /-nuː-/ n an inflammation of both the pleura and the lung.

Plexiglas /'plɛksɪ‚glæs/ n (trademark) a transparent thermoplastic.

plexor /'plɛksər/ n (med) a small hammer used in percussion and for testing reflexes.—also **plessor**.

plexus /'plɛksəs/ n (pl **plexuses, plexus**) a network, esp of nerves or blood vessels.

pliable /'plaɪəbəl/ adj easily bent or moulded; easily influenced.—**pliability** n. —**pliably** adv.

pliant /'plaɪənt/ adj easily bent or influenced; supple; flexible, yielding.—**pliancy** n.—**pliantly** adv.

plicate /'plaɪkeɪt/, **plicated** /plɪ'keɪtɪd/ adj pleated; folded in the form of a fan.

pliers /'plaɪərz/ npl a tool with hinged arms and jaws for cutting, shaping wire.

plight¹ /plaɪt/ n a dangerous situation; a predicament.

plight² vt to pledge, vow solemnly. • n a pledge; an engagement.—**plighter** n.

Plimsoll line /'plɪmsəl/ n a system of markings on the hull of ships to ensure there is no overloading and that cargo is balanced.—also **load line**.

plimsolls /'plɪmsəlz/, **plimsoles** /-soːlz/ npl (Brit) rubber-soled canvas shoes, sneakers.

Pliocene /'plaɪə‚siːn/ adj (geol) pertaining to the latest division of the Tertiary Period.

PLO abbr = Palestine Liberation Organization.

plod /plɒd/ vi (**plodding, plodded**) to walk heavily and slowly, to trudge; to work or study slowly and laboriously.—**plodder** n.—**ploddingly** adv.

plop /plɒp/ vti (**plopping, plopped**) to fall into water without a splash. • n the sound of this. • adv with a plop.

plot /plɒt/ n a small piece of land; a secret plan or conspiracy; the story in a play or novel, etc. • vt (**plotting, plotted**) to conspire; (route) to mark on a map; (points) to mark (on a graph) with coordinates.—**plotter** n.

plough /plaʊ/, **plow** n a farm implement for turning up soil; any implement like this, as a snowplough. • vt to cut and turn up with a plough; to make a furrow (in), to wrinkle; to force a way through; to work at laboriously; (with **into**) to run into; (with **back**) to reinvest; (sl) to fail an examination.—**ploughable** adj.—**plougher** n.

ploughman, plowman /'plaʊmən/ n (pl **ploughmen, plowmen**) one who ploughs; a farmworker.

ploughshare, plowshare /'plaʊʃər/ n the part of a plough which cuts the soil.

plover /'plʌvər/ n a wading bird with a short tail and a straight bill.

ploy /plɔɪ/ n a tactic or manoeuvre to outwit an opponent; an occupation or job; an escapade.

pluck /plʌk/ vt to pull off or at; to snatch; to strip off feathers; (fruit, flowers, etc) to pick; (person) to remove from one situation in life and transfer to another. • vi to make a sharp pull or twitch. • n a pull or tug; heart, courage; dogged resolution.—**plucker** n.

plucky /'plʌki/ adj (**pluckier, pluckiest**) brave, spirited.—**pluckily** adv.—**pluckiness** n.

plug /plʌg/ n a stopper used for filling a hole; a device for connecting an appliance to an electricity supply; a cake of tobacco; a kind of fishing lure; (inf) a free advertisement usu incorporated in other matter. • vti (**plugging, plugged**) to stop up with a plug; (sl) to shoot or punch; (inf) to seek to advertise by frequent repetition; (with **at**) (inf) to work doggedly.

plug-in adj able to be connected by a plug. • n a device or unit able to be connected by a plug.

plum /plʌm/ n an oval smooth-skinned sweet stone-fruit; a tree bearing it; a reddish-purple colour; a choice thing.

plumage /'pluːmɪdʒ/ n a bird's feathers.

plumb /plʌm/ n a lead weight attached to a line, used to determine how deep water is or whether a wall is vertical; any of various weights. • adj perfectly vertical. • adv vertically; in a direct manner; (inf) entirely. • vt to test by a plumb line; to examine minutely and critically; to weight with lead; to seal with lead; to supply with or install as plumbing. • vi to work as a plumber.

plumbago /plʌm'beɪgoː/ n (pl **plumbagos**) graphite; one of a genus of flowering plants.

plumber /'plʌmər/ n a person who installs and repairs water or gas pipes.

plumbing /'plʌmɪŋ/ n the system of pipes used in water or gas supply, or drainage; the plumber's craft.

plumbism /'plʌmbɪzəm/ n lead poisoning.

plume /pluːm/ *n* a large or ornamental bird's feather; a feathery ornament or thing; something resembling a feather in structure or density. • *vt* (*feathers*) to preen; to adorn with feathers; to indulge (oneself) with an obvious display of self-satisfaction.

plummet /'plɛmət/ *n* a plumb. • *vi* (**plummeting, plumeted**) to fall in a perpendicular manner; to drop sharply and abruptly.

plummy /'plɛmi/ *adj* (**plummier, plummiest**) like, full of, plums; (*inf*) rich, desirable; (*inf*) (*voice*) deep, drawling, rich-sounding.

plump[1] /plɛmp/ *adj* rounded, chubby. • *vti* to make or become plump; to swell.—**plumply** *adv*.—**plumpness** *n*.

plump[2] *vti* to fall, drop or sink, or come into contact suddenly and heavily; (*someone, something*) to favour or give support. • *n* a sudden drop or plunge or the sound of this. • *adv* straight down, straight ahead; abruptly; bluntly.

plum pudding *n* a rich boiled or steamed pudding with suet, dried fruit, spices, etc.

plumule /'pluːmjuːl/ *n* (*zool*) a down feather; (*bot*) the embryonic stem of a plant.

plumy /'pluːmi/ *adj* (**plumier, plumiest**) feathery; feathered.

plunder /'plɛndər/ *vt* to steal goods by force, to loot. • *n* plundering; booty.—**plunderer** *n*.

plunge /plɛndʒ/ *vti* to immerse, dive suddenly; to penetrate quickly; to hurl oneself or rush; (*horse*) to start violently forward.

plunger /'plɛndʒər/ *n* a solid cylinder that operates with a plunging motion, as a piston; a larger rubber suction cup used to free clogged drains.

plunk /plɛŋk/ *vt* (*mus*) to pluck. • *vti* to throw or fall heavily. *n* the sound produced by something being plucked, or falling in this way.

pluperfect /pluːˈpɜːfɪkt/ *adj, n* (*gram*) (a tense) denoting an action completed before a past point of time.

plural /'pluːrəl/ *adj* more than one; consisting of or containing more than one kind or class. • *n* (*gram*) the form referring to more than one person or thing.—**plurally** *adv*.

pluralism /'pluːrə‚lɪzəm/ *n* the simultaneous holding of more than one office or benefice; a theory that reality is composed of a plurality of entities; a theory that there are at least two levels of ultimate reality; the coexistence in society of people of distinct ethnic, cultural or religious groups, each preserving their own traditions; a doctrine or policy advocating this condition.—**pluralist** *n*.—**pluralistic** *adj*.—**pluralistically** *adv*.

plurality /pluːˈrælɪti/ *n* (*pl* **pluralities**) being plural; a majority; a large number; another term for pluralism.

plus /plɛs/ *prep* added to; in addition to. • *adj* indicating addition; positive. • *n* the sign (+) indicating a value greater than zero; an advantage or benefit; an extra.

plush /plɛʃ/ *n* a velvet-like fabric with a nap. • *adj* made of plush; (*inf*) luxurious.

Pluto /'pluːtoː/ *n* (*Greek myth*) the god of the underworld; (*astron*) the planet farthest from the sun, discovered in 1930.

plutocracy /pluːˈtɒkrəsi/ *n* (*pl* **plutocracies**) government or rule by the wealthy; a wealthy class.—**plutocratic** *adj*.—**plutocratically** *adv*.

plutocrat /'pluːtə‚kræt/ *n* a person who has power through wealth; a rich person.

Plutonian /pluːˈtoːniən/ *adj* pertaining to Pluto or the underworld; infernal.

plutonic /pluːˈtɒnɪk/ *adj* (*geol*) formed from magma cooling beneath the earth's surface.

plutonium /pluːˈtoːniəm/ *n* a highly toxic transuranic element used as fuel in nuclear power stations and in nuclear weapons.

pluvial /'pluːviəl/ *adj* caused by the action of rain; rainy.

pluviometer /‚pluːviˈɒmətər/ *n* an instrument used to measure rainfall.—*also* **rain gauge**.

ply[1] /plaɪ/ *vti* (**plying, plied**) to work at diligently and energetically; to wield; to subject to persistently; (*goods*) to sell; to go to and fro, run regularly; to keep busy.

ply[2] *n* (*pl* **plies**) a layer or thickness, as of cloth, plywood, etc; any of the twisted strands in a yarn, etc. • *vt* (**plying, plied**) to twist together.

plywood /'plaɪwʊd/ *n* a building material consisting of several thin layers of wood glued together.

PM *abbr* = post-mortem; Prime Minister.

Pm (*chem symbol*) promethium.

p.m. *abbr* = post meridiem.

PMS *abbr* = premenstrual syndrome.

PMT *abbr* = premenstrual tension.

pneumatic /nuːˈmætɪk/ or /njuː-/ *adj* concerning wind, air, or gases; operated by or filled with compressed air.—**pneumatically** *adv*.

pneumatics /nuːˈmætɪks/ or /njuː-/ *n sing* the science dealing with the mechanical properties of air.

pneumatology /‚nuːməˈtɒlədʒi/ or /‚njuː-/ *n* the theological study of the Holy Spirit.

pneumatometer /‚nuːməˈtɒmətər/ or/‚njuː-/ *n* an instrument for measuring the amount of air exhaled in one breath.

pneumatophore /'nuːmətə‚fɔr/ or /'njuː-/ *n* the breathing organ of a marsh plant.

pneumonia /nuːˈmoːniə/ or /njuː-/, /nə-/ *n* acute inflammation of the lungs.—**pneumonic** *adj*.

PO *abbr* = Personnel Officer; Petty Officer; Pilot Officer; post office; postal order.

Po (*chem symbol*) polonium.

poach[1] /poːtʃ/ *vt* to cook (an egg without its shell, fish, etc) in or over boiling water.

poach[2] *vti* to catch game or fish illegally; to trespass for this purpose; to encroach on, usurp another's rights, etc; to steal another's idea, employee, etc.—**poaching** *n*.

poacher[1] /-ər/ *n* a pan with shallow cups for poaching eggs; a dish for poaching fish, etc.

poacher[2] *n* a person who poaches another's property.

pochard /'poːtʃərd/ or /-kərd/ *n* (*pl* **pochards, pochard**) a red-headed European duck.

pock /pɒk/ *n* an eruptive pustule on the skin, *esp* as a result of smallpox.

pocket /'pɒkət/ *n* a small bag or pouch, *esp* in a garment, for carrying small articles; an isolated or enclosed area; a deposit (as of gold, water, or gas). • *adj* small enough to put in a pocket. • *vt* to put in one's pocket, to steal; (*ball*) to put in a pocket; to envelop; to enclose; (*money*) to take dishonestly; to suppress.

pocketbook /'pɒkət‚bʊk/ *n* in the US, a small folder or case for letters, money, credit cards, etc.

pocketful /'pɒkɪt‚fuːl/ *n* (*pl* **pocketfuls**) as much as a pocket holds.

pocketknife /'pɒkɪt‚naɪf/ *n* (*pl* **pocketknives**) a small knife with one or more blades that fold into the handle.

pocket money *n* money for occasional expenses; a child's allowance.

poco /'poːkoː/ *adv* (*mus*) a little.

pococurante /‚poːkoːkuːˈrænti/ or /-kjuː-/ *n, adj* (someone who is) indifferent.

pod /pɒd/ *n* a dry fruit or seed vessel, as of peas, beans, etc; a protective container or housing; a detachable compartment on a spacecraft. • *vi* (**podding, podded**) to remove the pod from.

podagra /pəˈdægrə/ or /'pədəgrə/ *n* gout, *esp* in the feet.—**podagral, podagric, podagrous** *adj*.

podgy /'pɒdʒi/ *adj* (**podgier, podgiest**) short and fat, squat.—*also* **pudgy**.—**podginess** *n*.

podium /'poːdiəm/ *n* (*pl* **podiums, podia**) a platform used by lecturers, etc; a low wall around the arena of an amphitheatre.

podophyllin /‚pɒdəˈfɪlɪn/ *n* a purgative resin obtained from the root of the May apple and mandrake.

poem /'poːəm/ or /poːm/ *n* an arrangement of words, *esp* in metre, often rhymed, in a style more imaginative than ordinary speech; a poetic thing.

poesy /'poːəzi/ *n* (*pl* **poesies**) the art of writing poetry.

poet /'poːət/ *n* the writer of a poem; a person with imaginative power and a sense **of beauty**.—**poetess** *nf*.

poetaster /‚poːəˈtæstər/ *n* an inferior poet.

poetic /poːˈɛtɪk/, **poetical** *adj* of poets or poetry; written in verse; imaginative, romantic, like poetry.—**poetically** *adv*.

poetic justice *n* an outcome in which vice is punished and virtue rewarded in an appropriate manner.

poetic licence *n* latitude allowed to a poet in grammar, facts, etc.

poetics /poːˈɛtɪks/ *n sing* the theory, or study, of poetry.

poetize /'poːə‚taɪz/ *vt* to make poetic; to compose poetry about. • *vi* to compose poetry.

poet laureate *n* (*pl* **poets laureate**) a poet officially appointed by the British sovereign to write poems celebrating national events, etc.

poetry /'poːətri/ *n* the art of writing poems; poems collectively; poetic quality or spirit.

pogo stick /'poːgoː/ *n* a stilt with a powerful spring used to hop along the ground.

pogrom /poː'grɒm/ or /'pɒgrəm/ n an organized extermination of a minority group.

poignant /'pɔɪnjənt/ adj piercing; incisive; deeply moving.— **poignancy** n.—**poignantly** adv.

poinsettia /pɔɪn'setə/ or /-setiə/ n a South American plant, widely cultivated as a house plant for its red bracts, which resemble petals.

point /pɔɪnt/ n a dot or tiny mark used in writing or printing (eg a decimal point, a full stop); a location; a place in a cycle, course, or scale; a unit in scoring or judging; the sharp end of a knife or pin; a moment of time; one of thirty-two divisions of the compass; a fundamental reason or aim; the tip; a physical characteristic; a railway switch; a unit of size in printing equal to one seventy-second of an inch; a unit used in quoting the prices of stocks, bonds and commodities; a headland or cape. • vti to give point to; to sharpen; to aim (at); to extend the finger (at or to); to indicate something; to call attention (to).

point-blank /pɔɪnt'blæŋk/ adj aimed straight at a mark; direct, blunt.—also adv.

pointed /'pɔɪntəd/ adj having a point; pertinent; aimed at a particular person or group; conspicuous.—**pointedly** adv.— **pointedness** n.

pointer /'pɔɪntər/ n a rod or needle for pointing; an indicator; a breed of hunting dog.

pointillism /'pwæntɪ.lɪzəm/ n in painting, the practice of applying small strokes or dots of colour to a surface so that from a distance they blend together.—**pointillist** n, adj.

pointless /'pɔɪntləs/ adj without a point; irrelevant, aimless.— **pointlessly** adv.—**pointlessness** n.

poise¹ /pɔɪz/ vt to balance; to hold supported without motion; (the head) to hold in a particular way; to put into readiness. • vi to become drawn up into readiness; to hover. • n a balanced state; self-possessed assurance of manner; gracious tact; bearing, carriage.

poise² n a centimetre-gram-second unit of viscosity equivalent to one dyne-second per square metre.

poison /'pɔɪzən/ n a substance that through its chemical action usu destroys or injures an organism; any corrupt influence; an object of aversion or abhorrence. • vt to administer poison in order to kill or injure; to put poison into; to influence wrongfully.—**poisoner** n.

poison gas n a poisonous gas, or a liquid or solid giving off poisonous vapours, used in warfare.

poison ivy n a climbing plant with ivory-coloured berries and an acutely irritating oil that causes an intensely itchy skin rash; the rash caused by poison ivy.

poisonous /'pɔɪzənəs/ adj being or containing poison; toxic; having a harmful influence; (inf) unpleasant.—**poisonously** adv.— **poisonousness** n.

poke /poːk/ vt to thrust (at), jab or prod; (hole, etc) to make by poking; (sl) to hit. • vi to jab (at); to pry or search (about or around). • n a jab; a prod or nudge; a thrust.

poker¹ /'poːkər/ n a metal rod for poking or stirring fire.

poker² n a card game in which a player bets that the value of his hand is higher than that of the hands held by others.

poker face n an expressionless face, concealing a person's thoughts or feelings.—**poker-faced** adj.

poky, pokey /'poːki/ adj (**pokier, pokiest**) small and uncomfortable.—**pokily** adv.—**pokiness** n.

polar /'poːlər/ adj of or near the North or South Pole; of a pole; having positive and negative electricity; directly opposite.

polar angle n the angle between the positive (polar) axis and the radius vector in polar coordinates.

polar bear n a large creamy-white bear that inhabits arctic regions.

polar coordinates npl either of a pair of coordinates that determine the position of points in space by measuring their distance along a fixed line from the origin or other given point and their angle, which lies between the fixed line and a single axis.

polarimeter /ˌpoːlə'rɪmɪtər/ n an instrument for measuring the polarization of light.

Polaris /poː'lɑrəs/ or /pə-/ n (astron) the brightest star in the Ursa Minor constellation, also known as the Pole Star.

polariscope /poː'leɪrɪˌskoːp/ n an instrument used to detect polarized light.

polarity /pə'leɪrɪti/ n (pl **polarities**) the condition of being polar; the magnet's property of pointing north; attraction towards a particular object or in a specific direction; (elect) the state, positive or negative, of a body; diametrical opposition; an instance of such opposition.

polarization /ˌpoːləraɪ'zeɪʃən/ n the production or acquirement of polarity; (optics) the process of causing light waves to vibrate in a uniform circular, elliptical or linear pattern; (elect) the separation of positive and negative charges; the grouping about opposing factions.

polarize /'poːləˌraɪz/ vt (light waves) to cause to vibrate in a definite pattern; to give physical polarity to; to break up into opposing factions; to concentrate.—**polarizable** adj.—**polarizer** n.

Polaroid /'poːləˌrɔɪd/ n (trademark) a transparent material used esp in sunglasses and lamps to prevent glare; a camera that produces a print in seconds.

polder /'poːldər/ n (Netherlands) a piece of land reclaimed from the sea.

pole¹ /poːl/ n a long slender piece of wood, metal, etc; a flagstaff. • vt to propel, support with a pole.

pole² n either end of an axis, esp of the earth; either of two opposed forces, parts, etc, as the ends of a magnet, terminals of a battery, etc; either of two opposed principles.

poleaxe /'poːlæks/, **poleax** n a long-handled battle axe; a type of axe used to slaughter cattle. • vt to hit or knock down with, or as if with, such an axe.

pole bean n a climbing plant that produces long green edible pods, a runner bean.

polecat /'poːlkæt/ n (pl **polecats, polecat**) a small, dark-brown animal, found in Europe, North Africa and Asia, related to the weasel and known for its unpleasant smell.

polemic /pə'lemɪk/ n a controversy or argument over doctrine; strong criticism; a controversialist. • adj involving dispute; controversial.—also **polemical.**—**polemically** adv.— **polemicist** n.

polemics /poː'lemɪks/ or /pə-/ n sing the art of controversial debate.

polenta /pə'lentə/ n an Italian porridge of maize, barley or chestnut meal.

pole vault n a field event in which competitors jump over a high bar using a long flexible pole.—**pole-vault** vi.—**pole-vaulter** n.

police /pə'liːs/ n the government department for keeping order, detecting crime, law enforcement, etc; (pl) the members of such a department; any similar organization. • vt to control, protect, etc with police or a similar force.

policeman /pə'liːsmən/ n (pl **policemen**) a member of a police force.—**policewoman** nf (pl **policewomen**).

police officer n a policeman or policewoman.

policy¹ /'pɒləsi/ n (pl **policies**) a written insurance contract.

policy² n (pl **policies**) political wisdom, statecraft; a course of action selected from among alternatives; a high-level overall plan embracing the general principles and aims of an organization, esp a government.

policyholder /'pɒləsiˌhoːldər/ n a person who has an insurance policy.

polio /'poːlioː/ n poliomyelitis.

poliomyelitis /ˌpoːlioːˌmaɪə'laɪtɪs/ n an acute infectious virus disease marked by inflammation of nerve cells in the spinal cord, causing paralysis.

Polish /'poːlɪʃ/ adj of or pertaining to Poland, its inhabitants, language or culture. • n the Slavic language of Poland.

polish /'pɒlɪʃ/ vti to make or become smooth and shiny by rubbing (with a cloth and polish); to give elegance or culture to; (with off) (inf) to finish completely. • n smoothness; elegance of manner; a finish or gloss; a substance, such as wax, used to polish.—**polisher** n.

polished /'pɒlɪʃt/ adj accomplished; smoothly or professionally done or performed; (rice) having had the husk removed.

polite /pə'laɪt/ adj courteous; well-bred; refined.—**politely** adv.—**politeness** n.

politesse /ˌpɒli'tes/ n (excessively) formal politeness.

politic /'pɒlətɪk/ adj expedient; shrewdly tactful; prudent.

political /pə'lɪtɪkəl/ adj relating to politics or government; characteristic of political parties or politicians.—**politically** adv.

political correctness n a movement aimed at removing discrimination against women, ethnic minorities, gays and lesbians, etc by combating sexist and racist language or policies in education, the arts, media and government.—**politically correct** adj.

political economy n the former name for the science of economics.

politician /ˌpɒlɪˈtɪʃən/ n a person engaged in politics, often used with implications of seeking personal or partisan gain, scheming, etc.

politico /pəˈlɪtɪˌkoː/ n (sl) a politician.

politics /ˈpɒlɪtɪks/ n (sing or pl) the science and art of government; political activities, beliefs or affairs; factional scheming for power.

polity /ˈpɒlɪti/ n (pl **polities**) the form or constitution of the government of a state; a constitution.

polka /ˈpoːlkə/ or /ˈpoːkə/ n a lively dance; the music for this. • vi to dance the polka.

polka dot n any of a pattern of small round dots forming a pattern on cloth.

poll /poːl/ n a counting, listing, etc of persons, esp of voters; the number of votes recorded; an opinion survey; (pl) a place where votes are cast. • vti to receive the votes (of); to cast a vote; to canvass or question in a poll.—**poller** n.

pollack /ˈpɒlək/ n (pl **pollacks, pollack**) a type of food fish.—also **pollock** (pl **pollocks, pollock**).

pollan /ˈpɒlən/ n an Irish freshwater fish.

pollard /ˈpɒlərd/ n a tree with its branches pruned to encourage growth; an animal which has cast its horns or antlers, or had them removed.

pollen /ˈpɒlən/ n the yellow dust, containing male spores, that is formed in the anthers of flowers.—**pollinic** adj.

pollex /ˈpɒlɛks/ n (pl **pollices**) a thumb or similar first digit.

pollinate /ˈpɒlɪˌneɪt/ vti to fertilize by uniting pollen with seed.—**pollinator** n.

pollination /pɒlɪˈneɪʃən/ n the transfer of pollen from the anthers of a flower to the stigma, esp by insects.

polliwog, pollywog /ˈpɒliˌwɒg/ or /-ˌwɒg/ n a tadpole.

pollock /ˈpɒlək/ see **pollack**.

pollster /ˈpoːlstər/ n a person who conducts a poll or compiles data obtained from a poll.

poll tax n a tax of a fixed amount per person levied on adults.

pollute /pəˈluːt/ vt to contaminate with harmful substances; to make corrupt; to profane.—**polluter** n.

pollution /pəˈluːʃən/ n the act of polluting; the state of being polluted; contamination by chemicals, noise, etc.

polo /ˈpoːloː/ n a game played on horseback by two teams, using a wooden ball and long-handled mallets.

polonaise /ˌpɒləˈneɪz/ n a slow, stately dance in three-four time; the music for such a dance; an outfit with a one-piece bodice and a skirt looped up at the sides.

polo shirt n a sports shirt made of a knitted fabric.

polonium /pəˈloːniəm/ n a radioactive element.

poltergeist /ˈpoːltərˌgaɪst/ n a spirit believed to move heavy objects about and to make noises.

poltroon /pɒlˈtruːn/ n (arch) a coward.

poly- /ˈpɒli/ prefix many.

polyandry /ˈpɒliˌændri/ n the practice of a woman having more than one husband at the same time.—**polyandrous** adj.

polyanthus /ˌpɒliˈænθəs/ n (pl **polyanthuses**) a hybrid garden primrose; a narcissus with small yellow or white flowers in clusters.

polyatomic /ˌpɒliəˈtɒmɪk/ adj with more than two atoms in the molecule.

polybasic /ˌpɑlɪˈbeɪsɪk/ adj (chem) having more than two bases or atoms of a base.

polychaete /ˈpɒliˌkiːt/, **poltchete** n a type of marine worm. • adj pertaining to this type of worm.—also **polychaetous**.

polychromatic /ˌpɒlikroˈmætɪk/ **polychromic, polychromous** adj having many colours; exhibiting a play of colours; (physics) (light, etc) having a mixture of wavelengths.—**polychromatism** n.

polychrome /ˈpɒliˌkroːm/ adj made with, or decorated in, many colours. • n a work of art in several colours; a painted statue.

polyclinic /ˈpɒliˌklɪni/ n a general hospital.

polydactyl /ˌpɒliˈdæktɪl/ n, adj (an animal or person) with more than the normal number of fingers or toes.

polyester /ˌpɒliˈɛstər/ n any of a number of synthetic polymeric resins used for adhesives, plastics, and textiles.

polyethylene /ˌpɒliˈɛθɪˌliːn/ n a light, plastic, multipurpose synthetic material resistant to moisture and chemicals.—also **polythene**.

polygamist /pəˈlɪgəməst/ n a person who advocates or practises polygamy.

polygamy /pəˈlɪgəmi/ or /poː-/ n the practice of being married to more than one person at a time; (bot) the condition of having staminate, pistillate and hermaphrodite flowers on one plant; (zool) the practice of having more than one mate.—**polygamous** adj.—**polygamously** adv.

polygenesis /ˌpɒliˈdʒɛnɪsɪs/ n the derivation of a species or race from many origins.—**polygenetic** adj.

polyglot /ˈpɒliˌglɒt/ adj having command of many languages; composed of numerous languages; containing matter in several languages; composed of elements from different languages. • n a person who speaks several languages.

polygon /ˈpɒliˌgɒn/ n a closed plane figure bound by three or more straight lines.—**polygonal** adj.

polygonum /pəˈlɪgənəm/ n one of a family of flowering plants including knotgrass.

polygraph /ˈpɒliˌgræf/ n an instrument for detecting and measuring involuntary changes in blood pressure, breathing, etc, often used as a lie detector.—**polygraphic** adj.

polygyny /pəˈlɪdʒɪni/ n the practice of a man having more than one wife at the same time.—**polygynous** adj.

polyhedron /ˌpɒliˈhiːdrən/ or /-ˈhɛdrən/ n (pl **polyhedrons, polyhedra**) a solid with many (usu more than six) plane faces.—**polyhedral** adj.

polymath /ˈpɒliˌmæθ/ n someone learned in many subjects.

polymer /ˈpɒləmər/ n (chem) a compound that has large molecules composed of many simpler molecules.—**polymeric** adj.—**polymerism** n.

polymerize /-aɪz/ vti to (cause to) form a polymer.

polymorph /ˌpɒliˈmɔrf/ n a polymorphous organism.

polymorphous /ˌpɒliˈmɔrfəs/, **polymorphic** adj having, or assuming, many different forms.

polynomial /ˌpɒliˈnoːmiəl/ n (math) an expression consisting of a sum of terms each of which is a product of a constant and one or more variables raised to a positive or zero integral power; (biol) a species name of more than two terms. • adj composed of or expressed as one or more polynomials.

polyp /ˈpɒlɪp/ n a small water animal with tentacles at the top of a tube-like body; a growth on mucous membrane.—**polypoid** adj.

polyphagous /pəˈlɪfəgəs/ adj voracious; (zool) feeding on various kinds of food.

polyphone /ˈpɒliˌfoːn/ n (linguistics) a polyphonic letter or symbol

polyphonic /ˌpɒliˈfɒnɪk/ adj many-voiced; (mus) contrapuntal; (phonetics) representing more than one sound.

polyphony /pəˈlɪfəni/ n (pl **polyphonies**) being polyphonic; using polyphones; (mus) counterpoint.

polypod /ˈpɒliˌpɒd/ n adj (an animal) with many legs.

polypody /ˈpɒliˌpoːdi/ n (pl **polypodies**) a type of fern.

polypus /ˈpɒlɪpəs/ n (pl **polypi**) (med) a tumour with branching roots, found in the nose or womb.

polystyrene /ˌpɒliˈstaɪˌriːn/ n a rigid plastic material used for packing, insulating, etc.

polysyllable /ˈpɒliˌsɪləbəl/ n a word of many syllables.—**polysyllabic** adj.—**polysyllabically** adv.

polytechnic /ˌpɒliˈtɛknɪk/ n an institution that provides instruction in many applied sciences and technical subjects.

polytheism /ˈpɒliθiːˌɪzəm/ n belief in many gods, or more than one god.—**polytheist** n.—**polytheistic** adj.

polythene /ˈpɒliˌθiːn/ see **polyethylene**.

polyunsaturated /ˌpɒliənˈsætʃəˌreɪtəd/ or /-tjuˌreɪtəd/ adj denoting any of certain plant and animal fats and oils with a low cholesterol content.

polyurethane /ˌpɒliˈjuərəˌθeɪn/ n any of various polymers that are used esp in flexible and rigid foams, resins, etc.

pomace /ˈpɒmɪs/ n crushed apples for making cider; the crushed apples left after making cider.

pomaceous /poːˈmeɪʃəs/ adj pertaining to pomes.

pomade /pəˈmeɪd/ or /-ˈmɒd/ n a scented ointment for the hair.

pomander /pəˈmændər/ n an aromatic ball or powder formerly carried for its pleasant smell or as protection against infection; a container for this.

pome /poːm/ n the stoneless fruit of the apple and related plants.

pomegranate /ˈpɒməˌgrænɪt/ or /ˈpɒmˌgrænɪt/ n an edible fruit with many seeds; the widely cultivated tropical tree bearing it.

Pomeranian /ˌpɒməˈreɪniə/ n a breed of small dog.

pomiculture /ˈpɒmiˌkəltʃər/ n fruit growing.

pommel /ˈpʌməl/ n the rounded, upward-projecting front part of a saddle; a knob on the hilt of a sword. • vt (**pommelling, pommelled** or **pommeling, pommeled**) to pummel.

pommy, pommie /ˈpʌmi/ n (pl **pommies**) (*Austral sl*) a British person.

pomology /pəˈmɒlədʒi/ n the study of fruit growing.—**pomological** adj.—**pomologist** n.

Pomona /pəˈmoːnə/ n (*Roman myth*) the goddess of fruit trees.

pomp /pɒmp/ n stately ceremony; ostentation.

pompadour /ˈpɒmpəˌdɔr/ or /-dur/ n an 18th century hairstyle.

pompano /ˈpɒmpənoː/ n (pl **pompano, pompanos**) an edible American sea fish.

pom-pom /ˈpɒmpɒm/ n a quick-firing automatic anti-aircraft gun.

pompon, pompom /ˈpɒmpɒm/ n an ornamental ball or tuft of fabric strands used on clothing as an ornament; a small tufted flower on some varieties of chrysanthemum and dahlia.

pomposity /pɒmˈpɒsɪti/ n (pl **pomposities**) the state of being pompous; self-importance; a pompous utterance or act.

pompous /ˈpɒmpəs/ adj stately; self-important.—**pompously** adv.—**pompousness** n.

poncho /ˈpɒntʃoː/ n (pl **ponchos**) a blanket-like cloak with a hole in the centre for the head.

pond /pɒnd/ n a body of standing water smaller than a lake.

ponder /ˈpɒndər/ vti to think deeply; to consider carefully.

ponderable /-əbəl/ adj capable of being evaluated; capable of being weighed.—**ponderability** n.

ponderous /ˈpɒndərəs/ adj heavy; awkward; dull; lifeless.—**ponderously** adv.—**ponderousness** n.

pong /pɒŋ/ n (sl) an unpleasant smell. • vi (sl) to stink.

pongee /pɒnˈdʒiː/ n a thin, unbleached, Chinese silk.

pontifex /ˈpɒntɪˌfɛks/ n (pl **pontifices**) (*ancient Rome*) a pontiff or high priest.

pontiff /ˈpɒntɪf/ n the Pope; a bishop; a pontifex.

pontifical /pɒnˈtɪfɪkəl/ adj of a pontiff; pompous. • npl a bishop's robes.—**pontifically** adv.

pontificate /pɒnˈtɪfɪˌkeɪt/ vi to speak sententiously, pompously or dogmatically; to officiate at a pontifical mass.—**pontificator** n.

pontoon¹ /pɒnˈtuːn/ n a boat or cylindrical float forming a support for a bridge.

pontoon² n a card game.

pony /ˈpoːni/ n (pl **ponies**) a small horse, a bronco, mustang, etc; (*inf*) a racehorse.

ponytail /ˈpoːniˌteɪl/ n a style of arranging hair to resemble a pony's tail.

poodle /ˈpuːdəl/ n a breed of dog of various sizes with a curly coat.

pool¹ /puːl/ n a small pond; a puddle; a small collection of liquid; a swimming pool.

pool² n a game played on a billiards table with six pockets; a combination of resources, funds, supplies, people, etc for some common purpose; the parties forming such a combination. • vti to contribute to a common fund, to share.

poop /puːp/ n (*naut*) the stern of a ship; the raised deck in the stern of a ship.

poor /pur/ or /pɔr/ adj having little money, needy; deserving pity, unfortunate; deficient; disappointing; inferior. • n those who have little.—**poorness** n.

poorhouse /ˈpurhʌus/ n (*formerly*) a public institution housing poor people.

poorly /ˈpurli/ adv insufficiently, badly. • adj not in good health.

pop¹ /pɒp/ n a short, explosive sound, a shot; any carbonated, nonalcoholic beverage. • vti (**popping, popped**) to make or cause a pop; to shoot; to go or come quickly (in, out, up); (*corn, maize*) to roast until it pops; to put suddenly; (*eyes*) to bulge.

pop² adj in a popular modern style. • n pop music; pop art; pop culture.

pop³ n (*inf*) father; (*inf*) a name used to address an old man.

pop art n a realistic art style using techniques and subjects from commercial art, comic strips, posters, etc.

popcorn /ˈpɒpkɔrn/ n a kind of corn or maize, which when heated pops or puffs up.

pope /poːp/ n the bishop of Rome, head of the RC Church.—**popedom** n.

pop-eyed /ˈpɒpaɪd/ adj with bulging eyes; (*fig*) astonished.

popgun /ˈpɒpgʌn/ n a toy gun that fires pellets or cork with a popping noise.

popinjay /ˈpɒpɪnˌdʒeɪ/ n a conceited person.

poplar /ˈpɒplər/ n a slender, quick-growing tree of the willow family.

poplin /ˈpɒplɪn/ n a sturdy corded fabric.

poppet /ˈpɒpət/ n a term of endearment.

poppet valve n a valve opened by being lifted from its seat.

poppy /ˈpɒpi/ n (pl **poppies**) an annual or perennial plant with showy flowers, one of which yields opium; a strong reddish colour.

poppycock /ˈpɒpiˌkɒk/ n (*inf*) nonsense.

populace /ˈpɒpjuləs/ n the common people; the masses; all the people in a country, region, etc.

popular /ˈpɒpjulər/ adj of the people; well liked; pleasing to many people; easy to understand.—**popularly** adv.

popularity /-ˈlɛrɪti/ n the condition or quality of being popular.

popularize /ˈpɒpjuləˌraɪz/ vt to make popular; to make generally accepted or understood.—**popularization** n.—**popularizer** n.

populate /ˈpɒpjuˌleɪt/ vt to inhabit; to supply with inhabitants.

population /ˌpɒpjuˈleɪʃən/ n all the inhabitants or the number of people in an area.

populism /ˌpɒpjuˈlɪzəm/ n any movement based on belief in the rights, wisdom, or virtue of the common people.

populist /ˈpɒpjulɪst/ n an advocate of populism; one who claims to represent the people; (*with cap*) a member of the Populist or People's Party in the US (1891–1904) aiming at public control of utilities, etc.

populous /ˈpɒpjuləs/ adj densely inhabited.—**populously** adv.—**populousness** n.

porbeagle /ˈpɔrˌbiːgəl/ n a type of shark.

porcelain /ˈpɔrsələn/ n a hard, white, translucent variety of ceramic ware. • adj made of porcelain.—**porcellaneous** adj.

porch /pɔrtʃ/ n a covered entrance to a building; an open or enclosed gallery or room on the outside of a building.

porcupine /ˈpɔrkjuˌpaɪn/ n a large rodent covered with protective quills.

pore¹ /pɔr/ n a tiny opening, as in the skin, plant leaves, stem, etc, for absorbing and discharging fluids.

pore² vti (*with over*) to look with steady attention; to study closely.

porgy /ˈpɔrgi/ n (pl **porgy, porgies**) an edible sea fish.

pork /pɔrk/ n the flesh of a pig used as food.

porker /ˈpɔrkər/ n a pig, *esp* a fattened one.

porky /ˈpɔrki/ adj (**porkier, porkiest**) of or like pork; (*sl*) impertinent; (*sl*) obese, fat.—**porkiness** n.

porno /ˈpɔrnə/ n (*sl*) pornography—*also* **porn**. • adj pornographic.

pornography /pɔrˈnɒgrəfi/ n writings, pictures, films, etc, intended primarily to arouse sexual desire.—**pornographer** n.—**pornographic** adj.—**pornographically** adv.

porous /ˈpɔrəs/ adj having pores; able to absorb air and fluids, etc.—**porously** adv.—**porousness** n.

porphyry /ˈpɔrfɪri/ n (pl **porphyry**) a reddish igneous rock, containing crystals of feldspar.

porpoise /ˈpɔrpəs/ n (pl **porpoise, porpoises**) any of several small whales, *esp* a black blunt-nosed whale of the north Atlantic and Pacific; any of several bottle-nosed dolphins.

porridge /ˈpɒrɪdʒ/ or /ˈpɒr-/ n a thick food, *usu* made by boiling oats or oatmeal in water or milk.

porringer /ˈpɒrɪndʒər/ n a small dish for porridge, etc.

port¹ /pɔrt/ n a harbour; a town with a harbour where ships load and unload cargo; airport; a place where goods may be cleared through customs.

port² n a porthole; an opening, as in a valve face, for the passage of steam, etc; a hole in an armoured vehicle for firing a weapon; a circuit in a computer for inputting or outputting data.

port³ n the left of an aircraft or ship looking forward.—*also* adj.

port⁴ n a strong, sweet, fortified dark red wine.

portable /ˈpɔrtəbəl/ adj capable of being carried or moved about easily.—**portability** n.

portage /pɔrˈtɒdʒ/ n a carrying of boats and supplies overland between navigable rivers, lakes, etc; any route over which this is done. • vti (*boats, etc*) to carry over a portage.

portal /ˈpɔrtəl/ n an impressive gate or doorway.

portamento /ˌpɔrtəˈmɛntoː/ n (*mus*) a continuous glide from one note to another.

portcullis /pɔrtˈkʌlɪs/ n a grating that can be lowered to bar entrance to a castle.

portend /pɔrˈtɛnd/ vt to give warning of, to foreshadow.

portent /ˈpɔrtɛnt/ or /-tənt/ n an omen, warning.

portentous /pɔr'tentəs/ *adj* ominous; pompous, self-important.—**portentously** *adv*.—**portentousness** *n*.

porter[1] /'pɔrtər/ *n* a doorman or gatekeeper.

porter[2] *n* a person who carries luggage, etc, for hire at a station, airport, etc; a railway attendant for passengers; a dark brown beer.

porterage /'pɔrtərədʒ/ *n* the hire of a porter; the charge for this.

porterhouse /'pɔrtər,hɛus/ *n* a choice cut of beef steak; (*formerly*) an eating place.

portfolio /pɔrt'fo:lio:/ *n* (*pl* **portfolios**) a flat case for carrying papers, drawings, etc; a collection of work; the office of a cabinet minister or minister of state; a list of stocks, shares, etc.

porthole /'pɔrtho:l/ *n* an opening (as a window) with a cover or closure *esp* in the side of a ship or aircraft; a port through which to shoot; an opening for intake or exhaust of a fluid.

portico /'pɔrtiko:/ *n* (*pl* **porticoes, porticos**) a covered walkway with columns supporting the roof.

portière /pɔrt'jɛr/ *n* a heavy curtain over a door or doorway.

portion /'pɔrʃən/ *n* a part, a share, *esp* an allotted part; a helping of food; destiny. • *vt* to share out.

portly /'pɔrtli/ *adj* (**portlier, portliest**) dignified; stout.—**portliness** *n*.

portmanteau /pɔrt'mæntɔ:/ *n* (*pl* **portmanteaus, portmanteaux**) a large oblong travelling case with two compartments.

portmanteau word *n* a word combining the sound and sense of two other words, *eg* brunch.

portrait /'pɔrtrət/ *n* a painting, photograph, etc, of a person, *esp* of the face; (*of person*) a likeness; a vivid description.

portraitist /'pɔrtrətist/ *n* a maker of portraits by painting, photography, etc.

portraiture /'pɔrtrətʃər/ *n* the drawing of portraits; a portrait; a description in words; portraits collectively.

portray /pɔr'trei/ *vt* to make a portrait of; to depict in words; to play the part of in a play, film, etc.—**portrayable** *adj*.—**portrayer** *n*.

portrayal /pɔr'treiəl/ *n* the act or process of portraying; a description; a representation.

portress /'pɔrtris/ *n* a female porter.

pose /po:z/ *n* a position or attitude, *esp* one held for an artist or photographer; an attitude deliberately adopted for effect. • *vti* to propound, assert; to assume an attitude for effect; to sit for a painting, photograph; to set oneself up (as).

poser /'po:zər/ *n* a person who poses; a difficult problem.

poseur /po:'zər/ *n* an affected, insincere person.

posh /pɒʃ/ *adj* (*inf*) elegant; fashionable.

posit /'pɒzit/ *vt* to assume as fact, postulate.

position /pə'zɪʃən/ *n* place, situation; a position occupied; posture; a job; state of affairs; point of view. • *vt* to place or locate.

positional /-əl/ *adj* related to, or fixed by position; involving little movement; dependent on context, environment or position.

positive /'pɒzitiv/ *adj* affirmative; definite; sure; marked by presence, not absence, of qualities; expressed clearly, or in a confident manner; constructive; empirical; (*elect*) charged with positive electricity; (*math*) greater than zero, plus; (*gram*) of adjective or adverb, denoting the simple form; (*photog*) having light, shade, colour as in the original. • *n* a positive quality or quantity; a photographic print made from a negative.

positively /-li/ *adv* in a positive way; decidedly.

positiveness /-nəs/ *n* the condition or quality of being positive; confidence; certainty.

positivism /'pɒzitivizəm/ *n* a philosophy recognizing only matters of fact and experience; the quality of being positive.—**positivist** *n*, *adj*.—**positivistic** *adj*.—**positivistically** *adv*.

positron /'pɒzi,trɒn/ *n* (*physics*) a particle of the same size as an electron, but with a positive charge.

posology /pə'sɒlədʒi/ *n* the area of medicine dealing with evaluation of doses.

posse /'pɒsi/ *n* in the US, a body of people summoned by a sheriff to assist in keeping the peace, etc; (*sl*) a group of criminals, *usu* of Jamaican origin and in New York.

possess /pə'zɛs/ *vt* to own, have, keep; to dominate or control the mind of.—**possessor** *n*.—**possessory** *adj*.

possessed /pə'zɛst/ *adj* owned; controlled as if by a demon.

possession /pə'zɛʃən/ *n* ownership; something possessed; (*pl*) property.

possessive /pə'zɛsiv/ *adj* of or indicating possession; (*gram*) denoting a case, form or construction expressing possession; having an excessive desire to possess or dominate.—**possessively** *adv*.—**possessiveness** *n*.

posset /'pɒsət/ *n* a hot drink of milk curdled with wine or ale.

possibility /,pɒsɪ'bɪlɪti/ *n* (*pl* **possibilities**) the state of being possible; a possible occurrence, a contingency.

possible /'pɒsibəl/ *adj* that may be or may happen; feasible, practicable.—**possibly** *adv*.

possum /'pɒsəm/ *n* (*inf*) an opossum; a phalanger; **play possum** to pretend to be asleep or dead; to remain silent.

post[1] /po:st/ *n* a piece of wood, metal, etc, set upright to support a building, sign, etc; the starting or finishing point of a race. • *vt* (*poster, etc*) to put up; to announce by posting notices; (*name*) to put on a posted or published list.

post[2] *n* a fixed position, *esp* where a sentry or group of soldiers is stationed; a position or job; a trading post; a settlement. • *vt* to station in a given place.

post[3] *n* the official conveyance of letters and parcels, mail; letters, parcels, etc, so conveyed; collection or delivery of post, mail. • *vt* to send a letter or parcel; to keep informed.—**postal** *adj*.

post- /po:st/ *prefix* after.

postage /'po:stidʒ/ *n* the charge for sending a letter, etc, as represented by stamps.

postage stamp *n* an adhesive or imprinted stamp issued or authorized by a government and used on mail as evidence of prepayment of postage.

postcard /'po:stkɑrd/ *n* a card, *usu* decorative, for sending messages by post.

post chaise *n* (*formerly*) a light, closed, horse-drawn carriage used for carrying both post and passengers.

postcode /'po:stko:d/ *n* letters and digits to denote an address and assist sorting.

postdate /po:st'deit/ *vt* to write a future date on a letter or cheque.

postdiluvian /,po:stdə'lu:viən/, **postdiluvial** *adj* occurring after the Flood (of the Old Testament).

poster /'po:stər/ *n* a *usu* decorative or ornamental printed sheet for advertising.

poste restante /,po:stre'stɑ:t/ *n* the department of a post office that will hold mail until it is called for, general delivery.

posterior /pɒ'sti:riər/ *adj* later in time or order; at the rear. • *n* the buttocks.—**posteriorly** *adv*.

posterity /pɒ'steriti/ *n* future generations; all of a person's descendants.

postern /'pɒstərn/ *n* a back or side entrance; a small private door.

postfix /po:st'fiks/ *vt* to append as a suffix. • *n* a suffix.

post-free /'po:st'fri:/ *adj* postpaid.

postglacial /po:st'gleiʃəl/ or /-siəl/ *adj* existing after a glacial period.

postgraduate /,po:st'grædʒu:it/ *n* a person pursuing study after graduating from a high school or college. • *adj* (*study*) continued after the taking of a degree.

posthaste /'po:st'heist/ *adv* with all possible speed.

posthumous /'pɒstjəmos/ or /-ju:məs/, /'pɒstʃəməs/ *adj* (*child*) born after its father's death; (*award, etc*) given after one's death.—**posthumously** *adv*.

postiche *Fr* /po'sti:ʃ/ *adj* artificial; superfluous; inappropriate. • *n* an ornament added, *esp* inappropriately, to finished work; a wig; an imitation.

postilion, postillion /pɒ'stiljən/ *n* someone who rides one of the horses drawing a carriage and guiding the team.

postimpressionism /,po:stim'preʃən,izəm/ *n* a 19th-century school of painting which sought to express the artist's conception of things rather than their outward appearance.—**postimpressionist** *n*, *adj*.

postliminium, postliminy /,po:stli'miniəm/ *n* (*law*) the right of a prisoner of war or exile to resume his or her former privileges on return to his or her own country.

postlude /'po:stlu:d/ *n* (*mus*) a closing movement.

postman /'po:stmæn/ or /-mən/ *n* (*pl* **postmen**) a person who delivers mail as a profession.

postmark /'po:stmɑrk/ *n* the post office mark cancelling the stamp on a letter by showing the date, place of posting.

postmaster /'po:st,mæstər/ *n* the manager of a post office.

postmeridian /,po:stmə'ridiən/ *adj* of or taking place in the afternoon.

post meridiem /,po:stmə'ridiəm/ = p.m. (Latin for *after noon*).

postmortem /po:st'mɔrtəm/ *n* an examination of a corpse to determine the cause of death; an autopsy.—*also adj*.

postnatal /poːstˈneɪtəl/ *adj* occurring immediately after birth.

post-obit /-ˈoːbɪt/ *adj* (*law*) after death. • *n* a bond in which a borrower undertakes to repay a loan on the death of someone from whom he or she expects to receive a legacy.

post office *n* the building where postage stamps are sold and other postal business conducted; a public department handling the transmission of mail.

postpaid /ˈpoːstpeɪd/ *adj* with a charge for postage, post free.

postpone /poːstˈpoːn/ or /poːsˈpoːn/ *vt* to put off, delay to a future date.—**postponable** *adj*.—**postponement** *n*.—**postponer** *n*.

postprandial /-ˈprændɪəl/ *adj* after-dinner.

postscript /ˈpoːstskrɪpt/ or /ˈpoːsskrɪpt/ *n* a note added to a letter after completion.

postulant /ˈpɒstjʊlənt/ or /ˈpɒstʃʊ-/ *n* someone making a request; a candidate for admission to a religious order.

postulate /ˈpɒstjʊ‚leɪt/ or /ˈpɒstʃʊ-/ *vt* to assume to be true; to demand or claim. • *n* a position taken as self-evident; (*math*) an unproved assumption taken as basic; an axiom.—**postulation** *n*.

posture /ˈpɒstʃər/ *n* a pose; a body position; an attitude of mind; an official stand or position. • *vti* to pose in a particular way; to assume a pose.—**postural** *adj*.—**posturer** *n*.

post-viral syndrome *n* the viral condition myalgic encephalomyelitis that affects the nervous system.

posy /ˈpoːzi/ *n* (*pl* **posies**) a small bunch of flowers.

pot[1] /pɒt/ *n* a deep, round cooking vessel; an earthenware or plastic container for plants; a framework for catching fish or lobsters; (*inf*) a large amount (as of money); (*inf*) all the money bet at a single time. • *vb* (**potting, potted**) *vt* to put or preserve in a pot. • *vi* to take a pot shot, shoot.

pot[2] *n* (*sl*) cannabis.

potable /ˈpoːtəbəl/ *adj* drinkable.

potash /ˈpɒtæʃ/ *n* potassium carbonate.

potassium /pəˈtæsɪəm/ *n* a soft silvery-white metallic element.—**potassic** *adj*.

potation /poːˈteɪʃən/ *n* the act of drinking; a draught or drink.

potato /pəˈteɪtoː/ *n* (*pl* **potatoes**) a starchy, oval tuber eaten as a vegetable.

potbelly /-‚beli/ *n* (*pl* **potbellies**) a protruding belly.—**potbellied** *adj*.

potboiler /ˈpɒtbɔɪlər/ *n* an inferior literary or artistic work done simply to earn money.

potboy /ˈpɒtbɔɪ/ *n* (*formerly*) in UK, an assistant in a public house.

poteen /pɒˈtiːn/ *n* (*Irish*) illicitly distilled whiskey.

potency /ˈpoːtənsi/ *n* (*pl* **potencies**) the quality or condition of being potent; power; strength.

potent /ˈpoːtənt/ *adj* powerful; influential; intoxicating; (*a male*) able to have sexual intercourse.—**potently** *adv*.

potentate /ˈpoːtən‚teɪt/ *n* a person with great power; a ruler; a monarch.

potential /pəˈtenʃəl/ *adj* possible, but not yet actual. • *n* the unrealized ability to do something.—**potentially** *adv*.

potentiality /-ʃiˈælɪti/ *n* (*pl* **potentialities**) latent capacity for development or growth; something with this.

potentiate /pəˈtenʃi‚eɪt/ *vt* to make possible; to give power to.

potentilla /‚poːtənˈtɪlə/ *n* a flowering plant of the rose family.

pother /ˈpɒðər/ *n* a bustle or turmoil; a turmoil.

pothole /ˈpɒthoːl/ *n* a hole worn in a road by traffic; (*geol*) a deep hole or cave in rock caused by the action of water.

pothouse /ˈpɒt‚haʊs/ *n* (*formerly*) in UK, a public house.

pothunter /ˈpɒt‚hʌntər/ *n* someone who hunts for the sake of the game caught, not for the sport.

potion /ˈpoːʃən/ *n* a mixture of liquids, such as poison.

potpourri /poːpuˈriː/ *n* (*pl* **potpourris**) a mixture of scented, dried flower petals; a collection; a medley or miscellany.

potsherd /ˈpɒtʃərd/, **potshard** *n* a piece of broken earthenware.

pot shot /ˈpɒtʃɒt/ *n* a random or easy shot.

pottage /ˈpɒtɪdʒ/ *n* a thick broth.

potted /ˈpɒtəd/ *adj* in a pot; preserved (in a pot); (*version, history*) abridged.

potter[1] /ˈpɒtər/ *n* a person who makes earthenware vessels.

potter[2] *vi* to busy oneself idly; (*US*) to putter.—**potterer** *n*.

pottery /ˈpɒtəri/ *n* (*pl* **potteries**) earthenware vessels; a workshop where such articles are made.

potto /ˈpɒtoː/ *n* (*pl* **pottos**) a West African lemur; a kinkajou.

potty[1] /ˈpɒti/ *adj* (**pottier, pottiest**) (*inf*) slightly crazy; trivial, petty.—**pottiness** *n*.

potty[2] *n* (*pl* **potties**) (*inf*) a chamber pot.

pouch /paʊtʃ/ *n* a small bag or sack; a bag for mail; a sacklike structure, as that on the abdomen of a kangaroo, etc, for carrying young.—**pouched** *adj*.

poult /poːlt/ *n* a young fowl.

poultice /ˈpoːltɪs/ *n* a hot moist dressing applied to a sore part of the body.

poultry /ˈpoːltri/ *n* domesticated birds kept for meat or eggs.

pounce /paʊns/ *vi* to swoop or spring suddenly (upon) in order to seize; to make a sudden assault or approach.—*also n*.

pound[1] /paʊnd/ *n* a unit of weight equal to 16 ounces; a unit of money in the UK and other countries, symbol £.

pound[2] *vt* to beat into a powder or a pulp; to hit hard. • *vi* to deliver heavy blows repeatedly (at or on); to move with heavy steps; to throb; (*with* **away**) to work hard and continuously.—**pounder** *n*.

pound[3] *n* a municipal enclosure for stray animals; a depot for holding impounded personal property until claimed; a place or condition of confinement.

poundage /ˈpaʊndɪdʒ/ *n* a charge per pound of weight; weight in pounds; the act of impounding; the state of being impounded.

poundal /ˈpaʊndəl/ *n* a unit of force, giving to a mass of one pound an acceleration of one foot per second per second.

pour /pɔr/ *vti* to cause to flow in a stream; to flow continuously; to rain heavily; to serve tea or coffee.—**pourer** *n*.

pourboire *Fr.* /puːrˈbwaːr/ *n* a tip or gratuity.

pout /paʊt/ *vti* to push out (the lips); to look sulky. • *n* a thrusting out of the lips; (*pl*) a fit of pique.—**poutingly** *adv*.

pouter /ˈpaʊtər/ *n* someone who pouts; a breed of pigeon with a prominent crop.

poverty /ˈpɒvərti/ *n* the condition of being poor; scarcity.

poverty-stricken *adj* very poor, impoverished.

POW *abbr* = prisoner of war.

powder /ˈpaʊdər/ *n* any substance in tiny, loose particles; a specific kind of powder, *esp* for medicinal or cosmetic use; fine dry light snow. • *vti* to sprinkle or cover with powder; to reduce to powder.—**powderer** *n*.

powdered /ˈpaʊdərd/ *adj* sprinkled or covered with powder; reduced to power.

powdered sugar *n* (*US*) icing sugar.

powdery /ˈpaʊdəri/ *adj* like powder; easily crumbled.

power /ˈpaʊər/ *n* ability to do something; political, social or financial control or force; a person or state with influence over others; legal force or authority; physical force; a source of energy; (*math*) the result of continued multiplication of a quantity by itself a specified number of times. • *adj* operated by electricity, a fuel engine, etc; served by an auxiliary system that reduces effort; carrying electricity. • *vt* to supply with a source of power.—**powered** *adj*.

powerful /ˈpaʊər‚ful/ *adj* mighty; strong; influential.—**powerfully** *adv*.—**powerfulness** *n*.

powerhouse /ˈpaʊər‚haʊs/ *n* a power station; (*inf*) a strong or energetic person, team, etc.

powerless /ˈpaʊərləs/ *adj* without power; helpless; feeble.—**powerlessly** *adv*.—**powerlessness** *n*.

power station, power plant *n* a building where electric power is generated.

power-walking *n* brisk walking as a means of improving fitness.

powwow /ˈpaʊwaʊ/ *n* an American Indian ceremony (as for invoking victory in war); (*inf*) any conference or get-together. • *vi* to confer, chat.

pox /pɒks/ *n* a virus disease marked by pustules; (*arch*) smallpox; syphilis; a plague; a curse.

pozzuolana, pozzolana /‚pɒtswoːˈlɒnə/ *n* volcanic ashes used in hydraulic cement.

pp *abbr* = past participle; (*mus*) pianissimo.

pp. *abbr* = pages.

p.p. *abbr* = per pro.

ppm *abbr* (*chem*) parts per million.

PPS *abbr* = post (additional) postscript.

PR *abbr* = public relations; proportional representation.

Pr (*chem symbol*) praseodymium.

practicable /ˈpræktɪkəbəl/ *adj* able to be practised; possible, feasible.—**practicability** *n*.—**practicably** *adv*.

practical /ˈpræktɪkəl/ *adj* concerned with action, not theory; workable; suitable; trained by practice; virtual, in effect.

practicality /-'kælıti/ *n* (*pl* **practicalities**) the condition of being practical; a practical feature or aspect.

practical joke *n* a prank intended to embarrass or to cause discomfort.

practically /'præktıklı/ *adv* in a practical manner; virtually.

practice /'præktıs/ *n* action; habit, custom; repetition and exercise to gain skill; the exercise of a profession.

practise /'præktıs/ *vti* to repeat an exercise to acquire skill; to put into practice; to do habitually or frequently; (*profession*) to work at.

practised /-tıst/ *adj* acquired by practice; proficient; experienced.

practitioner /præk'tıʃənər/ *n* a person who practises a profession.

praedial /'pri:dıəl/ *adj* pertaining to land or landed property.— *also* **predial**.

praetor /'pri:tər/ or /-tɔr/ *n* (*ancient Rome*) a magistrate, ranking next to a consul.

pragmatic /præg'mætık/ *adj* practical; testing the validity of all concepts by their practical results.—**pragmatically** *adv*.

pragmatics /præg'mætıks/ *n sing* the study of the relationship of signs and symbols and their use; (*linguistics*) the study of meaning derived from context.

pragmatism /'prægmə,tızəm/ *n* the judging of events or actions by their results, *esp* in politics; pragmatic behaviour; (*philos*) a theory that judges the truth of a doctrine by the conduct resulting from belief in it.—**pragmatist** *n*.—**pragmatistic** *adj*.

prairie /'preri/ *n* a large area of level or rolling land predominantly in grass; a dry treeless plateau; (*usu pl*) the region of central US and southern Canada that consists of such land.

prairie chicken *n* a grouse of the North American prairies.

prairie dog *n* a burrowing rodent related to the marmot.

prairie wolf *n* the coyote.

praise /preız/ *vt* to express approval of, to commend; to glorify, to worship. • *vi* to express praise. • *n* commendation; glorification.—**praiser** *n*.

praiseworthy /'preız,wərðı/ *adj* deserving praise; commendable.—**praiseworthily** *adv*.—**praiseworthiness** *n*.

praline /'preıli:n/ or /'prɒ-/ *n* a confection made of nuts and sugar.

prance /præns/ *vi* (*horse*) to spring on the hind legs, bound; (*person*) to walk or ride in a showy manner; to swagger. • *n* a prancing; a caper.—**prancer** *n*.—**prancingly** *adv*.

prank[1] /præŋk/ *n* a mischievous trick or joke; a ludicrous act.—**prankster** *n*.

prank[2] *vti* to adorn, to deck; to dress up showily.

prase /preız/ *n* a green, transparent form of quartz.

praseodymium /,preızıə'dımıəm/ *n* a silvery-white metallic element.

prate /preıt/ *vti* to chatter, talk idly.—**prater** *n*.

pratincole /'præntıŋ,koːl/ *n* a bird resembling a swallow.

prattle /'prætəl/ *vti* to talk in a childish manner; to babble. • *n* empty chatter.—**prattler** *n*.

prawn /prɒn/ *n* an edible marine shrimp-like crustacean. • *vi* to fish for prawns.—**prawner** *n*.

praxis /'præksıs/ *n* (*pl* **praxises, praxes**) practice; an example, or set of examples, for an exercise.

pray /preı/ *vti* to offer prayers to God; to implore.

prayer[1] /prer/ *n supplication*, entreaty, praise or thanks to God; the form of this; the act of praying; (*pl*) devotional services; something prayed for.

prayer[2] *n* one who prays.

prayerful /'prer,ful/ *adj* given to prayer; devout.—**prayerfully** *adv*.

pre- /pri/ *prefix* before, beforehand; previous to; surpassingly.

preach /pri:tʃ/ *vi* to advocate in an earnest or moralizing way. • *vt* to deliver a sermon; (*patience, etc*) to advocate.

preacher /'pri:tʃər/ *n* one who preaches, *esp* a Protestant clergyman.

preachify /'pri:tʃı,faı/ *vi* (*inf*) to hold forth tediously.—**preachification** *n*.

preachy /'pri:tʃı/ *adj* (**preachier, preachiest**) (*inf*) fond of moralizing or preaching.

preamble /pri:'æmbəl/ or /'pri:-/ *n* an introductory part to a document, speech, or story, stating its purpose.—**preambulary** *adj*.

prearrange /,pri:ə'reındʒ/ *vt* to arrange beforehand.—**prearrangement** *n*.

prebend /'prebənd/ *n* a stipend granted to a canon or member of the chapter by a cathedral.—**prebendal** *adj*.

prebendary /'prebəndərı/ *n* (*pl* **prebendaries**) someone who holds a prebend.

precancerous /pri:'kænsərəs/ *adj* likely to become cancerous.

precarious /prı'kerıəs/ *adj* dependent on chance; insecure; dangerous.—**precariously** *adv*.—**precariousness** *n*.

precatory /'prekə,tɔ:rı/, **precative** /'prekə,tıv/ *adj* suppliant, expresssing a wish.

precaution /prı'kɒʃən/ *n* a preventive measure; care taken beforehand; careful foresight.—**precautionary** *adj*.

precede /prı'si:d/ *vti* to be, come or go before in time, place, order, rank, or importance.

precedence /'presıdəns/ *n* priority; the right of higher rank.

precedent /'presıdənt/ *n* a previous and parallel case serving as an example; (*law*) a decision, etc, serving as a rule. • *adj* preceding; previous.—**precedented** *adj*.—**precedently** *adv*.

precedential /-ʃəl/ *adj* serving as a precedent; having precedence.

preceding /-ıŋ/ *adj* coming or going before; former.

precentor /prı'sentər/ *n* the leader of a choir in a cathedral or church.

precept /'pri:sept/ *n* a rule of moral conduct; a maxim; an order issued by a legally constituted authority to a subordinate.

preceptive /-tıv/ *adj* of or using precepts; didactic.—**preceptively** *adv*.

preceptor /-ər/ *n* an instructor or teacher.—**preceptress** *nf*.

precession /prı'seʃən/ *n* going before, in advance of—**precessional** *adj*.

precinct /'pri:sıŋkt/ *n* (*usu pl*) an enclosure between buildings, walls, etc; a limited area; an urban area where traffic is prohibited; (*pl*) environs; (*US*) a police district or a subdivision of a voting ward.

precious /'preʃəs/ *adj* of great cost or value; beloved; very fastidious; affected; thoroughgoing. • *adv* (*sl*) very.—**preciously** *adv*.—**preciousness** *n*.

precious metal *n* gold, silver, or platinum.

precious stone *n* a diamond, emerald, ruby, sapphire, pearl, and sometimes black opal; a gem.

precipice /'presıpıs/ *n* a cliff or overhanging rock face.

precipitant /prı'sıpıtənt/ *adj* falling headlong; hasty, impetuous. • *n* (*chem*) a substance causing precipitation.—**precipitance, precipitancy** *n*.

precipitate /prı'sıpı,teıt/ *vti* to throw from a height; to cause to happen suddenly or too soon; (*chem*) to separate out; to rain; to fall as rain, snow, dew, etc.—**precipitately** *adv*.—**precipitateness** *n*.—**precipitator** *n*.

precipitation /prı,sıpı'teıʃən/ *n* the act of precipitating; undue haste; rain, snow, etc; the amount of this.

precipitous /prı'sıpıtəs/ *adj* of or like a precipice; sheer, steep.—**precipitously** *adv*.—**precipitousness** *n*.

précis /'preısi:/ *n* (*pl* **précis**) a summary or abstract. • *vt* to make a précis of.

precise /prı'saıs/ *adj* clearly defined, exact; accurate; punctilious; particular.—**precisely** *adv*.—**preciseness** *n*.

precision /prı'sıʒən/ *n* the quality of being precise; accuracy. • *adj* (*machines*) having a high degree of accuracy.

preclude /prı'klu:d/ *vt* to rule out in advance; to make impossible.—**preclusion** *n*.—**preclusive** *adj*.

precocious /prı'koːʃəs/ *adj* prematurely ripe or developed.—**precociously** *adv*.—**precociousness** *n*.

precocity /-'kɒsıtı/ *n* the condition of being precocious, precociousness; early development, *esp* of a child's mind.

precognition /,pri:kɒg'nıʃən/ *n* the supposed extrasensory perception of a future event; clairvoyance.—**precognitive** *adj*.

pre-Columbian /,pri:kə'lʌmbıən/ *adj* of or originating in the Americas before their discovery by Christopher Columbus.

preconceive /,pri:kən'si:v/ *vt* to form an idea or opinion of before actual experience.

preconception /,pri:kən'sepʃən/ *n* the act of preconceiving; an opinion formed without actual knowledge.

precondition /,pri:kən'dıʃən/ *n* a requirement that must be met beforehand, a prerequisite. • *vt* (*an organism, a patient*) to prepare to behave or react in a certain way under certain conditions.

precursor /prı'kərsər/ *n* a predecessor; a substance from which another substance is formed.—**precursory** *adj*.

predacious, predaceous /prı'deıʃəs/ *adj* living on prey.—**predaciousness, predaceousness, predacity** *n*.

predate /pri:'deıt/ *vt* to antedate.

predator /'predətər/ n a person who preys, plunders or devours; a carnivorous animal.

predatory /'predətəri/ adj living on prey, of or relating to a predator; characterized by hunting or plundering.—**predatorily** adv.—**predatoriness** n.

predecease /ˌpriːdɪˈsiːs/ vt to die before (another).

predecessor /'priːdəˌsesər/ or /'priː-/ n a former holder of a position or office; an ancestor.

predella /prɪˈdelə/ n (pl **predellae**) a platform for, or shelf upon, an altar; a painting, or sculpture, on such a platform or shelf.

predestinarian /priːˌdestɪˈneriən/ adj pertaining to predestination. • n someone who believes in the doctrine of predestination.

predestinate /prɪˈdestɪˌneɪt/ adj predestined. • vt to predestine.

predestination /priːˌdestɪˈneɪʃən/ n a predestining or being predestined; destiny; (theol) the doctrine that God has from all eternity decreed the salvation or damnation of each soul.

predestine /prɪˈdestɪn/ vt to foreordain; to destine beforehand.

predeterminate /ˌpriːdɪˈtɜːmɪnət/ adj predetermined.

predetermine /ˌpriːdɪˈtɜːmɪn/ vt to decide beforehand.—**predetermination** n.

predicable /'predɪkəbəl/ adj which can be predicated.

predicament /prɪˈdɪkəmənt/ n a difficult or embarrassing situation.

predicant /'predɪkənt/ adj pertaining to preaching. • n a preaching friar, esp a Dominican.

predicate /'predɪˌkeɪt/ vt to state as a quality or attribute; to base (on facts, conditions etc). • n (gram) that which is stated about the subject.—**predication** n.

predicative /prɪˈdɪkətɪv/ adj (gram) (adjective, etc) making a statement about the subject of a verb. • n a predicative construction.

predicatory /'predɪkəˌtɔːri/ adj of or given to preaching.

predict /prɪˈdɪkt/ vt to foretell; to state (what one believes will happen).—**predictor** n.

predictable /prɪˈdɪktəbəl/ adj able to be predicted or anticipated; lacking originality.—**predictability** n.—**predictably** adv.

prediction /prɪˈdɪkʃən/ n the act of predicting; that which is predicted; a forecast or prophecy.—**predictive** adj.—**predictively** adv.

predigest /ˌpriːdaɪˈdʒest/ vt to treat (food) artificially to make easily digestible.

predilection /ˌpriːdɪˈlekʃən/ n partiality, liking for.

predispose /ˌpriːdɪˈspoːz/ vt to incline beforehand; (disease, etc) to make susceptible to.—**predisposition** n.

predominant /prɪˈdɒmɪnənt/ adj ruling over, controlling; influencing.—**predominance, predominancy** n.

predominantly /-li/ adv mainly.

predominate /prɪˈdɒmɪˌneɪt/ vt to rule over; to have influence or control over; to prevail; to be greater in number, intensity, etc.—**predomination** n.—**predominator** n.

pre-eminent, preeminent /prɪˈemɪnənt/ adj distinguished above others; outstanding.—**pre-eminence, preeminence** n.—**pre-eminently, preeminently** adv.

pre-empt, preempt /prɪˈempt/ or /-ˈemt/ vt to take action to check other action beforehand; in the US, to gain the right to buy (public land) by settling on it; to seize before anyone else can; to replace; (in bridge) to bid highly to exclude bids from opponents.—**pre-emptor, preemptor** n.—**pre-emptory, preemptory** adj.

pre-emption, preemption /prɪˈempʃən/ n a pre-empting or being pre-empted; a buying or the right to buy before the opportunity is given to others; such a purchase.

pre-emptive /prɪˈemptɪv/ adj (bridge) denoting a high bid to exclude bids from the opposition.—**pre-emptively** adv.

preen /priːn/ vti (birds) to clean and trim the feathers; to congratulate (oneself) for achievement; to groom (oneself); to gloat.—**preener** n.

prefab /'priːfæb/ n (inf) a prefabricated part or building.

prefabricate /priːˈfæbrɪˌkeɪt/ vt (house, etc) to build in standardized sections for shipment and quick assembly; to produce artificially.—**prefabrication** n.—**prefabricator** n.

preface /'prefəs/ n an introduction or preliminary explanation; a foreword or introduction to a book; a preamble. • vt to serve as a preface; to introduce.—**prefacer** n.

prefatory /'prefəˌtɔːri/ adj of or pertaining to a preface; introductory.—**prefatorily** adv.

prefect /'priːfekt/ n a person placed in authority over others; a student monitor in a school; in some countries, an administrative official.—**prefectorial** adj.

prefecture /'priːfektʃʊr/ n the office, district, residence, or tenure of a prefect.—**prefectural** adj.

prefer /prɪˈfɜːr/ vt (**preferring, preferred**) to like better; to promote, advance; to put before a court, etc, for consideration.—**preferrer** n.

preferable /'prefərəbəl/ or /'prefrəbəl/, /prəˈfɜːrəbəl/ adj deserving preference; superior; more desirable.—**preferably** adv.

preference /'prefərəns/ n the act of preferring, choosing, or favouring one above another; that which is chosen or preferred; prior right; advantage given to one person, country, etc, over others.

preferential /ˌprefəˈrenʃəl/ adj giving or receiving preference.—**preferentialism** n.—**preferentially** adv.

preferment /prɪˈfɜːrmənt/ n advancement; promotion to a higher post.

prefiguration /ˌpriːfɪɡjʊˈreɪʃən/ n the act of prefiguring.—**prefigurative** adj.

prefigure /priːˈfɪɡjʊr/ vt to suggest in advance, foreshadow; to imagine beforehand.

prefix /'priːfɪks/ vt to put at the beginning of or before; to put as an introduction. • n a syllable or group of syllables placed at the beginning of a word, affecting its meaning.—**prefixal** adj.—**prefixally** adv.

preglacial /priːˈɡleɪʃəl/ or /-sɪəl/ adj existing before a glacial period.

pregnable /'preɡnəbəl/ adj capable of being attacked and captured.

pregnancy /'preɡnənsi/ n (pl **pregnancies**) the state of being pregnant; the period of this.

pregnant /'preɡnənt/ adj having a foetus in the womb; significant, meaningful; imaginative; filled (with) or rich (in).—**pregnantly** adv.

prehensile /prɪˈhensaɪl/ adj capable of grasping, esp by wrapping around.—**prehensility** n.

prehension /prɪˈhenʃən/ n grasping; the ability to grasp.

prehistoric /ˌpriːhɪˈstɒrɪk/, **prehistorical** /-kəl/ adj of the period before written records began; (inf) old-fashioned.—**prehistorically** adv.

prehistory /priːˈhɪstəri/ n (pl **prehistories**) events that took place before recorded history; the study of prehistoric events; the history of the earlier background of an incident, etc.—**prehistorian** n.

prejudge /priːˈdʒʌdʒ/ vt to pass judgment on before a trial; to form a premature opinion.—**prejudger** n.—**prejudgment, prejudgement** n.

prejudice /'predʒʊdɪs/ n a judgment or opinion made without adequate knowledge; bias; intolerance or hatred of other races, etc; (law) injury or disadvantage due to another's action. • vt to affect or injure through prejudice.—**prejudiced** adj.

prejudicial /ˌpredʒʊˈdɪʃəl/ adj causing prejudice; detrimental, damaging.—**prejudicially** adv.

prelacy /'preləsi/ n (pl **prelacies**) the office or status of a prelate; prelates collectively; church government by prelates.

prelate /'prelət/ n a church dignity with episcopal authority.—**prelatic** adj.

prelature /-lətʃər/ n the office or status of a prelate.

preliminary /prɪˈlɪmɪneri/ adj preparatory; introductory. • n (pl **preliminaries**) an event preceding another; a preliminary step or measure; (in school) a preparatory examination.—**preliminarily** adv.

prelims /'priːlɪmz/ or /prɪˈlɪmz/ npl the front matter of a book, before the main text; preliminary school exams.

prelude /'preɪluːd/ or /-ljuːd/, /'prel-/ n an introductory act or event; an event preceding another of greater importance; (mus) a movement which acts as an introduction. • vti to serve as a prelude to, to usher in; to play a prelude.—**preludial** adj.—**prelusion** n.—**prelusive, prelusory** adj.

premarital /prɪˈmerɪtəl/ adj (sex) taking place before marriage.

premature /priːməˈtʃʊr/ or /'prem-/ adj occurring before the expected or normal time; too early, hasty.—**prematurely** adv.—**prematurity** n.

premeditate /prɪˈmedɪteɪt/ vt (crime, etc) to plan in advance.—**premeditatedly** adv.—**premeditative** adj.—**premeditator** n.

premeditation /-ˈteɪʃən/ n deliberation or thought before doing something; (law) the plotting of a crime beforehand, demonstrating intent to commit it.

premier /'pri:mjiːr/ or /'pri:mjər/, /'pri:miːr/, /'premjər/ *adj* principal; first. • *n* the head of a government, a prime minister.— **premiership** *n*.

premiere, première /prem'jer/ or /prə'mjer/, /'premjer/, /'pri:mjiːr/, /-'mjiːr/ *n* the first public performance of a play, film, etc. • *vt* to give a premiere of. • *vi* to have a first performance; to appear for the first time as a star performer.

premise /'premis/ *n* a proposition on which reasoning is based; something assumed or taken for granted.—*also* **premiss**; *(pl)* a piece of land and its buildings. • *vt* to state as an introduction; to postulate; to base on certain assumptions.

premium /'pri:miəm/ *n* a reward, *esp* an inducement to buy; a periodical payment for insurance; excess over an original price; something given free or at a reduced price with a purchase; a high value or value in excess of expectation. • *adj (goods)* high quality.

premonition /ˌpremə'nɪʃən/ *n* a foreboding; a feeling of something about to happen.—**premonitory** *adj*.

prenatal /pri'neɪtəl/ or /'pri:-/ *adj* before birth.

preoccupation /priɒkjʊ'peɪʃən/ *n* a concern that prevents thought of other things; mental absorption; business that takes precedence; preoccupancy.

preoccupied /pri'ɒkjʊpaɪd/ *adj* absent-minded, lost in thought; *(with* **with***)* having one's attention completely taken up by.

preoccupy /pri'ɒkjʊˌpaɪ/ *vt* (**preoccupying, preoccupied**) to take possession of beforehand; to engross, fill the thoughts of.

preordain /ˌpri:ɔr'deɪn/ *vt* to ordain beforehand.—**preordination** *n*.

prep /prep/ *abbr* = preparatory school; preparation; preposition.

prep school *see* **preparatory school.**

prepaid *see* **prepay.**

preparation /ˌprepə'reɪʃən/ *n* the act of preparing; a preparatory measure; something prepared, as a medicine, cosmetic, etc.

preparative /prɪ'perətɪv/ *adj* preparatory. • *n* something that prepares the way.—**preparatively** *adv*.

preparatory /'prepərəˌtɔri/ or /prə'perətɔri/ *adj* serving to prepare; introductory. • *adv* by way of preparation; in a preparatory manner.—**preparatorily** *adv*.

preparatory school *n* a private school for children aged 6 to 13 that prepares pupils for public school; in the US, a private secondary school that prepares students for college.—*also* **prep (school).**

prepare /prə'per/ *vt* to make ready in advance; to fit out, equip; to cook; to instruct, teach; to put together. • *vi* to make oneself ready.—**preparedly** *adv*.

prepared /prə'perd/ *adj* subjected to a special process or treatment.

preparedness /-nəs/ *n* the state of being prepared, *esp* for waging war.

prepay /pri'peɪ/ *vt* (**prepaying, prepaid**) to pay in advance.— **prepayment** *n*.

prepense /prɪ'pens/ *adj* premeditated.

preponderant /prə'pɒndərənt/ *adj* being greater in number, amount, importance, weight, etc; predominant.—**preponderance, preponderancy** *n*.—**preponderantly** *adv*.

preponderate /prɪ'pɒndəˌreɪt/ *vi* to be greater in number, amount, influence, etc; to predominate, prevail; to weigh more.—**preponderation** *n*.

preposition /ˌprepə'zɪʃən/ *n* a word used before a noun or pronoun to show its relation to another part of the sentence.— **prepositional** *adj*.

prepositive /pri'pɒzɪtɪv/ *adj, n (gram)* (a particle or word) which can be attached as a prefix to a word.

prepossess /ˌpri:pə'zes/ *vt* to impress favourably; to prejudice.

prepossessing /-ɪŋ/ *adj* impressing favourably; attractive.—**prepossessingly** *adv*.

prepossession /-'zeɪʃən/ *n* a prepossessed state; a preconceived opinion or judgement.

preposterous /prɪ'pɒstərəs/ *adj* ridiculous; laughable; absurd.— **preposterously** *adv*.—**preposterousness** *n*.

prepotency /pri'po:tənsi/ *n* the state of being prepotent; *(biol)* a dominant hereditary influence.

prepotent /prɪ'po:tənt/ *adj* very or more powerful; *(biol)* having a dominant hereditary influence.

prepuce /'pri:pju:s/ *n* the loose skin at the end of the penis.—*also* **foreskin.**

pre-Raphaelite /pri'ræfiəˌlaɪt/ *adj, n* (a member) of a 19th-century school of artists who imitated the Italian style of painting before Raphael, using brilliant colour and minute detail.

prerecord /ˌpri:rɪ'kɔrd/ *vt (radio, TV programme)* to record in advance for later broadcasting.—**prerecorded** *adj*.

prerequisite /pri'rekwɪzɪt/ *n* a condition, etc, that must be fulfilled prior to something else. • *adj* required beforehand.

prerogative /prə'rɒgətɪv/ *n* a privilege or right accorded through office or hereditary rank.

presage /'presədʒ/ *n* a foreboding or presentiment; an omen. • *vt* to foretell; to have a presentiment of.

presbyopia /ˌprezbi:'opiːə/ *n* a condition of long-sightedness, *usu* progressing with age, in which near objects are seen indistinctly, caused by a change in the refractive power of the eye due to the flattening of the lens.

presbyter /'presbɪtər/ or /'prez-/ *n* in the Presbyterian Church, an elder; in the Episcopal Church, a priest or minister.—**presbyterial** *adj*.

presbyterian /ˌprezbɪ'ti:riən/ or /'prez-/ *adj* of or denoting government by presbyteries; *(with cap)* of a Presbyterian Church. • *n* a member of a Presbyterian Church.—**Presbyterianism** *n*.

presbytery /'presbɪtri/ or /'prez-/ *n (pl* **presbyteries***)* in a Presbyterian Church a court composed of ministers and one elder from each church within a district; a district so represented; the eastern part of the chancel of a church; a Roman Catholic priest's house.

preschool /'pri:sku:l/ *adj* of or for a child between infancy and school age.

prescience /'presiəns/ *n* foreknowledge.—**prescient** *adj*.

prescribe /prə'skraɪb/ *vt* to designate; to ordain; *(rules)* to lay down; *(medicine, treatment)* to order, advise.—**prescriber** *n*.

prescript /'priskrɪpt/ *n* an ordnance or decree. • *adj* prescribed, directed.

prescription /prə'skrɪpʃən/ *n* act of prescribing; *(med)* a written instruction by a physician for the preparation of a drug; *(law)* establishment of a right or title through long use.

prescriptive /prɪ'skrɪptɪv/ *adj* prescribing, ordering, advising; based on long use, traditional.—**prescriptively** *adv*.

preselect /ˌpri:sɪ'lekt/ *vt* to select beforehand, *usu* according to a particular criterion.—**preselection** *n*.—**preselective** *adj*.

presence /'prezəns/ *n* being present; immediate surroundings; personal appearance and bearing; impressive bearing, personality, etc; something (as a spirit) felt or believed to be present.

presence of mind *n* readiness of resource in an emergency, etc; the ability to say the right thing.

present[1] /'prezənt/ *adj* being at the specified place; existing or happening now; *(gram)* denoting action or state now or action that is always true. • *n* the time being; now; the present tense.

present[2] *n* a gift.

present[3] /prə'zent/ *vt* to introduce someone, *esp* socially; *(a play, etc)* to bring before the public, exhibit; to make a gift or award; to show; to perform; *(law)* to lay a charge before a court; *(weapon)* to point in a particular direction. • *vi* to present a weapon; to become manifest; to come forward as a patient.

presentable /prɪ'zentəbəl/ *adj* of decent appearance; fit to go into company.—**presentability** *n*.—**presentably** *adv*.

presentation /ˌprezən'teɪʃən/ or /ˌpri:-/ *n* act of presenting; a display or exhibition; style of presenting; something offered or given; a description or persuasive account; *(med)* the position of a foetus in the uterus.—**presentational** *adj*.

presentative /-'teɪtɪv/ *adj (of benefice)* admitting presentation by patron; *(philos)* able to be apprehended directly by the mind.

presenter /-ər/ *n* a person who presents someone or something; *(radio, TV)* a person who introduces a show; an announcer.

presentiment /prɪ'zentɪmənt/ or /-'sentɪmənt/ *n* a premonition, apprehension, *esp* of evil.

presently /'prezəntli/ *adv* in a short while, soon.

presentment /prɪ'zentmənt/ *n* the act of presenting; something which is presented; a representation or delineation; the laying of a formal statement before a court or authority.

preservation /ˌprezər'veɪʃən/ *n* the act of preserving or securing; a state of being preserved or repaired.

preservationist /-ɪst/ *n* someone who undertakes or advocates preservation (as of a biological species or a historic landmark).

preservative /prə'zərvətɪv/ *adj* preserving. • *n* something that preserves or has the power of preserving, *esp* an additive.

preserve /prəˈzərv/ *vt* to keep safe from danger; to protect; (*food*) to can, pickle, or prepare for future use; to keep or reserve for personal or special use. • *vi* to make preserves; to raise and protect game for sport. • *n* (*usu pl*) fruit preserved by cooking in sugar; an area restricted for the protection of natural resources, *esp* one used for regulated hunting, etc; something regarded as reserved for certain persons.—**preservable** *adj*.—**preserver** *n*.

preset /priˈset/ *vt* (**presetting, preset**) to set (the controls of an electrical device) in advance.

preside /prɪˈzaɪd/ *vi* to take the chair or hold the position of authority; to take control or exercise authority.—**presider** *n*.

presidency /ˈprezɪdənsi/ *n* (*pl* **presidencies**) the office, dignity, term, jurisdiction or residence of a president.

president /ˈprezɪdənt/ *n* the head of state of a republic; the highest officer of a company, club, etc.—**presidential** *adj*.—**presidentially** *adv*.

president-elect *n* a president who has been elected to office but has not yet taken up the post.

presidio /priˈsɪdɪˌoː/ *n* (*pl* **presidios**) (*Spain*) a fort or military establishment.

presidium /prɪˈzɪdɪəm/ or /-ˈsɪdɪəm/ *n* (*pl* **presidiums, presidia**) a presiding committee in a communist organization.

press /pres/ *vt* to act on with steady force or weight; to push against, squeeze, compress, etc; to squeeze the juice, etc from; (*clothes, etc*) to iron; to embrace closely; to force, compel; to entreat; to emphasize; to trouble; to urge on; (*record*) to make from a matrix. • *vi* to weigh down; to crowd closely; to go forward with determination. • *n* pressure, urgency, etc; a crowd; a machine for crushing, stamping, etc; a machine for printing; a printing or publishing establishment; the gathering and distribution of news and those who perform these functions; newspapers collectively; any of various pressure devices; an upright closet for storing clothes.

press conference *n* a group interview given to members of the press by a politician, celebrity, etc.

pressing /ˈpresɪŋ/ *adj* urgent; calling for immediate attention; importunate. • *n* a number of records made at one time from a master.—**pressingly** *adv*.

pressman /ˈpresmən/ *n* (*pl* **pressmen**) a journalist; an operator of a printing press.

pressmark /ˈpresˌmɑrk/ *n* a number showing a book's place in a library.

press secretary *n* a person officially in charge of relations with the press for a *usu* prominent public figure.

press-up *n* an exercise involving raising and lowering the body with the arms.

pressure /ˈpreʃər/ *n* the act of pressing; a compelling force; a moral force; compression; urgency; constraint; (*physics*) force per unit of area. • *vt* to pressurize.

pressure cooker *n* a strong, sealed pan in which food can be cooked quickly by steam under pressure; (*inf*) a situation beset with emotional or social pressure.

pressure group *n* a group of people organized to alert public opinion, legislators, etc, to a particular area of interest.

pressure point *n* a point on the body where a blood vessel can be compressed to check bleeding.

pressurize /ˈpreʃəˌraɪz/ *vt* to keep nearly normal atmospheric pressure inside an aeroplane, etc, as at high altitudes; to exert pressure on; to attempt to compel, press.—**pressurization** *n*.—**pressurizer** *n*.

prestidigitation /ˌprestɪˈdɪdʒɪˌteɪʃən/ *n* sleight of hand.—**prestidigitator** *n*.

prestige /preˈstiːdʒ/ or /-ˈstiːʒ/ *n* standing in the eyes of people; commanding position in people's minds.

prestigious /preˈstiːdʒəs/ or /-ˈstɪdʒəs/ *adj* imparting prestige or distinction.

prestissimo /preˈstɪsˌmoː/ *adj, adv* (*mus*) very fast.

presto /ˈprestoː/ *adj, adv* (*mus*) quick; immediately. • *n* (*pl* **prestos**) (*mus*) a lively passage.

presumable /prɪˈzuːməbəl/ or /-zjuː-/ *adj* that may be presumed or taken to be true.

presumably /-məbli/ *adv* as may be presumed.

presume /prɪˈzuːm/ or /-ˈzjuːm/ *vt* to take for granted, suppose. • *vi* to assume to be true; to act without permission; to take liberties; (*with* **on, upon**) to take advantage of.—**presumedly** *adv*.—**presumer** *n*.

presuming /-ɪŋ/ *adj* venturing without permission; presumptuous.—**presumingly** *adv*.

presumption /prɪˈzempʃən/ *n* a supposition; a thing presumed; a strong probability; effrontery.

presumptive /prɪˈzemptɪv/ *adj* assumed in the absence of contrary evidence; probable.—**presumptively** *adv*.

presumptuous /prɪˈzemptʃuːəs/ *adj* tending to presume; bold; forward.—**presumptuously** *adv*.—**presumptuousness** *n*.

presuppose /ˌpriːsəˈpoːz/ *vt* to assume beforehand; to involve as a necessary prior condition.—**presupposition** *n*.

pretence /ˈpriːtens/ or /prɪˈtens/ *n* the act of pretending; a hypocritical show; a fraud, a sham.—*also* **pretense**.

pretend /prɪˈtend/ *vti* to claim, represent, or assert falsely; to feign, make believe; to lay claim (to).

pretended /prɪˈtendɪd/ *adj* feigned; ostensible; untrue; insincerely asserted or claimed.—**pretendedly** *adv*.

pretender /prɪˈtendər/ *n* a person who makes a pretence; a claimant to a title.

pretense *see* **pretence**.

pretension /prɪˈtenʃən/ *n* a false claim; affectation; assumption of superiority.

pretentious /prɪˈtenʃəs/ *adj* claiming great importance; ostentatious.—**pretentiously** *adv*.—**pretentiousness** *n*.

preterit, preterite /ˈpretərɪt/ (*gram*) *adj* denoting past action. • *n* the past tense.

preterition /ˌpretəˈrɪʃən/ *n* omission; (*theology*) the doctrine of the passing over of the non-elect by God.

preternatural /ˌpriːtərˈnætʃərəl/ or /-nætʃrəl/ *adj* out of the regular course of things, abnormal.

pretext /ˈpriːtekst/ *n* a pretended reason to conceal a true one; an excuse.

prettify /ˈprɪtɪˌfaɪ/ *vt* (**prettifying, prettified**) to make pretty.—**prettifaction** *n*.

pretty /ˈprɪti/ *adj* (**prettier, prettiest**) attractive in a dainty, graceful way. • *adv* (*inf*) fairly, moderately. • *n* (*pl* **pretties**) (*inf*) a pretty or pleasing person or thing. • *vt* (**prettying, prettied**) (*with* **up**) (*inf*) to make pretty.—**prettily** *adv*.—**prettiness** *n*.

pretzel /ˈpretsəl/ *n* a hard, brittle, salted biscuit, often formed in a loose knot.

prevail /prɪˈveɪl/ *vi* to overcome; to predominate; to be customary or in force.

prevailing /-ɪŋ/ *adj* generally accepted, widespread; predominant.—**prevailingly** *adv*.

prevalent /ˈprevələnt/ *adj* current; predominant; widely practised or experienced.—**prevalence** *n*.—**prevalently** *adv*.

prevaricate /prɪˈverɪˌkeɪt/ *vi* to make evasive or misleading statements.—**prevarication** *n*.—**prevaricator** *n*.

prevenient /prɪˈviːnɪənt/ *adj* preceding; anticipating; aiming at prevention.

prevent /prɪˈvent/ *vt* to keep from happening; to hinder.—**preventable, preventible** *adj*.—**preventably, preventibly** *adv*.—**preventer** *n*.

prevention /prɪˈvenʃən/ *n* a preventing or being prevented; a hindrance; a preventive.

preventive /prɪˈventɪv/, **preventative** /prɪˈventətɪv/ *adj* serving to prevent, precautionary. • *n* something used to prevent disease.—**preventively** *adv*.—**preventiveness** *n*.

preview /ˈpriːvjuː/ *n* an advance, restricted showing, as of a film; a showing of scenes from a film to advertise it. • *vt* to view or show in advance of public presentation; to give a preliminary survey.

previous /ˈpriːvɪəs/ *adj* coming before in time or order; prior, former.—**previously** *adv*.—**previousness** *n*.

prewar *adj* before a war.

prey /preɪ/ *n* an animal killed for food by another; a victim. • *vi* (*with* **on, upon**) to seize and devour prey; (*person*) to victimize; to weigh heavily on the mind.

priapism /ˈpraɪəˌpɪzəm/ *n* (*med*) abnormally prolonged penile erection.

price /praɪs/ *n* the amount, *usu* in money, paid for anything; the cost of obtaining some benefit; value, worth. • *vt* to set the price of something; to estimate a price; (*with* **out of the market**) to deprive by raising prices excessively.

priceless /-ləs/ *adj* very expensive; invaluable; (*inf*) very amusing, odd, or absurd.—**pricelessly** *adv*.

price war *n* a period of commercial competition marked by repeated cutting of prices among competitors.

pricey /'praɪsi/ *adj* (**pricier, priciest**) (*inf*) expensive.—*also* **pricy**.

prick /prɪk/ *n* a sharp point; a puncture or piercing made by a sharp point; the wound or sensation inflicted; a qualm (of conscience); (*offensive*) a spiteful person *usu* with authority. • *vti* to affect with anguish, grief, or remorse; to pierce slightly; to cause a sharp pain to; to goad, spur; (*the ears*) to erect; (*with* **out**) to transfer seedlings.

pricker /-ər/ *n* a thing that pricks, *esp* a prickle or thorn.

pricket /'prɪkɪt/ *n* a buck in its second year.

prickle /'prɪkəl/ *n* a thorn, spine or bristle; a pricking sensation. • *vti* to feel or cause to feel a pricking sensation.

prickly /'prɪkli/ *adj* (**pricklier, prickliest**) having prickles; tingling; irritable.—**prickliness** *n*.

prickly heat *n* a skin eruption caused by inflammation of the sweat glands.

pride /praɪd/ *n* feeling of self-worth or esteem; excessive self-esteem; conceit; a sense of one's own importance; a feeling of elation due to success; the cause of this; splendour; a herd (of lions). • *vti* (*reflex*) (*with* **in** *or* **on**)to be proud of; to take credit for.—**prideful** *adj*.

priedieu /'priːdjuː/ *or* /-duː/ *n* a desk with a low rest for kneeling upon while working or praying.

prier /'praɪər/ *n* one who pries.—*also* **pryer**.

priest /priːst/ *n* in various churches, a person authorized to perform sacred rites; an Anglican, Eastern Orthodox, or Roman Catholic clergyman ranking below a bishop.

priestcraft /'priːstkræft/ *n* the work of a priest and its related skills; (*derog*) the schemes used by priests to get power and wealth.

priestess /'priːstes/ *n* a priest who is a woman; a woman regarded as a leader (as of a movement).

priesthood /'priːsthʊd/ *n* the office of priest; priests collectively.

priestly /'priːstli/ *adj* (**priestlier, priestliest**) of or befitting a priest.—**priestliness** *n*.

prig /prɪg/ *n* a smug, self-righteous person.—**priggery, priggism** *n*.

priggish /-ɪʃ/ *adj* tiresomely precise; strait-laced.—**priggishly** *adv*.—**priggishness** *n*.

prim /prɪm/ *adj* (**primmer, primmest**) proper, formal and precise in manner; demure. • *vti* (**primming, primmed**) to make prim; to assume a prim expression.—**primly** *adv*.—**primness** *n*.

prima ballerina /ˌpriːməˌbæləˈriːnə/ *n* (*pl* **prima ballerinas**) the principal female dancer in a ballet company.

primacy /'praɪməsi/ *n* (*pl* **primacies**) the office of primate; the state of being first.

prima donna /ˌpriːməˈdɒnə/ *n* (*pl* **prima donnas**) the leading female singer in an opera; (*inf*) a temperamental person.

prima facie /ˌpraɪməˈfeɪʃi/ *adv* at first sight. • *adj* true, valid, or sufficient at first impression; self-evident; legally sufficient to establish a fact unless disproved.

primal /'praɪməl/ *adj* primeval; original; primitive; fundamental.

primarily /praɪˈmerɪli/ *adv* mainly.

primary /'praɪməri/ *or* /'praɪməri/ *adj* first; earliest; original; first in order of time; chief; elementary. • *n* (*pl* **primaries**) a person or thing that is highest in rank, importance, etc; a preliminary election at which candidates are chosen for the final election.

primary colour *n* one of the three colours from which all others except black can be obtained: red, blue, and yellow.

primary school *n* a school for children below age 11; in the US, a school for children up to the third or fourth grade of elementary school and sometimes kindergarten.

primate[1] /'praɪmeɪt/ *n* any of the highest order of mammals, including man.—**primatial** *adj*.

primate[2] /'praɪmət/ *n* an archbishop or the highest ranking bishop in a province, etc.—**primateship** *n*.

prime[1] /praɪm/ *adj* first in rank, importance, or quality; chief; (*math*) of a number, divisible only by itself and 1. • *n* the best time; the height of perfection; full maturity; full health and strength.—**primeness** *n*.

prime[2] *vt* to prepare or make something ready; to pour liquid into (a pump) or powder into (a firearm); to paint on a primer.

prime minister *n* the head of the government in a parliamentary democracy.

primer[1] /'praɪmər/ *n* a simple book for teaching; a small introductory book on a subject.

primer[2] *n* a detonating device; a first coat of paint or oil.

prime time *n* (*radio, TV*) the hours when the largest audience is available.

primeval /praɪˈmiːvəl/ *adj* of the first age of the world; primitive.

priming /'praɪmɪŋ/ *n* a preliminary coating (of paint); a powder used to explode a charge.

primipara /ˌpraɪˈmɪpərə/ *n* (*pl* **primiparas, primiparae**) (*obstetrics*) a woman due to give birth to her first child, or who has given birth to only one child.—**primiparous** *adj*.

primitive /'prɪmɪtɪv/ *adj* of the beginning or the earliest times; crude; simple; basic. • *n* a primitive person or thing.—**primitively** *adv*.—**primitiveness** *n*.

primo /'priːmoː/ *n* (*pl* **primos, primi**) (*mus*) the leading part in a duet or ensemble.

primogenitor /ˌpraɪmoˈdʒenɪtər/ *n* an ancestor or forefather; an earliest ancestor.

primogeniture /ˌpraɪmoˈdʒenɪtʃər/ *n* the condition of being the first-born child; (*law*) the right of inheritance of the eldest child.—**primogenitary** *adj*.

primordial /praɪˈmɔːdiəl/ *adj* earliest; primeval; fundamental; primitive.—**primordially** *adv*.

primp /prɪmp/ *vti* to dress (oneself) up.

primrose /'prɪmroːz/ *n* a perennial plant with pale yellow flowers.

primula /'prɪmjulə/ *n* any of a genus of plants that includes the primrose, cowslip, etc.

primum mobile /ˌpriːmʊmˈmoːbɪli/ *n* the first movement or cause of motion; (*astron*) the tenth and outermost of the imaginary spheres in the Ptolemaic system, which was supposed to revolve from East to West once every 24 hours, carrying the other spheres with it.

prince /prɪns/ *n* the son of a sovereign; a ruler ranking below a king; the head of a principality; any pre-eminent person.—**princedom** *n*.

princeling /'prɪnslɪŋ/ *n* a young prince; a petty ruler.

princely /'prɪnsli/ *adj* (**princelier, princeliest**) of or like a prince; lavish, generous; regal.—**princeliness** *n*.

princess /'prɪnses/ *or* /-'ses/ *n* a daughter of a sovereign; the wife of a prince; one outstanding in a specified respect.

principal /'prɪnsɪpəl/ *adj* first in rank or importance; chief. • *n* a principal person; a person who organizes; the head of a college or school; the leading player in a ballet, opera, etc; (*law*) the person who commits a crime; a person for whom another acts as agent; a capital sum lent or invested; a main beam or rafter.—**principalship** *n*.

principality /ˌprɪnsɪˈpælɪti/ *n* (*pl* **principalities**) the position of responsibility of a principal; the rank and territory of a prince.

principally /'prɪnsɪpæli/ *adv* mainly.

principle /'prɪnsɪpəl/ *n* a basic truth; a law or doctrine used as a basis for others; a moral code of conduct; a chemical constituent with a characteristic quality; a scientific law explaining a natural action; the method of a thing's working.

principled /'prɪnsɪpəld/ *adj* having, or acting in line with, moral principles.

prink /prɪŋk/ *vti* to dress (oneself) up; to preen oneself.

print /prɪnt/ *vti* to stamp (a mark, letter, etc) on a surface; to produce (on paper, etc) the impressions of inked type, etc; to produce (a book, etc); to write in letters resembling printed ones; to make (a photographic print). • *n* a mark made on a surface by pressure; the impression of letters, designs, etc, made from inked type, a plate, or block; an impression made by a photomechanical process; a photographic copy, *esp* from a negative.

printable /'prɪntəbəl/ *adj* able or fit to be printed.—**printability** *n*.

printed circuit *n* an electronic circuit whose connections are printed on metal-coated board.

printer /'prɪntər/ *n* a person engaged in printing; a machine for printing from; a device that produces printout.

printing /'prɪntɪŋ/ *n* the activity, skill, or business of producing printed matter; a style of writing using capital letters; the total number of books, etc, printed at one time.—*also* **impression**.

printout /'prɪntaʊt/ *n* the printed output of a computer.

prior[1] /'praɪər/ *adj* previous; taking precedence (as in importance).

prior[2] *n* the superior ranking below an abbot in a monastery; the head of a house or group of houses in a religious community.—**prioress** *nf*.

priorate /-rət/ *n* the office or status of a prior.

priority /praɪˈɒrɪti/ *n* (*pl* **priorities**) precedence in rank, time, or place; preference; something requiring specified attention.

priory /'praɪəri/ *n* (*pl* **priories**) a religious house under a prior or prioress.

prise, prize /praɪz/ *vt* to force (open, up) with a lever, etc.

prism /'prɪzəm/ n (geom) a solid whose ends are similar, equal, and parallel plane figures and whose sides are parallelograms; a transparent body of this form usu with triangular ends used for dispersing or reflecting light.

prismatic /prɪz'mætɪk/ adj of or like a prism; (colours) formed by a prism; brilliant.—**prismatically** adv.

prison /'prɪzən/ n a building used to house convicted criminals for punishment and suspects remanded in custody while awaiting trial; a penitentiary or jail.

prisoner /'prɪznər/ n a person held in prison or under arrest; a captive; a person confined by a restraint.

prisoner of war n a member of a military force taken prisoner by the enemy during combat.

pristine /'prɪstiːn/ or /-'stiːn/ adj pure; in an original, unspoiled condition.

prithee /'prɪðiː/ interj (arch) pray, please (= "I pray thee").

privacy /'praɪvəsɪ/ or /'prɪ-/ n (pl **privacies**) being private; seclusion; secrecy; one's private life.

private /'praɪvət/ adj of or concerning a particular person or group; not open to or controlled by the public; for an individual person; not holding public office; secret. • n (pl) the genitals; an enlisted man of the lowest military rank in the army.—**privately** adv.

private enterprise n an economic system in which business activity is operated by private individuals or companies under private not state control.

privateer /ˌpraɪvə'tiːr/ n a privately owned ship commissioned by a government to seize and plunder enemy vessels; a captain or crew member of such a ship.

privation /praɪ'veɪʃən/ n being deprived; want of comforts or necessities; hardship.

privative /'prɪvətɪv/ adj depriving; denoting the absence of something.

privatize /'praɪvəˌtaɪz/ vt to restore private ownership by buying back publicly owned stock in a company.

privet /'prɪvət/ n a white-flowered evergreen shrub used for hedges.

privilege /'prɪvɪlɪdʒ/ or /'prɪvlɪdʒ/ n a right or special benefit enjoyed by a person or a small group; a prerogative. • vt to bestow a privilege on.

privileged /'prɪvəlɪdʒd/ or /'prɪvlɪdʒd/ adj having or enjoying privileges; not subject to disclosure in a court of law.

privity /'prɪvɪtɪ/ n (pl **privities**) private knowledge; (law) a legally recognized relationship.

privy /'prɪvɪ/ adj private; having access to confidential information. • n (pl **privies**) a latrine; (law) a person with an interest in an action.—**privily** adv.

prize /praɪz/ n an award won in competition or a lottery; a reward given for merit; a thing worth striving for. • adj given as, rewarded by, a prize. • vt to value highly.

prizefight /'praɪzfaɪt/ n a professional boxing match.—**prizefighter** n.

PRO abbr = public relations officer.

pro[1] /proː/ adv, prep in favour of. • n (pl **pros**) an argument for a proposal or motion.

pro[2] adj professional. • n (pl **pros**) a professional.

pro- prefix acting; vice-; favouring; before; forth; according to.

proa /'proːə/ n a long, narrow, Malay boat propelled by oars and sails.

probability /ˌprobə'bɪlɪtɪ/ n (pl **probabilities**) that which is probable; likelihood; (math) the ratio of the chances in favour of an event to the total number.

probable /'probəbəl/ adj likely; to be expected.

probably /-lɪ/ adv without much doubt.

probang /'proːbæŋ/ n (med) a flexible rod with a sponge at the end, used to clear obstructions from, or apply medication to, the gullet.

probate /'proːbeɪt/ n the validating of a will; the certified copy of a will.

probation /proː'beɪʃən/ n testing of character or skill; release from prison under supervision by a probation officer; the state or period of being on probation.—**probationary, probational** adj.

probation officer n an official who watches over prisoners on probation.

probationer /proː'beɪʃənər/ n a person (as a newly admitted student nurse or teacher) whose fitness is being tested during a trial period; a convicted offender on probation.

probe /proːb/ n a flexible surgical instrument for exploring a wound; a device, as an unmanned spacecraft, used to obtain information about an environment; an investigation. • vt to explore with a probe; to examine closely; to investigate.—**prober** n.

probity /'proːbɪtɪ/ or /'prɒb-/ n honesty, integrity, uprightness.

problem /'probləm/ n a question for solution; a person, thing or matter difficult to cope with; a puzzle; (math) a proposition stating something to be done; an intricate unsettled question.

problematical /ˌproblə'mætɪk/, **problematic** /-kəl/ adj presenting a problem; questionable; uncertain.—**problematically** adv.

proboscidian, proboscidean /ˌprobə'sɪdɪən/ adj pertaining to the class of mammals which includes the elephant. • n an animal with a proboscis.

proboscis /proː'boskɪs/ or /-'bosɪs/ n (pl **proboscises, proboscides**) an elephant's trunk; a long snout; an insect's sucking organ; (humorous) a (large) nose.

procedure /prə'siːdʒər/ n an established mode of conducting business, esp in law or in a meeting; a practice; a prescribed or traditional course; a step taken as part of an established order of steps.—**procedural** adj.—**procedurally** adv.

proceed /prə'siːd/ or /'proː-/ vi to go on, esp after stopping; to come from; to continue; to carry on; to issue; to take action; to go to law.

proceeding /-ɪŋ/ n an advance or going forward; (pl) steps, action, in a lawsuit; (pl) published records of a society, etc.

proceeds /'proːsiːdz/ npl the total amount of money brought in; the net amount received.

process /'proːses/ or /'prɒ-/ n a course or state of going on; a series of events or actions; a method of operation; forward movement; (law) a court summons; the whole course of proceedings in a legal action. • vt to handle something following set procedures; (food, etc) to prepare by a special process; (law) to take action; (film) to develop.

procession /proː'seʃən/ or /prə-/ n a group of people marching in order, as in a parade.

processional /proː'seʃənəl/ or /prə-/ adj pertaining to, or used in, processions. • n a processional hymn or hymn book.

processor /'proːsesər/ or /prɒ-/ n one who or that which processes; (comput) a central processing unit.

pro-choice /proː'tʃɔɪs/ adj supporting a woman's right to choose whether or not to have an abortion.

proclaim /prə'kleɪm/ vt to announce publicly and officially; to tell openly; to praise.—**proclaimer** n.

proclamation /'prokləmeɪʃən/ n the act of proclaiming; an official notice to the public.—**proclamatory** adj.

proclitic /prə'klɪtɪk/ n, adj (a word) so closely connected with the following word as to lose its accent.

proclivity /prə'klɪvɪtɪ/ n (pl **proclivities**) a tendency or inclination.

proconsul /proː'konsəl/ n a governor of a colony or province.—**proconsular** adj.—**proconsulate, proconsulship** n.

procrastinate /prə'kræstɪˌneɪt/ vti to defer action, to delay.—**procrastination** n.—**procrastinator** n.

procreate /'proːkriˌeɪt/ vt to bring into being, to engender offspring.—**procreation** n.—**procreant, procreative** adj.—**procreator** n.

Procrustean /proː'krʌstɪən/ adj compelling uniformity by violent means.

proctor /'proktər/ n a member of the teaching staff of certain universities having the duty of enforcing discipline; in the US, a person who supervises dormitories and examinations in a school.—**proctorial** adj.

procumbent /prə'kʌmbənt/ adj lying face down, prone; (bot) trailing.

procuration /ˌprokju'reɪʃən/ n procuring; (law) the authorization to act on behalf of someone else.

procurator /'prokjuˌreɪtər/ n an agent; (ancient Rome) a provincial governor or treasurer.

procuratory /'prokjurəˌtɔrɪ/ n (law) the authorization to act on another person's behalf.

procure /prə'kjur/ vt to obtain by effort; to get and make available for sexual intercourse; to bring about. • vi to procure women.—**procurable** adj.—**procurement** n.

procurer /prə'kjurər/ n one who procures, esp one who supplies prostitutes.—**procuress** nf.

prod /prod/ vt (**prodding, prodded**) to poke or jab, as with a pointed stick; to rouse into activity. • n the action of prodding; a sharp object; a stimulus.—**prodder** n.

prodigal /ˈprɒdɪgəl/ *adj* wasteful; extravagant; open-handed. • *n* a wastrel; a person who squanders money.—**prodigally** *adv*.

prodigality /ˌprɒdɪˈgælɪti/ *n* (*pl* **prodigalities**) the state or quality of being prodigal; extravagance, wastefulness; lavishness.

prodigious /prəˈdɪdʒəs/ *adj* enormous, vast; amazing.—**prodigiously** *adv*.—**prodigiousness** *n*.

prodigy /ˈprɒdɪdʒi/ *n* (*pl* **prodigies**) an extraordinary person, thing or act; a gifted child.

produce /prəˈdjuːs/ *vt* to bring about; to bring forward, show; to yield; to cause; to manufacture, make; to give birth to; (*play, film*) to put before the public. • *vi* to yield something. • *n* that which is produced, *esp* agricultural products.—**producible** *adj*.—**producibility** *n*.

producer /ˈprɒdjusər/ *n* someone who produces, *esp* a farmer or manufacturer; a person who finances or supervises the putting on of a play or making of a film; an apparatus or plant for making gas.

product /ˈprɒdʌkt/ *n* a thing produced by nature, industry or art; a result; an outgrowth; (*math*) the number obtained by multiplying two or more numbers together.

production /prəˈdʌkʃən/ *n* the act of producing; a thing produced; a work presented on the stage or screen or over the air.—**productional** *adj*.

productive /prəˈdʌktɪv/ *adj* producing or capable of producing; fertile.—**productively** *adv*.—**productiveness** *n*.

productivity /-vɪti/ *n* the state of being productive; the ratio of the output of a manufacturing business to the input of materials, labour, etc.

proem /ˈprəʊəm/ *n* a preface or introduction.

Prof. /prɒf/ *abbr* = professor.

profane /prəˈfeɪn/ *adj* secular, not sacred; showing no respect for sacred things; irreverent; blasphemous; not possessing esoteric or expert knowledge. • *vt* to desecrate; to debase by a wrong, unworthy or vulgar use.—**profanation** *n*.—**profanely** *adv*.—**profaneness** *n*.—**profaner** *n*.

profanity /prəˈfænɪti/ *n* (*pl* **profanities**) irreverence; a profane act; blasphemy, swearing.

profess /prəˈfes/ *vt* to affirm publicly, declare; to claim to be expert in; to declare in words or appearance only.

professed /prəˈfest/ *adj* openly acknowledged.—**professedly** *adv*.

profession /prəˈfeʃən/ *n* an act of professing; avowal, *esp* of religious belief; an occupation requiring specialized knowledge and often long and intensive academic preparation; the people engaged in this; affirmation; entry into a religious order.

professional /-əl/ *adj* of or following a profession; conforming to the technical or ethical standards of a profession; earning a livelihood in an activity or field often engaged in by amateurs; having a specified occupation as a permanent career; engaged in by persons receiving financial return; pursuing a line of conduct as though it were a profession. • *n* one who follows a profession; a professional sportsman; one highly skilled in a particular occupation or field.—**professionally** *adv*.

professionalism /-əˌlɪzəm/ *n* the methods of professionals; the pursuit of an activity, *eg* a sport, for financial gain.

professor /prəˈfesər/ *n* a teacher of the highest rank at an institution of higher education; a teacher.—**professorial** *adj*.—**professorship** *n*.

professoriate, professorate /-ˌreɪt/ *n* a body of professors.

proffer /ˈprɒfər/ *vt* to offer, *usu* something intangible.

proficiency /prəˈfɪʃənsi/ *n* (*pl* **proficiencies**) a being proficient; competence; skill.

proficient /prəˈfɪʃənt/ *adj* skilled, competent.—**proficiently** *adv*.

profile /ˈprəʊfaɪl/ *n* a side view of the head as in a portrait, drawing, etc; a biographical sketch; a graph representing a person's abilities. • *vt* to represent in profile; to produce (as by writing, drawing, etc) a profile of.

profit /ˈprɒfɪt/ *n* gain; the excess of returns over expenditure; the compensation to entrepreneurs resulting from the assumption of risk; (*pl*) the excess returns from a business; advantage, benefit. • *vti* to be of advantage (to), benefit; to gain.—**profitless** *adj*.

profitable /-təbəl/ *adj* yielding profit, lucrative; beneficial; useful.—**profitably** *adv*.—**profitability** *n*.

profit and loss *n* a statement at the end of an accounting period that summarizes the revenue and expenditure of a business and shows the consequent profit or loss.

profiteer /ˌprɒfɪˈtiːr/ *vi* to make exorbitant profits, *esp* in wartime. • *n* a person who profiteers.—**profiteering** *n*.

profitless /ˈprɒfɪtləs/ *adj* without profit; useless.

profit sharing *n* a system by which employees share in the profits of a business.—**profit-sharing** *adj*.

profligate /ˈprɒflɪgət/ *adj* dissolute; immoral; extravagant. • *n* a profligate person, a libertine.—**profligacy** *n*.—**profligately** *adv*.

pro forma /prəʊˈfɔːmə/ *adj* made or carried out as a formality; provided in advance to prescribe form or describe items.

profound /prəˈfaʊnd/ *adj* at great depth; intellectually deep; abstruse, mysterious.—**profoundly** *adv*.—**profoundness** *n*.

profundity /prəˈfɛndɪti/ *n* (*pl* **profundities**) great depth of place, knowledge, skill, etc; a profound or abstruse thing.

profuse /prəˈfjuːz/ *adj* abundant; generous; extravagant.—**profusely** *adv*.—**profuseness** *n*.

profusion /prəˈfjuːʒən/ *n* an abundance.

progenitive /prəʊˈdʒenɪtɪv/ *adj* able to bear offspring.

progenitor /prəʊˈdʒenɪtər/ *n* an ancestor.

progeny /ˈprəʊdʒeni/ *n* (*pl* **progenies**) offspring; descendants; outcome.

prognathous /prɒgˈneɪθəs/ or /ˈprɒgnəθəs/, **prognathic** /prɒgˈnæθɪk/ *adj* having projecting lower jaw.—**prognathism** *n*.

prognosis /prɒgˈnəʊsɪs/ *n* (*pl* **prognoses**) a prediction; (*med*) a forecast of the course of a disease.

prognostic /prɒgˈnɒstɪk/ *adj* predictive (of); foretelling. • *n* a prediction; an omen; a forewarning symptom.

prognosticate /-ˌkeɪt/ *vt* to predict; to presage.—**prognostication** *n*.—**prognosticator** *n*.

programme /ˈprəʊgræm/ *n* (*US and comput*) **program** a printed list containing details of a ceremony, of the actors in a play, etc; a scheduled radio or television broadcast; a curriculum or syllabus for a course of study; a plan or schedule; a sequence of instructions fed into a computer. • *vti* (**programming, programmed** *or* **programing, programed**) to prepare a plan or schedule; to prepare a plan or schedule to feed a program into a computer; to write a programme.—**programmable** *adj*.—**programmer, programer** *adj*.—**programmatic** *adj*.

progress /ˈprəʊgrəs/ *n* a movement forwards or onwards, advance; satisfactory growth or development; a tour from place to place in stages. • *vi* to move forward, advance; to improve. • *vt* (*project*) to take to completion.

progression /prəˈgreʃən/ *n* progress; advancement by degrees; (*math*) a series of numbers, each differing from the succeeding according to a fixed law; (*mus*) a regular succession of chords.—**progressional** *adj*.

progressive /prəˈgresɪv/ *adj* advancing, improving; proceeding by degrees; continuously increasing; aiming at reforms; (*with cap*) denoting a broadly liberal Progressive Party. • *n* a person who believes in moderate political change, *esp* social improvement by government action; (*with cap*) a member of a Progressive Party.—**progressively** *adv*.—**progressiveness** *n*.—**progressivism** *n*.

prohibit /prəˈhɪbɪt/ *vt* to forbid by law; to prevent.

prohibition /prəˈhɪbɪʃən/ *n* the act of forbidding; an order that forbids; a legal ban on the manufacture and sale of alcoholic drinks; (*with cap*) the period (1920–33) when there was a legal ban of alcohol in the US.

prohibitionist *n* an advocate of legally prohibiting the sale of alcohol; (*with cap*) a member of the Prohibition Party in the US.

prohibitive /prəˈhɪbɪtɪv/, **prohibitory** /-ˌtɔri/ *adj* forbidding; so high as to prevent purchase, use, etc, of something.—**prohibitively** *adv*.

project /prəˈdʒekt/ or /ˈprəʊ-/ *n* a plan, scheme; an undertaking; a task carried out by students, etc, involving research. • *vt* to throw forward; (*light, shadow, etc*) to produce an outline of on a distance surface; to make objective or externalize; (*one's voice*) to make heard at a distance; (*feeling, etc*) to attribute to another; to imagine; to estimate, plan, or figure for the future. • *vi* to jut out; to come across vividly; to make oneself heard clearly.

projectile /prəˈdʒektaɪl/ or /-tɪl/ *n* a missile; something propelled by force. • *adj* throwing forward; capable of being thrown forward.

projection /prəˈdʒekʃən/ *n* the act of projecting or the condition of being projected; a thing projecting; the representation on a plane surface of part of the earth's surface; a projected image; an estimate of future possibilities based on a current trend; a mental image externalized; an unconscious attribution to another of one's own feelings and motives.—**projectional** adj.

projectionist n a person who operates a projector.

projective /prə'dʒɛktɪv/ adj (geom) pertaining to projection.

projector /prə'dʒɛktər/ n an instrument that projects images from transparencies or film; an instrument that projects rays of light; a person who promotes enterprises.

prolapse /pro:'læps/ vi (med) to fall or slip out of place. • n a prolapsed condition.

prolate /pro:'leɪt/ adj extended; (spheroid) elongated at the poles.

prolegomenon /ˌpro:lə'gɒmənən/ n (pl **prolegomena**) a critical introduction to a text.

proletariat /ˌpro:lə'tɛrɪət/ n the lowest social or economic class of a community; wage earners; the industrial working class.—**proletarian** adj, n.

proliferate /prə'lɪfəreɪt/ vi to grow or reproduce rapidly.—**proliferation** n.—**proliferative** adj.

proliferous /prə'lɪfərəs/ adj reproducing by budding; producing many offshoots.

prolific /prə'lɪfɪk/ adj producing abundantly; fruitful.—**prolificacy** n.—**prolifically** adv.

prolix /'pro:lɪks/ or /prə'lɪks/ adj verbose, long-winded, tedious.—**prolixity, prolixness** n.

prolocutor /pro:'lɒkjutər/ n a chairman or speaker at a convocation, esp of the Anglican Church.

prologue, prolog /'pro:lɒg/ n the introductory lines of a play, speech, or poem; the reciter of these; a preface; an introductory event. • vt (**prologuing, prologued** or **prologing, prologed**) to provide with a prologue; to usher in.

prolong /prə'lɒŋ/ vt to extend or lengthen in space or time; to spin out.—**prolonger** n.

prolongation /prə'lɒŋgeɪʃən/ n the act of prolonging; an extension or continuation.

prolusion /prə'lju:ʒən/ n a preliminary essay or article.—**prolusory** adj.

prom /prɒm/ n a dance for a high school or college class.

promenade /ˌprɒmə'neɪd/ n an esplanade; a ball or dance; a leisurely walk. • vti to take a promenade (along or through).—**promenader** n.

Promethean /prə'mi:θɪən/ adj (myth) pertaining to Prometheus; life-giving.

prominence /'prɒmɪnəns/, **prominency** /-sɪ/ n the state of being prominent; a projection; relative importance; celebrity, fame.

prominent /'prɒmɪnənt/ adj jutting, projecting; standing out, conspicuous; widely and favourably known; distinguished.—**prominently** adv.

promiscuity /ˌprɒmɪ'skju:ɪti/ n (pl **promiscuities**) the state of being promiscuous; promiscuous sexual behaviour; an indiscriminate mixture.

promiscuous /prə'mɪskjuəs/ adj indiscriminate, esp in sexual liaisons.—**promiscuously** adv.—**promiscuousness** n.

promise /'prɒmɪs/ n a pledge; an undertaking to do or not to do something; an indication, as of a successful future. • vti to pledge; to undertake; to give reason to expect.—**promiser** n.

promisee /ˌprɒmɪ'si:/ n (law) someone to whom a promise is made.

promising /'prɒmɪsɪŋ/ adj likely to turn out well; hopeful.

promisor /-ər/ n (law) someone who makes a promise.

promissory /-sɔːrɪ/ adj of the nature of or containing a promise.

promontory /'prɒməntɔːrɪ/ n (pl **promontories**) a peak of high land that juts out into a body of water.

promote /'prəmo:t/ vt to encourage; to advocate; to raise to a higher rank; (employee, student) to advance from one grade to the next higher grade; (product) to encourage sales by advertising, publicity, or discounting.—**promotable** adj.

promoter /-ər/ n a person who promotes, esp one who organizes and finances a sporting event or pop concert; a substance that increases the activity of a catalyst.

promotion /'prəmo:ʃən/ n an elevation in position or rank; the furtherance of the sale of merchandise through advertising, publicity, or discounting.—**promotional** adj.

prompt /prɒmpt/ adj without delay; quick to respond; immediate; of or relating to prompting actors. • vt to urge; to inspire; (actor) to remind of forgotten words, etc (as in a play). • n something that reminds; a time limit for payment of an account; the contract by which this time is fixed.—**promptly** adv.

prompter /-ər/ n one that prompts, esp a person who sits offstage and reminds actors of forgotten lines.

promptitude n quickness of decision and action; readiness; alacrity; punctuality.

promptness n alacrity in action or decision; quickness; punctuality.

promulgate /'prɒmɛlˌgeɪt/ vt to publish, spread abroad; to put (a law) into effect; to proclaim as coming into force.—**promulgation** n.—**promulgator** n.

pronate /'pro:neɪt/ vt (hand, arm) to turn so that the palm is downwards.—**pronation** n.

pronator /-ər/ n a pronating muscle.

prone /pro:n/ adj face downwards; lying flat, prostrate; inclined or disposed (to).—**pronely** adv.—**proneness** n.

prong /prɒŋ/ n a spike of a fork or other forked object.—**pronged** adj.

pronominal /prə'nɒmɪnəl/ adj pertaining to pronouns; acting as a pronoun.

pronoun /'pro:naun/ n a word used to represent a noun (eg I, he, she, it).

pronounce /prə'nauns/ vt to utter, articulate; to speak officially, pass (judgment); to declare formally.—**pronounceable** adj.—**pronouncer** n.

pronounced /prə'naunst/ adj marked, noticeable.—**pronouncedly** adv.

pronouncement /prə'naunsmənt/ n a formal announcement, declaration; a confident assertion.

pronto /'prɒnto:/ adv (inf) quickly.

pronunciation /prəˌnʌnsɪ'eɪʃən/ n articulation; the way a word is pronounced.

proof /pru:f/ n evidence that establishes the truth; the fact, act, or process of validating; test; demonstration; a sample from type, etc, for correction; a trial print from a photographic negative; the relative strength of an alcoholic liquor. • adj resistant; impervious, impenetrable. • vt to make proof against (water).

proofread /'pru:fri:d/ vti (**proofreading, proofread**) to read and correct (printed proofs).—**proofreader** n.

prop[1] /prɒp/ vt (**propping, propped**) to support by placing something under or against. • n a rigid support; a thing or person giving support.

prop[2] see **property**.

prop[3] n a propeller.

propaedeutic /ˌpro:pɪ'du:tɪk/ or /-'dju:-/ adj pertaining to propaedeutics, the preliminary knowledge or instruction necessary for the study of any art or science.

propagable /'prɒpəgəbəl/ adj which can be propagated.

propaganda /ˌprɒpə'gændə/ n the organized spread of ideas, doctrines, etc, to promote a cause; the ideas, etc, so spread.—**propagandism** n.—**propagandist** n, adj.

propagandize /-ˌdaɪz/ vt to spread by propaganda; to use propaganda among. • vi to spread propaganda; to use propaganda.

propagate /'prɒpəgeɪt/ vti to cause (a plant or animal) to reproduce itself; (plant or animal) to reproduce; (ideas, customs, etc) to spread.—**propagation** n.—**propagative** adj.

propagator /-ər/ n a device consisting of a box with a ventilated lid, used to regulate growing conditions for seeds and young plants.

propane /'pro:peɪn/ n a colourless flammable gas obtained from petroleum and used as a fuel.

pro patria /pro:'pætrɪˌiː/ for one's country.

propel /prə'pɛl/ vt (**propelling, propelled**) to drive or move forward.

propellant, propellent /prə'pɛlənt/ n a thing that propels; an explosive charge; rocket fuel; the gas that activates an aerosol spray.

propeller, propellor /prə'pɛlər/ n a mechanism to impart drive; a device having two or more blades in a revolving hub for propelling a ship or aircraft.

propensity /prə'pɛnsɪti/ n (pl **propensities**) a natural inclination; disposition, tendency.

proper /'prɒpər/ adj own, individual, peculiar; appropriate, fit; correct, conventional; decent, respectable; in the most restricted sense; (sl) thorough.

properly /-li/ adv in the right way; justifiably; (sl) thoroughly.

proper noun n the name of a particular person, place, etc.

property /'prɒpərti/ n (pl **properties**) a quality or attribute; a distinctive feature or characteristic; one's possessions; real estate, land; a movable article used in a stage setting.—also **prop**.

prophecy /'prɒfəsi/ n (pl **prophecies**) a message of divine will and purpose; prediction.

prophesy /'prɒfə,saɪ/ *vti* (**prophesying, prophesied**) to predict with assurance or on the basis of mystic knowledge; to foretell.—**prophesier** *n*.

prophet /'prɒfət/ *n* a religious leader regarded as, or claiming to be, divinely inspired; one who predicts the future.—**prophetess** *nf*.

prophetic /prə'fetɪk/, **prophetical** /-əl/ *adj* of a prophet or prophecy; prophesying events.—**prophetically** *adv*.

prophylactic /ˌprɒfə'læktɪk/ *adj* guarding against disease. • *n* a medicine which guards against disease; a condom.

prophylaxis /ˌprɒfə'læksɪs/ *n* preventive treatment.

propinquity /prə'pɪŋkwɪti/ *n* nearness of time, place or relationship.

propitiate /prə'pɪʃɪ,eɪt/ *vt* to appease, conciliate.—**propitiation** *n*.—**propitiator** *n*.

propitious /prə'pɪʃəs/ *adj* favourable, encouraging; auspicious, opportune.—**propitiously** *adv*.—**propitiousness** *n*.

propolis /'prɒpəlɪs/ *n* a resin from tree buds, collected by bees.

proponent /prə'po:nənt/ *n* someone who makes a proposal, or proposition.

proportion /prə'pɔrʃən/ *n* the relationship between things in size, quantity, or degree; ratio; symmetry, balance; comparative part or share; (*math*) the equality of two ratios; a share or quota; (*pl*) dimensions. • *vt* to put in proper relation with something else; to make proportionate (to).—**proportionment** *n*.—**proportionable** *adj*.

proportional /-əl/ *adj* of proportion; aiming at due proportion; proportionate.—**proportionality** *n*.—**proportionally** *adv*.

proportional representation *n* an electoral system arranged so that minorities are represented in proportion to their strength.

proportionate /-nət/ *adj* in due proportion, corresponding in amount. • *vt* to make proportionate.—**proportionately** *adv*.

proposal /prə'po:zəl/ *n* a scheme, plan, or suggestion; an offer of marriage.

propose /prə'po:z/ *vt* to present for consideration; to suggest; to intend; to announce the drinking of a toast to; (*person*) to nominate; to move as a resolution. • *vi* to make an offer (of marriage).—**proposer** *n*.

proposition /ˌprɒpəzɪʃən/ *n* a proposal for consideration; a plan; a request for sexual intercourse; (*inf*) a proposed deal, as in business; (*inf*) an undertaking to be dealt with; (*math*) a problem to be solved.—**propositional** *adj*.

propound /prə'paʊnd/ *vt* to put forward (a question, suggestion, etc).

proprietary /pro:'praɪətəri/ or /prə-/, /-təri/ *adj* characteristic of a proprietor; privately owned and managed and run as a profit-making organization; (*drug*) made and distributed under a tradename. • *n* (*pl* **proprietaries**) proprietors collectively; a drug protected by secrecy, patent, or copyright against free competition.

proprietor /prə'praɪətər/ *n* one with legal title to something; an owner.—**proprietorial** *adj*.—**proprietorially** *adv*.

propriety /prə'praɪəti/ *n* (*pl* **proprieties**) correctness of conduct or taste; fear of offending against rules of behaviour, *esp* between the sexes; (*pl*) the customs and manners of polite society.

proptosis /'prɒptoːsɪs/ *n* (*pl* **proptoses**) (*med*) a prolapse, *esp* of the eyeball.

propulsion /prə'pʌlʃən/ *n* the act of propelling; something that propels.—**propulsive, propulsory** *adj*.

propylaeum /ˌprɒpɪ'liːəm/, **propylon** /-'lɒn/ *n* (*pl* **propylaea, propylons** *or* **propyla**) a porch or entrance to a temple.

pro rata /'pro:reɪtə/ *adj, adv* in proportion.

prorogue /prə'ro:g/ *vt* to terminate a session (of a parliament, etc) without dissolving it.

prosaic /prə'zeɪk/ or /pro:/ *adj* commonplace, matter-of-fact, dull.—**prosaically** *adv*.—**prosaicness** *n*.

prosaism /'pro:zeɪ,sɪzəm/ *n* the quality of being prosaic; a word, saying, etc demonstrating this.

proscenium /prə'si:nɪəm/ or /pro:-/ *n* (*pl* **prosceniums**) the part of a stage in front of the curtain.

proscribe /prə'skraɪb/ *vt* to outlaw; to denounce; to prohibit the use of.—**proscriber** *n*.

proscription /prə'skrɪpʃən/ *n* the act of proscribing; the condition of being proscribed; outlawry; interdiction.—**proscriptive** *adj*.—**proscriptively** *adv*.

prose /pro:z/ *n* ordinary language, as opposed to verse. • *adj* in prose; humdrum, dull. • *vti* to talk tediously; to turn into prose.

prosecute /'prɒsə,kju:t/ *vt* to bring legal action against; to pursue. • *vi* to institute and carry on a legal suit or prosecution.—**prosecutable** *adj*.

prosecution /ˌprɒsə'kju:ʃən/ *n* the act of prosecuting, *esp* by law; the prosecuting party in a legal case.

prosecutor /'prɒsə,kju:tər/ *n* a person who prosecutes, *esp* in a criminal court.

proselyte /'prɒsə,laɪt/ *n* a convert, *esp* to Judaism. • *vti* to proselytize.

proselytize /'prɒsələ,taɪz/ *vti* to try to make a convert (of).—**proselytizer** *n*.

prosenchyma /prɒ'seŋkɪmə/ *n* (*bot*) tissue of elongated cells with little protoplasm.—**prosenchymatous** *adj*.

prose poem *n* a prose work of poetic style.

prosody *n* the study of verse forms and metrical structure; a particular style, system, or theory of versification.—**prosodic** *adj*.—**prosodically** *adv*.—**prosodist** *n*.

prosopopoeia, prosopopeia /ˌprɒsəpə'piːə/ *n* (*rhetoric*) a figure of speech in which an absent, dead or inanimate figure is represented as present and speaking.

prospect /'prɒspekt/ *n* a wide view, a vista; (*pl*) measure of future success; future outlook; expectation; a likely customer, candidate, etc. • *vti* to explore or search (for).

prospective /prə'spektɪv/ *adj* likely; anticipated, expected.—**prospectively** *adv*.

prospector /prə'spekər/ *n* one who prospects for gold, etc.

prospectus /prə'spektəs/ *n* (*pl* **prospectuses**) a printed statement of the features of a new work, enterprise, etc; something (as a condition or statement) that forecasts the course or nature of a situation.

prosper /'prɒspər/ *vi* to thrive; to flourish; to succeed.

prosperity /prɒ'speriti/ *n* (*pl* **prosperities**) success; wealth.

prosperous /'prɒspərəs/ *adj* successful, fortunate, thriving; favourable.—**prosperously** *adv*.

prostate /'prɒsteɪt/ *n* (*also* **prostate gland**) a gland situated around the neck of a man's bladder.—**prostatic** *adj*.

prosthesis /'prɒs'θiːsɪs/ *n* (*pl* **prostheses**) (*med*) the replacement of a lost limb, tooth, etc with an artificial one; (*gram*) the addition of a letter or syllable at the beginning of a word.—**prosthetic** *adj*.

prostitute /'prɒstɪ,tuːt/ or /-,tjuːt/ *n* a person who has sexual intercourse for money; (*fig*) one who deliberately debases his or her talents (as for money). • *vt* to offer indiscriminately for sexual intercourse, *esp* for money; to devote to corrupt or unworthy purposes.—**prostitutor** *n*.

prostitution /ˌprɒstɪ'tuːʃən/ or /-'tjuː-/ *n* the act or activity of being a prostitute; sexual intercourse for money, etc.

prostrate /'prɒstreɪt/ *adj* lying face downwards; helpless; overcome; lying prone or supine. • *vt* to throw oneself down; to lie flat; to humble oneself.—**prostration** *n*.

prostyle /'pro:staɪl/ *adj* (*archit*) with columns in front. • *n* a building, *esp* a temple, with columns in front.

prosy /'pro:zi/ *adj* (**prosier, prosiest**) like prose; dull, dry, tedious.—**prosily** *adv*.—**prosiness** *n*.

protactinium /ˌpro:tæk'tɪnɪəm/ *n* a rare radioactive element similar to uranium.

protagonist /pro:'tægənɪst/ *n* the main character in a drama, novel, etc; a supporter of a cause.

protasis /'prɒtəsɪs/ *n* (*pl* **protases**) (*gram*) an introductory clause of a conditional sentence.

protean /'pro:tiən/ or /-'tiːən/ *adj* able to assume many shapes, versatile; variable.

protect /prə'tekt/ *vt* to defend from danger or harm; to guard; to maintain the status and integrity of, *esp* through financial guarantees; to foster or shield from infringement or restriction; to restrict competition through tariffs and trade controls.

protection /prə'tekʃən/ *n* the act of protecting; the condition of being protected; something that protects; shelter; defence; patronage; the taxing of competing imports to foster home industry; the advocacy or theory of this.—*also* **protectionism**; immunity from prosecution or attack obtained by the payment of money.

protectionist /-nɪst/ *n* a person who advocates the protection of home trade by taxing competitive imports. • *adj* serving to protect.—**protectionism** *n*.

protective /prə'tektɪv/ *adj* serving to protect, defend, shelter.—**protectively** *adv*.—**protectiveness** *n*.

protector /-ər/ *n* a person or thing that protects; (*with cap*) (*formerly*) a regent who ruled during the minority, absence or illness of a monarch.

protectorate /prə'tektərət/ *n* the administration of a weaker state by a powerful one; a state so controlled; a regency; (*with cap*) the English government under Oliver and Richard Cromwell (1653–9).

protégé /'prɒtə,ʒi:/ or /prɒ-/ *n* a person guided and helped in his career by another person.—**protégée** *nf*.

protein /'prɒti:n/ *n* a complex organic compound containing nitrogen that is an essential constituent of food.

pro tem /prɒ:'tem/, **pro tempore** /prɒ:'tempəri/ *adv* for the time being.

proteolysis /,prɒti'ɒlɪsɪs/ *n* the disintegration of protein, *esp* during digestion.—**proteolytic** *adj*.

proteose /'prɒti,o:z/ *n* a compound substance formed by proteolysis.

protest /'prɒtɛst/ *vi* to object to; to remonstrate. • *vt* to assert or affirm; to execute or have executed a formal protest against; to make a statement or gesture in objection to. • *n* public dissent; an objection; a complaint; a formal statement of objection.—**protester, protestor** *n*.—**protestingly** *adv*.

Protestant /'prɒtəstənt/ *n* a member or adherent of one of the Christian churches deriving from the Reformation; a Christian not of the Orthodox or Roman Catholic Church, who adheres to the principles of the Reformation.—**Protestantism** *n*.

protestation /,prɒtə'steɪʃən/ *n* a solemn declaration; a strong protest.

prothalamion /,prɒθə'leɪmiən/ *n* (*pl* **prothalamia**) a bridal song, sung before a marriage ceremony.

prothonotary /,prɒ:θə'no:təri/ or /prə'θɒnə,təri/ *n* (*pl* **prothonotaries**) (*formerly*) the principal clerk in certain courts.—*also* **protonotary** (*pl* **protonotaries**).

prothorax /prɒ:'θo:ræks/ *n* (*pl* **prothoraxes, prothoraces**) the first segment of an insect's thorax.

protist /'prɒtɪst/ *n* a single-celled organism, neither animal nor plant.

protocol /'prɒtə,kɒl/ *n* a note, minute or draft of an agreement or transaction; the ceremonial etiquette accepted as correct in official dealings, as between heads of state or diplomatic officials; the formatting of data in an electronic communications system; the plan of a scientific experiment or treatment.

proton /'prɒ:tɒn/ *n* an elementary particle in the nucleus of all atoms, carrying a unit positive charge of electricity.

protonotary *see* **prothonotary**.

protoplasm /'prɒ:tə:,plæzəm/ *n* a semi-fluid viscous colloid, the essential living matter of all plant and animal cells.—**protoplasmic** *adj*.

prototype /'prɒ:tə,taɪp/ *n* an original model or type from which copies are made.—**prototypal, prototypic, prototypical** *adj*.

protozoan /,prɒ:tə'zo:ən/, **protozoon** /-'zo:ɒn/ *n* (*pl* **protozoans, protozoa**) a microscopic animal consisting of a single cell or a group of cells.

protozoology *n* the study of protozoans.

protract /prə'trækt/ *vt* to draw out or prolong; to lay down the lines and angles of with scale and protractor; to extend forwards and outwards.—**protractible** *adj*.—**protraction** *n*.

protracted /prə'træktəd/ *adj* extended, prolonged; long-drawn-out.—**protractedly** *adv*.—**protractedness** *n*.

protractile /prə'træktaɪl/ *adj* (*zool*) able to be extended.—**protractility** *n*.

protractive /prə'træktɪv/ *adj* delaying; protracted.

protractor /prə'træktər/ or /'prɒtræktər/ *n* an instrument for measuring and drawing angles; a muscle that extends a limb.

protrude /prɒ:'tru:d/ or /prə-/ *vti* to thrust outwards or forwards; to obtrude; to jut out, project.

protrusile /prə'tru:saɪl/ *adj* (*zool*) which can be thrust forward.

protrusion /prɒ:'tru:ʒən/ or /prə-/ *n* the act of protruding; something that protrudes; a bulge, a lump; a projection.

protrusive /prɒ:'tru:zɪv/ or /prə-/ *adj* tending to protrude; bulging out; unduly conspicuous; obtrusive; (*arch*) thrusting or impelling forward.—**protrusively** *adv*.—**protrusiveness** *n*.

protuberance /prə'tu:bərəns/ or /-'tju:b-/, **protuberancy** /prə'tu:bərənsi/ or /-'tju:b-/ *n* (*pl* **protuberance, protuberancies**) something that protrudes; a swelling, prominence.

protuberant /prə'tu:bərənt/ or /-'tju:b-/ *adj* bulging out, prominent.—**protuberantly** *adv*.

proud /praud/ *adj* having too high an opinion of oneself; arrogant, haughty; having proper self-respect; satisfied with one's achievements.—**proudly** *adv*.—**proudness** *n*.

prove /pru:v/ *vti* (**proving, proved** *or* **proven**) to try out, test, by experiment; to establish or demonstrate as true using accepted procedures; to show (oneself) to be worthy or capable; to turn out (to be), *esp* after trial or test; to rise.—**provable** *adj*.—**provably** *adv*.—**prover** *n*.

provenance /'prɒvənəns/ *n* place of origin, source.

provender /'prɒvəndər/ *n* dry fodder for cattle; any food.

proverb /'prɒvərb/ *n* a short traditional saying expressing a truth or moral instruction; an adage.

proverbial /prɒ'vɜrbiəl/ *adj* of or like, a proverb; generally known.—**proverbially** *adv*.

provide /prə'vaɪd/ *vti* to arrange for; to supply; to prepare; to afford (an opportunity); to make provision for (financially).—**provider** *n*.

provided /-əd/, **providing** /-ɪŋ/ *conj* on condition (that).

providence /'prɒvɪdəns/ *n* foresight, prudence; God's care and protection.

provident /'prɒvɪdənt/ *adj* providing for the future; far-seeing; thrifty.—**providently** *adv*.

providential /,prɒvɪ'dɛnʃəl/ *adj* arranged by providence; very opportune or lucky.—**providentially** *adv*.

province /'prɒvɪns/ *n* an administrative district or division of a country; the jurisdiction of an archbishop; (*pl*) the parts of a country removed from the main cities; a department of knowledge or activity.

provincial /prə'vɪnʃəl/ *adj* of a province or provinces; having the way, speech, etc of a certain province; country-like; rustic; unsophisticated. • *n* an inhabitant of the provinces or country areas; a person lacking sophistication.—**provinciality** *n*.—**provincially** *adv*.

provincialism /prə'vɪnʃə,lɪzəm/ *n* provincial speech, phrases, or point of view; narrowness.

provision /prə'vɪʒən/ *n* a requirement; something provided for the future; a stipulation, condition; (*pl*) supplies of food, stores. • *vt* to supply with stores.—**provisioner** *n*.

provisional /-əl/, **provisionary** /-ɛri/ *adj* temporary; conditional.—**provisionally** *adv*.

proviso /prə'vaɪzo:/ *n* (*pl* **provisos, provisoes**) a condition, stipulation; a limiting clause in an agreement, etc.

provisory /prə'vaɪzəri/ *adj* conditional; making provision; temporary.—**provisorily** *adv*.

provocation /,prɒvə'keɪʃən/ *n* the act of provoking or inciting; a cause of anger, resentment, etc.

provocative /prə'vɒkətɪv/ *adj* intentionally provoking, *esp* to anger or sexual desire; (*remark*) stimulating argument or discussion.—**provocatively** *adv*.—**provocativeness** *n*.

provoke /prə'vo:k/ *vt* to anger, infuriate; to incite, to arouse; to give rise to; to irritate, exasperate.

provoking /-ɪŋ/ *adj* annoying, exasperating.—**provokingly** *adv*.

provost /'prɒvɒst/ *n* a high executive official, as in some churches, colleges, or universities; in Scotland, a mayor.

prow /prau/ *n* the forward part of a ship, bow.

prowess /'prau'ɛs/ or /'prauɛs/, /-əs/ *n* bravery, gallantry; skill.

prowl /praul/ *vi* to move stealthily, *esp* in search of prey.—*also n*.

prowler /-ər/ *n* one that moves stealthily, *esp* an opportunist thief.

proximal /'prɒksɪməl/ *adj* (*anat*) at the inner end, towards the centre of the body.

proximate /'prɒksɪmət/ *adj* nearest, next; approximate.

proximity /prɒk'sɪməti/ *n* nearness in place, time, series, etc.

proximo /'prɒksɪ,mo:/ *adv* next month.

proxy /'prɒksi/ *n* (*pl* **proxies**) the authority to vote or act for another; a person so authorized.—*also adj*.

prude /pru:d/ *n* a person who is overly modest or proper in behaviour, speech, attitudes to sex, etc.—**prudery** *n*.

prudence /'pru:dəns/ *n* the quality of being prudent; caution; discretion; common sense.

prudent /'pru:dənt/ *adj* cautious; sensible; managing carefully; circumspect.—**prudently** *adv*.

prudential /pru:'dɛnʃəl/ *adj* marked by prudence.—**prudentially** *adv*.

prudish /'pru:dɪʃ/ *adj* over-correct in behaviour.—**prudishly** *adv*.—**prudishness** *n*.

pruinose /'pru:ɪ,no:s/ *adj* (*bot*) covered with a whitish dust or bloom.

prune[1] /pru:n/ *n* a dried plum.

prune² *vti* (*plant*) to remove dead or living parts from; to cut away what is unwanted or superfluous.—**pruner** *n*.

prunella /pru:'nelə/ *n* a strong silk or worsted fabric, used in shoes.

prurient /'pruriənt/ *adj* tending to excite lust; having lewd thoughts.—**prurience** *n*.—**pruriently** *adv*.

prurigo /pruə'raigo:/ *n* a skin disease causing violent itching.

pruritus /pruə'raitəs/ *n* a strong sensation of itching.

Prussian blue /'prʌʃən/ *n* a deep blue.

prussic acid /'prʌsɪk/ *n* a solution of hydrogen and cyanide that makes a deadly poison.

pry¹ /prai/ *vi* (**prying, pried**) to snoop into other people's affairs; to inquire impertinently. • *n* (*pl* **pries**) close inspection; impertinent peeping; a highly inquisitive person.

pry² *vt* (**prying, pried**) to raise with a lever, to prise.

pryer /'praiər/ *see* **prier**.

PS /ˌpiː'ɛs/ *abbr* = postscript.

psalm /sɒm/ *n* a sacred song or hymn, *esp* one from the Book of Psalms in the Bible.

psalmist /'sɒmɪst/ *n* a writer of psalms.

psalmody /'sɒmədi/ or /'sæm-/ *n* (*pl* **psalmodies**) the art or practice of singing psalms or hymns.—**psalmodic** *adj*.—**psalmodist** *n*.

Psalter, psalter /'sɒltər/ *n* the Book of Psalms, *esp* as found in a prayer book.

psaltery /-i/ *n* (*pl* **psalteries**) an ancient stringed musical instrument.

Pseudepigrapha /ˌsuːdɪ'pɪgrəfə/ or /ˌsjuː-/ *npl* spurious writings falsely ascribed to Biblical figures or times; Jewish writings of the first century BC and first century AD, allegedly by various prophets and kings of the Hebrew scriptures.

pseudo /'suːdoː/ or /'sjuː-/ *adj* false, pretended.

pseudocarp /'suːdoːˌkɑrp/ or /'sjuː-/ *n* (*bot*) a fruit formed from parts other than the ovary.

pseudomorph /'suːdəˌmɔrf/ or /'sjuː-/ *n* (*geol*) a mineral with the crystalline shape of another mineral.—**pseudomorphic, pseudomorphous** *adj*.—**pseudomorphism** *n*.

pseudonym /'suːdəˌnɪm/ or /'sjuː-/ *n* a false name adopted as by an author.—**pseudonymity** *n*.

pseudonymous /suː'dɒnɪməs/ or /sjuː-/ *adj* written or writing under an assumed name.—**pseudonymously** *adv*.

pshaw /pʃɔ/ or /ʃɔ/ *interj* an exclamation of disgust, disbelief, etc.

psittacine /'sɪtəˌsain/ *n* pertaining to parrots.

psittacosis /ˌsɪtə'koːsɪs/ *n* a contagious parrot disease transmissible to humans, in whom it causes pneumonia.

psoas /'soːəs/ *n* a muscle in the loin.

psoriasis /sə'raiəsɪs/ *n* a chronic skin disease marked by red scaly patches.—**psoriatic** *adj*.

psyche /'saiki/ *n* the spirit, soul; the mind, *esp* as a functional entity governing the total organism and its interactions with the environment.

psychedelic /ˌsaikə'dɛlɪk/ *adj* of or causing extreme changes in the conscious mind; of or like the auditory or visual effects produced by drugs (as LSD). • *n* a psychedelic drug.—**psychedelically** *adv*.

psychiatrist /saiki'ætrist/ or /saikai-/ *n* a specialist in psychiatric medicine.

psychiatry /sai'kaiətri/ *n* the branch of medicine dealing with disorders of the mind, including psychoses and neuroses.—**psychiatric** *adj*.—**psychiatrically** *adv*.

psychic /'saikik/ *adj* of the soul or spirit; of the mind; having sensitivity to, or contact with, forces that cannot be explained by natural laws.—*also* **psychical**. • *n* a person apparently sensitive to nonphysical forces; a medium; psychic phenomena.

psychoanalyse, psychoanalyze /ˌsaiko:'ænəˌlaiz/ *vt* to analyse and treat by psychoanalysis.

psychoanalysis /ˌsaiko:ə'næləsəs/ *n* a method of treating neuroses, phobias, and some other mental disorders by analysing emotional conflicts, repressions, etc.—**psychoanalytic, psychoanalytical** *adj*.

psychoanalyst /-'ænəˌlist/ *n* a specialist in psychoanalysis.

psychodynamics /ˌsaiko:dai'næmiks/ *n sing* the study of interaction of thoughts, motives, etc within an individual.—**psychodynamic** *adj*.

psychological /ˌsaiko:'lɒdʒikəl/ *adj* of or relating to psychology; of, relating to or coming from the mind or emotions; able to affect the mind or emotions.—**psychologically** *adv*.

psychologist /sai'kɒlədʒist/ *n* a person trained in psychology.

psychology /sai'kɒlədʒi/ *n* (*pl* **psychologies**) the science that studies the human mind and behaviour; mental state.

psychometrics /ˌsaiko:'metriks/ *n sing* the scientific measurement and testing of mental powers.—**psychometric, psychometrical** *adj*.—**psychometrician, psychometrist** *n*.

psychomotor /'saiko:ˌmoːtər/ *adj* denoting a physical action induced by a mental condition.

psychoneurosis /ˌsaiko:nju:'roːsɪs/ *n* (*pl* **psychoneuroses**) neurosis.

psychopath /'saiko:ˌpæθ/ or /'saikə-/ *n* a person suffering from a mental disorder that results in antisocial behaviour and lack of guilt.—**psychopathic** *adj*.

psychopathology /ˌsaiko:pə'θɒlədʒi/ *n* the study of mental disorders.

psychopathy /sai'kɒpəθi/ *n* mental disorder or disease.

psychophysiology /ˌsaiko:fizi'ɒlədʒi/ *n* the study of the relation between psychological and physiological processes.—**psychophysiological** *adj*.—**psychophysiologist** *n*.

psychosis /sai'koːsɪs/ *n* (*pl* **psychoses**) a mental disorder in which the personality is very seriously disorganized and contact with reality is *usu* impaired.

psychosomatic /ˌsaiko:sə'mætɪk/ *adj* of physical disorders that have a psychological or emotional origin.—**psychosomatically** *adv*.

psychotherapy /ˌsaiko:'θerəpi/ *n* the treatment of mental disorders by psychological methods.—**psychotherapeutic** *adj*.—**psychotherapist** *n*.

psychotic /sai'kɒtɪk/ *adj* of or like a psychosis; having a psychosis. • *n* a person suffering from a psychosis.—**psychotically** *adv*.

psychrometer /sai'krɒmɪtər/ *n* a type of hygrometer with both a wet and a dry bulb.

psychrophilic /sai'krɒfɪlɪk/ or /saɪ'kroː-/ *adj* (*biol*) thriving in the cold.

PT *abbr* = physical training.

Pt (*chem symbol*) platinum.

Pt. *abbr* = point (in place names).

pt *abbr* = pint.

PTA /ˌpiːtiː'ei/ *abbr* = Parent-Teacher Association.

ptarmigan /'tɑrmɪgən/ *n* (*pl* **ptarmigans, ptarmigan**) a species of grouse.

pteridology /ˌteri'dɒlədʒi/ *n* the study of ferns.

pterodactyl /ˌterə'dæktɪl/ *n* an extinct flying reptile with batlike wings.

pteropod /'terəpɒd/ *n* a small swimming mollusc with winglike lobes on its foot.

pterosaur /'terəˌsɔr/ *n* an extinct flying reptile.

pterygoid /'teriˌgɔid/ *adj* (*anat*) of or pertaining to either of the two processes in the skull attached like wings to the spheroid bone.

PTO /ˌpiːtiː'oː/ *abbr* = please turn over.

ptomaine, ptomain /'toːmein/ *n* a kind of alkaloid, often poisonous, found in decaying matter.

ptosis /'toːsɪs/ *n* (*pl* **ptoses**) drooping of the eyelid.

ptyalin /'taiəlɪn/ *n* an enzyme found in saliva.

ptyalism /'taiəˌlɪzəm/ *n* excessive salivation.

pub /pʌb/ *n* a public house, an inn.

puberty /'pjuːbərti/ *n* the stage at which the reproductive organs become functional.—**pubertal** *adj*.

pubescent /pjuː'besənt/ *adj* arriving at or having reached puberty; of or relating to puberty; covered with fine soft short hairs.—**pubescence** *n*.

pubic /'pjuːbɪk/ *adj* related to or situated near the pubis.

pubis /'pjuːbɪs/ *n* (*pl* **pubes**) the front part of the bones composing either half of the pelvis.

public /'pʌblɪk/ *adj* of, for, or by the people generally; performed in front of people; for the use of all people; open or known to all; acting officially for the people. • *n* the people in general; a particular section of the people, such as an audience, body of readers, etc; open observation.

public-address system *n* a system using microphones and loudspeakers to enable groups of people to hear clearly in an auditorium or out of doors.

publican /-ən/ *n* a person who keeps a public house; in ancient Rome, a collector of taxes.

publication /ˌpʌblə'keiʃən/ *n* public notification; the printing and distribution of books, magazines, etc; something published as a periodical, book, etc.

public health *n* the practice and science of protecting and improving community health by organized effort including sanitation, preventive medicine, etc.

publicist /'pʌblɔsɪst/ *n* a person who publicizes, *esp* one whose business it is; a political journalist.

publicity /pʌb'lɪsɪti/ *n* any information or action that brings a person or cause to public notice; work concerned with such promotional matter; notice by the public.

publicize /'pʌblɪˌsaɪz/ *vt* to give publicity to.

publicly /'pʌblɪkli/ *adv* in a public manner; openly; by the public; with the consent of the public.

public relations *n* relations with the general public of a company, institution, etc, as through publicity.

public school *n* a private secondary school, *usu* boarding; a school maintained by public money and supervised by local authorities.

public service *n* the supply of a commodity (gas, water, etc) or a service (transport, etc) to the community; a service in the public interest; employment in a government department, *esp* the civil service.

publish /'pʌblɪʃ/ *vt* to make generally known; to announce formally; (*book*) to issue for sale to the public. • *vi* to put out an edition; to have one's work accepted for publication.—**publishable** *adj.*

publisher /-ɔr/ *n* a person or company that prints and issues books, magazines, etc.

publishing /-ɪŋ/ *n* the business of the production and distribution of books, magazines, recordings, etc.

puce /pju:s/ *n, adj* (a) purplish brown.

puck /pʌk/ *n* a hard rubber disc used in ice hockey.

pucker /'pʌkɔr/ *vti* to draw together in creases, to wrinkle; (*with* **up**) to contract the lips ready to kiss. • *n* a wrinkle or fold.

puckish /'pʌkɪʃ/ *adj* impish, irresponsible.—**puckishly** *adv.*—**puckishness** *n.*

pudding /'pʊdɪŋ/ *n* a dessert; a steamed or baked dessert; a suet pie.

puddle /'pʌdɔl/ *n* a small pool of water, *esp* stagnant, spilled, or muddy water; a rough cement of kneaded clay. • *vti* to dabble in mud, to make muddy; to make or line with puddle; to stir (molten iron) to free it from carbon.—**puddler** *n.*

pudency /'pju:dɔnsi/ *n* modesty, sense of shame.

pudendum /pju:'dɛndɔm/ *n* (*pl* **pudenda**) (*usu pl*) the external reproductive organs, *esp* of a woman.—**pudendal** *adj.*

pudgy /'pʌdʒi/ *adj* (**pudgier, pudgiest**) short and fat, squat.—**pudginess** *n.*

pueblo /'pwɛbloʊ/ *n* an Indian settlement in Mexico and the South West United States.

puerile /'pjuɔraɪl/ *adj* juvenile; childish.—**puerilely** *adv.*—**puerility** *n.*

puerilism /pjuɔ'rɪlɪzɔm/ *n* a psychiatric condition of adults characterized by infantile or childish behaviour.

puerperal /pju:'ɔrpɔrɔl/ *adj* pertaining to, or following, childbirth.

puff /pʌf/ *n* a sudden short blast or gust; an exhalation of air or smoke; a light pastry; a pad for applying powder; a flattering notice, advertisement. • *vti* to emit a puff; to breathe hard, pant; to put out of breath; to praise with exaggeration; to swell; to blow, smoke, etc, with puffs.

puffball /'pʌfbɔːl/ *n* a round fungus which emits dustlike spores when broken.

puffer /'pʌfɔr/ *n* someone who, or something which puffs; a tropical fish with a spiny body which can be puffed up to form a globe.

puffiness /'pʌfɪˌnɛs/ *n* the state of being puffy or swollen.

puffy /'pʌfi/ *adj* (**puffier, puffiest**) inflated, swollen; panting.—**puffily** *adv.*

pug /pʌg/ *n* a breed of small dog with a face and nose like a bulldog. • *vt* (**pugging, pugged**) to mix (clay) for making bricks; to fill (a space) with clay or mortar.

pug nose *n* a nose having a slightly concave bridge and flattened nostrils.—**pug-nosed** *adj.*

pugilism /ˌpju:dʒɪ'lɪzɔm/ *n* the practice of fighting with the fists; boxing; skill in doing this.

pugilist /'pju:dʒɪlɪst/ *n* a boxer; a prizefighter.—**pugilistic** *adj.*—**pugilistically** *adv.*

pugnacious /pʌg'neɪʃɔs/ *adj* fond of fighting, belligerent.—**pugnacity, pugnaciousness** *n.*

puisne /'pju:ni/ *adj* (*judge*) lower in rank.

puissance /'pju:ɪsɔns/ or /'pwɪs-/ *n* (*arch*) power; (*showjumping*) an event in which a horse attempts particularly large jumps.—**puissant** *adj.*

puke /pju:k/ *vti* (*inf*) to vomit.—*also n.*

pukka /'pʌkɔ/ *adj* (*Anglo-Indian*) genuine, real; reliable, sound.

pulchritude /'pʌlkrɪˌtju:d/ *n* beauty.

pule /pju:l/ *vi* to whine, whimper.

pull /pʊl/ *vt* to tug at; to pluck; to move or draw towards oneself; to drag; to rip; to tear; (*muscle*) to strain; (*inf*) to carry out, perform; (*inf*) to restrain; (*inf: gun, etc*) to draw out; (*inf*) to attract. • *vi* to carry out the action of pulling something; to be capable of being pulled; to move (away, ahead, etc). • *n* the act of pulling or being pulled; a tug; a device for pulling; (*inf*) influence; (*inf*) drawing power.

pullet /'pʊlɔt/ *n* a young hen.

pulley /'pʊli/ *n* a wheel with a grooved rim for a cord, etc, used to raise weights by downward pull or change of direction of the pull; a group of these used to increase applied force; a wheel driven by a belt.

Pullman /'pʊlmɔn/ *n* (*pl* **Pullmans**) a railway carriage offering luxury accommodation, *usu* with sleeping berths.

pullover /'pʊlˌoʊvɔr/ *n* a buttonless garment with or without sleeves pulled on over the head.

pullulate /'pʌljʊˌleɪt/ *vi* to sprout, grow; to multiply quickly; to spring up.—**pullulation** *n.*

pulmonary /'pʌlmɔnɛri/ *adj* of, relating to or affecting the lungs; having lungs; denoting the artery that conveys deoxygenated blood directly to the lungs from the right ventricle of the heart.

pulp /pʌlp/ *n* a soft, moist, sticky mass; the soft, juicy part of a fruit or soft pith of a plant stem; ground-up, moistened fibres of wood, rags, etc, used to make paper; a book or magazine printed on cheap paper and often dealing with sensational material. • *vti* to make or become pulp or pulpy; to produce or reproduce (written matter) in pulp form.

pulpit /'pʊlpɪt/ or /'pʌl-/ *n* a raised enclosed platform, *esp* in a church, from which a clergyman preaches; preachers as a group.

pulpy /'pʌlpi/ *adj* (**pulpier, pulpiest**) consisting of or like pulp; soft.—**pulpiness** *n.*

pulque /'pu:lkeɪ/ *n* a Mexican alcoholic drink made from the fermented juice of the agave.

pulsar /'pʌlsɑr/ *n* any of several very small stars that emit radio pulses at regular intervals.

pulsate /'pʌlseɪt/ *vi* to beat or throb rhythmically; to vibrate, quiver.—**pulsative** *adj.*

pulsation /'pʌlseɪʃɔn/ *n* a pulsating; a single beat or throb; rhythmic throbbing.

pulsatory /'pʌlsɔtɔri/ *adj* pertaining to pulsation; pulsating.

pulse[1] /pʌls/ *n* a rhythmic beat or throb, as of the heart; a place where this is felt; an underlying opinion or sentiment or an indication of it; a short radio signal. • *vti* to throb, pulsate.

pulse[2] *n* the edible seeds of several leguminous plants, such as beans, peas and lentils; the plants producing them.

pulsimeter, pulsometer /pʌl'sɪmɔtɔr/ *n* (*med*) an instrument used to measure pulse rate and strength.

pulverize /'pʌlvɔˌraɪz/ *vti* to reduce to a fine powder; to demolish, smash; to crumble.—**pulverization** *n.*—**pulverizer** *n.*

pulverulent /pʌl'vɛrjuːlɔnt/ or /-jɔ-/ *adj* covered with dust; powdery; crumbling to dust.

pulvinate /'pʌlvɔˌneɪt/ or /-nɪt/ **pulvinated** *adj* (*archit*) curved convexly; (*bot*) having a cushionlike pad or swelling.

puma /'pju:mɔ/ *n* a mountain lion.

pumice /'pʌmɪs/ *n* a light, porous volcanic rock, used for scrubbing, polishing, etc.—**pumiceous** *adj.*

pummel /'pʌmɔl/ *vt* (**pummelling, pummelled** *or* **pummeling, pummeled**) to strike repeatedly with the fists, to thump.

pump[1] /pʌmp/ *n* a device that forces a liquid or gas into, or draws it out of, something. • *vti* to move (fluids) with a pump; to remove water, etc, from; to drive air into with a pump; to draw out, move up and down, pour forth, etc, as a pump does; (*inf*) to obtain information through questioning.

pump[2] *n* a light low shoe or slipper; a rubber-soled shoe.

pumpernickel /'pʌmpɔrˌnɪkɔl/ *n* a coarse rye bread.

pumpkin /'pʌmpkɪn/ *n* a large, round, orange fruit of the gourd family widely cultivated as food.

pun /pʌn/ *n* a play on words of the same sound but different meanings, *usu* humorous. • *vi* (**punning, punned**) to make a pun.—**punningly** *adv*.

punch[1] /pʌntʃ/ *vt* to strike with the fist; to prod or poke; to stamp, perforate with a tool; (*US*) (*cattle*) to herd. • *n* a blow with the fist; (*inf*) vigour; a machine or tool for punching.

punch[2] *n* a hot, sweet drink made with fruit juices, often mixed with wine or spirits.

punchbowl *n* a bowl for mixing punch; a bowl-shaped hollow.

punch card, punched card *n* in data processing, a card with a series of holes representing data.

puncheon /ˈpʌntʃən/ *n* a large cask holding between 70 and 120 gallons.

Punchinello /ˌpʌntʃɪˈnɛloː/ *n* the figure of the clown in Italian puppet theatre; a grotesque character.

punch line /ˈpʌntʃlaɪn/ *n* the last line of a joke or story, that conveys its humour or point.

punctate /ˈpʌŋkteɪt/ **punctated** *adj* marked with dots or points.—**punctation** *n*.

punctilio /pʌŋkˈtɪlioː/ *n* (*pl* **punctilios**) a fine point of etiquette; petty formality.

punctilious /pʌŋkˈtɪliəs/ *adj* very formal in conduct; scrupulously exact.

punctual /ˈpʌŋktʃʊəl/ *adj* being on time; prompt.—**punctuality** *n*.—**punctually** *adv*.

punctuate /ˈpʌŋktʃʊˌeɪt/ *vt* to use certain standardized marks in (written matter) to clarify meaning; to interrupt; to emphasize. • *vi* to use punctuation marks.—**punctuator** *n*.

punctuation /ˌpʌŋktʃʊˈeɪʃən/ *n* the act of punctuating; the state of being punctuated; a system of punctuation.

punctuation mark *n* one of the standardized symbols used in punctuation, as the period, colon, semicolon, comma, etc.

puncture /ˈpʌŋktʃər/ *n* a small hole made by a sharp object; the deflation of a tyre caused by a puncture. • *vt* to make useless or ineffective as if by a puncture; to deflate. • *vi* to become punctured.—**puncturable** *adj*.

pundit /ˈpʌndɪt/ *n* a learned person; an expert; a critic, *esp* one who writes in a daily newspaper.—*also* **pandit**.

pungent /ˈpʌndʒənt/ *adj* having an acrid smell or a sharp taste; caustic; bitter.—**pungency** *n*.—**pungently** *adv*.

punish /ˈpʌnɪʃ/ *vt* to subject a person to a penalty for a crime or misdemeanour; to chastise; to handle roughly.—**punisher** *n*.

punishable /ˈpʌnɪʃəbəl/ *adj* liable to legal punishment.—**punishability** *n*.

punishing /-ɪŋ/ *adj* causing retribution; (*inf*) arduous, gruelling, exhausting.—**punishingly** *adv*.

punishment /ˈpʌnɪʃmənt/ *n* a penalty for a crime or misdemeanour; rough treatment; the act of punishing or being punished.

punitive /ˈpjuːnɪtɪv/ **punitory** *adj* involving the inflicting of punishment.—**punitively** *adv*.—**punitiveness** *n*.

punk /pʌŋk/ *adj* (*sl*) inferior, of low quality. • *n* a young gangster or hoodlum; a follower of punk rock.

punka, punkah /ˈpʌŋkə/ *n* a palm-leaf fan; (*Anglo-Indian*) a large swinging fan suspended from the ceiling of a room and worked by an attendant.

punk rock *n* an aggressive form of rock music *usu* performed in a coarse, offensive way.

punster /ˈpʌnstər/ *n* a person who makes puns.

punt[1] /pʌnt/ *n* a long flat-bottomed square-ended river boat *usu* propelled with a pole. • *vti* to propel or convey in a punt.

punt[2] *vt* to kick a dropped ball before it reaches the ground. • *n* such a kick.

punter /ˈpʌntər/ *n* a person who gambles; (*sl*) a consumer; a customer.

punty /ˈpʌnti/ *n* (*pl* **punties**) an iron rod used in glass-blowing.

puny /ˈpjuːni/ *adj* (**punier, puniest**) of inferior size, strength, or importance; feeble.—**puniness** *n*.

pup /pʌp/ *n* a young dog, a puppy; a young fox, seal, rat, etc. • *vi* (**pupping, pupped**) to give birth to pups.

pupa /ˈpjuːpə/ *n* (*pl* **pupae, pupas**) an insect at the quiescent stage between the larva and the adult.—**pupal** *adj*.

pupate /ˈpjuːpeɪt/ *vi* (*entomology*) to become a pupa.—**pupation** *n*.

pupil[1] /ˈpjuːpəl/ *n* a child or young person taught under the supervision of a teacher or tutor; a person who has been taught or influenced by a famous or distinguished person.

pupil[2] *n* the round, dark opening in the centre of the iris of the eye through which light passes.

pupillage, pupilage /ˈpjuːpəlɪdʒ/ *n* the state of being a pupil; the period of time during which someone is a pupil.

pupillary /ˈpjuːpəˌlɛri/ *adj* pertaining to a pupil, or to a legal ward.

pupiparous /pjuːˈpɪpərəs/ *adj* (*entomology*) producing young in the pupal state.

puppet /ˈpʌpɪt/ *n* a doll moved by strings attached to its limbs or by a hand inserted in its body; a person controlled by another. • *adj* of or relating to puppets; acting in response to the controls of another while appearing independent.

puppeteer /ˌpʌpɪˈtiːr/ *n* a person who controls and entertains with puppets.

puppetry /ˈpʌpətri/ *n* the art of making and entertaining with puppets; stilted presentation.

puppy /ˈpʌpi/ *n* (*pl* **puppies**) a young domestic dog less than a year old.—**puppyhood** *n*.—**puppyish** *adj*.

Purana /puːˈrɒnə/ *n* a book of Hindu scriptures, written in Sanskrit.

purblind /ˈpərblaɪnd/ *adj* half-blind; (*fig*) obtuse, dull.

purchase /ˈpərtʃəs/ *vt* to buy; to obtain by effort or suffering. • *n* the act of purchasing; an object bought; leverage for raising or moving loads; means of achieving advantage.—**purchasable** *adj*.—**purchaser** *n*.

purdah /ˈpərdə/ *n* the custom among Muslims and some Hindus of secluding women from public observation.

pure /pjʊr/ or /pjər/ *adj* clean; not contaminated; not mixed; chaste, innocent; free from taint or defilement; mere; that and that only; abstract and theoretical; (*mus*) not discordant, perfectly in tune.—**pureness** *n*.

purée /ˈpjʊreɪ/ or /ˈpjʊr/ *n* cooked food sieved or pulped in a blender; a thick soup of this. • *vt* (**puréeing, puréed**) to prepare food in this way.

purely /ˈpjʊrli/ or /ˈpjərli/ *adv* in a pure way; solely, entirely.

purgation /pərˈgeɪʃən/ *n* a purging or purifying.

purgative /ˈpərgətɪv/ *adj* purging, cleansing; • *n* a drug or agent that purges the bowels.

purgatorial /-ˈtəriəl/ *adj* of, relating to or like purgatory; serving to purify of sin.

purgatory /ˈpərgəˌtori/ *n* a place of suffering or purification; (*with cap*: *RC church*) the intermediate place between death and heaven, where venial sins are purged.

purge /pərdʒ/ *vt* to cleanse, purify; (*nation, party, etc*) to rid of troublesome people; to clear (oneself) of a charge; to clear out the bowels of. • *n* the act or process of purging; a purgative; the removal of persons believed to be disloyal from an organization, *esp* a political party.—**purger** *n*.

purificator /ˈpjʊrəfɪˌkeɪtər/ *n* (*Christian Church*) a cloth used to wipe the chalice during Holy Communion.

purify /ˈpjʊrɪˌfaɪ/ *vti* (**purifying, purified**) to make or become pure; to cleanse; to make ceremonially clean; to free from harmful matter.—**purification** *n*.—**purificatory** *adj*.—**purifier** *n*.

Purim /ˈpʊrɪm/ or /puːˈriːm/ *n* a Jewish holiday celebrated yearly in February or March, to commemorate the deliverance of the Jews from massacre at the hands of Haman.

purine /ˈpʊriːn/ *n* a white crystalline compound found in uric acid.

purism /ˈpjʊrˌɪzəm/ *n* insistence on correctness in language, form, style, etc.

purist /ˈpjʊrɪst/ *n* someone who is a stickler for correctness in language, style, etc.—**purism** *n*.—**puristic** *adj*.—**puristically** *adv*.

puritan /ˈpjʊrɪtən/ or /ˈpjər/ *adj* a person who is extremely strict in religion or morals; (*with cap*) an extreme English Protestant of Elizabethan or Stuart times. • *adj* of or like a puritan; (*with cap*) of the Puritans.—**puritanism, Puritanism** *n*.

puritanical /ˌpjʊrɪˈtænɪkəl/ or /pjər/ *adj* rigorously strict in religious or moral matters; (*with cap*) of the Puritans or Puritanism.—**puritanically** *adv*.—**puritanicalness** *n*.

purity /ˈpjʊrɪti/ *n* the state of being pure.

purl /pərl/ *vt* to knit a stitch by drawing its base loop from front to back of the fabric. • *n* a stitch made in this way.

purlieu /ˈpərljuː/ *n* (*usu pl*) adjacent or outlying areas.

purlin /ˈpərlɪn/ **purline** *n* a piece of timber lying horizontally to support rafters.

purloin /pərˈlɔɪn/ *vt* to steal.—**purloiner** *n*.

purple /ˈpərpəl/ *n* a dark, bluish red; crimson cloth or clothing, *esp* as a former emblem of royalty. • *adj* purple-coloured; royal; (*writing style*) over-elaborate. • *vti* to make or become purple.

purport /pər'pɔrt/ *vt* to claim to be true; to imply; to be intended to seem. • *n* significance; apparent meaning.—**purportedly** *adv*.

purpose /'pərpəs/ *n* objective; intention; aim; function; resolution, determination. • *vti* to intend, design.

purposeful /'pərpəs,fʊl/ *adj* determined, resolute; intentional.—**purposefully** *adv*.—**purposefulness** *n*.

purposeless /'pərpəsləs/ *adj* lacking purpose; pointless.—**purposelessly** *adv*.—**purposelessness** *n*.

purposely /'pərpəsli/ *adv* deliberately; on purpose.

purposive /'pərpəsɪv/ *adj* having or serving a purpose.—**purposively** *adv*.

purpura /'pərpjʊrə/ *n* a blood disease causing the eruption of small purple spots.

purr /pər/ *vi* (*cat*) to make a low, murmuring sound of pleasure.—**purring** *n*.

purse /pərs/ *n* a small pouch or bag for money; finances, money; a sum of money for a present or a prize; (*US*) a woman's handbag. • *vt* to pucker, wrinkle up.

purser /'pərsər/ *n* an officer on a passenger ship in charge of accounts, tickets, etc; an airline official responsible for the comfort and welfare of passengers.

purslane /'pərslein/ *n* a flowering plant with fleshy leaves, used in salads.

pursuance /pər'suːəns/ or /-'sjuːəns/ *n* the pursuing or performance of an action.

pursuant /pər'suːənt/ or /-'sjuːənt/ *adj* (*law*) according; (*arch*) pursuing.

pursue /pər'suː/ or /-'sjuː/ *vb* (**pursuing, pursued**) *vt* to follow; to chase; to strive for; to seek to attain; to engage in; to proceed with. • *vi* to follow in order to capture.—**pursuer** *n*.

pursuit /pər'suːt/ or /-'sjuːt/ *n* the act of pursuing; an occupation; a pastime.

pursuivant /'pərsɪvənt/ or /-swɪ-/ *n* a low-ranking officer of the British College of Heralds; (*formerly*) an attendant or state messenger.

purulent /'pjʊrʊlənt/ or /'pjʊrjʊ-/ *adj* pertaining to pus.—**purulence, purulency** *adj*.—**purulently** *adv*.

purvey /'pərveɪ/ *vti* to procure and supply (provisions).

purveyance /pər'veɪəns/ *n* the procuring of provisions; the provisions provided; (*formerly*) the right accorded to royalty to buy up provisions without the owner's consent.

purveyor /-ər/ *n* a person who, or an organization which, supplies provisions.

pus /pʊs/ *n* a yellowish fluid produced by infected sores.

push /pʊʃ/ *vti* to exert pressure so as to move; to press against or forward; to impel forward, shove; to urge the use, sale, etc, of; (*inf*) to approach an age; (*inf*) to sell drugs illegally; to make an effort. • *n* a thrust, shove; an effort; an advance against opposition; (*inf*) energy and drive.

push button *n* a knob that activates an electrical switch which opens or closes a circuit to operate a radio, bell, etc.

pushchair /'pʊʃtʃər/ *n* a wheeled metal and canvas chair for a small child.—*also* **stroller**.

pusher /'pʊʃər/ *n* that which pushes; (*inf*) a person who sells illegal drugs.

pushing /'pʊʃɪŋ/ *adj* go-ahead, energetic; ambitious; assertive.

pushover /'pʊʃ,oːvər/ *n* (*inf*) something easily done, as a victory over an opposing team; (*inf*) a person easily taken advantage of.

pushy /'pʊʃi/ *adj* (**pushier, pushiest**) (*inf*) assertive; forceful; aggressively ambitious.—**pushily** *adv*.—**pushiness** *n*.

pusillanimous /,pjuːsə'lænəməs/ *adj* faint-hearted, cowardly.—**pusillanimity** *n*.

puss[1] /pʊs/ *n* (*inf*) a cat; (*sl*) a girl.

puss[2] *n* (*sl*) the mouth; the face.

pussy[1] /'pʊsi/ *n* (*pl* **pussies**) (*inf*) a cat, a pussycat.

pussy[2] *adj* (*pl* **pussier, pussiest**) like or containing pus.

pussycat /'pʊsikæt/ *n* (*inf*) a cat; an amiable person.

pussyfoot /'pʊsi,fʊt/ *vi* to move stealthily; to be evasive.—**pussyfooter** *n*.

pustule /'pʊstʃuːl/ *n* a blister or swelling containing pus.—**pustular** *adj*.—**pustulation** *n*.

put /pʊt/ *vti* (**putting, put**) to place, set; to cast, throw; to apply, direct; to bring into a specified state; to add (to); to subject to; to submit; to estimate; to stake; to express; to translate; to propose; (*a weight*) to hurl; (*with* **about**) to change the course of (a ship); to worry; (*with* **across**) to effect successfully; (*with* **away**) to remove; to lay by; (*sl*) to consume; (*arch*) to divorce;

(*with* **back**) to replace; to return to land; (*with* **by**) to thrust aside; to store up; (*with* **down**) to suppress; to silence; to kill or have killed; to write or enter; to reckon; to assign; (*with* **forth**) to exert; to bud or shoot; to set out; (*with* **in**) to interpose; to spend (time); to apply (for); to call (at); (*with* **off**) to doff, discard; to postpone; to evade; to get rid of; to discourage, repel; to foist (upon); to leave shore; (*with* **on**) to don; to assume, pretend; to increase; to add; to advance; (*with* **out**) to eject; to extend; to exert; to dislocate; to quench; to publish; to place (money) at interest; to disconcert, to anger; to leave shore; (*with* **over**) to succeed in, to carry through; (*with* **up**) to rouse; to offer (prayer); to propose as a candidate; to pack; to sheathe; to lodge; (*with* **up with**) to endure, to tolerate; (*with* **upon**) to impose upon; (*with* **wise**) to disabuse, to enlighten. • *adj* fixed.

putative /'pjuːtətɪv/ *adj* reputed, supposed.—**putatively** *adv*.

putrefy /'pjuːtrə,faɪ/ *vti* (**putrefying, putrefied**) to make or become putrid; to rot, decompose.—**putrefaction** *n*.—**putrefactive** *adj*.—**putrefier** *n*.

putrescent /pjuː'tresənt/ *adj* decaying, rotting.—**putrescence** *n*.

putrid /'pjuːtrɪd/ *adj* rotten or decayed and foul-smelling.—**putridity** *n*.—**putridly** *adv*.

putsch /pʊtʃ/ *n* an uprising or revolt.

putt /pʊt/ *vti* (*golf*) to hit (a ball) with a putter. • *n* in golf, a stroke to make the ball roll into the hole.

puttee /'pʊti/ *n* a legging made from a strip of cloth wound spirally from the ankle to the knee.

putter[1] /'pʊtər/ *n* (*golf*) a straight-faced club used in putting.

putter[2] *vi* the US word for potter.

putter[3] *n* one who or that which puts; an athlete who puts the shot.

putto /'pʊtoː/ *n* (*pl* **putti**) (*art*) a figure of cupid and representations of children.—*also* **amoretto, amorino**.

putty /'pʊti/ *n* (*pl* **putties**) a soft, plastic mixture of powdered chalk and linseed oil used to fill small cracks, fix glass in window frames, etc. • *vt* (**puttying, puttied**) to fix or fill with putty.

puzzle /'pʊzəl/ *vt* to bewilder; to perplex. • *vi* to be perplexed; to exercise one's mind, as over a problem. • *n* bewilderment; a difficult problem; a toy or problem for testing skill or ingenuity; a conundrum.—**puzzlement** *n*.—**puzzler** *n*.

puzzling /-lɪŋ/ *adj* perplexing, bewildering, inexplicable.—**puzzlingly** *adv*.

PVC *abbr* = polyvinyl chloride.

PWA *abbr* = person with AIDS.

pyaemia, pyemia /paɪ'iːmiə/ *n* blood poisoning.—**pyaemic** *adj*.

pycnometer /pɪk'nɒmətər/ *n* an instrument for measuring densities or specific gravities.

pygmy /'pɪgmi/ *n* (*pl* **pygmies**) an undersized person.—*also* **pigmy** (*pl* **pigmies**).

pyjamas /pə'dʒæməz/ or /-'dʒɒməz/ *npl* a loosely fitting sleeping suit of jacket and trousers.—*also* (*US*) **pajamas**.

pylon /'paɪlɒn/ *n* a tower-like structure supporting electric power lines.

pylorus /paɪ'lɔrəs/ *n* (*pl* **pylori**) (*anat*) the opening from the stomach into the intestine.

pyorrhoea, pyorrhea /,paɪə'riːə/ *n* inflammation of the gums and tooth sockets.

pyracantha /,paɪrə'kænθə/ *n* a small, flowering, evergreen shrub.

pyramid /'pɪrəmɪd/ *n* (*geom*) a solid figure having a polygon as base, and whose sides are triangles sharing a common vertex; a huge structure of this shape, as a royal tomb of ancient Egypt; an immaterial structure built on a broad supporting base and narrowing gradually to an apex.—**pyramidal, pyramidical, pyramidic** *adj*.—**pyramidally, pyramidically** *adv*.

pyre /paɪr/ *n* a pile of wood for cremating a dead body.

pyrethrum /paɪ'riːθrəm/ *n* a type of chrysanthemum with showy flowers; an insecticide made from this plant.

pyretic /paɪ'retɪk/ *adj* pertaining to, or causing, fever.

Pyrex /'paɪreks/ *n* (*trademark*) heat-resistant glassware.

pyrexia /paɪ'reksiə/ *n* fever.—**pyrexial, pyrexic** *adj*.

pyrheliometer /paɪr,hiːli'ɒmətər/ or /pɪr-/ *n* an instrument for measuring the sun's heat.

pyrites /paɪ'raɪtiːz/ or /'paɪraɪts/ *n* (*pl* **pyrites**) a sulphide of a metal, *esp* iron.

pyroelectric /,paɪroːɪ'lektrɪk/ *adj* becoming electric as a result of heat.

pyrogenic /ˌpaɪroˈdʒɛnɪk/, **pyrogenous** *adj* caused by, or causing, heat, or fever.

pyrolisis /paɪˈrɒləsɪs/ *n* decomposition by heat.

pyromania /ˌpaɪroˈmeɪnɪə/ *n* (*psychol*) an uncontrollable urge to set things on fire.

pyrometer /paɪˈrɒmɪtər/ *n* an instrument used to measure very high temperatures.—**pyrometry** *n*.

pyrope /ˈpaɪroːp/ *n* a deep red variety of garnet.

pyrophoric /ˌpaɪroˈfɒrɪk/ *adj* igniting when exposed to air.

pyrosis /paɪˈroːsɪs/ *n* heartburn.

pyrotechnics /ˌpaɪroˈtɛknɪks/ *n sing* the art of making or setting off fireworks; (*sing or pl*) a fireworks display; a brilliant display of virtuosity.—**pyrotechnic, pyrotechnical** *adj*.

pyroxylin /paɪˈrɒksəlɪn/, **pyroxyline** *n* a substance derived from cellulose, used in making plastics.

pyrrhic /ˈpɪrɪk/ *adj* (*victory*) so costly as to be equal to defeat.

pyrrhic /ˈpɪrɪk/ *n* a metrical foot of two syllables.

Pythagorean /pɪˌθægəˈriːən/ or /paɪ-/ *adj* pertaining to, or characteristic of, the Greek philosopher Pythagoras.

python /ˈpaɪθɒn/ *n* a large, nonpoisonous snake that kills by constriction.—**pythonic** *adj*.

pythoness /ˈpaɪθənəs/ *n* a priestess in the temple of Apollo at Delphi, in ancient Greece; a (female) soothsayer; a witch.

pyuria /paɪˈjurɪə/ *n* (*med*) the discharge of pus into the urine.

pyx /pɪks/ *n* (*Christian Church*) a container in which consecrated bread is kept.

pyxidium /pɪkˈsɪdɪəm/ *n* (*pl* **pyxidia**) (*bot*) a pyxis.

pyxis /ˈpɪksɪs/ *n* (*pl* **pyxides**) a seed capsule with a lid that falls off to release the seeds.

Q

QC /ˈkjuːˈsiː/ *abbr* = Queen's Counsel.

QED /ˌkjuːiːˈdiː/ *abbr* = quod erat demonstratum.

q.t. *abbr* = (*inf*) quiet.

qt *abbr* = quart.

qty *abbr* = quantity.

qua /kweɪ/ or /kwɐ/ *prep* as, in the character of, because.

quack[1] /kwæk/ *n* the cry of a duck. • *vi* to make a sound like a duck.

quack[2] *n* an untrained person who practises medicine fraudulently; a person who pretends to have knowledge and skill he does not have.—*also adj.*

quackery /ˈkwækəri/ *n* (*pl* **quackeries**) pretence of medical or other skill; imposture.

quacksalver /ˈkwæksælvər/ *n* (*arch*) a quack who deals in ointments, etc; a charlatan.

quad /kwɒd/ *n* quadrangle; quadruplet.

quadr- /kwɒdr/, **quadri-** /ˈkwɒdri/, **quadru-** /ˈkwɒdru/ *prefix* four.

quadragenarian /ˌkwɒdrədʒəˈnɛriən/ *n, adj* (a person) forty to forty-nine years old.

Quadragesima (Sunday) /ˌkwɒdrəˈdʒəsimə/ *n* the first Sunday in Lent.

Quadragesimal /ˌkwɒdrəˈdʒəsiməl/ *adj* pertaining to, or used in, Lent.

quadrangle /ˈkwɒdˌræŋɡəl/ *n* (*geom*) a plane figure with four sides and four angles, a rectangle; a court enclosed by buildings.—**quadrangular** *adj.*

quadrant /ˈkwɒdrənt/ *n* (*geom*) a quarter of the circumference of a circle; an arc of 90 degrees; an instrument with such an arc for measuring angles, altitudes, or elevations; a curved street.—**quadrantal** *adj.*

quadraphonic /ˌkwɒdrəˈfɒnik/ *adj* using four channels to record and reproduce sound.—**quadraphonics, quadraphony** *n.*

quadrate /ˈkwɒdrət/ *adj* (*zool*) of or pertaining to one of a pair of bones found in the skulls of fishes, reptiles and some birds; (*anat*) of or pertaining to the middle bone of the middle ear in mammals; (*arch*) square or rectangular. • *vt* to square or make rectangular; (*often with* **with**) to cause to conform; to correspond. • *n* a quadrate bone; a square or cube.

quadratic /kwɒˈdrætik/ *adj* square; (*math*) involving the square but no higher power. • *n* a quadratic equation.

quadratic equation *n* an equation in which the highest power of the unknown is the square.

quadratics /-tiks/ *n sing* the branch of algebra dealing with quadratic equations.

quadrature /ˈkwɒdrətʃər/ *n* the act of squaring; the reduction of a figure to a square, exactly or approximately; (*astron*) the position of a heavenly body when distant 90 degrees from another, usually the earth, said *esp* of the position of the moon from the sun; (*math*) the finding of square with an area exactly equal to a circle or other figure or a surface; (*electronics*) the state between two waves of being 90 degrees out of phase.

quadrennial /kwɒˈdrɛniəl/ *adj* lasting or occurring every four years.—**quadrennially** *adv.*

quadricentennial /ˌkwɒdrɒˌsɛnˈtiːniəl/ *n* a four hundredth anniversary.—*also adj.*

quadrifid /ˈkwɒdrifid/ *adj* with four parts, four-cleft.

quadriga /kwɒˈdriɡə/ *n* (*pl* **quadrigas, quadrigae**) an ancient Roman two-wheeled chariot drawn by four horses abreast.

quadrilateral /ˌkwɒdrəˈlætərəl/ *adj* having four sides. • *n* (*geom*) a plane figure of four sides; a combination or group that involves four parts or individuals.

quadrille /kwɒˈdril/ *n* a square dance for four or more couples; the music for this.

quadrillion /kwɒˈdriljən/ *n* in Europe, the fourth power of a million, ie 1 with 24 zeros; in US, the fifth power of a thousand, ie, 1 with 15 zeros.—*also adj.*—**quadrillionth** *adj.*

quadrinomial /ˌkwɒdrəˈnoːmiəl/ *n* an algebraic expression consisting of four terms.

quadripartite /ˌkwɒdrəˈpɑːtəit/ *adj* of four parts; shared by four.

quadriplegia /ˌkwɒdrəˈpliːdʒə/ *n* paralysis of all four limbs.—**quadriplegic** *adj, n.*

quadrivalent /ˌkwɒdrəˈveɪlənt/ *adj* (*chem*) with four valencies; with a valency of four, tetravalent.— **quadrivalency, quadrivalence**.

quadrivial /ˌkwɒˈdriviəl/ *adj* pertaining to a quadrivium; (*roads, etc*) leading in four ways; coming from four directions and meeting at the same point.

quadrivium /ˌkwɒˈdriviəl/ *n* (*pl* **quadrivia**) a medieval course of study comprising arithmetic, geometry, astronomy, and music.

quadroon /ˌkwɒˈdruːn/ *n* the child of one white and one half Negro parent, a person one quarter black.

quadrumanous /ˌkwɒˈdruːmənəs/, **quadrumanal** /ˌkwɒˈdruːmənəl/ *adj* (*monkeys and apes*) having two feet and two hands that are specialized for grasping.

quadruped /ˈkwɒdruˌped/ *n* a four-footed animal.—**quadrupedal** *adj.*

quadruple /kwɒˈdruːpəl/ or /-ˈdrʊ-/ *adj* four times as much or as many; made up of or consisting of four; having four divisions or parts. • *vti* to make or become four times as many.

quadruplet /kwɒˈdruːplət/ or /-ˈdrʊplət/ *n* one of four children born at one birth.

quadruplicate /kwɒˈdruːpliˌkeit/ *vt* to multiply by four; to make four copies of. • *adj* fourfold.—**quadruplication** *n.*

quadruplicity /kwɒˈdruːpliˌsiti/ *n* (*pl* **quadruplicities**) four-fold nature.

quaestor, questor /ˈkwiːstər/ *n* in ancient Rome, the public treasurer, or sometimes one of the other public officials.

quaff /kwɒf/ *vti* to take large drinks (of), drain.—**quaffer** *n.*

quagga /ˈkwægə/ *n* (*pl* **quaggas, quagga**) an extinct striped South African animal like a sand-coloured zebra.

quaggy /ˈkwægi/ *adj* (**quaggier, quaggiest**) of or like a bog or marsh.

quagmire /ˈkwægˌmaɪr/ or /ˈkwɒg-/ *n* soft, wet ground; a difficult situation.

quahog /ˈkwɒhɒɡ/ or /ˈkwæ-/ *n* an edible North American clam, found on the Atlantic coast.

quail[1] /kweɪl/ *vi* to cower, to shrink back with fear.

quail[2] *n* (*pl* **quails, quail**) a small American game bird.

quaint /kweɪnt/ *adj* attractive or pleasant in an odd or old-fashioned style.—**quaintly** *adv.*—**quaintness** *n.*

quake /kweɪk/ *vi* to tremble or shiver, *esp* with fear or cold; to quiver. • *n* a shaking or tremor; (*inf*) an earthquake.

Quaker /ˈkweɪkər/ *n* a popular name for a member of the Society of Friends, a religious sect advocating peace and simplicity.— **Quakerism** *n.*

quaky /ˈkweɪki/ *adj* (**quakier, quakiest**) shaky; trembling; unstable.—**quakily** *adv.*—**quakiness** *n.*

qualifiable /ˈkwɒliˌfaɪəbəl/ *adj* that may be qualified.

qualification /ˌkwɒləfɪˈkeɪʃən/ *n* qualifying; a thing that qualifies; a quality or acquirement that makes a person fit for a post, etc; modification; limitation; (*pl*) academic achievements.

qualifier /ˈkwɒlɪfaɪr/ *n* one that qualifies; an adjective or adverb.

qualify /ˈkwɒlɪfaɪ/ *vti* (**qualifying, qualified**) to restrict; to describe; to moderate; to modify, limit; to make or become capable or suitable; to fulfil conditions; to pass a final examination; (*gram*) to limit the meaning of.—**qualificatory** *adj.*—**qualifyingly** *adv.*

qualitative /ˈkwɒlɪˌteɪtɪv/ *adj* of or depending on quality; determining the nature, not the quality, of components.—**qualitatively** *adv.*

quality /ˈkwɒliti/ *n* (*pl* **qualities**) a characteristic or attribute; degree of excellence; high standard. • *adj* of high quality.

qualm /kwɒm/ or /kwɒlm/ *n* a doubt; a misgiving; a scruple; a sudden feeling of faintness or nausea.—**qualmish** *adj.*

quandary /ˈkwɒndri/ or /-dəri/ *n* (*pl* **quandaries**) a predicament; a dilemma.

quango /ˈkwæŋgo:/ *n* (*pl* **quangos**) (*acronym*) quasi-autonomous non-governmental organization.

quant /ˈkwænt/ or /ˈkwɒnt/ *n* a long pole, used in punting, with a disc on the end to prevent it from sinking when pushed into mud etc in a river. • *vt, vi* to punt with a quant.

quantify /ˈkwɒntɪˌfaɪ/ *vt* (**quantifying, quantified**) to express as a quantity; to determine the amount of.—**quantifiable** *adj.*—**quantification** *n.*

quantitative /ˈkwɒntɪˌteɪtɪv/ *adj* capable of being measured; relating to size or amount.—**quantitatively** *adv.*

quantity /ˈkwɒntɪti/ *n* (*pl* **quantities**) an amount that can be measured, counted or weighed; a large amount; the property by which a thing can be measured; a number or symbol expressing this property.

quantum /ˈkwɒntəm/ *n* (*pl* **quanta**) a quantity, share or portion; a fixed, elemental unit of energy. • *adj* large, significant.

quantum leap *n* an abrupt transition from one energy state to another; a sudden or noticeable change or increase.—*also* **quantum jump**.

quaquaversal /ˌkweɪkwəˈvɜrsəl/ *adj* (*geol*) pointing in every direction.

quarantine /ˈkwɒrənˌtiːn/ or /ˌkwɒrənˈtiːn/ *n* a period of isolation imposed to prevent the spread of disease; the time or place of this. • *vt* to put or keep in quarantine.

quark /kwɒrk/ or /kwɑrk/ *n* (*physics*) a hypothetical elementary particle.

quarrel /ˈkwɒrəl/ *n* an argument; an angry dispute; a cause of dispute. • *vi* (**quarrelling, quarrelled** *or* **quarreling, quarreled**) to argue violently; to fall out (with); to find fault (with).—**quarreller, quarreler** *n.*

quarrelsome /-səm/ *adj* contentious; apt to quarrel.

quarrier /ˈkwɒriər/, **quarryman** /ˈkwɒrimən/ *n* (*pl* **quarriers, quarrymen**) one who works in a quarry.

quarry[1] /ˈkwɒri/ *n* (*pl* **quarries**) an excavation for the extraction of stone, slate, etc; a place from which stone is excavated; a source of information, etc. • *vti* (**quarrying, quarried**) to excavate (from) a quarry; to research.

quarry[2] *n* (*pl* **quarries**) a hunted animal, prey.

quart /ˈkwɔrt/ or /ˈkɔrt/ *n* a liquid measure equal to a quarter of a gallon or two pints; a dry measure equal to two pints.

quartan /ˈkwɔrtən/ *adj* recurring every third day, said of a fever, *esp* malaria.

quarter /ˈkwɔrtər/ *n* a fourth of something; one fourth of a year; one fourth of an hour; (*US*) 25 cents, or a coin of this value; any leg of a four-legged animal with the adjoining parts; a particular district or section; (*pl*) lodgings; a particular source; an unspecified person or group; a compass point other than the cardinal points; mercy; (*her*) any of four quadrants of a shield. • *vti* to share or divide into four; to provide with lodgings; to lodge; to range over (an area) in search (of). • *adj* constituting a quarter.

quarterage /ˈkwɔrtəridʒ/ *n* a quarterly payment; (*rare*) a shelter.

quarterback /ˈkwɔrtərˌbæk/ *n* (*American football*) a player directly behind forwards and the centre, who directs play. • *vt* to direct the attacking play of (a football team); to manage, direct. • *vi* to play quarterback.

quarterbound /ˈkwɔrtərˌbaʊnd/ *adj* a book bound on the spine only in leather, or another material more expensive than the rest of the binding.

quarterdeck /ˈkwɔrtərˌdek/ *n* the stern area of the upper deck of a ship.

quartered /ˈkwɔrtərd/ *adj* divided into four quarters, sawn along two diameters, said of logs; (*her*) a shield divided into four parts, each with different arms, or with two sets of arms repeated at diagonally opposite corners; stationed or billeted, said especially of soldiers in civilian lodgings.

quarterfinal /ˈkwɔrtərˌfaɪnəl/ *n* one of four matches held before the semifinals in a tournament.—*also adj.*

quartering /ˈkwɔrtəriŋ/ *n* the assignment of quarters to soldiers etc; (*her*) the division of a shield that contains several coats, often denoting family's alliances and intermarriages; any coat of arms so treated.

quarterlight /ˈkwɔrtərˌlaɪt/ *n* a *usu* triangular section within the window of a car.

quarterly /ˈkwɔrtərli/ *adj* occurring, issued, or spaced at three-month intervals; (*her*) divided into quarters. • *adv* once every three months; (*her*) in quarters. • *n* (*pl* **quarterlies**) a publication issued four times a year.

quartermaster /ˈkwɔrtərˌmæstər/ *n* (*mil*) an officer in charge of stores; (*naut*) a petty officer in charge of steering, etc.

quarter note *n* (*mus*) a note having one fourth the duration of a whole note.

quarters *npl* lodgings, *esp* for soldiers; action stations, *esp* used in reference to each member of the crew of a battleship; in India, accommodation provided by an employer or by the government; (*sl used by soldiers*) (*sing*) a quartermaster.

quarterstaff /ˈkwɔrtərˌstæf/ *n* (*pl* **quarterstaves**) a staff 6 to 8 feet long and shod with iron, formerly used as a two-handed weapon of defence; the use of one of these.

quartet, quartette /kwɔrˈtet/ *n* a set or group of four; a piece of music composed for four instruments or voices; a group of four instrumentalists or voices.

quartic /ˈkwɑrtɪk/ *adj* (*math*) pertaining to the fourth power, biquadratic. • *n* the fourth power, arising from the multiplication of a square number or quantity by itself, biquadratic.

quartile /ˈkwɔrtaɪl/ *n* (*statistics*) one of three values of a variable that separates its distribution into four sets with equal frequencies. • *adj* (*statistics*) pertaining, or referring, to a quartile; (*astrol*) referring to an aspect of planets separated by 90 degree longitude.

quarto /ˈkwɔrto:/ *n* (*pl* **quartos**) a page size, approx 9 by 12 inches; a book of this size of page.

quartz /kwɔrts/ *n* a crystalline mineral, a form of silica, *usu* colourless and transparent.

quartzite /ˈkwɔrtsaɪt/ *n* a very hard quartz rock; a light-coloured quartz sandstone.

quasar /ˈkweɪzɑr/ or /-sɑr/ *n* a distant, starlike, celestial object that emits much light and powerful radio waves.

quash /kwɒʃ/ *vt* (*rebellion etc*) to put down; to suppress; to make void.

quasi /ˈkwɒzi/ *adv* seemingly; as if. • *prefix* almost, apparently.

quassia /ˈkwɒʃə/ *n* a South American tree yielding bark and wood of excessive bitterness; the bark and wood from a tree of the same family, used to make furniture; formerly a bitter tonic drug obtained from this, which is now used as an ingredient in insecticides.

quatercentenary /ˌkwætərsenˈtenəri/ or /-ˈtiːnəri/ *n* (*pl* **quatercentenaries**) a 400th anniversary, or the entire year of celebrations etc of a 400th anniversary.

quaternary /ˈkwɒtərˌneri/ or /kwəˈtɜrnəri/ *adj* consisting of, arranged in, or by, fours; of the number 4; (*chem*) an atom bound to four other atoms or groups, or containing such an atom; (*math*) with four variables. (*with cap*) denoting strata more recent than the Upper Tertiary, ie the most recent geological period, of less than 1 million years ago. • *n* (*pl* **quaternaries**) (*with* **the**) this geological rock system, consisting of Pleistocene and Holocene (recent) epochs.

quaternion /kwəˈtɜrniən/ *n* the number 4; a set of 4; (*maths*) a calculus or method of mathematical investigation using a generalized complex number with four components.

quaternity /kwəˈtɜrniti/ *n* (*pl* **quaternities**) four persons regarded as one, *esp* in relation to God.

quatrain /ˈkwɒtreɪn/ *n* a four-line stanza, rhymed alternately.

quatrefoil /ˈkætrəˌfɔɪl/ *n* a four-leaved plant, such as certain clovers; an ornamental figure in architectural tracery divided by cusps into four leaves.

quattrocento /ˌkwætroːˈtʃento:/ *n* the fifteenth century, *esp* in connection with Italian art and literature.

quaver /ˈkweɪvər/ *vi* to tremble, vibrate; to speak or sing with a quivering voice. • *n* a trembling sound or note; (*mus*) an eighth note.—**quaveringly** *adv.*—**quavery** *adj.*

quay /kiː/ *n* a loading wharf or landing place for vessels.

quayage /ˈkiːədʒ/ *n* an interconnected network of quays; quay dues.

queasy /ˈkwiːzi/ *adj* (**queasier, queasiest**) nauseous; easily upset; over-scrupulous.—**queasily** *adv.*—**queasiness** *n.*

quebracho /keɪˈbrɒtʃoː/ *n* (*pl* **quebrachos**) one of two types of South American tree with a hard timber rich in tannin, and used in tanning and dyeing; the medicinal bark of a South American tree, the alkaloids from the bark of which are also used in tanning; the wood or bark from any of these trees; any South American tree yielding a hard wood.

queen /kwiːn/ *n* a female sovereign and head of state; the wife or widow of a king; a woman considered pre-eminent; the egg-laying female of bees, wasps, etc; a playing card with a picture of a queen; (*chess*) the most powerful piece; (*sl*) a male homosexual, *esp* one who ostentatiously takes a feminine role. • *vi* (*with* **it**) to act like a queen, *esp* to put on airs. • *vt* (a pawn) to promote to a queen in chess.—**queendom** *n*.

queencake /'kwi:nkeɪk/ *n* a small currant cake.

queenly /'kwi:nlɪ/ *adj* (**queenlier, queenliest**) like or having the character or attributes of a queen; regal.—**queenliness** *n*.

queen mother *n* a queen dowager who is the mother of a ruling sovereign.

queer /kwɪːr/ *adj* strange, odd, curious; (*inf*) eccentric; (*sl*) homosexual. • *n* a (male) homosexual. •*vt* (*sl*) to spoil the success of.—**queerness** *n*.

quell /kwɛl/ *vt* to suppress; to allay.—**queller** *n*.

quench /kwɛntʃ/ *vt* (*thirst*) to satisfy or slake; (*fire*) to put out, extinguish; (*steel*) to cool; to suppress.—**quenchable** *adj*.—**quencher** *n*.

quenelle /kə'nɛl/ *n* a ball of savoury cooked meat, formed into various shapes and boiled in stock or fried.

quercine /kwər'siːn/ *adj* of the oak.

querist /'kwɛrɪst/ *n* one who asks questions.

quern /kwərn/ *n* a kind of stone handmill for grinding corn.

querulous /'kwɛrʊləs/ *adj* complaining, fretful, peevish.—**querulously** *adv*.

query /'kwiːrɪ/ or /'kwɛrɪ/ *n* (*pl* **queries**) a question; a question mark; doubt. • *vti* (**querying, queried**) to question; to doubt the accuracy of.

quest /kwɛst/ *n* a search, seeking, *esp* involving a journey. • *vti* to search (about) for, seek.—**quester** *n*.—**questingly** *adv*.

question /'kwɛstʃən/ *n* an interrogative sentence; an inquiry; a problem; a doubtful or controversial point; a subject of debate before an assembly; a part of a test or examination. • *vti* to ask questions (of); to interrogate intensively; to dispute; to subject to analysis.—**questioner** *n*.

questionable /-əbəl/ *adj* doubtful; not clearly true or honest.—**questionability** *n*. —**questionably** *adv*.

question mark *n* a punctuation mark (?) used at the end of a sentence to indicate a question, or to express doubt about something; something unknown.

questionnaire /-nɛr/ *n* a series of questions designed to collect statistical information; a survey made by the use of questionnaire.

quetzal /'kwɛtzəl/ or /'kɛtsəl/ *n* a large brilliantly coloured Central or Southern American bird, the male having long tail feathers; a Guatemalan coin.

queue /kjuː/ *n* a line of people, vehicles, etc awaiting a turn. • *vi* (**queuing, queued**) to wait in turn.

quibble /'kwɪbəl/ *n* a minor objection or criticism. • *vi* to argue about trifling matters.—**quibbler** *n*.—**quibblingly** *adv*.

quiche /kiːʃ/ *n* a savoury tart filled with onions and a cheese and egg custard.

quick /kwɪk/ *adj* rapid, speedy; nimble; prompt; responsive; alert; eager to learn. • *adv* (*inf*) in a quick manner. • *n* the sensitive flesh below a fingernail or toenail; the inmost sensibilities.—**quickly** *adv*.—**quickness** *n*.

quicken /'kwɪkən/ *vti* to speed up or accelerate; to make alive; to come to life; to invigorate.—**quickener** *n*.

quickie /'kwɪkɪ/ *n* (*inf*) anything done rapidly or in haste.

quicklime /'kwɪklaɪm/ *n* calcium oxide.

quicksand /'kwɪksænd/ *n* loose wet sand easily yielding to pressure in which persons, animals, etc may be swallowed up.

quicksilver /'kwɪkˌsɪlvər/ *n* mercury.

quickstep /'kwɪkstɛp/ *n* a ballroom dance in quick time; the music for this. • *vi* (**quickstepping, quickstepped**) to do this dance.

quick-tempered *adj* easily angered.

quick-witted *adj* mentally alert; quick in repartee.—**quick-wittedness** *n*.

quid /kwɪd/ *n* (*pl* **quid**) (*sl*) a pound (sterling).

quiddity /'kwɪdɪtɪ/ *n* (*pl* **quiddities**) (*philos*) the essence of a thing; captious subtlety, a quibble.

quidnunc /'kwɪdnʌŋk/ *n* one who is curious to know everything that happens; a gossip, a busybody.

quid pro quo /ˌkwɪdprɔːˈkwoː/ *n* (*pl* **quid pro quos**) something equivalent given in exchange for something else.

quiescent /kwɪ'ɛsənt/ *adj* dormant, inactive, inert; silent.—**quiescence** *n*.

quiet /'kwaɪət/ *adj* silent, not noisy; still, not moving; gentle, not boisterous; unobtrusive, not showy; placid, calm; monotonous,

uneventful; undisturbed. • *n* stillness, peace, repose; an undisturbed state. • *vti* to quieten.—**quietly** *adv*.—**quietness** *n*.

quieten /-ən/ *vti* to make or become quiet; to calm, soothe.

quietism /'kwaɪəˌtɪzəm/ *n* a mental tranquillity and passive attitude towards life; a form of religious mysticism, founded in 17th-century Spain, in which the cultivation of this attitude with reference to God's will is to be attained.

quietize, quietise /'kwaɪəˌtaɪz/ *vt* to insulate something from sound; to soundproof.

quietness /'kwaɪətnəs/ *n* repose.

quietude /'kwaɪəˌtuːd/ or /-ˌtjuːd/ *n* repose; tranquillity.

quietus /kwaɪ'iːtəs/ *n* (*pl* **quietuses**) death; the final settlement or discharge of debts etc; anything that results in death or annihilation.

quiff /kwɪf/ *n* (*Brit*) a curl plastered up above the forehead.

quill /kwɪl/ *n* the hollow stem of a feather; anything made of this, as a pen; a stiff, hollow spine of a hedgehog or porcupine.

quilt /kwɪlt/ *n* a thick, warm bedcover; a bedspread; a coverlet of two cloths sewn together with padding between. • *vti* to stitch together like a quilt; to make a quilt.—**quilter** *n*.—**quilting** *n*.

quin /kwɪn/ *n* a quintuplet.

quinary /'kwaɪnərɪ/ *adj* (*pl* **quinaries**) consisting of, or arranged in, fives; a number system with a base of the number 5; having five parts; the fifth member of something.

quinate /'kwɪneɪt/ *adj* (*bot*) with five leaflets on a petiole; said of a digitate leaf.

quince /kwɪns/ *n* a hard-fleshed yellow Asian fruit used in preserves; the tree it grows on.

quincentenary /ˌkwɪnsɛn'tɛnərɪ/ or /-'tiːnərɪ/ *n* (*pl* **quincentenaries**) a 500th anniversary, or the entire year of celebration, etc, of the 500th anniversary.

quincunx /'kwɪnkʌŋks/ *n* an arrangement of five things in form of four corners and centre of a square; (*bot*) such an arrangement of petals or sepals in bud; (*astrol*) two planets with an aspect of 150 degrees.

quindecagon /kwɪn'dɛkəɡən/ *n* a plane figure with 15 angles and 15 sides.

quinine /'kwɪnaɪn/ or /'kwaɪnaɪn/, /'kwɪniːn/ *n* a bitter crystalline alkaloid used in medicine; one of its salts used *esp* as an antimalarial and a bitter tonic.

quinqu-, quinque- /'kwɪŋkwɪ/ *prefix* five.

quinquagenarian /ˌkwɪŋkwədʒɪ'nɛrɪən/ *adj n* (a person) fifty to fifty-nine years old; relating to such a person.

Quinquagesima (Sunday) /ˌkwɪŋkwə'dʒɛsɪmə/ *n* the Sunday before Lent.

quinquennial /kwɪn'kwɛnɪəl/ *adj* lasting five years or occurring every five years.—**quinquennially** *adv*.

quinquennium /kwɪn'kwɛnɪəm/ *n* (*pl* **quinquennia**) a period of five years.

quinquepartite /'kwɪnkwɛˌpartaɪt/ *adj* of five parts; shared by five.

quinquereme /'kwɪnkwəˌriːm/ *n* in ancient Rome, a galley with five banks of oars on each side.

quinquevalent /ˌkwɪnkwə'veɪlənt/ *adj* (*chem*) having a valency of five, pentavalent.—**quinquevalency, quinquevalence** *n*.

quinsy /'kwɪnzɪ/ *n* a severe infection of the throat or adjacent parts causing swelling and fever.

quint /kwɪnt/ *n* (*US*) a quintuplet.

quintain /'kwɪntɪn/ *n* a post with a sandbag on a pivot, or other object, used for practising the medieval sport of tilting; tilting at this.

quintal /'kwɪntəl/ *n* a measure of weight, 100 lb; a measure of weight of 100 kilograms.

quintan /'kwɪntən/ *adj* said of an intermittent fever which recurs every fourth day.

quintessence /kwɪn'tɛsəns/ *n* the purest form or most typical representation of anything, the embodiment.

quintessential /ˌkwɪntə'sɛnʃəl/ *adj* most typical; fundamental.—**quintessentially** *adv*.

quintet, quintette /kwɪn'tɛt/ *n* a set or group of five; a piece of music composed for five instruments or voices; a group of five instrumentalists or voices.

quintillion /kwɪn'tɪljən/ *n* (*pl* **quintillions, quintillion**) in Western Europe, a million raised to the fifth power (1,000,0005), known in North America as a nonillion; in North America the sixth power of thousand, known as a trillion in Britain.—**quintillionth** *adj*.

quintuple /kwɪn'tʊpəl/ *adj* fivefold; having five divisions or parts; five times as much or as many. • *vti* to multiply by five. • *n* a number five times greater than another.

quintuplet /kwɪn'tʊplət/ *n* one of five offspring produced at one birth.

quintuplicate /kwɪn'tʊplɪˌkeɪt/ *vt* to multiply by five; to make five copies of.• *adj* five-fold. • *n* a set of five objects.—**quintuplication** *n*.

quip /kwɪp/ *n* a witty remark; a gibe. • *vt* (**quipping, quipped**) to make a clever or sarcastic remark.—**quipster** *n*.

quire /'kwaɪr/ *n* a set of 24 sheets of paper; one twentieth of a ream; a section of folded sheets sewn together in bookbinding.

quirk /kwərk/ *n* an unexpected turn or twist; a peculiarity of character or mannerism.

quirky /'kwərki/ *adj* (**quirkier, quirkiest**) odd or unusual in character, behaviour or appearance.—**quirkily** *adv*.—**quirkiness** *n*.

quirt /kwərt/ *n* a riding whip of plaited leather with a leather thong at the end. • *vt* to lash with this.

quisling /'kwɪzlɪŋ/ *n* a traitor who aids an invading enemy to regularize their conquest of his country; a collaborator.

quit /kwɪt/ *vti* (**quitting, quitted** *or* **quit**) to leave; to stop or cease; to resign; to free from obligation; to admit defeat. • *adj* free from; released from.

quitch (grass) /kwɪtʃ/ *n* couchgrass.

quite /kwaɪt/ *adv* completely; somewhat, fairly; really.

quits /kwɪts/ *adj* even; on equal terms by payment or revenge.

quittance /'kwɪtəns/ *n* a release from debt or obligation.

quitter /'kwɪtər/ *n* a person who gives up easily.

quiver[1] /'kwɪvər/ *vi* to shake; to tremble, shiver. • *n* a shiver, vibration.—**quiveringly** *adv*.—**quivery** *adj*.

quiver[2] *n* a case for holding arrows.—**quiverful** *n*.

qui vive /kiː'viːv/ *n* **on the qui vive** on the alert.

quixotic /kwɪk'sɒtɪk/, **quixotical** /-əl/ *adj* chivalrous or romantic to extravagance; unrealistically idealistic.—**quixotically** *adv*.

quixotism /'kwɪksəˌtɪzəm/, **quixotry** /-tri/ *n* romantic or extravagant notions or schemes; quixotic conduct or ideals.

quiz /kwɪz/ *n* (*pl* **quizzes**) a form of entertainment where players are asked questions of general knowledge; a short written or oral test. • *vt* (**quizzing, quizzed**) to interrogate; to make fun of.—**quizzer** *n*.

quizmaster /'kwɪzˌmæstər/ *n* a person who puts the questions to a contestant in a quiz show.

quiz show *n* an entertainment programme on television or radio in which contestants answer questions to win prizes.

quizzical /'kwɪzɪkəl/ *adj* humorous and questioning.—**quizzicality** *n*.—**quizzically** *adv*.

quod erat demonstrandum /kwɒdˌɛrætˌdemən'strændum/ (*Latin*) that which was to be proved.

quodlibet /'kwɒdlɪˌbet/ *n* a subtle or moot point, *esp* as part of a theological argument; (*mus*) a light musical medley.—**quodlibetical** *adj* **quodlibetically** *adv*.

quoin /kɔɪn/ *n* a wedge of wood or metal used to support and steady something (*esp* formerly a gun or cannon); a keystone; an external angle of a building; the stone forming this, the cornerstone; a wedge-shaped wooden block to tighten the pages of type within a chase.

quoit /kɔɪt/ *n* a ring of metal, plastic, etc thrown in quoits; (*pl*) a game in which rings are thrown at or over a peg.

quondam /'kwɒndæm/ *adj* that was, former.

quorum /'kwɔrəm/ *n* the minimum number that must be present at a meeting or assembly to make its proceedings valid.

quota /'kwoːtə/ *n* a proportional share; a prescribed amount; a part to be contributed.

quotable /'kwoːtəbəl/ *adj* worthy or fit to be quoted.—**quotability** *n*.

quotation /kwoː'teɪʃən/ *n* the act of quoting; the words quoted; an estimated price.

quotation mark *n* a punctuation mark to indicate the beginning (' *or* ") and the end (' *or* ") of a quoted passage.

quote /kwoːt/ *vt* to cite; to refer to; to repeat the words of a novel, play, poem, speech, etc exactly; to adduce by way of authority; to set off by quotation marks; to state the price of (something). • *n* (*inf*) something quoted; a quotation mark.

quoth /kwoːθ/ *vt* (*arch*) said, used with nouns and all pronouns except thou and you.

quotidian /kwoː'tɪdiən/ *adj* daily; recurring every day, occurring every day; belonging to each day; commonplace, routine, everyday, trivial. • *n* a fever, *esp* malaria, recurring every day.

quotient /'kwoːʃənt/ *n* (*math*) the result obtained when one number is divided by another.

quo warranto /'kwoːwəˈrænto/ *or* /-'ræn-/ *n* (*law*) a proceeding set in motion to determine the authority by which someone claims an office or privilege; (*formerly*) the title of a writ issued to a person to try the question of title to any public office or privilege.

qwerty, QWERTY /'kwərti/ *n* (*inf*) a standard typewriter or computer keyboard.

R

R, r /ɑr/ *n* the 18th letter of the English alphabet.
R. *abbr* = rabbi; Regiment; Regina (*Latin* Queen); Republican; Rex (*Latin King*); River; Royal.
RA *abbr* = Royal Academy or Royal Academician.
Ra (*chem symbol*) radium.
RAAF *abbr* = Royal Australian Air Force.
rabbet, rebate /ˈræbɪt/ *n* a recess or groove cut in a surface (*eg* wood) to receive another piece. • *vt* to cut a rabbet in; to join (pieces of wood, etc) using a rabbet.
rabbi /ˈræbaɪ/ *n* (*pl* **rabbis**) the religious and spiritual leader of a Jewish congregation.
rabbinate /ˈræbɪneɪt/ *n* the position or tenure of a rabbi; rabbis collectively.
rabbinical /rəˈbɪnɪkəl/ *adj* of or pertaining to rabbis, their office, writings, etc.—**rabbinically** *adv*.
rabbit /ˈræbɪt/ *n* a small burrowing mammal of the hare family with long ears, a short tail, and long hind legs; their flesh as food; their fur.
rabbit punch *n* a sharp blow to the back of the neck.
rabble /ˈræbəl/ *n* a disorderly crowd, a mob; the common herd.
rabble-rouser *n* a person who excites a mob to violent action; a demagogue.
Rabelasian /ˌræbəˈleɪziən/ *adj* of, pertaining to, or resembling the coarse, satirical humour of the French writer François Rabelais (1494–1553).
rabid /ˈræbɪd/ *adj* infected with rabies; raging; fanatical.
rabies /ˈreɪbiːz/ *n* an acute, infectious, viral disease transmitted by the bite of an infected animal.—*also* **hydrophobia**.
raccoon /rəˈkuːn/ *n* a small nocturnal carnivore of North America that lives in trees; its yellowish grey fur.
race[1] /reɪs/ *n* any of the divisions of humankind distinguished *esp* by colour of skin; any geographical, national, or tribal ethnic grouping; a subspecies of plants or animals; distinctive flavour or taste.
race[2] *n* a contest of speed, as in running, swimming, cycling, etc; a rapid current or channel of water. • *vi* to run at top speed or out of control; to compete in a race; (*engine*) to run without a working load or with the transmission disengaged. • *vt* to cause to race; to contest against.
racecourse /ˈreɪskɔrs/ *n* a track over which races are run, *esp* an oval track for racing horses.—*also* **racetrack**.
racehorse /ˈreɪshɔrs/ *n* a horse bred and trained for racing.
raceme /rəˈsiːm/ *n* (*bot*) an arrangement of flowers directly on a main stem, as in the lily of the valley.
racer /ˈreɪsər/ *n* a person who races; a machine used for racing, *esp* a bicycle; a kind of American snake.
race relations *npl* the relationship between different races in a community or nation; the sociological study of such relations.
racetrack /ˈreɪstræk/ *see* **racecourse**.
rachis, rhachis /ˈreɪkɪs/ *n* (*pl* **rachises, rhachises** or **rachides, rhachides**) the main stem of a plant's flower-head; the shaft of a feather; the spinal column.
rachitis /rəˈkaɪtɪs/ *n* rickets.
racial /ˈreɪʃəl/ *adj* of or relating to any of the divisions of humankind distinguished by colour, etc.
racism /ˈreɪsɪzəm/, **racialism** /ˈreɪʃəlɪzəm/ *n* a belief in the superiority of some races over others; prejudice against or hatred of other races; discriminating behaviour towards people of another race.—**racist** *n*.
rack /ræk/ *n* a framework for holding or displaying articles; an instrument for torture by stretching; the triangular frame for setting up balls in snooker; a toothed bar to engage with the teeth of a wheel pinion or worm gear; extreme pain or anxiety. • *vt* (*person*) to stretch on a rack; to arrange in or on a rack; to torture, torment; to move parts of machinery with a toothed rack.
racket[1], **racquet** /ˈrækət/ *n* a bat strung with nylon, for playing tennis, etc. (*pl*) a game for two or four players played in a four-walled court.
racket[2] *n* noisy confusion; din; an obtaining of money illegally; any fraudulent business.

racketeer /ˌrækəˈtiːr/ *n* a person who extorts money by threat or engages in an illegal profit-making enterprise.
rack railway *n* a railway on a steep incline that has a rack or cog between the rails to engage with a pinion on a locomotive.
rack-rent *n* an extortionate rent.—*also vt*.—**rack-renter** *n*.
racconteur /ˌrækɒnˈtɔr/ *n* a person who excels in relating anecdotes.
racquet *see* **racket**[1].
racy /ˈreɪsi/ *adj* (**racier, raciest**) lively, spirited; risqué.—**racily** *adv*.
rad[1] /ræd/ *n* a unit of absorbed dose of ionizing radiation.
rad[2] (*symbol*) radian.
radar /ˈreɪdɑr/ *n* a system or device for detecting objects such as aircraft by using the reflection of radio waves.
radar beacon *n* a fixed radio transmitter that sends out a signal which allows a ship or an aircraft to determine its own position.
radarscope /-ˌskoʊp/ *n* a cathode-ray oscilloscope which displays radar signals.
radial /ˈreɪdiəl/ *adj* like a radius; branching from a common centre.
radial ply *adj* (*tyre*) having the fabric cords of the outer casing lying radial to the hub for greater flexibility.
radial symmetry *n* the state of having similar parts arranged symmetrically around a common axis.
radian /ˈreɪdiən/ *n* the SI unit of plane angle, equal to the angle at the centre of a circle formed by radii of an arc equal in length to the radius.
radiance /ˈreɪdiəns/ *n* the condition of being radiant; brilliant light; dazzling beauty.
radiant /ˈreɪdiənt/ *adj* shining; beaming with happiness; sending out rays; transmitted by radiation.—**radiantly** *adv*.
radiant energy *n* energy in the form of electromagnetic radiation, such as heat or light.
radiant heat *n* heat conveyed by electromagnetic radiation rather than conduction or convection.
radiate /ˈreɪdiˌeɪt/ *vt* (*light, heat, etc*) to emit in rays; (*happiness, love, etc*) to give forth. • *vi* to spread out as if from a centre; to shine; to emit rays.
radiation /ˌreɪdiˈeɪʃən/ *n* radiant particles emitted as energy; rays emitted in nuclear decay; (*med*) treatment using a radioactive substance.
radiation sickness *n* an illness caused by excessive exposure to radiation from radioactive materials.
radiator /ˈreɪdiˌeɪtər/ or /ˈræd-/ *n* an apparatus for heating a room; a cooling device for a vehicle engine.
radical /ˈrædɪkəl/ *adj* of or relating to the root or origin; fundamental; favouring basic change. • *n* a person who advocates fundamental political or social change.—**radicalism** *n*.
radically /-li/ *adv* fundamentally.
radical sign *n* the symbol √ placed before a number to show that the square root (or a higher root denoted by an index number over the sign) is to be extracted.
radicchio /rəˈdiːkio/ *n* (*pl* **radicchios**) a type of Italian chicory with white-veined purple leaves eaten raw in salads.
radices /ˈrædɪsəz/ *see* **radix**.
radicle /ˈrædɪkəl/ *n* the part of a seed that develops into a root; a root-like subdivision of a nerve or vein.
radii /ˈreɪdiˌaɪ/ *see* **radius**.
radio- /ˈreɪdio/ *prefix* radial; radio; using radiant energy.
radio *n* the transmission of sounds or signals by electromagnetic waves through space, without wires, to a receiving set; such a set; broadcasting by radio as an industry, entertainment, etc. • *adj* of, using, used in, or sent by radio. • *vti* to transmit, or communicate with, by radio.
radioactive /ˌreɪdioˈæktɪv/ *adj* giving off radiant energy in the form of particles or rays caused by the disintegration of atomic nuclei.—**radioactivity** *n*.
radioactive decay *n* the disintegration of a nucleus as the result of electron capture.
radioactive waste *n* any waste products that contain radioactive materials.—*also* **nuclear waste**.

radio astronomy *n* astronomy dealing with radio waves in space in order to obtain information about the universe.

radio beacon *n* a radio transmitter that sends out signals as an aid to navigation.

radiocarbon /ˌreɪdɪoˈkɑːbən/ *n* a radioisotope of carbon used in carbon dating.

radiocarbon dating *n* carbon dating.

radio compass *n* a navigational device which can determine the direction of radio waves from a specific radio beacon.

radio control *n* remote control using radio signals.—**radio-controlled** *adj*.

radioelement /ˌreɪdɪoˈɛləmənt/ *n* a radioactive chemical element.

radio frequency *n* a frequency intermediate between audio frequencies and infrared frequencies used *esp* in radio and television transmission.

radiogram /ˈreɪdɪoˌgræm/ *n* a combined radio and record player.

radiograph /ˈreɪdɪoˌgrɑːf/ *n* an image produced on sensitive photographic film or plate by radiation other than light, *esp* X-rays.

radiography /ˌreɪdɪˈɒgræfɪ/ *n* the production of X-ray photographs for use in medicine, industry, etc.—**radiographer** *n*.

radioisotope /ˌreɪdɪoˈaɪsətəʊp/ *n* a radioactive isotope.

radiology /ˌreɪdɪˈɒlədʒɪ/ *n* a branch of medicine concerned with the use of radiant energy (as X-rays and radium) in the diagnosis and treatment of disease.—**radiologist** *n*.

radiometer /ˌreɪdɪˈɒmɪtər/ *n* an instrument for measuring radiant energy.—**radiometric** *adj*.

radiopaging /ˌreɪdɪoˈpeɪdʒɪŋ/ *n* a system for alerting a person using a small radio transmitter which beeps in response to a signal from a distance.

radiosonde /ˈreɪdɪoˌsɒnd/ *n* a small radio transmitter carried by a probe for sending back data on atmospheric conditions.

radio source *n* any celestial object, such as a supernova, that emits radio waves.

radio spectrum *n* that range of frequencies, between 10 kHz and 300,000 MHz, used in radio transmission.

radiotelegraphy /ˌreɪdɪoteˈlɒgrəfɪ/ *n* telegraphy that uses radio waves to transmit messages.—**radiotelegraph** *n*.—**radiotelegraphic** *adj*.

radiotelephone /ˌreɪdɪoˈtelɪfoʊn/ *n* a device for transmitting telephone messages using radio waves. • *vt* to transmit by radiotelephone. • *vi* to operate a radiotelephone.—**radiotelephony** *n*.

radio telescope *n* an instrument used in radio astronomy to receive and analyse radio waves.

radiotherapy *n* the medical treatment of disease, *esp* cancer, by X-rays or other radioactive substances.—**radiotherapist** *n*.

radio wave *n* an electromagnetic wave having radio frequency.

radish /ˈrædɪʃ/ *n* a pungent root eaten raw as a salad vegetable.

radium /ˈreɪdɪəm/ *n* a highly radioactive metallic element.

radium therapy *n* the treatment of cancer by exposure to radiation from radium.

radius /ˈreɪdɪəs/ *n* (*pl* **radii**) (*geom*) a straight line joining the centre of a circle or sphere to its circumference; a thing like this, a spoke; a sphere of activity; (*anat*) the thicker of the two bones of the forearm.

radix /ˈreɪdɪks/ *n* (*pl* **radices, radixes**) (*maths*) a number that is the base of a number system or for computation of logarithms.

radome /ˈreɪdoʊm/ *n* a protective housing for a radar antenna constructed from material which is transparent to radio waves.

radon /ˈreɪdɒn/ *n* a gaseous radioactive element.—*also* **niton**.

radula /ˈrædjʊlə/ *n* (*pl* **radulae**) a horny strip covered with minute teeth on the tongue of certain molluscs.

RAF /ræf/ or /ˌɑːreɪˈef/ *abbr* = Royal Air Force.

raffia /ˈræfɪə/ *n* a kind of palm; fibre from its leaves used in basket-making, etc.

raffish /ˈræfɪʃ/ *adj* untidy, disreputable, rakish; vulgarly flashy.

raffle /ˈræfəl/ *n* a lottery with prizes. • *vt* to offer as a prize in a raffle.

raft /rɑːft/ *n* a platform of logs, planks, etc strapped together to float on water.

rafter /ˈrɑːftər/ *n* one of the inclined, parallel beams that support a roof.

rag[1] /ræg/ *n* a torn or waste scrap of cloth; a shred; (*inf*) a sensationalist newspaper; (*pl*) tattered or shabby clothing.

rag[2] *vt* (**ragging, ragged**) to tease; to play practical jokes on. • *n* a practical joke; a series of boisterous stunts staged by British students to raise money for charity.

rag[3] *n* ragtime music.

raga /ˈrɑːgə/ *n* (a composition based on) any of various conventional melodic or rhythmic patterns in Indian music used as the basis for improvisation.

ragamuffin /ˈrægəmʌfɪn/ *n* an unkempt dirty person, *esp* a child.

rag and bone man *n* a man who buys and sells discarded clothing, furniture etc; (*US*) a junkman.

ragbag /ˈrægbæg/ *n* a bag for scraps; a miscellaneous collection, jumble.

rage /reɪdʒ/ *n* violent anger; passion; frenzy; fashion, craze. • *vi* to behave with violent anger; to storm; to spread rapidly; to be prevalent.

ragged /ˈrægɪd/ *adj* jagged; uneven; irregular; worn into rags; tattered.—**raggedly** *adv*.—**raggedness** *n*.

ragged robin *n* a Eurasian plant of the pink family with tattered looking pink or white flowers.

raggedy /ˈrægədɪ/ *adj* (*inf*) tattered.

ragi, raggee /ˈrægɪ/ *n* a cereal grass cultivated in Asia and Africa.

raging /ˈreɪdʒɪŋ/ *adj* violent; intense.

raglan /ˈræglən/ *n* a type of loose sleeve cut in one piece with the shoulder of a garment.

ragout /ˈræˈguː/ *n* a stew of meat and vegetables, highly seasoned.

ragtime /ˈrægtaɪm/ *n* quick tempo jazz piano music.

ragwort /ˈrægwɜːt/ *n* a European composite plant with yellow flowers.

rah /rɒ/ *interj* hurrah.

raid /reɪd/ *n* a sudden attack to assault or seize. • *vt* to make a raid on; to steal from.—**raider** *n*.

rail[1] /reɪl/ *n* a horizontal bar extending from one post to another, as in a fence, etc; one of a pair of parallel steel lines forming a track for the wheels of a train; a railroad.

rail[2] *vi* to speak angrily.

railhead /ˈreɪlhed/ *n* the furthest point reached by the tracks of an uncompleted railway; a terminus.

railing /ˈreɪlɪŋ/ *n* a fence of rails and posts; rails collectively.

raillery /ˈreɪlərɪ/ *n* (*pl* **railleries**) good-humoured banter, mockery.

railroad /ˈreɪlroʊd/ *n* railway. • *vt* to force unduly; (*bill, etc*) to push forward fast; to imprison hastily, *esp* unjustly.

railway /ˈreɪlweɪ/ *n* a track of parallel steel rails along which carriages are drawn by locomotive engines; a complete system of such tracks.

raiment /ˈreɪmənt/ *n* (*poet*) clothing.

rain /reɪn/ *n* water that falls from the clouds in the form of drops; a shower; a large quantity of anything falling like rain; (*pl*) the rainy season in the tropics. • *vti* (*of rain*) to fall; to fall like rain; (*rain, etc*) to pour down.

rainbow /ˈreɪnboʊ/ *n* the arc containing the colours of the spectrum formed in the sky by the refraction of the sun's rays in falling rain or in mist. • *adj* many-coloured.

rainbow trout *n* a large freshwater trout of Europe and North America with bright markings.

rain check *n* the postponement of acceptance of an offer or invitation; in the US, a ticket stub allowing future admission to an event in the case of it being rained off; .

raincoat /ˈreɪnkoʊt/ *n* a waterproof coat.

raindrop /-drɒp/ *n* a drop of rain.

rainfall /-fɔːl/ *n* a fall of rain; the amount of rain that falls on a given area in a specified time.

rain forest *n* a dense, evergreen forest in a tropical area with much rainfall.

rain gauge *n* an instrument for measuring rainfall.

rainproof /-pruːf/ *adj* rain-resisting.

rain shadow *n* the leeward side of a hill or mountain where the rain is relatively lighter.

rainy /ˈreɪnɪ/ *adj* (**rainier, rainiest**) full of rain; wet.

rainy day *n* a future need, *esp* financial.

raise /reɪz/ *vt* to elevate; to lift up; to set or place upright; to stir up, rouse; to increase in size, amount, degree, intensity, etc; to breed, bring up; (*question, etc*) to put forward; to collect or levy; (*siege*) to abandon. • *n* a rise in wages.

raisin /ˈreɪzən/ *n* a sweet, dried grape.

raison d'être *Fr.* /ˌreɪzɔ̃ˈdɛtr/ *n* (*pl* **raisons d'être**) reason for existence; justification.

raj /rɒdʒ/ or /rɒʒ/, /rɑːdʒ/ *n* the period of British rule in India.

rajah, raja /ˈrɒdʒə/ or /ˈrɒʒə/, /ˈrædʒə/ *n* (*formerly*) an Indian ruler; an Indian or Malayan chief or prince.

rake[1] /reɪk/ *n* a tool with a row of teeth and a handle for gathering together, scraping (leaves, hay, etc) or for smoothing gravel, etc. • *vt* to scrape, gather as with a rake; to sweep with gaze or gunshot; (*with* in: *money*, *etc*) to gather a great amount rapidly; (*with* up: *past misdemeanours*, *etc*) to bring to light.

rake[2] *n* the incline or slope of a mast, stern, etc.

rake[3] *n* a dissolute, debauched man, a libertine.

raki, rakee /rɑˈkiː/ or /ˈræki/ *n* a strong aromatic spirit distilled from grain in Turkey.

rakish /ˈreɪkɪʃ/ *adj* jaunty, dashing; dissolute.—**rakishly** *adv*.—**rakishness** *n*.

rale /ræl/ *n* a wheezing rattle detectable with a stethoscope in the chest of patients with lung disorders.

rallentando /ˌrælənˈtændo/ *adv* (*mus*) gradually slower.

rally /ˈræli/ *vti* (**rallying, rallied**) to bring or come together; to recover strength, revive; to take part in a motor rally; (*with* round) to help (a person); to support financially or morally. • *n* (*pl* **rallies**) a large assembly of people for a political purpose; a recovery (after illness); (*stock exchange*) a sharp increase in price after a decline; (*tennis*) a lengthy exchange of shots; a competitive test of driving and navigational skills.

RAM /ræm/ *abbr* = random-access memory.

ram /ræm/ *n* a male sheep; a battering device; a piston; (*with cap*) Aries, the first sign of the zodiac. • *vt* (**ramming, rammed**) to force or drive; to crash; to cram; to thrust violently.

Ramadan /ˈræməˌdæn/ *n* the ninth month of the Islamic year; the great fast during it.

ramble /ˈræmbəl/ *vi* to wander or stroll about for pleasure; (*plant*) to straggle; to write or talk aimlessly. • *n* a leisurely walk in the countryside.

rambler /ˈræmblər/ *n* a person who rambles; a climbing rose.

rambling /-ɪŋ/ *adj* spread out, straggling; circuitous; disconnected; disjointed.

Ramboesque /ˈræmboˌɛsk/ *adj* in the aggressive, mindless style of the fictional character Rambo, an indestructible one-man army who featured in several violent action films in the 1980s.

rambunctious /ræmˈbʌŋkʃəs/ *adj* (*inf*) boisterous, unruly.—**rambunctiously** *adv*.—**rambunctiousness** *n*.

rambutan /ræmˈbuːtən/ *n* (a Malaysian tree bearing) a hairy red edible fruit.

ramekin /ˈræmkɪn/ *n* a baked dish of cheese, breadcrumbs, etc; the small pot in which this is cooked.

ramification /ˌræməfɪˈkeɪʃən/ *n* a branching out; an offshoot; a consequence.

ramify /ˈræməˌfaɪ/ *vti* to (cause to) divide into branches or constituent parts.

ramjet /ˈræmdʒɛt/ *n* (an aircraft having) a type of jet engine that uses compressed air from the forward movement to burn the fuel.

ramose /ˈreɪmoːs/ or /rəˈmoːs/ *adj* composed of or having branches.—**ramosely** *adv*.

ramp /ræmp/ *n* a sloping walk or runway joining different levels; a wheeled staircase for boarding a plane; a sloping runway for launching boats, as from trailers.

rampage /ˈræmpeɪdʒ/ *n* angry or violent behaviour. • *vi* to rush about in an angry or violent manner.

rampant /ˈræmpənt/ *adj* dominant; luxuriant, unrestrained; violent; rife, prevalent; (*her*) (of a beast) standing on its hind legs.

rampart /ˈræmpɑrt/ *n* an embankment surrounding a fortification; a protective wall.

rampion /ˈræmpiən/ *n* a Eurasian plant with bell-shaped red or purple flowers whose root is sometimes used in salads.

ramrod /ˈræmrɒd/ *n* a rod for ramming home a charge in a muzzle-loading gun. • *adj* denoting a stiff, inflexible person.

ramshackle /ˈræmʃækəl/ *adj* dilapidated.

RAN *abbr* = Royal Australian Navy.

ran /ræn/ *see* **run**.

ranch /ræntʃ/ *n* in the US, a large farm for raising cattle, horses, or sheep; a style of house with all the rooms on one floor. • *vi* to own, manage, or work on a ranch.—**rancher** *n*.

rancid /ˈrænsɪd/ *adj* having an unpleasant smell and taste, as stale fats or oil.—**rancidity, rancidness** *n*.

rancour, rancor /ˈræŋkər/ *n* bitter hate or spite.—**rancorous** *adj*.—**rancorously** *adv*.

rand /rænd/ *n* a unit of money in South Africa, divided into 100 cents.

R & B *abbr* = rhythm and blues.

R & D /ˌɑrəndˈdiː/ *abbr* = research and development.

random /ˈrændəm/ *adj* haphazard; left to chance.

random-access *adj* (*comput*) direct access to data in any desired order.

randomize /ˈrændəmaɪz/ *vt* to arrange (*eg* a survey, samples) in a random way to obtain unbiased statistical results.—**randomization** *n*.—**randomizer** *n*.

R and R /ˌɑrəndˈɑr/ *abbr* = rest and recreation.

randy /ˈrændi/ *adj* (**randier, randiest**) (*sl*) lustful, sexually aroused.

ranee *see* **rani**.

rang /ræŋ/ *see* **ring**[2].

range /reɪndʒ/ *n* a row; a series of mountains, etc; scope, compass; the distance a ship, aircraft, or motor vehicle can travel without refuelling; the distance a gun, etc can fire, a projectile can be thrown, or from gun to target; fluctuation; a large open area for grazing livestock; a place for testing rockets in flight; a place for shooting or golf practice; a large cooking stove. • *vt* to place in order or a row; to establish the range of; (*livestock*) to graze on a range. • *vi* to be situated in a line; to rank or classify; (*gun*) to point or aim; to vary (inside limits).

range finder *n* an instrument for determining the range of a target.

ranger /ˈreɪndʒər/ *n* a forest or park warden.

rangy /ˈreɪndʒi/ *adj* (**rangier, rangiest**) tall and slim; long-limbed.—**ranginess** *n*.

rani, ranee /ˈræni/ *n* in India, a queen or princess; the wife of a rajah.

rank[1] /ræŋk/ *n* a line of objects; a line of soldiers standing abreast; high standing or position; status; (*pl*) ordinary members of the armed forces. • *vti* to arrange in a line; to have a specific position in an organization or on a scale; to outrank; (*with* with) to be counted among.

rank[2] *adj* growing uncontrollably; utter, flagrant; offensive in odour or flavour.

rank and file *n* ordinary soldiers; ordinary members, as distinguished from their leaders.

ranking /ˈræŋkɪŋ/ *n* a listing of things or people in order of importance. • *adj* of the highest rank; outstanding.

rankle /ˈræŋkəl/ *vi* to fester; to cause continuous resentment or irritation.

ransack /ˈrænˌsæk/ *vt* to plunder; to search thoroughly.

ransom /ˈrænsəm/ *n* the release of a captured person or thing; the price paid for this. • *vt* to secure release of by payment.

rant /rænt/ *vi* to speak loudly or violently; to preach noisily. • *n* loud, pompous talk.

ranunculus /rəˈnʌŋjʊləs/ *n* (*pl* **ranunculuses, ranunculi**) a common genus of *usu* yellow-flowered plants including the buttercup.

rap[1] /ræp/ *n* a sharp blow; a knock; (*inf*) talk, conversation; (*sl*) arrest for a crime. • *vti* (**rapping, rapped**) to strike lightly or sharply; to knock; (*sl*) to criticize sharply; (*with* out) to utter abruptly; (*sl*) to speak in a fast and rhythmic manner to a musical backing.

rap[2] *n* a style of popular music in which (*usu* rhyming) words and phrases are spoken in a rapidly spoken rhythmic chant over an instrumental backing.—**rapper** *n*.

rapacious *adj* grasping; extortionate.—**rapaciously** *adv*.—**rapacity** *n*.

rape[1] /reɪp/ *n* the act of forcing a person to have sexual intercourse against his or her will; the plundering (of a city, etc) as in warfare. • *vti* to commit rape (upon).

rape[2] *n* a bright yellow plant of the mustard family grown for its leaves and oily seeds.

rapid /ˈræpɪd/ *adj* at great speed; fast; sudden; steep. • *npl* a part of a river where the current flows swiftly.—**rapidity** *n*.—**rapidly** *adv*.

rapid eye movement *n* the rapid jerky movements of the eyeballs associated with dreaming while asleep.

rapier /ˈreɪpiər/ *n* a straight, two-edged sword with a narrow pointed blade.

rapine /ˈreɪpaɪn/ or /-pɪn/ *n* plunder, pillage.

rapist /ˈreɪpɪst/ *n* a person who commits rape.

rappel /ræˈpɛl/ *vi* to abseil.

rapport /rəˈpɔr/ *n* a sympathetic relationship; accord.

rapprochement *Fr.* /raproʃˈmɑ̃/ *n* re-establishment of cordial relations; reconciliation.

rapscallion /ræpˈskæljən/ *n* a rascal.

rapt /ræpt/ *adj* carried away, enraptured; absorbed, intent.

raptor /'ræptər/ *n* a bird of prey.

raptorial /ræp'tɔriəl/ *adj* of or pertaining to birds of prey; (*birds' feet*) adapted for seizing prey.

rapture /'ræptʃər/ *n* the state of being carried away with love, joy, etc; intense delight, ecstasy.—**rapturous** *adj.*—**rapturously** *adv.*

rara avis /ˌrerə'eɪvɪs/ or /ˌrɑrə'ævɪs/ *n* a rare or unique person or thing.

rare[1] /rer/ *adj* unusual; seldom seen; exceptionally good; (*gas*) of low density, thin. *adv.*—**rareness** *n.*

rare[2] *adj* not completely cooked, partly raw; underdone.

rare earth *n* (an oxide of) any of the lanthanide series of chemical elements.

rarefy /'rerɪfaɪ/ *vti* (**rarefying, rarefied**) to make or become less dense; to thin out; to expand without the addition of matter; to make more spiritual, abstruse or refined.—**rarefied** *adj.*

rare gas *n* an inert gas.

rarely /'rerli/ *adv* almost never, seldom; exceptionally, unusually.

raring /'rerɪŋ/ *adj* (*inf*) eager, enthusiastic.

rarity /'rerɪti/ *n* (*pl* **rarities**) rareness; a rare person or thing.

rasbora /'ræsbərə/ *n* any of various small brightly-coloured tropical fishes popular for aquariums.

rascal /'ræskəl/ *n* a rogue; a villain; a mischievous person.

rase /reɪs/ *see* **raze**.

rash[1] /ræʃ/ *adj* reckless; impetuous.—**rashly** *adv.*—**rashness** *n.*

rash[2] *n* a skin eruption of spots, etc.

rasher /'ræʃər/ *n* a thin slice of bacon or ham.

rasp /ræsp/ *n* a coarse file; a grating sound. • *vt* to scrape with a rasp. • *vi* to produce a grating sound.

raspberry /'ræzˌberi/ or /-bəri/, /-bri/ *n* (*pl* **raspberries**) a shrub with white flowers and red berry-like fruits; the fruit produced; (*inf*) a sound of dislike or derision.

Rastafarian /ˌræstə'feriən/, **Rasta** /'ræstə/ *n* a member of a largely Jamaican religious and political movement that worships Ras Tafari, the former Emperor of Ethiopia, Haile Selassie, as God.—*also adj.*

raster /'ræstər/ *n* a grid of lines scanned by an electron beam to make up an image, *esp* on a television screen.

rat /ræt/ *n* a long-tailed rodent similar to a mouse but larger; (*sl*) a sneaky, contemptible person, *esp* an informer; a scab. • *vi* (**ratting, ratted**) to hunt or catch rats; to betray or inform on someone; to work as a scab.

ratafia /ˌrætə'fiːə/ *n* a liqueur flavoured with fruit kernels, such as cherry, peach or almond; a sweet biscuit flavoured with coconut and almond.

ratatouille /ˌrætə'tuːi/ or /-'twiː/ *n* a dish consisting of a thick stew of roughly chopped vegetables such as onions, peppers, courgettes, aubergine, and tomatoes.

ratchet /'rætʃət/ *n* a device with a toothed wheel that moves in one direction only.

rate /reɪt/ *n* the amount, degree, etc of something in relation to units of something else; price, *esp* per unit; degree. • *vt* to fix the value of; to rank; to regard or consider; (*sl*) to think highly of. • *vi* to have value or status.

ratel /'reɪtəl/ *n* a carnivorous nocturnal mammal of Africa and Asia resembling the badger.

ratepayer /'reɪtpeɪər/ *n* a person who pays rates, a householder.

rather /'ræðər/ *adv* more willingly; preferably; somewhat; more accurately; on the contrary; (*inf*) yes, certainly.

ratify /'rætɪˌfaɪ/ *vt* (**ratifying, ratified**) to approve formally; to confirm.

rating /'reɪtɪŋ/ *n* an assessment; an evaluation, an appraisal, as of credit worthiness; classification by grade, as of military personnel; (*radio, TV*) the relative popularity of a programme according to sample polls.

ratio /'reɪʃoː/ or /-ʃoː/ *n* (*pl* **ratios**) the number of times one thing contains another; the quantitative relationship between two classes of objects; proportion.

ratiocinate /ˌrætɪ'ɒsɪˌneɪt/ or /ˌræʃi-/ *vi* to reason or argue systematically.—**ratiocination** *n.*

ration /'ræʃən/ *n* (*food, petrol*) a fixed amount or portion; (*pl*) food supply. • *vt* to supply with rations; (*food, petrol*) to restrict the supply of.

rational /'ræʃənəl/ *adj* of or based on reason; reasonable; sane.—**rationally** *adv.*

rationale /ˌræʃə'næl/ *n* the reason for a course of action; an explanation of principles.

rationalism /'ræʃənəˌlɪzəm/ *n* dependence on reason and rejection of intuition or the supernatural to justify ideas and beliefs, *esp* with regard to religion; the belief that reason can supply knowledge independently of personal experience.

rationality /ˌræʃə'nælɪti/ *n* (*pl* **rationalities**) the condition of being rational; the practice of being reasonable.

rationalize /'ræʃənəˌlaɪz/ *vti* to make rational; to justify one's reasons for an action; to cut down on personnel or equipment; to substitute a natural for a supernatural explanation.—**rationalization** *n.*

rational number *n* a number that can be expressed as the ratio of two integers.

ratline /'rætlɪn/ *n* any of the short ropes fastened between the shrouds of a sailing ship to form rungs.

ratoon, rattoon /rə'tuːn/ *n* a new shoot sprouting from the root of a perennial plant, *esp* sugarcane, after it has been cut back. • *vt* to encourage growth in this way.

rat race *n* continual hectic competitive activity.

rattan /rə'tæn/ *n* a climbing palm with a jointed stem; cane made of this.

rattle /'rætəl/ *vi* to clatter. • *vt* to make a series of sharp, quick noises; to clatter; to recite rapidly; to chatter; (*inf*) to disconcert, fluster. • *n* a rattling sound; a baby's toy that makes a rattling sound; a voluble talker; the rings on the tail of a rattlesnake.

rattler /'rætlər/ or /'rætələr/ *n* a rattlesnake.

rattlesnake /'rætəlˌsneɪk/ *n* a venomous American snake with a rattle in its tail.

rattling /'rætlɪŋ/ or /'rætəlɪŋ/ *adj* brisk, vigorous; first-rate. • *adv* to an extreme degree; very.

ratty /'ræti/ *adj* (**rattier, rattiest**) like or full of rats; (*sl*) angry, irritable, snappish.

raucous /'rɒkəs/ *adj* hoarse and harsh-sounding; loud and rowdy.

raunchy /'rɒntʃi/ *adj* (**raunchier, raunchiest**) (*sl*) coarse, earthy; careless, slovenly; cheap, inferior.

rauwolfia /rɔ'wulfiə/ or /roː-/ *n* a tropical flowering shrub of Southeast Asia; an extract from the root of this used in various drugs.

ravage /'rævɪdʒ/ *vt* to ruin, destroy; to plunder, lay waste. • *n* destruction; ruin; (*pl*) the effects of this.

rave /reɪv/ *vi* to speak wildly or as if delirious; (*inf*) to enthuse. • *n* enthusiastic praise.—**raving** *adj.*

ravel /'rævəl/ *vti* (**ravelling, ravelled** or **raveling, raveled**) to entangle or disentangle; to fray; to unwind; to make or become complicated.

raven /'rævən/ *n* a large crow-like bird with glossy black feathers. • *adj* of the colour or sheen of a raven.

ravenous /'rævənəs/ *adj* famished; voracious.—**ravenously** *adv.*

ravine /rə'viːn/ *n* a deep, narrow gorge, a large gully.

ravioli /ˌrævɪ'oːli/ *n* small cases of pasta filled with highly seasoned chopped meat or vegetables.

ravish /'rævɪʃ/ *vt* to violate; to rape; to enrapture.

ravishing /'rævɪʃɪŋ/ *adj* charming, captivating.

raw /rɒ/ *adj* uncooked; unrefined; in a natural state, crude; untrained, inexperienced; sore, skinned; damp, chilly; (*inf*) harsh or unfair.—**rawness** *n.*

rawhide /'rɒhaɪd/ *n* (a whip made from strips of) untanned leather.

raw material *n* something out of which a finished article is made; something with a potential for development, improvement, etc.

ray[1] /reɪ/ *n* a beam of light that comes from a bright source; any of several lines radiating from a centre; a beam of radiant energy, radioactive particles, etc; a tiny amount.

ray[2] *n* any of various fishes with a flattened body and the eyes on the upper surface.

rayon /'reɪɒn/ *n* a textile fibre made from a cellulose solution; a fabric of such fibres.

raze /reɪz/ *vt* to demolish; to erase; to level to the ground.—*also* **rase**.

razor /'reɪzər/ *n* a sharp-edged instrument for shaving.

razorbill /'reɪzərbɪl/ *n* a North Atlantic auk with a flattened sharp-edged bill.

razor clam, razor-shell *n* any of various bivalve marine molluscs with curved sharp shells.

razz /ræz/ *vt* (*inf*) to deride, heckle.

razzle-dazzle /'ræzəlˌdæzəl/, **razzmatazz** /'ræzməˌtæz/ *n* (*inf*) exciting, exuberant or colourful activity or atmosphere.

Rb (*chem symbol*) rubidium.

RC *abbr* = Roman Catholic.
RCA *abbr* = Radio Corporation of America.
RCAF *abbr* = Royal Canadian Air Force.
RCCh *abbr* = Roman Catholic Church.
RCMP *abbr* = Royal Canadian Mounted Police.
RCN *abbr* = Royal Canadian Navy.
RCP *abbr* = Royal College of Physicians.
RCS *abbr* = Royal College of Surgeons.
Rd *abbr* = road.
Re (*chem symbol*) rhenium.
re- /ri:/ *prefix* again, anew; back.
re[1] /ri:/ *prep* concerning, with reference to.
re[2] *n* the second note of a major scale in solmization.
reach /ri:tʃ/ *vti* to arrive at; to extend as far as; to make contact with; to pass, hand over; to attain, realize; to stretch out the hand; to extend in influence, space, etc; to carry, as sight, sound, etc; to try to get. • *n* the act or power of reaching; extent; mental range; scope; a continuous extent, *esp* of water.
react /ri:'ækt/ *vi* to act in response to a person or stimulus; to have a mutual or reverse effect; to revolt; (*chem*) to undergo a chemical reaction.
reaction /ri'ækʃən/ *n* an action in response to a stimulus; a revulsion of feeling; exhaustion after excitement, etc; opposition to new ideas; (*chem*) an action set up by one substance in another.
reactionary /-ˌɛri/ *adj, n* (a person) opposed to political or social change.
reactive /ri'æktiv/ *adj* of or relating to reaction; reacting to stimuli; caused by stress.
reactor /ri'æktər/ *n* a person or substance that undergoes a reaction; (*chem*) a vessel in which a reaction occurs; a nuclear reactor.
read /ri:d/ *vti* (**reading, read**) to understand something written; to speak aloud (from a book); to study by reading; to interpret, divine; to register, as a gauge; to foretell; (of a computer) to obtain (information) from; (*sl*) to hear and understand (a radio communication, etc); (*with* **about, of**) to learn by reading; to be phrased in certain words. • *adj* well-informed.
readable /'ri:dəbəl/ *adj* legible; pleasantly written.
readdress /ˌri:ə'drɛs/ *vt* to address again; (*letter*) to change the address when forwarding.
reader /'ri:dər/ *n* a person who reads; one who reads aloud to others; a proofreader; a person who evaluates manuscripts; a textbook, *esp* on reading; a unit that scans material for computation or storage; a senior lecturer.
readership /'ri:dərʃip/ *n* all the readers of a certain publication, author, etc.
readily /'rɛdili/ *adv* in a ready manner; willingly, easily.
reading /'ri:diŋ/ *n* the act of one who reads; any material to be read; the amount measured by a barometer, meter, etc; a particular interpretation of a play, etc.
readjust /ˌri:ə'dʒʌst/ *vt* to adjust again.
read-only memory *n* a small computer memory that cannot be changed by the computer and that contains a special-purpose program.
read-out /'ri:dʌut/ *n* the retrieval of information from a computer memory; the information retrieved.
read-write head *n* (*comput*) an electromagnetic head that can read and write data on a magnetic disc.
ready /'rɛdi/ *adj* (**readier, readiest**) prepared; fit for use; willing; inclined, apt; prompt, quick; handy. • *n* the state of being ready, *esp* the position of a firearm aimed for firing. • *vt* (**readying, readied**) to make ready.—**readiness** *n*.
ready-made *adj* made in standard sizes, not to measure.
reagent /ri:'eɪdʒənt/ *n* (*chem*) a substance used to detect, measure, or react with other substances.
real /ri:l/ *adj* existing, actual, not imaginary; true, genuine, not artificial; (*law*) immovable, consisting of land or houses. • *adv* (*sl*) very; really.
real estate *n* property; land.
realgar /ri'ælgər/ *n* a reddish mineral composed of arsenic sulphide.
realign /ˌri:ə'laɪn/ *vti* to align again; (*politics, diplomacy*) to readjust alliances, policies, etc.—**realignment** *n*.
realism /'ri:əˌlɪzəm/ *n* practical outlook; (*art, literature*) the ability to represent things as they really are without concealment; (*philos*) the doctrine that the physical world has an objective existence; the doctrine that general ideas have an objective existence.—**realist** *n*.

realistic /riə'lɪstɪk/ *adj* matter-of-fact, not visionary; lifelike; of or relating to realism.—**realistically** *adv*.
reality /ri'æliti/ *n* (*pl* **realities**) the fact or condition of being real; an actual fact or thing; truth.
realization /ˌriəlaɪ'zeɪʃən/ *n* the action of realizing; something comprehended or achieved.
realize /'riəlaɪz/ *vt* to become fully aware of; (*ambition, etc*) to make happen; to cause to appear real; to convert into money, be sold for.
really /'ri:li/ *adv* in fact, in reality; positively, very. • *interj* indeed.
realm /rɛlm/ *n* a kingdom, country; domain, region; sphere.
real number *n* any rational or irrational number.
real tennis *n* an early form of tennis played in a walled indoor court.
real-time *adj* involving the continual processing, manipulation and presentation of data by a computer as it is generated.
realtor /'ri:əltər/ *n* a person whose business is selling and leasing property, an estate agent.
realty /'ri:əlti/ *n* real estate.
ream /ri:m/ *n* a quantity of paper varying from 480 to 516 sheets; (*pl: inf*) a great amount.
reap /ri:p/ *vti* to harvest; to gain (a benefit).
reaper /'ri:pər/ *n* a person who or a machine that reaps.
rear[1] /rɪr/ *n* the back part or position, *esp* of an army; (*sl*) the rump. • *adj* of, at, or in the rear.
rear[2] *vt* to raise; (*children*) to bring up; to educate, nourish, etc. • *vi* (*horse*) to stand on the hind legs.
rear guard *n* a military detachment assigned to guard the rear of a body of troops. • *adj* relating to determined defensive resistance.
rear admiral *n* a naval officer next below in rank to a vice admiral.
rear light, rear lamp *n* a taillight.
rearm /ri:'ɑrm/ *vti* to arm or become armed again, *esp* with better weapons.—**rearmament** *n*.
rearview mirror *n* a mirror in a motor vehicle that allows the driver to see following traffic.
rearward /'ri:rwərd/ *adj, adv* at or towards the rear.—**rearwards** *adv*.
reason /'ri:zən/ *n* motive or justification (of an action or belief); the mental power to draw conclusions and determine truth; a cause; moderation; sanity; intelligence. • *vti* to think logically (about); to analyse; to argue or infer.
reasonable /-əbəl/ *adj* able to reason or listen to reason; rational; sensible; not expensive; moderate, fair.—**reasonableness** *n*.—**reasonably** *adv*.
reasoned /'ri:zənd/ *adj* convincingly argued.
reassure /ˌri:ə'ʃər/ or /-'ʃʊr/ *vt* to hearten; to give confidence to; to free from anxiety.—**reassurance** *n*.
rebate[1] /'ri:beɪt/ *n* a refund of part of an amount paid; discount.
rebate[2] see **rabbet**.
rebec, rebeck /'ri:bɛk/ *n* a medieval stringed instrument shaped like a lute and played with a bow.
rebel /'rɛbəl/ *n* a person who refuses to conform with convention. • *vi* (**rebelling, rebelled** *or* **rebeling, rebeled**) (*army*) to rise up against the authorities or the government; to dissent.
rebellion /rə'bɛljən/ or /rɪ-/ *n* armed resistance to an established government, insurrection; defiance of authority.
rebellious /rə'bɛljəs/ or /rɪ-/ *adj* of or engaged in rebellion; tending to rebel; stubborn.—**rebelliously** *adv*.
rebirth /ri:'bɜrθ/ or /'ri:-/ *n* a second or new birth; a revival, renaissance; spiritual regeneration.
rebound /'ri:baʊnd/ or /ri'baʊnd/ *vi* to spring back after impact; to bounce back; to recover. • *n* a recoil; an emotional reaction.
rebounder /-ər/ *n* a small trampoline used for keep-fit exercises.
rebuff /ri:'bʌf/ or /rə'bʌf/ *vt* to snub, repulse; to refuse unexpectedly.—*also n.*
rebuke /rə'bju:k/ or /ri:-/ *vt* to reprimand, chide. • *n* a reproof, reprimand.
rebus /'ri:bəs/ *n* (*pl* **rebuses**) a puzzle using images to represent the sound of words or syllables.
rebut /rə'bʌt/ or /ri:-/ *vt* (**rebutting, rebutted**) to disprove or refute by argument, etc.—**rebuttal** *n*.
rec *abbr* = receipt; recipe; record.
recalcitrant /rə'kælsitrənt/ or /ri:-/ *adj* refusing to obey authority, etc; actively disobedient.—**recalcitrance** *n*.
recall /rə'kɒl/ or /ri:-/ *vt* to call back; to bring to mind, remember; to revoke. • *n* remembrance; a summons to return; the removal from office by popular vote.

recant /rəˈkænt/ or /ri-/ *vti* to repudiate or retract a former opinion, declaration, or belief.—**recantation** *n*.

recap /ˈriːkæp/ *vti* (**recapping, recapped**) to recapitulate. • *n* (*inf*) recapitulation.

recapitulate /ˌriːkəˈpɪtʃʊˌleɪt/ *vt* to restate the main points of, to summarize.—**recapitulation** *n*.

recapture /riːˈkæptʃər/ *vt* to capture again; (*a lost feeling, etc*) to discover anew, regain. • *n* the act of recapturing; a thing or feeling recaptured.

recd, rec'd *abbr* = received.

recede /rəˈsiːd/ or /ri-/ *vi* to move back; to withdraw, retreat; to slope backwards; to grow less; to decline in value.

receding /-ɪŋ/ *adj* sloping backwards; disappearing from view; (*hair*) ceasing to grow at the temples.

receipt /rəˈsiːt/ or /ri-/ *n* the act of receiving; a written proof of this; (*pl*) amount received from business. • *vt* to acknowledge and mark as paid; to write a receipt for.

receive /rəˈsiːv/ or /ri-/ *vt* to acquire, be given; to experience, be subjected to; to admit, allow; to greet on arrival; to accept as true; (*stolen goods*) to take in; to transfer electrical signals. • *vi* to be a recipient; to convert radio waves into perceptible signals.

received /rəˈsiːvd/ or /ri-/ *adj* accepted, recognized.

Received Pronunciation *n* the unlocalized accent of British English, regarded as standard.

receiver /rəˈsiːvər/ or /ri-/ *n* a person who receives; equipment that receives electronic signals, *esp* on a telephone; (*law*) a person appointed to manage or hold in trust property in bankruptcy or pending a lawsuit.

receivership /-ʃɪp/ *n* the status of a business in the hands of a receiver.

recent /ˈriːsənt/ *adj* happening lately, fresh; not long established, modern.—**recently** *adv*.

receptacle /rəˈsəptəkəl/ or /ri-/ *n* a container.

reception /rəˈsepʃən/ or /ri-/ *n* the act of receiving or being received; a welcome; a social gathering, often to extend a formal welcome; a response, reaction; the quality of the sound or image produced by a radio or television set.

receptionist /-ɪst/ *n* a person employed to receive visitors to an office, hotel, hospital, etc.

receptive /rəˈseptɪv/ or /ri-/ *adj* able or quick to take in ideas or impressions.

recess /ˈriːses/ *n* a temporary halting of work, a vacation; a hidden or inner place; an alcove or niche. • *vti* to place in a recess; to form a recess in; to take a recess.

recession /rəˈseʃən/ or /ri-/ *n* the act of receding; a downturn in economic activity; an indentation.

recharge /riːˈtʃɑrdʒ/ or /ri-/ *vi* to renew the electric charge in (a battery, etc); to recover one's energies.

recherché /rəˈʃerʃeɪ/ *adj* uncommon, choice; refined, precious.

recidivism /rəˈsɪdɪvɪzəm/ *n* inevitable relapse into crime.—**recidivist** *n*.

recipe /ˈresɪpiː/ *n* a list of ingredients and directions for preparing food; a method for achieving an end.

recipient /rəˈsɪpiənt/ or /ri-/ *n* a person who receives.

reciprocal /rəˈsɪprəkəl/ or /ri-/ *adj* done by each to the other; mutual; complementary; interchangeable; (*gram*) expressing a mutual relationship. • *n* (*math*) an expression so related to another that their product is 1.—**reciprocally** *adv*.—**reciprocity** *n*.

reciprocate /rəˈsɪprəˌkeɪt/ or /ri-/ *vti* to give in return; to repay; (*mech*) to move alternately backwards and forwards.—**reciprocating** *adj*.—**reciprocation** *n*.

recital /rəˈsaɪtəl/ or /ri-/ *n* the act of reciting; a detailed account, narrative; a statement of facts; (*mus*) a performance given by an individual musician.

recitation /ˌresəˈteɪʃən/ *n* the act of reciting; something recited, as a poem, etc.

recitative /ˌresətəˈtiːv/ *n* a narrative part of an opera sung in the rhythms of ordinary speech.

recite /rəˈsaɪt/ or /ri-/ *vti* to repeat aloud from memory, declaim; to recount, enumerate; to repeat (a lesson).

reckless /ˈrekləs/ *adj* rash, careless, incautious.—**recklessly** *adv*.—**recklessness** *n*.

reckon /ˈrekən/ *vti* to count; to regard or consider; to think; to calculate; (*with* **with**) to take into account.

reckoning /-ɪŋ/ *n* a calculation; the settlement of an account.

reclaim /rəˈkleɪm/ or /ri-/ *vt* to recover, win back from a wild state or vice; (*wasteland*) to convert into land fit for cultivation;

(*plastics, etc*) to obtain from waste materials.—**reclaimable** *adj*.—**reclamation** *n*.

recline /rəˈklaɪn/ *vti* to cause or permit to lean or bend backwards; to lie down on the back or side.—**reclinable** *adj*.

recluse /rəˈkluːs/ or /ri-/ *n* a person who lives in solitude; a hermit.

recognition /ˌrekəgˈnɪʃən/ *n* the act of recognizing; identification; acknowledgment, admission; the sensing and encoding of printed and written data by a machine.

recognizance /rəˈkɒgnɪzəns/ or /-ˈkɒn-/ *n* (*law*) a bond by which a person undertakes before a court to observe some condition; the sum pledged as surety for this.

recognize /ˈrekəgˌnaɪz/ *vt* to know again, identify; to greet; to acknowledge formally; to accept, admit.—**recognizable** *adj*.

recoil /rəˈkɔɪl/ or /ri-/ *vti* to spring back, kick, as a gun; to shrink or flinch. • *n* the act of recoiling, a rebound.

recollect /ˌrekəˈlekt/ *vti* to recall; to remind (oneself) of something temporarily forgotten; to call something to mind.

recollection /ˌrekəˈlekʃən/ *n* the act of recalling to mind; a memory, impression; something remembered; tranquillity of mind; religious contemplation.

recombinant DNA /riːˈkɒmbɪnənt-/ *n* molecules of DNA from different sources spliced together in the laboratory.

recombination /riːˌkɒmbəˈneɪʃən/ *n* the combination of genetic material from different sources.

recommend /ˌrekəˈmend/ *vt* to counsel or advise; to commend or praise; to introduce favourably.—**recommendable** *adj*.—**recommendation** *n*.

recompense /ˈrekəmpens/ *n* to reward or pay an equivalent; to compensate. • *n* reward; repayment; compensation.

reconcile /ˈrekənˌsaɪl/ *vt* to re-establish friendly relations; to bring to agreement; to make compatible; to resolve; to settle; to make resigned (to); (*financial account*) to check with another account for accuracy.—**reconcilable** *adj*.—**reconciliation** *n*.

recondite /ˈrekənˌdaɪt/ or /rɪˈkɒn-/ *adj* needing specialized training or knowledge; complex, obscure.

recondition /riːkənˈdɪʃən/ *vt* to repair and restore to good working order.

reconnaissance /rəˈkɒnəsəns/ or /ri-/ *n* a survey of an area, *esp* for obtaining military information about an enemy.

reconnoitre, reconnoiter /ˌrekəˈnɔɪtər/ *vti* to make a reconnaissance (of).

reconsider /ˌriːkənˈsiːdər/ *vt* to consider afresh, review; to modify.—**reconsideration** *n*.

reconstitute /riːˈkɒnstɪˌtuːt/ or /-ˌtjuːt/ *vt* (*a dried or condensed substance*) to constitute again, *esp* to restore to its original form by adding water.—**reconstitution** *n*.

reconstruct /ˌriːkənˈstrʌkt/ *vt* to build again; to build up, as from remains, an image of the original; to supply missing parts by conjecture.—**reconstruction** *n*.

record /ˈrekərd/ or /ˈrekɔrd/ *vt* to preserve evidence of; to write down; to chart; to register, enrol; to register permanently by mechanical means; (*sound or visual images*) to register on a disc, tape, etc for later reproduction; to celebrate; to make a recording. • *vi* to record something. • *adj* being the best, largest, etc. • *n* a written account; a register; a report of proceedings; the known facts about anything or anyone; an outstanding performance or achievement that surpasses others previously recorded; a grooved vinyl disc for playing on a record player; (*comput*) data in machine-readable form.

recorder /-ər/ *n* an official who keeps records; a machine or device that records; a tape recorder; a wind instrument of the flute family.

recording /-ɪŋ/ *n* what is recorded, as on a disc or tape; the record.

recordist /-ɪst/ *n* a person who records sound.

record player *n* an instrument for playing records through a loudspeaker.

recount[1] /rəˈkaʊnt/ or /ri-/ *vt* to narrate the details of; to narrate.

recount[2] /riːˈkaʊnt/ or /ˈriː-/ *vt* to count again. • *n* a second counting of election votes.

recoup /rəˈkuːp/ or /ri-/ *vti* to make good (financial losses); to regain; to make up for something lost.

recourse /ˈriːkɔrs/ or /rɪˈkɔrs/ *n* a resort for help or protection when in danger; that to which one turns when seeking help.

re-cover /riːˈkʌvər/ *vt* to put a new cover on.

recover /rəˈkʌvər/ or /ri-/ *vti* to regain after losing; to reclaim; to regain health or after losing emotional control.—**recoverable** *adj*.

recovery /rə'kʌvəri/ or /ri-/ *n* (*pl* **recoveries**) the act or process of recovering; the condition of having recovered; reclamation; restoration; a retrieval of a capsule, etc after a space flight.

recreate /ˌriːkri'eɪt/ *vt* to create over again, *esp* mentally.

recreation /ˌrɛkri'eɪʃən/ *n* relaxation of the body or mind; a sport, pastime or amusement.—**recreational** *adj*.

recreational vehicle *n* a vehicle for camping out such as a motor home, camper, etc.

recreation room *n* a room used for relaxation, recreation, or social activities, *esp* in a hospital, etc.

recriminate /rə'krɪmɪˌneɪt/ or /ri-/ *vi* to return an accusation, make a counter-charge.—**recrimination** *n*.—**recriminatory** *adj*.

recrudesce /ˌriːkruː'dɛs/ or /ˌrɛk-/ *vi* (*esp disease*) to reappear again.—**recrudescence** *n*.

recruit /rə'kruːt/ or /ri-/ *n* a soldier newly enlisted; a member newly joined; a beginner. • *vti* to enlist (military personnel); to enlist (new members) for an organization; to increase or maintain the numbers of; to restore, reinvigorate.—**recruitment** *n*.

rectal /'rɛktəl/ *adj* of, for, or near the rectum.

rectangle /'rɛkˌtæŋgəl/ *n* a parallelogram with all its angles right angles.

rectangular /rɛk'tæŋgjʊlər/ *adj* having the shape of a rectangle; crossing, meeting, or lying at a right angle; having faces or surfaces shaped like right angles.

rectifier /'rɛktəˌfaɪr/ *n* a device that converts alternating current to direct current.

rectify /'rɛktəˌfaɪ/ *vt* (**rectifying, rectified**) to put right, correct; to amend; (*chem*) to refine by repeated distillation; (*elect*) to convert to direct current.—**rectifiable** *adj*.

rectilinear /ˌrɛktɪ'lɪniər/, **rectilineal** /-niəl/ *adj* of or bounded by straight lines; straight.

rectitude /'rɛktɪˌtuːd/ or /-ˌtjuːd/ *n* moral uprightness; probity; a being correct in judgment or procedure.

recto /'rɛktoː/ *n* (*pl* **rectos**) the right-hand page of an open book.

rector /'rɛktər/ *n* in some churches, a clergyman in charge of a parish; the head of certain schools, colleges, etc.—**rectorial** *adj*.

rectory /-ri/ *n* (*pl* **rectories**) the house of a minister or priest.

rectrix /'rɛktrɪks/ *n* (*pl* **rectrices**) any of the tail feathers of a bird, used for controlling the direction of flight.

rectum /'rɛktəm/ *n* (*pl* **rectums, recta**) the part of the large intestine leading to the anus.

rectus /'rɛktəs/ *n* (*pl* **recti**) any of various straight muscles, *esp* of the abdomen.

recumbent /rə'kʌmbənt/ or /ri-/ *adj* leaning, resting; lying down.

recuperate /rə'kuːpəˌreɪt/ or /ri-/ *vti* to get well again; to recover (losses, etc).—**recuperation** *n*.

recur /rə'kər/ or /ri-/ *vi* (**recurring, recurred**) to be repeated in thought, talk, etc; to occur again or at intervals.—**recurrence** *n*.—**recurrent** *adj*.

recycle /riː'saɪkəl/ *vti* (*a substance*) to pass through a process again; (*used matter*) to process to regain re-usable material; to save from loss and restore to usefulness.—**recyclable** *adj*.

red /rɛd/ *adj* (**redder, reddest**) of the colour of blood; politically left-wing. • *n* the colour of blood; any red pigment; a communist.

redact /rə'dækt/ or /ri-/ *vt* to edit (a manuscript, etc) for publication.—**redaction** *n*.—**redactor** *n*.

red admiral *n* a common butterfly of Europe and North America with black and red markings.

redback /'rɛdbæk/ *n* (*Austral*) a poisonous spider with red spots on its back.

red blood cell *n* any blood cell containing haemoglobin that conveys oxygen to the tissues.

red-blooded *adj* (*inf*) vigorous, virile.

redbreast /'rɛdˌbrɛst/ *n* a robin.

redbrick /'rɛdbrɪk/ *adj, n* a British university founded after 1945.

red card *n* (*soccer*) a red card held up by the referee indicating that a player is to be sent off.

red carpet *n* a strip of red carpet for dignitaries to walk on; a grand or impressive welcome or entertainment.

red cedar *n* (the reddish wood of) a North American juniper tree.

red cent *n* (*inf*) a trivial quantity of money.

red corpuscle *n* a red blood cell.

Red Crescent *n* the Red Cross in Muslim countries.

Red Cross *n* a red cross on a white ground, the symbol of the International Red Cross, a society for the relief of suffering in time of war and disaster.

red deer *n* a large deer with a reddish brown coat.

redden /'rɛdən/ *vti* to make or become red; to blush.

reddish /'rɛdɪʃ/ *adj* tinged with red.—**reddishness** *n*.

red dwarf *n* a star with a relatively small mass and low luminosity.

redeem /rə'diːm/ or /ri-/ *vt* to recover by payment; to regain; to deliver from sin; to pay off; to restore to favour; to make amends for.—**redeemable** *adj*.—**redeemer** *n*.

redemption /rə'dɛmpʃən/ or /ri-/ *n* the act of redeeming or the state of being redeemed; recovery; repurchase; salvation.

redeploy /ˌriː'dɪplɔɪ/ *vt* (*troops, workers*) to assign to new positions or activities.—**redeployment** *n*.

red flag *n* a symbol of communism or revolution; a sign of danger.

red fox *n* the common European fox with reddish fur.

red giant *n* a giant star with a relatively low surface temperature that emits a red glow.

red-handed *adj* caught in the act of committing a crime.

redhead /'rɛdhɛd/ *n* a person having red hair.—**redheaded** *adj*.

red herring *n* a herring cured to a dark brown colour; something that diverts attention from the real issue.

red-hot *adj* glowing with heat; extremely hot; very excited, angry, etc; very new.

redirect /ˌriː'dɪrɛkt/ or /-daɪrɛkt/ *vt* to change the direction or course of; to readdress.—**redirection** *n*.

red lead *n* a poisonous red oxide of lead used as a pigment.

red-letter *adj* of special significance.

red light *n* a warning signal, a cautionary sign; a deterrent.

red-light *adj* (*of a district*) containing brothels.

red mullet *n* a food fish of European waters, a goatfish.

redneck /'rɛdnɛk/ *n* (*derog*) a poor white farm labourer in the US South. • *adj* racist, reactionary.

redo /riː'duː/ *vt* (**redoing, redid,** *pp* **redone**) to do again; to redecorate.

red ochre *n* any of several types of reddish earth used as pigments.

redolent /'rɛdələnt/ *adj* having a strong scent, fragrant; reminiscent (of).—**redolence** *n*.

redouble /riː'dʌbəl/ *vti* to double again; to make or become twice as much.

redoubt /rɪ'daʊt/ *n* a detached outpost of a fortification.

redoubtable /rɪ'daʊtəbəl/ *adj* formidable.

redound /rə'daʊnd/ or /ri-/ *vi* to have a directly positive or negative effect (on); to rebound (on or upon).

red pepper *n* a variety of pepper grown for its spicy red fruit, capsicum; its fruit; the fruit of the sweet pepper when ripe and red; cayenne pepper.

red pine *n* a pine with reddish wood, *esp* of northeast North America.

redress /rə'drɛs/ or /ri-/ *vt* to put right, adjust; to compensate, make up for. • *n* remedy; compensation.

red salmon *n* any salmon with pinkish flesh, *esp* the sockeye.

redshank /'rɛdʃæŋk/ *n* a type of large European sandpiper.

red squirrel *n* a squirrel with reddish-brown fur of Europe, North America and Asia.

red tape *n* rigid adherence to bureaucratic routine and regulations, causing delay.

reduce /rə'djuːs/ or /ri-/, /-'djuːs/ *vt* to diminish or make smaller in size, amount, extent, or number; to lower in price; to simplify; to make thin; to subdue; to bring or convert (to another state or form).—**reducible** *adj*.

reductio ad absurdum /rɪˌdʌktioːædæb'zərdəm/ *n* a proof of the falsity of a proposition by demonstrating the absurdity of its logical consequences.

reduction /rə'dʌkʃən/ or /ri-/ *n* the act or process of reducing or being reduced; something reduced; the amount by which a thing is reduced; (*math*) the conversion of a fraction into decimal form.—**reductional** *adj*.—**reductive** *adj*.

redundant /rɪ'dʌndənt/ or /ri-/ *adj* surplus to requirements; (*Brit person*) deprived of one's job as being no longer necessary; excessive, wordy; (*words*) unnecessary to the meaning.—**redundancy** *n*.

reduplicate /rə'duːplɪˌkeɪt/ or /ri-/, /-'djuː-/ *vt* to make double, to repeat; (*gram*) to repeat (syllable or letter), to form (word) thus. • *adj* doubled, repeated.—**reduplication** *n*.—**reduplicative** *adj*.

red wine *n* wine made from black grapes with the skins left on.

redwood /'rɛdwʊd/ *n* an important timber tree of California that can reach a height of 360 feet; any of various trees yielding a red dye or reddish wood.

reed /riːd/ *n* a tall grass found in marshes; a thin piece of cane in the mouthpiece of a musical instrument; a person or thing too weak to rely on; one easily swayed or overcome.

redbird /ˈriːdbərd/ *see* **bobolink**.

re-educate, reeducate /ˌriːˈedʒuːkeɪt/ or /-ˈdʒuː-/ *vt* to educate again in order to adapt to changing circumstances.—**re-education, reeducation** *n*.

reedy /ˈriːdi/ *adj* (**reedier, reediest**) filled with reeds; resembling a reed; shrill, piping, as in the sound of a reed.—**reedily** *adv*.—**reediness** *n*.

reef /riːf/ *n* a ridge of rocks, sand, or coral at or just below the surface of water; a hazardous obstruction; a lode or vein of ore.

reefer /ˈriːfər/ *n* a thick double-breasted jacket, formerly worn by sailors; (*inf*) a cigarette containing cannabis.

reef knot *n* a symmetrical double knot.

reek /riːk/ *n* a strong smell. • *vi* to give off smoke, fumes or a strong or offensive smell.

reel[1] /riːl/ *n* a winding device; a spool or bobbin; thread wound on this; a length of film, about 300m (1,000ft). • *vt* to wind on to a reel; (*with* **in**) to draw in by means of a reel; (*with* **off**) to tell, write, etc with fluency; (*with* **out**) to unwind from a reel.

reel[2] *vi* to stagger or sway about; to be dizzy or in a whirl. • *n* a staggering motion.

reel[3] *n* a lively Scottish or Irish dance; the music for it. • *vi* to dance a reel.

re-enter /riːˈentər/ *vti* to enter again.

re-entry /riːˈentri/ *n* (*pl* **re-entries**) the act of entering or possessing again; the return of a spacecraft to the earth's atmosphere.

ref /ref/ *n* (*inf*) a referee.

ref. *abbr* = with reference to.

refectory /rəˈfektəri/ or /ri-/ *n* (*pl* **refectories**) the dining hall of a monastery, college, etc.

refer /rɪˈfər/ *vti* (**referring, referred**) to attribute, assign (to); (*with* **to**) to direct, have recourse (to); to relate to; to mention or allude to; to direct attention (to).—**referable** *adj*.

referee /ˌreˈfəriː/ *n* an adjudicator, arbitrator; an umpire; a judge.

reference /ˈrefərəns/ *n* the act of referring; a mention or allusion; a testimonial; a person who gives a testimonial; a direction to a passage in a book; a passage in a book referred to.

reference book *n* a book for reference rather than general reading, *eg* a yearbook, directory.

reference library *n* a library whose books may be consulted but not borrowed.

referendum /ˌrefəˈrendəm/ *n* (*pl* **referendums, referenda**) the submission of an issue directly to the vote of the electorate, a plebiscite.

referral /rəˈfərəl/ or /ri-/ *n* the act of referring or instance of being referred.

refill /riːˈfɪl/ *vt* to fill again. • *n* a replacement pack for an empty permanent container; a providing again.

refine /rəˈfaɪn/ or /ri-/ *vti* to purify; to make free from impurities or coarseness; to make or become cultured.

refined /riˈfaɪnd/ *adj* polished, cultured; affected.

refinement /rəˈfaɪnmənt/ or /ri-/ *n* fineness of manners or taste; an improvement; a fine distinction.

refinery /rəˈfaɪnəri/ or /ri-/ *n* (*pl* **refineries**) a plant where raw materials, *eg* sugar, oil, are refined.

refit /riˈfɪt/ *vti* (**refitting, refitted**) to make or become functional again by repairing, re-equipping, etc.—*also n*.

reflation /riˈfleɪʃən/ *n* the restoration of deflated prices to a desirable level.—**reflationary** *adj*.

reflect /rəˈflekt/ or /ri-/ *vt* (*light, heat, etc*) to throw back; to bend aside or back; to show an image of, as a mirror; to express. • *vi* to reproduce to the eye or mind; to mirror; to meditate; (*with* **upon**) to ponder; (*with* **on**) to discredit, disparage.

reflected /-əd/ *adj* thrown or cast back; mirrored; bent or folded back.

reflecting telescope *n* a telescope operated by a series of mirrors.

reflection /rəˈflekʃən/ or /ri-/ *n* a reflecting back, turning aside; the action of changing direction when a ray strikes and is thrown back; reflected heat, light or colour; a reflected image; meditation, thought; reconsideration; reproach.—*also* **reflexion**.

reflective /rəˈflektɪv/ or /ri-/ *adj* meditative; concerned with ideas.—**reflectively** *adv*.—**reflectiveness** *n*.

reflector /rəˈflektər/ or /ri-/ *n* a disc, instrument, strip or other surface that reflects light or heat.

reflex /ˈriːfleks/ *n* an involuntary response to a stimulus. • *adj* (*angle*) of more than 180 degrees; (*camera*) with a full-size viewfinder using the main lens.

reflex camera *n* a camera in which the image from the lens is conveyed by an angled mirror to a viewfinder for composition and focusing.

reflexion *see* **reflection**.

reflexive /rəˈfleksɪv/ or /ri-/ *adj* (*pron, verb*) referring back to the subject.—**reflexively** *adv*.

reflexology /ˌriːfleksˈɒlədʒi/ *n* (*alternative medicine*) a technique of applying pressure to specific points on the hands and feet to stimulate the blood supply to other areas of the body and help relieve stress.—**reflexologist** *n*.

reform /rəˈfɔrm/ or /ri-/ *vti* to improve; to make or become better by the removal of faults; to amend; to abolish abuse. • *n* improvement or transformation, *esp* of an institution; removal of social ills.—**reformed** *adj*.

re-form /riːˈfɔrm/ *vti* to form again.

reformation /ˌrefərˈmeɪʃən/ *n* the act of reforming or the state of being reformed; improvement; (*with cap*) the 16th-century religious revolt that resulted in the formation of Protestant churches.

reformatory /ˌrəˈfɔrmətəri/ or /ri-/ *adj* reforming. • *n* (*pl* **reformatories**) an institution for reforming young criminals; a prison for women.

reformer /rɪˈfɔrmər/ *n* a person who advocates or works for reform; an apparatus for changing the molecular structure of a hydrocarbon to form specialized products.

reform school *n* a reformatory for young people.

refract /rəˈfrækt/ or /ri-/ *vt* to cause (a ray of light, etc) to undergo refraction.

refracting telescope *n* a type of telescope in which the image is formed by a series of lenses.

refraction /rəˈfrækʃən/ or /ri-/ *n* the bending of a ray or wave of light, heat, or sound as it passes from one medium into another.

refractory /rəˈfræktəri/ or /ri-/ *adj* obstinate; (*disease, etc*) resistant to treatment; (*muscle*) unresponsive to stimuli; able to withstand high temperatures. • *n* (*pl* **refractories**) a heat-resistant material.

refrain[1] /rəˈfreɪn/ *vi* to abstain (from).

refrain[2] *n* recurring words in a song or poem, *esp* at the end of a stanza; a chorus.

refrangible /rəˈfrændʒəbəl/ or /ri-/ *adj* able to be refracted.

refresh /rəˈfreʃ/ or /ri-/ *vt* to revive; to give new energy to; to make cool; to take a drink.

refresher /-ər/ *n* something that refreshes, *esp* a drink; a reminder; a training course to renew one's skill or knowledge.

refresher course *n* a course designed to keep professionals informed of recent developments in their field of knowledge or expertise.

refreshing /-ɪŋ/ *adj* invigorating, reviving; pleasing because unsophisticated.

refreshment /rɪˈfreʃmənt/ *n* the act of refreshing; a restorative; (*pl*) food and drink; a light meal.

refrigerate /rəˈfrɪdʒəˌreɪt/ or /ri-/ *vti* to make, become, or keep cold; to preserve by keeping cold.—**refrigeration** *n*.

refrigerator /-ər/ *n* something that refrigerates; a chamber for keeping food, etc, cool; an apparatus for cooling.—*also* **fridge, icebox**.

refuel /riːˈfjuːəl/ *vti* (**refuelling, refuelled** *or* **refueling, refueled**) to supply with or take on fresh fuel.

refuge /reˈfjuːdʒ/ *n* a protection or shelter from danger; a retreat, sanctuary.

refugee /ˌrəfjuːˈdʒiː/ *n* a person who flees to another country to escape political or religious persecution.

refund /rəˈfend/ or /ri-/ *vti* to repay; to reimburse. • *n* a refunding or the amount refunded.

refurbish /riːˈfərbɪʃ/ *vt* to renovate or re-equip.—**refurbishment** *n*.

refusal /rəˈfjuːzəl/ or /ri-/ *n* the act or process of refusing; the choice of refusing or accepting.

refuse[1] /ˈrefjuːs/ *n* garbage, waste, rubbish.

refuse[2] *vt* to decline, reject; to withhold, deny. • *vi* (*horse*) to decline to jump.

refute /rəˈfjuːt/ or /ri-/ *vt* to rebut; to disprove.—**refutable** *adj*.—**refutably** *adv*.—**refutation** *n*.

regain /rəˈgeɪn/ or /ri-/ *vt* to get back, recover; to reach again.

regal /ˈriːgəl/ *adj* royal; relating to a king or queen.

regale /rəˈgeɪl/ or /ri-/ *vt* to entertain, as with a feast; to delight.

regalia /rə'geɪlɪə/ or /-'geɪljə/ *npl* royal insignia or prerogatives; the insignia of an order, office, or membership; finery.

regard /rə'gɑrd/ or /rɪ-/ *vt* to gaze at, observe; to hold in respect; to consider; to heed, take into account. • *n* a look; attention; reference; respect, esteem; (*pl*) good wishes, greetings.

regarding /-ɪŋ/ *prep* with reference to, about.

regardless /-ləs/ *adj* having no regard to. • *adv* (*inf*) in spite of everything; without heeding the cost, consequences, etc.

regatta /rə'gætə/ or /rɪ-/ *n* a meeting for yacht or boat races.

regency /'riːdʒənsɪ/ *n* (*pl* **regencies**) the status or authority of a regent; a regent's period of office; a body entrusted with the duties of a regent; rule; (*with cap*) in British history, the period 1810-20.

regenerate /rɪ'dʒɛnəˌreɪt/ *vti* to renew, give new life to; to be reborn spiritually; to reorganize; to produce anew.—**regeneration** *n*.

regent /'riːdʒənt/ *n* a person who rules or administers a country during the sovereign's minority, absence, or incapacity; a member of a governing board (as of a university).

reggae /'rɛgeɪ/ *n* a strongly accented West Indian musical form with four beats to the bar.

regicide /'rɛdʒɪˌsaɪd/ *n* the killer or the killing or a king.

regime, régime /reɪ'ʒiːm/ *n* a political or ruling system.

regimen /'rɛdʒɪˌmɛn/ *n* a system of diet, exercise, etc, for improving the health; a regular course of training.

regiment /'rɛdʒɪmənt/ *n* a military unit, smaller than a division, consisting *usu* of a number of battalions. • *vt* to organize in a strict manner; to subject to order or conformity.—**regimental** *adj*.

regimentation /ˌrɛdʒɪmən'teɪʃən/ *n* the act of regimenting; excessive orderliness.

Regina /rə'dʒaɪnə/ or /rɛ'dʒiːnə/ *n* a reigning queen.

region /'riːdʒən/ *n* a large, indefinite part of the earth's surface; one of the zones into which the atmosphere is divided; an administrative area of a country; a part of the body.—**regional** *adj*.

register /'rɛdʒɪstər/ *n* an official list; a written record, as for attendance; the book containing such a record or list; a tone of voice; a variety of language appropriate to a subject or occasion; (*comput*) a device in which data can be stored and operated on; (*print*) exact alignment; a device for indicating speed, etc; a plate regulating draught. • *vti* to record; to enter in or sign a register; to correspond exactly; to entrust a letter to the post with special precautions for safety; to express emotion facially; to make or convey an impression.

registered /-stərd/ *adj* recorded officially; qualified formally or officially.

registrar /'rɛdʒɪsˌtrɑr/ *n* a person who keeps records, *esp* one in an educational institution in charge of student records; a hospital doctor below a specialist in rank.

registration /ˌrɛdʒɪ'streɪʃən/ *n* the act of registering; the condition of having registered.

registry /'rɛdʒɪstrɪ/ *n* (*pl* **registries**) registration; a place where records are kept; an official record book.

regius professor *n* a person appointed to a university chair founded by the Crown.

regnal /'rɛgnəl/ *adj* pertaining to a sovereign or reign, *esp* designating a year of a reign calculated from the date of accession.

regress /rə'grɛs/ or /rɪ-/ *vi* to move backwards; to revert to a former condition.—**regressive** *adj*.—**regressively** *adv*.

regression /rə'grɛʃən/ or /rɪ-/ *n* the act of regressing; a relapse, reversion; a return to an earlier time or stage; (*psychoanal*) a retreat of the personality.

regret /rə'grɛt/ or /rɪ-/ *vt* (**regretting, regretted**) to feel sorrow, grief, or loss; to remember with longing; (*with* **that**) to repent of. • *n* disappointment; sorrow; grief; (*pl*) polite refusal.—**regretful** *adj*.—**regretfully** *adv*.

regrettable /-əbəl/ *adj* to be regretted; deserving reproof.—**regrettably** *adv*.

regroup /rɪ'gruːp/ *vti* to group again; (*mil*) to reorganize (troops, etc) following action.

regular /'rɛgjʊlər/ *adj* normal; habitual, not casual; at fixed intervals; according to rule, custom, or the accepted practice; uniform, consistent; symmetrical; fully qualified; belonging to a standing army; (*inf*) thorough, complete; (*inf*) pleasant, friendly. • *n* a professional soldier; (*inf*) a person who attends regularly.—**regularity** *n*.—**regularly** *adv*.

regular army *n* a permanent army.

regularize /-ˌraɪz/ *vt* to make regular or correct.—**regularization** *n*.

regulate /'rɛgjʊleɪt/ *vt* to control according to a rule; to cause to conform to a standard or needs; to adjust so as to put in good order.—**regulatory** *adj*.

regulation /ˌrɛgjʊ'leɪʃən/ *n* the act of regulating or state of being regulated; a prescribed rule, ordinance. • *adj* normal, standard.

regulator /'rɛgjʊleɪtər/ *n* one who or that which regulates; a regulating device; a lever in a watch that adjusts its speed.

regurgitate /rɪ'gɜrdʒɪˌteɪt/ *vti* to pour back, cast up again, *esp* from the stomach to the mouth.—**regurgitation** *n*.

rehabilitate /ˌriːhə'bɪlɪteɪt/ *vt* (*prisoner etc*) to help adapt to society after a stay in an institution; to put back in good condition; to restore to rights or privileges; (*sick person etc*) to help to adjust to normal conditions after illness.—**rehabilitation** *n*.

rehash /'riːhæʃ/ *n* old materials put in a new form. • *vt* to dish up again.

rehearse /rɪ'hɜrs/ *vti* to practise repeatedly before public performance; to recount, narrate in detail.—**rehearsal** *n*.

rehoboam /ˌriːhə'boːm/ *n* a wine bottle that holds six times the amount of a standard bottle.

reify /'riːɪfaɪ/ *vt* (**reifying, reified**) to make (something abstract) real or concrete.

reign /reɪn/ *n* the rule of a sovereign; the period of this; influence; domination. • *vi* to rule; to prevail.

reimburse /ˌriːm'bɜrs/ *vt* to repay; to refund (for expense or loss).—**reimbursable** *adj*.—**reimbursement** *n*.

rein /reɪn/ *n* the strap of a bridle for guiding or restraining a horse; (*pl*) a means of control or restraint. • *vt* to control with the rein; to restrain.

reincarnation /ˌriːɪnkɑr'neɪʃən/ *n* the incarnation of the soul after death in another body.—**reincarnate** *adj, vt*.

reindeer /'reɪndɪːr/ *n* a large deer with branched antlers found in northern regions.

reindeer moss *n* a lichen of northern regions that provides food for reindeer.

reinforce /riːm'fɔrs/ *vt* (*army etc*) to strengthen with fresh troops; (*a material*) to add to the strength of.

reinforced concrete *n* concrete with metal bars, wire, etc inserted in it for strength.

reinforcement /ˌriːɪn'fɔrsmənt/ *n* the act of reinforcing; additional support; (*pl*) additional troops.

reinstate /ˌriːɪn'steɪt/ *vt* to restore to a former position, rank, or condition.—**reinstatement** *n*.

reinterpret /ˌriːɪntər'prɛt/ *vt* to interpret again; to give a new explanation of.—**reinterpretation** *n*.

reissue /riː'ɪʃuː/ *vt* to issue again; to republish. • *n* a new issue; a reprint.

reiterate /riː'ɪtəreɪt/ *vt* to repeat; to say or do again or many times.—**reiteration** *n*.

reject /rə'dʒɛkt/ or /rɪ-/ *vt* to throw away, to discard; to refuse to accept, to decline; to rebuff. • *n* a thing or person rejected.—**rejection** *n*.

rejoice /rə'dʒɔɪs/ or /ri-/ *vi* to feel joyful or happy.

rejoin /rɪ'dʒɔɪn/ or /'riː-/ *vt* to join again; to return to.

rejoinder /rə'dʒɔɪndər/ or /rɪ-/ *n* a retort, a reply.

rejuvenate /rɪ'dʒuːvəˌneɪt/ or /ri-/ *vt* to give youthful vigour to.—**rejuvenation** *n*.

relapse /rɪ'læps/ *vi* to fall back into a worse state after improvement; to return to a former vice, to backslide. • *n* the recurrence of illness after apparent recovery.

relate /rə'leɪt/ *v* or /ri-/ *vt* to narrate, recount; to show a connection (between two or more things). • *vi* to have a formal relationship (with).

related /-əd/ *adj* connected, allied; akin.

relation /rə'leɪʃən/ or /rɪ-/ *n* the way in which one thing stands in respect to another, footing; reference, regard; connection by blood or marriage; a relative; a narration, a narrative; (*pl*) the connections between or among persons, nations, etc; (*pl*) one's family and in-laws.

relationship /rɪ'leɪʃənʃɪp/ *n* the tie or degree of kinship or intimacy; affinity; (*inf*) an affair.

relative /'rɛlətɪv/ *adj* having or expressing a relation; corresponding; pertinent; comparative, conditional; respective; meaningful only in relationship; (*gram*) referring to an antecedent. • *n* a person related by blood or marriage.—**relatively** *adv*.

relative molecular mass *n* the total of the atomic weights of all the atoms present in a molecule; the average mass per molecule of any substance relative to one-twelfth the mass of an atom of carbon-12.—*also* **molecular weight**.

relative pronoun *n* a pronoun that is used to connect a dependent clause to a main clause and that refers to a noun in the main clause.

relativity /ˌrɛlə'tɪvɪti/ *n* the state of being relative; the relation between one thing and another; (*physics*) the theory of the relative, rather than absolute, character of motion, velocity, mass, etc, and the interdependence of time, matter, and space.

relax /rə'læks/ or /ri-/ *vti* to slacken; to make or become less severe or strict; to make (the muscles) less rigid; to take a rest.

relaxant /-ənt/ *n* a drug that relieves muscular tension.

relaxation /ˌriːlæk'seɪʃən/ *n* the act of relaxing; the condition of being relaxed; recreation.

relay /'riːleɪ/ *n* a team of fresh horses, men, etc to relieve others; a race between teams, each member of which goes a part of the distance; (*elect*) a device for enabling a weak current to control others; a relayed broadcast. • *vt* (**relaying, relayed**) (*news, etc*) to spread in stages; to broadcast signals.

relay race *n* a race between teams in which each member does part of the distance.

release /ri'liːs/ *vt* to set free; to let go; to relinquish; (*film, etc*) to issue for public exhibition; (*information*) to make available; (*law*) to make over to another. • *n* a releasing, as from prison, work, etc; a device to hold or release a mechanism; a news item, etc, released to the public; (*law*) a written surrender of a claim.

relegate /'rɛlə,geɪt/ *vt* to move to an inferior position; to demote; to banish.—**relegation** *n*.

relent /rə'lent/ or /ri-/ *vi* to soften in attitude; to become less harsh or severe.

relentless /-ləs/ *adj* pitiless; unremitting.

relevant /'rɛləvənt/ *adj* applying to the matter in hand, pertinent; to the point.—**relevance, relevancy** *n*.

reliable /rə'laɪəbəl/ or /ri-/ *adj* dependable, trustworthy.—**reliability** *n*.—**reliably** *adv*.

reliance /rə'laɪəns/ or /ri-/ *n* trust; dependence; a thing relied on.—**reliant** *adj*.

relic /'rɛlɪk/ *n* an object, fragment, or custom that has survived from the past; part of a saint's body or belongings; (*pl*) remains of the dead.

relief /rə'liːf/ or /ri-/ *n* the sensation following the easing or lifting of discomfort or stress; release from a duty by another person; a person who takes the place of another on duty; that which relieves; aid; assistance to the needy or victims of a disaster; the projection of a carved design from its ground; distinctness, vividness. • *adj* providing relief in disasters etc.

relief map *n* a map in which topographic relief is represented by shading, colours, etc.

relieve /rə'liːv/ or /ri-/ *vt* to bring relief or assistance to; to release from obligation or duty; to ease; (*with* **oneself**) to empty the bladder or bowels. • *vi* to give relief; to break the monotony of; to bring into relief, to stand out.

relieved /rə'liːvd/ or /ri-/ *adj* having or showing relief, *esp* from anxiety or repressed emotions.

religion /rɪ'lɪdʒən/ *n* a belief in God or gods; a system of worship and faith; a formalized expression of belief.

religiosity /rɪˌlɪdʒɪ'ɒsɪti/ *n* the condition of being religious, *esp* excessively or sentimentally so.—**religiose** *adj*.

religious /rɪ'lɪdʒəs/ or /ri-/ *adj* of or conforming to religion; devout, pious; scrupulously and conscientiously faithful.—**religiously** *adv*.

relinquish /rə'lɪŋkwɪʃ/ or /ri-/ *vt* to give up; to renounce or surrender.—**relinquishment** *n*.

reliquary /'rɛlɪkwəri/ *n* (*pl* **reliquaries**) a container or shrine for sacred relics.

relish /'rɛlɪʃ/ *n* an appetizing flavour; a distinctive taste; enjoyment of food or an experience; a spicy accompaniment to food; gusto, zest. • *vt* to like the flavour of; to enjoy, appreciate.

relocate /'riːlɒ:ˌkeɪt/ or /ˌriːlɒ:'keɪt/, /riːlɒ:keɪt/ *vti* to set up in a new place; to place (an employee) in a different job; (*business*) to move to a new location.—**relocation** *n*.

reluctant /rə'lʌktənt/ or /ri-/ *adj* unwilling, loath; offering resistance.—**reluctance** *n*.—**reluctantly** *adv*.

rely /rə'laɪ/ or /ri-/ *vi* (**relying, relied**) to depend on; to trust.

REM /rɛm/ *abbr* = rapid eye movement.

remain /rə'meɪn/ or /ri-/ *vi* to stay behind or in the same place; to continue to be; to survive, to last; to be left over. • *npl* anything left after use; a corpse.

remainder /-dər/ *n* what is left, the rest; (*math*) the result of subtraction; the quantity left over after division; unsold stock, *esp* of books; (*law*) the residual interest in an estate.

remake /ri'meɪk/ or /'riːmeɪk/ *vt* (**remaking, remade**) to make again. • *n* a new version of an old film.

remand /rə'mænd/ *vt* to send back into custody for further evidence.—*also n*.

remark /rə'mɑrk/ or /ri-/ *vti* to notice; to observe; to pass a comment (upon). • *n* a brief comment.

remarkable /-əbəl/ *adj* unusual; extraordinary; worthy of comment.—**remarkably** *adv*.

remaster /ri:'mæstər/ *vt* to make a new (digital) master recording from an original (analogue) recording to provide improved sound quality on vinyl records or compact discs.

remedial /ri'miːdiəl/ *adj* providing a remedy; corrective; relating to the teaching of people with learning difficulties.

remedy /'rɛmɪdi/ *n* a medicine or any means to cure a disease; anything that puts something else to rights. • *vt* (**remedying, remedied**) to cure; to put right.

remember /rə'membər/ or /ri-/ *vti* to recall; to bear in mind; to mention (a person) to another as sending regards; to exercise or have the power of memory.

remembrance /rə'membrəns/ or /ri-/ *n* a reminiscence; a greeting or gift recalling or expressing friendship or affection; the extent of memory; an honouring of the dead or a past event.

Remembrance Sunday *n* the Sunday nearest November 11, on which the dead of the two World Wars are commemorated.

remind /rə'maɪnd/ or /ri-/ *vt* to cause to remember.

reminder /-ər/ *n* a thing that reminds, *esp* a letter from a creditor.

reminisce /ˌrɛmɪ'nɪs/ *vi* to think, talk, or write about past events.

reminiscence /-əns/ *n* the recalling of a past experience; (*pl*) memoirs.

reminiscent /-ənt/ *adj* reminding, suggestive (of); recalling the past.

remiss /rə'mɪs/ or /ri-/ *adj* negligent, slack.

remission /rə'mɪʃən/ or /ri-/ *n* the act of remitting; the reduction in length of a prison term; the lessening of the symptoms of a disease; pardon, forgiveness.

remit /rə'mɪt/ or /ri-/ *vti* (**remitting, remitted**) to forgive; to refrain from inflicting (a punishment) or exacting (a debt); to abate, moderate; to send payment (by post); (*law*) to refer to a lower court for reconsideration. • *n* the act of referring; an area of authority.

remittance /rə'mɪtəns/ or /ri-/ *n* the sending of money or a payment (by post); the payment or money sent.

remix /'riːmɪks/ or /ri'mɪks/ *vt* to adjust the balance and separation of a recording.—*also n*.

remnant /'rɛmnənt/ *n* a small remaining fragment or number; an oddment or scrap; a trace; an unsold or unused end of piece goods.

remodel /ri:'mɒdəl/ *vt* (**remodelling, remodelled** *or* **remodeling, remodeled**) to fashion afresh; to recast.

remonstrate /'rɛmən,streɪt/ *vi* to protest, to make a complaint (against).—**remonstrance** *n*.

remorse /rə'mɔrs/ *n* regret and guilt for a misdemeanour; compassion.—**remorseful** *adj*.—**remorsefully** *adv*.

remorseless /-ləs/ *adj* ruthless, cruel; relentless.—**remorselessly** *adv*.—**remorselessness** *n*.

remote /rə'mɒ:t/ *adj* far apart or distant in time or place; out of the way; not closely related; secluded; aloof; vague, faint.—**remotely** *adv*.

remote control *n* the control of a device or activity from a distance, *usu* by means of an electric circuit or the making or breaking of radio waves.

removal /rɪ'muːvəl/ *n* the act of removing; a change of home or office; dismissal.

remove /rɪ'muːv/ or /rə-/ *vti* to take away and put elsewhere; to dismiss, as from office; to get rid of; to kill; to go away. • *n* a stage in gradation; a degree in relationship.—**removable** *adj*.

removed /rɪ'muːvd/ or /rə-/ *adj* remote; separated by a specified degree, as of relationship; of a younger or older relationship.

remunerate /rɪ'mjuːnəˌreɪt/ *vt* to pay for a service; to reward.—**remuneration** *n*.

renaissance /ˈrɛnəˌsɒns/ or /rəˈneɪ-/, *Fr.* /ʀɛneɪˈsɔ̃s/ *n* a rebirth or revival; (*with cap*) the revival of European art and literature under the influence of classical study during the 14th-16th centuries.—*also adj.*

renal /ˈriːnəl/ *adj* relating to or near the kidneys.

renascent /rɪˈneɪsənt/ or /rɪˈnæsənt/ *adj* becoming active again, reviving.

rend /rɛnd/ *vti* (**rending, rent**) to tear, to wrench (apart); to be torn apart.

render /ˈrɛndər/ *vt* (*payments, accounts, etc*) to submit, as for approval; to give back; to pay back; to perform; to represent as by drawing; to translate, interpret; to cause to be; (*fat*) to melt down.

rendering /-ɪŋ/ *n* interpretation, translation.

rendezvous /ˈrɒndeɪˌvuː/ *n* (*pl* **rendezvous**) an arranged meeting; a place to meet; a popular haunt; the process of bringing two spacecraft together. • *vi* to meet by appointment.

rendition /rɛnˈdɪʃən/ *n* an interpretation; performance.

renegade /ˈrɛnəˌɡeɪd/ *n* a deserter; a person who is faithless to a principle, party, religion, or cause.

renege /rəˈneɡ/ or /rɪ-/, /-ˈneɪɡ/ *vti* to go back on, or fail to keep, a promise or agreement.

renegotiate /ˌriːnɪˈɡoʊʃɪˌeɪt/ *vti* to negotiate again, *esp* to improve the terms of a contract.—**renegotiable** *adj.*—**renegotiation** *n.*

renew /rɪˈnuː/ or /-ˈnjuː/ *vti* to restore to freshness or vigour; to begin again; to make or get anew; to replace; to grant or obtain an extension of.—**renewable** *adj.*—**renewal** *n.*

rennet /ˈrɛnət/ *n* an extract from the stomach of calves, etc, used to curdle milk.

renounce /rəˈnaʊns/ or /rɪ-/ *vt* to abandon formally; to give up; to disown.

renovate /ˈrɛnəˌveɪt/ *vt* to renew; to restore to good condition; to do up, repair.—**renovation** *n.*—**renovator** *n.*

renown /rɪˈnaʊn/ or /rə-/ *n* fame, celebrity.

renowned /rɪˈnaʊnd/ or /rə-/ *adj* famous, illustrious.

rent[1] /rɛnt/ *see* **rend**.

rent[2] /rɛnt/ *n* regular payment to another for the use of a house, machinery, etc. • *vti* to occupy as a tenant; to hire; to let for rent.

rental /ˈrɛntəl/ *n* an amount paid or received as rent; a house, car, etc, for rent; an act of renting; a business that rents something.

rent boy *n* a young male prostitute.

renunciation /rəˌnʌnsɪˈeɪʃən/ *n* the act of renouncing; formal abandonment; repudiation.

reopen /riˈoʊpən/ *vti* to open again; to resume.

reorganize /riˈɔrɡəˌnaɪz/ *vti* to organize again; to bring about a reorganization.—**reorganization** *n.*

Rep. *abbr* = Representative; Republic; Republican.

rep /rɛp/ *abbr* = repeat; report; reporter.

repair /rɪˈpɛr/ or /rə-/ *vt* to mend; to restore to good working order; to make amends for. • *n* the act of repairing; a place repaired; condition as to soundness.

reparable /rɪˈpɛrəbəl/ or /rə-/ *adj* capable of being repaired.

reparation /ˌrɛpəˈreɪʃən/ *n* amends; (*pl*) compensation, as for war damage.

repartee /reˈpɑrteɪ/ or /-tiː/ *n* a witty reply; skill in making such replies.

repast /rɪˈpæst/ *n* a meal.

repatriate /rɪˈpeɪtriˌeɪt/ *vt* to send back or restore to one's country of origin or citizenship.—**repatriation** *n.*

repay /rɪˈpeɪ/ *vt* (**repaying, repaid**) to pay back; to refund.—**repayable** *adj.*—**repayment** *n.*

repeal /rɪˈpiːl/ *vt* to annul, to rescind; to revoke.—*also n.*

repeat /rɪˈpiːt/ *vti* to say, write, or do again; to reiterate; to recite after another or from memory; to reproduce; to recur. • *n* a repetition, encore; anything said or done again, as a re-broadcast of a television programme; (*mus*) a passage to be repeated; the sign for this.—**repeatable** *adj.*

repeated /rɪˈpiːtəd/ *adj* frequent; done, seen, etc, again.

repeatedly /-li/ *adv* many times, over and over again.

repeater /rɪˈpiːtər/ *n* a clock or watch with a striking mechanism; a device for receiving and amplifying electronic communication signals; a firearm that has a repeating mechanism for reloading; a habitual violator of the laws.

repeating firearm *n* a firearm designed to load cartridges from a magazine.

repel /rəˈpɛl/ *vt* (**repelling, repelled**) to drive back; to beat off, repulse; to reject; to hold off; to cause distaste; (*water, dirt*) to be resistant to.

repellent /rəˈpɛlənt/ *adj* distasteful, unattractive; capable of repelling; impermeable. • *n* a substance that repels, *esp* a spray for protection against insects.

repent /rəˈpɛnt/ *vi* to wish one had not done something; to feel remorse or regret (for); to change and regret from evil ways.—**repentant** *adj.*

repentance /rəˈpɛntəns/ *n* penitence; contrition.

repercussion /ˌriːpərˈkʌʃən/ or /ˌrɛp/ *n* a rebound; a reverberation; a far-reaching, often indirect reaction to an event.

repertoire /ˈrɛpərˌtwɑr/ or /ˌrɛpərˈtwɑr/ *n* the stock of plays, songs, etc, that a company, singer, etc, can perform.

repertory /ˈrɛpərtɔri/ or /ˈrɛpətɔri/ *n* (*pl* **repertories**) a repertoire; the system of alternating several plays through a season with a permanent acting group.

repetition /ˌrɛpəˈtɪʃən/ *n* the act of repeating; something repeated, a copy.—**repetitive** *adj.*

repetitious /ˌrɛpəˈtɪʃəs/ *adj* full of repetition; boring.—**repetitiously** *adv.*—**repetitiousness** *n.*

rephrase /riˈfreɪz/ *vt* to phrase (a statement) in a different way.

replace /riˈpleɪs/ *vt* to put back; to take the place of, to substitute for; to supersede.—**replaceable** *adj.*

replacement /riˈpleɪsmənt/ *n* the act or process of replacing; a person or thing that replaces another.

replenish /rəˈplɛnɪʃ/ *vt* to stock again, refill.—**replenishment** *n.*

replete /rəˈpliːt/ *adj* filled, well provided; stuffed, gorged.

repletion /rəˈpliːʃən/ *n* complete fullness; satisfaction.

replica /ˈrɛplɪkə/ *n* an exact copy; a reproduction.

reply /rəˈplaɪ/ or /rɪ-/ *vti* (**replying, replied**) to answer, respond; to give as an answer. • *n* an answer.

repo-man /ˈriːpoʊ/ *n* (*pl* **repo-men**) (*sl*) a person who repossesses (*eg* a motor car).

report /rəˈpɔrt/ or /rɪ-/ *vti* to give an account of; to tell as news; to take down and describe for publication; to make a formal statement of; to complain about or against; to inform against; to present oneself (for duty). • *n* an account of facts; the formal statement of the findings of an investigation; a newspaper, radio or television account of an event; a rumour; a sharp, loud noise, as of a gun.

reportage /ˈrɛpɔrtɪdʒ/ *n* the art of reporting on current events; an accurate, observant and well-written account of an event.

report card *n* a report on a pupil or student that is periodically given to his or her parent; an evaluation of performance.

reportedly /rəˈpɔrtədli/ *adv* as reported, not directly.

reporter /rəˈpɔrtər/ *n* a person who gathers and reports news for a newspaper, radio or television; a person authorized to make statements concerning law decisions or legislative proceedings.

repose /rɪˈpoʊz/ *n* rest, sleep; stillness, peace; composure, serenity. • *vti* to lie down or lay at rest; to place (trust, etc) in someone; to rest; to lie dead.

reposition /ˌriːpəˈzɪʃən/ *vt* to place in a different or new position.

repository /rɪˈpɒzɪtəri/ *n* (*pl* **repositories**) a receptacle; a storehouse, warehouse; a confidant.

repossess /ˌriːpəˈzɛs/ *vt* to possess again; to restore possession of (property), *esp* for nonpayment of debt.—**repossession** *n.*

reprehend /ˌrɛprɪˈhɛnd/ *vt* to rebuke, to find fault with, to criticize.

reprehensible /ˌrɛprɪˈhɛnsɪbəl/ *adj* blameworthy, culpable.

reprehension /ˌrɛprɪˈhɛnʃən/ *n* blame, censure.

re-present /ˌriːprɪˈzɛnt/ *vt* to present again.

represent /ˌrɛprɪˈzɛnt/ *vt* to portray; to describe; to typify; to stand for, symbolize; to point out; to perform on the stage; to act as an agent for; to deputize for; to serve as a specimen, example, etc, of.—**representable** *adj.*

representation /ˌrɛprɪzɛnˈteɪʃən/ *n* the act of representing or being represented, as in a parliamentary assembly; a portrait, reproduction; (*pl*) a presentation of claims, protests, views, etc.

representative /ˌrɛprɪˈzɛntətɪv/ *adj* typical; portraying; consisting of or based on representation of the electorate by delegates. • *n* an example or type; a person who acts for another; a delegate, agent, salesman, etc.

repress /rɪˈprɛs/ *vt* to suppress, restrain; (*emotions*) to keep under control; to exclude involuntarily from the conscious mind.—**repressive** *adj.*—**represser, repressor** *n.*

repression /rɪˈprɛʃən/ *n* the act of repressing; the condition of being repressed; domination, tyranny.

reprieve /rɪˈpriːv/ *vt* to postpone or commute the punishment of; to give respite to.—*also n.*

reprimand /ˈreprɪˌmænd/ *n* a formal rebuke. • *vt* to reprove formally.

reprint /riˈprɪnt/ *vt* to print again. • *n* a book or article that has appeared in print before.

reprisal /rɪˈpraɪzəl/ *n* an act of retaliation for an injury done.

reprise /rɪˈpraɪz/ or /-priːz/ *n* (*mus*) the repetition of an earlier theme or passage.—*also vt*.

reproach /rɪˈproʊtʃ/ *vt* to accuse of a fault; to blame. • *n* a reproof; a source of shame or disgrace.—**reproachful** *adj*.

reprobate /ˈreprəˌbeɪt/ *n* a depraved person; a hardened sinner; a scoundrel.

reproduce /ˌriːprəˈduːs/ or /-proʊ-/, /-ˈdjuːs/ *vti* to make a copy, duplicate, or likeness of; to propagate; to produce offspring; to multiply.

reproduction /ˌriːprəˈdʌkʃən/ *n* the act of reproducing; the process by which plants and animals breed; a copy or likeness; a representation.—**reproductive** *adj*.

reprography /rɪˈprɒɡrəfi/ *n* the process of reproducing printed material, as by photocopying.—**reprographic** *adj*.

reproof /rɪˈpruːf/ *n* a rebuke, blame.

reprove /rɪˈpruːv/ *vt* to rebuke, censure.—**reprovingly** *adv*.

reptile /ˈreptaɪl/ *n* any of a class of cold-blooded, air-breathing vertebrates with horny scales or plates, as turtles, crocodiles, snakes, lizards, etc; a grovelling or despised person.—**reptilian** *adj*.

republic /rəˈpʌblɪk/ *n* a government in which the people elect the head of state, *usu* called president, and in which the people and their elected representatives have supreme power; a country governed in this way; a body of persons freely engaged in a specified activity.

republican /rəˈpʌblɪkən/ *adj* of, characteristic of, or supporting a republic. • *n* an advocate of republican government; (*with cap*) a member of the US Republican party.—**republicanism** *n*.

republish /riːˈpʌblɪʃ/ *vt* to publish again; to issue a new edition of (a book).—**republication** *n*.

repudiate /rəˈpjuːdieɪt/ or /rɪ-/ *vt* to reject, disown; to refuse to acknowledge or pay; to deny; (a treaty, etc) to disavow.—**repudiation** *n*.

repugnant /rəˈpʌɡnənt/ *adj* distasteful, offensive; contradictory; incompatible.—**repugnance** *n*.

repulse /rəˈpʌls/ *vt* to drive back; to repel; to reject. • *n* a rebuff, rejection; a defeat, check.

repulsion /rəˈpʌlʃən/ or /rɪ-/ *n* a feeling of disgust; aversion; (*physics*) the tendency of bodies to repel each other.

repulsive /rəˈpʌlsɪv/ *adj* disgusting; loathsome; exercising repulsion.—**repulsively** *adv*.

reputable /rəˈpjuːtəbəl/ *adj* of good repute, respectable.—**reputably** *adv*.

reputation /ˌrepjuˈteɪʃən/ *n* the estimation in which a person or thing is held; good name, honour.

repute /rəˈpjuːt/ *vt* to consider to be, to deem. • *n* reputation.

reputed /rəˈpjuːtəd/ *adj* generally reported; supposed, putative.

reputedly *adv* in common estimation; by repute.

request /-li/ *n* an asking for something; a petition; a demand; the thing asked for. • *vt* to ask for earnestly.

request stop *n* a place where a bus, etc stops only if signalled to do so.—*also* **flag stop**.

requiem *n* a mass for the dead; music for this.

require /ˈrɪkwiəm/ or /-iəm/ *vt* to demand; to need, call for; to order, command.

requirement /rəˈkwaɪrmənt/ *n* a need or want; an essential condition.

requisite /ˈrekwəzɪt/ *adj* needed; essential, indispensable. • *n* something required or indispensable.

requisition /ˈrekwəzɪʃən/ *n* a formal request, demand, or order, as for military supplies; the taking over of private property, etc, for military use. • *vt* to order; to take by requisition.

reredos /ˈriːrdɒs/ or /ˈriːrɪ-/ *n* a screen or partition separating the altar from the choir.

rerun /riːˈrʌn/ *vt* to run (a race, etc) again; to show a television programme, film, etc again.—*also n*.

resale /riːˈseɪl/ *n* the selling again (of something) *usu* to a new buyer; a repeat sale to a customer; a second-hand sale.

reschedule /riːˈskedʒʊəl/ or /-ˈskedʒuːl/, /-ˈʃedjuːl/, /-ˈʃedʒuːl/ *vt* (*debt*) to postpone or extend repayment terms.

rescind /rəˈsɪnd/ or /rɪ-/ *vt* to annul, cancel.

rescue /ˈreskjuː/ *vt* to save (a person, thing) from captivity, danger, or harm; to free forcibly from legal custody.—*also n*.—**rescuer** *n*.

research /ˈriːsɜːrtʃ/ or /rɪˈsɜːrtʃ/ *n* a diligent search; a systematic and careful investigation of a particular subject; a scientific study. • *vi* to carry out an investigation; to study.—**researcher** *n*.

resemble /rəˈzembəl/ *vt* to be like, to have a similarity to.—**resemblance** *n*.

resent /rəˈzent/ or /rɪ-/ *vt* to be indignant about; to begrudge; to take badly.—**resentful** *adj*.—**resentfully** *adv*.—**resentment** *n*.

reserpine /ˈrezərpiːn/ *n* an alkaloid extracted from the roots of a rauwolfia, used to treat high blood pressure and as a sedative.

reservation /ˌrezərˈveɪʃən/ *n* the act of reserving; (*of tickets, accommodation, etc*) a holding until called for; a limitation or proviso; (*pl*) doubt, scepticism; land set aside for a special purpose.

reserve /rəˈzɜːrv/ or /rɪ-/ *vt* to hold back for future use; to retain; to have set aside; (*tickets, hotel room, etc*) to book. • *n* something put aside for future use; land set aside for wild animals; (*sport*) a substitute; (*mil*) a force supplementary to a regular army; a restriction or qualification; reticence of feelings; caution.

reserved /rəˈzɜːrvd/ or /rɪ-/ *adj* set apart, booked; uncommunicative, lacking cordiality.—**reservedly** *adv*.

reservist /-vɪst/ *n* a member of a military reserve force.

reservoir /ˈrezərˌvwɑːr/ or /ˈrezəˌvwɑːr/ *n* a tank or artificial lake for storing water; an extra supply or store.

reset[1] /riːˈset/ *vt* (**resetting, reset**) to set (a bone, gem, type) over again; to place in a new setting; to change the reading of.

reset[2] *vt* (**resetting, reset**) (*Scots law*) to receive (stolen goods).—*also n*.

reshape /riːˈʃeɪp/ *vti* to shape anew.

reside /rəˈzaɪd/ or /rɪ-/ *vi* to live in a place permanently; to be vested or present in.

residence /ˈrezɪdəns/ *n* the act of living in a place; the period of residing; the house where one lives permanently; the status of a legal resident; a building used as a home.

residency /ˈrezɪdənsi/ *n* (*pl* **residencies**) a *usu* official place of residence, *eg* of a governor; a period of advanced training in medicine.

resident /ˈrezɪdənt/ *adj* residing; domiciled; living at one's place of work. • *n* a permanent inhabitant; a doctor who is serving a residency.

residential /ˌrezɪˈdenʃəl/ *adj* of or relating to residence; used for private homes.

residual /reˈzɪdʒʊəl/ *adj* left over; remaining as a residue.

residuary /ˈrezɪdʒʊəri/ *adj* of or relating to the residue of an estate.

residue /ˈrezɪˌduː/ or /-ˌdjuː/ *n* a remainder; a part left over; what is left of an estate after payment of debts and legacies.

resign /rəˈzaɪn/ or /rɪ-/ *vti* to give up (employment, etc); to relinquish; to yield to; to reconcile (oneself).

resignation /ˌrezɪɡˈneɪʃən/ *n* the resigning of office, etc; the written proof of this; patient endurance.

resigned /rəˈzaɪnd/ *adj* submissive, acquiescent; accepting the inevitable.

resilience /rəˈzɪljəns/, or /rɪ-/, /-ɪəns/, **resiliency** /-si/ *n* the quality of being resilient; physical or mental stamina.

resilient /rəˈzɪljənt/, or /rɪ-/, /-ɪənt/ *adj* elastic, springing back; buoyant; (*person*) capable of carrying on after suffering hardship.

resin /ˈrezɪn/ *n* a sticky substance exuded in the sap of trees and plants and used in medicines, varnishes, etc; rosin; a similar synthetic substance used in plastics.—**resinous** *adj*.

resist /rəˈzɪst/ or /rɪ-/ *vti* to fight against; to be proof against; to oppose or withstand.

resistance /rəˈzɪstəns/ or /rɪ-/ *n* the act of resisting; the power to resist, as to ward off disease; opposition, *esp* to an occupying force; hindrance; (*elect*) non-conductivity, opposition to a steady current.

resistant /rəˈzɪstənt/ or /rɪ-/ *adj* capable of resisting; (*with* **to**) immune to.

resistor /rəˈzɪstər/ or /rɪ-/ *n* an electrical device that resists current in a circuit.

resolute /ˈrezəˌluːt/ *adj* determined; firm of purpose, steadfast.—**resolutely** *adv*.—**resoluteness** *n*.

resolution /ˌrezəˈluːʃən/ *n* the act of resolving or the state of being resolved; determination; a fixed intention; the formal decision or opinion of a meeting; analysis, disintegration; (*med*) the dispersion of a tumour, etc; the picture definition in a TV; (*mus*) the relieving of a discord by a following concord; (*physics*) the process or capability of making distinguishable closely adjacent optical images or sources of light.

resolve /rə'zɒlv/ *vt* to break into component parts, dissolve; to convert or be converted (into); to analyse; to determine, make up one's mind; to solve, settle; to vote by resolution; to dispel (doubt); to explain; to conclude; (*med: tumour*) to disperse; (*mus: discord*) to convert into concord. • *n* a fixed intention; resolution; courage.

resolving power *n* the ability of a microscope or telescope to produce distinct images of objects in close proximity.

resonance /'rezənəns/ *n* resounding quality; vibration.

resonant /'rezənənt/ *adj* ringing; resounding, echoing.

resonator /,rezə'neitər/ *n* a device that produces or increases sound by resonance.

resort /rə'zɔrt/ or /ri-/ *n* a popular holiday location; a source of help, support, etc; recourse. • *vi* to have recourse to; to turn (to) for help, etc.

resound /rə'zaund/ or /ri-/ *vti* to echo; to reverberate; to go on sounding; to be much talked of; to spread (fame).

resounding /-ɪŋ/ *adj* echoing; notable; thorough.

resource /riː'zɔrs/ or /rɪ-/, /-sɔrs/ *n* source of help; an expedient; the ability to cope with a situation; a means of diversion; (*pl*) wealth; assets; raw materials.

resourceful /-fʊl/ *adj* able to cope in difficult situations; ingenious.—**resourcefulness** *n*.

respect /rə'spɛkt/ or /ri-/ *n* esteem; consideration; regard; (*pl*) good wishes; reference; relation. • *vt* to feel or show esteem or regard to; to treat considerately.

respectable /rə'spɛktəbəl/ or /ri-/ *adj* worthy of esteem; well-behaved; proper, correct, well-conducted; of moderate quality or size.—**respectability** *n*.—**respectably** *adv*.

respectful /-fʊl/ *adj* deferential.—**respectfully** *adv*.

respecting /-ɪŋ/ *prep* concerning.

respective /-tɪŋ/ *adj* proper to each, several.

respectively /-tɪvli/ *adv* in the indicated order.

respiration /,respə'reɪʃən/ *n* the act or process of breathing.

respirator /,respə'reɪtər/ *n* an apparatus to maintain breathing by artificial means; a device or mask to prevent the inhalation of harmful substances.

respiratory /'resprə,tori / or /'respərə-/ *adj* of or for respiration.

respire /rə'spaɪr/ *vti* to breathe.

respite /rə'spaɪt/ *n* a temporary delay; a period of rest or relief; a reprieve.

resplendent /rə'splɛndənt/ *adj* dazzling, shining brilliantly; magnificent.

respond /rə'spɒnd/ or /ri-/ *vti* to answer; to reply; to show a favourable reaction; to be answerable; (*with* **to**) to react.

respondent /rə'spɒndənt/ or /ri-/ *n* a defendant, *esp* in a divorce suit; one who answers.

response /rə'spɒns/ or /ri-/ *n* an answer; a reaction to stimulation.

responsibility /rə,spɒnsə'bɪlɪti/ or /ri-/ *n* (*pl* **responsibilities**) being responsible; a moral obligation or duty; a charge or trust; a thing one is responsible for.

responsible /rə'spɒnsəbəl/ or /ri-/ *adj* having control (over); (*with* **for**) accountable (for); capable of rational conduct; trustworthy; involving responsibility.—**responsibly** *adv*.

responsive /rə'spɒnsɪv/ or /ri-/ *adj* responding; sensitive to influence or stimulus; sympathetic.

rest¹ /rɛst/ *n* stillness, repose, sleep; inactivity; the state of not moving; relaxation; tranquillity; a support or prop; a pause in music, metre, etc; a place of quiet. • *vti* to take a rest; to give rest to; to be still; to lie down; to relax; to be fixed (on); to lean, support or be supported; to put one's trust (in).

rest² *n* the remainder; the others. • *vi* to remain.

restate /ri:'steɪt/ *vt* to state over again; to put differently.—**restatement** *n*.

restaurant /'restə,rɒnt/ or /'restrɒnt/ *n* a place where meals can be bought and eaten.

restaurateur /,restərə'tər/ *n* the keeper of a restaurant.

restful /'restfʊl/ *adj* peaceful.—**restfully** *adv*.—**restfulness** *n*.

rest home *n* an old people's home; a convalescent home.

restitution /,restə'tuːʃən/ or /-'tjuː-/ *n* the restoring of something to its owner; a reimbursement, as for loss.

restive /'restɪv/ *adj* impatient; fidgety.

restless /'restləs/ *adj* unsettled; agitated.—**restlessly** *adv*.—**restlessness** *n*.

restoration /,restər'eɪʃən/ *n* the act of restoring; reconstruction; renovation; (*with cap*) the re-establishment of the monarchy in Britain in 1660 under Charles II.

restorative /rə'storətɪv/ *adj* tending to restore health and strength. • *n* a medicine or food that reinvigorates.

restore /rə'stor/ or /ri-/ *vt* to give or put back; to re-establish; to repair; to renovate; to bring back to the original condition.—**restorer** *n*.

restrain /rə'strain/ or /ri-/ *vt* to hold back; to restrict; (*person*) to deprive of freedom.

restrained /rə'straind/ or /ri-/ *adj* moderate; self-controlled; without exuberance.

restraint /rə'straint/ or /ri-/ *n* the ability to hold back; something that restrains; control of emotions, impulses, etc.

restrict /rə'strikt/ or /ri-/ *vt* to keep within limits, circumscribe.

restricted /rə'striktəd/ or /ri-/ *adj* affected by restriction; limited; not generally available.

restriction /rə'strikʃən/ or /ri-/ *n* restraint; limitation; a limiting regulation.—**restrictive** *adj*.

restroom /'restruːm/ *n* a room equipped with toilets, washbowls, etc for the use of the public.

result /rə'zɛlt/ or /ri-/ *vi* to have as a consequence; to terminate in. • *n* a consequence; an outcome; a value obtained by mathematical calculation; (*sport*) the final score; (*pl*) a desired effect.

resultant /rə'zɛltənt/ or /ri-/ *adj* derived from or resulting from something else.

resume /rə'zuːm/ or /-'zjuːm/, /ri-/ *vti* to begin again; to continue after a stop or pause; to proceed after interruption.—**resumption** *n*.

résumé /'rezə,mei/ or /-zjʊ-/ *n* a summary, *esp* of employment experience; a curriculum vitae.

resurgence /rə'sərdʒəns/ or /ri-/ *n* a revival; a renewal of activity.—**resurgent** *adj*.

resurrect /,rezə'rɛkt/ *vt* to bring back into use; (*a custom*) to revive; to restore to life.

resurrection *n* a revival; a rising from the dead; (*with cap*) the rising of Christ from the dead.

resuscitate /rə'sʌsə,teit/ or /ri-/ *vti* to revive when apparently dead or unconscious.—**resuscitation** *n*.

resuscitator /-,teitər/ *n* an apparatus for forcing oxygen into the lungs; a person who resuscitates.

retable /rə'teibəl/ or /ri-/ *n* a step or ledge behind the altar of a church, slightly raised above it for the reception of lights, flowers, and other symbolical ornaments.

retail /rə'teil/ or /ri-/ *n* selling directly to the consumer in small quantities. • *adv* at a retail price. • *vti* to sell or be sold by retail.—*also adj*.—**retailer** *n*.

retain /rə'teil/ or /ri-/ *vt* to keep possession of; to keep in the mind, to remember; to keep in place, support; to hire the services of.

retainer /rə'teinər/ or /ri-/ *n* that which returns; (*formerly*) a servant to a family, a dependant; a fee to retain the services of.

retaining wall *n* a wall built to hold back earth or water.

retake /rə'teik/ or /ri-/ *vt* (**retaking, retook,** *pp* **retaken**) to capture again; to shoot a film scene again. • *n* a scene that has been reshot.

retaliate /rə'tæli,eit/ or /ri-/ *vti* to revenge oneself, *usu* by returning like for like; to strike back; to cast back (an accusation).—**retaliation** *n*.—**retaliatory** *adj*.

retard /rə'tard/ or /ri-/ *vti* to slow down, to delay; to make slow or late.—**retardation** *n*.

retardant /rə'tardənt/ or /ri-/ *n* a substance that retards, *esp* a chemical reaction. • *adj* retarding.

retarded /rə'tardəd/ or /ri-/ *adj* slow in physical or mental development.

retch /rɛtʃ/ *vi* to heave as if to vomit.

retention /rə'tenʃən/ or /ri-/ *n* the act of retaining; the capacity to retain; memory; (*med*) the abnormal retaining of fluid in a body cavity.

retentive /rə'tentiv/ or /ri-/ *adj* capable of retaining; keeping, holding. • *n* one who retains.—**retentiveness** *n*.

rethink /ri:'θɪŋk/ *vt* (**rethinking, rethought**) to consider or think about again, *esp* with a change in mind.

reticent /'retɪsənt/ *adj* reserved in speech; uncommunicative.—**reticence** *n*.

reticle /'retikəl/ *n* a network of fine wires, threads, etc placed in the focal plane of an optical instrument.

reticulate /rɪtɪ'kjuːleɪt/ *adj* resembling a network.—*also* **reticular**. • *vti* to arrange or be arranged into a network.—**reticulation** *n*.

retina /'retɪnə/ *n* (*pl* **retinas, retinae**) the innermost part of the eye, on which the image is formed.

retinue /ˈrɛtənju:/ or /-ˌnu:/ *n* a body of attendants.

retire /rəˈtaɪr/ or /rɪ-/ *vi* to give up one's work when pensionable age is reached; to withdraw; to retreat; to go to bed. • *vt* (*troops*) to withdraw from use; to compel to retire from a position, work, etc.

retirement /rəˈtaɪrmənt/ or /rɪ-/ *n* the act of retiring or the state of being retired; seclusion; privacy.

retiring /rəˈtaɪrɪŋ/ or /rɪ-/ *adj* unobtrusive; shy.

retort /rəˈtɔrt/ or /rɪ-/ *vi* to reply sharply or wittily. • *n* a sharp or witty reply; a vessel with a funnel bent downwards used in distilling; a receptacle used in making gas and steel.

retouch /ri:ˈtʌtʃ/ *vt* (*photograph, etc*) to improve or change by touching up; (*new growth of hair*) to colour to match other hair.

retrace /ri:ˈtreɪs/ *vt* to go back over; to trace back to a source.—**retraceable** *adj*.

retract /rəˈtrækt/ or /rɪ-/ *vti* to draw in or back; to withdraw (a statement, opinion, etc); to recant.—**retractable** *adj*.—**retraction** *n*.

retreat /rəˈtri:t/ or /rɪ-/ *vi* to withdraw, retire; to recede. • *n* a withdrawal, *esp* of troops; a sign for retiring; a quiet or secluded place, refuge; seclusion for religious devotion.

retrench /rəˈtrentʃ/ or /rɪ-/ *vti* to cut down (*esp* expenses); to economize.—**retrenchment** *n*.

retrial /ri:ˈtraɪəl/ *n* a second trial.

retribution /ˌrɛtrəˈbju:ʃən/ *n* deserved reward; something given or exacted in compensation, *esp* punishment.

retrieve /rəˈtri:v/ or /rɪ-/ *vt* to recover; to revive; (*a loss*) to make good; (*comput*) to obtain information from data stored in a computer. • *vi* (*dogs*) to retrieve game.—**retrievable** *adj*.—**retrieval** *n*.

retriever /rəˈtri:vər/ or /rɪ-/ *n* any of several breeds of dogs capable of being trained for retrieving.

retro /ˈrɛtrəʊ/ *n* (*pl* **retros**) a retrorocket. • *adj* denoting a fashion or style (in music, clothes, etc) that pays homage to the past.

retro- /ˈrɛtrəʊ/ *prefix* backwards; behind.

retroactive /ˌrɛtrəʊˈæktɪv/ *adj* having an effect on things that are already past.

retrograde /ˌrɛtrəˈgreɪd/ *adj* going backwards; passing from better to worse.

retrogression /ˌrɛtrəˈgreʃən/ *n* going backwards, *usu* a return to a former, less complex, level of development.

retrorocket /ˌrɛtrəʊˈrɒkət/ *n* a small rocket on an aircraft or spacecraft that produces thrust in the opposite direction to the line of flight to slow it down.

retrospect /ˈrɛtrəˌspɛkt/ *n* a looking back; a mental review of the past.—**retrospection** *n*.

retrospective /ˌrɛtrəˈspɛktɪv/ *adj* looking backwards; relating to the past. • *n* an exhibition of an artist's lifetime work.—**retrospectively** *adv*.

retroussé /ˌrɛtru:ˈseɪ/ *adj* turned upwards (*esp* of the nose).

retroversion /ˈrɛtrəʊˌvɜrʒən/ *n* the act of turning or state of being turned backwards.—**retroverted** *adj*.

Retrovir *n* (*trademark*) AZT.

retrovirus /ˈrɛtrəʊˌvaɪrəs/ *n* any of various viruses that use RNA to synthesize DNA, reversing the normal process in cells of transcription from DNA to RNA, which includes HIV.

retsina /rɛtˈsi:nə/ *n* a Greek white wine flavoured with resin.

return /rəˈtɜrn/ or /rɪ-/ *vi* to come or go back; to reply; to recur. • *vt* to give or send back; to repay; to yield; to answer; to elect. • *n* something returned; a recurrence; recompense; (*pl*) yield, revenue; a form for computing (income) tax.

returnable /rəˈtɜrnəbəl/ or /rɪ-/ *adj* required to be returned; capable of being returned (for reuse).

return ticket *n* (*Brit etc*) a ticket whose price includes the cost of the journey to and back from a destination.

reunion /ri:ˈju:nɪən/ *n* a meeting following separation; a social gathering of former colleagues.

reunite /ri:ˈju:naɪt/ *vt* to unite again; to reconcile. • *vi* to become reunited.

reusable /ri:ˈju:zəbəl/ *adj* able to be used again; renewable.

Rev. *abbr* = Reverend.

rev /rɛv/ *vt* (**revving, revved**) (*inf*) (*with* **up**) to increase the speed of an engine. • *n* revolution per minute.

revaluate /ri:ˈvælju:ˌeɪt/ *vt* to reassess the value of; to change (*esp* increase) the exchange value of (a currency).

revamp /ri:ˈvæmp/ *vt* to renovate, to rework, remodel; to transform. • *n* the process of revamping; something revamped.

revanchism /rəˈvæntʃɪzəm/ or /ri-/ *n* (support for) a policy aimed at regaining lost territory or possessions.—**revanchist** *n, adj*.

reveal /rəˈvi:l/ or /ri-/ *vt* (*something hidden or secret*) to make known; to expose; to make visible.

reveille /ˈrɛvəli/ *n* a morning bugle call to wake soldiers.

revel /ˈrɛvəl/ *vi* (**reveling, revelled** *or* **reveling, reveled**) (*with* **in**) to take pleasure or delight in; to make merry. • *n* (*pl*) merrymaking; entertainment.—**reveler, reveller** *n*.

revelry /ˈrɛvəlri/ *n* (*pl* **revelries**) the act of revelling; noisy festivity.

revelation /ˌrɛvəˈleɪʃən/ *n* the act of revealing; the disclosure of something secret; a communication from God to man; an illuminating experience.

revenge /rəˈvɛndʒ/ or /ri-/ *vt* to inflict punishment in return for; to satisfy oneself by retaliation; to avenge. • *n* the act of revenging; retaliation; a vindictive feeling.—**revenger** *n*.

revengeful /ˈrəvɛndʒfʊl/ or /ri-/ *adj* keen for revenge; vindictive.

revenue /ˈrɛvəˌnju:/ or /-ˌnu:/ *n* the total income produced by taxation; gross income from a business or investment.

reverb /rɪˈvɜrb/ or /ˈri:vɜrb/ *n* (*mus*) an electronic device for producing an artificial echo.

reverberate /rɪˈvɜrbəˌreɪt/ *vi* to rebound, recoil; to be reflected in; to resound, to echo.—**reverberation** *n*.

revere /rəˈvi:r/ *vt* to regard with great respect or awe; to venerate.

reverence /ˈrɛvərəns/ *n* profound respect; devotion; a gesture of respect (such as a bow). • *vt* to hold in respect.

reverend /ˈrɛvərənd/ *adj* worthy of reverence; of or relating to the clergy; (*with cap*) a title for a member of the clergy.

reverent /ˈrɛvərənt/ *adj* feeling or expressing reverence.—**reverently** *adv*.

reverie /ˈrɛvəri/ *n* a daydream; (*mus*) a dreamy piece.—*also* **revery** (*pl* **reveries**).

revers /rɪˈvi:rz/ *n* (*pl* **revers**) a lapel, *esp* on a woman's garment.

reversal /rəˈvɜrsəl/ *n* the act or process of reversing.

reverse /rəˈvɜrs/ *vti* to turn in the opposite direction; to turn outside in, upside down, etc; to move backwards; (*law*) to revoke or annul. • *n* the contrary or opposite of something; the back, *esp* of a coin; a setback; a mechanism for reversing. • *adj* opposite, contrary; causing movement in the opposite direction.

reverse video *n* a technique for highlighting on a computer monitor by reversing the normal text and background colours.

reversible /rəˈvɜrsəbəl/ *adj* with both sides usable; wearable with either side out; able to undergo a series of changes either backwards or forwards. • *n* a reversible cloth or article of clothing.

reversion /rəˈvɜrʒən/ or /ri-/ *n* return to a former condition or type; right to future possession; the return of an estate to the grantor or his heirs.—**reversionary** *adj*.

revert /rəˈvɜrt/ or /ri-/ *vi* to go back (to a former state); to take up again (a former subject); (*biol*) to return to a former or primitive type; (*law*) to go back to a former owner or his heirs.—**revertible** *adj*.

revery /ˈrɛvəri/ *see* **reverie**.

review /rəˈvju:/ *n* an evaluation; a survey; a reconsideration; a critical assessment, a critique; a periodical containing critical essays; an official inspection of ships or troops. • *vt* to re-examine; to inspect formally; to write a critique on.

reviewer /rəˈvju:ər/ *n* a person who writes a review, *esp* for a newspaper, a critic.

revile /rəˈvaɪl/ *vti* to use abusive language (to or about).

revise /rəˈvaɪz/ *vt* to correct and amend; to prepare a new, improved version of; to study again (for an examination).—**revision** *n*.

revitalize /rɪˈvaɪtəˌlaɪz/ *vt* to put new life into.—**revitalization** *n*.

revival /rɪˈvaɪvəl/ *n* the act of reviving; recovery from a neglected or depressed state; renewed performance (of a play); renewed interest in; religious awakening.

revivalist /rɪˈvaɪvəˌlɪst/ *n* a person who encourages religious practice.—**revivalism** *n*.

revive /rɪˈvaɪv/ *vti* to return to life; to make active again; to take up again.—**reviver** *n*.

revivify /rɪˈvɪvɪˌfaɪ/ *vt* to put new life into; to reanimate; to revive.—**revivification** *n*.—**revivifier** *n*.

revoke /rɪˈvəʊk/ or /ri-/ *vt* to cancel; to rescind. • *vi* (*cards*) to fail to follow suit.—**revocable** *adj*.—**revocation** *n*.

revolt /rɪˈvəʊlt/ or /ri-/ *vt* to rebel; to overturn; to shock. • *vi* to feel great disgust. • *n* rebellion; uprising; loathing.

revolting /rɪˈvəʊltɪŋ/ or /ri-/ *adj* extremely offensive.—**revoltingly** *adv*.

revolution /ˌrevə'luːʃən/ *n* the act of revolting; a motion round a centre or axis; a single completion of an orbit or rotation; a great change; an overthrow of a government, social system, etc.

revolutionary *adj* of or advocating revolution; radically new. • *n* a person who takes part in, or favours, revolution.

revolutionize /ˌrevə'luːʃə,naɪz/ *vt* to cause a complete change in.

revolve /rɪ'vɒlv/ or /ri-/ *vt* to travel or cause to travel in a circle or orbit; to rotate.

revolver /rɪ'vɒlvər/ or /ri-/ *n* a handgun with a magazine that revolves to reload.

revolving door *n* a door of two or four panels rotating around a central axis within a round chamber and operated electrically or manually.

revue /rɪ'vjuː/ or /ri-/ *n* a musical show with skits, dances, etc, often satirizing recent events.

revulsion /rɪ'vʌlʒən/ or /ri-/ *n* disgust; aversion; a sudden change or reversal of feeling, *esp* withdrawal with a sense of utter distaste.

reward /rɪ'wɔrd/ or /ri-/ *n* something that is given in return for something done; money offered, as for the capture of a criminal. • *vt* to give a reward.

rewarding /rɪ'wɔrdɪŋ/ or /ri-/ *adj* (*experience, activity, etc*) pleasing, profitable.

rewind /ri'waɪnd/ *vt* to wind again; to wind (an audiotape, etc) back to the beginning. • *n* the act of rewinding.

rewire /ri'waɪr/ *vt* to put new wiring into an electrical system.

reword /ri'wɔrd/ *vt* to change the wording of.

rework /ri'wɔrk/ *vt* to use again in a different form; to rewrite; to remodel.

rewrite /ri'raɪt/ *vt* to write again; to revise. • *n* something rewritten; revision.

Rex /reks/ *n* a reigning king.

rf *abbr* = radio frequency.

Rh *abbr* = rhesus.

rhachis /'reɪkɪs/ *see* **rachis**.

rhapsodize /'ræpsə,daɪz/ *vi* to speak or write (about) with enthusiasm or emotion.—**rhapsodist** *n*.

rhapsody /'ræpsədi/ *n* (*pl* **rhapsodies**) an enthusiastic speech or writing; (*mus*) an irregular instrumental composition of an epic, heroic or national character.

rhea /'riːə/ *n* any of several large flightless birds of South America resembling ostriches but smaller.

rhenium /'riːniəm/ *n* a hard heat-resistant metallic element.

rheo- /'riːoː/ *prefix* flow, current.

rheology /ri:'ɒlədʒi/ *n* the physics of the flow and deformation of matter.—**rheologist** *n*.—**rheological** *adj*.

rheostat /'riːə,stæt/ *n* a device that regulates electric current by varying the resistance to it.—**rheostatic** *adj*.

rhesus factor /'riːsəs/ *n* a substance usually present in the red blood cells of humans and higher animals.

rhesus monkey *n* a type of southern Asian macaque with light brown fur.

rhesus negative *adj* lacking the rhesus factor in the blood.

rhesus positive *adj* containing the rhesus factor in the blood.

rhetoric /'retərɪk/ *n* the art of effective speaking and writing; skill in using speech; insincere language.

rhetorical /rɪ'tɒrɪkəl/ *adj* of or relating to rhetoric; high-flown, bombastic.—**rhetorically** *adv*.

rhetorical question *n* a question asked for effect, to which no answer is expected.

rheum /'ruːm/ *n* a watery discharge from the mucous membranes of the nose, eyes, etc.—**rheumy** *adj*.

rheumatic /ruː'mætɪk/ *adj* of, relating to or suffering from rheumatism. • *n* a person who has rheumatism.

rheumatic fever *n* a disease characterized by inflammation and pain in the joints.

rheumatism /'ruːmə,tɪzəm/ *n* a disorder causing pain in muscles and joints.

rheumatoid /ruːmə,tɔɪd/ *adj* of or like rheumatism.

rheumatoid arthritis *n* a *usu* chronic disease characterized by inflammation, pain, and swelling of the joints.

rheumatology /ˌruːmə'tɒlədʒi/ *n* the study of rheumatic diseases.—**rheumatologist** *n*.

rhinal /'raɪnəl/ *adj* of or pertaining to the nose.

rhinestone /'raɪnstoːn/ *n* a colourless imitation precious stone made from paste, glass, or quartz.

Rhine wine *n* any of several wines from the valley of the River Rhine in Germany; a light dry wine from the Rhine valley or elsewhere.

rhinitis /raɪ'naɪtɪs/ *n* inflammation of the mucous membrane of the nose.

rhino- /'raɪnoː/, **rhin-** /raɪn/ *prefix* nose.

rhino /'raɪnoː/ *n* (*pl* **rhinos, rhino**) (*inf*) a rhinoceros.

rhinoceros /raɪ'nɒsərəs/ *n* (*pl* **rhinoceroses, rhinoceros**) a large, thick-skinned mammal with one or two horns on the nose.

rhinology /raɪ'nɒlədʒi/ *n* the branch of medicine dealing with the nose.—**rhinologist** *n*.

rhinoplasty /'raɪnoː,plæsti/ *n* plastic surgery of the nose.—**rhinoplastic** *adj*.

rhizo- /'raɪzoː/, **rhiz-** /'raɪz/ *prefix* root.

rhizome /'raɪzoːm/ *n* a stem on or below ground that produces roots below and shoots above; a rootstock.

rho /roː/ *n* (*pl* **rhos**) the 17th letter of the Greek alphabet.

Rhode Island Red *n* an American breed of domestic fowl with reddish-brown plumage.

rhodium /'roːdiəm/ *n* a hard white metallic element similar to platinum.

rhododendron /ˌroːdə'dendrən/ *n* an evergreen shrub with large flowers.

rhomb /rɒm/ *n* a rhombus.

rhombohedron /ˌrɒmbə'hedrən/ *n* (*pl* **rhombohedrons, rhombohedra**) a six-sided solid figure whose sides are rhombuses.—**rhombohedral** *adj*.

rhomboid /'rɒmbɔɪd/ *n* a parallelogram whose adjacent sides are unequal and whose angles are not right angles.—*also adj*.

rhombus /'rɒmbəs/ *n* (*pl* **rhombuses, rhombi**) a diamond shape.

rhubarb /'ruːbɑrb/ *n* a plant with large leaves and edible (when cooked) pink stalks; (*inf*) a noisy quarrel.

rhumb /rʌm/ *n* an imaginary line crossing all meridians at the same angle; a course navigated by a ship or aircraft that maintains a fixed compass bearing.—*also* **rhumb line**.

rhyme /raɪm/ *n* the repetition of sounds *usu* at the ends of lines in verse; such poetry or verse; a word corresponding with another in end sound. • *vti* to form a rhyme (with); to versify, put into rhyme.

rhyming slang *n* a type of slang that substitutes the original (often indecent) word with a word or phrase that rhymes with it, *eg loaf of bread = head*.

rhythm /'rɪðəm/ *n* a regular recurrence of beat, accent or silence in the flow of sound, *esp* of words and music; a measured flow; cadence.—**rhythmic, rhythmical** *adj*.—**rhythmically** *adv*.

rhythm and blues *n* a type of music that fuses elements of folk, blues and rock.

rhythm method *n* a method of contraception that relies on abstinence from sexual intercourse during the period when ovulation is most likely to occur.

rhythm section *n* those instruments in a band or group whose main role is to supply the rhythm, such as the double bass and drums.

rib /rɪb/ *n* one of the curved bones of the chest attached to the spine; any rib-like structure; a leaf vein; a vein of an insect's wing; a ridge or raised strip, as of knitting; a ridge of a mountain. • *vt* (**ribbing, ribbed**) to provide with ribs; to form vertical ridges in knitting; (*inf*) to tease or ridicule.

ribald /rɪ'bɔld/ or /raɪ-/ *adj* irreverent; humorously vulgar.

riband /'rɪbənd/ *n* a ribbon.

ribbon /rɪbən/ *n* silk, satin, velvet, etc, woven into a narrow band; a piece of this; a strip of cloth, etc, inked for use, as in a typewriter; (*pl*) torn shreds.

rib cage *n* the bony framework of ribs enclosing the wall of the chest.

riboflavin /ˌraɪboː'fleɪvɪn/ *n* a factor of the vitamin B complex found in milk, eggs, fruits, etc.

ribonuclease /ˌraɪboː'nuːkli,eɪs/ or /-'njuː-/ *n* any of several enzymes that act as catalytic triggers of RNA hydrolosis.

ribonucleic acid /ˌraɪboː'nuːkliːɪk/ or /-njuː-/, /-kleɪk/ *n* any of a group of nucleic acids found in all living cells, where they are essential to protein development.—**RNA** *abbr*.

ribose /'raɪboːs/ *n* a sugar occurring in RNA and riboflavin.

ribosome /'raɪbə,soːm/ *n* any of the tiny particles containing RNA and protein in cells where protein synthesis takes place.—**ribosomal** *adj*.

rice /rəɪs/ *n* an annual cereal grass cultivated in warm climates; its starchy food grain.

ricebird /ˈrəɪsˌbərd/ *see* **bobolink**.

rice paper *n* a delicate paper prepared from pith.

rich /rɪtʃ/ *adj* having much money, wealthy; abounding in natural resources, fertile; costly, fine; (*food*) sweet or oily, highly flavoured; deep in colour; (*inf*) full of humour. • *n* wealthy people collectively; (*pl* **riches**) wealth, abundance.—**richly** *adv*.—**richness** *n*.

Richter scale /ˈrɪktər/ *n* a scale ranging from 1 to 10 for measuring the intensity of an earthquake.

rick[1] /rɪk/ *n* a stack or large pile of hay, etc, in the open.

rick[2] *vt* (*Brit etc*) to sprain or strain slightly. • *n* such an injury.—*also* **wrick**.

rickets /ˈrɪkɪts/ *n* a children's disease marked by softening of the bones, caused by vitamin D deficiency.

rickettsia /rɪˈkɛtsɪə/ *n* (*pl* **rickettsiae, rickettsias**) any of a genus of microorganisms that inhabit mites, ticks, etc and cause serious diseases, such as typhus.—**rickettsial** *adj*.

rickety /ˈrɪkɪti/ *adj* shaky, unsteady.

rickrack /ˈrɪkræk/ *n* a zigzag braid for trimming clothing.

rickshaw, ricksha /ˈrɪkʃɔ/ *n* a light, two-wheeled man-drawn vehicle, orig used in Japan.

ricochet /ˈrɪkəˌʃeɪ/ *vi* (**ricocheting, ricocheted** *or* **ricochetting, ricochetted**) (*bullet*) to rebound or skip along ground or water. • *n* a rebound or glancing off; (*bullet*) a hit made after ricocheting.

ricotta /rɪˈkɒtə/ *n* a mildly-flavoured Italian soft white cheese made from sheep's milk.

rictus /ˈrɪktəs/ *n* (*pl* **rictus, rictuses**) the gap in an open mouth or beak; a fixed grimace, *esp* in horror.—**rictal** *adj*.

rid /rɪd/ *vt* (**ridding, rid** *or* **ridded**) to free from; to dispose (of).

riddance /ˈrɪdəns/ *n* clearance; disposal.

ridden[1] /ˈrɪdən/ *see* **ride**.

ridden[2] *adj* oppressed by; full of.

riddle[1] /ˈrɪdəl/ *n* a puzzling question; an enigma; a mysterious person or thing.

riddle[2] *n* a coarse sieve. • *vt* to sieve or sift; to perforate with holes; to spread through, permeate.

ride /rəɪd/ *vb* (**riding, rode**, *pp* **ridden**) *vti* to be carried along or travel in a vehicle or on an animal, bicycle, etc; to be supported or move on the water; to lie at anchor; to travel over a surface; to move on the body; (*inf*) to continue undisturbed. • *vt* (*horse, bicycle etc*); to sit on and control; to oppress, dominate; (*inf*) to torment. • *n* a trip or journey in a vehicle or on horseback, on a bicycle, etc; a thing to ride at a fairground.

rider /ˈrəɪdər/ *n* a person who rides; an addition to a document, amending a clause; an additional statement; something used to move along another piece.

ridge /rɪdʒ/ *n* a narrow crest or top; the ploughed earth thrown up between the furrows; a line where two slopes meet; (*of land etc*) a raised strip or elevation; a range of hills. • *vti* to form into ridges, wrinkle.—**ridged** *adj*.

ridgepole /ˈrɪdʒpoːl/ *n* the horizontal pole along the top of a tent.

ridicule /ˈrɪdɪˌkjuːl/ *n* mockery, derision. • *vt* to make fun of, to mock.

ridiculous /rɪˈdɪkjʊləs/ *adj* deserving ridicule; preposterous, silly.—**ridiculously** *adv*.—**ridiculousness** *n*.

riesling /ˈriːzlɪŋ/ *or* /-slɪŋ/ *n* (the grape that produces) a dry white wine.

rife /rəɪf/ *adj* widespread; prevalent.

riff /rɪf/ *n* (*jazz, rock*) a musical phrase played repeatedly, *esp* as the background to an extended solo improvisation.—*also vi*.

riffle /ˈrɪfəl/ *vt* to leaf or flick rapidly through (pages, files, etc); to shuffle cards by dividing the deck and then flicking the corners together with the thumbs. • *vi* to flick cursorily (through). • *n* (the sound of) an act or instance of riffling; a ripple in a stream or the small obstruction causing this; grooves, etc at the bottom of a sluice to trap gold particles.

riffraff /ˈrɪfræf/ *n* disreputable persons; refuse, rubbish.

rifle[1] /ˈrəɪfəl/ *n* a shoulder gun with a spirally grooved bore.

rifle[2] *vti* to steal; to look through (a person's papers or belongings).

rifling /ˈrəɪflɪŋ/ *n* (the cutting of) spiral grooves in the bore of a firearm that spin the projectile.

rift /rɪft/ *n* a split; a cleft; a fissure. • *vti* to split.

rift valley *n* a narrow valley caused by land subsiding between two parallel faults.

rig /rɪg/ *vt* (**rigging, rigged**) (*naut*) to equip with sails and tackle; to set up in working order; to manipulate fraudulently. • *n* the way sails, etc, are rigged; equipment or gear for a special purpose, such as oil drilling; a type of truck.

rigging /ˈrɪgɪŋ/ *n* the ropes for supporting masts and sails; (*in theatre*) a network of ropes and pulleys to support and maintain scenery.

right /rəɪt/ *adj* correct, true; just or good; appropriate; fit, recovered; opposite to left; conservative; designating the side meant to be seen. • *adv* straight; directly; completely, exactly; correctly, properly; to or on the right side. • *n* that which is just or correct; truth; fairness; justice; privilege; just or legal claim; (*pl*) the correct condition. • *vti* to set or become upright; to correct; to redress.—**rightness** *n*.

right angle *n* an angle of 90 degrees.

righteous /ˈrəɪtʃəs/ *adj* moral, virtuous.—**righteously** *adv*.—**righteousness** *n*.

rightful /ˈrəɪtfʊl/ *adj* legitimate; having a just claim.—**rightfully** *adv*.—**rightfulness** *n*.

right-hand *adj* of or towards the right side of a person or thing; for use by the right hand.

right-handed /rəɪtˈhændɪd/ *adj* using the right hand; done or made for use with the right hand. • *adv* with the right hand.

rightist /ˈrəɪtɪst/ *adj* politically conservative. • *n* a person belonging to or supporting a conservative political party.

rightly /ˈrəɪtli/ *adv* in truth; in the right; with good reason; properly.

right-minded *adj* having principles in accordance with standard notions of what is right.

right of way *n* a public path over private ground; the right to use this; precedence over other traffic.

right-on /ˈrəɪtˌɒn/ *adj* (*inf*) fashionable, trendy.

right-thinking *adj* holding generally acceptable views.

right-wing *adj* of or relating to the conservative faction of a political party, organization, etc.—**right-winger** *n*.

rigid /ˈrɪdʒɪd/ *adj* stiff, inflexible; severe, strict.—**rigidity** *n*.—**rigidly** *adv*.—**rigidness** *n*.

rigmarole /ˈrɪgməˌroːl/ *n* nonsense; a foolishly involved procedure.—*also* **rigamarole**.

rigor mortis /ˌrɪgərˈmɔrtɪs/ *n* the stiffening of the body after death.

rigorous *adj* stern, severe, strict.—**rigorously** *adv*.—**rigorousness** *n*.

rigour /ˈrɪgər/ *n* harsh inflexibility; severity; strictness.—*also US* **rigor**.

rile /rəɪl/ *vt* (*inf*) to irritate, to annoy, to anger.

rill /rɪl/ *n* a small brook or stream.

rim /rɪm/ *n* a border or raised edge, *esp* of something circular; the outer part of a wheel. • *vt* (**rimming, rimmed**) to supply or surround with a rim; to form a rim.

rimless /ˈrɪmləs/ *adj* lacking a rim; (*glasses*) without a frame.

rind /rəɪnd/ *n* crust; peel; bark.

rinderpest /ˈrɪndərˌpɛst/ *n* an acute viral disease of cattle.

ring[1] /rɪŋ/ *n* a circular band, *esp* of metal, worn on the finger, in the ear, etc; a hollow circle; a round enclosure; an arena for boxing, etc; a group of people engaged in secret or criminal activity to control a market, etc. • *vt* (**ringing, ringed**) to encircle, surround; to fit with a ring.

ring[2] *vti* (**ringing, rang** *or* **rung**, *pp* **rung**) to emit a bell-like sound; to resound; to peal; to sound a bell; to telephone; (*with up*) to total and record *esp* by means of a cash register; to achieve. • *n* a ringing sound; a resonant note; a set of church bells.

ringdove *n* another name for wood pigeon.

ringed /rɪŋd/ *adj* wearing rings; forming rings; having ring-like markings; surrounded by.

ringer /ˈrɪŋər/ *n* a person that rings bells; (*sl*) a person or thing closely resembling another; a horse entered into a race under a false name, weight, etc.

ring finger *n* the third finger, *esp* of the left hand, on which a wedding ring is traditionally worn.

ringhals /ˈrɪŋhælz/ *n* a poisonous African snake that spits venom at its victims.

ringleader /ˈrɪŋˌliːdər/ *n* a person who takes the lead in mischievous or unlawful behaviour.

ringlet /ˈrɪŋlət/ *n* a curling lock of hair.

ringmaster /ˈrɪŋˌmæstər/ *n* a master of ceremonies in a circus.

ringworm /ˈrɪŋˌwɔrm/ *n* a contagious skin infection.

rink /rɪŋk/ *n* an expanse of ice for skating; a smooth floor for roller skating; an alley for bowling.

rinse /rɪns/ *vt* to wash lightly; to flush under clean water to remove soap. • *n* the act of rinsing; a preparation for tinting the hair.

rioja /rɪˈoːhə/ *n* a type of Spanish red or white wine.

riot /ˈraɪət/ *n* violent public disorder; uproar; unrestrained profusion; (*inf*) something very funny. • *vi* to participate in a riot.—**rioter** *n*.—**rioting** *n*.

riotous /ˈraɪətəs/ *adj* disorderly, tumultuous, seditious; luxurious, wanton.—**riotously** *adv*.—**riotousness** *n*.

RIP *abbr* = rest in peace.

rip[1] /rɪp/ *vti* (**ripping, ripped**) to cut or tear apart roughly; to split; (*with* **off, out**) to remove in a violent or rough manner; (*inf*) to rush, speed; (*with* **into**) to attack, *esp* verbally. • *n* a tear; a split.

rip[2] *n* a stretch of broken water caused by currents and tides.

rip cord *n* a cord for releasing a parachute.

ripe /raɪp/ *adj* ready to be eaten or harvested; fully developed; mature.—**ripely** *adv*.—**ripeness** *n*.

ripen /ˈraɪpən/ *vt* to grow or make ripe.

rip-off *n* (*sl*) the act or a means of stealing; plagiarizing, cheating, etc.

riposte, ripost /rɪˈpɒst/ *n* a counterstroke; a retort; a retaliatory manoeuvre. • *vi* to make a riposte.

ripple /ˈrɪpəl/ *n* a little wave or undulation on the surface of water; the sound of this. • *vti* to have or form little waves on the surface (of).

rip-roaring /ˈrɪpˌrɔːrɪŋ/ *adj* (*inf*) exuberant, boisterous, thrilling.

ripsaw /ˈrɪpsɔː/ *n* a handsaw for cutting wood in the direction of the grain.

riptide *n* a powerful current flowing outwards from the shore.

RISC /rɪsk/ (*abbr*) = Reduced Instruction Set Computer: a computer with advanced yet simplified internal circuitry that allows a significant increase in processing speed over standard designs.

rise /raɪz/ *vi* (**rising, rose,** *pp* **risen**) to get up; to stand up; to ascend; to increase in value or size; to swell; to revolt; to be provoked; to originate; to tower; to slope up; (*voice*) to reach a higher pitch; to ascend from the grave; (*fish*) to come to the surface. • *n* an ascent; origin; an increase in price, salary, etc; an upward slope.

risible /ˈrɪzɪbəl/ *adj* tending to laugh; provoking laughter, derisory.—**risibility** *n*.

rising /ˈraɪzɪŋ/ *n* a revolt, insurrection. • *adj* ascending; approaching.

risk /rɪsk/ *n* chance of loss or injury; hazard; danger, peril. • *vt* to expose to possible danger or loss; to take the chance of.

risk capital *n* venture capital.

risky /ˈrɪski/ *adj* (**riskier, riskiest**) dangerous; uncertain; not secure.

risotto /rɪˈzɒtoː/ *n* (*pl* **risottos**) a dish of onions, rice, butter, etc, cooked in meat stock.

risqué /ˈrɪskeɪ/ *adj* verging on indecency; slightly offensive.

rissole /ˈrɪsoːl/ *n* a fried cake of minced meat, egg, and breadcrumbs.

rite /raɪt/ *n* a ceremonial practice or procedure, *esp* religious.

rite of passage *n* a ritual indicating a change in an individual's status, as at puberty or marriage.

ritual /ˈrɪtʃʊəl/ *adj* relating to rites or ceremonies. • *n* a fixed (religious) ceremony.—**ritually** *adv*.

ritzy /ˈrɪtsi/ *adj* (**ritzier, ritziest**) (*sl*) luxurious, smart.

rival /ˈraɪvəl/ *n* one of two or more people, organizations or teams competing with each other for the same goal. • *adj* competing; having comparable merit or claim. • *vt* (**rivalling, rivalled**) to strive to equal or excel; to be comparable to; to compete.

rivalry /ˈraɪvəlri/ *n* (*pl* **rivalries**) emulation; competition.

river /ˈrɪvər/ *n* a large natural stream of fresh water flowing into an ocean, lake, etc; a copious flow.

river basin *n* land drained by a river and its tributaries.

riverbed /ˈrɪvərbɛd/ *n* the channel formed by a river.

riverfront /ˈrɪvərˌfrʌnt/ *n* the land or an area along a river.

riverine /ˈrɪvəraɪn/ *adj* of, like, or produced by a river; living or located on the banks of a river.

riverside /ˈrɪvərsaɪd/ *n* the bank of a river.

rivet /ˈrɪvət/ *n* a short, metal bolt for holding metal plates together, the headless end being hammered flat. • *vt* to join with rivets; to fix one's eyes upon immovably; to engross one's attention.

riveter /ˈrɪvətər/ *n* a person who rivets; a machine that rivets.

Riviera /ˌrɪvɪˈɛrə/ *n* the coast of the northern Mediterranean from southeast France to northwest Italy.

rivulet /ˈrɪvjʊlət/ *n* a little stream.

riyal /ˈriːɒl/ *or* /ˈraɪəl/ *n* the standard currency unit of Saudi Arabia, Yemen, Quatar, or Dubai.

RMA /ˈɑːrɛmˈeɪ/ *abbr* = Royal Military Academy.

rms *abbr* = root mean square.

RN *abbr* = Registered Nurse; Royal Navy.

Rn (*chem symbol*) radon.

RNA /ˈɑːrɛnˈeɪ/ *abbr* = ribonucleic acid.

roach /roːtʃ/ *n* a small silvery freshwater fish.

road /roːd/ *n* a track, surfaced with tarmac or concrete, made for travelling; a highway; a street; a way or route.

road block /ˈroːdblɒk/ *n* a barrier erected across a road to halt traffic.

road hog *n* a selfish or aggressive car driver.

roadhouse /-hʊs/ *n* a tavern *usu* outside city limits providing meals, etc.

roadie /ˈroːdi/ *n* (*inf*) a person with responsibility for transporting and setting up stage equipment for a rock group, etc on tour.

road map *n* a map for motorists that gives information on the roads of a particular area.

road metal *n* broken stone and cinders used in making road and railway foundations.

road movie *n* a film genre in which the main characters are on a journey, both in a real and figurative sense.

roadrunner /ˈroːdˌrʌnər/ *n* a long-tailed, swift-running, terrestrial North American cuckoo.

roadshow *n* a group of touring entertainers; a radio or television show presented from a touring outside-broadcasting unit.

roadside /-saɪd/ *n* the border of a road.—*also adj*.

road-test *vt* to test (a vehicle) under practical operating conditions.—**road test** *n*.

roadway /ˈroːdweɪ/ *n* the strip of land over which a road passes; the main part of a road, used by vehicles.

roadwork /ˈroːdwərk/ *n* conditioning for an athletic contest consisting mainly of long runs.

roam /roːm/ *vti* to wander about, to rove.

roan /roːn/ *adj* having a base colour thickly sprinkled with white or grey. • *n* a horse with a roan coat, *esp* when the base colour is red.

roar /rɔr/ *vti* to make a loud, full, growling sound, as a lion, wind, fire, the sea; to utter loudly, as in a rage; to bellow; to guffaw.—*also n*.

roaring /ˈrɔrɪŋ/ *adj* boisterous, noisy; brisk.

roast /roːst/ *vti* (*meat, etc*) to cook with little or no moisture, as before a fire or in an oven; (*coffee, etc*) to process by exposure to heat; to expose to great heat; (*inf*) to criticize severely; to undergo roasting. • *n* roasted meat; a cut of meat for roasting; a picnic at which food is roasted.

rob /rɒb/ *vb* (**robbing, robbed**) *vt* to seize forcibly; to steal from; to plunder. • *vi* to commit robbery.—**robber** *n*.

robbery /ˈrɒbəri/ *n* (*pl* **robberies**) theft from a person by intimidation or by violence.

robe /roːb/ *n* a long flowing outer garment; the official dress of a judge, academic, etc; a bathrobe or dressing gown; a covering or wrap; (*pl*) ceremonial vestments. • *vti* to put on or dress in robes.

robin /ˈrɒbɪn/ *n* a songbird with a dull red breast.

robot /ˈroːbɒt/ *n* a mechanical device that acts in a seemingly human way; a mechanism guided by automatic controls.

robotics /roːˈbɒtɪks/ *n* (*used as sing*) the science of designing and using robots.

robust *adj* strong, sturdy, vigorous.—**robustly** *adv*.—**robustness** *n*.

roc /rɒk/ *n* (*Arabian legend*) a giant bird of enormous strength.

rock[1] /rɒk/ *n* a large stone or boulder; a person or thing providing foundation or support; (*geol*) a natural mineral deposit including sand, clay, etc; a hard sweet; (*inf*) a diamond, ice.

rock[2] *vti* to move to and fro, or from side to side; to sway strongly; to shake. • *n* a rocking motion; rock and roll.

rockabilly /ˈrɒkəˌbɪli/ *n* a type of fast-paced rock and country music originating in the US South in the 1950s.

rock-and-roll *n* popular music that incorporates country and blues elements and is *usu* played on electronic instruments with a heavily accented beat.

rock bottom *n* the lowest or most fundamental part or level. • *adj* very lowest.

rock crystal *n* transparent colourless quartz used in electronic and optical equipment.

rocker /ˈrɒkər/ *n* a rocking chair; a curved support on which a cradle, etc, rocks.

rockery /ˈrɒkəri/ *n* (*pl* **rockeries**) a garden among rocks for alpine plants.—*also* **rock garden**.

rocket /ˈrɒkət/ *n* any device driven forward by gases escaping through a rear vent, such as a firework, distress signal, or the propulsion mechanism of a spacecraft. • *vi* to move in or like a rocket; to soar.

rocket launcher *n* a device for launching rockets; an aircraft or motor vehicle equipped to launch rockets.

rocketry /ˈrɒkətri/ *n* the science of building and launching rockets.

rock garden *see* **rockery**.

rock house *n* (*sl*) a place where the drug crack is made available by dealers.

rocking chair *n* a chair mounted on rockers.

rocking horse *n* a toy horse fixed on rockers or springs.

rock salt *n* common salt in solid form or in large crystals.

rocky /ˈrɒki/ *adj* (**rockier, rockiest**) having many rocks; like rock; rugged, hard; shaky, unstable.

rococo /rəˈkoːkoː/ *adj* (*often cap*) elaborately ornate, as in an architectural style of 18th-century Europe.—*also n*.

rod /rɒd/ *n* a stick; a thin bar of metal or wood; a staff of office; a wand; a fishing rod; (*sl*) a pistol.

rode /roːd/ *see* **ride**.

rodent /ˈroːdənt/ *n* any of several relatively small gnawing animals with two strong front teeth.

rodeo /ˈroːdioː/ *n* (*pl* **rodeos**) (*US and Canada*) the rounding up of cattle; a display of cowboy skill.

roe[1] /roː/ *n* the eggs of fish.

roe[2] *n* a small reddish brown deer.—*also* **roe deer**; the female red deer.

roebuck /ˈroːbʌk/ *n* the male roe deer.

roe deer /ˌroːˈdiːr/ *n* a small graceful deer of European and Asian woodlands.

roentgen /ˈrɒntdʒən/ *n* the unit of measuring X-rays or gamma rays.—*also* **röntgen**.

roger /ˈrɒdʒər/ *interj* used in radio communications, etc to indicate message received and understood.

rogue /roːg/ *n* a scoundrel; a rascal; a mischievous person; a wild animal that lives apart from the herd.—**roguish** *adj*.—**roguishly** *adv*.

role, rôle /roːl/ *n* a part in a film or play taken by an actor; a function.

role model *n* a person who inspires others to emulate him or her.

role-playing *n* (*psychol*) a technique in which participants take on and act out roles in order to rehearse a situation or resolve a conflict.

roll /roːl/ *n* a scroll; anything wound into cylindrical form; a list or register; a turned-over edge; a rolling movement; a small cake of bread; a trill of some birds; an undulation; the sound of thunder; the beating of drumsticks. • *vi* to move by turning over or from side to side; to move like a wheel; to curl; to move in like waves; to flow. • *vt* to cause to roll; to turn on its axis; to move on wheels; to press with a roller; (*dice*) to throw; to beat rapidly, as a drum.

roll bar *n* a bar that reinforces the frame of a racing or sports car to protect the driver should the vehicle overturn.

roll call *n* the reading aloud of a list of names to check attendance.

roller /ˈroːlər/ *n* a revolving cylinder used for spreading paint, flattening surfaces, moving paper, etc; a large wave.

roller coaster *n* an elevated amusement ride in which small cars move on tracks that curve and dip sharply.—*also* **big dipper**.

roller skate *n* a four-wheeled skate strapped on to shoes.—**roller skating** *n*.

roller towel *n* a towel without ends on a roller.

rolling pin *n* a wooden, plastic or stone cylinder for rolling out pastry.

rolling stock *n* all the vehicles of a railway.

rolling stone *n* a person who cannot settle in one place; a free spirit.

rollmop /ˈroːlmɒp/ *n* a fillet of herring rolled up and pickled in brine or spiced vinegar.

roll-on/roll-off *adj* pertaining to a cargo ship or passenger ferry designed so that vehicles can be driven straight on and off.

roll-top desk /ˈroːltɒp/ *n* a writing desk with a flexible sliding cover of slats.

roly-poly /ˈroːliˌpoːli/ *n* (*pl* **roly-polies**) a pudding of pastry covered with jam and rolled up; a round and plump person.

ROM /rɒm/ *abbr* (*comput*) = read-only memory.

Roman /ˈroːmən/ *adj* of or relating to the city of Rome or its ancient empire, or the Latin alphabet; Roman Catholic. • *n* an inhabitant or citizen of Rome; a Roman Catholic.

roman /ˈroːmən/ *adj* ordinary type, not italic.

Roman candle *n* a type of cylindrical firework that emits coloured sparks.

Roman Catholic *adj* belonging to the Christian church that is headed by the Pope.—*also n*.

romance /ˈroːmæns/ or /roːˈmæns/ *n* a prose narrative; a medieval tale of chivalry; a series of unusual adventures; a novel dealing with this; an atmosphere of awe or wonder; a love story; a love affair; a picturesque falsehood. • *vi* to write romantic fiction; to exaggerate.

Romanesque /ˌroːməˈnesk/ *adj, n* (in) the style of round-arched and vaulted architecture prevalent between the Classical and Gothic periods.

Roman holiday *n* a holiday or entertainment at the expense of others' suffering.

Roman nose *n* a nose with a slender prominent ridge.

Roman numerals *n* the letters I, V, X, L, C, D, and M used to represent numbers in the manner of the ancient Romans.

romantic /roːˈmæntɪk/ *adj* of or given to romance; strange and picturesque; imaginative; sentimental; (*art, literature*) preferring passion and imagination to proportion and finish, subordinating form to content.—**romantically** *adv*.

romanticism /roːˈmæntəˌsɪzəm/ *n* a 19th-century philosophical and cultural movement characterized by the desire to bring nature and man into unity through the shaping power of the imagination; romantic approach, quality, or ideals.

romanticize /roːˈmæntəˌsaɪz/ *vt* to imbue (a person, concept, etc) with a romantic character. • *vi* to have romantic ideas.—**romanticization** *n*.

Romany /ˈrɒməni/ or /ˈroː-/ *n* a Gypsy; the Indic language of Gypsies.

romp /rɒmp/ *vi* to play boisterously. • *n* a noisy game; a frolic; an easy win.

rompers /ˈrɒmpərz/ *npl* a child's one-piece garment; a jumpsuit.

rondo /ˈrɒndoː/ *n* (*pl* **rondos**) a musical form with a leading theme to which return is made.

röntgen /ˈrɒntdʒən/ *see* **roentgen**.

roof /ruːf/ *n* (*pl* **roofs**) the upper covering of a building; the top of a vehicle; an upper limit. • *vt* to provide with a roof, to cover.

roof garden *n* a garden on a flat roof or balcony; a top floor decorated as a garden, *esp* if used as a restaurant.

roofing /ˈruːfɪŋ/ *n* materials for a roof.

rook[1] /rʊk/ *n* a crow-like bird.

rook[2] *n* (*chess*) a piece with the power to move horizontally or vertically, a castle.

rookery /ˈrʊkəri/ *n* (*pl* **rookeries**) a colony of rooks; a breeding ground or haunt of other birds or mammals; a crowded place.

rookie /ˈrʊki/ *n* (*sl*) an inexperienced army recruit; any novice.—*also adj*.

room /ruːm/ *n* space; unoccupied space; adequate space; a division of a house, a chamber; scope or opportunity; those in a room; (*pl*) lodgings. • *vi* to lodge.

room clerk *n* a receptionist in a hotel who books in guests and allocates rooms, etc.

rooming house *n* a house with individual rooms to let.

roommate *n* a person with whom one shares a room or rooms.

roomy /ˈruːmi/ *adj* (**roomier, roomiest**) having ample space; wide.—**roominess** *n*.

roost /ruːst/ *n* a bird's perch or sleeping-place; a place for resting. • *vi* to rest or sleep on a roost; to settle down, as for the night.

rooster /ˈruːstər/ *n* an adult male domestic fowl, a cockerel.

root[1] /ruːt/ *n* the part of a plant, *usu* underground, that anchors the plant, draws water from the soil, etc; the embedded part of a tooth, a hair, etc; a supporting or essential part; something that is an origin or source; (*math*) the factor of a quantity which multiplied by itself gives the quantity; (*mus*) the fundamental note of a chord; (*pl*) plants with edible roots. • *vti* to take root; to become established; (*with* **out**) to tear up, to eradicate.

root[2] *vti* to dig up with the snout; to search about, rummage; (*with* **for**) (*inf*) to encourage a team by cheering.

root beer *n* a carbonated drink flavored with extracts of certain roots and barks.

root crop *n* a crop, such as turnips, sugar beet, cultivated for its edible roots.

rooted /'ruːtəd/ *adj* firmly fixed; planted.

root mean square *n* the square root of the average of the squares of a set of numbers.

rootstock /'ruːtstɒk/ *n* an underground stem, rhizome; a stock for grafting, having a root or a piece of root.

rope /roːp/ *n* a thick cord or thin cable made of twisted fibres or wires; a string or row of things braided, intertwined or threaded together; a viscous thickening in a liquid. • *vt* to tie, bind, divide or enclose with a rope; to lasso; (*liquid*) to become ropy.—**ropy** *adj*.

Roquefort /'rɒkfər/ or /roːk-/, /-fərt/ *n* a French blue-veined cheese with a strong flavour.

rorqual /'rɔːrkwəl/ *n* any of several large whalebone whales with dorsal fins and deep furrows on the skin of the throat and chest.—*also* **finback**.

rosaceous /roːˈzeɪʃəs/ *adj* of or belonging to the large family of plants that includes the rose; resembling a rose; rose-coloured.

rosary /'roːzəri/ *n* (*pl* **rosaries**) a string of beads for keeping count of prayers; a series of prayers.

rose[1] /roːz/ *see* **rise**.

rose[2] *n* a prickly-stemmed plant with fragrant flowers of many delicate colours; its flower; a rosette; a perforated nozzle; a pinkish red or purplish red.

rosé /roːˈzeɪ/ *n* a pink wine made from skinless red grapes or by mixing white and red wine.

rose-coloured *adj* rosy; overly optimistic.

rosemary /'roːzɪˌmeri/ *n* a fragrant shrubby mint used in cookery and perfumery.

rosette /roːˈzet/ *n* a rose-shaped bunch of ribbon; a carving, etc, in the shape of a rose.

rosewater /'roːzwɒtər/ *n* water scented with rose petals.

rose window *n* a circular window filled with tracery.

rosewood /'roːzwʊd/ *n* (any of various tropical trees yielding) a fragrant dark wood used in making furniture.

rosin /'rɒzɪn/ *n* a pine-wood resin, *esp* in solid form, used in varnishes, etc, and for waxing the bows of stringed instruments.

roster /'rɒstər/ *n* a list or roll, as of military personnel; a list of duties.

rostrum /'rɒstrəm/ *n* (*pl* **rostrums, rostra**) a platform or stage for public speaking.

rosy /'roːzi/ *adj* (**rosier, rosiest**) of the colour of roses; having pink, healthy cheeks; optimistic, hopeful.

rot /rɒt/ *vti* (**rotting, rotted**) to decompose; to decay; to become degenerate. • *n* decay; corruption; several different diseases affecting timber or sheep; (*inf*) nonsense.

rota /'roːtə/ *n* a turn in succession; a list or roster of duties.

rotary /'roːtəri/ *adj* revolving; turning like a wheel.

Rotary Club *n* a club belonging to an international organization of business people for promoting community service.—**Rotarian** *n*.

rotate /'roːteɪt/ or /roːˈteɪt/ *vti* to turn around an axis like a wheel; to follow a sequence.

rotation /roːˈteɪʃən/ *n* the action of rotating; a regular succession, as of crops to avoid exhausting the soil.

rote /roːt/ *n* a fixed, mechanical way of doing something.

rotgut /'rɒtgət/ *n* (*sl*) alcoholic drink, *esp* spirits, of inferior quality and *usu* cheap.

rotisserie /roːˈtɪsəri/ *n* a large rotating spit on which poultry is roasted; a place where such food is prepared.

rotor /'roːtər/ *n* a rotating part of a machine or engine.

rotten /'rɒtən/ *adj* decayed, decomposed; corrupt; (*inf*) bad, nasty.—**rottenness** *n*.

rotund /roːˈtʌnd/ *adj* rounded; spherical; plump.

rotunda /roːˈtʌndə/ *n* a circular, *esp* domed, building or chamber.

rouble /'ruːbəl/ *n* a coin and monetary unit of Russia.—*also* **ruble**.

rouge /ruːʒ/ *n* a red cosmetic for colouring the cheeks; a red powder for polishing jewellery, etc. • *vti* to colour (the face) with rouge.

rough /rʌf/ *adj* uneven; not smooth; ill-mannered; violent; rude, unpolished; shaggy; coarse in texture; unrefined; violent, boisterous; stormy; wild; harsh, discordant; crude, unfinished; approximate; (*inf*) difficult. • *n* rough ground; (*golf*) any part of a

course with grass, etc, left uncut; a first sketch. • *vt* to make rough; to sketch roughly; (*with* **up**) (*inf*) to injure violently, beat up. • *adv* in a rough manner.—**roughly** *adv*.—**roughness** *n*.

roughage /'rʌfɪdʒ/ *n* rough or coarse food or fodder, as bran, etc.

rough-and-ready *adj* unfinished but sufficient; prepared hastily.

rough-and-tumble *n* a scuffle; confusion.

roughcast /'rʌfkæst/ *n* a mixture of lime and gravel for coating buildings; a rough surface finish. • *vt* (**roughcasting, roughcast**) to coat with roughcast.

rough-cut *n* an early version of a film with the scenes edited together in sequence and a soundtrack added.

roughen /'rʌfən/ *vti* to make or become rough.

roughhouse /'rʌfhʊs/ *n* (*sl*) (an instance of) noisy, boisterous or violent behaviour.

roughneck /-nek/ *n* (*sl*) a coarse person.

roughshod /-ʃɒd/ *adj* marked by force without consideration.

rough stuff *n* (*inf*) violent behaviour.

rough trade *n* (*sl*) a homosexual partner who is tough and possibly violent.

roulade /ruːˈlɒd/ *n* food in the shape of a roll, such as cheese or meat; (*mus*) a run of notes on one syllable.

roulette /ruːˈlet/ *n* a gambling game played with a revolving disc and a ball; a toothed wheel for making dots or perforations.

round /raʊnd/ *adj* circular, spherical, or cylindrical in form; curved; plump; (*math*) expressed to the nearest ten, hundred, etc, not fractional; considerable; candid; (*style*) flowing, balanced; (*vowel*) pronounced with rounded lips. • *adv* circularly; on all sides; from one side to another; in a ring; by indirect way; through a recurring period of time; in circumference; in a roundabout way; about; near; here and there; with a rotating movement; in the opposite direction; around. • *prep* encircling; on every side of; in the vicinity of; in a circuit through; around. • *n* anything round; a circuit; (*shots*) a volley; a unit of ammunition; a series or sequence; a bout, turn; (*golf*) a circuit of a course; a stage of a contest; (*mus*) a kind of canon. • *vt* to make or become round or plump; (*math*) to express as a round number; to complete; to go or pass around. • *vi* to make a circuit; to turn; to reverse direction.—**roundly** *adv*.—**roundness** *n*.

roundabout /'raʊndəˌbaʊt/ *adj* indirect, circuitous. • *n* a circuitous route; a merry-go-round; a traffic circle.

rounded /'raʊndəd/ *adj* curved or round; flowing, not angular.

roundhouse /'raʊndhʊs/ *n* a circular building for repairing and servicing railway locomotives.

round robin *n* a document with signatures in a circle to conceal their order; any document or letter signed by a number of people.

round-shouldered *adj* with bent shoulders; stooping.

round-table conference *n* a conference with all the parties on an equal footing.

round trip *n* a journey to a place and back again.

round-trip ticket *n* a ticket whose price includes the cost of the journey to and back from a destination.

roundup /'raʊndʌp/ *n* a driving together of livestock; (*inf*) the detention of several prisoners; a summary, as of news.

roundworm /'raʊndwərm/ *n* a nematode parasitic in people and pigs.

rouse /raʊz/ *vti* to provoke; to stir up; to awaken; to wake up; to become active.

rousing /'raʊzɪŋ/ *adj* stirring; vigorous.

rout[1] /raʊt/ *n* a noisy crowd, a rabble; a disorderly retreat. • *vt* to defeat and put to flight.

rout[2] *vti* to grub up, as a pig; to search haphazardly; to gouge out or make a furrow in (as wood or metal); to cause to emerge, *esp* from bed; to come up with; to uncover.

route /ruːt/ *n* a course to be taken; the roads travelled on a journey. • *vt* to plan the route of; to send (by a specified route).

routine /ruːˈtiːn/ *n* a procedure that is regular and unvarying; a sequence of set movements, as in a dance, skating, etc.—*also adj*.

roux /ruː/ *n* a mixture of equal quantities of flour and melted fat used as the basis for sauces.

rove /roːv/ *vti* to wander about, roam (over).

rover /'roːvər/ *n* a wanderer; a fickle person.

Rover, Rover Scout *n* the former name for a **Venture Scout**.

row[1] /roː/ *n* a line of persons or things; a line of seats (in a theatre, etc).

row[2] *vti* to propel with oars; to transport by rowing. • *n* an act or instance of rowing.—**rower** *n*.

row[3] *n* a noisy quarrel or dispute; a scolding; noise, disturbance. • *vi* to quarrel; to scold.

rowan /'roːən/ or /'rau-/ *n* a tree producing white flowers followed by small red berries.

rowdy /'raudi/ *adj* (**rowdier, rowdiest**) rough and noisy, disorderly. • *n* (*pl* **rowdies**) a rowdy person, a hooligan.—**rowdiness, rowdyism** *n*.

rowel /'rauəl/ *n* a spiked revolving disc at the end of a spur.

rowing boat *n* a small boat made for rowing.—*also US* **rowboat**.

rowing machine *n* an exercise machine with oars and a sliding seat that simulates a rowing action.

rowlock /'rolək/ or /'rʌ-/ *n* a fitting on the side of a boat that holds an oar in place and serves as its fulcrum.

royal /'rɔɪəl/ *adj* relating to or fit for a king or queen; regal; under the patronage of a king or queen; founded by a king or queen; of a kingdom, its government, etc. • *n* a type of topsail; a stag with a head of twelve points; (*inf*) a member of a royal family.—**royally** *adv*.

royal blue *n*, *adj* deep blue.

royal flush *n* (*poker*) a straight flush headed by an ace.

royalist /'rɔɪəlɪst/ *n* a person who advocates monarchy.

royal jelly *n* a nutritious secretion of the honeybee which is fed to larvae, *esp* those destined to become queens; a preparation of this sold as a health product.

royalty /'rɔɪəlti/ *n* (*pl* **royalties**) the rank or power of a king or queen; a royal person or persons; a share of the proceeds from a patent, book, song, etc, paid to the owner, author, composer, etc.

rpm /'ɑr'piː'em/ *abbr* = revolutions per minute.

-rrhagia *n suffix* denoting an abnormal discharge.

-rrhoea, -rrhea *n suffix* a flow.

RSVP /'ɑr'es'viː'piː/ *abbr* = répondez s'il vous plaît.

Ru (*chem symbol*) ruthenium.

rub /rʌb/ *vti* (**rubbing, rubbed**) to move (a hand, cloth, etc) over the surface of with pressure; to wipe, scour; to clean or polish; (*with* **away, off, out**) to remove or erase by friction; to chafe, grate; to fret; to take a rubbing of; (*with* **along**) to manage somehow; (*with* **down**) to rub vigorously with a towel; to smooth down. • *n* the act or process of rubbing; a drawback, difficulty.

rubber[1] /'rʌbər/ *n* an elastic substance made synthetically or from the sap of various tropical plants; an eraser; (*sl*) a condom; (*US:pl*) galoshes.

rubber[2] *n* a group of three games at whist, bridge, etc; the deciding game.

rubberize /'rʌbəraɪz/ *vt* to coat with rubber to make waterproof.

rubberneck /'rʌbər,nek/ *n* (*sl*) a person who gapes, *esp* intrusively; a sightseer.—*also vi*.

rubber plant *n* an Asian plant related to the fig with shiny leaves, popular as a houseplant.

rubber-stamp *vt* (*inf*) to give automatic approval without investigation.

rubber tree *n* a tree native to South America and widely cultivated in the tropics as a source of latex to make rubber.

rubbing /'rʌbɪŋ/ *n* an impression of an inscribed brass plate, etc, obtained by rubbing a wax substance on paper laid over it.

rubbish /'rʌbɪʃ/ *n* refuse; garbage, trash; nonsense.—**rubbishy** *adj*.

rubble /'rʌbəl/ *n* rough broken stone or rock; builders' rubbish.

rubella /ruː'belə/ *n* a mild contagious viral disease that may cause damage to an unborn child; also called **German measles**.

Rubenesque /,ruːbə'nesk/ *adj* of, like or pertaining to the art of the Florentine painter Peter Paul Rubens (1577-1640); opulent, colourful; (*woman's figure*) full-breasted and shapely.

rubidium /ruː'bɪdiəm/ *n* a soft radioactive metallic element.

ruble /'ruːbəl/ *see* **rouble**.

rubric /'ruːbrɪk/ *n* a heading or line marked out in red; any rule, explanatory comment, etc.

ruby /'ruːbi/ *n* (*pl* **rubies**) a deep red, transparent, valuable precious stone. • *adj* of the colour of a ruby.

ruby orange *n* an orange with red juice.

ruche /ruːʃ/ *vt* to pleat, gather, or flute fabric for use as a trimming. • *n* ruched fabric.

rucksack /'ruksæk/ *n* a bag worn on the back by hikers, used to carry camping or climbing equipment.

ruction /'rʌkʃən/ *n* (*inf*) a disturbance, a row, uproar.

rudder /'rʌdər/ *n* a flat vertical piece of wood or metal hinged to the stern of a ship or boat or the rear of an aircraft to steer by; a guiding principle.

ruddy /'rʌdi/ *adj* (**ruddier, ruddiest**) reddish pink; (*complexion*) of a healthy, red colour.

rude /ruːd/ *adj* uncivil, ill-mannered; uncultured, coarse; harsh, brutal; crude, roughly made; in a natural state, primitive; vigorous, hearty.—**rudely** *adv*.—**rudeness** *n*.

rudiment /'ruːdɪmənt/ *n* a first stage; a first slight beginning of something; an imperfectly developed organ; (*pl*) elements, first principles.

rudimentary /'ruːdɪmentri/ or /-təri/ *adj* elementary; imperfectly developed or represented only by a vestige.

rue /ruː/ *vti* (**rueing, rued**) to feel remorse for (a sin, fault, etc); to regret (an act, etc). • *n* (*arch*) sorrow.

rueful /'ruːful/ *adj* regretful; dejected; showing good-humoured self-pity.—**ruefully** *adv*.

ruff /rʌf/ *n* a pleated collar or frill worn round the neck; a fringe of feathers or fur round the neck of a bird or animal.

ruffian /'rʌfiən/ *n* a brutal lawless person; a villain.

ruffle /'rʌfəl/ *vti* to disturb the smoothness of, disarrange; to irritate; to agitate; to upset; to swagger about; to be quarrelsome; to flutter. • *n* pleated material used as a trim; a frill; a bird's ruff; a dispute, quarrel.

rug /rʌg/ *n* a thick heavy fabric used as a floor covering; a thick woollen wrap or coverlet.

rugby /'rʌgbi/ *n* a football game for two teams of 15 players played with an oval ball.

rugged /'rʌgəd/ *adj* rocky; rough, uneven; strong; stern; robust.—**ruggedly** *adv*.—**ruggedness** *n*.

rugger /'rʌgər/ *n* (*inf*) rugby.

ruin /'ruːɪn/ *n* destruction; downfall, wrecked state; the cause of this; a loss of fortune; (*pl*) the remains of something destroyed, decayed, etc. • *vti* to destroy; to spoil; to bankrupt; to come to ruin.

ruinous /'ruːənəs/ *adj* in ruins, tumbledown; causing ruin, disastrous.

rule /ruːl/ *n* a straight-edged instrument for drawing lines and measuring; government; the exercise of authority; a regulation, an order; a principle, a standard; habitual practice; the code of a religious order; a straight line. • *vti* to govern, to exercise authority over; to manage; to draw (lines) with a ruler; (*with* **out**) to exclude, to eliminate; to make impossible.

rule of thumb *n* a rough commonsense approach as opposed to a precise or theoretical one.

ruler /'ruːlər/ *n* a person who governs; a strip of wood, metal, etc, with a straight edge, used in drawing lines, measuring, etc.

ruling /'ruːlər/ *adj* governing; reigning; dominant. • *n* an authoritative pronouncement.

rum /rʌm/ *n* a spirit made from sugar cane.

rumba /'rʌmbə/ *n* a dance of Cuban origin with a complex rhythm. • *vi* to dance the rumba.

rumble /'rʌmbəl/ *vti* to make a low heavy rolling noise (as thunder); to move with such a sound; (*sl*) to see through, find out. • *n* the dull deep vibrant noise of thunder, etc.

rumbustious /rʌm'bʌstʃəs/ *adj* unruly, boisterous.

rumen /'ruːmən/ *n* (*pl* **rumens, rumina**) the first compartment of the stomach of a ruminant mammal.

ruminant /'ruːmənənt/ *n* a cud-chewing animal, such as cattle, deer, camels, etc. • *adj* chewing the cud; thoughtful.

ruminate /'ruːmɪ,neɪt/ *vi* to regurgitate food after it has been swallowed, chew cud; to ponder deeply, muse (on).

rummage /'rʌmɪdʒ/ *n* odds and ends; a search by ransacking. • *vti* to search thoroughly; to ransack; to fish (out).

rummage sale *n* a sale of second-hand clothes, books, etc to raise money for charity.—*also* **jumble sale**.

rummy /'rʌmi/ *n* a card game whose object is to form sets and sequences.

rumour, rumor /'ruːmər/ *n* hearsay, gossip; common talk not based on definite knowledge; an unconfirmed report, story. • *vt* to report by way of rumour.

rump /rʌmp/ *n* the hindquarters of an animal's body; the buttocks; the back end.

rumple /'rʌmpəl/ *n* a crease or wrinkle. • *vti* to crease; to disarrange, tousle.

rumpus /'rʌmpəs/ *n* (*pl* **rumpuses**) a commotion; a din.

run /rʌn/ *vi* (**running, ran** *or* **run**, *pp* **run**) to go by moving the legs faster than in walking; to hurry; to flee; to flow; to move; to be valid; to compete in a race, election, etc; (*colours*), to merge; (*with* across) to meet by accident; (*with* **around** *vi* (*inf*) to associate (with); to behave evasively or promiscuously; (*with* **away** *vi* to take flight, escape; to go out of control; (*with* **away with**) to abscond, elope; to steal; to win easily; (*with* **down**) (*engine, etc*) to cease to operate through lack of power; to become tired or exhausted; (*with* **off**) to leave hastily; to decide (a race) with a run-off; (*with* **through**) to use up (money, etc) completely; to read quickly. • *vt* (*a car, etc*) to drive; (*a business, etc*) to manage; (*a story*) to publish in a newspaper; (*temperature*) to suffer from a fever; (*with* **down**) to knock down with a moving vehicle; to collide with and cause to sink; to chase and capture; to tire, exhaust; to investigate, find; to criticize persistently; (*engine, etc*) to allow to gradually lose power; to reduce in quantity; (*with* **in**) to run a new car engine gently to start with; (*inf*) to arrest; (*with* **off**) to compose and talk glibly; to produce quickly, as copies on a photocopier; (*liquid*) to drain off; (*with* **out**) to exhaust a supply; (*inf*) to desert; (*with* **over**) (*vehicle*) to knock down a person or animal; to overflow; to exceed a limit; to rehearse quickly; (*with* **through**) to pierce with a sword or knife; to rehearse; (*with* **up**) to incur or amass. • *n* an act of running; a trip; a flow; a series; prevalence; a trend; an enclosure for chickens, etc; free and unrestricted access to all parts; (*in tights, etc*) a hole, a ladder.

run-around *n* deceitful or evasive behaviour towards someone.

runaway /ˈrʌnəweɪ/ *n* a person or thing that runs away; a fugitive. • *adj* out of control; (*inflation*) rising uncontrollably; (*race, etc*) easily won.

run-down /ˈrʌndaʊn/ *adj* dilapidated; ill; tired.

rundown /ˈrʌndaʊn/ *n* a brief summary; the process of going into a decline.

rune /ruːn/ *n* a letter of a primitive Teutonic alphabet; a magic mark or sign.—**runic** *adj*.

run-in /ˈrʌnɪn/ *n* (*inf*) a quarrel.

rung[1] /rʌŋ/ *see* **ring**[2].

rung[2] *n* the step of a ladder; the crossbar of a chair.

runner /ˈrʌnər/ *n* an athlete; a person who runs; a smuggler; a groove or strip on which something glides.

runner bean *n* a climbing plant that produces long green edible pods.

runner-up *n* (*pl* **runners-up**) the competitor who finishes second in a race, contest, etc.

running /ˈrʌnɪŋ/ *n* the act of moving swiftly; that which runs or flows; a racing, managing, etc. • *adj* moving swiftly; kept for a race; being in motion; continuous; discharing pus. • *adv* in succession.

running commentary *n* a verbal description on TV or radio of an event as it happens, *esp* sport.

running mate *n* the candidate in a US election standing for the less important of two positions in a linked office.

runny /ˈrʌni/ *adj* (**runnier, runniest**) tending to flow.

run-off /ˈrʌnɒf/ *n* a final deciding race, contest, etc.

run-of-the-mill *adj* average, mediocre.

runt /rʌnt/ *n* an unusually small animal, *esp* the smallest of a litter of pigs; a person of small stature.

run-through *n* a rehearsal; a cursory reading.

run-up *n* a preliminary period.

runway /ˈrʌnweɪ/ *n* a landing strip for aircraft.

rupee /ruːˈpiː/ *n* a unit of money in India, Pakistan, Sri Lanka, Seychelles, Mauritius, and Nepal.

rupiah /ruːˈpiːə/ *n* (*pl* **rupiah, rupiahs**) the standard currency unit of Indonesia.

rupture /ˈrʌptʃər/ *n* a breach; a severance, quarrel; the act of bursting or breaking; hernia. • *vti* to cause or suffer a rupture.

rural /ˈrʊrəl/ *adj* relating to the country or agriculture, rustic.—**rurally** *adv*.

ruse /ruːz/ *n* a trick or stratagem.

rush[1] /rʌʃ/ *vti* to move, push, drive, etc, swiftly or impetuously; to make a sudden attack (on); to do with unusual haste; to hurry. • *adj* marked by or needing extra speed or urgency. • *n* a sudden surge; a sudden demand; a press, as of business, requiring unusual haste; an unedited film print.

rush[2] *n* a marsh plant; its slender pithy stem; a worthless thing.

rush hour *n* the time at the beginning and end of the working day when traffic is at its heaviest.

rusk /rʌsk/ *n* a sweet or plain bread sliced and rebaked until dry and crisp.

russet /ˈrʌsət/ *adj* reddish-brown. • *n* a russet colour; a winter apple with a rough russet skin; a homespun russet cloth.

Russian /ˈrʌʃən/ *n* a native or inhabitant of Russia; the Slavonic language of Russians.—*also adj*.

Russian roulette *n* an act of bravado in which the cylinder of a revolver loaded with a single bullet is spun and the muzzle then pointed at the head and fired.

Russo- /ˈrʌsəʊ/ *prefix* Russia; Russian.

rust /rʌst/ *n* a reddish oxide coating formed on iron or steel when exposed to moisture; a reddish brown colour; a red mould on plants; the fungus causing this. • *vti* to form rust (on); to deteriorate, as through disuse.

rustic /ˈrʌstɪk/ *n* pertaining to or characteristic of the country; rural; simple, unsophisticated. • *n* a person from the country; a simple country dweller.

rustle /ˈrʌsəl/ *n* a crisp, rubbing sound as of dry leaves, paper, etc. • *vti* to make or move with a rustle; to hustle; to steal (cattle); (*with* **up**) (*inf*) to collect or get together.

rustler /ˈrʌslər/ *n* mainly in the US, a person who steals livestock, *esp* cattle; a hustler.

rusty /ˈrʌsti/ *adj* (**rustier, rustiest**) coated with rust; rust-coloured, faded; out of practice; antiquated.—**rustiness** *n*.

rut[1] *n* a track worn by wheels; an undeviating mechanical routine. • *vt* (**rutting, rutted**) to mark with ruts.

rut[2] *n* the seasonal period of sexual excitement in male ruminants, such as deer. • *vi* (**rutting, rutted**) to be in rut.

rutabaga /ˈruːtəˌbeɪgə/ *n* a swede.

ruthenium *n* a rare metallic element of the platinum group.

ruthless /ˈruːθləs/ *adj* cruel; merciless.—**ruthlessly** *adv*.—**ruthlessness** *n*.

RV /ˈɑːrˈviː/ *abbr* = recreational vehicle.

rye /raɪ/ *n* a hardy annual grass; its grain, used for making flour and whiskey; a whiskey made from rye.

S

S *abbr* = Saint; siemens; small; South, Southern; (*chem symbol*) sulphur.

S, s /ɛs/ *n* the 19th letter of the English alphabet; something shaped like an S.

SA *abbr* = South Africa; South America; Salvation Army.

Sabbatarian /ˌsæbəˈteɪrɪən/ *n* a strict observer of the sabbath.— **Sabbatarianism** *n*.

Sabbath /ˈsæbəθ/ *n* a day of rest and worship observed on a Saturday by Jews, Sunday by Christians and Friday by Muslims.

Sabbatical /səˈbætɪkəl/ *adj* of, pertaining to, or resembling the Sabbath.

sabbatical *n* a year's leave from a teaching post, often paid, for research or travel.

SABC *abbr* = South African Broadcasting Corporation.

saber *see* **sabre**.

sabin /ˈseɪbɪn/ *n* (*physics*) a unit of acoustic absorption.

Sabine /ˈsæbaɪn/ *n* a member of an ancient people who lived in the central Apennines in Italy.—*also adj*.

sable /ˈseɪbəl/ *n* a carnivorous mammal of arctic regions valued for its luxuriant dark brown fur; its fur.

sabot /ˈsæˈboː/ or /ˈsæboː/ *n* a shoe made from a single piece of wood; a shoe with a wooden sole and cloth upper.

sabotage /ˈsæbəˌtɒʒ/ *n* deliberate damage of machinery, or disruption of public services, by enemy agents, disgruntled employees, etc, to prevent their effective operation. • *vt* to practise sabotage on; to spoil, disrupt.

saboteur /ˌsæbəˈtɜr/ *n* a person who engages in sabotage.

sabra /ˈsæbrə/ *n* a Jew born in Israel.

sabre /ˈseɪbər/ *n* a cavalry sword with a curved blade; a light fencing sword.—*also* **saber**.

sabre-rattling *n* (*inf*) a conspicuous display of military power or aggression.

sabre-toothed tiger *n* an extinct species of large cat with long curved upper canine teeth.

sac /sæk/ *n* a bag-like part or cavity in a plant or animal.

saccate /ˈsækət/ *adj* in the shape of a sac or pouch.

saccharide /ˈsækəˌraɪd/ *n* a sugar.

saccharimeter /səˈkærɪmətər/ *n* an instrument for measuring the concentration of sugar solutions.

saccharin /ˈsækərɪn/ or /ˈsækrɪn/ *n* a non-fattening sugar substitute.

saccharine /ˈsækəˌrɪn/ or /ˈsækrɪn/ *adj* containing sugar; excessively sweet.

saccharo-, sacchar- /ˈsækərɒ/ *prefix* sugar.

sacerdotal /ˌsæsərˈdoːtəl/ *adj* relating to priests or the priesthood.—**sacerdotalism** *n*.—**sacerdotally** *adv*.

sachem /ˈseɪtʃəm/ *n* an American Indian chief of certain tribes; a political boss.

sachet /ˈsæˈʃeɪ/ *n* a sealed envelope or packet; a small perfumed bag or pad used to perfume clothes.

sack[1] /sæk/ *n* a large bag made of coarse cloth used as a container; the contents of this; a loose-fitting dress or coat; (*baseball*) a bag serving as a base; (*sl: with* **the**) dismissal. • *vt* to put into sacks; (*sl*) to dismiss.

sack[2] *n* the plunder or destruction of a place. • *vt* to plunder or loot.

sackbut /ˈsækbʌt/ *n* a type of medieval trombone.

sackcloth /ˈsækklɒθ/ *n* a coarse fabric for sacks, etc; penitential clothing.

sacking[1] /ˈsækɪŋ/ *n* the coarse cloth used for sacks.

sacking[2] /ˈsækɪŋ/ *n* the storming and plundering of a place.

sack race *n* a jumping race in which the participants' legs and lower bodies are enclosed in sacks.

sacra *see* **sacrum**.

sacrament /ˈsækrəmənt/ *n* a religious ceremony forming outward and visible sign of inward and spiritual grace, *esp* baptism and the Eucharist; the consecrated elements in the Eucharist, *esp* the bread; a sacred symbol or pledge.

sacramental /ˌsækrəˈmentəl/ *adj* of, pertaining to, or like a sacrament. • *n* (*RC Church*) a rite recognized as similar to a sacrament, *eg* the use of holy water.—**sacramentally** *adv*.

sacred /ˈseɪkrəd/ *adj* regarded as holy; consecrated to a god or God; connected with religion; worthy of or regarded with reverence, sacrosanct.

sacred cow *n* (*inf*) a person or thing regarded as above criticism.

sacrifice /ˈsækrɪˌfaɪs/ *n* the act of offering ceremonially to a deity; the slaughter of an animal (or person) to please a deity; the surrender of something valuable for the sake of something more important or worthy; loss without return; something sacrificed, an offering. • *vt* to slaughter or give up as a sacrifice; to give up for a higher good; to sell at a loss.—**sacrificial** *adj*.

sacrilege /ˈsækrɪlɪdʒ/ *n* violation of anything holy or sacred.

sacrilegious /-ˈlɪdʒəs/ *adj* guilty of sacrilege; irreverent.—**sacrilegiously** *adv*.—**sacrilegiousness** *n*.

sacristan /ˈsækrɪstən/ *n* a person in charge of the contents of a church; a sexton.

sacristy /ˈsækrɪsti/ *n* (*pl* **sacristies**) a room in a church where the sacred vessels, etc are kept.

sacrosanct /ˈsækrɒˌsæŋkt/ *adj* inviolable; very holy.

sacrum /ˈsækrəm/ or /ˈseɪkrəm/ *n* (*pl* **sacra**) a compound bone at the base of the spine forming the back of the pelvis.

sad /sæd/ *adj* (**sadder, saddest**) expressing grief or unhappiness; sorrowful; deplorable.—**sadly** *adv*.—**sadness** *n*.

sadden /ˈsædən/ *vti* to make or become sad.

saddle /ˈsædəl/ *n* a seat, *usu* of leather, for a rider on a horse, bicycle, etc; a ridge connecting two mountain peaks; a joint of mutton or venison consisting of the two loins; **in the saddle** mounted on a saddle; in control. • *vt* to put a saddle on; to burden, encumber.

saddlebag /ˈsædəlˌbæg/ *n* a bag hung from the saddle of a horse or bicycle.

saddlebow /-ˌboː/ *n* the arched front of a saddle.

saddlecloth /-ˌklɒθ/ or /-ˌklɒθ/ *n* a piece of cloth placed under a horse's saddle to prevent chafing.

saddler /ˈsædlər/ *n* a person who makes or sells saddles, harness, etc.

saddlery /ˈsædləri/ *n* (*pl* **saddleries**) articles made by a saddler; the business or premises of a saddler.

saddle soap *n* an oily soap for cleaning and preserving leather.

saddletree /ˈsædlˌtriː/ *n* the frame of a saddle.

sadhu, saddhu /ˈsɒduː/ *n* a Hindu holy man.

sadism /ˈseɪdɪzəm/ *n* sexual pleasure obtained from inflicting cruelty upon another; extreme cruelty.—**sadist** *n*.—**sadistic** *adj*.—**sadistically** *adv*.

sadomasochism /ˌseɪdoːˈmæsəˌkɪzəm/ *n* sexual pleasure obtained from inflicting cruelty upon oneself and receiving it from another.—**sadomasochist** *n*.—**sadomasochistic** *adj*.

s.a.e. *abbr* = stamped addressed envelope.

safari /səˈfɑri/ *n* (*pl* **safaris**) a journey or hunting expedition, *esp* in Africa.

safari jacket *n* a belted shirt jacket with pleated pockets.

safari suit *n* a safari jacket and matching trousers or skirt made from denim or similar hard-wearing material.

safe /seɪf/ *adj* unhurt; out of danger; reliable; secure; involving no risk; trustworthy; giving protection; prudent; sure; incapable of doing harm. • *n* a locking metal box or compartment for valuables.—**safely** *adv*.

safe-conduct *n* written permission for the holder to travel safely through hostile country.

safecracker *n* a person who opens and robs safes.—*also* **safebreaker**.—**safecracking** *n*.

safe-deposit *adj* (*box, room, etc*) designed for the protective storage of valuables, deeds, etc. • *n* a building with safes for renting—*also* **safety deposit**.

safeguard /ˈseɪfgɑrd/ *n* anything that protects against injury or danger; a proviso against foreseen risks. • *vt* to protect.

safe house *n* a refuge for victims of domestic violence, sexual abuse, etc run by social welfare organizations; a clandestine place used by intelligence services, terrorists, etc as a refuge.

safekeeping /ˌseɪfˈkiːpɪŋ/ *n* the act or process of keeping safely; protection.

safe period *n* the time in a woman's menstrual cycle when she is least likely to conceive.

safe seat *n* a parliamentary constituency in which the sitting MP enjoys a substantial majority and can be assured of re-election.

safe sex *n* sex in which precautions are taken to lessen the risk of catching HIV or other sexually transmitted diseases.

safety /'seɪfti/ *n* (*pl* **safeties**) freedom from danger; the state of being safe.

safety belt *n* a belt worn by a person working at a great height to prevent falling; a seatbelt in a car.

safety curtain *n* a fireproof curtain that can be lowered to separate a theatre stage from the auditorium.

safety deposit *see* **safe-deposit**.

safety glass *n* shatterproof glass.

safety lamp *n* a miner's lamp in which the flame is enclosed by a protective gauze to prevent it igniting combustible gases.

safety match *n* a match that will only ignite on a particular surface.

safety net *n* a net suspended beneath acrobats, etc; any protection against loss.

safety pin *n* a pin with a guard to cover the point.

safety razor *n* a razor with a guard that covers the blade to protect the skin from accidental cuts.

safety valve *n* an automatic valve for relieving excess pressure of steam, etc; a harmless outlet for emotion.

saffian /'sæfiən/ *n* a brightly dyed leather made from the skin of goats or sheep.

safflower /'sæflaʊr/ *n* (a red dye and oil derived from) a thistle-like plant with large orange or red flowers.

saffron /'sæfrən/ *n* a crocus whose bright yellow stigmas are used as a food colouring and flavouring; an orange-yellow colour.

sag /sæg/ *vi* (**sagging, sagged**) to droop downward in the middle; to sink or hang down unevenly under pressure.

saga /'sægə/ or /'sɒgə/ *n* a long story of heroic deeds.

sagacious /sə'geɪʃəs/ *adj* mentally acute, shrewd; wise.—**sagaciously** *adv.*—**sagaciousness** *n*.

sagacity /sə'gæsɪti/ *n* (*pl* **sagacities**) readiness of apprehension; discriminating intelligence; acute practical judgment.

sagamore /'sægə,mɔr/ *n* an American Indian chief of certain tribes.

sage[1] /seɪdʒ/ *adj* wise through reflection and experience. • *n* a person of profound wisdom.—**sagely** *adv.*—**sagely** *adv*.

sage[2] *n* a herb with leaves used for flavouring food; sagebrush.

sagebrush /'seɪdʒbrʌʃ/ *n* a low shrub of the alkaline plains of North America.

sagger, saggar /'sægər/ *n* a fireproof clay case in which procelain is put for baking.

sagittate /'sædʒɪ,teɪt/ *adj* (*leaf*) shaped like an arrowhead.

Sagittarius /sædʒɪ'teriəs/ *n* the Archer, ninth sign of the zodiac; in astrology, operative November 22–December 20.—**Sagittarian** *adj, n*.

sago /'seɪgoʊ/ *n* (*pl* **sagos**) a type of Asian palm; its starchy pith used in puddings.

saguaro /sə'gwɑroʊ/ *n* (*pl* **saguaros**) a large cactus of North American and Mexican desert areas bearing white flowers and edible fruit.

sahib /'sɒhɪb/ or /'sɒɪb/ *n* a form of polite address formerly used by Indians to European men.

said /sed/ *see* **say**.

saiga /'saɪgə/ or /'seɪ-/ *n* a stocky antelope of the Russian steppes.

sail /seɪl/ *n* a piece of canvas used to catch the wind to propel or steer a vessel; sails collectively; anything like a sail; an arm of a windmill; a voyage in a sailing vessel; **under sail** with the sails set; under way. • *vt* to navigate a vessel; to manage (a vessel); **to set sail** to spread the sails; to begin a voyage. • *vi* to be moved by sails; to travel by water; to glide or pass smoothly; to walk in a stately manner.

sailboard /'seɪlbɔrd/ *n* a type of large surfboard with a sail used in windsurfing.

sailboat /'seɪlboʊt/ *n* the US word for a sailing boat.

sailcloth /'seɪlklɒθ/ *n* canvas used for sails; a strong, durable fabric for clothing.

sailer /'seɪlər/ *n* a sailing vessel.

sailfish /'seɪlfɪʃ/ *n* (*pl* **sailfish, sailfishes**) a large game fish of tropical waters with a long sail-like dorsal fin.

sailing /'seɪlɪŋ/ *n* the act of sailing; the motion or direction of a ship, etc on water; a departure from a port.

sailing boat *n* a boat that is propelled by a sail or sails.

sailor /'seɪlər/ *n* a person who sails; one of a ship's crew.

sailoring /'seɪlərɪŋ/ *n* a sailor's life.

sailplane *n* a type of light glider. • *vi* to fly a sailplane.

sain /seɪn/ *vt* (*arch*) to make the sign of the cross on; to bless in order to protect from evil.

sainfoin /'seɪnfɔɪn/ or /'sæn-/ *n* a Eurasian leguminous plant with pink flowers, grown for fodder.

saint /seɪnt/ *n* a person who is very patient, charitable, etc; a person who is canonized by the Roman Catholic Church; one of the blessed in heaven.—**sainthood** *n*.

Saint Bernard *n* a breed of large dog with a reddish brown coat, often used as a rescue dog.

sainted /'seɪntəd/ *adj* canonized; holy; dead; much admired.

saintly /'seɪntli/ *adj* (**saintlier, saintliest**) of, like, or relating to a saint.—**saintliness** *n*.

Saint Patrick's Day *n* March 17, observed by the Irish in honour of the patron saint of Ireland.

saint's day *n* a day in the church calender which is devoted to the commemoration of a particular saint.

sake[1] /seɪk/ *n* behalf; purpose; benefit; interest.

sake[2] /'sɒki/ **saké, saki** *n* a Japanese alcoholic drink made from fermented rice and drunk warm.

sal /sɒl/ *n* (*chem*) a salt.

salaam /sə'lɒm/ *n* a form of ceremonial greeting in Muslim countries. • *vti* to make a salaam (to).

salacious /sə'leɪʃəs/ *adj* lustful; obscene.—**salaciously** *adv.*—**salaciousness** *n*.

salad /'sæləd/ *n* a dish, *usu* cold, of vegetables, fruits, meat, eggs, etc; lettuce, etc, used for this.

salad bar *n* a buffet in a restaurant at which diners choose their own salads.

salad days *npl* a time of youth and inexperience.

salad dressing *n* a cooked or uncooked sauce of oil, vinegar, spices, etc, to put on a salad.

salade niçoise *n* a salad of various ingredients, including tomatoes, hard-boiled eggs, and anchovy fillets or tuna fish.

salamander /'sælə,mændər/ *n* any of various lizard-like amphibians; a mythical lizard-like creature that was supposedly impervious to fire.

salami /sə'lɒmi/ *n* a highly seasoned Italian sausage.

salaried /'sælərɪd/ *adj* receiving a salary.

salary /'sæləri/ *n* (*pl* **salaries**) fixed, regular payment for non-manual work, *usu* paid monthly.

salchow /'saʊkaʊ/ *n* (*ice-skating*) a jump incorporating turns in the air.

sale /seɪl/ *n* the act of selling; the exchange of goods or services for money; the market or opportunity of selling; an auction; the disposal of goods at reduced prices; the period of this.

saleable /'seɪləbəl/ *adj* marketable; in good demand.—*also US* **salable**.

salep /'sæləp/ *n* (food made from) the starchy dried roots of various orchidaceous plants.

saleratus /,sɒlə'rætəs/ *n* sodium bicarbonate used in cooking.

saleroom /'seɪlruːm/ *n* a salesroom; an auction room.

salesclerk /'seɪlz,klɜrk/ *n* a person who sells goods in a store.

salesman /'seɪlzmən/ *n* (*pl* **salesmen**) a person who sells either in a given territory or in a store.—**saleswoman** *nf* (*pl* **saleswomen**).

salesmanship /-ʃɪp/ *n* the art or skill of selling.

salesperson /'seɪlz,pɜrsən/ *n* (*pl* **salespeople**) a salesman or saleswoman.

sales representative *n* a person who travels to sell within a given territory.

salesroom /'seɪlzruːm/ *n* a place where goods are displayed for sale; a saleroom.

sales talk *n* talk aimed at selling something; any talk to persuade.

sales tax *n* a tax levied (*usu* as a percentage) on the price of an object bought by a consumer.

Salic /'sælɪk/ or /'seɪ-/ *adj* of or pertaining to the Franks; relating to the Salic law.

Salic law *n* the law of the Franks excluding females from the succession to the French throne.

salicin /'sælɪsɪn/ *n* a bitter compound obtained from the bark of willows and poplars, used in medicine.

salient /'seɪliənt/ *adj* projecting outward; conspicuous; noteworthy; leaping, gushing.—**salience, saliency** *n.*—**saliently** *adv*.

salify /'sælɪ,faɪ/ *vt* to make salty; (*chem*) to convert into a salt.—**salification** *n*.

salimeter /ˈsælɪˌmɪtər/ *n* a device for measuring the amount of salt in a solution.

saline /ˈseɪliːn/ *adj* of or impregnated with salt or salts; salty. • *n* a solution of salt and water.—**salinity** *n*.

saliva /səˈlaɪvə/ *n* the liquid secreted by glands in the mouth that aids digestion.—**salivary** *adj*.

salivate /ˈsælɪveɪt/ *vi* to secrete saliva, *esp* excessively.—**salivation** *n*.

sallenders /ˈsæləndərz/ *npl* an eczematous rash on a horse's hock.

sallet /ˈsælət/ *n* a light helmet of the 15th century.

sallow /ˈsæloʊ/ *adj* (*complexion*) an unhealthy yellow colour, a pale brown colour.—**sallowness** *n*.

sally /ˈsæli/ *n* (*pl* **sallies**) a sudden attack; an outburst; a lively remark, quip. • *vi* (**sallying, sallied**) to make a sally; to go (forth).

salmagundi /ˌsælməˈgʌndi/ *n* a mixed dish of chopped meat, anchovies, eggs, vegetables, etc; a miscellany.

salmi /ˈsɒlmi/ *n* (*pl* **salmis**) a casserole of game-birds in a rich wine sauce.

salmon /ˈsæmən/ *n* (*pl* **salmon, salmons**) a large silvery edible fish that lives in salt water and spawns in fresh water; salmon pink.

salmonella /ˌsælməˈnelə/ *n* (*pl* **salmonellae, salmonella, salmonellas**) any of a genus of bacteria that causes food poisoning and diseases of the genital tract.

salmon ladder *n* a series of steps (*eg* in a waterfall or dam) to allow salmon to swim upstream to their breeding grounds.

salmon pink *adj* a yellowish pink colour.

salmon trout *n* a large trout resembling a salmon.

salon /səˈlɒn/ *n* a large reception hall or drawing room for receiving guests; the shop of a hairdresser, beautician, or couturier; an art gallery.

saloon /səˈluːn/ *n* a large reception room; a large cabin for the social use of a ship's passengers; a four-seater car with a boot; in the US, a place where alcoholic drinks are sold and consumed.

saloon bar *n* a comfortably furnished bar.

salopettes /ˌsæləˈpets/ *npl* thick quilted trousers with shoulder straps, worn for skiing.

salsa /ˈsælsə/ *n* (the music for) a type of Puerto Rican dance.

salsify /ˈsælsəˌfi/ *n* (*pl* **salsifies**) a purple-flowered plant with an edible root.

SALT /sɒlt/ *abbr* = Strategic Arms Limitation Talks *or* Treaty.

salt /sɒlt/ *n* a white crystalline substance (sodium chloride) used as a seasoning or preservative; piquancy, wit; (*chem*) a compound of an acid and a base; (*pl*) mineral salt as an aperient. • *adj* containing or tasting of salt; preserved with salt; pungent. • *vt* to flavour, pickle or sprinkle with salt; to give flavour or piquancy to (as a story); (*with* **away**) to hoard; to keep for the future.

saltbush /ˈsɒltbʊʃ/ *n* a shrub-like plant which provides grazing in dry regions.

salt cellar /ˈsɒltˌselər/ *n* a vessel for salt at the table.

salter /ˈsɒltər/ *n* someone who deals in or manufactures salt.

saltire /ˈsɒlˌtaɪr/ *n* an X-shaped cross dividing a shield, flag, etc, into four compartments.

salt lick *n* an area where animals go to lick salt residue; a block of salt for animals to lick.

salt marsh *n* an area regularly flooded by seawater.

saltpan *n* a hollow or depression where salt is deposited by evaporating seawater.

saltpetre, saltpeter /ˌsɒltˈpiːtər/ *n* a white powder (potassium nitrate) used in making gunpowder, etc.

saltshaker *n* a container for salt with a perforated top.

saltwater *adj* of or living in salt water or the sea.

salty /ˈsɒlti/ *adj* (**saltier, saltiest**) of, containing or tasting of salt; witty; earthy, coarse.

salubrious /səˈluːbriəs/ *adj* health-giving; wholesome.—**salubriously** *adv*.—**salubriousness** *n*.

saluki /səˈluːki/ *n* a breed of tall, slender hounds with long silky coats.

salutary /ˈsæljʊˌteri/ *adj* beneficial, wholesome.—**salutarily** *adv*.—**salutariness** *n*.

salutation /ˌsæljuːˈteɪʃən/ *n* a greeting; the words used in it.

salute /səˈluːt/ *n* a gesture of respect or greeting; (*mil*) a motion of the right hand to the head, or to a rifle; a discharge of guns, etc, as a military mark of honour. • *vti* to make a salute (to); to greet; to kiss; to praise or honour.

salvable /ˈsælvəbəl/ *adj* able to be salvaged.

salvage /ˈsælvɪdʒ/ *n* the rescuing of a ship or property from loss at sea, by fire, etc; the reward paid for this; the thing salvaged; waste material intended for further use. • *vt* to save from loss or danger.—**salvageable** *adj*.—**salvager** *n*.

salvation /sælˈveɪʃən/ *n* the act of saving or the state of being saved; in Christianity, the deliverance from evil; a means of preservation.—**salvational** *adj*.

Salvation Army *n* an international religious and charitable group organized on military lines founded by William Booth in 1865.—**Salvationist** *n*.

salve¹ /sælv/ *or* /sæv/ *n* a healing ointment or balm; a soothing influence. • *vt* to apply ointment to; to smooth over; to soothe.

salve² *vt* to salvage; (*arch*) to save.

salver /ˈsælvər/ *n* a small tray.

salvia /ˈsælviə/ *n* any of a genus of plants or small shrubs with red or purple flowers.

salvo¹ /ˈsælvoʊ/ *n* (**salvoes, salvos**) a firing of several guns or missiles simultaneously; a sudden burst; a spirited verbal attack.

salvo² *n* (*pl* **salvos**) an exception or reservation.

sal volatile /ˌsælvəˈlætɪli/ *n* a solution of ammonium carbonate in alcohol used as a remedy for faintness.

salvor /ˈsælvər/ *n* a person or vessel effecting a salvage at sea.

SAM (*abbr*) surface-to-air missile.

samara /səˈmɑːrə/ *or* /səˈmɑːrə/ *n* a dry winged single-seeded fruit produced by the ash, elm, etc.

Samaritan /səˈmærɪtən/ *n* a native or inhabitant of Samaria in ancient Palestine; a compassionate person; a Good Samaritan; a member of a voluntary organization that helps people in distress or despair.

samarium /səˈmeriəm/ *n* a silvery metallic element used in lasers and alloys.

samba /ˈsæmbə/ *n* a Brazilian dance of African origin; the music for this. • *vi* to dance the samba.

same /seɪm/ *adj* identical; exactly similar; unchanged; uniform, monotonous; previously mentioned. • *pron* the same person or thing. • *adv* in like manner.

sameness /-nəs/ *n* the state of being the same; monotony.

Samian /ˈseɪmiən/ *n* a native or inhabitant of the Aegean island of Samos in Greece. • *adj* of or pertaining to Samos or its people.

Samian ware *n* a type of red or black pottery from Samos.

samisen /ˈsæmɪsɪn/ *n* a Japanese guitar-like instrument with three strings.

samite /ˈsæmaɪt/ *or* /ˈseɪ-/ *n* a medieval heavy silken fabric.

samizdat /ˈsæmɪzˌdæt/ *or* /-ˈdæt/ *n* in the former Soviet Union, a system for the clandestine printing and distribution of banned literature.

Samoan /səˈmoʊən/ *n* a native or inhabitant of Samoa, a group of islands in the South Pacific; the Polynesian language of Samoa. • *adj* of or pertaining to Samoa, its people or language.

samosa /səˈmoʊsə/ *n* (*pl* **samosas, samosa**) an Indian savoury pasty with a spicy meat or vegetable filling.

samovar /ˈsæməˌvɑːr/ *n* a metal urn with an internal element used for boiling water for tea, *esp* in Russia.

Samoyed /ˈsæməˌjed/ *n* a member of a people of the northern Urals; the language of these people; a breed of sledge-dog with a thick creamy coat and a tightly curled tail.—**Samoyedic** *adj*.

sampan /ˈsæmˌpæn/ *n* a small flat-bottomed Chinese river boat.

samphire /ˈsæmˌfaɪr/ *n* a Eurasian coastal rock plant with edible fleshy leaves.

sample /ˈsæmpəl/ *n* a specimen; a small part representative of the whole; an instance. • *vt* (*food, drink*) to taste a small quantity of; to test by taking a sample.

sampler /ˈsæmplər/ *n* a person who takes samples; something containing a representative selection (as a record, book); an assortment; a piece of ornamental embroidery showing different stitches and patterns as an example of skill.

sampling /ˈsæmplɪŋ/ *n* (*mus industry*) the practice of extracting phrases from several recorded songs and putting them together electronically to make a new one.

samurai /ˈsæmʊˌraɪ/ *n* (*pl* **samurai**) a member of an ancient Japanese warrior caste.

samurai bond *n* a financial bond issued in yen by a non-Japanese company.

-san *suffix* a Japanese title of respect similar to Mr, Mrs, etc.

sanatorium /ˌsænəˈtoriəm/ *n* an establishment for the treatment of convalescents or the chronically ill.

sancta *see* **sanctum**.

sanctified /ˈsæŋktɪˌfaɪd/ *adj* hallowed; consecrated; sanctimonious.

sanctify /'sæŋktɪˌfaɪ/ *vt* (**sanctifying, sanctified**) to make holy; to purify from sin or evil; (*the Church*) to give official approval.—**sanctification** *n*.—**sanctifier** *n*.

sanctimonious /ˌsæŋktɪ'mo:niəs/ *adj* pretending to be holy; hypocritically pious or righteous.—**sanctimoniously** *adv*.—**sanctimoniousness** *n*.

sanctimony /'sæŋktɪˌmo:ni/ *n* self-righteousness; hypocrisy.

sanction /'sæŋkʃən/ *n* express permission, authorization; a binding influence; a penalty by which a law is enforced, *esp* a prohibition on trade with a country that has violated international law. • *vt* to permit; to give authority.—**sanctionable** *adj*.

sanctity /'sæŋktɪti/ *n* (*pl* **sanctities**) the condition of being holy or sacred; inviolability.

sanctuary /'sæŋktʃuːˌeri/ *n* (*pl* **sanctuaries**) a sacred place; the part of a church around the altar; a place where one is free from arrest or violence, an asylum; a refuge; an animal reserve.

sanctum /'sæŋktəm/ *n* (*pl* **sanctums, sancta**) a holy place; a private room where one is not to be disturbed.

Sanctus /'sæŋktəs/ *n* (*Christianity*) the hymn "Holy, holy, holy" used in communion; an orchestral setting of this.

sand /sænd/ *n* very fine rock particles; (*pl*) a desert; a sandy beach. • *vt* to smooth or polish with sand or sandpaper; to sprinkle with sand. • *adj* reddish yellow.

sandal[1] /'sændəl/ *n* a shoe consisting of a sole strapped to the foot; a low slipper or shoe.—**sandalled, sandaled** *adj*.

sandal[2] *n* sandalwood.

sandalwood /'sændəlˌwʊd/ *n* the yellow, scented wood of an Asian tree; the tree.

sandbag /'sændbæg/ *n* a bag of sand used for ballast or to protect against floodwater. • *vt* (**sandbagging, sandbagged**) to protect by laying sandbags; to hit with a sandbag; (*inf*) to coerce; (*sl*) to deceive.—**sandbagger** *n*.

sandbank /'sændbæŋk/ *n* a sand bar; a large deposit of sand forming a hill or mound.

sand bar /'sændbɑr/ *n* a ridge of sand built up in a river, a lake, or coastal waters by currents.

sandblast /'sændblæst/ *vt* (*a building*) to clean by blasting with sand at high velocity.—*also n*.

sand castle /'sændˌkæsəl/ *n* a model of a castle moulded from damp sand, as made at the seaside by children.

sander /'sændər/ *n* a power-driven tool for sanding wood or other surfaces.

sanderling /'sændərlɪŋ/ *n* a small wading bird.

sandglass /'sændglæs/ *n* an instrument that measures time by the running of sand through a narrow aperture.

S & L *abbr* = savings and loan association.

S & M *abbr* = sadomasochism.

sandman /'sændmæn/ *n* (*pl* **sandmen**) (*folklore*) an imaginary being who sends children to sleep by sprinkling sand in their eyes.

sand martin *n* a small European songbird that nests in holes in sandy riverbanks, etc.

sandpaper /'sændˌpeɪpər/ *n* a paper coated on one side with sand or another abrasive, used to smooth or polish. • *vt* to rub with sandpaper.

sandpiper /'sændˌpaɪpər/ *n* any of numerous small wading birds.

sandpit /'sændpɪt/ *n* a small enclosure filled with sand for children to play in.

sandstone /'sændsto:n/ *n* a sedimentary rock of compacted sand.

sandstorm /'sændstɔrm/ *n* a windstorm in a desert carrying clouds of sand.

sand trap *n* (*golf*) a pit of sand forming an obstacle on a golf course, a bunker.

sand wedge *n* (*golf*) a club for hitting the ball out of a sand trap.

sandwich /'sændwɪtʃ/ or /'sænwɪtʃ/, /'sæm-/ *n* two slices of bread with meat, cheese, or other filling between; anything in a sandwich-like arrangement. • *vt* to place between two things or two layers; to make such a place for.

sandwich board *n* two *usu* hinged boards hanging from the shoulders, one in front and one at the back, carried by a sandwich man.

sandwich man *n* a person who advertises by wearing a sandwich board.

sandy /'sændi/ *adj* (**sandier, sandiest**) of, like, or sprinkled with sand; yellowish grey.—**sandiness** *n*.

sane /seɪn/ *adj* mentally sound, not mad; reasonable, sensible.—**sanely** *adv*.—**saneness** *n*.

sang *see* **sing**.

sangfroid /sæŋ'frwɒ/ or /sɑ̃-/, /-fwɒ/ *n* coolness in danger, imperturbability.

Sangreal /'sæŋgriəl/ *n* the Holy Grail.

sangria /sæŋ'griːə/ *n* a Spanish drink made with red wine, orange juice and fresh fruit laced with brandy.

sanguinary /'sæŋgwɪnˌeri/ *adj* accompanied by bloodshed; bloodthirsty.—**sanguinarily** *adv*.

sanguine /'sæŋgwɪn/ *adj* confident, hopeful; blood-red; (*complexion*) ruddy.—**sanguineness** *n*.

sanguinely /-li/ *adv* confidently, hopefully.

sanguineous /-nəs/ *adj* of or relating to blood; full-blooded; blood-red; sanguinary; sanguine.

sanies /'seɪniːz/ *n* a watery mixture of blood and pus discharged from a sore or wound.—**sanious** *adj*.

sanitarian /ˌsænɪ'teriən/ *adj* hygienic. • *n* a specialist in matters of public health.

sanitarium *n* the US word for **sanatorium**.

sanitary /'sænɪˌteri/ *adj* relating to the promotion and protection of health; relating to the supply of water, drainage, and sewage disposal; hygienic.—**sanitarily** *adv*.—**sanitariness** *n*.

sanitary cordon *n* a cordon sanitaire.

sanitary engineering *n* the design, construction and installation of water and sewage systems.—**sanitary engineer** *n*.

sanitary towel, sanitary napkin *n* an absorbent pad worn externally during menstruation.

sanitation /ˌsænɪ'teɪʃən/ *n* the science and practice of achieving hygienic conditions; drainage and disposal of sewage.

sanitize /'sænəˌtaɪz/ *vt* to clean or sterilize; to make (language, etc) more respectable or acceptable.

sanity /'sænɪti/ *n* the condition of being sane; mental health; common sense.

sank *see* **sink**.

Sans. *abbr* = Sanskrit.

sans /sɒnz/ or /sɑ̃/ *prep* without.

sansculotte /ˌsækjuː'lɒt/ *n* in the French Revolution, a man without breeches, a term of contempt applied to a revolutionary who wore pantaloons instead of knee breeches; any revolutionary.

sans doute *Fr*. /sɒn'duːt/ doubtless; certainly.

Sansk. *abbr* = Sanskrit.

Sanskrit /'sænskrɪt/ *n* the ancient language used in Indian and Hindu sacred literature.—**Sanskrit** *adj*.—**Sanskritic** *adj*.

sans-serif, sanserif *n* (*print*) a character or typeface with no serifs.

sans souci *Fr*. /sɒnsuː'siː/ free from care.

Santa /'sæntə/ *n* Santa Claus. • *adj* sainted, holy.

Santa Claus /'sæntəˌklɔz/ *n* a legendary fat, white-bearded old man who brings presents to children at Christmas.—*also* **Father Christmas**.

sap[1] /sæp/ *n* the vital juice of plants; energy and health; (*inf*) a fool. • *vt* (**sapping, sapped**) to drain of sap; to exhaust the energy of.

sap[2] *n* a narrow or covered siege trench; the digging of this, undermining. • *vti* (**sapping, sapped**) to attack by or dig a sap; to undermine insidiously.

saphead /'sæpˌhed/ *n* (*sl*) a fool, a stupid person.

sapid /'sæpɪd/ *adj* having a pleasing flavour; agreeable.—**sapidity** *n*.

sapient /'seɪpiənt/ *adj* (*often ironical*) wise, discerning.—**sapience** *n*.—**sapiently** *adv*.

sapling /'sæplɪŋ/ *n* a young tree; a youth.

saponify /sə'pɒnɪˌfaɪ/ *vt* (**saponifying, saponified**) (*chem*) to convert (fat, oil, etc) into soap by combination with an alkali. • *vi* to undergo this process.—**saponification** *n*.—**saponifier** *n*.

sapor /'seɪpər/ *n* taste, flavour.

sapper /'sæpər/ *n* one who or that which saps; a soldier who lays, detects or disarms mines.

sapphire /'sæfaɪr/ *n* a transparent blue precious stone; a deep pure blue.—*also adj*.

sapro-, sapr- /'sæpro:/ *prefix* dead or decaying matter.

saprogenic /ˌsæprə'dʒenɪk/, **saprogenous** /-'dʒənəs/ *adj* producing or caused by putrefaction.

saprophagous /sæ'prɒfəgəs/ *adj* feeding on decaying matter.

saprophyte /'sæprəˌfaɪt/ *n* a plant or fungus that grows on dead organic matter.—**saprophytic** *adj*.

Saracen /'særəsən/ *n* a member of a nomadic people of the Syrian desert; a Muslim at the time of the Crusades. • *adj* of or pertaining to Saracens.—**Saracenic** *adj*.

sarcasm /ˈsɑːˌkæzəm/ *n* a scornful or ironic remark; the use of this.—**sarcastic** *adj*.—**sarcastically** *adv*.

sarco- /ˈsɑːkoː/, **sarc-** /sɑːk/ *prefix* flesh.

sarcoma /sɑːˈkoːmə/ *n* (*pl* **sarcomas, sarcomata**) a malignant tumour of connective tissue.—**sarcomatous** *adj*.

sarcophagus /sɑːˈkɒfəgəs/ *n* (*pl* **sarcophagi, sarcophaguses**) a large stone coffin or tomb.

sard /sɑːd/ *n* an orange-red variety of chalcedony.

sardine /sɑːˈdiːn/ *n* (*pl* **sardines, sardine**) a small, edible seafish.

sardonic /sɑːˈdɒnɪk/ *adj* (*smile, etc*) derisive, mocking, maliciously jocular.—**sardonically** *adv*.

sardonyx /ˈsɑːdənɪks/ *n* an onyx with alternate layers of white chalcedony and orange sard.

sargasso /sɑːˈɡæsoː/ *n* (*pl* **sargassos**) a large mass of floating sargassum.

sargassum /sɑːˈɡæsəm/ *n* any of a genus of tropical seaweed with air bladders that form to float in large masses.

sarge /sɑːdʒ/ *n* (*sl*) sergeant.

sari, saree /ˈsɑːri/ *n* a Hindu woman's principal garment, consisting of a long piece of cloth wrapped around the waist and across the shoulder.

sark /sɑːk/ *n* (*Scot*) a shirt.

sarong /səˈrɒŋ/ *n* a long strip of cloth wrapped around the lower body, worn *esp* in the Malay archipelago and the Pacific Islands.

sarsaparilla /ˌsæspəˈrɪlə/ *n* any of various tropical American trailing plants; the dried roots of these used as a flavouring and (formerly) in medicine; a soft drink flavoured with these roots.

sartorial /sɑːˈtɔːriəl/ *adj* of or relating to the making of men's clothing.—**sartorially** *adv*.

sartorius /sɑːˈtɔːriəs/ *n* (*pl* **sartorii**) a muscle that helps flex the knee.

SASE *abbr* = self-addressed stamped envelope.

sash[1] /sæʃ/ *n* a band of satin or ribbon worn around the waist or over the shoulder, often as a badge of honour.

sash[2] *n* a frame for holding the glass of a window, *esp* one that slides vertically.

sashay /sæˈʃeɪ/ *n* (*inf*) to walk in a casual manner, saunter; to swagger.

sash cord *n* a cord used to attach a sash weight to a sash.

sashimi /sæˈʃiːmi/ *n* a Japanese dish of thin strips of raw fish.

sash weight *n* a weight used to balance a sliding sash in an open position.

sash window *n* a window with sliding sashes.

sass /sæs/ *n* (*US inf*) rudeness, impudence. • *vt* to talk rudely or impudently to.

sassafras /ˈsæsəˌfræs/ *n* a North American tree of the laurel family; the aromatic dried root of this used as a flavouring.

Sassenach /ˈsæsəˌnæx/ or /-ˌnæk/ *n* (*Scot, Irish*) an English person.

sassy /ˈsæsi/ *adj* (**sassier, sassiest**) (*US sl*) rude; cheeky.

Sat *abbr* = Saturday; Saturn.

sat *see* **sit**.

Satan /ˈseɪtən/ *n* the devil, the adversary of God.

satanic /səˈtænɪk/, **satanical** /-kəl/ *adj* of or relating to Satan, devilish; marked by viciousness or cruelty.—**satanically** *adv*.

Satanism /ˈseɪtəˌnɪzəm/ *n* the worship of Satan; the perversion of Christian ceremonial forms associated with this.—**Satanist** *n*.

satay, saté /ˈsæˌteɪ/ or /ˈsæteɪ/ *n* an Indonesian dish of cubed chicken, beef, etc served with a piquant peanut sauce.

satchel /ˈsætʃəl/ *n* a bag with shoulder straps for carrying school books, etc.

sate /seɪt/ *vt* to satisfy to repletion, to satiate.

sateen /sæˈtiːn/ *n* a closely woven fabric with a glossy surface made in imitation of satin.

satellite /ˈsætəˌlaɪt/ *n* a planet orbiting another; a man-made object orbiting the earth, moon, etc, to gather scientific information or for communication; a nation economically dependent on a more powerful one.

satellite broadcasting, satellite television *n* the transmission of television programmes via an orbiting satellite to subscribers in possession of a receiving satellite dish aerial.

sati *see* **suttee**.

satiable /ˈseɪʃəbəl/ *adj* able to be satiated or sated.—**satiability** *n*.—**satiably** *adv*.

satiate /ˈseɪʃiˌeɪt/ *vt* to provide with more than enough so as to weary or disgust; to gorge.—**satiation** *n*.

satiety /səˈtaɪti/ *n* the state of being sated; a feeling of having had too much.

satin /ˈsætən/ *n* a fabric of woven silk with a smooth, shiny surface on one side. • *adj* of or resembling satin.

satinwood /ˈsætɪnˌwʊd/ *n* a smooth yellowish brown hard wood; a tree that yields such wood.

satiny /-ni/ *adj* smooth and lustrous, like satin.

satire /ˈsætaɪr/ *n* a literary work in which folly or evil in people's behaviour are held up to ridicule; trenchant wit, sarcasm.—**satirical** *adj*.—**satirically** *adv*.

satirist /ˈsætərɪst/ *n* a writer of satires.

satirize /ˈsætəraɪz/ *vt* to attack with satire.—**satirizer** *n*.

satisfaction /ˌsætɪsˈfækʃən/ *n* the act of satisfying or the condition of being satisfied; that which satisfies; comfort; atonement, reparation.

satisfactory /ˌsætɪsˈfæktəri/ or /-ˈfæktri/ *adj* giving satisfaction; adequate; acceptable; convincing.—**satisfactorily** *adv*.—**satisfactoriness** *n*.

satisfy /ˈsætəsˌfaɪ/ *vb* (**satisfying, satisfied**) *vi* to be enough for; to fulfil the needs or desires of. • *vt* to give enough to; (*hunger, desire etc*.) to appease; to please; to gratify; to comply with; (*creditor*) to discharge, to pay in full; to convince; to make reparation to; (*guilt, etc*) to atone for.

satori /səˈtɒri/ *n* (*Zen Buddhism*) a state of intuitive enlightenment.

satsuma /ˈsætsumə/ or /sætˈsuːmə/ *n* a loose-skinned, seedless, small orange; (*with cap*) a glazed yellow Japanese pottery.

saturate /ˈsætʃəˌreɪt/ *vt* to soak thoroughly; to fill completely.—**saturator** *n*.

saturated /ˈsætʃəˌreɪt/ *adj* (*chem*) absorbing the maximum amount possible of a substance; pure in colour.

saturation /ˌsætʃəˈreɪʃən/ *n* the act of saturating or the condition of being saturated; the supplying of a market with all the goods it will absorb; an overwhelming concentration of military power.

Saturday /ˈsætərˌdeɪ/ or /-di/ *n* the seventh and last day of the week.

Saturn /ˈsætərn/ *n* (*Roman myth*) the god of agriculture; (*astron*) the second largest planet in the solar system, with three rings revolving about it.—**Saturnian** *adj*.

Saturnalia /ˌsætərˈneɪliə/ *n* (*pl* **Saturnalias, Saturnalia**) in ancient Rome, a festival held in December in honour of Saturn; (*without cap*) a wild, unrestrained celebration.—**Saturnalian** *n*.

saturnine /ˈsætərˌnaɪn/ *adj* sullen, morose.—**saturninely** *adv*.

satyagraha /sætˈjɒɡrəˌhə/ *n* the principle and practice of passive resistance as adopted by Mahatma Gandhi in opposition to British colonial rule in India.

satyr /ˈsætər/ or /ˈseɪtər/ *n* (*Greek myth*) a woodland god in human form but with goat's ears, tail, and legs; a man with strong sexual appetites; a man with satyriasis.—**satyric** *adj*.

satyriasis /ˌsætɪˈraɪəsɪs/ *n* excessive sexual desire in men.

sauce /sɒs/ *n* a liquid or dressing served with food to enhance its flavour; stewed or preserved fruit eaten with other food or as a dessert; (*inf*) impudence. • *vt* to season with sauce; to make piquant; (*sl*) to cheek.

saucepan /ˈsɒspæn/ *n* a deep cooking pan with a handle and lid.

saucer /ˈsɒsər/ *n* a round shallow dish placed under a cup; a shallow depression; a thing shaped like a saucer.

saucy /ˈsɒsi/ *adj* (**saucier, sauciest**) rude, impertinent; sprightly.—**saucily** *adv*.—**sauciness** *n*.

sauerkraut /ˈsauərˌkraʊt/ *n* a German dish of chopped pickled cabbage.

sauna /ˈsɒnə/ *n* exposure of the body to hot steam, followed by cold water; the room where this is done.

saunter /ˈsɒntər/ *vi* to walk in a leisurely or idle way. • *n* a stroll.—**saunterer** *n*.

-saur /sɔr/ *n* *suffix* (*scientific*) reptiles.

saurian /ˈsɔriən/ *adj* of or resembling a lizard. • *n* (*formerly*) lizard.

sauro- /ˈsɔroː/ *prefix* lizard.

saury /ˈsɔri/ *n* (*pl* **sauries**) an Atlantic fish with a long body and elongated jaws.

sausage /ˈsɒsɪdʒ/ *n* minced seasoned meat, *esp* pork, packed into animal gut or other casing.

sauté /ˈsɒteɪ/ or /-ˈteɪ/, /soː-/ *adj* fried quickly and lightly. • *vt* (**sautéing, sautéed**) to fry in a small amount of oil or fat. • *n* a sautéed dish.

sauve qui peut /səvkiˈpœ/ *n* a precipitate flight, a general stampede.

savage /'sævɪdʒ/ *adj* fierce; wild; untamed; uncivilized; ferocious; primitive. • *n* a member of a primitive society; a brutal, fierce person or animal.—**savagely** *adv*.—**savageness** *n*.

savagery /'sævədʒəri/ *n* (*pl* **savageries**) the state of being a savage; an act of violence or cruelty; an uncivilized state.

savanna, savannah /sə'vænə/ *n* a treeless plain; an area of tropical or subtropical grassland.

savant /sæ'vɑ̃/ or /-'vɑ̃t/ *n* (*pl* **savants**) a person with extensive knowledge, *esp* in a certain discipline.

savate /sə'væt/ *n* a form of boxing using both the fists and the feet.

save[1] /seɪv/ *vt* to rescue from harm or danger; to keep, to accumulate; to set aside for future use; to avoid the necessity of; (*energy etc*) to prevent waste of; (*theol*) to deliver from sin. • *vi* to avoid waste, expense, etc; to economize; to store up money or goods; (*sports*) to keep an opponent from scoring or winning. • *n* (*sports*) the act of preventing one's opponent from scoring.—**savable, saveable** *adj*.

save[2] *conj, prep* except, but.

saveloy /'sævə,lɔɪ/ *n* a type of highly-seasoned smoked sausage.

saver /'seɪvər/ *n* a person who saves money in a bank or building society.

savin, savine /'sævɪn/ *n* a small Eurasian juniper bush with dark fruit the oil from which was once used medicinally.

saving[1] /'seɪvɪŋ/ *adj* thrifty, economical; (*clause*) containing a reservation; redeeming. • *n* what is saved; (*pl*) money saved for future use.

saving[2] *prep* except; with apology to.

savings and loan association *n* a company that pays interest on deposits and issues loans to enable people to buy their own houses, a building society.

savings account *n* a bank account that earns interest.

savings bank *n* a bank receiving small deposits and holding them in interest-bearing accounts.

saviour, savior /'seɪvjər/ *n* a person who saves another from harm or danger; (*with cap*) Jesus Christ.

savory /'seɪvəri/ *n* (*pl* **savories**) any of various Mediterranean aromatic plants used as herbs for flavouring.

savoir-faire *n* the skill of knowing the right thing to do; tact.

savour, savor /'seɪvjər/ *n* the flavour or smell of something; a distinctive quality. • *vti* to season; to enjoy; to have a specified taste or smell; to smack (of); to appreciate critically.—**savourer, savorer** *n*.

savoury, savory /'seɪvəri/ *adj* having a good taste or smell; spicy, not sweet; reputable. • *n* (*pl* **savouries, savories**) a savoury dish at the beginning or end of dinner; (*pl*) snacks served with drinks.—**savourily, savorily** *adv*.—**savouriness, savoriness** *n*.

savoy (cabbage) /'sævɔɪ/ or /sə'vɔɪ/ *n* a variety of cabbage with wrinkled leaves.

savvy /'sævi/ *vti* (**savvying, savvied**) (*sl*) to understand. • *n* (*sl*) understanding, know-how. • *adj* (**savvier, savviest**) (*sl*) shrewd.

saw[1] *see* **see**[1].

saw[2] /sɒ/ *n* a tool with a toothed edge for cutting wood, etc. • *vti* (**sawing, sawed**, *pp* **sawed** *or* **sawn**) to cut or shape with a saw; to use a saw; to make a to-and-fro motion.—**sawer** *n*.

saw[3] *n* a wise saying, a proverb.

sawbill /'sɔbɪl/ *n* a large, diving, fish-eating duck with a long narrow bill with serrated edges.

sawbones /'sɒbo:nz/ *n* (*sl*) a doctor or surgeon.

sawbuck /'sɒbʌk/ *n* a sawhorse.

sawdust /'sɒdʌst/ *n* fine particles of wood caused by sawing.

sawed-off *see* **sawn-off**.

sawfish /'sɒfɪʃ/ *n* (*pl* **sawfish, sawfishes**) a large ray with a serrated snout.

sawfly /'sɒflaɪ/ *n* (*pl* **sawflies**) any of various insects with a sawlike ovipositor.

sawhorse /'sɒhɔrs/ *n* a trestle, etc on which wood is laid for sawing.

sawmill /'sɒmɪl/ *n* a mill where timber is cut into logs or planks.

sawn *see* **saw**[2].

sawn-off *adj* (*shotgun*) having the barrel shortened to aid concealment; (*person*) (*sl*) small.—*also* **sawed-off**.

saw set /sɒ'set/ *n* an instrument for setting the teeth of a saw by bending each tooth to the left or right alternately.

sawyer /'sɔɪər/ or /'sɒjər/ *n* a person employed to saw timber.

sax /sæks/ *n* saxophone.

saxatile /'sæksə,taɪl/ or /-tɪl/ *adj* saxicolous.

saxe blue /,sæks'blu:/ *n* a light greyish-blue.—*also adj*.

saxhorn /'sækshɔrn/ *n* a brass musical instrument resembling a tuba.

saxicolous /sæk'sɪkə,ləs/, **saxicoline** /sæk'sɪkə,laɪn/ *adj* living among or on rocks.

saxifrage /'sæksɪfreɪdʒ/ or /-frədʒ/ *n* any of a genus of plants with small flowers and tufted leaves, popular in rock gardens.

Saxon /'sæksən/ *adj, n* (of) a member of a North German people that settled the southern part of Britain in the 5th-6th century.

saxony /'sæksəni/ *n* a fine wool; cloth made from it.

saxophone /'sæksə,fo:n/ *n* a brass wind instrument with a single reed and about twenty finger-keys.—**saxophonic** *adj*.—**saxophonist** *n*.

say /seɪ/ *vb* (**says, saying, said**) *vt* to speak, to utter; to state in words; to affirm, declare; to recite; to estimate; to assume. • *vi* to tell; to express in words. • *n* (*pl* **says**) the act of uttering; the right or opportunity to speak; a share in a decision. • *adv* for example. • *interj* expressing admiration, surprise, etc.

saying /'seɪɪŋ/ *n* a common remark; a proverb or adage.

say-so *n* (*inf*) an unfounded assertion; an authorization; the right to authorize.

sayyid, sayid /'seɪɪd/ *n* a Muslim title of respect applied to descendants of Mohammed's daughter Fatima.

Sb (*chem symbol*) antimony.

Sc (*chem symbol*) scandium.

sc. *abbr* = scene; science; scilicet; (*weight*) scruple; (*print*) small capitals.

scab /skæb/ *n* a dry crust on a wound or sore; a plant disease characterized by crustaceous spots; a worker who refuses to join a strike or who replaces a striking worker. • *vi* (**scabbing, scabbed**) to form a scab; to be covered with scabs; to work as a scab.—**scabby** *adj*.

scabbard /'skæbərd/ *n* a sheath for a sword or dagger. • *vt* to sheathe.

scabies /'skeɪbi:z/ *n* a contagious, itching skin disease.

scabiosa /skæbi'o:sə/ *n* any of a genus of Mediterranean plants with tightly clustered blue, red or white flowers.—*also* **scabious**.

scabious[1] /'skeɪbɪəs/ *adj* covered with scabs; of or resembling scabies.

scabious[2] *n* a scabiosa.

scabrous /'skæbrəs/ *adj* (*surface*) rough, scaly; indecent, offensive; intractable, difficult to manage.—**scabrously** *adv*.—**scabrousness** *n*.

scaffold /'skæfo:ld/ or /-fəld/ *n* a raised platform for the execution of a criminal; capital punishment; scaffolding.

scaffolding /'skæfo:ldɪŋ/ or /-fəldɪŋ/ *n* a temporary framework of wood and metal for use by workmen constructing a building, etc; materials for a scaffold.

scalable /'skeɪləbəl/ *adj* able to be scaled or climbed.

scalar /'skeɪlər/ *n* (*math*) having magnitude but not direction. • *n* a scalar quantity, *eg* time, mass.

scalar product *n* a scalar produced by multiplying together the magnitudes of two vectors and the cosine of the angle between them.

scald /skɒld/ *vt* to burn with hot liquid or steam; to heat almost to boiling point; to immerse in boiling water (to sterilize). • *n* an injury caused by hot liquid or steam.

scale[1] /skeɪl/ *n* (*pl*) a machine or instrument for weighing; one of the pans or the tray of a set of scales; (*pl*) (*with cap*) Libra, the seventh sign of the zodiac. • *vti* to weigh in a set of scales; to have a specified weight on a set of scales.

scale[2] *n* one of the thin plates covering a fish or reptile; a flake (of dry skin); an incrustation on teeth, etc. • *vti* to remove the scales from; to flake off.

scale[3] *n* a graduated measure; an instrument so marked; (*math*) the basis for a numerical system, 10 being that in general use; (*mus*) a series of tones from the keynote to its octave, in order of pitch; the proportion that a map, etc, bears to what it represents; a series of degrees classified by size, amount, etc; relative scope or size. • *vt* (*wall*) to go up or over; (*model*) to make or draw to scale; to increase or decrease in size.

scaled /'skeɪld/ *adj* (*reptile, etc*) covered with or having scales.

scale insect *n* any of various small insects that feed on host plants and secrete a waxy covering for protection.

scalene /skeɪ'li:n/ or /skeɪ'li:n/ *adj* (*geom*) having three sides of unequal length. • *n* a scalene triangle.

scallion /'skæljən/ n a young onion with a small bulb and long shoots eaten raw in salads, a spring onion or shallot.

scallop /'skæləp/ or /'skɒləp/ n an edible shellfish with two fluted, fan-shaped shells; one of a series of curves in an edging. • vt to cut into scallops.—**scalloped** adj.

scallywag /'skælə,wæg/ n (inf) a rascal; a scamp; a Southern white who supported the Republicans after the American Civil War.—also **scalawag, scallawag**.

scalp /skælp/ n the skin covering the skull, usu covered with hair. • vti to cut the scalp from; to criticize sharply; (inf) (tickets, etc) to buy and resell at higher prices.

scalpel /'skælpəl/ n a short, thin, very sharp knife used esp for surgery.

scaly /'skeɪli/ adj (**scalier, scaliest**) (reptile etc) like or covered with scales.—**scaliness** n.

scaly anteater n a pangolin.

scamp /skæmp/ n a rascal; a mischievous child.

scamper /'skæmpər/ vi to run away quickly or playfully. • n a brisk or playful run or movement.

scampi /'skæmpi/ n a dish of large shrimps or prawns cooked in breadcrumbs or prepared with a flavoured dressing.

scan /skæn/ vb (**scanning, scanned**) vt (page etc) to look through quickly; to scrutinize; (med) to examine with a radiological device; (TV) to pass an electronic beam over; (radar) to detect with an electronic beam; (poem) to conform to a rhythmical pattern; to check for recorded data by means of a mechanical or electronic device; (human body) to make a scan of in a scanner. • vi to analyse the pattern of verse. • n the act of scanning or an instance of being scanned.

scandal /'skændəl/ n a disgraceful event or action; talk arising from immoral behaviour; a feeling of moral outrage; the thing or person causing this; disgrace; malicious gossip.

scandalize /-aɪz/ vt to shock the moral feelings of; to defame.—**scandalization** n.—**scandalizer** n.

scandalmonger /'skændəl,mʌŋgər/ or /-,mʌŋgər/ n a person who spreads scandal or malicious gossip.—**scandalmongering** n.

scandalous /'skændələs/ adj causing scandal; shameful; spreading slander.—**scandalously** adv.—**scandalousness** n.

Scandinavian /,skændi'neiviən/ adj of or pertaining to Scandinavia, the region comprising Norway, Sweden, and Denmark, and sometimes Iceland, or its people. • n a native or inhabitant of Scandinavia.

scandium /,skændiəm/ n a rare metallic element present in small quantities in various minerals.

scanner /'skænər/ n a person or thing that scans; an electronic device that monitors or scans; a device for receiving or transmitting radar signals; a device for scanning the human body to obtain an image of an internal part.

scanning electron microscope n an electron microscope which scans an object to produce a three-dimensional image.

scansion /'skænʃən/ n the analysis of verse to show its metre.

scant /skænt/ adj limited; meagre; insufficient; scanty; grudging.

scantling /'skæntlɪŋ/ n a small piece of timber; the dimensions of timber and stone for a building or of a component for a ship or aircraft; a small quantity.

scanty /'skænti/ adj (**scantier, scantiest**) barely adequate; insufficient; small.—**scantily** adv.—**scantiness** n.

scapegoat /'skeɪpgoːt/ n a person who bears the blame for others; one who is the object of irrational hostility.

scapegrace /'skeɪpgreɪs/ n a graceless, hare-brained person; an incorrigible scamp.

scapula /'skæpjulə/ n (pl **scapulae**) the shoulder blade.

scapular /'skæpjulər/ adj of or relating to the scapula. • n a monastic robe worn in various Christian religious orders, consisting of a wide piece of cloth worn over the shoulders and hanging down at the front and back; any of the feathers along the base of a bird's wing.

scar[1] /skɑr/ n a mark left after the healing of a wound or sore; a blemish resulting from damage or wear. • vti (**scarring, scarred**) to mark with or form a scar.

scar[2] n a protruding or isolated rock; a precipitous crag; a rocky part of a hillside.

scarab /'skærəb/ or /'skæ-/ n a dung-beetle held to be sacred in ancient Egypt; a gem or seal in the shape of this.

scarabaeid /,skærə'biːɪd/ n any of a family of beetles including the dung beetle.—also adj.

scarce /skers/ adj not in abundance; hard to find; rare.—**scarceness** n.

scarcely /'skersli/ adv hardly, only just; probably not or certainly not.

scarcity /'skersiti/ n (**scarcities**) the state of being scarce; a dearth, deficiency.

scare /sker/ vti to startle; to frighten or become frightened; to drive away by frightening. • n a sudden fear; a period of general fear; a false alarm.

scarecrow /'skerkroː/ n a wooden figure dressed in clothes for scaring birds from crops; a thin or tattered person; something frightening but harmless.

scaremonger /'sker,mʌŋgər/ or /-mʌŋgər/ n a person who causes fear or panic by spreading rumours; an alarmist.

scarf /skɑrf/ n (pl **scarves**) a rectangular or square piece of cloth worn around the neck, shoulders or head for warmth or decoration.

scarfskin /'skɑrfskɪn/ n the outer layer of skin; cuticle.

scarify /'skerɪ,faɪ/ or /'skæ-/ vt (**scarifying, scarified**) to make cuts in, to scratch; to criticize savagely; to loosen the surface of (soil); to hasten germination by softening the wall (of a hard seed).—**scarification** n.

scarlatina /,skɑrlə'tiːnə/ n scarlet fever.

scarlet /'skɑrlət/ n a bright red with a tinge of orange; scarlet cloth or clothes. • adj scarlet coloured; immoral or sinful.

scarlet fever n an acute contagious disease marked by a sore throat, fever, and a scarlet rash.

scarlet pimpernel n a plant with red, purple or white flowers that close in dull weather.

scarlet runner n a climbing bean plant with scarlet flowers and elongated edible pods.—also **runner bean**.

scarlet woman n (arch) a prostitute.

scarp /skɑrp/ n a low steep slope; the inner face of a ditch in a fortification.

scarper /'skɑrpər/ vi (inf) to run away.

scarves see scarf.

scary /'skeri/ adj (**scarier, scariest**) frightening, alarming.—**scariness** n.

scat[1] /skæt/ vi (**scatting, scatted**) (inf) to leave hastily.

scat[2] n (jazz) a form of improvised singing without words. • vi (**scatting, scatted**) to sing in this way.

scathing /'skeɪðɪŋ/ adj bitterly critical; cutting, withering.—**scathingly** adv.

scatology /skə'tɒlədʒi/ n the scientific study of fossil and human excrement; a preoccupation with excrement or obscenity.—**scatological** adj.

scatter /'skætər/ vti to throw loosely about; to sprinkle; to dissipate; to put or take to flight; to disperse; to occur at random. • n a scattering or sprinkling.

scatterbrain /'skætər,breɪn/ n a frivolous, heedless person.—**scatterbrained** adj.

scattered /'skætər,breɪn/ adj dispersed widely, spaced out; straggling.

scattering /'skætərɪŋ/ n a small amount spread over a large area; a dispersion.

scatty /'skæti/ adj (**scattier, scattiest**) (inf) thoughtless, absent-minded, crazy.—**scattily** adv.—**scattiness** n.

scaup (duck) /skɒp/ n a diving duck of Europe and America.

scavenge /'skævəndʒ/ vi to gather things discarded by others; (animal) to eat decaying matter.—**scavenger** n.

ScD abbr = Doctor of Science.

scenario /sə'nerioː/ or /-'ɑrioː/ n (pl **scenarios**) an outline of events, real or imagined; the plot or script of a film, etc.

scene /siːn/ n the place in which anything occurs; the place in which the action of a play or a story occurs; a section of a play, a division of an act; the stage of a theatre; a painted screen, etc, used on this; an unseemly display of strong emotion; a landscape; surroundings; a place of action; (inf) an area of interest or activity (eg the music scene).

scene dock n (theatre) a storage area for scenery near the stage.

scenery /'siːnəri/ n (pl **sceneries**) painted screens, etc, used to represent places, as in a play, film, etc; an aspect of a landscape, esp of beautiful or impressive countryside.

scenic /'siːnɪk/ adj relating to natural scenery; picturesque; of or used on the stage.—**scenically** adv.

scenic railway n a miniature railway at an amusement park, etc.

scent /sɛnt/ *n* a perfume; an odour left by an animal, by which it can be tracked; the sense of smell; a line of pursuit or discovery. • *vt* to recognize by the sense of smell; to track by smell; to impart an odour to, to perfume; to get wind of, to detect.

scented /'sɛntəd/ *adj* perfumed.

sceptic *n* a person who questions opinions generally accepted; a person who doubts religious dectrines, an agnostic; an adherent of scepticism.—also **skeptic**.

sceptical *adj* doubting; questioning.—*also* **skeptical**.—**sceptically, skeptically** *adv*.

scepticism *n* an attitude of questioning criticism, doubt; (*philos*) the doctrine that absolute knowledge is unattainable.—*also* **skepticism**.

sceptre, scepter /'sɛptər/ *n* the staff of office held by a monarch on a ceremonial occasion; sovereignty.

schedule /'skɛdʒʊəl/ or /'skɛdʒuːl/, /'ʃɛdjuːl/, /'ʃɛdʒuːl/ *n* a timetable; a list, inventory or tabulated statement; a timed plan for a project. • *vt* to make a schedule; to plan.

scheelite /'ʃiːlaɪt/ *n* a mineral consisting of calcium tungstate.

schema /'skiːmə/ *n* (*pl* **schemata**) a plan or diagram.

schematic /ski:'mætɪk/ or /skɪ-/ *adj* of or like a scheme or diagram.—**schematically** *adv*.

schematize /'skiːmətaɪz/ *vt* to form into or express as a scheme.—**schematization** *n*.

scheme /skiːm/ *n* a plan; a project; a systematic arrangement; a diagram; an underhand plot. • *vti* to devise or plot.—**schemer** *n*.

scheming /'skiːmɪŋ/ *adj* cunning, intriguing.

scherzando /skɛrt'sændoʊ/ *adj, adv* (*mus*) to be performed lightheartedly. • *n* (*pl* **scherzandi**) a piece of music played in this manner.

scherzo /'skɛrtsoʊ/ *n* (*pl* **scherzos, scherzi**) a lively musical passage or movement, *usu* in triple time.

schilling /'ʃɪlɪŋ/ *n* the standard monetary unit of Austria.

schism /'skɪzəm/ *n* a division or separation into two parties, *esp* of a church; the sin of this; discord, disharmony.

schismatic /skɪz'mætɪk/, **schismatical** /-kəl/ *adj* of or creating schism. • *n* a person who creates schism or supports schism.—**schismatically** *adv*.

schist /ʃɪst/ *n* a type of crystalline rock in thin layers.—**schistose** *adj*.

schistosome /'ʃɪstəˌsoʊm/ *n* any of a genus of parasitic worms that infest the blood vessels of humans and animals.

schistosomiasis /ˌʃɪstəsoʊ'maɪəsɪs/ *n* a disease caused by infestation with schistosomes.

schizo /'skɪtsoʊ/ *n* (*pl* **schizos**) (*inf*) a schizophrenic person. • *adj* schizophrenic.

schizo- /'skɪtsoʊ/, **schiz-** /skɪts/ *prefix* split, division.

schizocarp /'skɪtsəˌkɑrp/ *n* a dry fruit that splits into single-seeded parts.

schizoid /'skɪtsɔɪd/ *adj* mildly schizophrenic.—*also n*.

schizomycete /'skɪtsəməˌsiːt/ *n* any microscopic organism such as a bacterium.

schizophrenia /skɪtsoʊ'friːniə/ or /-'friːnjə/ *n* a mental disorder characterized by withdrawal from reality and deterioration of the personality; the presence of mutually contradictory qualities or parts.—**schizophrenic** *adj, n*.

schlieren /'ʃliːrən/ *n* (*physics*) visible streaks in a transparent medium caused by variations in its density.

schmaltz, schmalz /ʃmɒlts/ *n* overly sentimental music, art, film, etc.—**schmaltzy, schmalzy** *adj*.

schnapps /ʃnæps/ or /ʃnɒps/ *n* (*pl* **schnapps**) a Dutch spirit distilled from potatoes; (*Germany*) any strong spirit.

schnauzer /'ʃnaʊzər/ or /'ʃnʊtsər/ *n* an orig German breed of terrier with a short wiry coat.

schnitzel /'ʃnɪtsəl/ *n* a cutlet of veal.

schnorkle *see* **snorkel**.

schnozzle /'ʃnɒzəl/ *n* (*sl*) nose.

scholar /'skɒlər/ *n* a pupil, a student; a learned person; the holder of a scholarship.

scholarly /-li/ *adj* learned, erudite, academic.

scholarship /'skɒlərʃɪp/ *n* an annual grant to a scholar or student, *usu* won by competitive examination; learning, academic achievement.

scholastic /skə'læstɪk/ *adj* of or relating to schools, scholars, or education; academic.—**scholastically** *adv*.

school[1] /skuːl/ *n* a shoal of porpoises, whales, or other aquatic animals of one kind swimming together.

school[2] *n* an educational establishment; its teachers and students; a regular session of teaching; formal education, schooling; a particular division of a university; a place or means of discipline; a group of thinkers, artists, writers, holding similar principles. • *vt* to train; to teach; to control or discipline.

schoolboy /'skuːlbɔɪ/ *n* a boy who attends school.

schoolchild /'skuːltʃaɪld/ *n* (*pl* **schoolchildren**) a child who attends school.

schoolgirl /'skuːlɡɜrl/ *n* a girl who attends school.

schoolhouse /'skuːlhɵʊs/ *n* a building used as a school.

schooling /'skuːlɪŋ/ *n* instruction in school.

schoolmaster /'skuːlˌmæstər/ *n* a man who teaches in school.

schoolmate /'skuːlmeɪt/ *n* a companion at school.—*also* **schoolfellow**.

schoolmistress /'skuːlˌmɪstrəs/ *n* a woman who teaches in school.

schoolroom /'skuːlruːm/ *n* a room in which pupils are taught, as in a school.

schoolteacher /'skuːlˌtiːtʃər/ *n* a person who teaches in school.

schooner /'skuːnər/ *n* a sailing ship with two or more masts rigged with fore-and-aft sails; a large drinking glass for sherry or beer.

schottische /ʃɒ'tiːʃ/ *n* (music for) a type of slow dance resembling a polka.

schuss /ʃʊs/ *n* (*skiing*) a fast straight downhill run. • *vi* to ski down this.

sci. *abbr* = science; scientific.

sciatic /saɪ'ætɪk/ *adj* of the hip.

sciatica /saɪ'ætɪkə/ *n* pain along the sciatic nerve, *esp* in the back of the thigh; (*loosely*) pain in the lower back or adjacent parts.

sciatic nerve *n* a long nerve running from the pelvic region to the back of the thigh.

science /'saɪəns/ *n* knowledge gained by systematic experimentation and analysis, and the formulation of general principles; a branch of this; skill or technique.

science fiction *n* highly imaginative fiction typically involving actual or projected scientific phenomena.

science park *n* an area where scientific discoveries are translated into commercial products and applications.

scientific /ˌsaɪən'tɪfɪk/ *adj* of or concerned with science; based on or using the principles and methods of science; systematic and exact; having or showing expert skill.—**scientifically** *adv*.

scientism /'saɪənˌtɪzəm/ *n* the use of scientific methods; the inappropriate use of or reliance on scientific methods.

scientist /'saɪəntɪst/ *n* a specialist in a branch of science, as in chemistry, etc.

Scientology /ˌsaɪən'tɒlədʒi/ *n* (*trademark*) a religious philosophy founded by L. Ron Hubbard in 1951.

sci-fi /'saɪfaɪ/ or /saɪ'faɪ/ *n* science fiction.

scilicet /'sɪləˌsɛt/ *adv* namely, that is to say.

scilla /'sɪlə/ *n* any of a genus of plants with small pink, blue or white flowers grown from bulbs.

scimitar /'sɪmɪtər/ *n* an Oriental curved sword, broadest near the point.

scintigraphy /sɪn'tɪɡrəfi/ *n* the production of images of internal body parts by detecting high-energy particles from a radioactive tracer administered to a patient.

scintilla /sɪn'tɪlə/ *n* an iota, tiny amount.

scintillate /'sɪntɪˌleɪt/ *vti* to give off sparks; to sparkle.—**scintillation** *n*.

scintillating /-ɪŋ/ *adj* sparkling; amusing.

scintillation counter *n* an instrument for registering the intensity of a radioactive source by recording the flashes of light produced by the impact of emitted photons on a phospor.

scion /'saɪən/ *n* a shoot for grafting; a young member of a family, a descendant.

scirrhus /'sɪrəs/ or /'skɪ-/ *n* (*pl* **scirrhi, scirrhuses**) a cancerous tumour consisting of fibrous tissue.

scission /'sɪʃən/ *n* the act of cutting or dividing; a cut, divide, or split.

scissor /'sɪzər/ *vt* to cut with scissors, to clip. • *npl* a tool for cutting paper, hair, etc, consisting of two fastened pivoted blades whose edges slide past each other; a gymnastic feat in which the leg movements resemble the opening and closing of scissors.

scissors kick *n* (*swimming*) a kick in which the legs move from the hip in a scissoring motion.

sciurine /'saɪəˌrin/ *adj* of or resembling a family of rodents which include squirrels and marmots.

sclera /'sklɪərə/ *n* the opaque outer covering of the eyeball excluding the cornea.

sclerenchyma /sklɪˈrɛŋkɪmə/ *n* a tissue forming the hard fibrous parts of plants.

sclero- /ˈsklɛroː/, **scler-** /sklɛr/ *prefix* hardness.

scleroderma /skliːrəˈdɜːmə/ or /sklɛr-/ *n* (*med*) a chronic disease in women causing thickening and hardening of the skin.

sclerodermatous /-təs/ *adj* (*zool*) covered with a hard layer of tissue, *eg* scales.

sclerosis /sklɔˈroːsɪs/ *n* a pathological hardening of body tissue; a disease marked by this.

sclerotic /sklɔˈrɒtɪk/ *adj* pertaining to the sclera; of or affected by sclerosis. • *n* the sclera.

sclerous /ˈskliːrəs/ or /ˈsklɛr-/ *adj* hard, bony.

scoff[1] /skɒf/ *vti* to jeer (at) or mock. • *n* an expression or object of derision; mocking words, a taunt.

scoff[2] *vt* (*sl*) to eat quickly and greedily.

scold /skoːld/ *vi* to reprove angrily; to tell off.

scolding /-ɪŋ/ *n* a harsh reprimand.

scoliosis /ˌskoːliˈoːsɪs/ *n* (*med*) lateral curvature of the spine.

scollop *see* **scallop**.

scombroid /ˈskɒmbrɔɪd/ *n* any member of a suborder of spiny-finned marine fishes used for food, such as the mackerel and tuna.—*also adj.*

sconce[1] /skɒns/ *n* a bracket on a wall for holding candles or electric lights.

sconce[2] *n* a defensive fortification, a bulwark.

scone /skuːn/ *n* a small, round cake made from flour and fat which is baked and spread with butter, etc.

scoop /skuːp/ *n* a small shovel-like utensil as for taking up flour, ice cream, etc; the bucket of a dredge, etc; the act of scooping or the amount scooped up at one time; (*inf*) a piece of exclusive news; (*inf*) the advantage gained in being the first to publish or broadcast this. • *vt* to shovel, lift or hollow out with a scoop; (*inf*) to obtain as a scoop; (*inf: rival newspaper etc*) to forestall with a news item.

scoot /skuːt/ *vti* to run quickly; to hurry (off).

scooter /ˈskuːtər/ *n* a child's two-wheeled vehicle with a footboard and steering handle; a motor scooter.

scope /skoːp/ *n* the opportunity to use one's abilities; extent; range; an instrument for viewing.

scopolamine /skəˈpɒləˌmiːn/ *n* an alkaloid extracted from certain plants, used as a sedative and for travel sickness.—*also* **hyoscine**.

scorbutic /skɔrˈbjuːtɪk/ *adj* of, suffering from, or resembling scurvy.—**scorbutically** *adv*.

scorch /skɔrtʃ/ *vti* to burn or be burned on the surface; to wither from over-exposure to heat; to singe; (*inf*) to drive or cycle furiously.

scorcher /ˈskɔrtʃər/ *n* (*inf*) a very hot day.

scorching /-ɪŋ/ *adj* (*inf: weather*) very hot; scathing.

score /skɔr/ *n* the total number of points made in a game or examination; a notch or scratch; a line indicating deletion or position; a group of twenty; a written copy of a musical composition showing the different parts; the music composed for a film; a grievance for settling; a reason or motive; (*inf*) the real facts; a bill or reckoning; (*pl*) an indefinite, large number. • *vt* to mark with cuts; (*mus*) to arrange in a score, to orchestrate; to gain or record points, as in a game; to evaluate in testing. • *vi* to make points, as in a game; to keep the score of a game; to gain an advantage, a success, etc; (*sl*) to be successful in seduction; (*with* **off**) to get the better of someone.—**scorer** *n*.

scoreboard /ˈskɔrbɔrd/ *n* a large manually or electronically operated board showing the score in a game or match.

scorecard /ˈskɔrkɑrd/ *n* (*golf, etc*) a card on which scores are recorded.

scorn /skɔrn/ *n* extreme contempt or disdain; the object of this. • *vt* to treat with contempt, to despise; to reject or refuse as unworthy.—**scornful** *adj*.—**scornfully** *adv*.

Scorpio /ˌskɔrpioː/ *n* the eighth sign of the zodiac in astrology, operative October 23-November 21.—**Scorpionic** *adj*.

scorpion /ˈskɔrpiən/ *n* a small, tropical, insect-like animal with pincers and a jointed tail with a poisonous sting.

scorpion fish *n* any of a genus of fish with poisonous spines on the dorsal fins.

Scot /skɒt/ *n* a native or inhabitant of Scotland; a member of a Celtic people from Ireland who settled in northern Britain in the 5th-6th centuries.

scotch /skɒtʃ/ *vt* (*a rumour*) to stamp out.

Scotch[1] *adj* another word for Scottish.

Scotch[2] *n* whisky made in Scotland.

Scotch broth *n* a thick soup made from beef or mutton with vegetables and pearl barley.

Scotch egg *n* a hard-boiled egg enclosed in sausagemeat, coated in breadcrumbs, and fried.

Scotchman /ˈskɒtʃmən/ *n* (*pl* **Scotchmen**) another word for Scotsman.—**Scotchwoman** (*pl* **Scotchwomen**) *nf*.

Scotch mist *n* a dense, wet mist; fine drizzle.

Scotch terrier *n* another name for a Scottish terrier.

scoter /ˈskoːtər/ *n* (*pl* **scoters, scoter**) a large sea duck with black plumage.

scot-free *adj* without penalty or injury.

Scotland Yard /ˈskɒtlənd/ *n* the headquarters of the London metropolitan police force.

scotoma /skɒˈtoːmə/ *n* (*pl* **scotomas, scotomata**) a blind spot in the visual field.

Scots /skɒts/ *adj* of or pertaining to Scotland, its law, money, and people, and the Scots language. • *n* the dialect of English developed in Lowland Scotland.

Scotsman /ˈskɒtsmən/ *n* (*pl* **Scotsmen**) a native or inhabitant of Scotland.—**Scotswoman** *n* (*pl* **Scotswomen**) *nf*.

Scots pine /-paɪn/ *n* (the wood of) a European pine with needle-like leaves.

Scotticism /ˈskɒtɪˌsɪzəm/ *n* a Scottish word or idiom.

Scottie /ˈskɒti/ *n* (*inf*) a Scottish terrier.

Scottish /ˈskɒtɪʃ/ *adj* of or relating to Scotland and its people.

Scottish deerhound *n* a large rough-haired greyhound, a deerhound.

Scottish National Party *n* a political party seeking independence for Scotland.

Scottish terrier *n* a small terrier with short legs and a wiry coat.

scoundrel /ˈskaundrəl/ *n* a rascal; a dishonest person.

scour[1] /ˈskaur/ *vt* to clean by rubbing with an abrasive cloth; to flush out with a current of water; to purge. • *n* the act or process of scouring; a place scoured by running water; scouring action (as of a glacier); damage done by scouring action.

scour[2] *vt* to hasten over or along, to range over, *esp* in search or pursuit.

scourge /skɔrdʒ/ *n* a whip; a means of inflicting punishment; a person who harasses and causes widespread and great affliction; a pest. • *vt* to flog; to punish harshly.

Scouse /skaus/ *n* (*inf*) a person from Liverpool; the dialect of Liverpool.—*also adj.*

scout /skaut/ *n* a person, plane, etc, sent to observe the enemy's strength, etc; a person employed to find new talent or survey a competitor, etc; (*with cap*) a member of the Scouting Association, an organization for young people. • *vti* to reconnoitre; to go in search of (something).

scouting /skautɪŋ/ *n* the act of one who scouts; (*with cap*) the activities of the Scouting Association.

Scouting Association *n* (*formerly* Boy Scouts, Girl Guides) an organization to develop in young people self-reliance and initiative, moral and physical courage and a courteous spirit.

scoutmaster /ˈskautˌmæstər/ *n* (*formerly*) the adult leader of a troop of Scouts.

scow /skau/ *n* an unpowered flat-bottomed boat for carrying freight, refuse, etc.

scowl /skaul/ *n* a contraction of the brows in an angry or threatening manner; a sullen expression. • *vi* to make a scowl; to look sullen.

Scrabble /ˈskræbəl/ *n* (*trademark*) a game in which words are formed from individual lettered tiles on a grid.

scrabble *vi* to scratch or grope about; to struggle; to scramble. • *n* a repeated scratching or clawing; a scramble; a scribble.

scrag /skræg/ *n* a scrawny person or animal; the lean end of a neck of mutton or veal; (*loosely*) neck.

scraggly /ˈskrægli/ *adj* (**scragglier, scraggliest**) untidy, uneven.

scraggy /ˈskrægi/ *adj* (**scraggier, scraggiest**) thin and bony, gaunt.

scram /skræm/ *vi* (**scramming, scrammed**) (*sl*) to get out, to go away at once.

scramble /ˈskræmbəl/ *vi* to move or climb hastily on all fours; to scuffle or struggle for something; to move with urgency or panic. • *vt* to mix haphazardly; to stir (slightly beaten eggs) while cooking; (*transmitted signals*) to make unintelligible in transit. • *n* a hard climb or advance; a disorderly struggle; a rapid emergency take-off of fighter planes; a motorcycle rally over rough ground.—**scrambler** *n*.

scrap¹ /skræp/ *n* a small piece; a fragment of discarded material; (*pl*) bits of food. • *adj* in the form of pieces, leftovers, etc; used and discarded. • *vt* (**scrapping, scrapped**) to discard; to make into scraps.

scrap² *n* (*inf*) a fight or quarrel. • *vi* (**scrapping, scrapped**) to have a scrap.

scrapbook /'skræpbʊk/ *n* a book for pasting clippings, etc, in.

scrape /skreɪp/ *vt* to rub with a sharp or abrasive object so as to clean, smooth or remove; to eke out or to be economical; to amass in small portions; to draw along with a grating or vibration; to get narrowly past, to graze; to draw back the foot in making a bow; (*with* **together**) to save or collect with difficulty. • *vi* (*with* **through**) to manage or succeed with difficulty or by a slim margin. • *n* the act of scraping; a grating sound; an abrasion, scratch; an awkward predicament.

scraper /'skreɪpər/ *n* an instrument for scraping; a grating or edge for scraping mud from boots.

scraperboard /'skræpbɔrd/ *n* a board with a black surface which can be scraped off with a special tool to form a design.

scrapheap *n* a pile of discarded material or things.

scraping /'skreɪpɪŋ/ *n* a piece scraped off.

scrappy /'skræpi/ *adj* (**scrappier, scrappiest**) disjointed; fragmentary; full of gaps.—**scrappily** *adv*.—**scrappiness** *n*.

scratch /skrætʃ/ *vt* to mark with a sharp point; to scrape with the nails or claws; to rub to relieve an itch; to chafe; to write awkwardly; (*writing etc*) to strike out; to withdraw from a race, etc. • *vi* to use nails or claws to tear or dig. • *n* the act of scratching; a mark or sound made by this; a slight injury; a starting line for a race; a scribble. • *adj* taken at random, haphazard, impromptu; without a handicap.

scratch pad *n* a notebook.

scratch video *n* a collage of images from existing television or cinema film.

scratchy /'skrætʃi/ *adj* (**scratchier, scratchiest**) making a scratching noise; uneven, ragged.—**scratchily** *adv*.—**scratchiness** *n*.

scrawl /skrɒl/ *n* careless or illegible handwriting; a scribble. • *vti* to draw or write carelessly.

scrawny /'skrɔni/ *adj* (**scrawnier, scrawniest**) skinny; bony.—**scrawniness** *n*.

scream /skriːm/ *vti* to utter a piercing cry, as of pain, fear, etc; to shout; to shriek. • *n* a sharp, piercing cry; (*inf*) a very funny person or thing.

scree /skriː/ *n* loose shifting stones; a slope covered with these.

screech /skriːtʃ/ *n* a harsh, high-pitched cry. • *vti* to utter a screech, to shriek.

screed /skriːd/ *n* a long, tedious letter or speech; an informal piece of writing.

screen /skriːn/ *n* a movable partition or framework to conceal, divide, or protect; a shelter or shield from heat, danger or view; an electronic display (as in a television set, computer terminal, etc); a surface on which films, slides, etc are projected; the motion picture industry; a coarse wire mesh over a window or door to keep out insects; a sieve. • *vt* to conceal or shelter; to grade by passing through a screen; to separate according to skill, etc; (*a film*) to show on a screen.

screening /'skriːnɪŋ/ *n* a showing of a film; a metal or plastic mesh, as for window screens; the refuse matter after sieving.

screenplay /'skriːnpleɪ/ *n* a story written in a form suitable for a film.

screenwriter /ˌskriːnˌraɪtər/ *n* a person who writes screenplays.

screw /skruː/ *n* a metal cylinder or cone with a spiral thread around it for fastening things by being turned; any spiral thing like this; a twist or turn of a screw; a twist of paper; pressure; a propeller with revolving blades on a shaft. • *vt* to fasten, tighten etc with a screw; to oppress; to extort, to cheat out of something due; (*sl, vulg*) to have sexual intercourse with; (*with* **up**) to gather (courage, etc). • *vi* to go together or come apart by being turned like a screw; to twist or turn with a writhing movement; (*sl, vulg*) to have sexual intercourse; (*with* **up**) to bungle.

screwball /'skruːbɔl/ *n* (*sl*) an odd or eccentric person. • *adj* whimsical, zany.

screwdriver /'skruːdraɪvər/ *n* a tool like a blunt chisel for turning screws; a drink of vodka and orange juice.

screwed /skruːd/ *adj* fastened by a screw; (*sl*) drunk.

screw eye *n* a metal screw with a ring instead of a slotted head.

screw pine *n* any of various tropical plants with slender stems and clusters of spiral leaves.

screw propeller *n* an early form of propeller based on the Archimedes screw.

screw top *n* a cap that screws onto the top of a bottle or other container; a bottle, etc having this.

screwy /'skruːi/ *adj* (**screwier, screwiest**) (*sl*) eccentric, odd.—**screwiness** *n*.

scribble /'skrɪbəl/ *vti* to draw or write hastily or carelessly, to scrawl; to be a writer. • *n* hasty writing, a scrawl.—**scribbler** *n*.

scribe /skraɪb/ *n* a person who copies (documents); an author or journalist; (*Bible*) an expounder of Jewish law. • *vt* to draw a line on by cutting with a pointed instrument.

scriber /'skraɪbər/ *n* a pointed tool used to score or mark lines (e.g on metal) as guides for cutting.

scrim /skrɪm/ *n* a light open-weave fabric used in upholstery, lining, and theatre sets.

scrimmage /'skrɪmɪdʒ/ *n* a confused struggle; a skirmish; (*football*) the period between the ball entering play and it being declared dead. • *vi* to engage in a scrimmage.

scrimp /skrɪmp/ *vti* to be sparing or frugal (with); to make too small, to skimp.

scrimshank /'skrɪmʃæŋk/ *vi* (*inf*) to shirk work, *esp* military duties.

scrimshaw /'skrɪmʃɔ/ *n* carvings made from shells, whalebone, ivory, etc, *usu* by sailors; the art of producing such carvings.

scrip /skrɪp/ *n* a written list; a certificate entitling the holder to a share of company stock.

Script. *abbr* = Scripture(s).

script /skrɪpt/ *n* handwriting; a style of writing; the text of a stage play, screenplay or broadcast; a plan of action; (*print*) type that resembles handwriting. • *vt* to write a script (for).

scriptural /'skrɪptʃərəl/ *adj* of or based on the Bible or Scripture.

scripture /'skrɪptʃər/ *n* any sacred writing; (*with cap, often pl*) the Jewish Bible or Old Testament; the Christian Bible or Old and New Testaments. • *adj* contained in or quoted from the Bible.

scriptwriter /'skrɪptˌraɪtər/ *n* a writer of screenplays for films, TV, etc; a screenwriter.—**scriptwriting** *n*.

scrofula /'skrɒfjʊlə/ *n* tuberculosis of the lymph glands in the neck.—**scrofulous** *adj*.

scroll /skroʊl/ *n* a roll of parchment or paper with writing on it; an ornament like this; (*her*) a ribbon with a motto; a list. • *vti* (*comput*) to move text across a screen; to decorate with scrolls.

scroll saw *n* a thin saw for cutting intricate designs.

Scrooge /skruːdʒ/ *n* (*also without cap*) a miserly, miserable person (after the character in *A Christmas Carol* by Charles Dickens).

scrotum /'skroʊtəm/ *n* (*pl* **scrota, scrotums**) the pouch of skin containing the testicles.

scrounge /skraʊndʒ/ *vti* (*inf*) to seek or obtain (something) for nothing.—**scrounger** *n*.

scrub¹ /skrʌb/ *n* an arid area of stunted trees and shrubs; such vegetation; anything small or mean. • *adj* small, stunted, inferior, etc.

scrub² *vti* (**scrubbing, scrubbed**) to clean vigorously, to scour; to rub hard; (*inf*) to remove, to cancel. • *n* the act of scrubbing.

scrubber /'skrʌbər/ *n* a person or thing that scrubs; (*sl*) a promiscuous woman.

scrubby /'skrʌbi/ *adj* (**scrubbier, scrubbiest**) stunted; paltry; unkempt.—**scrubbily** *adv*.—**scrubbiness** *n*.

scruff¹ /skrʌf/ *n* the back of the neck, the nape.

scruff² *n* (*inf*) a shabbily dressed person.

scruffy /'skrʌfi/ *adj* (**scruffier, scruffiest**) shabby; unkempt.—**scruffily** *adv*.—**scruffiness** *n*.

scrum /skrʌm/ *n* a scrummage.

scrum half *n* (*rugby*) (the position held by) the player who puts the ball into the scrum.

scrummage /'skrʌmɪdʒ/ *n* (*rugby*) a play consisting of a tussle between rival forwards in a compact mass for possession of the ball. • *vi* to form a scrum(mage).

scrump /skrʌmp/ *vt* (*dial*) to steal apples from an orchard or garden.

scrumptious /'skrʌmpʃəs/ *adj* (*inf*) delicious; very pleasing.—**scrumptiously** *adv*.—**scrumptiousness** *n*.

scrunch /skrʌntʃ/ *vti* to crumple, *esp* the hair when drying; to crunch; to be crumpled or crunched. • *n* a crunching sound; the act of scrunching.

scruple /'skru:pəl/ *n* (*usu pl*) a moral principle or belief causing one to doubt or hesitate about a course of action. • *vti* to hesitate owing to scruples.

scrupulous /'skru:pjuləs/ *adj* careful; conscientious; thorough.—**scrupulously** *adv.*—**scrupulousness** *n.*

scrutineer /skru:tɪ'nɪːr/ *n* a person who scrutinizes, *esp* an inspector of ballot papers.

scrutinize /'skru:tɪˌnaɪz/ *vti* to look closely at, to examine narrowly; to make a scrutiny.—**scrutinizer** *n.*

scrutiny /'skru:tɪni/ *n* (*pl* **scrutinies**) a careful examination; a critical gaze; an official inspection of votes cast in an election.

scuba /'sku:bə/ *n* a diver's apparatus with compressed-air tanks for breathing underwater.

scud /skʌd/ *vti* (**scudding, scudded**) to go along swiftly; to be driven before the wind. • *n* an act of scudding; light clouds, etc, driven by wind; a type of missile.

scuff /skʌf/ *vti* to drag the feet, to shuffle; to wear or mark the surface of by doing this.

scuffle /'skʌfəl/ *n* a confused fight; the sound of shuffling. • *vi* to fight confusedly; to move by shuffling.

scull /skʌl/ *n* an oar worked from side to side over the stern of a boat; a light rowing boat for racing. • *vti* to propel with a scull.

scullery /'skʌləri/ *n* (*pl* **sculleries**) a room for storage or kitchen work, such as washing dishes, etc.

sculpt /skʌlpt/ *vt* to carve, to sculpture.

sculptor /'skʌlptər/ *n* a person skilled in sculpture.

sculptress /'skʌlptrəs/ *n* a woman skilled in sculpture.

sculpture /'skʌlptʃər/ *n* the art of carving wood or forming clay, stone, etc, into figures, statues, etc; a three-dimensional work of art; a sculptor's work. • *vt* to carve, adorn or portray with sculptures; to shape, mould or form like sculpture.—**sculptural** *adj.*

scum /skʌm/ *n* a thin layer of impurities on top of a liquid; refuse; despicable people.

scumbag /'skʌmbæg/ *n* (*sl*) a disgusting or despicable person.

scumble /'skʌmbəl/ *vt* (*drawing and painting*) to soften lines or colours by applying a thin coat of opaque colour. • *n* the upper layer of colour applied for this purpose.

scunner /'skʌnər/ *n* (*Scot*) disgust. • *vti* to feel or cause to feel disgust.—**scunnered** *adj*

scupper /'skʌpər/ *n* a hole in a ship's side that lets water run from the deck into the sea. • *vt* (*sl*) to sink deliberately; to disable.

scurf /skɜːf/ *n* small flakes of dead skin (as dandruff); any scaly coating.

scurrilous /'skʌrɪləs/ *adj* abusive; grossly offensive.

scurry /'skʌri/ *vi* (**scurrying, scurried**) to hurry with quick, short steps, to scamper. • *n* (*pl* **scurries**) a bustle; a flurry (as of snow).

scurvy /'skɜːvi/ *n* a disease caused by a deficiency of vitamin C. • *adj* base; contemptible.

scut /skʌt/ *n* the short tail of certain animals, such as the deer or hare.

scute /skju:t/, **scutum** /-təm/ *n* an external scales or plate on the bodies of animals such as the armadillo, turtle, etc.

scutellum /sku'tɛləm/ *n* (*pl* **scutella**) any of the small horny scales or plates on a plant or animal.

scuttle[1] /'skʌtəl/ *vi* to run quickly; to hurry away. • *n* a short swift run; a hurried pace.

scuttle[2] *n* a bucket with a lip for storing coal.

scuttle[3] *n* (*naut*) a hatchway, a hole with a cover in a ship's deck or side. • *vt* to sink a ship by making holes in the bottom.

scuttlebut /'skʌtəlˌbʌt/ *n* (*formerly*) a cask containing drinking water on the deck of a ship; (*sl*) gossip.

scuzzy /'skʌzi/ *adj* (**scuzzier, scuzziest**) (*sl*) filthy, squalid.

scythe /saɪð/ *n* a two-handed implement with a large curved blade for cutting grass, etc. • *vti* to cut with a scythe; to mow down.

SDI *abbr* = Strategic Defense Initiative.

SE *abbr* = southeast(ern).

Se (*chem symbol*) selenium.

sea /si:/ *n* the ocean; a section of this; a vast expanse of water; a heavy wave, the swell of the ocean; something like the sea in size; the seafaring life. • *adj* marine, of the sea.

sea anchor *n* a device dragged behind a vessel to slow the rate of drifting or keep it heading into the wind.

sea anemone *n* any of various solitary brightly coloured polyps with a ring of petal-like tentacles surrounding the mouth.

sea bass *n* any of numerous American marine fishes with a long body and a spiny dorsal fin.

seaboard /'si:bɔːrd/ *n, adj* (land) bordering on the sea.

seaborne /'si:bɔːrn/ *adj* conveyed by the sea; carried on a ship.

sea bream *n* any of numerous marine food fishes of European seas.

sea breeze *n* a wind that blows from the sea to the land.

sea change *n* a radical transformation.

seacock /'si:kɒk/ *n* a valve in the hull of a vessel through which water can pass in or out.

sea cow *see* **dugong**.

sea cucumber *n* an echinoderm with an elongated body, leathery skin and an oral ring of tentacles at one end.

sea dog *n* an old sailor.

sea eagle *n* any of various fish-eating eagles.

seafarer /'si:ˌfɛrər/ *n* a sailor; a person who travels by sea.

seafaring /'si:ˌfɛrɪŋ/ *n* travelling by sea, *esp* the work of a sailor.—*also adj.*

seafood /'si:fu:d/ *n* edible fish or shellfish from the sea.

sea front /'si:frʌnt/ *n* the waterfront of a seaside place.

sea green *adj, n* (a) pale bluish green.

seagoing /-gəʊɪŋ/ *adj* (*ship*) made for use on the open sea.

seagull /'si:gʌl/ *n* a gull.

sea holly *n* a European coastal plant with blue flowers.

sea horse *n* a small bony-plated fish with a horselike head and neck and a long tail, that swims in an upright position; in fable, a horse with the tail of a fish.

sea kale /'si:keɪl/ *n* a European coastal plant with fleshy leaves and edible shoots.

seal[1] /si:l/ *n* an engraved stamp for impressing wax, lead, etc; wax, lead, etc, so impressed; that which authenticates or pledges; a device for closing or securing tightly. • *vt* to fix a seal to; to close tightly or securely; to shut up; to mark as settled, to confirm.

seal[2] *n* an aquatic mammal with four webbed flippers; the fur of some seals; a dark brown. • *vi* to hunt seals.

sea lane *n* a route for ships.

sealant /'si:lənt/ *n* a thing that seals, as wax, etc; a substance for stopping a leak, making watertight, etc.

sea lavender *n* any of a genus of coastal plants with white, pink or purple flowers.

sealed-beam *adj* (*car headlight*) having the reflector incorporated in the lamp.

sea legs *npl* (*inf*) the ability to walk steadily on a moving ship and to be free from seasickness.

sealer /'si:lər/ *n* a person or a ship whose business is hunting seals.

sea level *n* the level of the surface of the sea in relation to the land.

sea lily *n* an echinoderm with a thin elongated body topped by petal-like tentacles.

sealing wax *n* a resinous compound that is plastic when warm and used for sealing letters, etc.

sea lion *n* a large seal of the Pacific Ocean that has a loud roar and, in the male, a mane.

sealskin /'si:lskɪn/ *n* the fur of a seal; a coat of this.

Sealyham terrier /'si:lɪhæm/ *n* a breed of wire-haired terrier with short legs and a longish, *usu* white, coat.

seam /si:m/ *n* the line where two pieces of cloth are stitched together; (*geol*) a stratum of coal, oil, etc, between thicker ones; a line or wrinkle. • *vt* to join with a seam; to furrow.

seaman /'si:mən/ *n* (*pl* **seamen**) a sailor; a naval rank.

seamanship /'si:mənʃɪp/ *n* the skill of handling, working and navigating a ship.

sea mile *n* a nautical mile.

sea mouse *n* a marine worm with a broad body covered in hairlike bristles.

seamstress /'si:mstrəs/ or /'sɛm-/ *n* a woman who sews for a living.

seamy /'si:mi/ *adj* (**seamier, seamiest**) unpleasant or sordid.

seance, séance /'seɪɒns/ or /-ɑ̃s/ *n* a meeting of spiritualists to try to communicate with the dead.

sea otter *n* a large marine otter of North Pacific coasts that feeds on shellfish.

sea pink *n* the plant thrift.

seaplane /'si:pleɪn/ *n* an aeroplane with floats that allow it to take off from and land on water.

seaport /'si:pɔːrt/ *n* a port, harbour or town accessible to oceangoing ships.

sear /sɪr/ *vt* to burn or scorch the surface of; to brand with a heated iron; to wither up.

search /sɜːrtʃ/ *vi* to look around to find something; to explore. • *vt* to examine or inspect closely; to probe into. • *n* the act of searching; an investigation; a quest.—**searcher** *n.*

search engine *n* (*comput*) a tool that is used to look for and retrieve information on the Web.

searching /ˈsɜːtʃɪŋ/ *adj* keen, piercing; examining thoroughly.—**searchingly** *adv*.

searchlight /ˈsɜːtʃlaɪt/ *n* a powerful ray of light projected by an apparatus on a swivel; the apparatus.

search party *n* a group of people organized to locate a missing person or thing.

search warrant *n* a legal document that authorizes a police search.

seascape /ˈsiːskeɪp/ *n* a picture of a scene at sea.

Sea Scout *n* a member of a Scout troop specializing in sailing, canoeing, diving, etc.

sea serpent *n* a legendary sea-dwelling monster resembling a snake or dragon.

seashell /ˈsiːʃel/ *n* the discarded or empty shell of a marine mollusc.

seashore /ˈsiːʃɔr/ *n* land beside the sea or between high and low water marks; the beach.

seasick /ˈsiːsɪk/ *adj* affected with nausea brought on by the motion of a ship.—**seasickness** *n*.

seaside /ˈsiːsaɪd/ *n* seashore.

sea snail *n* a spiral-shelled marine mollusc, such as a whelk; a small slimy fish with pelvic fins formed into a sucker.

sea snake *n* a venomous snake of tropical waters with an oar-shaped tail.

season /ˈsiːzən/ *n* one of the four equal parts into which the year is divided: spring, summer, autumn, or winter; a period of time; a time when something is plentiful or in use; a suitable time; (*inf*) a season ticket. • *vt* (*food*) to flavour by adding salt, spices, etc; to make mature or experienced; (*wood*) to dry until ready for use. • *vi* to become experienced.

seasonable /ˈsiːzənəbəl/ *adj* suitable for the season; timely, opportune.—**seasonableness** *n*.—**seasonably** *adv*.

seasonal /ˈsiːzənəl/ *adj* of or relating to a particular season.—**seasonally** *adv*.

seasonal affective disorder *n* a state of depression that affects some people in the winter months, thought to be caused by a lack of sunlight.

seasoning /ˈsiːzənɪŋ/ *n* salt, spices, etc, used to enhance the flavour of food; the process of making something fit for use.

season ticket *n* a ticket or set of tickets valid for a number of concerts, games, journeys, etc, during a specified period.

seat /siːt/ *n* a piece of furniture for sitting on, such as a chair, bench, etc; the part of a chair on which one sits; the buttocks, the part of the trousers covering them; a way of sitting (on a horse, etc); the chief location, or centre; a part at or forming a base; the right to sit as a member; a parliamentary constituency; a large country house. • *vt* to place on a seat; to provide with seats; to settle.

seat belt *n* an anchored strap worn in a car or aeroplane to secure a person to a seat.

seated /ˈsiːtəd/ *adj* provided with a seat or seats; fixed, confirmed; located.

seating /ˈsiːtɪŋ/ *n* the arrangement or provision of seats.

sea trout *n* a marine variety of brown trout that migrates to fresh water to spawn.

sea urchin *n* a small marine animal with a round body enclosed in a shell covered with sharp spines.

sea wall /ˈsiːwɒl/ *n* a barrier or embankment to prevent erosion by the sea.

seaward /ˈsiːwərd/ *adj* toward the sea. • *adv* toward or in the direction of the sea.—**seawards** *adv*.

seaway /ˈsiːweɪ/ *n* an ocean traffic lane; a waterway for seagoing traffic to an inland port.

seaweed /ˈsiːwiːd/ *n* a mass of plants growing in or under water; a sea plant, *esp* a marine alga.

seaworthy /ˈsiːˌwɜrði/ *adj* fit to go to sea; able to withstand sea water, watertight.—**seaworthiness** *n*.

sebaceous /səˈbeɪʃəs/ *adj* of, secreting, containing, or producing oily or fatty matter.

sebaceous glands *npl* the small skin glands that secrete sebum onto the skin surface.

seborrhoea, seborrhea /ˌsebəˈriə/ *n* the excessive secretion of sebum.—**seborrhoeic, seborrheic** *adj*.

sebum /ˈsiːbəm/ *n* a fatty substance secreted by the sebaceous glands to lubricate the hair and skin.

SEC *abbr* = Securities and Exchange Commission.

sec[1] /sek/ *adj* (*wine*) dry; (*champagne*) medium sweet.

sec[2] *n* (*inf*) a second.

sec[3] *abbr* = secant.

sec. *abbr* = second.

secant /ˈsiːkənt/ *n* a trigonometrical function that is the reciprocal of the cosine; a straight line that intersects a curve.

secateurs /ˈsekəˌtɜrz/ *npl* a pair of small shears with curved blades for pruning, etc.

secede /səˈsiːd/ *vi* to withdraw formally one's membership from a society or organization.—**seceder** *n*.

secession /səˈseʃən/ *n* the act or an instance of seceding; a breaking away.—**secessional** *adj*.

seclude /səˈkluːd/ *vt* to keep (a person, etc) separate from others; to remove or screen from view.

secluded /səˈkluːdəd/ *adj* private; sheltered; kept from contact with other people.

seclusion /səˈkluːʒən/ *n* the state of being secluded; privacy, solitude.

second /ˈsekənd/ *adj* next after first; alternate; another of the same kind; next below the first in rank, value, etc. • *n* a person or thing coming second; another; an article of merchandise not of first quality; an aid or assistant, as to a boxer, duellist; the gear after low gear; one sixtieth of a minute of time or of an angular degree; (*pl*) (*inf*) another helping of food. • *adv* in the second place, group, etc. • *vt* to act as a second (to); (*a motion, resolution, etc*) to support; (*mil*) to place on temporary service elsewhere.

secondary /ˈsekəndˌeri/ *adj* subordinate; second in rank or importance; in the second stage; derived, not primary; relating to secondary school. • *n* (*pl* **secondaries**) that which is secondary; a delegate, a deputy.—**secondarily** *adv*.

secondary cell *n* a battery that can convert chemical energy to electrical energy by reversible chemical reactions and so be recharged.

secondary colour *n* a colour formed by mixing two primary colours.

secondary emission *n* (*physics*) the emission of secondary electrons from a solid surface due to bombardment by a beam of primary electrons or other elementary particles.

secondary school *n* a school between elementary or primary school and college or university.

secondary sexual characteristic *n* an attribute of a human being or animal that is characteristic of a particular sex but is not directly concerned with reproduction.

second best *adj* next to the best; inferior. • *adv* in second place. • *n* next to the best; an inferior alternative.

second chamber *n* the upper house in a legislative assembly with two chambers.

second childhood *n* dotage, senility.

second class *n* the class next to the first in a classification. • *adj* (second-class) relating to a second class; inferior, mediocre; (*seating, accommodation*) next in price and quality to first class; (*mail*) less expensive and handled more slowly (than first class).

Second Coming *n* (*Christianity*) the return to earth of Christ at the Last Judgment as prophesied.

second cousin *n* a child of the first cousin of one's parent.

second-degree burn *n* a burn which causes blistering of the skin.

second fiddle *n* (the musical part for) a second violin in an orchestra or string quartet; (*inf*) a person of secondary importance.

second hand *n* the moving pointer in a clock or watch that indicates the seconds.

second-hand *adj* bought after use by another; derived, not original.—*also adv*.

secondly *adv* in the second place.

second nature *n* a long-established habit, etc, deeply fixed in a person's nature.

second person *n* that form of a pronoun (as *you*) or verb (as *are*) that refers to the person spoken to.

second-rate *adj* of inferior quality.

second sight *n* the supposed faculty of seeing events before they occur.

second string *n* a reserve or substitute player in a team.

second thought *n* a change in thought or decision after consideration.

second wind *n* a return to regular breathing after a bout of exercise; renewed energy or enthusiasm.

secrecy /ˈsiːkrəsi/ *n* (*pl* **secrecies**) the state of being secret; the ability to keep secret.

secret /ˈsiːkrət/ *adj* not made public; concealed from others; hidden; private; remote. • *n* something hidden; a mystery; a hidden cause.

secret agent *n* a spy.

secretaire /ˌsekrəˈter/ *n* a writing desk with an upper section for books and documents.

secretariat /ˌsekrəˈteriət/ *n* an administrative office or staff, as in a government.

secretary /ˈsekrəˌteri/ *n* (*pl* **secretaries**) a person employed to deal with correspondence, filing, telephone calls of another or of an association; the head of a state department.—**secretarial** *adj*.

secretary bird *n* a large long-legged African bird of prey that eats mostly snakes.

secretary-general *n* (*pl* **secretaries-general**) the chief administrator of a large organization (*eg* the United Nations).

secretary of state *n* in the UK, any of various ministers in charge of government departments; (*with caps*) in the US, the minister in charge of foreign affairs.

secrete / səˈkriːt/ *vt* to conceal; to hide; (*cell, gland, etc*) to produce and release (a substance) out of blood or sap.

secretion /səˈkriːʃən/ *n* the process of secreting; a substance secreted by an animal or plant.

secretive /ˈsiːkrətɪv/ *adj* given to secrecy; uncommunicative, reticent.—**secretively** *adv*.—**secretiveness** *n*.

secretly /-li/ *adv* in a secret way; unknown to others.

secretory /sɪˈkriːtəri/ *adj* having the function of secreting, as a gland.

secret police *n* a police force that operates covertly to suppress political dissent rather than criminal activity.

secret service *n* a government agency that gathers intelligence, infiltrates terrorist or subversive organizations, conducts espionage, etc in the interests of national security.

sect /sekt/ *n* a religious denomination; a group of people united by a common interest or belief; a faction.

sectarian /sekˈterɪən/ *adj* of or confined to a religious sect; bigoted. • *n* a member or adherent of a sect.

sectarianism /-ɪzəm/ *n* devotion to a sect; religious narrowness.

section /ˈsekʃən/ *n* the act of cutting; a severed or separable part; a division; a distinct portion; a slice; a representation of anything cut through to show its interior; (*geom*) the cutting of a solid by a plane; a plane figure formed by this. • *vti* to cut or separate into sections; to represent in sections; to become separated or cut into parts.

sectional /ˈsekʃənəl/ *adj* of a section; made up of several sections; local rather than general in character.—**sectionally** *adv*.

sector /ˈsektər/ *n* (*geom*) a space enclosed by two radii of a circle and the arc they cut off; a distinctive part (as of an economy); a subdivision; (*mil*) an area of activity.

secular /ˈsekjʊlər/ *adj* having no connection with religion or the church; worldly.—**secularly** *adv*.

secularize /ˈsekjʊlərˌaɪz/ *vt* to change from religious to civil use or control.—**secularization** *n*.

secure /səˈkjuːər/ or /-ˈkjər/ *adj* free from danger, safe; stable; firmly held or fixed; confident, assured (of); reliable. • *vt* to make safe; to fasten firmly; to protect; to confine; to fortify; to guarantee; to gain possession of, to obtain.—**securely** *adv*.

security /səˈkjʊriti/ or /-kjər-/ *n* (*pl* **securities**) the state of being secure; a financial guarantee, surety; a pledge for repayment, etc; a protection or safeguard; a certificate of shares or bonds.

Security Council *n* the principal council of the United Nations charged with maintaining world peace.

security guard *n* a person employed to protect public buildings, banks, offices, etc and to transport large sums of money.

security police *n* a police force whose function is to prevent espionage; the military police of an air force.

security risk *n* a person or thing regarded as a potential threat to security.

sedan /sɪˈdæn/ *n* a car with no division between driver and passengers; a covered chair for one person with poles carried by two bearers.

sedate[1] /səˈdeɪt/ *adj* calm; composed; serious and unemotional.—**sedately** *adv*.—**sedateness** *n*.

sedate[2] *vti* to calm or become calm by the administration of a sedative.

sedation /səˈdeɪʃən/ *n* the act of calming or the condition of being calmed, *esp* by sedatives; the administration of sedatives to calm a patient.

sedative /ˈsedətɪv/ *n* a drug with a soothing, calming effect. • *adj* having a soothing, calming effect.

sedentary /ˈsedənˌteri/ *adj* requiring a sitting position; inactive; not migratory.

Seder /ˈseɪdər/ *n* a Jewish ceremonial meal held on the first night of Passover.

sedge /sedʒ/ *n* a grass-like plant that grows in marshes or beside water.

sedge warbler *n* a European songbird that inhabits marshy areas.

sediment /ˈsedəmənt/ *n* matter that settles at the bottom of a liquid; (*geol*) matter deposited by water or wind.

sedimentary /ˌsedəˈmentəri/ *adj* relating to or formed by sediment.

sedition /səˈdɪʃən/ *n* incitement to rebel against the government.—**seditious** *adj*.—**seditiously** *adv*.

seduce /səˈduːs/ or /-ˈdjuːs/ *vt* to lead astray; to corrupt; to entice into unlawful sexual intercourse.—**seducer** *n*.

seduction /səˈdʌkʃən/ *n* the act of seducing; temptations; attraction.

seductive /səˈdʌktɪv/ *adj* tending to seduce; enticing, alluring.—**seductively** *adv*.—**seductiveness** *n*.

sedulous /ˈsedjʊləs/ *adj* diligent; persevering.—**sedulously** *adv*.—**sedulousness** *n*.

see[1] /siː/ *vt* (**seeing, saw**, *pp* **seen**) to perceive with the eyes; to observe; to grasp with the intelligence; to ascertain; to take care (that); to accompany; to visit; to meet; to consult; (*guests*) to receive; (*with* **through**) to persist or endure to the end; to assist (*eg* a friend) during a crisis, difficulty, etc. • *vi* to have the faculty of sight; to make inquiry; to consider, to reflect; to understand; (*with* **about**) to deal with; to consider in detail; (*with* **off**) to be present when someone leaves on a journey, etc; (*inf*) to repel, get rid of; (*with* **through**) to recognize the true character of.

see[2] *n* the diocese of a bishop.

seed /siːd/ *n* the small, hard part (ovule) of a plant from which a new plant grows; such seeds collectively; the source of anything; sperm or semen; descendants; (*tennis*) a seeded tournament player. • *vti* to sow (seed); to produce or shed seed; to remove seeds from; (*tennis*) to arrange (a tournament) so that the best players cannot meet until later rounds.

seedbed /ˈsiːdbed/ *n* a nursery bed for a plant; a place or source of growth or development.

seed cake /ˈsiːdkeɪk/ *n* a sweet cake flavoured with aromatic (*usu* caraway) seeds.

seed coral *n* small pieces of coral used in jewellery.

seed corn *n* corn reserved for sowing; assets promising future earning potential.

seedless /ˈsiːdləs/ *adj* without seeds.

seedling /ˈsiːdlɪŋ/ *n* a young plant raised from seed, not from a cutting; a young tree before it is a sapling.

seed money *n* money used to start a new project or enterprise.

seed oyster *n* a young oyster ready for transplantation to a new bed.

seed pearl *n* a very small pearl.

seed potato *n* a potato tuber ready for planting.

seed vessel *n* a pericarp.

seedy /ˈsiːdi/ *adj* (**seedier, seediest**) full of seeds; out of sorts, indisposed; shabby; rundown.—**seedily** *adv*.—**seediness** *n*.

seeing /ˈsiːɪŋ/ *n* vision, sight. • *adj* having sight; observant. • *conj* in view of the fact that; since.

seek /siːk/ *vti* (**seeking, sought**) to search for; to try to find, obtain, or achieve; to resort to; (*with* **to**) to try to, to endeavour; (*with* **out**) to search for and locate a person or thing; to try to secure the society of.—**seeker** *n*.

seem /siːm/ *vi* to appear (to be); to give the impression of; to appear to oneself.

seeming /ˈsiːmɪŋ/ *adj* that seems real, true; ostensible, apparent.—**seemingly** *adv*.

seemly /ˈsiːmli/ *adj* (**seemlier, seemliest**) proper, fitting.—**seemliness** *n*.

seen /siːn/ *see* **see**[1].

seep /siːp/ *vi* to ooze gently, to leak through.

seepage /ˈsiːpədʒ/ *n* the act of seeping; the liquid that has seeped.

seer /ˈsiːər/ or /siːr/ *n* a person who sees visions, a prophet.

seersucker /ˈsiːrˌsʌkər/ *n* a light, *usu* cotton, fabric with a puckered surface.

seesaw /ˈsiːsɒ/ *n* a plank balanced across a central support so that it is tilted up and down by a person sitting on each end; an up-and-down movement like this; vacillation. • *vi* to move up and down; to fluctuate. • *adj, adv* alternately rising and falling.

seethe /si:ð/ *vi* to be very angry inwardly; to swarm (with people).

segment /'segmənt/ *n* a section; a portion; one of the two parts of a circle or sphere when a line is drawn through it. • *vti* to cut or separate into segments.—**segmentation** *n*.

segregate /'segrə,geɪt/ *vti* to set apart from others, to isolate; to separate racial or minority groups.

segregation /,segrə'geɪʃən/ *n* the act of segregating or the condition of being segregated; the policy of compelling racial groups to live apart.

seguidilla /,segə'di:ljə/ or /,seɪgə-/, /'di:jə/ *n* (the music for) a lively Spanish dance in triple time.

seiche /seɪʃ/ *n* an undulation of the surface of a lake, caused by earth tremors or changes in barometric pressure.

seigneur /si:'njər/ *n* a feudal lord.—**seigneurial** *adj*.

seigneury /'si:njəri/ *n* (*pl* **seigneuries**) the estate or authority of a seigneur.

seine /seɪn/ *n* a large fishing net that hangs vertically by means of floats along the top and weights along the bottom. • *vi* to catch fish with this.

seismic /'saɪzmɪk/ *adj* of or caused by earthquakes.—**seismically** *adv*.

seismo- /'saɪzmoʊ/, **seism-** /'saɪzm/ *prefix* earthquake.

seismograph /'saɪzmə,græf/ *n* an instrument for recording the direction, intensity, and time of an earthquake.—**seismographer** *n*.—**seismographic** *adj*.—**seismography** *n*.

seismology /saɪz'mɒlədʒi/ *n* the scientific study of earthquakes.—**seismologic, seismological** *adj*.—**seismologist** *n*.

seize /si:z/ *vt* to grasp; to capture; to take hold of suddenly or forcibly; to attack or afflict suddenly. • *vi* (*machinery*) to become jammed.—**seizable** *adj*.

seizure /'si:ʒər/ *n* the act of seizing; what is seized; a sudden attack of illness, an apoplectic stroke.

seldom /'seldəm/ *adv* not often, rarely.

select /sə'lekt/ *vti* to choose or pick out. • *adj* excellent; choice; limited (*eg* in membership); exclusive.

select committee *n* a parliamentary committee established to investigate and report on a particular subject.

selection /sə'lekʃən/ *n* the act of selecting; what is or are selected; the process by which certain animals or plants survive while others are eliminated, natural selection.

selective /sə'lektɪv/ *adj* having the power of selection; highly specific in activity or effect.—**selectively** *adv*.—**selectiveness** *n*.

selenium /sə'li:nɪəm/ *n* a nonmetallic solid chemical element with semiconductive and photoconductive properties that has various uses in electronics.

seleno- /sə'li:noʊ/, **selen-** /sə'li:n/ *prefix* the moon.

selenography /,si:lə'nɒgrəfi/ *n* the study and mapping of the physical features of the moon.—**selenographer** *n*.—**selenographic** *adj*.

self- /self/ *prefix* of itself or oneself; by, for, in relation to, itself or oneself; automatic.

self *n* (*pl* **selves**) the identity, character, etc, of any person or thing; one's own person as distinct from all others; one's own interests or advantage. • *adj* (*colour*) matching, uniform.

self-abnegation /self,æbnə'geɪʃən/ *n* denial of one's own interests or desires in favour of those of others.

self-absorption /,selfəb'zɔrpʃən/ *n* preoccupation with one's own interests and welfare.

self-abuse /,selfə'bju:s/ *n* disparagement or misuse of one's own abilities; a censorius term for masturbation.

self-acting /self'æktɪŋ/ *adj* automatic.

self-addressed /,selfə'drest/ *adj* addressed to return to the sender; intended for oneself.

self-aggrandizement /,selfə'grændaɪzmənt/ or /-dɪzmənt/ *n* acting to increase one's own power and importance at the expense of others.—**self-aggrandizing** *adj*.

self-approbation /selfæprəbeɪʃən/ *n* satisfaction with one's own actions or accomplishments, *esp* to excess.

self-assertion /,selfə'sərʃən/ *n* the act of asserting one's own opinions, ideas, or rights, *esp* determinedly.—**self-assertive** *adj*.

self-assured /-ə'ʃʊrd/ *adj* confident.—**self-assurance** *n*.

self-catering /self'keɪtərɪŋ/ *adj* catering for oneself.

self-centred, self-centered /self'sentərd/ *adj* preoccupied with one's own affairs.—**self-centerdly, self-centeredly** *adv*.—**self-centredness, self-centeredness** *n*.

self-coloured, self-colored /,self'kələrd/ *adj* of a single colour.

self-confessed /,selfkən'fest/ *adj* according to one's own testimony.

self-confident /self'kɒnfɪdənt/ *adj* sure of one's own powers.—**self-confidence** *n*.—**self-confidently** *adv*.

self-conscious /self'kɒnʃəs/ *adj* embarrassed or awkward in the presence of others, ill at ease.—**self-consciously** *adv*.—**self-consciousness** *n*.

self-contained /,selfkən'teɪnd/ *adj* complete in itself; showing self-control; uncommunicative.—**self-containment** *n*.

self-control /,selfkən'troʊl/ *n* control of one's emotions, desires, etc, by the will.—**self-controlled** *adj*.

self-deception /,selfdə'sepʃən/ or /-di-/ *n* the act or state of deceiving oneself.

self-defence, self-defense /,selfdə'fens/ or /-di-/ *n* the act of defending oneself; (*law*) a plea for the justification for the use of force.

self-denial /,selfdə'naɪəl/ or /-di-/ *n* abstention from pleasure, etc; unselfishness.

self-determination /,selfdə,tərmə'neɪʃən/ or /-di-/ *n* free will; the choice of action without compulsion; the right of a nation to choose its own form of government.

self-drive /-draɪv/ *adj* (*hired vehicle*) driven by the hirer.

self-educated /self'edju:,keɪtəd/ *adj* educated without benefit of formal instruction; educated at one's own expense.

self-effacement /,selfə'feɪsɪŋ/ *n* the act of making oneself or one's actions inconspicuous, due to modesty or timidity.

self-employed /,selfem'ploɪd/ *adj* earning one's living in one's own business or profession, not employed by another; working freelance.

self-esteem /,selfe'sti:m/ *n* confidence and respect for oneself; an exaggerated opinion of oneself.

self-evident /self'evɪdənt/ *adj* evident without proof or explanation.—**self-evidently** *adv*.

self-explanatory /,selfɪk'splænətəri/ *adj* easily understood without explanation.

self-expression /,selfɪk'spreʃən/ *n* the expression of one's own personality, as in creative art.

self-governing /self'gʌvərnɪŋ/ *adj* autonomous; (*colony, etc*) having an elective legislation.—**self-government** *n*.

self-help /self'help/ *n* the provision of means to help oneself, instead of relying on others.

self-image /self'ɪmɪdʒ/ *n* one's sense of oneself or one's importance.

self-importance /,selfɪm'pɔrtəns/ *n* an exaggerated estimate of one's own worth; pompousness.—**self-important** *adj*.

self-induced /,selfɪn'du:st/ or /-'dju:st/ *adj* brought on by oneself or itself.

self-induction /,selfɪn'dʌkʃən/ *n* the production of an electromotive force in a circuit by a variation in the electric current in the same circuit.

self-indulgence /,selfɪn'dʌldʒəns/ *n* undue gratification of one's desires, appetites, or whims.—**self-indulgent** *adj*.

self-inflicted /,selfɪn'flɪktəd/ *adj* (*wound, etc*) caused to a person by himself.

self-interest /self'ɪntrəst/ *n* regard to one's own advantage.

selfish /'selfɪʃ/ *adj* chiefly concerned with oneself; lacking in consideration for others.—**selfishly** *adv*.—**selfishness** *n*.

self-justification /self,dʒestɪfɪ'keɪʃən/ *n* the act or instance of making excuses for one's actions, etc.

selfless /'selfləs/ *adj* with no thought of self, unselfish.—**selflessly** *adv*.—**selflessness** *n*.

self-loading /self'loʊdɪŋ/ *n* (*firearm*) semiautomatic.—**self-loader** *n*.

self-love /self'lʌv/ *n* conceit; selfishness.

self-made /'selfmeɪd/ *adj* having achieved status or wealth by one's own efforts.

self-opinionated /selfə'pɪnjə,neɪtɪd/ *adj* conceited; stubborn.

self-pity /self'pɪti/ *n* pity for oneself.—**self-pitying** *adj*.

self-pollination /self,pɒlɪ'neɪʃən/ *n* the transfer of pollen from the anther to the stigma in the same flower.

self-portrait /self'pɔrtrət/ *n* an artist or author's painting or account of himself or herself.

self-possessed /,self/ *adj* cool and collected.

self-preservation /self,prezər'veɪʃən/ *n* the instinct to protect oneself from injury or death.

self-propelled /,selfprə'peld/ *adj* (*vehicle*) moving under its own power.

self-raising /self'reɪzɪŋ/ *adj* (*flour*) self-rising.

self-realization /ˌsɛlfˌriːəlaɪˈzeɪʃən/ n the understanding or achievement of one's own potential or desires.

self-regard /ˌsɛlfrəˈgɑrd/ or /-riˈgɑrd/ n concern for one's own interests; respect for oneself.

self-reliant /ˌsɛlfrɪˈlaɪənt/ adj relying on one's own powers; confident.—**self-reliance** n.

self-reproach /ˌsɛlfrɪˈproːtʃ/ n the act of blaming oneself.

self-respect /ˌsɛlfrɪˈspɛkt/ n proper respect for oneself, one's standing and dignity.—**self-respecting** adj.

self-righteous /sɛlfˈraɪtʃəs/ adj thinking oneself better than others; priggish.—**self-righteousness** n.

self-rising /sɛlfˈraɪzɪŋ/ adj (flour) containing a raising agent, self-raising.

self-rule /sɛlfˈruːl/ n self-government.

self-sacrifice /sɛlfˈsækrɪˌfaɪs/ n the sacrifice of one's own interests, welfare, etc, to secure that of others.

selfsame /ˈsɛlfseɪm/ adj identical, the very same.

self-satisfied /sɛlfˈsætɪsˌfaɪd/ adj smugly conceited.

self-seeking /ˈsɛlfˌsiːkɪŋ/ adj preoccupied with securing one's own well-being or interest; selfish.—**self-seeker** n.

self-service /sɛlfˈsɜrvəs/ adj serving oneself in a cafe, shop, filling station, etc.

self-serving /sɛlfˈsɜrvɪŋ/ adj always seeking to protect or further one's own interests.

self-sown /sɛlfˈsoːn/ adj (plants) grown from seeds that were planted or deposited naturally without intervention by humans or animals.

self-starter /sɛlfˈstɑrtər/ n an electric device for starting an engine; a motivated employee who requires little supervision.

self-styled /ˈsɛlfstaɪld/ adj called by oneself; pretended.

self-sufficient /ˌsɛlfsəˈfɪʃənt/ adj independent; supporting oneself (eg in growing food) without the help of others.—**self-sufficiency** n.

self-supporting /ˌsɛlfsəˈpɔrtɪŋ/ adj able to manage without help from others; able to stand unaided.

self-will /sɛlfˈwɪl/ n fixed adherence to one's own desires, intentions, etc; obstinacy.

self-winding /sɛlfˈwaɪndɪŋ/ adj (watch) wound automatically by an internal mechanism.

sell /sɛl/ vb (**selling, sold**) vt to exchange (goods, services, etc) for money or other equivalent; to offer for sale; to promote; to deal in; (with **up**) to sell all the goods of (a debtor) to clear the debt. • vi (with **off**) to clear out (stock) at bargain prices; (with **out**) to sell off, to betray for money or reward; (inf) to disappoint, to trick; to make sales; to attract buyers; (with **up**) to sell one's house, business, etc. • n an act or instance of selling; (inf) a disappointment, a trick, a fraud.—**seller** n.

Sellotape /ˈsɛləˌteɪp/ n (trademark) a transparent adhesive tape. • vt to seal or stick (something) using adhesive tape.

sellout n a show, game, etc, for which all the tickets are sold; (inf) a betrayal.

salvage, selvedge /ˈsɛlvɪdʒ/ n the edge of cloth so finished as to prevent unravelling.

selves /sɛlvz/ see **self**.

Sem abbr = Seminary; Semitic.

sem abbr = semester; semicolon.

semantic /səˈmæntɪk/ adj relating to the meaning of words. • npl the study of word meanings and changes.

semaphore /ˈsɛməˌfɔr/ n a system of visual signalling using the operator's arms, flags, etc; a signalling device consisting of a post with movable arms.

sematic /sɪˈmætɪk/ adj (animal colouration) warning of danger.

semblance /ˈsɛmbləns/ n likeness, resemblance; an outward, sometimes deceptive appearance.

semen /ˈsiːmən/ n the fluid that carries sperm in men and male animals.

semester /sɛˈmɛstər/ n an academic or school half-year.

semi /ˈsɛmi/ n (pl **semis**) (inf) a semidetached house; a semifinal.

semi- /ˈsɛmi/ or /-maɪ/ prefix half; not fully; twice in a (specified period).

semiannual /ˌsɛmiˈænjuəl/ adj happening twice a year, or lasting for six months.—also **semiyearly**.

semiautomatic /ˌsɛmiˌɒtəˈmætɪk/ or /ˌsɛmaɪ-/ adj partly automatic; (firearm) self-loading but discharging in single shots only as the trigger is pulled.

semibreve /ˈsɛmiˌbriːv/ or /ˌsɛmaɪ-/ n (mus) a note equal to two minims.—also **whole note**.

semicircle /ˈsɛmiˌsɜrkəl/ or /ˈsɛmaɪ-/ n half of a circle.—**semicircular** adj.

semicircular canal n any of the three fluid-filled tubes in the inner ear concerned with maintaining balance.

semicolon /ˌsɛmiˈkoːlən/ or /ˌsɛmaɪ-/ n the punctuation mark (;) of intermediate value between a comma and a full stop.

semiconductor /ˌsɛmikənˈdʌktər/ or /ˌsɛmaɪ-/ n a substance in a transmitter, as silicon, used to control the flow of current.

semiconscious /ˌsɛmiˈkɒnʃəs/ or /ˌsɛmaɪ-/ adj not fully conscious.—**semiconsciousness** n.

semi-detached /ˌsɛmidəˈtætʃt/ or /ˌsɛmaɪ-/ adj (house) with another joined to it on one side.—also n.

semifinal /ˌsɛmiˈfaɪnəl/ or /ˌsɛmaɪ-/ adj, n (the match or round) before the final in a knockout tournament.—**semifinalist** n.

semifluid /ˌsɛmiˈfluːɪd/ or /ˌsɛmaɪ-/ n having qualities between those of a fluid and a solid; viscous.

semiliterate /ˌsɛmiˈlɪtərɪt/ n barely able to read or write.

semilunar /ˌsɛmiˈluːnər/ or /ˌsɛmaɪ-/ adj in the shape of a crescent.

semilunar valve n either one of the two crescent-shaped valves in the heart.

seminal /ˈsɛmənəl/ adj of, relating to, or containing semen; promising or contributing to further development; original, influential.—**seminally** adv.

seminar /ˈsɛməˌnɑr/ n a group of students engaged in study or research under supervision; any group meeting to pool and discuss ideas.

seminary /ˈsɛməˌnɛri/ n (pl **seminaries**) a training college for priests, ministers, etc; a school for young women.

seminiferous /ˌsɛmiˈnɪfərəs/ adj producing or containing semen; (plants) bearing seeds.

semiology /ˌsiːmiˈɒlədʒi/ or /ˌsɛm-/ n the study of signs and symbols.—**semiologic, semiological** adj.—**semiologist** n.

semiotics /ˌsiːmiˈɒtɪks/ or /ˌsɛm-/ n sing the study of signs and symbols, esp their use in language and relationship to the world of things and ideas; the study of the symptoms of disease.—**semiotic, semiotical** adj.—**semiotician** n.

semiprecious /ˌsɛmiˈprɛʃəs/ or /ˌsɛmaɪ-/ adj denoting gems of lower value than precious stones.

semiprofessional /ˌsɛmiprəˈfɛʃənəl/ adj taking part in sport for pay, but not on a fulltime basis.—**semiprofessionally** adv.

semiquaver /ˈsɛmiˌkweɪvər/ n (mus) a sixteenth note.

semirigid /ˌsɛmiˈrɪdʒəd/ or /ˌsɛmaɪ-/ adj (airship) having a flexible gas container attached to a rigid keel.

semiskilled /ˌsɛmiˈskɪld/ or /ˌsɛmaɪ-/ adj partly skilled or trained.

semiskimmed /ˈsɛmiˌskɪmd/ adj (milk) having the cream partially removed.

semisolid /ˌsɛmiˈsɒləd/ or /ˌsɛmaɪ-/ adj having the properties between that of a liquid and a solid; extremely viscous.

Semite /ˈsɛmaɪt/ or /ˈsiːm-/ n a member of the group of peoples including Arabs and Jews.

Semitic /səˈmɪtɪk/ adj of or belonging to Semites; Jewish.

Semitism /ˈsɛməˌtɪzəm/ n any political or economic policy relating to Jews.

semitone /ˈsɛmiˌtoːn/ n (mus) an interval equal to half a tone.

semitrailer /ˈsɛmiˌtreɪlər/ or /ˌsɛmaɪ-/ n a trailer that has wheels at the back but is supported at the front by the towing vehicle.

semivowel /ˈsɛmiˌvaʊəl/ or /ˌsɛmaɪ-/ n (phon) a consonant that sound like a vowel (eg y or j), a glide.

semiyearly /-ˌjiːrli/ see **semiannual**.

semolina /ˌsɛməˈliːnə/ n coarse particles of grain left after the sifting of wheat.

sempre /ˈsɛmpreɪ/ or /-ri/ adv (mus) always.

Sen abbr = senator; senior.

senate /ˈsɛnət/ n a legislative or governing body; (with cap) the upper branch of a two-body legislature in France, the US, etc; the governing body of some universities.

senator /ˈsɛnətər/ n a member of a senate.—**senatorial** adj.

send /sɛnd/ vti (**sending, sent**) to cause or enable to go; to have conveyed, to dispatch (a message or messenger); to cause to move, to propel; to grant; to cause to be; (sl) to move (a person) to ecstasy; (with **down**) to expel from university; (with **for**) to order to be brought, to summon; (with **up**) (inf) to send to prison; to imitate or make fun of.—**sender** n.

send-off n a friendly demonstration at a departure; a start given to someone or something.

senescent /səˈnɛsənt/ adj growing old.—**senescence** n.

seneschal /'sɛnəʃəl/ n (hist) a steward in the house of a feudal lord.

senile /'siːnaɪl/ or /'sɛn-/ adj of or relating to old age; weakened, esp mentally, by old age.—**senility** n.

senior /'siːnjər/ adj higher in rank; of or for seniors; longer in service; older (when used to distinguish between father and son with the same first name). • n one's elder or superior in standing; a person of advanced age; a student in the last year of college or high school.

senior citizen n an elderly person, esp a retired one.

senior common room n a staffroom in a British college or university.

seniority /sɪn'jɔrəti/ or /-'jɑr-/ n (pl **seniorities**) the condition of being senior; status, priority, etc, in a given job.

sensation /sɛn'seɪʃən/ n awareness due to stimulation of the senses; an effect on the senses; a thrill; a state of excited interest; the cause of this.

sensational /sɛn'seɪʃənəl/ adj of or relating to sensation; exciting violent emotions; melodramatic.—**sensationally** adv.

sensationalism /sɛn'seɪʃənə,lɪzəm/ n the use of sensational writing, language, etc; the doctrine that all knowledge is obtained from sense impressions.—**sensationalist** adj.

sense /sɛns/ n one of the five human and animal faculties by which objects are perceived: sight, hearing, smell, taste, and touch; awareness; moral discernment; soundness of judgment; meaning, intelligibility; (pl) conscious awareness. • vt to perceive; to become aware of; to understand; to detect.

senseless /'sɛnsləs/ adj stupid, foolish; meaningless, purposeless; unconscious.—**senselessly** adv.—**senselessness** n.

sense organ n a bodily structure that reacts to stimuli and transmits them to the brain as nerve impulses.

sensibility /,sɛnsə'bɪlɪti/ n (pl **sensibilities**) the capacity to feel; over-sensitiveness; susceptibility; (pl) sensitive awareness or feelings.

sensible /'sɛnsəbəl/ adj having good sense or judgment; reasonable; practical; perceptible by the senses, appreciable; conscious (of); sensitive.—**sensibleness** n.—**sensibly** adv.

sensitive /'sɛnsətɪv/ adj having the power of sensation; feeling readily and acutely, keenly perceptive; (skin) delicate, easily irritated; (wound etc) still in a painful condition; easily hurt or shocked, tender, touchy; highly responsive to slight changes; sensory; (photog) reacting to light.—**sensitively** adj.—**sensitiveness** n.

sensitive plant n a tropical American plant whose leaves and stems fold when touched.

sensitivity /,sɛnsə'tɪvɪti/ n (pl **sensitivities**) the condition of being sensitive; awareness of changes or differences; responsiveness to stimuli or feelings, esp to excess.

sensitize /'sɛnsə,taɪz/ vt to make or become sensitive; (person) to render sensitive to an antigen, etc; (photog: paper etc) to render sensitive to light.—**sensitization** n.—**sensitizer** n.

sensitometer /,sɛnsə'tɒmɪtər/ n a device for measuring the sensitivity to light of a photographic medium.

sensor /'sɛnsər/ n a device for detecting, recording, or measuring physical phenomena, as heat, pulse, etc; a sense organ.

sensorium /sɛn'sɔriəm/ n (pl **sensoriums, sensoria**) the area of the brain regarded as responsible for receiving and processing external stimulii; the body's entire sensory apparatus.

sensory /'sɛnsəri/ adj of or relating to the senses, sensation, or the sense organs; conveying nerve impulses to the brain.

sensual /'sɛnʃʊəl/ adj bodily, relating to the senses rather than the mind; arousing sexual desire.—**sensuality** n.—**sensually** adv.

sensuous /'sɛnʃʊəs/ adj giving pleasure to the mind or body through the senses.—**sensuously** adv.—**sensuousness** n.

sent /sɛnt/ see **send**.

sentence /'sɛntəns/ n a court judgment; the punishment imposed; (gram) a series of words conveying a complete thought. • vt (a convicted person) to pronounce punishment upon; to condemn (to).

sententious /sɛn'tɛnʃəs/ adj terse, pithy; making frequent use of axioms and maxims; exhibiting a pompous, moralizing tone.—**sententiously** adv.—**sententiousness** n.

sentient /'sɛnʃənt/ adj making use of the senses, conscious.—**sentiently** adv.

sentiment /'sɛntəmənt/ n a feeling, awareness, or emotion; the thought behind something; an attitude of mind; a tendency to be swayed by feeling rather than reason; an exaggerated emotion.

sentimental /,sɛntə'mɛntəl/ adj of or arising from feelings; foolishly emotional; nostalgic.—**sentimentally** adv.

sentimentality /-'tælɪti/ n (pl **sentimentalities**) the quality or state of being sentimental; an affected or extreme tenderness.

sentinel /'sɛntɪnəl/ n a sentry or guard.

sentry /'sɛntri/ n (pl **sentries**) a soldier on guard to give warning of danger and to prevent unauthorized access.

sentry box n a shelter for a sentry.

senza /'sɛnzə/ prep (mus) without.

señor /se'njɔr/ n (pl **señors, señores**) the title of a Spanish-speaking man, equivalent to Mr or sir.

señora /se'njɔrə/ n (pl **señoras**) the title of a Spanish-speaking married woman, equivalent to Mrs or madam.

señorita /,sɛnjɔ'riːtə/ n (pl **señoritas**) the title of a Spanish-speaking unmarried woman, equivalent to Miss or madam.

Sep. abbr = September; Septuagint.

sepal /'siːpəl/ or /'sɛp-/ n any of the individual parts of the calyx of a flower.

separable /'sɛpərəbəl/ adj able to be separated or parted.—**separability** n.—**separably** adv.

separate /'sɛprət/ or /'sɛpərət/ vt to divide or part; to sever; to set or keep apart; to sort into different sizes. • vi to go different ways; to cease to live together as man and wife. • adj divided; distinct, individual; not shared. • n (pl) articles of clothing designed to be interchangeable with others to form various outfits.—**separately** adv.—**separateness** n.

separation /,sɛpə'reɪʃən/ n the act of separating or the state of being separate; a formal arrangement of husband and wife to live apart.

separatist /'sɛprətɪst/ or /'sɛpə-/ n a person who advocates or practises separation from an organization, church, or government; a person who advocates racial or political separation.—also adj.—**separatism** n.

separator /'sɛpə,reɪtər/ n one who separates; a machine that separates liquids from solids or liquids of different specific gravities.

Sephardi /sə'fɑrdi/ n (pl **Sephardim**) a Jew of Spanish, Portuguese or North African descent.—**Sephardic** adj.

sepia /'siːpiə/ adj, n (a) dark reddish brown.

sepoy /'siːpɔɪ/ n (formerly) an Indian soldier employed by the British.

seppuku /sə'puːkuː/ n harakiri.

sepsis /'sɛpsɪs/ n a septic state or agency; blood poisoning.

Sept. abbr = September.

septa /'sɛptə/ see **septum**.

September /sɛp'tɛmbər/ n the ninth month of the year, having 30 days.

septennial /sɛp'tɛniəl/ adj occuring every, or lasting, seven years. • n a seven-year period.—**septennially** adv.

septet /sɛp'tɛt/ n a set of seven singers or players; a musical composition for seven instruments or voices.

septic /'sɛptɪk/ adj infected by microorganisms; causing or caused by putrefaction.—**septically** adv.—**septicity** n.

septicaemia, septicemia /,sɛptə'siːmiə/ n a disease caused by poisonous bacteria in the blood.—**septicaemic, septicemic** adj.

septic tank n an underground tank in which sewage is decomposed by the action of bacteria.

septuagenarian /,sɛptuː:ədʒə'nɛriən/ or /,sɛptəgə'nɛriən/, /,sɛptʃuːə-/ n a person in his or her seventies.

Septuagesima /,sɛptjuː:ə'dʒɛsɪmə/ n the third Sunday before Lent.

Septuagint /'sɛptuː:ə,dʒɪnt/ or /,sɛp'tuː:ədʒɪnt/, /'sɛptʃuː:-/ n the Greek version of the Old Testament including the Apocrypha (said to have been translated by 70 scholars).

septum /'sɛptəm/ n (pl **septa**) a dividing membrane between two bodily cavities or parts.—**septal** adj.

septuplet /sɛp'tʌplɪt/ or /-'tuːplɪt/, /'sɛptə,plɛt/ n one of seven offspring produced at one birth.

sepulchral /sɪ'pʌlkrəl/ adj of or like a sepulchre; dismal, funereal; (sound) deep and hollow.

sepulchre, sepulcher /'sɛpəlkər/ n a tomb, a burial vault.

sequel /'siːkwəl/ n something that follows, the succeeding part; a consequence; the continuation of a story begun in an earlier literary work, film, etc.

sequela /sɪ'kwiːlə/ n (pl **sequelae**) (med) a condition arising from an existing disease; any complication of a disease or injury.

sequence /'siːkwəns/ n order of succession; a series of succeeding things; a single, uninterrupted episode, as in a film.

sequential /sɪ'kwɛnʃəl/ *adj* arranged in a sequence; following in sequence; consecutive.—**sequentially** *adv*.

sequester /sɪ'kwɛstər/ *vt* to place apart; to retire in seclusion; (*law*) to remove from one's possession until the claims of one's creditors are satisfied.

sequestrate /sɪ'kwɛstreɪt/ *vt* to sequester.—**sequestration** *n*.

sequin /'si:kwɪn/ *n* a shiny round piece of metal or foil sewn on clothes for decoration.

sequoia /sə'kwɔɪə/ *n* a lofty coniferous Californian tree.

sera /'sɪrə/ *see* serum.

sérac /se'ræk/ *n* a pinnacle or tower-shaped mass of ice among the crevasses of a glacier.

seraglio /sə'rælio:/ *n* (*pl* **seraglios**) a harem in a Muslim household or palace.

seraph /'sɛrəf/ *n* (*pl* **seraphs, seraphim**) (*theol*) a member of the highest order of angels.—**seraphic** *adj*.

Serb /sɜrb/, **Serbian** /'sɜrbiən/ *n* a native or inhabitant of Serbia; the Serbo-Croatian language of Serbia.—*also adj*.

Serbo-Croatian /,sɜrbo:kro:'eɪʃən/, **Serbo-Croat** /,sɜrbo:'kro:æt/ *n* the Slavonic language of the Serbs and Croatians.—*also adj*.

serenade /,sɛrə'neɪd/ *n* music sung or played at night beneath a person's window, *esp* by a lover. • *vt* to entertain with a serenade.

serendipity /,sɛrən'dɪpɪti/ *n* the faculty of making fortunate finds by chance.

serene /sə'ri:n/ *adj* calm; untroubled; tranquil; clear and unclouded; (*with cap*) honoured (used as part of certain royal titles).—**serenely** *adv*.—**serenity** *n*.

serf /sɜrf/ *n* (*pl* **serfs**) a labourer in feudal service who was bound to, and could be sold with, the land he worked; a drudge.—**serfdom** *n*.

serge /sɜrdʒ/ *n* a hard-wearing twilled woollen fabric.

sergeant /'sɑrdʒənt/ *n* a noncommissioned officer ranking above a corporal in the army, air force, and marine corps; a police officer ranking above a constable.

sergeant-at-arms *n* (*pl* **sergeants-at-arms**) an official in various legislative assemblies responsible for enforcing discipline.

sergeant major *n* a noncommissioned officer in the army, air force, marine corps serving as chief administrative assistant in a headquarters.

Sergt. *abbr* = Sergeant.

serial /'si:rɪəl/ *adj* of or forming a series; published, shown or broadcast by instalments at regular intervals. • *n* a story presented in regular instalments with a connected plot.

serialism /'si:rɪəlɪsm/ *n* (*mus*) the use of the twelve notes of the chromatic scale in a fixed order in a composition.

serialize /'si:rɪə,laɪz/ *vt* to arrange, publish or broadcast in serial form.—**serialization** *n*.

serial killer *n* one who commits over a period of time a number of killings often with a trademark method or pattern.

serial number *n* one of a series of numbers given for identification.

seriatim /,si:rɪ'eɪtɪm/ or /,sɛr-/ *adv* consecutively.

sericeous /sɪ'rɪʃəs/ *adj* (*bot*) covered in fine hairs

sericulture /'sɛrɪ,kʌltʃər/ *n* the breeding of silkworms to produce raw silk.—**sericultural** *adj*.—**sericulturist** *n*.

series /'si:ri:z/ *n sing, pl* a succession of items or events; a succession of things connected by some likeness; a sequence, a set; a radio or television serial whose episodes have self-contained plots; a set of books issued by one publisher; (*math*) a progression of numbers or quantities according to a certain law.

serif /'sɛrɪf/ *n* (*print*) a small line at the top or the bottom of the main stroke of a letter.

serigraph /'sɛrɪgræf/ *n* a print made using the silk-screen technique.—**serigraphy** *n*.

serin /'sɛrɪn/ *n* any of various small European finches related to the canary.

seriocomic /,si:rio:'kɒmɪk/ *adj* combining humour and seriousness.—**seriocomically** *adv*.

serious /'si:rɪəs/ *adj* grave, solemn, not frivolous; meaning what one says, sincere, earnest; requiring close attention or thought; important; critical.—**seriously** *adv*.—**seriousness** *n*.

sermon /'sɜrmən/ *n* a speech on religion or morals, *esp* by a clergyman; a long, serious talk of reproof, *esp* a tedious one.

sermonize /'sɜrmə,naɪz/ *vti* to compose sermons; to preach at or to at length.—**sermonizer** *n*.

sero- /si:ro:/ *prefix* serum.

serology /sɪ'rɒlədʒi/ *n* the scientific study of serums.—**serological** *adj*.—**serologist** *n*.

seropositive /,si:ro:'pɒzɪtɪv/ *adj* having a particular disease (*eg* HIV) for which one's blood has been tested.

serotinin /,sɛro:'tɪnɪn/ *n* a substance occurring in various body tissues that induces vasoconstriction.

serous /'si:rəs/ *adj* of or producing serum.

serous membrane *n* a thin membrane lining a body cavity that secretes a thin lubricant.

serpent /'sɜrpənt/ *n* a snake; a venomous or treacherous person.

serpentine /'sɜrpən,taɪn/ or /-ti:n/ *adj* like a serpent; twisting, tortuous; crooked, treacherous.

serpigo /sər'paɪgo:/ *n* a spreading skin complaint such as ringworm or herpes.

SERPS (*abbr*) = state earnings-related pension scheme.

serrate /se'reɪt/ *adj* (*leaves, etc*) having toothed edges; notched like a saw. • *vt* to make serrate.

serrated /-əd/ *adj* having an edge notched like the teeth of a saw.

serration /ser'eɪʃən/ *n* the state of being serrated; a saw-like edge; a single notch in a serrated edge.

serried /'sɛri:d/ *adj* packed closely, in compact order.

serum /'si:rəm/ *n* (*pl* **serums, sera**) the watery part of bodily fluid, *esp* liquid that separates out from the blood when it coagulates; such fluid taken from the blood of an animal immune to a disease, used as an antitoxin.

serum albumin *n* the principal blood protein.

serum hepatitis *n* a former name for hepatitis B, a viral disease, characterized by acute inflammation of the liver and jaundice, transmitted by contact with infected blood.

serval /'sɜrvəl/ *n* (*pl* **servals, serval**) an African cat with long legs and a tawny coat with black spots.

servant /'sɜrvənt/ *n* a personal or domestic attendant; one in the service of another.

serve /sɜrv/ *vt* to work for; to do military or naval service (for); to be useful to; to meet the needs (of), to suffice; (*a customer*) to wait upon; (*food, etc*) to hand round; (*a sentence*) to undergo; to be a soldier, sailor, etc; (*of a male animal*) to copulate with; (*law*) to deliver (a summons, etc); (*naut*) to bind (a rope) with thin cord to prevent fraying; (*tennis*) to put (the ball) into play. • *vi* to be employed as a servant; to be enough. • *n* the act of serving in tennis, etc.

server /'sɜrvər/ *n* one who serves, *esp* at tennis; something used in serving food and drink; a person who serves legal processes on another; the celebrant's assistant at mass; (*comput*) a computer used in a local area network that is the main source of programs or shared data.

service /'sɜrvɪs/ *n* the act of serving; the state of being a servant; domestic employment; a department of state employ; the people engaged in it; military employment or duty; work done for others; use, assistance; attendance in a hotel, etc; a facility providing a regular supply of trains, etc; a set of dishes; any religious ceremony; an overhaul of a vehicle; (*tennis*) the act or manner of seving; (*pl*) friendly help or professional aid; a system of providing a utility, as water, gas, etc. • *vt* to provide with assistance; to overhaul.

serviceable /'sɜrvɪsəbəl/ *adj* useful; durable.—**serviceably** *adv*.—**serviceableness** *n*.

service area *n* a place offering a range of services such as restaurants, toilet facilities, and petrol.

service charge *n* a sum added to a restaurant or hotel bill, etc for service.

serviceman /'sɜrvɪsmən/ *n* (*pl* **servicemen**) a member of the armed services; a person whose work is repairing something.—**servicewoman** *nf* (*pl* **servicewomen**)

service road *n* a minor road beside a main route that provides access to local shops, housing, etc.

service station *n* a place selling fuel, etc, for motor vehicles; a place at which some service is offered.

serviette /,sɜrvi'ɛt/ *n* a small napkin.

servile /'sɜrvaɪl/ *adj* of or like a slave; subservient; submissive; menial.—**servilely** *adv*.—**servility** *n*.

serving /'sɜrvɪŋ/ *n* a portion of food or drink.

servitude /'sɜrvɪ,tu:d/ or /-,tju:d/ *n* slavery, bondage; work imposed as punishment for a crime.

servo /'sɜrvo:/ *n* (*pl* **servos**) (*inf*) a servomotor or servomechanism. • *adj* activated by a servomechanism.

servomechanism /ˌsɜːvoʊˈmɛkəˌnɪzəm/ *n* an automatic device which uses small amounts of power to control a system of much greater power.

servomotor /ˈsɜːvoʊˌmoʊtər/ *n* a motor that supplies power to a servomechanism.

sesame /ˈsɛsəmi/ *n* an Asian plant that yields oil-bearing seeds; its seeds, also used for flavouring.

sesamoid /ˈsɛsəˌmɔɪd/ *adj* of or pertaining to the small bones or lumps of cartilage in a tendon.

sesqui- /ˈsɛskwi/ or /-kwə/ *prefix* one and a half; (*chem*) a ratio of two to three.

sesquicentenniel /ˌsɛskwɪsɛnˈtɛniəl/ or /ˌsɛskwə-/ *n* a period of 150 years; (the celebration of) a 150th anniversary.—*also adj*.

sessile /ˈsɛsaɪl/ *adj* (*leaves*) without a stalk; permanently attached.

session /ˈsɛʃən/ *n* the meeting of a court, legislature, etc; a series of such meetings; a period of these; a period of study, classes, etc; a university year; a period of time passed in an activity.

sesterce /ˈsɛstərs/, **sestertius** /sɛˈstərʃəs/ or /-ˈstərtiəs/ *n* in ancient Rome, a coin worth a quarter of a denarius.

sestet /sɛsˈtɛt/ *n* a poem or stanza of six lines, *esp* the last six lines of a sonnet.

set /sɛt/ *vb* (**setting, set**) *vt* to put in a specified place, condition, etc; (*trap for animals*) to fix; (*clock etc*) to adjust; (*table*) to arrange for a meal; (*hair*) to fix in a desired style; (*bone*)to put into normal position, etc; to make settled, rigid, or fixed; (*gems*) to mount; to direct; to furnish (an example) for others; to fit (words to music or music to words); (*type*) to arrange for printing; (*with* **against**) to weigh up, compare; to cause to be opposed to; (*with* **aside**) to discard; to reserve for a particular reason; (*with* **down**) to place (something) on a surface; to record, put in writing; to regard; to attribute (to); to allow to alight from (a vehicle); (*with* **out**) to present or display; to explain in detail; to plan, lay out. • *vi* to become firm, hard or fixed; to begin to move (out, forth, off, etc); (*sun*) to sink below the horizon; (*with* **about**) to begin; to abuse physically or verbally; (*with* **in**) to stitch (a sleeve) within a garment; to become established; (*with* **off**) to show up by contrast; to set in motion; to cause to explode; (*with* **on**) to urge (as a dog) to attack or pursue; to go on, advance; (*with* **out**) to begin a journey, career, etc; (*with* **to**) to start working, *esp* eagerly; to start fighting; (*with* **up**) to erect; to establish, to found; (*with* **upon**) to attack, *usu* with violence. • *adj* fixed, established; intentional; rigid, firm; obstinate; ready. • *n* a number of persons or things classed or belonging together; a group, a clique; the way in which a thing is set; direction; the scenery for a play, film, etc; assembled equipment for radio or television reception, etc; (*math*) the totality of points, numbers, or objects that satisfy a given condition; (*tennis*) a series of games forming a unit of a match; a rooted cutting of a plant ready for transplanting; a badger's burrow.—*also* **sett**.

seta /ˈsiːtə/ *n* (*pl* **setae**) a bristle or similar appendage of an animal or plant.

setback /ˈsɛtbæk/ *n* misfortune; a reversal.

setline /ˈsɛtlaɪn/ *n* a long fishing line with hooked shorter lines attached at regular intervals.

set piece *n* a formal or elaborate performance, *esp* of a work of art, music, etc; an elaborate fireworks display; (*sport*) a carefully rehearsed team move *usu* aimed at gaining the ball when play resumes.

setscrew /ˈsɛtˌskruː/ *n* a screw which when tightened prevents parts of a machine from moving relative to one another.

set-square *n* a flat triangular instrument for drawing angles.

settee /sɛˈtiː/ *n* a sofa for two people.

setter /ˈsɛtər/ *n* a large breed of gundog trained to stand rigid when spotting game.

set theory *n* the branch of mathematics concerned with the relations and properties of sets.

setting /ˈsɛtɪŋ/ *n* a background, scene, surroundings, environment; a mounting, as for a gem; the music for a song, etc.

settle /ˈsɛtəl/ *vti* to put in order; to pay (an account); to clarify; to decide, to come to an agreement; to make or become quiet or calm; to make or become firm; to establish or become established in a place, business, home, etc; to colonize (a country); to take up residence; to come to rest; (*dregs*) to fall to the bottom; to stabilize; to make or become comfortable (for resting); (*bird*) to alight; to bestow legally for life; (*with* **for**) to be content with.

settlement /ˈsɛtəlmənt/ *n* the act of settling; a sum settled, *esp* on a woman at her marriage; an arrangement; a small village; a newly established colony; subsidence (of buildings).

settler /ˈsɛtlər/ *n* a person who settles; an early colonist.

set-to *n* (*inf*) a squabble, fight.

set-up *n* the plan, makeup, etc, of equipment used in an organization; the details of a situation, plan, etc; (*inf*) a contest, etc, arranged to result in an easy win.

seven /ˈsɛvən/ *adj, n* one more than six. • *n* the symbol for this (7, VII, vii); the seventh in a series or set; something having seven units as members.

sevenfold /ˈsɛvənˌfoʊld/ *adj* having seven units or members; being seven times as great or as many.

seven seas *npl* all the world's oceans.

seventeen /ˌsɛvənˈtiːn/ *adj, n* one more than sixteen. • *n* the symbol for this (17, XVII, xvii).—**seventeenth** *adj*.

seventh /ˈsɛvənθ/ *adj, n* next after sixth; one of seven equal parts of a thing. • *n* (*mus*) an interval of seven diatonic degrees; the leading note.

seventh heaven *n* perfect happiness.

seventy /ˈsɛvənti/ *adj, n* seven times ten. • *n* the symbol for this (70, LXX, lxx); (in *pl*) **seventies** (70s) the numbers for 70 to 79; the same numbers in a life or century.—**seventieth** *adj*.

sever /ˈsɛvər/ *vti* to separate, to divide into parts; to break off.—**severance** *n*.

several /ˈsɛvrəl/ *adj* more than two but not very many; various; separate, distinct; respective. • *pron* (*with pl vb*) a few. • *n* (*with pl vb*) a small number (of).

severe /sɪˈviːr/ *adj* harsh, not lenient; very strict; stern; censorious; exacting, difficult; violent, not slight; (*illness*) critical; (*art*) plain, not florid.—**severely** *adv*.—**severity** *n*.

Seville orange /ˈsɛvɪl/ *n* (an orange tree bearing) a fruit with bitter flesh used to make marmalade.

Sèvres /sɛvr/ *n* a type of fine porcelain made in France.

sew /soʊ/ *vti* (**sewing, sewn** *or* **sewed**) to join or stitch together with needle and thread; to make, mend, etc, by sewing; (*with* **up**) to get full control of; (*inf*) to make sure of success in.—**sewing** *n*.

sewage /ˈsuːɪdʒ/ *n* waste matter carried away in a sewer.

sewage farm *n* a place where sewage is treated for use as manure.

sewer[1] /ˈsuːər/ *n* one who sews.

sewer[2] *n* an underground pipe or drain for carrying off liquid waste matter, etc; a main drain.

sewerage /ˈsuːərɪdʒ/ *n* a system of drainage by sewers; sewage.

sewing machine *n* a machine for sewing or stitching *usu* driven by an electric motor.

sewn /soʊn/ *see* **sew**.

sex /sɛks/ *n* the characteristics that distinguish male and female organisms on the basis of their reproductive function; either of the two categories (male and female) so distinguished; males or females collectively; the state of being male or female; the attraction between the sexes; (*inf*) sexual intercourse.

sex- *prefix* six.

sexagenarian /ˌsɛksədʒɪˈnɛriən/ *n* a person in the age range 60–69.—*also adj*.

Sexagesima /ˌsɛksəˈdʒɛsɪmə/ *n* the second Sunday before Lent.

sexagesimal /ˌsɛksəˈdʒɛsɪməl/ *adj* of or based on the number 60.

sex appeal *n* what makes a person sexually desirable.

sex chromosome *n* a chromosome that determines the sex of an animal.

sexed /sɛkst/ *adj* having a certain amount of sex or sexuality.

sex hormone *n* a hormone affecting the development of sexual organs and characteristics.

sexism /ˈsɛksɪzəm/ *n* exploitation and domination of one sex by the other, *esp* of women by men.—**sexist** *adj, n*.

sexless /ˈsɛksləs/ *adj* without sexual intercourse; sexually unappealing.—**sexlessly** *adv*.—**sexlessness** *n*.

sex object *n* a person regarded solely in terms of their sexual attractiveness.

sexology /sɛkˈsɒlədʒi/ *n* the study of human sexuality.—**sexologist** *n*.—**sexological** *adj*.

sex shop *n* a shop specializing in sex aids, pornographic magazines, etc.

sextant /ˈsɛkstənt/ *n* a navigator's instrument for measuring the altitude of the sun, etc, to determine position at sea.

sextet /sɛksˈtɛt/ *n* a set of six singers or players; a musical composition for six instruments or voices.

sexton /'sɛkstən/ *n* an officer in charge of the maintenance of church property.

sextuple /'sɛks,tʊpəl/ *adj* having six units or members; being six times as much or as many.—*also n.*

sextuplet /'sɛks,tʊplət/ *n* one of six offspring produced at one birth.

sexual /'sɛkʃʊəl/ *adj* of sex or the sexes; having sex.—**sexually** *adj.*

sexual harassment *n* frequent unwelcome attention from the opposite sex in the form of suggestive remarks, fondling, etc.

sexual intercourse the act of copulating.

sexuality /,sɛkʃʊ'ælɪti/ *n* sexual activity; expression of sexual interest, *esp* when excessive.

sexually transmitted disease *n* any of various diseases, such as syphilis or HIV, transmitted by sexual contact.—*also* **venereal disease**.

sexy /'sɛksi/ *adj* (**sexier, sexiest**) (*inf*) exciting, or intending to excite, sexual desire; attractive, entertaining; fashionable or stylish and as a result worthwhile.—**sexily** *adv.*—**sexiness** *n.*

SF *abbr* = science fiction.

sf, sfz *abbr* = sforzando.

sforzando /sfɔr'tsændo:/, **sforzato** /-'tsɒto:/ *adv* (*mus*) with vigour at the start. • *n* a notation indicating this.

sgd *abbr* = signed.

SGM *abbr* = Sergeant Major.

sgraffito /sgrɒ'fi:to:/ *n* (*pl* **sgraffiti**) (an example of) a technique in ceramic or mural design in which the surface layer (of glaze, plaster, etc) is scraped away to expose a contrasting background.

Sgt *abbr* = sergeant

Sgt Maj *abbr* = sergeant major.

sh /ʃ/ *interj* used to command silence.

shabby /'ʃæbi/ *adj* (**shabbier, shabbiest**) (*clothes*) threadbare, worn, or dirty; run-down, dilapidated; (*act, trick*) mean, shameful.—**shabbily** *adv.*—**shabbiness** *n.*

shack /ʃæk/ *n* a small, crudely built house or cabin; a shanty. • *vi* (*with* **up**) (*sl*) to cohabit (with); to spend the night (with), *esp* a person of the opposite sex.

shackle /'ʃækəl/ *n* a metal fastening, *usu* in pairs, for the wrists or ankles of a prisoner; a staple; anything that restrains freedom; (*pl*) fetters. • *vt* to fasten or join by a shackle; to hamper, to impede.

shad /ʃæd/ *n* (*pl* **shad, shads**) any of various fishes of the herring family used as food.

shade /ʃeɪd/ *n* relative darkness; dimness; the darker parts of anything; shadow; a shield or screen protecting from bright light; a ghost; a place sheltered from the sun; degree of darkness of a colour, *esp* when made by the addition of black; a minute difference; a blind; (*pl*) the darkness of approaching night; (*pl: sl*) sunglasses. • *vti* to screen from light; to overshadow; to make dark; to pass by degrees into another colour; to change slightly or by degrees.

shading /'ʃeɪdɪŋ/ *n* the fine gradations of colour, line, tone, etc, creating light and dark in a painting, etc; a shielding against light; nuances.

shadow /'ʃædo:/ *n* a patch of shade; darkness, obscurity; the dark parts of a painting, etc; shelter, protection; the dark shape of an object produced on a surface by intercepted light; an inseparable companion; a person (as a detective, etc) who shadows; an unsubstantial thing, a phantom; a mere remnant, a slight trace; gloom, affliction. • *vt* to cast a shadow over; to cloud; to follow and watch, *esp* in secret. • *adj* having an indistinct pattern or darker section; (*opposition party*) matching a function or position of the party in power.

shadow-box *vi* (*boxing*) to practice blows against an invisible opponent.

shadowy /'ʃædo:i/ *adj* full of shadows; dim, indistinct; unsubstantial.

shady /'ʃeɪdi/ *adj* (**shadier, shadiest**) giving or full of shade; sheltered from the sun; (*inf*) of doubtful honesty, disreputable.

SHAEF (*abbr*) = (*World War II*) Supreme Headquarters Allied Expeditionary Forces.

shaft /ʃæft/ *n* a straight rod, a pole; a stem, a shank; the main part of a column; an arrow or spear, or its stem; anything hurled like a missile; a ray of light, a stroke of lightning; a revolving rod for transmitting power, an axle; one of the poles between which a horse is harnessed; a hole giving access to a mine; a vertical opening through a building, as for a lift; a critical remark or attack; (*sl*) harsh or unfair treatment.

shag /ʃæg/ *n* a coarse tobacco cut into long pieces; a rough mop of hair, etc; a crested cormorant. • *adj* (*carpet*) having long, thick, woollen threads.

shaggy /'ʃægi/ *adj* (**shaggier, shaggiest**) (*hair, fur, etc*) long and unkempt; rough; untidy.—**shagginess** *n.*

shaggy-dog story *n* (*inf*) a long joke with a punch line that is a deliberate anticlimax.

shagreen /ʃæ'gri:n/ *n* the rough skin of certain sharks and rays; a type of leather with a gritty surface made from the hides of certain animals.

shah /ʃɒ/ *n* the title of the former ruler of Iran.

shake /ʃeɪk/ *vti* (**shaking, shook**, *pp* **shaken**) to move to and fro with quick short motions, to agitate; to tremble or vibrate; to jar or jolt; to brandish; to make or become unsteady; to weaken; to unsettle; to unnerve or become unnerved; to clasp (another's hand) as in greeting; (*with* **down**) to cause to subside by shaking; to obtain makeshift accommodation; (*sl*) to extort money from; (*with* **off**) to get rid of; (*with* **out**) to empty by shaking; to spread (a sail); (*with* **up**) to shake together, to mix; to upset. • *n* the act of shaking or being shaken; a jolt; a shock; a milkshake; (*inf*) a deal; (*pl inf*) a convulsive trembling.

shakedown /'ʃeɪkdaʊn/ *n* a makeshift or improvised bed; (*sl*) extortion of money, as by blackmail; a thorough search.

shaker /'ʃeɪkər/ *n* a container for holding condiments; a container in which cocktail ingredients are mixed.

shakers /-kərz/ *see* **movers and shakers**.

Shakespearean, Shakespearian /ʃeɪk'spiːriən/ *adj* of, pertaining to, or characteristic of William Shakespeare (1564-1616) or his works.

shako /'ʃeɪko:/ *n* (*pl* **shakos, shakoes**) a cylindrical military cap with a high crown and tall plume.

shake-up /'ʃeɪk,ʌp/ *n* an extensive reorganization.

shaky /'ʃeɪki/ *adj* (**shakier, shakiest**) unsteady; infirm; unreliable.—**shakily** *adv.*—**shakiness** *n.*

shale /ʃeɪl/ *n* a kind of clay rock like slate but softer.

shall /ʃæl/ or /ʃəl/ *vb aux* (*pt* **should**) used formally to express the future in the 1st person and determination, obligation or necessity in the 2nd and 3rd person; the more common form is **will**.

shallot /'ʃælət/ or /ʃə'lɒt/ *n* a small onion.

shallow /'ʃælo:/ *adj* having little depth; superficial, trivial. • *n* a shallow area in otherwise deep water.—**shallowness** *n.*

shalt /ʃælt/ (*arch*) *the 2nd person sing of* **shall**.

sham /ʃæm/ *n* a pretence; a person or thing that is a fraud. • *adj* counterfeit; fake.

shaman /'ʃeɪmən/ *n* a priest of shamanism believed to possess magical powers which allow him to communicate with and influence the spirit world.

shamanism /-ˌɪzəm/ *n* a religion of northern Asia which views the world as dominated by good and evil spirits that can be influenced only by the shamans.

shamateur /'ʃæmə,tʃər/ or /-tər/ *n* (*sport*) a player, athlete, etc who is officially classed as an amateur but who accepts payment.

shamble /'ʃæmbəl/ *vi* to walk with an ungainly stumbling gait.—*also n.*

shambles /'ʃæmbəlz/ *npl* a scene of great disorder; a slaughterhouse.

shambolic /ʃæm'bɒlɪk/ *adj* (*inf*) disorganized; utterly confused.

shame /ʃeɪm/ *n* a painful emotion arising from guilt or impropriety; modesty; disgrace, dishonour; the cause of this; (*sl*) a piece of unfairness. • *vti* to cause to feel shame; to bring disgrace on; to force by shame (into); to humiliate by showing superior qualities.

shamefaced /'ʃeɪmfeɪst/ *adj* bashful or modest; sheepish; showing shame; ashamed.—**shamefacedly** *adv.*—**shamefacedness** *n.*

shameful /'ʃeɪmfʊl/ *adj* disgraceful; outrageous.—**shamefully** *adv.*—**shamefulness** *n.*

shameless /'ʃeɪmləs/ *adj* immodest; impudent, brazen.—**shamelessly** *adv.*—**shamelessness** *n.*

shammy (leather) /'ʃæmi/ *see* **chamois leather**.

shampoo /ʃæm'puː/ *n* a liquid cleansing agent for washing the hair; the process of washing the hair or a carpet, etc. • *vt* to wash with shampoo.—**shampooer** *n.*

shamrock /'ʃæmrɒk/ *n* a three-leaved cloverlike plant, the national emblem of Ireland.

shan't /ʃænt/ = shall not.

shandy /'ʃændi/ *n* (*pl* **shandies**) beer diluted with a non-alcoholic drink (as lemonade).

shanghai /ʃæŋ'haɪ/ *vt* (**shanghaiing, shanghaied**) to force (a sailor, etc) to join a ship's crew, *esp* by kidnapping or drugging; to trick or force (a person) into doing something.— **shanghaier** *n*.

Shangri-la /ʃæŋgrɪ'lɒ/ *n* an imaginary utopia.

shank /ʃæŋk/ *n* the leg from the knee to the ankle, the shin; a shaft, stem, or handle.

shanks's pony, shanks's mare *n* one's own legs as used for walking.

shantung /ʃæn'tʊŋ/ *n* a coarse kind of silk.

shanty[1] /'ʃæntɪ/ *n* (*pl* **shanties**) a crude hut built from corrugated iron or cardboard.

shanty[2] *n* (*pl* **shanties**) (*formerly*) a song sung by sailors in the rhythm of their work, a chantey.

shantytown /'ʃæntɪˌtaʊn/ *n* a community of poor people living in shanties.

SHAPE /ʃeɪp/ (*abbr*) = Supreme Headquarters Allied Powers Europe.

shape /ʃeɪp/ *n* the external appearance, outline or contour of a thing; a figure; a definite form; an orderly arrangement; a mould or pattern; (*inf*) condition. • *vt* to give shape to; to form; to model, to mould; to determine; (*with* **up**) to develop to a definite or satisfactory form.

shapeless /'ʃeɪpləs/ *adj* lacking definite form; baggy.—**shapelessly** *adv*.—**shapelessness** *n*.

shapely /'ʃeɪplɪ/ *adj* (**shapelier, shapeliest**) well-proportioned.—**shapeliness** *n*.

shard /ʃɑrd/ *n* a fragment or broken piece, *esp* of pottery.

share /ʃer/ *n* an allotted portion, a part; one of the parts into which a company's capital stock is divided, entitling the holder to a share of profits. • *vti* to distribute, to apportion (out); to have or experience in common with others; to divide into portions; to contribute or receive a share of; to use jointly.

sharecropper /'ʃer,krɒpər/ *n* in the US, a tenant farmer who hands over a portion of the crop as rent.—**sharecrop** *vi*.

shareholder /'ʃerhoˌldər/ *n* a holder of shares in a property, *esp* a company.

share option *n* an option open to employees to buy shares in the company they work for.

shark /ʃɑrk/ *n* a large voracious marine fish; an extortioner, a swindler; (*sl*) an expert in a given activity.

sharkskin /'ʃɑrkskɪn/ *n* a rayon fabric with a smooth shiny finish.

sharp /ʃɑrp/ *adj* having a keen edge or fine point; pointed, not rounded; clear-cut; distinct; intense, piercing; cutting, severe; keen, biting; clever, artful; alert, mentally acute; (*mus*) raised a semitone in pitch; out of tune by being too high; (*sl*) smartly dressed. • *adv* punctually; quickly; (*mus*) above the right pitch. • *n* (*mus*) a note that is a semitone higher than the note denoted by the same letter; the symbol for this.—**sharply** *adv*.—**sharpness** *n*.

sharpen /'ʃɑrpən/ *vti* to make or become sharp or sharper.

sharpener /-ər/ *n* something that sharpens.

sharpshooter /'ʃɑrp,ʃuːtər/ *n* a marksman.

sharp-tongued /-,tʌŋd/ *adj* sarcastic; quick to criticize.

sharp-witted /'ʃɑrp'wɪtɪd/ *adj* thinking quickly and effectively.—**sharp-wittedly** *adv*.—**sharp-wittedness** *n*.

shatter /'ʃætər/ *vti* to reduce to fragments suddenly; to smash; to damage or be damaged severely.

shatterproof /'ʃætərpruːf/ *adj* resistant to shattering.

shave /ʃeɪv/ *vti* to remove facial or body hair with a razor; to cut away thin slices, to pare; to miss narrowly, to graze. • *n* the act or process of shaving; narrow escape or miss; a paring.

shaven /'ʃeɪvən/ *adj* shaved.

shaver /'ʃeɪvər/ *n* one who shaves; an instrument for shaving, *esp* an electrical one.

Shavian /'ʃeɪvɪən/ *adj* of, relating to, or resembling the works of the writer George Bernard Shaw (1856–1950).

shaving /'ʃeɪvɪŋ/ *n* the act of using a razor or scraping; a thin slice of wood, metal, etc, shaved off.

shawl /ʃɒl/ *n* a large square or oblong cloth worn as a covering for the head or shoulders or as a wrapping for a baby.

shawm /ʃɒm/ *n* a medieval woodwind instrument resembling an oboe.

she /ʃiː/ *pron* (*obj* **her**, *poss* **her, hers**) the female person or thing named before or in question. • *n* a female person or animal.

shea /ʃiː/ or /'ʃiːə/ *n* a tropical African tree with seeds that yield a butter-like fat used as food.

sheaf /ʃiːf/ *n* (*pl* **sheaves**) a bundle of reaped corn bound together; a collection of papers, etc, tied in a bundle.

shear /ʃiːr/ *vti* (**shearing, sheared** *or* **shorn**) to clip or cut (through); to remove (a sheep's fleece) by clipping; to divest; (*metal*) to break off because of a heavy force or twist. • *n* a stress acting sideways on a rivet and causing a break, etc; a machine for cutting metal; (*pl*) large scissors; (*pl*) a tool for cutting hedges, etc.

shearling /'ʃiːrlɪŋ/ *n* (the fleece of) a sheep after its first shearing.

shearwater /'ʃiːr,wɒtər/ *n* any of various seabirds that often glide close to the water.

sheath /ʃiːθ/ *n* (*pl* **sheaths**) a close-fitting cover, *esp* for a blade; a condom; a closefitting dress *usu* worn without a belt.

sheathe /ʃiːð/ *vt* to put into a sheath; to encase, to protect with a casing; (*cat*) to withdraw its claws.

sheath-knife *n* a knife with a fixed blade covered by a sheath.

sheave[1] /ʃiːv/ *vt* to gather into sheaves.

sheave[2] *n* a grooved wheel, *esp* in a pulley.

sheaves /ʃiːvz/ *see* **sheaf**.

shebang /ʃə'bæŋ/ *n* (*inf*) affair, business.

shebeen /ʃə'biːn/ *n* an unlicensed or illegal drinking den.

she'd /ʃiːd/ = she had; she would.

shed[1] /ʃed/ *n* a hut for storing garden tools; a large roofed shelter often with one or more sides open; a warehouse.

shed[2] *vt* (**shedding, shed**) (*tears*) to let fall; (*skin, etc*) to lose or cast off; to allow or cause to flow; to diffuse, radiate. • *n* a parting in the hair.

sheen /ʃiːn/ *n* a gloss, lustre; brightness.

sheep /ʃiːp/ *n* (*pl* **sheep**) a cud-chewing four-footed animal with a fleece and edible flesh called mutton; a bashful, submissive person.

sheepcote /-,kot/ *n* a sheepfold.

sheep-dip /-,dɪp/ *n* a liquid disinfectant or insecticide into which sheep are plunged to destroy parasites.

sheepdog /'ʃiːpdɒg/ *n* a dog trained to tend, drive, or guard sheep.

sheepfold /'ʃiːpfoːld/ *n* an enclosure for sheep.

sheepish /'ʃiːpɪʃ/ *adj* bashful, embarrassed.—**sheepishly** *adv*.—**sheepishness** *n*.

sheep's eyes *npl* (*arch*) amorous glances.

sheepshank /'ʃiːpʃæŋk/ *n* a knot in a rope to shorten it temporarily.

sheepskin /'ʃiːpskɪn/ *n* the skin of a sheep, *esp* with the fleece; a rug, parchment, or leather made from it; a garment made of or lined with sheepskin.

sheepwalk /'ʃiːpwɒk/ *n* an area of pasture for sheep.

sheer[1] /ʃiːr/ *adj* pure, unmixed; downright, utter; perpendicular, extremely steep; (*fabric*) delicately fine, transparent. • *adv* outright; perpendicularly, steeply.

sheer[2] *vti* to deviate or cause to deviate from a course; to swerve. • *n* the act of sheering; the upward curve of a deck toward bow or stern; a change in a ship's course.

sheerlegs /'ʃiːrlegz/ *n sing* a hoisting device comprising two or more upright poles crossed at the top from which lifting gear is suspended.

sheet[1] /ʃiːt/ *n* a broad thin piece of any material, as glass, plywood, metal, etc; a large rectangular piece of cloth used as inner bed clothes; a single piece of paper; (*inf*) a newspaper; a broad, flat expanse; a suspended or moving expanse (as of fire or rain).

sheet[2] *n* a rope that controls the angle of a sail in relation to the wind.

sheet anchor *n* a large anchor used only in emergencies; a support in extremity.

sheet bend *n* a knot for joining ropes of different thicknesses.

sheet glass *n* glass made in large sheets directly from the furnace or by making a cylinder and then flattening it.

sheeting /'ʃiːtɪŋ/ *n* fabric for sheets.

sheet lightning *n* lightning that has the appearance of a broad sheet due to reflection and diffusion by the clouds and sky.

sheet metal *n* metal rolled out in the form of a thin sheet.

sheet music *n* music printed on unbound sheets of paper.

sheikh /ʃiːk/ or /ʃeɪk/ *n* an Arab chief.

sheila /'ʃiːlə/ *n* (*Austral, NZ sl*) a girl or woman.

shekel /'ʃekəl/ *n* the unit of money in Israel; an old Jewish weight or silver coin; (*pl*) (*sl*) money.

shelduck /'ʃeldʌk/, **sheldrake** /-,dreɪk/ *n* any of several Old World brightly plumaged ducks.

shelf /ʃɛlf/ n (pl **shelves**) a board fixed horizontally on a wall or in a cupboard for holding articles; a ledge on a cliff face; a reef, a shoal.

shelf life n the length of time for which something may be stored without deterioration.

shell /ʃɛl/ n a hard outside covering of a nut, egg, shellfish, etc; an explosive projectile; an external framework; a light racing boat; outward show; a cartridge. • vt to remove the shell from; to bombard (with shells); (with **out**) (inf) to pay out (money).

she'll /ʃiːl/ or /ʃɪl/ = she will; she shall.

shellac, shellack /ʃə'læk/ n a resin usu produced in thin, flaky layers or shells; a thin varnish containing this and alcohol.

shellfish /'ʃɛlfɪʃ/ n an aquatic animal, esp an edible one, with a shell.

shellproof /'ʃɛlˌpruːf/ adj impervious to artillery shells, rockets and bombs.

shell shock n a nervous disorder caused by the shock of being under fire.—**shell-shocked** adj.

shelter /'ʃɛltər/ n a structure that protects, esp against weather; a place giving protection, a refuge; protection. • vti to give shelter to, to shield, to cover; to take shelter.

sheltie, shelty /'ʃɛlti/ n (pl **shelties**) a Shetland pony or Shetland sheepdog.

shelve /ʃɛlv/ vti to place on a shelf; to defer consideration, to put aside; to slope gently, to incline.

shelves /ʃɛlvz/ see **shelf**.

shelving /'ʃɛlvɪŋ/ n material for making shelves; shelves collectively.

shemozzle /ʃə'mɒzəl/ n (inf) a scene of confusion; a brawl.

shenanigan /ʃə'nænɪɡən/ n (often pl) trickery, deception; mischief, boisterous high spirits.

shepherd /'ʃɛpərd/ n a person who looks after sheep; a pastor. • vt to look after, as a shepherd; to manoeuvre or marshal in a particular direction.—**shepherdess** nf.

shepherd dog n a sheepdog.

shepherd's pie n a dish of minced meat covered with a mashed potato crust.

shepherd's purse n an annual plant with small white flowers and heart-shaped seed pods.

sherbet /'ʃɜːbət/ n a fruit-flavoured powder that can be used to make a slightly sparkling drink; a sorbet.

sheriff /'ʃɛrɪf/ n in US, the chief law enforcement officer of a county; in Scotland, a judge in an intermediate law court; in England and Wales, the chief officer of the Crown, a ceremonial post.

sheriff court n (Scot) the court dealing with the majority of criminal and civil cases.

Sherpa /'ʃɜːpə/ n (pl **Sherpas, Sherpa**) a member of a people living on the southern slopes of the Himalayas on the borders of Nepal and Tibet.

sherry /'ʃɛri/ n (pl **sherries**) a fortified wine originally made in Spain.

she's /ʃiːz/ = she is; she has.

Shetland pony /'ʃɛtlənd/ n a breed of small sturdy pony with a shaggy mane.

Shetland sheepdog n a breed of dog resembling a collie but smaller.

SHF, shf abbr = superhigh frequency.

Shiah, Shia /'ʃiə/ n a member of the main branch of Islam who acknowledge Mohammed's cousin Ali and his successors as the true imams.—also adj.

shibboleth /'ʃɪbəˌlɛθ/ n a slogan or catchword, esp that regarded as outmoded or identified with a particular group or culture; a custom or linguistic usage which identifies members of a particular group, party, class, etc.

shied /ʃaɪd/ see **shy**[1], **shy**[2].

shield /ʃiːld/ n a broad piece of armour carried for defence, usu on the left arm; a protective covering or guard; a thing or person that protects; a trophy in the shape of a shield. • vti to defend; to protect; to screen.

shier /'ʃaɪər/, **shiest** /-əst/ see **shy**[1].

shift /ʃɪft/ vti to change position (of); to contrive, to manage; to remove, to transfer; to replace by another or others; (gears) to change the arrangement of. • n a change in position; an expedient; a group of people working in relay with others; the time worked by them; a change or transfer; a straight dress.

shiftless /'ʃɪftləs/ adj incapable; feckless.—**shiftlessly** adv.—**shiftlessness** n.

shifty /'ʃɪfti/ adj (**shiftier, shiftiest**) artful, tricky; evasive.—**shiftily** adv.—**shiftiness** n.

shigella /ʃɪ'ɡɛlə/ n any of a genus of rod-shaped bacteria causing dysentery in humans and animals.

Shiite /'ʃiːəɪt/, **Shiah** /'ʃiə/ n a follower of Shiah.—also adj.

shillelagh /'ʃiləˌleɪ/ n an Irish club or cudgel.

shilling /'ʃɪlɪŋ/ n a former unit of currency of the UK and other countries, worth one twentieth of a pound.

shillyshally /'ʃiliˌʃæli/ vi (**shillyshallying, shillyshallied**) to vacillate, to hesitate. • n (pl **shillyshallies**) the inability to make up one's mind.

shim /ʃɪm/ n a thin washer or spacer used to tighten or space out joints, etc. • vt (**shimming, shimmed**) to space out, etc using shims.

shimmer /'ʃɪmər/ vi to glisten softly, to glimmer.—also n.—**shimmery** adj.

shimmy /'ʃɪmi/ n (pl **shimmies**) a jazz dance involving rapid movements of the upper body; an abnormal vibration in a vehicle or aircraft. • vi (**shimmying, shimmied**) to dance a shimmy; to vibrate.

shin /ʃɪn/ n the front part of the leg from the knee to the ankle; the shank. • vi (with **up**) to climb (a pole, etc) by gripping with legs and hands.

shinbone /'ʃɪnˌbəʊn/ n the tibia.

shindig /'ʃɪndɪɡ/ n (inf) a lively, noisy celebration; an uproar.

shine /ʃaɪn/ vti (**shining, shone**) to emit light; to be bright, to glow; to be brilliant or conspicuous; to direct the light of; to cause to gleam by polishing. • n a lustre, a gloss; (sl) a liking.

shiner /'ʃaɪnər/ n (inf) a black eye.

shingle[1] /'ʃɪŋɡəl/ n a thin wedge-shaped roof tile; a small signboard.

shingle[2] n waterworn pebbles as on a beach; an area covered with these.—**shingly** adj.

shingles /'ʃɪŋɡəlz/ npl a virus disease marked by a painful rash of red spots on the skin.

Shinto /'ʃɪntəʊ/ n the indigenous religion of Japan, involving veneration of the emperor, and the worship of ancestors and various natural deities.—**Shintoism** n.—**Shintoist** n.

shinty /'ʃɪnti/ n a game similar to hockey and hurling, played with a ball and curved sticks.

shiny /'ʃaɪni/ adj (**shinier, shiniest**) glossy, polished; worn smooth.

ship /ʃɪp/ n a large vessel navigating deep water; its officers and crew; a spacecraft. • vti (**shipping, shipped**) to transport by any carrier; to take in (water) over the side; to lay (oars) inside a boat; to go on board; to go or travel by ship.

shipboard /'ʃɪpbɔːd/ n the side of a ship.

shipbuilder /'ʃɪpˌbɪldər/ n a person or company that designs or constructs ships.—**shipbuilding** n.

ship chandler n an individual or business that provides essential supplies for ships.

shipload /'ʃɪpləʊd/ n as much as a ship can carry.

shipmaster /'ʃɪpˌmɑːstər/ n the captain or master of a ship.

shipmate /'ʃɪpmeɪt/ n a fellow sailor.

shipment /'ʃɪpmənt/ n goods shipped; a consignment.

ship of the line n (formerly) a warship large enough to fight in the first line of battle.

shipowner /'ʃɪpˌəʊnər/ n a person who owns (or has shares in) a ship.

shipper /'ʃɪpər/ n an individual or company that ships goods.

shipping /'ʃɪpɪŋ/ n the business of transporting goods; ships collectively.

ship's biscuit n a type of hard biscuit that was formerly part of a sailor's diet.

shipshape /'ʃɪpˌʃeɪp/ adj in good order, tidy.

shipworm /'ʃɪpwɜːm/ n any of a genus of worm-like molluscs that burrow in submerged wood.

shipwreck /'ʃɪprɛk/ n the loss of a vessel at sea; the remains of a wrecked ship; ruin, destruction. • vti to destroy by or suffer shipwreck; to ruin.

shipwright /'ʃɪpraɪt/ n a person skilled in constructing and repairing ships.

shipyard /'ʃɪpjɑːd/ n a yard or shed where ships are built or repaired.

shire /ʃaɪr/ n a county; a large powerful breed of draught horse.

shirk /ʃɜːk/ vti to neglect or avoid work; to refuse to face (duty, danger, etc).—**shirker** n.

shirr /ʃər/ *vt* to gather (fabric) with parallel threads run through it; to bake (eggs) in buttered dishes.

shirring /ʃiːrɪŋ/ or /ʃərɪŋ/ *n* a gathering made in cloth by drawing the material up on parallel rows of short stitches.

shirt /ʃərt/ *n* a sleeved garment of cotton, etc, for the upper body, typically having a fitted collar and cuffs and front buttons; (*inf*) one's money or resources.

shirtdress /ʃərtˌdres/ *n* a long shirt worn as a dress.

shirting /-ɪŋ/ *n* a fabric suitable for men's shirts.

shirtsleeve /-ˌsliːv/ *n* the sleeve of a shirt.

shirt-tail /-ˌteɪl/ *n* the flap of material at the back of a shirt below the waist.

shirtwaister, shirtwaist /-ˌweɪst/ *n* a woman's dress tailored in front in style similar to a shirt.

shirty /ʃərtɪ/ *adj* (**shirtier, shirtiest**) (*sl*) irritable, rude.

shish kebab /ʃɪʃkəˈbɒb/ or /-bæb/ *n* a kebab.

shit[1], shite /ʃɪt/ *n* (*vulg*) waste matter from humans or animals; excrement; heroin; something that is worthless. • *vti* to defecate (on). • *interj* (*sl*) an expression of strong disgust or disapproval.

shit[2] *n* (*sl*) something that is good.

shivaree /ʃɪvəri/ *see* **charivari**.

shiver[1] /ʃɪvər/ *n* a small fragment, a splinter.

shiver[2] *vi* to shake or tremble, as with cold or fear, to shudder.— *also n.*—**shivery** *adj.*

shoal[1] /ʃoːl/ *n* a large number of fish swimming together; a large crowd. • *vi* to form shoals.

shoal[2] *n* a submerged sandbank, *esp* one that shows at low tide; a shallow place; a hidden danger. • *vti* to come to a less deep part; to become shallower.

shock[1] /ʃɒk/ *n* a shaggy mass of hair.

shock[2] *n* a violent jolt or impact; a sudden disturbance to the emotions; the event or experience causing this; the nerve sensation caused by an electrical charge through the body; a disorder of the blood circulation, produced by displacement of body fluids (due to injury); (*sl*) a paralytic stroke. • *vt* to outrage, horrify. • *vi* to experience extreme horror, outrage, etc.

shock absorber *n* a device, as on the springs of a car, that absorbs the force of bumps and jars.

shocker /ʃɒkər/ *n* a sensational novel, play, etc; anything that shocks; (*sl*) a very bad specimen.

shock-jock *n* a disc-jockey at a radio station deliberately provocative in presentation, particularly when airing controversial issues.

shocking /ʃɒkɪŋ/ *adj* revolting; scandalous, improper; very bad.—**shockingly** *adv.*

shockproof /ʃɒkpruːf/ *adj* capable of withstanding shock without damage.

shock therapy, shock treatment *n* the treatment of certain mental illnesses by inducing convulsions using drugs or by passing electricity through the brain.

shock troops *npl* a highly disciplined force trained to lead an attack.

shock wave *n* the violent effect in the vicinity of an explosion caused by the change in atmospheric pressure; the compressed wave built up when the speed of a body or fluid exceeds that at which sound can be transmitted in the medium in which it is travelling.

shod /ʃɒd/ **shodden** *see* **shoe**.

shoddy /ʃɒdɪ/ *adj* (**shoddier, shoddiest**) made of inferior material; cheap and nasty, trashy.—**shoddily** *adv.*—**shoddiness** *n.*

shoe /ʃuː/ *n* an outer covering for the foot not enclosing the ankle; a thing like a shoe, a partial casing; a horseshoe; a drag for a wheel; a device to guide movement, provide contact, or protect against wear or slipping; a dealing box that holds several decks of cards. • *vt* (**shoeing, shod** *or* **shoed,** *pp* **shod, shoed** *or* **shodden**) to provide with shoes; to cover for strength or protection.

shoehorn /ʃuːhɔrn/ *n* a curved piece of plastic, metal, or horn used for easing the heel into a shoe.

shoelace /ʃuːleɪs/ *n* a cord that passes through eyelets in a shoe and is tied to keep the shoe on the foot.

shoemaker /ʃuːˌmeɪkər/ *n* a person who makes or mends shoes.

shoestring /ʃuːstrɪŋ/ *n* a shoelace; (*inf*) a small amount of money.

shoetree /ʃuːtriː/ *n* a block of wood, plastic or metal for preserving the shape of a shoe.

shogun /ʃoːgən/ *n* the hereditary commander of the army in feudal Japan.

shone /ʃɒn/ *see* **shine**.

shoo /ʃuː/ *interj* used to frighten (animals, people) away. • *vt* (**shooing, shooed**) to frighten away (as if) by shouting "shoo". • *vi* to cry "shoo".

shoo-in /ʃuːˌɪn/ *n* (*inf*) a person or thing certain to win or succeed.

shook /ʃʊk/ *see* **shake**.

shoot /ʃuːt/ *vb* (**shooting, shot**) *vt* to discharge or fire (a gun etc); to hit or kill with a bullet, etc; (*rapids*) to be carried swiftly over; to propel quickly; to thrust out; (*bolt*) to slide home; to variegate (with another colour, etc); (*a film scene*) to photograph; (*sport*) to kick or drive (a ball, etc) at goal; (*with* **down**) to disprove (an argument); (*with* **up**) to grow rapidly, to rise abruptly. • *vi* to move swiftly, to dart; to emit; to put forth buds, to sprout; to attack or kill indiscriminately; • *n* a contest, a shooting trip, etc; a new growth or sprout.

shooting /ʃuːtɪŋ/ *n* the act of firing a gun or letting off an arrow.

shooting star *n* a meteor.

shooting stick *n* a spiked stick with a handle that folds out into a small seat.

shop /ʃɒp/ *n* a building were retail goods are sold or services provided; a factory; a workshop; the details and technicalities of one's own work, and talk about these. • *vti* (**shopping, shopped**) to visit shops to examine or buy; (*sl*) to inform on (a person) to the police; (*with* **around**) to hunt for the best buy.

shop assistant *n* a person who serves customers in a retail shop.

shop floor *n* the part of a factory where goods are manufactured; the work force employed there, *usu* unionized.

shopkeeper /ʃɒpˌkiːpər/ *n* a person who owns or runs a shop.— **shopkeeping** *n.*

shoplifter /ʃɒplɪftər/ *n* a person who steals goods from shops.

shoplifting /-ɪŋ/ *n* stealing from a shop during shopping hours.—**shoplifter** *n.*

shopper /ʃɒpər/ *n* a person who shops; a bag for carrying shopping.

shopping /ʃɒpɪŋ/ *n* the act of shopping; the goods bought.—*also adj.*

shopping centre *n* a complex of shops, restaurants, and service establishments with a common parking area.—*also* **shopping plaza**.

shopping mall *n* a large enclosed shopping centre.

shopsoiled /ʃɒpsɔɪld/ *adj* shopworn.

shoptalk /-ˌtɔk/ *n* the specialized vocabulary of those in the same line of work or sharing an area of interest; talk about work after hours.

shopwalker /-ˌwɔkər/ *n* a person employed in large shop who oversees shop assistants, helps customers, etc.

shopworn /-ˌwɔrn/ *adj* faded, etc, from being on display in a shop.

shore[1] /ʃɔr/ *n* land beside the sea or a large body of water; beach.

shore[2] *n* a prop or beam used for support. • *vt* to prop (up), to support with a shore.

shoreline /ʃɔrlaɪn/ *n* the edge of an expanse of water.

shorn /ʃɔrn/ *see* **shear**.

short /ʃɔrt/ *adj* not measuring much; not long or tall; not great in range or scope; brief; concise; not retentive; curt; abrupt; less than the correct amount; below standard; deficient, lacking; (*pastry*) crisp or flaky; (*vowel*) not prolonged, unstressed; (*drink*) undiluted, neat. • *n* something short; (*pl*) trousers not covering the knee; (*pl*) an undergarment like these; a short circuit. • *adv* abruptly; concisely; without reaching the end. • *vti* to give less than what is needed; to short-change; to short-circuit.—**shortness** *n.*

shortage /ʃɔrtədʒ/ *n* a deficiency.

shortbread /ʃɔrtbred/ *n* a rich, crumbly cake or biscuit made with much shortening.

short-change /-ˌtʃeɪndʒ/ *vt* to give back less than the correct change; (*sl*) to cheat.

short-circuit /-ˈsərkɪt/ *n* the deviation of an electric current by a path of small resistance; an interrupted electric current. • *vti* to establish a short-circuit in; to cut off electric current; to provide with a short cut.

shortcoming /ʃɔrtˌkʌmɪŋ/ *n* a defect or inadequacy.

shortcrust pastry *n* a firm but crumbly pastry made with half as much fat as flour.

short cut /ʃɔrtkʌt/ *n* a shorter route; any way of saving time, effort, etc.

shorten /ʃɔrtən/ *vt* to make or become short or shorter; to reduce the amount of (sail) spread; to make (pastry, etc) crisp and flaky by adding fat.

shortening /'ʃɔrtənɪŋ/ n the act of shortening; the state of becoming shortened; a fat used for making pastry, etc, crisp and flaky.

shortfall /'ʃɔrtfɔl/ n (the amount or degree of) a deficit or deficiency.

shorthand /'ʃɔrthænd/ n a method of rapid writing using signs or contractions.—also adj.

short-handed /-ɪd/ adj not having the usual number of assistants.

shorthand typist n a person who produces typewritten documents from shorthand notes.—also **stenographer**.

short head /'ʃɔrt,hed/ n (horse racing) a distance less than a horse's head.

shorthorn /'ʃɔrthɔrn/ n one of a breed of large heavy cattle with short curved horns.

short list /'ʃɔrt,lɪst/ n a selected list of qualified applicants from which a choice must be made.

short-list vt to place (a person) on a short list.

short-lived /'ʃɔrt'laɪvd/ or /-'lɪvd/ adj not lasting or living for long.

shortly /'ʃɔrtli/ adv soon, in a short time; briefly; rudely.

short-range adj having a limited range in time or distance.

short shrift n curt, dismissive treatment.

short-sighted /ʃɔrt'saɪtəd/ or /'ʃɔrt-/ adj not able to see well at a distance; lacking foresight.—**short-sightedly** adv.—**short-sightedness** n.

short-tempered adj easily annoyed.

short-term adj of or for a limited time.

short time n a reduction in working hours due to recession, etc.

short-winded adj easily becoming breathless; (speech, writing) brief, to the point.

shortwave n a radio wave 60 metres or less in length.

shot[1] /ʃɒt/ see **shoot**.

shot[2] n the act of shooting; range, scope; an attempt; a solid projectile for a gun; projectiles collectively; small lead pellets for a shotgun; a marksman; a photograph or a continuous film sequence; a hypodermic injection, as of vaccine; a drink of alcohol.

shotgun /'ʃɒtɡʌn/ n a smooth-bore gun for firing small shot at close range.

shotgun wedding n (inf) an enforced wedding, usu because the bride is pregnant.

shot put n a field event in which a heavy metal ball is propelled with an overhand thrust from the shoulder.—**shot-putter** n.

shotten /'ʃɒtən/ adj (fish) having spawned recently.

should /ʃʊd/ vb aux used to express obligation, duty, expectation or probability, or a future condition.—also pt of **shall**.

shoulder /'ʃoʊldər/ n the joint connecting the arm with the trunk; a part like a shoulder; (pl) the upper part of the back; (pl) the capacity to bear a task or blame; a projecting part; the strip of land bordering a road. • vti to place on the shoulder to carry; to assume responsibility; to push with the shoulder, to jostle.

shoulder blade n the large flat triangular bone on either side of the back part of the human shoulder.

shoulder strap n a strap over the shoulders to hold up a garment, bag, etc.

shouldn't /ʃʊdənt/ = should not.

shout /ʃaʊt/ n a loud call; a yell. • vti to call loudly, to yell; (with **down**) to drown out or silence (a person speaking) by shouting.

shove /ʃʌv/ vti to drive forward; to push; to jostle; (with **off**) to push (a boat) off from the shore; (inf) to depart, leave. • n a forceful push.

shove-halfpenny n a game in which coins or discs are slid across a board marked with a scoring grid.

shovel /'ʃʌvəl/ n a broad tool like a scoop with a long handle for moving loose material. • vt (**shovelling, shovelled** or **shoveling, shoveled**) to move or lift with a shovel.

shoveller, shoveler /'ʃʌvələr/ n any of several pond and marsh ducks with a broad beak.

shovelhead n a breed of shark with a shovel-shaped head.

show /ʃoʊ/ vti (**showing, showed** or **shown**) to present to view, to exhibit; to demonstrate, to make clear; to prove; to manifest, to disclose; to direct, to guide; to appear, to be visible; to finish third in a horse race; (inf) to arrive; (with **off**) to display to advantage; to try to attract admiration; to behave pretentiously; (with **up**) to put in an appearance, to arrive; to expose to ridicule. • n a display, an exhibition; an entertainment; a theatrical performance; a radio or television programme; third place at the finish (as a horse race).

show business, show biz /'ʃoʊ,bɪz/ n the entertainment industry.

showcase /'ʃoʊkeɪs/ n a glass case or cabinet for displaying items in a shop or museum; a setting or situation designed to exhibit something to best advantage.—also vt.

showdown /'ʃoʊdaʊn/ n (inf) a final conflict; a disclosure of cards at poker.

shower /ʃaʊr/ n a brief period of rain, hail, or snow; a similar fall, as of tears, meteors, arrows, etc; a great number; a method of cleansing in which the body is sprayed with water from above; a wash in this; a party for the presentation of gifts, esp to a bride. • vt to pour copiously; to sprinkle; to bestow (with gifts). • vi to cleanse in a shower.

showgirl /'ʃoʊɡərl/ n a girl who appears in a chorus line, variety act, etc.

show house n a house on a new housing estate used as a sample for prospective buyers.

showjumping n the competitive riding of horses to demonstrate their skill in jumping.

showman /'ʃoʊmən/ n (pl **showmen**) a man who manages or presents a theatrical show, circus, etc; a person skilled in presentation.

shown /ʃoʊn/ see **show**.

showpiece /'ʃoʊpiːs/ n an exhibit; a perfect example of something.

showplace /-pleɪs/ n a place (eg tourist attraction, historic site) regarded as of exemplary interest or beauty.

showroom /-ruːm/ n a room where goods for sale are displayed.

showy /'ʃoʊi/ adj (**showier, showiest**) bright, colourful; ostentatious.—**showily** adv.—**showiness** n.

shrank /ʃræŋk/ see **shrink**.

shrapnel /'ʃræpnəl/ n an artillery shell filled with small pieces of metal that scatter on impact.

shred /ʃred/ n a strip cut or torn off; a fragment, a scrap. • vt (**shredding, shredded**) to cut or tear into small pieces.

shrew /ʃruː/ n a small, brown, nocturnal mouse-like animal with a long snout; a bad-tempered, nagging woman.

shrewd /ʃruːd/ adj astute, having common sense; keen, penetrating.—**shrewdly** adv.—**shrewdness** n.

shrewish /'ʃruːɪʃ/ adj sharp-tongued, nagging.

shriek /ʃriːk/ n a loud, shrill cry, a scream. • vti to screech, to scream.

shrieval /'ʃriːvəl/ adj of or pertaining to a sheriff.

shrievalty /'ʃriːvəlti/ n (pl **shrievalties**) the office, term of office or jurisdiction of a sheriff.

shrike /ʃraɪk/ n a bird with a hooked beak that impales its prey, mainly insects and small animals, on thorns.

shrill /ʃrɪl/ adj high-pitched and piercing in sound; strident.

shrimp /ʃrɪmp/ n a small edible shellfish with a long tail; (sl) a small or unimportant person. • vt to fish for shrimp.

shrine /ʃraɪn/ n a container for sacred relics; a saint's tomb; a place of worship; a hallowed place.

shrink /ʃrɪŋk/ vti (**shrinking, shrank** or **shrunk**, pp **shrunk** or **shrunken**) to become smaller, to contract as from cold, wetting, etc; to recoil (from), to flinch; to cause (cloth, etc) to contract by soaking. • n (sl) a psychiatrist.—**shrinkable** adj.

shrinkage /'ʃrɪŋkɪdʒ/ n contraction; diminution.

shrinking violet n a very shy or unassuming person.

shrink-wrap /'ʃrɪŋk,ræp/ vt (**shrink-wrapping, shrink-wrapped**) (book etc) to wrap in plastic film that is then shrunk by heat to form a tightly fitting package.

shrive /ʃraɪv/ vb (**shriving, shrived** or **shrove**, pp **shriven** or **shrived**) vt (arch) to hear the confession of; to impose penance on and absolve. • vi to confess, do penance and receive absolution.

shrivel /'ʃrɪvəl/ vti (**shrivelling, shrivelled** or **shriveling, shriveled**) to dry up or wither and become wrinkled; to curl up with heat, etc.

shroud /ʃraʊd/ n a burial cloth; anything that envelops or conceals; (naut) a supporting rope for a mast. • vt to wrap in a shroud; to envelop or conceal.

shrove /ʃroʊv/ see **shrive**.

Shrovetide /'ʃroʊvtaɪd/ n the three days before Ash Wednesday.

Shrove Tuesday n the last day before Lent.

shrub /ʃrʌb/ n a woody plant smaller than a tree with several stems rising from the same root; a bush.—**shrubby** adj.

shrubbery /'ʃrʌbəri/ n (pl **shrubberies**) an area of land planted with shrubs.

shrug /ʃrʌɡ/ vti (**shrugging, shrugged**) to draw up and contract (the shoulders) as a sign of doubt, indifference, etc; (*with* **off**) to brush aside; to shake off; (*a garment*) to remove by wriggling out. • *n* the act of shrugging.

shrunk /ʃrʌŋk/ *see* **shrink**.

shrunken /'ʃrʌŋkən/ *adj* shrivelled, pinched; reduced.

shtoom /ʃtuːm/ *n* (*sl*) silent, dumb.

shuck /ʃʌk/ *n* a husk, pod or shell. • *vt* to remove the shucks from.

shucks /ʃʌks/ *interj* used to express disappointment, irritation, etc.

shudder /'ʃʌdər/ *vi* to tremble violently, to shiver; to feel strong repugnance. • *n* a convulsive shiver of the body; a vibration.

shuffle /'ʃʌfəl/ *vt* to scrape (the feet) along the ground; to walk with dragging steps; (*playing cards*) to change the order of, to mix; to intermingle, to mix up; (*with* **off**) to get rid of.—*also n*.

shuffleboard /'ʃʌfəlbɔrd/ *n* a game in which players propel plastic or wooden discs into numbered scoring areas marked on a large flat surface.

shufty, shufti /'ʃʌfti/ *n* (*pl* **shufties**) (*sl*) a peek, a glance.

shun /ʃʌn/ *vt* (**shunning, shunned**) to avoid scrupulously; to keep away from.

shunt /ʃʌnt/ *vti* to move to a different place; to put aside, to shelve; (*trains*) to switch from one track to another; (*sl*) to collide.—*also n*.

shush /ʃʌʃ/ or /ʃʊʃ/ *interj* used to demand silence; peace, silence. • *vt* to demand silence (as if) by saying "shush".

shut /ʃʌt/ *vti* (**shutting, shut**) to close; to lock, to fasten; to close up parts of, to fold together; to bar; (*with* **down**) to (cause to) stop working or operating; (*with* **in**) to confine; to enclose; to block the view from; (*with* **off**) to check the flow of; to debar; (*with* **out**) to exclude; (*with* **up**) to confine; (*inf*) to stop talking; (*inf*) to silence.

shutdown /'ʃʌtdaʊn/ *n* a stoppage of work or activity, as in a factory.

shuteye /-aɪ/ *n* (*inf*) sleep.

shutter /'ʃʌtər/ *n* a movable cover for a window; a flap device for regulating the exposure of light to a camera lens.

shuttle /'ʃʌtəl/ *n* a device in a loom for holding the weft thread and carrying it between the warp threads; a bus, aircraft, etc, making back-and-forth trips over a short route. • *vti* to move back and forth rapidly.

shuttlecock¹ /'ʃʌtəlˌkɒk/ *n* a cork stuck with feathers, or a plastic imitation, hit with a racket in badminton.

shuttlecock² *see* **battledore**.

shy¹ /ʃaɪ/ *adj* (**shyer, shyest** *or* **shier, shiest**) very self-conscious, timid; bashful; wary, suspicious (of); (*sl*) lacking. • *vi* (**shying, shied**) to move suddenly, as when startled; to be or become cautious, etc. • *n* (*pl* **shies**) a sudden movement.— **shyly** *adv*.—**shyness** *n*.

shy² *vt* (**shying, shied**) to throw (something). • *n* (*pl* **shies**) a throw; (*inf*) an attempt, try.

shyster /'ʃaɪstər/ *n* (*inf*) a person, *esp* a lawyer, who is manipulative and disreputable.

SI *n* (Système International d'Unités) the universally used system of units based on the metre, second, kilogram, ampere, kelvin, candela, siemens, tesla, weber and mole.

Si (*chem symbol*) silicon.

si /siː/ *n* (*mus*) ti.

sial /'saɪˌæl/ *n* the outer layer of the earth's crust composed mostly of rock rich in silicon and aluminium.

Siamese cat /saɪˈmiːz/ or /ˌsaɪəˈmiːz/ *n* a breed of domestic shorthaired cat with a fawn or grey coat, darker ears, paws, tail and face, and blue eyes.

Siamese fighting fish *n* an aggressive brightly coloured freshwater fish.

Siamese twins *npl* twin babies born with the bodies joined together at some point, *esp* the hip.

sib /sɪb/ *n* a sibling.

sibilant /'sɪbɪlənt/ *adj* hissing. • *n* a sibilant letter, *eg* s, z.—**sibilance** *n*.

sibling /'sɪblɪŋ/ *n* a brother or sister.

sibyl /'sɪbəl/ *n* in ancient Greece and Rome, a female prophet or oracle.

sic /sɪk/ *adv* as written (used in text to indicate that an error or doubtful usage is reproduced from the original).

sick /sɪk/ *adj* unhealthy, ill; having nausea, vomiting; thoroughly tired (of); disgusted by or suffering from an excess; (*inf*) of humour, sadistic, gruesome.—**sickness** *n*.

sick bay *n* an area in a ship used as a hospital or dispensary; a room used for the treatment of the sick.

sickbed /'sɪkbɛd/ *n* the bed where one lies sick.

sick building syndrome *n* a collection of symptoms, including lethargy, headache and eye irritation, that affect those who work in totally air-conditioned buildings.

sicken /'sɪkən/ *vti* to make or become sick or nauseated; to show signs of illness; to nauseate.

sickening /'sɪkənɪŋ/ *adj* disgusting.—**sickeningly** *adv*.

sickle /'sɪkəl/ *n* a tool with a crescent-shaped blade for cutting tall grasses; anything shaped like this.

sick leave *n* absence from work due to illness.

sickle cell anaemia *n* a form of anaemia that is hereditary and marked by the presence of sickle-shaped red blood cells.

sick list *n* a list of employees, soldiers, etc who are absent due to illness.

sickly /'sɪkli/ *adj* (**sicklier, sickliest**) inclined to be ill; unhealthy; causing nausea; mawkish; pale, feeble.—**sickliness** *n*.

sick-making *adj* (*inf*) nauseating, galling.

sick pay *n* wages or salaries paid to an employee while he or she is off sick.

sickroom /'sɪkruːm/ *n* the room to which a patient is confined while sick.

side /saɪd/ *n* a line or surface bounding anything; the left or right part of the body; the top or underneath surface; the slope of a hill; an aspect, a direction; a party or faction; a cause; a team; a line of descent; (*sl*) conceit. • *adj* toward or at the side, lateral; incidental. • *vi* to associate with a particular faction.

side arms /'saɪdɑrmz/ *n* weapons (*eg* a pistol, dagger) worn in a belt or holster at the side of the waist.

sideboard /-bɔrd/ *n* a long table or cabinet for holding cutlery, crockery, etc; (*pl*) two strips of hair growing down a man's cheeks.—*also* **sideburns**.

sidecar /-kɑr/ *n* a small car attached to the side of a motor cycle; a cocktail of brandy, liqueur, and lemon juice.

sided /'saɪdəd/ *adj* having sides of a specified number or kind.

side dish *n* food accompanying a main course at a meal.

side drum *n* a small double-headed drum with snares, carried and played at the side.

side effect *n* a secondary and *usu* adverse effect, as of a drug or medical treatment.

side-glance *n* a look directed to one side; a slight reference.

sidekick /'saɪdkɪk/ *n* (*sl*) a confederate; a partner; a close friend.

sidelight /-laɪt/ *n* light coming from the side; a light on the side of a car, etc; incidental information.

sideline /-laɪn/ *n* a line marking the side limit of a playing area; a minor branch of business; a subsidiary interest.

sidelong /-lɒŋ/ *adj* oblique, not direct. • *adv* obliquely.

sidereal /saɪˈdiːriəl/ *adj* of or by reference to stars and constellations.

siderite /'sɪdəˌraɪt/ *n* a mineral composed mainly of ferrous carbonate used as a source of iron.

sidero-, sider- /'sɪdərəʊ/ or /'saɪ-/ *prefix* iron.

siderosis /ˌsaɪdəˈrəʊsɪs/ *n* a lung disease caused by inhalation of iron or other types of metallic particles.

side-saddle /'saɪdsædəl/ *n* a saddle that enables a rider to sit with both feet on the same side of a horse. • *adv* as if sitting on a side-saddle.

sideshow /-ʃəʊ/ *n* a minor attraction at a fair, etc; a subsidiary event.

sidesman /'saɪdzmən/ *n* (*pl* **sidesmen**) (*Anglican Church*) an officer assisting the churchwardens.

side-splitting /'saɪdˌsplɪtɪŋ/ *adj* uproariously funny.

sidestep /-step/ *vti* to take a step to one side; to avoid or dodge.—*also n*.

sidestroke /-ˌstrəʊk/ *n* (*swimming*) a stroke used while swimming on one's side.

sideswipe /-ˌswaɪp/ *n* a glancing blow; (*inf*) an incidental jibe or criticism.

sidetrack /-træk/ *vt* to prevent action by diversionary tactics; to shunt aside, to shelve. • *n* a railroad siding.

sidewalk /-wɒk/ *n* a path, *usu* paved, at the side of a street.

sidewall /-wɒl/ *n* either of the sides of a pneumatic tyre.

sideward /'saɪdwərd/, **sidewards** /-wərdz/ *adj*, *adv* sideways.

sideways /'saɪdweɪz/, **sideway** /-weɪ/ *adj*, *adv* toward or from one side; facing to the side.

side whiskers *n* sideboards or sideburns.

sidewinder /'saɪdˌwaɪndər/ *n* a North American rattlesnake that moves in a twisting sideways motion.

sidewise /'saɪdwaɪz/ *adv* sideways.

siding /'saɪdɪŋ/ *n* a short line beside a main railway track for use in shunting; a covering as of boards for the outside of a frame building.

sidle /'saɪdəl/ *vi* to move sideways, *esp* to edge along.

SIDS /sɪdz/ *abbr* = sudden infant death syndrome.

siege /siːdʒ/ *n* the surrounding of a fortified place to cut off supplies and compel its surrender; the act of besieging; a continued attempt to gain something.

siemens /'siːmənz/ *n* (*pl* **siemens**) the SI unit of electrical conductance.

sienna /sɪˈenə/ *n* an earthy pigment, either yellowish brown (raw sienna) or reddish brown (burnt sienna).

sierra /sɪˈɛrə/ *n* a range of mountains with jagged peaks.

siesta /sɪˈestə/ *n* a midday nap, *esp* in hot countries.

sieve /sɪv/ *n* a utensil with a meshed wire bottom for sifting and straining; a person who cannot keep secrets. • *vt* to put through a sieve, to sift.

sift /sɪft/ *vti* to separate coarser parts from finer with a sieve; to sort out; to examine critically; to pass as through a sieve.

sigh /saɪ/ *vti* to draw deep audible breath as a sign of weariness, relief, etc; to make a sound like this; to pine or lament (for); to utter with a sigh.—*also n.*

sight /saɪt/ *n* the act or faculty of seeing; what is seen or is worth seeing, a spectacle; a view or glimpse; range of vision; a device on a gun etc to guide the eye in aiming it; aim taken with this; (*inf*) anything that looks unpleasant, odd, etc. • *vti* to catch sight of; to aim through a sight.

sighted /'saɪtəd/ *adj* having sight, *esp* of a particular character, *eg* shortsighted.

sightless /-ləs/ *adj* without sight, blind.—**sightlessly** *adv.*—**sightlessness** *n.*

sightly /-li/ *adj* (**sightlier, sightliest**) pleasing to the eye; comely.—**sightliness** *n.*

sight-read /-riːd/ *vt* (**sight-reading, sight-read**) to play or sing from a piece of printed music without previous preparation. • *vi* to read at sight.

sightseeing /-ˌsiːɪŋ/ *n* the viewing or visiting of places of interest.—**sightseer** *n.*

sigma /'sɪgmə/ *n* the 18th letter of the Greek alphabet; (*math*) the symbol S indicating summation.

sigmoid /'sɪgmɔɪd/, **sigmoidal** /-əl/ *adj* curved like the letter S.

sign /saɪn/ *n* a mark or symbol; a gesture; an indication, token, trace, or symptom (of); an omen; (*math*) a conventional mark used to indicate an operation to be performed; a board or placard with publicly displayed information. • *vi* to append one's signature; to ratify thus. • *vt* to engage by written contract; to write one's name on; to make or indicate by a sign; to signal; to communicate by sign language; (*with* **away**) to relinquish by signing a deed, etc; (*with* **on**) to accept employment; to register; (*with* **off**) to complete a broadcast.

signal /'sɪgnəl/ *n* a sign, device or gesture to intimate a warning or to give information, *esp* at a distance; a message so conveyed; a semaphore system used by railways; in radio, etc, the electrical impulses transmitted or received; a sign or event that initiates action. • *vti* (**signalling, signalled** *or* **signaling, signaled**) to make a signal or signals (to); to communicate by signals. • *adj* striking, notable.—**signaller, signaler** *n.*

signalize /'sɪgnəˌlaɪz/ *vt* to point out; distinguish.—**signalization** *n.*

signally /'sɪgnəli/ *adv* remarkably; notably.

signalman /'sɪgnəlmən/ *n* (*pl* **signalmen**) a person who works signals or transmits signals.

signatory /'sɪgnəˌtɔri/ *n* (*pl* **signatories**) a party or state that has signed an agreement or treaty; the person who signs on behalf of their government.

signature /'sɪgnətʃər/ *n* a person's name written by himself or herself; the act of signing one's own name; a characteristic mark; (*mus*) the flats and sharps after the clef showing the key; (*print*) a mark on the first pages of each sheet of a book as a guide to the binder; such a sheet when folded.

signature tune *n* a tune associated with a performer or a TV, radio programme, etc.

signboard /'saɪnbɔrd/ *n* a board with a sign or inscription in front of a business, shop, etc.

signet /'sɪgnət/ *n* a small seal, *esp* one set in a ring; an official seal used in lieu of a signature in authenticating documents; the impression made by this.

signet ring *n* a ring with a seal set in it.

significant /sɪgˈnɪfɪkənt/ *adj* full of meaning, *esp* a special or hidden one; momentous, important; highly expressive; indicative (of).—**significance** *n.*—**significantly** *adv.*

signify /'sɪgnəˌfaɪ/ *vti* (**signifying, signified**) to mean; to be a sign of; to indicate; to represent; to matter, to be important; to make a sign.—**signification** *n.*

sign language *n* a system of manual signs and gestures for conveying meaning, used *esp* by the deaf.

signor, signior /siˈnjɔr/ *n* (*pl* **signors, signori**) an Italian man—equivalent to Mr.

signora /siˈnjɔrə/ *n* (*pl* **signoras, signore**) a married Italian woman—equivalent to Mrs or madam.

signore /-ˈnjɔːre/ *n* (*pl* **signori**) an Italian man—equivalent to sir.

signorina /ˌsiːnjəˈriːnə/ *n* (*pl* **signorinas, signorine**) an unmarried Italian woman—equivalent to Miss.

signpost /'saɪnpoːst/ *n* a post with signs on it to direct travellers; a beacon, a guide.—*also vt.*

Sikh /siːk/ *n* a member of an Indian sect, founded in the 16th century, that teaches monotheism and rejects idolatry and caste. • *adj* of or pertaining to the Sikhs or their beliefs.

silage /'saɪlədʒ/ *n* green fodder preserved for the winter in a silo.

sild /sɪld/ *n* (*pl* **silds, sild**) a young herring, *esp* when canned in Norway.

silence /'saɪləns/ *n* absence of sound; the time this lasts; refusal to speak or make a sound; secrecy. • *vt* to cause to be silent. • *interj* be silent!

silencer /'saɪlənsər/ *n* a device for reducing the noise of a vehicle exhaust or gun, a muffler.

silent /'saɪlənt/ *adj* not speaking; taciturn; noiseless; still.—**silently** *adv.*

silent majority *n* those who rarely assert their views but are presumed to be moderates.

silhouette /ˌsɪluːˈet/ *n* the outline of a shape against light or a lighter background; a solid outline drawing, *usu* in solid black on white, *esp* of a profile. • *vt* to show up in outline; to depict in silhouette.

silica /'sɪləkə/ *n* a hard mineral, a compound of oxygen and silicon, found in quartz and flint.

silicate /'sɪləˌkət/ *n* a salt containing silicon.

siliceous, silicious /sɪˈlɪʃəs/ *adj* of or containing silica.

silicon /'sɪlɪkən/ *n* a metalloid element occuring in silica and used extensively in transistors, etc, and as a compound in glass, etc. • *adj* of an area in which there are a number of computer software and hardware companies.

silicon chip *n* a microchip.

silicone /'sɪləˌkoːn/ *n* an organic polymer compound with good lubricating and insulating properties, used widely as a repellent, resin, etc.

silicosis /ˌsɪləˈkoːsɪs/ *n* a disease of the lungs caused by prolonged inhalation of silica particles.

silk /sɪlk/ *n* a fibre produced by silkworms; lustrous textile cloth, thread or a garment made of silk; (*pl*) silk garments; (*pl*) the colours of a racing stable, worn by a jockey, etc. •*adj* of, relating to or made of silk.

silk cotton *n* kapok.

silken /'sɪlkən/ *adj* made of or like silk; silky.

silk hat *n* a top hat covered in silk.

silk screen /'sɪlkskriːn/ *n* a stencil method of printing a colour design through the meshes of a fabric, as silk; a print so produced.—**silk-screen** *vt.*

silkweed /-wiːd/ *see* **milkweed**.

silkworm /'sɪlkwɜrm/ *n* a caterpillar of various moths that feeds on mulberry leaves and produces a strong fibre to construct its cocoon.

silky /'sɪlki/ *adj* (**silkier, silkiest**) soft and smooth like silk; glossy; suave.—**silkiness** *n.*

sill /sɪl/ *n* a heavy, horizontal slab of wood or stone at the bottom of a window frame or door.

sillabub /'sɪləˌbʌb/ *see* **syllabub**.

silly /'sɪli/ *adj* (**sillier, silliest**) foolish, stupid; frivolous; lacking in sense or judgment; being stunned or dazed. • *n* (*pl* **sillies**) a silly person.—**silliness** *n.*

silo /'saɪloː/ *n* (*pl* **silos)** an airtight pit or tower for storing fodder in a green compressed state; a deep pit for storing cement, coal, etc; an underground structure from which a missile can be fired.

silt /sɪlt/ *n* a fine-grained sandy sediment carried or deposited by water. • *vti* to fill or choke up with silt.

Silurian /sə'lʊriən/ *adj* (*geol*) of or pertaining to the division of Palaeozoic rocks between Ordovician and Devonian. • *n* this period.

silver /'sɪlvər/ *n* a ductile, malleable, greyish-white metallic element used in jewellery, cutlery, tableware, coins, etc; a lustrous, greyish white. • *adj* made of or plated with silver; silvery; (*hair*) grey; marking the 25th in a series. • *vt* to coat with silver or a substance resembling silver; to make or become silvery or grey.

silver birch *n* a Eurasian birch tree with silvery bark.

silver fox *n* (the pelt of) a red fox in a colour phase when its fur is black with silver-tipped hairs.

silver-gilt *n* gilded silver.

silver lining *n* a more favourable aspect of an otherwise hopeless situation.

silver paper *n* a metallic paper coated or laminated to resemble silver, tinfoil.

silver plate *n* a plating of silver; domestic utensils made of silver or of silver-plated metal.—**silver-plate** *vt.*

silver screen *n* (*inf*) (*with* **the**) the film industry; the screen on which a film is projected.

silver service *n* (*in restaurants*) a manner of serving food using a spoon and fork in one hand.

silverside /'sɪlvərsaɪd/ *n* a joint of beef cut from the upper haunch.

silversmith /-smɪθ/ *n* a worker in silver.

silver-tongued /-təŋd/ *adj* plausible, eloquent.

silverware /-ˌwer/ *n* items, such as serving plates, cutlery, etc made from silver or silver plate.

silver wedding *n* the 25th anniversary of a marriage.

silverweed /'sɪlvərwiːd/ *n* any of various plants with silvery leaves or hairs.

silvery /'sɪlvəri/ *adj* white and lustrous like silver; covered with silver; resembling silver in colour; (*sound*) soft and clear.

silviculture /'sɪlvəˌkʌltʃər/ *n* the branch of forestry dealing with the care and development of forests.

simian /'sɪmiən/ *adj* of or like an ape or monkey.

simian immunodeficiency virus *n* a virus, similar to human immunodeficiency virus, that interferes with the ability of the immune system of monkeys to resist disease.

similar /'sɪmələr/ *adj* having a resemblance to, like; nearly corresponding; (*geom*) corresponding exactly in shape if not size.—**similarity** *n.*—**similarly** *adv.*

simile /'sɪmɪli/ *n* a figure of speech likening one thing to another by the use of like, as, etc.

similitude /sɪ'mɪləˌtuːd/ or /-tjuːd/ *n* the state of being similar; guise, likeness.

simmer /'sɪmər/ *vti* to boil gently; to be or keep on the point of boiling; to be in a state of suppressed rage or laughter; (*with* **down**) to abate. • *n* the state of simmering.

simnel cake /'sɪmnəl/ *n* a rich fruit cake with marzipan and decorations traditionally eaten during Lent or Easter.

simony /'saɪməni/ or /'sɪm-/ *n* the buying and selling of ecclesiastical offices.

simoom /sə'muːm/, **simoon** /-muːn/ *n* a strong, hot, dry wind of the Arabian and North African deserts.

simpatico /sɪm'pætɪkoː/ *adj* (*inf*) agreeable, sympathetic.

simper /'sɪmpər/ *vi* to smile in a silly or self-conscious way.—*also n.*

simple /'sɪmpəl/ *adj* single, uncompounded; plain, not elaborate; clear, not complicated; easy to do, understand, or solve; artless, not sophisticated; weak in intellect; unsuspecting, credulous; sheer, mere.—**simpleness** *n.*

simple fraction *n* a fraction in which both the numerator and denominator are whole numbers.

simple-hearted /-ˌhɑrtɪd/ *adj* sincere, honest.

simple interest *n* interest paid on the principal of a loan only.

simple-minded /-'maɪndɪd/ *adj* foolish; mentally retarded.

simpleton /'sɪmpəltən/ *n* a foolish, weak-minded person.

simplicity /sɪm'plɪsɪti/ *n* (*pl* **simplicities)** the quality or state of being simple; absence of complications; easiness; lack of ornament, plainness, restraint; artlessness; directness; guilelessness, openness, naivety.

simplification /ˌsɪmplɪfɪ'keɪʃən/ *n* the act or result of making less complicated.

simplify /'sɪmplɪˌfaɪ/ *vt* (**simplifying, simplified**) to make simple or easy to understand.

simplistic /sɪm'plɪstɪk/ *adj* oversimplified; uncomplicated.—**simplistically** *adv.*

simply /'sɪmpli/ *adv* in a simple way; plainly; merely; absolutely.

simulacrum /ˌsɪmjʊ'leɪkrəm/ *n* (*pl* **simulacra**) a likeness or representation, *esp* a superficial one.

simulate /'sɪmjʊleɪt/ *vt* to pretend to have or feel, to feign; (*conditions*) to reproduce in order to conduct an experiment; to imitate.—**simulation** *n.*

simulator /'sɪmjʊˌleɪtər/ *n* a device that simulates specific conditions in order to test actions or reactions.

simulcast /'saɪməlˌkæst/ or /sɪm-/ *n* a simultaneous radio and television broadcast.—*also vt.*

simultaneous /ˌsaɪməl'teɪnɪəs/ or /ˌsɪm-/ *adj* done or occurring at the same time.—**simultaneity** *n.*—**simultaneously** *adv.*

sin[1] /sɪn/ *n* an offence against a religious or moral principle; transgression of the law of God; a wicked act, an offence; a misdeed, a fault. • *vi* (**sinning, sinned**) to commit a sin; to offend (against).

sin[2] *abbr* = sine.

sin bin /'sɪnˌbɪn/ *n* (*ice hockey, etc*) (*sl*) an enclosure off the playing area where players guilty of fouls are temporarily sent.

since /sɪns/ *adv* from then until now; subsequently; ago. • *prep* during, or continously from (then) until now; after. • *conj* from the time that; because, seeing that.

sincere /sɪn'siːr/ *adj* genuine, real, not pretended; honest, straightforward.—**sincerely** *adv.*

sincerity /-'serɪti/ *n* the quality or state of being sincere; genuineness, honesty, seriousness.

sinciput /'sɪnsɪˌpʊt/ *n* (*pl* **sinciputs, sincipita**) the front part of the skull; forehead.

sine /saɪn/ *n* (*trig*) a function that in a right-angled triangle is equal to the ratio of the length of the side opposite the angle to that of the hypotenuse.

sinecure /'sɪnəˌkjʊr/ *n* a position or office that provides an income without involving duties.

sine die /ˌsaɪnɪ'daɪɪ/ or /ˌsɪneɪ'diːeɪ/ *adv* without a date, indefinitely.

sine qua non /ˌsɪneɪkwɒ'nɒn/ or /-noːn/ *n* an essential condition, a necessity.

sinew /'sɪnjuː/ *n* a cord of fibrous tissue, a tendon; (*usu pl*) the chief supporting force, a mainstay; (*pl*) muscles, brawn.

sinewy /'sɪnjuːi/ *adj* having a lean body and strong muscles; tough, stringy.

sinfonia /ˌsɪnfə'niːə/ or /sɪn'foːniə/ *n* (*pl* **sinfonie, sinfonias**) a symphony.

sinfonietta /ˌsɪnfə'njetə/ *n* a short symphony; a small orchestra.

sinful /'sɪnfəl/ *adj* guilty of sin, wicked.—**sinfully** *adv.*—**sinfulness** *n.*

sing /sɪŋ/ *vti* (**singing, sang,** *pp* **sung**) to utter (words) with musical modulations; (*a song*) to perform; to hum, to ring; to write poetry (about), to praise; (*with* **out**) to shout, call out.—**singer** *n.*—**singing** *n.*

sing. *abbr* = singular.

singe /sɪndʒ/ *vt* (**singeing, singed**) to burn slightly; to scorch, *esp* to remove feathers, etc.—*also n.*

Singhalese /ˌsɪŋgə'liːz/ or /-'liːs/ *see* **Sinhalese.**

singing /'sɪŋɪŋ/ *n* the art or an act of singing.

singing telegram *n* (a service that provides) a greetings message delivered in song, *usu* by a person in fancy dress.

single /'sɪŋgəl/ *adj* one only, not double; individual; composed of one part; alone, sole; separate; unmarried; for one; with one contestant on each side; simple; whole, unbroken; (*tennis*) played between two persons only; (*ticket*) for the outward journey only. • *n* a single ticket; a game between two players; a hit scoring one; a record with one tune on each side. • *vt* (*with* **out**) to pick out, to select.

single blessedness *n* the unmarried state.

single-breasted /'sɪŋgəl'brestɪd/ *adj* (*suit, etc*) fastening in the centre with a single row of buttons.

single cream *n* cream with a low fat content.

single-decker *n* a bus with only one level of passenger accommodation.

single entry *n* (*book-keeping*) a system in which transactions are kept in one account only.

single figures *npl* the numbers less than 10, ie 1 to 9.

single file *n* a single column of persons or things, one behind the other.

single-handed /-'hændɪd/ *adj*, *adv* without assistance, unaided.—**single-handedly** *adv*.—**single-handedness** *n*.

single-lens reflex *n* a camera whose lens allows the photographer to see the same image as it exposes.

single-minded /-'maɪndɪd/ *adj* having only one aim in mind.—**single-mindedly** *adv*.—**single-mindedness** *n*.

singles bar *n* a bar or social club for single people only.

singlestick /-,stɪk/ *n* fencing with wooden sticks instead of swords; the stick used for this.

singlet /'sɪŋglət/ *n* an undervest.

single ticket *n* a ticket for a one-way journey only.

singleton /'sɪŋgəltən/ *n* a playing card that is the only one of its suit in a hand.

singly /'sɪŋgli/ *adv* alone; one by one.

singsong /'sɪŋsɒŋ/ *n* a droning monotonous utterance; a verse with a regular, marked rhythm and rhyme; (*inf*) a party where everyone sings. • *adj* having a regular or monotonous rhythm.

singular /'sɪŋjulər/ *adj* remarkable; exceptional; unusual; eccentric, odd; (*gram*) referring to only one person or thing. • *n* (*gram*) the singular number or form of a word.

singularity /,sɪŋgjuˈlɛrɪti/ or /-ˈlæ-/ *n* (*pl* **singularities**) the state of being singular; uniqueness; an odd trait, a peculiarity.

singularly /'sɪŋjulərli/ *adv* unusually; exceptionally.

Sinhalese /,sɪnhəˈliːz/ or /,sɪnəˈliːz/ *n* a member of a people who form the largest community in Sri Lanka; the language of these people.—*also adj*.—*also* **Singhalese**.

sinister /'sɪnɪstər/ *adj* inauspicious; ominous; ill-omened; evil-looking; malignant; wicked; left; (*her*) on the left side of the shield.

sinistral /'sɪnɪstrəl/ *adj* of or on the left; left-handed.—**sinistrally** *adv*.

sink /sɪŋk/ *vti* (**sinking, sank** *or* **sunk**, *pp* **sunk**) to go under the surface or to the bottom (of a liquid); to submerge in water; to go down slowly; (*wind*) to subside; to pass to a lower state; to droop, to decline; to grow weaker; to become hollow; to lower, to degrade; to cause to sink; to make by digging out; to invest; (*with* **in**) to penetrate; to thrust into; (*inf*) to be understood in full. • *n* a basin with an outflow pipe, *usu* in a kitchen; a cesspool; an area of sunken land.—**sinking** *n*.

sinker /'sɪŋkər/ *n* a weight used to submerge a fishing line.

sinkhole /-hoːl/ *n* a hole in rock strata, *esp* limestone, though which water sinks or runs underground; a hole into which foul waste matter is discharged.

sinking fund *n* money put aside for gradual payment of a debt.

Sinn Fein /ʃɪnˈfeɪn/ *n* a republican party in Ireland which is the political wing of the IRA.

sinner /'sɪnər/ *n* a person who sins.

Sino- /'saɪnoː/ *prefix* Chinese.

Sino-Tebetan /,saɪnoːtɪˈbetən/ *n* a family of languages that includes all the Chinese languages, Burmese and Tibetan.—*also adj*.

Sinology /saɪˈnɒlədʒi/ or /sɪ-/ *n* the study of Chinese language, history, society, etc.—**Sinologist** *n*.—**Sinological** *adj*.

sinsemilla /sɪnsəˈmɪlə/ *n* (a plant which produces) a highly potent type of marijuana.

sinter /'sɪntər/ *n* a white silicious deposit formed by the evaporation of hot mineral waters. • *vt* to form (metal or glass powder) into lumps by the application of heat and pressure.

sinuate /'sɪnjuət/ *adj* (*leaf*) having a wavy edge.—**sinuately** *adv*.

sinuous /'sɪnjuəs/ *adj* curving; winding; tortuous.—**sinuously** *adv*.—**sinuousness** *n*.

sinus /'saɪnəs/ *n* (*pl* **sinuses**) an air cavity in the skull that opens in the nasal cavities.

sinusitis /,saɪnəˈsaɪtɪs/ *n* inflammation of a sinus.

Siouan /'suːən/ *n* a family of North American Indian languages.

Sioux /suː/ *n* (*pl* **Sioux**) a member of various North American Indian peoples who speak Siouan.

sip /sɪp/ *vti* (**sipping, sipped**) to drink in small mouthfuls. • *n* the act of sipping; the quantity sipped.

siphon /'saɪfən/ *n* a bent tube for drawing off liquids from a higher to a lower level by atmospheric pressure; a bottle with an internal tube and tap at the top for aerated water. • *vti* to draw off, or be drawn off, with a siphon.—*also* **syphon**.

siphon bottle *n* a soda siphon.

sir /sər/ *n* a title of respect used to address a man in speech or correspondence; (*with cap*) a title preceding the first name of a knight or baronet. • *vt* to address as "sir".

sire /'saɪr/ *n* a father; a male ancestor; the male parent of an animal; a form of address to a king. • *vt* (*animal*) to beget.

siren /'saɪrən/ *n* a device producing a loud wailing sound as a warning signal; a fabled sea nymph who lured sailors to destruction with a sweet song; a seductive or alluring woman.

sirenian /saɪˈriːnɪən/ *n* a member of an order of plant-eating mammals that live in water, comprising the dugong and the manatee.—*also adj*.

sirloin /'sɜːlɔɪn/ *n* the upper part of a loin of beef.

sirocco /sɪˈrɒkoː/ *n* a hot, oppressive wind that blows across southern Europe from North Africa.

sirree /səˈriː/ *interj* (*inf*) sir – used for emphasis, *esp* after *yes* or *no*.

sis /sɪs/ *n* (*inf*) sister.

sisal /'saɪsəl/ *n* (a tropical agave plant whose leaves yield) a tough fibre used to make rope.

siskin /'sɪskɪn/ *n* a Eurasian songbird with greenish plumage related to the goldfinch.

sissy /'sɪsi/ *n* (*pl* **sissies**) an effeminate, feeble or cowardly boy or man.—*also adj*.

sister /'sɪstər/ *n* a female sibling, a daughter of the same parents; a female member or associate of the same race, creed, trade union, etc; a member of a religious sisterhood; one of the same kind, model, etc; a senior nurse. • *adj* (*ship, etc*) belonging to the same type.

sisterhood /-hud/ *n* a female religious or charitable order; the state of being a sister.

sister-in-law /-ɪn,lɔ/ *n* (*pl* **sisters-in-law**) the sister of a husband or wife; the wife of a brother.

sisterly /-li/ *adj* like a sister, kind, affectionate.

sistrum /'sɪstrəm/ *n* (*pl* **sistra**) an ancient Egyptian metal rattle used as a percussion instrument.

sit /sɪt/ *vti* (**sitting, sat**) to rest oneself on the buttocks, as on a chair; (*bird*) to perch; (*hen*) to cover eggs for hatching; (*legislator, etc*) to occupy a seat; (*court*) to be in session; to pose, as for a portrait; to ride (a horse); to press or weigh (upon); to be located; to rest or lie; to take an examination; to take care of a child, pet, etc, while the parents or owners are away; to cause to sit; to provide seats or seating room for; (*with* **down**) to take a seat; (*with* **for**) to represent in parliament; (*with* **in**) to attend a discussion or a musical session; to participate in a sit-in; (*with* **on**) to hold a meeting to discuss; to delay action on something; (*inf*) to suppress; to rebuke; (*with* **out**) to sit through the whole; to abstain from dancing; (*with* **up**) to straighten the back while sitting; not to go to bed; (*inf*) to be astonished.

sitar /sɪˈtɑr/ or /ˈsɪtər/ *n* an Indian musical instrument similar to a lute with a long neck.

sitcom /'sɪtkɒm/ *see* **situation comedy**.

site /saɪt/ *n* a space occupied or to be occupied by a building; a situation; the place or scene of something. • *vt* to locate, to place.

sit-in /'sɪtɪn/ *n* a strike in which the strikers refuse to leave the premises; civil disobedience in which demonstrators occupy a public place and refuse to leave voluntarily.

sitka spruce /'sɪtkə/ *n* a tall North American spruce tree.

sitter /'sɪtər/ *n* a person who looks after a child, dog, house, etc, while the parents or owners are away.

sitting /'sɪtɪŋ/ *n* the state of being seated; a period of being seated, as for a meal, a portrait; a session, as of a court; a clutch of eggs. • *adj* that is sitting; being in a judicial or legislative seat; used in or for sitting; performed while sitting.

sitting duck, sitting target *n* (*inf*) a person or thing that is an easy target for attack, criticism, etc.

sitting room /-ruːm/ *n* a room other than a bedroom or kitchen; a parlour.

sitting tenant *n* a tenant in occupation of a property.

situate /'sɪtʃueɪt/ *vt* to place in a site, situation, or category.

situated /-ɪd/ *adj* having a site, located; placed; provided with money, etc.

situation /sɪtʃuˈeɪʃən/ *n* a place, a position; a state of affairs, circumstances; a job or post.

situation comedy *n* a comic television or radio series made up of episodes involving the same group of characters.—*also* **sitcom**.

sit-up /'sɪt,ʌp/ *n* an exercise of sitting up from a prone position without using hands or legs.

SIV *abbr* = simian immunodeficiency virus.

six /sɪks/ *adj, n* one more than five. • *n* the symbol for this (6, VI, vi); the sixth in a series or set; something having six units as members.

sixer /'sɪksər/ *n* a leader of a group of six Brownies or Cub Scouts.

sixfold /'sɪksfoːld/ *adj* having six units or members; being six times as great or as many.

six-pack /-pæk/ *n* a pack of six units, as of cans of beer, etc, sold together.

sixpence /-pəns/ *n* (*formerly*) a British coin worth six old pennies.

six-shooter /-ˌʃuːtər/ *n* (*inf*) a six-chambered revolver.

sixteen /ˌsɪks'tiːn/ or /'sɪks-/ *adj, n* one more than fifteen. • *n* the symbol for this (16, XVI, xvi).—**sixteenth** *adj, n*.

sixteenth note *n* a musical note with a sixteenth the time value of a whole note, a semiquaver.

sixth /sɪksθ/ *n* one of six equal parts of a thing; (*mus*) an interval of six diatonic degrees; the sixth tone of a diatonic scale.—*also adv*. • *adj* next after fifth.—**sixthly** *adv*.

sixth sense *n* intuitive power.

sixty /'sɪksti/ *n* six times ten. • *n* (*pl* **sixties**) the symbol for this (60, LX, lx); (in *pl*) sixties (60s), the numbers for 60 to 69; the same numbers in a life or century.—**sixtieth** *adj, adv*.

sixty-fourth note *n* a musical note with the time value of one sixty-fourth of a whole note; a hemidemisemiquaver.

sixty-nine /ˌsɪksti'naɪn/ *n* soixante-neuf.

sizable, sizeable /'saɪzəbəl/ *adj* of some size; large.—**sizably, sizeably** *adv*.—**sizableness, sizeableness** *n*.

size[1] /saɪz/ *n* magnitude; the dimensions or proportions of something; a graduated measurement, as of clothing or shoes. • *vt* to sort according to size; to measure; (*with* **up**) (*inf*) to make an estimate or judgment of; to meet requirements.

size[2] *n* a thin pasty substance used to glaze paper, stiffen cloth, etc. • *vt* to treat with size.

sized /'saɪzd/ *adj* having a specified size.

sizzle /'sɪzəl/ *vti* to make a hissing spluttering noise, as of frying; to be extremely hot; to be very angry; to scorch, sear or fry with a sizzling sound. • *n* a hissing sound.

SJ *abbr* = Society of Jesus.

sjambok /'ʃæmbɒk/ *n* (*in S Africa*) a heavy whip made from rhinoceros hide.

ska /skɑː/ *n* a form of West Indian pop music, a precursor of reggae.

skate[1] /skeɪt/ *n* a steel blade attached to a boot for gliding on ice; a boot with such a runner; a roller skate. • *vi* to move on skates; (*with* **over**) to avoid dealing with (an issue, problem, etc) directly.—**skater** *n*.

skate[2] *n* an edible fish of the ray family with a broad, flat body and short, spineless tail.

skateboard /'skeɪtbɔrd/ *n* a short, oblong board with two wheels at each end for standing on and riding.—*also vi*.

skean-dhu /skiːn'duː/ or /'skiː ən-/ *n* (*Scot*) a dagger worn in the stocking as part of Highland dress.

skedaddle /skɪ'dædəl/ *vi* (*inf*) to run away.—*also n*.

skeet /skiːt/ *n* a type of clay-pigeon shooting in which clay targets are hurled into range at varying speeds and trajectories from two traps.

skein /skeɪn/ *n* a folded coil of yarn, thread, etc; a tangle; a flight of wild fowl, *esp* geese.

skeleton /'skɛlətən/ *n* the bony framework of the body of a human, an animal or plant; the bones separated from flesh and preserved in their natural position; a supporting structure, a framework; an outline, an abstract; a very thin person; something shameful kept secret. • *adj* (*staff, crew, etc*) reduced to the lowest possible level.—**skeletal** *adj*.

skeleton key *n* a key with a slender bit that can open many simple locks.

skeptic /'skɛptɪk/ *see* **sceptic**.

skeptical /-əl/ *see* **sceptical**.

skepticism /'skɛptəˌsɪzəm/ *see* **scepticism**.

skerry /'skɛri/ *n* (*pl* **skerries**) a rocky isle or reef.

sketch /skɛtʃ/ *n* a rough drawing, quickly made; a preliminary draft; a short literary piece or essay; a short humorous item for a revue, etc; a brief outline. • *vti* to make a sketch (of); to plan roughly.

sketchy /'skɛtʃi/ *adj* (**sketchier, sketchiest**) incomplete; vague; inadequate.—**sketchily** *adv*.—**sketchiness** *n*.

skew /skjuː/ *adj* slanting, oblique, set at an angle. • *adv* at a slant. • *vti* to slant or set at a slant; to swerve.

skewbald /'skjuːbɔld/ *adj* marked with patches of white and another colour except black. • *n* an animal, *esp* a horse, with such markings.

skewer /'skjuːər/ *n* a long wooden or metal pin on which pieces of meat and vegetables are cooked. • *vt* to pierce and fasten on a skewer; to transfix.

skewwhiff /skjuː'wɪf/ *adj* (*inf*) askew, not straight.

ski /skiː/ *n* (*pl* **skis**) a long narrow runner of wood, metal or plastic that is fastened to a boot for moving across snow; a water-ski. • *vi* (**skiing, skied**) to travel on skis.—**skier** *n*.

skibob /-bɒb/ *n* a snow vehicle similar to a bicycle with a low seat and steering handle mounted on two skis instead of wheels.

skid /skɪd/ *vti* (**skidding, skidded**) to slide without rotating; to slip sideways; (*vehicle*) to slide sideways out of control; to cause (a vehicle) to skid. • *n* the act of skidding; a drag to reduce speed; a ship's fender; a movable support for a heavy object; a runner on an aircraft's landing gear.

skid row, skid road *n* (*sl*) a shabby district where vagrants, etc, live.

skied /skiːd/ *see* **ski**.

skiff /skɪf/ *n* a small light boat for rowing.

skiffle /'skɪfəl/ *n* a type of music using guitars and makeshift instruments (*eg* washboards) which became popular in the 1950s.

ski jump *n* a long ramp surmounting a slope from which skiers jump in competition.—**ski-jump** *vi*.

skilful, skillful /'skɪlful/ *adj* having skill; proficient, adroit.—**skilfully, skillfully** *adv*.—**skilfulness, skillfulness** *n*.

ski lift *n* any of various devices for conveying skiers up a slope, such as a chair lift.

skill /skɪl/ *n* proficiency; expertness, dexterity; a developed aptitude or ability; a type of work or craft requiring specialist training.

skilled /skɪld/ *adj* fully trained, expert.

skillet /'skɪlət/ *n* a frying pan.

skim /skɪm/ *vti* (**skimming, skimmed**) to remove (cream, scum) from the surface of; to glide lightly over, to brush the surface of; to read superficially.

skimmer /'skɪmər/ *n* that which skims, *esp* a perforated utensil for skimming milk.

skimmia /'skɪmiə/ *n* any of a genus of evergreen shrubs with red berries.

skim milk, skimmed milk *n* milk from which the cream has been removed.

skimp /skɪmp/ *vti* to give scant measure (of), to stint; to be sparing or frugal (with).

skimpy /'skɪmpi/ *adj* (**skimpier, skimpiest**) small in size; inadequate, scant, meagre.—**skimpily** *adv*.—**skimpiness** *n*.

skin /skɪn/ *n* the tissue forming the outer covering of the body; a hide; the rind of a fruit; an outer layer or casing; a film on the surface of a liquid; a vessel for water, etc, made of hide. • *vti* (**skinning, skinned**) to remove the skin from, to peel; to injure by scraping (the knee, etc); to cover or become covered with skin; (*inf*) to swindle.

skin-deep *adj* superficial.

skin diving *n* the sport of swimming underwater with scuba equipment.—**skin-diver** *n*.

skinflint /-flɪnt/ *n* a stingy person.

skinful /-ful/ *n* (*pl* **skinfuls**) (*sl*) as much alcoholic drink as one can take.

skin graft *n* a piece of skin taken from one part of the body to replace damaged skin elsewhere.

skinhead /-hɛd/ *n* a British youth with cropped hair, large boots and braces, often belonging to an aggressive gang.

skink /skɪŋk/ *n* a small lizard of tropical Asia and Africa.

skinned /skɪnd/ *adj* having skin of a specified kind.

skinny /'skɪni/ *adj* (**skinnier, skinniest**) very thin; emaciated.—**skinniness** *n*.

skint /skɪnt/ *adj* (*sl*) having no money.

skintight /'skɪnˌtaɪt/ *adj* (*clothing*) fitting tightly; clinging.

skip[1] /skɪp/ *vti* (**skipping, skipped**) to leap or hop lightly over; to keep jumping over a rope as it is swung under one; to make omissions, to pass over, *esp* in reading; (*inf*) to leave (town) hurriedly, to make off; (*inf*) to miss deliberately. • *n* a skipping movement; a light jump.

skip[2] *n* a large metal container for holding building debris; a cage or bucket for hoisting workers or materials in a mine, quarry, etc.

ski pants *npl* fashion trousers worn tight with a strap that fits under the foot.

skipjack /'skɪpdʒæk/ *n* (*pl* **skipjack, skipjacks**) any of various food fishes including two varieties of tuna, one striped (skipjack) and the other spotted (black skipjack).

skiplane /'skiː,pleɪn/ *n* a light aircraft fitted with skis for taking off and landing on snow.

ski pole *n* one of a pair of pointed metal sticks used by skiers to provide forward thrust and to aid stability.—*also* **ski stick**.

skipper /'skɪpər/ *n* the captain of a boat, aircraft, or team. • *vt* to act as skipper; to captain.

skipping rope *n* a light rope, *usu* with a handle at each end, that is swung over the head and under the feet while jumping.

skirl /skɜrl/ *n* (*Scot*) the shrill wailing sound characteristic of bagpipes.—*also vi*.

skirmish /'skɜrmɪʃ/ *n* a minor fight in a war; a conflict or clash. • *vi* to take part in a skirmish.

skirt /skɜrt/ *n* a woman's garment that hangs from the waist; the lower part of a dress or coat; an outer edge, a border; (*sl*) a woman. • *vti* to border; to move along the edge (of); to evade.

skirting /'skɜrtɪŋ/ *n* a border, an edging; fabric for skirts.

skirting board *n* a narrow panel of wood at the foot of an interior wall.

ski stick *see ski pole*.

skit /skɪt/ *n* a short humorous sketch, as in the theatre.

ski tow *n* a motor-driven device that pulls skiers uphill.

skitter /'skɪtər/ *vti* to move or cause to move quickly or to skim across a surface.

skittish /'skɪtɪʃ/ *adj* (*animal*) frisky, easily frightened; (*person*) playful, frivolous, lively.—**skittishly** *adv*.—**skittishness** *n*.

skittles /'skɪtəls/ *n* a game in which a wooden or plastic bottle-shaped pin is knocked down by a ball.—*also* **ninepins**.

skive /skaɪv/ *vi* (*inf*) to avoid work or duties because of laziness.

skivvy /'skɪvi/ *n* (*pl* **skivvies**) a female domestic servant. • *vi* (**skivvying, skivvied**) to perform menial domestic duties.

skol, skoal /skɒl/ *or* /skoːl/ *interj* good health, cheers (*used in a toast*).

skua /'skjuːə/ *n* any of various large predatory seabirds with dark plumage.

skulduggery, skullduggery /skʌl'dʌgəri/ *n* (*inf*) deceit, underhand dealing.

skulk /skʌlk/ *vi* to move in a stealthy manner; to lurk.

skull /skʌl/ *n* the bony casing enclosing the brain; the cranium.

skull and crossbones *n* (*pl* **skulls and crossbones**) an image of a human skull and crossed thighbones used as a warning of danger.

skunk /skʌŋk/ *n* a small black-and-white mammal that emits a foul-smelling liquid when frightened; its fur; (*sl*) an obnoxious or mean person.

sky /skaɪ/ *n* (*pl* **skies**) the apparent vault over the earth; heaven; the upper atmosphere; weather, climate.

sky-blue *adj, n* (of) a bright pure blue, azure.

sky-diving /'skaɪ,daɪvɪŋ/ *n* the sport of parachute jumping involving free-fall manoeuvres.—**sky-diver** *n*.

Skye terrier /skaɪ/ *n* a breed of short-legged terrier with long hair and a long body.

sky-high /'skaɪ'haɪ/ *adj, adv* very high; in an enthusiastic manner; extremely expensive.

skyjack /-dʒæk/ *vt* to hijack an aircraft.

skylark /-lɑrk/ *n* a lark famous for its song as it soars.

skylight /-laɪt/ *n* a window in the roof or ceiling.

skyline /-laɪn/ *n* the visible horizon; the outline, as of mountains, buildings, etc, seen against the sky.

skyrocket /-rɒkət/ *n* a rocket. • *vi* to rise rapidly (*eg* in price, status, etc).

skyscraper /-,skreɪpər/ *n* a very tall building.

skyward /-,wərd/ *adj, adv* toward the sky.—**skywards** *adv*.

skywriting /-,raɪtɪŋ/ *n* (the act of creating) writing in the sky formed by smoke or vapour emitted from an aircraft.

slab /slæb/ *n* a flat, broad, thick piece (as of stone, wood, or bread, etc); something resembling this. • *vt* to cut or form into slabs; to cover or support with slabs; to put on thickly.

slack /slæk/ *adj* loose, relaxed, not tight; (*business*) slow, not brisk; sluggish; inattentive, careless. • *n* the part (of a rope, etc) that hangs loose; a dull period; a lull; (*pl*) trousers for casual wear. • *vti* to neglect (one's work, etc), to be lazy; (*with* **off**) to slacken (a rope, etc).—**slackness** *n*.

slacken /'slækən/ *vti* to make or become less active, brisk, etc; to loosen or relax, as a rope; to diminish, to abate.—**slackening** *n, adj*.

slacker /'slækər/ *n* a lazy person; a person who shirks.

slack water *n* the turn of the tide; a slow-moving stretch of water.

slag /slæg/ *n* the waste product from the smelting of metals; volcanic lava.

slain /sleɪn/ *see* **slay**.

slake /sleɪk/ *vt* to quench or satisfy (thirst, etc); to mix (lime) with water.

slalom /'slɒləm/ *n* downhill skiing in a zigzag course between upright markers; (*skiing, canoeing, etc*) a timed race over a slalom course. • *vi* to move over a zigzag course.

slam /slæm/ *vti* (**slamming, slammed**) to shut with a loud noise, to bang; to throw (down) violently; (*inf*) to criticize severely. • *n* a sound or the act of slamming, a bang; (*inf*) severe criticism; (*bridge*) the taking of 12 or 13 tricks.

slammer /'slæmər/ *n* (*sl*) a prison or jail.

slander /'slændər/ *n* a false and malicious statement about another; the uttering of this. • *vt* to utter a slander about, to defame.—**slanderous** *adj*.

slang /slæŋ/ *n* words or expressions used in familiar speech but not regarded as standard English; jargon of a particular social class, age group, etc. • *adj* relating to slang.

slant /slænt/ *vti* to incline, to slope; to tell in such a way as to have a bias. • *n* a slope; an oblique position; a bias, a point of view. • *adj* sloping.—**slantly** *adv*.

slanted /'slæntɪŋ/ *adj* prejudiced, biased; sloping.

slantwise /-waɪz/ *adv* at a slant.

slap /slæp/ *n* a smack with the open hand; an insult; a rebuff. • *vt* (**slapping, slapped**) to strike with something flat; to put, hit, etc, with force. • *adv* directly, full.

slapdash /'slæpdæʃ/ *adj* impetuous, hurried; careless; haphazard. • *adv* carelessly.

slaphappy *adj* (**slaphappier, slaphappiest**) casually or cheerfully irresponsible; giddy, punch-drunk.

slapstick /-stɪk/ *n* boisterous humour of a knockabout kind.

slap-up *adj* (*inf*) (*meals, entertainment*) lavish, luxury.

slash /slæʃ/ *vti* to cut gashes in, to slit; to strike fiercely (at) with a sword, etc; to reduce (prices) sharply. • *n* a cutting blow; a long slit, a gash.

slat /slæt/ *n* a thin, flat, narrow strip of wood, etc.

slate[1] /sleɪt/ *vt* to criticize or punish severely.

slate[2] *n* a fine-grained rock easily split into thin layers; a flat plate of this or other material used in roofing; a tablet (as of slate) for writing on; a list of proposed candidates. • *adj* the colour of slate, a deep bluish-grey colour; made of slate. • *vt* to cover with slates; to suggest as a political candidate.

slater /'sleɪtər/ *n* a person trained in roofing with slates; a wood louse.

slatted /'slætəd/ *adj* having slats.

slattern /'slætərn/ *n* a slovenly woman; a slut.

slaughter /'slɔːtər/ *n* the butchering of animals for food; a wholesale killing, a massacre.—*also vt*.—**slaughterer** *n*.

slaughterhouse /-,haʊs/ *n* a place where animals are slaughtered, an abattoir.

Slav /slæv/ *n* any person who speaks a Slavonic language.

slave /sleɪv/ *n* a person without freedom or personal rights, who is legally owned by another; a person under domination, *esp* of a habit or vice; a person who works like a slave, a drudge. • *vti* to toil hard, as a slave.

slave driver *n* a supervisor of slaves at work; a hard taskmaster.

slaveholder /'sleɪv,hoːldər/ *n* a person who owns slaves.

slaver[1] /'sleɪvər/ *n* a person engaged in the buying and selling of slaves.

slaver[2] /'slævər/ *vti* to dribble, to cover with saliva; to fawn upon, to flatter.

slavery /'sleɪvəri/ *n* the condition of being a slave; bondage; drudgery; slave-owning as an institution.

slave ship *n* a ship used in the slave trade.

Slave State *n* (*hist*) any of the Southern states of the US where slavery was legal until the Civil War.

slave trade *n* commercial traffic in slaves, *esp* the transport of Black Africans to Europe and America in the 16th to 19th centuries.

Slavic /'slævɪk/ *see* **Slavonic**.

slavish /'sleɪvɪʃ/ *adj* servile, abject; unoriginal.—**slavishly** *adv*.—**slavishness** *n*.

Slavonic /slə'vɒnɪk/, **Slavic** *adj* of or characteristic of the Slavs. • *n* a branch of the Indo-European family of languages, including Russian, Bulgarian, Polish and Czech.

slaw /slɔː/ *n* coleslaw.

slay /sleɪ/ *vti* (**slaying, slew,** *pp* **slain**) to kill in great numbers; to murder; (*sl*) to overwhelm, to affect in a powerful way.— **slayer** *n*.

sleaze /sli:z/ *n* (*inf*) sleaziness.

sleazy /'sli:zɪ/ *adj* (**sleazier, sleaziest**) disreputable, squalid.— **sleaziness** *n*.

sled /slɛd/, **sledge** /slɛdʒ/ *n* a framework on runners for travelling over snow or ice; a toboggan; a sleigh. • *vti* to go or convey by sledge.

sledgehammer /'slɛdʒˌhæmər/ *n* a large, heavy hammer for two hands.

sleek /sli:k/ *adj* smooth, glossy; having a prosperous or well-groomed appearance; plausible.

sleep /sli:p/ *n* a natural, regularly recurring rest for the body, with little or no consciousness; a period spent sleeping; a state of numbness followed by tingling. • *vti* (**sleeping, slept**) to rest in a state of sleep; to be inactive; to provide beds for; (*with* **around**) (*inf*) to be sexually promiscuous; (*with* **in**) to sleep on the premises; to sleep too long in the morning; (*with* **on**) to have a night's rest before making a decision; (*with* **off**) to get rid of by sleeping; (*with* **over**) to pass the night in someone else's house; (*with* **with**) to have sexual relations with.

sleeper /'sli:pər/ *n* a person or thing that sleeps; a horizontal beam that carries and spreads a weight; a sleeping car; something that suddenly attains prominence or value.

sleeping bag *n* a padded bag for sleeping in, *esp* outdoors.

sleeping car *n* a railway carriage with berths.

sleeping partner *n* a partner in a business who takes no part in its management.

sleeping pill *n* a pill that induces sleep.

sleeping sickness *n* a serious infectious disease marked by lethargy, coma.

sleepless /'sli:pləs/ *adj* without sleep; unable to sleep.

sleepwalker /-ˌwɒkər/ *n* a person who walks while asleep, a somnambulist.—**sleepwalking** *n*.

sleepy /'sli:pɪ/ *adj* (**sleepier, sleepiest**) drowsy; tired; lazy, not alert.—**sleepily** *adv*.—**sleepiness** *n*.

sleepyhead /-ˌhed/ *n* a tired or lazy person.

sleet /sli:t/ *n* snow or hail mixed with rain. • *vi* to rain in the form of sleet.

sleeve /sli:v/ *n* the part of a garment enclosing the arm; (*mech*) a tube that fits over a part; an open-ended cover, *esp* a paperboard envelope for a record.

sleeveless /'sli:vlɪs/ *adj* (*garment*) without sleeves.

sleigh /sleɪ/ *n* a light vehicle on runners for travelling over snow; a sledge.

sleight of hand *n* manual dexterity, such as in conjuring or juggling; a deception.

slender /'slendər/ *adj* thin; slim; slight; scanty.—**slenderly** *adv*.—**slenderness** *n*.

slept /slept/ *see* **sleep**.

sleuth /slu:θ/ *n* (*inf*) a detective.

sleuthhound *n* a bloodhound; (*inf*) a detective.

slew[1] /slu:/ *see* **slay**.

slew[2], **slue** *vti* to twist or be twisted sideways.

slew[3], **slue** *n* (*inf*) a great quantity.

slice /slaɪs/ *n* a thin flat piece cut from something (as bread, etc); a wedge-shaped piece (of cake, pie, etc); a portion, a share; a broad knife for serving fish, cheese, etc; (*golf*) a stroke that makes the ball curl to the right. • *vti* to divide into parts; to cut into slices; to strike (a ball) so that it curves.—**slicer** *n*.—**slicing** *adj, n*.

slick /slɪk/ *adj* clever, deft; smart but unsound; insincere; wily; (*inf*) smooth but superficial, tricky, etc. • *n* a patch or area of oil floating on water. • *vt* to make glossy; (*with* **up**) (*inf*) to make smart, neat, etc.

slicker /'slɪkər/ *n* a loose waterproof coat.

slide /slaɪd/ *vti* (**sliding, slid**) to move along in constant contact with a smooth surface, as on ice, to glide; to coast over snow and ice; to pass gradually (into); to move (an object) unobtrusively. • *n* the act of sliding, a glide; a strip of smooth ice for sliding on; a chute; the glass plate of a microscope; a photographic transparency; a landslide.

slide rule *n* a ruler with a graduated sliding part for making calculations.

sliding scale /'slaɪdɪŋ/ *n* a schedule for automatically varying one thing (*eg* wages) according to the fluctuations of another thing (*eg* cost of living); a flexible scale.

slier /slaɪər/, **sliest** /-əst/ *see* **sly**.

slight /slaɪt/ *adj* small, inconsiderable; trifling; slim; frail, flimsy. • *vt* to disregard as insignificant; to treat with disrespect, to snub. • *n* intentional indifference or neglect, discourtesy.

slighting /'slaɪtɪŋ/ *adj* disparaging; hurtful.

slightly /-lɪ/ *adv* to a small degree; slenderly.

slightness /-nəs/ *n* frailness or slenderness; lack of weight, solidity, importance, or thoroughness.

slim /slɪm/ *adj* slender, not stout; small in amount, degree, etc; slight. • *vti* (**slimming, slimmed**) to make or become slim; to reduce one's weight by diet, etc.—**slimness** *n*.

Slim *n* the name used in East Africa for AIDS.

slime /slaɪm/ *n* a sticky, slippery, half-liquid substance; a glutinous mud; mucus secreted by various animals (*eg* slugs).

slimmer /'slɪmmər/ *n* a person who controls their diet to lose weight.

slimming /-ɪŋ/ *n* the process of losing weight by dieting.

slimy /'slaɪmɪ/ *adj* (**slimier, slimiest**) like or covered with slime; repulsive; fawning.—**sliminess** *n*.

sling[1] /slɪŋ/ *n* a loop of leather with a string attached for hurling stones; a rope for lifting or hoisting weights; a bandage suspended from the neck for supporting an injured arm. • *vt* (**slinging, slung**) to throw, lift, or suspend (as) with a sling; to hurl.

sling[2] *n* a drink of sweetened water mixed with a spirit such as gin.

slingback /'slɪŋbæk/ *n* a shoe whose back consists of a strap.

slingshot /'slɪŋʃɒt/ *n* a contraption with elastic for shooting small stones, a catapult.

slink /slɪŋk/ *vi* (**slinking, slinked** *or* **slunk**) to move stealthily or furtively, to sneak.

slinky /'slɪŋkɪ/ *adj* (**slinkier, slinkiest**) (*inf*) sinuous in line or movement; (*clothes*) hugging the figure.

slip[1] /slɪp/ *vti* (**slipping, slipped**) to slide, to glide; to lose one's foothold and slide; to go or put quietly or quickly; to let go, to release; to escape from; (*with* **up**) to make a slight mistake. • *n* the act of slipping; a mistake, a lapse; a woman's undergarment; a pillowcase; a slipway.

slip[2] *n* a small piece of paper; a young, slim person; a long seat or narrow pew; a shoot for grafting, a cutting; a descendant, an offspring.

slip[3] *n* a mixture of watery clay used for coating or decorating pottery.

slipcase /'slɪpkeɪs/ *n* a protective case for one or more books with an open end to reveal the spines.

slipknot /-nɒt/ *n* a knot that slips along the rope around which it is tied; a knot that can be undone at a pull.

slip-on /-ˌɒn/ *adj* (*garment or shoe*) easy to put on or take off.— *also n*.

slippage /'slɪpədʒ/ *n* a slipping, as of one gear past another.

slipped disc *n* a ruptured cartilaginous disc between vertebrae.

slipper /'slɪpər/ *n* a light, soft, shoe worn in the house.

slippery /-ɪ/ or /-prɪ/ *adj* so smooth as to cause slipping; difficult to hold or catch; evasive, unreliable, shifty.

slippy /'slɪpɪ/ *adj* (**slippier, slippiest**) slippery.

slip road *n* a road that gives access to a main road or motorway.

slipshod /'slɪpʃɒd/ *adj* having the shoes down at heel; slovenly, careless.

slip stitch /-stɪtʃ/ *n* a concealed stitch used for hemming; an unworked stitch in knitting.—**slipstitch** *vt*.

slipstream /-stri:m/ *n* a stream of air driven astern by the engine of an aircraft; an area of forward suction immediately behind a rapidly moving racing car.

slip-up /-ʌp/ *n* (*inf*) an error, a lapse.

slipway /-weɪ/ *n* an inclined surface for launching or repairing ships; a sloped landing stage.

slit /slɪt/ *vt* (**slitting, slit**) to cut open or tear lengthways; to slash or tear into strips. • *n* a long cut, a slash; a narrow opening.— **slitter** *n*.

slither /'slɪðər/ *vi* to slide, as on a loose or wet surface; to slip or slide like a snake.—**slithery** *adj*.

slit trench *n* a narrow trench to provide shelter during battle.

sliver /'slɪvər/ *n* a small narrow piece torn off, a splinter; a thin slice.

slivovitz, slivowitz /'slɪvəvɪts/ *n* plum brandy.

slob /slɒb/ *n* (*sl*) a coarse or sloppy person.

slobber /'slɒbər/ *vti* to drool; to run at the mouth; to smear with dribbling saliva or food. • *n* dribbling saliva; maudlin talk.

sloe /sləʊ/ *n* (the dark fruit of the) blackthorn.

sloe-eyed /'sləʊˌaɪd/ *adj* having almond-shaped dark or black eyes.

sloe gin /-ˌdʒɪn/ *n* a gin flavoured with sloes.

slog /slɒg/ *vti* (slogging, slogged) to hit hard and wildly; to work laboriously; to trudge doggedly. • *n* a hard, boring spell of work; a strenuous walk or hike; a hard, random hit.—**slogger** *n*.

slogan /ˈsloːgən/ *n* a catchy phrase used in advertising or as a motto by a political party, etc.

sloop /sluːp/ *n* a small sailing vessel with one mast and a jib.

slop /slɒp/ *n* a puddle of spilled liquid; unappetizing semi-liquid food; (*pl*) liquid kitchen refuse. • *vti* (**slopping, slopped**) to spill or be spilled; (*with* **out**) (*prisoners*) to empty slop from chamber pots in the morning.

slope /sloːp/ *n* rising or falling ground; an inclined line or surface; the amount or degree of this. • *vti* to incline, to slant; (*inf*) to make off, to go.

sloppy /ˈslɒpɪ/ *adj* (**sloppier, sloppiest**) slushy; (*inf*) maudlin, sentimental; (*inf*) careless, untidy.—**sloppily** *adv*.—**sloppiness** *n*.

slosh /slɒʃ/ *n* watery snow, slush; (*inf*) a heavy blow; the sound of liquid splashing. • *vi* to walk (through) or splash (around) in liquid, mud, etc; (*of liquid*) to splash. • *vt* to throw or splash liquid, etc at someone or something; (*inf*) to hit somebody.

sloshed /slɒʃd/ *adj* (*inf*) drunk.

slot /slɒt/ *n* a long narrow opening in a mechanism for inserting a coin, a slit. • *vt* (**slotting, slotted**) to fit into a slot; to provide with a slot; (*inf*) to place in a series.

sloth /sloːθ/ *n* laziness, indolence; a slow-moving South American animal.—**slothful** *adj*.

slot machine *n* a machine operated by the insertion of a coin, used for gambling or dispensing drinks, etc.

slouch /slaʊtʃ/ *vti* to sit, stand or move in a drooping, slovenly way. • *n* a drooping slovenly posture or gait; the downward droop of a hat brim; (*inf*) a poor performer, a lazy or incompetent person.

slouch hat *n* a hat with a soft wide brim that can be pulled down to cover the ears.

slough[1] /slaʊ/ *n* a bog; deep, hopeless dejection.

slough[2] *n* the dead, outer skin of a snake. • *vti* to cast off, as a dead skin.

Slovak /ˈsloːvæk/ *n* a native or inhabitant of Slovakia, formerly part of Czechoslovakia; the language of Slovakia.—*also adj*.

Slovene /ˌsləˈviːn/ *n* a native or inhabitant of Slovenia, formerly part of Yugoslavia; the Slavonic language of Slovenia.—*also adj*.

slovenly /ˈslʌvənli/ or /ˈslɛv-/ *adj* untidy, dirty; careless.—**slovenliness** *n*.

slow /sloː/ *adj* moving at low speed, not fast; gradual; not quick in understanding; reluctant, backward; dull, sluggish; not progressive; (*clock*) behind in time; tedious, boring; (*surface*) causing slowness. • *vti* (*also with* **up, down**) to reduce the speed (of).—**slowly** *adv*.—**slowness** *n*.

slowcoach /ˈsloːkoːtʃ/ *n* (*inf*) a person who moves, works or thinks slowly.

slow handclap *n* slow regular clapping expressive of audience dissatisfaction.

slow match, slow fuse *n* a slow-burning match or fuse for igniting explosives.

slow-motion /-ˈmoːʃən/ *adj* moving slowly; denoting a filmed or taped scene with the original action slowed down.

slowworm /-wɜːrm/ *n* a legless European lizard with a greyish elongated body and very small eyes.

SLR *abbr* = single-lens reflex.

slub /slʌb/ *n* a lump in a piece of yarn or thread.

sludge /slʌdʒ/ *n* soft mud or snow; sediment; sewage.

slue /sluː/ *see* **slew**[2].

slug[1] /slʌg/ *n* a mollusc resembling a snail but with no outer shell.

slug[2] *n* a small bullet; a disc for inserting into a slot machine; a line of type; (*inf*) a hard blow; a drink of spirits. • *vt* (**slugging, slugged**) (*inf*) to hit hard with a fist or a bat.

sluggard /ˈslʌgərd/ *n* a lazy person. • *adj* lazy.

sluggish /ˈslʌgɪʃ/ *adj* slow, inactive; unresponsive.—**sluggishly** *adv*.—**sluggishness** *n*.

sluice /sluːs/ *n* a gate regulating a flow of water; the water passing through this; an artificial water channel. • *vti* to draw off through a sluice; to wash with a stream of water; to stream out as from a sluice.

slum /slʌm/ *n* a squalid, rundown house; (*usu pl*) an overcrowded area characterized by poverty, etc. • *vi* (**slumming, slummed**) to make do with less comfort.

slumber /ˈslʌmbər/ *vi* to sleep. • *n* a light sleep.

slump /slʌmp/ *n* a sudden fall in value or slackening in demand; (*sport*) a period of poor play. • *vi* to fall or decline suddenly; to sink down heavily; to collapse; to slouch.

slung /slʌŋ/ *see* **sling**.

slunk /slʌŋk/ *see* **slink**.

slur /slɜːr/ *vti* (**slurring, slurred**) to pronounce or speak indistinctly; (*letters, words*) to run together; (*mus*) to produce by gliding without a break; to make disparaging remarks. • *n* the act of slurring; a stigma, an imputation of disgrace; (*mus*) a curved line over notes to be slurred.

slurp /slɜːrp/ *vti* (*sl*) to drink or eat noisily. • *n* a loud sipping or sucking sound.

slurry /ˈslɜːri/ *n* (*pl* **slurries**) a liquid mixture of insoluble matter (as mud, lime, manure, etc).

slush /slʌʃ/ *n* liquid mud; melting snow; (*inf*) sentimental language.—**slushy** *adj*.

slush fund *n* a fund of money used secretly to bribe, etc.

slut /slʌt/ *n* a slovenly or immoral woman.—**sluttish** *adj*.

sly /slaɪ/ *adj* (**slyer, slyest** *or* **slier, sliest**) secretively cunning, wily; underhand; knowing.—**slyly** *adv*.—**slyness** *n*.

SM *abbr* = sergeant major; sadomasochism.

Sm (*chem symbol*) samarium.

smack[1] /smæk/ *n* a taste; a distinctive smell or flavour; small quantity, a trace. • *vi* to have a smell or taste (of); to have a slight trace of something.

smack[2] *vt* to strike or slap with the open hand; to kiss noisily; to make a sharp noise with the lips.—*also n*.

smack[3] *n* a small fishing vessel used in coastal waters.

smacker /ˈsmækər/ *n* (*sl*) a noisy kiss; (*sl*) a pound note or dollar bill.

small /smɔːl/ *adj* little in size, number, importance, etc; modest, humble; operating on a minor scale; young; petty. • *adv* in small pieces. • *n* the narrow, curving part of the back.

small arms *npl* portable firearms, such as handguns.

small beer *n* (*inf*) people or things regarded as trivial.

small change *n* coins of low value.

small fry *npl* people or things of little significance.

smallholding /ˈsmɔːlˌhoːldɪŋ/ *n* a small piece of agricultural land, *usu* between one and fifty acres.—**smallholder** *n*.

small hours *npl* the period between midnight and dawn.

small intestine *n* the section of the alimentary canal between the stomach and the colon.

small-minded /-ˌmaɪndɪd/ *adj* intolerant, narrow-minded; mean, vindictive.—**small-mindedly** *adv*.—**small-mindedness** *n*.

smallpox /-pɒks/ *n* an acute contagious viral disease, now rare, causing the eruption of pustules which leave the skin scarred and pitted.

small print *n* small type that is difficult to read in a contract or other document, *esp* conditions and limitations made deliberately inconspicuous.

small-scale /-skeɪl/ *adj* small in size or scope.

small screen *n* a television.

small talk *n* light, social conversation.

small-time /-taɪm/ *adj* (*inf*) unimportant.

smalt /smɒlt/ *n* a blue pigment used in colouring glass and ceramics.

smarmy /ˈsmɑːrmi/ *adj* (**smarmier, smarmiest**) (*inf*) obsequious, unpleasantly smooth and flattering.

smart /smɑːrt/ *n* a sudden, stinging pain. • *vi* to have or cause a sharp, stinging pain (as by a slap); to feel distress. • *adj* stinging; astute; clever, witty; fashionable; neatly dressed; (*equipment, etc*) capable of seemingly intelligent action through computer control; (*bombs, missiles*) guided to the target by lasers ensuring pinpoint accuracy.—**smartly** *adv*.—**smartness** *n*.

smart aleck /ˈsmɑːrtˌælək/ *n* (*inf*) an annoyingly clever person, a know-all.

smart card *n* a credit card containing a memory chip that records transactions made with the card.

smarten /ˈsmɑːrtən/ *vti* to make or become smart.

smart money *n* money invested or bet by experienced gamblers or financiers; money paid to secure release from an unpleasant situation, or obligation, *esp* military service.

smart set *n sing* or *pl* fashionable people or society.

smash /smæʃ/ *vti* to break into pieces with noise or violence; to hit, collide, or move with force; to destroy or be destroyed. • *n* a hard, heavy hit; a violent, noisy breaking; a violent collision; total failure, *esp* in business; (*inf*) a popular success.

smashed /smæʃd/ *adj* (*sl*) drunk or under the influence of drugs.

smasher /'smæʃər/ *n* (*inf*) an attractive or excellent person or thing.

smashing /-ɪŋ/ *n* (*inf*) excellent.

smash-up /-ʌp/ *n* (*inf*) a serious collision, a crash.

smattering /'smætərɪŋ/ *n* a slight superficial knowledge; a small number.

smear /smɪːr/ *vt* to cover with anything greasy or sticky; to make a smudge; to slander. • *n* a smudge; a slanderous attack; a deposit of blood, secretion, etc on a glass slide for examination under a microscope.

smear test *n* microscopic analysis of a smear of bodily cells, *esp* from the cervix, for cancer.

smegma /'smegmə/ *n* a sebaceous secretion which accumulates as solid matter in the folds of the skin, *esp* under the foreskin.

smell /smɛl/ *n* the sense by which odours are perceived with the nose; a scent, odour, or stench; a trace. • *vti* (**smelling, smelt** *or* **smelled**) to have or perceive an odour.—**smelly** *adj*.

smelling salts *npl* a preparation of ammonia used as a stimulant in cases of faintness, etc.

smelt[1] /smelt/ *vt* to extract ore from metal by melting.

smelt[2] *n* any of various small marine or freshwater food fishes related to the salmon.

smelt[3] *see* **smell**.

smidgen, smidgin /'smɪdʒən/ *n* (*inf*) a small amount.

smilax /'smaɪlæks/ *n* any of a genus of climbing plants bearing red berries that includes the sarsaparilla; an African vine cultivated for its decorative green leaves.

smile /smaɪl/ *vti* to express amusement, friendship, pleasure, etc, by a slight turning up of the corners of the mouth. • *n* the act of smiling; a bright aspect.—**smilingly** *adv*.

smirch /smɜːtʃ/ *vt* to dishonour; to soil, stain, or sully. • *n* a stain on reputation; a smudge, smear.

smirk /smɜːk/ *vi* to smile in an expression of smugness or scorn. • *n* a smug or scornful smile.—**smirkingly** *adv*.

smite /smaɪt/ *vb* (**smiting, smote,** *pp* **smitten** *or* **smote**) *vt* (*arch*) to strike hard; to kill or injure; to have a powerful affect on. • *vi* to strike, beat or come down (on) with force.—**smiter** *n*.

smith /smɪθ/ *n* a person who works in metal; a blacksmith.

smithereens /smɪðə'riːnz/ *npl* (*inf*) fragments.

smithery /'smɪθəri/ *n* the trade of a blacksmith.

smithy /'smɪθi/ *or* /'smɪði/ *n* (*pl* **smithies**) a blacksmith's workshop.

smitten /'smɪtən/ *see* **smite**.

smock /smɒk/ *n* a loose shirtlike outer garment to protect the clothes.

smocking /'smɒkɪŋ/ *n* ornamental stitching in a honeycomb pattern.

smog /smɒg/ *n* a mixture of fog and smoke; polluted air.—**smoggy** *adj*.

smoke /smoːk/ *n* a cloud or plume of gas and small particles emitted from a burning substance; any similar vapour; an act of smoking tobacco, etc; (*inf*) a cigar or cigarette. • *vi* to give off smoke; to (habitually) draw in and exhale the smoke of tobacco, etc. • *vt* to fumigate; to cure food by treating with smoke; to darken (*eg* glass) using smoke; (*with* **out**) to flush out using smoke; to bring into public view.—**smokable, smokeable** *adj*.

smoke detector *n* an electrical device that sets off an alarm when smoke is detected.

smokeless /'smoːkləs/ *adj* giving off little or no smoke.

smoker /-ər/ *n* a person who habitually smokes tobacco; a smoking car; (*formerly*) a gathering of men to smoke.

smoke screen /-skriːn/ *n* dense smoke used to conceal military movements, etc; something designed to obscure, conceal, or disguise the truth.

smokestack /-stæk/ *n* a tall chimney or funnel which discharges smoke or exhaust gases into the air.

smoky /'smoːki/ *adj* (**smokier, smokiest**) emitting smoke, *esp* excessively; filled with smoke; resembling smoke in appearance, flavour, smell, colour, etc.—**smokily** *adv*.—**smokiness** *n*.

smoky quartz *n* cairngorm.

smolt /smoːlt/ *n* a young salmon, about two years old, at the stage where it migrates to the sea for the first time.

smooch /smuːtʃ/ *vi* (*sl*) to kiss and cuddle, *esp* while dancing as a couple. • *n* (*sl*) a long kiss, an embrace.—**smoochy** *adj*.

smooth /smuːð/ *adj* having an even or flat surface; silky; not rough or lumpy; hairless; of even consistency; calm, unruffled; gently flowing in rhythm or sound. • *vti* to make smooth; to calm; to make easier.—**smoothly** *adv*.—**smoothness** *n*.

smoothbore /'smuːðbor/ *n* (*firearm*) not rifled. • *n* such a gun.

smoothen /'smuːðən/ *vti* to make or become smooth.

smooth-faced /'smuːð,feɪst/ *adj* shaven; having a smooth surface; hypocritical.

smoothie /'smuːði/ *n* (*sl*) a person, *esp* a man, who is excessively suave and self-assured in speech and appearance; a health drink made with liquidized fruit and (sometimes) yoghurt.

smooth muscle *n* a muscle capable of regular involuntary contractions, as in the walls of the stomach and gut.

smooth-tongued /-,tʌŋd/ *adj* persuasive in speech.

smoothy /'smuːði/ *n* (*pl* **smoothies**) (*sl*) a smoothie.

smorgasbord, smörgåsbord /'smɔrgəsbɔrd/ *n* a type of buffet or hors d'œuvres of various cold dishes of cheese, fish, salads, etc, served in Scandinavia; a restaurant specializing in this.

smote /smoːt/ *see* **smite**.

smother /'smʌðər/ *vt* to stifle, to suffocate; to put out a fire by covering it to remove the air supply; to cover over thickly; to hold back, suppress. • *vi* to undergo suffocation.—*also n*.

smoulder /'smoːldər/ *vi* to burn slowly or without flame; (*feelings*) to linger on in a suppressed state; to have concealed feelings of anger, jealousy, etc.—*also* **smolder**.

smudge /smʌdʒ/ *n* a dirty or blurred spot or area; a fire made to produce dense smoke. • *vt* to make a smudge; to smear; to blur; to produce smoke to protect against insects, etc. • *vi* to become smudged.

smudgy /'smʌdʒi/ *adj* blurred or dirty, smeared.—**smudgily** *adv*.—**smudginess** *n*.

smug /smʌg/ *adj* (**smugger, smuggest**) complacent, self-satisfied.—**smugly** *adv*.—**smugness** *n*.

smuggle /'smʌgəl/ *vt* to import or export (goods) secretly without paying customs duties; to convey or introduce secretly.—**smuggler** *n*.

smut /smʌt/ *n* a speck or smudge of dirt, soot, etc; indecent talk, writing, or pictures; a fungal disease of crop plants that covers the leaves in sooty spores. • *vti* (**smutting, smutted**) to stain or become stained with smut; (*crops, etc*) to infect or become infected with smut.

smut disease *n* a disease of wheat caused by fungi.

smutty /'smʌti/ *adj* (**smuttier, smuttiest**) soiled with smuts; obscene, filthy.—**smuttily** *adv*.—**smuttiness** *n*.

Sn (*chem symbol*) tin.

snack /snæk/ *n* a light meal between regular meals.

snaffle /'snæfəl/ *n* a jointed bit for a bridle.—*also* **snaffle bit**. • *vt* (*inf*) to snatch or steal for oneself.

snafu /snæ'fuː/ *or* /'snæfuː/ *n* (*sl*) (*situation normal all fucked up*) a state of utter confusion. • *adj* confused, chaotic. • *vt* (**snafuing, snafued**) to cause a state of confusion or chaos.

snag /snæg/ *n* a sharp point or projection; a tear, as in cloth, made by a snag, etc; an unexpected or hidden difficulty. • *vti* (**snagging, snagged**) to tear, etc, on a snag; to clear of snags.

snail /sneɪl/ *n* a mollusc having a wormlike body and a spiral protective shell; a slow-moving or sluggish person or thing.

snail-paced /'sneɪl,peɪst/ *adj* moving very slowly.

snail's pace *n* a very slow speed or rate of progress.

snake /sneɪk/ *n* a limbless, scaly reptile with a long, tapering body and with salivary glands often modified to produce venom; a sly, treacherous person. • *vt* to twist along like a snake. • *vi* to crawl silently and stealthily.

snake charmer *n* a person who entertains by appearing to mesmerize venomous snakes by playing music.

snakeroot /'sneɪkruːt/ *n* any of various North American plants whose roots have been used to treat snakebites; bistort.—*also* **snakeweed**.

snakes and ladders *n* a British board game in which counters are moved on a grid of squares, some of which have ladders leading nearer the finish, and others snakes leading back toward the start.

snakeskin /-skɪn/ *n* the skin of a snake as used to make handbags, shoes, etc.

snakestone /-stoːn/ *n* an ammonite twisted like a ram's horn.

snaky /'sneɪki/ *adj* (**snakier, snakiest**) like or full of snakes; treacherous looking.—**snakily** *adv*.—**snakiness** *n*.

snap /snæp/ *vti* (**snapping, snapped**) to break suddenly; to make or cause to make a sudden, cracking sound; to close, fasten, etc with this sound; (*with* **at**) to bite or grasp suddenly; to speak or utter sharply. • *adj* sudden. • *n* a sharp, cracking sound; a fastener that closes with a snapping sound; a crisp biscuit; a snapshot; a sudden spell of cold weather; (*inf*) vigour, energy.

snapdragon /'snæp,drægən/ *n* any of several plants of the figwort family with showy white, red or yellow flowers shaped like small jaws.

snap fastener *n* a press stud.

snapper /-ər/ *n* one who or that which snaps; (*pl* **snapper, snappers**) any of various sea fishes used as food; a snapping turtle.

snapping turtle *n* a large North American turtle with powerful jaws, a snapper.

snappy /'snæpi/ *adj* (**snappier, snappiest**) speaking sharply; brisk; lively; smart, fashionable.—**snappily** *adv.*—**snappiness** *n*.

snapshot /-ʃɒt/ *n* a photograph taken casually with a simple camera.

snare /snɛr/ *n* a loop of string or wire for trapping birds or animals; something that catches one unawares, a trap; a loop of gut wound with wire stretched around a snare drum that produces a rattling sound. • *vt* to trap using a snare.

snare drum *n* a double-headed drum with snares.

snarl[1] /snɑrl/ *vi* to growl with bared teeth; to speak in a rough, angry manner. • *vt* to express in a snarling manner. • *n* the act of snarling; the sound of this.

snarl[2] *vti* to make or become entangled or complicated. • *n* a tangle; disorder.

snarl-up /'snɑrlʌp/ *n* (*inf*) an instance or state of blockage or disorder, *esp* a traffic jam.

snatch /snætʃ/ *vt* to seize or grasp suddenly; to take as opportunity occurs. • *n* the act of snatching; a brief period; a fragment; (*inf*) a robbery.

snazzy /'snæzi/ *adj* (**snazzier, snazziest**) (*inf*) stylish, fashionable; flashy.

sneak /sni:k/ *vti* (**sneaking, sneaked**, *pp* (*sl*) **snuck**) to move, act, give, put, take, etc, secretly or stealthily. • *n* a person who acts secretly or stealthily; (*inf*) a person who tells or informs on others. • *adj* without warning.

sneaker /'sni:kər/ *n* one who or that which sneaks; a shoe with a cloth upper and soft rubber sole, worn informally.

sneaking /-ɪŋ/ *adj* underhand; secret; (*suspicion, admiration, etc*) felt or thought, but not openly expressed.—**sneakingly** *adv*.

sneaky /'sni:ki/ *adj* (**sneakier, sneakiest**) like a sneak; furtive; underhand.—**sneakily** *adv.*—**sneakiness** *n*.

sneer /snɪr/ *vi* to show scorn or contempt by curling up the upper lip. • *n* a derisive look or remark.—**sneerer** *n.*—**sneeringly** *adv*.

sneeze /sni:z/ *vi* to expel air through the nose violently and audibly. • *n* the act of sneezing.—**sneezy** *adj*.

snick /snɪk/ *n* a tiny cut or notch; (*cricket*) a stroke of the edge of the bat. • *vt* to make a tiny cut or notch in something; to hit (a ball) with a snick.

snicker /'snɪkər/ *vi* to laugh furtively and slyly, to snigger; to neigh, to whinny. • *n* a half-suppressed laugh, a giggle.—**snickeringly** *adv*.

snide /snaɪd/ *adj* malicious; superior in attitude; sneering.—**snidely** *adv.*—**snideness** *n*.

sniff /snɪf/ *vti* to inhale through the nose audibly; to smell by sniffing; to scoff; (*with* **at**) to express dislike or contempt for. • *n* the act of sniffing; the sound of this; a smell.—**sniffer** *n*.

sniffer dog *n* a police dog trained to locate hidden drugs or explosives by smell.

sniffle /'snɪfəl/ *vi* to sniff repeatedly. • *n* the act or sound of sniffling.

sniffy /'snɪfi/ *adj* (**sniffier, sniffiest**) (*inf*) disdainful, dismissive.—**sniffily** *adv.*—**sniffiness** *n*.

snifter /'snɪftər/ *n* a glass with a wide body and narrow top to preserve the aroma of brandy or other spirits; (*inf*) a small amount of alcoholic drink.

snigger /'snɪgər/ *vti* to laugh disrespectfully, to snicker.—*also n*.

snip /snɪp/ *vti* (**snipping, snipped**) to cut or clip with a single stroke of the scissors, etc. • *n* a small piece cut off; the act or sound of snipping; (*inf*) a bargain; (*inf*) a certainty, cinch.

snipe /snaɪp/ *n* (*pl* **snipes, snipe**) any of various birds with long straight flexible bills. • *vi* to shoot snipe; to shoot at individuals from a hidden position; to make sly criticisms of.—**sniper** *n*.

snippet /'snɪpət/ *n* a scrap of information.

snitch /snɪtʃ/ *vi* (*sl*) to inform, betray. • *vt* (*sl*) to steal, pilfer. • *n* (*sl*) an informer; the nose.—**snitcher** *n*.

snivel /'snɪvəl/ *vi* (**snivelling, snivelled** *or* **sniveling, sniveled**) to whine or whimper; to have a runny nose.—**sniveler, sniveller** *n*.

snob /snɒb/ *n* a person who wishes to be associated with those of a higher social status, whilst acting condescendingly to those whom he or she regards as inferior.

snobbery /'snɒbəri/ *n* (*pl* **snobberies**) snobbish behaviour or attitude; a snobbish act.

snobbish /-ɪʃ/ *adj* pertaining to, characteristic of, or like a snob.—**snobbishly** *adv.*—**snobbishness** *n*.

SNOBOL /'sno:bɒl/ *n* (*comput*) String Orientated Symbolic Language: a computer programming language used for text (ie strings of characters) retrieval and manipulation.

Sno-cat *n* (*trademark*) a vehicle designed for travelling on snow; a snowmobile

snog /snɒg/ *vi* (**snogging, snogged**) (*Brit sl*) to kiss and cuddle.—*also n*.

snood /snu:d/ *n* a small net or fabric pouch for holding a woman's hair at the back of the head; (*Scot*) a ribbon around the hair formerly worn by unmarried girls.

snook /snu:k/ *n* (*sl*) a gesture of contempt with the thumb to the nose and fingers spread.

snooker /'snʊkər/ *or* /'snu:k-/ *n* a game played on a billiard table with 15 red balls, 6 variously coloured balls, and a white cue ball; a position in the game where a ball lies directly between the cue ball and target ball. • *vt* to place in a snooker; (*inf*) to obstruct, thwart.

snoop /snu:p/ *vi* (*inf*) to pry about in a sneaking way. • *n* an act of snooping; a person who pries into other people's business.—**snooper** *n*.

snooperscope /'snu:pər,sko:p/ *n* an infrared night-vision device used by the police and military services.

snoot /snu:t/ *n* (*sl*) the nose.

snooty /'snu:ti/ *adj* (**snootier, snootiest**) haughty, snobbish.—**snootily** *adv.*—**snootiness** *n*.

snooze /snu:z/ *vi* (*inf*) to sleep lightly. • *n* (*inf*) a nap.

snore /snor/ *vi* to breathe roughly and noisily while asleep. • *n* the act or sound of snoring.

snorkel /'snorkəl/ *n* a breathing tube extending above the water, used in swimming just below the surface. • *vi* (**snorkelling, snorkelled** *or* **snorkeling, snorkeled**) to swim using a snorkel.—**snorkeler** *n*.

snort /snort/ *vi* to exhale noisily through the nostrils, *esp* as an expression of contempt or scorn. • *vt* to inhale (a drug) through the nose.

snorter /'snortər/ *n* (*sl*) something remarkable for its size, strength, difficulty, etc.

snot /snɒt/ *n* (*sl*) nasal mucus; (*sl*) a snotty person.

snotty /'snɒti/ *adj* (**snottier, snottiest**) covered with snot; (*sl*) irritatingly unpleasant; snobbish.—**snottily** *adv.*—**snottiness** *n*.

snout /snɐʊt/ *n* the nose or muzzle of an animal.

snow /sno:/ *n* frozen water vapour in the form of white flakes; a snowfall; a mass of snow. • *vi* to fall as snow; to deceive with smooth talk.

snowball /'sno:bɒl/ *n* snow pressed together in a ball for throwing; a drink made with advocaat and lemonade. • *vi* to throw snowballs; to increase rapidly in size.

snowberry /-beri/ *n* (*pl* **snowberries**) any of various shrubs bearing white berries.

snowbird /'sno:bərd/ *n* a small, mainly white bird of the finch or junco family, *esp* the snow bunting

snow-blind /-,blaɪnd/ *adj* temporarily blinded or dazzled by the intense glare of sunlight reflected from snow.—**snow-blindness** *n*.

snowblower /-,blo:ər/ *n* a machine for clearing snow from roads by sucking it up and blowing it off to the side.

snowboard /-bord/ *n* a board shaped like a large ski on which a person can stand to slide across snow.

snowbound /-baʊnd/ *adj* trapped by or covered in snow.

snowcap /-kæp/ *n* a covering of snow, as on a mountain peak.—**snowcapped** *adj*.

snowdrift /-drɪft/ *n* a bank of drifted snow.

snowdrop /-drɒp/ *n* a Eurasian plant of the daffodil family with white flowers that appears in early spring.

snowfall /-fɒl/ *n* a fall of snow; the amount of snow in a given time or area.

snowflake /-fleɪk/ *n* a fragile cluster of ice crystals.

snow goose n a large white North American goose with black-tipped wings.

snow leopard n a large cat of the central Asian mountains with a tawny coat that becomes white in winter.

snow line, snow limit n the lowest limit in altitude of permanent snow.

snowman /-mæn/ n (pl **snowmen**) snow piled into the shape of a human figure.

snowmobile /-mə͵biːl/ n a motor vehicle for travelling at speed over snow.

snowplough, snowplow /-plaʊ/ n a vehicle designed for clearing away snow.

snowshoe /-ʃuː/ n footwear in the shape of a racket-like frame with thongs for walking on soft snow. • vi (**snowshoeing, snowshoed**) to walk on snow using snowshoes.

snowstorm /-stɔrm/ n a storm with heavy snow.

snow tyre n a heavy tyre with deep treads for improved traction on snow and ice.

snow-white /-ˈwaɪt/ or /-ˈhwaɪt/ adj pure white.

snowy /ˈsnoʊi/ adj (**snowier, snowiest**) covered with snow; white or pure, like snow.—**snowily** adv.—**snowiness** n.

snowy owl n a large owl with white plumage of northern regions.

Snr, snr abbr = senior.

snub /snʌb/ vt (**snubbing, snubbed**) to insult by ignoring or making a cutting remark. • n the act of snubbing; an intentional slight.

snub-nosed /ˈsnʌbˌnoʊzd/ adj having a short upturned nose; (pistol) having a very short barrel.

snuck /snʌk/ see **sneak**.

snuff[1] /snʌf/ n a powdered preparation of tobacco inhaled through the nostrils.

snuff[2] n the charred portion of a wick. • vt to extinguish (a candle flame).

snuffbox /ˈsnʌfbɒks/ n a small box for snuff.

snuffer /ˈsnʌfər/ n a cone-shaped device for putting out a candle.

snuffle /ˈsnʌfəl/ vi to make sniffing noises, as when suffering from a cold or crying. • n the act of snuffling; (pl) a form of catarrh.

snuff movie n a pornographic film which ends by depicting the brutal murder of an unsuspecting participant.

snug /snʌg/ adj (**snugger, snuggest**) cosy; warm; close-fitting.—**snugly** adv.—**snugness** n.

snuggle /ˈsnʌgəl/ vi to nestle, cuddle. • vt to cuddle.

so[1] /soʊ/ adv in this way; as shown; as stated; to such an extent; very; (inf) very much; therefore; more or less; also, likewise; then.

so[2] see **sol**.

soak /soʊk/ vt to submerge in a liquid; to take in, absorb; (sl) to extract large amounts of money from. • vi to become saturated; to penetrate. • n the act or process of soaking.

so-and-so /ˈsoʊənˌsoʊ/ n (pl **so-and-sos**) an unspecified person or thing; (inf) (euphemism) an unpleasant or disliked person or thing.

soap /soʊp/ n a substance used with water to produce suds for washing; (inf) a soap opera. • vt to rub with soap.—**soapy** adj.

soapberry /ˈsoʊpˌbɛri/ n (pl **soapberries**) any of various tropical American trees bearing fruit which are rich in saponin.

soapbox /-bɒks/ n a temporary platform from which to deliver informal speeches.

soap opera n (inf) a daytime radio or television serial melodrama.

soapstone /-stoʊn/ n a type of soft grey-green stone with a soapy texture.—also **steatite**.

soapwort /-wərt/ n a Eurasian herbaceous plant of the pink family whose leaves form a soapy lather with water.

soapy /ˈsoʊpi/ adj (**soapier, soapiest**) like or full of soap; flattering, unctuous.—**soapily** adv.—**soapiness** n.

soar /sɔr/ vi to rise high in the air; to glide along high in the air; to increase; to rise in status.—**soarer** n.

sob /sɒb/ vb (**sobbing, sobbed**) vi to weep with convulsive gasps. • vt to speak while sobbing.

sober /ˈsoʊbər/ adj not drunk; serious and thoughtful; realistic, rational; subdued in colour. • vt (often with **up** or **down**) to make or become sober.—**soberly** adv.—**soberness** n.

sobriety /səˈbraɪəti/ n soberness; temperance; seriousness.

sobriquet, soubriquet. /ˌsoʊbrɪˈkeɪ/ or /ˈsoʊbrɪˌkeɪ/, /-ˈkɛt/ n a nickname.

sob story n (inf) a tale of distress intended to arouse sympathy.

Soc., soc. abbr = socialist; society.

so-called /ˈsoʊˈkɔld/ adj commonly named or known as.

soccer /ˈsɒkər/ n a football game played on a field by two teams of 11 players with a round inflated ball, association football.

sociable /ˈsoʊʃəbəl/ adj friendly; companionable.—**sociability** n.—**sociably** adv.

social /ˈsoʊʃəl/ adj living or organized in a community, not solitary; relating to human beings living in society; of or intended for communal activities; sociable. • n an informal gathering of people, such as a party.—**socially** adv.

social anthropology n the branch of anthropology that studies social and cultural systems and beliefs.

social climber n a person who strives to attain a higher social position.

social contract, social compact n a tacit agreement between individuals in society and between individuals and the government which defines the rights and duties of each.

Social Democratic Party n a political party that advocates the transition from capitalism to socialism in a gradual manner.—**Social Democrat** n.—**Social Democratic** adj.

socialism /ˈsoʊʃəˌlɪzəm/ n (a system based on) a political and economic theory advocating state ownership of the means of production and distribution.—**socialist** n, adj.—**socialistic** adj.—**socialistically** adv.

socialite /-ˌlaɪt/ n a person active or prominent in fashionable society.

socialize /-ˌlaɪz/ vt to meet other people socially.—**socialization** n.—**socializer** n.

social science n the study of human social organization and relationships using scientific methods.

social security n financial assistance for the unemployed, the disabled, etc to alleviate economic distress.

social service n a welfare service provided by the state, such as housing, education, and health.—**social-service** adj.

social work n any of various professional welfare services to aid the underprivileged in society.—**social worker** n.

society /səˈsaɪti/ n (pl **societies**) the social relationships between human beings or animals organized collectively; the system of human institutional organization; a community with the same language and customs; an interest group or organization; the fashionable or privileged members of a community; companionship.—**societal** adj.

Society of Friends n the official name for the Quakers.

Society of Jesus n the Roman Catholic religious order of the Jesuits.

socio- /ˈsoʊsio/ or /-ˈʃio/ prefix society; social.

socioeconomic /ˌsoʊsioˌiːkəˈnɒmɪk/ or /ˌsoʊˈʃio-/ adj of or involving social and economic aspects.

sociolinguistics /-lɪŋˈgwɪstɪk/ n sing the study of the social and cultural context of language.—**sociolinguist** n.

sociology /ˌsoʊsiˈɒlədʒi/ or /ˌsoʊˈʃi-/ n the study of the development and structure of society and social relationships.—**sociological** adj.—**sociologically** adv.—**sociologist** n.

sociometry /-ˈɒmɪtri/ or /ˌsoʊˈʃi-/ n the study of social relations within small groups.—**sociometric** adj.

sociopath /ˈsoʊsiəˌpæθ/ or /ˈsoʊsio-/, /ˈsoʊˈʃi-/ n a person suffering from a mental disorder that results in antisocial behaviour and lack of guilt.—**sociopathic** adj.

sociopolitical /ˌsoʊsioˈpəˈlɪtɪkəl/ adj of or involving social and political aspects.

sock[1] /sɒk/ n a kind of short stocking covering the foot and lower leg.

sock[2] vt (sl) to punch hard. • n a blow.

socket /ˈsɒkət/ n a hollow part into which something is inserted, such as an eye, a bone, a tooth, an electric plug, etc.

sockeye /ˈsɒkaɪ/ n a Pacific salmon valued as a food fish.—also **red salmon**.

Socratic /səˈkrætɪk/ adj of or relating to Socrates (c.470-399BC), the Greek philosopher, or his methods. • n an adherent of Socrates or his philosophy.

Socratic irony n feigning ignorance when posing questions to expose the real ignorance of the person responding.

Socratic method n philosophical instruction by means of question and answer.

sod[1] /sɒd/ n a lump of earth covered with grass; turf. • vt (**sodding, sodded**) to cover with turf.

sod[2] n (sl) an obnoxious person; (loosely) a person, man. • vi (**sodding, sodded**) (Brit sl) to damn; (with **off**) (sl) to go away.—also interj.

soda /ˈsoʊdə/ n sodium bicarbonate; sodium carbonate; soda water.

soda bread *n* bread made with baking soda instead of yeast.

soda fountain *n* in the US, a counter selling soft drinks, ice cream, snacks, etc; a device that dispenses soda water.

soda siphon *n* a pressurized container that dispenses soda water.

soda water *n* a fizzy drink made by charging water with carbon dioxide under pressure.

sodden /'sɒdən/ *adj* completely soaked through.—**soddenly** *adv.*

sodium /'soːdiəm/ *n* a metallic element.

sodium bicarbonate *n* a white soluble alkaline powder used in baking powder, fire extinguishers and in antacid medicines.

sodium chloride *n* salt.

sodium hydroxide *n* a white alkaline solid used in the manufacture of soap, paper and rayon.

sodium nitrate *n* a white crystalline compound used in fertilizers, matches and explosives, and as a food preservative.

sodium-vapour lamp *n* an electric lamp using sodium vapour through which a current is passed to produce an orange light, *esp* used for street lighting.

Sodom /'sɒdəm/ *n* (*Bible*) a wicked city destroyed by God; a wicked and depraved place.

sodomite /'sɒdəˌmaɪt/ *n* a person who practises sodomy.

sodomy /'sɒdəmi/ *n* anal sexual intercourse between males or between a man and woman.

sofa /'soːfə/ *n* an upholstered couch or settee with fixed back and arms.

soffit /'sɒfɪt/ *n* the underside of a structural element, such as an arch, stairway, balcony, etc.

soft /sɒft/ *adj* malleable; easily cut, shaped, etc; not as hard as normal, desirable, etc; smooth to the touch; (*drinks*) nonalcoholic; mild, as a breeze; lenient; (*sl*) easy, comfortable; (*colour, light*) not bright; (*sound*) gentle, low; (*drugs*) non-addictive.—**softly** *adv.*—**softness** *n.*

softball /'sɒftbɔːl/ *n* a game similar to baseball, but played with a larger, softer ball.

soft-boiled /-bɔɪld/ *adj* (*egg*) boiled so that the white hardens while the yolk remains soft.

soft-core /'sɒftkɔr/ *adj* (*pornography*) not sexually explicit.

softcover /-kʌvər/ *adj* paperback. • *n* a paperback book.

soft drink *n* a nonalcoholic drink.

soften /'sɒfən/ *vti* to make or become soft or softer.—**softener** *n.*

soft-focus *adj* (*lens*) designed to produce a slightly blurred image.

soft furnishings *npl* items such as curtains, carpets, rugs, etc.

soft goods /'sɒftgʊdz/ *npl* textile and clothing products.

softheaded /-ˌhedɪd/ *adj* stupid, feeble-minded.—**softheadedly** *adv.*—**softheadedness** *n.*

softhearted /-ˌhɑrtɪd/ *adj* kind; sentimental.—**softheartedly** *adv.*—**softheartedness** *n.*

soft landing *n* a landing by a spacecraft which leaves the vehicle and occupants undamaged.

soft option *n* the easiest choice in a range of alternatives.

soft palate *n* the fleshy area at the back of the roof of the mouth.

soft paste *n* a type of translucent porcelain made from refined clay, ground glass, bone ash, etc.

soft-pedal /-pedəl/ *n* a pedal on a piano for muting the tone. • *vt* (*inf*) (**soft-pedalling, soft-pedalled** *or* **soft-pedaling, soft-pedaled**) to avoid direct reference to, *esp* something embarrassing or unpleasant.

soft porn *n* (*inf*) soft-core pornography.

soft sell *n* selling by gentle persuasion.—**soft-sell** *adj.*

soft soap *n* a type of semisolid or liquid soap; (*inf*) flattery.

soft-soap *vt* (*inf*) to flatter.—**soft-soaper** *n.*

soft spot *n* a sentimental fondness (for).

soft touch *n* (*inf*) a person who is easily persuaded or exploited.

software /-wer/ *n* the programs used in computers.

softwood /-wʊd/ *n* the wood of any coniferous tree.

softy /'sɒfti/ *n* (*pl* **softies**) (*inf*) a person regarded as sentimental or physically weak.

soggy /'sɒgi/ *adj* (**soggier, soggiest**) soaked with water; moist and heavy.—**soggily** *adv.*—**sogginess** *n.*

soi-disant *Fr.* /swædiːˈzɑ̃/ *adj* self-styled.

soigné, soignée /'swɒnjeɪ/ *adj* well-groomed; elegant.

soil[1] /sɔɪl/ *n* the ground or earth in which plants grow; territory.

soil[2] *vt* to make or become dirty or stained.

soil pipe *n* a sewage or waste-water pipe.

soiree, soirée /swɑrˈeɪ/ *or* /ˈswɑr/ *n* an evening party of music in a private house.

soixante-neuf /ˌswɛsɑ̃ˈnəf/ *n* a sexual position that facilitates mutual cunnilingus and fellatio; sixty-nine.

sojourn /'sɒdʒərn/ *n* a temporary stay. • *vi* to stay for a short time.—**sojourner** *n.*

sol[1] /sɒl/ *n* (*mus*) the name for the fifth note of the diatonic scale —*also* **so.**

sol[2] *n* liquid in which a colloid is dissolved or suspended.

sol. *abbr* = soluble; solution.

solace /'sɒləs/ *n* comfort in misery; consolation. • *vt* to bring solace to.

solar /soːlər/ *adj* of or from the sun; powered by light or heat from the sun; reckoned by the sun.

solar cell *n* a cell that converts the sun's rays into electricity.

solar constant *n* the quantity of sun's energy radiated onto a given area of the earth's surface in a prescribed period.

solar day *n* the period of time during which the earth makes a complete revolution relative to the sun.

solar flare *n* a sudden brief eruption of intense energy from the sun's surface.

solarium /səˈlɛriəm/ *n* (*pl* **solariums, solaria**) a glass-enclosed room for sunbathing or exposure to the sun for medical treatment.

solar month *n* the period of time taken for the moon to make one complete revolution around the earth (approx. 27 days).

solar panel *n* a large thin panel that absorbs energy from sunlight and regenerates it.

solar plexus *n* the network of nerves behind the stomach; (*inf*) the pit of the stomach.

solar pond *n* a shallow artificial pond of salt water covered by fresh water, which absorbs heat from the sun's rays and converts it to electricity.

solar system *n* the sun and those bodies moving about it under the attraction of gravity.

solar wind *n* the constant flow of charged particles from the sun into outer space.

solar year *n* the period of time taken for the earth to make one revolution around the sun.

sold /soːld/ *see* **sell.**

solder /'sɒdər/ *n* a metal alloy used when melted to join or patch metal parts, etc. • *vti* to join or be joined with solder.

soldering iron *n* an electrically heated tool for melting and applying solder.

soldier /'soːldʒər/ *n* a person who serves in an army, *esp* a non-commissioned officer or private. • *vi* to serve as a soldier; (*with* **on**) to continue regardless of difficulties or dangers.—**soldierly** *adj.*

soldier of fortune *n* a man in constant search of military adventure; a mercenary.

soldiery /'soːldʒəri/ *n* (*pl* **soldieries**) soldiers collectively; a body of soldiers; the profession of being a soldier.

sole[1] /soːl/ *n* the underside of the foot or shoe. • *vt* to put a new sole on (a shoe).

sole[2] *n* (*pl* **sole, soles**) a type of flatfish used as food.

sole[3] *adj* only, being the only one; exclusive.—**solely** *adv.*

solecism /'sɒləˌsɪzəm/ *n* an error in speech or writing; a breach of etiquette or good manners.

solemn /'sɒləm/ *adj* serious; formal; sacred; performed with religious ceremony.—**solemnly** *adv.*—**solemnness** *n.*

solemnity /səˈlɛmnɪti/ *n* (*pl* **solemnities**) solemnness; a formal rite.

solenoid /'sɒləˌnɔɪd/ *or* /'sɒl-/ *n* a coil of wire that produces a magnetic field when an electric current is passed through it.—**solenoidal** *adj.*

sol-fa /sɒlˈfɒ/ *see* tonic sol-fa.

sol-fa syllable *n* any of the syllables (*do, re, mi,* etc) used to represent the notes of the musical scale in tonic sol-fa or solmization.

solfatara /ˌsoːlfəˈtɑrə/ *n* a volcanic outlet that emits only (sulphurous) gases and (water) vapours.

solfeggio /sɒlˈfedʒioː/ *n* (*pl* **solfeggi, solfeggios**) (*singing using*) the application of the sol-fa syllables to musical scales or melody.

solicit /səˈlɪsɪt/ *vti* to make a request or application to (a person for something); (*prostitute*) to offer sexual services for money.—**solicitation** *n.*

solicitor /-ər/ *n* a lawyer.

solicitous /-əs/ *adj* showing concern or attention.—**solicitously** *adv.*—**solicitousness** *n.*

solicitude /sə'lɪsɪˌtuːd/ or /-ˌtjuːd/ *n* the state of being solicitous; concern; anxiety; carefulness.

solid /'sɒlɪd/ *adj* firm; compact; not hollow; strongly constructed; having three dimensions; neither liquid nor gaseous; unanimous. • *n* a solid substance (not liquid or gas); a three-dimensional figure.—**solidly** *adv.*—**solidness** *n.*

solidarity /ˌsɒlɪ'dɛrɪti/ *n* (*pl* **solidarities**) unity of interest and action.

solid geometry *n* geometry of three-dimensional figures.

solidi /'sɒlɪdi/ *see* **solidus**.

solidify /sə'lɪdəˌfaɪ/ *vti* (**solidifying, solidified**) to make or become solid, compact, hard, etc.—**solidification** *n.*

solidity /sə'lɪdɪti/ *n* the state of being solid; density; compactness; stability; truth; moral firmness.

solid-state *adj* (*electronic devices*) using components, such as transistors, in which the current flow is through solid materials as opposed to a vacuum; of or relating to solids or their properties and characteristics.

solid-state physics *n sing* the physics of the properties of solids.

solidus /'sɒlɪdəs/ *n* (*pl* **solidi**) an oblique stroke (/) used to separate items of text as in dates, alternative words, lists, or the terms of fractions.

soliloquize /sə'lɪləˌkwaɪz/ *vt* to utter a soliloquy. • *vi* to talk to oneself.—**soliloquist** *n.*

soliloquy /sə'lɪləkwi/ *n* (*pl* **soliloquies**) the act of talking to oneself; an act or speech in a play that takes this form.

solipsism /'sɒlɪpˌsɪzəm/ *n* (*philos*) the theory that the only possible true knowledge is of self-existence.—**solipsistic** *adj.*—**solipsist** *n.*

solitaire /'sɒlɪˌtɛr/ *n* a single gemstone, *esp* a diamond; a card game for one, patience.

solitary /'sɒlɪtəri/ *adj* alone; only; single; living alone; lonely. • *n* (*pl* **solitaries**) a recluse.—**solitarily** *adv.*—**solitariness** *n.*

solitude /'sɒlɪˌtuːd/ or /-ˌtjuːd/ *n* the state of being alone; lack of company; a lonely place.—**solitudinous** *adj.*

solmization /ˌsɒlmə'zeɪʃən/ *n* (*mus*) the use of syllables to name the notes or degrees of a musical scale.

solo /'soːloː/ *n* (*pl* **solos**) a musical composition for one voice or instrument; a flight by a single person in an aircraft, *esp* a first flight. • *vi* to perform by oneself. • *adv* alone. • *adj* unaccompanied.—**soloist** *n.*

so long *interj* (*inf*) goodbye, farewell.

solo whist *n* a form of whist in which any player may bid independently to win or lose a prescribed number of tricks.

solstice /'soːlstɪs/ or /'sɒl-/ *n* either of the two times in the year at which the sun is farthest from the equator (June 21 and December 21).—**solsticial** *adj.*

soluble /'sɒljubəl/ *adj* capable of being dissolved (*usu* in water); capable of being solved or answered.—**solubility** *n.*—**solubly** *adv.*

solute /-juːt/ *n* a dissolved substance in a solution.

solution /sə'luːʃən/ *n* the act or process of answering a problem; the answer found; the dispersion of one substance in another, *usu* a liquid, so as to form a homogeneous mixture.

solvable /'sɒlvəbəl/ or /-sɒl-/ *adj* capable of being solved.—**solvability** *n.*

solve /sɒlv/ *vt* to work out the answer to; to clear up, resolve.

solvent /'sɒlvənt/ *adj* capable of dissolving a substance; able to pay all debts. • *n* a liquid that dissolves substances.—**solvency** *n.*

solvent abuse *n* the deliberate inhalation of fumes from solvents (such as in glue and polish) to become intoxicated.

soma /'soːmə/ *n* (*pl* **somatas, somas**) all of an organism except the germ cells.

Somali /sə'mɒli/ or /-'mæli/ *n* (*pl* **Somalis, Somali**) a native or inhabitant of Somalia; the Somali language.—*also adj.*—**Somalian** *adj.*

somatic /sə'mætɪk/ *adj* of or relating to the body, as opposed to the mind.—**somatically** *adv.*

somato-, somat- /'soːmətoː/ *prefix* body.

somatotype /'soːmətoːˌtaɪp/ *n* physical build, body type.

sombre, somber /'sɒmbər/ *adj* dark, gloomy or dull; dismal; sad.—**sombrely, somberly** *adv.*—**sombreness, somberness** *n.*

sombrero /sɒm'brɛroː/ *n* (*pl* **sombreros**) a wide-brimmed hat with a high crown, worn *esp* in Spanish-speaking countries.

some /sʌm/ *adj* certain but not specified or known; of a certain unspecified quantity, degree, etc; a little; (*inf*) remarkable, striking, etc. • *pron* a certain unspecified quantity, number, etc.

-some /-səm/ *adj suffix* apt to, *eg tiresome*. • *n suffix* a group of, *eg foursome*.

somebody /'sʌmˌbɛdi/ or /-bədi/ *n* (*pl* **somebodies**) an unspecified person; an important person. • *pron* someone.

someday /-deɪ/ *adv* at some future day or time.

somehow /-haʊ/ *adv* in a way or by a method not known or stated.

someone /-wʌn/ *n* somebody.—*also pron*.

someplace /-pleɪs/ *adv* somewhere.

somersault /'sʌmərˌsɒlt/ *n* a forward or backward roll head over heels along the ground or in mid-air.—*also vi*.

something /-θɪŋ/ *n pron* a thing not definitely known, understood, etc; an important or notable thing. • *adv* to some degree.

sometime /-taɪm/ *adj* former. • *adv* at some unspecified future date. • *adj* having been formerly; being so occasionally or in only some respects.

sometimes /-taɪmz/ *adv* at times, now and then.

someway /-weɪ/ *adv* in a certain unspecified manner.

somewhat /-wɒt/ or /-wɒt/ *adv* to some extent, degree, etc; a little.

somewhere /-wɛr/, **somewheres** /-wɛrz/ *adv* in, to or at some place not known or specified.

sommelier /ˌsɒməl'jeɪ/ *n* a wine waiter.

somnambulate /sɒm'næmbjuˌleɪt/ *vi* to get up and walk while asleep.—**somnambulant** *adj.*—**somnambulation** *n.*

somnambulism /sɒm'næmbjuˌlɪzəm/ *n* the practice of walking in one's sleep.—**somnambulist** *n.*—**somnambulistic** *adj.*

somnolent /'sɒmnələnt/ *adj* sleepy, drowsy.—**somnolence, somnolency** *n.*

son /sʌn/ *n* a male offspring or descendant.

sonar /'soːnɑr/ *n* an apparatus that detects underwater objects by means of reflecting sound waves.

sonata /sə'nɒtə/ or /-'nætə/ *n* (*mus*) a composition for a solo instrument, *usu* the piano.

sondage /'sɒndɒʒ/ *n* (*archaeol*) a deep inspection trench.

sonde /sɒnd/ *n* a device for collecting scientific data in the upper atmosphere.

sone /soːn/ *n* a unit of loudness equivalent to 40 phons.

son et lumière /ˌsɒneɪ'luːmjɛr/ *n* an evening entertainment staged at historical sites and buildings using lighting displays, music and recorded speech to illuminate the history of the place.

song /sɒŋ/ *n* a piece of music composed for the voice; the act or process of singing; the call of certain birds.

song and dance *n* (*inf*) a fuss; a long involved story.

songbird /'sɒŋbərd/ *n* a bird with a musical call.

songster /'sɒŋstər/ *n* a singer; a songbird—**songstress** *nf*.

sonic /'sɒnɪk/ *adj* of, producing, or involving sound waves.—**sonically** *adv.*

sonic barrier *n* the increase in air resistance experienced by objects travelling close to the speed of sound, the sound barrier.

sonic boom *n* an explosive sound produced by the shockwave when an aircraft, etc reaches supersonic speed.

son-in-law /'sʌnɪnˌlɒ/ *n* (*pl* **sons-in-law**) a daughter's husband.

sonnet /'sɒnət/ *n* a rhyming poem in a single stanza of fourteen lines.

sonneteer /ˌsɒnə'tiːr/ *n* a composer of sonnets.

sonny /'sʌni/ *n* (*pl* **sonnies**) a patronizing form of address to a boy.

sonobuoy /'sɒnəˌbɔɪ/ *n* a buoy used to detect underwater sounds and transmit them by radio to surface vessels.

sonorous /'sɒnərəs/ or /'soːn-/, /sə'nɔrəs/ *adj* giving out sound; full, rich, or deep in sound.—**sonorously** *adv.*—**sonorousness** *n.*

soon /suːn/ *adv* in a short time; before long; **sooner** *or* **later** at some future unspecified time, eventually.

soot /sʊt/ *n* a black powder produced from flames.—**sooty** *adj.*

soothe /suːð/ *vt* to calm or comfort; to alleviate; to relieve (pain, etc).—**soothing** *adj.*—**soothingly** *adv.*

soothsayer /'suːθˌseɪər/ *n* a person who predicts events.

SOP *abbr* = standard operating procedure.

sop. *abbr* = soprano.

sop /sɒp/ *n* a piece of bread or other food dipped in liquid before being eaten; a concession, bribe offered to appease or cajole. • *vt* (**sopping, sopped**) to dip (bread, etc) into liquid. • *vi* to be soaked.

sophism /'sɒfɪzəm/ *n* a clever but fallacious argument.—**sophistry** *n*.—**sophist** *n*.—**sophistic, sophistical** *adj*.

sophisticated /sə'fɪstɪkeɪtəd/ *adj* refined; worldly-wise; intelligent; complex.—**sophistication** *n*.

sophomore /'sɒfmɔr/ or /'sɒfə,mɔr/ *n* in the US, a second-year student at college or high school.—**sophomoric** *adj*.

soporific /,sɒpə'rɪfɪk/ *adj* inducing sleep; sleepy.

sopping /'sɒpɪŋ/ *adj* wet through.

soppy /'sɒpi/ *adj* (**soppier, soppiest**) wet; (*inf*) sickly sentimental.—**soppily** *adv*.—**soppiness** *n*.

sopranino /,sɒprə'ni:no:/ *n* (*pl* **sopraninos**) a musical instrument of the highest pitch in its class.

soprano /sə'prænɔː/ *n* (*pl* **sopranos, soprani**) the highest singing voice of females or boys; a person who sings soprano.

sorbet /sɔr'beɪ/ or /'sɔrbət/ *n* a flavoured water ice; sherbet.

sorcerer /'sɔrsərər/ *n* person who uses magic powers; a magician or wizard.—**sorceress** *nf*.

sorcery /-ri/ *n* (*pl* **sorceries**) the practice of magic, *esp* with the assistance of evil spirits.

sordid /'sɔrdɪd/ *adj* filthy, squalid; vile; base; selfish.—**sordidly** *adv*.—**sordidness** *n*.

sordino /sɔr'di:no:/ *n* (*pl* **sordini**) a mute for a stringed or brass musical instrument.

sore /sɔr/ *n* a painful or tender injury or wound; an ulcer or boil; grief; a cause of distress. • *adj* painful; tender; distressed.—**soreness** *n*.

sorehead /'sɔrhɛd/ *n* (*inf*) an angry, disgruntled person.

sorely /'sɔrli/ *adv* seriously, urgently.

sorghum /-gəm/ *n* any of a genus of tropical cereal grasses grown for fodder.

sorority /sə'rɔriti/ *n* (*pl* **sororities**) in the US, a society of women university students.

sorrel[1] /'sɔrəl/ *n* a colour between orange-brown and light brown; an animal, *esp* a horse, of this colour.

sorrel[2] *n* a herb with bitter leaves used in salads.

sorrow /'sɔroː/ or /'sɒ-/ *n* sadness; regret; an expression of grief. • *vi* to mourn, to grieve.

sorrowful /-,fʊl/ *adj* full of, showing or causing sorrow.—**sorrowfully** *adv*.—**sorrowfulness** *n*.

sorry /'sɔri/ or /'sɒ-/ *adj* (**sorrier, sorriest**) feeling pity, sympathy, remorse or regret; pitiful; poor.—**sorrily** *adv*.—**sorriness** *n*.

sort /sɔrt/ *n* a class, kind, or variety; quality or type. • *vt* to arrange according to kind; to classify; (*with out*) to find a solution to, resolve; to disentangle; to organize, discipline; (*inf*) to punish, to attack violently.—**sorter** *n*.

sorted /-ɪd/ *adj* (*sl*) the state of being fully prepared or organized; put in order.

sortie /'sɔrti/ *n* a sudden attack by troops from a besieged position; one mission by a single military plane.

SOS /,ɛsoː'ɛs/ *n* an international signal code of distress; an urgent call for help or rescue.

so-so *adj* not good but not bad, middling. • *adv* average, indifferently.

sot /sɒt/ *n* a habitual drunkard.

soteriology /so:,ti:ri:'ɒlədʒi/ or /sɒ-/ *n* (*theol*) the doctrine of salvation, *esp* through Jesus Christ.—**soteriological** *adj*.

sotto voce /,sɒtoː'voːtʃi/ *adv* in an undertone.

sou /su:/ *n* (*pl* **sous**) (*formerly*) a French coin of little value; a very small sum of money.

soubrette /su:'brɛt/ *n* a minor female role in a comedy, *esp* a pert lady's maid; a saucy girl.

soubriquet /,so:bri'keɪ/ or /'so:bri,keɪ/, /-'kɛt/ *see* **sobriquet**.

soufflé /'su:fleɪ/ *n* a baked dish made light and puffy by adding beaten egg whites before baking.—*also adj*.

sough /saʊ/ or /sʌf/ *vi* to make a moaning sound like the wind.—*also n*.

sought /sɔt/ *see* **seek**.

souk /su:k/ *n* an open-air market in Muslim countries.

soul /soːl/ *n* a person's spirit; the seat of the emotions, desires; essence; character; a human being. • *adj* characteristic of American Blacks.

soul-destroying *adj* extremely boring, depressing.

soul food *n* (*inf*) traditional food (*eg* yams, chitterlings) eaten by Blacks of the Southern US.

soulful /'soːlfʊl/ *adj* expressing profound sentiment.—**soulfully** *adv*.—**soulfulness** *n*.

soulless /'soːlləs/ *adj* devoid of emotion; bleak; dull.

soul mate /'soːlmeɪt/ *n* a person, such as a lover or close friend, with whom one bonds deeply.

soul music *n* music derived from Afro-American gospel singing marked by intensity of feeling and closely related to rhythm and blues.

soul-searching *n* close examination of one's conscience, motives, etc.

sound[1] /saʊnd/ *adj* healthy; free from injury or damage; substantial; stable; deep (as sleep) solid; thorough.—**soundly** *adv*.—**soundness** *n*.

sound[2] *n* a narrow channel of water connecting two seas or between a mainland and an island.

sound[3] *n* vibrations transmitted through the air and detected by the ear; the sensation of hearing; any audible noise; the impression given by something. • *vi* to make a sound; to give a summons by sound. • *vt* to cause to make a sound; to voice; to make a signal or order by sound; (*with* **off**) (*inf*) to complain loudly.

sound[4] *vt* to measure the depth of; (*often with* **out**) to attempt to discover the opinions and intentions of (someone).

sound barrier *n* the increase in air resistance experienced by objects travelling close to the speed of sound, the sonic barrier.

sound board *n* a thin board in certain musical instruments that resonates to enhance the sound; a sounding board.

soundbox *n* the hollow resonating cavity of a musical instrument such as a guitar or violin.

sound effects *npl* artificial sounds used for dramatic purposes in plays, television programmes, films, etc.

sounding[1] /'saʊndɪŋ/ *n* measurement of the depth of water; a test, sampling, *eg* of public opinion.

sounding[2] *adj* resounding.

sounding board *n* a thin board placed behind a platform to direct the sound at the audience; a sound board; a person or thing used to test reaction to a new idea or plan.

sounding line *n* a line marked at regular intervals for sounding to determine the depth of the water.

soundproof /'saʊndpru:f/ *adj* unable to be penetrated by sound. • *vt* to make soundproof by insulation, etc.

soundtrack /'saʊndtræk/ *n* the sound accompanying a film; the area on cinema film that carries the sound recording.

soup /su:p/ *n* a liquid food made from boiling meat, fish, vegetables, etc, in water; (*inf*) a difficult or embarrassing **situation**. • *vt* (with *up*) (*inf*) to increase the power and performance of an engine.—**soupy** *adj*.

soupçon /'su:psõ/ *n* a slight flavour; a trace.

soup kitchen *n* a place where soup and other food is dispensed to the homeless and destitute.

sour /'saʊr/ *adj* having a sharp, biting taste; spoiled by fermentation; cross; bad-tempered; distasteful or unpleasant; (*soil*) acid in reaction. • *vti* to make or become sour.—**sourly** *adv*.—**sourness** *n*.

source /sɔrs/ *n* a spring forming the head of a stream; an origin or cause; a person, book, etc, that provides information. • *vti* (*inf*) to find a supplier; to identify a source.

source program *n* (*comput*) an original program that has been translated into machine code.

sour cream *n* cream deliberately soured by bacteria and used in sauces, dressings, etc.

sourdough /'saʊrdoː/ *n* dough used in more than one baking to save on fresh yeast; a prospector in North America who lived on bread made from sourdough.

sour grapes *n sing* pretending to dislike something because it cannot be obtained or achieved by oneself.

sourpuss /'saʊr,pʊs/ *n* (*inf*) a gloomy person.

souse /saʊs/ *vt* to immerse in water or other liquid; to saturate; to pickle or steep in a marinade; (*sl*) to make drunk. • *vi* to become saturated or immersed. • *n* the act of sousing; something pickled; pickling liquid; (*sl*) a drunkard.

soutane /su:tæn/ *n* a cassock.

south /saʊθ/ *n* the direction to one's right when facing the direction of the rising sun; the region, country, continent, etc, lying relatively in that direction. • *adj, adv* facing toward or situated in the south.

Southdown *n* a breed of hornless sheep that yields wool and *esp* meat.

southeast /sɐʊθ'i:st/ *n* the point on a compass midway between south and east. • *adj, adv* at, toward, or from the southeast.

southeasterly /sɐʊθ'i:stərnli/ *adj, adv* toward or from the southeast. • *n* (*pl* **southeasterlies**) a wind from the southeast.

southeastern /sɐʊθ'i:stərn/ *adj* in, toward, or from the southeast; inhabiting or characteristic of the southeast.—**southeasterner** *n*.

southerly /'sɐðərli/ *adj* in, toward, or from the south. • *n* (*pl* **southerlies**) a wind from the south.

southern /'sɐðərn/ *adj* in, toward, or from the south; inhabiting or characteristic of the south.—**southernmost** *adj*.

southerner /'sɐðərnər/ *n* an inhabitant of the south.

southern lights *npl* the aurora australis.

southpaw /'sɐθpɒ/ *n* (*inf*) a left-handed boxer; a left-handed person.—*also adj*.

South Pole *n* the most southerly point on the earth's axis; the most southerly point on the celestial sphere; (*without caps*) the pole of a magnet that points south.

southward /'sɐʊθwərd/ *adj* toward the south.—**southwards** *adv*.

southwest /'sɐʊθwɛst/ *n* the point on a compass midway between south and west. • *adj, adv* at, toward, or from the southwest.

southwester /'sɐʊθwɛstʊərnəʊr/ *n* a strong wind from the southwest.

southwesterly *adj, adv* toward or from the southwest. • *n* (*pl* **southwesterlies**) a wind from the southwest.

southwestern *adj* in, toward, or from the southwest; inhabiting or characteristic of the southwest.—**southwesterner** *n*.

souvenir /ˌsu:və'ni:r/ *n* a keepsake, a memento.

sou'wester /saʊ'wɛstər/ *n* a waterproof hat with a wide brim at the back worn by sailors.

sovereign /'sɒvrən/ *adj* supreme in authority or rank; (*country, state, etc*) independent. • *n* a supreme ruler; a monarch.—**sovereignty** *n*.

soviet /'soʊvɪət/ *n* a workers' council in the former USSR.

sovietism /-ɪzəm/ *n* a political system of which the soviet is the unit.

sow[1]/saʊ/ *n* an adult female pig.

sow[2] /soʊ/ *vt* (**sowing, sowed**, *pp* **sown** *or* **sowed**) to plant or scatter seed on or in the ground; to disseminate; to implant.—**sower** *n*.

soya bean, soybean /'sɔɪbi:n/ *n* a type of bean (orig from Asia) used as a source of food and oil.

soy sauce, soya sauce *n* a dark, salty sauce made from fermented soybeans.

sozzled /'sɒzəld/ *adj* (*inf*) drunk.

sp *abbr* = species.

Sp. *abbr* = Spain; Spaniard; Spanish.

spa /spɒ/ *n* a mineral spring; a resort where there is a mineral spring.

space /speɪs/ *n* the limitless three-dimensional expanse within which all objects exist; outer space; a specific area; an interval, empty area; room; an unoccupied area or seat. • *vt* to arrange at intervals.

space age *n* the era when space exploration has become possible.

space-age *adj* of or pertaining to the space age; modern.

space bar *n* the long bar on a typewriter or computer keyboard for inserting spaces.

spacecraft /'speɪskræft/ *n* a vehicle for travel in outer space.

spaced-out, spaced /speɪst/ *adj* (*sl*) high on drugs.

spaceman /speɪsmæn/ *n* (*pl* **spacemen**) a person who travels in outer space; an alien.—**spacewoman** (*pl* **spacewomen**) *nf*.

space probe *n* an unmanned rocket equipped for exploring outer space.

spaceship /'speɪsʃɪp/ *n* a crewed spacecraft.

space shuttle *n* a manned spacecraft designed as a reusable ferry between the earth and a space station.

space station, space platform *n* a manned artificial satellite designed to orbit the earth and serve as a permanent base for space exploration.

spacesuit /'speɪsu:t/ *n* a sealed and pressurized suit worn by astronauts in space.

space-time (continuum) *n* (*physics*) the four-dimensional coordinate system comprising the three spatial and one temporal coordinates which together define a continuum in which any particle or event may be located.

spacewalk /'speɪswɒk/ *n* a period of time spent by an astronaut floating in space outside a spacecraft. • *vi* to walk in space.—**spacewalker** *n*.

spacious /'speɪʃəs/ *adj* large in extent; roomy.—**spaciously** *adv*.—**spaciousness** *n*.

spade[1] /speɪd/ *n* a tool with a broad blade and a handle, used for digging.

spade[2] *n* a black symbol resembling a stylized spearhead marking one of the four suits of playing cards; a card of this suit.

spadework /'speɪdwərk/ *n* routine preliminary work.

spadix /'speɪdɪks/ *n* (*pl* **spadixes, spadices**) a spike of flowers clustered around a fleshy stem and enclosed in a spathe.

spaghetti /spə'geti/ *n* pasta made in thin, solid strings.

spaghetti western *n* a type of violent cowboy film, *usu* shot on location in Italy or Spain, which became popular in the 1960s.

spake /speɪk/ (*arch*) *pt of* **speak**.

Spam /spæm/ *n* (*trademark*) tinned pork luncheon meat.

spam *n* the term given to junk mail in email transmissions.

span /spæn/ *n* a unit of length equal to a hand's breadth (about 9 inches/23 cm); the full extent between any two limits, such as the ends of a bridge or arch. • *vt* (**spanning, spanned**) to extend across.

Span. *abbr* = Spanish.

spandrel /'spændrəl/ *n* the space between the right or left shoulder of an arch and the rectangular wall or moulding enclosing it.

spangle /'spæŋgəl/ *n* a sequin or other small piece of shiny decoration; any small glittering particle. • *vt* to decorate with spangles. • *vi* to sparkle with or like spangles.—**spangly** *adj*.

Spaniard /'spænjərd/ *n* a native or inhabitant of Spain.

spaniel /'spænjəl/ *n* any of various breeds of dog with large drooping ears and a long silky coat.

Spanish /'spænɪʃ/ *adj* of or pertaining to Spain. • *n* the language of Spain and Spanish Americans; the people of Spain.

Spanish-American *adj* of or pertaining to the countries in America where Spanish is spoken. • *n* a native or inhabitant of a Spanish-American country.

Spanish fly *n* a European blister beetle; a substance prepared from dried Spanish fly (cantharides) which purportedly acts as an aphrodisiac.

Spanish guitar *n* a type of classical acoustic guitar music; the guitar used to play this.

Spanish omelette *n* an omelette containing chopped vegetables such as onions, tomatoes, pimentoes, etc.

spank /spæŋk/ *vt* to slap with the flat of the hand, *esp* on the buttocks.—*also n*.

spanking /'spæŋkɪŋ/ *adj* (*inf*) very impressive, large, smart, etc; (*inf*) brisk, lively.—*also adv*.

spanner /'spænər/ *n* a tool with a hole or (often adjustable) jaws to grip and turn nuts or bolts, a wrench.

spar[1] /spɑr/ *n* a pole supporting the rigging of a ship; one of the main structural members of the wing of an airplane.

spar[2] *vi* to box using gentle blows, as in training; to argue.—*also n*.

spare /spɛr/ *vt* to refrain from harming or killing; to afford; to make (something) available (*eg* time). • *adj* kept as an extra, additional; scanty. • *n* a spare part; a spare tyre.—**sparely** *adv*.—**spareness** *n*.

sparerib /'spɛrrɪb/ *n* a pork rib with most of the meat cut away.

spare tyre *n* (*inf*) a roll of excess fat around the waist.

sparing /'spɛrɪŋ/ *adj* frugal, economical.—**sparingly** *adv*.—**sparingness** *n*.

spark /spɑrk/ *n* a fiery or glowing particle thrown off by burning material or by friction; a flash of light from an electrical discharge; a trace. • *vt* to stir up; to activate. • *vi* to give off sparks.

sparkle /'spɑrkəl/ *n* a spark; vivacity. • *vi* to shine; to glitter; (*water, wine*) to effervesce; to be lively or witty.

sparkler /'spɑrklər/ *n* a handheld firework that throws off brilliant sparks; (*inf*) a diamond.

spark plug *n* a device that produces a spark to ignite the explosive mixture in an internal combustion engine.—*also* **sparking plug**.

sparring partner *n* (*boxing*) a partner who stands in as an opponent for training purposes; a person with whom one regularly argues.

sparrow /'sperǝʊ/ or /'spærǝʊ/ *n* any of various small brownish songbirds related to the finch.

sparse /spɑrs/ *adj* spread out thinly; scanty.—**sparsely** *adv.*—**sparseness, sparsity** *n*.

Spartan /'spɑrtǝn/ *adj* of or pertaining to Sparta in ancient Greece; rigourously severe.

spasm /'spæzǝm/ *n* a sudden, involuntary muscular contraction; any sudden burst (of emotion or activity).—**spasmodic** *adj* intermittent; of or like a spasm.—**spasmodically** *adv*.

spastic /'spæstɪk/ *n* a person who suffers from cerebral palsy. • *adj* affected by muscle spasm.—**spasticity** *n*.

spat[1] *see* **spit**[2].

spat[2] /spæt/ *n* a gaiter covering the ankle and instep and fastening under the shoe.

spat[3] *n* a young oyster or other bivalve mollusc.

spat[4] *n* a petty argument, or quarrel. • *vi* to have a petty argument.

spate /speɪt/ *n* a large amount; a sudden outburst (as of words); a sudden flood.

spathe /speɪð/ *n* a leafy part that encloses the floral spikes of certain flowers.

spatial /'speɪʃǝl/ *adj* relating to space.—**spatially** *adv*.

spatiotemporal /ˌspeɪʃiǝʊ'tempǝrǝl/ *adj* of, involving, or occurring in both space and time; of or pertaining to space-time.

spatter /'spætǝr/ *vti* to scatter or spurt out in drops; to splash.—*also* *n*.

spatula /'spætʃʊlǝ/ *n* a tool with a broad, flexible blade for spreading or mixing foods, paints, etc.

spatulate /'spætʃʊlǝt/ *adj* shaped like a spatula.

spawn /spɒn/ *n* a mass of eggs deposited by fish, frogs, or amphibians; offspring. • *vti* to lay eggs; to produce, *esp* in great quantity.

spay /speɪ/ *vt* (*female animals*) to sterilize by removing the ovaries from.

speak /spiːk/ *vi* (**speaking, spoke,** *pp* **spoken**) to utter words; to talk; to converse with; to deliver a speech; to be suggestive of something; to produce a characteristic sound; (*with* **out, up**) to speak loudly; to express an opinion frankly.—**speakable** *adj*.

speakeasy /'spiːkˌiːzi/ *n* (*pl* **speakeasies**) a club where alcoholic drink was sold illegally during the Prohibition era in the US in the 1920s.

speaker /'spiːkǝr/ *n* a person who speaks, *esp* before an audience; the presiding official in a legislative assembly; a loudspeaker.

speaking clock *n* a recorded telephone message which gives the time.

spear /spiːr/ *n* a weapon with a long shaft and a sharp point; a blade or shoot (of grass, broccoli, etc). • *vt* to pierce with a spear.

spearhead /'spiːrhed/ *n* the pointed head of a spear; the leading person or group in an attack or other action. • *vt* to serve as a leader of.

spearmint /'spiːrmɪnt/ *n* a common mint plant which yields an oil used for flavouring.

special /'speʃǝl/ *adj* distinguished; uncommon; designed for a particular purpose; peculiar to one person or thing.—**specially** *adv*.

Special Branch *n* the division of the British police force that deals with political security.

specialist /'speʃǝlɪst/ *n* a person who concentrates on a particular area of study or activity, *esp* in medicine.

speciality /ˌspeʃi'ælɪti/ *n* (*pl* **specialities**) a special skill or interest; a special product.—*also* US **specialty**.

specialize /'speʃǝlaɪz/ *vi* to concentrate on a particular area of study or activity. • *vt* to adapt to a particular use or purpose.—**specialization** *n*.

special licence *n* a licence allowing a marriage to take place without regard to the normal legal requirements.

special pleading *n* (*law*) the allegation of new facts in an action as opposed to a direct denial or admission of the opposition evidence; arguments that concentrate on the positive as opposed to the negative aspects of a case.

specialty /'speʃǝlti/ *see* **speciality**.

speciation /spiːʃi'eɪʃǝn/ or /spiːs-/ *n* the evolution of a species.—**speciate** *vi*.

specie /'spiːʃi/ *n* money in coin.

species /'spiːsiːz/ or /'spiːʃ-/ *n* (*pl* **species**) a class of plants or animals with the same main characteristics, enabling interbreeding; a distinct kind or sort.

specific /spǝ'sɪfɪk/ *adj* explicit; definite; of a particular kind. • *n* a characteristic quality or influence; a drug effective in treating a particular disease.—**specifically** *adv.*—**specificity** *n*.

specification /ˌspesɪfɪ'keɪʃǝn/ *n* a requirement; (*pl*) detailed description of dimensions, materials, etc of something.

specific gravity *n* the ratio of the density of a substance to that of the same volume of water.

specific heat capacity *n* the heat required to raise the temperature of a unit of mass of a given substance by one degree.

specify /'spesɪˌfaɪ/ *vt* (**specifying, specified**) to state specifically; to set down as a condition.—**specifier** *n*.

specimen /'spesɪmǝn/ *n* (*plant, animal, etc*) an example of a particular species; a sample; (*inf*) a person.

specious /'spiːʃǝs/ *adj* apparently true, but in fact false.—**speciously** *adv.*—**speciousness** *n*.

speck /spek/ *n* a small spot; a fleck.

speckle /'spekǝl/ *n* a small mark of a different colour. • *vt* to mark with speckles.

specs /speks/ *npl* specifications; (*inf*) spectacles.

spectacle /'spektǝkǝl/ *n* an unusual or interesting scene; a large public show; an object of derision or ridicule; (*pl*) a pair of glasses.—**spectacled** *adj*.

spectacular /spek'tækjʊlǝr/ *adj* impressive; astonishing.—**spectacularly** *adv*.

spectate /'spekteɪt/ *vi* to be a spectator.

spectator /spek'teɪtǝr/ *n* an onlooker.

specter *see* **spectre**.

spectra *see* **spectrum**.

spectral /'spektrǝl/ *adj* of or like a spectre; of or produced by a spectrum.—**spectrality** *adv.*—**spectrally** *adv*.

spectre /'spektǝr/ *n* an apparition or ghost; a haunting mental image.—*also* **specter**.

spectro- /'spektrǝʊ/ *prefix* spectrum.

spectrograph /'spektrǝʊˌgrɑːf/ *n* a device for producing and recording spectra.—**spectrographic** *adj*.

spectrometer /spek'trɒmǝtǝr/ *n* a spectroscope used to measure spectra.—**spectrometric** *adj.*—**spectrometry** *n*.

spectroscope /'spektrǝˌskǝʊp/ *n* an instrument for generating and examining spectra.—**spectroscopic** *adj.*—**spectroscopically** *adv.*—**spectroscopy** *n*.

spectrum /'spektrǝm/ *n* (*pl* **spectra**) the range of colour which is produced when a white light is passed through a prism; any similar distribution of wave frequencies; a broad range.

speculate /'spekjʊˌleɪt/ *vi* to theorize, to conjecture; to make investments in the hope of making a profit.—**speculation** *n.*—**speculator** *n*.

speculative /'spekjʊlǝtɪv/ *adj* of or based on speculation; engaging in speculation in finance, etc.—**speculatively** *adv.*—**speculativeness** *n*.

speculum /'spekjʊlǝm/ *n* (*pl* **specula, speculums**) a medical instrument for dilating and examining a bodily passage or cavity; a mirror used as a reflector in an optical instrument such as a telescope.

sped *see* **speed**.

speech /spiːtʃ/ *n* the action or power of speaking; a public address or talk; language, dialect.

speechify /'spiːtʃɪˌfaɪ/ *vi* (**speechifying, speechified**) to make a speech or speeches, *esp* in a dull or pompous manner.—**speechifier** *n*.

speechless /'spiːtʃlǝs/ *adj* unable to speak; silent, as from shock; impossible to express in words.—**speechlessly** *adv.*—**speechlessness** *n*.

speed /spiːd/ *n* quickness; rapidity or rate of motion; (*photog*) the sensitivity of film to light; (*sl*) an amphetamine drug. • *vi* (**speeding, sped** *or* **speeded**) to go quickly, to hurry; to drive (a vehicle) at an illegally high speed.

speeding /'spiːdɪŋ/ *n* the driving of a vehicle at an illegally high or dangerous speed.

speedometer /spǝ'dɒmǝtǝr/ *n* an instrument in a motor vehicle for measuring its speed.

speedway /'spiːdweɪ/ n the sport of racing light motorcycles around dirt or cinder tracks; a stadium for motorcycle racing; in the US, a road reserved for fast traffic.

speedwell /'spiːdwɛl/ n any of various plants of the figwort family with small blue or white flowers.

speedy /'spiːdi/ adj (**speedier, speediest**) quick; prompt.—**speedily** adv.—**speediness** n.

speleology /ˌspiːlɪˈɒlədʒi/ n the scientific study of caves.—**speleological** adj.—**speleologist** n.

spell[1] /spɛl/ n a sequence of words used to perform magic; fascination.

spell[2] vb (**spelling, spelt** or **spelled**) vt to name or write down in correct order the letters to form a word; (letters) to form a word when placed in the correct order; to indicate; (with **out**) to read slowly and painstakingly; to explain in detail; to discern, realize the meaning of. • vi to spell words.

spell[3] n a usu indefinite period of time; a period of duty in a certain occupation or activity. • vt to relieve, stand in for.

spellbound /'spɛlbaʊnd/ adj entranced, enthralled.

spelling bee n a spelling contest.

spelt see **spell**[2].

spelunker /spɪˈlʌŋkər/ n a person whose hobby is exploring caves.—**spelunking** n.

spend /spɛnd/ vb (**spending, spent**) vt to pay out (money); to concentrate (one's time or energy) on an activity; to pass, as time; to use up. • vi to pay out money.—**spender** n.

spendthrift /'spɛndθrɪft/ n a person who spends money wastefully or extravagantly.

spent[1] see **spend**.

spent[2] adj consumed, used up; physically drained, exhausted.

sperm /spɜːm/ n semen; the male reproductive cell.

spermaceti /ˌspɜːməˈsɛti/ n a waxy substance derived from the oil in the head of a sperm whale.

spermat(o)-, sperm(o)- /spɜːrˈmætoː/ prefix sperm.

spermatic /spərˈmætɪk/ adj pertaining to, consisting of, or conveying, sperm.

spermatid /'spɜːmətɪd/ n any of the four male gametes that form into a spermatozoon.

spermatocyte /spərˈmætoːˌsaɪt/ n a cell that develops into a male germ cell.

spermatogenesis /spərˌmætoːˈdʒɛnɪsɪs/ n the formation and development of spermatozoa in the testis.—**spermatogenetic** adj.

spermatogonium /spərˌmætoːˈɡoːniəm/ n (pl **spermatogonia**) an immature male germ cell.

spermatophyte /spərˈmætoːˌfaɪt/ n a plant that produces seeds.—**spermatophytic** adj.

spermatozoon /spərˌmætoːˈzoːɒn/ n (pl **spermatozoa**) any of the male reproductive cells present in the semen.

spermicide /'spɜːrməˌsaɪd/ n a substance that destroys sperm.—**spermicidal** adj.

sperm oil n oil obtained from the head of the sperm whale.

sperm whale n a large whale with a blunt head which is hunted for its oil and spermaceti.

spew /spjuː/ vti to vomit; to flow or gush forth. • n something spewed.

sphagnum /'sfæɡnəm/ or /'spæɡ/ n a genus of moss which grows in bogs and is a major constituent of peat.

sphalerite /'sfælʌˌraɪt/ see **blende**.

sphenoid /'sfiːnɔɪd/ adj wedge-shaped; of or pertaining to the sphenoid bone. • n a sphenoid bone.

sphenoid bone n a wedge-shaped bone found at the base of the skull.

sphere /sfɪːr/ n a ball, globe or other perfectly round object; a field of activity or interest; a social class.—**spherical, spheric** adj.—**spherically** adv.

spheroid /'sfɪːrɔɪd/ n a figure that is nearly a sphere.

spherometer /sfɪˈrɒmətər/ n an instrument for measuring the curvature of spherical surfaces.

spherule /'sferuːl/ n a small sphere.

sphincter /'sfɪŋktər/ n a ring-shaped muscle controlling the opening and closing of an orifice.

sphinx /sfɪŋks/ n (with cap) (Greek myth) a monster with a lion's body and human head which killed travellers who gave the wrong answer to a riddle; (without cap) any of various massive statues with a lion's body and human head erected by the ancient Egyptians; a mysterious or enigmatic person.

sphygmograph /ˈsfɪɡmoˌɡræf/ n a device that records variations in blood pressure and pulse.—**sphygmographic** adj.—**sphygmography** n.

sphygmomanometer /ˈsfɪɡmoməˈnɒmətər/ n a device for measuring arterial blood pressure.

spicate /'spaɪkeɪt/ adj (flowers, leaves) spiked, pointed.

spicatto /spɪˈkætoː/ or /-ˈkɒtoː/ n (pl **spicattos**) (mus) (a musical piece or passage played using) a technique in which the bow is made to rebound lightly off the strings of an instrument.—also adj.

spice /spaɪs/ n an aromatic vegetable substance used for flavouring and seasoning food; these substances collectively; something that adds zest or interest. • vt to flavour with spice; to add zest to.

spicebush /'spaɪsbʊʃ/ n an aromatic North American plant.

spick-and-span adj scrupulously clean and tidy.

spicule /'spaɪkjuːl/ n a small needle-like body in the skeleton of sponges, corals, etc; a jet of hot gas erupting from the surface of the sun.

spicy /'spaɪsi/ adj (**spicier, spiciest**) flavoured with spice; pungent; (inf) somewhat scandalous or indecent.—**spicily** adv.—**spiciness** n.

spider /'spaɪdər/ n a small wingless creature (arachnid) with eight legs, and abdominal spinnerets for spinning silk threads to make webs.

spider crab n any of various crabs with triangular bodies and very long legs.

spider monkey n a monkey of South and Central America with a slender body and long limbs.

spiderwort /'spaɪdərˌwɔːt/ n tradescantia.

spidery /'spaɪdəri/ adj thin, and angular, like a spider's legs.

spied see **spy**.

spiel /ʃpiːl/ or /spiːl/ n glib talk intended to cajole or persuade.—also vi.

spiffing /'spɪfɪŋ/ n (sl) (arch) excellent.

spiffy /'spɪfi/ adj (**spiffier, spiffiest**) smart, elegant.

spigot /'spɪɡət/ n a small stopper or tap for a cask; a tap.

spike /spaɪk/ n long heavy nail; a sharp-pointed projection, as on a shoe to prevent slipping; an ear of corn, etc; a cluster of stalkless flowers arranged on a long stem. • vt to pierce with a spike.—**spiky** adj

spikenard /'spaɪknɑːd/ n (a fragrant oil derived from) an Indian aromatic plant.

spilikin /'spɪlɪkɪn/ see **spillikin**

spill[1] /spɪl/ vti (**spilling, spilled** or **spilt**) to cause, esp unintentionally, to flow out of a container; to shed (blood). • n something spilled.—**spillage** n.

spill[2] n a splinter or thin strip of wood or twisted paper for lighting a fire, etc.

spillikin n a sliver of wood, cardboard or plastic.—also **spilikin**.

spillway /'spɪlweɪ/ n a channel that carries away surplus water from a dam, etc.

spilt see **spill**[1].

spin /spɪn/ vb (**spinning, spun**) vt to rotate rapidly; to draw out and twist fibres into thread or yarn; (spiders, silkworm, etc) to make a web or cocoon; to draw out (a story) to a great length; (with **out**) to prolong, extend; to cause to last longer, eg money. • vi to seem to be spinning from dizziness; (wheels) to turn rapidly without imparting forward motion. • n a swift rotation; (inf) a brief, fast ride in a vehicle; an emphasis or slant imparted to information, proposals or policies.

spina bifida /ˌspaɪnəˈbɪfɪdə/ n a congenital abnormality in the formation of the spine causing the meninges to protrude, and associated with partial paralysis.

spinach /'spɪnɪtʃ/ n a plant with large, green edible leaves.

spinal /'spaɪnəl/ adj of or relating to the spine or spinal cord.—**spinally** adv.

spinal column n the skeleton of jointed vertebrae and interconnecting cartilaginous tissue that surrounds and protects the spinal cord.—also **spine, backbone.**

spinal cord n the cord of nerves enclosed by the spinal column.

spindle /'spɪndəl/ n the notched rod by which thread is twisted in spinning; a pin around which machinery turns.

spindly /'spɪndli/ adj (**spindlier, spindliest**) tall and slender; frail.

spindrift /'spɪndrɪft/ n sea spray.

spine /spaɪn/ n a sharp, stiff projection, as a thorn of the cactus or quill of a porcupine; a spinal column; the backbone of a book.

spine-chiller *n* a book, film, etc that inspires terror.—**spine-chilling** *adj*.

spineless /'spaɪnləs/ *adj* lacking a spine; weak-willed; irresolute.—**spinelessly** *adv*.—**spinelessness** *n*.

spinet /'spɪnət/ *or* /spɪ'nət/ *n* a type of small harpsichord.

spinifex /'spɪnɪˌfɛks/ *n* any of several coarse Australian grasses with spiny seed heads or spiked leaves.

spinnaker /'spɪnəkər/ *n* a large triangular sail sometimes carried by racing yachts.

spinner /'spɪnər/ *n* a revolving fishing lure; (*cricket*) a ball bowled with a spin, or a bowler who does this.

spinneret /'spɪnəˌrɛt/ *n* an organ in spiders and other insects for producing silk threads.

spinning wheel *n* a small household machine with a wheel-driven spindle for spinning yarn from fibre.

spin-off /'spɪnɒf/ *n* a product or benefit derived incidentally from existing research and development.

spinose /'spaɪnoːs/ *adj* (*plants*) spiny.

spinster /'spɪnstər/ *n* an unmarried woman.

spiny /spaɪni/ *adj* (**spinier, spiniest**) covered with spines or thorns; troublesome.

spiny anteater *n* the echidna.

spiny lobster *n* any of several large edible crustaceans with a spiny shell.

spiracle /'spaɪrəkəl/ *n* a respiratory aperture in various insects and some fishes; the blowhole in whales.

spiraea, spirea /ˌspaɪ'riːə/ *n* any of various plants of the rose family having clusters of small white or pink flowers.

spiral /'spaɪrəl/ *adj* winding round in a continuous curve up or down a centre or pole. • *n* a helix; a spiral line or shape; a continuous expansion or decrease, *eg* in inflation. • *vi* (**spiralling, spiralled** *or* **spiraling, spiraled**) to move up or down in a spiral curve; to increase or decrease steadily.

spiral galaxy *n* a galaxy in which two arms consisting of new stars spiral outward from an ellipsoidal nucleus of old stars.

spire /'spaɪr/ *n* the tapering point of a steeple.

spirillum /ˌspaɪ'rɪləm/ *n* (*pl* **spirilla**) a bacterium with a curved or spiral body.

spirit /'spɪːrɪt/ *or* /'spɪrɪt/ *n* soul; a supernatural being, as a ghost, angel, etc; (*pl*) disposition; mood; vivacity, courage, etc; real meaning; essential quality; (*usu pl*) distilled alcoholic liquor. • *vt* to carry (away, off, etc) secretly and swiftly.

spirited /'spɪrɪtəd/ *adj* full of life; animated.—**spiritedly** *adv*.—**spiritedness** *n*.

spirit level *n* a glass tube filled with liquid containing an air bubble and mounted in a frame, used for testing whether a surface is level.

spiritual /'spɪrɪtʃʊəl/ *adj* of the soul; religious; sacred. • *n* an emotional religious song, originating among the Black slaves in the American South.—**spirituality** *n*.—**spiritually** *adv*.

spiritualism /'spɪrɪtʃʊəˌlɪzəm/ *n* the belief that the spirits of the dead can communicate with the living, as through mediums.—**spiritualist** *n*.

spirochaete, spirochete /'spaɪrəˌkiːt/ *n* any of a genus of slender spiral-shaped bacteria that includes those causing syphilis.

spirograph /'spaɪroːˌgræf/ *n* a device that records respiratory movements.—**spirographic** *adj*.

spirt *see* **spurt**.

spit[1] /spɪt/ *n* a pointed iron rod on which meat is roasted; a long narrow strip of land projecting into the water. • *vt* (**spitting, spitted**) to fix as on a spit, impale.

spit[2] *vb* (**spitting, spat** *or* **spit**) *vt* to eject from the mouth; to utter with scorn. • *vi* to expel saliva from the mouth; (*hot fat*) to splutter; to rain lightly. • *n* saliva.

spit and polish *n* (*inf*) obsession with neatness and cleanliness, *esp* in the military services.

spite /spaɪt/ *n* ill will; malice. • *vt* to annoy spitefully, to vex.—**spiteful** *adj*.

spitting image *n* (*inf*) a person who almost exactly resembles another.

spittle /'spɪtəl/ *n* saliva ejected from the mouth.

spittoon /spɪ'tuːn/ *n* a *usu* metal pan for spitting into, a cuspidor.

spiv /spɪv/ *n* (*sl*) a person of smart appearance who lives by shady dealings, *esp* on the black market.

splake /spleɪk/ *n* a hybrid trout that is a cross between a lake trout and a brook trout.

splanchnic /'splæŋknɪk/ *adj* of or pertaining to the viscera.

splash /splæʃ/ *vti* to spatter with liquid; to move with a splash; to display prominently; (*with* **down**) to land (a spacecraft) on water. • *n* something splashed; a patch of colour; a small amount, *esp* of a mixer added to an alcoholic drink.—**splashy** *adj*.

splashdown /'splæʃdaʊn/ *n* (the scheduled time of) the landing of a spacecraft on the ocean.

splatter /'splætər/ *vti* to splash, spatter.—*also n*.

splay /spleɪ/ *vti* to turn out at an angle; to spread out.

spleen /spliːn/ *n* a large lymphatic organ in the upper left part of the abdomen which modifies the blood structure; spitefulness; ill humour.

splendid /'splendɪd/ *adj* brilliant; magnificent; (*inf*) very good.—**splendidly** *adv*.—**splendidness** *n*.

splendiferous /splen'dɪfərəs/ *adj* (*inf*) splendid.

splendour, splendor /'splendər/ *n* brilliance; magnificence; grandeur.—**splendorous, splendrous** *adj*.

splenetic /splɪ'netɪk/ *adj* of or pertaining to the spleen; spiteful, irritable.—**splenetically** *adv*.

splenic /'spliːnɪk/ *or* /'splɛnɪk/ *n* of, pertaining to, or in the spleen.

splenius /'spliːniəs/ *n* (*pl* **splenii**) either of the two muscles at either side of the back of the neck that move the head.—**splenial** *adj*.

splenomegaly /ˌspliːnoː'mɛgəli/ *n* distension of the spleen.

splice /splaɪs/ *vt* to unite (two ends of a rope) by intertwining the strands; to connect (two pieces of timber) by overlapping.—*also n*.

spline /splaɪn/ *n* a key or slot in a shaft that fits into grooves in a surrounding sleeve and locks the two together.

splint /splɪnt/ *n* a rigid structure used to immobilize and support a fractured limb; a splinter of wood for lighting fires. • *vt* to put in splints.

splinter /'splɪntər/ *n* a thin, sharp piece of wood, glass, or metal broken off. • *vti* to break off into splinters.—**splintery** *adj*.

splinter group *n* a small group that has split off from the main body.

split /splɪt/ *vti* (**splitting, split**) to break apart (*usu* into two pieces); to separate into factions; to divide into shares; to burst or tear. • *n* the act or process of splitting; a narrow gap made (as if) by splitting; a dessert consisting of sliced fruit, *esp* banana, with ice cream, nuts, etc; (*often pl*) the act of extending the legs in opposite directions and lowering the the body to the floor. • *adj* divided; torn; fractured.

split infinitive *n* (*gram*) an infinitive with another word between *to* and the verb.

split-level /-'levəl/ *adj* (*building*) having rooms or areas in one part less than a full story higher than another that adjoins them.

split personality *n* unstable in mood or behaviour; having two or more distinct personalities.

split-screen *n* (*cinema, television*) a technique involving the simultaneous projection of different images onto separate areas of the screen.

split second *n* a very brief moment, an instant.—**split-second** *adj*.

split shift *n* a shift in which the working hours are divided into two distinct periods.

splodge /splɒdʒ/, **splotch** *n* a large irregular spot, stain or smear. • *vt* to mark with a splodge or splotch.—**splodgy, splotchy** *adj*.

splurge /splɜːrdʒ/ *vi* to spend lavishly (on); to show off. • *n* an extravagant display, *esp* of wealth.

splutter /'splʌtər/ *vi* to spit out food or drops of liquid noisily; to utter words confusedly and hurriedly.—*also n*.

spoil /spɔɪl/ *vb* (**spoiling, spoiled** *or* **spoilt**) *vt* to damage as to make useless, etc; to impair the enjoyment, etc, of; to overindulge (a child). • *vi* to become spoiled; to decay, etc, as food. • *npl* booty, valuables seized in war; the opportunities for financial gain from holding public office.

spoiler /'spɔɪlər/ *n* a projecting structure on an aircraft wing that increases drag to reduce lift; any similar structure for increasing the stability of vehicles at high speed.

spoil-sport /'spɔɪlspɔːrt/ *n* (*inf*) a person who spoils the fun of others.

spoilt /spɔɪlt/ *see* **spoil**.

spoke[1] /spoːk/ **spoken** *see* **speak**.

spoke[2] *n* any of the braces extending from the hub to the rim of a wheel.

spokeshave /ˈspoːkʃeɪv/ *n* a small two-handled plane used for smoothing curved surfaces.

spokesman /ˈspoːksmən/ *n* (*pl* **spokesmen**) a person authorized to speak on behalf of others.—**spokeswoman** *nf* (*pl* **spokeswomen**).

spondylitis /ˌspɒndɪˈlaɪtɪs/ *n* inflammation of the vertebrae.

sponge /spʌndʒ/ *n* a plantlike marine animal with an internal skeleton of elastic interlacing horny fibres; a piece of natural or manmade sponge for washing or cleaning. • *vt* to wipe with a sponge. • *vi* (*inf*) to scrounge.—**sponginess** *n*.—**spongy** *adj*.

sponge bag *n* a small waterproof bag for toilet articles, a wash-bag.

sponge cake *n* a sweet cake with a light porous texture.

sponson /ˈspɒnsən/ *n* a projecting gun-mounting on a ship or tank, etc to allow forward fire; an air-filled projection on the hull of a seaplane to provide stability.

sponsor /ˈspɒnsər/ *n* a person or organization that pays the expenses connected with an artistic production or sports event in return for advertising; a business firm, etc that pays for a radio or TV programme advertising its product. • *vt* to act as sponsor for.—**sponsorship** *n*.

spontaneity /ˌspɒntəˈneɪɪti/ *n* (*pl* **spontaneities**) the quality of being spontaneous; a spontaneous action, etc.

spontaneous /spɒnˈteɪnɪəs/ *adj* arising naturally; unpremeditated.—**spontaneously** *adv*.—**spontaneousness** *n*.

spontaneous combustion *n* the self-igniting of a substance through internal chemical processes such as oxidation.

spontaneous generation *n* abiogenesis.

spoof /spuːf/ *n* (*sl*) a hoax or joke; a light satire.—*also vti*.

spook /spuːk/ *n* (*inf*) a ghost; (*inf*) a spy. • *vt* to frighten.—**spooky** *adj*.

spool /spuːl/ *n* a cylinder, bobbin, or reel, upon which thread, photographic film, etc, are wound. • *vt* to wind on a spool.

spoon /spuːn/ *n* a utensil with a shallow bowl and a handle, for eating, stirring, etc.—**spoonful** *n*.

spoonbill /ˈspuːnbɪl/ *n* any of various wading birds with flattened bills.

spoonerism /ˈspuːnəˌrɪzəm/ *n* the accidental transposition of the initial letters or opening syllables of two or more words with amusing results, *eg half-warmed fish* for *half-formed wish*.

spoor /spʊr/ *n* a trail, *esp* of a wild animal. • *vti* to track (something) by a spoor.

sporadic /spəˈrædɪk/ *adj* occurring here and there; intermittent.—**sporadically** *adv*.

sporangium /spəˈrændʒɪəm/ *n* (*pl* **sporangia**) (*in fungi, etc*) an organ or part in which asexual spores are produced.

spore /spɔr/ *n* an asexual reproductive body produced by algae, fungae and ferns capable of giving rise to new individuals.

sporogenesis /ˌspɔrəˈdʒenəsɪs/ *n* the formation of spores in plants and animals.—**sporogenous** *adj*.

sporozoan /ˌspɔrəˈzoːən/ *n* any of a group of spore-producing parasitic protozoans that includes the malaria parasite.

sporran /ˈspɒrən/ *n* an ornamental pouch worn in front of the kilt as part of traditional Highland dress in Scotland.

sport /spɔrt/ *n* an athletic game or pastime, often competitive and involving physical capability; good-humoured joking; (*inf*) a person regarded as fair and abiding by the rules. • *vi* to play, to frolic. • *vt* (*inf*) to display, flaunt.

sporting /ˈspɔrtɪŋ/ *adj* interested in, concerned with, or suitable for sport; exhibiting sportsmanship; willing to take a risk.—**sportingly** *adv*.

sportive /ˈspɔrtɪv/ *adj* playful.—**sportively** *adv*.—**sportiveness** *n*.

sportscast /ˈspɔrtskæst/ *n* a sports broadcast.—**sportscaster** *n*.

sportsman /ˈspɔrtsmən/ *n* (*pl* **sportsmen**) a person engaged in sport; a person who plays by the rules, is fair, is a good loser, etc.—**sportswoman** *nf* (*pl* **sportswomen**).—**sportsmanlike, sportsmanly** *adj*.—**sportsmanship** *n*.

sports medicine *n* the branch of medicine dealing with sports injuries.

sporty /ˈspɔrti/ *adj* (**sportier, sportiest**) (*inf*) fond of sport; flashy, ostentatious.—**sportily** *adv*.—**sportiness** *n*.

sporule /ˈspɔruːl/ *n* a tiny spore.

spot /spɒt/ *n* a small area differing in colour, etc, from the surrounding area; a stain, speck, etc; a taint on character or reputation; a small quantity or amount; a locality; (*inf*) a difficult or embarrassing situation; a place on an entertainment programme; a spotlight. • *vt* (**spotting, spotted**) to mark with spots; (*inf*) to identify or recognise; to glimpse.

spot check /ˈspɒtʧek/ *n* a sudden random examination.—**spot-check** *vt*.

spotless /ˈspɒtləs/ *adj* immaculate.—**spotlessly** *adv*.—**spotlessness** *n*.

spotlight /ˈspɒtlaɪt/ *n* a powerful light used to illuminate a small area; intense public attention. • *vt* (**spotlighting, spotlighted** *or* **spotlit**) to illuminate with a spotlight; to focus attention on.

spot on *adj* (*inf*) absolutely right.

spotted dick /ˈspɒtɪd/ *n* a steamed pudding made with suet and currants.

spotty /ˈspɒti/ *adj* (**spottier, spottiest**) marked with spots, *esp* on the skin; intermittent, uneven.—**spottily** *adv*.—**spottiness** *n*.

spot-weld *vt* to join two pieces of metal with circular welds.—**spot-welder** *n*.—**spot welding** *n*.

spouse /spɛʊs/ *n* (one's) husband or wife.

spout /spɛʊt/ *vti* to eject in a strong jet or spurts; (*inf*) to drone on boringly. • *n* a projecting lip or tube for pouring out liquids.

spp *abbr* = species (*pl*).

SPQR *abbr* = *Senatus Populusque Romanus* (the Senate and People of Rome).

sprain /spreɪn/ *n* a wrenching of a joint by sudden twisting or tearing of ligaments.—*also vt*.

sprang /spræŋ/ *see* **spring**.

sprat /spræt/ *n* a small food fish related to the herring; a small or young herring.

sprawl /sprɔl/ *vi* to lie down with the limbs stretched out in an untidy manner; to spread out in a straggling way. • *n* a sprawling position.

spray[1] /spreɪ/ *n* fine particles of a liquid; mist; an aerosol or atomizer. • *vti* to direct a spray (on); to apply as a spray.

spray[2] *n* a number of flowers on one branch; a decorative flower arrangement; an ornament resembling this.

spray gun *n* a device for applying paint, varnish, etc in the form of a spray.

spread /spred/ *vt* (**spreading, spread**) to extend; to unfold or open; to disseminate; to distribute; to apply a coating (*eg* butter). • *vi* to expand in all directions. • *n* an expanse; (*inf*) a feast; food which can be spread on bread; a bed cover.

spread eagle *n* an emblem of an eagle with wings and legs stretched out.

spread-eagle /ˈspredˌiːgəl/ *vt* to stand or lie with the limbs outstretched.—**spread-eagled** *adj*.

spreadsheet /ˈspredʃiːt/ *n* a computer program that allows easy entry and manipulation of text and figures, used for accounting and financial planning.

spree /spriː/ *n* (*inf*) excessive indulgence, *eg* in spending money, alcohol consumption, etc.

spree killer *n* one who kills a group or number of people in an unpremeditated at a single site or location.

sprier /spraɪər/ *see* **spry**.

sprig /sprɪg/ *n* a twig with leaves on it.

sprightly /ˈspraɪtli/ *adj* (**sprightlier, sprightliest**) full of life or energy.—**sprightliness** *n*.

spring /sprɪŋ/ *vb* (**springing, sprang** *or* **sprung**, *pp* **sprung**) *vi* to move suddenly, as by elastic force; to arise suddenly; to originate. • *vt* to cause to spring up, to cause to operate suddenly. • *n* a leap; the season between winter and summer; a coiled piece of wire that springs back to its original shape when stretched; the source of a stream.

spring balance *n* a device that measures weight by the tension of a spring linked to a pointer on a calibrated scale.—*also* **spring scale**.

springboard /ˈsprɪŋbɔrd/ *n* a flexible board used by divers and in gymnastics to provided added height or impetus.

springbok /ˈsprɪŋbɒk/ *n* a South African gazelle.

spring chicken *n* a young chicken from two to ten months old; (*inf*) a young inexperienced person.

spring-clean /-'kli:n/ *vi* to clean (a house, etc) thoroughly.— **spring clean** *n*.

springe /sprɪndʒ/ *n* a snare for catching small animals.

spring onion *n* a scallion.

spring roll *n* a Chinese savoury snack comprising a mixture of beansprouts, chopped meat, etc rolled in a thin pancake and fried.

spring scale *see* **spring balance**.

springtail /'sprɪŋteɪl/ *n* any of various small wingless leaping insects.

spring tide *n* a high tide that occurs at the full or new moon.

springtime /'sprɪŋtaɪm/ *n* the season of spring; the earliest and most promising period in the life of something or someone.

springy /'sprɪŋi/ *adj* (**springier, springiest**) elastic, resilient; light, spongy.—**springily** *adv*.—**springiness** *n*.

sprinkle /'sprɪŋkəl/ *vt* to scatter in droplets or particles (on something).—*also n*.

sprinkler /'sprɪŋklər/ *n* a nozzle for spraying water; a fire-extinguishing system that operates automatically on detection of smoke or heat.

sprinkling /'sprɪŋklɪŋ/ *n* a small quantity scattered randomly.

sprint /sprɪnt/ *n* a short run or race at full speed. • *vi* to go at top speed.—**sprinter** *n*.

sprit /sprɪt/ *n* a small spar which runs from the mast to the outer upper corner of a sail.

sprite /spraɪt/ *n* an elf or imp; a dainty person.

spritsail /'sprɪtsəl/ or /-seɪl/ *n* a sail extended by a sprit.

spritzer /'sprɪtsər/ *n* a drink made with wine, *usu* white, and soda water.

sprocket /'sprɒkət/ *n* a wheel with a row of teeth which engage the holes in a chain, or a reel of film, in order to turn it.

sprout /spraʊt/ *n* a new shoot on a plant; a small cabbage-like vegetable. • *vt* to put forth (shoots). • *vi* to begin to grow.

spruce[1] /spru:s/ *adj* smart, neat, trim. • *vt* to smarten.

spruce[2] *n* an evergreen tree of the pine family with a conical head and soft light wood.

sprung /sprʌŋ/ *see* **spring**.

spry /spraɪ/ *adj* (**sprier, spriest** *or* **spryer, spryest**) vigorous, agile.—**spryly** *adv*.—**spryness** *n*.

spud /spʌd/ *n* a small narrow digging tool; (*inf*) a potato. • *vt* (**spudding, spudded**) to dig with a spud.—**spudder** *n*.

spume /spju:m/ *n* foam; surf; froth.

spun /spʌn/ *see* **spin**.

spunk /spʌŋk/ *n* a spark, a match; (*sl*) pluck, courage.

spunky /'spʌŋki/ *adj* (**spunkier, spunkiest**) full of courage; spirited.—**spunkily** *adv*.—**spunkiness** *n*.

spun silk *n* a shiny material made from silk waste.

spur /spər/ *n* a small metal wheel on a rider's heel, with sharp points for urging on the horse; encouragement, stimulus; a hard sharp projection. • *vt* (**spurring, spurred**) to urge on.

spurge /spərdʒ/ *n* any of various plants that produce a bitter milky juice.

spurious /'spəriəs/ or /'spjʊr-/ *adj* not legitimate or genuine; false.—**spuriously** *adv*.—**spuriousness** *n*.

spurn /spərn/ *vt* to reject with disdain. • *n* disdainful rejection.

spurt /spərt/ *vt* to gush forth in a sudden stream or jet. • *n* a sudden stream or jet; a burst of activity.—*also* **spirt**.

sputnik /'spʌtnɪk/ or /'spʊt-/ *n* the name used for series of artificial satellites launched by the former Soviet Union in the 1950s and 1960s (Russian for *travelling companion*).

sputter /'spʌtər/ *vi* to splutter.—*also n*.

sputum /'spju:təm/ *n* (*pl* **sputa**) saliva and mucus.

spy /spaɪ/ *n* (*pl* **spies**) a secret agent employed to collect information on rivals. • *vb* (**spying, spied**) *vt* to keep under secret surveillance, act as a spy (*usu with* **on**). • *vt* to catch sight of.

spyglass /'spaɪglæs/ *n* a small telescope.

sq *abbr* = sequence; squadron; square.

squab /skwɒb/ *n* (*pl* **squabs, squab**) a young bird, *esp* a pigeon; a stuffed cushion; a short fat person. • *adj* (*birds*) unfledged; short and fat.

squabble /'skwɒbəl/ *vi* to quarrel noisily. • *n* a noisy, petty quarrel.—*also n*.

squad /skwɒd/ *n* a small group of soldiers which form a working unit; a section of a police force; (*sport*) a group of players from which a team is selected.

squadron /'skwɒdrən/ *n* a unit of warships, cavalry, military aircraft, etc.

squalid /'skwɒlɪd/ *adj* filthy; neglected, sordid; degrading.—**squalidly** *adv*.—**squalidness** *n*.

squall /skwɔ:l/ *vi* to cry out loudly (like a baby). • *n* a loud cry; a violent gust of wind.

squalor /'skwɒlər/ *n* foulness; dirt, filth.

squama /'skweɪmə/ *n* (*pl* **squamae**) (*biol*) (something resembling) a scale.

squander /'skwɒndər/ *vt* to spend extravagantly or wastefully.

square /skwɛr/ *n* a shape with four sides of equal length and four right angles; an open space in a town, surrounded by buildings; (*inf*) an old-fashioned person; an instrument for drawing right angles; the product of a number multiplied by itself. • *adj* square-shaped; forming a square; forming a right angle (with); (*financial account*) settled; fair, honest; equal in score; (*inf*) old-fashioned. • *vt* to make square; to multiply (a quantity) by itself; (*with* **away**) (*inf*) to put in order, tidy up. • *vi* to agree.—**squarely** *adv*.—**squareness** *n*.

square bracket *n* either of a pair of written or printed characters [ ] used to enclose text or in mathematical expressions.

square dance *n* any of various dances in which the participants join hands to form squares.—**square-dance** *vi*.

square meal *n* a meal of satisfying quantity.

square measure *n* the measure of an area; the square of a lineal measure.

square root *n* a number that when multiplied by itself produces a given number (*2 is the square root of 4*).

squash[1] /skwɒʃ/ *vt* to squeeze, press, or crush; to suppress. • *vi* to squelch; to crowd. • *n* a crushed mass; a crowd of people pressed together; a fruit-flavoured drink; a game played in a walled court with rackets and rubber ball.—**squashy** *adj*.

squash[2] *n* (*pl* **squashes, squash**) a marrow or gourd eaten as a vegetable.

squat /skwɒt/ *vi* (**squatting, squatted**) to crouch down upon the heels; to occupy land or property, without permission or title. • *adj* short and dumpy. • *n* the act of squatting; a house that is occupied by squatters.

squatter /'skwɒtər/ *n* a person who squats.

squaw /skwɔ:/ *n* a North American Indian woman.

squawk /skwɔːk/ *n* a loud, raucous call or cry, as of a bird; (*inf*) loud protest.—*also vi*.

squeak /skwiːk/ *vi* to make a high-pitched cry. • *n* a squeaky noise.—**squeaker** *n*.—**squeaky** *adj*.

squeaky-clean /'skwiːki/ *adj* spotless; above reproach.

squeal /skwiːl/ *vi* to make a shrill and prolonged cry or sound; (*sl*) to be an informer; to protest.

squeamish /'skwiːmɪʃ/ *adj* easily nauseated; easily shocked or disgusted.—**squeamishly** *adv*.—**squeamishness** *n*.

squeegee /'skwiːdʒiː/ *n* a tool with a rubber-edged blade for scraping away excess water from a surface, *esp* a window. • *vt* (**squeegeeing, squeegeed**) to wipe clean with a squeegee.

squeeze /skwiːz/ *vt* to press firmly, compress; to grasp tightly; to hug; to force (through, into) by pressing; to extract liquid, juice, from by pressure; to obtain (money, etc) by force, to harass. • *n* squeezing or being squeezed; a hug; a small amount squeezed from something; a crowding together; financial pressure or hardship.—**squeezable** *adj*.

squelch /skwɛltʃ/ *vi* to walk through soft, wet ground, making a sucking noise. • *vt* to crush or squash completely. • *n* a squelching sound.

squib /skwɪb/ *n* a small firework that fizzes then explodes; a short, witty attack in speech or writing, a lampoon.

squid /skwɪd/ *n* (*pl* **squids, squid**) an edible mollusc, related to the cuttlefish, with a long body and ten arms.

squiffy /'skwɪfi/ *adj* (**squiffier, squiffiest**) slightly drunk.

squiggle /'skwɪgəl/ *n* a short wavy line, *esp* handwritten. • *vi* to squirm; to wriggle.—**squiggly** *adj*.

squill /skwɪl/ *n* a Mediterranean plant of the lilly family; a seashore variety of this whose bulbs were formerly used medicinally.

squint /skwɪnt/ *vi* to half close or cross the eyes; to glance sideways. • *n* crossed eyes, as caused by a visual disorder; a glance sideways; (*inf*) a look. • *adj* squinting; (*inf*) crooked.

squire /'skwaɪr/ *n* a country gentleman, *esp* the leading landowner in a district.

squirm /skwərm/ *vi* to writhe; to wriggle; to feel embarrassed or ashamed.

squirrel /'skwɔrəl/ n (pl **squirrels, squirrel**) a bushy tailed rodent with grey or reddish fur which lives in trees and feeds on nuts. • vt (**squirrelling, squirrelled** or **squirreling, squirreled**) (usu with **away**) to hoard.

squirrel cage n a small cylindrical cage which is rotated by a small animal running inside; the rotor of an induction motor with cylindrically arranged copper bars.

squirt /skwɔrt/ vt to eject liquid in a jet. • vi to spurt. • n a jet of liquid; (inf) an insignificant person.

squish /skwɪʃ/ vt to crush, esp so as to produce a squelching sound. • vi to make or move with a squelching sound. • n a soft squelching sound.—**squishy** adj.

Sr[1] (chem symbol) strontium.

Sr[2] abbr = Senior; Señor; sir; sister (religious).

SRO abbr = standing room only.

SS[1] abbr = Saints; steamship; Sunday School.

SS[2] abbr = Schutzstaffel, the Nazi paramilitary police force elite guard.

SSRI abbr = selective serotonin reuptake inhibitor, a type of drug used to treat depression.

SSSI abbr = site of special scientific interest.

St abbr = Saint.

St. abbr = Street.

stab /stæb/ vt (**stabbing, stabbed**) to injure with a knife or pointed weapon; to pain suddenly and sharply. • vi to thrust at (as if) with a pointed weapon. • n an act or instance of stabbing; a wound made by stabbing; a sudden sensation, as of emotion, pain, etc; (inf) an attempt.

stabile /'steɪbaɪl/ n an abstract sculpture resembling a mobile but stationary.

stabilize /'steɪbɪˌlaɪz/ vti to make or become stable or steady.—**stabilization** n.

stabilizer /'steɪbɪlaɪzər/ n a device for stabilizing (an aircraft, ship, bicycle, etc).

stable[1] /'steɪbəl/ adj steady or firm; firmly established; permanent; not decomposing readily.—**stability** n.

stable[2] n a building where horses or cattle are kept; a group of racehorses belonging to one owner; a group of people working for or trained by a specific establishment, as writers, performers, etc. • vti to put, keep, or live in a stable.

staccato /stə'kɑːto/ or /-'kɒto/ adj (musical notes) short, abrupt; (speech) sharp, abrupt, disconnected. • adv in a staccato manner.

stack /stæk/ n a large neatly arranged pile (of hay, papers, records, etc); a chimney stack; (inf) a large amount of; a number of aircraft circling an airport waiting for permission to land. • vt to pile, arrange in a stack.

stadia /'steɪdɪə/ see **stadium**.

stadium /'steɪdɪəm/ n (pl **stadium, stadia**) a sports ground surrounded by tiers of seats.

staff /stæf/ n (pl **staves**) a strong stick or pole; (mus) one of the five horizontal lines upon which music is written.—also **stave**; (pl **staffs**) a body of officers who help a commanding officer, or perform special duties; the workers employed in an establishment; the teachers or lecturers of an educational institution. • vt to provide with a staff.

stag /stæg/ n a full-grown male deer. • adj (party) for men only.

stag beetle n any of various beetles with large pincer-like mandibles.

stage /steɪdʒ/ n a degree or step in a process; a raised platform, esp for acting on; (with **the**) the theatre, the theatrical calling; any field of action or setting; a portion of a journey; a propulsion unit of a space rocket discarded when its fuel is spent. • vt to perform a play on the stage; to plan, organize (an event).

stagecoach /'steɪdʒkoːtʃ/ n a four-wheeled vehicle drawn by horses, that formerly carried passengers or mail.

stagecraft /'steɪdʒkræft/ n skill in writing or staging plays.

stage direction n an instruction in the text of a play (regarding characterization, movement, lighting, etc) for an actor or director.

stage door n the back entrance to a theatre used by the staff and players.

stage fright n nervousness at appearing before an audience.

stage left n the area of a stage to the left of an actor facing the audience.

stage-manage vt to act as a stage-manager; to organize or direct from behind the scenes.

stage manager n a person responsible for the stage arrangements prior to and during the performance of a play.

stage right n the area of a stage to the right of an actor facing the audience.

stage-struck adj obsessed with theatre and the idea of becoming an actor.

stage whisper n a loud whisper made by an actor and intentionally audible to the audience.

stagflation /stæg'fleɪʃən/ n an economic situation characterized by a combination of high inflation and stagnant or declining output and employment.

stagger /'stægər/ vi to walk unsteadily, to totter. • vt to astound; to give a shock to; to arrange so as not to overlap; to alternate.

staggering /'stægərɪŋ/ adj astounding.—**staggeringly** adv.

staging /'steɪdʒɪŋ/ n a temporary platform, esp horizontal planking supported by scaffolding.

staging area n an assembly point for troops in transit.

staging post n a regular stopover point on a long route.

stagnant /'stægnənt/ adj (water) not flowing, standing still with a revolting smell; unchanging, dull.—**stagnancy** n.

stagnate /'stægneɪt/ vi to be, or become, stagnant.—**stagnation** n.

stag party n a party for men only, usu given for one who is due to be married shortly.

stagy /'steɪdʒi/, **stagey** adj (**stagier, stagiest**) theatrical, dramatic.

staid /steɪd/ adj sober; sedate; old-fashioned.—**staidly** adv.—**staidness** n.

stain /steɪn/ vt to dye; to discolour with spots of something which cannot be removed. • vi to become stained; to produce stains. • n a discoloured mark; a moral blemish; a dye or liquid for staining materials, eg wood.

stained glass n coloured glass used in windows.

stainless /'steɪnləs/ adj free from stain; (materials) resistant to staining.—**stainlessly** adv.

stainless steel n a type of steel resistant to tarnishing and corrosion.

stair /steər/ n a flight of stairs; a single step; (pl) a stairway.

staircase /'steəkeɪs/ n a flight of stairs with banisters.

stairway /'steəweɪ/ n a staircase.

stairwell /'steəwel/ n the vertical shaft for a staircase.

stake[1] /steɪk/ n a sharpened metal or wooden post driven into the ground, as a marker or fence post; a post to which persons were tied for execution by burning; this form of execution. • vt to support with, tie or tether to a stake; to mark out (land) with stakes; (with **out**) to put under surveillance.

stake[2] vt to bet; (inf) to provide with money or resources. • n a bet; a financial interest; (pl) money risked on a race; (pl) the prize in a race.

stakeout /'steɪkʊt/ n surveillance, esp by police; premises under surveillance.

stalactite /stə'læktaɪt/ or /'stælək-/ n an icicle-like calcium deposit hanging from the roof of a cave.

stalag /'stælæg/ n a German prisoner-of-war camp in World War II.

stalagmite /stə'lægmaɪt/ or /'stæ-/ n a cylindrical deposit projecting upward from the floor of a cave, caused by the dripping of water and lime from the roof.

stale /steɪl/ adj deteriorated from age; tainted; musty; stagnant; jaded.—**staleness** n.

stalemate /'steɪlmeɪt/ n (chess) a situation in which a king can only be moved in and out of check, thus causing a draw; a deadlock.—also vt.

Stalinism /'stælɪˌnɪzəm/ n the theory and practice of authoritarian rule associated with the Soviet dictator Joseph Stalin (1879–1953).—**Stalinist** n, adj.

stalk[1] /stɔk/ n the stem of a plant.

stalk[2] vi to stride in a stiff or angry way; to hunt (game, prey) stealthily.—**stalker** n.

stalking-horse n a means of concealing true intentions; a candidate standing in an election to confuse the opposition or test the amount of prospective support for the real candidate in whose favour the stand-in then withdraws.

stall[1] /stɔl/ n a compartment for one animal in a stable; a table or stand for the display or sale of goods; a stalling of an engine; (aircraft) a loss of lift and downward plunge due to an excessive decrease in airspeed; (pl) the seats on the ground floor of a theatre. • vti (car engine) to stop or cause to stop suddenly, eg by misuse of the clutch; (aircraft) to lose or cause to lose lift because of an excessive reduction in airspeed.

stall[2] *vti* to play for time; to postpone or delay. • *n* (*inf*) any action used in stalling.

stallion /'stæljən/ *n* an uncastrated male horse, *esp* one kept for breeding.

stalwart /'stɒlwərt/ *adj* strong, sturdy; resolute; dependable. • *n* a loyal, hardworking supporter.

stamen /'steɪmən/ *n* (*pl* **stamens, stamina**) the pollen-bearing part of a flower.

stamina /'stæmɪnə/ *n* strength; staying power.

staminate /'stæmɪnət/ or /-neɪt/ *adj* (*plants*) having or producing stamens.

stammer /'stæmər/ *vti* to pause or falter in speaking; to stutter.— *also n.*—**stammerer** *n.*

stamp /stæmp/ *vt* to put a mark on; to imprint with an official seal; to affix a postage stamp; (*with* **out**) to extinguish by stamping; to suppress, eradicate, by force. • *vi* to bring the foot down heavily (on). • *n* a postage stamp; the mark cancelling a postage stamp; a block for imprinting.

stamp duty, stamp tax *n* a tax on some types of legal documents.

stampede /stæm'piːd/ *n* an impulsive rush of a panic-stricken herd; a rush of a crowd.—*also vti.*

stamping ground *n* (*inf*) a favourite or habitual meeting place.

stance /stæns/ *n* posture; the attitude taken in a given situation.

stanch /stɑːntʃ/ *see* **staunch**[2].

stanchion /'stæntʃən/ *n* an upright post, pillar, rod or similar support. • *vt* to provide with a stanchion.

stand /stænd/ *vb* (**standing, stood**) *vi* to be in an upright position; to be on, or rise to one's feet; to make resistance; to remain unchanged; to endure, tolerate; to reach a deadlock; (*with* **by**) to look on without interfering; to be available for use if required; (*with* **down**) to withdraw, resign; to leave a witness box after testifying in court; (*soldier*) to go off duty; (*with* **off**) to remain at a distance; to reach a stalemate; (*with* **up**) to rise to one's feet. • *vt* to put upright; to endure, tolerate; (*with* **by**) to remain loyal to, to defend; (*with* **off**) to (cause to) keep at a distance; to lay off (employees) temporarily; (*with* **up**) to resist; to withstand criticism, close examination, etc; (*inf*) to fail to keep an appointment with. • *n* a strong opinion; a standing position; a standstill; a place for taxis awaiting hire; (*pl*) a structure for spectators; the place taken by a witness for testifying in court; a piece of furniture for hanging things from; a stall or booth for a small retail business.

standard /'stændərd/ *n* a flag, banner, or emblem; an upright pole, pillar; an authorized weight or measure; a criterion; an established or accepted level of achievement; (*pl*) moral principles. • *adj* serving as a standard; typical.

standard-bearer *n* a person who carries a standard; the leader of a particular cause or party.

standardize /'stændərdaɪz/ *vt* to make standard; to reduce to a standard.—**standardization** *n.*—**standardizer** *n.*

standard of living *n* the level of material comforts enjoyed by an individual, family, group or community.

stand-by /'stændbaɪ/ *n* (*pl* **stand-bys**) a person or thing held in readiness for use in an emergency, etc.—*also adj.*

stand-in *n* a substitute; a person who takes the place of an actor during the preparation of a scene or in stunts.—*also vi.*

standing /'stændɪŋ/ *n* status or reputation; length of service, duration. • *adj* upright; permanent; (*jump*) performed from a stationary position.

standing army *n* a permanent body of paid soldiers as maintained by a nation.

standing order *n* an instruction to a bank by a depositor to pay fixed amounts at regular intervals (for bills, etc); a regulation governing conduct, procedure, etc in an organization or assembly.

standoff /'stændɒf/ *n* a deadlock, stalemate.

standoffish /stænd'ɒfɪʃ/ *adj* aloof, reserved.

standpipe /'stændpaɪp/ *n* a vertical pipe with a tap providing an external water supply.

standpoint /'stændpɔɪnt/ *n* a point of view, opinion.

stand-up *adj* (*collar*) upright; (*fight*) furious; (*comedian*) telling jokes standing alone in front of an audience.

standstill /'stændstɪl/ *n* a complete halt.

stank /stæŋk/ *see* **stink**.

stannic /'stænɪk/ *adj* of or containing (tetravalent) tin.

stannous /'stænəs/ *adj* of or containing (bivalent) tin.

stanza /'stænzə/ *n* a group of lines which form a division of a poem.

staple[1] /'steɪpəl/ *n* a principal commodity of trade or industry of a region or nation; a main constituent. • *adj* chief.

staple[2] *n* a U-shaped thin piece of wire for fastening. • *vt* to fasten with a staple.

star /stɑr/ *n* any one of the celestial bodies, *esp* those visible by night which appear as small points of light, including planets, comets, meteors, and less commonly the sun and moon; a figure with five points; an exceptionally successful or skilful person; a famous actor, actress, musician, etc. • *vti* (**starring, starred**) to feature or be featured as a star.

starboard /'stɑrbərd/ or /-bɔrd/ *n* the right side of a ship or aircraft when facing the bow.

starch /stɑrtʃ/ *n* a white, tasteless, food substance found in potatoes, cereal, etc; a fabric stiffener based on this. • *vt* to stiffen with starch.—**starchy** *adj.*

star-crossed /'stɑr,krɒst/ *adj* ill-fated; unfortunate.

stardom /-dəm/ *n* the fame and status enjoyed by celebrities or stars.

stardust /'stɑrdʌst/ *n* a large cluster of distant stars appearing as dust; a feeling of romance.

stare /stɛr/ *vi* to gaze fixedly, as in horror, astonishment, etc; to glare. • *n* a fixed gaze.

starfish /'stɑrfɪʃ/ *n* (*pl* **starfish, starfishes**) an echinoderm consisting of a central disc from which five arms radiate outward.

stargaze /'stɑrgeɪz/ *vi* to look at the stars; to daydream.

stark /stɑrk/ *adj* bare; plain; blunt; utter. • *adv* completely.— **starkly** *adv.*—**starkness** *n.*

starkers /'stɑrkərz/ *adj* (*inf*) completely naked.

starlet /'stɑrlət/ *n* a young actress regarded as a potential star.

starling /'stɑrlɪŋ/ *n* any of a family of small songbirds, *esp* a common European bird with black plumage tinged with green that congregates in large groups.

Star of David a six-pointed star formed by two intersecting triangles, a hexagram.

starry-eyed /'stɑriaɪd/ *adj* dreamy, impractical, overly optimistic.

Stars and Stripes *n sing* (*with* **the**) the national flag of the USA consisting of 13 alternate red and white stripes and a blue square filled with white stars representing the individual states.—*also* **Star-Spangled Banner.**

Star Spangled Banner *n* (*with* **the**) the national anthem of the USA; the Stars and Stripes.

star-studded *adj* featuring many celebrities.

start /stɑrt/ *vi* to commence, begin; to jump involuntarily, from fright. • *vt* to begin. • *n* a beginning; a slight involuntary body movement; a career opening.

starter /'stɑrtər/ *n* a person who starts something, *esp* an official who signals the beginning of a race; a competitor in a race; the first course of a meal; a small electric motor used to start an internal combustion engine.—*also* **self-starter.**

starting block *n* one of a pair of angled wooden or metal pads or blocks against which a sprinter braces the feet in crouch starts.

starting gate *n* (*horseracing*) a removable barrier holding each horse in line and which is raised to start a race.

starting grid *n* (*motor racing*) the numbered grid where drivers line up at the start of a race, position being determined by the times gained in practice laps.

starting price *n* (*esp horseracing*) the final odds on a horse offered by bookmakers at the start of a race.

starting stalls *npl* the metal enclosures for horses at the starting line with gates that spring open simultaneously to start the race.

startle /'stɑrtəl/ *vti* to be, or cause to be, frightened or surprised.—**startling** *adj.*

starve /stɑrv/ *vi* to die or suffer from a lack of food. • *vt* deprive (a person) of food; to deprive (of) anything necessary.—**starvation** *n.*

Star Wars *n sing* in the US, the popular name for the Strategic Defense Initiative.

stash /stæʃ/ *vt* to hide (money, etc) for future use. • *n* a hiding place; something hidden; (*sl*) drugs hidden for personal consumption.

state /steɪt/ *n* condition; frame of mind; position in society; ceremonious style; (*with cap*) an area or community with its own government, or forming a federation under a sovereign government. • *adj* of the state or State; public; ceremonial. • *vt* to express in words; to specify, declare officially.

statecraft /'steɪtkræft/ n the art of government; statesmanship.

State Department n the US government department that handles foreign affairs.

statehouse /'steɪthɐʊs/ n in the US, the building which houses a state legislature.

stateless /'steɪtləs/ adj not having a nationality.—**statelessness** n.

stately /'steɪtli/ adj (**statelier, stateliest**) dignified; majestic.—**stateliness** n.

stately home n a large country mansion, usu of historical interest, which is open to the public.

statement /'steɪtmənt/ n a formal announcement; a declaration; a document showing one's bank balance.

state-of-the-art adj using the most advanced technology yet possible.

stateroom /'steɪtruːm/ n a luxury private cabin in a ship; a large room in a palace used for state occasions.

States n sing or pl the USA.

state school n any school funded by the state which provides free education.

stateside /'steɪtsaɪd/ adj of, in, or to the US.—also adv.

statesman /'steɪtsmən/ n (pl **statesmen**) a well-known and experienced politician.—**statesmanship** n.

static /'stætɪk/ adj fixed; stationary; at rest. • n electrical interference causing noise on radio or TV.

static electricity n electricity which is stationary as opposed to flowing in a current.

statics /'stætɪks/ n sing the branch of mechanics dealing with the forces that produce a state of equilibrium.

station /'steɪʃən/ n a railway or bus terminal or stop; headquarters (of the emergency services); military headquarters; (inf) a TV channel; position in society, standing. • vt to assign to a post, place, office.

stationary /'steɪʃənˌeri/ adj not moving.

stationer /'steɪʃənər/ n a dealer in stationery, office supplies, etc.

stationery /'steɪʃənˌeri/ or /'steɪʃənriː/ n writing materials, esp paper and envelopes.

station house n in the US, a building that houses police or fire services.

stationmaster /'steɪʃənˌmæstər/ or /-ˌmɒstər/ n the senior official in charge of a railway station.

station wagon n in the US, a car with extra carrying space reached through a rear door.

statism /'steɪtɪzəm/ n the concentration of economic and political power in the state.—**statist** n.

statistic /stə'tɪstɪk/ n a fact obtained from analysing information expressed in numbers.

statistics /stə'tɪstɪks/ n sing the branch of mathematics dealing with the collection, analysis and presentation of numerical data.—**statistical** adj.—**statistician** n.

stator /'steɪtər/ n the stationary part of a motor or generator.

statoscope /'stætəˌskoːp/ n a sensitive aneroid barometer for indicating minute fluctuations in pressure, used in altimeters in aircraft.

statuary /'stætʃuːˌeri/ n (pl **statuaries**) statues collectively.

statue /'stætʃuː/ n a representation of a human or animal form that is carved or moulded.

statuesque /ˌstætʃuː'esk/ adj like a statue.—**statuesquely** adv.—**statuesqueness** n.

statuette /ˌstætʃuː'et/ n a small statue, figurine.

stature /'stætʃər/ n the standing height of a person; level of attainment.

status /'steɪtəs/ or /'steɪt-/ n (pl **statuses**) social or professional position or standing; prestige; condition or standing from the point of view of the law, position of affairs.

status quo /ˌsteɪtəs 'kwoː/ or /ˌsteɪt-/ n the existing state of affairs.

status symbol n a possession that indicates high social standing, wealth, etc.

statute /'stætʃuːt/ n a law enacted by a legislature; a regulation.

statute book n a register of statutes enacted by a legislature.

statute law n law enacted by a legislature.

statute mile n (formal) a mile.

statute of limitations n a statute that restricts the period of time in which proceedings may be brought to enforce a right or punish an offence.

statutory /'statʃətəri/ or /'statʃuːtəri/ adj established, regulated, or required by statute.

staunch[1] /stɔːntʃ/ adj loyal; dependable.—**staunchly** adv.—**staunchness** n.

staunch[2] vt to stem the flow of, as blood. • vi to cease to flow.—also **stanch**.

stave /steɪv/ n a piece of wood of a cask or barrel; (mus) a staff. • vt (**staving, staved** or **stove**) (usu with **in**) to smash or dent inward.

staves /steɪvz/ see **staff**.

stay[1] /steɪ/ n a rope supporting a mast.

stay[2] vi to remain in a place; to wait; to reside temporarily. • vt to support; to endure; to stop, restrain. • n a suspension of legal proceedings; a short time spent as a visitor or guest.

stay-at-home n a quiet, placid, unadventurous person.—also adj.

staying power n stamina.

St Bernard n a Saint Bernard dog.

STD abbr = sexually transmitted disease; subscriber trunk dialling.

steadfast /'stedfæst/ or /'stedfəst/ adj firm, fixed; resolute.—**steadfastly** adv.—**steadfastness** n.

steady /'stedi/ adj (**steadier, steadiest**) firm, stable; regular, constant; calm, unexcitable. • n (pl **steadies**) (inf) a regular boyfriend or girlfriend. • vti (**steadying, steadied**) to make or become steady.—**steadily** adv.—**steadiness** n.

steady-state theory n the theory that the universe remains in a steady equilibrium as matter is continuously created as it expands.

steak /steɪk/ n a slice of meat, esp beef or fish, for grilling or frying.

steakhouse /'steɪkˌhaʊs/ n a restaurant that specializes in steaks.

steal /stiːl/ vt (**stealing, stole**, pp **stolen**) to take (from someone) dishonestly; to obtain secretly. • n (inf) an unbelievable bargain.

stealth /stelθ/ n a manner of moving quietly and secretly.

Stealth technology n the development, in great secrecy, of a new type of military aircraft.

stealthy /'stelθi/ adj (**stealthier, stealthiest**) acting or performed in a quiet, secret manner; unobtrusive, furtive.—**stealthily** adv.—**stealthiness** n.

steam /stiːm/ n the hot mist or vapour created by boiling water. • vi to give off steam; to move by steam power; to cook with steam; (sl) to take part in illegal steaming; (with **up**) (glasses, windows) to become covered in condensation. • adj driven by steam.

steamboat /'stiːmboːt/ n a boat powered by steam.

steam engine n a stationary or locomotive engine powered by steam.

steamer /'stiːmər/ n a pan with a perforated bottom for cooking by steam; a ship propelled by steam engines; (sl) one who takes part in steaming.

steaming /'stiːmɪŋ/ n (sl) the practice of multiple mugging by a gang of youths who move rapidly down a street, mugging and shiplifting.

steam iron n an electric iron that can heat water to use as steam which is emitted through the face to improve pressing.

steamroller /'stiːmˌroːlər/ n a vehicle with heavy rollers for pressing down road surfaces; an overpowering person or thing. • vt to crush (as if) with a steamroller; to obtain or influence by overpowering force.

steamy /'stiːmi/ adj (**steamier, steamiest**) full of steam; (inf) erotic.—**steamily** adv.—**steaminess** n.

stearic acid /'stiːrɪk/ or /stiːˈarɪk/ n a fatty acid derived from solid fats and used for making candles and soap.

steatite /'stiːətaɪt/ n soapstone.

steato- /'stiːtoː/ prefix fat.

steed /stiːd/ n (arch, poet) a horse.

steel /stiːl/ n an alloy of iron and carbon; strength or courage. • adj of, or like, steel. • vt to cover with steel; to harden; to nerve (oneself).

steel band n a band that uses percussion instruments made from oil drums.

steel grey n a bluish-grey colour.

steel wool n a compact mass of steel fibres used for scouring and polishing.

steely /'stiːli/ adj (**steelier, steeliest**) of or like steel; hard, relentless.—**steeliness** n.

steelyard /'stiːljɑrd/ n a balance using a pivoted graduated arm along which a weight slides.

steenbok /'sti:nbɒk/ or /'steɪn-/ n (pl **steenboks, steenbok**) any of a genus of small antelopes of central and southern Africa.

steep[1] /sti:p/ adj sloping sharply; (inf) excessive, exorbitant.— **steeply** adv.—**steepness** n.

steep[2] vti to soak or be soaked in a liquid; to saturate; to imbue.— also n.

steepen /-ən/ vti to make or become steeper.

steeple /'sti:pəl/ n a tower of a church, with or without a spire; the spire alone.

steeplechase /'sti:pəl,tʃeɪs/ n a horse race across country or on a course over jumps; a track race over hurdles and water jumps.—**steeplechaser** n.

steeplejack /'sti:pəl,dʒæk/ n a person who climbs and repairs tall chimneys.

steer[1] /stɪr/ n a castrated male of the cattle family.

steer[2] vti to direct (a vehicle, ship, bicycle, etc) in the correct direction of travel.

steerage /'stɪrɪdʒ/ n the cheapest berths on a passenger ship.

steerageway /-,weɪ/ n a rate of forward motion that allows a vessel to be steered.

steering n the mechanism that controls the direction of a ship, vehicle, etc; the practice of manoeuvring non-white house buyers or tenants away from white areas.

steering committee n a committee that organizes the content and order of business for a legislative assembly or other body.

stegosaur, stegosaurus /,stegə'sɔrəs/ n (pl **stegosaurs, stegosauri**) any of various plant-eating dinosaurs with armoured body plates.

stein /staɪn/ n an earthenware beer mug, often with a hinged lid.

stele /sti:l/ or /'sti:li/ n (pl **stelae, steles**) an upright slab of stone with inscriptions dating from prehistoric times; an inscribed commemorative slab placed on the front of a building; the vascular tissue in the stems and roots of plants.

stellar /'stelər/ adj of, or composed of stars.

stellate /'stelaɪt/ or /-lət/ **stellated** adj of, resembling or composed of stars.

stellular /'steljulər/ adj filled with or composed of small stars; star-shaped.

St Elmo's fire n a flame-like electric discharge from a ship's mast and rigging, and church spires, in thundery weather.—also **corposant**.

stem[1] /stem/ n a plant stalk; the upright slender part of anything, such as a wineglass; the root of a word. • vi (**stemming, stemmed**) to originate (from).

stem[2] vt (**stemming, stemmed**) to stop, check (the flow or tide).

stench /stentʃ/ n a foul odour.

stencil /'stensəl/ n a pierced sheet of card or metal for reproducing letters by applying paint; a design so made. • vti (**stencilling, stencilled** or **stenciling, stenciled**) to produce (letters, etc) or designs using a stencil.—**stenciller, stenciler** n.

Sten gun /stengən/ n a light sub-machine gun.

stenography /stə'nɒgrəfi/ n shorthand.—**stenographer** n.

stenosis /stɪ'nəʊsɪs/ n (pl **stenoses**) an abnormal narrowing of a bodily passage or orifice.—**stenotic** adj.

stentorian /sten'tɔriən/ adj (voice) loud, booming.

step /step/ n one movement of the foot ahead in walking, running, or dancing; a pace; a grade or degree; a stage toward a goal; the tread of a stair, rung of a ladder. • vti (**stepping, stepped**) to take a step or a number of paces.

step- /step/ prefix related by remarriage of a spouse or parent.

stepbrother /'step,brʌðər/ n a son of one's step-parent from a former marriage.

stepchild /'steptʃaɪld/ n (pl **stepchildren**) a stepson or stepdaughter.

stepdaughter /'step,dɒtər/ n the daughter of one's spouse from a former marriage.

stepfather /'step,fɑðər/ n the husband of one's remarried mother.

stephanotis /,stefə'nəʊtɪs/ n a tropical climbing plant with fragrant white flowers.

stepladder /'step,lædər/ n a short portable ladder with flat steps fixed within a frame.

stepmother /'step,mʌðər/ n the wife of one's remarried father.

step-parent n stepfather or stepmother.

steppe /step/ n a vast grassy treeless plain.

stepping stone n a stone or stones allowing a stream, puddle, etc to be crossed by foot; a means of advancing toward some end.

stepsister /'step,sɪstər/ n the daughter of one's step-parent from a former marriage.

stepson /'stepsən/ n the son of one's spouse from a former marriage.

steradian /stə'reɪdiən/ n a unit of solid angular measurement.

stere /stɪr/ n a unit equal to one cubic metre (35.3 cubic feet), used for measuring timber.

stereo /'steriə/ n (pl **stereos**) a hi-fi or record player with two loudspeakers; stereophonic sound. • adj stereophonic.

stereochemistry /,steriə'kemɪstri/ n the study of the composition and properties of matter in relation to the spatial arrangement of atoms in molecules.

stereograph /'steriə,græf/ n two almost identical images that when superimposed and viewed through a stereoscope produce a three-dimensional picture.

stereophonic /,steriə'fɒnɪk/ adj (sound reproduction system) using two separate channels for recording and transmission to create a spatial effect.—**stereophonically** adv.—**stereophony** n.

stereoscope /'steriə,skəʊp/ n an optical device which blends two images viewed from a slightly different aspect into a single three-dimensional picture.—**stereoscopic** adj.

stereoscopy /-'ɒskəpi/ n viewing objects in three dimensions.

stereotype /'steriə,taɪp/ n a fixed, general image of a person or thing shared by many people.—also vt.

steric /'stɪrɪk/ adj of or pertaining to the spatial arrangement of atoms in a molecule.

sterile /'steraɪl/ or /'sterɪl/ adj unable to produce offspring, fruit, seeds, or spores; fruitless; free from germs.—**sterility** n.

sterilize /'sterə,laɪz/ vt to render incapable of reproduction; to free from germs.—**sterilization** n.—**sterilizer** n.

sterling /'stɜrlɪŋ/ n the British system of money. • adj of excellent character.

stern[1] /stɜrn/ adj severe; austere, harsh.—**sternly** adv.—**sternness** n.

stern[2] n the rear part of a boat or ship.

sternum /'stɜrnəm/ n (pl **sterna, sternums**) the breastbone.

sternutation /,stɜrnju:'teɪʃən/ n sneezing.

sternutator /'stɜrnju:,teɪtər/ n a substance that induces sneezing, tears, etc, such as a gas used in riot control.

steroid /'sterɔɪd/ or /'stɪrɔɪd/ n any of a large number of compounds sharing the same chemical structure, including sterols and many hormones.

sterol /'sterɒl/ n any of various solid steroid alcohols, such as cholesterol, found in plants and animals.

stertorous /'stɜrtərəs/ adj characterized by heavy breathing or snoring sounds.—**stertorously** adv.—**stertorousness** n.

stet /stet/ vt a proofreading direction meaning that deleted matter marked by a row of dots should remain. • vt (**setting, stetted**) to mark (text) in this way.

stethoscope /'steθə,skəʊp/ n an instrument used to detect body sounds.—**stethoscopic** adj.

stetson /'stetsən/ n a man's felt hat with a broad brim and high crown.

stevedore /'sti:və,dɒr/ n a labourer who loads and unloads ships.

stew /stu:/ or /stju:/ n a meal of cooked meat with vegetables. • vt to cook slowly.

steward /'stu:ərd/ or /'stju:-/ n a manager (of property); a race organizer; a person who serves food on an aircraft or ship and looks after passengers.

stewardess /'stu:ərdes/ or /'stju:-/ n a woman steward on an aircraft or ship.

stick[1] /stɪk/ vb (**sticking, stuck**) vt to pierce or stab; to attach with glue, adhesive tape, etc; (with **up**) (inf) to rob at gunpoint. • vi to cling to, to adhere; to stay close to; to be held up; (with **around**) (inf) to wait in the vicinity, to linger; (with **by**) to remain faithful to; to stay close to.

stick[2] n a broken off shoot or branch of a tree; a walking stick; a hockey stick; a rod.

sticker /'stɪkər/ n an adhesive label or poster.

sticking plaster n a thin strip of cloth with an adhesive backing for covering small cuts and abrasions.

stick insect n a wingless insect with a long thin body resembling a twig.

stick-in-the-mud /'stɪk'nðə,mʌd/ n (inf) a person who feels threatened by new ideas or situations.

stickleback /'stɪkəl,bæk/ n any of various small freshwater fishes with sharp spines on the back.

stickler /'stɪklər/ n a person who is scrupulous or obstinate about something.

stick-up /'stɪkʌp/ n (inf) a robbery at gunpoint.

sticky /'stɪki/ adj (**stickier, stickiest**) covered with adhesive or something sweet; (weather) warm and humid; (inf) difficult.—**stickily** adv.—**stickiness** n.

sticky end n (inf) an unpleasant death.

sticky wicket n (cricket) a damp wicket that is difficult to bat on; (inf) an awkward or unpleasant situation.

stiff /stɪf/ adj not flexible or supple; rigid; firm; moving with difficulty; having aching joints and muscles; formal, unfriendly; (drink) potent; (breeze) strong; (penalty) severe. • n (sl) a corpse. • adv utterly.—**stiffly** adv.—**stiffness** n.

stiffen /'stɪfən/ vti to make or become stiff.—**stiffener** n.

stiff-necked /'stɪf,nɛkt/ adj stubborn, aloof.

stifle /'staɪfəl/ vt to suffocate; to smother; to suppress, hold back.

stifling /'staɪfəlɪŋ/ adj excessively hot and stuffy.

stigma /'stɪgmə/ n (pl **stigmas, stigmata**) a social disgrace; the part of a flower that receives pollen; (Christianity) marks resembling the wounds of Christ thought to appear on the bodies of saintly people.

stigmatize /'stɪgmə,taɪz/ vt to brand as bad or disgraceful.—**stigmatization** n.

stile /staɪl/ n a step, or set of steps, for climbing over a wall or fence.

stiletto /stɪ'letoː/ n (pl **stilettos**) a small slender dagger; a pointed tool for piercing holes in leather, etc; a high heel tapering to a point on a woman's shoe. • vt (**stilettoeing, stilettoed**) to stab with a stiletto.

still[1] /stɪl/ adj motionless; calm; silent; (drink) not carbonated. • n a single photograph taken from a cinema film. • vti to make or become still. • adv continuously; nevertheless.—**stillness** n.

still[2] n an apparatus for distilling liquids, esp spirits.

stillborn /'stɪlbɔrn/ adj born dead; (idea, project, etc) a failure from the start, abortive.

still life n (pl **still lives**) a painting of inanimate objects, such as flowers, fruit, etc.

stilt /stɪlt/ n either of a pair of poles with footrests on which one can walk, as in a circus; a supporting column.

stilted /'stɪltɪd/ adj (speech, writing) pompous, unnaturally formal; (conversation) forced, intermittent.

Stilton /'stɪltən/ n a blue-veined cheese with a strong flavour.

stimulant /'stɪmjulənt/ n a drug, drink, or food that increases one's heart rate and body activity.

stimulate /'stɪmjuleɪt/ vt to excite, arouse.—**stimulation** n.

stimulus /'stɪmjuləs/ n (pl **stimuli**) something that acts as an incentive; an agent that arouses or provokes a response in a living organism.

sting /stɪŋ/ n a sharp pointed organ of a bee, wasp, etc, or hair on a plant, used for injecting poison; a skin wound caused by injected poison from an insect or plant; (sl) a swindle. • vt to wound with a sting; to cause to suffer mentally; to goad, incite; (sl) to cheat by overcharging. • vi to feel a sharp pain.

stingray /'stɪŋreɪ/ n any of various rays with a whiplike tail bearing sharp venomous spines.

stingy /'stɪndʒi/ adj (**stingier, stingiest**) miserly, mean.—**stingily** adv.—**stinginess** n.

stink /stɪŋk/ vi (**stinking, stank** or **stunk, pp stunk**) to give out an offensive smell; (sl) to possess something in an excessive amount; (sl) to be extremely bad in quality. • n a foul smell.

stink bomb n a small glass capsule which releases a foul smell when broken, used for practical jokes.

stinker /'stɪŋkər/ n (inf) an offensive person or thing; (inf) something difficult or unpleasant.

stinkhorn /'stɪŋkhɔrn/ n a type of foul-smelling fungus.

stinko /'stɪŋkoː/ adj (sl) drunk.

stinkweed /'stɪŋkwiːd/ n any of various plants with pungent scents.

stint /stɪnt/ vt to be frugal in the supply or allowance of something. • vi to be frugal, miserly. • n a fixed period or quantity of work; a limitation, restriction.

stipe /staɪp/ n a short stalk or stem of a plant, esp of a mushroom.

stipend /'staɪpend/ n a regular payment of money as wages or for expenses, esp to a clergyman.

stipendiary /stɪ'pendjəri/ or /-iːeri/, /staɪ-/ adj of or receiving a stipend. • n (pl **stipendiaries**) a person who receives a stipend.

stipple /'stɪpəl/ vt to engrave, paint, draw, etc, in tiny dots.

stipulate /'stɪpjuˌleɪt/ vt to specify as a condition of an agreement.—**stipulation** n.

stir[1] /stər/ vb (**stirring, stirred**) vt to mix, as with a spoon; to rouse; to stimulate or excite; (with up) to agitate, instigate. • vi to be disturbed; to move oneself; to be active. • n a stirring movement; tumult.

stir[2] n (sl) prison.

stir-fry /'stərˌfraɪ/ vt to cook (chopped vegetables, etc) by stirring rapidly in hot oil in a wok or frying pan.

stirring /'stərɪŋ/ adj rousing, exciting.—**stirringly** adv.

stirrup /'stərəp/ n a strap and flat-bottomed ring hanging from a saddle, for a rider's foot.

stirrup cup n a farewell drink, orig given to a rider on horseback before departure.

stirrup pump n a small portable water pump held steady by a stirrup-shaped foot bracket, used for fire-fighting.

stitch /stɪtʃ/ n a single in-and-out movement of a threaded needle in sewing; a single loop of a yarn in knitting or crocheting; a sudden, sharp pain, esp in the side. • vti to sew.

stoat /stoːt/ n a small European mammal related to the weasel.

stochastic /stə'kæstɪk/ adj random; involving chance or probability.

stock /stɒk/ n raw material; goods on hand; shares of corporate capital, or the certificates showing such ownership; lineage, family, race; a store; the cattle, horses, etc, kept on a farm; the broth obtained by boiling meat, bones, and vegetables as a foundation for soup, etc. • vt to supply; to keep in store. • adj standard; hackneyed.

stockade /stɒ'keɪd/ n a defensive enclosure or barrier of stakes fixed in the ground.

stockbroker /'stɒkˌbroːkər/ n a person who deals in stocks.

stock car n a standard production saloon car modified for racing.

stockholder /'stɒkˌhoːldər/ n an owner of corporate stock.

stocking filler n a gift suitable for a Christmas stocking.

stocking /'stɒkɪŋ/ n a sock; a nylon covering for a woman's leg, supported by suspenders.

stock market, stock exchange n the market for dealing in stocks and shares.

stockpile /'stɒkpaɪl/ n a reserve supply of essentials.—also vt.

stock-still /'stɒk'stɪl/ adv motionless.

stocktaking /'stɒkˌteɪkɪŋ/ n making an inventory of goods on hand (in a shop, warehouse, etc); evaluating one's present condition, resources, etc.

stocky /'stɒki/ adj (**stockier, stockiest**) short and sturdy.—**stockily** adv.—**stockiness** n.

stockyard /'stɒkjɑrd/ n a yard for holding cattle, sheep, pigs, etc before they are sold, transported, or slaughtered.

stodge /stɒdʒ/ n (inf) heavy, starchy food.

stodgy /'stɒdʒi/ adj (**stodgier, stodgiest**) (food) thick, heavy and indigestible; uninteresting.—**stodgily** adv.—**stodginess** n.

stoic /'stoːɪk/ n a person who suffers hardship without showing emotion.—**stoical** adj.—**stoically** adv.—**stoicism** n.

stoke /stoːk/ vt to stir and feed (a fire) with fuel.

STOL /stɒl/ abbr = short take-off and landing, a system that allows an aircraft to take off and land within a short distance.

stole[1] /stoːl/ see **steal**.

stole[2] n a long scarf or piece of fur worn on the shoulders.

stolen /'stoːlən/ see **steal**.

stolid /'stɒlɪd/ adj impassive; unemotional.—**stolidity** n.—**stolidly** adv.

stoma /'stoːmə/ n (pl **stomata**) a minute aperture in the epidermis of a plant for the passage of gases; an orifice or mouthlike opening; a permanent surgical opening, esp in the abdominal wall.

stomach /'stʌmək/ n the organ where food is digested; the belly. • vt to put up with.

stomach pump n a suction pump that empties the contents of the stomach through a long tube inserted orally.

stomata /'stoːmætə/ see **stoma**.

stomatitis /ˌstɒmə'taɪtəs/ n inflammation of the mouth.

stomatology /ˌstoːmə'tɒlədʒi/ n the branch of medicine concerned with the mouth.—**stomatological** adj.

stomp /stɒmp/ vti to walk with heavy steps; to stamp. • n an early jazz dance.

stone /stoːn/ *n* a small lump of rock; a precious stone or gem; the hard seed of a fruit; (*pl* **stone**) a unit of weight (14 lb./6.35 kg). • *vt* to throw stones at; to remove stones from (fruit).

Stone Age *n* the prehistoric age of human culture characterized by the use of stone tools and weapons.

stoned /stoːnd/ *adj* (*inf*) under the influence of drink or drugs.

stonefish /'stoːnfɪʃ/ *n* (*pl* **stonefish, stonefishes**) a venomous tropical fish with markings that resemble a stone on the seabed.

stone's throw *n* a short distance.

stonewall /'stoːnwɒl/ *vi* to obstruct or hinder, *esp* in politics and government.

stonewashed /'stoːnwɒʃd/ *adj* (*clothes*) made to appear worn and faded by the abrasive action of pumice particles.

stony, stoney /'stoːni/ *adj* (**stonier, stoniest**) of, like, or full of stones; unfeeling, heartless.—**stonily** *adv*.—**stoniness** *n*.

stony-broke *adj* (*inf*) completely without money.

stony-hearted *adj* unfeeling, cruel.—**stony-heartedness** *n*.

stood /stuːd/ *see* **stand**.

stooge /stuːdʒ/ *n* (*sl*) a performer who feeds lines to a comedian; a person subordinate to or dominated by another; a stool pigeon. • *vi* to act as a stooge.

stool /stuːl/ *n* a seat or a support for the back when sitting, with no back or arms; matter evacuated from the bowels.

stool pigeon *n* a police informer.

stoop[1] /stuːp/ *vti* to bend the body forward and downward; to degrade oneself; to deign.—*also n.*

stoop[2] *n* a porch or small landing with stairs at the entrance to a house or building.

stooped /stuːpt/ *adj* hunched.

stop /stɒp/ *vb* (**stopping, stopped**) *vt* to halt; to prevent; to intercept; to plug or block. • *vi* to cease; to come to an end; to stay. • *n* an act or instance of stopping; an impediment; (a knob controlling) a set of organ pipes; any of the standard settings of the aperture in a camera lens, f-stop; a regular stopping place for a bus or train; a punctuation mark, *esp* full stop.

stop bath *n* a mildly acidic solution used to halt the development of a negative print, plate, etc.

stopcock /'stɒpkɒk/ *n* a device for regulating the flow of liquid in a pipe.

stopgap /'stɒpɡæp/ *n* a temporary substitute, expedient.

stoplight /'stɒplaɪt/ *n* a red light on a traffic signal warning vehicles to halt; a brake light.

stopover /'stɒpˌoːvər/ *n* a short break in a journey.

stoppage /'stɒpɪdʒ/ *n* stopping or being stopped; an obstruction; a deduction from pay; a concerted cessation of work by employees, as during a strike.

stopper /'stɒpər/ *n* a cork or bung.

stop press *n* (the space reserved for) an item of last minute news added to a newspaper after printing has begun.

stopwatch /'stɒpwɒtʃ/ *n* a watch that can be started and stopped, used for timing sporting events.

storage /'stɔːrɪdʒ/ *n* storing or being stored; an area reserved for storing; (*comput*) the storing of data in a computer memory or on disk, tape, etc.

storage battery *n* an accumulator.

storage capacity *n* the maximum amount of information that can be held in computer memory or a storage device.

storage device *n* a piece of computer equipment, such as a hard disk, used to store data.

storage heater *n* a radiator which accumulates heat during periods of off-peak electricity.

store /stɔːr/ *n* a large supply of goods for future use; a warehouse; a shop. • *vt* to set aside; to put in a warehouse, etc; (*comput*) to put (data) into a computer memory or onto a storage device.

store card *n* a charge card issued by a store or chain of stores for the purchase of goods there only.

storehouse /'stɔːrhʌʊs/ *n* a place for storing things; a rich source or supply.

storey /'stɔːri/ *n* (*pl* **storeys**) a horizontal division of a building, a story.

stork /stɔːrk/ *n* any large wading bird of the family *Ciconiidae* with long legs and a long neck with a long pointed bill.

storksbill /'stɔːrksˌbɪl/ *n* any of several plants of the geranium family with pink or purple flowers.

storm /stɔːrm/ *n* a heavy fall of rain, snow, etc with strong winds; a violent commotion; a furore; (mil) an attack on a fortified place. • *vt* to rush, invade. • *vi* to be angry; to rain, snow hard.—**stormy** *adj*.

stormbound /'stɔːrmbaʊnd/ *adj* affected, confined or harassed by storms.

storm trooper *n* a member of the Sturmabteilung, a semi-military group of the German Nazi party (1924–45) notorious for its violence; a member of a shock troop.

Storting /'stɔːrtɪŋ/, **Storthing** *n* the parliament of Norway.

story[1] /'stɔːri/ *n* (*pl* **stories**) a narrative of real or imaginary events; a plot of a literary work; an anecdote; an account; (*inf*) a lie; a news article.

story[2] *n* (*pl* **stories**) a horizontal division of a building, a storey; a set of rooms occupying this space.

storyboard /'stɔːriˌbɔːrd/ *n* (*films, television*) a sequence of drawings or photographs showing the images to be shot to film for a particular story.

stout /staʊt/ *adj* strong; short and plump; sturdy. • *n* strong dark beer.—**stoutly** *adv*.—**stoutness** *n*.

stouthearted /-ˌhɑːrtɪd/ *adj* brave.—**stoutheartedly** *adv*.

stove[1] /stoːv/ *n* a cooker; heating apparatus.

stove[2] *see* **stave**.

stow /stoː/ *vt* to store, pack, in an orderly way.

stowage /'stoːɪdʒ/ *n* stowing or being stowed; goods in storage; a place for storage or the charge for this.

stowaway /'stoːəˌweɪ/ *n* a person who hides on a ship, car, aircraft, etc to avoid paying the fare.

strabismus /strəˈbɪzməs/ *n* a squint.

straddle /'strædəl/ *vt* to have one leg or support on either side of something.

strafe /streɪf/ *vt* to machine-gun (troops, vehicles, etc) from the air.—*also n.*

straggle /'stræɡəl/ *vi* to stray; to wander.—**straggler** *n*.—**straggly** *adj*.

straight /streɪt/ *adj* (*line*) continuing in one direction, not curved or bent; direct; honest; (*sl*) heterosexual; (*alcoholic drinks*) neat, not diluted. • *adv* directly; without delay. • *n* being straight; a straight line, form, or position; a straight part of a racetrack; (*poker*) a hand containing five cards in sequence.—**straightness** *n*.

straight and narrow *n* (*inf*) the honest and virtuous way of life.

straight angle *n* an angle of 180°.

straightaway /'streɪtəˌweɪ/ *adv* without delay.

straightedge /'streɪtedʒ/ *n* a length of wood, metal, etc used to rule or test for accurate straight lines.

straighten /'streɪtən/ *vti* to make or become straight; (*with* **out**) to make or become less confused or entangled; to resolve.

straight face *n* a face betraying no signs of emotion, *esp* amusement.—**straight-faced** *adj*.

straight fight *n* a contest between only two candidates.

straight flush *n* (*poker*) five cards of the same suit in sequence.

straightforward /streɪtˈfɔːrwərd/ *adj* honest, open; simple; easy.—**straightforwardly** *adv*.—**straightforwardness** *n*.

straightjacket /'streɪtˌdʒækɪt/ *see* **straitjacket**.

straight-laced /-'leɪst/ *see* **strait-laced**.

straight man *n* a person who acts as a stooge to a comedian.

straight-out *adj* (*inf*) honest, direct; thorough.

strain[1] /streɪn/ *vt* to tax; to stretch; to overexert; to stress; to injure (a muscle) by overstretching; (food) to drain or sieve. • *n* overexertion; tension; an injury from straining.

strain[2] *n* a plant or animal within a species having a common characteristic; a trait; a trace.

strained /streɪnd/ *adj* (*action, behaviour*) produced by excessive effort; (*mood, atmosphere*) tense, worried.

strainer /'streɪnər/ *n* a sieve or colander used for straining liquids, pasta, tea, etc.

strait /streɪt/ *n* a channel of sea linking two larger seas; (*usu pl*) difficulty, distress.

straitjacket /'streɪtˌdʒækət/ *n* a coatlike device for restraining violent people; something that restricts or limits.—*also vt.* — *also* **straightjacket**.

strait-laced /'streɪtˌleɪsd/ *adj* prim, morally strict.—*also* **straight-laced**.

strand[1] /strænd/ *vt* to run aground; to leave helpless, without transport or money.

strand[2] *n* a single piece of thread or wire twisted together to make a rope or cable; a tress of hair.—*also vt.*

strange /streɪndʒ/ *adj* peculiar; odd; unknown; unfamiliar.—**strangely** *adv.*—**strangeness** *n.*

stranger /ˈstreɪndʒər/ *n* a person who is unknown; a new arrival to a place, town, social gathering, etc; a person who is unfamiliar with or ignorant of something.

strangle /ˈstræŋgəl/ *vt* to kill by compressing the windpipe, to choke; to stifle, suppress.—**strangler** *n.*

stranglehold /ˈstræŋgəlˌhoːld/ *n* (*wrestling*) a grip that presses an opponent's windpipe; a powerful restrictive force or influence.

strangles /ˈstræŋgəlz/ *n sing* an infectious bacterial disease of horses that inflames the respiratory tract, equine distemper.

strangulate /ˈstræŋgjʊˌleɪt/ *vt* to strangle; to compress (*eg* a blood vessel or the intestine) so as to cause a blockage. • *vi* to become strangulated.—**strangulatation** *n.*

strangury /ˈstræŋgjʊri/ *n* slow, painful urination.

strap /stræp/ *n* a narrow strip of leather or cloth for carrying or holding (a bag, etc); a fastening, as on a shoe, wristwatch. • *vti* (**strapping, strapped**) to fasten with a strap; to beat with a strap.

straphanger /ˈstræpˌhæŋər/ *n* (*inf*) a standing passenger in a bus or train, etc.

strapping /ˈstræpɪŋ/ *adj* tall, well-built.

strata /ˈstrɑːtə/ *see* **stratum**.

stratagem /ˈstrætədʒəm/ *n* a clever action planned to deceive or outwit an enemy.

strategic /strəˈtiːdʒɪk/ **strategical** *adj* of, relating to, or important in strategy; (*weapons*) designed to strike at the enemy's homeland, not for use on the battlefield.—**strategically** *adv.*

Strategic Defense Initiative *n* the US government's proposed deployment of satellites armed with laser devices to destroy enemy missiles.

strategy /ˈstrætədʒi/ *n* (*pl* **strategies**) the planning and conduct of war; a political, economic, or business policy.—**strategist** *n.*

strath /stræθ/ *n* (*Scot*) a wide, flat river valley.

strathspey /stræθˈspeɪ/ *n* (the music for) a type of Scottish dance with slow gliding steps.

straticulate /strætɪˈkjuleɪt/ *n* (*rocks*) having thin strata.

stratified /ˈstrætɪˌfaɪd/ *adj* arranged or deposited in strata or layers.—**stratification** *n.*

stratigraphy /strəˈtɪgrəfi/ *n* (the scientific study of) the composition and order of rock strata.—**stratigraphic** *adj.*

stratocumulus /ˌstræːtoˈkjuːmjʊləs/ *n* (*pl* **stratocumuli**) layers of dark cloud in dense round masses.

stratosphere /ˈstrætəˌsfiːr/ *n* a layer of the earth's atmosphere above 10 km (6 miles) in which temperature increases with height.—**stratospheric** *adj.*

stratum /ˈstrætəm/ *n* (*pl* **strata, stratums**) a layer of sedimentary rock; a level (of society).

stratus /ˈstrætəs/ *n* (*pl* **strati**) a continuous horizontal layer of cloud.

straw /strɔː/ *n* the stalks of threshed grain; a tube for sucking up a drink.

strawberry /ˈstrɔːberi/ or /-bəri/ *n* (*pl* **strawberries**) a soft red fruit used in desserts and jam.

strawberry blonde *adj* (*hair*) reddish blonde. • *n* a woman with hair of this colour.

strawberry mark *n* an irregular blood-coloured birth mark.

strawberry tree *n* a European evergreen tree bearing fruit resembling strawberries.

straw poll *n* an unofficial poll to assess public opinion.

stray /streɪ/ *vi* to wander; to deviate; to digress. • *n* a domestic animal that has become lost. • *adj* random.

streak /striːk/ *n* a line or long mark of contrasting colour; a flash of lightning; a characteristic, a trace. • *vti* to mark with or form streaks; to run naked in public as a prank.—**streaker** *n.*

streaky /ˈstriːki/ *adj* (**streakier, streakiest**) marked with streaks; (*bacon*) having alternate layers of fat and lean.

stream /striːm/ *n* a small river, brook, etc; a flow of liquid; anything flowing and continuous. • *vi* to flow, gush.

streamer /ˈstriːmər/ *n* a banner; a long decorative ribbon.

streamline /ˈstriːmlaɪn/ *vt* to shape (a car, boat, etc) in a way that lessens resistance through air or water; to make more efficient, to simplify.—**streamlined** *adj.*

street /striːt/ *n* a public road in a town or city lined with houses; such a road with its buildings and pavements; the people living, working, etc, along a given street. • *adj* pertaining to urban youth culture.

streetcar /ˈstriːtkɑr/ *n* ; the US word for a tram, an electrically powered vehicle for public transport, which travels along rails set into the ground.

street cred, street credibility *n* the mastery of the style and ways or urban culture.

street fighter *n* (*sl*) a person who is tough and combative.

street value *n* the value of a commodity, *esp* an illegal drug, in terms of the price charged to the ultimate users.

streetwalker /ˈstriːtˌwɒkər/ *n* a prostitute who solicits in the streets.

streetwise /ˈstriːtwaɪz/ *adj* (*inf*) experienced in surviving or avoiding the potential dangers of urban life.

strength /streŋθ/ or /strenθ/ *n* the state or quality of being physically or mentally strong; power of exerting or withstanding pressure, stress, force; potency; effectiveness.

strengthen /ˈstreŋθən/ or /ˈstrenθən/ *vti* to make or become stronger.

strenuous /ˈstrenjʊəs/ *adj* vigorous; requiring exertion.—**strenuously** *adv.*—**strenuousness** *n.*

strep /strep/ *n* (*inf*) a streptococcus.

strepitoso /ˌstrepɪˈtoːsoː/ *adv* (*mus*) in a boisterous manner.

streptococcus /ˌstreptoˈkɒkəs/ *n* (*pl* **streptococci**) any of a genus of spherical bacteria occurring in chains of different length.

streptomycin /ˌstreptoˈmaɪsɪn/ *n* an antibiotic derived from a soil bacterium, used in the treatment of infections such as tuberculosis.

stress /stres/ *n* pressure; mental or physical tension or strain; emphasis; (*physics*) a system of forces producing or sustaining a strain. • *vt* to exert pressure on; to emphasize.

stretch /stretʃ/ *vt* to extend, to draw out. • *vi* to extend, spread; to extend (the limbs, body); to be capable of expanding, as in elastic material. • *n* the act of stretching or instance of being stretched; the capacity for being stretched; an expanse of time or space; (*sl*) a period of imprisonment.—**stretchy** *adj.*

stretcher /ˈstretʃər/ *n* a portable frame for carrying the sick or injured.

strew /struː/ *vt* (**strewing, strewed**, *pp* **strewn** *or* **strewed**) to scatter; to spread.

strewth /struːθ/ *interj* used to express surprise or alarm.

striation /straɪˈeɪʃən/ *n* any of a series of parallel grooves, scratches, ridges or lines on a surface.—**striated** *adj.*

stricken /ˈstrɪkən/ *adj* suffering (from an illness); afflicted, as by something painful.

strict /strɪkt/ *adj* harsh, firm; enforcing rules rigorously; rigid.—**strictly** *adv.*—**strictness** *n.*

stricture /ˈstrɪktʃər/ *n* harsh criticism, censure.

stride /straɪd/ *vi* (**striding, strode**, *pp* **stridden**) to walk with long steps. • *vt* to straddle.—*also n.*

strident /ˈstraɪdənt/ *adj* loud and harsh.—**stridency** *n.*—**stridently** *adv.*

stridulate /ˈstrɪdjʊˌleɪt/ *vi* (of insects) to make a chirping or scraping sound.

strife /straɪf/ *n* a fight, quarrel; struggle.

strike /straɪk/ *vb* (**striking, struck**) *vt* to hit; to crash into; (*mil*) to attack; to ignite (a match) by friction; (*disease, etc*) to afflict suddenly; to come upon, *esp* unexpectedly; to delete; (*clock*) to indicate by sounding; to assume (*eg* an attitude); to occur to; (*medal, coin*) to produce by stamping; (*flag, tent*) to lower, take down; to come upon (oil, ore, etc) by drilling or excavation; (*with* **down**) to afflict or cause to die suddenly; (*with* **off**) to delete or erase from (a list, etc); to prevent from continuing in a profession, *esp* due to malpractice; to sever or separate from (as if) with a blow; (*with* **out**) to erase or delete; (*with* **up**) to cause to begin, to bring about. • *vi* to cease work to enforce a demand (for higher wages or better working conditions). • *n* a stoppage of work; a military attack; (*with* **out**) to begin on a journey; (*baseball*) to be put out on strikes; (*inf*) to be completely unsuccessful; (*with* **up**) (*orchestra, band*) to begin to play or sing.

strikebound /ˈstraɪkbaʊnd/ *adj* (*factory, etc*) closed or paralysed by striking workers.

strikebreaker /ˈstraɪkˌbreɪkər/ *n* a person who continues work whilst colleagues are on strike; a person hired to replace a striking worker.—**strikebreaking** *n, adj.*

strike pay *n* money paid to workers on strike from trade union funds.

striker /'straɪkər/ *n* a worker who is on strike; a mechanism that strikes, as in a clock; (*soccer*) a forward player whose primary role is to score goals.

striking /'straɪkɪŋ/ *adj* impressive.—**strikingly** *adv*.

Strine /straɪn/ *n* Australian English (a humorous rendering of Australian pronunciation).

string /strɪŋ/ *n* a thin length of cord or twine used for tying, fastening, etc; a stretched length of catgut, wire, or other material in a musical instrument; (*pl*) the stringed instruments in an orchestra; their players; a line or series of things. • *vt* (**stringing, strung**) to thread on a string; (*with* **up**) (*sl*) to kill by hanging. • *vi* (*with* **along**) (*inf*) to appear to agree (with); to accompany; to deceive, *esp* to gain time.

stringed /strɪŋd/ *adj* (*musical instruments*) having strings.

stringent /'strɪndʒənt/ *adj* strict.—**stringently** *adv*.—**stringency** *n*.

stringer /'strɪŋər/ *n* a horizontal support in a structure; a long horizontal brace to strengthen a framework, as in an aircraft fuselage; a journalist or photographer temporarily employed by a newspaper, magazine or news service to cover a particular area.

string quartet *n* (a piece of music written for) a musical ensemble comprising two violins, one viola, and one cello.

string tie *n* a narrow tie.

stringy /'strɪŋi/ *adj* (**stringier, stringiest**) of or resembling string; (*meat, etc*) fibrous, chewy; (*physique*) sinewy.

strip /strɪp/ *vb* (**stripping, stripped**) *vt* to peel off; to divest; to take away removable parts. • *vi* to undress. • *n* a long, narrow piece (of cloth, land, etc); an airstrip or runway.

strip cartoon *n* a series of drawings in a newspaper, etc which tell a story.

strip club *n* a nightclub which features striptease artists.

stripe /straɪp/ *n* a narrow band of a different colour from the background; a chevron worn on a military uniform to indicate rank. • *vt* to mark with a stripe.—**striped** *adj*.—**stripy** *adj*.

strip lighting *n* lighting using long fluorescent tubes.

stripling /'strɪplɪŋ/ *n* a youth, boy.

strip mining *n* mining by surface excavation, opencast mining.

stripper /'strɪpər/ *n* a striptease artist; a device or solvent that removes paint.

striptease /'strɪptiːz/ *n* an erotic show where a person removes their clothes slowly and seductively to music.

strive /straɪv/ *vi* (**striving, strove,** *pp* **striven**) to endeavour earnestly, labour hard, to struggle, contend.

strobe /stroːb/ *n* (*inf*) a stroboscope.

strobe lighting *n* (the equipment used to produce) high-intensity flashing light.

stroboscope /'stroːbəˌskoːp/ *n* a device for observing motion by making the subject visible at prescribed intervals using a synchronized flashing light.

strode /stroːd/ *see* **stride**.

stroganoff /'stroːɡəˌnɒf/ *n* sliced beef cooked with mushrooms and onions in a sour cream sauce.

stroke[1] /stroːk/ *n* a blow or hit; (*med*) a seizure; the sound of a clock; (*sport*) an act of hitting a ball; a manner of swimming; the sweep of an oar in rowing; a movement of a pen, pencil, or paintbrush.

stroke[2] *vt* to caress; to do so as a sign of affection.

stroke play *n* (*golf*) scoring by the number of strokes taken.

stroll /stroːl/ *vi* to walk leisurely, to saunter. • *n* a leisurely walk for pleasure.

stroller /'stroːlər/ *n* a wheeled metal and canvas chair for a small child, a pushchair.

strong /strɒŋ/ *adj* physically or mentally powerful; potent; intense; healthy; convincing; powerfully affecting the sense of smell or taste, pungent. • *adv* effectively, vigorously.—**strongly** *adv*.

strong-arm *adj* using unwarranted physical force.

strongbox /'strɒŋbɒks/ *n* a solid, secure container for valuables.

strong drink *n* alcoholic drink.

stronghold /'strɒŋhoːld/ *n* a fortress; a centre of strength or support.

strong-minded *adj* resolute, determined.—**strong-mindedly** *adv*.—**strong-mindedness** *n*.

strong point *n* something at which one excels.

strongroom /'strɒŋruːm/ *n* a room specially designed to keep money and valuables secure from theft or fire, etc.

strontium /'strɒnʃɪəm/ or /-ʃəm/, /-tɪəm/ *n* a soft metallic element.

strop /strɒp/ *n* a strip of leather for sharpening a razor. • *vt* (**stropping, stropped**) to sharpen using a strop.

strophe /'stroːfi/ *n* a stanza or movement of a Greek chorus alternating with the antistrophe sung when moving to the left.—**strophic** *adj*.

stroppy /'strɒpi/ *adj* (**stroppier, stroppiest**) (*inf*) surly, angry; quarrelsome.

strove /stroːv/ *see* **strive**.

struck /strʌk/ *see* **strike**.

structuralism /'strʌktʃərəˌlɪzəm/ *n* a view of the social sciences, literature, linguistics, etc, which stresses the importance of inherent underlying hierarchical structures, interrelationships and patterns of organization.—**structuralist** *n*.

structure /'strʌktʃər/ *n* organization; construction; arrangement of parts in an organism, or of atoms in a molecule of a substance; system, framework; order. • *vt* to organize, to arrange; to build up.—**structural** *adj*.—**structurally** *adv*.

strudel /'struːdəl/ *n* very thin pastry rolled up with a fruit filling and baked.

struggle /'strʌɡəl/ *vi* to move strenuously so as to escape; to strive; to fight; to exert strength; to make one's way (along, through, up, etc) with difficulty. • *n* a violent effort; a fight.

strum /strʌm/ *vt* (**strumming, strummed**) to play on (a guitar, etc), by moving the thumb across the strings.

struma /'struːmə/ *n* (*pl* **strumae**) enlargement of the thyroid gland; goitre.

strumpet /'strʌmpət/ *n* (*arch*) a prostitute.

strung /strʌŋ/ *see* **string**.

strung-up *adj* (*inf*) tense, anxious.

strut[1] /strʌt/ *vi* (**strutting, strutted**) to walk in a proud or pompous manner.

strut[2] *n* a brace or structural support. • *vt* to brace.

struthious /'struːθɪəs/ *adj* (*birds*) related to or resembling the ostrich.

strychnine /'strɪknaɪn/ or /-niːn/, /-nɪn/ *n* a poison used in very small quantities as a stimulant.

stub /stʌb/ *n* a short piece left after the larger part has been removed or used; the counterfoil of a cheque, receipt, etc. • *vt* (**stubbing, stubbed**) to knock (one's toe or foot) painfully; to extinguish (a cigarette).

stubble /'stʌbəl/ *n* the stubs or stumps left in the ground when a crop has been harvested; any short, bristly growth, as of beard.—**stubbly** *adj*.

stubborn /'stʌbərn/ *adj* obstinate; persevering; determined, inflexible.—**stubbornly** *adv*.—**stubbornness** *n*.

stubby /'stʌbi/ *adj* (**stubbier, stubbiest**) short and thick; (*Austral sl*) a small bottle of beer.

stucco /'stʌkoː/ *n* (*pl* **stuccoes, stuccos**) a type of cement or plaster used to coat and decorate outside surfaces of walls. • *vt* (**stuccoing, stuccoed**) to decorate or finish with stucco.

stuck /stʌk/ *see* **stick**.

stuck-up *adj* (*inf*) conceited; proud; snobbish.

stud[1] /stʌd/ *n* a male animal, *esp* a horse, kept for breeding; a collection of horses and mares for breeding; a farm or stable for stud animals.

stud[2] *n* a large-headed nail; an ornamental fastener. • *vt* (**studding, studded**) to cover with studs.

studbook *n* a written record of the pedigree of a thoroughbred horse, dog, etc.

student /'stuːdənt/ or /'stjuː-/ *n* a person who studies or investigates a particular subject; a person who is enrolled for study at a school, college, university, etc.

studied /'stʌdiːd/ *adj* carefully planned.—**studiedly** *adv*.—**studiedness** *n*.

studio /'stuːdiːoː/ or /'stjuː-/ *n* (*pl* **studios**) the workshop of an artist, photographer or musician; (*pl*) a building where motion pictures are made; a room where television or radio programmes are recorded.

studio couch *n* a couch resembling a divan that can be converted into a bed.

studio flat *n* a small flat with one main room, a kitchen and a bathroom.

studious /'stuːdiəs/ or /'stjuː-/ *adj* given to study; careful.—**studiously** *adv*.—**studiousness** *n*.

study /'stʌdi/ *vt* (**studying, studied**) to observe and investigate (*eg* phenomena) closely; to learn (*eg* a language); to scrutinize; to follow a course (at college, etc). • *n* (*pl* **studies**) the process of studying; a detailed investigation and analysis of a subject; the written report of a study of something; a room for studying.

stuff /stʌf/ *n* material; matter; textile fabrics; cloth, *esp* when woollen; personal possessions generally. • *vt* to cram or fill completely.

stuffed shirt *n* (*inf*) a pretentious or pompous person.

stuffing /'stʌfɪŋ/ *n* material used to stuff or fill anything; a seasoned mixture put inside poultry, meat, vegetables etc before cooking.

stuffy /'stʌfi/ *adj* (**stuffier, stuffiest**) badly ventilated; lacking in fresh air; dull, uninspired.—**stuffily** *adv.*—**stuffiness** *n*.

stultify /'stʌltɪˌfaɪ/ *vt* (**stultifying, stultified**) to make ineffectual or futile.—**stultification** *n*.

stumble /'stʌmbəl/ *vi* to trip up or lose balance when walking; to falter; to discover by chance (*with* **across** *or* **on**). • *n* a trip; a blunder.

stumbling block *n* an obstacle to further progress.

stump /stʌmp/ *n* the part of a tree remaining in the ground after the trunk has been felled; the part of a limb, tooth, that remains after the larger part is cut off or destroyed. • *vt* (*inf*) to confuse, baffle; to campaign for an election.

stumpy /'stʌmpi/ *adj* (**stumpier, stumpiest**) short and thick.—**stumpiness** *n*.

stun /stʌn/ *vt* (**stunning, stunned**) to render unconscious due to a fall or heavy blow; to surprise completely; to shock.

stung /stʌŋ/ *see* **sting**.

stun gun *n* a type of gun that emits high-voltage electricity to stun victims.

stunk /stʌŋk/ *see* **stink**.

stunner /'stʌnər/ *n* (*inf*) a strikingly attractive or impressive person or thing.

stunning /'stʌnɪŋ/ *adj* (*inf*) strikingly attractive.—**stunningly** *adv*.

stunt[1] /stʌnt/ *vt* to prevent the growth of, to dwarf.

stunt[2] *n* a daring or spectacular feat; a project designed to attract attention. • *vi* to carry out stunts.

stupa /'stu:pə/ *n* a domed shrine holding Buddhist relics.

stupefy /'stu:pəfaɪ/ *or* /'stju:-/ *vt* (**stupefying, stupefied**) to dull the senses of.—**stupefaction** *n*.

stupendous /stu:'pendəs/ *or* /stju:-/ *adj* wonderful, astonishing.—**stupendously** *adv*.

stupid /'stu:pɪd/ *or* /'stju:-/ *adj* lacking in understanding or common sense; silly; foolish; stunned.—**stupidity** *n*.—**stupidly** *adv*.

stupor /'stu:pər/ *or* /'stju:-/ *n* extreme lethargy; mental dullness.

sturdy /'stɜrdi/ *adj* (**sturdier, sturdiest**) firm; strong, robust.—**sturdily** *adv.*—**sturdiness** *n*.

sturgeon /'stɜrdʒən/ *n* any of various large food fishes whose roe is also eaten as caviare.

Sturmabteilung *see* **storm trooper**.

stutter /'stʌtər/ *vi* to stammer.—*also n*.

sty[1] /staɪ/, **stye** *n* (*pl* **sties**) an inflamed swelling on the eyelid.

sty[2] *n* (*pl* **sties**) a pen for pigs; any filthy place.

style /staɪl/ *n* the manner of writing, painting, composing music peculiar to an individual or group; fashion, elegance. • *vt* to design or shape (*eg* hair).—**styler** *n*.

stylish /'staɪlɪʃ/ *adj* having style; fashionable.—**stylishly** *adv.*—**stylishness** *n*.

stylist /'staɪlɪst/ *n* a person who writes, paints, etc, with attention to style; a designer; a hairdresser.

stylistic /staɪ'lɪstɪk/ *adj* of literary or artistic style.—**stylistically** *adv*.

stylize /'staɪlaɪz/ *vt* to give a conventional style to.—**stylization** *n.*—**stylizer** *n*.

stylus /'staɪləs/ *n* (*pl* **styluses, styli**) the device attached to the cartridge on the arm of a record-player that rests in the groove of a record and transmits the vibrations that are converted to sound.

stymie /'staɪmi/ *n* (*pl* **stymies**) (*golf*) a situation in which a ball is obstructed by another ball between it and the hole. • *vt* (**stymieing, stymied**) to obstruct, hinder.

styptic /'stɪptɪk/ *adj* acting to stop bleeding by contracting the blood vessels. • *n* a styptic drug.

styrene /'staɪri:n/ *n* a liquid hydrocarbon used in making rubber and plastics.

suave /swɒv/ *adj* charming, polite.—**suavely** *adv.*—**suaveness** *n*.

suavity /-vɪti/ *n* (*pl* **suavities**) politeness; urbanity; a suave action, comment, etc.

sub /sʌb/ *n* (*inf*) a submarine; a substitute; a subscription; a subeditor.

sub- /sʌb/ *or* /səb/ *prefix* under, below; subordinate, next in rank to.

subaltern /sʌb'ɒltərn/ *or* /'sʌbəltərn/ *n* a commissioned officer in the British army ranking below captain. • *adj* inferior in rank or status.

subaqua /ˌsʌbə'kwɒ/ *adj* of or pertaining to underwater sports.

subatomic /ˌsʌbə'tɒmɪk/ *adj* smaller than an atom; occurring within an atom.

subconscious /sʌb'kɒnʃəs/ *adj* happening without one's awareness. • *n* the part of the mind that is active without one's conscious awareness.—**subconsciously** *adv.*—**subconsciousness** *n*.

subcontinent /'sʌbˌkɒntɪnənt/ *n* a land mass having great size but smaller than any of the *usu* recognized continents.

subcontract /'sʌbˌkɒntrækt/ *or* /ˌsʌb'kɒn-/ *n* a secondary contract, under which work or supply of materials is let out to a firm other than the main party of the contract.—*also vt.*—**subcontractor** *n*.

subculture /'sʌbˌkʌltʃər/ *n* a distinct group with its own customs, language, dress, etc within an existing culture.

subcutaneous /ˌsʌbkju:'teɪniəs/ *adj* under the skin.—**subcutaneously** *adv*.

subdivide /ˌsʌbdɪ'vaɪd/ *vt* to further divide what has already been divided. • *vi* to divide or be divided into parts.—**subdivision** *n*.

subdue /səb'du:/ *or* /-'dju:/ *vt* to dominate; to render submissive; to repress (*eg* a desire, impulse); to soften, tone down (*eg* colour, etc).

subeditor /sʌb'edɪtər/ *n* a person who checks and corrects newspaper articles.—**subedit** *vt*.

subhead /'sʌbhed/, **subheading** /'sʌbhedɪŋ/ *n* a heading associated with a subdivision of a text.

subhuman /sʌb'hju:mən/ *adj* (*animals*) lower down the evolutionary scale than mankind; less than human.

subject /'sʌbdʒəkt/ *adj* under the power of; liable. • *n* a person under the power of another; a citizen; a topic; a theme; the scheme or idea of a work of art. • *vt* to bring under control; to make liable; to cause to undergo something.—**subjection** *n*.

subjective /səb'dʒektɪv/ *adj* determined by one's own mind or consciousness; relating to reality as perceived and not independent of the mind; arising from one's own thoughts and emotions; personal.—**subjectively** *adv.*—**subjectivity** *n*.

sub judice /sʌb 'dʒu:dəsi/ *or* /sʊb 'ju:dɪˌkeɪ/ *adv* being decided by a court.

subjugate /'sʌbdʒʊˌgeɪt/ *vt* to overpower, to conquer.—**subjugation** *n*.

subjunctive /səb'dʒʌŋktɪv/ *adv* denoting that mood of a verb which expresses doubt, condition, wish, or hope. • *n* the subjunctive mood.

sublet /sʌb'let/ *vt* (**subletting, sublet**) to let (a property which one is renting) to another.

sublime /sə'blaɪm/ *adj* noble; exalted.—**sublimely** *adv.*—**sublimity** *n*.

subliminal /səb'lɪmənəl/ *adj* beneath or beyond the conscious awareness.—**subliminally** *adv*.

subliminal advertising *n* advertising using subliminal images to influence the viewer unconsciously.

sub-machine gun /ˌsʌbmə'ʃi:n/ *n* a light automatic or semi-automatic gun designed to be fired from the hip or shoulder.

submarine /ˌsʌbmə'ri:n/ *or* /'sʌb-/ *adj* underwater, *esp* under the sea. • *n* a naval vessel capable of being propelled under water, *esp* for firing torpedoes or missiles.

submerge /səb'mɜrdʒ/, **submerse** *vt* to plunge, sink or dive below the surface of water; to cover, hide, supress.—**submergence, submersion** *n*.

submersible /səb'mɜrsɪbəl/ *adj* capable of being submerged. • *n* an underwater vessel used for exploration or construction work.

submission /səb'mɪʃən/ n an act of submitting; something submitted, as an idea or proposal; the state of being submissive, compliant; the act of referring something for another's consideration, criticism, etc.—**submissively** adv.—**submissiveness** n.

submit /səb'mɪt/ vb (**submitting, submitted**) vt to surrender (oneself) to another person or force; to refer to another for consideration or judgment; to offer as an opinion. • vi to yield, to surrender.

subnormal /sʌb'nɔːməl/ adj less than normal; having low intelligence.—**subnormality** n.—**subnormally** adv.

subordinate /sə'bɔːdənət/ adj secondary; lower in order, rank. • n a subordinate person. • vt to put in a lower position or rank.—**subordination** n.

suborn /sə'bɔːn/ vt to persuade to commit perjury or some other illegal act.

subpoena /sə'piːnə/ n a written legal order requiring the attendance of a person in court. • vt (**subpoenaing, subpoenaed**) to serve with a subpoena.

sub rosa /sʌb'rəʊzə/ adv in secret.

subroutine /'sʌbruːˌtiːn/ n a self-contained section of a computer program that performs a particular task as many times as required by the main program.

subscribe /səb'skraɪb/ vt to pay to receive regular copies (of a magazine, etc); to donate money (to a charity, campaign); to support or agree with (an opinion, faith).—**subscriber** n.—**subscription** n.

subscriber trunk dialling n a service that allows users to dial long-distance calls directly.

subscript /'sʌbskrɪpt/ n a character written or printed below another character.—also adj.

subsequent /'sʌbsəkwent/ adj occurring or following after.—**subsequently** adv.

subservient /səb'sɜːviənt/ adj obsequious; servile; subordinate.—**subservience** n.—**subserviently** adv.

subside /səb'saɪd/ vi to sink or fall to the bottom; to settle; to diminish; to abate.—**subsidence** n.

subsidiarity /səbˌsɪdiˈɛriti/ or /səbˌsɪdʒəriti/ n the devolution of decision making or control to the lowest effective level.

subsidiary /səb'sɪdieri/ or /səb'sɪdʒəri/ adj secondary; supplementary; (company) owned or controlled by another. • n (pl subsidiaries) an accessory, an auxiliary; a business owned by another.—**subsidiarily** adv.

subsidize /'sʌbsɪˌdaɪz/ vt to aid or support with a subsidy.—**subsidization** n.—**subsidizer** n.

subsidy /'sʌbsɪdi/ n (pl **subsidies**) government financial aid to a private person or company to assist an enterprise.

subsist /səb'sɪst/ vi to exist; to continue; to manage to keep oneself alive (on).

subsistence /səb'sɪstəns/ n existence; livelihood.—**subsistent** adj.

subsoil /'sʌbsɔɪl/ n the layer of soil lying immediately beneath the surface soil.

subsonic /sʌb'sɒnɪk/ adj travelling at a speed less than that of sound.

substance /'sʌbstəns/ n matter (such as powder, liquid); the essential nature or part; significance.

substantial /səb'stænʃəl/ adj of considerable value or size; important; strongly built.—**substantiality** n.—**substantially** adv.

substantiate /səb'stænʃiˌeɪt/ vt to prove, to verify.—**substantiation** n.

substitute /'sʌbstiˌtuːt/ or /-ˌtjuːt/ vt to put or act in place of another person or thing (with for); to replace (by). • n a person or thing that serves in place of another.—also adj.—**substitution** n.

substructure /'sʌbˌstrʌktʃər/ n a foundation or supporting framework.

subsume /səb'suːm/ or /-'sjuːm/ vt to include in a larger group or category.

subterfuge /'sʌbtərˌfjuːdʒ/ n a trick employed to conceal something.

subterranean /ˌsʌbtə'reɪniən/ adj below the surface of the earth; concealed.

subtitle /'sʌbˌtaɪtəl/ n an explanatory, usu secondary, title to a book; a printed translation superimposed on a foreign language film.—also vt.

subtle /'sʌtəl/ adj delicate; slight; not noticeable; difficult to define, put into words; ingenious.—**subtleness** n.—**subtly** adv.

subtlety /'sʌtəlti/ n (pl **subtleties**) subtleness; a fine distinction.

subtotal /'sʌbˌtəʊtəl/ n the sum of part of a series of figures. • vt (**subtotalling, subtotalled** or **subtotaling, subtotaled**) to sum in part.

subtract /səb'trækt/ vti to take away or deduct, as one quantity from another.—**subtraction** n.

subtropical /sʌb'trɒpɪkəl/ adj of, characteristic of, the regions bordering on the tropics.

suburb /'sʌbɜːb/ n a residential district on the outskirts of a large town or city.—**suburban** adj.—**suburbia** n.

suburbanite /-ənaɪt/ n a person who lives in a suburb.

subversion /sʌb'vɜːʒən/ n the act of undermining the authority of a government, institution, etc; collapse, ruin.

subversive /sʌb'vɜːsɪv/ adj liable to subvert established authority. • n a person who engages in subversive activities.—**subversively** adv.—**subversiveness** n.

subvert /sʌb'vɜːt/ vt to overthrow, to ruin (something established); to corrupt, as in morals.

subway /'sʌbweɪ/ n a passage under a street; an underground metropolitan electric railway.

succeed /sək'siːd/ vt to come after, to follow; to take the place of. • vi to accomplish what is attempted; to prosper.

success /sək'sɛs/ n the gaining of wealth, fame, etc; the favourable outcome (of anything attempted); a successful person or action.

successful /-fʊl/ adj having success.—**successfully** adv.—**successfulness** n.

succession /sək'sɛʃən/ n following in sequence; a number of persons or things following in order; the act or process of succeeding to a title, throne, etc; the line of descent to succeed to something.

successive /sək'sɛsɪv/ adj following in sequence.—**successively** adv.—**successiveness** n.

successor /sək'sɛsər/ n a person who succeeds another, as to an office.

succinct /sə'sɪŋkt/ or /sʌk-/ adj clear, concise.—**succinctly** adv.—**succinctness** n.

succotash /sʌ'kəˌtæʃ/ n in the US, a cooked mixture of sweetcorn and lima beans.

succour, succor /'sʌkər/ n (a person or thing that provides) help, support, esp in time of need. • vt to provide such help.

succubus /'sʌkjʊbəs/, **succuba** n (pl **succubi, succubae**) a female demon thought to have sexual intercourse with sleeping men.

succulent /'sʌkjʊlənt/ adj juicy; moist and tasty; (plant) having fleshy tissue. • n a succulent plant (as a cactus).—**succulence, succulency** n.—**succulently** adv.

succumb /sə'kʌm/ vi to yield to superior strength or overpowering desire; to die.

such /sʌtʃ/ adj of a specified kind (eg such people, such a film); so great. • adv so; very.

suchlike /'sʌtʃlaɪk/ adj of similar kind.

suck /sʌk/ vt to draw (a liquid, air) into the mouth; to dissolve or roll about in the mouth (as a sweet); to draw in as if by sucking (with in, up, etc).—also n.

sucker /'sʌkər/ n (sl) a person who is easily taken in or deceived; a cup-shaped piece of rubber that adheres to surfaces.

suckle /'sʌkəl/ vt to feed at the breast or udder.

suckling /'sʌklɪŋ/ n a young animal that is not yet weaned.

sucks /sʌks/ interj (sl) used to express disappointment.

sucre /'suːkər/ n the monetary unit of Ecuador.

sucrose /'suːkrəʊs/ n sugar.

suction /'sʌkʃən/ n the act or process of sucking; the exertion of a force to form a vacuum.

sudden /'sʌdən/ adj happening quickly and unexpectedly, abrupt.—**suddenly** adv.—**suddenness** n.

sudden death n (sport) extra time in a tied match, the winner being the next to score or take a point.

suds /sʌds/ npl the bubbles or foam on the surface of soapy water.—**sudsy** adj.

sue /suː/ vt (**suing, sued**) to bring a legal action against.

suede, suède /sweɪd/ n leather finished with a soft nap.

suet /'suːət/ n white, solid fat in animal tissue, used in cooking.

suffer /'sʌfər/ vt to undergo; to endure; to experience. • vi to feel pain or distress.—**sufferer** n.—**suffering** n.

sufferable /-əbəl/ adj endurable.—**sufferably** adv.

sufferance /-rəns/ *n* reluctant tolerance, tacit permission; endurance.

suffice /sə'faɪs/ *vi* to be sufficient, adequate (for some purpose).

sufficient /sə'fɪʃənt/ *adj* enough; adequate.—**sufficiency** *n.*—**sufficiently** *adv.*

suffix /'sʌfɪks/ *n* (*pl* **suffixes**) a letter, syllable, or syllables added to the end of a word to modify its meaning or to form a new derivative.

suffocate /'sʌfəkeɪt/ *vti* to kill or be killed by depriving of oxygen, or by inhaling a poisonous gas; to feel hot and uncomfortable due to lack of air; to prevent from developing.—**suffocation** *n.*

suffrage /'sʌfrɪdʒ/ *n* the right to vote.

suffuse /sə'fjuːz/ *vt* to spread over or fill, as with colour or light.—**suffusion** *n.*

sugar /'ʃʊɡər/ *n* a sweet white, crystalline substance obtained from sugar cane and sugar beet. • *vi* to sweeten.

sugar beet *n* a type of beet from which sugar is extracted.

sugar cane *n* a tall grass with stout canes grown as a source of sugar.

sugar daddy *n* a wealthy and *usu* elderly man who lavishes gifts on an attractive young woman.

sugar maple *n* a North American maple from which sap is tapped to make maple syrup.

sugary /'ʃʊɡəri/ *adj* resembling or containing sugar; cloyingly sweet in manner, content, etc.—**sugariness** *n.*

suggest /sə'dʒɛst/ *vt* to put forward for consideration; to bring to one's mind; to evoke.—**suggestion** *n.*

suggestible /sə'dʒɛstəbəl/ *adj* easily influenced by others.—**suggestibility** *n.*

suggestive /-tɪv/ *adj* evocative; rather indecent, risqué.—**suggestively** *adv.*—**suggestiveness** *n.*

suicidal /ˌsuːɪ'saɪdəl/ *adj* of, pertaining to, suicide; liable to commit suicide; destructive of one's own interests.—**suicidally** *adv.*

suicide /'suːɪˌsaɪd/ *n* a person who kills himself intentionally; the act or instance of killing oneself intentionally; ruin of one's own interests.

suicide gene *n* a gene having bacteria that end its life cycle.

sui generis /suːɪ'dʒɛnərɪs/ *adj* unique.

suit /suːt/ *n* a set of matching garments, such as a jacket and trousers or skirt; one of the four sets of thirteen playing cards; a lawsuit. • *vt* to be appropriate; to be convenient or acceptable to.

suitable /'suːtəbəl/ *adj* fitting; convenient (to, for).—**suitably** *adv.*—**suitability** *n.*

suitcase /-keɪs/ *n* a portable, oblong travelling case.

suite /swiːt/ *n* a number of followers or attendants; a set, *esp* of rooms, furniture, pieces of music.

suitor /'suːtər/ *n* a man who courts a woman; (*law*) a person who brings a lawsuit.

sukiyaki /ˌsʊkɪ'jɒki/ *n* a Japanese dish of thinly sliced beef, vegetables and seafood cooked rapidly in soy sauce, saké, etc, at the table.

sulfa /'sʌlfə/ *see* **sulpha**.

sulfate /'sʌlfeɪt/ *see* **sulphate**.

sulfonamide /ˌsʌl'fɒnəˌmaɪd/ *see* **sulphonamide**.

sulfur /'sʌlfər/ *see* **sulphur**.

sulfuric /'sʌlfjʊrɪk/ *see* **sulphuric**.

sulk /sʌlk/ *vi* to be sullen.

sulky /'sʌlki/ *adj* (**sulkier, sulkiest**) bad-tempered, quiet and sullen, because of resentment.—**sulkily** *adv.*—**sulkiness** *n.*

sullen /'sʌlən/ *adj* moody and silent; gloomy, dull.—**sullenly** *adv.*—**sullenness** *n.*

sully /'sʌli/ *vt* (**sullying, sullied**) to blemish, to defile the purity of. • *n* (*pl* **sullies**) a tarnish or stain.

sulph-, sulf- /sʌlf/ *prefix* sulphur.

sulpha drug *n* any of various sulphonamide drugs used for treating bacterial infections.

sulphate /'sʌlfeɪt/ *n* a salt of sulphuric acid.—*also* **sulfate**.

sulphonamide /ˌsʌl'fɒnəˌmaɪd/ *n* any of a group of compounds that are amides of sulphonic acid, such as the sulfa drugs.—*also* **sulfonamide**.

sulphonic acid *n* any of a group strong organic acids used in the manufacture of drugs, dyes and detergents.

sulphur /'sʌlfər/ *n* a yellow nonmetallic element that is inflammable and has a strong odour.—*also* **sulfur**.—**sulphuric, sulfuric** *adj.*

sulphur dioxide *n* a pungent toxic gas used in various industrial processes that is a major air pollutant.

sulphuric acid *n* a powerfully corrosive acid.

sultan /'sʌltən/ *n* a ruler, *esp* of a Muslim state.

sultana /sʌl'tænə/ *n* a dried, white grape used in cooking; the wife or female relative of a sultan.

sultanate /'sʌltənət/ *n* a country or region ruled by a sultan; the office or authority of a sultan.

sultry /'sʌltri/ *adj* (**sultrier, sultriest**) (*weather*) very hot, humid and close; sensual; passionate.—**sultrily** *adv.*—**sultriness** *n.*

sum /sʌm/ *n* the result of two or more things added together; the total, aggregate; a quantity of money; essence, gist. • *vt* (**summing, summed**) to add (*usu with* up); to encapsulate; to summarize.

summarize /'sʌməˌraɪz/ *vt* to make or be a summary of.—**summarization** *n.*—**summarizer** *n.*

summary /'sʌməri/ *adj* concise; performed quickly, without formality. • *n* (*pl* **summaries**) a brief account of the main points of something.—**summarily** *adv.*—**summariness** *n.*

summation /sʌ'meɪʃən/ *n* the act of finding a sum or total; the result of summation; a summary; the summing up of an argument, *esp* by a lawyer before a jury.

summer /'sʌmər/ *n* the warmest season of the year, between spring and autumn.—**summery** *adj.*

summerhouse *n* a small building in a garden used as a shady retreat in summer.

summer school *n* an academic course held during the summer.

summing-up *n* a concluding summary of the points in a speech, argument, etc; a review of the main evidence made by a judge to the jury before it considers its verdict.

summit /'sʌmɪt/ *n* the highest point, the peak; a meeting of world leaders.

summitry /-ri/ *n* the practice of convening, or style of conducting, summit conferences.

summon /'sʌmən/ *vt* to order to appear, *esp* in court; to convene; to gather (strength, enthusiasm, etc).

summons /'sʌmənz/ *n* (*pl* **summonses**) a call to appear (in court). • *vt* to serve with a summons.

sumo /'suːmɔ/ *n* traditional Japanese wrestling.

sump /sʌmp/ *n* a section of the crankcase under an engine for the oil to drain into to form a reservoir.

sumptuous /'sʌmpʃuːəs/ *adj* lavish; luxurious.—**sumptuously** *adv.*—**sumptuousness** *n.*

sun /sʌn/ *n* the star around which the earth and other planets revolve which gives light and heat to the solar system; the sunshine. • *vi* (**sunning, sunned**) to expose oneself to the sun's rays.

Sun. *abbr* = Sunday.

sunbaked *adj* baked hard by exposure to the sun.

sunbathe /'sʌnbeɪð/ *vi* to lie in the rays of the sun or a sun lamp to get a suntan.—**sunbather** *n.*

sunbeam /-biːm/ *n* a ray of sunlight.

sunburn /-bərn/ *n* inflammation of the skin from exposure to sunlight.—*also vti.*

sunburst /-bərst/ *n* a sudden flash of sunlight; a pattern resembling the sun surrounded by rays; a brooch with a design resembling this.

sundae /'sʌndeɪ/ *n* a serving of ice cream covered with a topping of fruit, syrup, nuts, etc.

Sunday /'sʌndeɪ/ *n* the day of the week after Saturday, regarded as a day of worship by Christians; a newspaper published on a Sunday.

Sunday best *n* best clothes kept for wearing on Sundays.

Sunday school *n* a class for religious instruction held on Sundays.

sundew *n* any of various bog plants with sticky hairs that trap insects.

sundial *n* a device that shows the time by casting a shadow on a graduated dial.

sundown /'sʌndaʊn/ *n* sunset.

sundry /'sʌndri/ *adj* miscellaneous, various. • *n* (*pl* **sundries**) (*pl*) miscellaneous small things.

sunflower /'sʌnˌflaʊr/ *n* a tall plant with large yellow flowers whose seeds yield oil.

sung /sʌŋ/ *see* **sing**.

sunglasses /'sʌnˌɡlæsəz/ *npl* tinted glasses to protect the eyes from sunlight.

sunk /'sʌŋk/ *see* **sink**.

sunlamp *n* an electric lamp that produces ultra-violet rays for tanning the skin.

Sunna /'sʌnə/ *n* the body of Islamic doctrine accepted by orthodox Muslims as based on the life and teachings of Mohammed.

Sunni /'sʌni/ *n* the branch of Islam that accepts the orthodoxy of the Sunna.—**Sunnite** *n*.

sunny /'sʌni/ *adj* (**sunnier, sunniest**) (*weather*) bright with sunshine; (*person, mood*) cheerful.—**sunnily** *adv*.—**sunniness** *n*.

sunrise /'sʌnraɪz/ *n* dawn.

sunrise industry *n* a high-technology industry with a bright future.

sunroof /'sʌnru:f/ *n* a panel in the roof of a car that slides open.

sunset /-set/ *n* dusk.

sunshine /-ʃaɪn/ *n* the light and heat from the sun.

sunspot /-spɒt/ *n* a dark patch sometimes visible on the sun's surface; (*inf*) a holiday resort with guaranteed sunshine.

sunstroke /-strɔːk/ *n* illness caused by exposure to the sun.

suntan /-tæn/ *n* browning of the skin by the sun.—**suntanned** *adj*.

suntrap /-træp/ *n* a sunny sheltered spot.

super /'su:pər/ *adj* (*inf*) fantastic, excellent; (*inf*) a superintendent, as in the police. • *n* a variety of high-octane petrol.

super- /'su:pər/ *prefix* above, on the top of; extremely, excessively, greater in size, quality, etc.

superable *adj* able to be overcome.—**superably** *adv*.

superannuate /ˌsu:pər'ænjuˌeɪt/ *vt* to pension off on account of old age or illness.

superannuation /ˌsu:pərˌænju'eɪʃən/ *n* regular contributions from employees' wages toward a pension scheme.

superb /'su:pərb/ *adj* grand; excellent; of the highest quality.—**superbly** *adv*.

supercharge /'su:pərˌtʃɑrdʒ/ *vt* to increase the power of an engine by using a device that supplies air or fuel in increased quantities by raising the intake pressure; to charge (the atmosphere, a conversation, etc) with excess tension or emotion.—**supercharger** *n*.

supercilious /ˌsu:pər'siliəs/ *adj* arrogant; haughty, disdainful.—**superciliously** *adv*.—**superciliousness** *n*.

superconductivity /ˌsu:pərˌkɒndʌk'tɪvɪti/ *n* (*physics*) the complete loss of electrical resistance exhibited by certain materials at very low temperatures.—**superconducting, superconductive** *adj*.—**superconduction** *n*.—**superconductor** *n*.

supercool /'su:pərˌku:l/ *vt* to cool (a liquid, etc) below freezing without solidification or crystallization.

superdelegate *n* in US, a delegate to a Democratic party convention, appointed rather than elected.

superego /ˌsu:pər'i:goʊ/ *n* (*pl* **superegos**) (*psychol*) the division of the unconscious mind that functions as a conscience.

superficial /ˌsu:pər'fɪʃəl/ *adj* near the surface; slight, not profound; (*person*) shallow in nature.—**superficiality** *n*.—**superficially** *adv*.

superfluous /su:'pərflʊəs/ *adj* exceeding what is required; unnecessary.—**superfluity** *n*.

supergiant /'su:pərˌdʒaɪənt/ *n* a star of enormous size and brightness with a low density.

superglue /'su:pərˌglu:/ *n* an adhesive that forms strong bonds instantly.

supergrass *n* an informer who incriminates a large number of people.

superheat /ˌsu:pər'hi:t/ *vt* to heat above boiling point without vaporization; to heat a vapour above boiling point without boiling occurring.

superhigh frequency *n* a radio frequency between 30,000 and 3,000 megahertz.

superhuman /-'hju:mən/ *adj* surpassing normal human strength or abilities; divine.

superimpose /-ɪm'po:z/ *vt* to put or lay upon something else.

superintend /-ɪn'tend/ *vt* to have the charge and direction of; to control, manage.

superintendent /-ɪn'tendənt/ *n* a person who manages or supervises; a director; a British police officer next above the rank of inspector.

superior /su:'piːriər/ or /sʊ-/ *adj* higher in place, quality, rank, excellence; greater in number, power. • *n* a person of higher rank.—**superiority** *n*.

superiority complex *n* an inflated opinion of one's own abilities and merits.

superl. *abbr* = superlative.

superlative /su:'pərlətɪv/ *adj* of outstanding quality; (*gram*) denoting the extreme degree of comparison of adjectives and adverbs.—**superlatively** *adv*.

superman /'su:pərˌmæn/ *n* (*pl* **supermen**) a person of outstanding abilities and achievements.

supermarket /ˌsu:pər'mɑrkət/ *n* a large self-service shop selling food and household goods.

supernatural /-'nætʃərəl/ *adj* relating to things that cannot be explained by nature; involving ghosts, spirits, etc.—**supernaturally** *adv*.

supernova /-'no:və/ *n* (*pl* **supernovae, supernovas**) a star that explodes temporarily burning with an intensity one hundred million times that of the sun.

supernumerary /ˌsu:pər'nu:mərˌeri/ or /-nju:-/ *adj* extra; beyond the usual number. • *n* (*pl* **supernumeraries**) an extra person or thing.

superpose /ˌsu:pər'po:z/ *vt* to place (a geometric figure) on top of another so that their outlines coincide; to lay on top of.—**superposition** *n*.

superpower /'su:pərˌpaʊər/ *n* a nation with great economic and military strength.

superscript /'su:pərskrɪpt/ *n* a character written or printed above another character.—*also adj*.

supersede /ˌsu:pər'si:d/ *vt* to take the place of, replace.

supersmart card *n* a smart card equipped with a screen and a keyboard, allowing interaction with the user.

supersonic /ˌsu:pər'sɒnɪk/ *adj* faster than the speed of sound.—**supersonically** *adv*.

superstar /'su:pərˌstɑr/ *n* (*inf*) a sporting celebrity; a famous film actor or musician.

superstition /ˌsu:pər'stɪʃən/ *n* irrational belief based on ignorance or fear.—**superstitious** *adj*.

superstore /'su:pərˌstɔr/ *n* a very large supermarket.

superstructure /-ˌstrʌktʃər/ *n* a structure above or on something else, as above the base or foundation, as above the main deck of a ship.

Super Tuesday *n* in US politics, the Tuesday, *usu* in March, on which a number of states, with over half of all the delegates, hold primary elections for the selection of Presidential candidates.

supervise /-ˌvaɪz/ *vti* to have charge of, direct, to superintend.—**supervision** *n*.

supervisor /-ˌvaɪzər/ *n* one who supervises; an overseer, an inspector.—**supervisory** *adj*.

supine /'su:paɪn/ *adj* lying on the back; lazy, indigent.—**supinely** *adv*.

supper /'sʌpər/ *n* a meal taken in the evening, *esp* when dinner is eaten at midday; an evening social event; the food served at a supper; a light meal served late in the evening.

supplant /sə'plænt/ *vt* to replace; to remove in order to replace with something else.

supple /'sʌpəl/ *adj* flexible, easily bent; lithe; (*mind*) adaptable.—**suppleness** *n*.

supplement /'sʌpləmənt/ *n* an addition or extra amount (*usu* of money); an additional section of a book, periodical or newspaper. • *vt* to add to.—**supplemental** *adj*.

supply /'sʌplaɪ/ *vt* (**supplying, supplied**) to provide, meet (a deficiency, a need); to fill (a vacant place). • *n* (*pl* **supplies**) a stock; (*pl*) provisions.—**supplier** *n*.

support /sə'pɔrt/ *vt* to hold up, bear; to tolerate, withstand; to assist; to advocate (a cause, policy); to provide for (financially). • *n* a means of support; maintenance.

supporter /-ər/ *n* a person who backs a political party, sports team, etc.

suppose /sə'po:z/ *vt* to assume; to presume as true without definite knowledge; to think probable; to expect. • *vi* to conjecture.

supposed /sə'po:zd/ *adj* believed to be on available evidence.

supposedly /sə'po:zədli/ *adv* allegedly.

supposition /ˌsʌpə'zɪʃən/ *n* an assumption, hypothesis.

supposititious /ˌsʌpə'zɪʃəs/ *adj* hypothetical.

suppository /sə'pɒzɪˌtɔri/ *n* (*pl* **suppositories**) a cone or cylinder of medicated soluble material for insertion into the rectum or vagina.

suppress /sə'pres/ *vt* to crush, put an end to (*eg* a rebellion); to restrain (a person); to subdue.—**suppression** *n*.—**suppressor** *n*.

suppurate /ˈsʌpjəˌreɪt/ *vi* (*med*) to form or discharge pus.—**suppuration** *n*.—**suppurative** *adj*.

supra /ˈsuːprə/ *prefix* above, situated above; over; beyond.

supranational /ˌsuːprəˈnæʃənəl/ *adj* transcending national boundaries or interests.

supremacist /səˈprɛməsɪst/ or /suː-/ *n* a person who advocates the supremacy of a particular group.

supreme /suːˈpriːm/ or /sə-/ *adj* of highest power; greatest; final; ultimate.—**supremacy** *n*.

Supreme Court *n* in the US, the highest federal court.

supremo /səˈpriːmoː/ or /suː-/ *n* (*pl* **supremos**) (*inf*) the person in overall charge, a boss.

Supt *abbr* = superintendent.

surcharge /sərˈtʃɑrdʒ/ *vt* to overcharge (a person); to charge an additional sum; to overload. • *n* an additional tax or charge; an additional or excessive load.

surd /sərd/ *n* (*math*) a number containing an irrational root; an irrational number.

sure /ʃər/ or /ʃʊr/ *adj* certain; without doubt; reliable, inevitable; secure; safe; dependable. • *adv* certainly.

sure-fire /ˈʃərfaɪr/ or /ˈʃʊr-/ *adj* (*inf*) certain to succeed.

sure-footed *adj* not liable to slip or fall; unlikely to make a mistake.

surely /ˈʃərli/ or /ˈʃʊr-/ *adv* certainly; securely; it is to be hoped or expected that.

sure thing *n* (*inf*) something assured of success. • *interj* yes, of course.

surety /ˈʃərəti/ or /ˈʃʊr-/ *n* (*pl* **sureties**) a person who undertakes responsibility for the fulfilment of another's debt; security given as a guarantee of payment of a debt.

surf /sərf/ *n* the waves of the sea breaking on the shore or a reef.

surface /ˈsərfəs/ *n* the exterior face of an object; any of the faces of a solid; the uppermost level of sea or land; a flat area, such as the top of a table; superficial features. • *adj* superficial; external. • *vt* to cover with a surface, as in paving. • *vi* to rise to the surface of water.

surfboard /ˈsərfbɔrd/ *n* a long, narrow board used in the sport of surfing.

surfeit /ˈsərfiːt/ *n* an excessive amount.

surfing /ˈsərfɪŋ/ *n* the sport of riding in toward shore on the crest of a wave, *esp* on a surfboard.

surg. *abbr* = surgeon; surgery; surgical.

surge /sərdʒ/ *n* the rolling of the sea, as after a large wave; a sudden, strong increase, as of power.—*also vi*.

surgeon /ˈsərdʒən/ *n* a medical specialist who practises surgery.

surgery /ˈsərdʒəri/ *n* (*pl* **surgeries**) the treatment of diseases or injuries by manual or instrumental operations; the consulting room of a doctor or dentist; the daily period when a doctor is available for consultation; the regular period when an MP, lawyer, etc is available for consultation.—**surgical** *adj*.—**surgically** *adv*.

surgical spirit *n* methylated spirit used for sterilizing.

surly /ˈsərli/ *adj* (**surlier, surliest**) ill-tempered or rude.—**surlily** *adv*.—**surliness** *n*.

surmise /sərˈmaɪz/ *n* guess, conjecture. • *vt* to infer the existence of from partial evidence.

surmount /sərˈmaʊnt/ *vt* to overcome; to rise above.

surname /ˈsərneɪm/ *n* the family name. • *vt* to give a surname to.

surpass /sərˈpæs/ *vt* to outdo, to outshine; to excel; to exceed.

surpassing /-ɪŋ/ *adj* exceptional; greatly exceeding others.—**surpassingly** *adv*.

surplice /ˈsərplɪs/ or /-pləs/ *n* a loose, white, wide-sleeved clerical garment worn by clergymen and choristers.

surplus /ˈsərpləs/ *n* (*pl* **surpluses**) an amount in excess of what is required; an excess of revenues over expenditure in a financial year.

surprise /ˈsərpraɪz/ *n* the act of catching unawares; an unexpected gift, event; astonishment. • *vt* to cause to feel astonished; to attack unexpectedly; to take unawares.—**surprising** *adj*.—**surprisingly** *adv*.

surreal /səˈriːəl/ *adj* bizarre.

surrealism /-ˌlɪzəm/ *n* a movement in art characterized by the expression of the activities of the unconscious mind and dream elements.—**surrealist** *n*.—**surrealistic** *adj*.

surrender /səˈrɛndər/ *vt* to relinquish or give up possession or power. • *vi* to give oneself up (to an enemy).—*also n*.

surreptitious /ˌsʌrəpˈtɪʃəs/ *adj* done by stealth; clandestine, secret.—**surreptitiously** *adv*.

surrogacy /ˈsʌrəgəsi/, **surrogate motherhood** *n* a practice in which a woman bears a child for a childless couple.—**surrogate mother** *n*.

surrogate /ˈsʌrəgət/ *n* a person or thing acting as a substitute for another person or thing.—*also adj*.

surrogate mother *n* a woman who bears a child on behalf of a childless couple.

surround /səˈraʊnd/ *vt* to encircle on all or nearly all sides; (*mil*) to encircle. • *n* a border around the edge of something.

surroundings /-ɪŋz/ *npl* the conditions, objects, etc around a person or thing; the environment.

surtax /ˈsərtæks/ *n* an additional tax, *esp* on income above a prescribed level.—*also vt*.

surtitle /ˈsərˌtaɪtəl/ *n* a caption projected onto a screen above the stage during an opera as a translation of the libretto or to explain some detail of the action.—*also vt*.

surveillance /sərˈveɪləns/ *n* a secret watch kept over a person, *esp* a suspect.

survey /ˈsərveɪ/ *vt* (**surveying, surveyed**) to take a general view of; to appraise; to examine carefully; to measure and make a map of an area. • *n* (*pl* **surveys**) a detailed study, as by gathering information and analysing it, a general view; the process of surveying an area or a house.

surveyor /sərˈveɪər/ or /ˈsər-/ *n* a person who surveys land or buildings.

survival /sərˈvaɪvəl/ *n* surviving; a person or thing that survives; a relic.

survive /sərˈvaɪv/ *vt* to live after the death of another person; to continue, endure; to come through alive. • *vi* to remain alive (after experiencing a dangerous situation).—**survivor** *n*.

susceptible /səˈsɛptəbəl/ *adj* ready or liable to be affected by; impressionable.—**susceptibility** *n*.—**susceptibly** *adv*.

sushi /ˈsuːʃi/ *n* a Japanese dish of small cakes of cold rice with various toppings, *esp* raw fish.

suspect /səˈspɛkt/ *vt* to mistrust; to believe to be guilty; to think probable. • *n* a person under suspicion. • *adj* open to suspicion.

suspend /səˈspɛnd/ *vt* to hang; to discontinue, or cease temporarily; to postpone; to debar temporarily from a privilege, etc.

suspended animation *n* a cessation of the vital functions in an organism, *esp* though freezing.

suspended sentence *n* a sentence that does not come into force unless a further offence is committed.

suspender /-ər/ *n* a fastener for holding up stockings; (*pl*) the US name for braces.

suspender belt *n* a belt with suspenders to hold up a woman's stockings.

suspense /səˈspɛns/ *n* mental anxiety or uncertainty; excitement.

suspension /səˈspɛnʃən/ *n* suspending or being suspended; a temporary interruption or postponement; a temporary removal from office, privileges, etc; the system of springs, shock absorbers, etc that support a vehicle on its axles; (*chem*) a dispersion of fine particles in a liquid.

suspension bridge *n* a bridge carrying a roadway suspended by cables anchored to towers at either end.

suspicion /səˈspɪʃən/ *n* act of suspecting; a belief formed or held without sure proof; mistrust; a trace.—**suspicious** *adj*.—**suspiciously** *adv*.

sustain /səˈsteɪn/ *vt* hold up, support; to maintain; to suffer (*eg* an injury); to nourish.

sustenance /ˈsʌstənəns/ *n* nourishment.

suttee /sʌˈtiː/ or /ˈsʌti/ *n* (*Hinduism*) (*formerly*) the practice of a widow throwing herself on her husband's funeral pyre; this custom.—*also sati*.

suture /ˈsuːtʃər/ *n* a stitch holding together a wound after surgery.—*also vt*.

svelte /svɛlt/ *adj* slim and elegant.

SW *abbr* = southwest(ern); short wave.

swab /swɒb/ *n* a wad of absorbent material, *usu* cotton, used to clean wounds, take specimens, etc; a mop.—*also vt*.

swaddle /ˈswɒdəl/ *vt* to bind tightly, envelop; to wrap a baby in swaddling clothes.

swaddling clothes *npl* narrow strips of cloth used to wrap and restrain an infant.

swag /swæg/ *n* (*sl*) loot.

swagger /ˈswægər/ *vi* to strut; to brag loudly. • *n* boastfulness; swinging gait.

Swahili /swɔˈhiːli/ or /swɒ-/ *n* a language spoken in Kenya, Tanzania and other parts of east Africa; (*pl* **Swahilis, Swahili**) a member of a people speaking this language who live mainly in Zanzibar.

swain /sweɪn/ *n* (*poet*) a male suitor or lover.

swallow[1] /ˈswɒloː/ *n* a small migratory bird with long wings and a forked tail.

swallow[2] *vt* to cause food and drink to move from the mouth to the stomach; to endure; to engulf; (*inf*) to accept gullibly; (*emotion, etc*) to repress.—*also n.*

swallow dive *n* a dive executed with the back arched and arms outstretched at the start.

swam /swæm/ *see* **swim.**

swami /ˈswɒmi/ *n* (*pl* **swamies, swamis**) a Hindu religious teacher.

swamp /swæmp/ *n* wet, spongy land; bog. • *vt* to overwhelm; to flood as with water.—**swampy** *adj*.

swan /swɒn/ *n* a large, *usu* white, bird with a very long neck that lives on rivers and lakes. • *vi* (**swanning, swanned**) (*inf*) to wander aimlessly.

swan dive *n* a swallow dive.

swank /swæŋk/ *vi* (*inf*) to show off.—*also n.*—**swanky** *adj*.

swan song *n* a final appearance, performance, etc by a person facing retirement or death.

swap /swɒp/ *vti* (**swapping, swapped**) (*inf*) to trade, barter. • *n* (*inf*) the act of exchanging one thing for another.—*also* **swop.**

SWAPO, Swapo /ˈswɒpoː/ *abbr* = South West Africa People's Organization.

sward /sword/ *n* (an area of land with) a surface of short grass.

swarm /swɔrm/ *n* a colony of migrating bees; a moving mass, crowd or throng. • *vi* to move in great numbers; to teem.

swarthy /ˈswɔrði/ *adj* (**swarthier, swarthiest**) dark-complexioned.—**swarthiness** *n*.

swashbuckling /ˈswɒʃbʌklɪŋ/ *adj* swaggering; exciting, adventurous.—**swashbuckler** *n*.

swastika /ˈswɒsˈtiːkə/ or /ˈswɒstɪkə/ *n* an ancient symbol formed by a cross with the ends of the arms bent at right-angles, used by Nazi Germany.

swat /swɒt/ *vt* (**swatting, swatted**) (*inf*) to hit with a sharp blow; to swipe.—*also n.*—**swatter** *n*.

swath /swɒθ/ *n* the width of one sweep of a scythe or other mowing device; a strip, row, etc, mowed; a broad strip.

swathe /swɒθ/ or /sweɪð/ *vt* to bind or wrap round, as with a bandage; to envelop, enclose.

sway /sweɪ/ *vi* to swing or move from one side to the other or to and fro; to lean to one side; to vacillate in judgment or opinion. • *n* influence; control.

swear /swɛr/ *vi* (**swearing, swore,** *pp* **sworn**) to make a solemn affirmation, promise, etc, calling God as a witness; to give evidence on oath; to curse, blaspheme or use obscene language; to vow; (*with* **off**) to promise abstinence from. • *vt* (*with* **in**) to appoint to an office by the administration of an oath.

swearword *n* a profane or obscene expression.

sweat /swɛt/ *n* perspiration; (*inf*) hard work; (*inf*) a state of eagerness, anxiety.—*also vti.*—**sweaty** *adj*.

sweatband /ˈswɛtbænd/ *n* a strip of material in a hat, or worn on the wrist or around the forehead, to absorb sweat.

sweater /ˈswɛtər/ *n* a knitted pullover.

sweatshirt /-ʃərt/ *n* a loose, collarless, heavy cotton jersey.

sweatshop /-ʃɒp/ *n* a small factory or workshop where employees work long hours at low wages in poor conditions.

Swede /swiːd/ *n* a native of Sweden.

swede /swiːd/ *n* a round root vegetable with yellow flesh.

Swedish /ˈswiːdɪʃ/ *adj* pertaining to Sweden, its people or language. • *n* the language of Sweden.

sweep /swiːp/ *vb* (**sweeping, swept**) *vt* to clean with a broom; to remove (rubbish, dirt) with a brush. • *vi* to pass by swiftly. • *n* a movement, *esp* in an arc; a stroke; scope, range; a sweepstake.

sweeper /ˈswiːpər/ *n* a person who sweeps, *esp* the roads; (*soccer*) (*inf*) a player positioned before the goalkeeper to collect loose balls, tackle attacking players, etc.

sweeping /-ɪŋ/ *adj* wide-ranging; indiscriminate.—**sweepingly** *adv*.

sweepstake /-steɪk/, **sweepstakes** /-steɪks/ *n* a lottery in which the prize constitutes all the money staked; a horserace, etc in which the winner receives the entire prize.

sweet /swiːt/ *adj* having a taste like sugar; pleasing to other senses; gentle; kind. • *n* a small piece of confectionery; a dessert.—**sweetly** *adv*.—**sweetness** *n*.

sweet-and-sour *adj* (*food*) cooked in a sauce containing sugar and vinegar or lemon juice.

sweet brier *n* a Eurasian rose with pink flowers.

sweetbread /ˈswiːtbrɛd/ *n* the pancreas or thymus gland of an animal, cooked as food.

sweet cicely *n* an aromatic European plant with small white flowers; the aniseed-flavoured leaves of this once used in cookery.

sweet clover *n* a species of sweet-scented trefoil or clover, with clusters of small yellow or white flowers; melilot.

sweetcorn /ˈswiːtkɔrn/ *n* a variety of maize, corn on the cob.

sweeten /ˈswiːtən/ *vti* to make or become sweet or sweeter; to mollify.

sweetener /-ər/ *n* a sweetening substance that contains no sugar; (*sl*) a bribe.

sweetheart /ˈswiːthɑrt/ *n* a lover.

sweetie /ˈswiːti/ *n* (*inf*) a sweet; (*inf*) sweetheart, darling; a kindly, pleasant person.

sweetmeat /ˈswiːtmiːt/ *n* a sweet, preserve, small cake, or other sugary delicacy.

sweet pea *n* a climbing garden plant cultivated for its large fragrant blooms.

sweet pepper *n* (a plant bearing) a large fruit with thick fleshy walls eaten ripe (red) or unripe (green).

sweet potato *n* (a tropical climbing plant with) a large edible tuberous root.

sweet-talk *vt* (*inf*) to flatter, cajole.—**sweet talk** *n*.

sweet william *n* a widely grown Eurasian plant with clusters of white, red, pink, or purple flowers.

swell /swɛl/ *vi* (**swelling, swelled,** *pp* **swollen** *or* **swelled**) to increase in size or volume; to rise into waves; to bulge out. • *n* the movement of the sea; a bulge; a gradual increase in the loudness of a musical note; (*inf*) a socially prominent person. • *adj* excellent.

swelling /ˈswɛlɪŋ/ *n* inflammation.

swelter /ˈswɛltər/ *vi* to suffer from heat. • *n* humid, oppressive heat.

sweltering /-ɪŋ/ *adj* uncomfortably hot.

swept /swɛpt/ *see* **sweep.**

sweptback *adj* (*aircraft wing*) slanting backward.

sweptwing *adj* (*aircraft*) having sweptback wings.

swerve /swɔrv/ *vi* to turn aside suddenly from a line or course; to veer.—*also n.*

swift /swɪft/ *adj* moving with great speed; rapid. • *n* a swallow-like bird.—**swiftly** *adv*.—**swiftness** *n*.

swig /swɪg/ *vt* (*inf*) to take a long drink, *esp* from a bottle.—*also n.*

swill /swɪl/ *vti* to drink greedily; to guzzle; to rinse with a large amount of water. • *n* liquid refuse fed to pigs.

swim /swɪm/ *vi* (**swimming, swam,** *pp* **swum**) to move through water by using limbs or fins; to be dizzy; to be flooded with. • *n* the act of swimming.—**swimmer** *n*.

swimming costume, swimsuit /ˈswɪmsuːt/ *n* a one-piece garment for swimming in.

swimmingly /ˈswɪmɪŋli/ *adv* (*inf*) easily, without effort.

swindle /ˈswɪndəl/ *vti* to cheat (someone) of money or property.—*also n.*—**swindler** *n*.

swindle sheet *n* (*sl*) an expenses form.

swine /swaɪn/ *n* (*pl* **swine**) a pig; (*inf*) an contemptible person; (*inf*) an unpleasant thing.

swine fever *n* a viral infection of pigs.

swineherd /ˈswaɪnhərd/ *n* a person who looks after pigs.

swing /swɪŋ/ *vb* (**swinging, swung**) *vi* to sway or move to and fro, as an object hanging in the air; to pivot; to shift from one mood or opinion to another; (*music*) to have a lively rhythm; (*sl*) to be hanged. • *vt* to whirl; to play swing music; to influence; to achieve, bring about. • *n* a swinging, curving or rhythmic movement; a suspended seat for swinging in; a shift from one condition to another; a type of popular jazz played by a large band and characterized by a lively, steady rhythm.

swingeing /ˈswɪndʒɪŋ/ *adj* drastic, severe.

swinging /ˈswɪŋɪŋ/ *adj* (*inf*) up-to-date; lively.

swing-wing *adj* of or pertaining to an aircraft with movable wings that are swept back at high speeds and moved forward for approach and landing.—*also n.*

swipe /swaɪp/ *n* (*inf*) a hard, sweeping blow. • *vt* (*inf*) to hit with a swipe; (*sl*) to steal.

swirl /swɜrl/ *vti* to turn with a whirling motion.—*also n.*

swish /swɪʃ/ *vi* to move with a soft, whistling, hissing sound. • *n* a swishing sound. • *adj* (*inf*) smart, fashionable.

Swiss /swɪs/ *adj* of or belonging to Switzerland. • *n* (*pl* **Swiss**) a native of Switzerland.

swiss roll *n* a thin sponge cake spread with a layer of jam and rolled up.

switch /swɪtʃ/ *n* a control for turning on and off an electrical device; a sudden change; a swap. • *vt* to shift, change, swap; to turn on or off (as of an electrical device).

switchback /'swɪtʃbæk/ *n* a zigzag road in a mountain region; a roller coaster.

switchblade /-bleɪd/ *n* a flick knife.

switchboard /-bɔrd/ *n* an installation in a building where telephone calls are connected.

swivel /'swɪvəl/ *n* a coupling that permits parts to rotate. • *vi* (**swivelling, swivelled** *or* **swiveling, swiveled**) to turn (as if) on a pin or pivot.

swollen /'swoːlən/ *see* **swell**.

swoon /swuːn/ *vt* to faint.—*also n.*

swoop /swuːp/ *vt* to carry off abruptly. • *vi* to make a sudden attack (*usu with* **down**) as a bird in hunting.—*also n.*

swop /swɒp/ *see* **swap**.

sword /sɔrd/ *n* a weapon with a long blade and a handle at one end.

sword dance *n* a dance in which swords are brandished or placed on the ground and stepped between.

swordfish /'sɔrdfɪʃ/ *n* a large marine fish with a sword-like upper jaw.

swordplay /'sɔrdpleɪ/ *n* fighting with swords; verbal combat.

swordsman /'sɔrdsmən/ *n* (*pl* **swordsmen**) a person skilled in the use of a sword.

swordstick *n* a walking stick concealing a sword.

swore /swɔːr/ *see* **swear**.

sworn /swɔrn/ *see* **swear**.

swot /swɒt/ *vi* (*inf*) to study hard for an examination. • *n* (*inf*) a person who studies hard.

swum /swʌm/ *see* **swim**.

swung /swʌŋ/ *see* **swing**.

sycamore /'sɪkəmɔr/ *n* a Eurasian maple tree; an American plane tree; a tree of Africa and Asia bearing a fruit resembling a fig.

sycophant /'sɪkəfænt/ *or* /'saɪk-/, /-fənt/ *n* a person who flatters and praises powerful people to win their favour.—**sycophancy** *n.*—**sycophantic** *adj.*

syllabi /'sɪləbaɪ/ *see* **syllabus**.

syllabic /sɪ'læbɪk/ *adj* consisting of syllables; articulated in syllables.

syllable /'sɪləbəl/ *n* word or part of a word uttered in a single sound; one or more letters written to represent a spoken syllable.

syllabub, sillabub /'sɪləbʌb/ *n* a cold dessert made with sweetened whipped cream flavoured with sherry, wine, lemon juice, etc.

syllabus /'sɪləbəs/ *n* (*pl* **syllabuses, syllabi**) a summary or outline of a course of study or of examination requirements; the subjects studied for a particular course.

syllogism /'sɪlɒdʒɪzəm/ *n* a form of reasoning consisting of a major premise, a minor premise and a conclusion, *eg All men must die; I am a man; therefore I must die.*

sylph /sɪlf/ *n* a slim girl or woman.

symbiosis /ˌsɪmbaɪ'oːsɪs/ *n* a mutually advantageous partnership between two interdependent plant or animal species.—**symbiotic** *adj.*

symbol /'sɪmbəl/ *n* a representation; an object used to represent something abstract; an arbitrary or conventional sign standing for a quality, process, relation, etc as in music, chemistry, mathematics, etc.

symbolic /sɪm'bɒlɪk/, **symbolical** /-əl/ *adj* of, using, or constituting a symbol.—**symbolically** *adv.*

symbolism /-'bɒlɪzəm/ *n* the use of symbols; a system of symbolic representation.—**symbolist** *n.*

symbolize /'sɪmbəlaɪz/ *vt* to be a symbol; to represent by a symbol.—**symbolization** *n.*—**symbolizer** *n.*

symmetrical /sɪ'metrɪkəl/, **symmetric** /sɪ'metrɪk/ *adj* having symmetry.—**symmetrically** *adv.*

symmetry /'sɪmɪtri/ *n* (*pl* **symmetries**) the corresponding arrangement of one part to another in size, shape and position; balance or harmony of form resulting from this.

sympathetic /ˌsɪmpə'θetɪk/ *adj* having sympathy; compassionate.—**sympathetically** *adv.*

sympathize /'sɪmpəθaɪz/ *vi* feel sympathy for; to commiserate; to be in sympathy (with).—**sympathizer** *n.*—**sympathizingly** *adv.*

sympathy /'sɪmpəθi/ *n* (*pl* **sympathies**) agreement of ideas and opinions; compassion; (*pl*) support for an action or cause.

symphony /'sɪmfəni/ *n* (*pl* **symphonies**) an orchestral composition in several movements; a large orchestra for playing symphonic works.—**symphonic** *adj.*—**symphonically** *adv.*

symposium /sɪm'poːzɪəm/ *n* (*pl* **symposiums, symposia**) a conference at which several specialists deliver short addresses on a topic; an anthology of scholarly essays.

symptom /'sɪmptəm/ *n* a bodily sensation experienced by a patient indicative of a particular disease; an indication.

symptomatic /ˌsɪmptə'mætɪk/ *adj* of, being, or relating to symptoms; indicative.—**symptomatically** *adv.*

syn- /sɪn/ *prefix* together.

synagogue /'sɪnəɡɒɡ/ *n* the building where Jews assemble for worship and religious study.

synapse /'sɪnæps/ *or* /-'næps/, /'saɪn-/ *n* the point at which a nerve impulse is transmitted between neurons.

sync, synch /sɪnk/ *n* (*inf*) synchronization. • *vti* (*inf*) to synchronize.

synchromesh /'sɪnkroːˌmeʃ/ *adj* (*gear system*) incorporating a device that regulates the revolving parts in a gear so that they are at the same speed when brought into contact. • *n* a gear system using this.

synchronize /'sɪnkrənaɪz/ *vti* to occur at the same time and speed; (*watches*) to adjust to show the same time.—**synchronization** *n.*—**synchronizer** *n.*

synchronous /'sɪnkrənəs/ *adj* occurring at the same time.—**synchronously** *adv.*—**synchronousness** *n.*

syncopate /'sɪnkəpeɪt/ *vt* (*mus*) to modify beats (in a musical piece) by displacing the rhythmical accents from strong beats to weak ones and vice versa.—**syncopation** *n.*

syndicate /'sɪndɪkət/ *n* an association of individuals or corporations formed for a project requiring much capital; any group, as of criminals, organized for some undertaking; an organization selling articles or features to many newspapers, etc. • *vt* to manage as or form into a syndicate; to sell (an article, etc) through a syndicate. • *vi* to form a syndicate.—**syndication** *n.*

syndrome /'sɪndroːm/ *or* /-drəm/ *n* a characteristic pattern of signs and symptoms of a disease.

synergist /'sɪnərdʒɪst/ *n* a muscle that works in conjunction with another muscle; a drug that combines with another drug, the two having a greater effect when taken together than separately.—**synergism** *n.*—**synergistic** *adj.*

synergy /'sɪnərdʒi/ *n* synergism; in business, the possibility that the merger of two individual companies will produce a combined operation of greater productivity and efficiency.—**synergetic, synergistic** *adj.*

synesis /'sɪnəsɪs/ *n* (*gram*) a construction in harmony with its sense rather than with strict syntax, *eg* "a large number were present."

synod /'sɪnəd/ *n* a council of members of a church that meets to discuss religious issues.

synonym /'sɪnənɪm/ *n* a word that has the same, or similar, meaning as another or others in the same language.

synonymous /sɪ'nɒnɪməs/ *adj* having the same meaning; equivalent.—**synonymously** *adv.*

synonymy /sɪ'nɒnɪmi/ *n* (*pl* **synonymies**) the condition of being synonymous; a system or collection of synonyms; the use of synonyms for emphasis, *eg* "in any shape or form".

synopsis /sɪ'nɒpsɪs/ *n* (*pl* **synopses**) a summary or brief review of a subject.

synovia /saɪ'noːvɪə/ *or* /sɪn-/ *n* a thick fluid that lubricates the joints and tendons.—**synovial** *adj.*

synovitis /ˌsaɪnə'vaɪtɪs/ *n* inflammation of the membrane around a joint.

syntax /'sɪntæks/ *n* (*gram*) the arrangement of words in the sentences and phrases of language; the rules governing this.—**syntactic** *adj.*—**syntactically** *adv.*

synth /sɪnθ/ *n* short for synthesizer.

synthesis /'sɪnθəsɪs/ *n* (*pl* **syntheses**) the process of combining separate elements of thought into a whole; the production of a compound by a chemical reaction.

synthesize /'sɪnθə‚saɪz/ *vti* to combine into a whole.

synthesizer /-ər/ *n* an electronic device producing music and sounds by using a computer to combine individual sounds previously recorded.

synthetic /sɪn'θɛtɪk/ *adj* produced by chemical synthesis; artificial.—**synthetically** *adv*.

syphilis /'sɪfɪlɪs/ *n* a venereal disease caused by infection with a microorganism and characterized by an ulcerating chancre, *usu* on the genitals, and over time producing serious clinical manifestations.—**syphilitic** *adj*.

syphon /'saɪfən/ *see* **siphon**.

Syrian /'sɪrɪən/ *n* a native or inhabitant of Syria; the Arabic dialect spoken there.—*also adj*.

syringe /sɪ'rɪndʒ/ or /'sɪr-/ *n* a hollow tube with a plunger at one end and a sharp needle at the other by which liquids are injected or withdrawn, *esp* in medicine. • *vt* to inject or cleanse with a syringe.

syrinx /'sɪrɪŋks/ *n* (*pl* **syringes**) the vocal organ in birds.

syrup /'sɪrəp/ *n* a thick sweet substance made by boiling sugar with water; the concentrated juice of a fruit or plant.—**syrupy** *adj*.

systaltic /sɪ'stæltɪk/ or /-'stɒl-/ *adj* (*heart, etc*) alternately expanding and contracting; pulsating.

system /'sɪstəm/ *n* a method of working or organizing by following a set of rules; routine; organization; structure; a political regime; an arrangement of parts fitting together.

systematic /‚sɪstə'mætɪk/ *adj* constituting or based on a system; according to a system.—**systematically** *adv*.

systematize /‚sɪstəmə'taɪz/ *vt* to arrange according to a system.—**systematization** *n*.—**systematizer** *n*.

systemic /sɪ'stɛmɪk/ *adj* (*poison, infection, etc*) of or affecting the entire body; (*insecticide, etc*) designed to be taken up into the plant tissues.—**systemically** *adv*.

systemize /‚sɪstə'maɪz/ *vt* to systematize.—**systemization** *n*.

systems analysis *n* analysis of a particular task or operation to determine how computer hardware and software may best perform it.—**systems analyst** *n*.

systole /'sɪstəli/ *n* the regular contractions of the chambers of the heart by which the circulation of blood is maintained.—**systolic** *adj*.

T

T (*chem symbol*) tritium.

T, t /ti:/ *n* the 20th letter of the English alphabet; something shaped like a T.

t *abbr* = ton.

Ta (*chem symbol*) tantalum.

tab[1] /tæb/ *n* tabulator; tablet. • *vt* (**tabbing, tabbed**) to tabulate.

tab[2] *n* a small tag, label or flap; (*inf*) a bill, as for expenses. • *vt* (**tabbing, tabbed**) to fix a tab on.

tabard /'tæbərd/ *n* a short armless tunic, *esp* one bearing a coat of arms and worn by a herald or by a knight over his armour; a sleeveless garment shaped like this worn by women.

Tabasco /tə'bæsko:/ *n* (*trademark*) a very hot red pepper sauce.

tabbouleh /tə'bu:lei/ *n* an Arabic salad made with vegetables, spices, lemon juice and cracked wheat.

tabby /'tæbi/ *n* (*pl* **tabbies**) a domestic cat with a striped coat, *esp* a female; a heavy watered silk. • *adj* striped in brown or grey. • *vt* (**tabbying, tabbied**) to pattern (silk) with a wavy pattern.

tabernacle /'tæbər,nækəl/ *n* (*Bible*) the portable tent carried by Jews through the desert containing their sacred writings; a place of worship.—**tabernacular** *adj*.

tabes /'teibi:z/ *n* (*pl* **tabes**) wasting caused by chronic disease.—**tabetic** *adj, n*.

tabes dorsalis /-'dɔrsəlis/ *n* paralysis caused by syphilis at an advanced stage when it attacks the spinal cord.

tablature /'tæblətʃər/ *n* musical notation indicating the strings, frets, fingering, rhythm, etc, to be used, *esp* for the lute.

table /'teibəl/ *n* a piece of furniture consisting of a slab or board on legs; the people seated round a table; supply of food; a flat surface; a level area; a slab or tablet in a wall; an inscription on this; a list of facts and figures arranged in columns for reference or comparison; a folding leaf of a backgammon board; **at table** having a meal; **on the table** (*legislative bill, etc*) postponed, often indefinitely; **to turn the tables on** to put (an opponent) in a position of disadvantage previously held by oneself. • *vt* to submit, to put forward; to postpone indefinitely; to lay on a table. • *adj* of, on or at a table.

tableau /'tæblo:/ *n* (*pl* **tableaux, tableaus**) a dramatic or graphic representation of a group or scene; a tableau vivant.

tableau vivant /,tæblə'vi:vã/ *n* (*pl* **tableaux vivants**) a representation of an historical scene by people in costume posed silently and motionless.

tablecloth /'teibəl,klɒθ/ *n* a cloth for covering a table.

table d'hôte /,tæblə'do:t/ *n* (*pl* **tables d'hôte**) a meal at a fixed price for a set number of courses.—*also adj*.

tableland /'teibəl,lænd/ *n* an expanse of flat elevated land, a plateau.

tablespoon /'teibəl,spu:n/ *n* a large serving spoon; a unit of measure in cooking.

tablespoonful /-ful/ *n* (**tablespoonfuls**) the amount a tablespoon holds.

tablet /'tæblət/ *n* a pad of paper; a medicinal pill; a cake of solid substance, such as soap; a slab of stone.

table tennis *n* a game like tennis played on a table with small bats and a ball.

tableware /'teibəl,wer/ *n* dishes, cutlery, etc for use at mealtimes.

tabloid /'tæblɔid/ *n* a small-format newspaper characterized by emphasis on photographs and news in condensed form.

taboo, tabu /tə'bu:/ or /tæ-/ *n* (*pl* **taboos, tabus**) a religious or social prohibition of the use or practice of something; the thing prohibited. • *adj* forbidden from use, mention, etc. • *vt* (**tabooing, tabooed** *or* **tabuing, tabued**) to forbid by social or personal influence the use, practice or mention of something or contact with someone.

tabor, tabour /'teibər/ *n* a small drum formerly used to accompany a pipe, both instruments being played by the same person.

tabular /'tæbjulər/ *adj* like a table, flat; arranged in the form of a table; calculated with a table.—**tabularly** *adv*.

tabula rasa /,tæbjulə'ræzə/ *n* (*pl* **tabulae rasae**) the mind when regarded as in its original state and clear of impressions; a fresh start.

tabulate /'tæbju,leit/ *vt* to arrange (written material) in tabular form.—**tabulation** *n*.

tabulator /-ər/ *n* a device that sets stops to locate columns on a typewriter or word processor.

tacamahac /'tækmə,hæk/ *n* (any tree yielding) any of various pungent gum resins used *esp* in incense.

tacet /'tæsət/ or /'tei-/ *vi* a direction on a musical score indicating that from this point a particular instrument is not to play.

tachism /'tæʃizəm/ *n* a form of action painting using random blobs of colour.

tachistoscope /tə'kistə,sko:p/ *n* a device for projecting visual information onto a screen for a split second only, used in the study of perception and learning.

tacho- /'tæko:/ *prefix* speed.

tachograph /'tækə,græf/ *n* a device in motor vehicles, *esp* lorries, to record speed and time of travel.

tachometer /tə'kɒmətər/ *n* an instrument for measuring the speed of rotation of a shaft, as in a vehicle engine.

tachy- /'tæki/ *prefix* rapid or accelerated.

tachycardia /,tæki'kardiə/ *n* an abnormally fast heartbeat, *esp* over 100 beats per minute.

tachygraphy /tə'kigrəfi/ *n* shorthand, *esp* as used in ancient Greece and Rome.

tachymeter /tə'kimətər/ *n* a surveying instrument for measuring long distances rapidly.

tachyon /'tækiɒn/ *n* (*physics*) a theoretical elementary particle that can travel faster than light.

tacit /'tæsit/ *adj* implied without really being spoken; understood.—**tacitly** *adv*.—**tacitness** *n*.

taciturn /'tæsi,tərn/ *adj* habitually silent and reserved.—**taciturnity** *n*.

tack[1] /tæk/ *n* a short, sharp-pointed nail with a flat head; a long loose temporary stitch in dressmaking, etc; the course of a sailing ship; a course of action, approach; stickiness, adhesiveness. • *vt* to fasten with tacks. • *vi* to change direction.

tack[2] *n* (*inf*) food.

tack[3] *n* riding equipment for horses.

tackle /'tækəl/ *n* a system of ropes and pulleys for lifting; equipment; rigging; (*sport*) an act of grabbing and stopping an opponent. • *vt* (*task, etc*) to attend to, undertake; (*a person*) to confront; (*sport*) to challenge with a tackle.

tacky[1] /'tæki/ *adj* (**tackier, tackiest**) (*paint, etc*) sticky.

tacky[2] *adj* (**tackier, tackiest**) (*inf*) shabby; ostentatious and vulgar; seedy.—**tackiness** *n*.

tact /tækt/ *n* discretion in managing the feelings of others.—**tactful** *adj*.—**tactless** *adj*.

tactical voting *n* the strategy in elections of voting for the candidate most likely to defeat the favourite, rather than voting for one's preferred choice.

tactics /'tæktiks/ *n sing* stratagem; ploy; the science or art of manoeuvring troops in the presence of the enemy.—**tactical** *adj*.—**tactician** *n*.

tactile /'tæktail/ *adj* relating to, or having a sense of touch.

tad /tæd/ *n* (*inf*) a small boy; (*inf*) a tiny quantity; a bit.

tadpole /'tædpo:l/ *n* the larva of a frog or toad, *esp* at the stage when the head and tail have developed.

taeniasis /'ti:nai,əsis/ *n* infestation with tapeworms.—*also* **teniasis**.

taffeta /'tæfətə/ *n* a thin glossy fabric with a silky lustre.

taffrail /'tæfreil/ *n* the rail at the stern of a ship.

tag[1] /tæg/ *n* a strip or label for identification. • *vt* to attach a tag; to mark with a tag. • *vi* (*with* **onto, after, along**) to trail along (behind).

tag[2] *n* a children's chasing game; (*baseball*) the putting out of a runner by touching him with the ball. • *vt* (**tagging, tagged**) to touch another player in a game of tag; (*baseball*) to put a runner out by touching him with the ball.

tag end *n* the final part of something.

tagliatelle /ˌtæljəˈtɛli/ *n* pasta in narrow ribbons.

tahini /təˈhiːni/ *n* a thick paste of ground sesame seeds.

tahr /tɑr/ *n* a type of Himalayan wild goat.

Tahitian /təˈhiːʃən/ or /-tiən/ *adj* of or pertaining to the South Pacific island of Tahiti, its people or language. • *n* a native of Tahiti; the Polynesian language spoken in Tahiti.

t'ai chi ch'uan /taɪˈtʃiːˌtʃwɒn/ *n* a Chinese form of exercise using movements designed to improve balance and coordination.—*also* **t'ai chi**.

taiga /ˈtaɪɡə/ *n* coniferous forests dominated by spruces and firs extending across the subarctic regions of Eurasia and North America.

tail /teɪl/ *n* the appendage of an animal growing from the rear, generally hanging loose; the rear part of anything; (*pl*) the side of a coin without a head on it; (*inf*) a person who keeps another under surveillance, *esp* a detective. • *vti* to follow closely, to shadow; (*with* **off, away**) to (cause to) dwindle.

tailback /ˈteɪlbæk/ *n* a long queue of traffic behind an obstruction.

tailboard /ˈteɪlbɔrd/ *n* a hinged or removable section at the rear of a motor vehicle.

tail coat *n* a man's black or grey coat cut horizontally just below the waist at the front with two long tails at the back and worn as part of full evening dress.

tail-end *adj* tardy; being the last in line. • *n* the last.

tailgate /ˈteɪlɡeɪt/ *n* the hinged board at the rear of a truck which can be let down or removed. • *vti* to drive dangerously close behind (another vehicle).—**tailgater** *n*.

taillight /ˈteɪllaɪt/ *n* a red warning light at the rear of a motor vehicle.

tailor /ˈteɪlər/ *n* a person who makes and repairs outer garments, *esp.* men's suits. • *vi* to work as a tailor. • *vt* to adapt to fit a particular requirement.

tailor-made *adj* specially designed for a particular purpose or person.

tailpipe /ˈteɪlpaɪp/ *n* a pipe at the rear of jet engine or motor vehicle for discharging exhaust gases.

tailplane /ˈteɪlpleɪn/ *n* a small stabilizing wing at the rear of an aircraft, a horizontal stabilizer.

tail rotor *n* the small propeller at the rear of a helicopter that counteracts the tendency of the body to spin in the opposite direction to the main rotor blades.

tailspin /ˈteɪlspɪn/ *n* a spiralling nose dive; (*inf*) a state of confusion or panic.

tailstock /ˈteɪlstɒk/ *n* the adjustable part of a lathe that supports the free end of a workpiece.

tailwind /ˈteɪlwɪnd/ *n* a wind in the same direction as a ship or aircraft is travelling.

taint /teɪnt/ *vt* to contaminate; to infect. • *vi* to be corrupted or disgraced. • *n* a stain; corruption.

taipan[1] /ˈtaɪpæn/ *n* the foreign head of a business in China.

taipan[2] *n* a venomous Australian snake.

take /teɪk/ *vb* (**taking, took**, *pp* **taken**) *vt* to lay hold of; to grasp or seize; to gain, win; to choose, select; (*attitude, pose*) to adopt; to understand; to consume; to accept or agree to; to lead or carry with one; to use as a means of travel; (*math*) to subtract (from); to use; to steal; (*gram*) to be used with; to endure calmly; (*with* **apart**) to dismantle; to criticize; (*with* **back**) to retract, withdraw (a promise, etc); (*with* **down**) to write down; to dismantle; to humiliate; (*with* **for**) (*inf*) to mistakenly believe to be; (*with* **in**) to understand, perceive; to include; to make a garment smaller by altering seams, etc; to offer accommodation to; (*inf*) to swindle, deceive; (*with* **on**) to employ as labour; to assume or acquire; to agree to do (something); to fight against; (*with* **out**) to extract; to obtain, procure; to escort; (*sl*) to kill; (*with* **up**) to begin as a business or hobby; to accept an offer or invitation; to occupy (time or space); to act as a patron to; to shorten (a garment); to interrupt or criticize; to absorb. • *vi* (*plant, etc*) to start growing successfully; to become effective; to catch on; to have recourse to; to go to; (*with* **after**) to resemble in appearance, character, etc; (*with* **on**) (*inf*) to become upset or distraught; (*with* **to**) to escape to as a refuge; to acquire a liking for; to adopt as a habit; (*with* **up**) to

resume, continue further. • *n* (*film, TV*) the amount of film used without stopping the camera when shooting.

takeaway /ˈteɪkəˌweɪ/ *n* a takeout.

take-home pay *n* pay remaining after all deductions, such as income tax, have been made.

taken /ˈteɪkən/ *see* **take**.

takeoff /ˈteɪkɒf/ *n* the process of an aircraft becoming airborne; (*inf*) an amusing impression or caricature of another person.

takeout, take-out /ˈteɪkaʊt/ *n* a cooked meal that is sold for consumption outside the premises; a shop or restaurant that provides such meals.—*also adj.*

takeover /ˈteɪkoːvər/ *n* the taking over of control, as in business.—*also adj.*

taking /ˈteɪkɪŋ/ *adj* attractive, charming; (*inf*) catching, contagious. • *n* the act of one that takes; (*pl*) earnings; profits.

talc /tælk/ *n* a type of smooth mineral used in ceramics and talcum powder; short for talcum powder.

talcum powder /ˈtælkəm/ *n* perfumed powdered talc for the skin.

tale /teɪl/ *n* a narrative or story; a fictitious account, a lie; idle or malicious gossip.

talent /ˈtælənt/ *n* any innate or special aptitude.—**talented** *adj*.

talent scout *n* a person employed to recruit talented people for professional careers in sport, entertainment, etc.

talent show *n* a show which gives amateurs a chance to perform in the hope of attracting interest from professionals for permanent engagements.

talipot /ˈtælɪˌpɒt/ *n* a palm tree of the East Indies with large leaves used for roofing, umbrellas, etc.

talisman /ˈtælɪzmən/ or /ˈtælɪs-/ *n* (*pl* **talismans**) an object or charm supposed to ward off evil and bring good luck; an amulet.

talk /tɒk/ *vt* to speak; to know how to speak (a language); to discuss or speak of (something); to influence by talking; (*with* **down**) to silence or override (a speaker, argument, etc) by talking loudly; to radio instructions to (an aircraft) so that it may land safely; (*with* **into**) to persuade by argument or talking; (*with* **out**) to resolve by discussion; (*with* **round**) to persuade by talking. • *vi* to converse; to discuss; to gossip; to divulge information; (*with* **back**) to reply impudently; (*with* **down**) to speak in a condescending manner (to); (*with* **round**) to discuss (a subject) without reaching any conclusion; (*with* **shop**) to discuss work, *esp* after working hours. • *n* a discussion; a lecture; gossip; (*pl*) negotiations.

talkative /ˈtɒkətɪv/ *adj* given to talking a great deal.

talkie /ˈtɒki/ *n* (*inf*) an early motion-picture film with sound.

Talking Book *n* (*trademark*) a recording of a book for the blind.

talking head *n* the head and shoulders of a person on television talking directly to the camera without using visual material.

talking picture *n* a talkie.

talking point *n* a subject for conversation or discussion; something that lends support to an argument.

talking-to *n* a reprimand, lecture.

talk show *n* a television or radio programme with informal interviews and conversation, a chat show.

tall /tɒl/ *adj* above average in height; (*inf*) (*story*) exaggerated.—**tallness** *n*.

tallboy /ˈtɒlbɔɪ/ *n* a high chest of drawers on legs, a highboy.

tallith /ˈtælɪθ/ *n* (*pl* **tallithim**) a fringed shawl worn by Jewish men during religious services.

tall order *n* (*inf*) a request that is difficult to fulfil.

tallow /ˈtæloː/ *n* solid animal fat used to make soap, candles, etc.

tall ship *n* a square-rigged sailing vessel.

tall story *n* (*inf*) an exaggerated or unbelievable account.

tally /ˈtæli/ *n* (*pl* **tallies**) reckoning, account; one score in a game. • *vi* (**tallying, tallied**) to correspond; to keep score.

tally-ho *n* the cry of a person at a fox hunt when sighting the quarry.—*also vti.*

Talmud /ˈtælmʊd/ or /-məd/ *n* the body of Jewish law.—**Talmudic** *adj*.

talon /ˈtælən/ *n* a claw of an animal, *esp* a bird of prey.

talus[1] /ˈteɪləs/ *n* (*pl* **tali**) the anklebone.

talus[2] *n* (*pl* **taluses**) scree; the sloping side of a wall.

tamale /təˈmɒli/ or /-ˈmæli/ *n* a Mexican dish of minced meat with crushed maize and seasonings.

tamandua /təˈmændjuːə/ *n* a small tree-dwelling anteater of Central and South America.

tamarack /'tæmə,ræk/ *n* (the wood of) any of various North American larches.

tamarin /'tæmərɪn/ *n* any of numerous small monkeys of South America resembling marmosets.

tamarind /'tæmərɪnd/ *n* a tropical evergreen tree bearing a pulpy fruit used for food, in beverages and in laxative preparations.

tamarisk /'tæmərɪsk/ *n* any of a genus of evergreen trees and shrubs of Mediterranean and tropical regions with tiny leaves and numerous clusters of pink or white flowers.

tambour /'tæmbʊr/ *n* a drum; (an embroidery produced on) a circular frame for holding fabric taut during embroidery; a rolling top on a desk or cabinet made from thin strips of wood on a canvas backing. • *vt* to embroider using a tambour.

tamboura, tambura /tæm'bʊrə/ *n* an Indian stringed instrument used to provide a drone as accompaniment to singing.

tambourin /ˌtæmbə'riːn/ *n* a dance of Provence in France; the music for this; a long drum used in Provence.

tambourine *n* a percussion hand instrument made of skin stretched over a circular frame with small jingling metal discs around the edge.

tambura *see* **tamboura**.

tame /teɪm/ *adj* (*animal*) not wild, domesticated; compliant; dull, uninteresting. • *vt* (*animal*) to domesticate; to subdue; to soften.

Tamil /'tæmɪl/ *n* a member of a people inhabiting southeastern India and Sri Lanka; the language they speak.—*also adj*.

tam-o'-shanter /'tæmə,ʃæntər/ *n* a tight-fitting Scottish woollen or cloth beret with a full crown and a pompom on top.

tamp /tæmp/ *vt* to pack down firmly with a series of blows; to pack (a blast-hole) with sand or earth above the explosive charge.

tamper /'tæmpər/ *vi* to meddle (with); to interfere (with).

tampion /'tæmpɪən/ *n* a plug for the muzzle of a gun.

tampon /'tæmpɒn/ *n* a firm plug of cotton wool inserted in the vagina during menstruation.

tam-tam /'tæmtæm/ *n* a gong.

tan[1] /tæn/ *n* a yellowish-brown colour; suntan. • *vti* (**tanning, tanned**) to acquire a suntan through sunbathing; (*skin, hide*) to convert into leather using tannin; (*inf*) to thrash.

tan[2] *abbr* = tangent.

tanager /'tænədʒər/ *n* any of numerous American woodland songbirds, the male of which has vividly coloured plumage.

tanbark /'tænbɑrk/ *n* bark, *esp* from the oak, used as a source of tannin.

tandem /'tændəm/ *n* a bicycle for two riders, sitting one behind the other.

tandoori /tæn'dʊri/ *n* an Indian method of cooking meat, vegetables and bread using a large clay oven.

tang /tæŋ/ *n* sharp smell or a strong taste.—**tangy** *adj*.

tangent /'tændʒənt/ *n* a line that touches a curve or circle at one point, without crossing it. • *adj* touching at one point.

tangential /tæn'dʒənʃəl/ *adj* of superficial relevance; digressive.

tangerine /tændʒə'riːn/ *n* a small, sweet orange with a loose skin; the colour of this.—*also adj*.

tangible /'tændʒɪbəl/ *adj* capable of being felt, seen or noticed; substantial; real.—**tangibility** *n*.

tangle /'tæŋgəl/ *n* a mass of hair, string or wire knotted together confusedly; a complication. • *vt* to intertwine in a mass, to snarl; to entangle, complicate. • *vi* to become tangled or complicated; (*with* **with**) to become involved in argument with.

tango /'tæŋgoː/ *n* (*pl* **tangos**) a Latin American ballroom dance. • *vi* (**tangoing, tangoed**) to dance the tango.

tangram /'tæŋgræm/ *n* a Chinese puzzle made from a square cut into a rhomboid, a square and five triangles, which can be combined to produce different figures.

tank /tæŋk/ *n* a large container for storing liquids or gases; an armoured combat vehicle, mounted with guns and having caterpillar tracks.

tanka /'tæŋkə/ *n* (*pl* **tankas, tanka**) a Japanese verse form with five lines.

tankage /'tæŋkɪdʒ/ *n* the capacity of a tank; the storing of oil, etc in tanks.

tankard /'tæŋkərd/ *n* a tall, one-handled drinking mug, often with a hinged lid.

tanked /'tæŋkt/ *adj* (*sl*) extremely drunk.

tank engine *n* a steam locomotive that carries its own water supplies instead of using a tender.

tanker /'tæŋkər/ *n* a large ship or truck for transporting oil and other liquids.

tank top *n* a sleeveless pullover with a low neck.

tanner /'tænər/ *n* a person who tans skins.

tannery /-i/ *n* (*pl* **tanneries**) a place where hides are tanned.

tannic /'tænɪk/ *adj* of, resembling, or derived from tan or tannin.

tannic acid *n* tannin.

tannin /'tænɪn/ *n* a yellow or brown chemical found in plants or tea, used in tanning.

tansy /'tænzi/ *n* (*pl* **tansies**) any of numerous aromatic plants with yellow flowers and finely-divided leaves, once used for seasoning and as a medicine.

tantalize /'tæntə,laɪz/ *vt* to tease or torment by presenting something greatly desired, but keeping it inaccessible.

tantalum /'tæntələm/ *n* a hard metallic element of the vanadium family, *esp* used for hardening alloys.

tantalus /'tæntələs/ *n* a cabinet or case where bottles of spirit may be locked up yet remain visible.

tantamount /'tæntə,maʊnt/ *adj* equivalent (to) in effect; as good as.

tantara /'tæntərə/ *n* the sound of a horn or trumpet playing a fanfare.

tantrum /'tæntrəm/ *n* a childish fit of bad temper.

Tao /tau/ or /dau/ *n* (*Taoism*) the spirit of creative harmony in the universe; the path of virtuous conduct in harmony with the natural order.

Taoiseach /'tiːʃəx/ *n* the Prime Minister of the Republic of Ireland.

Taoism /'tauɪzəm/ or /'dau-/ *n* a Chinese religious and philosophical system advocating a simple passive life in harmony with the natural order.

tap[1] /tæp/ *n* a quick, light blow or touch; a piece of metal attached to the heel or toe of a shoe for reinforcement or to tap-dance. • *vti* (**tapping, tapped**) to strike lightly; to make a tapping sound.

tap[2] *n* a device controlling the flow of liquid through a pipe or from a container, a faucet. • *vt* (**tapping, tapped**) to pierce in order to draw fluid from; to connect a secret listening device to a telephone; (*inf*) to ask for money from; (*resources, etc*) to draw on.

tap-dance *vi* to perform a step dance in shoes with taps.—**tap-dancer** *n*.—**tap-dancing** *n*.

tape /teɪp/ *n* a strong, narrow strip of cloth, paper, etc, used for tying, binding, etc; tape measure; magnetic tape, as in a cassette or videotape. • *vt* to wrap with tape; to record on magnetic tape.

tape deck *n* a tape recorder in a hi-fi system.

tape measure *n* a tape marked in inches or centimetres for measuring.

tape player *n* a self-contained tape recorder.

tape recorder *n* a machine used for recording and reproducing sounds or music on magnetic tape, *esp* as part of a hi-fi system, a tape deck.

tape recording *n* a recording made on magnetic tape.

taper /'teɪpər/ *n* a long thin candle. • *vti* to make or become gradually narrower toward one end.—**tapering** *adj*.

tapestry /'tæpəstri/ *n* (*pl* **tapestries**) a heavy fabric woven with patterns or figures, used for wall hangings and furnishings.

tapeworm /'teɪpwɜrm/ *n* a tape-like, parasitic, intestinal worm.

tapioca /ˌtæpi'oːkə/ *n* a glutinous starch extracted from the root of the cassava and used in puddings, etc.

tapir /'teɪpər/ *n* or /-piːr/ *n* (*pl* **tapirs, tapir**) a South American hoofed mammal with a short flexible proboscis.

tappet /'tæpət/ *n* a projecting arm or lever (*eg* a cam) that moves or is moved by another part in a machine.

taproom /'tæpruːm/ *n* a bar.

taps /tæps/ *n sing* in the US, a call on a bugle at a military camp signalling lights out; any similar signal, as at a military funeral.

tar[1] /tɑr/ *n* a thick, dark, viscous substance obtained from wood, coal, peat, etc., used for surfacing roads. • *vt* to coat with tar.—**tarry** *adj*.

tar[2] *n* a (*inf*) a sailor.

taramasalata /ˌtærəməsə'lætə/ *n* a pale pink fish-roe paste served as a starter.

tarantella /ˌtærən'telə/ *n* (the music for) a lively peasant dance of southern Italy.

tarantula /tə'ræntʃulə/ *n* (*pl* **tarantulas, tarantulae**) a large, hairy spider with a poisonous bite that is painful but not deadly.

tarboosh, tarbush /tɑr'buːʃ/ *n* a brimless red cap resembling a fez worn by Muslim men.

tardy /'tɑrdi/ *adj* (**tardier, tardiest**) slow; later than expected.—**tardily** *adv*.—**tardiness** *n*.

tare[1] /ter/ *n* (the seed of) a type of vetch plant.

tare[2] *n* (an allowance for) the weight of the wrapping or container in which goods are packed; the weight of an unloaded goods vehicle. • *vt* to weigh in order to calculate the tare.

target /'tɑrgət/ *n* a mark to aim at, *esp* in shooting; an objective or ambition.

tariff /'tɛrɪf/ or /'tærɪf/ *n* a tax on imports or exports; (*in a hotel*) a list of prices; the rate of charge for public services, such as gas or electricity.

tarlatan, tarletan /'tɑrlətən/ *n* a type of thin stiff cotton fabric.

tarmac /'tɑrmæk/, **tarmacadam** /,tɑrmə'kædəm/ *n* a material for surfacing roads made from crushed stones and tar; an airport runway. • *vti* (**tarmacking, tarmacked**) to lay down a tarmac surface.

tarn /tɑrn/ *n* a small mountain lake.

tarnish /'tɑrnɪʃ/ *vi* (*metal*) to lose its lustre or discolour due to exposure to the air. • *vt* (*reputation*) to taint.—*also n*.

taro /'tɑro/ *n* (*pl* **taros**) (the edible root of) a tropical Asian plant.

tarot /'tæro/ *n* a game played with 22 pictorial cards, which are also used for fortune-telling.

tarpaulin /tɑr'pɔlən/ *n* canvas cloth coated with a waterproof substance.

tarragon /'tɛrə,gɒn/ *n* an aromatic herb used for flavouring.

tarry /'tɛri/ *vi* (**tarrying, tarried**) to delay or dawdle; to linger; to wait briefly.

tarsus /'tɑrsəs/ *n* (*pl* **tarsi**) the small bones of the ankle and the heel in vertebrates; the plate of tissue that stiffens the eyelid.— **tarsal** *adj, n*.

tart[1] /tɑrt/ *adj* having a sour, sharp taste; (*speech*) sharp, severe. —**tartly** *adv*.—**tartness** *n*.

tart[2] *n* an open pastry case containing fruit, jam or custard; (*inf*) a prostitute. • *vt* (*with* **up**) (*inf*) to dress cheaply and gaudily; to decorate, *esp* cheaply.

tartan /'tɑrtən/ *n* a woollen cloth with a chequered pattern, having a distinctive design for each Scottish clan.

tartar /'tɑrtər/ *n* a hard, yellow, crusty deposit which forms on the teeth; a salty deposit on the sides of wine casks.

tartaric acid *n* an organic acid obtained from grapes and many other fruits.

tartar sauce *n* a mayonnaise sauce with chopped capers, herbs, etc, eaten *esp* with fish.

task /tæsk/ *n* a specific amount of work to be done; a chore.

task force *n* a small unit with a specific mission, *usu* military.

taskmaster /'tæsk,mæstər/ *n* a person who demands constant hard work.

Tasmanian devil *n* a burrowing flesh-eating marsupial of Tasmania with a black coat and long tail.

tassel /'tɛsəl/ *n* an ornamental tuft of silken threads decorating soft furnishings, clothes, etc; a growth that looks like this, *esp* on corn. • *vb* (**tasselling, tasselled** *or* **tasseling, tasseled**) *vt* to decorate with tassels. • *vi* (*plant*) to grow tassels.

taste /teɪst/ *vt* to perceive (a flavour) by taking into the mouth; to try by eating and drinking a little; to sample; to experience. • *vi* to try by the mouth; to have a specific flavour. • *n* the sense by which flavours are perceived; a small portion; the ability to recognize what is beautiful, attractive, etc; liking; a brief experience.

taste bud *n* any of the small projecting sensory organs on the tongue's surface by which taste is perceived.

tasteful /'teɪstfʊl/ *adj* showing good taste.—**tastefully** *adv*.— **tastefulness** *n*.

tasteless /'teɪstləs/ *adj* without taste, bland; in bad taste.—**tastelessly** *adv*.

taster /'teɪstər/ *n* a person skilled in determining the balance of flavours in a product, *esp* tea, wine; a device for tasting or sampling; (*formerly*) a person who tasted food before it was served to a king, etc.

tasty /'teɪsti/ *adj* (**tastier, tastiest**) savoury; having a pleasant flavour.

ta-ta /tæ'tɑ/ *interj* (*inf*) goodbye.

tatami /tə'tɒmi/ *n* (*pl* **tatamis, tatami**) straw matting used as a floor covering, *esp* in Japan.

tatter /'tætər/ *n* a torn or ragged piece of cloth.—**tattered** *adj*.

tatterdemalion /,tætərdɪ'mæljən/ or /-meɪl-/ *n* a person wearing ragged clothes, a ragamuffin.—*also adj*.

tatting /'tætɪŋ/ *n* (the process of making) a type of delicate handmade lace.

tattle /'tætəl/ *vi* to gossip. • *vt* to reveal (secrets, etc) by gossiping. • *n* (a) gossip.

tattletale /'tætəl,teɪl/ *n* a gossip. • *adj* telltale.

tattoo[1] /tæ'tu:/ *n* (*pl* **tattoos**) a continuous beating of a drum; a military display of exercises and music.

tattoo[2] *vt* (**tattooing, tattooed**) to make permanent patterns or pictures on the skin by pricking and marking with dyes. • *n* (*pl* **tattoos**) marks made on the skin in this way.

tatty /'tæti/ *adj* (**tattier, tattiest**) shabby, ragged.

tau /taʊ/ or /tɒ/ *n* the 19th letter of the Greek alphabet.

taught /tɒt/ *see* **teach**.

taunt /tɒnt/ *vt* to provoke with mockery or contempt; to tease. • *n* an insult.

taupe /toːp/ *n, adj* (a) brownish-grey.

taurine /'tɔriːn/ or /-raɪn/ *n* of or like a bull.

tauromachy /tɔ'rɒməki/ *n* the art or practice of bullfighting.

Taurus /'tɔrəs/ *n* the Bull, the second sign of the zodiac.—**Taurean** *adj*.

taut /tɒt/ *adj* stretched tight; tense; stressed.

tauten /'tɒt'n/ *vti* to make or become taut.

tauto-, taut- /'tɒto:/ *prefix* same.

tautog /tɒ'tɒg/ *n* a large North American food fish related to the wrasse.

tautology /tɒ'tɒlədʒi/ *n* (*pl* **tautologies**) a statement which uses different words to repeat the same thing.—**tautological, tautologous** *adj*.

tavern /'tævərn/ *n* a place licensed to sell alcoholic drinks; an inn.

taverna /tə'vɜrnə/ *n* a Greek hotel with its own bar; a Greek restaurant.

tawdry /'tɒdri/ *adj* (**tawdrier, tawdriest**) showy, cheap, and of poor quality.

tawny /'tɒni/ *adj* yellowish brown.

tawny owl *n* a European owl with brown plumage.

tawse /tɒz/ *n* (*Scot*) a leather strap with a slit end formerly used for punishing schoolchildren.

tax /tæks/ *n* a rate imposed by the government on property or persons to raise revenues; a strain. • *vt* to impose a tax (upon); to strain.

taxa /'tæksə/ *see* **taxon**.

taxable /'tæksəbəl/ *adj* able or liable to be taxed.

taxation /tæk'seɪʃən/ *n* the act of levying taxes; the amount raised as tax.

tax avoidance *n* avoiding paying tax using legal means.

tax-deductible *adj* (*expenses, etc*) legitimately deducted from income before tax assessment.

tax evasion *n* avoiding paying tax using illegal methods.

tax exile *n* a person who lives abroad to avoid paying high taxes.

tax haven *n* a place where taxes are lower than average.

taxi /'tæksi/ *n* (*pl* **taxis**) a car, *usu* fitted with a taximeter, that may be hired to transport passengers. • *vi* (**taxiing** *or* **taxying, taxied**) (*aircraft*) to move along the runway before takeoff or after landing.

taxicab /'tæksikæb/ *n see* **taxi**.

taxidermy /'tæksi,dɜrmi/ *n* the art of preparing and stuffing the skins of animals ready for exhibiting.—**taxidermist** *n*.

taximeter /'tæksi,mi:tər/ *n* a meter fitted into a taxi to record the time taken for a journey.

taxis /'tæksɪs/ *n* a movement in a simple organism (*eg* a bacterium) in response to certain external stimulii; (*surgery*) the restoration of a displaced part by manual pressure.

taxiway /'tæksiweɪ/ *n* a marked route from a terminal to a runway along which an aircraft taxis.

taxon /'tæksən/ *n* (*pl* **taxa**) any taxonomic group or category.

taxonomy /tæk'sɒnəmi/ *n* (the science of) the classification of living things into groups based on similarities of biological origin, design, function, etc.

taxpayer /'tæks,peɪər/ *n* a person who or an organization that pays taxes.

tax return *n* a statement of a person's income for the purposes of tax assessment.

tax shelter *n* a financial arrangement to minimize tax liability.

tax therapist *n* a tax adviser who helps with the completion of income tax forms.

TB *abbr* = tuberculosis.

Tb (*chem symbol*) terbium.

T-bone steak *n* a large sirloin steak containing a T-shaped bone.

tbs., tbsp. *abbr* = tablespoon; tablespoonful.

Tc (*chem symbol*) technetium.

T-cell *n* a lymphocyte that kills cells infected with a virus.—*also* **T-lymphocyte**.

Te (*chem symbol*) tellurium.

tea /tiː/ *n* a shrub growing in China, India, Sri Lanka, etc; its dried, shredded leaves, which are infused in boiling water for a beverage; in UK, a light meal taken in mid-afternoon; a main meal taken in the early evening.

tea bag *n* a small porous bag containing tea leaves for infusing.

tea ball *n* a perforated metal ball which holds tea leaves to make tea.

tea biscuit *n* a semi-sweet, plain biscuit.

tea caddy *n* an airtight container for storing tea.

teach /tiːtʃ/ *vb* (**teaching, taught**) *vt* to impart knowledge to; to give lessons (to); to train; to help to learn. • *vi* to give instruction, *esp* as a profession.—**teachable** *adj*.

tea chest *n* a large wooden box used to transport tea.

teacher /ˈtiːtʃər/ *n* a person who instructs others, *esp* as an occupation.

teach-in *n* an informal conference at a university or college with lectures and discussions on a topical issue.

teaching /ˈtiːtʃɪŋ/ *n* the profession or practice of being a teacher; the act of giving instruction.

tea cloth *n* a tea towel for drying dishes; a dishtowel.

tea cosy *n* a cover for a teapot to keep the contents warm.

teacup /ˈtiːkʌp/ *n* a small cup for drinking tea.

teak /tiːk/ *n* a type of hard wood from an East Indian tree.

teal /tiːl/ *n* (*pl* **teal, teals**) a small freshwater duck; a dark greenish blue.

team /tiːm/ *n* a group of people participating in a sport together; a group of people working together; two or more animals pulling a vehicle. • *vi* (*with* **up**) to join in cooperative activity.

team-mate /ˈtiːmmeɪt/ *n* a colleague, a fellow team member.

team spirit *n* willingness to work harmoniously within a group.

teamster /ˈtiːmstər/ *n* a truck driver.

teamwork /ˈtiːmwərk/ *n* cooperation of individuals for the benefit of the team; the ability of a team to work together.

teapot /ˈtiːpɒt/ *n* a vessel in which tea is made.

teapoy /ˈtiːpɔɪ/ *n* a three-legged stand or table.

tear[1] /tɪər/ *n* a drop of salty liquid appearing in the eyes when crying or when the eyes are smarting; anything tear-shaped.

tear[2] *vb* (**tearing, tore,** *pp* **torn**) *vt* to pull apart by force; to split; to lacerate; (*with* **down**) to destroy, demolish. • *vi* to move with speed; (*with* **into**) (*inf*) to attack physically or verbally. • *n* a hole or split.

tearaway /ˈtɛrəˌweɪ/ *n* an impetuous, violent person.

tearful /ˈtɪərfʊl/ *adj* weeping; sad.—**tearfully** *adv*.

tear gas *n* gas that irritates the eyes and nasal passages, used in riot control.

tearing /ˈtɛrɪŋ/ *adj* overwhelming, violent.

tear-jerker /ˈtɪərˌdʒɜrkər/ *n* a strongly sentimental book, film, play, etc.

tearoom /ˈtiːˌruːm/ **teashop** *n* a restaurant where tea and light refreshments are served.

tea rose *n* any of numerous garden bush roses descended from a Chinese rose and valued for their large tea-scented blooms.

tease /tiːz/ *vt* to separate the fibres of; to torment or irritate; to taunt playfully. • *n* a person who teases or torments; (*inf*) a flirt.—**teaser** *n*.

teasel, teazel, teazle /ˈtiːzəl/ *n* any of various plants with prickly leaves and flower heads formerly dried and used to raise a nap on woollen cloth; an implement used for this purpose.

tea service, tea set *n* the set of cups and saucers, etc for serving tea.

teashop *n* a tearoom.

teaspoon /ˈtiːspuːn/ *n* a small spoon for use with a teacup or as a measure; the amount measured by this.—**teaspoonful** *n*.

teat /tiːt/ *or* /tɪt/ *n* the mouthpiece of a baby's feeding bottle; the nipple on a breast or udder.

tea towel, tea cloth *n* a towel for drying dishes; a dishtowel.

tech. /tɛk/ *abbr* = technical; technology.

technetium /tɛkˈniːʃɪəm/ *or* /-ʃəm/ *n* an artificially produced metallic element whose radioisotope is used in radiotherapy.

technical /ˈtɛknɪkəl/ *adj* relating to, or specializing in practical, industrial, mechanical or applied sciences; (*expression, etc*) belonging to or peculiar to a particular field of activity.—**technically** *adv*.

technicality /ˌtɛknɪˈkælɪti/ *n* (*pl* **technicalities**) a petty formality or technical point.

technical knockout *n* (*boxing*) a decision by a referee to end a fight because a boxer is too badly hurt to continue.

technician /tɛkˈnɪʃən/ *n* a person skilled in the practice of any art, *esp* in practical work with scientific equipment.

Technicolor /ˈtɛknɪˌkʌlər/ *n* (*trademark*) the production of colour film by combining identical scenes with different primary colours into a single print.

technique /tɛkˈniːk/ *n* method of performing a particular task; knack.

techno- /ˈtɛknəʊ/ *prefix* technical; technological.

technocracy /tɛkˈnɒkrəsi/ *n* (*pl* **technocracies**) government by technical experts.—**technocrat** *n*.—**technocratic** *adj*.

technology /tɛkˈnɒlədʒi/ *n* (*pl* **technologies**) the application of mechanical and applied sciences to industrial use.—**technological** *adj*.—**technologist** *n*.

techy /ˈtɛtʃi/ *see* **tetchy**.

tectonic /tɛkˈtɒnɪk/ *adj* of or relating to building or construction; (*geological structures or forces*) resulting from deformation of the earth's crust.

tectonics /tɛkˈtɒnɪks/ *n sing* the art or science of constructing buildings, etc; the study of the forces which shape the earth's geological structure.

teddy /ˈtɛdi/ *n* (*pl* **teddies**) a woman's one-piece undergarment.

teddy bear *n* a stuffed toy bear.

Te Deum /tiːˈdiːəm/ *or* /teɪ ˈdeɪəm/ *n* a Latin hymn used in services of thanksgiving to God.

tedious /ˈtiːdiəs/ *adj* monotonous; boring.—**tediously** *adv*.—**tedium** *n*.

tee /tiː/ *n* (*golf*) the place from where the first stroke is played at each hole; a small peg from which the ball is driven. • *vti* to position (the ball) on the tee; (*with* **off**) to hit a golf ball from a tee.

teem[1] /tiːm/ *vi* (*with* **with**) to be prolific or abundant in.

teem[2] *vi* to pour (with rain).

teen /tiːn/ *n* a teenager. • *adj* teenage.

teenager /ˈtiːnˌeɪdʒər/ *n* (*inf*) a person who is in his or her teens.

teens /tiːnz/ *npl* the years of one's life from thir*teen* to nine*teen*.—**teenage, teenaged** *adj*.

teeny /ˈtiːni/ *adj* (**teenier, teeniest**) (*inf*) tiny.

teenybopper /ˈtiːniˌbɒpər/ *n* a young girl who avidly follows the latest fashions in clothes and pop music.

teepee /ˈtiːpiː/ *see* **tepee**.

tee-shirt *see* **T-shirt**.

teeter /ˈtiːtər/ *vi* to move or stand unsteadily.

teeth /tiːθ/ *see* **tooth**.

teethe /tiːð/ *vi* to cut one's first teeth.

teething /ˈtiːðɪŋ/ *n* the condition in babies of the first growth of teeth.

teething ring *n* a hard ring for a teething baby to chew on.

teething troubles *npl* problems encountered in the early stages of a project, etc; pain caused by growing teeth.

teetotaller, teetotaler /tiːˈtoʊtələr/ *n* a person who abstains from alcoholic drinks.—**teetotal** *adj*.

TEFL /ˈtɛfəl/ *abbr* = Teaching English as a Foreign Language.

Teflon /ˈtɛflɒn/ *n* (*trademark*) polytetrafluoroethylene, a coating for pots and pans that prevents food sticking. • *adj* (*inf*) able to avoid (political) scandal by claiming ignorance or blaming others.

tegument /ˈtɛɡjʊmənt/ *n* an outer covering; an integument.

tektite /ˈtɛktaɪt/ *n* a spherical glassy object found in various parts of the world and thought to be of meteoric origin.

tel. *abbr* = telephone.

tel-, tele- /ˈtɛli/ *prefix* at a distance; television.

telaesthesia /ˌtɛləsˈθiːsɪə/ *n* supposed perception of objects or events beyond the normal range of the senses.—*also* **telesthesia**.—**telaesthetic, telesthetic** *adj*.

telamon /ˈtɛləmən/ *or* /-mɒːn/ *n* (*archit*) a figure or half-figure of a man, used in place of a column or pilaster to support an entablature, an atlas.

telecast /ˈtɛləˌkæst/ *vt* to broadcast by television. • *n* a television broadcast.—**telecaster** *n*.

telecom /ˈtɛləkɒm/ **telecoms** *n* short for telecommunications.

telecommunication /ˌtɛləkəˌmjuːnɪˈkeɪʃən/ *n* communication of information over long distances by telephone and radio; (*pl*) the technology of telephone and radio communication.

teledu /ˈtɛləˌduː/ *n* a mammal of Java and Sumatra resembling the badger and related to the skunk, which releases a foul-smelling liquid when threatened.

telefilm /ˈtɛləfɪlm/ *n* a motion picture produced for television.

telegenic /ˌtɛlə'dʒɛnɪk/ *adj* suitable for television in content or appearance.

telegram /'tɛlə.græm/ *n* a message sent by telegraph.

telegraph /'tɛlə.grɑːf/ *n* a system for transmitting messages over long distances using electricity, wires and a code. • *vt* to transmit by telegraph.—**telegraphic** *adj.*—**telegraphy** *n.*

telekinesis /ˌtɛlɪkɪ'niːsɪs/ *n* the movement of objects using pure thought without the application of physical force.—**telekinetic** *adj.*

telemark /'tɛlə.mɑːk/ *n* (*skiing*) a turn in which one ski is placed ahead of the other and then angled gradually inward.

telemeter /'tɛlə.miːtər/ or /tə'lɛmɪtər/ *n* any instrument that measures or records events and transmits the data to a distant receiver; (*surveying*) a device for measuring distances. • *vt* to gather and transmit data from a distance.

telemetry /tɪ'lɛmətri/ *n* the use of radio waves to transmit, register and record the readings of an instrument at a distance.

telencephalon /ˌtɛlɛn'sɛfə.lɒn/ *n* the frontal brain including the cerebrum, parts of the hypothalamus and the third ventricle.—**telencephalic** *adj.*

teleology /ˌtɛli'ɒlədʒi/ or /ˌtiː-/ *n* the philosophical doctrine that explains nature or natural processes in terms of purpose or design.—**teleological** *adj.*—**teleologist** *n.*

telepathy /tə'lɛpəθi/ *n* the communication between people's minds of thoughts and feelings, without the need for speech or proximity.—**telepathic** *adj.*

telephone /'tɛlə.fəʊn/ *n* an instrument for transmitting speech at a distance, *esp* by means of electricity. • *vt* (*someone*) to call by telephone.

telephone book *n* a book listing the names, addresses and telephone numbers of subscribers in a given area.

telephone booth *n* a cubicle for paid public use of a telephone.

telephone directory *n* a telephone book.

telephone operator, telephonist *n* a person who operates a telephone switchboard.

telephony /tɪ'lɛfəni/ *n* the system by which sounds are transmitted by telephone.—**telephonic** *adj.*

telephotography /ˌtɛləfə'tɒgrəfi:/ *n* the use of a telephoto lens to photograph distant objects.

telephoto lens /ˌtɛlə'fəʊtəʊ.lɛns/ *n* a camera lens that magnifies distant objects.

teleprinter /'tɛlə.prɪntər/ *n* a teletypewriter.

Teleprompter /'tɛlə.prɒmptər/ *n* (*trademark*) a prompting device used in TV, etc, which provides speakers with a script that remains invisible to the audience, an autocue.

telesales /'tɛlə.seɪlz/ *npl* selling products and services by telephone.

telescope /'tɛlə.skəʊp/ *n* a tubular optical instrument for viewing objects at a distance.

telescopic /ˌtɛlə'skɒpɪk/ *adj* of or like a telescope; that can be viewed by through a telescope.—**telescopically** *adv.*

telesthesia /ˌtɛlɛs'θiːʒə/ or /-ziə/ *see* **telaesthesia**.

Teletext /'tɛlə.tɛkst/ *n* (*trademark*) written information transmitted non-interactively to television viewers.

telethon /'tɛlə.θɒn/ *n* a long television extravaganza which encourages viewers to send in money for a charitable cause.

Teletype /'tɛlə.taɪp/ *n* (*trademark*) a teleprinter.

teletypewriter /ˌtɛlə'taɪp.raɪtər/ *n* a telegraph apparatus with a keyboard that transmits and a printer that receives messages over a distance.

televangelist /tɛlə'vændʒəlɪst/ *n* a person, *usu* a minister of the Christian Pentecostal church, who conducts television shows to preach the church's message and seek donations.

televise /'tɛlə.vaɪz/ *vt* (*a programme*) to transmit by television.

television /'tɛlə.vɪʒən/ *n* the transmission of visual images and accompanying sound through electrical and sound waves; a television receiving set; television broadcasting.

telex /'tɛlɛks/ *n* a communication system whereby subscribers hire teletypewriters for transmitting messages. • *vt* to transmit by telex.

tell /tɛl/ *vb* (**telling, told**) *vt* to narrate; to disclose; to inform; to notify; to instruct; to distinguish; (*with* **off**) (*inf*) to reprimand; to count off and assign to a duty. • *vi* to tell tales, to inform on; to produce a marked effect.

teller /'tɛlər/ *n* a bank clerk; a person appointed to count votes in an election.

telling /'tɛlɪŋ/ *adj* having great impact.

telltale /'tɛlteɪl/ *n* a person who tells tales about others. • *adj* revealing what is meant to be hidden.

tellurian /tɛ'lʊriən/ or /tə-/ *adj* of the earth. • *n* an inhabitant of the earth.

telluric /tɛ'lʊrɪk/ *adj* of or in the earth or soil; of or containing (high valency) tellurium.

tellurium /tɛ'lʊriəm/ *n* a brittle nonmetallic element related to sulphur and selenium.

tellurometer /tɛ'lʊrə.miːtər/ *n* (*surveying*) an electronic instrument for measuring distances using microwaves.

telly /'tɛli/ *n* (*pl* **tellies**) (*inf*) television.

telo- /'tɛlə/ or /-oː/, **tel-** *prefix* end.

temerity /tə'mɛriti/ *n* rashness.

temp /tɛmp/ *n* (*inf*) a temporary employee.

temp. /tɛmp/ *abbr* = temperature.

temper /'tɛmpər/ *n* a frame of mind; a fit of anger. • *vt* to tone down, moderate; (*steel*) to heat and cool repeatedly to bring to the correct hardness.

tempera /'tɛmpərə/ *n* (a method of painting using) powdered pigments mixed with an emulsion, *esp* egg yolk and water; a painting done in tempera; opaque watercolour used for posters.

temperament /'tɛmprəmənt/ or /-pərmənt/ *n* one's disposition.

temperamental /ˌtɛmprə'mɛntəl/ or /-pər-/ *adj* easily irritated; erratic.—**temperamentally** *adv.*

temperance /'tɛmprəns/ or /-pərəns/ *n* moderation; abstinence from alcohol.

temperate /'tɛmprət/ or /-pərət/ *adj* mild or moderate in temperature; (*behaviour*) moderate, self-controlled.

temperature /'tɛmprətʃər/ or /-pərtʃər/ *n* degree of heat or cold; body heat above the normal.

tempest /'tɛmpəst/ *n* a violent storm.

tempestuous /tɛm'pɛstʃuəs/ *adj* stormy; violent; passionate.

tempi /'tɛmpi/ *see* **tempo**.

template /'tɛmpleɪt/ or /-plət/ *n* a pattern, gauge or mould used as a guide *esp* in cutting metal, stone or plastic.

temple[1] /'tɛmpəl/ *n* a place of worship.

temple[2] *n* the region on either side of the head above the cheekbone.

tempo /'tɛmpoː/ *n* (*pl* **tempos, tempi**) (*mus*) the speed at which music is meant to be played; rate of any activity.

temporal[1] /'tɛmpərəl/ *adj* relating to time; secular, civil.

temporal[2] *adj* of or relating to the temples of the head.

temporality /ˌtɛmpə'ræliti/ *n* (*pl* **temporalities**) the state or condition of being temporal; a secular or civil authority or power.

temporal lobe *n* a lobe on each side of the cerebral hemisphere associated with hearing and speech.

temporary /'tɛmpəreri/ *adj* lasting or used for a limited time only; not permanent.—**temporarily** *adv.*

temporize /'tɛmpə.raɪz/ *vi* to delay in order to gain time; to act to fit the occasion.—**temporization** *n.*—**temporizer** *n.*

tempt /tɛmpt/ *vt* to entice to do wrong; to invite, attract, induce.—**tempter** *n.*—**temptress** *nf.*

temptation /tɛmp'teɪʃən/ *n* the act of tempting or the state of being tempted; something or someone that tempts.

tempting /'tɛmptɪŋ/ *adj* attractive, inviting.

tempura /tɛm'pʊrə/ *n* a Japanese dish of seafood or vegetables fried in batter.

ten /tɛn/ *adj, n* the cardinal number next above nine. • *n* the symbol for this (10, X, x).

tenable /'tɛnəbəl/ *adj* capable of being believed, held, or defended.

tenacious /tə'neɪʃəs/ *adj* grasping firmly; persistent; retentive; adhesive.

tenacity /tə'næsiti/ *n* the state or quality of being tenacious; doggedness, obstinacy; adhesiveness, stickiness.

tenaculum /tə'nækjuləm/ *n* (*pl* **tenacula**) a hooked surgical instrument for seizing and holding parts, such as arteries.

tenancy /'tɛnənsi/ *n* (*pl* **tenancies**) the temporary possession by a tenant of another's property; the period of this.

tenant /'tɛnənt/ *n* a person who pays rent to occupy a house or flat or for the use of land or buildings; an occupant.

tenant farmer *n* a farmer who works land owned by someone else to whom he pays rent.

tench /tɛntʃ/ *n* (*pl* **tench**) a freshwater fish of the carp family.

tend[1] /tɛnd/ *vt* to take care of; to attend (to).

tend[2] *vi* to be inclined; to move in a specific direction.

tendency /'tɛndənsi/ *n* (*pl* **tendencies**) an inclination or leaning.

tendentious, tendencious /tɛnˈdɛnʃəs/ *adj* showing bias, not impartial.—**tendentiousness, tendenciousness** *n*.

tender[1] /ˈtɛndər/ *n* a railroad car attached to locomotives to carry fuel and water; a small ship that brings stores to a larger one.

tender[2] *vt* to present for acceptance; to offer as payment. • *vi* to make an offer. • *n* an offer to provide goods or services at a fixed price.

tender[3] *adj* soft, delicate; fragile; painful, sore; sensitive; sympathetic.—**tenderly** *adv*.—**tenderness** *n*.

tenderfoot /ˈtɛndərˌfʊt/ *n* a newcomer to rough, outdoor life; an inexperienced beginner.

tenderhearted *n* having a compassionate, loving or sensitive disposition.—**tenderheartedly** *adv*.—**tenderheartedness** *n*.

tenderize /ˈtɛndəˌraɪz/ *vt* (*meat*) to make more tender by pounding or by adding a substance that softens.—**tenderization** *n*.—**tenderizer** *n*.

tenderloin /ˈtɛndərˌlɔɪn/ *n* a cut of meat from between the ribs and sirloin.

tendon /ˈtɛndən/ *n* fibrous tissue attaching a muscle to a bone.

tendril /ˈtɛndrɪl/ *n* a thread-like shoot of a climbing plant by which it attaches itself for support.

tenement /ˈtɛnəmənt/ *n* a building divided into flats, each occupied by a separate owner or tenant.

tenesmus /təˈnɛzməs/ *n* (*med*) an urgent but ineffectual attempt to urinate or void the bowels.

tenet /ˈtɛnət/ *n* any belief or doctrine.

tenfold /ˈtɛnfoːld/ *adj, adv* 10 times as much or as many; composed of 10 parts.

ten-gallon hat /ˈtɛnˈgælən/ *n* a wide-brimmed hat with a high crown, *esp* worn by cowboys.

teniasis /ˈtiːnɪəsɪs/ *see* **taeniasis**.

tenner /ˈtɛnər/ *n* (*inf*) a ten-pound note; a ten-dollar bill.

tennis /ˈtɛnɪs/ *n* a game for two or four people, played by hitting a ball over a net with a racket.

tennis court *n* a court surfaced with clay, asphalt or grass on which tennis is played.

tennis elbow *n* stiffness and pain in the elbow joint due to excessive exercise, such as playing tennis.

tenon /ˈtɛnən/ *n* a projection on the end of a piece of wood for connecting with a mortise. • *vt* to form a tenon; to connect using a tenon and mortise.

tenon saw *n* a fine-toothed saw with a sturdy back used for cutting tenons, etc.

tenor /ˈtɛnər/ *n* a general purpose or intent; the highest regular adult male voice, higher than a baritone and lower than an alto; a man who sings tenor.

tenor clef *n* a C clef placed so as to designate the fourth line of the staff as middle C.

tenosynovitis /ˌtɛnoːˌsaɪnoːˈvaɪtɪs/ *n* inflammation of the tendons in a joint through repetitive movements of the joint concerned.

tenpin /ˈtɛnpɪn/ *n* a bowling pin used in tenpins.

tenpin bowling *n* a bowling game involving the rolling of a large bowl along a lane to knock over as many as possible of tenpins.

tenpins /ˈtɛnpɪnz/ *n sing* US word for **tenpin bowling**.

tenrec /ˈtɛnrɛk/ *n* any of various related mammals of Madagascar resembling shrews.

tense[1] /tɛns/ *n* (*gram*) the verb form that indicates the time of an action or the existence of a state.

tense[2] *adj* stretched, taut; apprehensive; nervous and highly strung. • *vti* to make or become tense.—**tensely** *adv*.—**tenseness** *n*.

tensile /ˈtɛnsaɪl/ or /-səl/ *adj* of or relating to tension; stretchable.

tensile strength *n* the greatest stress a material can bear without breaking.

tensimeter /tɛnˈsɪmətər/ *n* an instrument that measures differences in vapour pressures.

tensiometer /ˌtɛnsiˈɒmətər/ *n* an instrument for measuring tensile strength; an instrument for comparing vapour pressures in different liquids; an instrument for measuring the surface tension of a liquid; an instrument for measuring the moisture content of soil.

tension /ˈtɛnʃən/ *n* the act of stretching; the state of being stretched; (*between forces, etc*) opposition; stress; mental strain.

tensor /ˈtɛnsər/ *n* any muscle that stretches or tightens a body part.

tent /tɛnt/ *n* a portable shelter of canvas, plastic or other waterproof fabric, which is erected on poles and fixed to the ground by ropes and pegs.

tentacle /ˈtɛntəkəl/ *n* a long, slender, flexible growth near the mouth of invertebrates, used for feeling, grasping or handling.

tentative /ˈtɛntətɪv/ *adj* provisional; not definite.—**tentatively** *adv*.—**tentativeness** *n*.

tenterhook /ˈtɛntərˌhʊk/ *n* one of a series of hooks on which cloth is stretched to dry; (*pl*) (*with* **on**) in a tense or anxious state.

tenth /tɛnθ/ *adj* the last of ten; being one of ten equal parts. • *n* one of ten equal parts.

tenuous /ˈtɛnjus/ *adj* slight, flimsy, insubstantial.—**tenuousness** *n*.

tenure /ˈtɛnjər/ *n* the holding of property or a position; the period of time which a position lasts; a permanent position, *usu* granted after holding a job for a number of years.—**tenured** *adj*.

tenuto /təˈnuːtoː/ *adv, adj* (*mus*) (*note*) sustained for its full time value.

teocalli /ˌtiːəˈkæli/ *n* (*pl* **teocallis**) the pyramid-shaped bases supporting Aztec temples.

tepee /ˈtiːpi/ *n* a cone-shaped, North American Indian tent formed of skins; a wigwam.—*also* **teepee**.

tepid /ˈtɛpɪd/ *adj* slightly warm, lukewarm.

tequila /təˈkiːlə/ *n* a spirit distilled from a Mexican agave plant; the plant itself.

ter. *abbr* = terrace; territory.

ter- /tər/ *prefix* three times; third; three.

tera- /ˈtɛrə/ *prefix* ten to the power of 12.

terbium /ˈtɜrbiəm/ *n* a metallic element of the rare earth group.

tercel /ˈtɜrsəl/ *see* **tiercel**.

tercentenary /ˌtɜrsɛnˈtɛnəri/ *n* (*pl* **tercentenaries**) a three hundredth anniversary.—*also adj*.

terebene /ˈtɛrəˌbiːn/ *n* a liquid hydrocarbon derived from oil of turpentine and sulphuric acid used in making varnishes, as an antiseptic and in medicines.

terebinth /ˈtɛrəbɪnθ/ *n* a European tree that yields a resinous liquid.

terebinthine /ˌtɛrəˈbɪnθɪn/ or /-ˌθɪn/, /-ˌθaɪn/ *n* or or pertaining to the terebinth; of or like turpentine.

teredo /təˈriːdoː/ *n* (*pl* **teredos, teredines**) a burrowing mollusc, the shipworm.

terete /təˈriːt/ *adj* (*plant, animal part*) having a smooth cylindrical shape.

tergiversate /ˈtɜrdʒɪvərseɪt/ *vi* to switch allegiances; to be evasive, to equivocate.

term /tɜrm/ *n* a limit; any prescribed period of time; a division of an academic year; a word or expression, *esp* in a specialized field of knowledge; (*pl*) mutual relationship between people; (*pl*) conditions of a contract, etc. • *vt* to call, designate.

termagant /ˈtɜrməgənt/ *n* (*arch*) a shrewish, nagging woman.

terminal /ˈtɜrmɪnəl/ *adj* being or situated at the end or extremity; (*disease*) fatal, incurable. • *n* a bus, coach or railroad station at the end of the line; the point at which an electrical current enters or leaves a device; a device with a keyboard and monitor for inputting or viewing data from a computer.—**terminally** *adv*.

terminate /ˈtɜrmɪneɪt/ *vti* to bring or come to an end.—**termination** *n*.

terminology /ˌtɜrmɪˈnɒlədʒi/ *n* (*pl* **terminologies**) the terms used in any specialized subject.

terminus /ˈtɜrmɪnəs/ *n* (*pl* **termini, terminuses**) the final part; a limit; end of a transportation line.

termitarium /ˌtɜrmɪˈtɛriəm/ *n* (*pl* **termitaria**) a termites' nest.

termite /ˈtɜrmaɪt/ *n* a wood-eating, white, ant-like insect.

tern /tɜrn/ *n* a small, black and white sea bird.

ternary /ˈtɜrnəri/ *adj* in three parts; (*number system*) using three as a base.

terpene /ˈtɜrpiːn/ *n* any of various hydrocarbons present in the essential oils of plants, *esp* conifers.

Terpsichorean /ˌtɜrpsɪˈkɔriən/ or /-kɔˈriːən/ *adj* pertaining to dancing, or to Terpsichore, the Muse of dancing and choral song in classical myth.

terrace /ˈtɛrəs/ *n* a raised level area of earth, often part of a slope; an unroofed paved area adjoining a house; a row of houses; a patio or balcony. • *vt* to make into a terrace.

terracotta /ˌtɛrəˈkɒtə/ *n* a brownish-red clay used for making flower pots and statues, which is baked but not glazed; a brown-red colour.

terra firma /ˌtɛrəˈfɜrmə/ *n* solid ground; the earth.

terrain /təˈreɪn/ n the surface features of a tract of land; (fig) field of activity.

terra incognita /ˌterəɪŋkɒgˈniːtə/ or /ɪnˈkɒgnɪtə/ n an unexplored or unknown area or country.

terrapin /ˈterəpɪn/ n an aquatic North American turtle.

terrarium /təˈreəriəm/ n (pl **terraria, terrariums**) an enclosure for small land animals; a glass container for plants.

terrazzo /teˈrætsoː/ or /-ˈræzoː/ n mosaic flooring in the form of marble chips set in mortar and highly polished.

terrestrial /təˈrestriəl/ adj relating to, or existing on, the earth; earthly; representing the earth.

terrible /ˈterɪbəl/ adj causing great fear; dreadful; (inf) very unpleasant.

terribly /ˈterɪbli/ adv frighteningly; (inf) very.

terrier /ˈteriər/ n a type of small, active dog.

terrific /təˈrɪfɪk/ adj of great size; (inf) excellent.

terrify /ˈterɪfaɪ/ vt (**terrifying, terrified**) to fill with terror, to frighten greatly.

terrine /təˈriːn/ n an earthenware dish for pâté; pâté or similar food served in this.

territorial /ˌterəˈtoːriəl/ adj relating to or owned by a territory. • n (with cap) a member of the Territorial Army, a British volunteer reserve force.

territorial waters npl the coastal and inland waters under the jurisdiction of a nation.

territory /ˈterətəri/ n (pl **territories**) an area under the jurisdiction of a city or state; a wide tract of land; an area assigned to a salesman; an area of knowledge.

terror /ˈterər/ n great fear; an object or person inspiring fear or dread.

terrorism /ˈterərˌɪzəm/ n the use of terror and violence to intimidate.— **terrorist** n.

terrorize /ˈterəˌraɪz/ vt to terrify; to control by terror.—**terrorization** n.

terry /ˈteri/ n (pl **terries**) a cloth with an uncut pile made of looped threads.

terse /tɜːs/ adj abrupt, to the point, concise.—**tersely** adv.

tertian /ˈtɜːʃən/ adj (fever) occurring on alternate days.

tertiary /ˈtɜːʃəri/ adj third.

tesla /ˈteslə/ n the SI unit of magnetic flux density.

tessellated /ˈtesəˌleɪtəd/ adj resembling mosaic.

tessera /ˈtesərə/ n (pl **tesserae**) a piece of marble, glass, etc used in a mosaic.

tessitura /ˌtesəˈtʊrə/ n (mus) the natural pitch of a voice or instrument.

test /test/ n an examination; trial; a chemical reaction to test a substance or to test for an illness; a series of questions or exercises. • vt to examine critically.

testament /ˈtestəmənt/ n a will; proof; tribute; (arch) a covenant made by God with men; (with cap) one of the two main parts of the Bible.

testate /ˈtesteɪt/ adj having made and left a will.

testator /təˈsteɪtər/ n a person who leaves a will.

test ban n an agreement between nations to limit or abandon tests of nuclear weapons.

test-bed n an area designed for testing machinery.

test case n a legal action that establishes a precedent.

testes /ˈtesˌtiːz/ see **testis**.

testicle /ˈtestɪkəl/ n either of the two male reproductive glands that produce sperm, a testis.

testify /ˈtestəˌfaɪ/ vb (**testifying, testified**) vi to give evidence under oath; to serve as witness (to); (with **to**) to be evidence of. • vt to be evidence of.

testimonial /ˌtestəˈmoːniəl/ adj relating to a testimony. • n a recommendation of one's character or abilities.

testimony /ˈtestəˌmoːni/ n (pl **testimonies**) evidence; declaration of truth or fact.

testis /ˈtestɪs/ n (pl **testes**) a testicle.

test match n one of a series of international cricket or Rugby football matches.

testosterone /teˈstɒstəˌroːn/ n a steroid hormone secreted by the testes.

test pilot n someone who flies new types of aircraft to test their performance and characteristics.

test tube n a cylinder of thin glass closed at one end, used in scientific experiments.

test-tube baby n a baby which develops from an ovum fertilized outside the mother's body and replaced in the womb.

testy /ˈtesti/ adj (**testier, testiest**) touchy, irritable.

tetanus /ˈtetnəs/ or /ˈtetənəs/ n an intense and painful spasm of muscles, caused by the infection of a wound by bacteria; lockjaw.

tetchy /ˈtetʃi/ adj (**tetchier, tetchiest**) irritable, touchy.—also **techy**.—**tetchily** adv.—**tetchiness** n.

tête-à-tête /ˌtetæˈtet/ n (pl **tête-à-têtes, tête-à-tête**) a private conversation between two people.

tether /ˈteðər/ n a rope or chain for tying an animal; the limit of one's endurance. • vt to fasten with a tether; to limit.

tetra- /ˈtetrə/, **tetr-** prefix four.

tetrahedron /ˌtetrəˈhiːdrən/ or /-ˈhedrən/ n (pl **tetrahedrons, tetrahedra**) a solid figure enclosed by four plane faces of triangular shape.

tetrahydroamino-acridine /ˌtetrəˌhaɪdroːˌmiːnoˈækrɪˌdiːn/ n a drug currently being tried out for use in the treatment of Alzheimer's disease.

tetrahydrocannabinol /ˌtetrəˌhaɪdrəkəˈnæbɪnɒl/ n a natural compound that is the main intoxicant in cannabis and can also be produced synthetically.

tetralogy /teˈtrælədʒi/ or /-ˈtrɒlədʒi/ n (pl **tetralogies**) a series of four related works, such as novels or plays.

tetravalent /ˌtetrəˈveɪlənt/ adj (chem) having a valency of four.

Teutonic /tuːˈtɒnɪk/ or /tjuː-/ adj of Germanic peoples or their language.

Tex-Mex /teksˈmeks/ adj of or pertaining to a Texan version of something Mexican, such as food or music.

text /tekst/ n the main part of a printed work; the original or exact wording; a passage from the Bible forming the basis of a sermon; a subject or topic; a textbook.

textbook /ˈtekstbuk/ n a book used as a basis for instruction.

textile /ˈtekstaɪl/ n a woven fabric or cloth. • adj relating to the making of fabrics.

textual /ˈtekstʃuəl/ adj of or relating to a text; contained in or based on a text; (operation, etc) exactly as planned according to theory or calculation.

textual criticism n the study of a written work (eg the Bible) to establish the original text; the close reading and analysis of any literary work.

texture /ˈtekstʃər/ n the characteristic appearance, arrangement or feel of a thing; the way in which threads in a material are interwoven.—**textural** adj.

TGIF abbr = thank God it's Friday.

Th (chem symbol) thorium.

Th. abbr = Thursday.

THA abbr = tetrahydroamino-acridine.

Thai /taɪ/ n (pl **Thais, Thai**) a native or inhabitant of Thailand; the language of Thailand.—also adj.

thalamus /ˈθæləməs/ n (pl **thalami**) either of the two masses of tissue which sit close together at the base of the brain.

thalidomide /θəˈlɪdəˌmaɪd/ n a sedative drug withdrawn from use when it was discovered to cause malformation in unborn babies.

thallium /ˈθæliəm/ n a soft white poisonous metallic element.

than /ðən/ or /ðæn/ conj introducing the second element of a comparison.

thanatology /ˌθænəˈtɒlədʒi/ n the scientific study of death.

thank /θæŋk/ vt to express gratitude to or appreciation for. • npl an expression of gratitude.—**thankful** adj.—**thankfully** adv.

thankless /ˈθæŋkləs/ adj without thanks; unappreciated; fruitless, unrewarding.—**thanklessness** n.

thanksgiving /ˌθæŋksˈgɪvɪŋ/ n the act of giving thanks; a prayer of gratitude to God; (with cap) Thanksgiving Day.

Thanksgiving Day n a legal holiday observed on the fourth Thursday of November in the US, and on the second Monday of October in Canada.

thank-you n an expression of gratitude.

that /ðæt/ or /ðət/ demons adj, pron (pl **those**) the (one) there or then, esp the latter or more distant thing. • rel pron who or which. • conj introducing noun clause or adverbial clause of purpose or consequence; because; in order that; (preceded by **so, such**) as a result.

thatch /θætʃ/ n roofing straw. • vt to cover a roof with thatch.

thaumatology /ˌθɔːməˈtɒlədʒi/ n (pl **thaumatologies**) the study of miracles; a discourse on miracles.

thaumaturge /ˈθɔːməˌtɜːdʒ/, **thaumaturgist** /ˈθɔːməˌtɜːdʒəst/ n a miracle-worker; a magician.—**thaumaturgy** n.

thaw /θɒ/ *vi* to melt or grow liquid; to become friendly. •*vt* to cause to melt. • *n* the melting of ice or snow by warm weather.

THC *abbr* = tetrahydrocannabinol.

the /ði/ (before vowels) or /ðə/ (before consonants), /ˈði:/ *demons adj* denoting a particular person or thing. • *adv* used before comparative adjectives or adverbs for emphasis.

theatre, theater /ˈθɪətər/ *n* a building where plays and operas are performed; the theatrical world as a whole; a setting for important events; field of operations.

theatre-in-the-round *n* a theatre with seats arranged in a circle around the stage area.

theatrical /θiːˈætrɪkəl/ *adj* relating to the theatre; melodramatic, affected.—**theatrically** *adv*.

theatricals /θiːˈætrɪkəlz/ *npl* performances of drama, *esp* by amateurs.

thee /ði/ *pron* the objective case of **thou**.

theft /θɛft/ *n* act or crime of stealing.

theine /ˈθiːiːn/ *n* caffeine.

their /ðer/ *poss adj* of or belonging to them; his, hers, its.

theirs /ðerz/ *poss pron* of or belonging to them; his, hers, its.

theism /ˈθiːɪzəm/ *n* belief in the existence of a God or gods, *esp* God as the supernatural Creator of the universe.—**theist** *n*.— **theistic** *adj*.

them /ðem/ or /ðəm/ *pron* the objective case of **they**.

theme /θiːm/ *n* the main subject of a discussion; an idea or motif in a work; a short essay; a leading melody; a style adopted for an exhibition, activity, etc.—**thematic** *adj*.

theme park *n* a leisure area in which the buildings and settings follow a particular theme, *eg* a period in history.

theme song *n* a recurring melody in a film score or musical that is associated with the work or a particular character; a signature tune.

themselves /ðəmˈsɛlvz/ *pron* the reflexive form of **they** or **them**.

then /ðen/ *adv* at that time; afterward; immediately; next in time. • *conj* for that reason; in that case.

thenar /ˈθiːnər/ or /ˈθiːnɑr/ *n* the ball of the thumb; the palm of the hand.

thence /ðens/ *adv* from that time or place; for that reason.

thenceforth /ðensˈfɔːθ/ *adv* from that time on; thereafter.

thenceforward /ðensˈfɔːwərd/, **thenceforwards** *adv* thenceforth.

theo- /ˈθiːɔː/, **the-** *prefix* god.

theobromine /θiːəˈbroːmiːn/ *n* an alkaloid similar to caffeine present in cacao beans and tea, used in treating heart disease.

theocracy /θiːˈɒkrəsi/ *n* (*pl* **theocracies**) (a state having) government by a deity or priesthood.—**theocrat** *n*.—**theocratic** *adj*.

theodolite /θiːˈɒdəˌlaɪt/ *n* a surveying instrument for measuring angles.

theol. *abbr* = theologian; theological; theology.

theologian /θiːəˈloːdʒən/ *n* a person who studies and interprets religious texts; a teacher of theology.

theology /θiːˈɒlədʒi/ *n* (*pl* **theologies**) the study of God and of religious doctrine and matters of divinity.—**theological, theologic** *adj*.—**theologically** *adv*.

theorem /ˈθiːrəm/ or /ˈθiːərəm/ *n* a proposition that can be proved from accepted principles; law or principle.

theoretical /θiːəˈrɛtɪkəl/, **theoretic** /θiːəˈrɛtɪk/ *adj* of or based on theory, not practical application; hypothetical; conjectural.— **theoretically** *adv*.

theoretician /ˌθiːrəˈtɪʃən/ *n* a person who concentrates on the theoretical basis of a subject.

theoretics /θiːəˈrɛtɪks/ *npl* the speculative parts of a science.

theorize /ˈθiːəraɪz/ or /ˈθiːraɪz/ *vi* to form theories; to speculate.—**theorist, theorizer** *n*.—**theorization** *n*.

theory /ˈθiːri/ or /θiːˈɒri/ *n* (*pl* **theories**) an explanation or system of anything; ideas and abstract principles of a science or art; speculation; a hypothesis.

therapeutic /ˌθerəˈpjuːtɪk/, **therapeutical** *adj* relating to the treatment of disease; beneficial.—**therapeutically** *adv*.

therapeutics /ˌθerəˈpjuːtɪks/ *npl* the curative branch of medicine.

therapy /ˈθerəpi/ *n* (*pl* **therapies**) the treatment of physical or mental illness.—**therapist** *n*.

there /ðer/ *adv* in, at or to, that place or point; in that respect; in that matter.

thereabout, thereabouts /ˈðerəˌbʊts/ or /-ˈbʊts/ *adv* at or near that place or number.

thereafter /ðerˈæftər/ *adv* after that; according to that.

thereagainst /ˌðerəˈgɛnst/ *adv* in opposition to; contrary to.

thereat /ðerˈæt/ *adv* at that place; at such time.

thereby /ˈðerbaɪ/ or /-ˈbaɪ/ *adv* by that means.

therefore /ˈðerfɔr/ *adv* for that or this reason; consequently.

therein /ðerˈɪn/ *adv* in that place or respect.

thereof /ðerˈɒv/ *adv* of this or that; because of that.

thereon /ðerˈɒn/ *adv* on that or it; immediately following that.

thereupon /ˈθerəpɒn/ or /ˌðerəˈpɒn/ *adv* immediately after that.

therm /θɜrm/ *n* a measurement of heat.

thermal /ˈθɜrməl/, **thermic** /ˈθɜrmɪk/ *adj* generating heat; hot; warm; (*underwear*) of a knitted material with air spaces for insulation. • *n* a rising current of warm air.

thermion /ˈθɜrmiˌɒn/ *n* an electron emitted by a material at high temperature.

thermionic /ˌθɜrmiˈɒnɪk/ *adj* of, pertaining to, or worked by thermions, *esp* a tube.

thermistor /θɜrˈmɪstər/ *n* a semicondoctor device whose resistance varies inversely with a change in temperature.

thermo- /ˈθɜrmoː/, **therm-** *prefix* heat.

thermocouple /ˈθɜrmoːˌkʌpəl/ *n* a device which generates a thermoelectric effect between two dissimilar semiconductors, used in measuring temperature differences.

thermodynamics /ˌθɜrmoːdaɪˈnæmɪks/ *n sing* the branch of physics concerned with the relationship between heat and other forms of energy.

thermoelectric /ˌθɜrmoːɪˈlɛktrɪk/, **thermoelectrical** /-kəl/ *adj* of or derived from electricity generated by difference of temperature.—**thermoelectricity** *n*.

thermometer /θɜrˈmɒmɪtər/ *n* an instrument for measuring temperature.

thermonuclear /ˌθɜrmoːˈnuːkliər/ or /-ˈnjuː-/ *adj* of or relating to nuclear fusion or nuclear weapons that utilize fusion reactions.

thermoplastic /ˌθɜrmoːˈplæstɪk/ *adj* becoming soft and malleable when heated. • *n* a resin or synthetic plastic that can be heated, moulded and cooled without appreciable change of its properties.

Thermos /ˈθɜrməs/ *n* (*trademark*) a brand of vacuum bottle.

thermostat /ˈθɜrməˌstæt/ *n* an automatic device for regulating temperatures.

thesaurus /θəˈsɔrəs/ *n* (*pl* **thesauri, thesauruses**) a reference book of synonyms and antonyms.

these /ði:z/ *see* **this**.

thesis /ˈθiːsɪs/ *n* (*pl* **theses**) a dissertation written as part of an academic degree; a theory expressed as a statement for discussion.

thespian /ˈθespiən/ *adj* of or pertaining to drama. • *n* an actor or actress.

theta /ˈθeɪtə/ *n* the eighth letter of the Greek alphabet.

they /ðeɪ/ *pers pron, pl of* **he, she** *or* **it**.

they'd /ðeɪd/ = they would; they had.

they'll /ðeɪl/ or /ðel/ = they will; they shall.

they're /ðer/ = they are.

they've /ðeɪv/ = they have.

thiamine, thiamin /ˈθaɪəmɪn/ *n* vitamin B, present in a wide variety of plants and animals and essential for normal metabolism and nerve function.

thick /θɪk/ *adj* dense; viscous; fat, broad; abundant, closely set; in quick succession; crowded; (*inf*) stupid. • *adv* closely; frequently.

thicken /ˈθɪkən/ *vti* to make or become thick.—**thickener** *n*.

thicket /ˈθɪkət/ *n* a small group of trees or shrubs growing thickly and closely together.

thickhead /ˈθɪkhed/ *n* (*inf*) an ignorant person, an idiot.—**thick-headed** *adj*.

thickness /ˈθɪknəs/ *n* being thick; the dimension other than length or width; a layer.

thickset /θɪkˈset/ *adj* having a short, stocky body.

thick-skinned /ˈθɪkˈskɪnd/ *adj* not sensitive; not easily offended.

thick-witted /ˈθɪkˌwɪtɪd/ *adj* stupid.

thief /θiːf/ *n* (*pl* **thieves**) a person who steals.

thieve /θiːv/ *vti* to steal.

thigh /θaɪ/ *n* the thick fleshy part of the leg from the hip to the knee.

thighbone /ˈθaɪˌboːn/ *n* the femur.

thimble /ˈθɪmbəl/ *n* a cap or cover worn to protect the finger when sewing.

thimbleful /ˈθɪmbəlˌfʊl/ *n* what a thimble contains, a tiny amount.

thin /θɪn/ *adj* (**thinner, thinnest**) narrow; slim; lean; sparse, weak, watery; (*material*) fine; not dense. • *vt* to make thin; to make less crowded; to water down.—**thinly** *adv*.—**thinness** *n*.

thine /ðaɪn/ *pron* an old-fashioned word for **yours**.

thing /θɪŋ/ *n* an inanimate object; an event; an action; (*pl*) possessions; (*inf*) an obsession.

thingamabob, thingumabob /ˈθɪŋəməˌbɒb/ *n* (*inf*) something or someone the name of which has been forgotten, is unknown or is hard to categorize, etc.—*also* **thingamajig, thingumajig, thingummy, thingie.**

think /θɪŋk/ *vb* (**thinking, thought**) *vi* to exercise the mind in order to make a decision; to revolve ideas in the mind, to ponder; to remember; to consider. • *vt* to judge, to believe or consider; (*with* **up**) to concoct, devise; (*with* **over**) to ponder, to consider the costs and benefits of.—**thinker** *n*.

thinking /ˈθɪŋkɪŋ/ *adj* capable of using thought, rational; intelligent. • *n* the process of using thought; opinion, reasoning.

think-tank /ˈθɪŋktæŋk/ *n* (*inf*) a group of experts convened to analyse and advise on ways of handling a particular problem.

thinner /ˈθɪnər/ *n* a substance, such as turpentine, added to paint, varnish, etc, to thin it.

thin-skinned /ˈθɪnˈskɪnd/ *adj* overly sensitive to criticism; easily offended.

third /θɜrd/ *adj* the last of three; being one of three equal parts. • *n* one of three equal parts.

third degree *n* the use of torture, bullying or rough questioning to obtain information.

third-degree burn *n* a severe burn which destroys surface and underlying tissue and may involve loss of fluid and shock.

thirdly /ˈθɜrdli/ *adv* in the third place; as a third point.

third person *n* grammatical forms, such as pronouns and verbs, used when referring to the person or thing spoken or written of, not to the person speaking or writing or to the person or persons addressed.

third-rate *adj* inferior.

Third World *n* the underdeveloped countries of the world (*usu* refers to Africa, Asia and South America).

thirst /θɜrst/ *n* a craving for drink; a longing. • *vi* to feel thirst; to have a longing.

thirsty /ˈθɜrsti/ *adj* (**thirstier, thirstiest**) having a desire to drink; dry, arid; longing or craving for.—**thirstily** *adv*.—**thirstiness** *n*.

thirteen /θɜrˈtiːn/ *adj, n* three and ten.—**thirteenth** *adj, n*.

thirty /ˈθɜrti/ *adj, n* (*pl* **thirties**) three times ten.—**thirtieth** *adj, n*.

thirty-second note *n* (*mus*) a note with a time value of one thirty-secondth of a whole note, a demisemiquaver.

this /ðɪs/ *demons pron* (*pl* **these**) *or adj* denoting a person or thing near, just mentioned, or about to be mentioned.

thistle /ˈθɪsəl/ *n* a wild plant with prickly leaves and a purple flower.

thistledown /ˈθɪsəlˌdaʊn/ *n* the feathery cluster of seeds produced by the thistle.

thither /ˈðɪðər/ *adv* (*arch*) to or toward that place.

tho, tho' /ðoː/ *conj, adv* (*inf*) though.

thong /θɒŋ/ *n* a piece or strap of leather to lash things together; the lash of a whip; a sandal held on the foot by a thong passing between the toes and fixed to a strap passing over the top of the foot.

Thor /ˈθɔr/ *n* (*Norse myth*) the god of thunder.

thorax /ˈθɔræks/ *n* (*pl* **thoraxes, thoraces**) the part of the body enclosed by the ribs; the chest; (*in insects*) the middle one of the three chief divisions of the body.—**thoracic** *adj*.

thorium /ˈθɔrɪəm/ *n* a radioactive metallic element used in industry and as a nuclear fuel.

thorn /θɔrn/ *n* a shrub or small tree having thorns, *esp* hawthorn; a sharp point or prickle on the stem of a plant or the branch of a tree.

thorny /ˈθɔrni/ *adj* (**thornier, thorniest**) prickly; (*problem*) knotty.

thoron /ˈθɔrˌɒn/ *n* a gas that is a radioactive isotope of radon.

thorough /ˈθɜroː/ *or* /ˈθɜroː/, /ˈθɜrə/ *adj* complete, very detailed and painstaking, exhaustive.—**thoroughness** *n*.

thoroughbred /ˈθɜroːbred/ *or* /ˈθɜroː-/, /ˈθɜrə-/ *adj* bred from pure stock. • *n* a pedigree animal, *esp* a horse.

thoroughfare /ˈθɜroːˌfer/ *or* /ˈθɜroː-/, /ˈθɜrə-/ *n* a way through; a public highway, road; right of passing through.

thoroughgoing /ˈθɜroːˌgoːɪŋ/ *or* /ˈθɜroː-/, /ˈθɜrə-/ *adj* very thorough; out-and-out.

thoroughly /-li/ *adv* completely, fully; entirely, absolutely.

those /ðoːz/ *adj, pron* plural of **that**.

thou¹ /ðaʊ/ *pron* an old-fashioned word for **you**.

thou² *n* (*pl* **thous, thou**) (*inf*) a thousand; a thousandth of an inch.

though /ðoː/ *conj* yet, even if. • *adv* however; nevertheless.

thought /θɒt/ *n* the act of thinking; reasoning; serious consideration; an idea; opinions collectively; design, intention. • *pt, pp* of **think**.

thoughtful /ˈθɒtfʊl/ *adj* pensive; considerate.

thoughtless /ˈθɒtləs/ *adj* without thought; inconsiderate.

thousand /ˈθaʊzənd/ *adj* ten times one hundred; (*pl*) denoting any large but unspecified number. • *n* the number 1000.—**thousandth** *adj, n*.

thrash /θræʃ/ *vt* to beat soundly; to defeat; (*with* **out**) to discuss thoroughly, until agreement is reached. • *vi* to thresh grain; to writhe.

thrashing /-ɪŋ/ *n* a beating or flogging; punishment.

thread /θred/ *n* a fine strand or filament; a long thin piece of cotton, silk or nylon for sewing; the spiral part of a screw; (*of reasoning*) a line. • *vt* to pass a thread through the eye of a needle; to make one's way (through).

threadbare /ˈθredber/ *adj* worn, shabby.

threadworm /ˈθredwɜrm/ *n* a long slender worm, parasitic in humans and pigs.

threat /θret/ *n* a declaration of an intention to inflict harm or punishment upon another.

threaten /ˈθretən/ *vti* to utter threats to; to portend.

threatening /ˈθretənɪŋ/ *adj* menacing, intimidating; warning; ominous, sinister.—**threateningly** *adv*.

three /θriː/ *adj, n* the cardinal number next above two. • *n* the symbol (3, III, iii) expressing this.

three-D, 3-D /ˈθriːˌdi/ *n* a three-dimensional effect.

three-dimensional /-dəˈmenʃənəl/ *adj* having three dimensions.

threefold /ˈθriːfoːld/ *adj, adv* three times as much or as many; composed of three parts.

three-quarter /ˈθriːˈkwɔrtər/ *adj* being three quarters of the normal size or length. • *n* (*Rugby football*) one of *usu* four attacking players used particularly for running with the ball.

three Rs *npl* reading, writing and arithmetic, regarded as the basis of learning.

threescore /ˈθriːˈskɔr/ *n* (*arch*) sixty.—*also adj*.

threesome /ˈθriːsəm/ *n* a group of three; a game for three people.

threnody /ˈθrenədi/, **threnode** *n* (*pl* **threnodies, threnodes**) a song or speech of lamentation, *esp* on a person's death.

thresh /θreʃ/ *or* /θræʃ/ *vti* to beat out (grain) from (husks).

threshold /ˈθreʃoːld/ *or* /-hoːld/ *n* the sill at the door of a building; doorway, entrance; the starting point, beginning.

threw /θruː/ *see* **throw**.

thrice /θraɪs/ *adv* three times.

thrift /θrɪft/ *n* careful management of money.—**thrifty** *adj*.

thrill /θrɪl/ *vti* to tingle with pleasure or excitement. • *n* a sensation of pleasure and excitement; a trembling or quiver.

thriller /ˈθrɪlər/ *n* a novel, film or play depicting an exciting story of mystery and suspense.

thrilling /-ɪŋ/ *adj* exciting, gripping.

thrips /θrɪps/ *n* (*pl* **thrips**) any of various small insects with sucking mouthparts that feed on and damage plants.

thrive /θraɪv/ *vi* (**thriving, thrived** *or* **throve**, *pp* **thrived** *or* **thriven**) to prosper, to be successful; to grow vigorously.—**thriving** *adj*.

thro', thro /θruː/ *prep, adv* (*inf*) through.

throat /θroːt/ *n* the front part of the neck; the passage from the back of the mouth to the top part of the tubes into the lungs and stomach; an entrance.

throaty /ˈθroːti/ *adj* (**throatier, throatiest**) hoarse; guttural; deep, husky.—**throatily** *adv*.

throb /θrɒb/ *vi* (**throbbing, throbbed**) to beat or pulsate rhythmically, with more than usual force; to vibrate, beat.—*also n*.

throes /θroːz/ *npl* violent pangs or pain.

thrombin /ˈθrɒmbɪn/ *n* an enzyme that contributes to blood clotting.

thrombocyte /ˈθrɒmbəˌsaɪt/ *n* a blood platelet.

thrombosis /θrɒmˈboːsɪs/ *n* (*pl* **thromboses**) the forming of a blood clot in the heart or in a blood-vessel.

thrombus /ˈθrɒmbəs/ *n* (*pl* **thrombi**) the blood clot that blocks a vessel in thrombosis.

throne /θroːn/ *n* a chair of state occupied by a monarch; sovereign power. • *vt* to place on a throne.

throng /θrɒŋ/ *n* a crowd. • *vti* to crowd, congregate.

throstle /'θrɒsəl/ *n* a poetic name for a thrush.

throttle /'θrɒtəl/ *n* a valve controlling the flow of fuel or steam to an engine. • *vt* to regulate the speed of (an engine) using a throttle; to choke or strangle.

through /θru:/ *prep* from one side or end to the other; into and then out of; covering all parts; from beginning to end of; by means of; in consequence of; up to and including. • *adv* from one end or side to the other; completely. • *adj* going without interruption; unobstructed.

throughout /θru:'ʊt/ *prep* in every part of; from beginning to end. • *adv* everywhere; at every moment.

throughput /'θru:pʊt/ *n* the amount of material processed in a particular period, *esp* by a computer.

throughway /'θru:weɪ/ *see* **thruway**.

throve /θroːv/ *see* **thrive**.

throw /θroː/ *vb* (**throwing, threw,** *pp* **thrown**) *vt* to hurl, to fling; to cast off; (*party*) to hold; (*inf*) to confuse or disconcert; (*with* **off**) to cast off, discard, abandon; to distract, elude; to produce in a casual manner; to confuse, disconcert; (*with* **out**) to discard, reject; to dismiss or eject, *esp* forcibly; to emit, give forth; to construct out from a main section; to confuse, distract; (*with* **over**) to abandon, jilt; (*with* **together**) to assemble hurriedly or carelessly; to bring (people) into casual contact; (*with* **up**) to raise quickly; to resign from, abandon; to build hurriedly; to produce; (*inf*) to vomit. • *vi* to cast or hurl through the air (with the arm and wrist); to cast dice; (*with* **up**) (*inf*) to vomit. • *n* the act of throwing; the distance to which anything can be thrown; a cast of dice.

throwaway /'θroːəweɪ/ *adj* disposable.

throwback /'θroːbæk/ *n* a reversion to an earlier or more primitive type.

throw-in *n* (*soccer*) a throw from touch to resume play.

thrown /θroːn/ *see* **throw**.

thru /θru:/ *prep* (*sl*) through.

thrum /θrʌm/ *vi* (**thrumming, thrummed**) to strum; to beat incessantly.

thrush[1] /θrʌʃ/ *n* a songbird with a brown back and spotted breast.

thrush[2] *n* a fungal infection occurring in the mouths of babies or in women's vaginas.

thrust /θrʌst/ *vti* (**thrusting, thrust**) to push with force; to stab, pierce; to force into a situation. • *n* a forceful push or stab; pressure; the driving force of a propeller; forward movement; the point or basic meaning.

thruway /'θru:ˌweɪ/ *n* an expressway.—*also* **throughway**.

thud /θʌd/ *n* a dull, heavy sound, caused by a blow or a heavy object falling. • *vi* (**thudding, thudded**) to make such a sound.

thug /θʌg/ *n* a violent and rough person, *esp* a criminal.

thuggery /'θʌgəri/ *n* rough and violent behaviour.

thulium /'θu:liəm/ or /'θju:-/ *n* a malleable metallic element of the rare-earth group.

thumb /θʌm/ *n* the first, short, thick finger of the human hand. • *vt* (*book*) to turn (the pages) idly.

thumbed /θʌmd/ *adj* worn by use.

thumb index *n* a series of semicircular notches cut in the edge of a book for easier reference to particular parts.

thumbnail /'θʌmneɪl/ *n* the nail of the thumb. • *adj* concise.

thumbnut /'θʌmnʌt/ *n* a wing nut.

thumbscrew /'θʌmskru:/ *n* an instrument of torture that crushes the thumbs; a screw with a modified head for tightening with the finger and thumb.

thumbtack /'θʌmtæk/ *n* a flat-headed pin used for fastening paper, drawings, etc, a drawing pin.

thump /θʌmp/ *n* a heavy blow; a thud. • *vt* to strike with something heavy. • *vi* to throb or beat violently.

thumping /'θʌmpɪŋ/ *adj* (*inf*) very great.

thunder /'θʌndər/ *n* the deep rumbling or loud cracking sound after a flash of lightning; any similar sound. • *vi* to sound as thunder. • *vt* (*words*) to utter loudly.

thunderbolt /'θʌndərboːlt/ *n* a flash of lightning accompanied by thunder; anything sudden and shocking.

thunderclap /'θʌndərˌklæp/ *n* a loud bang of thunder.

thundering /'θʌndərɪŋ/ *adj* (*inf*) unusually great, excessive.

thunderous /'θʌndərəs/ *adj* very loud; producing thunder.

thunderstorm /'θʌndərˌstɔːrm/ *n* a storm with thunder and lightning.

thunderstruck /'θʌndərˌstrʌk/ *adj* astonished.

thundery /'θʌndəri/ *adj* indicating thunder.

Thur., Thurs. *abbr* = Thursday.

thurible /'θɜːrəbəl/ *n* a container for burning incense; another word for a censer.

Thursday /'θɜːrzdeɪ/ or /-di/ *n* the fifth day of the week.

thus /ðʌs/ *adv* in this or that way; to this degree or extent; so; therefore.

thwack /θwæk/ *vti* to hit hard, whack. • *n* a heavy blow, whack; the sound of this.

thwart /θwɔːrt/ *vt* to prevent, to frustrate.

thy /ðaɪ/ *poss adj* an old-fashioned word for **your**.

thyme /taɪm/ *n* a herb with small leaves used for flavouring savoury food.

thymol /'θaɪmɒl/ *n* a substance obtained from thyme and used as a fungicide and antiseptic.

thymus /'θaɪməs/ *n* (*pl* **thymuses, thymi**) a gland near the base of the neck that shrivels after puberty.

thyristor /θaɪ'rɪstər/ *n* any of various semiconductor devices that act as switches or rectifiers.

thyroid /'θaɪrɔɪd/ *n* the gland in the neck affecting growth and metabolism.

thyrotropin /ˌθaɪrə'troːpɪn/ or /θaɪ'rɒtrəpɪn/, **thyrotrophin** *n* a hormone secreted by the pituitary gland that stimulates the thyroid gland.

thyroxine, thyroxin /θaɪ'rɒksən/ *n* the main hormone produced by the thyroid gland.

Tl (*chem symbol*) thallium.

Ti (*chem symbol*) titanium.

ti /ti:/ *n* the seventh note of the scale in solmization.

tiara /ti'erə/ or /-'ɑːrə/ *n* a semicircular crown decorated with jewels.

tibia /'tɪbiə/ *n* (*pl* **tibiae, tibias**) the inner and thicker of the two bones between the knee and the ankle; the shinbone.

tic /tɪk/ *n* any involuntary, regularly repeated, spasmodic contraction of a muscle.

tick[1] /tɪk/ *n* a small bloodsucking insect that lives on people and animals.

tick[2] *vi* to make a regular series of short sounds; to beat, as a clock; (*inf*) to work, function; (*with* **over**) (*engine*) to idle; to function routinely. • *n* the sound of a clock; (*sl*) a moment.

tick[3] *vt* (*often with* **off**) to check off, as items in a list. • *n* a check mark (√) to check off items on a list or to indicate correctness.

ticker /'tɪkər/ *n* a telegraphic device that receives and outputs stock-market prices on a paper tape; any similar device operated electronically and outputting to a display monitor; (*inf*) the heart; (*inf*) a watch.

ticker tape *n* a continuous length of paper tape output from a telegraphic ticker.

ticket /'tɪkət/ *n* a printed card, etc, that gives one a right of travel or entry; a label on merchandise giving size, price, etc.

tickle /'tɪkəl/ *vt* to touch lightly to provoke pleasure or laughter; to please or delight.

ticklish /'tɪkəlɪʃ/ or /'tɪklɪʃ/, **tickly** *adj* sensitive to being tickled; easily offended; difficult or delicate.

tick-tack-toe /tɪktæk'toː/ *n sing* the US word for **noughts and crosses**.

ticktock *n* a ticking sound, *esp* of a clock. • *vi* to make such a sound.

tidal /'taɪdəl/ *adj* relating to, or having, tides.

tidal wave *n* a large wave as a result of high winds with spring tides; a huge destructive wave caused by earthquakes; something overwhelming.

tidbit /'tɪdbɪt/ *see* **titbit**.

tiddly /'tɪdli/ or /'tɪdəli/ *adj* (**tiddlier, tiddliest**) (*inf*) very small; (*inf*) slightly drunk.

tiddlywinks, tiddledywinks /'tɪdliwɪŋks/ or /'tɪdəli-/ *npl* a game whose object is to flick small plastic discs into a container by snapping them with a larger disc.

tide /taɪd/ *n* the regular rise and fall of the seas, oceans, etc *usu* twice a day; a current of water; a tendency; a flood. • *vt* (*with* **over**) to help along temporarily.

tidemark /'taɪdmɑːrk/ *n* the highest or lowest point reached by the sea.

tide rip *n* another word for a rip tide.

tidewater /'taɪdˌwɔːtər/ *n* water overflowing land at flood tide; water that is affected by the tide.

tidings /'taɪdɪŋz/ *npl* news, information.

tidy /'taɪdi/ *adj* (**tidier, tidiest**) neat; orderly. • *vt* to make neat; to put things in order.—**tidily** *adv.*—**tidiness** *n.*

tie /taɪ/ *vb* (**tying, tied**) *vt* to bind; to fasten with a string or thread; to make a bow or knot in; to restrict; (*with* **in**) to link with something; (*with* **up**) to fasten tightly (as if) with cord, string, etc; to connect, link; to invest money, etc, so as to make it unavailable for alternative uses; to preoccupy, distract. • *vi* to score the same number of points (as an opponent); (*with* **in**) to be linked in a certain way; (*with* **up**) to dock (a vessel). • *n* a knot, bow, etc; a bond; a long narrow piece of cloth worn with a shirt; necktie; an equality in score.

tiebreaker /ˈtaɪˌbreɪkər/, **tiebreak** /ˈtaɪbreɪk/ *n* any means of deciding a contest which has ended in a draw, such as an extra game, hole, question, etc.

tie-dyeing, tie-dye *n* a method of producing patterns on textiles by tying or knotting parts of the fabric to limit the amount of dye absorbed.

tie-in *n* a link or connection; a book linked to a film or TV series.

tie line *n* a telephone link between two private branch exchanges.

tiepin *n* a decorative pin used to secure the ends of a tie to a shirt.

tier /tiːr/ *n* a row or rank in a series when several rows are placed one above another.

tiercel /ˈtɪrsəl/ *n* a male of various hawks, *esp* as used in falconry.—*also* **tercel**.

tie-up *n* a link, connection; a standstill.

tiff /tɪf/ *n* a petty quarrel or disagreement. • *vi* to quarrel; to be in a huff.

tiger /ˈtaɪɡər/ *n* a large, fierce carnivorous animal of the cat family, having orange and black stripes.—**tigress** *nf*.

tiger beetle *n* any of numerous predatory beetles with powerful mandibles and spotted wing cases.

tiger cat *n* an ocelot or similar medium-sized wildcat with a striped coat.

tiger lily *n* a lily of China and Japan cultivated for its dark-spotted orange flowers.

tiger moth *n* any of various large moths marked with stripes or spots.

tiger's eye, tigereye *n* a brownish-yellow gemstone.

tiger shark *n* a large shark of warm waters with a striped or spotted skin.

tiger snake *n* an aggressive poisonous Australian snake with striped markings.

tight /taɪt/ *adj* taut; fitting closely; not leaky; constricted; miserly; difficult; providing little space or time for variance; (*contest*) close; (*inf*) drunk.

tighten /ˈtaɪtən/ *vti* to make or grow tight or tighter.

tightfisted /ˈtaɪtˌfɪstɪd/ *adj* miserly.

tightknit /ˈtaɪtˌnɪt/ *adj* tightly integrated.

tight-lipped /ˈtaɪtˈlɪpt/ *adj* having the lips firmly pressed together, as from annoyance; taciturn.

tightrope /ˈtaɪtrɔːp/ *n* a taut rope on which acrobats walk.

tights /taɪts/ *npl* a one-piece garment covering the legs and lower body; panty hose.

tigon /ˈtaɪɡən/, **tiglon** /ˈtaɪɡlən/ *n* the hybrid offspring of a tiger and a lioness.

tike /ˈtaɪk/ *see* **tyke**.

tilde /ˈtɪldə/ *n* a sign ~ placed above a letter to indicate a nasal sound, as in Spanish *señor*.

tile /taɪl/ *n* a thin slab of baked clay used for covering roofs, floors, etc. • *vt* to cover with tiles.

till[1] /tɪl/ *n* a drawer inside a cash register for keeping money.

till[2] *prep* until. • *conj* until.

till[3] *vt* (*land*) to cultivate for raising crops, as by ploughing.

tiller /ˈtɪlər/ *n* the handle or lever for turning a rudder in order to steer a boat.

tilt /tɪlt/ *vi* to slope, incline, slant. • *vt* to raise one end of. • *n* a slope or angle.

timbale *Fr.* /tɑ̃ˈbæl/ *n* a mixture of meat or fish with cream cooked in a mould lined with vegetables or pastry.

timber /ˈtɪmbər/ *n* wood when used as building material; a beam; trees collectively. • *vt* to provide with timber or beams.

timbered /ˈtɪmbərd/ *adj* (*building*) having wooden beams on the exterior.

timber hitch *n* a knot used to tie a rope, etc to a log or spar.

timber line /ˈtɪmbərˌlaɪn/ *see* **tree line**.

timber wolf *n* a type of large grey North American wolf.

timbre /ˈtæmbər/ or *Fr.* /ˈtæbrə/ *n* the quality of sound of a voice or musical instrument.

time /taɪm/ *n* the past, present and future; a particular moment; hour of the day; an opportunity; the right moment; duration; occasion; musical beat. • *vt* to regulate as to time; to measure or record the duration of.

time and motion study *n* the study of working procedures to improve efficiency.

time bomb *n* a bomb designed to explode at a predetermined time; something with a potentially delayed reaction.

time clock *n* a device that records the times of arrival and departure of an employee on a card.

time-consuming *adj* using up or taking a lot of time.

time exposure *n* exposure of a photographic film for *usu* several seconds; a photograph taken in this way.

time-honoured *adj* traditional, in accordance with venerable customs.

time immemorial *n* the far distant past beyond memory or record.

timekeeper /ˈtaɪmˌkiːpər/ *n* a person or instrument that records or keeps time; an employee who records the hours worked by others.—**timekeeping** *n*.

time lag *n* the interval between two connected events.

time-lapse photography *n* a technique of filming very slow action, such as plant growth, by taking single frames at fixed intervals and then running them at normal speed.

timeless /ˈtaɪmləs/ *adj* eternal; ageless.

timely /ˈtaɪmli/ *adj* at the right time, opportune.—**timeliness** *n*.

time-out *n* (*sport*) a suspension of play to rest, discuss tactics, etc; a brief rest period.

timepiece /ˈtaɪmpiːs/ *n* a clock or watch.

timer /ˈtaɪmər/ *n* a device for measuring, recording or controlling time; a device for controlling lights, heating, etc by setting an electrical clock to regulate their operations.

timeserver *n* a person whose opinions, behaviour, etc, follow current fashions.—**timeserving** *adj, n*.

timeshare *n* joint ownership of holiday accommodation by several people with each occupying the same premises in turn for short periods.

time signature *n* a sign on a musical staff indicating the number of beats per bar and time value of each beat.

timetable /ˈtaɪmˌteɪbəl/ *n* a list of times of arrivals and departures of trains, aeroplanes, etc; a schedule showing a planned order or sequence.

timeworn *adj* dilapidated; old-fashioned, hackneyed.

time zone *n* a geographical region throughout which the same standard time is used.

timid /ˈtɪmɪd/ *adj* shy; lacking confidence.—**timidity** *n*.—**timidly** *adv*.

timing /ˈtaɪmɪŋ/ *n* the control and expression of speech or actions to create the best effect, *esp* in the theatre, etc.

timocracy /taɪˈmɒkrəsi/ *n* (*pl* **timocracies**) a form of government in which ownership of property is required to hold office.

timorous /ˈtɪmərəs/ *adj* timid, fearful.—**timorously** *adv*.—**timorousness** *n*.

timpani /ˈtɪmpəni/ *npl* a set of kettledrums.—**timpanist** *n*.—*also* **tympani, tympany**.

tin /tɪn/ *n* a malleable metallic element; a container of tin, a can. • *adj* made of tin or tin plate. • *vt* (**tinning, tinned**) to put food into a tin.

tinctorial /tɪŋkˈtɔːriəl/ *adj* pertaining to colouring, dyeing or staining.

tincture /ˈtɪŋktʃər/ *n* an extract of a substance in a solution of alcohol for medicinal use; a colour, hue, tint; a hint of flavour or aroma; an heraldic colour. • *vt* to tint with a colour.

tinder /ˈtɪndər/ *n* dry wood for lighting a fire from a spark.

tinderbox /ˈtɪndərbɒks/ *n* a metal box with tinder, flint and steel for making a spark; an unstable or potentially explosive person, thing or situation.

tine /taɪn/ *n* a slender projecting point, as the prong of a fork or point of an antler.

tinea /ˈtɪniə/ *n* a fungal skin condition, *esp* ringworm.

tinfoil /ˈtɪnfɔɪl/ *n* baking foil for wrapping food; silver paper.

ting /tɪŋ/ *n* a high sharp ringing sound. • *vi* to make this sound.

tinge /tɪndʒ/ *vt* to tint or colour. • *n* a slight tint, colour or flavour.

tingle /ˈtɪŋɡəl/ *vi* to feel a prickling, itching or stinging sensation. • *n* a prickling sensation; a thrill.—**tinglingly** *adv*.—**tingly** *adj*.

tin god *n* a self-important person; a person who is undeservedly venerated.

tinker /ˈtɪŋkər/ n (formerly) a travelling mender of pots and pans. • vi to fiddle with; to attempt to repair.

tinkle /ˈtɪŋkəl/ vi to make a sound like a small bell ringing; to clink, to jingle; to clink repeatedly. • n a tinkling sound; (inf) a telephone call.

tinnitus /tɪˈnɑɪtəs/ n a continuous ringing or roaring sound in the ears caused by an infection, etc.

tinny /ˈtɪni/ adj (**tinnier, tinniest**) of or resembling tin; flimsy in construction or appearance; (food) having a metallic taste; having a high metallic sound.

tin plate n thin sheets of iron or steel plated with tin.—**tin-plate** adj.

tinsel /ˈtɪnsəl/ n a shiny Christmas decoration made of long pieces of thread wound round with thin strips of metal or plastic foil; something showy but of low value. • adj cheaply showy, flashy. • vt (**tinselling, tinselled** or **tinseling, tinseled**) to adorn with tinsel.

Tinseltown /ˈtɪnsəlˌtaʊn/ n (inf) Hollywood.

tint /tɪnt/ n a shade of any colour, esp a pale one; a tinge; a hair dye. • vt to colour or tinge.

tintinnabulation /ˌtɪntɪˌnæbjuˈleɪʃən/ n (the sound of) a ringing of bells.

tiny /ˈtaɪni/ adj (**tinier, tiniest**) very small.

tip[1] /tɪp/ n the pointed end of anything; the end, as of a billiard cue, etc. • vt (**tipping, tipped**) to put a tip on.

tip[2] vti (**tipping, tipped**) to tilt or cause to tilt; to overturn; to empty (out, into, etc); to give a gratuity to, as a waiter, etc; (rubbish) to dump; to give a helpful hint or inside information to. • n a light tap; a gratuity; a rubbish dump; an inside piece of information; a helpful hint.

tip-off /ˈtɪpɒf/ n a warning based on inside information.

tipple /ˈtɪpəl/ vi to drink alcohol regularly in small quantities. • n an alcoholic drink.

tipster /ˈtɪpstər/ n a person who gives horse-racing tips.

tipsy /ˈtɪpsi/ adj (**tipsier, tipsiest**) slightly drunk.

tiptoe /ˈtɪptoʊ/ vi (**tiptoeing, tiptoed**) to walk very quietly or carefully.

tiptop /ˈtɪptɒp/ adj excellent. • adv at the peak of condition. • n the best; the highest point.

tirade /ˈtaɪreɪd/ n a long and very angry speech of censure or criticism.

tire[1] /taɪr/ vt to exhaust the strength of, to weary. • vi to become weary; to lose patience; to become bored.

tire[2] /taɪr/ see **tyre**.

tired /taɪrd/ adj weary, sleepy; hackneyed, conventional, flat; (with of) exasperated by, bored with.

tireless /ˈtaɪrləs/ adj never wearying.—**tirelessly** adv.—**tirelessness** n.

tiresome /ˈtaɪrsəm/ adj tedious.

tiro /ˈtaɪroʊ/ see **tyro**.

'tis /tɪz/ (poet) = it is.

tissue /ˈtɪʃuː/ or /ˈtɪʃjuː/ n thin, absorbent paper used as a disposable handkerchief, etc; a very finely woven fabric; a mass of organic cells of a similar structure and function.

tit[1] /tɪt/ n a songbird such as a blue tit or great tit.

tit[2] n (vulg) a woman's breast.

titan /ˈtaɪtən/ n a person of enormous strength, size or ability.

titanic /taɪˈtænɪk/ adj monumental; huge.

titanium /taɪˈteɪniəm/ or /tɪ-/ n a strong metallic element used to make lightweight alloys.

titanium dioxide n a white powder used chiefly as a pigment.

titbit /ˈtɪtbɪt/ n a tasty morsel of food; a choice item of information.—also **tidbit**.

titer /ˈtaɪtər/ or /ˈtiːt-/ see **titre**.

tit for tat n an equivalent given in retaliation.

tithe /taɪð/ n a tenth part of agricultural produce, formerly allotted for the maintenance of the clergy and other church purposes. • vti to pay a tithe.

titillate /ˈtɪtəˌleɪt/ vt to tickle; to arouse or excite pleasurably.

titillation /-ˈleɪʃən/ n the act of titillating; the condition of being titillated; a pleasurable feeling, esp sexual.

titivate, tittivate /ˈtɪtɪˌveɪt/ vti to smarten up.

title /ˈtaɪtəl/ n the name of a book, play, piece of music, work of art, etc; the heading of a section of a book; a name denoting nobility or rank or office held, or attached to a personal name; (law) that which gives a legal right (to possession).

titled /ˈtaɪtəld/ adj having a title.

title deed n a deed or document proving a title or right to possession.

title page n the page of a book containing its title and usually the author's and publisher's names.

title role n the character in a play, film, etc after whom it is named.

titrate /ˈtaɪtreɪt/ vt to measure by titration.

titration /-ˈtreɪʃən/ n a method of determining the amount of a constituent in a solution by adding a known quantity of a reagent.

titre /ˈtaɪtər/ n the concentration of a substance in a solution as determined by titration.

titter /ˈtɪtər/ vi to giggle, snigger. • n a suppressed laugh.

tittle-tattle /ˈtɪtəlˌtætəl/ n idle chat, empty gossip.

titular /ˈtɪtjʊlər/ adj having, or relating to, a title; existing in name or title only.

tizzy /ˈtɪzi/ n (inf) a state of confusion or agitation.

TKO /ˈtiːˌkeɪoʊ/ abbr = technical knockout.

TLC abbr = tender loving care.

T-lymphocyte /ˈtiːˌlɪmfəsɑɪt/ see **T-cell**.

TM abbr = trademark; transcendental meditation.

Tm (chem symbol) thulium.

TNT abbr = trinitrotoluene.

to /tuː/ prep in the direction of; toward; as far as; expressing the purpose of an action; indicating the infinitive; introducing the indirect object; in comparison with. • adv toward.

toad /toʊd/ n an amphibious reptile, like a frog, but having a drier skin and spending less time in water.

toadflax /ˈtoʊdflæks/ n a common perennial plant with yellow and orange flowers.

toadstool /ˈtoʊdstuːl/ n a mushroom, esp a poisonous or inedible one.

toady /ˈtoʊdi/ n (pl **toadies**) a person who flatters insincerely, a sycophant. • vi (**toadying, toadied**) (with **to**) to act in a servile manner.

to and fro adj forward and backward; here and there.—**toing and froing** n.

toast /toʊst/ vt to brown over a fire or in a toaster; to warm; to drink to the health of. • n toasted bread; the sentiment or person to which one drinks.

toaster /ˈtoʊstər/ n a person who toasts; a thing that toasts, esp an electrical appliance for toasting.

toastmaster /ˈtoʊstˌmæstər/ n the proposer of toasts at public dinners.—**toastmistress** nf.

tobacco /təˈbækoʊ/ n (pl **tobaccos, tobaccoes**) a plant whose dried leaves are used for smoking, chewing or snuff.

tobacconist /təˈbækənɪst/ n a person or shop that sells cigarettes, etc.

toboggan /təˈbɒgən/ n a sledge.

toby (jug) /ˈtoʊbi/ n (pl **tobies, toby jugs**) a mug in the shape of a man with a three-cornered hat.

toccata /təˈkætə/ n a piece of music for keyboard in a free style with rapid runs.

tocopherol /ˌtoʊkɒˈfərɒl/ n vitamin E, present in wheat-germ oil, egg yolk, etc.

tocsin /ˈtɒksɪn/ n an alarm bell; a warning signal.

today /təˈdeɪ/ n this day; the present age. • adv on this day; nowadays.

toddle /ˈtɒdəl/ vi to walk with short, unsteady, steps, as a child who is learning to walk.

toddler /ˈtɒdlər/ n a young child.

toddy /ˈtɒdi/ n (pl **toddies**) a drink of whisky or brandy, sugar, and hot water.

to-do /təˈduː/ n (pl **to-dos**) (inf) a fuss, commotion, quarrel.

toe /toʊ/ n one of the five digits on the foot; the part of the shoe or sock that covers the toes.

toe cap /ˈtoʊkæp/ n a reinforced covering on the toe of a shoe or boot.

toehold /ˈtoʊhoʊld/ n a small ledge, crack, etc used in climbing; any slight means of support or access; (wrestling) a hold in which an opponent's foot is twisted.

toenail /ˈtoʊneɪl/ n the thin, hard covering on the end of the toes.

toffee, toffy /ˈtɒfi/ n (pl **toffees, toffies**) a sweet of brittle but tender texture made by boiling sugar and butter together.

toffee apple n an apple coated with toffee and eaten from a stick.

toffee-nosed adj (inf) pretentious, patronizing, arrogant.

tofu /ˈtoʊfuː/ n unfermented soya bean curd, used in cooking.

tog[1] /tɒg/ n (pl) (inf) clothes. • vt (**togging, togged**) (inf) to dress.

tog[2] *n* a unit of thermal resistance used to measure the power of insulation of a duvet, garment, etc.

toga /'toːgə/ *n* a piece of cloth draped around the body, as worn by citizens in ancient Rome.

together /tə'geðər/ *adv* in one place or group; in cooperation with; in unison; jointly.

toggle /'tɒgəl/ *n* a peg attached to a rope to prevent it from passing through a loop or knot; a button of this form; (*comput*) a software instruction for starting or stopping a style, etc. • *vt* to fasten with a toggle.

toggle switch *n* an electrical device for opening or closing a circuit.

toil /tɔɪl/ *vi* to work strenuously; to move with great effort. • *n* hard work.

toilet /'tɔɪlət/ *n* a lavatory; the room containing a lavatory; the act of washing and dressing oneself.

toilet paper, toilet tissue *n* an absorbent paper for cleansing after urination, etc, *usu* wound around a cardboard cylinder.

toiletry /'tɔɪlətri/ *n* (*pl* **toiletries**) a lotion, perfume, etc used in washing and dressing oneself.

toilet water *n* a diluted perfume.

token /'toːkən/ *n* a symbol, sign; an indication; a metal disc for a slot machine; a souvenir; a gift voucher. • *adj* nominal; symbolic.

tokenism /'toːkən,ɪzəm/ *n* the making of only a token effort.

tolbooth /'toːl,buːθ/ *n* (*Scot*) a town hall; a jail.

told /toːld/ *see* **tell**.

tolerable /'tɒlərəbəl/ *adj* bearable; fairly good.—**tolerably** *adv*.

tolerance /'tɒlərəns/ *n* open-mindedness; forbearance; (*med*) ability to resist the action of a drug, etc; ability of a substance to endure heat, stress, etc without damage.

tolerant /'tɒlərənt/ *adj* able to put up with the beliefs, actions, etc of others; broad-minded; showing tolerance to a drug, etc; capable of enduring stress, etc.

tolerate /'tɒlə,reɪt/ *vt* to endure, put up with, suffer.

toll[1] /toːl/ *n* money levied for passing over a bridge or road; a charge for a service, such as a long-distance telephone call; the number of people killed in an accident or disaster.

toll[2] *vt* (*bell*) to ring slowly and repeatedly, as a funeral bell. • *vi* to sound, as a bell. • *n* the sound of a bell when tolling.

tollbooth *n* a booth where money is paid to pass over a , road, etc.—*also* **tolbooth**.

toll call *n* a telephone call charged at higher than the standard or local rate.

tollgate /'toːl,geɪt/ *n* a gate where money is paid to pass over a bridge, road, etc.

toluene /'tɒlju,iːn/ *n* a flammable hydrocarbon derived from petroleum and coal tar used as a solvent and in organic synthesis.

tom /tɒm/ *n* a male animal, *esp* a cat.

tomahawk /'tɒmə,hɒk/ *n* a light axe used by North American Indians.

tomato /tə'meɪtoː/ *or* /-'mætoː/ *n* (*pl* **tomatoes**) a plant with red pulpy fruit used as a vegetable.

tomb /tuːm/ *n* a vault in the earth for the burial of the dead.

tomboy /'tɒmbɔɪ/ *n* a girl who likes rough outdoor activities.

tombstone /'tuːmstoːn/ *n* a memorial stone over a grave.

tomcat /'tɒmkæt/ *n* a male cat.

Tom, Dick and Harry /,tɒm dɪk ənd 'heri/ *n* an ordinary person, anybody taken at random.

tome /toːm/ *n* a large, heavy book, *esp* a scholarly one.

-tome /toːm/ *n suffix* a cutting instrument.

tomfool /tɒm'fuːl/ *n* a fool.

tomfoolery /tɒm'fuːləri/ *n* (*pl* **tomfooleries**) foolish behaviour; nonsense.

Tommy /'tɒmi/ *n* (*pl* **Tommies**) (*inf*) a private in the British army.

tommy gun *n* a (Thompson) sub-machine gun.

tommyrot /'tɒmi,rɒt/ *n* complete nonsense.

tomography /tə'mɒgrəfi/ *n* a process which produces an x-ray photograph of a plane section of the body or other object.

tomorrow /tə'mɒroː/ *or* /-mɒroː/ *n* the day after today; the future.—*also adv*.

tomtit /tɒm'tɪt/ *or* /'tɒm,tɪt/ *n* any of various small tits, *esp* a blue tit.

tom-tom /'tɒm,tɒm/ *n* a long small-headed drum usually beaten with the hands.

-tomy /təmi/ *n suffix* surgical incision.

ton /tʌn/ *n* a unit of weight equivalent to 2,240 pounds in UK, 2,000 pounds in US; (*pl*) (*inf*) a great quantity.

tonal /'toːnəl/ *n* of or pertaining to tone; having a key.

tonality /toː'næliti/ *n* (*pl* **tonalities**) the character of a musical composition in relation to scale or key; a system of tones; the scheme of colours and tones in a painting.

tone /toːn/ *n* the quality of a sound; pitch or inflection of the voice; colour, shade; body condition. • *vti* to give tone to; to harmonize (with); (*with* **down**) to (become) moderate in tone; (*with* **up**) to make or become healthier, tighter, etc.

tone arm *n* the tracking arm in a record player that holds the cartridge and stylus.

tone-deaf *adj* insensitive to differences in musical pitch.

tone poem *n* a symphonic poem.

toner /'toːnər/ *n* a cosmetic used on the skin for various effects; a chemical used to alter the tone of a photograph; the ink particles used in various reprographic devices such as laser printers and photocopiers.

tong /tɒŋ/ *n* (*formerly*) a Chinese-American secret society.

tongs /tɒŋgz/ *npl* an instrument consisting of two arms that are hinged, used for grasping and lifting.

tongue /tʌŋ/ *n* the soft, moveable organ in the mouth, used in tasting, swallowing, and speech; the ability to speak; a language; (*shoe*) a piece of leather under the laces; a jet of flame; the tongue of an animal served as food; the catch of a buckle.

tongue-lash /'tʌŋ,læʃ/ *vt* to scold, rebuke severely.—**tongue lashing** *n*.

tongue-tied /-,taɪd/ *adj* speechless.

tongue-twister *n* a sequence of words that it is difficult to pronounce quickly and clearly.

tonic /'tɒnɪk/ *n* a medicine that improves physical well-being; something that imparts vigour; a carbonated mineral water with a bitter taste. • *adj* relating to tones or sounds.

tonic sol-fa *n* the system of sol-fa or solmization syllables used to represent the notes of the musical scale.

tonight /tə'naɪt/ *n* this night; the night or evening of the present day.—*also adv*.

tonnage /'tʌnɪdʒ/ *n* a merchant ship's capacity measured in tons; the weight of its cargo; the amount of shipping of a country or port; merchant ships collectively; a duty levied on ships based on tonnage or capacity.

tonne /tʌn/ *n* metric ton, 1,000 kg.

tonometer /toː'nɒmətər/ *n* a device, such as a tuning fork, for measuring the pitch of tones.

tonsil /'tɒnsɪl/ *n* one of the two oval organs of soft tissue situated one on each side of the throat.

tonsillectomy /,tɒnsə'lektəmi/ *n* (*pl* **tonsillectomies**) a surgical operation to remove the tonsils.

tonsillitis /,tɒnsə'laɪtɪs/ *n* inflammation of the tonsils.

tonsure /'tɒnʃər/ *n* shaving part of the head to denote a clerical state in certain churches and religious orders; the shaved area itself. • *vt* to give a tonsure to (a monk, etc).—**tonsured** *adj*.

Tony /'toːni/ *n* (*pl* **Tonys, Tonies**) in the US, an annual award for excellence in the theatre.

too /tuː/ *adv* in addition; also; likewise; extremely; very.

took /tʊk/ *see* **take**.

tool /tuːl/ *n* an implement that is used by hand; a means for achieving any purpose.

tooling /'tuːlɪŋ/ *n* a design or decoration made with a tool, as on leather.

tool-maker /'tuːl,meɪkər/ *n* a person who repairs and maintains precision machine tools.

toolroom /-,ruːm/ *n* an area in a factory, machine shop, etc where tools are kept or repaired.

toot /tuːt/ *vi* to hoot a car horn, whistle, etc in short blasts. • *n* a hoot.—*also vt*.

tooth /tuːθ/ *n* (*pl* **teeth**) one of the white, bone-like structures arranged in rows in the mouth, used in biting and chewing; the palate; a tooth-like projection on a comb, saw, or wheel.

toothache /'tuːθeɪk/ *n* a pain in a tooth.

toothbrush /-brʌʃ/ *n* a small brush for cleaning teeth.

toothed whale *n* any of various whales with simple teeth, such as dolphins.

toothpaste /-peɪst/ *n* a paste for cleaning teeth, used with a toothbrush.

toothpick /-pɪk/ *n* a sliver of wood or plastic for removing food particles from between the teeth.

tooth powder *n* a powder used for cleaning the teeth.

toothsome /-səm/ *adj* appetizing.

toothy /'tu:θi/ *adj* (**toothier, toothiest**) having or revealing prominent teeth.

top[1] /tɒp/ *n* the highest, or uppermost, part or surface of anything; the highest in rank; the crown of the head; the lid. • *adj* highest; greatest. • *vt* to cover on the top; to remove the top of or from; to rise above; to surpass; (*with* **up**) to raise up to the full capacity or amount.

top[2] *n* a child's toy, which is spun on its pointed base.

topaz /'to:pæz/ *n* any of various yellow gems.

top brass *npl* (*inf*) the highest-ranking military or other officials.

topcoat /'tɒpko:t/ *n* an overcoat.

top dog *n* (*inf*) the leader, the most important person.

top drawer *n* the most prominent people in society.

tope[1] /to:p/ *vi* to consume alcoholic drink in excessive quantities.—**toper** *n*.

tope[2] *n* a small grey European shark.

topee /'to:pi/ *n* a pith helmet.—*also* **topi**.

top flight *adj* excellent, of the highest quality.

topgallant /tɒp'gælənt/ *or* /tə'gælənt/ *n* a mast or sail above a topmast.—*also adj*.

top gear *n* the highest gear in a motor vehicle; maximum speed or activity.

top hat *n* a man's tall, silk hat.

top-heavy *adj* having an upper part too heavy for the lower, causing instability.

topi /'to:pi/ *see* **topee**.

topiary /'to:pi‚ɛri/ *adj* pertaining to the art or practice of trimming bushes and trees into ornamental shapes. • *n* (**topiaries**) a tree or bush shaped in this way.

topic /'tɒpik/ *n* a subject for discussion; the theme of a speech or writing.

topical /-əl/ *adj* of current interest.

topknot /'tɒpnɒt/ *n* a tuft of hair or knot of ribbons on the head.

topless /-ləs/ *adj* lacking a top; (*garment*) revealing the breasts; wearing such a garment.

topmast /-mæst/ *n* a mast next above the lowest mast.

topmost /mo:st/ *adj* nearest the top, highest.

topnotch /-nɒtʃ/ *adj* (*inf*) excellent.

topo- /'to:po:/, **top-** /to:p/ *prefix* place; locality.

topography /tə'pɒgrəfi/ *n* (*pl* **topographies**) the study or description of surface features of a place on maps or charts.—**topographer** *n*.—**topographical** *adj*.

topology /tə'pɒlədʒi/ *n* the study of the properties of geometric figures that are unaffected by distortion.—**topological** *adj*.—**topologist** *n*.

topping /'tɒpiŋ/ *n* a top layer, *esp* a sauce for food.

topple /'tɒpəl/ *vi* to fall over. • *vt* to cause to overbalance and fall; (*government*) to overthrow.

topsail /'tɒpseil/ *or* /-səl/ *n* a square sail next above the lowest sail on a mast.

top secret *adj* highly confidential.

topside /-said/ *n* the upper side; a boneless cut of beef; the open or upper decks of a ship. • *adv* on top.

topsoil /-soil/ *n* the surface layer of soil.

topspin /-spin/ *n* a spin imparted to a ball that makes it travel faster or higher.

topsy-turvy /'tɛpsi‚tɜrvi/ *adj, adv* turned upside down; in confusion.

toque /tu:k/ *n* a small brimless hat for women; in Canada, a close-fitting, stretchable knitted hat (*also* **tuque**).

tor /tɔr/ *n* a high, rocky hill.

Torah /'tɔrə/ *n* (a scroll containing) the Pentateuch; Jewish sacred writings and teachings collectively.

torch /tɔrtʃ/ *n* a flashlight; a device for giving off a hot flame.—**torchlight** *n*.

torchbearer /'tɔrtʃ‚bɛrər/ *n* a person carrying a torch; a leader, source of inspiration.

torch song /tɔrtʃsɒŋ/ *n* a sentimental song about the sufferings of love.—**torch singer** *n*.

tore /tɔr/ *see* **tear**.

toreador /'tɔriə‚dɔr/ *n* a bullfighter, *esp* on horseback.

torero /tə'rɛro:/ *n* (*pl* **toreros**) a bullfighter, *esp* one who fights on foot.

torii /'tɔrii/ *n* (*pl* **torii**) a gateway to a Japanese Shinto temple.

torment /'tɔrmɛnt/ *n* torture, anguish; a source of pain. • *vt* to afflict with extreme pain, physical or mental.—**tormentor, tormenter** *n*.

torn /tɔrn/ *see* **tear**[2].

tornado /tɔr'neido:/ *n* (*pl* **tornadoes, tornados**) a violently whirling column of air seen as a funnel-shaped cloud that *usu* destroys everything in its narrow path.

toroid /'tɔrɔid/ *n* (a solid enclosed by) a surface generated by a circle rotated about a line in the same plane as but not intersecting the circle.—**toroidal** *adj*.

torpedo /tɔr'pi:do:/ *n* (*pl* **torpedoes**) a self-propelled submarine offensive weapon, carrying an explosive charge. • *vt* to attack, hit, or destroy with torpedo(es).

torpedo boat *n* a small high-speed warship from which torpedoes are launched.

torpid /'tɔrpid/ *adj* lethargic, sluggish.—**torpidity** *n*.

torpor /'tɔrpər/ *n* a state of lethargy.

torque /tɔrk/ *n* (*physics*) a force that causes rotation around a central point, such as an axle.

torr /tɔr/ *n* (*pl* **torr**) a unit of pressure equal to 133.322 newtons per square metre.

torrent /'tɔrənt/ *n* a rushing stream; a flood of words.—**torrential** *adj*.

torrid /'tɔrid/ *adj* burning, parched or scorched with heat; passionate.—**torridity, torridness** *n*.

torsi /'tɔrsi/ *see* **torso**.

torsion /'tɔrʃən/ *n* a twisting effect on an object when equal forces are applied at both ends but in opposite directions.

torsk /tɔrsk/ *n* (*pl* **torsk, torsks**) a large marine food fish related to the cod.

torso /'tɔrso:/ *n* (*pl* **torsos, torsi**) the trunk of the human body.

tort /tɔrt/ *n* (*law*) a private or civil wrong.

torte /tɔrt/ *n* a rich cake or tart filled with cream, fruit, etc.

tortellini /‚tɔrtə'li:ni/ *n* small stuffed pasta shapes.

tortilla /tɔr'ti:ə/ *n* a round thin maize pancake usually eaten hot with a topping or filling.

tortoise /'tɔrtəs/ *n* a slow-moving reptile with a dome-shaped shell into which it can withdraw.

tortoiseshell /'tɔrtəs‚ʃɛl/ *n* a brown and yellow colour.

tortricid /'tɔrtrisid/ *n* any of a family of moths whose larvae live in nests of rolled-up leaves.

tortuous /'tɔrtʃəs/ *adj* full of twists, involved.—**tortuously** *adv*.

torture /'tɔrtʃər/ *n* subjection to severe physical or mental pain to extort a confession, or as a punishment.—*also vt*.—**torturer** *n*.

torus /'tɔrəs/ *n* a convex semicircular moulding, *esp* at the base of a column; a toroid.—**toric** *adj*.

Tory /'tɔri/ *n* (*pl* **Tories**) a member of the Conservative Party in UK and Canadian politics; an American supporter of the British during the American Revolution.—*also adj*.

tosh /tɒʃ/ *n* (*sl*) nonsense.

toss /tɒs/ *vt* to throw up; to pitch; to fling; (*head*) to throw back; (*with* **off**) to produce, write, perform, etc, quickly and easily; to drink in one gulp. • *vi* to be tossed about; to move restlessly; (*with* **up**) to spin a coin to decide a question by the side that falls uppermost. • *n* the act of tossing or being tossed; a pitch; a fall.

toss-up *n* the throwing of a coin to decide a question; an even chance.

tot[1] /tɒt/ *n* anything little, *esp* a child; a small measure of spirits.

tot[2] *vt* (**totting, totted**) (*with* **up**) to add up or total.

total /'to:təl/ *adj* whole, complete; absolute. • *n* the whole sum; the entire amount. • *vt* (**totalling, totalled** *or* **totaling, totaled**) to add up.—**totally** *adv*.

totalitarian /to:‚tæli'tɛriən/ *adj* relating to a system of government in which one political group maintains complete control, *esp* under a dictator.—**totalitarianism** *n*.

totality /to:'tæliti/ *n* (*pl* **totalities**) the whole amount.

totalizator /'to:təlai‚zeitər/ *n* a machine for registering bets and computing the odds and payoff, as at a racetrack.

tote[1] /to:t/ *n* (*inf*) totalizator.

tote[2] *vt* to carry.

tote bag *n* (*inf*) a large bag for shopping or other items.

totem /'to:təm/ *n* an object regarded as a symbol and treated with respect by a particular group of people.

totem pole *n* a large pole carved with totemic symbols used in rituals by certain North American Indian tribes.

totter /'tɒtər/ *vi* to walk unsteadily; to shake or sway as if about to fall.—**tottery** *adj*.

toucan /'tu:kən/ *n* a fruit-eating South American bird with an immense, brightly coloured beak.

touch /tʌtʃ/ *vt* to come in contact with, *esp* with the hand or fingers; to reach; to affect with emotion; to tinge or tint; to border on; (*sl*) to ask for money (from); (*with* **off**) to cause to explode, as with a lighted match; to cause (violence, a riot, etc) to start; (*with* **up**) to improve by making minor alterations or additions to. • *vi* to be in contact; to be adjacent; to allude to. • *n* the act of touching; the sense by which something is perceived through contact; a trace; understanding; a special quality or skill.

touch-and-go *adj* precarious, risky.

touchdown /'tʌtʃdaʊn/ *n* the moment when an aircraft or space-ship lands; (*rugby, American football*) a placing of the ball on the ground to score.

touché /tu:'ʃeɪ/ *interj* (*fencing*) used to acknowledge an opponent's hit; an acknowledgement of a valid or accomplished reply, remark, witty comment, etc.

touched /tʌtʃt/ *adj* emotionally affected; mentally disturbed.

touching /'tʌtʃɪŋ/ *adj* affecting, moving.

touch judge *n* a linesman in Rugby football.

touchline /'tʌtʃlaɪn/ *n* (*football, etc*) the side boundary of a pitch.

touchmark /-mɑrk/ *n* a maker's distinguishing mark on pewter.

touchpaper /-peɪpər/ *n* paper impregnated with a slow-burning substance used to ignite fireworks.

touchstone /-stoːn/ *n* a siliceous stone used to test gold and silver from the marks they make on it; any test or standard of genuineness.

touch-type *vi* to type quickly and accurately without looking at the keyboard.—**touch-typist** *n*.

touchwood /-wʊd/ *n* dry rotten wood useful for tinder.

touchy /'tʌtʃi/ *adj* (**tochier, touchiest**) irritable; very risky.

tough /tʌf/ *adj* strong; durable; hardy; rough and violent; difficult; (*inf*) unlucky.—**toughen** *vti*.—**toughness** *n*.

tough-minded *adj* realistic; unsentimental.

toupee /tu:'pi:/ *n* a wig or section of hair to cover a bald spot, *esp* worn by men.

tour /tur/ *n* a turn, period, etc as of military duty; a long trip, as for sightseeing. • *vti* to go on a tour (through).

touraco /'turə,ko:/ *n* (*pl* **touracos**) any of a family of brightly coloured crested birds native to Africa.

tour de force /turdə'fɔrs/ *n* (*pl* **tours de force**) an outstanding achievement or performance.

tourism /'turizəm/ *n* travelling for pleasure; the business of catering for people who do this; the encouragement of touring.

tourist /'turizəm/ *n* one who makes a tour, a sightseer, travelling for pleasure.—*also adj*.

tourist class *n* economy accommodation, as on a ship, aircraft, etc.

touristy /'turisti/ *adj* (*inf*) full of or designed for tourists.

tourmaline /'turmə,li:n/ *n* a silicate mineral of various colours used in jewellery and electronic equipment.

tournament /'tɜrnəmənt/ *or* /'tur-/ *n* a sporting event involving a number of competitors and a series of games.

tournedos /'tɜrnə,do:/ *n* (*pl* **tournedos**) a thick round fillet of beef steak.

tourniquet /'tɜrnəkət/ *or* /'tur-/, /-,keɪ/, /-,ki:/ *n* a device for compressing a blood vessel to stop bleeding.

tour operator *n* a company that specializes in offering package tours.

tousle /'teʊsəl/ *or* /-zəl/ *vt* to make untidy, ruffle, make tangled (*esp* hair).

tout /'teʊt/ *vti* (*inf*) to praise highly; (*inf*) to sell betting tips on (race horses); (*inf*) to solicit business in a brazen way. • *n* (*inf*) a person who does so.

tovarish, tovarich /tə'vɑrɪʃ/ *n* a comrade.

tow /taʊ/ *vt* to pull or drag with a rope. • *n* the act of towing; a towrope.

towage /'to:ɪdʒ/ *n* the act of towing; the charge made for it.

toward /tə'wɔrd/ *or* /twɔrd/, **towards** /-wɔrdz/ *prep* in the direction of; concerning; just before; as a contribution to.

towel /'taʊəl/ *n* an absorbent cloth for drying the skin after it is washed, and for other purposes; **to throw in the towel** to admit defeat. • *vti* (**towelling, towelled** *or* **toweling, toweled**) to rub (oneself) with a towel.

towelette /'taʊəl,ɛt/ *n* a small moistened tissue for cleaning the face, etc.

towelling, toweling /'taʊəlɪŋ/ *n* cloth for towels; a rubbing with a towel.

tower /'taʊər/ *n* a tall, narrow building, standing alone or forming part of another; a fortress. • *vi* (*with* **over**) to rise above; to loom.

tower block *n* a skyscraper.

towering /'taʊərɪŋ/ *adj* immensely tall; powerful, impressive; intense.

town /taʊn/ *n* a densely populated urban centre, smaller than a city and larger than a village; the people of a town.

townie /'taʊni/ *n* (*pl* **townies**) a person who lives in a city or town as opposed to the countryside.—*also* **towny**.

town hall *n* a large building housing the offices of the town council, often with a hall for public meetings.

town house /'taʊnhaʊs/ *n* a two or three-story house with a garage below, *usu* one of a row; a house in a fashionable area; one's house in town.

township /'taʊnʃɪp/ *n* a division of a county in many US states, constituting a unit of local government; (*formerly*) in South Africa, an urban area reserved for Blacks.

towny /'taʊni/ *see* **townie**.

towpath /'to:pæθ/ *n* the footpath beside a river or canal.

towrope, towline *n* a strong rope or cable for towing a wheeled vehicle, ship, etc.

tox- /tɒks/, **toxic-** /'tɒksɪk/, **toxico-** /'tɒksɪko:/ *prefix* poison.

toxaemia, toxemia /tɒk'si:miə/ *n* a type of blood poisoning.—**toxaemic, toxemic** *adj*.

toxic /'tɒksɪk/ *adj* poisonous; harmful; deadly.—**toxicity** *n*.

toxicant /-ənt/ *n* a poison. • *adj* poisonous.

toxicology /tɒksɪ'kɒlədʒi/ *n* the scientific study of poisons, their effects and antidotes.—**toxicologic, toxicological** *adj*.—**toxicologist** *n*.

toxin /'tɒksɪn/ *n* a poison produced by microorganisms and causing certain diseases.

toxocariasis /ˌtɒksə'kærɪeɪsɪs/ *n* a disease in humans caused by the larvae of a parasitic roundworm found in dogs and cats.

toxoid /'tɒksɔɪd/ *n* a toxin of reduced power used in vaccines to stimulate the production of antitoxins.

toxoplasmosis /ˌtɒkso:plæz'mo:sɪs/ *n* a disease affecting the central nervous system caused by a parasitic worm.

toy /tɔɪ/ *n* an object for children to play with; a replica; a miniature. • *vi* to trifle; to flirt.

toyboy *n* the younger male lover of an older woman.

trace /treɪs/ *n* a mark etc left by a person, animal or thing; a barely perceptible footprint; a small quantity. • *vt* to follow by tracks; to discover the whereabouts of; (*map, etc*) to copy by following the lines on transparent paper.

traceable /'treɪsəbəl/ *adj* able to be traced.—**traceably** *adv*.

trace element *n* a chemical element, as copper, zinc, etc, essential in nutrition but only in minute amounts.

tracer /'treɪsər/ *n* a projectile which glows or leaves a smoke trail allowing its flight to be observed; a radioisotope introduced into the body whose course can be traced by a detector for diagnostic purposes.

trachea /'treɪkiə/ *or* /trə'ki:ə/ *in* (*pl* **tracheae**) the air passage from the mouth to the lungs, the windpipe.

tracheo- /'treɪkio:/, **trache-** /'treɪki/ *prefix* trachea.

tracheotomy /ˌtreɪki'ɒtəmi/ *n* (*pl* **tracheotomies**) an incision into the trachea, *esp* to bypass a blockage in the air passage.

trachoma /trə'ko:mə/ *n* an infectious eye disease caused by a virus that leads to scarring and eventual blindness.—**trachomatous** *adj*.

trachyte /'treɪkaɪt/ *or* /'træk-/ *n* a type of light-coloured volcanic rock.

tracing /'treɪsɪŋ/ *n* a copy of a drawing, etc made by tracing.

tracing paper *n* transparent paper used for tracing.

track /træk/ *vt* to follow the tracks of; (*satellite, etc*) to follow by radar and record position; (*with* **down**) to find by tracking. • *n* a mark left; a footprint; parallel steel rails on which trains run; a course for running or racing; sports performed on a track, as running, hurdling; the band on which the wheels of a tractor or tank run; one piece of music on a record; a sound track.

track-and-field *adj* denoting various competitive athletic events (as running, jumping, weight-throwing) performed on a track and adjacent field.

tracker /'trækər/ *n* a person who follows by tracking footprints, etc; a dog that follows a scent.

track event *n* an athletic event that takes place on a running track.

tracking station *n* a place that uses radio or radar antennae to follow the course of objects in space or the atmosphere.

tracklaying *adj* (*vehicle*) having an endless loop of metal track around the wheels.

track record *n* (*inf*) a record of the past achievements or failures of someone or something.

track shoe *n* a spiked running shoe.

tracksuit *n* a loose suit worn by athletes to keep warm.

tract[1] /trækt/ *n* an expanse of land or water; a part of a bodily system or organ.

tract[2] *n* a treatise.

tractable /'træktəbəl/ *adj* easily worked; easily taught; docile.

traction /'trækʃən/ *n* act or state of drawing and pulling; (*med*) the using of weights to pull on a muscle, etc, to correct an abnormal condition.

tractor /'træktər/ *n* a motor vehicle for pulling heavy loads and farming machinery.

trad /træd/ *adj* (*inf*) traditional. • *n* traditional jazz.

trade /treid/ *n* buying and selling (of commodities); commerce; occupation; customers; business. • *vi* to buy and sell; to exchange; (*with* **on**) to take advantage of.—**trader** *n*.

trade cycle *n* a recurrent fluctuation in economic activity between boom and slump.

trade gap *n* the amount by which the value of a country's visible imports exceeds its visible exports.

trade-in *n* a used item given in part payment when buying a replacement.

trade-off *n* the exchange or substitution of one thing or priority for another, often as a compromise.

trademark /'treidmɑrk/ *n* a name used on a product by a manufacturer to distinguish it from its competitors, *esp* when legally protected.—*also vt*.

tradescantia /ˌtrædə'skæntiə/ *n* any of a genus of common houseplants cultivated for their variegated foliage.

tradesman /'treidzmən/ *n* (*pl* **tradesmen**) a shopkeeper; a skilled worker.

trade union, trades union *n* an organized association of employees of any trade or industry for the protection of their income and working conditions.

trade wind *n* a wind that blows toward the equator at either side of it.

trading /'treidiŋ/ *n* the act of buying and selling (goods, etc).—*also adj*.

tradition /trə'diʃən/ *n* the handing down from generation to generation of opinions and practices; the belief or practice thus passed on; custom.—**traditional** *adj*.—**traditionally** *adv*.

traduce /trə'djuːs/ or /-'djuːs/ *vt* to speak badly of; to misrepresent.

traffic /'træfik/ *n* trade; the movement or number of vehicles, pedestrians, etc, along a street, etc. • *vi* (**trafficking, trafficked**) to do business (*esp.* in illegal drugs).

traffic circle *n* a junction of thoroughfares where traffic circulates one way to ease progress, a roundabout.

traffic island *n* a raised area in the centre of a road to guide traffic and provide refuge for pedestrians crossing.

traffic light *n* one of a set of coloured lights used to control traffic at street crossings, etc.

traffic pattern *n* a network of airlanes above an airport to which aircraft are restricted.

tragacanth /'trægəˌkænθ/ *n* a gum obtained from a species of spiny leguminous plants used in pharmacy and in calico printing.

tragedian /trə'dʒiːdiən/ *n* an actor who plays mainly tragic roles.—**tragedienne** *nf*.

tragedy /'trædʒədi/ *n* (*pl* **tragedies**) a play or drama that is serious and sad, and the climax a catastrophe; an accident or situation involving death or suffering.—**tragic** *adj*.—**tragically** *adv*.

tragicomedy /ˌtrædʒɪ'kɒmədi/ *n* a dramatic or literary work which combines tragic and comic elements; a situation or event with tragic and comic aspects.

trail /treil/ *vt* to drag along the ground; to have in its wake; to follow behind; to advertise a film, event or programme beforehand. • *vi* to hang or drag loosely behind; (*plant*) to climb; (*with* **off** *or* **away**) to grow weaker or dimmer. • *n* a path or track; the scent of an animal; something left in the wake (*eg a trail of smoke*).

trailblazer /'treilˌbleizər/ *n* a person who blazes a trail; a pioneer in a particular field.

trailer /-ər/ *n* a large vehicle designed to be towed by a truck; etc; in the US, a motor home; an advertisement for a film or television programme.

trailer park *n* in the US, an area available for rent to motor homes, caravans, etc, *usu* with electricity, water, etc, piped in.

trailing edge *n* the rear edge of an aerofoil.

train /trein/ *vt* to teach, to guide; to tame for use, as animals; to prepare for racing, etc; (*gun, etc*) to aim. • *vi* to do exercise or preparation. • *n* a series of railroad cars pulled by a locomotive; a sequence; the back part of a dress that trails along the floor; a retinue.

trained /treind/ *adj* skilled.

trainee /trei'niː/ *n* a person who is being trained.

trainer /'treinər/ *n* a coach or instructor in sports; a person who prepares horses for racing.

training /-iŋ/ *n* practical instruction; a course of physical exercises.

training school *n* an institution for training in vocational subjects, *eg* teaching, nursing.

training ship *n* a moored vessel on which people are taught seamanship.

train oil *n* oil obtained from whale blubber.

train surfing *n* the practice of clinging onto the outside of a moving train for kicks.—**train surfer** *n*.

traipse /treips/ *vi* to walk wearily, trudge about. • *n* a tiring walk, a trudge.

trait /treit/ *n* a characteristic feature.

traitor /'treitər/ *n* a person who commits treason or betrays his country, friends, etc.—**traitorous** *adj*.

trajectory /trə'dʒektəri/ *n* (*pl* **trajectories**) the path of an object, such as a bullet, moving through space.

tram[1] /træm/ *n* a small wagon running on rails in a mine; a streetcar; a cable car.

tram[2] *n* a double twisted thread used in some silks.

trammel /'træməl/ *n* a type of net for catching birds or fish; (*often pl*) a hindrance to freedom of movement or action; an instrument for drawing ellipses. • *vt* (**trammelling, trammeling, trammeled**) to trap, catch; to hinder, restrict.

tramp /træmp/ *vti* to walk heavily; to tread or trample; to wander about as a tramp. • *n* a vagrant; (*sl*) a prostitute.

trample /'træmpəl/ *vti* to tread under foot.

trampoline /ˌtræmpə'liːn/ *n* a sheet of strong canvas stretched tightly on a frame, used in acrobatic tumbling.

trance /træns/ *n* a state of unconsciousness, induced by hypnosis, in which some of the powers of the waking body, such as response to commands, may be retained.

tranche /trɑːntʃ/ *n* a portion of something, *esp* a sum of money or issue of shares.

tranquil /'træŋkwil/ *adj* quiet, calm, peaceful.—**tranquilly** *adv*.

tranquillize, tranquilize /'træŋkwiˌlaiz/ *vt* to make tranquil, *esp* by administering a drug.—**tranquillization, tranquilization** *n*.

tranquillizer, tranquilizer /ˌtræŋkwi'laizər/ *n* a drug that calms.

tranquillity, tranquility /træŋ'kwiliti/ *n* the state of being tranquil; calmness.

trans. *abbr* = transitive; translated; translation; translator.

trans- /trænz/ *prefix* through; across; on the other side of.

transact /træn'zækt/ *vt* (*business*) to conduct or carry out.

transaction /træn'zækʃən/ *n* the act of transacting; something transacted, *esp* a business deal; (*pl*) a record of the proceedings of a society.

transalpine /trænz'ælpain/ *adj* beyond (*usu* north) of the Alps.

transatlantic /ˌtrænzət'læntik/ *adj* crossing the Atlantic Ocean; across, beyond the Atlantic.

transceiver /træn'siːvər/ *n* a combined radio transmitter and receiver.

transcend /træn'send/ *vt* to rise above or beyond; to surpass.—**transcendent** *adj*.

transcendental /ˌtrænsen'dentəl/ *adj* beyond physical experience; surpassing; supernatural.—**transcendentally** *adv*.

transcendental meditation *n* a technique for emptying and refreshing the mind by repeating a mantra.

transcontinental /ˌtrænskɒnti'nentəl/ *adj* extending or travelling across a continent.—**transcontinentally** *adv*.

transcribe /træn'skraib/ *vt* to write out fully from notes or a tape recording; to make a phonetic transcription; to arrange a piece of music for an instrument other than the one it was written for.

transcript /træn'skript/ *n* a written or printed copy made by transcribing; an official copy of proceedings, etc.

transcription /træn'skripʃən/ *n* the act of transcribing; something transcribed, *esp* a piece of music; a transcript; a recording made for broadcasting.

transducer /træns'du:sər/ or /-'dju:s/ *n* a device that converts energy from one form into another.

transept /'træn'sept/ *n* one of the two wings of a church, at right angles to the nave.

transfer /'trænsfər/ *vb* (**transferring, transferred**) *vt* to carry, convey, from one place to another; (*law*) to make over (property) to another; (*money*) to move from the control of one institution to another. • *vi* to change to another bus, etc. • *n* the act of transferring; the state of being transferred; someone or something that is transferred; a design that can be moved from one surface to another.—**transferable** *adj*.

transference /'trænsfərəns/ *n* the act of transferring; the state of being transferred; (*psychoanal*) the redirection of emotion under analysis, *usu* toward the analyst.

transfer RNA *n* a form of RNA that carries an amino acid to a ribosome in protein synthesis.

transfiguration /ˌtrænsfɪgəˈreɪʃən/ *n* a change in appearance, *esp* to a more spiritual or exalted form; (*with cap*) (the festival commemorating) the change in the appearance of Christ as described in the Gospels.

transfigure /'trænsfɪgər/ *vt* to transform or become transformed in appearance, *esp* for the better.

transfix /'trænsfɪks/ *vt* to impale with a sharp weapon; to paralyse with shock or horror.

transform /'trænsfɔrm/ *vti* to change the shape, appearance, or condition of; to convert.—**transformation** *n*.

transformer /-ər/ *n* a device for changing alternating current with an increase or decrease of voltage.

transfusion /træns'fjuːʒən/ *n* the injection of blood into the veins of a sick or injured person.—**transfuse** *vt*.

transgress /-'gres/ *vti* to break or violate (a moral law or code of behaviour); to overstep (a limit).—**transgressor** *n*.

transgression /-'greʃən/ *n* the act of transgressing; infringement of a rule, etc; a sin.

transhumance /-'hjuːməns/ *n* the seasonal movement of livestock to new grazing areas.

transient /'trænziənt/ *adj* temporary; of short duration, momentary.—**transience** *n*.

transistor /'trænzɪstər/ *n* a device using a semiconductor to amplify sound, as in a radio or television; a small portable radio.

transit /'trænzɪt/ *n* a passing over or through; conveyance of people or goods.

transit camp *n* temporary accommodation for soldiers, refugees, etc.

transition /træn'zɪʃən/ *n* passage from one place or state to another; change.—**transitional** *adj*.

transitive /'trænzɪtɪv/ *adj* (*gram*) denoting a verb that requires a direct object; of or relating to transition.—**transitively** *adv*.—**transitivity** *n*.

transitory /'trænzɪˌtɔri/ *adj* lasting only a short time.—**transitorily** *adv*.——**transitoriness** *n*.

translate /'trænzleɪt/ or /-'leɪt/ *vti* to express in another language; to explain, interpret.—**translator** *n*.

translation /trænz'leɪʃən/ *n* the act of translating; something that has been translated into another language or state; an interpretation.

transliterate /-'lɪtəˌreɪt/ *vt* to convert a word, etc into the corresponding characters of another alphabet.—**transliteration** *n*.

translucent /-'luːsənt/ *adj* allowing light to pass through, but not transparent.—**translucence** *n*.

transmigrate /ˌtrænzmaɪ'greɪt/ *vi* (*soul*) to pass into the body of another person after death; to migrate.

transmission /trænz'mɪʃən/ *n* the act of transmitting; something transmitted; a system using gears, etc, to transfer power from an engine to a moving part, *esp* wheels of a vehicle; a radio or television broadcast.

transmit /'trænzmɪt/ *vt* (**transmitting, transmitted**) to send from one place or person to another; to communicate; to convey; (*radio or television signals*) to send out.

transmitter /-ər/ *n* an apparatus for broadcasting television or radio programmes.

transmogrify /trænz'mɒgrɪˌfaɪ/ *vt* (**transmogrifying, transmogrified**) to change shape, *esp* in a bizarre or comic manner.—**transmogrification** *n*.

transmute /-'mjuːt/ *vt* to change into a different form or substance.—**transmutation** *n*.

transnational /-'næʃənəl/ *n* extending beyond national boundaries.

transoceanic /-ˌoʃɪ'ænɪk/ *adj* on or from the other side of ocean; crossing the ocean.

transom /'trænsəm/ *n* a horizontal bar across a window or between a door and a window over it; a fanlight; any of several transverse beams supporting and strengthening the stern of a vessel.

transparency /'trænspərənsi/ *n* (*pl* **transparencies**) the state of being transparent; (*photog*) a slide.

transparent /'træns'perənt/ *adj* that may be easily seen through; clear, easily understood.—**transparently** *adv*.—**transparentness** *n*.

transpire /træn'spaɪr/ *vti* to emit, to pass off through the pores of the skin; to exhale (moisture); (*news*) to become known, to leak out; (*inf*) to happen.—**transpiration** *n*.

transplant /-'plænt/ *vt* (*plant*) to remove and plant in another place; (*med*) to remove an organ from one person and transfer it to another.—*also n*.

transport /-'pɔrt/ *vt* to convey from one place to another; to enrapture. • *n* the system of transporting goods or passengers; the conveyance of troops and their equipment by sea or land; a vehicle for this purpose.—**transportable** *adj*.—**transportation** *n*.

transpose /-'pozz/ *vt* to put into a different order; to interchange; (*mus*) to change the key of.—**transposition** *n*.

transputer /-'pjutər/ *n* (*comput*) a fast microchip comprising a 32-bit microprocessor which is used as a component in compact supercomputers.

transsexual /-'sekʃuəl/ *n* a person born of one sex who identifies psychologically with the opposite sex.—**transsexualism** *n*.

transubstantiation /ˌtrænsəbˌstænsɪ'eɪʃən/ *n* (*esp in RC Church*) the doctrine that the bread and wine of the communion are wholly transformed into the body and blood of Christ when consecrated, although their appearance remains unchanged.

transuranic /-juː'rænɪk/ *adj* (*element*) having an atomic number greater than that of uranium.

transverse /'trænzvərs/ *adj* crosswise.—**transversely** *adv*.

transvestite /trænz'vestaɪt/ *n* a person who gains sexual pleasure from wearing the clothes of the opposite sex.—**transvestism** *n*.

trap /træp/ *n* a mechanical device or pit for snaring animals; an ambush; a trick to catch someone out; a two-wheeled horse-drawn carriage. • *vt* (**trapping, trapped**) to catch in a trap; to trick.

trapdoor *n* a hinged or sliding door in a roof, ceiling or floor.

trapeze /trə'piːz/ *n* a gymnastic apparatus consisting of a horizontal bar suspended by two parallel ropes.

trapezium /trə'piːzɪəm/ *n* (*pl* **trapeziums, trapezia**) a quadrilateral in which two of the sides are parallel; in US, a quadrilateral in which none of the sides are parallel.—**trapezial** *adj*.

trapezoid /'træpəˌzɔɪd/ *n* a quadrilateral in which none of the sides are parallel. In the US, a quadrilateral with two sides parallel.

trapper /'træpər/ *n* a person who traps animals, *esp* for their skins.

trappings /-ɪŋz/ *npl* trimmings; additions; ornaments.

trash /træʃ/ *n* nonsense; refuse; rubbish.

trash can *n* a container for household refuse, a dustbin, garbage can.

trashy /'træʃi/ *adj* (**trashier, trashiest**) of poor quality.—**trashiness** *n*.

trattoria /ˌtrætə'riːə/ *n* (*pl* **trattorias, trattorie**) an Italian restaurant.

trauma /'trɔmə/ *n* an emotional shock that may cause long-term psychological damage; an upsetting experience.—**traumatic** *adj*.

travel /'trævəl/ *vb* (**travelling, travelled** *or* **traveling, traveled**) *vi* to journey or move from one place to another. • *vt* to journey across, through. • *n* journey.

travel agency *n* an agency through which one can book travel.—**travel agent** *n*.

traveller, traveler /-ər/ *n* a person who travels; a salesman who travels for a company.

traveller's cheque *n* a draft purchased from a bank, etc signed at the time of purchase and signed again at the time of cashing.

travelogue, travelog /-lɒg/ *n* a film or illustrated lecture on travel.

traverse /trə'vərs/ or /'trævərs/ *n* a horizontal move in rock climbing, skiing, etc. • *vt* to cross.

travertine /'trævərˌtiːn/ *n* a mineral comprising mostly calcium carbonate, used for building.

travesty /'trævəsti/ *n* (*pl* **travesties**) a misrepresentation; a poor imitation; a parody.

trawl /'trɒl/ *vti* to fish by dragging a large net behind a fishing boat.

trawler /-ər/ *n* a boat used for trawling.

tray /treɪ/ *n* a flat board, or sheet of metal or plastic, surrounded by a rim, used for carrying food or drink.

treacherous /'tretʃərəs/ *adj* untrustworthy, disloyal; unstable, dangerous.

treachery /-ri/ *n* (*pl* **treacheries**) disloyalty, betrayal of trust.

treacle /'tri:kəl/ *n* a thick sticky substance obtained during the refining of sugar.—**treacly** *adj*.

tread /tri:d/ *vti* (**treading, trod,** *pp* **trodden**) to step or walk on, along, in, over or across; to crush or squash (with the feet); to trample (on). • *n* a step, way of walking; the part of a shoe, wheel, or tire that touches the ground.

treadle /'tri:dəl/ *n* a foot lever or pedal on a machine.

treadmill /'tredmɪl/ *n* a grind; a monotonous routine.

treas. *abbr* = treasurer, treasury.

treason /'tri:zən/ *n* the crime of betraying one's government or attempting to overthrow it; treachery.—**treasonable** *adj*.

treasure /'treʒər/ *n* wealth and riches hoarded up; a person or thing much valued. • *vt* to hoard up; to prize greatly.

treasurer /-ər/ *n* a person appointed to take charge of the finances of a society, government or city.

treasure hunt *n* a game in which players follow clues to locate a hidden object.

treasure-trove *n* (*law*) valuable items such as gold and silver found buried and of unknown ownership; any valuable find.

treasury /-ri/ *n* (*pl* **treasuries**) a place where valuable objects are deposited; the funds or revenues of a government.

treat /tri:t/ *vt* to deal with or regard; to subject to the action of a chemical; to apply medical treatment to; to pay for another person's entertainment; to deal with in speech or writing. • *n* an entertainment paid for by another person; a pleasure seldom indulged; a unusual cause of enjoyment.

treatise /'tri:tɪs/ *n* a formal essay in which a subject is treated systematically.

treatment /'tri:tmənt/ *n* the application of drugs, etc, to a patient; the manner of dealing with a person or thing, *esp* in a novel or painting; behaviour toward someone.

treaty /'tri:ti/ *n* (*pl* **treaties**) a formal agreement between states.

treble /'trebəl/ *adj* triple, threefold; (*mus*) denoting the treble. • *n* the highest range of musical notes in singing. • *vti* to make or become three times as much.

treble clef *n* (*mus*) a clef that places G above middle C on the second line of the staff.

trebuchet /'trebjuˌʃet/ or /-bəʃət/ *n* a type of medieval military catapult used in sieges.

trecento /treɪ'tʃento:/ *n* the 14th century, *esp* in reference to Italian art and literature.

tree /tri:/ *n* a tall, woody, perennial plant having a single trunk, branches and leaves.

tree creeper /'tri:ˌkri:pər/ *n* any of various small songbirds with curved beaks for prising insects from tree trunks.

tree fern *n* a large tropical fern with a woody stem.

tree frog *n* any of various frogs that inhabit trees.

tree line /'tri:laɪn/ *n* the height or latitude beyond which no trees grow on mountains or in cold regions.—*also* **timber line**.

tree surgeon *n* a person skilled in saving diseased or damaged trees.—**tree surgery** *n*.

tree toad *n* a tree frog.

trefoil /'trefɔɪl/ *n* any of various plants with three leaflets; an ornament or design resembling this.

trek /trek/ *vi* (**trekking, trekked**) to travel slowly or laboriously; (*inf*) to go on foot (to). • *n* a long and difficult journey; a migration.

trellis /'trelɪs/ *n* a structure of latticework, for supporting climbing plants, etc.—**trelliswork** *n*.

tremble /'trembəl/ *vi* to shake, shiver from cold or fear; to quiver.—*also n*.

trembler /'tremblər/ *n* a device that makes or breaks an electric circuit when subject to vibration.

tremendous /trɪ'mendəs/ *adj* awe-inspiring; very large or great; (*inf*) wonderful; marvellous.

tremolo /'tremo:lo:/ *n* (*pl* **tremolos**) a tremulous effect in playing or singing; a device that produces this effect, as in an organ.

tremor /'tremər/ *n* a vibration; an involuntary shaking.

tremulous /'tremjuləs/ *adj* quivering; agitated.

trench /trentʃ/ *n* a long narrow channel in the earth, used for drainage; such an excavation made for military purposes.

trenchant /'trentʃənt/ *adj* keen; incisive; effective.

trench coat *n* a waterproof coat.

trencher /'trentʃər/ *n* a wooden board formerly used for serving food.

trencherman /-mən/ *n* a person who eats heartily.

trench fever *n* an infectious disease characterized by fever and muscular pains that is transmitted by lice.

trench foot *n* a degenerative condition of the feet caused by prolonged immersion in cold water.

trend /trend/ *n* tendency; a current style or fashion.

trendsetter *n* a person who starts a new fashion.

trendy /'trendi/ *adj* (**trendier, trendiest**) (*inf*) fashionable. • *n* (*pl* **trendies**) (*inf*) a person who tries to be fashionable.—**trendily** *adv*.—**trendiness** *n*.

trepan /trɪ'pæn/ *n* a primitive form of trephine. • *vt* (**trepanning, trepanned**) to cut with a trepan.

trepang /trɪ'pæŋ/ *n* a type of large sea cucumber dried and used in Chinese cookery, bêche-de-mer.

trephine /trɪ'faɪn/ *n* a surgical saw for removing circular sections of bone, *esp* from the skull. • *vt* to cut with a trephine.

trepidation /ˌtrepɪ'deɪʃən/ *n* a state of fear or anxiety.

trespass /'trespəs/ *vi* to intrude upon another person's property without their permission; to encroach upon, or infringe, another's rights. • *n* act of trespassing.—**trespasser** *n*.

tress /tres/ *n* a lock, braid, or plait of hair.

trestle /'tresəl/ *n* a wooden framework for supporting a table top or scaffold boards.

trews /tru:z/ *npl* tight-fitting tartan trousers.

trey /treɪ/ *n* three spots or the number three on a dice, domino or playing card.

tri- /traɪ/ *prefix* having, made up of, or containing three or three parts; every third.

triad /'traɪæd/ *n* a group or set of three, a trio.

triage /'triːɑʒ/ or /-ɒʒ/, /-'æz/, /-'ɒʒ/ *n* the sorting and treatment of the wounded according to chance of survival.

trial /'traɪəl/ *n* a test or experiment; judicial examination; an attempt; a preliminary race, game in a competition; suffering; hardship; a person causing annoyance.

trial and error *n* solving problems through trying various solutions and rejecting the least successful.

trial run *n* an opportunity to test something before purchase, as a vehicle; a rehearsal.

triangle /'traɪˌæŋgəl/ *n* (*math*) a plane figure with three angles and three sides; a percussion instrument consisting of a triangular metal bar beaten with a metal stick.—**triangular** *adj*.

triangulate /traɪ'æŋgjuˌleɪt/ *vt* to divide into triangles; to make triangular; to survey by dividing an area into a network of triangles.—**triangulation** *n*.

triathlon /traɪ'æθlən/ *n* an athletic event in which all contestants compete in swimming, cycling and running.

triatomic /ˌtraɪə'tɒmɪk/ *adj* (*chem*) having three atoms in the molecule.

tribadism /'traɪˌbædɪzəm/ *n* simulated heterosexual intercourse by lesbians, with one partner lying on top of the other.

tribe /traɪb/ *n* a group of people of the same race, sharing the same customs, religion, language or land.—**tribal** *adj*.—**tribesman** *n*.

tribo- /'traɪbo:/ *prefix* friction.

triboelectricity /ˌtraɪbo:ˌiːlek'trɪsɪti/ *n* electricity generated by friction.

tribology /traɪ'bɒlədʒi/ *n* the study of friction, wear and lubrication between moving surfaces, as gearing systems.

triboluminescence /ˌtraɪbo:ˌluːmɪ'nesəns/ *n* luminescence caused by friction.—**triboluminescent** *adj*.

tribulation /'trɪbjuleɪʃən/ *n* distress, difficulty, hardship.

tribunal /traɪ'bjuːnəl/ or /trɪ-/ *n* a court of justice; a committee that investigates and decides on a particular problem.

tribune[1] /trɪ'bjuːn/ *n* in ancient Rome, a magistrate appointed to protect the rights of common people; a champion of the people.

tribune[2] *n* a raised platform or dais from which speeches are delivered.

tributary /trɪ'bjuːˌteri/ *n* (*pl* **tributaries**) a stream or river flowing into a larger one.

tribute /trɪˈbjuːt/ *n* a speech, gift or action to show one's respect or thanks to someone; a payment made at certain intervals by one nation to another in return for peace.

tricentenary /traɪˌsentəˈneri/ *n* (*pl* **tricentenaries**) a tricentennial.—*also adj.*

tricentennial /ˌtraɪsenˈteniəl/ *adj* lasting, or happening every, 300 years. • *n* an anniversary of 300 years; a period of 300 years.

triceps /ˈtraɪseps/ *n* (*pl* **tricepses, triceps**) any three-headed muscle, *esp* the large muscle that extends the forearm.

trichiasis /trɪˈkaɪəsɪs/ *n* a condition of having in-growing eyelashes which irritate the eyeball.

trichina /trɪˈkiːnə/ *n* (*pl* **trichinae**) a hair-like parasitic worm that infests the intestines and muscles of pigs and humans.

trichinosis /ˌtrɪkəˈnoːsɪs/ *n* a disease in humans caused by infestation of muscular tissues by trichinae.

tricho- /ˈtrɪko/, **trich-** /trɪk/ *prefix* hair; filament.

trichology /trɪˈkɒlədʒi/ *n* the medical study and treatment of hair diseases.—**trichologist** *n*.

trichosis /trɪˈkoːsɪs/ *n* any disease of the hair.

trichotomy /trɪˈkɒtəmi/ *n* (*pl* **trichotomies**) a division into three parts or categories.—**trichotomous** *adj.*

trichromatic /ˌtraɪkrəˈmætɪk/ *adj* of, involving, or combining three colours; of or having normal colour vision.—**trichromatism** *n*.

trick /trɪk/ *n* fraud; deception; a mischievous plan or joke; a magical illusion; a clever feat; skill, knack; the playing cards won in a round. • *adj* using fraud or clever contrivance to deceive. • *vt* to deceive, cheat.—**trickster** *n*.

trickery /ˈtrɪkəri/ *n* (*pl* **trickeries**) the practice or an act of using underhand methods to achieve an aim; deception.

trickle /ˈtrɪkəl/ *vti* to flow or cause to flow in drops or in a small stream.—*also n.*

trickle-down *adj* denoting a theory in economics that financial incentives to big business will percolate through to small businesses and individuals.

trick or treat *n* a Halloween tradition (*chiefly* in the US) in which children dress in costumes, call on their neighbours and threaten to do mischief if refused presents of sweets, apples, nuts, money, etc.

tricky /ˈtrɪki/ *adj* (**trickier, trickiest**) complicated, difficult to handle; risky; cunning, deceitful.—**trickily** *adv*.—**trickiness** *n*.

tricolour, tricolor /ˈtraɪˌkʌlər/ *n* a flag with three stripes of different colours.

tricorn /ˈtraɪkɔrn/ *adj* having three horns or corners. • *n* a three-cornered hat.

tricuspid /traɪˈkʌspid/ *adj* having three cusps, flaps, points, or segments. • *n* a tooth with three cusps.

tricycle /ˈtraɪˌsaɪkəl/ *n* a three-wheeled pedal cycle, *esp* for children.

trident /ˈtraɪdənt/ *n* three-pronged spear.

tridentate /traɪˈdenteɪt/, **tridental** /-ˈdentəl/ *adj* having three teeth or prongs.

tried[1] /traɪd/ *see* **try**.

tried[2] *adj* tested; trustworthy.

triennial /traɪˈeniəl/ *adj* happening every third year; lasting for three years.

triennium /traɪˈeniəm/ *n* (*pl* **trienniums, triennia**) a period of three years.

trier /ˈtraɪər/ *n* one who tries.

trifle /ˈtraɪfəl/ *vi* to treat lightly; to dally. • *n* anything of little value; a dessert of whipped cream, custard, sponge cake, sherry, etc.

trifling /ˈtraɪflɪŋ/ *adj* insignificant.

trifocal /traɪˈfoːkəl/ *adj* having three focuses or focal lengths. • *npl* glasses with trifocal lenses.

trifurcate /traɪˈfərkət/, **trifurcated** /-əd/ *adj* having three branches or forks.

trig. *abbr* = trigonometrical; trigonometry.

trigeminal /traɪˈdʒemɪnəl/ *adj* pertaining to the trigeminal nerve.

trigeminal nerve *n* either of a pair of cranial nerves that supply various facial muscles.

trigger /ˈtrɪɡər/ *n* a catch that when pulled activates the firing mechanism of a gun. • *vt* (*with* **off**) to initiate; to set (off).

trigger-happy *adj* too eager to resort to firearms or violence; rash, aggressive.

trigonometric function *n* any of various functions (*eg* sine, cosine, tangent) expressed as ratios of the sides of a right-angled triangle.

trigonometry /ˌtrɪɡəˈnɒmətri/ *n* the branch of mathematics concerned with calculating the angles of triangles or the lengths of their sides.

trike /traɪk/ *n* (*inf*) a tricycle.

trilateral /traɪˈlætərəl/ *adj* having three sides.

trilby /ˈtrɪlbi/ *n* (*pl* **trilbies**) a soft felt hat with a fold in the crown.

trilingual /traɪˈlɪŋɡwəl/ or /-juːəl/ *adj* speaking three languages; written in three languages.—**trilingualism** *n*.

trill /trɪl/ *vti* to sing or play with a tremulous tone; (*a bird*) to make a shrill, warbling sound.—*also n.*

trillion /ˈtrɪliən/ *n* a million million (1012); (*formerly*) in UK, a million million million (1018); (*inf*) (*pl*) a very large number.

trilobite /ˈtraɪləˌbaɪt/ *n* any of a group of extinct Palaeozoic marine arthropods with a body in three sections.

trilogy /ˈtrɪlədʒi/ *n* (*pl* **trilogies**) any series of three related literary or operatic works.

trim /trɪm/ *adj* (**trimmer, trimmest**) in good condition; tidy; neat; slim. • *vt* to neaten; to cut or prune; to decorate; (*ship, aircraft*) to balance the weight of cargo in. • *n* a decorative edging; a haircut that tidies.

trimaran /ˈtraɪməˌræn/ *n* a boat with three hulls.

trimester /ˈtraɪˌmestər/ or /traɪˈmestər/ *n* a period of three months; a division of the academic year in certain North American colleges and universities.

trimming /trɪmɪŋ/ *n* decorative part of clothing; (*pl*) accompaniments.

trinitrotoluene /traɪˌnaɪtrəˈtɒljuːˌiːn/ *n* a solid yellow chemical substance used as a high explosive.

trinity /ˈtrɪnɪti/ *n* (*pl* **trinities**) a group of three; (*with cap*) in Christianity, the union of Father, Son and Holy Spirit in one God.

trinket /ˈtrɪŋkət/ *n* a small or worthless ornament.

trinomial /traɪˈnoːmiəl/ *adj* having three terms. • *n* (*math*) a polynomial consisting of three terms.

trio /ˈtriːoː/ *n* (*pl* **trios**) a set of three; (*mus*) a group of three singers or instrumentalists.

triode /ˈtraɪoːd/ *n* an electronic valve or semiconductor device with three electrodes.

trip /ˈtrɪp/ *vb* (**tripping, tripped**) *vi* to move or tread lightly; to stumble and fall; to make a blunder. • *vt* (*often with* **up**) to cause to stumble; to activate a trip. • *n* a stumble; a journey, tour, or voyage; a slip; a mistake; a light step; a mechanical switch; (*sl*) a hallucinatory experience under the influence of a drug.

tripartite /traɪˈpartaɪt/ *adj* made up of or divided into three parts; involving or binding three parties.

tripe /traɪp/ *n* the stomach lining of a ruminant, prepared for cooking; (*inf*) rubbish, nonsense.

triplane /ˈtraɪˌpleɪn/ *n* an aircraft with three wings positioned one above the other.

triple /ˈtrɪpəl/ *adj* threefold; three times as many. • *vti* to treble.

triple jump *n* an athletic event in which a competitor makes a hop, step and jump in succession.

triplet /ˈtrɪplət/ *n* one of three children born at one birth.

triplicate /ˈtrɪplɪkət/ *adj* threefold.

tripod /ˈtraɪpɒd/ *n* a three-legged stand, as for supporting a camera.

tripper /ˈtrɪpər/ *n* a tourist; a trip switch.

triptych /ˈtrɪptɪk/ *n* a picture consisting of three panels fixed or hinged side by side.

tripwire /ˈtrɪpwaɪr/ *n* a concealed wire that sets off a bomb, booby trap, etc when tripped over.

trireme /ˈtraɪriːm/ *n* an ancient Greek galley with three banks of oars.

trisect /ˈtraɪsekt/ *vt* to divide into three (equal) parts.—**trisection** *n*.

trishaw /ˈtraɪʃɒ/ *n* a rickshaw.

triskelion /traɪˈskeliən/ *n* (*pl* **triskelia**) a symbol consisting of three bent limbs or branches radiating from a centre.

trismus /ˈtrɪzməs/ *n* lockjaw.

trisyllable /ˌtraɪˈsɪləbəl/ *n* a word of three syllables.

trite /traɪt/ *adj* dull; hackneyed.

tritium /ˈtrɪtiəm/ *n* a radioactive isotope of hydrogen.

triton /ˈtraɪtən/ *n* any of various marine gastropod molluscs having a heavy spiral shell; (*with cap*) (*Greek myth*) a sea-god depicted as half man and half fish blowing a spiral shell.

triturate /'trɪtʃəˌreɪt/ *vt* to crush or grind into a fine powder.— **trituration** *n*.

triumph /'traɪəmf/ *n* a victory; success; a great achievement. • *vi* to win a victory or success; to rejoice over a victory.—**triumphal** *adj*.

triumphant /traɪˈæmfənt/ *adj* feeling or showing triumph; celebratory; victorious.—**triumphantly** *adv*.

triumvir /traɪˈæmvər/ *n* (*pl* **triumvirs, triumviri**) a member of a ruling body of three persons.

triumvirate /traɪˈæmvərət/ *n* the office of a triumvir; joint rule by three persons.

trivalent /traɪˈvælənt/ *adj* having a valency of three.

trivet /'trɪvət/ *n* a three-legged metal stand for supporting hot dishes.

trivia /'trɪvɪə/ *npl* unimportant details.

trivial /-əl/ *adj* unimportant; commonplace.

triviality /ˌtrɪvɪˈælɪtɪ/ *n* (*pl* **trivialities**) a trifle, detail; the state of being trivial.

-trix /trɪks/ *n suffix* female.

t-RNA *abbr* = transfer RNA.

trocar /'troːkɑr/ *n* a pointed instrument for inserting drainage tubes into bodily cavities.

trochal /'troːkəl/ *adj* wheel-shaped.

troche /'troːkɪ/ *n* a medicinal lozenge.

trochee /'troːkɪ/ *n* a metrical foot comprising one long syllable followed by one short syllable.

trod /trɒd/, **trodden** /'trɒdn/ *see* **tread**.

troglodyte /'trɒɡləˌdaɪt/ *n* a cave dweller.

troika /'trɔɪkə/ *n* (a Russian vehicle drawn by) three horses harnessed abreast; a triumvirate.

troll /troːl/ *n* a supernatural creature, dwelling in a cave, hill, etc.

trolley /'trɒlɪ/ *n* (*pl* **trolleys**) a table on wheels for carrying or serving food; a cart for transporting luggage; a cart for carrying shopping in a supermarket; a device that transmits electric current from an overhead wire to a motor vehicle, such as a trolleybus.

trolleybus, trolley car *n* a bus that sometimes runs on rails and is powered by electricity from overhead wires.

trollop /'trɒləp/ *n* a slovenly woman; a prostitute.—**trollopy** *adj*.

trombone /trɒmˈboːn/ *n* a brass musical wind instrument whose length is varied with a U-shaped sliding section.

troop /truːp/ *n* a crowd of people; a group of soldiers within a cavalry regiment; (*pl*) armed forces; soldiers. • *vi* to go in a crowd.

trooper /'truːpər/ *n* a soldier in a cavalry regiment; in the US, a mounted policeman or a state policeman.

troopship /'truːpʃɪp/ *n* a ship used to transport military forces.

trope /troːp/ *n* a word or phrase used in a figurative sense.

-trope /troːp/ *n suffix* turning, being attracted toward.

trophic /'troːfɪk/ or /'trɒfɪk/ *adj* pertaining to nutrition.

tropho- /'trɒfoː/, **troph-** *prefix* nutrition.

trophy /'troːfɪ/ *n* (*pl* **trophies**) a cup or shield won as a prize in a competition or contest; a memento, as taken in battle or hunting.

-trophy /'troːfɪ/ *n suffix* growth, nutrition.

tropic /'trɒpɪk/ *n* one of the two parallel lines of latitude north and south of the equator; (*pl*) the regions lying between these lines.

-tropic /'trɒpɪk/ *adj suffix* turning to or responding to an external stimulus.

tropical /'trɒpɪkəl/ *adj* relating to the tropics; (*weather*) hot and humid.

tropism /'troːpɪzəm/ *n* the involuntary direction of growth of a plant due to an external stimulus.

-tropism /trəˌpɪzəm/, **-tropy** *n suffix* turning or developing in response to an external stimulus.

tropo- /trɒpə/ *prefix* turning or changing.

-tropous /'trɒpoːz/ *adj suffix* turning away.

tropopause /'trɒpəˌpɔːz/ or /'troː-/ *n* the region between the troposphere and stratosphere.

troposphere /'trɒpəˌsfɪːr/ or /'troː-/ *n* the region of the atmosphere below the stratosphere which varies in temperature and in which clouds form.

trot /trɒt/ *vb* (**trotting, trotted**) *vi* (*horse*) to go, lifting the feet higher than in walking and moving at a faster rate. • *vt* (*with* **out**) (*inf*) to produce or display repeatedly, *esp* for others' approval; to produce in a trite or careless manner. • *n* the gait of a horse; a brisk pace.

trotter /'trɒtər/ *n* a horse trained for fast trotting; the foot of an animal, *esp* a pig.

troubadour /'truːbəˌdɔr/ *n* a minstrel; a poet or singer.

trouble /'trʌbəl/ *vti* to cause trouble to; to worry; to pain; to upset; to cause inconvenience; to take pains (to). • *n* an anxiety; a medical condition causing pain; a problem; unrest or disturbance.—**troublesome** *adj*.

troubleshooter /'trʌbəlˌʃuːtər/ *n* a person whose work is to locate and eliminate a source of trouble or conflict.—**troubleshooting** *n*.

trough /trɒf/ *n* a long, narrow container for water or animal feed; a channel in the ground; an elongated area of low barometric pressure.

trounce /traʊns/ *vt* to defeat completely.

troupe /truːp/ *n* a travelling company, *esp* of actors, dancers or acrobats.—**trouper** *n*.

trousers /'traʊzərz/ *npl* an item of clothing covering the body from waist to ankle, with two tubes of material for the legs; in the US, pants.

trousseau /'truːsoː/ or /truːˈsoː/ *n* (*pl* **trousseaux, trousseaus**) the clothes and linen a bride collects for her marriage.

trout /traʊt/ *n* (*pl* **trout**) a game fish of the salmon family living in fresh water.

trove /troːv/ *see* **treasure trove**.

trowel /'traʊəl/ *n* a hand tool for gardening; a flat-bladed tool for spreading cement, etc.

troy (weight) /trɔɪ/ *n* a system for weighing precious stones and metals, in which one pound = 12 ounces and one ounce = 20 pennyweights or 480 grains.

truant /'truːənt/ *n* a pupil who is absent from school without permission. • *vi* to play truant.—*also adj.*—**truancy** *n*.

truce /truːs/ *n* an agreement between two armies or states to suspend hostilities.

truck /trʌk/ *n* a heavy motor vehicle for transporting goods; another name for lorry; a vehicle open at the back for moving goods or animals. • *vt* (*goods*) to convey by truck. • *vi* to drive a truck.

trucker /'trʌkər/ *n* a truck driver.

truculent /'trʌkjʊlənt/ *adj* sullen; aggressive.—**truculence** *n*.—**truculently** *adv*.

trudge /trʌdʒ/ *vti* to travel on foot, heavily or wearily. • *n* a tiring walk.

true /truː/ *adj* (**truer, truest**) conforming with fact; correct, accurate; genuine; loyal; perfectly in tune. • *adv* truthfully; rightly.

true-blue /'truːˈbluː/ *adj* staunchly loyal or committed.—**true blue** *n*.

truelove /'truːˌlʌv/ *n* a sweetheart.

truffle /'trʌfəl/ *n* a round, edible underground fungus; a sweet made with chocolate, butter and sugar.

truism /'truːɪzəm/ *n* a self-evident truth.

truly /'truːlɪ/ *adv* completely; genuinely; to a great degree.

trump /trʌmp/ *n* (*cards*) the suit that is chosen to have the highest value in one game. • *vt* to play a trump card on; (*with* **up**) to invent maliciously, fabricate (an accusation, etc).

trumpery /'trʌmpərɪ/ *adj* worthless. • *n* (*pl* **trumperies**) foolish talk, nonsense; a worthless article.

trumpet /'trʌmpət/ *n* a brass wind instrument consisting of a long tube with a flared end and three buttons. • *vti* to proclaim loudly.—**trumpeter** *n*.

trumpeter swan *n* a rare wild North American swan with a black bill.

truncate /'trʌŋkeɪt/ or /trʌŋˈkeɪt/ *vt* to cut the top end off; to shorten.—**truncation** *n*.

truncheon /'trʌntʃən/ *n* a short, thick club carried by a policeman.

trundle /'trʌndəl/ *vt* (*an object*) to push or pull on wheels. • *vi* to move along slowly.

trunk /trʌŋk/ *n* the main stem of a tree; the torso; the main body of anything; the proboscis of an elephant; a strong box or chest for clothes, etc, *esp* on a journey; storage space at the rear of an automobile; (*pl*) a man's short, light pants specially for swimming.

trunk line *n* a transportation system handling through traffic; a communications system.

trunk road *n* a main road.

truss /trʌs/ *n* a supporting framework for a roof or bridge; a hernia brace. • *vt* to bind (up).

trust /trʌst/ *n* firm belief in the truth of anything, faith in a person; confidence in; custody; a financial arrangement of investing money for another person; a business syndicate. • *adj* held in trust. • *vti* to have confidence in; to believe.—**trustful** *adj*.

trustee /trʌsˈtiː/ *n* a person who has legal control of money or property that they are keeping or investing for another person, or for an organization or institution.—**trusteeship** *n*.

trustworthy /ˈtrʌstˌwɜrði/ *adj* reliable, dependable.

trusty /ˈtrʌsti/ *adj* (**trustier, trustiest**) trustworthy, faithful. • *n* a prisoner granted special privileges as a trustworthy person.—**trustily** *adv*.—**trustiness** *n*.

truth /truːθ/ *n* that which is true, factual or genuine; agreement with reality.

truthful /ˈtruːθfʊl/ *adj* telling the truth; accurate, realistic; honest, frank.—**truthfulness** *n*.

try /traɪ/ *vb* (**trying, tried**) *vt* to test the result or effect by experiment; to determine judicially; to put strain on; (*with* **on**) to put (a garment) on to check the fit, etc; (*inf*) to attempt to deceive somebody; (*with* **out**) to test (someone) for a job, etc. • *vi* to attempt; to make an effort; (*with* **out**) to undergo a test (for a job, team, etc). • *n* (*pl* **tries**) an attempt, an effort; (*rugby football*) a score made with a touchdown.

trying /ˈtraɪɪŋ/ *adj* causing annoyance, exasperating.—**tryingly** *adv*.—**tryingness** *n*.

try-on /ˈtraɪɒn/ *n* (*inf*) a trying on of clothes to check the fit; an attempt to deceive.

tryout /ˈtraɪaʊt/ *n* an experimental test; an audition for a theatrical part; (*sports, etc*) a test for a position in a team.

trypanosome /ˈtrɪpənəˌsoːm/ or /trɪˈpænə-/ *n* any of genus of parasitic worms that infest the blood of animals and humans and can cause sleeping sickness.

trypanosomiasis /ˌtrɪpənəsəˈmaɪəsɪs/ or /trɪˈpænə-/ *n* (a disease caused by) infection with trypanosomes.

trypsin /ˈtrɪpsɪn/ *n* an enzyme in the pancreas involved in digestion.—**tryptic** *adj*.

tryptophan /ˈtrɪptəˌfæn/, **tryptophane** *n* an amino acid found in proteins which is essential to life.

try square *n* an L-shaped instrument for drawing and testing right angles.

tryst /trɪst/ *n* an appointment to meet secretly.

tsar /tsɑr/ or /zɑr/ *n* (*formerly*) the title of the emperors of Russia (until 1917) and sovereigns of certain other Slav nations; a powerful person.—*also* **czar**.

tsarevitch /ˈtsɑrəvɪtʃ/ or /ˈzɑr-/ *n* the eldest son of a tsar.—*also* **czarevitch**.

tsarina /tsɑˈriːnə/ or /zɑ-/, **tsaritsa** /tsɑˈriːtzə/ or /zɑ-/ *n* the wife of a tsar; an empress.—*also* **czarina**.

tsetse fly /ˈtsiːtsi/ or /ˈtiːtsi/ *n* a fly that feeds on blood and transmits diseases.

T-shirt /ˈtiːʃərt/ *n* a short-sleeved casual cotton top.—*also* **tee-shirt**.

tsp. *abbr* = teaspoon.

T-square /ˈtiːskwer/ *n* a T-shaped instrument for drawing and determining right angles.

Tu. *abbr* = Tuesday.

tub /tʌb/ *n* a circular container, made of staves and hoops; a bathtub.

tuba /ˈtuːbə/ or /ˈtjuːbə/ *n* a large brass instrument of bass pitch.

tubby /ˈtʌbi/ *adj* (**tubbier, tubbiest**) plump.

tube /tuːb/ or /ˈtjuːb/ *n* a long, thin, hollow pipe; a soft metal or plastic cylinder in which thick liquids or pastes, such as toothpaste, are stored; (*inf*) the underground railway system, *esp* that in London.—**tubular** *adj*.

tubeless tire /ˈtuːblɪs/ or /ˈtjuːb-/ *n* a tire that remains airtight without requiring an inner tube.

tuber /ˈtuːbər/ or /ˈtjuːbər/ *n* the swollen, fleshy root of a plant where reserves of food are stored up, as a potato.

tubercle /ˈtuːbərkəl/ or /ˈtjuː-/ *n* a small round swelling or nodule, *esp* on bone, skin or a plant; an abnormal lump, *esp* one characteristic of tuberculosis.

tubercle bacillus *n* a bacterium that causes tuberculosis.

tuberculate /tuːˈbərkjuˌleɪt/ or /-lɪt/ *adj* affected with tubercles.—**tuberculation** *n*.

tuberculin /tuːˈbərkjulɪn/ *n* a sterile liquid prepared with weakened tubercle bacillus and used in the diagnosis of tuberculosis.

tuberculosis /tuˌbərkjuˈloːsɪs/ *n* an infectious disease of the lungs.—**tubercular** *adj*.

tuberose /ˈtuːbəˌroːz/ or /ˈtuːbroːz/, /ˈtjuː-/ *n* a bulbous Mexican plant with fragrant white flowers.

tuberous /ˈtuːbərəs/ or /ˈtjuːbərəs/ *adj* (*plants*) forming or resembling tubers.

tubing /ˈtuːbɪŋ/ or /ˈtjuːbɪŋ/ *n* tubes collectively; a length of tube; the material from which tubes are made; a circular fabric.

tub-thumper /ˈtʌbˌθʌmpər/ *n* a passionate or aggressive public speaker.

tubular bells /ˈtuːbjələr/ or /ˈtjuː-/ *npl* an orchestral percussion instrument consisting of a set of long metal tubes played with a mallet to simulate the sounds of bells.

tuck /tʌk/ *vt* to draw or gather together in a fold; (*with* **up**) to wrap snugly. • *vi* (*inf*) (*with* **into**) to eat greedily. • *n* a fold in a garment.

tucker /ˈtʌkər/ *vt* (*inf*) in the US, to exhaust, tire (out).

Tue., Tues. *abbr* = Tuesday.

Tuesday /ˈtuːzdeɪ/ or /ˈtjuːz-/, /-di/ *n* the third day of the week.

tufa /ˈtuːfə/ or /ˈtjuː-/ *n* a type of porous rock deposited from springs.

tuff /tʌf/ *n* a type of volcanic rock composed of fused lava ash.

tuffet /ˈtʌfɪt/ *n* a small low seat; a clump of grass.

tuft /tʌft/ *n* a bunch of grass, hair or feathers held together at the base; a clump.

tug /tʌg/ *vti* (**tugging, tugged**) to pull with effort or to drag along. • *n* a strong pull; a tugboat.

tugboat /ˈtʌgboːt/ *n* a small powerful boat for towing ships.

tug of love *n* a conflict over the custody of a child between separated parents, etc.

tug of war *n* a contest in which two teams tug on opposite ends of a rope to pull the opposing team over a central line; a struggle for supremacy between two opponents.

tuition /tuːˈɪʃən/ or /tjuː-/ *n* teaching, instruction.

tulip /ˈtuːlɪp/ or /ˈtjuː-/ *n* a highly-coloured cup-shaped flower grown from bulbs.

tulip tree *n* a North American tree with large tulip-shaped flowers.

tulipwood /ˈtuːlɪpˌwʊd/ *n* the soft white wood of the tulip tree used in making furniture.

tulle /tuːl/ *n* a delicate semi-transparent fabric of rayon, silk, etc, used for scarfs and veils.

tumble /ˈtʌmbəl/ *vi* to fall over; to roll or to twist the body, as an acrobat; (*with* **to**) (*inf*) to discover (a secret, etc); to understand. • *vt* to push or cause to fall. • *n* a fall; a somersault.

tumbledown /ˈtʌmbəldaʊn/ *adj* dilapidated, crumbling.

tumble-dry *vt* (*clothes*) to dry by rotating with warm air in a machine.—**tumble dryer** *n*.

tumbler /ˈtʌmblər/ *n* a large drinking glass without a handle or stem; an acrobat.

tumbler switch *n* a simple electrical switch used in lighting.

tumbleweed /ˈtʌmbəlˌwiːd/ *n* a plant that detaches from its roots and is blown around by the wind.

tumbrel /ˈtʌmbrəl/, **tumbril** /-rɪl/ *n* a farm cart that tips up to deposit its load; a cart of similar design used to carry prisoners to the guillotine during the French Revolution.

tumescent /tjuːˈmesənt/ or /tjuː-/ *adj* swollen or beginning to swell.

tumid /ˈtuːmɪd/ or /ˈtjuː-/ *adj* swollen, distended; pompous, bombastic.—**tumidly** *adv*.—**tumidity** *n*.

tummy /ˈtʌmi/ *n* (*pl* **tummies**) (*inf*) stomach.

tumour, tumor /ˈtuːmər/ or /ˈtjuː-/ *n* an abnormal growth of tissue in any part of the body.

tumult /ˈtjuːmʌlt/ or /ˈtuː-/, /-mʌlt/, /ˈtʌmʌlt/ *n* a commotion; an uproar.

tumultuous /təˈmʌltʃuəs/ or /tuː-/, /tjuː-/, /-tjuəs/ *adj* disorderly; rowdy, noisy; restless.—**tumultuously** *adv*.—**tumultuousness** *n*.

tun /tʌn/ *n* a large wine or beer cask; a unit of capacity equal to about 252 wine gallons (954 litres).

tuna /ˈtuːnə/ or /ˈtjuː-/ *n* (*pl* **tuna, tunas**) a large ocean fish of the mackerel group.

tundra /ˈtʌndrə/ *n* a vast treeless arctic plain.

tune /tuːn/ or /ˈtjuːn/ *n* a melody; correct musical pitch; harmony. • *vt* (*musical instrument*) to adjust the notes of; (*radio, TV etc*) to adjust the resonant frequency, etc, to a particular value; (*with* **up**) to adjust an engine to improve its performance. • *vi* (*with* **up**) to adjust (musical instruments) to a common pitch before playing.—**tuneful** *adj*.—**tunefully** *adv*.

tune-up /tuːnʌp/ or /tjuː-/ *n* an adjustment of a musical instrument to correct pitch or of an engine to improve its performance.

tungsten /ˈtʌŋstən/ *n* a hard malleable greyish white metallic element used in lamps, etc, and in alloys with steel.

tunic /ˈtuːnɪk/ or /ˈtjuː-/ *n* a hip or knee-length loose, *usu* belted blouse-like garment; a close-fitting jacket worn by soldiers and policemen.

tunicate /ˈtuːnɪkət/ or /ˈtjuː-/, /-ˌkeɪt/ *n* any of a group of small primitive marine animals with sac-shaped bodies enclosed in a thick membrane. • *adj* having or enclosed in a membrane; (*bulbs*) made up from concentric layers of tissue.

tuning fork *n* a two-pronged steel fork that produces a fixed note when struck and is used to tune musical instruments or set a pitch for singing.

tunnel /ˈtʌnəl/ *n* an underground passage, *esp* one for cars or trains underneath a river or town centre. • *vb* (**tunnelling, tunnelled** *or* **tunneling, tunneled**) *vt* to make a way through. • *vi* to make a tunnel.

tunnel vision *n* a condition in which peripheral vision is impaired; a narrowness of viewpoint due to preoccupation with a single idea, plan, etc.

tunny /ˈtʌni/ *n* (*pl* **tunnies, tunny**) tuna.

tuppence /ˈtʌpəns/ *n* twopence.

turban /ˈtɜːbən/ *n* a headdress consisting of cloth wound in folds around the head worn by men; a woman's hat of this shape.

turbid /ˈtɜːbɪd/ *adj* muddy; dense; thick.—**turbidity** *n*.—**turbidly** *adv*.

turbine /ˈtɜːbaɪn/ *n* a machine in which power is produced when the forced passage of steam, water, etc causes the blades to rotate.

turbo- /ˈtɜːboː/ *prefix* of, driven or powered by a turbine.

turbofan /ˈtɜːboːˌfæn/ *n* a jet engine with a large fan that forces air out with the exhaust gases to increase thrust; an aircraft with such engines; the fan in such an engine.

turbojet /ˈtɜːboːˌdʒet/ *n* (an aircraft with) a turbojet engine.

turbojet engine *n* a gas turbine that provides propulsive power from a jet of hot exhaust gases.

turboprop /ˈtɜːboːˌprɒp/ *n* a jet aircraft engine that also operates a turbine-driven air compressor.

turbot /ˈtɜːbət/ *n* (*pl* **turbot, turbots**) a large, flat, round edible fish.

turbulence /ˈtɜːbjʊləns/ *n* a state of confusion and disorder; (*weather*) instability causing gusty air currents.

turbulent /ˈtɜːbjʊlənt/ *adj* disturbed, in violent commotion.

turd /tɜːd/ *n* (*vulg*) a piece of excrement; (*vulg sl*) a despicable person.

tureen /təˈriːn/ or /tjʊ-/ *n* a large dish for serving soup, etc.

turf /tɜːf/ *n* (*pl* **turfs, turves**) the surface layer of grass and its roots; (*with* **the**) horse racing; a racetrack. • *vt* to cover with turf; (*with* **out**) (*inf*) to eject forcibly, throw out.

turf war *n* a dispute over an area, or land claimed by one party as being under control in the face of the claims of another individual or group.

turgid /ˈtɜːdʒɪd/ *adj* swollen; pompous, bombastic.—**turgidity** *n*.—**turgidly** *adv*.

Turk /tɜːk/ *n* a native or inhabitant of Turkey; any speaker of a Turkic language.

Turk. /tɜːk/ *abbr* = Turkey; Turkish.

turkey /ˈtɜːki/ *n* (*pl* **turkeys, turkey**) a large bird farmed for its meat.

turkey buzzard *n* an American vulture.

turkey cock /ˈtɜːkiˌkɒk/ *n* a male turkey.

Turkey red *n* (a cotton fabric of) a bright red colour.

Turki /ˈtɜːki/ *adj* of, being or pertaining to the Turkic languages or speakers of these languages; the Turkic languages collectively.

Turkic /ˈtɜːkɪk/ *n* a branch of the Altaic family of languages including Turkish, Tartar, etc.

Turkish /ˈtɜːkɪʃ/ *adj* pertaining to Turkey, its people or their language. • *n* the official language of Turkey.

Turkish bath *n* a bath with steam rooms, showers, massage, etc.

Turkish coffee *n* strong black (*usu* sweetened) coffee.

Turkish delight *n* a jelly-like flower-flavoured sweet covered with icing sugar.

Turk's-cap lily *n* a variety of lily with purple-red flowers found in Europe and Asia; martagon lily.

turmeric /ˈtɜːmərɪk/ *n* a tropical Indian plant; the powdered stem of this plant used as a yellow colouring agent and curry spice.

turmoil /ˈtɜːmɔɪl/ *n* agitation; disturbance, confusion.

turn /tɜːn/ *vi* to revolve; to go in the opposite direction; to depend on; to appeal (to) for help; to direct (thought or attention) away from; to change in character; to be shaped on the lathe; (*with* **off**) to leave or deviate from a road, etc; (*with* **in**) (*inf*) to retire to bed for the night; (*with* **on**) to depend on; (*with* **to**) to begin a task; (*with* **up**) to appear, arrive; to find unexpectedly; to happen without warning. • *vt* to change the position or direction of by revolving; to reverse; to transform; (*age, etc*) to have just passed; to change or convert; to invert; (*with* **off**) to cause to cease operating (as if) by flicking a switch, turning a knob, etc; (*inf*) to cause a person to lose interest in or develop a dislike for something; (*with* **down**) to reduce the volume or intensity of (sound, brightness, etc); to refuse, decline; to fold down (sheets, a collar, etc); (*with* **in**) to deliver; to produce, record (a performance, score, etc); (*with* **on**) to cause to begin operating (as if) by flicking a switch, turning a knob, etc; (*sl*) to arouse or excite, *esp* sexually; (*with* **up**) to discover, uncover; to increase the volume or intensity of (sound, brightness, etc). • *n* a rotation; new direction or tendency; a place in sequence; a turning point, crisis; performer's act; an act of kindness or malice; a bend.

turnabout /ˈtɜːnəbʊt/ *n* a reversal of position, opinion, attitude, etc.

turncoat /ˈtɜːnkoːt/ *n* a deserter, renegade.

turner /ˈtɜːnər/ *n* a person who operates a lathe.

turning /ˈtɜːnɪŋ/ *n* a road, path, etc that leads off from a main way; the point where it leads off; a bend; the art of shaping objects on a lathe; an object so made; (*pl*) waste produced on a lathe.

turning point *n* the point at which a significant change occurs.

turnip /ˈtɜːnəp/ or /-nɪp/ *n* a plant with a large white or yellow root, cultivated as a vegetable.

turnout /ˈtɜːnʊt/ *n* a gathering of people.

turnover /ˈtɜːnˌoːvər/ *n* the volume of business transacted in a given period; a fruit or meat pasty; the rate of replacement of workers.

turnpike /ˈtɜːnpaɪk/ *n* a toll road, *esp* one that is an expressway.

turnround /ˈtɜːnraʊnd/ *n* (the time required to complete) the unloading and reloading of a ship, aircraft, etc.

turnstile /ˈtɜːnstaɪl/ *n* a mechanical gate across a footpath or entrance which admits only one person at a time.

turntable /ˈtɜːnˌteɪbəl/ *n* a circular, horizontal revolving platform, as in a record player.

turn-up /ˈtɜːnˌʌp/ *n* the cuff of a trouser; (*inf*) a surprise.

turpentine /ˈtɜːpəntaɪn/ *n* an oily resin secreted by coniferous trees, used as a solvent and thinner for paints.—*also* **turps**.

turpentine tree *n* a terebinth or related tree that yields a turpentine.

turpitude /ˈtɜːpɪˌtuːd/ or /-ˌtjuːd/ *n* depravity; wickedness.

turps /tɜːps/ *n sing* (*inf*) turpentine.

turquoise /ˈtɜːkɔɪz/ or /-kwɔɪz/ *n* an opaque greenish-blue mineral, valued as a gem; the colour of turquoise.—*also adj*.

turret /ˈtɛrɪt/ *n* a small tower on a building rising above it; a dome or revolving structure for guns, as on a warship, tank or aeroplane.—**turreted** *adj*.

turtle /ˈtɜːtəl/ *n* any of an order of land, freshwater or marine reptiles having a soft body encased in a hard shell; **to turn turtle** to turn upside down.

turtledove /ˈtɜːtəlˌdʌv/ *n* a brown dove with speckled wings and a dark tail, noted for its cooing and its care for its partner and young.

turtleneck /ˈtɜːtəlnɛk/ *n* a high close-fitting neckline on a sweater.

turves /tɜːvz/ *see* **turf**.

tusk /tʌsk/ *n* a long, projecting tooth on either side of the mouth, as of the elephant.—**tusked** *adj*.

tusker /ˈtʌskər/ *n* an animal with tusks.

tussle /ˈtʌsəl/ *n* a scuffle.

tussock /ˈtʌsək/ *n* a dense tuft of grass.

tutelage /ˈtuːtələdʒ/ or /ˈtjuː-/ *n* guardianship; guidance by a tutor.

tutor /ˈtuːtər/ or /ˈtjuː-/ *n* a private teacher who instructs pupils individually; a member of staff responsible for the supervision and teaching of students in a British university. • *vt* to instruct; to act as a tutor.

tutorial /tuːˈtɔːriəl/ or /tjuː-/ *n* a period of tuition by a tutor to an individual or a small group. • *adj* of or pertaining to a tutor.

tutti /ˈtuːti/ *adj, adv* (*mus*) all together, to be performed by the whole orchestra. • *n* a musical piece or passage so performed.

tutti-frutti /ˌtuːtiˈfruːti/ *n* (*pl* **tutti-fruttis**) a type of ice cream containing pieces of chopped candied fruits.

tut-tut /tʌtˈtʌt/ *interj* an exclamation of impatience or mild disapproval. • *vi* (**tut-tutting, tut-tutted**) to express disapproval or impatience by uttering "tut-tut".

tutu /ˈtuːtuː/ *n* a short, projecting, layered skirt worn by a ballerina.

tu-whit tu-whoo /tuˌwɪttuˈwuː/ *interj* an imitation of the cry of an owl.

tuxedo /tʌkˈsiːdoː/ *n* a man's semi-formal suit with a tailless jacket.—*also* **dinner jacket**.

TV /tiːˈviː/ *abbr* = television.

TVP *abbr* = textured vegetable protein; a meat substitute used in vegetarian dishes.

twaddle /ˈtwɒdəl/ *n* utter rubbish in speech or writing. • *vi* to speak or write twaddle.

twain /tweɪn/ *adj, n* (*arch*) two.

twang /twæŋ/ *n* a sharp, vibrant sound, as of a taut string when plucked; a nasal tone of voice. • *vt* to make a twanging sound.

'twas /twəz/ or /twɒz/ (*poet*) = it was.

tweak /twiːk/ *vt* to twist, pinch or pull with sudden jerks. • *n* a sharp pinch or twist.

twee /twiː/ *adj* (*inf*) excessively quaint, affected.

tweed /twiːd/ *n* a twilled woollen fabric used in making clothes.

'tween /twiːn/ *prep* (*arch*) between.

tweet /twiːt/ *interj* an imitation of the chirp of a small bird. • *vi* to make this sound.

tweeter /ˈtwiːtər/ *n* a small loudspeaker for reproducing high-frequency sounds.

tweezers /ˈtwiːzərz/ *n sing* small pincers used for plucking.

twelfth /twelfθ/ or /twelθ/ *adj* the last of twelve; being one of twelve equal parts.

Twelfth Day *n* Epiphany.

twelfth man *n* the reserve member of a cricket team.

Twelfth Night *n* the evening of Epiphany, the twelfth day after Christmas, 6 January; the eve of Epiphany, 5th January.

twelve /twelv/ *adj* the cardinal number next after eleven. • *n* the symbol for this (12, XII, xii).

twelve-tone /twelvˈtoːn/ *adj* pertaining to a type of serial music using only the twelve semitones of the chromatic scale as a tone row for compositions.

twelvemo /ˈtwelvmoː/ *n* a book of sheets folded into twelve leaves; this book size.—*also* **duodecimo**.

twenty /ˈtwenti/ *adj, n* two times ten. • *n* (*pl* **twenties**) the symbol for this (20, XX, xx).—**twentieth** *adj*.

twenty-one /ˈtwentiˈwʌn/ *n* pontoon (card game); blackjack.

twenty-twenty, 20/20 /ˌtwentiˈtwenti/ *adj* (*vision*) normal.

'twere /twər/ (*poet*) = it were.

twerp /twərp/ *n* (*inf*) a foolish or contemptible person.—*also* **twirp**.

twice /twaɪs/ *adv* two times; two times as much; doubly.

twiddle /ˈtwɪdəl/ *vt* to twirl or fiddle with idly.

twig[1] /twɪg/ *n* a small branch or shoot of a tree.—**twiggy** *adj*.

twig[2] *vti* (**twigging, twigged**) (*inf*) to grasp the meaning of.

twilight /ˈtwaɪlaɪt/ *n* the dim light just after sunset and before sunrise; the final stages of something.

twilit /ˈtwaɪlɪt/ *adj* lit by twilight.

twill /twɪl/ *n* a cloth woven in such a way as to produce diagonal lines across it.—**twilled** *adj*.

twin /twɪn/ *n* either of two persons or animals born at the same birth; one thing resembling another. • *adj* double; very like another; consisting of two parts nearly alike. • *vt* (**twinning, twinned**) to pair together.

twin bed *n* one of a pair of single beds.

twine /twaɪn/ *n* a string of twisted fibres or hemp. • *vti* to twist together; to wind around.

twin-engined /ˈtwɪnˈendʒənd/ *adj* (*aircraft*) having two engines.

twinge /twɪndʒ/ *n* a sudden, stabbing pain; an emotional pang.

twinkle /ˈtwɪŋkəl/ *vi* to sparkle; to flicker.

twinkling /ˈtwɪŋklɪŋ/ *n* a wink; an instant; the shining of the stars.

twin-screw /ˈtwɪnˈskruː/ *adj* (*vessel*) having two propellers.

twinset *n* a jumper and cardigan designed to be worn together.

twin-tub *n* a washing machine with two drums, one for washing and the other for spin-drying.

twirl /twərl/ *vt* to whirl; to rotate; to wind or twist. • *vi* to turn around rapidly.

twirp /twərp/ *see* **twerp**.

twist /twɪst/ *vt* to unite by winding together; to coil; to confuse or distort (the meaning of); to bend. • *vi* to revolve; to writhe. • *n* the act or result of twisting; a twist of thread; a curve or bend; an unexpected event; a wrench.

twister /ˈtwɪstər/ *n* a tornado; (*inf*) a dishonest person, a swindler.

twisty /ˈtwɪsti/ *adj* (**twistier, twistiest**) winding.

twit[1] /twɪt/ *vt* (**twitting, twitted**) to tease or reproach. • *n* a nervous state.

twit[2] *n* (*inf*) a silly or foolish person.

twitch /twɪtʃ/ *vt* to pull with a sudden jerk. • *vi* to be suddenly jerked. • *n* a sudden muscular spasm.

twitter /ˈtwɪtər/ *n* a chirp, as of a bird. • *vi* to chirp.

two /tuː/ *adj, n* the cardinal number next above one. • *n* the symbol for this (2, II, ii).

two-cycle /ˈtuːˈsaɪkəl/ *see* **two-stroke**.

two-dimensional /ˈtuːdəˈmenʃənəl/ *adj* of or having two dimensions; lacking (the illusion of) depth.

two-edged /ˈtuːˈedʒd/ *adj* having two cutting edges; (*remark, etc*) double-edged.

two-faced /ˈtuːˈfeɪst/ *adj* deceitful, hypocritical.

twofold /ˈtuːfoːld/ *adj* multiplied by two; double. • *adv* doubly.

two-handed /ˈtuːˈhændɪd/ *adj* having or needing two hands; ambidextrous; requiring two people.

twopence /ˈtʌpəns/ *n* the sum of two pence; in UK, a coin of this value; something of little value.—*also* **tuppence**.

two-piece /ˈtuːˈpiːs/ *n* a garment consisting of two separate matching bits.—*also adj*.

two-ply /ˈtuːˈplaɪ/ *adj* made of two thicknesses or strands.

twosome /ˈtuːsəm/ *n* a group of two; a game for two people.

two-step /ˈtuːˈstep/ *n* (the music for) a ballroom dance in duple time.

two-stroke /ˈtuːˈstroːk/ *n, adj* (an internal combustion engine) having a piston which makes two strokes for every explosion.—*also* **two-cycle**.

two-time /ˈtuːˈtaɪm/ *vti* (*sl*) to be unfaithful to (a lover, etc); to double-cross.—**two-timer** *n*.

two-tone /ˈtuːˈtoːn/ *adj* of two colours or shades of the same colour; (*sirens, etc*) having two notes.

two-way /ˈtuːˈweɪ/ *adj* allowing movement or operation in two (opposite) directions; involving two participants; involving mutual obligation; (*radio, telephone*) capable of transmitting and receiving messages.

two-way mirror *n* a sheet of glass that reflects as a mirror on one side but can be seen through from the other.

'twould /twʊd/ (*poet*) = it would.

tycoon /taɪˈkuːn/ *n* a powerful industrialist, etc.

tyke /taɪk/ *n* a (mongrel) dog; (*inf*) a cheeky child.—*also* **tike**.

tympani, tympany /ˈtɪmpəni/ *see* **timpani**.

tympanic bone *n* a bone enclosing part of the middle ear and supporting the tympanic membrane.

tympanic membrane *n* the eardrum.

tympanites /ˌtɪmpəˈnaɪtiːz/ *n* distension of the abdomen caused by the accumulation of gas in the intestine.—**tympanitic** *adj*.

tympanitis /ˌtɪmpəˈnaɪtɪs/ *n* inflammation of the eardrum.

tympanum /ˈtɪmpənəm/ *n* (*pl* **tympanums, tympana**) the cavity of the middle ear; the tympanic membrane, eardrum; the space between the lintel of a doorway and the enclosing arch; the (recessed) triangular face of a pediment.

type /taɪp/ *n* a kind, class or group; sort; model; a block of metal for printing letters; style of print. • *vt* to write by means of a typewriter; to classify.

-type /taɪp/ *n suffix* of the form specified; printing process.

typecast /ˈtaɪpkæst/ *vt* (**typecasting, typecast**) (*actor*) to cast in the same role repeatedly because of physical appearance, etc.

typeface /ˈtaɪpfeɪs/ *n* the printing surface of a type character; a particular design of a set of type characters.

typescript /ˈtaɪpskrɪpt/ *n* a typed copy of a book, document, etc.

typeset /ˈtaɪpˌset/ *vt* (**typesetting, typeset**) to set in type.—**typesetter** *n*.

typewriter /ˈtaɪpˌraɪtər/ *n* a keyboard machine for printing characters.

typhoid /ˈtaɪfɔɪd/ *n* typhoid fever. • *adj* of or pertaining to typhoid fever.—*also* **typhoidal**.

typhoid fever *n* an acute infectious disease acquired by ingesting contaminated food or water.

typhoon /taɪˈfuːn/ *n* a violent tropical cyclone originating in the western Pacific.

typhus /ˈtɔɪfəs/ *n* a highly contagious acute disease spread by body lice and characterized by fever, a rash and headache.—**typhous** *adj*.

typical /ˈtɪpɪkəl/ *adj* representative of a particular type; characteristic.—**typicality** *n*.—**typically** *adv*.

typify /ˈtɪpɪˌfaɪ/ *vt* (**typifying, typified**) to characterize.—**typification** *n*.

typist /ˈtəɪpɪst/ *n* a person who types or uses a typewriter, *esp* as a job.

typo /ˈtəɪpoː/ *n* (*pl* **typos**) (*inf*) a typographical error.

typography /taɪˈpɒɡrəfi/ *n* the way in which printed material is designed or set for printing.—**typographic, typographical** *adj*.

tyrannicide /tiˈrænəˌsaɪd/ or /tə-/, /taɪ-/ *n* (a person responsible for) the killing of a tyrant.

tyrannize /ˈtirəˌnaɪz/ *vi* to exercise power (over) in a vicious and oppressive manner. • *vt* to crush, oppress.—**tyrannizer** *n*.

tyrannosaur /təˈrænəsɔr/ or /taɪ-/, /ti-/, **tyrannosaurus** /-ˌrænəˈsɔrəs/ *n* a large carnivorous dinosaur of the Cretaceous period which stood on powerful hind legs.

tyranny /ˈtirəni/ *n* (*pl* **tyrannies**) the government or authority of a tyrant; harshness; oppression.

tyrant /ˈtaɪrənt/ *n* a person who uses his or her power arbitrarily and oppressively; a despot.—**tyrannical** *adj*.

tyre /taɪr/ *n* a rubber ring, *usu* hollow and inflated, covering the rim of a wheel.

tyro /ˈtaɪˌroː/ *n* (*pl* **tyros**) a novice, a beginner.—*also* **tiro**.

tzar /tsɑr/ or /zɑr/ *n* a czar.—**tzarevitch** *n*.—**tzarina** *n*.

tzatsiki /tsætˈsiːki/ *n* a Greek dip made from plain yogurt, shredded cucumber, and mint.

U

U /juː/ *abbr* = uranium; (*cinema*) universal (suitable for all age groups).

U, u *n* the 21st letter of the English alphabet; something shaped like a U.

UAE *abbr* = United Arab Emirates.

ubiety /juːˈbaɪətɪ/ *n* the state of being in a specific place.

ubiquitous /juːˈbɪkwɪtəs/ *adj* existing, or seeming to exist everywhere at once.—**ubiquity** *n*.

U-boat /ˈjuːbəʊt/ *n* a German submarine.

uc *abbr* = upper case.

udder /ˈʌdər/ *n* a milk-secreting organ containing two or more teats, as in cows.

UFO *abbr* = unidentified flying object.

ufology /juːˈfɒlədʒɪ/ *n* the study of UFOs.—**ufologist** *n*.

ugh /ə/ or /ʌg/, /ʌx/ *interj* an expression of disgust, dislike or horror.

ugli /ˈʌglɪ/, **ugli fruit** *n* (*pl* **uglis, uglies**) a citrus fruit that is a cross between a grapefruit and a tangerine.

ugly /ˈʌglɪ/ *adj* (**uglier, ugliest**) unsightly; unattractive; repulsive; ill tempered.—**ugliness** *n*.

ugly duckling *n* an initially unpromising person or thing that turns out successfully.

UHF *abbr* = ultrahigh frequency.

uh-huh /ˈəˈhʌ/ *interj* used to indicate assent or agreement.

UHT *abbr* = ultra-heat treated (milk or cream).

UK *abbr* = United Kingdom.

ukelele, ukulele /ˌjuːkəˈleɪlɪ/ *n* a small, four-stringed guitar.

ulcer /ˈʌlsər/ *n* an open sore on the surface of the skin or a mucous membrane.—**ulcerous** *adj*.

ulcerate /ˈʌlsəˌreɪt/ *vti* to make or become ulcerous.

-ule /juːl/ or /jʊl/ *n suffix* smallness.

ulema /ˈuːlɪmə/ *n* (a member of) a body of Muslim theologians and religious scholars.

-ulent /jʊlənt/ *adj suffix* abundant.

ullage /ˈʌlɪdʒ/ *n* the amount by which a container (*eg*. a barrel) is less than full.

ulna /ˈʌlnə/ *n* (*pl* **ulnas, ulnae**) the longer and thinner of the two bones in the human forearm; the corresponding bone in the forelimb of other vertebrates.—**ulnar** *adj*.

ulnar nerve /ˈʌlnər/ *n* a nerve in the forearm that passes close to the skin surface at the elbow.

ulotrichous /juːˈlɒtrɪkəs/ *adj* having woolly or curly hair.

ulster /ˈʌlstər/ *n* a long heavy double-breasted overcoat with a belt.

Ulsterman /ˈʌlstərmən/ *n* (*pl* **Ulstermen**) a native or inhabitant of Ulster (a former province of Ireland now divided between Northern Ireland and the Republic of Ireland).—**Ulsterwoman** (*pl* **Ulsterwomen**) *nf*.

ulterior /ʌlˈtiːrɪər/ *adj* (*motives*) hidden, not evident; subsequent.

ultima /ˈʌltɪmə/ *n* the last syllable of a word.

ultimate /ˈʌltɪmət/ *adj* last; final; most significant; essential. • *n* the most significant thing.—**ultimately** *adv*.

ultimatum /ˌʌltɪˈmeɪtəm/ *n* (*pl* **ultimatums, ultimata**) the final proposal, condition or terms in negotiations.

ultimogeniture /ˌʌltɪmoˈdʒenɪtʃər/ *n* (*law*) inheritance by the youngest son.

ultra /ˈʌltrə/ *adj* extreme, uncompromising. • *n* an extremist.

ultra- /ˈʌltrə/ *prefix* beyond.

ultraconservative /ˌʌltrəkənˈsɜːvətɪv/ *adj* deeply conservative or reactionary. • *n* a reactionary person.

ultrafiche /ˈʌltrəˌfiːʃ/ *n* a type of high-density microfiche containing a very large number of microcopies.

ultrahigh frequency /ˌʌltrəˈhaɪ/ *n* a radio frequency in the range between 300 megahertz and 3000 megahertz.

ultraism /ˈʌltrəɪzəm/ *n* the advocacy of extreme action.—**ultraist** *n*.

ultramarine /ˌʌltrəməˈriːn/ *adj* deep blue. • *n* a blue pigment; a vivid, deep blue.

ultramicroscope /ˌʌltrəˈmaɪkrəˌskoːp/ *n* an optical device for viewing tiny particles undetectable by a conventional microscope.—**ultramicroscopic** *adj*.

ultrashort /ˌʌltrəˈʃɔːt/ *adj* (*radio wave*) having a wavelength less than 10 metres.

ultrasonic /ˌʌltrəˈsɒnɪk/ *adj* (*waves, vibrations*) having a frequency beyond the human ear's audible range.

ultrasound /ˈʌltrəˌsaʊnd/ *n* ultrasonic waves used in medical diagnosis and therapy.

ultraviolet /ˌʌltrəˈvaɪələt/ *adj* of light waves, shorter than the wavelengths of visible light and longer than X-rays.

ultraviolet light /ʌltrəˈvaɪələt laɪt/ *n* ultraviolet radiation.

ultravirus /ˌʌltrəˈvaɪrəs/ *n* a virus small enough to pass through the finest filter.

ululate /ˈʌljʊˌleɪt/ or /ˈjuːl-/ *vi* to howl or wail, as with pain or grief.—**ululant** *adj*.—**ululation** *n*.

umbel /ˈʌmbəl/ *n* a flower-cluster characteristic of plants of the carrot family, in which the stalks grow from the same place on the main stem producing an umbrella effect.—**umbellate** *adj*.

umbelliferous /ˌʌmbəˈlɪfərəs/ *adj* of or pertaining to a family of plants and shrubs bearing umbels, including carrots, parsley and fennel.—**umbellifer** *n*.

umber /ˈʌmbər/ *n* a brown pigment. • *adj* dark brown.

umbilical /ʌmˈbɪlɪkəl/ *n* of, pertaining to, near, or resembling the navel.

umbilical cord *n* the vascular tube connecting a foetus with the placenta through which oxygen and nutrients are passed.

umbilicate /ʌmˈbɪlɪkət/, **umbilicated** *n* depressed or shaped like a navel; having an umbilicus.—**umbilication** *n*.

umbilicus /ʌmˈbɪlɪkəs/ or /ˌʌmbɪˈlaɪkəs/ *n* (*pl* **umbilici**) the navel; a navel-shaped depression on a plant or animal.

umbo /ˈʌmboː/ *n* (*pl* **umbones, umbos**) the boss in the centre of a shield; a rounded anatomical protrusion.

umbra /ˈʌmbrə/ *n* (*pl* **umbrae, umbras**) an area of total shadow, *esp* during an eclipse; the dark centre of a sunspot.—**umbral** *adj*.

umbrage /ˈʌmbrɪdʒ/ *n* resentment; offence.

umbrella /ʌmˈbrelə/ *n* a cloth-covered collapsible frame carried in the hand for protection from rain or sun; a general protection.

umiak /ˈuːmɪˌæk/ *n* a large open Eskimo boat made from hide stretched over a wooden frame.—*also* **oomiak**.

umlaut /ˈʊmlaʊt/ *n* the mark (¨) placed over a vowel in German and other languages to modify its sound; the change of a vowel brought about by its assimilation to another vowel.

umpire /ˈʌmpaɪr/ *n* an official who enforces the rules in sport; an arbitrator.—*also vti*.

umpteen /ˈʌmptiːn/ or /-ˈtiːn/ *adj* (*inf*) an undetermined large number.—**umpteenth** *adj*.

UN *abbr* = United Nations.

un- /ʌn/ *prefix* not; opposite of; contrary to; reversal of an action or state.

'un, un /ən/ *pron* (*dial*) one.

unable /ʌnˈeɪbəl/ *adj* not able; lacking the strength, skill, power or opportunity (to do something).

unaccountable /ˌʌnəˈkaʊntəbəl/ *adj* inexplicable, puzzling; not to be called to account for one's actions.

unaccustomed /ˌʌnəˈkʌstəmd/ *adj* (*with* **to**) not used (to); not usual or familiar.

una corda /ˈuːnə ˈkɔːdə/ *adj, adv* (*mus*) (*piano*) to be played with the soft pedal depressed.

unadulterated /ˌʌnəˈdʌltəˌreɪtəd/ *adj* pure, unmixed.

unadvised /ˌʌnədˈvaɪzd/ *adj* unwise, imprudent; not advised.—**unadvisedly** *adv*.

unaffected /ˌʌnəˈfektəd/ *adj* sincere, frank, without pretension; not influenced or affected.—**unaffectedly** *adv*.

un-American *adj* contrary to US customs, ideals or interests.—**un-Americanism** *n*.

unanimous /juːˈnænɪməs/ *adj* showing complete agreement.—**unanimity** *n*.—**unanimously** *adv*.

unapproachable /ˌʌnəˈproːtʃəbəl/ *adj* aloof, unfriendly; impossible to reach; not to be equalled or rivalled.

unarmed /ʌnˈɑrmd/ *adj* not in possession of weapons; defenceless.

unasked /ʌnˈæskt/ *adj* not asked or asked for; not invited or requested; spontaneous. • *adv* of one's own accord; without prompting.

unassailable /ˌʌnəˈseɪləbəl/ *adj* not open to attack; not open to criticism or doubt.

unassuming /ˌʌnəˈsuːmɪŋ/ or /-sjuː-/ *adj* unpretentious; modest.

unattached /ˌʌnəˈtætʃt/ *adj* unmarried, not engaged to be married; not belonging to a particular group, organization, etc.

unattended /ˌʌnəˈtendəd/ *adj* not supervised; not accompanied.

unauthorized /ʌnˈɒθəˌraɪzd/ *adj* not endorsed by authority.

unavailing /ˌʌnəˈveɪlɪŋ/ *adj* futile, hopeless.—**unavailingly** *adv*.

unavoidable /ˌʌnəˈvoɪdəbəl/ *adj* bound to happen, inevitable; necessary, compulsory.—**unavoidably** *adv*.

unaware /ˌʌnəˈwer/ *adj* not conscious or aware (of); ignorant (of).

unawares /ˌʌnəˈwerz/ *adv* by surprise; unexpectedly, without warning.

unbalanced /ʌnˈbælənsd/ *adj* mentally unstable; having bias or over-representing a particular view, group, interest, etc; (*bookkeeping*) not having equal debit and credit totals.

·unbearable /ʌnˈberəbəl/ *adj* intolerable, not able to be endured.—**unbearably** *adv*.

unbeatable /ʌnˈbiːtəbəl/ *adj* impossible to beat; outstanding, excellent.

unbeaten /ʌnˈbiːtən/ *adj* not beaten, unsurpassed.

unbecoming /ˌʌnbɪˈkʌmɪŋ/ *adj* (*clothes, make-up, etc*) not enhancing the wearer's appearance; (*behaviour*) not suitable or seemly.

unbeknown /ˌʌnbɪˈnoːn/ *adj* (*with* **to**) happening without (a person's) knowledge.

unbelief /ʌnbɪˈliːf/ *n* disbelief, scepticism, *esp* in religious matters.

unbelievable /ˌʌnbɪˈliːvəbəl/ *adj* not able to be believed; incredible.—**unbelievably** *adv*.

unbeliever /ˌʌnbɪˈliːvər/ *n* a person who does not believe, *esp* in a religion.

unbelieving /ˌʌnbɪˈliːvɪŋ/ *adj* lacking belief; sceptical.—**unbelievingly** *adv*.

unbend /ʌnˈbend/ *vb* (**unbending, unbent**) *vt* to straighten from a bent shape; to release or untie (*eg* a rope). • *vi* to become more relaxed, affable or informal in manner.

unbending /ʌnˈbendɪŋ/ *adj* severe, stern; inflexible, unchanging; rigid in behaviour or attitude.

unbiased, unbiassed /ʌnˈbaɪəst/ *adj* without prejudice or bias; impartial, even-handed, disinterested.

unbidden /ʌnˈbɪdən/ *adj* not commanded, asked for or invited.

unblushing /ʌnˈblʌʃɪŋ/ *adj* shameless, impudent.—**unblushingly** *adv*.

unborn /ʌnˈbɔrn/ *adj* not yet born; still to appear or happen in the future.

unbosom /ʌnˈbuzəm/ *vt* to reveal the thoughts or feelings of (oneself).

unbounded /ʌnˈbaʊndəd/ *adj* without limits.

unbowed /ʌnˈbaud/ *adj* not bowed; not subdued, free.

unbridled /ʌnˈbraɪdəld/ *adj* unrestrained; (*horse*) having no bridle.

unbroken /ʌnˈbroːkən/ *adj* whole, in one piece; continuous, uninterrupted; (*record*) not yet beaten; (*horses, etc*) wild, untamed; organized, disciplined.

unburden /ʌnˈbɔrdən/ *vt* to reveal or confess one's troubles, secrets etc to another in order to relieve the mind; to take off a burden.

unbutton /ʌnˈbʌtən/ *vt* to unfasten the buttons of (a garment).

unbuttoned /ʌnˈbʌtənd/ *adj* unfastened; (*inf*) free, uninhibited.

uncalled-for /ʌnˈkɒld fɔr/ *adj* unnecessary, unwanted, unwarranted.

uncanny /ʌnˈkæni/ *adj* (**uncannier, uncanniest**) odd; unexpected; suggestive of supernatural powers; unearthly.

unceremonious /ˌʌnserəˈmoːniəs/ *adj* without ceremony, informal; abrupt, rude.—**unceremoniously** *adv*.

uncertain /ʌnˈsɔrtən/ *adj* not knowing accurately, doubtful; (*with* **of**) not confident or sure; not fixed, variable, changeable.—**uncertainty** *n*.

uncertainty principle *n* (*phys*) the principle that it is impossible to determine accurately both the position and momentum of an elementary particle simultaneously.—*also* **Heisenberg uncertainty principle**.

uncharted /ʌnˈtʃɑrtəd/ *adj* not marked on a map; unsurveyed, unexplored.

unchristian /ʌnˈkrɪstʃən/ *adj* contrary to Christian belief or principle; savage, pagan.

uncial /ˈʌnsiəl/ or /-ʃəl/ *adj* written in or resembling large rounded capital letters as used in early medieval Greek and Latin manuscripts. • *n* an uncial character or manuscript.

uncinate /ˈʌnsɪnət/ *adj* (*plant, animal*) having a hook-shaped part.

uncircumcised /ʌnˈsɜrkəmˌsaɪzd/ *adj* not circumcised; not Jewish; impure.—**uncircumcision** *n*.

uncivil /ʌnˈsɪvəl/ *adj* lacking in manners, impolite.—**uncivility** *n*.

uncivilized /ʌnˈsɪvəˌlaɪzd/ *adj* not civilized, unsophisticated; remote, wild.

uncle /ˈʌŋkəl/ *n* the brother of one's father or mother; the husband of one's aunt.

unclean /ʌnˈkliːn/ *adj* not clean, contaminated; ceremonially defiled.

Uncle Sam *n* the government of the US personified.

unclothe /ʌnˈkloːð/ *vt* (**unclothing, unclothed** or **unclad**) to remove the clothes from; to uncover.

uncoil /ʌnˈkɔɪl/ *vti* to (cause to) unwind.

uncomfortable /ʌnˈkʌmftərbəl/ or /-fərtəbəl/, /-frtəbəl/ *adj* causing discomfort; feeling discomfort or unease.

uncommitted /ˌʌnkəˈmɪtəd/ *adj* not bound to a particular cause, belief or course of action.

uncommon /ʌnˈkɒmən/ *adj* rare, unusual; extraordinary.

uncommonly /-li/ *adv* hardly ever; exceptionally, particularly.

uncommunicative /ˌʌnkəˈmjuːnɪkətɪv/ *adj* not willing to talk or express an opinion, etc; reserved.

uncompromising /ʌnˈkɒmprəˌmaɪzɪŋ/ *adj* not prepared to compromise; inflexible, obstinate.

unconcern /ˌʌnkənˈsɔrn/ *n* indifference.

unconcerned /-d/ *adj* not involved in or concerned with; not troubled.

unconditional /ˌʌnkənˈdɪʃənəl/ *adj* without restrictions or conditions, absolute.

unconscionable /ʌnˈkɒnʃənəbəl/ *adj* unscrupulous; unreasonable.—**unconscionably** *adv*.

unconscious /ʌnˈkɒnʃəs/ *adj* not aware (of); lacking normal perception by the senses, insensible; unintentional. • *n* the deepest level of mind containing feelings and emotions of which one is unaware and unable to control.—**unconsciously** *adv*.

unconsciousness /-nəs/ *n* the state of being without the senses, as when knocked out.

unconstitutional /ˌʌnkɒnstɪˈtuːʃənəl/ or /-ˈtjuː-/ *adj* contrary to the constitution of a country.—**unconstitutionality** *n*.

unconventional /ˌʌnkənˈvenʃənəl/ *adj* not bound by social rules or conventions.—**unconventionally** *adv*.

uncork /ʌnˈkɔrk/ *vt* to pull the cork from a bottle; (*emotions, desires, etc*) to unleash, give vent to.

uncouple /ʌnˈkʌpəl/ *vti* to disconnect or become disconnected.

uncouth /ʌnˈkuːθ/ *adj* lacking in manners; rough; rude.—**uncouthness** *n*.

uncover /ʌnˈkʌvər/ *vt* to remove the cover from; to reveal or expose; to remove one's hat in greeting or out of respect.

uncovered /ʌnˈkʌvərd/ *adj* not having a cover; revealed; not having any insurance or security; with one's hat removed out of respect, etc.

UNCTAD /ˈjuːˌenˌsiːˌtiːˌæˌdiː/ *abbr* = United Nations Conference on Trade and Development.

unction /ˈʌŋkʃən/ *n* an anointing, as for medical or religious purposes; anything that soothes or comforts; affected sincerity.

unctuous /ˈʌŋktʃʊəs/ *adj* oily; smarmy; too suave; insincerely charming.—**unctuously** *adv*.—**unctuousness** *n*.

uncurl /ʌnˈkɜrl/ *vti* to straighten; to straighten up, relax.

uncut /ʌnˈkʌt/ *adj* not cut; (*book*) not having the folds of the leaves trimmed or slit; (*gemstone*) not cut into shape; not abridged.

undaunted /ʌnˈdɒntəd/ *adj* fearless; not discouraged.—**undauntedly** *adv*.

undecagon /ˌʌnˈdekəˌɡɒn/ *n* a polygon with eleven sides.

undeceive /ˌʌndɪˈsiːv/ *vt* to free from deception or error.

undecided /ˌʌndɪˈsaɪdəd/ *adj* doubtful, hesitant; (*solution, etc*) not determined.—**undecidedly** *adv*.

undeniable /ˌʌndəˈnaɪəbəl/ *adj* readily apparent, obviously true; unquestionably excellent.

under /'ʌndər/ *prep* lower than; beneath the surface of; below; covered by; subject to; less than, falling short of. • *adv* beneath, below, lower down. • *adj* lower in position, degree or rank; subordinate.

under- /'ʌndər/ *prefix* beneath, below.

underachieve /ˌʌndərə'tʃiːv/ *vi* to perform less well than expected given one's potential.—**underachiever** *n*.

underact /ˌʌndər'ækt/ *vt* to perform (a dramatic role) without proper conviction or emphasis.

underage /ˌʌndər'eɪdʒ/ *adj* below the normal or legal age.

underarm /'ʌndərɑrm/ *adj* of, for, in, or used on the area under the arm, or armpit; done with the hand below the level of the elbow or shoulder.

underbelly /'ʌndərˌbɛli/ *n* (*pl* **underbellies**) the underside of an animal, etc; the most vulnerable part of something.

underbid /ˌʌndər'bɪd/ *vb* (**underbidding, underbid**) *vt* to bid a lower amount than (rivals); (*bridge, etc*) to bid less than the strength of the hand merits. • *vi* to bid too low.

undercapitalized /ˌʌndər'kæpɪtəlaɪz/ *adj* (*business*) having insufficient capital to operate efficiently.

undercarriage /'ʌndərˌkɛrɪdʒ/ *n* the landing gear of an aeroplane; a car's supporting framework.

undercharge /ˌʌndər'tʃɑrdʒ/ *vt* to charge below the fair price.

underclass /'ʌndərˌklæs/ *n* those least privileged people in society who fall outside the normal social scale, characterized by poverty, unemployment, poor education, social instability, etc.

underclothes /'ʌndərˌkloːz/ or /-ˌkloːðz/ *npl* underwear.—*also* **underclothing**.

undercoat /'ʌndərˌkoːt/ *n* a coat of paint, etc, applied as a base below another; a growth of hair or fur under another; a coat worn under an overcoat.

undercover /ˌʌndər'kʌvər/ or /'ʌn-/ *adj* done or operating secretly.

undercurrent /'ʌndərˌkʌrənt/ *n* a hidden current under water; an emotion, opinion, etc, not apparent.

undercut /ˌʌndər'kʌt/ *vt* (**undercutting, undercut**) to charge less than a competitor; to undermine.

underdeveloped /ˌʌndərdə'vɛləpt/ *adj* not fully grown, immature; (*societies*) having an inadequate social and political infrastructure for sustained economic growth; (*film*) not processed long enough to form a proper image.

underdog /'ʌndərˌdɒg/ *n* the loser in an encounter, contest, etc; a person in an inferior position.

underdone /ˌʌndər'dʌn/ *adj* not sufficiently or completely cooked.

underdressed /ˌʌndər'drɛst/ *adj* wearing clothes that are too informal for a particular occasion.

underemployed /ˌʌndərəm'plɔɪd/ *adj* not fully or most efficiently employed.

underestimate /ˌʌndər'ɛstəˌmeɪt/ *vti* to set too low an estimate on or for. • *n* too low an estimate.

underexpose /ˌʌndərək'spoːz/ *vt* (*photog*) to fail to expose (film) to light sufficiently long to produce a good image.—**underexposed** *adj*.—**underexposure** *n*.

underfelt /ˌʌndər'fɛlt/ *n* a layer of thick felt between a carpet and floor.

underfoot /ˌʌndər'fut/ *adv* underneath the foot or feet; on the ground.

undergarment /'ʌndərˌgɑrmənt/ *n* a piece of underwear or clothing worn beneath other outer clothing.

undergo /ˌʌndər'goː/ *vt* (**undergoing, underwent,** *pp* **undergone**) to experience, suffer, endure.

undergraduate /ˌʌndər'grædʒʊət/ *n* a student at a college or university studying for a first degree.

underground /ˌʌndər'graʊnd/ *adj* situated under the surface of the ground; secret; of noncommercial newspapers, movies, etc that are unconventional, radical, etc. • *n* a secret group working for the overthrow of the government or the expulsion of occupying forces; an underground railway system.

undergrowth /'ʌndərˌgroːθ/ *n* shrubs, plants, etc growing beneath trees.

underhand /'ʌndərˌhænd/ *adv* (*sport*) with an underarm motion; underhandedly.

underhanded /'ʌndərˌhændəd/ *adj* sly, secret, deceptive.—**underhandedly** *adv*.

underlay /ˌʌndər'leɪ/ *n* a material, lining laid beneath another for support; felt or rubber laid beneath a carpet for insulation, etc.

underlie /ˌʌndər'laɪ/ *vt* (**underlying, underlay,** *pp* **underlain**) to be situated under; to form the basis of.

underline /'ʌndərˌlaɪn/ *vt* to put a line underneath; to emphasize.

underling /'ʌndərlɪŋ/ *n* a person of inferior rank or status to someone else; a subordinate.

underlying /'ʌndərˌlaɪɪŋ/ *adj* existing, but hard to detect; fundamental, supporting.

undermentioned /'ʌndərˌmɛnʃənd/ *adj* mentioned below or later in the text.

undermine /'ʌndərˌmaɪn/ *vt* to wear away, or weaken; to injure or weaken, *esp* by subtle or insidious means.

underneath /ˌʌndər'niːθ/ *adv* under. • *adj* lower. • *n* the underside.—*also prep*.

undernourished /ˌʌndər'nərɪʃt/ *adj* consuming or supplied with less than the minimum quantity of food necessary for normal health and growth.

underpants /'ʌndərˌpænts/ *npl* pants worn as an undergarment by men and boys.

underpass /'ʌndərˌpæs/ *n* a section of road running beneath another road, a railway, etc.

underpin /ˌʌndər'pɪn/ *vt* to strengthen or support from beneath.

underpinning /'ʌndərpɪnɪŋ/ *n* the material used to support a structure, the foundation.

underplay /'ʌndərˌpleɪ/ *vt* to perform (a dramatic role) with restraint; to play down the importance of.

underprivileged /ˌʌndər'prɪvlɪdʒd/ or /-'prɪvəlɪdʒd/ *adj* lacking the basic rights of other members of society; poor.

underproof /ˌʌndər'pruːf/ *adj* containing less alcohol per volume than proof spirit.

underrate /ˌʌndər'reɪt/ *vt* to undervalue, to underestimate.

underscore /'ʌndərˌskɔr/ *vt* to draw a line under; to emphasize.

undersea /'ʌndərˌsiː/ *adj, adv* below the surface of the sea.

underseal /'ʌndərˌsiːl/ *n* a protective layer of tar, etc applied to the underside of a vehicle. • *vt* to apply this protective layer.

undersecretary /ˌʌndər'sɛkrəˌteri/ *n* (*pl* **undersecretaries**) a senior civil servant in Great Britain; in US, a secretary immediately subordinate to a principal.

undersell /ˌʌndər'sɛl/ *vt* (**underselling, undersold**) to sell at a reduced price; to sell at a price lower than (someone else); to promote with moderation.

undersexed /ˌʌndər'sɛksd/ *adj* having a weaker than normal sex drive.

undershirt /ˌʌndər'ʃərt/ *n* a vest.

undershoot /ˌʌndər'ʃuːt/ *vti* (**undershooting, undershot**) to (cause to) land short of a runway; to shoot short of a target.

underside /'ʌndərˌsaɪd/ *n* the lower surface.

undersigned /'ʌndərˌsaɪnd/ *adj* signed at the end. • *n* a person who signs his or her name at the end of a document.

undersized /'ʌndərˌsaɪzd/ *adj* less than usual size.

underskirt /'ʌndərˌskərt/ *n* a woman's undergarment worn beneath the skirt, a petticoat.

underslung /'ʌndərˌslʌŋ/ *adj* suspended from above; (*vehicle chassis*) suspended below the axles.

understand /ˌʌndər'stænd/ *vb* (**understanding, understood**) *vt* to comprehend; to realize; to believe; to assume; to know thoroughly (*eg* a language); to accept; to be sympathetic with. • *vi* to comprehend; to believe.—**understandable** *adj*.

understanding /ˌʌndər'stændɪŋ/ *n* comprehension; compassion; sympathy; personal opinion, viewpoint; mutual agreement. • *adj* sympathetic.

understate /ˌʌndər'steɪt/ *vt* to state something in restrained terms; to represent as less than is the case.—**understatement** *n*.

understudy /'ʌndərˌstɛdi/ *vti* (**understudying, understudied**) to learn a role or part so as to be able to replace (the actor playing it); to act as an understudy (to).—*also n*.

undertake /ˌʌndər'teɪk/ *vt* (**undertaking, undertook,** *pp* **undertaken**) to attempt to; to agree to; to commit oneself to; to promise; to guarantee.

undertaker /'ʌndərˌteɪkər/ *n* a funeral director.

undertaking /'ʌndərˌteɪkɪŋ/ *n* enterprise; task; promise; obligation.

underthings /'ʌndərθɪŋz/ *npl* underwear.

undertone /'ʌndərˌtoːn/ *n* a hushed tone of voice; an undercurrent of feeling; a pale colour.

undertow /'ʌndərˌtoː/ *n* the backwash from a breaking wave; an undercurrent moving in a different direction from the surface current.

undervalue /ˌʌndər'vælju:/ *vt* (**undervaluing, undervalued**) to put too low a price or value on.—**undervaluation** *n*.

underwater /ˌʌndər'wɒtər/ *adj* being carried on under the surface of the water, *esp* the sea; submerged; below the water line of a vessel.—*also adv*.

under way /ˌʌndər'weɪ/ *adv* in or into motion or progress.

underwear /'ʌndər,wer/ *n* garments worn underneath one's outer clothes, next to the skin.

underweight /ˌʌndər'weɪt/ *adj* weighing less than normal or necessary.

underwent /ˌʌndər'wɛnt/ *see* **undergo**.

underwhelm /ˌʌndər'wɛlm/ *vt* to disappoint.

underworld /'ʌndər,wɜrld/ *n* criminals as an organized group; (*myth*) Hades.

underwrite /'ʌndər,raɪt/ or /ˌʌn-/ *vt* to agree to finance (an undertaking, etc); to sign one's name to (an insurance policy), thus assuming liability. • *vi* to work as an underwriter.—**underwriter** *n*.

undesirable /ˌʌndə'zaɪrəbəl/ *adj* not desirable; not pleasant; objectionable.—**undesirability** *n*.—**undesirably** *adv*.

undetermined /ˌʌndə'tɜrmənd/ *adj* not yet decided; not discovered.

undies /'ʌndiːz/ *npl* (*inf*) women's underwear.

undo /ʌn'duː/ *vt* (**undoing, undid,** *pp* **undone**) to untie or unwrap; to reverse (what has been done); to bring ruin on.

undone /ʌn'dʌn/ *adj* not done; not fastened or tied.

undoubted /ʌn'daʊtəd/ *adj* without doubt; definite, certain.—**undoubtedly** *adv*.

undreamed /ʌn'driːmd/, **undreamt** /ʌn'drɛmt/ *n* (*with* **of**) not thought of or imagined.

undress /ʌn'drɛs/ *vt* to remove the clothes from. • *vi* to take off one's clothes.

undressed /ʌn'drɛsd/ *adj* not dressed, partially or informally clothed; (*wound*) not bandaged; (*food*) not prepared for serving; (*hides*) not processed.

undue /ʌn'duː/ or /-'djuː/ *adj* improper; excessive.

undulate /'ʌndju,leɪt/ or /-dʒu,leɪt/ *vti* to move or cause to move like waves; to have or cause to have a wavy form or surface.

undulation /ˌʌndju'leɪʃən/ or /-dʒʊ-/ *n* a wavelike form or motion.

unduly /ʌn'duːli/ or /-'djuː-/ *adv* too; excessively; improperly.

undying /ʌn'daɪɪŋ/ *adj* eternal.

unearned /ʌn'ɜrnd/ *adj* (*income*) not earned by labour or skill; undeserved.

unearth /ʌn'ɜrθ/ *vt* to dig up from the earth; to discover; to reveal.

unearthly /ʌn'ɜrθli/ *adj* mysterious; eerie; supernatural; absurd; unreasonable.

uneasy /ʌn'iːzi/ *adj* uncomfortable; restless; anxious; disquieting.—**uneasily** *adv*.—**uneasiness** *n*.

uneatable /ʌn'iːtəbəl/ *adj* (*food*) not edible, *esp* because of its condition or appearance.

uneconomic /ˌʌnekə'nɒmɪk/ or /ˌʌniːk-/ *adj* wasteful; unprofitable.

unemployable /ˌʌnəm'plɔɪəbəl/ *adj* not fit or acceptable for work.

unemployed /ʌnəm'plɔɪd/ *adj* not having a job, out of work.—**unemployment** *n*.

unequal /ʌn'iːkwəl/ *adj* not equal; not regular or uniform; not sufficiently strong or able.—**unequally** *adv*.

unequalled, unequaled /ʌn'iːkwəld/ *adj* not equalled; supreme.

unequivocal /ˌʌnə'kwɪvəkəl/ *adj* unambiguous; plain; clear.—**unequivocally** *adv*.

unerring /ʌn'ɛrɪŋ/ or /-'ɜrɪŋ/ *adj* sure, unfailing.

UNESCO /juː'nɛskoʊ/ *abbr* = United Nations Educational, Scientific and Cultural Organization.

uneven /ʌn'iːvən/ *adj* not level or smooth; variable; not divisible by two without leaving a remainder.—**unevenness** *n*.

uneventful /ˌʌnə'ventfʊl/ *adj* ordinary, routine.—**uneventfully** *adv*.

unexampled /ˌʌnəg'zæmpəld/ *adj* without precedent or comparison.

unexceptionable /ˌʌnɪk'sepʃənəbəl/ *adj* irreproachable.

unexceptional /ˌʌnək'sepʃənəl/ *adj* ordinary, normal.

unexpected /ˌʌnək'spɛktəd/ *adj* not looked for, unforeseen.—**unexpectedly** *adv*.

unfailing /ʌn'feɪlɪŋ/ *adj* not failing or giving up; persistent; constant, dependable.—**unfailingly** *adv*.

unfair /ʌn'fɛr/ *adj* unjust; unequal; against the rules.—**unfairly** *adv*.—**unfairness** *n*.

unfaithful /ʌn'feɪθfʊl/ *adj* disloyal; not abiding by a promise; adulterous.—**unfaithfully** *adv*.—**unfaithfulness** *n*.

unfamiliar /ˌʌnfə'mɪljər/ *adj* not known, strange; (*with* **with**) not familiar.

unfasten /ʌn'fæsən/ *vt* to open or become opened; to undo or become undone; to loose, loosen.

unfathomable /ʌn'fæðəməbəl/ *adj* not able to be measured; incomprehensible.

unfavourable, unfavorable /ʌn'feɪvərəbəl/ *adj* negative, disapproving; adverse.

unfeeling /ʌn'fiːlɪŋ/ *adj* callous, hardhearted.—**unfeelingly** *adv*.

unfinished /ʌn'fɪnɪʃt/ *adj* not finished, incomplete; in the making; crude, sketchy.

unfit /ʌn'fɪt/ *adj* unsuitable; in bad physical condition.

unflappable /ʌn'flæpəbəl/ *adj* (*inf*) calm, not easily agitated.

unflinching /ʌn'flɪntʃɪŋ/ *adj* calm, steadfast.—**unflinchingly** *adv*.

unfold /ʌn'foʊld/ *vti* to open or spread out; to become revealed; to develop.

unforeseen /ˌʌnfor'siːn/ *adj* unsuspected.

unforgettable /ˌʌnfər'getəbəl/ or /-for-/ *adj* never to be forgotten; fixed in the mind; impressive, exceptional.—**unforgettably** *adv*.

unfortunate /ʌn'fortʃənət/ *adj* unlucky; disastrous; regrettable. • *n* an unlucky person.

unfortunately /ʌn'fortʃənətli/ *adv* regrettably, unluckily, unhappily.

unfounded /ʌn'faʊndəd/ *adj* groundless; baseless.

unfreeze /ʌn'friːz/ *vti* (**unfreezing, unfroze, unfrozen**) to (cause to) thaw; to remove restrictions on (wage or price rises, etc).

unfrock /ʌn'frɒk/ *vt* to remove (a person in holy orders) from ecclesiastical office.

unfurl /ʌn'fɜrl/ *vti* to open; to unfold.

ungainly /ʌn'geɪnli/ *adj* (**ungainlier, ungainliest**) awkward; clumsy.—**ungainliness** *n*.

ungodly /ʌn'gɒdli/ *adj* (**ungoldier, ungodliest**) not religious; sinful; wicked; (*inf*) outrageous.

ungovernable /ʌn'gʌvərnəbəl/ *adj* not able to be controlled or restrained.

unguarded /ʌn'gardəd/ *adj* without protection, vulnerable; open to attack; careless; candid, frank.—**unguardedly** *adv*.

unguent /'ʌŋgwənt/ *n* a lubricant or ointment.

ungulate /'ʌŋgjʊlət/ *n adj* (an animal) having hooves.

unhallowed /ʌn'hæloːd/ *adj* not consecrated; sinful.

unhappy /ʌn'hæpi/ *adj* (**unhappier, unhappiest**) not happy or fortunate; sad; wretched; not suitable.—**unhappily** *adv*.—**unhappiness** *n*.

unhealthy /ʌn'hɛlθi/ *adj* (**unhealthier, unhealthiest**) not healthy or fit, sick; encouraging or resulting from poor health; harmful, degrading; dangerous.—**unhealthily** *adv*.—**unhealthiness** *n*.

unheard /ʌn'hɜrd/ *adj* not heard; not listened to.

unheard-of *adj* not known before; without precedent.

unhinge /ʌn'hɪndʒ/ *vt* to make crazy, derange.

unholy /ʌn'hoːli/ *adj* (**unholier, unholiest**) wicked; (*inf*) outrageous, enormous.

unhook /ʌn'hʊk/ *vt* to remove from a hook; to unfasten the hooks of (a garment).

uni /'juː,nɪ/ *n* (*inf*) university.

uni- /'juːnɪ/ *prefix* one; single.

unicameral /ˌjuːnɪ'kæmərəl/ *adj* of or having only one legislative chamber.—**unicamerally** *adv*.

UNICEF /'juːnə,sef/ *abbr* = United Nations International Children's Emergency Fund, now United Nations Children's Fund.

unicellular /ˌjuːnɪ'seljələr/ *adj* (*microorganisms, etc*) consisting of a single cell.—**unicellularity** *n*.

unicorn /'juːnɪkorn/ *n* an imaginary creature with a body like a horse and a single horn on the forehead.

unicycle /'juːnɪ,saɪkəl/ *n* a pedal-driven cycle with a single wheel, used by circus and street entertainers.

unidirectional /ˌjuːnɪdɪ'rekʃənəl/ or /ˌjuːnɪdaɪ-/ *adj* involving, going in, or operating in one direction only.

uniform /'juːnɪ,form/ *adj* unchanging in form; consistent; identical. • *n* the distinctive clothes worn by members of the same organization, such as soldiers, schoolchildren.—**uniformly** *adv*.

uniformity /ˌjuːnɪ'formiti/ *n* (*pl* **uniformities**) the state of being consistent or the same; dullness, monotony.

unify /'juːnɪ,faɪ/ *vt* (**unifying, unified**) to make into one; to unite.—**unification** *n*.

unilateral /juːnɪˈlætərəl/ *adj* involving one only of several parties; not reciprocal.—**unilateralism** *n*.—**unilaterally** *adv*.

unimpeachable /ˌʌnɪmˈpiːtʃəbəl/ *adj* completely honest, truthful, etc; irreproachable.—**unimpeachably** *adv*.

uninhibited /ˌʌnɪnˈhæbɪtəd/ *adj* not repressed or restrained; relaxed, spontaneous.—**uninhibitedly** *adv*.

uninterested /ʌnˈɪntrəstəd/ or /-tərestəd/ *adj* lacking interest; not concerned, indifferent.—**uninterestedly** *adv*.

union /ˈjuːnjən/ *n* the act of uniting; a combination of several things; a confederation of individuals or groups; marriage; a trades union.

unionist /ˈjuːnjənɪst/ *n* an advocate or supporter of union or unionism.—**unionism** *n*.

unionize /ˈjuːnjəˌnaɪz/ *vt* to organize (employees) into a trade union.—**unionization** *n*.

Union Jack *n* the national flag of the UK.

unipolar /ˌjuːnɪˈpoʊlər/ *adj* of, produced by, or having a single electric or magnetic pole.—**unipolarity** *n*.

unique /juːˈniːk/ *adj* without equal; the only one of its kind.—**uniquely** *adv*.

unisex /ˈjuːnɪˌseks/ *adj* of a style that can be worn by both sexes.

unisexual /juːnɪˈseksʊəl/ *adj* of one sex only; having male or female sex organs but not both.—**unisexually** *adv*.—**unisexuality** *n*.

unison /ˈjuːnɪsən/ *n* accordance of sound, concord, harmony; **in unison** simultaneously, in agreement, in harmony.

unit /ˈjuːnɪt/ *n* the smallest whole number, one; a single or whole entity; (*measurement*) a standard amount; an establishment or group of people who carry out a specific function; a piece of furniture fitting together with other pieces.—**unitary** *adj*.

unite /jʊˈnaɪt/ or /juː-/ *vti* to join into one, to combine; to be unified in purpose.

United Kingdom *n* Great Britain and Northern Ireland.

United Nations *n sing or pl* an international organization of nations for world peace and security formed in 1945.

United States *n* a federation of states, *esp* the United States of America.

unit trust /ˈjuːnɪt trest/ *n* a company that manages a range of investments on behalf of members of the public whose interests are looked after by an independent trust.

unity /ˈjuːnɪti/ *n* (*pl* **unities**) oneness; harmony; concord.

Univ. *abbr* = university.

universal /juːnɪˈvɜrsəl/ *adj* widespread; general; relating to all the world or the universe; relating to or applicable to all mankind.—**universally** *adv*.—**universality** *n* (*pl* **universalities**).

universe /ˈjuːnɪˌvɜrs/ *n* all existing things; (*astron*) the totality of space, stars, planets and other forms of matter and energy; the world.

university /ˌjuːnɪˈvɜrsɪti/ *n* (*pl* **universities**) an institution of higher education which confers bachelors' and higher degrees; the campus or staff of a university.

unjust /ʌnˈdʒest/ *adj* not characterized by justice; not fair.—**unjustly** *adv*.—**unjustness** *n*.

unkempt /ʌnˈkempt/ *adj* uncombed; slovenly, dishevelled.

unkind /ʌnˈkaɪnd/ *adj* lacking in kindness or sympathy; harsh; cruel.—**unkindly** *adv*.—**unkindness** *n*.

unknown /ʌnˈnoːn/ *adj* not known; not famous; not understood; with an unknown value. • *n* an unknown person or thing.

unleaded /ʌnˈledəd/ *adj* (*petrol*) not mixed with tetraethyl lead.

unleash /ʌnˈliːʃ/ *vt* to release from a leash; to free from restraint.

unleavened /ʌnˈlevənd/ *adj* (*bread, etc*) made without yeast or other raising agent.

unless /ʌnˈles/ or /ʌnˈles/ *conj* if not; except that.

unlettered /ʌnˈletərd/ *adj* illiterate.

unlike /ʌnˈlaɪk/ *adj* not the same, dissimilar. • *prep* not like; not characteristic of.—**unlikeness** *n*.

unlikely /ʌnˈlaɪkli/ *adj* improbable; unpromising.

unlimited /ʌnˈlɪmɪtəd/ *adj* without limits; boundless; not restricted.—**unlimitedly** *adv*.

unlisted /ʌnˈlɪstəd/ *adj* not on a list; ex-directory.

unload /ʌnˈloːd/ *vti* to remove a load, discharge freight from a truck, ship, etc; to relieve of or express troubles, etc; to dispose of, dump; to empty, *esp* a gun.

unlock /ʌnˈlɒk/ *vt* (*door, lock, etc*) to unfasten; to let loose; to reveal; to release.

unloose /ʌnˈluːs/, **unloosen** /ʌnˈluːsən/ *vt* to relax (a grip, etc); to release, free; to untie.

unlovely /ʌnˈlʌvli/ *n* ugly, unpleasant.—**unloveliness** *n*.

unlucky /ʌnˈlʌki/ *adj* (**unluckier, unluckiest**) not lucky, not fortunate; likely to bring misfortune; regrettable.

unman /ʌnˈmæn/ *vt* (**unmanning, unmanned**) to weaken the nerve or courage of; to make effeminate.

unmanly /ʌnˈmænli/ *adj* weak, cowardly; effeminate.—**unmanliness** *n*.

unmanned /ʌnˈmænd/ *adj* (*spacecraft, etc*) not manned, operated by remote control.

unmannerly /ʌnˈmænərli/ *adj* lacking good manners; rude.—**unmannerliness** *n*.

unmask /ʌnˈmæsk/ *vti* to remove the mask from; to expose, show up.

unmentionable /ʌnˈmenʃənəbəl/ *adj* too bad, shocking, embarrassing, etc to be mentioned.

unmentionables /ʌnˈmenʃənəbəls/ *npl* underwear.

unmistakable, unmistakeable /ˌʌnmɪˈsteɪkəbəl/ *adj* obvious, clear.—**unmistakably, unmistakeably** *adv*.

unmitigated /ʌnˈmɪtɪˌɡeɪtəd/ *adj* unqualified, absolute.

unmoved /ʌnˈmuːvd/ *adj* not touched by emotion, calm.

unnatural /ʌnˈnætʃərəl/ *adj* abnormal; contrary to nature; artificial; affected; strange; wicked.—**unnaturally** *adv*.

unnecessary /ʌnˈnesəseri/ *adj* not necessary.—**unnecessarily** *adv*.—**unnecessariness** *n*.

unnerve /ʌnˈnɜrv/ *vt* to cause to lose courage, strength, confidence; to frighten.

unnumbered /ʌnˈnembərd/ *adj* countless; not having a number.

UNO /ˈjuːnoː/ *abbr* = United Nations Organization.

unobtrusive /ˌʌnəbˈtruːsɪv/ *adj* modest, staying in the background.

unoccupied /ʌnˈɒkjuˌpaɪd/ *adj* not occupied, empty; unemployed.

unpack /ʌnˈpæk/ *vti* (*suitcase, etc*) to remove the contents of; (*container, etc*) to take things out of; to unload.

unparalleled /ʌnˈperəˌleld/ *adj* having no equal, unmatched.

unparliamentary /ˌʌnpɑrləˈmentri/ *adj* contrary to parliamentary procedure or practice.

unperson /ˈʌnˌpɜrsən/ *n* a person (*eg*. a political dissident) whose existence is officially ignored or denied.

unpick /ʌnˈpɪk/ *vt* to undo the stitching of.

unplaced /ʌnˈpleɪst/ *adj* not placed; not among the first three at the end of a race.

unpleasant /ʌnˈplezənt/ *adj* not pleasing or agreeable; nasty; objectionable.—**unpleasantly** *adv*.—**unpleasantness** *n*.

unplumbed /ʌnˈplʌmd/ *adj* not plumbed; not fully investigated or explored.

unpopular /ʌnˈpɒpjʊlər/ *adj* disliked; lacking general approval.—**unpopularity** *n*.

unprecedented /ʌnˈpresəˌdentəd/ *adj* having no precedent; unparalleled.

unprejudiced /ʌnˈpredʒʊdɪst/ *adj* not prejudiced, impartial.

unprepossessing /ˌʌnpriːpəˈzesɪŋ/ *adj* unattractive, repellent.

unpretentious /ˌʌnprəˈtenʃəs/ *adj* modest, not boasting.

unprincipled /ʌnˈprɪnsɪpəld/ *adj* lacking scruples.

unprintable /ʌnˈprɪntəbəl/ *adj* too bad, libellous, obscene, etc to be printed.

unprofessional /ˌʌnprəˈfeʃənəl/ *adj* contrary to professional etiquette.—**unprofessionally** *adv*.

unputdownable /ˌʌnpʊtˈdaʊnəbəl/ *adj* (*book*) grippingly readable.

unqualified /ʌnˈkwɒlɪfaɪd/ *adj* lacking recognized qualifications; not equal to; not restricted, complete.

unquestionable /ʌnˈkwestʃənəbəl/ *adj* certain, not disputed.—**unquestionably** *adv*.

unquestioned /ʌnˈkwestʃənd/ *adj* not called into question; indisputable.

unquiet /ʌnˈkwaɪət/ *adj* turbulent, disordered; nervous, agitated.—**unquietly** *adv*.—**unquietness** *n*.

unquote /ˈʌnkwoːt/ *interj* used when speaking to indicate the end of a direct quotation.

unravel /ʌnˈrævəl/ *vt* (**unravelling, unravelled** *or* **unraveling, unraveled**) to disentangle; to solve.

unread /ʌnˈred/ *adj* not read (yet); unfamiliar with a specified subject; illiterate.

unreadable /ʌnˈriːdəbəl/ *adj* illegible; not worth reading.

unreal /ʌnˈriːl/ *adj* not real; imaginary, fanciful; false, insincere.

unreason /ʌnˈriːzən/ *n* absence of reason in thought or action.

unreasonable /ʌn'ri:zənəbəl/ *adj* contrary to reason; lacking reason; immoderate; excessive.—**unreasonably** *adv.*

unreasoning /ʌn'ri:zənɪŋ/ *adj* lacking reason, irrational.

unrelenting /ˌʌnrɪ'lentɪŋ/ *adj* relentless; continuous.—**unrelentingly** *adv.*

unremitting /ˌʌnrɪ'mɪtɪŋ/ *adj* incessant.

unrequited /ˌʌnrɪ'kwaɪtɪd/ *adj* not reciprocated, not returned.

unreserved /ˌʌnrɪ'zɜrvd/ *adj* not reserved; frank, demonstrative; absolute, entire; not booked.

unreservedly /-vədli/ *adv* without conditions; openly.

unrest /ʌn'rest/ *n* uneasiness; anxiety; angry discontent verging on revolt.

unrighteous /ʌn'raɪtʃəs/ *adj* sinful, wicked.

unrivalled, unrivaled /ʌn'raɪvəld/ *adj* without equal, peerless.

unroll /ʌn'roːl/ *vti* to open out or down from a roll; to unfold; to straighten out; to reveal or become revealed.

unruffled /ʌn'rʌfəld/ *adj* cool and calm; still, smooth.

unruly /ʌn'ruːli/ *adj* (**unrulier, unruliest**) hard to control, restrain, or keep in order; disobedient.

unsaddle /ʌn'sædəl/ *vt* to take the saddle from; to unseat. • *vi* to remove the saddle from a horse.

unsaid /ʌn'sed/ *adj* not said or expressed.

unsaturated /ʌn'sætʃəˌreɪtəd/ or /-tjuˌreɪtəd/ *adj* (*chemical substance*) having double or triple bonds and therefore able to form products by chemical addition; (*vegetable fats*) containing fatty acids with double bonds.—**unsaturation** *n.*

unsavoury, unsavory /ʌn'seɪvəri/ *adj* distasteful; disagreeable; offensive.

unscathed /ʌn'skeɪðd/ *adj* unharmed.

unscramble /ʌn'skræmbəl/ *vt* to disentangle; (*a scrambled message*) to make intelligible.

unscrew /ʌn'skruː/ *vti* to remove a screw from; (*lid, etc*) to loosen by turning.

unscrupulous /ʌn'skruːpjuləs/ *adj* without principles.

unseasonable /ʌn'siːzənəbəl/ *n* (*weather*) unusual for the season of the year; untimely.—**unseasonableness** *n.*—**unseasonably** *adv.*

unseat /ʌn'siːt/ *vt* to dislodge from a seat, saddle, etc; to remove from office.

unseeded /ʌn'siːdəd/ *adj* (*tennis players, etc*) not ranked among the top players in the preliminary rounds of a competition.

unseemly /ʌn'siːmli/ *adj* unbecoming; inappropriate.

unseen /ʌn'siːn/ *adj* concealed, hidden; not seen or read beforehand.

unselfish /ʌn'selfɪʃ/ *adj* not selfish; thinking of others before oneself.—**unselfishly** *adv.*—**unselfishness** *n.*

unsettle /ʌn'setəl/ *vti* to disturb, disrupt, or disorder.

unsettled /ʌn'setəld/ *adj* changeable; lacking stability; unpredictable; not concluded.

unsheathe /ʌn'ʃiːð/ *vt* to draw (a weapon) from a sheath.

unsightly /ʌn'saɪtli/ *adj* unattractive; ugly.

unskilful, unskillful /ʌn'skɪlful/ *adj* clumsy, awkward.

unskilled /ʌn'skɪld/ *adj* without special skill or training.

unsociable /ʌn'soːʃəbəl/ *n* antisocial; reserved.

unsocial /ʌn'soːʃəl/ *n* averse to social activities; (*working hours*) outwith the normal working day.

unsolicited /ˌʌnsə'lɪsɪtəd/ *adj* not asked for.

unsophisticated /ˌʌnsə'fɪstɪˌkeɪtəd/ *adj* naïve, inexperienced; simple; pure, unadulterated.

unsound /ʌn'saʊnd/ *adj* flimsy, not stable; defective, flawed; in poor health; not sane.—**unsoundly** *adv.*—**unsoundness** *n.*

unsparing /ʌn'speərɪŋ/ *adj* profuse, lavish; severe.

unspeakable /ʌn'spiːkəbəl/ *adj* bad beyond words, indescribable.

unstable /ʌn'steɪbəl/ *adj* easily upset; mentally unbalanced; irresolute.

unsteady /ʌn'stedi/ *adj* (**unsteadier, unsteadiest**) shaky, reeling; vacillating.—**unsteadily** *adv.*

unstop /ʌn'stɒp/ *vt* (**unstopping, unstopped**) to remove the stopper from; to free from an obstruction.

unstrung /ʌn'strʌŋ/ *adj* emotionally distressed.

unstudied /ʌn'stʌdɪd/ *adj* natural; unaffected in manner.

unsubstantial /ˌʌnsəb'stænʃəl/ *adj* lacking weight, flimsy; of doubtful factual validity.

unsullied /ʌn'sʌlɪd/ *adj* not stained, pure.

unsung /ʌn'sʌŋ/ *adj* not acclaimed or celebrated.

unswerving /ʌn'swɜrvɪŋ/ *adj* not deviating; constant, unchanging.

untangle /ʌn'tæŋgəl/ *vt* to rid of tangles, unravel; to sort out.

untaught /ʌn'tɒt/ *adj* not educated or trained; not acquired by teaching.

untenable /ʌn'tenəbəl/ *adj* not able to be justified or defended.—**untenability** *n.*

unthinkable /ʌn'θɪŋkəbəl/ *adj* inconceivable; out of the question; improbable.—**unthinkably** *adv.*

unthinking /ʌn'θɪŋkɪŋ/ *adj* unable to think; thoughtless, inconsiderate.—**unthinkingly** *adv.*

untidy /ʌn'taɪdi/ *adj* (**untidier, untidiest**) not neat, disordered. • *vt* (**untidying, untidied**) to make untidy.—**untidily** *adv.*

untie /ʌn'taɪ/ *vt* (**untying, untied**) to undo a knot in, unfasten.

until /ən'tɪl/ or /ʌn-/ *prep* up to the time of; before. • *conj* up to the time when or that; to the point, degree, etc that; before.

untimely /ʌn'taɪmli/ *adj* premature; inopportune.

unto /'ʌntu/ or /'ʌntə/ *prep* (*arch*) to.

untold /ʌn'toːld/ *adj* not told; too great to be counted; immeasurable.

untouchable /ʌn'tʌtʃəbəl/ *adj* unable to be touched or handled; exempt from criticism or control; lying beyond reach.

untoward /ˌʌntə'wɔrd/ *adj* unseemly; unfavourable; adverse.

untrue /ʌn'truː/ *adj* incorrect, false; not faithful, disloyal; inaccurate.

untruth /ʌn'truːθ/ *n* falsehood; a lie.

untruthful /ʌn'truːθful/ *adj* telling lies; false.

untutored /ʌn'tuːtərd/ or /-'tjuːtərd/ *adj* lacking (refined) education.

unused /ʌn'juːzd/ *adj* not (yet) used; (*with to*) not accustomed (to something).

unusual /ʌn'juːʒuəl/ *adj* uncommon; rare.

unutterable /ʌn'ʌtərəbəl/ *adj* impossible to express in words.—**unutterably** *adv.*

unvarnished /ʌn'vɑrnɪʃt/ *adj* not varnished; plain, direct; not embellished.

unveil /ʌn'veɪl/ *vt* to reveal; to disclose.

unwaged /ʌn'weɪdʒd/ *adj* not paid a wage; unemployed.

unwarrantable /ʌn'wɔrəntəbəl/ *adj* indefensible.

unwarranted /ʌn'wɔrəntəd/ *adj* not authorized.

unwary /ʌn'weəri/ *adj* lacking caution; heedless, gullible; unguarded.—**unwarily** *adv.*

unwelcome /ʌn'welkəm/ *adj* not welcome, not invited; disagreeable; unpleasant.

unwell /ʌn'wel/ *adj* ill, not well; (*inf*) suffering from a hangover.

unwholesome /ʌn'hoːlsəm/ *adj* harmful to physical, mental or moral health and well-being; ill-looking; (*food*) of poor quality.—**unwholesomeness** *n.*

unwieldy /ʌn'wiːldi/ *adj* not easily moved or handled, as because of large size; awkward.—**unwieldily** *adv.*—**unwieldiness** *n.*

unwilling /ʌn'wɪlɪŋ/ *adj* not willing, reluctant; said or done with reluctance.—**unwillingly** *adv.*—**unwillingness** *n.*

unwind /ʌn'waɪnd/ *vt* to untangle; to undo. • *vi* to relax.

unwise /ʌn'waɪz/ *adj* lacking wisdom; imprudent.—**unwisely** *adv.*

unwitting /ʌn'wɪtɪŋ/ *adj* not knowing; unintentional.—**unwittingly** *adv.*

unworldly /ʌn'wɜrldli/ *adj* spiritual, not concerned with the material world.

unworthy /ʌn'wɜrði/ *adj* (**unworthier, unworthiest**) not deserving.

unwritten /ʌn'rɪtən/ *adj* not written or printed; traditional; oral.

unwritten law *n* law based on custom or mores rather than legislative enactment.

up /ʌp/ *adv* to, toward, in or on a higher place; to a later period; so as to be even with in time, degree, etc. • *prep* from a lower to a higher point on or along. • *adj* moving or directed upward; at an end; (*inf*) well-informed. • *vt* (**upping, upped**) to raise; to increase; to take up. • *n* ascent; high point.

up-and-coming *adj* promising for the future; likely to succeed.

upas /'juːpəs/ *n* a Javanese tree that yields a poisonous sap.

upbeat /'ʌpbiːt/ *n* (*mus*) an unaccented beat in the last bar. • *adj* (*inf*) cheerful, optimistic.

upbraid /ʌp'breɪd/ *vt* to rebuke severely; to reproach.

upbringing /'ʌpˌbrɪŋɪŋ/ *n* the process of educating and nurturing (a child).

upcountry /ʌp'kʌntri/ or /'ʌp-/ *adv* towards the interior of a country, inland.

update /'ʌpdeɪt/ *vt* to bring up to date.

updraught, updraft /'ʌpdræft/ *n* a upward flow of air or other gas.

upend /ʌpˈɛnd/ *vti* to turn or become turned on end; to upset or transform completely.

upfront /ʌpˈfrʌnt/ or /ˈʌp-/ *adj* honest, open. • *adv* (*money*) paid in advance.

upgrade /ˈʌpɡreɪd/ *vt* to improve, raise to a higher grade.

upheaval /ʌpˈhiːvəl/ *n* radical or violent change.

uphill /ˈʌphɪl/ *adj* ascending, rising; difficult, arduous. • *adv* up a slope or hill; against difficulties.

uphold /ʌpˈhoːld/ *vt* (**upholding, upheld**) to support, sustain; to defend.

upholster /ʌpˈoːlstər/ or /ʌpˈhoːl-/ *vt* (*furniture*) to fit with stuffing, springs, covering, etc.—**upholsterer** *n*.

upholstery /ʌpˈoːlstəri/ or /ʌpˈhoːl-/ *n* (*pl* **upholsteries**) materials used to make a soft covering *esp* for a seat.

upkeep /ˈʌpkiːp/ *n* maintenance; the cost of it.

upland /ˈʌplænd/ or /-lənd/ *n* an area of high ground. • *adj* of or pertaining to uplands.

uplift /ʌpˈlɪft/ *vt* to raise, lift up; to improve the moral, cultural, spiritual, etc standard or condition of. • *n* a moral, cultural, spiritual, etc improvement.

upmarket /ˈʌpmɑrkət/ *adj* of or appealing to wealthier buyers.

upmost /ˈʌpˌmoːst/ *see* **uppermost**.

upon /əˈpɒn/ *prep* on, on top of.

upper /ˈʌpər/ *adj* farther up; higher in position, rank, status. • *n* the part of a boot or shoe above the sole; (*sl*) a drug used as a stimulant.

upper case *n* capital letters.—**upper-case** *adj*.

upper class *n* people occupying the highest social rank.—*also adj*.

upper crust *n* (*inf*) the aristocracy.

uppercut /ˈʌpərkʌt/ *n* an upward swinging punch to the chin.—*also vb*.

upper hand *n* the position of control, advantage.

upper house, chamber *n* one of the two houses of a bicameral legislature, such as the British House of Lords or US Senate.

uppermost /ˈʌpərˌmoːst/ *adj* at the top; highest in importance. • *adv* into the highest position, etc.—*also* **upmost**.

uppity /ˈʌpɪti/ *adj* (*inf*) snobbish, arrogant.

upright /ˈʌpraɪt/ *adj* vertical, in an erect position; righteous, honest, just. • *n* a vertical post or support. • *adv* vertically.

uprising /ˈʌpˌraɪzɪŋ/ *n* a revolt; a rebellion.

uproar /ˈʌprɔr/ *n* a noisy disturbance; a commotion; an outcry.

uproarious /ʌpˈrɔriəs/ *adj* making or marked by an uproar; extremely funny; (*laughter*) boisterous.—**uproariously** *adv*.

uproot /ʌpˈruːt/ or /ˈʌp-/ *vt* to tear out by the roots; to remove from established surroundings.

upset[1] /ʌpˈsɛt/ or /ˈʌp-/ *vt* (**upsetting, upset**) to overturn; to spill; to disturb; to put out of order; to distress; to overthrow; to make physically sick.

upset[2] *n* an unexpected defeat; distress or its cause. • *adj* distressed; confused; defeated.

upshot /ˈʌpʃɒt/ *n* the conclusion; the result.

upside down /ˌʌpsaɪdˈdaun/ *adj* inverted; the wrong way up; (*inf*) topsy turvy.

upsilon /ˈjuːpsɪˌlɒn/ or /ʌpˈsaɪlən/ *n* the 20th letter of the Greek alphabet.

upstage /ʌpˈsteɪdʒ/ *vt* to draw attention to oneself. • *adv* to the rear of the stage.

upstairs /ʌpˈstɛrz/ or /ˈʌp-/ *adv* up the stairs; to an upper level or storey. • *n* an upper floor.

upstanding /ʌpˈstændɪŋ/ *adj* honest; of good character; in a standing position.

upstart /ˈʌpstɑrt/ *n* a person who has suddenly risen to a position of wealth and power; an arrogant person.

upstate /ˈʌpsteɪt/ *n* the mostly northern areas of a US state. • *adv, adj* towards, in, or pertaining to this area of a US state.

upstream /ˈʌpstriːm/ *adv, adj* in the direction from which a stream is flowing.

upstroke /ˈʌpˌstroːk/ *n* an upward stroke, as of a pen, paintbrush, piston, etc.

upsurge /ˈʌpsərdʒ/ *n* a sudden rise or swell.

upswing /ˈʌpswɪŋ/ *n* an upward swing or movement; an improvement, *esp* in the state of the economy.

uptake /ˈʌpteɪk/ *n* a taking up; a shaft or pipe for carrying smoke upwards; (*inf*) understanding.

uptight /ʌpˈtaɪt/ or /ˈʌptaɪt/ *adj* (*inf*) very tense, nervous, etc.

up-to-date /ˌʌptəˈdeɪt/ *adj* modern; fashionable.

upturn /ˈʌptərn/ *n* an upward trend; an (economic) improvement. • *vt* to turn upside down.

upward /ˈʌpwərd/, **upwards** /-z/ *adj* from a lower to a higher place.—*also adv*.

upwardly-mobile *adj* aspiring to improve one's social and economic status.—**upward mobility** *n*.

upwind /ˈʌpwɪnd/ or /-ˈwɪnd/ *adj, adv* in the direction from which the wind is blowing.

uraemia, uremia /juˈriːmiə/ *n* the accumulation of waste products in the blood that are normally passed in the urine.

uranium /juˈreɪniəm/ *n* a metallic element used as a source of nuclear energy.

urano- /ˈjurənoː/ *prefix* sky; the heavens.

uranography /ˌjurəˈnɒɡrəfi/ *n* the description and mapping of the stars, etc by astronomers.—**uranographer** *n*.—**uranographic** *adj*.

Uranus /ˈjurənəs/ or /ˈjurən-/ *n* the seventh planet from the sun.

urate /ˈjureɪt/ *n* a salt or ester of uric acid.—**uratic** *adj*.

urban /ˈərbən/ *adj* of or relating to a city.—**urbanization, urbanisation** *n*.

urbane /ərˈbeɪn/ *adj* sophisticated; refined.—**urbanity** *n*.

urban guerrilla *n* a terrorist who operates in a town or city.

urbanite /ˈərbəˌnaɪt/ *n* a person who lives in a town or city.

urban renewal *n* rehabilitation of dilapidated city areas, as by housing construction and slum clearance.

urchin /ˈərtʃɪn/ *n* a raggedly dressed mischievous child; a sea urchin.

urea /juˈriːə/ *n* a soluble crystalline compound present in urine produced by protein metabolism.

ureter /juˈriːtər/ *n* a tube that carries urine from the kidney to the bladder or cloaca.

urethra /juˈriːθrə/ *n* the duct carrying urine out of the bladder.

urethritis /ˌjurɪˈθraɪtɪs/ *n* inflammation of the urethra.

uretic /juˈrɛtɪk/ *adj* of or pertaining to the urine.

urge /ərdʒ/ *vt* to drive forward; to press, plead with. • *n* an impulse, yearning.

urgency /ˈərdʒənsi/ *n* (*pl* **urgencies**) the quality or condition of being urgent; compelling need; importance.

urgent /ˈərdʒənt/ *adj* impelling; persistent; calling for immediate attention.—**urgently** *adv*.

-urgy /ərdʒi/ *n suffix* technology; technique.

-uria /ˈjuri/ *n suffix* diseased condition of the urine.

uric /ˈjurɪk/ *adj* of, present in, or derived from urine.

uric acid *n* a white odourless substance found in the urine of birds, reptiles and some mammals.

urinal /ˈjurənəl/ *n* a bowl or trough for urination in public lavatories.

urinalysis /ˌjurɪˈnælɪsɪs/ *n* (*pl* **urinalyses**) the chemical analysis of urine for signs of disease.

urinate /ˈjurəˌneɪt/ *vi* to pass urine.

urine /ˈjurɪn/ *n* a yellowish fluid excreted by the kidneys and conveyed to the bladder.—**urinary** *adj*.

urinogenital /ˌjurənoːˈdʒɛnɪtəl/ *adj* urogenital.

urn /ərn/ *n* a vase or large vessel; a receptacle for preserving the ashes of the dead; a large metal container for boiling water for tea or coffee.

uro- /ˈjuroː/, **ur-** *prefix* urine; urinary tract.

urogenital /ˌjuroːˈdʒɛnɪtəl/, **urinogenital** *adj* of or pertaining to the urinary and reproductive organs.—*also* **genitourinary**.

urology /juˈrɒlədʒi/ *n* the medical study and treatment of urogenital diseases.—**urologist** *n*.—**urological** *adj*.

uroscopy /juˈrɒskəpi/ *n* the diagnosis of diseases by the examination of the patient's urine.

ursine /ˈərsaɪn/ *adj* of or resembling a bear.

urticaria /ˌərtɪˈkɛriə/ *n* an allergic reaction which produces raised itchy whitish patches on the skin.—*also* **hives, nettle rash**.

us /ɛs/ or /əs/ *pron* the objective case of **we**.

US *abbr* = United States.

USA *abbr* = United States of America.

USAF *abbr* = United States Air Force.

usage /ˈjuːsədʒ/ *n* customary use; practice, custom; use of language.

use[1] /juːz/ *vt* to put to some purpose; to utilize; to exploit (a person); to partake of (drink, drugs, tobacco, etc).—**usable, useable** *adj*.

use[2] *n* act of using or putting to a purpose; usage; usefulness; need (for); advantage; practice, custom.

used /juːzd/ *adj* not new; second-hand.

useful /'ju:sfʊl/ *adj* able to be used to good effect; (*inf*) capable, commendable.—**usefully** *adv*.

useless /'ju:sləs/ *adj* having no use.—**uselessly** *adv*.—**uselessness** *n*.

user /'ju:zər/ *n* one who uses; (*inf*) a drug addict.

user-friendly *adj* easy to understand and operate.

usher /'ʌʃər/ *n* one who shows people to their seats in a theatre, church, etc; a doorkeeper in a law court. • *vt* to escort to seats, etc.

usherette /ˌʌʃər'ɛt/ *nf* a woman who directs people to their seats in a cinema.

USN *abbr* = United States Navy.

USSR *abbr* = (*formerly*) Union of Soviet Socialist Republics.

usual /'ju:ʒuːəl/ *adj* customary; ordinary; normal.—**usually** *adv*.

usurer /'ju:ʒərər/ *n* a person who lends money at an excessively high rate of interest.

usurp /jʊ'sɔrp/ or /-zɔrp/ *vt* to seize or appropriate unlawfully.—**usurper** *n*.

usury /'ju:ʒəri/ *n* (*pl* **usuries**) the practice of taking excessive interest on a loan; an excessive interest rate.

utensil /ju:'tɛnsəl/ *n* an implement or container, *esp* one for use in the kitchen.

uterus /'ju:tərəs/ *n* (*pl* **uteri**) the female organ in which offspring are developed until birth, the womb.—**uterine** *adj*.

utilitarian /ˌju:tɪlɪ'teriən/ *adj* designed to be of practical use.

utility /ju:'tɪlɪti/ *n* (*pl* **utilities**) usefulness; a public service, such as telephone, electricity, etc; a company providing such a service.

utility room *n* a room containing laundry appliances, heating equipment, etc.

utilize /'ju:təˌlaɪz/ *vt* to make practical use of.—**utilization** *n*.

utmost /'ʌtmoːst/ *adj* of the greatest degree or amount; furthest. • *n* the most possible.

utopia /ju:'to:piə/ *n* a imaginary society or place considered to be ideal or perfect.—**utopian** *adj, n*.

utter[1] /'ʌtər/ *adj* absolute; complete.

utter[2] *vt* to say; to speak.—**utterance** *n*.

utterly /-li/ *adv* completely.

UV *abbr* = ultraviolet.

uvula /'ju:vjʊlə/ *n* (*pl* **uvulas, uvulae**) the fleshy tissue suspended in the back of the throat over the back part of the tongue.

uxorious /ʌk'zɔriəs/ *adj* excessively fond of one's wife; doting.—**uxoriously** *adv*.—**uxoriousness** *n*.

V

V *abbr* = volt(s).

V, v /viː/ *n* the 22nd letter of the English alphabet; something shaped like a V.

v *abbr* = velocity; *versus* against; *vide* see; verb.

vac /væk/ *abbr* = vacuum.

vacancy /ˈveɪkənsi/ *n* (*pl* **vacancies**) emptiness; an unoccupied job or position.

vacant /ˈveɪkənt/ *adj* empty; unoccupied; (*expression*) blank.—**vacantly** *adv*.—**vacantness** *n*.

vacate /ˈveɪkeɪt/ or /vəˈkeɪt/ *vt* to leave empty; to give up possession of.

vacation /veɪˈkeɪʃən/ *n* a period of the year when universities, colleges and law courts are closed; another word *esp* in the US for holiday;. • *vi* in the US, to go on holiday.

vacationer /-ər/, **vacationist** /-ɪst/ *n* the US word for a person on holiday, a holiday-maker.

vaccinal /ˈvæksɪnəl/ *adj* pertaining to or caused by a vaccine or vaccination.

vaccinate /ˈvæksɪˌneɪt/ *vt* to inoculate with vaccine as a protection against a disease.—**vaccinator** *n*.

vaccination /ˌvæksɪˈneɪʃən/ *n* inoculation with a vaccine; the resulting scar.

vaccine /vækˈsiːn/ or /ˈvæksiːn/ *n* a modified and hence harmless virus or other microorganism used for inoculation to give immunity from certain diseases by stimulating antibody production; cowpox virus used in this way against smallpox.

vaccinia /vækˈsɪniə/ *n* (*med*) cowpox.—**vaccinial** *adj*.

vacillate /ˈvæsɪˌleɪt/ *vi* to waver, to show indecision; to fluctuate.—**vacillation** *n*.—**vacillator** *n*.

vacuity /vəˈkjuːɪti/ *n* (*pl* **vacuities**) emptiness; a vacant state of mind or expression; absence of matter; a vacuum; idleness; lack; an inane remark.

vacuole /ˈvækjuˌʊl/ *n* (*biol*) a small cell or cavity filled with fluid in the interior of organic cells or protoplasm.—**vacuolate, vacuolated** *adj*.

vacuous /ˈvækjuːəs/ *adj* empty; lacking intelligence, mindless.—**vacuously** *adv*.—**vacuousness** *n*.

vacuum /ˈvækjuːm/ *n* (*pl* **vacuums, vacua**) a region devoid of all matter; a region in which gas is present at low pressure; a vacuum cleaner. • *vt* to clean with a vacuum cleaner. • *adj* of, having or creating a vacuum; working by suction or maintenance of a partial vacuum.

vacuum cleaner *n* an electrical appliance for removing dust from carpets, etc, by suction.—**vacuum-clean** *vt*.

vacuum bottle, vacuum flask *n* a container for keeping liquids hot or cold.

vacuum-packed /ˈvækjuːmˌpækt/ *adj* sealed in an airtight packet from which the air has been removed.

vade mecum /ˌveɪdiˈmiːkəm/ or /ˌveɪdiˈmeɪkəm/ *n* (*pl* **vade mecums**) a handbook or manual, etc, for ready reference, *usu* of a size to fit in a pocket.

vagabond /ˈvægəˌbɒnd/ *n* a vagrant; a wandering, homeless person.—**vagabondage** *n*.—**vagabondism** *n*.

vagal /ˈveɪgəl/ *adj* of, pertaining to, affected or controlled by the vagus nerve.

vagary /ˈveɪgəri/ *n* (*pl* **vagaries**) unpredictable or erratic behaviour or actions; a whim.—**vagarious** *adj*.

vagina /vəˈdʒaɪnə/ *n* (**vaginas, vaginae**) in female mammals and humans, the canal connecting the uterus and the external sex organs.—**vaginal** *adj*.

vaginate /ˈvædʒənɪt/ or /-ˌneɪt/, **vaginated** *adj* (*bot*) (*plant parts*) sheathed; with a vagina or sheath.

vagrancy /ˈveɪgrənsi/ (*pl* **vagrancies**) the habits and life of a vagrant; a wandering without a settled home.

vagrant /ˈveɪgrənt/ *n* a person who has no settled home, a tramp. • *adj* wandering, roaming; wayward.—**vagrantly** *adv*.

vague /veɪg/ *adj* unclear; indistinct, imprecise; (*person*) absentminded.—**vaguely** *adv*.—**vagueness** *n*.

vagus /ˈveɪgəs/ *n* (*pl* **vagi**) vagus nerve.

vagus nerve *n* either of a pair of cranial nerves supplying the larynx, heart, lungs, etc.

vail[1] /veɪl/ *vti* (*arch*) to lower, to let fall; to take off (a hat) in respect.

vail[2] *n* (*arch*) a gratuity, a tip.

vain /veɪn/ *adj* conceited; excessively concerned with one's appearance; senseless; futile; worthless; **in vain** to no purpose.—**vainly** *adv*.—**vainness** *n*.

vainglorious /veɪnˈglɔːriəs/ *adj* elated by one's achievements; boastful; showy.—**vaingloriously** *adv*.—**vaingloriousness** *n*.

vainglory /ˈveɪnglɔːri/ or /-ˈglɔːri/ *n* (*pl* **vainglories**) excessive vanity; boastfulness; showiness.

vair /vɛr/ *n* a fur trimming on medieval robes, probably of Russian squirrel; (*her*) fur represented by small shields, coloured white and blue alternately.

valance /ˈvæləns/ or /veɪl-/ *n* a decorative cover for the base of a bed; a canopy for a window frame to hide rods, etc; a pelmet.—**valanced** *adj*.

vale[1] /veɪl/ *n* a valley.

vale[2] *interj, n* (*arch*) farewell.

valediction /ˌvælɪˈdɪkʃən/ *n* a saying farewell; a taking leave; an instance of this; a speech made at this time.

valedictorian /ˌvælədɪkˈtɔːriən/ *n* a in the US, a college student appointed on grounds of merit to deliver the valedictory oration.

valedictory /ˌvæləˈdɪktəri/ *adj* uttered or bestowed on saying farewell; shown, performed or done by way of valediction. • *n* (*pl* **valedictories**) a statement or speech made on leaving a position, etc; in the US, a valedictory oration.

valence /ˈveɪləns/, **valency** /-si/ *n* (*pl* **valences, valencies**) (*chem*) the power of elements to combine; the number of atoms of hydrogen that an atom or group can combine with to form a compound.

valence electron, valency electron *n* (*chem*) one of the electrons present in the outermost shell of an atom of a corresponding element.

Valenciennes (lace) /væˌlɑːsiˈɛn/ *n* an ornate type of bobbin lace, formerly made of linen, now *usu* of cotton.

-valent /ˈvælənt/ *adj suffix* having a specified number of valences, *eg* univalent.

valentine /ˈvæləntaɪn/ *n* a lover or sweetheart chosen on St Valentine's Day, February 14; a card or gift sent on that day.

valerian /vəˈliːriən/ *n* a herb with a root formerly used for medicinal purposes; the root of this used as a sedative.

valet /væˈleɪ/ or /ˈvæ-/ *n* a manservant; a steward in a hotel or on board ship. • *vt* to attend (someone) as a valet. • *vi* to work as a valet.

valetudinarian /ˌvælɪˌtjuːdɪˈnɛriən/, **valetudinary** /-ri/ *n* (*pl* **valetudinarians, valetudinaries**) a person who is overly preoccupied with his or her own health, a hypochondriac; a chronic invalid. • *adj* of ill health; sickly; seeking to recover health—**valetudinarianism** *n*.

valgus /ˈvælgəs/ *adj* (*med*) deviating outwards from the vertical middle line of the body. • *n* (*pl* **valguses**) a deformity caused by a twisting from the middle line of the body, *eg* bow-legs.

Valhalla /vælˈhælə/ *n* (*Scandinavian myth*) the palace or hall of immortality in which the souls of heroes slain in battle dwell.—*also* **Walhalla**.

valiant /ˈvæljənt/ *adj* courageous; brave.—**valiance, valiancy** *n*.—**valiantly** *adv*.

valid /ˈvælɪd/ *adj* based on facts; (*objection, etc*) sound; legally acceptable; binding.—**validity** *n*.—**validly** *adv*.

validate /ˈvælɪˌdeɪt/ *vt* to corroborate; to legalize.—**validation** *n*.

valine /ˈvæliːn/ or /veɪ-/ *n* an amino acid formed by the digestion of protein.

valise /vəˈliːs/ *n* a small case, *usu* of a size large enough to carry what is needed for an overnight visit.

Valkyrie /vælˈkiːri/ or /ˈvælkɪri/ *n* (*Scandinavian myth*) one of the twelve Norse war goddesses, handmaidens of Odin, who selected those who were worthy to be slain in battle and led them to Valhalla.—*also* **Walkyrie**.

vallation /væ'leɪʃən/ *n* a defensive wall; a rampart; the act of building this.

vallecula /və'lɛkjulə/ *n* (*pl* **valleculae**) (*anat*) a cleft or depressed area; (*bot*) a groove, a deep wrinkle.—**vallecular, valleculate** *adj.*

valley /'væli/ *n* (*pl* **valleys**) low land between hills or mountains *usu* with a river or stream flowing along its bottom; something resembling a valley, *eg* the angle where two sloping sides of a roof meet.

valonia /və'loːniə/ *n* a large, dried acorn cup, or unripened acorn, from a particular kind of oak tree, used in tanning, dyeing, ink-making, etc.

valor /'vælər/ *see* **valour**.

valorize /'vælə,raɪz/ *vt* to give an arbitrary price to (something) under government control.—**valorization** *n.*

valorous /'vælərəs/ *adj* (*person*) valiant, courageous; (*action*) characterized by valour.—**valorously** *adv.*—**valorousness** *n.*

valour /'vælər/ *n* courage; bravery (in battle).—*also US* **valor**.

valse *Fr.* /vals/ *n* a waltz, often used in the titles of musical compositions.

valuable /'væljuːəbəl/ or /'væljəbəl/ *adj* having considerable importance or monetary worth. • *n* a personal possession of value, *esp* jewellery; (*pl*) valuable possessions.—**valuably** *adv.*

valuate /'væljuːeɪt/ *vt* to estimate the worth of, to value.—**valuator** *n.*

valuation /,væljuː'eɪʃən/ *n* the act of valuing or valuating; an estimated price or worth; an estimation.—**valuational** *adj.*

value /'væljuː/ *n* worth, merit, importance; market value; purchasing power; relative worth; (*pl*) moral principles. • *vt* (**valuing, valued**) to estimate the worth of; to regard highly; to prize.—**valuer** *n.*

value-added tax *n* a tax levied on the difference between the production cost of an item and its selling price.

valued /'væljuːd/ *adj* estimated; esteemed, prized.

value judgment *n* a subjective or unwarranted judgment.

valueless /'væljuːləs/ *adj* without value; worthless.—**valuelessness** *n.*

valuta /və'luːtə/ *n* the value of one currency in terms of another.

valvar /'vælvjʊlər/ *see* **valvular**.

valvate /'væl,veɪt/ *adj* having, resembling, or operating by means of a valve or valves; (*bot*) (*petals*) meeting at the edges without overlapping.

valve /vælv/ *n* a device for controlling the flow of a gas or liquid through a pipe; (*anat*) a tube allowing blood to flow in one direction only; (*mus*) a device on a brass instrument for increasing the length of the tube and thus altering the pitch being played.

valvular /'vælvjʊlər/ *adj* of, affecting a valve or valves, *esp* of the heart; acting like a valve; shaped like a valve; operating by means of a valve or valves.

valvule /'væl,vjuːl/, **valvelet** /'vælvɛlət/ *n* a little valve; anything resembling this.

valvulitis /,vælvjəlaɪtəs/ *n* inflammation of the valves, *esp* of the heart.

vambrace /'væmbreɪs/ *n* plate armour for the forearm.

vamoose, vamose /væ'muːs/ *vi* (*sl*) to make off quickly, to decamp.

vamp[1] /væmp/ *n* the part of a sock, boot or shoe covering the front of the foot; anything patched up or refurbished; an improvised musical accompaniment made up of chords. • *vt* to provide with a (new) vamp; to mend or repair; (*with* **up**) to renovate; (*mus*) to improvise.—**vamper** *n.*

vamp[2] *n* a seductive woman. • *vt* to fascinate or exploit by seducing. • *vi* to act as a vamp.

vampire /'væmpaɪr/ *n* (*folklore*) a dead creature that by night leaves its grave to suck the blood of living people; a person who preys on others, an extortioner; a vampire bat.—**vampiric** *adj.*

vampire bat *n* a tropical American blood-sucking bat.

vampirism /'væmpaɪr,ɪzəm/ *n* belief in vampires; bloodsucking, or other acts associated with vampires.

van[1] /væn/ *n* a covered motor vehicle for transporting goods, etc.

van[2] *n* the vanguard.

vanadium /və'neɪdiəm/ *n* a rare soft white metallic element used in steel alloys.—**vanadic** *adj.*

vandal /'vændəl/ *n* a person who wilfully or ignorantly damages property; (*with cap*) a member of a Germanic tribe that sacked Rome (455AD). • *adj* of acting like a vandal; characterized by vandalism or lack of culture.

vandalism /'vændə,lɪzm/ *n* the ruthless destruction or spoiling of anything beautiful or venerable; barbarous, ignorant or inartistic treatment.—**vandalistic** *adj.*

vandalize /'vændə,laɪz/ *vt* to carry out an act of vandalism.—**vandalization** *n.*

Van de Graaf generator /,vændə'græf/ *n* a machine that continuously separates electrostatic charges and in so doing produces a very high voltage.

van der Waals' force /vændər'wɒls/ *n* a weak attractive force between two neighbouring atoms.

Vandyke beard /væn'daɪk/ *n* a small pointed beard.

Vandyke collar *n* a wide, white collar of lace or sewed work, with a deeply indented edge.

vane /veɪn/ *n* a blade at the top of a spire, etc to show wind direction; a weather vane; a blade on a windmill or propeller.

vang /væŋ/ *n* (*naut*) a guy rope from the end of a gaff to the deck, used for steadying the extremity of the peak of a gaff to the side of a ship; a rope running from the boom of a mainsail to the deck, used to keep the boom lowered.

vanguard /'vængɑrd/ *n* the front part of an army; the leading position of any movement.

vanilla /və'nɪlə/ or /-'nɛlə/ *n* extract from the orchid pod used as a flavouring.—**vanillic** *adj* from vanilla.

vanish /'vænɪʃ/ *vi* to disappear from sight, to become invisible, *esp* in a rapid and mysterious manner; to fade away; to cease to exist; (*math*) (*numbers, quantities*) to become zero.—**vanisher** *n.*

vanishing cream *n* a cleansing or foundation cream for make-up that is colourless when applied to the face.

vanity /'vænɪti/ *n* (*pl* **vanities**) a fruitless endeavour; worthlessness; empty pride or conceit; love of indiscriminate admiration; an idle matter or show; a worthless or unfounded idea or statement; emptiness, lightness.

vanity case, vanity box *n* a small case used for carrying cosmetics, etc.

vanquish /'væŋkwɪʃ/ *vt* to conquer; to defeat; to overcome, to subdue.—**vanquisher** *n.*—**vanquishment** *n.*

vantage /'væntɪdʒ/ *n* a favourable position; a position allowing a clear view or understanding.

vanward /'vænwərd/ *adj* towards the front, in the van. • *adv* forward, towards the front.

vapid /'væpɪd/ *adj* flavourless, flat, insipid; dull, lifeless.—**vapidity** *n.*—**vapidly** *adv.*

vapor /'veɪpər/ *see* **vapour**.

vaporish /-ɪʃ/ *see* **vapourish**.

vaporize /'veɪpə,raɪz/ *vt* to change into vapour.—**vaporization** *n.*—**vaporizer** *n.*

vaporous /'veɪpərəs/ *adj* in the form of or like vapour; foggy, steamy; unreal, fanciful.—**vaporously** *adv.*—**vaporosity** *n.*

vapour /'veɪpər/ *n* the gaseous state of a substance normally liquid or solid; particles of water or smoke in the air; (*pl*) hysteria. • *vi* to pass off in vapour, vaporize; to boast.—*also US* **vapor**.

vapourish /-ɪʃ/ *adj* like vapour; full of vapour; (*arch*) in a state of depression and lethargy.—*also US* **vaporish**.—**vapourishness, vapurishness** *n.*

vapour trail *n* condensed vapour left in the wake of an aircraft exhaust appearing as a white trail in the sky.

varec /'værɛk/ *n* the ash left after burning kelp.

variable /'veriəbəl/ *adj* liable to change; not constant. • *n* (*math*) a changing quantity that can have different values, as opposed to a constant.—**variability** *n.*—**variably** *adv.*

variance /'veriəns/ *n* disagreement, dissension; variation; tendency to vary; (*law*) a discrepancy between two statements or documents; **at variance** in conflict.

variant /'veriənt/ *adj* different; differing from an accepted or normal type, text, etc. • *n* a variant form or reading.

variation /,veri'eɪʃən/ *n* a varying or being varied; alteration; deviation from a standard or type; diversity; deviation of the magnetic needle from true north; the measure of this; (*gram*) inflexion; (*mus*) repetition of a theme or melody with modifications.—**variational** *adj.*

varicella /,værɪ'sɛlə/ *n* (*med*) chickenpox.—**varicelloid** *adj.*

varices /'værə,siːz/ *see* **varix**.

varicocele /'værɪkə,siːl/ *n* a swelling of the veins of the scrotum or of the spermatic cord.

varicoloured, varicolored /'veri,kələrd/ *adj* variegated, particoloured; of several colours.

varicose /'veri,koːs/ *adj* (*veins*) abnormally swollen and dilated.—**varicosis** *n.*—**varicosity** *n.*

varied /'vɛrɪːd/ *adj* showing variety, changing; partially changed; various; variegated.—**variedly** *adv*.

variegate /'vɛrəˌgeɪt/ or /-rɪəˌgeɪt/ *vt* to mark with different colours or tints; to dapple, streak; to cause to diversify.

variegated /'vɛrəˌgeɪtəd/ or /-rɪəˌgeɪtəd/ *adj* marked with different colours.

variegation /ˌvɛrəˈgeɪʃən/ *n* the condition of being variegated; diversity of colours.

variety /vəˈraɪətɪ/ *n* (*pl* **varieties**) diversity; an assortment.—**varietal** *adj*.

variety show *n* an entertainment made up of various acts, such as songs, comedy turns, etc.

variform /'vɛrɪˌfɔrm/ *adj* having various forms.

variola /vəˈraɪələ/ *n* (*med*) smallpox.—**variolar** *adj*.

variolate /vəˈraɪəleɪt/ *adj* having shallow, pitted depressions similar to those left on the skin after smallpox. • *vt* to inoculate with smallpox virus.—**variolation** *n*.

variole /'vɛrɪˌoːl/ *n* a whitish spot or round mass consisting of radiating threads of crystal.

variolite /'vɛrɪəˌlaɪt/ *n* a kind of igneous rock with whitish spots, made up of clustered varioles.—**variolitic** *adj*.

varioloid /'vɛrɪəˌlɔɪd/ *n* smallpox modified by vaccination or other means of acquired partial immunity. • *adj* like smallpox.

variorum /ˌvɛrɪˈɔrəm/ *n* an edition of the works of an author with notes by various commentators.—*also adj*.

various /'vɛrɪəs/ *adj* varied, different; several.—**variously** *adv*.

varix /'vɛrɪks/ *n* (*pl* **varices**) (*med*) a varicose vein; a twisted, dilated artery.

varlet /'vɑrlət/ *n* a scoundrel; (*arch*) a servant, attendant, or page of a knight.

varmint /'vɑrmɪnt/ *n* (*dial*) a rascal; an offensive or trying person or animal.

varnish /'vɑrnɪʃ/ *n* a sticky liquid which dries and forms a hard, glossy coating. • *vt* to coat with varnish.—**varnisher** *n*.

varsity /'vɑrsɪtɪ/ *n* (*pl* **varsities**) (*inf*) university.

varus /'vɛrəs/ *n* (*pl* **varuses**) a deformity caused by a turning in towards the vertical midline of the body, *eg* pigeon toes.

vary /'vɛrɪ/ *vti* (**varying, varied**) to change, to diversify, modify; to become altered.—**varyingly** *adv*.

vascular /'væskjʊlər/ *adj* (*biol*) of, consisting of, or containing vessels as part of a structure of animal and vegetable organisms for conveying blood, sap, etc.—**vascularity** *n*.

vasculum /'væskjʊləm/ *n* (*pl* **vascula, vasculums**) a botanist's specimen box.

vas deferens /væsˈdɛfəˌrɛnz/ *n* (*pl* **vasa deferentia**) the spermatic duct.

vase /vɒz/ or /veɪz/, /veɪs/ *n* a vessel for displaying flowers.

vasectomy /vəˈsɛktəmɪ/ *n* (*pl* **vasectomies**) male sterilization involving the cutting of the sperm-carrying tube.

Vaseline /'væsəˌliːn/ *n* (*trademark*) petroleum jelly used as a lubricant.

vasoconstrictor /ˌveɪzoːkənˈstrɪktər/ *n* a nerve, drug, etc, that constricts blood vessels.—**vasoconstrictive** *adj*.

vasodilator /ˌveɪzoːdaɪˈleɪtər/ *n* a nerve, drug etc that dilates blood vessels.—**vasodilative** *adj*.

vasomotor /'veɪzoːˌmoːtər/ *adj* (*nerve, drug, etc*) pertaining to or controlling the diameter of blood vessels.

vassal /'væsəl/ *n* a servant, dependant; subordinate.

vassalage /'væsəlɪdʒ/ *n* the state of being a vassal; the obligations associated with such a state; servitude; dependence; (*rare*) vassals collectively.

vast /vɑːst/ *adj* immense.—**vastly** *adv*.—**vastness** *n*.

vasty (**vastier, vastiest**) /'vɑːstɪ/ *adj* (*arch*) vast.

VAT /ˌviːeɪˈtiː/ or /væt/ *abbr* = value added tax.

vat /væt/ *n* a large barrel or tank. • *vt* (**vatting, vatted**) to put in a vat; to treat in a vat.

vatic /'vætɪk/, **vatical** /'vætɪkəl/ *adj* of or relating to a prophet or prophecy.

Vatican /'vætɪkən/ *n* the residence of the pope in Rome; papal authority.

Vaticanism /'vætɪkənˌɪzəm/ *n* (*often derog*) the doctrine of Papal supremacy and infallibility.

vaticination /væˌtɪsɪˈneɪʃən/ *n* a prophecy.

vaudeville /'vɒdvɪl/ or /'vɒdəˌvɪl/ *n* a stage show consisting of various acts, such as singing, dancing and comedy.

vault[1] /vɒlt/ *n* an arched ceiling or roof; a burial chamber; a strongroom for valuables; a cellar.—**vaulted** *adj*.

vault[2] *vti* to leap or jump over an obstacle. • *n* a leap.—**vaulter** *n*.

vaulting[1] /'vɒltɪŋ/ *n* (*arch*) arched work in a building, etc.

vaulting[2] *adj* overly confident; to an exaggerated degree; used in the act of leaping over.

vaunt /vɒnt/ *vti* to display boastfully; to brag. • *n* a boast.—**vaunter** *n*.—**vauntingly** *adv*.

vavasour, vavasor, vavassor /'vævəˌsʊr/ *n* (*feudalism*) the tenant of a baron or lord who is that lord's vassal and who in turn has other vassals under him.

VC *abbr* = Victoria Cross; vice-chairman; Vietcong.

VCR *abbr* = video cassette recorder.

VD *abbr* = venereal disease.

VDU *abbr* = video display unit.

veal /viːl/ *n* the edible flesh of a calf.

vector /'vɛktər/ *n* (*physics*) a physical quantity having both direction and magnitude, *eg* displacement, acceleration, etc; an aircraft's or missile's course; (*biol*) a piece of DNA that transmits a parasitic disease.—**vectorial** *adj*.

Veda /'veɪdə/ or /'viː-/ *n* (any of) the oldest sacred books or collection of hymns of the Hindus, written in old Sanskrit and of great antiquity.—**Vedic** *adj*.

Vedanta /vɪˈdænt/ or /veˈdɒ-/ *n* a Hindu philosophy based on the Veda, postulating that the world of the senses is based on an illusion.—**Vedantic** *adj*.

vedette /veˈdet/ *n* a small patrol boat.—*also* **vedette boat**; a mounted sentry in advance of an outpost.—*also* **vidette**.

Vedic /'veɪdɪk/ or /'viː-/ *adj* pertaining to the Veda, or to the old Sanskrit in which these were written; pertaining to the original Indo-Europeans of India.

veer /viːr/ *vi* (*wind*) to change direction; to swing around; to change from one mood or opinion to another.—**veeringly** *adv*.

veery /'viːrɪ/ *n* (*pl* **veeries**) a tawny North American thrush.

veg. /vɛdʒ/ *abbr* = vegetable(s).

vegan /'viːgən/ or /'veɪ-/, /'vɛdʒən/ *n* a strict vegetarian who consumes no animal or dairy products.

vegetable /'vɛdʒtəbəl/ or /'vɛdʒətəbəl/ *n* a herbaceous plant grown for food. • *adj* of, relating to or derived from plants.

vegetal /'vɛdʒətəl/ *adj* of growth and vital functions; vegetable.

vegetarian /ˌvɛdʒəˈtɛrɪən/ *n* a person who consumes a diet that excludes meat and fish. • *adj* of vegetarians; consisting wholly of vegetables.

vegetarianism /-ˌɪzəm/ *n* the doctrine or practice of vegetarians; abstention from meating meat, fish, or other animal products.

vegetate /'vɛdʒəˌteɪt/ *vi* to grow like a plant; to sprout; to lead a mentally inactive, aimless life.

vegetation /ˌvɛdʒəˈteɪʃən/ *n* vegetable growth; plants in general.—**vegetational** *adj*.

vegetative /'vɛdʒəˌteɪtɪv/, **vegetive** /'vɛdʒətɪv/ *adj* (*plants*) growing or having the power of growing, or producing growth in; (*way of life*) dull, passive, uneventful; (*reproduction*) asexual; referring to functions other than sexual reproduction.

vehement /'viːəmənt/ *adj* passionate; forceful; furious.—**vehemence, vehemency** *n*.—**vehemently** *adv*.

vehicle /'viːəkəl/ *n* a conveyance, such as a car, bus or truck, for carrying people or goods on land; a means of transmission for ideas, impressions, etc, a medium; (*med*) a substance in which a strong medicine can be administered palatably.—**vehicular** *adj*.

veil /veɪl/ *n* a thin fabric worn over the head or face of a woman; a nun's headdress; anything that conceals; a velum. • *vt* to put on a veil; to cover; to conceal, dissemble.

veiled /'veɪld/ *adj* covered with or wearing a veil; shrouded in a veil; concealed, hidden; covert; not openly declared; (*sound, voice*) indistinct, muffled.

vein /veɪn/ *n* (*anat*) one of the vessels that convey the blood back to the heart; (*geol*) a seam of a mineral within a rock; (*bot*) a branching rib in a leaf; a streak of different colour, as in marble, cheese, etc; a style or mood (*serious vein*). • *vt* to streak.—**veiny** *adj*.

veinlet /'veɪnlɪt/ *n* a small vein.

veinprint /'veɪnˌprɪnt/ *n* the pattern of veins on the back of the hand, which is unique to an individual.

velamen /vɪˈleɪmən/ *n* (*pl* **velamina**) (*anat*) an outer membrane or epidermis; a velum; (*bot*) a thick, moisture-absorbing aerial root, consisting of dead cells, found on some plants.

velar /'viːlər/ *adj* of the velum or soft palate; (*phonetics*) pronounced with the back of the tongue touching the soft palate. • *n* a velar sound.

velarium /vəˈlɛriəm/ *n* (*pl* **velaria**) in ancient Rome, the great awning that stretched over open theatres.

Velcro /ˈvɛlkrəʊ/ *n* (*trademark*) a nylon material made of matching strips of tiny hooks and pile that are easily pressed together or pulled apart.

veld, veldt /vɛlt/ *n* in South Africa, open grass country.

velites /ˈviːlɪˌtiːz/ *n* in ancient Rome, a lightly armed soldier, *usu* from the poorer section of society.

velleity /vəˈliːəti/ *n* (*pl* **velleities**) (*arch*) the lowest degree of desire, mere inclination.

vellum /ˈvɛləm/ *n* fine parchment; a good quality writing paper.

veloce /ˈvɛlɒs/ *adv* (*mus*) very quickly.

velocipede /vəˈlɒsɪˌpiːd/ *n* an early form of bicycle, propelled by striking the toes on the road; any early form of bicycle or tricycle.

velocity /vəˈlɒsɪti/ *n* (*pl* **velocities**) the rate of change of position of any object; speed.

velour /vəˈlʊr/, **velours** /vəˈlʊrz/ *n* a velvet-like fabric.

velouté /vəluːˈteɪ/ *n* a rich white sauce or soup, with a basis of egg yolks, cream and stock.

velum /ˈviːləm/ *n* (*pl* **vela**) (*anat*) the soft palate; any body structure resembling a veil; (*bot, zool*) a membranous covering or organ, such as the membranous covering of certain molluscs or that covering a developing mushroom.

velure /vəˈlʊr/ *n* a kind of plush or velvet-like material; a velvet pad for smoothing a silk hat.

velutinous /vəˈluːtɪnəs/ *adj* (*bot*) thickly covered with short hairs, velvety.

velvet /ˈvɛlvət/ *n* a fabric made from silk, rayon, etc with a soft, thick pile; anything like velvet in texture.

velveteen /ˌvɛlvəˈtiːn/ *n* a cotton cloth with a pile like velvet.

velvety /ˈvɛlvəti/ *adj* soft to the touch; mellow.

vena /ˈviːnə/ *n* (*pl* **venae**) (*anat*) a vein.

vena cava /ˌviːnəˈkeɪvə/ *n* (*pl* **venae cavae**) one of the two major veins that empty blood into the right chamber of the heart in air-breathing vertebrates.

venal /ˈviːnəl/ *adj* corrupt; willing to accept bribes.—**venality** *n*.—**venally** *adv*.

venatic /vɪˈnætɪk/, **venatical** /vɪˈnætɪkəl/ *adj* of or pertaining to hunting; (*people*) likely to engage in hunting.

venation /vɪˈneɪʃən/ *n* the arrangement of veins in a leaf or an insect's wing; these veins collectively.—**venational** *adj*.

vend /vɛnd/ *vt* to sell, to offer for sale; to peddle; (*rare*) to state or disseminate (an opinion, etc).

vendace /ˈvɛnˌdeɪs/ *n* (*pl* **vendaces, vendace**) either of two types of small European freshwater fish.

vendee /vɛnˈdiː/ *n* (*law*) a buyer; someone to whom something has been sold.

vendetta /vɛnˈdɛtə/ *n* the taking of private vengeance; a feud.—**vendettist** *n*.

vendible /ˈvɛndəbəl/ *adj* saleable; (*arch*) venal. • *n* (*usu pl*) something that is saleable.

vending machine *n* a coin-operated machine which dispenses goods.

vendor, vender /ˈvɛndər/ or /-dɔr/ *n* a seller; a machine that ejects goods, etc, after a required amount of coins has been inserted.

veneer /vəˈniːr/ *n* an overlay of fine wood or plastic; a superficial appearance. • *vt* to cover with veneer.

venerable /ˈvɛnərəbəl/ *adj* worthy of reverence or respect.—**venerability** *n*.—**venerably** *adv*.

venerate /ˈvɛnəˌreɪt/ *vt* to revere; to respect.—**venerator** *n*.

veneration /ˌvɛnəˈreɪʃən/ *n* a venerating or being venerated; respect mingled with awe, deep reverence.

venereal /vəˈniːriəl/ *adj* (*disease*) resulting from sexual intercourse.

venereal disease *n* any of various diseases, such as syphilis or HIV, transmitted by sexual intercourse.— *also* **sexually transmitted disease** or **infection**.

venery[1] /ˈvɛnəri/ *n* (*arch*) hunting, *usu* with hounds, the chase.

venery[2] *n* (*arch*) sexual indulgence, the pursuit of sexual gratification.

venesection /ˈviːnəˌsɛkʃən/ *n* the operation of opening a vein; phlebotomy.

Venetian blind *n* a window blind formed of long thin horizontal slips of wood that can be pivoted.

vengeance /ˈvɛndʒəns/ *n* the act of taking revenge; retribution; **with a vengeance** to a high degree; and no mistake.

vengeful /ˈvɛndʒfʊl/ *adj* bent on vengeance; vindictive.—**vengefully** *adv* **vengefulness** *n*.

venial /ˈviːniəl/ *adj* (*sin*) forgivable, excusable, not very wrong; (*sin*) not entailing damnation.—**veniality** *n*.—**venially** *adv*.

venison /ˈvɛnɪsən/ or /-zən/ *n* the edible flesh of the deer.

Venite /vɪˈneɪti/ *n* (*Anglican church*) the 95th Psalm, used as a canticle at Matins; the music for this.

venom /ˌvɛnəm/ *n* the poison of a snake, wasp, etc; spite, malice, rancour.

venomous /ˈvɛnəməs/ *adj* secreting venom; malicious, spiteful.—**venomously** *adv*.—**venomousness** *n*.

venose /ˈviːnəʊs/ *adj* having many veins, veiny; venous; (*plant*) with a surface of vein-like ridges.

venosity /vɪˈnɒsəti/ *n* the state of being abnormally venose; (*blood vessels, organs*) the condition of containing too much blood.

venous /ˈviːnəs/ *adj* pertaining to, contained in, or consisting of veins or blood.—**venously** *adv*.—**venousness** *n*.

vent[1] /vɛnt/ *n* a small opening or slit; an outlet or flue for the escape of fumes. • *vt* to release; (*temper*) to give expression to.—**venter** *n*

vent[2] *n* a slit in the back of a coat, often forming a flap; an opening in a battlemented wall.

ventage /ˈvɛntɪdʒ/ *n* a finger-hole of a flute or similar instrument; a small opening, an outlet.

ventail /ˈvɛnˌteɪl/ *n* the part of a helmet protecting the lower part of the face.

venter /ˈvɛntər/ *n* (*anat, zool*) the belly or abdomen of vertebrates; the part of a muscle that swells outwards; (*bot*) the swollen base of that part of some plants containing the egg cell; (*law*) the womb.

ventilate /ˈvɛntɪˌleɪt/ *vt* to supply with fresh air; to oxygenate (the blood); to make public, to submit to discussion.—**ventilative** *adj*.

ventilation /ˌvɛntɪˈleɪʃən/ *n* the act of ventilating; the state of being ventilated; free discussion.

ventilator /ˈvɛntɪˌleɪtər/ *n* an appliance for ventilating a room, etc; (*med*) a device for enabling a patient to breathe normally.

ventral /ˈvɛntrəl/ *adj* (*anat*) of or on the belly, abdominal; (*bot*) of, pertaining to, or located on that part of a plant facing towards the stem, *esp* a leaf.

ventricle /ˈvɛntrɪkəl/ *n* a small cavity; one of the lower chambers of the heart, which pumps blood; one of the four cavities of the brain.—**ventricular** *adj*.

ventricose, ventricous /ˈvɛntrɪˌkəʊs/ *adj* (*biol*) swelling, *esp* on one side only.—**ventricosity** *n*.

ventriloquism /vɛnˈtrɪləˌkwɪzəm/, **ventriloquy** /vɛnˈtrɪləkwi/ *n* the act or art of speaking so that the sounds appear to come from a source other than the actual speaker.—**ventriloquial** *adj*.—**ventriloquist** *n*.—**ventriloquistic** *adj*.

ventriloquize /vɛnˈtrɪləˌkwiːz/ *vi* to practise ventriloquism.

venture /ˈvɛntʃər/ *n* a dangerous expedition; a risky undertaking. • *vti* to risk; to dare.—**venturer** *n*.

venture capital *n* capital available for investment in risky but potentially very profitable enterprises and repayable at higher than normal interest rates, risk capital.

Venture Scout, Venturer *n* a young man or woman who is a member of the senior branch of the Scouts.

venturesome /ˈvɛntʃərsəm/ *adj* daring, rash; risky, hazardous.—**venturesomely** *adv*.—**venturesomeness** *n*.

venue /ˈvɛnjuː/ *n* the place of an action or event.

Venus /ˈviːnəs/ *n* (*Roman myth*) the goddess of love; (*astron*) the planet second from the sun, that can sometimes be seen as a bright star in the morning or evening; a beautiful woman.

veracious /vəˈreɪʃəs/ *adj* observant of the truth, truthful; honest; true, accurate.—**veraciously** *adv*.—**veraciousness** *n*.

veracity /vəˈræsɪti/ *n* (*pl* **veracities**) habitual observance of the truth; correspondence with the truth or facts; a truthful statement, a truth.

veranda, verandah /vəˈrændə/ *n* a roofed porch, supported by light pillars.

veratrine /ˈvɛrəˌtriːn/ or /-trɪn/ *n* a poisonous mixture of alkaloids from plants of the hellebore family, formerly used medically, to relieve neuralgia or as a counter-irritant.

verb /vɜːb/ *n* (*gram*) the part of speech that expresses an action, a process, state or condition or mode of being.

verbal /'vɜrbəl/ *adj* of, concerned with or expressed in words; spoken, not written; literal; (*gram*) of, pertaining to or characteristic of a verb.—**verbally** *adv*.

verbalism /'vɜrbə,lɪzəm/ *n* something expressed in words; a word or phrase; excessive attention to wording rather than content; meaningless phrases or sentences resulting from this.

verbalist /,vɜrbə'lɪst/ *n* one skilled with words; one who concentrates on words rather than content.—**verbalistic** *adj*.

verbalize /'vɜrbə,laɪz/ *vt* to put into words; to make into a verb.—**verbalization** *n*.

verbatim /vɜr'beɪtɪm/ *adj, adv* word for word.

verbena /vɜr'biːnə/ *n* any of various kinds of ornamental fragrant plant, *usu* found in America, with red, white or purple flowers; any similar type of plant.

verbiage /'vɜrbiədʒ/ *n* more words than are needed for clarity, wordiness; the use of too many words.

verbify /'vɜrbə,faɪ/ *vti* (**verbifying, verbified**) to convert (a noun, etc) into a verb; to be verbose.

verbose /vɜr'boːs/ *adj* using more words than are necessary; overloaded with words.—**verbosely** *adv*.—**verbosity** *n*.

verdant /'vɜrdənt/ *adj* (*grass, foliage*) green and fresh; covered with grass; inexperienced, gullible.—**verdancy** *n*.—**verdantly** *adv*.

verderer /'vɜrdərər/ *n* (*formerly*) in England, an official who had charge of the royal forests and was responsible for maintaining peace in them.

verdict /'vɜrdɪkt/ *n* the decision of a jury at the end of a trial; decision, judgment.

verdigris /'vɜrdɪgrɪs/ or /-,griːs/ *n* a greenish deposit that forms on copper or brass.

verdure /'vɜrdjər/ or /-dʒər/ *n* green vegetation; greenness; freshness; the freshness and healthy growth of vegetation.—**verdurous** *adj*.—**verdurousness** *n*.

verge[1] /vɜrdʒ/ *n* the brink; the extreme edge or margin; a grass border beside a road; a staff or wand as an emblem of office; the spindle of a watch balance; (*archit*) a projecting edge of roof tiles or slates.

verge[2] *vi* to incline, descend; (*with* **on**) to border on, to be on the verge of.

verger /'vɜrdʒər/ *n* an official who has care of the interior of a church; a staff bearer of a bishop, etc.

veridical /və'rɪdɪkəl/ *adj* truthful, veracious; (*psychol*) of or pertaining to events in dreams that in retrospect appear to have foretold the future.

verifiable /,vɛrɪ'faɪəbəl/ *adj* capable of being verified.—**verifiability** *n*.

verification /,vɛrɪfɪ'keɪʃən/ *n* the act of proving to be true; confirmation; the state of being verified; a marshalling of facts, etc that proves the truth of, *eg* a theory; (*law*) (*formerly*) a short affidavit at the end of a pleading indicating that the pleader is willing to supply proof.

verify /'vɛrɪfaɪ/ *vt* (**verifying, verified**) to confirm the truth of, to check; to substantiate, to bear out; (*law*) to authenticate or support by proofs.—**verifiable** *adj*.—**verification** *n*.—**verifier** *n*.

verily /'vɛrɪli/ *adv* (*arch*) in truth, certainly.

verisimilitude /,vɛrɪsɪ'mɪlɪ,tuːd/ or /-,tjuːd/ *n* the appearance of truth, probability.—**verisimilar** *adj*.

verismo /ve'rɪzmoː/ *n* a type of opera concerned with representing contemporary life of ordinary people in an honest and realistic way.

veritable /'vɛrɪtəbəl/ *adj* real, genuine.—**veritably** *adv*.

verity /'vɛrɪti/ *n* (*pl* **verities**) the quality or state of being true; a truth; a true fact, reality.

verjuice /'vɜrdʒuːs/ *n* an acidic liquor expressed from unripe grapes, apples, etc, formerly used in sauces; sourness, tartness.

vermeil /'vɜrmeɪl/ or /-mɪl/ *n* silver-gilt, or any other metal gilded; (*poet*) vermilion. • *adj* of a bright red colour.

vermicelli /,vɜrmɪ'tʃeli/ *n* a pasta similar to spaghetti but in finer strings.

vermicide /'vɜrmɪ,saɪd/ *n* a substance for killing worms.—**vermicidal** *adj*.

vermicular /vɜrmɪkjʊlər/ *adj* vermiform; vermiculate; wormlike; pertaining to or caused by worms.

vermiculate /vɜr'mɪkjʊlət/ *adj* moving like a worm; worm-eaten; adorned with wavy lines; (*thoughts*) constantly recurring, casuistic. • *vt* to mark with close wavy lines.—**vermiculation** *n*.

vermiform /'vɜrmɪ,fɔrm/ *adj* worm-shaped.

vermiform appendix *n* the worm-shaped structure attached to the caecum vestigially in humans and certain other mammals, the appendix.

vermifuge /'vɜrmɪ,fjuːdʒ/ *n* a drug, etc, that expels intestinal worms.

vermilion, vermillion /vɜr'mɪljən/ *n* a bright scarlet colour. • *adj* of this colour.

vermin /'vɜrmɪn/ *n* (*used as pl*) pests, such as insects and rodents; persons dangerous to society.

vermination /,vɜrmɪ'neɪʃən/ *n* the breeding or spread of vermin, worms or larvae; infestation with vermin, worms or larvae.

verminous /'vɜrmɪnəs/ *adj* infested with, caused by, or like vermin.

vermouth /vɜr'muːθ/ *n* a white wine flavoured with herbs, used in cocktails and as an aperitif.

vernacular /vɜr'nækjʊlər/ *n* the commonly spoken language or dialect of a country or region. • *adj* native.—**vernacularly** *adv*.

vernacularism /-ɪzəm/ *n* vernacular usage; a vernacular word or expression.

vernal /'vɜrnəl/ *adj* of, appearing in, relating to, or suggestive of the spring.—**vernally** *adv*.

vernation /vɜr'neɪʃən/ *n* (*bot*) the arrangement of leaves within a bud.

vernier /'vɜrniər/ *n* a small sliding scale attached to a larger fixed scale, with gradations to indicate minute subdivisions of the smallest divisions on the main fixed scale; an additional apparatus used to finetune or adjust an instrument. • *adj* of, pertaining to, or having a vernier.

Veronal /'vɛrənəl/ (*trademark*) *n* a sedative or hypnotic drug; barbitone.

veronica[1] /və'rɒnɪkə/ *n* any of several plants with blue, pink or white flowers, incl speedwell.

veronica[2] *n* (*RC Church*) the image of Christ's face that in legend appeared on a handkerchief given to him by St Veronica as he went to his crucifixion; this handkerchief; any similar image of Christ's face on a cloth.

veronica[3] *n* (*bullfighting*) a manoeuvre by a matador in which he swings the cape slowly before the bull while standing still.

verruca /və'ruːkə/ *n* (*pl* **verrucae, verrucas**) a wart on the hand or foot; (*biol*) a wart-like excrescence.—**verrucose, verrucous** *adj*.

versatile /'vɜrsə,taɪl/ *adj* turning readily from one occupation to another, adaptable; talented in many different ways; variable, fickle, changeable; (*biol*) able to move or turn freely.—**versatilely** *adv*.—**versatility** *n*.

verse /vɜrs/ *n* a line of poetry; a stanza of a poem; a metrical composition, *esp* of a light nature; a short section of a chapter in the Bible. • *vti* to make verses (about).

versed /vɜrst/ *adj* skilled or learned in a subject.

versicle /'vɜrsɪkəl/ *n* a short verse or text sung by priest and congregation alternately in a liturgical service.

versicolour, versicolor /'vɜrsɪ,kʊlər/ *adj* parti-coloured; changeable in colour, iridescent.

versification /,vɜrsɪfɪ'keɪʃən/ *n* verse-making; the metre or verses of a poem; the conversion of prose into verse.

versify /'vɜrsɪ,faɪ/ *vti* (**versifying, versified**) to write poetry or verse; to turn into verse.—**versifier** *n*.

version /'vɜrʒən/ *n* a translation from one language into another; a particular account or description.—**versional** *adj*.

vers libre /veːr'liːbrə/ *n* verse with no regular metrical system; free verse.

verso /'vɜrsoː/ *n* (*pl* **versos**) a left-hand, even-numbered page of a book, the back of the recto; the back of a printed sheet; the reverse of a coin.

versus /'vɜrsəs/ *prep* against; in contrast to.

vert /vɜrt/ *n* (*English law*) (*formerly*) the right to collect whatever grows and bears a green leaf in a forest; green vegetation; (*her*) green.

vert. /vɜrt/ *abbr* = vertical.

vertebra /'vɜrtəbrə/ *n* (*pl* **vertebrae, vertebras**) one of the interconnecting bones of the spinal column.—**vertebral** *adj*.

vertebrate /'vɜrtə,breɪt/ or /-brət/ *n* an animal with a backbone. • *adj* having a backbone; of the vertebrates.

vertebration /,vɜrtə'breɪʃən/ *n* division into vertebrae or vertebrae-like segments.

vertex /'vɜrtɛks/ *n* (*pl* **vertexes, vertices**) the topmost point; apex; (*anat*) the crown of the head; (*geom*) the point at which two sides of a polygon or the planes of a solid intersect.

vertical /'vɜrtɪkəl/ *adj* perpendicular to the horizon; upright. • *n* a vertical line or plane.—**verticality** *n*.—**vertically** *adv*.

verticil /'vɜrtɪsɪl/ *n* a whorl-like arrangement of leaves or flowers around a stem.

verticillate /ˌvɜr'tɪsɪlət/ *adj* (*biol*) arranged in a whorl-like pattern.—**verticillately** *adv*.—**verticillation** *n*.

vertiginous /vɜr'tɪdʒɪnəs/ *adj* revolving, rotary; giddy; causing giddiness; whirling.—**vertiginously** *adv*.—**vertiginousness** *n*.

vertigo /'vɜrtɪgoʊ/ *n* (*pl* **vertigoes, vertigines**) a sensation of dizziness and sickness caused by a disorder of the sense of balance.—**vertiginous** *adj*.

vertu /vɜr'tuː/ or /'vɜrˌtuː/ *see* **virtu**.

vervain /'vɜrveɪn/ *n* a perennial European with clusters of tiny bluish-purple flowers.

verve /vɜrv/ *n* enthusiasm; liveliness; energy.

vervet /'vɜrvət/ *n* a small African monkey with dark hands and feet and yellowish or greenish coat.

very /'veri/ *adj* complete; absolute; same. • *adv* extremely; truly; really.

Very light *n* a coloured flare fired from a Very pistol as a signal at sea or to give temporary light.

vesica /'vesɪkə/ *n* (*pl* **vesicae**) (*anat*) the bladder, *esp* the urinary bladder; (art) a pointed oval halo used as an aureole in medieval sculpture or painting.—**vesical** *adj*.

vesicant /'vesɪkənt/, **vesicatory** /'vesɪkəˌtɔri/ *n* (*pl* **vesicants, vesicatories**) a substance (*eg* mustard gas) that causes blistering, with applications in chemical warfare. • *adj* raising blisters.

vesicate /'vesɪˌkeɪt/ *vt* to raise blisters on. • *vi* to become blistered.—**vesication** *n*.

vesicle /'vesɪkəl/ *n* a small blister; a small cyst or sac; (*anat*) a bladder-like vessel or cavity, *esp* one filled with serous fluid; (*geol*) a cavity in rock formed by gases during solidification; (*bot*) a small sac found in some seaweeds and aquatic plants.—**vesicular** *adj*.

vesper /'vespər/ *n* (*arch*) evening; (*with cap*) the evening star; (*Anglican Church*) evensong; (*RC Church*) the sixth of the canonical hours. • *adj* pertaining to evening or vespers.

vespertine /'vespərˌtaɪn/ or /-tɪn/, **vespertinal** /-əl/ *adj* of evening; (*bot*) opening in the evening; (*zool*) active in the evening; (*astron*) setting about sunset.

vespiary /'vespiˌeri/ *n* (*pl* **vespiaries**) a nest of wasps or hornets.

vespine /'vespaɪn/ *adj* of, pertaining to, or like a wasp or wasps.

vessel /'vesəl/ *n* a container; a ship or boat; a tube in the body along which fluids pass.

vest /vest/ *n* a sleeveless undergarment worn next to the skin, a singlet; a waistcoat. • *vt* to place or settle (power, authority, etc.); (*with* in) to confer or be conferred on; to invest with a right to.

Vesta /'vestə/ *n* (*astron*) a bright asteroid; (*Roman myth*) the goddess of the hearth and the household fire.

vesta /'vestə/ *n* a short match of wax or wood, lit by friction.

vestal /'vestəl/ *adj* pertaining to or sacred to the goddess Vesta; vowed to chastity, pure. • *n* a vestal virgin; a virgin.

vestal virgin *n* one of the six virgin priestesses who tended the sacred fire on the altar of the temple of Vesta, in ancient Rome.

vested /'vestəd/ *adj* (*law*) having permanent entitlement to the possession or use of property, now and in the future, ratified by law or custom; (*priest, etc*) clothed in ecclesiastical vestments.

vested interest *n* (*law*) a permanent entitlement to the possession and use of property, now and in the future; a strong reason for acting in a certain way, *usu* for personal gain; (*usu pl*) people in such a state.

vestibule /'vestɪˌbjuːl/ *n* an entrance hall or lobby; a covered entrance at the end of a rail carriage; (*anat*) a communicating channel.—**vestibular** *adj*.

vestige /'vestɪdʒ/ *n* a hint; a trace; a rudimentary survival of a former organ; a particle.—**vestigial** *adj*.—**vestigially** *adv*.

vestment /'vestmənt/ *n* a garment or robe, *esp* that worn by a priest or official.—**vestmental** *adj*.

vestry /'vestri/ *n* (*pl* **vestries**) a room in a church where vestments, etc, are kept and parochial meetings held; a meeting for parish business.—**vestral** *adj*.

vestryman /'vestrimən/ *n* (*pl* **vestrymen**) a member of a vestry elected by the parishioners.

vesture /'vestʃər/ *n* (*arch*) clothing; something that clothes, a covering; (*law*) everything growing on someone's land apart from trees; something obtained from land, such as wheat. • (*arch*) *vt* to clothe.

vesuvianite /və'suːviəˌnaɪt/ *n* a mineral of a green, brown or yellow colour, similar to the garnet, idocrase.

vet /vet/ *n* a veterinary surgeon. • *vt* (**vetting, vetted**) to examine, check for errors, etc.

vetch /vetʃ/ *n* a common leguminous climbing plant with blue or purple flowers and a stem with tendrils, found in temperate climates and used for green fodder; any similar plant.

vetchling /'vetʃlɪŋ/ *n* a climbing plant like a vetch mainly found in northern temperate regions with angled or winged stems with tendrils and gaudy flowers.

veteran /'vetərən/ or /'vetrən/ *adj* old, experienced; having served in the armed forces. • *n* a person who has served in the armed forces; a person who has given long service in a particular activity.

veterinary /'vetrɪˌneri/ or /'vetərɪ-/ *adj* of or dealing with diseases of domestic animals.

veterinarian /ˌvetrɪ'neriən/ or /ˌvetərɪ-/, **veterinary surgeon** *n* a person trained in treating sick or injured animals.

veto /'viːtoʊ/ *n* (*pl* **vetoes**) the right of a person or group to prohibit an action or legislation; a prohibition. • *vt* (**vetoing, vetoed**) to refuse to agree to; to prohibit.—**vetoer** *n*.

vex /veks/ *vt* to annoy; to puzzle, confuse.—**vexer** *n*.—**vexingly** *adv*.

vexation /vek'seɪʃən/ *n* a vexing or being vexed; an annoying thing; irritation, distress.

vexatious /vek'seɪʃəs/ *adj* causing vexation; annoying; troublesome; harassing; (*litigation*) designed merely to annoy.—**vexatiously** *adv*.

vexed /vekst/ *adj* annoyed; (*question*) much debated.—**vexedly** *adv*.—**vexedness** *n*.

vexillum /vek'sɪləm/ *n* (*pl* **vexilla**) (*bot*) the largest petal found on flowers of the plant family to which the sweet pea and similar plants belong; (*zool*) the vane of a feather.

VHF *abbr* = very high frequency.

via /'viːə/ or /'vaɪə/ *prep* by way of.

viable /'vaɪəbəl/ *adj* capable of growing or developing; workable; practicable.—**viability** *n*.—**viably** *adv*.

viaduct /'vaɪəˌdʌkt/ *n* a road or railway carried by a bridge with arches over a valley, river, etc.

vial /'vaɪəl/ *n* a small bottle for medicines, etc; a phial.

via media /ˌviːə'miːdiə/ or /-'miːdiə/, /ˌvaɪə-/ *n* a middle course between extremes; a compromise.

viand /'vaɪənd/ *n* an article of food. (*pl*) meat ready to be cooked; food.

viaticum /vaɪ'ætɪkəm/ *n* (*pl* **viatica, viaticums**) (*RC Church*) the Eucharist administered to someone whose death is or might be imminent; (*rare*) an allowance or provisions given to a person setting out on a journey.

vibes /vaɪbz/ *npl* (*sl*) vibrations; vibraphone.

vibraculum /vaɪ'brækjʊləm/ *n* (*pl* **vibracula**) (*zool*) a whip-like appendage by which some polyzoans ward off parasites.

vibrant /'vaɪbrənt/ *adj* vibrating; resonant; bright; lively.—**vibrancy** *n*.—**vibrantly** *adv*.

vibraphone /'vaɪbrəˌfoʊn/ *n* a percussion instrument that produces a vibrato by resonating metal bars.—**vibraphonist** *n*.

vibrate /'vaɪbreɪt/ *vti* to shake; to move quickly backwards and forwards; to quiver; to oscillate; to resound.—**vibratingly** *adv*.

vibratile /'vaɪbrəˌtaɪl/ *adj* capable of or characterized by vibrating.—**vibratility** *n*.

vibration /vaɪ'breɪʃən/ *n* a vibrating or being vibrated; oscillation; resonance; vacillation; (*usu pl*) an emotional reaction instinctively sensed; (*physics*) the rapid alternating of particles caused by the disturbance of equilibrium.—**vibrational** *adj*.

vibrative /'vaɪbrəˌtɪv/ *adj* vibratory.

vibrato /vɪ'brɔːtoʊ/ *n* (*pl* **vibratos**) (*mus*) a pulsating effect obtained by rapid variation of emphasis on the same tone.

vibrator /'vaɪbreɪtər/ *n* the vibrating part in various instruments; a dildo.

vibratory /'vaɪbrəˌtɔri/ *adj* vibrating; consisting of or causing vibrations.

vibrio /'vɪbriːoʊ/ *n* (*pl* **vibrios**) a spiral or curved, rod-like bacillus.—**vibrioid** *adj*.

vibrissa /vaɪ'brɪsə/ *n* (*pl* **vibrissae**) a sensitive whisker on an animal's face; any of the bristle-like feathers found in the beak area of certain insect-eating birds.

viburnum /vaɪˈbɜːnəm/ *n* any of several shrubs or trees, incl the guelder rose, with red or black berry-like fruits, found in various temperate and sub-tropical regions; the dried bark from some of these, sometimes used medicinally.

vicar /ˈvɪkər/ *n* a parish priest; a clergyman in charge of a chapel.

vicarage /ˈvɪkərɪdʒ/ *n* the residence of a vicar.

vicarial /vəˈkeərɪəl/ *adj* of, pertaining to, or acting as a vicar, vicars or a vicariate; (*ecclesiastical functions*) delegated, vicarious.

vicariate, vicarate /vəˈkeərɪət/ *n* the rank, office, or district of a vicar.

vicarious /vɪˈkeərɪəs/ or /vaɪ-/ *adj* substitute; obtained second-hand by listening to or watching another person's experiences.—**vicariously** *adv*.—**vicariousness** *n*.

vice[1] /vaɪs/ *n* an evil action or habit; a grave moral fault; great wickedness; a serious defect, a blemish.

vice[2] *n* a clamping device with jaws, used for holding objects firmly.—*also US* **vise**.

vice- /prefix* one who acts in place of or as a deputy to another.

vice admiral /vaɪsˈædmərəl/ *n* a rank of naval officer next below admiral.

vice-chairman *n* (*pl* **vice-chairmen**) one who takes the chair in a chairman's absence.

vice chancellor /vaɪsˈtʃænsələr/ *n* the chief executive officer of a university.

vice consul *n* a person who acts in place of a consul in a subordinate district, etc.

vicegerent /vaɪsˈdʒerənt/ *n adj* a person holding delegated power or ruling as another's deputy.—*also adj*.—**vicegerency** *n*.

vicennial /vaɪˈsenɪəl/ *adj* lasting twenty years; happening every twenty years.

vice president /vaɪsˈprezɪdənt/ *n* a deputy or assistant president.

viceregal /vaɪsˈriːɡəl/ *adj* of or relating to a viceroy; (*Austral, NZ*) of or relating to a governor general.

vicereine /ˈvaɪsreɪn/ *n* a viceroy's wife.

viceroy /ˈvaɪsrɔɪ/ *n* one who rules a country or province as a representative of a king or queen.

viceroyalty /-ˈrɔɪəlti/, **viceroyship** /-ʃɪp/ *n* (*pl* **viceroyalties, viceroyships**) the office or term of a viceroy.

vice versa /ˌvaɪsˈvɜːsə/ or /ˌvaɪsə-/ *adv* conversely; the other way round.

vichyssoise /ˌviːʃiːˈswɒz/ or /ˈvɪ-/ *n* leek and potato soup consumed cold.

Vichy water /ˈviːʃiː/ *n* a mineral water from Vichy in France.

vicinage /ˈvɪsɪnɪdʒ/ *n* a surrounding district, a neighbourhood; the people of a neighbourhood; proximity.

vicinal /ˈvɪsɪnəl/ *adj* neighbouring; adjacent; (*chem*) resembling or substituting for a crystal face or form; denoting substituted atoms on adjacent atoms in a molecule.

vicinity /vəˈsɪnɪti/ *n* (*pl* **vicinities**) a nearby area; proximity.

vicious /ˈvɪʃəs/ *adj* cruel; violent; malicious; ferocious.—**viciously** *adv*.—**viciousness** *n*.

vicissitude /vɪˈsɪsɪˌtjuːd/ or /-ˌtʃuːd/ *n* a change of circumstances or fortune; (*pl*) ups and downs.—**vicissitudinary, vicissitudinous** *adj*.

victim /ˈvɪktəm/ or /-tɪm/ *n* a person who has been killed or injured by an action beyond his or her control; a dupe.

victimize /-ˌaɪz/ or /-tɪm-/ *vt* to make a victim of, to cause to suffer.—**victimization** *n*.—**victimizer** *n*.

victor /ˈvɪktər/ *n* a winner; a conqueror.

victoria /vɪkˈtɔːrɪə/ *n* a light, open, four-wheeled, two-seater carriage; a giant South American water-lily; a victoria plum.

Victorian /vɪkˈtɔːrɪən/ *adj* of or living in the reign of Queen Victoria; old-fashioned, prudish.

victoria plum *n* a large purplish-red sweet variety of plum.

victorious /vɪkˈtɔːrɪəs/ *adj* having won in battle or contest; emblematic of victory; triumphant.—**victoriously** *adv*.

victory /ˈvɪktəri/ *n* (*pl* **victories**) triumph in battle; success; achievement.

victual /ˈvɪtəl/ *n* (*usu pl*) food, provisions. • *vt* (**victualling, victualled** *or* **victualing, victualed**) to supply with food; to take in provisions.

victualler, victualer /ˈvɪtlər/ *n* (*formerly*) a supplier of provisions, *esp* to an army; a provision ship; an innkeeper.

vicuña, vicuna /vɪˈkjuːnə/ *n* a South American animal similar to the llama with a fine, long, reddish silky fleece; cloth made from this fleece.

vide /ˈviːdeɪ/ (*Latin*) see.

vide infra /ˈɪnfrə/ (*Latin*) see later (in this book).

videlicet /vəˈdeɪlɪˌset/ *adv* that is to say, namely.

video /ˈvɪdɪəʊ/ *n* (*pl* **videos**) the transmission or recording of television programmes or films, using a television set and a video recorder and tape. • *vt* (**videoing, videoed**) to record on video tape.

video cassette *n* a cassette containing video tape.

video recorder *n* the machine on which video cassettes are played or recorded.

video tape /ˈvɪdɪəʊteɪp/ *n* a magnetic tape on which images and sounds can be recorded for reproduction on television.—**video-tape** *vt*.

vide supra /ˈviːdeɪˈsuːprə/ (*Latin*) see earlier (in this book).

vidette /vɪˈdet/ *see* **vedette**.

vidkid /ˈvɪdˈkɪd/ *n* a child who is addicted to watching television or video.

vie /vaɪ/ *vi* (**vying, vied**) to contend or strive for superiority.—**vier** *n*.

view /vjuː/ *n* sight; range of vision; inspection, examination; intention; scene; opinion. • *vt* to see; to consider; to examine intellectually.

viewer /ˈvjuːər/ *n* a person who views, *esp* television; an optical device used in viewing.

viewfinder /ˈvjuːˌfaɪndər/ *n* a device in a camera showing the view to be photographed.

viewless /ˈvjuːləs/ *adj* without a view; (*poet*) invisible, unseen.

viewpoint /ˈvjuːpɔɪnt/ *n* opinion; a place from which something can be viewed, *esp* a scenic panorama.

vigil /ˈvɪdʒəl/ *n* keeping watch at night.

vigilance /ˈvɪdʒələns/ *n* a being vigilant; watchfulness; alertness.

vigilant /ˈvɪdʒələnt/ *adj* on the watch to discover and avoid danger, watchful; alert; cautious.—**vigilantly** *adv*.

vigilante /ˌvɪdʒəˈlænti/ *n* a self-appointed law enforcer.

vignette /vɪnˈjet/ *n* a small picture or design in a book without a line framing it; a picture, the edges of which shade off gradually into the background; a short word sketch. • *vt* to depict in vignette; to shade off into the background.—**vignettist** *n*.

vigor /ˈvɪgər/ *see* **vigour**.

vigoroso /ˌvɪgəˈrɔːsɔː/ or It. /ˌviːgɔˈrɔsɔ/ *adv* (*mus*) with vigour.

vigorous /ˈvɪgərəs/ *adj* full of vigour; powerful; lusty.—**vigorously** *adv*.—**vigorousness** *n*.

vigour /ˈvɪgər/ *n* physical or mental strength; vitality.—*also* **vigor**.

Viking /ˈvaɪkɪŋ/ *n* one of the Norse pirates who ravaged the coasts of Europe from the 8th–10th centuries.

vilayet /ˈviːləˌjet/ *n* a province of Turkey.

vile /vaɪl/ *adj* wicked; evil; offensive; very bad.—**vilely** *adv*.—**vileness** *n*.

vilify /ˈvɪləˌfaɪ/ *vt* (**vilifying, vilified**) to malign.—**vilification** *n*.—**vilifier** *n*.

villa /ˈvɪlə/ *n* a large country or suburban house.

village /ˈvɪlɪdʒ/ *n* a collection of houses smaller than a town.

villager /-ər/ *n* an inhabitant of a village.

villain /ˈvɪlən/ *n* a scoundrel; the main evil character in a play, film or novel; (*arch*) a boor.

villainous /-əs/ *adj* depraved, evil, wicked; very bad, wretched.—**villainously** *adv*.—**villainousness** *n*.

villainy /-i/ *n* (*pl* **villainies**) great wickedness; an atrocious crime.

villanella /ˌvɪləˈnelə/ *n* (*pl* **villanelle**) a popular part-song of 17th-century Italy.

villanelle /ˌvɪləˈnel/ *n* a poem of 19 lines in six stanzas rhymed aba aba aba aba abaa, the 6th, 12th and 18th lines being the same as the first, and the 9th, 15th and 19th the same as the third.

villein /ˈvɪlən/ *n* (*hist*) a feudal tenant of the lowest class, a serf.

villi /ˈvɪlˌaɪ/ *see* **villus**.

villous, villose /ˈvɪləʊs/ *adj* covered with villi; (*bot*) covered with long, thin, soft hairs.

villus /ˈvɪləs/ *n* (*pl* **villi**) (*biol*) the velvety fibre of the mucous membrane of the intestine; (*bot*) the soft hair covering a fruit or flower.—**villosity**.

vim /vɪm/ (*sl*) energy, force.

vimineous /vəˈmɪnɪəs/ *adj* (*bot*) of or producing long flexible shoots.

vina /ˈviːnɒ/ *n* a seven-stringed Indian musical instrument.

vinaceous /vaɪˈneɪʃəs/ *adj* of the colour of wine; wine-red.

vinaigrette /ˌvɪnəˈɡret/ *n* a salad dressing made from oil, vinegar and seasoning.

vincible /'vɪnsəbəl/ *adj* capable of being conquered or overcome.—**vincibility** *n*.

vinculum /'vɪŋkjuləm/ *n* (*pl* **vincula**) (*anat*) a ligament; (*math*) a horizontal line over quantities having the effect of a parenthesis; (*print*) a brace; a bond of union, a tie.

vindicate /'vɪndɪˌkeɪt/ *vt* to establish the existence or truth of, to justify; to clear of charges, to absolve from blame.—**vindicable** *adj*.—**vindicator** *n*.—**vindicatory** *adj*.

vindication /-'keɪʃən/ *n* a vindicating or being vindicated; an event, fact, evidence, etc, that justifies a deed or claim.

vindictive /vɪn'dɪktɪv/ *adj* vengeful; spiteful; (*damages*) exemplary, punitive.—**vindictively** *adv*.—**vindictiveness** *n*.

vine /'vaɪn/ *n* any climbing plant, or its stem; a grapevine; a sphere of activity, *esp* spiritual or mental endeavour.

vinedresser /'vaɪnˌdresər/ *n* a person who cultivates vines.

vinegar /'vɪnəgər/ *n* a sour-tasting liquid containing acetic acid, used as a condiment and preservative.

vinegary /'vɪnəgəri/ *adj* of or like vinegar; sour; ill-tempered.

vinery /'vaɪnəri/ *n* (*pl* **vineries**) a place where grapes are grown or wine is made.

vineyard /'vɪnjərd/ *n* a plantation of grapevines.

vingt-et-un *Fr.* /væteɪˈœ̃/ *n* a gambling game with cards in which players try to obtain points better than the banker's but not more than 21.—*also* **blackjack, pontoon, twenty-one**.

vinic /'vaɪnɪk/ or /'vɪnɪk/ *adj* contained in or obtained from wine.

viniculture /'vɪnɪˌkʌltʃər/ *n* the cultivation of vines and manufacture of wine, viticulture.—**vinicultural** *adj*.—**viniculturist** *n*.

viniferous /vaɪˈnɪfərəs/ *adj* wine-producing.

vinificator /'vɪnɪˌfɪˈkeɪtər/ *n* in winemaking, an apparatus for collecting alcoholic vapours.

vin ordinaire *Fr.* /ˌvæ̃ ɔrdɪˈnɛr/ *n* (*pl* **vins ordinaires**) the ordinary table wine of France.

vinous /'vaɪnəs/ *adj* of, pertaining to, or having the qualities of wine; like wine; wine-coloured; inspired by wine.—**vinosity** *n*.

vintage /'vɪntɪdʒ/ *n* the grape harvest of one season; wine, *esp* of good quality, made in a particular year; wine of a particular region; the product of a particular period. • *adj* (*cars*) classic; (*wine*) of a specified year and of good quality; (*play*) characteristic of the best.

vintager /'vɪntədʒər/ *n* a gatherer of grapes in a wine harvest.

vintner /'vɪntnər/ *n* a wine merchant.

vinyl /'vaɪnəl/ *n* a strong plastic used in floor coverings, furniture and records, etc.

viol /'vaɪəl/ *n* a family of medieval six-stringed instruments played with a bow, similar to a violin but with a softer sound.

viola[1] /vɪˈoːlə/ *n* a stringed instrument of the violin family, and tuned a fifth below it.

viola[2] /vaɪoːlə/ or /viː-/ *n* any of several plants of the genus that includes violets and pansies.

violable /'vaɪələbəl/ *adj* capable of being violated or broken.

violaceous /ˌvaɪəˈleɪʃəs/ *adj* of violet colour or family.

viola da gamba /viˌoːlədəˈgæmbə/ *n* the bass viol.

viola d'amore /viˌoːlədæˈmɔreɪ/ *n* a tenor viol with seven strings and a sweet tone.

violate /'vaɪəˌleɪt/ *vt* to break or infringe (an agreement); to rape; to disturb (one's privacy).—**violative** *adj*.—**violator** *n*.

violation /-'leɪʃən/ *n* the act of violating, infringing, or injuring; rape; outrage; an act of irreverence or profanation.

violence /'vaɪələns/ *n* physical force intended to cause injury or destruction; natural force; passion, intensity.

violent /'vaɪələnt/ *adj* urged or driven by force; vehement; impetuous; forcible; furious; severe.—**violently** *adv*.

violet /'vaɪələt/ or /'vaɪlət/ *n* a small plant with bluish-purple flowers; a bluish-purple colour.

violin /ˌvaɪəˈlɪn/ *n* a four-stringed musical instrument, played with a bow.

violinist /-ɪst/ *n* a person who plays the violin.

violist /viˈoːləst/ *n* a player of a viol or viola.

violoncellist /ˌviːəˌlɒnˈtʃɛlɪst/ or /ˌvaɪə-/ *n* a performer on the violoncello.

violoncello /ˌviːələnˈtʃɛloː/ *n* (*pl* **violoncellos**) the full name for a **cello**.

violone /vjoˈloːneɪ/ *n* the largest type of viol, corresponding to the double-bass.

VIP /ˌviːaɪˈpiː/ *abbr* = Very Important Person.

viper /'vaɪpər/ *n* a common European venomous snake.—**viperine** *adj*.

viperous /-əs/, **viperish** /-ɪʃ/ *adj* viper-like; malignant.

virago /vɪˈrɒɡoː/ or /-ˈreɪɡoː/ *n* (*pl* **viragoes, viragos**) a bad-tempered woman.

viral /'vaɪːrəl/ *adj* of or caused by a virus.

virelay, virelai /'vɪrəˌleɪ/ *n* an old French form of poem with short lines and two rhymes variously arranged.

vireo /'vɪrioː/ *n* (*pl* **vireos**) a small greenish American singing bird.

virescence /vɪrˈesəns/ *n* the state of being virescent, *esp* in place of the normal colour of petals.

virescent /vaɪˈresənt/ or /vɪ-/ *adj* beginning to be green; greenish.

virgate[1] /'vərgət/ *adj* (*bot*) slim and straight.

virgate[2] *n* an old English unit of land equal to approx 30 acres.

virgin /'vərdʒɪn/ *n* a person (*esp* a woman) who has never had sexual intercourse; (*with cap*) Mary, the mother of Christ; a painting or statue of her. • *adj* chaste; pure; untouched.

virginal[1] /-əl/ *adj* of or pertaining to a virgin or virginity; befitting a virgin; chaste, pure, innocent; fresh, unsullied, untouched.

virginal[2] *n* a small rectangular keyed musical instrument resembling a harpsichord but without legs.

virginity /vərˈdʒɪnɪti/ *n* the state of being a virgin; the state of being chaste, untouched, etc.

Virgo /'vərɡoː/ *n* the Virgin, the 6th sign of the zodiac.—**Virgoan** *adj*.

virgo intacta *n* (*pl* **virgines intactae**) (*law*) a girl or woman who is a virgin.

virgulate /'vərɡjuːlɪt/ or /-ˌleɪt/ *adj* rod-shaped.

virgule /'vərɡjuːl/ *n* a small rod; a slanting punctuation mark (/), a solidus.

viridescent /ˌvɪrəˈdesənt/ *adj* greenish; turning green.— **viridescence** *n*.

viridity /vəˈrɪdəti/ *n* greenness; freshness.

virile /'vɪraɪl/ or /-əl/ *adj* of a mature man, manly; strong, forceful; sexually potent.—**virility** *n*.

virtu /vərˈtuː/ *n* a love or knowledge of the fine arts, connoisseurship; artistic excellence, fine workmanship; the quality of appealing to a collector; artistic objects, antiques, curios, etc, collectively.—*also* **vertu**.

virtual /'vərtʃuːəl/ *adj* in effect or essence, though not in fact or strict definition; (*comput*) denoting memory, making use of an external memory to increase capacity.

virtually /-i/ or /-tjuː-/ *adv* to all intents and purposes, practically.

virtue /'vərtʃuː/ *n* moral excellence; any admirable quality; chastity; merit.

virtuoso /ˌvərtʃuːˈoːsoː/ or /-tjuː-/, /-zoː/ *n* (*pl* **virtuosos, virtuosi**) a person highly skilled in an activity, *esp* in playing a musical instrument. • *adj* skilled, masterly in technique.—**virtuosic** *adj*.—**virtuosity** *n*.

virtuous /-əs/ or /-tjuːəs-/ *adj* righteous; upright; pure.—**virtuously** *adv*.—**virtuousness** *n*.

virulent /'vɪrulənt/ or /'vɪrjuː/ *adj* (*disease*) deadly; extremely poisonous; hostile; vicious.—**virulence** *n*.—**virulently** *adv*.

virus /'vaɪrəs/ *n* a microorganism capable of causing ill-health; illness caused by virus; (*comput*) an unauthorized computer program which inserts itself into computer systems and causes disruption to existing software.

visa /'viːzə/ *n* an endorsement on a passport allowing the bearer to travel in the country of the government issuing it. • *vt* (**visaing, visaed**) to mark with a visa; to grant a visa to.

visage /'vɪzɪdʒ/ *n* the face; the countenance; appearance.

visard /'vɪzərd/ *see* **vizard**.

vis-à-vis /ˌviːzæˈviː/ *prep* opposite to; in face of. • *adj, adv* facing. • *n* the person opposite; a counterpart.

viscacha /vɪsˈkæʃə/ *n* a South American burrowing rodent, that looks like a large chinchilla.—*also* **vizcacha**.

viscera /'vɪsərə/ *npl* (*sing* **viscus**) the large internal organs of the animal body, the entrails.

visceral /-l/ *adj* of, pertaining to, or affecting the viscera; pertaining to or touching deeply inward feelings.—**viscerally** *adv*.

viscid /'vɪsɪd/ *adj* (*leaves*) covered with a sticky layer; (*fluids*) thick, glutinous.—**viscidity** *n*—**viscidly** *adv*.

viscometer /vɪsˈkɒmɪtər/, **viscosimeter** /vɪˈskɒsɪ-/ *n* an instrument for measuring viscosity.

viscose /'vɪskoːs/, or /-koːz/ *n* a form of cellulose used in making artificial silk.

viscosity /vɪ'skɒsiti/ n (pl **viscosities**) the property or state of being sticky or glutinous; (physics) a property of fluids that indicates their resistance to flow.

viscount /'vaɪkaʊnt/ n in Britain, a title of nobility next below an earl.—**viscountess** nf.

viscountcy /-si/ n (pl **viscountcies**) the rank of a viscount.

viscous /'vɪskəs/ adj sticky, thick; having viscosity.—**viscously** adv.—**viscousness** n.

viscus /'vɪskəs/ see **viscera**.

visibility /ˌvɪzɪ'bɪlɪti/ n (pl **visibilities**) clearness of seeing or being seen; the degree of clearness of the atmosphere.

visible /'vɪzɪbəl/ adj able to be seen, perceptible; apparent, evident.—**visibleness** n.—**visibly** adv.

visible speech n a phonetic alphabet representing the actual movements of the vocal organs and used in teaching the deaf.

vision /'vɪʒən/ n the power of seeing, sight; a supernatural appearance; a revelation; foresight; imagination; a mental concept; a person, scene, etc of unusual beauty; something seen in a dream or trance.—**visional** adj.

visionary /-ˌɛri/ adj imaginative; having foresight; existing in imagination only, not real. • n (pl **visionaries**) an imaginative person; a dreamer; an idealist, a mystic.

visit /'vɪzɪt/ vt to go to see; to pay a call upon a person or place; to stay with or at; to punish or reward with. • vi to see or meet someone regularly. • n the act of going to see, a call.—**visitable** adj.

visitant /'vɪzɪtənt/ n a migratory bird; a visitor, esp a pilgrim; a ghost. • adj (arch) visiting.

visitation /ˌvɪzɪ'teɪʃən/ n a visit by a superior; a punitive act of God; an official visit; right of access of a divorced parent to his or her children; a large migration of animals; (with cap) the visit paid by the Virgin Mary to Elizabeth (Luke 1:39ff), a picture representing the event; the day on which this is commemorated, 2 July.—**visitational** adj.

visiting card n a small card with a person's name on it, left when paying visits.

visitor /'vɪzɪtər/ n a person who visits; a caller; a tourist; a migratory bird pausing in transit; an official acting as an inspector and adviser.

visor /'vaɪzər/ n a movable part of a helmet protecting the face; the peak of a cap.—also **vizor**.—**visored** adj.

vista /'vɪstə/ n a view, as from a high place; a mental picture.—**vistaed, vista'd** adj.

visual /'vɪʒʊəl/ or /'vɪʒj-/ adj having, producing, or relating to vision or sight; perceptible, visible; (knowledge) attained by sight or vision; (impressions, etc) based upon something seen; of the nature of, producing or conveying a picture in the mind; (physics) optical. • n a piece of graphic material used for display or to convey a concept, etc; (pl) the visual aspect of a film, etc.—**visually** adv.

visual aid n a film, slide or overhead projector, etc used to aid teaching.

visualize /'vɪʒʊəˌlaɪz/ vt to form a mental picture of; to make visible to the mind or imagination. • vi to construct a visual image in the mind.—**visualization** n.—**visualizer** n.

vital /'vaɪtəl/ adj of, connected with or necessary to life; essential; lively, animated; fundamental; (wound, error) fatal. • n (pl) the bodily organs essential for life.—**vitally** adv.

vitalism /'vaɪtəˌlɪzəm/ n the belief that life cannot be explained as resulting wholly from physical and chemical processes, but must include some other vital non-material force or process.—**vitalist** n.—**vitalistic** adj.

vitality /vaɪ'tælɪti/ n (pl **vitalities**) vigour, hold on life; spirits; animation; capacity to last, durability.

vitalize /'vaɪtəˌlaɪz/ vt to give life to; to animate; to make vigorous.—**vitalization** n.

vital statistics npl data recording births, deaths, marriages, etc used in compiling population statistics; (inf) the measurements of a woman's figure.

vitamin /'vaɪtəmɪn/ n one of several organic substances occurring naturally in foods, which are essential for good health.—**vitaminic** adj.

vitellin /vɪ'tɛlɪn/ or /vaɪ-/ n a protein forming the major component in the yolk of birds' eggs.

vitelline /vɪ'tɛlaɪn/ or /vaɪ-/, /-lɪn/ adj of or pertaining to egg yolk; of a yellow colour close to the shade of egg yolk.

vitiate /'vɪʃiˌeɪt/ vt to make faulty or ineffective; to taint; to deprave; to invalidate or annul (a legal document, etc).—**vitiation** n.—**vitiator** n.

viticulture /'vɪtɪˌkʌltʃər/ n the science of grapes and grape-growing.—**viticulturer, viticulturist** n.—**viticultural** adj.

vitreous /'vɪtriəs/ adj of like or obtained from glass; of the vitreous body.—**vitreousness** n.

vitreous body, vitreous humour n the transparent tissue of the eyeball.

vitrescence /vɪ'trɛsəns/ n the quality of being vitrescent; the process of changing something, such as a crystalline material, into glass.

vitrescent /-ənt/ adj capable of being made into or becoming like glass.

vitric /'vɪtrɪk/ adj glass-like.

vitrify /'vɪtrɪˌfaɪ/ vt (**vitrifying, vitrified**) to convert into glass or a glass-like substance.—**vitrifiable** adj.—**vitrification, vitrifaction** n.

vitriol /'vɪtriˌɒl/ or /'vɪtriəl/ n sulphuric acid; savage criticism. • vt (**vitrioling, vitrioled** or **vitriolling, vitriolled**) to throw vitriol over, to poison with vitriol.

vitriolic /ˌvɪtri'ɒlɪk/ adj of or relating to vitriol; scathing, bitter.

vitriolize /'vɪtriəˌlaɪz/ vt to harm by throwing vitriol over; to change into vitriol; to use vitriol in or as a part of the processing of something.—**vitriolization** n.

vitta /'vɪtə/ n (pl **vittae**) (bot) an oil tube in the fruit of some plants, eg parsley; (zool) a coloured stripe.—**vittate** adj.

vituline /'vɪtə/ adj of, like, calves or veal.

vituperate /vɪtu:pəˌreɪt/ or /-'tju:/, /vaɪ-/ vt to berate; to abuse verbally.—**vituperative** adj.—**vituperator** n.

vituperation /-'reɪʃən/ n the act of vituperating; blame, censure, reproof; the expression of this in abusive or violent language.

viva[1] /'vi:və/ interj long live, hurrah for.

viva[2] /'vaɪvə/ n an oral examination, a viva voce. • vt (**vivas** or **viva's, vivaing, vivaed** or **viva'd**) to examine orally.

vivace /vɪ'vɒtʃeɪ/ adv (mus) in a lively manner; with spirit.

vivacious /vɪ'veɪʃəs/ or /vaɪ-/ adj lively; animated; spirited.—**vivaciously** adv.—**vivaciousness** n.

vivacity /vɪ'væsiti/ n (pl **vivacities**) vivaciousness; animation of the mind or disposition; liveliness of conception or perception; spirited conduct, manner or speech; brilliancy of light or colour.

vivarium /vaɪ'vɛriəm/ or /vɪ-/ n (pl **vivariums, vivaria**) a place for keeping animals in their natural state for research or observation.

viva voce /ˌviːvə'vɒtʃeɪ/ or /'vo:tʃeɪ/ adj, adv orally, by word of mouth. • n an oral examination, a viva.

vivid /'vɪvɪd/ adj brightly coloured; graphic; lively; intense.—**vividly** adv.—**vividness** n.

vivify /'vɪvɪˌfaɪ/ vt (**vivifying, vivified**) to give life to; to make more lively or more vivid.—**vivification** n.—**vivifier** n.

viviparous /vɪ'vɪpərəs/ adj (zool) giving birth to young that have developed inside the body, as do most mammals.—**viviparity** n.—**viviparously** adv.

vivisect /'vɪvɪˌsɛkt/ or /-'sɛkt/ vt to subject to vivisection.—**vivisector** n.

vivisection /ˌvɪvɪ'sɛkʃən/ n the practice of performing surgical operations on living animals for scientific research.—**vivisectional** adj.

vivisectionist /-ɪst/ n a person who practises or approves of vivisection.

vixen /'vɪksən/ n a female fox; a malicious or shrewish woman.—**vixenish** adj.

viz. /vɪz/ abbr = videlicet namely.

vizard /'vɪzərd/ n (arch) a mask or other object that disguises; a visor.—also **visard**.

vizcacha /vɪs'kɒtʃə/ see **vischacha**.

vizier, vizir /'vɪziːər/ or /vɪ'ziːri/ n a minister of state or high official in Muslim countries, esp in the Ottoman Empire.

vizierate /-rət/ n the status, authority or (term of) office of a vizier.

vizor /vaɪ'zər/ see **visor**.

vocable /'voːkəbəl/ n (linguistics) a word looked on as a pattern of characters or sounds with no regard to meaning; a sound; a vowel. • adj able to be spoken.

vocabulary /və'kæbjuˌlɛri/ n (pl **vocabularies**) an alphabetical list of words with their meanings; the words of a language; an individual's command or use of particular words.

vocal /'vo:kəl/ *adj* of, for, endowed with, relating to, or produced by the voice; outspoken, noisy; (*phonetics*) having a vowel function. • *n* a vowel; (*pl*) music for the voice, not another instrument.—**vocally** *adv*.

vocal chords *npl* either of two pairs of elastic membranous folds in the larynx, *esp* the lower pair, which vibrate and produce sound.

vocalic /vo:'kælɪk/ *adj* of, like or containing vowels.

vocalise /vo:kə'li:z/ *n* a vocal exercise to improve flexibility and control of the voice in which a singer sings to one vowel sound.

vocalist /'vo:kəlɪst/ *n* a singer.

vocalize /'vo:kə,laɪz/ *vti* to express with the voice; to articulate, utter distinctly; to use the singing voice; to sing to vowel sounds; to write with vowels or vowel points.—**vocalization** *n*.—**vocalizer** *n*.

vocation /vo:'keɪʃən/ *n* a calling to a particular career or occupation, *esp* to a religious life; a sense of fitness for a particular career.

vocational /-əl/ *adj* of or relating to a vocation or occupation; providing special training for a particular career.—**vocationally** *adv*.

vocative /'vɒkətɪv/ *adj* used, involved in or pertaining to loud utterances to attract attention; (*gram*) denoting the case of a noun, adjective, or pronoun used in addressing a person in some inflected languages, *eg* Latin. • *n* (*gram*) a vocative case or form.

vociferant /vo:'sɪfər,ənt/ *adj* clamorous, noisy. • *n* a clamorous, noisy person.

vociferate /və'sɪfə,reɪt/ *vti* to speak loudly and insistently, to clamour; to shout, to bawl.—**vociferation** *n*.—**vociferator** *n*.

vociferous /vo:'sɪfərəs/ *adj* clamorous, noisy.—**vociferously** *adv*.—**vociferousness** *n*.

vodka /'vɒdkə/ *n* a spirit distilled from rye, potatoes, etc.

vogue /vo:g/ *n* the fashion at a specified time; popularity. • *adj* fashionable, in vogue.—**voguish** *adj*.

voice /vɔɪs/ *n* sound from the mouth; sound produced by speaking or singing; the quality of this; the power of speech; utterance; expressed opinion, vote; (*gram*) the forms of a verb showing the relation of subject to action; (*phonetics*) a sound uttered with vibration of the vocal chords not with mere breath. • *vt* to express; to speak; (*mus*) to regulate so as to give the correct tone; (*phonetics*) to utter with the voice, to make sonant.—**voicer** *n*.

voiced /-t/ *adj* having a voice, *esp* of a specified kind, quality or tone; (*phonetics*) uttered with the voice or vibration of the vocal chords, sonant.

voiceful /'vɔɪsful/ *adj* (*poet*) having a voice; sonorous.

voiceless /'vɔɪsləs/ *adj* speechless, dumb; (*phonetics*) not voiced.—**voicelessly** *adv*.—**voicelessness** *n*.

voice-over *n* the voice of an unseen narrator, *esp* in a film, TV commercial, etc.

void /vɔɪd/ *adj* unoccupied, empty; not legally binding; having no cards of a particular suit. • *n* an empty space, a vacuum; vacancy, sense of loss. • *vt* to discharge, to emit; empty; to make invalid.—**voidable** *adj*.—**voider** *n*.

voidance /'vɔɪdəns/ *n* the act of voiding or evacuating; emptiness; the annulment of a legal deed.

voided /-'vɔɪdɪd/ *adj* (*her*) having the inner part of a figure cut away, leaving only the outer edges; being, or having been caused to be, empty.

voile /vɔɪl/ or /vwɒl/ *n* a light, sheer fabric of silk, rayon, etc, used for dresses, scarves, etc.

volant /'vo:lənt/ *adj* flying; able to fly; (*her*) appearing to fly; (*poet*) nimble.

Volapuk, Volapük /'vo:lə,puk/ or /'vɒlə-/ *n* an artificial language taking elements from English, French, German, Latin. etc, invented in 1880 and intended for international commercial use.—**Volapukist, Volapükist** *n*.

volar /'vo:lər/ *adj* (*anat*) of the palm of the hand or sole of the foot.

volatile /'vɒlə,taɪl/ *adj* evaporating very quickly; changeable, fickle; unstable; light-hearted, mercurial; flighty; (*comput*) having a memory that loses data when power is disconnected.—**volatility** *n*.

volatilize /vɒ'lætɪ,laɪz/ *vti* to turn into vapour, to (cause to) evaporate.—**volatilization** *n*.

vol-au-vent /'vɒlo:,võ/ *n* a case of light puff pastry filled with a savoury sauce.

volcanic /vɒl'kænɪk/ *adj* of, like or due to the action of a volcano; violent, intense.—**volcanically** *adv*.

volcanism /'vɒlkənɪzəm/ *n* volcanic action.—*also* **vulcanism**.

volcanize /'vɒlkə,naɪz/ *vt* to subject to volcanic heat; to cause to change by means of volcanic heat.—**volcanization** *n*.

volcano /vɒl'keɪno:/ *n* (*pl* **volcanoes, volcanos**) a hill or mountain formed by ejection of lava, ashes, etc through an opening in the earth's crust.

volcanology /,vɒlkə'nɒlədʒi/ *n* the science of volcanoes and the occurrences associated with them.—*also* **vulcanology**.—**volcanological, vulcanological** *adj*.—**volcanologist, vulcanologist** *n*.

vole[1] /vo:l/ *n* a small rat-like rodent with a short tail.

vole[2] *vt* to win all the tricks in a deal. • *n* a slam.

volitant /'vɒlɪtənt/ *adj* able to fly, volant; flying, or otherwise moving about, in a rapid, nimble fashion.

volition /və'lɪʃən/ *n* the exercise of the will; choice.—**volitional** *adj*.

volitive /'vɒlɪtɪv/ *adj* pertaining to or having the power of will; (*gram*) desiderative; expressing a wish or intention.

volley /'vɒli/ *n* (*pl* **volleys**) the multiple discharge of many missiles or small arms; a barrage; (*tennis, volleyball*) the return of the ball before it reaches the ground. • *vt* (**volleying, volleyed**) to return (a ball) before it hits the ground.—**volleyer** *n*.

volleyball /-,bɒl/ *n* a team game played by hitting a large inflated ball over a net with the hands; the ball used.

volt[1] /vo:lt/ *n* the circular gait of a horse in dressage; (*fencing*) a leap to avoid a thrust.

volt[2] *n* the unit of measure of the force of an electrical current.

volta /'vo:ltə/ or /'vɒl/ *n* (*pl* **volte**) a lively 16th-century Italian dance; (*mus*) music in triple time, originally written to accompany such a dance; (*mus*) a particular time as specified.

voltage /'vo:ltɪdʒ/ *n* electrical energy that moves a charge around a circuit, measured in volts.

voltaic /vɒl'teɪɪk/ *adj* pertaining to electricity generated by chemical action or galvanism; galvanic.

voltaism /'vɒltə,ɪzəm/ *n* galvanism; electricity generated by chemical action.

voltameter /vɒl'tæmɪtər/ *n* an instrument for measuring an electric charge; a coulombmeter.

volte-face /vo:ltə'fæs/ *n* (*pl* **volte-faces, volte-face**) a change to an opposite opinion or direction.

voltmeter /'vo:lt,mi:tər/ *n* an instrument for measuring voltage.

voluble /'vɒljubəl/ *adj* speaking with a great flow of words, fluent; (*arch*) revolving, rotating; (*bot*) twining.—**volubility** *n*.—**volubly** *adv*.

volubleness /'vɒljubəlnəs/ *n* excessive fluency of speech.

volume /'vɒlju:m/ *n* the amount of space occupied by an object; quantity, amount; intensity of sound; a book; one book of a series.—**volumed** *adj*.

volumeter /vo:'ju:mətər/ *n* an instrument for measuring the volume of a gas, liquid, or solid.

volumetric /,vɒlju'metrɪk/ *adj* of or relating to measurement by volume.—**volumetrically** *adv*.

voluminous /və'lu:mɪnəs/ *adj* of great size or bulk; (*writings*) capable of filling many volumes; (*clothes*) ample, loose.—**voluminosity** *n*.—**voluminously** *adv*.

voluntarism /'vɒləntə,rɪzəm/ *n* the theory that the will is dominant over the intellect; a belief in voluntary participation not compulsion in a course of action; voluntaryism.—**voluntaryist** *n*.

voluntary /'vɒlən,teri/ *adj* spontaneous, deliberate; without remuneration; supported by voluntary effort; having free will; (*law*) acting gratuitously or from choice, not because of any legal compulsion or argument; (*muscles*) controlled by conscious effort; designed; pertaining to voluntaryism. • *n* (*pl* **voluntaries**) an organ solo, often improvised, played before or after a church service; (*arch*) a volunteer.—**voluntarily** *adv*.—**voluntariness** *n*.

voluntaryism /-təri,ɪzəm/ *n* the theory that churches, schools, etc, should depend on voluntary contributions, not state aid.—**voluntarist** *n*.—**voluntaristic** *adj*.

volunteer /,vɒlən'ti:r/ *n* a person who carries out work on a voluntary basis; a person who freely undertakes military service. • *vti* to offer unasked; to come forward, enlist or serve voluntarily.

voluptuary /vəˈlɛptʃʊˌɛri/ n (pl **voluptuaries**) a person given up to bodily pleasures or the enjoyment of luxury, a sensualist. • adj exciting sensual desire; devoted to pleasures of the senses; voluptuous; luxurious.

voluptuous /vəˈlɛptʃʊəs/ adj excessively fond of pleasure; having an attractive figure; luxurious; exciting sensual desire.— **voluptuously** adv.—**voluptuousness** n.

volute /ˈvɒljuːt/ or /vəˈljuːt/, /-ˈluːt/ n a spiral; a whorl; anything shaped to resemble a spiral or otherwise convoluted form; a spiral, scroll-shaped ornament, esp on an Ionic capital, a helix; a tropical shellfish with a spiral shell; any of the whorls found on the shells of snails; an auxiliary curved part of an engine that collects waste gases or liquids from that engine. • adj spiral-shaped; (machinery) moving spirally; (bot) rolled up.—also **voluted**.

volution /vəˈluːʃən/ n a spiral; a convoluted or turning shape or movement; any of the whorls of a shell.

volvox /ˈvɒlˌvɒks/ n a genus of round, hollow microscopic plants having a rotatory motion, found in ponds, etc.

vomer /ˈvoːmər/ n the flat, slender bone separating the nostrils in mammals.

vomit /ˈvɒmɪt/ vi to eject the contents of the stomach through the mouth, to spew. • n matter ejected from the stomach when vomiting.—**vomiter** n.

vomitive /ˈvɒmətɪv/ adj of or causing vomiting. • n an emetic.

vomitory /ˈvɒmɪtəri/ adj vomitive. • n (pl **vomitories**) an emetic; an aperture for vomited matter; any opening through which something is ejected; in ancient Rome, a corridor from a street entrance to a tier of seats in an amphitheatre.—also **vomitorium**.

vomiturition /ˌvɒmɪtjuːˈrɪʃən/ n violent retching; repeated vomiting.

voodoo /ˈvuːduː/ n (pl **voodoos**) a religious cult in the West Indies, based on a belief in sorcery, etc; one who practises voodoo. • vt (**voodooing, voodooed**) to affect by voodoo.

voodooism /-ˌɪzəm/ n the beliefs and practices of voodoo.— **voodooist** n.—**voodooistic** adj.

voracious /vəˈreɪʃəs/ adj eager to devour (food, literature etc); very greedy.—**voraciously** adv.—**voracity** n.

vortex /ˈvɔːteks/ n (pl **vortexes, vortices**) a whirlpool; a powerful eddy; a whirlwind; a whirling motion or mass.—**vortical** adj.—**vortically** adv.

vorticella /ˌvɔːtɪˈsɛlə/ n (pl **vorticellae**) any of a genus of ciliated, bell-shaped animalcules.

vorticism /ˈvɔːtəˌsɪzəm/ n an art movement in which cubist techniques were amalgamated with that aspect of futurism expressing reservations about the quality of contemporary life, and its reliance on machines, so that objects were presented so as to give the effect of an assemblage of vortices.—**vorticist** n.

vortiginous /vɔːˈtɪdʒənəs/ adj whirling, vortical; vortex-like.

votary /ˈvoːtəri/ n (pl **votaries**) a person vowed to religious service or worship; an ardent follower, a devotee of a person, religion, occupation, idea, etc.—also **votarist**. • adj ardently devoted to a deity or saint.

vote /voːt/ n an indication of a choice or opinion as to a matter on which one has a right to be consulted; a ballot; decision by a majority; the right to vote; franchise. • vi to cast one's vote. • vt to elect (to office).—**votable, voteable** adj.

voter /ˈvoːtər/ n a person with a right to vote, esp one who uses it.

votive /ˈvoːtɪv/ adj given, consecrated, or promised by vow; (RC Church) voluntary, given by free will not by prescription.

vouch /vaʊtʃ/ vt to provide evidence or proof of. • vi to give assurance; to guarantee.

voucher /ˈvaʊtʃər/ n a written record of a transaction; a receipt; a token that can be exchanged for something else.

vouchsafe /-ˈseɪf/ vt to give, to grant; to condescend (to).— **vouchsafement** n.

voussoir /ˈvuːswɒr/ n any of the wedge-shaped stones forming the arch of a bridge or vault.

vow /vaʊ/ n a solemn or binding promise. • vt to promise; to resolve.—**vower** n.

vowel /ˈvaʊəl/ n an open speech sound produced by continuous passage of the breath; a letter representing such a sound, as a, e, i, o, u. • adj of or constituting a vowel.—**vowelless** adj.

vowelize /ˈvaʊəlˌaɪz/ vt to insert vowel points in (usu something written in Hebrew).—**vowelization** n.

vowel point n a diacritical mark indicating a vowel in Hebrew, Arabic, etc.

vox /vɒks/ n (pl **voces**) a voice; a sound.

vox humana n an organ stop with tones like the human voice.

vox populi /ˌvɒksˈpɒpjuˌli/ n popular opinion; the voice of the people.

voyage /ˈvɔɪədʒ/ n a long journey, esp by ship or spacecraft. • vi to journey.—**voyager** n.

voyeur /vɔɪˈjɜr/ n a person who is sexually gratified from watching sexual acts or objects; a peeping Tom.—**voyeurism** n.— **voyeuristic** adj.

VP abbr = vice-president.

vraisemblance /vəˈraɪsɛmˌblɒns/ n an appearance of truth, verisimilitude.

vs abbr = versus against.

VSO abbr = Voluntary Service Overseas.

vug, vugh /vʌg/ n (mining) a small cavity, often crystal-lined, in a lode or rock.

Vulcan /ˈvʌlkən/ n (Roman myth) the god of fire and smiths; (arch) a planet once thought to orbit Mercury.

vulcanism /ˈvʌlkəˌnɪsm/ see **volcanism**.

vulcanite /ˈvʌlkəˌnaɪt/ n a hard, vulcanized rubber, which is resistant to the effects of chemicals, ebonite.

vulcanize /ˈvʌlkəˌnaɪz/ vt to treat (rubber) with sulphur, white lead and other substances at high temperatures under pressure to improve its strength and elasticity or render it hard and non-elastic; to change the properties of (any material) in a similar way.—**vulcanization** n.

vulcanology /ˌvʌlkəˈnɒlədʒi/ see **volcanology**.

vulgar /ˈvʌlgər/ adj of the common people; vernacular; unrefined, in bad taste; coarse; offensive, indecent.—**vulgarly** adv.—**vulgarness** n.

vulgarian /vʌlˈgeɪriən/ n a vulgar pretentious person, esp one who shows of his or her wealth.

vulgarism /ˈvʌlgəˌrɪzəm/ n a crude expression; coarseness.

vulgarity /vʌlˈgerɪti/ n (pl **vulgarities**) coarseness of manners or language; a vulgar phrase, expression, act, etc.

vulgarize /ˈvʌlgəˌraɪz/ vt to debase; to popularize.—**vulgarization** n.—**vulgarizer** n.

Vulgate /ˈvʌlgeɪt/ n a 4th-century Latin version of the Bible made by St Jerome, by combining text from the original language material and an earlier Latin text derived from the Greek; (RC Church) a revised form of this used as the authorized version. • adj pertaining to, or contained in, the Vulgate.

vulnerable /ˈvʌlnərəbəl/ adj capable of being wounded physically or mentally; open to persuasion; easily influenced; open to attack, assailable; (contract bridge) having won one game and liable to doubled penalties.—**vulnerability** n.—**vulnerably** adv.

vulnerary /ˈvʌlnərˌeri/ adj used for healing wounds. • n (pl **vulneraries**) a drug, ointment, etc, used in this way.

vulpine /ˈvʌlpaɪn/, **vulpecular** /vʌlˈpɛkjuːlər/ adj pertaining to, like, or characteristic of a fox; cunning.

vulture /ˈvʌltʃər/ n a large bird of prey having no feathers on the neck or head and feeding chiefly on carrion; a rapacious person.

vulturine /-ˌriːn/, **vulturous** /-əs/ adj vulture-like.

vulva /ˈvʌlvə/ n (pl **vulvae, vulvas**) the external genitals of human females.—**vulval, vulvar, vulvate** adj.

vulviform /ˈvʌlvəˌfɔrm/ adj like a cleft with projecting edges.

vulvitis /vʌlˈvaɪtɪs/ n inflammation of the vulva.

vying /ˈvaɪɪŋ/ see **vie**.

W

W (*chem symbol*) tungsten.

w *abbr* = watt(s); west.

W, w *n* the 23rd letter of the English alphabet.

WAAC *abbr* = (*formerly*) Women's Army Auxiliary Corps.

WAAF *abbr* = (*formerly*) Women's Auxiliary Air Force.

wacky /'wæki/ *adj* (**wackier, wackiest**) (*sl*) crazy, eccentric.—**wackily** *adv*.—**wackiness** *n*.

wad /wɒd/ *n* a small, soft mass, as of cotton or paper; a bundle of paper money.

wadding /'wɒdɪŋ/ *n* any soft material for use in padding, packing, etc.

waddle /'wɒdəl/ *vi* to walk with short steps and sway from side to side, as a duck.—*also n*.

waddy /wɒdiː/ *n* (*pl* **waddies**) a club with a thickened head used as a weapon by Australian Aborigines. • *vt* (**waddying, waddied**) to hit with a waddy.

wade /weɪd/ *vti* to walk through water; to pass (through) with difficulty.

wader /'weɪdər/ *n* a bird that wades, *eg* the heron; (*pl*) high waterproof boots worn by anglers.

wadi, wady /'wɒdi/ *n* a channel of a stream in North Africa which is dry except in the rainy season.

wafer /'weɪfər/ *n* a thin crisp cracker or biscuit; (*Christianity*) the disc of unleavened bread used in the Eucharist.

waffle[1] /'wɒfəl/ *n* a thick, crisp pancake baked in a waffle iron.

waffle[2] *vi* (*esp Brit inf*) to speak or write at length without saying anything substantial.

waffle iron *n* a metal cooking utensil with two hinged metal parts that close and impress a square pattern on a waffle.

waft /wɒft/ *or* /wæft/ *vt* to drift or float through the air. • *n* a breath, scent or sound carried through the air.

wag[1] /wæg/ *vti* (**wagging, wagged**) to move rapidly from side to side or up and down (as of a finger, tail).—*also n*.

wag[2] *n* a joker, a wit.

wage /weɪdʒ/ *vt* to carry on, *esp* war. • *n* (*often pl*) payment for work or services.

wage earner *n* a person who works for wages.

wager /'weɪdʒər/ *n* a bet. • *vti* to bet.

waggle /'wægəl/ *vti* to wag.—*also n*.

Wagnerian /vɒg'nɪərɪən/ *n* of or resembling the music of Richard Wagner (1813–83), characterized by dramatic grandeur and emotional intensity.

wagon /'wægən/ *n* a four-wheeled vehicle pulled by a horse or tractor, for carrying heavy goods.

wagoner /-ər/ *n* a driver of a wagon.

wagon-lit /-lit/ *n* (*pl* **wagons-lits**) a sleeping-car on a European train.

wagtail /'wægteɪl/ *n* any of numerous small birds with tails that jerk constantly.

wah-wah /'wɒwɒ/ *n* the sound of a trumpet, etc when alternately muted and unmuted; a pedal or lever used with an electric guitar, etc to imitate this sound.

waif /weɪf/ *n* a homeless, neglected child.

wail /weɪl/ *vi* to make a long, loud cry of sorrow or grief; to howl, to moan.—*also n*.

wain /weɪn/ *n* (*poet*) a farm wagon.

wainscot /'weɪnskɒt/ *n* wooden panelling on the interior of a wall.—*also* **wainscoting**. • *vt* to line (a wall) with a wainscot.

wainwright /-raɪt/ *n* a person who builds wagons.

waist /weɪst/ *n* the narrowest part of the human trunk, between the ribs and the hips; the narrow part of anything that is wider at the ends; the part of a garment covering the waist.

waistband /'weɪstbænd/ *n* a band of material (on a skirt, trousers, etc) that strengthens and completes the waist.

waistcoat /-kəʊt/ *n* a waist-length, sleeveless garment worn immediately under a suit jacket; a vest.

waistline /-laɪn/ *n* the narrowest part of the waist; its measurement; the seam that joins the bodice and skirt of a dress, etc; the level of this.

wait /weɪt/ *vti* to stay, or to be, in expectation or readiness; to defer or to be postponed; to remain; (*with* **at** *or* **on**) to serve food at a meal. • *n* act or period of waiting.

waiter /'weɪtər/ *n* a man or woman who serves at table, as in a restaurant.—**waitress** *nf*.

waiting /-ɪŋ/ *n* the act of remaining inactive or stationary; a period of waiting. • *adj* of or pertaining to a wait; in attendance.

waiting game *n* a delay in acting or deciding in order to benefit from more favourable circumstances later.

waiting list *n* a list of people applying for or waiting to obtain something.

waiting room *n* a room for people to wait in at a station, hospital, etc.

waive /weɪv/ *vt* to refrain from enforcing; to relinquish voluntarily.

waiver /'weɪvər/ *n* (*law*) a waiving of a right, claim etc.

wake[1] /weɪk/ *vb* (**waking, woke**, *pp* **woken**) *vi* to emerge from sleep; to become awake. • *vt* to rouse from sleep. • *n* a watch or vigil beside a corpse, on the eve of the burial.—**wakeful** *adj*.—**waken** *vti*.

wake[2] *n* the waves or foamy water left in the track of a ship; a trail.

wale /weɪl/ *n* a ridge or mark on the body, a weal; a ridge on a ribbed material such as corduroy; a heavy plank along a ship's side.

Walhalla /vælhæl'ə/ *or* /vɒlhɒl'ə/ *see* **Valhalla**.

walk /wɒk/ *vi* to travel on foot with alternate steps; (*with* **out**) to leave suddenly; to go on strike; (*with* **on**) to abandon, jilt. • *vt* to pass through or over; (*a dog*) to exercise; to escort on foot. • *n* the act of walking; distance walked over; gait; a ramble or stroll; a profession.—**walker** *n*.

walkabout /'wɔːkəbaʊt/ *n* a ceremonial wander through the Australian bush made periodically by an Aborigine; an informal stroll through a crowd by a politician, celebrity, etc.

walkie-talkie, walky-talky /ˌwɒkiˈtɒki/ *n* (*pl* **walkie-talkies, walky-talkies**) a portable two-way radio transmitter and receiver.

walk-in *adj* (*cupboard*) large enough to enter and move around in.

walking /'wɔːkɪŋ/ *adj* able to walk; appearing to walk; ambulatory; marked by travelling on foot (*walking holiday*); intended for walkers (*walking boots*); in animate form (*walking bomb*). • *n* the act of walking; gait; the condition of a track, etc.

walking papers *n* (*sl*) notice of dismissal.

walking stick *n* a stick used in walking, a cane.

Walkman /'wɔːkmən/ *n* (*trademark*) a small portable cassette player (and sometimes radio) used with earphones.

walk-on *n* a small (*esp* non-speaking) part in a play.

walkout /'wɔːkaʊt/ *n* a strike; a sudden departure.

walkover /-əʊvər/ *n* an unopposed or easy victory; a horse race with only one starter.

walk-through *n* a rehearsal.

walkway /'wɔːkweɪ/ *n* road, path, etc, for pedestrians only.

Walkyrie /vælˈkɪriː/ *or* /ˈvælkəriː/ *see* **Valkyrie**.

wall /wɒl/ *n* a vertical structure of brick, stone, etc for enclosing, dividing or protecting. • *vt* to enclose with a wall; to close up with a wall.

wallaby /'wɒləbi/ *n* (*pl* **wallabies, wallaby**) a small kangaroo-like animal.

wallah, walla /'wɒlə/ *n* (*inf*) a person with a specified job or responsibility.

wallaroo /ˌwɒləˈruː/ *n* (*pl* **wallaroos, wallaroo**) a type of large kangaroo.

walled /wɒld/ *adj* having walls; surrounded or protected as if by walls; fortified.

wallet /'wɒlət/ *n* a small folding case for paper money, cards etc.

walleye /'wɒlaɪ/ *n* an eye with an opaque cornea; any eye with a pale or white iris; a squint in which an eye turns outward; a large North American freshwater fish with prominent eyes.

wallflower /'wɒlˌflaʊr/ *n* a fragrant plant with red or yellow flowers; a person who does not dance for lack of a partner.

Walloon /wɒ'luːn/ *n* a member of a French-speaking people of southern Belgium and adjacent areas of France; the French dialect of Walloons.—*also adj*.

wallop /'wɒləp/ vt (inf) to beat or defeat soundly; (inf) to strike hard. • n (inf) a hard blow.

walloping /-ɪŋ/ adj (inf) large, massive. • n (inf) a thrashing, a defeat.

wallow /'wɒloː/ vi (animal) to roll about in mud; to indulge oneself in emotion.—also n.

wallpaper /'wɒl͵peɪpər/ n decorated paper for covering the walls of a room.

Wall Street n a street in New York where the Stock Exchange is situated; the centre of American finance.

wall-to-wall /'wɒltuːˈwɒl/ adj (carpet) covering the whole area of a room; (inf) nonstop, continuous.

wally /'wɒli/ n (pl wallies) (sl) an idiot.

walnut /-nʌt/ n a tree producing an edible nut with a round shell and wrinkled seed; its nut; its wood used for furniture.

walrus /-rəs/ n (pl walruses, walrus) a large, thick-skinned aquatic animal, related to the seals, having long canine teeth and coarse whiskers.

walrus moustache n a thick drooping moustache.

waltz /wɒlts/ n a piece of music with three beats to the bar; a whirling or slowly circling dance. • vi to dance a waltz.

wampum /'wɒmpəm/ n polished shells strung like beads formerly used as money by North American Indians.

wan /wɒn/ adj (wanner, wannest) pale and sickly; feeble or weak.—wanly adv.—wanness n.

wand /wɒnd/ n a magician's rod.

wander /'wɒndər/ vi to ramble with no definite destination; to go astray; to lose concentration.—also n.

wandering Jew n any of various trailing or climbing plants; (with cap) a legendary figure condemned by Christ to roam the world until the Day of Judgement as punishment for an insult.

wanderlust /-͵lʌst/ n a compelling desire for travel.

wane /weɪn/ vi to decrease, esp of the moon; to decline. • n decrease, decline.

wangle /'wæŋɡəl/ vti (inf) to achieve (something) by devious means.

wannabe, wannabee /'wɒnəbi/ n someone who aspires to be like someone else (who is usu successful or famous) perhaps in appearance, mode of dress etc. • adj would-be, aspiring.

want /wɒnt/ n lack; poverty. • vt to need; to require; to lack; to wish (for).

want ad n (inf) a newspaper or magazine advertisement requesting an item, job, etc.

wanted /'wɒntəd/ adj sought after.

wanting /-ɪŋ/ adj lacking.

wanton /-ən/ adj malicious; wilful; sexually provocative.

wapiti /'wɒpɪti/ n (pl wapitis) a large deer of North America.

war /wɔr/ n military conflict between nations or parties; a conflict; a contest. • vi (warring, warred) to make war.

warble /'wɔrbəl/ vi to sing with trills and runs; to sing like a bird.

warble fly n a species of fly the larvae of which burrow under the skin of cattle causing painful lumps.

warbler /wɔrblər/ n any of a family of small Old World songbirds which includes the nightingale and robin.

war crime n a crime committed in wartime (such as mistreatment of prisoners) which violates conventional notions of decency.

war cry n a rallying call in battle; a party catchword.

ward /wɔrd/ n a section of a hospital; an electoral district; a division of a prison; a child placed under the supervision of a court. • vt (with off) to repel; to fend off.—wardship n.

-ward /wərd/, **-wards** /-z/ adj suffix indicating a certain direction.

war dance n a ritual dance before or after battle as practised by certain North American Indian tribes.

warden /'wɔrdən/ n an official; a person in charge of a building or home; a prison governor.

warder /-ər/ n (Brit) a prison officer.

ward heeler n (sl) a local political hanger-on for a politician.

wardrobe /-roːb/ n a cupboard for clothes; one's clothes.

wardroom /-ruːm/ n a room in a warship for use by officers with the exception of the captain.

ware /wɛr/ n (pl) merchandise, goods for sale; pottery.

warehouse /'wɛrhʊs/ n a building for storing goods.

warfare /'wɔrfɛr/ n armed hostilities; conflict.

warfarin /-fərɪn/ n a crystalline substance used in medicine as an anticoagulant and also as a poison to kill rodents.

war game n a simulated battle or tactical exercise using models or computers for military training; a re-enactment of a battle using model soldiers.

warhead /-hed/ n the section of a missile containing the explosive.

warhorse /-hors/ n a horse used in battle; (inf) a veteran of military or political conflict.

warlike /-laɪk/ adj hostile.

warlock /-lɒk/ n a sorcerer, a magician.

warlord /-lord/ n a military leader or ruler of (part of) a country.

warm /wɔrm/ adj moderately hot; friendly, kind; (colours) rich; enthusiastic. • vt to make warm. • vi to become enthusiastic (about). —warmly adv.—warmth n.

warm-blooded /-blʌdɪd/ adj having a constant and relatively high temperature; passionate.

warm front n the edge of an advancing mass of warm air.

warm-hearted /-ˈhɑrtəd/ adj kind, sympathetic; affectionate.

warming pan n a long-handled (usu copper) pan filled with hot coals and formerly used to warm a bed.

warmonger /'wɔr͵mɒŋɡər/ or /-͵mʌŋɡər/ n a person who incites war, esp for personal gain; warrior, a fighting soldier.

warm-up /-ʌp/ n a period of exercise or practice before a race, etc.

warn /wɔrn/ vt to notify of danger; to caution or advise (against).—warning n.

warp /wɔrp/ vti to twist out of shape; to distort; to corrupt. • n the threads arranged lengthwise on a loom across which other threads are passed.

war paint n paint smeared on the face and body by North American Indians before entering battle; (inf) formal or ceremonial dress, regalia; (inf) cosmetics.

warpath /'wɔrpæθ/ n the route used by a war party of North American Indians; (with on the) on a hostile expedition; (with on the) (inf) angry.

warped /wɔrpt/ adj distorted, twisted; embittered.

warplane /'wɔrpleɪn/ n an aircraft for use in combat.

warrant /'wɔrənt/ vt to guarantee; to justify. • n a document giving authorization; a writ for arrest.

warrantee /͵wɔrənˈtiː/ n somebody to whom a warrant is given.

warrant officer n a person in the armed services holding a rank between commissioned officers and NCOs.

warrantor /-ər/ n a person or company that offers a warranty.

warranty /'wɔrənti/ n (pl warranties) a pledge to replace something if it is not as represented, a guarantee.

warren /'wɔrən/ n an area in which rabbits breed.

warring /-ɪŋ/ adj engaged in war.

warrior /-ɪər/ n a soldier, fighter.

warship /-ʃɪp/ n a ship equipped for war.

wart /wɔrt/ n a small, hard projection on the skin.—warty adj.

wart hog n an African wild pig with warty lumps on the face, large tusks and thick course hair.

wartime /-taɪm/ adj, n (of) a period or time of war.

wary /'wɛri/ adj (warier, wariest) watchful; cautious.—warily adv.—wariness n.

was /wɒz/ or /wəz/ see be.

wash /wɒʃ/ vti to cleanse with water and soap; to flow against or over; to sweep along by the action of water; to separate gold, etc, from earth by washing; to cover with a thin coat of metal or paint; (with down) to wash thoroughly from top to bottom; to take a drink of liquid to help in swallowing food. • n a washing; the break of waves on the shore; the waves left behind by a boat; a liquid used for washing.

washable /'wɒʃəbəl/ adj able to be washed without damage.—washability n.

washboard /-bord/ n a corrugated board used (esp formerly) for scrubbing clothes.

washbowl /'wɒʃboːl/, **washbasin** /-beɪsɪn/ n a basin or bowl, esp a bathroom fixture, for use in washing one's hands, etc.—also wash-hand basin.

washcloth /-klɒθ/ n the US word for a face cloth or flannel.

washed-out adj faded in colour; fatigued.

washed-up adj unsuccessful, ineffective; unpromising.

washer /-ər/ n a flat ring of metal, rubber, etc, to give tightness to joints; a washing machine.

washing /-ɪŋ/ n the act of cleansing with water; a number of items washed together.

washing machine n a device for washing clothes.

washing powder n a powdered detergent formulated for washing fabrics.

washing soda *n* sodium carbonate dissolved in water used for washing and cleaning.

washing-up *n* the washing of dishes and cutlery after a meal; the dishes and cutlery waiting to be washed.

washout /-ɐʊt/ *n* (*sl*) a failure.

washroom /-ruːm/ *n* cloakroom; a US word for the lavatory.

washstand /-stænd/ *n* a piece of furniture for holding a bowl and jug of water used for washing.

washtub /-tʌb/ *n* a large tub used for washing clothes.

washy /-i/ *adj* (**washier, washiest**) weak, watery; pale; lacking in strength or vigour.—**washiness** *n*.

wasn't /'wɛzənt/ = was not.

wasp /wɒsp/ *n* a winged insect with a black and yellow striped body, which can sting.

Wasp, WASP *n* an American of northern European, *esp* British, descent and Protestant upbringing, regarded as belonging to the most privileged group in American society (*White Anglo-Saxon Protestant*).

waspish /'wɒspɪʃ/ *adj* sharp in speech or manner; irritable.

wasp waist *n* a very slender waist.

wassail /'wɒseɪl/ or /'wɒsəl/ *n* (*formerly*) a toast made at festivities; a festive celebration with a lot of drinking and merriment; spiced ale or mulled wine served (*esp* formerly) at Christmas or other festive occasions. • *vi* to make merry.

Wassermann test /'wɒsərmən/ *n* a blood test used to diagnose syphilis.

wastage /'weɪstɪdʒ/ *n* anything lost by use or natural decay; wasteful or avoidable loss of something valuable.

waste /weɪst/ *adj* useless; left over; uncultivated or uninhabited. • *vt* to ravage; to squander; to use foolishly; to fail to use. • *vi* to lose strength, etc as by disease. • *n* uncultivated or uninhabited land; discarded material, garbage, excrement.—**wasteful** *adj*.—**wastefully** *adv*.—**wastefulness** *n*.

wasted /'weɪstəd/ *adj* ravaged, devastated; not used to best advantage; weak, emaciated; (*sl*) dead, killed; (*sl*) showing the effects of alcohol or drug abuse.

wasteland /-lænd/ *n* a piece of barren or uncultivated land; a desolate region; something (*eg* a period of time, relationship) lacking in moral, spiritual, emotional, etc vitality.

wastepaper /-peɪpər/ *n* paper discarded as waste.

wastepipe /-paɪp/ *n* a pipe carrying off used water from sinks, baths, etc.

waster /-ər/ *n* a wasteful person or thing; a good-for-nothing.

wasting asset *n* a non-renewable resource such as a coal mine.

wastrel /-rəl/ *n* a vagabond; a waster, idler.

watch /wɒtʃ/ *n* surveillance; close observation; vigil; guard; a small timepiece worn on the wrist, etc; a period of duty on a ship. • *vi* to look with attention; to wait for; to keep vigil. • *vt* to keep one's eyes fixed on; to guard; to tend; to observe closely; (*chance, etc*) to wait for.—**watcher** *n*.—**watchful** *adj*.—**watchfully** *adv*.—**watchfulness** *n*.

watchband /'wɒtʃbænd/ *n* a strap of leather, etc, for securing a watch to the wrist.

watchcase /'wɒtʃkeɪs/ *n* a protective metal casing for a watch mechanism.

watchdog /-dɒg/ *n* a dog that guards property; a person or group that monitors safety, standards, etc.

watchmaker /-meɪkər/ *n* a person who makes and repairs watches.

watchman /-mən/ *n* (*pl* **watchmen**) a person who guards a building or other property.

watch night *n* a religious service on New Year's Eve.

watchtower /-tauər/ *n* a tower for a sentry to keep watch from.

watchword /-wərd/ *n* a password.

water /'wɒtər/ *n* the substance H_2O, a clear, thin liquid, lacking taste or smell, and essential for life; any body of it, as the ocean, a lake, river, etc; bodily secretions such as tears, urine. • *vt* to moisten with water; to irrigate; to dilute with water; (*with down*) to dilute; to reduce in strength or effectiveness. • *vi* (*eyes*) to smart; to salivate; to take in water.

water bed /-bed/ *n* a bed with a water-filled mattress.

water bird *n* any swimming or wading bird.

water biscuit *n* a thin, crisp biscuit, *usu* served with cheese.

water blister *n* a blister on the skin filled with watery fluid instead of blood.

water boatman *n* any of various aquatic bugs adapted for swimming.

waterborne /-bɔrn/ *adj* floating on or travelling by water.

waterbuck /-bʌk/ *n* an African antelope which lives in swampy areas.

water buffalo *n* a common domesticated Asian buffalo.

water cannon *n* an apparatus for pumping water at high pressure to disperse crowds.

water chestnut *n* an Asian aquatic plant with edible nutlike fruit; (the edible tuber of) a Chinese plant with a succulent root.

water clock *n* a clock with a mechanism operated by flowing or dripping water.

water-closet *n* a lavatory.

watercolour, watercolor /-kələr/ *n* a water-soluble paint; a picture painted with watercolours.

water-cooled *adj* (*engine etc*) cooled by the circulation of water.

watercourse /-kɔrs/ *n* (a channel for) a stream, river or canal.

watercraft /-kræft/ *n* skill in handling boats and other vessels; a vessel travelling by water.

watercress /-krɛs/ *n* a plant growing in ponds and streams, used in a salad.

water cure *n* hydropathy.

water diviner *n* a person who searches for water using a divining rod.

waterfall /-fɔl/ *n* a fall of water over a precipice or down a hill.

water flea *n* any of numerous tiny freshwater crustaceans.

waterfowl /-faʊl/ *n* (*pl* **waterfowl**) a bird that frequents lakes, rivers, etc, esp a duck.

waterfront /-frʌnt/ *n* an area alongside a body of water, *esp* a docks.

water gas *n* a toxic inflammable mixture of carbon monoxide and hydrogen produced by passing steam over hot carbon, used as a fuel.

water glass /-glæs/ *n* a solution of sodium or potassium silicate in water used as a protective coating and to preserve eggs.

water hammer *n* (the sound of) the concussion of water in a pipe when a blockage is suddenly dislodged.

water hole *n* a water-filled hollow where animals drink.

water hyacinth *n* a floating aquatic plant of tropical America that often blocks waterways with its dense growth.

water ice *n* an iced dessert made from frozen water, sugar and a flavouring.

watering can *n* a container with a spout for watering plants.

watering hole *n* (*inf*) a bar or pub.

watering place *n* a place where animals or people can obtain water; a spa resort.

water jacket *n* a casing filled with water used for cooling machinery.

water jump *n* a ditch filled with water used as an obstacle in a steeplechase and other sporting contests.

water level *n* the surface level of water in a reservoir, etc.

water lily *n* any of a family of plants with large floating leaves and showy flowers.

waterline /-laɪn/ *n* a line up to which a ship's hull is submerged.

waterlogged /-lɒgd/ *adj* soaked or saturated with water.

water main *n* a main pipe or conduit for carrying water.

watermark /-mɑrk/ *n* a line marking the height to which water has risen; a mark impressed on paper which can only be seen when held up to the light.

watermelon /-mɛlən/ *n* a large fruit with a hard green rind and edible red watery flesh.

water mill /-mɪl/ *n* a mill operated by a water wheel.

water pistol *n* a toy gun that shoots a stream of water.

water polo *n* a game played in water by two teams of seven swimmers with the aim of scoring by hitting a ball into the opponents' goal.

water power *n* the power of falling or moving water used to operate machinery or generate electricity.

waterproof /-pruːf/ *adj* impervious to water; watertight.—*also vt*.

water-repellent *adj* (*fabrics, etc*) treated with a substance that prevents penetration by water.

water-resistant *adj* (*fabrics, etc*) designed to resist water penetration as long as possible.

watershed /-ʃed/ *n* a turning point.

waterside /-saɪd/ *n* the edge of a body of water.

water-skiing *n* the sport of planing on water by being towed by a motorboat.—**water-skier** *n*.

water softener *n* a device or chemical designed to counteract chemicals that cause hardness in water.

water-soluble *adj* capable of dissolving in water.

water spaniel *n* a breed of large curly-coated spaniel used in hunting waterfowl.

waterspout /-,spɐʊt/ *n* a pipe for draining water; a tall column of water formed by a whirlwind and reaching from the sea to the clouds.

water table *n* the level below which the ground is saturated with water.

watertight /-,təɪt/ *adj* not allowing water to pass through; foolproof.

water tower *n* an elevated tank or reservoir to allow water to be supplied under pressure.

waterway /-,weɪ/ *n* a navigable channel of water.

water wheel *n* a wheel designed to be turned by running water and used to drive machinery; a wheel used for raising water.

water wings *npl* inflatable rubber floats worn on the arms of those learning to swim.

waterworks /-,wɜrks/ *n* (*as sing*) an establishment that supplies water to a district; (*pl: inf*) the urinary system; (*inf*) tears.

waterworn /-wɔrn/ *adj* rubbed smooth by the action of water.

watery /-i/ *adj* thin, diluted.

watt /ˈwɒt/ *n* a unit of electrical power.

wattage /-ɪdʒ/ *n* amount of electrical power.

wattle /ˈwɒtəl/ *n* (material for) a framework of stakes or poles interwoven with thin branches, twigs, etc formerly used for fencing and building; a loose flap of skin hanging from the necks of certain birds and lizards; an Australian acacia tree with small brightly-coloured flowers. • *vt* to build of or with wattle; to interweave or interlace (with sticks, etc) to make a light frame.

wave /weɪv/ *n* an undulation travelling on the surface of water; the form in which light and sound are thought to travel; an increase or upsurge (*eg* of crime); a hair curl; a movement of the hand in greeting or farewell. • *vti* to move freely backward and forward; to flutter; to undulate; to move the hand to and fro in greeting, farewell, etc; (*with* **down**) to signal (a vehicle, etc) to stop with a wave.—**wavy** *adj*.

wave band /ˈweɪvbænd/ *n* a range of radio frequencies or wavelengths.

waveguide /-gaɪd/ *n* a metal tube used to guide microwaves along a particular path.

wavelength /-leŋθ/ or /-leŋkθ/ *n* the distance between the crests of successive waves of light or sound; radio frequency.

wavelet /-lət/ *n* a small wave.

wave mechanics *n sing* (*physics*) the theory in quantum mechanics that describes the behaviour of elementary particles in terms of their wave properties.

waver /ˈweɪvər/ *vi* to hesitate; to falter.—**waverer** *n*.

wax[1] /wæks/ *n* beeswax; an oily substance used to make candles, polish, etc. • *vt* to rub, polish, cover or treat with wax.

wax[2] *vi* to increase in strength, size, etc.

waxen /ˈwæksən/ *adj* made of wax; pale and smooth like wax.

wax paper *n* paper that has been rendered moistureproof by treating with wax.

waxwork /-wɜrk/ *n* a figure or model formed of wax; (*pl*) an exhibition of such figures.

waxy /-i/ *adj* (**waxier, waxiest**) consisting of or like wax; adhesive.—**waxily** *adv*.—**waxiness** *n*.

way /weɪ/ *n* path, route; road; distance; room to advance; direction; state; means; possibility; manner of living; (*pl*) habits.

waybill /ˈweɪbɪl/ *n* a document with list of goods and shipping instructions accompanying a shipment.

wayfarer /-,ferər/ *n* a traveller.

waylay /weɪˈleɪ/ *vt* (**waylaying, waylaid**) to lie in wait for; to accost.

way-out /-aʊt/ *adj* (*inf*) unconventional, unusual; amazing.

-ways /-z/ *adv suffix* indicating a certain direction or manner.

ways and means *npl* the methods used to accomplish something; the revenues and means of raising revenues for the use of government.

wayside /ˈweɪsaɪd/ *n* the side of or land adjacent to a road.

wayward /-wərd/ *adj* wilful, stubborn; unpredictable.—**waywardness** *n*.

WBA *abbr* = World Boxing Association.

WBC *abbr* = World Boxing Council.

WC *abbr* = water-closet.

we /wiː/ *pron pl* of I; I and others.

weak /wiːk/ *adj* lacking power or strength; feeble; ineffectual.—**weakness** *n*.

weaken /ˈwiːkən/ *vti* to make or grow weaker.

weak interaction *n* (*physics*) an interaction between elementary particles that is responsible for certain particle decay processes.

weak-kneed /ˈwiːk,niːd/ *adj* (*inf*) submissive, easily intimidated.

weakling /-lɪŋ/ *n* a person who lacks strength of character.

weakly /-li/ *adj* (**weaklier, weakliest**) not robust; sickly. • *adv* in a weak manner, feebly.

weak-minded /-,maɪndɪd/ *adj* lacking in determination; feeble-minded.

weal /wiːl/ *n* a raised mark on the skin left by a blow with a lash.

wealth /welθ/ *n* a large amount of possessions or money; affluence; an abundance (of).—**wealthy** *adj*.

wean /wiːn/ *vt* (*baby, animal*) to replace the mother's milk with other nourishment; to dissuade (from indulging a habit).

weapon /ˈwepən/ *n* any instrument used in fighting.

weaponry /-ri/ *n* weapons collectively.

wear /wer/ *vb* (**wearing, wore**, *pp* **worn**) *vt* to have on the body as clothing; (*hair, etc*) to arrange in a particular way; to display; to rub away; to impair by use; to exhaust, tire; (*with* **down**) to overcome gradually through persistent pressure; (*with* **out**) to tire or exhaust. • *vi* to be impaired by use or time; to be spent tediously; (*with* **off**) to become gradually weaker in effect; (*with* **out**) to make or become worthless through prolonged use. • *n* deterioration from frequent use; articles worn.—**wearer** *n*.

wearable /ˈwerəbəl/ *adj* suitable to be worn.

wear and tear *n* deterioration or depreciation from everyday use.

wearing /-ɪŋ/ *adj* exhausting, tiresome, oppressive.

weary /ˈwiːri/ *adj* (**wearier, weariest**) tired; bored. • *vti* (**wearying, wearied**) to make or become tired.—**weariness** *n*.—**wearisome** *adj*.

weasel /ˈwiːzəl/ *n* a small carnivorous animal with a long slender body and reddish fur.

weasel words *npl* (*inf*) evasive or misleading talk.

weather /ˈweðər/ *n* atmospheric conditions, such as temperature, rainfall, cloudiness, etc. • *vt* to expose to the action of the weather; to survive. • *vi* to withstand the weather.

weather-beaten /-,biːtən/ *adj* worn or damaged by the weather; hardened or bronzed through exposure to the weather.

weatherboard /-,bɔrd/ *n* a sloping, *usu* overlapping, timber board used as external cladding for a wall or roof.—**weatherboarding** *n*.

weather-bound /-,baʊnd/ *adj* delayed or postponed due to bad weather.

weathercock /-,kɒk/ *n* a weather vane in the form of a cock to show the wind direction.

weathered /ˈweðərd/ *adj* affected or seasoned by exposure to the weather; (*rocks*) altered in shape by erosion; (*roof*) having a sloped surface to allow rainwater to escape.

weather eye *n* an eye trained to observe changes in the weather; (*inf*) an alert or watchful gaze.

weatherglass *n* a barometer.

weathering /-ɪŋ/ *n* the erosion of rocks through the action of the wind, rain, frost, etc.

weatherman /-,mæn/ *n* (*pl* **weathermen**) a weather forecaster on radio or television who is usually also a professional meteorologist.

weather map *n* a chart showing weather conditions over a particular area for a specified period.

weatherproof /-pruːf/ *adj* designed to withstand exposure to weather without damage or deterioration.—*also vt*.

weather station *n* a meteorological post for collecting, recording and transmitting data on weather conditions.

weather vane *n* a device attached to a tall structure to indicate wind direction.

weave /wiːv/ *vb* (**weaving, wove**, *pp* **woven**) *vt* to interlace threads in a loom to form fabric; to construct. • *vi* to make a way through (*eg* a crowd), to zigzag.—**weaver** *n*.

weaverbird /ˈwiːvərbərd/ *n* any of various Old World songbirds that build nests of interwoven grass, twigs, etc, including the house sparrow.

Web *n* short for Worldwide Web.

web /web/ *n* a woven fabric; the fine threads spun by a spider; the membrane joining the digits of birds, animals.

webbed /-d/ *adj* (*ducks, etc*) having the digits connected by a fold of skin.

webbing /ˈwebɪŋ/ *n* a strong narrow woven fabric of jute, cotton, etc, used for straps and belts; anything forming a web.

weber /'veɪbər/ *n* the SI unit of magnetic flux.

wed /wɛd/ *vti* (**wedding, wedded** *or* **wed**) to marry; to join closely.

Wed *abbr* = Wednesday.

we'd /wi:d/ = we had; we would.

wedded /'wɛdɪd/ *adj* of or resulting from marriage; devoted (to art, etc).

wedding /-ɪŋ/ *n* marriage; the ceremony of marriage.

wedding cake *n* an ornately decorated rich fruit cake, *usu* in three tiers, served at a wedding.

wedding ring *n* a band of gold or platinum used at a wedding and worn to show marital status.

wedge /wɛdʒ/ *n* a v-shaped block of wood or metal for splitting or fastening; a wedge-shaped object. • *vti* to split or secure with a wedge; to thrust (in) tightly; to become fixed tightly.

wedlock /'wɛdlɒk/ *n* marriage.

Wednesday /'wɛnzdeɪ/ *or* /-di/ *n* fourth day of the week, between Tuesday and Thursday.

wee[1] /wi:/ *adj* (*Scot*) small, tiny.

wee[2] *n* (*inf*) the act of passing urine; urine. • *vt* (*inf*) to pass urine.—*also* **wee-wee**.

weed /wi:d/ *n* any undesired plant, *esp* one that crowds out desired plants; (*sl*) marijuana; (*pl*) a widow's black mourning clothes. • *vt* to remove weeds; (*with* **out**) to remove or eliminate (something superfluous or harmful).

weedkiller /'wi:dkɪlər/ *n* a chemical or hormonal substance used to kill weeds.

weedy /'wi:di/ *adj* (**weedier, weediest**) full of weeds; (*inf*) thin and scrawny.

week /wi:k/ *n* the period of seven consecutive days, *esp* from Sunday to Sunday.

weekday /'wi:kdeɪ/ *n* a day of the week other than Saturday or Sunday.

weekend, week-end /-ɛnd/ *or* /-'ɛnd/ *n* the period from Friday night to Sunday night.—*also adj*.

weekly /-li/ *adj* happening once a week or every week.

weeknight /-naɪt/ *n* the evening or night of a weekday.

weeny /'wi:ni/ *adj* (**weenier, weeniest**) (*inf*) tiny, minute.

weep /wi:p/ *vti* (**weeping, wept**) to shed tears, to cry; (*wound*) to ooze.

weepie /'wi:pi/ *n* (*inf*) a sentimental film.

weeping /-ɪŋ/ *n* the act of weeping. • *adj* shedding tears; exuding moisture; (*tree*) with drooping branches.—**weepingly** *adv*.

weeping willow *n* a Chinese willow tree with slender drooping branches.

weepy /'wi:pi/ *adj* (**weepier, weepiest**) tearful; prone to crying.—**weepily** *adv*.—**weepiness** *n*.

weevil /'wi:vəl/ *n* a beetle which feeds on plants and crops.

wee-wee /'wi:wi:/ *see* **wee**[2].

weft /wɛft/ *n* the yarn woven across the lengthwise threads in a loom.—*also* **woof**.

weigh /weɪ/ *vt* to measure the weight of; to consider carefully; (*with* **down**) to weight; to oppress; (*with* **up**) to assess, make a judgment about (a person, thing, etc). • *vi* to have weight; to be burdensome; (*with* **in**) (*boxer, wrestler*) to be weighed before a bout; (*jockey*) to be weighed after a race; (*inf*) to make a contribution to (*eg* an argument).

weighbridge *n* a large scale consisting of a metal plate set into the road onto which vehicles are driven to be weighed.

weigh-in /'weɪˌɪn/ *n* (*sports*) the checking of the weight of a contestant, *esp* of a jockey after a race or of a boxer before a bout.

weight /weɪt/ *n* the amount which anything weighs; influence; any unit of heaviness. • *vt* to attach a weight to.

weightlessness /'weɪtləsˌnəs/ *n* the state of having no or little reaction to gravity, *esp* in space travel.

weight lifting /-ˌlɪftɪŋ/ *n* the sport of lifting weights of a specific amount in a particular way.—**weight lifter** *n*.

weight training *n* physical exercise involving lifting heavy weights.

weight watcher *n* a person on a diet to lose weight.

weighty /'weɪti/ *adj* (**weightier, weightiest**) heavy; serious.—**weightily** *adv*.

weir /wɪr/ *n* a low dam across a river which controls the flow of water.

weird /wɪrd/ *adj* unearthly, mysterious; eerie; bizarre.—**weirdly** *adv*.

weirdo /'wɪrdoː/, **weirdie** /'wɪrdiː/ *n* (*pl* **weirdos, weirdies**) (*inf*) an eccentric person.

welch /wɛlʃ/ *see* **welsh**.

welcome /'wɛlkəm/ *adj* gladly received; pleasing. • *n* reception of a person or thing. • *vt* to greet kindly.

weld /wɛld/ *vt* to unite, as metal by heating until fused or soft enough to hammer together; to join closely. • *n* a welded joint.

welfare /'wɛlfər/ *n* wellbeing; health; assistance or financial aid granted to the poor, the unemployed, etc.

welfare state *n* a state in which the government assumes responsibility for the health and social security of its citizens.

well[1] /wɛl/ *n* a spring; a hole bored in the ground to provide a source of water, oil, gas, etc; the open space in the middle of a staircase. • *vi* to pour forth.

well[2] *adj* (**better, best**) agreeable; comfortable; in good health. • *adv* in a proper, satisfactory, or excellent manner; thoroughly; prosperously; with good reason; to a considerable degree; fully. • *interj* an expression of surprise, etc.

we'll /wi:l/ *or* /wɪl/ = we will; we shall.

well-advised /ˌwɛləd'vaɪzd/ *adj* acting with good sense; carefully thought out.

well-appointed /-ə'pɔɪntɪd/ *adj* fully equipped or furnished.

well-balanced /'wɛl'bælənst/ *adj* sensible, sane.

well-being /-ˌbiːɪŋ/ *n* condition of being well or contented; welfare.

well-bred /-'brɛd/ *adj* well brought up; of good stock.

well-connected /-'kənɛktɪd/ *adj* having powerful friends or relatives.

well-disposed /-dɪs'poːzd/ *adj* favourable, feeling kindly (toward).

well-done /-'dʌn/ *adj* performed with skill; thoroughly cooked, as meat.

well-favoured, well-favored /-feɪvərd/ *adj* attractive.

well-found /-'faʊnd/ *adj* fully equipped.

well-founded /-'faʊndɪd/ *adj* borne out by facts.

well-groomed /-'gruːmd/ *adj* clean and tidy in dress and appearance.

well-grounded /-'graʊndɪd/ *adj* well instructed in a subject.

wellhead /-hɛd/ *n* the source of a stream, spring, etc; a source, origin.

well-heeled /-'hiːld/ *adj* (*inf*) wealthy.

wellies /'wɛliːz/ *npl* (*inf*) wellingtons.

well-informed /-ɪn'fɔːrmd/ *adj* knowledgeable on a wide range of subjects; possessing reliable information on a specific matter.

wellington (boot) /'wɛlɪŋtən/ *n* a rubber, waterproof boot.

well-intentioned /-ɪn'tɛnʃənd/ *adj* having good intentions (but often without producing good results).

well-knit /'wɛl'nɪt/ *adj* firm, compact.

well-known /-'noːn/ *adj* widely known, famous; known fully.

well-mannered /-mænərd/ *adj* having or showing good manners; polite.

well-meaning /-'miːnɪŋ/ *adj* having good intentions (but often without producing good results).

well-nigh /-'naɪ/ *adv* almost.

well-off /-'ɔf/ *adj* in comfortable circumstances; prosperous.

well-preserved /-prɪ'zɜːrvd/ *adj* well looked after; remaining youthful in appearance.

well-read /'wɛl'rɛd/ *adj* having read widely and deeply.

well-rounded /-'raʊndɪd/ *adj* having a pleasantly curved or rounded shape; full, complete.

well-spoken /-'spoːkən/ *adj* spoken clearly and eloquently; spoken in a pleasing manner.

well-thought-of /-'θɔtˌɒv/ *adj* having a good reputation.

well-thumbed *adj* (*book*) marked by frequent handling.

well-to-do /-tə'duː/ *adj* prosperous.

well-wisher /-ˌwɪʃər/ *n* a person who is sympathetic to another person, cause, etc.

well-worn /-'wɔrn/ *adj* showing signs of wear; (*phrase, etc*) trite, hackneyed.

Welsh /wɛlʃ/ *adj* relating to the people of Wales or their language.—*also n*.

welsh *vti* to avoid paying a gambling debt; to run off without paying.—*also* **welch.**—**welsher, welcher** *n*.

Welsh corgi /-'kɔrgiː/ *n* a corgi.

Welsh dresser *n* a dresser with drawers and cupboards below and open shelves above.

Welsh rabbit, Welsh rarebit *n* melted cheese on toast.

welt /wɛlt/ *n* a band or strip to strengthen a seam; a weal.

welter /'wɛltər/ *vi* to roll or wallow. • *n* a jumble.

welterweight /-ˌweɪt/ *n* a professional boxer weighing 140–147 pounds; a wrestler weighing 154–172 pounds.

wench /wɛntʃ/ *n* (*used facetiously*) a girl or young woman.

wend /wɛnd/ *vt* to amble, to saunter.

Wendy house /'wɛndɪhʊs/ *n* (*Brit*) a toy house for children to play in.

Wensleydale /'wɛnzlɪ,deɪl/ *n* a mild crumbly English cheese.

went /wɛnt/ *see* **go**.

wept /wɛpt/ *see* **weep**.

were /wɜr/ *see* **be**.

we're /wiːr/ = we are.

weren't /wɜrnt/ = were not.

werewolf /'wɛrwʊlf/ or /'wiːr-/ *n* (*pl* **werewolves**) an imaginary person able to transform himself for a time into a wolf.

west /'wɛst/ *n* the direction of the sun at sunset; one of the four points of the compass; the region in the west of any country; (*with cap*) Europe and the Western Hemisphere. • *adj* situated in, or toward the west. • *adv* in or to the west.

westerly /'wɛstərlɪ/ *adj* toward the west; blowing from the west. • *n* (*pl* **westerlies**) a wind blowing from the west.—*also adv.*

western /'wɛstərn/ *adj* of or in the west. • *n* a film, novel, etc about the *usu* pre-20th century American West.

westerner /-ər/ *n* a person from the west.

Western Hemisphere *n* that half of the earth containing North and South America.

westernize /'wɛstər,naɪz/ *vti* to make or become familiar with the ideas, institutions, customs, etc of the West.—**westernization** *n*.

westernmost /'wɛstərn,moːst/ *adj* farthest west.

westward /-wərd/ *adj* toward the west.—*also adv.*—**westwards** *adv*.

wet /wɛt/ *adj* (**wetter, wettest**) covered or saturated with water or other liquid; rainy; misty; not yet dry. • *n* water or other liquid; rain or rainy weather. • *vti* (**wetting, wet** *or* **wetted**) to soak; to moisten.—**wetness** *n*.

wet blanket *n* (*inf*) a person who dampens the enthusiasm of others.

wet dream *n* (*inf*) an erotic dream causing orgasm.

wet nurse *n* a woman employed to care for or suckle another's child.

wet-nurse /-,nərs/ *vt* to act as a wet nurse; (*inf*) to devote constant attention to (a person).

wet rot *n* (*Brit*) decay in timber caused by a fungus; any of various fungi that cause rot in damp timber.

wet suit /'wɛtsuːt/ *n* a close-fitting suit worn by divers, etc, to retain body heat.

we've /wiːv/ = we have.

whack /wæk/ *vti* (*inf*) to strike sharply, *esp* making a sound. • *n* (*inf*) a sharp blow.

whacking /'wækɪŋ/ *adj* (*Brit inf*) enormous. • *adv* (*inf*) very, extremely.

whale /weɪl/ *n* a very large sea mammal that breathes through a blowhole, and resembles a fish in shape. • *vi* to hunt whales.

whalebone /'weɪlboːn/ *n* a horny substance forming plates in the upper jaws of toothless whales; a piece of this formerly used for stiffening undergarments.

whalebone whale *n* any of various large whales that have whalebone plates instead of teeth which are used to filter plankton for food.

whaler /'weɪlər/ *n* a person or a ship employed in hunting whales.

whaling /-ɪŋ/ *n* the practice of hunting whales for food, oil, etc.

wham /wæm/ *n* (the sound of) a heavy blow. • *vti* (**whamming, whammed**) to hit or cause to hit with a loud noise.

whang /wæŋ/ *n* (the sound of) a forceful blow. • *vti* to hit or cause to hit with force.

wharf /wɔrf/ *n* (*pl* **wharfs, wharves**) a platform for loading and unloading ships in harbour.

wharfage /'wɔrfɪdʒ/ *n* (the charge for) the use of a wharf; wharves collectively.

wharfinger /-fɪndʒər/ *n* the owner or manager of a wharf.

what /wɛt/ or /wɒt/ *adj* of what sort, how much, how great. • *relative pron* that which; as much or many as. • *interj* used as an expression of surprise or astonishment.

whatever /wɛt'ɛvər/ or /wɒt-/ *pron* anything that; no matter what.

whatnot /'wɛtnɒt/ or /wɒt-/ *n* (*inf*) something or someone the name of which has been forgotten, is unknown or is hard to categorize; a set of open shelves for ornaments, photographs, etc.

whatsit /'wɛtzɪt/ or /wɒt-/ *n* (*inf*) something or someone the name of which has been forgotten, is unknown or is hard to categorize.

whatsoever /,wɛtso:'ɛvər/ or /wɒt-/ *adj* whatever.

wheat /wiːt/ *n* a cereal grain *usu* ground into flour for bread.

wheatear /'wiːtiːr/ *n* a small grey and white migratory thrush.

wheaten /'wiːtən/ *adj* made from the grain or flour of wheat; pale yellow in colour.

wheat germ *n* the kernel of a grain of wheat, high in nutritive value.

wheatmeal /-miːl/ *adj, n* (made from) brown flour with a high proportion of wheat grain.

whee /wiː/ *interj* used to express joy or delight.

wheedle /'wiːdəl/ *vt* to persuade, to cajole (into); to coax with flattery.

wheel /wiːl/ *n* a solid disc or circular rim turning on an axle; a steering wheel; (*pl*) the moving forces. • *vt* to transport on wheels. • *vi* to turn round or on an axis; to move in a circular direction, as a bird.

wheelbarrow /'wiːl,bɛroː/ *n* a cart with one wheel in front and two handles and legs at the rear.

wheelbase /-beɪs/ *n* the distance between the front and rear axles of a vehicle.

wheelchair /-tʃɛr/ *n* a chair with large wheels for invalids.

wheel clamp *n* a device that prevents an illegally parked car from being driven away until a fine is paid to release it.—*also vt.*

wheeler-dealer /-ər'diːlər/ *n* (*inf*) a shrewd operator in business, politics, etc.

wheelie /'wiːlɪ/ *n* a stunt in which a bicycle or motorcycle is ridden for a distance with the front wheel off the ground.

wheelie bin *n* a large container for domestic rubbish often on wheels.

wheelwright /-raɪt/ *n* a person who makes and repairs wheels for a living.

wheeze /wiːz/ *vi* to breathe with a rasping sound; to breathe with difficulty.—*also n.*

wheezy /'wiːzɪ/ *adj* (**wheezier, wheeziest**) making a wheezing sound.—**wheezily** *adv*.—**wheeziness** *n*.

whelk /wɛlk/ *n* a shellfish with a snail-like shell.

whelp /wɛlp/ *n* the young of various animals, *esp* a dog; an impudent child. • *vt* to give birth to (a puppy, etc). • *vi* (*bitch*) to bring forth young.

when /wɛn/ *adv* at what or which time. • *conj* at the time at which; although; *relative pron* at which.

whence /wɛns/ *adv* from what place.—*also conj.*

whenever /wɛn'ɛvər/ *adv, conj* at whatever time.

whensoever /,wɛnso:'ɛvər/ *conj, adv* whenever.

where /wɛr/ *adv* at which or what place; to which place; from what source; *relative pron* in or to which.

whereabouts /'wɛrə'baʊts/ *adv* near or at what place; about where. • *n* approximate location.

whereas /wɛr'æz/ *conj* since; on the contrary.

whereby /-'baɪ/ *adv* by which.—*also conj.*

wherein /-'ɪn/ *adv* (*formal*) in what; how. • *conj* in which; where.

whereof /-ɛv/ *adv, conj* (*arch*) of what or which.

whereon /-'ɒn/ *adv, conj* (*arch*) on what or which.

wheresoever /,wɛrso:'ɛvər/ *adv* (*emphatic*) wherever.

whereto /wɛr'tuː/ *adv, conj* (*formal*) to what or which.

whereupon /'wɛrə,pɒn/ or /,wɛrə'pɒn/ *adv* at which point; upon which.

wherever /wɛr'ɛvər/ *adv* at or to whatever place.

wherewithal /'wɛrwɪ,θɒl/ or /-,ðɒl/ *n* the means or resources.

whet /wɛt/ *vt* (**whetting, whetted**) to sharpen by rubbing, to stimulate.

whether /'wɛðər/ *conj* introducing an alternative possibility or condition.

whetstone /'wɛtstoːn/ *n* a stone for sharpening the edges of tools; something that sharpens or stimulates.

whew /hwjuː/ *interj* an exclamation of astonishment, amazement, relief, etc.

whey /weɪ/ *n* the watery part of milk that is separated from the curds in sour milk.

which /wɪtʃ/ *adj* what one (of). • *pron* which person or thing; that. • *relative pron* person or thing referred to.

whichever /-'ɛvər/ *pron* whatever one that; whether one or the other; no matter which.—*also adj.*

whichsoever /,wɪtʃso:'ɛvər/ *adj, pron* (*arch*) whichever.

whiff /wɪf/ *n* a sudden puff of air, smoke or odour.

while /waɪl/ *n* a period of time. • *conj* during the time that; whereas; although. • *vt* to pass (the time) pleasantly.

whilst /waɪlst/ *conj* (*esp Brit*) while.

whim /wɪm/ *n* a fancy; an irrational thought.

whimper /'wɪmpər/ *vi* to make a low, unhappy cry.—*also n.*

whimsical /-zəkəl/ *adj* unusual, odd, fantastic.—**whimsicality** *n*.

whimsy, whimsey /-zi/ *n* (*pl* **whimsies, whimseys**) a fanciful notion, a whim.

whine /wain/ *vi* (*dog*) to make a long, high-pitched cry; (*person*) to complain childishly. • *n* a plaintive cry.

whinge /windʒ/ *vi* to moan, complain.—*also n*.

whinny /'wini/ *vi* (**whinnying, whinnied**) to neigh softly.—*also n*.

whip /wip/ *n* a piece of leather attached to a handle used for punishing people or driving on animals; an officer in parliament who maintains party discipline. • *vb* (**whipping, whipped**) *vt* to move, pull, throw, etc suddenly; to strike, as with a lash; (*eggs, etc*) to beat into a froth; (*with* **up**) to stir into action, excite; (*inf*) to produce in a hurry. • *vi* to move rapidly.

whipcord /'wipkord/ *n* a strong cord of tightly twisted strands used for whips; a cotton or worsted fabric with diagonal ridges.

whip hand *n* (*usu with* **the**) the dominant position.

whiplash /-læʃ/ *n* a stroke with a whip; a neck injury when the head is jerked forward and backward.

whipped cream *n* cream that has been stiffened by beating, used as a topping for desserts, etc.

whippersnapper /'wipər,snæpər/ *n* an insignificant but impudent young person.

whippet /'wipit/ *n* a small racing dog like a greyhound.

whipping boy *n* a person who is constantly punished for the mistakes of others, a scapegoat.

whippoorwill /-ər,wil/ *n* a nocturnal American bird with a distinctive call.

whip-round *n* (*inf*) an appeal among friends for contributions.

whipsaw /-sɒ/ *n* any of various types of saw with a long flexible blade.

whipstock /-stɒk/ *n* the handle of a whip.

whir, whirr /wər/ or /hwər/ *n* a humming or buzzing sound. • *vti* (**whirring, whirred**) to revolve with a buzzing noise.

whirl /wərl/ *n* a swift turning; confusion, commotion; (*inf*) an attempt or try. • *vti* to turn around rapidly; to spin.

whirligig /'wərligig/ *n* a spinning top.

whirlpool /-puːl/ *n* a circular current or vortex of water.

whirlpool bath *n* a bath with a device that swirls water.

whirlwind /-wind/ *n* a whirling column of air; rapid activity.

whisk /wisk/ *vt* to make a quick sweeping movement; (*eggs, cream*) to beat, whip. • *vi* to move nimbly and efficiently. • *n* a kitchen utensil for whisking; (*inf*) a small amount.

whisker /'wiskər/ *n* any of the sensory bristles on the face of a cat, etc; (*pl*) the hair growing on a man's face, *esp* the cheeks.—**whiskered** *adj*.

whiskey /-ki/ *n* whisky distilled in the US or Ireland.

whisky *n* (*pl* **whiskies**) a spirit distilled from barley or rye.

whisper /'wispər/ *vti* to speak softly; to spread a rumour. • *n* a hushed tone; a hint, trace.

whist /wist/ *n* a card game for four players in two sides, each side attempting to win the greater number of the 13 tricks.

whistle /'wisəl/ *vti* to make a shrill sound by forcing the breath through the lips; to make a similar sound with a whistle; (*wind*) to move with a shrill sound; (*with* **for**) (*inf*) to demand or hope for in vain. • *n* a whistling sound; a musical instrument; a metal tube that is blown to make a shrill warning sound.

whistle stop *n* a minor railroad station where trains stop only on signal; a brief appearance by a candidate on tour during an election campaign.

Whit /wit/ *see* **Whitsuntide**.

whit *n* the tiniest possible amount.

white /'wait/ *adj* of the colour of snow; pure; bright; (*skin*) light-coloured. • *n* the colour white; the white part of an egg or the eye.

white ant *n* a termite.

whitebait /-beit/ *n* (*pl* **whitebait**) the edible young of the herring and sprat.

white blood cell *n* a leucocyte.

whitecap /-kæp/ *n* a wave with a white foamy crest.

white-collar /-kɒlər/ *adj* of office and professional workers.

white dwarf *n* a small faint star of high density.

white elephant *n* a thing of little use.

white feather *n* a symbol of cowardice.

whitefish *n* (*pl* same or **whitefishes**) a freshwater fish of the trout family in northern North America.

white flag *n* a flag of plain white material used to signify surrender or arrange a truce.

whitefly /'waitflai/ *n* (*pl* **whiteflies**) any of various small insects that feed on and injure plants.

white gold *n* a pale alloy of gold chiefly with platinum and palladium.

white goods *npl* household appliances, as refrigerators, etc; household linen, as sheets, towels, etc.

Whitehall /-hɒl/ *n* the British government; departmental government.

white heat *n* an intense heat accompanied by the emission of white light from a substance; (*inf*) intense excitement or emotion.

white-hot /-hɒt/ *adj* of a temperature so hot that white light is emitted; intensely passionate.

White House *n* the official residence of the president of the US; the US presidency.

white lead *n* a white solid of mostly lead carbonate, *esp* used in pigments.

white lie *n* a harmless lie, *esp* as uttered out of politeness.

white light *n* light, *eg* sunlight, that contains approximately equal proportions of the whole spectrum of visible radiation.

white matter *n* whitish tissue in the brain and spinal cord composed of nerve fibres.

white meat *n* a light-coloured meat such as poultry or veal.

white metal *n* an alloy, *esp* of tin, used in bearings, domestic utensils, etc.

whiten /'waitən/ *vti* to make or become white; to bleach.

white noise *n* sound that contains approximately equal proportions of all the audible frequencies.

whiteout /-ɐut/ *n* a weather condition when heavy cloud and snow reflect most of the available light and greatly reduce visibility.

white paper *n* a government document detailing proposed legislation.

white sauce *n* a sauce made with butter, flour and seasonings mixed with milk, cream or stock.

white slave *n* a woman or girl held against her will and forced into prostitution.

white spirit *n* a colourless inflammable liquid distilled from petroleum and used as a solvent and thinner for paint.

white tie *n* a white bow tie worn as part of a man's formal evening dress.—**white-tie** *adj*.

whitewash /'waitwɒʃ/ *n* a mixture of lime and water, used for whitening walls; concealment of the truth.—*also vt*.

white water *n* water with a foaming surface, as in rapids.

white whale *n* the beluga.

white wine *n* wine made from green grapes or from skinned black grapes.

whitewood /-wʊd/ *n* (any of various trees yielding) a light-coloured wood.

whither /'wiðər/ *adv* to what or which place.

whiting /'waitiŋ/ *n* (*pl* **whitings, whiting**) an edible saltwater fish of the cod family.

whitlow /'witloː/ *n* a painful inflammation at the end of a finger or toe.

Whitsun /-sən/ *adj* (*Christianity*) of, observed on, or pertaining to Whit Sunday or Whitsuntide. • *n* Whitsuntide.

Whit Sunday *n* (*Christianity*) the seventh Sunday after Easter, Pentecost.

Whitsuntide /'witsən,taid/ *n* (*Christianity*) the week beginning with Whit Sunday.—*also* **Whit**.

whittle /-əl/ *vt* to pare or cut thin shavings from (wood); (*with* **away** *or* **down**) to reduce.

whiz, whizz /wiz/ *vi* (**whizzing, whizzed**) to make a humming sound. • *n* (*pl* **whizzes**) a humming sound; (*inf*) an expert.

whiz kid, whizz kid *n* (*inf*) a person of extraordinary achievements given their relatively young age.

WHO *abbr* = World Health Organization.

who /huː/ *pron* what or which person; that.

whoa /woː/ *interj* a command given, *esp* to a horse, to slow down or come to a halt.

who'd /huːd/ = who would.

whodunit, whodunnit /huːˈdɪnit/ *n* (*inf*) a detective novel, play, etc.

whoever /huːˈɛvər/ *pron* anyone who; whatever person.

whole /hoːl/ *adj* not broken, intact; containing the total amount, number, etc.; complete. • *n* the entire amount; a thing complete in itself.

wholefood *n* unrefined food, free from additives.

wholehearted /'hoːlˌhɑrtəd/ *adj* sincere, single-minded, enthusiastic.—**wholeheartedly** *adv.*

whole hog /'hoːl'hɒg/ *n* (*inf*) the complete amount or extent.

wholemeal /'hoːlmiːl/ *adj see* **wholewheat**.

whole note *n* (*mus*) a note with a time value equal to two half notes.—*also* **semibreve**

whole number *n* a number without fractions; an integer.

wholesale /-seɪl/ *n* selling of goods, *usu* at lower prices and in quantity, to a retailer.

wholesome /-səm/ *adj* healthy; mentally beneficial.—**wholesomeness** *n.*

wholewheat /-wiːt/ *or* /hwiːt/ *adj* made from the entire wheat kernel.—*also* **wholemeal**.

who'll /huːl/ *or* /'huːəl/ = who will; who shall.

wholly /'hoːlli/ *adv* completely.

whom /huːm/ *pron* objective case of **who**.

whomever /-'ɛvər/ *pron* the objective form of **whoever**.

whoop /wuːp/ *or* /wʊp/, /huːp/ *n* a loud cry of excitement.

whoopee /'huːpiː/ *or* /'wʊpiː/, /'wuːpiː/ *interj* used to express wild excitement. • *n* boisterous fun.

whoopee cushion *n* a joke cushion that emits a rude noise when sat on.

whooping cough /'wuːpɪŋ/ *or* /'huːpɪŋ/ *n* an infectious disease, *esp* of children, causing coughing spasms.

whoops /wʊps/ *interj* (*inf*) an exclamation of surprise or apology.

whoosh /wuːʃ/ *or* /wʊʃ/ *n* a rushing or hissing sound. • *vi* to make or move with such a sound.

whop /wɒp/ *or* /hwɒp/ *vt* (**whopping, whopped**) to beat, thrash; to defeat completely.

whopper /'wɒpər/ *n* (*inf*) a large specimen.—**whopping** *adj.*

whore /hɔr/ *or* /hʊr/ *n* a prostitute.

whorehouse /'hɔrhəʊs/ *or* /'hur-/ *n* a brothel.

whoremonger /-ˌmɒŋgər/ *or* /-mʌŋgər/, /'hur-/ *n* a person who uses the services of whores.—*also* **whoremaster**.

whorl /wɔrl/ *or* /wɜrl/ *n* a ring of leaves or petals round a stem; a single turn of a spiral; something shaped like a spiral; the central ridges of a fingerprint forming a complete circle.

whortleberry /'wɔrtəlˌbɛri/ *n* a bilberry.

who's /huːz/ = who is.

whose /huːz/ *pron* the possessive case of **who** or **which**.

whosoever /ˌhuːsoːˈɛvər/ *pron* (*arch*) whoever.

who's who *n* a reference book containing the names and brief biographical details of famous or important people.

why /waɪ/ *adv* for what cause or reason? • *interj* exclamation of surprise. • *n* (*pl* **whys**) a cause.

whydah /'wɪdə/ *n* any of various African weaverbirds with black and white plumage.

WI *abbr* = West Indies; Women's Institute.

wick /wɪk/ *n* a cord, as in a candle or lamp, that supplies fuel to the flame.

wicked /'wɪkɪd/ *adj* evil, immoral, sinful.—**wickedly** *adv.*— **wickedness** *n.*

wicker /-ər/ *n* a long, thin, flexible twig; such twigs woven together, as in making baskets.—**wickerwork** *n.*

wicket /-ɪt/ *n* a small door or gate; (*croquet*) any of the small wire arches through which the balls must be hit; (*cricket*) the stumps at which the bowler aims the ball; the area between the bowler and the batsman; a batsman's innings.

wicketkeeper /'wɪkɪtˌkiːpər/ *n* (*cricket*) the fielder standing immediately behind the wicket.

widdershins /'wɪdərˌʃɪnz/ *see* **withershins**.

wide /waɪd/ *adj* broad; extensive; of a definite distance from side to side; (*with* **of**) far from the aim; open fully. • *n* (*cricket*) a ball bowled beyond the reach of the batsman.—**widely** *adv.*

wide-angle /'waɪdˌæŋgəl/ *adj* (*photog*) with an angle of view of 60 degrees or more.

wide-awake /-əˌweɪk/ *adj* fully awake; ready, alert.

wide-eyed /-ˌaɪd/ *adj* astonished; innocent.

widen /'waɪdən/ *vti* to make or grow wide or wider.

widespread /-spred/ *or* /-'spred/ *adj* widely extended; general.

widget /'wɪdʒɪt/ *n* (*inf*) a small device or gadget the name of which is lost or forgotten; a whatsit.

widow /'wɪdoː/ *n* a woman whose husband has died. • *vt* to cause to become a widow.—**widowhood** *n.*

widower /-ər/ *n* a man whose wife has died.

widow's peak *n* a pointed growth of hair in the middle of the forehead.

width /wɪdθ/ *or* /wɪtθ/ *n* breadth.

wield /wiːld/ *vt* (*a weapon, etc*) to brandish; to exercise power.

wife /waɪf/ *n* (*pl* **wives**) a married woman.

wig /wɪg/ *n* an artificial covering of real or synthetic hair for the head.

wigeon, widgeon /'wɪdʒən/ *n* a Eurasian wild duck the male of which has a gingery head.

wigging /'wɪgɪŋ/ *n* (*Brit inf*) a severe reprimand.

wiggle /'wɪgəl/ *vti* to move from side to side with jerky movements.

wigwag /-wæg/ *vb* (**wigwagging, wigwagged**) *vi* to move back and forth; to send a signal by means of flag semaphore. • *vt* to signal by wigwagging; to cause (something) to move back and forth. • *n* (the message sent using) a system of signalling with flags.

wigwam /-wæm/ *n* a North American Indian conical shelter.

wilco /'wɪlkoː/ *interj* used in telecommunications to indicate that a message is received and being acted upon.

wild /waɪld/ *adj* in its natural state; not tamed or cultivated; uncivilized; lacking control; disorderly; furious.—**wildly** *adv.*— **wildness** *n.*

wild boar *n* a wild pig with tusks, of Europe and Asia.

wild card *n* (*card games*) a card with an arbitrary value determined by the holder; (*sport*) a team that has not qualified for a competition but is allowed to take part; (*sl*) an unpredictable element.

wildcat /'waɪldkæt/ *adj* (*strike*) unofficial. • *n* a fierce, undomesticated cat.

wildebeest /'wɪldəˌbiːst/ *or* /'vɪl-/ *n* (*pl* **wildebeests, wildebeest**) a gnu.

wilderness /-ərnəs/ *n* an uncultivated and desolate place.

wild-eyed /'waɪdˌaɪd/ *adj* staring angrily or crazily.

wildfire /-ˌfaɪr/ *n* a fire that spreads fast and is hard to put out.

wildfowl /-faʊl/ *n* any bird that is hunted for game, *esp* waterbirds such as ducks and geese.

wild-goose chase *n* a futile pursuit of something.

wilding /'waɪldɪŋ/ *n* (the fruit of) any uncultivated plant; a wild animal; (*sl*) a violent rampage though the streets by a teenage gang.

wildlife /-laɪf/ *n* animals in the wild.

wild oat *n* (*usu pl*) a Eurasian grass related to cultivated oats; (*pl*) youthful excesses.

wild rice *n* a North American grass that bears edible grains; its grain.

Wild West *n* the western US during the lawless period of early settlement.

wile /waɪl/ *n* a trick, craftiness.

wilful /'wɪlfʊl/ *adj* stubborn; done intentionally.—*also* **willful**.— **wilfully, willfully** *adv.*—**wilfulness, willfulness** *n.*

will[1] /wɪl/ *n* power of choosing or determining; desire; determination; attitude, disposition; a legal document directing the disposal of one's property after death. • *vt* to bequeath; to command.

will[2] *aux vb* used in constructions with 2nd and 3rd persons; used to show futurity, determination, obligation.

willful /'wɪlfəl/ *see* **wilful**.

willies /'wɪliːz/ *npl* (with **the**) nervousness, jumpiness.

willing /-ɪŋ/ *adj* ready, inclined; eager.—**willingly** *adv.*—**willingness** *n.*

will-o'-the-wisp /ˌwɪləðəˈwɪsp/ *n* a pale phosphorescent glow sometimes seen over marshy areas and thought to be caused by combustion of gas from decaying organic matter; an elusive person or thing.

willow /'wɪloː/ *n* a tree or shrub with slender, flexible branches; the wood of the willow.

willowherb /-hɔrb/ *or* /-ɔrb/ *n* any of various plants of the evening-primrose family with pink or white flowers.

willow pattern *n* a traditional oriental-style design on china tableware consisting of a scene with figures and a willow tree, *usu* in blue on a white background.

willowy /-i/ *adj* flexible, graceful.

willpower /'wɪlˌpaʊər/ *n* the ability to control one's emotions and actions.

willy-nilly /ˌwɪliˈnɪli/ *adv* whether desired or not.

wilt /wɪlt/ *vi* to become limp, as from heat; (*plant*) to droop; to become weak or faint.

wily /'waɪli/ *adj* (**wilier, wiliest**) crafty; sly.—**wiliness** *n.*

WIMP, Wimp /wɪmp/ (*acronym*) (*comput*) a graphical interface using Windows, Icons, Mice and Pull-down menus that makes a computer easier to use.

wimp *n* (*inf*) a weak or ineffectual person.

wimple /'wɪmpəl/ *n* a linen or silk cloth draped round the head and neck but leaving the face uncovered, worn by women in medieval times and still used by some nuns.

win /wɪn/ *vti* (**winning, won**) to gain with effort; to succeed in a contest; to gain *eg* by luck; to achieve influence over; (*with* **over**) to gain the support or affection of (someone). • *n* a success.

wince /wɪns/ *vi* to shrink back; to flinch (as in pain).—*also n*.

winch /wɪntʃ/ *n* a hoisting machine. • *vt* to hoist or lower with a winch.

wind[1] /wɪnd/ *n* a current of air; breath; scent of game; (*inf*) flatulence; tendency; (*mus*) wind instrument(s). • *vt* (**winding, winded**) to cause to be short of breath; to perceive by scent.

wind[2] *vb* (**winding, wound**) *vt* to turn by cranking; to tighten the spring of a clock; to coil around something else; to encircle or cover, as with a bandage; (*with* **down**) to lower by winding a handle, etc. • *vi* to turn, to twist, to meander; (*with* **down**) to diminish in power or intensity; to slacken; to relax.

windage /'wɪndɪdʒ/ *n* the difference between the bore of a gun and the diameter of the projectile; (an allowance for) the deflection of a projectile caused by the wind.

windbag /-bæg/ *n* (*inf*) a person who talks a lot of rubbish.

windblown /-bloʊn/ *adj* blown or shaped by the wind.

windbreak /-breɪk/ *n* a shelter that breaks the force of the wind, as a line of trees.

windburn /-bɜrn/ *n* redness and soreness of the skin due to the wind.

windcheater /-ˌtʃiːtər/ *n* a warm hooded jacket of windproof material.

wind-chill /-ˌtʃɪl/ *n* a measure of the effect of low temperature combined with wind.

winded /'wɪndɪd/ *adj* out of breath.

winder /-ər/ *n* one who or that which winds; a winding apparatus; a key for winding a spring-driven mechanism; a step in a spiral staircase.

windfall /-fɒl/ *n* fruit blown off a tree; any unexpected gain, *esp* financial.

winding /-ɪŋ/ *adj* meandering.

winding sheet *n* a sheet used to wrap a body for burial.

wind instrument *n* a musical instrument played by blowing into it or passing an air current through it.

windjammer /'wɪndˌdʒæmər/ *n* a large fast merchant sailing vessel.

windlass /-ləs/ *n* any of various devices for hoisting, hauling or lifting using a rope or chain wound round a motorized drum. • *vt* to hoist, etc using a windlass.

wind machine *n* a device used in film and theatre to produce realistic wind effects.

windmill /-mɪl/ *n* a machine operated by the force of the wind turning a set of sails.

window /'wɪndoʊ/ *n* a framework containing glass in the opening in a wall of a building, or in a vehicle, etc, for air and light.

window box *n* a narrow box on a windowsill for growing flowers, etc.

windowdressing *n* the arrangement of goods in a shop window; ornamentation intended to disguise the true nature of something.

windowpane /-peɪn/ *n* the glass in a window.

window-shopping /-ˌʃɒpɪŋ/ *n* the occupation of looking at goods for sale without buying them.—**window-shopper** *n*.

windowsill /-sɪl/ *n* a sill beneath a window.

windpipe /'wɪndpaɪp/ *n* the air passage from the mouth to the lungs, the trachea.

windrow /'wɪndroʊ/ *n* a row of leaves or pile of soil heaped up by or as if by the wind.

windscreen /-skriːn/, (*US*) **windshield** /-ʃiːld/ *n* a protective shield of glass in the front of a vehicle.

windscreen wiper, (*US*) **windshield wiper** *n* a metal blade with a rubber edge that removes rain, etc, from a windscreen.

windsock /-sɒk/ *n* a canvas cylinder flown from an airport mast to show the direction of the wind.—*also* **drogue**.

windsurfing /-ˌsɜrfɪŋ/ *n* the sport of skimming along the surface of the water standing on a surfboard fitted with a sail.

windswept /-swept/ *adj* exposed to the wind; dishevelled.

wind tunnel *n* an apparatus for maintaining a constant force of air current to test the aerodynamics of an aircraft, etc.

wind-up /'waɪndʌp/ *n* the conclusion.

windward /'wɪndwərd/ *adv, adj* toward the direction where the wind blows from.

windy /'wɪndi/ or /waɪndi/ *adj* (**windier, windiest**) exposed to the winds; stormy; verbose.

wine /waɪn/ *n* fermented grape juice used as an alcoholic beverage; the fermented juice of other fruits or plants.

wine bar *n* a bar that serves wine and food.

wine box *n* wine sold in a box with a small tap for pouring.

wine cellar *n* a place for storing wines, ideally a cool cellar; a stock of stored wines.

wine-coloured /'waɪnˌkʌlərd/ *adj* dark purplish-red.

wine cooler *n* a vessel that is filled with ice for cooling wine bottles.

wineglass /-glæs/ *n* a glass, *usu* with a stem, for drinking wine.

winegrower /-groʊər/ *n* a person who grows vines and makes wine.

wine press /-pres/ *n* (a place containing) equipment for squeezing juice from grapes to make wine.

winery /'waɪnəri/ *n* (*pl* **wineries**) a place where wine is made.

wineskin /-skɪn/ *n* the skin of an animal, *esp* a goat, sewn into a bag for holding wine.

wing /wɪŋ/ *n* the forelimb of a bird, bat or insect, by which it flies; the main lateral surface of an aeroplane; a projecting part of a building; the side of a stage; a section of a political party. • *vti* to make one's way swiftly; to wound without killing.

wing chair *n* an armchair with high sides for excluding draughts.

wing collar *n* a stiff upturned shirt collar with the points turned down.

wingding /'wɪŋdɪŋ/ *n* (*inf*) a wild party; a real or pretended fit.

wing nut *n* a nut that is tightened manually using flat wings that project on each side.

wingspan /-spæn/, **wingspread** /-spred/ *n* the width of a bird or aeroplane between the tips of the wings.

wink /wɪŋk/ *vi* to quickly open and close one's eye; to give a hint by winking; (*with* **at**) to disregard; to allow (something normally prohibited) to happen. • *n* the act of winking; an instant.

winkle[1] /'wɪŋkəl/ *n* a periwinkle.

winkle[2] *n* an edible sea snail. • *vt* (*with* **out**) (*inf*) to extract, prise out; to uncover, disclose.

winkle-pickers /-ˌpɪkərs/ *npl* shoes or boots with sharp pointed toes.

winner /'wɪnər/ *n* one that wins; (*inf*) a person or thing that is assured of success.

winning /-ɪŋ/ *n* a victory; (*pl*) money won in gambling. • *adj* charming.

winnow /'wɪnoʊ/ *vt* to separate out the chaff from (the grain) by blowing air across it; to analyze.

wino /'waɪnoʊ/ *n* (*pl* **winos**) (*inf*) a down-and-out addicted to cheap wine.

winsome /'wɪnsəm/ *adj* charming, pleasing.

winter /-tər/ *n* the coldest season of the year: in the northern hemisphere from November or December to January or February. • *vi* to spend the winter.

wintergreen /'wɪntərˌgriːn/ *n* any of various evergreen plants or shrubs; an aromatic essential oil from these formerly used in medicine.

winterize /-ˌaɪz/ *vt* to prepare something (*eg* a car) to withstand winter weather.—**winterization** *n*.

winter sports *npl* sports that take place on ice or snow, such as skiing.

wintry, wintery /-ri/ *adj* (**wintrier, wintriest**) typical of winter, cold, stormy, snowy; unfriendly, frigid.

winy /'waɪni/ *adj* (**winier, winiest**) tasting like or resembling wine.

wipe /waɪp/ *vt* to rub a surface with a cloth in order to clean or dry it; (*with* **out**) to remove; to erase; to kill off; to destroy. • *n* a wiping.

wiper /'waɪpər/ *n* a person or thing that wipes; a windscreen wiper.

wire /waɪr/ *n* a flexible thread of metal; a length of this; (*horse racing*) the finish line of a race; a telegram. • *adj* formed of wire. • *vt* to fasten, furnish, connect, etc, with wire; to send a telegram.

wired /-d/ *adj* (*sl*) wearing a hidden electronic recording or listening device; (*sl*) nervous or edgy, *esp* as a result of taking a stimulating drug.

wire-haired /'waɪrˌherd/ *adj* (*dogs, etc*) having a coat of stiff hairs.

wireless /-ləs/ *n* (*formerly*) a radio.

wire service *n* in the US, a news agency that sends out news to television and radio stations.

wiretap /-tæp/ *vb* (**wiretapping, wiretapped**) *vi* to connect to a telephone wire in order to listen in to a private conversation. • *vt* to tap (a telephone).—**wiretapper** *n*.

wireworm /-wɔrm/ *n* the filament-like larva of certain beetles which infest and destroy plant roots.

wiring /-ɪŋ/ *n* a system of wires used in an electrical device or circuit.

wiry /'waɪri/ *adj* (**wirier, wiriest**) lean, supple and sinewy.—**wiriness** *n*.

wisdom /'wɪzdəm/ *n* the ability to use knowledge; sound judgment.

wisdom tooth *n* one of four teeth set at the end of each side of the upper and lower jaw in humans and grown last.

wise /waɪz/ *adj* having knowledge or common sense; learned; prudent. • *vti* (*with* **up**) (*inf*) (to cause) to become informed or aware.— **wisely** *adv*.

-wise /waɪz/ *adv suffix* direction or manner; concerning.

wiseacre /'waɪzˌeɪkər/ *n* a person who pretends to be clever or wise, a know-all.

wisecrack /-kræk/ *n* (*inf*) a witty or sarcastic remark.—*also vi*.

wise guy /-gaɪ/ *n* (*inf*) a person who is always making critical or sarcastic comments.

wise use *n* a policy designed to protect the use of natural resources and promote environmental awareness.

wish /wɪʃ/ *vti* to long for; to express a desire. • *n* desire; thing desired.

wishbone /'wɪʃboːn/ *n* the forked bone at the front of the breastbone of a bird consisting of the fused clavicles.

wishful /-fʊl/ *adj* having a wish; hopeful.

wishful thinking *n* the mistaken belief that one's wishes correspond to reality.

wishy-washy /'wɪʃiːˌwɒʃi/ *adj* weak, thin, feeble.

wisp /wɪsp/ *n* a thin strand; a small bunch, as of hay; anything slender.—**wispy** *adj*.

wisteria, wistaria /wɪ'stiːriə/ *n* a purple-flowered climbing plant.

wistful /'wɪstfʊl/ *adj* pensive; sad; yearning.—**wistfully** *adv*.—**wistfulness** *n*.

wit /wɪt/ *n* (*speech, writing*) the facility of combining ideas with humorous effect; a person with this ability; (*pl*) ability to think quickly.

witch /wɪtʃ/ *n* a woman who practises magic and is considered to a have dealings with the devil.

witchcraft /'wɪtʃkræft/ *n* the practice of magic.

witch doctor *n* a man in certain tribes who appears to be able to cure sickness or cause harm to people.

witchery /-əri/ *n* (*pl* **witcheries**) witchcraft; fascination.

witch hazel *n* any of a genus of North American shrubs with yellow flowers; a soothing lotion made from the bark of this applied to lumps, bruises, skin rashes, etc.

witch hunt *n* a campaign of harassment of those with dissenting opinions; the search for and persecution of those accused of witchcraft.

witching /-ɪŋ/ *adj* of or suitable for witchcraft.

with /wɪθ/ or /wɪð/ *prep* denoting nearness or agreement; in the company of; in the same direction as; among; by means of; possessing.

withal /wɪ'ðɔl/ *adv* (*arch*) as well; moreover.

withdraw /wɪθ'drɔ/ or /wɪð-/ *vb* (**withdrawing, withdrew,** *pp* **withdrawn**) *vt* to draw back or away; to remove; to retract. • *vi* to retire; to retreat.—**withdrawal** *n*.

withdrawn /wɪθdrɒn/ or /wɪð/ *adj* introverted, reserved; remote.

wither /'wɪðər/ *vi* to fade or become limp or dry, as of a plant. • *vt* to cause to dry up or fade.

withers /-z/ *npl* the ridge between the shoulder blades of a horse.

withershins /-ʃɪnz/ *adv* counter-clockwise.—*also* **widdershins**.

withhold /wɪθ'hoːld/ *vt* (**withholding, withheld**) to hold back; to deduct; to restrain; to refuse to grant.

within /wɪθɪn/ or /-ˈðɪn/ *prep* inside; not exceeding; not beyond.

without /wɪ'θɛʊt/ or /-ðɛʊt/ *prep* outside or out of, beyond; not having, lacking. • *adv* outside.

withstand /wɪθ'stænd/ or /wɪð-/ *vt* (**withstanding, withstood**) to oppose or resist, *esp* successfully; to endure.

witless /'wɪtləs/ *adj* foolish, stupid; not witty.

witness /-nəs/ *n* a person who gives evidence or attests a signing; testimony (of a fact). • *vt* to have first-hand knowledge of; to see; to be the scene of; to serve as evidence of; to attest a signing. • *vi* to testify.

witness stand, witness box *n* an enclosure for witnesses in a court of law.

witticism /'wɪtɪsɪzəm/ *n* a witty remark.

wittingly /'wɪtɪŋli/ *adv* knowingly.

witty /'wɪti/ *adj* (**wittier, wittiest**) full of wit.—**wittily** *adv*.—**wittiness** *n*.

wives /waɪvz/ *see* **wife**.

wizard /'wɪzərd/ *n* a magician; a man who practises witchcraft or magic; an expert.—**wizardry** *n*.

wizened /-ənd/ *adj* dried up, wrinkled, shrivelled.

wk *abbr* = week.

woad /woːd/ *n* (a blue dye obtained from the leaves of) a European plant of the mustard family.

wobble /'wɒbəl/ *vi* to sway unsteadily from side to side; to waver, to hesitate.—**wobbly** *adj*.

wodge /wɒdʒ/ *n* (*inf*) a thick slice or chunk of something.

woe /woː/ *n* grief, misery; (*pl*) misfortune.—**woeful** *adj*.—**woefully** *adv*.

woebegone /'woːbəˌgɒn/ *adj* sorrowful.

wok /wɒk/ *n* a large, metal, hemispherical pan used for Chinese-style cooking.

woke /woːk/, **woken** /'woːkən/ *see* **wake**[1].

wolf /wʊlf/ *n* (*pl* **wolves**) a wild animal of the dog family that hunts in packs; a flirtatious man.

wolfhound /'wʊlfhɛʊnd/ *n* any of several types of large dog formerly used to hunt wolves.

wolfram /-rəm/ *n* tungsten; wolframite.

wolframite /-rəˌmɛɪt/ *n* a mineral that is the chief ore of tungsten and also contains iron and manganese.

wolf whistle *n* a whistle made by a man when seeing an attractive woman.

wolverine /ˌwʊlvər'iːn/ or /'wʊlvərˌiːn/ *n* a voracious carnivorous animal of northern forests of Europe, North America and Asia with thick black fur.

wolves /wʊlvz/ *see* **wolf**.

woman /'wʊmən/ *n* (*pl* **women**) an adult human female; the female sex.

womanhood /-ˌhʊd/ *n* the state of being a woman.

womanish /-ɪʃ/ *n* resembling a woman; suitable for women.

womanize /'wʊməˌnaɪz/ *vi* to pursue women for sex.—**womanizer** *n*.

womankind /'wʊmənˌkaɪnd/ *n* female human beings; women collectively, *esp* as distinct from men.

womanly /-li/ *adj* having the qualities of a woman.

womb /wuːm/ *n* the female organ in which offspring are developed until birth, the uterus; any womb-like cavity; a place where something is produced.

wombat /'wɒmbæt/ *n* an Australian marsupial mammal resembling a small bear.

women /'wɪmɪn/ *see* **woman**.

womenfolk /-ˌfoːk/ *npl* women collectively; the female members of a family, group or community.

Women's Institute *n* a mainly British organization for women which engages in various social and cultural activities.

Women's Movement *n* a feminist movement seeking to end male domination of women in society.

won /wɒn/ *see* **win**.

wonder /'wʌndər/ *n* a feeling of surprise or astonishment; something that excites such a feeling; a prodigy. • *vi* to feel wonder; to be curious; to speculate; to marvel.

wonderful /-ˌfʊl/ *adj* marvellous.—**wonderfully** *adv*.

wonderland /-ˌlænd/ *n* a land full of marvels.

wonderment /-mənt/ *n* astonishment, awe; curiosity.

wondrous /-əs/ *adj* (*poet*) wonderful, marvellous.

wonky /'wɒŋki/ *adj* (**wonkier, wonkiest**) (*sl*) crooked, unsteady.

wont /wɒnt/ *adj* accustomed; inclined. • *n* habit.

won't /woːnt/ = will not.

woo /wuː/ *vt* (**wooing, wooed**) to seek to attract with a view to marriage; to court; to solicit eagerly.—**wooer** *n*.

wood /wʊd/ *n* the hard fibrous substance under the bark of trees; trees cut or sawn, timber; a thick growth of trees.

wood alcohol *n* methanol.

woodbine /'wʊdbaɪn/ *n* wild honeysuckle.

woodchuck /-tʃʌk/ *n* a North American marmot with thick reddish-brown fur.—*also* **groundhog**.

woodcock /-kɒk/ *n* a game bird related to the snipe.

woodcraft /-kræft/ *n* skill in living and surviving in the forest, *esp* hunting; skill at woodwork.

woodcut /-kʌt/ *n* an engraving made on wood; a print made from this.

woodcutter /-ˌkʌtər/ *n* a person whose job is to cut down trees.

wooded /'wʊdɪd/ *adj* covered with trees.

wooden /-ən/ *adj* made of wood; stiff.

wood engraving *n* the art of engraving illustrations on wood; (a print taken from) a piece of engraved wood.

woodenhead /'wʊdənˌhed/ *n* (*inf*) a foolish person.

woodland /-lənd/ *n* land covered with trees.

woodlouse /-lʊs/ *n* (*pl* **woodlice**) a small ground-dwelling wingless crustacean with a segmented body that can roll itself into a ball.

woodman /-mən/ *n* (*pl* **woodmen**) a forester or woodcutter.

wood nymph *n* (*Greek myth*) a nymph of the woods, a dryad.

woodpecker /-ˌpekər/ *n* a bird that pecks holes in trees to extract insects.

wood pigeon *n* a large European wild pigeon with white patches of feathers on the body and neck.

woodpile /-paɪl/ *n* a pile of wood, *esp* firewood.

wood pulp *n* wood that has been pulped and treated for paper-making.

wood screw *n* a pointed metal screw with an external thread and slotted head designed to be driven into wood with a screwdriver.

woodshed /-ʃed/ *n* a small shed for storing wood (*eg* firewood), tools, gardening equipment, etc.

woodsman /'wʊdzmən/ *n* (*pl* **woodsmen**) a person who lives and works in a wood; a woodman.

woodwind /-wɪnd/ *n* section of an orchestra in which wind instruments, originally made of wood, are played.

woodwork /-wɜːk/ *n* carpentry.

woodworm /-wɜːm/ *n* (*esp Brit*) an insect larva that bores into wood; the damage in furniture so caused.

woody /-wʊdi/ *adj* (**woodier, woodiest**) covered in trees.

woof[1] /wʊf/ *n* the horizontal threads crossing the warp in a woven fabric.

woof[2] /wʊf/ or /wuːf/ *interj* a noise like the bark of a dog. • *vi* to make this sound.

woofer /'wuːfər/ *n* a loudspeaker.

wool /wʊl/ *n* the fleece of sheep and other animals; thread or yarn spun from the coats of sheep; cloth made from this yarn.

woollen, woolen /'wʊlən/ *adj* made of wool.

woolly bear *n* a large furry caterpillar produced by the tiger moth.

woolly, wooly /'wʊli/ *adj* (**woollier, woolliest** *or* **woolier, wooliest**) of, like or covered with wool; indistinct, blurred; muddled. • *n* (*pl* **woollies**) (*inf*) a woollen garment.—**woolliness, wooliness** *n*.

woolsack /-sæk/ *n* the official seat of the Lord Chancellor in the British House of Lords (formerly made from a large sack of wool).

woozy /'wuːzi/ *adj* (**woozier, wooziest**) (*inf*) mentally confused, dazed; dizzy, nauseous.

word /wɜːd/ *n* a single unit of language in speech or writing; talk, discussion; a message; a promise; a command; information; a password; (*pl*) lyrics; (*pl*) a quarrel. • *vt* to put into words, to phrase; to flatter.

word blindness *n* alexia or dyslexia.

word for word /'wɜːdfər'wɜːd/ *adj, adv* (*a translation, etc*) using exactly the same words, verbatim.

wording /'wɜːdɪŋ/ *n* the way in which words are used, *esp* in written form; a choice of words.

word-perfect *adj* able to repeat something without mistake.—*also* **letter-perfect**.

wordplay /-pleɪ/ *n* verbal wit or repartee.

word processor *n* computer software that allows the input, formatting, storage and printing of text electronically; the hardware, including microprocessor, monitor, keyboard and printer, required to operate word-processing software.

wordy /'wɜːdi/ *adj* (**wordier, wordiest**) verbose.

wore /wɔːr/ *see* **wear**.

work /wɜːk/ *n* employment, occupation; a task; the product of work; manner of working; place of work; a literary composition; (*pl*) a factory, plant. • *vi* to be employed, to have a job; to operate (a machine, etc); to produce effects; (*with* **on**) to (attempt to) persuade by persistent effort; (*with* **out**) to undertake a regular, planned series of exercises. • *vt* to effect, to achieve;

(*with* **off**) to eliminate though effort; (*with* **over**) to examine closely; (*inf*) to assault violently. —**workable** *adj*.—**worker** *n*.

workaday /'wɜːkəˌdeɪ/ *adj* suited for working days; ordinary, mundane.

workaholic /ˌwɜːkə'hɒlɪk/ *n* a person with a compulsive need to work.

workbench /'wɜːkbentʃ/ *n* a bench designed for woodworking, metalworking, etc.

workbook /-bʊk/ *n* an exercise book with spaces for answers to set questions.

workbox /-bɒks/ *n* a box for holding material and tools for work.

workday /-deɪ/ *see* **working day**.

work force /-fɔːs/ *n* the number of workers who are engaged in a particular industry; the total number of workers who are potentially available.

workhorse /-hɔːs/ *n* a horse used for work on a farm; (*inf*) a person or thing that works the hardest in an organization, business, etc.

workhouse /-hɑʊs/ *n* (*formerly*) in UK, a public institution for paupers; in US, a prison for petty offenders whose sentences are served by manual labour.

working /'wɜːkɪŋ/ *adj* spent in or used for work; functioning. • *n* operation; mode of operation; (*pl*) the manner of functioning or operating; (*pl*) the parts of a mine that are worked.

working capital *n* liquid capital available for the daily operation of a business.

working class *n* people who work for wages, *esp* manual workers; proletariat.—*also adj*.

working day, workday *n* a day for working as opposed to a holiday; the number of hours spent working during the day.

working drawing *n* a plan or drawing used to guide a builder, engineer, etc during the actual construction.

working party *n* (*esp Brit*) a committee established to investigate a particular problem.

workload /-ləʊd/ *n* the amount of work done or required to be done in a particular period.

workman /-mən/ *n* (*pl* **workmen**) a person employed in manual labour; a person who works in a particular manner.

workmanlike /-mənˌlaɪk/ *adj* skilful.

workmanship /-mənʃɪp/ *n* technical skill; the way a thing is made, style.

workmate /-meɪt/ *n* a colleague with whom one works.

work of art *n* a fine painting, sculpture, building, etc; something that has the aesthetic qualities of a work of art.

work-out /'wɜːkɑʊt/ *n* a session of strenuous physical exercises.

workroom /-ruːm/ *n* a room for work, a workshop.

workshop /-ʃɒp/ *n* a room or building where work is done; a seminar for specified intensive study, work, etc.

workshy /-ʃaɪ/ *adj* disinclined to work.

work station /-ˌsteɪʃən/ *n* a place in an office, *esp* a desk equipped with a computer terminal, where a single person works.

work-to-rule *n* industrial action in which employees adhere strictly to rules and regulations in the workplace with the aim of slowing production.—**work to rule** *vi*.

worktop /-tɒp/ *n* an area in a kitchen, *usu* with a laminated surface, where food is prepared.

world /wɜːld/ *n* the planet earth and its inhabitants; mankind; the universe; a sphere of existence; the public.

worldbeater /'wɜːldˌbiːtər/ *n* someone or something surpassing all others, a champion.—**worldbeating** *adj*.

world-class /-'klæs/ *adj* of the highest quality in the world.

worldly /-li/ *adj* (**worldlier, worldliest**) earthly, rather than spiritual; material; experienced.

world music *n* popular music of or combining ethnic styles from various different countries around the world.

world power *n* a country that is powerful enough to influence international politics.

World Series *n* in the US, an annual competition (best of seven games) between the winning teams of the two major North American baseball leagues.

world-shaking *adj* of momentous significance.

World War I *n* a war (1914–18) in which Belgium, France, Italy, Japan, Russia, UK, US, and other allies defeated Germany, Austria, Bulgaria, and Turkey.

World War II *n* a war (1939–45) in which France, UK, US, USSR, and other allies defeated Germany, Italy, and Japan.

world-weary /-ˌwɪriː/ *adj* tired of life.

worldwide /-waɪd/ or /-'waɪd/ *adj* universal.

World Wide Web *n* (*comput*) a hypertext-based document retrieval system linked to the Internet that allows easy access to information on a huge variety of subjects.—*also* **worldwide web.**

WORM *abbr* (*comput*) = Write Once Read Many Times: an optical disk that stores information which cannot then be over-written, used for data archiving and backup.

worm /wɜrm/ *n* an earthworm; an insect larva; the thread of a screw; (*comput*) a virus in the form of a program that makes copies of itself from one disk drive to another or through email and may cause serious damage. • *vt* to work (oneself into a position) slowly or secretly; to extract information by slow and persistent means.

worm-eaten /'wɜrm,iːtən/ *adj* eaten into (as if) by worms; decayed; antiquated.

worms /-z/ *or* /vɔrmz/ *n sing* any disease or condition caused by infestation with parasitic worms.

worm's-eye view /'wɜrmz,aɪ/ *n* the view from the very bottom or humblest position.

wormwood /-wʊd/ *n* a European plant that yields a bitter oil used in making absinthe; (something causing) bitterness.

wormy /'wɜrmi/ *adj* (**wormier, wormiest**) infested with or eaten by worms; resembling a worm; full of holes caused by burrowing worms.

worn /wɔrn/ *see* **wear.**

worn-out /-aʊt/ *adj* (*machine, etc*) past its useful life; (*person*) depressed, tired.

worriment /'wɜrimənt/ *n* (*inf*) worry, anxiety.

worrisome /-səm/ *adj* causing worry; prone to anxiety.

worry /'wɜri/ *vb* (**worrying, worried**) *vt* to bother, pester, harass. • *vi* to be uneasy or anxious; to fret. • *n* (*pl* **worries**) a cause or feeling of anxiety.—**worrier** *n.*

worry beads *npl* a string of beads fiddled with for comfort or to relieve tension.

worse /wɜrs/ *adj* (*compar of* **bad** *and* **ill**) less favourable; not so well as before. • *adv* with great severity.—**worsen** *vti.*

worship /'wɜrʃɪp/ *n* religious adoration; a religious ritual, *eg* prayers; devotion. • *vb* (**worshipping, worshipped** *or* **worshiping, worshiped**) *vt* to adore or idolize. • *vi* to participate in a religious service.—**worshipper, worshiper** *n.*

worshipful /-,fʊl/ *adj* feeling or displaying worship or respect; (*with cap*) in UK, used as a title of respect for various high-ranking officials.

worst /wɜrst/ *adj* (*superl of* **bad** *or* **ill;** *see also* **worse**) bad or ill in the highest degree; of the lowest quality. • *adv* to the worst degree. • *n* the least good part.

worst-case /'wɜrst,keɪs/ *adj* being, or taking account of, the worst possible situation or outcome (*worst-case scenario*).

worsted /- əd/ *n* twisted thread or yarn made from long, combed wool.

worth /wɜrθ/ *n* value; price; excellence; importance. • *adj* equal in value to; meriting.

worthless /'wɜrθləs/ *adj* valueless; useless; of bad character.—**worthlessness** *n.*

worthwhile /-waɪl/ *or* /-'waɪl/ *adj* important or rewarding enough to justify the effort.

worthy /'wɜrði/ *adj* (**worthier, worthiest**) virtuous; deserving. • *n* (*pl* **worthies**) a worthy person, a local celebrity.—**worthily** *adv.*

would /wʊd/ *or* /wəd/ *see* **will**².

would-be /'wʊdbiː/ *adj* aspiring or professing to be.

wouldn't /-ənt/ = would not.

wound¹ /wuːnd/ *n* any cut, bruise, hurt, or injury caused to the skin; hurt feelings. • *vt* to injure.

wound² *see* **wind**².

wove /wəʊv/, **woven** /'wəʊvən/ *see* **weave.**

wow /waʊ/ *interj* exclamation of astonishment. • *n* (*sl*) a success.

wp, WP *abbr* = word processing; word processor.

wpm *abbr* = words per minute.

wrack¹ /ræk/ *n* destruction; **wrack and ruin** (the remains of) something destroyed.

wrack² *n* seaweed deposited on the shore.

wraith /reɪθ/ *n* an apparition of a living person, supposedly a sign of impending death; any ghost.

wrangle /'ræŋgəl/ *vi* to argue; to dispute noisily. • *n* a noisy argument.

wrap /ræp/ *vt* (**wrapping, wrapped**) to fold (paper) around (a

present, purchase etc); to wind (around); to enfold; (*with* **up**) to enclose in paper; (*inf*) to make the final arrangements for. • *vi* (*with* **up**) to put warm clothes on; (*inf*) to be quiet. • *n* a shawl.

wrapper /'ræpər/ *n* one who or that which wraps; a book jacket; a light dressing gown.

wrasse /ræs/ *n* a marine food fish with thick lips and brilliant colouration.

wrath /ræθ/ *n* intense anger; rage.—**wrathful** *adj.*

wreak /riːk/ *vt* to inflict or exact (*eg* vengeance, havoc).

wreath /riːθ/ *n* (*pl* **wreaths**) a twisted ring of leaves, flowers, etc; something like this in shape.

wreathe /riːð/ *vti* to form into a wreath; to decorate with wreaths; to move or coil in wreaths.

wreck /rɛk/ *n* accidental destruction of a ship; a badly damaged ship; a run-down person or thing. • *vt* to destroy; to ruin.

wreckage /'rɛkɪdʒ/ *n* the process of wrecking; remnants from a wreck.

wrecked /-t/ *adj* (*sl*) intoxicated by alcohol or drugs; exhausted.

wrecker /'rɛkər/ *n* a person who causes a wreck; a demolition worker; a breakdown van.

wren /rɛn/ *n* small brownish songbird, with a short erect tail.

wrench /-tʃ/ *vt* to give something a violent pull or twist; to injure with a twist, to sprain; to distort. • *n* a forceful twist; a sprain; a spanner; emotional upset caused by parting.

wrest /rɛst/ *vt* to take with force (from); to seize; to obtain by toil.

wrestle /'rɛsəl/ *vti* to fight by holding and trying to throw one's opponent down; to struggle. • *n* a contest in which the opponents wrestle.—**wrestler** *n.*

wrestling /-ɪŋ/ *n* the skill or sport of fighting by grappling and trying to throw each other to the ground.

wretch /rɛtʃ/ *n* a miserable or pitied person; a despised and scorned person.

wretched /'rɛtʃəd/ *adj* very miserable; in poor circumstances; despicable.—**wretchedly** *adv.*—**wretchedness** *n.*

wrier /raɪər/, **wriest** /-əst/ *see* **wry.**

wriggle /'rɪgəl/ *vi* to move with a twisting motion; to squirm, to writhe; to use evasive tricks.—*also n.*—**wriggler** *n.*—**wriggly** *adj.*

wright /raɪt/ *n* a maker (*eg playwright*), a builder (*eg shipwright*).

wring /rɪŋ/ *vt* (**wringing, wrung**) to twist; to compress by twisting in order to squeeze water from; to pain; to obtain forcibly.

wrinkle /'rɪŋkəl/ *n* a small crease or fold on a surface. • *vti* to make or become wrinkled.

wrist /rɪst/ *n* the joint connecting the hand with the forearm.

wristband /'rɪstbænd/ *n* the cuff of a sleeve that covers the wrist; a band round the wrist that absorbs sweat.

wristwatch /-wɒtʃ/ *n* a watch worn on a bracelet or strap around the wrist.

writ /rɪt/ *n* (*law*) a written court order.

write /raɪt/ *vb* (**writing, wrote,** *pp* **written**) *vt* to form letters on paper with a pen or pencil; to express in writing; to compose (a letter, music, literary work, etc); to communicate by letter; (*with* **off**) to cancel a bad debt as a loss; (*inf*) to damage (a vehicle) beyond repair; (*with* **down**) *vt* to put in writing; to harm or demean (a person) in writing; (*with* **up**) to describe, update, or put into finished form by writing; to praise or publicize in writing. • *vi* to be a writer; (*with* **down to** *or* **for**) to write in a simplified style for a less educated taste.

write-off /'raɪt,ɒf/ *n* a debt cancelled as a loss; (*inf*) a badly damaged car.

writer /'r aɪtər/ *n* an author; a scribe or clerk.

writer's cramp *n* painful spasms or paralysis in the thumb and fingers from excessive writing.

write-up *n* a published report or review, *esp* a favourable one.

writhe /raɪð/ *vi* to twist the body violently, as in pain; to squirm (under, at).

writing /'raɪtɪŋ/ *n* the act of forming letters on paper, etc; a written document; authorship; (*pl*) literary works.

writing paper *n* paper treated to accept ink and used *esp* for letters.

written /'rɪtən/ *see* **write.**

wrong /rɒŋ/ *adj* not right, incorrect; mistaken, misinformed; immoral. • *n* harm; injury done to another. • *adv* incorrectly. • *vt* to do wrong to.—**wrongly** *adv.*

wrongdoer /'rɒŋ,duːər/ *n* a person who breaks (moral) laws.—**wrongdoing** *n.*

wrongful /-fʊl/ *adj* unwarranted, unjust.—**wrongfully** *adv.*

wrong-headed /-'hɛdɪd/ *adj* stubborn; of poor judgment.

wrote /rəʊt/ *see* **write**.

wrought /rɒt/ *adj* formed; made; (*metals*) shaped by hammering, etc.

wrought iron *n* iron that is forged or rolled, not cast.

wrung /rɛŋ/ *see* **wring**.

wry /raɪ/ *adj* (**wryer, wryest** *or* **wrier, wriest**) twisted, contorted; ironic.—**wryly** *adv*.—**wryness** *n*.

wt *abbr* = weight.

wunderkind /'vʊndər,kɪnd/ *n* (*pl* **wunderkinder, wunderkinds**) a child prodigy; a whizz kid.

wurst /wərst/ or /wʊrst/ *n* any of various types of spicy sausage from Germany or Austria.

WWI *abbr* = World War I.

WWII *abbr* = World War II.

WWF *abbr* = Worldwide Fund for Nature.

WWW *abbr* = World Wide Web.

WYSIWYG /'wɪzi,wɪɡ/ *adj* (*acronym*) (*comput*) what you see is what you get: meaning that the layout and style of text, etc, on screen will be exactly as printed out.

X

X, x /ɛks/ *n* the 24th letter of the English alphabet; something shaped like an X; the mark used by an illiterate person to represent a signature; a mark (on a map) to show a particular spot.

X, x *symbol* (*math*) unknown quantity; the figure 10. • *n* an unknown or mysterious factor.

xanth- /zænθ/, **xantho-** /zænθo:/ or /-θə/ *prefix* yellow.

xanthein /ˈzænθiin/ *n* a soluble yellow pigment found in plant tissue.

xanthic /-ɪk/ *adj* yellowish; of or relating to xanthine.

xanthine /-ɪːn/ *n* a yellowish-white crystalline compound allied to uric acid; a derivative of this.

Xanthippe /zænˈθɪpi/ *n* the wife of Socrates (*fl* 5th century BC); a quarrelsome scolding wife.

xantho-, xanth- /ˈzænθo:/ or /-θə/ *prefix* yellow.

xanthochroid /ˈzænθəˌkrɔɪd/ *adj* blond and blue-eyed with fair white skin. • *n* an xanthochroid person.

xanthoma /zænˈθoːmə/ *n* (*pl* **xanthomas, xanthomata**) a small yellow tumour in the skin caused by deposits of lipids.— **xanthomatous** *adj*.

xanthophyll /ˈzænθə fɪl/ *n* (*bot*) an orange or yellow pigment in autumn leaves.—**xanthophyllous** *adj*.

xanthopsia /ˈzænθoːpsɪə/ *n* a disturbance in vision causing everything to appear yellow.

xanthosis /ˈzænθoːsɪs/ *n* a yellow pigmentation of the skin in diabetes, etc.

xanthous /ˈzænθəs/ *adj* yellow.

x-axis /ˈɛksˌæksɪs/ *n* (*pl* **x-axes**) the reference axis of a graph along which the x coordinate is measured.

X-chromosome *n* one of the pair (*with* the Y-chromosome) of sex chromosomes that occur in females.

Xe (*chem symbol*) xenon.

xebec /ˈziːbɛk/ *n* a small three-masted Mediterranean sailing vessel with lateen sails.

xeno- /ˈzɛnoː/ or /ˈziːnoː/, **xen-** /ˈzɛn/ or /ziːn/ *prefix* strange; foreign.

xenolith /ˈzɛnəliθ/ or /ˈziːn-/ *n* (*geol*) a rock occuring in a system of rocks to which it does not belong.

xenomorphic /ˈzɛnoˌmɔrfɪk/ *adj* (*mineral grain*) abnormal in shape owing to the pressure of adjacent minerals in rock.

xenon /ˈzɛnɒn/ *n* a heavy inert colourless odourless gaseous element found in tiny quantities in the atmosphere.

xenophobia /ˌzɛnəˈfoːbiə/ or /ˌziːn-/ *n* fear or dislike of strangers or foreigners.—**xenophobe** *n*.—**xenophobic** *adj*.

xer-, xero- /ˈziːroː/ or /ˈzɛroː/ *prefix* dryness.

xeroderma /ˌziːrəˈdərmə/, **xerodermia** /ˌziːrəˈdərmiə/ *n* dryness of the skin caused by a deficiency in secretions from the sebaceous glands.

xerography /ziːˈrɒɡrəfi/ or /zɛ-/ *n* photocopying by using light to form an electrostatic image on a photoconductive plate to which toner powder adheres, the particles then being fused by heat and the image transferred onto paper.—**xerographic** *adj*.—**xerographically** *adv*.

xerophilous /ziːˈrɒfɪləs/ or /zɛ-/ *adj* (*plant*) drought-loving; adapted to a dry climate.—**xerophily** *n*.

xerophthalmia /ˌzɪrɒfˈθælmiə/ *n* a disease of the eye with dryness and ulceration of the cornea, caused by vitamin deficiency.—**xerophthalmic** *adj*.

xerophyte /ˈziːrəˌfaɪt/ or /zɛ-/ *n* a xerophilous plant, *eg* cactus, that has adapted for growth with a limited water supply.—**xerophytic** *adj*.

xerostomia /ˌziːrɒsˌtəmiə/ *n* abnormal dryness of the mouth caused by failure of the salivary glands.

Xerox /ˈziːrɒks/ *n* (*trademark*) a photocopying process using xerography; the copy produced by this. • *vt* to produce a copy in this way.

x-height *n* (*print*) the height of the letter x in lowercase.

xi /saɪ/ or /ɡzaɪ/, /zaɪ/ *n* (*pl* **xis**) the 14th letter of the Greek alphabet.

xiphisternum /ˌzɪfəˈstərnəm/ *n* (*pl* **xiphisterna**) (*anat, zool*) the lowest part of the breastbone, the xiphoid process.—**xiphisternal** *adj*.

xiphoid /ˈzɪfɔɪd/ *adj* sword-shaped. • *n* the xiphoid process.

xiphoid process *n* the xiphisternum.

Xmas /ˈkrɪsməs/ or /ˈɛksməs/ *abbr* = Christmas.

X-ray, x-ray /ˈɛksreɪ/ *n* radiation of very short wavelengths, capable of penetrating solid bodies, and printing on a photographic plate a shadow picture of objects not permeable by light rays. • *vt* to photograph by x-rays.

xylem /ˈzaɪlɛm/ *n* the woody vegetable tissue in plants that conducts water and gives support.

xylo- /ˈzaɪloː/, **xyl-** /ˈzaɪl/ *prefix* wood.

xylograph /ˈzaɪləˌɡræf/ *n* a wood engraving; an impression made from a wood block.

xylography /zaɪˈlɒɡrəfi/ *n* the art of making wood engravings or making woodcuts; the art of printing from wood blocks.—**xylographer** *n*.—**xylographic** *adj*.—**xylographically** *adv*.

xyloid /ˈzaɪˌlɔɪd/ *adj* like wood.

xylophagous /zaɪˈlɒfəɡəs/ *adj* (*insects*) wood-eating.

xylophone /ˈzaɪləˌfoːn/ *n* a percussion instrument consisting of a series of wooden bars which are struck with small hammers.—**xylophonic** *adj*.

xylophonist /ˈzaɪləˌfoːnɪst/ *n* a performer on a xylophone.

xylotomous /zaɪˈlɒtəməs/ *adj* (*insects*) boring into or cutting wood.

Y

Y (*chem symbol*) yttrium.

Y /waɪ/ *abbr* = yen (Japanese currency).

Y, y *n* the 25th letter of the English alphabet; something shaped like a Y.

Y, y *symbol* (*math*) the second unknown quantity.

y *abbr* = year; yard.

yabber /ˈjæbər/ *n* (*Austral sl*) talk, *esp* in broken English. • *vti* to talk.

yacht /jɒt/ *n* a sailing or mechanically driven vessel, used for pleasure cruises or racing. • *vi* to race or cruise in a yacht.—**yachting** *n*.—**yachtsman** *n* (*pl* **yachtsmen**).—**yachtswoman** *nf* (*pl* **yachtswomen**).

yackety-yak (*var. of* **yak²**) *n* (*sl*) persistent trivial chatter.

yah /jæ/ *interj* expressing derision.

yahoo /ˈjæhuː/ *n* (*pl* **yahoos**) a crude, vicious person.

Yahweh, Yahveh /ˈjɒweɪ/ *n* Jehovah.

yak¹ /jæk/ *n* a domesticated species of ox found in Tibet having horns and long hair.

yak² *n* (*sl*) persistent trivial talk or chatter. • *vi* (**yakking, yakked**) to talk in this way.

Yale lock *n* (*trademark*) a type of cylinder lock for doors.

yam /jæm/ *n* the edible, starchy tuberous root of a tropical climbing plant; sweet potato.

yamen /ˈjɑmən/ *n* (*formerly*) in Imperial China, the official residence of a Chinese official.

yammer /ˈjæmər/ *vi* (*inf*) to whimper or whine constantly; (*inf*) to complain loudly and persistently. • *n* (*inf*) a whining or complaining sound.

Yank /jæŋk/ *n* (*inf*) a Yankee.

yank *vti* to pull suddenly, to jerk. • *n* a sudden sharp pull.

Yankee /ˈjæŋki/ *n* (*inf*) a citizen of the US, an American.

yap /jæp/ *vi* (**yapping, yapped**) to yelp, bark; (*sl*) to talk constantly, *esp* in a noisy or irritating manner.

yapok, yapock /ˈjæpɒk/ *n* a tropical American aquatic marsupial with webbed hind feet, thick fur, and a long tail.

yard¹ /jɑrd/ *n* a unit of measure of three feet and equivalent to 0.9144 metres; (*naut*) a spar hung across a mast to support a sail.

yard² *n* an enclosed concrete area, *esp* near a building; an enclosure for a commercial activity (*eg* a shipyard); an area of ground for growing herbs, fruits, flowers, or vegetables, *usu* attached to a house, a garden; an area with tracks for the making up of trains, servicing of locomotives, etc.

yardage¹ /ˈjɑrdɪdʒ/ *n* a length measured in yards.

yardage² *n* the use of a yard; the charge made for this.

yardarm /ˈjɑrdɑrm/ *n* (*naut*) either half of a yard.

yardstick /-stɪk/ *n* a standard used in judging.

yare /jər/ *adj* ready; active, brisk; (*yacht, etc*) easily handled.

yarmulke /ˈjɑrməlkə/ *n* a skullcap worn by Jewish men at prayer and by Orthodox male Jews at all times.

yarn /jɑrn/ *n* fibres of wool, cotton etc spun into strands for weaving, knitting, etc; (*inf*) a tale or story. • *vi* to tell a yarn; to talk at length.

yarrow /ˈjæroː/ *n* a strongly scented astringent herb with clusters of small flowers.

yashmak, yashmac /ˈjæʃmæk/ *n* a veil worn by Muslim women, showing only the eyes.

yataghan, yatagan /ˈjætəˌɡæn/ *or* /-ɡən/ *n* a short curved Turkish sword without a guard.

yatter /ˈjætər/ *vi* (*sl*) to gabble, to chatter.—*also n*.

yauld /jɔːd/ *or* /jɒd/, /jɒld/ *adj* (*Scot*) active; alert.

yaupon /jɔːpən/ *n* an American evergreen shrub of the holly family.

yaw /jɒ/ *vi* (*ship, aircraft*) to deviate from a course; (*aircraft*) to turn from side to side about the vertical axis. • *vt* to cause to yaw. • *n* a yawing movement or course.

yawl /jɒl/ *n* a two-masted sailing vessel with its aftermast at the stern.

yawn /jɒn/ *vi* to open the jaws involuntarily and inhale, as from drowsiness; to gape.—*also n*.

yawning /ˈjɒnɪŋ/ *adj* gaping; wide-open; drowsy.—**yawningly** *adv*.

yawp /jɒp/ *vi* to cry harshly, to scream; (*sl*) to speak foolishly. • *n* such a cry or talk.

yaws /jɒz/ *n sing* a tropical disease causing ulceration of the skin, framboesia.

y-axis /ˈwaɪˌæksɪs/ *n* (*pl* **y-axes**) the reference axis of a graph along which the y coordinate is measured.

Yb (*chem symbol*) ytterbium.

Y-chromosome *n* one of the pair (with the X-chromosome) of sex chromosomes that occur in males.

yclept /ɪˈklɛpt/ *adj* (*arch*) named.

yd., yds *abbr* = yard(s).

ye¹ /jiː/ *pron* (*arch*) you (the person addressed and others) the old method of printing the.

ye² *definite article* (*arch*) the.

yea /jeɪ/ *adv, n* (*arch*) yes.

yeah /jæ/ *or* /jɛ/ *adv* (*inf*) yes.

yean /jiːn/ *vi* (*sheep, goat*) to bring forth (a lamb or kid).

yeanling /ˈjiːlɪŋ/ *n* a lamb or kid.

year /jiːr/ *n* a period of twelve months, or 365 or 366 days, beginning with 1 January and ending with 31 December; a period of approximately twelve months.

yearbook /ˈjiːrbʊk/ *n* an annual publication reviewing the events of the previous year or bringing information up to date.

yearling /-lɪŋ/ *n* an animal a year old or in its second year.

yearlong /-lɒŋ/ *adj* lasting a year.

yearly /-li/ *adj* occurring every year; lasting a year. • *adv* once a year; from year to year.

yearn /jɜrn/ *vi* to feel desire (for); to long for.—**yearning** *n*.

yeast /jiːst/ *n* a fungus that causes alcoholic fermentation, used in brewing and baking.

yeasty /ˈjiːsti/ *adj* (**yeastier, yeastiest**) smelling of or containing yeast.—**yeastiness** *n*.

yegg /jɛɡ/, **yegman** /-mən/ *n* (*pl* **yeggs, yegmen**) (*US sl*) a safecracker, a criminal.

yeld /jɛld/ *adj* (*Scot*) barren, giving no milk.

yell /jɛl/ *vti* to shout loudly; to scream; to emit a yell. • *n* a loud shout; a concerted cheer by supporters, students, etc, at a game.

yellow /ˈjɛloː/ *adj* of the colour of lemons, egg yolk, etc; having a yellowish skin; (*inf*) cowardly. • *n* the colour yellow. • *vi* to become or turn yellow.

yellow-belly /-bɛli/ *n* (*pl* **yellow-bellies**) (*sl*) a coward.—**yellow-bellied** *adj*.

yellow fever *n* an infectious tropical fever caused by a virus transmitted by certain mosquitoes.

yellowhammer /-ˌhæmər/ *n* a small European bird with a yellow head, neck, and breast.

yellow jacket *n* in the US, a hornet or wasp with yellow markings.

yellow pages *npl* (part of) a telephone directory that lists business subscribers under different categories according to the type of service offered.

yellow spot *n* (*anat*) the point of acutest vision in the retina.

yellow streak *n* (*inf*) a cowardly nature.

yellowwood /-wʊd/ *n* an American tree; its wood, which yields a yellow dye.

yelp /jɛlp/ *vti* to utter a sharp, shrill cry or bark.—*also n*.

yen¹ /jɛn/ *n* (*pl* **yen**) the monetary unit of Japan.

yen² *n* (*inf*) a yearning, an ambition.

yeoman /ˈjoːmən/ *n* (*pl* **yeomen**) (*formerly*) a farmer who cultivated his own land; a non-commissioned officer in the navy, marines.

yeomanly /-li/ *adj* of or like a yeoman; workmanlike.—*also adv*.

yeoman of the guard *n* a member of the British sovereign's veteran bodyguard.

yeomanry /-ri/ *n* yeomen collectively; a volunteer cavalry force raised from country districts as a home guard (1761–1907) now part of the Territorial Army.

yeoman service *n* effective assistance.

yep /jɛp/ *adv* (*inf*) yes.

yerba (maté) /'jɛrbə/ *n* an infusion of dried leaves of the maté, which makes a mildly stimulating tea.

yes /jɛs/ *adv* a word of affirmation or consent.

yes man *n* a servile, fawning, sycophantic person.

yester /'jɛstər/ *adv* (*rare*) of yesterday.

yesterday /'jɛstərdeɪ/ *n* the day before today; the recent past. • *adv* on the day before today; recently.

yet /jɛt/ *adv* still; so far; even. • *conj* nevertheless; however; still.

yeti /'jɛti/ *n* a mysterious animal thought to live high in the Himalayan mountains but never seen.—*also* **abominable snowman**.

yew /ju:/ *n* an evergreen tree or shrub with thin, sharp leaves and red berries.

Y-fronts /'wɔɪfrɛnts/ *npl* (*trademark*) men's underpants with an inverted Y-shaped opening at the front.

Ygdrasil, Yggdrasil /'ɪgdrəsɪl/ *n* (*Norse myth*) an ash tree whose roots and branches bind together earth, heaven, and hell.

yid /jɪd/ *n* (*derog*) a Jew.

Yiddish /'jɪdɪʃ/ *n* a mixed German and Hebrew dialect spoken by European Jews.

yield /ji:ld/ *vt* to resign; to give forth, to produce, as a crop, result, profit, etc. • *vi* to submit; to give way to physical force, to surrender. • *n* the amount yielded; the profit or return on a financial investment.

yip /jɪp/ *n* a cry, an exclamation. • *vi* (**yipping, yipped**) to utter a yip.

yippee /'jɪpi:/ or /-'pi:/ *interj* used to express exuberant delight.

ylang-ylang /'i:læŋˌi:læŋ/ *n* a Malaysian tree with fragrant flowers; a perfume made from the flowers.

YMCA *abbr* = Young Men's Christian Association.

YMHA *abbr* = Young Men's Hebrew Association.

yob /jɒb/, **yobbo** /'jɒbo:/ *n* (*pl* **yobs, yobbos**) (*sl*) a young lout, a hooligan.

yodel /'jo:dəl/ *vti* (**yodelling, yodelled** or **yodeling, yodeled**) to sing, alternating from the ordinary voice to falsetto.—**yodeller, yodeler** *n*.

yoga /'jo:gə/ *n* a system of exercises for attaining bodily and mental control and well-being.—**yogic** *adj*.

yogi /'jo:gi/ *n* (*pl* **yogis, yogin**) a person skilled in yoga.

yoghurt, yogurt /'jɒgərt/ *n* a semi-liquid food made from milk curdled by bacteria.

yo-heave-ho /'jo:hi:vˌho:/ *interj* (*formerly*) a cry made by sailors while heaving anchor, etc.

yoicks /jɔɪks/ *interj* a foxhunting cry urging on the hounds.

yoke /jo:k/ *n* a bond or tie; slavery; the wooden frame joining oxen to make them pull together; part of a garment that is fitted below the neck. • *vt* to put a yoke on; to join together.

yokel /'jo:kəl/ *n* (*derog*) country people who are regarded as unsophisticated and simple-minded.

yolk /jo:k/ *n* the yellow part of an egg.

yolk sac *n* the membrane enclosing an egg yolk.

Yom Kippur /jɒmkɪ'pur/ *n* an annual Jewish holiday marked by fasting and prayer.—*also* **Day of Atonement**.

yomp /jɒmp/ *vi* to march laboriously carrying heavy equipment, *esp* over rough terrain.

yon /jɒn/ *adj, adv* (*dial*) yonder, over there.

yonder /'jɒndər/ *adv* over there.

yore /jɔr/ *n* time long past.

Yorkist /'jɔrkɪst/ *n* an adherent of the royal house of York in England, *esp* during the Wars of the Roses (1455-85).—*also adj*.

Yorkshire pudding *n* a baked pudding made from batter and traditionally eaten with roast beef.

Yorkshire terrier *n* a small shaggy breed of terrier with a long coat of bluish grey and tan hair.

you /ju:/ *pron* (*gram*) 2nd person singular or plural; the person or persons spoken to.

you'd /ju:d/ or /jud/ = you would; you had.

you'll /ju:l/ or /jul/ = you will; you shall.

young /jɛŋ/ *adj* in the early period of life; in the first part of growth; new; inexperienced. • *n* young people; offspring.

youngling /-lɪŋ/ *n* (*poet*) a young child or animal.

youngster /jɛŋ'stər/ *n* a young person; a youth.

your /jɔr/ or /jur/ *poss adj* of or belonging to or done by you.

you're /jur/ or /jɔr/, /jɔr/ = you are.

yours /jurz/ or /jɔrz/ *poss pron* of or belonging to you.

yourself /jɔrˌsɛlf/ or /jur-/ *pron* (*pl* **yourselves**) the emphatic and reflexive form of **you**.

youth /ju:θ/ *n* the period between childhood and adulthood; young people collectively; the early stages of something; a young man or boy.—**youthful** *adj*.—**youthfully** *adv*.

youth hostel *n* a supervised lodging for *usu* young travellers.

you've /ju:v/ or /juv/ = you have.

yowl /jaul/ *n* a loud mournful cry, *esp* from pain.—*also vi*.

yo-yo /'jo:jo:/ *n* (*pl* **yo-yos**) a hand-held toy made of a flat spool which can be made to wind up and down a piece of string.

yr *abbr* = year; younger; your.

yrs *abbr* = years; yours.

ytterbium /ɪ'tərbiəm/ *n* a soft metallic element of the lanthanide series.

yttrium /'ɪtriəm/ *n* a metallic element used in alloys and lasers.

yuan /ju:'ɒn/ *n* (*pl* **yuan**) the monetary unit of the People's Republic of China.

yucca /'jɛkə/ *n* a plant with stiff, spear-like leaves and white flowers.

yuck /jɛk/ *interj* (*sl*) expressing disgust.

yucky /'jɛki/ *adj* (**yuckier, yuckiest**) (*sl*) disgusting.

yule /ju:l/ *n* Christmas.

yule log /'ju:llɒg/ *n* a large log traditionally burnt in the fire on Christmas Eve.

yuletide /'ju:ltaɪd/ *n* the Christmas festival or season.

yummy /'jɛmi/ *adj* (**yummier, yummiest**) (*inf*) tasty, pleasing. • *interj* yum-yum.

yum-yum /'jɛmˌjɛm/ *interj* used to express pleasure, *esp* when eating.

yup /jɛp/ *adv* (*inf*) yes.

yuppie /'jɛpi/ *n* (*inf*) any young professional regarded as affluent, ambitious, materialistic, etc.

yurt /jurt/ or /jɔrt/ *n* a circular portable tent of skins used by the Mongolian nomads of Siberia.

YWCA *abbr* = Young Women's Christian Association.

YWHA *abbr* = Young Women's Hebrew Association.

Z

Z /zɛd/ or /ziː/ (*symbol*) (*physics*) impedance; (*chem*) atomic number.

z /zɛd/ (*symbol*) (*math*) an algebraic variable; the z-axis.

Z, z /zɛd/ *n* the 26th letter of the English alphabet; something shaped like a Z; (*math*) the third unknown quantity.

z. *abbr* = zero; zone.

zabaglione /ˌzɒbɒˈloːneɪ/ *n* a dessert of whipped egg yolks, sugar and marsala wine.

Zaïrese /zaɪrˈiːz/ *n* a native or inhabitant of the former African republic of Zaïre.—*also adj*.

zamindar /zəˈmiːndər/ *n* (*hist*) in India, a district tax collector under the Mogul empire; a landowner paying land tax.—*also* **zemindar**.

zany /ˈzeɪni/ *adj* (**zanier, zaniest**) comical; eccentric.—**zanily** *adv*.—**zaniness** *n*.

zap /zæp/ *vb* (**zapping, zapped**) *vt* to attack; to kill; to bombard; (*comput*) to get rid of data. • *vi* to rush around.

zappy /ˈzæpi/ *adj* (**zappier, zappiest**) (*sl*) energetic, snappy.

zareba, zariba /zəˈriːbə/ *n* in northern East Africa, a stockade made of thorn hedges as a protection against wild animals or enemies; a place so protected.

zarf /zɑrf/ *n* an ornamental holder for a coffee cup used in Arab countries.

zarzuela /zɑrˈzweɪlə/ *n* a traditional Spanish one-act comic opera with a satirical theme and including dialogue.

z-axis /ˈziːæksɪs/ *n* the reference axis of a three-dimensional coordinate system, along which the z-coordinate is measured.

zeal /ziːl/ *n* fervent devotion; fanaticism.

zealot /ˈzɛlət/ *n* an extreme partisan, a fanatic.

zealous /ˈzɛləs/ *adj* full of zeal; ardent.—**zealously** *adv*.—**zealousness** *n*.

zebra /ˈziːbrə/ or /ˈzɛb-/ *n* (*pl* **zebras, zebra**) a black and white striped wild animal of southern and eastern Africa related to the horse.—**zebrine** *adj*.

zebra crossing *n* a street crossing for pedestrians marked by black and white strips on the road.

zebu /ˈziːbuː/ *n* (*pl* **zebus, zebu**) an Asian and African ox with a prominent hump and a large dewlap.

zee /ziː/ *n* (*pl* **zees**) in US, the letter z.

zedoary /ˈzɛdoˌɛri/ *n* an aromatic substance like ginger made from the root stock of an Indian plant.

Zeitgeist /ˈtsɔɪtˌgaɪst/ *n* the spirit of the time; the beliefs, attitudes, tastes, etc, of a particular period.

zemindar /zɪˌmiːnˈdɑr/ *see* **zamindar**.

zemstvo /ˈzɛmstvo/ *n* (*pl* **zemstvos, zemstva**) a local elective assembly in the old Russian empire.

Zen /zɛn/ *n* a Japanese Buddhist sect that emphasizes self-awareness and self-mastery as the means to enlightenment.

zenana /zeˈnɒnə/ *n* the part of the house reserved for women and girls in a Muslim household.

Zend-Avesta /ˌzɛndəˈvɛstə/ *n* the sacred writings of the Zoroastrians.

zenith /ˈziːnɪθ/ or /ˈzɛn/ *n* the point at which the sun or moon appears to be exactly overhead; peak, summit (of ambition, etc).

zephyr /ˈzɛfər/ *n* a soft, gentle breeze; a very thin woollen material; a garment made of this.

zeppelin /ˈzɛpəlɪn/ *n* a rigid, cigar-shaped airship.

zero /ˈziːroː/ *n* (*pl* **zeros, zeroes**) the symbol 0; nothing; the lowest point; freezing point, 0 degrees Celsius. • *vi* (*with* **in**) (*inf*) to focus attention on (a problem, subject, etc); (*inf*) to converge upon; (*with* **in on**) to concentrate fire (from a weapon) on a specific target.

zero gravity *n* weightlessness.

zero hour *n* the time at which something is scheduled to begin.

zest /zɛst/ *n* the outer part of the skin of an orange or lemon used to give flavour; enthusiasm; excitement.—**zestful** *adj*.—**zestfully** *adv*.—**zestfulness** *n*.

zeta /ˈziːtə/ *n* the sixth letter of the Greek alphabet.

zeugma /ˈzuːgmə/ or /ˈzjuː-/ *n* a figure of speech in which a word is used with two others, to only one of which it properly applies.—**zeugmatic** *adj*.

Zeus /ˈzuːs/ or /ˈzjuːs/ *n* (*Greek myth*) the king of the gods.

zigzag /ˈzɪgzæg/ *n* a series of short, sharp angles in alternate directions. • *adj* having sharp turns. • *vti* (**zigzagging, zigzagged**) to move or form in a zigzag.

zilch /zɪltʃ/, **zilcho** *n* (*sl*) nothing.

zillah /ˈzɪlə/ *n* (*hist*) an administrative district in India during British rule.

zillion /ˈzɪljən/ *n* (*pl* **zillion, zillions**) (*inf*) an indefinitely large number or quantity.

Zimb *abbr* = Zimbabwe.

Zimbabwean /zɪmˈbɒbwiən/ or /-weɪən/ *n* a native or inhabitant of the African republic of Zimbabwe.—*also adj*.

Zimmer /ˈzɪmər/ *n* (*trademark*) a frame of tubular metal used by the infirm as a walking aid.

zinc /zɪŋk/ *n* a bluish-white metallic element used in alloys and batteries. • *vt* (**zincing, zinced** *or* **zincking, zincked**) to coat with zinc.—**zincic** *adj*.

zincograph /ˈzɪŋkəˌgræf/ *n* a design in relief on a zinc plate; a print made from this. • *vti* to etch on zinc; to reproduce in this way.—**zincographer** *n*.—**zincographic** *adj*.—**zincography** *n*.

zing /zɪŋ/ *n* (*inf*) a high-pitched buzz; (*inf*) vitality, exuberance. • *vi* (*inf*) to move with a zinging sound.

zinnia /ˈzɪnjə/ *n* a tropical American plant with showy flowers.

Zionism /ˈzaɪəˌnɪzəm/ *n* a movement formerly to resettle Jews in Palestine as their national home, now concerned with the development of Israel.—**Zionist** *n, adj*.—**Zionistic** *adj*.

zip /zɪp/ *n* a light whizzing sound of a bullet, etc; (*sl*) brisk energy; a fastener on clothing, bags, etc with interlocking teeth. • *vb* (**zipping, zipped**) *vi* to move at high speed, to dart. • *vt* to fasten with a zip.—*also* **zip fastener**.

zip code *n* the US equivalent of a postcode that uses digits to denote an area.

zipper /ˈzɪpər/ *n* the US word for a zip.

zippy /-i/ *adj* (**zippier, zippiest**) speedy; energetic.

zircon /ˈzɜrkɒn/ *n* a variously coloured hard translucent mineral, some varieties of which are cut as gemstones.

zirconium /zərˈkoːniəm/ *n* a metallic element found in zircon and used in alloys.

zit /zɪt/ *n* (*sl*) a pimple, spot.

zither /ˈzɪðər/ *n* a musical instrument with 30–45 strings over a shallow sounding box played by plucking.—**zitherist** *n*.

zloty /ˈzlɒti/ *n* (*pl* **zlotys, zloty**) the monetary unit of Poland.

Zn (*chem symbol*) zinc.

zodiac /ˈzoːdiˌæk/ *n* an imaginary belt in the heavens along which the sun, moon, and chief planets appear to move, divided crosswise into twelve equal areas, called "signs of the zodiac," each named after a constellation; a diagram representing this.—**zodiacal** *adj*.

zodiacal light *n* a luminous triangular tract of sky sometimes seen before dawn or after dusk, *esp* in the tropics.

zoetrope /ˈzoːɪtrup/ *n* a toy with a revolving cylinder showing a series of pictures in apparent motion.

-zoic /ˈzoɪk/ *adj suffix* (*animal*) having a specified kind of existence; (*geol*) belonging to an era with a particular form of life.

Zollverein /ˈtsɒlfəˌraɪn/ *n* in 19th century, a union of German states with common customs tariffs against outside countries and free trade among themselves.

zombie, zombi /ˈzɒmbi/ *n* (*pl* **zombies**) a person who is lifeless and apathetic; an automaton.

zonate /ˈzoːneɪt/, **zonated** *adj* (*bot, zool*) marked with bands.

zone /zoːn/ *n* a region, area; a subdivision; any area with a specified use or restriction. • *vt* to divide or mark off into zones; to designate as a zone; to encircle with a zone.—**zonal** *adj*.

zonked /zɒŋt/ *adj* (*sl*) intoxicated by drugs or alcohol; (*sl*) exhausted.

zoo /zu:/ *n* (*pl* **zoos**) a place where a collection of living wild animals is kept for public showing.

zoo-, zo- /ˈzoːə/ or /ˈzuːə/ *prefix* animals.

zoochemistry /ˈzoːəˌkɛməstri/ *n* the chemistry of the constituents of animal bodies.—**zoochemical** *adj*.

zoogeography /ˌzoːədʒiˈɒgrəfi/ or /ˌzuːə-/ *n* the science of the geographical distribution of animals.—**zoogeographer** *n*.—**zoogeographic, zoogeographical** *adj*.

zoography /zoːˈɒgrəfi/ or /zuː-/ *n* descriptive zoology.—**zoographic, zoographical** *adj*.

zooid /ˈzoːɔɪd/ or /ˈzuː/ *adj* resembling but not completely being an animal or plant. • *n* a zooid organism; an animal organism produced by fission; (*corals, etc*) a member of a compound organism.

zool. *abbr* = zoological; zoology.

zoological garden /ˌzoːəˈlɒdʒɪkəlˈgɑːdən/ *n* a zoo.

zoologist /ˌzoːˈɒlədʒɪst/ *n* a person who studies animals and animal behaviour.

zoology /-dʒi/ or /zuː/ *n* (*pl* **zoologies**) the study of animals with regard to their classification, structure and habits.—**zoological** *adj*.—**zoologically** *adv*.

zoom /zu:m/ *vi* to go quickly, to speed; to climb upward sharply in an aeroplane; to rise rapidly; (*photog*) to focus in on an object using a zoom lens. • *n* the act of zooming; a zoom lens.

zoom lens *n* (*photog*) a camera lens that makes distant objects appear closer without moving the camera.

zoomorphism /ˌzoːəˈmɔrfɪzəm/ or /ˌzuːə/, /zuːˈmɔrfɪzəm/ *n* the representation (*esp* of a deity) in the form of or with the attributes of an animal.—**zoomorphic** *adj*.

zoophyte /ˈzoːəˌfaɪt/ or /ˈzuːə/ *n* any animal (*eg* coral, a sponge) that resembles a plant.—**zoophytic** *adj*.

zootomy /zoːˈɒtəmi/ *n* animal anatomy; the dissection of animals.—**zootomical** *adj*.—**zootomist** *n*.

zorille, zoril /ˈzɒrɪl/ *n* a small African mammal that resembles and smells like a skunk.

Zoroastrianism /ˌzɔroːˈæstriənɪzəm/ *n* a religious system founded by the Persian prophet Zoroaster (*c*.628–551 BC), based on the recognition of the dual principle of good and evil.—**Zoroastrian** *n, adj*.

Zouave /zuːˈɒv/ or /zwɒv/ *n* (*formerly*) a soldier in a French-Algerian infantry unit characterized by a colourful eastern-style uniform; a soldier in a similiar unit, *esp* a Union Army unit of the American Civil War.

zounds /zaʊndz/ *interj* (*arch*) expressing anger and astonishment.

Zr (*chem symbol*) zirconium.

zucchetto /zuːˈkɛtoː/ or /tsuː-/ *n* (*pl* **zucchettos**) a skullcap worn by Roman Catholic ecclesiastics, which varies in colour according to rank (black for a priest, purple for a bishop, red for a cardinal, white for the Pope).

zucchini /zuːˈkiːni/ *npl n* a type of small vegetable marrow.—*also* **courgette**.

Zulu /ˈzuːluː/ *n* (*pl* **Zulus, Zulu**) a member of a Negroid people of South Africa, or their language.—*also adj*.

zwieback /ˈzwiːbæk/ *n* a thin rusk.

zyg-, zygo- /ˈzaɪgoː/ *prefix* yoked, paired.

zygodactyl /ˌzaɪgoːˈdæktɪl/ *adj* (*bird*) with the toes in pairs, two pointing forward and two backward. • *n* a zygodactyl bird, *eg* the parrot.—**zygodactylous** *adj*.

zygomorphic /ˌzaɪgəˈmɔrfɪk/, **zygomorphous** /-ˈmɔrfəs/ *adj* (*flowers*) bilaterally symmetrical.—**zygomorphism, zygomorphy** *n*.

zygospore /ˌzaɪgəˈspoːr/ *n* a spore formed from the fusion of gametes.—**zygosporic** *adj*.

zygote /ˌzaɪˈgoːt/ *n* the cell formed by the union of an ovum and a sperm; the developing organism from such a cell.

zymosis /zaɪˈmoːsɪs/ or /zɪ-/ *n* (*pl* **zymoses**) an infectious disease caused by a virus or organism that acts like a ferment; fermentation.

zymotic /zaɪˈmɒtɪk/ or /zɪ-/ *adj* caused by or relating to an infection or an infectious disease; producing fermentation.

zymurgy /ˈzaɪmərdʒi/ *n* the chemistry of fermentation in brewing, etc.

THESAURUS

A

aback *adv* back, backward, rearward, regressively.

abaft *prep* (*naut*) aft, astern, back of, behind.

abandon *vb* abdicate, abjure, desert, drop, evacuate, forsake, forswear, leave, quit, relinquish, yield; cede, forgo, give up, let go, renounce, resign, surrender, vacate, waive. • *n* careless freedom, dash, impetuosity, impulse, wildness.

abandoned *adj* depraved, derelict, deserted, discarded, dropped, forsaken, left, outcast, rejected, relinquished; corrupt, demoralized, depraved, dissolute, graceless, impenitent, irreclaimable, lost, obdurate, profligate, reprobate, shameless, sinful, unprincipled, vicious, wicked.

abandonment *n* desertion, dereliction, giving up, leaving, relinquishment, renunciation, surrender.

abase *vb* depress, drop, lower, reduce, sink; debase, degrade, disgrace, humble, humiliate.

abasement *n* abjection, debasement, degradation, disgrace, humbleness, humiliation, shame.

abash *vb* affront, bewilder, confound, confuse, dash, discompose, disconcert, embarrass, humiliate, humble, shame, snub.

abashment *n* confusion, embarrassment, humiliation, mortification, shame.

abate *vb* diminish, decrease, lessen, lower, moderate, reduce, relax, remove, slacken; allow, bate, deduct, mitigate, rebate, remit; allay, alleviate, appease, assuage, blunt, calm, compose, dull, mitigate, moderate, mollify, pacify, qualify, quiet, quell, soften, soothe, tranquillize.

abatement *n* alleviation, assuagement, decrement, decrease, extenuation, mitigation, moderation, remission; cessation, decline, diminution, ebb, fading, lowering, sinking, settlement; allowance, deduction, rebate, reduction.

abbey *n* convent, monastery, priory.

abbreviate *vb* abridge, compress, condense, contract, cut, curtail, epitomize, reduce, retrench, shorten.

abbreviation *n* abridgment, compression, condensation, contraction, curtailment, cutting, reduction, shortening.

abdicate *vb* abandon, cede, forgo, forsake, give up, quit, relinquish, renounce, resign, retire, surrender.

abdication *n* abandonment, abdicating, relinquishment, renunciation, resignation, surrender.

abdomen *n* belly, gut, paunch, stomach.

abduct *vb* carry off, kidnap, spirit away, take away.

abduction *n* carrying off, kidnapping, removal, seizure, withdrawal.

aberrant *adj* deviating, devious, divergent, diverging, erratic, rambling, wandering; abnormal, anomalistic, anomalous, disconnected, eccentric, erratic, exceptional, inconsequent, peculiar, irregular, preternatural, singular, strange, unnatural, unusual.

aberration *n* departure, deviation, divergence, rambling, wandering; abnormality, anomaly, eccentricity, irregularity, peculiarity, singularity, unconformity; delusion, disorder, hallucination, illusion, instability.

abet *vb* aid, assist, back, help, support, sustain, uphold; advocate, condone, countenance, encourage, favour, incite, sanction.

abettor *n* ally, assistant; adviser, advocate, promoter; accessory, accomplice, associate, confederate.

abeyance *n* anticipation, calculation, expectancy, waiting; dormancy, inactivity, intermission, quiescence, remission, reservation, suppression, suspension.

abhor *vb* abominate, detest, dislike intensely, execrate, hate, loathe, nauseate, view with horror.

abhorrence *n* abomination, antipathy, aversion, detestation, disgust, hatred, horror, loathing.

abhorrent *adj* abominating, detesting, hating, loathing; hateful, horrifying, horrible, loathsome, nauseating, odious, offensive, repellent, repugnant, repulsive, revolting, shocking.

abide *vb* lodge, rest, sojourn, stay, wait; dwell, inhabit, live, reside; bear, continue, persevere, persist, remain; endure, last,

suffer, tolerate; (*with* **by**) act up to, conform to, discharge, fulfil, keep, persist in.

abiding *adj* changeless, constant, continuing, durable, enduring, immutable, lasting, permanent, stable, unchangeable.

ability *n* ableness, adroitness, aptitude, aptness, cleverness, dexterity, efficacy, efficiency, facility, might, ingenuity, knack, power, readiness, skill, strength, talent, vigour; competency, qualification; calibre, capability, capacity, expertness, faculty, gift, parts.

abject *adj* base, beggarly, contemptible, cringing, degraded, despicable, dirty, grovelling, ignoble, low, mean, menial, miserable, paltry, pitiful, poor, servile, sneaking, slavish, vile, worthless, wretched.

abjectness *n* abasement, abjection, baseness, contemptibleness, meanness, pitifulness, servility, vileness.

abjuration *n* abandonment, abnegation, discarding, disowning, rejection, relinquishment, renunciation, repudiation; disavowal, disclaimer, disclaiming, recall, recantation, repeal, retraction, reversal, revocation.

abjure *vb* abandon, discard, disclaim, disown, forgo, forswear, give up, reject, relinquish, renounce, repudiate; disavow, disclaim, recall, recant, renounce, repeal, retract, revoke, withdraw.

able *adj* accomplished, adroit, apt, clever, expert, ingenious, practical, proficient, qualified, quick, skilful, talented, versed; competent, effective, efficient, fitted, quick; capable, gifted, mighty, powerful, talented; athletic, brawny, muscular, robust, stalwart, strong, vigorous.

ablution *n* baptism, bathing, cleansing, lavation, purification, washing.

abnegation *n* abandonment, denial, renunciation, surrender.

abnormal *adj* aberrant, anomalous, divergent, eccentric, exceptional, peculiar, odd, singular, strange, uncomfortable, unnatural, unusual, weird.

abnormality *n* abnormity, anomaly, deformity, idiosyncrasy, irregularity, monstrosity, peculiarity, oddity, singularity, unconformity.

aboard *adv* inside, within, on.

abode *n* domicile, dwelling, habitation, home, house, lodging, quarters, residence, residency, seat.

abolish *vb* abrogate, annul, cancel, eliminate, invalidate, nullify, quash, repeal, rescind, revoke; annihilate, destroy, end, eradicate, extirpate, extinguish, obliterate, overthrow, suppress, terminate.

abolition *n* abrogation, annulling, annulment, cancellation, cancelling, nullification, repeal, rescinding, rescission, revocation; annihilation, destruction, eradication, extinction, extinguishment, extirpation, obliteration, overthrow, subversion, suppression.

abominable *adj* accursed, contemptible, cursed, damnable, detestable, execrable, hellish, horrid, nefarious, odious; abhorrent, detestable, disgusting, foul, hateful, loathsome, nauseous, obnoxious, shocking, revolting, repugnant, repulsive; shabby, vile, wretched.

abominate *vb* abhor, detest, execrate, hate, loathe, recoil from, revolt at, shrink from, shudder at.

abomination *n* abhorrence, antipathy, aversion, detestation, disgust, execration, hatred, loathing, nauseation; contamination, corruption, corruptness, defilement, foulness, impurity, loathsomeness, odiousness, pollution, taint, uncleanness; annoyance, curse, evil, infliction, nuisance, plague, torment.

aboriginal *adj* autochthonal, autochthonous, first, indigenous, native, original, primary, prime, primeval, primitive, pristine.

abortion *n* miscarriage, premature labour; disappointment, failure.

abortive *adj* immature, incomplete, rudimental, rudimentary, stunted, untimely; futile, fruitless, idle, ineffectual, inoperative, nugatory, profitless, unavailing, unsuccessful, useless, vain.

abound *vb* flow, flourish, increase, swarm, swell; exuberate, luxuriate, overflow, proliferate, swarm, teem.

about *prep* around, encircling, surrounding, round; near; concerning, referring to, regarding, relating to, relative to, respecting, touching, with regard to, with respect to; all over, over, through. • *adv* around, before; approximately, near, nearly.

above *adj* above-mentioned, aforementioned, aforesaid, foregoing, preceding, previous, prior. • *adv* aloft, overhead; before, previously; of a higher rank. • *prep* higher than, on top of; exceeding, greater than, more than, over; beyond, superior to.

above-board *adj* candid, frank, honest, open, straightforward, truthful, upright. • *adv* candidly, fairly, openly, sincerely.

abrade *vb* erase, erode, rub off, scrape out, wear away.

abrasion *n* attrition, disintegration, friction, wearing down; scrape, scratch.

abreast *adv* aligned, alongside.

abridge *vb* abbreviate, condense, compress, shorten, summarize; contract, diminish, lessen, reduce.

abridgment *n* compression, condensation, contraction, curtailment, diminution, epitomizing, reduction, shortening; abstract, brief, compendium, digest, epitome, outline, précis, summary, syllabus, synopsis; deprivation, limitation, restriction.

abroad *adv* expansively, unrestrainedly, ubiquitously, widely; forth, out of doors; overseas; extensively, publicly.

abrogate *vb* abolish, annul, cancel, invalidate, nullify, overrule, quash, repeal, rescind, revoke, set aside, vacate, void.

abrogation *n* abolition, annulling, annulment, cancellation, cancelling, repeal rescinding, rescission, revocation, voidance, voiding.

abrupt *adj* broken, craggy, jagged, rough, rugged; acclivous, acclivitous, precipitous, steep; hasty, ill-timed, precipitate, sudden, unanticipated, unexpected; blunt, brusque, curt, discourteous; cramped, harsh, jerky, stiff.

abscess *n* boil, fester, pustule, sore, ulcer.

abscond *vb* bolt, decamp, elope, escape, flee, fly, retreat, run off, sneak away, steal away, withdraw.

absence *n* nonappearance, nonattendance; abstraction, distraction, inattention, musing, preoccupation, reverie; default, defect, deficiency, lack, privation.

absent *adj* abroad, away, elsewhere, gone, not present, otherwhere; abstracted, dreaming, inattentive, lost, musing, napping, preoccupied.

absolute *adj* complete, ideal, independent, perfect, supreme, unconditional, unconditioned, unlimited, unqualified, unrestricted; arbitrary, authoritative, autocratic, despotic, dictatorial, imperious, irresponsible, tyrannical, tyrannous; actual, categorical, certain, decided, determinate, genuine, positive, real, unequivocal, unquestionable, veritable.

absolutely *adv* completely, definitely, unconditionally; actually, downright, indeed, indubitably, infallibly, positively, really, truly, unquestionably.

absoluteness *n* actuality, completeness, ideality, perfection, positiveness, reality, supremeness; absolutism, arbitrariness, despotism, tyranny.

absolution *n* acquittal, clearance, deliverance, discharge, forgiveness, liberation, pardon, release, remission, shrift, shriving.

absolutism *n* absoluteness, arbitrariness, autocracy, despotism, tyranny.

absolve *vb* acquit, clear, deliver, discharge, exculpate, excuse, exonerate, forgive, free, liberate, loose, pardon, release, set free, shrive.

absorb *vb* appropriate, assimilate, drink in, imbibe, soak up; consume, destroy, devour, engorge, engulf, exhaust, swallow up, take up; arrest, engage, engross, fix, immerse, occupy, rivet.

absorbent *adj* absorbing, imbibing, penetrable, porous, receptive.

absorption *adj* appropriation, assimilation, imbibing, osmosis, soaking up; consumption, destroying, devouring, engorgement, engulfing, exhaustion, swallowing up; concentration, engagement, engrossment, immersion, occupation, preoccupation.

abstain *vb* avoid, cease, deny oneself, desist, forbear, refrain, refuse, stop, withhold.

abstemious *adj* abstinent, frugal, moderate, self-denying, sober, temperate.

abstinence *n* abstemiousness, avoidance, forbearance, moderation, self-restraint, soberness, sobriety, teetotalism, temperance.

abstinent *adj* abstaining, fasting; abstemious, restraining, self-denying, self-restraining, sober, temperate.

abstract *vb* detach, disengage, disjoin, dissociate, disunite, isolate, separate; appropriate, purloin, seize, steal, take; abbreviate, abridge, epitomize. • *adj* isolated, separate, simple, unrelated; abstracted, occult, recondite, refined, subtle, vague; nonobjective, nonrepresentational. • *n* abridgment, condensation, digest, excerpt, extract, précis, selection, summary, synopsis.

abstracted *adj* absent, absent-minded, dreaming, inattentive, lost, musing, preoccupied; abstruse, refined, subtle.

abstraction *n* absence, absent-mindedness, brown study, inattention, muse, musing, preoccupation, reverie; disconnection, disjunction, isolation, separation; abduction, appropriation, pilfering, purloining, seizure, stealing, taking.

abstruse *adj* abstract, attenuated, dark, difficult, enigmatic, hidden, indefinite, mysterious, mystic, mystical, obscure, occult, profound, recondite, remote, subtle, transcendental, vague.

absurd *adj* egregious, fantastic, foolish, incongruous, ill-advised, ill-judged, irrational, ludicrous, nonsensical, nugatory, preposterous, ridiculous, self-annulling, senseless, silly, stupid, unreasonable.

absurdity *n* drivel, extravagance, fatuity, folly, foolery, foolishness, idiocy, nonsense.

abundance *n* affluence, amplitude, ampleness, copiousness, exuberance, fertility, flow, flood, largeness, luxuriance, opulence, overflow, plenitude, profusion, richness, store, wealth.

abundant *adj* abounding, ample, bountiful, copious, exuberant, flowing, full, good, large, lavish, rich, liberal, much, overflowing, plentiful, plenteous, replete, teeming, thick.

abuse *vb* betray, cajole, deceive, desecrate, dishonour, misapply, misemploy, misuse, pervert, pollute, profane, prostitute, violate, wrong; harm, hurt, ill-use, ill-treat, injure, maltreat, mishandle; asperse, berate, blacken, calumniate, defame, disparage, lampoon, lash, malign, revile, reproach, satirize, slander, traduce, upbraid, vilify. • *n* desecration, dishonour, illuse, misuse, perversion, pollution, profanation; ill-treatment, maltreatment, outrage; malfeasance, malversation; aspersion, defamation, disparagement, insult, invective, obloquy, opprobrium, railing, rating, reviling, ribaldry, rudeness, scurrility, upbraiding, vilification, vituperation.

abusive *adj* calumnious, carping, condemnatory, contumelious, damnatory, denunciatory, injurious, insolent, insulting, offensive, opprobrious, reproachful, reviling, ribald, rude, scurrilous, vilificatory, vituperative.

abut *vb* adjoin, border, impinge, meet, project.

abutment *n* bank, bulwark, buttress, embankment, fortification; abutting, abuttal, adjacency, contiguity, juxtaposition.

abuttal *n* adjacency, boundary, contiguity, juxtaposition, nearness, next, terminus.

abyss *n* abysm, chasm, gorge, gulf, pit.

academic *adj* collegiate, lettered, scholastic. • *n* academician, classicist, doctor, fellow, pundit, savant, scholar, student, teacher.

academy *n* college, high school, institute, school.

accede *vb* accept, acquiesce, agree, assent to, comply with, concur, consent, yield.

accelerate *vb* dispatch, expedite, forward, hasten, hurry, precipitate, press on, quicken, speed, urge on.

acceleration *n* expedition, hastening, hurrying, quickening, pickup, precipitation, speeding up, stepping up.

accent *vb* accentuate, emphasize, stress. • *n* cadence, inflection, intonation, tone; beat, emphasis, ictus.

accentuate *vb* accent, emphasize, mark, point up, punctuate, stress; highlight, overemphasize, overstress, underline, underscore.

accept *vb* acquire, derive, get, gain, obtain, receive, take; accede to, acknowledge, acquiesce in, admit, agree to, approve, assent to, avow, embrace; estimate, construe, interpret, regard, value.

acceptable *adj* agreeable, gratifying, pleasant, pleasing, pleasurable, welcome.

acceptance *n* accepting, acknowledgment, receipt, reception, taking; approbation, approval, gratification, satisfaction.

acceptation *n* construction, import, interpretation, meaning, sense, significance, signification, understanding; adoption, approval, currency, vogue.

access *vb* broach, enter, open, open up. • *n* approach, avenue, entrance, entry, passage, way; admission, admittance, audience, interview; addition, accession, aggrandizement, enlargement, gain, increase, increment; (*med*) attack, fit, onset, recurrence.

accession *n* addition, augmentation, enlargement, extension, increase; succession.

accessory *adj* abetting, additional, additive, adjunct, aiding, ancillary, assisting, contributory, helping, subsidiary, subordinate, supplemental. • *n* abettor, accomplice, assistant, associate, confederate, helper; accompaniment, attendant, concomitant, detail, subsidiary.

accident *n* calamity, casualty, condition, contingency, disaster, fortuity, incident, misadventure, miscarriage, mischance, misfortune, mishap; affection, alteration, chance, contingency, mode, modification, property, quality, state.

accidental *adj* casual, chance, contingent, fortuitous, undesigned, unintended; adventitious, dispensable, immaterial, incidental, nonessential.

acclamation *n* acclaim, applause, cheer, cry, plaudit, outcry, salutation, shouting.

acclimatization, acclimation *n* adaptation, adjustment, conditioning, familiarization, habituation, inurement, naturalization.

acclimatize, acclimate *vb* accustom, adapt, adjust, condition, familiarize, habituate, inure, naturalize, season.

acclivity *n* ascent, height, hill, rising ground, steep, upward slope.

accommodate *vb* contain, furnish, hold, oblige, serve, supply; adapt, fit, suit; adjust, compose, harmonize, reconcile, settle.

accommodation *n* advantage, convenience, privilege; adaptation, agreement, conformity, fitness, suitableness; adjustment, harmonization, harmony, pacification, reconciliation, settlement.

accompaniment *n* adjunct, appendage, attachment, attendant, concomitant.

accompany *vb* attend, chaperon, convoy, escort, follow, go with.

accomplice *n* abettor, accessory, ally, assistant, associate, confederate, partner.

accomplish *vb* achieve, bring about, carry, carry through, complete, compass, consummate, do, effect, execute, perform, perfect; conclude, end, finish, terminate.

accomplished *adj* achieved, completed, done, effected, executed, finished, fulfilled, realized; able, adroit, apt, consummate, educated, experienced, expert, finished, instructed, practised, proficient, qualified, ripe, skilful, versed; elegant, fashionable, fine, polished, polite, refined.

accomplishment *n* achievement, acquirement, attainment, qualification; completion, fulfilment.

accord *vb* admit, allow, concede, deign, give, grant, vouchsafe, yield; agree, assent, concur, correspond, harmonize, quadrate, tally. • *n* accordance, agreement, concord, concurrence, conformity, consensus, harmony, unanimity, unison.

accordant *adj* agreeable, agreeing, congruous, consonant, harmonious, suitable, symphonious.

accordingly *adv* agreeably, conformably, consistently, suitably; consequently, hence, so, thence, therefore, thus, whence, wherefore.

accost *vb* address, confront, greet, hail, salute, speak to, stop.

account *vb* assess, appraise, estimate, evaluate, judge, rate; (*with* **for**) assign, attribute, explain, expound, justify, rationalize, vindicate. • *n* inventory, record, register, score; bill, book, charge; calculation, computation, count, reckoning, score, tale, tally; chronicle, detail, description, narration, narrative, portrayal, recital, rehearsal, relation, report, statement, tidings, word; elucidation, explanation, exposition; consideration, ground, motive, reason, regard, sake; consequence, consideration, dignity, distinction, importance, note, repute, reputation, worth.

accountable *adj* amenable, answerable, duty-bound, liable, responsible.

accoutre *vb* arm, dress, equip, fit out, furnish.

accredit *vb* authorize, depute, empower, entrust.

accrue *vb* arise, come, follow, flow, inure, issue, proceed, result.

accumulate *vb* agglomerate, aggregate, amass, bring together, collect, gather, grow, hoard, increase, pile, store.

accumulation *n* agglomeration, aggregation, collection, heap, hoard, mass, pile, store.

accuracy *n* carefulness, correctness, exactness, fidelity, precision, strictness.

accurate *adj* close, correct, exact, faithful, nice, precise, regular, strict, true, truthful.

accusation *n* arraignment, charge, incrimination, impeachment, indictment.

accuse *vb* arraign, charge, censure, impeach, indict, tax.

accustom *vb* discipline, drill, familiarize, habituate, harden, inure, train, use.

ace *n* (*cards, dice*) one spot, single pip, single point; atom, bit, grain, iota, jot, particle, single, unit, whit; expert, master, virtuoso. • *adj* best, expert, fine, outstanding, superb.

acerbity *n* acidity, acridity, acridness, astringency, bitterness, roughness, sourness, tartness; acrimony, bitterness, harshness, severity, venom.

achieve *vb* accomplish, attain, complete, do, effect, execute, finish, fulfil, perform, realize; acquire, gain, get, obtain, win.

achievement *n* accomplishment, acquirement, attainment, completion, consummation, performance, realization; deed, exploit, feat, work.

acid *adj* pungent, sharp, sour, stinging, tart, vinegary.

acknowledge *vb* recognize; accept, admit, accept, allow, concede, grant; avow, confess, own, profess.

acme *n* apex, climax, height, peak, pinnacle, summit, top, vertex, zenith.

acquaint *vb* familiarize; announce, apprise, communicate, enlighten, disclose, inform, make aware, make known, notify, tell.

acquaintance *n* companionship, familiarity, fellowship, intimacy, knowledge; associate, companion, comrade, friend.

acquiesce *vb* bow, comply, consent, give way, rest, submit, yield; agree, assent, concur, consent.

acquire *vb* achieve, attain, earn, gain, get, have, obtain, procure, realize, secure, win; learn thoroughly, master.

acquirement *n* acquiring, gaining, gathering, mastery; acquisition, accomplishment, attainment.

acquit *vb* absolve, clear, discharge, exculpate, excuse, exonerate, forgive, liberate, pardon, pay, quit, release, set free, settle.

acquittal *n* absolution, acquittance, clearance, deliverance, discharge, exoneration, liberation, release.

acquittance *n* discharge; quittance, receipt.

acrid *adj* biting, bitter, caustic, pungent, sharp.

acrimonious *adj* acrid, bitter, caustic, censorious, crabbed, harsh, malignant, petulant, sarcastic, severe, testy, virulent.

acrimony *n* causticity, causticness, corrosiveness, sharpness; abusiveness, acridity, asperity, bitterness, churlishness, harshness, rancour, severity, spite, venom.

act *vb* do, execute, function, make, operate, work; enact, feign, perform, play. • *n* achievement, deed, exploit, feat, performance, proceeding, turn; bill, decree, enactment, law, ordinance, statute; actuality, existence, fact, reality.

acting *adj* interim, provisional, substitute, temporary. • *n* enacting, impersonation, performance, portrayal, theatre; counterfeiting, dissimulation, imitation, pretence.

action *n* achievement, activity, agency, deed, exertion, exploit, feat; battle, combat, conflict, contest, encounter, engagement, operation; lawsuit, prosecution.

active *adj* effective, efficient, influential, living, operative; assiduous, bustling, busy, diligent, industrious, restless; agile, alert, brisk, energetic, lively, nimble, prompt, quick, smart, spirited, sprightly, supple; animated, ebullient, fervent, vigorous.

actual *adj* certain, decided, genuine, objective, real, substantial, tangible, true, veritable; perceptible, present, sensible, tangible; absolute, categorical, positive.

actuate *vb* impel, incite, induce, instigate, move, persuade, prompt.

acumen *n* acuteness, astuteness, discernment, ingenuity, keenness, penetration, sagacity, sharpness, shrewdness.

acute *adj* pointed, sharp; astute, bright, discerning, ingenious, intelligent, keen, quick, penetrating, piercing, sagacious, sage, sharp, shrewd, smart, subtle; distressing, fierce, intense, piercing, pungent, poignant, severe, violent; high, high-toned, sharp, shrill; (*med*) sudden, temporary, violent.

adage *n* aphorism, dictum, maxim, proverb, saw, saying.

adapt *vb* accommodate, adjust, conform, coordinate, fit, qualify, proportion, suit, temper.

add *vb* adjoin, affix, annex, append, attach, join, tag; sum, sum up, total.

addict *vb* accustom, apply, dedicate, devote, habituate. • *n* devotee, enthusiast, fan; head, junkie, user.

addicted *adj* attached, devoted, given up to, inclined, prone, wedded.

addition *n* augmentation, accession, enlargement, extension, increase, supplement; adjunct, appendage, appendix, extra.

address *vb* accost, apply to, court, direct. • *n* appeal, application, entreaty, invocation, memorial, petition, request, solicitation, suit; discourse, oration, lecture, sermon, speech; ability, adroitness, art, dexterity, expertness, skill; courtesy, deportment, demeanour, tact.

adduce *vb* advance, allege, assign, offer, present; cite, mention, name.

adept *adj* accomplished, experienced, practised, proficient, skilled. • *n* expert, master, virtuoso.

adequate *adj* able, adapted, capable, competent, equal, fit, requisite, satisfactory, sufficient, suitable.

adhere *vb* cling, cleave, cohere, hold, stick; appertain, belong, pertain.

adherent *adj* adhering, clinging, sticking. • *n* acolyte, dependant, disciple, follower, partisan, supporter, vassal.

adhesion *n* adherence, attachment, clinging, coherence, sticking.

adhesive *adj* clinging, sticking; glutinous, gummy, sticky, tenacious, viscous. • *n* binder, cement, glue, paste.

adieu *n* farewell, goodbye, parting, valediction.

adipose *adj* fat, fatty, greasy, oily, oleaginous, sebaceous.

adjacent *adj* adjoining, bordering, conterminous, contiguous, near, near to, neighbouring, touching.

adjoin *vb* abut, add, annex, append, border, combine, neighbour, unite, verge.

adjourn *vb* defer, delay, postpone, procrastinate; close, dissolve, end, interrupt, prorogue, suspend.

adjudge *vb* allot, assign, award; decide, decree, determine, settle.

adjunct *n* addition, advantage, appendage, appurtenance, attachment, attribute, auxiliary, dependency, help.

adjure *vb* beg, beseech, entreat, pray, supplicate.

adjust *vb* adapt, arrange, dispose, rectify; regulate, set right, settle, suit; compose, harmonize, pacify, reconcile, settle; accommodate, adapt, fit, suit.

administer *vb* contribute, deal out, dispense, supply; conduct, control, direct, govern, manage, oversee, superintend; conduce, contribute.

admirable *adj* astonishing, striking, surprising, wonderful; excellent, fine, rare, superb.

admiration *n* affection, approbation, approval, astonishment, delight, esteem, pleasure, regard.

admirer *n* beau, gallant, suitor, sweetheart; fan, follower, supporter.

admissible *adj* allowable, lawful, permissible, possible.

admission *n* access, admittance, entrance, introduction; acceptance, acknowledgement, allowance, assent, avowal, concession.

admit *vb* give access to, let in, receive; agree to, accept, acknowledge, concede, confess; allow, bear, permit, suffer, tolerate.

admonish *vb* censure, rebuke, reprove; advise caution, counsel, enjoin, forewarn, warn; acquaint, apprise, inform, instruct, notify, remind.

admonition *n* censure, rebuke, remonstrance; advice, caution, chiding, counsel, instruction, monition.

adolescence *n* minority, nonage, teens, youth.

adolescent *adj* juvenile, young, youthful. • *n* minor, teenager, youth.

adopt *vb* appropriate, assume; accept, approve, avow, espouse, maintain, support; affiliate, father, foster.

adore *vb* worship; esteem, honour, idolize, love, revere, venerate.

adorn *vb* beautify, decorate, embellish, enrich, garnish, gild, grace, ornament.

adroit *adj* apt, dextrous, expert, handy, ingenious, ready, skilful.

adulation *n* blandishment, cajolery, fawning, flattery, flummery, praise, sycophancy.

adult *adj* grown-up, mature, ripe, ripened. • *n* grown-up person.

adulterate *vb* alloy, contaminate, corrupt, debase, deteriorate, vitiate.

advance *adj* beforehand, forward, leading. • *vb* propel, push, send forward; aggrandize, dignify, elevate, exalt, promote; benefit, forward, further, improve, promote; adduce, allege, assign, offer, propose, propound; augment, increase; proceed, progress; grow, improve, prosper, thrive. • *n* march, progress; advancement, enhancement, growth, promotion, rise; offer, overture, proffering, proposal, proposition, tender; appreciation, rise.

advancement *n* advance, benefit, gain, growth, improvement, profit.

advantage *n* ascendancy, precedence, pre-eminence, superiority, upper-hand; benefit, blessing, emolument, gain, profit, return; account, behalf, interest; accommodation, convenience, prerogative, privilege.

advantageous *adj* beneficial, favourable, profitable.

advent *n* accession, approach, arrival, coming, visitation.

adventitious *adj* accidental, extraneous, extrinsic, foreign, fortuitous, nonessential.

adventure *vb* dare, hazard, imperil, peril, risk, venture. • *n* chance, contingency, experiment, fortuity, hazard, risk, venture; crisis, contingency, event, incident, occurrence, transaction.

adventurous *adj* bold, chivalrous, courageous, daring, doughty; foolhardy, headlong, precipitate, rash, reckless; dangerous, hazardous, perilous.

adversary *n* antagonist, enemy, foe, opponent.

adverse *adj* conflicting, contrary, opposing; antagonistic, harmful, hostile, hurtful, inimical, unfavourable, unpropitious; calamitous, disastrous, unfortunate, unlucky, untoward.

adversity *n* affliction, calamity, disaster, distress, misery, misfortune, sorrow, suffering, woe.

advertise *vb* advise, announce, declare, inform, placard, proclaim, publish.

advertisement *n* announcement, information, notice, proclamation.

advice *n* admonition, caution, counsel, exhortation, persuasion, suggestion, recommendation; information, intelligence, notice, notification; care, counsel, deliberation, forethought.

advisable *adj* advantageous, desirable, expedient, prudent.

advise *vb* admonish, counsel, commend, recommend, suggest, urge; acquaint, apprise, inform, notify; confer, consult, deliberate.

adviser *n* counsellor, director, guide, instructor.

advocate *vb* countenance, defend, favour, justify, maintain, support, uphold, vindicate. • *n* apologist, counsellor, defender, maintainer, patron, pleader, supporter; attorney, barrister, counsel, lawyer, solicitor.

aegis *n* defence, protection, safeguard, shelter.

aesthetic *adj* appropriate, beautiful, tasteful.

affable *adj* accessible, approachable, communicative, conversable, cordial, easy, familiar, frank, free, sociable, social; complaisant, courteous, civil, obliging, polite, urbane.

affair *n* business, circumstance, concern, matter, office, question; event, incident, occurrence, performance, proceeding, transaction; battle, combat, conflict, encounter, engagement, skirmish.

affairs *npl* administration, relations; business, estate, finances, property.

affect *vb* act upon, alter, change, influence, modify, transform; concern, interest, regard, relate; improve, melt, move, overcome, subdue, touch; aim at, aspire to, crave, yearn for; adopt, assume, feign.

affectation *n* affectedness, airs, artificiality, foppery, pretension, simulation.

affected *adj* artificial, assumed, feigned, insincere, theatrical; assuming, conceited, foppish, vain.

affection *n* bent, bias, feeling, inclination, passion, proclivity, propensity; accident, attribute, character, mark, modification, mode, note, property; attachment, endearment, fondness, goodwill, kindness, partiality, love.

affectionate *adj* attached, devoted, fond, kind, loving, sympathetic, tender.

affiliate *vb* ally, annex, associate, connect, incorporate, join, unite. • *n* ally, associate, confederate.

affinity *n* connection, propinquity, relationship; analogy, attraction, correspondence, likeness, relation, resemblance, similarity, sympathy.

affirm *vb* allege, assert, asseverate, aver, declare, state; approve, confirm, establish, ratify.

affix *vb* annex, attach, connect, fasten, join, subjoin, tack.

afflict *vb* agonize, distress, grieve, pain, persecute, plague, torment, trouble, try, wound.

affliction *n* adversity, calamity, disaster, misfortune, stroke, visitation; bitterness, depression, distress, grief, misery, plague, scourge, sorrow, trial, tribulation, wretchedness, woe.

affluent *adj* abounding, abundant, bounteous, plenteous; moneyed, opulent, rich, wealthy.

afford *vb* furnish, produce, supply, yield; bestow, communicate, confer, give, grant, impart, offer; bear, endure, support.

affray *n* brawl, conflict, disturbance, feud, fight, quarrel, scuffle, struggle.

affright *vb* affray, alarm, appal, confound, dismay, shock, startle. • *n* alarm, consternation, fear, fright, panic, terror.

affront *vb* abuse, insult, outrage; annoy, chafe, displease, fret, irritate, offend, pique, provoke, vex. • *n* abuse, contumely, insult, outrage, vexation, wrong.

afraid *adj* aghast, alarmed, anxious, apprehensive, frightened, scared, timid.

after *prep* later than, subsequent to; behind, following; about, according to; because of, in imitation of. • *adj* behind, consecutive, ensuing, following, later, succeeding, successive, subsequent; aft, back, hind, rear, rearmost, tail.• *adv* afterwards, later, next, since, subsequently, then, thereafter.

again *adv* afresh, anew, another time, once more; besides, further, in addition, moreover.

against *prep* adverse to, contrary to, in opposition to, resisting; abutting, close up to, facing, fronting, off, opposite to, over; in anticipation of, for, in expectation of; in compensation for, to counterbalance, to match.

age *vb* decline, grow old, mature. • *n* aeon, date, epoch, period, time; decline, old age, senility; antiquity, oldness.

agency *n* action, force, intervention, means, mediation, operation, procurement; charge, direction, management, superintendence, supervision.

agent *n* actor, doer, executor, operator, performer; active element, cause, force; attorney, broker, commissioner, deputy, factor, intermediary, manager, middleman.

agglomeration *n* accumulation, aggregation, conglomeration, heap, lump, pile.

agglutinate *vb* cement, fasten, glue, unite.

aggrandize *vb* advance, dignify, elevate, enrich, exalt, promote.

aggravate *vb* heighten, increase, worsen; colour, exaggerate, magnify, overstate; enrage, irritate, provoke, tease.

aggravation *n* exaggeration, heightening, irritation.

aggregate *vb* accumulate, amass, collect, heap, pile. • *adj* collected, total. • *n* amount, gross, total, whole.

aggressive *adj* assailing, assailant, assaulting, attacking, invading, offensive; pushing, self-assertive.

aggressor *n* assailant, assaulter, attacker, invader.

aggrieve *vb* afflict, grieve, pain; abuse, ill-treat, impose, injure, oppress, wrong.

aghast *adj* appalled, dismayed, frightened, horrified, horror-struck, panic-stricken, terrified; amazed, astonished, startled, thunderstruck.

agile *adj* active, alert, brisk, lively, nimble, prompt, smart, ready.

agitate *vb* disturb, jar, rock, shake, trouble; disquiet, excite, ferment, rouse, trouble; confuse, discontent, flurry, fluster, flutter; canvass, debate, discuss, dispute, investigate.

agitation *n* concussion, shake, shaking; commotion, convulsion, disturbance, ferment, jarring, storm, tumult, turmoil; discomposure, distraction, emotion, excitement, flutter, perturbation, ruffle, tremor, trepidation; controversy, debate, discussion.

agnostic *n* doubter, empiricist, sceptic.

agonize *vb* distress, excruciate, rack, torment, torture.

agony *n* anguish, distress, pangs.

agree *vb* accord, concur, harmonize, unite; accede, acquiesce, assent, comply, concur, subscribe; bargain, contract, covenant, engage, promise, undertake; compound, compromise; chime, cohere, conform, correspond, match, suit, tally.

agreeable *adj* charming, pleasant, pleasing.

agreement *n* accordance, compliance, concord, harmony, union; bargain, compact, contract, pact, treaty.

agriculture *n* cultivation, culture, farming, geoponics, husbandry, tillage.

aid *vb* assist, help, serve, support; relieve, succour; advance, facilitate, further, promote. • *n* assistance, cooperation, help, patronage; alms, subsidy, succour, relief.

ailment *n* disease, illness, sickness.

aim *vb* direct, level, point, train; design, intend, mean, purpose, seek. • *n* bearing, course, direction, tendency; design, object, view, reason.

air *vb* expose, display, ventilate. • *n* atmosphere, breeze; appearance, aspect, manner; melody, tune.

aisle *n* passage, walk.

akin *adj* allied, kin, related; analogous, cognate, congenial, connected.

alacrity *n* agility, alertness, activity, eagerness, promptitude; cheerfulness, gaiety, hilarity, liveliness, vivacity.

alarm *vb* daunt, frighten, scare, startle, terrify. • *n* alarm-bell, tocsin, warning; apprehension, fear, fright, terror.

alert *adj* awake, circumspect, vigilant, watchful, wary; active, brisk, lively, nimble, quick, prompt, ready, sprightly. • *vb* alarm, arouse, caution, forewarn, signal, warn. • *n* alarm, signal, warning.

alertness *n* circumspection, vigilance, watchfulness, wariness; activity, briskness, nimbleness, promptness, readiness, spryness.

alien *adj* foreign, not native; differing, estranged, inappropriate, remote, unallied, separated. • *n* foreigner, stranger.

alienate *vb* (*legal*) assign, demise, transfer; disaffect, estrange, wean, withdraw.

alienation *n* (*legal*) assignment, conveyance, transfer; breach, disaffection, division, estrangement, rupture; (*med*) aberration, delusion, derangement, hallucination, insanity, madness.

alike *adj* akin, analogous, duplicate, identical, resembling, similar. • *adv* equally.

aliment *n* diet, fare, meat, nutriment, provision, rations, sustenance.

alive *adj* animate, breathing, live; aware, responsive, sensitive, susceptible; brisk, cheerful, lively, sprightly.

allay *vb* appease, calm, check, compose; alleviate, assuage, lessen, moderate, solace, temper.

allege *vb* affirm, assert, declare, maintain, say; adduce, advance, assign, cite, plead, produce, quote.

allegiance *n* duty, homage, fealty, fidelity, loyalty, obligation.

allegory *n* apologue, fable, myth, parable, story, tale.

alleviate *vb* assuage, lighten, mitigate, mollify, moderate, quell, quiet, quieten, soften, soothe.

alliance *n* affinity, intermarriage, relation; coalition, combination, confederacy, league, treaty, union; affiliation, connection, relationship, similarity.

allot *vb* divide, dispense, distribute; assign, fix, prescribe, specify.

allow *vb* acknowledge, admit, concede, confess, grant, own; authorize, grant, let, permit; bear, endure, suffer, tolerate; grant, yield, relinquish, spare; approve, justify, sanction; abate, bate, deduct, remit.

allude *vb* glance, hint, mention, imply, insinuate, intimate, refer, suggest, touch.

allure *vb* attract, beguile, cajole, coax, entice, lure, persuade, seduce, tempt. • *n* appeal, attraction, lure, temptation.

allusion *n* hint, implication, intimation, insinuation, mention, reference, suggestion.

ally *vb* combine, connect, join, league, marry, unite. • *n* aider, assistant, associate, coadjutor, colleague, friend, partner.

almighty *adj* all-powerful, omnipotent.

alms *npl* benefaction, bounty, charity, dole, gift, gratuity.

alone *adj* companionless, deserted, forsaken, isolated, lonely, only, single, sole, solitary.

along *adv* lengthways, lengthwise; forward, onward; beside, together, simultaneously.

aloud *adv* audibly, loudly, sonorously, vociferously.

alter *vb* change, conform, modify, shift, turn, transform, transmit, vary.

altercation *n* bickering, contention, controversy, dispute, dissension, strife, wrangling.

alternating *adj* intermittent, interrupted.

alternative *adj* another, different, second, substitute. • *n* choice, option, preference.

although *conj* albeit, even if, for all that, notwithstanding, though.

altitude *n* elevation, height, loftiness.

altogether *adv* completely, entirely, totally, utterly.

always *adv* continually, eternally, ever, evermore, perpetually, unceasingly.

amalgamate *vb* blend, combine, commingle, compound, incorporate, mix.

amass *vb* accumulate, aggregate, collect, gather, heap, scrape together.

amateur *n* dilettante, nonprofessional.

amaze *vb* astonish, astound, bewilder, confound, confuse, dumbfound, perplex, stagger, stupefy.

amazement *n* astonishment, bewilderment, confusion, marvel, surprise, wonder.

ambassador *n* deputy, envoy, legate, minister, plenipotentiary.

ambiguous *adj* dubious, doubtful, enigmatic, equivocal, uncertain, indefinite, indistinct, obscure, vague.

ambition *n* aspiration, emulation, longing, yearning.

ambitious *adj* aspiring, avid, eager, intent.

ameliorate *vb* amend, benefit, better, elevate, improve, mend.

amenability *n* amenableness, responsiveness; accountability, liability, responsibility.

amenable *adj* acquiescent, agreeable, persuadable, responsive, susceptible; accountable, liable, responsible.

amend *vb* better, correct, improve, mend, redress, reform.

amends *npl* atonement, compensation, expiation, indemnification, recompense, reparation, restitution.

amenity *n* agreeableness, mildness, pleasantness, softness; affability, civility, courtesy, geniality, graciousness, urbanity.

amiable *adj* attractive, benign, charming, genial, good-natured, harmonious, kind, lovable, lovely, pleasant, pleasing, sweet, winning, winsome.

amicable *adj* amiable, cordial, friendly, harmonious, kind, kindly, peaceable.

amiss *adj* erroneous, inaccurate, incorrect, faulty, improper, wrong. • *adv* erroneously, inaccurately, incorrectly, wrongly.

amnesty *n* absolution, condonation, dispensation, forgiveness, oblivion.

amorous *adj* ardent, enamoured, fond, longing, loving, passionate, tender; erotic, impassioned.

amorphous *adj* formless, irregular, shapeless, unshapen; noncrystalline, structureless; chaotic, characterless, clumsy, disorganized, misshapen, unorganized, vague.

amount *n* aggregate, sum, total.

ample *adj* broad, capacious, extended, extensive, great, large, roomy, spacious; abounding, abundant, copious, generous, liberal, plentiful; diffusive, unrestricted.

amputate *vb* clip, curtail, prune, lop, remove, separate, sever.

amuse *vb* charm, cheer, divert, enliven, entertain, gladden, relax, solace; beguile, cheat, deceive, delude, mislead.

amusement *n* diversion, entertainment, frolic, fun, merriment, pleasure.

analeptic *adj* comforting, invigorating, restorative.

analogy *n* correspondence, likeness, parallelism, parity, resemblance, similarity.

analysis *n* decomposition, dissection, resolution, separation.

anarchy *n* chaos, confusion, disorder, misrule, lawlessness, riot.

anathema *n* ban, curse, denunciation, excommunication, execration, malediction, proscription.

anatomy *n* dissection; form, skeleton, structure.

ancestor *n* father, forebear, forefather, progenitor.

ancestry *n* family, house, line, lineage; descent, genealogy, parentage, pedigree, stock.

anchor *vb* fasten, fix, secure; cast anchor, take firm hold. • *n* (*naut*) ground tackle; defence, hold, security, stay.

ancient *adj* old, primitive, pristine; antiquated, antique, archaic, obsolete.

ancillary *adj* accessory, auxiliary, contributory, helpful, instrumental.

angelic *adj* adorable, celestial, cherubic, heavenly, saintly, seraphic; entrancing, enrapturing, rapturous, ravishing.

anger *vb* chafe, displease, enrage, gall, infuriate, irritate, madden. • *n* choler, exasperation, fury, gall, indignation, ire, passion, rage, resentment, spleen, wrath.

angle *vb* fish. • *n* divergence, flare, opening; bend, corner, crotch, cusp, point; fish-hook, hook.

angry *adj* chafed, exasperated, furious, galled, incensed, irritated, nettled, piqued, provoked, resentful.

anguish *n* agony, distress, grief, pang, rack, torment, torture.

anile *adj* aged, decrepit, doting, imbecile, senile.

animadversion *n* comment, notice, observation, remark; blame, censure, condemnation, reproof, stricture.

animate *vb* inform, quicken, vitalize, vivify; fortify, invigorate, revive; activate, enliven, excite, heat, impel, kindle, rouse, stimulate, stir, waken; elate, embolden, encourage, exhilarate, gladden, hearten. • *adj* alive, breathing, live, living, organic, quick.

animosity *n* bitterness, enmity, grudge, hatred, hostility, rancour, rankling, spleen, virulence.

annals *npl* archives, chronicles, records, registers, rolls.

annex *vb* affix, append, attach, subjoin, tag, tack; connect, join, unite.

annihilate *vb* abolish, annul, destroy, dissolve, exterminate, extinguish, kill, obliterate, raze, ruin.

annotation *n* comment, explanation, illustration, note, observation, remark.

announce *vb* advertise, communicate, declare, disclose, proclaim, promulgate, publish, report, reveal, trumpet.

announcement *n* advertisement, annunciation, bulletin, declaration, manifesto, notice, notification, proclamation.

annoy *vb* badger, chafe, disquiet, disturb, fret, hector, irk, irritate, molest, pain, pester, plague, trouble, vex, worry, wound.

annul *vb* abolish, abrogate, cancel, countermand, nullify, overrule, quash, repeal, recall, reverse, revoke.

anoint *vb* consecrate, oil, sanctify, smear.

anonymous *adj* nameless, unacknowledged, unsigned.

answer *vb* fulfil, rejoin, reply, respond, satisfy. • *n* rejoinder, reply, response, retort; confutation, rebuttal, refutation.

answerable *adj* accountable, amenable, correspondent, liable, responsible, suited.

antagonism *n* contradiction, discordance, disharmony, dissonant, incompatibility, opposition.

antecedent *adj* anterior, foregoing, forerunning, precedent, preceding, previous. • *n* forerunner, precursor.

anterior *adj* antecedent, foregoing, preceding, previous, prior; fore, front.

anticipate *vb* antedate, forestall, foretaste, prevent; count upon, expect, forecast, foresee.

anticipation *n* apprehension, contemplation, expectation, hope, prospect, trust; expectancy, forecast, foresight, foretaste, preconception, presentiment.

antidote *n* corrective, counteractive, counter-poison; cure, remedy, restorative, specific.

antipathy *n* abhorrence, aversion, disgust, detestation, hate, hatred, horror, loathing, repugnance.

antique *adj* ancient, archaic, bygone, old, old-fashioned.

anxiety *n* apprehension, care, concern, disquiet, fear, foreboding, misgiving, perplexity, trouble, uneasiness, vexation, worry.

anxious *adj* apprehensive, restless, solicitous, uneasy, unquiet, worried.

apart *adv* aloof, aside, separately; asunder.

apathetic *adj* cold, dull, impassive, inert, listless, obtuse, passionless, sluggish, torpid, unfeeling.

ape *vb* counterfeit, imitate, mimic; affect. • *n* simian, troglodyte; imitator, mimic; image, imitation, likeness, type.

aperture *n* chasm, cleft, eye, gap, opening, hole, orifice, passage.

aphorism *n* adage, apothegm, byword, maxim, proverb, saw, saying.

apish *adj* imitative, mimicking; affected, foppish, trifling.

aplomb *n* composure, confidence, equanimity, self-confidence.

apocryphal *adj* doubtful, fabulous, false, legendary, spurious, uncanonical.

apologetic *adj* exculpatory, excusatory; defensive, vindictive.

apology *n* defence, justification, vindication; acknowledgement, excuse, explanation, plea, reparation.

apostate *adj* backsliding, disloyal, faithless, false, perfidious, recreant, traitorous, untrue. • *n* backslider, deserter, pervert, renegade, turncoat.

apostle *n* angel, herald, messenger, missionary, preacher; advocate, follower, supporter.

apothegm *n* aphorism, byword, dictum, maxim, proverb, saw, saying.

appal *vb* affright, alarm, daunt, dismay, frighten, horrify, scare, shock.

apparel *n* attire, array, clothes, clothing, dress, garments, habit, raiment, robes, suit, trappings, vestments.

apparent *adj* discernible, perceptible, visible; conspicuous, evident, legible, manifest, obvious, open, patent, plain, unmistakable; external, ostensible, seeming, superficial.

apparition *n* appearance, appearing, epiphany, manifestation; being, form; ghost, phantom, spectre, spirit, vision.

appeal *vb* address, entreat, implore, invoke, refer, request, solicit. • *n* application, entreaty, invocation, solicitation, suit.

appear *vb* emerge, loom; break, open; arise, occur, offer; look, seem, show.

appearance *n* advent, arrival, apparition, coming; form, shape; colour, face, fashion, feature, guise, pretence, pretext; air, aspect, complexion, demeanour, manner, mien.

appease *vb* abate, allay, assuage, calm, ease, lessen, mitigate, pacify, placate, quell, soothe, temper, tranquillize.

appellation *n* address, cognomen, denomination, epithet, style, title.

append *vb* attach, fasten, hang; add, annex, subjoin, tack, tag.

appendix *n* addition, adjunct, appurtenance, codicil; excursus, supplement.

appetite *n* craving, desire, longing, lust, passion; gusto, relish, stomach, zest; hunger.

applaud *vb* acclaim, cheer, clap, compliment, encourage, extol, magnify.

applause *n* acclamation, approval, cheers, commendation, plaudit.

applicable *adj* adapted, appropriate, apt, befitting, fitting, germane, pertinent, proper, relevant.

application *n* emollient, lotion, ointment, poultice, wash; appliance, exercise, practice, use; appeal, petition, request, solicitation, suit; assiduity, constancy, diligence, effort, industry.

apply *vb* bestow, lay upon; appropriate, convert, employ, exercise, use; addict, address, dedicate, devote, direct, engage.

appoint *vb* determine, establish, fix, prescribe; bid, command, decree, direct, order, require; allot, assign, delegate, depute, detail, destine, settle; constitute, create, name, nominate; equip, furnish, supply.

apportion *vb* allocate, allot, allow, assign, deal, dispense, divide, share.

apposite *adj* apt, fit, germane, pertinent, relevant, suitable, pertinent.

appraise *vb* appreciate, estimate, prize, rate, value.

appreciate *vb* appreciate, esteem, estimate, rate, realize, value.

apprehend *vb* arrest, catch, detain, seize, take; conceive, imagine, regard, view; appreciate, perceive, realize, see, take in; fear, forebode; conceive, fancy, hold, imagine, presume, understand.

apprehension *n* arrest, capture, seizure; intellect, intelligence, mind, reason; discernment, intellect, knowledge, perception, sense; belief, fancy, idea, notion, sentiment, view; alarm, care, dread, distrust, fear, misgiving, suspicion.

apprise *vb* acquaint, inform, notify, tell.

approach *vb* advance, approximate, come close; broach; resemble. • *n* advance, advent; approximation, convergence, nearing, tendency; entrance, path, way.

approbation *n* approval, commendation, liking, praise; assent, concurrence, consent, endorsement, ratification, sanction.

appropriate *vb* adopt, arrogate, assume, set apart; allot, apportion, assign, devote; apply, convert, employ, use. • *adj* adapted, apt, befitting, fit, opportune, seemly, suitable.

approve *vb* appreciate, commend, like, praise, recommend, value; confirm, countenance, justify, ratify, sustain, uphold.

approximate *vb* approach, resemble. • *adj* approaching, proximate; almost exact, inexact, rough.

apt *adj* applicable, apposite, appropriate, befitting, fit, felicitous, germane; disposed, inclined, liable, prone, subject; able, adroit, clever, dextrous, expert, handy, happy, prompt, ready, skilful.

aptitude *n* applicability, appropriateness, felicity, fitness, pertinence, suitability; inclination, tendency, turn; ability, address, adroitness, quickness, readiness, tact.

arbitrary *adj* absolute, autocratic, despotic, domineering, imperious, overbearing, unlimited; capricious, discretionary, fanciful, voluntary, whimsical.

arcade *n* colonnade, loggia.

arch[1] *adj* cunning, knowing, frolicsome, merry, mirthful, playful, roguish, shrewd, sly; consummate, chief, leading, pre-eminent, prime, primal, principal.

arch[2] *vb* span, vault; bend, curve. • *n* archway, span, vault.

archaic *adj* ancient, antiquated, antique, bygone, obsolete, old.

archives *npl* documents, muniments, records, registers, rolls.

ardent *adj* burning, fiery, hot; eager, earnest, fervent, impassioned, keen, passionate, warm, zealous.

ardour *n* glow, heat, warmth; eagerness, enthusiasm, fervour, heat, passion, soul, spirit, warmth, zeal.

arduous *adj* high, lofty, steep, uphill; difficult, fatiguing, hard, laborious, onerous, tiresome, toilsome, wearisome.

area *n* circle, circuit, district, domain, field, range, realm, region, tract.

argue *vb* plead, reason upon; debate, dispute; denote, evince, imply, indicate, mean, prove; contest, debate, discuss, sift.

arid *adj* barren, dry, parched, sterile, unfertile; dry, dull, jejune, pointless, uninteresting.

aright *adv* correctly, justly, rightly, truly.

arise *vb* ascend, mount, soar, tower; appear, emerge, rise, spring; begin, originate; rebel, revolt, rise; accrue, come, emanate, ensue, flow, issue, originate, proceed, result.

aristocracy *n* gentry, nobility, noblesse, peerage.

arm[1] *n* bough, branch, limb, protection; cove, creek, estuary, firth, fjord, frith, inlet.

arm[2] *vb* array, equip, furnish; clothe, cover, fortify, guard, protect, strengthen.

arms *npl* accoutrements, armour, array, harness, mail, panoply, weapons; crest, escutcheon.

army *n* battalions, force, host, legions, troops; host, multitude, throng, vast assemblage.

around *prep* about, encircling, encompassing, round, surrounding. • *adv* about, approximately, generally, near, nearly, practically, round, thereabouts.

arouse *vb* animate, awaken, excite, incite, kindle, provoke, rouse, stimulate, warm, whet.

arraign *vb* accuse, censure, charge, denounce, impeach, indict, prosecute, tax.

arrange *vb* array, class, classify, dispose, distribute, group, range, rank; adjust, determine, fix upon, settle; concoct, construct, devise, plan, prepare, project.

arrant *adj* bad, consummate, downright, gross, notorious, rank, utter.

array *vb* arrange, dispose, place, range, rank; accoutre, adorn, attire, decorate, dress, enrobe, embellish, equip, garnish, habit, invest. • *n* arrangement, collection, disposition, marshalling, order; apparel, attire, clothes, dress, garments; army, battalions, soldiery, troops.

arrest *vb* check, delay, detain, hinder, hold, interrupt, obstruct, restrain, stay, stop, withhold; apprehend, capture, catch, seize, take; catch, engage, engross, fix, occupy, secure, rivet. • *n* check, checking, detention, hindrance, interruption, obstruction, restraining, stay, staying, stopping; apprehension, capture, detention, seizure.

arrive *vb* attain, come, get to, reach.

arrogance *n* assumption, assurance, disdain, effrontery, haughtiness, loftiness, lordliness, presumption, pride, scornfulness, superciliousness.

arrogate *vb* assume, claim unduly, demand, usurp.

arrow *n* bolt, dart, reed, shaft.

art *n* business, craft, employment, trade; address, adroitness, aptitude, dexterity, ingenuity, knack, readiness, sagacity, skill; artfulness, artifice, astuteness, craft, deceit, duplicity, finesse, subtlety.

artful *adj* crafty, cunning, disingenuous, insincere, sly, tricky, wily.

article *n* branch, clause, division, head, item, member, paragraph, part, point, portion; essay, paper, piece; commodity, substance, thing.

artifice *n* art, chicanery, contrivance, cunning, deception, deceit, duplicity, effort, finesse, fraud, imposture, invention, stratagem, subterfuge, trick, trickery.

artificial *adj* counterfeit, sham, spurious; assumed, affected, constrained, fictitious, forced, laboured, strained.

artless *adj* ignorant, rude, unskilful, untaught; natural, plain, simple; candid, fair, frank, guileless, honest, plain, unaffected, simple, sincere, truthful, unsuspicious.

ascend *vb* arise, aspire, climb, mount, soar, tower.

ascendancy, ascendency *n* authority, control, domination, mastery, power, predominance, sovereignty, superiority, sway.

ascertain *vb* certify, define, determine, establish, fix, settle, verify; discover, find out, get at.

ashamed *adj* abashed, confused.

ask *vb* interrogate, inquire, question; adjure, beg, conjure, crave, desire, dun, entreat, implore, invite, inquire, petition, request, solicit, supplicate, seek, sue.

aspect *n* air, bearing, countenance, expression, feature, look, mien, visage; appearance, attitude, condition, light, phase, position, posture, situation, state, view; angle, direction, outlook, prospect.

asperity *n* ruggedness, roughness, unevenness; acrimony, causticity, corrosiveness, sharpness, sourness, tartness; acerbity, bitterness, churlishness, harshness, sternness, sullenness, severity, virulence.

aspersion *n* abuse, backbiting, calumny, censure, defamation, detraction, slander, vituperation, reflection, reproach.

aspiration *n* aim, ambition, craving, hankering, hope, longing.

aspire *vb* desire, hope, long, yearn; ascend, mount, rise, soar, tower.

assail *vb* assault, attack, invade, oppugn; impugn, malign, maltreat; ply, storm.

assassinate *vb* dispatch, kill, murder, slay.

assault *vb* assail, attack, charge, invade. • *n* aggression, attack, charge, incursion, invasion, onset, onslaught; storm.

assemble *vb* call, collect, congregate, convene, convoke, gather, levy, muster; converge, forgather.

assembly *n* company, collection, concourse, congregation, gathering, meeting, rout, throng; caucus, congress, conclave, convention, convocation, diet, legislature, meeting, parliament, synod.

assent *vb* accede, acquiesce, agree, concur, subscribe, yield. • *n* accord, acquiescence, allowance, approval, approbation, consent.

assert *vb* affirm, allege, aver, asseverate, declare, express, maintain, predicate, pronounce, protest; claim, defend, emphasize, maintain, press, uphold, vindicate.

assertion *n* affirmation, allegation, asseveration, averment, declaration, position, predication, remark, statement, word; defence, emphasis, maintenance, pressing, support, vindication.

assess *vb* appraise, compute, estimate, rate, value; assign, determine, fix, impose, levy.

asseverate *vb* affirm, aver, avow, declare, maintain, protest.

assiduous *adj* active, busy, careful, constant, diligent, devoted, indefatigable, industrious, sedulous, unremitting, untiring.

assign *vb* allot, appoint, apportion, appropriate; fix, designate, determine, specify; adduce, advance, allege, give, grant, offer, present, show.

assist *vb* abet, aid, befriend, further, help, patronize, promote, second, speed, support, sustain; aid, relieve, succour; alternate with, relieve, spell.

associate *vb* affiliate, combine, conjoin, couple, join, link, relate, yoke; consort, fraternize, mingle, sort. • *n* chum, companion, comrade, familiar, follower, mate; ally, confederate, friend, partner, fellow.

association *n* combination, company, confederation, connection, partnership, society.

assort *vb* arrange, class, classify, distribute, group, rank, sort; agree, be adapted, consort, suit.

assuage *vb* allay, alleviate, appease, calm, ease, lessen, mitigate, moderate, mollify, pacify, quell, relieve, soothe, tranquillize.

assume *vb* take, undertake; affect, counterfeit, feign, pretend, sham; arrogate, usurp; beg, hypothesize, imply, postulate, posit, presuppose, suppose, simulate.

assurance *n* assuredness, certainty, conviction, persuasion; pledge, security, surety, warrant; engagement, pledge, promise; averment, assertion, protestation; audacity, confidence, courage, firmness, intrepidity; arrogance, brass, boldness, effrontery, face, front, impudence.

assure *vb* encourage, embolden, hearten; certify, insure, secure against loss, vouch for.

astonish *vb* amaze, astound, confound, daze, dumbfound, overwhelm, startle, stun, stupefy, surprise.

astute *adj* acute, cunning, deep, discerning, ingenious, intelligent, penetrating, perspicacious, quick, sagacious, sharp, shrewd.

asylum *n* refuge, retreat, sanctuary, shelter.

athletic *adj* brawny, lusty, muscular, powerful, robust, sinewy, stalwart, stout, strapping, strong, sturdy.

athletics *npl* aerobics, eurythmics, exercise, exercising, gymnastics, sports, track and field, workout.

atom *n* bit, molecule, monad, particle, scintilla.

atone *vb* answer, compensate, expiate, satisfy.

atonement *n* amends, expiation, propitiation, reparation, satisfaction.

atrocity *n* depravity, enormity, flagrancy, ferocity, savagery, villainy.

attach *vb* affix, annex, connect, fasten, join, hitch, tie; charm, captivate, enamour, endear, engage, win; (*legal*) distress, distrain, seize, take.

attack *vb* assail, assault, charge, encounter, invade, set upon, storm, tackle; censure, criticise, impugn. • *n* aggression, assault, charge, offence, onset, onslaught, raid, thrust.

attain *vb* accomplish, achieve, acquire, get, obtain, secure; arrive at, come to, reach.

attempt *vb* assail, assault, attack; aim, endeavour, seek, strive, try. • *n* effort, endeavour, enterprise, experiment, undertaking, venture; assault, attack, onset.

attend *vb* accompany, escort, follow; guard, protect, watch; minister to, serve, wait on; give heed, hear, harken, listen; be attendant, serve, tend, wait.

attention *n* care, circumspection, heed, mindfulness, observation, regard, watch, watchfulness; application, reflection, study; civility, courtesy, deference, politeness, regard, respect; addresses, courtship, devotion, suit, wooing.

attentive *adj* alive, awake, careful, civil, considerate, courteous, heedful, mindful, observant, watchful.

attenuate *vb* contract, dilute, diminish, elongate, lengthen, lessen, rarefy, reduce, slim, thin, weaken.

attest *vb* authenticate, certify, corroborate, confirm, ratify, seal, vouch; adjure, call to witness, invoke; confess, display, exhibit, manifest, prove, show, witness.

attic *n* garret, loft, upper storey.

Attic *adj* delicate, subtle, penetrating, pointed, pungent; chaste, classic, correct, elegant, polished, pure.

attire *vb* accoutre, apparel, array, clothe, dress, enrobe, equip, rig, robe. • *n* clothes, clothing, costume, dress, garb, gear, habiliment, outfit, toilet, trapping, vestment, vesture, wardrobe.

attitude *n* pose, position, posture; aspect, conjuncture, condition, phase, prediction, situation, standing, state.

attract *vb* draw, pull; allure, captivate, charm, decoy, enamour, endear, entice, engage, fascinate, invite, win.

attraction *n* affinity, drawing, pull; allurement, charm, enticement, fascination, magnetism, lure, seduction, witchery.

attribute *vb* ascribe, assign, impute, refer. • *n* characteristic, mark, note, peculiarity, predicate, property, quality.

attrition *n* abrasion, friction, rubbing.

attune *vb* accord, harmonize, modulate, tune; accommodate, adapt, adjust, attempt.

audacity *n* boldness, courage, daring, fearlessness, intrepidity; assurance, brass, effrontery, face, front, impudence, insolence, presumption, sauciness.

audience *n* assemblage, congregation; hearing, interview, reception.

augment *vb* add to, enhance, enlarge, increase, magnify, multiply, swell.

augmentation *n* accession, addition, enlargement, extension, increase.

augury *n* prediction, prognostication, prophecy, soothsaying; auspice, forerunner, harbinger, herald, omen, precursor, portent, sign.

august *adj* awe-inspiring, awful, dignified, grand, imposing, kingly, majestic, noble, princely, regal, solemn, stately, venerable.

auspicious *adj* fortunate, happy, lucky, prosperous, successful; bright, favourable, golden, opportune, promising, prosperous.

austere *adj* ascetic, difficult, formal, hard, harsh, morose, relentless, rigid, rigorous, severe, stern, stiff, strict, uncompromising, unrelenting.

authentic *adj* genuine, pure, real, true, unadulterated, uncorrupted, veritable; accurate, authoritative, reliable, true, trustworthy.

authority *n* dominion, empire, government, jurisdiction, power, sovereignty; ascendency, control, influence, rule, supremacy, sway; authorization, liberty, order, permit, precept, sanction, warranty; testimony, witness; connoisseur, expert, master.

authorize *vb* empower, enable, entitle; allow, approve, confirm, countenance, permit, ratify, sanction.

auxiliary *adj* aiding, ancillary, assisting, helpful, subsidiary. • *n* ally, assistant, confederate, help.

avail *vb* assist, benefit, help, profit, use, service.

available *adj* accessible, advantageous, applicable, beneficial, profitable, serviceable, useful.

avarice *n* acquisitiveness, covetousness, greediness, penuriousness, rapacity.

avaricious *adj* grasping, miserly, niggardly, parsimonious.

avenge *vb* punish, retaliate, revenge, vindicate.

avenue *n* access, entrance, entry, passage; alley, path, road, street, walk; channel, pass, route, way.

aver *vb* allege, assert, asseverate, avouch, declare, pronounce, protest, say.

averse *adj* adverse, backward, disinclined, indisposed, opposed, unwilling.

aversion *n* abhorrence, antipathy, disgust, dislike, hate, hatred, loathing, reluctance, repugnance.

avid *adj* eager, greedy, voracious.

avocation *n* business, calling, employment, occupation, trade, vocation; distraction, hindrance, interruption.

avoid *vb* dodge, elude, escape, eschew, shun; forebear, refrain from.

avouch *vb* allege, assert, declare, maintain, say.

avow *vb* admit, acknowledge, confess, own.

awaken *vb* arouse, excite, incite, kindle, provoke, spur, stimulate; wake, waken; begin, be excited.

award *vb* adjudge, allot, assign, bestow, decree, grant. • *n* adjudication, allotment, assignment, decision, decree, determination, gift, judgement.

aware *adj* acquainted, apprised, conscious, conversant, informed, knowing, mindful, sensible.

away *adv* absent, not present. • *adj* at a distance; elsewhere; out of the way.

awe *vb* cow, daunt, intimidate, overawe. • *n* abashment, fear, reverence; dread, fear, fearfulness, terror.

awful *adj* august, awesome, dread, grand, inspired; abashed, alarming, appalled, dire, frightful, portentous, tremendous.

awkward *adj* bungling, clumsy, inept, maladroit, unskilful; lumbering, unfit, ungainly, unmanageable; boorish; inconvenient, unsuitable.

axiom *n* adage, aphorism, apothegm, maxim, postulation, truism.

axis *n* axle, shaft, spindle.

azure *adj* blue, cerulean, sky-coloured.

B

babble *vb* blather, chatter, gibber, jabber, prate, prattle. • *n* chat, gossip, palaver, prate, tattle.

babel *n* clamour, confusion, din, discord, disorder, hubbub, jargon, pother.

baby *vb* coddle, cosset, indulge, mollycoddle, pamper, spoil. • *adj* babyish, childish, infantile, puerile; diminutive, doll-like, miniature, pocket, pocket-sized, small-scale. • *n* babe, brat, child, infant, suckling, nursling; chicken, coward, milksop, namby-pamby, sad sack, weakling; miniature; innocent.

bacchanal *n* carouse, debauchery, drunkenness, revelry, roisterousness.

back *vb* abet, aid, countenance, favour, second, support, sustain; go back, move back, retreat, withdraw. • *adj* hindmost. • *adv* in return, in consideration; ago, gone, since; aside, away, behind, by; abaft, astern, backwards, hindwards, rearwards. • *n* end, hind part, posterior, rear.

backbite *vb* abuse, asperse, blacken, defame, libel, malign, revile, scandalize, slander, traduce, vilify.

backbone *n* chine, spine; constancy, courage, decision, firmness, nerve, pluck, resolution, steadfastness.

backslider *n* apostate, deserter, renegade.

backward *adj* disinclined, hesitating, indisposed, loath, reluctant, unwilling, wavering; dull, slow, sluggish, stolid, stupid. • *adv* aback, behind, rearward.

bad *adj* baleful, baneful, detrimental, evil, harmful, hurtful, injurious, noxious, pernicious, unwholesome, vicious; abandoned, corrupt, depraved, immoral, sinful, unfair, unprincipled, wicked; unfortunate, unhappy, unlucky, miserable; disappointing, discouraging, distressing, sad, unwelcoming; abominable, mean, shabby, scurvy, vile, wretched; defective, inferior, imperfect, incompetent, poor, unsuitable; hard, heavy, serious, severe.

badge *n* brand, emblem, mark, sign, symbol, token.

badger *vb* annoy, bait, bother, hector, harry, pester, persecute, tease, torment, trouble, vex, worry.

baffle *vb* balk, block, check, circumvent, defeat, foil, frustrate, mar, thwart, undermine, upset; bewilder, confound, disconcert, perplex.

bait *vb* harry, tease, worry. • *n* allurement, decoy, enticement, lure, temptation.

balance *vb* equilibrate, pose, (*naut*) trim; compare, weigh; compensate, counteract, estimate; adjust, clear, equalize, square. • *n* equilibrium, liberation; excess, remainder, residue, surplus.

bald *adj* bare, naked, uncovered, treeless; dull, inelegant, meagre; prosaic, tame, unadorned, vapid.

baleful *adj* baneful, deadly, calamitous, hurtful, injurious, mischievous, noxious, pernicious, ruinous.

balk *vb* baffle, defeat, disappoint, disconcert, foil, frustrate, thwart.

ball *n* drop, globe, orb, pellet, marble, sphere; bullet, missile, projectile, shot; assembly, dance.

balmy *adj* aromatic, fragrant, healing, odorous, perfumed.

ban *vb* anathematize, curse, execrate; interdict, outlaw. • *n* edict, proclamation; anathema, curse, denunciation, execration; interdiction, outlawry, penalty, prohibition

band[1] *vb* belt, bind, cinch, encircle, gird, girdle; ally, associate, combine, connect, join, league; bar, marble, streak, stripe, striate, vein. • *n* crew, gang, horde, society, troop; ensemble, group, orchestra.

band[2] *n* ligament, ligature, tie; bond, chain, cord, fetter, manacle, shackle, trammel; bandage, belt, binding, cincture, girth, tourniquet.

bandit *n* brigand, freebooter, footpad, gangster, highwayman, outlaw, robber.

baneful *adj* poisonous, venomous; deadly, destructive, hurtful, mischievous, noxious, pernicious.

bang *vb* beat, knock, maul, pommel, pound, strike, thrash, thump; slam; clatter, rattle, resound, ring. • *n* clang, clangour, whang; blow, knock, lick, thump, thwack, whack.

banish *vb* exile, expatriate, ostracize; dismiss, exclude, expel.

bank[1] *vb* incline, slope, tilt; embank. • *n* dike, embankment, escarpment, heap, knoll, mound; border, bound, brim, brink, margin, rim, strand; course, row, tier.

bank[2] *vb* deposit, keep, save. • *n* depository, fund, reserve, savings, stockpile.

banner *n* colours, ensign, flag, standard, pennon, standard, streamer.

banter *vb* chaff, deride, jeer, joke, mock, quiz, rally, ridicule. • *n* badinage, chaff, derision, jesting, joking, mockery, quizzing, raillery, ridicule.

bar *vb* exclude, hinder, obstruct, prevent, prohibit, restrain, stop. • *n* grating, pole, rail, rod; barricade, hindrance, impediment, obstacle, obstruction, stop; bank, sand bar, shallow, shoal, spit; (*legal*) barristers, counsel, court, judgement, tribunal.

barbarian *adj* brutal, cruel, ferocious, fierce, fell, inhuman, ruthless, savage, truculent, unfeeling. • *n* brute, ruffian, savage.

barbaric *adj* barbarous, rude, savage, uncivilized, untamed; capricious, coarse, gaudy, riotous, showy, outlandish, uncouth, untamed, wild.

bare *vb* denude, depilate, divest, strip, unsheathe; disclose, manifest, open, reveal, show. • *adj* denuded, exposed, naked, nude, stripped, unclothed, uncovered, undressed, unsheltered; alone, mere, sheer, simple; bald, meagre, plain, unadorned, uncovered, unfurnished; empty, destitute, indigent, poor.

bargain *vb* agree, contract, covenant, stipulate; convey, sell, transfer. • *n* agreement, compact, contract, covenant, convention, indenture, transaction, stipulation, treaty; proceeds, purchase, result.

barren *adj* childless, infecund, sterile; (*bot*) acarpous, sterile; bare, infertile, poor, sterile, unproductive; ineffectual, unfruitful, uninstructive.

barricade *vb* block up, fortify, protect, obstruct. • *n* barrier, obstruction, palisade, stockade.

barrier *n* bar, barricade, hindrance, impediment, obstacle, obstruction, stop.

barter *vb* bargain, exchange, sell, trade, traffic.

base[1] *adj* cheap, inferior, worthless; counterfeit, debased, false, spurious; baseborn, humble, lowly, mean, nameless, plebeian, unknown, untitled, vulgar; abject, beggarly, contemptible, degraded, despicable, low, menial, pitiful, servile, sordid, sorry, worthless.

base[2] *vb* establish, found, ground. • *n* foundation, fundament, substructure, underpinning; pedestal, plinth, stand; centre, headquarters, HQ, seat; starting point; basis, cause, grounds, reason, standpoint; bottom, foot, foundation, ground.

bashful *adj* coy, diffident, shy, timid.

basis n base, bottom, foundation, fundament, ground, groundwork.

bastard *adj* adulterated, baseborn, counterfeit, false, illegitimate, sham. • *n* love child.

batch *vb* assemble, bunch, bundle, collect, gather, group. • *n* amount, collection, crowd, lot, quantity.

bathe *vb* immerse, lave, wash; cover, enfold, enwrap, drench, flood, infold, suffuse. • *n* bath, shower, swim.

batter[1] *vb* beat, pelt, smite; break, bruise, demolish, destroy, shatter, shiver, smash; abrade, deface, disfigure, indent, mar; incline, recede, retreat, slope. • *n* batsman, striker.

batter[2] *n* dough, goo, goop, gunk, paste, pulp.

battle *vb* contend, contest, engage, fight, strive, struggle. • *n* action, affair, brush, combat, conflict, contest, engagement, fight, fray.

bauble *n* gewgaw, gimcrack, knick-knack, plaything, toy, trifle, trinket.

bawdy *adj* obscene, filthy, impure, indecent, lascivious, lewd, smutty, unchaste.

bawl *vb* clamour, cry, hoot, howl, roar, shout, squall, vociferate, yell.

bay[1] *vb* bark, howl, wail, yell, yelp.

bay[2] *n* alcove, compartment, niche, nook, opening, recess.

bay[3] *n* bight, cove, gulf, inlet.

bays *npl* applause, chaplet, fame, garland, glory, honour, plaudits, praise, renown.

beach *vb* ground, maroon, strand. • *n* coast, margin, rim, sands, seashore, seaside, shore, shoreline, strand, waterfront.

beacon *vb* brighten, flame, shine, signal; enlighten, illuminate, illumine, guide, light, signal. • *n* lighthouse, pharos, watchtower; sign, signal.

beadle *n* apparitor, church officer, crier, servitor, summoner.

beak *n* bill, mandible, (*sl*) nose; (*naut*) bow, prow, stem.

beam *vb* beacon, gleam, glisten, glitter, shine. • *n* balk, girder, joist, scantling, stud; gleam, pencil, ray, streak.

bear *vb* support, sustain, uphold; carry, convey, deport, transport, waft; abide, brook, endure, stand, suffer, tolerate, undergo; carry on, keep up, maintain; cherish, entertain, harbour; produce; cast, drop, sustain; endure, submit, suffer; act, operate, work. • *n* growler, grumbler, moaner, snarler; speculator.

bearable *adj* endurable, sufferable, supportable, tolerable.

bearing *n* air, behaviour, demeanour, deportment, conduct, carriage, conduct, mien, port; connection, dependency, relation; endurance, patience, suffering; aim, course, direction; bringing forth, producing; bed, receptacle, socket.

beastly *adj* abominable, brutish, ignoble, low, sensual, vile.

beat *vb* bang, baste, belabour, buffet, cane, cudgel, drub, hammer, hit, knock, maul, pound, pummel, punch, strike, thrash, thump, thwack, whack, whip; bray, bruise, pound, pulverize; batter, pelt; conquer, defeat, overcome, rout, subdue, surpass, vanquish; pulsate, throb; dash, strike. • *adj* baffled, bamboozled, confounded, mystified, nonplussed, perplexed, puzzled, stumped; done, dog-tired, exhausted, tired out, worn out; beaten, defeated, licked, worsted. • *n* blow, striking, stroke; beating, pulsation, throb; accent, metre, rhythm; circuit, course, round.

beatific *adj* ecstatic, enchanting, enraptured, ravishing, rapt.

beatitude *n* blessing, ecstasy, felicity, happiness.

beau *n* coxcomb, dandy, exquisite, fop, popinjay; admirer, lover, suitor, sweetheart.

beautiful *adj* charming, comely, fair, fine, exquisite, handsome, lovely, pretty.

beautify *vb* adorn, array, bedeck, deck, decorate, embellish, emblazon, garnish, gild, grace, ornament, set.

beauty *n* elegance, grace, symmetry; attractiveness, comeliness, fairness, loveliness, seemliness; belle.

become *vb* change to, get, go, wax; adorn, befit, set off, suit.

becoming *adj* appropriate, apt, congruous, decent, decorous, due, fit, proper, right, seemly, suitable; comely, graceful, neat, pretty.

bed *vb* embed, establish, imbed, implant, infix, inset, plant; harbour, house, lodge. • *n* berth, bunk, cot, couch; channel, depression, hollow; base, foundation, receptacle, support, underlay; accumulation, layer, seam, stratum, vein.

bedim *vb* cloud, darken, dim, obscure.

befall *vb* betide, overtake; chance, happen, occur, supervene.

befitting *adj* appropriate, apt, becoming, decorous, fit, proper, right, suitable, seemly.

befool *vb* bamboozle, beguile, cheat, circumvent, delude, deceive, dupe, fool, hoax, hoodwink, infatuate, stupefy, trick.

befriend *vb* aid, benefit, countenance, encourage, favour, help, patronize.

beg *vb* adjure, ask, beseech, conjure, crave, entreat, implore, importune, petition, pray, request, solicit, supplicate.

beggarly *adj* destitute, needy, poor; abject, base, despicable, grovelling, low, mean, miserable, miserly, paltry, pitiful, scant, servile, shabby, sorry, stingy, vile, wretched.

begin *vb* arise, commence, enter, open; inaugurate, institute, originate, start.

beginning *n* arising, commencement, dawn, emergence, inauguration, inception, initiation, opening, outset, start, rise; origin, source.

beguile *vb* cheat, deceive, delude; amuse, cheer, divert, entertain, solace.

behaviour *n* air, bearing, carriage, comportment, conduct, demeanour, deportment, manner, manners, mien.

behest *n* bidding, charge, command, commandment, direction, hest, injunction, mandate, order, precept.

behind *prep* abaft, after, following. • *adv* abaft, aft, astern, rearward. • *adj* arrested, backward, checked, detained, retarded; after, behind. • *n* afterpart, rear, stern, tail; back, back side, reverse; bottom, buttocks, posterior, rump.

behold *vb* consider, contemplate, eye, observe, regard, see, survey, view.

behoove *vb* become, befit, suit; be binding, be obligatory.

being *n* actuality, existence, reality, subsistence; core, essence, heart, root.

beleaguer *vb* besiege, blockade, invest; beset, block, encumber, encompass, encounter, obstruct, surround.

belief *n* assurance, confidence, conviction, persuasion, trust; acceptance, assent, credence, credit, currency; creed, doctrine, dogma, faith, opinion, tenet.

bellow *vb* bawl, clamour, cry, howl, vociferate, yell.

belt *n* band, cincture, girdle, girth, zone; region, stretch, strip.

bemoan *vb* bewail, deplore, lament, mourn.

bemused *adj* bewildered, confused, fuddled, muddled, muzzy, stupefied, tipsy.

bend *vb* bow, crook, curve, deflect, draw; direct, incline, turn; bend, dispose, influence, mould, persuade, subdue; (*naut*) fasten, make fast; crook, deflect, deviate, diverge, swerve; bow, lower, stoop; condescend, deign. • *n* angle, arc, arcuation, crook, curvature, curve, elbow, flexure, turn.

beneath *prep* below, under, underneath; unbecoming, unbefitting, unworthy. • *adv* below, underneath.

benediction *n* beatitude, benefit, benison, blessing, boon, grace, favour.

benefaction *n* alms, boon, charity, contribution, donation, favour, gift, grant, gratuity, offering, present.

beneficent *adj* benevolent, bounteous, bountiful, charitable, generous, kind, liberal.

beneficial *adj* advantageous, favourable, helpful, profitable, salutary, serviceable, useful, wholesome.

benefit *vb* befriend, help, serve; advantage, avail, profit. • *n* favour, good turn, kindness, service; account, advantage, behalf, gain, good, interest, profit, utility.

benevolence *n* beneficence, benignity, generosity, goodwill, humanity, kindliness, kindness.

benevolent *adj* altruistic, benign, charitable, generous, humane, kind, kind-hearted, liberal, obliging, philanthropic, tender, unselfish.

benign *adj* amiable, amicable, beneficent, benevolent, complaisant, friendly, gentle, good, gracious, humane, kind, kindly, obliging.

bent *adj* angled, angular, bowed, crooked, curved, deflected, embowed, flexed, hooked, twisted; disposed, inclined, prone, minded; (*with* **on**) determined, fixed on, resolved, set on. • *n* bias, inclination, leaning, partiality, penchant, predilection, prepossession, proclivity, propensity.

bequeath *vb* devise, give, grant, leave, will; impart, transmit.

berate *vb* chide, rate, reprimand, reprove, scold.

bereave *vb* afflict, deprive of, despoil, dispossess, divest, rob, spoil, strip.

beseech *vb* beg, conjure, entreat, implore, importune, petition, supplicate; ask, beg, crave, solicit.

beset *vb* besiege, encompass, enclose, environ, encircle, hem in, surround; decorate, embarrass, embellish, entangle, garnish, ornament, perplex, set.

beside[1] *prep* at the side of, by the side of, close to, near; aside from, not according to, out of the course of, out of the way of; not in possession of, out of.

besides[1] *prep* barring, distinct from, excluding, except, excepting, in addition to, other than, over and above, save.

beside[2], **besides**[2] *adv* additionally, also, further, furthermore, in addition, more, moreover, over and above, too, yet.

besiege *vb* beset, blockade, encircle, encompass, environ, invest, surround.

besot *vb* drench, intoxicate, soak, steep; befool, delude, infatuate, stultify, stupefy.

bespatter *vb* bedaub, befoul, besmirch, smear, spatter.

bespeak *vb* accost, address, declare, evince, forestall, imply, indicate, prearrange, predict, proclaim, solicit.

best *vb* better, exceed, excel, predominate, rival, surpass; beat, defeat, outdo, worst. • *adj* chief, first, foremost, highest, leading, utmost. • *adv* advantageously, excellently; extremely, greatly. • *n* choice, cream, flower, pick.

bestial *adj* beast-like, beastly, brutal, degraded, depraved, irrational, low, vile; sensual.

bestow *vb* deposit, dispose, put, place, store, stow; accord, give, grant, impart.

bet *vb* gamble, hazard, lay, pledge, stake, wage, wager. • *n* gamble, hazard, stake, wager.

bethink *vb* cogitate, consider, ponder, recall, recollect, reflect, remember.

betide *vb* befall, happen, occur, overtake.

betimes *adv* beforehand, early, forward, soon.

betoken *vb* argue, betray, denote, evince, imply, indicate, prove, represent, show, signify, typify.

betray *vb* be false to, break, violate; blab, discover, divulge, expose, reveal, show, tell; argue, betoken, display, evince, expose, exhibit, imply, indicate, manifest, reveal; beguile, delude, ensnare, lure, mislead; corrupt, ruin, seduce, undo.

betroth *vb* affiance, engage to marry, pledge in marriage, plight.

better *vb* advance, amend, correct, exceed, improve, promote, rectify, reform. • *adj* bigger, fitter, greater, larger, less ill, preferable. • *n* advantage, superiority, upper hand, victory; improvement, greater good.

between *prep* amidst, among, betwixt.

bewail *vb* bemoan, deplore, express, lament, mourn over, rue, sorrow.

beware *vb* avoid, heed, look out, mind.

bewilder *vb* confound, confuse, daze, distract, embarrass, entangle, muddle, mystify, nonplus, perplex, pose, puzzle, stagger.

bewitch *vb* captivate, charm, enchant, enrapture, entrance, fascinate, spellbind, transport.

beyond *prep* above, before, farther, over, past, remote, yonder.

bias *vb* bend, dispose, incline, influence, predispose, prejudice. • *n* bent, inclination, leaning, partiality, penchant, predilection, prepossession, proclivity, propensity, slant, tendency, turn.

bicker *vb* argue, dispute, jangle, quarrel, spar, spat, squabble, wrangle.

bid *vb* charge, command, direct, enjoin, order, require, summon; ask, call, invite, pray, request, solicit; offer, propose, proffer, tender. • *n* bidding, offer, proposal.

big *adj* bumper, bulking, bulky, great, huge, large, massive, monstrous; important, imposing; distended, inflated, full, swollen, tumid; fecund, fruitful, productive, teeming.

bigoted *adj* dogmatic, hidebound, intolerant, obstinate, narrow-minded, opinionated, prejudiced.

bill[1] *vb* charge, dun, invoice; programme, schedule; advertise, boost, plug, promote, publicize. • *n* account, charges, reckoning, score; advertisement, banner, hoarding, placard, poster; playbill, programme, schedule; bill of exchange, certificate, money; account, reckoning, statement.

bill[2] *n* beak, mandible, (*sl*) nose; billhook, brush-cutter, hedgebill, hedging knife; caress, fondle, kiss, toy.

billet *vb* allot, apportion, assign, distribute, quarter, station. • *n* accommodation, lodgings, quarters.

billow *vb* surge, wave; heave, roll; bag, balloon, bulge, dilate, swell. • *n* roller, surge, swell, wave.

bin *n* box, bunker, crib, frame, receptacle.

bind *vb* confine, enchain, fetter, restrain, restrict; bandage, tie up, wrap; fasten, lash, pinion, secure, tie, truss; engage, hold, oblige, obligate, pledge; contract, harden, shrink, stiffen.

birth *n* ancestry, blood, descent, extraction, lineage, race; being, creation, creature, offspring, production, progeny.

bit *n* crumb, fragment, morsel, mouthful, piece, scrap; atom, grain, jot, mite, particle, tittle, whit; instant, minute, moment, second.

bite *vb* champ, chew, crunch, gnaw; burn, make smart, sting; catch, clutch, grapple, grasp, grip; bamboozle, cheat, cozen, deceive, defraud, dupe, gull, mislead, outwit, overreach, trick. • *n* grasp, hold; punch, relish, spice, pungency, tang, zest; lick, morsel, sip, taste; crick, nip, pain, pang, prick, sting.

bitter *adj* acrid; dire, fell, merciless, relentless, ruthless; harsh, severe, stern; afflictive, calamitous, distressing, galling, grievous, painful, poignant, sore, sorrowful.

black *adj* dark, ebony, inky, jet, sable, swarthy; dingy, dusky, lowering, murky, pitchy; calamitous, dark, depressing, disastrous, dismal, doleful, forbidding, gloomy, melancholy, mournful, sombre, sullen.

blacken *vb* darken; deface, defile, soil, stain, sully; asperse, besmirch, calumniate, defame, malign, revile, slander, traduce, vilify.

blamable *adj* blameable, blameworthy, censurable, culpable, delinquent, faulty, remiss, reprehensible.

blame *vb* accuse, censure, condemn, disapprove, reflect upon, reprehend, reproach, reprove, upbraid. • *n* animadversion, censure, condemnation, disapproval, dispraise, disapprobation, reprehension, reproach, reproof; defect, demerit, fault, guilt, misdeed, shortcoming, sin, wrong.

blameless *adj* faultless, guiltless, inculpable, innocent, irreproachable, unblemished, undefiled, unimpeachable, unspotted, unsullied, spotless, stainless.

blanch *vb* bleach, fade, etiolate, whiten.

bland *adj* balmy, demulcent, gentle, mild, soothing, soft; affable, amiable, complaisant, kindly, mild, suave.

blandishment *n* cajolery, coaxing, compliment, fascination, fawning, flattery, wheedling.

blank *adj* bare, empty, vacuous, void; amazed, astonished, confounded, confused, dumbfounded, nonplussed; absolute, complete, entire, mere, perfect, pure, simple, unabated, unadulterated, unmitigated, unmixed, utter, perfect.

blare *vb* blazon, blow, peal, proclaim, trumpet. • *n* blast, clang, clangour, peal.

blasphemy *n* impiousness, sacrilege; cursing, profanity, swearing.

blast *vb* annihilate, blight, destroy, kill, ruin, shrivel, wither; burst, explode, kill. • *n* blow, gust, squall; blare, clang, peal; burst, discharge, explosion.

blaze *vb* blazon, proclaim, publish; burn, flame, glow. • *n* flame, flare, flash, glow, light.

bleach *vb* blanch, etiolate, render white, whiten.

bleak *adj* bare, exposed, unprotected, unsheltered, storm-beaten, windswept; biting, chill, cold, piercing, raw; cheerless, comfortless, desolate, dreary, uncongenial.

blemish *vb* blur, injure, mar, spot, stain, sully, taint, tarnish; asperse, calumniate, defame, malign, revile, slander, traduce, vilify. • *n* blot, blur, defect, disfigurement, fault, flaw, imperfection, soil, speck, spot, tarnish; disgrace, dishonour, reproach, stain, taint.

blend *vb* amalgamate, coalesce, combine, commingle, fuse, mingle, mix, unite. • *n* amalgamation, combination, compound, fusion, mix, mixture, union.

bless *vb* beatify, delight, gladden; adore, celebrate, exalt, extol, glorify, magnify, praise.

blessedness *n* beatitude, bliss, blissfulness, felicity, happiness, joy.

blight *vb* blast, destroy, kill, ruin, shrivel, wither; annihilate, annul, crush, disappoint, frustrate. • *n* blast, mildew, pestilence.

blind *vb* blear, darken, deprive of sight; blindfold, hoodwink. • *adj* eyeless, sightless, stone-blind, unseeing; benighted, ignorant, injudicious, purblind, undiscerning, unenlightened; concealed, confused, dark, dim, hidden, intricate, involved, labyrinthine, obscure, private, remote; careless, headlong, heedless, inconsiderate, indiscriminate, thoughtless; blank, closed, shut. • *n* cover, curtain, screen, shade, shutter; blinker; concealment, disguise, feint, pretence, pretext, ruse, stratagem, subterfuge.

blink *vb* nictate, nictitate, wink; flicker, flutter, gleam, glitter, intermit, twinkle; avoid, disregard, evade, gloss over, ignore, overlook, pass over. • *n* glance, glimpse, sight, view, wink; gleam, glimmer, sheen, shimmer, twinkle.

bliss *n* beatification, beatitude, blessedness, blissfulness, ecstasy, felicity, happiness, heaven, joy, rapture, transport.

blithe *adj* airy, animated, blithesome, buoyant, cheerful, debonair, elated, happy, jocund, joyful, joyous, lively, mirthful, sprightly, vivacious.

bloat *vb* dilate, distend, inflate, swell.

block *vb* arrest, bar, blockade, check, choke, close, hinder, impede, jam, obstruct, stop; form, mould, shape; brace, stiffen. • *n* lump, mass; blockhead, dunce, fool, simpleton; pulley, tackle; execution, scaffold; jam, obstruction, pack, stoppage.

blood *n* children, descendants, offspring, posterity, progeny; family, house, kin, kindred, line, relations; consanguinity, descent, kinship, lineage, relationship; courage, disposition, feelings, mettle, passion, spirit, temper.

bloom *vb* blossom, blow, flower; thrive, prosper. • *n* blossom, blossoming, blow, efflorescence, florescence, flowering; delicacy, delicateness, flush, freshness, heyday, prime, vigour; flush, glow, rose.

blossom *vb* bloom, blow, flower. • *n* bloom, blow, efflorescence, flower.

blot *vb* cancel, efface, erase, expunge, obliterate, rub out; blur, deface, disfigure, obscure, spot, stain, sully; disgrace, dishonour, tarnish. • *n* blemish, blur, erasure, spot, obliteration, stain; disgrace, dishonour, stigma.

blow[1] *n* bang, beat, buffet, dab, impact, knock, pat, punch, rap, slam, stroke, thump, wallop, buffet, impact; affliction, calamity, disaster, misfortune, setback.

blow[2] *vb* breathe, gasp, pant, puff; flow, move, scud, stream, waft. • *n* blast, gale, gust, squall, storm, wind.

blue *adj* azure, cerulean, cobalt, indigo, sapphire, ultramarine; ghastly, livid, pallid; dejected, depressed, dispirited, downcast, gloomy, glum, mopey, melancholic, melancholy, sad.

bluff[1] *adj* abrupt, blunt, blustering, coarse, frank, good-natured, open, outspoken; abrupt, precipitous, sheer, steep. • *n* cliff, headland, height.

bluff[2] *vb* deceive, defraud, lie, mislead. • *n* deceit, deception, feint, fraud, lie.

blunder *vb* err, flounder, mistake; stumble. • *n* error, fault, howler, mistake, solecism.

blunt *adj* dull, edgeless, obtuse, pointless, unsharpened; insensible, stolid, thick-witted; abrupt, bluff, downright, plainspoken, outspoken, unceremonious, uncourtly. • *vb* deaden, dull, numb, weaken.

blur *vb* bedim, darken, dim, obscure; blemish, blot, spot, stain, sully, tarnish. • *n* blemish, blot, soil, spot, stain, tarnish; disgrace, smear.

blush *vb* colour, flush, glow, redden. • *n* bloom, flush, glow, colour, reddening, suffusion.

bluster *vb* boast, brag, bully, domineer, roar, swagger, swell, vaunt. • *n* boisterousness, noise, tumult, turbulence; braggadocio, bravado, boasting, gasconade, swaggering.

board *n* deal, panel, plank; diet, entertainment, fare, food, meals, provision, victuals; cabinet, conclave, committee, council; directorate; panel.

boast *vb* bluster, brag, crack, flourish, crow, vaunt. • *n* blustering, boasting, bombast, brag, braggadocio, bravado, bombast, swaggering, vaunt.

bode *vb* augur, betoken, forebode, foreshadow, foretell, portend, predict, prefigure, presage, prophesy.

bodily *adj* carnal, corporeal, fleshly, physical. • *adv* altogether, completely, entirely, wholly.

body *n* carcass, corpse, remains; stem, torso, trunk; aggregate, bulk, corpus, mass; being, individual, mortal creature, person; assemblage, association, band, company, corporation, corps, coterie, force, party, society, troop; consistency, substance, thickness.

boggle *vb* demur, falter, hang fire, hesitate, shrink, vacillate, waver.

boil[1] *vb* agitate, bubble, foam, froth, rage, seethe, simmer. • *n* ebullience, ebullition.

boil[2] (*med*) gathering, pimple, pustule, swelling, tumour.

boisterous *adj* loud, roaring, stormy; clamouring, loud, noisy, obstreperous, tumultuous, turbulent.

bold *adj* adventurous, audacious, courageous; brave, daring, dauntless, doughty, fearless, gallant, hardy, heroic, intrepid, mettlesome, manful, manly, spirited, stouthearted, undaunted, valiant, valorous; assured, confident, self-reliant; assuming, forward, impertinent, impudent, insolent, push, rude, saucy; conspicuous, projecting, prominent, striking; abrupt, precipitous, prominent, steep.

bolster *vb* aid, assist, defend, help, maintain, prop, stay, support. • *n* cushion, pillow; prop, support.

bolt *vb* abscond, flee, fly. • *n* arrow, dart, missile, shaft; thunderbolt.

bombast *n* bluster, brag, braggadocio, fustian, gasconade, mouthing, pomposity, rant.

bond *vb* bind, connect, fuse, glue, join. • *adj* captive, enslaved, enthralled, subjugated. • *n* band, cord, fastening, ligament, ligature, link, nexus; bondage, captivity, chains, constraint, fetters, prison, shackle; attachment, attraction, connection, coupling, link, tie, union; compact, obligation, pledge, promise.

bondage *n* captivity, confinement, enslavement, enthralment, peonage, serfdom, servitude, slavery, thraldom, vassalage.

bonny *adj* beautiful, handsome, fair, fine, pretty; airy, blithe, buoyant, buxom, cheerful, jolly, joyous, merry, playful, sporty, sprightly, winsome.

bonus *n* gift, honorarium, premium, reward, subsidy.

booby *n* blockhead, dunce, fool, idiot, simpleton.

book *vb* bespeak, engage, reserve; programme, schedule; list, log, record, register. • *n* booklet, brochure, compendium, handbook, manual, monograph, pamphlet, textbook, tract, treatise, volume, work.

bookish *adj* erudite, learned, literary, scholarly, studious.

boon *adj* convivial, jolly, jovial, hearty; close, intimate. • *n* benefaction, favour, grant, gift, present; advantage, benefit, blessing, good, privilege.

boor *n* bumpkin, clodhopper, clown, lout, lubber, peasant, rustic, swain.

boorish *adj* awkward, bearish, clownish, course, gruff, ill-bred, loutish, lubberly, rude, rustic, uncivilized, uncouth, uneducated.

bootless *adj* abortive, fruitless, futile, profitless, vain, worthless, useless.

booty *n* loot, pillage, plunder, spoil.

border *vb* bound, edge, fringe, line, march, rim, skirt, verge; abut, adjoin, butt, conjoin, connect, neighbour. • *n* brim, brink, edge, fringe, hem, margin, rim, skirt, verge; boundary, confine, frontier, limit, march, outskirts.

bore[1] *vb* annoy, fatigue, plague, tire, trouble, vex, weary, worry. • *n* bother, nuisance, pest, worry.

bore[2] *vb* drill, perforate, pierce, sink, tunnel. • *n* calibre, hole, shaft, tunnel.

borrow *vb* take and return, use temporarily; adopt, appropriate, imitate; dissemble, feign, simulate.

boss[1] *vb* emboss, stud; • *n* knob, protuberance, stud.

boss[2] *vb* command, direct, employ, run. • *n* employer, foreman, master, overseer, superintendent.

botch *vb* blunder, bungle, cobble, mar, mend, mess, patch, spoil. • *n* blotch, pustule, sore; failure, miscarriage.

bother *vb* annoy, disturb, harass, molest, perplex, pester, plague, tease, trouble, vex, worry. • *n* annoyance, perplexity, plague, trouble, vexation.

bottom *vb* build, establish, found. • *adj* base, basic, ground, lowermost, lowest, nethermost, undermost. • *n* base, basis, foot, foundation, groundwork; dale, meadow, valley; buttocks, fundament, seat; dregs, grounds, lees, sediment.

bounce *vb* bound, jump, leap, rebound, recoil, spring. • *n* knock, thump; bound, jump, leap, spring, vault.

bound[1] *adj* assured, certain, decided, determined, resolute, resolved; confined, hampered, restricted, restrained; committed, contracted, engaged, pledged, promised; beholden, dutybound, obligated, obliged.

bound[2] *vb* border, delimit, circumscribe, confine, demarcate, limit, restrict, terminate. • *n* boundary, confine, edge, limit, march, margin, periphery, term, verge.

bound[3] *vb* jump, leap, spring. • *n* bounce, jump, leap, spring, vault.

boundary *n* border, bourn, circuit, circumference, confine, limit, march, periphery, term, verge.

boundless *adj* endless, immeasurable, infinite, limitless, unbounded, unconfined, undefined, unlimited, vast.

bountiful *adj* beneficent, bounteous, generous, liberal, munificent, princely.

bounty *n* beneficence, benevolence, charity, donation, generosity, gift, kindness, premium, present, reward.

bourn *n* border, boundary, confine, limit; brook, burn, rill, rivulet, stream, torrent.

bow[1] *n* (*naut*) beak, prow, stem.

bow[2] *vb* arc, bend, buckle, crook, curve, droop, flex, yield; crush, depress, subdue; curtsy, genuflect, kowtow, submit. • *n* arc, bend, bilge, bulge, convex, curve, flexion; bob, curtsy, genuflection, greeting, homage, obeisance; coming out, debut, introduction; curtain call, encore.

bowels *npl* entrails, guts, insides, viscera; compassion, mercy, pity, sympathy, tenderness.

box[1] *vb* fight, hit, mill, spar. • *n* blow, buffet, fight, hit, spar.

box[2] *vb* barrel, crate, pack, parcel. • *n* case, chest, container, crate, portmanteau, trunk.

boy *n* lad, stripling, youth.

brace *vb* make tight, tighten; buttress, fortify, reinforce, shore, strengthen, support, truss. • *n* couple, pair; clamp, girder, prop, shore, stay, support, tie, truss.

brag *vb* bluster, boast, flourish, gasconade, vaunt.

branch *vb* diverge, fork, bifurcate, ramify, spread. • *n* bough, offset, limb, shoot, sprig, twig; arm, fork, ramification, spur; article, department, member, part, portion, section, subdivision.

brand *vb* denounce, stigmatize, mark. • *n* firebrand, torch; bolt, lightning flash; cachet, mark, stamp, tally; blot, reproach, stain, stigma.

brave *vb* dare, defy. • *adj* bold, courageous, fearless, heroic, intrepid, stalwart.

bravery *n* courage, daring, fearlessness, gallantry, valour.

brawl *vb* bicker, dispute, jangle, quarrel, squabble. • *n* broil, dispute, feud, fracas, fray, jangle, quarrel, row, scuffle, squabble, uproar, wrangle.

brawny *adj* athletic, lusty, muscular, powerful, robust, sinewy, stalwart, strapping, strong, sturdy.

bray *vb* clamour, hoot, roar, trumpet, vociferate. • *n* blare, crash, roar, shout.

breach *n* break, chasm, crack, disruption, fissure, flaw, fracture, opening, rent, rift, rupture; alienation, difference, disaffection, disagreement, split.

bread *n* aliment, diet, fare, food, nourishment, nutriment, provisions, regimen, victuals.

break *vb* crack, disrupt, fracture, part, rend, rive, sever; batter, burst, crush, shatter, smash, splinter; cashier, degrade, discard, discharge, dismiss; disobey, infringe, transgress, violate; intermit, interrupt, stop; disclose, open, unfold. • *n* aperture, breach, chasm, fissure, gap, rent, rip, rupture; break-up, crash, debacle.

breast *vb* face, oppose, resist, stem, withstand. • *n* bosom, chest, thorax; affections, conscience, heart; mammary gland, mammary organ, pap, udder.

breath *n* exhaling, inhaling, pant, sigh, respiration, whiff; animation, existence, life; pause, respite, rest; breathing space, instant, moment.

breathe *vb* live, exist; emit, exhale, give out; diffuse, express, indicate, manifest, show.

breed *vb* bear, beget, engender, hatch, produce; bring up, foster, nourish, nurture, raise, rear; discipline, educate, instruct, nurture, rear, school, teach, train; generate, originate. • *n* extraction, family, lineage, pedigree, progeny, race, strain.

brevity *n* briefness, compression, conciseness, curtness, pithiness, shortness, terseness, transiency.

brew *vb* concoct, contrive, devise, excite, foment, instigate, plot. • *n* beverage, concoction, drink, liquor, mixture, potation.

bribe *vb* buy, corrupt, influence, pay off, suborn. • *n* allurement, corruption, enticement, graft, pay-off, subornation.

bridle *vb* check, curb, control, govern, restrain. • *n* check, control, curb.

brief *vb* direct, give directions, instruct; capsulate, summarize, delineate, describe, draft, outline, sketch; (*law*) retain. • *adj* concise, curt, inconsiderable, laconic, pithy, short, succinct, terse; fleeting, momentary, short, temporary, transient. • *n* abstract, breviary, briefing, epitome, compendium, summary, syllabus; (*law*) precept, writ.

brigand *n* bandit, footpad, freebooter, gangster, highwayman, marauder, outlaw, robber, thug.

bright *adj* blazing, brilliant, dazzling, gleaming, glowing, light, luminous, radiant, shining, sparkling, sunny; clear, cloudless, lambent, lucid, transparent; famous, glorious, illustrious; acute, discerning, ingenious, intelligent, keen; auspicious, cheering, encouraging, exhilarating, favourable, inspiring, promising, propitious; cheerful, genial, happy, lively, merry, pleasant, smiling, vivacious.

brilliant *adj* beaming, bright, effulgent, gleaming, glistening, glittering, lustrous, radiant, resplendent, shining, sparkling splendid; admirable, celebrated, distinguished, famous, glorious, illustrious, renowned; dazzling, decided, prominent, signal, striking, unusual.

brim *n* border, brink, edge, rim, margin, skirt, verge; bank, border, coast, margin, shore.

bring *vb* bear, convey, fetch; accompany, attend, conduct, convey, convoy, guide, lead; gain, get, obtain, procure, produce.

brisk *adj* active, alert, agile, lively, nimble, perky, quick, smart, spirited, spry.

brittle *adj* brash, breakable, crisp, crumbling, fragile, frangible, frail, shivery.

broach *vb* open, pierce, set; approach, break, hint, suggest; proclaim, publish, utter.

broad *adj* ample, expansive, extensive, large, spacious, sweeping, vast, wide; enlarged, hospitable, liberal, tolerant; diffused, open, spread; coarse, gross, indecent, indelicate, unrefined, vulgar.

broaden *vb* augment, enlarge, expand, extend, increase, spread, stretch, widen.

broken *adj* fractured, rent, ruptured, separated, severed, shattered, shivered, torn; exhausted, feeble, impaired, shaken, shattered, spent, wasted; defective, halting, hesitating, imperfect, stammering, stumbling; contrite, humble, lowly, penitent; abrupt, craggy, precipitous, rough.

broker *n* agent, factor, go-between, middleman.

brood *vb* incubate, sit. • *n* issue, offspring, progeny; breed, kind, line, lineage, sort, strain.

brook *vb* abide, bear, endure, suffer, tolerate. • *n* burn, beck, creek, rill, rivulet, run, streamlet.

brotherhood *n* association, clan, clique, coterie, fraternity, junta, society.

brotherly *adj* affectionate, amicable, cordial, friendly, kind.

browbeat *vb* bully, intimidate, overawe, overbear.

bruise *vb* contuse, crunch, squeeze; batter, break, maul, pound, pulverize; batter, deface, indent. • *n* blemish, contusion, swelling.

brush[1] *n* brushwood, bush, scrub, scrubwood, shrubs, thicket, wilderness.

brush[2] *vb* buff, clean, polish, swab, sweep, wipe; curry, groom, rub down; caress, flick, glance, graze, scrape, skim, touch. • *n* besom, broom; action, affair, collision, contest, conflict, encounter, engagement, fight, skirmish.

brutal *adj* barbaric, barbarous, brutish, cruel, ferocious, inhuman, ruthless, savage; bearish, brusque, churlish, gruff, impolite, harsh, rude, rough, truculent, uncivil.

brute *n* barbarian, beast, monster, ogre, savage; animal, beast, creature. • *adj* carnal, mindless, physical; bestial, coarse, gross.

bubble *vb* boil, effervesce, foam. • *n* bead, blob, fluid, globule; bagatelle, trifle; cheat, delusion, hoax.

buccaneer *n* corsair, freebooter, pirate.

buck *vb* jump, leap. • *n* beau, blade, blood, dandy, fop, gallant, spark; male.

bud *vb* burgeon, germinate, push, shoot, sprout, vegetate. • *n* burgeon, gem, germ, gemmule, shoot, sprout.

budget *vb* allocate, cost, estimate. • *n* account, estimate, financial statement; assets, finances, funds, means, resources; bag, bundle, pack, packet, parcel, roll; assortment, batch, collection, lot, set, store.

buffet[1] *vb* beat, box, cuff, slap, smite, strike; resist, struggle against. • *n* blow, box, cuff, slap, strike;

buffet[2] *n* cupboard, sideboard; refreshment counter.

buffoon *n* antic, clown, droll, fool, harlequin, jester, mountebank.

build *vb* construct, erect, establish, fabricate, fashion, model, raise, rear. • *n* body, figure, form, frame, physique; construction, shape, structure.

building *n* construction, erection, fabrication; edifice, fabric, house, pile, substructure, structure.

bulk *n* dimension, magnitude, mass, size, volume; amplitude, bulkiness, massiveness; body, majority, mass.

bully *vb* browbeat, bulldoze, domineer, haze, hector, intimidate, overbear. • *n* blusterer, browbeater, bulldozer, hector, swaggerer, roisterer, tyrant.

bulwark *n* barrier, fortification, parapet, rampart, wall; palladium, safeguard, security.

bump *vb* collide, knock, strike, thump. • *n* blow, jar, jolt, knock, shock, thump; lump, protuberance, swelling.

bunch *vb* assemble, collect, crowd, group, herd, pack. • *n* bulge, bump, bundle, hump, knob, lump, protuberance; cluster, hand, fascicle; assortment, batch, collection, group, lot, parcel, set; knot, tuft.

bundle *vb* bale, pack, package, parcel, truss, wrap. • *n* bale, batch, bunch, collection, heap, pack, package, packet, parcel, pile, roll, truss.

bungler *n* botcher, duffer, fumbler, lout, lubber, mis-manager, muddler.

burden *vb* encumber, grieve, load, oppress, overlay, overload, saddle, surcharge, try. • *n* capacity, cargo, freight, lading, load, tonnage, weight; affliction, charge, clog, encumbrance, impediment, grievance, sorrow, trial, trouble; drift, point, substance, tenor, surcharge.

bureau *n* chest of drawers, dresser; counting room, office.

burial *n* burying, entombment, inhumation, interment, sepulture.

burlesque *vb* ape, imitate, lampoon, mock, ridicule, satirize. • *n* caricature, extravaganza, parody, send-up, take-off, travesty.

burn[1] *n* beck, brook, gill, rill, rivulet, runnel, runlet, stream water.

burn[2] *vb* blaze, conflagrate, enflame, fire, flame, ignite, kindle, light, smoulder; cremate, incinerate; scald, scorch, singe; boil, broil, cook, roast, seethe, simmer, stew, swelter, toast; bronze, brown, sunburn, suntan, tan; bake, desiccate, dry, parch, sear, shrivel, wither; glow, incandesce, tingle, warm. • *n* scald, scorch, singe; sunburn.

burning *adj* aflame, fiery, hot, scorching; ardent, earnest, fervent, fervid, impassioned, intense.

burnish *vb* brighten, buff, furbish, polish, shine. • *n* glaze, gloss, patina, polish, shine.

burst *vb* break open, be rent, explode, shatter, split open. • *adj* broken, kaput, punctured, ruptured, shattered, split. • *n* break, breakage, breach, fracture, rupture; blast, blowout, blowup, discharge, detonation, explosion; spurt; blaze, flare, flash; cloudburst, downpour; bang, crack, crash, report, sound; fusillade, salvo, spray, volley, outburst, outbreak flare-up, blaze, eruption.

bury *vb* entomb, inearth, inhume, inter; conceal, hide, secrete, shroud.

business *n* calling, employment, occupation, profession, pursuit, vocation; commerce, dealing, trade, traffic; affair, concern, engagement, matter, transaction, undertaking; duty, function, office, task, work.

bustle *vb* fuss, hurry, scurry. • *n* ado, commotion, flurry, fuss, hurry, hustle, pother, stir, tumult.

busy *vb* devote, employ, engage, occupy, spend, work. • *adj* employed, engaged, occupied; active, assiduous, diligent, engrossed, industrious, sedulous, working; agile, brisk, nimble, spry, stirring; meddling, officious.

but *conj* except, excepting, further, howbeit, moreover, still, unless, yet. • *adv* all the same, even, notwithstanding, still, yet.

butchery *n* massacre, murder, slaughter.

butt[1] *vb* bunt, push, shove, shunt, strike; encroach, impose, interfere, intrude, invade, obtrude. • *n* buck, bunt, push, shove, shunt, thrust.

butt[2] *n* barrel, cask.

butt[3] *n* aim, goal, mark, object, point, target; dupe, gull, victim.

butt[4] *vb* abut, adjoin, conjoin, connect, neighbour. • *n* end, piece, remainder, stub, stump; buttocks, posterior, rump.

buttonhole *vb* bore, catch, detain in conversation, importune.

buttress *vb* brace, prop, shore, stay, support. • *n* brace, bulwark, prop, stay, support.

buxom *adj* comely, fresh, healthy, hearty, plump, rosy, ruddy, vigorous.

byword *n* adage, aphorism, apothegm, dictum, maxim, proverb, saying, saw.

C

cabal *vb* conspire, intrigue, machinate, plot. • *n* clique, combination, confederacy, coterie, faction, gang, junta, league, party, set; conspiracy, intrigue, machination, plot.

cabbalistic, cabalistic *adj* dark, fanciful, mysterious, mystic, occult, secret.

cabaret *n* tavern, inn, public house, wine shop.

cabin *n* berth, bunk, cot, cottage, crib, dwelling, hovel, hut, shack, shanty, shed.

cabinet *n* apartment, boudoir, chamber, closet; case, davenport, desk, escritoire; council, ministry.

cachinnation *n* guffaw, laugh, laughter.

cackle *vb* giggle, laugh, snicker, titter; babble, chatter, gabble, palaver, prate, prattle, titter. • *n* babble, chatter, giggle, prate, prattle, snigger, titter.

cacophonous *adj* discordant, grating, harsh, inharmonious, jarring, raucous.

cadaverous *adj* bloodless, deathlike, ghastly, pale, pallid, wan.

cage *vb* confine, immure, imprison, incarcerate. • *n* coop, pen, pound.

caitiff *adj* base, craven, pusillanimous, rascally, recreant. • *n* coward, knave, miscreant, rascal, rogue, scoundrel, sneak, traitor, vagabond, villain, wretch.

cajole *vb* blandish, coax, flatter, jolly, wheedle; beguile, deceive, delude, entrap, inveigle, tempt.

calamity *n* adversity, affliction, blow, casualty, cataclysm, catastrophe, disaster, distress, downfall, evil, hardship, mischance, misery, misfortune, mishap, reverse, ruin, stroke, trial, visitation.

calculate *vb* cast, compute, count, estimate, figure, rate, reckon, weigh; tell.

calculating *adj* crafty, designing, scheming, selfish; careful, cautious, circumspect, far-sighted, politic, sagacious, wary.

calefaction *n* heating, warming; hotness, incandescence, warmth.

calendar *n* almanac, ephemeris, register; catalogue, list, schedule.

calibre *n* bore, capacity, diameter, gauge; ability, capacity, endowment, faculty, gifts, parts, scope, talent.

call *vb* christen, denominate, designate, dub, entitle, name, phrase, style, term; bid, invite, summons; assemble, convene, convoke, muster; cry, exclaim; arouse, awaken, proclaim, rouse, shout, waken; appoint, elect, ordain. • *n* cry, outcry, voice; appeal, invitation, summons; claim, demand, summons; appointment, election, invitation.

calling *n* business, craft, employment, occupation, profession, pursuit, trade.

callous *adj* hard, hardened, indurated; apathetic, dull, indifferent, insensible, inured, obdurate, obtuse, sluggish, torpid, unfeeling, unsusceptible.

callow *adj* naked, unfeathered, unfledged; green, immature, inexperienced, sappy, silly, soft, unfledged, unsophisticated.

calm *vb* allay, becalm, compose, hush, lull, smooth, still, tranquillize; alleviate, appease, assuage, moderate, mollify, pacify, quiet, soften, soothe, tranquillize. • *adj* halcyon, mild, peaceful, placid, quiet, reposeful, serene, smooth, still, tranquil, unruffled; collected, cool, composed, controlled, impassive, imperturbable, sedate, self-possessed, undisturbed, unperturbed, unruffled, untroubled. • *n* lull; equanimity, peace, placidity, quiet, repose, serenity, stillness, tranquillity.

calorific *adj* heat, heat-producing.

calumniate *vb* abuse, asperse, backbite, blacken, blemish, defame, discredit, disparage, lampoon, libel, malign, revile, slander, traduce, vilify.

calumny *n* abuses, aspersion, backbiting, defamation, detraction, evil-speaking, insult, libel, lying, obloquy, slander, vilification, vituperation.

camarilla *n* cabal, clique, junta, ring.

camber *vb* arch, bend, curve. • *n* arch, arching, convexity.

camp[1] *vb* bivouac, encamp, lodge, pitch, tent. • *n* bivouac, cantonment, encampment, laager; cabal, circle, clique, coterie, faction, group, junta, party, ring, set.

camp[2] *adj* affected, artificial, effeminate, exaggerated, mannered, theatrical.

canaille *n* mob, populace, proletariat, rabble, ragbag, riffraff, scum.

canal *n* channel, duct, pipe, tube.

cancel *vb* blot, efface, erase, expunge, obliterate; abrogate, annul, countermand, nullify, quash, repeal, rescind, revoke.

candelabrum *n* candlestick, chandelier, lustre.

candid *adj* fair, impartial, just, unbiased, unprejudiced; artless, frank, free, guileless, honest, honourable, ingenuous, naive, open, plain, sincere, straightforward.

candidate *n* applicant, aspirant, claimant, competitor, probationer.

candour *n* fairness, impartiality, justice; artlessness, frankness, guilelessness, honesty, ingenuousness, openness, simplicity, sincerity, straightforwardness, truthfulness.

canker *vb* corrode, erode, rot, rust, waste; blight, consume, corrupt, embitter, envenom, infect, poison, sour. • *n* gangrene, rot; bale, bane, blight, corruption, infection, irritation.

canon *n* catalogue, criterion, formula, formulary, law, regulation, rule, standard, statute.

canorous *adj* musical, tuneful.

cant[1] *vb* whine. • *adj* current, partisan, popular, rote, routine, set; argotic, slangy. • *n* hypocrisy; argot, jargon, lingo, slang.

cant[2] *vb* bevel, incline, list, slant, tilt, turn. • *n* bevel, inclination, leaning, list, pitch, slant, tilt, turn.

cantankerous *adj* contumacious, crabbed, cross-grained, dogged, headstrong, heady, intractable, obdurate, obstinate, perverse, refractory, stiff, stubborn, wilful, unyielding.

canting *adj* affected, pious, sanctimonious, whining.

canvas *n* burlap, scrim, tarpaulin.

canvass *vb* discuss, dispute; analyze, consider, examine, investigate, review, scrutinize, sift, study; campaign, electioneer, solicit votes. • *n* debate, discussion, dispute; examination, scrutiny, sifting.

canyon *n* gorge, gulch, ravine.

cap *vb* cover, surmount; complete, crown, finish; exceed, overtop, surpass, transcend; match, parallel, pattern. • *n* beret, head-cover, head-dress; acme, chief, crown, head, peak, perfection, pitch, summit, top.

capability *n* ability, brains, calibre, capableness, capacity, competency, efficiency, faculty, force, power, scope, skill.

capable *adj* adapted, fitted, qualified, suited; able, accomplished, clever, competent, efficient, gifted, ingenious, intelligent, sagacious, skilful.

capacious *adj* ample, broad, comprehensive, expanded, extensive, large, roomy, spacious, wide.

capacitate *vb* enable, qualify.

capacity *n* amplitude, dimensions, magnitude, volume; aptitude, aptness, brains, calibre, discernment, faculty, forte, genius, gift, parts, power, talent, turn, wit; ability, capability, calibre, cleverness, competency, efficiency, skill; character, charge, function, office, position, post, province, service, sphere.

caparison *vb* accoutre, costume, equip, outfit, rig out. • *n* accoutrements, armour, get-up, harness, housing, livery, outfit, panoply, tack, tackle, trappings, turnout.

caper *vb* bound, caracole, frisk, gambol, hop, leap, prank, romp, skip, spring. • *n* bound, dance, gambol, frisk, hop, jump, leap, prance, romp, skip.

capillary *adj* delicate, fine, minute, slender.

capital *adj* cardinal, chief, essential, important, leading, main, major, pre-eminent, principal, prominent; fatal; excellent, first-class, first-rate, good, prime, splendid. • *n* chief city, metropolis, seat; money, estate, investments, shares, stock.

caprice *n* crotchet, fancy, fickleness, freak, humour, inconstancy, maggot, phantasy, quirk, vagary, whim, whimsy.

capricious *adj* changeable, crotchety, fanciful, fantastical, fickle, fitful, freakish, humoursome, odd, puckish, queer, uncertain, variable, wayward, whimsical.

capsize *vb* overturn, upset.

capsule *n* case, covering, envelope, sheath, shell, wrapper: pericarp, pod, seed-vessel.

captain *vb* command, direct, head, lead, manage, officer, preside. • *n* chief, chieftain, commander, leader, master, officer, soldier, warrior.

captious *adj* carping, cavilling, censorious, critical, fault-finding, hypercritical; acrimonious, cantankerous, contentious, crabbed, cross, snappish, snarling, splenetic, testy, touchy, waspish; ensnaring, insidious.

captivate *vb* allure, attract, bewitch, catch, capture, charm, enamour, enchant, enthral, fascinate, gain, hypnotize, infatuate, win.

captivity *n* confinement, durance, duress, imprisonment; bondage, enthralment, servitude, slavery, subjection, thraldom, vassalage.

capture *vb* apprehend, arrest, catch, seize. • *n* apprehension, arrest, catch, catching, imprisonment, seizure; bag, prize.

carcass *n* body, cadaver, corpse, corse, remains.

cardinal *adj* capital, central, chief, essential, first, important, leading, main, pre-eminent, primary, principal, vital.

care *n* anxiety, concern, perplexity, trouble, solicitude, worry; attention, carefulness, caution, circumspection, heed, regard, vigilance, wariness, watchfulness; charge, custody, guardianship, keep, oversight, superintendence, ward; burden, charge, concern, responsibility.

careful *adj* anxious, solicitous, concerned, troubled, uneasy; attentive, heedful, mindful, regardful, thoughtful; cautious, canny, circumspect, discreet, leery, vigilant, watchful.

careless *adj* carefree, nonchalant, unapprehensive, undisturbed, unperplexed, unsolicitous, untroubled; disregardful, heedless, inattentive, incautious, inconsiderate, neglectful, negligent, regardless, remiss, thoughtless, unobservant, unconcerned, unconsidered, unmindful, unthinking.

carelessness *n* heedlessness, inadvertence, inattention, inconsiderateness, neglect, negligence, remissness, slackness, thoughtlessness, unconcern.

caress *vb* coddle, cuddle, cosset, embrace, fondle, hug, kiss, pet. • *n* cuddle, embrace, fondling, hug, kiss.

caressing *n* blandishment, dalliance, endearment, fondling.

cargo *n* freight, lading, load.

caricature *vb* burlesque, parody, send-up, take-off, travesty. • *n* burlesque, farce, ludicrous, parody, representation, take-off, travesty.

carious *adj* decayed, mortified, putrid, rotten, ulcerated.

cark *vb* annoy, fret, grieve, harass, perplex, worry.

carnage *n* bloodshed, butchery, havoc, massacre, murder, slaughter.

carnal *adj* animal, concupiscent, fleshly, lascivious, lecherous, lewd, libidinous, lubricous, lustful, salacious, sensual, voluptuous; bodily, earthy, mundane. natural, secular, temporal, unregenerate, unspiritual.

carol *vb* chant, hum, sing, warble. • *n* canticle, chorus, ditty, hymn, lay, song, warble.

carousal *n* banquet, entertainment, feast, festival, merry-making, regale; bacchanal, carouse, debauch, jamboree, jollification, orgy, revel, revelling, revelry, saturnalia, spree, wassail.

carp *vb* cavil, censure, criticize, fault.

carping *adj* captious, cavilling, censorious, hypercritical. • *n* cavil, censure, fault-finding, hypercriticism.

carriage *n* conveyance, vehicle; air, bearing, behaviour, conduct, demeanour, deportment, front, mien, port.

carry *vb* bear, convey, transfer, transmit, transport; impel, push forward, urge; accomplish, compass, effect, gain, secure; bear up, support, sustain; infer, involve, imply, import, signify.

cart *n* conveyance, tumbril, van, vehicle, wagon.

carte-blanche *n* authority, power.

carve *vb* chisel, cut, divide, engrave, grave, hack, hew, indent, incise, sculpt, sculpture; fashion, form, mould, shape.

cascade *vb* cataract, descend, drop, engulf, fall, inundate, overflow, plunge, tumble. • *n* cataract, fall, falls, force, linn, waterfall.

case[1] *vb* cover, encase, enclose, envelop, protect, wrap; box, pack. • *n* capsule, covering, sheathe; box, cabinet, container, holder, receptacle.

case[2] *n* condition, plight, predicament, situation, state; example, instance, occurrence; circumstance, condition, contingency, event; action, argument, cause, lawsuit, process, suit, trial.

case-hardened *adj* hardened, indurated, steeled; brazen, brazen-faced, obdurate, reprobate.

cash *n* banknotes, bullion, coin, currency, money, payment, specie.

cashier *vb* break, discard, discharge, dismiss.

cast *vb* fling, hurl, pitch, send, shy, sling, throw, toss; drive, force, impel, thrust; lay aside, put off, shed; calculate, compute, reckon; communicate, diffuse, impart, shed, throw. • *n* fling, throw, toss; shade, tinge, tint, touch; air, character, look, manner, mien, style, tone, turn; form, mould.

castaway *adj* abandoned, cast-off, discarded, rejected. • *n* derelict, outcast, reprobate, vagabond.

caste *n* class, grade, lineage, order, race, rank, species, status.

castigate *vb* beat, chastise, flog, lambaste, lash, thrash, whip; chaste, correct, discipline, punish; criticize, flagellate, upbraid.

castle *n* citadel, fortress, stronghold.

castrate *vb* caponize, emasculate, geld; mortify, subdue, suppress, weaken.

casual *adj* accidental, contingent, fortuitous, incidental, irregular, occasional, random, uncertain, unforeseen, unintentional, unpremeditated; informal, relaxed.

casualty *n* chance, contingency, fortuity, mishap; accident, catastrophe, disaster, mischance, misfortune.

cat *n* grimalkin, kitten, puss, tabby, tomcat.

cataclysm *n* deluge, flood, inundation; disaster, upheaval.

catacomb *n* crypt, tomb, vault.

catalogue *vb* alphabetize, categorize, chronicle, class, classify, codify, file, index, list, record, tabulate. • *n* enumeration, index, inventory, invoice, list, record, register, roll, schedule.

cataract *n* cascade, fall, waterfall.

catastrophe *n* conclusion, consummation, denouement, end, finale, issue, termination, upshot; adversity, blow, calamity, cataclysm, debacle, disaster, ill, misfortune, mischance, mishap, trial, trouble.

catch *vb* clutch, grasp, gripe, nab, seize, snatch; apprehend, arrest, capture; overtake; enmesh, ensnare, entangle, entrap, lime, net; bewitch, captivate, charm, enchant, fascinate, win; surprise, take unawares. • *n* arrest, capture, seizure; bag, find, haul, plum, prize; drawback, fault, hitch, obstacle, rub, snag; captive, conquest.

catching *adj* communicable, contagious, infectious, pestiferous, pestilential; attractive, captivating, charming, enchanting, fascinating, taking, winning, winsome.

catechize *adj* examine, interrogate, question, quiz.

catechumen *n* convert, disciple, learner, neophyte, novice, proselyte, pupil, tyro.

categorical *adj* absolute, direct, downright, emphatic, explicit, express, positive, unconditional, unqualified, unreserved, utter.

category *n* class, division, head, heading, list, order, rank, sort.

catenation *n* conjunction, connection, union.

cater *vb* feed, provide, purvey.

cathartic *adj* abstergent, aperient, cleansing, evacuant, laxative, purgative. • *n* aperient, laxative, physic, purgative, purge.

catholic *adj* general, universal, world-wide; charitable, liberal, tolerant, unbigoted, unexclusive, unsectarian.

cause *vb* breed, create, originate, produce; effect, effectuate, occasion, produce. • *n* agent, creator, mainspring, origin, original, producer, source, spring; account, agency, consideration, ground, incentive, incitement, inducement, motive, reason; aim, end, object, purpose; action, case, suit, trial.

caustic *adj* acrid, cathartic, consuming, corroding, corrosive, eating, erosive, mordant, virulent; biting, bitter, burning, cutting, sarcastic, satirical, scalding, scathing, severe, sharp, stinging.

caution *vb* admonish, forewarn, warn. • *n* care, carefulness, circumspection, discretion, forethought, heed, heedfulness, providence, prudence, wariness, vigilance, watchfulness; admonition, advice, counsel, injunction, warning.

cautious *adj* careful, chary, circumspect, discreet, heedful, prudent, wary, vigilant, wary, watchful.

cavalier *adj* arrogant, curt, disdainful, haughty, insolent, scornful, supercilious; debonair, gallant, gay. • *n* chevalier, equestrian, horseman, horse-soldier, knight.

cave *n* cavern, cavity, den, grot, grotto.

cavil *vb* carp, censure, hypercriticize, object.

cavilling *adj* captious, carping, censorious, critical, hypercritical.

cavity *n* hollow, pocket, vacuole, void.

cease *vb* desist, intermit, pause, refrain, stay, stop; fail; discontinue, end, quit, terminate.

ceaseless *adj* continual, continuous, incessant, unceasing, unintermitting, uninterrupted, unremitting; endless, eternal, everlasting, perpetual.

cede *vb* abandon, abdicate, relinquish, resign, surrender, transfer, yield; convey, grant.

celebrate *vb* applaud, bless, commend, emblazon, extol, glorify, laud, magnify, praise, trumpet; commemorate, honour, keep, observe; solemnize.

celebrated *adj* distinguished, eminent, famed, famous, glorious, illustrious, notable, renowned.

celebrity *n* credit, distinction, eminence, fame, glory, honour, renown, reputation, repute; lion, notable, star.

celerity *n* fleetness, haste, quickness, rapidity, speed, swiftness, velocity.

celestial *adj* empyreal, empyrean; angelic, divine, god-like, heavenly, seraphic, supernal, supernatural.

celibate *adj* single, unmarried. • *n* bachelor, single, virgin.

cellular *adj* alveolate, honeycombed.

cement *vb* attach, bind, join, combine, connect, solder, unite, weld; cohere, stick. • *n* glue, paste, mortar, solder.

cemetery *n* burial-ground, burying-ground, churchyard, god's acre, graveyard, necropolis.

censor *vb* blue-pencil, bowdlerize, cut, edit, expurgate; classify, kill, quash, squash, suppress. • *n* caviller, censurer, faultfinder.

censorious *adj* captious, carping, cavilling, condemnatory, faultfinding, hypercritical, severe.

censure *vb* abuse, blame, chide, condemn, rebuke, reprehend, reprimand, reproach, reprobate, reprove, scold, upbraid. • *n* animadversion, blame, condemnation, criticism, disapprobation, disapproval, rebuke, remonstrance, reprehension, reproach, reproof, stricture.

ceremonious *adj* civil, courtly, lofty, stately; formal, studied; exact, formal, punctilious, precise, starched, stiff.

ceremony *n* ceremonial, etiquette, form, formality, observance, solemnity, rite; parade, pomp, show, stateliness.

certain *adj* absolute, incontestable, incontrovertible, indisputable, indubitable, positive, undeniable, undisputed, unquestionable, unquestioned; assured, confident, sure, undoubting; infallible, never-failing, unfailing; actual, existing, real; constant, determinate, fixed, settled, stated.

certainty *n* indubitability, indubitableness, inevitableness, inevitability, surety, unquestionability, unquestionableness; assurance, assuredness, certitude, confidence, conviction, surety.

certify *vb* attest, notify, testify, vouch; ascertain, determine, verify, show.

cerulean *adj* azure, blue, sky-blue.

cessation *n* ceasing, discontinuance, intermission, pause, remission, respite, rest, stop, stoppage, suspension.

cession *n* abandonment, capitulation, ceding, concession, conveyance, grant, relinquishment, renunciation, surrender, yielding.

chafe *vb* rub; anger, annoy, chagrin, enrage, exasperate, fret, gall, incense, irritate, nettle, offend, provoke, ruffle, tease, vex; fret, fume, rage.

chaff *vb* banter, deride, jeer, mock, rally, ridicule. scoff. • *n* glumes, hulls, husks; refuse, rubbish, trash, waste.

chaffer *n* bargain, haggle, higgle, negotiate.

chagrin *vb* annoy, chafe, displease, irritate, mortify, provoke, vex. • *n* annoyance, displeasure, disquiet, dissatisfaction, fretfulness, humiliation, ill-humour, irritation, mortification, spleen, vexation.

chain *vb* bind, confine, fetter, manacle, restrain, shackle, trammel; enslave. • *n* bond, fetter, manacle, shackle, union.

chalice *n* bowl, cup, goblet.

challenge *vb* brave, call out, dare, defy, dispute; demand, require. • *n* defiance, interrogation, question; exception, objection.

chamber *n* apartment, hall, room; cavity, hollow.

champion *vb* advocate, defend, uphold. • *n* defender, promoter, protector, vindicator; belt-holder, hero, victor, warrior, winner.

chance *vb* befall, betide, happen, occur. • *adj* accidental, adventitious, casual, fortuitous, incidental, unexpected, unforeseen. • *n* accident, cast, fortuity, fortune, hap, luck; contingency, possibility; occasion, opening, opportunity; contingency, fortuity, gamble, peradventure, uncertainty; hazard, jeopardy, peril, risk.

change *vb* alter, fluctuate, modify, vary; displace, remove, replace, shift, substitute; barter, commute, exchange. • *n* alteration, mutation, revolution, transition, transmutation, turning, variance, variation; innovation, novelty, variety, vicissitude.

changeable *adj* alterable, inconstant, modifiable, mutable, uncertain, unsettled, unstable, unsteadfast, unsteady, variable,

variant; capricious, fickle, fitful, flighty, giddy, mercurial, vacillating, volatile, wavering.

changeless *adj* abiding, consistent, constant, fixed, immutable, permanent, regular, reliable, resolute, settled, stationary, unalterable, unchanging.

channel *vb* chamfer, cut, flute, groove. • *n* canal, conduit, duct, passage; aqueduct, canal, chute, drain, flume, furrow; chamfer, groove, fluting, furrow, gutter.

chant *vb* carol, sing, warble; intone, recite; canticle, song.

chaos *n* anarchy, confusion, disorder.

chapfallen *adj* blue, crest-fallen, dejected, depressed, despondent, discouraged, disheartened, dispirited, downcast, downhearted, low-spirited, melancholy, sad.

chaplet *n* coronal, garland, wreath.

char *vb* burn, scorch.

character *n* emblem, figure, hieroglyph, ideograph, letter, mark, sign, symbol; bent, constitution, cast, disposition, nature, quality; individual, original, person, personage; reputation, repute; nature, traits; eccentric, trait.

characteristic *adj* distinctive, peculiar, singular, special, specific, typical. • *n* attribute, feature, idiosyncrasy, lineament, mark, peculiarity, quality, trait.

charge *vb* burden, encumber, freight, lade, load; entrust; ascribe, impute, lay; accuse, arraign, blame, criminate, impeach, inculpate, indict, involve; bid, command, exhort, enjoin, order, require, tax; assault, attack bear down. • *n* burden, cargo, freight, lading, load; care, custody, keeping, management, ward; commission, duty, employment, office, trust; responsibility, trust; command, direction, injunction, mandate, order, precept; exhortation, instruction; cost, debit, expense, expenditure, outlay; price, sum; assault, attack, encounter, onset, onslaught.

charger *n* dish, platter; mount, steed, war-horse.

charily *adv* carefully, cautiously, distrustfully, prudently, sparingly, suspiciously, warily.

charitable *adj* beneficial, beneficent, benignant, bountiful, generous, kind, liberal, open-handed; candid, considerate, lenient, mild.

charity *n* benevolence, benignity, fellow-feeling, good-nature, goodwill, kind-heartedness, kindness, tenderheartedness; beneficence, bounty, generosity, humanity, philanthropy. liberality.

charlatan *n* cheat, empiric, impostor, mountebank, pretender, quack.

charm *vb* allure, attract, becharm, bewitch, captivate, catch, delight, enamour, enchain, enchant, enrapture, enravish, fascinate, transport, win. • *n* enchantment, incantation, magic, necromancy, sorcery, spell, witchery; amulet, talisman; allurement, attraction, attractiveness, fascination.

charming *adj* bewitching, captivating, delightful, enchanting, enrapturing, fascinating, lovely.

charter *vb* incorporate; hire, let. • *n* franchise, immunity, liberty, prerogation, privilege, right; bond, deed, indenture, instrument, prerogative.

chary *adj* careful, cautious, circumspect, shy, wary; abstemious, careful, choice, economical, frugal, provident, saving, sparing, temperate, thrifty, unwasteful.

chase *vb* follow, hunt, pursue, track; emboss. • *n* course, field-sport, hunt, hunting.

chasm *n* cavity, cleft, fissure, gap, hollow, hiatus, opening.

chaste *adj* clean, continent, innocent, modest, pure, pure-minded, undefiled, virtuous; chastened, pure, simple, unaffected, uncorrupt.

chasten *vb* correct, humble; purify, refine, render, subdue.

chastening *n* chastisement, correction, discipline, humbling.

chastise *vb* castigate, correct, flog, lash, punish, whip; chasten, correct, discipline, humble, punish, subdue.

chastity *n* abstinence, celibacy, continence, innocence, modesty, pure-mindedness, purity, virtue; cleanness, decency; chasteness, refinement, restrainedness, simplicity, sobriety, unaffectedness.

chat *vb* babble, chatter, confabulate, gossip, prate, prattle. • *n* chit-chat, confabulation, conversation, gossip, prattle.

chatter *vb* babble, chat, confabulate, gossip, prate, prattle. • *n* babble, chat, gabble, jabber, patter, prattle.

cheap *adj* inexpensive, low-priced; common, indifferent, inferior, mean, meretricious, paltry, poor.

cheapen *vb* belittle, depreciate.

cheat *vb* cozen, deceive, dissemble, juggle, shuffle; bamboozle, befool, beguile, cajole, circumvent, deceive, defraud, chouse, delude, dupe, ensnare, entrap, fool, gammon, gull, hoax, hoodwink, inveigle, jockey, mislead, outwit, overreach, trick. • *n* artifice, beguilement, blind, catch, chouse, deceit, deception, fraud, imposition, imposture, juggle, pitfall, snare, stratagem, swindle, trap, trick, wile; counterfeit, deception, delusion, illusion, mockery, paste, sham, tinsel; beguiler, charlatan, cheater, cozener, impostor, jockey, knave, mountebank, trickster, rogue, render, sharper, seizer, shuffler, swindler, taker, tearer.

check *vb* block, bridle, control, counteract, curb, hinder, obstruct, repress, restrain; chide, rebuke, reprimand, reprove. • *n* bar, barrier, block, brake, bridle, clog, control, curb, damper, hindrance, impediment, interference, obstacle, obstruction, rebuff, repression, restraint, stop, stopper.

cheep *vb* chirp, creak, peep, pipe, squeak.

cheer *vb* animate, encourage, enliven, exhilarate, gladden, incite, inspirit; comfort, console, solace; applaud, clap. • *n* cheerfulness, gaiety, gladness, glee, hilarity, jollity, joy, merriment, mirth; entertainment, food, provision, repast, viands, victuals; acclamation, hurrah, huzza.

cheerful *adj* animated, airy, blithe, buoyant, cheery, gay, glad, gleeful, happy, joyful, jocund, jolly, joyous, light-hearted, lightsome, lively, merry, mirthful, sprightly, sunny; animating, cheering, cheery, encouraging, enlivening, glad, gladdening, gladsome, grateful, inspiriting, jocund, pleasant.

cheerless *adj* dark, dejected, desolate, despondent, disconsolate, discouraged, dismal, doleful, dreary, forlorn, gloomy, joyless, low-spirited, lugubrious, melancholy, mournful, rueful, sad, sombre, spiritless, woe-begone.

cherish *vb* comfort, foster, nourish, nurse, nurture, support, sustain; treasure; encourage, entertain, indulge, harbour.

chest *n* box, case, coffer; breast, thorax, trunk.

chew *vb* crunch, manducate, masticate, munch; bite, champ, gnaw; meditate, ruminate.

chicanery *n* chicane, deception, duplicity, intrigue, intriguing, sophistication, sophistry, stratagems, tergiversation, trickery, wiles, wire-pulling.

chide *vb* admonish, blame, censure, rebuke, reprimand, reprove, scold, upbraid; chafe, clamour, fret, fume, scold.

chief *adj* first, foremost, headmost, leading, master, supereminent, supreme, top; capital, cardinal, especial, essential, grand, great, main, master, paramount, prime, principal, supreme, vital. • *n* chieftain, commander; head, leader.

chiffonier *n* cabinet, sideboard.

child *n* babe, baby, bairn, bantling, brat, chit, infant, nursling, suckling, wean; issue, offspring, progeny.

childbirth *n* child-bearing, delivery, labour, parturition, travail.

childish *adj* infantile, juvenile, puerile, tender, young; foolish, frivolous, silly, trifling, weak.

childlike *adj* docile, dutiful, gentle, meek, obedient, submissive; confiding, guileless, ingenuous, innocent, simple, trustful, uncrafty.

chill *vb* dampen, depress, deject, discourage, dishearten. • *adj* bleak, chilly, cold, frigid, gelid. • *n* chilliness, cold, coldness, frigidity; ague, rigour, shiver; damp, depression.

chime *vb* accord, harmonize. • *n* accord, consonance.

chimera *n* crochet, delusion, dream, fantasy, hallucination, illusion, phantom.

chimerical *adj* delusive, fanciful, fantastic, illusory, imaginary, quixotic, shadowy, unfounded, visionary, wild.

chink[1] *vb* cleave, crack, fissure, crevasse, incise, split, slit. • *n* aperture, cleft, crack, cranny, crevice, fissure, gap, opening, slit.

chink[2] *vb, n* jingle, clink, ring, ting, tink, tinkle.

chip *vb* flake, fragment, hew, pare, scrape. • *n* flake, fragment, paring, scrap.

chirp *vb* cheep, chirrup, peep, twitter.

chirrup *vb* animate, cheer, encourage, inspirit.

chisel *vb* carve, cut, gouge, sculpt, sculpture.

chivalrous *adj* adventurous, bold, brave, chivalric, gallant, knightly, valiant, warlike; gallant, generous, high-minded, magnanimous.

chivalry *n* knighthood, knight-errantry; courtesy, gallantry, politeness; courage, valour.

choice *adj* excellent, exquisite, precious, rare, select, superior, uncommon, unusual, valuable; careful, chary, frugal, sparing. • *n* alternative, election, option, selection; favourite, pick, preference.

choke *vb* gag, smother, stifle, strangle, suffocate, throttle; overcome, overpower, smother, suppress; bar, block, close, obstruct, stop.

choleric *adj* angry, fiery, hasty, hot, fiery, irascible, irritable, passionate, petulant, testy, touchy, waspish.

choose *vb* adopt, co-opt, cull, designate, elect, pick, predestine, prefer, select.

chop *vb* cut, hack, hew; mince; shift, veer. • *n* slice; brand, quality; chap, jaw.

chouse *vb* bamboozle, beguile, cheat, circumvent, cozen, deceive, defraud, delude, dupe, gull, hoodwink, overreach, swindle, trick, victimize. • *n* cully, dupe, gull, simpleton, tool; artifice, cheat, circumvention, deceit, deception, delusion, double-dealing, fraud, imposition, imposture, ruse, stratagem, trick, wile.

christen *vb* baptize; call, dub, denominate, designate, entitle, name, style, term, title.

chronic *adj* confirmed, continuing, deep-seated, inveterate, rooted.

chronicle *vb* narrate, record, register. • *n* diary, journal, register; account, annals, history, narration, recital, record.

chuckle *vb* crow, exult, giggle, laugh, snigger, titter. • *n* giggle, laughter, snigger, titter.

chum *n* buddy, companion, comrade, crony, friend, mate, pal.

churl *n* boor, bumpkin, clodhopper, clown, countryman, lout, peasant, ploughman, rustic; curmudgeon, hunks, miser, niggard, scrimp, skinflint.

churlish *adj* brusque, brutish, cynical, harsh, impolite, rough, rude, snappish, snarling, surly, uncivil, waspish; crabbed, ill-tempered, morose, sullen; close, close-fisted, illiberal, mean, miserly, niggardly, penurious, stingy.

churn *vb* agitate, jostle.

cicatrice *n* cicatrix, mark, scar, seam.

cicesbeo *n* beau, escort, gallant, gigolo.

cincture *n* band, belt, cestos, cestus, girdle.

cipher *n* naught, nothing, zero; character, device, monogram, symbol; nobody, nonentity.

circle *vb* compass, encircle, encompass, gird, girdle, ring; gyrate, revolve, rotate, round, turn. • *n* circlet, corona, gyre, hoop, ring, rondure; circumference, cordon, periphery; ball, globe, orb, sphere; compass, enclosure; class, clique, company, coterie, fraternity, set, society; bounds, circuit, compass, field, province, range, region, sphere.

circuit *n* ambit, circumambience, circumambiency, cycle, revolution, turn; bounds, district, field, province, range, region, space, sphere, tract; boundary, compass; course, detour, perambulation, round, tour.

circuitous *adj* ambiguous, devious, indirect, roundabout, tortuous, turning, winding.

circulate *vb* diffuse, disseminate, promulgate, propagate, publish, spread.

circumference *n* bound, boundary, circuit, girth, outline, perimeter, periphery.

circumlocution *n* circuitousness, obliqueness, periphrase, periphrasis, verbosity, wordiness.

circumscribe *vb* bound, define, encircle, enclose, encompass, limit, surround; confine, restrict.

circumspect *adj* attentive, careful, cautious, considerate, discreet, heedful, judicious, observant, prudent, vigilant, wary, watchful.

circumstance *n* accident, incident; condition, detail, event, fact, happening, occurrence, position, situation.

circumstantial *adj* detailed, particular; indirect, inferential, presumptive.

circumvent *vb* check, checkmate, outgeneral, thwart; bamboozle, beguile, cheat, chouse, cozen, deceive, defraud, delude, dupe, gull, hoodwink, inveigle, mislead, outwit, overreach, trick.

circumvention *n* cheat, cheating, chicanery, deceit, deception, duplicity, fraud, guile, imposition, imposture, indirection, trickery, wiles.

cistern *n* basin, pond, reservoir, tank.

citation *n* excerpt, extract, quotation; enumeration, mention, quotation, quoting.

cite *vb* adduce, enumerate, extract, mention, name, quote; call, summon.

citizen *n* burgess, burgher, denizen, dweller, freeman, inhabitant, resident, subject, townsman.

civil *adj* civic, municipal, political; domestic; accommodating, affable, civilized, complaisant, courteous, courtly, debonair, easy, gracious, obliging, polished, polite, refined, suave, urbane, well-bred, well-mannered.

civility *n* affability, amiability, complaisance, courteousness, courtesy, good-breeding, politeness, suavity, urbanity.

civilize *vb* cultivate, educate, enlighten, humanize, improve, polish, refine.

claim *vb* ask, assert, challenge, demand, exact, require. • *n* call, demand, lien, requisition; pretension, privilege, right, title.

clammy *adj* adhesive, dauby, glutinous, gummy, ropy, smeary, sticky, viscid, viscous; close, damp, dank, moist, sticky, sweaty.

clamour *vb* shout, vociferate. • *n* blare, din, exclamation, hullabaloo, noise, outcry, uproar, vociferation.

clan *n* family, phratry, race, sect, tribe; band, brotherhood, clique, coterie, fraternity, gang, set, society, sodality.

clandestine *adj* concealed, covert, fraudulent, furtive, hidden, private, secret, sly, stealthy, surreptitious, underhand.

clap *vb* pat, slap, strike; force, slam; applaud, cheer. • *n* blow, knock, slap; bang, burst, explosion, peal, slam.

clarify *vb* cleanse, clear, depurate, purify, strain.

clash *vb* collide, crash, strike; clang, clank, clatter, crash, rattle; contend, disagree, interfere. • *n* collision; clang, clangour, clank, clashing, clatter, crash, rattle; contradiction, disagreement, interference, jar, jarring, opposition.

clasp *vb* clutch, entwine, grasp, grapple, grip, seize; embrace, enfold, fold, hug. • *n* buckle, catch, hasp, hook; embrace, hug.

class *vb* arrange, classify, dispose, distribute, range, rank. • *n* form, grade, order, rank, status; group, seminar; breed, kind, sort; category, collection, denomination, division, group, head.

classical *adj* first-rate, master, masterly, model, standard; Greek, Latin, Roman; Attic, chaste, elegant, polished, pure, refined.

classify *vb* arrange, assort, categorize, class, dispose, distribute, group, pigeonhole, rank, systematize, tabulate.

clatter *vb* clash, rattle; babble, clack, gabble, jabber, prate, prattle. • *n* clattering, clutter, rattling.

clause *n* article, condition, provision, stipulation.

claw *vb* lacerate, scratch, tear. • *n* talon, ungula.

clean *vb* cleanse, clear, purge, purify, rinse, scour, scrub, wash, wipe. • *adj* immaculate, spotless, unsmirched, unsoiled, unspotted, unstained, unsullied, white; clarified, pure, purified, unadulterated, unmixed; adroit, delicate, dextrous, graceful, light, neat, shapely; complete, entire, flawless, faultless, perfect, unabated, unblemished, unimpaired, whole; chaste, innocent, moral, pure, undefiled. • *adv* altogether, completely, entirely, perfectly, quite, thoroughly, wholly.

cleanse *vb* clean, clear, elutriate, purge, purify, rinse, scour, scrub, wash, wipe.

clear *vb* clarify, cleanse, purify, refine; emancipate, disenthral, free, liberate, loose; absolve, acquit, discharge, exonerate, justify, vindicate; disembarrass, disengage, disentangle, extricate, loosen, rid; clean up, scour, sweep; balance; emancipate, free, liberate. • *adj* bright, crystalline, light, limpid, luminous, pellucid, transparent; pure, unadulterated, unmixed; free, open, unencumbered, unobstructed; cloudless, fair, serene, sunny, unclouded, undimmed, unobscured; net; distinct, intelligible, lucid, luminous, perspicuous; apparent, conspicuous, distinct, evident, indisputable, manifest, obvious, palpable, unambiguous, undeniable, unequivocal, unmistakable, unquestionable, visible; clean, guiltless, immaculate, innocent, irreproachable, sinless, spotless, unblemished, undefiled, unspotted, unsullied; unhampered, unimpeded, unobstructed; euphonious, fluty, liquid, mellifluous, musical, silvery, sonorous.

cleave¹ *vb* crack, divide, open, part, rend, rive, sever, split, sunder.

cleave² *vb* adhere, cling, cohere, hold, stick.

cleft *adj* bifurcated, cloven, forked. • *n* breach, break, chasm, chink, cranny, crevice, fissure, fracture, gap, interstice, opening, rent, rift.

clemency *n* mildness, softness; compassion, fellow-feeling, forgivingness, gentleness, kindness, lenience, leniency, lenity, mercifulness, mercy, mildness, tenderness.

clement *adj* compassionate, forgiving, gentle, humane, indulgent, kind, kind-hearted, lenient, merciful, mild, tender, tender-hearted.

clench *vb* close tightly, grip; fasten, fix, rivet, secure.

clergy *n* clergymen, the cloth, ministers.

clever *adj* able, apt, gifted, talented; adroit, capable, dextrous, discerning, expert, handy, ingenious, knowing, quick, ready, skilful, smart, talented.

click *vb* beat, clack, clink, tick. • *n* beat, clack, clink, tick; catch, detent, pawl, ratchet.

cliff *n* crag, palisade, precipice, scar, steep.

climate *n* clime, temperature, weather; country, region.

climax *vb* consummate, crown, culminate, peak. • *n* acme, consummation, crown, culmination, head, peak, summit, top, zenith.

clinch *vb* clasp, clench, clutch, grapple, grasp, grip; fasten, secure; confirm, establish, fix. • *n* catch, clutch, grasp, grip; clincher, clamp, cramp, holdfast.

cling *vb* adhere, clear, stick; clasp, embrace, entwine.

clink *vb, n* chink, jingle, ring, tinkle; chime, rhyme.

clip *vb* cut, shear, snip; curtail, cut, dock, pare, prune, trim. • *n* cutting, shearing; blow, knock, lick, rap, thump, thwack, thump.

clique *n* association, brotherhood, cabal, camarilla, clan, club, coterie, gang, junta, party, ring, set, sodality.

cloak *vb* conceal, cover, dissemble, hide, mask, veil. • *n* mantle, surcoat; blind, cover, mask, pretext, veil.

clock *vb* mark time, measure, stopwatch; clock up, record, register. • *n* chronometer, horologue, timekeeper, timepiece, timer, watch.

clog *vb* fetter, hamper, shackle, trammel; choke, obstruct; burden, cumber, embarrass, encumber, hamper, hinder, impede, load, restrain, trammel. • *n* dead-weight, drag-weight, fetter, shackle, trammel; check, drawback, encumbrance, hindrance, impediment, obstacle, obstruction.

cloister *n* abbey, convent, monastery, nunnery, priory; arcade, colonnade, piazza.

close¹ *adj* closed, confined, snug, tight; hidden, private, secret; incommunicative, reserved, reticent, secretive, taciturn; concealed, retired, secluded, withdrawn; confined, motionless, stagnant; airless, oppressive, stale, stifling, stuffy, sultry; compact, compressed, dense, form, solid, thick; adjacent, adjoining, approaching, immediately, near, nearly, neighbouring; attached, dear, confidential, devoted, intimate; assiduous, earnest, fixed, intense, intent, unremitting; accurate, exact, faithful, nice, precise, strict; churlish, close-fisted, curmudgeonly, mean, illiberal, miserly, niggardly, parsimonious, penurious, stingy, ungenerous. • *n* courtyard, enclosure, grounds, precinct, yard.

close² *vb* occlude, seal, shut; choke, clog, estop, obstruct, stop; cease, complete, concede, end, finish, terminate; coalesce, unite; cease, conclude, finish, terminate; clinch, grapple; agree. • *n* cessation, conclusion, end, finish, termination.

closet *n* cabinet, retiring-room; press, store-room.

clot *vb* coagulate, concrete. • *n* coagulation, concretion, lump.

clothe *vb* array, attire, deck, dress, rig; cover,endow, envelop, enwrap, invest with, swathe.

clothes *n* apparel, array, attire, clothing, costume, dress, garb, garments, gear, habiliments, habits, raiment, rig, vestments, vesture.

cloud *vb* becloud, obnubilate, overcast, overspread; befog, darken, dim, obscure, shade, shadow. • *n* cirrus, cumulus, fog, haze, mist, nebulosity, scud, stratus, vapour; army, crowd, horde, host, multitude, swarm, throng; darkness, eclipse, gloom, obscuration, obscurity.

cloudy *adj* clouded, filmy, foggy, hazy, lowering, lurid, murky, overcast; confused, dark, dim, obscure; depressing, dismal, gloomy, sullen; clouded, mottled; blurred, dimmed, lustreless, muddy.

clown *n* churl, clod-breaker, clodhopper, hind, husbandman, lubber; boor, bumpkin, churl, fellow, lout; blockhead, dolt, clodpoll, dunce, dunderhead, numbskull, simpleton, thickhead; buffoon, droll, farceur, fool, harlequin, jack-a-dandy, jack-pudding, jester, merry-andrew, mime, pantaloon, pickle-herring, punch, scaramouch, zany.

clownish *adj* awkward, boorish, clumsy, coarse, loutish, ungainly, rough, rustic; churlish, ill-bred, ill-mannered, impolite, rude, uncivil.

cloy *vb* glut, pall, sate, satiate, surfeit.

club *vb* combine, unite; beat, bludgeon, cudgel. • *n* bat, bludgeon, cosh, cudgel, hickory, shillelagh, stick, truncheon; association, company, coterie, fraternity, set, society, sodality.

clump *vb* assemble, batch, bunch, cluster, group, lump; lumber, stamp, stomp, stump, trudge. • *n* assemblage, bunch, cluster, collection, group, patch, tuft.

clumsy *adj* botched, cumbrous, heavy, ill-made, ill-shaped, lumbering, ponderous, unwieldy; awkward, blundering, bungling, elephantine, heavy-handed, inapt, mal adroit, unhandy, unskilled.

cluster *vb* assemble, batch, bunch, clump, collect, gather, group, lump, throng. • *n* agglomeration, assemblage, batch, bunch, clump, collection, gathering, group, throng.

clutch[1] *vb* catch, clasp, clench, clinch, grab, grapple, grasp, grip, hold, seize, snatch, squeeze. • *n* clasp, clench, clinch, grasp, grip, hold, seizure, squeeze.

clutch[2] *n* aerie, brood, hatching, nest.

clutches *npl* claws, paws, talons; hands, power.

clutter *vb* confuse, disarrange, disarray, disorder, jumble, litter, mess, muss; clatter. • *n* bustle, clatter, clattering, racket; confusion, disarray, disorder, jumble, litter, mess, muss.

coadjutor *n* abettor, accomplice, aider, ally, assistant, associate, auxiliary, collaborator, colleague, cooperator, fellow-helper, helper, helpmate, partner.

coagulate *vb* clot, congeal, concrete, curdle, thicken.

coalesce *vb* amalgamate, blend, cohere, combine, commix, incorporate, mix, unite; concur, fraternize.

coalition *n* alliance, association, combination, compact, confederacy, confederation, conjunction, conspiracy, co-partnership, federation, league, union.

coarse *adj* crude, impure, rough, unpurified; broad, gross, indecent, indelicate, ribald, vulgar; bearish, bluff, boorish, brutish, churlish, clownish, gruff, impolite, loutish, rude, unpolished; crass, inelegant.

coast *vb* flow, glide, roll, skim, sail, slide, sweep. • *n* littoral, seaboard, sea-coast, seaside, shore, strand; border.

coat *vb* cover, spread. • *n* cut-away, frock, jacket; coating, cover, covering; layer.

coax *vb* allure, beguile, cajole, cog, entice, flatter, persuade, soothe, wheedle.

cobble *vb* botch, bungle; mend, patch, repair, tinker.

cobweb *adj* flimsy, gauzy, slight, thin, worthless. • *n* entanglement, meshes, snare, toils.

cochleate *adj* cochlear, cochleary, cochleous, cochleated, spiral, spiry.

cockle *vb* corrugate, pucker, wrinkle.

coddle *vb* caress, cocker, fondle, humour, indulge, nurse, pamper, pet.

codger *n* churl, curmudgeon, hunks, lick-penny, miser, niggard, screw, scrimp, skinflint.

codify *vb* condense, digest, summarize, systematize, tabulate.

coerce *vb* check, curb, repress, restrain, subdue; compel, constrain, drive, force, urge.

coercion *n* check, curb, repression, restraint; compulsion, constraint, force.

coeval *adj* coetaneous, coexistent, contemporaneous, contemporary, synchronous.

coexistent *adj* coetaneous, coeval, simultaneous, synchronous.

coffer *n* box, casket, chest, trunk; money-chest, safe, strongbox; caisson.

cogent *adj* compelling, conclusive, convincing, effective, forcible, influential, irresistible, persuasive, potent, powerful, resistless, strong, trenchant, urgent.

cogitate *vb* consider, deliberate, meditate, ponder, reflect, ruminate, muse, think, weigh.

cognate *adj* affiliated, affined, akin, allied, alike, analogous, connected, kindred, related, similar.

cognizance *n* cognition, knowing, knowledge, notice, observation.

cohere *vb* agree, coincide, conform, fit, square, suit.

coherence *n* coalition, cohesion, connection, dependence, union; agreement, congruity, consistency, correspondence, harmony, intelligibility, intelligible, meaning, rationality, unity.

coherent *adj* adherent, connected, united; congruous, consistent, intelligible, logical.

cohort *n* band, battalion, line, squadron.

coil *vb* curl, twine, twirl, twist, wind. • *n* convolution, curlicue, helix, knot, roll, spiral, tendril, twirl, volute, whorl; bustle, care, clamour, confusion, entanglements, perplexities, tumult, turmoil, uproar.

coin *vb* counterfeit, create, devise, fabricate, forge, form, invent, mint, originate, mould, stamp. • *n* coign, corner, quoin; key, plug, prop, wedge; cash, money, specie.

coincide *vb* cohere, correspond, square, tally; acquiesce, agree, harmonize, concur.

coincidence *n* corresponding, squaring, tallying; agreeing, concurrent, concurring.

cold *adj* arctic, biting, bleak, boreal, chill, chilly, cutting, frosty, gelid, glacial, icy, nipping, polar, raw, wintry; frost-bitten, shivering; apathetic, cold-blooded, dead, freezing, frigid, indifferent, lukewarm, passionless, phlegmatic, sluggish, stoical, stony, torpid, unconcerned, unfeeling, unimpressible, unresponsive, unsusceptible, unsympathetic; dead, dull, spiritless, unaffecting, uninspiring, uninteresting. • *n* chill, chilliness, coldness.

collapse *vb* break down, fail, fall. • *n* depression, exhaustion, failure, faint, prostration, sinking, subsidence.

collar *vb* apprehend, arrest, capture, grab, nab, seize. • *n* collarette, gorget, neckband, ruff, torque; band, belt, fillet, guard, ring, yoke.

collate *vb* adduce, collect, compare, compose.

collateral *adj* contingent, indirect, secondary, subordinate; concurrent, parallel; confirmatory, corroborative; accessory, accompanying, additional, ancillary, auxiliary, concomitant, contributory, simultaneous, supernumerary; consanguineous, related. • *n* guarantee, guaranty, security, surety, warranty; accessory, extra, nonessential, unessential; consanguinean, relative.

collation *n* luncheon, repast, meal.

colleague *n* aider, ally, assistant, associate, auxiliary, coadjutor, collaborator, companion, confederate, confrere, cooperator, helper, partner.

collect *vb* assemble, compile, gather, muster; accumulate, aggregate, amass, garner.

collected *adj* calm, composed, cool, placid, self-possessed, serene, unperturbed.

collection *n* aggregation, assemblage, cluster, crowd, drove, gathering, group, pack; accumulation, congeries, conglomeration, heap, hoard, lot, mass, pile, store; alms, contribution, offering, offertory.

colligate *vb* bind, combine, fasten, unite.

collision *n* clash, concussion, crash, encounter, impact, impingement, shock; conflict, crashing, interference, opposition.

collocate *vb* arrange, dispose, place, set.

colloquy *n* conference, conversation, dialogue, discourse, talk.

collude *vb* concert, connive, conspire.

collusion *n* connivance, conspiracy, coven, craft, deceit.

collusive *adj* conniving, conspiratorial, , dishonest, deceitful, deceptive, fraudulent.

colossal *adj* Cyclopean, enormous, gigantic, Herculean, huge, immense, monstrous, prodigious, vast.

colour *vb* discolour, dye, paint, stain, tinge, tint; disguise, varnish; disguise, distort, garble, misrepresent, pervert; blush, flush, redden, show. • *n* hue, shade, tinge, tint, tone; paint, pigment, stain; redness, rosiness, ruddiness; complexion; appearance, disguise, excuse, guise, plea, pretence, pretext, semblance.

colourless *adj* achromatic, uncoloured, untinged; blanched, hueless, livid, pale, pallid; blank, characterless, dull, expressionless, inexpressive, monotonous.

colours *n* banner, ensign, flag, standard.

column *n* pillar, pilaster; file, line, row.

coma *n* drowsiness, lethargy, somnolence, stupor, torpor; bunch, clump, cluster, tuft.

comatose *adj* drowsy, lethargic, sleepy, somnolent, stupefied.

comb *vb* card, curry, dress, groom, rake, unknot, untangle; rake, ransack, rummage, scour, search. • *n* card, hatchel, ripple; harrow, rake.

combat *vb* contend, contest, fight, struggle, war; battle, oppose, resist, struggle, withstand. • *n* action, affair, battle, brush, conflict, contest, encounter, fight, skirmish.

combative *adj* belligerent, contentious, militant, pugnacious, quarrelsome.

combination *n* association, conjunction, connection, union; alliance, cartel, coalition, confederacy, consolidation, league, merger, syndicate; cabal, clique, conspiracy, faction, junta, ring; amalgamation, compound, mixture.

combine *vb* cooperate, merge, pool, unite; amalgamate, blend, incorporate, mix.

combustible *adj* consumable, inflammable.

come *vb* advance, approach; arise, ensue, flow, follow, issue, originate, proceed, result; befall, betide, happen, occur.

comely *adj* becoming, decent, decorous, fitting, seemly, suitable; beautiful, fair, graceful, handsome, personable, pretty, symmetrical.

comfort *vb* alleviate, animate, cheer, console, encourage, enliven, gladden, inspirit, invigorate, refresh, revive, solace, soothe, strengthen. • *n* aid, assistance, countenance, help, support, succour; consolation, solace, encouragement, relief; ease, enjoyment, peace, satisfaction.

comfortable *adj* acceptable, agreeable, delightful, enjoyable, grateful, gratifying, happy, pleasant, pleasurable, welcome; commodious, convenient, easeful, snug; painless.

comfortless *adj* bleak, cheerless, desolate, drear, dreary, forlorn, miserable, wretched; broken-hearted, desolate, disconsolate, forlorn, heart-broken, inconsolable, miserable, woe-begone, wretched.

comical *adj* amusing, burlesque, comic, diverting, droll, farcical, funny, humorous, laughable, ludicrous, sportive, whimsical.

coming *adj* approaching, arising, arriving, ensuing, eventual, expected, forthcoming, future, imminent, issuing, looming, nearing, prospective, ultimate; emergent, emerging, successful; due, owed, owing. • *n* advent, approach, arrival; imminence, imminency, nearness; apparition, appearance, disclosure, emergence, manifestation, materialization, occurrence, presentation, revelation, rising.

comity *n* affability, amenity, civility, courtesy, politeness, suavity, urbanity.

command *vb* bid, charge, direct, enjoin, order, require; control, dominate, govern, lead, rule, sway; claim, challenge, compel, demand, exact. • *n* behest, bidding, charge, commandment, direction, hest, injunction, mandate, order, requirement, requisition; ascendency, authority, dominion, control, government, power, rule, sway, supremacy.

commander *n* captain, chief, chieftain, commandment, head, leader.

commemorate *vb* celebrate, keep, observe, solemnize.

commence *vb* begin, inaugurate, initiate, institute, open, originate, start.

commend *vb* assign, bespeak, confide, recommend, remit; commit, entrust, yield; applaud, approve, eulogize, extol, laud, praise.

commendation *n* approbation, approval, good opinion, recommendation; praise, encomium, eulogy, panegyric.

commensurate *adj* commeasurable, commensurable; coextensive, conterminous, equal; adequate, appropriate, corresponding, due, proportionate, proportioned, sufficient.

comment *vb* animadvert, annotate, criticize, explain, interpret, note, remark. • *n* annotation, elucidation, explanation, exposition, illustration, commentary, note, gloss; animadversion, observation, remark.

commentator *n* annotator, commentator, critic, expositor, expounder, interpreter.

commerce *n* business, exchange, dealing, trade, traffic; communication, communion, intercourse.

commercial *adj* mercantile, trading.

commination *n* denunciation, menace, threat, threatening.

commingle *vb* amalgamate, blend, combine, commix, intermingle, intermix, join, mingle, mix, unite.

comminute *vb* bray, bruise, grind, levigate, powder, pulverize, triturate.

commiserate *vb* compassionate, condole, pity, sympathize.

commiseration *n* compassion, pitying; condolence, pity, sympathy.

commission *vb* authorize, empower; delegate, depute. • *n* doing, perpetration; care, charge, duty, employment, errand, office, task, trust; allowance, compensation, fee, rake-off.

commissioner *n* agent, delegate, deputy.

commit *vb* confide, consign, delegate, entrust, remand; consign, deposit, lay, place, put, relegate, resign; do, enact, perform, perpetrate; imprison; engage, implicate, pledge.

commix *vb* amalgamate, blend, combine, commingle, compound, intermingle, mingle, mix, unite.

commodious *adj* advantageous, ample, comfortable, convenient, fit, proper, roomy, spacious, suitable, useful.

commodity *n* goods, merchandise, produce, wares.

common *adj* collective, public; general, useful; common-place, customary, everyday, familiar, frequent, habitual, usual; banal, hackneyed, stale, threadbare, trite; indifferent, inferior, low, ordinary, plebeian, popular, undistinguished, vulgar.

commonplace *adj* common, hackneyed, ordinary, stale, threadbare, trite. • *n* banality, cliché, platitude; jotting, memoir, memorandum, note, reminder.

common-sense, common-sensical *adj* practical, sagacious, sensible, sober.

commotion *n* agitation, disturbance, ferment, perturbation, welter; ado, bustle, disorder, disturbance, hurly-burly, pother, tumult, turbulence, turmoil.

communicate *vb* bestow, confer, convey, give, impart, transmit; acquaint, announce, declare, disclose, divulge, publish, reveal, unfold; commune, converse, correspond.

communication *n* conveyance, disclosure, giving, imparting, transmittal; commence, conference, conversation, converse, correspondence, intercourse; announcement, dispatch, information, message, news.

communicative *adj* affable, chatty, conversable, free, open, sociable, unreserved.

communion *n* converse, fellowship, intercourse, participation; Eucharist, holy communion, Lord's Supper, sacrament.

community *n* commonwealth, people, public, society; association, brotherhood, college, society; likeness, participancy, sameness, similarity.

compact[1] *n* agreement, arrangement, bargain, concordant, contract, covenant, convention, pact, stipulation, treaty.

compact[2] *vb* compress, condense, pack, press; bind, consolidate, unite. • *adj* close, compressed, condensed, dense, firm, solid; brief, compendious, concise, laconic, pithy, pointed, sententious, short, succinct, terse.

companion *n* accomplice, ally, associate, comrade, compeer, confederate, consort, crony, friend, fellow, mate; partaker, participant, participator, partner, sharer.

companionable *adj* affable, conversable, familiar, friendly, genial, neighbourly, sociable.

companionship *n* association, fellowship, friendship, intercourse, society.

company *n* assemblage, assembly, band, bevy, body, circle, collection, communication, concourse, congregation, coterie, crew, crowd, flock, gang, gathering, group, herd, rout, set, syndicate, troop; party; companionship, fellowship, guests, society, visitor, visitors; association, copartnership, corporation, firm, house, partnership.

compare *vb* assimilate, balance, collate, parallel; liken, resemble.

comparison *n* collation, compare, estimate; simile, similitude.

compartment *n* bay, cell, division, pigeonhole, section.

compass *vb* embrace, encompass, enclose, encircle, environ, surround; beleaguer, beset, besiege, block, blockade, invest; accomplish, achieve, attain, carry, consummate, effect, obtain, perform, procure, realize; contrive, devise, intend, meditate, plot, purpose. • *n* bound, boundary, extent, gamut, limit, range, reach, register, scope, stretch; circuit, round.

compassion *n* clemency, commiseration, condolence, fellow-feeling, heart, humanity, kind-heartedness, kindness, kindliness, mercy, pity, rue, ruth, sorrow, sympathy, tenderheartedness, tenderness.

compassionate *adj* benignant, clement, commiserative, gracious, kind, merciful, pitying, ruthful, sympathetic, tender.

compatible *adj* accordant, agreeable to, congruous, consistent, consonant, reconcilable, suitable.

compeer *n* associate, comrade, companion, equal, fellow, mate, peer.

compel *vb* constrain, force, coerce, drive, necessitate, oblige; bend, bow, subdue, subject.

compend *n* abbreviation, abridgement, abstract, breviary, brief, compendium, conspectus, digest, epitome, précis, summary, syllabus, synopsis.

compendious *adj* abbreviated, abridged, brief, comprehensive, concise, short, succinct, summary.

compensate *vb* counterbalance, counterpoise, countervail; guerdon, recompense, reimburse, remunerate, reward; indemnify, reimburse, repay, requite; atone.

compensation *n* pay, payment, recompense, remuneration, reward, salary; amends, atonement, indemnification, indemnity, reparation, requital, satisfaction; balance, counterpoise, equalization, offset.

compete *vb* contend, contest, cope, emulate, rival, strive, struggle, vie.

competence *n* ability, capability, capacity, fitness, qualification, suitableness; adequacy, adequateness, enough, sufficiency.

competent *adj* able, capable, clever, equal, endowed, qualified; adapted, adequate, convenient, fit, sufficient, suitable.

competition *n* contest, emulation, rivalry, rivals.

competitor *n* adversary, antagonist, contestant, emulator, opponent.

compile *vb* compose, prepare, write; arrange, collect, select.

complacency *n* content, contentment, gratification, pleasure, satisfaction; affability, civility, complaisance, courtesy, politeness.

complacent *adj* contented, gratified, pleased, satisfied; affable, civil, complaisant, courteous, easy, gracious, grateful, obliging, polite, urbane.

complain *vb* bemoan, bewail, deplore, grieve, groan, grouch, grumble, lament, moan, murmur, repine, whine.

complainant *n* accuser, plaintiff.

complaining *adj* fault-finding, murmuring, querulous.

complaint *n* grievance, gripe, grumble, lament, lamentation, plaint, murmur, wail; ail, ailment, annoyance, disease, disorder, illness, indisposition, malady, sickness; accusation, charge, information.

complete *vb* accomplish, achieve, conclude, consummate, do, effect, effectuate, end, execute, finish, fulfil, perfect, perform, realize, terminate. • *adj* clean, consummate, faultless, full, perfect, perform, thorough; all, entire, integral, total, unbroken, undiminished, undivided, unimpaired, whole; accomplished, achieved, completed, concluded, consummated, ended, finished.

completion *n* accomplishing, accomplishment, achieving, conclusion, consummation, effecting, effectuation, ending, execution, finishing, perfecting, performance, termination.

complex *adj* composite, compound, compounded, manifold, mingled, mixed; complicate, complicated, entangled, intricate, involved, knotty, mazy, tangled. • *n* complexus, complication, involute, skein, tangle; entirety, integration, network, totality, whole; compulsion, fixation, obsession, preoccupation, prepossession; prejudice.

complexion *n* colour, hue, tint.

complexity *n* complication, entanglement, intricacy, involution.

compliance *n* concession, obedience, submission; acquiescence, agreement, assent, concurrence, consent; compliancy, yieldingness.

complicate *vb* confuse, entangle, interweave, involve.

complication *n* complexity, confusion, entanglement, intricacy; combination, complexus, mixture.

compliment *vb* commend, congratulate, eulogize, extol, flatter, laud, praise. • *n* admiration, commendation, courtesy, encomium, eulogy, favour, flattery, honour, laudation, praise, tribute.

complimentary *adj* commendatory, congratulatory, encomiastic, eulogistic, flattering, laudatory, panegyrical.

comply *vb* adhere to, complete, discharge, fulfil, meet, observe, perform, satisfy; accede, accord, acquiesce, agree to, assent, consent to, yield.

component *adj* composing, constituent, constituting. • *n* constituent, element, ingredient, part.

comport *vb* accord, agree, coincide, correspond, fit, harmonize, square, suit, tally.

compose *vb* build, compact, compound, constitute, form, make, synthesize; contrive, create, frame, imagine, indite, invent, write; adjust, arrange, regulate, settle; appease, assuage, calm, pacify, quell, quiet, soothe, still, tranquillize.

composed *adj* calm, collected, cool, imperturbable, placid, quiet, sedate, self-possessed, tranquil, undisturbed, unmoved, unruffled.

composite *adj* amalgamated, combined, complex, compounded, mixed; integrated, unitary. • *n* admixture, amalgam, blend, combination, composition, compound, mixture, unification.

composition *n* constitution, construction, formation, framing, making; compound, mixture; arrangement, combination, conjunction, make-up, synthesize, union; invention, opus, piece, production, writing; agreement, arrangement, compromise.

compost *n* fertilizer, fertilizing, manure, mixture.

composure *n* calmness, coolness, equanimity, placidity, sedateness, quiet, self-possession, serenity, tranquillity.

compotation *n* conviviality, frolicking, jollification, revelling, revelry, rousing, wassailling; bacchanal, carousal, carouse, debauch, orgy, revel, saturnalia, wassail.

compound[1] *vb* amalgamate, blend, combine, intermingle, intermix, mingle, mix, unite; adjust, arrange, compose, compromise, settle. • *adj* complex, composite. • *n* combination, composition, mixture; farrago, hodgepodge, jumble, medley, mess, olio.

compound[2] *n* enclosure, garden, yard.

comprehend *vb* comprise, contain, embrace, embody, enclose, include, involve; apprehend, conceive, discern, grasp, know, imagine, master, perceive, see, understand.

comprehension *n* comprising, embracing, inclusion; compass, domain, embrace, field, limits, province, range, reach, scope, sphere, sweep; connotation, depth, force, intention; conception, grasp, intelligence, understanding; intellect, intelligence, mind, reason, understanding.

comprehensive *adj* all-embracing, ample, broad, capacious, compendious, extensive, full, inclusive, large, sweeping, wide.

compress *vb* abbreviate, condense, constrict, contract, crowd, press, shorten, squeeze, summarize.

compression *n* condensation, confining, pinching, pressing, squeezing; brevity, pithiness, succinctness, terseness.

comprise *vb* comprehend, contain, embody, embrace, enclose, include, involve.

compromise *vb* adjust, arbitrate, arrange, compose, compound, settle; imperil, jeopardize, prejudice; commit, engage, implicate, pledge; agree, compound. • *n* adjustment, agreement, composition, settlement.

compulsion *n* coercion, constraint, force, forcing, pressure, urgency.

compulsory *adj* coercive, compelling, constraining; binding, enforced, imperative, necessary, obligatory, unavoidable.

compunction *n* contrition, misgiving, penitence, qualm, regret, reluctance, remorse, repentance, sorrow.

computable *adj* calculable, numerable, reckonable.

computation *n* account, calculation, estimate, reckoning, score, tally.

compute *vb* calculate, count, enumerate, estimate, figure, measure, number, rate, reckon, sum.

comrade *n* accomplice, ally, associate, chum, companion, compatriot, compeer, crony, fellow, mate, pal.

concatenate *vb* connect, join, link, unite.

concatenation *n* connection; chain, congeries, linking, series, sequence, succession.

concave *adj* depressed, excavated, hollow, hollowed, scooped.

conceal *vb* bury, cover, screen, secrete; disguise, dissemble, mask.

concede *vb* grant, surrender, yield; acknowledge, admit, allow, confess, grant.

conceit *n* belief, conception, fancy, idea, image, imagination, notion, thought; caprice, illusion, vagary, whim; estimate, estimation, impression, judgement, opinion; conceitedness, egoism, self-complacency, priggishness, priggery, self-conceit, self-esteem, self-sufficiency, vanity; crotchet, point, quip, quirk.

conceited *adj* egotistical, opinionated, opinionative, overweening, self-conceited, vain.

conceivable *adj* imaginable, picturable; cogitable, comprehensible, intelligible, rational, thinkable.

conceive *vb* create, contrive, devise, form, plan, purpose; fancy, imagine; comprehend, fathom, think, understand; assume, imagine, suppose; bear, become pregnant.

concern *vb* affect, belong to, interest, pertain to, regard, relate to, touch; disquiet, disturb, trouble. • *n* affair, business, matter, transaction, concernment, consequence, importance, interest, moment, weight; anxiety, care, carefulness, solicitude, worry; business, company, establishment, firm, house.

concert *vb* combine, concoct, contrive, design, devise, invent, plan, plot, project. • *n* agreement, concord, concordance, cooperation, harmony, union, unison.

concession *n* acquiescence, assent, cessation, compliance, surrender, yielding; acknowledgement, allowance, boon, confession, grant, privilege.

conciliate *vb* appease, pacify, placate, propitiate, reconcile; engage, gain, secure, win, win over.

concise *adj* brief, compact, compendious, comprehensive, compressed, condensed, crisp, laconic, pithy, pointed, pregnant, sententious, short, succinct, summary, terse.

conclave *n* assembly, cabinet, council.

conclude *vb* close, end, finish, terminate; deduce, gather, infer, judge; decide, determine, judge; arrange, complete, settle; bar, hinder, restrain, stop; decide, determine, resolve.

conclusion *n* deduction, inference; decision, determination, judgement; close, completion, end, event, finale, issue, termination, upshot; arrangement, closing, effecting, establishing, settlement.

conclusive *adj* clinching, convincing, decisive, irrefutable, unanswerable; final, ultimate.

concoct *vb* brew, contrive, design, devise, frame, hatch, invent, mature, plan, plot, prepare, project.

concomitant *adj* accessory, accompanying, attendant, attending, coincident, concurrent, conjoined. • *n* accessory, accompaniment, attendant.

concord *n* agreement, amity, friendship, harmony, peace, unanimity, union, unison, unity; accord, adaptation, concordance, consonance, harmony.

concordant *adj* accordant, agreeable, agreeing, harmonious.

concordat *n* agreement, bargain, compact, convention, covenant, stipulation, treaty.

concourse *n* confluence, conflux, congress; assemblage, assembly, collection, crowd, gathering, meeting, multitude, throng.

concrete *vb* cake, congeal, coagulate, harden, solidify, thicken. • *adj* compact, consolidated, firm, solid, solidified; agglomerated, complex, conglomerated, compound, concreted; completely, entire, individualized, total. • *n* compound, concretion, mixture; cement.

concubine *n* hetaera, hetaira, mistress, paramour.

concupiscence *n* lasciviousness, lechery, lewdness, lust, pruriency.

concupiscent *adj* carnal, lascivious, lecherous, lewd, libidinous, lustful, prurient, rampant, salacious, sensual.

concur *vb* accede, acquiesce, agree, approve, assent, coincide, consent, harmonize; combine, conspire, cooperate, help.

concurrent *adj* agreeing, coincident, harmonizing, meeting, uniting; associate, associated, attendant, concomitant, conjoined, united.

concussion *n* agitation, shaking; clash, crash, shock.

condemn *vb* adjudge, convict, doom, sentence; disapprove, proscribe, reprobate; blame, censure, damn, deprecate, disapprove, reprehend, reprove, upbraid.

condemnation *n* conviction, doom, judgement, penalty, sentence; banning, disapproval, proscription; guilt, sin, wrong; blame, censure, disapprobation, disapproval, reprobation, reproof.

condemnatory *adj* blaming, censuring, damnatory, deprecatory, disapproving, reproachful.

condense *vb* compress, concentrate, consolidate, densify, thicken; abbreviate, abridge, contract, curtail, diminish, epitomize, reduce, shorten, summarize; liquefy.

condescend *vb* deign, vouchsafe; descend, stoop, submit.

condescension *n* affability, civility, courtesy, deference, favour, graciousness, obeisance.

condign *adj* adequate, deserved, just, merited, suitable.

condiment *n* appetizer, relish, sauce, seasoning.

condition *vb* postulate, specify, stipulate; groom, prepare, qualify, ready, train; acclimatize, accustom, adapt, adjust, familiarize, habituate, naturalize; attune, commission, fix, overhaul, prepare, recondition, repair, service, tune. • *n* case, circumstances, plight, predicament, situation, state; class, estate, grade, rank, station; arrangement, consideration, provision, proviso, stipulation; attendant, necessity, postulate, precondition, prerequisite.

condole *vb* commiserate, compassionate, console, sympathize.

condonation *n* forgiveness, overlooking, pardon.

condone *vb* excuse, forgive, pardon.

conduce *vb* contribute, lead, tend; advance, aid.

conducive *adj* conducting, contributing, instrumental, promotive, subservient, subsidiary.

conduct *vb* convoy, direct, escort, lead; administer, command, govern, lead, preside, superintend; manage, operate, regulate; direct, lead. • *n* administration, direction, guidance, leadership, management; convoy, escort, guard; actions, bearing, behaviour, career, carriage, demeanour, deportment, manners.

conductor *n* guide, lead; director, leader, manager; propagator, transmitter.

conduit *n* canal, channel, duct, passage, pipe, tube.

confederacy *n* alliance, coalition, compact, confederation, covenant, federation, league, union.

confer *vb* advise, consult, converse, deliberate, discourse, parley, talk; bestow, give, grant, vouchsafe.

confess *vb* acknowledge, admit, avow, own; admit, concede, grant, recognize; attest, exhibit, manifest, prove, show; shrive.

confession *n* acknowledgement, admission, avowal.

confide *vb* commit, consign, entrust, trust.

confidence *n* belief, certitude, dependence, faith, reliance, trust; aplomb, assurance, boldness, cocksureness, courage, firmness, intrepidity, self-reliance; secrecy.

confident *adj* assured, certain, cocksure, positive, sure; bold, presumptuous, sanguine, undaunted.

confidential *adj* intimate, private, secret; faithful, trustworthy.

configuration *n* conformation, contour, figure, form, gestalt, outline, shape.

confine *vb* restrain, shut in, shut up; immure, imprison, incarcerate, impound, jail, mew; bound, circumscribe, limit, restrict. • *n* border, boundary, frontier, limit.

confinement *n* restraint; captivity, duress, durance, immurement, imprisonment, incarceration; childbed, childbirth, delivery, lying-in, parturition.

confines *npl* borders, boundaries, edges, frontiers, limits, marches, precincts.

confirm *vb* assure, establish, fix, settle; strengthen; authenticate, avouch, corroborate, countersign, endorse, substantiate, verify; bind, ratify, sanction.

confirmation *n* establishment, settlement; corroboration, proof, substantiation, verification.

confiscate *vb* appropriate, forfeit, seize.

conflict *vb* clash, combat, contend, contest, disagree, fight, interfere, strive, struggle. • *n* battle, collision, combat, contention, contest, encounter, fight, struggle; antagonism, clashing, disagreement, discord, disharmony, inconsistency, interference, opposition.

confluence *n* conflux, junction, meeting, union; army, assemblage, assembly, concourse, crowd, collection, horde, host, multitude, swarm.

confluent *adj* blending, concurring, flowing, joining, meeting, merging, uniting.

conform *vb* accommodate, adapt, adjust; agree, comport, correspond, harmonize, square, tally.

conformation *n* accordance, agreement, compliance, conformity; configuration, figure, form, manner, shape, structure.

confound *vb* confuse; baffle, bewilder, embarrass, flurry, mystify, nonplus, perplex, pose; amaze, astonish, astound, bewilder, dumfound, paralyse, petrify, startle, stun, stupefy, surprise; annihilate, demolish, destroy, overthrow, overwhelm, ruin; abash, confuse, discompose, disconcert, mortify, shame.

confront *vb* face; challenge, contrapose, encounter, oppose, threaten.

confuse *vb* blend, confound, intermingle, mingle, mix; derange, disarrange, disorder, jumble, mess, muddle; darken, obscure, perplex; befuddle, bewilder, embarrass, flabbergast, flurry, fluster, mystify, nonplus, pose; abash, confound, discompose, disconcert, mortify, shame.

confusion *n* anarchy, chaos, clutter, confusedness, derangement, disarrangement, disarray, disorder, jumble, muddle; agitation, commotion, ferment, stir, tumult, turmoil; astonishment, bewilderment, distraction, embarrassment, fluster, fuddle, perplexity; abashment, discomfiture, mortification, shame; annihilation, defeat, demolition, destruction, overthrow, ruin.

confute *vb* disprove, oppugn, overthrow, refute, silence.

congeal *vb* benumb, condense, curdle, freeze, stiffen, thicken.

congenial *adj* kindred, similar, sympathetic; adapted, agreeable, natural, suitable, suited; agreeable, favourable, genial.

congenital *adj* connate, connatural, inborn.

congeries *n* accumulation, agglomeration, aggregate, aggregation, collection, conglomeration, crowd, cluster, heap, mass.

congratulate *vb* compliment, felicitate, gratulate, greet, hail, salute.

congregate *vb* assemble, collect, convene, convoke, gather, muster; gather, meet, swarm, throng.

congregation *n* assemblage, assembly, collection, gathering, meeting.

congress *n* assembly, conclave, conference, convention, convocation, council, diet, meeting.

congruity *n* agreement, conformity, consistency, fitness, suitableness.

congruous *adj* accordant, agreeing, compatible, consistent, consonant, suitable; appropriate, befitting, fit, meet, proper, seemly.

conjecture *vb* assume, guess, hypothesize, imagine, suppose, surmise, suspect; dare say, fancy, presume. • *n* assumption, guess, hypothesis, supposition, surmise, theory.

conjoin *vb* associate, combine, connect, join, unite.

conjugal *adj* bridal, connubial, hymeneal, matrimonial, nuptial.

conjuncture *n* combination, concurrence, connection; crisis, emergency, exigency, juncture.

conjure *vb* adjure, beg, beseech, crave, entreat, implore, invoke, pray, supplicate; bewitch, charm, enchant, fascinate; juggle.

connect *vb* associate, conjoin, combine, couple, hyphenate, interlink, join, link, unite; cohere, interlock.

connected *adj* associated, coupled, joined, united; akin, allied, related; communicating.

connection *n* alliance, association, dependence, junction, union; commerce, communication, intercourse; affinity, relationship; kindred, kinsman, relation, relative.

connive *vb* collude, conspire, plot, scheme.

connoisseur *n* critic, expert, virtuoso.

connotation *n* comprehension, depth, force, intent, intention, meaning.

connubial *adj* bridal, conjugal, hymeneal, matrimonial, nuptial.

conquer *vb* beat, checkmate, crush, defeat, discomfit, humble, master, overcome, overpower, overthrow, prevail, quell, reduce, rout, subdue, subjugate, vanquish; overcome, surmount.

conqueror *n* humbler, subduer, subjugator, vanquisher; superior, victor, winner.

conquest *n* defeat, discomfiture, mastery, overthrow, reduction, subjection, subjugation; triumph, victor; winning.

consanguinity *n* affinity, kinship, blood-relationship, kin, kindred, relationship.

conscientious *adj* careful, exact, fair, faithful, high-principled, honest, honourable, incorruptible, just, scrupulous, straightforward, uncorrupt, upright.

conscious *adj* intelligent, knowing, percipient, sentient; intellectual, rational, reasoning, reflecting, self-conscious, thinking; apprised, awake, aware, cognizant, percipient, sensible; self-admitted, self-accusing.

consecrate *vb* dedicate, devote, ordain; hallow, sanctify, venerate.

consecutive *adj* following, succeeding.

consent *vb* agree, allow, assent, concur, permit, yield; accede, acquiesce, comply. • *n* approval, assent, concurrence, permission; accord, agreement, consensus, concord, cooperation, harmony, unison; acquiescence, compliance.

consequence *n* effect, end, event, issue, result; conclusion, deduction, inference; concatenation, connection, consecution; concern, distinction, importance, influence, interest, moment, standing, weight.

consequential *adj* consequent, following, resulting, sequential; arrogant, conceited, inflated, pompous, pretentious, self-important, self-sufficient, vainglorious.

conservation *n* guardianship, maintenance, preservation, protection.

conservative *adj* conservatory, moderate, moderationist; preservative; reactionary, unprogressive. • *n* die-hard, reactionary, redneck, rightist, right-winger; moderate; preservative.

conserve *vb* keep, maintain, preserve, protect, save, sustain, uphold. • *n* confit, confection, jam, preserve, sweetmeat.

consider *vb* attend, brood, contemplate, examine, heed, mark, mind, ponder, reflect, revolve, study, weigh; care for, consult, envisage, regard, respect; cogitate, deliberate, mediate, muse, ponder, reflect, ruminate, think; account, believe, deem, hold, judge, opine.

considerate *adj* circumspect, deliberate, discrete, judicious, provident, prudent, serious, sober, staid, thoughtful; charitable, forbearing, patient.

consideration *n* attention, cogitation, contemplation, deliberation, notice, heed, meditation, pondering, reflection, regard; consequence, importance, important, moment, significant, weight; account, cause, ground, motive, reason, sake, score.

consign *vb* deliver, hand over, remand, resign, transfer, transmit; commit, entrust; ship.

consignor *n* sender, shipper, transmitter.

consistency *n* compactness, consistence, density, thickness; agreement, compatibility, conformableness, congruity, consonance, correspondence, harmony.

consistent *adj* accordant, agreeing, comfortable, compatible, congruous, consonant, correspondent, harmonious, logical.

consolation *n* alleviation, comfort, condolence, encouragement, relief, solace.

console *vb* assuage, calm, cheer, comfort, encourage, solace, relieve, soothe.

consolidate *vb* cement, compact, compress, condense, conduce, harden, solidify, thicken; combine, conjoin, fuse, unite.

consolidation *n* solidification; combination, union.

consonance *n* accord, concord, conformity, harmony; accord, accordance, agreement, congruence, congruity, consistency, unison.

consonant *adj* accordant, according, harmonious; compatible, congruous, consistent. • *n* articulation, letter-sound.

consort *vb* associate, fraternize. • *n* associate, companion, fellow, husband, spouse, partner.

conspectus *n* abstract, brief, breviary, compend, compendium, digest, epitome, outline, precis, summary, syllabus, synopsis.

conspicuous *adj* apparent, clear, discernible, glaring, manifest, noticeable, perceptible, plain, striking, visible; celebrated, distinguished, eminent, famed, famous, illustrious, marked, noted, outstanding. pre-eminent, prominent, remarkable, signal.

conspiracy *n* cabal, collusion, confederation, intrigue, league, machination, plot, scheme.

conspire *vb* concur, conduce, cooperate; combine, compass, contrive, devise, project; confederate, contrive, hatch, plot, scheme.

constancy *n* immutability, permanence, stability, unchangeableness; regularity, unchangeableness; decision, determination, firmness, inflexibility, resolution, steadfastness, steadiness; devotion, faithfulness, fidelity, loyalty, trustiness, truth.

constant *adj* abiding, enduring, fixed, immutable, invariable, invariant, permanent, perpetual, stable, unalterable, unchanging, unvaried; certain, regular, stated, uniform; determined, firm, resolute, stanch, steadfast, steady, unanswering, undeviating, unmoved, unshaken, unwavering; assiduous, diligent, persevering, sedulous, tenacious, unremitting; continual, continuous, incessant, perpetual, sustained, unbroken, uninterrupted; devoted, faithful, loyal, true, trusty.

consternation *n* alarm, amazement, awe, bewilderment, dread, fear, fright, horror, panic, terror.

constituent *adj* component, composing, constituting, forming; appointing, electoral. • *n* component, element, ingredient, principal; elector, voter.

constitute *vb* compose, form, make; appoint, delegate, depute, empower; enact, establish, fix, set up.

constitution *n* establishment, formation, make-up, organization, structure; character, characteristic, disposition, form, habit, humour, peculiarity, physique, quality, spirit, temper, temperament.

constitutional *adj* congenital, connate, inborn, inbred, inherent, innate, natural, organic; lawful, legal, legitimate. • *n* airing, exercise, promenade, stretch, walk.

constrain *vb* coerce, compel, drive, force; chain, confine, curb, enthral, hold, restrain; draw, impel, urge.

constriction *n* compression, constraint, contraction.

construct *vb* build, fabricate, erect, raise, set up; arrange, establish, form, found, frame, institute, invent, make, organize, originate.

construction *n* building, erection, fabrication; configuration, conformation, figure, form, formation, made, shape, structure; explanation, interpretation, rendering, version.

construe *vb* analyse, explain, expound, interpret, parse, render, translate.

consult *vb* advise, ask, confer, counsel, deliberate, interrogate, question; consider, regard.

consume *vb* absorb, decay, destroy, devour, dissipate, exhaust, expend, lavish, lessen, spend, squander, vanish, waste.

consummate[1] *vb* accomplish, achieve, compass, complete, conclude, crown, effect, effectuate, end, execute, finish, perfect, perform.

consummate[2] *adj* complete, done, effected, finished, fulfilled, perfect, supreme.

consumption *n* decay, decline, decrease, destruction, diminution, expenditure, use, waste; atrophy, emaciation.

contact *vb* hit, impinge, touch; approach, be heard, communicate with, reach. • *n* approximation, contiguity, junction, juxtaposition, taction, tangency, touch.

contagion *n* infection; contamination, corruption, infection, taint.

contagious *adj* catching, epidemic, infectious; deadly, pestiferous, pestilential, poisonous.

contain *vb* accommodate, comprehend, comprise, embody, embrace, enclose, include; check, restrain.

contaminate *vb* corrupt, defile, deprave, infect, poison, pollute, soil, stain, sully, taint, tarnish, vitiate.

contamination *n* contaminating, defilement, defiling, polluting, pollution; abomination, defilement, impurity, foulness, infection, pollution, stain, taint, uncleanness.

contemn *vb* despise, disdain, disregard, neglect, scorn, scout, slight, spurn.

contemplate *vb* behold, gaze upon, observe, survey; consider, dwell on, meditate on, muse on, ponder, reflect upon, study, survey, think about; design, intend, mean, plan, purpose.

contemplation *n* cogitation, deliberation, meditation, pondering, reflection, speculation, study, thought; prospect, prospective, view; expectation.

contemporaneous *adj* coetaneous, coeval, coexistent, coexisting, coincident, concomitant, contemporary, simultaneous, synchronous.

contemporary *adj* coetaneous, coeval, coexistent, coexisting, coincident, concomitant, concurrent, contemporaneous, current, present, simultaneous, synchronous; advanced, modern, modernistic, progressive, up-to-date. • *n* coeval, coexistent, compeer, fellow.

contempt *n* contumely, derision, despite, disdain, disregard, misprision, mockery, scorn, slight.

contemptible *adj* abject, base, despicable, haughty, insolent, insulting, low, mean, paltry, pitiful, scurvy, sorry, supercilious, vile, worthless.

contemptuous *adj* arrogant, contumelious, disdainful, haughty, insolent, insulting, scornful, sneering, supercilious.

contend *vb* battle, combat, compete, contest, fight, strive, struggle, vie; argue, debate, dispute, litigate; affirm, assert, contest, maintain.

content[1] *n* essence, gist, meaning, meat, stuff, substance; capacity, measure, space, volume.

content[2] *vb* appease, delight, gladden, gratify, humour, indulge, please, satisfy, suffice. • *adj* agreeable, contented, happy, pleased, satisfied. • *n* contentment, ease, peace, satisfaction.

contention *n* discord, dissension, feud, squabble, strife, quarrel, rapture, wrangle, wrangling; altercation, bickering, contest, controversy, debate, dispute, litigation, logomachy.

contentious *adj* belligerent, cross, litigious, peevish, perverse, petulant, pugnacious, quarrelsome, wrangling; captious, cavilling, disputatious.

conterminous *adj* adjacent, adjoining, contiguous; co-extensive, coincident, commensurate.

contest *vb* argue, contend, controvert, debate, dispute, litigate, question; strive, struggle; compete, cope, fight, vie. • *n* altercation, contention, controversy, difference, dispute, debate, quarrel; affray, battle, bout, combat, conflict, encounter, fight, match, scrimmage, struggle, tussle; competition, contention, rivalry.

contexture *n* composition, constitution, framework, structure, texture.

contiguous *adj* abutting, adjacent, adjoining, beside, bordering, conterminous, meeting, near, neighbouring, touching.

continent[1] *n* mainland, mass, tract.

continent[2] *adj* abstemious, abstinent, chaste, restrained, self-commanding, self-controlled, moderate, sober, temperate.

contingency *n* accidentalness, chance, fortuity, uncertainty; accident, casualty, event, incident, occurrence.

contingent *adj* accidental, adventitious, casual, fortuitous, incidental; conditional, dependent, uncertain. • *n* proportion, quota, share.

continual *adj* constant, constant, perpetual, unceasing, uninterrupted, unremitting; endless, eternal, everlasting, interminable, perennial, permanent, perpetual, unending; constant, oft-repeated.

continuance *n* abiding, continuation, duration, endurance, lasting, persistence, stay; continuation, extension, perpetuation, prolongation, protraction; concatenation, connection, sequence, succession; constancy, endurance, perseverance, persistence.

continue *vb* endure, last, remain; abide, linger, remain, stay, tarry; endure, persevere, persist, stick; extend, prolong, perpetuate, protract.

continuous *adj* connected, continued, extended, prolonged, unbroken, unintermitted, uninterrupted.

contour *n* outline, profile.

contraband *adj* banned, forbidden, illegal, illicit, interdicted, prohibited, smuggled, unlawful.

contract *vb* abbreviate, abridge, condense, confine, curtail, diminish, epitomize, lessen, narrow, reduce, shorten; absorb, catch, incur, get, make, take; constrict, shrink, shrivel, wrinkle; agree, bargain, covenant, engage, pledge, stipulate. • *n* agreement, arrangement, bargain, bond, compact, concordat, covenant, convention, engagement, pact, stipulation, treaty.

contradict *vb* assail, challenge, controvert, deny, dispute, gainsay, impugn, traverse; abrogate, annul, belie, counter, disallow, negative, contravene, counteract, oppose, thwart.

contradiction *n* controversion, denial, gainsaying; antinomy, clashing, contrariety, incongruity, opposition.

contradictory *adj* antagonistic, contrary, incompatible, inconsistent, negating, opposed, opposite, repugnant.

contrariety *n* antagonism, clashing, contradiction, contrast, opposition, repugnance.

contrary *adj* adverse, counter, discordant, opposed, opposing, opposite; antagonistic, conflicting, contradictory, repugnant, retroactive; forward, headstrong, obstinate, refractory, stubborn, unruly, wayward, perverse. • *n* antithesis, converse, obverse, opposite, reverse.

contrast *vb* compare, differentiate, distinguish, oppose. • *n* contrariety, difference, opposition; comparison, distinction.

contravene *vb* abrogate, annul, contradict, counteract, countervail, cross, go against, hinder, interfere, nullify, oppose, set aside, thwart.

contravention *n* abrogation, contradiction, interference, opposition, transgression, traversal, violation.

contretemps *n* accident, mischance, mishap.

contribute *vb* bestow, donate, give, grant, subscribe; afford, aid, furnish, supply; concur, conduce, conspire, cooperate, minister, serve, tend.

contribution *n* bestowal, bestowment, grant; donation, gift, offering, subscription.

contrite *adj* humble, penitent, repentant, sorrowful.

contrition *n* compunction, humiliation, penitence, regret, remorse, repentance, self-condemnation, self-reproach, sorrow.

contrivance *n* design, inventive, inventiveness; contraption, device, gadget, invention, machine; artifice, device, fabrication, machination, plan, plot, scheme, shift, stratagem.

contrive *vb* arrange, brew, concoct, design, devise, effect, form, frame, hatch, invent, plan, project; consider, plan, plot, scheme; manage, make out.

control *vb* command, direct, dominate, govern, manage, oversee, sway, regulate, rule, superintend; bridle, check, counteract, curb, check, hinder, repress, restrain. • *n* ascendency, command, direction, disposition, dominion, government, guidance, mastery, oversight, regiment, regulation, rule, superintendence, supremacy, sway.

controversy *n* altercation, argument, contention, debate, discussion, disputation, dispute, logomachy, polemics, quarrel, strife; lawsuit.

contumacious *adj* disobedient, cross-grained, disrespectful, haughty, headstrong, intractable, obdurate, obstinate, pertinacious, perverse, rebellious, refractory, stiff-necked, stubborn.

contumacy *n* doggedness, haughtiness, headiness, obduracy, obstinacy, pertinacity, perverseness, stubbornness; contempt, disobedience, disrespect, insolence, insubordination, rebelliousness.

contumelious *adj* abusive, arrogant, calumnious, contemptuous, disdainful, insolent, insulting, opprobrious, overbearing, rude, scornful, supercilious.

contumely *n* abuse, affront, arrogance, contempt, contemptuousness, disdain, indignity, insolence, insult, obloquy, opprobrium, reproach, rudeness, scorn, superciliousness.

contuse *vb* bruise, crush, injure, knock, squeeze, wound.

contusion *n* bruise, crush, injury, knock, squeeze, wound.

convalescence *n* recovery, recuperation.

convene *vb* assemble, congregate, gather, meet, muster; assemble, call, collect, convoke, muster, summon.

convenience *n* fitness, propriety, suitableness; accessibility, accommodation, comfort, commodiousness, ease, handiness, satisfaction, serviceability, serviceableness.

convenient *adj* adapted, appropriate, fit, fitted, proper, suitable, suited; advantageous, beneficial, comfortable, commodious, favourable, handy, helpful, serviceable, timely, useful.

convent *n* abbey, cloister, monastery, priory.

convention *n* assembly, congress, convocation, meeting; agreement, bargain, compact, contract, pact, stipulation, treaty; custom, formality, usage.

conventional *adj* agreed on, bargained for, stipulated; accustomed, approved, common, customary, everyday, habitual, ordinary, orthodox, regular, standard, traditional, usual, wonted.

conversable *adj* affable, communicative, free, open, sociable, social, unreversed.

conversation *n* chat, colloquy, communion, confabulation, conference, converse, dialogue, discourse, intercourse, interlocution, parley, talk.

converse[1] *vb* commune; chat, confabulate, discourse, gossip, parley, talk. • *n* commerce, communication, intercourse; colloquy, conversation, talk.

converse[2] *adj* adverse, contradictory, contrary, counter, opposed, opposing, opposite; *n* antithesis, contrary, opposite, reverse.

conversion *n* change, reduction, resolution, transformation, transmutation; interchange, reversal, transposition.

convert *vb* alter, change, transform, transmute; interchange, reverse, transpose; apply, appropriate, convince. • *n* catechumen, disciple, neophyte, proselyte.

convey *vb* bear, bring, carry, fetch, transmit, transport, waft; abalienate, alienate, cede, consign, deliver, demise, devise, devolve, grant, sell, transfer.

conveyance *n* alienation, cession, transfer, transference, transmission; carriage, carrying, conveying, transfer, transmission.

convict *vb* condemn, confute, convince, imprison, sentence. • *n* criminal, culprit, felon, malefactor, prisoner.

convivial *adj* festal, festive, gay, jolly, jovial, merry, mirthful, social.

convocation *n* assembling, convening, convoking, gathering, summoning; assembly, congress, convention, council, diet, meeting, synod.

convoke *vb* assemble, convene, muster, summon.

convoy *vb* accompany, attend, escort, guard, protect. • *n* attendance, attendant, escort, guard, protection.

convulse *vb* agitate, derange, disorder, disturb, shake, shatter.

convulsion *n* cramp, fit, spasm; agitation, commotion, disturbance, shaking, tumult.

cook *vb* bake, boil, broil, fry, grill, microwave, roast, spit-roast, steam, stir-fry; falsify, garble.

cool *vb* chill, ice, refrigerate; abate, allay, calm, damp, moderate, quiet, temper. • *adj* calm, collected, composed, dispassionate, placid, sedate, self-possessed, quiet, staid, unexcited, unimpassioned, undisturbed, unruffled; cold-blooded, indifferent, lukewarm, unconcerned; apathetic, chilling, freezing, frigid, repellent; bold, impertinent, impudent, self-possessed, shameless. • *n* chill, chilliness, coolness; calmness, composure, coolheadedness, countenance, equanimity, poise, self-possession, self-restraint.

coop *vb* cage, confine, encage, immure, imprison. • *n* barrel, box, cage, pen.

cooperate *vb* abet, aid, assist, co-act, collaborate, combine, concur, conduce, conspire, contribute, help, unite.

cooperation *n* aid, assistance, co-action, concert, concurrence, collaboration, synergy.

coordinate *vb* accord, agree, arrange, equalize, harmonize, integrate, methodize, organize, regulate, synchronize, systematize. • *adj* coequal, equal, equivalent, tantamount; coincident, synchronous. • *n* complement, counterpart, like, pendant; companion, fellow, match, mate.

copartnership *n* association, fraternity, partnership; company, concern, establishment, firm, house.

cope *vb* combat, compete, contend, encounter, engage, strive, struggle, vie.

copious *adj* abundant, ample, exuberant, full, overflowing, plenteous, plentiful, profuse, rich.

copiousness *n* abundance, exuberance, fullness, plenty, profusion, richness.

copse *n* coppice, grove, thicket.

copulation *n* coition, congress, coupling.

copy *vb* duplicate, reproduce, trace, transcribe; follow, imitate, pattern. • *n* counterscript, duplicate, facsimile, off-print, replica, reproduction, transcript; archetype, model, original, pattern; manuscript, typescript.

cord *n* braid, gimp, line, string.

cordate *adj* cordiform, heart-shaped.

cordial *adj* affectionate, ardent, earnest, heartfelt, hearty, sincere, warm, warm-hearted; grateful, invigorating, restorative, pleasant, refreshing. • *n* balm, balsam, elixir, tisane, tonic; liqueur.

core *n* centre, essence, heart, kernel.

corner *vb* confound, confuse, nonplus, perplex, pose, puzzle. • *n* angle, bend, crutch, cusp, elbow, joint, knee; niche, nook, recess, retreat.

corollary *n* conclusion, consequence, deduction, induction, inference.

coronal *n* bays, chaplet, crown, garland, laurel, wreath.

corporal *adj* bodily; corporeal, material, physical.

corporeal *adj* bodily, fleshly, substantial; corporal, material, nonspiritual, physical.

corps *n* band, body, company, contingent, division, platoon, regiment, squad, squadron, troop.

corpse *n* body, carcass, corse, remains; ashes, dust.

corpulent *adj* big, burly, fat, fleshy, large, lusty, obese, plump, portly, pursy, rotund, stout.

corpuscle *n* atom, bit, grain, iota, jot, mite, molecule, monad, particle, scintilla, scrap, whit.

correct *vb* adjust, amend, cure, improve, mend, reclaim, rectify, redress, reform, regulate, remedy; chasten, discipline, punish. • *adj* accurate, equitable, exact, faultless, just, precise, proper, regular, right, true, upright.

correction *n* amendment, improvement, redress; chastening, discipline, punishment.

corrective *adj* alternative, correctory, counteractive, emendatory, improving, modifying, rectifying, reformative, reformatory.

correctness *n* accuracy, exactness, faultlessness, nicety, precision, propriety, rectitude, regularity, rightness, truth.

correlate *n* complement, correlative, counterpart.

correspond *vb* accord, agree, answer, comport, conform, fit, harmonize, match, square, suit, tally; answer, belong, correlate; communicate.

correspondence *n* accord, agreement, coincidence, concurrence, conformity, congruity, fitness, harmony, match; correlation, counterposition; communication, letters, writing.

corroborate *vb* confirm, establish, ratify, substantiate, support, sustain, strengthen.

corrode *vb* canker, erode, gnaw; consume, deteriorate, rust, waste; blight, embitter, envenom, poison.

corrosive *adj* acrid, biting, consuming, cathartic, caustic, corroding, eroding, erosive, violent; consuming, corroding, gnawing, mordant, wasting, wearing; blighting, cankerous, carking, embittering, envenoming, poisoning.

corrugate *vb* cockle, crease, furrow, groove, pucker, rumple, wrinkle.

corrupt *vb* putrefy, putrid, render; contaminate, defile, infect, pollute, spoil, taint, vitiate; degrade, demoralize, deprave, pervert; adulterate, debase, falsify, sophisticate; bribe, entice. • *adj* contaminated, corrupted, impure, infected, putrid, rotten, spoiled, tainted, unsound; abandoned, debauched, depraved, dissolute, profligate, reprobate, vicious, wicked; bribable, buyable.

corruption *n* putrefaction, putrescence, rottenness; adulteration, contamination, debasement, defilement, infection, perversion, pollution, vitiation; demoralization, depravation, depravity, immorality, laxity, sinfulness, wickedness; bribery, dishonesty.

corsair *n* buccaneer, picaroon, pirate, rover, sea-robber, sea-rover.

corset *n* bodice, girdle, stays.

cosmonaut *n* astronaut, spaceman.

cosmos *n* creation, macrocosm, universe, world; harmony, order, structure.

cost *vb* absorb, consume, require. • *n* amount, charge, expenditure, expense, outlay, price; costliness, preciousness, richness, splendour, sumptuousness; damage, detriment, loss, pain, sacrifice, suffering.

costly *adj* dear, expensive, high-priced; gorgeous, luxurious, precious, rich, splendid, sumptuous, valuable.

costume *n* apparel, attire, dress, robes, uniform.

cosy, cozy *adj* comfortable, easy, snug; chatty, conversable, social, talkative.

coterie *n* association, brotherhood, circle, club, set, society, sodality.

cottage *n* cabin, chalet, cot, hut, lodge, shack, shanty.

couch *vb* lie, recline; crouch, squat; bend down, stoop; conceal, cover up, hide; lay, level. • *n* bed, davenport, divan, lounge, seat, settee, settle, sofa.

council *n* advisers, cabinet, ministry; assembly, congress, conclave, convention, convocation, diet, husting, meeting, parliament, synod.

counsel *vb* admonish, advise, caution, recommend, warm. • *n* admonition, advice, caution, instruction, opinion, recommendation, suggestion; deliberation, forethought; advocate, barrister, counsellor, lawyer.

count *vb* enumerate, number, score; calculate, cast, compute, estimate, reckon; account, consider, deem, esteem, hold, judge, regard, think; tell. • *n* reckoning, tally.

countenance *vb* abet, aid, approve, assist, befriend, encourage, favour, patronize, sanction, support. • *n* aspect, look, men; aid, approbation, approval, assistance, encouragement, favour, patronage, sanction, support.

counter[1] *n* abacus, calculator, computer, meter, reckoner, tabulator, totalizator; bar, buffet, shopboard, table; (*naut*) end, poop, stern, tail; chip, token.

counter[2] *vb* contradict, contravene, counteract, oppose, retaliate. • *adj* adverse, against, contrary, opposed, opposite. • *adv* contrariwise, contrary. • *n* antithesis, contrary, converse, opposite, reverse; counterblast, counterblow, retaliation.

counteract *vb* check, contrapose, contravene, cross, counter, counterpose, defeat, foil, frustrate, hinder, oppose, resist, thwart, traverse; annul, countervail, counterbalance, destroy, neutralize, offset.

counteractive *adj* antidote, corrective, counteragent, medicine, remedy, restorative.

counterbalance *vb* balance, counterpoise; compensate, countervail.

counterfeit *vb* forge, imitate; fake, feign, pretend, sham, simulate; copy, imitate. • *adj* fake, forged, fraudulent, spurious, supposititious; false, feigned, hypocritical, mock, sham, simulated, spurious; copied, imitated, resembling. • *n* copy, fake, forgery, sham.

countermand *vb* abrogate, annul, cancel, recall, repeal, rescind, revoke.

counterpane *n* coverlet, duvet, quilt.

counterpart *n* copy, duplicate; complement, correlate, correlative, reverse, supplement; fellow, mate, match, tally, twin.

counterpoise *vb* balance, counteract, countervail, counterbalance, equilibrate, offset. • *n* balance, counterweight.

countersign *n* password, watchword.

countervail *vb* balance, compensate, counterbalance.

country *n* land, region; countryside; fatherland, home, kingdom, state, territory; nation, people, population. • *adj* rural, rustic; countrified, rough, rude, uncultivated, unpolished, unrefined.

countryman *n* compatriot, fellow-citizen; boor, clown, farmer, hind, husbandman, peasant, rustic, swain.

couple *vb* pair, unite; copulate, embrace; buckle, clasp, conjoin, connect, join, link, pair, yoke. • *n* brace, pair, twain, two; bond, coupling, lea, link, tie.

courage *n* audaciousness, audacity, boldness, bravery, daring, derring-do, dauntlessness, fearlessness, firmness, fortitude, gallantry, hardihood, heroism, intrepidity, manhood, mettle, nerve, pluck, prowess, resolution, spirit, spunk, valorousness, valour.

courageous *adj* audacious, brave, bold, chivalrous, daring, dauntless, fearless, gallant, hardy, heroic, intrepid, lion-hearted, mettlesome, plucky, resolute, reliant, staunch, stout, undismayed, valiant, valorous.

course *vb* chase, follow, hunt, pursue, race, run. • *n* career, circuit, race, run; road, route, track, way; bearing, direction, path, tremor, track; ambit, beat, orbit, round; process, progress, sequence; order, regularity, succession, turn; behaviour, conduct, deportment; arrangement, series, system.

court *vb* coddle, fawn, flatter, ingratiate; address, woo; seek; invite, solicit. • *n* area, courtyard, patio, quadrangle; addresses, civilities, homage, respects, solicitations; retinue, palace, tribunal.

courteous *adj* affable, attentive, ceremonious, civil, complaisant, courtly, debonair, elegant, gracious, obliging, polished, polite, refined, respected, urbane, well-bred, well-mannered.

courtesan *n* harlot, prostitute, strumpet, vamp, wanton, wench, whore.

courtesy *n* affability, civility, complaisance, courteousness, elegance, good-breeding, graciousness, polish, politeness, refine, urbanity.

courtly *adj* affable, ceremonious, civil, elegant, flattering, lordly, obliging, polished, polite, refined, urbane.

courtyard *n* area, court, patio, quadrangle, yard.

cove[1] *n* anchorage, bay, bight, creek, firth, fjord, inlet.

cove[2] *n* bloke, chap, character, customer, fellow, type.

covenant *vb* agree, bargain, contract, stipulate. • *n* bond, deed; arrangement, bargain, compact, concordat, contract, convention, pact, stipulation, treaty.

cover *vb* overlay, overspread; cloak, conceal, curtain, disguise, hide, mask, screen, secrete, shroud, veil; defend, guard, protect, shelter, shield; case, clothe, envelop, invest, jacket, sheathe; comprehend, comprise, contain, embody, embrace, include. • *n* capsule, case, covering, integument, tegument, top; cloak, disguise, screen, veil; guard, defence, protection, safeguard, shelter, shield; shrubbery, thicket, underbrush, undergrowth, underwood, woods.

covert *adj* clandestine, concealed, disguised, hidden, insidious, private, secret, sly, stealthy, underhand. • *n* coppice, shade, shrubbery, thicket, underwood; asylum; defence, harbour, hiding-place, refuge, retreat, sanctuary, shelter.

covet *vb* aim after, desire, long for, yearn for; hanker after, lust after.

covetous *adj* acquisitive, avaricious, close-fisted, grasping, greedy, miserly, niggardly, parsimonious, penurious, rapacious.

cow[1] *n* bovine, heifer.

cow[2] *vb* abash, break, daunt, discourage, dishearten, frighten, intimidate, overawe, subdue.

coward *adj* cowardly, timid. • *n* caitiff, craven, dastard, milksop, poltroon, recreant, skulker, sneak, wheyface.

cowardly *adj* base, chicken-hearted, coward, craven, dastardly, faint-hearted, fearful, lily-livered, mean, pusillanimous, timid, timorous, white-livered, yellow.

cower *vb* bend, cringe, crouch, fawn, shrink, squat, stoop.

coxcomb *n* beau, dandy, dude, exquisite, fop, jackanapes, popinjay, prig.

coy *adj* backward, bashful, demure, diffident, distant, modest, reserved, retiring, self-effacing, shrinking, shy, timid.

coyness *n* affectation, archness, backwardness, bashfulness, coquettishness, demureness, diffidence, evasiveness, modesty, primness, reserve, shrinking, shyness, timidity.

cozen *vb* beguile, cheat, chouse, circumvent, deceive, defraud, diddle, dupe, gull, overreach, swindle, trick, victimize.

cozy *see* **cosy**.

crabbed *adj* acrid, rough, sore, tart; acrimonious, cantankerous, captious, caustic, censorious, churlish, cross, growling, harsh, ill-tempered, morose, peevish, petulant, snappish, snarling, splenetic, surly, testy, touchy, waspish; difficult, intractable, perplexing, tough, trying, unmanageable.

crabbedness *n* acridity, acridness, roughness, sourness, tartness; acerbity, acrimonious, asperity, churlishness, harshness, ill-tempered, moodiness, moroseness, sullenness; difficulty, intractability, perplexity.

crack *vb* break; chop, cleave, split; snap; craze, madden; boast, brag, bluster, crow, gasconade, vapour, vaunt. • *adj* capital, excellent, first-class, first-rate, tip-top. • *n* breach, break, chink, cleft, cranny, crevice, fissure, fracture, opening, rent, rift, split; burst, clap, explosion, pop, report; snap.

cracked *adj* broken, crackled, split; crack-brained, crazed, crazy, demented, deranged, flighty, insane.

crackle *vb* crepitate, decrepitate, snap.

craft *n* ability, aptitude, cleverness, dexterity, expertness, power, readiness, skill, tact, talent; artifice, artfulness, cunning, craftiness, deceitfulness, deception, guile, shrewdness, subtlety; art, avocation, business, calling, employment, handicraft, trade, vocation; vessel.

crafty *adj* arch, artful, astute, cunning, crooked, deceitful, designing, fraudulent, guileful, insidious, intriguing, scheming, shrewd, sly, subtle, tricky, wily.

crag *n* rock; neck, throat.

craggy *adj* broken, cragged, jagged, rough, rugged, scraggy, uneven.

cram *vb* fill, glut, gorge, satiate, stuff; compress, crowd, overcrowd, press, squeeze; coach, grind.

cramp *vb* convulse; check, clog, confine, hamper, hinder, impede, obstruct, restrain, restrict. • *n* convulsion, crick, spasm; check, restraint, restriction, obstruction.

crank *vb* bend, crankle, crinkle, turn, twist, wind. • *n* bend, quirk, turn, twist, winding.

cranny *n* breach, break, chink, cleft, crack, crevice, fissure, gap, hole, interstice, nook, opening, rift.

crapulous *adj* crapulent, drunk, drunken, inebriated, intoxicated, tipsy.

crash *vb* break, shatter, shiver, smash, splinter. • *adj* emergency, fast, intensive, rushed, speeded-up. • *n* clang, clash, collision concussion, jar.

crass *adj* coarse, gross, raw, thick, unabated, unrefined.

cravat *n* neckcloth, neckerchief, necktie.

crave *vb* ask, beg, beseech, entreat, implore, petition, solicit, supplicate; desire, hanker after, long for, need, want, yearn for.

craven *n* coward, dastard, milk-sop, poltroon, recreant. • *adj* cowardly, chicken-hearted, lily-livered, pusillanimous, yellow.

craving *n* hankering, hungering, longing, yearning.

craw *n* crop, gullet, stomach, throat.

craze *vb* bewilder, confuse, dement, derange, madden; disorder, impair, weaken. • *n* fashion, mania, mode, novelty.

crazy *adj* broken, crank, rickety, shaky, shattered, tottering; crack-brained, delirious, demented, deranged, distracted, idiotic, insane, lunatic, mad, silly.

create *vb* originate, procreate; cause, design, fashion, form, invent, occasion, produce; appoint, constitute, make.

creation *n* formation, invention, origination, production; cosmos, universe; appointment, constitution, establishment, nomination.

creator *n* author, designer, inventor, fashioner, maker, originator; god.

creature *n* animal, beast, being, body, brute, man, person; dependant, hanger-on, minion, parasite, retainer, vassal; miscreant, wretch.

credence *n* acceptance, belief, confidence, credit, faith, reliance, trust.

credentials *npl* certificate, diploma, missive, passport, recommendation, testament, testimonial, title, voucher, warrant.

credibility *n* believability, plausibility, tenability, , trustworthiness.

credit *vb* accept, believe, trust; loan, trust. • *n* belief, confidence, credence, faith, reliance, trust; esteem, regard, reputableness, reputation; influence, power; honour, merit; loan, trust.

creditable *adj* estimable, honourable, meritorious, praiseworthy, reputable, respectable.

credulity *n* credulousness, gullibility, silliness, simplicity, stupidity.

credulous *adj* dupable, green, gullible, naive, over-trusting, trustful, uncritical, unsuspecting, unsuspicious.

creed *n* belief, confession, doctrine, dogma, opinion, profession, tenet.

creek *n* bay, bight, cove, fjord, inlet; rivulet, streamlet.

creep *vb* crawl; steal upon; cringe, fawn, grovel, insinuate. • *n* crawl, scrabble, scramble; fawner, groveller, sycophant, toady.

crenate *adj* indented, notched, scalloped.

crepitate *vb* crack, crackle, decrepitate, snap.

crest *n* comb, plume, topknot, tuft; apex, crown, head, ridge, summit, top; arms, badge, bearings.

crestfallen *adj* chap-fallen, dejected, depressed, despondent, discouraged, disheartened, dispirited, downcast, downhearted, low-spirited, melancholy, sad.

crevice *n* chink, cleft, crack, cranny, fissure, fracture, gap, hole, interstice, opening, rent, rift.

crew *n* company, complement, hands; company, corps, gang, horde, mob, party, posse, set, squad, team, throng.

crib *vb* cage, confine, encage, enclose, imprison; pilfer, purloin. • *n* manger, rack; bin, bunker; plagiarism, plunder, theft.

crick *vb* jar, rick, wrench, wrick. • *n* convulsion, cramp, jarring, spasm, rick, wrench, wrick.

crime *n* felony, misdeed, misdemeanour, offence, violation; delinquency, fault, guilt, iniquity, sin, transgression, unrighteousness, wickedness, wrong.

criminal *adj* culpable, felonious, flagitious, guilty, illegal, immoral, iniquitous, nefarious, unlawful, vicious, wicked, wrong. • *n* convict, culprit, delinquent, felon, malefactor, offender, sinner, transgressor.

criminate *vb* accuse, arraign, charge, convict, impeach, indict; implicate, involve.

crimp *vb* crisp, curl.

cringe *vb* bend, bow, cower, crouch, fawn, grovel, kneel, sneak, stoop, truckle.

cripple *vb* cramp, destroy, disable, enfeeble, impair, lame, maim, mutilate, paralyse, ruin, weaken.

crisis *n* acme, climax, height; conjuncture, emergency, exigency, juncture, pass, pinch, push, rub, strait, urgency.

crisp *adj* brittle, curled, friable, frizzled.

criterion *n* canon, gauge, measure, principle, proof, rule, standard, test, touchstone.

critic *n* arbiter, caviller, censor, connoisseur, judge, nit-picker, reviewer.

critical *adj* accurate, exact, nice; captious, carping, cavilling, censorious, exacting; crucial, decisive, determining, important, turning: dangerous, dubious, exigent, hazardous, imminent, momentous, precarious, ticklish.

criticism *n* analysis, animadversion, appreciation, comment, critique, evaluation, judgement, review, strictures.

criticize *vb* appraise, evaluate, examine, judge.

croak *vb* complain, groan, grumble, moan, mumble, repine; die.

crone *n* hag, witch.

crony *n* ally, associate, chum, friend, mate, mucker, pal.

crook *vb* bend, bow, curve, incurvate, turn, wind. • *n* bend, curvature, flexion, turn; artifice, machination, trick; criminal, thief, villain.

crooked *adj* angular, bent, bowed, curved, winding, zigzag; askew, aslant, awry, deformed, disfigured, distorted, twisted, wry; crafty, deceitful, devious, dishonest, dishonourable, fraudulent,

insidious, intriguing, knavish, tricky, underhanded, unfair, unscrupulous.

crop *vb* gather, mow, pick, pluck, reap; browse, nibble; clip, curtail, lop, reduce, shorten. • *n* harvest, produce, yield.

cross *vb* intersect, pass over, traverse; hinder, interfere, obstruct, thwart; interbred, intermix. • *adj* transverse; cantankerous, captious, crabbed, churlish, crusty, cynical, fractious, fretful, grouchy, ill-natured, ill-tempered, irascible, irritable, morose, peevish, pettish, petulant, snappish, snarling, sour, spleeny, splenetic, sulky, sullen, surly, testy, touchy, waspish. • *n* crucifix, gibbet, rood; affliction, misfortune, trial, trouble, vexation; cross-breeding, hybrid, intermixture.

cross-grained *adj* cantankerous, headstrong, obdurate, peevish, perverse, refractory, stubborn, untractable, wayward.

crossing *n* intersection, overpass, traversing, under-pass.

crossways, crosswise *adv* across, over, transversely.

crotchet *n* caprice, fad, fancy, freak, quirk, vagary, whim, whimsy.

crouch *vb* cower, cringe, fawn, truckle; crouch, kneel, stoop, squat; bow, curtsy, genuflect.

croup *n* buttocks, crupper, rump.

crow *vb* bluster, boast, brag, chuckle, exult, flourish, gasconade, swagger, triumph, vapour, vaunt.

crowd *vb* compress, cram, jam, pack, press; collect, congregate, flock, herd, huddle, swarm. • *n* assembly, company, concourse, flock, herd, horde, host, jam, multitude, press, throng; mob, pack, populace, rabble, rout.

crown *vb* adorn, dignify, honour; recompense, requite, reward; cap, complete, consummate, finish, perfect. • *n* bays, chaplet, coronal, coronet, garland, diadem, laurel, wreath; monarchy, royalty, sovereignty; diadem; dignity, honour, recompense, reward; apex, crest, summit, top.

crowning *adj* completing, consummating, dignifying, finishing, perfecting.

crucial *adj* intersecting, transverse; critical, decisive, searching, severe, testing, trying.

crude *adj* raw, uncooked, undressed, unworked; harsh, immature, rough, unripe; crass, coarse, unrefined; awkward, immature, indigestible, rude, uncouth, unpolished, unpremeditated.

cruel *adj* barbarous, blood-thirsty, dire, fell, ferocious, inexorable, hard-hearted, inhuman, merciless, pitiless, relentless, ruthless, sanguinary, savage, truculent, uncompassionate, unfeeling, unmerciful, unrelenting; bitter, cold, hard, severe, sharp, unfeeling.

crumble *vb* bruise, crush, decay, disintegrate, perish, pound, pulverize, triturate.

crumple *vb* rumple, wrinkle.

crush *vb* bruise, compress, contuse, squash, squeeze; bray, comminute, crumble, disintegrate, mash; demolish, raze, shatter; conquer, overcome, overpower, overwhelm, quell, subdue.

crust *n* coat, coating, incrustation, outside, shell, surface.

crusty *adj* churlish, crabbed, cross, cynical, fretful, forward, morose, peevish, pettish, petulant, snappish, snarling, surly, testy, touchy, waspish; friable, hard, short.

cry *vb* call, clamour, exclaim; blubber, snivel, sob, wail, weep, whimper; bawl, bellow, hoot, roar, shout, vociferate, scream, screech, squawk, squall, squeal, yell; announce, blazon, proclaim, publish. • *n* acclamation, clamour, ejaculation, exclamation, outcry; crying, lament, lamentation, plaint, weeping; bawl, bellow, howl, roar, scream, screech, shriek, yell; announcement, proclamation, publication.

crypt *n* catacomb, tomb, vault.

cuddle *vb* cosset, nestle, snuggle, squat; caress, embrace, fondle, hug, pet. • *n* caress, embrace, hug.

cudgel *vb* bang, baste, batter, beat, cane, drub, thrash, thump. • *n* bastinado, baton, bludgeon, club, shillelagh, stick, truncheon.

cue *vb* intimate, prompt, remind, sign, signal. • *n* catchword, hint, intimation, nod, prompting, sign, signal, suggestion.

cuff *vb* beat, box, buffet, knock, pummel, punch, slap, smack, strike, thump. • *n* blow, box, punch, slap, smack, strike, thump.

cul-de-sac *n* alley, dead end, impasse, pocket.

cull *vb* choose, elect, pick, select; collect, gather, glean, pluck.

culmination *n* acme, apex, climax, completion, consummation, crown, summit, top, zenith.

culpability *n* blame, blameworthiness, criminality, culpableness, guilt, remissness, sinfulness.

culpable *adj* blameable, blameworthy, censurable, faulty, guilty, reprehensible, sinful, transgressive, wrong.

culprit *n* delinquent, criminal, evil-doer, felon, malefactor, offender.

cultivate *vb* farm, fertilize, till, work; civilize, develop, discipline, elevate, improve, meliorate, refine, train; investigate, prosecute, pursue, search, study; cherish, foster, nourish, patronize, promote.

culture *n* agriculture, cultivation, farming, husbandry, tillage; cultivation, elevation, improvement, refinement.

cumber *vb* burden, clog, encumber, hamper, impede, obstruct, oppress, overload; annoy, distract, embarrass, harass, perplex, plague, torment, trouble, worry.

cumbersome *adj* burdensome, clumsy, cumbrous, embarrassing, heavy, inconvenient, oppressive, troublesome, unmanageable, unwieldy, vexatious.

cuneiform *adj* cuneate, wedge-shaped.

cunning *adj* artful, astute, crafty, crooked, deceitful, designing, diplomatic, foxy, guileful, intriguing, machiavellian, sharp, shrewd, sly, subtle, tricky, wily; curious, ingenious. • *n* art, artfulness, artifice, astuteness, craft, shrewdness, subtlety; craftiness, chicane, chicanery, deceit, deception, intrigue, slyness.

cup *n* beaker, bowl, chalice, goblet, mug; cupful, draught, potion.

cupboard *n* buffet, cabinet, closet.

cupidity *n* avidity, greed, hankering, longing, lust; acquisitiveness, avarice, covetousness, greediness, stinginess.

curative *adj* healing, medicinal, remedial, restorative.

curator *n* custodian, guardian, keeper, superintendent.

curb *vb* bridle, check, control, hinder, moderate, repress, restrain. • *n* bridle, check, control, hindrance, rein, restraint.

cure *vb* alleviate, correct, heal, mend, remedy, restore; kipper, pickle, preserve. • *n* antidote, corrective, help, remedy, reparative, restorative, specific; alleviation, healing, restorative.

curiosity *n* interest, inquiringness, inquisitiveness; celebrity, curio, marvel, novelty, oddity, phenomenon, rarity, sight, spectacle, wonder.

curious *adj* interested, inquiring, inquisitive, meddling, peering, prying, scrutinizing; extraordinary, marvellous, novel, queer, rare, singular, strange, unique, unusual; cunning, elegant, fine, finished, neat, skilful, well-wrought.

curl *vb* coil, twist, wind, writhe; bend, buckle, ripple, wave. • *n* curlicue, lovelock, ringlet; flexure, sinuosity, undulation, wave, waving, winding.

curmudgeon *n* churl, lick-penny, miser, niggard, screw, scrimp, skinflint.

currency *n* publicity; acceptance, circulation, transmission; bills, coins, money, notes.

current *adj* common, general, popular, rife; circulating, passing; existing, instant, present, prevalent, widespread. • *n* course, progression, river, stream, tide, undertow. • *adv* commonly, generally, popularly, publicly.

curry *vb* comb, dress; beat, cudgel, drub, thrash.

curse *vb* anathematize, damn, denounce, execrate, imprecate, invoke, maledict; blast, blight, destroy, doom; afflict, annoy, harass, injure, plague, scourge, torment, vex; blaspheme, swear. • *n* anathema, ban, denunciation, execration, fulmination, imprecation, malediction, malison; affliction, annoyance, plague, scourge, torment, trouble, vexation; ban, condemnation, penalty, sentence.

cursed *adj* accursed, banned, blighted, curse-laden, unholy; abominable, detestable, execrable, hateful, villainous; annoying, confounded, plaguing, scourging, tormenting, troublesome, vexatious.

cursory *adj* brief, careless, desultory, hasty, passing, rapid, slight, summary, superficial, transient, transitory.

curt *adj* brief, concise, laconic, short, terse; crusty, rude, snappish, tart.

curtail *vb* abridge, dock, lop, retrench, shorten; abbreviate, contract, decrease, diminish, lessen.

curtain *vb* cloak, cover, drape, mantle, screen, shade, shield, veil. • *n* arras, drape, drop, portière, screen, shade.

curvature *n* arcuation, bend, bending, camber, crook, curve, flexure, incurvation.

curve *vb* bend, crook, inflect, turn, twist, wind. • *n* arcuation, bend, bending, camber, crook, flexure, incurvation.

curvet *vb* bound, leap, vault; caper, frisk.

cushion *vb* absorb, damp, dampen, deaden, dull, muffle, mute, soften, subdue, suppress; cradle, pillow, support. • *n* bolster, hassock, pad, pillow, woolsack.

cusp *n* angle, horn, point.

custodian *n* curator, guardian, keeper, sacristan, superintendent, warden.

custody *n* care, charge, guardianship, keeping, safe-keeping, protection, watch, ward; confinement, durance, duress, imprisonment, prison.

custom *n* consuetude, convention, fashion, habit, manner, mode, practice, rule, usage, use, way; form, formality, observation; patronage; duty, impost, tax, toll, tribute.

customary *adj* accustomed, common, consuetudinary, conventional, familiar, fashionable, general, habitual, gnomic, prescriptive, regular, usual, wonted.

cut *vb* chop, cleave, divide, gash, incise, lance, sever, slice, slit, wound; carve, chisel, sculpture; hurt, move, pierce, touch; ignore, slight; abbreviate, abridge, curtail, shorten. • *n* gash, groove, incision, nick, slash, slice, slit; channel, passage; piece, slice; fling, sarcasm, taunt; fashion, form, mode, shape, style.

cutthroat *adj* barbarous, cruel, ferocious, murderous; competitive, exacting, exorbitant, extortionate, rivalling, ruthless, usurious, vying.• *n* assassin, murderer, ruffian.

cutting *adj* keen, sharp; acid, biting, bitter, caustic, piercing, sarcastic, sardonic, satirical, severe, trenchant, wounding.

cycle *n* age, circle, era, period, revolution, round.

Cyclopean *adj* colossal, enormous, gigantic, Herculean, immense, vast.

cynical *adj* captious, carping, censorious, churlish, crabbed, cross, crusty, fretful, ill-natured, ill-tempered, morose, peevish, pettish, petulant, sarcastic, satirical, snappish, snarling, surly, testy, touchy, waspish; contemptuous, derisive, misanthropic, pessimistic, scornful.

cynosure *n* attraction, centre.

cyst *n* pouch, sac.

D

dab *vb* box, rap, slap, strike, tap touch; coat, daub, smear. • *adj* adept, expert, proficient; pat. • *n* lump, mass, pat.

dabble *vb* dip, moisten, soak, spatter, splash, sprinkle, wet; meddle, tamper, trifle.

daft *adj* absurd, delirious, foolish, giddy, idiotic, insane, silly, simple, stupid, witless; frolicsome, merry, mirthful, playful, sportive.

dagger *n* bayonet, dirk, poniard, stiletto.

dainty *adj* delicate, delicious, luscious, nice, palatable, savoury, tender, toothsome; beautiful, charming, choice, delicate, elegant, exquisite, fine, neat; fastidious, finical, finicky, over-nice, particular, scrupulous, squeamish. • *n* delicacy, titbit, treat.

dale *n* bottom, dell, dingle, glen, vale, valley.

dalliance *n* caressing, endearments, flirtation, fondling.

dally *vb* dawdle, fritter, idle, trifle, waste time; flirt, fondle, toy.

damage *vb* harm, hurt, impair, injure, mar. • *n* detriment, harm, hurt, injury, loss, mischief.

damages *npl* compensation, fine, forfeiture, indemnity, reparation, satisfaction.

dame *n* babe, baby, broad, doll, girl; lady, madam, matron, mistress.

damn *vb* condemn, doom, kill, ruin. • *n* bean, curse, fig, hoot, rap, sou, straw, whit.

damnable *adj* abominable, accursed, atrocious, cursed, detestable, hateful, execrable, odious, outrageous.

damp *vb* dampen, moisten; allay, abate, check, discourage, moderate, repress, restrain; chill, cool, deaden, deject, depress, dispirit. • *adj* dank, humid, moist, wet. • *n* dampness, dank, fog, mist, moisture, vapour; chill, dejection, depression.

damper *n* check, hindrance, impediment, obstacle; damp, depression, discouragement, wet blanket.

dandle *vb* amuse, caress, fondle, pet, toss; dance.

danger *n* jeopardy, insecurity, hazard, peril, risk, venture.

dangerous *adj* critical, hazardous, insecure, perilous, risky, ticklish, unsafe.

dangle *vb* drape, hang, pend, sway, swing; fawn.

dank *adj* damp, humid, moist, wet.

dapper *adj* active, agile, alert, brisk, lively, nimble, quick, ready, smart, spry; neat, nice, pretty, spruce, trim.

dapple *vb* diversify, spot, variegate. • *adj* dappled, spotted, variegated.

dare *vb* challenge, defy, endanger, hazard, provoke, risk. • *n* challenge, defiance, gage.

daring *adj* adventurous, bold, brave, chivalrous, courageous, dauntless, doughty, fearless, gallant, heroic, intrepid, valiant, valorous. • *n* adventurousness, boldness, bravery, courage, dauntlessness, doughtiness, fearlessness, intrepidity, undauntedness, valour.

dark *adj* black, cloudy, darksome, dusky, ebony, inky, lightless, lurid, moonless, murky, opaque, overcast, pitchy, rayless, shady, shadowy, starless, sunless, swart, tenebrous, umbrageous, unenlightened, unilluminated; abstruse, cabbalistic, enigmatical, incomprehensible, mysterious, mystic, mystical, obscure, occult, opaque, recondite, transcendental, unillumined, unintelligible; cheerless, discouraging, dismal, disheartening, funereal, gloomy; benighted, darkened, ignorant, rude, unlettered, untaught; atrocious, damnable, infamous, flagitious, foul, horrible, infernal, nefarious, vile, wicked. • *n* darkness, dusk, murkiness, obscurity; concealment, privacy, secrecy; blindness, ignorance.

darken *vb* cloud, dim, eclipse, obscure, shade, shadow; chill, damp, depress, gloom, sadden; benight, stultify, stupefy; obscure, perplex; defile, dim, dull, stain, sully.

darkness *n* blackness, dimness, gloom, obscurity; blindness, ignorance; cheerlessness, despondency, gloom, joylessness; privacy, secrecy.

darling *adj* beloved, cherished, dear, loved, precious, treasured. • *n* dear, favourite, idol, love, sweetheart.

dart *vb* ejaculate, hurl, launch, propel, sling, throw; emit, shoot, dash, rush, scoot, spring.

dash *vb* break, destroy, disappoint, frustrate, ruin, shatter, spoil, thwart; abash, confound, disappoint, surprise; bolt, dart, fly, run, speed, rush. • *n* blow, stroke; advance, onset, rush; infusion, smack, spice, sprinkling, tincture, tinge, touch; flourish, show.

dashing *adj* headlong, impetuous, precipitate, rushing; brilliant, gay, showy, spirited.

dastardly *adj* base, cowardly, coward, cowering, craven, pusillanimous, recreant. • *n* coward, craven, milksop, poltroon, recreant.

data *npl* conditions, facts, information, premises.

date *n* age, cycle, day, generation, time; epoch, era, period; appointment, arrangement, assignation, engagement, interview, rendezvous, tryst; catch, steady, sweetheart.

daub *vb* bedaub, begrime, besmear, blur, cover, deface, defile, grime, plaster, smear, smudge, soil, sully. • *n* smear, smirch, smudge.

daunt *vb* alarm, appal, check, cow, deter, discourage, frighten, intimate, scare, subdue, tame, terrify, thwart.

dauntless *adj* bold, brave, chivalrous, courageous, daring, doughty, gallant, heroic, indomitable, intrepid, unaffrighted, unconquerable, undaunted, undismayed, valiant, valorous.

dawdle *vb* dally, delay, fiddle, idle, lag, loiter, potter, trifle.

dawn *vb* appear, begin, break, gleam, glimmer, open, rise. • *n* daybreak, dawning, cockcrow, sunrise, sun-up.

day *n* daylight, sunlight, sunshine; age, epoch, generation, lifetime, time.

daze *vb* blind, dazzle; bewilder, confound, confuse, perplex, stun, stupefy. • *n* bewilderment, confusion, discomposure, perturbation, pother; coma, stupor, swoon, trance.

dazzle *vb* blind, daze; astonish, confound, overpower, surprise. • *n* brightness, brilliance, splendour.

dead *adj* breathless, deceased, defunct, departed, gone, inanimate, lifeless; apathetic, callous, cold, dull, frigid, indifferent, inert, lukewarm, numb, obtuse, spiritless, torpid, unfeeling; flat, insipid, stagnant, tasteless, vapid; barren, inactive, sterile, unemployed, unprofitable, useless. • *adv* absolutely, completely, downright, fundamentally, quite; direct, directly, due, exactly, just, right, squarely, straight. • *n* depth, midst; hush, peace, quietude, silence, stillness.

deaden *vb* abate, damp, dampen, dull, impair, muffle, mute, restrain, retard, smother, weaken; benumb, blunt, hebetate, obtund, paralyse.

deadly *adj* deleterious, destructive, fatal, lethal, malignant, mortal, murderous, noxious, pernicious, poisonous, venomous; implacable, mortal, rancorous, sanguinary.

deal *vb* allot, apportion, assign, bestow, dispense, distribute, divide, give, reward, share; bargain, trade, traffic, treat with. • *n* amount, degree, distribution, extent, lot, portion, quantity, share; bargain, transaction.

dear *adj* costly, expensive, high-priced; beloved, cherished, darling, esteemed, precious, treasured. • *n* beloved, darling, deary, honey, love, precious, sweet, sweetie, sweetheart.

dearth *n* deficiency, insufficiency, scarcity; famine, lack, need, shortage, want.

death *n* cessation, decease, demise, departure, destruction, dissolution, dying, end, exit, mortality, passing.

deathless *adj* eternal, everlasting, immortal, imperishable, undying; boring, dull, turgid.

debacle *n* breakdown, cataclysm, collapse; rout, stampede.

debar *vb* blackball, deny, exclude, hinder, prevent, prohibit, restrain, shut out, stop, withhold.

debase *vb* adulterate, alloy, depress, deteriorate; impair, injure, lower, pervert, reduce, vitiate; abase, degrade, disgrace, dishonour, humble, humiliate, mortify, shame; befoul, contaminate, corrupt, defile, foul, pollute, soil, taint.

debate *vb* argue, canvass, contest, discuss, dispute; contend, deliberate, wrangle. • *n* controversy, discussion, disputation; altercation, contention, contest, dispute, logomachy.

debauch *vb* corrupt, deprave, pollute, vitiate; deflower, ravish, seduce, violate. • *n* carousal, orgy, revel, saturnalia.

debauchery *n* dissipation, dissoluteness, excesses, intemperance; debauch, excess, intemperance, lewdness, licentiousness, lust; bacchanal, carousal, compotation, indulgence, orgies, potation, revelry, revels, saturnalia, spree.

debilitate *vb* enervate, enfeeble, exhaust, prostrate, relax, weaken.

debility *n* enervation, exhaustion, faintness, feebleness, frailty, imbecility, infirmity, languor, prostration, weakness.

debonair *adj* affable, civil, complaisant, courteous, easy, gracious, kind, obliging, polite, refined, urbane, well-bred.

debris *n* detritus, fragments, remains, rubbish, rubble, ruins, wreck, wreckage.

debt *n* arrears, debit, due, liability, obligation; fault, misdoing, offence, shortcoming, sin, transgression, trespass.

decadence *n* caducity, decay, declension, decline, degeneracy, degeneration, deterioration, fall, retrogression.

decamp *vb* abscond, bolt, escape, flee, fly.

decapitate *vb* behead, decollate, guillotine.

decay *vb* decline, deteriorate, disintegrate, fail, perish, wane, waste, wither; decompose, putrefy, rot. • *n* caducity, decadence, declension, decline, decomposition, decrepitude, degeneracy, degeneration, deterioration, dilapidation, disintegration, fading, failing, perishing, putrefaction, ruin, wasting, withering.

deceased *adj* dead, defunct, departed, gone, late, lost.

deceit *n* artifice, cheating, chicanery, cozenage, craftiness, deceitfulness, deception, double-dealing, duplicity, finesse, fraud, guile, hypocrisy, imposition, imposture, pretence, sham, treachery, tricky, underhandedness, wile.

deceitful *adj* counterfeit, deceptive, delusive, fallacious, hollow, illusive, illusory, insidious, misleading; circumventive, cunning, designing, dissembling, dodgy, double-dealing, evasive, false, fraudulent, guileful, hypocritical, insincere, tricky, underhanded, wily.

deceive *vb* befool, beguile, betray, cheat, chouse, circumvent, cozen, defraud, delude, disappoint, double-cross, dupe, ensnare, entrap, fool, gull, hoax, hoodwink, humbug, mislead, outwit, overreach, trick.

deceiver *n* charlatan, cheat, humbug, hypocrite, knave, impostor, pretender, rogue, sharper, trickster.

decent *adj* appropriate, becoming, befitting, comely, seemly, decorous, fit, proper, seemly; chaste, delicate, modest, pure; moderate, passable, respectable, tolerable.

deception *n* artifice, cheating, chicanery, cozenage, craftiness, deceitfulness, deception, double-dealing, duplicity, finesse, fraud, guile, hoax, hypocrisy, imposition, imposture, pretence, sham, treachery, trick, underhandedness, wile; cheat, chouse, ruse, stratagem, wile.

deceptive *adj* deceitful, deceiving, delusive, disingenuous, fallacious, false, illusive, illusory, misleading.

decide *vb* close, conclude, determine, end, settle, terminate; resolve; adjudge, adjudicate, award.

decided *adj* determined, firm, resolute, unhesitating, unwavering; absolute, categorical, positive, unequivocal; certain, clear, indisputable, undeniable, unmistakable, unquestionable.

deciduous *adj* caducous, nonperennial, temporary.

decipher *vb* explain, expound, interpret, reveal, solve, unfold, unravel; read.

decision *n* conclusion, determination, judgement, settlement; adjudication, award, decree, pronouncement, sentence; firmness, resolution.

decisive *adj* conclusive, determinative, final.

deck *vb* adorn, array, beautify, decorate, embellish, grace, ornament; apparel, attire, bedeck, clothe, dress, robe.

declaim *vb* harangue, mouth, rant, speak, spout.

declamation *n* declaiming, haranguing, mouthing, ranting, spouting.

declamatory *adj* bombastic, discursive, fustian, grandiloquent, high-flown, high-sounding, incoherent, inflated, pompous, pretentious, rhetorical, swelling, turgid.

declaration *n* affirmation, assertion, asseveration, averment, avowal, protestation, statement; announcement, proclamation, publication.

declaratory *adj* affirmative, annunciatory, assertive, declarative, definite, enunciative, enunciatory, expressive; explanatory, expository.

declare *vb* advertise, affirm, announce, assert, asseverate, aver, blazon, bruit, proclaim, promulgate, pronounce, publish, state, utter.

declension *n* decadence, decay, decline, degeneracy, deterioration, diminution; inflection, variation; declination, nonacceptance, refusal.

declination *n* bending, descent, inclination; decadence, decay, decline, degeneracy, degeneration, degradation, deterioration, diminution; aberration, departure, deviation, digression, divagation, divergence; declinature, nonacceptance, refusal.

decline *vb* incline, lean, slope; decay, droop, fail, flag, languish, pine, sink; degenerate, depreciate, deteriorate; decrease, diminish, dwindle, fade, ebb, lapse, lessen, wane; avoid, refuse, reject; inflect, vary. • *n* decadence, decay, declension, declination, degeneracy, deterioration, diminution, wane; atrophy, consumption, marasmus, phthisis; declivity, hill, incline, slope.

declivity *n* declination, descent, incline, slope.

decompose *vb* analyse, disintegrate, dissolve, distil, resolve, separate; corrupt, decay, putrefy, rot.

decomposition *n* analysis, break-up, disintegration, resolution; caries, corruption, crumbling, decay, disintegration, dissolution, putrescence, rotting.

decorate *vb* adorn, beautify, bedeck, deck, embellish, enrich, garnish, grace, ornament.

decoration *n* adorning, beautifying, bedecking, decking, enriching, garnishing, ornamentation, ornamenting; adornment, enrichment, embellishment, ornament.

decorous *adj* appropriate, becoming, befitting, comely, decent, fit, suitable, proper, sedate, seemly, staid.

decorum *n* appropriate behaviour, courtliness, decency, deportment, dignity, gravity, politeness, propriety, sedateness, seemliness.

decoy *vb* allure, deceive, ensnare, entice, entrap, inveigle, lure, seduce, tempt. • *n* allurement, lure, enticement.

decrease *vb* abate, contract, decline, diminish, dwindle, ebb, lessen, subside, wane; curtail, diminish, lessen, lower, reduce, retrench. • *n* abatement, contraction, declension, decline, decrement, diminishing, diminution, ebb, ebbing, lessening, reduction, subsidence, waning.

decree *vb* adjudge, appoint, command, decide, determine, enact, enjoin, order, ordain. • *n* act, command, edict, enactment, fiat, law, mandate, order, ordinance, precept, regulation, statute.

decrement *n* decrease, diminution, lessening, loss, waste.

decrepit *adj* feeble, effete, shattered, wasted, weak; aged, crippled, superannuated.

decry *vb* abuse, belittle, blame, condemn, denounce, depreciate, detract, discredit, disparage, run down, traduce, underrate, undervalue.

dedicate *vb* consecrate, devote, hallow, sanctify; address, inscribe.

deduce *vb* conclude, derive, draw, gather, infer.

deducible *adj* derivable, inferable.

deduct *vb* remove, subtract, withdraw; abate, detract.

deduction *n* removal, subtraction, withdrawal; abatement, allowance, defalcation, discount, rebate, reduction, reprise; conclusion, consequence, corollary, inference.

deed *n* achievement, act, action, derring-do, exploit, feat, performance; fact, truth, reality; charter, contract, document, indenture, instrument, transfer.

deem *vb* account, believe, conceive, consider, count, estimate, hold, imagine, judge, regard, suppose, think; fancy, opine.

deep *adj* abysmal, extensive, great, profound; abstruse, difficult, hard, intricate, knotty, mysterious, recondite, unfathomable; astute, cunning, designing, discerning, intelligent, insidious, penetrating, sagacious, shrewd; absorbed, engrossed; bass, grave, low; entire, great, heartfelt, thorough. • *n* main, ocean, water, sea; abyss, depth, profundity; enigma, mystery, riddle; silence, stillness.

deeply *adv* profoundly; completely, entirely, extensively, greatly, thoroughly; affectingly, distressingly, feelingly, mournfully, sadly.

deface *vb* blotch, deform, disfigure, injure, mar, mutilate, obliterate, soil, spoil, sully, tarnish.

de facto *adj* actual, real. • *adv* actually, in effect, in fact, really, truly.

defalcate *vb* abate, curtail, retrench, lop.

defalcation *n* abatement, deduction, diminution, discount, reduction; default, deficiency, deficit, shortage, shortcoming; embezzlement, fraud.

defamation *n* abuse, aspersion, back-biting, calumny, detraction, disparagement, libel, obloquy, opprobrium, scandal, slander.

defamatory *adj* abusive, calumnious, libellous, slanderous.

defame *vb* abuse, asperse, blacken, belie, besmirch, blemish, calumniate, detract, disgrace, dishonour, libel, malign, revile, slander, smirch, traduce, vilify.

default *vb* defalcate, dishonour, fail, repudiate, welsh. • *n* defalcation, failure, lapse, neglect, offence, omission, oversight, shortcoming ; defect, deficiency, deficit, delinquency, destitution, fault, lack, want.

defaulter *n* delinquent, embezzler, offender, peculator.

defeat *vb* beat, checkmate, conquer, discomfit, overcome, overpower, overthrow, repulse, rout, ruin, vanquish; baffle, balk, block, disappoint, disconcert, foil, frustrate, thwart. • *n* discomfiture, downfall, overthrow, repulse, rout, vanquishment; bafflement, checkmate, frustration.

defect *vb* abandon, desert, rebel, revolt. • *n* default, deficiency, destitution, lack, shortcoming, spot, taint, want; blemish, blotch, error, flaw, imperfection, mistake; failing, fault, foible.

defection *n* abandonment, desertion, rebellion, revolt; apostasy, backsliding, dereliction.

defective *adj* deficient, inadequate, incomplete, insufficient, scant, short; faulty, imperfect, marred.

defence *n* defending, guarding, holding, maintaining, maintenance, protection; buckler, bulwark, fortification, guard, protection, rampart, resistance, shield; apology, excuse, justification, plea, vindication.

defenceless *adj* exposed, helpless, unarmed, unprotected, unguarded, unshielded, weak.

defend *vb* cover, fortify, guard, preserve, protect, safeguard, screen, secure, shelter, shield; assert, espouse, justify, maintain, plead, uphold, vindicate.

defender *n* asserter, maintainer, pleader, upholder; champion, protector, vindicator.

defer[1] *vb* adjourn, delay, pigeonhole, procrastinate, postpone, prorogue, protract, shelve, table.

defer[2] *vb* abide by, acknowledge, bow to, give way, submit, yield; admire, esteem, honour, regard, respect.

deference *n* esteem, homage, honour, obeisance, regard, respect, reverence, veneration; complaisance, consideration; obedience, submission.

deferential *adj* respectful, reverential.

defiance *n* challenge, daring; contempt, despite, disobedience, disregard, opposition, spite.

defiant *adj* contumacious, recalcitrant, resistant; bold, courageous, resistant.

deficiency *n* dearth, default, deficit, insufficiency, lack, meagreness, scantiness, scarcity, shortage, shortness, want; defect, error, failing, falling, fault, foible, frailty, imperfection, infirmity, weakness.

deficient *adj* defective, faulty, imperfect, inadequate, incomplete, insufficient, lacking, scant, scanty, scarce, short, unsatisfactory, wanting.

deficit *n* deficiency, lack, scarcity, shortage, shortness.

defile[1] *vb* dirty, foul, soil, stain, tarnish; contaminate, debase, poison, pollute, sully, taint, vitiate; corrupt, debauch, deflower, ravish, seduce, violate.

defile[2] *vb* file, march, parade, promenade. • *n* col, gorge, pass, passage, ravine, strait.

define *vb* bound, circumscribe, designate, delimit, demarcate, determine, explain, limit, specify.

definite *adj* defined, determinate, determined, fixed, restricted; assured, certain, clear, exact, explicit, positive, precise, specific, unequivocal.

definitive *adj* categorical, determinate, explicit, express, positive, unconditional; conclusive, decisive, final.

deflect *vb* bend, deviate, diverge, swerve, turn, twist, waver, wind.

deflower *vb* corrupt, debauch, defile, seduce.

deform *vb* deface, disfigure, distort, injure, mar, misshape, ruin, spoil.

deformity *n* abnormality, crookedness, defect, disfigurement, distortion, inelegance, irregularity, malformation, misproportion, misshapenness, monstrosity, ugliness.

defraud *vb* beguile, cheat, chouse, circumvent, cozen, deceive, delude, diddle, dupe, embezzle, gull, overreach, outwit, pilfer, rob, swindle, trick.

defray *vb* bear, discharge, liquidate, meet, pay, settle.

deft *adj* adroit, apt, clever, dab, dextrous, expert, handy, ready, skilful.

defunct *adj* dead, deceased, departed, extinct, gone; abrogated, annulled, cancelled, inoperative.

defy *vb* challenge, dare; brave, contemn, despise, disregard, face, flout, provoke, scorn, slight, spurn.

degeneracy *n* abasement, caducity, corruption, debasement, decadence, decay, declension, decline, decrease, degenerateness, degeneration, degradation, depravation, deterioration; inferiority, meanness, poorness.

degenerate *vb* decay, decline, decrease, deteriorate, retrograde, sink. • *adj* base, corrupt, decayed, degenerated, deteriorated, fallen, inferior, low, mean, perverted.

degeneration *n* debasement, decline, degeneracy, deterioration.

degradation *n* deposition, disgrace, dishonour, humiliation, ignominy; abasement, caducity, corruption, debasement, decadence, decline, degeneracy, degeneration, deterioration, perversion, vitiation.

degrade *vb* abase, alloy, break, cashier, corrupt, debase, demote, discredit, disgrace, dishonour, disparage, downgrade, humiliate, humble, lower, pervert, vitiate; deteriorate, impair, lower, sink.

degree *n* stage, step; class, grade, order, quality, rank, standing, station; extent, measure; division, interval, space.

deify *vb* apotheosize, idolize, glorify, revere; elevate, ennoble, exalt.

deign *vb* accord, condescend, grant, vouchsafe.

deject *vb* depress, discourage, dishearten, dispirit, sadden.

dejected *adj* blue, chapfallen, crestfallen, depressed, despondent, disheartened, dispirited, doleful, downcast, downhearted, gloomy, low-spirited, miserable, sad, wretched.

delay *vb* defer, postpone, procrastinate; arrest, detain, check, hinder, impede, retard, stay, stop; prolong, protract; dawdle, linger, loiter, tarry. • *n* deferment, postponement, procrastination; check, detention, hindrance, impediment, retardation, stoppage; prolonging, protraction; dallying, dawdling, lingering, tarrying, stay, stop.

delectable *adj* agreeable, charming, delightful, enjoyable, gratifying, pleasant, pleasing.

delectation *n* delight, ecstasy, gladness, joy, rapture, ravishment, transport.

delegate *vb* appoint, authorize, mission, depute, deputize, transfer; commit, entrust. • *n* ambassador, commissioner, delegate, deputy, envoy, representative.

delete *vb* cancel, efface, erase, expunge, obliterate, remove.

deleterious *adj* deadly, destructive, lethal, noxious, poisonous; harmful, hurtful, injurious, pernicious, unwholesome.

deliberate *vb* cogitate, consider, consult, meditate, muse, ponder, reflect, ruminate, think, weigh. • *adj* careful, cautious, circumspect, considerate, heedful, purposeful, methodical, thoughtful, wary; well-advised, well-considered; aforethought, intentional, premeditated, purposed, studied.

deliberation *n* caution, circumspection, cogitation, consideration, coolness, meditation, prudence, reflection, thought, thoughtfulness, wariness; purpose.

delicacy *n* agreeableness, daintiness, deliciousness, pleasantness, relish, savouriness; bonne bouche, dainty, tidbit; elegance, fitness, lightness, niceness, nicety, smoothness, softness, tenderness; fragility, frailty, slenderness, slightness, tenderness, weakness; carefulness, discrimination, fastidiousness, finesse, nicety, scrupulousness, sensitivity, subtlety, tact; purity, refinement, sensibility.

delicate *adj* agreeable, delicious, pleasant, pleasing, palatable, savoury; elegant, exquisite, fine, nice; careful, dainty, discriminating, fastidious, scrupulous; fragile, frail, slender, slight, tender, delicate; pure, refined.

delicious *adj* dainty, delicate, luscious, nice, palatable, savoury; agreeable, charming, choice, delightful, exquisite, grateful, pleasant.

delight *vb* charm, enchant, enrapture, gratify, please, ravish, rejoice, satisfy, transport. • *n* charm, delectation, ecstasy, enjoyment, gladness, gratification, happiness, joy, pleasure, rapture, ravishment, satisfaction, transport.

delightful *adj* agreeable, captivating, charming, delectable, enchanting, enjoyable, enrapturing, rapturous, ravishing, transporting.

delineate *vb* design, draw, figure, paint, sketch, trace; depict, describe, picture, portray.

delineation *n* design, draught, drawing, figure, outline, sketch; account, description, picture, portrayal.

delinquency *n* crime, fault, misdeed, misdemeanour, offence, wrong-doing.

delinquent *adj* negligent, offending. • *n* criminal, culprit, defaulter, malefactor, miscreant, misdoer, offender, transgressor, wrong-doer.

delirious *adj* crazy, demented, deranged, frantic, frenzied, light-headed, mad, insane, raving, wandering.

delirium *n* aberration, derangement, frenzy, hallucination, incoherence, insanity, lunacy, madness, raving, wandering.

deliver *vb* emancipate, free, liberate, release; extricate, redeem, rescue, save; commit, give, impart, transfer; cede, grant, relinquish, resign, yield; declare, emit, promulgate, pronounce, speak, utter; deal, discharge.

deliverance *n* emancipation, escape, liberation, redemption, release.

delivery *n* conveyance, surrender; commitment, giving, rendering, transference, transferral, transmission; elocution, enunciation, pronunciation, speech, utterance; childbirth, confinement, labour, parturition, travail.

dell *n* dale, dingle, glen, valley, ravine.

delude *vb* beguile, cheat, chouse, circumvent, cozen, deceive, dupe, gull, misguide, mislead, overreach, trick.

deluge *vb* drown, inundate, overflow, overwhelm, submerge. • *n* cataclysm, downpour, flood, inundation, overflow, rush.

delusion *n* artifice, cheat, clap-trap, deceit, dodge, fetch, fraud, imposition, imposture, ruse, snare, trick, wile; deception, error, fallacy, fancy, hallucination, illusion, mistake, mockery, phantasm.

delusive *adj* deceitful, deceiving, deceptive, fallacious, illusional, illusionary, illusive.

demand *vb* challenge, exact, require; claim, necessitate, require; ask, inquire. • *n* claim, draft, exaction, requirement, requisition; call, want; inquiry, interrogation, question.

demarcation *n* bound, boundary, confine, distinction, division, enclosure, limit, separation.

demeanour *n* air, bearing, behaviour, carriage, deportment, manner, mien.

demented *adj* crack-brained, crazed, crazy, daft, deranged, dotty, foolish, idiotic, infatuated, insane, lunatic.

dementia *n* idiocy, insanity, lunacy.

demerit *n* delinquency, fault, ill-desert.

demise *vb* alienate, consign, convey, devolve, grant, transfer; bequeath, devise, leave, will. • *n* alienation, conveyance, transfer, transference, transmission; death, decease.

demolish *vb* annihilate, destroy, dismantle, level, over-throw, overturn, pulverize, raze, ruin.

demon *n* devil, fiend, kelpie, goblin, troll.

demoniac, demoniacal *adj* demonic, demonical, devilish, diabolic, diabolical, fiendish, hellish, infernal, Mephistophelean, Mephistophelian, satanic; delirious, distracted, frantic, frenzied, feverish, hysterical, mad, overwrought, rabid.

demonstrate *vb* establish, exhibit, illustrate, indicate, manifest, prove, show.

demonstration *n* display, exhibition, manifestation, show.

demonstrative *adj* affectionate, communicative, effusive, emotional, expansive, expressive, extroverted, open, outgoing, passionate, sentimental, suggestive, talkative, unreserved; absolute, apodictic, certain, conclusive, probative; exemplificative, illustrative.

demoralize *vb* corrupt, debase, debauch, deprave, vitiate; depress, discourage, dishearten, weaken.

demulcent *adj* emollient, lenitive, mild, mollifying, sedative, soothing.

demur *vb* halt, hesitate, pause, stop, waver; doubt, object, scruple. • *n* demurral, hesitance, hesitancy, hesitation, objection, pause, qualm, scruple.

demure *adj* prudish; coy, decorous, grave, modest, priggish, prudish, sedate, sober, staid.

den *n* cavern, cave; haunt, lair, resort, retreat.

denial *n* contradiction, controverting, negation; abjuration, disavowal, disclaimer, disowning; disallowance, refusal, rejection.

denizen *n* citizen, dweller, inhabitant, resident.

denominate *vb* call, christen, designate, dub, entitle, name, phrase, style, term.

denomination *n* appellation, designation, name, style, term, title; class, kind, sort; body, persuasion, school, sect.

denote *vb* betoken, connote, designate, imply, indicate, mark, mean, note, show, signify, typify.

dénouement *n* catastrophe, unravelling; consummation, issue, finale, upshot, conclusion, termination.

denounce *vb* menace, threaten; arraign, attack, brand, censure, condemn, proscribe, stigmatize, upbraid; accuse, inform, denunciate.

dense *adj* close, compact, compressed, condensed, thick; dull, slow, stupid.

dent *vb* depress, dint, indent, pit. • *n* depression, dint, indentation, nick, notch.

dentate *adj* notched, serrate, toothed.

denude *vb* bare, divest, strip.

denunciation *n* menace, threat; arraignment, censure, fulmination, invective; exposure.

deny *vb* contradict, gainsay, oppose, refute, traverse; abjure, abnegate, disavow, disclaim, disown, renounce; disallow, refuse, reject, withhold.

depart *vb* absent, disappear, vanish; abandon, decamp, go, leave, migrate, quit, remove, withdraw; decease, die; deviate, diverge, vary.

department *n* district, division, part, portion, province; bureau, function, office, province, sphere, station; branch, division, subdivision.

departure *n* exit, leaving, parting, removal, recession, removal, retirement, withdrawal; abandonment, forsaking; death, decease, demise, deviation, exit.

depend *vb* hang, hinge, turn.

dependant *n* client, hanger-on, henchman, minion, retainer, subordinate, vassal; attendant, circumstance, concomitant, consequence, corollary.

dependence *n* concatenation, connection, interdependence; confidence, reliance, trust; buttress, prop, staff, stay, support, supporter; contingency, need, subjection, subordination.

dependency *n* adjunct, appurtenance; colony, province.

dependent *adj* hanging, pendant; conditioned, contingent, relying, subject, subordinate.

depict *vb* delineate, limn, outline, paint, pencil, portray, sketch; describe, render, represent.

deplete *vb* drain, empty, evacuate, exhaust, reduce.

deplorable *adj* calamitous, distressful, distressing, grievous, lamentable, melancholy, miserable, mournful, pitiable, regrettable, sad, wretched.

deplore *vb* bemoan, bewail, grieve for, lament, mourn, regret.

deploy *vb* display, expand, extend, open, unfold.

deportment *n* air, bearing, behaviour, breeding, carriage, comportment, conduct, demeanour, manner, mien, port.

depose *vb* break, cashier, degrade, dethrone, dismiss, displace, oust, reduce; avouch, declare, depone, testify.

deposit *vb* drop, dump, precipitate; lay, put; bank, hoard, lodge, put, save, store; commit, entrust. • *n* diluvium, dregs, lees, precipitate, precipitation, sediment, settlement, settlings, silt; money, pawn, pledge, security, stake.

depositary *n* fiduciary, guardian, trustee.

deposition *n* affidavit, evidence, testimony; deposit, precipitation, settlement; dethroning, displacement, removal.

depository *n* deposit, depot, storehouse, warehouse.

depot *n* depository, magazine, storehouse, warehouse.

depravation *n* abasement, corruption, deterioration, impairing, injury, vitiation; debasement, degeneracy, degeneration, depravity, impairment.

depraved *adj* abandoned, corrupt, corrupted, debased, debauched, degenerate, dissolute, evil, graceless, hardened, immoral, lascivious, lewd, licentious, lost, perverted, profligate, reprobate, shameless, sinful, vicious, wicked.

depravity *n* corruption, degeneracy, depravedness; baseness, contamination, corruption, corruptness, criminality, demoralization, immorality, iniquity, license, perversion, vice, viciousness, wickedness.

depreciate *vb* underestimate, undervalue, underrate; belittle, censure, decry, degrade, disparage, malign, traduce.

depreciation *n* belittling, censure, derogation, detraction, disparagement, maligning, traducing.

depredation *n* despoiling, devastation, pilfering, pillage, plunder, rapine, robbery, spoliation, theft.

depress *vb* bow, detrude, drop, lower, reduce, sink; abase, abash, degrade, debase, disgrace, humble, humiliate; chill, damp, dampen, deject, discourage, dishearten, dispirit, sadden; deaden, lower.

depression *n* cavity, concavity, dent, dimple, dint, excavation, hollow, hollowness, indentation, pit; blues, cheerlessness, dejection, dejectedness, despondency, disconsolateness, disheartenment, dispiritedness, dole, dolefulness, downheartedness, dumps, gloom, gloominess, hypochondria, melancholy, sadness, vapours; inactivity, lowness, stagnation; abasement, debasement, degradation, humiliation.

deprivation *n* bereavement, dispossession, loss, privation, spoliation, stripping.

deprive *vb* bereave, denude, despoil, dispossess, divest, rob, strip.

depth *n* abyss, deepness, drop, profundity; extent, measure; middle, midst, stillness; astuteness, discernment, penetration, perspicacity, profoundness, profundity, sagacity, shrewdness.

deputation *n* commission, delegation; commissioners, deputies, delegates, delegation, embassies, envoys, legation.

depute *vb* accredit, appoint, authorize, charge, commission, delegate, empower, entrust.

deputy *adj* acting, assistant, vice, subordinate. • *n* agent, commissioner, delegate, envoy, factor, legate, lieutenant, proxy, representative, substitute, viceregent.

derange *vb* confound, confuse, disarrange, disconcert, disorder, displace, madden, perturb, unsettle; discompose, disconcert, disturb, perturb, ruffle, upset; craze, madden, unbalance, unhinge.

derangement *n* confusion, disarrangement, disorder, irregularity; discomposure, disturbance, perturbation; aberration, alienation, delirium, dementia, hallucination, insanity, lunacy, madness, mania.

derelict *adj* abandoned, forsaken, left, relinquished; delinquent, faithless, guilty, neglectful, negligent, unfaithful. • *n* castaway, castoff, outcast, tramp, vagrant, wreck, wretch.

dereliction *n* abandonment, desertion, relinquishement, renunciation; delinquency, failure, faithlessness, fault, neglect, negligence.

deride *vb* chaff, flout, gibe, insult, jeer, lampoon, mock, ridicule, satirize, scoff, scorn, sneer, taunt.

derision *n* contempt, disrespect, insult, laughter, mockery, ridicule, scorn.

derisive *adj* contemptuous, contumelious, mocking, ridiculing, scoffing, scornful.

derivation *n* descent, extraction, genealogy; etymology; deducing, deriving, drawing, getting, obtaining; beginning, foundation, origination, source.

derive *vb* draw, get, obtain, receive; deduce, follow, infer, trace.

derogate *vb* compromise, depreciate, detract, diminish, disparage, lessen.

derogatory *adj* belittling, depreciative, deprecatory, detracting, dishonouring, disparaging, injurious.

descant *vb* amplify, animadvert, dilate, discourse, discuss, enlarge, expatiate. • *n* melody, soprano, treble; animadversion, commentary, remarks; discourse, discussion.

descend *vb* drop, fall, pitch, plunge, sink, swoop; alight, dismount; go, pass, proceed, devolve; derive, issue, originate.

descendants *npl* offspring, issue, posterity, progeny.

descent *n* downrush, drop, fall; descending; decline, declivity, dip, pitch, slope; ancestry, derivation, extraction, genealogy, lineage, parentage, pedigree; assault, attack, foray, incursion, invasion, raid.

describe *vb* define, delineate, draw, illustrate, limn, sketch, specify, trace; detail; depict, explain, narrate, portray, recount, relate, represent; characterize.

description *n* delineation, tracing; account, depiction, explanation, narration, narrative, portrayal, recital, relation, report, representation; class, kind, sort, species.

descry *vb* behold, discover, discern, distinguish, espy, observe, perceive, see; detect, recognize.

desecrate *vb* abuse, pervert, defile, pollute, profane, violate.

desert[1] *n* due, excellence, merit, worth; punishment, reward.

desert[2] *vb* abandon, abscond, forsake, leave, quit, relinquish, renounce, resign, quit, vacate.

desert[3] *adj* barren, desolate, forsaken, lonely, solitary, uncultivated, uninhabited, unproductive, untilled, waste, wild.

deserted *adj* abandoned, forsaken, relinquished.

deserter *n* abandoner, forsaker, quitter, runaway; apostate, backslider, fugitive, recreant, renegade, revolter, traitor, turncoat.

desertion *n* abandonment, dereliction, recreancy, relinquishment.

deserve *vb* earn, gain, merit, procure, win.

desiderate *vb* desire, lack, miss, need, want.

design *vb* brew, concoct, contrive, devise, intend, invent, mean, plan, project, scheme; intend, mean, purpose; delineate, describe, draw, outline, sketch, trace. • *n* aim, device, drift, intent,

intention, mark, meaning, object, plan, proposal, project, purport, purpose, scheme, scope; delineation, draught, drawing, outline, plan, sketch; adaptation, artifice, contrivance, invention, inventiveness.

designate *vb* denote, distinguish, indicate, particularize, select, show, specify, stipulate; characterize, define, describe; call, christen, denominate, dub, entitle, name, style; allot, appoint, christen.

designation *n* indication, particularization, selection, specification; class, description, kind; appellation, denomination, name, style, title.

designing *adj* artful, astute, crafty, crooked, cunning, deceitful, insidious, intriguing, Machiavellian, scheming, sly, subtle, treacherous, trickish, tricky, unscrupulous, wily.

desirable *adj* agreeable, beneficial, covetable, eligible, enviable, good, pleasing, preferable.

desire *vb* covet, crave, desiderate, fancy, hanker after, long for, lust after, want, wish, yearn for; ask, entreat, request, solicit. • *n* eroticism, lasciviousness, libidinousness, libido, lust, lustfulness, passion; eagerness, fancy, hope, inclination, mind, partiality, penchant, pleasure, volition, want, wish.

desirous *adj* avid, eager, desiring, longing, solicitous, wishful.

desist *vb* cease, discontinue, forbear, pause, stay, stop.

desolate *vb* depopulate, despoil, destroy, devastate, pillage, plunder, ravage, ruin, sack. • *adj* bare, barren, bleak, desert, forsaken, lonely, solitary, unfrequented, uninhabited, waste, wild; companionable, lonely, lonesome, solitary; desolated, destroyed, devastated, ravaged, ruined; cheerless, comfortless, companionless, disconsolate, dreary, forlorn, forsaken, miserable, wretched.

desolation *n* destruction, devastation, havoc, ravage, ruin; barrenness, bleakness, desolateness, dreariness, loneliness, solitariness, solitude, wildness; gloom, gloominess, misery, sadness, unhappiness, wretchedness.

despair *vb* despond, give up, lose hope. • *n* dejection, desperation, despondency, disheartenment, hopelessness.

despatch *see* **dispatch**.

desperado *n* daredevil, gangster, marauder, ruffian, thug, tough.

desperate *adj* despairing, despondent, desponding, hopeless; forlorn, irretrievable; extreme; audacious, daring, foolhardy, frantic, furious, headstrong, precipitate, rash, reckless, violent, wild, wretched; extreme, great, monstrous, prodigious, supreme.

desperation *n* despair, hopelessness; fury, rage.

despicable *adj* abject, base, contemptible, degrading, low, mean, paltry, pitiful, shameful, sordid, vile, worthless.

despise *vb* contemn, disdain, disregard, neglect, scorn, slight, spurn, undervalue.

despite *n* malevolence, malice, malignity, spite; contempt, contumacy, defiance. • *prep* notwithstanding.

despoil *vb* bereave, denude, deprive, dispossess, divest, strip; devastate, fleece, pillage, plunder, ravage, rifle, rob.

despond *vb* despair, give up, lose hope, mourn, sorrow.

despondency *n* blues, dejection, depression, discouragement, gloom, hopelessness, melancholy, sadness.

despondent *adj* dejected, depressed, discouraged, disheartened, dispirited, low-spirited, melancholy.

despot *n* autocrat, dictator; oppressor, tyrant.

despotic *adj* absolute, arrogant, autocratic, dictatorial, imperious; arbitrary, oppressive, tyrannical, tyrannous.

despotism *n* absolutism, autocracy, dictatorship; oppression, tyranny.

destination *n* appointment, decree, destiny, doom, fate, foreordainment, foreordination, fortune, lot, ordination, star; aim, design, drift, end, intention, object, purpose, scope; bourne, goal, harbour, haven, journey's end, resting-place, terminus.

destine *vb* allot, appoint, assign, consecrate, devote, ordain; design, intend, predetermine; decree, doom, foreordain, predestine.

destitute *adj* distressed, indigent, moneyless, necessitous, needy, penniless, penurious, pinched, poor, reduced, wanting.

destitution *n* indigence, need, penury, poverty, privation, want.

destroy *vb* demolish, overthrow, overturn, subvert, raze, ruin; annihilate, dissolve, efface, quench; desolate, devastate, devour, ravage, waste; eradicate, extinguish, extirpate, kill, uproot, slay.

destruction *n* demolition, havoc, overthrow, ruin, subversion; desolation, devastation, holocaust, ravage; annihilation, eradication, extinction, extirpation; death, massacre, murder, slaughter.

destructive *adj* baleful, baneful, deadly, deleterious, detrimental, fatal, hurtful, injurious, lethal, mischievous, noxious, pernicious, ruinous; annihilatory, eradicative, exterminative, extirpative.

desultory *adj* capricious, cursory, discursive, erratic, fitful, inconstant, inexact, irregular, loose, rambling, roving, slight, spasmodic, unconnected, unmethodical, unsettled, unsystematic, vague, wandering.

detach *vb* disengage, disconnect, disjoin, dissever, disunite, divide, part, separate, sever, unfix; appoint, detail, send.

detail *vb* delineate, depict, describe, enumerate, narrate, particularize, portray, recount, rehearse, relate, specify; appoint, detach, send. • *n* account, narration, narrative, recital, relation; appointment, detachment; item, part.

details *npl* facts, minutiae, particulars, parts.

detain *vb* arrest, check, delay, hinder, hold, keep, restrain, retain, stay, stop; confine.

detect *vb* ascertain, catch, descry, disclose, discover, expose, reveal, unmask.

detention *n* confinement, delay, hindrance, restraint, withholding.

deter *vb* debar, discourage, frighten, hinder, prevent, restrain, stop, withhold.

deteriorate *vb* corrupt, debase, degrade, deprave, disgrace, impair, spoil, vitiate; decline, degenerate, depreciate, worsen.

deterioration *n* corruption, debasement, degradation, depravation, vitiation, perversion; caducity, decadence, decay, decline, degeneracy, degeneration, impairment.

determinate *adj* absolute, certain, definite, determined, established, explicit, express, fixed, limited, positive, settled; conclusive, decided, decisive, definitive.

determination *n* ascertainment, decision, deciding, determining, fixing, settlement, settling; conclusion, judgment, purpose, resolution, resolve, result; direction, leaning, tendency; firmness, constancy, effort, endeavour, exertion, grit, persistence, stamina, resoluteness; definition, limitation, qualification.

determine *vb* adjust, conclude, decide, end, establish, fix, resolve, settle; ascertain, certify, check, verify; impel, incline, induce, influence, lead, turn; decide, resolve; condition, define, limit; compel, necessitate.

detest *vb* abhor, abominate, despise, execrate, hate, loathe, nauseate, recoil from.

detestable *adj* abhorred, abominable, accursed, cursed, damnable, execrable, hateful, odious; disgusting, loathsome, nauseating, offensive, repulsive, sickening, vile.

dethrone *vb* depose, uncrown.

detract *vb* abuse, asperse, belittle, calumniate, debase, decry, defame, depreciate, derogate, disparage, slander, traduce, vilify; deprecate, deteriorate, diminish, lessen.

detraction *n* abuse, aspersion, calumny, censure, defamation, depreciation, derogation, disparagement, slander.

detriment *n* cost, damage, disadvantage, evil, harm, hurt, injury, loss, mischief, prejudice.

detrimental *adj* baleful, deleterious, destructive, harmful, hurtful, injurious, mischievous, pernicious, prejudicial.

devastate *vb* desolate, despoil, destroy, lay waste, harry, pillage, plunder, ravage, sack, spoil, strip, waste.

devastation *n* despoiling, destroying, harrying, pillaging, plundering, ravaging, sacking, spoiling, stripping, wasting; desolation, destruction, havoc, pillage, rapine, ravage, ruin, waste.

develop *vb* disentangle, disclose, evolve, exhibit, explicate, uncover, unfold, unravel; cultivate, grow, mature, open, progress.

development *n* disclosure, disentanglement, exhibition, unfolding, unravelling; growth, increase, maturation, maturing; evolution, growth, progression; elaboration, expansion, explication.

deviate *vb* alter, deflect, digress, diverge, sheer off, slew, tack, turn aside, wheel, wheel about; err, go astray, stray, swerve, wander; differ, vary.

deviation *n* aberration, departure, depression, divarication, divergence, turning; alteration, change, difference, variance, variation.

device *n* contraption, contrivance, gadget, invention; design, expedient, plan, project, resort, resource, scheme, shift; artifice, evasion, fraud, manoeuvre, ruse, stratagem, trick, wile; blazon, emblazonment, emblem, sign, symbol, type.

devil *n* archfiend, demon, fiend, goblin; Apollyon, Belial, Deuce, Evil One, Lucifer, Old Harry, Old Nick, Old Serpent, Prince of Darkness, Satan.

devilish *adj* demon, demonic, demonical, demoniac, demoniacal, diabolic, diabolical, fiendish, hellish, infernal, Mephistophelean, Mephistophelian, satanic; atrocious, barbarous, cruel, malevolent, malicious, malign, malignant, wicked.

devilry *n* devilment, diablerie, mischief; devilishness, fiendishness, wickedness.

devious *adj* deviating, erratic, roundabout, wandering; circuitous, confusing, crooked, labyrinthine, mazy, obscure; crooked, disingenuous, misleading, treacherous.

devise *vb* brew, compass, concert, concoct, contrive, dream up, excogitate, imagine, invent, plan, project, scheme; bequeath, demise, leave, will.

devoid *adj* bare, destitute, empty, vacant, void.

devolve *vb* alienate, consign, convey, deliver over, demise, fall, hand over, make over, pass, transfer.

devote *vb* appropriate, consecrate, dedicate, destine; set apart; addict, apply, give up, resign; consign, doom, give over.

devoted *adj* affectionate, attached, loving; ardent, assiduous, earnest, zealous.

devotee *n* bigot, enthusiast, fan, fanatic, zealot.

devotion *n* consecration, dedication, duty; devotedness, devoutness, fidelity, godliness, holiness, piety, religion, religiousness, saintliness, sanctity; adoration, prayer, worship; affection, attachment, love; ardour, devotedness, eagerness, earnestness, fervour, passion, spirit, zeal.

devotional *adj* devout, godly, pious, religious, saintly.

devour *vb* engorge, gorge, gulp down, raven, swallow eagerly, wolf; annihilate, consume, destroy, expend, spend, swallow up, waste.

devout *adj* devotional, godly, holy, pious, religious, saint-like, saintly; earnest, grave, serious, sincere, solemn.

dexterity *n* ability, address, adroitness, aptitude, aptness, art, cleverness, expertness, facility, knack, quickness, readiness, skilfulness, skill, tact.

dexterous, dextrous *adj* able, adept, adroit, apt, deft, clever, expert, facile, handy, nimble-fingered, quick, ready, skilful.

diabolic, diabolical *adj* atrocious, barbarous, cruel, devilish, fiendish, hellish, impious, infernal, malevolent, malign, malignant, satanic, wicked.

diagram *n* chart, delineation, figure, graph, map, outline, plan, sketch.

dialect *n* idiom, localism, provincialism; jargon, lingo, patois, patter; language, parlance, phraseology, speech, tongue.

dialectal *adj* idiomatic, local, provincial.

dialectic, dialectical *adj* analytical, critical, logical, rational, rationalistic.

dialogue *n* colloquy, communication, conference, conversation, converse, intercourse, interlocution; playbook, script, speech, text, words.

diaphanous *adj* clear, filmy, gossamer, pellucid, sheer, translucent, transparent.

diarrhoea *n* (*med*) flux, looseness, purging, relaxation.

diary *n* chronicle, daybook, journal, register.

diatribe *n* disputation, disquisition, dissertation; abuse, harangue, invective, philippic, reviling, tirade.

dictate *vb* bid, direct, command, decree, enjoin, ordain, order, prescribe, require. • *n* bidding, command, decree, injunction, order; maxim, precept, rule.

dictation *n* direction, order, prescription.

dictator *n* autocrat, despot, tyrant.

dictatorial *adj* absolute, unlimited, unrestricted; authoritative, despotic, dictatory, domineering, imperious, overbearing, peremptory, tyrannical.

dictatorship *n* absolutism, authoritarianism, autocracy, despotism, iron rule, totalitarianism, tyranny.

diction *n* expression, language, phraseology, style, vocabulary, wording.

dictionary *n* glossary, lexicon, thesaurus, vocabulary, wordbook; cyclopedia, encyclopedia.

dictum *n* affirmation, assertion, saying; (*law*) award, arbitrament, decision, opinion.

didactic, didactical *adj* educational, instructive, pedagogic, preceptive.

die *vb* decease, demise, depart, expire, pass on; decay, decline, fade, fade out, perish, wither; cease, disappear, vanish; faint, fall, sink.

diet[1] *vb* eat, feed, nourish; abstain, fast, regulate, slim. • *n* aliment, fare, food, nourishment, nutriment, provision, rations, regimen, subsistence, viands, victuals.

diet[2] *n* assembly, congress, convention, convocation, council, parliament.

differ *vb* deviate, diverge, vary; disagree, dissent; bicker, contend, dispute, quarrel, wrangle.

difference *n* contrariety, contrast, departure, deviation, disagreement, disparity, dissimilarity, dissimilitude, divergence, diversity, heterogeneity, inconformity, nuance, opposition, unlikeness, variation; alienation, altercation, bickering, breach, contention, contest, controversy, debate, disaccord, disagreement, disharmony, dispute, dissension, embroilment, falling out, irreconcilability, jarring, misunderstanding, quarrel, rupture, schism, strife, variance, wrangle; discrimination, distinction.

different *adj* distinct, nonidentical, separate, unlike; contradistinct, contrary, contrasted, deviating, disagreeing, discrepant, dissimilar, divergent, diverse, incompatible, incongruous, unlike, variant, various; divers, heterogeneous, manifold, many, sundry.

difficult *adj* arduous, exacting, hard, Herculean, stiff, tough, uphill; abstruse, complex, intricate, knotty, obscure, perplexing; austere, rigid, unaccommodating, uncompliant, unyielding; dainty, fastidious, squeamish.

difficulty *n* arduousness, laboriousness; bar, barrier, crux, deadlock, dilemma, embarrassment, emergency, exigency, fix, hindrance, impediment, knot, obstacle, obstruction, perplexity, pickle, pinch, predicament, stand, standstill, thwart, trial, trouble; cavil, objection; complication, controversy, difference, embarrassment, embroilment, imbroglio, misunderstanding.

diffidence *n* distrust, doubt, hesitance, hesitancy, hesitation, reluctance; bashfulness, modesty, sheepishness, shyness, timidity.

diffident *adj* distrustful, doubtful, hesitant, hesitating, reluctant; bashful, modest, over-modest, sheepish, shy, timid.

diffuse[1] *vb* circulate, disperse, disseminate, distribute, intermingle, propagate, scatter, spread, strew.

diffuse[2] *adj* broadcast, dispersed, scattered, sparse, sporadic, widespread; broad, extensive, liberal, profuse, wide; copious, loose, prolix, rambling, verbose, wordy.

diffusion *n* circulation, dispersion, dissemination, distribution, extension, propagation, spread, strewing.

diffusive *adj* expansive, permeating, wide-reaching; spreading, dispersive, disseminative, distributive, distributory.

dig *vb* channel, delve, excavate, grub, hollow out, quarry, scoop, tunnel. • *n* poke, punch, thrust.

digest[1] *vb* arrange, classify, codify, dispose, methodize, systemize, tabulate; concoct; assimilate, consider, contemplate, meditate, ponder, reflect upon, study; master; macerate, soak, steep.

digest[2] *n* code, system; abridgement, abstract, brief, breviary, compend, compendium, conspectus, epitome, summary, synopsis.

dignified *adj* august, courtly, decorous, grave, imposing, majestic, noble, stately.

dignify *vb* advance, aggrandize, elevate, ennoble, exalt, promote; adorn, grace, honour.

dignity *n* elevation, eminence, exaltation, excellence, glory, greatness, honour, place, rank, respectability, standing, station; decorum, grandeur, majesty, nobleness, stateliness; preferment; dignitary, magistrate; elevation, height.

digress *vb* depart, deviate, diverge, expatiate, wander.

digression *n* departure, deviation, divergence; episode, excursus.

dilapidate *vb* demolish, destroy, disintegrate, ruin, waste.

dilapidated *adj* decayed, ruined, run down, wasted.

dilapidation *n* decay, demolition, destruction, disintegration, disrepair, dissolution, downfall, ruin, waste.

dilate *vb* distend, enlarge, expand, extend, inflate, swell, tend, widen; amplify, descant, dwell, enlarge, expatiate.

dilation *n* amplification, bloating, distension, enlargement, expanding, expansion, spreading, swelling.

dilatory *adj* backward, behind-hand, delaying, laggard, lagging, lingering, loitering, off-putting, procrastinating, slack, slow, sluggish, tardy.

dilemma *n* difficulty, fix, plight, predicament, problem, quandary, strait.

diligence *n* activity, application, assiduity, assiduousness, attention, care, constancy, earnestness, heedfulness, industry, laboriousness, perseverance, sedulousness.

diligent *adj* active, assiduous, attentive, busy, careful, constant, earnest, hard-working, indefatigable, industrious, laborious, notable, painstaking, persevering, persistent, sedulous, tireless.

dilly-dally *vb* dally, dawdle. delay, lag, linger, loiter, saunter, trifle.

dilute *vb* attenuate, reduce, thin, weaken. • *adj* attenuated, diluted, thin, weak, wishy-washy.

dim *vb* blur, cloud, darken, dull, obscure, sully, tarnish. • *adj* cloudy, dark, dusky, faint, ill-defined, indefinite, indistinct, mysterious, obscure, shadowy; dull, obtuse; clouded, confused, darkened, faint, obscured; blurred, dulled, sullied, tarnished.

dimension *n* extension, extent, measure.

dimensions *npl* amplitude, bigness, bulk, capacity, greatness, largeness, magnitude, mass, massiveness, size, volume; measurements.

diminish *vb* abate, belittle, contract, decrease, lessen, reduce; curtail, cut, dwindle, melt, narrow, shrink, shrivel, subside, taper off, weaken.

diminution *n* abatement, abridgement, attenuation, contraction, curtailment, decrescendo, cut, decay, decrease, deduction, lessening, reduction, retrenchment, weakening.

diminutive *adj* contracted, dwarfish, little, minute, puny, pygmy, small, tiny.

din *vb* beat, boom, clamour, drum, hammer, pound, repeat, ring, thunder. • *n* bruit, clamour, clash, clatter, crash, crashing, hubbub, hullabaloo, hurly-burly, noise, outcry, racket, row, shout, uproar.

dingle *n* dale, dell, glen, vale, valley.

dingy *adj* brown, dun, dusky; bedimmed, colourless, dimmed, dulled, faded, obscure, smirched, soiled, sullied.

dint *n* blow, stroke; dent, indentation, nick, notch; force, power.

diocese *n* bishopric, charge, episcopate, jurisdiction, see.

dip *vb* douse, duck, immerse, plunge, souse; bail, ladle; dive, pitch; bend, incline, slope. • *n* decline, declivity, descent, drop, fall; concavity, depression, hole, hollow, pit, sink; bathe, dipping, ducking, sousing, swim.

diplomat *n* diplomatist, envoy, legate, minister, negotiator.

dire *adj* alarming, awful, calamitous, cruel, destructive, disastrous, dismal, dreadful, fearful, gloomy, horrible, horrid, implacable, inexorable, portentous, shocking, terrible, terrific, tremendous, woeful.

direct *vb* aim. cast, level, point, turn; advise, conduct, control, dispose, guide, govern, manage, regulate, rule; command, bid, enjoin, instruct, order; lead, show; address, superscribe. • *adj* immediate, straight, undeviating; absolute, categorical, express, plain, unambiguous; downright, earnest, frank, ingenuous, open, outspoken, sincere, straightforward, unequivocal.

direction *n* aim; tendency; bearing, course; administration, conduct, control, government, management, oversight, superintendence; guidance, lead; command, order, prescription; address, superscription.

directly *adv* absolutely, expressly, openly, unambiguously; forthwith, immediately, instantly, quickly, presently, promptly, soon, speedily.

director *n* boss, manager, superintendent; adviser, counsellor, guide, instructor, mentor, monitor.

direful *adj* awful, calamitous, dire, dreadful, fearful, gloomy, horrible, shocking, terrible, terrific, tremendous.

dirge *n* coronach, elegy, lament, monody, requiem, threnody.

dirty *vb* befoul, defile, draggle, foul, pollute, soil, sully. • *adj* begrimed, defiled, filthy, foul, mucky, nasty, soiled, unclean; clouded, cloudy, dark, dull, muddy, sullied; base, beggarly, contemptible, despicable, grovelling, low, mean, paltry, pitiful, scurvy, shabby, sneaking, squalid; disagreeable, rainy, sloppy, uncomfortable.

disability *n* disablement, disqualification, impotence, impotency, inability, incapacity, incompetence, incompetency, unfitness, weakness.

disable *vb* cripple, enfeeble, hamstring, impair, paralyse, unman, weaken; disenable, disqualify, incapacitate, unfit.

disabuse *vb* correct, undeceive.

disadvantage *n* disadvantageousness, inconvenience, unfavourableness; damage, detriment, disservice, drawback, harm, hindrance, hurt, injury, loss, prejudice.

disadvantageous *adj* inconvenient, inexpedient, unfavourable; deleterious, detrimental, harmful, hurtful, injurious, prejudicial.

disaffect *vb* alienate, disdain, dislike, disorder, estrange.

disaffected *adj* alienated, disloyal, dissatisfied, estranged.

disaffection *n* alienation, breach, disagreement, dislike, disloyalty, dissatisfaction, estrangement, repugnance, ill will, unfriendliness.

disagree *vb* deviate, differ, diverge, vary; dissent; argue, bicker, clash, debate, dispute, quarrel, wrangle.

disagreeable *adj* contrary, displeasing, distasteful, nasty, offensive, unpleasant, unpleasing, unsuitable.

disagreement *n* deviation, difference, discrepancy, dissimilarity, dissimilitude, divergence, diversity, incongruity, unlikeness; disaccord, dissent; argument, bickering, clashing, conflict, contention, dispute, dissension, disunion, disunity, jarring, misunderstanding, quarrel, strife, variance, wrangle.

disallow *vb* forbid, prohibit; disapprove, reject; deny, disavow, disclaim, dismiss, disown, repudiate.

disappear *vb* depart, fade, vanish; cease, dissolve.

disappoint *vb* baffle, balk, deceive, defeat, delude, disconcert, foil, frustrate, mortify, tantalize, thwart, vex.

disappointment *n* baffling, balk, failure, foiling, frustration, miscarriage, mortification, unfulfilment.

disapprobation *n* blame, censure, condemnation, disapproval, dislike, displeasure, reproof.

disapprove *vb* blame, censure, condemn, deprecate, dislike; disallow, reject.

disarrange *vb* agitate, confuse, derange, disallow, dishevel, dislike, dislocate, disorder, disorganize, disturb, jumble, reject, rumple, tumble, unsettle.

disarray *n* confusion, disorder; dishabille.

disaster *n* accident, adversity, blow, calamity, casualty, catastrophe, misadventure, mischance, misfortune, mishap, reverse, ruin, stroke.

disastrous *adj* adverse, calamitous, catastrophic, destructive, hapless, ill-fated, ill-starred, ruinous, unfortunate, unlucky, unpropitious, unprosperous, untoward.

disavow *vb* deny, disallow, disclaim, disown.

disband *vb* break up, disperse, scatter, separate.

disbelief *n* agnosticism, doubt, nonconviction, rejection, unbelief.

disburden *vb* alleviate, diminish, disburden, discharge, disencumber, ease, free, relieve, rid.

disbursement *n* expenditure, spending.

discard *vb* abandon, cast off, lay aside, reject; banish, break, cashier, discharge, dismiss, remove, repudiate.

discern *vb* differentiate, discriminate, distinguish, judge; behold, descry, discover, espy, notice, observe, perceive, recognize, see.

discernible *adj* detectable, discoverable, perceptible.

discerning *adj* acute, astute, clear-sighted, discriminating, discriminative, eagle-eyed, ingenious, intelligent, judicious, knowing, perspicacious, piercing, sagacious, sharp, shrewd.

discernment *n* acumen, acuteness, astuteness, brightness, cleverness, discrimination, ingenuity, insight, intelligence, judgement, penetration, perspicacity, sagacity, sharpness, shrewdness; beholding, descrying, discerning, discovery, espial, notice, perception.

discharge *vb* disburden, unburden, unload; eject, emit, excrete, expel, void; cash, liquidate, pay; absolve, acquit, clear, exonerate, free, release, relieve; cashier, discard, dismiss, sack; destroy, remove; execute, perform, fulfil, observe; annul, cancel, invalidate, nullify, rescind. • *n* disburdening, unloading; acquittal, dismissal, displacement, ejection, emission, evacuation, excretion, expulsion, vent, voiding; blast, burst, detonation, explosion, firing; execution, fulfilment, observance; annulment, clearance, liquidation, payment, satisfaction, settlement; exemption, liberation, release; flow, flux, execration.

disciple *n* catechumen, learner, pupil, scholar, student; adherent, follower, partisan, supporter.

discipline *vb* breed, drill, educate, exercise, form, instruct, teach, train; control, govern, regulate, school; chasten, chastise, punish. • *n* culture, drill, drilling, education, exercise, instruction, training; control, government, regulation, subjection; chastisement, correction, punishment.

disclaim *vb* abandon, disallow, disown, disavow; reject, renounce, repudiate.

disclose *vb* discover, exhibit, expose, manifest, uncover; bare, betray, blab, communicate, divulge, impart, publish, reveal, show, tell, unfold, unveil, utter.

disclosure *n* betrayal, discovery, exposé, exposure, revelation, uncovering. discolour *vb* stain, tarnish, tinge.

discomfit *vb* beat, checkmate, conquer, defeat, overcome, overpower, overthrow, rout, subdue, vanquish, worst; abash, baffle, balk, confound, disconcert, foil, frustrate, perplex, upset.

discomfiture *n* confusion, defeat, frustration, overthrow, rout, vexation.

discomfort *n* annoyance, disquiet, distress, inquietude, malaise, trouble, uneasiness, unpleasantness, vexation.

discommode *vb* annoy, disquiet, disturb, harass, incommode, inconvenience, molest, trouble.

discompose *vb* confuse, derange, disarrange, disorder, disturb, embroil, jumble, unsettle; agitate, annoy, chafe, displease, disquiet, fret, harass, irritate, nettle, plague, provoke, ruffle, trouble, upset, vex, worry; abash, bewilder, disconcert, embarrass, fluster, perplex.

disconcert *vb* baffle, balk, contravene, defeat, disarrange, frustrate, interrupt, thwart, undo, upset; abash, agitate, bewilder, confuse, demoralize, discompose, disturb, embarrass, faze, perplex, perturb, unbalance, worry.

disconnect *vb* detach, disengage, disjoin, dissociate, disunite, separate, sever, uncouple, unlink.

disconsolate *adj* broken-hearted, cheerless, comfortless, dejected, desolate, forlorn, gloomy, heartbroken, inconsolable, melancholy, miserable, sad, sorrowful, unhappy, woeful, wretched.

discontent *n* discontentment, displeasure, dissatisfaction, inquietude, restlessness, uneasiness.

discontinuance *n* cessation, discontinuation, disjunction, disruption, intermission, interruption, separation, stop, stoppage, stopping, suspension.

discontinue *vb* cease, intermit, interrupt, quit, stop.

discord *n* contention, difference, disagreement, dissension, opposition, quarrelling, rupture, strife, variance, wrangling; cacophony, discordance, dissonance, harshness, jangle, jarring.

discordance *n* conflict, disagreement, incongruity, inconsistency, opposition, repugnance; discord, dissonance.

discordant *adj* contradictory, contrary, disagreeing, incongruous, inconsistent, opposite, repugnant; cacophonous, dissonant, harsh, inharmonious, jangling, jarring.

discount *vb* allow for, deduct, lower, rebate, reduce, subtract; disregard, ignore, overlook. • *n* abatement, drawback; allowance, deduction, rebate, reduction.

discourage *vb* abase, awe, damp, daunt, deject, depress, deject, dismay, dishearten, dispirit, frighten, intimidate; deter, dissuade, hinder; disfavour, discountenance.

discouragement *n* disheartening; dissuasion; damper, deterrent, embarrassment, hindrance, impediment, obstacle, wet blanket.

discourse *vb* expiate, hold forth, lucubrate, sermonize, speak; advise, confer, converse, parley, talk; emit, utter. • *n* address, disquisition, dissertation, homily, lecture, preachment, sermon, speech, treatise; colloquy, conversation, converse, talk.

discourteous *adj* abrupt, brusque, curt, disrespectful, ill-bred, ill-mannered, impolite, inurbane, rude, uncivil, uncourtly, ungentlemanly, unmannerly.

discourtesy *n* abruptness, brusqueness, ill-breeding, impoliteness, incivility, rudeness.

discover *vb* communicate, disclose, exhibit, impart, manifest, show, reveal, tell; ascertain, behold, discern, espy, see; descry, detect, determine, discern; contrive, invent, originate.

discredit *vb* disbelieve, doubt, question; depreciate, disgrace, dishonour, disparage, reproach. • *n* disbelief, distrust; disgrace, dishonour, disrepute, ignominy, notoriety, obloquy, odium, opprobrium, reproach, scandal.

discreditable *adj* derogatory, disgraceful, disreputable, dishonourable, ignominious, infamous, inglorious, scandalous, unworthy.

discreet *adj* careful, cautious, circumspect, considerate, discerning, heedful, judicious, prudent, sagacious, wary, wise.

discrepancy *n* contrariety, difference, disagreement, discordance, dissonance, divergence, incongruity, inconsistency, variance, variation.

discrete *adj* discontinuous, disjunct, distinct, separate; disjunctive.

discretion *n* care, carefulness, caution, circumspection, considerateness, consideration, heedfulness, judgement, judicious, prudence, wariness; discrimination, maturity, responsibility; choice, option, pleasure, will.

discrimination *n* difference, distinction; acumen, acuteness, discernment, in-sight, judgement, penetration, sagacity.

discriminatory *adj* characteristic, characterizing, discriminating, discriminative, distinctive, distinguishing.

discursive *adj* argumentative, reasoning; casual, cursory, desultory, digressive, erratic, excursive, loose, rambling, roving, wandering, wave.

discus *n* disk, quoit.

discuss *vb* agitate, argue, canvass, consider, debate, deliberate, examine, sift, ventilate.

disdain *vb* contemn, deride, despise, disregard, reject, scorn, slight, scout, spurn. • *n* arrogance, contempt, contumely, haughtiness, hauteur, scorn, sneer, superciliousness.

disdainful *adj* cavalier, contemptuous, contumelious, haughty, scornful, supercilious.

disease *n* affection, affliction, ail, ailment, complaint, disorder, distemper, illness, indisposition, infirmity, malady, sickness.

disembarrass *vb* clear, disburden, disencumber, disengage, disentangle, extricate, ease, free, release, rid.

disembodied *adj* bodiless, disincarnate, immaterial, incorporeal, spiritual, unbodied.

disembowel *vb* degut, embowel, eviscerate.

disengage *vb* clear, deliver, discharge, disembarrass, disembroil, disencumber, disentangle, extricate, liberate, release; detach, disjoin, dissociate, disunite, divide, separate; wean, withdraw.

disentangle *vb* loosen, separate, unfold, unravel, untwist; clear, detach, disconnect, disembroil, disengage, extricate, liberate, loose, unloose.

disfavour *n* disapproval, disesteem, dislike, disrespect; discredit, disregard, disrepute, unacceptableness; disservice, unkindness. • *vb* disapprove, dislike, object, oppose.

disfigure *vb* blemish, deface, deform, injure, mar, spoil.

disfigurement *n* blemishing, defacement, deforming, disfiguration, injury, marring, spoiling; blemish, defect, deformity, scar, spot, stain.

disgorge *vb* belch, cast up, spew, throw up, vomit; discharge, eject; give up, relinquish, surrender, yield.

disgrace *vb* degrade, humble, humiliate; abase, debase, defame, discredit, disfavour, dishonour, disparage, reproach, stain, sully, taint, tarnish. • *n* abomination, disrepute, humiliation, ignominy, infamy, mortification, shame, scandal.

disgraceful *adj* discreditable, dishonourable, disreputable, ignominious, infamous, opprobrious, scandalous, shameful.

disguise *vb* cloak, conceal, cover, dissemble, hide, mask, muffle, screen, secrete, shroud, veil. • *n* concealment, cover, mask, veil; blind, cloak, masquerade, pretence, pretext, veneer.

disguised *adj* cloaked, masked, veiled.

disgust *vb* nauseate, sicken; abominate, detest, displease, offend, repel, repulse, revolt. • *n* disrelish, distaste, loathing, nausea; abhorrence, abomination, antipathy, aversion, detestation, dislike, repugnance, revulsion.

dish *vb* deal out, give, ladle, serve; blight, dash, frustrate, mar, ruin, spoil. • *n* bowl, plate, saucer, vessel.

dishearten *vb* cast down, damp, dampen, daunt, deject, depress, deter, discourage, dispirit.

dished *adj* baffled, balked, disappointed, disconcerted, foiled, frustrated, upset.

dishevelled *adj* disarranged, disordered, messed, tousled, tumbled, unkempt, untidy, untrimmed.

dishonest *adj* cheating, corrupt, crafty, crooked, deceitful, deceiving, deceptive, designing, faithless, false, falsehearted, fraudulent, guileful, knavish, perfidious, slippery, treacherous, unfair, unscrupulous.

dishonesty *n* deceitfulness, faithlessness, falsehood, fraud, fraudulence, fraudulency, improbity, knavery, perfidious, treachery, trickery.

dishonour *vb* abase, defame, degrade, discredit, disfavour, dishonour, disgrace, disparage, reproach, shame, taint. • *n* abasement, basement, contempt, degradation, discredit, disesteem, disfavour, disgrace, dishonour, disparagement, disrepute, ignominy, infamy, obloquy, odium, opprobrium, reproach, scandal, shame.

dishonourable *adj* discreditable, disgraceful, disreputable, ignominious, infamous, scandalous, shameful; base, false, falsehearted, shameless.

disinclination *n* alienation, antipathy, aversion, dislike, indisposition, reluctance, repugnance, unwillingness.

disinfect *vb* cleanse, deodorize, fumigate, purify, sterilize.

disingenuous *adj* artful, deceitful, dishonest, hollow, insidious, insincere, uncandid, unfair, wily.

disintegrate *vb* crumble, decompose, dissolve, disunite, pulverize, separate.

disinter *vb* dig up, disentomb, disinhume, exhume, unbury.

disinterested *adj* candid, fair, high-minded, impartial, indifferent, unbiased, unselfish, unprejudiced; generous, liberal, magnanimous.

disjoin *vb* detach, disconnect, dissever, dissociate, disunite, divide, part, separate, sever, sunder.

disjointed *adj* desultory, disconnected, incoherent, loose.

disjunction *n* disassociation, disconnection, disunion, isolation, parting, separation, severance.

dislike *vb* abominate, detest, disapprove, disrelish, hate, loathe. • *n* antagonism, antipathy, aversion, disapproval, disfavour, disgust, disinclination, displeasure, disrelish, distaste, loathing, repugnance.

dislocate *vb* disarrange, displace, disturb; disarticulate, disjoint, luxate, slip.

dislodge *vb* dismount, dispel, displace, eject, expel, oust, remove.

disloyal *adj* disaffected, faithless, false, perfidious, traitorous, treacherous, treasonable, undutiful, unfaithful, unpatriotic, untrue.

disloyalty *n* faithlessness, perfidy, treachery, treason, undutifulness, unfaithfulness.

dismal *adj* cheerless, dark, dreary, dull, gloomy, lonesome; blue, calamitous, doleful, dolorous, funereal, lugubrious, melancholy, mournful, sad, sombre, sorrowful.

dismantle *vb* divest, strip, unrig.

dismay *vb* affright, alarm, appal, daunt, discourage, dishearten, frighten, horrify, intimidate, paralyse, scare, terrify. • *n* affright, alarm, consternation, fear, fright, horror, terror.

dismember *vb* disjoint, dislimb, dislocate, mutilate; divide, separate, rend, sever.

dismiss *vb* banish, cashier, discard, discharge, disperse, reject, release, remove.

dismount *vb* alight, descend, dismantle, unhorse; dislodge, displace.

disobedient *adj* froward, noncompliant, noncomplying, obstinate, rebellious, refractory, uncomplying, undutiful, unruly, unsubmissive.

disobey *vb* infringe, transgress, violate.

disobliging *adj* ill-natured, unaccommodating, unamiable, unfriendly, unkind.

disorder *vb* confound, confuse, derange, disarrange, discompose, disorganize, disturb, unsettle, upset. • *n* confusion, derangement, disarrangement, disarray, disorganization, irregularity, jumble, litter, mess, topsy-turvy; brawl, commotion, disturbance, fight, quarrel, riot, tumult; riotousness, tumultuousness, turbulence; ail, ailment, complaint, distemper, illness, indisposition, malady, sickness.

disorderly *adj* chaotic, confused, intemperate, irregular, unmethodical, unsystematic, untidy; lawless, rebellious, riotous, tumultuous, turbulent, ungovernable, unmanageable, unruly.

disorganization *n* chaos, confusion, demoralization, derangement, disorder.

disorganize *vb* confuse, demoralize, derange, disarrange, discompose, disorder, disturb, unsettle, upset.

disown *vb* disavow, disclaim, reject, renounce, repudiate; abnegate, deny, disallow.

disparage *vb* belittle, decry, depreciate, derogate from, detract from, doubt, question, run down, underestimate, underpraise, underrate, undervalue; asperse, defame, inveigh against, reflect on, reproach, slur, speak ill of, traduce, vilify.

disparagement *n* belittlement, depreciation, derogation, detraction, underrating, undervaluing; derogation, detraction, diminution, harm, impairment, injury, lessening, prejudice, worsening; aspersion, calumny, defamation, reflection, reproach, traduction, vilification; blackening, disgrace, dispraise, indignity, reproach.

disparity *n* difference, disproportion, inequality; dissimilarity, dissimilitude, unlikeness.

dispassionate *adj* calm, collected, composed, cool, imperturbable, inexcitable, moderate, quiet, serene, sober, staid, temperate, undisturbed, unexcitable, unexcited, unimpassioned, unruffled; candid, disinterested, fair, impartial, neutral, unbiased.

dispatch, despatch *vb* assassinate, kill, murder, slaughter, slay; accelerate, conclude, dismiss, expedite, finish, forward, hasten, hurry, quicken, speed. • *n* dispatching, sending; diligence, expedition, haste, rapidity, speed; completion, conduct, doing, transaction; communication, document, instruction, letter, message, missive, report.

dispel *vb* banish, disperse, dissipate, scatter.

dispensation *n* allotment, apportioning, apportionment, dispensing, distributing, distribution; administration, stewardship; economy, plan, scheme, system; exemption, immunity, indulgence, licence, privilege.

dispense *vb* allot, apportion, assign, distribute; administer, apply, execute; absolve, excuse, exempt, exonerate, release, relieve.

disperse *vb* dispel, dissipate, dissolve, scatter, separate; diffuse, disseminate, spread; disappear, vanish.

dispirit *vb* damp, dampen, depress, deject, discourage, dishearten.

dispirited *adj* chapfallen, dejected, depressed, discouraged, disheartened, down-cast, down-hearted.

displace *vb* dislocate, mislay, misplace, move; dislodge, remove; cashier, depose, discard, discharge, dismiss, oust, replace, unseat.

display *vb* expand, extend, open, spread, unfold; exhibit, show; flaunt, parade. • *n* exhibition, manifestation, show; flourish, ostentation, pageant, parade, pomp.

displease *vb* disgruntle, disgust, disoblige, dissatisfy, offend; affront, aggravate, anger, annoy, chafe, chagrin, fret, irritate, nettle, pique, provoke, vex.

displeasure *n* disaffection, disapprobation, disapproval, dislike, dissatisfaction, distaste; anger, annoyance, indignation, irritation, pique, resentment, vexation, wrath; injury, offence.

disport *vb* caper, frisk, frolic, gambol, play, sport, wanton; amuse, beguile, cheer, divert, entertain, relax, solace.

disposal *n* arrangement, disposition; conduct, control, direction, disposure, government, management, ordering, regulation; bestowment, dispensation, distribution.

dispose *vb* arrange, distribute, marshal, group, place, range, rank, set; adjust, determine, regulate, settle; bias, incline, induce, lead, move, predispose; control, decide, regulate, rule, settle; arrange, bargain, compound; alienate, convey, demise, sell, transfer.

disposed *adj* apt, inclined, prone, ready, tending.

disposition *n* arrangement, arranging, classification, disposing, grouping, location, placing; adjustment, control, direction, disposure, disposal, management, ordering, regulation; aptitude, bent, bias, inclination, nature, predisposition, proclivity, proneness, propensity, tendency; character, constitution, humour, native, nature, temper, temperament, turn; inclination, willingness; bestowal, bestowment, dispensation, distribution.

dispossess *vb* deprive, divest, expropriate, strip; dislodge, eject, oust; disseise, disseize, evict, oust.

dispraise *n* blame, censure; discredit, disgrace, dishonour, disparagement, opprobrium, reproach, shame.

disproof *n* confutation, rebuttal, refutation.

disproportion *n* disparity, inadequacy, inequality, insufficiency, unsuitableness; incommensurateness.

disprove *vb* confute, rebel, rebut.

disputable *adj* controvertible, debatable, doubtful, questionable.

disputation *n* argumentation, controversy, debate, dispute.

disputatious *adj* argumentative, bickering, captious, cavilling, contentious, dissentious, litigious, polemical, pugnacious, quarrelsome.

dispute *vb* altercate, argue, debate, litigate, question; bicker, brawl, jangle, quarrel, spar, spat, squabble, tiff, wrangle; agitate, argue, debate, ventilate; challenge, contradict, controvert, deny, impugn; contest, struggle for. • *n* controversy, debate, discussion, disputation; altercation, argument, bickering, brawl, disagreement, dissension, spat, squabble, tiff, wrangle.

disqualification *n* disability, incapitation.

disqualify *vb* disable, incapacitate, unfit; disenable, preclude, prohibit.

disquiet *vb* agitate, annoy, bother, discompose, disturb, excite, fret, harass, incommode, molest, plague, pester, trouble, vex, worry. • *n* anxiety, discomposure, disquietude, disturbance, restlessness, solicitude, trouble, uneasiness, unrest, vexation, worry.

disquisition *n* dissertation, discourse, essay, paper, thesis, treatise.

disregard *vb* contemn, despise, disdain, disobey, disparage, ignore, neglect, overlook, slight. • *n* contempt, ignoring, inattention, neglect, pretermit, oversight, slight; disesteem, disfavour, indifference.

disrelish *vb* dislike, loathe. • *n* dislike, distaste; flatness, insipidity, insipidness, nauseousness; antipathy, aversion, repugnance.

disreputable *adj* derogatory, discreditable, dishonourable, disgraceful, infamous, opprobrious, scandalous, shameful; base, contemptible, low, mean, vicious, vile, vulgar.

disrepute *n* abasement, degradation, derogation, discredit, disgrace, dishonour, ill-repute, odium.

disrespect *n* disesteem, disregard, irreverence, neglect, slight.

disrespectful *adj* discourteous, impertinent, impolite, rude, uncivil, uncourteous.

dissatisfaction *n* discontent, disquiet, inquietude, uneasiness; disapprobation, disapproval, dislike, displeasure.

dissect *vb* analyze, examine, explore, investigate, scrutinize, sift; cut apart.

dissemble *vb* cloak, conceal, cover, disguise, hide; counterfeit, dissimulate, feign, pretend.

dissembler *n* dissimulator, feigner, hypocrite, pretender, sham.

disseminate *vb* circulate, diffuse, disperse, proclaim, promulgate, propagate, publish, scatter, spread.

dissension *n* contention, difference, disagreement, discord, quarrel, strife, variance.

dissent *vb* decline, differ, disagree, refuse. • *n* difference, disagreement, nonconformity, opposition, recusancy, refusal.

dissentient *adj* disagreeing, dissenting, dissident, factious.

dissertation *n* discourse, disquisition, essay, thesis, treatise.

disservice *n* disadvantage, disfavour, harm, hurt, ill-turn, injury, mischief.

dissidence *n* disagreement, dissent, nonconformity, sectarianism.

dissimilar *adj* different, divergent, diverse, heterogeneous, unlike, various.

dissimilarity *n* dissimilitude, disparity, divergent, diversity, unlikeness, variation.

dissimulation *n* concealment, deceit, dissembling, double-dealing, duplicity, feigning, hypocrisy, pretence.

dissipate *vb* dispel, disperse, scatter; consume, expend, lavish, spend, squander, waste; disappear, vanish.

dissipation *n* dispersion, dissemination, scattering, vanishing; squandering, waste; crapulence, debauchery, dissoluteness, drunkenness, excess, profligacy.

dissociate *vb* disjoin, dissever, disunite, divide, separate, sever, sunder.

dissolute *adj* abandoned, corrupt, debauched, depraved, disorderly, dissipated, graceless, lax, lewd, licentious, loose, profligate, rakish, reprobate, shameless, vicious, wanton, wild.

dissolution *n* liquefaction, melting, solution; decomposition, putrefaction; death, disease; destruction, overthrow, ruin; termination.

dissolve *vb* liquefy, melt; disorganize, disunite, divide, loose, separate, sever; destroy, ruin; disappear, fade, scatter, vanish; crumble, decompose, disintegrate, perish.

dissonance *n* cacophony, discord, discordance, harshness, jarring; disagreement, discrepancy, incongruity, inconsistency.

dissonant *adj* discordant, grating, harsh, jangling, jarring, unharmonious; contradictory, disagreeing, discrepant, incongruous, inconsistent.

distance *vb* excel, outdo, outstrip, surpass. • *n* farness, remoteness; aloofness, coldness, frigidity, reserve, stiffness, offishness; absence, separation, space.

distant *adj* far, far-away, remote; aloof, ceremonious, cold, cool, frigid, haughty, reserved, stiff, uncordial; faint, indirect, obscure, slight.

distaste *n* disgust, disrelish; antipathy, aversion, disinclination, dislike, displeasure, dissatisfaction, repugnance.

distasteful *adj* disgusting, loathsome, nauseating, nauseous, unpalatable, unsavoury; disagreeable, displeasing, offensive, repugnant, repulsive, unpleasant.

distemper *n* ail, ailment, complaint, disease, disorder, illness, indisposition, malady, sickness.

distempered *adj* diseased, disordered; immoderate, inordinate, intemperate, unregulated.

distend *vb* bloat, dilate, enlarge, expand, increase, inflate, puff, stretch, swell, widen.

distil *vb* dribble, drip, drop; extract, separate.

distinct *adj* definite, different, discrete, disjunct, individual, separate, unconnected; clear, defined, manifest, obvious, plain, unconfused, unmistakable, well-defined.

distinction *n* discernment, discrimination, distinguishing; difference; account, celebrity, credit, eminence, fame, name, note, rank, renown, reputation, repute, respectability, superiority.

distinctive *adj* characteristic, differentiating, discriminating, distinguishing.

distinctness *n* difference, separateness; clearness, explicitness, lucidity, lucidness, perspicuity, precision.

distinguish *vb* characterize, mark; differentiate, discern, discriminate, perceive, recognize, see, single out, tell; demarcate, divide, separate; celebrate, honour, signalize.

distinguished *adj* celebrated, eminent, famous, illustrious, noted; conspicuous, extraordinary, laureate, marked, shining, superior, transcendent.

distort *vb* contort, deform, gnarl, screw, twist, warp, wrest; falsify, misrepresent, pervert.

distortion *n* contortion, deformation, deformity, twist, wryness; falsification, misrepresentation, perversion, wresting.

distract *vb* divert, draw away; bewilder, confound, confuse, derange, discompose, disconcert, disturb, embarrass, harass, madden, mystify, perplex, puzzle.

distracted *adj* crazed, crazy, deranged, frantic, furious, insane, mad, raving, wild.

distraction *n* abstraction, bewilderment, confusion, mystification, embarrassment, perplexity; agitation, commotion, discord, disorder, disturbance, division, perturbation, tumult, turmoil; aberration, alienation, delirium, derangement, frenzy, hallucination, incoherence, insanity, lunacy, madness, mania, raving, wandering.

distress *vb* afflict, annoy, grieve, harry, pain, perplex, rack, trouble; distrain, seize, take. • *n* affliction, calamity, disaster, misery, misfortune, adversity, hardship, perplexity, trial, tribulation; agony, anguish, dolour, grief, sorrow, suffering; gnawing, gripe, griping, pain, torment, torture; destitution, indigence, poverty, privation, straits, want.

distribute *vb* allocate, allot, apportion, assign, deal, dispense, divide, dole out, give, mete, partition, prorate, share; administer, arrange, assort, class, classify, dispose.

distribution *n* allocation, allotment, apportionment, assignment, assortment, dispensation, dispensing; arrangement, disposal, disposition, classification, division, dole, grouping, partition, sharing.

district *n* circuit, department, neighbourhood, province, quarter, region, section, territory, tract, ward.

distrust *vb* disbelieve, discredit, doubt, misbelieve, mistrust, question, suspect. • *n* doubt, misgiving, mistrust, question, suspicion.

distrustful *adj* doubting, dubious, suspicious.

disturb *vb* agitate, shake, stir; confuse, derange, disarrange, disorder, unsettle, upset; annoy, discompose, disconcert, disquiet, distract, fuss, incommode, molest, perturb, plague, trouble, ruffle, vex, worry; impede, interrupt, hinder.

disturbance *n* agitation, commotion, confusion, convulsion, derangement, disorder, perturbation, unsettlement; annoyance, discomposure, distraction, excitement, fuss; hindrance, interruption, molestation; brawl, commotion, disorder, excitement, fracas, hubbub, riot, rising, tumult, turmoil, uproar.

disunion *n* disconnection, disjunction, division, separation, severance; breach, feud, rupture, schism.

disunite *vb* detach, disconnect, disjoin, dissever, dissociate, divide, part, rend, separate, segregate, sever, sunder; alienate, estrange.

disuse *n* desuetude, discontinuance, disusage, neglect, nonobservance.

ditch *vb* canalize, dig, excavate, furrow, gouge, trench; abandon, discard, dump, jettison, scrap. • *n* channel, drain, fosse, moat, trench.

divagation *n* deviation, digression, rambling, roaming, straying, wandering.

divan *n* bed, chesterfield, couch, settee, sofa.

divaricate *vb* diverge, fork, part.

dive *vb* explore, fathom, penetrate, plunge, sound. • *n* drop, fall, header, plunge; bar, den, dump, joint, saloon.

diverge *vb* divide, radiate, separate; divaricate, separate; deviate, differ, disagree, vary.

divers *adj* different, manifold, many, numerous, several, sundry, various.

diverse *adj* different, differing, disagreeing, dissimilar, divergent, heterogeneous, multifarious, multiform, separate, unlike, variant, various, varying.

diversion *n* deflection, diverting; amusement, delight, distraction, enjoyment, entertainment, game, gratification, pastime, play, pleasure, recreation, sport; detour, digression.

diversity *n* difference, dissimilarity, dissimilitude, divergence, unlikeness, variation; heterogeneity, manifoldness, multifariousness, multiformity, variety.

divert *vb* deflect, distract, disturb; amuse, beguile, delight, entertain, exhilarate, give pleasure, gratify, recreate, refresh, solace.

divest *vb* denude, disrobe, strip, unclothe, undress; deprive, dispossess, strip.

divide *vb* bisect, cleave, cut, dismember, dissever, disunite, open, part, rend, segregate, separate, sever, shear, split, sunder; allocate, allot, apportion, assign, dispense, distribute, dole, mete, portion, share; compartmentalize, demarcate, partition; alienate, disunite, estrange.

divination *n* augury, divining, foretelling, incantation, magic, sooth-saying, sorcery; prediction, presage, prophecy.

divine *vb* foretell, predict, presage, prognosticate, vaticinate, prophesy; believe, conjecture, fancy, guess, suppose, surmise, suspect, think. • *adj* deiform, godlike, superhuman, supernatural; angelic, celestial, heavenly, holy, sacred, seraphic, spiritual; exalted, exalting, rapturous, supreme, transcendent. • *n* churchman, clergyman, ecclesiastic, minister, parson, pastor, priest.

division *n* compartmentalization, disconnection, disjunction, dismemberment, segmentation, separation, severance; category, class, compartment, head, parcel, portion, section, segment; demarcation, partition; alienation, allotment, apportionment, distribution; breach, difference, disagreement, discord, disunion, estrangement, feud, rupture, variance.

divorce *vb* disconnect, dissolve, disunite, part, put away, separate, sever, split up, sunder, unmarry. • *n* disjunction, dissolution, disunion, division, divorcement, parting, separation, severance.

divulge *vb* communicate, declare, disclose, discover, exhibit, expose, impart, proclaim, promulgate, publish, reveal, tell, uncover.

dizzy *adj* giddy, vertiginous; careless, heedless, thoughtless.

do *vb* accomplish, achieve, act, commit, effect, execute, perform; complete, conclude, end, finish, settle, terminate; conduct, transact; observe, perform, practice; translate, render; cook, prepare; cheat, chouse, cozen, hoax, swindle; serve, suffice. • *n* act, action, adventure, deed, doing, exploit, feat, thing; banquet, event, feast, function, party.

docile *adj* amenable, obedient, pliant, teachable, tractable, yielding.

dock¹ *vb* clip, curtail, cut, deduct, truncate; lessen, shorten.

dock² *vb* anchor, moor; join, meet. • *n* anchorage, basin, berth, dockage, dockyard, dry dock, harbour, haven, marina, pier, shipyard, wharf.

doctor *vb* adulterate, alter, cook, falsify, manipulate, tamper with; attend, minister to, cure, heal, remedy, treat; fix, mend, overhaul, repair, service. • *n* general practitioner, GP, healer, leech, medic, physician; adept, savant.

doctrinaire *adj* impractical, theoretical. • *n* ideologist, theorist, thinker.

doctrine *n* article, belief, creed, dogma, opinion, precept, principle, teaching, tenet.

dodge *vb* equivocate, evade, prevaricate, quibble, shuffle. • *n* artifice, cavil, evasion, quibble, subterfuge, trick.

dogged *adj* cantankerous, headstrong, inflexible, intractable, mulish, obstinate, pertinacious, perverse, resolute, stubborn, tenacious, unyielding, wilful; churlish, morose, sour, sullen, surly.

dogma *n* article, belief, creed, doctrine, opinion, precept, principle, tenet.

dogmatic *adj* authoritative, categorical, formal, settled; arrogant, confident, dictatorial, imperious, magisterial, opinionated, oracular, overbearing, peremptory, positive; doctrinal.

dole *vb* allocate, allot, apportion, assign, deal, distribute, divide, share. • *n* allocation, allotment, apportionment, distribution; part, portion, share; alms, donation, gift, gratuity, pittance; affliction, distress, grief, sorrow, woe.

doleful *adj* lugubrious, melancholy, piteous, rueful, sad, sombre, sorrowful, woebegone, woeful; cheerless, dark, dismal, dolorous, dreary, gloomy.

dolorous *adj* cheerless, dark, dismal, gloomy; doleful, lugubrious, mournful, piteous, rueful, sad, sorrowful, woeful.

dolt *n* blockhead, booby, dullard, dunce, fool, ignoramus, simpleton.

domain *n* authority, dominion, jurisdiction, province, sway; empire, realm, territory; lands, estate; branch, department, region.

domestic *n* charwoman, help, home help, maid, servant. • *adj* domiciliary, family, home, household, private; domesticated; internal, intestine.

domesticate *vb* tame; adopt, assimilate, familiarize, naturalize.

domicile *vb* domiciliate, dwell, inhabit, live, remain, reside. • *n* abode, dwelling, habitation, harbour, home, house, residence.

dominant *adj* ascendant, ascending, chief, controlling, governing, influential, outstanding, paramount, predominant, pre-eminent, preponderant, presiding, prevailing, ruling.

dominate *vb* control, rule, sway; command, overlook, overtop, surmount.

domineer *vb* rule, tyrannize; bluster, bully, hector, menace, swagger, swell, threaten.

dominion *n* ascendancy, authority, command, control, domain, domination, government, jurisdiction, mastery, rule, sovereign, sovereignty, supremacy, sway; country, kingdom, realm, region, territory.

donation *n* alms, benefaction, boon, contribution, dole, donative, gift, grant, gratuity, largesse, offering, present, subscription.

done *adj* accomplished, achieved, effected, executed, performed; completed, concluded, ended, finished, terminated; carried on, transacted; rendered, translated; cooked, prepared; cheated, cozened, hoaxed, swindled; (*with* **for**) damned, dished, *hors de combat*, ruined, shelved, spoiled, wound up.

donkey *n* ass, mule; dunce, fool, simpleton.

donor *n* benefactor, bestower, giver; donator.

double *vb* fold, plait; duplicate, geminate, increase, multiply, repeat; return. • *adj* binary, coupled, geminate, paired; dual, twice, twofold; deceitful, dishonest, double-dealing, false, hollow, insincere, knavish, perfidious, treacherous, two-faced. • *adv* doubly, twice, twofold. • *n* doubling, fold, plait; artifice, manoeuvre, ruse, shift, stratagem, trick, wile; copy, counterpart, twin.

doublet *n* jacket, jerkin.

doubt *vb* demur, fluctuate, hesitate, vacillate, waver; distrust, mistrust, query, question, suspect. • *n* dubiety, dubiousness, dubitation, hesitance, hesitancy, hesitation, incertitude, indecision, irresolution, question, suspense, uncertainty, vacillation; distrust, misgiving, mistrust, scepticism, suspicion.

doubtful *adj* dubious, hesitating, sceptical, undecided, undetermined, wavering; ambiguous, dubious, enigmatical, equivocal, hazardous, obscure, problematical, unsure; indeterminate, questionable, undecided, unquestioned.

doubtless *adv* certainly, unquestionably; clearly, indisputably, precisely.

doughty *adj* adventurous, bold, brave, chivalrous, courageous, daring, dauntless, fearless, gallant, heroic, intrepid, redoubtable, valiant, valorous.

douse *see* **dowse**.

dowdy *adj* awkward, dingy, ill-dressed, shabby, slatternly, slovenly; old-fashioned, unfashionable.

dowel *n* peg, pin, pinion, tenon.

dower *n* endowment, gift; dowry; portion, share.

downcast *adj* chapfallen, crestfallen, dejected, depressed, despondent, discouraged, disheartened, dispirited, downhearted, low-spirited, sad, unhappy.

downfall *n* descent, destruction, fall, ruin.

downhearted *adj* chapfallen, crestfallen, dejected, depressed, despondent, discouraged, disheartened, dispirited, downcast, low-spirited, sad, unhappy.

downright *adj* absolute, categorical, clear, explicit, plain, positive, sheer, simple, undisguised, unequivocal, utter; aboveboard, artless, blunt, direct, frank, honest, ingenuous, open, sincere, straightforward, unceremonious.

downy *adj* lanate, lanated, lanose.

dowse, douse *vb* dip, immerse, plunge, souse, submerge.

doxy *n* mistress, paramour; courtesan, drab, harlot, prostitute, strumpet, streetwalker, whore.

doze *vb* drowse, nap, sleep, slumber. • *n* drowse, forty-winks, nap.

dozy *adj* drowsy, heavy, sleepy, sluggish.

draft *vb* detach, select; commandeer, conscript, impress; delineate, draw, outline, sketch. • *n* conscription, drawing, selection; delineation, outline, sketch; bill, cheque, order.

drag *vb* draw, haul, pull, tow, tug; trail; linger, loiter. • *n* favour, influence, pull; brake, check, curb, lag, resistance, retardation, scotch, skid, slackening, slack-off, slowing.

draggle *vb* befoul, bemire, besmirch, dangle, drabble, trail.

dragoon *vb* compel, drive, force, harass, harry, persecute. • *n* cavalier, equestrian, horse-soldier.

drain *vb* milk, sluice, tap; empty, evacuate, exhaust; dry. • *n* channel, culvert, ditch, sewer, sluice, trench, watercourse; exhaustion, withdrawal.

draught *n* current, drawing, pulling, traction; cup, dose, drench, drink, potion; delineation, design, draft, outline, sketch.

draw *vb* drag, haul, tow, tug, pull; attract; drain, suck, syphon; extract, extort; breathe in, inhale, inspire; allure, engage, entice, induce, influence, lead, move, persuade; extend, protract, stretch; delineate, depict, sketch; deduce, derive, infer; compose, draft, formulate, frame, prepare; blister, vesicate, write.

drawback *n* defect, deficiency, detriment, disadvantage, fault, flaw, imperfection, injury; abatement, allowance, deduction, discount, rebate, reduction.

drawing *n* attracting, draining, inhaling, pulling, traction; delineation, draught, outline, picture, plan, sketch.

dread *vb* apprehend, fear. • *adj* dreadful, frightful, horrible, terrible; awful, venerable. • *n* affright, alarm, apprehension, fear, terror; awe, veneration.

dreadful *adj* alarming, appalling, awesome, dire, direful, fearful, formidable, frightful, horrible, horrid, terrible, terrific, tremendous; awful, venerable.

dream *vb* fancy, imagine, think. • *n* conceit, day-dream, delusion, fancy, fantasy, hallucination, illusion, imagination, reverie, vagary, vision.

dreamer *n* enthusiast, visionary.

dreamy *adj* absent, abstracted, fanciful, ideal, misty, shadowy, speculative, unreal, visionary.

dreary *adj* cheerless, chilling, comfortless, dark, depressing, dismal, drear, gloomy, lonely, lonesome, sad, solitary, sorrowful; boring, dull, monotonous, tedious, tiresome, uninteresting, wearisome.

dregs *npl* feculence, grounds, lees, off-scourings, residuum, scourings, sediment, waste; draff, dross, refuse, scum, trash.

drench *vb* dowse, drown, imbrue, saturate, soak, souse, steep, wet; physic, purge.

dress *vb* align, straighten; adjust, arrange, dispose; fit, prepare; accoutre, apparel, array, attire, clothe, robe, rig; adorn, bedeck, deck, decorate, drape, embellish, trim. • *n* apparel, attire, clothes, clothing, costume, garb, guise, garments, habiliment, habit, raiment, suit, toilet, vesture; bedizenment, bravery; frock, gown, rob.

dressing *n* compost, fertilizer, manure; forcemeat, stuffing.

dressy *adj* flashy, gaudy, showy.

driblet *n* bit, drop, fragment, morsel, piece, scrap.

drift *vb* accumulate, drive, float, wander. • *n* bearing, course, direction; aim, design, intent, intention, mark, object, proposal, purpose, scope, tendency; detritus, deposit, diluvium; gallery, passage, tunnel; current, rush, sweep; heap, pile.

drill[1] *vb* bore, perforate, pierce; discipline, exercise, instruct, teach, train. • *n* borer; discipline, exercise, training.

drill[2] *n* channel, furrow, trench.

drink *vb* imbibe, sip, swill; carouse, indulge, revel, tipple, tope; swallow, quaff; absorb. • *n* beverage, draught, liquid, potation, potion; dram, nip, sip, snifter, refreshment.

drip *vb* dribble, drop, leak, trickle; distil, filter, percolate; ooze, reek, seep, weep. • *n* dribble, drippings, drop, leak, leakage, leaking, trickle, tricklet; bore, nuisance, wet blanket.

drive *vb* hurl, impel, propel, send, shoot, thrust; actuate, incite, press, urge; coerce, compel, constrain, force, harass, oblige, overburden, press, rush; go, guide, ride, travel; aim, intend. • *n* effort, energy, pressure; airing, ride; road.

drivel *vb* babble, blether, dote, drool, slaver, slobber. • *n* balderdash, drivelling, fatuity, nonsense, prating, rubbish, slaver, stuff, twaddle.

drizzle *vb* mizzle, rain, shower, sprinkle. • *n* haar, mist, mizzle, rain, sprinkling.

droll *adj* comic, comical, farcical, funny, jocular, ludicrous, laughable, ridiculous; amusing, diverting, facetious, odd, quaint, queer, waggish. • *n* buffoon, clown, comedian, fool, harlequin, jester, punch, Punchinello, scaramouch, wag, zany.

drollery *n* archness, buffoonery, fun, humour, jocularity, pleasantry, waggishness, whimsicality.

drone *vb* dawdle, drawl, idle, loaf, lounge; hum. • *n* idler, loafer, lounger, sluggard.

drool *vb* drivel, slaver.

droop *vb* fade, wilt, wither; decline, fail, faint, flag, languish, sink, weaken; bend, hang.

drop *vb* distil, drip, shed; decline, depress, descend, dump, lower, sink; abandon, desert, forsake, forswear, leave, omit, relinquish, quit; cease, discontinue, intermit, remit; fall, precipitate. • *n* bead, droplet, globule; earring, pendant.

dross *n* cinder, lees, recrement, scoria, scum, slag; refuse, waste.

drought *n* aridity, drouth, dryness, thirstiness.

drove *n* flock, herd; collection, company, crowd.

drown *vb* deluge, engulf, flood, immerse, inundate, overflow, sink, submerge, swamp; overcome, overpower, overwhelm.

drowse *vb* doze, nap, sleep, slumber, snooze. • *n* doze, forty winks, nap, siesta, sleep, snooze.

drowsy *adj* dozy, sleepy; comatose, lethargic, stupid; lulling, soporific.

drub *vb* bang, beat, cane, cudgel, flog, hit, knock, pommel, pound, strike, thrash, thump, whack.

drubbing *n* beating, caning, cudgelling, flagellation, flogging, pommelling, pounding, thrashing, thumping, whacking.

drudge *vb* grub, grind, plod, slave, toil, work. • *n* grind, hack, hard worker, menial, plodder, scullion, servant, slave, toiler, worker.

drug *vb* dose, medicate; disgust, surfeit. • *n* medicine, physic, remedy; poison.

drunk *adj* boozed, drunken, inebriated, intoxicated, maudlin, soaked, tipsy; ablaze, aflame, delirious, fervent, suffused. • *n* alcoholic, boozer, dipsomaniac, drunkard, inebriate, lush, soak; bacchanal, bender, binge.

drunkard *n* alcoholic, boozer, carouser, dipsomaniac, drinker, drunk, inebriate, reveller, sot, tippler, toper.

dry *vb* dehydrate, desiccate, drain, exsiccate, parch. • *adj* desiccated, dried, juiceless, sapless, unmoistened; arid, droughty, parched; drouthy, thirsty; barren, dull, insipid, jejune, plain, pointless, tame, tedious, tiresome, unembellished, uninteresting, vapid; cutting, keen, sarcastic, severe, sharp, sly.

dub *vb* call, christen, denominate, designate, entitle, name, style, term.

dubious *adj* doubtful, fluctuating, hesitant, irresolute, sceptical, uncertain, undecided, unsettled, wavering; ambiguous, doubtful, equivocal, improbable, questionable, uncertain.

duck *vb* dip, dive, immerse, plunge, submerge, souse; bend, bow, dodge, stoop.

duct *n* canal, channel, conduit, pipe, tube; blood-vessel.

ductile *adj* compliant, docile, facile, tractable, yielding; flexible, malleable, pliant; extensible, tensile.

dudgeon *n* anger, indignation, ill will, ire, malice, resentment, umbrage, wrath.

due *adj* owed, owing; appropriate, becoming, befitting, bounden, fit, proper, suitable, right. • *adv* dead, direct, directly, exactly, just, right, squarely, straight. • *n* claim, debt, desert, right.

dulcet *adj* delicious, honeyed, luscious, sweet; harmonious, melodious; agreeable, charming, delightful, pleasant, pleasing.

dull *vb* blunt; benumb, besot, deaden, hebetate, obtund, paralyse, stupefy; dampen, deject, depress, discourage, dishearten, dispirit; allay, alleviate, assuage, mitigate, moderate, quiet, soften; deaden, dim, sully, tarnish. • *adj* blockish, brutish, doltish, obtuse, stolid, stupid, unintelligent; apathetic, callous, dead, insensible, passionless, phlegmatic, unfeeling, unimpassioned, unresponsive; heavy, inactive, inanimate, inert, languish, lifeless, slow, sluggish, torpid; blunt, dulled, hebetate, obtuse; cheerless, dismal, dreary, gloomy, sad, sombre; dim, lack-lustre, lustreless,

matt, obscure, opaque, tarnished; dry, flat, insipid, irksome, jejune, prosy, tedious, tiresome, uninteresting, wearisome.

duly *adv* befittingly, decorously, fitly, properly, rightly; regularly.

dumb *adj* inarticulate, mute, silent, soundless, speechless, voiceless.

dumbfound, dumfound *vb* amaze, astonish, astound, bewilder, confound, confuse, nonplus, pose.

dumps *npl* blues, dejection, depression, despondency, gloom, gloominess, melancholy, sadness.

dun[1] *adj* greyish-brown, brown, drab.

dun[2] *vb* beset, importune, press, urge.

dunce *n* ass, block, blockhead, clodpole, dolt, donkey, dullard, dunderhead, fool, goose, halfwit, ignoramus, jackass, lackwit, loon, nincompoop, numskull, oaf, simpleton, thickhead, witling.

dupe *vb* beguile, cheat, chouse, circumvent, cozen, deceive, delude, gull, hoodwink, outwit, overreach, swindle, trick. • *n* gull, simpleton.

duplicate *vb* copy, double, repeat, replicate, reproduce. • *adj* doubled, twofold. • *n* copy, counterpart, facsimile, replica, transcript.

duplicity *n* artifice, chicanery, circumvention, deceit, deception, dishonesty, dissimulation, double-dealing, falseness, fraud, guile, hypocrisy, perfidy.

durable *adj* abiding, constant, continuing, enduring, firm, lasting, permanent, persistent, stable.

duration *n* continuance, continuation, permanency, perpetuation, prolongation; period, time.

duress *n* captivity, confinement, constraint, durance, hardship, imprisonment, restraint; compulsion.

dusky *adj* cloudy, darkish, dim, murky, obscure, overcast, shady, shadowy; dark, swarthy, tawny.

dutiful *adj* duteous, obedient, submissive; deferential, respectful, reverential.

duty *n* allegiance, devoirs, obligation, responsibility, reverence; business, engagement, function, office, service; custom, excise, impost, tariff, tax, toll.

dwarf *vb* lower, stunt. • *n* bantam, homunculus, manikin, midget, pygmy.

dwarfish *adj* diminutive, dwarfed, little, low, pygmy, small, stunted, tiny, undersized.

dwell *vb* abide, inhabit, live, lodge, remain, reside, rest, sojourn, stay, stop, tarry, tenant.

dwelling *n* abode, cot, domicile, dugout, establishment, habitation, home, house, hutch, lodging, mansion, quarters, residence.

dwindle *vb* decrease, diminish, lessen, shrink; decay, decline, deteriorate, pine, sink, waste away.

dye *vb* colour, stain, tinge. • *n* cast, colour, hue, shade, stain, tinge, tint.

dying *adj* expiring; mortal, perishable. • *n* death, decease, demise, departure, dissolution, exit.

dynasty *n* dominion, empire, government, rule, sovereignty.

dyspepsia *n* indigestion.

E

eager *adj* agog, avid, anxious, desirous, fain, greedy, impatient, keen, longing, yearning; animated, ardent, earnest, enthusiastic, fervent, fervid, forward, glowing, hot, impetuous, sanguine, vehement, zealous.

eagerness *n* ardour, avidity, earnestness, enthusiasm, fervour, greediness, heartiness, hunger, impatience, impetuosity, intentness, keenness, longing, thirst, vehemence, yearning, zeal.

eagle-eyed *adj* discerning, hawk-eyed, sharp-sighted.

ear[1] *n* attention, hearing, heed, regard.

ear[2] *n* head, spike.

early *adj* opportune, seasonable, timely; forward, premature; dawning, matutinal. • *adv* anon, beforehand, betimes, ere, seasonably, shortly, soon.

earn *vb* acquire, gain, get, obtain, procure, realize, reap, win; deserve, merit.

earnest *adj* animated, ardent, eager, cordial, fervent, fervid, glowing, hearty, impassioned, importune, warm, zealous; fixed, intent, steady; sincere, true, truthful; important, momentous, serious, weighty. • *n* reality, seriousness, truth; foretaste, pledge, promise; handsel, payment.

earnings *npl* allowance, emoluments, gains, income, pay, proceeds, profits, remuneration, reward, salary, stipend.

earth *n* globe, orb, planet, world; clay, clod, dirt, glebe, ground, humus, land, loam, sod, soil, turf; mankind, world.

earthborn *adj* abject, base, earthly, grovelling, low, mean, unspiritual.

earthly *adj* terrestrial; base, carnal, earthborn, low, gross, grovelling, sensual, sordid, unspiritual, worldly; bodily, material, mundane, natural, secular, temporal.

earthy *adj* clayey, earth-like, terrene; earthly, terrestrial; coarse, gross, material, unrefined.

ease *vb* disburden, disencumber, pacify, quiet, relieve, still; abate, allay, alleviate, appease, assuage, diminish, mitigate, soothe; loosen, release; facilitate, favour. • *n* leisure, quiescence, repose, rest; calmness, content, contentment, enjoyment, happiness, peace, quiet, quietness, quietude, relief, repose, satisfaction, serenity, tranquillity; easiness, facility, readiness; flexibility, freedom, liberty, lightness, naturalness, unconcern, unconstraint; comfort, elbowroom.

easy *adj* light; careless, comfortable, contented, effortless, painless, quiet, satisfied, tranquil, untroubled; accommodating, complaisant, compliant, complying, facile, indolent, manageable, pliant, submissive, tractable, yielding; graceful, informal, natural, unconstrained; flowing, ready, smooth, unaffected; gentle, lenient, mild, moderate; affluent, loose, unconcerned, unembarrassed.

eat *vb* chew, consume, devour, engorge, ingest, ravage, swallow; corrode, demolish, erode; breakfast, dine, feed, lunch, sup.

eatable *adj* edible, esculent, harmless, wholesome.

ebb *vb* abate, recede, retire, subside; decay, decline, decrease, degenerate, deteriorate, sink, wane. • *n* refluence, reflux, regress, regression, retrocedence, retrocession, retrogression, return; caducity, decay, decline, degeneration, deterioration, wane, waning; abatement, decrease, decrement, diminution.

ebullition *n* ebullition, effervescence; burst, bursting, overenthusiasm, overflow, rush, vigour.

ebullition *n* boiling, bubbling; effervescence, fermentation; burst, fit, outbreak, outburst, paroxysm.

eccentric *adj* decentred, parabolic; aberrant, abnormal, anomalous, cranky, erratic, fantastic, irregular, odd, outlandish, peculiar, singular, strange, uncommon, unnatural, wayward, whimsical. • *n* crank, curiosity, original.

eccentricity *n* ellipticity, flattening, flatness, oblateness; aberration, irregularity, oddity, oddness, peculiarity, singularity, strangeness, waywardness.

ecclesiastic[1], **ecclesiastical** *adj* churchish, churchly, clerical, ministerial, nonsecular, pastoral, priestly, religious, sacerdotal.

ecclesiastic[2] *n* chaplain, churchman, clergyman, cleric, clerk, divine, minister, parson, pastor, priest, reverend, shepherd.

echo *vb* reply, resound, reverberate, ring; re-echo, repeat. • *n* answer, repetition, reverberation; imitation.

éclat *n* acclamation, applause, brilliancy, effect, glory, lustre, pomp, renown, show, splendour.

eclipse *vb* cloud, darken, dim, obscure, overshadow, veil; annihilate, annul, blot out, extinguish. • *n* clouding, concealment, darkening, dimming, disappearance, hiding, obscuration, occultation, shrouding, vanishing, veiling; annihilation, blotting out, destruction, extinction, extinguishment, obliteration.

eclogue *n* bucolic, idyl, pastoral.

economize *vb* husband, manage, save; retrench.

economy *n* frugality, husbandry, parsimony, providence, retrenchment, saving, skimping, stinginess, thrift, thriftiness; administration, arrangement, management, method, order, plan, regulation, system; dispensation.

ecstasy *n* frenzy, madness, paroxysm, trance; delight, gladness, joy, rhapsody, rapture, ravishment, transport.

eddy *vb* gurgle, surge, spin, swirl, whirl. • *n* countercurrent; swirl, vortex, whirlpool.

edge *vb* sharpen; border, fringe, rim. • *n* border, brim, brink, bound, crest, fringe, hem, lip, margin, rim, verge; animation, intensity, interest, keenness, sharpness, zest; acrimony, bitterness, gall, sharpness, sting.

edging *n* border, frill, fringe, trimming.

edible *adj* eatable, esculent, harmless, wholesome.

edict *n* act, command, constitution, decision, decree, law, mandate, manifesto, notice, order, ordinance, proclamation, regulation, rescript, statute.

edifice *n* building, fabric, habitation, house, structure.

edify *vb* educate, elevate, enlightenment, improve, inform, instruct, nurture, teach, upbuild.

edition *n* impression, issue, number.

educate *vb* breed, cultivate, develop, discipline, drill, edify, exercise, indoctrinate, inform, instruct, mature, nurture, rear, school, teach, train.

educated *adj* cultured, lettered, literate.

education *n* breeding, cultivation, culture, development, discipline, drilling, indoctrination, instruction, nurture, pedagogics, schooling, teaching, training, tuition.

educe *vb* bring out, draw out, elicit, evolve, extract.

eerie *adj* awesome, fearful, frightening, strange, uncanny, weird.

efface *vb* blot, blot out, cancel, delete, destroy, erase, expunge, obliterate, remove, sponge.

effect *vb* cause, create, effectuate, produce; accomplish, achieve, carry, compass, complete, conclude, consummate, contrive, do, execute, force, negotiate, perform, realize, work. • *n* consequence, event, fruit, issue, outcome, result; efficiency, fact, force, power, reality; validity, weight; drift, import, intent, meaning, purport, significance, tenor.

effective *adj* able, active, adequate, competent, convincing, effectual, sufficient; cogent, efficacious, energetic, forcible, potent, powerful.

effects *npl* chattels, furniture, goods, movables, property.

effectual *adj* operative, successful; active, effective, efficacious, efficient.

effectuate *vb* accomplish, achieve, complete, do, effect, execute, fulfil, perform, secure.

effeminate *adj* delicate, feminine, soft, tender, timorous, unmanly, womanish, womanlike, womanly; camp.

effervesce *vb* bubble, ferment, foam, froth.

effete *adj* addle, barren, fruitless, sterile, unfruitful, unproductive, unprolific; decayed, exhausted, spent, wasted.

efficacious *adj* active, adequate, competent, effective, effectual, efficient, energetic, operative, powerful.

efficacy *n* ability, competency, effectiveness, efficiency, energy, force, potency, power, strength, vigour, virtue.

efficient *adj* active, capable, competent, effective, effectual, efficacious, operative, potent; able, energetic, ready, skilful.

effigy *n* figure, image, likeness, portrait, representation, statue.

effloresce *vb* bloom, flower.

efflorescence *n* blooming, blossoming, flowering.

effluence *n* discharge, efflux, effluvium, emanation, emission, flow, outflow, outpouring.

effort *n* application, attempt, endeavour, essay, exertion, pains, spurt, strain, strife, stretch, struggle, trial, trouble.

effrontery *n* assurance, audacity, boldness, brass, disrespect, hardihood, impudence, incivility, insolence, presumption, rudeness, sauciness, shamelessness.

effulgent *adj* burning, beaming, blazing, bright, brilliant, dazzling, flaming, glowing, lustrous, radiant, refulgent, resplendent, shining, splendid.

effusion *n* discharge, efflux, emission, gush, outpouring; shedding, spilling, waste; address, speech, talk, utterance.

egg *vb* (*with* **on**) encourage, incite, instigate, push, stimulate, urge; harass, harry, provoke.

ego *n* id, self, me, subject, superego.

egotism *n* self-admiration, self-assertion, self-commendation, self-conceit, self-esteem, self-importance, self-praise; egoism, selfishness.

egotistic, egotistical *adj* bumptious, conceited, egoistical, opinionated, self-asserting, self-admiring, self-centred, self-conceited, self-important, self-loving, vain.

egregious *adj* conspicuous, enormous, extraordinary, flagrant, great, gross, huge, monstrous, outrageous, prodigious, remarkable, tremendous.

egress *n* departure, emergence, exit, outlet, way out.

eject *vb* belch, discharge, disgorge, emit, evacuate, puke, spew, spit, spout, spurt, void, vomit; bounce, cashier, discharge, dismiss, disposes, eliminate, evict, expel, fire, oust; banish, reject, throw out.

elaborate *vb* develop, improve, mature, produce, refine, ripen. • *adj* complicated, decorated, detailed, dressy, laboured, laborious, ornate, perfected, studied.

elapse *vb* go, lapse, pass.

elastic *adj* rebounding, recoiling, resilient, springy; buoyant, recuperative.

elated *adj* animated, cheered, elate, elevated, excited, exhilarated, exultant, flushed, puffed up, roused.

elbow *vb* crowd, force, hustle, jostle, nudge, push, shoulder. • *n* angle, bend, corner, flexure, joining, turn.

elder *adj* older, senior; ranking; ancient, earlier, older. • *n* ancestor, senior; presbyter, prior, senator.

elect *vb* appoint, choose, cull, designate, pick, prefer, select. • *adj* choice, chosen, picked, selected; appointed, elected; predestinated, redeemed.

election *n* appointment, choice, preference, selection; alternative, freedom, freewill, liberty; predestination.

elector *n* chooser, constituent, selector, voter.

electrify *vb* charge, galvanize; astonish, enchant, excite, rouse, startle, stir, thrill.

elegance, elegancy *n* beauty, grace, propriety, symmetry; courtliness, daintiness, gentility, nicety, polish, politeness, refinement, taste.

elegant *adj* beautiful, chaste, classical, dainty, graceful, fine, handsome, neat, symmetrical, tasteful, trim, well-made, well-proportioned; accomplished, courtly, cultivated, fashionable, genteel, polished, polite, refined.

elegiac *adj* dirgeful, mournful, plaintive, sorrowful.

elegy *n* dirge, epicedium, lament, ode, threnody.

element *n* basis, component, constituent, factor, germ, ingredient, part, principle, rudiment, unit; environment, milieu, sphere.

elementary *adj* primordial, simple, uncombined, uncomplicated, uncompounded; basic, component, fundamental, initial, primary, rudimental, rudimentary.

elevate *vb* erect, hoist, lift, raise; advance, aggrandize, exalt, promote; dignify, ennoble, exalt, greaten, improve, refine; animate, cheer, elate, excite, exhilarate, rouse.

elfin *adj* elflike, elvish, mischievous, weird.

elicit *vb* draw out, educe, evoke, extort, fetch, obtain, pump, wrest, wring; deduce, educe.

eligible *adj* desirable, preferable; qualified, suitable, worthy.

eliminate *vb* disengage, eradicate, exclude, expel, remove, separate; ignore, omit, reject.

ellipsis *n* gap, hiatus, lacuna, omission.

elliptical *adj* oval; defective, incomplete.

elocution *n* declamation, delivery, oratory, rhetoric, speech, utterance.

elongate *vb* draw, draw out, extend, lengthen, protract, stretch.

elope *vb* abscond, bolt, decamp, disappear, leave.

eloquence *n* fluency, oratory, rhetoric.

else *adv* besides, differently, otherwise.

elucidate *vb* clarify, demonstrate, explain, expound, illuminate, illustrate, interpret, unfold.

elucidation *n* annotation, clarification, comment, commentary, elucidating, explaining, explanation, exposition, gloss, scholium.

elude *vb* avoid, escape, evade, shun, slip; baffle, balk, disappoint, disconcert, escape, foil, frustrate, thwart.

elusive *adj* deceptive, deceitful, delusive, evasive, fallacious, fraudulent, illusory; equivocatory, equivocating, shuffling.

Elysian *adj* blissful, celestial, delightful, enchanting, heavenly, ravishing, seraphic.

emaciation *n* attenuation, lankness, leanness, meagreness, tabes, tabescence, thinness.

emanate *vb* arise, come, emerge, flow, issue, originate, proceed, spring.

emancipate *vb* deliver, discharge, disenthral, enfranchise, free, liberate, manumit, release, unchain, unfetter, unshackle.

emancipation *n* deliverance, enfranchisement, deliverance, freedom, liberation, manumission, release.

emasculate *vb* castrate, geld; debilitate, effeminize, enervate, unman, weaken.

embalm *vb* cherish, consecrate, conserve, enshrine, preserve, store, treasure; perfume, scent.

embargo *vb* ban, bar, blockade, debar, exclude, prohibit, proscribe, restrict, stop, withhold. • *n* ban, bar, blockade, exclusion, hindrance, impediment, prohibition, prohibitory, proscription, restraint, restriction, stoppage.

embark *vb* engage, enlist.

embarrass *vb* beset, entangle, perplex; annoy, clog, bother, distress, hamper, harass, involve, plague, trouble, vex; abash, confound, confuse, discomfit, disconcert, dumbfound, mortify, nonplus, pose, shame.

embellish *vb* adorn, beautify, bedeck, deck, decorate, emblazon, enhance, enrich, garnish, grace, ornament.

embellishment *n* adornment, decoration, enrichment, ornament, ornamentation.

embezzle *vb* appropriate, defalcate, filch, misappropriate, peculate, pilfer, purloin, steal.

embitter *vb* aggravate, envenom, exacerbate; anger, enrage, exasperate, madden.

emblem *n* badge, cognizance, device, mark, representation, sign, symbol, token, type.

embody *vb* combine, compact, concentrate, incorporate; comprehend, comprise, contain, embrace, include; codify, methodize, systematize.

embolden *vb* animate, cheer, elate, encourage, gladden, hearten, inspirit, nerve, reassure.

embosom *vb* bury, cherish, clasp, conceal, enfold, envelop, enwrap, foster, hide, nurse, surround.

embrace *vb* clasp; accept, seize, welcome; comprehend, comprise, contain, cover, embody, encircle, enclose, encompass, enfold, hold, include. • *n* clasp, fold, hug.

embroil *vb* commingle, encumber, ensnarl, entangle, implicate, involve; confuse, discompose, disorder, distract, disturb, perplex, trouble.

embryo *n* beginning, germ, nucleus, root, rudiment.

embryonic *adj* incipient, rudimentary, undeveloped.

emendation *n* amendment, correction, improvement, rectification.

emerge *vb* rise; emanate, escape, issue; appear, arise, outcrop.

emergency *n* crisis, difficulty, dilemma, exigency, extremity, necessity, pass, pinch, push, strait, urgency; conjuncture, crisis, juncture, pass.

emigration *n* departure, exodus, migration, removal.

eminence *n* elevation, hill, projection, prominence, protuberance; celebrity, conspicuousness, distinction, exaltation, fame, loftiness, note, preferment, reputation, repute, renown.

eminent *adj* elevated, high, lofty; celebrated, conspicuous, distinguished, exalted, famous, illustrious, notable, prominent, remarkable, renowned.

emissary *n* messenger, scout, secret agent, spy.

emit *vb* breathe out, dart, discharge, eject, emanate, exhale, gust, hurl, jet, outpour, shed, shoot, spurt, squirt.

emollient *adj* relaxing, softening, soothing. • *n* softener.

emolument *n* compensation, gain, hire, income, lucre, pay, pecuniary, profits, salary, stipend, wages; advantage, benefit, profit, perquisites.

emotion *n* agitation, excitement, feeling, passion, perturbation, sentiment, sympathy, trepidation.

emphasis *n* accent, stress; force, importance, impressiveness, moment, significance, weight.

emphatic *adj* decided, distinct, earnest, energetic, expressive, forcible, impressive, intensive, positive, significant, strong, unequivocal.

empire *n* domain, dominion, sovereignty, supremacy; authority, command, control, government, rule, sway.

empirical, empiric *adj* experimental, experiential; hypothetical, provisional, tentative; charlatanic, quackish.

employ *vb* busy, devote, engage, engross, enlist, exercise, occupy, retain; apply, commission, use. • *n* employment, service.

employee *n* agent, clerk, employee, hand, servant, workman.

employment *n* avocation, business, calling, craft, employ, engagement, occupation, profession, pursuit, trade, vocation, work.

emporium *n* market, mart, shop, store.

empower *vb* authorize, commission, permit, qualify, sanction, warrant; enable.

empty *vb* deplete, drain, evacuate, exhaust; discharge, disembogue; flow, embogue. • *adj* blank, hollow, unoccupied, vacant, vacuous, void; deplete, destitute, devoid, hungry; unfilled, unfurnished, unsupplied; unsatisfactory, unsatisfying, unsubstantial, useless, vain; clear, deserted, desolate, exhausted, free, unburdened, unloaded, waste; foolish, frivolous, inane, senseless, silly, stupid, trivial, weak.

empyrean, empyreal *adj* aerial, airy, ethereal, heavenly, refined, sublimated, sublimed.

emulation *n* competition, rivalry, strife, vying; contention, envy, jealousy.

enable *vb* authorize, capacitate, commission, empower, fit, permit, prepare, qualify, sanction, warrant.

enact *vb* authorize, command, decree, establish, legislate, ordain, order, sanction; act, perform, personate, play, represent.

enactment *n* act, decree, law, edict, ordinance.

enamour *vb* bewitch, captivate, charm, enchant, endear, fascinate.

enchain *vb* bind, confine, enslave, fetter, hold, manacle, restrain, shackle.

enchant *vb* beguile, bewitch, charm, delude, fascinate; captivate, catch, enamour, win; beatify, delight, enrapture, rapture, ravish, transport.

enchanting *adj* bewitching, blissful, captivating, charming, delightful, enrapturing, fascinating, rapturous, ravishing.

enchantment *n* charm, conjuration, incantation, magic, necromancy, sorcery, spell, witchery; bliss, delight, fascination, rapture, ravishment, transport.

encase *vb* encircle, enclose, incase, infix, set; chase, emboss, engrave, inlay, ornament.

encage *vb* confine, coop up, impound, imprison, shut up.

encircle *vb* belt, circumscribe, encompass, enclose, engird, enring, environ, gird, ring, span, surround, twine; clasp, embrace, enfold, fold.

enclose, inclose *vb* circumscribe, corral, coop, embosom, encircle, encompass, environ, fence in, hedge, include, pen, shut in, surround; box, cover, encase, envelop, wrap.

encomium *n* applause, commendation, eulogy, laudation, panegyric, praise.

encompass *vb* belt, compass, encircle, enclose, engird, environ, gird, surround; beset, besiege, hem in, include, invest, surround.

encounter *vb* confront, face, meet; attack, combat, contend, engage, strive, struggle. • *n* assault, attack, clash, collision, meeting, onset; action, affair, battle, brush, combat, conflict, contest, dispute, engagement, skirmish.

encourage *vb* animate, assure, cheer, comfort, console, embolden, enhearten, fortify, hearten, incite, inspirit, instigate, reassure, stimulate, strengthen; abet, aid, advance, approve, countenance, favour, foster, further, help, patronize, promote, support.

encroach *vb* infringe, invade, intrude, tench, trespass, usurp.

encumber *vb* burden, clog, hamper, hinder, impede, load, obstruct, overload, oppress, retard; complicate, embarrass, entangle, involve, perplex.

encumbrance *n* burden, clog, deadweight, drag, embarrassment, hampering, hindrance, impediment, incubus, load; claim, debt, liability, lien.

end *vb* abolish, close, conclude, discontinue, dissolve, drop, finish, stop, terminate; annihilate, destroy, kill; cease, terminate. • *n* extremity, tip; cessation, close, denouement, ending, expiration, finale, finis, finish, last, period, stoppage, wind-up; completion, conclusion, consummation; annihilation, catastrophe, destruction, dissolution; bound, limit, termination, terminus; consequence, event, issue, result, settlement, sequel, upshot; fragment, remnant, scrap, stub, tag, tail; aim, design, goal, intent, intention, object, objective, purpose.

endanger *vb* compromise, hazard, imperil, jeopardize, peril, risk.

endear *vb* attach, bind, captivate, charm, win.

endearment *n* attachment, fondness, love, tenderness; caress, blandishment, fondling.

endeavour *vb* aim, attempt, essay, labour, seek, strive, struggle, study, try. • *n* aim, attempt, conatus, effort, essay, exertion, trial, struggle, trial.

endless *adj* boundless, illimitable, immeasurable, indeterminable, infinite, interminable, limitless, unlimited; dateless, eternal, everlasting, never-ending, perpetual, unending; deathless, ever-enduring, ever-living, immortal, imperishable, undying.

endorse, indorse *vb* approve, back, confirm, guarantee, ratify, sanction, superscribe, support, visé, vouch for, warrant; superscribe.

endow *vb* bequeath, clothe, confer, dower, endue, enrich, gift, indue, invest, supply.

endowment *n* bequest, boon, bounty, gift, grant, largesse, present; foundation, fund, property, revenue; ability, aptitude, capability, capacity, faculty, genius, gift, parts, power, qualification, quality, talent.

endurance *n* abiding, bearing, sufferance, suffering, tolerance, toleration; backbone, bottom, forbearance, fortitude, guts, patience, resignation.

endure *vb* bear, support, sustain; experience, suffer, undergo, weather; abide, brook, permit, pocket, swallow, tolerate, stomach, submit, withstand; continue, last, persist, remain, wear.

enemy *n* adversary, foe; antagonist, foeman, opponent, rival.

energetic *adj* active, effective, efficacious, emphatic, enterprising, forceful, forcible, hearty, mettlesome, potent, powerful, strenuous, strong, vigorous.

energy *n* activity, dash, drive, efficacy, efficiency, force, go, impetus, intensity, mettle, might, potency, power, strength, verve, vim; animation, life, manliness, spirit, spiritedness, stamina, vigour, zeal.

enervate *vb* break, debilitate, devitalize, emasculate, enfeeble, exhaust, paralyse, relax, soften, unhinge, unnerve, weaken.

enfeeble *vb* debilitate, devitalize, enervate, exhaust, relax, unhinge, unnerve, weaken.

enfold, infold *vb* enclose, envelop, fold, enwrap, wrap; clasp, embrace.

enforce *vb* compel, constrain, exact, force, oblige, require, urge.

enfranchise *vb* emancipate, free, liberate, manumit, release.

engage *vb* bind, commit, obligate, pledge, promise; affiance, betroth, plight; book, brief, employ, enlist, hire, retain; arrest, allure, attach, draw, entertain, fix, gain, win; busy, commission, contract, engross, occupy; attack, encounter; combat, contend, contest, fight, interlock, struggle; embark, enlist; agree, promise, stipulate, undertake, warrant.

engagement *n* appointment, assurance, contract, obligation, pledge, promise, stipulation; affiancing, betrothment, betrothal, plighting; avocation, business, calling, employment, enterprise, occupation; action, battle, combat, encounter, fight.

engender *vb* bear, beget, breed, create, generate, procreate, propagate; cause, excite, incite, occasion, produce.

engine *n* invention, machine; agency, agent, device, implement, instrument, means, method, tool, weapon.

engorge *vb* bolt, devour, eat, gobble, gorge, gulp, swallow; glut, obstruct, stuff.

engrave *vb* carve, chisel, cut, etch, grave, hatch, incise, sculpt; grave, impress, imprint, infix.

engross *vb* absorb, engage, occupy, take up; buy up, forestall, monopolize.

engrossment *n* absorption, forestalling, monopoly.

engulf, ingulf *vb* absorb, overwhelm, plunge, swallow up.

enhance *vb* advance, aggravate, augment, elevate, heighten, increase, intensify, raise, swell.

enhearten *vb* animate, assure, cheer, comfort, console, embolden, encourage, hearten, incite, inspirit, reassure, stimulate.

enigma *n* conundrum, mystery, problem, puzzle, riddle.

enigmatic, enigmatical *adj* ambiguous, dark, doubtful, equivocal, hidden, incomprehensible, mysterious, mystic, obscure, occult, perplexing, puzzling, recondite, uncertain, unintelligible.

enjoin *vb* admonish, advise, urge; bid, command, direct, order, prescribe, require; prohibit, restrain.

enjoy *vb* like, possess, relish.

enjoyment *n* delight, delectation, gratification, happiness, indulgence, pleasure, satisfaction; possession.

enkindle *vb* inflame, ignite, kindle; excite, incite, instigate, provoke, rouse, stimulate.

enlarge *vb* amplify, augment, broaden, develop, dilate, distend, expand, extend, grow, increase, magnify, widen; aggrandize, engreaten, ennoble, expand, exaggerate, greaten; swell.

enlighten *vb* illume, illuminate, illumine; counsel, educate, civilize, inform, instruct, teach.

enlist *vb* enrol, levy, recruit, register; enrol, list; embark, engage.

enliven *vb* animate, invigorate, quicken, reanimate, rouse, wake; exhilarate, cheer, brighten, delight, elate, gladden, inspire, inspirit, rouse.

enmity *n* animosity, aversion, bitterness, hate, hatred, hostility, ill-will, malevolence, malignity, rancour.

ennoble *vb* aggrandize, dignify, elevate, engreaten, enlarge, exalt, glorify, greaten, raise.

ennui *n* boredom, irksomeness, languor, lassitude, listlessness, tedium, tiresomeness, weariness.

enormity *n* atrociousness, atrocity, depravity, flagitiousness, heinousness, nefariousness, outrageousness, villainy, wickedness.

enormous *adj* abnormal, exceptional, inordinate, irregular; colossal, Cyclopean, elephantine, Herculean, huge, immense, monstrous, vast, gigantic, prodigious, titanic, tremendous.

enough *adj* abundant, adequate, ample, plenty, sufficient. • *adv* satisfactorily, sufficiently. • *n* abundance, plenty, sufficiency.

enquire *see* **inquire.**

enrage *vb* anger, chafe, exasperate, incense, inflame, infuriate, irritate, madden, provoke.

enrapture *vb* beatify, bewitch, delight, enchant, enravish, entrance, surpassingly, transport.

enrich *vb* endow; adorn, deck, decorate, embellish, grace, ornament.

enrobe *vb* clothe, dress, apparel, array, attire, invest, robe.

enrol *vb* catalogue, engage, engross, enlist, list, register; chronicle, record.

ensconce *vb* conceal, cover, harbour, hide, protect, screen, secure, settle, shelter, shield, snugly.

enshrine *vb* embalm, enclose, entomb; cherish, treasure.

ensign *n* banner, colours, eagle, flag, gonfalcon, pennon, standard, streamer; sign, signal, symbol; badge, hatchment.

enslave *vb* captivate, dominate, master, overmaster, overpower, subjugate.

ensnare *vb* catch, entrap; allure, inveigle, seduce; bewilder, confound, embarrass, encumber, entangle, perplex.

ensue *vb* follow, succeed; arise, come, flow, issue, proceed, result, spring.

entangle *vb* catch, ensnare, entrap; confuse, enmesh, intertwine, intertwist, interweave, knot, mat, ravel, tangle; bewilder, embarrass, encumber, ensnare, involve, nonplus, perplex, puzzle.

enterprise *n* adventure, attempt, cause, effort, endeavour, essay, project, undertaking, scheme, venture; activity, adventurousness, daring, dash, energy, initiative, readiness, push.

enterprising *adj* adventurous, audacious, bold, daring, dashing, venturesome, venturous; active, adventurous, alert, efficient, energetic, prompt, resourceful, smart, spirited, stirring, strenuous, zealous.

entertain *vb* fete, receive, regale, treat; cherish, foster, harbour, hold, lodge, shelter; admit, consider; amuse, cheer, divert, please, recreate.

entertainment *n* hospitality; banquet, collation, feast, festival, reception, treat; amusement, diversion, pastime, recreation, sport.

enthusiasm *n* ecstasy, exaltation, fanaticism; ardour, earnestness, devotion, eagerness, fervour, passion, warmth, zeal.

enthusiast *n* bigot, devotee, fan, fanatic, freak, zealot; castle-builder, dreamer, visionary.

entice *vb* allure, attract, bait, cajole, coax, decoy, inveigle, lure, persuade, prevail on, seduce, tempt, wheedle, wile.

enticement *n* allurement, attraction, bait, blandishment, inducement, inveiglement, lure, persuasion, seduction.

entire *adj* complete, integrated, perfect, unbroken, undiminished, undivided, unimpaired, whole; complete, full, plenary, thorough; mere, pure, sheer, unalloyed, unmingled, unmitigated, unmixed.

entitle *vb* call, characterize, christen, denominate, designate, dub, name, style; empower, enable, fit for, qualify for.

entomb *vb* bury, inhume, inter.

entrails *npl* bowels, guts, intestines, inwards, offal, viscera.

entrance[1] *n* access, approach, avenue, incoming, ingress; adit, avenue, aperture, door, doorway, entry, gate, hallway, inlet, lobby, mouth, passage, portal, stile, vestibule; beginning, commencement, debut, initiation, introduction; admission, entrée.

entrance[2] *vb* bewitch, captivate, charm, delight, enchant, enrapture, fascinate, ravish, transport.

entrap *vb* catch, ensnare; allure, entice, inveigle, seduce; embarrass, entangle, involve, nonplus, perplex, pose, stagger.

entreat *vb* adjure, beg, beseech, crave, enjoin, implore, importune, petition, pray, solicit, supplicate.

entreaty *n* adjuration, appeal, importunity, petition, prayer, request, solicitation, suit, supplication.

entrée *n* access, admission, admittance.

entrench, intrench *vb* furrow; circumvallate, fortify; encroach, infringe, invade, trench, trespass.

entrenchment, intrenchment *n* entrenching; earthwork, fortification; defence, protection, shelter; encroachment, inroad, invasion.

entrust *vb* commit, confide, consign.

entwine *vb* entwist, interlace, intertwine, interweave, inweave, twine, twist, weave; embrace, encircle, encumber, interlace, surround.

enumerate *vb* calculate, cite, compute, count, detail, mention, number, numerate, reckon, recount, specify, tell.

enunciate *vb* articulate, declare, proclaim, promulgate, pronounce, propound, publish, say, speak, utter.

envelop *vb* encase, enfold, enwrap, fold, pack, wrap; cover, encircle, encompass, enshroud, hide, involve, surround.

envelope *n* capsule, case, covering, integument, shroud, skin, wrapper, veil, vesture, wrap.

envenom *vb* poison, taint; embitter, malign; aggravate, enrage, exasperate, incense, inflame, irritate, madden, provoke.

environ *vb* begird, belt, embrace, encircle, encompass, enclose, engird, envelop, gird, hedge, hem, surround; beset, besiege, encompass, invest.

environs *npl* neighbourhood, vicinage, vicinity.

envoy *n* ambassador, legate, minister, plenipotentiary; courier, messenger.

envy *vb* hate; begrudge, grudge; covet, emulate, desire. • *n* enviousness, hate, hatred, ill-will, jealousy, malice, spite; grudge, grudging.

enwrap *vb* absorb, cover, encase, engross, envelop, infold, involve, wrap, wrap up.

ephemeral *adj* brief, diurnal, evanescent, fleeting, flitting, fugacious, fugitive, momentary, occasional, short-lived, transient, transitory.

epic *adj* Homeric, heroic, narrative.

epicure *n* gastronome, glutton, gourmand, gourmet; epicurean, sensualist, Sybarite, voluptuary.

epidemic *adj* general, pandemic, prevailing, prevalent. • *n* outbreak, pandemia, pestilence, plague, spread, wave.

epidermis *n* cuticle, scarf-skin.

epigrammatic *adj* antithetic, concise, laconic, piquant, poignant, pointed, pungent, sharp, terse.

episcopal *adj* Episcopalian, pontifical, prelatic.

epistle *n* communication, letter, missive, note.

epithet *n* appellation, description, designation, name, predicate, title.

epitome *n* abbreviation, abridgement, abstract, breviary, brief, comment, compendium, condensation, conspectus, digest, summary, syllabus, synopsis.

epitomize *vb* abbreviate, abridge, abstract, condense, contract, curtail, cut, reduce, shorten, summarize.

epoch *n* age, date, era, period, time.

equable *adj* calm, equal, even, even-tempered, regular, steady, uniform, serene, tranquil, unruffled.

equal *vb* equalize, even, match. • *adj* alike, coordinate, equivalent, like, tantamount; even, level, equable, regular, uniform; equitable, even-handed, fair, impartial, just, unbiased; co-extensive, commensurate, corresponding, parallel, proportionate; adequate, competent, fit, sufficient. • *n* compeer, fellow, match, peer; rival.

equanimity *n* calmness, composure, coolness, peace, regularity, self-possession, serenity, steadiness.

equestrian *adj* equine, horse-like, horsy. • *n* horseman, rider; cavalier, cavalryman, chevalier, horse soldier, knight.

equilibrist *n* acrobat, balancer, funambulist, rope-walker.

equip *vb* appoint, arm, furnish, provide, rig, supply; accoutre, array, dress.

equipage *n* accoutrements, apparatus, baggage, effects, equipment, furniture; carriage, turnout, vehicle; attendance, procession, retinue, suite, train.

equipment *n* accoutrement, apparatus, baggage, equipage, furniture, gear, outfit, rigging.

equipoise *n* balance, equilibrium.

equitable *adj* even-handed, candid, honest, impartial, just, unbiased, unprejudiced, upright; adequate, fair, proper, reasonable, right.

equity *n* just, right; fair play, fairness, impartiality, justice, rectitude, reasonableness, righteousness, uprightness.

equivalent *adj* commensurate, equal, equipollent, tantamount; interchangeable, synonymous. • *n* complement, coordinate, counterpart, double, equal, fellow, like, match, parallel, pendant, quid pro quo.

equivocal *adj* ambiguous; doubtful, dubious, enigmatic, indeterminate, problematical, puzzling, uncertain.

equivocate *vb* dodge, evade, fence, palter, prevaricate, shuffle, quibble.

equivocation *n* evasion, paltering, prevarication, quibbling, shuffling; double entendre, double meaning, quibble.

era *n* age, date, epoch, period, time.

eradicate *vb* extirpate, root, uproot; abolish, annihilate, destroy, obliterate.

erase *vb* blot, cancel, delete, efface, expunge, obliterate, scrape out.

erasure *n* cancellation, cancelling, effacing, expunging, obliteration.

erect *vb* build, construct, raise, rear; create, establish, form, found, institute, plant. • *adj* standing, unrecumbent, uplifted, upright; elevated, vertical, perpendicular, straight; bold, firm, undaunted, undismayed, unshaken, unterrified.

erelong *adv* early, quickly, shortly, soon, speedily.

eremite *n* anchoret, anchorite, hermit, recluse, solitary.

ergo *adv* consequently, hence, therefore.

erode *vb* canker, consume, corrode, destroy, eat away, fret, rub.

erosive *adj* acrid, cathartic, caustic, corroding, corrosive, eating, virulent.

erotic *adj* amorous, amatory, arousing, seductive, stimulating, titillating.

err *vb* deviate, ramble, rove, stray, wander; blunder, misjudge, mistake; fall, lapse, nod, offend, sin, stumble, trespass, trip.

errand *n* charge, commission, mandate, message, mission, purpose.

errant *adj* adventurous, rambling, roving, stray, wandering.

erratic *adj* nomadic, rambling, roving, wandering; moving, planetary; abnormal, capricious, deviating, eccentric, irregular, odd, queer, strange.

erratum *n* correction, corrigendum, error, misprint, mistake.

erroneous *adj* false, incorrect, inaccurate, inexact, mistaken untrue, wrong.

error *n* blunder, fallacy, inaccuracy, misapprehension, mistake, oversight; delinquency, fault, iniquity, misdeed, misdoing, misstep, obliquity, offence, shortcoming, sin, transgression, trespass, wrongdoing.

erudition *n* knowledge, learning, lore, scholarship.

eruption *n* explosion, outbreak, outburst; sally; rash.

escape *vb* avoid, elude, evade, flee from, shun; abscond, bolt, decamp, flee, fly; slip. • *n* flight; release; passage, passing; leakage.

eschew *vb* abstain, avoid, elude, flee from, shun.

escort *vb* convey, guard, protect; accompany, attend, conduct. • *n* attendant, bodyguard, cavalier, companion, convoy, gallant, guard, squire; protection, safe conduct, safeguard; attendance, company.

esculent *adj* eatable, edible, wholesome.

esoteric *adj* hidden, inmost, inner, mysterious, private, recondite, secret.

especial *adj* absolute, chief, distinct, distinguished, marked, particular, peculiar, principal, singular, special, specific, uncommon, unusual; detailed, minute, noteworthy.

espousal *n* affiancing, betrothing, espousing, plighting; adoption, defence, maintenance, support.

espouse *vb* betroth, plight, promise; marry, wed; adopt, champion, defend, embrace, maintain, support.

espy *vb* descry, detect, discern, discover, observe, perceive, spy, watch.

esquire *n* armiger, attendant, escort, gentleman, squire.

essay¹ *vb* attempt, endeavour, try. • *n* aim, attempt, effort, endeavour, exertion, struggle, trial.

essay² *n* article, composition, disquisition, dissertation, paper, thesis.

essence *n* nature, quintessence, substance; extract, part; odour, perfume, scent; being, entity, existence, nature.

essential *adj* fundamental, indispensable, important, inward, intrinsic, necessary, requisite, vital; diffusible, pure, rectified, volatile.

establish *vb* fix, secure, set, settle; decree, enact, ordain; build, constitute, erect, form, found, institute, organize, originate, pitch, plant, raise; ensconce, ground, install, place, plant, root, secure; approve, confirm, ratify, sanction; prove, substantiate, verify.

estate *n* condition, state; position, rank, standing; division, order; effects, fortune, possessions, property; interest.

esteem *vb* appreciate, estimate, rate, reckon, value; admire, honour, like, prize, respect, revere, reverence, value, venerate, worship; account, believe, consider, deem, fancy, hold, imagine, suppose, regard, think. • *n* account, appreciation, consideration, estimate, estimation, judgement, opinion, reckoning, valuation; credit, honour, regard, respect, reverence.

estimable *adj* appreciable, calculable, computable; admirable, credible, deserving, excellent, good, meritorious, precious, respectful, valuable, worthy.

estimate *vb* appraise, appreciate, esteem, prise, rate, value; assess, calculate, compute, count, gauge, judge, reckon. • *n* estimation, judgement, valuation; calculation, computation.

estimation *n* appreciation, estimate, valuation; esteem, estimate, judgement, opinion; honour, reckoning, regard, respect, reverence.

estop *vb* bar, impede, preclude, stop.

estrange *vb* withdraw, withhold; alienate, divert; disaffect, destroy.

estuary *n* creek, inlet, fiord, firth, frith, mouth.

etch *vb* corrode, engrave.

eternal *adj* absolute, inevitable, necessary, self-active, self-existent, self-originated; abiding, ceaseless, endless, ever-enduring, everlasting, incessant, interminable, never-ending, perennial, permanent, perpetual, sempiternal, unceasing, unending; deathless, immortal, imperishable, incorruptible, indestructible, never-dying, undying; immutable, unchangeable; constant, continual, continuous, incessant, persistent, unbroken, uninterrupted.

ethereal *adj* aerial, airy, celestial, empyreal, heavenly, unworldly; attenuated, light, subtle, tenuous, volatile; delicate, fairy, flimsy, fragile, rare, refined, subtle.

eulogize *vb* applaud, commend, extol, laud, magnify, praise.

eulogy *n* discourse, eulogium, panegyric, speech; applause, encomium, commendation, laudation, praise.

euphonious *adj* clear, euphonic, harmonious, mellifluous, mellow, melodious, musical, silvery, smooth, sweet-toned.

evacuant *adj* abstergent, cathartic, cleansing, emetic, purgative. • *n* cathartic, purgative.

evacuate *vb* empty; discharge, clean out, clear out, eject, excrete, expel, purge, void; abandon, desert, forsake, leave, quit, relinquish, withdraw.

evade *vb* elude, escape; avoid, decline, dodge, funk, shun; baffle, elude, foil; dodge, equivocate, fence, palter, prevaricate, quibble, shuffle.

evanescence *n* disappearance, evanishing, evanishment, vanishing; transience, transientness, transitoriness.

evanescent *adj* ephemeral, fleeting, flitting, fugitive, passing, short-lived, transient, transitory, vanishing.

evaporate *vb* distil, volatilize; dehydrate, dry, vaporize; disperse, dissolve, fade, vanish.

evaporation *n* distillation, volatilization; dehydration, drying, vaporization; disappearance, dispersal, dissolution.

evasion *n* artifice, avoidance, bluffing, deceit, dodge, equivocation, escape, excuse, funking, prevarication, quibble, shift, subterfuge, shuffling, sophistical, tergiversation.

evasive *adj* elusive, elusory, equivocating, prevaricating, shuffling, slippery, sophistical.

even *vb* balance, equalize, harmonize, symmetrize; align, flatten, flush, level, smooth, square. • *adj* flat, horizontal, level, plane, smooth; calm, composed, equable, equal, peaceful, placid, regular, steady, uniform, unruffled; direct, equitable, fair, impartial, just, straightforward. • *adv* exactly, just, verily; likewise. • *n* eve, evening, eventide, vesper.

evening *n* dusk, eve, even, eventide, nightfall, sunset, twilight.

event *n* circumstance, episode, fact, happening, incident, occurrence; conclusion, consequence, end, issue, outcome, result, sequel, termination; adventure, affair.

eventful *adj* critical, important, memorable, momentous, remarkable, signal, stirring.

eventual *adj* final, last, ultimate; conditional, contingent, possible. • *adv* always, aye, constantly, continually, eternally, ever evermore, forever, incessantly, perpetually, unceasingly.

everlasting *adj* ceaseless, constant, continual, endless, eternal, ever-during, incessant, interminable, never-ceasing, never-ending, perpetual, unceasing, unending, unintermitting, uninterrupted; deathless, ever-living, immortal, imperishable, never-dying, undying.

evermore *adv* always, constantly, continually, eternally, ever, forever, perpetually.

everyday *adj* accustomed, common, commonplace, customary, habitual, routine, usual, wonted.

evict *vb* dispossess, eject, thrust out.

evidence *vb* evince, make clear, manifest, prove, show, testify, vouch. • *n* affirmation, attestation, averment, confirmation, corroboration, deposition, grounds, indication, proof, testimony, token, trace, voucher, witness.

evident *adj* apparent, bald, clear, conspicuous, distinct, downright, incontestable, indisputable, manifest, obvious, open, overt, palpable, patent, plain, unmistakable.

evil *adj* bad, ill; base, corrupt, malicious, malevolent, malign, nefarious, perverse, sinful, vicious, vile, wicked, wrong; bad, deleterious, baleful, baneful, destructive, harmful, hurtful, injurious, mischievous, noxious, pernicious, profane; adverse, calamitous, diabolic, disastrous, unfortunate, unhappy, unpropitious, woeful. • *n* calamity, disaster, ill, misery, misfortune, pain, reverse, sorrow, suffering, woe; badness, baseness, corruption, depravity, malignity, sin, viciousness, wickedness; bale, bane, blast, canker, curse, harm, injury, mischief, wrong.

evince *vb* establish, evidence, manifest, prove, show; disclose, display, exhibit, indicate, reveal.

eviscerate *vb* disembowel, embowel, gut.

evoke *vb* arouse, elicit, excite, provoke, rouse.

evolve *vb* develop, educe, exhibit, expand, open, unfold, unroll.

exacerbate *vb* aggravate, embitter, enrage, exasperate, excite, inflame, infuriate, irritate, provoke, vex.

exact *vb* elicit, extort, mulch, require, squeeze; ask, claim, compel, demand, enforce, requisition, take. • *adj* rigid, rigorous, scrupulous, severe, strict; diametric, express, faultless, precise, true; accurate, close, correct, definite, faithful, literal, undeviating; accurate, critical, delicate, fine, nice, sensitive; careful, methodical, punctilious, orderly, punctual, regular.

exacting *adj* critical, difficult, exactive, rigid, extortionary.

exaction *n* contribution, extortion, oppression, rapacity, tribute.

exactness *n* accuracy, correctness, exactitude, faithfulness, faultlessness, fidelity, nicety, precision, rigour; carefulness, method, precision, regularity, rigidness, scrupulosity, scrupulousness, strictness.

exaggerate *vb* enlarge, magnify, overcharge, overcolour, overstate, romance, strain, stretch.

exalt *vb* elevate, erect, heighten, lift up, raise; aggrandize, dignify, elevate, ennoble; bless, extol, glorify, magnify, praise.

exalted *adj* elated, elevated, high, highflown, lofty, lordly, magnificent.

examination *n* inspection, observation; exploration, inquiry, inquisition, investigation, perusal, research, search, scrutiny, survey; catechism, probation, review, test, trial.

examine *vb* inspect, observe; canvass, consider, explore, inquire, investigate, scrutinize, study, test; catechize, interrogate.

example *n* archetype, copy, model, pattern, piece, prototype, representative, sample, sampler, specimen, standard; exemplification, illustration, instance, precedent, warning.

exanimate *adj* dead, defunct, inanimate, lifeless; inanimate, inert, sluggish, spiritless, torpid.

exasperate *vb* affront, anger, chafe, enrage, incense, irritate, nettle, offend, provoke, vex; aggravate, exacerbate, inflame, rouse.

exasperation *n* annoyance, exacerbation, irritation, pro- vocation; anger, fury, ire, passion, rage, wrath; aggravation, heightening, increase, worsening.

excavate *vb* burrow, cut, delve, dig, hollow, hollow out, scoop, trench.

exceed *vb* cap, overstep, surpass, transcend; excel, outdo, outstrip, outvie, pass.

excel *vb* beat, eclipse, outdo, outrival, outstrip, outvie, surpass; cap, exceed, transcend.

excellence *n* distinction, eminence, pre-eminence, superiority, transcendence; fineness, fitness, goodness, perfection, purity, quality, superiority; advantage; goodness, probity, uprightness, virtue, worth.

excellent *adj* admirable, choice, crack, eminent, first-rate, prime, sterling, superior, tiptop, transcendent; deserving, estimable, praiseworthy, virtuous, worthy.

except *vb* exclude, leave out, omit, reject. • *conj* unless. • *prep* bar, but, excepting, excluding, save.

exceptional *adj* aberrant, abnormal, anomalous, exceptive, irregular, peculiar, rare, special, strange, superior, uncommon, unnatural, unusual.

excerpt *vb* cite, cull, extract, quote, select, take. • *n* citation, extract, quotation, selection.

excess *adj* excessive, unnecessary, redundant, spare, superfluous, surplus. • *n* disproportion, fulsomeness, glut, oversupply, plethora, redundance, redundancy, surfeit, superabundance, superfluity; overplus, remainder, surplus; debauchery, dissipation, dissoluteness, intemperance, immoderation, overindulgence, unrestraint; extravagance, immoderation, overdoing.

excessive *adj* disproportionate, exuberant, superabundant, superfluous, undue; extravagant, enormous, inordinate, outrageous, unreasonable; extreme, immoderate, intemperate; vehement, violent.

exchange *vb* barter, change, commute, shuffle, substitute, swap, trade, truck; bandy, interchange. • *n* barter, change, commutation, dealing, shuffle, substitution, trade, traffic; interchange, reciprocity; bazaar, bourse, fair, market.

excise[1] *n* capitation, customs, dues, duty, tariff, tax, taxes, toll.

excise[2] *vb* cancel, cut, delete, edit, efface, eradicate, erase, expunge, extirpate, remove, strike out.

excision *n* destruction, eradication, extermination, extirpation.

excitable *adj* impressible, nervous, sensitive, susceptible; choleric, hasty, hot-headed, hot-tempered, irascible, irritable, passionate, quick-tempered.

excite *vb* animate, arouse, awaken, brew, evoke, impel, incite, inflame, instigate, kindle, move, prompt, provoke, rouse, spur, stimulate; create, elicit, evoke, raise; agitate, discompose, disturb, irritate.

excitement *n* excitation, exciting; incitement, motive, stimulus; activity, agitation, bustle, commotion, disturbance, ferment, flutter, perturbation, sensation, stir, tension; choler, heat, irritation, passion, violence, warmth.

exclaim *vb* call, cry, declare, ejaculate, shout, utter, vociferate.

exclude *vb* ban, bar, blackball, debar, ostracize, preclude, reject; hinder, prevent, prohibit, restrain, withhold; except, omit; eject, eliminate, expel, extrude.

exclusive *adj* debarring, excluding; illiberal, narrow, narrow-minded, selfish, uncharitable; aristocratic, choice, clannish, cliquish, fastidious, fashionable, select, snobbish; only, sole, special.

excommunicate *vb* anathematize, ban, curse, denounce, dismiss, eject, exclude, expel, exscind, proscribe, unchurch.

excoriate *vb* abrade, flay, gall, scar, scarify, score, skin, strip.

excrement *n* dejections, dung, faeces, excreta, excretion, ordure, stool.

excrescence *n* fungus, growth, knob, lump, outgrowth, protuberance, tumour, wart.

excrete *vb* discharge, eject, eliminate, separate.

excruciate *vb* agonize, rack, torment, torture.

exculpate *vb* absolve, acquit, clear, discharge, exonerate, free, justify, release, set right, vindicate.

excursion *n* drive, expedition, jaunt, journey, ramble, ride, sally, tour, trip, voyage, walk; digression, episode.

excursive *adj* devious, diffuse, digressive, discursive, erratic, rambling, roaming, roving, wandering.

excusable *adj* allowable, defensible, forgivable, justifiable, pardonable, venial, warrantable.

excursus *n* discussion, disquisition, dissertation.

excuse *vb* absolve, acquit, exculpate, exonerate, forgive, pardon, remit; extenuate, justify; exempt, free, release; overlook. • *n* absolution, apology, defence, extenuation, justification, plea; colour, disguise, evasion, guise, pretence, pretext, makeshift, semblance, subterfuge.

execrable *adj* abhorrent, abominable, accursed, cursed, damnable, detestable, hateful, odious; disgusting, loathsome, nauseating, nauseous, obnoxious, offensive, repulsive, revolting, sickening, vile.

execrate *vb* curse, damn, imprecate; abhor, abominate, detest, hate, loathe.

execute *vb* accomplish, achieve, carry out, complete. consummate, do, effect, effectuate, finish, perform, perpetrate; administer, enforce, seal, sign; behead, electrocute, guillotine, hang.

execution *n* accomplishment, achievement, completion, consummation, operation, performance; warrant, writ; beheading, electrocution, hanging.

executive *adj* administrative, commanding, controlling, directing, managing, ministerial, officiating, presiding, ruling. • *n* administrator, director, manager.

exegetic, exegetical *adj* explanatory, explicative, explicatory, expository, hermeneutic, interpretative.

exemplary *adj* assiduous, close, exact, faithful, punctual, punctilious, rigid, rigorous, scrupulous; commendable, correct, good, estimable, excellent, praiseworthy, virtuous; admonitory, condign, monitory, warning.

exemplify *vb* evidence, exhibit, illustrate, manifest, show.

exempt *vb* absolve, except, excuse, exonerate, free, release, relieve. • *adj* absolved, excepted, excused, exempted, free, immune, liberated, privileged, released.

exemption *n* absolution, dispensation, exception, immunity, privilege, release.

exercise *vb* apply, busy, employ, exert, praxis, use; effect, exert, produce, wield; break in, discipline, drill, habituate, school, train; practise, prosecute, pursue; task, test, try; afflict, agitate, annoy, burden, pain, trouble. • *n* appliance, application, custom, employment, operation, performance, play, plying, practice, usage, use, working; action, activity, effort, exertion, labour, toil, work; discipline, drill, drilling, schooling, training; lesson, praxis, study, task, test, theme.

exert *vb* employ, endeavour, exercise, labour, strain, strive, struggle, toil, use, work.

exertion *n* action, exercise, exerting, use; attempt, effort, endeavour, labour, strain, stretch, struggle, toil, trial.

exhalation *n* emission, evaporation; damp, effluvium, fog, fume, mist, reek, smoke, steam, vapour.

exhale *vb* breathe, discharge, elect, emanate, emit, evaporate, reek; blow, expire, puff.

exhaust *vb* drain, draw, empty; consume, destroy, dissipate, expend, impoverish, lavish, spend, squander, waste; cripple, debilitate, deplete, disable, enfeeble, enervate, overtire, prostrate, weaken.

exhaustion *n* debilitation, enervation, fatigue, lassitude, weariness.

exhibit *vb* demonstrate, disclose, display, evince, expose, express, indicate, manifest, offer, present, reveal, show; offer, present, propose.

exhibition *n* demonstration, display, exposition, manifestation, representation, spectacle, show; allowance, benefaction, grant, pension, scholarship.

exhilarate *vb* animate, cheer, elate, enliven, gladden, inspire, inspirit, rejoice, stimulate.

exhilaration *n* animating, cheering, elating, enlivening, gladdening, rejoicing, stimulating; animation, cheer, cheerfulness, gaiety, gladness, glee, good spirits, hilarity, joyousness.

exhort *vb* advise, caution, encourage, incite, persuade, stimulate, urge, warm; preach.

exhume *vb* disentomb, disinhume, disinter, unbury, unearth.

exigency, exigence *n* demand, necessity, need, requirement, urgency, want; conjuncture, crisis, difficulty, distress, emergency, extremity, juncture, nonplus, quandary, pass, pinch, pressure, strait.

exiguous *adj* attenuated, diminutive, fine, small, scanty, slender, tiny.

exile *vb* banish, expatriate, expel, ostracize, proscribe. • *n* banishment, expatriation, expulsion, ostracism, proscription, separation; outcast, refugee.

exist *vb* be, breathe, live; abide, continue, endure, last, remain.

existence *n* being, subsisting, subsistence; being, creature, entity, essence, thing; animation, continuation, life, living, vitality, vivacity.

exit *vb* depart, egress, go, leave. • *n* departure, withdrawal; death, decrease, demise, end; egress, outlet.

exonerate *vb* absolve, acquit, clear, exculpate, justify, vindicate; absolve, discharge, except, exempt, free, release.

exorbitant *adj* enormous, excessive, extravagant, inordinate, unreasonable.

exorcise *vb* cast out, drive away, expel; deliver, purify; address, conjure.

exordium *n* introduction, opening, preamble, preface, prelude, proem, prologue.

exotic *adj* extraneous, foreign; extravagant.

expand *vb* develop, open, spread, unfold, unfurl; diffuse, enlarge, extend, increase, stretch; dilate, distend, enlarge.

expanse *n* area, expansion, extent, field, stretch.

expansion *n* expansion, opening, spreading; diastole, dilation, distension, swelling; development, diffusion, enlargement, increase; expanse, extent, stretch.

ex parte *adj* biased, one-sided, partisan.

expatiate *vb* amplify, decant, dilate, enlarge, range, rove.

expatriate *vb* banish, exile, expel, ostracize, proscribe. • *adj* banished, exiled, refugee. • *n* displaced person, emigrant, exile.

expect *vb* anticipate, await, calculate, contemplate, forecast, foresee, hope, reckon, rely.

expectancy *n* expectance, expectation; abeyance, prospect.

expectation *n* anticipation, expectance, expectancy, hope, prospect; assurance, confidence, presumption, reliance, trust.

expedient *adj* advisable, appropriate, convenient, desirable, fit, proper, politic, suitable; advantageous, profitable, useful. • *n* contrivance, device, means, method, resort, resource, scheme, shift, stopgap, substitute.

expedite *vb* accelerate, advance, dispatch, facilitate, forward, hasten, hurry, precipitate, press, quicken, urge.

expedition *n* alacrity, alertness, celerity, dispatch, haste, promptness, quickness, speed; enterprise, undertaking; campaign, excursion, journey, march, quest, voyage.

expeditious *adj* quick, speedy, swift, rapid; active, alert, diligent, nimble, prompt, punctual, swift.

expel *vb* dislodge, egest, eject, eliminate, excrete; discharge, eject, evacuate, void; bounce, discharge, exclude, exscind, fire, oust, relegate, remove; banish, disown, excommunicate, exile, expatriate, ostracize, proscribe, unchurch.

expend *vb* disburse, spend; consume, employ, exert, use; dissipate, exhaust, scatter, waste.

expenditure *n* disbursement, outlay, outlaying, spending; charge, cost, expenditure, outlay.

expensive *adj* costly, dear, high-priced; extravagant, lavish, wasteful.

experience *vb* endure, suffer; feel, know; encounter, suffer, undergo. • *n* endurance, practice, trial; evidence, knowledge, proof, test, testimony.

experienced *adj* able, accomplished, expert, instructed, knowing, old, practised, qualified, skilful, trained, thoroughbred, versed, veteran, wise.

experiment *vb* examine, investigate, test, try. • *n* assay, examination, investigation, ordeal, practice, proof, test, testimony, touchstone, trial.

expert *adj* able, adroit, apt, clever, dextrous, proficient, prompt, quick, ready, skilful. • *n* adept, authority, connoisseur, crack, master, specialist.

expertise *n* adroitness, aptness, dexterity, facility, promptness, skilfulness, skill.

expiate *vb* atone, redeem, satisfy.

expiration *n* death, decease, demise, departure, exit; cessation, close, conclusion, end, termination.

expire *vb* cease, close, conclude, end, stop, terminate; emit, exhale; decease, depart, die, perish.

explain *vb* demonstrate, elucidate, expound, illustrate, interpret, resolve, solve, unfold, unravel; account for, justify, warrant.

explanation *n* clarification, description, elucidation, exegesis, explication, exposition, illustration, interpretation; account, answer, deduction, justification, key, meaning, secret, solution, warrant.

explicit *adj* absolute, categorical, clear, definite, determinate, exact, express, plain, positive, precise, unambiguous, unequivocal, unreserved.

explode *vb* burst, detonate, discharge, displode, shatter, shiver; contemn, discard, repudiate, scorn, scout.

exploit *vb* befool, milk, use, utilize. • *n* achievement, act, deed, feat.

explore *vb* examine, fathom, inquire, inspect, investigate, prospect, scrutinize, seek.

explosion *n* blast, burst, bursting, clap, crack, detonation, discharge, displosion, fulmination, pop.

exponent *n* example, illustration, index, indication, specimen, symbol, type; commentator, demonstrator, elucidator, expounder, illustrator, interpreter.

expose *vb* bare, display, uncover; descry, detect, disclose, unearth; denounce, mask; subject; endanger, jeopardize, risk, venture.

exposé *n* exhibit, exposition, manifesto; denouncement, divulgement, exposure, revelation.

exposition *n* disclosure, interpretation; commentary, critique, elucidation, exegesis, explanation, explication, interpretation; display, show.

expound *vb* develop, present, rehearse, reproduce, unfold; clear, elucidate, explain, interpret.

express *vb* air, assert, asseverate, declare, emit, enunciate, manifest, utter, vent, signify, speak, state, voice; betoken, denote, equal, exhibit, indicate, intimate, present, represent, show, symbolize. • *adj* categorical, clear, definite, determinate, explicit, outspoken, plain, positive, unambiguous; accurate, close, exact, faithful, precise, true; particular, special; fast, nonstop, quick, rapid, speedy, swift. • *n* dispatch, message.

expression *n* assertion, asseveration, communication, declaration, emission, statement, utterance, voicing; language, locution, phrase, remark, saying, term, word; air, aspect, look, mien.

expressive *adj* indicative, meaningful, significant; demonstrative, eloquent, emphatic, energetic, forcible, lively, strong, vivid; appropriate, sympathetic, well-modulated.

expulsion *n* discharge, eviction, expelling, ousting; elimination, evacuation, excretion; ejection, excision, excommunication, extrusion, ostracism, separation.

expunge *vb* annihilate, annul, cancel, delete, destroy, efface, erase, obliterate, wipe out.

expurgate *vb* clean, cleanse, purge, purify; bowdlerize, emasculate.

exquisite *adj* accurate, delicate, discriminating, exact, fastidious, nice, refined; choice, elect, excellent, precious, rare, valuable; complete, consummate, matchless, perfect; acute, keen, intense, poignant. • *n* beau, coxcomb, dandy, fop, popinjay.

extant *adj* existent, existing, present, surviving, undestroyed, visible.

extempore *adj* extemporaneous, extemporary, impromptu, improvised. • *adv* offhand, suddenly, unpremeditatedly, unpreparedly.

extend *vb* reach, stretch; continue, elongate, lengthen, prolong, protract, widen; augment, broaden, dilate, distend, enlarge, expand, increase; diffuse, spread; give, impart, offer, yield; lie, range.

extensible *adj* ductile, elastic, extendible, extensile, protractible, protractile.

extension *n* augmentation, continuation, delay, dilatation, dilation, distension, enlargement, expansion, increase, prolongation, protraction.

extensive *adj* broad, capacious, comprehensive, expanded, extended, far-reaching, large, wide, widespread.

extent *n* amplitude, expanse, expansion; amount, bulk, content, degree, magnitude, size, volume; compass, measure, length, proportions, reach, stretch; area, field, latitude, range, scope; breadth, depth, height, width.

extenuate *vb* diminish, lessen, reduce, soften, weaken; excuse, mitigate, palliate, qualify.

exterior *adj* external, outer, outlying, outside, outward, superficial, surface; extrinsic, foreign. • *n* outside, surface; appearance.

exterminate *vb* abolish, annihilate, destroy, eliminate, eradicate, extirpate, uproot.

external *adj* exterior, outer, outside, outward, superficial; extrinsic, foreign; apparent, visible.

extinct *adj* extinguished, quenched; closed, dead, ended, lapsed, terminated, vanished.

extinction *n* death, extinguishment; abolishment, abolition, annihilation, destruction, excision, extermination, extirpation.

extinguish *vb* choke, douse, put out, quell, smother, stifle, suffocate, suppress; destroy, nullify, subdue; eclipse, obscure.

extirpate *vb* abolish, annihilate, deracinate, destroy, eradicate, exterminate, uproot, weed.

extol *vb* celebrate, exalt, glorify, laud, magnify, praise; applaud, commend, eulogize, panegyrize.

extort *vb* elicit, exact, extract, force, squeeze, wrench, wrest, wring.

extortion *n* blackmail, compulsion, demand, exaction, oppression, overcharge, rapacity, tribute; exorbitance.

extortionate *adj* bloodsucking, exacting, hard, harsh, oppressive, rapacious, rigorous, severe; exorbitant, unreasonable.

extra *adj* accessory, additional, auxiliary, collateral; another, farther, fresh, further, more, new, other, plus, ulterior; side, spare, supernumerary, supplemental, supplementary, surplus; extraordinary, extreme, unusual. • *adv* additionally, also, beyond, farthermore, furthermore, more, moreover, plus. • *n* accessory, appendage, collateral, nonessential, special, supernumerary, supplement; bonus, premium; balance, leftover, remainder, spare, surplus.

extract *vb* extort, pull out, remove, withdraw; derive, distil, draw, express, squeeze; cite, determine, derive, quote, select. • *n* citation, excerpt, passage, quotation, selection; decoction, distillation, essence, infusion, juice.

extraction *n* drawing out, derivation, distillation, elicitation, essence, pulling out; birth, descent, genealogy, lineage, origin, parentage.

extraneous *adj* external, extrinsic, foreign; additional, adventitious, external, superfluous, supplementary, unessential.

extraordinary *adj* abnormal, amazing, distinguished, egregious, exceptional, marvellous, monstrous, particular, peculiar, phenomenal, prodigious, rare, remarkable, signal, singular, special, strange, uncommon, unprecedented, unusual, unwonted, wonderful.

extravagance *n* excess, enormity, exorbitance, preposterousness, unreasonableness; absurdity, excess, folly, irregularity, wildness; lavishness, prodigality, profuseness, profusion, superabundance; waste.

extravagant *adj* excessive, exorbitant, inordinate, preposterous, unreasonable; absurd, foolish, irregular, wild; lavish, prodigal, profuse, spendthrift.

extreme *adj* farthest, outermost, remotest, utmost, uttermost; greatest, highest; final, last, ultimate; drastic, egregious, excessive, extravagant, immoderate, intense, outrageous, radical, unreasonable. • *n* end, extremity, limit; acme, climax, degree, height, pink; danger, distress.

extremity *n* border, edge, end, extreme, limb, termination, verge.

extricate *vb* clear, deliver, disembarrass, disengage, disentangle, liberate, release, relieve.

extrinsic *adj* external, extraneous, foreign, outside, outward, superabundance, superfluity.

exuberance *n* abundance, copiousness, flood, luxuriance, plenitude; excess, lavishness, overabundance, overflow, overgrowth, over-luxuriance, profusion, rankness, redundancy, superabundance, superfluity.

exuberant *adj* abounding, abundant, copious, fertile, flowing, luxuriant, prolific, rich; excessive, lavish, overabundant, overflowing, over-luxuriant, profuse, rank, redundant, superabounding, superabundant, wanton.

exude *vb* discharge, excrete, secrete, sweat; infiltrate, ooze, percolate.

exult *vb* gloat, glory, jubilate, rejoice, transport, triumph, taunt, vault.

exultation *n* delight, elation, joy, jubilation, transport, triumph.

eye *vb* contemplate, inspect, ogle, scrutinize, survey, view, watch. • *n* estimate, judgement, look, sight, vision, view; inspection, notice, observation, scrutiny, sight, vigilance, watch; aperture, eyelet, peephole, perforation; bud, shoot.

F

fable *n* allegory, legend, myth, parable, story, tale; fabrication, falsehood, fiction, figment, forgery, untruth.

fabric *n* building, edifice, pile, structure; conformation, make, texture, workmanship; cloth, material, stuff, textile, tissue, web.

fabricate *vb* build, construct, erect, frame; compose, devise, fashion, make, manufacture; coin, fake, feign, forge, invent.

fabrication *n* building, construction, erection; manufacture; fable, fake, falsehood, fiction, figment, forgery, invention, lie.

fabulous *adj* amazing, apocryphal, coined, fabricated, feigned, fictitious, forged, imaginary, invented, legendary, marvellous, mythical, romancing, unbelievable, unreal.

façade *n* elevation, face, front.

face *vb* confront; beard, buck, brave, dare, defy, front, oppose; dress, level, polish, smooth; cover, incrust, veneer. • *n* cover, facet, surface; breast, escarpment, front; countenance, features, grimace, physiognomy, visage; appearance, expression, look, semblance; assurance, audacity, boldness, brass, confidence, effrontery, impudence.

facet *n* cut, face, lozenge, surface.

facetious *adj* amusing, comical, droll, funny, humorous, jocose, jocular, pleasant, waggish, witty; entertaining, gay, lively, merry, sportive, sprightly.

facile *adj* easy; affable, approachable, complaisant, conversable, courteous, mild; compliant, ductile, flexible, fluent, manageable, pliable, pliant, tractable, yielding; dextrous, ready, skilful.

facilitate *vb* expedite, help.

facility *n* ease, easiness; ability, dexterity, expertness, knack, quickness, readiness; ductility, flexibility, pliancy; advantage, appliance, convenience, means, resource; affability, civility, complaisance, politeness.

facsimile *n* copy, duplicate, fax, reproduction.

fact *n* act, circumstance, deed, event, incident, occurrence, performance; actuality, certainty, existence, reality, truth.

faction *n* cabal, clique, combination, division, junta, party, side; disagreement, discord, disorder, dissension, recalcitrance, recalcitrancy, refractoriness, sedition, seditiousness, tumult, turbulence, turbulency.

factious *adj* litigious, malcontent, rebellious, recalcitrant, refractory, seditious. turbulent.

factitious *adj* artful, artificial, conventional, false, unnatural, unreal.

factor *n* agent, bailiff, broker, consignee, go-between, steward, component, element, ingredient; influence, reason.

factory *n* manufactory, mill, work, workshop.

faculty *n* ability, capability, capacity, endowment, power, property, quality; ableness, address, adroitness, aptitude, aptness, clearness, competency, dexterity, efficiency, expertness, facility, forte, ingenuity, knack, qualification, quickness, readiness, skill, skilfulness, talent, turn; body, department, profession; authority, prerogative, license, privilege, right.

fade *vb* disappear, die, evanesce, fall, faint, perish, vanish; decay, decline, droop, fall, languish, wither; bleach, blanch, pale; disperse, dissolve.

faeces *npl* dregs, lees, sediment, settlings; dung, excrement, ordure, settlings.

fag *vb* droop, flag, sink; drudge, toil; fatigue, jade, tire, weary. • *n* drudgery, fatigue, work; drudge, grub, hack; cigarette, smoke.

fail *vb* break, collapse, decay, decline, fade, sicken, sink, wane; cease, disappear; fall, miscarry, miss; neglect, omit; bankrupt, break.

failing *adj* deficient, lacking, needing, wanting; declining, deteriorating, fading, flagging, languishing, sinking, waning, wilting; unsuccessful. • *prep* lacking, needing, wanting. • *n* decay, decline; failure, miscarriage; defect, deficiency, fault, foible, frailty, imperfection, infirmity, shortcoming, vice, weakness; error, lapse, slip; bankruptcy, insolvency.

failure *n* defectiveness, deficiency, delinquency, shortcoming; fail, miscarriage, negligence, neglect, nonobservance, nonperformance, omission, slip; abortion, botch, breakdown, collapse, fiasco, fizzle; bankruptcy, crash, downfall, insolvency, ruin; decay, declension, decline, loss.

fain *adj* anxious, glad, inclined, pleased, rejoiced, well-pleased. • *adv* cheerfully, eagerly, gladly, joyfully, willingly.

faint *vb* swoon; decline, fade, fail, languish, weaken. • *adj* swooning; drooping, exhausted, feeble, languid, listless, sickly, weak; gentle, inconsiderable, little, slight, small, soft, thin; dim, dull, indistinct, perceptible, scarce, slight; cowardly, dastardly, faint-hearted, fearful, timid, timorous; dejected, depressed, discouraged, disheartened, dispirited. • *n* blackout, swoon.

faint-hearted *adj* cowardly, dastardly, faint, fearful, timid, timorous.

fair¹ *adj* spotless, unblemished, unspotted, unstained, untarnished; blond, light, white; beautiful, comely, handsome, shapely; clear, cloudless, pleasant, unclouded; favourable, prosperous; hopeful, promising, propitious; clear, distinct, open, plain, unencumbered, unobstructed; candid, frank, honest, honourable, impartial, ingenuous, just, unbiased, upright; equitable, proper; average, decent, indifferent, mediocre, moderate, ordinary, passable, reasonable, respectful, tolerable.

fair² *n* bazaar, carnival, exposition, festival, fete, funfair, gala, kermess.

fairy *n* brownie, elf, demon, fay, sprite.

faith *n* assurance, belief, confidence, credence, credit, dependence, reliance, trust; creed, doctrine, dogma, persuasion, religion, tenet; constancy, faithfulness, fidelity, loyalty, truth, truthfulness.

faithful *adj* constant, devoted, loyal, staunch, steadfast, true; honest, upright, reliable, trustworthy, trusty; reliable, truthful; accurate, close, conscientiousness, exact, nice, strict.

faithless *adj* unbelieving; dishonest, disloyal, false, fickle, fluctuating, inconstant, mercurial, mutable, perfidious, shifting, treacherous, truthless, unsteady, untruthful, vacillating, variable, wavering.

fall *vb* collapse, depend, descend, drop, sink, topple, tumble; abate, decline, decrease, depreciate, ebb, subside; err, lapse, sin, stumble, transgress, trespass, trip; die, perish; befall, chance, come, happen, occur, pass; become, get; come, pass. • *n* collapse, comedown, descent, downcome, dropping, falling, flop, plop, tumble; cascade, cataract, waterfall; death, destruction, downfall, overthrow, ruin, surrender; comeuppance, degradation; apostasy, declension, failure, lapse, slip; decline, decrease, depreciation, diminution, ebb, sinking, subsidence; cadence, close; declivity, inclination, slope.

fallacious *adj* absurd, deceptive, deceiving, delusive, disappointing, erroneous, false, illusive, illusory, misleading; paralogistic, sophistical, worthless.

fallacy *n* aberration, deceit, deception, delusion, error, falsehood, illusion, misapprehension, misconception, mistake, untruth; non sequitur, paralogism, sophism, sophistry.

fallibility *n* frailty, imperfection, uncertainty.

fallible *adj* erring, frail, ignorant, imperfect, uncertain, weak.

fallow *adj* left, neglected, uncultivated, unsowed, untilled; dormant, inactive, inert.

false *adj* lying, mendacious, truthless, untrue, unveracious; dishonest, dishonourable, disingenuous, disloyal, double-faced, double-tongued, faithless, false-hearted, perfidious, treacherous, unfaithful; fictitious, forged, made-up, unreliable, untrustworthy; artificial, bastard, bogus, counterfeit, factitious, feigned, forged, hollow, hypocritical, make-believe, pretended, pseudo, sham, spurious, suppositious; erroneous, improper, incorrect, unfounded, wrong; deceitful, deceiving, deceptive, disappointing, fallacious, misleading.

false-hearted *adj* dishonourable, disloyal, double, double-tongued, faithless, false, perfidious, treacherous.

falsehood *n* falsity; fabrication, fib, fiction, lie, untruth; cheat, counterfeit, imposture, mendacity, treachery.

falsify *vb* alter, adulterate, belie, cook, counterfeit, doctor, fake, falsely, garble, misrepresent, misstate, represent; disprove; violate.

falsity *n* falsehood, untruth, untruthfulness.

falter *vb* halt, hesitate, lisp, quaver, stammer, stutter; fail, stagger, stumble, totter, tremble, waver; dodder.

fame *n* bruit, hearsay, report, rumour; celebrity, credit, eminence, glory, greatness, honour, illustriousness, kudos, lustre, notoriety, renown, reputation, repute.

familiar *adj* acquainted, aware, conversant, well-versed; amicable, close, cordial, domestic, fraternal, friendly, homely, intimate, near; affable, accessible, companionable, conversable, courteous, civil, friendly, kindly, sociable, social; easy, free and easy, unceremonious, unconstrained; common, frequent, well-known. • *n* acquaintance, associate, companion, friend, intimate.

familiarity *n* acquaintance, knowledge, understanding; fellowship, friendship, intimacy; closeness, friendliness, sociability; freedom, informality, liberty; disrespect, overfreedom, presumption; intercourse.

familiarize *vb* accustom, habituate, inure, train, use.

family *n* brood, household, people; ancestors, blood, breed, clan, dynasty, kindred, house, lineage, race, stock, strain, tribe; class, genus, group, kind, subdivision.

famine *n* dearth, destitution, hunger, scarcity, starvation.

famish *vb* distress, exhaust, pinch, starve.

famous *adj* celebrated, conspicuous, distinguished, eminent, excellent, fabled, famed, far-famed, great, glorious, heroic, honoured, illustrious, immortal, notable, noted, notorious, remarkable, renowned, signal.

fan[1] *vb* agitate, beat, move, winnow; blow, cool, refresh, ventilate; excite, fire, increase, rouse, stimulate. • *n* blower, cooler, punkah, ventilator.

fan[2] *n* admirer, buff, devotee, enthusiast, fancier, follower, pursuer, supporter.

fanatic *n* bigot, devotee, enthusiast, visionary, zealot.

fanatical *adj* bigoted, enthusiastic, frenzied, mad, rabid, visionary, wild, zealous.

fanciful *adj* capricious, crotchety, imaginary, visionary, whimsical; chimerical, fantastical, ideal, imaginary, wild.

fancy *vb* apprehend, believe, conjecture, imagine, suppose, think; conceive, imagine. • *adj* elegant, fine, nice, ornamented; extravagant, fanciful, whimsical. • *n* imagination; apprehension, conceit, conception, impression, idea, image, notion, thought; approval, fondness, inclination, judgement, liking, penchant, taste; caprice, crotchet, fantasy, freak, humour, maggot, quirk, vagary, whim, whimsy; apparition, chimera, daydream, delusion, hallucination, megrim, phantasm, reverie, vision.

fanfaron *n* blatherskite, blusterer, braggadocio, bully, hector, swaggerer, vapourer.

fang *n* claw, nail, talon, tooth; tusk.

fantastic *adj* chimerical, fanciful, imaginary, romantic, unreal, visionary; bizarre, capricious, grotesque, odd, quaint, queer, strange, whimsical, wild.

far *adj* distant, long, protracted, remote; farther, remoter; alienated, estranged, hostile. • *adv* considerably, extremely, greatly, very much; afar, distantly, far away, remotely.

farce *n* burlesque, caricature, parody, travesty; forcemeat, stuffing.

farcical *adj* absurd, comic, droll, funny, laughable, ludicrous, ridiculous.

fardel *n* bundle, burden, load, pack; annoyance, burden, ill, trouble.

fare *vb* go, journey, pass, travel; happen, prosper, prove; feed, live, manage, subsist. • *n* charge, price, ticket money; passenger, traveller; board, commons, food, table, victuals, provisions; condition, experience, fortune, luck, outcome.

farewell *n* adieu, leave-taking, valediction; departure, leave, parting, valedictory.

far-fetched *adj* abstruse, catachrestic, forced, recondite, strained.

farrago *n* gallimaufry, hodgepodge, hotchpotch, jumble, medley, miscellany, mixture, potpourri, salmagundi.

farther *adj* additional; further, remoter, ulterior. • *adv* beyond, further; besides, furthermore, moreover.

farthingale *n* crinoline, hoop, hoop skirt.

fascinate *vb* affect, bewitch, overpower, spellbind, stupefy, transfix; absorb, captivate, catch, charm, delight, enamour, enchant, enrapture, entrance.

fascination *n* absorption, charm, enchantment, magic, sorcery, spell, witchcraft, witchery.

fash *vb* harass, perplex, plague, torment, trouble, vex, worry. • *n* anxiety, care, trouble, vexation.

fashion *vb* contrive, create, design, forge, form, make, mould, pattern, shape; accommodate, adapt, adjust, fit, suit. • *n* appearance, cast, configuration, conformation, cut, figure, form, make, model, mould, pattern, shape, stamp; manner, method, sort, wake; conventionalism, conventionality, custom, fad, mode, style, usage, vogue; breeding, gentility; quality.

fashionable *adj* modish, stylish; current, modern, prevailing, up-to-date; customary, usual; genteel, well-bred.

fast[1] *adj* close, fastened, firm, fixed, immovable, tenacious, tight; constant, faithful, permanent, resolute, staunch, steadfast, unswerving, unwavering; fortified, impregnable, strong; deep, profound, sound; fleet, quick, rapid, swift; dissipated, dissolute, extravagant, giddy, reckless, thoughtless, thriftless, wild. • *adv* firmly, immovably, tightly; quickly, rapidly, swiftly; extravagantly, prodigally, reckless, wildly.

fast[2] *vb* abstain, go hungry, starve. • *n* abstention, abstinence, diet, fasting, starvation.

fasten *vb* attach, bind, bolt, catch, chain, cleat, fix, gird, lace, lock, pin, secure, strap, tether, tie; belay, bend; connect, hold, join, unite.

fastidious *adj* critical, dainty, delicate, difficult, exquisite, finical, hypercritical, meticulous, overdelicate, overnice, particular, precise, precious, punctilious, queasy, squeamish.

fat *adj* adipose, fatty, greasy, oily, oleaginous, unctuous; corpulent, fleshy, gross, obese, paunchy, portly, plump, pudgy, pursy; coarse, dull, heavy, sluggish, stupid; lucrative, profitable, rich; fertile, fruitful, productive, rich. • *n* adipose tissue, ester, grease, oil; best part, cream, flower; corpulence, fatness, fleshiness, obesity, plumpness, stoutness.

fatal *adj* deadly, lethal, mortal; baleful, baneful, calamitous, catastrophic, destructive, mischievous, pernicious, ruinous; destined, doomed, foreordained, inevitable, predestined.

fatality *n* destiny, fate; mortality; calamity, disaster.

fate *n* destination, destiny, fate; cup, die, doom, experience, lot, fortune, portion, weird; death, destruction, ruin.

fated *adj* appointed, destined, doomed, foredoomed, predetermined, predestinated, predestined, preordained.

fatherly *adj* benign, kind, paternal, protecting, tender.

fathom *vb* comprehend, divine, penetrate, reach, understand; estimate, gauge, measure, plumb, probe, sound.

fathomless *adj* abysmal, bottomless, deep, immeasurable, profound; impenetrable, incomprehensible, obscure.

fatigue *vb* exhaust, fag, jade, tire, weaken, weary. • *n* exhaustion, lassitude, tiredness, weariness; hardship, labour, toil.

fatuity *n* foolishness, idiocy, imbecility, stupidity; absurdity, folly, inanity, infatuation, madness.

fatuous *adj* dense, drivelling, dull, foolish, idiotic, stupid, witless; infatuated, mad, senseless, silly, weak.

fault *n* blemish, defect, flaw, foible, frailty, imperfection, infirmity, negligence, obliquity, offence, shortcoming, spot, weakness; delinquency, error, indiscretion, lapse, misdeed, misdemeanour, offence, peccadillo, slip, transgression, trespass, vice, wrong; blame, culpability.

faultless *adj* blameless, guiltless, immaculate, innocent, sinless, spotless, stainless; accurate, correct, perfect, unblemished.

faulty *adj* bad, defective, imperfect, incorrect; blameable, blameworthy, censurable, culpable, reprehensible.

faux pas *n* blunder, indiscretion, mistake.

favour *vb* befriend, countenance, encourage, patronize; approve, ease, facilitate; aid, assist, help, oblige, support; extenuate, humour, indulge, palliate, spare. • *n* approval, benignity, countenance, esteem, friendless, goodwill, grace, kindness, benefaction, benefit, boon, dispensation, kindness; championship, patronage, popularity, support; gift, present, token; badge, decoration, knot, rosette; leave, pardon, permission; advantage, cover, indulgence, protection; bias, partiality, prejudice.

favourable *adj* auspicious, friendly, kind, propitious, well-disposed, willing; conductive, contributing, propitious; adapted, advantage, beneficial, benign, convenient, fair, fit, good, helpful, suitable.

favourite *adj* beloved, darling, dear; choice, fancied, esteemed, pet, preferred.

fawn *vb* bootlick, bow, creep, cringe, crouch, dangle, kneel, stoop, toady, truckle.

fealty *n* allegiance, homage, loyalty, obeisance, submission; devotion, faithfulness, fidelity, honour, loyalty.

fear *vb* apprehend, dread; revere, reverence, venerate. • *n* affright, alarm, apprehension, consternation, dismay, dread, fright, horror, panic, phobia, scare, terror; disquietude, flutter, perturbation, palpitation, quaking, quivering, trembling, tremor, trepidation; anxiety, apprehension, concern, misdoubt, misgiving, qualm, solicitude; awe, dread, reverence, veneration.

fearful *adj* afraid, apprehensive, haunted; chicken-hearted, chicken-livered, cowardly, faint-hearted, lily-livered, nervous, pusillanimous, timid, timorous; dire, direful, dreadful, frightful, ghastly, horrible, shocking, terrible.

fearless *adj* bold, brave, courageous, daring, dauntless, doughty, gallant, heroic, intrepid, unterrified, valiant, valorous.

feasible *adj* achievable, attainable, possible, practicable, suitable.

feast *n* delight, gladden, gratify, rejoice. • *n* banquet, carousal, entertainment, regale, repast, revels, symposium, treat; celebration, festival, fete, holiday; delight, enjoyment, pleasure.

feat *n* accomplishment, achievement, act, deed, exploit, performance, stunt, trick.

feather *n* plume; kind, nature, species.

featly *adv* adroitly, dextrously, nimbly, skilfully.

feature *vb* envisage, envision, picture, visualize; imagine; specialize; appear in, headline, star. • *n* appearance, aspect, component; conformation, fashion, make; characteristic, item, mark, particularity, peculiarity, property, point, trait; leader, lead item, special; favour, expression, lineament; article, film, motion picture, movie, story; highlight, high spot.

fecund *adj* fruitful, impregnated, productive, prolific, rich.

fecundity *n* fertility, fruitfulness, productiveness.

federation *n* alliance, allying, confederation, federating, federation, leaguing, union, uniting; affiliation, coalition, combination, compact, confederacy, entente, federacy, league, copartnership.

fee *vb* pay, recompense, reward. • *n* account, bill, charge, compensation, honorarium, remuneration, reward, tip; benefice, fief, feud.

feeble *adj* anaemic, debilitated, declining, drooping, enervated, exhausted, frail, infirm, languid, languishing, sickly; dim, faint, imperfect, indistinct.

feed *vb* contribute, provide, supply; cherish, eat, nourish, subsist, sustain. • *n* fodder, food, foodstuff, forage, provender.

feel *vb* apprehend, intuit, perceive, sense; examine, handle, probe, touch; enjoy, experience, suffer; prove, sound, test, try; appear, look, seem; believe, conceive, deem, fancy, infer, opine, suppose, think. • *n* atmosphere, feeling, quality; finish, surface, texture.

feeling *n* consciousness, impression, notion, perception, sensation; atmosphere, sense, sentience, touch; affecting, emotion, heartstrings, impression, passion, soul, sympathy; sensibility, sentiment, susceptibility, tenderness; attitude, impression, opinion.

feign *vb* devise, fabricate, forge, imagine, invent; affect, assume, counterfeit, imitate, pretend, sham, simulate.

feint *n* artifice, blind, expedient, make-believe, pretence, stratagem, trick.

felicitate *vb* complicate, congratulate; beatify, bless, delight.

felicitous *adj* appropriate, apt, fit, happy, ingenious, inspired, opportune, pertinent, seasonable, skilful, well-timed; auspicious, fortunate, prosperous, propitious, successful.

felicity *n* blessedness, bliss, blissfulness, gladness, happiness, joy; appropriateness, aptitude, aptness, felicitousness, fitness, grace, propriety, readiness, suitableness; fortune, luck, success.

fell[1] *vb* beat, knock down, level, prostrate; cut, demolish, hew.

fell[2] *adj* barbarous, bloodthirsty, bloody, cruel, ferocious, fierce, implacable, inhuman, malicious, malign, malignant, pitiless, relentless, ruthless, sanguinary, savage, unrelenting, vandalistic; deadly, destructive.

fellow *adj* affiliated, associated, joint, like, mutual, similar, twin. • *n* associate, companion, comrade; compeer, equal, peer; counterpart, mate, match, partner; member; boy, character, individual, man, person.

fellowship *n* brotherhood, companionship, comradeship, familiarity, intimacy; participation; partnership; communion, converse, intercourse; affability, kindliness, sociability, sociableness.

felon *n* convict, criminal, culprit, delinquent, malefactor, outlaw; inflammation, whitlow.

felonious *adj* atrocious, cruel, felon, heinous, infamous, malicious, malign, malignant, nefarious, perfidious, vicious, villainous.

female *adj* delicate, gentle, ladylike, soft; fertile, pistil-bearing, pistillate.

feminine *adj* affectionate, delicate, gentle, graceful, modest, soft, tender; female, ladylike, maidenly, womanish, womanly; effeminateness, effeminacy, softness, unmanliness, weakness, womanliness.

fen *n* bog, marsh, moor, morass, quagmire, slough, swamp.

fence *vb* defend, enclose, fortify, guard, protect, surround; circumscribe, evade, equivocate, hedge, prevaricate; guard, parry. • *n* barrier, hedge, hoarding, palings, palisade, stockade, wall; defence, protection, guard, security, shield; fencing, swordplay, swordsmanship; receiver.

fenny *adj* boggy, fennish, swampy, marshy.

feral, ferine *adj* ferocious, fierce, rapacious, ravenous, savage, untamed, wild.

ferment *vb* agitate, excite, heat; boil, brew, bubble, concoct, heat, seethe. • *n* barm, leaven, yeast; agitation, commotion, fever, glow, heat, tumult.

ferocious *adj* feral, fierce, rapacious, ravenous, savage, untamed, wild; barbarous, bloody, bloodthirsty, brutal, cruel, fell, inhuman, merciless, murderous, pitiless, remorseless, ruthless, sanguinary, truculent, vandalistic, violent.

ferocity *n* ferociousness, ferocity, fierceness, rapacity, savageness, wildness; barbarity, cruelty, inhumanity.

fertile *adj* bearing, breeding, fecund, prolific; exuberant, fruitful, luxuriant, plenteous, productive, rich, teeming; female, fruit-bearing, pistillate.

fertility *n* fertileness, fertility; abundance, exuberant, fruitfulness, luxuriance, plenteousness, productiveness, richness.

fervent *adj* burning, hot, glowing, melting, seething; animated, ardent, earnest, enthusiastic, fervid, fierce, fiery, glowing, impassioned, intense, passionate, vehement, warm, zealous.

fervour *n* heat, warmth; animation, ardour, eagerness, earnestness, excitement, fervency, intensity, vehemence, zeal.

fester *vb* corrupt, rankle, suppurate, ulcerate; putrefy, rot. • *n* abscess, canker, gathering, pustule, sore, suppination; festering, rankling.

festival *n* anniversary, carnival, feast, fete, gala, holiday, jubilee; banquet, carousal, celebration, entertainment, treat.

festive *adj* carnival, convivial, festal, festival, gay, jolly, jovial, joyful, merry, mirthful, uproarious.

festivity *n* conviviality, festival, gaiety, jollity, joviality, joyfulness, joyousness, merrymaking, mirth.

festoon *vb* adorn, decorate, embellish, garland, hoop, ornament. • *n* decoration, embellishment, garland, hoop, ornament, ornamentation.

fetch *vb* bring, elicit, get; accomplish, achieve, effect, perform; attain, reach. • *n* artifice, dodge, ruse, stratagem, trick.

fetid *adj* foul, malodorous, mephitic, noisome, offensive, rancid, rank, rank-smelling, stinking, strong-smelling.

fetish *n* charm, medicine, talisman.

fetter *vb* clog, hamper, shackle, trammel; bind, chain, confine, encumber, hamper, restrain, tie, trammel. • *n* bond, chain, clog, hamper, shackle.

feud *vb* argue, bicker, clash, contend, dispute, quarrel. • *n* affray, argument, bickering, broil, clashing, contention, contest, discord, dissension, enmity, fray, grudge, hostility, jarring, quarrel, rupture, strife, vendetta.

fever *n* agitation, excitement, ferment, fire, flush, heat, passion.

fey *adj* clairvoyant, ethereal, strange, unusual, whimsical; death-smitten, doomed.

fiasco *n* failure, fizzle.

fiat *n* command, decree, order, ordinance.

fibre *n* filament, pile, staple, strand, texture, thread; stamina, strength, toughness.

fickle *adj* capricious, changeable, faithless, fitful, inconstant, irresolute, mercurial, mutable, shifting, unsettled, unstable, unsteady, vacillating, variable, veering, violate, volatile, wavering.

fiction *n* fancy, fantasy, imagination, invention; novel, romance; fable, fabrication, falsehood, figment, forgery, invention, lie.

fictitious *adj* assumed, fabulous, fanciful, feigned, imaginary, invented, mythical, unreal; artificial, counterfeit, dummy, false, spurious, supposititious.

fiddle *vb* dawdle, fidget, interfere, tinker, trifle; cheat, swindle, tamper. • *n* fraud, swindle; fiddler, violin, violinist.

fiddle-de-dee *interj* fudge, moonshine, nonsense, stuff.

fiddle-faddle *n* frivolity, gabble, gibberish, nonsense, prate, stuff, trifling, trivia, twaddle.

fidelity *n* constancy, devotedness, devotion, dutifulness, faithfulness, fealty, loyalty, true-heartedness, truth; accuracy, closeness, exactness, faithfulness, precision.

fidget *vb* chafe, fret, hitch, twitch, worry. • *n* fidgetiness, impatience, restlessness, uneasiness.

fiduciary *adj* confident, fiducial, firm, steadfast, trustful, undoubting, unwavering; reliable, trustworthy. • *n* depositary, trustee.

field *n* clearing, glebe, meadow; expanse, extent, opportunity, range, room, scope, surface; department, domain, province, realm, region.

fiendish *adj* atrocious, cruel, demoniac, devilish, diabolical, hellish, implacable, infernal, malevolent, malicious, malign, malignant.

fierce *adj* barbarous, brutal, cruel, fell, ferocious, furious, infuriate, ravenous, savage; fiery, impetuous, murderous, passionate, tearing, tigerish, truculent, turbulent, uncurbed, untamed, vehement, violent.

fiery *adj* fervent, fervid, flaming, heated, hot, glowing, lurid; ardent, fierce, impassioned, impetuous, inflamed, passionate, vehement.

fight *vb* battle, combat, war; contend, contest, dispute, feud, oppose, strive, struggle, wrestle; encounter, engage; handle, manage, manoeuvre. • *n* affair, affray, action, battle, brush, combat, conflict, confrontation, contest, duel, encounter, engagement, melée, quarrel, struggle, war; brawl, broil, riot, row, skirmish; fighting, pluck, pugnacity, resistance, spirit, temper.

figment *n* fable, fabrication, falsehood, fiction, invention.

figurative *adj* emblematical, representative, symbolic, representative, typical; metaphorical, tropical; florid, flowery, ornate, poetical.

figure *vb* adorn, diversify, ornament, variegate; delineate, depict, represent, signify, symbolize, typify; conceive, image, imagine, picture; calculate, cipher, compute; act, appear, perform. • *n* configuration, conformation, form, outline, shape; effigy, image, likeness, representative; design, diagram, drawing, pattern; image, metaphor, trope; emblem, symbol, type; character, digit, number, numeral.

filament *n* cirrus, fibre, fibril, gossamer, hair, strand, tendril, thread.

filch *vb* crib, nick, pilfer, purloin, rob, snitch, seal, thieve.

file[1] *vb* order, pigeonhole, record, tidy. • *n* data, dossier, folder, portfolio; column, line, list, range, rank, row, series, tier.

file[2] *vb* burnish, furbish, polish, rasp, refine, smooth.

filibuster *vb* delay, frustrate, obstruct, play for time, stall, temporize. • *n* frustrater, obstructionist, thwarter; adventurer, buccaneer, corsair, freebooter, pirate.

fill *vb* occupy, pervade; dilate, distend, expand, stretch, trim; furnish, replenish, stock, store, supply; cloy, congest, content, cram, glut, gorge, line, pack, pall, sate, satiate, satisfy, saturate, stuff, suffuse, swell; engage, fulfil, hold, occupy, officiate, perform.

film *vb* becloud, cloud, coat, cover, darken, fog, mist, obfuscate, obscure, veil; photograph, shoot, take. • *n* cloud, coating, gauze, membrane, nebula, pellicle, scum, skin, veil; thread.

filter *vb* filtrate, strain; exude, ooze, percolate, transude. • *n* diffuser, colander, riddle, sieve, sifter, strainer.

filth *n* dirt, nastiness, ordure; corruption, defilement, foulness, grossness, impurity, obscenity, pollution, squalor, uncleanness, vileness.

filthy *adj* defiled, dirty, foul, licentious, nasty, obscene, pornographic, squalid, unclean; corrupt, gross, impure, unclean; miry, mucky, muddy.

final *adj* eventual, extreme, last, latest, terminal, ultimate; conclusive, decisive, definitive, irrevocable.

finale *n* conclusion, end, termination.

finances *npl* funds, resources, revenues, treasury; income, property.

find *vb* discover, fall upon; gain, get, obtain, procure; ascertain, notice, observe, perceive, remark; catch, detect; contribute, furnish, provide, supply. • *n* acquisition, catch, discovery, finding, plum, prize, strike.

fine[1] *vb* filter, purify, refine. • *adj* comminuted, little, minute, small; capillary, delicate, small; choice, light; exact, keen, sharp; attenuated, subtle, tenuous, thin; exquisite, fastidious, nice, refined, sensitive, subtle; dandy, excellent, superb, superior; beautiful, elegant, handsome, magnificent, splendid; clean, pure, unadulterated.

fine[2] *vb* amerce, mulct, penalize, punish. • *n* amercement, forfeit, forfeiture, mulct, penalty, punishment.

finery *n* decorations, frippery, gewgaws, ornaments, splendour, showiness, trappings, trimmings, trinkets.

finesse *vb* manipulate, manoeuvre. • *n* artifice, contrivance, cunning, craft, manipulation, manoeuvre, manoeuvring, ruses, stratagems, strategy, wiles.

finger *vb* handle, manipulate, play, purloin.

finical *adj* critical, dainty, dapper, fastidious, foppish, jaunty, overnice, overparticular, scrupulous, spruce, squeamish, trim.

finish *vb* accomplish, achieve, complete, consummate, execute, fulfil, perform; elaborate, perfect, polish; close, conclude, end, terminate. • *n* elaboration, elegance, perfection, polish; close, end, death, termination, wind-up.

finite *adj* bounded, circumscribed, conditioned, contracted, definable, limited, restricted, terminable.

fire *vb* ignite, kindle, light; animate, enliven, excite, inflame, inspirit, invigorate, rouse, stir up; discharge, eject, expel, hurl. • *n* combustion; blaze, conflagration; discharge, firing; animation, ardour, enthusiasm, fervour, fervency, fever, force, heat, impetuosity, inflammation, intensity, passion, spirit, vigour, violence; light, lustre, radiance, splendour; imagination, imaginativeness, inspiration, vivacity; affliction, persecution, torture, trouble.

firm[1] *adj* established, coherent, confirmed, consistent, fast, fixed, immovable, inflexible, rooted, secure, settled, stable; compact, compressed, dense, hard, solid; constant, determined, resolute, staunch, steadfast, steady, unshaken; loyal, robust, sinewy, stanch, stout, sturdy, strong.

firm[2] *n* association, business, company, concern, corporation, house, partnership.

firmament *n* heavens, sky, vault, welkin.

firmness *n* compactness, fixedness, hardness, solidity; stability, strength; constancy, soundness, steadfastness, steadiness.

first *adj* capital, chief, foremost, highest, leading, prime, principal; earliest, eldest, original; maiden; elementary, primary, rudimentary; aboriginal, primal, primeval, primitive, pristine. • *adv* chiefly, firstly, initially, mainly, primarily, principally; before, foremost, headmost; before, rather, rather than, sooner, sooner than. • *n* alpha, initial, prime.

first-rate *adj* excellent, prime, superior.

fissure *n* breach, break, chasm, chink, cleft, crack, cranny, crevice, fracture, gap, hole, interstice, opening, rent, rift.

fit[1] *vb* adapt, adjust, suit; become, conform; accommodate, equip, prepare, provide, qualify. • *adj* capacitated, competent, fitted; adequate, appropriate, apt, becoming, befitting, consonant, convenient, fitting, good, meet, pertinent, proper, seemly, suitable.

fit[2] *n* convulsion, fit, paroxysm, qualm, seizure, spasm, spell; fancy, humour, whim; mood, pet, tantrum; interval, period, spell, turn.

fitful *adj* capricious, changeable, convulsive, fanciful, fantastic, fickle, humoursome, impulsive, intermittent, irregular, odd, spasmodic, unstable, variable, whimsical; checkered, eventful.

fitness *n* adaptation, appropriateness, aptitude, aptness, pertinence, propriety, suitableness; preparation, qualification.

fix *vb* establish, fasten, place, plant, set; adjust, correct, mend, repair; attach, bind, clinch, connect, fasten, lock, rivet, stay, tie; appoint, decide, define, determine, limit, seal, settle; consolidate, harden, solidify; abide, remain, rest; congeal, stiffen. • *n* difficulty, dilemma, quandary, pickle, plight, predicament.

flabbergast *vb* abash, amaze, astonish, astound, confound, confuse, disconcert, dumbfound, nonplus.

flabby *adj* feeble, flaccid, inelastic, limp, soft, week, yielding.

flaccid *adj* baggy, drooping, flabby, inelastic, lax, limber, limp, loose, pendulous, relaxed, soft, weak, yielding.

flag[1] *vb* droop, hang, loose; decline, droop, fail, faint, lag, languish, pine, sink, succumb, weaken, weary; stale, pall.

flag[2] *vb* indicate, mark, semaphore, sign, signal. • *n* banner, colours, ensign, gonfalon, pennant, pennon, standard, streamer.

flagellate *vb* beat, castigate, chastise, cudgel, drub, flog, scourge, thrash, whip.

flagitious *adj* abandoned, atrocious, corrupt, flagrant, heinous, infamous, monstrous, nefarious, profligate, scandalous, villainous, wicked.

flagrant *adj* burning, flaming, glowing, raging; crying, enormous, flagitious, glaring, monstrous, nefarious, notorious, outrageous, shameful, wanton, wicked.

flake *vb* desquamate, scale. • *n* lamina, layer, scale.

flamboyant *adj* bright, gorgeous, ornate, rococo.

flame *vb* blaze, shine; burn, flash, glow, warm. • *n* blaze, brightness, fire, flare, vapour; affection, ardour, enthusiasm, fervency, fervour, keenness, warmth.

flaming *adj* blazing; burning, bursting, exciting, glowing, intense, lambent, vehement, violent.

flap *vb* beat, flutter, shake, vibrate, wave. • *n* apron, fly, lap, lappet, tab; beating, flapping, flop, flutter, slap, shaking, swinging, waving.

flare *vb* blaze, flicker, flutter, waver; dazzle, flame, glare; splay, spread, widen. • *n* blaze, dazzle, flame, glare.

flash *vb* blaze, glance, glare, glisten, light, shimmer, scintillate, sparkle, twinkle. • *n* instant, moment, twinkling.

flashy *adj* flaunting, gaudy, gay, loud, ostentatious, pretentious, showy, tinsel.

flat *adj* champaign, horizontal, level; even, plane, smooth, unbroken; low, prostrate, overthrow; dull, frigid, jejune, lifeless, monotonous, pointless, prosaic, spiritless, tame, unanimated, uniform, uninteresting; dead, flashy, insipid, mawkish, stale, tasteless, vapid; absolute, clear, direct, downright, peremptory, positive. • *adv* flatly, flush, horizontally, level. • *n* bar, sandbank, shallow, shoal, strand; champaign, lowland, plain; apartment, floor, lodging, storey.

flatter *vb* compliment, gratify, praise; blandish, blarney, butter up, cajole, coax, coddle, court, entice, fawn, humour, inveigle, wheedle.

flattery *n* adulation, blandishment, blarney, cajolery, fawning, obsequiousness, servility, sycophancy, toadyism.

flaunt *vb* boast, display, disport, flourish, parade, sport, vaunt; brandish.

flaunting *adj* flashy, garish, gaudy, ostentatious, showy, tawdry.

flavour *n* gust, gusto, relish, savour, seasoning, smack, taste, zest; admixture, lacing, seasoning; aroma, essence, soul, spirit.

flaw *n* break, breach, cleft, crack, fissure, fracture, gap, rent, rift; blemish, defect, fault, fleck, imperfection, speck, spot.

flay *vb* excoriate, flay; criticize.

fleck *vb* dapple, mottle, speckle, spot, streak, variegate. • *n* speckle, spot, streak.

flecked *adj* dappled, mottled, piebald, spotted, straked, striped, variegated.

flee *vb* abscond, avoid, decamp, depart, escape, fly, leave, run, skedaddle.

fleece *vb* clip, shear; cheat, despoil, pluck, plunder, rifle, rob, steal, strip.

fleer *vb* mock, jeer, gibe, scoff, sneer.

fleet[1] *n* armada, escadrille, flotilla, navy, squadron; company, group.

fleet[2] *adj* fast, nimble, quick, rapid, speedy, swift.

fleeting *adj* brief, caducous, ephemeral, evanescent, flitting, flying, fugitive, passing, short-lived, temporary, transient, transitory.

fleetness *n* celerity, nimbleness, quickness, rapidity, speed, swiftness, velocity.

flesh *n* food, meat; carnality, desires; kindred, race, stock; man, mankind, world.

fleshly *adj* animal, bodily, carnal, lascivious, lustful, lecherous, sensual.

fleshy *adj* corpulent, fat, obese, plump, stout.

flexibility *n* flexibleness, limbersome, lithesome, pliability, pliancy, suppleness; affability, complaisance, compliance, disposition, ductility, pliancy, tractableness, tractability, yielding.

flexible *adj* flexible, limber, lithe, pliable, pliant, supple, willowy; affable, complaisant, ductile, docile, gentle, tractable, tractile, yielding.

flexose, flexuous *adj* bending, crooked, serpentine, sinuate, sinuous, tortuous, waxy, winding.

flibbertigibbet *n* demon, imp, sprite.

flight[1] *n* flying, mounting, soaring, volition; shower, flight; steps, stairs.

flight[2] *n* departure, fleeing, flying, retreat, rout, stampede; exodus, hegira.

flighty *adj* capricious, deranged, fickle, frivolous, giddy, light-headed, mercurial, unbalanced, volatile, wild, whimsical.

flimsy *adj* slight, thin, unsubstantial; feeble, foolish, frivolous, light, puerile, shallow, superficial, trashy, trifling, trivial, weak; insubstantial, sleazy.

flinch *vb* blench, flee, recoil, retreat, shirk, shrink, swerve, wince, withdraw.

fling *vb* cast, chuck, dart, emit, heave, hurl, pitch, shy, throw, toss; flounce, wince. • *n* cast, throw, toss.

flippancy *n* volubility; assuredness, glibness, pertness.

flippant *adj* fluent, glib, talkative, voluble; bold, forward, frivolous, glib, impertinent, inconsiderate, irreverent, malapert, pert, saucy, trifling.

flirt *vb* chuck, fling, hurl, pitch, shy, throw, toss; flutter, twirl, whirl, whisk; coquet, dally, philander. • *n* coquette, jilt, philanderer; jerk.

flirtation *n* coquetry, dalliance, philandering.

flit *vb* flicker, flutter, hover; depart, hasten, pass.

flitting *adj* brief, ephemeral, evanescent, fleeting, fugitive, passing, short, transient, transitory.

float *vb* drift, glide, hang, ride, sail, soar, swim, waft; launch, support.

flock *vb* collect, congregate, gather, group, herd, swarm, throng. • *n* collection, group, multitude; bevy, company, convoy, drove, flight, gaggle, herd, pack, swarm, team, troupe; congregation.

flog *vb* beat, castigate, chastise, drub, flagellate, lash, scourge, thrash, whip.

flood *vb* deluge, inundate, overflow, submerge, swamp. • *n* deluge, freshet, inundation, overflow, tide; bore, downpour, eagre, flow, outburst, spate, rush; abundance, excess.

floor *vb* deck, pave; beat, confound, conquer, overthrow, prevail, prostrate, puzzle; disconcert, nonplus. • *n* storey; bottom, deck, flooring, pavement, stage.

florid *adj* bright-coloured, flushed, red-faced, rubicund; embellished, figurative, luxuriant, ornate, rhetorical, rococo.

flounce[1] *vb* fling, jerk, spring, throw, toss, wince. • *n* jerk, spring.

flounce[2] *n* frill, furbelow, ruffle.

flounder *vb* blunder, flop, flounce, plunge, struggle, toss, tumble, wallow.

flourish *vb* grow, thrive; boast, bluster, brag, gasconade, show off, vaunt, vapour; brandish, flaunt, swing, wave. • *n* dash, display, ostentation, parade, show; bombast, fustian, grandiloquence; brandishing, shake, waving; blast, fanfare, tantivy.

flout *vb* chaff, deride, fleer, gibe, insult, jeer, mock, ridicule, scoff, sneer, taunt. • *n* gibe, fling, insult, jeer, mock, mockery, mocking, scoff, scoffing, taunt.

flow *vb* pour, run, stream; deliquesce, liquefy, melt; arise, come, emanate, follow, grow, issue, proceed, result, spring; glide; float, undulate, wave, waver; abound, run. • *n* current, discharge, flood, flux, gush, rush, stream, trickle; abundance, copiousness.

flower *vb* bloom, blossom, effloresce; develop. • *n* bloom, blossom; best, cream, elite, essence, pick; freshness, prime, vigour.

flowery *adj* bloomy, florid; embellished, figurative, florid, ornate, overwrought.

flowing *adj* abundant, copious, fluent, smooth.

fluctuate *vb* oscillate, swing, undulate, vibrate, wave; change, vary; vacillate, waver.

flue *n* chimney, duct; flew, fluff, nap, floss, fur.

fluency *n* liquidness, smoothness; affluence, copiousness; ease, facility, readiness.

fluent *adj* current, flowing, gliding, liquid; smooth; affluent, copious, easy, facile, glib, ready, talkative, voluble.

fluff *vb* blunder, bungle, forget, fumble, mess up, miscue, misremember, muddle, muff. • *n* down, flew, floss, flue, fur, lint, nap; cobweb, feather, gossamer, thistledown; blunder, bungle, fumble, muff.

flume *n* channel, chute, mill race, race.

flummery *n* chaff, frivolity, froth, moonshine, nonsense, trash, trifling; adulation, blandishment, blarney, flattery; brose, porridge, sowens.

flunky, flunkey *n* footman, lackey, livery servant, manservant, valet; snob, toady.

flurry *vb* agitate, confuse, disconcert, disturb, excite, fluster, hurry, perturb. • *n* gust, flaw, squall; agitation, bustle, commotion, confusion, disturbance, excitement, flutter, haste, hurry, hurry-scurry, perturbation, ruffle, scurry.

flush[1] *vb* flow, rush, start; glow, mantle, redden; animate, elate, elevate, erect, excite; cleanse, drench. • *adj* bright, fresh, glowing, vigorous; abundant, affluent, exuberant, fecund, fertile, generous, lavish, liberal, prodigal, prolific, rich, wealthy, well-supplied; even, flat, level, plane. • *adv* evenly, flat, level; full, point-blank, right, square, squarely, straight. • *n* bloom, blush, glow, redness, rosiness, ruddiness; impulse, shock, thrill.

flush[2] *vb* disturb, rouse, start, uncover.

fluster *vb* excite, flush, heat; agitate, disturb, flurry, hurry, perturb, ruffle; confound, confuse, discompose, disconcert. • *n* glow, heat; agitation, flurry, flutter, hurry, hurry-scurry, perturbation, ruffle.

fluted *adj* channelled, corrugated, grooved.

flutter *vb* flap, hover; flirt, flit; beat, palpitate, quiver, tremble; fluctuate, oscillate, vacillate, waver. • *n* agitation, tremor; hurry, commotion, confusion, excitement, flurry, fluster, hurry-scurry, perturbation, quivering, tremble, tumult, twitter.

flux *n* flow, flowing; change, mutation, shifting, transition; diarrhoea, dysentery, looseness; fusing, melting, menstruum, solvent.

fly[1] *vb* aviate, hover, mount, soar; flap, float, flutter, play, sail, soar, undulate, vibrate, wave; burst, explode; abscond, decamp, depart, flee, vanish; elapse, flit, glide, pass, slip.

fly[2] *adj* alert, bright, sharp, smart, wide-awake; astute, cunning, knowing, sly; agile, fleet, nimble, quick, spry.

foal *n* colt, filly.

foam *vb* cream, froth, lather, spume; boil, churn, ferment, fume, seethe, simmer, stew. • *n* bubbles, cream, froth, scum, spray, spume, suds.

fodder *n* feed, food, forage, provender, rations.

foe *n* adversary, antagonist, enemy, foeman, opponent.

fog *vb* bedim, bemist, blear, blur, cloud, dim, enmist, mist; addle, befuddle, confuse, fuddle, muddle. • *n* blear, blur, dimness, film, fogginess, haze, haziness, mist, smog, vapour; befuddlement, confusion, fuddle, maze, muddle.

foggy *adj* blurred, cloudy, dim, dimmed, hazy, indistinct, misty, obscure; befuddled, bewildered, confused, dazed, muddled, muddy, stupid.

foible *n* defect, failing, fault, frailty, imperfection, infirmity, penchant, weakness.

foil[1] *vb* baffle, balk, check, checkmate, circumvent, defeat, disappoint, frustrate, thwart.

foil[2] *n* film, flake, lamina; background, contrast.

foist *vb* impose, insert, interpolate, introduce, palm off, thrust.

fold[1] *vb* bend, cover, double, envelop, wrap; clasp, embrace, enfold, enwrap, gather, infold, interlace; collapse, fail. • *n* double, doubling, gather, plait, plicature.

fold[2] *n* cot, enclosure, pen.

foliaceous *adj* foliate, leafy; flaky, foliated, lamellar, lamellate, lamellated, laminated, scaly, schistose.

folk *n* kindred, nation, people.

follow *vb* ensue, succeed; chase, dog, hound, pursue, run after, trail; accompany, attend; conform, heed, obey, observe; cherish, cultivate, seek; practise, pursue; adopt, copy, imitate; arise, come, flow, issue, proceed, result, spring.

follower *n* acolyte, attendant, associate, companion, dependant, retainer, supporter; adherent, admirer, disciple, partisan, pupil; copier, imitator.

folly *n* doltishness, dullness, imbecility, levity, shallowness; absurdity, extravagance, fatuity, foolishness, imprudence, inanity, indiscretion, ineptitude, nonsense, senselessness; blunder, faux pas, indiscretion, unwisdom.

foment *vb* bathe, embrocate, stupe; abet, brew, encourage, excite, foster, instigate, promote, stimulate.

fond *adj* absurd, baseless, empty, foolish, senseless, silly, vain, weak; affectionate, amorous, doting, loving, overaffectionate, tender.

fondle *vb* blandish, caress, coddle, cosset, dandle, pet.

fondness *n* absurdity, delusion, folly, silliness, weakness; liking, partiality, predilection, preference, propensity; appetite, relish, taste.

food *n* aliment, board, bread, cheer, commons, diet, fare, meat, nourishment, nutriment, nutrition, pabulum, provisions, rations, regimen, subsistence, sustenance, viands, victuals; feed, fodder, forage, provender.

fool *vb* jest, play, toy, trifle; beguile, cheat, circumvent, cozen, deceive, delude, dupe, gull, hoodwink, overreach, trick. • *n* blockhead, dolt, driveller, idiot, imbecile, nincompoop, ninny, nitwit, simpleton; antic, buffoon, clown, droll, harlequin, jester, merry-andrew, punch, scaramouch, zany; butt, dupe.

foolery *n* absurdity, folly, foolishness, nonsense; buffoonery, mummery, tomfoolery.

foolhardy *adj* adventurous, bold, desperate, harebrained, headlong, hot-headed, incautious, precipitate, rash, reckless, venturesome, venturous.

foolish *adj* brainless, daft, fatuous, idiotic, inane, inept, insensate, irrational, senseless, shallow, silly, simple, thick-skulled, vain, weak, witless; absurd, ill-judged, imprudent, indiscreet, nonsensical, preposterous, ridiculous, unreasonable, unwise; childish, contemptible, idle, puerile, trifling, trivial, vain.

foolishness *n* doltishness, dullness, fatuity, folly, imbecility, shallowness, silliness, stupidity; absurdity, extravagance, imprudence, indiscretion, nonsense; childishness, puerility, triviality.

footing *n* foothold, purchase; basis, foundation, groundwork, installation; condition, grade, rank, standing, state, status; settlement, establishment.

footman *n* footboy, menial, lackey, runner, servant.

footpad *n* bandit, brigand, freebooter, highwayman, robber.

footpath *n* footway, path, trail.

footprint *n* footfall, footmark, footstep, trace, track.

footstep *n* footmark, footprint, trace, track; footfall, step, tread; mark, sign, token, trace, vestige.

fop *n* beau, coxcomb, dandy, dude, exquisite, macaroni, popinjay, prig, swell.

foppish *adj* coxcombical, dandified, dandyish, dressy, finical, spruce, vain.

forage *vb* feed, graze, provender, provision, victual; hunt for, range, rummage, search, seek; maraud, plunder, raid. • *n* feed, fodder, food, pasturage, provender; hunt, rummage, search.

foray *n* descent, incursion, invasion, inroad, irruption, raid.

forbear *vb* cease, desist, hold, pause, stop, stay; abstain, refrain; endure, tolerate; avoid, decline, shun; abstain, omit, withhold.

forbearance *n* abstinence, avoidance, forbearing, self-restraint, shunning, refraining; indulgence, leniency, long-suffering, mildness, moderation, patience.

forbid *vb* ban, debar, disallow, embargo, enjoin, hinder, inhibit, interdict, prohibit, proscribe, taboo, veto.

forbidding *adj* abhorrent, disagreeable, displeasing, odious, offensive, repellant, repulsive, threatening, unpleasant.

force *vb* coerce, compel, constrain, necessitate, oblige; drive, impel, overcome, press, urge; ravish, violate. • *n* emphasis, energy, head, might, pith, power, strength, stress, vigour, vim; agency, efficacy, efficiency, cogency, potency, validity, virtue; coercion, compulsion, constraint, enforcement, vehemence, violence; army, array, battalion, host, legion, phalanx, posse, soldiery, squadron, troop.

forcible *adj* all-powerful, cogent, impressive, irresistible, mighty, potent, powerful, strong, weighty; impetuous, vehement, violent, unrestrained; coerced, coercive, compulsory; convincing, energetic, effective, efficacious, telling, vigorous.

forcibly *adv* mightily, powerfully; coercively, compulsorily, perforce, violently; effectively, energetically, vigorously.

ford *n* current, flood, stream; crossing, wading place.

fore *adj* anterior, antecedent, first, foregoing, former, forward, preceding, previous, prior; advanced, foremost, head, leading.

forebode *vb* augur, betoken, foreshow, foretell, indicate, portend, predict, prefigure, presage, prognosticate, promise, signify.

foreboding *n* augury, omen, prediction, premonition, presage, presentiment, prognostication.

forecast *vb* anticipate, foresee, predict; calculate, contrive, devise, plan, project, scheme. • *n* anticipation, foresight, forethought, planning, prevision, prophecy, provident.

foreclose *vb* debar, hinder, preclude, prevent, stop.

foredoom *vb* foreordain, predestine, preordain.

forego *see* **forgo.**

foregoing *adj* antecedent, anterior, fore, former, preceding, previous, prior.

foregone *adj* bygone, former, past, previous.

foreign *adj* alien, distant, exotic, exterior, external, outward, outlandish, remote, strange, unnative; adventitious, exterior, extraneous, extrinsic, inappropriate, irrelevant, outside, unnatural, unrelated.

foreknowledge *n* foresight, prescience, prognostication.

foremost *adj* first, front, highest, leading, main, principal.

foreordain *vb* appoint, foredoom, predestinate, predetermine, preordain.

forerunner *n* avant-courier, foregoer, harbinger, herald, precursor, predecessor; omen, precursor, prelude, premonition, prognosticate, sign.

foresee *vb* anticipate, forebode, forecast, foreknow, foretell, prognosticate, prophesy.

foreshadow *vb* forebode, predict, prefigure, presage, presignify, prognosticate, prophesy.

foresight *n* foreknowledge, prescience, prevision; anticipation, care, caution, forecast, forethought, precaution, providence, prudence.

forest *n* wood, woods, woodland.

forestall *vb* hinder, frustrate, intercept, preclude, prevent, thwart; antedate, anticipate, foretaste; engross, monopolize, regrate.

foretaste *n* anticipation, forestalling, prelibation.

foretell *vb* predict, prophesy; augur, betoken, forebode, forecast, foreshadow, foreshow, portend, presage, presignify, prognosticate, prophesy.

forethought *n* anticipation, forecast, foresight, precaution, providence, prudence.

forever *adv* always, constantly, continually, endlessly, eternally, ever, evermore, everlastingly, perpetually, unceasingly.

forewarn *vb* admonish, advise, caution, dissuade.

forfeit *vb* alienate, lose. • *n* amercement, damages, fine, forfeiture, mulct, penalty.

forfend *vb* avert, forbid, hinder, prevent, protect.

forge *vb* beat, fabricate, form, frame, hammer; coin, devise, frame, invent; counterfeit, falsify, feign. • *n* furnace, ironworks, smithy.

forgery *n* counterfeit, fake, falsification, imitation.

forgetful *adj* careless, heedless, inattentive, mindless, neglectful, negligent, oblivious, unmindful.

forgive *vb* absolve, acquit, condone, excuse, exonerate, pardon, remit.

forgiveness *n* absolution, acquittal, amnesty, condoning. exoneration, pardon, remission, reprieve.

forgiving *adj* absolutory, absolvatory, acquitting, clearing, excusing, pardoning, placable, releasing.

forgo *vb* abandon, cede, relinquish, renounce, resign, surrender, yield.

fork *vb* bifurcate, branch, divaricate, divide. • *n* bifurcation, branch, branching, crotch, divarication, division.

forked *adj* bifurcated, branching, divaricated, furcate, furcated.

forlorn *adj* abandoned, deserted, forsaken, friendless, helpless, lost, solitary; abject, comfortless, dejected, desolate, destitute, disconsolate, helpless, hopeless, lamentable, pitiable, miserable, woebegone, wretched.

form *vb* fashion model, mould, shape; build, conceive, construct, create, fabricate, make, produce; contrive, devise, frame, invent; compose, constitute, develop, organize; discipline, educate, teach, train. • *n* body, build, cast, configuration, conformation, contour, cut, fashion, figure, format, mould, outline, pattern, shape; formula, formulary, method, mode, practice, ritual; class, kind, manner, model, order, sort, system, type; arrangement, order, regularity, shapeliness; ceremonial, ceremony, conventionality, etiquette, formality, observance, ordinance, punctilio, rite, ritual; bench, seat; class, rank; arrangement, combination, organization.

formal *adj* explicit, express, official, positive, strict; fixed, methodical, regular, rigid, set, stiff; affected, ceremonious, exact, precise, prim, punctilious, starchy. starched; constitutive, essential; external, outward, perfunctory; formative, innate, organic, primordial.

formality *n* ceremonial, ceremony, conventionality, etiquette, punctilio, rite, ritual.

formation *n* creation, genesis, production; composition, constitution; arrangement, combination, disposal, disposition.

formative *adj* creative, determinative, plastic, shaping; derivative, inflectional, nonradical.

former *adj* antecedent, anterior, earlier, foregoing, preceding, previous, prior; late, old-time, quondam; by, bygone, foregone, gone, past.

formidable *adj* appalling, dangerous, difficult, dreadful, fearful, frightful, horrible, menacing, redoubtable, shocking, terrible, terrific, threatening, tremendous.

forsake *vb* abandon, desert, leave, quit; drop, forgo, forswear, relinquish, renounce, surrender, yield.

forsooth *adv* certainly, indeed, really, surely, truly.

forswear *vb* abandon, desert, drop, forsake, leave, quit, reject, renounce; abjure, deny, eschew, perjure, recant, repudiate, retract.

fort *n* bulwark, castle, citadel, defence, fastness, fortification, fortress, stronghold.

forthwith *adv* directly, immediately, instantly, quickly, straightaway.

fortification *n* breastwork, bulwark, castle, citadel, defence, earthwork, fastness, fort, keep, rampart, redoubt, stronghold, tower.

fortify *vb* brace, encourage, entrench, garrison, protect, reinforce, stiffen, strengthen; confirm, corroborate.

fortitude *n* braveness, bravery, courage, determination, endurance, firmness, hardiness, patience, pluck, resolution, strength, valour.

fortuitous *adj* accidental, casual, chance, contingent, incidental.

fortunate *adj* favoured, happy, lucky, prosperous, providential, successful; advantageous, auspicious, favourable, happy, lucky, propitious, timely.

fortune *n* accident, casualty, chance, contingency, fortuity, hap, luck; estate, possessions, property, substance; affluence, felicity, opulence, prosperity, riches, wealth; destination, destiny, doom, fate, lot, star; event, issue, result; favour, success.

forward *vb* advance, aid, encourage, favour, foster, further, help, promote, support; accelerate, dispatch, expedite, hasten, hurry, quicken, speed; dispatch, post, send, ship, transmit. • *adj* ahead, advanced, onward; anterior, front, fore, head; prompt, eager, earnest, hasty, impulsive, quick, ready, willing, zealous; assuming, bold, brazen, brazen-faced, confident, flippant, impertinent, pert, presumptuous, presuming; advanced, early, premature. • *adv* ahead, onward.

foster *vb* cosset, feed, nurse, nourish, support, sustain; advance, aid, breed, cherish, cultivate, encourage, favour, foment, forward, further, harbour, patronize, promote, rear, stimulate.

foul *vb* besmirch, defile, dirty, pollute, soil, stain, sully; clog, collide, entangle, jam. • *adj* dirty, fetid, filthy, impure, nasty, polluted, putrid, soiled, stained, squalid, sullied, rank, tarnished, unclean; disgusting, hateful, loathsome, noisome, odious, offensive; dishonourable, underhand, unfair, sinister; abominable, base, dark, detestable, disgraceful, infamous, scandalous, scurvy, shameful, wile, wicked; coarse, low, obscene, vulgar; abusive, foul-mouthed, foul-spoken, insulting, scurrilous; cloudy, rainy, rough, stormy, wet; feculent, muddy, thick, turbid; entangled, tangled.

foul-mouthed *adj* abusive, blackguardly, blasphemous, filthy, foul, indecent, insolent, insulting, obscene, scurrilous.

found *vb* base, fix, ground, place, rest, set; build, construct, erect, raise; colonize, establish, institute, originate, plant; cast, mould.

foundation *n* base, basis, bed, bottom, footing, ground, groundwork, substructure, support; endowment, establishment, settlement.

founder[1] *n* author, builder, establisher, father, institutor, originator, organizer, planter.

founder[2] *n* caster, moulder.

founder[3] *vb* sink, swamp, welter; collapse, fail, miscarry; fall, stumble, trip.

fountain *n* fount, reservoir, spring, well; jet, upswelling; cause, fountainhead, origin, original, source.

foxy *adj* artful, crafty, cunning, sly, subtle, wily.

fracas *n* affray, brawl, disturbance, outbreak, quarrel, riot, row, uproar, tumult.

fractious *adj* captious, cross, fretful, irritable, peevish, pettish, perverse, petulant, querulous, snappish, splenetic, touchy, testy, waspish.

fracture *vb* break, crack, split. • *n* breaking, rupture; breach, break, cleft, crack, fissure, flaw, opening, rift, rent.

fragile *adj* breakable, brittle, delicate, frangible; feeble, frail, infirm, weak.

fragility *n* breakability, breakableness, brittleness, frangibility, frangibleness; feebleness, frailty, infirmity, weakness.

fragment *vb* atomize, break, fracture, pulverize, splinter. • *n* bit, chip, fraction, fracture, morsel, part, piece, remnant, scrap.

fragrance *n* aroma, balminess, bouquet, odour, perfume, redolence, scent, smell.

fragrant *adj* ambrosial, aromatic, balmy, odoriferous, odorous, perfumed, redolent, spicy, sweet, sweet-scented, sweet-smelling.

frail *adj* breakable, brittle, delicate, fragile, frangible, slight; feeble, infirm, weak.

frailty *n* feebleness, frailness, infirmity, weakness; blemish, defect, failing, fault, foible, imperfection, peccability, shortcoming.

frame *vb* build, compose, constitute, construct, erect, form, make, mould, plan, shape; contrive, devise, fabricate, fashion, forge, invest, plan. • *n* body, carcass, framework, framing, shell, skeleton; constitution, fabric, form, structure, scheme, system; condition, humour, mood, state, temper.

franchise *n* privilege, right; suffrage, vote; exemption, immunity.

frangible *adj* breakable, brittle, fragile.

frank *adj* artless, candid, direct, downright, frank-hearted, free, genuine, guileless, ingenuous, naive, open, outspoken, outright, plain, plain-spoken, point-blank, sincere, straightforward, truthful, unequivocal, unreserved, unrestricted.

frankness *n* candour, ingenuousness, openness, outspokenness, plain speaking, truth, straightforwardness.

frantic *adj* crazy, distracted, distraught, frenzied, furious, infuriate, mad. outrageous, phrenetic, rabid, raging, raving, transported, wild.

fraternity *n* association, brotherhood, circle, clan, club, company, fellowship, league, set, society, sodality; brotherliness.

fraternize *vb* associate, coalesce, concur, consort, cooperate, harmonize, sympathize, unite.

fraud *n* artifice, cheat, craft, deception, deceit, duplicity, guile, hoax, humbug, imposition, imposture, sham, stratagem, treachery, trick, trickery, wile.

fraudulent *adj* crafty, deceitful, deceptive, dishonest, false, knavish, treacherous, trickish, tricky, wily.

fraught *adj* abounding, big, burdened, charged, filled, freighted, laden, pregnant, stored, weighted.

fray[1] *n* affray, battle, brawl, broil, combat, fight, quarrel, riot.

fray[2] *vb* chafe, fret, rub, wear; ravel, shred.

freak *adj* bizarre, freakish, grotesque, monstrous, odd, unexpected, unforeseen. • *n* caprice, crotchet, fancy, humour, maggot, quirk, vagary, whim, whimsey; antic, caper, gambol; abnormality, abortion, monstrosity.

freakish *adj* capricious, changeable, eccentric, erratic, fanciful, humoursome, odd, queer, whimsical.

free *vb* deliver, discharge, disenthral, emancipate, enfranchise, enlarge, liberate, manumit, ransom, release, redeem, rescue, save; clear, disencumber, disengage, extricate, rid, unbind, unchain, unfetter, unlock; exempt, immunize, privilege. • *adj* bondless, independent, loose, unattached, unconfined, unentangled, unimpeded, unrestrained, untrammelled; autonomous, delivered, emancipated, freeborn, liberated, manumitted, ransomed, released, self-governing; clear, exempt, immune, privileged; allowed, permitted; devoid, empty, open, unimpeded, unobstructed, unrestricted; affable, artless, candid, frank, ingenuous, sincere, unreserved; bountiful, charitable, free-hearted, generous, hospitable, liberal, munificent, openhanded; immoderate, lavish, prodigal; eager, prompt, ready, willing; available, gratuitous, spontaneous; careless, lax, loose; bold, easy, familiar, informal, overfamiliar, unconstrained. • *adv* openly, outright, unreservedly, unrestrainedly, unstintingly; freely, gratis, gratuitously.

freebooter *n* bandit, brigand, despoiler, footpad, gangster, highwayman, marauder, pillager, plunderer, robber; buccaneer, pirate, rover.

freedom *n* emancipation, independence, liberation, liberty, release; elbowroom, margin, play, range, scope, swing; franchise, immunity, privilege; familiarity, laxity, license, looseness.

freethinker *n* agnostic, deist, doubter, infidel, sceptic, unbeliever.

freeze *vb* congeal, glaciate, harden, stiffen; benumb, chill.

freight *vb* burden, charge, lade, load. • *n* burden, cargo, lading, load.

frenzy *n* aberration, delirium, derangement, distraction, fury, insanity, lunacy, madness, mania, paroxysm, rage, raving, transport.

frequent *vb* attend, haunt, resort, visit. • *adj* iterating, oft-repeated; common, customary, everyday, familiar, habitual, persistent, usual; constant, continual, incessant.

fresh *adj* new, novel, recent; renewed, revived; blooming, flourishing, green, undecayed, unimpaired, unfaded, unobliterated, unwilted, unwithered, well-preserved; sweet; delicate, fair, fresh-coloured, ruddy, rosy; florid, hardy, healthy, vigorous, strong; active, energetic, unexhausted, unfatigued, unwearied, vigorous; keen, lively, unabated, undecayed, unimpaired, vivid; additional, further; uncured, undried, unsalted, unsmoked; bracing, health-giving, invigorating, refreshing, sweet; brisk, stiff, strong; inexperienced, raw, uncultivated, unpracticed, unskilled, untrained, unused.

freshen *vb* quicken, receive, refresh, revive.

fret[1] *vb* abrade, chafe, fray, gall, rub, wear; affront, agitate, annoy, gall, harass, irritate, nettle, provoke, ruffle, tease, vex, wear, worry; ripple, roughen; corrode; fume, peeve, rage, stew. • *n* agitation, fretfulness, fretting, irritation, peevishness, vexation.

fret[2] *vb* diversify, interlace, ornament, variegate. • *n* fretwork, interlacing, ornament; ridge, wale, whelk.

fretful *adj* captious, cross, fractious, ill-humoured, ill-tempered, irritable, peevish, pettish, petulant, querulous, short-tempered, snappish, spleeny, splenetic, testy, touchy, uneasy, waspish.

friable *adj* brittle, crisp, crumbling, powdery, pulverable.

friction *n* abrasion, attrition, grating, rubbing; bickering, disagreement, dissension, wrangling.

friend *adj* benefactor, chum, companion, comrade, crony, confidant, intimate; adherent, ally, associate, confrere, partisan; advocate, defender, encourager, favourer, patron, supporter, well-wisher.

friendly *adj* affectionate, amiable, benevolent, favourable, kind, kind-hearted, kindly, well-disposed; amicable, cordial, fraternal, neighbourly; conciliatory, peaceable, unhostile.

friendship *n* affection, attachment, benevolence, fondness, goodness, love, regard; fellowship, intimacy; amicability, amicableness, amity, cordiality, familiarity, fraternization, friendliness, harmony.

fright *n* affright, alarm, consternation, dismay, funk, horror, panic, scare, terror.

frighten *vb* affright, alarm, appal, daunt, dismay, intimidate, scare, stampede, terrify.

frightful *adj* alarming, awful, dire, direful, dread, dreadful, fearful, horrible, horrid, shocking, terrible, terrific; ghastly, grim, grisly, gruesome, hideous.

frigid *adj* cold, cool, gelid; dull, lifeless, spiritless, tame, unanimated, uninterested, uninteresting; chilling, distant, forbidding, formal, freezing, prim, repellent, repelling, repulsive, rigid, stiff.

frill *n* edging, frilling, furbelow, gathering, ruche, ruching, ruffle; affectation, mannerism.

fringe *vb* border, bound, edge, hem, march, rim, skirt, verge. • *n* border, edge, edging, tassel, trimming. • *adj* edging, extra, unofficial.

frisk *vb* caper, dance, frolic, gambol, hop, jump, play, leap, romp, skip, sport, wanton.

frisky *adj* frolicsome, coltish, gay, lively, playful, sportive.

frivolity *n* flummery, folly, fribbling, frippery, frivolousness, levity, puerility, trifling, triviality.

frivolous *adj* childish, empty, flighty, flimsy, flippant, foolish, giddy, idle, light, paltry, petty, puerile, silly, trashy, trifling, trivial, unimportant, vain, worthless.

frolic *vb* caper, frisk, gambol, lark, play, romp, sport. • *n* escapade, gambol, lark, romp, skylark, spree, trick; drollery, fun, play, pleasantry, sport.

frolicsome *adj* coltish, fresh, frolic, gamesome, gay, lively, playful, sportive.

front *vb* confront, encounter, face, oppose. • *adj* anterior, forward; foremost, frontal, headmost. • *n* brow, face, forehead; assurance, boldness, brass, effrontery, impudence; breast, head, van, vanguard; anterior, face, forepart, obverse; facade, frontage.

frontier *n* border, boundary, coast, confine, limits, marches.

frosty *adj* chill, chilly, cold, icy, stinging, wintry; cold, cold-hearted, frigid, indifferent, unaffectionate, uncordial, unimpassioned, unloving; dull-hearted, lifeless, spiritless, unanimated; frosted, grey-hearted, hoary, white.

froth *vb* bubble, cream, foam, lather, spume. • *n* bubbles, foam, lather, spume; balderdash, flummery, nonsense, trash, triviality.

frothy *adj* foamy, spumy; empty, frivolous, light, trifling, trivial, unsubstantial, vain.

froward *adj* captious, contrary, contumacious, cross, defiant, disobedient, fractious, impudent, intractable, obstinate, peevish, perverse, petulant, refractory, stubborn, ungovernable, untoward, unyielding, wayward, wilful.

frown *vb* glower, lower, scowl.

frowzy, frowsy *adj* fetid, musty, noisome, rancid, rank, stale; disordered, disorderly, dowdy, slatternly, slovenly.

frugal *adj* abstemious, careful, chary, choice, economical, provident, saving, sparing, temperate, thrifty, unwasteful.

fruit *n* crop, harvest, produce, production; advantage, consequence, effect, good, outcome, product, profit, result; issue, offspring, young.

fruitful *adj* abounding, productive; fecund, fertile, prolific; abundant, exuberant, plenteous, plentiful, rich, teeming.

fruition *n* completion, fulfilment, perfection; enjoyment.

fruitless *adj* acarpous, barren, sterile, infecund, unfertile, unfruitful, unproductive, unprolific; abortive, bootless, futile, idle, ineffectual, profitless, unavailing, unprofitable, useless, vain.

frumpish, frumpy *adj* cross, cross-grained, cross-tempered, dowdy, grumpy, irritable, shabby, slatternly, snappish.

frustrate *vb* baffle, balk, check, circumvent, defeat, disappoint, disconcert, foil, thwart; cross, hinder, outwit.

frustrated *adj* balked, blighted, dashed, defeated, foiled, thwarted; ineffectual, null, useless, vain.

fuddled *adj* befuddled, boozy, corned, crapulous, drunk, groggy, high, inebriated, intoxicated, muddled, slewed, tight, tipsy.

fugacious *adj* evanescent, fleeting, fugitive, transient, transitory.

fugitive *adj* escaping, fleeing, flying; brief, ephemeral, evanescent, fleeting, flitting, fugacious, momentary, short, short-lived, temporal, temporary, transient, transitory, uncertain, unstable, volatile. • *n* émigré, escapee, evacuee, fleer, outlaw, refugee, runaway.

fulfil *vb* accomplish, complete, consummate, effect, effectuate, execute, realize; adhere, discharge, do, keep, obey, observe, perform; answer, fill, meet, satisfy.

full *adj* brimful, filled, flush, replete; abounding, replete, well-stocked; bagging, flowing, loose, voluminous; chock-full, cloyed, crammed, glutted, gorged, overflowing, packed, sated, satiated, saturated, soaked, stuffed, swollen; adequate, complete, entire, mature, perfect; abundant, ample, copious, plenteous, plentiful, sufficient; clear, deep, distinct, loud, rounded, strong; broad, large, capacious, comprehensive, extensive, plump; circumstantial, detailed, exhaustive. • *adv* completely, fully; directly, exactly, precisely.

fullness *n* abundance, affluence, copiousness, plenitude, plenty, profusion; glut, satiety, sating, repletion; completeness, completion, entireness, perfection; clearness, loudness, resonance, strength; dilation, distension, enlargement, plumpness, rotundity, roundness, swelling.

fully *adv* abundantly, amply, completely, copiously, entirely, largely, plentifully, sufficiently.

fulminate *vb* detonate, explode; curse, denounce, hurl, menace, threaten, thunder.

fulsome *adj* excessive, extravagant, fawning; disgusting, nauseous, nauseating, offensive, repulsive; coarse, gross, lustful, questionable.

fumble *vb* bungle, grope, mismanage, stumble; mumble, stammer, stutter.

fume *vb* reek, smoke, vaporize. • *n* effluvium exhalation, reek, smell, smoke, steam, vapour; agitation, fret, fry, fury, passion, pet, rage, storm.

fun *adj* amusing, diverting, droll, entertaining. • *n* amusement, diversion, drollery, frolic, gaiety, humour, jesting, jocularity, jollity, joy, merriment, mirth, play, pranks, sport, pleasantry, waggishness.

function *vb* act, discharge, go, operate, officiate, perform, run, serve, work. • *n* discharge, execution, exercise, operation, performance, purpose, use; activity, business, capacity, duty, employment, occupation, office, part, province, role; ceremony, rite; dependant, derivative.

fund *vb* afford, endow, finance, invest, provide, subsidise, support; garner, hoard, stock, store. • *n* accumulation, capital, endowment, reserve, stock; store, supply; foundation.

fundament *n* bottom, buttocks, seat.

fundamental *adj* basal, basic, bottom, cardinal, constitutional, elementary, essential, indispensable, organic, principal, primary, radical. • *n* essential, principal, rule.

funeral *n* burial, cremation, exequies, internment, obsequies.

funereal *adj* dark, dismal, gloomy, lugubrious, melancholy, mournful, sad, sepulchral, sombre, woeful.

funk *vb* blanch, shrink, quail. • *n* stench, stink; fear, fright, panic.

funny *adj* amusing, comic, comical, diverting, droll, facetious, farcical, humorous, jocose, jocular, laughable, ludicrous, sportive, witty; curious, odd, queer, strange. • *n* jest, joke; cartoon, comic.

furbish *vb* burnish, brighten, polish, renew, renovate, rub, shine.

furious *adj* angry, fierce, frantic, frenzied, fuming, infuriated, mad, raging, violent, wild; boisterous, fierce, impetuous, stormy, tempestuous, tumultuous, turbulent, vehement.

furnish *vb* appoint, endow, provide, supply; decorate, equip, fit; afford, bestow, contribute, give, offer, present, produce, yield.

furniture *n* chattels, effects, household goods, movables; apparatus, appendages, appliances, equipment, fittings, furnishings; decorations, embellishments, ornaments.

furore *n* commotion, craze, enthusiasm, excitement, fad, fury, madness, mania, rage, vogue.

furrow *vb* chamfer, channel, cleave, corrugate, cut, flute, groove, hollow; pucker, seam, wrinkle. • *n* chamfer, channel, cut, depression, fluting, groove, hollow, line, seam, track, trench, rot, wrinkle.

further *vb* advance, aid, assist, encourage, help, forward, promote, succour, strengthen. • *adj* additional. • *adv* also, besides, farther, furthermore, moreover.

furtive *adj* clandestine, hidden, secret, sly, skulking, sneaking, sneaky, stealthy, stolen, surreptitious.

fury *n* anger, frenzy, fit, furore, ire, madness, passion, rage; fierceness, impetuosity, turbulence, turbulency, vehemence; bacchant, bacchante, bedlam, hag, shrew, termagant, virago, vixen.

fuse *vb* dissolve, melt, liquefy, smelt; amalgamate, blend, coalesce, combine, commingle, intermingle, intermix, merge, unite. • *n* match.

fusion *n* liquefaction, melting; amalgamation, blending, commingling, commixture, intermingling, intermixture, union; coalition, merging.

fuss *vb* bustle, fidget; fret, fume, worry. • *n* ado, agitation, bother, bustle, commotion, disturbance, excitement, fidget, flurry, fluster, fret, hurry, pother, stir, worry.

fustian *n* bombast, claptrap, rant, rodomontade; balderdash, inanity, nonsense, stuff, trash, twaddle.

fusty *adj* ill-smelling, malodorous, mildewed, mouldy, musty, rank.

futile *adj* frivolous, trifling, trivial; bootless, fruitless, idle, ineffectual, profitless, unavailing, unprofitable, useless, vain, valueless, worthless.

futility *n* frivolousness, triviality; bootlessness, fruitlessness, uselessness, vanity, worthlessness.

future *adj* coming, eventual, forthcoming, hereafter, prospective, subsequent. • *n* hereafter, outlook, prospect.

G

gabble *vb* babble, chatter, clack, gibber, gossip, prate, prattle. • *n* babble, chatter, clack, gap, gossip, jabber, palaver, prate, prattle, twaddle.

gadabout *n* idler, loafer, rambler, rover, vagrant; gossip, talebearer, vagrant.

gaffer *n* boss, foreman, overseer, supervisor.

gag[1] *n* jape, jest, joke, stunt, wisecrack.

gag[2] *vb* muffle, muzzle, shackle, silence, stifle, throttle; regurgitate, retch, throw up, vomit; choke, gasp, pant. • *n* muzzle.

gage *n* pawn, pledge, security, surety; challenge, defiance, gauntlet, glove.

gaiety *n* animation, blithesomeness, cheerfulness, glee, hilarity, jollity, joviality, merriment, mirth, vivacity.

gain *vb* achieve, acquire, earn, get, obtain, procure, reap, secure; conciliate, enlist, persuade, prevail, win; arrive, attain, reach; clear, net, profit. • *n* accretion, addition, gainings, profits, winnings; acquisition, earnings, emolument, lucre; advantage, benefit, blessing, good, profit.

gainful *adj* advantageous, beneficial, profitable; lucrative, paying, productive, remunerative.

gainsay *vb* contradict, controvert, deny, dispute, forbid.

gait *n* carriage, pace, step, stride, walk.

galaxy *n* assemblage, assembly, cluster, collection, constellation, group.

gale *n* blast, hurricane, squall, storm, tempest, tornado, typhoon.

gall[1] *n* effrontery, impudence; bile; acerbity, bitterness, malice, maliciousness, malignity, rancour, spite.

gall[2] *vb* chafe, excoriate, fret, hurt; affront, annoy, exasperate, harass, incense, irritate, plague, provoke, sting, tease, vex.

gallant *adj* fine, magnificent, showy, splendid, well-dressed; bold, brave, chivalrous, courageous, daring, fearless, heroic, high-spirited, intrepid, valiant, valorous; chivalrous, fine, honourable, high-minded, lofty, magnanimous, noble. • *n* beau, blade, spark; lover, suitor, wooer.

gallantry *n* boldness, bravery, chivalry, courage, courageousness, fearlessness, heroism, intrepidity, prowess, valour; courtesy, courteousness, elegance, politeness.

galling *adj* chafing, irritating, vexing.

gallop *vb* fly, hurry, run, rush, scamper, speed.

gamble *vb* bet, dice, game, hazard, plunge, speculate, wager. • *n* chance, risk, speculation; bet, punt, wager.

gambol *vb* caper, cut, frisk, frolic, hop, jump, leap, romp, skip. • *n* frolic, hop, jump, skip.

game[1] *vb* gamble, sport, stake. • *n* amusement, contest, diversion, pastime, play, sport; adventure, enterprise, measure, plan, project, scheme, stratagem, undertaking; prey, quarry, victim.

game[2] *adj* brave, courageous, dauntless, fearless, gallant, heroic, intrepid, plucky, unflinching, valorous; enduring, persevering, resolute, undaunted; ready, eager, willing.

game[3] *adj* crippled, disabled, halt, injured, lame.

gameness *n* bravery, courage, grit, heart, mettle, nerve, pith, pluck, pluckiness, spirit, stamina.

gamesome *adj* frisky, frolicsome, lively, merry, playful, sportive, sprightly, vivacious.

gammon *vb* bamboozle, beguile, cheat, circumvent, deceive, delude, dupe, gull, hoax, humbug, inveigle, mislead, overreach, outwit. • *n* bosh, hoax, humbug, imposition, nonsense.

gang *n* band, cabal, clique, company, coterie, crew, horde, party, set, troop.

gaol *see* **jail**.

gap *n* breach, break, cavity, chasm, chink, cleft, crack, cranny, crevice, hiatus, hollow, interval, interstice, lacuna, opening, pass, ravine, rift, space, vacancy.

gape *vb* burst open, dehisce, open, stare, yawn.

garb *vb* attire, clothe, dress. • *n* apparel, attire, clothes, costume, dress, garments, habiliment, habit, raiment, robes, uniform, vestment.

garbage *n* filth, offal, refuse, remains, rubbish, trash, waste.

garble *vb* corrupt, distort, falsify, misquote, misrepresent, mutilate, pervert.

gargantuan *adj* big, Brobdingnagian, colossal, enormous, gigantic, huge, prodigious, tremendous.

garish *adj* bright, dazzling, flashy, flaunting, gaudy, glaring, loud, showy, staring, tawdry.

garland *vb* adorn, festoon, wreathe. • *n* chaplet, coronal, crown, festoon, wreath.

garment *n* clothes, clothing, dress, habit, vestment.

garner *vb* accumulate, collect, deposit, gather, hoard, husband, reserve, save, store, treasure.

garnish *vb* adorn, beautify, bedeck, decorate, deck, embellish, grace, ornament, prank, trim. • *n* decoration, enhancement, ornament, trimming.

garrulous *adj* babbling, loquacious, prating, prattling, talkative.

gasconade *n* bluster, boast, brag, bravado, swagger, vaunt, vapouring.

gasp *vb* blow, choke, pant, puff. • *n* blow, exclamation, gulp, puff.

gather *vb* assemble, cluster, collect, convene, group, muster, rally; accumulate, amass, garner, hoard, huddle, lump; bunch, crop, cull, glean, pick, pluck, rake, reap, shock, stack; acquire, gain, get, win; conclude, deduce, derive, infer; fold, plait, pucker, shirr, tuck; condense, grow, increase, thicken.

gathering *n* acquisition, collecting, earning, gain, heap, pile, procuring; assemblage, assembly, collection, company, concourse, congregation, meeting, muster; abscess, boil, fester, pimple, pustule, sore, suppuration, tumour, ulcer.

gauche *adj* awkward, blundering, bungling, clumsy, inept, tactless, uncouth.

gaudy *adj* bespangled, brilliant, brummagem, cheap, flashy, flaunting, garish, gimcrack, glittering, loud, ostentatious, overdecorated, sham, showy, spurious, tawdry, tinsel.

gauge *vb* calculate, check, determine, weigh; assess, estimate, guess, reckon. • *n* criterion, example, indicator, measure, meter, touchstone, yardstick; bore, depth, height, magnitude, size, thickness, width.

gaunt *adj* angular, attenuated, emaciated, haggard, lank, lean, meagre, scraggy, skinny, slender, spare, thin.

gawky *adj* awkward, boorish, clownish, clumsy, green, loutish, raw, rustic, uncouth, ungainly.

gay *adj* bright, brilliant, dashing, fine, showy; flashy, flaunting, garish, gaudy, glittering, loud, tawdry, tinsel; airy, blithe, blithesome, cheerful, festive, frivolous, frolicsome, gladsome, gleeful, hilarious, jaunty, jolly, jovial, light-hearted, lively, merry, mirthful, sportive, sprightly, vivacious.

gear *vb* adapt, equip, fit, suit, tailor. • *n* apparel, array, clothes, clothing, dress, garb; accoutrements, appliances, appointments, appurtenances, array, harness, goods, movables, subsidiaries; harness, rigging, tackle, trappings; apparatus, machinery, mechanics.

gelid *adj* chill, chilly, cold, freezing, frigid, icy.

gem *n* jewel, stone, treasure.

genealogy *n* ancestry, descent, lineage, pedigree, stock.

general *adj* broad, collective, generic, popular, universal, widespread; catholic, ecumenical; common, current, ordinary, usual; inaccurate, indefinite, inexact, vague.

generally *adv* commonly, extensively, universally, usually.

generate *vb* beget, breed, engender, procreate, propagate, reproduce, spawn; cause, form, make, produce.

generation *n* creation, engendering, formation, procreation, production; age, epoch, era, period, time; breed, children, family, kind, offspring, progeny, race, stock.

generosity *n* disinterestedness, high-mindedness, magnanimity, nobleness, bounteousness, bountifulness, bounty, charity, liberality, openhandedness.

generous *adj* high-minded, honourable, magnanimous, noble; beneficent, bountiful, charitable, free, hospitable, liberal, munificent, open-handed; abundant, ample, copious, plentiful, rich.

genial *adj* cheering, encouraging, enlivening, fostering, inspiring, mild, warm; agreeable, cheerful, cordial, friendly, hearty, jovial, kindly, merry, mirthful, pleasant.

genius *n* aptitude, aptness, bent, capacity, endowment, faculty, flair, gift, talent, turn; brains, creative power, ingenuity, inspiration, intellect, invention, parts, sagacity, wit; adeptness, master, master hand, proficiency; character, disposition, naturalness, nature; deity, demon, spirit.

genteel *adj* aristocratic, courteous, gentlemanly, lady-like, polished, polite, refined, well-bred; elegant, fashionable, graceful, stylish.

gentility *n* civility, courtesy, good breeding, politeness, refinement, urbanity.

gentle *adj* amiable, bland, clement, compassionate, humane, indulgent, kind, kindly, lenient, meek, merciful, mild, moderate, soft, tender, tender-hearted; docile, pacific, peaceable, placid, quiet, tame, temperate, tractable; bland, easy, gradual, light, slight; soft; high-born, noble, well-born; chivalrous, courteous, cultivated, knightly, polished, refined, well-bred.

gentlemanly *adj* civil, complaisant, courteous, cultivated, delicate, genteel, honourable, polite, refined, urbane, well-bred.

genuine *adj* authentic, honest, proper, pure, real, right, true, unadulterated, unalloyed, uncorrupted, veritable; frank, native, sincere, unaffected.

genus *n* class, group, kind, order, race, sort, type.

germ *n* embryo, nucleus, ovule, ovum, seed, seed-bud; bacterium, microbe, microorganism; beginning, cause, origin, rudiment, source.

germane *adj* akin, allied, cognate, related; apposite, appropriate, fitting, pertinent, relevant, suitable.

germinate *vb* bud, burgeon, develop, generate, grow, pollinate, push, shoot, sprout, vegetate.

gesture *vb* indicate, motion, signal, wave. • *n* action, attitude, gesticulation, gesturing, posture, sign, signal.

get *vb* achieve, acquire, attain, earn, gain, obtain, procure, receive, relieve, secure, win; finish, master, prepare; beget, breed, engender, generate, procreate.

gewgaw *n* bauble, gimcrack, gaud, kickshaw, knick-knack, plaything, trifle, toy, trinket.

ghastly *adj* cadaverous, corpse-like, death-like, deathly, ghostly, lurid, pale, pallid, wan; dismal, dreadful, fearful, frightful, grim, grisly, gruesome, hideous, horrible, shocking, terrible.

ghost *n* soul, spirit; apparition, phantom, revenant, shade, spectre, spook, sprite, wraith.

giant *adj* colossal, enormous, Herculean, huge, large, monstrous, prodigious, vast. • *n* colossus, cyclops, Hercules, monster.

gibberish *n* babble, balderdash, drivel, gabble, gobbledygook, jabber, nonsense, prate, prating.

gibe, jibe *vb* deride, fleer, flout, jeer, mock, ridicule, scoff, sneer, taunt. • *n* ridicule, sneer, taunt.

giddiness *n* dizziness, head-spinning, vertigo.

giddy *adj* dizzy, head-spinning, vertiginous; careless, changeable, fickle, flighty, frivolous, hare-brained, headlong, heedless, inconstant, irresolute, light-headed, thoughtless, unsteady, vacillating, wild.

gift *n* alms, allowance, benefaction, bequest, bonus, boon, bounty, contribution, donation, dowry, endowment, favour, grant, gratuity, honorarium, largesse, legacy, offering, premium, present, prize, subscription, subsidy, tip; faculty, talent.

gifted *adj* able, capable, clever, ingenious, intelligent, inventive, sagacious, talented.

gigantic *adj* colossal, Cyclopean, enormous, giant, herculean, huge, immense, prodigious, titanic, tremendous, vast.

giggle *vb, n* cackle, grin, laugh, snigger, snicker, titter.

gild *vb* adorn, beautify, bedeck, brighten, decorate, embellish, grace, illuminate.

gimcrack *adj* flimsy, frail, puny; base, cheap, paltry, poor. • *n* bauble, knick-knack, toy, trifle.

gird *vb* belt, girdle; begird, encircle, enclose, encompass, engird, environ, surround; brace, support. • *n* band, belt, cincture, girdle, girth, sash, waistband.

gist *n* basis, core, essence, force, ground, marrow, meaning, pith, point, substance.

give *vb* accord, bequeath, bestow, confer, devise, entrust, present; afford, contribute, donate, furnish, grant, proffer, spare, supply; communicate, impart; deliver, exchange, pay, requite; allow, permit, vouchsafe; emit, pronounce, render, utter; produce,

yield; cause, occasion; apply, devote, surrender; bend, sink, recede, retire, retreat, yield.

glad *adj* delighted, gratified, happy, pleased, rejoicing, well-contented; animated, blithe, cheerful, cheery, elated, gladsome, jocund, joyful, joyous, light, light-hearted, merry, playful, radiant; animating, bright, cheering, exhilarating, gladdening, gratifying, pleasing.

gladden *vb* bless, cheer, delight, elate, enliven, exhilarate, gratify, please, rejoice.

gladiator *n* prize-fighter, sword-player, swordsman.

gladness *n* animation, cheerfulness, delight, gratification, happiness, joy, joyfulness, joyousness, pleasure.

gladsome *adj* airy, blithe, blithesome, cheerful, delighted, frolicsome, glad, gleeful, jocund, jolly, jovial, joyful, joyous, light-hearted, lively, merry, pleased, sportive, sprightly, vivacious.

glamour *n* bewitchment, charm, enchantment, fascination, spell, witchery.

glance *vb* coruscate, gleam, glisten, glister, glitter, scintillate, shine; dart, flit; gaze, glimpse, look, view. • *n* gleam, glitter; gleam, look, view.

glare *vb* dazzle, flame, flare, gleam, glisten, glitter, sparkle; frown, gaze, glower. • *n* flare, glitter.

glaring *adj* dazzling, gleaming, glistening, glittering; barefaced, conspicuous, extreme, manifest, notorious, open.

glassy *adj* brilliant, crystal, crystalline, gleaming, lucent, shining, transparent.

glaze *vb* burnish, calender, furbish, gloss, polish. • *n* coat, enamel, finish, glazing, polish, varnish.

gleam *vb* beam, coruscate, flash, glance, glimmer, glitter, shine, sparkle. • *n* beam, flash, glance, glimmer, glimmering, glow, ray; brightness, coruscation, flashing, gleaming, glitter, glittering, lustre, splendour.

glean *vb* collect, cull, gather, get, harvest, pick, select.

glee *n* exhilaration, fun, gaiety, hilarity, jocularity, jollity, joviality, joy, liveliness, merriment, mirth, sportiveness, verve.

glib *adj* slippery, smooth; artful, facile, flippant, fluent, ready, talkative, voluble.

glide *vb* float, glissade, roll on, skate, skim, slide, slip; flow, lapse, run, roll. • *n* gliding, lapse, sliding, slip.

glimmer *vb* flash, flicker, gleam, glitter, shine, twinkle. • *n* beam, gleam, glimmering, ray; glance, glimpse.

glimpse *vb* espy, look, spot, view. • *n* flash, glance, glimmering, glint, look, sight.

glitter *vb* coruscate, flare, flash, glance, glare, gleam, glisten, glister, scintillate, shine, sparkle. • *n* beam, beaming, brightness, brilliancy, coruscation, gleam, glister, lustre, radiance, scintillation, shine, sparkle, splendour.

gloaming *n* dusk, eventide, nightfall, twilight.

gloat *vb* exult, gaze, rejoice, stare, triumph.

globe *n* ball, earth, orb, sphere.

globular *adj* globate, globated, globe-shaped, globose, globous, round, spheral, spheric, spherical.

globule *n* bead, drop, particle, spherule.

gloom *n* cloud, darkness, dimness, gloominess, obscurity, shade, shadow; cheerlessness, dejection, depression, despondency, downheartedness, dullness, melancholy, sadness.

gloomy *adj* dark, dim, dusky, obscure; cheerless, dismal, lowering, lurid; crestfallen, dejected, depressed, despondent, disheartened, dispirited, downcast, downhearted, glum, melancholy, morose, sad, sullen; depressing, disheartening, dispiriting, heavy, saddening.

glorify *vb* adore, bless, celebrate, exalt, extol, honour, laud, magnify, worship; adorn, brighten, elevate, ennoble, make bright.

glorious *adj* celebrated, conspicuous, distinguished, eminent, excellent, famed, famous, illustrious, pre-eminent, renowned; brilliant, bright, grand, magnificent, radiant, resplendent, splendid; consummate, exalted, high, lofty, noble, supreme.

glory *vb* boast, exult, vaunt. • *n* celebrity, distinction, eminence, fame, honour, illustriousness, praise, renown; brightness, brilliancy, effulgence, lustre, pride, resplendence, splendour; exaltation, exceeding, gloriousness, greatness, grandeur, nobleness; bliss, happiness.

gloss[1] *vb* coat, colour, disguise, extenuate, glaze, palliate, varnish, veneer, veil. • *n* coating, lustre, polish, sheen, varnish, veneer; pretence, pretext.

gloss[2] *vb* annotate, comment, elucidate, explain, interpret. • *n* annotation, comment, commentary, elucidation, explanation, interpretation, note.

glove *n* gantlet, gauntlet, handwear, mitt, mitten; challenge.

glow *vb* incandesce, radiate, shine; blush, burn, flush, redden. • *n* blaze, brightness, brilliance, burning, incandescence, luminosity, reddening; ardour, bloom, enthusiasm, fervency, fervour, flush, impetuosity, vehemence, warmth.

glower *vb* frown, glare, lower, scowl, stare. • *n* frown, glare, scowl.

glum *adj* churlish, crabbed, crestfallen, cross-grained, crusty, depressed, frowning, gloomy, glowering, moody, morose, sour, spleenish, spleeny, sulky, sullen, surly.

glut *vb* block up, cloy, cram, gorge, satiate, stuff. • *n* excess, saturation, surfeit, surplus.

glutinous *adj* adhesive, clammy, cohesive, gluey, gummy, sticky, tenacious, viscid, viscous.

glutton *n* gobbler, gorger, gourmand, gormandizer, greedy-guts, lurcher, pig.

gnarled *adj* contorted, cross-grained, gnarly, knotted, knotty, snaggy, twisted.

go *vb* advance, move, pass, proceed, progress repair; act, operate; be about, extravagate, fare, journey, roam, rove, travel, walk, wend; depart, disappear, cease; elapse, extend, lead, reach, run; avail, concur, contribute, tend, serve; eventuate, fare, turn out; afford, bet, risk, wager. • *n* action, business, case, chance, circumstance, doings, turn; custom, fad, fashion, mode, vogue; energy, endurance, power, stamina, verve, vivacity.

goad *vb* annoy, badger, harass, irritate, sting, worry; arouse, impel, incite, instigate, prod, spur, stimulate, urge. • *n* incentive, incitement, pressure, stimulation.

goal *n* bound, home, limit, mark, mete, post; end, object; aim, design, destination.

gobble *vb* bolt, devour, gorge, gulp, swallow.

goblin *n* apparition, elf, bogey, demon, gnome, hobgoblin, phantom, spectre, sprite.

god *n* almighty, creator, deity, divinity, idol, Jehovah, omnipotence, providence.

godless *adj* atheistic, impious, irreligious, profane, ungodly, wicked.

godlike *adj* celestial, divine, heavenly, supernal.

godly *adj* devout, holy, pious, religious, righteous, saint-like, saintly.

godsend *n* fortune, gift, luck, present, windfall.

golden *adj* aureate, brilliant, bright, gilded, resplendent, shining, splendid; excellent, precious; auspicious, favourable, opportune, propitious; blessed, delightful, glorious, halcyon, happy.

good *adj* advantageous, beneficial, favourable, profitable, serviceable, useful; adequate, appropriate, becoming, convenient, fit, proper, satisfactory, suitable, well-adapted; decorous, dutiful, honest, just, pious, reliable, religious, righteous, true, upright, virtuous, well-behaved, worthy; admirable, capable, excellent, genuine, healthy, precious, sincere, sound, sterling, valid, valuable; benevolent, favourable, friendly, gracious, humane, kind, merciful, obliging, well-disposed; fair, honourable, immaculate, unblemished, unimpeachable, unimpeached, unsullied, untarnished; cheerful, companionable, lively, genial, social; able, competent, dextrous, expert, qualified, ready, skilful, thorough, well-qualified; credit-worthy; agreeable, cheering, gratifying, pleasant. • *n* advantage, benefit, boon, favour, gain, profit, utility; interest, prosperity, welfare, weal; excellence, righteousness, virtue, worth.

good breeding *n* affability, civility, courtesy, good manners, polish, politeness, urbanity.

goodbye *n* adieu, farewell, parting.

goodly *adj* beautiful, comely, good-looking, graceful; agreeable, considerate, desirable, happy, pleasant.

good-natured *adj* amiable, benevolent, friendly, kind, kind-hearted, kindly.

goodness *n* excellence, quality, value, worth; honesty, integrity, morality, principle, probity, righteousness, uprightness, virtue; benevolence, beneficence, benignity, good-will, humaneness, humanity, kindness.

goods *npl* belongings, chattels, effects, furniture, movables; commodities, merchandise, stock, wares.

goodwill *n* benevolence, kindness, good nature; ardour, earnestness, heartiness, willingness, zeal; custom, patronage.

gore *vb* horn, pierce, stab, wound.

gorge[1] *vb* bolt, devour, eat, feed, swallow; cram, fill, glut, gormandize, sate, satiate, stuff, surfeit. • *n* craw, crop, gullet, throat.

gorge[2] *n* canyon, defile, fissure, notch, ravine.

gorgeous *adj* bright, brilliant, dazzling, fine, glittering, grand, magnificent, resplendent, rich, shining, showy, splendid, superb.

Gorgon *n* bugaboo, fright, hobgoblin, hydra, ogre, spectre.

gory *adj* bloody, ensanguined, sanguinary.

gospel *n* creed, doctrine, message, news, revelation, tidings.

gossip *vb* chat, cackle, clack, gabble, prate, prattle, tattle. • *n* babbler, busybody, chatterer, gossipmonger, newsmonger, quidnunc, tale-bearer, tattler, tell-tale; cackle, chat, chit-chat, prate, prattle, tattle.

gourmet *n* connoisseur, epicure, epicurean.

govern *vb* administer, conduct, direct, manage, regulate, reign, rule, superintend, supervise; guide, pilot, steer; bridle, check, command, control, curb, restrain, rule, sway.

government *n* autonomy, command, conduct, control, direction, discipline, dominion, guidance, management, regulation, restraint, rule, rulership, sway; administration, cabinet, commonwealth, polity, sovereignty, state.

governor *n* commander, comptroller, director, head, headmaster, manager, overseer, ruler, superintendent, supervisor; chief magistrate, executive; guardian, instructor, tutor.

grab *vb* capture, clutch, seize, snatch.

grace *vb* adorn, beautify, deck, decorate, embellish; dignify, honour. • *n* benignity, condescension, favour, good-will, kindness, love; devotion, efficacy, holiness, love, piety, religion, sanctity, virtue; forgiveness, mercy, pardon, reprieve; accomplishment, attractiveness, charm, elegance, polish, propriety, refinement; beauty, comeliness, ease, gracefulness, symmetry; blessing, petition, thanks.

graceful *adj* beautiful, becoming, comely, easy, elegant; flowing, natural, rounded, unlaboured; appropriate; felicitous, happy, tactful.

graceless *adj* abandoned, corrupt, depraved, dissolute, hardened, incorrigible, irreclaimable, lost, obdurate, profligate, reprobate, repugnant, shameless.

gracious *adj* beneficent, benevolent, benign, benignant, compassionate, condescending, favourable, friendly, gentle, good-natured, kind, kindly, lenient, merciful, mild, tender; affable, civil, courteous, easy, familiar, polite.

grade *vb* arrange, classify, group, order, rank, sort. • *n* brand, degree, intensity, stage, step, rank; gradient, incline, slope.

gradual *adj* approximate, continuous, gentle, progressive, regular, slow, successive.

graduate *vb* adapt, adjust, proportion, regulate. • *n* alumna, alumnus, laureate, postgraduate.

graft *vb* ingraft, inoculate, insert, transplant. • *n* bud, scion, shoot, slip, sprout; corruption, favouritism, influence, nepotism.

grain *n* kernel, ovule, seed; cereals, corn, grist; atom, bit, glimmer, jot, particle, scintilla, scrap, shadow, spark, tittle, trace, whit; disposition, fibre, humour, temper, texture; colour, dye, hue, shade, stain, texture, tincture, tinge.

granary *n* corn-house, garner, grange, store-house.

grand *adj* august, dignified, elevated, eminent, exalted, great, illustrious, lordly, majestic, princely, stately, sublime; fine, glorious, gorgeous, magnificent, pompous, lofty, noble, splendid, superb; chief, leading, main, pre-eminent, principal, superior.

grandee *n* lord, noble, nobleman.

grandeur *n* elevation, greatness, immensity, impressiveness, loftiness, vastness; augustness, dignity, eminence, glory, magnificence, majesty, nobility, pomp, splendour, state, stateliness.

grandiloquent *adj* bombastic, declamatory, high-minded, high-sounding, inflated, pompous, rhetorical, stilted, swelling, tumid, turgid.

grant *vb* accord, admit, allow, sanction; cede, concede, give, impart, indulge; bestow, confer, deign, invest, vouchsafe; convey, transfer, yield. • *n* admission, allowance, benefaction, bestowal, boon, bounty, concession, donation, endowment, gift, indulgence, largesse, present; conveyance, cession.

graphic *adj* descriptive, diagrammatic, figural, figurative, forcible, lively, pictorial, picturesque, striking, telling, vivid, well-delineated, well-drawn.

grapple *vb* catch, clutch, grasp, grip, hold, hug, seize, tackle, wrestle.

grasp *vb* catch, clasp, clinch, clutch, grapple, grip, seize; comprehend, understand. • *n* clasp, grip, hold; comprehension, power, reach, scope, understanding.

grasping *adj* acquisitive, avaricious, covetous, exacting, greedy, rapacious, sordid, tight-fisted.

grate *vb* abrade, rub, scrape, triturate; comminute, rasp; creak, fret, grind, jar, vex. • *n* bars, grating, latticework, screen; basket, fire bed.

grateful *adj* appreciative, beholden, indebted, obliged, sensible, thankful; pleasant, welcome.

gratification *n* gratifying, indulgence, indulging, pleasing, satisfaction, satisfying; delight, enjoyment, fruition, pleasure, reward.

gratify *vb* delight, gladden, please; humour, fulfil, grant, indulge, requite, satisfy.

gratifying *adj* agreeable, delightful, grateful, pleasing, welcome.

grating *adj* disagreeable, displeasing, harsh, irritating, offensive. • *n* grate, partition.

gratis *adv* freely, gratuitously.

gratitude *n* goodwill, gratitude, indebtedness, thankfulness.

gratuitous *adj* free, spontaneous, unrewarded, voluntary; assumed, baseless, groundless, unfounded, unwarranted, wanton.

gratuity *n* benefaction, bounty, charity, donation, endowment, gift, grant, largesse, present.

grave[1] *n* crypt, mausoleum, ossuary, pit, sepulchre, sepulture, tomb, vault.

grave[2] *adj* cogent, heavy, important, momentous, ponderous, pressing, serious, weighty; dignified, sage, sedate, serious, slow, solemn, staid, thoughtful; dull, grim, plain, quiet, sober, sombre, subdued; cruel, hard, harsh, severe; despicable, dire, dismal, gross, heinous, infamous, outrageous, scandalous, shameful, shocking; heavy, hollow, low, low-pitched, sepulchral.

grave[3] *vb* engrave, impress, imprint, infix; carve, chisel, cut, sculpt.

gravel *vb* bewilder, embarrass, nonplus, perplex, pose, puzzle, stagger. • *n* ballast, grit, sand, shingle.

graveyard *n* burial ground, cemetery, churchyard, god's acre, mortuary, necropolis.

gravity *n* heaviness, weight; demureness, sedateness, seriousness, sobriety, thoughtfulness; importance, moment, momentousness, weightiness.

graze *vb* brush, glance, scrape, scratch; abrade, shave, skim; browse, crop, feed, pasture. • *n* abrasion, bruise, scrape, scratch.

great *adj* ample, big, bulky, Cyclopean, enormous, gigantic, Herculean, huge, immense, large, pregnant, vast; decided, excessive, high, much, pronounced; countless, numerous; chief, considerable, grand, important, leading, main, pre-eminent, principal, superior, weighty; celebrated, distinguished, eminent, exalted, excellent, famed, famous, far-famed, illustrious, noted, prominent, renowned; august, dignified, elevated, grand, lofty, majestic, noble, sublime; chivalrous, generous, high-minded, magnanimous; fine, magnificent, rich, sumptuous.

greatness *n* bulk, dimensions, largeness, magnitude, size; distinction, elevation, eminence, fame, importance, renown; augustness, dignity, grandeur, majesty, loftiness, nobility, nobleness, sublimity; chivalry, generosity, magnanimity, spirit.

greed, greediness *n* gluttony, hunger, omnivorousness, ravenousness, voracity; avidity, covetousness, desire, eagerness, longing; avarice, cupidity, graspingness, grasping, rapacity, selfishness.

greedy *adj* devouring, edacious, gluttonous, insatiable, insatiate, rapacious, ravenous, voracious; desirous, eager; avaricious, grasping, selfish.

green *adj* aquamarine, emerald, olive, verdant, verdure, viridescent, viridian; blooming, flourishing, fresh, undecayed; fresh, new, recent; immature, unfledged, unripe; callow, crude, inexpert, ignorant, inexperienced, raw, unskilful, untrained, verdant, young; unseasoned; conservationist, ecological, environmentalist. • *n* common, grass plot, lawn, sward, turf, verdure.

greenhorn *n* beginner, novice, tyro.

greet *vb* accost, address, complement, hail, receive, salute, welcome.

greeting *n* compliment, salutation, salute, welcome.

grief *n* affliction, agony, anguish, bitterness, distress, dole, heartbreak, misery, regret, sadness, sorrow, suffering, tribulation, mourning, woe; grievance, trial; disaster, failure, mishap.

grievance *n* burden, complaint, hardship, injury, oppression, wrong; affliction, distress, grief, sorrow, trial, woe.

grieve *vb* afflict, aggrieve, agonize, discomfort, distress, hurt, oppress, pain, sadden, wound; bewail, deplore, mourn, lament, regret, sorrow, suffer.

grievous *adj* afflicting, afflictive, burdensome, deplorable, distressing, heavy, lamentable, oppressive, painful, sad, sorrowful; baleful, baneful, calamitous, destructive, detrimental, hurtful, injurious, mischievous, noxious, troublesome; aggravated, atrocious, dreadful, flagitious, flagrant, gross, heinous, iniquitous, intense, intolerable, severe, outrageous, wicked.

grill *vb* broil, griddle, roast, toast; sweat; cross-examine, interrogate, question; torment, torture. • *n* grating, gridiron; cross-examination, cross-questioning.

grim *adj* cruel, ferocious, fierce, harsh, relentless, ruthless, savage, stern, unyielding; appalling, dire, dreadful, fearful, frightful, grisly, hideous, horrid, horrible, terrific.

grimace *vb, n* frown, scowl, smirk, sneer.

grime *n* dirt, filth, foulness, smut.

grimy *adj* begrimed, defiled, dirty, filthy, foul, soiled, sullied, unclean.

grind *vb* bruise, crunch, crush, grate, grit, pulverize, rub, triturate; sharpen, whet; afflict, harass, oppress, persecute, plague, trouble. • *n* chore, drudgery, labour, toil.

grip *vb* clasp, clutch, grasp, hold, seize. • *n* clasp, clutch, control, domination, grasp, hold.

grisly *adj* appalling, frightful, dreadful, ghastly, grim, grey, hideous, horrible, horrid, terrible, terrific.

grit *vb* clench, grate, grind. • *n* bran, gravel, pebbles, sand; courage, decision, determination, firmness, perseverance, pluck, resolution, spirit.

groan *vb* complain, lament, moan, whine; creak. • *n* cry, moan, whine; complaint; grouse, grumble.

groom *vb* clean, dress, tidy; brush, tend; coach, educate, nurture, train. • *n* equerry, hostler, manservant, ostler, servant, stablehand, valet, waiter.

groove *n* channel, cut, furrow, rabbet, rebate, recess, rut, scoring; routine.

gross *vb* accumulate, earn, make. • *adj* big, bulky, burly, fat, great, large; dense, dull, stupid, thick; beastly, broad, carnal, coarse, crass, earthy, impure, indelicate, licentious, low, obscene, unbecoming, unrefined, unseemly, vulgar, rough, sensual; aggravated, brutal, enormous, flagrant, glaring, grievous, manifest, obvious, palpable, plain, outrageous, shameful; aggregate, entire, total, whole. • *n* aggregate, bulk, total, whole.

grossness *n* bigness, bulkiness, greatness; density, thickness; coarseness, ill-breeding, rudeness, vulgarity; bestiality, brutality, carnality, coarseness, impurity, indelicacy, licentiousness, sensuality.

grotesque *adj* bizarre, extravagant, fanciful, fantastic, incongruous, odd, strange, unnatural, whimsical, wild; absurd, antic, burlesque, ludicrous, ridiculous.

ground *vb* fell, place; base, establish, fix, found, set; instruct, train. • *n* area, clod, distance, earth, loam, mould, sod, soil, turf; country, domain, land, region, territory; acres, estate, field, property; base, basis, foundation, groundwork, support; account, consideration, excuse, gist, motive, opinion, reason.

groundless *adj* baseless, causeless, false, gratuitous, idle, unauthorized, unfounded, unjustifiable, unsolicited, unsought, unwarranted.

grounds *npl* deposit, dregs, grouts, lees, precipitate, sediment, settlings; accounts, arguments, considerations, reasons, support; campus, gardens, lawns, premises, yard.

group *vb* arrange, assemble, dispose, order. • *n* aggregation, assemblage, assembly, body, combination, class, clump, cluster, collection, order.

grove *n* copse, glade, spinney, thicket, wood, woodland.

grovel *vb* cower, crawl, creep, cringe, fawn, flatter, sneak.

grovelling *adj* creeping, crouching, squat; abject, base, beggarly, cringing, fawning, low, mean, servile, slavish, sneaking, undignified, unworthy, vile.

grow *vb* enlarge, expand, extend, increase, swell; arise, burgeon, develop, germinate, shoot, sprout, vegetate; advance, extend, improve, progress, thrive, wax; cultivate, produce, raise.

growl *vb* complain, croak, find fault, gnarl, groan, grumble, lament, murmur, snarl. • *n* croak, grown, snarl; complaint.

growth *n* augmentation, development, expansion, extension, growing, increase; burgeoning, excrescence, formation, germination, pollution, shooting, sprouting, vegetation; cultivation, produce, product, production; advance, advancement, development, improvement, progress; adulthood, maturity.

grub *vb* clear, dig, eradicate, root. • *n* caterpillar, larvae, maggot; drudge, plodder.

grudge *vb* begrudge, envy, repine; complain, grieve, murmur. • *n* aversion, dislike, enmity, grievance, hate, hatred, ill-will, malevolence, malice, pique, rancour, resentment, spite, venom.

gruff *adj* bluff, blunt, brusque, churlish, discourteous, grumpy, harsh, impolite, rough, rude, rugged, surly, uncivil, ungracious.

grumble *vb* croak, complain, murmur, repine; gnarl, growl, snarl; roar, rumble. • *n* growl, murmur, complaint, roar, rumble.

grumpy *adj* crabbed, cross, glum, moody, morose, sour, sullen, surly.

guarantee *vb* assure, insure, pledge, secure, warrant. • *n* assurance, pledge, security, surety, warrant, warranty.

guard *vb* defend, keep, patrol, protect, safeguard, save, secure, shelter, shield, watch. • *n* aegis, bulwark, custody, defence, palladium, protection, rampart, safeguard, security, shield; keeper, guardian, patrol, sentinel, sentry, warden, watch, watchman; conduct, convoy, escort; attention, care, caution, circumspection, heed, watchfulness.

guarded *adj* careful, cautious, circumspect, reserved, reticent, wary, watchful.

guardian *n* custodian, defender, guard, keeper, preserver, protector, trustee, warden.

guerdon *n* recompense, remuneration, requital, reward.

guess *vb* conjecture, divine, mistrust, surmise, suspect; fathom, find out, penetrate, solve; believe, fancy, hazard, imagine, reckon, suppose, think. • *n* conjecture, divination, notion, supposition, surmise.

guest *n* caller, company, visitant.

guidance *n* conduct, control, direction, escort, government, lead, leadership, pilotage, steering.

guide *vb* conduct, escort, lead, pilot; control, direct, govern, manage, preside, regulate, rule, steer, superintend, supervise. • *n* cicerone, conductor, director, monitor, pilot; adviser, counsellor, instructor, mentor; clew, directory, index, key, thread; guidebook, itinerary, landmark.

guild *n* association, brotherhood, company, corporation, fellowship, fraternity, society, union.

guile *n* art, artfulness, artifice, craft, cunning, deceit, deception, duplicity, fraud, knavery, ruse, subtlety, treachery, trickery, wiles, wiliness.

guileless *adj* artless, candid, frank, honest, ingenuous, innocent, open, pure, simple-minded, sincere, straightforward, truthful, undesigning, unsophisticated.

guilt *n* blame, criminality, culpability, guiltless; ill-desert, iniquity, offensiveness, wickedness, wrong; crime, offence, sin.

guiltless *adj* blameless, immaculate, innocent, pure, sinless, spotless, unpolluted, unspotted, unsullied, untarnished.

guilty *adj* criminal, culpable, evil, sinful, wicked, wrong.

guise *n* appearance, aspect, costume, dress, fashion, figure, form, garb, manner, mode, shape; air, behaviour, demeanour, mien; cover, custom, disguise, habit, pretence, pretext, practice.

gulf *n* abyss, chasm, opening; bay, inlet; whirlpool.

gull *vb* beguile, cheat, circumvent, cozen, deceive, dupe, hoax, overreach, swindle, trick. • *n* cheat, deception, hoax, imposition, fraud, trick; cat's paw, dupe.

gullibility *n* credulity, naiveness, naivety, overtrustfulness, simplicity, unsophistication.

gullible *adj* confiding, credulous, naive, over-trustful, simple, unsophisticated, unsuspicious.

gumption *n* ability, astuteness, cleverness, capacity, common sense, discernment, penetration, power, sagacity, shrewdness, skill; courage, guts, spirit.

gun *n* blunderbuss, cannon, carbine, firearm, musket, pistol, revolver, rifle, shotgun.

gurgle *vb* babble, bubble, murmur, purl, ripple. • *n* babbling, murmur, ripple.

gush *vb* burst, flood, flow, pour, rush, spout, stream; emotionalize, sentimentalize. • *n* flow, jet, onrush, rush, spurt, surge; effusion, effusiveness, loquacity, loquaciousness, talkativeness.

gushing *adj* flowing, issuing, rushing; demonstrative, effusive, sentimental.

gust *vb* blast, blow, puff. • *n* blast, blow, squall; burst, fit, outburst, paroxysm.

gusto *n* enjoyment, gust, liking, pleasure, relish, zest.

gusty *adj* blustering, blustery, puffy, squally, stormy, tempestuous, unsteady, windy.

gut *vb* destroy, disembowel, embowel, eviscerate, paunch. • *n* bowels, entrails, intestines, inwards, viscera.

gutter *n* channel, conduit, kennel, pipe, tube.

guttural *adj* deep, gruff, hoarse, thick, throaty.

guy *vb* caricature, mimic, ridicule. • *n* boy, man, person; dowdy, eccentric, fright, scarecrow.

guzzle *vb* carouse, drink, gorge, gormandize, quaff, swill, tipple, tope.

gyrate *vb* revolve, rotate, spin, whirl.

H

habiliment *n* apparel, attire, clothes, costume, dress, garb, garment, habit, raiment, robes, uniform, vesture, vestment.

habit *vb* accoutre, array, attire, clothe, dress, equip, robe. • *n* condition, constitution, temperament; addiction, custom, habitude, manner, practice, rule, usage, way, wont; apparel, costume, dress, garb, habiliment.

habitation *n* abode, domicile, dwelling, headquarters, home, house, lodging, quarters, residence.

habitual *adj* accustomed, common, confirmed, customary, everyday, familiar, inveterate, ordinary, regular, routine, settled, usual, wonted.

habituate *vb* accustom, familiarize, harden, inure, train, use.

habitude *n* custom, practice, usage, wont.

hack[1] *vb* chop, cut, hew, mangle, mutilate, notch; cough, rasp. • *n* cut, cleft, incision, notch; cough, rasp.

hack[2] *vb* ride. • *adj* hired, mercenary; banal, hackneyed, pedestrian, uninspired, unoriginal. • *n* horse, nag, pony; hireling, mercenary; journalist, scribbler, writer.

hackneyed *adj* banal, common, commonplace, overworked, pedestrian, stale, threadbare, trite.

hag *n* beldame, crone, fury, harridan, jezebel, she-monster, shrew, termagant, virago, vixen, witch.

haggard *adj* intractable, refractory, unruly, untamed, wild, wayward; careworn, emaciated, gaunt, ghastly, lank, lean, meagre, raw, spare, thin, wasted, worn.

haggle *vb* argue, bargain, cavil, chaffer, dispute, higgle, stickle; annoy, badger, bait, fret, harass, tease, worry.

hail[1] *vb* acclaim, greet, salute, welcome; accost, address, call, hallo, signal. • *n* greeting, salute.

hail[2] *vb* assail, bombard, rain, shower, storm, volley. • *n* bombardment, rain, shower, storm, volley.

halcyon *adj* calm, golden, happy, palmy, placid, peaceful, quiet, serene, still, tranquil, unruffled, undisturbed.

hale *adj* hardy, healthy, hearty, robust, sound, strong, vigorous, well.

halfwit *n* blockhead, dunce, moron, simpleton.

halfwitted *adj* doltish, dull, dull-witted, feeble-minded, foolish, sappy, shallow, silly, simple, soft, stolid, stupid, thick.

hall *n* chamber, corridor, entrance, entry, hallway, lobby, passage, vestibule; manor, manor-house; auditorium, lecture-room.

halloo *vb* call, cry, shout. • *n* call, cry, hallo, holla, hollo, shout.

hallow *vb* consecrate, dedicate, devote, revere, sanctify, solemnize; enshrine, honour, respect, reverence, venerate.

hallowed *adj* blessed, holy, honoured, revered, sacred.

hallucination *n* blunder, error, fallacy, mistake; aberration, delusion, illusion, phantasm, phantasy, self-deception, vision.

halo *n* aura, aureole, glory, nimbus.

halt[1] *vb* cease, desist, hold, rest, stand, stop. • *n* end, impasse, pause, standstill, stop.

halt[2] *vb* hesitate, pause, stammer, waver; falter, hobble, limp. • *adj* crippled, disabled, lame. • *n* hobble, limp.

hammer *vb* beat, forge, form, shape; excogitate, contrive, invent.

hammer and tongs *adv* earnestly, energetically, resolutely, strenuously, vigorously, zealously.

hamper *vb* bind, clog, confine, curb, embarrass, encumber, entangle, fetter, hinder, impede, obstruct, prevent, restrain, restrict, shackle, trammel. • *n* basket, box, crate, picnic basket; embarrassment, encumbrance, fetter, handicap, impediment, obstruction, restraint, trammel.

hand *vb* deliver, give, present, transmit; conduct, guide, lead. • *n* direction, part, side; ability, dexterity, faculty, skill, talent; course, inning, management, turn; agency, intervention, participation, share; control, possession, power; artificer, artisan, craftsman, employee, labourer, operative, workman; index, indicator, pointer; chirography, handwriting.

handbook *n* guidebook, manual.

handcuff *vb* bind, fetter, manacle, shackle. • *n* fetter, manacle, shackle.

handful *n* fistful, maniple, smattering.

handicap *vb* encumber, hamper, hinder, restrict. • *n* disadvantage, encumbrance, hampering, hindrance, restriction.

handicraft *n* hand manufacture, handwork, workmanship.

handle *vb* feel, finger, manhandle, paw, touch; direct, manage, manipulate, use, wield; discourse, discuss, treat. • *n* haft, helve, hilt, stock.

handsome *adj* admirable, comely, fine-looking, stately, well-formed, well-proportioned; appropriate, suitable, becoming, easy, graceful; generous, gracious, liberal, magnanimous, noble; ample, large, plentiful, sufficient.

handy *adj* adroit, clever, dextrous, expert, ready, skilful, skilled; close, convenient, near.

hang *vb* attach, swing; execute, truss; decline, drop, droop, incline; adorn, drape; dangle, depend, impend, suspend; rely; cling, loiter, rest, stick; float, hover, pay.

hangdog *adj* ashamed, base, blackguard, low, villainous, scurvy, sneaking.

hanger-on *n* dependant, minion, parasite, vassal.

hanker *vb* covet, crave, desire, hunger, long, lust, want, yearn.

hap *n* accident, chance, fate, fortune, lot.

haphazard *adj* aimless, chance, random.

hapless *adj* ill-fated, ill-starred, luckless, miserable, unfortunate, unhappy, unlucky, wretched.

happen *vb* befall, betide, chance, come, occur.

happily *adv* fortunately, luckily; agreeably, delightfully, prosperously, successfully.

happiness *n* brightness, cheerfulness, delight, gaiety, joy, light-heartedness, merriment, pleasure; beatitude, blessedness, bliss, felicity, enjoyment, welfare, well-being.

happy *adj* blessed, blest, blissful, cheerful, contented, joyful, joyous, light-hearted, merry; charmed, delighted, glad, gladdened, gratified, pleased; fortunate, lucky, prosperous, successful; able, adroit, apt, dextrous, expert, ready, skilful; befitting, felicitous, opportune, pertinent, seasonable, well-timed; auspicious, bright, favourable, propitious.

harangue *vb* address, declaim, spout. • *n* address, bombast, declamation, oration, rant, screed, speech, tirade.

harass *vb* exhaust, fag, fatigue, jade, tire, weary; annoy, badger, distress, gall, heckle, disturb, harry, molest, pester, plague, tantalize, tease, torment, trouble, vex, worry.

harbour *vb* protect, lodge, shelter; cherish, entertain, foster, indulge. • *n* asylum, cover, refuge, resting place, retreat, sanctuary, shelter; anchorage, destination, haven, port.

hard *adj* adamantine, compact, firm, flinty, impenetrable, marble, rigid, solid, resistant, stony, stubborn, unyielding; difficult, intricate, knotty, perplexing, puzzling; arduous, exacting, fatiguing, laborious, toilsome, wearying; austere, callous, cruel, exacting, hard-hearted, incorrigible, inflexible, insensible, insensitive, obdurate, oppressive, reprobate, rigorous, severe, unfeeling, unkind, unsusceptible, unsympathetic, unyielding, untender; calamitous, disagreeable, distressing, grievous, painful, unpleasant; acid, alcoholic, harsh, rough, sour; excessive, intemperate. • *adv* close, near; diligently, earnestly, energetically, incessantly, laboriously; distressfully, painfully, rigorously, severely; forcibly, vehemently, violently.

harden *vb* accustom, discipline, form, habituate, inure, season, train; brace, fortify, indurate, nerve, steel, stiffen, strengthen.

hardened *adj* annealed, case-hardened, tempered, indurated; abandoned, accustomed, benumbed, callous, confirmed, deadened, depraved, habituated, impenitent, incorrigible, inured, insensible, irreclaimable, lost, obdurate, reprobate, seared, seasoned, steeled, trained, unfeeling.

hard-headed *adj* astute, collected, cool, intelligent, sagacious, shrewd, well-balanced, wise.

hardhearted *adj* cruel, fell, implacable, inexorable, merciless, pitiless, relentless, ruthless, unfeeling, uncompassionate, unmerciful, unpitying, unrelenting.

hardihood *n* audacity, boldness, bravery, courage, decision, firmness, fortitude, intrepidity, manhood, mettle, pluck, resolution, stoutness; assurance, audacity, brass, effrontery, impudence.

hardly *adv* barely, scarcely; cruelly, harshly, rigorously, roughly, severely, unkindly.

hardship *n* fatigue, toil, weariness; affliction, burden, calamity, grievance, hardness, injury, misfortune, privation, suffering, trial, trouble.

hardy *adj* enduring, firm, hale, healthy, hearty, inured, lusty, rigorous, robust, rugged, sound, stout, strong, sturdy, tough; bold, brave, courageous, daring, heroic, intrepid, manly, resolute, stout-hearted, valiant.

harebrained *adj* careless, changeable, flighty, giddy, harumscarum, headlong, heedless, rash, reckless, unsteady, volatile, wild.

hark *interj* attend, hear, hearken, listen.

harlequin *n* antic, buffoon, clown, droll, fool, jester, punch, fool.

harm *vb* damage, hurt, injure, scathe; abuse, desecrate, ill-use, ill-treat, maltreat, molest. • *n* damage, detriment, disadvantage, hurt, injury, mischief, misfortune, prejudice, wrong.

harmful *adj* baneful, detrimental, disadvantageous, hurtful, injurious, mischievous, noxious, pernicious, prejudicial.

harmless *adj* innocent, innocuous, innoxious; inoffensive, safe, unoffending.

harmonious *adj* concordant, consonant, harmonic; dulcet, euphonious, mellifluous, melodious, musical, smooth, tuneful; comfortable, congruent, consistent, correspondent, orderly, symmetrical; agreeable, amicable, brotherly, cordial, fraternal, friendly, neighbourly.

harmonize *vb* adapt, attune, reconcile, unite; accord, agree, blend, chime, comport, conform, correspond, square, sympathize, tally, tune.

harmony *n* euphony, melodiousness, melody; accord, accordance, agreement, chime, concord, concordance, consonance, order, unison; adaptation, congruence, congruity, consistency, correspondence, fairness, smoothness, suitableness; amity, friendship, peace.

harness *vb* hitch, tackle. • *n* equipment, gear, tackle, tackling; accoutrements, armour, array, mail, mounting.

harp *vb* dwell, iterate, reiterate, renew, repeat.

harping *n* dwelling, iteration, reiteration, repetition.

harrow *vb* harass, lacerate, rend, tear, torment, torture, wound.

harry *vb* devastate, pillage, plunder, raid, ravage, rob; annoy, chafe, disturb, fret, gall, harass, harrow, incommode, pester, plague, molest, tease, torment, trouble, vex, worry.

harsh *adj* acid, acrid, astringent, biting, caustic, corrosive, crabbed, rough, sharp, sour, tart; cacophonous, discordant, grating, jarring, metallic, raucous, strident, unmelodious; abusive, austere, crabbed, crabby, cruel, disagreeable, hard, ill-natured, ill-tempered, morose, rigorous, severe, stern, unfeeling; bearish, bluff, blunt, brutal, gruff, rude, uncivil, ungracious.

harshness *n* roughness; acerbity, asperity, austerity, churlishness, crabbedness, hardness, ill-nature, ill-temper, moroseness, rigour, severity, sternness, unkindness; bluffness, bluntness, churlishness, gruffness, incivility, ungraciousness, rudeness.

harum-scarum *adj* hare-brained, precipitate, rash, reckless, volatile, wild.

harvest *vb* gather, glean, reap. • *n* crops, produce, yield; consequence, effect, issue, outcome, produce, result.

haste *n* alacrity, celerity, dispatch, expedition, nimbleness, promptitude, quickness, rapidity, speed, urgency, velocity; flurry, hurry, hustle, impetuosity, precipitateness, precipitation, press, rashness, rush, vehemence.

hasten *vb* haste, hurry; accelerate, dispatch, expedite, precipitate, press, push, quicken, speed, urge.

hasty *adj* brisk, fast, fleet, quick, rapid, speedy, swift; cursory, hurried, passing, slight, superficial; ill-advised, rash, reckless; headlong, helter-skelter, pell-mell, precipitate; abrupt, choleric, excitable, fiery, fretful, hot-headed, irascible, irritable, passionate, peevish, peppery, pettish, petulant, testy, touchy, waspish.

hatch *vb* brew, concoct, contrive, excogitate, design, devise, plan, plot, project, scheme; breed, incubate.

hate *vb* abhor, abominate, detest, dislike, execrate, loathe, nauseate. • *n* abomination, animosity, antipathy, detestation, dislike, enmity, execration, hatred, hostility, loathing.

hateful *adj* malevolent, malicious, malign, malignant, rancorous, spiteful; abhorrent, abominable, accursed, damnable, detestable, execrable, horrid, odious, shocking; disgusting, foul, loathsome, nauseous, obnoxious, offensive, repellent, repugnant, repulsive, revolting, vile.

hatred *n* animosity, enmity, hate, hostility, ill-will, malevolence, malice, malignity, odium, rancour; abhorrence, abomination, antipathy, aversion, detestation, disgust, execration, horror, loathing, repugnance, revulsion.

haughtiness *n* arrogance, contempt, contemptuousness, disdain, hauteur, insolence, loftiness, pride, self-importance, snobbishness, stateliness, superciliousness.

haughty *adj* arrogant, assuming, contemptuous, disdainful, imperious, insolent, lofty, lordly, overbearing, overweening, proud, scornful, snobbish, supercilious.

haul *vb* drag, draw, lug, pull, tow, trail, tug. • *n* heaving, pull, tug; booty, harvest, takings, yield.

haunt *vb* frequent, resort; follow, importune; hover, inhabit, obsess. • *n* den, resort, retreat.

hauteur *n* arrogance, contempt, contemptuousness, disdain, haughtiness, insolence, loftiness, pride, self-importance, stateliness, superciliousness.

have *vb* cherish, exercise, experience, keep, hold, occupy, own, possess; acquire, gain, get, obtain, receive; accept, take.

haven *n* asylum, refuge, retreat, shelter; anchorage, harbour, port.

havoc *n* carnage, damage, desolation, destruction, devastation, ravage, ruin, slaughter, waste, wreck.

hawk-eyed *adj* eagle-eyed, sharp-sighted.

hazard *vb* adventure, risk, venture; endanger, imperil, jeopardize. • *n* accident, casualty, chance, contingency, event, fortuity, stake; danger, jeopardy, peril, risk, venture.

hazardous *adj* dangerous, insecure, perilous, precarious, risky, uncertain, unsafe.

haze *n* fog, har, mist, smog; cloud, dimness, fume, miasma, obscurity, pall.

hazy *adj* foggy, misty; cloudy, dim, nebulous, obscure; confused, indefinite, indistinct, uncertain, vague.

head *vb* command, control, direct, govern, guide, lead, rule; aim, point, tend; beat, excel, outdo, precede, surpass. • *adj* chief, first, grand, highest, leading, main, principal; adverse, contrary. • *n* acme, summit, top; beginning, commencement, origin, rise, source; chief, chieftain, commander, director, leader, master, principal, superintendent, superior; intellect, mind, thought, understanding; branch, category, class, department, division, section, subject, topic; brain, crown, headpiece, intellect, mind, thought, understanding; cape, headland, point, promontory.

headiness *n* hurry, precipitation, rashness; obstinacy, stubbornness.

headless *adj* acephalous, beheaded; leaderless, undirected; headstrong, heady, imprudent, obstinate, rash, senseless, stubborn.

headlong *adj* dangerous, hasty, heady, impulsive, inconsiderate, perilous, precipitate, rash, reckless, ruinous, thoughtless; perpendicular, precipitous, sheer, steep. • *adv* hastily, headfirst, helter-skelter, hurriedly, precipitately, rashly, thoughtlessly.

headstone *n* cornerstone, gravestone.

headstrong *adj* cantankerous, cross-grained, dogged, forward, headless, heady, intractable, obstinate, self-willed, stubborn, ungovernable, unruly, violent, wayward.

heady *adj* hasty, headlong, impetuous, impulsive, inconsiderate, precipitate, rash, reckless, rushing, stubborn, thoughtless; exciting, inebriating, inflaming, intoxicating, spirituous, strong.

heal *vb* amend, cure, remedy, repair, restore; compose, harmonize, reconcile, settle, soothe.

healing *adj* curative, palliative, remedial, restoring, restorative; assuaging, assuasive, comforting, composing, gentle, lenitive, mild, soothing.

health *n* healthfulness, robustness, salubrity, sanity, soundness, strength, tone, vigour.

healthy *adj* active, hale, hearty, lusty, sound, vigorous, well; bracing, healthful, health-giving, hygienic, invigorating, nourishing, salubrious, salutary, wholesome.

heap *vb* accumulate, augment, amass, collect, overfill, pile up, store. • *n* accumulation, collection, cumulus, huddle, lot, mass, mound, pile, stack.

hear *vb* eavesdrop, hearken, heed, listen, overhear; ascertain, discover, gather, learn, understand; examine, judge.

heart *n* bosom, breast; centre, core, essence, interior, kernel, marrow, meaning, pith; affection, benevolence, character, disposition, feeling, inclination, love, mind, passion, purpose, will; affections, ardour, emotion, feeling, love; boldness, courage, fortitude, resolution, spirit.

heartache *n* affliction, anguish, bitterness, distress, dole, grief, heartbreak, sorrow, woe.

heartbroken *adj* broken-hearted, cheerless, comfortless, desolate, disconsolate, forlorn, inconsolable, miserable, woebegone, wretched.

hearten *vb* animate, assure, cheer, comfort, console, embolden, encourage, enhearten, incite, inspire, inspirit, reassure, stimulate.

heartfelt *adj* cordial, deep, deep-felt, hearty, profound, sincere, warm.

hearth *n* fireplace, fireside, forge, hearthstone.

heartily *adv* abundantly, completely, cordially, earnestly, freely, largely, sincerely, vigorously.

heartless *adj* brutal, cold, cruel, hard, harsh, merciless, pitiless, unfeeling, unsympathetic; spiritless, timid, timorous, uncourageous.

heart-rending *adj* affecting, afflicting, anguishing, crushing, distressing.

hearty *adj* cordial, deep, earnest, fervent, heartfelt, profound, sincere, true, unfeigned, warm; active, animated, energetic, fit, vigorous, zealous; convivial, hale, healthy, robust, sound, strong, warm; abundant, full, heavy; nourishing, nutritious, rich.

heat *vb* excite, flush, inflame; animate, rouse, stimulate, stir. • *n* calorie, caloricity, torridity, warmth; excitement, fever, flush, impetuosity, passion, vehemence, violence; ardour, earnestness, fervency, fervour, glow, intensity, zeal; exasperation, fierceness, frenzy, rage.

heath *n* field, moor, wasteland, plain.

heathen *adj* animist, animistic; pagan, paganical, paganish, paganistic, unconverted; agnostic, atheist, atheistic, gentile, idolatrous, infidel, irreligious; barbarous, cruel, inhuman, savage. • *n* atheist, gentile, idolater, idolatress, infidel, pagan, unbeliever; barbarian, philistine, savage.

heave *vb* elevate, hoist, lift, raise; breathe, exhale; cast, fling, hurl, send, throw, toss; dilate, expand, pant, rise, swell; retch, throw up; strive, struggle.

heaven *n* empyrean, firmament, sky, welkin; bliss, ecstasy, elysium, felicity, happiness, paradise, rapture, transport.

heavenly *adj* celestial, empyreal, ethereal; angelic, beatific, beatified, cherubic, divine, elysian, glorious, god-like, sainted, saintly, seraphic; blissful, delightful, divine, ecstatic, enrapturing, enravishing, exquisite, golden, rapturous, ravishing, exquisite, transporting.

heaviness *n* gravity, heft, ponderousness, weight; grievousness, oppressiveness, severity; dullness, languor, lassitude, sluggishness, stupidity; dejection, depression, despondency, gloom, melancholy, sadness, seriousness.

heavy *adj* grave, hard, onerous, ponderous, weighty; afflictive, burdensome, crushing, cumbersome, grievous, oppressive, severe, serious, dilatory, dull, inactive, inanimate, indolent, inert, lifeless, listless, sleepy, slow, sluggish, stupid, torpid; chapfallen, crestfallen, crushed, depressed, dejected, despondent, disconsolate, downhearted, gloomy, low-spirited, melancholy, sad, sobered, sorrowful; difficult, laborious, tedious, tiresome, wearisome, weary; burdened, encumbered, loaded; clammy, clayey, cloggy, ill-raised, miry, muddy, soggy; boisterous, deep, energetic, loud, roaring, severe, stormy, strong, tempestuous, violent; cloudy, dark, dense, gloomy, lowering, overcast.

hebetate *adj* blunt; dull, obtuse, sluggish, stupid, stupefied.

hectic *adj* animated, excited, fevered, feverish, flushed, heated, hot.

hector *vb* bluster, boast, bully, menace, threaten; annoy, fret, harass, harry, irritate, provoke, tease, vex, worry. • *n* blusterer, bully, swaggerer.

hedge *vb* block, encumber, hinder, obstruct, surround; enclose, fence, fortify, guard, protect; disappear, dodge, evade, hide, skulk, temporize. • *n* barrier, hedgerow, fence, limit.

heed *vb* attend, consider, mark, mind, note, notice, observe, regard. • *n* attention, care, carefulness, caution, circumspection, consideration, heedfulness, mindfulness, notice, observation, regard, wariness, vigilance, watchfulness.

heedful *adj* attentive, careful, cautious, circumspect, mindful, observant, observing, provident, regardful, watchful, wary.

heedless *adj* careless, inattentive, neglectful, negligent, precipitate, rash, reckless, thoughtless, unmindful, unminding, unobserving, unobservant.

heft *n* handle, haft, helve; bulk, weight.

hegemony *n* ascendancy, authority, headship, leadership, predominance, preponderance, rule.

height *n* altitude, elevation, tallness; acme, apex, climax, eminence, head, meridian, pinnacle, summit, top, vertex, zenith; eminence, hill, mountain; dignity, exaltation, grandeur, loftiness, perfection.

heighten *vb* elevate, raise; ennoble, exalt, magnify, make greater; augment, enhance, improve, increase, strengthen; aggravate, intensify.

heinous *adj* aggravated, atrocious, crying, enormous, excessive, flagitious, flagrant, hateful, infamous, monstrous, nefarious, odious, villainous.

heir *n* child, inheritor, offspring, product.

helical *adj* screw-shaped, spiral, winding.

hellish *adj* abominable, accursed, atrocious, curst, damnable, damned, demoniacal, detestable, devilish, diabolical, execrable, fiendish, infernal, monstrous, nefarious, satanic.

helm *n* rudder, steering-gear, tiller, wheel; command, control, direction, rein, rule.

help *vb* relieve, save, succour; abet, aid, assist, back, cooperate, second, serve, support, sustain, wait; alleviate, ameliorate, better, cure, heal, improve, remedy, restore; control, hinder, prevent, repress, resist, withstand; avoid, forbear, control. • *n* aid, assistance, succour, support; relief, remedy; assistant, helper, servant.

helper *adj* aider, abettor, ally, assistant, auxiliary, coadjutor, colleague, helpmate, partner, supporter.

helpful *adj* advantageous, assistant, auxiliary, beneficial, contributory, convenient, favourable, kind, profitable, serviceable, useful.

helpless *adj* disabled, feeble, imbecile, impotent, infirm, powerless, prostrate, resourceless, weak; abandoned, defenceless, exposed, unprotected; desperate, irremediable, remediless.

helpmate *n* companion, consort, husband, partner, wife; aider, assistant, associate, helper.

helter-skelter *adj* disorderly, headlong, irregular, pell-mell, precipitate. • *adv* confusedly, hastily, headlong, higgledy-piggledy, pell-mell, precipitately, wildly.

hem *vb* border, edge, skirt; beset, confine, enclose, environ, surround, sew; hesitate. • *n* border, edge, trim.

henchman *n* attendant, follower, retainer, servant, supporter.

herald *vb* announce, proclaim, publish. • *n* announcer, crier, publisher; harbinger, precursor, proclaimer.

heraldry *n* blazonry, emblazonry.

herbage *n* greenery, herb, pasture, plants, vegetation.

herculean *adj* able-bodied, athletic, brawny, mighty, muscular, powerful, puissant, sinewy, stalwart, strong, sturdy, vigorous; dangerous, difficult, hard, laborious, perilous, toilsome, troublesome; colossal, Cyclopean, gigantic, great, strapping.

herd *vb* drive, gather, lead, tend; assemble, associate, flock. • *n* drover, herder, herdsman, shepherd; crowd, multitude, populace, rabble; assemblage, assembly, collection, drove, flock, pack.

hereditary *adj* ancestral, inheritable, inherited, patrimonial, transmitted.

heresy *n* dissent, error, heterodoxy, impiety, recusancy, unorthodoxy.

heretic *n* dissenter, dissident, nonconformist, recusant, schismatic, sectarian, sectary, separatist, unbeliever.

heretical *adj* heterodox, impious, schismatic, schismatical, sectarian, unorthodox.

heritage *n* estate, inheritance, legacy, patrimony, portion.

hermetic *adj* airtight, impervious; cabbalistic, emblematic, emblematical, magical, mysterious, mystic, mystical, occult, secret, symbolic, symbolical.

hermit *n* anchoress, anchoret, anchorite, ascetic, eremite, monk, recluse, solitaire, solitary.

heroic *adj* bold, brave, courageous, daring, dauntless, fearless, gallant, illustrious, intrepid, magnanimous, noble, valiant; desperate, extravagant, extreme, violent.

heroism *n* boldness, bravery, courage, daring, endurance, fearlessness, fortitude, gallantry, intrepidity, prowess, valour.

hesitate *vb* boggle, delay, demur, doubt, pause, scruple, shilly-shally, stickle, vacillate, waver; falter, stammer, stutter.

hesitation *n* halting, misgiving, reluctance; delay, doubt, indecision, suspense, uncertainty, vacillation; faltering, stammering, stuttering.

heterodox *adj* heretical, recusant, schismatic, unorthodox, unsound; apocryphal, uncanonical.

heterogeneous *adj* contrasted, contrary, different, dissimilar, diverse, incongruous, indiscriminate, miscellaneous, mixed, opposed, unhomogeneous, unlike.

hew *vb* chop, cut, fell, hack; fashion, form, shape, smooth.

hiatus *n* blank, break, chasm, gap, interval, lacuna, opening, rift.

hidden *adj* blind, clandestine, cloaked, close, concealed, covered, covert, enshrouded, latent, masked, occult, private, secluded, secret, suppressed, undiscovered, veiled; abstruse, cabbalistic, cryptic, dark, esoteric, hermetic, inward, mysterious, mystic, mystical, obscure, oracular, recondite.

hide *vb* bury, conceal, cover, secrete, suppress, withhold; cloak, disguise, eclipse, hoard, mask, screen, shelter, veil.

hideous *adj* abominable, appalling, awful, dreadful, frightful, ghastly, ghoulish, grim, grisly, horrible, horrid, repulsive, revolting, shocking, terrible, terrifying.

hie *vb* hasten, speed.

hieratic *adj* consecrated, devoted, priestly, sacred, sacerdotal.

hieroglyph *n* picture-writing, rebus, sign, symbol.

hieroglyphic *adj* emblematic, emblematical, figurative, obscure, symbolic, symbolical.

higgle *vb* hawk, peddle; bargain, chaffer, haggle, negotiate.

higgledy-piggledy *adj* chaotic, confused, disorderly, jumbled. • *adv* confusedly, in disorder, helter-skelter, pell-mell.

high *adj* elevated, high-reaching, lofty, soaring, tall, towering; distinguished, eminent, pre-eminent, prominent, superior; admirable, dignified, exalted, great, noble; arrogant, haughty, lordly, proud, supercilious; boisterous, strong, tumultuous, turbulent, violent; costly, dear, pricey; acute, high-pitched, high-toned, piercing, sharp, shrill; tainted, malodorous. • *adv* powerfully, profoundly; eminently, loftily; luxuriously, richly.

high-flown *adj* elevated, presumptuous, proud, lofty, swollen; extravagant, high-coloured, lofty, overdrawn, overstrained; bombastic, inflated, pompous, pretentious, strained, swollen, turgid.

high-handed *adj* arbitrary, despotic, dictatorial, domineering, oppressive, overbearing, self-willed, violent, wilful.

highly strung *adj* ardent, excitable, irascible, nervous, quick, tense; high-spirited, sensitive.

high-minded *adj* arrogant, haughty, lofty, proud; elevated, high-toned; generous honourable, magnanimous, noble, spiritual.

highwayman *n* bandit, brigand, footpad, freebooter, marauder, outlaw, robber.

hilarious *adj* boisterous, cheerful, comical, convivial, riotous, uproarious, jovial, joyful, merry, mirthful, noisy.

hilarity *n* cheerfulness, conviviality, exhilarated, gaiety, glee, jollity, joviality, joyousness, merriment, mirth.

hill *n* ascent, ben, elevation, eminence, hillock, knoll, mount, mountain, rise, tor.

hind *adj* back, hinder, hindmost, posterior, rear, rearward.

hinder *vb* bar, check, clog, delay, embarrass, encumber, impede, interrupt, obstruct, oppose, prevent, restrain, retard, stop, thwart.

hindrance *n* check, deterrent, encumbrance, hitch, impediment, interruption, obstacle, obstruction, restraint, stop, stoppage.

hinge *vb* depend, hang, rest, turn.

hint *vb* allude, glance, imply, insinuate, intimate, mention, refer, suggest. • *n* allusion, clue, implication, indication, innuendo, insinuation, intimation, mention, reminder, suggestion, taste, trace.

hire *vb* buy, rent, secure; charter, employ, engage, lease, let. • *n* allowance, bribe, compensation, pay, remuneration, rent, reward, salary, stipend, wages.

hireling *n* employee, mercenary, myrmidon.

hirsute *adj* bristled, bristly, hairy, shaggy; boorish, course, ill-bred, loutish, rough, rude, rustic, uncouth, unmannerly.

hiss *vb* shrill, sibilate, whistle, whir, whiz; condemn, damn, ridicule. • *n* fizzle, hissing, sibilant, sibilation, sizzle.

historian *n* annalist, autobiographer, biographer, chronicler, narrator, recorder.

history *n* account, autobiography, annals, biography, chronicle, genealogy, memoirs, narration, narrative, recital, record, relation, story.

hit *vb* discomfit, hurt, knock, strike; accomplish, achieve, attain, gain, reach, secure, succeed, win; accord, fit, suit; beat, clash, collide, contact, smite. • *n* blow, collision, strike, stroke; chance, fortune, hazard, success, venture.

hitch *vb* catch, impede, stick, stop; attach, connect, fasten, harness, join, tether, tie, unite, yoke. • *n* catch, check, hindrance, impediment, interruption, obstacle; knot, noose.

hoar *adj* ancient, grey, hoary, old, white.

hoard *vb* accumulate, amass, collect, deposit, garner, hive, husband, save, store, treasure. • *n* accumulation, collection, deposit, fund, mass, reserve, savings, stockpile, store.

hoarse *adj* discordant, grating, gruff, guttural, harsh, husky, low, raucous, rough.

hoary *adj* grey, hoar, silvery, white; ancient, old, venerable.

hoax *vb* deceive, dupe, fool, gammon, gull, hoodwink, swindle, trick. • *n* canard, cheat, deception, fraud, humbug, imposition, imposture, joke, trick, swindle.

hobble *vb* falter, halt, hop, limp; fasten, fetter, hopple, shackle, tie. • *n* halt, limp; clog, fetter, shackle; embarrassment, difficulty, perplexity, pickle, strait.

hobgoblin *n* apparition, bogey, bugbear, goblin, imp, spectre, spirit, sprite.

hobnail *n* bumpkin, churl, clodhopper, clown, lout, rustic.

hocus-pocus *n* cheater, impostor, juggler, sharper, swindler, trickster; artifice, cheat, deceit, deception, delusion, hoax, imposition, juggle, trick.

hodgepodge *n* farrago, hash, hotchpotch, jumble, medley, miscellany, mixture, ragout, stew.

hog *n* beast, glutton, pig; grunter, porker, swine.

hoggish *adj* brutish, filthy, gluttonish, piggish, swinish; grasping, greedy, mean, selfish, sordid.

hoist *vb* elevate, heave, lift, raise, rear. • *n* elevator, lift.

hold *vb* clasp, clinch, clutch, grasp, grip, seize; have, keep, occupy, possess, retain; bind, confine, control, detain, imprison, restrain, restrict; connect, fasten, fix, lock; arrest, check, stay, stop, suspend, withhold; continue, keep up, maintain, manage, prosecute, support, sustain; cherish, embrace, entertain; account, believe, consider, count, deem, entertain, esteem, judge, reckon, regard, think; accommodate, admit, carry, contain, receive, stow; assemble, conduct, convene; endure, last, persist, remain; adhere, cleave, cling, cohere, stick. • *n* anchor, bite, clasp, control, embrace, foothold, grasp, grip, possession, retention, seizure; prop, stay, support; claim, footing, vantage point; castle, fort, fortification, fortress, stronghold, tower; locker, storage, storehouse.

hole *n* aperture, opening, perforation; abyss, bore, cave, cavern, cavity, chasm, depression, excavation, eye, hollow, pit, pore, void; burrow, cover, lair, retreat; den, hovel, kennel.

holiday *n* anniversary, celebration, feast, festival, festivity, fete, gala, recess, vacation.

holiness *n* blessedness, consecration, devotion, devoutness, godliness, piety, purity, religiousness, righteousness, sacredness, saintliness, sanctity, sinlessness.

hollow *vb* dig, excavate, groove, scoop. • *adj* cavernous, concave, depressed, empty, sunken, vacant, void; deceitful, faithless, false, false-hearted, hollow-hearted, hypocritical, insincere, pharisaical, treacherous, unfeeling; deep, low, muffled, reverberating, rumbling, sepulchral. • *n* basin, bowl, depression; cave, cavern, cavity, concavity, dent, dimple, dint, depression, excavation, hole, pit; canal, channel, cup, dimple, dig, groove, pocket, sag.

holocaust *n* carnage, destruction, devastation, genocide, massacre.

holy *adj* blessed, consecrated, dedicated, devoted, hallowed, sacred, sanctified; devout, godly, pious, pure, religious, righteous, saintlike, saintly, sinless, spiritual.

homage *n* allegiance, devotion, fealty, fidelity, loyalty; court, deference, duty, honour, obeisance, respect, reverence, service; adoration, devotion, worship.

home *adj* domestic, family; close, direct, effective, penetrating, pointed. • *n* abode, dwelling, seat, quarters, residence.

homely *adj* domestic, familiar, house-like; coarse, commonplace, homespun, inelegant, plain, simple, unattractive, uncomely, unpolished, unpretentious.

homespun *adj* coarse, homely, inelegant, plain, rude, rustic, unpolished.

homicide *n* manslaughter, murder.

homily *n* address, discourse, lecture, sermon.

homogeneous *adj* akin, alike, cognate, kindred, similar, uniform.

honest *adj* equitable, fair, faithful, honourable, open, straight, straightforward; conscientious, equitable, reliable, sound, square, true, trustworthy, trusty, uncorrupted, upright, virtuous; above-board, faithful, genuine, thorough, unadulterated; creditable, decent, proper, reputable, respectable, suitable; chaste, decent; candid, direct, frank, ingenuous, sincere, unreserved.

honesty *n* equity, fairness, faithfulness, fidelity, honour, integrity, justice, probity, trustiness, trustworthiness, uprightness; truth, truthfulness, veracity; genuineness, thoroughness; candour, frankness, ingenuousness, openness, sincerity, straightforwardness, unreserve.

honorary *adj* formal, nominal, titular, unofficial, unpaid.

honour *vb* dignify, exalt, glorify, grace; respect, revere, reverence, venerate; adore, hallow, worship; celebrate, commemorate, keep, observe. • *n* civility, deference, esteem, homage, respect, reverence, veneration; dignity, distinction, elevation, nobleness; consideration, credit, fame, glory, reputation; high-mindedness, honesty, integrity, magnanimity, probity, uprightness; chastity, purity, virtue; boast, credit, ornament, pride.

honourable *adj* elevated, famous, great, illustrious, noble; admirable, conscientious, fair, honest, just, magnanimous, true, trustworthy, upright, virtuous, worshipful; creditable, esteemed, estimable, equitable, proper, respected, reputable, right.

honours *npl* dignities, distinctions, privilege, titles; adornments, beauties, decorations, glories; civilities.

hood *n* capuche, coif, cover, cowl, head.

hoodwink *vb* blind, blindfold; cloak, conceal, cover, hide; cheat, circumvent, cozen, deceive, delete, dupe, fool, gull, impose, overreach, trick.

hook *vb* catch, ensnare, entrap, hasp, snare; bend, curve. • *n* catch, clasp, fastener, hasp; snare, trap; cutter, grass-hook, reaper, reaping-hook, sickle.

hooked *adj* aquiline, bent, crooked, curved, hamate, unciform.

hoop *vb* clasp, encircle, enclose, surround. • *n* band, circlet, girdle, ring; crinoline, farthingale.

hoot *vb* boo, cry, jeer, shout, yell; condemn, decry, denounce, execrate, hiss. • *n* boo, cry, jeer, shout, yell.

hop *vb* bound, caper, frisk, jump, leap, skip, spring; dance, trip; halt, hobble, limp. • *n* bound, caper, dance, jump, leap, skip, spring.

hope *vb* anticipate, await, desire, expect, long; believe, rely, trust. • *n* confidence, belief, faith, reliance, sanguineness, sanguinity, trust; anticipation, desire, expectancy, expectation.

hopeful *adj* anticipatory, confident, expectant, fond, optimistic, sanguine; cheerful, encouraging, promising.

hopeless *adj* abject, crushed, depressed, despondent, despairing, desperate, disconsolate, downcast, forlorn, pessimistic, woebegone; abandoned, helpless, incurable, irremediable, remediless; impossible, impracticable, unachievable, unattainable.

horde *n* clan, crew, gang, troop; crowd, multitude, pack, throng.

horn *vb* gore, pierce. • *n* trumpet, wind instrument; beaker, drinking cup, cornucopia; spike, spur; cusp, prong, wing.

horrid *adj* alarming, awful, bristling, dire, dreadful, fearful, frightful, harrowing, hideous, horrible, horrific, horrifying, rough, terrible, terrific; abominable, disagreeable, disgusting, odious, offensive, repulsive, revolting, shocking, unpleasant, vile.

horrify *vb* affright, alarm, frighten, shock, terrify, terrorise.

horror *n* alarm, awe, consternation, dismay, dread, fear, fright, panic; abhorrence, abomination, antipathy, aversion, detestation, disgust, hatred, loathing, repugnance, revulsion; shuddering.

horse *n* charger, cob, colt, courser, filly, gelding, mare, nag, pad, palfrey, pony, stallion, steed; cavalry, horseman; buck, clotheshorse, frame, sawhorse, stand, support.

horseman *n* cavalier, equestrian, rider; cavalryman, chasseur, dragoon, horse-soldier.

hospitable *adj* attentive, bountiful, kind; bountiful, cordial, generous, liberal, open, receptive, sociable, unconstrained, unreserved.

host[1] *n* entertainer, innkeeper, landlord, master of ceremonies, presenter, proprietor, owner, receptionist.

host[2] *n* array, army, legion; assemblage, assembly, horde, multitude, throng.

host[3] *n* altar bread, bread, consecrated bread, loaf, wafer.

hostile *adj* inimical, unfriendly, warlike; adverse, antagonistic, contrary, opposed, opposite, repugnant.

hostilities *npl* conflict, fighting, war, warfare.

hostility *n* animosity, antagonism, enmity, hatred, ill-will, unfriendliness; contrariness, opposition, repugnance, variance.

hot *adj* burning, fiery, scalding; boiling, flaming, heated, incandescent, parching, roasting, torrid; heated, oppressive, sweltering, warm; angry, choleric, excitable, furious, hasty, impatient, impetuous, irascible, lustful, passionate, touchy, urgent, violent; animated, ardent, eager, fervent, fervid, glowing, passionate, vehement; acrid, biting, highly flavoured, highly seasoned, peppery, piquant, pungent, sharp, stinging.

hotchpotch *n* farrago, jumble, hodgepodge, medley, miscellany, stew.

hotel *n* inn, public house, tavern.

hot-headed *adj* furious, headlong, headstrong, hot-brained, impetuous, inconsiderate, passionate, precipitate, rash, reckless, vehement, violent.

hound *vb* drive, incite, spur, urge; bate, chase, goad, harass, harry, hunt, pursue.

house *vb* harbour, lodge, protect, shelter. • *n* abode, domicile, dwelling, habitation, home, mansion, residence; building, edifice; family, household; kindred, race, lineage, tribe; company, concern, firm, partnership; hotel, inn, public house, tavern.

housing *n* accommodation, dwellings, houses; casing, container, covering, protection, shelter.

hovel *n* cabin, cot, den, hole, hut, shed.

hover *vb* flutter; hang; vacillate, waver.

however *adv* but, however, nevertheless, notwithstanding, still, though, yet.

howl *vb* bawl, cry, lament, ululate, weep, yell, yowl. • *n* cry, yell, ululation.

hoyden *n* romp, tomboy.

hoydenish *adj* bad-mannered, boisterous, bold, ill-behaved, ill-taught, inelegant, romping, rough, rude, rustic, tomboyish, uncouth, ungenteel, unladylike, unruly.

hubbub *n* clamour, confusion, din, disorder, disturbance, hullabaloo, racket, riot, outcry, tumult, uproar.

huckster *n* hawker, peddler, retailer.

huddle *vb* cluster, crowd, gather; crouch, curl up, nestle, snuggle. • *n* confusion, crowd, disorder, disturbance, jumble, tumult.

hue *n* cast, colour, complexion, dye, shade, tinge, tint, tone.

huff *vb* blow, breathe, exhale, pant, puff. • *n* anger, fume, miff, passion, pet, quarrel, rage, temper, tiff.

hug *vb* clasp, cling, cuddle, embrace, grasp, grip, squeeze; cherish, nurse, retain. • *n* clasp, cuddle, embrace, grasp, squeeze.

huge *adj* bulky, colossal, Cyclopean, elephantine, enormous, gigantic, herculean, immense, stupendous, vast,

huggermugger *adj* clandestine, secret, sly; base, contemptible, mean, unfair; confused, disorderly, slovenly.

hull *vb* husk, peel, shell. • *n* covering, husk, rind, shell.

hullabaloo *n* clamour, confusion, din, disturbance, hubbub, outcry, racket, vociferation, uproar.

hum *vb* buzz, drone, murmur; croon, sing.

humane *adj* accommodating, benevolent, benign, charitable, clement, compassionate, gentle, good-hearted, kind, kind-hearted, lenient, merciful, obliging, tender, sympathetic; cultivating, elevating, humanizing, refining, rational, spiritual.

humanity *n* benevolence, benignity, charity, fellow-feeling, humaneness, kind-heartedness, kindness, philanthropy, sympathy, tenderness; humankind, mankind, mortality.

humanize *vb* civilize, cultivate, educate, enlighten, improve, polish, reclaim, refine, soften.

humble *vb* abase, abash, break, crush, debase, degrade, disgrace, humiliate, lower, mortify, reduce, sink, subdue. • *adj* meek, modest, lowly, simple, submissive, unambitious, unassuming, unobtrusive, unostentatious, unpretending; low, obscure, mean, plain, poor, small, undistinguished, unpretentious.

humbug *vb* cheat, cozen, deceive, hoax, swindle, trick. • *n* cheat, dodge, gammon, hoax, imposition, imposture, deception, fraud, trick; cant, charlatanism, charlatanry, hypocrisy, mummery, quackery; charlatan, impostor, fake, quack.

humdrum *adj* boring, dronish, dreary, dry, dull, monotonous, prosy, stupid, tedious, tiresome, wearisome.

humid *adj* damp, dank, moist, wet.

humiliate *vb* abase, abash, debase, degrade, depress, humble, mortify, shame.

humiliation *n* abasement, affront, condescension, crushing, degradation, disgrace, dishonouring, humbling, indignity, mortification, self-abasement, submissiveness, resignation.

humility *n* diffidence, humbleness, lowliness, meekness, modesty, self-abasement, submissiveness.

humorist *n* comic, comedian, droll, jester, joker, wag, wit.

humorous *adj* comic, comical, droll, facetious, funny, humorous, jocose, jocular, laughable, ludicrous, merry, playful, pleasant, sportive, whimsical, witty.

humour *vb* favour, gratify, indulge. • *n* bent, bias, disposition, predilection, prosperity, temper, vein; mood, state; caprice, crotchet, fancy, freak, vagary, whim, whimsy, wrinkle; drollery, facetiousness, fun, jocoseness, jocularity, pleasantry, wit; fluid, moisture, vapour.

hunch *vb* arch, jostle, nudge, punch, push, shove. • *n* bunch, hump, knob, protuberance; nudge, punch, push, shove; feeling, idea, intuition, premonition.

hungry *adj* covetous, craving, desirous, greedy; famished, starved, starving; barren, poor, unfertile, unproductive.

hunk *n* chunk, hunch, lump, slice.

hunt *vb* chase, drive, follow, hound, pursue, stalk, trap, trail; poach, shoot; search, seek. • *n* chase, field-sport, hunting, pursuit.

hurl *vb* cast, dart, fling, pitch, project, send, sling, throw, toss.

hurly-burly *n* bustle, commotion, confusion, disturbance, hurl, hurly, uproar, tumult, turmoil.

hurricane *n* cyclone, gale, storm, tempest, tornado, typhoon.

hurried *adj* cursory, hasty, slight, superficial.

hurry *vb* drive, precipitate; dispatch, expedite, hasten, quicken, speed; haste, scurry. • *n* agitation, bustle, confusion, flurry, flutter, perturbation, precipitation; celerity, haste, dispatch, expedition, promptitude, promptness, quickness.

hurt *vb* damage, disable, disadvantage, harm, impair, injure, mar; bruise, pain, wound; afflict, grieve, offend; ache, smart, throb. • *n* damage, detriment, disadvantage, harm, injury, mischief; ache, bruise, pain, suffering, wound.

hurtful *adj* baleful, baneful, deleterious, destructive, detrimental, disadvantageous, harmful, injurious, mischievous, noxious, pernicious, prejudicial, unwholesome.

husband *vb* economize, hoard, save, store.

husbandry *n* agriculture, cultivation, farming, geoponics, tillage; economy, frugality, thrift.

hush *vb* quiet, repress, silence, still, suppress; appease, assuage, calm, console, quiet, still. • *n* quiet, quietness, silence, stillness.

hypocrite *n* deceiver, dissembler, impostor, pretender.

hypocritical *adj* deceiving, dissembling, false, insincere, spurious, two-faced.

hypothesis *n* assumption, proposition, supposition, theory.

hypothetical *adj* assumed, imaginary, supposed, theoretical.

hysterical *adj* frantic, frenzied, overwrought, uncontrollable; comical, uproarious.

I

ice *vb* chill, congeal, freeze. • *n* crystal; frosting, sugar.

icy *adj* glacial; chilling, cold, frosty; cold-hearted, distant, frigid, indifferent, unemotional.

idea *n* archetype, essence, exemplar, ideal, model, pattern, plan, model; fantasy, fiction, image, imagination; apprehension, conceit, conception, fancy, illusion, impression, thought; belief, judgement, notion, opinion, sentiment, supposition.

ideal *adj* intellectual, mental; chimerical, fancied, fanciful, fantastic, illusory, imaginary, unreal, visionary, shadowy; complete, consummate, excellent, perfect; impractical, unattainable, utopian. • *n* criterion, example, model, standard.

identical *adj* equivalent, same, selfsame, tantamount.

identity *n* existence, individuality, personality, sameness.

ideology *n* belief, creed, dogma, philosophy, principle.

idiocy *n* fatuity, feebleness, foolishness, imbecility, insanity.

idiosyncrasy *n* caprice, eccentricity, fad, peculiarity, singularity.

idiot *n* blockhead, booby, dunce, fool, ignoramus, imbecile, simpleton.

idiotic *adj* fatuous, foolish, imbecile, irrational, senseless, sottish, stupid.

idle *adj* inactive, unemployed, unoccupied, vacant; indolent, inert, lazy, slothful, sluggish; abortive, bootless, fruitless, futile, groundless, ineffectual, unavailing, useless, vain; foolish, frivolous, trashy, trifling, trivial, unimportant, unprofitable. • *vb* dally, dawdle, laze, loiter, potter, waste; drift, shirk, slack.

idler *n* dawdler, doodle, drone, laggard, lazybones, loafer, lounger, slacker, slowcoach, sluggard, trifler.

idol *n* deity, god, icon, image, pagan, simulacrum, symbol; delusion, falsity, pretender, sham; beloved, darling, favourite, pet.

idolater *n* heathen, pagan; admirer, adorer, worshipper.

idolize *vb* canonize, deify; adore, honour, love, reverence, venerate.

idyll *n* eclogue, pastoral.

if *conj* admitting, allowing, granting, provided, supposing, though, whether. • *n* condition, hesitation, uncertainty.

igneous *adj* combustible, combustive, conflagrative, fiery, molten.

ignite *vb* burn, inflame, kindle, light, torch.

ignoble *adj* base-born, low, low-born, mean, peasant, plebeian, rustic, vulgar; contemptible, degraded, insignificant, mean, worthless; disgraceful, dishonourable, infamous, low, unworthy.

ignominious *adj* discreditable, disgraceful, dishonourable, disreputable, infamous, opprobrious, scandalous, shameful; base, contemptible, despicable.

ignominy *n* abasement, contempt, discredit, disgrace, dishonour disrepute, infamy, obloquy, odium, opprobrium, scandal, shame.

ignoramus *n* blockhead, duffer, dunce, fool, greenhorn, novice, numskull, simpleton.

ignorance *n* benightedness, darkness, illiteracy, nescience, rusticity; blindness, unawareness.

ignorant *adj* blind, illiterate, nescient, unaware, unconversant, uneducated, unenlightened, uninformed, uninstructed, unlearned, unread, untaught, untutored, unwitting.

ignore *vb* disregard, neglect, overlook, reject, skip.

ill *adj* bad, evil, faulty, harmful, iniquitous, naughty, unfavourable, unfortunate, unjust, wicked; ailing, diseased, disordered, indisposed, sick, unwell, wrong; crabbed, cross, hateful, malicious, malevolent, peevish, surly, unkind, ill-bred; ill-favoured, ugly, unprepossessing. • *adv* badly, poorly, unfortunately. • *n* badness, depravity, evil, mischief, misfortune, wickedness; affliction, ailment, calamity, harm, misery, pain, trouble.

ill-advised *adj* foolish, ill-judged, imprudent, injudicious, unwise.

ill-bred *adj* discourteous, ill-behaved, ill-mannered, impolite, rude, uncivil, uncourteous, uncouth.

illegal *adj* contraband, forbidden, illegitimate, illicit, prohibited, unauthorized, unlawful, unlicensed.

illegible *adj* indecipherable, obscure, undecipherable, unreadable.

illegitimate *adj* bastard, misbegotten, natural.

ill-fated *adj* ill-starred, luckless, unfortunate, unlucky.

ill-favoured *adj* homely, ugly, offensive, plain, unpleasant.

ill humour *n* fretfulness, ill-temper, peevishness, petulance, testiness.

illiberal *adj* close, close-fisted, covetous, mean, miserly, narrow, niggardly, parsimonious, penurious, selfish, sordid, stingy, ungenerous; bigoted, narrow-minded, uncharitable, ungentlemanly, vulgar.

illicit *adj* illegal, illegitimate, unauthorized, unlawful, unlegalized, unlicensed; criminal, guilty, forbidden, improper, wrong.

illimitable *adj* boundless, endless, immeasurable, immense, infinite, unbounded, unlimited, vast.

illiterate *adj* ignorant, uneducated, uninstructed, unlearned, unlettered, untaught, untutored.

ill-judged *adj* foolish, ill-advised, imprudent, injudicious, unwise.

ill-mannered *adj* discourteous, ill-behaved, ill-bred, impolite, rude, uncivil, uncourteous, uncourtly, uncouth, unpolished.

ill-natured *adj* disobliging, hateful, malevolent, unamiable, unfriendly, unkind; acrimonious, bitter, churlish, crabbed, cross, cross-grained, crusty, ill-tempered, morose, perverse, petulant, sour, spiteful, sulky, sullen, wayward.

illness *n* ailing, ailment, complaint, disease, disorder, distemper, indisposition, malady, sickness.

illogical *adj* absurd, fallacious, inconsistent, inconclusive, inconsequent, incorrect, invalid, unreasonable, unsound.

ill-proportioned *adj* awkward, ill-made, ill-shaped, misshapen, misproportioned, shapeless.

ill-starred *adj* ill-fated, luckless, unfortunate, unhappy, unlucky.

ill temper *n* bad temper, crabbedness, crossness, grouchiness, ill nature, moroseness, sulkiness, sullenness.

ill-tempered *adj* acrimonious, bad-tempered, crabbed, cross, grouchy, ill-natured, morose, sour, sulky, surly.

ill-timed *adj* inapposite, inopportune, irrelevant, unseasonable, untimely.

ill-treat *vb* abuse, ill-use, injure, maltreat, mishandle, misuse.

illude *vb* cheat, deceive, delude, disappoint, mock, swindle, trick.

illuminate *vb* illume, illumine, light; adorn, brighten, decorate, depict, edify, enlighten, inform, inspire, instruct, make wise.

illusion *n* chimera, deception, delusion, error, fallacy, false appearance, fantasy, hallucination, mockery, phantasm.

illusive, illusory *adj* barmecide, deceitful, deceptive, delusive, fallacious, imaginary, make-believe, mock, sham, unsatisfying, unreal, unsubstantial, visionary, tantalizing.

illustrate *vb* clarify, demonstrate, elucidate, enlighten, exemplify, explain; adorn, depict, draw.

illustration *n* demonstration, elucidation, enlightenment, exemplification, explanation, interpretation; adornment, decoration, picture.

illustrative *adj* elucidative, elucidatory, exemplifying.

illustrious *adj* bright, brilliant, glorious, radiant, splendid; celebrated, conspicuous, distinguished, eminent, famed, famous, noble, noted, remarkable, renowned, signal.

ill will *n* animosity, dislike, enmity, envy, grudge, hate, hatred, hostility, ill nature, malevolence, malice, malignity, rancour, spleen, spite, uncharitableness, unkindness, venom.

image *n* idol, statue; copy, effigy, figure, form, imago, likeness, picture, resemblance, representation, shape, similitude, simulacrum, statue, symbol; conception, counterpart, embodiment, idea, reflection.

imagery *n* dream, phantasm, phantom, vision.

imaginable *adj* assumable, cogitable, conceivable, conjecturable, plausible, possible, supposable, thinkable.

imaginary *adj* chimerical, dreamy, fancied, fanciful, fantastic, fictitious, ideal, illusive, illusory, invented, quixotic, shadowy, unreal, utopian, visionary, wild; assumed, conceivable, hypothetical, supposed.

imagination *n* chimera, conception, fancy, fantasy, invention, unreality; position; contrivance, device, plot, scheme.

imaginative *adj* creative, dreamy, fanciful, inventive, poetical, plastic, visionary.

imagine *vb* conceive, dream, fancy, imagine, picture, pretend; contrive, create, devise, frame, invent, mould, project; assume, suppose, hypothesize; apprehend, assume, believe, deem, guess, opine, suppose, think.

imbecile *adj* cretinous, drivelling, fatuous, feeble, feeble-minded, foolish, helpless, idiotic, imbecilic, inane, infirm, witless. • *n* dotard, driveller.

imbecility *n* debility, feebleness, helplessness, infirmity, weakness; foolishness, idiocy, silliness, stupidity, weak-mindedness.

imbibe *vb* absorb, assimilate, drink, suck, swallow; acquire, gain, gather, get, receive.

imbroglio *n* complexity, complication, embarrassment, entanglement, misunderstanding.

imbrue *vb* drench, embrue, gain, moisten, soak, stain, steep, wet.

imbue *vb* colour, dye, stain, tincture, tinge, tint; bathe, impregnate, infuse, inoculate, permeate, pervade, provide, saturate, steep.

imitate *vb* copy, counterfeit, duplicate, echo, emulate, follow, forge, mirror, reproduce, simulate; ape, impersonate, mimic, mock, personate; burlesque, parody, travesty.

imitation *adj* artificial, fake, man-made, mock, reproduction, synthetic. • *n* aping, copying, imitation, mimicking, parroting; copy, duplicate, likeness, resemblance; mimicry, mocking; burlesque, parody, travesty.

imitative *adj* copying, emulative, imitating, mimetic, simulative; apeish, aping, mimicking.

imitator *n* copier, copycat, copyist, echo, impersonator, mimic, mimicker, parrot.

immaculate *adj* clean, pure, spotless, stainless, unblemished, uncontaminated, undefiled, unpolluted, unspotted, unsullied, untainted, untarnished; faultless, guiltless, holy, innocent, pure, saintly, sinless, stainless.

immanent *adj* congenital, inborn, indwelling, inherent, innate, internal, intrinsic, subjective.

immaterial *adj* bodiless, ethereal, extramundane, impalpable, incorporeal, mental, metaphysical, spiritual, unbodied, unfleshly, unsubstantial; inconsequential, insignificant, nonessential, unessential, unimportant.

immature *adj* crude, green, imperfect, raw, rudimental, rudimentary, unfinished, unformed, unprepared, unripe, unripened, youthful; hasty, premature, unseasonable, untimely.

immaturity *n* crudeness, crudity, greenness, imperfection, rawness, unpreparedness, unripeness.

immeasurable *adj* bottomless, boundless, illimitable, immense, infinite, limitless, measureless, unbounded, vast.

immediate *adj* close, contiguous, near, next, proximate; intuitive, primary, unmeditated; direct, instant, instantaneous, present, pressing, prompt.

immediately *adv* closely, proximately; directly, forthwith, instantly, presently, presto, pronto.

immemorial *adj* ancient, hoary, olden.

immense *adj* boundless, illimitable, infinite, interminable, measureless, unbounded, unlimited; colossal, elephantine, enormous, gigantic, huge, large, monstrous, mountainous, prodigious, stupendous, titanic, tremendous, vast.

immensity *n* boundlessness, endlessness, limitlessness, infiniteness, infinitude, infinity; amplitude, enormity, greatness, hugeness, magnitude, vastness.

immerse *vb* baptize, bathe, dip, douse, duck, overwhelm, plunge, sink, souse, submerge; absorb, engage, engross, involve.

immersion *n* dipping, immersing, plunging; absorption, engagement; disappearance; baptism.

imminent *adj* close, impending, near, overhanging, threatening; alarming, dangerous, perilous.

immobile *adj* fixed, immovable, inflexible, motionless, quiescent, stable, static, stationary, steadfast; dull, expressionless, impassive, rigid, stiff, stolid.

immobility *n* fixedness, fixity, immovability, immovableness, motionlessness, stability, steadfastness, unmovableness; dullness, expressionlessness, inflexibility, rigidity, stiffness, stolidity.

immoderate *adj* excessive, exorbitant, extravagant, extreme, inordinate, intemperate, unreasonable.

immodest *adj* coarse, gross, indecorous, indelicate, lewd, shameless; bold, brazen, forward, impudent, indecent; broad, filthy, impure, indecent, obscene, smutty, unchaste.

immodesty *n* coarseness, grossness, indecorum, indelicacy, shamelessness; impurity, lewdness, obscenity, smuttiness, unchastity; boldness, brass, forwardness, impatience.

immolate *vb* kill, sacrifice.

immoral *adj* antisocial, corrupt, loose, sinful, unethical, vicious, wicked, wrong; bad, depraved, dissolute, profligate, unprincipled; abandoned, indecent, licentious.

immorality *n* corruption, corruptness, criminality, demoralization, depravity, impurity, profligacy, sin, sinfulness, vice, wickedness; wrong.

immortal *adj* deathless, ever-living, imperishable, incorruptible, indestructible, indissoluble, never-dying, undying, unfading; ceaseless, continuing, eternal, endless, everlasting, never-ending, perpetual, sempiternal; abiding, enduring, lasting, permanent. • *n* god, goddess; genius, hero.

immortality *n* deathlessness, incorruptibility, incorruptibleness, indestructibility; perpetuity.

immortalize *vb* apotheosize, enshrine, glorify, perpetuate.

immovable *adj* firm, fixed, immobile, stable, stationary; impassive, steadfast, unalterable, unchangeable, unshaken, unyielding.

immunity *n* exemption, exoneration, freedom, release; charter, franchise, liberty, license, prerogative, privilege, right.

immure *vb* confine, entomb, imprison, incarcerate.

immutability *n* constancy, inflexibility, invariability, invariableness, permanence, stability, unalterableness, unchangeableness.

immutable *adj* constant, fixed, inflexible, invariable, permanent, stable, unalterable, unchangeable, undeviating.

imp *n* demon, devil, elf, flibbertigibbet, hobgoblin, scamp, sprite; graft, scion, shoot.

impact *vb* collide, crash, strike. • *n* brunt, impression, impulse, shock, stroke, touch; collision, contact, impinging, striking.

impair *vb* blemish, damage, deface, deteriorate, injure, mar, ruin, spoil, vitiate; decrease, diminish, lessen, reduce; enervate, enfeeble, weaken.

impale *vb* hole, pierce, puncture, spear, spike, stab, transfix.

impalpable *adj* attenuated, delicate, fine, intangible; imperceptible, inapprehensible, incorporeal, indistinct, shadowy, unsubstantial.

impart *vb* bestow, confer, give, grant; communicate, disclose, discover, divulge, relate, reveal, share, tell.

impartial *adj* candid, disinterested, dispassionate, equal, equitable, even-handed, fair, honourable, just, unbiased, unprejudiced, unwarped.

impassable *adj* blocked, closed, impenetrable, impermeable, impervious, inaccessible, pathless, unattainable, unnavigable, unreachable.

impassioned *adj* animated, ardent, burning, excited, fervent, fervid, fiery, glowing, impetuous, intense, passionate, vehement, warm, zealous.

impassive *adj* calm, passionless; apathetic, callous, indifferent, insensible, insusceptible, unfeeling, unimpressible, unsusceptible.

impassivity *n* calmness, composure, indifference, insensibility, insusceptibility, passionlessness, stolidity.

impatience *n* disquietude, restlessness, uneasiness; eagerness, haste, impetuosity, precipitation, vehemence; heat, irritableness, irritability, violence.

impatient *adj* restless, uneasy, unquiet; eager, hasty, impetuous, precipitate, vehement; abrupt, brusque, choleric, fretful, hot, intolerant, irritable, peevish, sudden, testy, violent.

impeach *vb* accuse, arraign, charge, indict; asperse, censure, denounce, disparage, discredit, impair, impute, incriminate, lessen.

impeachment *n* accusation, arraignment, indictment; aspersion, censure, disparagement, imputation, incrimination, reproach.

impeccable *adj* faultless, immaculate, incorrupt, innocent, perfect, pure, sinless, stainless, uncorrupt.

impede *vb* bar, block, check, clog, curb, delay, encumber, hinder, interrupt, obstruct, restrain, retard, stop, thwart.

impediment *n* bar, barrier, block, check, curb, difficulty, encumbrance, hindrance, obstacle, obstruction, stumbling block.

impel *vb* drive, push, send, urge; actuate, animate, compel, constrain, embolden, incite, induce, influence, instigate, move, persuade, stimulate.

impend *vb* approach, menace, near, threaten.

impending *adj* approaching, imminent, menacing, near, threatening.

impenetrable *adj* impermeable, impervious, inaccessible; cold, dull, impassive, indifferent, obtuse, senseless, stolid, unsympathetic; dense, proof.

impenitence *n* hardheartedness, impenitency, impenitentness, obduracy, stubbornness.

impenitent *adj* hardened, hard-hearted, incorrigible, irreclaimable, obdurate, recusant, relentless, seared, stubborn, uncontrite, unconverted, unrepentant.

imperative *adj* authoritative, commanding, despotic, domineering, imperious, overbearing, peremptory, urgent; binding, obligatory.

imperceptible *adj* inaudible, indiscernible, indistinguishable, invisible; fine, impalpable, inappreciable, gradual, minute.

imperfect *adj* abortive, crude, deficient, garbled, incomplete, poor; defective, faulty, impaired.

imperfection *n* defectiveness, deficiency, faultiness, incompleteness; blemish, defect, fault, flaw, lack, stain, taint; failing, foible, frailty, limitation, vice, weakness.

imperial *adj* kingly, regal, royal, sovereign; august, consummate, exalted, grand, great, kingly, magnificent, majestic, noble, regal, royal, queenly, supreme, sovereign, supreme, consummate.

imperil *vb* endanger, expose, hazard, jeopardize, risk.

imperious *adj* arrogant, authoritative, commanding, compelling, despotic, dictatorial, domineering, haughty, imperative, lordly, magisterial, overbearing, tyrannical, urgent, compelling.

imperishable *adj* eternal, everlasting, immortal, incorruptible, indestructible, never-ending, perennial, unfading.

impermeable *adj* impenetrable, impervious.

impermissible *adj* deniable, insufferable, objectionable, unallowable, unallowed, unlawful.

impersonate *vb* act, ape, enact, imitate, mimic, mock, personate; embody, incarnate, personify, typify.

impersonation *n* incarnation, manifestation, personification; enacting, imitation, impersonating, mimicking, personating, representation.

impertinence *n* irrelevance, irrelevancy, unfitness, impropriety; assurance, boldness, brass, brazenness, effrontery, face, forwardness, impudence, incivility, insolence, intrusiveness, presumption, rudeness, sauciness, pertness.

impertinent *adj* inapplicable, inapposite, irrelevant; bold, forward, impudent, insolent, intrusive, malapert, meddling, officious, pert, rude, saucy, unmannerly.

imperturbability *n* calmness, collectedness, composure, dispassion, placidity, placidness, sedateness, serenity, steadiness, tranquility.

imperturbable *adj* calm, collected, composed, cool, placid, sedate, serene, tranquil, unmoved, undisturbed, unexcitable, unmoved, unruffled.

impervious *adj* impassable, impenetrable, impermeable.

impetuosity *n* force, fury, haste, precipitancy, vehemence, violence.

impetuous *adj* ardent, boisterous, brash, breakneck, fierce, fiery, furious, hasty, headlong, hot, hot-headed, impulsive, overzealous, passionate, precipitate, vehement, violent.

impetus *n* energy, force, momentum, propulsion.

impiety *n* irreverence, profanity, ungodliness; iniquity, sacreligiousness, sin, sinfulness, ungodliness, unholiness, unrighteousness, wickedness.

impinge *vb* clash, dash, encroach, hit, infringe, strike, touch.

impious *adj* blasphemous, godless, iniquitous, irreligious, irreverent, profane, sinful, ungodly, unholy, unrighteous, wicked.

implacable *adj* deadly, inexorable, merciless, pitiless, rancorous, relentless, unappeasable, unforgiving, unpropitiating, unrelenting.

implant *vb* ingraft, infix, insert, introduce, place.

implement *vb* effect, execute, fulfil. • *n* appliance, instrument, tool, utensil.

implicate *vb* entangle, enfold; compromise, concern, entangle, include, involve.

implication *n* entanglement, involvement, involution; connotation, hint, inference, innuendo, intimation; conclusion, meaning, significance.

implicit *adj* implied, inferred, understood; absolute, constant, firm, steadfast, unhesitating, unquestioning, unreserved, unshaken.

implicitly *adv* by implication, silently, tacitly, unspokenly, virtually, wordlessly.

implore *vb* adjure, ask, beg, beseech, entreat, petition, pray, solicit, supplicate.

imply *vb* betoken, connote, denote, import, include, infer, insinuate, involve, mean, presuppose, signify.

impolicy *n* folly, imprudence, ill-judgement, indiscretion, inexpediency.

impolite *adj* bearish, boorish, discourteous, disrespectful, ill-bred, insolent, rough, rude, uncivil, uncourteous, ungentle, ungentlemanly, ungracious, unmannerly, unpolished, unrefined.

impoliteness *n* boorishness, discourteousness, discourtesy, disrespect, ill-breeding, incivility, insolence, rudeness, unmannerliness.

impolitic *adj* ill-advised, imprudent, indiscreet, inexpedient, injudicious, unwise.

import *vb* bring in, introduce, transport; betoken, denote, imply, mean, purport, signify. • *n* goods, importation, merchandise; bearing, drift, gist, intention, interpretation, matter, meaning, purpose, sense, signification, spirit, tenor; consequence, importance, significance, weight.

importance *n* concern, consequence, gravity, import, moment, momentousness, significance, weight, weightiness; consequence, pomposity, self-importance.

important *adj* considerable, grave, material, momentous, notable, pompous, ponderous, serious, significant, urgent, valuable, weighty; esteemed, influential, prominent, substantial; consequential, pompous, self-important.

importunate *adj* busy, earnest, persistent, pertinacious, pressing, teasing, troublesome, urgent.

importune *vb* ask, beset, dun, ply, press, solicit, urge.

importunity *n* appeal, beseechment, entreaty, petition, plying, prayer, pressing, suit, supplication, urging; contention, insistence; urgency.

impose *vb* lay, place, put, set; appoint, charge, dictate, enjoin, force, inflict, obtrude, prescribe, tax; (*with* **on, upon**) abuse, cheat, circumvent, deceive, delude, dupe, exploit, hoax, trick, victimize.

imposing *adj* august, commanding, dignified, exalted, grand, grandiose, impressive, lofty, magnificent, majestic, noble, stately, striking.

imposition *n* imposing, laying, placing, putting; burden, charge, constraint, injunction, levy, oppression, tax; artifice, cheating, deception, dupery, fraud, imposture, trickery.

impossibility *n* hopelessness, impracticability, inability, infeasibility, unattainability; inconceivability.

impossible *adj* hopeless, impracticable, infeasible, unachievable, unattainable; inconceivable, self-contradictory, unthinkable.

impost *n* custom, duty, excise, rate, tax, toil, tribute.

impostor *n* charlatan, cheat, counterfeiter, deceiver, double-dealer, humbug, hypocrite, knave, mountebank, pretender, quack, rogue, trickster.

imposture *n* artifice, cheat, deceit, deception, delusion, dodge, fraud, hoax, imposition, ruse, stratagem, trick, wile.

impotence *n* disability, feebleness, frailty, helplessness, inability, incapability, incapacity, incompetence, inefficaciousness, inefficacy, inefficiency, infirmity, powerlessness, weakness.

impotent *adj* disabled, enfeebled, feeble, frail, helpless, incapable, incapacitated, incompetent, inefficient, infirm, nerveless, powerless, unable, weak; barren, sterile.

impound *vb* confine, coop, engage, imprison.

impoverish *vb* beggar, pauperize; deplete, exhaust, ruin.

impracticability *n* impossibility, impracticableness, impracticality, infeasibility, unpracticability.

impracticable *adj* impossible, infeasible; intractable, obstinate, recalcitrant, stubborn, thorny, unmanageable; impassable, insurmountable.

impracticality *n* impossibility, impracticableness, impractibility, infeasibility, unpracticability; irrationality, unpracticalness, unrealism, unreality, unreasonableness.

imprecate *vb* anathematize, curse, execrate, invoke, maledict.

imprecation *n* anathema, curse, denunciation, execration, invocation, malediction.

imprecatory *adj* appealing, beseeching, entreating, imploratory, imploring, imprecatory, pleading; cursing, damnatory, execrating, maledictory.

impregnable *adj* immovable, impenetrable, indestructible, invincible, inviolable, invulnerable, irrefrangible, secure, unconquerable, unassailable, unyielding.

impregnate *vb* fecundate, fertilize, fructify; dye, fill, imbrue, imbue, infuse, permeate, pervade, saturate, soak, tincture, tinge.

impress *vb* engrave, imprint, print, stamp; affect, move, strike; fix, inculcate; draft, enlist, levy, press, requisition. • *n* impression, imprint, mark, print, seal, stamp; cognizance, device, emblem, motto, symbol.

impressibility *n* affectibility, impressionability, pliancy, receptiveness, responsiveness, sensibility, sensitiveness, susceptibility.

impressible *adj* affectible, excitable, impressionable, pliant, receptive, responsive, sensitive, soft, susceptible, tender.

impression *n* edition, imprinting, printing, stamping; brand, dent, impress, mark, stamp; effect, influence, sensation; fancy, idea, instinct, notion, opinion, recollection.

impressive *adj* affecting, effective, emphatic, exciting, forcible, moving, overpowering, powerful, solemn, speaking, splendid, stirring, striking, telling, touching.

imprint *vb* engrave, mark, print, stamp; impress, inculcate. • *n* impression, mark, print, sign, stamp.

imprison *vb* confine, jail, immure, incarcerate, shut up.

imprisonment *n* captivity, commitment, confinement, constraint, durance, duress, incarceration, restraint.

improbability *n* doubt, uncertainty, unlikelihood.

improbable *adj* doubtful, uncertain, unlikely, unplausible.

improbity *n* dishonesty, faithlessness, fraud, fraudulence, knavery, unfairness.

impromptu *adj* extempore, improvised, offhand, spontaneous, unpremeditated, unprepared, unrehearsed. • *adv* extemporaneously, extemporarily, extempore, offhand, ad-lib.

improper *adj* immodest, inapposite, inappropriate, irregular, unadapted, unapt, unfit, unsuitable, unsuited; indecent, indecorous, indelicate, unbecoming, unseemly; erroneous, inaccurate, incorrect, wrong.

impropriety *n* inappropriateness, unfitness, unsuitability, unsuitableness; indecorousness, indecorum, unseemliness.

improve *vb* ameliorate, amend, better, correct, edify, meliorate, mend, rectify, reform; cultivate; gain, mend, progress; enhance, increase, rise.

improvement *n* ameliorating, amelioration, amendment, bettering, improving, meliorating, melioration; advancement, proficiency, progress.

improvidence *n* imprudence, thriftlessness, unthriftiness.

improvident *adj* careless, heedless, imprudent, incautious, inconsiderate, negligent, prodigal, rash, reckless, shiftless, thoughtless, thriftless, unthrifty, wasteful.

improvisation *n* ad-libbing, contrivance, extemporaneousness, extemporariness, extemporization, fabrication, invention; (*mus*) extempore, impromptu.

improvise *vb* ad-lib, contrive, extemporize, fabricate, imagine, invent.

imprudence *n* carelessness, heedlessness, improvidence, incautiousness, inconsideration, indiscretion, rashness.

imprudent *adj* careless, heedless, ill-advised, ill-judged, improvident, incautious, inconsiderate, indiscreet, rash, unadvised, unwise.

impudence *n* assurance, audacity, boldness, brashness, brass, bumptiousness, cheek, cheekiness, effrontery, face, flippancy, forwardness, front, gall, impertinence, insolence, jaw, lip, nerve, pertness, presumption, rudeness, sauciness, shamelessness.

impudent *adj* bold, bold-faced, brazen, brazen-faced, cool, flippant, forward, immodest, impertinent, insolent, insulting, pert, presumptuous, rude, saucy, shameless.

impugn *vb* assail, attack, challenge, contradict, dispute, gainsay, oppose, question, resist.

impulse *n* force, impetus, impelling, momentum, push, thrust; appetite, inclination, instinct, passion, proclivity; incentive, incitement, influence, instigation, motive, instigation.

impulsive *adj* impelling, moving, propulsive; emotional, hasty, heedless, hot, impetuous, mad-cap, passionate, quick, rash, vehement, violent.

impunity *n* exemption, immunity, liberty, licence, permission, security.

impure *adj* defiled, dirty, feculent, filthy, foul, polluted, unclean; bawdy, coarse, immodest, gross, immoral, indelicate, indecent, lewd, licentious, loose, obscene, ribald, smutty, unchaste; adulterated, corrupt, mixed.

impurity *n* defilement, feculence, filth, foulness, pollution, uncleanness; admixture, coarseness, grossness, immodesty, indecency, indelicacy, lewdness, licentiousness, looseness, obscenity, ribaldry, smut, smuttiness, unchastity, vulgarity.

imputable *adj* ascribable, attributable, chargeable, owing, referable, traceable, owing.

imputation *n* attributing, charging, imputing; accusation, blame, censure, charge, reproach.

impute *vb* ascribe, attribute, charge, consider, imply, insinuate, refer.

inability *n* impotence, incapacity, incapability, incompetence, incompetency, inefficiency; disability, disqualification.

inaccessible *adj* unapproachable, unattainable.

inaccuracy *n* erroneousness, impropriety, incorrectness, inexactness; blunder, defect, error, fault, mistake.

inaccurate *adj* defective, erroneous, faulty, incorrect, inexact, mistaken, wrong.

inaccurately *adv* carelessly, cursorily, imprecisely, incorrectly, inexactly, mistakenly, unprecisely, wrongly.

inactive *adj* inactive; dormant, inert, inoperative, peaceful, quiet, quiescent; dilatory, drowsy, dull, idle, inanimate, indolent, inert, lazy, lifeless, lumpish, passive, slothful, sleepy, stagnant, supine.

inactivity *n* dilatoriness, idleness, inaction, indolence, inertness, laziness, sloth, sluggishness, supineness, torpidity, torpor.

inadequacy *n* inadequateness, insufficiency; defectiveness, imperfection, incompetence, incompetency, incompleteness, insufficiency, unfitness, unsuitableness.

inadequate *adj* disproportionate, incapable, insufficient, unequal; defective, imperfect, inapt, incompetent, incomplete.

inadmissible *adj* improper, incompetent, unacceptable, unallowable, unqualified, unreasonable.

inadvertence, inadvertency *n* carelessness, heedlessness, inattention, inconsiderateness, negligence, thoughtlessness; blunder, error, oversight, slip.

inadvertent *adj* careless, heedless, inattentive, inconsiderate, negligent, thoughtless, unobservant.

inadvertently *adv* accidently, carelessly, heedlessly, inconsiderately, negligently, thoughtlessly, unintentionally.

inalienable *adj* undeprivable, unforfeitable, untransferable.

inane *adj* empty, fatuous, vacuous, void; foolish, frivolous, idiotic, puerile, senseless, silly, stupid, trifling, vain, worthless.

inanimate *adj* breathless, dead, extinct; dead, dull, inert, lifeless, soulless, spiritless.

inanition *n* emptiness, inanity, vacuity; exhaustion, hunger, malnutrition, starvation, want.

inanity *n* emptiness, foolishness, inanition, vacuity; folly, frivolousness, puerility, vanity, worthlessness.

inapplicable *adj* inapposite, inappropriate, inapt, irrelevant, unfit, unsuitable, unsuited.

inapposite *adj* impertinent, inapplicable, irrelevant, nonpertinent; inappropriate, unfit, unsuitable.

inappreciable *adj* impalpable, imperceptible, inconsiderable, inconspicuous, indiscernible, infinitesimal, insignificant, negligible, undiscernible, unnoticed.

inappropriate *adj* inapposite, unadapted, unbecoming, unfit, unsuitable, unsullied.

inapt *adj* inapposite, unapt, unfit, unsuitable; awkward, clumsy, dull, slow, stolid, stupid.

inaptitude *n* awkwardness, inapplicability, inappropriateness, inaptness, unfitness, unsuitableness.

inarticulate *adj* blurred, indistinct, thick; dumb, mute.

inartificial *adj* artless, direct, guileless, ingenuous, naive, simple, simple-minded, sincere, single-minded.

inasmuch as *conj* considering that, seeing that, since.

inattention *n* absent-mindedness, carelessness, disregard, heedlessness, inadvertence, inapplication, inconsiderateness, neglect, remissness, slip, thoughtlessness, unmindfulness, unobservance.

inattentive *adj* absent-minded, careless, disregarding, heedless, inadvertent, inconsiderate, neglectful, remiss, thoughtless, unmindful, unobservant.

inaudible *adj* faint, indistinct, muffled; mute, noiseless, silent, still.

inaugurate *vb* induct, install, introduce, invest; begin, commence, initiate, institute, originate.

inauguration *n* beginning, commencement, initiation, institution, investiture, installation, opening, origination.

inauspicious *adj* bad, discouraging, ill-omened, ill-starred, ominous, unfavourable, unfortunate, unlucky, unpromising, unpropitious, untoward.

inborn *adj* congenital, inbred, ingrained, inherent, innate, instinctive, native, natural.

incalculable *adj* countless, enormous, immense, incalculable, inestimable, innumerable, sumless, unknown, untold.

incandescence *n* candescence, glow, gleam, luminousness, luminosity.

incandescent *adj* aglow, candent, candescent, gleaming, glowing, luminous, luminant, radiant.

incantation *n* charm, conjuration, enchantment, magic, necromancy, sorcery, spell, witchcraft, witchery.

incapability *n* disability, inability, incapacity, incompetence.

incapable *adj* feeble, impotent, incompetent, insufficient, unable, unfit, unfitted, unqualified, weak.

incapacious *adj* cramped, deficient, incommodious, narrow, scant.

incapacitate *vb* cripple, disable; disqualify, make unfit.

incapacity *n* disability, inability, incapability, incompetence; disqualification, unfitness.

incarcerate *vb* commit, confine, immure, imprison, jail, restrain, restrict.

incarnate *vb* body, embody, incorporate, personify. • *adj* bodied, embodied, incorporated, personified.

incarnation *n* embodiment, exemplification, impersonation, manifestation, personification.

incautious *adj* impolitic, imprudent, indiscreet, uncircumspect, unwary; careless, headlong, heedless, inconsiderate, negligent, rash, reckless, thoughtless.

incendiary *adj* dissentious, factious, inflammatory, seditious. • *n* agitator, firebrand, fire-raiser.

incense[1] *vb* anger, chafe, enkindle, enrage, exasperate, excite, heat, inflame, irritate, madden, provoke.

incense[2] *n* aroma, fragrance, perfume, scent; admiration, adulation, applause, laudation.

incentive *n* cause, encouragement, goad, impulse, incitement, inducement, instigation, mainspring, motive, provocation, spur, stimulus.

inception *n* beginning, commencement, inauguration, initiation, origin, rise, start.

incertitude *n* ambiguity, doubt, doubtfulness, indecision, uncertainty.

incessant *adj* ceaseless, constant, continual, continuous, eternal, everlasting, never-ending, perpetual, unceasing, unending, uninterrupted, unremitting.

inchoate *adj* beginning, commencing, inceptive, incipient, initial.

incident *n* circumstance, episode, event, fact, happening, occurrence. • *adj* happening; belonging, pertaining, appertaining, accessory, relating, natural; falling, impinging.

incidental *adj* accidental, casual, chance, concomitant, contingent, fortuitous, subordinate; adventitious, extraneous, nonessential, occasional.

incinerate *vb* burn, char, conflagrate, cremate, incremate.

incipient *adj* beginning, commencing, inchoate, inceptive, originating, starting.

incised *adj* carved, cut, engraved, gashed, graved, graven.

incision *n* cut, gash, notch, opening, penetration.

incisive *adj* cutting; acute, biting, sarcastic, satirical, sharp; acute, clear, distinct, penetrating, sharp-cut, trenchant.

incite *vb* actuate, animate, arouse, drive, encourage, excite, foment, goad, hound, impel, instigate, prod, prompt, provoke, push, rouse, spur, stimulate, urge.

incitement *n* encouragement, goad, impulse, incentive, inducement, motive, provocative, spur, stimulus.

incivility *n* discourteousness, discourtesy, disrespect, ill-breeding, ill-manners, impoliteness, impudence, inurbanity, rudeness, uncourtliness, unmannerliness.

inclemency *n* boisterousness, cruelty, harshness, rigour, roughness, severity, storminess, tempestuousness, tyranny.

inclement *adj* boisterous, harsh, rigorous, rough, severe, stormy; cruel, unmerciful.

inclination *n* inclining, leaning, slant, slope; trending, verging; aptitude, bent, bias, disposition, penchant, predilection, predisposition, proclivity, proneness, propensity, tendency, turn, twist; desire, fondness, liking, taste, partiality, predilection, wish; bow, nod, obeisance.

incline *vb* lean, slant, slope; bend, nod, verge; tend; bias, dispose, predispose, turn; bow. • *n* ascent, descent, grade, gradient, rise, slope.

inclose *see* **enclose**.

include *vb* contain, hold; comprehend, comprise, contain, cover, embody, embrace, incorporate, involve, take in.

inclusive *adj* comprehending, embracing, encircling, enclosing, including, taking in.

incognito, incognita *adj* camouflaged, concealed, disguised, unknown. • *n* camouflage, concealment, disguise.

incoherent *adj* detached, loose, nonadhesive, noncohesive; disconnected, incongruous, inconsequential, inconsistent, uncoordinated; confused, illogical, irrational, rambling, unintelligible, wild.

income *n* earnings, emolument, gains, interest, pay, perquisite, proceeds, profits, receipts, rents, return, revenue, salary, wages.

incommensurate *adj* disproportionate, inadequate, insufficient, unequal.

incommode *vb* annoy, discommode, disquiet, disturb, embarrass, hinder, inconvenience, molest, plague, trouble, upset, vex.

incommodious *adj* awkward, cumbersome, cumbrous, inconvenient, unhandy, unmanageable, unsuitable, unwieldy; annoying, disadvantageous, harassing, irritating, vexatious.

incommunicative *adj* exclusive, unsociable, unsocial, reserved.

incomparable *adj* matchless, inimitable, peerless, surpassing, transcendent, unequalled, unparalleled, unrivalled.

incompatibility *n* contrariety, contradictoriness, discrepancy, incongruity, inconsistency, irreconcilability, unsuitability, unsuitableness

incompatible *adj* contradictory, incongruous, inconsistent, inharmonious, irreconcilable, unadapted, unsuitable.

incompetence *n* inability, incapability, incapacity, incompetency; inadequacy, insufficiency; disqualification, unfitness.

incompetent *adj* incapable, unable; inadequate, insufficient; disqualified, incapacitated, unconstitutional, unfit, unfitted.

incomplete *adj* defective, deficient, imperfect, partial; inexhaustive, unaccompanied, uncompleted, unexecuted, unfinished.

incomprehensible *adj* inconceivable, inexhaustible, unfathomable, unimaginable; inconceivable, unintelligible, unthinkable.

incomputable *adj* enormous, immense, incalculable, innumerable, prodigious.

inconceivable *adj* incomprehensible, incredible, unbelievable, unimaginable, unthinkable.

inconclusive *adj* inconsequent, inconsequential, indecisive, unconvincing, illogical, unproved, unproven.

incongruity *n* absurdity, contradiction, contradictoriness, contrariety, discordance, discordancy, discrepancy, impropriety, inappropriateness, incoherence, incompatibility, inconsistency, unfitness, unsuitableness.

incongruous *adj* absurd, contradictory, contrary, disagreeing, discrepant, inappropriate, incoherent, incompatible, inconsistent, inharmonious, unfit, unsuitable.

inconsequent *adj* desultory, disconnected, fragmentary, illogical, inconclusive, inconsistent, irrelevant, loose.

inconsiderable *adj* immaterial, insignificant, petty, slight, small, trifling, trivial, unimportant.

inconsiderate *adj* intolerant, uncharitable, unthoughtful; careless, heedless, giddy, hare-brained, hasty, headlong, imprudent, inadvertent, inattentive, indifferent, indiscreet, light-headed, negligent, rash, thoughtless.

inconsistency *n* incoherence, incompatibility, incongruity, unsuitableness; contradiction, contrariety; changeableness, inconstancy, instability, vacillation, unsteadiness.

inconsistent *adj* different, discrepant, illogical, incoherent, incompatible, incongruous, inconsequent, inconsonant, irreconcilable, unsuitable; contradictory, contrary; changeable, fickle, inconstant, unstable, unsteady, vacillating, variable.

inconsolable *adj* comfortless, crushed, disconsolate, forlorn, heartbroken, hopeless, woebegone.

inconstancy *n* changeableness, mutability, variability, variation, fluctuation, faithlessness, fickleness, capriciousness, vacillation, uncertainty, unsteadiness, volatility.

inconstant *adj* capricious, changeable, faithless, fickle, fluctuating, mercurial, mutable, unsettled, unsteady, vacillating, variable, varying, volatile, wavering; mutable, uncertain, unstable.

incontestable *adj* certain, incontrovertible, indisputable, indubitable, irrefrangible, sure, undeniable, unquestionable.

incontinence *n* excess, extravagance, indulgence, intemperance, irrepressibility, lasciviousness, lewdness, licentiousness, prodigality, profligacy, riotousness, unrestraint, wantonness, wildness.

incontinent *adj* debauched, lascivious, lewd, licentious, lustful, prodigal, unchaste, uncontrolled, unrestrained.

incontrovertible *adj* certain, incontestable, indisputable, indubitable, irrefutable, sure, undeniable, unquestionable.

inconvenience *vb* discommode; annoy, disturb, molest, trouble, vex. • *n* annoyance, disadvantage, disturbance, molestation, trouble, vexation; awkwardness, cumbersomeness, incommodiousness, unwieldiness; unfitness, unseasonableness, unsuitableness.

inconvenient *adj* annoying, awkward, cumbersome, cumbrous, disadvantageous, incommodious, inopportune, troublesome, uncomfortable, unfit, unhandy, unmanageable, unseasonable, unsuitable, untimely, unwieldy, vexatious.

incorporate *vb* affiliate, amalgamate, associate, blend, combine, consolidate, include, merge, mix, unite; embody, incarnate. • *adj* incorporeal, immaterial, spiritual, supernatural; blended, consolidated, merged, united.

incorporation *n* affiliation, alignment, amalgamation, association, blend, blending, combination, consolidation, fusion, inclusion, merger, mixture, unification, union, embodiment, incarnation, personification.

incorporeal *adj* bodiless, immaterial, impalpable, incorporate, spiritual, supernatural, unsubstantial.

incorrect *adj* erroneous, false, inaccurate, inexact, untrue, wrong; faulty, improper, mistaken, ungrammatical, unbecoming, unsound.

incorrectness *n* error, inaccuracy, inexactness, mistake.

incorrigible *adj* abandoned, graceless, hardened, irreclaimable, lost, obdurate, recreant, reprobate, shameless; helpless, hopeless, irremediable, irrecoverable, irreparable, irretrievable, irreversible, remediless.

incorruptibility *n* unpurchasableness; deathlessness, immortality, imperishableness, incorruptibleness, incorruption, indestructibility.

incorruptible *adj* honest, unbribable; imperishable, indestructible, immortal, undying, deathless, everlasting.

increase *vb* accrue, advance, augment, enlarge, extend, grow, intensify, mount, wax; multiply; enhance, greaten, heighten, raise, reinforce; aggravate, prolong. • *n* accession, accretion, accumulation, addition, augmentation, crescendo, development, enlargement, expansion, extension, growth, heightening, increment, intensification, multiplication, swelling; gain, produce, product, profit; descendants, issue, offspring, progeny.

incredible *adj* absurd, inadmissible, nonsensical, unbelievable.

incredulity *n* distrust, doubt, incredulousness, scepticism, unbelief.

incredulous *adj* distrustful, doubtful, dubious, sceptical, unbelieving.

increment *n* addition, augmentation, enlargement, increase.

incriminate *vb* accuse, blame, charge, criminate, impeach.

incubate *vb* brood, develop, hatch, sit.

inculcate *vb* enforce, implant, impress, infix, infuse, ingraft, inspire, instil.

inculpable *adj* blameless, faultless, innocent, irreprehensible, irreproachable, irreprovable, sinless, unblamable, unblameable.

inculpate *vb* accuse, blame, censure, charge, incriminate, impeach, incriminate.

inculpatory *adj* criminatory, incriminating.

incumbent *adj* binding, devolved, devolving, laid, obligatory; leaning, prone, reclining, resting. • *n* holder, occupant.

incur *vb* acquire, bring, contract.

incurable *adj* cureless, hopeless, irrecoverable, remediless; helpless, incorrigible, irremediable, irreparable, irretrievable, remediless.

incurious *adj* careless, heedless, inattentive, indifferent, uninquisitive, unobservant, uninterested.

incursion *n* descent, foray, raid, inroad, irruption.

incursive *adj* aggressive, hostile, invasive, predatory, raiding.

incurvate *vb* bend, bow, crook, curve. • *adj* (*bot*) aduncous, arcuate, bowed, crooked, curved, hooked.

indebted *adj* beholden, obliged, owing.

indecency *n* impropriety, indecorum, offensiveness, outrageousness, unseemliness; coarseness, filthiness, foulness, grossness, immodesty, impurity, obscenity, vileness.

indecent *adj* bold, improper, indecorous, offensive, outrageous, unbecoming, unseemly; coarse, dirty, filthy, gross, immodest, impure, indelicate, lewd, nasty, obscene, pornographic, salacious, shameless, smutty, unchaste.

indecipherable *adj* illegible, undecipherable, undiscoverable, inexplicable, obscure, unintelligible, unreadable.

indecision *n* changeableness, fickleness, hesitation, inconstancy, irresolution, unsteadiness, vacillation.

indecisive *adj* dubious, hesitating, inconclusive, irresolute, undecided, unsettled, vacillating, wavering.

indecorous *adj* coarse, gross, ill-bred, impolite, improper, indecent, rude, unbecoming, uncivil, unseemly.

indecorum *n* grossness, ill-breeding, ill manners, impoliteness, impropriety, incivility, indecency, indecorousness.

indeed *adv* absolutely, actually, certainly, in fact, in truth, in reality, positively, really, strictly, truly, verily, veritably. • *interj* really! you don't say so! is it possible!

indefatigable *adj* assiduous, never-tiring, persevering, persistent, sedulous, tireless, unflagging, unremitting, untiring, unwearied.

indefeasible *adj* immutable, inalienable, irreversible, irrevocable, unalterable.

indefensible *adj* censurable, defenceless, faulty, unpardonable, untenable; inexcusable, insupportable, unjustifiable, unwarrantable, wrong.

indefinite *adj* confused, doubtful, equivocal, general, imprecise, indefinable, indecisive, indeterminate, indistinct, inexact, inexplicit, lax, loose, nondescript, obscure, uncertain, undefined, undetermined, unfixed, unsettled, vague.

indelible *adj* fast, fixed, ineffaceable, ingrained, permanent.

indelicacy *n* coarseness, grossness, indecorousness, indecorum, impropriety, offensiveness, unseemliness, vulgarity; immodesty, indecency, lewdness, unchastity; foulness, obscenity.

indelicate *adj* broad, coarse, gross, indecorous, intrusive, rude, unbecoming, unseemly; foul, immodest, indecent, lewd, obscene, unchaste, vulgar.

indemnification *n* compensation, reimbursement, remuneration, security.

indemnify *vb* compensate, reimburse, remunerate, requite, secure.

indent *vb* bruise, jag, notch, pink, scallop, serrate; bind, indenture.

indentation *n* bruise, dent, depression, jag, notch.

indenture *vb* bind, indent. • *n* contract, instrument; indentation.

independence *n* freedom, liberty, self-direction; distinctness, nondependence, separation; competence, ease.

independent *adj* absolute, autonomous, free, self-directing, uncoerced, unrestrained, unrestricted, voluntary; (*person*) self-reliant, unconstrained, unconventional.

indescribable *adj* ineffable, inexpressible, nameless, unutterable.

indestructible *adj* abiding, endless, enduring, everlasting, fadeless, imperishable, incorruptible, undecaying.

indeterminate *adj* indefinite, uncertain, undetermined, unfixed.

index *vb* alphabetize, catalogue, codify, earmark, file, list, mark, tabulate. • *n* catalogue, list, register, tally; indicator, lead, mark, pointer, sign, signal, token; contents, table of contents; forefinger; exponent.

indicate *vb* betoken, denote, designate, evince, exhibit, foreshadow, manifest, mark, point out, prefigure, presage, register, show, signify, specify, tell; hint, imply, intimate, sketch, suggest.

indication *n* hint, index, manifestation, mark, note, sign, suggestion, symptom, token.

indicative *adj* significant, suggestive, symptomatic; (*gram*) affirmative, declarative.

indict *vb* (*law*) accuse, charge, present.

indictment *n* (*law*) indicting, presentment; accusation, arraignment, charge, crimination, impeachment.

indifference *n* apathy, carelessness, coldness, coolness, heedlessness, inattention, insignificance, negligence, unconcern, unconcernedness, uninterestedness; disinterestedness, impartiality, neutrality.

indifferent *adj* apathetic, cold, cool, dead, distant, dull, easygoing, frigid, heedless, inattentive, incurious, insensible, insouciant, listless, lukewarm, nonchalant, perfunctory, regardless, stoical, unconcerned, uninterested, unmindful, unmoved; equal; fair, medium, middling, moderate, ordinary, passable, tolerable; mediocre, so-so; immaterial, unimportant; disinterested, impartial, neutral, unbiased.

indigence *n* destitution, distress, necessity, need, neediness, pauperism, penury, poverty, privation, want.

indigenous *adj* aboriginal, home-grown, inborn, inherent, native.

indigent *adj* destitute, distressed, insolvent, moneyless, necessitous, needy, penniless, pinched, poor, reduced.

indigested *adj* unconcocted, undigested; crude, ill-advised, ill-considered, ill-judged; confused, disorderly, ill-arranged, unmethodical.

indigestion *n* dyspepsia, dyspepsy.

indignant *adj* angry, exasperated, incensed, irate, ireful, provoked, roused, wrathful, wroth.

indignation *n* anger, choler, displeasure, exasperation, fury, ire, rage, resentment, wrath.

indignity *n* abuse, affront, contumely, dishonour, disrespect, ignominy, insult, obloquy, opprobrium, outrage, reproach, slight.

indirect *adj* circuitous, circumlocutory, collateral, devious, oblique, roundabout, sidelong, tortuous; deceitful, dishonest, dishonorable, unfair; mediate, remote, secondary, subordinate.

indiscernible *adj* imperceptible, indistinguishable, invisible, undiscernible, undiscoverable.

indiscipline *n* laxity, insubordination.

indiscreet *adj* foolish, hasty, headlong, heedless, imprudent, incautious, inconsiderate, injudicious, rash, reckless, unwise.

indiscretion *n* folly, imprudence, inconsiderateness, rashness; blunder, faux pas, lapse, mistake, misstep.

indiscriminate *adj* confused, heterogeneous, indistinct, mingled, miscellaneous, mixed, promiscuous, undiscriminating, undistinguishable, undistinguishing.

indispensable *adj* essential, expedient, necessary, needed, needful, requisite.

indisputable *adj* certain, incontestable, indubitable, infallible, sure, undeniable, undoubted, unmistakable, unquestionable.

indisposed *adj* ailing, ill, sick, unwell; averse, backward, disinclined, loath, reluctant, unfriendly, unwilling.

indisposition *n* ailment, illness, sickness; aversion, backwardness, dislike, disinclination, reluctance, unwillingness.

indisputable *adj* certain, incontestable, indutitable, infallible, sure, undeniable, undoubted, unmistakable, unquestionable.

indissoluble *adj* abiding, enduring, firm, imperishable, incorruptible, indestructible, lasting, stable, unbreakable.

indistinct *adj* ambiguous, doubtful, uncertain; blurred, dim, dull, faint, hazy, misty, nebulous, obscure, shadowy, vague; confused, inarticulate, indefinite, indistinguishable, undefined, undistinguishable.

indistinguishable *adj* imperceptible, indiscernible, unnoticeable, unobservable; chaotic, confused, dim, indistinct, obscure, vague.

indite *vb* compose, pen, write.

individual *adj* characteristic, distinct, identical, idiosyncratic, marked, one, particular, personal, respective, separate, single, singular, special, unique; peculiar, proper; decided, definite, independent, positive, self-guided, unconventional. • *n* being, character, party, person, personage, somebody, someone; type, unit.

individuality *n* definiteness, indentity, personality; originality, self-direction, self-determination, singularity, uniqueness.

individualize *vb* individuate, particularize, singularize, specify.

indivisible *adj* incommensurable, indissoluble, inseparable, unbreakable, unpartiable.

indocile *adj* cantankerous, contumacious, dogged, froward, inapt, headstrong, intractable, mulish, obstinate, perverse, refractory, stubborn, ungovernable, unmanageable, unruly, unteachable.

indoctrinate *vb* brainwash, imbue, initiate, instruct, rehabilitate, teach.

indoctrination *n* grounding, initiation, instruction, rehabilitation.

indolence *n* idleness, inactivity, inertia, inertness, laziness, listlessness, sloth, slothfulness, sluggishness.

indolent *adj* easy, easy-going, inactive, inert, lazy, listless, lumpish, otiose, slothful, sluggish, supine.

indomitable *adj* invincible, unconquerable, unyielding.

indorse *see* **endorse**.

indubitable *adj* certain, evident, incontestable, incontrovertible, indisputable, sure, undeniable, unquestionable.

induce *vb* actuate, allure, bring, draw, drive, entice, impel, incite, influence, instigate, move, persuade, prevail, prompt, spur, urge; bring on, cause, effect, motivate, lead, occasion, produce.

inducement *n* allurement, draw, enticement, instigation, persuasion; cause, consideration, impulse, incentive, incitement, influence, motive, reason, spur, stimulus.

induct *vb* inaugurate, initiate, install, institute, introduce, invest.

induction *n* inauguration, initiation, institution, installation, introduction; conclusion, generalization, inference.

indue *vb* assume, endow, clothe, endue, invest, supply.

indulge *vb* gratify, license, revel, satisfy, wallow, yield to; coddle, cosset, favour, humour, pamper, pet, spoil; allow, cherish, foster, harbour, permit, suffer.

indulgence *n* gratification, humouring, pampering; favour, kindness, lenience, lenity, liberality, tenderness; (*theol*) absolution, remission.

indulgent *adj* clement, easy, favouring, forbearing, gentle, humouring, kind, lenient, mild, pampering, tender, tolerant.

indurate *vb* harden, inure, sear, strengthen.

induration *n* hardening, obduracy.

industrious *adj* assiduous, diligent, hard-working, laborious, notable, operose, sedulous; brisk, busy, persevering, persistent.

industry *n* activity, application, assiduousness, assiduity, diligence; perseverance, persistence, sedulousness, vigour; effort, labour, toil.

inebriated *adj* drunk, intoxicated, stupefied.

ineffable *adj* indescribable, inexpressible, unspeakable, unutterable.

ineffaceable *adj* indelible, indestructible, inerasable, inexpungeable, ingrained.

ineffectual *adj* abortive, bootless, fruitless, futile, inadequate, inefficacious, ineffective, inoperative, useless, unavailing, vain; feeble, inefficient, powerless, impotent, weak.

inefficacy *n* ineffectualness, inefficiency.

inefficient *adj* feeble, incapable, ineffectual, ineffective, inefficacious, weak.

inelastic *adj* flabby, flaccid, inductile, inflexible, irresilient.

inelegant *adj* abrupt, awkward, clumsy, coarse, constrained, cramped, crude, graceless, harsh, homely, homespun, rough, rude, stiff, tasteless, uncourtly, uncouth, ungainly, ungraceful, unpolished, unrefined.

ineligible *adj* disqualified, unqualified; inexpedient, objectionable, unadvisable, undesirable.

inept *adj* awkward, improper, inapposite, inappropriate, unapt, unfit, unsuitable; null, useless, void, worthless; foolish, nonsensical, pointless, senseless, silly, stupid.

ineptitude *n* inapposteness, inappropriateness, inaptitude, unfitness, unsuitability, unsuitable-ness; emptiness, nullity, uselessness, worthlessness; folly, foolishness, nonsense, pointlessness, senselessness, silliness, stupidity.

inequality *n* disproportion, inequitableness, injustice, unfairness; difference, disparity, dissimilarity, diversity, imparity, irregularity, roughness, unevenness; inadequacy, incompetency, insufficiency.

inequitable *adj* unfair, unjust.

inert *adj* comatose, dead, inactive, lifeless, motionless, quiescent, passive; apathetic, dronish, dull, idle, indolent, lazy, lethargic, lumpish, phlegmatic, slothful, sluggish, supine, torpid.

inertia *n* apathy, inertness, lethargy, passiveness, passivity, slothfulness, sluggishness.

inestimable *adj* incalculable, invaluable, precious, priceless, valuable.

inevitable *adj* certain, necessary, unavoidable, undoubted.

inexact *adj* imprecise, inaccurate, incorrect; careless, crude, loose.

inexcusable *adj* indefensible, irremissible, unallowable, unjustifiable, unpardonable.

inexhaustible *adj* boundless, exhaustless, indefatigable, unfailing, unlimited.

inexorable *adj* cruel, firm, hard, immovable, implacable, inflexible, merciless, pitiless, relentless, severe, steadfast, unbending, uncompassionate, unmerciful, unrelenting, unyielding.

inexpedient *adj* disadvantageous, ill-judged, impolitic, imprudent, indiscreet, injudicious, inopportune, unadvisable, unprofitable, unwise.

inexperience *n* greenness, ignorance, rawness.

inexperienced *adj* callow, green, raw, strange, unacquainted, unconversant, undisciplined, uninitiated, unpractised, unschooled, unskilled, untrained, untried, unversed, young.

inexpert *adj* awkward, bungling, clumsy, inapt, maladroit, unhandy, unskilful, unskilled.

inexpiable *adj* implacable, inexorable, irreconcilable, unappeasable; irremissible, unatonable, unpardonable.

inexplicable *adj* enigmatic, enigmatical, incomprehensible, inscrutable, mysterious, strange, unaccountable, unintelligible.

inexpressible *adj* indescribable, ineffable, unspeakable, unutterable; boundless, infinite, surpassing.

inexpressive *adj* blank, characterless, dull, unexpressive.

inextinguishable *adj* unquenchable.

in extremis *adv* moribund.

inextricable *adj* entangled, intricate, perplexed, unsolvable.

infallibility *n* certainty, infallibleness, perfection.

infallible *adj* certain, indubitable, oracular, sure, unerring, unfailing.

infamous *adj* abominable, atrocious, base, damnable, dark, detestable, discreditable, disgraceful, dishonorable, disreputable, heinous, ignominious, nefarious, odious, opprobrious, outrageous, scandalous, shameful, shameless, vile, villainous, wicked.

infamy *n* abasement, discredit, disgrace, dishonour, disrepute, ignominy, obloquy, odium, opprobrium, scandal, shame; atrocity, detestableness, disgracefulness, dishonorableness, odiousness, scandalousness, shamefulness, villainy, wickedness.

infancy *n* beginning, commencement; babyhood, childhood, minority, nonage, pupillage.

infant *n* babe, baby, bairn, bantling, brat, chit, minor, nursling, papoose, suckling, tot.

infantile *adj* childish, infantine, newborn, tender, young; babyish, childish, weak; babylike, childlike.

infatuate *vb* befool, besot, captivate, delude, prepossess, stultify.

infatuation *n* absorption, besottedness, folly, foolishness, prepossession, stupefaction.

infeasible *adj* impractical, unfeasible.

infect *vb* affect, contaminate, corrupt, defile, poison, pollute, taint, vitiate.

infection *n* affection, bane, contagion, contamination, corruption, defilement, pest, poison, pollution, taint, virus, vitiation.

infectious *adj* catching, communicable, contagious, contaminating, corrupting, defiling, demoralizing, pestiferous, pestilential, poisoning, polluting, sympathetic, vitiating.

infecund *adj* barren, infertile, sterile, unfruitful, unproductive, unprolific.

infecundity *n* unfruitfulness.

infelicitous *adj* calamitous, miserable, unfortunate, unhappy, wretched; inauspicious, unfavourable, unpropitious; ill-chosen, inappropriate, unfitting.

infer *vb* collect, conclude, deduce, derive, draw, gather, glean, guess, presume, reason.

inference *n* conclusion, consequence, corollary, deduction, generalization, guess, illation, implication, induction, presumption.

inferior *adj* lower, nether; junior, minor, secondary, subordinate; bad, base, deficient, humble, imperfect, indifferent, mean, mediocre, paltry, poor, second-rate, shabby.

inferiority *n* juniority, subjection, subordination, mediocrity; deficiency, imperfection, inadequacy, shortcoming.

infernal *adj* abominable, accursed, atrocious, damnable, dark, demoniacal, devilish, diabolical, fiendish, fiendlike, hellish, malicious, nefarious, satanic, Stygian.

infertility *n* barrenness, infecundity, sterility, unfruitfulness, unproductivity.

infest *vb* annoy, disturb, harass, haunt, molest, plague, tease, torment, trouble, vex, worry; beset, overrun, possess, swarm, throng.

infidel *n* agnostic, atheist, disbeliever, heathen, heretic, sceptic, unbeliever.

infidelity *n* adultery, disloyality, faithlessness, treachery, unfaithfulness; disbelief, scepticism, unbelief.

infiltrate *vb* absorb, pervade, soak.

infinite *adj* boundless, endless, illimitable, immeasurable, inexhaustible, interminable, limitless, measureless, perfect, unbounded, unlimited; enormous, immense, stupendous, vast; absolute, eternal, self-determined, self-existent, unconditioned.

infinitesimal *adj* infinitely small; microscopic, miniscule.

infinity *n* absoluteness, boundlessness, endlessness, eternity, immensity, infiniteness, infinitude, interminateness, self-determination, self-existence, vastness.

infirm *adj* ailing, debilitated, enfeebled, feeble, frail, weak, weakened; faltering, irresolute, vacillating, wavering; insecure, precarious, unsound, unstable.

infirmity *n* ailment, debility, feebleness, frailness, frailty, weakness; defect, failing, fault, foible, weakness.

infix *vb* fasten, fix, plant, set; implant, inculcate, infuse, ingraft, instil.

inflame *vb* animate, arouse, excite, enkindle, fire, heat, incite, inspirit, intensify, rouse, stimulate; aggravate, anger, chafe, embitter, enrage, exasperate, incense, infuriate, irritate, madden, nettle, provoke.

inflammability *n* combustibility, combustibleness, inflammableness.

inflammable *adj* combustible, ignitible; excitable.

inflammation *n* burning, conflagration; anger, animosity, excitement, heat, rage, turbulence, violence.

inflammatory *adj* fiery, inflaming; dissentious, incendiary, seditious.

inflate *vb* bloat, blow up, distend, expand, swell, sufflate; elate, puff up; enlarge, increase.

inflated *adj* bloated, distended, puffed-up, swollen; bombastic, declamatory, grandiloquent, high-flown, magniloquent, overblown, pompous, rhetorical, stilted, tumid, turgid.

inflation *n* enlargement, increase, overenlargement, overissue; bloatedness, distension, expansion, sufflation; bombast, conceit, conceitedness, self-conceit, self-complacency, self-importance, self-sufficiency, vaingloriousness, vainglory.

inflect *vb* bend, bow, curve, turn; *(gram)* conjugate, decline, vary.

inflection *n* bend, bending, crook, curvature, curvity, flexure; *(gram)* accidence, conjugation, declension, variation; *(mus)* modulation.

inflexibility *n* inflexibleness, rigidity, stiffness; doggedness, obstinacy, perinacity, stubbornness; firmness, perseverance, resolution, tenacity.

inflexible *adj* rigid, rigorous, stiff, unbending; cantankerous, cross-grained, dogged, headstrong, heady, inexorable, intractable, obdurate, obstinant, pertinacious, refractory, stubborn, unyielding, wilful; firm, immovable, persevering, resolute, steadfast, unbending.

inflict *vb* bring, impose, lay on.

infliction *n* imposition, inflicting; judgment, punishment.

inflorescence *n* blooming, blossoming, flowering.

influence *vb* affect, bias, control, direct, lead, modify, prejudice, prepossess, sway; actuate, arouse, impel, incite, induce, instigate, move, persuade, prevail upon, rouse. • *n* ascendancy, authority, control, mastery, potency, predominance, pull, rule, sway; credit, reputation, weight; inflow, inflowing, influx; magnetism, power, spell.

influential *adj* controlling, effective, effectual, potent, powerful, strong; authoritative, momentous, substantial, weighty.

influx *n* flowing in, introduction.

infold *see* **enfold**.

inform *vb* animate, inspire, quicken; acquaint, advise, apprise, enlighten, instruct, notify, teach, tell, tip, warn.

informal *adj* unceremonious, unconventional, unofficial; easy, familiar, natural, simple; irregular, nonconformist, unusual.

informality *n* unceremoniousness; unconventionality; ease, familiarity, naturalness, simplicity; noncomformity, irregularity, unusualness.

informant *n* advertiser, adviser, informer, intelligencer, newsmonger, notifier, relator; accuser, complainant, informer.

information *n* advice, data, intelligence, knowledge, notice; advertisement, enlightenment, instruction, message, tip, word, warning; accusation, complaint, denunciation.

informer *n* accuser, complainant, informant, snitch.

infraction *n* breach, breaking, disobedience, encroachment, infringement, nonobservance, transgression, violation.

infrangible *adj* inseparable, inviolable, unbreakable.

infrequency *n* rareness, rarity, uncommonness, unusualness.

infrequent *adj* rare, uncommon, unfrequent, unusual; occasional, scant, scarce, sporadic.

infringe *vb* break, contravene, disobey, intrude, invade, transgress, violate.

infringement *n* breach, breaking, disobedience, infraction, nonobservance, transgression, violation.

infuriated *adj* angry, enraged, furious, incensed, maddened, raging, wild.

infuse *vb* breathe into, implant, inculcate, ingraft, insinuate, inspire, instil, introduce; macerate, steep.

infusion *n* inculcation, instillation, introduction; infusing, macerating, steeping.

ingathering *n* harvest.

ingenious *adj* able, adroit, artful, bright, clever, fertile, gifted, inventive, ready, sagacious, shrewd, witty.

ingenuity *n* ability, acuteness, aptitude, aptness, capacity, capableness, cleverness, faculty, genius, gift, ingeniousness, inventiveness, knack, readiness, skill, turn.

ingenuous *adj* artless, candid, childlike, downright, frank, generous, guileless, honest, innocent, naive, open, open-hearted, plain, simple-minded, sincere, single-minded, straightforward, transparent, truthful, unreserved.

ingenuousness *n* artlessness, candour, childlikeness, frankness, guilelessness, honesty, naivety, open-heartedness, openness, sincerity, single-mindedness, truthfulness.

inglorious *adj* humble, lowly, mean, nameless, obscure, undistinguished, unhonoured, unknown, unmarked, unnoted; discreditable, disgraceful, humiliating, ignominous, scandalous, shameful.

ingloriousness *n* humbleness, lowliness, meanness, namelessness, obscurity; abasement, discredit, disgrace, dishonour, disrepute, humiliation, infamy, ignominousness, ignominy, obloquy, odium, opprobrium, shame.

ingraft *vb* graft, implant, inculcate, infix, infuse, instil.

ingrain *vb* dye, imbue, impregnate.

ingratiate *vb* insinuate.

ingratitude *n* thanklessness, ungratefulness, unthankfulness.

ingredient *n* component, constituent, element.

ingress *n* entrance, entré, entry, introgression.

ingulf *see* **engulf**.

inhabit *vb* abide, dwell, live, occupy, people, reside, sojourn.

inhabitable *adj* habitable, livable.

inhabitant *n* citizen, denizen, dweller, inhabiter, resident.

inhalation *n* breath, inhaling, inspiration; sniff, snuff.

inhale *vb* breathe in, draw in, inbreathe, inspire.

inharmonious *adj* discordant, inharmonic, out of tune, unharmonious, unmusical.

inhere *vb* cleave to, stick, stick fast; abide, belong, exist, lie, pertain, reside.

inherent *adj* essential, immanent, inborn, inbred, indwelling, ingrained, innate, inseparable, intrinsic, native, natural, proper; adhering, sticking.

inherit *vb* get, receive.

inheritance *n* heritage, legacy, patrimony; inheriting.

inheritor *n* heir, (*law*) parcener.

inhibit *vb* bar, check, debar, hinder, obstruct, prevent, repress, restrain, stop; forbid, interdict, prohibit.

inhibition *n* check, hindrance, impediment, obstacle, obstruction, restraint; disallowance, embargo, interdict, interdiction, prevention, prohibition.

inhospitable *adj* cool, forbidding, unfriendly, unkind; bigoted, illiberal, intolerant, narrow, prejudiced, ungenerous, unreceptive; barren, wild.

inhospitality *n* inhospitableness, unkindness; illiberality, narrowness.

inhuman *adj* barbarous, brutal, cruel, fell, ferocious, merciless, pitiless, remorseless, ruthless, savage, unfeeling; nonhuman.

inhumanity *n* barbarity, brutality, cruelty, ferocity, savageness; hard-heartedness, unkindness.

inhume *vb* bury, entomb, inter.

inimical *adj* antagonistic, hostile, unfriendly; adverse, contrary, harmful, hurtful, noxious, opposed, pernicious, repugnant, unfavourable.

inimitable *adj* incomparable, matchless, peerless, unequalled, unexampled, unmatched, unparagoned, unparalleled, unrivalled, unsurpassed.

iniquitous *adj* atrocious, criminal, flagitious, heinous, inequitable, nefarious, sinful, wicked, wrong, unfair, unjust, unrighteous.

iniquity *n* injustice, sin, sinfulness, unrighteousness, wickedness, wrong; crime, misdeed, offence.

initial *adj* first; beginning, commencing, incipient, initiatory, introductory, opening, original; elementary, inchoate, rudimentary.

initiate *vb* begin, commence, enter upon, inaugurate, introduce, open; ground, indoctrinate, instruct, prime, teach.

initiation *n* beginning, commencement, inauguration, opening; admission, entrance, introduction; indoctrinate, instruction.

initiative *n* beginning; energy, enterprise.

initiatory *adj* inceptive, initiative.

inject *vb* force in, interject, insert, introduce, intromit.

injudicious *adj* foolish, hasty, ill-advised, ill-judged, imprudent, incautious, inconsiderate, indiscreet, rash, unwise.

injunction *n* admonition, bidding, command, mandate, order, precept.

injure *vb* damage, disfigure, harm, hurt, impair, mar, spoil, sully, wound; abuse, aggrieve, wrong; affront, dishonour, insult.

injurious *adj* baneful, damaging, deadly, deleterious, destructive, detrimental, disadvantageous, evil, fatal, hurtful, mischievous, noxious, pernicious, prejudicial, ruinous; inequitable, iniquitous, unjust, wrongful; contumelious, detractory, libellous, slanderous.

injury *n* evil, ill, injustice, wrong; damage, detriment, harm, hurt, impairment, loss, mischief, prejudice.

injustice *n* inequity, unfairness; grievance, iniquity, injury, wrong.

inkhorn *n* inkbottle, inkstand.

inkling *n* hint, intimation, suggestion, whisper.

inky *adj* atramentous, black, murky.

inland *adj* domestic, hinterland, home, upcountry; interior, internal.

inlet *n* arm, bay, bight, cove, creek; entrance, ingress, passage.

inmate *n* denizen, dweller, guest, intern, occupant.

inmost *adj* deepest, innermost.

inn *n* hostel, hostelry, hotel, pub, public house, tavern.

innate *adj* congenital, constitutional, inborn, inbred, indigenous, inherent, inherited, instinctive, native, natural, organic.

inner *adj* interior, internal.

innermost *adj* deepest, inmost.

innkeeper *n* host, innholder, landlady, landlord, tavernkeeper.

innocence *n* blamelessness, chastity, guilelessness, guiltlessness, purity, simplicity, sinlessness, stainlessness; harmlessness, innocuousness, innoxiousness, inoffensiveness.

innocent *adj* blameless, clean, clear, faultless, guiltless, immaculate, pure, sinless, spotless, unfallen, upright; harmless, innocuous, innoxious, inoffensive; lawful, legitimate, permitted; artless, guileless, ignorant, ingenuous, simple. • *n* babe, child, ingénue, naif, naive, unsophisticate.

innocuous *adj* harmless, innocent, inoffensive, safe.

innovate *vb* change, introduce.

innovation *n* change, introduction; departure, novelty.

innuendo *n* allusion, hint, insinuation, intimation, suggestion.

innumerable *adj* countless, numberless.

inoculate *vb* infect, vaccinate.

inoffensive *adj* harmless, innocent, innocuous, innoxious, unobjectionable, unoffending.

inoperative *adj* inactive, ineffectual, inefficacious, not in force.

inopportune *adj* ill-timed, inexpedient, infelicitous, mistimed, unfortunate, unhappy, unseasonable, untimely.

inordinate *adj* excessive, extravagant, immoderate, intemperate, irregular.

inorganic *adj* inanimate, unorganized; mineral.

inquest *n* inquiry, inquisition, investigation, quest, search.

inquietude *n* anxiety, disquiet, disquietude, disturbance, restlessness, uneasiness.

inquire, enquire *vb* ask, catechize, interpellate, interrogate, investigate, query, question, quiz.

inquiry, enquiry *n* examination, exploration, investigation, research, scrutiny, study; interrogation, query, question, quiz.

inquisition *n* examination, inquest, inquiry, investigation, search.

inquisitive *adj* curious, inquiring, scrutinizing; curious, meddlesome, peeping, peering, prying.

inroad *n* encroachment, foray, incursion, invasion, irruption, raid.

insalubrious *adj* noxious, unhealthful, unhealthy, unwholesome.

insane *adj* abnormal, crazed, crazy, delirious, demented, deranged, distracted, lunatic, mad, maniacal, unhealthy, unsound.

insanity *n* craziness, delirium, dementia, derangement, lunacy, madness, mania, mental aberration, mental alienation.

insatiable *adj* greedy, rapacious, voracious; insatiate, unappeasable.

inscribe *vb* emblaze, endorse, engrave, enroll, impress, imprint, letter, mark, write; address, dedicate.

inscrutable *adj* hidden, impenetrable, incomprehensible, inexplicable, mysterious, undiscover-able, unfathomable, unsearchable.

inscrutableness *n* impenetrability, incomprehensibility, incomprehensibleness, inexplicability, inscrutability, mysteriousness, mystery, unfathomableness, unsearchableness.

insecure *adj* risky, uncertain, unconfident, unsure; exposed, ill-protected, unprotected, unsafe; dangerous, hazardous, perilous; infirm, shaking, shaky, tottering, unstable, weak, wobbly.

insecurity *n* riskiness, uncertainty; danger, hazardousness, peril; instability, shakiness, weakness, wobbliness.

insensate *adj* dull, indifferent, insensible, torpid; brutal, foolish, senseless, unwise; inanimate, insensible, insentient, nonpercipient, unconscious, unperceiving.

insensibility *n* dullness, insentience, lethargy, torpor; apathy, indifference, insusceptibility, unfeelingness, dullness, stupidity; anaesthesia, coma, stupor, unconsciousness.

insensible *adj* imperceivable, imperceptible, undiscoverable; blunted, brutish, deaf, dull, insensate, numb, obtuse, senseless, sluggish, stolid, stupid, torpid, unconscious; apathetic, callous, phlegmatic, impassive, indifferent, insensitive, insentient, unfeeling, unimpressible, unsusceptible.

insensibly *adv* imperceptibly.

insentient *adj* inert, nonsentient, senseless; inanimate, insensible, insensate, nonpercipient, unconscious, unperceiving.

inseparable *adj* close, friendly, intimate, together; indissoluble, indivisible, inseverable.

insert *vb* infix, inject, intercalate, interpolate, introduce, inweave, parenthesize, place, put, set.

inside *adj* inner, interior, internal; confidential, exclusive, internal, private, secret. • *adv* indoors, within. • *n* inner part, interior; nature.

insidious *adj* creeping, deceptive, gradual, secretive; arch, artful, crafty, crooked, cunning, deceitful, designing, diplomatic, foxy, guileful, intriguing, Machiavellian, sly, sneaky, subtle, treacherous, trickish, tricky, wily.

insight *n* discernment, intuition, penetration, perception, perspicuity, understanding.

insignia *npl* badges, marks.

insignificance *n* emptiness, nothingenss, paltriness, triviality, unimportance.

insignificant *adj* contemptible, empty, immaterial, inconsequential, inconsiderable, inferior, meaningless, paltry, petty, small, sorry, trifling, trivial, unessential, unimportant.

insincere *adj* deceitful, dishonest, disingenuous, dissembling, dissimulating, double-faced, double-tongued, duplicitous, empty, faithless, false, hollow, hypocritical, pharisaical, truthless, uncandid, untrue.

insincerity *n* bad faith, deceitfulness, dishonesty, disingenuousness, dissimulation, duplicity, falseness, faithlessness, hypocrisy.

insinuate *vb* hint, inculcate, infuse, ingratiate, instil, intimate, introduce, suggest.

insipid *adj* dead, dull, flat, heavy, inanimate, jejune, lifeless, monotonous, pointless, prosaic, prosy, spiritless, stupid, tame, unentertaining, uninteresting; mawkish, savourless, stale, tasteless, vapid, zestless.

insipidity, insipidness *n* dullness, heaviness, lifelessness, prosiness, stupidity, tameness; flatness, mawkishness, staleness, tastlessness, unsavouriness, vapidness, zestlessness.

insist *vb* demand, maintain, urge.

insistence *n* importunity, solicitousness, urging, urgency.

insnare *see* **ensnare**.

insolence *n* impertinence, impudence, malapertness, pertness, rudeness, sauciness; contempt, contumacy, contumely, disrespect, frowardness, insubordination.

insolent *adj* abusive, contemptuous, contumelious, disrespectful, domineering, insulting, offensive, overbearing, rude, supercilious; cheeky, impertinent, impudent, malapert, pert, saucy; contumacious, disobedient, froward, insubordinate.

insoluble *adj* indissoluble, indissolvable, irreducible; inexplicable, insolvable.

insolvable *adj* inexplicable.

insolvent *adj* bankrupt, broken, failed, ruined.

insomnia *n* sleeplessness, wakefulness.

inspect *vb* examine, investigate, look into, pry into, scrutinize; oversee, superintend, supervise.

inspection *n* examination, investigation, scrutiny; oversight, superintendence, supervision.

inspector *n* censor, critic, examiner, visitor; boss, overseer, superintendent, supervisor.

inspiration *n* breathing, inhalation; afflatus, fire, inflatus; elevation, exaltation; enthusiasm.

inspire *vb* breathe, inhale; infuse, instil; animate, cheer, enliven, inspirit; elevate, exalt, stimulate; fill, imbue, impart, inform, quicken.

inspirit *vb* animate, arouse, cheer, comfort, embolden, encourage, enhearten, enliven, fire, hearten, incite, invigorate, quicken, rouse, stimulate.

instable *see* **unstable**.

instability *n* changeableness, fickleness, inconstancy, insecurity, mutability.

install, instal *vb* inaugurate, induct, introduce; establish, place, set up.

installation *n* inauguration, induction, instalment, investiture.

instalment *n* earnest, payment, portion.

instance *vb* adduce, cite, mention, specify. • *n* case, example, exemplification, illustration, occasion; impulse, incitement, instigation, motive, prompting, request, solicitation.

instant *adj* direct, immediate, instantaneous, prompt, quick; current, present; earnest, fast, imperative, importunate, pressing, urgent; ready cooked. • *n* flash, jiffy, moment, second, trice, twinkling; hour, time.

instantaneous *adj* abrupt, immediate, instant, quick, sudden.

instantaneously *adv* forthwith, immediately, presto, quickly, right away.

instauration *n* reconstitution, reconstruction, redintegration, re-establishment, rehabilitation, reinstatement, renewal, renovation, restoration.

instead *adv* in lieu, in place, rather.

instigate *vb* actuate, agitate, encourage, impel, incite, influence, initiate, move, persuade, prevail upon, prompt, provoke, rouse, set on, spur on, stimulate, stir up, tempt, urge.

instigation *n* encouragement, incitement, influence, instance, prompting, solicitation, urgency.

instil, instill *vb* enforce, implant, impress, inculcate, ingraft; impart, infuse, insinuate.

instillation *n* infusion, insinuation, introduction.

instinct *n* natural impulse.

instinctive *adj* automatic, inherent, innate, intuitive, involuntary, natural, spontaneous; impulsive, unreflecting.

institute[1] *n* academy, college, foundation, guild, institution, school; custom, doctrine, dogma, law, maxim, precedent, principle, rule, tenet.

institute[2] *vb* begin, commence, constitute, establish, found, initial, install, introduce, organize, originate, start.

institution *n* enactment, establishment, foundation, institute, society; investiture; custom, law, practice.

instruct *vb* discipline, educate, enlighten, exercise, guide, indoctrinate, inform, initiate, school, teach, train; apprise, bid, command, direct, enjoin, order, prescribe to.

instruction *n* breeding, discipline, education, indoctrination, information, nurture, schooling, teaching, training, tuition; advice, counsel, precept; command, direction, mandate, order.

instructor *n* educator, master, preceptor, schoolteacher, teacher, tutor.

instrument *n* appliance, apparatus, contrivance, device, implement, musical instrument, tool, utensil; agent, means, medium; charter, deed, document, indenture, writing.

instrumental *adj* ancillary, assisting, auxiliary, conducive, contributory, helpful, helping, ministerial, ministrant, serviceable, subservient, subsidiary.

instrumentality *n* agency, intermediary; intervention, means, mediation.

insubordinate *adj* disobedient, disorderly, mutinous, refractory, riotous, seditious, turbulent, ungovernable, unruly.

insubordination *n* disobedience, insurrection, mutiny, revolt, riotousness, sedition; indiscipline, laxity.

insufferable *adj* intolerable, unbearable, unendurable, insupportable; abominable, detestable, disgusting, execrable, outrageous.

insufficiency *n* dearth, defectiveness, deficiency, lack, inadequacy, inadequateness, incapability, incompetence, paucity, shortage.

insufficient *adj* deficient, inadequate, incommensurate, incompetent, scanty; incapable, incompetent, unfitted, unqualified, unsuited, unsatisfactory.

insular *adj* contracted, illiberal, limited, narrow, petty, prejudiced, restricted; isolated, remote.

insulate *vb* detach, disconnect, disengage, disunite, isolate, separate.

insulation *n* disconnection, disengagement, isolation, separation.

insult *vb* abuse, affront, injure, offend, outrage, slander, slight. • *n* abuse, affront, cheek, contumely, indignity, insolence, offence, outrage, sauce, slight.

insulting *adj* abusive, arrogant, contumelious, impertinent, impolite, insolent, rude, vituperative.

insuperable *adj* impassable, insurmountable.

insupportable *adj* insufferable, intolerable, unbearable, unendurable.

insuppressible *adj* irrepressible, uncontrollable.

insurance *n* assurance, security.

insure *vb* assure, guarantee, indemnify, secure, underwrite.

insurgent *adj* disobedient, insubordinate, mutinous, rebellious, revolting, revolutionary, seditious. • *n* mutineer, rebel, revolter, revolutionary.

insurmountable *adj* impassable, insuperable.

insurrection *n* insurgence, mutiny, rebellion, revolt, revolution, rising, sedition, uprising.

intact *adj* scathless, unharmed, unhurt, unimpaired, uninjured, untouched; complete, entire, integral, sound, unbroken, undiminished, whole.

intangible *adj* dim, impalpable, imperceptible, indefinite, insubstantial, intactile, shadowy, vague; aerial, phantom, spiritous.

intangibility *n* imperceptibility, insubstantiality, intangibleness, shadowiness, vagueness.

integral *adj* complete, component, entire, integrant, total, whole.

integrity *n* goodness, honesty, principle, probity, purity, rectitude, soundness, uprightness, virtue; completeness, entireness, entirety, wholeness.

integument *n* coat, covering, envelope, skin, tegument.

intellect *n* brains, cognitive faculty, intelligence, mind, rational faculty, reason, reasoning, faculty, sense, thought, understanding, wit.

intellectual *adj* cerebral, intelligent, mental, scholarly, thoughtful. • *n* academic, highbrow, pundit, savant, scholar.

intelligence *n* acumen, apprehension, brightness, discernment, imagination, insight, penetration, quickness, sagacity, shrewdness, understanding, wits; information, knowledge; advice, instruction, news, notice, notification, tidings; brains, intellect, mentality, sense, spirit.

intelligent *adj* acute, alert, apt, astute, brainy, bright, clear-headed, clear-sighted, clever, discerning, keen-eyed, keen-sighted, knowing, long-headed, quick, quick-sighted, sagacious, sensible, sharp-sighted, sharp-witted, shrewd, understanding.

intelligibility *n* clarity, comprehensibility, intelligibleness, perspicuity.

intelligible *adj* clear, comprehensible, distinct, evident, lucid, manifest, obvious, patent, perspicuous, plain, transparent, understandable.

intemperate *adj* drunken; excessive, extravagant, extreme, immoderate, inordinate, unbridled, uncontrolled, unrestrained; self-indulgent.

intend *vb* aim at, contemplate, design, determine, drive at, mean, meditate, propose, purpose, think of.

intendant *n* inspector, overseer, superintendent, supervisor.

intense *adj* ardent, earnest, fervid, passionate, vehement; close, intent, severe, strained, stretched, strict; energetic, forcible, keen, potent, powerful, sharp, strong, vigorous, violent; acute, deep, extreme, exquisite, grievous, poignant.

intensify *vb* aggravate, concentrate, deepen, enhance, heighten, quicken, strengthen, whet.

intensity *n* closeness, intenseness, severity, strictness; excess, extremity, violence; activity, energy, force, power, strength, vigour; ardour, earnestness, vehemence.

intensive *adj* emphatic, intensifying.

intent *adj* absorbed, attentive, close, eager, earnest, engrossed, occupied, pre-occupied, zealous; bent, determined, decided, resolved, set. • *n* aim, design, drift, end, import, intention, mark, meaning, object, plan, purport, purpose, purview, scope, view.

intention *n* aim, design, drift, end, import, intent, mark, meaning, object, plan, purport, purpose, purview, scope, view.

intentional *adj* contemplated, deliberate, designed, intended, preconcerted, predetermined, premeditated, purposed, studied, voluntary, wilful.

inter *vb* bury, commit to the earth, entomb, inhume, inurn.

intercalate *vb* insert, interpolate.

intercede *vb* arbitrate, interpose, mediate; entreat, plead, supplicate.

intercept *vb* cut off, interrupt, obstruct, seize.

intercession *n* interposition, intervention, mediation; entreaty, pleading, prayer, supplication.

intercessor *n* interceder, mediator.

interchange *vb* alternate, change, exchange, vary. • *n* alternation.

interchangeableness *n* interchangeability.

interchangeably *adv* alternately.

intercourse *n* commerce, communication, communion, connection, converse, correspondence, dealings, fellowship, truck; acquaintance, intimacy.

interdict *vb* debar, forbid, inhibit, prohibit, prescribe, proscribe, restrain from. • *n* ban, decree, interdiction, prohibition.

interest *vb* affect, concern, touch; absorb, attract, engage, enlist, excite, grip, hold, occupy. • *n* advantage, benefit, good, profit, weal; attention, concern, regard, sympathy; part, participation, portion, share, stake; discount, premium, profit.

interested *adj* attentive, concerned, involved, occupied; biassed, patial, prejudiced; selfish, self-seeking.

interesting *adj* attractive, engaging, entertaining, pleasing.

interfere *vb* intermeddle, interpose, meddle; clash, collide, conflict.

interference *n* intermeddling, interposition; clashing, collision, interfering, opposition.

interim *n* intermediate time, interval, meantime.

interior *adj* inmost, inner, internal, inward; inland, remote; domestic, home. • *n* inner part, inland, inside.

interjacent *adj* intermediate, interposed, intervening, parenthetical.

interject *vb* comment, inject, insert, interpose.

interjection *n* exclamation.

interlace *vb* bind, complicate, entwine, intersperse, intertwine, interweave, inweave, knit, mix, plait, twine, twist, unite.

interlard *vb* diversify, interminate, intersperse, intertwine, mix, vary.

interline *vb* insert, write between.

interlineal *adj* interlinear, interlined.

interlink, interlock *vb* connect, interchain, interrelate, join.

interlocution *n* colloquy, conference, dialogue, interchange.

interlocutor *n* respondent, speaker.

interloper *n* intruder, meddler.

intermeddle *vb* interfere, interpose, meddle.

intermediary *n* go-between, mediator.

intermediate *adj* interjacent, interposed, intervening, mean, median, middle, transitional.

interment *n* burial, entombment, inhumation, sepulture.

interminable *adj* boundless, endless, illimitable, immeasurable, infinite, limitless, unbounded, unlimited; long-drawn-out, tedious, wearisome.

intermingle *vb* blend, commingle, commix, intermix, mingle, mix.

intermission *n* cessation, interruption, interval, lull, pause, remission, respite, rest, stop, stoppage, suspension.

intermit *vb* interrupt, intervene, stop, suspend; discontinue, give over, leave off; abate, subside.

intermittent *adj* broken, capricious, discontinuous, fitful, flickering, intermitting, periodic, recurrent, remittent, spasmodic.

intermix *vb* blend, commingle, commix, intermingle, mingle, mix.

internal *adj* inner, inside, interior, inward; incorporeal, mental, spiritual; deeper, emblematic, hidden, higher, metaphorical, secret, symbolical, under; genuine, inherent, intrinsic, real, true; domestic, home, inland, inside.

international *adj* cosmopolitan, universal.

internecine *adj* deadly, destructive, exterminating, exterminatory, interneciary, internecinal, internecive, mortal.

interpellate *vb* interrogate, question.

interpellation *n* interruption; intercession, interposition; interrogation, questioning.

interplay *n* interaction.

interpolate *vb* add, foist, insert, interpose; (*math*) intercalate, introduce.

interpose *vb* arbitrate, intercede, intervene, mediate; interfere, intermeddle, interrupt, meddle, tamper; insert, interject, put in, remark, sandwich, set between; intrude, thurst in.

interposition *n* intercession, interpellation, intervention, mediation.

interpret *vb* decipher, decode, define, elucidate, explain, expound, solve, unfold, unravel; construe, render, translate.

interpretation *n* meaning, sense, signification; elucidation, explanation, explication, exposition; construction, rendering, rendition, translation, version.

interpreter *n* expositor, expounder, translator.

interrogate *vb* ask, catechize, examine, inquire of, interpellate, question.

interrogation *n* catechizing, examination, examining, interpellation, interrogating, questioning; inquiry, query, question.

interrogative *adj* interrogatory, questioning.

interrupt *vb* break, check, disturb, hinder, intercept, interfere with, obstruct, pretermit, stop; break, cut, disconnect, disjoin, dissever, dissolve, disunite, divide, separate, sever, sunder; break off, cease, discontinue, intermit, leave off, suspend.

interruption *n* hindrance, impediment, obstacle, obstruction, stop, stoppage; cessation, discontinuance, intermission, pause, suspension; break, breaking, disconnecting, disconnection, disjunction, dissolution, disunion, disuniting, division, separation, severing, sundering.

intersect *vb* cross, cut, decussate, divide, interrupt.

intersection *n* crossing.

interspace *n* interlude, interstice, interval.

intersperse *vb* intermingle, scatter, sprinkle; diversify, interlard, mix.

interstice *n* interspace, interval, space; chink, crevice.

interstitial *adj* intermediate, intervening.

intertwine *vb* interlace, intertwine, interweave, inweave, twine.

interval *n* interim, interlude, interregnum, pause, period, recess, season, space, spell, term; interstice, skip.

intervene *vb* come between, interfere, mediate; befall, happen, occur.

intervening *adj* interjacent, intermediate; interstitial.

intervention *n* interference, interposition; agency, mediation.

interview *n* conference, consultation, parley; meeting.

interweave *vb* interlace, intertwine, inweave, weave; intermingle, intermix, mingle, mix.

intestinal *adj* domestic, interior, internal.

intestines *npl* bowels, entrails, guts, insides, inwards, viscera.

intimacy *n* close acquaintance, familiarity, fellowship, friendship; closeness, nearness.

intimate[1] *adj* close, near; familiar, friendly; bosom, chummy, close, dear, homelike, special; confidential, personal, private, secret; detailed, exhaustive, first-hand, immediate, penetrating, profound; cosy, warm. • *n* chum, confidant, companion, crony, friend.

intimate[2] *vb* allude to, express, hint, impart, indicate, insinuate, signify, suggest, tell.

intimately *adv* closely, confidentially, familiarly, nearly, thoroughly.

intimation *n* allusion, hint, innuendo, insinuation, suggestion.

intimidate *vb* abash, affright, alarm, appal, browbeat, bully, cow, daunt, dishearten, dismay, frighten, overawe, scare, subdue, terrify, terrorize.

intimidation *n* fear, intimidating, terror, terrorism.

intolerable *adj* insufferable, insupportable, unbearable, unendurable.

intolerance *n* bigotry, narrowness; impatience, rejection.

intolerant *adj* bigoted, narrow, proscriptive; dictatorial, impatient, imperious, overbearing, supercilious.

intonation *n* cadence, modulation, tone; musical recitation.

in toto *adv* entirely, wholly.

intoxicate *vb* fuddle, inebriate, muddle.

intoxicated *adj* boozy, drunk, drunken, fuddled, inebriated, maudlin, mellow, muddled, stewed, tight, tipsy.

intoxication *n* drunkenness, ebriety, inebriation, inebriety; excitement, exhilaration, infatuation.

intractability *n* cantankerousness, contrariety, inflexibility, intractableness, obduracy, obstinacy, perverseness, perversity, pig-headedness, stubbornness, wilfulness.

intractable *adj* cantankerous, contrary, contumacious, cross-grained, dogged, froward, headstrong, indocile, inflexible, mulish, obdurate, obstinate, perverse, pig-headed, refractory, restive, stubborn, tough, uncontrollable, ungovernable, unmanageable, unruly, unyielding, wilful.

intrench *see* **entrench**.

intrenchment *see* **entrenchment**.

intrepid *adj* bold, brave, chivalrous, courageous, daring, dauntless, doughty, fearless, gallant, heroic, unappalled, unawed, undaunted, undismayed, unterrified, valiant, valorous.

intrepidity *n* boldness, bravery, courage, daring, dauntlessness, fearlessness, gallantry, heroism, intrepidness, prowess, spirit, valour.

intricacy *n* complexity, complication, difficulty, entanglement, intricateness, involution, obscurity, perplexity.

intricate *adj* complicated, difficult, entangled, involved, mazy, obscure, perplexed.

intrigue *vb* connive, conspire, machinate, plot, scheme; beguile, bewitch, captivate, charm, fascinate. • *n* artifice, cabal, conspiracy, deception, finesse, Machiavelianism, machination, manoeuvre, plot, ruse, scheme, stratagem, wile; amour, liaison, love affair.

intriguing *adj* arch, artful, crafty, crooked, cunning, deceitful, designing, diplomatic, foxy, Machiavelian, insidious, politic, sly, sneaky, subtle, tortuous, trickish, tricky, wily.

intrinsic *adj* essential, genuine, real, sterling, true; inborn, inbred, ingrained, inherent, internal, inward, native, natural.

intrinsically *adv* essentially, really, truly; inherently, naturally.

introduce *vb* bring in, conduct, import, induct, inject, insert, lead in, usher in; present; begin, broach, commence, inaugurate, initiate, institute, start.

introduction *n* exordium, preface, prelude, proem; introducing, ushering in; presentation.

introductory *adj* precursory, prefatory, preliminary, proemial.

introspection *n* introversion, self-contemplation.

intrude *vb* encroach, impose, infringe, interfere, interlope, obtrude, trespass.

intruder *n* interloper, intermeddler, meddler, stranger.

intrusion *n* encroachment, infringement, intruding, obtrusion.

intrusive *adj* obtrusive, trespassing.

intuition *n* apprehension, cognition, insight, instinct; clairvoyance, divination, presentiment.

intuitive *adj* instinctive, intuitional, natural; clear, distinct, full, immediate.

intumesce *vb* bubble up, dilate, expand, swell.

intumescence *n* inturgescence, swelling, tumefaction, turgescence.

inundate *vb* deluge, drown, flood, glut, overflow, overwhelm, submerge.

inundation *n* cataclysm, deluge, flood, glut, overflow, superfluity.

inure *vb* accustom, discipline, familiarize, habituate, harden, toughen, train, use.

inutile *adj* bootless, ineffectual, inoperative, unavailing, unprofitable, useless.

invade *vb* encroach upon, infringe, violate; attack, enter in, march into.

invalid[1] *adj* baseless, fallacious, false, inoperative, nugatory, unfounded, unsound, untrue, worthless; (*law*) null, void.

invalid[2] *adj* ailing, bedridden, feeble, frail, ill, infirm, sick, sickly, valetudinary, weak, weakly. • *n* convalescent, patient, valetudinarian.

invalidate *vb* abrogate, annul, cancel, nullify, overthrow, quash, repeal, reverse, undo, unmake, vitiate.

invalidity *n* baselessness, fallaciousness, fallacy, falsity, unsoundness.

invaluable *adj* inestimable, priceless.

invariable *adj* changeless, constant, unchanging, uniform, unvarying; changeless, immutable, unalterable, unchangeable.

invariableness *n* changelessness, constancy, uniformity, unvaryingness; changelessness, immutability, unchangeableness, invariability.

invasion *n* encroachment, incursion, infringement, inroad; aggression, assault, attack, foray, raid.

invective *n* abuse, censure, contumely, denunciation, diatribe, railing, reproach, sarcasm, satire, vituperation.

inveigh *vb* blame, censure, condemn, declaim against, denounce, exclaim against, rail at, reproach, vituperate.

inveigle *vb* contrive, devise; concoct, conceive, create, design, excogitate, frame, imagine, originate; coin, fabricate, forge, spin.

invent *vb* concoct, contrive, design, devise, discover, fabricate, find out, frame, originate.

invention *n* creation, discovery, ingenuity, inventing, origination; contrivance, design, device; coinage, fabrication, fiction, forgery.

inventive *adj* creative, fertile, ingenious.

inventor *n* author, contriver, creator, originator.

inventory *n* account, catalogue, list, record, roll, register, schedule.

inverse *adj* indirect, inverted, opposite, reversed.

inversion *n* inverting, reversing, transposal, transposition.

invert *vb* capsize, overturn; reverse, transpose.

invertebrate *adj* invertebral; spineless.

invest *vb* put money into; confer, endow, endue; (*mil*) beset, besiege, enclose, surround; array, clothe, dress.

investigate *vb* canvass, consider, dissect, examine, explore, follow up, inquire into, look into, overhaul, probe, question, research, scrutinize, search into, search out, sift, study.

investigation *n* examination, exploration, inquiry, inquisition, overhauling, research, scrutiny, search, sifting, study.

investiture *n* habilitation, induction, installation, ordination.

investment *n* money invested; endowment; (*mil*) beleaguerment, siege; clothes, dress, garments, habiliments, robe, vestment.

inveteracy *n* inveterateness, obstinacy.

inveterate *adj* accustomed, besetting, chronic, confirmed, deep–seated, habitual, habituated, hardened, ingrained, long-established, obstinate.

invidious *adj* disagreeable, envious, hateful, odious, offensive, unfair.

invigorate *vb* animate, brace, energize, fortify, harden, nerve, quicken, refresh, stimulate, strengthen, vivify.

invincible *adj* impregnable, indomitable, ineradicable, insuperable, insurmountable, irrepressible, unconquerable, unsubduable, unyielding.

inviolable *adj* hallowed, holy, inviolate, sacramental, sacred, sacrosanct, stainless.

inviolate *adj* unbroken, unviolated; pure, stainless, unblemished, undefiled, unhurt, uninjured, unpolluted, unprofaned, unstained; inviolable, sacred.

invisibility *n* imperceptibility, indistinctness, invisibleness, obscurity.

invisible *adj* impalpable, imperceptible, indistinguishable, intangible, unapparent, undiscernable, unperceivable, unseen.

invitation *n* bidding, call, challenge, solicitation, summons.

invite *vb* ask, bid, call, challenge, request, solicit, summon; allure, attract, draw on, entice, lead, persuade, prevail upon.

inviting *adj* alluring, attractive, bewitching, captivating, engaging, fascinating, pleasing, winning; prepossessing, promising.

invocation *n* conjuration, orison, petition, prayer, summoning, supplication.

invoice *vb* bill, list. • *n* bill, inventory, list, schedule.

invoke *vb* adjure, appeal to, beseech, beg, call upon, conjure, entreat, implore, importune, pray, pray to, solicit, summon, supplicate.

involuntary *adj* automatic, blind, instinctive, mechanical, reflex, spontaneous, unintentional; compulsory, reluctant, unwilling.

involve *vb* comprise, contain, embrace, imply, include, lead to; complicate, compromise, embarrass, entangle, implicate, incriminate, inculpate; cover, envelop, enwrap, surround, wrap; blend, conjoin, connect, join, mingle; entwine, interlace, intertwine, interweave, inweave.

invulnerability *n* invincibility, invulnerableness.

invulnerable *adj* incontrovertible, invincible, unassailable, irrefragable.

inward[1] *adj* incoming, inner, interior, internal; essential, hidden, mental, spiritual; private, secret.

inward[2], **inwards** *adv* inwardly, towards the inside, within.

inweave *vb* entwine, interlace, intertwine, interweave, weave together.

iota *n* atom, bit, glimmer, grain, jot, mite, particle, scintilla, scrap, shadow, spark, tittle, trace, whit.

irascibility *n* hastiness, hot-headedness, impatience, irascibleness, irritability, peevishness, petulance, quickness, spleen, testiness, touchiness.

irascible *adj* choleric, cranky, hasty, hot, hot-headed, impatient, irritable, nettlesome, peevish, peppery, pettish, petulant, quick, splenetic, snappish, testy, touchy, waspish.

irate *adj* angry, incensed, ireful, irritated, piqued.

ire *n* anger, choler, exasperation, fury, indignation, passion, rage, resentment, wrath.

ireful *adj* angry, furious, incensed, irate, raging, passionate.

iridescent *adj* irisated, nacreous, opalescent, pavonine, prismatic, rainbow-like.

iris *n* rainbow; (*bot*) fleur-de-lis, flower-de-luce; diaphragm of the eye.

irksome *adj* annoying, burdensome, humdrum, monotonous, tedious, tiresome, wearisome, weary, wearying.

iron *adj* ferric, ferrous.

ironic, ironical *adj* mocking, sarcastic.

irons *npl* chains, fetters, gyves, hampers, manacles, shackles.

irony *n* mockery, raillery, ridicule, sarcasm, satire.

irradiate *vb* brighten, illume, illuminate, illumine, light up, shine upon.

irrational *adj* absurd, extravagant, foolish, injudicious, preposterous, ridiculous, silly, unwise; unreasonable, unreasoning, unthinking; brute, brutish; aberrant, alienated, brainless, crazy, demented, fantastic, idiotic, imbecilic, insane, lunatic.

irrationality *n* absurdity, folly, foolishness, unreasonableness; brutishness.

irreclaimable *adj* hopeless, incurable, irrecoverable, irreparable, irretrievable, irreversible, remediless; abandoned, graceless, hardened, impenitent, incorrigible, lost, obdurate, profligate, recreant, reprobate, shameless, unrepentant.

irreconcilable *adj* implacable, inexorable, inexpiable, unappeasable; incompatible, incongruous, inconsistent.

irrecoverable *adj* hopeless, incurable, irremediable, irreparable, irretrievable, remediless.

irrefragable *adj* impregnable, incontestable, incontrovertible, indisputable, invincible, irrefutable, irresistible, unanswerable, unassailable, undeniable.

irrefutable *adj* impregnable, incontestable, incontrovertible, indisputable, invincible, irrefragable, irresistible, unanswerable, unassailable, undeniable.

irregular *adj* aberrant, abnormal, anomalistic, anomalous, crooked, devious, eccentric, erratic, exceptional, heteromorphous, raged, tortuous, unconformable, unusual; capricious, changeable, desultory, fitful, spasmodic, uncertain, unpunctual, unsettled, variable; disordered, disorderly, improper, uncanonical, unparliamentary, unsystematic; asymmetric, uneven, unsymmetrical; disorderly, dissolute, immoral, loose, wild. • *n* casual, freelance, hireling, mercenary.

irregularity *n* aberration, abnormality, anomaly, anomalousness, singularity; capriciousness, changeableness, uncertainty, variableness; asymmetry; disorderliness, dissoluteness, immorality, laxity, looseness, wildness.

irrelevance, irrelevancy *n* impertinency, inapplicability, nonpertinency.

irrelevant *adj* extraneous, foreign, illogical, impertinent, inapplicable, inapposite, inappropriate, inconsequent, unessential, unrelated.

irreligion *n* atheism, godlessness, impiety, ungodliness.

irreligious *adj* godless, ungodly, undevout; blasphemous, disrespectful, impious, irreverent, profane, ribald, wicked.

irremediable *adj* hopeless, incurable, immedicable, irrecoverable, irreparable, remediless.

irremissible *adj* binding, inexpiable, obligatory, unatonable, unpardonable.

irreparable *adj* irrecoverable, irremediable, irretrievable, remediless.

irreprehensible *adj* blameless, faultless, inculpable, innocent, irreproachable, irreprovable, unblamable.

irrepressible *adj* insuppressible, uncontrollable, unquenchable, unsmotherable.

irreproachable *adj* blameless, faultless, inculpable, innocent, irreprehensible, irreprovable, unblamable.

irresistible *adj* irrefragable, irrepressible, overpowering, overwhelming, resistless.

irresolute *adj* changeable, faltering, fickle, hesitant, hesitating, inconstant, mutable, spineless, uncertain, undecided, undetermined, unsettled, unstable, unsteady, vacillating, wavering.

irrespective *adj* independent, regardless.

irresponsible *adj* unaccountable; untrustworthy.

irretrievable *adj* incurable, irrecoverable, irremediable, irreparable, remediless.

irreverence *n* blasphemy, impiety, profaneness, profanity; disesteem, disrespect.

irreverent *adj* blasphemous, impious, irreligious, profane; disrespectful, slighting.

irreversible *adj* irrepealable, irrevocable, unalterable, unchangeable; changeless, immutable, invariable.

irrevocable *adj* irrepealable, irreversible, unalterable, unchangeable.

irrigate *vb* moisten, wash, water, wet.

irrigation *n* watering.

irritability *n* excitability, fretfulness, irascibility, peevishness, petulance, snappishness, susceptibility, testiness.

irritable *adj* captious, choleric, excitable, fiery, fretful, hasty, hot, irascible, passionate, peppery, peevish, pettish, petulant, snappish, splenetic, susceptible, testy, touchy, waspish.

irritate *vb* anger, annoy, chafe, enrage, exacerbate, exasperate, fret, incense, jar, nag, nettle, offend, provoke, rasp, rile, ruffle, vex; gall, tease; (*med*) excite, inflame, stimulate.

irritation *n* irritating; anger, exacerbation, exasperation, excitement, indignation, ire, passion, provocation, resentment, wrath; (*med*) excitation, inflammation, stimulation; burn, itch.

irruption *n* breaking in, bursting in; foray, incursion, inroad, invasion, raid.

island *n* atoll, isle, islet, reef.

isochronal *adj* isochronous, uniform.

isolate *vb* detach, dissociate, insulate, quarantine, segregate, separate, set apart.

isolated *adj* detached, separate, single, solitary.

isolation *n* detachment, disconnection, insulation, quarantine, segregation, separation; loneliness, solitariness, solitude.

issue *vb* come out, flow out, flow forth, gush, run, rush out, spout, spring, spurt, well; arise, come, emanate, ensue, flow, follow, originate, proceed, spring; end, eventuate, result, terminate; appear, come out, deliver, depart, debouch, discharge, emerge, emit, put forth, send out; distribute, give out; publish, utter. • *n* conclusion, consequence, consummation, denouement, end, effect, event, finale, outcome, result, termination, upshot; antagonism, contest, controversy; debouchment, delivering, delivery, discharge, emergence, emigration, emission, issuance; flux, outflow, outpouring, stream; copy, edition, number; egress, exit, outlet, passage out, vent, way out; escape, sally, sortie; children, offspring, posterity, progeny.

itch *vb* tingle. • *n* itching; burning, coveting, importunate craving, teasing desire, uneasy hankering.

itching *n* itch; craving, longing, importunate craving, desire, appetite, hankering.

item *adv* also, in like manner. • *n* article, detail, entry, particular, point.

iterate *vb* reiterate, repeat.

itinerant *adj* nomadic, peripatetic, roaming, roving, travelling, unsettled, wandering.

itinerary *n* guide, guidebook; circuit, route.

J

jabber *vb* chatter, gabble, prate, prattle.

jacket *n* casing, cover, sheath; anorak, blazer coat, doublet, jerkin.

jaded *adj* dull, exhausted, fatigued, satiated, tired, weary.

jagged *adj* cleft, divided, indented, notched, serrated, ragged, uneven.

jail, gaol *n* bridewell, (*sl*) clink, dungeon, lockup, (*sl*) nick, penitentiary, prison.

jam *vb* block, crowd, crush, press. • *n* block, crowd, crush, mass, pack, press.

jangle *vb* bicker, chatter, dispute, gossip, jar, quarrel, spar, spat, squabble, tiff, wrangle. • *n* clang, clangour, clash, din, dissonance.

jar¹ *vb* clash, grate, interfere, shake; bicker, contend, jangle, quarrel, spar, spat, squabble, tiff, wrangle; agitate, jolt, jounce, shake. • *n* clash, conflict, disaccord, discord, jangle, dissonance; agitation, jolt, jostle, shake, shaking, shock, start.

jar² *n* can, crock, cruse, ewer, flagon.

jarring *adj* conflicting, discordant, inconsistent, inconsonant, wrangling.

jargon *n* gabble, gibberish, nonsense, rigmarole: argot, cant, lingo, slang; chaos, confusion, disarray, disorder, jumble.

jaundiced *adj* biased, envious, prejudiced.

jaunt *n* excursion, ramble, tour, trip.

jaunty *adj* airy, cheery, garish, gay, fine, fluttering, showy, sprightly, unconcerned.

jealous *adj* distrustful, envious, suspicious; anxious, apprehensive, intolerant, solicitous, zealous.

jealousy *n* envy, suspicion, watchfulness.

jeer *vb* deride, despise, flout, gibe, jape, jest, mock, scoff, sneer, spurn, rail, ridicule, taunt. • *n* abuse, derision, mockery, sneer, ridicule, taunt.

jeopardize *vb* endanger, hazard, imperil, risk, venture.

jeopardy *n* danger, hazard, peril, risk, venture.

jerk *vb, n* flip, hitch, pluck, tweak, twitch, yank.

jest *vb* banter, joke, quiz. • *n* fun, joke, pleasantry, raillery, sport.

jester *n* humorist, joker, wag; buffoon, clown, droll, fool, harlequin, punch.

jibe *see* **gibe**.

jiffy *n* instant, moment, second, twinkling, trice.

jilt *vb* break with, deceive, disappoint, discard. • *n* coquette, flirt, light-o'-love.

jingle *vb* chink, clink, jangle, rattle, tinkle. • *n* chink, clink, jangle, rattle, tinkle; chorus, ditty, melody, song.

jocose *adj* comical, droll, facetious, funny, humorous, jesting, jocular, merry, sportive, waggish, witty.

jocund *adj* airy, blithe, cheerful, debonair, frolicsome, jolly, joyful, joyous, lively, merry, playful.

jog *vb* jostle, notify, nudge, push, remind, warn; canter, run, trot. • *n* push, reminder.

join *vb* add, annex, append, attach; cement, combine, conjoin, connect, couple, dovetail, link, unite, yoke; amalgamate, assemble, associate, confederate, consolidate.

joint *vb* fit, join, unite. • *adj* combined, concerted, concurrent, conjoint. • *n* connection, junction, juncture, hinge, splice.

joke *vb* banter, jest, frolic, rally. • *n* crank, jest, quip, quirk, witticism.

jolly *adj* airy, blithe, cheerful, frolicsome, gamesome, facetious, funny, gay, jovial, joyous, merry, mirthful, jocular, jocund, playful, sportive, sprightly, waggish; bouncing, chubby, lusty, plump, portly, stout.

jolt *vb* jar, shake, shock. • *n* jar, jolting, jounce, shaking.

jostle *vb* collide, elbow, hustle, joggle, shake, shoulder, shove.

jot *n* ace, atom, bit, corpuscle, iota, grain, mite, particle, scrap, whit.

journal *n* daybook, diary, log; gazette, magazine, newspapers, periodical.

journey *vb* ramble, roam, rove, travel: fare, go, proceed. • *n* excursion, expedition, jaunt, passage, pilgrimage, tour, travel, trip, voyage.

jovial *adj* airy, convivial, festive, jolly, joyous, merry, mirthful.

joy *n* beatification, beatitude, delight, ecstasy, exultation, gladness, glee, mirth, pleasure, rapture, ravishment, transport; bliss, felicity, happiness.

joyful *adj* blithe, blithesome, buoyant, delighted, elate, elated, exultant, glad, happy, jocund, jolly, joyous, merry, rejoicing.

jubilant *adj* exultant, exulting, rejoicing, triumphant.

judge *vb* conclude, decide, decree, determine, pronounce; adjudicate, arbitrate, condemn, doom, sentence, try, umpire; account, apprehend, believe, consider, deem, esteem, guess, hold, imagine, measure, reckon, regard, suppose, think; appreciate, estimate. • *n* adjudicator, arbiter, arbitrator, bencher, justice, magistrate, moderator, referee, umpire, connoisseur, critic.

judgment, judgement *n* brains, ballast, circumspection, depth, discernment, discretion, discrimination, intelligence, judiciousness, penetration, prudence, sagacity, sense, sensibility, taste, understanding, wisdom, wit; conclusion, consideration, decision, determination, estimation, notion, opinion, thought; adjudication, arbitration, award, censure, condemnation, decree, doom, sentence.

judicious *adj* cautious, considerate, cool, critical, discriminating, discreet, enlightened, provident, politic, prudent, rational, reasonable, sagacious, sensible, sober, solid, sound, staid, wise.

jug *n* cruse, ewer, flagon, pitcher, vessel.

juicy *adj* lush, moist, sappy, succulent, watery; entertaining, exciting, interesting, lively, racy, spicy.

jumble *vb* confound, confuse, disarrange, disorder, mix, muddle. • *n* confusion, disarrangement, disorder, medley, mess, mixture, muddle.

jump *vb* bound, caper, clear, hop, leap, skip, spring, vault. • *n* bound, caper, hop, leak, skip, spring, vault; fence, hurdle, obstacle; break, gap, interruption, space; advance, boost, increase, rise; jar, jolt, shock, start, twitch.

junction *n* combination, connection, coupling, hook-up, joining, linking, seam, union; conjunction, joint, juncture.

junta *n* cabal, clique, combination, confederacy, coterie, faction, gang, league, party, set.

just *adj* equitable, lawful, legitimate, reasonable, right, rightful; candid, even-handed, fair, fair-minded, impartial; blameless, conscientious, good, honest, honourable, pure, square, straightforward, virtuous; accurate, correct, exact, normal, proper, regular, true; condign, deserved, due, merited, suitable.

justice *n* accuracy, equitableness, equity, fairness, honesty, impartiality, justness, right; judge, justiciary.

justifiable *adj* defensible, fit, proper, right, vindicable, warrantable.

justification *n* defence, exculpation, excuse, exoneration, reason, vindication, warrant.

justify *vb* approve, defend, exculpate, excuse, exonerate, maintain, vindicate, support, warrant.

justness *n* accuracy, correctness, fitness, justice, precision, propriety.

juvenile *adj* childish, immature, puerile, young, youthful. • *n* boy, child, girl, youth.

juxtaposition *n* adjacency, contiguity, contact, proximity.

K

keen[1] *adj* ardent, eager, earnest, fervid, intense, vehement, vivid; acute, sharp; cutting; acrimonious, biting, bitter, caustic, poignant, pungent, sarcastic, severe; astute, discerning, intelligent, quick, sagacious, sharp-sighted, shrewd.

keen[2] *vb* bemoan, bewail, deplore, grieve, lament, mourn, sorrow, weep. • *n* coronach, dirge, elegy, lament, lamentation, monody, plaint, requiem, threnody.

keenness *n* ardour, eagerness, fervour, vehemence, zest; acuteness, sharpness; rigour, severity, sternness; acrimony, asperity, bitterness, causticity, causticness, pungency; astuteness, sagacity, shrewdness.

keep *vb* detain, hold, retain; continue, preserve; confine, detain, reserve, restrain, withhold; attend, guard, preserve, protect; adhere to, fulfil; celebrate, commemorate, honour, observe, perform, solemnize; maintain, support, sustain; husband, save, store; abide, dwell, lodge, stay, remain; endure, last. • *n* board, maintenance, subsistence, support; donjon, dungeon, stronghold, tower.

keeper *n* caretaker, conservator, curator, custodian, defender, gaoler, governor, guardian, jailer, superintendent, warden, warder, watchman.

keeping *n* care, charge, custody, guard, possession; feed, maintenance, support; agreement, conformity, congruity, consistency, harmony.

keepsake *n* memento, souvenir, token.

ken *n* cognizance, sight, view.

key *adj* basic, crucial, essential, important, major, principal. • *n* lock-opener, opener; clue, elucidation, explanation, guide, solution, translation; (*mus*) keynote, tonic; clamp, lever, wedge.

kick *vb* boot, punt; oppose, rebel, resist, spurn. • *n* force, intensity, power, punch, vitality; excitement, pleasure, thrill.

kidnap *vb* abduct, capture, carry off, remove, steal away.

kill *vb* assassinate, butcher, dispatch, destroy, massacre, murder, slaughter, slay.

kin *adj* akin, allied, cognate, kindred, related. • *n* affinity, consanguinity, relationship; connections, family, kindred, kinsfolk, relations, relatives, siblings.

kind[1] *adj* accommodating, amiable, beneficent, benevolent, benign, bland, bounteous, brotherly, charitable, clement, compassionate, complaisant, gentle, good, good-natured, forbearing, friendly, generous, gracious, humane, indulgent, lenient, mild, obliging, sympathetic, tender, tender-hearted.

kind[2] *n* breed, class, family, genus, race, set, species, type; brand, character, colour, denomination, description, form, make, manner, nature, persuasion, sort, stamp, strain, style.

kindle *vb* fire, ignite, inflame, light; animate, awaken, bestir, exasperate, excite, foment, incite, provoke, rouse, stimulate, stir, thrill, warm.

kindliness *n* amiability, benevolence, benignity, charity, compassion, friendliness, humanity, kindness, sympathy; gentleness, mildness, softness.

kindly *adj* appropriate, congenial, kindred, natural, proper; benevolent, considerate, friendly, gracious, humane, sympathetic, well-disposed. • *adv* agreeably, graciously, humanely, politely, thoughtfully.

kindness *n* benefaction, charity, favour; amiability, beneficence, benevolence, benignity, clemency, generosity, goodness, grace, humanity, kindliness, mildness, philanthropy, sympathy, tenderness.

kindred *adj* akin, allied, congenial, connected, related, sympathetic. • *n* affinity, consanguinity, flesh, relationship; folks, kin, kinsfolk, kinsmen, relations, relatives.

king *n* majesty, monarch, sovereign.

kingdom *n* dominion, empire, monarchy, rule, sovereignty, supremacy; region, tract; division, department, domain, province, realm.

kingly *adj* imperial, kinglike, monarchical, regal, royal, sovereign; august, glorious, grand, imperial, imposing, magnificent, majestic, noble, splendid.

kink *n* cramp, crick, curl, entanglement, knot, loop, twist; crochet, whim, wrinkle.

kinsfolk *n* kin, kindred, kinsmen, relations, relatives.

kit *n* equipment, implements, outfit, set, working.

knack *n* ability, address, adroitness, aptitude, aptness, dexterity, dextrousness, expertness, facility, quickness, readiness, skill.

knave *n* caitiff, cheat, miscreant, rascal, rogue, scamp, scapegrace, scoundrel, sharper, swindler, trickster, villain.

knavery *n* criminality, dishonesty, fraud, knavishness, rascality, scoundrelism, trickery, villainy.

knavish *adj* dishonest, fraudulent, rascally, scoundrelly, unprincipled, roguish, trickish, tricky, villainous.

knell *vb* announce, peal, ring, toll. • *n* chime, peal, ring, toll.

knife *vb* cut, slash, stab. • *n* blade, jackknife, lance.

knit *vb* connect, interlace, join, unite, weave.

knob *n* boss, bunch, hunch, lump, protuberance, stud.

knock *vb* clap, cuff, hit, rap, rattle, slap, strike, thump; beat, blow, box. • *n* blow, slap, smack, thump; blame, criticism, rejection, setback.

knoll *n* hill, hillock, mound.

knot *vb* complicate, entangle, gnarl, kink, tie, weave. • *n* complication, entanglement; connection, tie; joint, node, knag; bunch, rosette, tuft; band, cluster, clique, crew, gang, group, pack, set, squad.

knotty *adj* gnarled, hard, knaggy, knurled, knotted, rough, rugged; complex, difficult, harassing, intricate, involved, perplexing, troublesome.

know *vb* apprehend, comprehend, cognize, discern, perceive, recognize, see, understand; discriminate, distinguish.

knowing *adj* accomplished, competent, experienced, intelligent, proficient, qualified, skilful, well-informed; aware, conscious, percipient, sensible, thinking; cunning, expressive, significant.

knowingly *adv* consciously, intentionally, purposely, wittingly.

knowledge *n* apprehension, command, comprehension, discernment, judgment, perception, understanding, wit; acquaintance, acquirement, attainments, enlightenment, erudition, information, learning, lore, mastery, scholarship, science; cognition, cognizance, consciousness, ken, notice, prescience, recognition.

knowledgeable *adj* aware, conscious, experienced, well-informed; educated, intelligent, learned, scholarly.

knuckle *vb* cringe, crouch, stoop, submit, yield.

L

laborious *adj* assiduous, diligent, hardworking, indefatigable, industrious, painstaking, sedulous, toiling; arduous, difficult, fatiguing, hard, Herculean, irksome, onerous, tiresome, toilsome, wearisome.

labour *vb* drudge, endeavour, exert, strive, toil, travail, work. • *n* drudgery, effort, exertion, industry, pains, toil, work; childbirth, delivery, parturition.

labyrinth *n* entanglement, intricacy, maze, perplexity, windings.

labyrinthine *adj* confused, convoluted, intricate, involved, labyrinthian, labyrinthic, perplexing, winding.

lace *vb* attach, bind, fasten, intertwine, tie, twine. • *n* filigree, lattice, mesh, net, netting, network, openwork, web.

lacerate *vb* claw, cut, lancinate, mangle, rend, rip, sever, slash, tear, wound; afflict, harrow, rend, torture, wound.

lack *vb* need, want. • *n* dearth, default, defectiveness, deficiency, deficit, destitution, insufficiency, need, scantiness, scarcity, shortcoming, shortness, want.

lackadaisical *adj* languishing, sentimental, pensive.

laconic *adj* brief, compact, concise, pithy, sententious, short, succinct, terse.

lad *n* boy, schoolboy, stripling, youngster, youth.

lading *n* burden, cargo, freight, load.

ladylike *adj* courtly, genteel, refined, well-bred.

lag *vb* dawdle, delay, idle, linger, loiter, saunter, tarry.

laggard *n* idler, lingerer, loiterer, lounger, saunterer, sluggard.

lair *n* burrow, couch, den, form, resting place.

lambent *adj* flickering, gliding, gleaming, licking, touching, twinkling.

lame *vb* cripple, disable, hobble. • *adj* crippled, defective, disabled, halt, hobbling, limping; feeble, insufficient, poor, unsatisfactory, weak.

lament *vb* complain, grieve, keen, moan, mourn, sorrow, wail, weep; bemoan, bewail, deplore, regret. • *n* complaint, lamentation, moan, moaning, plaint, wailing; coronach, dirge, elegy, keen, monody, requiem, threnody.

lamentable *adj* deplorable, doleful, grievous, lamented, melancholy, woeful; contemptible, miserable, pitiful, poor, wretched.

lamentation *n* dirge, grief, lament, moan, moaning, mourning, plaint, ululation, sorrow, wailing.

lampoon *vb* calumniate, defame, lash, libel, parody, ridicule, satirize, slander. • *n* calumny, defamation, libel, parody, pasquinade, parody, satire, slander.

land *vb* arrive, debark, disembark. • *n* earth, ground, soil; country, district, province, region, reservation, territory, tract, weald.

landlord *n* owner, proprietor; host, hotelier, innkeeper.

landscape *n* prospect, scene, view.

language *n* dialect, speech, tongue, vernacular; conversation; expression, idiom, jargon, parlance, phraseology, slang, style, terminology; utterance, voice.

languid *adj* drooping, exhausted, faint, feeble, flagging, languishing, pining, weak; dull, heartless, heavy, inactive, listless, lukewarm, slow, sluggish, spiritless, torpid.

languish *vb* decline, droop, fade, fail, faint, pine, sicken, sink, wither.

languor *n* debility, faintness, feebleness, languidness, languishment, weakness; apathy, ennui, heartlessness, heaviness, lethargy, listlessness, torpidness, torpor, weariness.

lank *adj* attenuated, emaciated, gaunt, lean, meagre, scraggy, slender, skinny, slim, starveling, thin.

lap¹ *vb* drink, lick, mouth, tongue; plash, ripple, splash, wash; quaff, sip, sup, swizzle, tipple. • *n* draught, dram, drench, drink, gulp, lick, swig, swill, quaff, sip, sup, suck; plash, splash, wash.

lap² *vb* cover, enfold, fold, turn, twist, swaddle, wrap; distance, pass, outdistance, overlap. • *n* fold, flap, lappet, lapel, ply, plait; ambit, beat, circle, circuit, cycle, loop, orbit, revolution, round, tour, turn, walk.

lapse *vb* glide, sink, slide, slip; err, fail, fall. • *n* course, flow, gliding; declension, decline, fall; error, fault, indiscretion, misstep, shortcoming, slip.

larceny *n* pilfering, robbery, stealing, theft, thievery.

large *adj* big, broad, bulky, colossal, elephantine, enormous, heroic, great, huge, immense, vast; broad, expanded, extensive, spacious, wide; abundant, ample, copious, full, liberal, plentiful; capacious, comprehensive.

lascivious *adj* concupiscent, immodest, incontinent, goatish, lecherous, lewd, libidinous, loose, lubricious, lustful, prurient, salacious, sensual, unchaste, voluptuous, wanton.

lash¹ *vb* belay, bind, strap, tie; fasten, join, moor, pinion, secure.

lash² *vb* beat, castigate, chastise, flagellate, flail, flay, flog, goad, scourge, swinge, thrash, whip; assail, censure, excoriate, lampoon, satirize, trounce. • *n* scourge, strap, thong, whip; cut, slap, smack, stroke, stripe.

lass *n* damsel, girl, lassie, maiden, miss.

lassitude *n* dullness, exhaustion, fatigue, languor, languidness, prostration, tiredness, weariness.

last¹ *vb* abide, carry on, continue, dwell, endure, extend, maintain, persist, prevail, remain, stand, stay, survive.

last² *adj* hindermost, hindmost, latest; conclusive, final, terminal, ultimate; eventual, endmost, extreme, farthest, ultimate; greatest, highest, maximal, maximum, most, supreme, superlative, utmost; latest, newest; aforegoing, foregoing, latter, preceding; departing, farewell, final, leaving, parting, valedictory. • *n* conclusion, consummation, culmination, end, ending, finale, finis, finish, termination.

last³ *n* cast, form, matrix, mould, shape, template.

lasting *adj* abiding, durable, enduring, fixed, perennial, permanent, perpetual, stable.

lastly *adv* conclusively, eventually, finally, ultimately.

late *adj* behindhand, delayed, overdue, slow, tardy; deceased, former; recent. • *adv* lately, recently, sometime; tardily.

latent *adj* abeyant, concealed, hidden, invisible, occult, secret, unseen, veiled.

latitude *n* amplitude, breadth, compass, extent, range, room, scope; freedom, indulgence, liberty; laxity.

latter *adj* last, latest, modern, recent.

lattice *n* espalier, grating, latticework, trellis.

laud *vb* approve, celebrate, extol, glorify, magnify, praise.

laudable *adj* commendable, meritorious, praiseworthy.

laugh *vb* cackle, chortle, chuckle, giggle, guffaw, snicker, snigger, titter. • *n* chortle, chuckle, giggle, guffaw, laughter, titter.

laughable *adj* amusing, comical, diverting, droll, farcical, funny, ludicrous, mirthful, ridiculous.

laughter *n* cackle, chortle, chuckle, glee, giggle, guffaw, laugh, laughing.

launch *vb* cast, dart, dispatch, hurl, lance, project, throw; descant, dilate, enlarge, expiate; begin, commence, inaugurate, open, start.

lavish *vb* dissipate, expend, spend, squander, waste. • *adj* excessive, extravagant, generous, immoderate, overliberal, prodigal, profuse, thriftless, unrestrained, unstinted, unthrifty, wasteful.

law *n* act, code, canon, command, commandment, covenant, decree, edict, enactment, order, precept, principle, statute, regulation, rule; jurisprudence; litigation, process, suit.

lawful *adj* constitutional, constituted, legal, legalized, legitimate; allowable, authorized, permissible, warrantable; equitable, rightful, just, proper, valid.

lawless *adj* anarchic, anarchical, chaotic, disorderly, insubordinate, rebellious, reckless, riotous, seditious, wild.

lawyer *n* advocate, attorney, barrister, counsel, counsellor, pettifogger, solicitor.

lax *adj* loose, relaxed, slow; drooping, flabby, soft; neglectful, negligent, remiss; dissolute, immoral, licentious, seditious, wild.

lay¹ *vb* deposit, establish, leave, place, plant, posit, put, set, settle, spread; arrange, dispose, locate, organize, position; bear, produce; advance, lodge, offer, submit; allocate, allot, ascribe, assign, attribute, charge, impute; concoct, contrive, design, plan, plot, prepare; apply, burden, encumber, impose, saddle, tax; bet, gamble, hazard, risk, stake, wager; allay, alleviate, appease, assuage, calm, relieve, soothe, still, suppress; disclose, divulge, explain, reveal, show, unveil; acquire, grab, grasp, seize; assault, attack, beat up; discover, find, unearth; bless, confirm, consecrate, ordain. • *n* arrangement, array, form, formation; attitude, aspect, bearing, demeanour, direction, lie, pose, position, posture, set.

lay[2] *adj* amateur, inexpert, nonprofessional; civil, laic, laical, nonclerical, nonecclesiastical, nonreligious, secular, temporal, unclerical.

lay[3] *n* ballad, carol, ditty, lied, lyric, ode, poem, rhyme, round, song, verse.

layer *n* bed, course, lay, seam, stratum.

laziness *n* idleness, inactivity, indolence, slackness, sloth, fulness, sluggishness, tardiness.

lazy *adj* idle, inactive, indolent, inert, slack, slothful, slow, sluggish, supine, torpid.

lead *vb* conduct, deliver, direct, draw, escort, guide; front, head, precede; advance, excel, outstrip, pass; allure, entice, induce, persuade, prevail; conduce, contribute, serve, tend. • *adj* chief, first, foremost, main, primary, prime, principal. • *n* direction, guidance, leadership; advance; precedence, priority.

leader *n* conductor, director, guide; captain, chief, chieftain, commander, head; superior, dominator, victor.

leading *adj* governing, ruling; capital, chief, first, foremost, highest, principal, superior.

league *vb* ally, associate, band, combine, confederate, unite. • *n* alliance, association, coalition, combination, combine, confederacy, confederation, consortium, union.

leak *vb* drip, escape, exude, ooze, pass, percolate, spill. • *n* chink, crack, crevice, hole, fissure, oozing, opening; drip, leakage, leaking, percolation.

lean[1] *adj* bony, emaciated, gaunt, lank, meagre, poor, skinny, thin; dull, barren, jejune, meagre, tame; inadequate, pitiful, scanty, slender; bare, barren, infertile, unproductive.

lean[2] *vb* incline, slope; bear, recline, repose, rest; confide, depend, rely, trust.

leaning *n* aptitude, bent, bias, disposition, inclination, liking, predilection, proneness, propensity, tendency.

leap *vb* bound, clear, jump, spring, vault; caper, frisk, gambol, hop, skip. • *n* bound, jump, spring, vault; caper, frisk, gambol, hop, skip.

learn *vb* acquire, ascertain, attain, collect, gain, gather, hear, memorize.

learned *adj* erudite, lettered, literate, scholarly, well-read; expert, experienced, knowing, skilled, versed, well-informed.

learner *n* beginner, novice, pupil, student, tyro.

learning *n* acquirements, attainments, culture, education, information, knowledge, lore, scholarship, tuition.

least *adj* meanest, minutest, smallest, tiniest.

leave[1] *vb* abandon, decamp, go, quit, vacate, withdraw; desert, forsake, relinquish, renounce; commit, consign, refer; cease, desist from, discontinue, refrain, stop; allow, let, let alone, permit; bequeath, demise, desist, will.

leave[2] *n* allowance, liberty, permission, licence, sufferance; departure, retirement, withdrawal; adieu, farewell, goodbye.

leaven *vb* ferment, lighten, raise; colour, elevate, imbue, inspire, lift, permeate, tinge; infect, vitiate. • *n* barm, ferment, yeast; influence, inspiration.

leavings *npl* bits, dregs, fragments, leftovers, pieces, relics, remains, remnants, scraps.

lecherous *adj* carnal, concupiscent, incontinent, lascivious, lewd, libidinous, lubricious, lustful, wanton, salacious, unchaste.

lechery *n* concupiscence, lasciviousness, lewdness, lubriciousness, lubricity, lust, salaciousness, salacity.

lecture *vb* censure, chide, reprimand, reprove, scold, sermonize; address, harangue, teach. • *n* censure, lecturing, lesson, reprimand, reproof, scolding; address, discourse, prelection.

ledge *n* projection, ridge, shelf.

lees *npl* dregs, precipitate, refuse, sediment, settlings.

leg *n* limb, prop.

legacy *n* bequest, gift, heirloom; heritage, inheritance, tradition.

legal *adj* allowable, authorized, constitutional, lawful, legalized, legitimate, proper, sanctioned.

legalize *vb* authorize, legitimate, legitimatize, legitimize, permit, sanction.

legend *n* fable, fiction, myth, narrative, romance, story, tale.

legendary *adj* fabulous, fictitious, mythical, romantic.

legible *adj* clear, decipherable, fair, distinct, plain, readable; apparent, discoverable, recognizable, manifest.

legion *n* army, body, cohort, column, corps, detachment, detail, division, force, maniple, phalanx, platoon; squad; army, horde, host, multitude, number, swarm, throng. • *adj* many, multitudinous, myriad, numerous.

legislate *vb* enact, ordain.

legitimacy *n* lawfulness, legality; genuineness.

legitimate *adj* authorized, lawful, legal, sanctioned; genuine, valid; correct, justifiable, logical, reasonable, warrantable, warranted.

leisure *n* convenience, ease, freedom, liberty, opportunity, recreation, retirement, vacation.

lend *vb* advance, afford, bestow, confer, furnish, give, grant, impart, loan, supply.

lengthen *vb* elongate, extend, produce, prolong, stretch; continue, protract.

lengthy *adj* diffuse, lengthened, long, long-drawn-out, prolix, prolonged, protracted.

lenience, leniency *n* clemency, compassion, forbearance, gentleness, lenity, mercy, mildness, tenderness.

lenient *adj* assuasive, lenitive, mitigating, mitigative, softening, soothing; clement, easy, forbearing, gentle, humouring, indulgent, long-suffering, merciful, mild, tender, tolerant.

lesion *n* derangement, disorder, hurt, injury.

less *adj* baser, inferior, lower, smaller; decreased, fewer, lesser, reduced, smaller, shorter; • *adv* barely, below, least, under; decreasingly. • *prep* excepting, lacking, minus, sans, short of, without.

lessen *vb* abate, abridge, contract, curtail, decrease, diminish, narrow, reduce, shrink; degrade, lower; dwindle, weaken.

lesson *n* exercise, task; instruction, precept; censure, chiding, lecture, lecturing, rebuke, reproof, scolding.

let[1] *vb* admit, allow, authorize, permit, suffer; charter, hire, lease, rent.

let[2] *vb* hinder, impede, instruct, prevent. • *n* hindrance, impediment, interference, obstacle, obstruction, restriction.

lethal *adj* deadly, destructive, fatal, mortal, murderous.

lethargic *adj* apathetic, comatose, drowsy, dull, heavy, inactive, inert, sleepy, stupid, stupefied, torpid.

lethargy *n* apathy, coma, drowsiness, dullness, hypnotism, inactiveness, inactivity, inertia, sleepiness, sluggishness, stupefaction, stupidity, stupor, torpor.

letter *n* epistle, missive, note.

lettered *adj* bookish, educated, erudite, learned, literary, versed, well-read.

levee *n* ceremony, entertainment, reception, party, soiree; embankment.

level *vb* equalize, flatten, horizontalize, smooth; demolish, destroy, raze; aim, direct, point. • *adj* equal, even, flat, flush, horizontal, plain, plane, smooth. • *n* altitude, degree, equality, evenness, plain, plane, smoothness; deck, floor, layer, stage, storey, tier.

levity *n* buoyancy, facetiousness, fickleness, flightiness, flippancy, frivolity, giddiness, inconstancy, levity, volatility.

levy *vb* collect, exact, gather, tax; call, muster, raise, summon. • *n* duty, tax.

lewd *adj* despicable, impure, lascivious, libidinous, licentious, loose, lustful, profligate, unchaste, vile, wanton, wicked.

liability *n* accountableness, accountability, duty, obligation, responsibility, tendency; exposedness; debt, indebtedness, obligation.

liable *adj* accountable, amenable, answerable, bound, responsible; exposed, likely, obnoxious, subject.

liaison *n* amour, intimacy, intrigue; connection, relation, union.

libel *vb* calumniate, defame, lampoon, satirize, slander, vilify. • *n* calumny, defamation, lampoon, satire, slander, vilification, vituperation.

liberal *adj* beneficent, bountiful, charitable, disinterested, free, generous, munificent, open-hearted, princely, unselfish; broad-minded, catholic, chivalrous, enlarged, high-minded, honourable, magnanimous, tolerant, unbiased, unbigoted; abundant, ample, bounteous, full, large, plentiful, unstinted; humanizing, liberalizing, refined, refining.

liberality *n* beneficence, bountifulness, bounty, charity, disinterestedness, generosity, kindness, munificence; benefaction, donation, gift, gratuity, present; broad-mindedness, catholicity, candour, impartiality, large-mindedness, magnanimity, toleration.

liberate *vb* deliver, discharge, disenthral, emancipate, free, manumit, ransom, release.

libertine *adj* corrupt, depraved, dissolute, licentious, profligate, rakish. • *n* debauchee, lecher, profligate, rake, roue, voluptuary.

liberty *n* emancipation, freedom, independence, liberation, self-direction, self-government; franchise, immunity, privilege; leave, licence, permission.

libidinous *adj* carnal, concupiscent, debauched, impure, incontinent, lascivious, lecherous, lewd, loose, lubricious, lustful, salacious, sensual, unchaste, wanton, wicked.

licence *n* authorization, leave, permission, privilege, right; certificate, charter, dispensation, imprimatur, permit, warrant; anarchy, disorder, freedom, lawlessness, laxity, liberty.

license *vb* allow, authorize, grant, permit, warrant; suffer, tolerate.

licentious *adj* disorderly, riotous, uncontrolled, uncurbed, ungovernable, unrestrained, unruly, wanton; debauched, dissolute, lax, libertine, loose, profligate, rakish; immoral, impure, lascivious, lecherous, lewd, libertine, libidinous, lustful, sensual, unchaste, wicked.

lick *vb* beat, flog, spank, thrash; lap, taste. • *n* blow, slap, stroke; salt-spring.

lie[1] *vb* couch, recline, remain, repose, rest; consist, pertain.

lie[2] *vb* equivocate, falsify, fib, prevaricate, romance. • *n* equivocation, falsehood, falsification, fib, misrepresentation, prevarication, untruth; delusion, illusion.

lief *adv* freely, gladly, willingly.

life *n* activity, alertness, animation, briskness, energy, sparkle, spirit, sprightliness, verve, vigour, vivacity; behaviour, conduct, deportment; being, duration, existence, lifetime; autobiography, biography, curriculum vitae, memoirs, story.

lifeless *adj* dead, deceased, defunct, extinct, inanimate; cold, dull, flat, frigid, inert, lethargic, passive, pulseless, slow, sluggish, tame, torpid.

lift *vb* elevate, exalt, hoist, raise, uplift. • *n* aid, assistance, help; elevator.

light[1] *vb* alight, land, perch, settle. • *adj* porous, sandy, spongy, well-leavened; loose, sandy; free, portable, unburdened, unencumbered; inconsiderable, moderate, negligible, slight, small, trifling, trivial, unimportant; ethereal, feathery, flimsy, gossamer, insubstantial, weightless; easy, effortless, facile; fickle, frivolous, unsettled, unsteady, volatile; airy, buoyant, carefree, light-hearted, lightsome; unaccented, unstressed, weak.

light[2] *vb* conflagrate, fire, ignite, inflame, kindle; brighten, illume, illuminate, illumine, luminate, irradiate, lighten. • *adj* bright, clear, fair, lightsome, luminous, pale, pearly, whitish. • *n* dawn, day, daybreak, sunrise; blaze, brightness, effulgence, gleam, illumination, luminosity, phosphorescence, radiance, ray; candle, lamp, lantern, lighthouse, taper, torch; comprehension, enlightenment, information, insight, instruction, knowledge; elucidation, explanation, illustration; attitude, construction, interpretation, observation, reference, regard, respect, view.

lighten[1] *vb* allay, alleviate, ease, mitigate, palliate; disburden, disencumber, relieve, unburden, unload.

lighten[2] *vb* brighten, gleam, shine; light, illume, illuminate, illumine, irradiate; enlighten, inform; emit, flash.

light-headed *adj* dizzy, giddy, vertiginous; confused, delirious, wandering; addle-pated, frivolous, giddy, heedless, indiscreet, light, rattle-brained, thoughtless, volatile.

light-hearted *adj* blithe, blithesome, carefree, cheerful, frolicsome, gay, glad, gladsome, gleeful, happy, jocund, jovial, joyful, lightsome, merry.

lightness *n* flightiness, frivolity, giddiness, levity, volatility; agility, buoyancy, facility.

like[1] *vb* approve, please; cherish, enjoy, love, relish; esteem, fancy, regard; choose, desire, elect, list, prefer, select, wish. • *n* liking, partiality, preference.

like[2] *adj* alike, allied, analogous, cognate, corresponding, parallel, resembling, similar; equal, same; likely, probable. • *adv* likely, probably. • *n* counterpart, equal, match, peer, twin.

likelihood *n* probability, verisimilitude.

likely *adj* credible, liable, possible, probable; agreeable, appropriate, convenient, likable, pleasing, suitable, well-adapted, well-suited. • *adv* doubtlessly, presumably, probably.

likeness *n* appearance, form, parallel, resemblance, semblance, similarity, similitude; copy, counterpart, effigy, facsimile, image, picture, portrait, representation.

liking *n* desire, fondness, partiality, wish; appearance, bent, bias, disposition, inclination, leaning, penchant, predisposition, proneness, propensity, tendency, turn.

limb *n* arm, extremity, leg, member; bough, branch, offshoot.

limit *vb* bound, circumscribe, define; check, condition, hinder, restrain, restrict. • *n* bound, boundary, bourn, confine, frontier, march, precinct, term, termination, terminus; check, hindrance, obstruction, restraint, restriction.

limitation *n* check, constraint, restraint, restriction.

limitless *adj* boundless, endless, eternal, illimitable, immeasurable, infinite, never-ending, unbounded, undefined, unending, unlimited.

limp[1] *vb* halt, hitch, hobble, totter. • *n* hitch, hobble, shamble, shuffle, totter.

limp[2] *adj* drooping, droopy, floppy, sagging, weak; flabby, flaccid, flexible, limber, pliable, relaxed, slack, soft.

limpid *adj* bright, clear, crystal, crystalline, lucid, pellucid, pure, translucent, transparent.

line *vb* align, line up, range, rank, regiment; border, bound, edge, fringe, hem, interline, march, rim, verge; seam, stripe, streak, striate, trace; carve, chisel, crease, cut, crosshatch; define, delineate, describe. • *n* mark, streak, stripe; cable, cord, rope, string, thread; rank, row; ancestry, family, lineage, race, succession; course, method; business, calling, employment, job, occupation, post, pursuit.

lineage *n* ancestry, birth, breed, descendants, descent, extraction, family, forebears, forefathers, genealogy, house, line, offspring, progeny, race.

lineament *n* feature, line, outline, trait.

linen *n* cloth, fabric, flax, lingerie.

linger *vb* dally, dawdle, delay, idle, lag, loiter, remain, saunter, stay, tarry, wait.

link *vb* bind, conjoin, connect, fasten, join, tie, unite. • *n* bond, connection, connective, copula, coupler, joint, juncture; division, member, part, piece.

liquefy *vb* dissolve, fuse, melt, thaw.

liquid *adj* fluid; clear, dulcet, flowing, mellifluous, mellifluent, melting, soft. • *n* fluid, liquor.

list[1] *vb* alphabetize, catalogue, chronicle, codify, docket, enumerate, file, index, inventory, record, register, tabulate, tally; enlist, enroll; choose, desire, elect, like, please, prefer, wish. • *n* catalogue, enumeration, index, inventory, invoice, register, roll, schedule, scroll, series, table, tally; border, bound, limit; border, edge, selvedge, strip, stripe; fillet, listel.

list[2] *vb* cant, heel, incline, keel, lean, pitch, tilt, tip. • *n* cant, inclination, incline, leaning, pitch, slope, tilt, tip.

listen *vb* attend, eavesdrop, hark, hear, hearken, heed, obey, observe.

listless *adj* apathetic, careless, heedless, impassive, inattentive, indifferent, indolent, languid, torpid, vacant, supine, thoughtless, vacant.

listlessness *n* apathy, carelessness, heedlessness, impassivity, inattention, indifference, indolence, languidness, languor, supineness, thoughtlessness, torpor, torpidity, vacancy.

literally *adv* actually, really; exactly, precisely, rigorously, strictly.

literary *adj* bookish, book-learned, erudite, instructed, learned, lettered, literate, scholarly, well-read.

literature *n* erudition, learning, letters, lore, writings.

lithe *adj* flexible, flexile, limber, pliable, pliant, supple.

litigation *n* contending, contest, disputing, lawsuit.

litigious *adj* contentious, disputatious, quarrelsome; controvertible, disputable.

litter *vb* derange, disarrange, disorder, scatter, strew; bear. • *n* bedding, couch, palanquin, sedan, stretcher; confusion, disarray, disorder, mess, untidiness; fragments, rubbish, shreds, trash.

little *adj* diminutive, infinitesimal, minute, small, tiny, wee; brief, short, small; feeble, inconsiderable, insignificant, moderate, petty, scanty, slender, slight, trivial, unimportant, weak; contemptible, illiberal, mean, narrow, niggardly, paltry, selfish, stingy. • *n* handful, jot, modicum, pinch, pittance, trifle, whit.

live[1] *vb* be, exist; continue, endure, last, remain, survive; abide, dwell, reside; fare, feed, nourish, subsist, support; continue, lead, pass.

live[2] *adj* alive, animate, living, quick; burning, hot, ignited; bright, brilliant, glowing, lively, vivid; active, animated, earnest, glowing, wide-awake.

livelihood *n* living, maintenance, subsistence, support, sustenance.

liveliness *n* activity, animation, briskness, gaiety, spirit, sprightliness, vivacity.

lively *adj* active, agile, alert, brisk, energetic, nimble, quick, smart, stirring, supple, vigorous, vivacious; airy, animated, blithe, blithesome, buoyant, frolicsome, gleeful, jocund, jolly, merry, spirited, sportive, sprightly, spry; bright, brilliant, clear, fresh, glowing, strong, vivid; dynamic, forcible, glowing, impassioned, intense, keen, nervous, piquant, racy, sparkling, strenuous, vigorous.

living *adj* alive, breathing, existing, live, organic, quick; active, lively, quickening. • *n* livelihood, maintenance, subsistence, support; estate, keeping; benefice.

load *vb* freight, lade; burden, cumber, encumber, oppress, weigh. • *n* burden, freightage, pack, weight; cargo, freight, lading; clog, deadweight, encumbrance, incubus, oppression, pressure.

loafer *n* (*sl*) bum, idler, lounger, vagabond, vagrant.

loath *adj* averse, backward, disinclined, indisposed, reluctant, unwilling.

loathe *vb* abhor, abominate, detest, dislike, hate, recoil.

loathing *n* abhorrence, abomination, antipathy, aversion, detestation, disgust, hatred, horror, repugnance, revulsion.

loathsome *adj* disgusting, nauseating, nauseous, offensive, palling, repulsive, revolting, sickening; abominable, abhorrent, detestable, execrable, hateful, odious, shocking.

local *adj* limited, neighbouring, provincial, regional, restricted, sectional, territorial, topical.

locality *n* location, neighbourhood, place, position, site, situation, spot.

locate *vb* determine, establish, fix, place, set, settle.

lock[1] *vb* bolt, fasten, padlock, seal; confine; clog, impede, restrain, stop; clasp, embrace, encircle, enclose, grapple, hug, join, press. • *n* bolt, fastening, padlock; embrace, grapple, hug.

lock[2] *n* curl, ringlet, tress, tuft.

lodge *vb* deposit, fix, settle; fix, place, plant; accommodate, cover, entertain, harbour, quarter, shelter; abide, dwell, inhabit, live, reside, rest; remain, rest, sojourn, stay, stop. • *n* cabin, cot, cottage, hovel, hut, shed; cave, den, haunt, lair; assemblage, assembly, association club, group, society.

lodging *n* abode, apartment, dwelling, habitation, quarters, residence; cover, harbour, protection, refuge, shelter.

loftiness *n* altitude, elevation, height; arrogance, haughtiness, pride, vanity; dignity, grandeur, sublimity.

lofty *adj* elevated, high, tall, towering; arrogant, haughty, proud; eminent, exalted, sublime; dignified, imposing, majestic, stately.

logical *adj* close, coherent, consistent, dialectical, sound, valid; discriminating, rational, reasoned.

loiter *vb* dally, dawdle, delay, dilly-dally, idle, lag, linger, saunter, stroll, tarry.

loneliness *n* isolation, retirement, seclusion, solitariness, solitude; desolation, dreariness, forlornness.

lonely *adj* apart, dreary, isolated, lonesome, remote, retired, secluded, separate, sequestrated, solitary; alone, lone, companionless, friendless, unaccompanied; deserted, desolate, forlorn, forsaken, withdrawn.

lonesome *adj* cheerless, deserted, desolate, dreary, gloomy, lone, lonely.

long[1] *vb* anticipate, await, expect; aspire, covet, crave, desire, hanker, lust, pine, wish, yearn.

long[2] *adj* drawn-out, extended, extensive, far-reaching, lengthy, prolonged, protracted, stretched; diffuse, long-winded, prolix, tedious, wearisome; backward, behindhand, dilatory, lingering, slack, slow, tardy.

longing *n* aspiration, coveting, craving, desire, hankering, hunger, pining, yearning.

long-suffering *adj* enduring, forbearing, patient. • *n* clemency, endurance, forbearing.

look *vb* behold, examine, notice, see, search; consider, inspect, investigate, observe, study, contemplate, gaze, regard, scan, survey, view; anticipate, await, expect; heed, mind, watch; face, front; appear, seem. • *n* examination, gaze, glance, peep, peer, search; appearance, aspect, complexion; air, aspect, manner, mien.

loophole *n* aperture, crenellation, loop, opening; excuse, plea, pretence, pretext, subterfuge.

loose *vb* free, liberate, release, unbind, undo, unfasten, unlash, unlock, untie; ease, loosen, relax, slacken; detach, disconnect, disengage. • *adj* unbound, unconfined, unfastened, unsewn, untied; disengaged, free, unattached; relaxed; diffuse, diffusive, prolix, rambling, unconnected; ill-defined, indefinite, indeterminate, indistinct, vague; careless, heedless, negligent, lax, slack; debauched, dissolute, immoral, licentious, unchaste, wanton.

loosen *vb* liberate, relax, release, separate, slacken, unbind, unloose, untie.

looseness *n* easiness, slackness; laxity, levity; lewdness, unchastity, wantonness, wickedness; diarrhoea, flux.

loot *vb* pillage, plunder, ransack, rifle, rob, sack. • *n* booty, plunder, spoil.

lop *vb* cut, truncate; crop, curtail, dock, prune; detach, dissever, sever.

loquacious *adj* garrulous, talkative, voluble, wordy; noisy, speaking, talking; babbling, blabbing, tattling, tell-tale.

loquacity *n* babbling, chattering, gabbling, garrulity, loquaciousness, talkativeness, volubility.

lord *n* earl, noble, nobleman, peer, viscount; governor, king, liege, master, monarch, prince, ruler, seigneur, seignior, sovereign, superior; husband, spouse.

lordly *adj* aristocratic, dignified, exalted, grand, lofty, majestic, noble; arrogant, despotic, domineering, haughty, imperious, insolent, masterful, overbearing, proud, tyrannical; large, liberal.

lordship *n* authority, command, control, direction, domination, dominion, empire, government, rule, sovereignty, sway; manor, domain, seigneury, seigniory.

lore *n* erudition, knowledge, learning, letters, scholarship; admonition, advice, counsel, doctrine, instruction, lesson, teaching, wisdom.

lose *vb* deprive, dispossess, forfeit, miss; dislodge, displace, mislay, misspend, squander, waste; decline, fall, succumb, yield.

loss *n* deprivation, failure, forfeiture, privation; casualty, damage, defeat, destruction, detriment, disadvantage, injury, overthrow, ruin; squandering, waste.

lost *adj* astray, missing; forfeited, missed, unredeemed; dissipated, misspent, squandered, wasted; bewildered, confused, distracted, perplexed, puzzled; absent, absent-minded, abstracted, dreamy, napping, preoccupied; abandoned, corrupt, debauched, depraved, dissolute, graceless, hardened, incorrigible, irreclaimable, licentious, profligate, reprobate, shameless, unchaste, wanton; destroyed, ruined.

lot *n* allotment, apportionment, destiny, doom, fate; accident, chance, fate, fortune, hap, haphazard, hazard; division, parcel, part, portion.

loth *adj* averse, disinclined, disliking, reluctant, unwilling.

loud *adj* high-sounding, noisy, resounding, sonorous; deafening, stentorian, strong, stunning; boisterous, clamorous, noisy, obstreperous, tumultuous, turbulent, uproarious, vociferous; emphatic, impressive, positive, vehement; flashy, gaudy, glaring, loud, ostentatious, showy, vulgar.

lounge *vb* loll, recline, sprawl; dawdle, idle, loaf, loiter.

love *vb* adore, like, worship. • *n* accord, affection, amity, courtship, delight, fondness, friendship, kindness, regard, tenderness, warmth; adoration, amour, ardour, attachment, passion; devotion, inclination, liking; benevolence, charity, goodwill.

lovely *adj* beautiful, charming, delectable, delightful, enchanting, exquisite, graceful, pleasing, sweet, winning; admirable, adorable, amiable.

loving *adj* affectionate, dear, fond, kind, tender.

low[1] *vb* bellow, moo.

low[2] *adj* basal, depressed, profound; gentle, grave, soft, subdued; cheap, humble, mean, plebeian, vulgar; abject, base, baseminded, degraded, dirty, grovelling, ignoble, low-minded, menial, scurvy, servile, shabby, slavish, vile; derogatory, disgraceful, dishonourable, disreputable, unbecoming, undignified, ungentlemanly, unhandsome, unmanly; exhausted, feeble, reduced, weak; frugal, plain, poor, simple, spare; lowly, reverent, submissive; dejected, depressed, dispirited.

lower[1] *vb* depress, drop, sink, subside; debase, degrade, disgrace, humble, humiliate, reduce; abate, decrease, diminish, lessen. • *adj* baser, inferior, less, lesser, shorter, smaller; subjacent, under.

lower[2] *vb* blacken, darken, frown, glower, threaten.

lowering *adj* dark, clouded, cloudy, lurid, murky, overcast, threatening.

lowliness *n* humbleness, humility, meekness, self-abasement, submissiveness.

lowly *adj* gentle, humble, meek, mild, modest, plain, poor, simple, unassuming, unpretending, unpretentious; low-born, mean, servile.

loyal *adj* constant, devoted, faithful, patriotic, true.

loyalty *n* allegiance, constancy, devotion, faithfulness, fealty, fidelity, patriotism.

lubricious *adj* slippery, smooth; uncertain, unstable, wavering; impure, incontinent, lascivious, lecherous, lewd, libidinous, licentious, lustful, salacious, unchaste, wanton.

lucid *adj* beaming, bright, brilliant, luminous, radiant, resplendent, shining, clear, crystalline, diaphanous, limpid, lucent, pellucid, pure, transparent; clear, distinct, evident, intelligible, obvious, perspicuous, plain; reasonable, sane, sober, sound.

luck *n* accident, casualty, chance, fate, fortune, hap, haphazard, hazard, serendipity, success.

luckless *adj* ill-fated, ill-starred, unfortunate, unhappy, unlucky, unpropitious, unprosperous, unsuccessful.

lucky *adj* blessed, favoured, fortunate, happy, successful; auspicious, favourable, propitious, prosperous.

lucrative *adj* advantageous, gainful, paying, profitable, remunerative.

ludicrous *adj* absurd, burlesque, comic, comical, droll, farcical, funny, laughable, odd, ridiculous, sportive.

lugubrious *adj* complaining, doleful, gloomy, melancholy, mournful, sad, serious, sombre, sorrowful.

lukewarm *adj* blood-warm, tepid, thermal; apathetic, cold, dull, indifferent, listless, unconcerned, torpid.

lull *vb* calm, compose, hush, quiet, still, tranquillize; abate, cease, decrease, diminish, subside. • *n* calm, calmness, cessation.

lumber[1] *vb* rumble, shamble, trudge.

lumber[2] *n* refuse, rubbish, trash, trumpery; wood.

luminous *adj* effulgent, incandescent, radiant, refulgent, resplendent, shining; bright, brilliant, clear; clear, lucid, lucent, perspicuous, plain.

lunacy *n* aberration, craziness, dementia, derangement, insanity, madness, mania.

lunatic *adj* crazy, demented, deranged, insane, mad, psychopathic. • *n* madman, maniac, psychopath.

lurch *vb* appropriate, filch, pilfer, purloin, steal; deceive, defeat, disappoint, evade; ambush, lurk, skulk; contrive, dodge, shift, trick; pitch, sway.

lure *vb* allure, attract, decoy, entice, inveigle, seduce, tempt. • *n* allurement, attraction, bait, decoy, enticement, temptation.

lurid *adj* dismal, ghastly, gloomy, lowering, murky, pale, wan; glaring, sensational, startling, unrestrained.

lurk *vb* hide, prowl, skulk, slink, sneak, snoop.

luscious *adj* delicious, delightful, grateful, palatable, pleasing, savoury, sweet.

lush *adj* fresh, juicy, luxuriant, moist, sappy, succulent, watery.

lust *vb* covet, crave, desire, hanker, need, want, yearn. • *n* cupidity, desire, longing; carnality, concupiscence, lasciviousness, lechery, lewdness, lubricity, salaciousness, salacity, wantonness.

lustful *adj* carnal, concupiscent, hankering, lascivious, lecherous, licentious, libidinous, lubricious, salacious.

lustily *adv* strongly, vigorously.

lustiness *n* hardihood, power, robustness, stoutness, strength, sturdiness, vigour.

lustre *n* brightness, brilliance, brilliancy, splendour.

lusty *adj* healthful, lively, robust, stout, strong, sturdy, vigorous; bulky, burly, corpulent, fat, large, stout.

luxuriance *n* exuberance, profusion, superabundance.

luxuriant *adj* exuberant, plenteous, plentiful, profuse, superabundant.

luxuriate *vb* abound, delight, enjoy, flourish, indulge, revel.

luxurious *adj* epicurean, opulent, pampered, self-indulgent, sensual, sybaritic, voluptuous.

luxury *n* epicureanism, epicurism, luxuriousness, opulence, sensuality, voluptuousness; delight, enjoyment, gratification, indulgence, pleasure; dainty, delicacy, treat.

lying *adj* equivocating, false, mendacious, untruthful, untrue.

lyric *adj* dulcet, euphonious, lyrical, mellifluous, mellifluent, melodic, melodious, musical, poetic, silvery, tuneful.

lyrical *adj* ecstatic, enthusiastic, expressive, impassion; dulcet, lyric, mellifluous, mellifluent, melodic, melodious, musical, poetic.

M

macabre *adj* cadaverous, deathlike, deathly, dreadful, eerie, frightening, frightful, ghoulish, grim, grisly, gruesome, hideous, horrid, morbid, unearthly, weird.

mace *n* baton, staff, truncheon.

macerate *vb* harass, mortify, torture; digest, soak, soften, steep.

Machiavellian *adj* arch, artful, astute, crafty, crooked, cunning, deceitful, designing, diplomatic, insidious, intriguing, shrewd, sly, subtle, tricky, wily.

machination *n* artifice, cabal, conspiracy, contrivance, design, intrigue, plot, scheme, stratagem, trick.

machine *n* instrument, puppet, tool; machinery, organization, system; engine.

mad *adj* crazed, crazy, delirious, demented, deranged, distracted, insane, irrational, lunatic, maniac, maniacal; enraged, furious, rabid, raging, violent; angry, enraged, exasperated, furious, incensed, provoked, wrathful; distracted, infatuated, wild; frantic, frenzied, raving.

madden *vb* annoy, craze, enrage, exasperate, inflame, infuriate, irritate, provoke.

madness *n* aberration, craziness, dementia, derangement, insanity, lunacy, mania; delirium, frenzy, fury, rage.

magazine *n* depository, depot, entrepot, receptacle, repository, storehouse, warehouse; pamphlet, paper, periodical.

magic *adj* bewitching, charming, enchanting, fascinating, magical, miraculous, spellbinding. • *n* conjuring, enchantment, necromancy, sorcery, thaumaturgy, voodoo, witchcraft; char, fascination, witchery.

magician *n* conjurer, enchanter, juggler, magus, necromancer, shaman, sorcerer, wizard.

magisterial *adj* august, dignified, majestic, pompous; authoritative, despotic, domineering, imperious, dictatorial.

magnanimity *n* chivalry, disinterestedness, forbearance, high-mindedness, generosity, nobility.

magnificence *n* brilliance, éclat, grandeur, luxuriousness, luxury, majesty, pomp, splendour.

magnificent *adj* elegant, grand, majestic, noble, splendid, superb; brilliant, gorgeous, imposing, lavish, luxurious, pompous, showy, stately.

magnify *vb* amplify, augment, enlarge; bless, celebrate, elevate, exalt, extol, glorify, laud, praise; exaggerate.

magnitude *n* bulk, dimension, extent, mass, size, volume; consequence, greatness, importance; grandeur, loftiness, sublimity.

maid *n* damsel, girl, lass, lassie, maiden, virgin; maidservant, servant.

maiden *adj* chaste, pure, undefiled, virgin; fresh, new, unused. • *n* girl, maid, virgin.

maidenly *adj* demure, gentle, modest, maidenlike, reserved.

maim *vb* cripple, disable, disfigure, mangle, mar, mutilate. • *n* crippling, disfigurement, mutilation; harm, hurt, injury, mischief.

main¹ *adj* capital, cardinal, chief, leading, principal; essential, important, indispensable, necessary, requisite, vital; enormous, huge, mighty, vast; pure, sheer; absolute, direct, entire, mere. • *n* channel, pipe; force, might, power, strength, violence.

main² *n* high seas, ocean; continent, mainland.

maintain *vb* keep, preserve, support, sustain, uphold; hold, possess; defend, vindicate, justify; carry on, continue, keep up; feed, provide, supply; allege, assert, declare; affirm, aver, contend, hold, say.

maintenance *n* defence, justification, preservation, support, sustenance, vindication; bread, food, livelihood, provisions, subsistence, sustenance, victuals.

majestic *adj* august, dignified, imperial, imposing, lofty, noble, pompous, princely, stately, regal, royal; grand, magnificent, splendid, sublime.

majesty *n* augustness, dignity, elevation, grandeur, loftiness, stateliness.

majority *n* bulk, greater, mass, more, most, plurality, preponderance, superiority; adulthood, manhood.

make *vb* create; fashion, figure, form, frame, mould, shape; cause, construct, effect, establish, fabricate, produce; do, execute, perform, practise; acquire, gain, get, raise, secure; cause, compel, constrain, force, occasion; compose, constitute; go, journey, move, proceed, tend, travel; conduce, contribute, effect, favour, operate; estimate, judge, reckon, suppose, think. • *n* brand, build, constitution, construction, form, shape, structure.

maker *n* creator, god; builder, constructor, fabricator, framer, manufacturer; author, composer, poet, writer.

maladministration *n* malversation, misgovernment, misrule.

maladroit *adj* awkward, bungling, clumsy, inept, inexpert, unhandy, unskilful, unskilled.

malady *n* affliction, ailment, complaint, disease, disorder, illness, indisposition, sickness.

malcontent *adj* discontented, dissatisfied, insurgent, rebellious, resentful, uneasy, unsatisfied. • *n* agitator, complainer, faultfinder, grumbler, spoilsport.

malediction *n* anathema, ban, curse, cursing, denunciation, execration, imprecation, malison.

malefactor *n* convict, criminal, culprit, delinquent, evildoer, felon, offender, outlaw.

malevolence *n* hate, hatred, ill-will, malice, malignity, rancour, spite, spitefulness, vindictiveness.

malevolent *adj* evil-minded, hateful, hostile, ill-natured, malicious, malignant, mischievous, rancorous, spiteful, venomous, vindictive.

malice *n* animosity, bitterness, enmity, grudge, hate, ill-will, malevolence, maliciousness, malignity, pique, rancour, spite, spitefulness, venom, vindictiveness.

malicious *adj* bitter, envious, evil-minded, ill-disposed, ill-natured, invidious, malevolent, malignant, mischievous, rancorous, resentful, spiteful, vicious.

malign *vb* abuse, asperse, blacken, calumniate, defame, disparage, revile, scandalize, slander, traduce, vilify. • *adj* malevolent, malicious, malignant, ill-disposed; baneful, injurious, pernicious, unfavourable, unpropitious.

malignant *adj* bitter, envious, hostile, inimical, malevolent, malicious, malign, spiteful, rancorous, resentful, virulent; heinous, pernicious; ill-boding, unfavourable, unpropitious; dangerous, fatal.

malignity *n* animosity, hatred, ill-will, malice, malevolence, maliciousness, rancour, spite; deadliness, destructiveness, fatality, harmfulness, malignancy, perniciousness, virulence; enormity, evilness, heinousness.

malpractice *n* dereliction, malversation, misbehaviour, misconduct, misdeed, misdoing, sin, transgression.

maltreat *vb* abuse, harm, hurt, ill-treat, ill-use, injure.

mammoth *adj* colossal, enormous, gigantic, huge, immense, vast.

man *vb* crew, garrison, furnish; fortify, reinforce, strengthen. • *n* adult, being, body, human, individual, one, person, personage, somebody, soul; humanity, humankind, mankind; attendant, butler, dependant, liege, servant, subject, valet, vassal; employee, workman.

manacle *vb* bind, chain, fetter, handcuff, restrain, shackle, tie. • *n* bond, chain, handcuff, gyve, hand-fetter, shackle.

manage *vb* administer, conduct, direct, guide, handle, operate, order, regulate, superintend, supervise, transact, treat; control, govern, rule; handle, manipulate, train, wield; contrive, economize, husband, save.

manageable *adj* controllable, docile, easy, governable, tamable, tractable.

management *n* administration, care, charge, conduct, control, direction, disposal, economy, government, guidance, superintendence, supervision, surveillance, treatment.

manager *n* comptroller, conductor, director, executive, governor, impresario, overseer, superintendent, supervisor.

mandate *n* charge, command, commission, edict, injunction, order, precept, requirement.

manful *adj* bold, brave, courageous, daring, heroic, honourable, intrepid, noble, stout, strong, undaunted, vigorous.

mangily *adv* basely, foully, meanly, scabbily, scurvily, vilely.

mangle[1] *vb* hack, lacerate, mutilate, rend, tear; cripple, crush, destroy, maim, mar, spoil.

mangle[2] *vb* calender, polish, press, smooth.

manhood *n* virility; bravery, courage, firmness, fortitude, hardihood, manfulness, manliness, resolution; human nature, humanity; adulthood, maturity.

mania *n* aberration, craziness, delirium, dementia, derangement, frenzy, insanity, lunacy, madness; craze, desire, enthusiasm, fad, fanaticism.

manifest *vb* declare, demonstrate, disclose, discover, display, evidence, evince, exhibit, express, reveal, show. • *adj* apparent, clear, conspicuous, distinct, evident, glaring, indubitable, obvious, open, palpable, patent, plain, unmistakable, visible.

manifestation *n* disclosure, display, exhibition, exposure, expression, revelation.

manifold *adj* complex, diverse, many, multifarious, multiplied, multitudinous, numerous, several, sundry, varied, various.

manipulate *vb* handle, operate, work.

manliness *n* boldness, bravery, courage, dignity, fearlessness, firmness, heroism, intrepidity, nobleness, resolution, valour.

manly *adj* bold, brave, courageous, daring, dignified, firm, heroic, intrepid, manful, noble, stout, strong, undaunted, vigorous; male, masculine, virile.

manner *n* fashion, form, method, mode, style, way; custom, habit, practice; degree, extent, measure; kind, kinds, sort, sorts; air, appearance, aspect, behaviour, carriage, demeanour, deportment, look, mien; mannerism, peculiarity; behaviour, conduct, habits, morals; civility, deportment.

mannerly *adj* ceremonious, civil, complaisant, courteous, polite, refined, respectful, urbane, well-behaved, well-bred.

manners *npl* conduct, habits, morals; air, bearing, behaviour, breeding, carriage, comportment, deportment, etiquette.

manoeuvre *vb* contrive, finesse, intrigue, manage, plan, plot, scheme. • *n* evolution, exercise, movement, operation; artifice, finesse, intrigue, plan, plot, ruse, scheme, stratagem, trick.

mansion *n* abode, dwelling, dwelling house, habitation, hall, residence, seat.

mantle *vb* cloak, cover, discover, obscure; expand, spread; bubble, cream, effervesce, foam, froth, sparkle. • *n* chasuble, cloak, toga; cover, covering, hood.

manufacture *vb* build, compose, construct, create, fabricate, forge, form, make, mould, produce, shape. • *n* constructing, fabrication, making, production.

manumission *n* deliverance, emancipation, enfranchisement, freedom, liberation, release.

manumit *vb* deliver, emancipate, enfranchise, free, liberate, release.

manure *vb* enrich, fertilize. • *n* compost, dressing, fertilizer, guano, muck.

many *adj* abundant, diverse, frequent, innumerable, manifold, multifarious, multifold, multiplied, multitudinous, numerous, sundry, varied, various. • *n* crowd, multitude, people.

map *vb* chart, draw up, plan, plot, set out, sketch. • *n* chart, diagram, outline, plot, sketch.

mar *vb* blot, damage, harm, hurt, impair, injure, ruin, spoil, stain; deface, deform, disfigure, maim, mutilate.

marauder *n* bandit, brigand, desperado, filibuster, freebooter, outlaw, pillager, plunderer, ravager, robber, rover.

march *vb* go, pace, parade, step, tramp, walk. • *n* hike, tramp, walk; parade, procession; gait, step, stride; advance, evolution, progress.

marches *npl* borders, boundaries, confines, frontiers, limits, precincts.

margin *n* border, brim, brink, confine, edge, limit, rim, skirt, verge; latitude, room, space, surplus.

marine *adj* oceanic, pelagic, saltwater, sea; maritime, naval, nautical. • *n* navy, shipping; sea-dog, sea soldier, soldier; sea piece, seascape.

mariner *n* navigator, sailor, salt, seafarer, seaman, tar.

marital *adj* connubial, conjugal, matrimonial.

maritime *adj* marine, naval, nautical, oceanic, sea, seafaring, seagoing; coastal, seaside.

mark *vb* distinguish, earmark, label; betoken, brand, characterize, denote, designate, engrave, impress, imprint, indicate, print, stamp; evince, heed, note, notice, observe, regard, remark, show, spot. • *n* brand, character, characteristic, impression, impress, line, note, print, sign, stamp, symbol, token,

race; evidence, indication, proof, symptom, trace, track, vestige; badge; footprint; bull's-eye, butt, object, target; consequence, distinction, eminence, fame, importance, notability, position, preeminence, reputation, significance.

marked *adj* conspicuous, distinguished, eminent, notable, noted, outstanding, prominent, remarkable.

marriage *n* espousals, nuptials, spousals, wedding; matrimony, wedlock; union; alliance, association, confederation.

marrow *n* medulla, pith; cream, essence, quintessence, substance.

marsh *n* bog, fen, mire, morass, quagmire, slough, swamp.

marshal *vb* arrange, array, dispose, gather, muster, range, order, rank; guide, herald, lead. • *n* conductor, director, master of ceremonies, regulator; harbinger, herald, pursuivant.

marshy *adj* boggy, miry, mossy, swampy, wet.

martial *adj* brave, heroic, military, soldier-like, warlike.

marvel *vb* gape, gaze, goggle, wonder. • *n* miracle, prodigy, wonder; admiration, amazement, astonishment, surprise.

marvellous *adj* amazing, astonishing, extraordinary, miraculous, prodigious, strange, stupendous, wonderful, wondrous; improbable, incredible, surprising, unbelievable.

masculine *adj* bold, hardy, manful, manlike, manly, mannish, virile; potent, powerful, robust, strong, vigorous; bold, coarse, forward.

mask *vb* cloak, conceal, cover, disguise, hide, screen, shroud, veil. • *n* blind, cloak, disguise, screen, veil; evasion, pretence, plea, pretext, ruse, shift, subterfuge, trick; masquerade; bustle, mummery.

masquerade *vb* cover, disguise, hide, mask, revel, veil. • *n* mask, mummery, revel, revelry.

Mass *n* communion, Eucharist.

mass *vb* accumulate, amass, assemble, collect, gather, rally, throng. • *adj* extensive, general, large-scale, widespread. • *n* cake, clot, lump; assemblage, collection, combination, congeries, heap; bulk, dimension, magnitude, size; accumulation, aggregate, body, sum, total, totality, whole.

massacre *vb* annihilate, butcher, exterminate, kill, murder, slaughter, slay. • *n* annihilation, butchery, carnage, extermination, killing, murder, pogrom, slaughter.

massive *adj* big, bulky, colossal, enormous, heavy, huge, immense, ponderous, solid, substantial, vast, weighty.

master *vb* conquer, defeat, direct, govern, overcome, overpower, rule, subdue, subjugate, vanquish; acquire, learn. • *adj* cardinal, chief, especial, grand, great, main, leading, prime, principal; adept, expert, proficient. • *n* director, governor, lord, manager, overseer, superintendent, ruler; captain, commander; instructor, pedagogue, preceptor, schoolteacher, teacher, tutor; holder, owner, possessor, proprietor; chief, head, leader, principal.

masterly *adj* adroit, clever, dextrous, excellent, expert, finished, skilful, skilled; arbitrary, despotic, despotical, domineering, imperious.

mastery *n* command, dominion, mastership, power, rule, supremacy, sway; ascendancy, conquest, leadership, preeminence, superiority, upper-hand, victory; acquisition, acquirement, attainment; ability, cleverness, dexterity, proficiency, skill.

masticate *vb* chew, eat, munch.

match *vb* equal, rival; adapt, fit, harmonize, proportion, suit; marry, mate; combine, couple, join, sort; oppose, pit; correspond, suit, tally. • *n* companion, equal, mate, tally; competition, contest, game, trial; marriage, union.

matchless *adj* consummate, excellent, exquisite, incomparable, inimitable, peerless, perfect, surpassing, unequalled, unmatched, unparalleled, unrivalled.

mate *vb* marry, match, wed; compete, equal, vie; appal, confound, crush, enervate, subdue, stupefy. • *n* associate, companion, compeer, consort, crony, friend, fellow, intimate; companion, equal, match; assistant, subordinate; husband, spouse, wife.

material *adj* bodily, corporeal, nonspiritual, physical, temporal; essential, important, momentous, relevant, vital, weighty. • *n* body, element, stuff, substance.

maternal *adj* motherlike, motherly.

matrimonial *adj* conjugal, connubial, espousal, hymeneal, marital, nuptial, spousal.

matrimony *n* marriage, wedlock.

matter *vb* import, signify, weigh. • *n* body, content, sense, substance; difficulty, distress, trouble; material, stuff; question, subject, subject matter, topic; affair, business, concern, event; consequence, import, importance, moment, significance; discharge, purulence, pus.

mature *vb* develop, perfect, ripen. • *adj* complete, fit, full-grown, perfect, ripe; completed, prepared, ready, well-considered, well-digested.

maturity *n* completeness, completion, matureness, perfection, ripeness.

mawkish *adj* disgusting, flat, insipid, nauseous, sickly, stale, tasteless, vapid; emotional, feeble, maudlin, sentimental.

maxim *n* adage, aphorism, apothegm, axiom, byword, dictum, proverb, saw, saying, truism.

maze *vb* amaze, bewilder, confound, confuse, perplex. • *n* intricacy, labyrinth, meander; bewilderment, embarrassment, intricacy, perplexity, puzzle, uncertainty.

mazy *adj* confused, confusing, intricate, labyrinthian, labyrinthic, labyrinthine, perplexing, winding.

meagre *adj* emaciated, gaunt, lank, lean, poor, skinny, starved, spare, thin; barren, poor, sterile, unproductive; bald, barren, dry, dull, mean, poor, prosy, feeble, insignificant, jejune, scanty, small, tame, uninteresting, vapid.

mean[1] *vb* contemplate, design, intend, purpose; connote, denote, express, imply, import, indicate, purport, signify, symbolize.

mean[2] *adj* average, medium, middle; intermediate, intervening. • *n* measure, mediocrity, medium, moderation; average; agency, instrument, instrumentality, means, measure, method, mode, way.

mean[3] *adj* coarse, common, humble, ignoble, low, ordinary, plebeian, vulgar; abject, base, base-minded, beggarly, contemptible, degraded, dirty, dishonourable, disingenuous, grovelling, low-minded, pitiful, rascally, scurvy, servile, shabby, sneaking, sorry, spiritless, unfair, vile; illiberal, mercenary, miserly, narrow, narrow-minded, niggardly, parsimonious, penurious, selfish, sordid, stingy, ungenerous, unhandsome; contemptible, despicable, diminutive, insignificant, paltry, petty, poor, small, wretched.

meaning *n* acceptation, drift, import, intention, purport, purpose, sense, signification.

means *npl* instrument, method, mode, way; appliance, expedient, measure, resource, shift, step; estate, income, property, resources, revenue, substance, wealth, wherewithal.

measure *vb* mete; adjust, gauge, proportion; appraise, appreciate, estimate, gauge, value. • *n* gauge, meter, rule, standard; degree, extent, length, limit; allotment, share, proportion; means, step; foot, metre, rhythm, tune, verse.

measureless *adj* boundless, endless, immeasurable, immense, limitless, unbounded, unlimited, vast.

meat *n* aliment, cheer, diet, fare, feed, flesh, food, nourishment, nutriment, provision, rations, regimen, subsistence, sustenance, viands, victuals.

mechanic *n* artificer, artisan, craftsman, hand, handicraftsman, machinist, operative, workman.

meddle *vb* interfere, intermeddle, interpose, intrude.

meddlesome *adj* interfering, intermeddling, intrusive, officious, prying.

mediate *vb* arbitrate, intercede, interpose, intervene, settle. • *adj* interposed, intervening, middle.

mediation *n* arbitration, intercession, interposition, intervention.

mediator *n* advocate, arbitrator, interceder, intercessor, propitiator, umpire.

medicine *n* drug, medicament, medication, physic; therapy.

mediocre *adj* average, commonplace, indifferent, mean, medium, middling, ordinary.

meditate *vb* concoct, contrive, design, devise, intend, plan, purpose, scheme; chew, contemplate, ruminate, study; cogitate, muse, ponder, think.

meditation *n* cogitation, contemplation, musing, pondering, reflection, ruminating, study, thought.

meditative *adj* contemplative, pensive, reflective, studious, thoughtful.

medium *adj* average, mean, mediocre, middle. • *n* agency, channel, intermediary, instrument, instrumentality, means, organ; conditions, environment, influences; average, means.

medley *n* confusion, farrago, hodgepodge, hotchpotch, jumble, mass, melange, miscellany, mishmash, mixture.

meed *n* award, guerdon, premium, prize, recompense, remuneration, reward.

meek *adj* gentle, humble, lowly, mild, modest, pacific, soft, submissive, unassuming, yielding.

meekness *n* gentleness, humbleness, humility, lowliness, mildness, modesty, submission, submissiveness.

meet *vb* cross, intersect, transact; confront, encounter, engage; answer, comply, fulfil, gratify, satisfy; converge, join, unite; assemble, collect, convene, congregate, forgather, muster, rally. • *adj* adapted, appropriate, befitting, convenient, fit, fitting, proper, qualified, suitable, suited.

meeting *n* encounter, interview; assemblage, assembly, audience, company, concourse, conference, congregation, convention, gathering; assignation, encounter, introduction, rendezvous; confluence, conflux, intersection, joining, junction, union; collision.

melancholy *adj* blue, dejected, depressed, despondent, desponding, disconsolate, dismal, dispirited, doleful, down, downcast, downhearted, gloomy, glum, hypochondriac, low-spirited, lugubrious, moody, mopish, sad, sombre, sorrowful, unhappy; afflictive, calamitous, unfortunate, unlucky; dark, gloomy, grave, quiet. • *n* blues, dejection, depression, despondency, dismals, dumps, gloom, gloominess, hypochondria, sadness, vapours.

melee *n* affray, brawl, broil, contest, fight, fray, scuffle.

mellifluous, mellifluent *adj* dulcet, euphonic, euphonical, euphonious, mellow, silver-toned, silvery, smooth, soft, sweet.

mellow *vb* mature, ripen; improve, smooth, soften, tone; pulverize; perfect. • *adj* mature, ripe; dulcet, mellifluous, mellifluent, rich, silver-toned, silvery, smooth, soft; delicate; genial, good-humoured, jolly, jovial, matured, softened; mellowy, loamy, unctuous; perfected, well-prepared; disguised, fuddled, intoxicated, tipsy.

melodious *adj* arioso, concordant, dulcet, euphonious, harmonious, mellifluous, mellifluent, musical, silvery, sweet, tuneful.

melody *n* air, descant, music, plainsong, song, theme, tune.

melt *vb* dissolve, fuse, liquefy, thaw; mollify, relax, soften, subdue; dissipate, waste; blend, pass, shade.

member *n* arm, leg, limb, organ; component, constituent, element, part, portion; branch, clause, division, head.

memento *n* memorial, remembrance, reminder, souvenir.

memoir *n* account, autobiography, biography, journal, narrative, record, register.

memorable *adj* celebrated, distinguished, extraordinary, famous, great, illustrious, important, notable, noteworthy, remarkable, signal, significant.

memorandum *n* minute, note, record.

memorial *adj* commemorative, monumental. • *n* cairn, commemoration, memento, monument, plaque, record, souvenir; memorandum, remembrance.

memory *n* recollection, remembrance, reminiscence; celebrity, fame, renown, reputation; commemoration, memorial.

menace *vb* alarm, frighten, intimidate, threaten. • *n* danger, hazard, peril, threat, warning; nuisance, pest, troublemaker.

menage *n* household, housekeeping, management.

mend *vb* darn, patch, rectify, refit, repair, restore, retouch; ameliorate, amend, better, correct, emend, improve, meliorate, reconcile, rectify, reform; advance, help; augment, increase.

mendacious *adj* deceitful, deceptive, fallacious, false, lying, untrue, untruthful.

mendacity *n* deceit, deceitfulness, deception, duplicity, falsehood, lie, untruth.

mendicant *n* beggar, pauper, tramp.

menial *adj* base, low, mean, servile, vile. • *n* attendant, bondsman, domestic, flunkey, footman, lackey, serf, servant, slave, underling, valet, waiter.

mensuration *n* measurement, measuring; survey, surveying.

mental *adj* ideal, immaterial, intellectual, psychiatric, subjective.

mention *vb* acquaint, allude, cite, communicate, declare, disclose, divulge, impart, inform, name, report, reveal, state, tell. • *n* allusion, citation, designation, notice, noting, reference.

mentor *n* adviser, counsellor, guide, instructor, monitor.

mephitic *adj* baleful, baneful, fetid, foul, mephitical, noisome, noxious, poisonous, pestilential.

mercantile *adj* commercial, marketable, trading.

mercenary *adj* hired, paid, purchased, venal; avaricious, covetous, grasping, mean, niggardly, parsimonious, penurious, sordid, stingy. • *n* hireling, soldier.

merchandise *n* commodities, goods, wares.

merchant *n* dealer, retailer, shopkeeper, trader, tradesman.

merciful *adj* clement, compassionate, forgiving, gracious, lenient, pitiful; benignant, forbearing, gentle, humane, kind, mild, tender, tender-hearted.

merciless *adj* barbarous, callous, cruel, fell, hard-hearted, inexorable, pitiless, relentless, remorseless, ruthless, savage, severe, uncompassionate, unfeeling, unmerciful, unrelenting, unrepenting, unsparing.

mercurial *adj* active, lively, nimble, prompt, quick, sprightly; cheerful, light-hearted; changeable, fickle, flighty, inconstant, mobile, volatile.

mercy *n* benevolence, clemency, compassion, gentleness, kindness, lenience, leniency, lenity, mildness, pity, tenderness; blessing, favour, grace; discretion, disposal; forgiveness, pardon.

mere *adj* bald, bare, naked, plain, sole, simple; absolute, entire, pure, sheer, unmixed. • *n* lake, pond, pool.

meretricious *adj* deceitful, brummagem, false, gaudy, make-believe, sham, showy, spurious, tawdry.

merge *vb* bury, dip, immerse, involve, lose, plunge, sink, submerge.

meridian *n* acme, apex, climax, culmination, summit, zenith; midday, noon, noontide.

merit *vb* deserve, earn, incur; acquire, gain, profit, value. • *n* claim, right; credit, desert, excellence, goodness, worth, worthiness.

meritorious *adj* commendable, deserving, excellent, good, worthy.

merriment *n* amusement, frolic, gaiety, hilarity, jocularity, jollity, joviality, laughter, liveliness, mirth, sport, sportiveness.

merry *adj* agreeable, brisk, delightful, exhilarating, lively, pleasant, stirring; airy, blithe, blithesome, buxom, cheerful, comical, droll, facetious, frolicsome, gladsome, gleeful, hilarious, jocund, jolly, jovial, joyous, light-hearted, lively, mirthful, sportive, sprightly, vivacious.

mess *n* company, set; farrago, hodgepodge, hotchpotch, jumble, medley, mass, melange, miscellany, mishmash, mixture; confusion, muddle, perplexity, pickle, plight, predicament.

message *n* communication, dispatch, intimation, letter, missive, notice, telegram, wire, word.

messenger *n* carrier, courier, emissary, envoy, express, mercury, nuncio; forerunner, harbinger, herald, precursor.

metamorphic *adj* changeable, mutable, variable.

metamorphose *vb* change, mutate, transfigure, transform, transmute.

metamorphosis *n* change, mutation, transfiguration, transformation, transmutation.

metaphorical *adj* allegorical, figurative, symbolic, symbolical.

metaphysical *adj* abstract, allegorical, figurative, general, intellectual, parabolic, subjective, unreal.

mete *vb* dispense, distribute, divide, measure, ration, share. • *n* bound, boundary, butt, limit, measure, term, terminus.

meteor *n* aerolite, falling star, shooting star.

method *n* course, manner, means, mode, procedure, process, rule, way; arrangement, classification, disposition, order, plan, regularity, scheme, system.

methodical *adj* exact, orderly, regular, systematic, systematical.

metropolis *n* capital, city, conurbation.

mettle *n* constitution, element, material, stuff; character, disposition, spirit, temper; ardour, courage, fire, hardihood, life, nerve, pluck, sprightliness, vigour.

mettlesome *adj* ardent, brisk, courageous, fiery, frisky, high-spirited, lively, spirited, sprightly.

mew *vb* confine, coop, encase, enclose, imprison; cast, change, mould, shed.

microscopic *adj* infinitesimal, minute, tiny.

middle *adj* central, halfway, mean, medial, mid; intermediate, intervening. • *n* centre, halfway, mean, midst.

middleman *n* agent, broker, factor, go-between, intermediary.

mien *n* air, appearance, aspect, bearing, behaviour, carriage, countenance, demeanour, deportment, look, manner.

might *n* ability, capacity, efficacy, efficiency, force, main, power, prowess, puissance, strength.

mighty *adj* able, bold, courageous, potent, powerful, puissant, robust, strong, sturdy, valiant, valorous, vigorous; bulky, enormous, huge, immense, monstrous, stupendous, vast.

migratory *adj* nomadic, roving, shifting, strolling, unsettled, wandering, vagrant.

mild *adj* amiable, clement, compassionate, gentle, good-natured, indulgent, kind, lenient, meek, merciful, pacific, tender; bland, pleasant, soft, suave; calm, kind, placid, temperate, tranquil; assuasive, compliant, demulcent, emollient, lenitive, mollifying, soothing.

mildness *n* amiability, clemency, gentleness, indulgence, kindness, meekness, moderation, mirth, softness, tenderness, warmth.

mildew *n* blight, blast, mould, must, mustiness, smut, rust.

milieu *n* background, environment, sphere, surroundings.

militant *adj* belligerent, combative, contending, fighting.

military *adj* martial, soldier, soldierly, warlike. • *n* army, militia, soldiers.

mill *vb* comminute, crush, grate, grind, levigate, powder, pulverize. • *n* factory, manufactory; grinder; crowd, throng.

mimic *vb* ape, counterfeit, imitate, impersonate, mime, mock, parody. • *adj* imitative, mock, simulated. • *n* imitator, impersonator, mime, mocker, parodist, parrot.

mince[1] *vb* chop, cut, hash, shatter. • *n* forcemeat, hash, mash, mincemeat.

mince[2] *vb* attenuate, diminish, extenuate, mitigate, palliate, soften; pose, sashay, simper, smirk.

mind[1] *vb* attend, heed, mark, note, notice, regard, tend, watch; obey, observe, submit; design, incline, intend, mean; recall, recollect, remember, remind; beware, look out, watch out. • *n* soul, spirit; brains, common sense, intellect, reason, sense, understanding; belief, consideration, contemplation, judgement, opinion, reflection, sentiment, thought; memory, recollection, remembrance; bent, desire, disposition, inclination, intention, leaning, purpose, tendency, will.

mind[2] *vb* balk, begrudge, grudge, object, resent.

mindful *adj* attentive, careful, heedful, observant, regardful, thoughtful.

mindless *adj* dull, heavy, insensible, senseless, sluggish, stupid, unthinking; careless, forgetful, heedless, neglectful, negligent, regardless.

mine *vb* dig, excavate, quarry, unearth; sap, undermine, weaken; destroy, ruin. • *n* colliery, deposit, lode, pit, shaft.

mingle *vb* blend, combine, commingle, compound, intermingle, intermix, join, mix, unite.

miniature *adj* bantam, diminutive, little, small, tiny.

minion *n* creature, dependant, favourite, hanger-on, parasite, sycophant; darling, favourite, flatterer, pet.

minister *vb* administer, afford, furnish, give, supply; aid, assist, contribute, help, succour. • *n* agent, assistant, servant, subordinate, underling; administrator, executive; ambassador, delegate, envoy, plenipotentiary; chaplain, churchman, clergyman, cleric, curate, divine, ecclesiastic, parson, pastor, preacher, priest, rector, vicar.

ministry *n* agency, aid, help, instrumentality, interposition, intervention, ministration, service, support; administration, cabinet, council, government.

minor *adj* less, smaller; inferior, junior, secondary, subordinate, younger; inconsiderable, petty, unimportant, small.

minstrel *n* bard, musician, singer, troubadour.

mint *vb* coin, stamp; fabricate, fashion, forge, invent, make, produce. • *adj* fresh, new, perfect, undamaged. • *n* die, punch, seal, stamp; fortune, (*inf*) heap, million, pile, wad.

minute[1] *adj* diminutive, fine, little, microscopic, miniature, slender, slight, small, tiny; circumstantial, critical, detailed, exact, fussy, meticulous, nice, particular, precise.

minute[2] *n* account, entry, item, memorandum, note, proceedings, record; instant, moment, second, trice, twinkling.

miracle *n* marvel, prodigy, wonder.

miraculous *adj* supernatural, thaumaturgic, thaumaturgical; amazing, extraordinary, incredible, marvellous, unaccountable, unbelievable, wondrous.

mirror *vb* copy, echo, emulate, reflect, show. • *n* looking-glass, reflector, speculum; archetype, exemplar, example, model, paragon, pattern, prototype.

mirth *n* cheerfulness, festivity, frolic, fun, gaiety, gladness, glee, hilarity, festivity, jollity, joviality, joyousness, laughter, merriment, merry-making, rejoicing, sport.

mirthful *adj* cheery, cheery, festive, frolicsome, hilarious, jocund, jolly, merry, jovial, joyous, lively, playful, sportive, vivacious; comic, droll, humorous, facetious, funny, jocose, jocular, ludicrous, merry, waggish, witty.

misadventure *n* accident, calamity, catastrophe, cross, disaster, failure, ill-luck, infelicity, mischance, misfortune, mishap, reverse.

misanthrope *n* cynic, egoist, egotist, man-hater, misanthropist.

misapply *vb* abuse, misuse, pervert.

misapprehend *vb* misconceive, mistake, misunderstand.

misbehaviour *n* ill-behaviour, ill-conduct, incivility, miscarriage, misconduct, misdemeanour, naughtiness, rudeness.

miscarriage *n* calamity, defeat, disaster, failure, mischance, mishap; misbehaviour, misconduct, ill-behaviour.

miscellaneous *adj* confused, diverse, diversified, heterogeneous, indiscriminate, jumbled, many, mingled, mixed, promiscuous, stromatic, stromatous, various.

miscellany *n* collection, diversity, farrago, gallimaufry, hodgepodge, hotchpotch, jumble, medley, mishmash, melange, miscellaneous, mixture, variety.

mischance *n* accident, calamity, disaster, ill-fortune, ill-luck, infelicity, misadventure, misfortune, mishap.

mischief *n* damage, detriment, disadvantage, evil, harm, hurt, ill, injury, prejudice; ill-consequence, misfortune, trouble; devilry, wrong-doing.

mischievous *adj* destructive, detrimental, harmful, hurtful, injurious, noxious, pernicious; malicious, sinful, vicious, wicked; annoying, impish, naughty, troublesome, vexatious.

misconceive *vb* misapprehend, misjudge, mistake, misunderstand.

misconduct *vb* botch, bungle, misdirect, mismanage. • *n* bad conduct, ill-conduct, misbehaviour, misdemeanour, rudeness, transgression; ill-management, mismanagement.

misconstrue *vb* misread, mistranslate; misapprehend, misinterpret, mistake, misunderstand.

miscreant *adj* corrupt, criminal, evil, rascally, unprincipled, vicious, villainous, wicked. • *n* caitiff, knave, ragamuffin, rascal, rogue, ruffian, scamp, scoundrel, vagabond, villain.

misdemeanour *n* fault, ill-behaviour, misbehaviour, misconduct, misdeed, offence, transgression, trespass.

miser *n* churl, curmudgeon, lickpenny, money-grabber, niggard, penny-pincher, pinch-fist, screw, scrimp, skinflint.

miserable *adj* afflicted, broken-hearted, comfortless, disconsolate, distressed, forlorn, heartbroken, unhappy, wretched; calamitous, hapless, ill-starred, pitiable, unfortunate, unlucky; poor, valueless, worthless; abject, contemptible, despicable, low, mean, worthless.

miserly *adj* avaricious, beggarly, close, close-fisted, covetous, grasping, mean, niggardly, parsimonious, penurious, sordid, stingy, tight-fisted.

misery *n* affliction, agony, anguish, calamity, desolation, distress, grief, heartache, heavy-heartedness, misfortune, sorrow, suffering, torment, torture, tribulation, unhappiness, woe, wretchedness.

misfortune *n* adversity, affliction, bad luck, blow, calamity, casualty, catastrophe, disaster, distress, hardship, harm, ill, infliction, misadventure, mischance, mishap, reverse, scourge, stroke, trial, trouble, visitation.

misgiving *n* apprehension, distrust, doubt, hesitation, suspicion, uncertainty.

mishap *n* accident, calamity, disaster, ill luck, misadventure, mischance, misfortune.

misinterpret *vb* distort, falsify, misapprehend, misconceive, misconstrue, misjudge.

mislead *vb* beguile, deceive, delude, misdirect, misguide.

mismanage *vb* botch, fumble, misconduct, mishandle, misrule.

misprize *vb* slight, underestimate, underrate, undervalue.

misrepresent *vb* belie, caricature, distort, falsify, misinterpret, misstate, pervert.

misrule *n* anarchy, confusion, disorder, malad-ministration, misgovernment, mismanagement.

miss[1] *vb* blunder, err, fail, fall short, forgo, lack, lose, miscarry, mistake, omit, overlook, trip; avoid, escape, evade, skip, slip; feel the loss of, need, want, wish. • *n* blunder, error, failure, fault, mistake, omission, oversight, slip, trip; loss, want.

miss[2] *n* damsel, girl, lass, maid, maiden.

misshapen *adj* deformed, ill-formed, ill-shaped, ill-proportioned, misformed, ugly, ungainly.

missile *n* projectile, weapon.

mission *n* commission, legation; business, charge, duty, errand, office, trust; delegation, deputation, embassy.

missive *n* communication, epistle, letter, message, note.

mist *vb* cloud, drizzle, mizzle, smog. • *n* cloud, fog, haze; bewilderment, obscurity, perplexity.

mistake *vb* misapprehend, miscalculate, misconceive, misjudge, misunderstand; confound, take; blunder, err. • *n* misapprehension, miscalculation, misconception, mistaking, misunderstanding; blunder, error, fault, inaccuracy, oversight, slip, trip.

mistaken *adj* erroneous, inaccurate, incorrect, misinformed, wrong.

mistrust *vb* distrust, doubt, suspect; apprehend, fear, surmise, suspect. • *n* doubt, distrust, misgiving, suspicion.

misty *adj* cloudy, clouded, dark, dim, foggy, obscure, overcast.

misunderstand *vb* misapprehend, misconceive, misconstrue, mistake.

misunderstanding *n* error, misapprehension, misconception, mistake; difference, difficulty, disagreement, discord, dissension, quarrel.

misuse *vb* desecrate, misapply, misemploy, pervert, profane; abuse, ill-treat, maltreat, ill-use; fritter, squander, waste. • *n* abuse, perversion, profanation, prostitution; ill-treatment, ill-use, ill-usage, misusage; misapplication, solecism.

mitigate *vb* abate, alleviate, assuage, diminish, extenuate, lessen, moderate, palliate, relieve; allay, appease, calm, mollify, pacify, quell, quiet, reduce, soften, soothe; moderate, temper.

mitigation *n* abatement, allaying, alleviation, assuagement, diminution, moderation, palliation, relief.

mix *vb* alloy, amalgamate, blend, commingle, combine, compound, incorporate, interfuse, interlard, mingle, unite; associate, join. • *n* alloy, amalgam, blend, combination, compound, mixture.

mixture *n* admixture, association, intermixture, union; compound, farrago, hash, hodgepodge, hotchpotch, jumble, medley, melange, mishmash; diversity, miscellany, variety.

moan *vb* bemoan, bewail, deplore, grieve, groan, lament, mourn, sigh, weep. • *n* groan, lament, lamentation, sigh, wail.

mob *vb* crowd, jostle, surround, swarm, pack, throng. • *n* assemblage, crowd, rabble, multitude, throng, tumult; dregs, canaille, populace, rabble, riffraff, scum.

mobile *adj* changeable, fickle, expressive, inconstant, sensitive, variable, volatile.

mock *vb* ape, counterfeit, imitate, mimic, take off; deride, flout, gibe, insult, jeer, ridicule, taunt; balk, cheat, deceive, defeat, disappoint, dupe, elude, illude, mislead. • *adj* assumed, claptrap, counterfeit, fake, false, feigned, make-believe, pretended, spurious. • *n* fake, imitation, phoney, sham; gibe, insult, jeer, scoff, taunt.

mockery *n* contumely, counterfeit, deception, derision, imitation, jeering, mimicry, ridicule, scoffing, scorn, sham, travesty.

mode *n* fashion, manner, method, style, way; accident, affection, degree, graduation, modification, quality, variety.

model *vb* design, fashion, form, mould, plan, shape. • *adj* admirable, archetypal, estimable, exemplary, ideal, meritorious, paradigmatic, perfect, praiseworthy, worthy. • *n* archetype, design, mould, original, pattern, protoplast, prototype; type; dummy, example, form; copy, facsimile, image, imitation, representation.

moderate *vb* abate, allay, appease, assuage, blunt, dull, lessen, soothe, mitigate, mollify, pacify, quell, quiet, reduce, repress, soften, still, subdue; diminish, qualify, slacken, temper; control, govern, regulate. • *adj* abstinent, frugal, sparing, temperate; limited, mediocre; abstemious, sober; calm, cool, judicious, reasonable, steady; gentle, mild, temperate, tolerable.

moderation *n* abstemiousness, forbearance, frugality, restraint, sobriety, temperance; calmness, composure, coolness, deliberateness, equanimity, mildness, sedateness.

modern *adj* fresh, late, latest, new, novel, present, recent, up-to-date.

modest *adj* bashful, coy, diffident, humble, meek, reserved, retiring, shy, unassuming, unobtrusive, unostentatious, unpretending, unpretentious; chaste, proper, pure, virtuous; becoming, decent, moderate.

modesty *n* bashfulness, coyness, diffidence, humility, meekness, propriety, prudishness, reserve, shyness, unobtrusiveness; chastity, purity, virtue; decency, moderation.

modification *n* alteration, change, qualification, reformation, variation; form, manner, mode, state.

modify *vb* alter, change, qualify, reform, shape, vary; lower, moderate, qualify, soften.

modish *adj* fashionable, stylish; ceremonious, conventional, courtly, genteel.

modulate *vb* attune, harmonize, tune; inflict, vary; adapt, adjust, proportion.

moiety *n* half; part, portion, share.

moil *vb* drudge, labour, toil; bespatter, daub, defile, soil, splash, spot, stain; fatigue, weary, tire.

moist *adj* damp, dank, humid, marshy, muggy, swampy, wet.

moisture *n* dampness, dankness, humidity, wetness.

mole *n* breakwater, dike, dyke, jetty, mound, pier, quay.

molecule *n* atom, monad, particle.

molest *vb* annoy, badger, bore, bother, chafe, discommode, disquiet, disturb, harass, harry, fret, gull, hector, incommode, inconvenience, irritate, oppress, pester, plague, tease, torment, trouble, vex, worry.

mollify *vb* soften; appease, calm, compose, pacify, quiet, soothe, tranquillize; abate, allay, assuage, blunt, dull, ease, lessen, mitigate, moderate, relieve, temper; qualify, tone down.

moment *n* flash, instant, jiffy, second, trice, twinkling, wink; avail, consequence, consideration, force, gravity, importance, significance, signification, value, weight; drive, force, impetus, momentum.

momentous *adj* grave, important, serious, significant, vital, weighty.

momentum *n* impetus, moment.

monarch *n* autocrat, despot; chief, dictator, emperor, king, potentate, prince, queen, ruler, sovereign.

monastery *n* abbey, cloister, convent, lamasery, nunnery, priory.

monastic *adj* coenobitic, coenobitical, conventual, monkish, secluded.

money *n* banknotes, cash, coin, currency, riches, specie, wealth.

moneyed, monied *adj* affluent, opulent, rich, well-off, well-to-do.

monitor *vb* check, observe, oversee, supervise, watch. • *n* admonisher, admonitor, adviser, counsellor, instructor, mentor, overseer.

monomania *n* delusion, hallucination, illusion, insanity, self-deception.

monopolize *vb* control, dominate, engross, forestall.

monotonous *adj* boring, dull, tedious, tiresome, undiversified, uniform, unvaried, unvarying, wearisome.

monotony *n* boredom, dullness, sameness, tedium, tiresomeness, uniformity, wearisomeness.

monster *adj* enormous, gigantic, huge, immense, mammoth, monstrous. • *n* enormity, marvel, prodigy, wonder; brute, demon, fiend, miscreant, ruffian, villain, wretch.

monstrous *adj* abnormal, preternatural, prodigious, unnatural; colossal, enormous, extraordinary, huge, immense, stupendous, vast; marvellous, strange, wonderful; bad, base, dreadful, flagrant, frightful, hateful, hideous, horrible, shocking, terrible.

monument *n* memorial, record, remembrance, testimonial; cairn, cenotaph, gravestone, mausoleum, memorial, pillar, tomb, tombstone.

mood *n* disposition, humour, temper, vein.

moody *adj* capricious, humoursome, variable; angry, crabbed, crusty, fretful, ill-tempered, irascible, irritable, passionate, pettish, peevish, petulant, snappish, snarling, sour, testy; crossgrained, dogged, frowning, glowering, glum, intractable, morose, perverse, spleeny, stubborn, sulky, sullen, wayward; abstracted, gloomy, melancholy, pensive, sad, saturnine.

moonshine *n* balderdash, fiction, flummery, fudge, fustian, nonsense, pretence, stuff, trash, twaddle, vanity.

moor[1] *vb* anchor, berth, fasten, fix, secure, tie.

moor[2] *n* bog, common, heath, moorland, morass, moss, wasteland.

moot *vb* agitate, argue, debate, discuss, dispute. • *adj* arguable, debatable, doubtful, unsettled.

mopish *adj* dejected, depressed, desponding, downcast, downhearted, gloomy, glum, sad.

moral *adj* ethical, good, honest, honourable, just, upright, virtuous; abstract, ideal, intellectual, mental. • *n* intent, meaning, significance.

morals *npl* ethics, morality; behaviour, conduct, habits, manners.

morass *n* bog, fen, marsh, quagmire, slough, swamp.

morbid *adj* ailing, corrupted, diseased, sick, sickly, tainted, unhealthy, unsound, vitiated; depressed, downcast, gloomy, pessimistic, sensitive.

mordacious *adj* acrid, biting, cutting, mordant, pungent, sharp, stinging; caustic, poignant, satirical, sarcastic, scathing, severe.

mordant *adj* biting, caustic, keen, mordacious, nipping, sarcastic.

moreover *adv, conj* also, besides, further, furthermore, likewise, too.

morning *n* aurora, daybreak, dawn, morn, morningtide, sunrise.

morose *adj* austere, churlish, crabbed, crusty, dejected, desponding, downcast, downhearted, gloomy, glum, melancholy, moody, sad, severe, sour, sullen, surly.

morsel *n* bite, mouthful, titbit; bit, fragment, part, piece, scrap.

mortal *adj* deadly, destructive, fatal, final, human, lethal, perishable, vital. • *n* being, earthling, human, man, person, woman.

mortality *n* corruption, death, destruction, fatality.

mortification *n* chagrin, disappointment, discontent, dissatisfaction, displeasure, humiliation, trouble, shame, vexation; humility, penance, self-abasement, self-denial; gangrene, necrosis.

mortify *vb* annoy, chagrin, depress, disappoint, displease, disquiet, dissatisfy, harass, humble, plague, vex, worry; abase, abash, confound, humiliate, restrain, shame, subdue; corrupt, fester, gangrene, putrefy.

mortuary *n* burial place, cemetery, churchyard, graveyard, necropolis; charnel house, morgue.

mostly *adv* chiefly, customarily, especially, generally, mainly, particularly, principally.

mote *n* atom, corpuscle, flaw, mite, particle, speck, spot.

motherly *adj* affectionate, kind, maternal, paternal, tender.

motion *vb* beckon, direct, gesture, signal. • *n* action, change, drift, flux, movement, passage, stir, transit; air, gait, port; gesture, impulse, prompting, suggestion; proposal, proposition.

motionless *adj* fixed, immobile, quiescent, stable, stagnant, standing, stationary, still, torpid, unmoved.

motive *adj* activating, driving, moving, operative. • *n* cause, consideration, ground, impulse, incentive, incitement, inducement, influence, occasion, prompting, purpose, reason, spur, stimulus.

motley *adj* coloured, dappled, mottled, speckled, spotted, variegated; composite, diversified, heterogeneous, mingled, mixed.

mottled *adj* dappled, motley, piebald, speckled, spotted, variegated.

mould[1] *vb* carve, cast, fashion, form, make, model, shape. • *n* cast, character, fashion, form, matrix, pattern, shape; material, matter, substance.

mould[2] *n* blight, mildew, mouldiness, must, mustiness, rot; fungus, lichen, mushroom, puffball, rust, smut, toadstool; earth, loam, soil.

moulder *vb* crumble, decay, perish, waste.

mouldy *adj* decaying, fusty, mildewed, musty.

mound *n* bank, barrow, hill, hillock, knoll, tumulus; bulwark, defence, rampart.

mount[1] *n* hill, mountain, peak.

mount[2] *vb* arise, ascend, climb, rise, soar, tower; escalate, scale; embellish, ornament; bestride, get upon. • *n* charger, horse, ride, steed.

mountain *n* alp, height, hill, mount, peak; abundance, heap, mound, stack.

mountebank *n* charlatan, cheat, impostor, pretender, quack.

mourn *vb* bemoan, bewail, deplore, grieve, lament, sorrow, wail.

mournful *adj* afflicting, afflictive, calamitous, deplorable, distressed, grievous, lamentable, sad, woeful; doleful, heavy, heavy-hearted, lugubrious, melancholy, sorrowful, tearful.

mouth *vb* clamour, declaim, rant, roar, vociferate. • *n* chaps, jaws; aperture, opening, orifice; entrance, inlet; oracle, mouthpiece, speaker, spokesman.

movables *npl* chattels, effects, furniture, goods, property, wares.

move *vb* dislodge, drive, impel, propel, push, shift, start, stir; actuate, incite, instigate, rouse; determine, incline, induce, influence, persuade, prompt; affect, impress, touch, trouble; agitate, awaken, excite, incense, irritate; propose, recommend, suggest; go, march, proceed, walk; act, live; flit, remove. • *n* action, motion, movement.

movement *n* change, move, motion, passage; emotion; crusade, drive.

moving *adj* impelling, influencing, instigating, persuading, persuasive; affecting, impressive, pathetic, touching.

mucous *adj* glutinous, gummy, mucilaginous, ropy, slimy, viscid.

mud *n* dirt, mire, muck, slime.

muddle *vb* confuse, disarrange, disorder; fuddle, inebriate, stupefy; muff, mull, spoil. • *n* confusion, disorder, mess, plight, predicament.

muddy *vb* dirty, foul, smear, soil; confuse, obscure. • *adj* dirty, foul, impure, slimy, soiled, turbid; bothered, confused, dull, heavy, stupid; incoherent, obscure, vague.

muffle *vb* cover, envelop, shroud, wrap; conceal, disguise, involve; deaden, soften, stifle, suppress.

mulish *adj* cross-grained, headstrong, intractable, obstinate, stubborn.

multifarious *adj* different, divers, diverse, diversified, manifold, multiform, multitudinous, various.

multiloquence *n* garrulity, loquacity, loquaciousness, talkativeness.

multiply *vb* augment, extend, increase, spread.

multitude *n* numerousness; host, legion; army, assemblage, assembly, collection, concourse, congregation, crowd, horde, mob, swarm, throng; commonality, herd, mass, mob, pack, populace, rabble.

mundane *adj* earthly, secular, sublunary, temporal, terrene, terrestrial, worldly.

munificence *n* benefice, bounteousness, bountifulness, bounty, generosity, liberality.

munificent *adj* beneficent, bounteous, bountiful, free, generous, liberal, princely.

murder *vb* assassinate, butcher, destroy, dispatch, kill, massacre, slaughter, slay; abuse, mar, spoil. • *n* assassination, butchery, destruction, homicide, killing, manslaughter, massacre.

murderer *n* assassin, butcher, cut-throat, killer, manslaughterer, slaughterer, slayer.

murderous *adj* barbarous, bloodthirsty, bloody, cruel, fell, sanguinary, savage.

murky *adj* cheerless, cloudy, dark, dim, dusky, gloomy, hazy, lowering, lurid, obscure, overcast.

murmur *vb* croak, grumble, mumble, mutter; hum, whisper. • *n* complaint, grumble, mutter, plaint, whimper; hum, undertone, whisper.

muscular *adj* sinewy; athletic, brawny, powerful, lusty, stalwart, stout, strong, sturdy, vigorous.

muse *vb* brood, cogitate, consider, contemplate, deliberate, dream, meditate, ponder, reflect, ruminate, speculate, think. • *n* abstraction, musing, reverie.

music *n* harmony, melody, symphony.

musical *adj* dulcet, harmonious, melodious, sweet, sweet-sounding, symphonious, tuneful.

musing *adj* absent-minded, meditative, preoccupied. • *n* absent-mindedness, abstraction, contemplation, daydreaming, meditation, muse, reflection, reverie, rumination.

muster *vb* assemble, collect, congregate, convene, convoke, gather, marshal, meet, rally, summon. • *n* assemblage, assembly, collection, congregation, convention, convocation, gathering, meeting, rally.

musty *adj* fetid, foul, fusty, mouldy, rank, sour, spoiled; hackneyed, old, stale, threadbare, trite; ill-favoured, insipid, vapid; dull, heavy, rusty, spiritless.

mutable *adj* alterable, changeable; changeful, fickle, inconstant, irresolute, mutational, unsettled, unstable, unsteady, vacillating, variable, wavering.

mutation *n* alteration, change, variation.

mute *vb* dampen, lower, moderate, muffle, soften. • *adj* dumb, voiceless; silent, speechless, still, taciturn.

mutilate *vb* cripple, damage, disable, disfigure, hamstring, injure, maim, mangle, mar.

mutinous *adj* contumacious, insubordinate, rebellious, refractory, riotous, tumultuous, turbulent, unruly; insurgent, seditious.

mutiny *vb* rebel, revolt, rise, resist. • *n* insubordination, insurrection, rebellion, revolt, revolution, riot, rising, sedition, uprising.

mutter *vb* grumble, muffle, mumble, murmur.

mutual *adj* alternate, common, correlative, interchangeable, interchanged, reciprocal, requited.

myopic *adj* near-sighted, purblind, short-sighted.

myriad *adj* innumerable, manifold, multitudinous, uncounted. • *n* host, million(s), multitude, score(s), sea, swarm, thousand(s).

mysterious *adj* abstruse, cabbalistic, concealed, cryptic, dark, dim, enigmatic, enigmatical, hidden, incomprehensible, inexplicable, inscrutable, mystic, mystical, obscure, occult, puzzling, recondite, secret, sphinx-like, unaccountable, unfathomable, unintelligible, unknown.

mystery *n* enigma, puzzle, riddle, secret; art, business, calling, trade.

mystical *adj* abstruse, cabbalistic, dark, enigmatical, esoteric, hidden, inscrutable, mysterious, obscure, occult, recondite, transcendental; allegorical, emblematic, emblematical, symbolic, symbolical.

mystify *vb* befog, bewilder, confound, confuse, dumbfound, embarrass, obfuscate, perplex, pose, puzzle.

myth *n* fable, legend, tradition; allegory, fiction, invention, parable, story; falsehood, fancy, figment, lie, untruth.

mythical *adj* allegorical, fabled, fabulous, fanciful, fictitious, imaginary, legendary, mythological.

N

nab vb catch, clutch, grasp, seize.

nag[1] vb carp, fuss, hector, henpeck, pester, torment, worry. • n nagger, scold, shrew, tartar.

nag[2] n bronco, crock, hack, horse, pony, scrag.

naive adj artless, candid, ingenuous, natural, plain, simple, unaffected, unsophisticated.

naked adj bare, nude, uncovered; denuded, unclad, unclothed, undressed; defenceless, exposed, open, unarmed, unguarded, unprotected; evident, manifest, plain, stark, unconcealed, undisguised; mere, sheer, simple; bare, destitute, rough, rude, unfurnished, unprovided; uncoloured, unexaggerated, unvarnished.

name vb call, christen, denounce, dub, entitle, phrase, style, term; mention; denominate, designate, indicate, nominate, specify. • n appellation, cognomen, denomination, designation, epithet, nickname, surname, sobriquet, title; character, credit, reputation, repute; celebrity, distinction, eminence, fame, honour, note, praise, renown.

narcotic adj stupefacient, stupefactive, stupefying. • n anaesthetic, anodyne, dope, opiate, sedative, stupefacient, tranquillizer.

narrate vb chronicle, describe, detail, enumerate, recite, recount, rehearse, relate, tell.

narration n account, description, chronicle, history, narrative, recital, rehearsal, relation, story, tale.

narrow vb confine, contract, cramp, limit, restrict, straiten. • adj circumscribed, confined, contracted, cramped, incapacious, limited, pinched, scanty, straitened; bigoted, hidebound, illiberal, ungenerous; close, near.

nastiness n defilement, dirtiness, filth, filthiness, foulness, impurity, pollution, squalor, uncleanness; indecency, grossness, obscenity, pornography, ribaldry, smut, smuttiness.

nasty adj defiled, dirty, filthy, foul, impure, loathsome, polluted, squalid, unclean; gross, indecent, indelicate, lewd, loose, obscene, smutty, vile; disagreeable, disgusting, nauseous, odious, offensive, repulsive, sickening; aggravating, annoying, pesky, pestering, troublesome.

nation n commonwealth, realm, state; community, people, population, race, stock, tribe.

native adj aboriginal, autochthonal, autochthonous, domestic, home, indigenous, vernacular; genuine, intrinsic, natural, original, real; congenital, inborn, inbred, inherent, innate, natal. • n aborigine, autochthon, inhabitant, national, resident.

natty adj dandyish, fine, foppish, jaunty, neat, nice, spruce, tidy.

natural adj indigenous, innate, native, original; characteristic, essential; legitimate, normal, regular; artless, authentic, genuine, ingenuous, unreal, simple, spontaneous, unaffected; bastard, illegitimate.

nature n universe, world; character, constitution, essence; kind, quality, species, sort; disposition, grain, humour, mood, temper; being, intellect, intelligence, mind.

naughty adj bad, corrupt, mischievous, perverse, worthless.

nausea n queasiness, seasickness; loathing, qualm; aversion, disgust, repugnance.

nauseous adj abhorrent, disgusting, distasteful, loathsome, offensive, repulsive, revolting, sickening.

naval adj marine, maritime, nautical.

navigate vb cruise, direct, guide, pilot, plan, sail, steer.

navy n fleet, shipping, vessels.

near vb approach, draw close. • adj adjacent, approximate, close, contiguous, neighbouring, nigh; approaching, forthcoming, imminent, impending; dear, familiar, friendly, intimate; direct, immediate, short, straight; accurate, literal; narrow, parsimonious.

nearly adv almost, approximately, well-nigh; closely, intimately, pressingly; meanly, parsimoniously, penuriously, stingily.

neat adj clean, cleanly, orderly, tidy, trim, unsoiled; nice, smart, spruce; chaste, pure, simple; excellent, pure, unadulterated; adroit, clever, exact, finished; dainty, nice.

nebulous adj cloudy, hazy, misty.

necessary adj inevitable, unavoidable; essential, expedient, indispensable, needful, requisite; compelling, compulsory, involuntary. • n essential, necessity, requirement, requisite.

necessitate vb compel, constrain, demand, force, impel, oblige.

necessitous adj destitute, distressed, indigent, moneyless, needy, penniless, pinched, poor, poverty-stricken; narrow, pinching.

necessity n inevitability, inevitableness, unavoidability, unavoidableness; compulsion, destiny, fatality, fate; emergency, urgency; exigency, indigence, indispensability, indispensableness, need, needfulness, poverty, want; essentiality, essentialness, requirement, requisite.

necromancy n conjuration, divination, enchantment, magic, sorcery, witchcraft, wizardry.

necropolis n burial ground, cemetery, churchyard, crematorium, graveyard, mortuary.

need vb demand, lack, require, want. • n emergency, exigency, extremity, necessity, strait, urgency, want; destitution, distress, indigence, neediness, penury, poverty, privation.

needful adj distressful, necessitous, necessary; essential, indispensable, requisite.

needless adj superfluous, unnecessary, useless.

needy adj destitute, indigent, necessitous, poor.

nefarious adj abominable, atrocious, detestable, dreadful, execrable, flagitious, heinous, horrible, infamous, iniquitous, scandalous, vile, wicked.

negation n denial, disavowal, disclaimer, rejection, renunciation.

neglect vb condemn, despise, disregard, forget, ignore, omit, overlook, slight. • n carelessness, default, failure, heedlessness, inattention, omission, remissness; disregard, disrespect, slight; indifference, negligence.

negligence n carelessness, disregard, heedlessness, inadvertency, inattention, indifference, neglect, remissness, slackness, thoughtlessness; defect, fault, inadvertence, omission, shortcoming.

negligent adj careless, heedless, inattentive, indifferent, neglectful, regardless, thoughtless.

negotiate vb arrange, bargain, deal, debate, sell, settle, transact, treat.

neighbourhood n district, environs, locality, vicinage, vicinity; adjacency, nearness, propinquity, proximity.

neighbourly adj attentive, civil, friendly, kind, obliging, social.

neophyte n beginner, catechumen, convert, novice, pupil, tyro.

nerve vb brace, energize, fortify, invigorate, strengthen. • n force, might, power, strength, vigour; coolness, courage, endurance, firmness, fortitude, hardihood, manhood, pluck, resolution, self-command, steadiness.

nervous adj forcible, powerful, robust, strong, vigorous; irritable, fearful, shaky, timid, timorous, weak, weakly.

nestle vb cuddle, harbour, lodge, nuzzle, snug, snuggle.

nettle vb chafe, exasperate, fret, harass, incense, irritate, provoke, ruffle, sting, tease, vex.

neutral adj impartial, indifferent; colourless, mediocre.

neutralize vb cancel, counterbalance, counterpoise, invalidate, offset.

nevertheless adv however, nonetheless, notwithstanding, yet.

new adj fresh, latest, modern, novel, recent, unused; additional, another, further; reinvigorated, renovated, repaired.

news n advice, information, intelligence, report, tidings, word.

nice adj accurate, correct, critical, definite, delicate, exact, exquisite, precise, rigorous, strict; dainty, difficult, exacting, fastidious, finical, punctilious, squeamish; discerning, discriminating, particular, precise, scrupulous; neat, tidy, trim; fine, minute, refined, subtle; delicate, delicious, luscious, palatable, savoury, soft, tender; agreeable, delightful, good, pleasant.

nicety n accuracy, exactness, niceness, precision, truth, daintiness, fastidiousness, squeamishness; discrimination, subtlety.

niggard n churl, curmudgeon, miser, screw, scrimp, skinflint.

niggardly adj avaricious, close, close-fisted, illiberal, mean, mercenary, miserly, parsimonious, penurious, skinflint, sordid, stingy.

nigh *adj* adjacent, adjoining, contiguous, near; present, proximate. • *adv* almost, near, nearly.

nimble *adj* active, agile, alert, brisk, lively, prompt, quick, speedy, sprightly, spry, swift, tripping.

nobility *n* aristocracy, dignity, elevation, eminence, grandeur, greatness, loftiness, magnanimity, nobleness, peerage, superiority, worthiness.

noble *adj* dignified, elevated, eminent, exalted, generous, great, honourable, illustrious, magnanimous, superior, worthy; choice, excellent; aristocratic, gentle, high-born, patrician; grand, lofty, lordly, magnificent, splendid, stately. • *n* aristocrat, grandee, lord, nobleman, peer.

noctambulist *n* sleepwalker, somnambulist.

noise *vb* bruit, gossip, repeat, report, rumour. • *n* ado, blare, clamour, clatter, cry, din, fuss, hubbub, hullabaloo, outcry, pandemonium, racket, row, sound, tumult, uproar, vociferation.

noiseless *adj* inaudible, quiet, silent, soundless.

noisome *adj* bad, baneful, deleterious, disgusting, fetid, foul, hurtful, injurious, mischievous, nocuous, noxious, offensive, pernicious, pestiferous, pestilential, poisonous, unhealthy, unwholesome.

noisy *adj* blatant, blustering, boisterous, brawling, clamorous, loud, uproarious, riotous, tumultuous, vociferous.

nomadic *adj* migratory, pastoral, vagrant, wandering.

nominal *adj* formal, inconsiderable, minimal, ostensible, pretended, professed, so-called, titular.

nominate *vb* appoint, choose, designate, name, present, propose.

nonchalant *adj* apathetic, careless, cool, indifferent, unconcerned.

nondescript *adj* amorphous, characterless, commonplace, dull, indescribable, odd, ordinary, unclassifiable, uninteresting, unremarkable.

nonentity *n* cipher, futility, inexistence, inexistency, insignificance, nobody, nonexistence, nothingness.

nonplus *vb* astonish, bewilder, confound, confuse, discomfit, disconcert, embarrass, floor, gravel, perplex, pose, puzzle.

nonsensical *adj* absurd, foolish, irrational, senseless, silly, stupid.

norm *n* model, pattern, rule, standard.

normal *adj* analogical, legitimate, natural, ordinary, regular, usual; erect, perpendicular, vertical.

notable *adj* distinguished, extraordinary, memorable, noted, remarkable, signal; conspicuous, evident, noticeable, observable, plain, prominent, striking; notorious, rare, well-known. • *n* celebrity, dignitary, notability, worthy.

note *vb* heed, mark, notice, observe, regard, remark; record, register; denote, designate. • *n* memorandum, minute, record; annotation, comment, remark, scholium; indication, mark, sign, symbol, token; account, bill, catalogue, reckoning; billet, epistle, letter; consideration, heed, notice, observation; celebrity, consequence, credit, distinction, eminence, fame, notability, notedness, renown, reputation, respectability; banknote, bill, promissory note; song, strain, tune, voice.

noted *adj* celebrated, conspicuous, distinguished, eminent, famed, famous, illustrious, notable, notorious, remarkable, renowned, well-known.

nothing *n* inexistence, nonentity, nonexistence, nothingness, nullity; bagatelle, trifle.

notice *vb* mark, note, observe, perceive, regard, see; comment on, mention, remark; attend to, heed. • *n* cognizance, heed, note, observation, regard; advice, announcement, information, intelligence, mention, news, notification; communication, intimation, premonition, warning; attention, civility, consideration, respect; comments, remarks.

notify *vb* advertise, announce, declare, publish, promulgate; acquaint, apprise, inform.

notion *n* concept, conception, idea; apprehension, belief, conceit, conviction, expectation, estimation, impression, judgement, opinion, sentiment, view.

notoriety *n* celebrity, fame, figure, name, note, publicity, reputation, repute, vogue.

notorious *adj* apparent, egregious, evident, notable, obvious, open, overt, manifest, patent, well-known; celebrated, conspicuous, distinguished, famed, famous, flagrant, infamous, noted, remarkable, renowned.

notwithstanding *conj* despite, however, nevertheless, yet. • *prep* despite.

nourish *vb* feed, nurse, nurture; maintain, supply, support; breed, educate, instruct, train; cherish, encourage, foment, foster, promote, succour.

nourishment *n* aliment, diet, food, nutriment, nutrition, sustenance.

novel *adj* fresh, modern, new, rare, recent, strange, uncommon, unusual. • *n* fiction, romance, story, tale.

novice *n* convert, proselyte; initiate, neophyte, novitiate, probationer; apprentice, beginner, learner, tyro.

noxious *adj* baneful, deadly, deleterious, destructive, detrimental, hurtful, injurious, insalubrious, mischievous, noisome, pernicious, pestilent, poisonous, unfavourable, unwholesome.

nude *adj* bare, denuded, exposed, naked, uncovered, unclothed, undressed.

nugatory *adj* frivolous, insignificant, trifling, trivial, vain, worthless; bootless, ineffectual, inefficacious, inoperative, null, unavailing, useless.

nuisance *n* annoyance, bore, bother, infliction, offence, pest, plague, trouble.

null *adj* ineffectual, invalid, nugatory, useless, void; characterless, colourless.

nullify *vb* abolish, abrogate, annul, cancel, invalidate, negate, quash, repeal, revoke.

numb *vb* benumb, deaden, stupefy. • *adj* benumbed, deadened, dulled, insensible, paralysed.

number *vb* calculate, compute, count, enumerate, numerate, reckon, tell; account, reckon. • *n* digit, figure, numeral; horde, multitude, numerousness, throng; aggregate, collection, sum, total.

numerous *adj* abundant, many, numberless.

nuncio *n* ambassador, legate, messenger.

nunnery *n* abbey, cloister, convent, monastery.

nuptial *adj* bridal, conjugal, connubial, hymeneal, matrimonial.

nuptials *npl* espousal, marriage, wedding.

nurse *vb* nourish, nurture; rear, suckle; cherish, encourage, feed, foment, foster, pamper, promote, succour; economize, manage; caress, dandle, fondle. • *n* auxiliary, orderly, sister; amah, *au pair*, babysitter, nanny, nursemaid, nurserymaid.

nurture *vb* feed, nourish, nurse, tend; breed, discipline, educate, instruct, rear, school, train. • *n* diet, food, nourishment; breeding, discipline, education, instruction, schooling, training, tuition; attention, nourishing, nursing.

nutriment *n* aliment, food, nourishment, nutrition, pabulum, subsistence, sustenance.

nutrition *n* diet, food, nourishment, nutriment.

nutritious *adj* invigorating, nourishing, strengthening, supporting, sustaining.

nymph *n* damsel, dryad, lass, girl, maid, maiden, naiad.

O

oaf *n* blockhead, dolt, dunce, fool, idiot, simpleton.

oath *n* blasphemy, curse, expletive, imprecation, malediction; affirmation, pledge, promise, vow.

obduracy *n* contumacy, doggedness, obstinacy, stubbornness, tenacity; depravity, impenitence.

obdurate *adj* hard, harsh, rough, rugged; callous, cantankerous, dogged, firm, hardened, inflexible, insensible, obstinate, pigheaded, unfeeling, stubborn, unbending, unyielding; depraved, graceless, lost, reprobate, shameless, impenitent, incorrigible, irreclaimable.

obedience *n* acquiescence, agreement, compliance, duty, respect, reverence, submission, submissiveness, subservience.

obedient *adj* acquiescent, compliant, deferential, duteous, dutiful, observant, regardful, respectful, submissive, subservient, yielding.

obeisance *n* bow, courtesy, curtsy, homage, reverence, salutation.

obelisk *n* column, pillar.

obese *adj* corpulent, fat, fleshy, gross, plump, podgy, portly, stout.

obesity *n* corpulence, corpulency, embonpoint, fatness, fleshiness, obeseness, plumpness.

obey *vb* comply, conform, heed, keep, mind, observe, submit, yield.

obfuscate *vb* cloud, darken, obscure; bewilder, confuse, muddle.

object[1] *vb* cavil, contravene, demur, deprecate, disapprove of, except to, impeach, oppose, protest, refuse.

object[2] *n* particular, phenomenon, precept, reality, thing; aim, butt, destination, end, mark, recipient, target; design, drift, goal, intention, motive, purpose, use, view.

objection *n* censure, difficulty, doubt, exception, protest, remonstrance, scruple.

objurgate *vb* chide, reprehend, reprove.

oblation *n* gift, offering, sacrifice.

obligation *n* accountability, accountableness, responsibility; agreement, bond, contract, covenant, engagement, stipulation; debt, indebtedness, liability.

obligatory *adj* binding, coercive, compulsory, enforced, necessary, unavoidable.

oblige *vb* bind, coerce, compel, constrain, force, necessitate, require; accommodate, benefit, convenience, favour, gratify, please; obligate, bind.

obliging *adj* accommodating, civil, complaisant, considerate, kind, friendly, polite.

oblique *adj* aslant, inclined, sidelong, slanting; indirect, obscure.

obliterate *vb* cancel, delete, destroy, efface, eradicate, erase, expunge.

oblivious *adj* careless, forgetful, heedless, inattentive, mindless, negligent, neglectful.

obloquy *n* aspersion, backbiting, blame, calumny, censure, contumely, defamation, detraction, disgrace, odium, reproach, reviling, slander, traducing.

obnoxious *adj* blameworthy, censurable, faulty, reprehensible; hateful, objectionable, obscene, odious, offensive, repellent, repugnant, repulsive, unpleasant, unpleasing.

obscene *adj* broad, coarse, filthy, gross, immodest, impure, indecent, indelicate, ribald, unchaste, lewd, licentious, loose, offensive, pornographic, shameless, smutty; disgusting, dirty, foul.

obscure *vb* becloud, befog, blur, cloud, darken, eclipse, dim, obfuscate, obnubilate, shade; conceal, cover, equivocate, hide. • *adj* dark, darksome, dim, dusky, gloomy, lurid, murky, rayless, shadowy, sombre, unenlightened, unilluminated; abstruse, blind, cabbalistic, difficult, doubtful, enigmatic, high, incomprehensible, indefinite, indistinct, intricate, involved, mysterious, mystic, recondite, undefined, unintelligible, vague; remote, secluded; humble, inglorious, nameless, renownless, undistinguished, unhonoured, unknown, unnoted, unnoticed.

obsequious *adj* cringing, deferential, fawning, flattering, servile, slavish, supple, subservient, sycophantic, truckling.

observant *adj* attentive, heedful, mindful, perceptive, quick, regardful, vigilant, watchful.

observation *n* attention, cognition, notice, observance; annotation, note, remark; experience, knowledge.

observe *vb* eye, mark, note, notice, remark, watch; behold, detect, discover, perceive, see; express, mention, remark, say, utter; comply, conform, follow, fulfil, obey; celebrate, keep, regard, solemnize.

obsolete *adj* ancient, antiquated, antique, archaic, disused, neglected, old, old-fashioned, obsolescent, out-of-date, past, passé, unfashionable.

obstacle *n* barrier, check, difficulty, hindrance, impediment, interference, interruption, obstruction, snag, stumbling block.

obstinacy *n* contumacy, doggedness, headiness, firmness, inflexibility, intractability, obduracy, persistence, perseverance, perversity, resoluteness, stubbornness, tenacity, wilfulness.

obstinate *adj* cross-grained, contumacious, dogged, firm, headstrong, inflexible, immovable, intractable, mulish, obdurate, opinionated, persistent, pertinacious, perverse, resolute, self-willed, stubborn, tenacious, unyielding, wilful.

obstreperous *adj* boisterous, clamorous, loud, noisy, riotous, tumultuous, turbulent, unruly, uproarious, vociferous.

obstruct *vb* bar, barricade, block, blockade, block up, choke, clog, close, glut, jam, obturate, stop; hinder, impede, oppose, prevent; arrest, check, curb, delay, embrace, interrupt, retard, slow.

obstruction *n* bar, barrier, block, blocking, check, difficulty, hindrance, impediment, obstacle, stoppage; check, clog, embarrassment, interruption, obturation.

obtain *vb* achieve, acquire, attain, bring, contrive, earn, elicit, gain, get, induce, procure, secure; hold, prevail, stand, subsist.

obtrude *vb* encroach, infringe, interfere, intrude, trespass.

obtrusive *adj* forward, interfering, intrusive, meddling, officious.

obtuse *adj* blunt; blockish, doltish, dull, dull-witted, heavy, stockish, stolid, stupid, slow, unintellectual, unintelligent.

obviate *vb* anticipate, avert, counteract, preclude, prevent, remove.

obvious *adj* exposed, liable, open, subject; apparent, clear, distinct, evident, manifest, palatable, patent, perceptible, plain, self-evident, unmistakable, visible.

occasion *vb* breed, cause, create, originate, produce; induce, influence, move, persuade. • *n* casualty, event, incident, occurrence; conjuncture, convenience, juncture, opening, opportunity; condition, necessity, need, exigency, requirement, want; cause, ground, reason; inducement, influence; circumstance, exigency.

occasional *adj* accidental, casual, incidental, infrequent, irregular, uncommon; causative, causing.

occasionally *adv* casually, sometimes.

occult *adj* abstruse, cabbalistic, hidden, latent, secret, invisible, mysterious, mystic, mystical, recondite, shrouded, undetected, undiscovered, unknown, unrevealed, veiled. • *n* magic, sorcery, witchcraft.

occupation *n* holding, occupancy, possession, tenure, use; avocation, business, calling, craft, employment, engagement, job, post, profession, trade, vocation.

occupy *vb* capture, hold, keep, possess; cover, fill, garrison, inhabit, take up, tenant; engage, employ, use.

occur *vb* appear, arise, offer; befall, chance, eventuate, happen, result, supervene.

occurrence *n* accident, adventure, affair, casualty, event, happening, incident, proceeding, transaction.

odd *adj* additional, redundant, remaining; casual, incidental; inappropriate, queer, unsuitable; comical, droll, erratic, extravagant, extraordinary, fantastic, grotesque, irregular, peculiar, quaint, singular, strange, uncommon, uncouth, unique, unusual, whimsical.

odds *npl* difference, disparity, inequality; advantage, superiority, supremacy.

odious *adj* abominable, detestable, execrable, hateful, shocking; hated, obnoxious, unpopular; disagreeable, forbidding, loathsome, offensive.

odium *n* abhorrence, detestation, dislike, enmity, hate, hatred; odiousness, repulsiveness; obloquy, opprobrium, reproach, shame.

odorous *adj* aromatic, balmy, fragrant, perfumed, redolent, scented, sweet-scented, sweet-smelling.

odour *n* aroma, fragrance, perfume, redolence, scent, smell.

offal *n* carrion, dregs, garbage, refuse, rubbish, waste.

offence *n* aggression, attack, assault; anger, displeasure, indignation, pique, resentment, umbrage, wrath; affront, harm, injury, injustice, insult, outrage, wrong; crime, delinquency, fault, misdeed, misdemeanour, sin, transgression, trespass.

offend *vb* affront, annoy, chafe, displease, fret, gall, irritate, mortify, nettle, provoke, vex; molest, pain, shock, wound; fall, sin, stumble, transgress.

offender *n* convict, criminal, culprit, delinquent, felon, malefactor, sinner, transgressor, trespasser.

offensive *adj* aggressive, attacking, invading; disgusting, loathsome, nauseating, nauseous, repulsive, sickening; abominable, detestable, disagreeable, displeasing, execrable, hateful, obnoxious, repugnant, revolting, shocking, unpalatable, unpleasant; abusive, disagreeable, impertinent, insolent, insulting, irritating, opprobrious, rude, saucy, unpleasant. • *n* attack, onslaught.

offer *vb* present, proffer, tender; exhibit; furnish, propose, propound, show; volunteer; dare, essay, endeavour, venture. • *n* overture, proffering, proposal, proposition, tender, overture; attempt, bid, endeavour, essay.

offhand *adj* abrupt, brusque, casual, curt, extempore, impromptu, informal, unpremeditated, unstudied. • *adv* carelessly, casually, clumsily, haphazardly, informally, slapdash; ad-lib, extemporaneously, extemporarily, extempore, impromptu.

office *n* duty, function, service, work; berth, place, position, post, situation; business, capacity, charge, employment, trust; bureau, room.

officiate *vb* act, perform, preside, serve.

officious *adj* busy, dictatorial, forward, impertinent, interfering, intermeddling, meddlesome, meddling, obtrusive, pushing, pushy.

offset *vb* balance, counteract, counterbalance, counterpoise. • *n* branch, offshoot, scion, shoot, slip, sprout, twig; counterbalance, counterpoise, set-off, equivalent.

offspring *n* brood, children, descendants, issue, litter, posterity, progeny; cadet, child, scion.

often *adv* frequently, generally, oftentimes, repeatedly.

ogre *n* bugbear, demon, devil, goblin, hobgoblin, monster, spectre.

old *adj* aged, ancient, antiquated, antique, archaic, elderly, obsolete, olden, old-fashioned, superannuated; decayed, done, senile, worn-out; original, primitive, pristine; former, preceding, pre-existing.

oleaginous *adj* adipose, fat, fatty, greasy, oily, sebaceous, unctuous.

omen *n* augury, auspice, foreboding, portent, presage, prognosis, sign, warning.

ominous *adj* inauspicious, monitory, portentous, premonitory, threatening, unpropitious.

omission *n* default, failure, forgetfulness, neglect, oversight.

omit *vb* disregard, drop, eliminate, exclude, miss, neglect, overlook, skip.

omnipotent *adj* almighty, all-powerful.

omniscient *adj* all-knowing, all-seeing, all-wise.

oneness *n* individuality, singleness, unity.

onerous *adj* burdensome, difficult, hard, heavy, laborious, oppressive, responsible, weighty.

one-sided *adj* partial, prejudiced, unfair, unilateral, unjust.

only *adj* alone, single, sole, solitary. • *adv* barely, merely, simply.

onset *n* assault, attack, charge, onslaught, storm, storming.

onus *n* burden, liability, load, responsibility.

ooze *vb* distil, drip, drop, shed; drain, exude, filter, leak, percolate, stain, transude. • *n* mire, mud, slime.

opaque *adj* dark, dim, hazy, muddy; abstruse, cryptic, enigmatic, enigmatical, obscure, unclear.

open *vb* expand, spread; begin, commence, initiate; disclose, exhibit, reveal, show; unbar, unclose, uncover, unlock, unseal, untie. • *adj* expanded, extended, unclosed, spread wide; aboveboard, artless, candid, cordial, fair, frank, guileless, hearty, honest, sincere, openhearted, single-minded, undesigning, undisguised, undissembling, unreserved; bounteous, bountiful, free, generous, liberal, munificent; ajar, uncovered; exposed, undefended, unprotected; clear, unobstructed; accessible, public, unenclosed, unrestricted; mild, moderate; apparent, debatable, evident, obvious, patent, plain, undetermined.

opening *adj* commencing, first, inaugural, initiatory, introductory. • *n* aperture, breach, chasm, cleft, fissure, flaw, gap, gulf, hole, interspace, loophole, orifice, perforation, rent, rift; beginning, commencement, dawn; chance, opportunity, vacancy.

openly *adv* candidly, frankly, honestly, plainly, publicly.

openness *n* candour, frankness, honesty, ingenuousness, plainness, unreservedness.

operate *vb* act, function, work; cause, effect, occasion, produce; manipulate, use, run.

operation *n* manipulation, performance, procedure, proceeding, process; action, affair, manoeuvre, motion, movement.

operative *adj* active, effective, effectual, efficient, serviceable, vigorous; important, indicative, influential, significant. • *n* artisan, employee, labourer, mechanic, worker, workman.

opiate *adj* narcotic, sedative, soporiferous, soporific. • *n* anodyne, drug, narcotic, sedative, tranquillizer.

opine *vb* apprehend, believe, conceive, fancy, judge, suppose, presume, surmise, think.

opinion *n* conception, idea, impression, judgment, notion, sentiment, view; belief, persuasion, tenet; esteem, estimation, judgment.

opinionated *adj* biased, bigoted, cocksure, conceited, dictatorial, dogmatic, opinionative, prejudiced, stubborn.

opponent *adj* adverse, antagonistic, contrary, opposing, opposite, repugnant. • *n* adversary, antagonist, competitor, contestant, counteragent, enemy, foe, opposite, opposer, party, rival.

opportune *adj* appropriate, auspicious, convenient, favourable, felicitous, fit, fitting, fortunate, lucky, propitious, seasonable, suitable, timely, well-timed.

opportunity *n* chance, convenience, moment, occasion.

oppose *vb* combat, contravene, counteract, dispute, obstruct, oppugn, resist, thwart, withstand; check, prevent; confront, counterpoise.

opposite *adj* facing, fronting; conflicting, contradictory, contrary, different, diverse, incompatible, inconsistent, irreconcilable; adverse, antagonistic, hostile, inimical, opposed, opposing, repugnant. • *n* contradiction, contrary, converse, reverse.

opposition *n* antagonism, antinomy, contrariety, inconsistency, repugnance; counteraction, counter-influence, hostility, resistance; hindrance, obstacle, obstruction, oppression, prevention.

oppress *vb* burden, crush, depress, harass, load, maltreat, overburden, overpower, overwhelm, persecute, subdue, suppress, tyrannize, wrong.

oppression *n* abuse, calamity, cruelty, hardship, injury, injustice, misery, persecution, severity, suffering, tyranny; depression, dullness, heaviness, lassitude.

oppressive *adj* close, muggy, stifling, suffocating, sultry.

opprobrious *adj* abusive, condemnatory, contemptuous, damnatory, insolent, insulting, offensive, reproachable, scandalous, scurrilous, vituperative; despised, dishonourable, disreputable, hateful, infamous, shameful.

opprobrium *n* contumely, scurrility; calumny, disgrace, ignominy, infamy, obloquy, odium, reproach.

oppugn *vb* assail, argue, attack, combat, contravene, oppose, resist, thwart, withstand.

option *n* choice, discretion, election, preference, selection.

optional *adj* discretionary, elective, nonobligatory, voluntary.

opulence *n* affluence, fortune, independence, luxury, riches, wealth.

opulent *adj* affluent, flush, luxurious, moneyed, plentiful, rich, sumptuous, wealthy.

oracular *adj* ominous, portentous, prophetic; authoritative, dogmatic, magisterial, positive; aged, grave, wise; ambiguous, blind, dark, equivocal, obscure.

oral *adj* nuncupative, spoken, verbal, vocal.

oration *n* address, declamation, discourse, harangue, speech.

orb *n* ball, globe, sphere; circle, circuit, orbit, ring; disk, wheel.

orbit *vb* circle, encircle, revolve around. • *n* course, path, revolution, track.

ordain *vb* appoint, call, consecrate, elect, experiment, constitute, establish, institute, regulate; decree, enjoin, enact, order, prescribe.

order *vb* adjust, arrange, methodize, regulate, systematize; carry on, conduct, manage; bid, command, direct, instruct, require. • *n* arrangement, disposition, method, regularity, symmetry, system; law, regulation, rule; discipline, peace, quiet; command, commission, direction, injunction, instruction, mandate, prescription; class, degree, grade, kind, rank; family, tribe; brotherhood, community, fraternity, society; sequence, succession.

orderly *adj* methodical, regular, systematic; peaceable, quiet, well-behaved; neat, shipshape, tidy.

ordinance *n* appointment, command, decree, edict, enactment, law, order, prescript, regulation, rule, statute; ceremony, observance, sacrament, rite, ritual.

ordinary *adj* accustomed, customary, established, everyday, normal, regular, settled, wonted, everyday, regular; common, frequent, habitual, usual; average, commonplace, indifferent, inferior, mean, mediocre, second-rate, undistinguished; homely, plain.

organization *n* business, construction, constitution, organism, structure, system.

organize *vb* adjust, constitute, construct, form, make, shape; arrange, coordinate, correlate, establish, systematize.

orgy *n* carousal, debauch, debauchery, revel, saturnalia.

orifice *n* aperture, hole, mouth, perforation, pore, vent.

origin *n* beginning, birth, commencement, cradle, derivation, foundation, fountain, fountainhead, original, rise, root, source, spring, starting point; cause, occasion; heritage, lineage, parentage.

original *adj* aboriginal, first, primary, primeval, primitive, primordial, pristine; fresh, inventive, novel; eccentric, odd, peculiar. • *n* cause, commencement, origin, source, spring; archetype, exemplar, model, pattern, prototype, protoplast, type.

originate *vb* arise, begin, emanate, flow, proceed, rise, spring; create, discover, form, invent, produce.

originator *n* author, creator, former, inventor, maker, parent.

orison *n* petition, prayer, solicitation, supplication.

ornament *vb* adorn, beautify, bedeck, bedizen, decorate, deck, emblazon, garnish, grace. • *n* adornment, bedizenment, decoration, design, embellishment, garnish, ornamentation.

ornate *adj* beautiful, bedecked, decorated, elaborate, elegant, embellished, florid, flowery, ornamental, ornamented.

orthodox *adj* conventional, correct, sound, true.

oscillate *vb* fluctuate, sway, swing, vacillate, vary, vibrate.

ostensible *adj* apparent, assigned, avowed, declared, exhibited, manifest, presented, visible; plausible, professed, specious.

ostentation *n* dash, display, flourish, pageantry, parade, pomp, pomposity, pompousness, show, vaunting; appearance, semblance, showiness.

ostentatious *adj* boastful, dashing, flaunting, pompous, pretentious, showy, vain, vainglorious; gaudy.

ostracize *vb* banish, boycott, exclude, excommunicate, exile, expatriate, expel, evict.

oust *vb* dislodge, dispossess, eject, evict, expel.

outbreak *n* ebullition, eruption, explosion, outburst; affray, broil, conflict, commotion, fray, riot, row; flare-up, manifestation.

outcast *n* exile, expatriate; castaway, pariah, reprobate, vagabond.

outcome *n* conclusion, consequence, event, issue, result, upshot.

outcry *n* cry, scream, screech, yell; bruit, clamour, noise, tumult, vociferation.

outdo *vb* beat, exceed, excel, outgo, outstrip, outvie, surpass.

outlandish *adj* alien, exotic, foreign, strange; barbarous, bizarre, uncouth.

outlaw *vb* ban, banish, condemn, exclude, forbid, make illegal, prohibit. • *n* bandit, brigand, crook, freebooter, highwayman, lawbreaker, marauder, robber, thief.

outlay *n* disbursement, expenditure, outgoings.

outline *vb* delineate, draft, draw, plan, silhouette, sketch. • *n* contour, profile; delineation, draft, drawing, plan, rough draft, silhouette, sketch.

outlive *vb* last, live longer, survive.

outlook *n* future, prospect, sight, view; lookout, watch-tower.

outrage *vb* abuse, injure, insult, maltreat, offend, shock, injure. • *n* abuse, affront, indignity, insult, offence.

outrageous *adj* abusive, frantic, furious, frenzied, mad, raging, turbulent, violent, wild; atrocious, enormous, flagrant, heinous, monstrous, nefarious, villainous; enormous, excessive, extravagant, unwarrantable.

outré *adj* excessive, exorbitant, extravagant, immoderate, inordinate, overstrained, unconventional.

outrun *vb* beat, exceed, outdistance, outgo, outstrip, outspeed, surpass.

outset *n* beginning, commencement, entrance, opening, start, starting point.

outshine *vb* eclipse, outstrip, overshadow, surpass.

outspoken *adj* abrupt, blunt, candid, frank, plain, plainspoken, unceremonious, unreserved.

outstanding *adj* due, owing, uncollected, ungathered, unpaid, unsettled; conspicuous, eminent, prominent, striking.

outward *adj* exterior, external, outer, outside.

outwit *vb* cheat, circumvent, deceive, defraud, diddle, dupe, gull, outmanoeuvre, overreach, swindle, victimize.

overawe *vb* affright, awe, browbeat, cow, daunt, frighten, intimidate, scare, terrify.

overbalance *vb* capsize, overset, overturn, tumble, upset; outweigh, preponderate.

overbearing *adj* oppressive, overpowering; arrogant, dictatorial, dogmatic, domineering, haughty, imperious, overweening, proud, supercilious.

overcast *vb* cloud, darken, overcloud, overshadow, shade, shadow. • *adj* cloudy, darkened, hazy, murky, obscure.

overcharge *vb* burden, oppress, overburden, overload, surcharge; crowd, overfill; exaggerate, overstate, overstrain.

overcome *vb* beat, choke, conquer, crush, defeat, discomfit, overbear, overmaster, overpower, overthrow, overturn, overwhelm, prevail, rout, subdue, subjugate, surmount, vanquish.

overflow *vb* brim over, fall over, pour over, pour out, shower, spill; deluge, inundate, submerge. • *n* deluge, inundation, profusion, superabundance.

overhaul *vb* overtake; check, examine, inspect, repair, survey. • *n* check, examination, inspection.

overlay *vb* cover, spread over; overlie, overpress, smother; crush, overpower, overwhelm; cloud, hide, obscure, overcast. • *n* appliqué, covering, decoration, veneer.

overlook *vb* inspect, oversee, superintend, supervise; disregard, miss, neglect, slight; condone, excuse, forgive, pardon, pass over.

overpower *vb* beat, conquer, crush, defeat, discomfit, overbear, overcome, overmaster, overturn, overwhelm, subdue, subjugate, vanquish.

overreach *vb* exceed, outstrip, overshoot, pass, surpass; cheat, circumvent, deceive, defraud.

override *vb* outride, outweigh, pass, quash, supersede, surpass.

overrule *vb* control, govern, sway; annul, cancel, nullify, recall, reject, repeal, repudiate, rescind, revoke, reject, set aside, supersede, suppress.

oversight *n* care, charge, control, direction, inspection, management, superintendence, supervision, surveillance; blunder, error, fault, inadvertence, inattention, lapse, miss, mistake, neglect, omission, slip, trip.

overt *adj* apparent, glaring, open, manifest, notorious, patent, public, unconcealed.

overthrow *vb* overturn, upset, subvert; demolish, destroy, level; beat, conquer, crush, defeat, discomfit, foil, master, overcome, overpower, overwhelm, rout, subjugate, vanquish, worst. • *n* downfall, fall, prostration, subversion; destruction, demolition, ruin; defeat, discomfiture, dispersion, rout.

overturn *vb* invert, overthrow, reverse, subvert, upset.

overture *n* invitation, offer, proposal, proposition.

overweening *adj* arrogant, conceited, consequential, egotistical, haughty, opinionated, proud, supercilious, vain, vainglorious.

overwhelm *vb* drown, engulf, inundate, overflow, submerge, swallow up, swamp; conquer, crush, defeat, overbear, overcome, overpower, subdue, vanquish.

overwrought *adj* overdone, overelaborate; agitated, excited, overexcited, overworked, stirred.

own[1] *vb* have, hold, possess; avow, confess; acknowledge, admit, allow, concede.

own[2] *adj* particular, personal, private.

owner *n* freeholder, holder, landlord, possessor, proprietor.

P

pace *vb* go, hasten, hurry, move, step, walk. • *n* amble, gait, step, walk.

pacific *adj* appeasing, conciliatory, ironic, mollifying, placating, peacemaking, propitiatory; calm, gentle, peaceable, peaceful, quiet, smooth, tranquil, unruffled.

pacify *vb* appease, conciliate, harmonize, tranquillize; allay, appease, assuage, calm, compose, hush, lay, lull, moderate, mollify, placate, propitiate, quell, quiet, smooth, soften, soothe, still.

pack *vb* compact, compress, crowd, fill; bundle, burden, load, stow. • *n* bale, budget, bundle, package, packet, parcel; burden, load; assemblage, assembly, assortment, collection, set; band, bevy, clan, company, crew, gang, knot, lot, party, squad.

pact *n* agreement, alliance, bargain, bond, compact, concordat, contract, convention, covenant, league, stipulation.

pagan *adj* heathen, heathenish, idolatrous, irreligious, paganist, paganistic. • *n* gentile, heathen, idolater.

pageantry *n* display, flourish, magnificence, parade, pomp, show, splendour, state.

pain *vb* agonize, bite, distress, hurt, rack, sting, torment, torture; afflict, aggrieve, annoy, bore, chafe, displease, disquiet, fret, grieve, harass, incommode, plague, tease, trouble, vex, worry; rankle, smart, shoot, sting, twinge. • *n* ache, agony, anguish, discomfort, distress, gripe, hurt, pang, smart, soreness, sting, suffering, throe, torment, torture, twinge; affliction, anguish, anxiety, bitterness, care, chagrin, disquiet, dolour, grief, heartache, misery, punishment, solicitude, sorrow, trouble, uneasiness, unhappiness, vexation, woe, wretchedness.

painful *adj* agonizing, distressful, excruciating, racking, sharp, tormenting, torturing; afflicting, afflictive, annoying, baleful, disagreeable, displeasing, disquieting, distressing, dolorous, grievous, provoking, troublesome, unpleasant, vexatious; arduous, careful, difficult, hard, severe, sore, toilsome.

pains *npl* care, effort, labour, task, toilsomeness, trouble; childbirth, labour, travail.

painstaking *adj* assiduous, careful, conscientious, diligent, hardworking, industrious, laborious, persevering, plodding, sedulous, strenuous.

paint *vb* delineate, depict, describe, draw, figure, pencil, portray, represent, sketch; adorn, beautify, deck, embellish, ornament. • *n* colouring, dye, pigment, stain; cosmetics, greasepaint, make-up.

pair *vb* couple, marry, mate, match. • *n* brace, couple, double, duo, match, twosome.

pal *n* buddy, chum, companion, comrade, crony, friend, mate, mucker.

palatable *adj* acceptable, agreeable, appetizing, delicate, delicious, enjoyable, flavourful, flavoursome, gustative, gustatory, luscious, nice, pleasant, pleasing, savoury, relishable, tasteful, tasty, toothsome.

palaver *vb* chat, chatter, converse, patter, prattle, say, speak, talk; confer, parley; blandish, cajole, flatter, wheedle. • *n* chat, chatter, conversation, discussion, language, prattle, speech, talk; confab, confabulation, conference, conclave, parley, powwow; balderdash, cajolery, flummery, gibberish.

pale *vb* blanch, lose colour, whiten. • *adj* ashen, ashy, blanched, bloodless, pallid, sickly, wan, white; blank, dim, obscure, spectral. • *n* picket, stake; circuit, enclosure; district, region, territory; boundary, confine, fence, limit.

pall¹ *n* cloak, cover, curtain, mantle, pallium, shield, shroud, veil.

pall² *vb* cloy, glut, gorge, satiate, surfeit; deject, depress, discourage, dishearten, dispirit; cloak, cover, drape, invest, overspread, shroud.

palliate *vb* cloak, conceal, cover, excuse, extenuate, hide, gloss, lessen; abate, allay, alleviate, assuage, blunt, diminish, dull, ease, mitigate, moderate, mollify, quell, quiet, relieve, soften, soothe, still.

pallid *adj* ashen, ashy, cadaverous, colourless, pale, sallow, wan, whitish.

palm¹ *vb* foist, impose, obtrude, pass off; handle, touch.

palm² *n* bays, crown, laurels, prize, trophy, victory.

palmy *adj* flourishing, fortunate, glorious, golden, halcyon, happy, joyous, prosperous, thriving, victorious.

palpable *adj* corporeal, material, tactile, tangible; evident, glaring, gross, intelligible, manifest, obvious, patent, plain, unmistakable.

palpitate *vb* flutter, pulsate, throb; quiver, shiver, tremble.

palter *vb* dodge, equivocate, evade, haggle, prevaricate, quibble, shift, shuffle, trifle.

paltry *adj* diminutive, feeble, inconsiderable, insignificant, little, miserable, petty, slender, slight, small, sorry, trifling, trivial, unimportant, wretched.

pamper *vb* baby, coddle, fondle, gratify, humour, spoil.

panacea *n* catholicon, cure-all, medicine, remedy.

panegyric *adj* commendatory, encomiastic, encomiastical, eulogistic, eulogistical, laudatory, panegyrical. • *n* eulogy, laudation, praise, paean, tribute.

pang *n* agony, anguish, distress, gripe, pain, throe, twinge.

panic *vb* affright, alarm, scare, startle, terrify; become terrified, overreact. • *n* alarm, consternation, fear, fright, jitters, terror.

pant *vb* blow, gasp, puff; heave, palpitate, pulsate, throb; languish; desire, hunger, long, sigh, thirst, yearn. • *n* blow, gasp, puff.

parable *n* allegory, fable, story.

paraclete *n* advocate, comforter, consoler, intercessor, mediator.

parade *vb* display, flaunt, show, vaunt. • *n* ceremony, display, flaunting, ostentation, pomp, show; array, pageant, review, spectacle; mall, promenade.

paradox *n* absurdity, contradiction, mystery.

paragon *n* flower, ideal, masterpiece, model, nonpareil, pattern, standard.

paragraph *n* clause, item, notice, passage, section, sentence, subdivision.

parallel *vb* be alike, compare, conform, correlate, match. • *adj* abreast, concurrent; allied, analogous, correspondent, equal, like, resembling, similar. • *n* conformity, likeness, resemblance, similarity; analogue, correlative, counterpart.

paramount *adj* chief, dominant, eminent, pre-eminent, principal, superior, supreme.

paraphernalia *n* accoutrements, appendages, appurtenances, baggage, belongings, effects, equipage, equipment, ornaments, trappings.

parasite *n* bloodsucker, fawner, flatterer, flunky, hanger-on, leech, spaniel, sycophant, toady, wheedler.

parcel *vb* allot, apportion, dispense, distribute, divide. • *n* budget, bundle, package; batch, collection, group, lot, set; division, part, patch, piece, plot, portion, tract.

parched *adj* arid, dry, scorched, shrivelled, thirsty.

pardon *vb* condone, forgive, overlook, remit; absolve, acquit, clear, discharge, excuse, release. • *n* absolution, amnesty, condonation, discharge, excuse, forgiveness, grace, mercy, overlook, release.

parentage *n* ancestry, birth, descent, extraction, family, lineage, origin, parenthood, pedigree, stock.

pariah *n* outcast, wretch.

parish *n* community, congregation, parishioners; district, subdivision.

parity *n* analogy, correspondence, equality, equivalence, likeness, sameness, similarity.

parody *vb* burlesque, caricature, imitate, lampoon, mock, ridicule, satirize, travesty. • *n* burlesque, caricature, imitation, ridicule, satire, travesty.

paroxysm *n* attack, convulsion, exacerbation, fit, outburst, seizure, spasm, throe.

parsimonious *adj* avaricious, close, close-fisted, covetous, frugal, grasping, grudging, illiberal, mean, mercenary, miserly, near, niggardly, penurious, shabby, sordid, sparing, stingy, tightfisted.

parson *n* churchman, clergyman, divine, ecclesiastic, incumbent, minister, pastor, priest, rector.

part *vb* break, dismember, dissever, divide, sever, subdivide, sunder; detach, disconnect, disjoin, dissociate, disunite, separate; allot, apportion, distribute, divide, mete, share; secrete. • *n* crumb, division, fraction, fragment, moiety, parcel, piece, portion, remnant, scrap, section, segment, subdivision; component, constituent, element, ingredient, member, organ; lot, share; concern, interest, participation; allotment, apportionment, dividend; business, charge, duty, function, office, work; faction, party; side; character, cue, lines, role; clause, paragraph, passage.

partake *vb* engage, participate, share; consume, eat, take;evince, evoke, show, suggest.

partial *adj* component, fractional, imperfect, incomplete, limited; biased, influential, interested, one-sided, prejudiced, prepossessed, unfair, unjust, warped; fond, indulgent.

participate *vb* engage in, partake, perform, share.

particle *n* atom, bit, corpuscle, crumb, drop, glimmer, grain, granule, iota, jot, mite, molecule, morsel, mote, scrap, shred, snip, spark, speck, whit.

particular *adj* especial, special, specific; distinct, individual, respective, separate, single; characteristic, distinctive, peculiar; individual, intimate, own, personal, private; notable, noteworthy; circumstantial, definite, detailed, exact, minute, narrow, precise; careful, close, conscientious, critical, fastidious, nice, scrupulous, strict; marked, odd, singular, strange, uncommon. • *n* case, circumstance, count, detail, feature, instance, item, particularity, point, regard, respect.

parting *adj* breaking, dividing, separating; final, last, valedictory; declining, departing. • *n* breaking, disruption, rupture, severing; detachment, division, separation; death, departure, farewell, leave-taking.

partisan *adj* biased, factional, interested, partial, prejudiced. • *n* adherent, backer, champion, disciple, follower, supporter, votary; baton, halberd, pike, quarterstaff, truncheon, staff.

partition *vb* apportion, distribute, divide, portion, separate, share. • *n* division, separation; barrier, division, screen, wall; allotment, apportionment, distribution.

partner *n* associate, colleague, copartner, partaker, participant, participator; accomplice, ally, coadjutor, confederate; companion, consort, spouse.

partnership *n* association, company, copartnership, firm, house, society; connection, interest, participation, union.

parts *npl* abilities, accomplishments, endowments, faculties, genius, gifts, intellect, intelligence, mind, qualities, powers, talents; districts, regions.

party *n* alliance, association, cabal, circle, clique, combination, confederacy, coterie, faction, group, junta, league, ring, set; body, company, detachment, squad, troop; assembly, gathering; partaker, participant, participator, sharer; defendant, litigant, plaintiff; individual, one, person, somebody; cause, division, interest, side.

pass[1] *vb* devolve, fall, go, move, proceed; change, elapse, flit, glide, lapse, slip; cease, die, fade, expire, vanish; happen, occur; convey, deliver, send, transmit, transfer; disregard, ignore, neglect; exceed, excel, surpass; approve, ratify, sanction; answer, do, succeed, suffice, suit; express, pronounce, utter; beguile, wile.

pass[2] *n* avenue, ford, road, route, way; defile, gorge, passage, ravine; authorization, licence, passport, permission, ticket; condition, conjecture, plight, situation, state; lunge, push, thrust, tilt; transfer, trick.

passable *adj* admissible, allowable, mediocre, middling, moderate, ordinary, so-so, tolerable; acceptable, current, receivable; navigable, traversable.

passage *n* going, passing, progress, transit; evacuation, journey, migration, transit, voyage; avenue, channel, course, pass, path, road, route, thoroughfare, way; access, entry, reception; act, deed, event, feat, incidence, occurrence, passion; corridor, gallery, gate, hall; clause, paragraph, sentence, text; course, death, decease, departure, expiration, lapse; affair, brush, change, collision, combat, conflict, contest, encounter.

passenger *n* fare, itinerant, tourist, traveller, voyager, wayfarer.

passionate *adj* animated, ardent, burning, earnest, enthusiastic, excited, fervent, fiery, furious, glowing, hot-blooded, impassioned, impetuous, impulsive, intense, vehement, warm, zealous; hot-headed, irascible, quick-tempered, tempestuous, violent.

passive *adj* inactive, inert, quiescent, receptive; apathetic, enduring, long-suffering, nonresistant, patient, stoical, submissive, suffering, unresisting.

past *adj* accomplished, elapsed, ended, gone, spent; ancient, bygone, former, obsolete, outworn. • *adv* above, extra, beyond, over. • *prep* above, after, beyond, exceeding. • *n* antiquity, heretofore, history, olden times, yesterday.

pastime *n* amusement, diversion, entertainment, hobby, play, recreation, sport.

pastor *n* clergyman, churchman, divine, ecclesiastic, minister, parson, priest, vicar.

pat[1] *vb* dab, hit, rap, tap; caress, chuck, fondle, pet. • *n* dab, hit, pad, rap, tap; caress.

pat[2] *adj* appropriate, apt, fit, pertinent, suitable. • *adv* aptly, conveniently, fitly, opportunely, seasonably.

patch *vb* mend, repair. • *n* repair; parcel, plot, tract.

patent *adj* expanded, open, spreading; apparent, clear, conspicuous, evident, glaring, indisputable, manifest, notorious, obvious, public, open, palpable, plain, unconcealed, unmistakable. • *n* copyright, privilege, right.

paternity *n* derivation, descent, fatherhood, origin.

path *n* access, avenue, course, footway, passage, pathway, road, route, track, trail, way.

pathetic *adj* affecting, melting, moving, pitiable, plaintive, sad, tender, touching.

patience *n* endurance, fortitude, long-sufferance, resignation, submission, sufferance; calmness, composure, quietness; forbearance, indulgence, leniency; assiduity, constancy, diligence, indefatigability, indefatigableness, perseverance, persistence.

patient *adj* meek, passive, resigned, submissive, uncomplaining, unrepining; calm, composed, contented, quiet; indulgent, lenient, long-suffering; assiduous, constant, diligent, indefatigable, persevering, persistent. • *n* case, invalid, subject, sufferer.

patrician *adj* aristocratic, blue-blooded, highborn, noble, senatorial, well-born. • *n* aristocrat, blue blood, nobleman.

patron *n* advocate, defender, favourer, guardian, helper, protector, supporter.

patronize *vb* aid, assist, befriend, countenance, defend, favour, maintain, support; condescend, disparage, scorn.

pattern *vb* copy, follow, imitate. • *n* archetype, exemplar, last, model, original, paradigm, plan, prototype; example, guide, sample, specimen; mirror, paragon; design, figure, shape, style, type.

paucity *n* deficiency, exiguity, insufficiency, lack, poverty, rarity, shortage.

paunch *n* abdomen, belly, gut, stomach.

pauperism *n* beggary, destitution, indigence, mendicancy, mendicity, need, poverty, penury, want.

pause *vb* breathe, cease, delay, desist, rest, stay, stop, wait; delay, forbear, intermit, stay, stop, tarry, wait; deliberate, demur, hesitate, waver. • *n* break, caesura, cessation, halt, intermission, interruption, interval, remission, rest, stop, stoppage, stopping, suspension; hesitation, suspense, uncertainty; paragraph.

pawn[1] *n* cat's-paw, dupe, plaything, puppet, stooge, tool, toy.

pawn[2] *vb* bet, gage, hazard, lay, pledge, risk, stake, wager. • *n* assurance, bond, guarantee, pledge, security.

pay *vb* defray, discharge, discount, foot, honour, liquidate, meet, quit, settle; compensate, recompense, reimburse, requite, reward; punish, revenge; give, offer, render. • *n* allowance, commission, compensation, emolument, hire, recompense, reimbursement, remuneration, requital, reward, salary, wages.

peace *n* calm, calmness, quiet, quietness, repose, stillness; accord, amity, friendliness, harmony; composure, equanimity, imperturbability, placidity, quietude, tranquillity; agreement, armistice.

peaceable *adj* pacific, peaceful; amiable, amicable, friendly, gentle, inoffensive, mild; placid, quiet, serene, still, tranquil, undisturbed, unmoved.

peaceful *adj* quiet, undisturbed; amicable, concordant, friendly, gentle, harmonious, mild, pacific, peaceable; calm, composed, placid, serene, still.

peak *vb* climax, culminate, top; dwindle, thin. • *n* acme, apex, crest, crown, pinnacle, summit, top, zenith.

peaked *adj* piked, pointed, thin.

peasant *n* boor, countryman, clown, hind, labourer, rustic, swain.

peculate *vb* appropriate, defraud, embezzle, misappropriate, pilfer, purloin, rob, steal.

peculiar *adj* appropriate, idiosyncratic, individual, proper; characteristic, eccentric, exceptional, extraordinary, odd, queer, rare, singular, strange, striking, uncommon, unusual; individual, especial, particular, select, special, specific.

peculiarity *n* appropriateness, distinctiveness, individuality, speciality; characteristic, idiosyncrasy, oddity, peculiarity, singularity.

pedantic *adj* conceited, fussy, officious, ostentatious, over-learned, particular, pedagogical, pompous, pragmatical, precise, pretentious, priggish, stilted.

pedlar *n* chapman, costermonger, hawker, packman, vendor.

pedigree *adj* purebred, thoroughbred. • *n* ancestry, breed, descent, extraction, family, genealogy, house, line, lineage, race, stock, strain.

peer[1] *vb* gaze, look, peek, peep, pry, squinny, squint; appear, emerge.

peer[2] *n* associate, co-equal, companion, compeer, equal, equivalent, fellow, like, mate, match; aristocrat, baron, count, duke, earl, grandee, lord, marquis, noble, nobleman, viscount.

peerless *adj* excellent, incomparable, matchless, outstanding, superlative, unequalled, unique, unmatched, unsurpassed.

peevish *adj* acrimonious, captious, churlish, complaining, crabbed, cross, crusty, discontented, fretful, ill-natured, ill-tempered, irascible, irritable, pettish, petulant, querulous, snappish, snarling, splenetic, spleeny, testy, waspish; forward, headstrong, obstinate, self-willed, stubborn; childish, silly, thoughtless, trifling.

pellucid *adj* bright, clear, crystalline, diaphanous, limpid, lucid, transparent.

pelt[1] *vb* assail, batter, beat, belabour, bombard, pepper, stone, strike; cast, hurl, throw; hurry, rush, speed, tear.

pelt[2] *n* coat, hide, skin.

pen[1] *vb* compose, draft, indite, inscribe, write.

pen[2] *vb* confine, coop, encage, enclose, impound, imprison, incarcerate. • *n* cage, coop, corral, crib, hutch, enclosure, paddock, pound, stall, sty.

penalty *n* chastisement, fine, forfeiture, mulct, punishment, retribution.

penance *n* humiliation, maceration, mortification, penalty, punishment.

penchant *n* bent, bias, disposition, fondness, inclination, leaning, liking, predilection, predisposition, proclivity, proneness, propensity, taste, tendency, turn.

penetrate *vb* bore, burrow, cut, enter, invade, penetrate, percolate, perforate, pervade, pierce, soak, stab; affect, sensitize, touch; comprehend, discern, perceive, understand.

penetrating *adj* penetrative, permeating, piercing, sharp, subtle; acute, clear-sighted, discerning, intelligent, keen, quick, sagacious, sharp-witted, shrewd.

penetration *n* acuteness, discernment, insight, sagacity.

penitence *n* compunction, contrition, qualms, regret, remorse, repentance, sorrow.

penitent *adj* compunctious, conscience-stricken, contrite, regretful, remorseful, repentant, sorrowing, sorrowful. • *n* penance-doer, penitentiary, repentant.

penniless *adj* destitute, distressed, impecunious, indigent, moneyless, pinched, poor, necessitous, needy, pensive, poverty-stricken, reduced.

pensive *adj* contemplative, dreamy, meditative, reflective, sober, thoughtful; grave, melancholic, melancholy, mournful, sad, serious, solemn.

penurious *adj* inadequate, ill-provided, insufficient, meagre, niggardly, poor, scanty, stinted; avaricious, close, close-fisted, covetous, illiberal, grasping, grudging, mean, mercenary, miserly, near, niggardly, parsimonious, sordid, stingy, tightfisted.

penury *n* beggary, destitution, indigence, need, poverty, privation, want.

people *vb* colonize, inhabit, populate. • *n* clan, country, family, nation, race, state, tribe; folk, humankind, persons, population, public; commons, community, democracy, populace, proletariat; mob, multitude, rabble.

perceive *vb* behold, descry, detect, discern, discover, discriminate, distinguish, note, notice, observe, recognize, remark, see, spot; appreciate, comprehend, know, understand.

perceptible *adj* apparent, appreciable, cognizable, discernible, noticeable, perceivable, understandable, visible.

perception *n* apprehension, cognition, discernment, perceiving, recognition, seeing; comprehension, conception, consciousness, perceptiveness, perceptivity, understanding, feeling.

perchance *adv* haply, maybe, mayhap, peradventure, perhaps, possibly, probably.

percolate *vb* drain, drip, exude, filter, filtrate, ooze, penetrate, stain, transude.

percussion *n* collision, clash, concussion, crash, encounter, shock.

perdition *n* damnation, demolition, destruction, downfall, hell, overthrow, ruin, wreck.

peremptory *adj* absolute, authoritative, categorical, commanding, decisive, express, imperative, imperious, positive; determined, resolute, resolved; arbitrary, dogmatic, incontrovertible.

perennial *adj* ceaseless, constant, continual, deathless, enduring, immortal, imperishable, lasting, never-failing, permanent, perpetual, unceasing, undying, unfailing, uninterrupted.

perfect *vb* accomplish, complete, consummate, elaborate, finish. • *adj* completed, finished; complete, entire, full, unqualified, utter, whole; capital, consummate, excellent, exquisite, faultless, ideal; accomplished, disciplined, expert, skilled; blameless, faultless, holy, immaculate, pure, spotless, unblemished.

perfection *n* completeness, completion, consummation, correctness, excellence, faultlessness, finish, maturity, perfection, perfectness, wholeness; beauty, quality.

perfidious *adj* deceitful, dishonest, disloyal, double-faced, faithless, false, false-hearted, traitorous, treacherous, unfaithful, untrustworthy, venal.

perfidy *n* defection, disloyalty, faithlessness, infidelity, perfidiousness, traitorousness, treachery, treason.

perforate *vb* bore, drill, penetrate, pierce, pink, prick, punch, riddle, trepan.

perform *vb* accomplish, achieve, compass, consummate, do, effect, transact; complete, discharge, execute, fulfil, meet, observe, satisfy; act, play, represent.

performance *n* accomplishment, achievement, completion, consummation, discharge, doing, execution, fulfilment; act, action, deed, exploit, feat, work; composition, production; acting, entertainment, exhibition, play, representation, hold; execution, playing.

perfume *n* aroma, balminess, bouquet, fragrance, incense, odour, redolence, scent, smell, sweetness.

perfunctory *adj* careless, formal, heedless, indifferent, mechanical, negligent, reckless, slight, slovenly, thoughtless, unmindful.

perhaps *adv* haply, peradventure, perchance, possibly.

peril *vb* endanger, imperil, jeopardize, risk. • *n* danger, hazard, insecurity, jeopardy, pitfall, risk, snare, uncertainty.

perilous *adj* dangerous, hazardous, risky, unsafe.

period *n* aeon, age, cycle, date, eon, epoch, season, span, spell, stage, term, time; continuance, duration; bound, conclusion, determination, end, limit, term, termination; clause, phrase, proposition, sentence.

periodical *adj* cyclical, incidental, intermittent, recurrent, recurring, regular, seasonal, systematic. • *n* magazine, paper, review, serial, weekly.

periphery *n* boundary, circumference, outside, perimeter, superficies, surface.

perish *vb* decay, moulder, shrivel, waste, wither; decease, die, expire, vanish.

perishable *adj* decaying, decomposable, destructible; dying, frail, mortal, temporary.

perjured *adj* false, forsworn, perfidious, traitorous, treacherous, untrue.

permanent *adj* abiding, constant, continuing, durable, enduring, fixed, immutable, invariable, lasting, perpetual, persistent, stable, standing, steadfast, unchangeable, unchanging, unfading, unmovable.

permissible *adj* admissible, allowable, free, lawful, legal, legitimate, proper, sufferable, unprohibited.

permission *n* allowance, authorization, consent, dispensation, leave, liberty, licence, permit, sufferance, toleration, warrant.

permit *vb* agree, allow, endure, let, suffer, tolerate; admit, authorize, consent, empower, license, warrant. • *n* leave, liberty, licence, passport, permission, sanction, warrant.

pernicious *adj* baleful, baneful, damaging, deadly, deleterious, destructive, detrimental, disadvantageous, fatal, harmful, hurtful, injurious, malign, mischievous, noisome, noxious, prejudicial, ruinous; evil-hearted, malevolent, malicious, malignant, mischief-making, wicked.

perpetrate *vb* commit, do, execute, perform.

perpetual *adj* ceaseless, continual, constant, endless, enduring, eternal, ever-enduring, everlasting, incessant, interminable, never-ceasing, never-ending, perennial, permanent, sempiternal, unceasing, unending, unfailing, uninterrupted.

perplex *vb* complicate, encumber, entangle, involve, snarl, tangle; beset, bewilder, confound, confuse, corner, distract, embarrass, fog, mystify, nonplus, pother, puzzle, set; annoy, bother, disturb, harass, molest, pester, plague, tease, trouble, vex, worry.

persecute *vb* afflict, distress, harass, molest, oppress, worry; annoy, beset, importune, pester, solicit, tease.

perseverance *n* constancy, continuance, doggedness, indefatigableness, persistence, persistency, pertinacity, resolution, steadfastness, steadiness, tenacity.

persevere *vb* continue, determine, endure, maintain, persist, remain, resolve, stick.

persist *vb* continue, endure, last, remain; insist, persevere.

persistent *adj* constant, continuing, enduring, fixed, immovable, persevering, persisting, steady, tenacious; contumacious, dogged, indefatigable, obdurate, obstinate, pertinacious, perverse, pigheaded, stubborn.

personable *adj* comely, good-looking, graceful, seemly, well-turned-out.

personal *adj* individual, peculiar, private, special; bodily, corporal, corporeal, exterior, material, physical.

personate *vb* act, impersonate, personify, play, represent; disguise, mast; counterfeit, feign, simulate.

perspective *n* panorama, prospect, view, vista; proportion, relation.

perspicacious *adj* keen-eyed, quick-sighted, sharp-sighted; acute, clever, discerning, keen, penetrating, sagacious, sharp-witted, shrewd.

perspicacity *n* acumen, acuteness, astuteness, discernment, insight, penetration, perspicaciousness, sagacity, sharpness, shrewdness.

perspicuity *n* clearness, distinctness, explicitness, intelligibility, lucidity, lucidness, perspicuousness, plainness, transparency.

perspicuous *adj* clear, distinct, explicit, intelligible, lucid, obvious, plain, transparent, unequivocal.

perspire *vb* exhale, glow, sweat, swelter.

persuade *vb* allure, actuate, entice, impel, incite, induce, influence, lead, move, prevail upon, urge; advise, counsel, convince, satisfy; inculcate, teach.

persuasion *n* exhortation, incitement, inducement, influence; belief, conviction, opinion; creed, doctrine, dogma, tenet; kind, sort, variety.

persuasive *adj* cogent, convincing, inducing, inducible, logical, persuading, plausible, sound, valid, weighty.

pert *adj* brisk, dapper, lively, nimble, smart, sprightly, perky; bold, flippant, forward, free, impertinent, impudent, malapert, presuming, smart, saucy.

pertain *vb* appertain, befit, behove, belong, concern, refer, regard, relate.

pertinacious *adj* constant, determined, firm, obdurate, persevering, resolute, staunch, steadfast, steady; dogged, headstrong, inflexible, mulish, intractable, obstinate, perverse, stubborn, unyielding, wayward, wilful.

pertinent *adj* adapted, applicable, apposite, appropriate, apropos, apt, fit, germane, pat, proper, relevant, suitable; appurtenant, belonging, concerning, pertaining, regarding.

perturb *vb* agitate, disquiet, distress, disturb, excite, trouble, unsettle, upset, vex, worry; confuse.

pervade *vb* affect, animate, diffuse, extend, fill, imbue, impregnate, infiltrate, penetrate, permeate.

perverse *adj* bad, disturbed, oblique, perverted; contrary, dogged, headstrong, mulish, obstinate, pertinacious, perversive, stubborn, ungovernable, intractable, unyielding, wayward, wilful; cantankerous, churlish, crabbed, cross, cross-grained, crusty, cussed, morose, peevish, petulant, snappish, snarling, spiteful, spleeny, surly, testy, touchy, wicked, wrong-headed; inconvenient, troublesome, untoward, vexatious.

perversion *n* abasement, corruption, debasement, impairment, injury, prostitution, vitiation.

perverted *adj* corrupt, debased, distorted, evil, impaired, misguiding, vitiated, wicked.

pessimistic *adj* cynical, dark, dejected, depressed, despondent, downhearted, gloomy, glum, melancholy, melancholic, morose, sad.

pest *n* disease, epidemic, infection, pestilence, plague; annoyance, bane, curse, infliction, nuisance, scourge, trouble.

pestilent *adj* contagious, infectious, malignant, pestilential; deadly, evil, injurious, malign, mischievous, noxious, poisonous; annoying, corrupt, pernicious, troublesome, vexatious.

petition *vb* ask, beg, crave, entreat, pray, solicit, sue, supplicate. • *n* address, appeal, application, entreaty, prayer, request, solicitation, supplication, suit.

petrify *vb* calcify, fossilize, lapidify; benumb, deaden; amaze, appal, astonish, astound, confound, dumbfound, paralyse, stun, stupefy.

petty *adj* diminutive, frivolous, inconsiderable, inferior, insignificant, little, mean, slight, small, trifling, trivial, unimportant.

petulant *adj* acrimonious, captious, cavilling, censorious, choleric, crabbed, cross, crusty, forward, fretful, hasty, ill-humoured, ill-tempered, irascible, irritable, peevish, perverse, pettish, querulous, snappish, snarling, testy, touchy, waspish.

phantom *n* apparition, ghost, illusion, phantasm, spectre, vision, wraith.

pharisaism *n* cant, formalism, hypocrisy, phariseeism, piety, sanctimoniousness, self-righteousness.

phenomenal *adj* marvellous, miraculous, prodigious, wondrous.

philanthropy *n* alms-giving, altruism, benevolence, charity, grace, humanitarianism, humanity, kindness.

philosophical, philosophic *adj* rational, reasonable, sound, wise; calm, collected, composed, cool, imperturbable, sedate, serene, stoical, tranquil, unruffled.

phlegmatic *adj* apathetic, calm, cold, cold-blooded, dull, frigid, heavy, impassive, indifferent, inert, sluggish, stoical, tame, unfeeling.

phobia *n* aversion, detestation, dislike, distaste, dread, fear, hatred.

phrase *vb* call, christen, denominate, designate, describe, dub, entitle, name, style. • *n* diction, expression, phraseology, style.

phraseology *n* diction, expression, language, phrasing, style.

physical *adj* material, natural; bodily, corporeal, external, substantial, tangible, sensible.

physiognomy *n* configuration, countenance, face, look, visage.

picaroon *n* adventurer, cheat, rogue; buccaneer, corsair, free-booter, marauder, pirate, plunderer, sea-rover.

pick *vb* peck, pierce, strike; cut, detach, gather, pluck; choose, cull, select; acquire, collect, get; pilfer, steal. • *n* pickaxe, pike, spike, toothpick.

picture *vb* delineate, draw, imagine, paint, represent. • *n* drawing, engraving, painting, print; copy, counterpart, delineation, embodiment, illustration, image, likeness, portraiture, portrayal, semblance, representation, resemblance, similitude; description.

picturesque *adj* beautiful, charming, colourful, graphic, scenic, striking, vivid.

piece *vb* mend, patch, repair; augment, complete, enlarge, increase; cement, join, unite. • *n* amount, bit, chunk, cut, fragment, hunk, part, quantity, scrap, shred, slice; portion; article, item, object; composition, lucubration, work, writing.

pied *adj* irregular, motley, mottled, particoloured, piebald, spotted, variegated.

pierce *vb* gore, impale, pink, prick, stab, transfix; bore, drill, excite, penetrate, perforate, puncture; affect, move, rouse, strike, thrill, touch.

piety *n* devotion, devoutness, holiness, godliness, grace, religion, sanctity.

pile[1] *vb* accumulate, amass; collect, gather, heap, load. • *n* accumulation, collection, heap, mass, stack; fortune, wad; building, edifice, erection, fabric, pyramid, skyscraper, structure, tower; reactor, nuclear reactor.

pile[2] *n* beam, column, pier, pillar, pole, post.

pile[3] *n* down, feel, finish, fur, fluff, fuzz, grain, nap, pappus, shag, surface, texture.

pilfer *vb* filch, purloin, rob, steal, thieve.

pilgrim *n* journeyer, sojourner, traveller, wanderer, wayfarer; crusader, devotee, palmer.

pilgrimage *n* crusade, excursion, expedition, journey, tour, trip.

pillage *vb* despoil, loot, plunder, rifle, sack, spoil, strip. • *n* depredation, destruction, devastation, plundering, rapine, spoliation; despoliation, plunder, rifling, sack, spoils.

pillar *n* column, pier, pilaster, post, shaft, stanchion; maintainer, prop, support, supporter, upholder.

pilot *vb* conduct, control, direct, guide, navigate, steer. • *adj* experimental, model, trial. • *n* helmsman, navigator, steersman; airman, aviator, conductor, director, flier, guide.

pinch *vb* compress, contract, cramp, gripe, nip, squeeze; afflict, distress, famish, oppress, straiten, stint; frost, nip; apprehend, arrest; economize, spare, stint. • *n* gripe, nip; pang, throe; crisis, difficulty, emergency, exigency, oppression, pressure, push, strait, stress.

pine *vb* decay, decline, droop, fade, flag, languish, waste, wilt, wither; desire, long, yearn.

pinion *vb* bind, chain, fasten, fetter, maim, restrain, shackle. • *n* pennon, wing; feather, quill, pen, plume, wing; fetter.

pinnacle *n* minaret, turret; acme, apex, height, peak, summit, top, zenith.

pious *adj* filial; devout, godly, holy, religious, reverential, righteous, saintly.

piquant *adj* biting, highly flavoured, piercing, prickling, pungent, sharp, stinging; interesting, lively, racy, sparkling, stimulating; cutting, keen, pointed, severe, strong, tart.

pique *vb* goad, incite, instigate, spur, stimulate, urge; affront, chafe, displease, fret, incense, irritate, nettle, offend, provoke, sting, vex, wound. • *n* annoyance, displeasure, irritation, offence, resentment, vexation.

pirate *vb* copy, crib, plagiarize, reproduce, steal. • *n* buccaneer, corsair, freebooter, marauder, picaroon, privateer, seadog, searobber, sea-rover, sea wolf.

pit *vb* match, oppose; dent, gouge, hole, mark, nick, notch, scar. • *n* cavity, hole, hollow; crater, dent, depression, dint, excavation, well; abyss, chasm, gulf; pitfall, snare, trap: auditorium, orchestra.

pitch *vb* fall, lurch, plunge, reel; light, settle, rest; cast, dart, fling, heave, hurl, lance, launch, send, toss, throw; erect, establish, fix, locate, place, plant, set, settle, station. • *n* degree, extent, height, intensity, measure, modulation, rage, rate; declivity, descent, inclination, slope; cast, jerk, plunge, throw, toss; place, position, spot; field, ground; line, patter.

piteous *adj* affecting, distressing, doleful, grievous, mournful, pathetic, rueful, sorrowful, woeful; deplorable, lamentable, miserable, pitiable, wretched; compassionate, tender.

pith *n* chief, core, essence, heart, gist, kernel, marrow, part, quintessence, soul, substance; importance, moment, weight; cogency, force, energy, strength, vigour.

pithy *adj* cogent, energetic, forcible, powerful; compact, concise, brief, laconic, meaty, pointed, short, sententious, substantial, terse; corky, porous.

pitiable *adj* deplorable, lamentable, miserable, pathetic, piteous, pitiable, woeful, wretched; abject, base, contemptible, despicable, disreputable, insignificant, low, paltry, mean, rascally, sorry, vile, worthless.

pitiably *adv* deplorably, distressingly, grievously, lamentably, miserably, pathetically, piteously, woefully, wretchedly.

pitiful *adj* compassionate, kind, lenient, merciful, mild, sympathetic, tender, tenderhearted; deplorable, lamentable, miserable, pathetic, piteous, pitiable, wretched; abject, base, contemptible, despicable, disreputable, insignificant, mean, paltry, rascally, sorry, vile, worthless.

pitiless *adj* cruel, hardhearted, implacable, inexorable, merciless, unmerciful, relentless, remorseless, unfeeling, unpitying, unrelenting, unsympathetic.

pittance *n* allowance, allotment, alms, charity, dole, gift; driblet, drop, insufficiency, mite, modicum, trifle.

pity *vb* commiserate, condole, sympathize. • *n* clemency, commiseration, compassion, condolence, fellow-feeling, grace, humanity, leniency, mercy, quarter, sympathy, tenderheartedness.

pivot *vb* depend, hinge, turn. • *n* axis, axle, centre, focus, hinge, joint.

place *vb* arrange, bestow, commit, deposit, dispose, fix, install, lay, locate, lodge, orient, orientate, pitch, plant, pose, put, seat, set, settle, situate, stand, station, rest; allocate, arrange, class, classify, identify, order, organize, recognize; appoint, assign, commission, establish, induct, nominate. • *n* area, courtyard, square; bounds, district, division, locale, locality, location, part, position, premises, quarter, region, scene, site, situation, spot, station, tract, whereabouts; calling, charge, employment, function, occupation, office, pitch, post; calling, condition, grade, precedence, rank, sphere, stakes, standing; abode, building, dwelling, habitation, mansion, residence, seat; city, town, village; fort, fortress, stronghold; paragraph, part, passage, portion; ground, occasion, opportunity, reason, room; lieu, stead.

placid *adj* calm, collected, composed, cool, equable, gentle, peaceful, quiet, serene, tranquil, undisturbed, unexcitable, unmoved, unruffled; halcyon, mild, serene.

plague *vb* afflict, annoy, badger, bore, bother, pester, chafe, disquiet, distress, disturb, embarrass, harass, fret, gall, harry, hector, incommode, irritate, molest, perplex, tantalize, tease, torment, trouble, vex, worry. • *n* disease, pestilence, pest; affliction, annoyance, curse, molestation, nuisance, thorn, torment, trouble, vexation, worry.

plain *adj* dull, even, flat, level, plane, smooth, uniform; clear, open, unencumbered, uninterrupted; apparent, certain, conspicuous, evident, distinct, glaring, manifest, notable, notorious, obvious, overt, palpable, patent, prominent, pronounced, staring, transparent, unmistakable, visible; explicit, intelligible, perspicuous, unambiguous, unequivocal; homely, ugly; aboveboard, blunt, crude, candid, direct, downright, frank, honest, ingenuous, open, openhearted, sincere, single-minded, straightforward, undesigning, unreserved, unsophisticated: artless, common, natural, simple, unaffected, unlearned; absolute, mere, unmistakable; clear, direct, easy; audible, articulate, definite; frugal, homely, unadorned, unfigured, unornamented, unvariegated. • *n* expanse, flats, grassland, pampas, plateau, prairie, steppe, stretch.

plaint *n* complaint, cry, lament, lamentation, moan, wail.

plaintiff *n* accuser, prosecutor.

plaintive *adj* dirge-like, doleful, grievous, melancholy, mournful, piteous, rueful, sad, sorrowful, woeful.

plan *vb* arrange, calculate, concert, delineate, devise, diagram, figure, premeditate, project, represent, study; concoct, conspire, contrive, design, digest, hatch, invent, manoeuvre, machinate, plot, prepare, scheme. • *n* chart, delineation, diagram, draught, drawing, layout, map, plot, sketch; arrangement, conception, contrivance, design, device, idea, method, programme, project, proposal, proposition, scheme, system; cabal, conspiracy, intrigue, machination; custom, process, way.

plane *vb* even, flatten, level, smooth; float, fly, glide, skate, skim, soar. • *adj* even, flat, horizontal, level, smooth. • *n* degree, evenness, level, levelness, smoothness; aeroplane, aircraft; groover, jointer, rabbet, rebate, scraper.

plant *vb* bed, sow; breed, engender; direct, point, set; colonize, furnish, inhabit, settle; establish, introduce; deposit, establish, fix, found, hide. • *n* herb, organism, vegetable; establishment, equipment, factory, works.

plaster *vb* bedaub, coat, cover, smear, spread. • *n* cement, gypsum, mortar, stucco.

plastic *adj* ductile, flexible, formative, mouldable, pliable, pliant, soft.

platitude *n* dullness, flatness, insipidity, mawkishness; banality, commonplace, truism; balderdash, chatter, flummery, fudge, jargon, moonshine, nonsense, palaver, stuff, trash, twaddle, verbiage.

plaudit *n* acclaim, acclamation, applause, approbation, clapping, commendation, encomium, praise.

plausible *adj* believable, credible, probable, reasonable; bland, fair-spoken, glib, smooth, suave.

play *vb* caper, disport, frisk, frolic, gambol, revel, romp, skip, sport; dally, flirt, idle, toy, trifle, wanton; flutter, hover, wave; act, impersonate, perform, personate, represent; bet, gamble, stake, wager. • *n* amusement, exercise, frolic, gambols, game, jest, pastime, prank, romp, sport; gambling, gaming; act, comedy, drama, farce, performance, tragedy; action, motion, movement; elbowroom, freedom, latitude, movement, opportunity, range, scope, sweep, swing, use.

playful *adj* frisky, frolicsome, gamesome, jolly, kittenish, merry, mirthful, rollicking, sportive; amusing, arch, humorous, lively, mischievous, roguish, skittish, sprightly, vivacious.

plead *vb* answer, appeal, argue, reason; argue, defend, discuss, reason, rejoin; beg, beseech, entreat, implore, petition, sue, supplicate.

pleasant *adj* acceptable, agreeable, delectable, delightful, enjoyable, grateful, gratifying, nice, pleasing, pleasurable, prepossessing, seemly, welcome; cheerful, enlivening, good-humoured, gracious, likable, lively, merry, sportive, sprightly, vivacious; amusing, facetious, humorous, jocose, jocular, sportive, witty.

please *vb* charm, delight, elate, gladden, gratify, pleasure, rejoice; content, oblige, satisfy; choose, like, prefer.

pleasure *n* cheer, comfort, delight, delectation, elation, enjoyment, exhilaration, joy, gladness, gratifying, gusto, relish, satisfaction, solace; amusement, diversion, entertainment, indulgence, refreshment, treat; gratification, luxury, sensuality, voluptuousness; choice, desire, preference, purpose, will, wish; favour, kindness.

plebeian *adj* base, common, ignoble, low, lowborn, mean, obscure, popular, vulgar. • *n* commoner, peasant, proletarian.

pledge *vb* hypothecate, mortgage, pawn, plight; affiance, bind, contract, engage, plight, promise. • *n* collateral, deposit, gage, pawn; earnest, guarantee, security; hostage, security.

plenipotentiary *n* ambassador, envoy, legate, minister.

plenitude *n* abundance, completeness, fullness, plenteousness, plentifulness, plenty, plethora, profusion, repletion.

plentiful *adj* abundant, ample, copious, full, enough, exuberant, fruitful, luxuriant, plenteous, productive, sufficient.

plenty *n* abundance, adequacy, affluence, amplitude, copiousness, enough, exuberance, fertility, fruitfulness, fullness, overflow, plenteousness, plentifulness, plethora, profusion, sufficiency, supply.

pleonastic *adj* circumlocutory, diffuse, redundant, superfluous, tautological, verbose, wordy.

plethora *n* fullness, plenitude, repletion; excess, redundance, redundancy, superabundance, superfluity, surfeit.

pliable *adj* flexible, limber, lithe, lithesome, pliable, pliant, supple; adaptable, compliant, docile, ductile, facile, manageable, obsequious, tractable, yielding.

plight[1] *n* case, category, complication, condition, dilemma, imbroglio, mess, muddle, pass, predicament, scrape, situation, state, strait.

plight[2] *vb* avow, contract, covenant, engage, honour, pledge, promise, propose, swear, vow. • *n* avowal, contract, covenant, oath, pledge, promise, troth, vow, word; affiancing, betrothal, engagement.

plod *vb* drudge, lumber, moil, persevere, persist, toil, trudge.

plot[1] *vb* connive, conspire, intrigue, machinate, scheme; brew, concoct, contrive, devise, frame, hatch, compass, plan, project; chart, map. • *n* blueprint, chart, diagram, draft, outline, plan, scenario, skeleton; cabal, combination, complicity, connivance, conspiracy, intrigue, plan, project, scheme, stratagem; script, story, subject, theme, thread, topic.

plot[2] *n* field, lot, parcel, patch, piece, plat, section, tract.

pluck[1] *vb* cull, gather, pick; jerk, pull, snatch, tear, tug, twitch.

pluck[2] *n* backbone, bravery, courage, daring, determination, energy, force, grit, hardihood, heroism, indomitability, indomitableness, manhood, mettle, nerve, resolution, spirit, valour.

plump[1] *adj* bonny, bouncing, buxom, chubby, corpulent, fat, fleshy, full-figured, obese, portly, rotund, round, sleek, stout, well-rounded; distended, full, swollen, tumid.

plump[2] *vb* dive, drop, plank, plop, plunge, plunk, put; choose, favour, support • *adj* blunt, complete, direct, downright, full, unqualified, unreserved.

plunder *vb* desolate, despoil, devastate, fleece, forage, harry, loot, maraud, pillage, raid, ransack, ravage, rifle, rob, sack, spoil, spoliate, plunge. • *n* freebooting, devastation, harrying, marauding, rapine, robbery, sack; booty, pillage, prey, spoil.

ply[1] *vb* apply, employ, exert, manipulate, wield; exercise, practise; assail, belabour, beset, press; importune, solicit, urge; offer, present.

ply[2] *n* fold, layer, plait, twist; bent, bias, direction, turn.

pocket *vb* appropriate, steal; bear, endure, suffer, tolerate. • *n* cavity, cul-de-sac, hollow, pouch, receptacle.

poignant *adj* bitter, intense, penetrating, pierce, severe, sharp; acrid, biting, mordacious, piquant, prickling, pungent, sharp, stinging; caustic, irritating, keen, mordant, pointed, satirical, severe.

point *vb* acuminate, sharpen; aim, direct, level; designate indicate, show; punctuate. • *n* apex, needle, nib, pin, prong, spike, stylus, tip; cape, headland, projection, promontory; eve, instant, moment, period, verge; place, site, spot, stage, station; condition, degree, grade, state; aim, design, end, intent, limit, object, purpose; nicety, pique, punctilio, trifle; position, proposition, question, text, theme, thesis; aspect, matter, respect; characteristic, peculiarity, trait; character, mark, stop; dot, jot, speck; epigram, quip, quirk, sally, witticism; poignancy, sting.

point-blank *adj* categorical, direct, downright, explicit, express, plain, straight. • *adv* categorically, directly, flush, full, plainly, right, straight.

pointless *adj* blunt, obtuse; aimless, dull, flat, fruitless, futile, meaningless, vague, vapid, stupid.

poise *vb* balance, float, hang, hover, support, suspend. • *n* aplomb, balance, composure, dignity, equanimity, equilibrium, equipoise, serenity.

poison *vb* adulterate, contaminate, corrupt, defile, embitter, envenom, impair, infect, intoxicate, pollute, taint, vitiate. • *adj* deadly, lethal, poisonous, toxic. • *n* bane, canker, contagion, pest, taint, toxin, venom, virulence, virus.

poisonous *adj* baneful, corruptive, deadly, fatal, noxious, pestiferous, pestilential, toxic, venomous.

poke *vb* jab, jog, punch, push, shove, thrust; interfere, meddle, pry, snoop. • *n* jab, jog, punch, push, shove, thrust; bag, pocket, pouch, sack.

pole[1] *n* caber, mast, post, rod, spar, staff, stick; bar, beam, pile, shaft; oar, paddle, scull.

pole[2] *n* axis, axle, hub, pivot, spindle.

poles *npl* antipodes, antipoles, counterpoles, opposites.

policy *n* administration, government, management, rule; plan, plank, platform, role; art, address, cunning, discretion, prudence, shrewdness, skill, stratagem, strategy, tactics; acumen, astuteness, wisdom, wit.

polish *vb* brighten, buff, burnish, furbish, glaze, gloss, scour, shine, smooth; civilize, refine. • *n* brightness, brilliance, brilliancy, lustre, splendour; accomplishment, elegance, finish, grace, refinement.

polished *adj* bright, burnished, glossed, glossy, lustrous, shining, smooth; accomplished, cultivated, elegant, finished, graceful, polite, refined.

polite *adj* attentive, accomplished, affable, chivalrous, civil, complaisant, courtly, courteous, cultivated, elegant, gallant, genteel, gentle, gentlemanly, gracious, mannerly, obliging, polished, refined, suave, urbane, well, well-bred, well-mannered.

politic *adj* civic, civil, political; astute, discreet, judicious, longheaded, noncommittal, provident, prudent, prudential, sagacious, wary, wise; artful, crafty, cunning, diplomatic, expedient, foxy, ingenious, intriguing, Machiavellian, shrewd, skilful, sly, subtle, strategic, timeserving, unscrupulous, wily; welladapted, well-devised.

political *adj* civic, civil, national, politic, public.

pollute *vb* defile, foul, soil, taint; contaminate, corrupt, debase, demoralize, deprave, impair, infect, pervert, poison, stain, tarnish, vitiate; desecrate, profane; abuse, debauch, defile, deflower, dishonour, ravish, violate.

pollution *n* abomination, contamination, corruption, defilement, foulness, impurity, pollutedness, taint, uncleanness, vitiation.

poltroon *n* coward, crave, dastard, milksop, recreant, skulk, sneak.

pomp *n* display, flourish, grandeur, magnificence, ostentation, pageant, pageantry, parade, pompousness, pride, show, splendour, state, style.

pompous *adj* august, boastful, bombastic, dignified, gorgeous, grand, inflated, lofty, magisterial, ostentatious, pretentious, showy, splendid, stately, sumptuous, superb, vainglorious.

ponder *vb* cogitate, consider, contemplate, deliberate, examine, meditate, muse, reflect, study, weigh.

ponderous *adj* bulky, heavy, massive, weighty; dull, laboured, slow-moving; important, momentous; forcible, mighty.

poniard *n* dagger, dirk, stiletto.

poor *adj* indigent, necessitous, needy, pinched, straitened; destitute, distressed, embarrassed, impecunious, impoverished, insolvent, moneyless, penniless, poverty-stricken, reduced, seedy, unprosperous; emaciated, gaunt, spare, lank, lean, shrunk, skinny, spare, thin; barren, fruitless, sterile, unfertile, unfruitful, unproductive, unprolific; flimsy, inadequate, insignificant, insufficient, paltry, slender, slight, small, trifling, trivial, unimportant, valueless, worthless; decrepit, delicate, feeble, frail, infirm, unsound, weak; inferior, shabby, valueless, worthless; bad, beggarly, contemptible, despicable, humble, inferior, low, mean, pitiful, sorry; bald, cold, dry, dull, feeble, frigid, jejune, languid, meagre, prosaic, prosing, spiritless, tame, vapid, weak; ill-fated, infirm, inauspicious, indifferent, luckless, miserable, pitiable, unfavourable, unfortunate, unhappy, unlucky, wretched; deficient, imperfect, inadequate, insufficient, mediocre, scant, scanty; faulty, unsatisfactory; feeble.

populace *n* citizens, crowd, inhabitants, masses, people, public, throng.

popular *adj* lay, plebeian, public; comprehensible, easy, familiar, plain; acceptable, accepted, accredited, admired, approved, favoured, liked, pleasing, praised, received; common, current, prevailing, prevalent; cheap, inexpensive.

pore[1] *n* hole, opening, orifice, spiracle.

pore[2] *vb* brood, consider, dwell, examine, gaze, read, study.

porous *adj* honeycombed, light, loose, open, penetrable, perforated, permeable, pervious, sandy.

porridge *n* broth, gruel, mush, pap, pottage, soup.

port[1] *n* anchorage, harbour, haven, shelter; door, entrance, gate, passageway; embrasure, porthole.

port[2] *n* air, appearance, bearing, behaviour, carriage, demeanour, deportment, mien, presence.

portable *adj* convenient, handy, light, manageable, movable, portative, transmissible.

portend *vb* augur, betoken, bode, forebode, foreshadow, foretoken, indicate, presage, procrastinate, signify, threaten.

portent *n* augury, omen, presage, prognosis, sign, warning; marvel, phenomenon, wonder.

portion *vb* allot, distribute, divide, parcel; endow, supply. • *n* bit, fragment, morsel, part, piece, scrap, section; allotment, contingent, dividend, division, lot, measure, quantity, quota, ration, share; inheritance.

portly *adj* dignified, grand, imposing, magisterial, majestic, stately; bulky, burly, corpulent, fleshy, large, plump, round, stout.

portray *vb* act, draw, depict, delineate, describe, paint, picture, represent, pose, position, sketch.

pose *vb* arrange, place, set; bewilder, confound, dumbfound, embarrass, mystify, nonplus, perplex, place, puzzle, set, stagger; affect, attitudinize. • *n* attitude, posture; affectation, air, facade, mannerism, pretence, role.

position *vb* arrange, array, fix, locate, place, put, set, site, stand. • *n* locality, place, post, site, situation, spot, station; relation; attitude, bearing, posture; affirmation, assertion, doctrine, predication, principle, proposition, thesis; caste, dignity, honour, rank, standing, status; circumstance, condition, phase, place, state; berth, billet, incumbency, place, post, situation.

positive *adj* categorical, clear, defined, definite, direct, determinate, explicit, express, expressed, precise, unequivocal, unmistakable, unqualified; absolute, actual, real, substantial, true, veritable; assured, certain, confident, convinced, sure; decisive, incontrovertible, indisputable, indubitable, inescapable; imperative, unconditional, undeniable; decided, dogmatic, emphatic, obstinate, overbearing, overconfident, peremptory, stubborn, tenacious.

possess *vb* control, have, hold, keep, obsess, obtain, occupy, own, seize.

possession *n* monopoly, ownership, proprietorship; control, occupation, occupancy, retention, tenancy, tenure; bedevilment, lunacy, madness, obsession; (*pl*) assets, effects, estate, property, wealth.

possessor *n* owner, proprietor.

possible *adj* conceivable, contingent, imaginable, potential; accessible, feasible, likely, practical, practicable, workable.

possibly *adv* haply, maybe, mayhap, peradventure, perchance, perhaps.

post[1] *vb* advertise, announce, inform, placard, publish; brand, defame, disgrace, vilify; enter, slate, record, register. • *n* column, picket, pier, pillar, stake, support.

post[2] *vb* establish, fix, place, put, set, station. • *n* billet, employment, office, place, position, quarter, seat, situation, station.

post[3] *vb* drop, dispatch, mail. • *n* carrier, courier, express, mercury, messenger, postman; dispatch, haste, hurry, speed.

posterior *adj* after, ensuing, following, later, latter, postprandial, subsequent. • *n* back, buttocks, hind, hinder, rump.

posterity *n* descendants, offspring, progeny, seed; breed, brood, children, family, heirs, issue.

postpone *vb* adjourn, defer, delay, procrastinate, prorogue, retard.

postscript *n* addition, afterthought, appendix, supplement.

postulate *vb* assume, presuppose; beseech, entreat, solicit, supplicate. • *n* assumption, axiom, conjecture, hypothesis, proposition, speculation, supposition, theory.

posture *vb* attitudinize, pose. • *n* attitude, pose, position; condition, disposition, mood, phase, state.

pot *n* kettle, pan, saucepan, skillet; can, cup, mug, tankard; crock, jar, jug.

potency *n* efficacy, energy, force, intensity, might, power, strength, vigour; authority, control, influence, sway.

potent *adj* efficacious, forceful, forcible, intense, powerful, strong, virile; able, authoritative, capable, efficient, mighty, puissant, strong; cogent, influential.

potentate *n* emperor, king, monarch, prince, sovereign, ruler.

potential *adj* able, capable, inherent, latent, possible. • *n* ability, capability, dynamic, possibility, potentiality, power.

pother *vb* beset, bewilder, confound, confuse, embarrass, harass, perplex, pose, puzzle, tease. • *n* bustle, commotion, confusion, disturbance, flutter, fuss, huddle, hurly-burly, rumpus, tumult, turbulence, turmoil.

pound[1] *vb* beat, strike, thump; bray, bruise, comminute, crush, levigate, pulverize, triturate; confound, coop, enclose, impound.

pound[2] *n* enclosure, fold, pen.

pour *vb* cascade, emerge, flood, flow, gush, issue, rain, shower, stream.

pouting *adj* bad-tempered, cross, ill-humoured, moody, morose, sulky, sullen.

poverty *n* destitution, difficulties, distress, impecuniosity, impecuniousness, indigence, necessity, need, neediness, penury, privation, straits, want; beggary, mendicancy, pauperism, pennilessness; dearth, jejuneness, lack, scantiness, sparingness, meagreness; exiguity, paucity, poorness, smallness; humbleness, inferiority, lowliness; barrenness, sterility, unfruitfulness, unproductiveness.

power *n* ability, ableness, capability, cogency, competency, efficacy, faculty, might, potency, validity, talent; energy, force, strength, virtue; capacity, susceptibility; endowment, faculty, gift, talent; ascendancy, authoritativeness, authority, carte blanche, command, control, domination, dominion, government, influence, omnipotence, predominance, prerogative, pressure, proxy, puissance, rule, sovereignty, sway, warrant; governor, monarch, potentate, ruler, sovereign; army, host, troop.

powerful *adj* mighty, potent, puissant; able-bodied, herculean, muscular, nervous, robust, sinewy, strong, sturdy, vigorous, vivid; able, commanding, dominating, forceful, forcible, overpowering; cogent, effective, effectual, efficacious, efficient, energetic, influential, operative, valid.

practicable *adj* achievable, attainable, bearable, feasible, performable, possible, workable; operative, passable, penetrable.

practical *adj* hardheaded, matter-of-fact, pragmatic, pragmatical; able, experienced, practised, proficient, qualified, trained, skilled, thoroughbred, versed; effective, useful, virtual, workable.

practice *n* custom, habit, manner, method, repetition; procedure, usage, use; application, drill, exercise, pursuit; action, acts, behaviour, conduct, dealing, proceeding.

practise *vb* apply, do, exercise, follow, observe, perform, perpetrate, pursue.

practised *adj* able, accomplished, experienced, instructed, practical, proficient, qualified, skilled, thoroughbred, trained, versed.

pragmatic *adj* impertinent, intermeddling, interfering, intrusive, meddlesome, meddling, obtrusive, officious, over-busy; earthy, hard-headed, matter-of-fact, practical, pragmatical, realistic, sensible, stolid.

praise *vb* approbate, acclaim, applaud, approve, commend; celebrate, compliment, eulogize, extol, flatter, laud; adore, bless, exalt, glorify, magnify, worship. • *n* acclaim, approbation, approval, commendation; encomium, eulogy, glorification, laud, laudation, panegyric; exaltation, extolling, glorification, homage, tribute, worship; celebrity, distinction, fame, glory, honour, renown; desert, merit, praiseworthiness.

praiseworthy *adj* commendable, creditable, good, laudable, meritorious.

prank *n* antic, caper, escapade, frolic, gambol, trick.

prate *vb* babble, chatter, gabble, jabber, palaver, prattle, tattle. • *n* chatter, gabble, nonsense, palaver, prattle, twaddle.

pray *vb* ask, beg, beseech, conjure, entreat, implore, importune, invoke, petition, request, solicit, supplicate.

prayer *n* beseeching, entreaty, imploration, petition, request, solicitation, suit, supplication; adoration, devotion(s), litany, invocation, orison, praise, suffrage.

preach *vb* declare, deliver, proclaim, pronounce, publish; inculcate, press, teach, urge; exhort, lecture, moralize, sermonize.

preamble *n* foreword, introduction, preface, prelude, prologue.

precarious *adj* critical, doubtful, dubious, equivocal, hazardous, insecure, perilous, unassured, riskful, risky, uncertain, unsettled, unstable, unsteady.

precaution *n* care, caution, circumspection, foresight, forethought, providence, prudence, safeguard, wariness; anticipation, premonition, provision.

precautionary *adj* preservative, preventative, provident.

precede *vb* antedate, forerun, head, herald, introduce, lead, utter.

precedence *n* advantage, antecedence, lead, pre-eminence, preference, priority, superiority, supremacy.

precedent *n* antecedent, authority, custom, example, instance, model, pattern, procedure, standard, usage.

precept *n* behest, bidding, canon, charge, command, commandment, decree, dictate, edict, injunction, instruction, law, mandate, ordinance, ordination, order, regulation; direction, doctrine, maxim, principle, teaching, rubric, rule.

preceptor *n* instructor, lecturer, master, pedagogue, professor, schoolteacher, teacher, tutor.

precinct *n* border, bound, boundary, confine, environs, frontier, enclosure, limit, list, march, neighbourhood, purlieus, term, terminus; area, district.

precious *adj* costly, inestimable, invaluable, priceless, prized, valuable; adored, beloved, cherished, darling, dear, idolized, treasured; fastidious, overnice, over-refined, precise.

precipice *n* bluff, cliff, crag, steep.

precipitate *vb* advance, accelerate, dispatch, expedite, forward, further, hasten, hurry, plunge, press, quicken, speed. • *adj* hasty, hurried, headlong, impetuous, indiscreet, overhasty, rash, reckless; abrupt, sudden, violent.

precipitous *adj* abrupt, cliffy, craggy, perpendicular, uphill, sheer, steep.

precise *adj* accurate, correct, definite, distinct, exact, explicit, express, nice, pointed, severe, strict, unequivocal, well-defined; careful, scrupulous; ceremonious, finical, formal, prim, punctilious, rigid, starched, stiff.

precision *n* accuracy, correctness, definiteness, distinctness, exactitude, exactness, nicety, preciseness.

preclude *vb* bar, check, debar, hinder, inhibit, obviate, prevent, prohibit, restrain, stop.

precocious *adj* advanced, forward, overforward, premature.

preconcert *vb* concoct, prearrange, predetermine, premeditate, prepare.

precursor *n* antecedent, cause, forerunner, predecessor; harbinger, herald, messenger, pioneer; omen, presage, sign.

precursory *adj* antecedent, anterior, forerunning, precedent, preceding, previous, prior; initiatory, introductory, precursive, prefatory, preliminary, prelusive, prelusory, premonitory, preparatory, prognosticative.

predatory *adj* greedy, pillaging, plundering, predacious, rapacious, ravaging, ravenous, voracious.

predestination *n* doom, fate, foredoom, foreordainment, foreordination, necessity, predetermination, preordination.

predicament *n* attitude, case, condition, plight, position, posture, situation, state; corner, dilemma, emergency, exigency, fix, hole, impasse, mess, pass, pinch, push, quandary, scrape.

predict *vb* augur, betoken, bode, divine, forebode, forecast, foredoom, foresee, forespeak, foretell, foretoken, forewarn, portend, prognosticate, prophesy, read, signify, soothsay.

predilection *n* bent, bias, desire, fondness, inclination, leaning, liking, love, partiality, predisposition, preference, prejudice, prepossession.

predisposition *n* aptitude, bent, bias, disposition, inclination, leaning, proclivity, proneness, propensity, willingness.

predominant *adj* ascendant, controlling, dominant, overruling, prevailing, prevalent, reigning, ruling, sovereign, supreme.

predominate *vb* dominate, preponderate, prevail, rule.

pre-eminent *adj* chief, conspicuous, consummate, controlling, distinguished, excellent, excelling, paramount, peerless, predominant, renowned, superior, supreme, surpassing, transcendent, unequalled.

preface *vb* begin, introduce, induct, launch, open, precede. • *n* exordium, foreword, induction, introduction, preamble, preliminary, prelude, prelusion, premise, proem, prologue, prolusion.

prefatory *adj* antecedent, initiative, introductory, precursive, precursory, preliminary, prelusive, prelusory, preparatory, proemial.

prefer *vb* address, offer, present, proffer, tender; advance, elevate, promote, raise; adopt, choose, elect, fancy, pick, select, wish.

preference *n* advancement, choice, election, estimation, precedence, priority, selection.

preferment *n* advancement, benefice, dignity, elevation, exaltation, promotion.

pregnant *adj* big, enceinte, parturient; fraught, full, important, replete, significant, weighty; fecund, fertile, fruitful, generative, potential, procreant, procreative, productive, prolific.

prejudice *vb* bias, incline, influence, turn, warp; damage, diminish, hurt, impair, injure. • *n* bias, intolerance, partiality, preconception, predilection, prejudgement, prepossession, unfairness; damage, detriment, disadvantage, harm, hurt, impairment, injury, loss, mischief.

prejudiced *adj* biased, bigoted, influenced, one-sided, partial, partisan, unfair.

preliminary *adj* antecedent, initiatory, introductory, precedent, precursive, precursory, prefatory, prelusive, prelusory, preparatory, previous, prior, proemial. • *n* beginning, initiation, introduction, opening, preamble, preface, prelude, start.

prelude *n* introduction, opening, overture, prelusion, preparation, voluntary; exordium, preamble, preface, preliminary, proem.

premature *adj* hasty, ill-considered, precipitate, unmatured, unprepared, unripe, unseasonable, untimely.

premeditation *n* deliberation, design, forethought, intention, prearrangement, predetermination, purpose.

premise *vb* introduce, preamble, preface, prefix. • *n* affirmation, antecedent, argument, assertion, assumption, basis, foundation, ground, hypothesis, position, premiss, presupposition, proposition, support, thesis, theorem.

premium *n* bonus, bounty, encouragement, fee, gift, guerdon, meed, payment, prize, recompense, remuneration, reward; appreciation, enhancement.

premonition *n* caution, foreboding, foreshadowing, forewarning, indication, omen, portent, presage, presentiment, sign, warning.

preoccupied *adj* absent, absentminded, abstracted, dreaming, engrossed, inadvertent, inattentive, lost, musing, unobservant.

prepare *vb* adapt, adjust, fit, qualify; arrange, concoct, fabricate, make, order, plan, procure, provide.

preponderant *adj* outweighing, overbalancing, preponderating.

prepossessing *adj* alluring, amiable, attractive, bewitching, captivating, charming, engaging, fascinating, inviting, taking, winning.

preposterous *adj* absurd, excessive, exorbitant, extravagant, foolish, improper, irrational, monstrous, nonsensical, perverted, ridiculous, unfit, unreasonable, wrong.

prerogative *n* advantage, birthright, claim, franchise, immunity, liberty, privilege, right.

presage *vb* divine, forebode; augur, betoken, bode, foreshadow, foretell, foretoken, indicate, portend, predict, prognosticate, prophesy, signify, soothsay. • *n* augury, auspice, boding, foreboding, foreshowing, indication, omen, portent, prognostication, sign, token; foreknowledge, precognition, prediction, premonition, presentiment, prophecy.

prescribe *vb* advocate, appoint, command, decree, dictate, direct, enjoin, establish, institute, ordain, order.

presence *n* attendance, company, inhabitance, inhabitancy, nearness, neighbourhood, occupancy, propinquity, proximity, residence, ubiquity, vicinity; air, appearance, carriage, demeanour, mien, personality.

present[1] *adj* near; actual, current, existing, happening, immediate, instant, living; available, quick, ready; attentive, favourable. • *n* now, time being, today.

present[2] *n* benefaction, boon, donation, favour, gift, grant, gratuity, largesse, offering.

present[3] *vb* introduce, nominate; exhibit, offer; bestow, confer, give, grant; deliver, hand; advance, express, prefer, proffer, tender.

presentiment *n* anticipation, apprehension, foreboding, forecast, foretaste, forethought, prescience.

presently *adv* anon, directly, forthwith, immediately, shortly, soon.

preservation *n* cherishing, conservation, curing, maintenance, protection, support; safety, salvation, security; integrity, keeping, soundness.

preserve *vb* defend, guard, keep, protect, rescue, save, secure, shield; maintain, uphold, sustain, support; conserve, economize, husband, retain. • *n* comfit, compote, confection, confiture, conserve, jam, jelly, marmalade, sweetmeat; enclosure, warren.

preside *vb* control, direct, govern, manage, officiate.

press *vb* compress, crowd, crush, squeeze; flatten, iron, smooth; clasp, embrace, hug; force, compel, constrain; emphasize, enforce, enjoin, inculcate, stress, urge; hasten, hurry, push, rush; crowd, throng; entreat, importune, solicit. • *n* crowd, crush, multitude, throng; hurry, pressure, urgency; case, closet, cupboard, repository.

pressing *adj* constraining, critical, distressing, imperative, importunate, persistent, serious, urgent, vital.

pressure *n* compressing, crushing, squeezing; influence, force; compulsion, exigency, hurry, persuasion, press, stress, urgency; affliction, calamity, difficulty, distress, embarrassment, grievance, oppression, straits; impression, stamp.

prestidigitation *n* conjuring, juggling, legerdemain, sleight-of-hand.

prestige *n* credit, distinction, importance, influence, reputation, weight.

presume *vb* anticipate, apprehend, assume, believe, conjecture, deduce, expect, infer, surmise, suppose, think; consider, presuppose; dare, undertake, venture.

presumption *n* anticipation, assumption, belief, concession, conclusion, condition, conjecture, deduction, guess, hypothesis, inference, opinion, supposition, understanding; arrogance, assurance, audacity, boldness, brass, effrontery, forwardness, haughtiness, presumptuousness; probability.

presumptuous *adj* arrogant, assuming, audacious, bold, brash, forward, irreverent, insolent, intrusive, presuming; foolhardy, overconfident, rash.

pretence *n* affectation, cloak, colour, disguise, mask, semblance, show, simulation, veil, window-dressing; excuse, evasion, fabrication, feigning, makeshift, pretext, sham, subterfuge; claim, pretension.

pretend *vb* affect, counterfeit, deem, dissemble, fake, falsify, feign, sham, simulate; act, imagine, lie, profess; aspire, claim.

pretension *n* assertion, assumption, claim, demand, pretence; affectation, airs, conceit, ostentation, pertness, pretentiousness, priggishness, vanity.

pretentious *adj* affected, assuming, conceited, conspicuous, ostentatious, presuming, priggish, showy, tawdry, unnatural, vain.

preternatural *adj* abnormal, anomalous, extraordinary, inexplicable, irregular, miraculous, mysterious, odd, peculiar, strange, unnatural.

pretext *n* affectation, appearance, blind, cloak, colour, guise, mask, pretence, semblance, show, simulation, veil; excuse, justification, plea, vindication.

pretty *adj* attractive, beautiful, bonny, comely, elegant, fair, handsome, neat, pleasing, trim; affected, foppish. • *adv* fairly, moderately, quite, rather, somewhat.

prevail *vb* overcome, succeed, triumph, win; obtain, predominate, preponderate, reign, rule.

prevailing *adj* controlling, dominant, effectual, efficacious, general, influential, operative, overruling, persuading, predominant, preponderant, prevalent, ruling, successful.

prevalent *adj* ascendant, compelling, efficacious, governing, predominant, prevailing, successful, superior; extensive, general, rife, widespread.

prevaricate *vb* cavil, deviate, dodge, equivocate, evade, palter, pettifog, quibble, shift, shuffle, tergiversate.

prevent *vb* bar, check, debar, deter, forestall, help, hinder, impede, inhibit, intercept, interrupt, obstruct, obviate, preclude, prohibit, restrain, save, stop, thwart.

prevention *n* anticipation, determent, deterrence, deterrent, frustration, hindrance, interception, interruption, obstruction, preclusion, prohibition, restriction, stoppage.

previous *adj* antecedent, anterior, earlier, foregoing, foregone, former, precedent, preceding, prior.

prey *vb* devour, eat, feed on, live off; exploit, intimidate, terrorize; burden, distress, haunt, oppress, trouble, worry. • *n* booty, loot, pillage, plunder, prize, rapine, spoil; food, game, kill, quarry, victim; depredation, ravage.

price *vb* assess, estimate, evaluate, rate, value. • *n* amount, cost, expense, outlay, value; appraisal, charge, estimation, excellence, figure, rate, quotation, valuation, value, worth; compensation, guerdon, recompense, return, reward.

priceless *adj* dear, expensive, precious, inestimable, invaluable, valuable; amusing, comic, droll, funny, humorous, killing, rich.

prick *vb* perforate, pierce, puncture, stick; drive, goad, impel, incite, spur, urge; cut, hurt, mark, pain, sting, wound; hasten, post, ride. • *n* mark, perforation, point, puncture; prickle, sting, wound.

pride *vb* boast, brag, crow, preen, revel in. • *n* conceit, egotism, self-complacency, self-esteem, self-exaltation, self-importance, self-sufficiency, vanity; arrogance, assumption, disdain, haughtiness, hauteur, insolence, loftiness, lordliness, pomposity, presumption, superciliousness, vainglory; decorum, dignity, elevation, self-respect; decoration, glory, ornament, show, splendour.

priest *n* churchman, clergyman, divine, ecclesiastic, minister, pastor, presbyter.

prim *adj* demure, formal, nice, precise, prudish, starch, starched, stiff, strait-laced.

primary *adj* aboriginal, earliest, first, initial, original, prime, primitive, primeval, primordial, pristine; chief, main, principal; basic, elementary, fundamental, preparatory: radical.

prime[1] *adj* aboriginal, basic, first, initial, original, primal, primary, primeval, primitive, primordial, pristine; chief, foremost,

highest, leading, main, paramount, principal; blooming, early; capital, cardinal, dominant, predominant; excellent, first-class, first-rate, optimal, optimum, quintessential, superlative; beginning, opening. • *n* beginning, dawn, morning, opening; spring, springtime, youth; bloom, cream, flower, height, heyday, optimum, perfection, quintessence, zenith.

prime[2] *vb* charge, load, prepare, undercoat; coach, groom, train, tutor.

primeval *adj* original, primitive, primordial, pristine.

primitive *adj* aboriginal, first, fundamental, original, primal, primary, prime, primitive, primordial, pristine; ancient, antiquated, crude, old-fashioned, quaint, simple, uncivilized, unsophisticated.

prince *n* monarch, potentate, ruler, sovereign; dauphin, heir apparent, infant; chief, leader, potentate.

princely *adj* imperial, regal, royal; august, generous, grand, liberal, magnanimous, magnificent, majestic, munificent, noble, pompous, splendid, superb, titled; dignified, elevated, high-minded, lofty, noble, stately.

principal *adj* capital, cardinal, chief, essential, first, foremost, highest, leading, main, pre-eminent, prime. • *n* chief, head, leader; head teacher, master.

principally *adv* chiefly, essentially, especially, mainly, particularly.

principle *n* cause, fountain, fountainhead, groundwork, mainspring, nature, origin, source, spring; basis, constituent, element, essence, substratum; assumption, axiom, law, maxim, postulation; doctrine, dogma, impulse, maxim, opinion, precept, rule, tenet, theory; conviction, ground, motive, reason; equity, goodness, honesty, honour, incorruptibility, integrity, justice, probity, rectitude, righteousness, trustiness, truth, uprightness, virtue, worth; faculty, power.

prink *vb* adorn, deck, decorate; preen, primp, spruce.

print *vb* engrave, impress, imprint, mark, stamp; issue, publish. • *n* book, periodical, publication; copy, engraving, photograph, picture; characters, font, fount, lettering, type, typeface.

prior *adj* antecedent, anterior, earlier, foregoing, precedent, preceding, precursory, previous, superior.

priority *n* antecedence, anteriority, precedence, pre-eminence, pre-existence, superiority.

priory *n* abbey, cloister, convent, monastery, nunnery.

prison *n* confinement, dungeon, gaol, jail, keep, lockup, penitentiary, reformatory; can, clink, cooler, jug.

pristine *adj* ancient, earliest, first, former, old, original, primary, primeval, primitive, primordial.

privacy *n* concealment, secrecy; retirement, retreat, seclusion, solitude.

private *adj* retired, secluded, sequestrated, solitary; individual, own, particular, peculiar, personal, special, unofficial; confidential, privy; clandestine, concealed, hidden, secret. • *n* GI, soldier, tommy.

privation *n* bereavement, deprivation, dispossession, loss; destitution, distress, indigence, necessity, need, want; absence, negation; degradation.

privilege *n* advantage, charter, claim, exemption, favour, franchise, immunity, leave, liberty, licence, permission, prerogative, right.

privy *adj* individual, particular, peculiar, personal, private, special; clandestine, secret; retired, sequestrated.

prize[1] *vb* appreciate, cherish, esteem, treasure, value.

prize[2] *adj* best, champion, first-rate, outstanding, winning. • *n* guerdon, honours, meed, premium, reward; cup, decoration, medal, laurels, palm, trophy; booty, capture, lot, plunder, spoil; advantage, gain, privilege.

probability *n* chance, prospect, likelihood, presumption; appearance, credibility, credibleness, likeliness, verisimilitude.

probable *adj* apparent, credible, likely, presumable, reasonable.

probably *adv* apparently, likely, maybe, perchance, perhaps, presumably, possibly, seemingly.

probation *n* essay, examination, ordeal, proof, test, trial; novitiate.

probe *vb* examine, explore, fathom, investigate, measure, prove, scrutinize, search, sift, sound, test, verify. • *n* examination, exploration, inquiry, investigation, scrutiny, study.

probity *n* candour, conscientiousness, equity, fairness, faith, goodness, honesty, honour, incorruptibility, integrity, justice, loyalty, morality, principle, rectitude, righteousness, sincerity, soundness, trustworthiness, truth, truthfulness, uprightness, veracity, virtue, worth.

problem *adj* difficult, intractable, uncontrollable, unruly. • *n* dilemma, dispute, doubt, enigma, exercise, proposition, puzzle, riddle, theorem.

problematic *adj* debatable, disputable, doubtful, dubious, enigmatic, problematical, puzzling, questionable, suspicious, uncertain, unsettled.

procedure *n* conduct, course, custom, management, method, operation, policy, practice, process; act, action, deed, measure, performance, proceeding, step, transaction.

proceed *vb* advance, continue, go, pass, progress; accrue, arise, come, emanate, ensue, flow, follow, issue, originate, result, spring.

proceeds *npl* balance, earnings, effects, gain, income, net, produce, products, profits, receipts, returns, yield.

process *vb* advance, deal with, fulfil, handle, progress; alter, convert, refine, transform. • *n* advance, course, progress, train; action, conduct, management, measure, mode, operation, performance, practice, procedure, proceeding, step, transaction; way; action, case, suit, trial; outgrowth, projection, protuberance.

procession *n* cavalcade, cortege, file, march, parade, retinue, train.

proclaim *vb* advertise, announce, blazon, broach, broadcast, circulate, cry, declare, herald, promulgate, publish, trumpet; ban, outlaw, proscribe.

proclamation *n* advertisement, announcement, blazon, declaration, promulgation, publication; ban, decree, edict, manifesto, ordinance.

proclivity *n* bearing, bent, bias, determination, direction, disposition, drift, inclination, leaning, predisposition, proneness, propensity, tendency, turn; aptitude, facility, readiness.

procrastinate *vb* adjourn, defer, delay, postpone, prolong, protract, retard; neglect, omit; lag, loiter.

procrastination *n* delay, dilatoriness, postponement, protraction, slowness, tardiness.

procreate *vb* beget, breed, engender, generate, produce, propagate.

procurable *adj* acquirable, compassable, obtainable.

procurator *n* agent, attorney, deputy, proctor, proxy, representative, solicitor.

procure *vb* acquire, gain, get, obtain; cause, compass, contrive, effect.

procurer *n* bawd, pander, pimp.

prodigal *adj* abundant, dissipated, excessive, extravagant, generous, improvident, lavish, profuse, reckless, squandering, thriftless, unthrifty, wasteful. • *n* spendthrift, squanderer, waster, wastrel.

prodigality *n* excess, extravagance, lavishness, profusion, squandering, unthriftiness, waste, wastefulness.

prodigious *adj* amazing, astonishing, astounding, extraordinary, marvellous, miraculous, portentous, remarkable, startling, strange, surprising, uncommon, wonderful, wondrous; enormous, huge, immense, monstrous, vast.

prodigy *n* marvel, miracle, phenomenon, portent, sign, wonder; curiosity, monster, monstrosity.

produce *vb* exhibit, show; bear, beget, breed, conceive, engender, furnish, generate, hatch, procreate, yield; accomplish, achieve, cause, create, effect, make, occasion, originate; accrue, afford, give, impart, make, render; extend, lengthen, prolong, protract; fabricate, fashion, manufacture. • *n* crop, fruit, greengrocery, harvest, product, vegetables, yield.

producer *n* creator, inventor, maker, originator; agriculturalist, farmer, greengrocer, husbandman, raiser.

product *n* crops, fruits, harvest, outcome, proceeds, produce, production, returns, yield; consequence, effect, fruit, issue, performance, production, result, work.

production *n* fruit, produce, product; construction, creation, erection, fabrication, making, performance; completion, fruition; birth, breeding, development, growth, propagation; opus, publication, work; continuation, extension, lengthening, prolongation.

productive *adj* copious, fertile, fruitful, luxuriant, plenteous, prolific, teeming; causative, constructive, creative, efficient, life-giving, producing.

proem *n* exordium, foreword, introduction, preface, prelims, prelude, prolegomena.

profane *vb* defile, desecrate, pollute, violate; abuse, debase. • *adj* blasphemous, godless, heathen, idolatrous, impious, impure, pagan, secular, temporal, unconsecrated, unhallowed, unholy, unsanctified, worldly, unspiritual; impure, polluted, unholy.

profanity *n* blasphemy, impiety, irreverence, profaneness, sacrilege.

profess *vb* acknowledge, affirm, allege, aver, avouch, avow, confess, declare, own, proclaim, state; affect, feign, pretend.

profession *n* acknowledgement, assertion, avowal, claim, declaration; avocation, evasion, pretence, pretension, protestation, representation; business, calling, employment, engagement, occupation, office, trade, vocation.

proffer *vb* offer, propose, propound, suggest, tender, volunteer. • *n* offer, proposal, suggestion, tender.

proficiency *n* advancement, forwardness, improvement; accomplishment, aptitude, competency, dexterity, mastery, skill.

proficient *adj* able, accomplished, adept, competent, conversant, dextrous, expert, finished, masterly, practised, skilled, skilful, thoroughbred, trained, qualified, well-versed. • *n* adept, expert, master, master-hand.

profit *vb* advance, benefit, gain, improve. • *n* aid, clearance, earnings, emolument, fruit, gain, lucre, produce, return; advancement, advantage, benefit, interest, perquisite, service, use, utility, weal.

profitable *adj* advantageous, beneficial, desirable, gainful, productive, useful; lucrative, remunerative.

profitless *adj* bootless, fruitless, unprofitable, useless, valueless, worthless.

profligate *adj* abandoned, corrupt, corrupted, degenerate, depraved, dissipated, dissolute, graceless, immoral, shameless, vicious, vitiated, wicked. • *n* debauchee, libertine, rake, reprobate, roué.

profound *adj* abysmal, deep, fathomless; heavy, undisturbed; erudite, learned, penetrating, sagacious, skilled; deeply felt, far-reaching, heartfelt, intense, lively, strong, touching, vivid; low, submissive; abstruse, mysterious, obscure, occult, subtle, recondite; complete, thorough.

profundity *n* deepness, depth, profoundness.

profuse *adj* abundant, bountiful, copious, excessive, extravagant, exuberant, generous, improvident, lavish, overabundant, plentiful, prodigal, wasteful.

profusion *n* abundance, bounty, copiousness, excess, exuberance, extravagance, lavishness, prodigality, profuseness, superabundance, waste.

progenitor *n* ancestor, forebear, forefather.

progeny *n* breed, children, descendants, family, issue, lineage, offshoot, offspring, posterity, race, scion, stock, young.

prognostic *adj* foreshadowing, foreshowing, foretokening. • *n* augury, foreboding, indication, omen, presage, prognostication, sign, symptom, token; foretelling, prediction, prophecy.

prognosticate *vb* foretell, predict, prophesy; augur, betoken, forebode, foreshadow, foreshow, foretoken, indicate, portend, presage.

prognostication *n* foreknowledge, foreshowing, foretelling, prediction, presage; augury, foreboding, foretoken, indication, portent, prophecy.

progress *vb* advance, continue, proceed; better, gain, improve, increase. • *n* advance, advancement, progression; course, headway, ongoing, passage; betterment, development, growth, improvement, increase, reform; circuit, procession.

prohibit *vb* debar, hamper, hinder, preclude, prevent; ban, disallow, forbid, inhibit, interdict.

prohibition *n* ban, bar, disallowance, embargo, forbiddance, inhibition, interdict, interdiction, obstruction, prevention, proscription, taboo, veto.

prohibitive *adj* forbidding, prohibiting, refraining, restrictive.

project *vb* cast, eject, fling, hurl, propel, shoot, throw; brew, concoct, contrive, design, devise, intend, plan, plot, purpose, scheme; delineate, draw, exhibit; bulge, extend, jut, protrude. • *n* contrivance, design, device, intention, plan, proposal, purpose, scheme.

projectile *n* bullet, missile, shell.

projection *n* delivery, ejection, emission, propulsion, throwing; contriving, designing, planning, scheming; bulge, extension, outshoot, process, prominence, protuberance, salience, saliency, salient, spur; delineation, map, plan.

proletarian *adj* mean, plebeian, vile, vulgar. • *n* commoner, plebeian.

proletariat *n* commonality, hoi polloi, masses, mob, plebs, working class.

prolific *adj* abundant, fertile, fruitful, generative, productive, teeming.

prolix *adj* boring, circumlocutory, discursive, diffuse, lengthy, long, long-winded, loose, prolonged, protracted, prosaic, rambling, tedious, tiresome, verbose, wordy.

prologue *n* foreword, introduction, preamble, preface, preliminary, prelude, proem.

prolong *vb* continue, extend, lengthen, protract, sustain; defer, postpone.

promenade *vb* saunter, walk. • *n* dance, stroll, walk; boulevard, esplanade, parade, walkway.

prominent *adj* convex, embossed, jutting, projecting, protuberant, raised, relieved; celebrated, conspicuous, distinguished, eminent, famous, foremost, influential, leading, main, noticeable, outstanding; conspicuous, distinctive, important, manifest, marked, principal, salient.

promiscuous *adj* confused, heterogeneous, indiscriminate, intermingled, mingled, miscellaneous, mixed; abandoned, dissipated, dissolute, immoral, licentious, loose, unchaste, wanton.

promise *vb* covenant, engage, pledge, subscribe, swear, underwrite, vow; assure, attest, guarantee, warrant; agree, bargain, engage, stipulate, undertake. • *n* agreement, assurance, contract, engagement, oath, parole, pledge, profession, undertaking, vow, word.

promising *adj* auspicious, encouraging, hopeful, likely, propitious.

promote *vb* advance, aid, assist, cultivate, encourage, further, help, promote; dignify, elevate, exalt, graduate, honour, pass, prefer, raise.

promotion *n* advancement, encouragement, furtherance; elevation, exaltation, preferment.

prompt *vb* actuate, dispose, impel, incite, incline, induce, instigate, stimulate, urge; remind; dictate, hint, influence, suggest. • *adj* active, alert, apt, quick, ready; forward, hasty; disposed, inclined, prone; early, exact, immediate, instant, precise, punctual, seasonable, timely. • *adv* apace, directly, forthwith, immediately, promptly. • *n* cue, hint, prompter, reminder, stimulus.

promptly *adv* apace, directly, expeditiously, forthwith, immediately, instantly, pronto, punctually, quickly, speedily, straightway, straightaway, summarily, swiftly.

promptness *n* activity, alertness, alacrity, promptitude, readiness, quickness.

promulgate *vb* advertise, announce, broadcast, bruit, circulate, declare, notify, proclaim, publish, spread, trumpet.

prone *adj* flat, horizontal, prostrate, recumbent; declivitous, inclined, inclining, sloping; apt, bent, disposed, inclined, predisposed, tending; eager, prompt, ready.

pronounce *vb* articulate, enunciate, frame, say, speak, utter; affirm, announce, assert, declare, deliver, state.

proof *adj* firm, fixed, impenetrable, stable, steadfast. • *n* essay, examination, ordeal, test, trial; attestation, certification, conclusion, conclusiveness, confirmation, corroboration, demonstration, evidence, ratification, substantiation, testimony, verification.

prop *vb* bolster, brace, buttress, maintain, shore, stay, support, sustain, truss, uphold. • *n* support, stay; buttress, fulcrum, pin, shore, strut.

propaganda *n* inculcation, indoctrination, promotion.

propagate *vb* continue, increase, multiply; circulate, diffuse, disseminate, extend, promote, promulgate, publish, spread, transmit; beget, breed, engender, generate, originate, procreate.

propel *vb* drive, force, impel, push, urge; cast, fling, hurl, project, throw.

propensity *n* aptitude, bent, bias, disposition, inclination, ply, proclivity, proneness, tendency.

proper *adj* individual, inherent, natural, original, particular, peculiar, special, specific; adapted, appropriate, becoming, befitting, convenient, decent, decorous, demure, fit, fitting, legitimate, meet, pertinent, respectable, right, seemly, suitable; accurate, correct, exact, fair, fastidious, formal, just, precise; actual, real.

property *n* attribute, characteristic, disposition, mark, peculiarity, quality, trait, virtue; appurtenance, assets, belongings, chattels, circumstances, effects, estate, goods, possessions, resources, wealth; ownership, possession, proprietorship, tenure; claim, copyright, interest, participation, right, title.

prophecy *n* augury, divination, forecast, foretelling, portent, prediction, premonition, presage, prognostication; exhortation, instruction, preaching.

prophesy *vb* augur, divine, foretell, predict, prognosticate.

propinquity *n* adjacency, contiguity, nearness, neighbourhood, proximity, vicinity; affinity, connection, consanguinity, kindred, relationship.

propitiate *vb* appease, atone, conciliate, intercede, mediate, pacify, reconcile, satisfy.

propitious *adj* benevolent, benign, friendly, gracious, kind, merciful; auspicious, encouraging, favourable, fortunate, happy, lucky, opportune, promising, prosperous, thriving, timely, well-disposed.

proportion *vb* adjust, graduate, regulate; form, shape. • *n* arrangement, relation; adjustment, commensuration, dimension, distribution, symmetry; extent, lot, part, portion, quota, ratio, share.

proposal *n* design, motion, offer, overture, proffer, proposition, recommendation, scheme, statement, suggestion, tender.

propose *vb* move, offer, pose, present, propound, proffer, put, recommend, state, submit, suggest, tender; design, intend, mean, purpose.

proposition *vb* accost, proffer, solicit. • *n* offer, overture, project, proposal, suggestion, tender, undertaking; affirmation, assertion, axiom, declaration, dictum, doctrine, position, postulation, predication, statement, theorem, thesis.

proprietor *n* lord, master, owner, possessor, proprietary.

propriety *n* accuracy, adaptation, appropriation, aptness, becomingness, consonance, correctness, fitness, justness, reasonableness, rightness, seemliness, suitableness; conventionality, decency, decorum, demureness, fastidiousness, formality, modesty, properness, respectability.

prorogation *n* adjournment, continuance, postponement.

prosaic *adj* commonplace, dull, flat, humdrum, matter-of-fact, pedestrian, plain, prolix, prosing, sober, stupid, tame, tedious, tiresome, unentertaining, unimaginative, uninspired, uninteresting, unromantic, vapid.

proscribe *vb* banish, doom, exile, expel, ostracize, outlaw; exclude, forbid, interdict, prohibit; censure, condemn, curse, denounce, reject.

prosecute *vb* conduct, continue, exercise, follow, persist, pursue; arraign, indict, sue, summon.

prospect *vb* explore, search, seek, survey. • *n* display, field, landscape, outlook, perspective, scene, show, sight, spectacle, survey, view, vision, vista; picture, scenery; anticipation, calculation, contemplation, expectance, expectancy, expectation, foreseeing, foresight, hope, presumption, promise, trust; likelihood, probability.

prospectus *n* announcement, conspectus, description, design, outline, plan, programme, sketch, syllabus.

prosper *vb* aid, favour, forward, help; advance, flourish, grow rich, thrive, succeed; batten, increase.

prosperity *n* affluence, blessings, happiness, felicity, good luck, success, thrift, weal, welfare, well-being; boom, heyday.

prosperous *adj* blooming, flourishing, fortunate, golden, halcyon, rich, successful, thriving; auspicious, booming, bright, favourable, good, golden, lucky, promising, propitious, providential, rosy.

prostrate *vb* demolish, destroy, fell, level, overthrow, overturn, ruin; depress, exhaust, overcome, reduce. • *adj* fallen, prostrated, prone, recumbent, supine; helpless, powerless.

prostration *n* demolition, destruction, overthrow; dejection, depression, exhaustion.

prosy *adj* prosaic, unpoetic, unpoetical; dull, flat, jejune, stupid, tedious, tiresome, unentertaining, unimaginative, uninteresting.

protect *vb* cover, defend, guard, shield; fortify, harbour, house, preserve, save, screen, secure, shelter; champion, countenance, foster, patronize.

protector *n* champion, custodian, defender, guardian, patron, warden.

protest *vb* affirm, assert, asseverate, attest, aver, avow, declare, profess, testify; demur, expostulate, object, remonstrate, repudiate. • *n* complaint, declaration, disapproval, objection, protestation.

prototype *n* archetype, copy, exemplar, example, ideal, model, original, paradigm, precedent, protoplast, type.

protract *vb* continue, extend, lengthen, prolong; defer, delay, postpone.

protrude *vb* beetle, bulge, extend, jut, project.

protuberance *n* bulge, bump, elevation, excrescence, hump, lump, process, projection, prominence, roundness, swelling, tumour.

proud *adj* assuming, conceited, contended, egotistical, overweening, self-conscious, self-satisfied, vain; arrogant, boastful, haughty, high-spirited, highly strung, imperious, lofty, lordly, presumptuous, supercilious, uppish, vainglorious.

prove *vb* ascertain, conform, demonstrate, establish, evidence, evince, justify, manifest, show, substantiate, sustain, verify; assay, check, examine, experiment, test, try.

proverb *n* adage, aphorism, apothegm, byword, dictum, maxim, precept, saw, saying.

proverbial *adj* acknowledged, current, notorious, unquestioned.

provide *vb* arrange, collect, plan, prepare, procure; gather, keep, store; afford, contribute, feed, furnish, produce, stock, supply, yield; cater, purvey; agree, bargain, condition, contract, covenant, engage, stipulate.

provided, providing *conj* granted, if, supposing.

provident *adj* careful, cautious, considerate, discreet, farseeing, forecasting, forehanded, foreseeing, prudent; economical, frugal, thrifty.

province *n* district, domain, region, section, territory, tract; colony, dependency; business, calling, capacity, charge, department, duty, employment, function, office, part, post, sphere; department, division, jurisdiction.

provincial *adj* annexed, appendant, outlying; bucolic, countrified, rude, rural, rustic, unpolished, unrefined; insular, local, narrow. • *n* peasant, rustic, yokel.

provision *n* anticipation, providing; arrangement, care, preparation, readiness; equipment, fund, grist, hoard, reserve, resources, stock, store, supplies, supply; clause, condition, prerequisite, proviso, reservation, stipulation.

provisions *npl* eatables, fare, food, provender, supplies, viands, victuals.

proviso *n* clause, condition, provision, stipulation.

provocation *n* incentive, incitement, provocativeness, stimulant, stimulus; affront, indignity, insult, offence; angering, vexation.

provoke *vb* animate, arouse, awaken, excite, impel, incite, induce, inflame, instigate, kindle, move, rouse, stimulate; affront, aggravate, anger, annoy, chafe, enrage, exacerbate, exasperate, incense, infuriate, irritate, nettle, offend, pique, vex; cause, elicit, evoke, instigate, occasion, produce, promote.

provoking *adj* aggravating, annoying, exasperating, irritating, offensive, tormenting, vexatious, vexing.

prowess *n* bravery, courage, daring, fearlessness, gallantry, heroism, intrepidity, valour; aptitude, dexterity, expertness, facility.

proximity *n* adjacency, contiguity, nearness, neighbourhood, propinquity, vicinage, vicinity.

proxy *n* agent, attorney, commissioner, delegate, deputy, lieutenant, representative, substitute.

prudence *n* carefulness, caution, circumspection, common sense, considerateness, discretion, forecast, foresight, judgment, judiciousness, policy, providence, sense, tact, wariness, wisdom.

prudent *adj* cautious, careful, circumspect, considerate, discreet, foreseeing, heedful, judicious, politic, provident, prudential, wary, wise.

prudish *adj* coy, demure, modest, precise, prim, reserved, straitlaced.

prune *vb* abbreviate, clip, cut, dock, lop, thin, trim; dress, preen.

prurient *adj* covetous, craving, desiring, hankering, itching, lascivious, libidinous, longing, lustful.

pry *vb* examine, ferret, inspect, investigate, peep, peer, question, scrutinize, search; force, lever, prise.

public *adj* civil, common, countrywide, general, national, political, state; known, notorious, open, popular, published, well-known. • *n* citizens, community, country, everyone, general public, masses, nation, people, population; audience, buyers, following, supporters.

publication *n* advertisement, announcement, disclosure, divulgement, divulgence, proclamation, promulgation, report; edition, issue, issuance, printing.

publicity *n* daylight, currency, limelight, notoriety, spotlight; outlet, vent.

publish *vb* advertise, air, bruit, announce, blaze, blazon, broach, communicate, declare, diffuse, disclose, disseminate, impart, placard, post, proclaim, promulgate, reveal, tell, utter, vent, ventilate.

pucker *vb* cockle, contract, corrugate, crease, crinkle, furrow, gather, pinch, purse, shirr, wrinkle. • *n* crease, crinkle, fold, furrow, wrinkle.

puerile *adj* boyish, childish, infantile, juvenile, youthful; foolish, frivolous, idle, nonsensical, petty, senseless, silly, simple, trifling, trivial, weak.

puffy *adj* distended, swelled, swollen, tumid, turgid; bombastic, extravagant, inflated, pompous.

pugnacious *adj* belligerent, bellicose, contentious, fighting, irascible, irritable, petulant, quarrelsome.

puissant *adj* forcible, mighty, potent, powerful, strong.

pull *vb* drag, draw, haul, row, tow, tug; cull, extract, gather, pick, pluck; detach, rend, tear, wrest. • *n* pluck, shake, tug, twitch, wrench; contest, struggle; attraction, gravity, magnetism; graft, influence, power.

pulsate *vb* beat, palpitate, pant, throb, thump, vibrate.

pulverize *vb* bruise, comminute, grind, levigate, triturate.

pun *vb* assonate, alliterate, play on words. • *n* assonance, alliteration, clinch, conceit, double-meaning, paranomasia, play on words, quip, rhyme, witticism, wordplay.

punctilious *adj* careful, ceremonious, conscientious, exact, formal, nice, particular, precise, punctual, scrupulous, strict.

punctual *adj* exact, nice, precise, punctilious; early, prompt, ready, regular, seasonable, timely.

puncture *vb* bore, penetrate, perforate, pierce, prick. • *n* bite, hole, sting, wound.

pungent *adj* acid, acrid, biting, burning, caustic, hot, mordant, penetrating, peppery, piercing, piquant, prickling, racy, salty, seasoned, sharp, smart, sour, spicy, stimulating, stinging; acute, acrimonious, cutting, distressing, irritating, keen, painful, peevish, poignant, pointed, satirical, severe, tart, trenchant, waspish.

punish *vb* beat, castigate, chasten, chastise, correct, discipline, flog, lash, scourge, torture, whip.

punishment *n* castigation, chastening, chastisement, correction, discipline, infliction, retribution, scourging, trial; judgment, nemesis, penalty.

puny *adj* feeble, inferior, weak; dwarf, dwarfish, insignificant, diminutive, little, petty, pygmy, small, stunted, tiny, underdeveloped, undersized.

pupil *n* beginner, catechumen, disciple, learner, neophyte, novice, scholar, student, tyro.

pupillage *n* minority, nonage, tutelage, wardship.

puppet *n* doll, image, manikin, marionette; cat's-paw, pawn, tool.

purchase *vb* buy, gain, get, obtain, pay for, procure; achieve, attain, earn, win. • *n* acquisition, buy, gain, possession, property; advantage, foothold, grasp, hold, influence, support.

pure *adj* clean, clear, fair, immaculate, spotless, stainless, unadulterated, unalloyed, unblemished, uncorrupted, undefiled, unpolluted, unspotted, unstained, unsullied, untainted, untarnished; chaste, continent, guileless, guiltless, holy, honest, incorrupt, innocent, modest, sincere, true, uncorrupt, upright, virgin, virtuous; genuine, perfect, real, simple, true, unadorned; absolute, essential, mere, sheer, thorough; classic, classical.

purge *vb* cleanse, clear, purify; clarify, defecate, evacuate; deterge, scour; absolve, pardon, shrive. • *n* elimination, eradication, expulsion, removal, suppression; cathartic, emetic, enema, laxative, physic.

purify *vb* clean, cleanse, clear, depurate, expurgate, purge, refine, wash; clarify, fine.

puritanical *adj* ascetic, narrow-minded, overscrupulous, prim, prudish, rigid, severe, strait-laced, strict.

purity *n* clearness, fineness; cleanness, correctness, faultlessness, immaculacy, immaculateness; guilelessness, guiltlessness, holiness, honesty, innocence, integrity, piety, simplicity, truth, uprightness, virtue; excellence, genuineness, homogeneity, simpleness; chasteness, chastity, continence, modesty, pudency, virginity.

purlieus *npl* borders, bounds, confines, environs, limits, neighbourhood, outskirts, precincts, suburbs, vicinage, vicinity.

purloin *vb* abstract, crib, filch, pilfer, rob, steal, thieve.

purport *vb* allege, assert, claim, maintain, pretend, profess; denote, express, imply, indicate, mean, signify, suggest. • *n* bearing, current, design, drift, gist, import, intent, meaning, scope, sense, significance, signification, spirit, tendency, tenor.

purpose *vb* contemplate, design, intend, mean, meditate; determine, resolve. • *n* aim, design, drift, end, intent, intention, object, resolution, resolve, view; plan, project; meaning, purport, sense; consequence, effect.

pursue *vb* chase, dog, follow, hound, hunt, shadow, track; conduct, continue, cultivate, maintain, practise, prosecute; seek, strive; accompany, attend.

pursuit *n* chase, hunt, race; conduct, cultivation, practice, prosecution, pursuance; avocation, calling, business, employment, fad, hobby, occupation, vocation.

pursy *adj* corpulent, fat, fleshy, plump, podgy, pudgy, short, thick; short-breathed, short-winded; opulent, rich.

purview *n* body, compass, extent, limit, reach, scope, sphere, view.

push *vb* elbow, crowd, hustle, impel, jostle, shoulder, shove, thrust; advance, drive, hurry, propel, urge; importune, persuade, tease. • *n* pressure, thrust; determination, perseverance; emergency, exigency, extremity, pinch, strait, test, trial; assault, attack, charge, endeavour, onset.

pusillanimous *adj* chicken, chicken-hearted, cowardly, dastardly, faint-hearted, feeble, lily-livered, mean-spirited, spiritless, timid, recreant, timorous, weak.

pustule *n* abscess, blain, blister, blotch, boil, fester, gathering, pimple, sore, ulcer.

put *vb* bring, collocate, deposit, impose, lay, locate, place, set; enjoin, impose, inflict, levy; offer, present, propose, state; compel, constrain, force, oblige; entice, incite, induce, urge; express, utter.

putative *adj* deemed, reckoned, reported, reputed, supposed.

putrefy *vb* corrupt, decay, decompose, fester, rot, stink.

putrid *adj* corrupt, decayed, decomposed, fetid, rank, rotten, stinking.

puzzle *vb* bewilder, confound, confuse, embarrass, gravel, mystify, nonplus, perplex, pose, stagger; complicate, entangle. • *n* conundrum, enigma, labyrinth, maze, paradox, poser, problem, riddle; bewilderment, complication, confusion, difficulty, dilemma, embarrassment, mystification, perplexity, point, quandary, question.

pygmy *adj* diminutive, dwarf, dwarfish, Lilliputian, little, midget, stunted, tiny. • *n* dwarf, Lilliputian, midget.

Q

quack[1] *vb, n* cackle, cry, squeak.

quack[2] *adj* fake, false, sham. • *n* charlatan, empiric, humbug, impostor, mountebank, pretender.

quadruple *adj* fourfold, quadruplicate.

quagmire *n* bog, fen, marsh, morass, slough, swamp; difficulty, impasse, muddle, predicament.

quail *vb* blench, cower, droop, faint, flinch, shrink, tremble.

quaint *adj* antiquated, antique, archaic, curious, droll, extraordinary, fanciful, odd, old-fashioned, queer, singular, uncommon, unique, unusual; affected, fantastic, far-fetched, whimsical; artful, ingenious.

quake *vb* quiver, shake, shiver, shudder; move, vibrate. • *n* earthquake, shake, shudder.

qualification *n* ability, accomplishment, capability, competency, eligibility, fitness, suitability; condition, exception, limitation, modification, proviso, restriction, stipulation; abatement, allowance, diminution, mitigation.

qualified *adj* accomplished, certificated, certified, competent, fitted, equipped, licensed, trained; adapted, circumscribed, conditional, limited, modified, restricted.

qualify *vb* adapt, capacitate, empower, entitle, equip, fit; limit, modify, narrow, restrain, restrict; abate, assuage, ease, mitigate, moderate, reduce, soften; diminish, modulate, temper, regulate, vary.

quality *n* affection, attribute, characteristic, colour, distinction, feature, flavour, mark, nature, peculiarity, property, singularity, timbre, tinge, trait; character, condition, disposition, humour, mood, temper; brand, calibre, capacity, class, description, excellence, grade, kind, rank, sort, stamp, standing, station, status, virtue; aristocracy, gentility, gentry, noblesse, nobility.

qualm *n* agony, pang, throe; nausea, queasiness, sickness; compunction, remorse, uneasiness, twinge.

quandary *n* bewilderment, difficulty, dilemma, doubt, embarrassment, perplexity, pickle, plight, predicament, problem, puzzle, strait, uncertainty.

quantity *n* content, extent, greatness, measure, number, portion, share, size; aggregate, batch, amount, bulk, lot, mass, quantum, store, sum, volume; duration, length.

quarrel *vb* altercate, bicker, brawl, carp, cavil, clash, contend, differ, dispute, fight, jangle, jar, scold, scuffle, spar, spat, squabble, strive, wrangle. • *n* altercation, affray, bickering, brawl, breach, breeze, broil, clash, contention, contest, controversy, difference, disagreement, discord, dispute, dissension, disturbance, feud, fight, fray, imbroglio, jar, miff, misunderstanding, quarrelling, row, rupture, spat, squabble, strife, tiff, tumult, variance, wrangle.

quarrelsome *adj* argumentative, choleric, combative, contentious, cross, discordant, disputatious, dissentious, fiery, irascible, irritable, petulant, pugnacious, ugly, wranglesome.

quarter *vb* billet, lodge, post, station; allot, furnish, share. • *n* abode, billet, dwelling, habitation, lodgings, posts, quarters, stations; direction, district, locality, location, lodge, position, region, territory; clemency, mercy, mildness.

quash *vb* abate, abolish, annul, cancel, invalidate, nullify, overthrow; crush, extinguish, repress, stop, subdue, suppress.

queasy *adj* nauseated, pukish, seasick, sick, squeamish.

queer *vb* botch, harm, impair, mar, spoil. • *adj* curious, droll, extraordinary, fantastic, odd, peculiar, quaint, singular, strange, uncommon, unusual, whimsical; gay, homosexual.

quell *vb* conquer, crush, overcome, overpower, subdue; bridle, check, curb, extinguish, lay, quench, rein in, repress, restrain, stifle; allay, calm, compose, hush, lull, pacify, quiet, quieten, still, tranquillize; alleviate, appease, blunt, deaden, dull, mitigate, mollify, soften, soothe.

quench *vb* extinguish, put out; check, destroy, repress, satiate, stifle, still, suppress; allay, cool, dampen, extinguish, slake.

querulous *adj* bewailing, complaining, cross, discontented, dissatisfied, fretful, fretting, irritable, mourning, murmuring, peevish, petulant, plaintive, touchy, whining.

query *vb* ask, enquire, inquire, question; dispute, doubt. • *n* enquiry, inquiry, interrogatory, issue, problem, question.

quest *n* expedition, journey, search, voyage; pursuit, suit; examination, enquiry, inquiry; demand, desire, invitation, prayer, request, solicitation.

question *vb* ask, catechize, enquire, examine, inquire, interrogate, quiz, sound out; doubt, query; challenge, dispute. • *n* examination, enquiry, inquiry, interpellation, interrogation; enquiry, inquiry, interrogatory, query; debate, discussion, disquisition, examination, investigation, issue, trial; controversy, dispute, doubt; motion, mystery, point, poser, problem, proposition, puzzle, topic.

questionable *adj* ambiguous, controversial, controvertible, debatable, doubtful, disputable, equivocal, problematic, problematical, suspicious, uncertain, undecided.

quibble *vb* cavil, equivocate, evade, prevaricate, shuffle. • *n* equivocation, evasion, pretence, prevarication, quirk, shift, shuffle, sophism, subtlety, subterfuge.

quick *adj* active, agile, alert, animated, brisk, lively, nimble, prompt, ready, smart, sprightly; expeditious, fast, fleet, flying, hurried, rapid, speedy, swift; adroit, apt, clever, dextrous, expert, skilful; choleric, hasty, impetuous, irascible, irritable, passionate, peppery, petulant, precipitate, sharp, unceremonious, testy, touchy, waspish; alive, animate, live, living.

quicken *vb* animate, energize, resuscitate, revivify, vivify; cheer, enliven, invigorate, reinvigorate, revive, whet; accelerate, dispatch, expedite, hasten, hurry, speed; actuate, excite, incite, kindle, refresh, sharpen, stimulate; accelerate, live, take effect.

quickly *adv* apace, fast, immediately, nimbly, quick, rapidly, readily, soon, speedily, swiftly.

quickness *n* celerity, dispatch, expedition, haste, rapidity, speed, swiftness, velocity; agility, alertness, activity, briskness, liveliness, nimbleness, promptness, readiness, smartness; adroitness, aptitude, aptness, dexterity, facility, knack; acumen, acuteness, keenness, penetration, perspicacity, sagacity, sharpness, shrewdness.

quiescent *adj* at rest, hushed, motionless, quiet, resting, still; calm, mute, placid, quiet, serene, still, tranquil, unagitated, undisturbed, unruffled.

quiet *adj* hushed, motionless, quiescent, still, unmoved; calm, contented, gentle, mild, meek, modest, peaceable, peaceful, placid, silent, smooth, tranquil, undemonstrative, unobtrusive, unruffled; patient; retired, secluded. • *n* calmness, peace, repose, rest, silence, stillness.

quieten *vb* arrest, discontinue, intermit, interrupt, still, stop, suspend; allay, appease, calm, compose, lull, pacify, sober, soothe, tranquillize; hush, silence; alleviate, assuage, blunt, dull, mitigate, moderate, mollify, soften.

quip *n* crank, flout, gibe, jeer, mock, quirk, repartee, retort, sarcasm, sally, scoff, sneer, taunt, witticism.

quit *vb* absolve, acquit, deliver, free, release; clear, deliver, discharge from, free, liberate, relieve; acquit, behave, conduct; carry through, perform; discharge, pay, repay, requite; relinquish, renounce, resign, stop, surrender; depart from, leave, withdraw from; abandon, desert, forsake, forswear. • *adj* absolved, acquitted, clear, discharged, free, released.

quite *adv* completely, entirely, exactly, perfectly, positively, precisely, totally, wholly.

quiver *vb* flicker, flutter, oscillate, palpitate, quake, play, shake, shiver, shudder, tremble, twitch, vibrate. • *n* shake, shiver, shudder, trembling.

quixotic *adj* absurd, chimerical, fanciful, fantastic, fantastical, freakish, imaginary, mad, romantic, utopian, visionary, wild.

quiz *vb* examine, question, test; peer at; banter, hoax, puzzle, ridicule. • *n* enigma, hoax, jest, joke, puzzle; jester, joker, hoax.

quota *n* allocation, allotment, apportionment, contingent, portion, proportion, quantity, share.

quotation *n* citation, clipping, cutting, extract, excerpt, reference, selection; estimate, rate, tender.

quote *vb* adduce, cite, excerpt, extract, illustrate, instance, name, repeat, take; estimate, tender.

R

rabble *n* commonality, horde, mob, populace, riffraff, rout, scum, trash.

rabid *adj* frantic, furious, mad, raging, wild; bigoted, fanatical, intolerant, irrational, narrow-minded, rampant.

race[1] *n* ancestry, breed, family, generation, house, kindred, line, lineage, pedigree, stock, strain; clan, folk, nation, people, tribe; breed, children, descendants, issue, offspring, progeny, stock.

race[2] *vb* career, compete, contest, course, hasten, hurry, run, speed. • *n* career, chase, competition, contest, course, dash, heat, match, pursuit, run, sprint; flavour, quality, smack, strength, taste.

rack *vb* agonize, distress, excruciate, rend, torment, torture, wring; exhaust, force, harass, oppress, strain, stretch, wrest. • *n* agony, anguish, pang, torment, torture; crib, manger; neck, crag; dampness, mist, moisture, vapour.

racket *n* clamour, clatter, din, dissipation, disturbance, fracas, frolic, hubbub, noise, outcry, tumult, uproar; game, graft, scheme, understanding.

racy *adj* flavoursome, palatable, piquant, pungent, rich, spicy, strong; forcible, lively, pungent, smart, spirited, stimulating, vigorous, vivacious.

radiance *n* brightness, brilliance, brilliancy, effluence, efflux, emission, glare, glitter, light, lustre, refulgence, resplendence, shine, splendour.

radiant *adj* beaming, brilliant, effulgent, glittering, glorious, luminous, lustrous, resplendent, shining, sparkling, splendid; ecstatic, happy, pleased.

radiate *vb* beam, gleam, glitter, shine; emanate, emit; diffuse, spread.

radical *adj* constitutional, deep-seated, essential, fundamental, ingrained, inherent, innate, native, natural, organic, original, uncompromising; original, primitive, simple, uncompounded, underived; complete, entire, extreme, fanatic, insurgent, perfect, rebellious, thorough, total. • *n* etymon, radix, root; fanatic, revolutionary.

rage *vb* bluster, boil, chafe, foam, fret, fume, ravage, rave. • *n* excitement, frenzy, fury, madness, passion, rampage, raving, vehemence, wrath; craze, fashion, mania, mode, style, vogue.

ragged *adj* rent, tattered, torn; contemptible, mean, poor, shabby; jagged, rough, rugged, shaggy, uneven; discordant, dissonant, inharmonious, unmusical.

raid *vb* assault, forage, invade, pillage, plunder. • *n* attack, foray, invasion, inroad, plunder.

rail *vb* abuse, censure, inveigh, scoff, scold, sneer, upbraid.

raillery *n* banter, chaff, irony, joke, pleasantry, ridicule, satire.

raiment *n* array, apparel, attire, clothes, clothing, costume, dress, garb, garments, habiliment, habit, vestments, vesture.

rain *vb* drizzle, drop, fall, pour, shower, sprinkle, teem; bestow, lavish. • *n* cloudburst, downpour, drizzle, mist, shower, sprinkling.

raise *vb* boost, construct, erect, heave, hoist, lift, uplift, upraise, rear; advance, elevate, ennoble, exalt, promote; aggravate, amplify, augment, enhance, heighten, increase, invigorate; arouse, awake, cause, effect, excite, originate, produce, rouse, stir up, occasion, start; assemble, collect, get, levy, obtain; breed, cultivate, grow, propagate, rear; ferment, leaven, work.

rake[1] *vb* collect, comb, gather, scratch; ransack, scour.

rake[2] *n* debauchee, libertine, profligate, roué.

rakish *adj* debauched, dissipated, dissolute, lewd, licentious; cavalier, jaunty.

ramble *vb* digress, maunder, range, roam, rove, saunter, straggle, stray, stroll, wander. • *n* excursion, rambling, roving, tour, trip, stroll, wandering.

rambling *adj* discursive, irregular; straggling, strolling, wandering.

ramification *n* arborescence, branching, divarication, forking, radiation; branch, division, offshoot, subdivision; consequence, upshot.

ramify *vb* branch, divaricate, extend, separate.

rampant *adj* excessive, exuberant, luxuriant, rank, wanton; boisterous, dominant, headstrong, impetuous, predominant, raging, uncontrollable, unbridled, ungovernable, vehement, violent.

rampart *n* bulwark, circumvallation, defence, fence, fortification, guard, security, wall.

rancid *adj* bad, fetid, foul, fusty, musty, offensive, rank, sour, stinking, tainted.

rancorous *adj* bitter, implacable, malevolent, malicious, malign, malignant, resentful, spiteful, vindictive, virulent.

rancour *n* animosity, antipathy, bitterness, enmity, gall, grudge, hate, hatred, ill-will, malevolence, malice, malignity, spite, venom, vindictiveness.

random *adj* accidental, casual, chance, fortuitous, haphazard, irregular, stray, wandering.

range *vb* course, cruise, extend, ramble, roam, rove, straggle, stray, stroll, wander; bend, lie, run; arrange, class, dispose, rank. • *n* file, line, row, rank, tier; class, kind, order, sort; excursion, expedition, ramble, roving, wandering; amplitude, bound, command, compass, distance, extent, latitude, reach, scope, sweep, view; register.

rank[1] *vb* arrange, class, classify, range. • *n* file, line, order, range, row, tier; class, division, group, order, series; birth, blood, caste, degree, estate, grade, position, quality, sphere, stakes, standing; dignity, distinction, eminence, nobility.

rank[2] *adj* dense, exuberant, luxuriant, overabundant, overgrown, vigorous, wild; excessive, extreme, extravagant, flagrant, gross, rampant, sheer, unmitigated, utter, violent; fetid, foul, fusty, musty, offensive, rancid; fertile, productive, rich; coarse, disgusting.

ransack *vb* pillage, plunder, ravage, rifle, sack, strip; explore, overhaul, rummage, search thoroughly.

ransom *vb* deliver, emancipate, free, liberate, redeem, rescue, unfetter. • *n* money, payment pay-off, price; deliverance, liberation, redemption, release.

rant *vb* declaim, mouth, spout, vociferate. • *n* bombast, cant, exaggeration, fustian.

rapacious *adj* predacious, preying, raptorial; avaricious, grasping, greedy, ravenous, voracious.

rapid *adj* fast, fleet, quick, swift; brisk, expeditious, hasty, hurried, quick, speedy.

rapine *n* depredation, pillage, plunder, robbery, spoliation.

rapt *adj* absorbed, charmed, delighted, ecstatic, engrossed, enraptured, entranced, fascinated, inspired, spellbound.

rapture *vb* enrapture, ravish, transport. • *n* delight, exultation, enthusiasm, rhapsody; beatification, beatitude, bliss, ecstasy, felicity, happiness, joy, spell, transport.

rare[1] *adj* sparse, subtle, thin; extraordinary, infrequent, scarce, singular, strange, uncommon, unique, unusual; choice, excellent, exquisite, fine, incomparable, inimitable.

rare[2] *adj* bloody, underdone.

rarity *n* attenuation, ethereality, etherealness, rarefaction, rareness, tenuity, tenuousness, thinness; infrequency, scarcity, singularity, sparseness, uncommonness, unwontedness.

rascal *n* blackguard, caitiff, knave, miscreant, rogue, reprobate, scallywag, scapegrace, scamp, scoundrel, vagabond, villain.

rash[1] *adj* adventurous, audacious, careless, foolhardy, hasty, headlong, headstrong, heedless, incautious, inconsiderate, indiscreet, injudicious, impetuous, impulsive, incautious, precipitate, quick, rapid, reckless, temerarious, thoughtless, unguarded, unwary, venturesome.

rash[2] *n* breaking-out, efflorescence, eruption; epidemic, flood, outbreak, plague, spate.

rashness *n* carelessness, foolhardiness, hastiness, heedlessness, inconsideration, indiscretion, precipitation, recklessness, temerity, venturesomeness.

rate[1] *vb* appraise, compute, estimate, value. • *n* cost, price; class, degree, estimate, rank, value, valuation, worth; proportion, ration; assessment, charge, impost, tax.

rate[2] *vb* abuse, berate, censure, chide, criticize, find fault, reprimand, reprove, scold.

ratify *vb* confirm, corroborate, endorse, establish, seal, settle, substantiate; approve, bind, consent, sanction.

ration *vb* apportion, deal, distribute, dole, restrict. • *n* allowance, portion, quota, share.

rational *adj* intellectual, reasoning; equitable, fair, fit, just, moderate, natural, normal, proper, reasonable, right; discreet, enlightened, intelligent, judicious, sagacious, sensible, sound, wise.

raucous *adj* harsh, hoarse, husky, rough.

ravage *vb* consume, desolate, despoil, destroy, devastate, harry, overrun, pillage, plunder, ransack, ruin, sack, spoil, strip, waste. • *n* desolation, despoilment, destruction, devastation, havoc, pillage, plunder, rapine, ruin, spoil, waste.

ravenous *adj* devouring, ferocious, gluttonous, greedy, insatiable, omnivorous, ravening, rapacious, voracious.

ravine *n* canyon, cleft, defile, gap, gorge, gulch, gully, pass.

raving *adj* delirious, deranged, distracted, frantic, frenzied, furious, infuriated, mad, phrenetic, raging. • *n* delirium, frenzy, fury, madness, rage.

ravish *vb* abuse, debauch, defile, deflower, force, outrage, violate; captivate, charm, delight, enchant, enrapture, entrance, overjoy, transport; abduct, kidnap, seize, snatch, strip.

raw *adj* fresh, inexperienced, unpractised, unprepared, unseasoned, untried, unskilled; crude, green, immature, unfinished, unripe; bare, chafed, excoriated, galled, sensitive, sore; bleak, chilly, cold, cutting, damp, piercing, windswept; uncooked.

ray *n* beam, emanation, gleam, moonbeam, radiance, shaft, streak, sunbeam.

raze *vb* demolish, destroy, dismantle, extirpate, fell, level, overthrow, ruin, subvert; efface, erase, obliterate.

reach *vb* extend, stretch; grasp, hit, strike, touch; arrive at, attain, gain, get, obtain, win. • *n* capability, capacity, grasp.

readily *adv* easily, promptly, quickly; cheerfully, willingly.

readiness *n* alacrity, alertness, expedition, quickness, promptitude, promptness; aptitude, aptness, dexterity, easiness, expertness, facility, quickness, skill; preparation, preparedness, ripeness; cheerfulness, disposition, eagerness, ease, willingness.

ready *vb* arrange, equip, organize, prepare. • *adj* alert, expeditious, prompt, quick, punctual, speedy; adroit, apt, clever, dextrous, expert, facile, handy, keen, nimble, prepared, prompt, ripe, quick, sharp, skilful, smart; cheerful, disposed, eager, free, inclined, willing; accommodating, available, convenient, near, handy; easy, facile, fluent, offhand, opportune, short, spontaneous.

real *adj* absolute, actual, certain, literal, positive, practical, substantial, substantive, veritable; authentic, genuine, true; essential, internal, intrinsic.

realize *vb* accomplish, achieve, discharge, effect, effectuate, perfect, perform; apprehend, comprehend, experience, recognize, understand; externalize, substantiate; acquire, earn, gain, get, net, obtain, produce, sell.

reality *n* actuality, certainty, fact, truth, verity.

really *adv* absolutely, actually, certainly, indeed, positively, truly, verily, veritably.

reap *vb* acquire, crop, gain, gather, get, harvest, obtain, receive.

rear[1] *adj* aft, back, following, hind, last. • *n* background, reverse, setting; heel, posterior, rear end, rump, stern, tail; path, trail, train, wake.

rear[2] *vb* construct, elevate, erect, hoist, lift, raise; cherish, educate, foster, instruct, nourish, nurse, nurture, train; breed, grow; rouse, stir up.

reason *vb* argue, conclude, debate, deduce, draw from, infer, intellectualize, syllogize, think, trace. • *n* faculty, intellect, intelligence, judgement, mind, principle, sanity, sense, thinking, understanding; account, argument, basis, cause, consideration, excuse, explanation, gist, ground, motive, occasion, pretence, proof; aim, design, end, object, purpose; argument, reasoning; common sense, reasonableness, wisdom; equity, fairness, justice, right; exposition, rationale, theory.

reasonable *adj* equitable, fair, fit, honest, just, proper, rational, right, suitable; enlightened, intelligent, judicious, sagacious, sensible, wise; considerable, fair, moderate, tolerable; credible, intellectual, plausible, well-founded; sane, sober, sound; cheap, inexpensive, low-priced.

rebate *vb* abate, bate, blunt, deduct, diminish, lessen, reduce; cut, pare, rabbet. • *n* decrease, decrement, diminution, lessening; allowance, deduction, discount, reduction.

rebel *vb* mutiny, resist, revolt, strike. • *adj* insubordinate, insurgent, mutinous, rebellious. • *n* insurgent, mutineer, traitor.

rebellion *n* anarchy, insubordination, insurrection, mutiny, resistance, revolt, revolution, uprising.

rebellious *adj* contumacious, defiant, disloyal, disobedient, insubordinate, intractable, obstinate, mutinous, rebel, refractory, seditious.

rebuff *vb* check, chide, oppose, refuse, reject, repel, reprimand, resist, snub. • *n* check, defeat, discouragement, opposition, rejection, resistance, snub.

rebuke *vb* blame, censure, chide, lecture, upbraid, reprehend, reprimand, reprove, scold, silence. • *n* blame, censure, chiding, expostulation, remonstrance, reprimand, reprehension, reproach, reproof, reproval; affliction, chastisement, punishment.

recall *vb* abjure, abnegate, annul, cancel, countermand, deny, nullify, overrule, recant, repeal, repudiate, rescind, retract, revoke, swallow, withdraw; commemorate, recollect, remember, retrace, review, revive. • *n* abjuration, abnegation, annulment, cancellation, nullification, recantation, repeal, repudiation, rescindment, retraction, revocation, withdrawal; memory, recollection, remembrance, reminiscence.

recant *vb* abjure, annul, disavow, disown, recall, renounce, repudiate, retract, revoke, unsay.

recapitulate *vb* epitomize, recite, rehearse, reiterate, repeat, restate, review, summarize.

recede *vb* desist, ebb, retire, regress, retreat, retrograde, return, withdraw.

receive *vb* accept, acquire, derive, gain, get, obtain, take; admit, shelter, take in; entertain, greet, welcome; allow, permit, tolerate; adopt, approve, believe, credit, embrace, follow, learn, understand; accommodate, carry, contain, hold, include, retain; bear, encounter, endure, experience, meet, suffer, sustain.

recent *adj* fresh, new, novel; latter, modern, young; deceased, foregoing, late, preceding, retiring.

reception *n* acceptance, receipt, receiving; entertainment, greeting, welcome; levee, soiree, party; admission, credence; belief, credence, recognition.

recess *n* alcove, corner, depth, hollow, niche, nook, privacy, retreat, seclusion; break, holiday, intermission, interval, respite, vacation; recession, retirement, retreat, withdrawal.

reciprocal *adj* alternate, commutable, complementary, correlative, correspondent, mutual.

recital *n* rehearsal, repetition, recitation; account, description, detail, explanation, narration, relation, statement, telling.

recite *vb* declaim, deliver, rehearse, repeat; describe, mention, narrate, recount, relate, tell; count, detail, enumerate, number, recapitulate.

reckless *adj* breakneck, careless, desperate, devil-may-care, flighty, foolhardy, giddy, harebrained, headlong, heedless, inattentive, improvident, imprudent, inconsiderate, indifferent, indiscreet, mindless, negligent, rash, regardless, remiss, thoughtless, temerarious, uncircumspect, unconcerned, unsteady, volatile, wild.

reckon *vb* calculate, cast, compute, consider, count, enumerate, guess, number; account, class, esteem, estimate, regard, repute, value.

reckoning *n* calculation, computation, consideration, counting; account, bill, charge, estimate, register, score; arrangement, settlement.

reclaim *vb* amend, correct, reform; recover, redeem, regenerate, regain, reinstate, restore; civilize, tame.

recline *vb* couch, lean, lie, lounge, repose, rest.

recluse *adj* anchoritic, anchoritical, cloistered, eremitic, eremitical, hermitic, hermitical, reclusive, solitary. • *n* anchorite, ascetic, eremite, hermit, monk, solitary.

reclusive *adj* recluse, retired, secluded, sequestered, sequestrated, solitary.

recognition *n* identification, memory, recollection, remembrance; acknowledgement, appreciation, avowal, comprehension, confession, notice; allowance, concession.

recognize *vb* apprehend, identify, perceive, remember; acknowledge, admit, avow, confess, own; allow, concede, grant; greet, salute.

recoil *vb* react, rebound, reverberate; retire, retreat, withdraw; blench, fail, falter, quail, shrink. • *n* backstroke, boomerang, elasticity, kick, reaction, rebound, repercussion, resilience, revulsion, ricochet, shrinking.

recollect *vb* recall, remember, reminisce.

recollection *n* memory, remembrance, reminiscence.

recommend *vb* approve, commend, endorse, praise, sanction; commit; advise, counsel, prescribe, suggest.

recommendation *n* advocacy, approbation, approval, commendation, counsel, credential, praise, testimonial.

recompense *vb* compensate, remunerate, repay, requite, reward, satisfy; indemnify, redress, reimburse. • *n* amends, compensation, indemnification, indemnity, remuneration, repayment, reward, satisfaction; requital, retribution.

reconcilable *adj* appeasable, forgiving, placable; companionable, congruous, consistent.

reconcile *vb* appease, conciliate, pacify, placate, propitiate, reunite; content, harmonize, regulate; adjust, compose, heal, settle.

recondite *adj* concealed, dark, hidden, mystic, mystical, obscure, occult, secret, transcendental.

record *vb* chronicle, enter, note, register. • *n* account, annals, archive, chronicle, diary, docket, enrolment, entry, file, list, minute, memoir, memorandum, memorial, note, proceedings, register, registry, report, roll, score; mark, memorial, relic, trace, track, trail, vestige; memory, remembrance; achievement, career, history.

recount *vb* describe, detail, enumerate, mention, narrate, particularize, portray, recite, relate, rehearse, report, tell.

recover *vb* recapture, reclaim, regain; rally, recruit, repair, retrieve; cure, heal, restore, revive; redeem, rescue, salvage, save; convalesce, recuperate.

recreant *adj* base, cowardly, craven, dastardly, faint-hearted, mean-spirited, pusillanimous, yielding; apostate, backsliding, faithless, false, perfidious, treacherous, unfaithful, untrue. • *n* coward, dastard; apostate, backslider, renegade.

recreation *n* amusement, cheer, diversion, entertainment, fun, game, leisure, pastime, play, relaxation, sport.

recreational *adj* amusing, diverting, entertaining, refreshing, relaxing, relieving.

recruit *vb* repair, replenish; recover, refresh, regain, reinvigorate, renew, renovate, restore, retrieve, revive, strengthen, supply. • *n* auxiliary, beginner, helper, learner, novice, tyro.

rectify *vb* adjust, amend, better, correct, emend, improve, mend, redress, reform, regulate, straighten.

rectitude *n* conscientiousness, equity, goodness, honesty, integrity, justice, principle, probity, right, righteousness, straightforwardness, uprightness, virtue.

recumbent *adj* leaning, lying, prone, prostrate, reclining; idle, inactive, listless, reposing.

recur *vb* reappear, resort, return, revert.

recusancy *n* dissent, heresy, heterodoxy, nonconformity.

redeem *vb* reform, regain, repurchase, retrieve; free, liberate, ransom, rescue, save; deliver, reclaim, recover, reinstate; atone, compensate for, recompense; discharge, fulfil, keep, perform, satisfy.

redemption *n* buying, compensation, recovery, repurchase, retrieval; deliverance, liberation, ransom, release, rescue, salvation; discharge, fulfilment, performance.

redolent *adj* aromatic, balmy, fragrant, odoriferous, odorous, scented, sweet, sweet-smelling.

redoubtable *adj* awful, doughty, dreadful, formidable, terrible, valiant.

redound *vb* accrue, conduce, contribute, result, tend.

redress *vb* amend, correct, order, rectify, remedy, repair; compensate, ease, relieve. • *n* abatement, amends, atonement, compensation, correction, cure, indemnification, rectification, repair, righting, remedy, relief, reparation, satisfaction.

reduce *vb* bring; form, make, model, mould, remodel, render, resolve, shape; abate, abbreviate, abridge, attenuate, contract, curtail, decimate, decrease, diminish, lessen, minimize, shorten, thin; abase, debase, degrade, depress, dwarf, impair, lower, weaken; capture, conquer, master, overpower, overthrow, subject, subdue, subjugate, vanquish; impoverish, ruin; resolve, solve.

redundant *adj* copious, excessive, exuberant, fulsome, inordinate, lavish, needless, overflowing, overmuch, plentiful, prodigal, superabundant, replete, superfluous, unnecessary, useless; diffuse, periphrastic, pleonastic, tautological, verbose, wordy.

reel[1] *n* capstan, winch, windlass; bobbin, spool.

reel[2] *vb* falter, flounder, heave, lurch, pitch, plunge, rear, rock, roll, stagger, sway, toss, totter, tumble, wallow, welter, vacillate; spin, swing, turn, twirl, wheel, whirl. • *n* gyre, pirouette, spin, turn, twirl, wheel, whirl.

re-establish *vb* re-found, rehabilitate, reinstall, reinstate, renew, renovate, replace, restore.

refer *vb* commit, consign, direct, leave, relegate, send, submit; ascribe, assign, attribute, impute; appertain, belong, concern, pertain, point, relate, respect, touch; appeal, apply, consult; advert, allude, cite, quote.

referee *vb* arbitrate, judge, umpire. • *n* arbiter, arbitrator, judge, umpire.

reference *n* concern, connection, regard, respect; allusion, ascription, citation, hint, intimation, mark, reference, relegation.

refine *vb* clarify, cleanse, defecate, fine, purify; cultivate, humanize, improve, polish, rarefy, spiritualize.

refined *adj* courtly, cultured, genteel, polished, polite; discerning, discriminating, fastidious, sensitive; filtered, processed, purified.

refinement *n* clarification, filtration, purification, sublimation; betterment, improvement; delicacy, cultivation, culture, elegance, elevation, finish, gentility, good breeding, polish, politeness, purity, spirituality, style.

reflect *vb* copy, imitate, mirror, reproduce; cogitate, consider, contemplate, deliberate, meditate, muse, ponder, ruminate, study, think.

reflection *n* echo, shadow; cogitation, consideration, contemplation, deliberation, idea, meditation, musing, opinion, remark, rumination, thinking, thought; aspersion, blame, censure, criticism, disparagement, reproach, slur.

reflective *adj* reflecting, reflexive; cogitating, deliberating, musing, pondering, reasoning, thoughtful.

reform *vb* amend, ameliorate, better, correct, improve, mend, meliorate, rectify, reclaim, redeem, regenerate, repair, restore; reconstruct, remodel, reshape. • *n* amendment, correction, progress, reconstruction, rectification, reformation.

reformation *n* amendment, emendation, improvement, reform; adoption, conversion, redemption; refashioning, regeneration, reproduction, reconstruction.

refractory *adj* cantankerous, contumacious, cross-grained, disobedient, dogged, headstrong, heady, incoercible, intractable, mulish, obstinate, perverse, recalcitrant, self-willed, stiff, stubborn, sullen, ungovernable, unmanageable, unruly, unyielding.

refrain[1] *vb* abstain, cease, desist, forbear, stop, withhold.

refrain[2] *n* chorus, song, undersong.

refresh *vb* air, brace, cheer, cool, enliven, exhilarate, freshen, invigorate, reanimate, recreate, recruit, reinvigorate, revive, regale, slake.

refreshing *adj* comfortable, cooling, grateful, invigorating, pleasant, reanimating, restful, reviving.

refuge *n* asylum, covert, harbour, haven, protection, retreat, safety, sanction, security, shelter.

refulgent *adj* bright, brilliant, effulgent, lustrous, radiant, resplendent, shining.

refund *vb* reimburse, repay, restore, return. • *n* reimbursement, repayment.

refuse[1] *n* chaff, discard, draff, dross, dregs, garbage, junk, leavings, lees, litter, lumber, offal, recrement, remains, rubbish, scoria, scum, sediment, slag, sweepings, trash, waste.

refuse[2] *vb* decline, deny, withhold; disallow, disavow, exclude, rebuff, reject, renege, renounce, repel, repudiate, repulse, revoke, veto.

refute *vb* confute, defeat, disprove, overcome, overthrow, rebut, repel, silence.

regain *vb* recapture, recover, re-obtain, repossess, retrieve.

regal *adj* imposing, imperial, kingly, noble, royal, sovereign.

regale *vb* delight, entertain, gratify, refresh; banquet, feast.

regard *vb* behold, gaze, look, notice, mark, observe, remark, see, view, watch; attend to, consider, heed, mind, respect; esteem, honour, revere, reverence, value; account, believe, estimate, deem, hold, imagine, reckon, suppose, think, treat, use. • *n* aspect, gaze, look, view; attention, attentiveness, care, concern, consideration, heed, notice, observance; account, reference, relation, respect; admiration, affection, attachment, deference, esteem, estimation, favour, honour, interest, liking, love, respect, reverence, sympathy, value; account, eminence, note, reputation, repute; condition, matter, point.

regardful *adj* attentive, careful, considerate, deferential, heedful, mindful, observing, thoughtful, watchful.

regarding *prep* concerning, respecting, touching.

regardless *adj* careless, disregarding, heedless, inattentive, indifferent, mindless, neglectful, negligent, unconcerned, unmindful, unobservant. • *adv* however, irrespectively, nevertheless, nonetheless, notwithstanding.

regenerate *vb* reproduce; renovate, revive; change, convert, renew, sanctify. • *adj* born-again, converted, reformed, regenerated.

regime n administration, government, rule.

region n climate, clime, country, district, division, latitude, locale, locality, province, quarter, scene, territory, tract; area, neighbourhood, part, place, portion, spot, space, sphere, terrain, vicinity.

register vb delineate, portray, record, show. • n annals, archive, catalogue, chronicle, list, record, roll, schedule; clerk, registrar, registry; compass, range.

regret vb bewail, deplore, grieve, lament, repine, sorrow; bemoan, repent, mourn, rue. • n concern, disappointment, grief, lamentation, rue, sorrow, trouble; compunction, contrition, penitence, remorse, repentance, repining, self-condemnation, self-reproach.

regular adj conventional, natural, normal, ordinary, typical; correct, customary, cyclic, established, fixed, habitual, periodic, periodical, recurring, reasonable, rhythmic, seasonal, stated, usual; steady, constant, uniform, even; just, methodical, orderly, punctual, systematic, unvarying; complete, genuine, indubitable, out-and-out, perfect, thorough; balanced, consistent, symmetrical.

regulate vb adjust, arrange, dispose, methodize, order, organize, settle, standardize, time, systematize; conduct, control, direct, govern, guide, manage, rule.

regulation adj customary, mandatory, official, required, standard. • n adjustment, arrangement, control, disposal, disposition, law, management, order, ordering, precept, rule, settlement.

rehabilitate vb reinstate, re-establish, restore; reconstruct, reconstitute, reintegrate, reinvigorate, renew, renovate.

rehearsal n drill, practice, recital, recitation, repetition; account, history, mention, narration, narrative, recounting, relation, statement, story, telling.

rehearse vb recite, repeat; delineate, depict, describe, detail, enumerate, narrate, portray, recapitulate, recount, relate, tell.

reign vb administer, command, govern, influence, predominate, prevail, rule. • n control, dominion, empire, influence, power, royalty, sovereignty, power, rule, sway.

reimburse vb refund, repay, restore; compensate, indemnify, requite, satisfy.

rein vb bridle, check, control, curb, guide, harness, hold, restrain, restrict. • n bridle, check, curb, harness, restraint, restriction.

reinforce vb augment, fortify, strengthen.

reinstate vb re-establish, rehabilitate, reinstall, replace, restore.

reject vb cashier, discard, dismiss, eject, exclude, pluck; decline, deny, disallow, despise, disapprove, disbelieve, rebuff, refuse, renounce, repel, repudiate, scout, slight, spurn, veto. • n cast-off, discard, failure, refusal, repudiation.

rejoice vb cheer, delight, enliven, enrapture, exhilarate, gladden, gratify, please, transport; crow, exult, delight, gloat, glory, jubilate, triumph, vaunt.

rejoin vb answer, rebut, respond, retort.

relate vb describe, detail, mention, narrate, recite, recount, rehearse, report, tell; apply, connect, correlate.

relation n account, chronicle, description, detail, explanation, history, mention, narration, narrative, recital, rehearsal, report, statement, story, tale; affinity, application, bearing, connection, correlation, dependency, pertinence, relationship; concern, reference, regard, respect; alliance, nearness, propinquity, rapport; blood, consanguinity, cousinship, kin, kindred, kinship, relationship; kinsman, kinswoman, relative.

relax vb loose, loosen, slacken, unbrace, unstrain; debilitate, enervate, enfeeble, prostrate, unbrace, unstring, weaken; abate, diminish, lessen, mitigate, reduce, remit; amuse, divert, ease, entertain, recreate, unbend.

release vb deliver, discharge, disengage, exempt, extricate, free, liberate, loose, unloose; acquit, discharge, quit, relinquish, remit. • n deliverance, discharge, freedom, liberation; absolution, dispensation, excuse, exemption, exoneration; acquaintance, clearance.

relentless adj cruel, hard, impenitent, implacable, inexorable, merciless, obdurate, pitiless, rancorous, remorseless, ruthless, unappeasable, uncompassionate, unfeeling, unforgiving, unmerciful, unpitying, unrelenting, unyielding, vindictive.

relevant adj applicable, appropriate, apposite, apt, apropos, fit, germane, pertinent, proper, relative, suitable.

reliable adj authentic, certain, constant, dependable, sure, trustworthy, trusty, unfailing.

reliance n assurance, confidence, credence, dependence, hope, trust.

relic n keepsake, memento, memorial, remembrance, souvenir, token, trophy; trace, vestige.

relics npl fragments, leavings, remainder, remains, remnants, ruins, scraps; body, cadaver, corpse, remains.

relict n dowager, widow.

relief n aid, alleviation, amelioration, assistance, assuagement, comfort, deliverance, ease, easement, help, mitigation, reinforcement, respite, rest, succour, softening, support; indemnification, redress, remedy; embossment, projection, prominence, protrusion; clearness, distinction, perspective, vividness.

relieve vb aid, comfort, help, spell, succour, support, sustain; abate, allay, alleviate, assuage, cure, diminish, ease, lessen, lighten, mitigate, remedy, remove, soothe; indemnify, redress, right, repair; disengage, free, release, remedy, rescue.

religious adj devotional, devout, god-fearing, godly, holy, pious, prayerful, spiritual; conscientious, exact, rigid, scrupulous, strict; canonical, divine, theological.

relinquish vb abandon, desert, forsake, forswear, leave, quit, renounce, resign, vacate; abdicate, cede, forbear, forgo, give up, surrender, yield.

relish vb appreciate, enjoy, like, prefer; season, flavour, taste. • n appetite, appreciation, enjoyment, fondness, gratification, gusto, inclination, liking, partiality, predilection, taste, zest; cast, flavour, manner, quality, savour, seasoning, sort, tang, tinge, touch; appetizer, condiment.

reluctance n aversion, backwardness, disinclination, dislike, loathing, repugnance, unwillingness.

reluctant adj averse, backward, disinclined, hesitant, indisposed, loath, unwilling.

rely vb confide, count, depend, hope, lean, reckon, repose, trust.

remain vb abide, continue, endure, last; exceed, persist, survive; abide, continue, dwell, halt, inhabit, rest, sojourn, stay, stop, tarry, wait.

remainder n balance, excess, leavings, remains, remnant, residue, rest, surplus.

remark vb heed, notice, observe, regard; comment, express, mention, observe, say, state, utter. • n consideration, heed, notice, observation, regard; annotation, comment, gloss, note, stricture; assertion, averment, comment, declaration, saying, statement, utterance.

remarkable adj conspicuous, distinguished, eminent, extraordinary, famous, notable, noteworthy, noticeable, pre-eminent, rare, singular, strange, striking, uncommon, unusual, wonderful.

remedy vb cure, heal, help, palliate, relieve; amend, correct, rectify, redress, repair, restore, retrieve. • n antidote, antitoxin, corrective, counteractive, cure, help, medicine, nostrum, panacea, restorative, specific; redress, reparation, restitution, restoration; aid, assistance, relief.

remembrance n recollection, reminiscence, retrospection; keepsake, memento, memorial, memory, reminder, souvenir, token; consideration, regard, thought.

reminiscence n memory, recollection, remembrance, retrospective.

remiss adj backward, behindhand, dilatory, indolent, languid, lax, lazy, slack, slow, tardy; careless, dilatory, heedless, idle, inattentive, neglectful, negligent, shiftless, slothful, thoughtless.

remission n abatement, decrease, diminution, lessening, mitigation, moderation, reduction, relaxation; cancellation, discharge, release, relinquishment; intermission, interruption, pause, rest, stop, stoppage, suspense, suspension; absolution, acquittal, excuse, exoneration, forgiveness, indulgence, pardon.

remit vb replace, restore, return; abate, bate, diminish, relax; release; absolve, condone, excuse, forgive, overlook, pardon; relinquish, resign, surrender; consign, forward, refer, send, transmit. • n authorization, brief, instructions, orders.

remnant n remainder, remains, residue, rest, trace; fragment, piece, scrap.

remorse n compunction, contrition, penitence, qualm, regret, repentance, reproach, self-reproach, sorrow.

remorseless adj cruel, barbarous, hard, harsh, implacable, inexorable, merciless, pitiless, relentless, ruthless, savage, uncompassionate, unmerciful, unrelenting.

remote adj distant, far, out-of-the-way; alien, far-fetched, foreign, inappropriate, unconnected, unrelated; abstracted, separated; inconsiderable, slight; isolated, removed, secluded, sequestrated.

removal n abstraction, departure, dislodgement, displacement, relegation, remove, shift, transference; elimination, extraction, withdrawal; abatement, destruction; discharge, dismissal, ejection, expulsion.

remove *vb* carry, dislodge, displace, shift, transfer, transport; abstract, extract, withdraw; abate, banish, destroy, suppress; cashier, depose, discharge, dismiss, eject, expel, oust, retire; depart, move.

remunerate *vb* compensate, indemnify, pay, recompense, reimburse, repay, requite, reward, satisfy.

remuneration *n* compensation, earnings, indemnity, pay, payment, recompense, reimbursement, reparation, repayment, reward, salary, wages.

remunerative *adj* gainful, lucrative, paying, profitable; compensatory, recompensing, remuneratory, reparative, requiting, rewarding.

rend *vb* break, burst, cleave, crack, destroy, dismember, dissever, disrupt, divide, fracture, lacerate, rive, rupture, sever, shiver, snap, split, sunder, tear.

render *vb* restore, return, surrender; assign, deliver, give, present; afford, contribute, furnish, supply, yield; construe, interpret, translate.

rendition *n* restitution, return, surrender; delineation, exhibition, interpretation, rendering, representation, reproduction; translation, version.

renegade *adj* apostate, backsliding, disloyal, false, outlawed, rebellious, recreant, unfaithful. • *n* apostate, backslider, recreant, turncoat; deserter, outlaw, rebel, revolter, traitor; vagabond, wretch.

renew *vb* rebuild, recreate, re-establish, refit, refresh, rejuvenate, renovate, repair, replenish, restore, resuscitate, revive; continue, recommence, repeat; iterate, reiterate; regenerate, transform.

renounce *vb* abjure, abnegate, decline, deny, disclaim, disown, forswear, neglect, recant, repudiate, reject, slight; abandon, abdicate, drop, forgo, forsake, desert, leave, quit, relinquish, resign.

renovate *vb* reconstitute, re-establish, refresh, refurbish, renew, restore, revamp; reanimate, recreate, regenerate, reproduce, resuscitate, revive, revivify.

renown *n* celebrity, distinction, eminence, fame, figure, glory, honour, greatness, name, note, notability, notoriety, reputation, repute.

renowned *adj* celebrated, distinguished, eminent, famed, famous, honoured, illustrious, remarkable, wonderful.

rent[1] *n* breach, break, crack, cleft, crevice, fissure, flaw, fracture, gap, laceration, opening, rift, rupture, separation, split, tear; schism.

rent[2] *vb* hire, lease, let. • *n* income, rental, revenue.

repair[1] *vb* mend, patch, piece, refit, retouch, tinker, vamp; correct, recruit, restore, retrieve. • *n* mending, refitting, renewal, reparation, restoration.

repair[2] *vb* betake oneself, go, move, resort, turn.

repairable *adj* curable, recoverable, reparable, restorable, retrievable.

reparable *adj* curable, recoverable, repairable, restorable, retrievable.

reparation *n* renewal, repair, restoration; amends, atonement, compensation, correction, indemnification, recompense, redress, requital, restitution, satisfaction.

repay *vb* refund, reimburse, restore, return; compensate, recompense, remunerate, reward, satisfy; avenge, retaliate, revenge.

repeal *vb* abolish, annul, cancel, recall, rescind, reverse, revoke. • *n* abolition, abrogation, annulment, cancellation, rescission, reversal, revocation.

repeat *vb* double, duplicate, iterate; cite, narrate, quote, recapitulate, recite, rehearse; echo, renew, reproduce. • *n* duplicate, duplication, echo, iteration, recapitulation, reiteration, repetition.

repel *vb* beat, disperse, repulse, scatter; check, confront, oppose, parry, rebuff, resist, withstand; decline, refuse, reject; disgust, revolt, sicken.

repellent *adj* abhorrent, disgusting, forbidding, repelling, repugnant, repulsive, revolting, uninviting.

repent *vb* atone, regret, relent, rue, sorrow.

repentance *n* compunction, contriteness, contrition, penitence, regret, remorse, self-accusation, self-condemnation, self-reproach.

repentant *adj* contrite, penitent, regretful, remorseful, rueful, sorrowful, sorry.

repercussion *n* rebound, recoil, reverberation; backlash, consequence, result.

repetition *n* harping, iteration, recapitulation, reiteration; diffuseness, redundancy, tautology, verbosity; narration, recital, rehearsal, relation, retailing; recurrence, renewal.

repine *vb* croak, complain, fret, grumble, long, mope, murmur.

replace *vb* re-establish, reinstate, reset; refund, repay, restore; succeed, supersede, supplant.

replenish *vb* fill, refill, renew, re-supply; enrich, furnish, provide, store, supply.

replete *adj* abounding, charged, exuberant, fraught, full, glutted, gorged, satiated, well-stocked.

repletion *n* abundance, exuberance, fullness, glut, profusion, satiation, satiety, surfeit.

replica *n* autograph, copy, duplicate, facsimile, reproduction.

reply *vb* answer, echo, rejoin, respond. • *n* acknowledgement, answer, rejoinder, repartee, replication, response, retort.

report *vb* announce, annunciate, communicate, declare; advertise, broadcast, bruit, describe, detail, herald, mention, narrate, noise, promulgate, publish, recite, relate, rumour, state, tell; minute, record. • *n* account, announcement, communication, declaration, statement; advice, description, detail, narration, narrative, news, recital, story, tale, talk, tidings; gossip, hearsay, rumour; clap, detonation, discharge, explosion, noise, repercussion, sound; fame, reputation, repute; account, bulletin, minute, note, record, statement.

repose[1] *vb* compose, recline, rest, settle; couch, lie, recline, sleep, slumber; confide, lean. • *n* quiet, recumbence, recumbency, rest, sleep, slumber; breathing time, inactivity, leisure, respite, relaxation; calm, ease, peace, peacefulness, quietness, quietude, stillness, tranquillity.

repose[2] *vb* place, put, stake; deposit, lodge, reposit, store.

repository *n* conservatory, depository, depot, magazine, museum, receptacle, repertory, storehouse, storeroom, thesaurus, treasury, vault.

reprehend *vb* accuse, blame, censure, chide, rebuke, reprimand, reproach, reprove, upbraid.

reprehensible *adj* blameable, blameworthy, censurable, condemnable, culpable, reprovable.

reprehension *n* admonition, blame, censure, condemnation, rebuke, reprimand, reproof.

represent *vb* exhibit, express, show; delineate, depict, describe, draw, portray, sketch; act, impersonate, mimic, personate, personify; exemplify, illustrate, image, reproduce, symbolize, typify.

representation *n* delineation, exhibition, show; impersonation, personation, simulation; account, description, narration, narrative, relation, statement; image, likeness, model, portraiture, resemblance, semblance; sight, spectacle; expostulation, remonstrance.

representative *adj* figurative, illustrative, symbolic, typical; delegated, deputed, representing. • *n* agent, commissioner, delegate, deputy, emissary, envoy, legate, lieutenant, messenger, proxy, substitute.

repress *vb* choke, crush, dull, overcome, overpower, silence, smother, subdue, suppress, quell; bridle, chasten, chastise, check, control, curb, restrain; appease, calm, quiet.

reprimand *vb* admonish, blame, censure, chide, rebuke, reprehend, reproach, reprove, upbraid. • *n* admonition, blame, censure, rebuke, reprehension, reproach, reprobation, reproof, reproval.

reprint *vb* republish. • *n* reimpression, republication; copy.

reproach *vb* blame, censure, rebuke, reprehend, reprimand, reprove, upbraid; abuse, accuse, asperse, condemn, defame, discredit, disparage, revile, traduce, vilify. • *n* abuse, blame, censure, condemnation, contempt, contumely, disapprobation, disapproval, expostulation, insolence, invective, railing, rebuke, remonstrance, reprobation, reproof, reviling, scorn, scurrility, upbraiding, vilification; abasement, discredit, disgrace, dishonour, disrepute, indignity, ignominy, infamy, insult, obloquy, odium, offence, opprobrium, scandal, shame, slur, stigma.

reproachful *adj* abusive, censorious, condemnatory, contemptuous, contumelious, damnatory, insolent, insulting, offensive, opprobrious, railing, reproving, sacrifice, scolding, scornful, scurrilous, upbraiding, vituperative; base, discreditable, disgraceful, dishonourable, disreputable, infamous, scandalous, shameful, vile.

reprobate *vb* censure, condemn, disapprove, discard, reject, reprehend; disallow; abandon, disown. • *adj* abandoned, base, castaway, corrupt, depraved, graceless, hardened, irredeemable, lost, profligate, shameless, vile, vitiated, wicked. • *n* caitiff, castaway, miscreant, outcast, rascal, scamp, scoundrel, sinner, villain.

reproduce *vb* copy, duplicate, emulate, imitate, print, repeat, represent; breed, generate, procreate, propagate.

reproof *n* admonition, animadversion, blame, castigation, censure, chiding, condemnation, correction, criticism, lecture, monition, objurgation, rating, rebuke, reprehension, reprimand, reproach, reproval, upbraiding.

reprove *vb* admonish, blame, castigate, censure, chide, condemn, correct, criticize, inculpate, lecture, objurgate, rate, rebuke, reprimand, reproach, scold, upbraid.

reptilian *adj* abject, crawling, creeping, grovelling, low, mean, treacherous, vile, vulgar.

repudiate *vb* abjure, deny, disavow, discard, disclaim, disown, nullify, reject, renounce.

repugnance *n* contrariety, contrariness, incompatibility, inconsistency, irreconcilability, irreconcilableness, unsuitability, unsuitableness; contest, opposition, resistance, struggle; antipathy, aversion, detestation, dislike, hatred, hostility, reluctance, repulsion, unwillingness.

repugnant *adj* incompatible, inconsistent, irreconcilable; adverse, antagonistic, contrary, hostile, inimical, opposed, opposing, unfavourable; detestable, distasteful, offensive, repellent, repulsive.

repulse *vb* check, defeat, refuse, reject, repel. • *n* repelling, repulsion; denial, refusal; disappointment, failure.

repulsion *n* abhorrence, antagonism, anticipation, aversion, discard, disgust, dislike, hatred, hostility, loathing, rebuff, rejection, repugnance, repulse, spurning.

repulsive *adj* abhorrent, cold, disagreeable, disgusting, forbidding, frigid, harsh, hateful, loathsome, nauseating, nauseous, odious, offensive, repellent, repugnant, reserved, revolting, sickening, ugly, unpleasant.

reputable *adj* creditable, estimable, excellent, good, honourable, respectable, worthy.

reputation *n* account, character, fame, mark, name, repute; celebrity, credit, distinction, eclat, esteem, estimation, glory, honour, prestige, regard, renown, report, respect; notoriety.

repute *vb* account, consider, deem, esteem, estimate, hold, judge, reckon, regard, think.

request *vb* ask, beg, beseech, call, claim, demand, desire, entreat, pray, solicit, supplicate. • *n* asking, entreaty, importunity, invitation, petition, prayer, requisition, solicitation, suit, supplication.

require *vb* beg, beseech, bid, claim, crave, demand, dun, importune, invite, pray, requisition, request, sue, summon; need, want; direct, enjoin, exact, order, prescribe.

requirement *n* claim, demand, exigency, market, need, needfulness, requisite, requisition, request, urgency, want; behest, bidding, charge, command, decree, exaction, injunction, mandate, order, precept.

requisite *adj* essential, imperative, indispensable, necessary, needful, needed, required. • *n* essential, necessity, need, requirement.

requite *vb* compensate, pay, remunerate, reciprocate, recompense, repay, reward, satisfy; avenge, punish, retaliate, satisfy.

rescind *vb* abolish, abrogate, annul, cancel, countermand, quash, recall, repeal, reverse, revoke, vacate, void.

rescue *vb* deliver, extricate, free, liberate, preserve, ransom, recapture, recover, redeem, release, retake, save. • *n* deliverance, extrication, liberation, redemption, release, salvation.

research *vb* analyse, examine, explore, inquire, investigate, probe, study. • *n* analysis, examination, exploration, inquiry, investigation, scrutiny, study.

resemblance *n* affinity, agreement, analogy, likeness, semblance, similarity, similitude; counterpart, facsimile, image, representation.

resemble *vb* compare, liken; copy, counterfeit, imitate.

resentful *adj* angry, bitter, choleric, huffy, hurt, irascible, irritable, malignant, revengeful, sore, touchy.

resentment *n* acrimony, anger, annoyance, bitterness, choler, displeasure, dudgeon, fury, gall, grudge, heartburning, huff, indignation, ire, irritation, pique, rage, soreness, spleen, sulks, umbrage, vexation, wrath.

reservation *n* reserve, suppression; appropriation, booking, exception, restriction, saving; proviso, salvo; custody, park, reserve, sanctuary.

reserve *vb* hold, husband, keep, retain, store. • *adj* alternate, auxiliary, spare, substitute. • *n* reservation; aloofness, backwardness,

closeness, coldness, concealment, constraint, suppression, reservedness, retention, restraint, reticence, uncommunicativeness, unresponsiveness; coyness, demureness, modesty, shyness, taciturnity; park, reservation, sanctuary.

reserved *adj* coy, demure, modest, shy, taciturn; aloof, backward, cautious, cold, distant, incommunicative, restrained, reticent, self-controlled, unsociable, unsocial; bespoken, booked, excepted, held, kept, retained, set apart, taken, withheld.

reside *vb* abide, domicile, domiciliate, dwell, inhabit, live, lodge, remain, room, sojourn, stay.

residence *n* inhabitance, inhabitancy, sojourn, stay, stop, tarrying; abode, domicile, dwelling, habitation, home, house, lodging, mansion.

residue *n* leavings, remainder, remains, remnant, residuum, rest; excess, overplus, surplus.

resign *vb* abandon, abdicate, abjure, cede, commit, disclaim, forego, forsake, leave, quit, relinquish, renounce, surrender, yield.

resignation *n* abandonment, abdication, relinquishment, renunciation, retirement, surrender; acquiescence, compliance, endurance, forbearance, fortitude, long-sufferance, patience, submission, sufferance.

resist *vb* assail, attack, baffle, block, check, confront, counteract, disappoint, frustrate, hinder, impede, impugn, neutralize, obstruct, oppose, rebel, rebuff, stand against, stem, stop, strive, thwart, withstand.

resolute *adj* bold, constant, decided, determined, earnest, firm, fixed, game, hardy, inflexible, persevering, pertinacious, relentless, resolved, staunch, steadfast, steady, stout, stouthearted, sturdy, tenacious, unalterable, unbending, undaunted, unflinching, unshaken, unwavering, unyielding.

resolution *n* boldness, disentanglement, explication, unravelling; backbone, constancy, courage, decision, determination, earnestness, energy, firmness, fortitude, grit, hardihood, inflexibility, intention, manliness, pluck, perseverance, purpose, relentlessness, resolve, resoluteness, stamina, steadfastness, steadiness, tenacity.

resolve *vb* analyse, disperse, scatter, separate, reduce; change, dissolve, liquefy, melt, reduce, transform; decipher, disentangle, elucidate, explain, interpret, unfold, solve, unravel; conclude, decide, determine, fix, intend, purpose, will. • *n* conclusion, decision, determination, intention, will; declaration, resolution.

resonant *adj* booming, clangorous, resounding, reverberating, ringing, roaring, sonorous, thundering, vibrant.

resort *vb* frequent, haunt; assemble, congregate, convene, go, repair. • *n* application, expedient, recourse; haunt, refuge, rendezvous, retreat, spa; assembling, confluence, concourse, meeting; recourse, reference.

resound *vb* echo, re-echo, reverberate, ring; celebrate, extol, praise, sound.

resource *n* dependence, resort; appliance, contrivance, device, expedient, instrumentality, means, resort.

resources *npl* capital, funds, income, money, property, reserve, supplies, wealth.

respect *vb* admire, esteem, honour, prize, regard, revere, reverence, spare, value, venerate; consider, heed, notice, observe. • *n* attention, civility, courtesy, consideration, deference, estimation, homage, honour, notice, politeness, recognition, regard, reverence, veneration; consideration, favour, goodwill, kind; aspect, bearing, connection, feature, matter, particular, point, reference, regard, relation.

respects *npl* compliments, greetings, regards.

respectable *adj* considerable, estimable, honourable, presentable, proper, upright, worthy; adequate, moderate; tolerable.

respectful *adj* ceremonious, civil, complaisant, courteous, decorous, deferential, dutiful, formal, polite.

respire *vb* breathe, exhale, live.

respite *vb* delay, relieve, reprieve. • *n* break, cessation, delay, intermission, interval, pause, recess, rest, stay, stop; forbearance, postponement, reprieve.

resplendent *adj* beaming, bright, brilliant, effulgent, lucid, glittering, glorious, gorgeous, luminous, lustrous, radiant, shining, splendid.

respond *vb* answer, reply, rejoin; accord, correspond, suit.

response *n* answer, replication, rejoinder, reply, retort.

responsible *adj* accountable, amenable, answerable, liable, trustworthy.

rest[1] *vb* cease, desist, halt, hold, pause, repose, stop; breathe, relax, unbend; repose, sleep, slumber; lean, lie, lounge, perch, recline, ride; acquiesce, confide, trust; confide, rely, trust; calm, comfort, ease. • *n* fixity, immobility, inactivity, motionlessness, quiescence, quiet, repose; hush, peace, peacefulness, quietness, relief, security, stillness, tranquillity; cessation, intermission, interval, lull, pause, relaxation, respite, stop, stay; siesta, sleep, slumber; death; brace, stay, support; axis, fulcrum, pivot.

rest[2] *vb* be left, remain. • *n* balance, remainder, remnant, residuum; overplus, surplus.

restaurant *n* bistro, café, cafeteria, chophouse, eatery, eating house, pizzeria, trattoria.

restitution *n* restoration, return; amends, compensation, indemnification, recompense, rehabilitation, remuneration, reparation, repayment, requital, satisfaction.

restive *adj* mulish, obstinate, stopping, stubborn, unwilling; impatient, recalcitrant, restless, uneasy, unquiet.

restless *adj* disquieted, disturbed, restive, sleepless, uneasy, unquiet, unresting; changeable, inconstant, irresolute, unsteady, vacillating; active, astatic, roving, transient, unsettled, unstable, wandering; agitated, fidgety, fretful, turbulent.

restoration *n* recall, recovery, re-establishment, reinstatement, reparation, replacement, restitution, return; reconsideration, redemption, reintegration, renewal, renovation, repair, resuscitation, revival; convalescence, cure, recruitment, recuperation.

restorative *adj* curative, invigorating, recuperative, remedial, restoring, stimulating. • *n* corrective, curative, cure, healing, medicine, remedy, reparative, stimulant.

restore *vb* refund, repay, return; caulk, cobble, emend, heal, mend, patch, reintegrate, re-establish, rehabilitate, reinstate, renew, repair, replace, retrieve; cure, heal, recover, revive; resuscitate.

restrain *vb* bridle, check, coerce, confine, constrain, curb, debar, govern, hamper, hinder, hold, keep, muzzle, picket, prevent, repress, restrict, rule, subdue, tie, withhold; abridge, circumscribe, narrow.

restraint *n* bridle, check, coercion, control, compulsion, constraint, curb, discipline, repression, suppression; arrest, deterrence, hindrance, inhibition, limitation, prevention, prohibition, restriction, stay, stop; confinement, detention, imprisonment, shackles; constraint, stiffness, reserve, unnaturalness.

restrict *vb* bound, circumscribe, confine, limit, qualify, restrain, straiten.

restriction *n* confinement, limitation; constraint, restraint; reservation, reserve.

result *vb* accrue, arise, come, ensue, flow, follow, issue, originate, proceed, spring, rise; end, eventuate, terminate. • *n* conclusion, consequence, deduction, inference, outcome; corollary, effect, end, event, eventuality, fruit, harvest, issue, product, sequel, termination; decision, determination, finding, resolution, resolve, solution, verdict.

resume *vb* continue, recommence, renew, restart, summarize.

résumé *n* abstract, curriculum vitae, epitome, recapitulation, summary, synopsis.

resuscitate *vb* quicken, reanimate, renew, resurrect, restore, revive, revivify.

retain *vb* detain, hold, husband, keep, preserve, recall, recollect, remember, reserve, save, withhold; engage, maintain.

retainer *n* adherent, attendant, dependant, follower, hanger-on, servant.

retaliate *vb* avenge, match, repay, requite, retort, return, turn.

retaliation *n* boomerang, counterstroke, punishment, repayment, requital, retribution, revenge.

retard *vb* check, clog, hinder, impede, obstruct, slacken; adjourn, defer, delay, postpone, procrastinate.

reticent *adj* close, reserved, secretive, silent, taciturn, uncommunicative.

retinue *n* bodyguard, cortege, entourage, escort, followers, household, ménage, suite, tail, train.

retire *vb* discharge, shelve, superannuate, withdraw; depart, leave, resign, retreat.

retired *adj* abstracted, removed, withdrawn; apart, private, secret, sequestrated, solitary.

retirement *n* isolation, loneliness, privacy, retreat, seclusion, solitude, withdrawal.

retiring *adj* coy, demure, diffident, modest, reserved, retreating, shy, withdrawing.

retort *vb* answer, rejoin, reply, respond. • *n* answer, rejoinder, repartee, reply, response; crucible, jar, vessel, vial.

retract *vb* reverse, withdraw; abjure, cancel, disavow, recall, recant, revoke, unsay.

retreat *vb* recoil, retire, withdraw; recede. • *n* departure, recession, recoil, retirement, withdrawal; privacy, seclusion, solitude; asylum, cove, den, habitat, haunt, niche, recess, refuge, resort, shelter.

retrench *vb* clip, curtail, cut, delete, dock, lop, mutilate, pare, prune; abridge, decrease, diminish, lessen; confine, limit; economize, encroach.

retribution *n* compensation, desert, judgement, nemesis, penalty, recompense, repayment, requital, retaliation, return, revenge, reward, vengeance.

retrieve *vb* recall, recover, recoup, recruit, re-establish, regain, repair, restore.

retrograde *vb* decline, degenerate, recede, retire, retrocede. • *adj* backward, inverse, retrogressive, unprogressive.

retrospect *n* recollection, re-examination, reminiscence, re-survey, review, survey.

return *vb* reappear, recoil, recur, revert; answer, reply, respond; recriminate, retort; convey, give, communicate, reciprocate, recompense, refund, remit, repay, report, requite, send, tell, transmit; elect. • *n* payment, reimbursement, remittance, repayment; recompense, recovery, recurrence, renewal, repayment, requital, restitution, restoration, reward; advantage, benefit, interest, profit, rent, yield.

reunion *n* assemblage, assembly, gathering, meeting, re-assembly; rapprochement, reconciliation.

reveal *vb* announce, communicate, confess, declare, disclose, discover, display, divulge, expose, impart, open, publish, tell, uncover, unmask, unseal, unveil.

revel *vb* carouse, disport, riot, roister, tipple; delight, indulge, luxuriate, wanton. • *n* carousal, feast, festival, saturnalia, spree.

revelry *n* bacchanal, carousal, carouse, debauch, festivity, jollification, jollity, orgy, revel, riot, rout, saturnalia, wassail.

revenge *vb* avenge, repay, requite, retaliate, vindicate. • *n* malevolence, rancour, reprisal, requital, retaliation, retribution, vengeance, vindictiveness.

revengeful *adj* implacable, malevolent, malicious, malignant, resentful, rancorous, spiteful, vengeful, vindictive.

revenue *n* fruits, income, produce, proceeds, receipts, return, reward, wealth.

reverberate *vb* echo, re-echo, resound, return.

revere *vb* adore, esteem, hallow, honour, reverence, venerate, worship.

reverence *vb* adore, esteem, hallow, honour, revere, venerate, worship. • *n* adoration, awe, deference, homage, honour, respect, veneration, worship.

reverential *adj* deferential, humble, respectful, reverent, submissive.

reverse *vb* invert, transpose; overset, overthrow, overturn, quash, subvert, undo, unmake; annul, countermand, repeal, rescind, retract, revoke; back, back up, retreat. • *adj* back, converse, contrary, opposite, verso. • *n* back, calamity, check, comedown, contrary, counterpart, defeat, opposite, tail; change, vicissitude; adversity, affliction, hardship, misadventure, mischance, misfortune, mishap, trial.

revert *vb* repel, reverse; backslide, lapse, recur, relapse, return.

review *vb* inspect, overlook, reconsider, re-examine, retrace, revise, survey; analyse, criticize, discuss, edit, judge, scrutinize, study. • *n* reconsideration, re-examination, re-survey, retrospect, survey; analysis, digest, synopsis; commentary, critique, criticism, notice, review, scrutiny, study.

revile *vb* abuse, asperse, backbite, calumniate, defame, execrate, malign, reproach, slander, traduce, upbraid, vilify.

revise *vb* reconsider, re-examine, review; alter, amend, correct, edit, overhaul, polish.

revive *vb* reanimate, reinspire, reinspirit, reinvigorate, resuscitate, revitalize, revivify; animate, cheer, comfort, invigorate, quicken, reawaken, recover, refresh, renew, renovate, rouse, strengthen; reawake, recall.

revocation *n* abjuration, recall, recantation, repeal, retraction, reversal.

revoke *vb* abolish, abrogate, annul, cancel, countermand, invalidate, quash, recall, recant, repeal, repudiate, rescind, retract.

revolt *vb* desert, mutiny, rebel, rise; disgust, nauseate, repel, sicken. • *n* defection, desertion, faithlessness, inconstancy;

disobedience, insurrection, mutiny, outbreak, rebellion, sedition, strike, uprising.

revolting *adj* abhorrent, abominable, disgusting, hateful, monstrous, nauseating, nauseous, objectionable, obnoxious, offensive, repulsive, shocking, sickening; insurgent, mutinous, rebellious.

revolution *n* coup, disobedience, insurrection, mutiny, outbreak, rebellion, sedition, strike, uprising; change, innovation, reformation, transformation, upheaval; circle, circuit, cycle, lap, orbit, rotation, spin, turn.

revolve *vb* circle, circulate, rotate, swing, turn, wheel; devolve, return; consider, mediate, ponder, ruminate, study.

revulsion *n* abstraction, shrinking, withdrawal; change, reaction, reversal, transition; abhorrence, disgust, loathing, repugnance.

reward *vb* compensate, gratify, indemnify, pay, punish, recompense, remember, remunerate, requite. • *n* compensation, gratification, guerdon, indemnification, pay, recompense, remuneration, requital; bounty, bonus, fee, gratuity, honorarium, meed, perquisite, premium, remembrance, tip; punishment, retribution.

rhythm *n* cadence, lilt, pulsation, swing; measure, metre, number.

ribald *adj* base, blue, coarse, filthy, gross, indecent, lewd, loose, low, mean, obscene, vile.

rich *adj* affluent, flush, moneyed, opulent, prosperous, wealthy; costly, estimable, gorgeous, luxurious, precious, splendid, sumptuous, superb, valuable; delicious, luscious, savoury; abundant, ample, copious, enough, full, plentiful, plenteous, sufficient; fertile, fruitful, luxuriant, productive, prolific; bright, dark, deep, exuberant, vivid; harmonious, mellow, melodious, soft, sweet; comical, funny, humorous, laughable.

riches *npl* abundance, affluence, fortune, money, opulence, plenty, richness, wealth, wealthiness.

rickety *adj* broken, imperfect, shaky, shattered, tottering, tumbledown, unsteady, weak.

rid *vb* deliver, free, release; clear, disburden, disencumber, scour, sweep; disinherit, dispatch, dissolve, divorce, finish, sever.

riddance *n* deliverance, disencumberment, extrication, escape, freedom, release, relief.

riddle¹ *vb* explain, solve, unriddle. • *n* conundrum, enigma, mystery, puzzle, rebus.

riddle² *vb* sieve, sift, perforate, permeate, spread. • *n* colander, sieve, strainer.

ridge *n* chine, hogback, ledge, saddle, spine, rib, watershed, weal, wrinkle.

ridicule *vb* banter, burlesque, chaff, deride, disparage, jeer, mock, lampoon, rally, satirize, scout, taunt. • *n* badinage, banter, burlesque, chaff, derision, game, gibe, irony, jeer, mockery, persiflage, quip, raillery, sarcasm, satire, sneer, squib, wit.

ridiculous *adj* absurd, amusing, comical, droll, eccentric, fantastic, farcical, funny, laughable, ludicrous, nonsensical, odd, outlandish, preposterous, queer, risible, waggish.

rife *adj* abundant, common, current, general, numerous, plentiful, prevailing, prevalent, replete.

riffraff *n* horde, mob, populace, rabble, scum, trash.

rifle *vb* despoil, fleece, pillage, plunder, ransack, rob, strip.

rift *vb* cleave, rive, split. • *n* breach, break, chink, cleft, crack, cranny, crevice, fissure, fracture, gap, opening, reft, rent.

rig *vb* accoutre, clothe, dress. • *n* costume, dress, garb; equipment, team.

right *vb* adjust, correct, regulate, settle, straighten, vindicate. • *adj* direct, rectilinear, straight; erect, perpendicular, plumb, upright; equitable, even-handed, fair, just, justifiable, honest, lawful, legal, legitimate, rightful, square, unswerving; appropriate, becoming, correct, conventional, fit, fitting, meet, orderly, proper, reasonable, seemly, suitable, well-done; actual, genuine, real, true, unquestionable; dexter, dextral, right-handed. • *adv* equitably, fairly, justly, lawfully, rightfully, rightly; correctly, fitly, properly, suitably, truly; actually, exactly, just, really, truly, well. • *n* authority, claim, liberty, permission, power, privilege, title; equity, good, honour, justice, lawfulness, legality, propriety, reason, righteousness, truth.

righteous *adj* devout, godly, good, holy, honest, incorrupt, just, pious, religious, saintly, uncorrupt, upright, virtuous; equitable, fair, right, rightful.

righteousness *n* equity, faithfulness, godliness, goodness, holiness, honesty, integrity, justice, piety, purity, right, rightfulness, sanctity, uprightness, virtue.

rightful *adj* lawful, legitimate, true; appropriate, correct, deserved, due, equitable, fair, fitting, honest, just, legal, merited, proper, reasonable, suitable.

rigid *adj* firm, hard, inflexible, permanent, stiff, stiffened, unbending, unpliant, unyielding; bristling, erect, precipitous, steep; austere, conventional, correct, exact, formal, harsh, meticulous, precise, rigorous, severe, sharp, stern, strict, unmitigated; cruel.

rigmarole *n* balderdash, flummery, gibberish, gobbledegook, jargon, nonsense, palaver, trash, twaddle, verbiage.

rigour *n* hardness, inflexibility, rigidity, rigidness, stiffness; asperity, austerity, harshness, severity, sternness; evenness, strictness; inclemency.

rile *vb* anger, annoy, irritate, upset, vex.

rim *n* brim, brink, border, confine, curb, edge, flange, girdle, margin, ring, skirt.

ring¹ *vb* circle, encircle, enclose, girdle, surround. • *n* circle, circlet, girdle, hoop, round, whorl; cabal, clique, combination, confederacy, coterie, gang, junta, league, set.

ring² *vb* chime, clang, jingle, knell, peal, resound, reverberate, sound, tingle, toll; call, phone, telephone. • *n* chime, knell, peal, tinkle, toll; call, phone call, telephone call.

riot *vb* carouse, luxuriate, revel. • *n* affray, altercation, brawl, broil, commotion, disturbance, fray, outbreak, pandemonium, quarrel, squabble, tumult, uproar; dissipation, excess, luxury, merrymaking, revelry.

riotous *adj* boisterous, luxurious, merry, revelling, unrestrained, wanton; disorderly, insubordinate, lawless, mutinous, rebellious, refractory, seditious, tumultuous, turbulent, ungovernable, unruly, violent.

ripe *adj* advanced, grown, mature, mellow, seasoned, soft; fit, prepared, ready; accomplished, complete, consummate, finished, perfect, perfected.

ripen *vb* burgeon, develop, mature, prepare.

rise *vb* arise, ascend, clamber, climb, levitate, mount; excel, succeed; enlarge, heighten, increase, swell, thrive; revive; grow, kindle, wax; begin, flow, head, originate, proceed, spring, start; mutiny, rebel, revolt; happen, occur. • *n* ascension, ascent, rising; elevation, grade, hill, slope; beginning, emergence, flow, origin, source, spring; advance, augmentation, expansion, increase.

risible *adj* amusing, comical, droll, farcical, funny, laughable, ludicrous, ridiculous.

risk *vb* bet, endanger, hazard, jeopardize, peril, speculate, stake, venture, wager. • *n* chance, danger, hazard, jeopardy, peril, venture.

rite *n* ceremonial, ceremony, form, formulary, ministration, observance, ordinance, ritual, rubric, sacrament, solemnity.

ritual *adj* ceremonial, conventional, formal, habitual, routine, stereotyped. • *n* ceremonial, ceremony, liturgy, observance, rite, sacrament, service; convention, form, formality, habit, practice, protocol.

rival *vb* emulate, match, oppose. • *adj* competing, contending, emulating, emulous, opposing. • *n* antagonist, competitor, emulator, opponent.

rive *vb* cleave, rend, split.

river *n* affluent, current, reach, stream, tributary.

road *n* course, highway, lane, passage, path, pathway, roadway, route, street, thoroughfare, track, trail, turnpike, way.

roam *vb* jaunt, prowl, ramble, range, rove, straggle, stray, stroll, wander.

roar *vb* bawl, bellow, cry, howl, vociferate, yell; boom, peal, rattle, resound, thunder. • *n* bellow, roaring; rage, resonance, storm, thunder; cry, outcry, shout; laugh, laughter, shout.

rob *vb* despoil, fleece, pilfer, pillage, plunder, rook, strip; appropriate, deprive, embezzle, plagiarize.

robber *n* bandit, brigand, desperado, depredator, despoiler, footpad, freebooter, highwayman, marauder, pillager, pirate, plunderer, rifler, thief.

robbery *n* depredation, despoliation, embezzlement, freebooting, larceny, peculation, piracy, plagiarism, plundering, spoliation, theft.

robe *vb* array, clothe, dress, invest. • *n* attire, costume, dress, garment, gown, habit, vestment; bathrobe, dressing gown, housecoat.

robust *adj* able-bodied, athletic, brawny, energetic, firm, forceful, hale, hardy, hearty, iron, lusty, muscular, powerful, seasoned, self-assertive, sinewy, sound, stalwart, stout, strong, sturdy, vigorous.

rock[1] *n* boulder, cliff, crag, reef, stone; asylum, defence, foundation, protection, refuge, strength, support; gneiss, granite, marble, slate, etc.

rock[2] *vb* calm, cradle, lull, quiet, soothe, still, tranquillize; reel, shake, sway, teeter, totter, wobble.

rogue *n* beggar, vagabond, vagrant; caitiff, cheat, knave, rascal, scamp, scapegrace, scoundrel, sharper, swindler, trickster, villain.

roguish *adj* dishonest, fraudulent, knavish, rascally, scoundrelly, trickish, tricky; arch, sportive, mischievous, puckish, waggish, wanton.

role *n* character, function, impersonation, part, task.

roll *vb* gyrate, revolve, rotate, turn, wheel; curl, muffle, swathe, wind; bind, involve, enfold, envelop; flatten, level, smooth, spread; bowl, drive; trundle, wheel; gybe, lean, lurch, stagger, sway, yaw; billow, swell, undulate; wallow, welter; flow, glide, run. • *n* document, scroll, volume; annals, chronicle, history, record, rota; catalogue, inventory, list, register, schedule; booming, resonance, reverberation, thunder; cylinder, roller.

rollicking *adj* frisky, frolicking, frolicsome, jolly, jovial, lively, swaggering.

romance *vb* exaggerate, fantasize. • *n* fantasy, fiction, legend, novel, story, tale; exaggeration, falsehood, lie; ballad, idyll, song.

romantic *adj* extravagant, fanciful, fantastic, ideal, imaginative, sentimental, wild; chimerical, fabulous, fantastic, fictitious, imaginary, improbable, legendary, picturesque, quixotic, sentimental. • *n* dreamer, idealist, sentimentalist, visionary.

romp *vb* caper, gambol, frisk, sport. • *n* caper, frolic, gambol.

room *n* accommodation, capacity, compass, elbowroom, expanse, extent, field, latitude, leeway, play, scope, space, swing; place, stead; apartment, chamber, lodging; chance, occasion, opportunity.

roomy *adj* ample, broad, capacious, comfortable, commodious, expansive, extensive, large, spacious, wide.

root[1] *vb* anchor, embed, fasten, implant, place, settle; confirm, establish. • *n* base, bottom, foundation; cause, occasion, motive, origin, reason, source; etymon, radical, radix, stem.

root[2] *vb* destroy, eradicate, extirpate, exterminate, remove, unearth, uproot; burrow, dig, forage, grub, rummage; applaud, cheer, encourage.

rooted *adj* chronic, confirmed, deep, established, fixed, radical.

roseate *adj* blooming, blushing, rose-coloured, rosy, rubicund; hopeful.

rostrum *n* platform, stage, stand, tribune.

rosy *adj* auspicious, blooming, blushing, favourable, flushed, hopeful, roseate, ruddy, sanguine.

rot *vb* corrupt, decay, decompose, degenerate, putrefy, spoil, taint. • *n* corruption, decay, decomposition, putrefaction.

rotary *adj* circular, rotating, revolving, rotatory, turning, whirling.

rotten *adj* carious, corrupt, decomposed, fetid, putrefied, putrescent, putrid, rank, stinking; defective, unsound; corrupt, deceitful, immoral, treacherous, unsound, untrustworthy.

rotund *adj* buxom, chubby, full, globular, obese, plump, round, stout; fluent, grandiloquent.

roué *n* debauchee, libertine, profligate, rake.

rough *vb* coarsen, roughen; manhandle, mishandle, molest. • *adj* bumpy, craggy, irregular, jagged, rugged, scabrous, scraggy, scratchy, stubby, uneven; approximate, cross-grained, crude, formless, incomplete, knotty, rough-hewn, shapeless, sketchy, uncut, unfashioned, unfinished, unhewn, unpolished, unwrought, vague; bristly, bushy, coarse, disordered, hairy, hirsute, ragged, shaggy, unkempt; austere, bearish, bluff, blunt, brusque, burly, churlish, discourteous, gruff, harsh, impolite, indelicate, rude, surly, uncivil, uncourteous, ungracious, unpolished, unrefined; harsh, severe, sharp, violent; astringent, crabbed, hard, sour, tart; discordant, grating, inharmonious, jarring, raucous, scabrous, unmusical; boisterous, foul, inclement, severe, stormy, tempestuous, tumultuous, turbulent, untamed, violent, wild; acrimonious, brutal, cruel, disorderly, riotous, rowdy, severe, uncivil, unfeeling, ungentle. • *n* bully, rowdy, roughneck, ruffian; draft, outline, sketch, suggestion; unevenness.

round *vb* curve; circuit, encircle, encompass, surround. • *adj* bulbous, circular, cylindrical, globular, orbed, orbicular, rotund, spherical; complete, considerable, entire, full, great, large, unbroken, whole; chubby, corpulent, plump, stout, swelling; continuous, flowing, harmonious, smooth; brisk, quick; blunt, candid, fair, frank, honest, open, plain, upright. • *adv* around, circularly, circuitously. • *prep* about, around. • *n*

bout, cycle, game, lap, revolution, rotation, succession, turn; canon, catch, dance; ball, circle, circumference, cylinder, globe, sphere; circuit, compass, perambulation, routine, tour, watch.

roundabout *adj* circuitous, circumlocutory, indirect, tortuous; ample, broad, extensive; encircling, encompassing.

rouse *vb* arouse, awaken, raise, shake, wake, waken; animate, bestir, brace, enkindle, excite, inspire, kindle, rally, stimulate, stir, whet; startle, surprise.

rout *vb* beat, conquer, defeat, discomfit, overcome, overpower, overthrow, vanquish; chase away, dispel, disperse, scatter. • *n* defeat, discomfiture, flight, ruin; concourse, multitude, rabble; brawl, disturbance, noise, roar, uproar.

route *vb* direct, forward, send, steer. • *n* course, circuit, direction, itinerary, journey, march, road, passage, path, way.

routine *adj* conventional, familiar, habitual, ordinary, standard, typical, usual; boring, dull, humdrum, predictable, tiresome. • *n* beat, custom, groove, method, order, path, practice, procedure, round, rut.

rove *vb* prowl, ramble, range, roam, stray, struggle, stroll, wander.

row[1] *n* file, line, queue, range, rank, series, string, tier; alley, street, terrace.

row[2] *vb* argue, dispute, fight, quarrel, squabble. • *n* affray, altercation, brawl, broil, commotion, dispute, disturbance, noise, outbreak, quarrel, riot, squabble, tumult, uproar.

royal *adj* august, courtly, dignified, generous, grand, imperial, kingly, kinglike, magnanimous, magnificent, majestic, monarchical, noble, princely, regal, sovereign, splendid, superb.

rub *vb* abrade, chafe, grate, graze, scrape; burnish, clean, massage, polish, scour, wipe; apply, put, smear, spread. • *n* caress, massage, polish, scouring, shine, wipe; catch, difficulty, drawback, impediment, obstacle, problem.

rubbish *n* debris, detritus, fragments, refuse, ruins, waste; dregs, dross, garbage, litter, lumber, scoria, scum, sweepings, trash, trumpery.

rubicund *adj* blushing, erubescent, florid, flushed, red, reddish, ruddy.

rude *adj* coarse, crude, ill-formed, rough, rugged, shapeless, uneven, unfashioned, unformed, unwrought; artless, barbarous, boorish, clownish, ignorant, illiterate, loutish, raw, savage, uncivilized, uncouth, uncultivated, undisciplined, unpolished, ungraceful, unskilful, unskilled, untaught, untrained, untutored, vulgar; awkward, barbarous, bluff, blunt, boorish, brusque, brutal, churlish, gruff, ill-bred, impertinent, impolite, impudent, insolent, insulting, ribald, saucy, uncivil, uncourteous, unrefined; boisterous, fierce, harsh, severe, tumultuous, turbulent, violent; artless, inelegant, rustic, unpolished; hearty, robust.

rudimentary *adj* elementary, embryonic, fundamental, initial, primary, rudimental, undeveloped.

rue *vb* deplore, grieve, lament, regret, repent.

rueful *adj* dismal, doleful, lamentable, lugubrious, melancholic, melancholy, mournful, penitent, regretful, sad, sorrowful, woeful.

ruffian *n* bully, caitiff, cutthroat, hoodlum, miscreant, monster, murderer, rascal, robber, roisterer, rowdy, scoundrel, villain, wretch.

ruffle *vb* damage, derange, disarrange, dishevel, disorder, ripple, roughen, rumple; agitate, confuse, discompose, disquiet, disturb, excite, harass, irritate, molest, plague, perturb, torment, trouble, vex, worry; cockle, flounce, pucker, wrinkle. • *n* edging, frill, ruff; agitation, bustle, commotion, confusion, contention, disturbance, excitement, fight, fluster, flutter, flurry, perturbation, tumult.

rugged *adj* austere, bristly, coarse, crabbed, cragged, craggy, hard, hardy, irregular, ragged, robust, rough, rude, scraggy, severe, seamed, shaggy, uneven, unkempt, wrinkled; boisterous, inclement, stormy, tempestuous, tumultuous, turbulent, violent; grating, harsh, inharmonious, unmusical, scabrous.

ruin *vb* crush, damn, defeat, demolish, desolate, destroy, devastate, overthrow, overturn, overwhelm, seduce, shatter, smash, subvert, wreck; beggar, impoverish. • *n* damnation, decay, defeat, demolition, desolation, destruction, devastation, discomfiture, downfall, fall, loss, perdition, prostration, rack, ruination, shipwreck, subversion, undoing, wrack, wreck; bane, mischief, pest.

ruination *n* demolition, destruction, overthrow, ruin, subversion.

ruinous *adj* decayed, demolished, dilapidated; baneful, calamitous, damnatory, destructive, disastrous, mischievous, noisome, noxious, pernicious, subversive, wasteful.

rule *vb* bridle, command, conduct, control, direct, domineer, govern, judge, lead, manage, reign, restrain; advise, guide, persuade; adjudicate, decide, determine, establish, settle; obtain, prevail, predominate. • *n* authority, command, control, direction, domination, dominion, empire, government, jurisdiction, lordship, mastery, mastership, regency, reign, sway; behaviour, conduct; habit, method, order, regularity, routine, system; aphorism, canon, convention, criterion, formula, guide, law, maxim, model, precedent, precept, standard, system, test, touchstone; decision, order, prescription, regulation, ruling.

ruler *n* chief, governor, king, lord, master, monarch, potentate, regent, sovereign; director, head, manager, president; controller, guide, rule; straight-edge.

ruminate *vb* brood, chew, cogitate, consider, contemplate, meditate, muse, ponder, reflect, think.

rumour *vb* bruit, circulate, report, tell. • *n* bruit, gossip, hearsay, report, talk; news, report, story, tidings; celebrity, fame, reputation, repute.

rumple *vb* crease, crush, corrugate, crumple, disarrange, dishevel, pucker, ruffle, wrinkle. • *n* crease, corrugation, crumple, fold, pucker, wrinkle.

run *vb* bolt, career, course, gallop, haste, hasten, hie, hurry, lope, post, race, scamper, scour, scud, scuttle, speed, trip; flow, glide, go, move, proceed, stream; fuse, liquefy, melt; advance, pass, proceed, vanish; extend, lie, spread, stretch; circulate, pass, press; average, incline, tend; flee; pierce, stab; drive, force, propel, push, thrust, turn; cast, form, mould, shape; follow, perform, pursue, take; discharge, emit; direct, maintain, manage. • *n* race, running; course, current, flow, motion, passage, progress, way, wont; continuance, currency, popularity; excursion, gallop, journey, trip, trot; demand, pressure; brook, burn, flow, rill, rivulet, runlet, runnel, streamlet.

rupture *vb* break, burst, fracture, sever, split. • *n* breach, break, burst, disruption, fracture, split; contention, faction, feud, hostility, quarrel, schism.

rural *adj* agrarian, bucolic, country, pastoral, rustic, sylvan.

ruse *n* artifice, deception, deceit, fraud, hoax, imposture, manoeuvre, sham, stratagem, trick, wile.

rush *vb* attack, career, charge, dash, drive, gush, hurtle, precipitate, surge, sweep, tear. • *n* dash, onrush, onset, plunge, precipitance, precipitancy, rout, stampede, tear.

rust *vb* corrode, decay, degenerate. • *n* blight, corrosion, crust, mildew, must, mould, mustiness.

rustic *adj* country, rural; awkward, boorish, clownish, countrified, loutish, outlandish, rough, rude, uncouth, unpolished, untaught; coarse, countrified, homely, plain, simple, unadorned; artless, honest, unsophisticated. • *n* boor, bumpkin, clown, countryman, peasant, swain, yokel.

ruthless *adj* barbarous, cruel, fell, ferocious, hardhearted, inexorable, inhuman, merciless, pitiless, relentless, remorseless, savage, truculent, uncompassionate, unmerciful, unpitying, unrelenting, unsparing.

S

sable *adj* black, dark, dusky, ebony, sombre.

sabulous *adj* gritty, sabulose, sandy.

sack[1] *n* bag, pouch.

sack[2] *vb* despoil, devastate, pillage, plunder, ravage, spoil. • *n* desolation, despoliation, destruction, devastation, havoc, ravage, sacking, spoliation, waste; booty, plunder, spoil.

sacred *adj* consecrated, dedicated, devoted, divine, hallowed, holy; inviolable, inviolate; sainted, venerable.

sacrifice *vb* forgo, immolate, surrender. • *n* immolation, oblation, offering; destruction, devotion, loss, surrender.

sacrilege *n* desecration, profanation, violation.

sacrilegious *adj* desecrating, impious, irreverent, profane.

sad *adj* grave, pensive, sedate, serious, sober, sombre, staid.

saddle *vb* burden, charge, clog, encumber, load.

sadly *adv* grievously, miserable, mournfully, sorrowfully; afflictively, badly, calamitously; darkly; gravely, seriously, soberly.

sadness *n* dejection, depression, despondency, melancholy, mournful, sorrow, sorrowfulness; dolefulness, gloominess, grief, mournfulness, sorrow; gravity, sedateness, seriousness.

safe *adj* undamaged, unharmed, unhurt, unscathed; guarded, protected, secure, snug, unexposed; certain, dependable, reliable, sure, trustworthy; good, harmless, sound, whole. • *n* chest, coffer, strongbox.

safeguard *vb* guard, protect. • *n* defence, protection, security; convoy, escort, guard, safe-conduct; pass, passport.

sagacious *adj* acute, apt, astute, clear-sighted, discerning, intelligent, judicious, keen, penetrating, perspicacious, rational, sage, sharp-witted, wise, shrewd.

sagacity *n* acuteness, astuteness, discernment, ingenuity, insight, penetration, perspicacity, quickness, readiness, sense, sharpness, shrewdness, wisdom.

sage *adj* acute, discerning, intelligent, prudent, sagacious, sapient, sensible, shrewd, wise; judicious, well-judged; grave, serious, solemn. • *n* philosopher, pundit, savant.

sailor *n* mariner, navigator, salt, seafarer, seaman, tar.

saintly *adj* devout, godly, holy, pious, religious.

sake *n* end, cause, purpose, reason; account, consideration, interest, regard, respect, score.

saleable *adj* marketable, merchantable, vendible.

salacious *adj* carnal, concupiscent, incontinent, lascivious, lecherous, lewd, libidinous, loose, lustful, prurient, unchaste, wanton.

salary *n* allowance, hire, pay, stipend, wages.

salient *adj* bounding, jumping, leaping; beating, springing, throbbing; jutting, projecting, prominent; conspicuous, remarkable, striking.

saline *adj* briny, salty.

sally *vb* issue, rush. • *n* digression, excursion, sortie, run, trip; escapade, frolic; crank, fancy, jest, joke, quip, quirk, sprightly, witticism.

salt *adj* saline, salted, salty; bitter, pungent, sharp. • *n* flavour, savour, seasoning, smack, relish, taste; humour, piquancy, poignancy, sarcasm, smartness, wit, zest; mariner, sailor, seaman, tar.

salubrious *adj* beneficial, benign, healthful, healthy, salutary, sanitary, wholesome.

salutary *adj* healthy, healthful, helpful, safe, salubrious, wholesome; advantageous, beneficial, good, profitable, serviceable, useful.

salute *vb* accost, address, congratulate, greet, hail, welcome. • *n* address, greeting, salutation.

salvation *n* deliverance, escape, preservation, redemption, rescue, saving.

same *adj* ditto, identical, selfsame; corresponding, like, similar.

sample *vb* savour, sip, smack, sup, taste; test, try; demonstrate, exemplify, illustrate, instance. • *adj* exemplary, illustrative, representative. • *n* demonstration, exemplification, illustration, instance, piece, specimen; example, model, pattern.

sanctify *vb* consecrate, hallow, purify; justify, ratify, sanction.

sanctimonious *adj* affected, devout, holy, hypocritical, pharisaical, pious, self-righteous.

sanction *vb* authorize, countenance, encourage, support; confirm, ratify. • *n* approval, authority, authorization, confirmation, countenance, endorsement, ratification, support, warranty; ban, boycott, embargo, penalty.

sanctity *n* devotion, godliness, goodness, grace, holiness, piety, purity, religiousness, saintliness.

sanctuary *n* altar, church, shrine, temple; asylum, protection, refuge, retreat, shelter.

sane *adj* healthy, lucid, rational, reasonable, sober, sound.

sang-froid *n* calmness, composure, coolness, imperturbability, indifference, nonchalance, phlegm, unconcern.

sanguinary *adj* bloody, gory, murderous; barbarous, bloodthirsty, cruel, fell, pitiless, savage, ruthless.

sanguine *adj* crimson, florid, red; animated, ardent, cheerful, lively, warm; buoyant, confident, enthusiastic, hopeful, optimistic; full-blooded.

sanitary *adj* clean, curative, healing, healthy, hygienic, remedial, therapeutic, wholesome.

sanity *n* normality, rationality, reason, saneness, soundness.

sapient *adj* acute, discerning, intelligent, knowing, sagacious, sage, sensible, shrewd, wise.

sarcastic *adj* acrimonious, biting, cutting, mordacious, mordant, sardonic, satirical, sharp, severe, sneering, taunting.

sardonic *adj* bitter, derisive, ironical, malevolent, malicious, malignant, sarcastic.

satanic *adj* devilish, diabolical, evil, false, fiendish, hellish, infernal, malicious.

satellite *adj* dependent, subordinate, tributary, vassal. • *n* attendant, dependant, follower, hanger-on, retainer, vassal.

satiate *vb* fill, sate, satisfy, suffice; cloy, glut, gorge, overfeed, overfill, pall, surfeit.

satire *n* burlesque, diatribe, invective, fling, irony, lampoon, pasquinade, philippic, ridicule, sarcasm, skit, squib.

satirical *adj* abusive, biting, bitter, censorious, cutting, invective, ironical, keen, mordacious, poignant, reproachful, sarcastic, severe, sharp, taunting.

satirize *vb* abuse, censure, lampoon, ridicule.

satisfaction *n* comfort, complacency, contentment, ease, enjoyment, gratification, pleasure, satiety; amends, appeasement, atonement, compensation, indemnification, recompense, redress, remuneration, reparation, requital, reward.

satisfactory *adj* adequate, conclusive, convincing, decisive, sufficient; gratifying, pleasing.

satisfy *vb* appease, content, fill, gratify, please, sate, satiate, suffice; indemnify, compensate, liquidate, pay, recompense, remunerate, requite; discharge, settle; assure, convince, persuade; answer, fulfil, meet.

saturate *vb* drench, fill, fit, imbue, soak, steep, wet.

saturnine *adj* dark, dull, gloomy, grave, heavy, leaden, morose, phlegmatic, sad, sedate, sombre; melancholic, mournful, serious, unhappy; mischievous, naughty, troublesome, vexatious, wicked.

sauce *n* cheekiness, impudence, insolence; appetizer, compound, condiment, relish, seasoning.

saucy *adj* bold, cavalier, disrespectful, flippant, forward, immodest, impertinent, impudent, insolent, pert, rude.

saunter *vb* amble, dawdle, delay, dilly-dally, lag, linger, loiter, lounge, stroll, tarry. • *n* amble, stroll, walk.

savage *vb* attack, lacerate, mangle, maul. • *adj* rough, uncultivated, wild; rude, uncivilized, unpolished, untaught; bloodthirsty, feral, ferine, ferocious, fierce, rapacious, untamed, vicious; beastly, bestial, brutal, brutish, inhuman; atrocious, barbarous, barbaric, bloody, brutal, cruel, fell, fiendish, hardhearted, heathenish, merciless, murderous, pitiless, relentless, ruthless, sanguinary, truculent; native, rough, rugged. • *n* barbarian, brute, heathen, vandal.

save *vb* keep, liberate, preserve, rescue; salvage, recover, redeem; economize, gather, hoard, husband, reserve, store; hinder, obviate, prevent, spare. • *prep* but, deducting, except.

saviour *n* defender, deliverer, guardian, protector, preserver, rescuer, saver.

savour *vb* affect, appreciate, enjoy, like, partake, relish; flavour, season. • *n* flavour, gusto, relish, smack, taste; fragrance, odour, smell, scent.

savoury *adj* agreeable, delicious, flavourful, luscious, nice, palatable, piquant, relishing.

saw *n* adage, aphorism, apothegm, axiom, byword, dictum, maxim, precept, proverb, sententious saying.

say *vb* declare, express, pronounce, speak, tell, utter; affirm, allege, argue; recite, rehearse, repeat; assume, presume, suppose. • *n* affirmation, declaration, speech, statement; decision, voice, vote.

saying *n* declaration, expression, observation, remark, speech, statement; adage, aphorism, byword, dictum, maxim, proverb, saw.

scale[1] *n* basin, dish, pan; balance.

scale[2] *n* flake, lamina, lamella, layer, plate.

scale[3] *vb* ascend, climb, escalate, mount. • *n* graduation.

scamp *n* cheat, knave, rascal, rogue, scapegrace, scoundrel, swindler, trickster, villain.

scamper *vb* haste, hasten, hie, run, scud, speed, trip.

scan *vb* examine, investigate, scrutinize, search, sift.

scandal *vb* asperse, defame, libel, traduce. • *n* aspersion, calumny, defamation, obloquy, reproach; discredit, disgrace, dishonour, disrepute, ignominy, infamy, odium, opprobrium, offence, shame.

scandalize *vb* offend; asperse, backbite, calumniate, decry, defame, disgust, lampoon, libel, reproach, revile, satirize, slander, traduce, vilify.

scandalous *adj* defamatory, libellous, opprobrious, slanderous; atrocious, disgraceful, disreputable, infamous, inglorious, ignominious, odious, shameful.

scanty *adj* insufficient, meagre, narrow, scant, small; hardly, scarce, short, slender; niggardly, parsimonious, penurious, scrimpy, skimpy, sparing.

scar[1] *vb* hurt, mark, wound. • *n* cicatrice, cicatrix, seam; blemish, defect, disfigurement, flaw, injury, mark.

scar[2] *n* bluff, cliff, crag, precipice.

scarce *adj* deficient, wanting; infrequent, rare, uncommon. • *adv* barely, hardly, scantily.

scarcely *adv* barely, hardly, scantily.

scarcity *n* dearth, deficiency, insufficiency, lack, want; infrequency, rareness, rarity, uncommonness.

scare *vb* affright, alarm, appal, daunt, fright, frighten, intimidate, shock, startle, terrify. • *n* alarm, fright, panic, shock, terror.

scathe *vb* blast, damage, destroy, injure, harm, haste. • *n* damage, harm, injury, mischief, waste.

scatter *vb* broadcast, sprinkle, strew; diffuse, disperse, disseminate, dissipate, distribute, separate, spread; disappoint, dispel, frustrate, overthrow.

scene *n* display, exhibition, pageant, representation, show, sight, spectacle, view; place, situation, spot; arena, stage.

scent *vb* breathe in, inhale, nose, smell, sniff; detect, smell out, sniff out; aromatize, perfume. • *n* aroma, balminess, fragrance, odour, perfume, smell, redolence.

sceptic *n* doubter, freethinker, questioner, unbeliever.

sceptical *adj* doubtful, doubting, dubious, hesitating, incredulous, questioning, unbelieving.

scepticism *n* doubt, dubiety, freethinking, incredulity, unbelief.

schedule *vb* line up, list, plan, programme, tabulate. • *n* document, scroll; catalogue, inventory, list, plan, record, register, roll, table, timetable.

scheme *vb* contrive, design, frame, imagine, plan, plot, project. • *n* plan, system, theory; cabal, conspiracy, contrivance, design, device, intrigue, machination, plan, plot, project, stratagem; arrangement, draught, diagram, outline.

schism *n* division, separation, split; discord, disunion, division, faction, separation.

scholar *n* disciple, learner, pupil, student; don, fellow, intellectual, pedant, savant.

scholarship *n* accomplishments, acquirements, attainments, erudition, knowledge, learning; bursary, exhibition, foundation, grant, maintenance.

scholastic *adj* academic, bookish, lettered, literary; formal, pedantic.

school *vb* drill, educate, exercise, indoctrinate, instruct, teach, train; admonish, control, chide, discipline, govern, reprove, tutor. • *adj* academic, collegiate, institutional, scholastic, schoolish. • *n* academy, college, gymnasium, institute, institution, kindergarten, lyceum, manège, polytechnic, seminary, university; adherents, camarilla, circle, clique, coterie, disciples, followers; body, order, organization, party, sect.

schooling *n* discipline, education, instruction, nurture, teaching, training, tuition.

scintillate *vb* coruscate, flash, gleam, glisten, glitter, sparkle, twinkle.

scoff *vb* deride, flout, jeer, mock, ridicule, taunt; gibe, sneer. • *n* flout, gibe, jeer, sneer, mockery, taunt; derision, ridicule.

scold *vb* berate, blame, censure, chide, rate, reprimand, reprove; brawl, rail, rate, reprimand, upbraid, vituperate. • *n* shrew, termagant, virago, vixen.

scope *n* aim, design, drift, end, intent, intention, mark, object, purpose, tendency, view; amplitude, field, latitude, liberty, margin, opportunity, purview, range, room, space, sphere, vent; extent, length, span, stretch, sweep.

scorch *vb* blister, burn, char, parch, roast, sear, shrivel, singe.

score *vb* cut, furrow, mark, notch, scratch; charge, note, record; impute, note; enter, register. • *n* incision, mark, notch; account, bill, charge, debt, reckoning; consideration, ground, motive, reason.

scorn *vb* condemn, despise, disregard, disdain, scout, slight, spurn. • *n* contempt, derision, disdain, mockery, slight, sneer; scoff.

scornful *adj* contemptuous, defiant, disdainful, contemptuous, regardless.

scot-free *adj* untaxed; clear, unhurt, uninjured, safe.

scoundrel *n* cheat, knave, miscreant, rascal, reprobate, rogue, scamp, swindler, trickster, villain.

scour[1] *vb* brighten, buff, burnish, clean, cleanse, polish, purge, scrape, scrub, rub, wash, whiten; rake; efface, obliterate, overrun.

scour[2] *vb* career, course, range, scamper, scud, scuttle; comb, hunt, rake, ransack, rifle, rummage, search.

scourge *vb* lash, whip; afflict, chasten, chastise, correct, punish; harass, torment. • *n* cord, cowhide, lash, strap, thong, whip; affliction, bane, curse, infliction, nuisance, pest, plague, punishment.

scout *vb* contemn, deride, disdain, despise, ridicule, scoff, scorn, sneer, spurn; investigate, probe, search. • *n* escort, lookout, precursor, vanguard.

scowl *vb* frown, glower, lower. • *n* frown, glower, lower.

scraggy *adj* broken, craggy, rough, rugged, scabrous, scragged, uneven; attenuated, bony, emaciated, gaunt, lank, lean, meagre, scrawny, skinny, thin.

scrap[1] *vb* discard, junk, trash. • *n* bit, fragment, modicum, particle, piece, snippet; bite, crumb, morsel, mouthful; debris, junk, litter, rubbish, rubble, trash, waste.

scrap[2] *vb* altercate, bicker, dispute, clash, fight, hassle, quarrel, row, spat, squabble, tiff, tussle, wrangle. • *n* affray, altercation, bickering, clash, dispute, fight, fray, hassle, melee, quarrel, row, run-in, set-to, spat, squabble, tiff, tussle, wrangle.

scrape *vb* bark, grind, rasp, scuff; accumulate, acquire, collect, gather, save; erase, remove. • *n* difficulty, distress, embarrassment, perplexity, predicament.

scream *vb* screech, shriek, squall, ululate. • *n* cry, outcry, screech, shriek, shrill, ululation.

screen *vb* cloak, conceal, cover, defend, fence, hide, mask, protect, shelter, shroud. • *n* blind, curtain, lattice, partition; defence, guard, protection, shield; cloak, cover, veil, disguise; riddle, sieve.

screw *vb* force, press, pressurize, squeeze, tighten, twist, wrench; oppress, rack; distort. • *n* extortioner, extortionist, miser, scrimp, skinflint; prison guard; sexual intercourse.

scrimmage *n* brawl, melee, riot, scuffle, skirmish.

scrimp *vb* contract, curtail, limit, pinch, reduce, scant, shorten, straiten.

scrimpy *adj* contracted, deficient, narrow, scanty.

scroll *n* inventory, list, parchment, roll, schedule.

scrub[1] *adj* contemptible, inferior, mean, niggardly, scrubby, shabby, small, stunted. • *n* brushwood, underbrush, underwood.

scrub[2] *vb* clean, cleanse, rub, scour, scrape, wash.

scruple *vb* boggle, demur, falter, hesitate, object, pause, stickle, waver. • *n* delicacy, hesitancy, hesitation, nicety, perplexity, qualm.

scrupulous *adj* conscientious, fastidious, nice, precise, punctilious, rigorous, strict; careful, cautious, circumspect, exact, vigilant.

scrutinize *vb* canvass, dissect, examine, explore, investigate, overhaul, probe, search, sift, study.

scrutiny *n* examination, exploration, inquisition, inspection, investigation, search, searching, sifting.

scud *vb* flee, fly, haste, hasten, hie, post, run, scamper, speed, trip.

scuffle *vb* contend, fight, strive, struggle. • *n* altercation, brawl, broil, contest, encounter, fight, fray, quarrel, squabble, struggle, wrangle.

sculpt *vb* carve, chisel, cut, sculpture; engrave, grave.

scurrilous *adj* abusive, blackguardly, contumelious, foul, foulmouthed, indecent, infamous, insolent, insulting, offensive, opprobrious, reproachful, ribald, vituperative; coarse, gross, low, mean, obscene, vile, vulgar.

scurry *vb* bustle, dash, hasten, hurry, scamper, scud, scutter. • *n* burst, bustle, dash, flurry, haste, hurry, scamper, scud, spurt.

scurvy *adj* scabbed, scabby, scurfy; abject, bad, base, contemptible, despicable, low, mean, pitiful, sorry, vile, vulgar, worthless; malicious, mischievous, offensive.

scuttle[1] *vb* hurry, hustle, run, rush, scamper, scramble, scud, scurry. • *n* dash, drive, flurry, haste, hurry, hustle, race, rush, scamper, scramble, scud, scurry.

scuttle[2] *vb* capsize, founder, go down, sink, overturn, upset. • *n* hatch, hatchway.

seal *vb* close, fasten, secure; attest, authenticate, confirm, establish, ratify, sanction; confine, enclose, imprison. • *n* fastening, stamp, wafer, wax; assurance, attestation, authentication, confirmation, pledge, ratification.

seamy *adj* disreputable, nasty, seedy, sordid, unpleasant.

sear *vb* blight, brand, cauterize, dry, scorch, wither. • *adj* dried up, dry, sere, withered.

search *vb* examine, explore, ferret, inspect, investigate, overhaul, probe, ransack, scrutinize, sift; delve, hunt, forage, inquire, look, rummage. • *n* examination, exploration, hunt, inquiry, inspection, investigation, pursuit, quest, research, seeking, scrutiny.

searching *adj* close, keen, penetrating, trying; examining, exploring, inquiring, investigating, probing, seeking.

seared *adj* callous, graceless, hardened, impenitent, incorrigible, obdurate, shameless, unrepentant.

season *vb* acclimatize, accustom, form, habituate, harden, inure, mature, qualify, temper, train; flavour, spice. • *n* interval, period, spell, term, time, while.

seasonable *adj* appropriate, convenient, fit, opportune, suitable, timely.

seasoning *n* condiment, flavouring, relish, salt, sauce.

seat *vb* establish, fix, locate, place, set, station. • *n* place, site, situation, station; abode, capital, dwelling, house, mansion, residence; bottom, fundament; bench, chair, pew, settle, stall, stool.

secede *vb* apostatize, resign, retire, withdraw.

secluded *adj* close, covert, embowered, isolated, private, removed, retired, screened, sequestrated, withdrawn.

seclusion *n* obscurity, privacy, retirement, secrecy, separation, solitude, withdrawal.

second[1] *n* instant, jiffy, minute, moment, trice.

second[2] *vb* abet, advance, aid, assist, back, encourage, forward, further, help, promote, support, sustain; approve, favour. • *adj* inferior, second-rate, secondary; following, next, subsequent; additional, extra, other; double, duplicate. • *n* another, other; assistant, backer, supporter.

secondary *adj* collateral, inferior, minor, subsidiary, subordinate. • *n* delegate, deputy, proxy.

secrecy *n* clandestineness, concealment, furtiveness, stealth, surreptitiousness.

secret *adj* close, concealed, covered, covert, cryptic, hid, hidden, mysterious, privy, shrouded, veiled, unknown, unrevealed, unseen; cabbalistic, clandestine, furtive, privy, sly, stealthy, surreptitious, underhand; confidential, private, retired, secluded, unseen; abstruse, latent, mysterious, obscure, occult, recondite, unknown. • *n* confidence, enigma, key, mystery.

secretary *n* clerk, scribe, writer; escritoire, writing-desk.

secrete[1] *vb* bury, cache, conceal, disguise, hide, shroud, stash; screen, separate.

secrete[2] *vb* discharge, emit, excrete, exude, release, secern.

secretive *adj* cautious, close, reserved, reticent, taciturn, uncommunicative, wary.

sect *n* denomination, faction, schism, school.

section *n* cutting, division, fraction, part, piece, portion, segment, slice.

secular *adj* civil, laic, laical, lay, profane, temporal, worldly.

secure *vb* guard, protect, safeguard; assure, ensure, guarantee, insure; fasten; acquire, gain, get, obtain, procure. • *adj* assured, certain, confident, sure; insured, protected, safe; fast, firm, fixed, immovable, stable; careless, easy, undisturbed, unsuspecting; heedless, inattentive, incautious, negligent, overconfident.

security *n* bulwark, defence, guard, palladium, protection, safeguard, safety, shelter; bond, collateral, deposit, guarantee, pawn, pledge, stake, surety, warranty; carelessness, heedlessness, overconfidence, negligence; assurance, assuredness, certainty, confidence, ease.

sedate *adj* calm, collected, composed, contemplative, cool, demure, grave, placid, philosophical, quiet, serene, serious, sober, still, thoughtful, tranquil, undisturbed, unemotional, unruffled.

sedative *adj* allaying, anodyne, assuasive, balmy, calming, composing, demulcent, lenient, lenitive, soothing, tranquillizing. • *n* anaesthetic, anodyne, hypnotic, narcotic, opiate.

sedentary *adj* inactive, motionless, sluggish, torpid.

sediment *n* dregs, grounds, lees, precipitate, residue, residuum, settlings.

sedition *n* insurgence, insurrection, mutiny, rebellion, revolt, riot, rising, treason, tumult, uprising, uproar.

seditious *adj* factious, incendiary, insurgent, mutinous, rebellious, refractory, riotous, tumultuous, turbulent.

seduce *vb* allure, attract, betray, corrupt, debauch, deceive, decoy, deprave, ensnare, entice, inveigle, lead, mislead.

seductive *adj* alluring, attractive, enticing, tempting.

sedulous *adj* active, assiduous, busy, diligent, industrious, laborious, notable, painstaking, persevering, unremitting, untiring.

see *vb* behold, contemplate, descry, glimpse, sight, spot, survey; comprehend, conceive, distinguish, espy, know, notice, observe, perceive, recognize, remark, understand; beware, consider, envisage, regard, visualize; experience, feel, suffer; examine, inspire, notice, observe; discern, look; call on, visit.

seed *n* semen, sperm; embryo, grain, kernel, matured ovule; germ, original; children, descendants, offspring, progeny; birth, generation, race.

seedy *adj* faded, old, shabby, worn; destitute, distressed, indigent, needy, penniless, pinched, poor.

seek *vb* hunt, look, search; court, follow, prosecute, pursue, solicit; attempt, endeavour, strive, try.

seem *vb* appear, assume, look, pretend.

seeming *adj* apparent, appearing, ostensible, specious. • *n* appearance, colour, guise, look, semblance.

seemly *adj* appropriate, becoming, befitting, congruous, convenient, decent, decorous, expedient, fit, fitting, meet, proper, right, suitable; beautiful, comely, fair, good-looking, graceful, handsome, pretty, well-favoured.

seer *n* augur, diviner, foreteller, predictor, prophet, soothsayer.

segment *n* bit, division, part, piece, portion, section, sector.

segregate *vb* detach, disconnect, disperse, insulate, part, separate.

segregation *n* apartheid, discrimination, insulation, separation.

seize *vb* capture, catch, clutch, grab, grapple, grasp, grip, snatch; confiscate, impress, impound; apprehend, comprehend; arrest, take.

seldom *adv* infrequently, occasionally, rarely.

select *vb* choose, cull, pick, prefer. • *adj* choice, chosen, excellent, exquisite, good, picked, rare, selected.

selection *n* choice, election, pick, preference.

self-conscious *adj* awkward, diffident, embarrassed, insecure, nervous.

self-control *n* restraint, willpower.

self-important *adj* assuming, consequential, proud, haughty, lordly, overbearing, overweening.

selfish *adj* egoistic, egotistical, greedy, illiberal, mean, narrow, self-seeking, ungenerous.

self-possessed *adj* calm, collected, composed, cool, placid, sedate, undisturbed, unexcited, unruffled.

self-willed *adj* contumacious, dogged, headstrong, obstinate, pig-headed, stubborn, uncompliant, wilful.

sell *vb* barter, exchange, hawk, market, peddle, trade, vend.

semblance *n* likeness, resemblance, similarity; air, appearance, aspect, bearing, exterior, figure, form, mien, seeming, show; image, representation, similitude.

seminal *adj* important, original; germinal, radical, rudimental, rudimentary, unformed.

seminary *n* academy, college, gymnasium, high school, institute, school, university.

send *vb* cast, drive, emit, fling, hurl, impel, lance, launch, project, propel, throw, toss; delegate, depute, dispatch; forward, transmit; bestow, confer, give, grant.

senile *adj* aged, doddering, superannuated; doting, imbecile.

senior *adj* elder, older; higher.

seniority *n* eldership, precedence, priority, superiority.

sensation *n* feeling, sense, perception; excitement, impression, thrill.

sensational *adj* exciting, melodramatic, startling, thrilling.

sense *vb* appraise, appreciate, estimate, notice, observe, perceive, suspect, understand. • *n* brains, intellect, intelligence, mind, reason, understanding; appreciation, apprehension, discernment, feeling, perception, recognition, tact; connotation, idea, implication, judgment, notion, opinion, sentiment, view; import, interpretation, meaning, purport, significance; sagacity, soundness, substance, wisdom.

senseless *adj* apathetic, inert, insensate, unfeeling; absurd, foolish, ill-judged, nonsensical, silly, unmeaning, unreasonable, unwise; doltish, foolish, simple, stupid, witless, weak-minded.

sensible *adj* apprehensible, perceptible; aware, cognizant, conscious, convinced, persuaded, satisfied; discreet, intelligent, judicious, rational, reasonable, sagacious, sage, sober, sound, wise; observant, understanding; impressionable, sensitive.

sensitive *adj* perceptive, sentient; affected, impressible, impressionable, responsive, susceptible; delicate, tender, touchy.

sensual *adj* animal, bodily, carnal, voluptuous; gross, lascivious, lewd, licentious, unchaste.

sentence *vb* condemn, doom, judge. • *n* decision, determination, judgment, opinion, verdict; doctrine, dogma, opinion, tenet; condemnation, conviction, doom; period, proposition.

sententious *adj* compendious, compact, concise, didactic, laconic, pithy, pointed, succinct, terse.

sentiment *n* judgment, notion, opinion; maxim, saying; emotion, tenderness; disposition, feeling, thought.

sentimental *adj* impressible, impressionable, over-emotional, romantic, tender.

sentinel *n* guard, guardsman, patrol, picket, sentry, watchman.

separate *vb* detach, disconnect, disjoin, disunite, dissever, divide, divorce, part, sever, sunder; eliminate, remove, withdraw; cleave, open. • *adj* detached, disconnected, disjoined, disjointed, dissociated, disunited, divided, parted, severed; discrete, distinct, divorced, unconnected; alone, segregated, withdrawn.

separation *n* disjunction, disjuncture, dissociation; disconnection, disseverance, disseveration, disunion, division, divorce; analysis, decomposition.

sepulchral *adj* deep, dismal, funereal, gloomy, grave, hollow, lugubrious, melancholy, mournful, sad, sombre, woeful.

sepulchre *n* burial place, charnel house, grave, ossuary, sepulture, tomb.

sequel *n* close, conclusion, denouement, end, termination; consequence, event, issue, result, upshot.

sequence *n* following, graduation, progression, succession; arrangement, series, train.

sequestrated *adj* hidden, private, retired, secluded, unfrequented, withdrawn; seized.

seraphic *adj* angelic, celestial, heavenly, sublime; holy, pure, refined.

serene *adj* calm, collected, placid, peaceful, quiet, tranquil, sedate, undisturbed, unperturbed, unruffled; bright, calm, clear, fair, unclouded.

serenity *n* calm, calmness, collectedness, composure, coolness, imperturbability, peace, peacefulness, quiescence, sedateness, tranquillity; brightness, calmness, clearness, fairness, peace, quietness, stillness.

serf *n* bondman, servant, slave, thrall, villein.

serfdom *n* bondage, enslavement, enthralment, servitude, slavery, subjection, thraldom.

series *n* chain, concatenation, course, line, order, progression, sequence, succession, train.

serious *adj* earnest, grave, demure, pious, resolute, sedate, sober, solemn, staid, thoughtful; dangerous, great, important, momentous, weighty.

sermon *n* discourse, exhortation, homily, lecture.

serpentine *adj* anfractuous, convoluted, crooked, meandering, sinuous, spiral, tortuous, twisted, undulating, winding.

servant *n* attendant, dependant, factotum, helper, henchman, retainer, servitor, subaltern, subordinate, underling; domestic, drudge, flunky, lackey, menial, scullion, slave.

serve *vb* aid, assist, attend, help, minister, oblige, succour; advance, benefit, forward, promote; content, satisfy, supply; handle, officiate, manage, manipulate, work.

service *vb* check, maintain, overhaul, repair. • *n* labour, ministration, work; attendance, business, duty, employ, employment, office; advantage, benefit, good, gain, profit; avail, purpose, use, utility; ceremony, function, observance, rite, worship.

serviceable *adj* advantageous, available, beneficial, convenient, functional, handy, helpful, operative, profitable, useful.

servile *adj* dependent, menial; abject, base, beggarly, cringing, fawning, grovelling, low, mean, obsequious, slavish, sneaking, sycophantic, truckling.

servility *n* bondage, dependence, slavery; abjection, abjectness, baseness, fawning, meanness, obsequiousness, slavishness, sycophancy.

servitor *n* attendant, dependant, footman, lackey, retainer, servant, squire, valet, waiter.

servitude *n* bondage, enslavement, enthralment, serfdom, service, slavery, thraldom.

set[1] *vb* lay, locate, mount, place, put, stand, station; appoint, determine, establish, fix, settle; risk, stake, wager; adapt, adjust, regulate; adorn, stud, variegate; arrange, dispose, pose, post; appoint, assign, predetermine, prescribe; estimate, prize, rate, value; embarrass, perplex, pose; contrive, produce; decline, sink; congeal, concern, consolidate, harden, solidify; flow, incline, run, tend; (*with* **about**) begin, commence; (*with* **apart**) appropriate, consecrate, dedicate, devote, reserve, set aside; (*with* **aside**) abrogate, annul, omit, reject; reserve, set apart; (*with* **before**) display, exhibit; (*with* **down**) chronicle, jot down, record, register, state, write down; (*with* **forth**) display, exhibit, explain, expound, manifest, promulgate, publish, put forward, represent, show; (*with* **forward**) advance, further, promote; (*with* **free**) acquit, clear, emancipate, liberate, release; (*with* **off**) adorn, decorate, embellish; define, portion off; (*with* **on**) actuate, encourage, impel, influence, incite, instigate, prompt, spur, urge; attack, assault, set upon; (*with* **out**) display, issue, publish, proclaim, prove, recommend, show; (*with* **right**) correct, put in order; (*with* **to rights**) adjust, regulate; (*with* **up**) elevate, erect, exalt, raise; establish, found, institute; (*with* **upon**) assail, assault, attack, fly at, rush upon. • *adj* appointed, established, formal, ordained, prescribed, regular, settled; determined, fixed, firm, obstinate, positive, stiff, unyielding; immovable, predetermined; located, placed, put. • *n* attitude, position, posture; scene, scenery, setting.

set[2] *n* assortment, collection, suit; class, circle, clique, cluster, company, coterie, division, gang, group, knot, party, school, sect.

setback *n* blow, hitch, hold-up, rebuff; defeat, disappointment, reverse.

set-off *n* adornment, decoration, embellishment, ornament; counterbalance, counterclaim, equivalent.

settle *vb* adjust, arrange, compose, regulate; account, balance, close up, conclude, discharge, liquidate, pay, pay up, reckon, satisfy, square; allay, calm, compose, pacify, quiet, repose, rest, still, tranquillize; confirm, decide, determine, make clear; establish, fix, set; fall, gravitate, sink, subside; abide, colonize, domicile, dwell, establish, inhabit, people, place, plant, reside; (*with* **on**) determine on, fix on, fix upon; establish. • *n* bench, seat, stool.

settled *adj* established, fixed, stable; decided, deep-rooted, steady, unchanging; adjusted, arranged; methodical, orderly, quiet; common, customary, everyday, ordinary, usual, wonted.

set-to *n* combat, conflict, contest, fight.

sever *vb* divide, part, rend, separate, sunder; detach, disconnect, disjoin, disunite.

several *adj* individual, single, particular; distinct, exclusive, independent, separate; different, divers, diverse, manifold, many, sundry, various.

severance *n* partition, separation.

severe *adj* austere, bitter, dour, hard, harsh, inexorable, morose, painful, relentless, rigid, rigorous, rough, sharp, stern, stiff, strait-laced, unmitigated, unrelenting, unsparing; accurate, exact, methodical, strict; chaste, plain, restrained, simple, unadorned; biting, caustic, cruel, cutting, harsh, keen, sarcastic, satirical, trenchant; acute, afflictive, distressing, excruciating, extreme, intense, stringent, violent; critical, exact.

severity *n* austerity, gravity, harshness, rigour, seriousness, sternness, strictness; accuracy, exactness, niceness; chasteness, plainness, simplicity; acrimony, causticity, keenness, sharpness; afflictiveness, extremity, keenness, stringency, violence; cruelty.

sew *vb* baste, bind, hem, stitch, tack.

sex *n* gender, femininity, masculinity, sexuality; coitus, copulation, fornication, love-making.

shabby *adj* faded, mean, poor, ragged, seedy, threadbare, worn, worn-out; beggarly, mean, paltry, penurious, stingy, ungentlemanly, unhandsome.

shackle *vb* chain, fetter, gyve, hamper, manacle; bind, clog, confine, cumber, embarrass, encumber, impede, obstruct, restrict, trammel. • *n* chain, fetter, gyve, hamper, manacle.

shade *vb* cloud, darken, dim, eclipse, obfuscate, obscure; cover, ensconce, hide, protect, screen, shelter. • *n* darkness, dusk, duskiness, gloom, obscurity, shadow; cover, protection, shelter; awning, blind, curtain, screen, shutter, veil; degree, difference, kind, variety; cast, colour, complexion, dye, hue, tinge, tint, tone; apparition, ghost, manes, phantom, shadow, spectre, spirit.

shadow *vb* becloud, cloud, darken, obscure, shade; adumbrate, foreshadow, symbolize, typify; conceal, cover, hide, protect, screen, shroud. • *n* penumbra, shade, umbra, umbrage; darkness, gloom, obscurity; cover, protection, security, shelter; adumbration, foreshadowing, image, prefiguration, representation; apparition, ghost, phantom, shade, spirit; image, portrait, reflection, silhouette.

shadowy *adj* shady, umbrageous; dark, dim, gloomy, murky, obscure; ghostly, imaginary, impalpable, insubstantial, intangible, spectral, unreal, unsubstantial, visionary.

shady *adj* shadowy, umbrageous; crooked.

shaft *n* arrow, missile, weapon; handle, helve; pole, tongue; axis, spindle; pinnacle, spire; stalk, stem, trunk.

shaggy *adj* rough, rugged.

shake *vb* quake, quaver, quiver, shiver, shudder, totter, tremble; agitate, convulse, jar, jolt, stagger; daunt, frighten, intimidate; endanger, move, weaken; oscillate, vibrate, wave; move, put away, remove, throw off. • *n* agitation, concussion, flutter, jar, jolt, quaking, shaking, shivering, shock, trembling, tremor.

shaky *adj* jiggly, quaky, shaking, tottering, trembling.

shallow *adj* flimsy, foolish, frivolous, puerile, trashy, trifling, trivial; empty, ignorant, silly, slight, simple, superficial, unintelligent.

sham *vb* ape, feign, imitate, pretend; cheat, deceive, delude, dupe, impose, trick. • *adj* assumed, counterfeit, false, feigned, mock, make-believe, pretended, spurious. • *n* delusion, feint, fraud, humbug, imposition, imposture, pretence, trick.

shamble *vb* hobble, shuffle.

shambles *npl* abattoir, slaughterhouse; confusion, disorder, mess.

shame *vb* debase, degrade, discredit, disgrace, dishonour, stain, sully, taint, tarnish; abash, confound, confuse, discompose, disconcert, humble, humiliate; deride, flout, jeer, mock, ridicule, sneer. • *n* contempt, degradation, derision, discredit, disgrace, dishonour, disrepute, ignominy, infamy, obloquy, odium, opprobrium; abashment, chagrin, confusion, embarrassment, humiliation, mortification; reproach, scandal; decency, decorousness, decorum, modesty, propriety, seemliness.

shamefaced *adj* bashful, diffident, overmodest.

shameful *adj* atrocious, base, disgraceful, dishonourable, disreputable, heinous, ignominious, infamous, nefarious, opprobrious, outrageous, scandalous, vile, villainous, wicked; degrading, indecent, unbecoming.

shameless *adj* assuming, audacious, bold-faced, brazen, brazen-faced, cool, immodest, impudent, indecent, indelicate, insolent, unabashed, unblushing; abandoned, corrupt, depraved, dissolute, graceless, hardened, incorrigible, irreclaimable, lost, obdurate, profligate, reprobate, sinful, unprincipled, vicious.

shape *vb* create, form, make, produce; fashion, model, mould; adjust, direct, frame, regulate; conceive, conjure up, figure, image, imagine. • *n* appearance, aspect, fashion, figure, form, guise, make; build, cast, cut, model, mould, pattern; apparition, image.

shapeless *adj* amorphous, formless; grotesque, irregular, rude, uncouth, unsymmetrical.

shapely *adj* comely, symmetrical, trim, well-formed.

share *vb* apportion, distribute, divide, parcel out, portion, split; partake, participate; experience, receive. • *n* part, portion, quantum; allotment, allowance, contingent, deal, dividend, division, interest, lot, proportion, quantity, quota.

sharer *n* communicant, partaker, participator.

sharp *adj* acute, cutting, keen, keen-edged, knife-edged, razor-edged, trenchant; acuminate, needle-shaped, peaked, pointed, ridged; apt, astute, canny, clear-sighted, clever, cunning, discerning, discriminating, ingenious, inventive, keen-witted, penetrating, perspicacious, quick, ready, sagacious, sharp-witted, shrewd, smart, subtle, witty; acid, acrid, biting, bitter, burning, high-flavoured, high-seasoned, hot, mordacious, piquant, poignant, pungent, sour, stinging; acrimonious, biting, caustic, cutting, harsh, mordant, sarcastic, severe, tart, trenchant; cruel, hard, rigid; afflicting, distressing, excruciating, intense, painful, piercing, shooting, sore, violent; nipping, pinching; ardent, eager, fervid, fierce, fiery, impetuous, strong; high, screeching, shrill; attentive, vigilant; severe; close, exacting, shrewd, cold, crisp, freezing, icy wintry. • *adv* abruptly, sharply, suddenly; exactly, precisely, punctually.

sharp-cut *adj* clear, distinct, well-defined.

sharpen *vb* edge, intensify, point.

sharper *n* cheat, deceiver, defrauder, knave, rogue, shark, swindler, trickster.

sharply *adv* rigorously, roughly, severely; acutely, keenly; vehemently, violently; accurately, exactly, minutely, trenchantly, wittily; abruptly, steeply.

sharpness *n* acuteness, keenness, trenchancy; acuity, spinosity; acumen, cleverness, discernment, ingenuity, quickness, sagacity, shrewdness, smartness, wit; acidity, acridity, piquancy, pungency, sting, tartness; causticness, incisiveness, pungency, sarcasm, satire, severity; afflictiveness, intensity, painfulness, poignancy; ardour, fierceness, violence; discordance, dissonance, highness, screechiness, squeakiness, shrillness.

sharp-sighted *adj* clear-sighted, keen, keen-eyed, keen-sighted.

sharp-witted *adj* acute, clear-sighted, cunning, discerning, ingenious, intelligent, keen, keen-sighted, long-headed, quick, sagacious, sharp, shrewd.

shatter *vb* break, burst, crack, rend, shiver, smash, splinter, split; break up, derange, disorder, overthrow.

shave *vb* crop, cut off, mow, pare; slice; graze, skim, touch.

shaver *n* boy, child, youngster; bargainer, extortioner, sharper.

shear *vb* clip, cut, fleece, strip; divest; break off.

sheath *n* case, casing, covering, envelope, scabbard, sheathing.

sheathe *vb* case, cover, encase, enclose.

shed[1] *n* cabin, cot, hovel, hut, outhouse, shack, shelter.

shed[2] *vb* effuse, let fall, pour out, spill; diffuse, emit, give out, scatter, spread; cast, let fall, put off, slough, throw off.

sheen *n* brightness, gloss, glossiness, shine, spendour.

sheep *n* ewe, lamb, ram.

sheepish *adj* bashful, diffident, overmodest, shamefaced, timid, timorous.

sheer[1] *adj* perpendicular, precipitous, steep, vertical; clear, downright, mere, pure, simple, unadulterated, unmingled, unmixed, unqualified, utter; clear; fine, transparent. • *adv* outright; perpendicularly, steeply.

sheer[2] *vb* decline, deviate, move aside, swerve. • *n* bow, curve.

shelf *n* bracket, console, ledge, mantelpiece.

shell *vb* exfoliate, fall off, peel off; bombard. • *n* carapace, case, covering, shard; bomb, grenade, sharpnel; framework.

shelter *vb* cover, defend, ensconce, harbour, hide, house, protect, screen, shield, shroud. • *n* asylum, cover, covert, harbour, haven, hideaway, refuge, retreat, sanctuary; defence, protection, safety, screen, security, shield; guardian, protector.

shelve *vb* dismiss, put aside; incline, slope.

shepherd *vb* escort, guide, marshal, usher; direct, drive, drove, herd, lead; guard, tend, watch over. • *n* drover, grazier, herder, herdsman; chaplain, churchman, clergyman, cleric, divine, ecclesiastic, minister, padre, parson, pastor; chaperon, duenna, escort, guide, squire, usher.

shield *vb* cover, defend, guard, protect, shelter; repel, ward off; avert, forbid, forfend. • *n* aegis, buckler, escutcheon, scutcheon, targe; bulwark, cover, defence, guard, palladium, protection, rampart, safeguard, security, shelter.

shift *vb* alter, change, fluctuate, move, vary; chop, dodge, swerve, veer; contrive, devise, manage, plan, scheme, shuffle. • *n* change, substitution, turn; contrivance, expedient, means, resort, resource; artifice, craft, device, dodge, evasion, fraud, mask, ruse, stratagem, subterfuge, trick, wile; chemise, smock.

shiftless *adj* improvident, imprudent, negligent, slack, thriftless, unresourceful.

shifty *adj* tricky, undependable, wily.

shillyshally *vb* hesitate, waver. • *n* hesitation, irresolute, wavering.

shimmer *vb* flash, glimmer, glisten, shine. • *n* blink, glimmer, glitter, twinkle.

shin *vb* climb, swarm. • *n* shinbone, tibia.

shindy *n* disturbance, riot, roughhouse, row, spree, uproar.

shine *vb* beam, blaze, coruscate, flare, give light, glare, gleam, glimmer, glisten, glitter, glow, lighten, radiate, sparkle; excel. • *n* brightness, brilliancy, glaze, gloss, polish, sheen.

shining *adj* beaming, bright, brilliant, effulgent, gleaming, glowing, glistening, glittering, luminous, lustrous, radiant, resplendent, splendid; conspicuous, distinguished, illustrious.

shiny *adj* bright, clear, luminous, sunshiny, unclouded; brilliant, burnished, glassy, glossy, polished.

ship *n* boat, craft, steamer, vessel.

shipshape *adj* neat, orderly, tidy, trim, well-arranged.

shipwreck *vb* cast away, maroon, strand, wreck. • *n* demolition, destruction, miscarriage, overthrow, perdition, ruin, subversion, wreck.

shirk *vb* avoid, dodge, evade, malinger, quit, slack; cheat, shark, trick.

shiver[1] *vb* break, shatter, splinter. • *n* bit, fragment, piece, slice, sliver, splinter.

shiver[2] *vb* quake, quiver, shake, shudder, tremble. • *n* shaking, shivering, shuddering, tremor.

shivery[1] *adj* brittle, crumbly, frangible, friable, shatterable, splintery.

shivery[2] *adj* quaking, quavering, quivering, shaky, trembly, tremulous; chilly, shivering.

shoal[1] *vb* crowd, throng. • *n* crowd, horde, multitude, swarm, throng.

shoal[2] *n* sandbank, shallows; danger.

shock *vb* appall, horrify; disgust, disquiet, disturb, nauseate, offend, outrage, revolt, scandalize, sicken; astound, stagger, stun; collide with, jar, jolt, shake, strike against; encounter, meet. • *n* agitation, blow, offence, stroke, trauma; assault, brunt, conflict; clash, collision, concussion, impact, percussion.

shocking *adj* abominable, detestable, disgraceful, disgusting, execrable, foul, hateful, loathsome, obnoxious, odious, offensive, repugnant, repulsive, revolting; appalling, awful, dire, dreadful, fearful, frightful, ghastly, hideous, horrible, horrid, horrific, monstrous, terrible.

shoot *vb* catapult, expel, hurl, let fly, propel; discharge, fire, let off; dart, fly, pass, pelt; extend, jut, project, protrude, protuberate, push, put forth, send forth, stretch; bud, germinate, sprout; (*with* **up**) grow increase, spring up, run up, start up. • *n* branch, offshoot, scion, sprout, twig.

shop *n* emporium, market, mart, store; workshop.

shore[1] *n* beach, brim, coast, seaboard, seaside, strand, waterside.

shore[2] *vb* brace, buttress, prop, stay, support. • *n* beam, brace, buttress, prop, stay, support.

shorn *adj* cut-off; deprived.

short *adj* brief, curtailed; direct, near, straight; compendious, concise, condensed, laconic, pithy, terse, sententious, succinct, summary; abrupt, curt, petulant, pointed, sharp, snappish, uncivil; defective, deficient, inadequate, insufficient, niggardly, scanty, scrimpy; contracted, desitute, lacking, limited, minus, wanting; dwarfish, squat, undersized; brittle, crisp, crumbling, friable. • *adv* abruptly, at once, forthwith, suddenly.

shortcoming *n* defect, deficiency, delinquency, error, failing, failure, fault, imperfection, inadequacy, remissness, slip, weakness.

shorten *vb* abbreviate, abridge, curtail, cut short; abridge, contract, diminish, lessen, retrench, reduce; cut off, dock, lop, trim; confine, hinder, restrain, restrict.

shortening *n* abbreviation, abridgment, contraction, curtailment, diminution, retrenchment, reduction.

shorthand *n* brachygraphy, stenography, tachygraphy.

short-lived *adj* emphemeral, transient, transitory.

shortly *adv* quickly, soon; briefly, concisely, succinctly, tersely.

short-sighted *adj* myopic, nearsighted, purblind; imprudent, indiscreet.

shot[1] *n* discharge; ball, bullet, missile, projectile; marksman, shooter.

shot[2] *adj* chatoyant, iridescent, irisated, moiré, watered; intermingled, interspersed, interwoven.

shoulder *vb* bear, bolster, carry, hump, maintain, pack, support, sustain, tote; crowd, elbow, jostle, press forward, push, thrust. • *n* projection, protuberance.

shoulder blade *n* blade bone, omoplate, scapula, shoulder bone.

shout *vb* bawl, cheer, clamour, exclaim, halloo, roar, vociferate, whoop, yell. • *n* cheer, clamour, exclamation, halloo, hoot, huzza, outcry, roar, vociferation, whoop, yell.

shove *vb* jostle, press against, propel, push, push aside; (*with* **off**) push away, thrust away.

show *vb* blazon, display, exhibit, flaunt, parade, present; indicate, mark, point out; disclose, discover, divulge, explain, make clear, make known, proclaim, publish, reveal, unfold; demonstrate, evidence, manifest, prove, verify; conduct, guide, usher; direct, inform, instruct, teach; expound, elucidate, interpret; (*with* **off**) display, exhibit, make a show, set off; (*with* **up**) expose. • *n* array, exhibition, representation, sight, spectacle; blazonry, bravery, ceremony, dash, demonstration, display, flourish, ostentation, pageant, pageantry, parade, pomp, splendour, splurge; likeness, resemblance, semblance; affectation, appearance, colour, illusion, mask, plausibility, pose, pretence, pretext, simulation, speciousness; entertainment, production.

showy *adj* bedizened, dressy, fine, flashy, flaunting, garish, gaudy, glaring, gorgeous, loud, ornate, smart, swanky, splendid; grand, magnificent, ostentatious, pompous, pretentious, stately, sumptuous.

shred *vb* tear. • *n* bit, fragment, piece, rag, scrap, strip, tatter.

shrew *n* brawler, fury, scold, spitfire, termagant, virago, vixen.

shrewd *adj* arch, artful, astute, crafty, cunning, Machiavellian, sly, subtle, wily; acute, astute, canny, discerning, discriminating, ingenious, keen, knowing, penetrating, sagacious, sharp, sharp-sighted.

shrewdness *n* address, archness, art, artfulness, astuteness, craft, cunning, policy, skill, slyness, subtlety; acumen, acuteness, discernment, ingenuity, keenness, penetration, perspicacity, sagacity, sharpness, wit.

shrewish *adj* brawling, clamorous, froward, peevish, petulant, scolding, vixenish.

shriek *vb* scream, screech, squeal, yell, yelp. • *n* cry, scream, screech, yell.

shrill *adj* acute, high, high-toned, high-pitched, piercing, piping, sharp.

shrine *n* reliquary, sacred tomb; altar, hallowed place, sacred place.

shrink *vb* contract, decrease, dwindle, shrivel, wither; balk, blench, draw back, flinch, give way, quail, recoil, retire, swerve, wince, withdraw.

shrivel *vb* dry, dry up, parch; contract, decrease, dwindle, shrink, wither, wrinkle.

shroud *vb* bury, cloak, conceal, cover, hide, mask, muffle, protect, screen, shelter, veil. • *n* covering, garment; grave clothes, winding sheet.

shrub *n* bush, dwarf tree, low tree.

shrubby *adj* bushy.

shudder *vb* quake, quiver, shake, shiver, tremble. • *n* shaking, shuddering, trembling, tremor.

shuffle *vb* confuse, disorder, intermix, jumble, mix, shift; cavil, dodge, equivocate, evade, prevaricate, quibble, vacillate; struggle. • *n* artifice, cavil, evasion, fraud, pretence, pretext, prevarication, quibble, ruse, shuffling, sophism, subterfuge, trick.

shun *vb* avoid, elude, eschew, escape, evade, get clear of.

shut *vb* close, close up, stop; confine, coop up, enclose, imprison, lock up, shut up; (*with* **in**) confine, enclose; (*with* **off**) bar, exclude, intercept; (*with* **up**) close up, shut; confine, enclose, fasten in, imprison, lock in, lock up.

shy *vb* cast, chuck, fling, hurl, jerk, pitch, sling, throw, toss; boggle, sheer, start aside. • *adj* bashful, coy, diffident, reserved, retiring, sheepish, shrinking, timid; cautious, chary, distrustful, heedful, wary. • *n* start; fling, throw.

sibilant *adj* buzzing, hissing, sibilous.

sick *adj* ailing, ill, indisposed, laid-up, unwell, weak; nauseated, queasy; disgusted, revolted, tired, weary; diseased, distempered, disordered, feeble, morbid, unhealthy, unsound, weak; languishing, longing, pining.

sicken *vb* ail, disease, fall sick, make sick; nauseate; disgust, weary; decay, droop, languish, pine.

sickening *adj* nauseating, nauseous, palling, sickish; disgusting, distasteful, loathsome, offensive, repulsive, revolting.

sickly *adj* ailing, diseased, faint, feeble, infirm, languid, languishing, morbid, unhealthy, valetudinary, weak, weakly.

sickness *n* ail, ailment, complaint, disease, disorder, distemper, illness, indisposition, invalidism, malady, morbidity; nausea, qualmishness, queasiness.

side *vb* border, bound, edge, flank, frontier, march, rim, skirt, verge; avert, turn aside; (*with* **with**) befriend, favour, flock to, join with, second, support. • *adj* flanking, later, skirting; indirect, oblique; extra, odd, off, spare. • *n* border, edge, flank, margin, verge; cause, faction, interest, party, sect.

sideboard *n* buffet, dresser.

side by side abreast, alongside, by the side.

sidelong *adj* lateral, oblique. • *adv* laterally, obliquely; on the side.

sidewalk *n* footpath, footway, pavement.

sideways, sidewise *adv* laterally. • *adv* athwart, crossways, crosswise, laterally, obliquely, sidelong, sidewards.

siesta *n* doze, nap.

sift *vb* part, separate; bolt, screen, winnow; analyse, canvass, discuss, examine, fathom, follow up, inquire into, investigate, probe, scrutinze, sound, try.

sigh *vb* complain, grieve, lament, mourn. • *n* long breath, sough, suspiration.

sight *vb* get sight of, perceive, see. • *n* cognizance, ken, perception, view; beholding, eyesight, seeing, vision; exhibition, prospect, representation, scene, show, spectacle, wonder; consideration, estimation, knowledge; examination, inspection.

sightless *adj* blind, eyeless, unseeing.

sightly *adj* beautiful, comely, handsome.

sign *vb* indicate, signal, signify; countersign, endorse, subscribe. • *n* emblem, index, indication, manifestation, mark, note, proof, signal, signification, symbol, symptom, token; beacon; augury, auspice, foreboding, miracle, omen, portent, presage, prodigy, prognostic, wonder; type; countersign, password.

signal *vb* flag, glance, hail, nod, nudge, salute, sign, signalize, sound, speak, touch, wave, wink. • *adj* conspicuous, eminent, extraordinary, memorable, notable, noteworthy, remarkable. • *n* cue, indication, mark, sign, token.

signalize *vb* celebrate, distinguish, make memorable.

signature *n* mark, sign, stamp; autograph, hand.

significance *n* implication, import, meaning, purport, sense; consequence, importance, moment, portent, weight; emphasis, energy, expressiveness, force, impressiveness.

significant *adj* betokening, expressive, indicative, significative, signifying; important, material, momentous, portentous, weighty; forcible, emphatic, expressive, telling.

signification *n* expression; acceptation, import, meaning, purport, sense.

signify *vb* betoken, communication, express, indicate, intimate; denote, imply, import, mean, purport, suggest; announce, declare, give notice of, impart, make known, manifest, proclaim, utter; augur, foreshadow, indicate, portend, represent; matter, weigh.

silence *vb* hush, muzzle, still; allay, calm, quiet. • *interj* be silent, be still, hush, soft, tush, tut, whist. • *n* calm, hush, lull, noiselessness, peace, quiet, quietude, soundlessness, stillness; dumbness, mumness, muteness, reticence, speechlessness, taciturnity.

silent *adj* calm, hushed, noiseless, quiet, soundless, still; dumb, inarticulate, mum, mute, nonvocal, speechless, tacit; reticent, taciturn, uncommunicative.

silken *adj* flossy, silky, soft.

silkiness *n* smoothness, softness.

silly *adj* brainless, childish, foolish, inept, senseless, shallow, simple, stupid, weak-minded, witless; absurd, extravagant, frivolous, imprudent, indiscreet, nonsensical, preposterous, trifling, unwise. • *n* ass, duffer, goose, idiot, simpleton.

silt *n* alluvium, deposit, deposition, residue, settlement, settlings, sediment.

silver *adj* argent, silvery; bright, silvery, white; clear, mellifluous, soft.

similar *adj* analogous, duplicate, like, resembling, twin; homogeneous, uniform.

similarity *n* agreement, analogy, correspondence, likeness, parallelism, parity, resemblance, sameness, semblance, similitude.

simile *n* comparison, metaphor, similitude.

similitude *n* image, likeness, resemblance; comparison, metaphor, simile.

simmer *vb* boil, bubble, seethe, stew.

simper *vb* smile, smirk.

simple *adj* bare, elementary, homogeneous, incomplex, mere, single, unalloyed, unblended, uncombined, uncompounded, unmingled, unmixed; chaste, plain, homespun, inornate, natural, neat, unadorned, unaffected, unembellished, unpretentious, unstudied, unvarnished; artless, downright, frank, guileless, inartificial, ingenuous, naive, open, simple-hearted, simple-minded, sincere, single-minded, straightforward, true, unconstrained, undesigning, unsophisticated; credulous, fatuous, foolish, shallow, silly, unwise, weak; clear, intelligible, understandable, uninvolved, unmistakable.

simple-hearted *adj* artless, frank, ingenuous, open, simple, single-hearted.

simpleton *n* fool, greenhorn, nincompoop, ninny.

simplicity *n* chasteness, homeliness, naturalness, neatness, plainness; artlessness, frankness, naivety, openness, simplesse, sincerity; clearness; gullibility, folly, silliness, weakness.

simply *adv* artlessly, plainly, sincerely, unaffectedly; barely, merely, of itself, solely; absolutely, alone.

simulate *vb* act, affect, ape, assume, counterfeit, dissemble, feign, mimic, pretend, sham.

simulation *n* counterfeiting, feigning, personation, pretence.

simultaneous *adj* coeval, coincident, concomitant, concurrent, contemporaneous, synchronous.

sin *vb* do wrong, err, transgress, trespass. • *n* delinquency, depravity, guilt, iniquity, misdeed, offence, transgression, unrighteousness, wickedness, wrong.

since *conj* as, because, considering, seeing that. • *adv* ago, before this; from that time. • *prep* after, from the time of, subsequently to.

sincere *adj* pure, unmixed; genuine, honest, inartificial, real, true, unaffected, unfeigned, unvarnished; artless, candid, direct, frank, guileless, hearty, honest, ingenuous, open, plain, single, straightforward, truthful, undissembling, upright, whole-hearted.

sincerity *n* artlessness, candour, earnestness, frankness, genuineness, guilelessness, honesty, ingenuousness, probity, truth, truthfulness, unaffectedness, veracity.

sinew *n* ligament, tendon; brawn, muscle, nerve, strength.

sinewy *adj* able-bodied, brawny, firm, Herculean, muscular, nervous, powerful, robust, stalwart, strapping, strong, sturdy, vigorous, wiry.

sinful *adj* bad, criminal, depraved, immoral, iniquitous, mischievous, peccant, transgressive, unholy, unrighteous, wicked, wrong.

sinfulness *n* corruption, criminality, depravity, iniquity, irreligion, ungodliness, unholiness, unrighteousness, wickedness.

sing *vb* cantillate, carol, chant, hum, hymn, intone, lilt, troll, warble, yodel.

singe *vb* burn, scorch, sear.

singer *n* cantor, caroler, chanter, gleeman, prima donna, minstrel, psalmodist, songster, vocalist.

single *vb* (*with* **out**) choose, pick, select, single. • *adj* alone, isolated, one only, sole, solitary; individual, particular, separate; celibate, unmarried, unwedded; pure, simple, uncompounded, unmixed; honest, ingenuous, sincere, unbiased, uncorrupt, upright.

single-handed *adj* alone, by one's self, unaided, unassisted.

single-minded *adj* artless, candid, guileless, ingenuous, sincere.

singleness *n* individuality, unity; purity, simplicity; ingenuousness, integrity, sincerity, uprightness.

singular *adj* eminent, exceptional, extraordinary, rare, remarkable, strange, uncommon, unusual, unwonted; particular, unexampled, unparalleled, unprecedented; unaccountable, bizarre, curious, eccentric, fantastic, odd, peculiar, queer; individual, single; not complex, single, uncompounded, unique.

singularity *n* aberration, abnormality, irregularity, oddness, rareness, rarity, strangeness, uncommonness; characteristic, idiosyncrasy, individuality, particularity, peculiarity; eccentricity, oddity.

sinister *adj* baleful, injurious, untoward; boding ill, inauspicious, ominous, unlucky; left, on the left hand.

sink *vb* droop, drop, fall, founder, go down, submerge, subside; enter, penetrate; collapse, fail; decay, decline, decrease, dwindle, give way, languish, lose strength; engulf, immerse, merge, submerge, submerse; dig, excavate, scoop out; abase, bring down, crush, debase, degrade, depress, diminish, lessen, lower, overbear; destroy, overthrow, overwhelm, reduce, ruin, swamp, waste. • *n* basin, cloaca, drain.

sinless *adj* faultless, guiltless, immaculate, impeccable, innocent, spotless, unblemished, undefiled, unspotted, unsullied, untarnished.

sinner *n* criminal, delinquent, evildoer, offender, reprobate, wrongdoer.

sinuosity *n* crook, curvature, flexure, sinus, tortuosity, winding.

sinuous *adj* bending, crooked, curved, curvilinear, flexuous, serpentine, sinuate, sinuated, tortuous, undulating, wavy, winding.

sip *vb* drink, suck up, sup; absorb, drink in. • *n* small draught, taste.

sire *vb* father, reproduce; author, breed, conceive, create, generate, originate, produce, propagate. • *n* father, male parent, progenitor; man, male person; sir, sirrah; author, begetter, creator, father, generator, originator.

siren *adj* alluring, bewitching, fascinating, seducing, tempting. • *n* mermaid; charmer, Circe, seducer, seductress, tempter, temptress.

sit *vb* be, remain, repose, rest, stay; bear on, lie, rest; abide, dwell, settle; perch; brood, incubate; become, be suited, fit.

site *vb* locate, place, position, situate, station. • *n* ground, locality, location, place, position, seat, situation, spot, station, whereabouts.

sitting *n* meeting, session.

situation *n* ground, locality, location, place, position, seat, site, spot, whereabouts; case, category, circumstances, condition, juncture, plight, predicament, state; employment, office, place, post, station.

size *n* amplitude, bigness, bulk, dimensions, expanse, greatness, largeness, magnitude, mass, volume.

skeleton *n* framework; draft, outline, sketch.

sketch *vb* design, draft, draw out; delineate, depict, paint, portray, represent. • *n* delineation, design, draft, drawing, outline, plan, skeleton.

sketchy *adj* crude, incomplete, unfinished.

skilful *adj* able, accomplished, adept, adroit, apt, clever, competent, conversant, cunning, deft, dexterous, dextrous, expert, handy, ingenious, masterly, practised, proficient, qualified, quick, ready, skilled, trained, versed, well-versed.

skill *n* ability, address, adroitness, aptitude, aptness, art, cleverness, deftness, dexterity, expertise, expertness, facility, ingenuity, knack, quickness, readiness, skilfulness; discernment, discrimination, knowledge, understanding, wit.

skim *vb* brush, glance, graze, kiss, scrape, scratch, sweep, touch lightly; coast, flow, fly, glide, sail, scud, whisk; dip into, glance at, scan, skip, thumb over, touch upon.

skin *vb* pare, peel; decorticate, excoriate, flay. • *n* cuticle, cutis, derm, epidermis, hide, integument, pellicle, pelt; hull, husk, peel, rind.

skinflint *n* churl, curmudgeon, lickpenny, miser, niggard, scrimp.

skinny *adj* emaciated, lank, lean, poor, shrivelled, shrunk, thin.

skip *vb* bound, caper, frisk, gambol, hop, jump, leap, spring; disregard, intermit, miss, neglect, omit, pass over, skim. • *n* bound, caper, frisk, gambol, hop, jump, leap, spring.

skirmish *vb* battle, brush, collide, combat, contest, fight, scuffle, tussle. • *n* affair, affray, battle, brush, collision, combat, conflict, contest, encounter, fight, scuffle, tussle.

skirt *vb* border, bound, edge, fringe, hem, march, rim; circumnavigate, circumvent, flank, go along. • *n* border, boundary, edge, margin, rim, verge; flap, kilt, overskirt, petticoat.

skittish *adj* changeable, fickle, inconstant; hasty, volatile, wanton; shy, timid, timorous.

skulk *vb* hide, lurk, slink, sneak.

skulker *n* lurker, sneak; shirk, slacker, malingerer.

skull *n* brain pan, cranium.

sky *n* empyrean, firmament, heaven, heavens, welkin.

sky-blue *adj* azure, cerulean, sapphire, sky-coloured.

skylarking *n* carousing, frolicking, sporting.

slab *adj* slimy, thick, viscous. • *n* beam, board, layer, panel, plank, slat, table, tablet; mire, mud, puddle, slime.

slabber *vb* drivel, slaver, slobber; drop, let fall, shed, spill.

slack *vb* ease off, let up; abate, ease up, relax, slacken; malinger, shirk; choke, damp, extinguish, smother, stifle. • *adj* backward, careless, inattentive, lax, negligent, remiss; abated, dilatory, diminished, lingering, slow, tardy; loose, relaxed; dull, idle, inactive, quiet, sluggish. • *n* excess, leeway, looseness, play; coal dust, culm, residue.

slacken *vb* abate, diminish, lessen, lower, mitigate, moderate, neglect, remit, relieve, retard, slack; loosen, relax; flag, slow down; bridle, check, control, curb, repress, restrain.

slackness *n* looseness; inattention, negligence, remissness; slowness, tardiness.

slander *vb* asperse, backbite, belie, brand, calumniate, decry, defame, libel, malign, reproach, scandalize, traduce, vilify; detract from, disparage. • *n* aspersion, backbiting, calumny, defamation, detraction, libel, obloquy, scandal, vilification.

slanderous *adj* calumnious, defamatory, false, libellous, malicious, maligning.

slang *n* argo, cant, jargon, lingo.

slant *vb* incline, lean, lie obliquely, list, slope. • *n* inclination, slope, steep, tilt.

slap *vb* dab, clap, pat, smack, spank, strike. • *adv* instantly, quickly, plumply. • *n* blow, clap.

slapdash *adv* haphazardly, hurriedly, precipitately.

slash *vb* cut, gash, slit. • *n* cut, gash, slit.

slashed *adj* cut, slit; (*bot*) jagged, laciniate, multifid.

slattern *adj* slatternly, slovenly, sluttish. • *n* drab, slut, sloven, trollop.

slatternly *adj* dirty, slattern, slovenly, sluttish, unclean, untidy. • *adv* carelessly, negligently, sluttishly.

slaughter *vb* butcher, kill, massacre, murder, slay. • *n* bloodshed, butchery, carnage, havoc, killing, massacre, murder, slaying.

slaughterer *n* assassin, butcher, cutthroat, destroyer, killer, murderer, slayer.

slave *vb* drudge, moil, toil. • *n* bondmaid, bondservant, bondslave, bondman, captive, dependant, henchman, helot, peon, serf, thrall, vassal, villein; drudge, menial.

slavery *n* bondage, bond-service, captivity, enslavement, enthralment, serfdom, servitude, thraldom, vassalage, villeinage; drudgery, mean labour.

slavish *adj* abject, beggarly, base, cringing, fawning, grovelling, low, mean, obsequious, servile, sycophantic; drudging, laborious, menial, servile.

slay *vb* assassinate, butcher, dispatch, kill, massacre, murder, slaughter; destroy, ruin.

slayer *n* assassin, destroyer, killer, murderer, slaughterer.

sledge *n* drag, sled; cutter, pung, sleigh.

sleek *adj* glossy, satin, silken, silky, smooth.

sleekly *adv* evenly, glossily, nicely, smoothly.

sleep *vb* catnap, doze, drowse, nap, slumber. • *n* dormancy, hypnosis, lethargy, repose, rest, slumber.

sleeping *adj* dormant, inactive, quiescent.

sleepwalker *n* night-walker, noctambulist, somnambulist.

sleepwalking *n* somnambulism.

sleepy *adj* comatose, dozy, drowsy, heavy, lethargic, nodding, somnolent; narcotic, opiate, slumberous, somniferous, somnific, soporiferous, soporific; dull, heavy, inactive, lazy, slow, sluggish, torpid.

sleight *n* adroitness, dexterity, manoeuvring.

sleight of hand *n* conjuring, hocus-pocus, jugglery, legerdemain, prestdigitation.

slender *adj* lank, lithe, narrow, skinny, slim, spindly, thin; feeble, fine, flimsy, fragile, slight, tenuous, weak; inconsiderable, moderate, small, trivial; exiguous, inadequate, insufficient, lean, meagre, pitiful, scanty; abstemious, light, simple, spare, sparing.

slice *vb* cut, divide, part, section; cut off, sever. • *n* chop, collop, piece.

slick *adj* glassy, glossy, polished, sleek, smooth; alert, clever, cunning, shrewd, slippery, unctuous. *vb* burnish, gloss, lacquer, polish, shine, sleek, varnish; grease, lubricate, oil.

slide *vb* glide, move smoothly, slip. • *n* glide, glissade, skid, slip.

sliding *adj* gliding, slippery, uncertain. • *n* backsliding, falling, fault, lapse, transgression.

slight *vb* cold-shoulder, disdain, disregard, neglect, snub; overlook; scamp, skimp, slur. • *adj* inconsiderable, insignificant, little, paltry, petty, small, trifling, trivial, unimportant, unsubstantial; delicate, feeble, frail, gentle, weak; careless, cursory, desultory, hasty, hurried, negligent, scanty, superficial; flimsy, perishable; slender, slim. • *n* discourtesy, disregard, disrespect, inattention, indignity, neglect.

slightingly *adv* contemptuously, disrespectfully, scornfully, slightly.

slightly *adv* inconsiderably, little, somewhat; feebly, slenderly, weakly; cursorily, hastily, negligently, superficially.

slim *vb* bant, diet, lose weight, reduce, slenderize. • *adj* gaunt, lank, lithe, narrow, skinny, slender, spare; inconsiderable, paltry, poor, slight, trifling, trivial, unsubstantial, weak; insufficient, meagre.

slime *n* mire, mud, ooze, sludge.

slimy *adj* miry, muddy, oozy; clammy, gelatinous, glutinous, gummy, lubricious, mucilaginous, mucous, ropy, slabby, viscid, viscous.

sling *vb* cast, fling, hurl, throw; hang up, suspend.

slink *vb* skulk, slip away, sneak, steal away.

slip *vb* glide, slide; err, mistake, trip; lose, omit; disengage, throw off; escape, let go, loose, loosen, release, . • *n* glide, slide, slipping; blunder, lapse, misstep, mistake, oversight, peccadillo, trip; backsliding, error, fault, impropriety, indiscretion, transgression; desertion, escape; cord, leash, strap, string; case, covering, wrapper.

slippery *adj* glib, slithery, smooth; changeable, insecure, mutable, perilous, shaky, uncertain, unsafe, unstable, unsteady; cunning, dishonest, elusive, faithless, false, knavish, perfidious, shifty, treacherous.

slipshod *adj* careless, shuffling, slovenly, untidy.

slit *vb* cut; divide, rend, slash, split, sunder. • *n* cut, gash.

slobber *vb* drivel, drool, slabber, slaver; daub, obscure, smear, stain.

slobbery *adj* dank, floody, moist, muddy, sloppy, wet.

slope *vb* incline, slant, tilt. • *n* acclivity, cant, declivity, glacis, grade, gradient, incline, inclination, obliquity, pitch, ramp.

sloping *adj* aslant, bevelled, declivitous, inclining, oblique, shelving, slanting.

sloppy *adj* muddy, plashy, slabby, slobbery, splashy, wet.

sloth *n* dilatoriness, slowness, tardiness; idleness, inaction, inactivity, indolence, inertness, laziness, lumpishness, slothfulness, sluggishness, supineness, torpor.

slothful *adj* dronish, idle, inactive, indolent, inert, lazy, lumpish, slack, sluggish, supine, torpid.

slouch *vb* droop, loll, slump; shamble, shuffle. • *n* malingerer, shirker, slacker; shamble, shuffle, stoop.

slouching *adj* awkward, clownish, loutish, lubberly, uncouth, ungainly.

slough[1] *n* bog, fen, marsh, morass, quagmire; dejection, depression, despondence, despondency.

slough[2] *vb* cast, desquamate, excuviate, moult, shed, throw off; cast off, discard, divest, jettison, reject. • *n* cast, desquamation.

sloven *n* slattern, slob, slouch, slut.

slovenly *adj* unclean, untidy; blowsy, disorderly, dowdy, frowsy, loose, slatternly, tacky, unkempt, untidy; careless, heedless, lazy, negligent, perfunctory.

slow *vb* abate, brake, check, decelerate, diminish, lessen, mitigate, moderate, modulate, reduce, weaken; delay,detain, retard; ease, ease up, relax, slack, slacken, slack off. • *adj* deliberate, gradual; dead, dull, heavy, inactive, inert, sluggish, stupid; behindhand, late, tardy, unready; delaying, dilatory, lingering, slack.

sludge *n* mire, mud; slosh, slush.

sluggard *n* dawdler, drone, idler, laggard, lounger, slug.

sluggish *adj* dronish, drowsy, idle, inactive, indolent, inert, languid, lazy, listless, lumpish, phlegmatic, slothful, torpid; slow; dull, stupid, supine, tame.

sluice *vb* drain, drench, flood, flush, irrigate. • *n* floodgate, opening, vent.

slumber *vb* catnap, doze, nap, repose, rest, sleep. • *n* catnap, doze, nap, repose, rest, siesta, sleep.

slumberous *adj* drowsy, sleepy, somniferous, somnific, soporific.

slump *vb* droop, drop, fall, flop, founder, sag, sink, sink down; decline, depreciate, deteriorate, ebb, fail, fall away, lose ground, recede, slide, slip, subside, wane. • *n* droop, drop, fall, flop, lowering, sag, sinkage; decline, depreciation, deterioration, downturn, downtrend, subsidence, ebb, falling off, wane; crash, recession, smash.

slur *vb* asperse, calumniate, disparage, depreciate, reproach, traduce; conceal, disregard, gloss over, obscure, pass over, slight. • *n* mark, stain; brand, disgrace, reproach, stain, stigma; innuendo.

slush *n* slosh, sludge.

slushy *vb* plashy, sloppy, sloshy, sludgy.

slut *n* drab, slattern, sloven, trollop.

sluttish *adj* careless, dirty, disorderly, unclean, untidy.

sly *adj* artful, crafty, cunning, insidious, subtle, wily; astute, cautious, shrewd; arch, knowing, clandestine, secret, stealthy, underhand.

smack[1] *vb* smell, taste. • *n* flavour, savour, tang, taste, tincture; dash, infusion, little, space, soupçon, sprinkling, tinge, touch; smattering.

smack[2] *vb* slap, strike; crack, slash, snap; buss, kiss. • *n* crack, slap, slash, snap; buss, kiss.

small *adj* diminutive, Lilliputian, little, miniature, petite, pygmy, tiny, wee; infinitesimal, microscopic, minute; inappreciable, inconsiderable, insignificant, petty, trifling, trivial, unimportant; moderate, paltry, scanty, slender; faint, feeble, puny, slight, weak; illiberal, mean, narrow, narrow-minded, paltry, selfish, sorded, ungenerous, unworthy.

small talk *n* chat, conversation, gossip.

smart[1] *vb* hurt, pain, sting; suffer. • *adj* keen, painful, poignant, pricking, pungent, severe, sharp, stinging.

smart[2] *adj* active, agile, brisk, fresh, lively, nimble, quick, spirited, sprightly, spry; effective, efficient, energetic, forcible, vigorous; adroit, alert, clever, dexterous, dextrous, expert, intelligent, stirring; acute, apt, pertinent, ready, witty; chic, dapper, fine, natty, showy, spruce, trim.

smartness *n* acuteness, keenness, poignancy, pungency, severity, sharpness; efficiency, energy, force, vigour; activity, agility, briskness, liveliness, nimbleness, sprightliness, spryness, vivacity; alertness, cleverness, dexterity, expertise, expertness, intelligence, quickness; acuteness, aptness, pertinency, wit, wittiness; chic, nattiness, spruceness, trimness.

smash *vb* break, crush, dash, mash, shatter. • *n* crash, debacle, destruction, ruin; bankruptcy, failure.

smattering *n* dabbling, smatter, sprinkling.

smear *vb* bedaub, begrime, besmear, daub, plaster, smudge; contaminate, pollute, smirch, smut, soil, stain, sully, tarnish. • *n* blot, blotch, daub, patch, smirch, smudge, spot, stain; calumny, defamation, libel, slander.

smell *vb* scent, sniff, stench, stink. • *n* aroma, bouquet, fragrance, fume, odour, perfume, redolence, scent, stench, stink; sniff, snuff.

smelt *vb* fuse, melt.

smile *vb* grin, laugh, simper, smirk. • *n* grin, simper, smirk.

smite *vb* beat, box, collide, cuff, knock, strike, wallop, whack; destroy, kill, slay; afflict, chasten, punish; blast, destroy.

smitten *adj* attracted, captivated, charmed, enamoured, fascinated, taken; destroyed, killed, slain; smit, struck; afflicted, chastened, punished.

smock *n* chemise, shift, slip; blouse, gaberdine.

smoke *vb* emit, exhale, reek, steam; fumigate, smudge; discover, find out, smell out. • *n* effluvium, exhalation, fume, mist, reek, smother, steam, vapour; fumigation, smudge.

smoky *adj* fuliginous, fumid, fumy, smudgy; begrimed, blackened, dark, reeky, sooty, tanned.

smooth *vb* flatten, level, plane; ease, lubricate; extenuate, palliate, soften; allay, alleviate, assuage, calm, mitigate, mollify. • *adj* even, flat, level, plane, polished, unruffled, unwrinkled; glabrous, glossy, satiny, silky, sleek, soft, velvet; euphonious, flowing, liquid, mellifluent; fluent, glib, voluble; bland, flattering, ingratiating, insinuating, mild, oily, smooth-tongued, soothing, suave, unctuous.

smoothly *adv* evenly; easily, readily, unobstructedly; blandly, flatteringly, gently, mildly, pleasantly, softly, soothingly.

smooth-tongued *adj* adulatory, cozening, flattering, plausible, smooth, smooth-spoken.

smother *vb* choke, stifle, suffocate; conceal, deaden, extinguish, hide, keep down, repress, suppress; smoke, smoulder.

smudge *vb* besmear, blacken, blur, smear, smut, smutch, soil, spot, stain. • *n* blur, blot, smear, smut, spot, stain.

smug *adj* complacent, self-satisfied; neat, nice, spruce, trim.

smuggler *n* contrabandist, runner.

smut *vb* blacken, smouch, smudge, soil, stain, sully, taint, tarnish. • *n* dirt, smudge, smutch, soot; nastiness, obscenity, ribaldry, smuttiness; pornography.

smutty *adj* coarse, gross, immodest, impure, indecent, indelicate, loose, nasty; dirty, foul, nasty, soiled, stained.

snack *n* bite, light meal, nibble.

snag *vb* catch, enmesh, entangle, hook, snare, sniggle, tangle. • *n* knarl, knob, knot, projection, protuberance, snub; catch, difficulty, drawback, hitch, rub, shortcoming, weakness; obstacle.

snaky *adj* serpentine, snaking, winding; artful, cunning, deceitful, insinuating, sly, subtle.

snap *vb* break, fracture; bite, catch at, seize, snatch at, snip; crack; crackle, crepitate, decrepitate, pop. • *adj* casual, cursory, hasty, offhand, sudden, superficial. • *n* bite, catch, nip, seizure; catch, clasp, fastening, lock; crack, fillip, flick, flip, smack; briskness, energy, verve, vim.

snappish *adj* acrimonious, captious, churlish, crabbed, cross, crusty, froward, irascible, ill-tempered, peevish, perverse, pettish, petulant, snarling, splenetic, surly, tart, testy, touchy, waspish.

snare *vb* catch, ensnare, entangle, entrap. • *n* catch, gin, net, noose, springe, toil, trap, wile.

snarl[1] *vb* girn, gnarl, growl, grumble, murmur. • *n* growl, grumble.

snarl[2] *vb* complicate, disorder, entangle, knot; confuse, embarrass, ensnare. • *n* complication, disorder, entanglement, tangle; difficulty, embarrassment, intricacy.

snatch *vb* catch, clutch, grasp, grip, pluck, pull, seize, snip, twich, wrest, wring, • *n* bit, fragment, part, portion; catch, effort.

sneak *vb* lurk, skulk, slink, steal; crouch, truckle. • *adj* clandestine, concealed, covert, hidden, secret, sly, underhand. • *n* informer, telltale; lurker, shirk.

sneaky *adj* furtive, skulking, slinking; abject, crouching, grovelling, mean; clandestine, concealed, covert, hidden, secret, sly, underhand.

sneer *vb* flout, gibe, jeer, mock, rail, scoff; (*with* **at**) deride, despise, disdain, laugh at, mock, rail at, scoff, spurn. • *n* flouting, gibe, jeer, scoff.

snicker *vb* giggle, laugh, snigger, titter.

sniff *vb* breathe, inhale, snuff; scent, smell.

snip *vb* clip, cut, nip; snap, snatch. • *n* bit, fragment, particle, piece, shred; share, snack.

snivel *vb* blubber, cry, fret, sniffle, snuffle, weep, whimper, whine.

snivelly *adj* snotty; pitiful, whining.

snob *n* climber, toady.

snooze *vb* catnap, doze, drowse, nap, sleep, slumber. • *n* catnap, nap, sleep, slumber.

snout *n* muzzle, nose; nozzle.

snowy *adj* immaculate, pure, spotless, unblemished, unstained, unsullied, white.

snub[1] *vb* abash, cold-shoulder, cut, discomfit, humble, humiliate, mortify, slight, take down. • *n* check, rebuke, slight.

snub[2] *vb* check, clip, cut short, dock, nip, prune, stunt. • *adj* pug, retroussé, snubbed, squashed, squat, stubby, turned-up.

snuff[1] *vb* breathe, inhale, sniff; scent, smell; snort.

snuff[2] *vb* (*with* **out**) annihilate, destroy, efface, extinguish, obliterate.

snuffle *vb* sniffle; snort, snuff.

snug *adj* close, concealed; comfortable, compact, convenient, neat, trim.

snuggle *vb* cuddle, nestle, nuzzle.

so *adv* thus, with equal reason; in such a manner; in this way, likewise; as it is, as it was, such; for this reason, therefore; be it so, thus be it. • *conj* in case that, on condition that, provided that.

soak *vb* drench, moisten, permeate, saturate, wet; absorb, imbibe; imbue, macerate, steep.

soar *vb* ascend, fly aloft, glide, mount, rise, tower.

sob *vb* cry, sigh convulsively, weep.

sober *vb* (*with* **up**) calm down, collect oneself, compose oneself, control oneself, cool off, master, moderate, simmer down. • *adj* abstemious, abstinent, temperate, unintoxicated; rational, reasonable, sane, sound; calm, collected, composed, cool, dispassionate, moderate, rational, reasonabler, regular, restrained, steady, temperate, unimpassioned, unruffled, well-regulated; demure, grave, quiet, sedate, serious, solemn, sombre, staid; dark, drab, dull-looking, quiet, sad, subdued.

sobriety *n* abstemiousness, abstinence, soberness, temperance; calmness, coolness, gravity, sedateness, sober-mindedness, staidness, thoughtfulness; gravity, seriousness, solemnity.

sobriquet *n* appellation, nickname, nom de plume, pseudonym.

sociability *n* companionableness, comradeship, good fellowship, sociality.

sociable *adj* accessible, affable, communicative, companionable, conversable, friendly, genial, neighbourly, social.

social *adj* civic, civil; accessible, affable, communicative, companionable, familiar, friendly, hospitable, neighbourly, sociable; convivial, festive, gregarious. • *n* conversazione, gathering, get-together, party, reception, soiree.

society *n* association, companionship, company, converse, fellowship; the community, populace, the public, the world; élite, *monde*; body, brotherhood, copartnership, corporation, club, fraternity, partnersnip, sodality, union.

sodden *adj* drenched, saturated, soaked, steeped, wet; boiled, decocted, seethed, stewed.

sofa *n* couch, davenport, divan, ottoman, settee.

soft *adj* impressible, malleable, plastic, pliable, yielding; downy, fleecy, velvety, mushy, pulpy, squashy; compliant, facile, irresolute, submissive, undecided, weak; bland, mild, gentle, kind, lenient, soft-hearted, tender; delicate; easy, even, quiet, smooth-going, steady; effeminate, luxurious, unmanly; dulcet, fluty, mellifluous, melodious, smooth. • *interj* hold, stop.

soften *vb* intenerate, mellow, melt, tenderize; abate, allay, alleviate, appease, assuage, attemper, balm, blunt, calm, dull, ease, lessen, make easy, mitigate, moderate, mollify, milden, qualify, quell, quiet, relent, relieve, soothe, still, temper; extenuate, modify, palliate, qualify; enervate, weaken.

soil[1] *n* earth, ground loam, mould; country, land.

soil[2] *vb* bedaub, begrime, bemire, besmear, bespatter, contaminate, daub, defile, dirty, foul, pollute, smirch, stain, sully, taint, tarnish. • *n* blemish, defilement, dirt, filth, foulness; blot, spot, stain, taint, tarnish.

sojourn *vb* abide, dwell, live, lodge, remain, reside, rest, stay, stop, tarry, visit. • *n* residence, stay.

solace *vb* cheer, comfort, console, soothe; allay, assuage, mitigate, relieve, soften. • *n* alleviation, cheer, comfort, consolation, relief.

soldier *n* fighting man, man-at-arms, warrior; GI, private.

soldierly *adj* martial, military, warlike; brave, courageous, gallant, heroic, honourable, intrepid, valiant.

sole *adj* alone, individual, one, only, single, solitary, unique.

solecism *n* barbarism, blunder, error, faux pas, impropriety, incongruity, mistake, slip.

solemn *adj* ceremonial, formal, ritual; devotional, devout, religious, reverential, sacred; earnest, grave, serious, sober; august, awe-inspiring, awful, grand, imposing, impressive, majestic, stately, venerable.

solemnity *n* celebration, ceremony, observance, office, rite; awfulness, sacredness, sanctity; gravity, impressiveness, seriousness.

solemnize *vb* celebrate, commemorate, honour, keep, observe.

solicit *vb* appeal to, ask, beg, beseech, conjure, crave, entreat, implore, importune, petition, pray, press, request, supplicate, urge; arouse, awaken, entice, excite, invite, summon; canvass, seek.

solicitation *n* address, appeal, asking, entreaty, imploration, importunity, insistence, petition, request, suit, supplication, urgency; bidding, call, invitation, summons.

solicitor *n* attorney, law agent, lawyer; asker, canvasser, drummer, petitioner, solicitant.

solicitous *adj* anxious, apprehensive, careful, concerned, disturbed, eager, troubled, uneasy.

solicitude *n* anxiety, care, carefulness, concern, perplexity, trouble.

solid *adj* congealed, firm, hard, impenetrable, rock-like; compact, dense, impermeable, massed; cubic; sound, stable, stout, strong, substantial; just, real, true, valid, weighty; dependable, faithful, reliable, safe, staunch, steadfast, trustworthy, well established.

solidarity *n* communion of interests, community, consolidation, fellowship, joint interest, mutual responsibility.

solidify *vb* compact, congeal, consolidate, harden, petrify.

solidity *n* compactness, consistency, density, firmness, hardness, solidness; fullness; massiveness, stability, strength; dependability, gravity, justice, reliability, soundness, steadiness, validity, weight; cubic content, volume.

soliloquy *n* monologue.

solitariness *n* isolation, privacy, reclusion, retirement, seclusion; loneliness, solitude.

solitary *adj* alone, companionless, lone, lonely, only, separate, unaccompanied; individual, single, sole; desert, deserted, desolate, isolated, lonely, remote, retired, secluded, unfrequented.

solitude *n* isolation, loneliness, privacy, recluseness, retiredness, retirement, seclusion, solitariness; desert, waste, wilderness.

solution *n* answer, clue, disentanglement, elucidation, explication, explanation, key, resolution, unravelling, unriddling; disintegration, dissolution, liquefaction, melting, resolution, separation; breach, disconnection, discontinuance, disjunction, disruption.

solve *vb* clear, clear up, disentangle, elucidate, explain, expound, interpret, make plain, resolve, unfold.

solvent *n* diluent, dissolvent, menstruum.

somatic *adj* bodily, corporeal.

sombre *adj* cloudy, dark, dismal, dull, dusky, gloomy, murky, overcast, rayless, shady, sombrous, sunless; doleful, funereal, grave, lugubrious, melancholy, mournful, sad, sober.

some *adj* a, an, any, one; about, near; certain, little, moderate, part, several.

somebody *n* one, someone, something; celebrity, VIP.

somehow *adv* in some way.

something *n* part, portion, thing; somebody; affair, event, matter.

sometime *adj* former, late. • *adv* formerly, once; now and then, at one time or other, sometimes.

sometimes *adv* at intervals, at times, now and then, occasionally; at a past period, formerly, once.

somewhat *adv* in some degree, more or less, rather, something. • *n* something, a little, more or less, part.

somewhere *adv* here and there, in one place or another, in some place.

somnambulism *n* sleepwalking, somnambulation.

somnambulist *n* night-walker, noctambulist, sleepwalker, somnambulator, somnambule.

somniferous *adj* narcotic, opiate, slumberous, somnific, soporific, soporiferous.

somnolence *n* doziness, drowsiness, sleepiness, somnolency.

somnolent *adj* dozy, drowsy, sleepy.

son *n* cadet, heir, junior, scion.

song *n* aria, ballad, canticle, canzonet, carol, ditty, glee, lay, lullaby, snatch; descant, melody; anthem, hymn, poem, psalm, strain; poesy, poetry, verse.

sonorous *adj* full-toned, resonant, resounding, ringing, sounding; high-sounding, loud.

soon *adv* anon, before long, by and by, in a short time, presently, shortly; betimes, early, forthwith, promptly, quick; gladly, lief, readily, willingly.

soot *n* carbon, crock, dust.

soothe *vb* cajole, flatter, humour; appease, assuage, balm, calm, compose, lull, mollify, pacify, quiet, soften, still, tranquillize; allay, alleviate, blunt, check, deaden, dull, ease, lessen, mitigate, moderate, palliate, qualify, relieve, repress, soften, subdue, temper.

soothsayer *n* augur, diviner, foreteller, necromancer, predictor, prophet, seer, sorcerer, vaticinator.

sooty *adj* black, dark, dusky, fuliginous, murky, sable.

sophism *n* casuistry, fallacy, paralogism, paralogy, quibble, specious argument.

sophist *n* quibbler.

sophistical *adj* casuistical, fallacious, illogical, quibbling, subtle, unsound.

soporific *adj* dormitive, hypnotic, narcotic, opiate, sleepy, slumberous, somnific, somniferous, soporiferous, soporous.

soppy *adj* drenched, saturated, soaked, sopped; emotional, mawkish, sentimental.

soprano *n* (*mus*) descant, discant, treble.

sorcerer *n* charmer, conjurer, diviner, enchanter, juggler, magician, necromancers, seer, shaman, soothsayer, thaumaturgist, wizard.

sorcery *n* black art, charm, divination, enchantment, necromancy, occultism, shamanism, spell, thaumaturgy, voodoo, witchcraft.

sordid *adj* base, degraded, low, mean, vile; avaricious, close-fisted, covetous, illiberal, miserly, niggardly, penurious, stingy, ungenerous.

sore *adj* irritated, painful, raw, tender, ulcerated; aggrieved, galled, grieved, hurt, irritable, vexed; afflictive, distressing, severe, sharp, violent. • *n* abscess, boil, fester, gathering, imposthume, pustule, ulcer; affliction, grief, pain, sorrow, trouble.

sorely *adv* greatly, grievously, severely, violently.

sorrily *adv* despicably, meanly, pitiably, poorly, wretchedly.

sorrow *vb* bemoan, bewail, grieve, lament, mourn, weep. • *n* affliction, dolour, grief, heartache, mourning, sadness, trouble, woe.

sorrowful *adj* afflicted, dejected, depressed, grieved, grieving, heartsore, sad; baleful, distressing, grievous, lamentable, melancholy, mournful, painful; disconsolate, dismal, doleful, dolorous, drear, dreary, lugubrious, melancholy, piteous, rueful, woebegone, woeful.

sorry *adj* afflicted, dejected, grieved, pained, poor, sorrowful; distressing, pitiful; chagrined, mortified, pained, regretful, remorseful, sad, vexed; abject, base, beggarly, contemptible, despicable, low, mean, paltry, insignificant, miserable, shabby, worthless, wretched.

sort *vb* arrange, assort, class, classify, distribute, order; conjoin, join, put together; choose, elect, pick out, select; associate, consort, fraternize; accord, agree with, fit, suit. • *n* character, class, denomination, description, kind, nature, order, race, rank, species, type; manner, way.

sortie *n* attack, foray, raid, sally.

so-so *adj* indifferent, mediocre, middling, ordinary, passable, tolerable.

sot *n* blockhead, dolt, dullard, dunce, fool, simpleton; drunkard, tippler, toper.

sottish *adj* doltish, dull, foolish, senseless, simple, stupid; befuddled, besotted, drunken, insensate, senseless, tipsy.

sotto voce *adv* in a low voice, in an undertone, softly.

sough *n* murmur, sigh; breath, breeze, waft.

soul *n* mind, psyche, spirit; being, person; embodiment, essence, personification, spirit, vital principle; ardour, energy, fervour, inspiration, vitality.

soulless *adj* dead, expressionless, lifeless, unfeeling.

sound[1] *adj* entire, intact, unbroken, unhurt, unimpaired, uninjured, unmutilated, whole; hale, hardy, healthy, hearty, vigorous; good, perfect, undecayed; sane, well-balanced; correct, orthodox, right, solid, valid, well-founded; legal; deep, fast, profound, unbroken, undisturbed; forcible, lusty, severe, stout.

sound[2] *n* channel, narrows, strait.

sound[3] *vb* resound; appear, seem; play on; express, pronounce, utter; announce, celebrate, proclaim, publish, spread. • *n* noise, note, tone, voice, whisper.

sound[4] *vb* fathom, gauge, measure, test; examine, probe, search, test, try.

sounding *adj* audible, resonant, resounding, ringing, sonorous; imposing, significant.

soundless *adj* dumb, noiseless, silent; abysmal, bottomless, deep, profound, unfathomable, unsounded.

soundly *adv* satisfactorily, thoroughly, well; healthily, heartily; forcibly, lustily, severely, smartly, stoutly; correctly, rightly, truly; firmly, strongly; deeply, fast, profoundly.

soundness *n* entireness, entirety, integrity, wholeness; healthiness, vigour, saneness, sanity; correctness, orthodoxy, rectitude, reliability, truth, validity; firmness, solidity, strength, validity.

soup *n* broth, consommé, purée.

sour *vb* acidulate; embitter, envenom. • *adj* acetose, acetous, acid, astringent, pricked, sharp, tart, vinegary; acrimonious, crabbed, cross, crusty, fretful, glum, ill-humoured, ill-natured, ill-tempered, peevish, pettish, petulant, snarling, surly; bitter, disagreeable, unpleasant; austere, dismal, gloomy, morose, sad, sullen; bad, coagulated, curdled, musty, rancid, turned.

source *n* beginning, fountain, fountainhead, head, origin, rise, root, spring, well; cause, original.

sourness *n* acidity, sharpness, tartness; acrimony, asperity, churlishness, crabbedness, crossness, discontent, harshness, moroseness, peevishness.

souse *vb* pickle; dip, douse, immerse, plunge, submerge.

souvenir *n* keepsake, memento, remembrance, reminder.

sovereign *adj* imperial, monarchical, princely, regal, royal, supreme; chief, commanding, excellent, highest, paramount, predominant, principal, supreme, utmost; efficacious, effectual. • *n* autocrat, monarch, suzerain; emperor, empress, king, lord, potentate, prince, princess, queen, ruler.

sovereignty *n* authority, dominion, empire, power, rule, supremacy, sway.

sow *vb* scatter, spread, strew; disperse, disseminate, propagate, spread abroad; plant; besprinkle, scatter.

space *n* expanse, expansion, extension, extent, proportions, spread; accommodation, capacity, room, place; distance, interspace, interval.

spacious *adj* extended, extensive, vast, wide; ample, broad, capacious, commodious, large, roomy, wide.

span *vb* compass, cross, encompass, measure, overlay. • *n* brief period, spell; pair, team, yoke.

spank *vb* slap, strike.

spar[1] *n* beam, boom, pole, sprit, yard.

spar[2] *vb* box, fight; argue, bicker, contend, dispute, quarrel, spat, squabble, wrangle.

spare *vb* lay aside, lay by, reserve, save, set apart, set aside; dispense with, do without, part with; forbear, omit, refrain, withhold; exempt, forgive, keep from; afford, allow, give, grant; save; economize, pinch. • *adj* frugal, scanty, sparing, stinted; chary, parsimonious; emaciated, gaunt, lank, lean, meagre, poor, thin, scraggy, skinny, raw-boned; additional, extra, supernumerary.

sparing *adj* little, scanty, scarce; abstemious, meagre, spare; chary, economical, frugal, parsimonious, saving; compassionate, forgiving, lenient, merciful.

spark *vb* scintillate, sparkle; begin, fire, incite, instigate, kindle, light, set off, start, touch off, trigger. • *n* scintilla, scintillation, sparkle; beginning, element, germ, seed.

sparkle *vb* coruscate, flash, gleam, glisten, glister, glitter, radiate, scintillate, shine, twinkle; bubble, effervesce, foam, froth. • *n* glint, scintillation, spark; luminosity, lustre.

sparkling *adj* brilliant, flashing, glistening, glittering, glittery, twinkling; bubbling, effervescing, eloquent, foaming, frothing, mantling; brilliant, glowing, lively, nervous, piquant, racy, spirited, sprightly, witty.

sparse *adj* dispersed, infrequent, scanty, scattered, sporadic, thin.

spartan *adj* bold, brave, chivalric, courageous, daring, dauntless, doughty, fearless, hardy, heroic, intrepid, lion-hearted, undaunted, valiant, valorous; austere, exacting, hard, severe, tough, unsparing; enduring, long-suffering, self-controlled, stoic.

spasm *n* contraction, cramp, crick, twitch; fit, paroxysm, seizure, throe.

spasmodic *adj* erratic, fitful, intermittent, irregular, sporadic; convulsive, paroxysmal, spasmodical, violent.

spat *vb* argue, bicker, dispute, jangle, quarrel, spar, squabble, wrangle.

spatter *vb* bespatter, besprinkle, plash, splash, sprinkle; spit, sputter.

spawn *vb* bring forth, generate, produce. • *n* eggs, roe; fruit, offspring, product.

speak *vb* articulate, deliver, enunciate, express, pronounce, utter; announce, confer, declare, disclose, mention, say, tell; celebrate, make known, proclaim, speak abroad; accost, address, greet, hail; exhibit; argue, converse, dispute, talk; declaim, discourse, hold forth, harangue, orate, plead, spout, treat.

speaker *n* discourse, elocutionist, orator, prolocutor, spokesman; chairman, presiding officer.

speaking *adj* rhetorical, talking; eloquent, expressive; lifelike. • *n* discourse, talk, utterance; declamation, elocution, oratory.

spear *n* dart, gaff, harpoon, javelin, lance, pike; shoot, spire.

special *adj* specific, specifical; especial, individual, particular, peculiar, unique; exceptional, extraordinary, marked, particular, uncommon; appropriate, express.

speciality, specialty *n* particularity; feature, forte, pet subject.

species *n* assemblage, class, collection, group; description, kind, sort, variety; (*law*) fashion, figure, form, shape.

specific *adj* characteristic, especial, particular, peculiar; definite, limited, precise, specified.

specification *n* characterization, designation; details, particularization.

specify *vb* define, designate, detail, indicate, individualize, name, show, particularize.

specimen *n* copy, example, model, pattern, sample.

specious *adj* manifest, obvious, open, showy; flimsy, illusory, ostensible, plausible, sophistical.

speck *n* blemish, blot, flaw, speckle, spot, stain; atom, bit, corpuscle, mite, mote, particle, scintilla.

spectacle *n* display, exhibition, pageant, parade, representation, review, scene, show, sight; curiosity, marvel, phenomenon, wonder.

spectacles *npl* glasses, goggles, shades.

spectator *n* beholder, bystander, observer, onlooker, witness.

spectral *adj* eerie, ghostlike, ghostly, phantomlike, shadowy, spooky, weird, wraithlike.

spectre, specter *n* apparition, banshee, ghost, goblin, hobgoblin, phantom, shade, shadow, spirit, sprite, wraith.

spectrum *n* appearance, image, representation.

speculate *vb* cogitate, conjecture, contemplate, imagine, meditate, muse, ponder, reflect, ruminate, theorize, think; bet, gamble, hazard, risk, trade, venture.

speculation *n* contemplation, intellectualization; conjecture, hypothesis, scheme, supposition, reasoning, reflection, theory, view.

speculative *adj* contemplative, philosophical, speculatory, unpractical; ideal, imaginary, theoretical; hazardous, risky, unsecured.

speculator *n* speculatist, theorist, theorizer; adventurer, dealer, gambler, trader.

speech *n* articulation, language, words; dialect, idiom, locution, tongue; conversation, oral communication, parlance, talk, verbal intercourse; mention, observation, remark, saying; address, declaration, discourse, harangue, oration, palaver.

speechless *adj* dumb, gagged, inarticulate, mute, silent; dazed, dumbfounded, flabbergasted, shocked.

speed *vb* hasten, hurry, rush, scurry; flourish, prosper, succeed, thrive; accelerate, expedite, hasten, hurry, quicken, press forward, urge on; carry through, dispatch, execute; advance, aid, assist, help; favour. • *n* acceleration, celerity, dispatch, expedition, fleetness, haste, hurry, quickness, rapidity, swiftness, velocity; good fortune, good luck, prosperity, success; impetuosity.

speedy *adj* fast, fleet, flying, hasty, hurried, hurrying, nimble, quick, rapid, swift; expeditious, prompt, quick; approaching, early, near.

spell[1] *n* charm, exorcism, hoodoo, incantation, jinx, witchery; allure, bewitchment, captivation, enchantment, entrancement, fascination.

spell[2] *vb* decipher, interpret, read, unfold, unravel, unriddle.

spell[3] *n* fit, interval, period, round, season, stint, term, turn.

spellbound *adj* bewitched, charmed, enchanted, entranced, enthralled, fascinated.

spend *vb* disburse, dispose of, expend, lay out, part with; consume, dissipate, exhaust, lavish, squander, use up, wear, waste; apply, bestow, devote, employ, pass.

spendthrift *n* prodigal, spender, squanderer, waster.

spent *adj* exhausted, fatigued, played out, used up, wearied, worn out.

spew *vb* cast up, puke, throw up, vomit; cast forth, eject.

spheral *adj* complete, perfect, symmetrical.

sphere *n* ball, globe, orb, spheroid; ambit, beat, bound, circle, circuit, compass, department, function, office, orbit, province, range, walk; order, rank, standing; country, domain, quarter, realm, region.

spherical *adj* bulbous, globated, globous, globular, orbicular, rotund, round, spheroid; planetary.

spice *n* flavour, flavouring, relish, savour, taste; admixture, dash, grain, infusion, particle, smack, soupçon, sprinkling, tincture.

spicily *adv* pungently, wittily.

spicy *adj* aromatic, balmy, fragrant; keen, piquant, pointed, pungent, sharp; indelicate, off-colour, racy, risqué, sensational, suggestive.

spill *vb* effuse, pour out, shed. • *n* accident, fall, tumble.

spin *vb* twist; draw out, extend; lengthen, prolong, protract, spend; pirouette, turn, twirl, whirl. • *n* drive, joyride, ride; autorotation, gyration, loop, revolution, rotation, turning, wheeling; pirouette, reel, turn, wheel, whirl.

spindle *n* axis, shaft.

spine *n* barb, prickle, thorn; backbone; ridge.

spinose *adj* briery, spinous, spiny, thorny.

spiny *adj* briery, prickly, spinose, spinous, thorny; difficult, perplexed, troublesome.

spiracle *n* aperture, blowhole, orifice, pore, vent.

spiral *adj* cochlear, cochleated, curled, helical, screw-shaped, spiry, winding. • *n* helix, winding, worm.

spire *n* curl, spiral, twist, wreath; steeple; blade, shoot, spear, stalk; apex, summit.

spirit *vb* animate, encourage, excite, inspirit; carry off, kidnap. • *n* immaterial substance, life, vital essence; person, soul;

angel, apparition, demon, elf, fairy, genius, ghost, phantom, shade, spectre, sprite; disposition, frame of mind, humour, mood, temper; spirits; ardour, cheerfulness, courage, earnestness, energy, enterprise, enthusiasm, fire, force, mettle, resolution, vigour, vim, vivacity, zeal; animation, cheerfulness, enterprise, esprit, glow, liveliness, piquancy, spice, spunk, vivacity, warmth; drift, gist, intent, meaning, purport, sense, significance, tenor; character, characteristic, complexion, essence, nature, quality, quintessence; alcohol, liquor; (*with* **the**) Comforter, Holy Ghost, Paraclete.

spirited *adj* active, alert, animated, ardent, bold, brisk, courageous, earnest, frisky, high-mettled, high-spirited, highstrung, lively, mettlesome, sprightly, vivacious.

spiritless *adj* breathless, dead, extinct, lifeless; dejected, depressed, discouraged, dispirited, low-spirited; apathetic, cold, dull, feeble, languid, phlegmatic, sluggish, soulless, torpid, unenterprising; dull, frigid, heavy, insipid, prosaic, prosy, stupid, tame, uninteresting.

spiritual *adj* ethereal, ghostly, immaterial incorporeal, psychical, supersensible; ideal, moral, unwordly; divine, holy, pure, sacred; ecclesiastical.

spiritualize *vb* elevate, etherealize, purify, refine.

spirituous *adj* alcoholic, ardent, spiritous.

spit[1] *vb* impale, thrust through, transfix.

spit[2] *vb* eject, throw out; drivel, drool, expectorate, salivate, slobber, spawl, splutter. • *n* saliva, spawl, spittle, sputum.

spite *vb* injure, mortify, thwart; annoy, offend, vex. • *n* grudge, hate, hatred, ill-nature, ill-will, malevolence, malice, maliciousness, malignity, pique, rancour, spleen, venom, vindictiveness.

spiteful *adj* evil-minded, hateful, ill-disposed, ill-natured, malevolent, malicious, malign, malignant, rancorous.

spittoon *n* cuspidor.

splash *vb* dabble, dash, plash, spatter, splurge, swash, swish. • *n* blot, daub, spot.

splay *adj* broad, spreading out, turned out, wide.

spleen *n* anger, animosity, chagrin, gall, grudge, hatred, illhumour, irascibility, malevolence, malice, malignity, peevishness, pique, rancour, spite.

spleeny *adj* angry, fretful, ill-tempered, irritable, peevish, spleenish, splenetic.

splendid *adj* beaming, bright, brilliant, effulgent, glowing, lustrous, radiant, refulgent, resplendent, shining; dazzling, gorgeous, imposing, kingly, magnificent, pompous, showy, sumptuous, superb; celebrated, conspicuous, distinguished, eminent, excellent, famous, glorious, illustrious, noble, preeminent, remarkable, signal; grand, heroic, lofty, noble, sublime.

splendour *n* brightness, brilliance, brilliancy, lustre, radiance, refulgence; display, éclat, gorgeousness, grandeur, magnificence, parade, pomp, show, showiness, stateliness; celebrity, eminence, fame, glory, grandeur, renown; grandeur, loftiness, nobleness, sublimity.

splenetic *adj* choleric, cross, fretful, irascible, irritable, peevish, pettish, petulant, snappish, testy, touchy, waspish; churlish, crabbed, morose, sour, sulky, sullen; gloomy, jaundiced.

splice *vb* braid, connect, join, knit, mortise.

splinter *vb* rend, shiver, sliver, split. • *n* fragment, piece.

split *vb* cleave, rive; break, burst, rend, splinter; divide, part, separate, sunder. • *n* crack, fissure, rent; breach, division, separation.

splotch *n* blot, daub, smear, spot, stain.

splutter *vb* sputter, stammer, stutter.

spoil *vb* despoil, fleece, loot, pilfer, plunder, ravage, rob, steal, strip, waste; corrupt, damage, destroy, disfigure, harm, impair, injure, mar, ruin, vitiate; decay, decompose. • *n* booty, loot, pillage, plunder, prey; rapine, robbery, spoliation, waste.

spoiler *n* pillager, plunderer, robber; corrupter, destroyer.

spokesman *n* mouthpiece, prolocutor, speaker.

spoliate *vb* despoil, destroy, loot, pillage, plunder, rob, spoil.

spoliation *n* depradation, deprivation, despoilation, destruction, robbery; destruction, devastation, pillage, plundering, rapine, ravagement.

sponge *vb* cleanse, wipe; efface, expunge, obliterate, rub out, wipe out.

sponger *n* hanger-on, parasite.

spongy *adj* absorbent, porous, spongeous; rainy, showery, wet; drenched, marshy, saturated, soaked, wet.

sponsor *vb* back, capitalize, endorse, finance, guarantee, patronize, promote, support, stake, subsidize, take up, underwrite. • *n* angel, backer, guarantor, patron, promoter, supporter, surety, underwriter; godfather, godmother, godparent.

spontaneity *n* improvisation, impulsiveness, spontaneousness.

spontaneous *adj* free, gratuitous, impulsive, improvised, instinctive, self-acting, self-moving, unbidden, uncompelled, unconstrained, voluntary, willing.

sporadic *adj* dispersed, infrequent, isolated, rare, scattered, separate, spasmodic.

sport *vb* caper, disport, frolic, gambol, have fun, make merry, play, romp, skip; trifle; display, exhibit. • *n* amusement, diversion, entertainment, frolic, fun, gambol, game, jollity, joviality, merriment, merry-making, mirth, pastime, pleasantry, prank, recreation; jest, joke; derision, jeer, mockery, ridicule; monstrosity.

sportive *adj* frisky, frolicsome, gamesome, hilarious, lively, merry, playful, prankish, rollicking, sprightly, tricksy; comic, facetious, funny, humorous, jocose, jocular, lively, ludicrous, mirthful, vivacious, waggish.

spot *vb* besprinkle, dapple, dot, speck, stud, variegate; blemish, disgrace, soil, splotch, stain, sully, tarnish; detect, discern, espy, make out, observe, see, sight. • *n* blot, dapple, fleck, freckle, maculation, mark, mottle, patch, pip, speck, speckle; blemish, blotch, flaw, pock, splotch, stain, taint; locality, place, site.

spotless *adj* perfect, undefaced, unspotted; blameless, immaculate, innocent, irreproachable, pure, stainless, unblemished, unstained, untainted, untarnished.

spotted *adj* bespeckled, bespotted, dotted, flecked, freckled, maculated, ocellated, speckled, spotty.

spousal *adj* bridal, conjugal, connubial, hymeneal, marital, matrimonial, nuptial, wedded.

spouse *n* companion, consort, husband, mate, partner, wife.

spout *vb* gush, jet, pour out, spirit, spurt, squirt; declaim, mouth, speak, utter. • *n* conduit, tube; beak, nose, nozzle, waterspout.

sprain *vb* overstrain, rick, strain, twist, wrench, wrick.

spray[1] *vb* atomize, besprinkle, douche, gush, jet, shower, splash, splatter, spout, sprinkle, squirt. • *n* aerosol, atomizer, douche, foam, froth, shower, sprinkler, spume.

spray[2] *n* bough, branch, shoot, sprig, twig.

spread *vb* dilate, expand, extend, mantle, stretch; diffuse, disperse, distribute, radiate, scatter, sprinkle, strew; broadcast, circulate, disseminate, divulge, make known, make public, promulgate, propagate, publish; open, unfold, unfurl; cover, extend over, overspread. • *n* compass, extent, range, reach, scope, stretch; expansion, extension; circulation, dissemination, propagation; cloth, cover; banquet, feast, meal.

spree *n* bacchanal, carousal, debauch, frolic, jollification, orgy, revel, revelry, saturnalia.

sprig *n* shoot, spray, twig; lad, youth.

sprightliness *n* animation, activity, briskness, cheerfulness, frolicsomeness, gaiety, life, liveliness, nimbleness, vigour, vivacity.

sprightly *adj* airy, animated, blithe, blithesome, brisk, buoyant, cheerful, debonair, frolicsome, joyous, lively, mercurial, vigorous, vivacious.

spring *vb* bound, hop, jump, leap, prance, vault; arise, emerge, grow, issue, proceed, put forth, shoot forth, stem; derive, descend, emanate, flow, originate, rise, start; fly back, rebound, recoil; bend, warp; grow, thrive, wax. • *adj* hopping, jumping, resilient, springy. • *n* bound, hop, jump, leap, vault; elasticity, flexibility, resilience, resiliency, springiness; fount, fountain, fountainhead, geyser, springhead, well; cause, origin, original, principle, source; seed time, springtime.

springe *n* gin, net, noose, snare, trap.

springiness *n* elasticity, resilience, spring; sponginess, wetness.

springy *adj* bouncing, bounding, elastic, rebounding, recoiling, resilient.

sprinkle *vb* scatter, strew; bedew, besprinkle, dust, powder, sand, spatter; wash, cleanse, purify, shower.

sprinkling *n* affusion, baptism, bedewing, spattering, splattering, spraying, wetting; dash, scattering, seasoning, smack, soupçon, suggestion, tinge, touch, trace, vestige.

sprite *n* apparition, elf, fairy, ghost, goblin, hobgoblin, phantom, pixie, shade, spectre, spirit.

sprout *vb* burgeon, burst forth, germinate, grow, pullulate, push, put forth, ramify, shoot, shoot forth. • *n* shoot, sprig.

spruce *vb* preen, prink; adorn, deck, dress, smarten, trim. • *adj* dandyish, dapper, fine, foppish, jaunty, natty, neat, nice, smart, tidy, trig, trim.

spry *adj* active, agile, alert, brisk, lively, nimble, prompt, quick, ready, smart, sprightly, stirring, supple.

spume *n* foam, froth, scum, spray.

spumy *adj* foamy, frothy, spumous.

spur *vb* gallop, hasten, press on, prick; animate, arouse, drive, goad, impel, incite, induce, instigate, rouse, stimulate, urge forward. • *n* goad, point, prick, rowel; fillip, impulse, incentive, incitement, inducement, instigation, motive, provocation, stimulus, whip; gnarl, knob, knot, point, projection, snag.

spurious *adj* bogus, counterfeit, deceitful, false, feigned, fictitious, make-believe, meretricious, mock, pretended, sham, supposititious, unauthentic.

spurn *vb* drive away, kick; contemn, despise, disregard, flout, scorn, slight; disdain, reject, repudiate.

spurt *vb* gush, jet, spirt, spout, spring out, stream out, well. • *n* gush, jet, spout, squirt; burst, dash, rush.

sputter *vb* spawl, spit, splutter, stammer.

spy *vb* behold, discern, espy, see; detect, discover, search out; explore, inspect, scrutinize, search; shadow, trail, watch. • *n* agent, detective, double agent, mole, scout, undercover agent.

squabble *vb* brawl, fight, quarrel, scuffle, struggle, wrangle; altercate, bicker, contend, dispute, jangle. • *n* brawl, dispute, fight, quarrel, rumpus, scrimmage.

squad *n* band, bevy, crew, gang, knot, lot, relay, set.

squalid *adj* dirty, filthy, foul, mucky, slovenly, unclean, unkempt.

squalidness *n* filthiness, foulness, squalidity, squalor.

squall *vb* bawl, cry, cry out, scream, yell. • *n* bawl, cry, outcry, scream, yell; blast, flurry, gale, gust, hurricane, storm, tempest.

squally *adj* blustering, blustery, gusty, stormy, tempestuous, windy.

squander *vb* dissipate, expend, lavish, lose, misuse, scatter, spend, throw away, waste.

squanderer *n* lavisher, prodigal, spendthrift, waster.

square *vb* make square, quadrate; accommodate, adapt, fit, mould, regulate, shape, suit; adjust, balance, close, make even, settle; accord, chime in, cohere, comport, fall in, fit, harmonize, quadrate, suit. • *adj* four-square, quadrilateral, quadrate; equal, equitable, exact, fair, honest, just, upright; adjusted, balanced, even, settled; true, suitable. • *n* four-sided figure, quadrate, rectangle, tetragon; open area, parade, piazza, plaza.

squash *vb* crush, mash.

squashy *adj* pulpy, soft.

squat *vb* cower, crouch; occupy, plant, settle. • *adj* cowering, crouching; dumpy, pudgy, short, stocky, stubby, thickset.

squeal *vb* creak, cry, howl, scream, screech, shriek, squawk, yell; betray, inform on. • *n* creak, cry, howl, scream, screech, shriek, squawk, yell.

squeamish *adj* nauseated, qualmish, queasy, sickish; dainty, delicate, fastidious, finical, hypercritical, nice, over-nice, particular, priggish.

squeeze *vb* clutch, compress, constrict, grip, nip, pinch, press; drive, force; crush, harass, oppress; crowd, force through; press; (*with* out) extract. • *n* congestion, crowd, crush, throng; compression.

squelch *vb* crush, quash, quell, silence, squash, suppress.

squib *n* firework, fuse; lampoon, pasquinade, satire.

squint *vb* look askance, look obliquely, peer. • *adj* askew, aslant, crooked, oblique, skew, skewed, twisted.

squire *vb* accompany, attend, escort, wait on.

squirm *vb* twist, wriggle, writhe.

squirt *vb* eject, jet, splash, spurt.

stab *vb* broach, gore, jab, pierce, pink, spear, stick, transfix, transpierce; wound. • *n* cut, jab, prick, thrust; blow, dagger-stroke, injury, wound.

stability *n* durability, firmness, fixedness, immovability, permanence, stableness, steadiness; constancy, firmness, reliability.

stable *adj* established, fixed, immovable, immutable, invariable, permanent, unalterable, unchangeable; constant, firm, staunch, steadfast, steady, unwavering; abiding, durable, enduring, fast, lasting, permanent, perpetual, secure, sure.

staff *n* baton, cane, pole, rod, stick, wand; bat, bludgeon, club, cudgel, mace; prop, stay, support; employees, personnel, team, workers, work force.

stage *vb* dramatize, perform, present, produce, put on. • *n* dais, platform, rostrum, scaffold, staging, stand; arena, field; boards, playhouse, theatre; degree, point, step; diligence, omnibus, stagecoach.

stagey *adj* bombastic, declamatory, dramatic, melodramatic, ranting, theatrical.

stagger *vb* reel, sway, totter; alternate, fluctuate, overlap, vacillate, vary; falter, hesitate, waver; amaze, astonish, astound, confound, dumbfound, nonplus, pose, shock, surprise.

stagnant *adj* close, motionless, quiet, standing; dormant, dull, heavy, inactive, inert, sluggish, torpid.

stagnate *vb* decay, deteriorate, languish, rot, stand still, vegetate.

staid *adj* calm, composed, demure, grave, sedate, serious, settled, sober, solemn, steady, unadventurous.

stain *vb* blemish, blot, blotch, discolour, maculate, smirch, soil, splotch, spot, sully, tarnish; colour, dye, tinge; contaminate, corrupt, debase, defile, deprave, disgrace, dishonour, pollute, taint. • *n* blemish, blot, defect, discoloration, flaw, imperfection, spot, tarnish; contamination, disgrace, dishonour, infamy, pollution, reproach, shame, taint, tarnish.

stainless *adj* spotless, unspotted, untarnished; blameless, faultless, innocent, guiltless, pure, spotless, uncorrupted, unsullied.

stairs *npl* flight of steps, staircase, stairway.

stake[1] *vb* brace, mark, prop, secure, support. • *n* pale, palisade, peg, picket, post, stick.

stake[2] *vb* finance, pledge, wager; hazard, imperil, jeopardize, peril, risk, venture. • *n* bet, pledge, wager; adventure, hazard, risk, venture.

stale *adj* flat, fusty, insipid, mawkish, mouldy, musty, sour, tasteless, vapid; decayed, effete, faded, old, time-worn, worn-out; common, commonplace, hackneyed, stereotyped, threadbare, trite.

stalk[1] *n* culm, pedicel, peduncle, petiole, shaft, spire, stem, stock.

stalk[2] *vb* march, pace, stride, strut, swagger; follow, hunt, shadow, track, walk stealthily.

stall[1] *n* stable; cell, compartment, recess; booth, kiosk, shop, stand.

stall[2] *vb* block, delay, equivocate, filibuster, hinder, postpone, procrastinate, temporize; arrest, check, conk out, die, fail, halt, stick, stop.

stalwart *adj* able-bodied, athletic, brawny, lusty, muscular, powerful, robust, sinewy, stout, strapping, strong, sturdy, vigorous; bold, brave, daring, gallant, indomitable, intrepid, redoubtable, resolute, valiant, valorous. • *n* backer, member, partisan, supporter.

stamina *n* energy, force, lustiness, power, stoutness, strength, sturdiness, vigour.

stammer *vb* falter, hesitate, stutter. • *n* faltering, hesitation, stutter.

stamp *vb* brand, impress, imprint, mark, print. • *n* brand, impress, impression, print; cast, character, complexion, cut, description, fashion, form, kind, make, mould, sort, type.

stampede *vb* charge, flee, panic. • *n* charge, flight, rout, running away, rush.

stanch *see* **staunch**[1].

stanchion *n* prop, shore, stay, support.

stand *vb* be erect, remain upright; abide, be fixed, continue, endure, hold good, remain; halt, pause, stop; be firm, be resolute, stand ground, stay; be valid, have force; depend, have support, rest; bear, brook, endure, suffer, sustain, weather; abide, admit, await, submit, tolerate, yield; fix, place, put, set upright; (*with* against) oppose, resist, withstand; (*with* by) be near, be present; aid, assist, defend, help, side with, support; defend, make good, justify, maintain, support, vindicate; (*naut*) attend, be ready; (*with* fast) be fixed, be immovable; (*with* for) mean, represent, signify; aid, defend, help, maintain, side with, support; (*with* off) keep aloof, keep off; not to comply; (*with* out) be prominent, jut, project, protrude; not comply, not yield, persist; (*with* up for) defend, justify, support, sustain, uphold; (*with* with) agree. • *n* place, position, post, standing place, station; halt, stay, stop; dais, platform, rostrum; booth, stall; opposition, resistance.

standard[1] *n* banner, colours, ensign, flag, gonfalon, pennon, streamer.

standard[2] *adj* average, conventional, customary, normal, ordinary, regular, usual; accepted, approved, authoritative, orthodox, received; formulary, prescriptive, regulation. • n canon, criterion, model, norm, rule, test, type; gauge, measure, model, scale; support, upright.

standing adj established, fixed, immovable, settled; durable, lasting, permanent; motionless, stagnant. • n position, stand, station; continuance, duration, existence; footing, ground, hold; condition, estimation, rank, reputation, status.

standpoint n point of view, viewpoint.

standstill n cessation, interruption, stand, stop; deadlock.

stanza n measure, staff, stave, strophe, verse.

staple adj basic, chief, essential, fundamental, main, primary, principal. • n fibre, filament, pile, thread; body, bulk, mass, substance.

star vb act, appear, feature, headline, lead, perform, play; emphasize, highlight, stress, underline. • adj leading, main, paramount, principal; celebrated, illustrious, well-known. • n heavenly body, luminary; asterisk, pentacle, pentagram; destiny, doom, fate, fortune, lot; diva, headliner, hero, heroine, lead, leading lady, leading man, prima ballerina, prima donna, principal, protagonist.

starchy adj ceremonious, exact, formal, precise, prim, punctilious, rigid, starched, stiff.

stare vb gape, gaze, look intently, watch.

stark adj rigid, stiff; absolute, bare, downright, entire, gross, mere, pure, sheer, simple. • adv absolutely, completely, entirely, fully, wholly.

starry adj astral, sidereal, star-spangled, stellar; bright, brilliant, lustrous, shining, sparkling, twinkling.

start vb begin, commence, inaugurate, initiate, institute; discover, invent; flinch, jump, shrink, startle, wince; alarm, disturb, fright, rouse, scare; depart, set off, take off; arise, call forth, evoke, raise; dislocate, move suddenly, spring. • n beginning, commencement, inauguration, outset; fit, jump, spasm, twitch; impulse, sally.

startle vb flinch, shrink, start, wince; affright, alarm, fright, frighten, scare, shock; amaze, astonish, astound.

startling adj abrupt, alarming, astonishing, shocking, sudden, surprising, unexpected, unforeseen, unheard of.

starvation n famine, famishment.

starve vb famish, perish; be in need, lack, want; kill, subdue.

starveling adj attenuated, emaciated, gaunt, hungry, lank, lean, meagre, scraggy, skinny, thin. • n beggar, mendicant, pauper.

state vb affirm, assert, aver, declare, explain, expound, express, narrate, propound, recite, say, set forth, specify, voice. • adj civic, national, public. • n case, circumstances, condition, pass, phase, plight, position, posture, predicament, situation, status; condition, guise, mode, quality, rank; dignity, glory, grandeur, magnificence, pageantry, parade, pomp, spendour; body politic, civil community, commonwealth, nation, realm.

statecraft n diplomacy, political subtlety, state management, statesmanship.

stated adj established, fixed, regular, settled; detailed, set forth, specified.

stately adj august, dignified, elevated, grand, imperial, imposing, lofty, magnificent, majestic, noble, princely, royal; ceremonious, formal, magisterial, pompous, solemn.

statement n account, allegation, announcement, communiqué, declaration, description, exposition, mention, narration, narrative, recital, relation, report, specification; assertion, predication, proposition, pronouncement, thesis.

statesman n politician.

station vb establish, fix, locate, place, post, set. • n location, place, position, lost, seat, situation; business, employment, function, occupation, office; character, condition, degree, dignity, footing, rank, standing, state, status; depot, stop, terminal.

stationary adj fixed, motionless, permanent, quiescent, stable, standing, still.

statuary n carving, sculpture, statues.

statue n figurine, image, statuette.

stature n height, physique, size, tallness; altitude, consequence, elevation, eminence, prominence.

status n caste, condition, footing, position, rank, standing, station.

statute n act, decree, edict, enactment, law, ordinance, regulation.

staunch¹, stanch vb arrest, block, check, dam, plug, stem, stop.

staunch² adj firm, sound, stout, strong; constant, faithful, firm, hearty, loyal, resolute, stable, steadfast, steady, strong, trustworthy, trusty, unwavering, zealous.

stave vb break, burst; (with **off**) adjourn, defer, delay, postpone, procrastinate, put off, waive.

stay vb abide, dwell, lodge, rest, sojourn, tarry; continue, halt, remain, stand still, stop; attend, delay, linger, wait; arrest, check, curb, hold, keep in, prevent, rein in, restrain, withhold; delay, detain, hinder, obstruct; hold up, prop, shore up, support, sustain, uphold. • n delay, repose, rest, sojourn; halt, stand, stop; bar, check, curb, hindrance, impediment, interruption, obstacle, obstruction, restraint, stumbling block; buttress, dependence, prop, staff, support, supporter.

stead n place, room.

steadfast adj established, fast, firm, fixed, stable; constant, faithful, implicit, persevering, pertinacious, resolute, resolved, staunch, steady, unhesitating, unreserved, unshaken, unwavering, wholehearted.

steadiness n constancy, firmness, perseverance, persistence, resolution, steadfastness; fixedness, stability.

steady vb balance, counterbalance, secure, stabilize, support. • adj firm, fixed, stable; constant, equable, regular, undeviating, uniform, unremitting; persevering, resolute, staunch, steadfast, unchangeable, unwavering.

steal vb burglarize, burgle, crib, embezzle, filch, peculate, pilfer, plagiarize, poach, purloin, shoplift, thieve; creep, sneak, pass stealthily.

stealing n burglary, larceny, peculation, shoplifting, robbery, theft, thievery.

stealth n secrecy, slyness, stealthiness.

stealthy adj clandestine, furtive, private, secret, skulking, sly, sneaking, surreptitious, underhand.

steam vb emit vapour, fume; evaporate, vaporize; coddle, cook, poach; navigate, sail; be hot, sweat. • n vapour; effluvium, exhalation, fume, mist, reek, smoke.

steamboat n steamer, steamship.

steamy adj misty, moist, vaporous; erotic, voluptuous.

steed n charger, horse, mount.

steel vb case-harden; edge; brace, fortify, harden, make firm, nerve, strengthen.

steep¹ adj abrupt, declivitous, precipitous, sheer, sloping, sudden. • n declivity, precipice.

steep² vb digest, drench, imbrue, imbue, macerate, saturate, soak.

steeple n belfry, spire, tower, turret.

steer vb direct, conduct, govern, guide, pilot, point.

steersman n conductor, guide, helmsman, pilot.

stellar adj astral, starry, star-spangled, stellary.

stem¹ vb (with **from**) bud, descend, generate, originate, spring, sprout. • n axis, stipe, trunk; pedicel, peduncle, petiole, stalk; branch, descendant, offspring, progeny, scion, shoot; ancestry, descent, family, generation, line, lineage, pedigree, race, stock; (naut) beak, bow, cutwater, forepart, prow; helm, lookout; etymon, radical, radix, origin, root.

stem² vb breast, oppose, resist, withstand; check, dam, oppose, staunch, stay, stop.

stench n bad smell, fetor, offensive odour, stink.

stenography n brachygraphy, shorthand, tachygraphy.

stentorian adj loud-voiced, powerful, sonorous, thundering, trumpet-like.

step vb pace, stride, tramp, tread, walk. • n footstep, pace, stride; stair, tread; degree, gradation, grade, interval; advance, advancement, progression; act, action, deed, procedure, proceeding; footprint, trace, track, vestige; footfall, gait, pace, walk; expedient, means, measure, method; round, rundle, rung.

steppe n pampa, prairie, savannah.

sterile adj barren, infecund, unfruitful, unproductive, unprolific; bare, dry, empty, poor; (bot) acarpous, male, staminate.

sterility n barrenness, fruitlessness, infecundity, unfruitfulness, unproductiveness.

sterling adj genuine, positive, pure, real, sound, standard, substantial, true.

stern¹ adj austere, dour, forbidding, grim, severe; bitter, cruel, hard, harsh, inflexible, relentless, rigid, rigorous, severe, strict, unrelenting; immovable, incorruptible, steadfast, uncompromising.

stern² n behind, breach, hind part, posterior, rear, tail; (naut) counter, poop, rudderpost, tailpost; butt, buttocks, fundament, rump.

sternness n austerity, rigidity, severity; asperity, cruelty, harshness, inflexibility, relentlessness, rigour.

sternum *n* (*anat*) breastbone, sternon.

stertorous *adj* hoarsely breathing, snoring.

stew *vb* boil, seethe, simmer, stive. • *n* ragout; confusion, difficulty, mess, scrape.

steward *n* chamberlain, majordomo, seneschal; manciple, purveyor.

stick[1] *vb* gore, penetrate, pierce, puncture, spear, stab, transfix; infix, insert, thrust; attach, cement, glue, paste; fix in, set; adhere, cleave, cling, hold; abide, persist, remain, stay, stop; doubt, hesitate, scruple, stickle, waver; (*with* **by**) adhere to, be faithful, support. • *n* prick, stab, thrust.

stick[2] *n* birch, rod, switch; bat, bludgeon, club, cudgel, shillelah; cane, staff, walking stick; cue, pole, spar, stake.

stickiness *n* adhesiveness, glutinousness, tenacity, viscosity, viscousness.

stickle *vb* altercate, contend, contest, struggle; doubt, hesitate, scruple, stick, waver.

sticky *adj* adhesive, clinging, gluey, glutinous, gummy, mucilaginous, tenacious, viscid, viscous.

stiff *adj* inflexible, rigid, stark, unbending, unyielding; firm, tenacious, thick; obstinate, pertinacious, strong, stubborn; absolute, austere, dogmatic, inexorable, peremptory, positive, rigorous, severe, straitlaced, strict, stringent, uncompromising; ceremonious, chilling, constrained, formal, frigid, prim, punctilious, stately, starchy, stilted; abrupt, cramped, crude, graceless, harsh, inelegant.

stiff-necked *adj* contumacious, cross-grained, dogged, headstrong, intractable, mulish, obdurate, obstinate, stubborn, unruly.

stiffness *n* hardness, inflexibility, rigidity, rigidness, rigour, starkness; compactness, consistence, denseness, density, thickness; contumaciousness, inflexibility, obstinacy, pertinacity, stubbornness; austerity, harshness, rigorousness, severity, sternness, strictness; constraint, formality, frigidity, precision, primness, tenseness.

stifle *vb* choke, smother, suffocate; check, deaden, destroy, extinguish, quench, repress, stop, suppress; conceal, gag, hush, muffle, muzzle, silence, smother, still.

stigma *n* blot, blur, brand, disgrace, dishonour, reproach, shame, spot, stain, taint, tarnish.

stigmatize *vb* brand, defame, discredit, disgrace, dishonour, post, reproach, slur, villify.

stiletto *n* dagger, dirk, poniard, stylet; bodkin, piercer.

still[1] *vb* hush, muffle, silence, stifle; allay, appease, calm, compose, lull, pacify, quiet, smooth, tranquillize; calm, check, immobilize, restrain, stop, subdue, suppress. • *adj* hushed, mum, mute, noiseless, silent; calm, placid, quiet, serene, stilly, tranquil, unruffled; inert, motionless, quiescent, stagnant, stationary. • *n* hush, lull, peace, quiet, quietness, quietude, silence, stillness, tranquillity; picture, photograph, shot.

still[2] *n* distillery, still-house; distillatory, retort, stillatory.

still[3] *adv, conj* till now, to this time, yet; however, nevertheless, notwithstanding; always, continually, ever, habitually, uniformly; after that, again, in continuance.

stilted *adj* bombastic, fustian, grandiloquent, grandiose, highflown, high-sounding, inflated, magniloquent, pompous, pretentious, stilty, swelling, tumid, turgid.

stimulant *adj* exciting, stimulating, stimulative. • *n* bracer, cordial, pick-me-up, tonic; fillip, incentive, provocative, spur, stimulus.

stimulate *vb* animate, arouse, awaken, brace, encourage, energize, excite, fire, foment, goad, impel, incite, inflame, inspirit, instigate, kindle, prick, prompt, provoke, rally, rouse, set on, spur, stir up, urge, whet, work up.

stimulus *n* encouragement, fillip, goad, incentive, incitement, motivation, motive, provocation, spur, stimulant.

sting *vb* hurt, nettle, prick, wound; afflict, cut, pain.

stinging *adj* acute, painful, piercing; biting, nipping, pungent, tingling.

stingy *adj* avaricious, close, close-fisted, covetous, grudging, mean, miserly, narrow-hearted, niggardly, parsimonious, penurious.

stink *vb* emit a stench, reek, smell bad. • *n* bad smell, fetor, offensive odour, stench.

stint *vb* bound, confine, limit, restrain; begrudge, pinch, scrimp, skimp, straiten; cease, desist, stop. • *n* bound, limit, restraint; lot, period, project, quota, share, shift, stretch, task, time, turn.

stipend *n* allowance, compensation, emolument, fee, hire, honorarium, pay, remuneration, salary, wages.

stipulate *vb* agree, bargain, condition, contract, covenant, engage, provide, settle terms.

stipulation *n* agreement, bargain, concordat, condition, contract, convention, covenant, engagement, indenture, obligation, pact.

stir *vb* budge, change place, go, move; agitate, bestir, disturb, prod; argue, discuss, moot, raise, start; animate, arouse, awaken, excite, goad, incite, instigate, prompt, provoke, quicken, rouse, spur, stimulate; appear, happen, turn up; get up, rise; (*with* **up**) animate, awaken, incite, instigate, move, provoke, quicken, rouse, stimulate. • *n* activity, ado, agitation, bustle, confusion, excitement, fidget, flurry, fuss, hurry, movement; commotion, disorder, disturbance, tumult, uproar.

stirring *adj* active, brisk, diligent, industrious, lively, smart; animating, arousing, awakening, exciting, quickening, stimulating.

stitch *vb* backstitch, baste, bind, embroider, fell, hem, seam, sew, tack, whip.

stive *vb* stow, stuff; boil, seethe, stew; make close, hot or sultry.

stock *vb* fill, furnish, store, supply; accumulate, garner, hoard, lay in, reposit, reserve, save, treasure up. • *adj* permanent, standard, standing. • *n* assets, capital, commodities, fund, principal, shares; accumulation, hoard, inventory, merchandise, provision, range, reserve, store, supply; ancestry, breed, descent, family, house, line, lineage, parentage, pedigree, race; cravat, neckcloth; butt, haft, hand; block, log, pillar, post, stake; stalk, stem, trunk.

stockholder *n* shareholder.

stocking *n* hose, sock.

stock market *n* stock exchange; cattle market.

stocks *npl* funds, public funds, public securities; shares.

stockstill *adj* dead-still, immobile, motionless, stationary, still, unmoving.

stocky *adj* chubby, chunky, dumpy, plump, short, stout, stubby, thickset.

stoic, stoical *adj* apathetic, cold-blooded, impassive, imperturbable, passionless, patient, philosophic, philosophical, phlegmatic, unimpassioned.

stoicism *n* apathy, coldness, coolness, impassivity, indifference, insensibility, nonchalance, phlegm.

stolen *adj* filched, pilfered, purloined; clandestine, furtive, secret, sly, stealthy, surreptitious.

stolid *adj* blockish, doltish, dull, foolish, heavy, obtuse, slow, stockish, stupid.

stolidity *n* doltishness, dullness, foolishness, obtuseness, stolidness, stupidity.

stomach *vb* abide, bear, brook, endure, put up with, stand, submit to, suffer, swallow, tolerate. • *n* abdomen, belly, gut, paunch, pot, tummy; appetite, desire, inclination, keenness, liking, relish, taste.

stone *vb* cover, face, slate, tile; lapidate, pelt. • *n* boulder, cobble, gravel, pebble, rock; gem, jewel, precious stone; cenotaph, gravestone, monument, tombstone; nut, pit; adamant, agate, flint, gneiss, granite, marble, slate, etc.

stony *adj* gritty, hard, lapidose, lithic, petrous, rocky; adamantine, flinty, hard, inflexible, obdurate; cruel, hard-hearted, inexorable, pitiless, stony-hearted, unfeeling, unrelenting.

stoop *vb* bend forward, bend down, bow, lean, sag, slouch, slump; abase, cower, cringe, give in, submit, succumb, surrender; condescend, deign, descend, vouchsafe; fall, sink. • *n* bend, inclination, sag, slouch, slump; descent, swoop.

stop *vb* block, blockade, close, close up, obstruct, occlude; arrest, check, halt, hold, pause, stall, stay; bar, delay, embargo, hinder, impede, intercept, interrupt, obstruct, preclude, prevent, repress, restrain, staunch, suppress, thwart; break off, cease, desist, discontinue, forbear, give over, leave off, refrain from; intermit, quiet, quieten, terminate; lodge, tarry. • *n* halt, intermission, pause, respite, rest, stoppage, suspension, truce; block, cessation, check, hindrance, interruption, obstruction, repression; bar, impediment, obstacle; full stop, point.

stopcock *n* cock, faucet, tap.

stoppage *n* arrest, block, check, closure, hindrance, interruption, obstruction, prevention.

stopper *n* cork, plug, stopple.

store *vb* accumulate, amass, cache, deposit, garner, hoard, husband, lay by, lay in, lay up, put by, reserve, save, store up, stow away, treasure up; furnish, provide, replenish, stock, supply.

• *n* accumulation, cache, deposit, fund, hoard, provision, reserve, stock, supply, treasure, treasury; abundance, plenty; storehouse; emporium, market, shop.

storehouse *n* depository, depot, godown, magazine, repository, store, warehouse.

storm *vb* assail, assault, attack; blow violently; fume, rage, rampage, rant, rave, tear. • *n* blizzard, gale, hurricane, squall, tempest, tornado, typhoon, whirlwind; agitation, clamour, commotion, disturbance, insurrection, outbreak, sedition, tumult, turmoil; adversity, affliction, calamity, distress; assault, attack, brunt, onset, onslaught; violence.

storminess *n* inclemency, roughness, tempestuousness.

stormy *adj* blustering, boisterous, gusty, squally, tempestuous, windy; passionate, riotous, rough, turbulent, violent, wild; agitated, furious.

story *n* annals, chronicle, history, record; account, narration, narrative, recital, record, rehearsal, relation, report, statement, tale; fable, fiction, novel, romance; anecdote, incident, legend, tale; canard, fabrication, falsehood, fib, figure, invention, lie, untruth.

storyteller *n* bard, chronicler, narrator, raconteur.

stout *adj* able-bodied, athletic, brawny, lusty, robust, sinewy, stalwart, strong, sturdy, vigorous; courageous, hardy, indomitable, stouthearted; contumacious, obstinate, proud, resolute, stubborn; compact, firm, solid, staunch; bouncing, bulky, burly, chubby, corpulent, fat, heavy, jolly, large, obese, plump, portly, stocky, strapping, thickset.

stouthearted *adj* fearless, heroic, redoubtable; bold, brave, courageous, dauntless, doughty, firm, gallant, hardy, indomitable, intrepid, resolute, valiant, valorous.

stow *vb* load, pack, put away, store, stuff.

straddle *vb* bestride.

straggle *vb* rove, wander; deviate, digress, ramble, range, roam, stray, stroll.

straggling *adj* rambling, roving, straying, strolling, wandering; scattered.

straight *adj* direct, near, rectilinear, right, short, undeviating, unswerving; erect, perpendicular, plumb, right, upright, vertical; equitable, fair, honest, honourable, just, square, straightforward. • *adv* at once, directly, forthwith, immediately, straightaway, straightway, without delay.

straightaway, straightway *adv* at once, directly, forthwith, immediately, speedily, straight, suddenly, without delay.

straighten *vb* arrange, make straight, neaten, order, tidy.

straight-laced *see* **strait-laced**.

strain[1] *vb* draw tightly, make tense, stretch, tighten; injure, sprain, wrench; exert, overexert, overtax, rack; embrace, fold, hug, press, squeeze; compel, constrain, force; dilute, distill, drain, filter, filtrate, ooze, percolate, purify, separate; fatigue, overtask, overwork, task, tax, tire. • *n* stress, tenseness, tension, tensity; effort, exertion, force, overexertion; burden, task, tax; sprain, wrech; lay, melody, movement, snatch, song, stave, tune.

strain[2] *n* manner, style, tone, vein; disposition, tendency, trait, turn; descent, extraction, family, lineage, pedigree, race, stock.

strait *adj* close, confined, constrained, constricted, contracted, narrow; rigid, rigorous, severe, strict; difficult, distressful, grievous, straitened. • *n* channel, narrows, pass, sound.

straits *npl* crisis, difficulty, dilemma, distress, embarrassment, emergency, exigency, extremity, hardship, pass, perplexity, pinch, plight, predicament.

straiten *vb* confine, constrain, constrict, contract, limit; narrow; intensify, stretch; distress, embarrass, perplex, pinch, press.

straitened *adj* distressed, embarrassed limited, perplexed, pinched.

strait-laced, straight-laced *adj* austere, formal, prim, rigid, rigorous, stern, stiff, strict, uncompromising.

straitness *n* narrowness, rigour, severity, strictness; difficulty, distress, trouble; insufficiency, narrowness, scarcity, want.

strand[1] *vb* abandon, beach, be wrecked, cast away, go aground, ground, maroon, run aground, wreck. • *n* beach, coast, shore.

strand[2] *n* braid, cord, fibre, filament, line, rope, string, tress.

stranded *adj* aground, ashore, cast away, lost, shipwrecked, wrecked.

strange *adj* alien, exotic, far-fetched, foreign, outlandish, remote; new, novel; curious, exceptional, extraordinary, irregular, odd, particular, peculiar, rare, singular, surprising, uncommon, unusual; abnormal, anomalous, extraordinary, inconceivable, incredible, inexplicable, marvellous, mysterious, preternatural, unaccountable, unbelievable, unheard of, unique, unnatural, wonderful; bizarre, droll, grotesque, quaint, queer; inexperienced, unacquainted, unfamiliar, unknown; bashful, distant, distrustful, reserved, shy, uncommunicative.

strangeness *n* foreignness; bashfulness, coldness, distance, reserve, shyness, uncommunicativeness; eccentricity, grotesqueness, oddness, singularity, uncommonness, uncouthness.

stranger *n* alien, foreigner, newcomer, immigrant, outsider; guest, visitor.

strangle *vb* choke, contract, smother, squeeze, stifle, suffocate, throttle, tighten; keep back, quiet, repress, still, suppress.

strap *vb* beat, thrash, whip; bind, fasten, sharpen, strop. • *n* thong; band, ligature, strip, tie; razor-strap, strop.

strapping *adj* big, burly, large, lusty, stalwart, stout, strong, tall.

stratagem *n* artifice, cunning, device, dodge, finesse, intrigue, machination, manoeuvre, plan, plot, ruse, scheme, trick, wile.

strategic, strategical *adj* calculated, deliberate, diplomatic, manoeuvering, planned, politic, tactical; critical, decisive, key, vital.

strategy *n* generalship, manoeuvering, plan, policy, stratagem, strategetics, tactics.

stratum *n* band, bed, layer.

straw *n* culm, stalk, stem; button, farthing, fig, penny, pin, rush, snap.

stray *vb* deviate, digress, err, meander, ramble, range, roam, rove, straggle, stroll, swerve, transgress, wander. • *adj* abandoned, lost, strayed, wandering; accidental, erratic, random, scattered.

streak *vb* band, bar, striate, stripe, vein; dart, dash, flash, hurtle, run, speed, sprint, stream, tear. • *n* band, bar, belt, layer, line, strip, stripe, thread, trace, vein; cast, grain, tone, touch, vein; beam, bolt, dart, dash, flare, flash, ray, stream.

streaky *adj* streaked, striped, veined.

stream *vb* course, flow, glide, pour, run, spout; emit, pour out, shed; emanate, go forth, issue, radiate; extend, float, stretch out, wave. • *n* brook, burn, race, rill, rivulet, run, runlet, runnel, trickle; course, current, flow, flux, race, rush, tide, torrent, wake, wash; beam, gleam, patch, radiation, ray, streak.

streamer *n* banner, colours, ensign, flag, pennon, standard.

street *n* avenue, highway, road, way.

strength *n* force, might, main, nerve, potency, power, vigour; hardness, solidity, toughness; impregnability, proof; brawn, grit, healthy, lustiness, muscle, robustness, sinew, stamina, thews, vigorousness; animation, courage, determination, firmness, fortitude, resolution, spirit; cogency, efficacy, soundness, validity; emphasis, energy; security, stay, support; brightness, brilliance, clearness, intensity, vitality, vividness; body, excellence, virtue; impetuosity, vehemence, violence; boldness.

strengthen *vb* buttress, recruit, reinforce; fortify; brace, energize, harden, nerve, steel, stimulate; freshen, invigorate, vitalize; animate, encourage; clench, clinch, confirm, corroborate, establish, fix, justify, sustain, support.

strenuous *adj* active, ardent, eager, earnest, energetic, resolute, vigorous, zealous; bold, determined, doughty, intrepid, resolute, spirited, strong, valiant.

stress *vb* accent, accentuate, emphasize, highlight, point up, underline, underscore; bear, bear upon, press, pressurize; pull, rack, strain, stretch, tense, tug. • *n* accent, accentuation, emphasis; effort, force, pull, strain, tension, tug; boisterousness, severity, violence; pressure, urgency.

stretch *vb* brace, screw, strain, tense, tighten; elongate, extend, lengthen, protract, pull; display, distend, expand, spread, unfold, widen; sprain, strain; distort, exaggerate, misrepresent. • *n* compass, extension, extent, range, reach, scope; effort, exertion, strain, struggle; course, direction.

strict *adj* close, strained, tense, tight; accurate, careful, close, exact, literal, particular, precise, scrupulous; austere, inflexible, harsh, orthodox, puritanical, rigid, rigorous, severe, stern, strait-laced, stringent, uncompromising, unyielding.

stricture *n* animadversion, censure, denunciation, criticism, compression, constriction, contraction.

strife *n* battle, combat, conflict, contention, contest, discord, quarrel, struggle, warfare.

strike *vb* bang, beat, belabour, box, buffet, cudgel, cuff, hit, knock, lash, pound, punch, rap, slap, slug, smite, thump, whip; impress, imprint, stamp; afflict, chastise, deal, give, inflict, punish; affect, astonish, electrify, stun; clash, collide, dash, touch; surrender, yield; mutiny, rebel, rise.

stringent *adj* binding, contracting, rigid, rigorous, severe, strict.

strip[1] *n* piece, ribbon, shred, slip.

strip[2] *vb* denude, hull, skin, uncover; bereave, deprive, deforest, desolate, despoil, devastate, disarm, dismantle, disrobe, divest, expose, fleece, loot, shave; plunder, pillage, ransack, rob, sack, spoil; disrobe, uncover, undress.

strive *vb* aim, attempt, endeavour, exert, labour, strain, struggle, toil; contend, contest, fight, tussle, wrestle; compete, cope.

stroke[1] *n* blow, glance, hit, impact, knock, lash, pat, percussion, rap, shot, switch, thump; attack, paralysis, stroke; affliction, damage, hardship, hurt, injury, misfortune, reverse, visitation; dash, feat, masterstroke, touch.

stroke[2] *vb* caress, feel, palpate, pet, knead, massage, nuzzle, rub, touch.

stroll *vb* loiter, lounge, ramble, range, rove, saunter, straggle, stray, wander. • *n* excursion, promenade, ramble, rambling, roving, tour, trip, walk, wandering.

strong *adj* energetic, forcible, powerful, robust, sturdy; able, enduring; cogent, firm, valid.

structure *vb* arrange, constitute, construct, make, organize. • *n* arrangement, conformation, configuration, constitution, construction, form, formation, make, organization; anatomy, composition, texture; building, edifice, fabric, framework, pile.

struggle *vb* aim, endeavour, exert, labour, strive, toil, try; battle, contend, contest, fight, wrestle; agonize, flounder, writhe. • *n* effort, endeavour, exertion, labour, pains; battle, conflict, contention, contest, fight, strife; agony, contortions, distress.

stubborn *adj* contumacious, dogged, headstrong, heady, inflexible, intractable, mulish, obdurate, obstinate, perverse, positive, refractory, ungovernable, unmanageable, unruly, unyielding, willful; constant, enduring, firm, hardy, persevering, persistent, steady, stoical, uncomplaining, unremitting; firm, hard, inflexible, stiff, strong, tough, unpliant, studied.

studious *adj* contemplative, meditative, reflective, thoughtful; assiduous, attentive, desirous, diligent, eager, lettered, scholarly, zealous.

study *vb* cogitate, lucubrate, meditate, muse, ponder, reflect, think; analyze, contemplate, examine, investigate, ponder, probe, scrutinize, search, sift, weigh. • *n* exercise, inquiry, investigation, reading, research, stumble; cogitation, consideration, contemplation, examination, meditation, reflection, thought; stun; model, object, representation, sketch; den, library, office, studio.

stunning *adj* deafening, stentorian; dumbfounding, stupefying.

stunted *adj* checked, diminutive, dwarfed, dwarfish, lilliputian, little, nipped, small, undersized.

stupendous *adj* amazing, astonishing, astounding, marvellous, overwhelming, surprising, wonderful; enormous, huge, immense, monstrous, prodigious, towering, tremendous, vast.

stupid *adj* brainless, crass, doltish, dull, foolish, idiotic, inane, inept, obtuse, pointless, prosaic, senseless, simple, slow, sluggish, stolid, tedious, tiresome, witless.

stupor *n* coma, confusion, daze, lethargy, narcosis, numbness, stupefaction, torpor.

sturdy *adj* bold, determined, dogged, firm, hardy, obstinate, persevering, pertinacious, resolute, stiff, stubborn, sturdy; athletic, brawny, forcible, lusty, muscular, powerful, robust, stalwart, stout, strong, thickset, vigorous, well-set.

style *vb* address, call, characterize, denominate, designate, dub, entitle, name, term. • *n* dedication, expression, phraseology, turn; cast, character, fashion, form, genre, make, manner, method, mode, model, shape, vogue, way; appellation, denomination, designation, name, title; chic, elegance, smartness; pen, pin, point, stylus.

stylish *adj* chic, courtly, elegant, fashionable, genteel, modish, polished, smart.

suave *adj* affable, agreeable, amiable, bland, courteous, debonair, delightful, glib, gracious, mild, pleasant, smooth, sweet, oily, unctuous, urbane.

subdue *vb* beat, bend, break, bow, conquer, control, crush, defeat, discomfit, foil, master, overbear, overcome, overpower, overwhelm, quell, rout, subject, subjugate, surmount, vanquish, worst; allay, choke, curb, mellow, moderate, mollify, reduce, repress, restrain, soften, suppress, temper.

subject *vb* control, master, overcome, reduce, subdue, subjugate, tame; enslave, enthral; abandon, refer, submit, surrender. • *adj* beneath, subjacent, underneath; dependent, enslaved, inferior, servile, subjected, subordinate, subservient; conditional, obedient, submissive; disposed, exposed to, liable, obnoxious, prone. • *n* dependent, henchman, liegeman, slave, subordinate; matter, point, subject matter, theme, thesis, topic; nominative, premise; case, object, patient, recipient; ego, mind, self, thinking.

subjoin *vb* add, affix, annex, append, join, suffix.

subjugate *vb* conquer, enslave, enthral, master, overcome, overpower, overthrow, subdue, subject, vanquish.

sublimate *vb* alter, change, repress.

sublime *adj* aloft, *elevated, high,* sacred; eminent, exalted, grand, great, lofty, mighty; august, glorious, magnificent, majestic, noble, stately, solemn, sublunary; elated, elevated, eloquent, exhilarated, raised.

submission *n* capitulation, cession, relinquishment, surrender, yielding; acquiescence, compliance, obedience, resignation; deference, homage, humility, lowliness, obeisance, passiveness, prostration, self-abasement, submissiveness.

submissive *adj* amenable, compliant, docile, pliant, tame, tractable, yielding; acquiescent, long-suffering, obedient, passive, patient, resigned, unassertive, uncomplaining, unrepining; deferential, humble, lowly, meek, obsequious, prostrate, self-abasing.

submit *vb* cede, defer, endure, resign, subject, surrender, yield; commit, propose, refer; offer; acquiesce, bend, capitulate, comply, stoop, succumb.

subordinate *adj* ancillary, dependent, inferior, junior, minor, secondary, subject, subservient, subsidiary. • *n* assistant, dependant, inferior, subject, underling.

subscribe *vb* accede, approve, agree, assent, consent, yield; contribute, donate, give, offer, promise.

subscription *n* aid, assistance, contribution, donation, gift, offering.

subsequent *adj* after, attendant, ensuing, later, latter, following, posterior, sequent, succeeding.

subservient *adj* inferior, obsequious, servile, subject, subordinate; accessory, aiding, auxiliary, conducive, contributory, helpful, instrumental, serviceable, useful.

subside *vb* settle, sink; abate, decline, decrease, diminish, drop, ebb, fall, intermit, lapse, lessen, lower, lull, wane.

subsidence *n* settling, sinking; abatement, decline, decrease, descent, ebb, diminution, lessening.

subsidiary *adj* adjutant, aiding, assistant, auxiliary, cooperative, corroborative, helping, subordinate, subservient.

subsidize *vb* aid, finance, fund, sponsor, support, underwrite.

subsidy *n* aid, bounty, grant, subvention, support, underwriting.

subsist *vb* be, breathe, consist, exist, inhere, live, prevail; abide, continue, endure, persist, remain; feed, maintain, ration, support.

subsistence *n* aliment, food, livelihood, living, maintenance, meat, nourishment, nutriment, provision, rations, support, sustenance, victuals.

substance *n* actuality, element, groundwork, hypostasis, reality, substratum; burden, content, core, drift, essence, gist, heart, import, meaning, pith, sense, significance, solidity, soul, sum, weight; estate, income, means, property, resources, wealth.

substantial *adj* actual, considerable, essential, existent, hypostatic, pithy, potential, real, subsistent, virtual; concrete, durable, positive, solid, tangible, true; corporeal, bodily, material; bulky, firm, goodly, heavy, large, massive, notable, significant, sizable, solid, sound, stable, stout, strong, well-made; cogent, just, efficient, influential, valid, weighty.

substantially *adv* adequately, essentially, firmly, materially, positively, really, truly.

substantiate *vb* actualize, confirm, corroborate, establish, prove, ratify, verify.

subterfuge *n* artifice, evasion, excuse, expedient, mask, pretence, pretext, quirk, shift, shuffle, sophistry, trick.

subtle *adj* arch, artful, astute, crafty, crooked, cunning, designing, diplomatic, intriguing, insinuating, sly, tricky, wily; clever, ingenious; acute, deep, discerning, discriminating, keen, profound, sagacious, shrewd; airy, delicate, ethereal, light, nice, rare, refined, slender, subtle, thin, volatile.

subtlety *n* artfulness, artifice, astuteness, craft, craftiness, cunning, guile, subtleness; acumen, acuteness, cleverness, discernment, intelligence, keenness, sagacity, sharpness, shrewdness; attenuation, delicacy, fitness, nicety, rareness, refinement.

subtract *vb* deduct, detract, diminish, remove, take, withdraw.

suburbs *npl* environs, confines, neighbourhood, outskirts, precincts, purlieus, vicinage.

subversive *adj* destructive, overthrowing, pervasive, ruining, upsetting. • *n* collaborator, dissident, insurrectionist, saboteur, terrorist, traitor.

subvert *vb* invert, overset, overthrow, overturn, reverse, upset; demolish, destroy, extinguish, raze, ruin; confound, corrupt, injure, pervert.

succeed *vb* ensue, follow, inherit, replace; flourish, gain, hit, prevail, prosper, thrive, win.

success *n* attainment, issue, result; fortune, happiness, hit, luck, prosperity, triumph.

successful *adj* auspicious, booming, felicitous, fortunate, happy, lucky, prosperous, victorious, winning.

succession *n* chain, concatenation, cycle, consecution, following, procession, progression, rotation, round, sequence, series, suite; descent, entail, inheritance, lineage, race, reversion.

succinct *adj* brief, compact, compendious, concise, condensed, curt, laconic, pithy, short, summary, terse.

succour *vb* aid, assist, help, relieve; cherish, comfort, encourage, foster, nurse. • *n* aid, assistance, help, relief, support.

succulent *adj* juicy, luscious, lush, nutritive, sappy.

succumb *vb* capitulate, die, submit, surrender, yield.

sudden *adj* abrupt, hasty, hurried, immediate, instantaneous, rash, unanticipated, unexpected, unforeseen, unusual; brief, momentary, quick, rapid.

sue *vb* charge, court, indict, prosecute, solicit, summon, woo; appeal, beg, demand, entreat, implore, petition, plead, pray, supplicate.

suffer *vb* feel, undergo; bear, endure, sustain, tolerate; admit, allow, indulge, let, permit.

sufferable *adj* allowable, bearable, endurable, permissible, tolerable.

sufferance *n* endurance, inconvenience, misery, pain, suffering; long-suffering, moderation, patience, submission; allowance, permission, toleration.

suffice *vb* avail, content, satisfy, serve.

sufficient *adj* adequate, ample, commensurate, competent, enough, full, plenteous, satisfactory; able, equal, fit, qualified, responsible.

suffocate *vb* asphyxiate, choke, smother, stifle, strangle.

suffrage *n* ballot, franchise, voice, vote; approval, attestation, consent, testimonial, witness.

suggest *vb* advise, allude, hint, indicate, insinuate, intimate, move, present, prompt, propose, propound, recommend.

suggestion *n* allusion, hint, indication, insinuation, intimation, presentation, prompting, proposal, recommendation, reminder.

suit *vb* accommodate, adapt, adjust, fashion, fit, level, match; accord, become, befit, gratify, harmonize, please, satisfy, tally. • *n* appeal, entreaty, invocation, petition, prayer, request, solicitation, supplication; courtship, wooing; action, case, cause, process, prosecution, trial; clothing, costume, habit.

suitable *adj* adapted, accordant, agreeable, answerable, apposite, applicable, appropriate, apt, becoming, befitting, conformable, congruous, convenient, consonant, correspondent, decent, due, eligible, expedient, fit, fitting, just, meet, pertinent, proper, relevant, seemly, worthy.

suite *n* attendants, bodyguard, convoy, cortege, court, escort, followers, staff, retainers, retinue, train; collection, series, set, suit; apartment, rooms.

sulky *adj* aloof, churlish, cross, cross-grained, dogged, grouchy, ill-humoured, ill-tempered, moody, morose, perverse, sour, spleenish, spleeny, splenetic, sullen, surly, vexatious, wayward.

sullen *adj* cross, crusty, glum, grumpy, ill-tempered, moody, morose, sore, sour, sulky; cheerless, cloudy, dark, depressing, dismal, foreboding, funereal, gloomy, lowering, melancholy, mournful, sombre; dull, heavy, slow, sluggish; intractable, obstinate, perverse, refractory, stubborn, vexatious; baleful, evil, inauspicious, malign, malignant, sinister, unlucky, unpropitious.

sully *vb* blemish, blot, contaminate, deface, defame, dirty, disgrace, dishonour, foul, smirch, soil, slur, spot, stain, tarnish.

sultry *adj* close, damp, hot, humid, muggy, oppressive, stifling, stuffy, sweltering.

sum *vb* add, calculate, compute, reckon; collect, comprehend, condense, epitomize, summarize. • *n* aggregate, amount, total,

totality, whole; compendium, substance, summary; acme, completion, height, summit.

summary *adj* brief, compendious, concise, curt, laconic, pithy, short, succinct, terse; brief, quick, rapid. • *n* abridgement, abstract, brief, compendium, digest, epitome, precis, résumé, syllabus, synopsis.

summit *n* acme, apex, cap, climax, crest, crown, pinnacle, top, vertex, zenith.

summon *vb* arouse, bid, call, cite, invite, invoke, rouse; convene, convoke; charge, indict, prosecute, subpoena, sue.

sumptuous *adj* costly, dear, expensive, gorgeous, grand, lavish, luxurious, magnificent, munificent, pompous, prodigal, rich, showy, splendid, stately, superb.

sunburnt *adj* bronzed, brown, ruddy, tanned.

sunder *vb* break, disconnect, disjoin, dissociate, dissever, disunited, divide, part, separate, sever.

sundry *adj* different, divers, several, some, various.

sunny *adj* bright, brilliant, clear, fine, luminous, radiant, shining, unclouded, warm; cheerful, genial, happy, joyful, mild, optimistic, pleasant, smiling.

superannuated *adj* aged, anile, antiquated, decrepit, disqualified, doting, effete, imbecile, passé, retired, rusty, time-worn, unfit.

superb *adj* august, beautiful, elegant, exquisite, grand, gorgeous, imposing, magnificent, majestic, noble, pompous, rich, showy, splendid, stately, sumptuous.

supercilious *adj* arrogant, condescending, contemptuous, dictatorial, domineering, haughty, high, imperious, insolent, intolerant, lofty, lordly, magisterial, overbearing, overweening, proud, scornful, vainglorious.

superficial *adj* external, flimsy, shallow, untrustworthy.

superfluity *n* excess, exuberance, redundancy, superabundance, surfeit.

superfluous *adj* excessive, redundant, unnecessary.

superintend *vb* administer, conduct, control, direct, inspect, manage, overlook, oversee, supervise.

superintendence *n* care, charge, control, direction, guidance, government, inspection, management, oversight, supervision, surveillance.

superior *adj* better, greater, high, higher, finer, paramount, supreme, ultra, upper; chief, foremost, principal; distinguished, matchless, noble, pre-eminent, preferable, sovereign, surpassing, unrivalled, unsurpassed; predominant, prevalent. • *n* boss, chief, director, head, higher-up, leader, manager, principal, senior, supervisor.

superiority *n* advantage, ascendency, lead, odds, predominance, pre-eminence, prevalence, transcendence; excellence, nobility, worthiness.

superlative *adj* consummate, greatest, incomparable, peerless, pre-eminent, supreme, surpassing, transcendent.

supernatural *adj* abnormal, marvellous, metaphysical, miraculous, otherworldly, preternatural, unearthly.

supernumerary *adj* excessive, odd, redundant, superfluous.

supersede *vb* annul, neutralize, obviate, overrule, suspend; displace, remove, replace, succeed, supplant.

supervise *vb* administer, conduct, control, direct, inspect, manage, overlook, oversee, superintend.

supine *adj* apathetic, careless, drowsy, dull, idle, indifferent, indolent, inert, languid, lethargic, listless, lumpish, lazy, negligent, otiose, prostrate, recumbent, sleepy, slothful, sluggish, spineless, torpid.

supplant *vb* overpower, overthrow, undermine; displace, remove, replace, supersede.

supple *adj* elastic, flexible, limber, lithe, pliable, pliant; compliant, humble, submissive, yielding; adulatory, cringing, fawning, flattering, grovelling, obsequious, oily, parasitical, servile, slavish, sycophantic.

supplement *vb* add, augment, extend, reinforce, supply. • *n* addendum, addition, appendix, codicil, complement, continuation, postscript.

suppliant *adj* begging, beseeching, entreating, imploring, precatory, praying, suing, supplicating. • *n* applicant, petitioner, solicitor, suitor, supplicant.

supplicate *vb* beg, beseech, crave, entreat, implore, importune, petition, pray, solicit.

supplication *n* invocation, orison, petition, prayer; entreaty, petition, prayer, request, solicitation.

supply *vb* endue, equip, furnish, minister, outfit, provide, replenish, stock, store; afford, accommodate, contribute, furnish, give, grant, yield. • *n* hoard, provision, reserve, stock, store.

support *vb* brace, cradle, pillow, prop, sustain, uphold; bear, endure, undergo, suffer, tolerate; cherish, keep, maintain, nourish, nurture; act, assume, carry, perform, play, represent; accredit, confirm, corroborate, substantiate, verify; abet, advocate, aid, approve, assist, back, befriend, champion, countenance, encourage, favour, float, hold, patronize, relieve, reinforce, succour, vindicate. • *n* bolster, brace, buttress, foothold, guy, hold, prop, purchase, shore, stay, substructure, supporter, underpinning; groundwork, mainstay, staff; base, basis, bed, foundation; keeping, living, livelihood, maintenance, subsistence, sustenance; confirmation, evidence; aid, assistance, backing, behalf, championship, comfort, countenance, encouragement, favour, help, patronage, succour.

suppose *vb* apprehend, believe, conceive, conclude, consider, conjecture, deem, imagine, judge, presume, presuppose, think; assume, hypothesize; imply, posit, predicate, think; fancy, opine, speculate, surmise, suspect, theorize, wean.

supposition *n* conjecture, guess, guesswork, presumption, surmise; assumption, hypothesis, postulation, theory, thesis; doubt, uncertainty.

suppress *vb* choke, crush, destroy, overwhelm, overpower, overthrow, quash, quell, quench, smother, stifle, subdue, withhold; arrest, inhibit, obstruct, repress, restrain, stop; conceal, extinguish, keep, retain, secret, silence, stifle, strangle.

supremacy *n* ascendancy, domination, headship, lordship, mastery, predominance, pre-eminence, primacy, sovereignty.

supreme *adj* chief, dominant, first, greatest, highest, leading, paramount, predominant, pre-eminent, principal, sovereign.

sure *adj* assured, certain, confident, positive; accurate, dependable, effective, honest, infallible, precise, reliable, trustworthy, undeniable, undoubted, unmistakable, well-proven; guaranteed, inevitable, irrevocable; fast, firm, safe, secure, stable, steady.

surely *adv* assuredly, certainly, infallibly, sure, undoubtedly; firmly, safely, securely, steadily.

surety *n* bail, bond, certainty, guarantee, pledge, safety, security.

surfeit *vb* cram, gorge, overfeed, sate, satiate; cloy, nauseate, pall. • *n* excess, fullness, glut, oppression, plethora, satiation, satiety, superabundance, superfluity.

surge *vb* billow, rise, rush, sweep, swell, swirl, tower. • *n* billow, breaker, roller, wave, white horse.

surly *adj* churlish, crabbed, cross, crusty, discourteous, fretful, gruff, grumpy, harsh, ill-natured, ill-tempered, morose, peevish, perverse, pettish, petulant, rough, rude, snappish, snarling, sour, sullen, testy, touchy, uncivil, ungracious, waspish; dark, tempestuous.

surmise *vb* believe, conclude, conjecture, consider, divine, fancy, guess, imagine, presume, suppose, think, suspect. • *n* conclusion, conjecture, doubt, guess, notion, possibility, supposition, suspicion, thought.

surmount *vb* clear, climb, crown, overtop, scale, top, vault; conquer, master, overcome, overpower, subdue, vanquish; exceed, overpass, pass, surpass, transcend.

surpass *vb* beat, cap, eclipse, exceed, excel, outdo, outmatch, outnumber, outrun, outstrip, override, overshadow, overtop, outshine, surmount, transcend.

surplus *adj* additional, leftover, remaining, spare, superfluous, supernumerary, supplementary. • *n* balance, excess, overplus, remainder, residue, superabundance, surfeit.

surprise *vb* amaze, astonish, astound, bewilder, confuse, disconcert, dumbfound, startle, stun. • *n* amazement, astonishment, blow, shock, wonder.

surprising *adj* amazing, astonishing, astounding, extraordinary, marvellous, unexpected, remarkable, startling, strange, unexpected, wonderful.

surrender *vb* cede, sacrifice, yield; abdicate, abandon, forgo, relinquish, renounce, resign, waive; capitulate, comply, succumb. • *n* abandonment, capitulation, cession, delivery, relinquishment, renunciation, resignation, yielding.

surreptitious *adj* clandestine, fraudulent, furtive, secret, sly, stealthy, unauthorized, underhand.

surround *vb* beset, circumscribe, compass, embrace, encircle, encompass, environ, girdle, hem, invest, loop.

surveillance *n* care, charge, control, direction, inspection, management, oversight, superintendence, supervision, surveyorship, vigilance, watch.

survey *vb* contemplate, observe, overlook, reconnoitre, review, scan, scout, view; examine, inspect, scrutinize; oversee, supervise; estimate, measure, plan, plot, prospect. • *n* prospect, retrospect, sight, view; examination, inspection, reconnaissance, review; estimating, measuring, planning, plotting, prospecting, work-study.

survive *vb* endure, last, outlast, outlive.

susceptible *adj* capable, excitable, impressible, impressionable, inclined, predisposed, receptive, sensitive.

suspect *vb* believe, conclude, conjecture, fancy, guess, imagine, judge, suppose, surmise, think; distrust, doubt, mistrust. • *adj* doubtful, dubious, suspicious.

suspend *vb* append, hang, sling, swing; adjourn, arrest, defer, delay, discontinue, hinder, intermit, interrupt, postpone, stay, withhold; debar, dismiss, rusticate.

suspicion *n* assumption, conjecture, dash, guess, hint, inkling, suggestion, supposition, surmise, trace; apprehension, distrust, doubt, fear, jealousy, misgiving, mistrust.

suspicious *adj* distrustful, jealous, mistrustful, suspect, suspecting; doubtful, questionable.

sustain *vb* bear, bolster, fortify, prop, strengthen, support, uphold; maintain, nourish, perpetuate, preserve; aid, assist, comfort, relieve; brave, endure, suffer, undergo; approve, confirm, ratify, sanction, validate; confirm, establish, justify, prove.

sustenance *n* maintenance, subsistence, support; aliment, bread, food, nourishment, nutriment, nutrition, provisions, supplies, victuals.

swagger *vb* bluster, boast, brag, bully, flourish, hector, ruffle, strut, swell, vapour. • *n* airs, arrogance, bluster, boastfulness, braggadocio, ruffling, strut.

swain *n* clown, countryman, hind, peasant, rustic; adorer, gallant, inamorata, lover, suitor, wooer.

swallow *vb* bolt, devour, drink, eat, englut, engorge, gobble, gorge, gulp, imbibe, ingurgitate, swamp; absorb, appropriate, arrogate, devour, engulf, submerge; consume, employ, occupy; brook, digest, endure, pocket, stomach; recant, renounce, retract. • *n* gullet, oesophagus, throat; inclination, liking, palate, relish, taste; deglutition, draught, gulp, ingurgitation, mouthful, taste.

swamp *vb* engulf, overwhelm, sink; capsize, embarrass, overset, ruin, upset, wreck. • *n* bog, fen, marsh, morass, quagmire, slough.

sward *n* grass, lawn, sod, turf.

swarm *vb* abound, crowd, teem, throng. • *n* cloud, concourse, crowd, drove, flock, hive, horde, host, mass, multitude, press, shoal, throng.

swarthy *adj* black, brown, dark, dark-skinned, dusky, tawny.

sway *vb* balance, brandish, move, poise, rock, roll, swing, wave, wield; bend, bias, influence, persuade, turn, urge; control, dominate, direct, govern, guide, manage, rule; hoist, raise; incline, lean, lurch, yaw. • *n* ascendency, authority, command, control, domination, dominion, empire, government, mastership, mastery, omnipotence, predominance, power, rule, sovereignty; bias, direction, influence, weight; preponderance, preponderation; oscillation, sweep, swing, wag, wave.

swear *vb* affirm, attest, avow, declare, depose, promise, say, state, testify, vow; blaspheme, curse.

sweep *vb* clean, brush; graze, touch; rake, scour, traverse. • *n* amplitude, compass, drive, movement, range, reach, scope; destruction, devastation, havoc, ravage; curvature, curve.

sweeping *adj* broad, comprehensive, exaggerated, extensive, extravagant, general, unqualified, wholesale.

sweet *adj* candied, cloying, honeyed, luscious, nectareous, nectarous, sugary, saccharine; balmy, fragrant, odorous, redolent, spicy; harmonious, dulcet, mellifluous, mellow, melodious, musical, pleasant, soft, tuneful, silver-toned, silvery; beautiful, fair, lovely; agreeable, charming, delightful, grateful, gratifying; affectionate, amiable, attractive, engaging, gentle, mild, lovable, winning, benignant, serene; clean, fresh, pure, sound. • *n* fragrance, perfume, redolence; blessing, delight, enjoyment, gratification, joy, pleasure; candy, treat.

swell *vb* belly, bloat, bulge, dilate, distend, expand, inflate, intumesce, puff, swell, tumefy; augment, enlarge, increase; heave, rise, surge; strut, swagger. • *n* swelling; augmentation, excrescence, protuberance; ascent, elevation, hill, rise; force, intensity, power; billows, surge, undulation, waves; beau, blade, buck, coxcomb, dandy, exquisite, fop, popinjay.

swerve *vb* deflect, depart, deviate, stray, turn, wander; bend, incline, yield; climb, swarm, wind.

swift *adj* expeditious, fast, fleet, flying, quick, rapid, speedy; alert, eager, forward, prompt, ready, zealous; instant, sudden.

swiftness *n* celerity, expedition, fleetness, quickness, rapidity, speed, velocity.

swindle *vb* cheat, con, cozen, deceive, defraud, diddle, dupe, embezzle, forge, gull, hoax, overreach, steal, trick, victimize. • *n* cheat, con, deceit, deception, fraud, hoax, imposition, knavery, roguery, trickery.

swindler *n* blackleg, cheat, defaulter, embezzler, faker, fraud, impostor, jockey, knave, peculator, rogue, sharper, trickster.

swing *vb* oscillate, sway, vibrate, wave; dangle, depend, hang; brandish, flourish, whirl; administer, manage. • *n* fluctuation, oscillation, sway, undulation, vibration; elbow-room, freedom, margin, play, range, scope, sweep; bias, tendency.

swoop *vb* descend, pounce, rush, seize, stoop, sweep. • *n* clutch, pounce, seizure; stoop, descent.

sword *n* brand, broadsword, claymore, cutlass, epee, falchion, foil, hanger, rapier, sabre, scimitar.

sybarite *n* epicure, voluptuary.

sycophancy *n* adulation, cringing, fawning, flattery, grovelling, obsequiousness, servility.

sycophant *n* cringer, fawner, flunky, hanger-on, lickspittle, parasite, spaniel, toady, wheedler.

syllabus *n* abridgement, abstract, breviary, brief, compendium, digest, epitome, outline, summary, synopsis.

symbol *n* badge, emblem, exponent, figure, mark, picture, representation, representative, sign, token, type.

symbolic, symbolical *adj* emblematic, figurative, hieroglyphic, representative, significant, typical.

symmetry *n* balance, congruity, evenness, harmony, order, parallelism, proportion, regularity, shapeliness.

sympathetic *adj* affectionate, commiserating, compassionate, condoling, kind, pitiful, tender.

sympathy *n* accord, affinity, agreement, communion, concert, concord, congeniality, correlation, correspondence, harmony, reciprocity, union; commiseration, compassion, condolence, fellow-feeling, kindliness, pity, tenderness, thoughtfulness.

symptom *n* diagnostic, indication, mark, note, prognostic, sign, token.

symptomatic *adj* characteristic, indicative, symbolic, suggestive.

synonymous *adj* equipollent, equivalent, identical, interchangeable, similar, tantamount.

synopsis *n* abridgement, abstract, compendium, digest, epitome, outline, precis, résumé, summary, syllabus.

system *n* method, order, plan.

systematic *adj* methodic, methodical, orderly, regular.

T

tabernacle *n* pavilion, tent; cathedral, chapel, church, minster, synagogue, temple.

table *vb* enter, move, propose, submit, suggest. • *n* plate, slab, tablet; board, counter, desk, stand; catalogue, chart, compendium, index, list, schedule, syllabus, synopsis, tabulation; diet, fare, food, victuals.

tableau *n* picture, scene, representation.

taboo *vb* forbid, interdict, prohibit, proscribe. • *adj* banned, forbidden, inviolable, outlawed, prohibited, proscribed. • *n* ban, interdict, prohibition, proscription.

tacit *adj* implicit, implied, inferred, silent, understood, unexpressed, unspoken.

taciturn *adj* close, dumb, laconic, mum, reserved, reticent, silent, tight-lipped, uncommunicative.

tack *vb* add, affix, append, attach, fasten, tag; gybe, yaw, zigzag. • *n* nail, pin, staple; bearing, course, direction, heading, path, plan, procedure.

tackle *vb* attach, grapple, seize; attempt, try, undertake. • *n* apparatus, cordage, equipment, furniture, gear, harness, implements, rigging, tackling, tools, weapons.

tact *n* address, adroitness, cleverness, dexterity, diplomacy, discernment, finesse, insight, knack, perception, skill, understanding.

tail *vb* dog, follow, shadow, stalk, track. • *adj* abridged, curtailed, limited, reduced. • *n* appendage, conclusion, end, extremity, stub; flap, skirt; queue, retinue, train.

taint *vb* imbue, impregnate; contaminate, corrupt, defile, inflect, mildew, pollute, poison, spoil, touch; blot, stain, sully, tarnish. • *n* stain, tincture, tinge, touch; contamination, corruption, defilement, depravation, infection, pollution; blemish, defect, fault, flaw, spot.

take *vb* accept, obtain, procure, receive; clasp, clutch, grasp, grip, gripe, seize, snatch; filch, misappropriate, pilfer, purloin, steal; abstract, apprehend, appropriate, arrest, bag, capture, ensnare, entrap; attack, befall, smite; capture, carry off, conquer, gain, win; allure, attract, bewitch, captivate, charm, delight, enchant, engage, fascinate, interest, please; consider, hold, interrupt, suppose, regard, understand; choose, elect, espouse, select; employ, expend, use; claim, demand, necessitate, require; bear, endure, experience, feel, perceive, tolerate; deduce, derive, detect, discover, draw; carry, conduct, convey, lead, transfer; clear, surmount; drink, eat, imbibe, inhale, swallow. • *n* proceeds, profits, return, revenue, takings, yield.

tale *n* account, fable, legend, narration, novel, parable, recital, rehearsal, relation, romance, story, yarn; catalogue, count, enumeration, numbering, reckoning, tally.

talent *n* ableness, ability, aptitude, capacity, cleverness, endowment, faculty, forte, genius, gift, knack, parts, power, turn.

talk *vb* chatter, communicate, confer, confess, converse, declaim, discuss, gossip, pontificate, speak. • *n* chatter, communication, conversation, diction, gossip, jargon, language, rumour, speech, utterance.

talkative *adj* chatty, communicative, garrulous, loquacious, voluble.

tally *vb* accord, agree, conform, coincide, correspond, harmonize, match, square, suit. • *n* match, mate; check, counterpart, muster, roll call; account, reckoning.

tame *vb* domesticate, reclaim, train; conquer, master, overcome, repress, subdue, subjugate. • *adj* docile, domestic, domesticated, gentle, mild, reclaimed; broken, crushed, meek, subdued, unresisting, submissive; barren, commonplace, dull, feeble, flat, insipid, jejune, languid, lean, poor, prosaic, prosy, spiritless, tedious, uninteresting, vapid.

tamper *vb* alter, conquer, dabble, damage, interfere, meddle; intrigue, seduce, suborn.

tang *n* aftertaste, flavour, relish, savour, smack, taste; keenness, nip, sting.

tangible *adj* corporeal, material, palpable, tactile, touchable; actual, certain, embodied, evident, obvious, open, perceptible, plain, positive, real, sensible, solid, stable, substantial.

tangle *vb* complicate, entangle, intertwine, interweave, mat, perplex, snarl; catch, ensnare, entrap, involve, catch; embarrass, embroil, perplex. • *n* complication, disorder, intricacy, jumble, perplexity, snarl; dilemma, embarrassment, quandary, perplexity.

tantalize *vb* balk, disappoint, frustrate, irritate, provoke, tease, torment, vex.

tantamount *adj* equal, equivalent, synonymous.

tantrum *n* fit, ill-humour, outburst, paroxysm, temper, whim.

tap[1] *vb* knock, pat, rap, strike, tip, touch. • *n* pat, tip, rap, touch.

tap[2] *vb* broach, draw off, extract, pierce; draw on, exploit, mine, use, utilize; bug, eavesdrop, listen in. • *n* faucet, plug, spigot, spout, stopcock, valve; bug, listening device, transmitter.

tardiness *n* delay, dilatoriness, lateness, procrastination, slackness, slowness.

tardy *adj* slow, sluggish, snail-like; backward, behindhand, dilatory, late, loitering, overdue, slack.

tarn *n* bog, fen, marsh, morass, swamp.

tarnish *vb* blemish, deface, defame, dim, discolour, dull, slur, smear, soil, stain, sully. • *n* blemish, blot, soiling, spot, stain.

tarry *vb* delay, dally, linger, loiter, remain, stay, stop, wait; defer; abide, lodge, rest, sojourn.

tart *adj* acid, acidulous, acrid, astringent, piquant, pungent, sharp, sour; acrimonious, caustic, crabbed, curt, harsh, ill-humoured, ill-tempered, keen, petulant, sarcastic, severe, snappish, testy.

task *vb* burden, overwork, strain, tax. • *n* drudgery, labour, toil, work; business, charge, chore, duty, employment, enterprise, job, mission, stint, undertaking; assignment, exercise, lesson.

taste *vb* experience, feel, perceive, undergo; relish, savour, sip. • *n* flavour, gusto, relish, savour, smack, piquancy; admixture, bit, dash, fragment, hint, infusion, morsel, mouthful, sample, shade, sprinkling, suggestion, tincture; appetite, desire, fondness, liking, partiality, predilection; acumen, cultivation, culture, delicacy, discernment, discrimination, elegance, fine-feeling, grace, judgement, polish, refinement; manner, style.

tasteful *adj* appetizing, delicious, flavoursome, palatable, savoury, tasty, toothsome; aesthetic, artistic, attractive, elegant.

tasteless *adj* flat, insipid, savourless, stale, watery; dull, mawkish, uninteresting, vapid.

tattle *vb* babble, chat, chatter, jabber, prate, prattle; blab, gossip, inform. • *n* gabble, gossip, prate, prattle, tittle-tattle, twaddle.

taunt *vb* censure, chaff, deride, flout, jeer, mock, scoff, sneer, revile, reproach, ridicule, twit, upbraid. • *n* censure, derision, gibe, insult, jeer, quip, quirk, reproach, ridicule, scoff.

taut *adj* strained, stretched, tense, tight.

tautology *n* iteration, pleonasm, redundancy, reiteration, repetition, verbosity, wordiness.

tavern *n* bar, chophouse, hostelry, inn, pub, public house.

tawdry *adj* flashy, gaudy, garish, glittering, loud, meretricious, ostentatious, showy.

tax *vb* burden, demand, exact, load, overtax, require, strain, task; accuse, charge. • *n* assessment, custom, duty, excise, impost, levy, rate, taxation, toll, tribute; burden, charge, demand, requisition, strain; accusation, censure.

teach *vb* catechize, coach, discipline, drill, edify, educate, enlighten, inform, indoctrinate, initiate, instruct, ground, prime, school, train, tutor; communicate, disseminate, explain, expound, impart, implant, inculcate, infuse, instil, interpret, preach, propagate; admonish, advise, counsel, direct, guide, signify, show.

teacher *n* coach, educator, inculcator, informant, instructor, master, pedagogue, preceptor, schoolteacher, trainer, tutor; adviser, counsellor, guide, mentor; pastor, preacher.

tear *vb* burst, slit, rive, rend, rip; claw, lacerate, mangle, shatter, rend, wound; sever, sunder; fume, rage, rant, rave. • *n* fissure, laceration, rent, rip, wrench.

tease *vb* annoy, badger, beg, bother, chafe, chagrin, disturb, harass, harry, hector, importune, irritate, molest, pester, plague, provoke, tantalize, torment, trouble, vex, worry.

tedious *adj* dull, fatiguing, irksome, monotonous, tiresome, trying, uninteresting, wearisome; dilatory, slow, sluggish, tardy.

teem *vb* abound, bear, produce, swarm; discharge, empty, overflow.

teeming *adj* abounding, fraught, full, overflowing, pregnant, prolific, replete, swarming.

tell *vb* compute, count, enumerate, number, reckon; describe, narrate, recount, rehearse, relate, report; acknowledge, announce, betray, confess, declare, disclose, divulge, inform, own, reveal; acquaint, communicate, instruct, teach; discern, discover, distinguish; express, mention, publish, speak, state, utter.

temper *vb* modify, qualify; appease, assuage, calm, mitigate, mollify, moderate, pacify, restrain, soften, soothe; accommodate, adapt, adjust, fit, suit. • *n* character, constitution, nature, organization, quality, structure, temperament, type; disposition, frame, grain, humour, mood, spirits, tone, vein; calmness, composure, equanimity, moderation, tranquillity; anger, illtemper, irritation, spleen, passion.

temperament *n* character, constitution, disposition, habit, idiosyncrasy, nature, organization, temper.

temperate *adj* abstemious, ascetic, austere, chaste, continent, frugal, moderate, self-controlled, self-denying, sparing; calm, cool, dispassionate, mild, sober, sedate.

tempest *n* cyclone, gale, hurricane, squall, storm, tornado; commotion, disturbance, excitement, perturbation, tumult, turmoil.

temporal *adj* civil, lay, mundane, political, profane, secular, terrestrial, worldly; brief, ephemeral, evanescent, fleeting, momentary, short-lived, temporal, transient, transitory.

temporary *adj* brief, ephemeral, evanescent, fleeting, impermanent, momentary, short-lived, transient, transitory.

tempt *vb* prove, test, try; allure, decoy, entice, induce, inveigle, persuade, seduce; dispose, incite, incline, instigate, lead, prompt, provoke.

tempting *adj* alluring, attractive, enticing, inviting, seductive.

tenable *adj* defensible, maintainable, rational, reasonable, sound.

tenacious *adj* retentive, unforgetful; adhesive, clinging, cohesive, firm, glutinous, gummy, resisting, retentive, sticky, strong, tough, unyielding, viscous; dogged, fast, obstinate, opinionated, opinionative, pertinacious, persistent, resolute, stubborn, unwavering.

tenacity *n* retentiveness, tenaciousness; adhesiveness, cohesiveness, glutinosity, glutinousness, gumminess, toughness, stickiness, strength, viscidity; doggedness, firmness, obstinacy, perseverance, persistency, pertinacity, resolution, stubbornness.

tend[1] *vb* accompany, attend, graze, guard, keep, protect, shepherd, watch.

tend[2] *vb* aim, exert, gravitate, head, incline, influence, lead, lean, point, trend, verge; conduce, contribute.

tendency *n* aim, aptitude, bearing, bent, bias, course, determination, disposition, direction, drift, gravitation, inclination, leaning, liability, predisposition, proclivity, proneness, propensity, scope, set, susceptibility, turn, twist, warp.

tender[1] *vb* bid, offer, present, proffer, propose, suggest, volunteer. • *n* bid, offer, proffer, proposal; currency, money.

tender[2] *adj* callow, delicate, effeminate, feeble, feminine, fragile, immature, infantile, soft, weak, young; affectionate, compassionate, gentle, humane, kind, lenient, loving, merciful, mild, pitiful, sensitive, sympathetic, tender-hearted; affecting, disagreeable, painful, pathetic, touching, unpleasant.

tenebrous *adj* cloudy, dark, darksome, dusky, gloomy, murky, obscure, shadowy, shady, sombre, tenebrious.

tenement *n* abode, apartment, domicile, dwelling, flat, house.

tenet *n* belief, creed, position, dogma, doctrine, notion, opinion, position, principle, view.

tenor *n* cast, character, cut, fashion, form, manner, mood, nature, stamp, tendency, trend, tone; drift, gist, import, intent, meaning, purport, sense, significance, spirit.

tense *vb* flex, strain, tauten, tighten. • *adj* rigid, stiff, strained, stretched, taut, tight; excited, highly strung, intent, nervous, rapt.

tentative *adj* essaying, experimental, provisional, testing, toying.

tenure *n* holding, occupancy, occupation, possession, tenancy, tenement, use.

term *vb* call, christen, denominate, designate, dub, entitle, name, phrase, style. • *n* bound, boundary, bourn, confine, limit, mete,

terminus; duration, period, season, semester, span, spell, termination, time; denomination, expression, locution, name, phrase, word.

termagant *n* beldam, hag, scold, shrew, spitfire, virago, vixen. •

terminal *adj* bounding, limiting; final, terminating, ultimate. • *n* end, extremity, termination; bound, limit; airport, depot, station, terminus.

terminate *vb* bound, limit; end, finish, close, complete, conclude; eventuate, issue, prove.

termination *n* ending, suffix; bound, extend, limit; end, completion, conclusion, consequence, effect, issue, outcome, result.

terms *npl* conditions, provisions, stipulations.

terrestrial *adj* earthly, mundane, subastral, subcelestial, sublunar, sublunary, tellurian, worldly. • *n* earthling, human.

terrible *adj* appalling, dire, dreadful, fearful, formidable, frightful, gruesome, hideous, horrible, horrid, shocking, terrific, tremendous; alarming, awe-inspiring, awful, dread; great, excessive, extreme, severe.

terrific *adj* marvellous, sensational, superb; immense, intense; alarming, dreadful, formidable, frightful, terrible, tremendous.

terrify *vb* affright, alarm, appal, daunt, dismay, fright, frighten, horrify, scare, shock, startle, terrorize.

territory *n* country, district, domain, dominion, division, land, place, province, quarter, region, section, tract.

terror *n* affright, alarm, anxiety, awe, consternation, dismay, dread, fear, fright, horror, intimidation, panic, terrorism.

terse *adj* brief, compact, concise, laconic, neat, pithy, polished, sententious, short, smooth, succinct.

test *vb* assay; examine, prove, try. • *n* attempt, essay, examination, experiment, ordeal, proof, trial; criterion, standard, touchstone; example, exhibition; discrimination, distinction, judgment.

testify *vb* affirm, assert, asseverate, attest, avow, certify, corroborate, declare, depose, evidence, state, swear.

testimonial *n* certificate, credential, recommendation, voucher; monument, record.

testimony *n* affirmation, attestation, confession, confirmation, corroboration, declaration, deposition, profession; evidence, proof, witness.

testy *adj* captious, choleric, cross, fretful, hasty, irascible, irritable, quick, peevish, peppery, pettish, petulant, snappish, splenetic, touchy, waspish.

tetchy *adj* crabbed, cross, fretful, irritable, peevish, sullen, touchy.

tether *vb* chain, fasten, picket, stake, tie. • *n* chain, fastening, rope.

text *n* copy, subject, theme, thesis, topic, treatise.

texture *n* fabric, web, weft; character, coarseness, composition, constitution, fibre, fineness, grain, make-up, nap, organization, structure, tissue.

thankful *adj* appreciative, beholden, grateful, indebted, obliged.

thankfulness *n* appreciation, gratefulness, gratitude.

thankless *adj* profitless, ungracious, ungrateful, unthankful.

thaw *vb* dissolve, liquefy, melt, soften, unbend.

theatre *n* opera house, playhouse; arena, scene, seat, stage.

theatrical *adj* dramatic, dramaturgic, dramaturgical, histrionic, scenic, spectacular; affected, ceremonious, meretricious, ostentatious, pompous, showy, stagy, stilted, unnatural.

theft *n* depredation, embezzlement, fraud, larceny, peculation, pilfering, purloining, robbery, spoliation, stealing, swindling, thieving.

theme *n* composition, essay, motif, subject, text, thesis, topic, treatise.

theoretical *adj* abstract, conjectural, doctrinaire, ideal, hypothetical, pure, speculative, unapplied.

theory *n* assumption, conjecture, hypothesis, idea, plan, postulation, principle, scheme, speculation, surmise, system; doctrine, philosophy, science; explanation, exposition, philosophy, rationale.

therefore *adv* accordingly, afterward, consequently, hence, so, subsequently, then, thence, whence.

thesaurus *n* dictionary, encyclopedia, repository, storehouse, treasure.

thick *adj* bulky, chunky, dumpy, plump, solid, squab, squat, stubby, thickset; clotted, coagulated, crass, dense, dull, gross, heavy, viscous; blurred, cloudy, dirty, foggy, hazy, indistinguishable, misty, obscure, vaporous; muddy, roiled, turbid; abundant, frequent, multitudinous, numerous; close, compact, crowded, set, thickset; confused, guttural, hoarse, inarticulate, indistinct; dim, dull, weak; familiar, friendly, intimate, neighbourly, well-acquainted. • *adv* fast, frequently, quick; closely, densely, thickly. • *n* centre, middle, midst.

thicket *n* clump, coppice, copse, covert, forest, grove, jungle, shrubbery, underbrush, undergrowth, wood, woodland.

thief *n* depredator, filcher, pilferer, lifter, marauder, purloiner, robber, shark, stealer; burglar, corsair, defaulter, defrauder, embezzler, footpad, highwayman, housebreaker, kidnapper, pickpocket, pirate, poacher, privateer, sharper, swindler, peculator.

thieve *vb* cheat, embezzle, peculate, pilfer, plunder, purloin, rob, steal, swindle.

thin *vb* attenuate, dilute, diminish, prune, reduce, refine, weaken. • *adj* attenuated, bony, emaciated, fine, fleshless, flimsy, gaunt, haggard, lank, lanky, lean, meagre, peaked, pinched, poor, scanty, scraggy, scrawny, slender, slight, slim, small, sparse, spindly.

thing *n* being, body, contrivance, creature, entity, object, something, substance; act, action, affair, arrangement, circumstance, concern, deed, event, matter, occurrence, transaction.

think *vb* cogitate, contemplate, dream, meditate, muse, ponder, reflect, ruminate, speculate; consider, deliberate, reason, undertake; apprehend, believe, conceive, conclude, deem, determine, fancy, hold, imagine, judge, opine, presume, reckon, suppose, surmise; design, intend, mean, purpose; account, count, deem, esteem, hold, regard; compass, design, plan, plot. • *n* assessment, contemplation, deliberation, meditation, opinion, reasoning, reflection.

thirst *n* appetite, craving, desire, hunger, longing, yearning; aridity, drought, dryness.

thirsty *adj* arid, dry, parched; eager, greedy, hungry, longing, yearning.

thorn *n* prickle, spine; annoyance, bane, care, evil, infliction, nettle, nuisance, plague, torment, trouble, scourge.

thorny *adj* briary, briery, prickly, spinose, spinous, spiny; acuminate, barbed, pointed, prickling, sharp, spiky; annoying, difficult, harassing, perplexing, rugged, troublesome, trying, vexatious.

thorough, thoroughgoing *adj* absolute, arrant, complete, downright, entire, exhaustive, finished, perfect, radical, sweeping, total unmitigated, utter; accurate, correct, reliable, trustworthy.

though *conj* admitting, allowing, although, granted, granting, if, notwithstanding, still. • *adv* however, nevertheless, still, yet.

thought *n* absorption, cogitation, engrossment, meditation, musing, reflection, reverie, rumination; contemplation, intellect, ratiocination, thinking, thoughtfulness; application, conception, consideration, deliberation, idea, pondering, speculation, study; consciousness, imagination, intellect, perception, understanding; conceit, fancy, notion; conclusion, judgment, motion, opinion, sentiment, supposition, view; anxiety, attention, care, concern, provision, regard, solicitude, thoughtfulness; design, expectation, intention, purpose.

thoughtful *adj* absorbed, contemplative, deliberative, dreamy, engrossed, introspective, pensive, philosophic, reflecting, reflective, sedate, speculative; attentive, careful, cautious, circumspect, considerate, discreet, heedful, friendly, kind-hearted, kindly, mindful, neighbourly, provident, prudent, regardful, watchful, wary; quiet, serious, sober, studious.

thoughtless *adj* careless, casual, flighty, heedless, improvident, inattentive, inconsiderate, neglectful, negligent, precipitate, rash, reckless, regardless, remiss, trifling, unmindful, unthinking; blank, blockish, dull, insensate, stupid, vacant, vacuous.

thraldom *n* bondage, enslavement, enthralment, serfdom, servitude, slavery, subjection, thrall, vassalage.

thrash *vb* beat, bruise, conquer, defeat, drub, flog, lash, maul, pommel, punish, thwack, trounce, wallop, whip.

thread *vb* course, direction, drift, tenor; reeve, trace. • *n* cord, fibre, filament, hair, line, twist; pile, staple.

threadbare *adj* napless, old, seedy, worn; common, commonplace, hackneyed, stale, trite, worn-out.

threat *n* commination, defiance, denunciation, fulmination, intimidation, menace, thunder, thunderbolt.

threaten *vb* denounce, endanger, fulminate, intimidate, menace, thunder; augur, forebode, foreshadow, indicate, portend, presage, prognosticate, warn.

threshold *n* doorsill, sill; door, entrance, gate; beginning, commencement, opening, outset, start.

thrift *n* economy, frugality, parsimony, saving, thriftiness; gain, luck, profit, prosperity, success.

thriftless *adj* extravagant, improvident, lavish, profuse, prodigal, shiftless, unthrifty, wasteful.

thrifty *adj* careful, economical, frugal, provident, saving, sparing; flourishing, prosperous, thriving, vigorous.

thrill *vb* affect, agitate, electrify, inspire, move, penetrate, pierce, rouse, stir, touch. • *n* excitement, sensation, shock, tingling, tremor.

thrilling *adj* affecting, exciting, gripping, moving, sensational, touching.

thrive *vb* advance, batten, bloom, boom, flourish, prosper, succeed.

throng *vb* congregate, crowd, fill, flock, pack, press, swarm. • *n* assemblage, concourse, congregation, crowd, horde, host, mob, multitude, swarm.

throttle *vb* choke, silence, strangle, suffocate.

throw *vb* cast, chuck, dart, fling, hurl, lance, launch, overturn, pitch, pitchfork, send, sling, toss, whirl. • *n* cast, fling, hurl, launch, pitch, sling, toss, whirl; chance, gamble, try, venture.

thrust *vb* clap, dig, drive, force, impel, jam, plunge, poke, propel, push, ram, run, shove, stick. • *n* dig, jab, lunge, pass, plunge, poke, propulsion, push, shove, stab, tilt.

thump *vb* bang, batter, beat, belabour, knock, punch, strike, thrash, thwack, whack. • *n* blow, knock, punch, strike, stroke.

thwart *vb* baffle, balk, contravene, counteract, cross, defeat, disconcert, frustrate, hinder, impede, oppose, obstruct, oppugn; cross, intersect, traverse.

tickle *vb* amuse, delight, divert, enliven, gladden, gratify, please, rejoice, titillate.

ticklish *adj* dangerous, precarious, risky, tottering, uncertain, unstable, unsteady; critical, delicate, difficult, nice.

tide *n* course, current, ebb, flow, stream.

tidings *npl* advice, greetings, information, intelligence, news, report, word.

tidy *vb* clean, neaten, order, straighten. • *adj* clean, neat, orderly, shipshape, spruce, trig, trim.

tie *vb* bind, confine, fasten, knot, lock, manacle, secure, shackle, fetter, yoke; complicate, entangle, interlace, knit; connect, hold, join, link, unite; constrain, oblige, restrain, restrict. • *n* band, fastening, knot, ligament, ligature; allegiance, bond, obligation; bow, cravat, necktie.

tier *n* line, rank, row, series.

tiff *n* fit, fume, passion, pet, miff, rage.

tight *adj* close, compact, fast, firm; taut, tense, stretched; impassable, narrow, strait.

till *vb* cultivate, plough, harrow.

tillage *n* agriculture, cultivation, culture, farming, geoponics, husbandry.

tilt *vb* cant, incline, slant, slope, tip; forge, hammer; point, thrust; joust, rush. • *n* awning, canopy, tent; lunge, pass, thrust; cant, inclination, slant, slope, tip.

time *vb* clock, control, count, measure, regulate, schedule. • *n* duration, interim, interval, season, span, spell, tenure, term, while; aeon, age, date, epoch, eon, era; term; cycle, dynasty, reign; confinement, delivery, parturition; measure, rhythm.

timely *adj* acceptable, appropriate, apropos, early, opportune, prompt, punctual, seasonable, well-timed.

timid *adj* afraid, cowardly, faint-hearted, fearful, irresolute, meticulous, nervous, pusillanimous, skittish, timorous, unadventurous; bashful, coy, diffident, modest, shame-faced, shrinking.

tincture *vb* colour, dye, shade, stain, tinge, tint; flavour, season; imbue, impregnate, impress, infuse. • *n* grain, hue, shade, stain, tinge, tint, tone; flavour, smack, spice, taste; admixture, dash, infusion, seasoning, sprinkling, touch.

tinge *vb* colour, dye, stain, tincture, tint; imbue, impregnate, impress, infuse. • *n* cast, colour, dye, hue, shade, stain, tincture, tint; flavour, smack, spice, quality, taste.

tint *n* cast, colour, complexion, dye, hue, shade, tinge, tone.

tiny *adj* diminutive, dwarfish, Lilliputian, little, microscopic, miniature, minute, puny, pygmy, small, wee.

tip[1] *n* apex, cap, end, extremity, peak, pinnacle, point, top, vertex.

tip[2] *vb* incline, overturn, tilt; dispose of, dump. • *n* donation, fee, gift, gratuity, perquisite, reward; inclination, slant; hint, pointer, suggestion; strike, tap.

tirade n abuse, denunciation, diatribe, harangue, outburst.

tire vb exhaust, fag, fatigue, harass, jade, weary; bore, bother, irk.

tiresome adj annoying, arduous, boring, dull, exhausting, fatiguing, fagging, humdrum, irksome, laborious, monotonous, tedious, wearisome, vexatious.

tissue n cloth, fabric; membrane, network, structure, texture, web; accumulation, chain, collection, combination, conglomeration, mass, series, set.

titanic adj colossal, Cyclopean, enormous, gigantic, herculean, huge, immense, mighty, monstrous, prodigious, stupendous, vast.

title vb call, designate, name, style, term. • n caption, legend, head, heading; appellation, application, cognomen, completion, denomination, designation, epithet, name; claim, due, ownership, part, possession, prerogative, privilege, right.

tittle n atom, bit, grain, iota, jot, mite, particle, scrap, speck, whit.

tittle-tattle vb, n babble, cackle, chatter, discourse, gabble, gossip, prattle.

toast vb brown, dry, heat; honour, pledge, propose, salute. • n compliment, drink, pledge, salutation, salute; favourite, pet.

toil vb drudge, labour, strive, work. • n drudgery, effort, exertion, exhaustion, grinding, labour, pains, travail, work; gin, net, noose, snare, spring, trap.

toilsome adj arduous, difficult, fatiguing, hard, laborious, onerous, painful, severe, tedious, wearisome.

token adj nominal, superficial, symbolic. • n badge, evidence, index, indication, manifestation, mark, note, sign, symbol, trace, trait; keepsake, memento, memorial, reminder, souvenir.

tolerable adj bearable, endurable, sufferable, supportable; fair, indifferent, middling, ordinary, passable, so-so.

tolerance n endurance, receptivity, sufferance, toleration.

tolerate vb admit, allow, indulge, let, permit, receive; abide, brook, endure, suffer.

toll¹ n assessment, charge, customs, demand, dues, duty, fee, impost, levy, rate, tax, tribute; cost, damage, loss.

toll² vb chime, knell, peal, ring, sound. • n chime, knell, peal, ring, ringing, tolling.

tomb n catacomb, charnel house, crypt, grave, mausoleum, sepulchre, vault.

tone vb blend, harmonize, match, suit. • n note, sound; accent, cadence, emphasis, inflection, intonation, modulation; key, mood, strain, temper; elasticity, energy, force, health, strength, tension, vigour; cast, colour, manner, hue, shade, style, tint; drift, tenor.

tongue n accent, dialect, language, utterance, vernacular; discourse, parlance, speech, talk; nation, race.

too adv additionally, also, further, likewise, moreover, overmuch.

toothsome adj agreeable, dainty, delicious, luscious, nice, palatable, savoury.

top vb cap, head, tip; ride, surmount; outgo, surpass. • adj apical, best, chief, culminating, finest, first, foremost, highest, leading, prime, principal, topmost, uppermost. • n acme, apex, crest, crown, head, meridian, pinnacle, summit, surface, vertex, zenith.

topic n business, question, subject, text, theme, thesis; division, head, subdivision; commonplace, dictum, maxim, precept, proposition, principle, rule; arrangement, scheme.

topple vb fall, overturn, tumble, upset.

torment vb annoy, agonize, distress, excruciate, pain, rack, torture; badger, fret, harass, harry, irritate, nettle, plague, provoke, tantalize, tease, trouble, vex, worry. • n agony, anguish, pang, rack, torture.

tornado n blizzard, cyclone, gale, hurricane, storm, tempest, typhoon, whirlwind.

torpid adj benumbed, lethargic, motionless, numb; apathetic, dormant, dull, inactive, indolent, inert, listless, sleepy, slothful, sluggish, stupid.

torpor n coma, insensibility, lethargy, numbness, torpidity; inaction, inactivity, inertness, sluggishness, stupidity.

torrid adj arid, burnt, dried, parched; burning, fiery, hot, parching, scorching, sultry, tropical, violent.

tortuous adj crooked, curved, curvilineal, curvilinear, serpentine, sinuate, sinuated, sinuous, twisted, winding; ambiguous, circuitous, crooked, deceitful, indirect, perverse, roundabout.

torture vb agonize, distress, excruciate, pain, rack, torment. • n agony, anguish, distress, pain, pang, rack, torment.

toss vb cast, fling, hurl, pitch, throw; agitate, rock, shake; disquiet, harass, try; roll, writhe. • n cast, fling, pitch, throw.

total vb add, amount to, reach, reckon. • adj complete, entire, full, whole; integral, undivided. • n aggregate, all, gross, lump, mass, sum, totality, whole.

totter vb falter, reel, stagger, vacillate; lean, oscillate, reel, rock, shake, sway, tremble, waver; fail, fall, flag.

touch vb feel, graze, handle, hit, pat, strike, tap; concern, interest, regard; affect, impress, move, stir; grasp, reach, stretch; melt, mollify, soften; afflict, distress, hurt, injure, molest, sting, wound. • n hint, smack, suggestion, suspicion, taste, trace; blow, contract, hit, pat, tap.

touchiness n fretfulness, irritability, irascibility, peevishness, pettishness, petulance, snappishness, spleen, testiness.

touching adj affecting, heart-rending, impressive, melting, moving, pathetic, pitiable, tender; abutting, adjacent, bordering, tangent.

touchy adj choleric, cross, fretful, hot-tempered, irascible, irritable, peevish, petulant, quick-tempered, snappish, splenetic, tetchy, testy, waspish.

tough adj adhesive, cohesive, flexible, tenacious; coriaceous, leathery; clammy, ropy, sticky, viscous; inflexible, intractable, rigid, stiff; callous, hard, obdurate, stubborn; difficult, formidable, hard, troublesome. • n brute, bully, hooligan, ruffian, thug.

tour vb journey, perambulate, travel, visit. • n circuit, course, excursion, expedition, journey, perambulation, pilgrimage, round.

tow vb drag, draw, haul, pull, tug. • n drag, lift, pull.

tower vb mount, rise, soar, transcend. • n belfry, bell tower, column, minaret, spire, steeple, turret; castle, citadel, fortress, stronghold; pillar, refuge, rock, support.

towering adj elevated, lofty; excessive, extreme, prodigious, violent.

toy vb dally, play, sport, trifle, wanton. • n bauble, doll, gewgaw, gimmick, knick-knack, plaything, puppet, trinket; bagatelle, bubble, trifle; play, sport.

trace vb follow, track, train; copy, deduce, delineate, derive, describe, draw, sketch. • n evidence, footmark, footprint, footstep, impression, mark, remains, sign, token, track, trail, vestige, wake; memorial, record; bit, dash, flavour, hint, suspicion, streak, tinge.

track vb chase, draw, follow, pursue, scent, track, trail. • n footmark, footprint, footstep, spoor, trace, vestige; course, pathway, rails, road, runway, trace, trail, wake, way.

trackless adj pathless, solitary, unfrequented, unused.

tract¹ n area, district, quarter, region, territory; parcel, patch, part, piece, plot, portion.

tract² n disquisition, dissertation, essay, homily, pamphlet, sermon, thesis, tractate, treatise.

tractable adj amenable, docile, governable, manageable, submissive, willing, yielding; adaptable, ductile, malleable, plastic, tractile.

trade vb bargain, barter, chaffer, deal, exchange, interchange, sell, traffic. • n bargaining, barter, business, commerce, dealing, traffic; avocation, calling, craft, employment, occupation, office, profession, pursuit, vocation.

traditional adj accustomed, apocryphal, customary, established, historic, legendary, old, oral, transmitted, uncertain, unverified, unwritten.

traduce vb abuse, asperse, blemish, brand, calumniate, decry, defame, depreciate, disparage, revile, malign, slander, vilify.

traducer n calumniator, defamer, detractor, slanderer, vilifier.

traffic vb bargain, barter, chaffer, deal, exchange, trade. • n barter, business, chaffer, commerce, exchange, intercourse, trade, transportation, truck.

tragedy n drama, play; adversity, calamity, catastrophe, disaster, misfortune.

tragic adj dramatic; calamitous, catastrophic, disastrous, dreadful, fatal, grievous, heart-breaking, mournful, sad, shocking, sorrowful.

trail vb follow, hunt, trace, track; drag, draw, float, flow, haul, pull. • n footmark, footprint, footstep, mark, trace, track.

train vb drag, draw, haul, trail, tug; allure, entice; discipline, drill, educate, exercise, instruct, school, teach; accustom, break in, familiarize, habituate, inure, prepare, rehearse, use. • n trail, wake; entourage, cortege, followers, retinue, staff, suite; chain, consecution, sequel, series, set, succession; course, method, order, process; allure, artifice, device, enticement, lure, persuasion, stratagem, trap.

trait *n* line, mark, stroke, touch; characteristic, feature, lineage, particularity, peculiarity, quality.

traitor *n* apostate, betrayer, deceiver, Judas, miscreant, quisling, renegade, turncoat; conspirator, deserter, insurgent, mutineer, rebel, revolutionary.

traitorous *adj* faithless, false, perfidious, recreant, treacherous; insidious, treasonable.

trammel *vb* clog, confine, cramp, cumber, hamper, hinder, fetter, restrain, restrict, shackle, tie. • *n* bond, chain, fetter, hindrance, impediment, net, restraint, shackle.

tramp *vb* hike, march, plod, trudge, walk. • *n* excursion, journey, march, walk; landloper, loafer, stroller, tramper, vagabond, vagrant.

trample *vb* crush, tread; scorn, spurn.

trance *n* dream, ecstasy, hypnosis, rapture; catalepsy, coma.

tranquil *adj* calm, hushed, peaceful, placid, quiet, serene, still, undisturbed, unmoved, unperturbed, unruffled, untroubled.

tranquillity *n* calmness, peace, peacefulness, placidity, placidness, quiet, quietness, serenity, stillness, tranquilness.

tranquillize *vb* allay, appease, assuage, calm, compose, hush, lay, lull, moderate, pacify, quell, quiet, silence, soothe, still.

transact *vb* conduct, dispatch, enact, execute, do, manage, negotiate, perform, treat.

transaction *n* act, action, conduct, doing, management, negotiation, performance; affair, business, deal, dealing, incident, event, job, matter, occurrence, procedure, proceeding.

transcend *vb* exceed, overlap, overstep, pass, transgress; excel, outstrip, outrival, outvie, overtop, surmount, surpass.

transcendent *adj* consummate, inimitable, peerless, pre-eminent, supereminent, surpassing, unequalled, unparalleled, unrivalled, unsurpassed; metempiric, metempirical, noumenal, super-sensible.

transcript *n* duplicate, engrossment, rescript.

transfer *vb* convey, dispatch, move, remove, send, translate, transmit, transplant, transport; abalienate, alienate, assign, cede, confer, convey, consign, deed, devise, displace, forward, grant, pass, relegate. • *n* abalienation, alienation, assignment, bequest, carriage, cession, change, conveyance, copy, demise, devisal, gift, grant, move, relegation, removal, shift, shipment, transference, transferring, transit, transmission, transportation.

transfigure *vb* change, convert, dignify, idealize, metamorphose, transform.

transform *vb* alter, change, metamorphose, transfigure; convert, resolve, translate, transmogrify, transmute.

transgress *vb* exceed, transcend, overpass, overstep; break, contravene, disobey, infringe, violate; err, intrude, offend, sin, slip, trespass.

transgression *n* breach, disobedience, encroachment, infraction, infringement, transgression, violation; crime, delinquency, error, fault, iniquity, misdeed, misdemeanour, misdoing, offence, sin, slip, trespass, wrongdoing.

transient *adj* diurnal, ephemeral, evanescent, fleeting, fugitive, impertinent, meteoric, mortal, passing, perishable, short-lived, temporary, transitory, volatile; hasty, imperfect, momentary, short.

transitory *adj* brief, ephemeral, evanescent, fleeting, flitting, fugacious, momentary, passing, short, temporary, transient.

translate *vb* remove, transfer, transport; construe, decipher, decode, interpret, render, turn.

translucent *adj* diaphanous, hyaline, pellucid, semi-opaque, semi-transparent.

transmit *vb* forward, remit, send; communicate, conduct, radiate; bear, carry, convey.

transparent *adj* bright, clear, diaphanous, limpid, lucid; crystalline, hyaline, pellucid, serene, translucent, transpicuous, unclouded; open, porous, transpicuous; evident, obvious, manifest, patent.

transpire *vb* befall, chance, happen, occur; evaporate, exhale.

transport *vb* bear, carry, cart, conduct, convey, fetch, remove, ship, take, transfer, truck; banish, expel; beatify, delight, enrapture, enravish, entrance, ravish. • *n* carriage, conveyance, movement, transportation, transporting; beatification, beatitude, bliss, ecstasy, felicity, happiness, rapture, ravishment; frenzy, passion, vehemence, warmth.

transude *vb* exude, filter, ooze, percolate, strain.

trap *vb* catch, ensnare, entrap, noose, snare, springe; ambush, deceive, dupe, trick; enmesh, tangle, trepan. • *n* gin, snare, springe, toil; ambush, artifice, pitfall, stratagem, trepan.

trappings *npl* adornments, decorations, dress, embellishments, frippery, gear, livery, ornaments, paraphernalia, rigging; accoutrements, caparisons, equipment, gear.

trash *n* dregs, dross, garbage, refuse, rubbish, trumpery, waste; balderdash, nonsense, twaddle.

travel *vb* journey, peregrinate, ramble, roam, rove, tour, voyage, walk, wander; go, move, pass. • *n* excursion, expedition, journey, peregrination, ramble, tour, trip, voyage, walk.

traveller *n* excursionist, explorer, globe-trotter, itinerant, passenger, pilgrim, rover, sightseer, tourist, trekker, tripper, voyager, wanderer, wayfarer.

traverse *vb* contravene, counteract, defeat, frustrate, obstruct, oppose, thwart; ford, pass, play, range.

travesty *vb* imitate, parody, take off. • *n* burlesque, caricature, imitation, parody, take-off.

treacherous *adj* deceitful, disloyal, faithless, false, false-hearted, insidious, perfidious, recreant, sly, traitorous, treasonable, unfaithful, unreliable, unsafe, untrustworthy.

treachery *n* betrayal, deceitfulness, disloyalty, double-dealing, faithlessness, foul play, infidelity, insidiousness, perfidiousness, treason, perfidy.

treason *n* betrayal, disloyalty, lèse-majesté, lese-majesty, perfidy, sedition, traitorousness, treachery.

treasonable *adj* disloyal, traitorous, treacherous.

treasure *vb* accumulate, collect, garner, hoard, husband, save, store; cherish, idolize, prize, value, worship. • *n* cash, funds, jewels, money, riches, savings, valuables, wealth; abundance, reserve, stock, store.

treasurer *n* banker, bursar, purser, receiver, trustee.

treat *vb* entertain, feast, gratify, refresh; attend, doctor, dose, handle, manage, serve; bargain, covenant, negotiate, parley. • *n* banquet, entertainment, feast; delight, enjoyment, entertainment, gratification, luxury, pleasure, refreshment.

treatise *n* commentary, discourse, dissertation, disquisition, monograph, tractate.

treatment *n* usage, use; dealing, handling, management, manipulation; doctoring, therapy.

treaty *n* agreement, alliance, bargain, compact, concordat, convention, covenant, entente, league, pact.

tremble *vb* quake, quaver, quiver, shake, shiver, shudder, vibrate, wobble. • *n* quake, quiver, shake, shiver, shudder, tremor, vibration, wobble.

tremendous *adj* colossal, enormous, huge, immense, excellent, marvellous, wonderful; alarming, appalling, awful, dreadful, fearful, frightful, horrid, horrible, terrible.

tremor *n* agitation, quaking, quivering, shaking, trembling, trepidation, tremulousness, vibration.

tremulous *adj* afraid, fearful, quavering, quivering, shaking, shaky, shivering, timid, trembling, vibrating.

trench *vb* carve, cut; ditch, channel, entrench, furrow. • *n* channel, ditch, drain, furrow, gutter, moat, pit, sewer, trough; dugout, entrenchment, fortification.

trenchant *adj* cutting, keen, sharp; acute, biting, caustic, crisp, incisive, pointed, piquant, pungent, sarcastic, sententious, severe, unsparing, vigorous.

trend *vb* drift, gravitate, incline, lean, run, stretch, sweep, tend, turn. • *n* bent, course, direction, drift, inclination, set, leaning, tendency, trending.

trepidation *n* agitation, quaking, quivering, shaking, trembling, tremor; dismay, excitement, fear, perturbation, tremulousness.

trespass *vb* encroach, infringe, intrude, trench; offend, sin, transgress. • *n* encroachment, infringement, injury, intrusion, invasion; crime, delinquency, error, fault, sin, misdeed, misdemeanour, offence, transgression; trespasser.

trial *adj* experimental, exploratory, testing. • *n* examination, experiment, test; experience, knowledge; aim, attempt, effort, endeavour, essay, exertion, struggle; assay, criterion, ordeal, prohibition, proof, test, touchstone; affliction, burden, chagrin, dolour, distress, grief, hardship, heartache, inclination, misery, mortification, pain, sorrow, suffering, tribulation, trouble, unhappiness, vexation, woe, wretchedness; action, case, cause, hearing, suit.

tribe *n* clan, family, lineage, race, sept, stock; class, distinction, division, order.

tribulation *n* adversity, affliction, distress, grief, misery, pain, sorrow, suffering, trial, trouble, unhappiness, woe, wretchedness.

tribunal *n* bench, judgement seat; assizes, bar, court, judicature, session.

tribute *n* subsidy, tax; custom, duty, excise, impost, tax, toll; contribution, grant, offering.

trice *n* flash, instant, jiffy, moment, second, twinkling.

trick *adj* cheat, circumvent, cozen, deceive, defraud, delude, diddle, dupe, fob, gull, hoax, overreach. • *n* artifice, blind, deceit, deception, dodge, fake, feint, fraud, game, hoax, imposture, manoeuvre, shift, ruse, swindle, stratagem, wile; antic, caper, craft, deftness, gambol, sleight; habit, mannerism, peculiarity, practice.

trickle *vb* distil, dribble, drip, drop, ooze, percolate, seep. • *n* dribble, drip, percolation, seepage.

tricky *adj* artful, cunning, deceitful, deceptive, subtle, trickish.

trifle *vb* dally, dawdle, fool, fribble, palter, play, potter, toy. • *n* bagatelle, bauble, bean, fig, nothing, triviality; iota, jot, modicum, particle, trace.

trifling *adj* empty, frippery, frivolous, inconsiderable, insignificant, nugatory, petty, piddling, shallow, slight, small, trivial, unimportant, worthless.

trill *vb* shake, quaver, warble. • *n* quaver, shake, tremolo, warbling.

trim *vb* adjust, arrange, prepare; balance, equalize, fill; adorn, array, bedeck, decorate, dress, embellish, garnish, ornament; clip, curtail, cut, lop, mow, poll, prune, shave, shear; berate, chastise, chide, rebuke, reprimand, reprove, trounce; fluctuate, hedge, shift, shuffle, vacillate. • *adj* compact, neat, nice, shapely, snug, tidy, well-adjusted, well-ordered; chic, elegant, finical, smart, spruce. • *n* dress, embellishment, gear, ornaments, trappings, trimmings; case, condition, order, plight, state.

trinket *n* bagatelle, bauble, bijoux, gewgaw, gimcrack, knickknack, toy, trifle.

trinkets *npl* bijouterie, jewellery, jewels, ornaments.

trip *vb* caper, dance, frisk, hop, skip; misstep, stumble; bungle, blunder, err, fail, mistake; overthrow, supplant, upset; catch, convict, detect. • *n* hop, skip; lurch, misstep, stumble; blunder, bungle, error, failure, fault, lapse, miss, mistake, oversight, slip; circuit, excursion, expedition, jaunt, journey, ramble, route, stroll, tour.

trite *adj* banal, beaten, common, commonplace, hackneyed, old, ordinary, stale, stereotyped, threadbare, usual, worn.

triturate *vb* beat, bray, bruise, grind, pound, rub, thrash; comminute, levigate, pulverize.

triumph *vb* exult, rejoice; prevail, succeed, win; flourish, prosper, thrive; boast, brag, crow, gloat, swagger, vaunt. • *n* celebration, exultation, joy, jubilation, jubilee, ovation; accomplishment, achievement, conquest, success, victory.

triumphant *adj* boastful, conquering, elated, exultant, exulting, jubilant, rejoicing, successful, victorious.

trivial *adj* frivolous, gimcrack, immaterial, inconsiderable, insignificant, light, little, nugatory, paltry, petty, small, slight, slim, trifling, trumpery, unimportant.

trollop *n* prostitute, slattern, slut, whore.

troop *vb* crowd, flock, muster, throng. • *n* company, crowd, flock, herd, multitude, number, throng; band, body, party, squad, troupe.

trophy *n* laurels, medal, palm, prize.

troth *n* candour, sincerity, truth, veracity, verity; allegiance, belief, faith, fidelity, word; betrothal.

trouble *vb* agitate, confuse, derange, disarrange, disorder, disturb; afflict, ail, annoy, badger, concern, disquiet, distress, fret, grieve, harass, molest, perplex, perturb, pester, plague, torment, vex, worry. • *n* adversity, affliction, calamity, distress, dolour, grief, hardship, misfortune, misery, pain, sorrow, suffering, tribulation, woe; ado, annoyance, anxiety, bother, care, discomfort, embarrassment, fuss, inconvenience, irritation, pains, perplexity, plague, torment, vexation, worry; commotion, disturbance, row; bewilderment, disquietude, embarrassment, perplexity, uneasiness.

troublesome *adj* annoying, distressing, disturbing, galling, grievous, harassing, painful, perplexing, vexatious, worrisome; burdensome, irksome, tiresome, wearisome; importunate, intrusive, teasing; arduous, difficult, hard, inconvenient, trying, unwieldy.

troublous *adj* agitated, disquieted, disturbed, perturbed, tumultuous, turbulent.

trough *n* hutch, manger; channel, depression, hollow, furrow.

truant *vb* be absent, desert, dodge, malinger, shirk, skive. • *n* absentee, deserter, idler, laggard, loiterer, lounger, malingerer, quitter, runaway, shirker, vagabond.

truce *n* armistice, breathing space, cessation, delay, intermission, lull, pause, recess, reprieve, respite, rest.

truck *vb* barter, deal, exchange, trade, traffic. • *n* lorry, van, wagon.

truckle *vb* roll, trundle; cringe, crouch, fawn, knuckle, stoop, submit, yield.

truculent *adj* barbarous, bloodthirsty, ferocious, fierce, savage; cruel, malevolent, relentless; destructive, deadly, fatal, ruthless.

true *adj* actual, unaffected, authentic, genuine, legitimate, pure, real, rightful, sincere, sound, truthful, veritable; substantial, veracious; constant, faithful, loyal, staunch, steady; equitable, honest, honourable, just, upright, trusty, trustworthy, virtuous; accurate, correct, even, exact, right, straight, undeviating. • *adv* good, well.

truism *n* axiom, commonplace, platitude.

trumpery *adj* pinchbeck, rubbishy, trashy, trifling, worthless. • *n* deceit, deception, falsehood, humbug, imposture; frippery, rubbish, stuff, trash, trifles.

truncheon *n* club, cudgel, nightstick, partisan, staff; baton, wand.

trunk *n* body, bole, butt, shaft, stalk, stem, stock, torso; box, chest, coffer.

trundle *vb* bowl, revolve, roll, spin, truckle, wheel.

truss *vb* bind, bundle, close, cram, hang, pack. • *n* bundle, package, packet; apparatus, bandage, support.

trust *vb* confide, depend, expect, hope, rely; believe, credit; commit, entrust. • *n* belief, confidence, credence, faith; credit, tick; charge, deposit; commission, duty, errand; assurance, conviction, expectation, hope, reliance, secutrity.

trustful *adj* confiding, trusting, unquestioning, unsuspecting; faithful, trustworthy, trusty.

trustworthy *adj* confidential, constant, credible, dependable, faithful, firm, honest, incorrupt, upright, reliable, responsible, straightforward, staunch, true, trusty, uncorrupt, upright.

truth *n* fact, reality, veracity; actuality, authenticity, realism; canon, law, oracle, principle; right, truthfulness, veracity; candour, fidelity, frankness, honesty, honour, ingenuousness, integrity, probity, sincerity, virtue; constancy, devotion, faith, fealty, loyalty, steadfastness; accuracy, correctness, exactitude, exactness, nicety, precision, regularity, trueness.

truthful *adj* correct, reliable, true, trustworthy, veracious; artless, candid, frank, guileless, honest, ingenuous, open, sincere, straightforward, trusty.

truthless *adj* canting, disingenuous, dishonest, false, faithless, hollow, hypocritical, insincere, pharisaical, treacherous, unfair, untrustworthy.

try *vb* examine, prove, test; attempt, essay; adjudicate, adjudge, examine, hear; purify, refine; sample, sift, smell, taste; aim, attempt, endeavour, seek, strain, strive. • *n* attempt, effort, endeavour, experiment, trial.

trying *adj* difficult, fatiguing, hard, irksome, tiresome, wearisome; afflicting, afflictive, calamitous, deplorable, dire, distressing, grievous, hard, painful, sad, severe.

tryst *n* appointment, assignation, rendezvous.

tube *n* bore, bronchus, cylinder, duct, hollow, hose, pipe, pipette, worm.

tuft *n* brush, bunch, crest, feather, knot, plume, topknot, tussock; clump, cluster, group.

tug *vb* drag, draw, haul, pull, tow, wrench; labour, strive, struggle. • *n* drag, haul, pull, tow, wrench.

tuition *n* education, instruction, schooling, teaching, training.

tumble *vb* heave, pitch, roll, toss, wallow; fall, sprawl, stumble, topple, trip; derange, disarrange, dishevel, disorder, disturb, rumple, tousle. • *n* collapse, drop, fall, plunge, spill, stumble, trip.

tumbler *n* acrobat, juggler; glass.

tumid *adj* bloated, distended, enlarged, puffed-up, swelled, swollen, turgid; bombastic, declamatory, fustian, grandiloquent, grandiose, high-flown, inflated, pompous, puffy, rhetorical, stilted, swelling.

tumour *n* boil, carbuncle, swelling, tumefaction.

tumult *n* ado, affray, agitation, altercation, bluster, brawl, disturbance, ferment, flurry, feud, fracas, fray, fuss, hubbub, huddle, hurly-burly, melee, noise, perturbation, pother, quarrel, racket, riot, row, squabble, stir, turbulence, turmoil, uproar.

tumultuous *adj* blustery, breezy, bustling, confused, disorderly, disturbed, riotous, turbulent, unruly.

tune *vb* accord, attune, harmonize, modulate; adapt, adjust, attune. • *n* air, aria, melody, strain, tone; agreement, concord, harmony; accord, order.

tuneful *adj* dulcet, harmonious, melodious, musical.

turbid *adj* foul, impure, muddy, thick, unsettled.

turbulence *n* agitation, commotion, confusion, disorder, disturbance, excitement, tumult, tumultuousness, turmoil, unruliness, uproar; insubordination, insurrection, mutiny, rebellion, riot, sedition.

turbulent *adj* agitated, disturbed, restless, tumultuous, wild; blatant, blustering, boisterous, brawling, disorderly, obstreperous, tumultuous, uproarious, vociferous; factious, insubordinate, insurgent, mutinous, raging, rebellious, refractory, revolutionary, riotous, seditious, stormy, violent.

turf *n* grass, greensward, sod, sward; horse racing, racecourse, race-ground.

turgid *adj* bloated, distended, protuberant, puffed-up, swelled, swollen, tumid; bombastic, declamatory, diffuse, digressive, fustian, high-flown, inflated, grandiloquent, grandiose, ostentatious, pompous, puffy, rhetorical, stilted.

turmoil *n* activity, agitation, bustle, commotion, confusion, disorder, disturbance, ferment, flurry, huddle, hubbub, hurly-burly, noise, trouble, tumult, turbulence, uproar.

turn *vb* revolve, rotate; bend, cast, defect, inflict, round, spin, sway, swivel, twirl, twist, wheel; crank, grind, wind; deflect, divert, transfer, warp; form, mould, shape; adapt, fit, manoeuvre, suit; alter, change, conform, metamorphose, transform, transmute, vary; convert, persuade, prejudice; construe, render, translate; depend, hang, hinge, pivot; eventuate, issue, result, terminate; acidify, curdle, ferment. • *n* cycle, gyration, revolution, rotation, round; bending, deflection, deviation, diversion, doubling, flection, flexion, flexure, reel, retroversion, slew, spin, sweep, swing, swirl, swivel, turning, twist, twirl, whirl, winding; alteration, change, variation, vicissitude; bend, circuit, drive, ramble, run, round, stroll; bout, hand, innings, opportunity, shift, spell; act, action, deed, office; convenience, occasion, purpose; cast, fashion, form, guise, manner, mould, phase, shape; aptitude, bent, bias, disposition, faculty, genius, gift, inclination, leaning, proclivity, proneness, propensity, talent, tendency.

turncoat *n* apostate, backslider, deserter, recreant, renegade, traitor, wretch.

turpitude *n* baseness, degradation, depravity, vileness, wickedness.

turret *n* cupola, minaret, pinnacle.

tussle *vb* conflict, contend, contest, scuffle, struggle, wrestle. • *n* conflict, contest, fight, scuffle, struggle.

tutelage *n* care, charge, dependence, guardianship, protection, teaching, tutorage, tutorship, wardship.

tutor *vb* coach, educate, instruct, teach; discipline, train. • *n* coach, governess, governor, instructor, master, preceptor, schoolteacher, teacher.

twaddle *vb* chatter, gabble, maunder, prate, prattle. • *n* balderdash, chatter, flummery, gabble, gibberish, gobbledegook, gossip, jargon, moonshine, nonsense, platitude, prate, prattle, rigmarole, stuff, tattle.

tweak *vb*, *n* jerk, pinch, pull, twinge, twitch.

twig[1] *n* bough, branch, offshoot, shoot, slip, spray, sprig, stick, switch.

twig[2] *vb* catch on, comprehend, discover, grasp, realize, recognize, see, understand.

twin *vb* couple, link, match, pair. • *adj* double, doubled, duplicate, geminate, identical, matched, matching, second, twain. • *n* corollary, double, duplicate, fellow, likeness, match.

twine *vb* embrace, encircle, entwine, interlace, surround, wreathe; bend, meander, wind; coil, twist. • *n* convolution, coil, twist; embrace, twining, winding; cord, string.

twinge *vb* pinch, tweak, twitch. • *n* pinch, tweak, twitch; gripe, pang, spasm.

twinkle *vb* blink, twink, wink; flash, glimmer, scintillate, sparkle. • *n* blink, flash, gleam, glimmer, scintillation, sparkle; flash, instant, jiffy, moment, second, tick, trice, twinkling.

twinkling *n* flashing, sparkling, twinkle; flash, instant, jiffy, moment, second, tick, trice.

twirl *vb* revolve, rotate, spin, turn, twist, twirl. • *n* convolution, revolution, turn, twist, whirling.

twist *vb* purl, rotate, spin, twine; complicate, contort, convolute, distort, pervert, screw, wring; coil, writhe; encircle, wind, wreathe. • *n* coil, curl, spin, twine; braid, roll; change, complication, development, variation; bend, convolution, turn; defect, distortion, flaw, imperfection; jerk, pull, sprain, wrench; aberration, characteristic, eccentricity, oddity, peculiarity, quirk.

twit[1] *vb* banter, blame, censure, reproach, taunt, tease, upbraid.

twit[2] *n* blockhead, fool, idiot, nincompoop, nitwit.

twitch *vb* jerk, pluck, pull, snatch. • *n* jerk, pull; contraction, pull, quiver, spasm, twitching.

type *n* emblem, mark, stamp; adumbration, image, representation, representative, shadow, sign, symbol, token; archetype, exemplar, model, original, pattern, prototype, protoplast, standard; character, form, kind, nature, sort; figure, letter, text, typography.

typical *adj* emblematic, exemplary, figurative, ideal, indicative, model, representative, symbolic, true.

typify *vb* betoken, denote, embody, exemplify, figure, image, indicate, represent, signify.

tyrannical *adj* absolute, arbitrary, autocratic, cruel, despotic, dictatorial, domineering, high, imperious, irresponsible, severe, tyrannical, unjust; galling, grinding, inhuman, oppressive, overbearing, severe.

tyranny *n* absolutism, autocracy, despotism, dictatorship, harshness, oppression.

tyrant *n* autocrat, despot, dictator, oppressor.

tyro *n* beginner, learner, neophyte, novice; dabbler, smatterer.

U

ubiquitous *adj* omnipresent, present, universal.

udder *n* nipple, pap, teat.

ugly *adj* crooked, homely, ill-favoured, plain, ordinary, unlovely, unprepossessing, unshapely, unsightly; forbidding, frightful, gruesome, hideous, horrible, horrid, loathsome, monstrous, shocking, terrible, repellent, repulsive; bad-tempered, cantankerous, churlish, cross, quarrelsome, spiteful, surly, spiteful, vicious.

ulcer *n* boil, fester, gathering, pustule, sore.

ulterior *adj* beyond, distant, farther; hidden, personal, secret, selfish, undisclosed.

ultimate *adj* conclusive, decisive, eventual, extreme, farthest, final, last. • *n* acme, consummation, culmination, height, peak, pink, quintessence, summit.

ultra *adj* advanced, beyond, extreme, radical.

umbrage *n* shadow, shade; anger, displeasure, dissatisfaction, dudgeon, injury, offence, pique, resentment.

umpire *vb* adjudicate, arbitrate, judge, referee. • *n* adjudicator, arbiter, arbitrator, judge, referee.

unabashed *adj* bold, brazen, confident, unblushing, undaunted, undismayed.

unable *adj* impotent, incapable, incompetent, powerless, weak.

unacceptable *adj* disagreeable, distasteful, offensive, unpleasant, unsatisfactory, unwelcome.

unaccommodating *adj* disobliging, noncompliant, uncivil, ungracious.

unaccomplished *adj* incomplete, unachieved, undone, unperformed, unexecuted, unfinished; ill-educated, uncultivated, unpolished.

unaccountable *adj* inexplicable, incomprehensible, inscrutable, mysterious, unintelligible; irresponsible, unanswerable.

unaccustomed *adj* uninitiated, unskilled, unused; foreign, new, strange, unfamiliar, unusual.

unaffected *adj* artless, honest, naive, natural, plain, simple, sincere, real, unfeigned; chaste, pure, unadorned; insensible, unchanged, unimpressed, unmoved, unstirred, untouched.

unanimity *n* accord, agreement, concert, concord, harmony, union, unity.

unanimous *adj* agreeing, concordant, harmonious, like-minded, solid, united.

unassuming *adj* humble, modest, reserved, unobtrusive, unpretending, unpretentious.

unattainable *adj* inaccessible, unobtainable.

unavailing *adj* abortive, fruitless, futile, ineffectual, ineffective, inept, nugatory, unsuccessful, useless, vain.

unbalanced *adj* unsound, unsteady; unadjusted, unsettled.

unbearable *adj* insufferable, insupportable, unendurable.

unbecoming *adj* inappropriate, indecent, indecorous, improper, unbefitting, unbeseeming, unseemly, unsuitable.

unbelief *n* disbelief, dissent, distrust, incredulity, incredulousness, miscreance, miscreancy, nonconformity; doubt, freethinking, infidelity, scepticism.

unbeliever *n* agnostic, deist, disbeliever, doubter, heathen, infidel, sceptic.

unbending *adj* inflexible, rigid, stiff, unpliant, unyielding; firm, obstinate, resolute, stubborn.

unbiased *adj* disinterested, impartial, indifferent, neutral, uninfluenced, unprejudiced, unwarped.

unbind *vb* loose, undo, unfasten, unloose, untie; free, unchain, unfetter.

unblemished *adj* faultless, guiltless, immaculate, impeccable, innocent, intact, perfect, pure, sinless, spotless, stainless, undefiled, unspotted, unsullied, untarnished.

unblushing *adj* boldfaced, impudent, shameless.

unbounded *adj* absolute, boundless, endless, immeasurable, immense, infinite, interminable, measureless, unlimited, vast; immoderate, uncontrolled, unrestrained, unrestricted.

unbridled *adj* dissolute, intractable, lax, licensed, licentious, loose, uncontrolled, ungovernable, unrestrained, violent, wanton.

unbroken *adj* complete, entire, even, full, intact, unimpaired; constant, continuous, fast, profound, sound, successive, undisturbed; inviolate, unbetrayed, unviolated.

unbuckle *vb* loose, unfasten, unloose.

uncanny *adj* inopportune, unsafe; eerie, eery, ghostly, unearthly, unnatural, weird.

unceremonious *adj* abrupt, bluff, blunt, brusque, course, curt, gruff, plain, rough, rude, ungracious; casual, familiar, informal, offhand, unconstrained.

uncertain *adj* ambiguous, doubtful, dubious, equivocal, indefinite, indeterminate, indistinct, questionable, unsettled; insecure, precarious, problematical; capricious, changeable, desultory, fitful, fluctuating, irregular, mutable, shaky, slippery, unreliable, variable.

unchaste *adj* dissolute, incontinent, indecent, immoral, lascivious, lecherous, libidinous, lewd, loose, obscene, wanton.

unchecked *adj* uncurbed, unhampered, unhindered, unobstructed, unrestrained, untrammelled.

uncivil *adj* bearish, blunt, boorish, brusque, discourteous, disobliging, disrespectful, gruff, ill-bred, ill-mannered, impolite, irreverent, rough, rude, uncomplaisant, uncourteous, uncouth, ungentle, ungracious, unmannered, unseemly.

unclean *adj* abominable, beastly, dirty, filthy, foul, grimy, grubby, miry, muddy, nasty, offensive, purulent, repulsive, soiled, sullied; improper, indecent, indecorous, obscene, polluted, risqué, sinful, smutty, unholy, uncleanly.

uncomfortable *adj* disagreeable, displeasing, disquieted, distressing, disturbed, uneasy, unpleasant, restless; cheerless, close, oppressive; dismal, miserable, unhappy.

uncommon *adj* choice, exceptional, extraordinary, infrequent, noteworthy, odd, original, queer, rare, remarkable, scarce, singular, strange, unexampled, unfamiliar, unusual, unwonted.

uncommunicative *adj* close, inconversable, reserved, reticent, taciturn, unsociable, unsocial.

uncomplaining *adj* long-suffering, meek, patient, resigned, tolerant.

uncompromising *adj* inflexible, narrow, obstinate, orthodox, rigid, stiff, strict, unyielding.

unconcerned *adj* apathetic, careless, indifferent.

unconditional *adj* absolute, categorical, complete, entire, free, full, positive, unlimited, unqualified, unreserved, unrestricted.

uncongenial *adj* antagonistic, discordant, displeasing, ill-assorted, incompatible, inharmonious, mismatched, unsuited, unsympathetic.

uncouth *adj* awkward, boorish, clownish, clumsy, gawky, inelegant, loutish, lubberly, rough, rude, rustic, uncourtly, ungainly, unpolished, unrefined, unseemly; odd, outlandish, strange, unfamiliar, unusual.

uncover *vb* denude, divest, lay bare, strip; disclose, discover, expose, reveal, unmask, unveil; bare, doff; open, unclose, unseal.

unctuous *adj* adipose, greasy, oily, fat, fatty, oleaginous, pinguid, sebaceous; bland, lubricious, smooth, slippery; bland, fawning, glib, obsequious, plausible, servile, suave, sycophantic; fervid, gushing.

uncultivated *adj* fallow, uncultured, unreclaimed, untilled; homely, ignorant, illiterate, rude, uncivilized, uncultured, uneducated, unfit, unlettered, unpolished, unread, unready, unrefined, untaught; rough, savage, sylvan, uncouth, wild.

undaunted *adj* bold, brave, courageous, dauntless, fearless, intrepid, plucky, resolute, undismayed.

undefiled *adj* clean, immaculate, pure, spotless, stainless, unblemished, unspotted, unsullied, untarnished; honest, innocent, inviolate, pure, uncorrupted, unpolluted, unstained.

undemonstrative *adj* calm, composed, demure, impassive, modest, placid, quiet, reserved, sedate, sober, staid, tranquil.

undeniable *adj* certain, conclusive, evident, incontestable, incontrovertible, indisputable, indubitable, obvious, unquestionable.

under *prep* below, beneath, inferior to, lower than, subordinate to, underneath. • *adv* below, beneath, down, lower.

underestimate *vb* belittle, underrate, undervalue.

undergo *vb* bear, endure, experience, suffer, sustain.

underhand *adj* clandestine, deceitful, disingenuous, fraudulent, hidden, secret, sly, stealthy, underhanded, unfair. • *adv* clandestinely, privately, secretly, slyly, stealthily, surreptitiously; fraudulently, unfairly.

underling *n* agent, inferior, servant, subordinate.

undermine *vb* excavate, mine, sap; demoralize, foil, frustrate, thwart, weaken.

understand *vb* apprehend, catch, comprehend, conceive, discern, grasp, know, penetrate, perceive, see, seize, twig; assume, interpret, take; imply, mean.

understanding *adj* compassionate, considerate, forgiving, kind, kindly, patient, sympathetic, tolerant. • *n* brains, comprehension, discernment, faculty, intellect, intelligence, judgement, knowledge, mind, reason, sense.

undertake *vb* assume, attempt, begin, embark on, engage in, enter upon, take in hand; agree, bargain, contract, covenant, engage, guarantee, promise, stipulate.

undertaking *n* adventure, affair, attempt, business, effort, endeavour, engagement, enterprise, essay, move, project, task, venture.

undesigned *adj* spontaneous, unintended, unintentional, unplanned, unpremeditated.

undigested *adj* crude, ill-advised, ill-considered, ill-judged; confused, disorderly, ill-arranged, unmethodical.

undivided *adj* complete, entire, whole; one, united.

undo *vb* annul, cancel, frustrate, invalidate, neutralize, nullify, offset, reverse; disengage, loose, unfasten, unmake, unravel, untie; crush, destroy, overturn, ruin.

undoubted *adj* incontrovertible, indisputable, indubitable, undisputed, unquestionable, unquestioned.

undress *vb* denude, dismantle, disrobe, unclothe, unrobe, peel, strip. • *n* disarray, nakedness, nudity; mufti, negligee.

undue *adj* illegal, illegitimate, improper, unlawful, excessive, disproportionate, disproportioned, immoderate, unsuitable; unfit.

undulation *n* billowing, fluctuation, pulsation, ripple, wave.

undying *adj* deathless, endless, immortal, imperishable.

unearthly *adj* preternatural, supernatural, uncanny, weird.

uneasy *adj* disquieted, disturbed, fidgety, impatient, perturbed, restless, restive, unquiet, worried; awkward, stiff, ungainly, ungraceful; constraining, cramping, disagreeable, uncomfortable.

unending *adj* endless, eternal, everlasting, interminable, neverending, perpetual, unceasing.

unequal *adj* disproportionate, disproportioned, ill-matched, inferior, irregular, insufficient, not alike, uneven.

unequalled *adj* exceeding, incomparable, inimitable, matchless, new, nonpareil, novel, paramount, peerless, pre-eminent, superlative, surpassing, transcendent, unheard of, unique, unparalleled, unrivalled.

unequivocal *adj* absolute, certain, clear, evident, incontestable, indubitable, positive; explicit, unambiguous, unmistakable.

uneven *adj* hilly, jagged, lumpy, ragged, rough, rugged, stony; motley, unequal, variable, variegated.

uneventful *adj* commonplace, dull, eventless, humdrum, quiet, monotonous, smooth, uninteresting.

unexceptionable *adj* excellent, faultless, good, irreproachable.

unexpected *adj* abrupt, sudden, unforeseen.

unfair *adj* dishonest, dishonourable, faithless, false, hypocritical, inequitable, insincere, oblique, one-sided, partial, unequal, unjust, wrongful.

unfaithful *adj* adulterous, derelict, deceitful, dishonest, disloyal, false, faithless, fickle, perfidious, treacherous, unreliable; negligent; changeable, inconstant, untrue.

unfamiliar *adj* bizarre, foreign, new, novel, outlandish, queer, singular, strange, uncommon, unusual.

unfashionable *adj* antiquated, destitute, disused, obsolete, oldfashioned, unconventional.

unfavourable *adj* adverse, contrary, disadvantageous, discouraging, ill, inauspicious, inimical, inopportune, indisposed, malign, sinister, unfriendly, unlucky, unpropitious, untimely; foul, inclement.

unfeeling *adj* apathetic, callous, heartless, insensible, numb, obdurate, torpid, unconscious, unimpressionable; adamantine, cold-blooded, cruel, hard, merciless, pitiless, stony, unkind, unsympathetic.

unfit *vb* disable, disqualify, incapacitate. • *adj* improper, inappropriate, incompetent, inconsistent, unsuitable; ill-equipped, inadequate, incapable, unqualified, useless; debilitated, feeble, flabby, unhealthy, unsound.

unflagging *adj* constant, indefatigable, never-ending, persevering, steady, unfaltering, unremitting, untiring, unwearied.

unflinching *adj* firm, resolute, steady, unshrinking.

unfold *vb* display, expand, open, separate, unfurl, unroll; declare, disclose, reveal, tell; decipher, develop, disentangle, evolve, explain, illustrate, interpret, resolve, unravel.

unfortunate *adj* hapless, ill-fated, ill-starred, infelicitous, luckless, unhappy, unlucky, unprosperous, unsuccessful, wretched; calamitous, deplorable, disastrous; inappropriate, inexpedient.

unfrequented *adj* abandoned, deserted, forsaken, lone, solitary, uninhabited, unoccupied.

unfruitful *adj* barren, fruitless, sterile; infecund, unprolific; unprofitable, unproductive.

ungainly *adj* awkward, boorish, clownish, clumsy, gawky, inelegant, loutish, lubberly, lumbering, slouching, stiff, uncourtly, uncouth, ungraceful.

ungentlemanly *adj* ill-bred, impolite, rude, uncivil, ungentle, ungracious, unmannerly.

unhappy *adj* afflicted, disastrous, dismal, distressed, drear, evil, inauspicious, miserable, painful, unfortunate, wretched.

unhealthy *adj* ailing, diseased, feeble, indisposed, infirm, poorly, sickly, toxic, unsanitary, unsound, toxic, venomous.

uniform *adj* alike, constant, even, equable, equal, smooth, steady, regular, unbroken, unchanged, undeviating, unvaried, unvarying. • *n* costume, dress, livery, outfit, regalia, suit.

uniformity *n* constancy, continuity, permanence, regularity, sameness, stability; accordance, agreement, conformity, consistency, unanimity.

unimportant *adj* immaterial, inappreciable, inconsequent, inconsequential, inconsiderable, indifferent, insignificant, mediocre, minor, paltry, petty, small, slight, trifling, trivial.

unintentional *adj* accidental, casual, fortuitous, inadvertent, involuntary, spontaneous, undesigned, unmeant, unplanned, unpremeditated, unthinking.

uninterrupted *adj* continuous, endless, incessant, perpetual, unceasing.

union *n* coalescence, coalition, combination, conjunction, coupling, fusion, incorporation, joining, junction, unification, uniting; agreement, concert, concord, concurrence, harmony, unanimity, unity; alliance, association, club, confederacy, federation, guild, league.

unique *adj* choice, exceptional, matchless, only, peculiar, rare, single, sole, singular, uncommon, unexampled, unmatched.

unison *n* accord, accordance, agreement, concord, harmony.

unite *vb* amalgamate, attach, blend, centralize, coalesce, confederate, consolidate, embody, fuse, incorporate, merge, weld; associate, conjoin, connect, couple, link, marry; combine, join; harmonize, reconcile; agree, concert, concur, cooperate, fraternize.

universal *adj* all-reaching, catholic, cosmic, encyclopedic, general, ubiquitous, unlimited; all, complete, entire, total, whole.

unjust *adj* inequitable, injurious, partial, unequal, unfair, unwarranted, wrong, wrongful; flagitious, heinous, influenced, iniquitous, nefarious, unrighteous, wicked; biased, prejudiced, uncandid.

unjustifiable *adj* indefensible, unjust, unreasonable, unwarrantable; inexcusable, unpardonable.

unknown *adj* unappreciated, unascertained; undiscovered, unexplored, uninvestigated; concealed, dark, enigmatic, hidden, mysterious, mystic; anonymous, incognito, inglorious, nameless, obscure, renownless, undistinguished, unheralded, unnoted.

unladylike *adj* ill-bred, impolite, rude, uncivil, ungentle, ungracious, unmannerly.

unlamented *adj* unmourned, unregretted.

unlimited *adj* boundless, infinite, interminable, limitless, measureless, unbounded; absolute, full, unconfined, unconstrained, unrestricted; indefinite, undefined.

unlucky *adj* baleful, disastrous, ill-fated, ill-starred, luckless, unfortunate, unprosperous, unsuccessful; ill-omened, inauspicious; miserable, unhappy.

unmanageable *adj* awkward, cumbersome, inconvenient, unwieldy; intractable, unruly, unworkable, vicious; difficult, impractical.

unmatched *adj* matchless, unequalled, unparalleled, unrivalled.

unmitigated *adj* absolute, complete, consummate, perfect, sheer, stark, thorough, unqualified, utter.

unnatural *adj* aberrant, abnormal, anomalous, foreign, irregular, prodigious, uncommon; brutal, cold, heartless, inhuman, unfeeling, unusual; affected, artificial, constrained, forced, insincere, self-conscious, stilted, strained; factitious.

unpleasant *adj* disagreeable, displeasing, distasteful, obnoxious, offensive, repulsive, unlovely, ungrateful, unacceptable, unpalatable, unwelcome.

unpremeditated *adj* extempore, impromptu, offhand, spontaneous, undesigned, unintentional, unstudied.

unprincipled *adj* bad, crooked, dishonest, fraudulent, immoral, iniquitous, knavish, lawless, profligate, rascally, roguish, thievish, trickish, tricky, unscrupulous, vicious, villainous, wicked.

unqualified *adj* disqualified, incompetent, ineligible, unadapted, unfit; absolute, certain, consummate, decided, direct, downright, full, outright, unconditional, unmeasured, unrestricted, unmitigated; exaggerated, sweeping.

unreal *adj* chimerical, dreamlike, fanciful, flimsy, ghostly, illusory, insubstantial, nebulous, shadowy, spectral, visionary, unsubstantial.

unreasonable *adj* absurd, excessive, exorbitant, foolish, illjudged, illogical, immoderate, impractical, injudicious, irrational, nonsensical, preposterous, senseless, silly, stupid, unfair, unreasoning, unwarrantable, unwise.

unreliable *adj* fallible, fickle, irresponsible, treacherous, uncertain, undependable, unstable, unsure, untrustworthy.

unremitting *adj* assiduous, constant, continual, diligent, incessant, indefatigable, persevering, sedulous, unabating, unceasing.

unrepentant *adj* abandoned, callous, graceless, hardened, impenitent, incorrigible, irreclaimable, lost, obdurate, profligate, recreant, seared, shameless.

unrequited *adj* unanswered, unreturned, unrewarded.

unreserved *adj* absolute, entire, full, unlimited; above-board, artless, candid, communicative, fair, frank, guileless, honest, ingenuous, open, sincere, single-minded, undesigning, undissembling; demonstrative, emotional, open-hearted.

unresisting *adj* compliant, long-suffering, non-resistant, obedient, passive, patient, submissive, yielding.

unresponsive *adj* irresponsive, unsympathetic.

unrestrained *adj* unbridled, unchecked, uncurbed, unfettered, unhindered, unobstructed, unreserved; broad, dissolute, incontinent, inordinate, lax, lewd, licentious, loose, wanton; lawless, wild.

unrestricted *adj* free, unbridled, unconditional, unconfined, uncurbed, unfettered, unlimited, unqualified, unrestrained; clear, open, public, unobstructed.

unrevealed *adj* hidden, occult, secret, undiscovered, unknown.

unrewarded *adj* unpaid, unrecompensed.

unriddle *vb* explain, expound, solve, unfold, unravel.

unrighteous *adj* evil, sinful, ungodly, unholy, vicious, wicked, wrong; heinous, inequitable, iniquitous, nefarious, unfair, unjust.

unripe *adj* crude, green, hard, immature, premature, sour; incomplete, unfinished.

unrivalled *adj* incomparable, inimitable, matchless, peerless, unequalled, unexampled, unique, unparalleled.

unrobe *vb* disrobe, undress.

unroll *vb* develop, discover, evolve, open, unfold; display, lay open.

unromantic *adj* literal, matter-of-fact, prosaic.

unroot *vb* eradicate, extirpate, root out, uproot.

unruffled *adj* calm, peaceful, placid, quiet, serene, smooth, still, tranquil; collected, composed, cool, imperturbable, peaceful, philosophical, placid, tranquil, undisturbed, unexcited, unmoved.

unruly *adj* disobedient, disorderly, fractious, headstrong, insubordinate, intractable, mutinous, obstreperous, rebellious, refractory, riotous, seditious, turbulent, ungovernable, unmanageable, wanton, wild; lawless, obstinate, rebellious, stubborn, vicious.

unsafe *adj* dangerous, hazardous, insecure, perilous, precarious, risky, treacherous, uncertain, unprotected.

unsaid *adj* tacit, unmentioned, unspoken, unuttered.

unsanctified *adj* profane, unhallowed, unholy.

unsatisfactory *adj* insufficient; disappointing; faulty, feeble, imperfect, poor, weak.

unsatisfied *adj* insatiate, unsated, unsatiated, unstaunched; discontented, displeased, dissatisfied, malcontent; undischarged, unpaid, unperformed, unrendered.

unsavoury *adj* flat, insipid, mawkish, savourless, tasteless, unflavoured, unpalatable, vapid; disagreeable, disgusting, distasteful, nasty, nauseating, nauseous, offensive, rank, revolting, sickening, uninviting, unpleasing.

unsay *vb* recall, recant, retract, take back.

unscathed *adj* unharmed, uninjured.

unschooled *adj* ignorant, uneducated, uninstructed; undisciplined, untrained.

unscrupulous *adj* dishonest, reckless, ruthless, unconscientious, unprincipled, unrestrained.

unsealed *adj* open, unclosed.

unsearchable *adj* hidden, incomprehensible, inscrutable, mysterious.

unseasonable *adj* ill-timed, inappropriate, infelicitous, inopportune, untimely; late, too late; inexpedient, undesireable, unfit, ungrateful, unsuitable, unwelcome; premature, too early.

unseasonably *adv* malapropos, unsuitably, untimely.

unseasoned *adj* inexperienced, unaccustomed, unqualified, untrained; immoderate, inordinate, irregular; green; fresh, unsalted.

unseeing *adj* blind, sightless.

unseemly *adj* improper, indecent, inappropriate, indecorous, unbecoming, uncomely, unfit, unmeet, unsuitable.

unseen *adj* undiscerned, undiscovered, unobserved, unperceived; imperceptible, indiscoverable, invisible, latent.

unselfish *adj* altruistic, devoted, disinterested, generous, highminded, impersonal, liberal, magnanimous, self-denying, selfforgetful, selfless, self-sacrificing.

unserviceable *adj* ill-conditioned, unsound, useless; profitless, unprofitable.

unsettle *vb* confuse, derange, disarrange, disconcert, disorder, disturb, trouble, unbalance, unfix, unhinge, upset.

unsettled *adj* changeable, fickle, inconstant, restless, transient, unstable, unsteady, vacillating, wavering; inequable, unequal; feculent, muddy, roiled, roily, turbid; adrift, afloat, homeless, unestablished, uninhabited; open, tentative, unadjusted, undecided, undetermined; due, outstanding, owing, unpaid; perturbed, troubled, unnerved.

unshackle *vb* emancipate, liberate, loose, release, set free, unbind, unchain, unfetter.

unshaken *adj* constant, firm, resolute, steadfast, steady, unmoved.

unshapen *adj* deformed, grotesque, ill-formed, ill-made, illshaped, misshapen, shapeless, ugly, uncouth.

unsheltered *adj* exposed, unprotected.

unshrinking *adj* firm, determined, persisting, resolute, unblenching, unflinching.

unshroud *vb* discover, expose, reveal, uncover.

unsightly *adj* deformed, disagreeable, hideous, repellent, repulsive, ugly.

unskilful, unskillful *adj* awkward, bungling, clumsy, inapt, inexpert, maladroit, rough, rude, unhandy, unskilled, unversed.

unskilled *adj* inexperienced, raw, undisciplined, undrilled, uneducated, unexercised, unpractised, unprepared, unschooled; unskilful.

unslaked *adj* unquenched, unslacked.

unsleeping *adj* unslumbering, vigilant, wakeful, watchful.

unsmirched *adj* undefiled, unpolluted, unspotted.

unsociable *adj* distant, reserved, retiring, segregative, shy, solitary, standoffish, taciturn, uncommunicative, uncompanionable, ungenial, unsocial; inhospitable, misanthropic, morose.

unsoiled *adj* clean, spotless, unspotted, unstained, unsullied, untarnished.

unsophisticated *adj* genuine, pure, unadulterated; good, guileless, innocent, undepraved, unpolluted, invitiated; artless, honest, ingenuous, naive, natural, simple, sincere, straightforward, unaffected, undesigning, unstudied.

unsound *adj* decayed, defective, impaired, imperfect, rotten, thin, wasted, weak; broken, disturbed, light, restless; diseased, feeble, infirm, morbid, poorly, sickly, unhealthy, weak; deceitful, erroneous, fallacious, false, faulty, hollow, illogical, incorrect, invalid, ill-advised, irrational, questionable, sophistical, unreasonable, unsubstantial, untenable, wrong; dishonest, false, insincere, unfaithful, untrustworthy, untrue; insubstantial, unreal; heretical, heterodox, unorthodox.

unsparing *adj* bountiful, generous, lavish, liberal, profuse, ungrudging; harsh, inexorable, relentless, rigorous, ruthless, severe, uncompromising, unforgiving.

unspeakable *adj* indescribable, ineffable, inexpressible, unutterable.

unspiritual *adj* bodily, carnal, fleshly, sensual.

unspotted *adj* clean, spotless, unsoiled, unstained, unsullied, untarnished; faultless, immaculate, innocent, pure, stainless, unblemished, uncorrupted, undefiled, untainted.

unstable *adj* infirm, insecure, precarious, top-heavy, tottering, unbalanced, unballasted, unreliable, unsafe, unsettled, unsteady; changeable, erratic, fickle, inconstant, irresolute, mercurial, mutable, vacillating, variable, wavering, weak, volatile.—*also* **instable**.

unstained *adj* colourless, uncoloured, undyed, untinged; clean, spotless, unspotted.

unsteady *adj* fluctuating, oscillating, unsettled; insecure, precarious, unstable; changeable, desultory, ever-changing, fickle, inconstant, irresolute, mutable, unreliable, variable, wavering; drunken, jumpy, tottering, vacillating, wobbly, tipsy.

unstinted *adj* abundant, ample, bountiful, full, large, lavish, plentiful, prodigal, profuse.

unstrung *adj* overcome, shaken, unnerved, weak.

unstudied *adj* extempore, extemporaneous, impromptu, offhand, spontaneous, unpremeditated; inexpert, unskilled, unversed.

unsubdued *adj* unbowed, unbroken, unconquered, untamed.

unsubmissive *adj* disobedient, contumacious, indocile, insubordinate, obstinate, perverse, refractory, uncomplying, ungovernable, unmanageable, unruly, unyielding.

unsubstantial *adj* airy, flimsy, gaseous, gossamery, light, slight, tenuous, thin, vaporous; apparitional, bodiless, chimerical, cloudbuilt, dreamlike, empty, fantastical, ideal, illusory, imaginary, imponderable, moonshiny, spectral, unreal, vague, visionary; erroneous, fallacious, flimsy, groundless, illogical, unfounded, ungrounded, unsolid, unsound, untenable, weak.

unsuccessful *adj* abortive, bootless, fruitless, futile, ineffectual, profitless, unavailing, vain; ill-fated, ill-starred, luckless, unfortunate, unhappy, unlucky, unprosperous.

unsuitable *adj* ill-adapted, inappropriate, malapropos, unfit, unsatisfactory, unsuited; improper, inapplicable, inapt, incongruous, inexpedient, infelicitous, unbecoming, unbeseeming, unfitting.

unsuited *adj* unadapted, unfitted, unqualified.

unsullied *adj* chaste, clean, spotless, unsoiled, unspotted, unstained, untarnished; immaculate, pure, stainless, unblemished, uncorrupted, undefiled, untainted, untouched, virginal.

unsupplied *adj* destitute, unfurnished, unprovided.

unsupported *adj* unaided, unassisted; unbacked, unseconded, unsustained, unupheld.

unsurpassed *adj* matchless, peerless, unequalled, unexampled, unexcelled, unmatched, unparagoned, unparalleled, unrivalled.

unsusceptible *adj* apathetic, cold, impassive, insusceptible, phlegmatic, stoical, unimpressible, unimpressionable.

unsuspecting *adj* confiding, credulous, trusting, unsuspicious.

unsuspicious *adj* confiding, credulous, gullible, simple, trustful, unsuspecting.

unsustainable *adj* insupportable, intolerable; controvertible, erroneous, unmaintainable, untenable.

unswerving *adj* direct, straight, undeviating; constant, determined, firm, resolute, staunch, steadfast, steady, stable, unwavering.

unsymmetrical *adj* amorphous, asymmetric, disproportionate, formless, irregular, unbalanced.

unsystematic, unsystematical *adj* casual, disorderly, haphazard, irregular, planless, unmethodical.

untainted *adj* chaste, clean, faultless, fresh, healthy, pure, sweet, wholesome; spotless, unsoiled, unstained, unsullied, untarnished; immaculate, stainless, unblemished, uncorrupted, undefiled, unspotted.

untamable *adj* unconquerable.

untamed *adj* fierce, unbroken, wild.

untangle *vb* disentangle, explain, explicate.

untarnished *adj* chaste, clean, spotless, unsoiled, unspotted, unstained, unsullied; immaculate, pure, spotless, stainless, unblemished, uncorrupted, undefiled, unspotted, unsullied, untainted, virginal, virtuous.

untaught *adj* illiterate, unenlightened, uninformed, unlettered; ignorant, inexperienced, undisciplined, undrilled, uneducated, uninitiated, uninstructed, untutored.

untenable *adj* indefensible, unmaintainable, unsound; fallacious, hollow, illogical, indefensible, insupportable, unjustifiable, weak.

untenanted *adj* deserted, empty, tenantless, uninhabited, unoccupied.

unterrified *adj* fearless, unappalled, unawed, undismayed, undaunted, unscared.

unthankful *adj* thankless, ungrateful.

unthinking *adj* careless, heedless, inconsiderate, thoughtless, unreasoning, unreflecting; automatic, mechanical.

unthoughtful *adj* careless, heedless, inconsiderate, thoughtless.

unthrifty *adj* extravagant, improvident, lavish, prodigal, profuse, thriftless, wasteful.

untidy *adj* careless, disorderly, dowdy, frumpy, mussy, slatternly, slovenly, unkempt, unneat.

untie *vb* free, loose, loosen, unbind, unfasten, unknot, unloose; clear, resolve, solve, unfold.

until *adv, conj* till, to the time when; to the place, point, state or degree that; • *prep* till, to.

untimely *adj* ill-timed, immature, inconvenient, inopportune, mistimed, premature, unseasonable, unsuitable; ill-considered, inauspicious, uncalled for, unfortunate. • *adv* unseasonably, unsuitably.

untinged *adj* achromatic, colourless, hueless, uncoloured, undyed, unstained.

untiring *adj* persevering, incessant, indefatigable, patient, tireless, unceasing, unfatiguable, unflagging, unremitting, unwearied, unwearying.

untold *adj* countless, incalculable, innumerable, uncounted, unnumbered; unrelated, unrevealed.

untouched *adj* intact, scatheless, unharmed, unhurt, uninjured, unscathed; insensible, unaffected, unmoved, unstirred.

untoward *adj* adverse, froward, intractable, perverse, refractory, stubborn, unfortunate; annoying, ill-timed, inconvenient, unmanageable, vexatious; awkward, uncouth, ungainly, ungraceful.

untrained *adj* green, ignorant, inexperienced, raw, unbroken, undisciplined, undrilled, uneducated, uninstructed, unpractised, unskilled, untaught, untutored.

untrammelled *adj* free, unhampered.

untried *adj* fresh, inexperienced, maiden, new, unassayed, unattempted, unattested, virgin; undecided.

untrodden *adj* pathless, trackless, unbeaten.

untroubled *adj* calm, careless, composed, peaceful, serene, smooth, tranquil, undisturbed, unvexed.

untrue *adj* contrary, false, inaccurate, wrong; disloyal, faithless, perfidious, recreant, treacherous, unfaithful.

untrustworthy *adj* deceitful, dishonest, inaccurate, rotten, slippery, treacherous, undependable, unreliable; disloyal, false; deceptive, fallible, illusive, questionable.

untruth *n* error, faithlessness, falsehood, falsity, incorrectness, inveracity, treachery; deceit, deception, fabrication, fib, fiction, forgery, imposture, invention, lie, misrepresentation, misstatement, story.

untutored *adj* ignorant, inexperienced, undisciplined, undrilled, uneducated, uninitiated, uninstructed, untaught; artless, natural, simple, unsophisticated.

untwist *vb* disentangle, disentwine, ravel, unravel, unwreathe.

unused *adj* idle, unemployed, untried; new, unaccustomed, unfamiliar.

unusual *adj* abnormal, curious, exceptional, extraordinary, odd, peculiar, queer, rare, recherché, remarkable, singular, strange, unaccustomed, uncommon, unwonted.

unutterable *adj* incommunicable, indescribable, ineffable, inexpressible, unspeakable.

unvarnished *adj* unpolished; candid, plain, simple, true, unadorned, unembellished.

unvarying *adj* constant, invariable, unchanging.

unveil *vb* disclose, expose, reveal, show, uncover, unmask.

unveracious *adj* false, lying, mendacious, untruthful.

unversed *adj* inexperienced, raw, undisciplined, undrilled, uneducated, unexercised, unpractised, unprepared, unschooled, unskilful.

unviolated *adj* inviolate, unbetrayed, unbroken.

unwarlike *adj* pacific, peaceful.

unwarped *adj* impartial, unbiased, undistorted, unprejudiced.

unwarrantable *adj* improper, indefensible, unjustifiable.

unwary *adj* careless, hasty, heedless, imprudent, incautious, indiscreet, precipitate, rash, reckless, remiss, uncircumspect, unguarded.

unwavering *adj* constant, determined, firm, fixed, resolute, settled, staunch, steadfast, steady, unhesitating.

unwearied *adj* unfatigued; constant, continual, incessant, indefatigable, persevering, persistent, unceasing, unremitting, untiring.

unwelcome *adj* disagreeable, unacceptable, ungrateful, unpleasant, unpleasing.

unwell *adj* ailing, delicate, diseased, ill, indisposed, sick.

unwept *adj* unlamented, unmourned, unregretted.

unwholesome *adj* baneful, deleterious, injurious, insalubrious, noisome, noxious, poisonous, unhealthful, unhealthy; injudicious, pernicious, unsound; corrupt, tainted.

unwieldy *adj* bulky, clumsy, cumbersome, cumbrous, elephantine, heavy, hulking, large, massy, ponderous, unmanageable, weighty.

unwilling *adj* averse, backward, disinclined, indisposed, laggard, loath, opposed, recalcitrant, reluctant; forced, grudging.

unwind *vb* unravel, unreel, untwine, wind off; disentangle.

unwise *adj* brainless, foolish, ill-advised, ill-judged, impolitic, imprudent, indiscreet, injudicious, inexpedient, senseless, silly, stupid, unwary, weak.

unwitnessed *adj* unknown, unseen, unspied.

unwittingly *adv* ignorantly, inadvertently, unconsciously, undesignedly, unintentionally, unknowingly.

unwonted *adj* infrequent, rare, uncommon, unusual; unaccustomed, unused.

unworthy *adj* undeserving; bad, base, blameworthy, worthless; shameful, unbecoming, vile; contemptible, derogatory, despicable, discreditable, mean, paltry, reprehensible, shabby.

unwrap *vb* open, unfold.

unwrinkled *adj* smooth, unforrowed.

unwritten *adj* oral, traditional, unrecorded; conventional, customary.

unwrought *adj* crude, rough, rude, unfashioned, unformed.

unyielding *adj* constant, determined, indomitable, inflexible, pertinacious, resolute, staunch, steadfast, steady, tenacious, uncompromising, unwavering; headstrong, intractable, obstinate, perverse, self-willed, stiff, stubborn, wayward, wilful; adamantine, firm, grim, hard, immovable, implastic, inexorable, relentless, rigid, unbending.

unyoke *vb* disconnect, disjoin, part, separate.

unyoked *adj* disconnected, separated; licentious, loose, unrestrained.

upbraid *vb* accuse, blame, chide, condemn, criticize, denounce, fault, reproach, reprove, revile, scold, taunt, twit.

upheaval *n* elevation, upthrow; cataclysm, convulsion, disorder, eruption, explosion, outburst, overthrow.

uphill *adj* ascending, upward; arduous, difficult, hard, laborious, strenuous, toilsome, wearisome.

uphold *vb* elevate, raise; bear up, hold up, support, sustain; advocate, aid, champion, countenance, defend, justify, maintain, vindicate.

upland *n* down, fell, ridge, plateau.

uplift *vb* raise, upraise; animate, elevate, inspire, lift, refine. • *n* ascent, climb, elevation, lift, rise, upthrust; exaltation, inspiration, uplifting; improvement, refinement.

upon *prep* on, on top of, over; about, concerning, on the subject of, relating to; immediately after, with.

upper hand *n* advantage, ascendancy, control, dominion, mastership, mastery, pre-eminence, rule, superiority, supremacy, whip hand.

uppermost *adj* foremost, highest, loftiest, supreme, topmost, upmost.

uppish *adj* arrogant, assuming, haughty, perky, proud, smart.

upright *adj* erect, perpendicular, vertical; conscientious, equitable, fair, faithful, good, honest, honourable, incorruptible, just, pure, righteous, straightforward, true, trustworthy, upstanding, virtuous.

uprightness *n* erectness, perpendicularity, verticality; equity, fairness, goodness, honesty, honour, incorruptibility, integrity, justice, probity, rectitude, righteousness, straightforwardness, trustiness, trustworthiness, virtue, worth.

uproar *n* clamour, commotion, confusion, din, disturbance, fracas, hubbub, hurly-burly, noise, pandemonium, racket, riot, tumult, turmoil, vociferation.

uproarious *adj* boisterous, clamorous, loud, noisy, obstreperous, riotous, tumultuous.

uproot *vb* eradicate, extirpate, root out.

upset *vb* capsize, invert, overthrow, overtumble, overturn, spill, tip over, topple, turn turtle; agitate, confound, confuse, discompose, disconcert, distress, disturb, embarrass, excite, fluster, muddle, overwhelm, perturb, shock, startle, trouble, unnerve, unsettle; checkmate, defeat, overthrow, revolutionize, subvert; foil, frustrate, nonplus, thwart. • *adj* disproved, exposed, overthrown; bothered, confused, disconcerted, flustered, mixed-up, perturbed; shocked, startled, unsettled; beaten, defeated, overcome, overpowered, overthrown; discomfited, distressed, discomposed, overexcited, overwrought, shaken, troubled, unnerved. • *n* confutation, refutation; foiling, frustration, overthrow, revolution, revulsion, ruin, subversion, thwarting.

upshot *n* conclusion, consummation, effect, end, event, issue, outcome, result, termination.

upside down *adj* bottom side up, bottom up, confused, head over heels, inverted, topsy-turvy.

upstart *n* adventurer, arriviste, parvenu, snob, social cimber, yuppie.

upturned *adj* raised, uplifted; retroussé.

upward *adj* ascending, climbing, mounting, rising, uphill. • *adv* above, aloft, overhead, up; heavenwards, skywards.

urbane *adj* civil, complaisant, courteous, courtly, elegant, mannerly, polished, polite, refined, smooth, suave, well-mannered.

urbanity *n* amenity, civility, complaisance, courtesy, politeness, smoothness, suavity.

urchin *n* brat, child, kid, ragamuffin, rascal, scrap, squirt, tad.

urge *vb* crowd, drive, force on, impel, press, press on, push, push on; beg, beseech, conjure, entreat, exhort, implore, importune, ply, solicit, tease; animate, egg on, encourage, goad, hurry, incite, instigate, quicken, spur, stimulate. • *n* compulsion, desire, drive, impulse, longing, pressure, wish, yearning.

urgency *n* drive, emergency, exigency, haste, necessity, press, pressure, push, stress; clamorousness, entreaty, insistence, importunity, instance, solicitation; goad, incitement, spur, stimulus.

urgent *adj* cogent, critical, crucial, crying, exigent, immediate, imperative, important, importunate, insistent, instant, pertinacious, pressing, serious.

urinal *n* chamber, chamber pot, lavatory, pot, potty, jordan, toilet.

urinate *vb* make water, pee, pee-pee, piddle, piss, stale, wee.

usage *n* treatment; consuetude, custom, fashion, habit, method, mode, practice, prescription, tradition, use.

use *vb* administer, apply, avail oneself of, drive, employ, handle, improve, make use of, manipulate, occupy, operate, ply, put into action, take advantage of, turn to account, wield, work; exercise, exert, exploit, practice, profit by, utilize; absorb, consume, exhaust, expend, swallow up, waste, wear out; accustom, familiarize, habituate, harden, inure, train; act toward, behave toward, deal with, manage, treat; be accustomed, be wont. • *n* appliance, application, consumption, conversion, disposal, exercise, employ, employment, practice, utilization; adaptability, advantage, avail, benefit, convenience, profit, service, usefulness, utility, wear; exigency, necessity, indispensability, need, occasion, requisiteness; custom, habit, handling, method, treatment, usage, way.

useful *adj* active, advantageous, available, availing, beneficial, commodious, conducive, contributory, convenient, effective, good, helpful, instrumental, operative, practical, profitable, remunerative, salutary, suitable, serviceable, utilitarian; available, helpful, serviceable, valuable.

usefulness *n* advantage, profit, serviceableness, utility, value.

useless *adj* abortive, bootless, fruitless, futile, helpless, idle, incapable, incompetent, ineffective, ineffectual, inutile, nugatory, null, profitless, unavailing, unprofitable, unproductive, unserviceable, valueless, worthless; good for nothing, waste.

usher *vb* announce, forerun, herald, induct, introduce, precede; conduct, direct, escort, shepherd, show. • *n* attendant, conductor, escort, shepherd, squire.

usual *adj* accustomed, common, customary, everyday, familiar, frequent, general, habitual, normal, ordinary, prevailing, prevalent, regular, wonted.

usurp *vb* appropriate, arrogate, assume, seize.

usurpation *n* assumption, dispossession, infringement, seizure.

usury *n* interest; exploitation, extortion, profiteering.

utensil *n* device, implement, instrument, tool.

utility *n* advantageousness, avail, benefit, profit, service, use, usefulness; happiness, welfare.

utilize *vb* employ, exploit, make use of, put to use, turn to account, use.

utmost *adj* extreme, farthest, highest, last, main, most distant, remotest; greatest, uttermost. • *n* best, extreme, maximum, most.

Utopian *adj* air-built, air-drawn, chimerical, fanciful, ideal, imaginary, visionary, unreal.

utricle *n* bladder, cyst, sac, vesicle.

utter[1] *adj* complete, entire, perfect, total; absolute, blank, diametric, downright, final, peremptory, sheer, stark, thorough, thoroughgoing, unconditional, unqualified, total.

utter[2] *vb* articulate, breathe, deliver, disclose, divulge, emit, enunciate, express, give forth, pronounce, reveal, speak, talk, tell, voice; announce, circulate, declare, issue, publish.

utterance *n* articulation, delivery, disclosure, emission, expression, pronouncement, pronunciation, publication, speech.

utterly *adv* absolutely, altogether, completely, downright, entirely, quite, totally, unconditionally, wholly.

uttermost *adj* extreme, farthest; greatest, utmost.

V

vacant *adj* blank, empty, unfilled, void; disengaged, free, unemployed, unoccupied, unencumbered; thoughtless, unmeaning, unthinking, unreflective; uninhabited, untenanted.

vacate *vb* abandon, evacuate, relinquish, surrender; abolish, abrogate, annul, cancel, disannul, invalidate, nullify, overrule, quash, rescind.

vacillate *vb* dither, fluctuate, hesitate, oscillate, rock, sway, waver.

vacillation *n* faltering, fluctuation, hesitation, inconstancy, indecision, irresolution, reeling, rocking, staggering, swaying, unsteadiness, wavering.

vacuity *n* emptiness, inanition, vacancy; emptiness, vacancy, vacuum, void; expressionlessness, inanity, nihility.

vacuous *adj* empty, empty-headed, unfilled, vacant, void; inane, unintelligent.

vacuum *n* emptiness, vacuity, void.

vagabond *adj* footloose, idle, meandering, rambling, roving, roaming, strolling, vagrant, wandering. • *n* beggar, castaway, landloper, loafer, lounger, nomad, outcast, tramp, vagrant, wanderer.

vagary *n* caprice, crotchet, fancy, freak, humour, whim.

vagrant *adj* erratic, itinerant, roaming, roving, nomadic, strolling, unsettled, wandering. • *n* beggar, castaway, landloper, loafer, lounger, nomad, outcast, tramp, vagabond, wanderer.

vague *adj* ambiguous, confused, dim, doubtful, indefinite, ill-defined, indistinct, lax, loose, obscure, uncertain, undetermined, unfixed, unsettled.

vain *adj* baseless, delusive, dreamy, empty, false, imaginary, shadowy, suppositional, unsubstantial, unreal, void; abortive, bootless, fruitless, futile, ineffectual, nugatory, profitless, unavailing, unprofitable; trivial, unessential, unimportant, unsatisfactory, unsatisfying, useless, vapid, worthless; arrogant, conceited, egotistical, flushed, high, inflated, opinionated, ostentatious, overweening, proud, self-confident, self-opinionated, vainglorious; gaudy, glittering, gorgeous, showy.

valediction *n* adieu, farewell, goodbye, leave-taking.

valet *n* attendant, flunky, groom, lackey, servant.

valetudinarian *adj* delicate, feeble, frail, infirm, sickly.

valiant *adj* bold, brave, chivalrous, courageous, daring, dauntless, doughty, fearless, gallant, heroic, intrepid, lion-hearted, redoubtable, Spartan, valorous, undaunted.

valid *adj* binding, cogent, conclusive, efficacious, efficient, good, grave, important, just, logical, powerful, solid, sound, strong, substantial, sufficient, weighty.

valley *n* basin, bottom, canyon, dale, dell, dingle, glen, hollow, ravine, strath, vale.

valorous *adj* bold, brave, courageous, dauntless, doughty, intrepid, stout.

valour *n* boldness, bravery, courage, daring, gallantry, heroism, prowess, spirit.

valuable *adj* advantageous, precious, profitable, useful; costly, expensive, rich; admirable, estimable, worthy. • *n* heirloom, treasure.

value *vb* account, appraise, assess, estimate, price, rate, reckon; appreciate, esteem, prize, regard, treasure. • *n* avail, importance, usefulness, utility, worth; cost, equivalent, price, rate; estimation, excellence, importance, merit, valuation.

valueless *adj* miserable, useless, worthless.

vandal *n* barbarian, destroyer, savage.

vandalism *n* barbarism, barbarity, savagery.

vanish *vb* disappear, dissolve, fade, melt.

vanity *n* emptiness, falsity, foolishness, futility, hollowness, insanity, triviality, unreality, worthlessness; arrogance, conceit, egotism, ostentation, self-conceit.

vanquish *vb* conquer, defeat, outwit, overcome, overpower, overthrow, subdue, subjugate; crush, discomfit, foil, master, quell, rout, worst.

vapid *adj* dead, flat, insipid, lifeless, savourless, spiritless, stale, tasteless; dull, feeble, jejune, languid, meagre, prosaic, prosy, tame.

vapour *n* cloud, exhalation, fog, fume, mist, rack, reek, smoke, steam; daydream, dream, fantasy, phantom, vagary, vision, whim, whimsy.

variable *adj* changeable, mutable, shifting; aberrant, alterable, capricious, fickle, fitful, floating, fluctuating, inconstant, mobile, mutable, protean, restless, shifting, unsteady, vacillating, wavering.

variance *n* disagreement, difference, discord, dissension, incompatibility, jarring, strife.

variation *n* alteration, change, modification; departure, deviation, difference, discrepancy, innovation; contrariety, discordance.

variegated *adj* chequered, dappled, diversified, flecked, kaleidoscopic, mottled, multicoloured, pied, spotted, striped.

variety *n* difference, dissimilarity, diversity, diversification, medley, miscellany, mixture, multiplicity, variation; kind, sort.

various *adj* different, diverse, manifold, many, numerous, several, sundry.

varnish *vb* enamel, glaze, japan, lacquer; adorn, decorate, embellish, garnish, gild, polish; disguise, excuse, extenuate, gloss over, palliate. • *n* enamel, lacquer, stain; cover, extenuation, gloss.

vary *vb* alter, metamorphose, transform; alternate, exchange, rotate; diversify, modify, variegate; depart, deviate, swerve.

vassal *n* bondman, liegeman, retainer, serf, slave, subject, thrall.

vassalage *n* bondage, dependence, serfdom, servitude, slavery, subjection.

vast *adj* boundless, infinite, measureless, spacious, wide; colossal, enormous, gigantic, huge, immense, mighty, monstrous, prodigious, tremendous; extraordinary, remarkable.

vaticination *n* augury, divination, prediction, prognostication, prophecy.

vault[1] *vb* arch, bend, curve, span. • *n* cupola, curve, dome; catacomb, cell, cellar, crypt, dungeon, tomb; depository, strongroom.

vault[2] *vb* bound, jump, leap, spring; tumble, turn. • *n* bound, leap, jump, spring.

vaunt *vb* advertise, boast, brag, display, exult, flaunt, flourish, parade.

veer *vb* change, shift, turn.

vegetate *vb* blossom, develop, flourish, flower, germinate, grow, shoot, sprout, swell; bask, hibernate, idle, stagnate.

vehemence *n* impetuosity, violence; ardour, eagerness, earnestness, enthusiasm, fervency, fervour, heat, keenness, passion, warmth, zeal; force, intensity.

vehement *adj* furious, high, hot, impetuous, passionate, rampant, violent; ardent, burning, eager, earnest, enthusiastic, fervid, fiery, keen, passionate, sanguine, zealous; forcible, mighty, powerful, strong.

veil *vb* cloak, conceal, cover, curtain, envelop, hide, invest, mask, screen, shroud. • *n* cover, curtain, film, shade, screen; blind, cloak, disguise, mask, muffler, visor.

vein *n* course, current, lode, seam, streak, stripe, thread, wave; bent, character, faculty, humour, mood, talent, turn.

velocity *n* acceleration, celerity, expedition, fleetness, haste, quickness, rapidity, speed, swiftness.

velvety *adj* delicate, downy, smooth, soft.

venal *adj* corrupt, mean, purchasable, sordid.

vend *vb* dispose, flog, hawk, retail, sell.

venerable *adj* grave, respected, revered, sage, wise; awful, dread, dreadful; aged, old, patriarchal.

venerate *vb* adore, esteem, honour, respect, revere.

veneration *n* adoration, devotion, esteem, respect, reverence, worship.

vengeance *n* retaliation, retribution, revenge.

venial *adj* allowed, excusable, pardonable, permitted, trivial.

venom *n* poison, virus; acerbity, acrimony, bitterness, gall, hate, ill-will, malevolence, malice, maliciousness, malignity, rancour, spite, virulence.

venomous *adj* deadly, poisonous, septic, toxic, virulent; caustic, malicious, malignant, mischievous, noxious, spiteful.

vent *vb* emit, express, release, utter. • *n* air hole, hole, mouth, opening, orifice; air pipe, air tube, aperture, blowhole, bunghole, hydrant, plug, spiracle, spout, tap, orifice; effusion, emission, escape, outlet, passage; discharge, expression, utterance.

ventilate *vb* aerate, air, freshen, oxygenate, purify; fan, winnow; canvass, comment, discuss, examine, publish, review, scrutinize.

venture *vb* adventure, dare, hazard, imperil, jeopardize, presume, risk, speculate, test, try, undertake. • *n* adventure, chance, hazard, jeopardy, peril, risk, speculation, stake.

venturesome *adj* adventurous, bold, courageous, daring, doughty, enterprising, fearless, foolhardy, intrepid, presumptuous, rash, venturous.

veracious *adj* reliable, straightforward, true, trustworthy, truthful; credible, genuine, honest, unfeigned.

veracity *n* accuracy, candour, correctness, credibility, exactness, fidelity, frankness, honesty, ingenuousness, probity, sincerity, trueness, truth, truthfulness.

verbal *adj* nuncupative, oral, spoken, unwritten.

verbose *adj* diffusive, long-winded, loquacious, talkative, wordy.

verdant *adj* fresh, green, verdure, verdurous; green, inexperienced, raw, unsophisticated.

verdict *n* answer, decision, finding, judgement, opinion, sentence.

verge *vb* bear, incline, lean, slope, tend; approach, border, skirt. • *n* mace, rod, staff; border, boundary, brink, confine, edge, extreme, limit, margin; edge, eve, point.

verification *n* authentication, attestation, confirmation, corroboration.

verify *vb* attest, authenticate, confirm, corroborate, prove, substantiate.

verily *adv* absolutely, actually, confidently, indeed, positively, really, truly.

verity *n* certainty, reality, truth, truthfulness.

vermicular *adj* convoluted, flexuose, flexuous, meandering, serpentine, sinuous, tortuous, twisting, undulating, waving, winding, wormish, wormlike.

vernacular *adj* common, indigenous, local, mother, native, vulgar. • *n* cant, dialect, jargon, patois, speech.

versatile *adj* capricious, changeable, erratic, mobile, variable; fickle, inconstant, mercurial, unsteady; adaptable, protean, plastic, varied.

versed *adj* able, accomplished, acquainted, clever, conversant, practised, proficient, qualified, skilful, skilled, trained.

version *n* interpretation, reading, rendering, translation.

vertex *n* apex, crown, height, summit, top, zenith.

vertical *adj* erect, perpendicular, plumb, steep, upright.

vertiginous *adj* rotatory, rotary, whirling; dizzy, giddy.

vertigo *n* dizziness, giddiness.

verve *n* animation, ardour, energy, enthusiasm, force, rapture, spirit.

very *adv* absolutely, enormously, excessively, hugely, remarkably, surpassingly. • *adj* actual, exact, identical, precise, same; bare, mere, plain, pure, simple.

vesicle *n* bladder, blister, cell, cyst, follicle.

vest *vb* clothe, cover, dress, envelop; endow, furnish, invest. • *n* dress, garment, robe, vestment, vesture, waistcoat.

vestibule *n* anteroom, entrance hall, lobby, porch.

vestige *n* evidence, footprint, footstep, mark, record, relic, sign, token.

veteran *adj* adept, aged, experienced, disciplined, seasoned, old. • *n* campaigner, old soldier; master, past master, old-timer, old-stager.

veto *vb* ban, embargo, forbid, interdict, negate, prohibit. • *n* ban, embargo, interdict, prohibition, refusal.

vex *vb* annoy, badger, bother, chafe, cross, distress, gall, harass, harry, hector, molest, perplex, pester, plague, tease, torment, trouble, roil, spite, worry; affront, displease, fret, irk, irritate, nettle, offend, provoke; agitate, disquiet, disturb.

vexation *n* affliction, agitation, chagrin, discomfort, displeasure, disquiet, distress, grief, irritation, pique, sorrow, trouble; annoyance, curse, nuisance, plague, torment; damage, troubling, vexing.

vexed *adj* afflicted, agitated, annoyed, bothered, disquieted, harassed, irritated, perplexed, plagued, provoked, troubled, worried.

vibrate *vb* oscillate, sway, swing, undulate, wave; impinge, quiver, sound, thrill; fluctuate, hesitate, vacillate, waver.

vibration *n* nutation, oscillation, vibration.

vicarious *adj* commissioned, delegated, indirect, second-hand, substituted.

vice *n* blemish, defect, failing, fault, imperfection, infirmity; badness, corruption, depravation, depravity, error, evil, immorality, iniquity, laxity, obliquity, sin, viciousness, vileness, wickedness.

vicinity *n* nearness, proximity; locality, neighbourhood, vicinage.

vicious *adj* abandoned, atrocious, bad, corrupt, degenerate, demoralized, depraved, devilish, diabolical, evil, flagrant, hellish, immoral, iniquitous, mischievous, profligate, shameless, sinful, unprincipled, wicked; malicious, spiteful, venomous; foul, impure; debased, faulty; contrary, refractory.

viciousness *n* badness, corruption, depravity, immorality, profligacy.

vicissitude *n* alteration, interchange; change, fluctuation, mutation, revolution, variation.

victim *n* martyr, sacrifice, sufferer; prey; cat's-paw, cull, cully, dupe, gull, gudgeon, puppet.

victimize *vb* bamboozle, befool, beguile, cheat, circumvent, cozen, deceive, defraud, diddle, dupe, fool, gull, hoax, hoodwink, overreach, swindle, trick.

victor *n* champion, conqueror, vanquisher, winner.

victorious *adj* conquering, successful, triumphant, winning.

victory *n* achievement, conquest, mastery, triumph.

victuals *npl* comestibles, eatables, fare, food, meat, provisions, repast, sustenance, viands.

vie *vb* compete, contend, emulate, rival, strive.

view *vb* behold, contemplate, eye, inspect, scan, survey; consider, inspect, regard, study. • *n* inspection, observation, regard, sight; outlook, panorama, perspective, prospect, range, scene, survey, vista; aim, intent, intention, design, drift, object, purpose, scope; belief, conception, impression, idea, judgement, notion, opinion, sentiment, theory; appearance, aspect, show.

vigilance *n* alertness, attentiveness, carefulness, caution, circumspection, observance, watchfulness.

vigilant *adj* alert, attentive, careless, cautious, circumspect, unsleeping, wakeful, watchful.

vigorous *adj* lusty, powerful, strong; active, alert, cordial, energetic, forcible, strenuous, vehement, vivid, virile; brisk, hale, hardy, robust, sound, sturdy, healthy; fresh, flourishing; bold, emphatic, impassioned, lively, nervous, piquant, pointed, severe, sparkling, spirited, trenchant.

vigour *n* activity, efficacy, energy, force, might, potency, power, spirit, strength; bloom, elasticity, haleness, health, heartiness, pep, punch, robustness, soundness, thriftiness, tone, vim, vitality; enthusiasm, freshness, fire, intensity, liveliness, piquancy, strenuousness, vehemence, verve, raciness.

vile *adj* abject, base, beastly, beggarly, brutish, contemptible, despicable, disgusting, grovelling, ignoble, low, odious, paltry, pitiful, repulsive, scurvy, shabby, slavish, sorry, ugly; bad, evil, foul, gross, impure, iniquitous, lewd, obscene, sinful, vicious, wicked; cheap, mean, miserable, valueless, worthless.

vilify *vb* abuse, asperse, backbite, berate, blacken, blemish, brand, calumniate, decry, defame, disparage, lampoon, libel, malign, revile, scandalize, slander, slur, traduce, vituperate.

villain *n* blackguard, knave, miscreant, rascal, reprobate, rogue, ruffian, scamp, scapegrace, scoundrel.

villainous *adj* base, mean, vile; corrupt, depraved, knavish, unprincipled, wicked; atrocious, heinous, outrageous, sinful; mischievous, sorry.

vindicate *vb* defend, justify, uphold; advocate, avenge, assert, maintain, right, support.

vindication *n* apology, excuse, defence, justification.

vindictive *adj* avenging, grudgeful, implacable, malevolent, malicious, malignant, retaliative, revengeful, spiteful, unforgiving, unrelenting, vengeful.

violate *vb* hurt, injure; break, disobey, infringe, invade; desecrate, pollute, profane; abuse, debauch, defile, deflower, outrage, ravish, transgress.

violent *adj* boisterous, demented, forceful, forcible, frenzied, furious, high, hot, impetuous, insane, intense, stormy, tumultuous, turbulent, vehement, wild; fierce, fiery, fuming, heady, heavy, infuriate, passionate, obstreperous, strong, raging, rampant, rank, rapid, raving, refractory, roaring, rough, tearing, towering, ungovernable; accidental, unnatural; desperate, extreme, outrageous, unjust; acute, exquisite, poignant, sharp.

virago *n* amazon, brawler, fury, shrew, tartar, vixen.

virgin *adj* chaste, maidenly, modest, pure, undefiled, stainless, unpolluted, vestal, virginal; fresh, maiden, untouched, unused. • *n* celibate, damsel, girl, lass, maid, maiden.

virile *adj* forceful, manly, masculine, robust, vigorous.

virtual *adj* constructive, equivalent, essential, implicit, implied, indirect, practical, substantial.

virtue *n* chastity, goodness, grace, morality, purity; efficacy, excellence, honesty, integrity, justice, probity, quality, rectitude, worth.

virtuous *adj* blameless, equitable, exemplary, excellent, good, honest, moral, noble, righteous, upright, worthy; chaste, continent, immaculate, innocent, modest, pure, undefiled; efficacious, powerful.

virulent *adj* deadly, malignant, poisonous, toxic, venomous; acrid, acrimonious, bitter, caustic.

visage *n* aspect, countenance, face, guise, physiognomy, semblance.

viscera *n* bowels, entrails, guts, intestines.

viscous *adj* adhesive, clammy, glutinous, ropy, slimy, sticky, tenacious.

visible *adj* observable, perceivable, perceptible, seeable, visual; apparent, clear, conspicuous, discoverable, distinct, evident, manifest, noticeable, obvious, open, palpable, patent, plain, revealed, unhidden, unmistakable.

vision *n* eyesight, seeing, sight; eyeshot, ken; apparition, chimera, dream, ghost, hallucination, illusion, phantom, spectre.

visionary *adj* imaginative, impractical, quixotic, romantic; chimerical, dreamy, fancied, fanciful, fantastic, ideal, illusory, imaginary, romantic, shadowy, unsubstantial, utopian, wild. • *n* dreamer, enthusiast, fanatic, idealist, optimist, theorist, zealot.

vital *adj* basic, cardinal, essential, indispensable, necessary, needful; animate, alive, existing, life-giving, living; paramount.

vitality *n* animation, life, strength, vigour, virility.

vitiate *vb* adulterate, contaminate, corrupt, debase, defile, degrade, deprave, deteriorate, impair, infect, injure, invalidate, poison, pollute, spoil.

vitiation *n* adulteration, corruption, degeneracy, degeneration, degradation, depravation, deterioration, impairment, injury, invalidation, perversion, pollution, prostitution.

vituperate *vb* abuse, berate, blame, censure, denounce, overwhelm, rate, revile, scold, upbraid, vilify.

vituperation *n* abuse, blame, censure, invective, reproach, railing, reviling, scolding, upbraiding.

vivacious *adj* active, animated, breezy, brisk, buxom, cheerful, frolicsome, gay, jocund, light-hearted, lively, merry, mirthful, spirited, sportive, sprightly.

vivacity *n* animation, cheer, cheerfulness, gaiety, liveliness, sprightliness.

vivid *adj* active, animated, bright, brilliant, clear, intense, fresh, lively, living, lucid, quick, sprightly, strong; expressive, graphic, striking, telling.

vivify *vb* animate, arouse, awake, quicken, vitalize.

vixen *n* brawler, scold, shrew, spitfire, tartar, virago.

vocabulary *n* dictionary, glossary, lexicon, wordbook; language, terms, words.

vocation *n* call, citation, injunction, summons; business, calling, employment, occupation, profession, pursuit, trade.

vociferate *vb* bawl, bellow, clamour, cry, exclaim, rant, shout, yell.

vociferous *adj* blatant, clamorous, loud, noisy, obstreperous, ranting, stunning, uproarious.

vogue *adj* fashionable, modish, stylish, trendy. • *n* custom, fashion, favour, mode, practice, repute, style, usage, way.

voice *vb* declare, express, say, utter. • *n* speech, tongue, utterance; noise, notes, sound; opinion, option, preference, suffrage, vote; accent, articulation, enunciation, inflection, intonation, modulation, pronunciation, tone; expression, language, words.

void *vb* clear, eject, emit, empty, evacuate. • *adj* blank, empty, hollow, vacant; clear, destitute, devoid, free, lacking, wanting, without; inept, ineffectual, invalid, nugatory, null; imaginary, unreal, vain. • *n* abyss, blank, chasm, emptiness, hole, vacuum.

volatile *adj* gaseous, incoercible; airy, buoyant, frivolous, gay, jolly, lively, sprightly, vivacious; capricious, changeable, fickle, flighty, flyaway, giddy, harebrained, inconstant, light-headed, mercurial, reckless, unsteady, whimsical, wild.

volition *n* choice, determination, discretion, option, preference, will.

volley *n* fusillade, round, salvo; blast, burst, discharge, emission, explosion, outbreak, report, shower, storm.

voluble *adj* fluent, garrulous, glib, loquacious, talkative.

volume *n* book, tome; amplitude, body, bulk, compass, dimension, size, substance, vastness; fullness, power, quantity.

voluminous *adj* ample, big, bulky, full, great, large; copious, diffuse, discursive, flowing.

voluntary *adj* free, spontaneous, unasked, unbidden, unforced; deliberate, designed, intended, purposed; discretionary, optional, willing.

volunteer *vb* offer, present, proffer, propose, tender.

voluptuary *n* epicure, hedonist, sensualist.

voluptuous *adj* carnal, effeminate, epicurean, fleshy, licentious, luxurious, sensual, sybaritic.

vomit *vb* discharge, eject, emit, puke, regurgitate, spew, throw up.

voracious *adj* devouring, edacious, greedy, hungry, rapacious, ravenous.

vortex *n* eddy, maelstrom, whirl, whirlpool.

votary *adj* devoted, promised. • *n* adherent, devotee, enthusiast, follower, supporter, votarist, zealot.

vote *vb* ballot, elect, opt, return; judge, pronounce, propose, suggest. • *n* ballot, franchise, poll, referendum, suffrage, voice.

vouch *vb* affirm, asseverate, attest, aver, declare, guarantee, support, uphold, verify, warrant.

vouchsafe *vb* accord, cede, deign, grant, stoop, yield.

vow *vb* consecrate, dedicate, devote; asseverate. • *n* oath, pledge, promise.

voyage *vb* cruise, journey, navigate, ply, sail. • *n* crossing, cruise, excursion, journey, passage, sail, trip.

vulgar *adj* base-born, common, ignoble, lowly, plebeian; boorish, cheap, coarse, discourteous, flashy, homespun, garish, gaudy, ill-bred, inelegant, loud, rustic, showy, tawdry, uncultivated, unrefined; general, ordinary, popular, public; base, broad, loose, low, gross, mean, ribald, vile; inelegant, unauthorized.

vulgarity *n* baseness, coarseness, grossness, meanness, rudeness.

vulnerable *adj* accessible, assailable, defenceless, exposed, weak.

W

waddle *vb* toddle, toggle, waggle, wiggle, wobble.

waft *vb* bear, carry, convey, float, transmit, transport. • *n* breath, breeze, draught, puff.

wag[1] *vb* shake, sway, waggle; oscillate, vibrate, waver; advance, move, progress, stir. • *n* flutter, nod, oscillation, vibration.

wag[2] *n* humorist, jester, joker, wit.

wage *vb* bet, hazard, lay, stake, wager; conduct, undertake.

wager *vb* back, bet, gamble, lay, pledge, risk, stake. • *n* bet, gamble, pledge, risk, stake.

wages *npl* allowance, compensation, earnings, emolument, hire, pay, payment, remuneration, salary, stipend.

waggish *adj* frolicsome, gamesome, mischievous, roguish, tricksy; comical, droll, facetious, funny, humorous, jocular, jocose, merry, sportive.

wagon *n* cart, lorry, truck, van, waggon, wain.

wail *vb* bemoan, deplore, lament, mourn; cry, howl, weep. • *n* complaint, cry, lamentation, moan, wailing.

waist *n* bodice, corsage, waistline.

wait *vb* delay, linger, pause, remain, rest, stay, tarry; attend, minister, serve; abide, await, expect, look for. • *n* delay, halt, holdup, pause, respite, rest, stay, stop.

waiter, waitress *n* attendant, lackey, servant, servitor, steward, valet.

waive *vb* defer, forgo, surrender, relinquish, remit, renounce; desert, reject.

wake[1] *vb* arise, awake, awaken; activate, animate, arouse, awaken, excite, kindle, provoke, stimulate. • *n* vigil, watch, watching.

wake[2] *n* course, path, rear, track, trail, wash.

wakeful *adj* awake, sleepless, restless; alert, observant, vigilant, wary, watchful.

wale *n* ridge, streak, stripe, welt, whelk.

walk *vb* advance, depart, go, march, move, pace, saunter, step, stride, stroll, tramp. • *n* amble, carriage, gait, step; beat, career, course, department, field, province; conduct, procedure; alley, avenue, cloister, esplanade, footpath, path, pathway, pavement, promenade, range, sidewalk, way; constitutional, excursion, hike, ramble, saunter, stroll, tramp, turn.

wall *n* escarp, parapet, plane, upright.

wallet *n* bag, knapsack, pocketbook, purse, sack.

wan *adj* ashen, bloodless, cadaverous, colourless, haggard, pale, pallid.

wand *n* baton, mace, truncheon, sceptre.

wander *vb* forage, prowl, ramble, range, roam, rove, stroll; deviate, digress, straggle, stray; moon, rave. • *n* amble, cruise, excursion, ramble, stroll.

wane *vb* abate, decrease, ebb, subside; decline, fail, sink. • *n* decrease, diminution, lessening; decay, declension, decline, failure.

want *vb* crave, desire, need, require, wish; fail, lack, neglect, omit. • *n* absence, defect, default, deficiency, lack; defectiveness, failure, inadequacy, insufficiency, meagreness, paucity, poverty, scantiness, scarcity, shortness; requirement; craving, desire, longing, wish; destitution, distress, indigence, necessity, need, penury, poverty, privation, straits.

wanton *vb* caper, disport, frisk, frolic, play, revel, romp, sport; dally, flirt, toy, trifle. • *adj* free, loose, unchecked, unrestrained, wandering; abounding, exuberant, luxuriant, overgrown, rampant; airy, capricious, coltish, frisky, playful, skittish, sportive; dissolute, irregular, licentious, loose; carnal, immoral, incontinent, lascivious, lecherous, lewd, libidinous, light, lustful, prurient, salacious, unchaste; careless, gratuitous, groundless, heedless, inconsiderate, needless, perverse, reckless, wayward, wilful. • *n* baggage, flirt, harlot, light-o'-love, prostitute, rake, roué, slut, whore.

war *vb* battle, campaign, combat, contend, crusade, engage, fight, strive. • *n* contention, enmity, hostility, strife, warfare.

warble *vb* sing, trill, yodel. • *n* carol, chant, hymn, hum.

ward *vb* guard, watch; defend, fend, parry, protect, repel. • *n* care, charge, guard, guardianship, watch; defender, guardian, keeper, protector, warden; custody; defence, garrison, protection; minor, pupil; district, division, precinct, quarter; apartment, cubicle.

warehouse *n* depot, magazine, repository, store, storehouse.

wares *npl* commodities, goods, merchandise, movables.

warfare *n* battle, conflict, contest, discord, engagement, fray, hostilities, strife, struggle, war.

warily *adv* carefully, cautiously, charily, circumspectly, heedfully, watchfully, vigilantly.

wariness *n* care, caution, circumspection, foresight, thought, vigilance.

warlike *adj* bellicose, belligerent, combative, hostile, inimical, martial, military, soldierly, watchful.

warm *vb* heat, roast, toast; animate, chafe, excite, rouse. • *adj* lukewarm, tepid; genial, mild, pleasant, sunny; close, muggy, oppressive; affectionate, ardent, cordial, eager, earnest, enthusiastic, fervent, fervid, glowing, hearty, hot, zealous; excited, fiery, flushed, furious, hasty, keen, lively, passionate, quick, vehement, violent.

warmth *n* glow, tepidity; ardour, fervency, fervour, zeal; animation, cordiality, eagerness, earnestness, enthusiasm, excitement, fervency, fever, fire, flush, heat, intensity, passion, spirit, vehemence.

warn *vb* caution, forewarn; admonish, advise; apprise, inform, notify; bid, call, summon.

warning *adj* admonitory, cautionary, cautioning, monitory. • *n* admonition, advice, caveat, caution, monition; information, notice; augury, indication, intimation, omen, portent, presage, prognostic, sign, symptom; call, summons; example, lesson, sample.

warp *vb* bend, bias, contort, deviate, distort, pervert, swerve, turn, twist. • *n* bent, bias, cast, crook, distortion, inclination, leaning, quirk, sheer, skew, slant, slew, swerve, twist, turn.

warrant *vb* answer for, certify, guarantee, secure; affirm, assure, attest, avouch, declare, justify, state; authorize, justify, license, maintain, sanction, support, sustain, uphold. • *n* guarantee, pledge, security, surety, warranty; authentication, authority, commission, verification; order, pass, permit, summons, subpoena, voucher, writ.

warrantable *adj* admissible, allowable, defensible, justifiable, lawful, permissible, proper, right, vindicable.

warrior *n* champion, captain, fighter, hero, soldier.

wary *adj* careful, cautious, chary, circumspect, discreet, guarded, heedful, prudent, scrupulous, vigilant, watchful.

wash *vb* purify, purge; moisten, wet; bathe, clean, flush, irrigate, lap, lave, rinse, sluice; colour, stain, tint. • *n* ablution, bathing, cleansing, lavation, washing; bog, fen, marsh, swamp, quagmire; bath, embrocation, lotion; laundry, washing.

washy *adj* damp, diluted, moist, oozy, sloppy, thin, watery, weak; feeble, jejune, pointless, poor, spiritless, trashy, trumpery, unmeaning, vapid, worthless.

waspish *adj* choleric, fretful, irascible, irritable, peevish, petulant, snappish, testy, touchy; slender, slim, small-waisted.

waste *vb* consume, corrode, decrease, diminish, emaciate, wear; absorb, deplete, devour, dissipate, drain, empty, exhaust, expend, lavish, lose, misspend, misuse, scatter, spend, squander; demolish, desolate, destroy, devastate, devour, dilapidate, harry, pillage, plunder, ravage, ruin, scour, strip; damage, impair, injure; decay, dwindle, perish, wither. • *adj* bare, desolated, destroyed, devastated, empty, ravaged, ruined, spoiled, stripped, void; dismal, dreary, forlorn; abandoned, bare, barren, uncultivated, unimproved, uninhabited, untilled, wild; useless, valueless, worthless; exuberant, superfluous. • *n* consumption, decrement, diminution, dissipation, exhaustion, expenditure, loss, wasting; destruction, dispersion, extravagance, loss, squandering, wanton; decay, desolation, destruction, devastation, havoc, pillage, ravage, ruin; chaff, debris, detritus, dross, excrement, husks, junk, matter, offal, refuse, rubbish, trash, wastrel, worthlessness; barrenness, desert, expanse, solitude, wild, wilderness.

wasteful *adj* destructive, ruinous; extravagant, improvident, lavish, prodigal, profuse, squandering, thriftless, unthrifty.

watch *vb* attend, guard, keep, oversee, protect, superintend, tend; eye, mark, observe. • *n* espial, guard, outlook, wakefulness, watchfulness, watching, vigil, ward; alertness, attention, inspection, observation, surveillance; guard, picket, sentinel, sentry, watchman; pocket watch, ticker, timepiece, wristwatch.

watchful *adj* alert, attentive, awake, careful, circumspect, guarded, heedful, observant, vigilant, wakeful, wary.

watchword *n* catchword, cry, motto, password, shibboleth, word.

waterfall *n* cascade, cataract, fall, linn.

watery *adj* diluted, thin, waterish, weak; insipid, spiritless, tasteful, vapid; moist, wet.

wave *vb* float, flutter, heave, shake, sway, undulate, wallow; brandish, flaunt, flourish, swing; beckon, signal. • *n* billow, bore, breaker, flood, flush, ripple, roll, surge, swell, tide, undulation; flourish, gesture, sway; convolution, curl, roll, unevenness.

waver *vb* flicker, float, undulate, wave; reel, totter; falter, fluctuate, flutter, hesitate, oscillate, quiver, vacillate.

wax *vb* become, grow, increase, mount, rise.

way *n* advance, journey, march, progression, transit, trend; access, alley, artery, avenue, beat, channel, course, highroad, highway, passage, path, road, route, street, track, trail; fashion, manner, means, method, mode, system; distance, interval, space, stretch; behaviour, custom, form, guise, habit, habitude, practice, process, style, usage; device, plan, scheme.

wayfarer *n* itinerant, nomad, passenger, pilgrim, rambler, traveller, walker, wanderer.

wayward *adj* capricious, captious, contrary, forward, headstrong, intractable, obstinate, perverse, refractory, stubborn, unruly, wilful.

weak *adj* debilitated, delicate, enfeebled, enervated, exhausted, faint, feeble, fragile, frail, infirm, invalid, languid, languishing, shaky, sickly, spent, strengthless, tender, unhealthy, unsound, wasted, weakly; accessible, defenceless, unprotected, vulnerable; light, soft, unstressed; boneless, cowardly, infirm; compliant, irresolute, pliable, pliant, undecided, undetermined, unsettled, unstable, unsteady, vacillating, wavering, yielding; childish, foolish, imbecile, senseless, shallow, silly, simple, stupid, weak-minded, witless; erring, foolish, indiscreet, injudicious, unwise; gentle, indistinct, low, small; adulterated, attenuated, diluted, insipid, tasteless, thin, watery; flimsy, frivolous, poor, sleazy, slight, trifling; futile, illogical, inconclusive, ineffective, ineffectual, inefficient, lame, unconvincing, unsatisfactory, unsupported, unsustained, vague, vain; unsafe, unsound, unsubstantial, untrustworthy; helpless, impotent, powerless; breakable, brittle, delicate, frangible; inconsiderable, puny, slender, slight, small.

weaken *vb* cramp, cripple, debilitate, devitalize, enervate, enfeeble, invalidate, relax, sap, shake, stagger, undermine, unman, unnerve, unstring; adulterate, attenuate, debase, depress, dilute, exhaust, impair, impoverish, lessen, lower, reduce.

weakness *n* debility, feebleness, fragility, frailty, infirmity, languor, softness; defect, failing, fault, flaw; fondness, inclination, liking.

weal *n* advantage, good, happiness, interest, profit, utility, prosperity, welfare; ridge, streak, stripe.

wealth *n* assets, capital, cash, fortune, funds, goods, money, possessions, property, riches, treasure; abundance, affluence, opulence, plenty, profusion.

wean *vb* alienate, detach, disengage, withdraw.

wear *vb* bear, carry, don; endure, last; consume, impair, rub, use, waste. • *n* corrosion, deterioration, disintegration, erosion, wear and tear; consumption, use; apparel, array, attire, clothes, clothing, dress, garb, gear.

wearied *adj* apathetic, bored, exhausted, fagged, fatigued, jaded, tired, weary, worn.

weariness *n* apathy, boredom, ennui, exhaustion, fatigue, languor, lassitude, monotony, prostration, sameness, tedium.

wearisome *adj* annoying, boring, dull, exhausting, fatiguing, humdrum, irksome, monotonous, prolix, prosaic, slow, tedious, tiresome, troublesome, trying, uninteresting, vexatious.

weary *vb* debilitate, exhaust, fag, fatigue, harass, jade, tire. • *adj* apathetic, bored, drowsy, exhausted, jaded, spent, tired, worn; irksome, tiresome, wearisome.

weave *vb* braid, entwine, interlace, lace, mat, plait, pleat, twine; compose, construct, fabricate, make.

wed *vb* contract, couple, espouse, marry, unite.

wedding *n* bridal, espousal, marriage, nuptials.

wedlock *n* marriage, matrimony.

ween *vb* fancy, imagine, suppose, think.

weep *vb* bemoan, bewail, complain, cry, lament, sob.

weigh *vb* balance, counterbalance, lift, raise; consider, deliberate, esteem, examine, study.

weight *vb* ballast, burden, fill, freight, load; weigh. • *n* gravity, heaviness, heft, tonnage; burden, load, pressure; consequence, efficacy, emphasis, importance, impressiveness, influence, moment, pith, power, significance, value.

weighty *adj* heavy, massive, onerous, ponderous, unwieldy; considerable, efficacious, forcible, grave, important, influential, serious, significant.

weird *adj* eerie, ghostly, strange, supernatural, uncanny, unearthly, witching.

welcome *vb* embrace, greet, hail, receive. • *adj* acceptable, agreeable, grateful, gratifying, pleasant, pleasing, satisfying. • *n* greeting, reception, salutation.

welfare *n* advantage, affluence, benefit, happiness, profit, prosperity, success, thrift, weal, wellbeing.

well[1] *vb* flow, gush, issue, jet, pour, spring. • *n* fount, fountain, reservoir, spring, wellhead, wellspring; origin, source; hole, pit, shaft.

well[2] *adj* hale, healthy, hearty, sound; fortunate, good, happy, profitable, satisfactory, useful. • *adv* accurately, adequately, correctly, efficiently, properly, suitably; abundantly, considerably, fully, thoroughly; agreeably, commendably, favourably, worthily.

wellbeing *n* comfort, good, happiness, health, prosperity, welfare.

welter *vb* flounder, roll, toss, wallow. • *n* confusion, jumble, mess.

wet *vb* dabble, damp, dampen, dip, drench, moisten, saturate, soak, sprinkle, water. • *adj* clammy, damp, dank, dewy, dripping, humid, moist; rainy, showery, sprinkly. • *n* dampness, humidity, moisture, wetness.

whack *vb*, *n* bang, beat, rap, strike, thrash, thump, thwack.

wharf *n* dock, pier, quay.

wheedle *vb* cajole, coax, flatter, inveigle, lure.

wheel *vb* gyrate, revolve, roll, rotate, spin, swing, turn, twist, whirl, wind. • *n* circle, revolution, roll, rotation, spin, turn, twirl.

whet *vb* grind, sharpen; arouse, awaken, excite, provoke, rouse, stimulate; animate, inspire, kindle, quicken, warm.

whiff *vb*, *n* blast, gust, puff.

whim *n* caprice, crotchet, fancy, freak, frolic, humour, notion, quirk, sport, vagary, whimsy, wish.

whimsical *adj* capricious, crotchety, eccentric, erratic, fanciful, frolicsome, odd, peculiar, quaint, singular.

whine *vb* cry, grumble, mewl, moan, snivel, wail, whimper. • *n* complaint, cry, grumble, moan, sob, wail, whimper.

whip *vb* beat, lash, strike; flagellate, flog, goad, horsewhip, scourge, slash; hurt, sting; jerk, snap, snatch, whisk. • *n* bullwhip, cane, crop, horsewhip, knout, lash, scourge, switch, thong.

whipping *n* beating, castigation, dusting, flagellation, flogging, thrashing.

whirl *vb* gyrate, pirouette, roll, revolve, rotate, turn, twirl, twist, wheel. • *n* eddy, flurry, flutter, gyration, rotation, spin, swirl, twirl, vortex.

whit *n* atom, bit, grain, iota, jot, mite, particle, scrap, speck, tittle.

white *adj* argent, canescent, chalky, frosty, hoary, ivory, milky, silver, snowy; grey, pale, pallid, wan; candid, clean, chaste, immaculate, innocent, pure, spotless, unblemished.

whole *adj* all, complete, entire, intact, integral, total, undivided; faultless, firm, good, perfect, strong, unbroken, undivided, uninjured; healthy, sound, well. • *adv* entire, in one. • *n* aggregate, all, amount, ensemble, entirety, gross, sum, total, totality.

wholesome *adj* healthy, healthful, invigorating, nourishing, nutritious, salubrious, salutary; beneficial, good, helpful, improving, salutary; fresh, sound, sweet.

wholly *adv* altogether, completely, entirely, fully, totally, utterly.

whoop *vb* halloo, hoot, roar, shout, yell. • *n* bellow, hoot, roar, shout, yell.

whore *n* bawd, courtesan, drab, harlot, prostitute, streetwalker, strumpet.

wicked *adj* abandoned, abominable, depraved, devilish, godless, graceless, immoral, impious, infamous, irreligious, irreverent, profane, sinful, ungodly, unholy, unprincipled, unrighteous, vicious, vile, worthless; atrocious, bad, black, criminal, dark, evil, heinous, ill, iniquitous, monstrous, nefarious, unjust, villainous.

wide *adj* ample, broad, capacious, comprehensive, distended, expanded, large, spacious, vast; distant, remote; prevalent, rife, widespread. • *adv* completely, farthest, fully.

wield *vb* brandish, flourish, handle, manipulate, ply, work; control, manage, sway, use.

wild *adj* feral, undomesticated, untamed; desert, desolate, native, rough, rude, uncultivated; barbarous, ferocious, fierce, savage, uncivilized; dense, luxuriant, rank; disorderly, distracted, frantic, frenzied, furious, impetuous, irregular, mad, outrageous, raving, turbulent, ungoverned, uncontrolled, violent; dissipated, fast, flighty, foolish, giddy, harebrained, heedless, ill-advised, inconsiderate, reckless, thoughtless, unwise; boisterous, rough, stormy; crazy, extravagant, fanciful, grotesque, imaginary, strange. • *n* desert, waste, wilderness.

wilderness *n* desert, waste, wild.

wilful *adj* cantankerous, contumacious, dogged, headstrong, heady, inflexible, intractable, mulish, obdurate, obstinate, perverse, pig-headed, refractory, self-willed, stubborn, unruly, unyielding; arbitrary, capricious; deliberate, intended, intentional, planned, premeditated.

will *vb* bid, command, decree, direct, enjoin, ordain; choose, desire, elect, wish; bequeath, convey, demise, devise, leave. • *n* decision, determination, resoluteness, resolution, self-reliance; desire, disposition, inclination, intent, pleasure, purpose, volition, wish; behest, command, decree, demand, direction, order, request, requirement.

willing *adj* adaptable, amenable, compliant, desirous, disposed, inclined, minded; deliberate, free, intentional, spontaneous, unasked, unbidden, voluntary; cordial, eager, forward, prompt, ready.

willingly *adv* cheerfully, gladly, readily, spontaneously, voluntarily.

wily *adj* arch, artful, crafty, crooked, cunning, deceitful, designing, diplomatic, foxy, insidious, intriguing, politic, sly, subtle, treacherous, tricky.

win *vb* accomplish, achieve, acquire, catch, earn, effect, gain, gather, get, make, obtain, procure, reach, realize, reclaim, recover; gain, succeed, surpass, triumph; arrive; allure, attract, convince, influence, persuade. • *n* conquest, success, triumph, victory.

wind[1] *n* air, blast, breeze, draught, gust, hurricane, whiff, zephyr; breath, breathing, expiration, inspiration, respiration; flatulence, gas, windiness.

wind[2] *vb* coil, crank, encircle, involve, reel, roll, turn, twine, twist; bend, curve, meander, zigzag. • *n* bend, curve, meander, twist, zigzag.

winding *adj* circuitous, devious, flexuose, flexuous, meandering, serpentine, tortuous, turning, twisting. • *n* bend, curve, meander, turn, twist.

windy *adj* breezy, blowy, blustering, boisterous, draughty, gusty, squally, stormy, tempestuous; airy, empty, hollow, inflated.

winning *adj* alluring, attractive, bewitching, brilliant, captivating, charming, dazzling, delightful, enchanting, engaging, fascinating, lovely, persuasive, pleasing, prepossessing; conquering, triumphant, victorious.

winnow *vb* cull, glean, divide, fan, part, select, separate, sift.

winsome *adj* blithe, blithesome, bonny, buoyant, charming, cheerful, debonair, jocund, light-hearted, lively, lovable, merry, pleasant, sportive, winning.

wintry *adj* arctic, boreal, brumal, cold, frosty, icy, snowy.

wipe *vb* clean, dry, mop, rub. • *n* mop, rub, blow, hit, strike; gibe, jeer, sarcasm, sneer, taunt.

wisdom *n* depth, discernment, far-sightedness, foresight, insight, judgement, judiciousness, prescience, profundity, prudence, sagacity, sapience, sense, solidity, understanding, wiseness; attainment, edification, enlightenment, erudition, information, knowledge, learning, lore, scholarship; reason.

wise *adj* deep, discerning, enlightened, intelligent, judicious, penetrating, philosophical, profound, rational, seasonable, sensible, sage, sapient, solid, sound; erudite, informed, knowing, learned, scholarly; crafty, cunning, designing, foxy, politic, sly, subtle, wary, wily.

wish *vb* covet, desire, hanker, list, long; bid, command, desire, direct, intend, mean, order, want. • *n* behest, desire, intention, mind, pleasure, want, will; craving, desire, hankering, inclination, liking, longing, want, yearning.

wistful *adj* contemplative, engrossed, meditative, musing, pensive, reflective, thoughtful; desirous, eager, earnest, longing.

wit *n* genius, intellect, intelligence, reason, sense, understanding; brightness, banter, cleverness, drollery, facetiousness, fun, humour, jocularity, piquancy, point, raillery, satire, sparkle, whim; conceit, epigram, jest, joke, pleasantry, quip, quirk, repartee, sally, witticism; humorist, joker, wag.

witch *n* charmer, enchantress, fascinator, sorceress; crone, hag, sibyl.

witchcraft *n* conjuration, enchantment, magic, necromancy, sorcery, spell.

withdraw *vb* abstract, deduct, remove, retire, separate, sequester, sequestrate, subduct, subtract; disengage, wean; abjure, recall, recant, relinquish, resign, retract, revoke; abdicate, decamp, depart, dissociate, retire, shrink, vacate.

wither *vb* contract, droop, dry, sear, shrivel, wilt, wizen; decay, decline, languish, pine, waste.

withhold *vb* check, detain, hinder, repress, restrain, retain, suppress.

withstand *vb* confront, defy, face, oppose, resist.

witless *adj* daft, dull, foolish, halfwitted, obtuse, senseless, shallow, silly, stupid, unintelligent.

witness *vb* corroborate, mark, note, notice, observe, see. • *n* attestation, conformation, corroboration, evidence, proof, testimony; beholder, bystander, corroborator, deponent, eyewitness, onlooker, spectator, testifier.

witty *adj* bright, clever, droll, facetious, funny, humorous, jocose, jocular, pleasant, waggish; alert, penetrating, quick, sparkling, sprightly.

wizard *n* charmer, diviner, conjurer, enchanter, magician, necromancer, seer, soothsayer, sorcerer.

woe *n* affliction, agony, anguish, bitterness, depression, distress, dole, grief, heartache, melancholy, misery, sorrow, torture, tribulation, trouble, unhappiness, wretchedness.

woeful *adj* afflicted, agonized, anguished, burdened, disconsolate, distressed, melancholy, miserable, mournful, piteous, sad, sorrowful, troubled, unhappy, wretched; afflicting, afflictive, calamitous, deplorable, depressing, disastrous, distressing, dreadful, tragic, tragical, grievous, lamentable, pitiable, saddening.

wonder *vb* admire, gape, marvel; conjecture, ponder, query, question, speculate. • *n* amazement, astonishment, awe, bewilderment, curiosity, marvel, miracle, prodigy, surprise, stupefaction, wonderment.

wonderful *adj* amazing, astonishing, astounding, awe-inspiring, awesome, awful, extraordinary, marvellous, miraculous, portentous, prodigious, startling, stupendous, surprising.

wont *adj* accustomed, customary, familiar, habitual, ordinary, usual. • *n* custom, habit, practice, rule, usage.

wonted *adj* accustomed, common, conventional, customary, everyday, familiar, frequent, habitual, ordinary, regular, usual.

wood *n* coppice, copse, covert, forest, greenwood, grove, spinney, thicket, woodland.

word *vb* express, phrase, put, say, state, term, utter. • *n* expression, name, phrase, term, utterance; account, advice, information, intelligence, message, news, report, tidings; affirmation, assertion, averment, avowal, declaration, statement; conversation, speech; agreement, assurance, engagement, parole, pledge, plight, promise; behest, bidding, command, direction, order, precept; countersign, password, signal, watchword.

wordy *adj* circumlocutory, diffuse, garrulous, inflated, lengthened, long-winded, loquacious, periphrastic, rambling, talkative, tedious, verbose, windy.

work *vb* act, operate; drudge, fag, grind, grub, labour, slave, sweat, toil; move, perform, succeed; aim, attempt, strive, try; effervesce, ferment, leaven, rise; accomplish, beget, cause, effect, engender, manage, originate, produce; exert, strain; embroider, stitch. • *n* exertion, drudgery, grind, labour, pain, toil; business, employment, function, occupation, task; action, accomplishment, achievement, composition, deed, feat, fruit, handiwork, opus, performance, product, production; fabric, manufacture; ferment, leaven; management, treatment.

workman *n* journeyman, employee, labourer, operative, worker, wright; artisan, craftsman, mechanic.

world *n* cosmos, creation, earth, globe, nature, planet, sphere, universe.

worldly *adj* common, earthly, human, mundane, sublunary, terrestrial; carnal, fleshly, profane, secular, temporal; ambitious, grovelling, irreligious, selfish, proud, sordid, unsanctified, unspiritual; sophisticated, worldly-wise.

worry *vb* annoy, badger, bait, beset, bore, bother, chafe, disquiet, disturb, fret, gall, harass, harry, hector, infest, irritate, molest, persecute, pester, plague, tease, torment, trouble, vex. • *n* annoyance, anxiety, apprehensiveness, care, concern, disquiet, fear, misgiving, perplexity, solicitude, trouble, uneasiness, vexation.

worship *vb* adore, esteem, honour, revere, venerate; deify, idolize; aspire, pray. • *n* adoration, devotion, esteem, homage, idolatry, idolizing, respect, reverence; aspiration, exultation, invocation, laud, praise, prayer, supplication.

worst *vb* beat, choke, conquer, crush, defeat, discomfit, foil, master, overpower, overthrow, quell, rout, subdue, subjugate, vanquish.

worth *n* account, character, credit, desert, excellence, importance, integrity, merit, nobleness, worthiness, virtue; cost, estimation, price, value.

worthless *adj* futile, meritless, miserable, nugatory, paltry, poor, trifling, unproductive, unsalable, unserviceable, useless, valueless, wretched; abject, base, corrupt, degraded, ignoble, low, mean, vile.

worthy *adj* deserving, fit, suitable; estimable, excellent, exemplary, good, honest, honourable, reputable, righteous, upright, virtuous. • *n* celebrity, dignitary, luminary, notability, personage, somebody, VIP.

wound *vb* damage, harm, hurt, injure; cut, gall, harrow, irritate, lacerate, pain, prick, stab; annoy, mortify, offend. • *n* blow, hurt, injury; damage, detriment; anguish, grief, pain, pang, torture.

wraith *n* apparition, ghost, phantom, spectre, vision.

wrangle *vb* argue, bicker, brawl, cavil, dispute, jangle, jar, quarrel, squabble, spar, spat. • *n* altercation, argument, bickering, brawl, contest, controversy, jar, quarrel, squabble.

wrap *vb* cloak, cover, encase, envelop, muffle, swathe, wind. • *n* blanket, cape, cloak, cover, overcoat, shawl.

wrath *n* anger, choler, exasperation, fury, heat, resentment, indignation, ire, irritation, offence, passion, rage.

wrathful *adj* angry, enraged, exasperated, furious, hot, indignant, infuriated, irate, mad, passionate, provoked, rageful.

wreak *vb* execute, exercise, indulge, inflict, work.

wreath *n* chaplet, curl, festoon, garland, ring, twine.

wreathe *vb* encircle, festoon, garland, intertwine, surround, twine, twist.

wreck *vb* founder, shipwreck, strand; blast, blight, break, devastate, ruin, spoil. • *n* crash, desolation, destruction, perdition, prostration, ruin, shipwreck, smash, undoing.

wrench *vb* distort, pervert, twist, wrest, wring; sprain, strain; extort, extract. • *n* twist, wring; sprain, strain; monkey wrench, spanner.

wrest *vb* force, pull, strain, twist, wrench, wring.

wrestle *vb* contend, contest, grapple, strive, struggle.

wretch *n* outcast, pariah, pilgarlic, troglodyte, vagabond, victim, sufferer; beggar, criminal, hound, knave, miscreant, rascal, ruffian, rogue, scoundrel, villain.

wretched *adj* afflicted, comfortless, distressed, forlorn, sad, unfortunate, unhappy, woebegone; afflicting, calamitous, deplorable, depressing, pitiable, sad, saddening, shocking, sorrowful; bad, beggarly, contemptible, mean, paltry, pitiful, poor, shabby, sorry, vile, worthless.

wring *vb* contort, twist, wrench; extort, force, wrest; anguish, distress, harass, pain, rack, torture.

wrinkle¹ *vb* cockle, corrugate, crease, gather, pucker, rumple. • *n* cockle, corrugation, crease, crimp, crinkle, crumple, fold, furrow, gather, plait, ridge, rumple.

wrinkle² *n* caprice, fancy, notion, quirk, whim; device, tip, trick.

writ *n* decree, order, subpoena, summons.

write *vb* compose, copy, indite, inscribe, pen, scrawl, scribble, transcribe.

writer *n* amanuensis, author, clerk, penman, scribe, secretary.

writhe *vb* contort, distort, squirm, twist, wriggle.

written *adj* composed, indited, inscribed, penned, transcribed.

wrong *vb* abuse, encroach, injure, maltreat, oppress. • *adj* inequitable, unfair, unjust, wrongful; bad, criminal, evil, guilty, immoral, improper, iniquitous, reprehensible, sinful, vicious, wicked; amiss, improper, inappropriate, unfit, unsuitable; erroneous, false, faulty, inaccurate, incorrect, mistaken, untrue. • *adv* amiss, erroneously, falsely, faultily, improperly, inaccurately, incorrectly, wrongly. • *n* foul, grievance, inequity, injury, injustice, trespass, unfairness; blame, crime, dishonesty, evil, guilt, immorality, iniquity, misdeed, misdoing, sin, transgression, unrighteousness, vice, wickedness, wrongdoing; error, falsity.

wroth *adj* angry, enraged, exasperated, furious, incensed, indignant, irate, passionate, provoked, resentful.

wrought *adj* done, effected, performed, worked.

wry *adj* askew, awry, contorted, crooked, distorted, twisted.

XYZ

xanthous *adj* blonde, fair, light-complexioned, xanthic, yellow.

xiphoid *adj* ensiform, gladiate, sword-like, sword-shaped.

Xmas *n* Christmas, Christmastide, Noel, Yule, Yuletide.

X-ray *n* roentgen ray, röntgen ray.

xylograph *n* cut, woodcut, wood engraving.

xylographer *n* wood engraver.

xylophagous *adj* wood-eating, wood-nourished.

yap *vb* bark, cry, yelp. • *n* bark, cry, yelp.

yard *n* close, compound, court, courtyard, enclosure, garden.

yarn *n* anecdote, boasting, fabrication, narrative, story, tale, untruth.

yawn *vb* dehisce, gape, open wide. • *n* gap, gape, gulf.

yearn *vb* crave, desire, hanker after, long for.

yell *vb* bawl, bellow, cry out, howl, roar, scream, screech, shriek, squeal. • *n* cry, howl, roar, scream, screech, shriek.

yellow *adj* aureate, gilded, gilt, gold, golden, lemon, primrose, saffron, xanthic, xanthous.

yelp *vb* bark, howl, yap; complain, bitch, grouse. • *n* bark, sharp cry, howl.

yet *adv* at last, besides, further, however, over and above, so far, still, thus far, ultimately. • *conj* moreover, nevertheless, notwithstanding, now.

yield *vb* afford, bear, bestow, communicate, confer, fetch, furnish, impart, produce, render, supply; accede, accord, acknowledge, acquiesce, allow, assent, comply, concede, give, grant, permit; abandon, abdicate, cede, forgo, give up, let go, quit, relax, relinquish, resign, submit, succumb, surrender, waive. • *n* earnings, income, output, produce, profit, return, revenue.

yielding *adj* accommodating, acquiescent, affable, compliant, complaisant, easy, manageable, obedient, passive, submissive, unresisting; bending, flexible, flexile, plastic, pliant, soft, supple, tractable; fertile, productive.

yoke *vb* associate, bracket, connect, couple, harness, interlink, join, link, unite. • *n* bond, chain, ligature, link, tie, union; bondage, dependence, enslavement, service, servitude, subjection, vassalage; couple, pair.

yokel *n* boor, bumpkin, countryman, peasant, rustic.

yore *adj* ancient, antique, old, olden. • *n* long ago, long since, olden times.

young *adj* green, ignorant, inexperienced, juvenile, new, recent, youthful. • *n* young people, youth; babies, issue, brood, offspring, progeny, spawn.

youngster *n* adolescent, boy, girl, lad, lass, stripling, youth.

youth *n* adolescence, childhood, immaturity, juvenile, juvenility, minority, nonage, pupillage, wardship; boy, girl, lad, lass, schoolboy, schoolgirl, slip, sprig, stripling, youngster.

youthful *adj* boyish, childish, girlish, immature, juvenile, puerile, young.

zany *adj* comic, comical, crazy, droll, eccentric, funny, imaginative, scatterbrained; clownish, foolish, ludicrous, silly. • *n* buffoon, clown, droll, fool, harlequin, jester, punch.

zeal *n* alacrity, ardour, cordiality, devotedness, devotion, earnestness, eagerness, energy, enthusiasm, fervour, glow, heartiness, intensity, jealousness, passion, soul, spirit, warmth.

zealot *n* bigot, devotee, fanatic, freak, partisan.

zealous *adj* ardent, burning, devoted, eager, earnest, enthusiastic, fervent, fiery, forward, glowing, jealous, keen, passionate, prompt, ready, swift, warm.

zenith *n* acme, apex, climax, culmination, heyday, pinnacle, prime, summit, top, utmost, height.

zero *n* cipher, naught, nadir, nil, nothing, nought.

zest *n* appetite, enjoyment, exhilaration, gusto, liking, piquancy, relish, thrill; edge, flavour, salt, savour, tang, taste; appetizer, sauce.

zone *n* band, belt, cincture, girdle, girth; circuit, clime, region.

zymotic *adj* bacterial, fermentative, germinating.

MAPS OF THE WORLD

Contents

Symbols for maps on pages:
8-22, 27-38, 40-54, 60-62

Inhabitants
More than 5 million **New York**

1 000 000 - 5 000 000 **Seattle**

250 000 - 1 000 000 ■ **Mexicali**

100 000 - 250 000 ● Tijuana

25 000 - 100 000 ● Sparks

Less than 25 000 •• Monterey

National capital (UPPERCASE) **OTTAWA**

State capital **Boise**

International boundary

Disputed international boundary

State boundary

Disputed state boundary

Major road

Other road

Road under construction

Seasonal road

Railway

Canal

Highest peak in continent ▲ McKinley

Highest peak in country △ Logan

Height in feet ▲ 17000ft

Depth in feet ▽ 185ft

Coral reef

Dam | Kainji Dam

Waterfall | Niagara Falls

Pass)(

International airport ⊕

National airport ✦

Historical site ⚎

Scientific site ⚐

Scale 1:20 000 000

| 0 | 200 | 400 | 600 km |

| 0 | 100 | 200 | 300 miles |

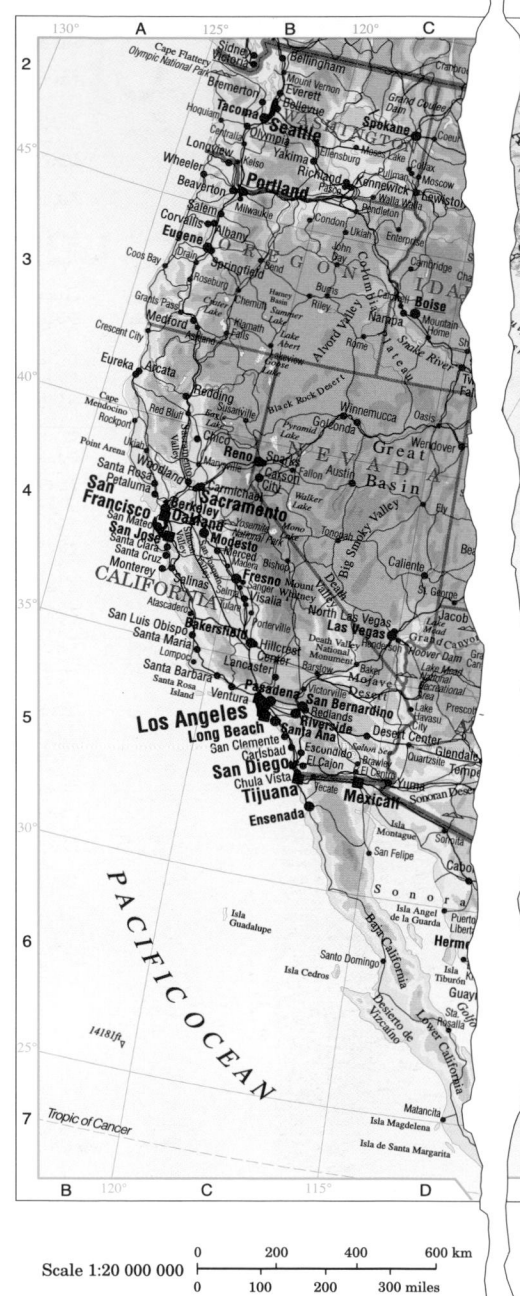

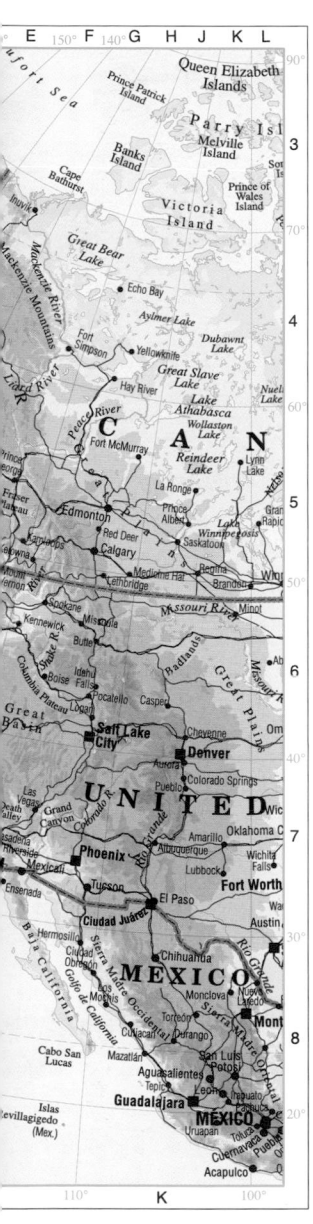

Symbols for maps on pages:
7, 24-25, 56-59

	Inhabitants
🐾 **Chicago**	More than 5 million
■ **Columbus**	1 000 000 - 5 000 000
• Quebec	250 000 - 1 000 000
• Halifax	100 000 - 250 000
•• Anderson	Less than 100 000
NASSAU	National capital (UPPERCASE)
<u>Sacramento</u>	State capital
	International boundary
	Disputed international boundary
	Major road
	Road under construction
	Major railway
	Canal
▲ McKinley	Highest peak in continent
▲ Logan	Highest peak in country
▲ 17000ft	Heights in feet
▽ 185ft	Depths in feet
	Coral reef
⬠	Scientific station
	Territorial claims in Antarctica
	Disputed territorial claims in Antarctica
| Grand Coulee Dam	Dam
| Virginia Falls	Waterfall

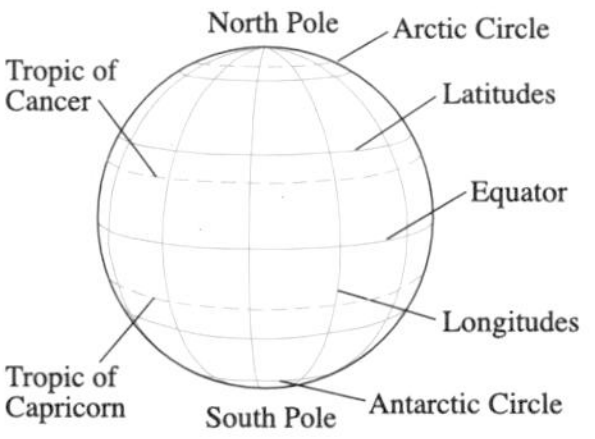

North Pole — Arctic Circle
Tropic of Cancer — Latitudes
— Equator
Longitudes
Tropic of Capricorn
South Pole — Antarctic Circle

Colour Key for Contours

	Glacier/ice cap
	6000m
	5000m
	4000m
	3000m
	2000m
	1000m
	500m
	200m
	0m

Marshland
Salt lake
Seasonal lake
Salt desert

Symbols for Political maps on pages:
5, 6, 23, 26, 39, 55

	Inhabitants
● **Lagos**	More than 5 million
● **Ibadan**	1 000 000 - 5 000 000
• Kano	250 000 - 1 000 000
• Gashua	100 000 - 250 000
• Maradi	25 000 - 100 000
■ ■ ▪	National Capital
● ●	State Capital
	International boundary
	Disputed International boundary
	State boundary
	Railway

The letters and numbers in the map edges are there to help you find names. Look for London in the index **29** D4. Turn to page 29 and look top or bottom for number 4 and left or right for letter D. In this blue grid square you will find the city of London.

Scale 1:50 000 000 means that a distance on the map is 50 000 000 times longer on the Earth's surface e.g. 1 cm on the map represents 500 km on the surface and 1 inch on the map represents 800 miles.

0   500   1000   1500 km
0   250   500   750 miles

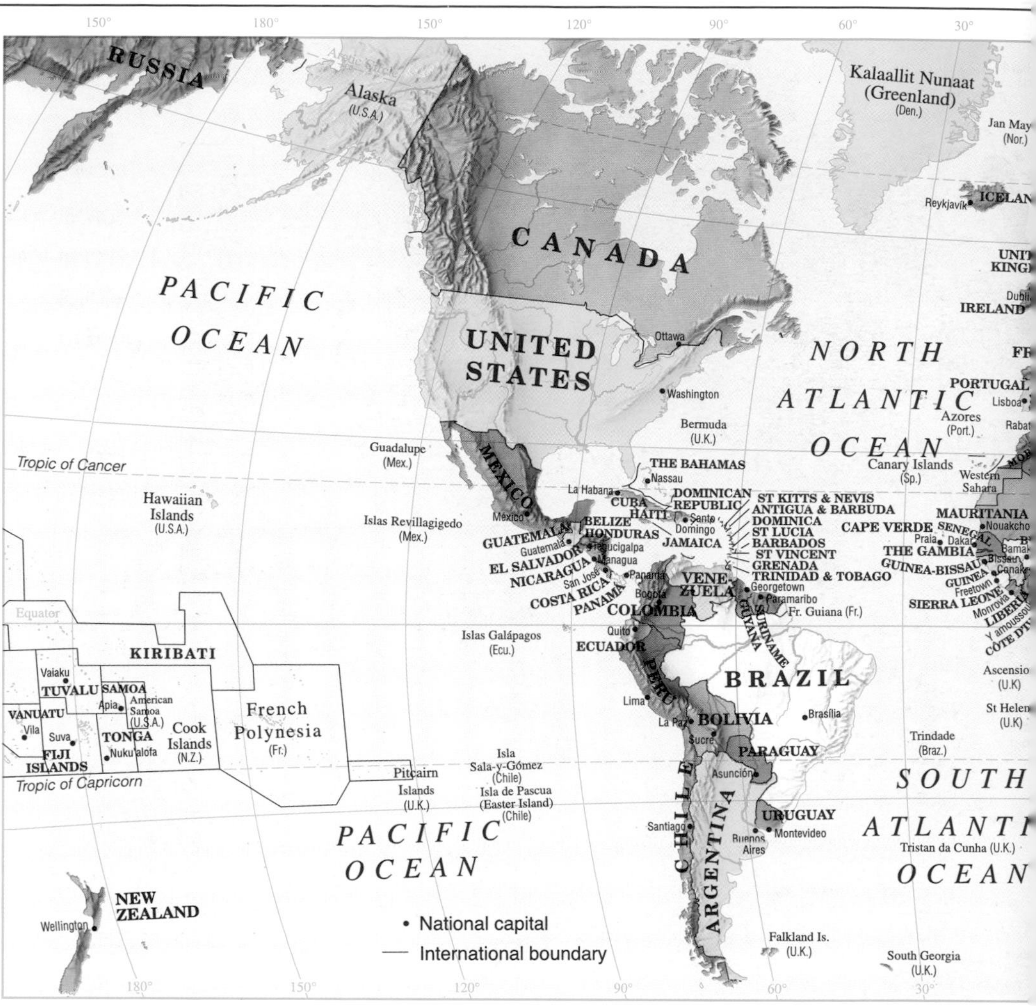

RUSSIA

Alaska
(U.S.A.)

Kalaallit Nunaat
(Greenland)
(Den.)

Jan Mayen
(Nor.)

ICELAND

Reykjavik

CANADA

UNITED
KINGD

Dublin
IRELAND

PACIFIC
OCEAN

UNITED
STATES

Ottawa

Washington

NORTH

FR

ATLANTIC

PORTUGAL

Lisboa

OCEAN

Azores
(Port.)

Rabat

MO

Bermuda
(U.K.)

Tropic of Cancer

Guadalupe
(Mex.)

Canary Islands
(Sp.)

Western
Sahara

Hawaiian
Islands
(U.S.A.)

Islas Revillagigedo
(Mex.)

MEXICO

THE BAHAMAS

Nassau

La Habana

CUBA

DOMINICAN
REPUBLIC

ST KITTS & NEVIS
ANTIGUA & BARBUDA

MAURITANIA

Nouakchott

México

HAITI

Santo
Domingo

DOMINICA

CAPE VERDE

SENEGA

BELIZE

GUATEMALA

Guatemala

HONDURAS

ST LUCIA
BARBADOS

Praia Dakar

THE GAMBIA

Bama

JAMAICA

ST VINCENT

GUINEA-BISSAU Bissau Conakr

Tegucigalpa

GRENADA

GUINEA

EL SALVADOR

Managua

TRINIDAD & TOBAGO

Freetown

San José

Panama

VENE-
ZUELA

Georgetown

SIERRA LEONE

Monrovia

LIBERIA

NICARAGUA

COSTA RICA

PANAMA

Bogotá

COLOMBIA

Paramaribo

Fr. Guiana (Fr.)

y amoussou

CÔTE D'IV

Equator

Islas Galápagos
(Ecu.)

Quito

ECUADOR

SURINAME

GUYANA

KIRIBATI

Vaiaku

TUVALU

SAMOA

Apia

American
Samoa
(U.S.A.)

French
Polynesia
(Fr.)

Lima

PERU

BRAZIL

Ascension
(U.K.)

La Paz

BOLIVIA

Brasília

St Helena
(U.K.)

VANUATU

Vila

Suva

TONGA

Cook
Islands
(N.Z.)

Sucre

PARAGUAY

Trindade
(Braz.)

FIJI
ISLANDS

Nuku'alofa

Pitcairn
Islands
(U.K.)

Isla
Sala-y-Gómez
(Chile)

Asunción

SOUTH

Tropic of Capricorn

Isla
de Pascua
(Easter Island)
(Chile)

URUGUAY

ATLANTI

PACIFIC
OCEAN

CHILE

ARGENTINA

Santiago

Buenos
Aires

Montevideo

Tristan da Cunha (U.K.)

OCEAN

NEW
ZEALAND

Wellington

• National capital

— International boundary

Falkland Is.
(U.K.)

South Georgia
(U.K.)

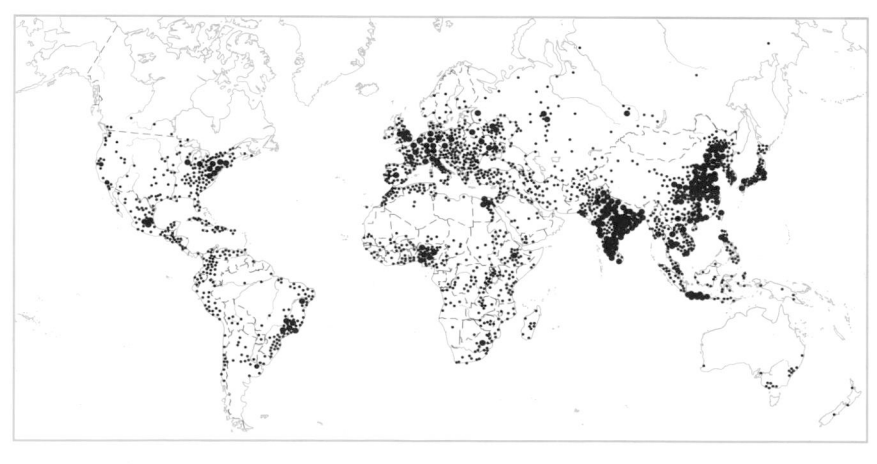

POPULATION

• 10 million inhabitan
· 1 million inhabitan

The density of popu
varies over the Earth's
surface. Some parts
sparsely populated bec
of geographical condi
high mountains, hot de
or cold tundra. Compa
maps on pages 8-9,1
Some parts are de
populated due to good
conditions, economica
physically convenient f
big cities, as well as
reasons such as religi
ethnic grouping. Popu
growth is mainly centre
the already densely
populated areas.

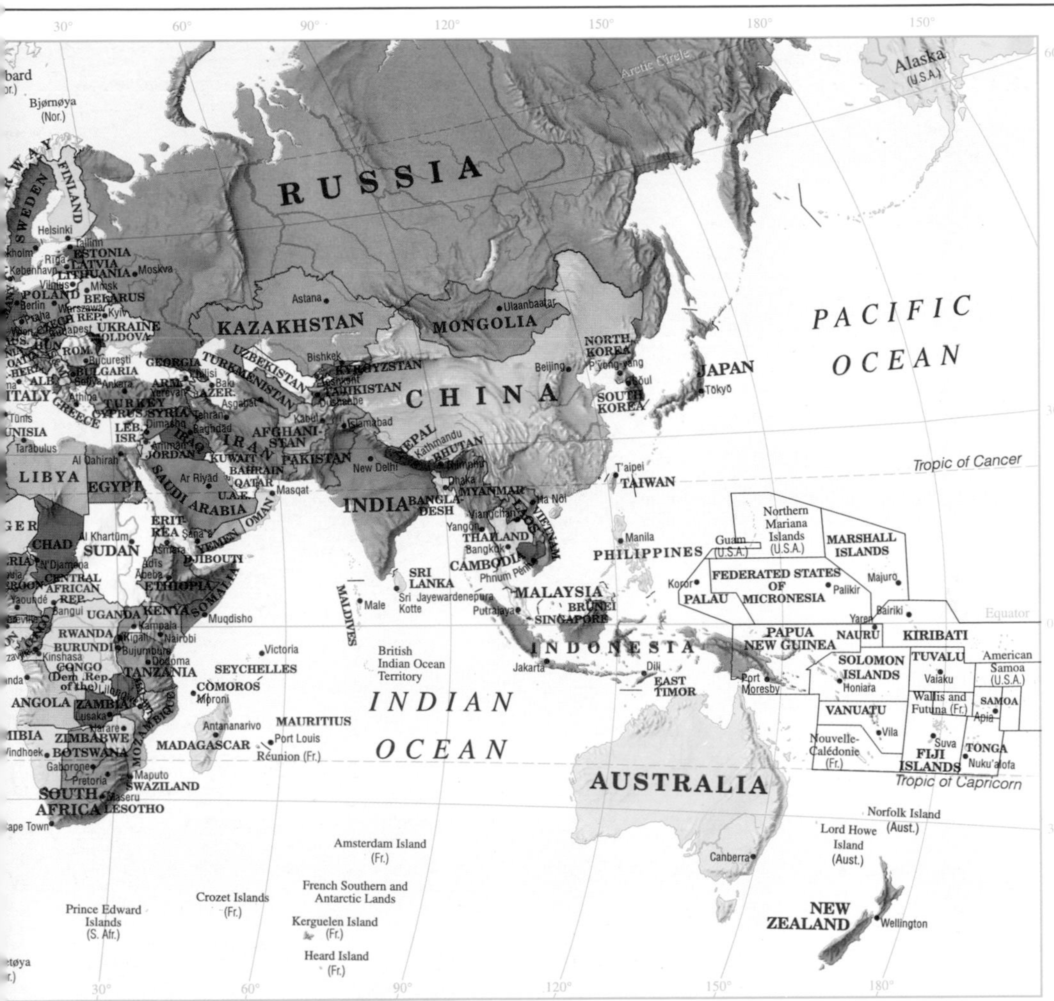

RUSSIA

PACIFIC OCEAN

SWEDEN FINLAND
Bjørnøya (Nor.)
Helsinki
Tallinn ESTONIA
Riga LATVIA Moskva
Vilnius LITHUANIA
Minsk
POLAND BELARUS
Warszawa
UKRAINE Kyïv
CZECH REP. MOLDOVA
BULGARIA
ROM. Bucuresti
ITALY ALB. GREECE Ankara TURKEY
TUNISIA Tarabulus

KAZAKHSTAN
Astana
Bishkek
UZBEKISTAN KYRGYZSTAN
Aşgabat TURKMENISTAN TAJIKISTAN
Dushanbe
Tehran
AFGHANI-STAN
Islamabad
IRAN PAKISTAN
New Delhi
NEPAL Kathmandu
BHUTAN
INDIA BANGLA-DESH Dhaka

MONGOLIA
Ulaanbaatar
CHINA
Beijing
NORTH KOREA P'yongyang
SOUTH KOREA Söul
JAPAN Tökyö
T'aipei TAIWAN

GEORGIA ARM. AZER.
Tbilisi Baku
SYRIA Baghdad
LEB. ISR. JORDAN Dimashq
IRAQ KUWAIT
Al Qahirah
SAUDI ARABIA Al Riyad
BAHRAIN QATAR
U.A.E. Masqat
OMAN
YEMEN

LIBYA EGYPT
NIGER CHAD SUDAN
Al Khartum
ERITREA
DJIBOUTI
ETHIOPIA
CENTRAL AFRICAN REP.
Bangui
UGANDA Kampala
CONGO (Dem.Rep.of the)
Kinshasa
RWANDA Nairobi
BURUNDI Bujumbura
TANZANIA Dodoma
ANGOLA ZAMBIA
Lusaka
ZIMBABWE BOTSWANA
Gaborone
Pretoria SWAZILAND
SOUTH AFRICA LESOTHO
Cape Town

SOMALIA Muqdisho
KENYA
SEYCHELLES Victoria
COMOROS Moroni
MAURITIUS Port Louis
Réunion (Fr.)
MADAGASCAR
Antananarivo
MALDIVES Male
SRI LANKA Sri Jayewardenepura Kotte
MYANMAR Yangon
THAILAND Bangkok
CAMBODIA Phnum Pénh
VIETNAM Ha Noi
MALAYSIA
BRUNEI
SINGAPORE Putrajaya
INDONESIA
Jakarta

PHILIPPINES Manila
Guam (U.S.A.)
Northern Mariana Islands (U.S.A.)
MARSHALL ISLANDS Majuro
PALAU Koror
FEDERATED STATES OF MICRONESIA Palikir
Yaren NAURU
PAPUA NEW GUINEA
Port Moresby
EAST TIMOR Dili
SOLOMON ISLANDS Honiara
VANUATU Vila
Nouvelle-Calédonie (Fr.)
FIJI ISLANDS Suva
TONGA Nuku'alofa
TUVALU Vaiaku
KIRIBATI Bairiki
Wallis and Futuna (Fr.)
SAMOA Apia
American Samoa (U.S.A.)

INDIAN OCEAN
British Indian Ocean Territory

AUSTRALIA
Canberra

NEW ZEALAND
Wellington

Norfolk Island (Aust.)
Lord Howe Island (Aust.)

Amsterdam Island (Fr.)
Crozet Islands (Fr.)
French Southern and Antarctic Lands
Kerguelen Island (Fr.)
Heard Island (Fr.)
Prince Edward Islands (S. Afr.)

Arctic Circle
Alaska (U.S.A.)
Tropic of Cancer
Equator
Tropic of Capricorn

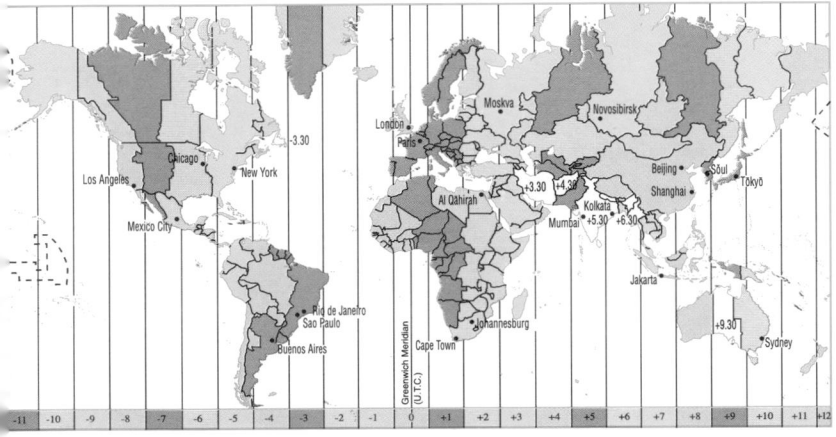

TIME ZONES

The Earth spins around its axis anticlockwise and completes one turn every 24 hours. As the world rotates it is day on the part facing the Sun and night on the side in shadow. As shown on this map, we have divided the Earth into 24 standard time zones. They are based upon lines of longitude at 15 degree intervals but mainly follow country or state boundaries. You can compare times around the world by using the map. For example; when it is 12 noon in London it is 5 hours earlier in New York or 7 am.

Los Angeles • Chicago • New York
Mexico City •
London Paris • Moskva • Novosibirsk
-3.30 Al Qahirah +3.30 +4.30
Beijing • Söul
Shanghai • Tökyö
Kolkata +5.30 +6.30
Mumbai
Jakarta
Rio de Janeiro
Sao Paulo
Buenos Aires
Johannesburg +9.30 • Sydney
Cape Town
Greenwich Meridian (U.T.C.)

-11 -10 -9 -8 -7 -6 -5 -4 -3 -2 -1 +1 +2 +3 +4 +5 +6 +7 +8 +9 +10 +11 +12

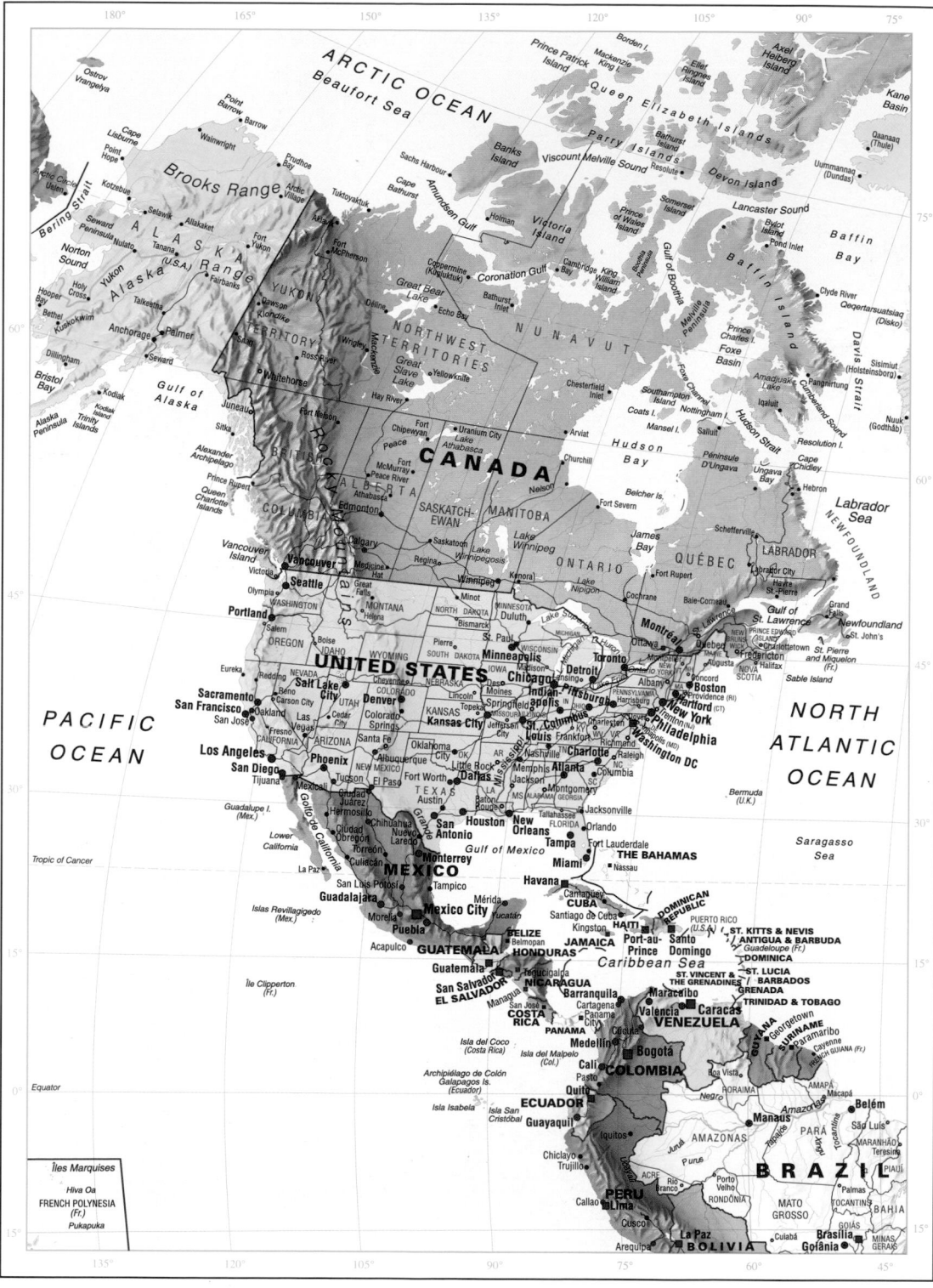

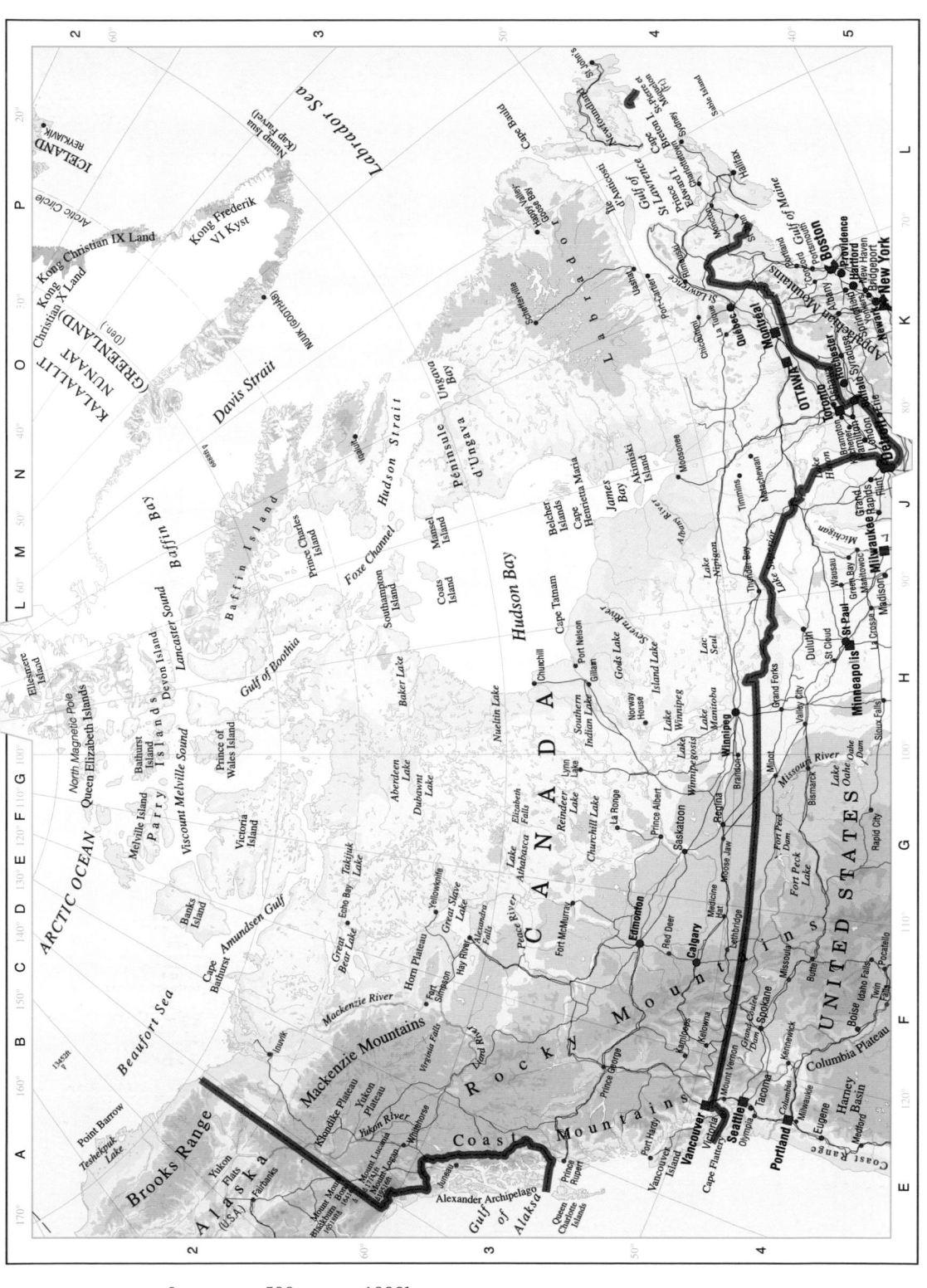

Scale 1: 31 250 000

| 0 | 500 | 1000km |

| 0 | 300 | 600miles |

© Geddes & Grosset

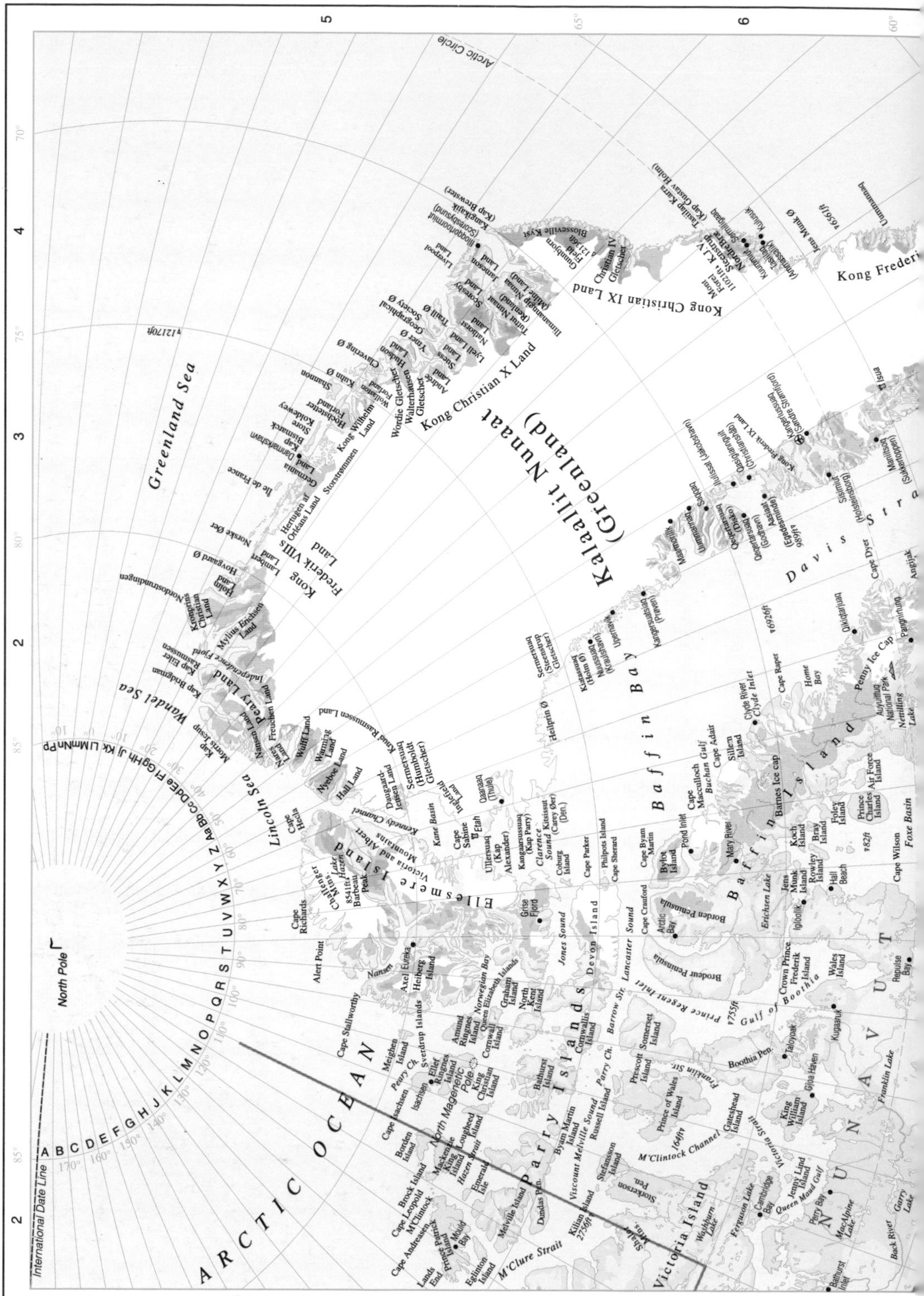

ARCTIC OCEAN

Kalaallit Nunaat
(Greenland)

Kong Christian X Land

Kong Christian IX Land

Greenland Sea

Wandel Sea

Lincoln Sea

Baffin Bay

Davis Strait

Ellesmere Island

Baffin Island

Devon Island

Victoria Island

Parry Islands

NUNAVUT

North Pole

International Date Line

Arctic Circle

Scale 1: 20 000 000

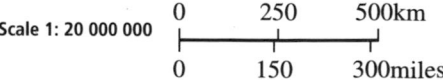

0   250   500km

0   150   300miles

ARCTIC OCEAN

North Pole

International Date Line

Kalaallit Nunaat (Greenland)

Wandel Sea

Lincoln Sea

Ellesmere Island

Victoria and Albert Mountains

Parry Islands

Baffin Bay

Baffin Island

NUNAVUT

Victoria Island

Banks Island

Beaufort Sea

Chukchi Sea

Vostochno-Sibirskoye More (East Siberian Sea)

Ostrov Genrijetty
Ostrov Zjannetty

Mys Blossom

Ostrov Vrangelya

ALASKA

U.S.A.

Brooks Range

North Slope

Alaska Range

Kuskokwim Mountains

YUKON

Mackenzie River

Anchorage

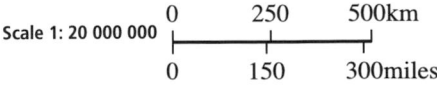

Scale 1: 20 000 000

| 0 | 250 | 500km |
| 0 | 150 | 300miles |

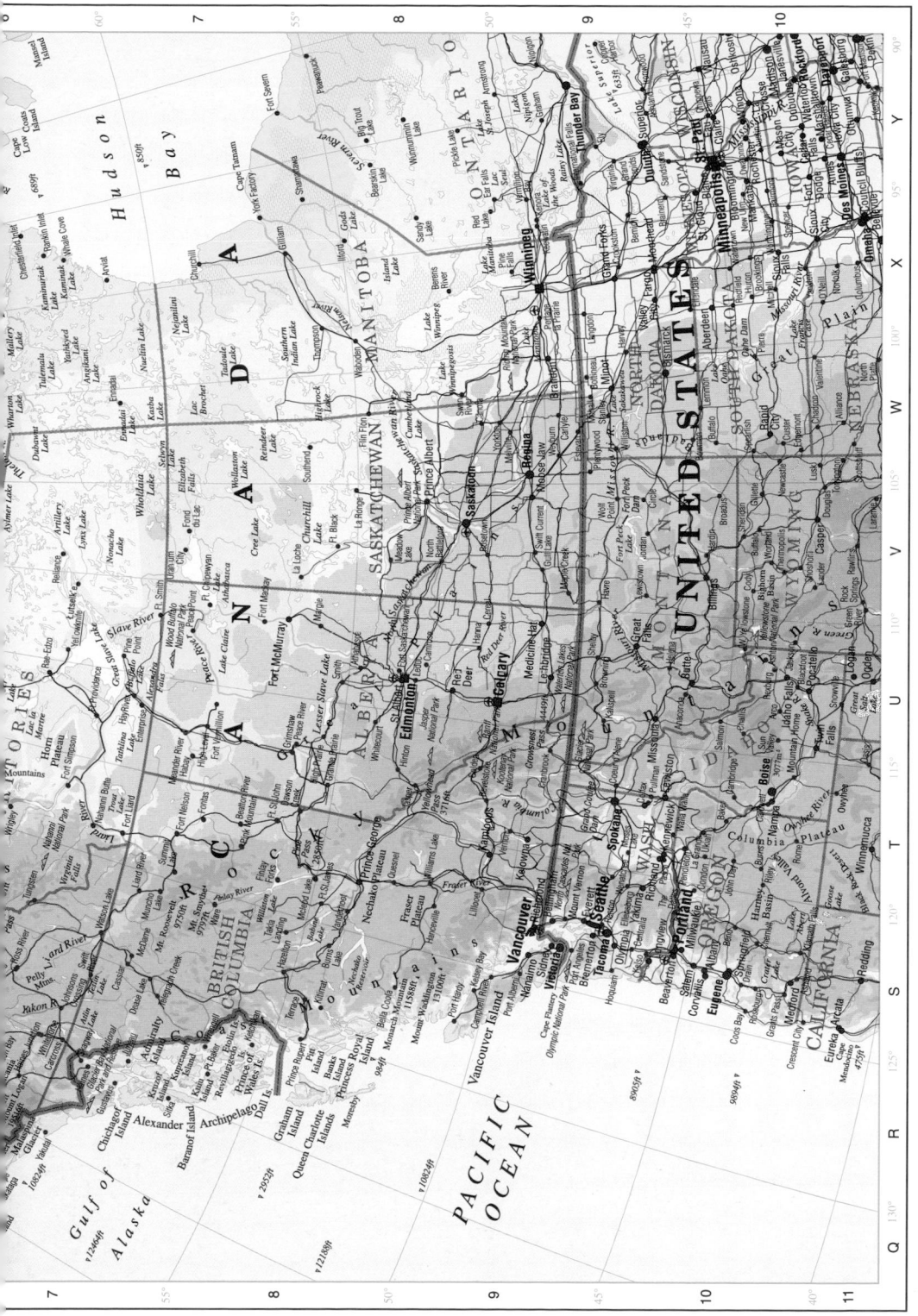

Scale 1: 19 231 000

```
0      200    400    600    800   1000km
0    100    200    300    400    500   600miles
```

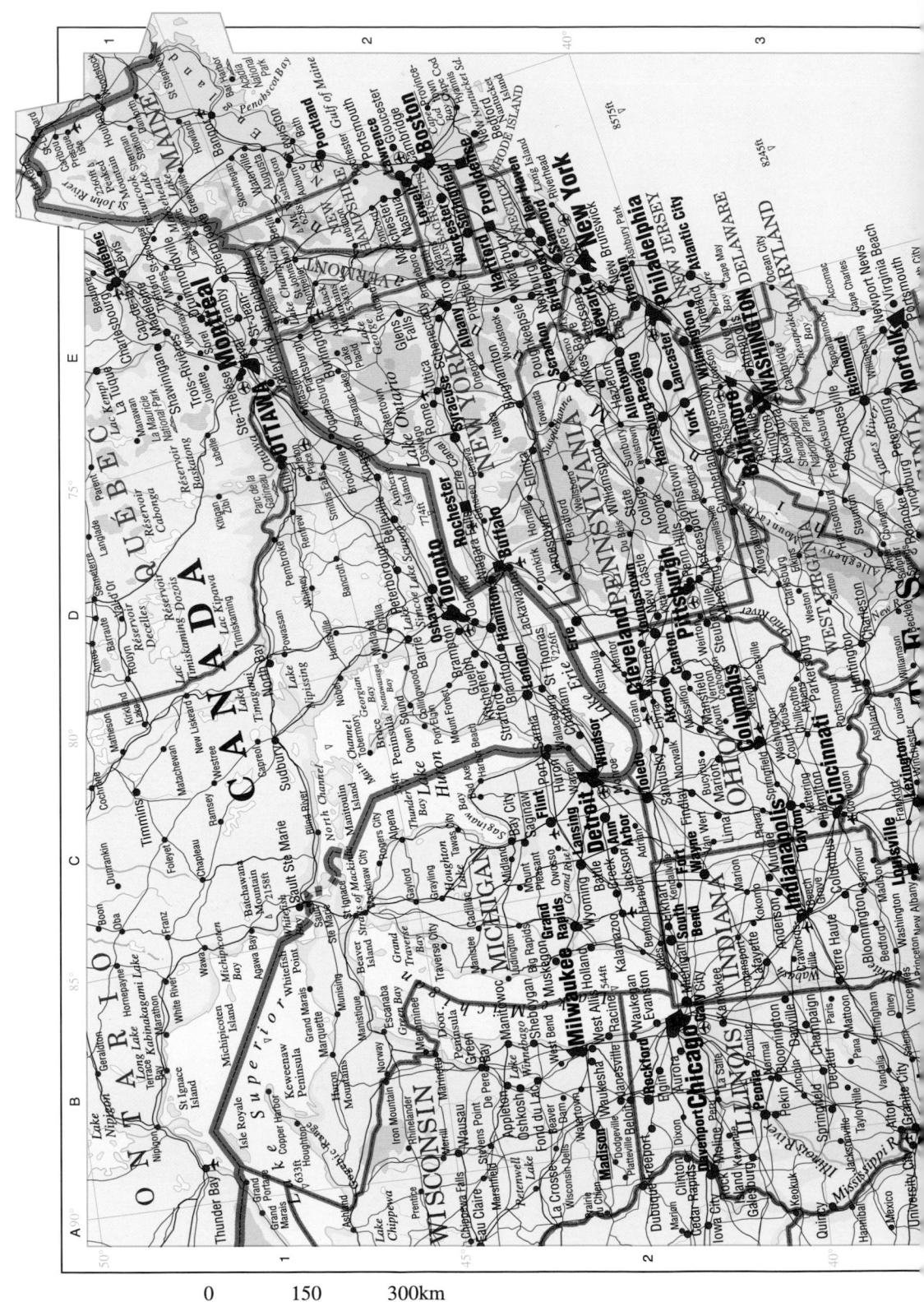

Scale 1: 10 000 000

| 0 | 150 | 300km |

| 0 | 75 | 150miles |

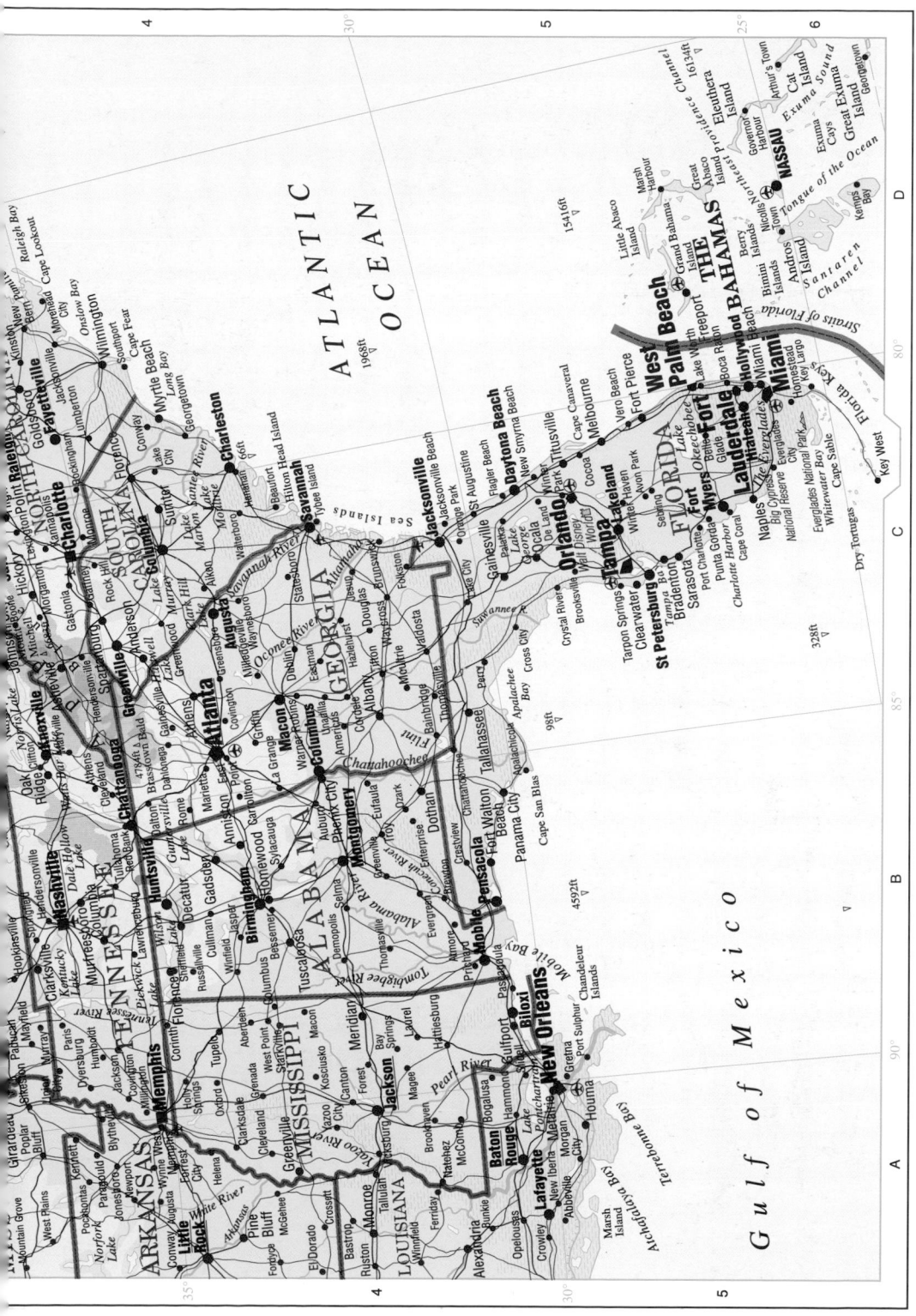

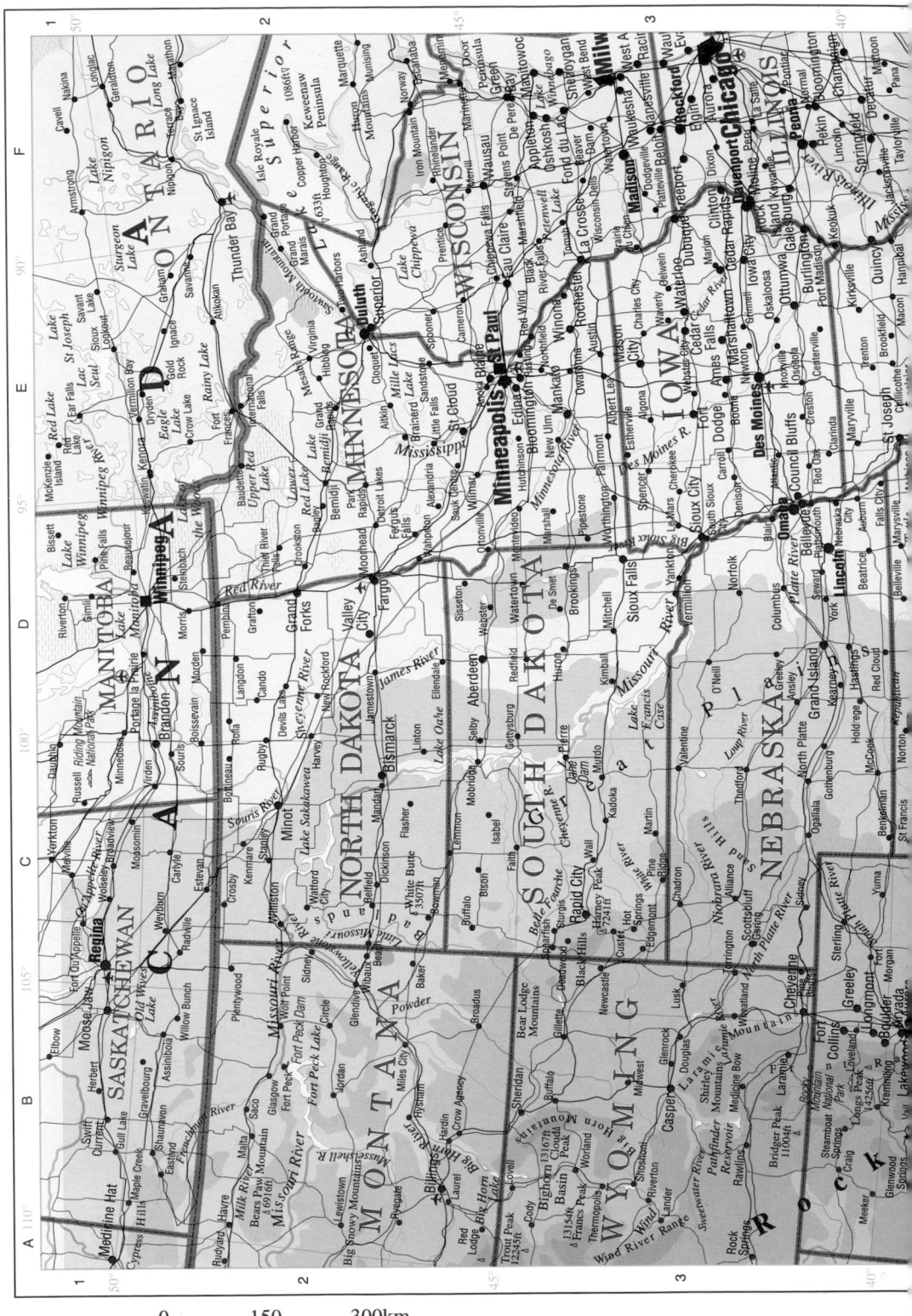

Scale 1: 10 000 000

0   150   300km

0   75   150miles

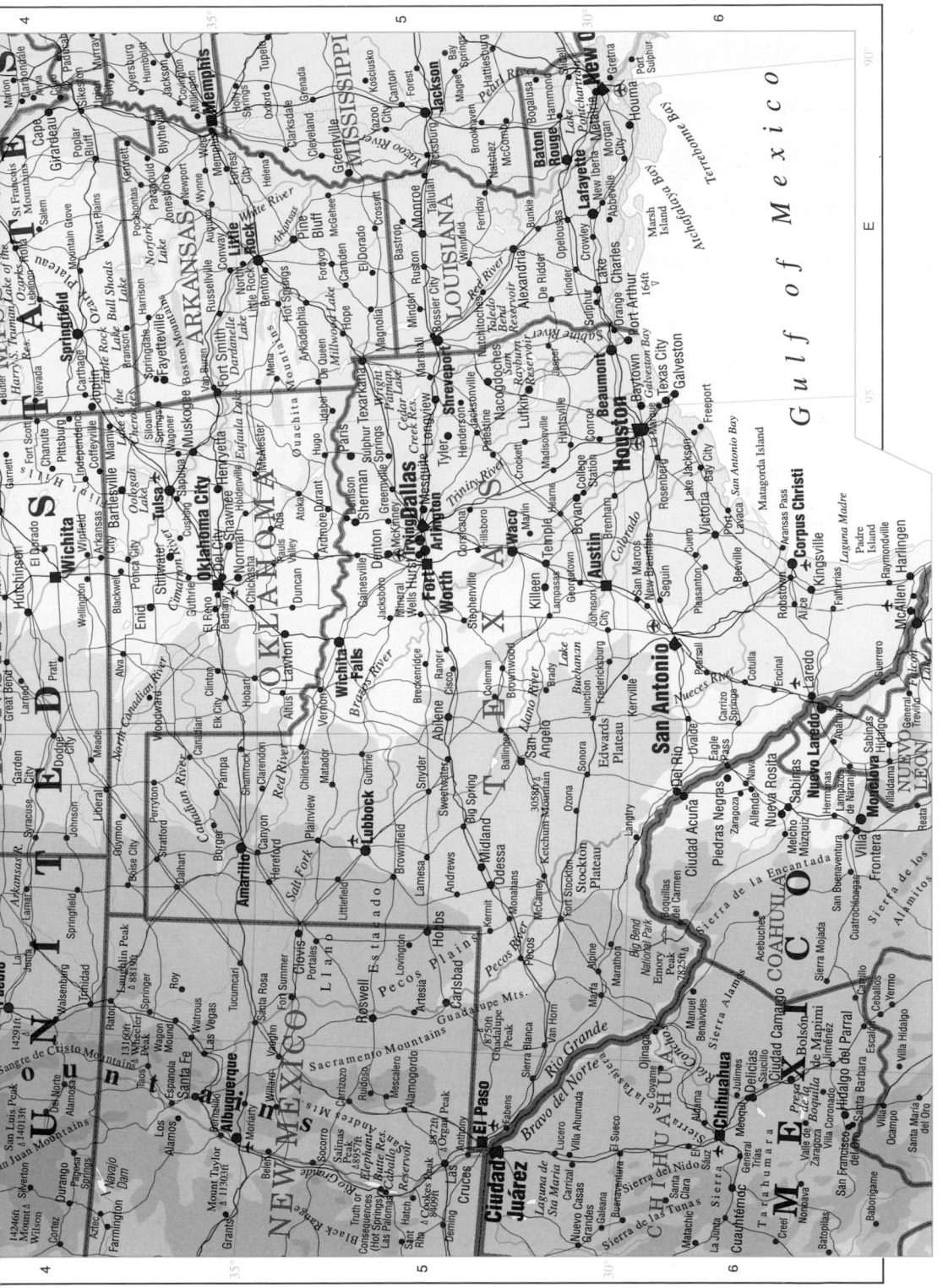

Scale 1: 10 000 000

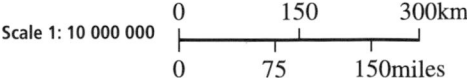

Scale 1: 12 800 000

| 0 | 200 | 400km |

| 0 | 100 | 200miles |

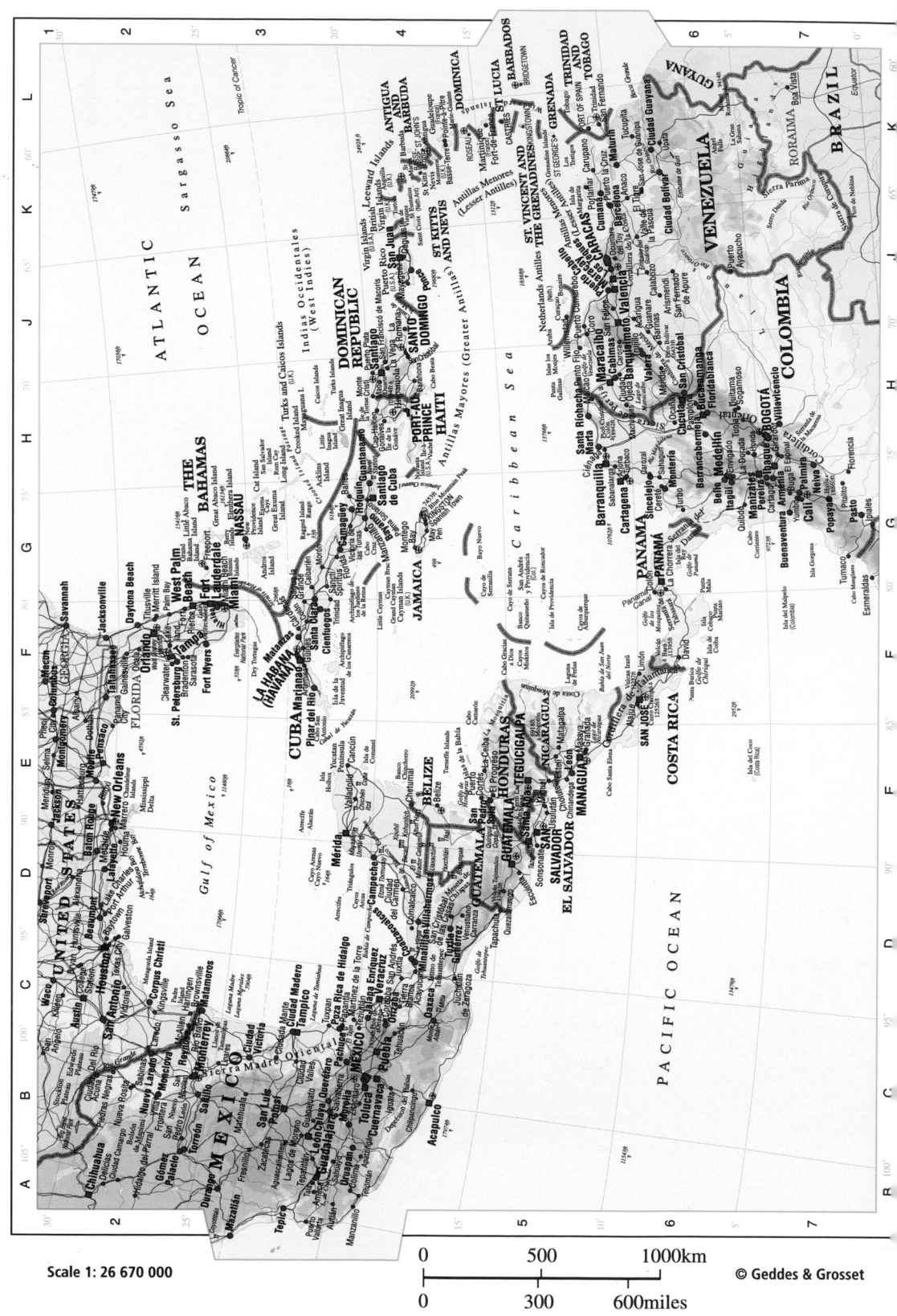

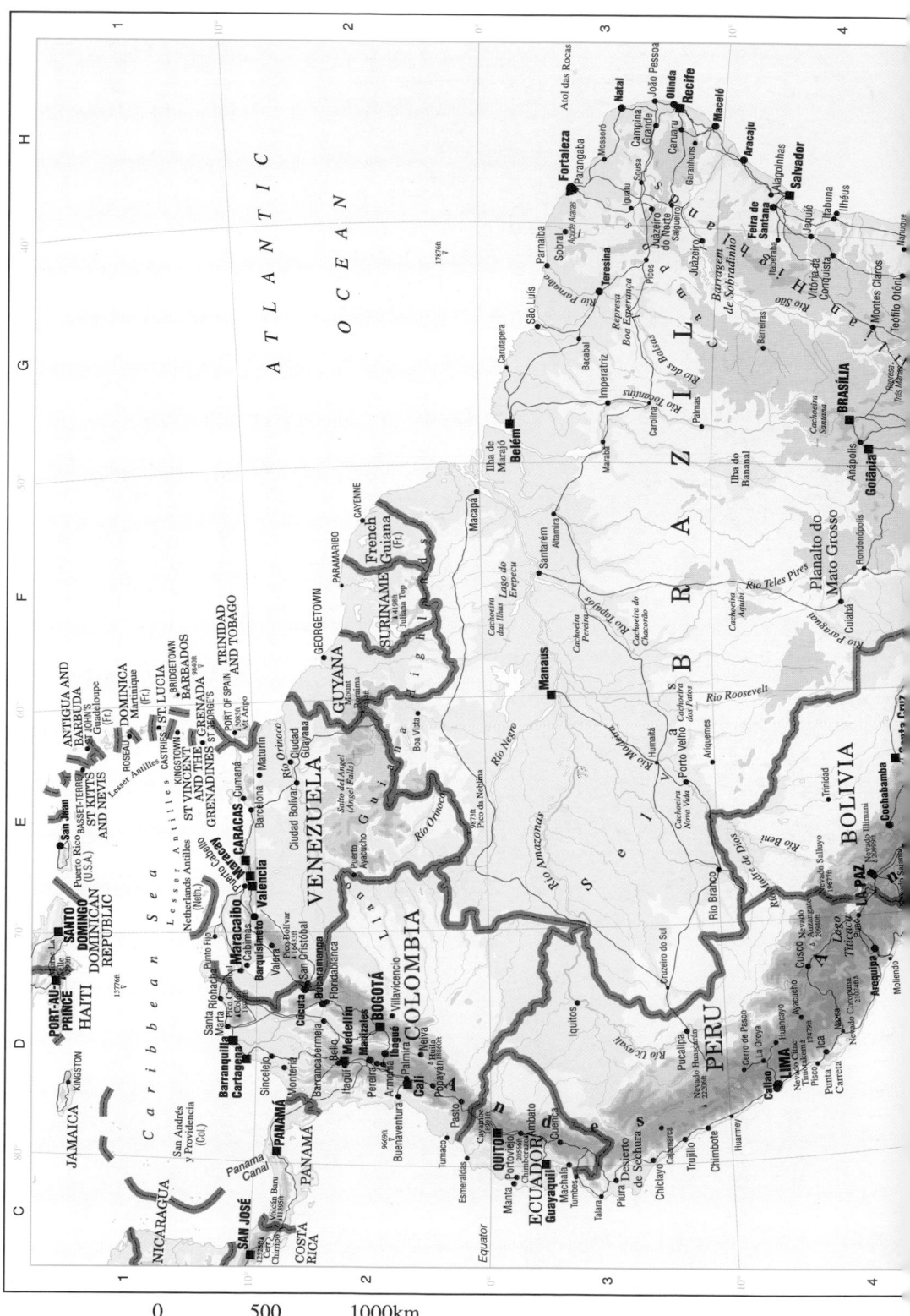

Scale 1: 31 250 000

0 500 1000km

0 250 500miles

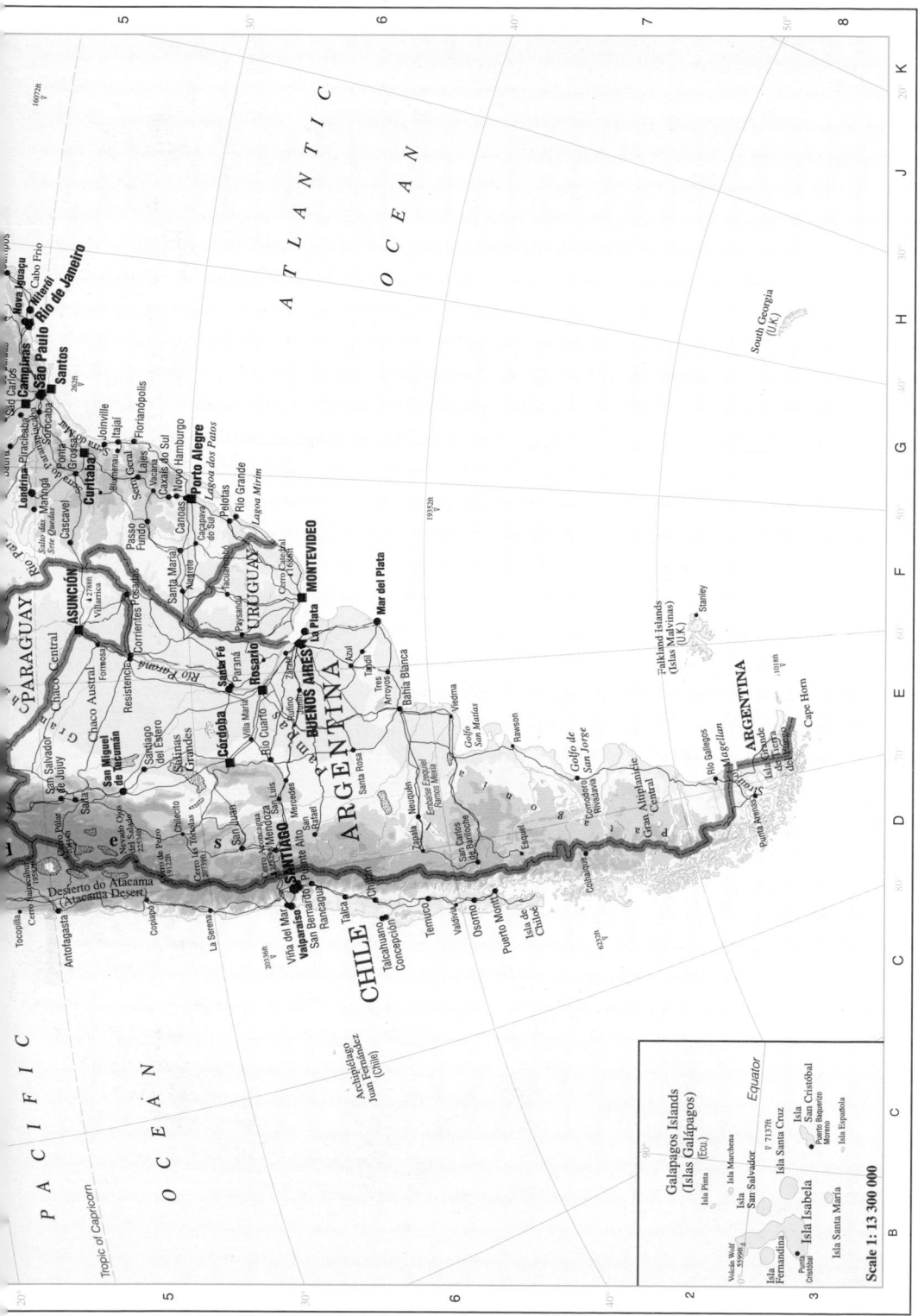

ATLANTIC

OCEAN

PACIFIC

OCEAN

Tropic of Capricorn

PARAGUAY

ASUNCIÓN

Gran Chaco

Chaco Austral

Chaco Central

San Salvador de Jujuy

Salta

San Miguel de Tucumán

Santiago del Estero

Salinas Grandes

San Juan

ARGENTINA

CHILE

Antofagasta

Tocopilla

Desierto do Atacama
(Atacama Desert)

Copiapó

La Serena

Archipiélago Juan Fernández
(Chile)

Valparaíso
Viña del Mar
SANTIAGO
San Bernardo
Rancagua

Talca

Talcahuano
Concepción

Temuco

Valdivia

Osorno

Puerto Montt

Isla de
Chiloé

Formosa

Resistencia

Corrientes

Posadas

Santa María

Paraná

Santa Fe

Rosario

Córdoba

Río Cuarto

Villa María

Mendoza

San Luis

San Rafael

Mercedes

Santa Rosa

Neuquén

San Carlos
de Bariloche

Esquel

URUGUAY

MONTEVIDEO

La Plata

BUENOS AIRES

Azul

Tandil

Tres
Arroyos

Bahía Blanca

Viedma

Rawson

Golfo
San Matías

Golfo
San Jorge

Comodoro
Rivadavia

Puerto Deseado

Río Gallegos

Punta Arenas

Mar del Plata

ARGENTINA

Cape Horn

Falkland Islands
(Islas Malvinas)
(U.K.)

Stanley

South Georgia
(U.K.)

Rio de Janeiro

Niterói

São Paulo

Santos

Campinas

Curitiba

Florianópolis

Joinville

Porto Alegre

Pelotas

Rio Grande

Lagoa dos Patos

Lagoa Mirim

Londrina

Galápagos Islands
(Islas Galápagos)
(Ecu.)

Equator

Isla Marchena

Isla San Salvador

Isla Santa Cruz

Isla
San Cristóbal

Puerto Baquerizo
Moreno

Isla Española

Isla Isabela

Isla Santa María

Isla
Fernandina

Isla Pinta

Scale 1: 13 300 000

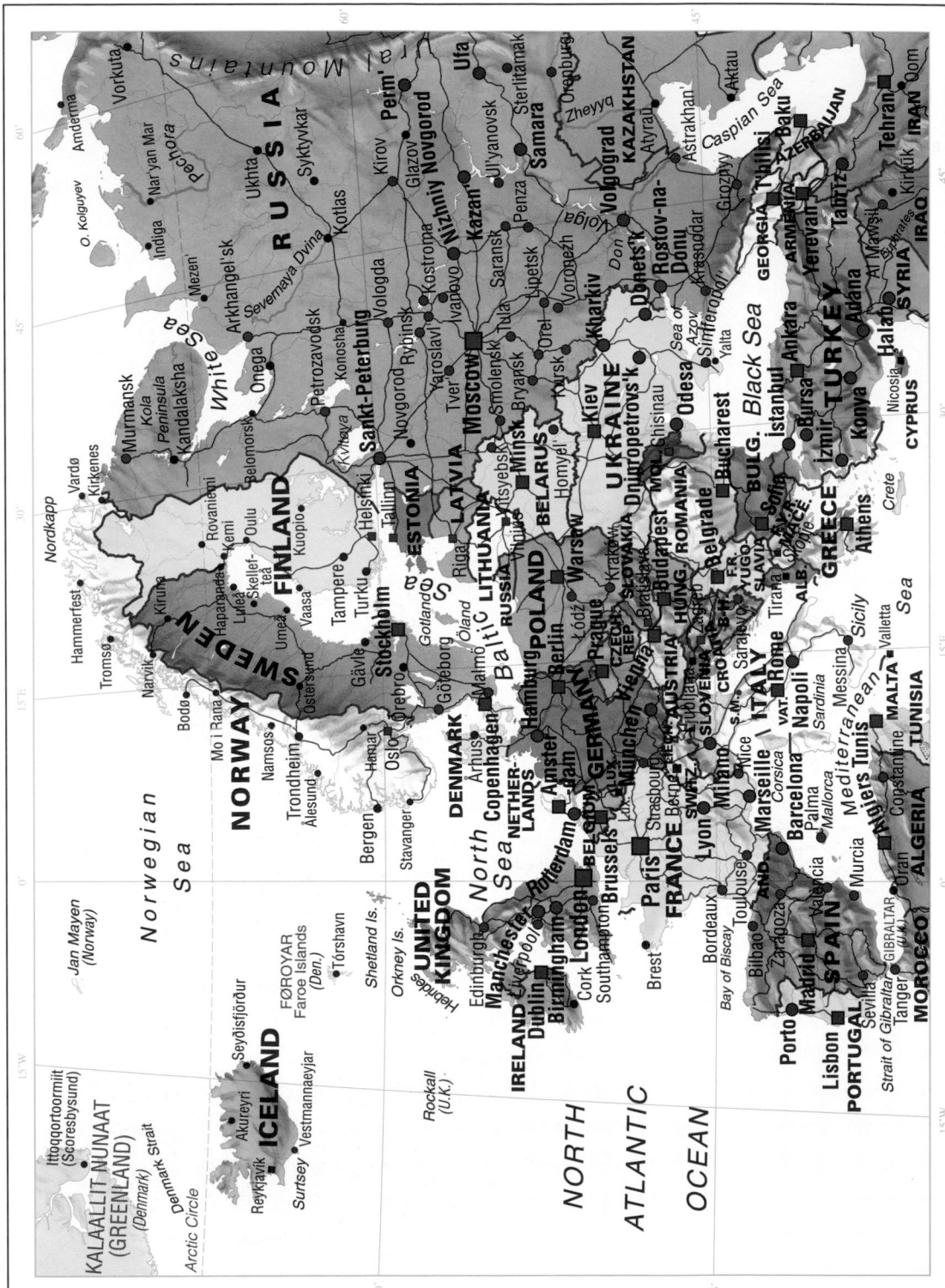

Scale 1: 6 670 000

| 0 | 100 | 200km |
| 0 | 50 | 100miles |

© Geddes & Grosset

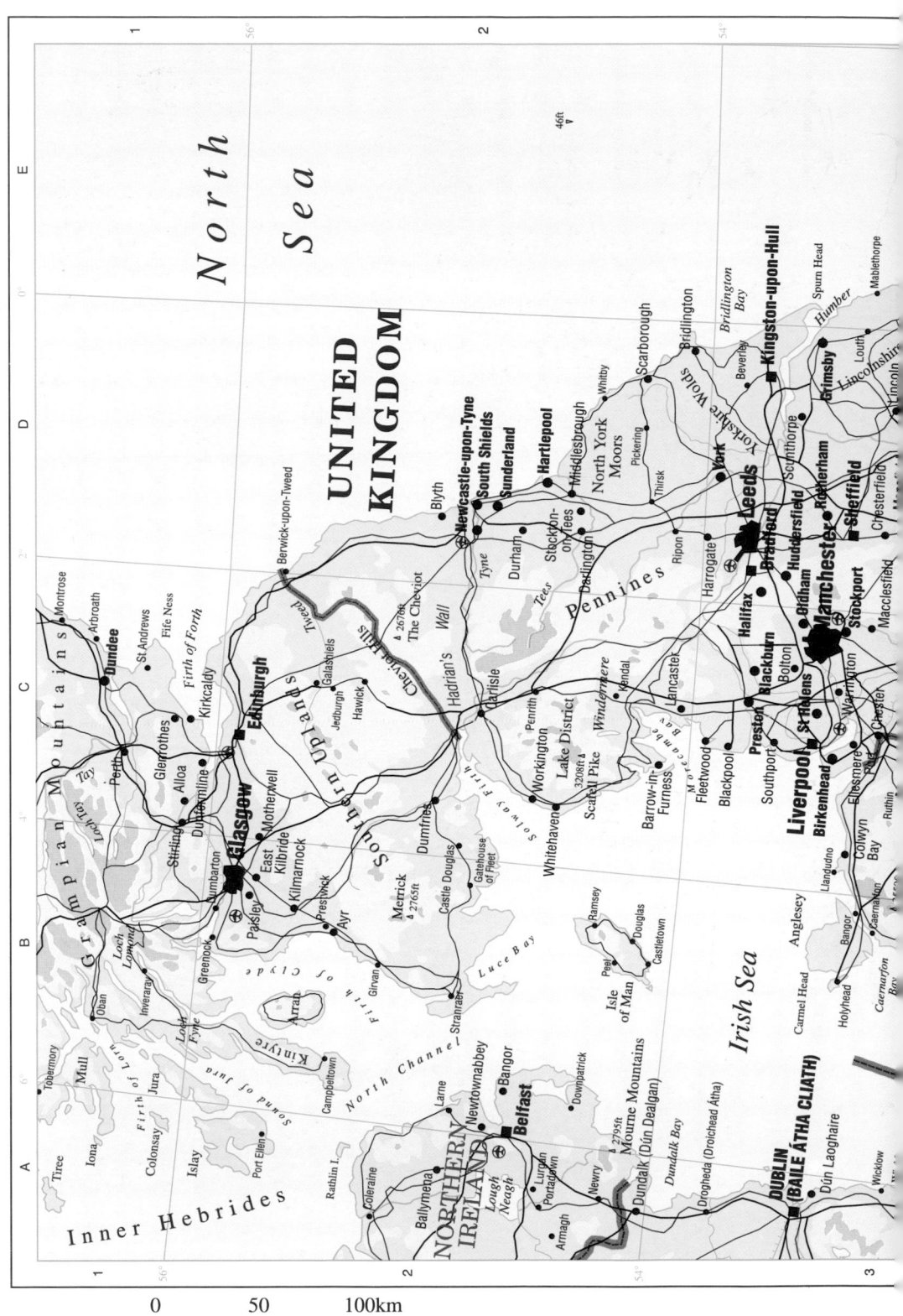

Scale 1: 3 335 000

0   50   100km

0   25   50miles

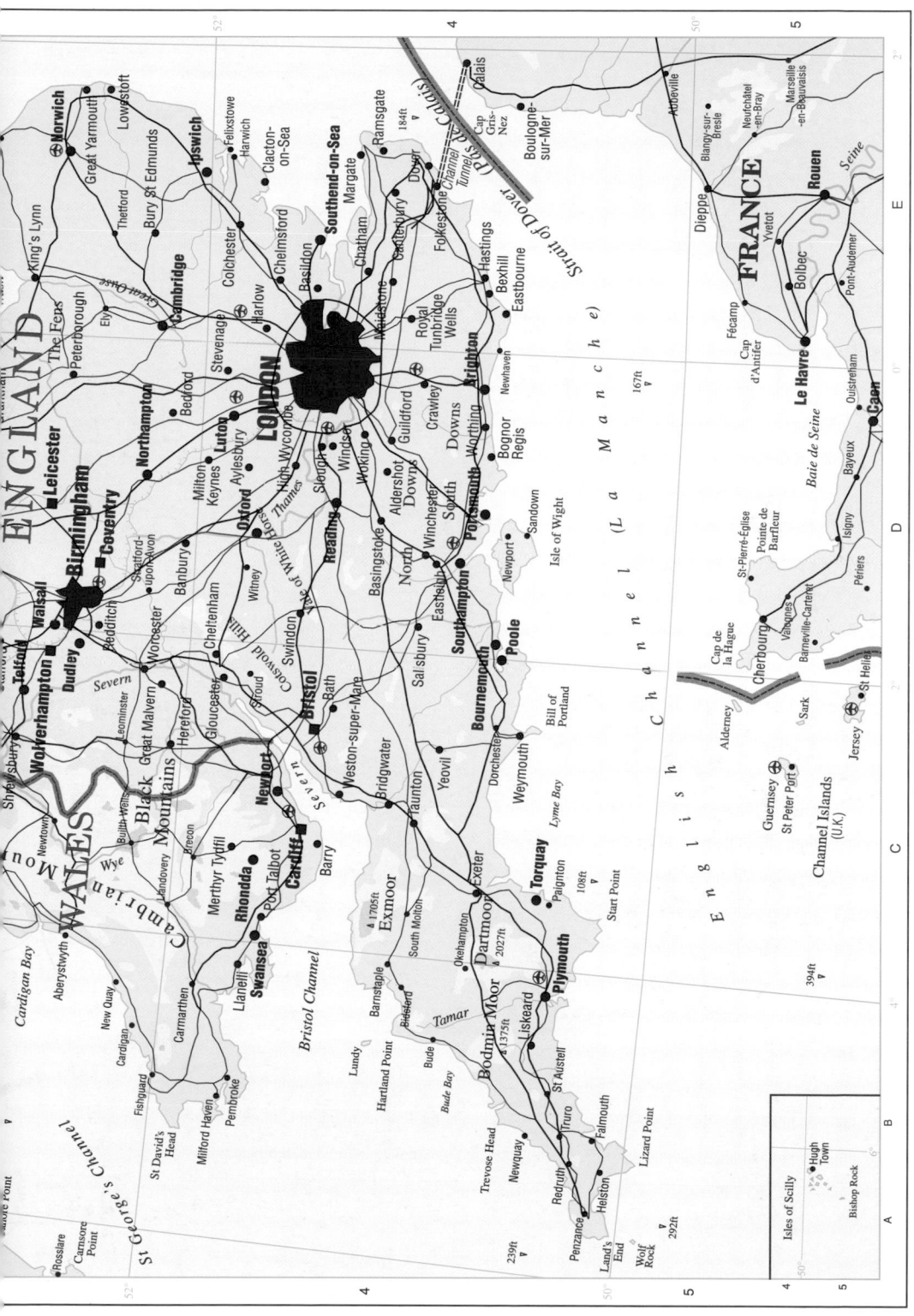

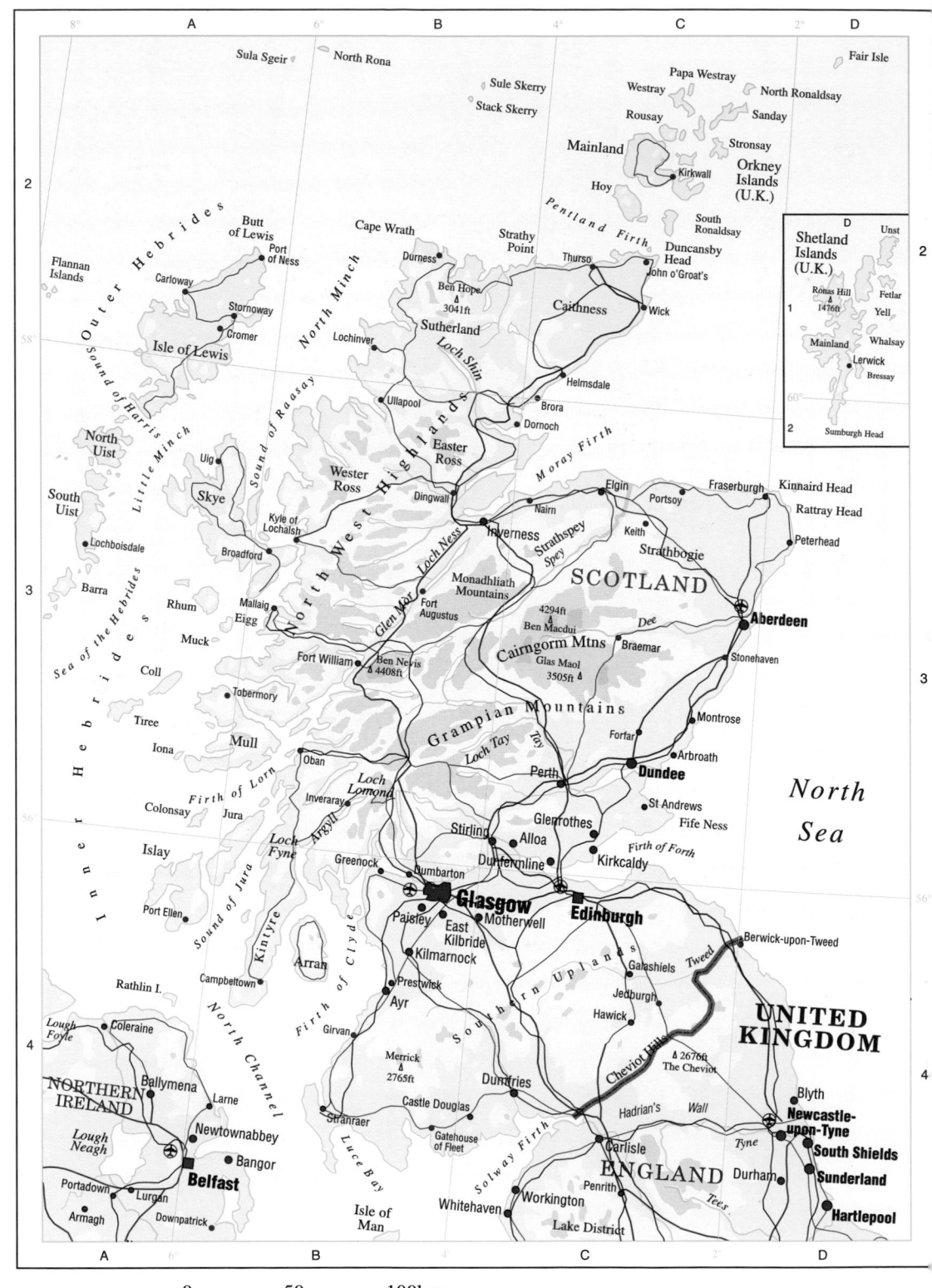

Sula Sgeir · North Rona
Fair Isle
Sule Skerry
Stack Skerry
Papa Westray
Westray · North Ronaldsay
Rousay · Sanday
Mainland · Stronsay
Orkney
Kirkwall · Islands
Hoy · (U.K.)
South
Ronaldsay
Flannan
Islands
Butt
of Lewis
Port
of Ness
Cape Wrath
Durness
Strathy
Point
Thurso
Duncansby
Head
John o'Groat's
Carloway
Stornoway
Cromer
Isle of Lewis
Lochinver
Ben Hope
3041ft
Sutherland
Loch Shin
Caithness
Wick
North
Uist
Uig
Wester
Ross
Easter
Ross
Ullapool
Brora
Dornoch
Helmsdale
Moray Firth
South
Uist
Lochboisdale
Skye
Kyle of
Lochalsh
Dingwall
Inverness
Nairn
Elgin
Portsoy
Fraserburgh
Kinnaird Head
Rattray Head
Peterhead
Barra
Broadford
Monadhliath
Mountains
Strathspey
Keith
Strathbogie
SCOTLAND
Rhum
Mallaig
Eigg
Glen Mor
Fort
Augustus
4294ft
Ben Macdui
Dee
Aberdeen
Muck
Fort William
Ben Nevis
4408ft
Cairngorm Mtns
Braemar
Glas Maol
3505ft
Stonehaven
Coll
Tobermory
Grampian Mountains
Forfar
Montrose
Tiree
Iona
Mull
Oban
Loch
Lomond
Loch Tay
Perth
Arbroath
Dundee
Colonsay
Jura
Inveraray
Stirling
Glenrothes
St Andrews
Fife Ness
Islay
Loch
Fyne
Greenock
Alloa
Firth of Forth
Dumbarton
Dunfermline
Kirkcaldy
Port Ellen
Kintyre
Arran
Paisley
Glasgow
East
Kilbride
Motherwell
Edinburgh
Berwick-upon-Tweed
Campbeltown
Kilmarnock
Galashiels
Tweed
UNITED
KINGDOM
Rathlin I.
Prestwick
Ayr
Jedburgh
Hawick
Cheviot Hills
2676ft
The Cheviot
Lough
Foyle
Coleraine
Merrick
2765ft
Dumfries
Hadrian's
Wall
Blyth
Newcastle-
upon-Tyne
NORTHERN
IRELAND
Ballymena
Larne
Castle Douglas
Stranraer
Girvan
Carlisle
ENGLAND
South Shields
Sunderland
Lough
Neagh
Newtownabbey
Bangor
Gatehouse
of Fleet
Solway Firth
Penrith
Durham
Hartlepool
Portadown
Lurgan
Belfast
Luce Bay
Whitehaven
Workington
Lake District
Armagh
Downpatrick
Isle of
Man

Inner Hebrides
Sea of the Hebrides
Sound of Jura
Firth of Clyde
North Channel
Southern Uplands
North Sea
North
Sea

Outer Hebrides
Sound of Harris
North Minch
Little Minch
Sound of Raasay
North West Highlands
Loch Ness
Pentland Firth

D
Shetland
Islands
(U.K.)
Unst
Rónas Hill
1476ft
Fetlar
Yell
Mainland
Whalsay
Lerwick
Bressay
Sumburgh Head

0 50 100km
0 25 50miles

© Geddes & Grosset

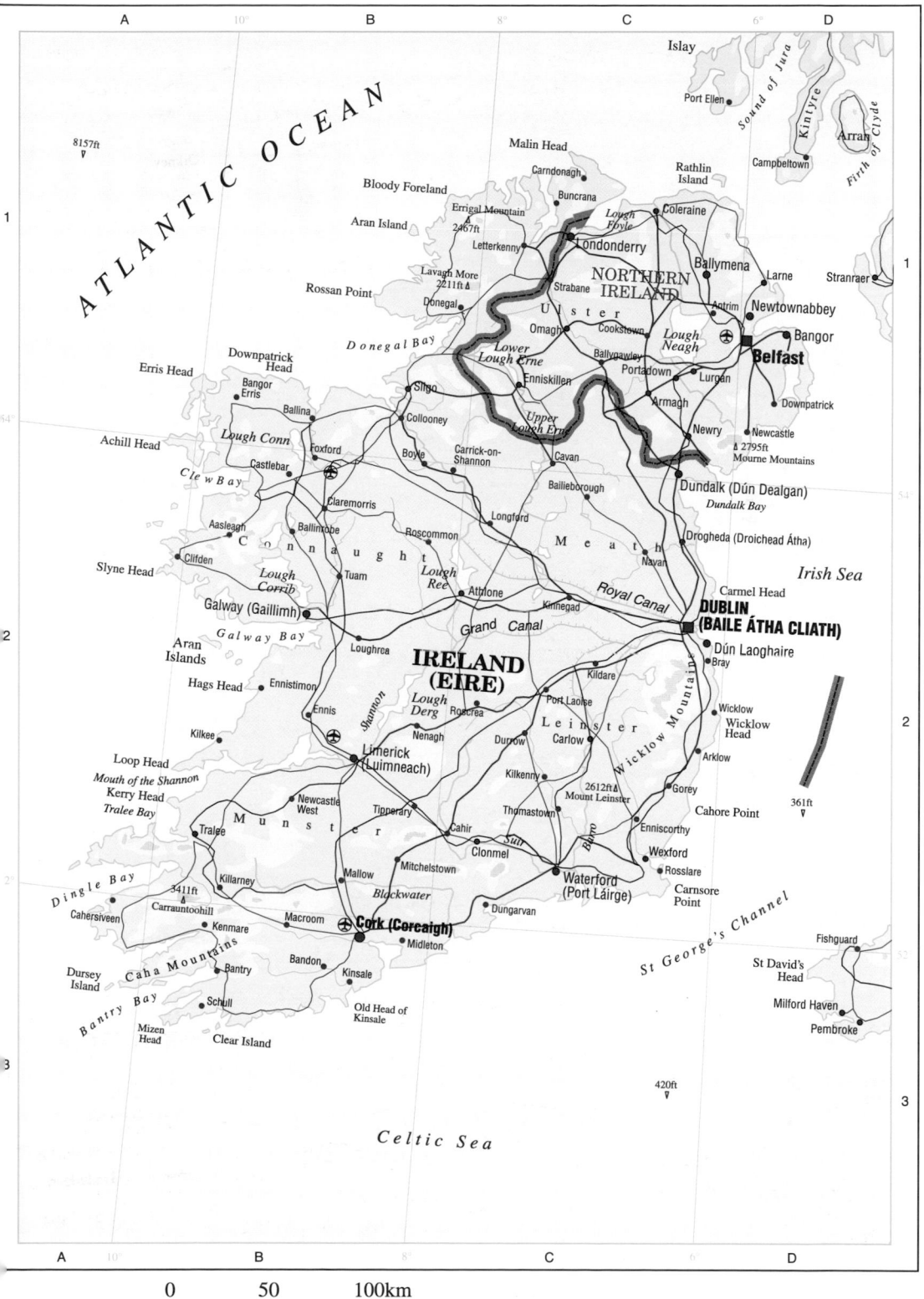

ATLANTIC OCEAN

8157ft ▽

Islay

Port Ellen

Sound of Jura

Kintyre

Arran

Firth of Clyde

Campbeltown

Stranraer

Malin Head

Carndonagh

Rathlin Island

Bloody Foreland

Buncrana

Coleraine

Aran Island

Errigal Mountain 2467ft

Lough Foyle

Letterkenny

Londonderry

Ballymena

Larne

Rossan Point

Lavagh More 2211ft ▲

Donegal

Strabane

NORTHERN IRELAND

Antrim

Newtownabbey

Bangor

Downpatrick Head

Ulster

Omagh

Cookstown

Lough Neagh

Belfast

Erris Head

Bangor Erris

Sligo

Lower Lough Erne

Enniskillen

Ballynahinch

Portadown

Lurgan

Downpatrick

Ballina

Colloney

Upper Lough Erne

Armagh

Newry

Newcastle

Donegal Bay

Lough Conn

Foxford

Boyle

Carrick-on-Shannon

Cavan

Mourne Mountains 2795ft ▲

Achill Head

Castlebar

Bailieborough

Dundalk (Dún Dealgan)

Clew Bay

Claremorris

Longford

Meath

Dundalk Bay

Drogheda (Droichead Átha)

Aasleagh

Ballinrobe

Roscommon

Connaught

Slyne Head

Clifden

Tuam

Lough Ree

Athlone

Navan

Irish Sea

Lough Corrib

Kinnegad

Royal Canal

Carmel Head

Galway (Gaillimh)

Galway Bay

Loughrea

Grand Canal

DUBLIN (BAILE ÁTHA CLIATH)

Aran Islands

IRELAND (EIRE)

Kildare

Dún Laoghaire

Bray

Hags Head

Ennistimon

Lough Derg

Roscrea

Port Laoise

Wicklow

Wicklow Head

Ennis

Leinster

Durrow

Carlow

Kilkee

Nenagh

Wicklow Mountains

Arklow

Loop Head

Shannon

Limerick (Luimneach)

Kilkenny

Mount Leinster 2612ft ▲

Gorey

Mouth of the Shannon

Cahore Point

Kerry Head

Newcastle West

Tipperary

Thomastown

Enniscorthy

361ft ▽

Tralee Bay

Munster

Cahir

Barrow

Wexford

Tralee

Clonmel

Waterford (Port Láirge)

Rosslare

Killarney

Mallow

Mitchelstown

Carnsore Point

Dingle Bay

3411ft ▲ Carrauntoohill

Macroom

Blackwater

Dungarvan

St George's Channel

Cahersiveen

Kenmare

Midleton

Cork (Corcaigh)

Fishguard

Dursey Island

Caha Mountains

Bantry

Bandon

Kinsale

St David's Head

Bantry Bay

Schull

Old Head of Kinsale

Milford Haven

Mizen Head

Clear Island

Pembroke

Celtic Sea

420ft ▽

Scale 1: 3 335 000

0   50   100km

0   25   50miles

© Geddes & Grosset

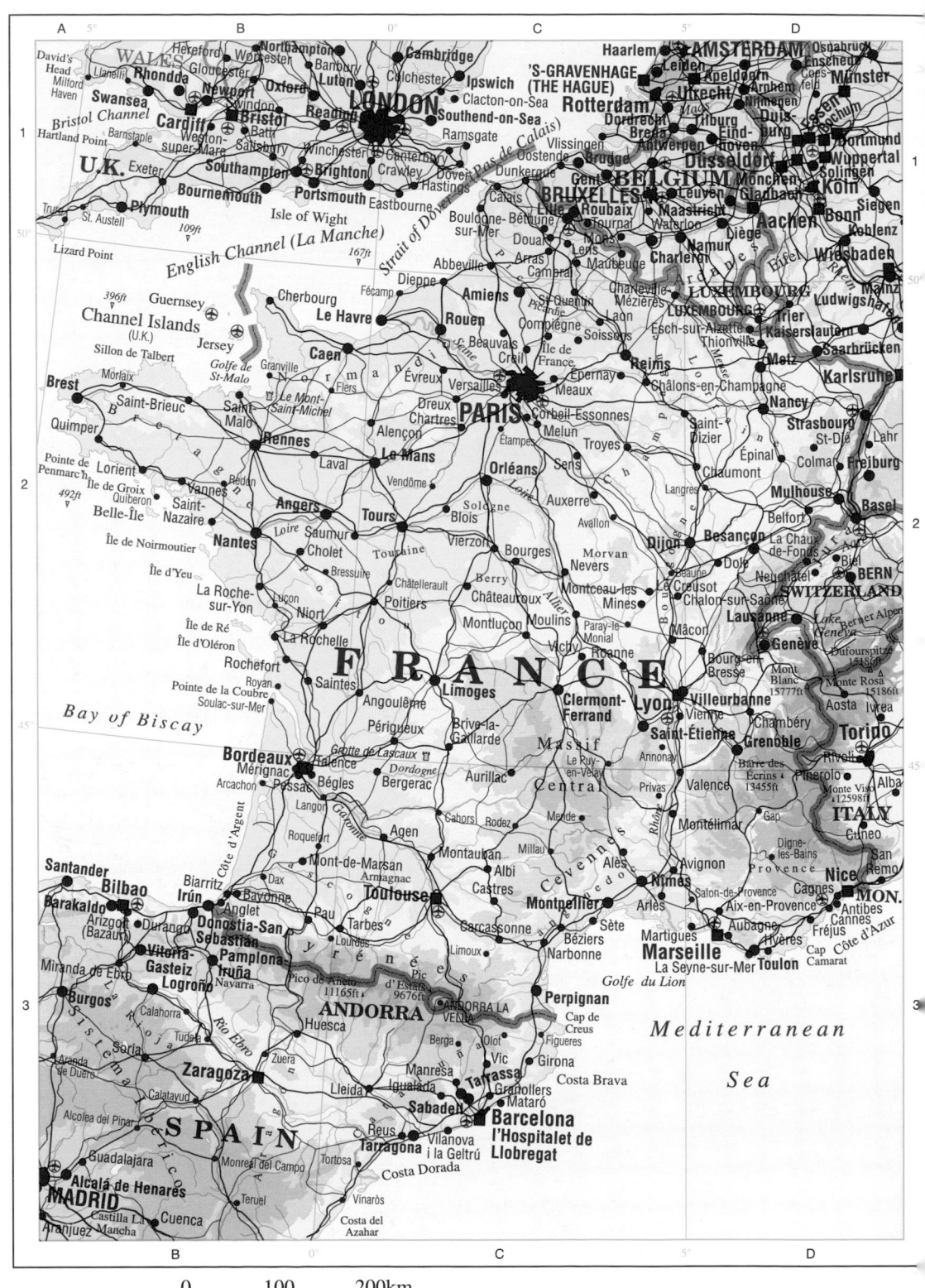

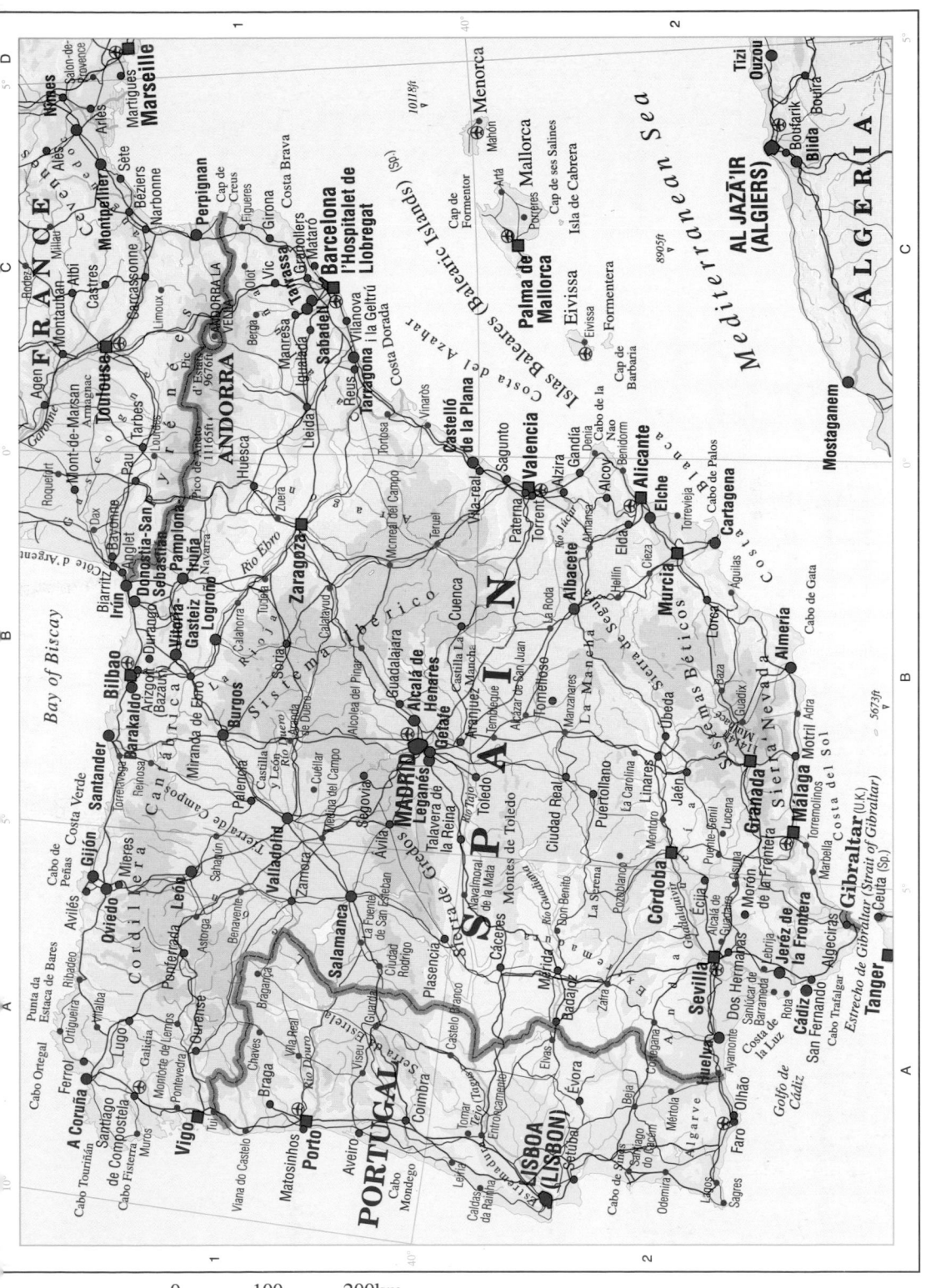

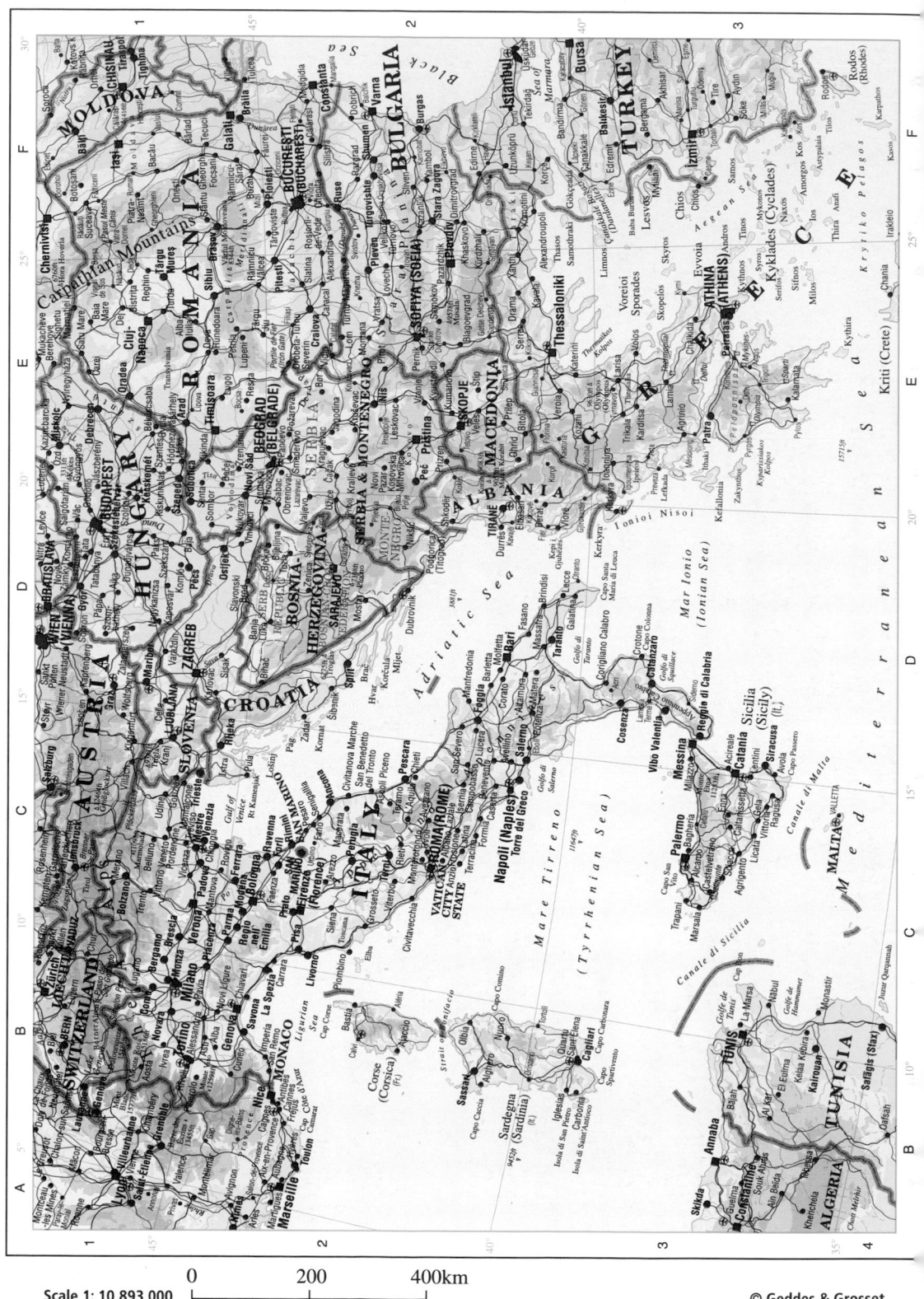

Scale 1: 10 893 000

0   200   400km

0   100   200miles

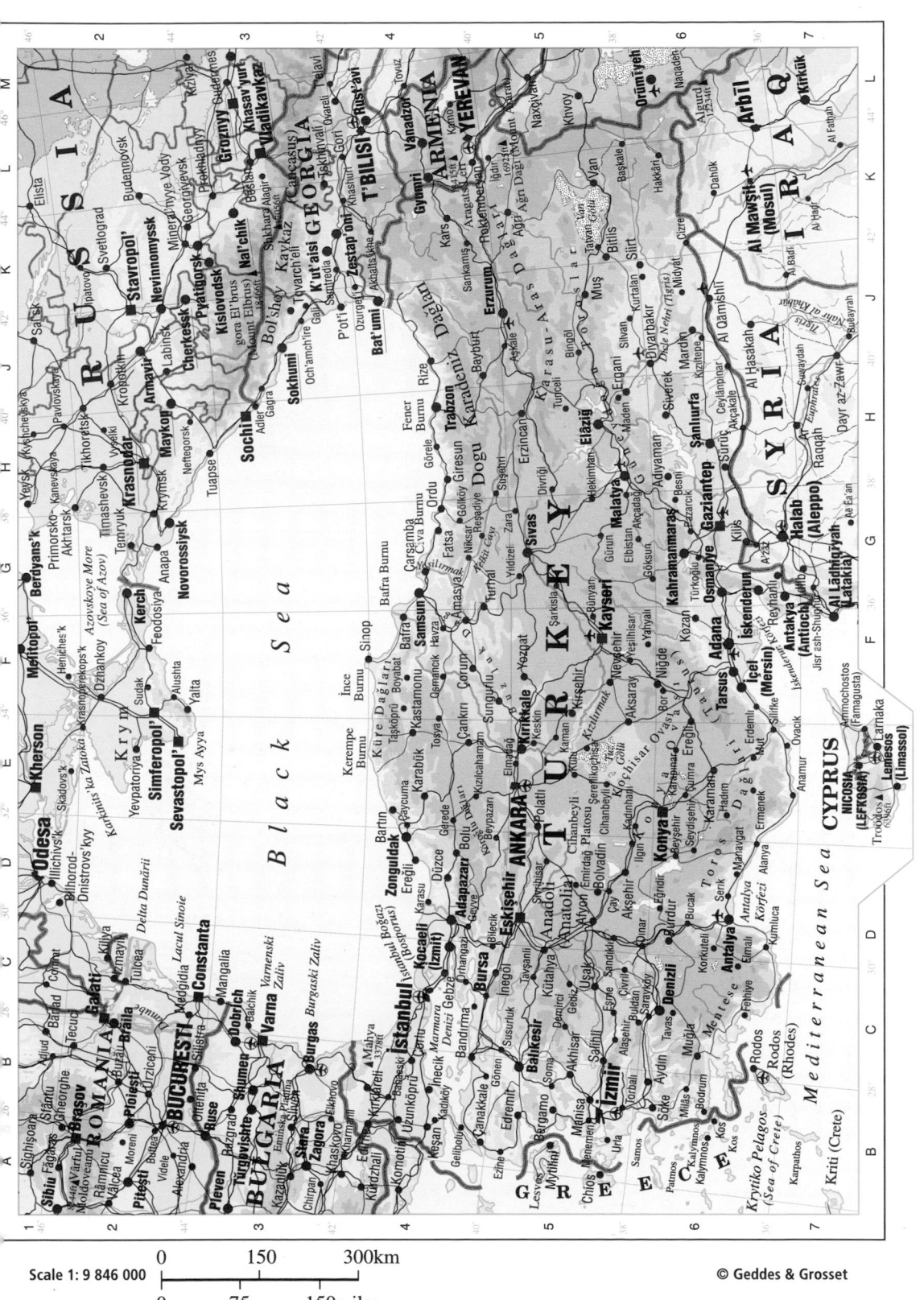

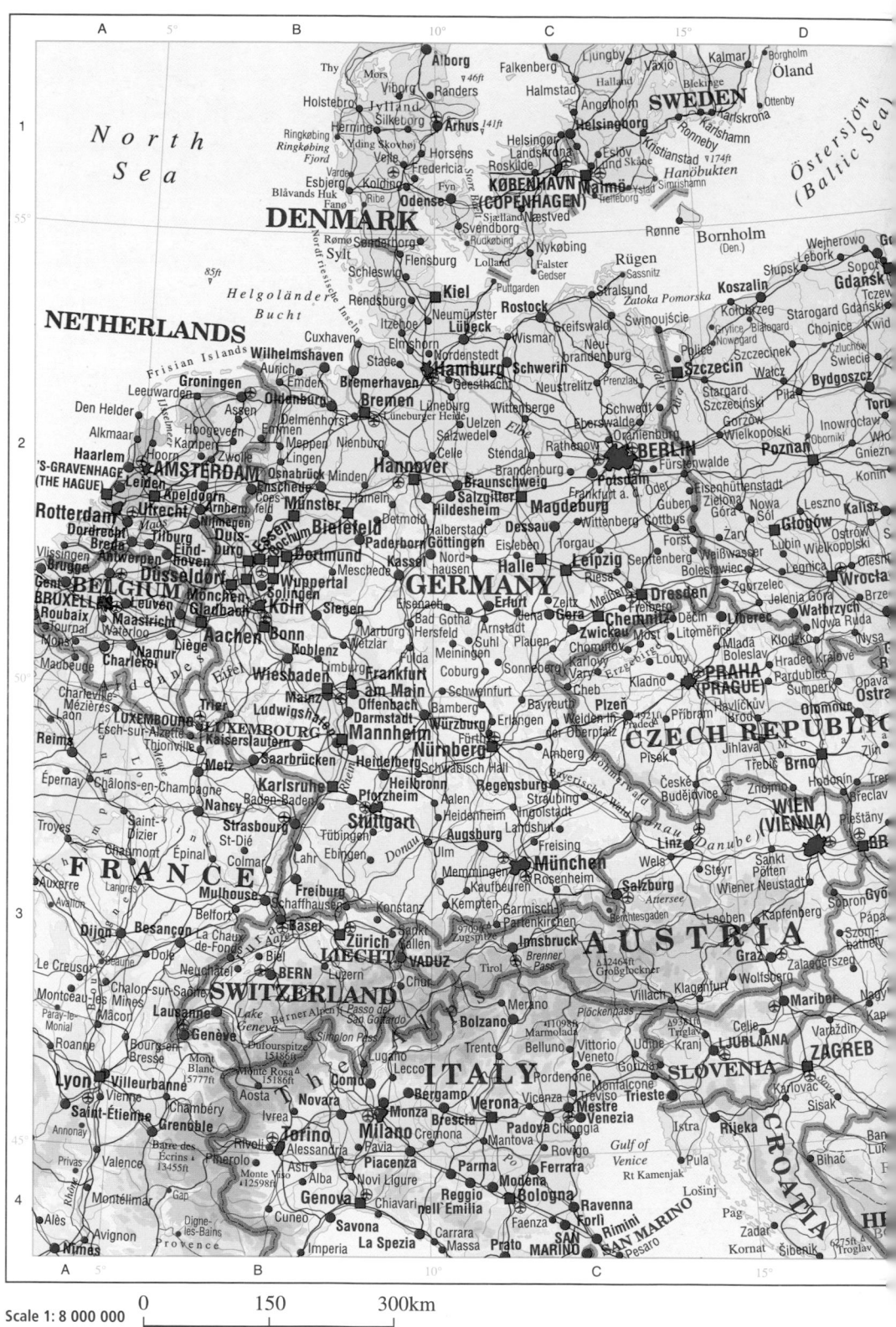

North Sea

Thy Mors Viborg Randers Ålborg Falkenberg Ljungby Vaxjo Kalmar Öland Borgholm

Holstebro Jylland Silkeborg Århus 141ft Halmstad Angaholm SWEDEN Ottenby

Ringkøbing Iding Skovho Horsens Helsingor Landskrona Helsingborg Karlshamn

Ringkøbing Fjord Velje Fredericia Roskilde Eslov Kristianstad ▼174ft *Östersjön (Baltic Sea)*

Esbjerg Kolding Fyn KØBENHAVN (COPENHAGEN) Malmö Ystad Simrishamn Hanöbukten

Blåvands Huk Fanø Ribe Odense

DENMARK Rømø Sønderborg Svendborg Næstved Rønne Bornholm (Den.)

Sylt Schleswig Flensburg Lolland Falster Nykøbing Wejherowo Gda

Rendsburg Kiel Putgarden Rügen Sassnitz Slupsk Sopo Gda

Helgoländer Bucht Neumünster Rostock Stralsund Zatoka Pomorska Koszalin Starogard Gda

Cuxhaven Itzehoe Lübeck Wismar Greifswald Swinoujście Kolobrzeg Chojnice Kwid

Wilhelmshaven Stade Elmshorn Nordenstedt brandenburg Szczecin Stargard Szczeciński Swiecie

NETHERLANDS Aurich Emden Bremerhaven **Hamburg** Schwerin Neustrelitz Prenzlau Szczecinek Walcz Bydgoszcz Toru

Groningen Assen Oldenburg Bremen Lüneburg Uelzen Eberswalde Oranienburg Wielkopolski Obomiki Inowroclaw Gniez

Leeuwarden Hoogeveen Emmen Meppen Nienburg Salzwedel Stendal Rathenow **BERLIN** Fürstenwalde Poznan Konin

Haarlem Hoorn Zwolle Osnabrück Minden **Hannover** Braunschweig Potsdam Eisenhüttenstadt Zielona Nowa Leszno Kalisz

'S-GRAVENHAGE (THE HAGUE) Leiden Apeldoorn Arnhem Coes Hameln Hildesheim Magdeburg Wittenberg Cottbus Góra Sól Glogów Ostrów Wielkopolski

AMSTERDAM Utrecht Nijmegen **Münster** Detmold Halberstadt Eisleben Torgau Weißwasser Lubin Wroclaw

Rotterdam Dordrecht Breda Duis- Bochum **Bielefeld** Paderborn Göttingen Nord- Dessau Forst Boleslawiec Legnica

Vlissingen Antwerpen Eindhoven burg **Dortmund** Kassel hausen **Halle** Riesa Meiben Weißwasser Zgorzelec Jelenia Góra

Brugge **BELGIUM** Solingen Wuppertal Meschede **GERMANY** **Leipzig** **Dresden** Décin Liberec Walbrzych Nowa Ruda

Gent BRUXELLES Mönchen **Köln** Siegen Eisenach Erfurt Jena Gera **Chemnitz** Most Litoměřice Mladá Klodzko Nysa

Roubaix Gladbach Bonn Marburg Bad Gotha Arnstadt Zwickau Chomutov Karlovy Loun Boleslav Hradec Králové

Tournal Maastricht Aachen Koblenz Wetzlar Hersfeld Suhl Plauen Vary Cheb Kladno **PRAHA (PRAGUE)** Pardubice Sumperk Opava Ostra

Mons Liège Eifel Limburg Fulda Meiningen Sonneberg Bayreuth Weiden Plzeň Pribram Havlíčkův Olomouc

Maubeuge Charleroi Namur Wiesbaden Frankfurt Schweinfurt Coburg in der Oberpfalz **CZECH REPUBLIC** Jihlava Brod Zlín

Charleville- Ardennes Mainz am Main Bamberg Erlangen Amberg Písek České Třebíč **Brno** Tren

Mézières Laon Trier **LUXEMBOURG** Ludwigshafen Offenbach Würzburg Fürth **Nürnberg** Budějovice Znojmo Hodonín Břeclav

Reims Esch-sur-Alzette Kaiserslautern Darmstadt Mannheim Schwäbisch Hall Regensburg Straubing Hodonín

Épernay Châlons-en-Champagne Metz Saarbrücken Heidelberg Heilbronn Aalen Ingolstadt Landshut Donau Linz **WIEN (VIENNA)** Piešťany öB

Nancy Karlsruhe Pforzheim **Stuttgart** Augsburg Freising München Wels Steyr Sankt Pölten Wiener Neustadt Sopron

Troyes Saint-Dizier Baden-Baden Tübingen Ebingen Ulm Memmingen **München** Rosenheim Salzburg **AUSTRIA** Graz

FRANCE Épinal Strasbourg St-Dié Colmar Lahr Donau Kaufbeuren Garmisch-Partenkirchen Berchtesgaden Attersee Leoben Kapfenberg Pápa

Auxerre Avallon Chaumont Langres Belfort Schaffhausen Konstanz Zugspitze Innsbruck Villach Klagenfurt Wolfsberg Maribor

Dijon Besançon La Chaux-de-Fonds Basel **Zürich** St. Gallen Tirol Brenner Pass Großglockner Celle Kranj LJUBLJANA Varaždin **ZAGREB**

Le Creusot Beaune Dole Neuchâtel Biel **BERN** Luzern Chur Bolzano Merano Plöckenpass **SLOVENIA** Karlovac

Montceau-les-Mines Chalon-sur-Saône **SWITZERLAND** Lausanne Lake Geneva Berner Alpen San Gottardo Trento Belluno Vittorio Veneto Udine Gorizia Trieste Istra Rijeka Sisak

Paray-le-Monial Mâcon **Genève** Simplon Pass Lugano Como Lecco Bergamo Vicenza Treviso Mestre Venezia Pula **CROATIA**

Lyon Villeurbanne Bourg-en-Bresse Mont Blanc Monte Rosa Aosta Ivrea Novara **Milano** Brescia Verona Padova Chioggia Rovigo Gulf of Venice Bihać

Saint-Étienne Chambéry Grenoble Barre des Écrins Pinerolo Rivoli **Torino** Monza Cremona Mantova Po Ferrara Ravenna Rt Kamenjak HI

Annonay Privas Valence Gap Digne-les-Bains Monte Viso Cuneo Alba Asti Alessandria Pavia Piacenza Parma Modena Bologna Pesaro Zadar Šibenik

Alès Montélimar Avignon Nîmes Provence Imperia La Spezia Carrara Massa Prato **ITALY** Reggio nell'Emilia Genova Chiavari Savona Faenza Forlì Rimini SAN MARINO Kornat Troglav

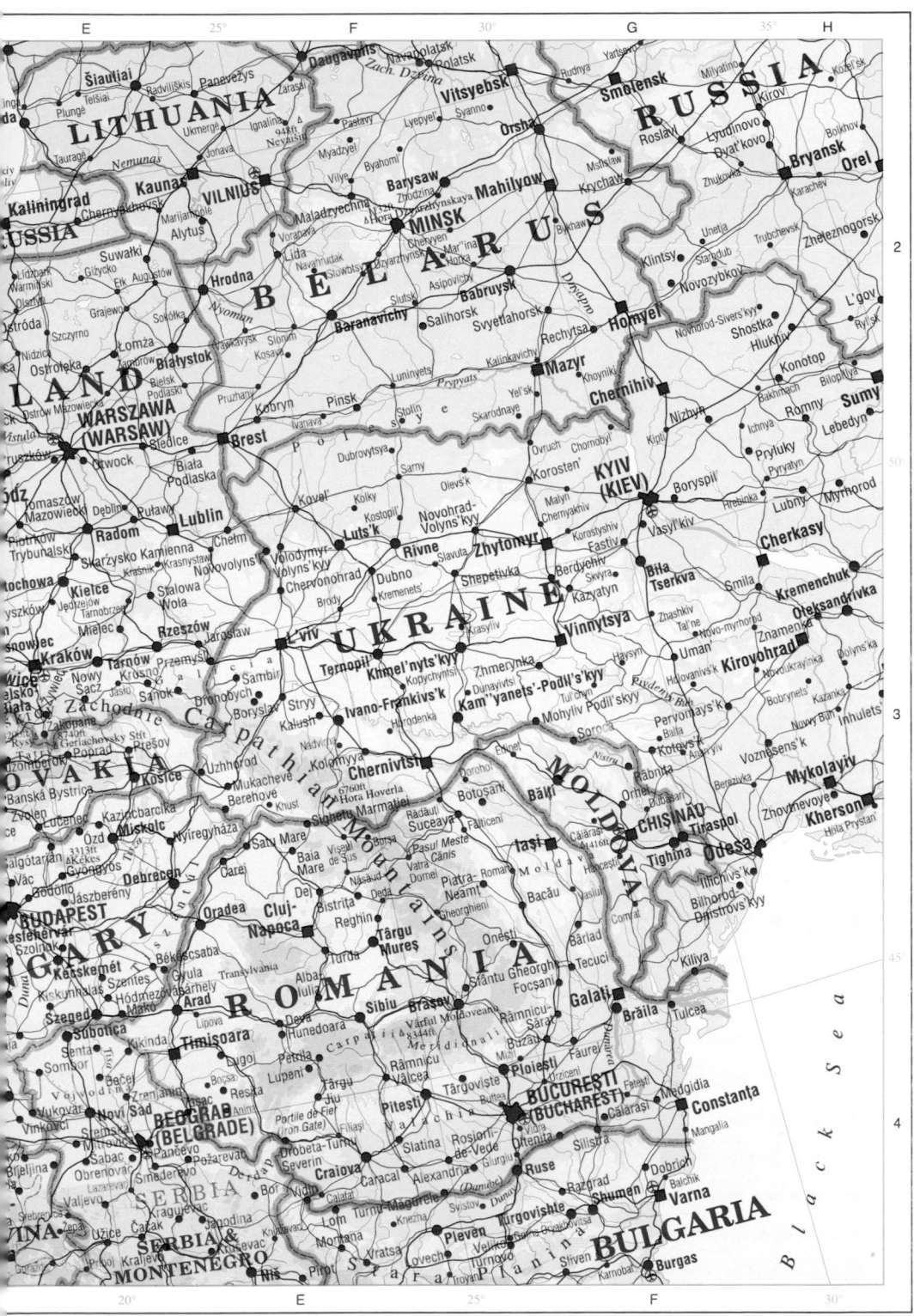

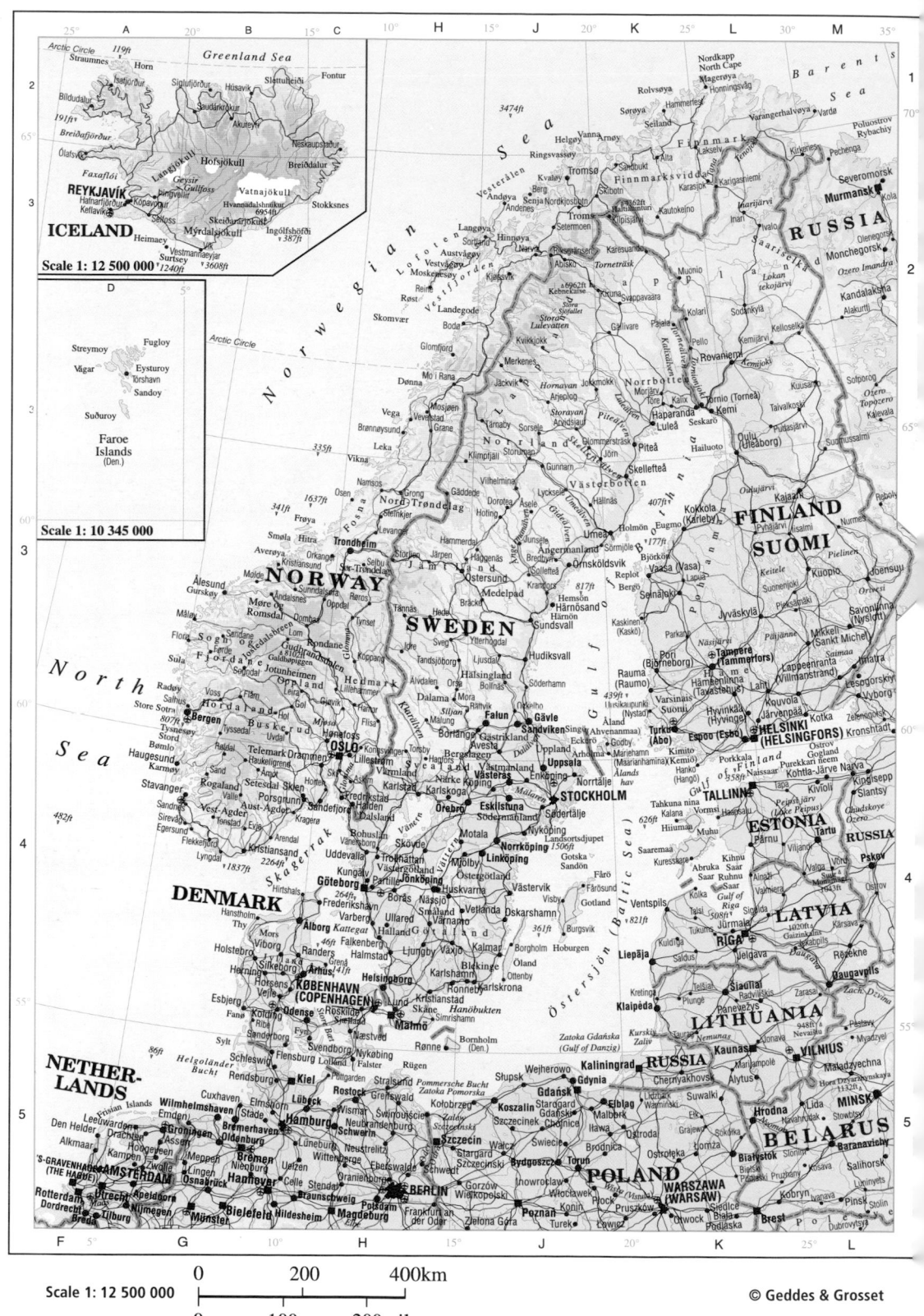

Scale 1: 12 500 000

0   200   400km

0   100   200miles

Scale 1: 18 100 000

| 0 | 250 | 500km |

| 0 | 150 | 300miles |

© Geddes & Grosset

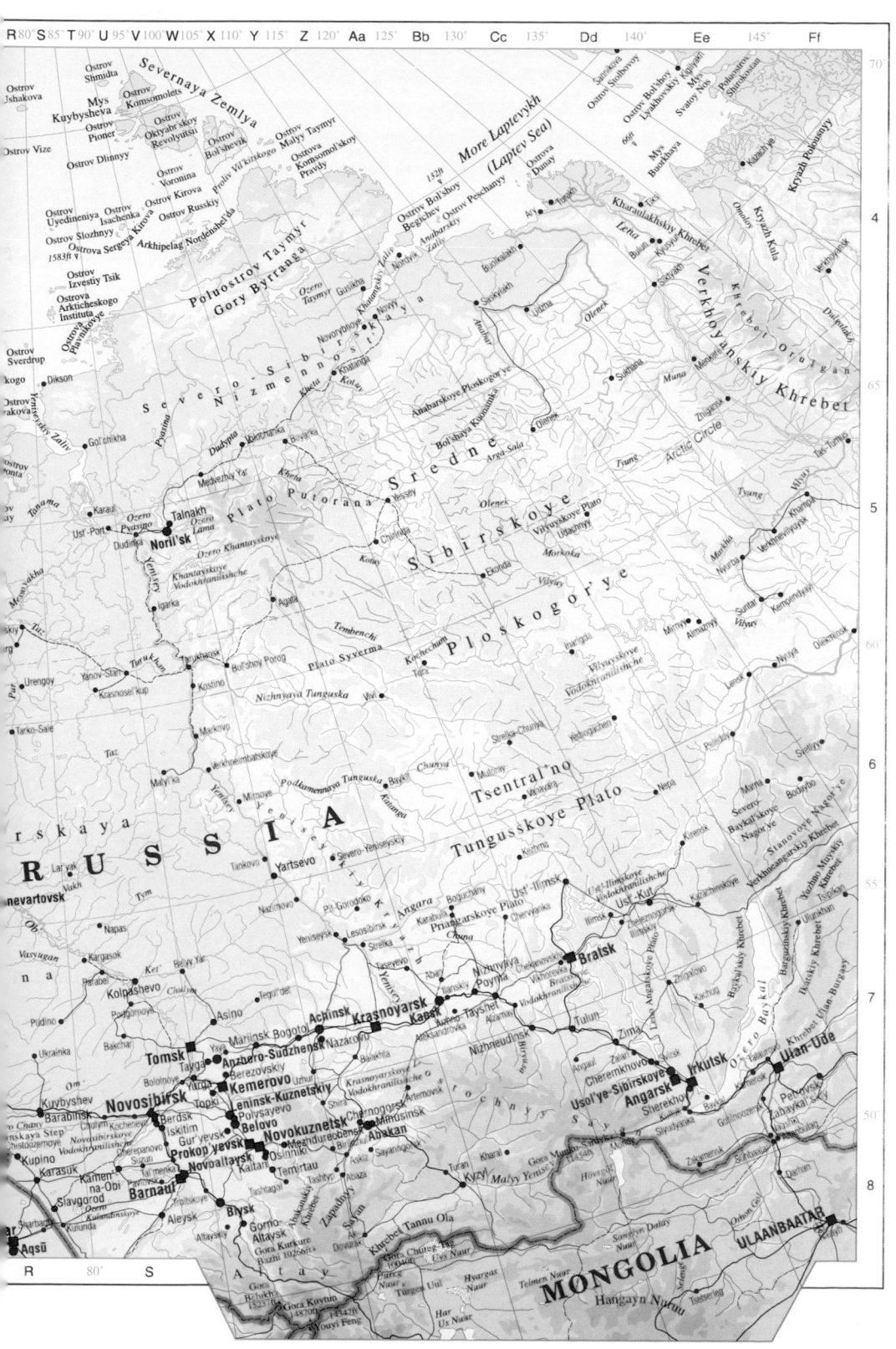

Ostrov Ushakova
Ostrov Shmidta
Mys Kuybysheva
Ostrov Komsomolets

Severnaya Zemlya

Ostrov Vize
Ostrov Pioner
Ostrov Oktyabr'skoy Revolyutsii

More Laptevykh
(Laptev Sea)

Ostrov Dlinnyy
Ostrov Voronina
Ostrov Bol'shevik
Proliv Vil'kitskogo
Malyy Taymyr
Ostrov Komsomol'skoy Pravdy

Ostrov Bol'shoy Begichev

Kharaulakhskiy Khrebet

Ostrov Uyedineniya
Ostrov Isachenka
Ostrova Sergeya Kirova
Ostrov Russkiy
Arkhipelag Nordenshel'da

Lena

Verkhoyanskiy Khrebet

Ostrov Slozhnyy
Ostrov Izvestiy Tsik
Ostrova Arkticheskogo Instituta
Ostrova Plavkovye

Poluostrov Taymyr
Gory Byrranga

Khrebet Orulgan

Ostrov Sverdrup
Dikson

Severo-Sibirskaya Nizmennost'

Srednе Sibirskoye Ploskogor'ye

Arctic Circle

Talnakh
Noril'sk
Dudinka
Ozero Pyasino

Plato Putorana

Ploskogor'ye

Tsentral'no Tungusskoye Plato

Stanovoye Nagor'ye

R U S S I A

Tankovo
Yartsevo
Severo-Yeniseyskiy

Ust'-Ilimskoye Vodokhranilishche
Ust'-Kut

Tomsk
Achinsk
Krasnoyarsk
Kansk
Tayshet
Bratsk

Ulan-Ude

Novosibirsk
Kemerovo
Leninsk-Kuznetskiy
Novokuznetsk
Abakan
Irkutsk
Angarsk
Usol'ye-Sibirskoye

Barnaul
Biysk

Aqsü

M O N G O L I A

ULAANBAATAR

Hangayn Nuruu

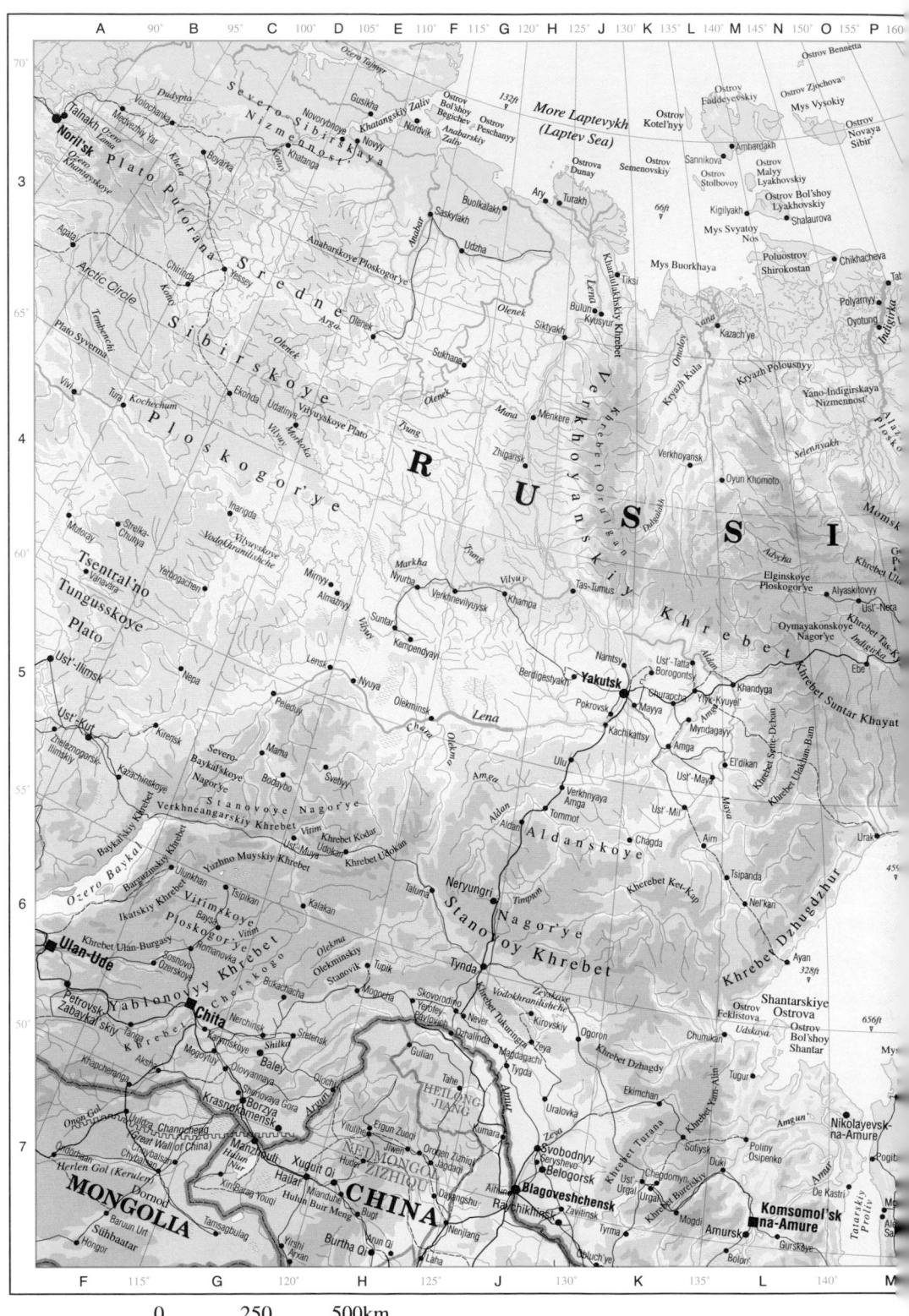

0   250   500km

0   150   300miles

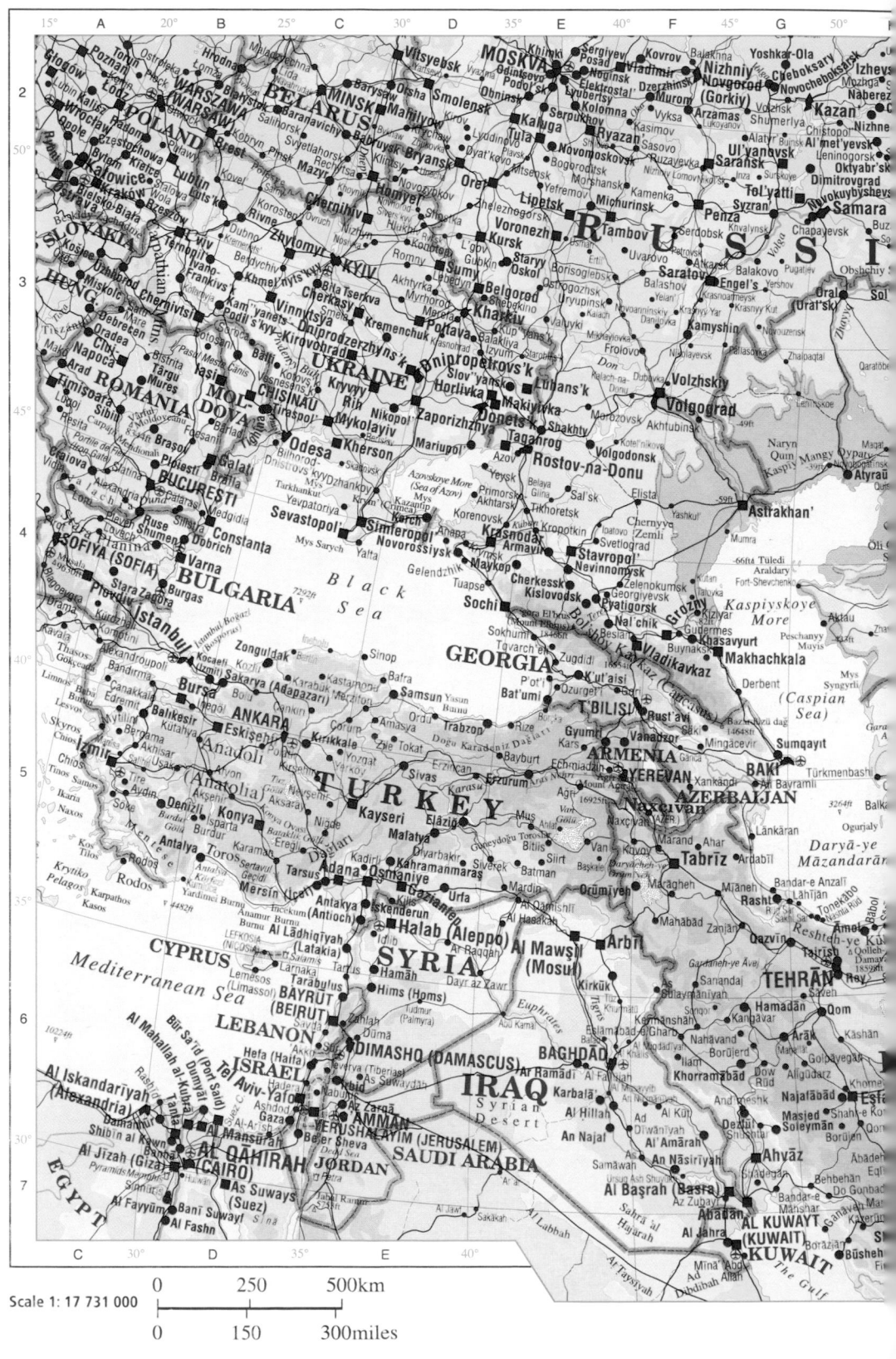

0   250   500km

0   150   300miles

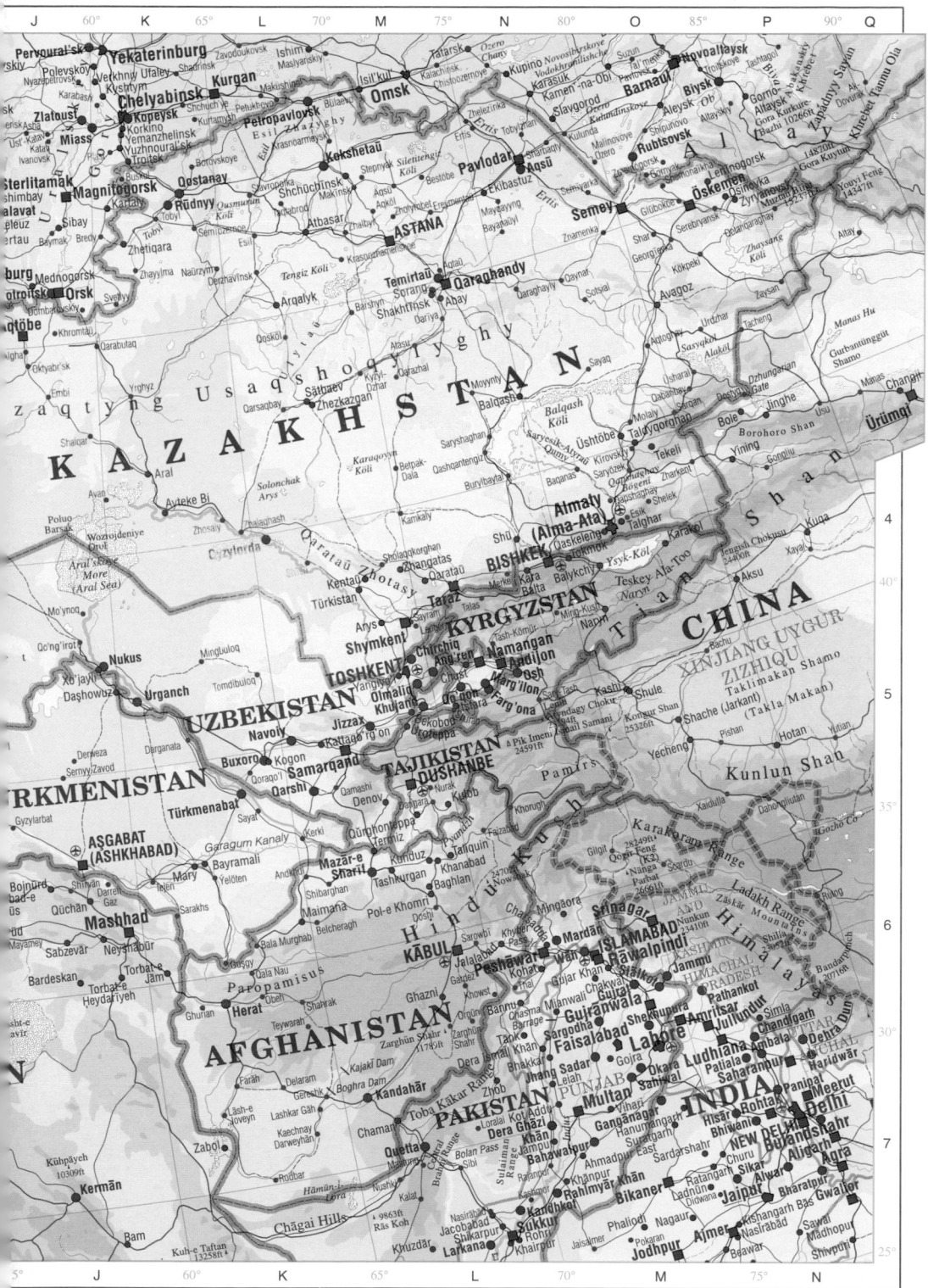

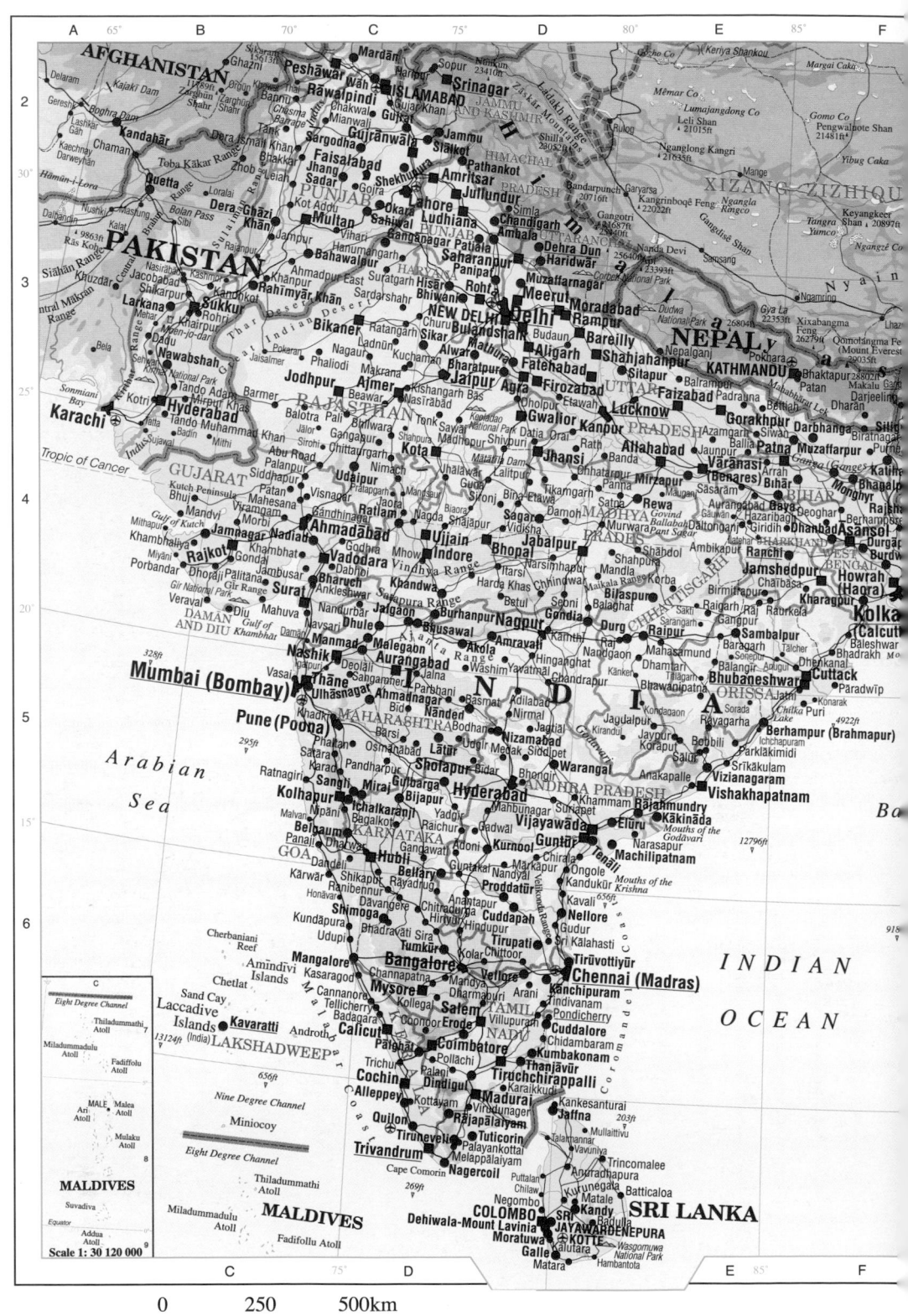

Scale 1: 30 120 000

MALDIVES

Scale 1: 17 705 000

| 0 | 250 | 500km |

| 0 | 150 | 300miles |

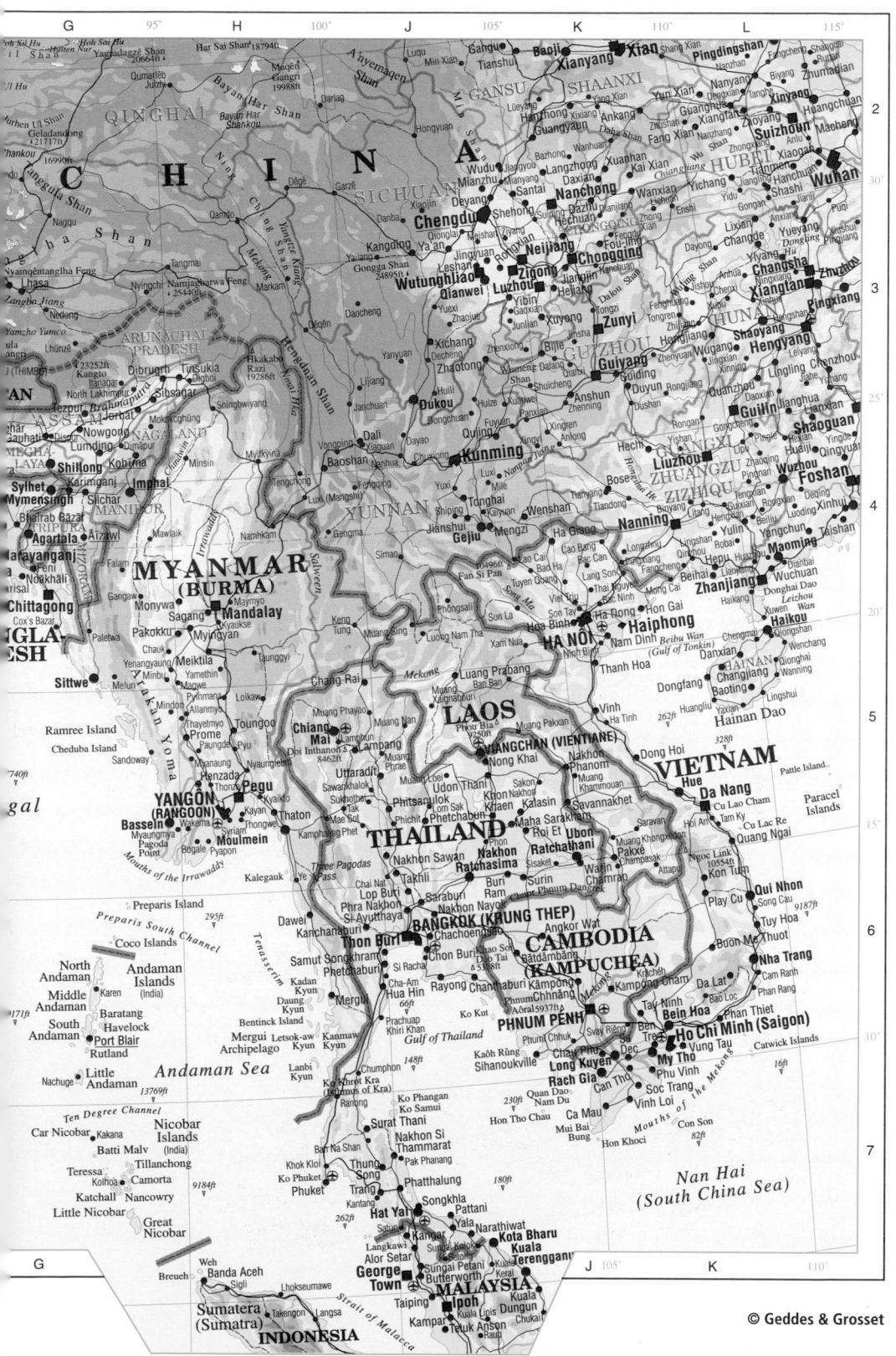

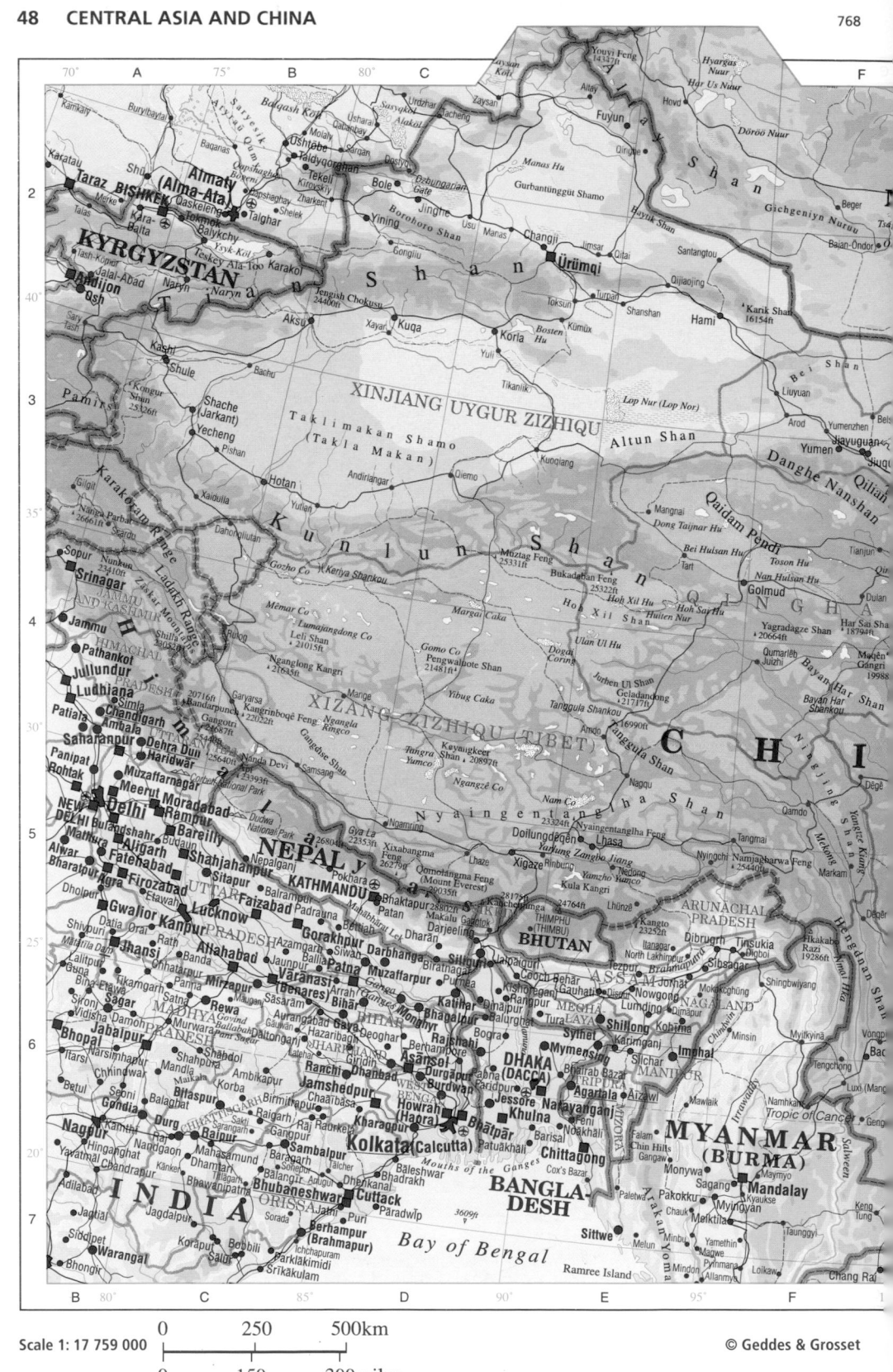

Scale 1: 17 759 000

| 0 | 250 | 500km |

| 0 | 150 | 300miles |

© Geddes & Grosset

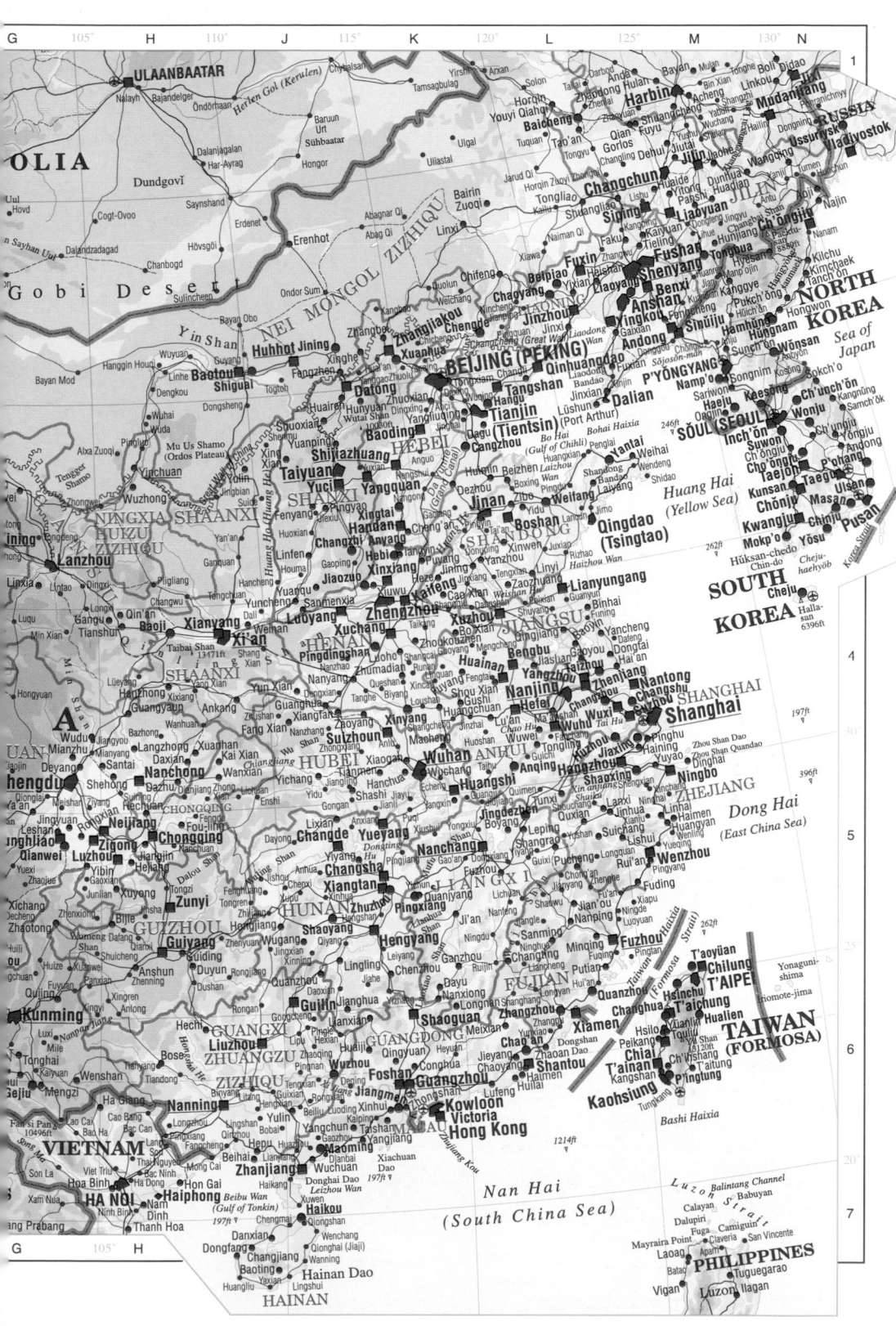

0   250   500km

0   150   300miles

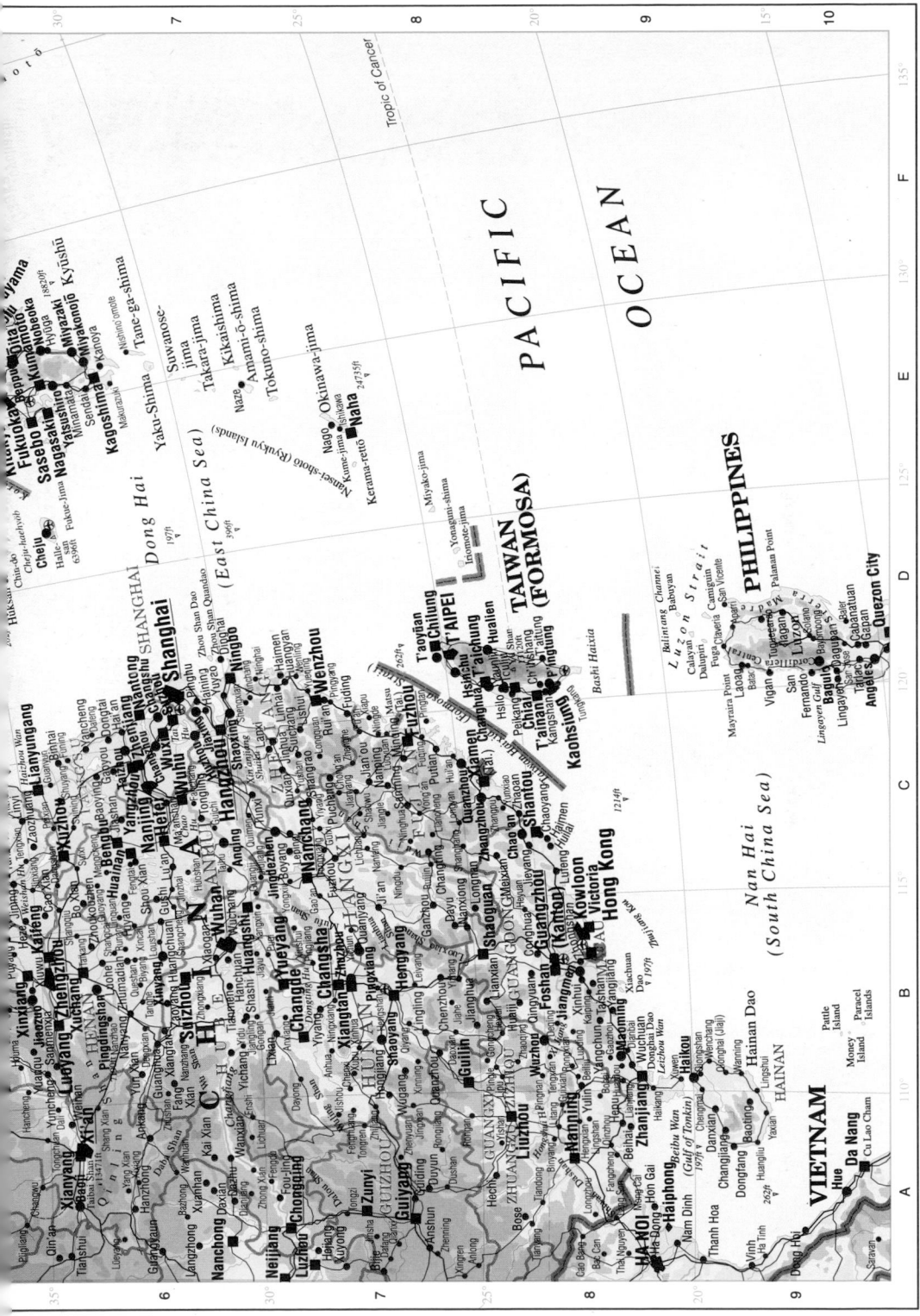

Scale 1: 17 778 000

```
0        250       500km
|____|____|____|____|
0        150       300miles
```

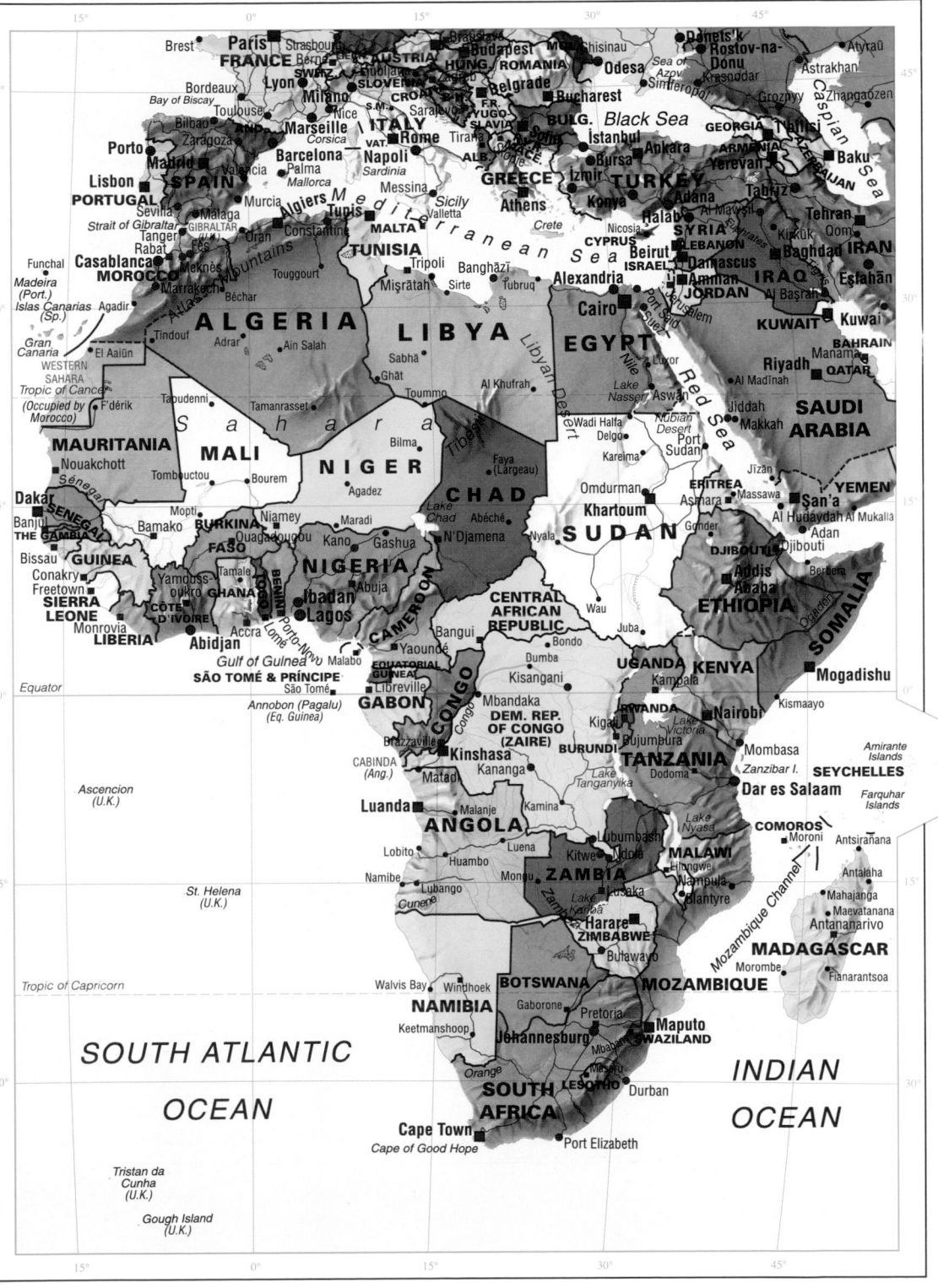

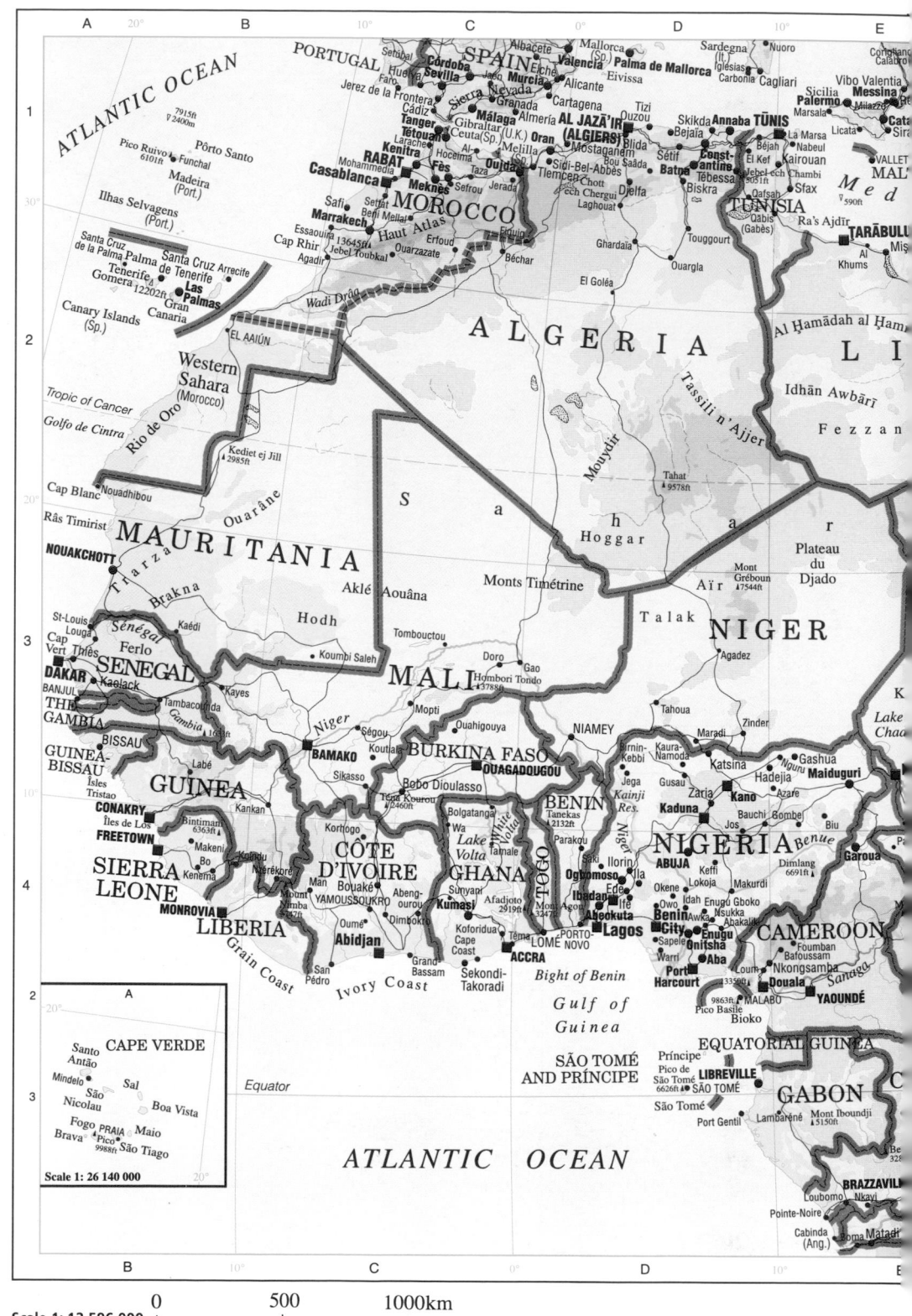

ATLANTIC OCEAN

7915ft
▽2400m

PORTUGAL

Albacete Mallorca Sardegna (It.) Nuoro
Setúbal Córdoba SPAIN Valencia Palma de Mallorca Carbonia Cagliari Coriglian Calabr
Sevilla Murcia Alicante Eivissa Iglesias
Jerez de la Frontera Sierra Nevada Granada Cartagena Palermo Messina Cata
Cádiz Málaga Almería AL JAZA'IR Skikda Annaba TÚNIS La Marsa Marsala Sira
Huelva Faro (ALGIERS) Bejaïa Nabeul Licata
Tanger Gibraltar Ceuta(Sp.) Melilla Mostaganem Sétif Constantine El Kef Kairouan MAL'
Tétouan Hoceima Oran Bou Saâda Sfax Chambi ▲VALLET
Larache Sidi-Bel-Abbès Batna Tébessa Qafsah ▽590m
RABAT Mohammedia Oujda Tlemcen Djelfa Biskra Gabès Med
Casablanca Meknès Jerada ech Chergui Chott Laghouat Touggourt Ra's Ajdir TARABULU
Fès Sefrou ech Chergui Ghardaïa Ouargla Al Khums
Safi Settat Beni Mellal Erfoud El Goléa
Marrakech Haut Atlas Ouarzazate Béchar
Essaouira 13645ft Jebel Toubkal
Cap Rhir Agadir

ALGERIA LI

Idhân Awbârî
Fezzan

MOROCCO

Santa Cruz Arrecife
de la Palma
Santa Cruz Palma de Tenerife
Tenerife 12202ft
Gomera Gran
Canaria
Las
Palmas

Canary Islands
(Sp.)

EL AAIÚN

Western
Sahara
(Morocco)

Rio de Oro

Golfo de Cintra

Tropic of Cancer

Kediet ej Jill
▲2985ft

Cap Blanc Nouadhibou
Râs Timirist

Ouarâne

Tassili n'Ajjer

Mouydir

Plateau
du
Djado

Hoggar

Tahat
▲9578ft

Mont
Gréboun
▲7544ft

MAURITANIA

NOUAKCHOTT

Aklé Aouâna

Monts Timétrine

Aïr

NIGER

Hodh

Tombouctou

Talak

St-Louis Senegal Kaédi
Louga Ferlo
Cap Vert Thiès
DAKAR Kaolack

SENEGAL

Koumbi Saleh

Doro
Hombori Tondo
▲37880

Gao

Agadez

Tahoua

K
Lake
Chaa

THE
GAMBIA BANJUL

GUINEA-
BISSAU BISSAU

Tambacounda Gambia 1641m

Kayes

Niger

MALI

Mopti

NIAMEY

Birnin-
Kebbi

Maradi

Zinder

Labé

Kankan

BAMAKO Ségou Koutiala Ouahigouya
Sikasso

BURKINA FASO

OUAGADOUGOU

Katsina

Zaria

Gashua

Maiduguri

Kaura-
Namoda

Nguru

Hadejia

Azare

GUINEA

CONAKRY
Îles de Los
FREETOWN

Bintimani
6363ft

SIERRA
LEONE

Bebo Dioulasso

Korhogo

Gusau

Kano

Bauchi Bombel

Biu

Bolgatanga

Wa

Lake
Volta

Tanekas

Parakou

Saki Ilorin

ABUJA

Kaduna

Jos Jega

Kainji
Res.

NIGERIA

Benue Garoua

CÔTE
D'IVOIRE

Bo Makeni
Kenema

YAMOUSSOUKRO

Bouaké

Sunyani

Tamale

GHANA

TOGO

Ogbomoso

Ibadan

BENIN

Keffi
Lokoja

Makurdi

Dimlang
6691ft▲

Man

Abeng-
ourou

Afadjoto
29198▲

Mango Agou

Edo

Ife

Owo Idah

Okene

Enugu Gboko

Abakaliki

Benin
City Awka

CAMEROON

Foumban
Bafoussam

MONROVIA

Oumé

Dimbok

Koforidua
Cape
Coast

PORTO
NOVO

LOMÉ

Abeokuta

Lagos

Sapele

Warri

Onitsha Enugu

Aba

Nkongsamba

Douala

LIBERIA

San
Pédro

Abidjan

Grand-
Bassam

Tema ACCRA

Sekondi-
Takoradi

Bight of Benin

Port
Harcourt

MALABO

Pico Basile
9863ft▲

Bioko

YAOUNDÉ

Grain Coast

Ivory Coast

Gulf of
Guinea

SÃO TOMÉ
AND PRÍNCIPE

EQUATORIAL GUINEA

Príncipe
Pico de
São Tomé
6626ft▲ SÃO TOMÉ

LIBREVILLE

GABON

Sanga

São Tomé

Port Gentil

Lambaréné

Mont Iboundji
▲5150m

ATLANTIC OCEAN

BRAZZAVIL

Loubomo Nkayi

Pointe-Noire

Cabinda
(Ang.)

Boma Matadi

CAPE VERDE

Santo
Antão
Mindelo Sal
São
Nicolau Boa Vista
Fogo PRAIA Maio
Brava Pico São Tiago
9888ft▲

Equator

Scale 1: 26 140 000

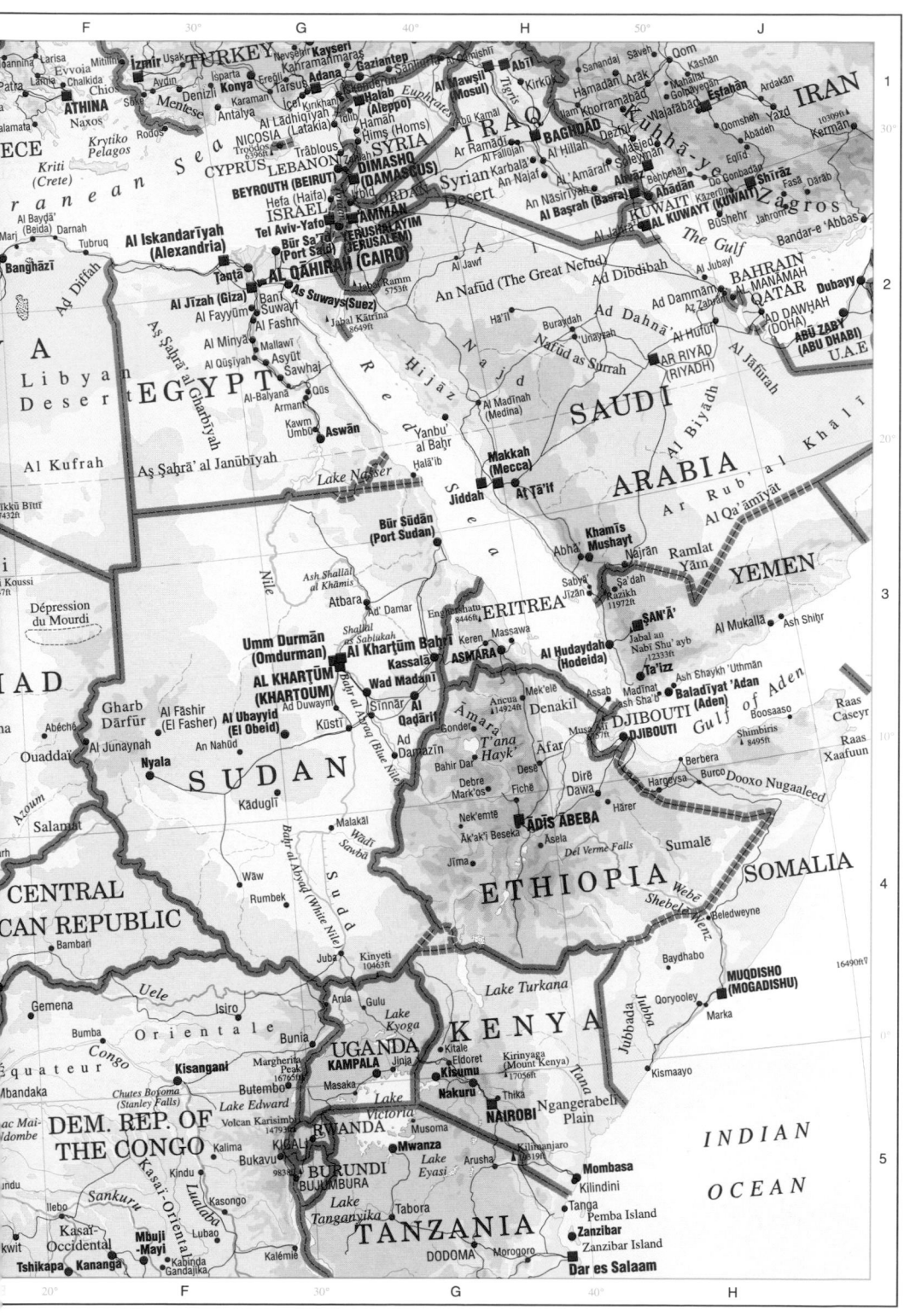

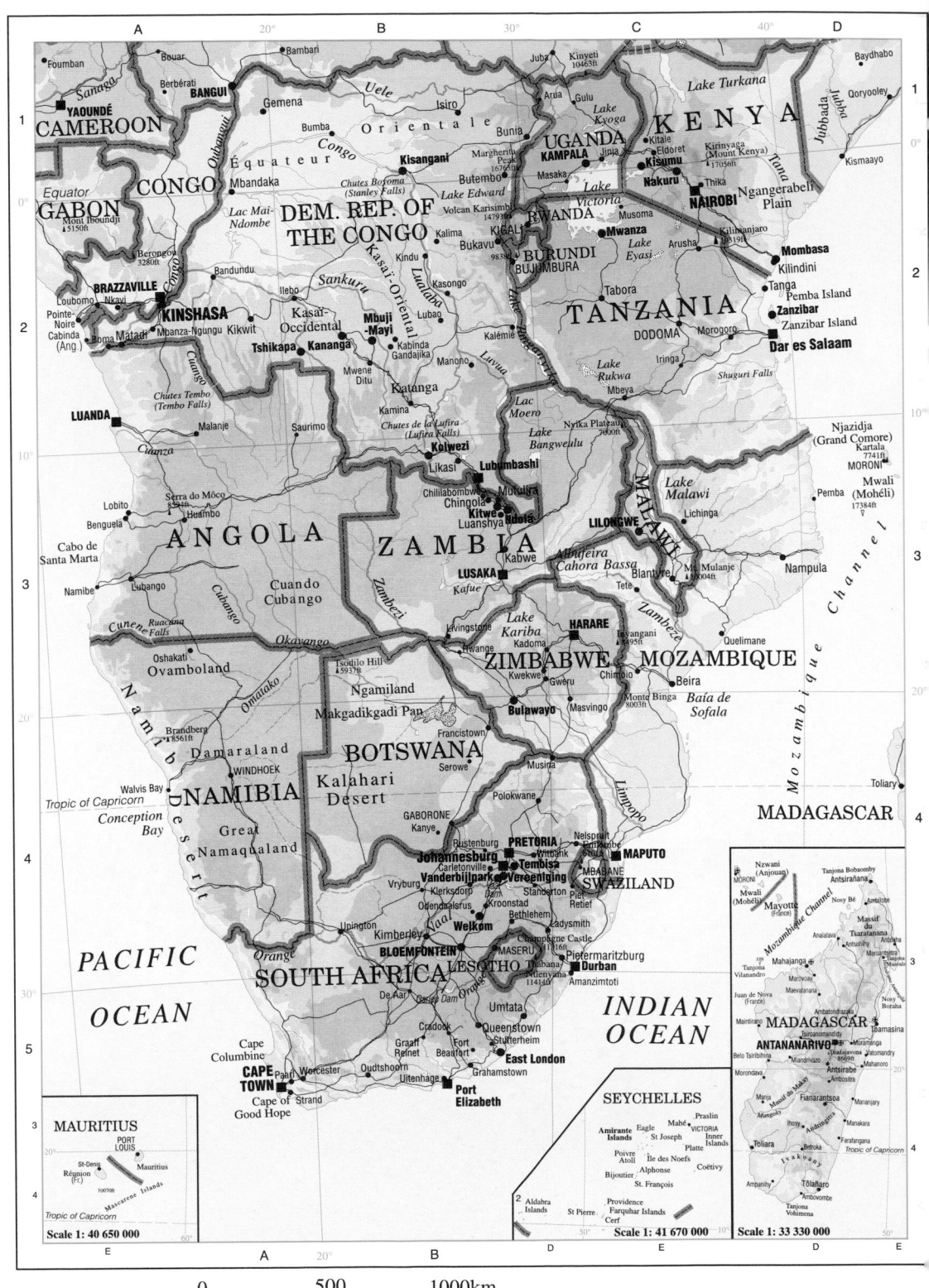

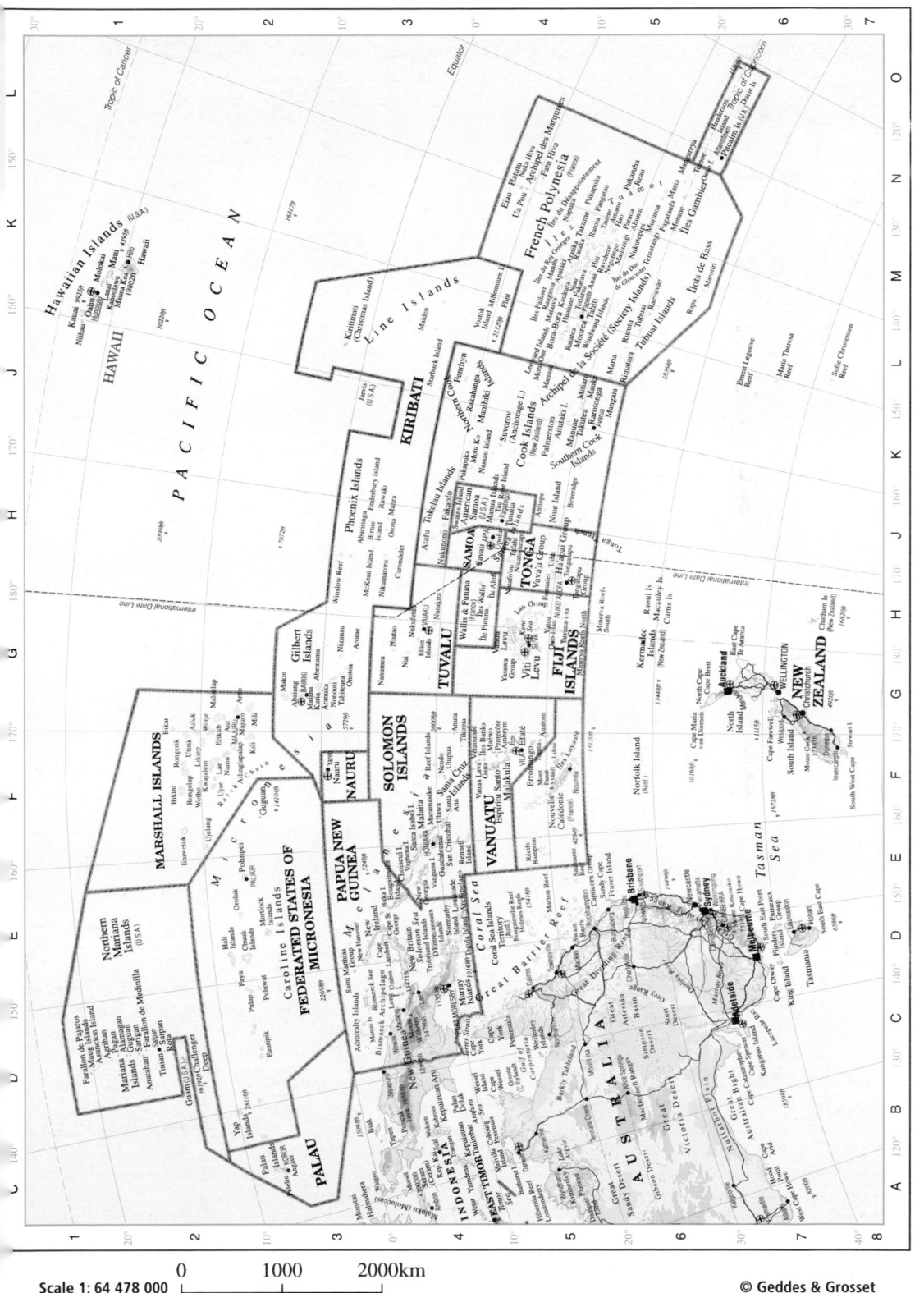

Scale 1: 64 478 000

| 0 | 1000 | 2000km |

| 0 | 600 | 1200miles |

© Geddes & Grosset

Bali Pulau Praya
Penida
Sumbawa Tanjung Karossa Memboro Payeti
Sumba Sawu Kupang Soe
9515ft Rote
Timor INDONESIA
Timor Sea

Cape Van Cape Croker
Diemen Croker Island
Dundee Str. Goulburn
Cobourg Island Elcho
Peninsula Island
82ft Cap

Bathurst Island
Melville Island Van Diemen
Charles Point Gulf
Darwin Arnhem Land

Ashmore Hibernia
Reef Reef
Cape Scott Pine Creek Numbulwar Mission
Cape M
Londonderry

Scott Joseph Daly Katherine
Reef Bonaparte Borrolo
Bonaparte Gulf
Archipelago
Drysdale River Kununurra Daly Waters
Adele National Park Wyndham Ord River Dam NORTHER
Island Buccaneer Lake Victoria Wave Hill Newcastle Waters
Archipelago Argyle River Downs Lake
Cape King Leopold Ranges Woods Bar
Lévêque Durack Ranges Tanami Desert Tennant Creek
Dampier Derby Fitzroy Kimberley Wildlife Sanctuary TERRITO
Land Crossing Plateau Halls Creek
Broome Fitzroy Lake
Edgar Range Gregory
Eighty Mile Beach McLarty Hills Lake Lucas AUSTRA
5178ft Great Sandy Lake Hazlett TERRITO
Port Hedland Desert Stuart Bluff Range Aileron
Barrow Island Dampier Lake Percival Lake
North West Cape Waukarlycarly Lakes Mackay Alice Springs
Onslow Chichester Range Lake Dora Lake Auld Macdonnell Ranges
National Park Lake George Lake Finke Gorge
Hamersley Range Lake Disappointment Macdonald National Park Simp
National Park Lake Des
Hamersley Range Newman WESTERN Neale Lake Finke
Barlee Range Gibson Desert Amadeus Ayers Rock-Mount
Collier Ranges Browne Range Olga National Park Kulgera
Tropic of Capricorn National Park Nature Reserve Petermann Ranges
Kennedy Range Barrow Range Tomkinson Ranges Musgrave Ranges
Carnarvon National Park Lake Lake Warburton Range Birksgate Range Everard Ranges
Shark Gascoyne Robinson Ranges Gregory Buchanan Lake Mt Willoughby
Bay Junction Macadam Plains Nabberu Gillen Baker
Lake Lake Lake
453ft Meekatharra Wiluna Carnegie A Cool
Yeo Great Victoria Everard
AUSTRALIA Lake Lake Lake Desert Serpentine
Shake Way Darlot Throssell Lake Lakes Lake Dey-Dey
Cue Lake Leonora Laverton Gidgi Lake Maurice SOUTH AU
Mount Austin Sandstone Lake Great Victoria Desert Ooldea
Magnet Carey Nature Reserve
Lake Lake Plumridge Tarcoola
Mullewa Barlee Menzies Ballard Minigwal Lakes Lake
Geraldton Paynes Find Lake Rawlinna Everard
Houtman Mongers Moore Lake Rebecca Nullarbor Plain Ceduna
Abrolhos Lake Lake Deborah Kalgoorlie Hampton Tableland Eucla Motel Penong
Dongara Moora West Coolgardie Great Streaky Bay
Beacon Lake Deborah Lake Lefroy 213ft Anxious Bay
Bullfinch East Lake Australian Bight Elliston
Merredin Southern Seabrook Cowan
Stirling Northam Cross Lake Dundas Balladonia Port L
Wanneroo The Johnston Morseman Cape Arid Catast
Perth Gosnells Lakes National Park Russell Range
13787ft Armadale Corrigin Fl
Fremantle Narrogin Lake Grace Cape Arid
Bunbury Katanning Stirling Range Ravensthorpe Esperance
Cape Naturaliste Wagin National Park Fitzgerald River
Busselton National Park Archipelago of
Augusta Manjimup Range Hood Point the Recherche
Cape Leeuwin Denmark Cheyne Bay Bremer Bay
West Cape Albany
Howe

INDIAN OCEAN

8200ft

Scale 1: 18 182 000

0 300 600km

0 150 300miles

Scale 1: 8 696 000

0   150   300km

0   75   150miles

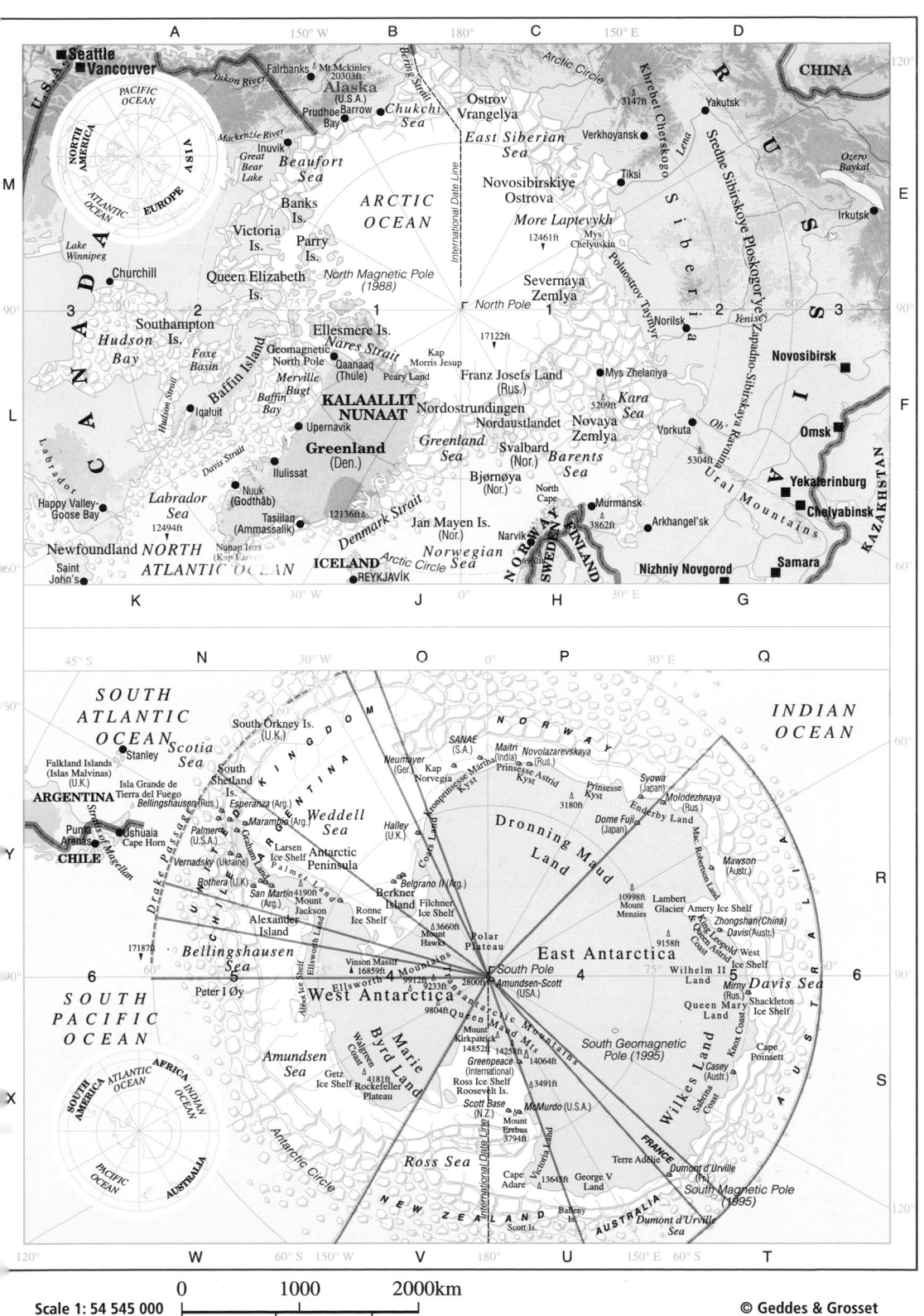

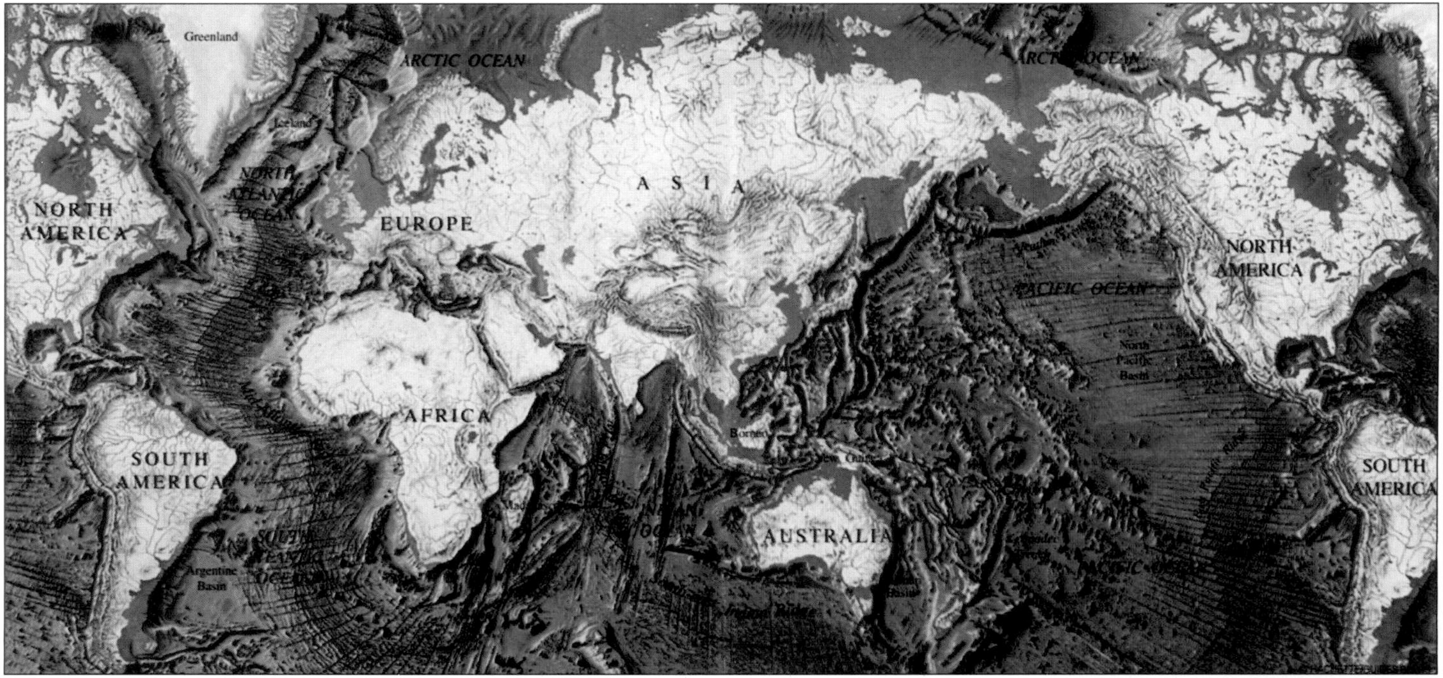

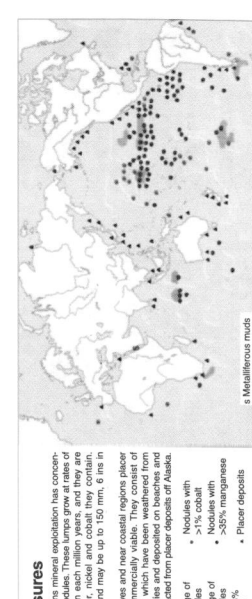

Seabed treasures

In the deeper sea regions mineral exploitation has concentrated on manganese nodules. These lumps grow at rates of between 3-8 mm, .25 in each million years, and they are valuable for the copper, nickel and cobalt they contain. Granules vary in size and may be up to 150 mm, 6 ins in diameter.

On the continental shelves and near coastal regions placer deposits are often commercially viable. They consist of heavy mineral particles which have been weathered from locally occuring ore bodies and deposited on beaches and in estuaries. Gold is extracted from placer deposits off Alaska.

☐ Moderate coverage of manganese nodules	• Nodules with >1% cobalt
▨ Extensive coverage of manganese nodules	• Nodules with >35% manganese
• Nodules with >1.8% nickel and copper	• Placer deposits

s Metalliferous muds

Underwater landscapes

Topography of the ocean floor can be divided into two distinct features: the continental margins and the deep sea basins.

The character of the ocean basin depends on the extent to which sediments mask the crust and also the degree of volcanic activity. The sediments may be either pelagic or terrigenous. The latter are brought down by turbidity currents which are avalanches of silt and sand from the continental shelf. These powerful currents can cut channels in the continental shelf such as the Hatteras Canyon off North America and transport material thousands of kilometres.

On the continental shelf, sediments are affected by waves, tidal currents and changes in sea level.

a. Shallow areas are most accessible, they may overlie oil and gas bearing rock.
b. The continental slope defines the edge of the continental block.
c. Deep sea floors can be very flat with gradients less than 1:1000.
d. A Guyot is a submarine volcanic mountain with a completely smooth top.
e. Volcanic islands can be higher above the seabed than Everest is above sea level.
f. Mid ocean ridges. New oceanic crust is formed along these.
g. Atolls are extinct volcanoes which have been colonized by coral.
h. Deep sea trenches. Oceanic crust is destroyed under neighbouring plates.

Map Index

APPENDICES

Appendix 1

World Facts

Afghanistan
Area: 251,772 sq mi/652,225 sq km
Population: 20,833,000
Capital: Kabul
Other cities: Herat, Kandahar, Mazar-i-Sharif
Form of government: Islamic Republic
Religions: Sunni Islam, Shia Islam
Currency: Afghani

Albania
Area: 11,100 sq mi/28,748 sq km
Population: 3,581,000
Capital: Tirana (Tiranè)
Other cities: Durrès, Shkodèr, Vlorë
Form of government: Republic
Religions: Sunni Islam, Albanian Orthodox, RC
Currency: Lek

Algeria
Area: 919,595 sq mi/2,381,741 sq km
Population: 29,168,000
Capital: Algiers (El Djazair, Alger)
Other cities: Oran, Constantine, 'Annaba
Form of government: Republic
Religion: Sunni Islam
Currency: Algerian Dinar

American Samoa *see* Samoa, American.

Andorra
Area: 175 sq mi/453 sq km
Population: 65,900
Capital: Andorra la Vella
Form of government: Republic
Religion: RC
Currency: Euro

Angola
Area: 481,354 sq mi/1,246,700 sq km
Population: 11,185,000
Capital: Luanda
Other cities: Huambo, Lobito, Benguela
Form of government: People's Republic
Religions: RC, traditional beliefs
Currency: Kwanza

Anguilla
Area: 37 sq mi/96 sq km
Population: 12,400
Capital: The Valley
Form of government: British Overseas Territory
Religion: Christianity
Currency: East Caribbean Dollar

Antigua and Barbuda
Area: 171 sq mi/442 sq km
Population: 66,000
Capital: St John's
Form of government: Constitutional Monarchy
Religion: Christianity (mainly Anglicanism)
Currency: East Caribbean Dollar

Argentina
Area: 1,073,518 sq mi/2,780,400 sq km
Population: 39,920,000
Capital: Buenos Aires
Other cities: Cordoba, Rosario, Mar del Plata, Mendoza, La Plata
Form of government: Republic
Religion: RC
Currency: Peso

Armenia
Area: 11,506 sq mi/29,800 sq km
Population: 2,796,000
Capital: Yerevan
Other major city: Kunmayr (Gyumri)
Form of government: Republic
Religion: Christianity
Currency: Dram

Aruba
Area: 75 sq mi/193 sq km
Population: 87,000
Capital: Oranjestad
Form of government: Self-governing Dutch Territory
Religion: Christianity
Currency: Aruban Florin

Australia
Area: 2,988,902 sq mi/7,741,220 sq km
Population: 20,264,000
Capital: Canberra
Other cities: Adelaide, Brisbane, Melbourne, Perth, Sydney
Form of government: Federal Parliamentary State
Religion: Christianity
Currency: Australian Dollar

Austria
Area: 32,378 sq mi/83,859 sq km
Population: 8,192,000
Capital: Vienna (Wien)
Other cities: Graz, Linz, Salzburg, Innsbruck
Form of government: Federal Republic
Religion: RC
Currency: Euro

Azerbaijan

Area: 33,436 sq mi/86,600 sq km
Population: 7,961,000
Capital: Baku
Other major city: Sumqayit
Form of government: Republic
Religions: Sunni Islam, Russian Orthodox
Currency: Azerbaijani Manat

Azores

Area: 901 sq mi/2,335 sq km
Population: 336,100
Capital: Ponta Delgada

Bahamas, The

Area: 5,358 sq mi/13,878 sq km
Population: 284,000
Capital: Nassau
Other important city: Freeport
Form of government: Constitutional Monarchy
Religion: Christianity
Currency: Bahamian Dollar

Bahrain

Area: 268 sq mi/694 sq km
Population: 698, 585
Capital: Manama (Al Manamah)
Form of government: Constitutional Hereditary Monarchy
Religions: Shia Islam, Sunni Islam, Christianity
Currency: Bahraini Dinar

Bangladesh

Area: 55,598 sq mi/143,998 sq km
Population: 147,365,000
Capital: Dhaka
Other cities: Chittagong, Khulna, Narayanganj, Saidpur
Form of government: Republic
Religions: Sunni Islam, Hindu
Currency: Taka

Barbados

Area: 166 sq mi/430 sq km
Population: 279,000
Capital: Bridgetown
Form of government: Parliamentary Democracy
Religion: Christianity
Currency: Barbados Dollar

Belarus (Belorussia, Byelorussia)

Area: 80,155 sq mi/207,600 sq km
Population: 10,293,000
Capital: Minsk
Other cities: Homyel (Gomel), Vitsyebsk, Mahilyov
Form of government: Republic
Religions: Eastern Orthodox, RC, Islam
Currency: Belarusian Ruble

Belau *see* **Palau**.

Belgium

Area: 11,783 sq mi/30,519 sq km
Population: 10,379,000
Capital: Brussels
Other cities: Antwerp, Charleroi, Ghent, Liège, Oostende
Form of government: Constitutional Monarchy
Religion: RC
Currency: Euro

Belize

Area: 8,763 sq mi/22,696 sq km
Population: 287,730
Capital: Belmopan
Other major city: Belize City
Form of government: Parliamentary Democracy
Religion: Christianity
Currency: Belizean Dollar

Belorussia *see* **Belarus**.

Benin

Area: 43,484 sq mi/112,622 sq km
Population: 7,862,000
Capital: Porto-Novo
Form of government: Republic
Religions: Traditional beliefs, RC, Sunni Islam
Currency: CFA Franc

Bermuda

Area: 20 sq mi/53 sq km
Population: 64,000
Capital: Hamilton
Form of government: British Overseas Territory
Religions: Protestantism, RC
Currency: Bermudan Dollar

Bhutan

Area: 18,147 sq mi/47,000 sq km
Population: 2,279,000
Capital: Thimphu (Thimbu)
Form of government: Constitutional Monarchy
Religions: Buddhism, Hinduism
Currency: Ngultrum, Indian Rupee

Bolivia

Area: 424,165 sq mi/1,098,581 sq km
Population: 8,989,000
Capital: La Paz(administrative), Sucre (legal)
Other major city: Cochabamba
Form of government: Republic
Religion: RC
Currency: Boliviano

Bosnia-Herzegovina

Area: 19,735 sq mi/51,129 sq km
Population: 4,510,000
Capital: Sarajevo
Other cities: Banja Luka, Mostar, Tuzla
Form of government: Republic
Religions: Eastern Orthodox, Sunni Islam, RC
Currency: Marka

Botswana

Area: 224,607 sq mi/581,730 sq km
Population: 1,639,000
Capital: Gaborone
Other cities: Francistown, Molepolole, Mahalapye
Form of government: Republic
Religions: Traditional beliefs, Christianity
Currency: Pula

Brazil

Area: 3,300,171 sq mi/8,547,403 sq km
Population: 188,078,000
Capital: Brasília
Other cities: Balem, Belo Horizonte, Curitiba, Porto
  Alegre, Recife, Rio de Janeiro, Salvador, São Paulo
Form of government: Federal Republic
Religion: RC
Currency: Real

British Indian Ocean Territory

The Chagos Archipelago is a group of five coral atolls in
the middle of the Indian Ocean. A British colony with an
area of 20 square miles/52 square kilometres.

Brunei

Area: 2,226 sq mi/5,765 sq km
Population: 379,444
Capital: Bandar Seri Begawan
Other cities: Kuala Belait, Seria
Form of government: Monarchy (Sultanate)
Religion: Sunni Islam
Currency: Bruneian Dollar

Bulgaria

Area: 42,823 sq mi/110,912 sq km
Population: 7,385,000
Capital: Sofia (Sofiya)
Other cities: Burgas, Plovdiv, Ruse, Varna
Form of government: Republic
Religion: Eastern Orthodox
Currency: Lev

Burkina Faso (Burkina)

Area: 105,792 sq mi/274,000 sq km
Population: 13,902,000
Capital: Ouagadougou
Other cities: Bobo-Dioulasso, Koudougou
Form of government: Republic
Religions: Traditional beliefs, Sunni Islam
Currency: CFA Franc

Burma *see* **Myanmar.**

Burundi

Area: 10,747 sq mi/27,834 sq km
Population: 8,090,000
Capital: Bujumbura
Form of government: Republic
Religions: Christianity, traditional beliefs
Currency: Burundi Franc

Byelorussia *see* **Belarus.**

Cambodia

Area: 69,898 sq mi/181,035 sq km
Population: 13,881,000
Capital: Phnom-Penh
Other cities: Battambang, Kampong Cham
Form of government: Constitutional Monarchy
Religion: Buddhism
Currency: Riel

Cameroon

Area: 183,569 sq mi/475,442 sq km
Population: 17,340,000
Capital: Yaoundé
Other major city: Douala
Form of government: Republic
Religions: Traditional beliefs, Christianity,
  Sunni Islam
Currency: CFA Franc

Canada

Area: 3,849,674 sq mi/9,970,610 sq km
Population: 33,098,000
Capital: Ottawa
Other cities: Calgary, Toronto, Montréal, Vancouver,
  Québec City, Winnipeg
Form of government: Federal Parliamentary State
Religions: RC, United Church of Canada,
  Anglicanism
Currency: Canadian Dollar

Canary Islands

Area: 2,808 sq mi/7,273 sq km
Population: 1,493,000
Capital: Las Palmas, on Gran Canaria
Currency: Euro

Cape Verde

Area: 1,557 sq mi/4,033 sq km
Population: 420,979
Capital: Praia
Form of government: Republic
Religion: RC
Currency: Cape Verdean Escudo

Cayman Islands
Area: 102 sq mi/264 sq km
Population: 45,436
Capital: George Town, on Grand Cayman
Form of government: British Overseas Territory
Religion: Christianity
Currency: Cayman Islands Dollar

Central African Republic
Area: 240,535 sq mi/622,984 sq km
Population: 4,303,000
Capital: Bangui
Other cities: Bambari, Bangassou
Form of government: Republic
Religions: Traditional beliefs, RC
Currency: CFA Franc

Chad
Area: 495,755 sq mi/1,284,000 sq km
Population: 9,944,000
Capital: N'Djamena
Other cities: Sarh, Moundou, Abéché
Form of government: Republic
Religions: Sunni Islam, Christianity, traditional beliefs
Currency: CFA Franc

Channel Islands
British Crown dependencies: the main islands are Jersey and Guernsey, but the group also includes Alderney, Sark, Herm and Brechou. The Channel Islands have an area of 75 square miles/194 square kilometres and a population of 143,000.

Chile
Area: 292,135 sq mi/756,626 sq km
Population: 16,134,000
Capital: Santiago
Other cities: Arica, Concepcion, Valparaiso, Viña del Mar
Form of government: Republic
Religion: RC
Currency: Chilean Peso

China
Area: 3,705,408 sq mi/9,596,961 sq km
Population: 1,313,973,000
Capital: Beijing (Peking)
Other cities: Chengdu, Guangzhou, Harbin, Shanghai, Tianjin, Wuhan
Form of government: People's Republic
Religions: Buddhism, Taoism (officially atheist)
Currency: Yuan

Colombia
Area: 439,737 sq mi/1,138,914 sq km
Population: 43,593,000
Capital: Bogotá
Other cities: Barranquilla, Cali, Cartagena, Medellin
Form of government: Republic
Religion: RC
Currency: Colombian Peso

Comoros
Area: 720 sq mi/1,865 sq km excluding Mayotte
Population: 690,948
Capital: Moroni
Other cities: Dornoni, Fomboni, Mutsamudu, Mitsamiouli
Form of government: Republic
Religion: Sunni Islam
Currency: Comoran Franc

Congo, Republic of
Area: 132,047 sq mi/342,000 sq km
Population: 3,702,000
Capital: Brazzaville
Other major city: Pointe-Noire
Form of government: Republic
Religions: Christianity, traditional beliefs
Currency: CFA Franc

Congo, Democratic Republic of
Area: 905,355 sq mi/2,344,858 sq km
Population: 62,660,000
Capital: Kinshasa
Other cities: Bukavu, Lubumbashi, Matadi, Mbuji-Mayi, Kananga, Kisangani
Form of government: Transitional
Religions: RC, Protestantism, Islam
Currency: Congolese Franc

Cook Islands
Area: 93 sq mi/240 sq km
Population: 21,388
Capital: Avarua, on Rarotonga
Form of government: Self-governing in association with New Zealand
Religion: Christianity
Currency: New Zealand Dollar

Costa Rica
Area: 19,730 sq mi/51,100 sq km
Population: 4,075,000
Capital: San José
Other cities: Alajuela, Límon, Puntarenas
Form of government: Republic
Religion: RC
Currency: Costa Rican Colon

Côte d'Ivoire
Area: 124,504 sq mi/322,463 sq km
Population: 17,654,000
Capital: Yamoussoukro
Other cities: Abidjan, Bouaké, Daloa
Form of government: Republic
Religions: Traditional beliefs, Sunni Islam, RC
Currency: CFA Franc

Croatia (Hrvatska)

Area: 21,824 sq mi/56,538 sq km
Population: 4,501,000
Capital: Zagreb
Other cities: Osijek, Rijeka, Split
Form of government: Republic
Religions: RC, Eastern Orthodox
Currency: Kuna

Cuba

Area: 42,804 sq mi/110,861 sq km
Population: 11,382,000
Capital: Havana (La Habana)
Other cities: Camaguey, Holguin, Santa Clara, Santiago de Cuba
Form of government: Socialist Republic
Religion: RC
Currency: Cuban Peso and Convertible Peso

Cyprus

Area: 3,572 sq mi/9,251 sq km
Population: 784,301
Capital: Nicosia (Lefkosia)
Other cities: Famagusta, Limassol, Larnaca
Form of government: Republic
Religions: Greek Orthodox, Sunni Islam
Currency: Cypriot Pound and Turkish New Lira

Czech Republic

Area: 30,450 sq mi/78,864 sq km
Population: 10,235,000
Capital: Prague (Praha)
Other cities: Brno, Olomouc, Ostrava, Plzen
Form of government: Republic
Religions: RC, Protestantism
Currency: Czech Koruna

Denmark

Area: 16,639 sq mi/43,094 sq km
Population: 5,450,000 (excluding the FAEROE ISLANDS)
Capital: Copenhagen (København)
Other cities: Ålborg, Århus, Odense
Form of government: Constitutional Monarchy
Religion: Lutheranism
Currency: Danish Krone

Djibouti

Area: 8,958 sq mi/23,200 sq km
Population: 486,530
Capital: Djibouti
Form of government: Republic
Religion: Sunni Islam
Currency: Djiboutian Franc

Dominica

Area: 290 sq mi/751 sq km
Population: 69,000
Capital: Roseau
Form of government: Republic
Religion: RC
Currency: East Caribbean Dollar

Dominican Republic

Area: 18,816 sq mi/48,734 sq km
Population: 9,183,000
Capital: Santo Domingo
Other cities: Barahona, Santiago, San Pedro de Macoris
Form of government: Republic
Religion: RC
Currency: Dominican Peso

Ecuador

Area: 109,484 sq mi/283,561 sq km
Population: 13,547,000
Capital: Quito
Other cities: Ambato, Guayaquil, Cuenca, Machala
Form of government: Republic
Religion: RC
Currency: US Dollar

Egypt

Area: 386,887 sq mi/1,001,449 sq km
Population: 78,603,000
Capital: Cairo (El Qâhira)
Other cities: Alexandria, Giza, Port Said, Suez
Form of government: Republic
Religions: Sunni Islam, Christianity
Currency: Egyptian Pound

El Salvador

Area: 8,124 sq mi/21,041 sq km
Population: 6,822,000
Capital: San Salvador
Other cities: Santa Ana, San Miguel
Form of government: Republic
Religion: RC
Currency: US Dollar

Equatorial Guinea

Area: 10,830 sq mi/28,051 sq km
Population: 540,100
Capital: Malabo
Other major city: Bata
Form of government: Republic
Religion: RC
Currency: CFA Franc

Eritrea

Area: 45,406 sq mi/117,600 sq km
Population: 4,786,000
Capital: Asmara
Other cities: Mitsiwa, Keren, Nak'fa, Ak'ordat
Form of government: Transitional Government
Religions: Sunni Islam, Christianity
Currency: Nakfa

Estonia

Area: 17,413 sq mi/45,227 sq km
Population: 1,324,000
Capital: Tallinn
Other cities: Tartu, Narva, Pärnu
Form of government: Republic
Religions: Eastern Orthodox, Lutheranism
Currency: Estonian Kroon

Ethiopia
Area: 426,373 sq mi/1,104,300 sq km
Population: 74,777,000
Capital: Addis Ababa (Adis Abeba)
Other cities: Dire Dawa, Gonder, Jima
Form of government: Federal Republic
Religions: Ethiopian Orthodox, Sunni Islam
Currency: Ethiopian Birr

Faeroe (Faroe) Islands (Føroyar)
Area: 540 sq mi/1,399 sq km
Population: 47,246
Capital: Tørshavn
Form of government: Self-governing Region of Denmark
Religion: Lutheranism
Currency: Danish Krone

Falkland Islands
Area: 4,700 sq mi/12,173 sq km
Population: 2,967
Capital: Stanley
Form of government: British Overseas Territory
Religion: Christianity
Currency: Falkland Pound

Fiji
Area: 7,056 sq mi/18,274 sq km
Population: 905,949
Capital: Suva
Form of government: Republic
Religions: Christianity, Hinduism
Currency: Fijian Dollar

Finland
Area: 130,559 sq mi/338,145 sq km
Population: 5,231,000
Capital: Helsinki (Helsingfors)
Other cities: Turku, Tampere
Form of government: Republic
Religion: Lutheranism
Currency: Euro

France
Area: 212,935 sq mi/551,500 sq km
Population: 60,876,000
Capital: Paris
Other cities: Bordeaux, Lyon, Marseille, Nantes, Nice,
Toulouse, Strasbourg
Form of government: Republic
Religion: RC
Currency: Euro

French Guiana (Guyane)
Area: 34,749 sq mi/90,000 sq km
Population: 199,509
Capital: Cayenne
Form of government: French Overseas Department
Religion: RC
Currency: Euro

French Polynesia
Area: 1,544 sq mi/4,000 sq km
Population: 274,578
Capital: Papeete
Form of government: Overseas Territory of France
Religions: Protestantism, RC
Currency: CFP Franc

French Southern and Antarctic Territories
Territories in Antarctica and the Antarctic Ocean administered by France that include the Crozet Islands and Kerguelen.

Gabon
Area: 103,347 sq mi/267,668 sq km
Population: 1,424,000
Capital: Libreville
Other major city: Port Gentile
Form of government: Republic
Religions: Christianity, traditional beliefs
Currency: CFA Franc

Gambia, The
Area: 4,361 sq mi/11,295 sq km
Population: 1,641,000
Capital: Banjul
Form of government: Republic
Religions: Sunni Islam, Christianity
Currency: Dalasi

Georgia
Area: 26,911 sq mi/69,700 sq km
Population: 4,661,000
Capital: T'bilisi
Other cities: Kutaisi, Rustavi, Batumi
Form of government: Republic
Religions: Georgian and Russian Orthodox, Islam
Currency: Lari

Germany
Area: 137,735 sq mi/356,733 sq km
Population: 82,422,000
Capital: Berlin
Other cities: Bonn, Cologne, Dortmund, Düsseldorf,
Essen, Frankfurt, Hamburg, Leipzig, Munich,
Stuttgart
Form of government: Federal Republic
Religions: Protestantism, RC
Currency: Euro

Ghana
Area: 92,100 sq mi/238,537 sq km
Population: 22,409,350
Capital: Accra
Other cities: Sekondi-Takoradi, Kumasi, Tamale
Form of government: Republic
Religions: Christianity, Islam, traditional beliefs
Currency: Cedi

Gibraltar

Area: 2.5 sq mi/6.5 sq km
Population: 27,928
Capital: Gibraltar
Form of government: British Overseas Territory
Religion: Christianity
Currency: Gibraltar Pound

Greece

Area: 50,949 sq mi/131,957 sq km
Population: 10,688,000
Capital: Athens (Athínai)
Other cities: Iráklian, Lárisa, Patras, Piraeus,
  Thessaloníki
Form of government: Republic
Religion: Greek Orthodox
Currency: Euro

Greenland (Kalaallit Nunaat)

Area: 840,000 sq mi/2,175,600 sq km
Population: 56,361
Capital: Gothåb (Nuuk)
Form of government: Self-governing Region of Denmark
Religion: Lutheranism
Currency: Danish Krone

Grenada

Area: 133 sq mi/344 sq km
Population: 89,703
Capital: Saint George's
Form of government: Independent State within the Com-
  monwealth
Religions: RC, Anglicanism, Methodism
Currency: East Caribbean Dollar

Guadeloupe

Area: 658 sq mi/1,705 sq km
Population: 431,000
Capital: Basse Terre
Other main town: Pointe-à-Pitre
Form of government: French Overseas Department
Religion: RC
Currency: Euro

Guam

Area: 212 sq mi/549 sq km
Population: 171,019
Capital: Agana
Form of government: Unincorporated Territory of the
  USA
Religion: RC
Currency: US dollar

Guatemala

Area: 42,042 sq mi/108,889 sq km
Population: 12,293,000
Capital: Guatemala City
Other cities: Cobán, Puerto Barrios, Quezaltenango
Form of government: Republic
Religion: RC
Currency: Quetzal, US Dollar

Guinea

Area: 94,926 sq mi/245,857 sq km
Population: 9,690,000
Capital: Conakry
Other cities: Kankan, Kindia, Labé
Form of government: Republic
Religion: Sunni Islam
Currency: Guinean Franc

Guinea-Bissau

Area: 13,948 sq mi/36,125 sq km
Population: 1,442,000
Capital: Bissau
Form of government: Republic
Religions: Traditional beliefs, Sunni Islam
Currency: CFA Franc

Guyana

Area: 83,000 sq mi/214,969 sq km
Population: 767,245
Capital: Georgetown
Other cities: Linden, New Amsterdam
Form of government: Republic
Religions: Christianity, Hinduism, Islam
Currency: Guyanese Dollar

Guyane *see* French Guiana.

Haiti

Area: 10,714 sq mi/27,750 sq km
Population: 8,308,000
Capital: Port-au-Prince
Other towns: Cap-Haïtien, Les Cayes, Gonaïves
Form of government: Republic
Religions: RC, Voodooism
Currency: Gourde

Honduras

Area: 43,277 sq mi/112,088 sq km
Population: 7,326,000
Capital: Tegucigalpa
Other cities: San Pedro Sula, La Ceiba, Puerto Cortès
Form of government: Republic
Religion: RC
Currency: Lempira

Hong Kong

Area: 415 sq mi/1,075 sq km
Population: 6,940,200
Form of government: Special Administrative Region of
  China
Religions: Buddhism, Taoism, Christianity
Currency: Hong Kong Dollar

Hungary

Area: 35,920 sq mi/93,032 sq km
Population: 9,981,000
Capital: Budapest
Other cities: Debrecen, Miskolc, Pécs, Szeged
Form of government: Republic
Religions: RC, Calvinism, Lutheranism
Currency: Forint

Iceland.
Area: 39,769 sq mi/103,000 sq km
Population: 299,388
Capital: Reykjavík
Other cities: Akureyri, Kópavogur
Form of government: Republic
Religion: Lutheranism
Currency: Icelandic Krona

India
Area: 1,269,346 sq mi/3,287,590 sq km
Population: 1,095,351,000
Capital: New Delhi
Other cities: Ahmadabad, Bangalore, Bombay, Calcutta,
Delhi, Madras, Hyderabad, Kanpur
Form of government: Federal Republic
Religions: Hinduism, Islam, Sikkism, Christianity,
Jainism, Buddhism
Currency: Indian Rupee

Indonesia
Area: 735,358 sq mi/1,904,569 sq km
Population: 245,452,000
Capital: Jakarta
Other cities: Bandung, Medan, Palembang, Semarang,
Surabaya
Form of government: Republic
Religions: Sunni Islam, Christianity, Hinduism
Currency: Indonesian Rupiah

Iran, Islamic Republic of
Area: 634,293 sq mi/1,648,195 sq km
Population: 68,688,000
Capital: Tehran
Other cities: Esfahan, Mashhad, Tabriz
Form of government: Republic
Religion: Shia Islam
Currency: Iranian Rial

Iraq
Area: 169,235 sq mi/438,317 sq km
Population: 26,783,000
Capital: Baghdad
Other cities: Al-Basrah, Al Mawsil
Form of government: Republic
Religions: Shia Islam, Sunni Islam
Currency: New Iraqi Dinar

Ireland, Republic of
Area: 27,137 sq mi/70,284 sq km
Population: 4,062,000
Capital: Dublin (Baile Atha Cliath)
Other cities: Cork, Galway, Limerick, Waterford
Form of government: Republic
Religion: RC
Currency: Euro

Israel
Area: 8,130 sq mi/21,056 sq km
Population: 6,352,000
Capital: Tel Aviv (Tel Aviv-Yafo)
Other cities: Jerusalem, Haifa
Form of government: Parliamentary Democracy
Religions: Judaism, Sunni Islam, Christianity
Currency: New Israeli Shekel

Italy
Area: 116,320 sq mi/301,268 sq km
Population: 58,133,000
Capital: Rome (Roma)
Other cities: Milan, Naples, Turin, Genoa, Palermo,
Florence
Form of government: Republic
Religion: RC
Currency: Euro

Jamaica
Area: 4,243 sq mi/10,990 sq km
Population: 2,758,000
Capital: Kingston
Other town: Montego Bay
Form of government: Parliamentary Democracy
Religions: Protestantism, Anglicanism, RC
Currency: Jamaican Dollar

Japan
Area: 145,870 sq mi/377,801 sq km
Population: 127,463,000
Capital: Tokyo
Other cities: Osaka, Nagoya, Sapporo, Kobe, Kyoto,
Yokohama
Form of government: Constitutional Monarchy
Religions: Shintoism, Buddhism, Christianity
Currency: Yen

Jordan
Area: 37,738 sq mi/97,740 sq km
Population: 5,906,000
Capital: Amman
Other cities: Aqaba, Irbid, Zarqa
Form of government: Constitutional Monarchy
Religion: Sunni Islam
Currency: Jordanian Dinar

Kazakhstan
Area:1,049,156 sq mi/2,717,300 sq km
Population: 15,671,000
Capital: Astana
Other major city: Almaty
Form of government: Republic
Religions: Sunni Islam, Russian Orthodox
Currency: Tenge

Kenya

Area: 224,081 sq mi/580,367 sq km
Population: 34,707,000
Capital: Nairobi
Other towns: Mombasa, Eldoret, Kisumu, Nakuru
Form of government: Republic
Religions: RC, Protestantism, Islam, traditional beliefs
Currency: Kenyan Shilling

Kiribati

Area: 280 sq mi/726 sq km
Population: 105,432,000
Capital: Tarawa
Government: Republic
Religions: RC, Protestantism
Currency: Australian Dollar

Korea, Democratic People's Republic of (North Korea)

Area: 46,540 sq mi/120,538 sq km
Population: 23,113,000
Capital: Pyongyang
Other cities: Chongjin, Wonsan, Hamhung
Form of government: Socialist Republic
Religions: Buddhism, Confucianism, Chondogyo (a combination of Taoism and Confucianism)
Currency: North Korean Won

Korea, Republic of (South Korea)

Area: 38,368 sq mi/99,373 sq km
Population: 48,846,000
Capital: Seoul
Other cities: Pusan, Taegu
Form of government: Republic
Religions: Buddhism, Christianity, Confucianism, Chondogyo (a combination of Taoism and Confucianism)
Currency: South Korean Won

Kuwait

Area: 6,880 sq mi/17,818 sq km
Population: 2,418,100
Capital: Kuwait City (Al Kuwayt)
Government: Constitutional Hereditary Emirate
Religions: Sunni Islam, Shia Islam
Currency: Kuwaiti Dinar

Kyrgyzstan

Area: 76,641 sq mi/198,500 sq km
Population: 5,213,000
Capital: Bishkek
Other major city: Osh
Form of government: Republic
Religions: Sunni Islam, Russian Orthodox
Currency: Som

Laos

Area: 91,429 sq mi/236,800 sq km
Population: 6,368,000
Capital: Vientiane
Other cities: Luang Prabang, Savannakhét, Paksé
Form of government: People's Democratic Republic
Religion: Buddhism, traditional beliefs
Currency: Kip

Latvia

Area: 24,942 sq mi/64,600 sq km
Population: 2,274,000
Capital: Riga
Other cities: Liepaja, Daugavpils
Form of government: Republic
Religion: Lutheranism, RC, Russian Orthodox
Currency: Latvian Lat

Lebanon

Area: 4,015 sq mi/10,400 sq km
Population: 3,874,900
Capital: Beirut (Beyrouth)
Other important cities: Tripoli, Sidon
Form of government: Republic
Religions: Shia Islam, Sunni Islam, Christianity
Currency: Lebanese Pound

Lesotho

Area: 11,720 sq mi/30,355 sq km
Population: 2,022,000
Capital: Maseru
Form of government: Constitutional Monarchy
Religions: Christianity, traditional beliefs
Currency: Loti, South African Rand

Liberia

Area: 43,000 sq mi/111,369 sq km
Population: 3,042,000
Capital: Monrovia
Other major city: Buchanan
Form of government: Republic
Religions: Traditional beliefs, Christianity, Sunni Islam
Currency: Liberian Dollar

Libya

Area: 679,362 sq mi/1,759,540 sq km
Population: 5,900,739
Capital: Tripoli (Tarabulus)
Other cities: Benghazi, Misrãta
Form of government: Socialist People's Republic
Religion: Sunni Islam
Currency: Libyan Dinar

Liechtenstein

Area: 62 sq mi/160 sq km
Population: 33,987
Capital: Vaduz
Form of government: Constitutional Monarchy
Religion: RC
Currency: Swiss Franc

Lithuania

Population: 3,585,00
Capital: Vilnius
Other cities: Kaunas, Klaipeda, Siauliai
Form of government: Republic
Religion: RC
Currency: Litas

Luxembourg, Grand Duchy of

Population: 474,400
Capital: Luxembourg City
Other cities: Esch-sur-Algette, Differdange,
  Dudelange
Form of government: Constitutional Monarchy
Religion: RC
Currency: Euro

Macau (Macao)

Area: 7 sq mi/18 sq km
Population: 453,125
Capital: Macao
Form of government: Special Administrative Region of
  China
Religions: Buddhism, RC
Currency: Pataca

Macedonia, The Former Yugoslav Republic of (FYROM)

Area: 9,928 sq mi/25,713 sq km
Population: 2,050,000
Capital: Skopje
Other cities: Kumanovo, Ohrid
Form of government: Republic
Religions: Eastern Orthodox, Islam
Currency: Macedonian Denar

Madagascar

Area: 226,658 sq mi/587,041 sq km
Population: 18,595,000
Capital: Antananarivo
Other cities: Fianarantsoa, Mahajanga, Toamasina,
  Toliara
Form of government: Republic
Religions: Traditional beliefs, Christianity,
  Islam
Currency: Madagascar Ariary

Malawi

Area: 45,747 sq mi/118,484 sq km
Population: 13,013,000
Capital: Lilongwe
Other cities: Blantyre, Zomba
Form of government: Republic
Religions: Christianity, Islam
Currency: Malawian Kwacha

Malaysia, The Federation of

Area: 127,320 sq mi/329,758 sq km
Population: 24,385,000
Capital: Kuala Lumpur
Other cities: Ipoh, George Town, Johor Baharu
Form of government: Constitutional Monarchy
Religions: Islam, Buddhism, Hinduism, Christianity
Currency: Ringgit

Maldives, Republic of

Area: 115 sq mi/298 sq km
Population: 359,000
Capital: Malé
Form of government: Republic
Religion: Sunni Islam
Currency: Rufiyaa

Mali

Area: 478,841 sq mi/1,240,192 sq km
Population: 11,716,000
Capital: Bamako
Other towns: Gao, Kayes, Ségou, Mopti, Sikasso
Form of government: Republic
Religions: Sunni Islam, traditional beliefs
Currency: CFA Franc

Malta

Area: 122 sq mi/316 sq km
Population: 400,214
Capital: Valletta
Form of government: Republic
Religion: RC
Currency: Maltese Lira

Marshall Islands

Area: 70 sq mi/181 sq km
Population: 60,422
Capital: Dalag-Uliga-Darrit (on Majuro Atoll)
Form of government: Republic in free association with
  the USA
Religion: Christianity
Currency: US Dollar

Martinique

Area: 425 sq mi/1,102 sq km
Population: 436,131
Capital: Fort-de-France
Form of government: Overseas Department of France
Religion: RC
Currency: Euro

Mauritania (The Islamic Republic of Mauritania)

Area: 395,956 sq mi/1,025,520 sq km
Population: 3,177,000
Capital: Nouakchott
Other cities: Kaédi, Nouadhibou
Form of government: Republic
Religion: Sunni Islam
Currency: Ouguiya

Mauritius

Area: 788 sq mi/2,040 sq km
Population: 1,240,000
Capital: Port Louis
Form of government: Republic
Religions: Hinduism, RC, Sunni Islam
Currency: Mauritian Rupee

Mexico

Area: 756,066 sq mi/1,958,201 sq km
Population: 107,449,000
Capital: México City
Other cities: Guadalajara, León, Monterrey, Puebla,
   Tijuana
Form of government: Federal Republic
Religion: RC
Currency: Mexican Peso

Micronesia, Federated States of

Area: 271 sq mi/702 sq km
Population: 108,000
Capital: Palikir
Form of government: Constitutional Government in free
   association with the USA
Religion: Christianity
Currency: US Dollar

Moldova (Moldavia)

Area: 13,012 sq mi/33,700 sq km
Population: 4,466,000
Capital: Chisinau
Other cities: Tiraspol, Tighina, Bel'tsy
Form of government: Republic
Religion: Eastern Orthodox
Currency: Moldovan Leu

Monaco

Area: 0.4 sq mile/1 sq kilometre
Population: 32,000
Capital: Monaco
Form of government: Constitutional Monarchy
Religion: RC
Currency: Euro

Mongolia

Area: 604,829 sq mi/1,566,500 sq km
Population: 2,832,000
Capital: Ulaanbaatar
Other cities: Altay, Saynshand, Hovd, Choybalsan,
   Tsetserleg
Form of government: Parliamentary/Presidential
Religions: Buddhism, Shamanism, Christianity,
   Islam
Currency: Togrok/Tugrik

Montenegro *(as from 2006)*

Area: 5,414 sq mi/14,026 sq km
Population: 630,548
Capitals: (capital) Cetinje, (administrative capital)
   Podgorica
Other cities: Bar, Berane, Pljevlja, Herceg Novi
Form of government: Republic
Religions: Orthodox, Islam, RC
Currency: Euro

Morocco

Area: 172,414 sq mi/446,550 sq km
Population: 33,241,000
Capital: Rabat
Other cities: Casablanca, Fès, Marrakech,
   Tangier
Form of government: Constitutional Monarchy
Religion: Sunni Islam
Currency: Moroccan Dirham

Mozambique

Area: 309,496 sq mi/799,380 sq km
Population: 19,686,000
Capital: Maputo
Other towns: Beira, Nampula
Form of government: Republic
Religions: RC, Sunni Islam
Currency: Metical

Myanmar, Union of (Burma)

Area: 261,228 sq mi/676,578 sq km
Population: 47,382,000
Capital: Rangoon (Yangon)
Other cities: Mandalay, Moulmein, Pegu
Form of government: Republic
Religion: Buddhism
Currency: Kyat

Namibia

Area: 318,261 sq mi/824,292 sq km
Population: 2,044,000
Capital: Windhoek
Form of government: Republic
Religions: Christianity, traditional beliefs
Currency: Namibian Dollar, South African
   Rand

Nauru

Area: 8 sq mi/21 sq km
Population: 13,287
Capital: Nauru
Form of government: Republic
Religions: Protestantism, RC
Currency: Australian Dollar

Nepal, Kingdom of
Area: 56,827 sq mi/147,181 sq km
Population: 28,287,000
Capital: Kathmandu
Other city: Biratnagar
Form of government: Constitutional Monarchy
Religions: Hinduism, Buddhism, Islam
Currency: Nepalese Rupee

Netherlands, The
Area: 15,770 sq mi/40,844 sq km
Population: 16,491,000
Capital: Amsterdam
Seat of government: The Hague (s'Gravenhage)
Other cities: Rotterdam, Eindhoven
Form of government: Constitutional Monarchy
Religions: RC, Dutch Reformed, Calvinism
Currency: Euro

Netherlands Antilles
Area: 309 sq mi/800 sq km
Population: 221,736
Capital: Willemstad
Form of government: Autonomous country within the
   Netherlands
Religion: RC
Currency: Netherlands Antillean Guilder

New Caledonia (Nouvelle Calédonie)
Area: 7,172 sq mi/18,575 sq km
Population: 219,246
Capital: Noumea
Form of government: Overseas Territory of
   France
Religions: RC, Protestantism
Currency: CFP Franc

New Zealand
Area: 104,454 sq mi/270,534 sq km
Population: 4,076,000
Capital: Wellington
Other cities: Auckland, Christchurch, Dunedin,
   Hamilton
Form of government: Parliamentary Democracy
Religions: Anglicanism, RC, Presbyterianism
Currency: New Zealand Dollar

Nicaragua
Area: 50,193 sq mi/130,668 sq km
Population: 5,570,000
Capital: Managua
Form of government: Republic
Religion: RC
Currency: Gold Cordoba

Niger
Area: 489,191 sq mi/1,267,000 sq km
Population: 12,525,000
Capital: Niamey
Other cities: Agadez, Maradi, Tahoua, Zinder
Form of government: Republic
Religion: Sunni Islam
Currency: CFA Franc

Nigeria
Area: 356,669 sq mi/923,768 sq km
Population: 131,859,000
Capital: Abuja
Other cities: Lagos, Onitsha, Enugu, Ibadan, Kano,
   Ogbomosho
Form of government: Federal Republic
Religions: Sunni Islam, Christianity, traditional
   beliefs
Currency: Naira

Northern Mariana Islands
Area: 179 sq mi/464 sq km
Population: 82,459
Capital: Saipan
Form of government: Commonwealth in political
   union with the USA
Religions: RC, traditional beliefs
Currency: US Dollar

Norway
Area: 125,050 sq mi/323,877 sq km
Population: 4,610,000
Capital: Oslo
Other cities: Bergen, Trondheim, Stavanger,
   Kristiansand, Tromsö
Form of government: Constitutional Monarchy
Religion: Church of Norway
Currency: Norwegian Krone

Oman (Sultanate of Oman)
Area: 119,498 sq mi/309,500 sq km
Population: 3,102,000
Capital: Mascat (Musqat)
Other towns: Salalah, Al Khaburah, Matrah
Form of government: Monarchy
Religions: Ibadhi Islam, Sunni Islam, Shia Islam
Currency: Omani Rial

Pakistan (Islamic Republic of Pakistan)
Area: 307,374 sq mi/796,095 sq km
Population: 165,803,000
Capital: Islamabad
Other cities: Faisalabad, Hyderabad, Karachi, Lahore,
   Rawalpindi
Form of government: Federal Republic
Religions: Sunni Islam, Shia Isla, Christianity,
   Hinduism
Currency: Pakistani Rupee

Palau

Area: 177 sq mi/459 sq km
Population: 20,579
Capital: Koror
Form of government: Republic in free association with
the USA
Religions: RC, Protestantism, Modekngei
Currency: US Dollar

Panama

Area: 29,157 sq mi/75,517 sq km
Population: 3,191,000
Capital: Panama City
Other cities: Colón, Puerto Armuelles, David
Form of government: Republic
Religion: RC
Currency: Balboa, US Dollar

Papua New Guinea

Area: 178,704 sq mi/462,840 sq km
Population: 5,670,000
Capital: Port Moresby
Form of government: Constitutional Parliamentary
Democracy
Religions: Christianity, traditional beliefs
Currency: Kina

Paraguay

Area: 157,048 sq mi/406,752 sq km
Population: 6,506,000
Capital: Asunción
Other cities: Concepción, Ciudad del Este,
Encarnación
Form of government: Republic
Religion: RC
Currency: Guarani

Peru

Area: 496,225 sq mi/1,285,216 sq km
Population: 28,302,000
Capital: Lima
Other cities: Arequipa, Callao, Chiclayo, Cuzco, Trujillo
Form of government: Republic
Religion: RC
Currency: Nuevo Sol

Philippines

Area: 115,813 sq mi/300,000 sq km
Population: 89,468,000
Capital: Manila
Other cities: Cebu, Davao, Quezon City,
Zamboanga
Form of government: Republic
Religions: Sunni Islam, RC
Currency: Philippine Peso

Pitcairn Islands

Area: 2 sq mi/5 sq km
Population: 50
Form of government: British Overseas Territory
Religion: Seventh Day Adventism
Currency: New Zealand dollar

Poland

Area: 124,808 sq mi/323,250 sq km
Population: 38,536,000
Capital: Warsaw (Warszawa)
Other cities: Gdansk, Kraków, Lódz, Poznan, Wroclaw
Form of government: Republic
Religion: RC
Currency: Zloty

Portugal

Area: 35,514 sq mi/91,982 sq km
Population: 10,605,800
Capital: Lisbon (Lisboa)
Other cities: Braga, Coimbra, Faro, Oporto, Setúbal
Form of government: Republic
Religion: RC
Currency: Euro

Puerto Rico

Area: 3,427 sq mi/8,875 sq km
Population: 3,927,000
Capital: San Juan
Form of government: Self-governing commonwealth in
association with the USA
Religion: RC
Currency: US Dollar

Qatar

Area: 4,247 sq mi/11,000 sq km)
Population: 885,359
Capital: Doha (Ad Dawhah)
Form of government: Traditional Emirate
Religion: Wahhabi Sunni Islam
Currency: Qatari Riyal

Réunion

Area: 969 sq mi/2,510 sq km
Population: 787,584
Capital: St Denis
Form of government: French Overseas Department
Religion: RC
Currency: Euro

Romania

Area: 92,043 sq mi/238,391 sq km
Population 22,303,000
Capital: Bucharest (Bucuresti)
Other cities: Brasov, Constanta, Galati, Iasi, Timisoara,
Craiova, Brâila, Arad, Ploiesti
Form of government: Republic
Religion: Eastern Orthodox
Currency: Leu (New Leu from 2006)

Russia (Russian Federation)

Area: 6,592,850 sq mi/17,075,400 sq km
Population: 142,893,000
Capital: Moscow (Moskva)
Other cities: St Petersburg, Nizhniy Novgorod,
    Novosibirsk, Samara
Form of government: Federation
Religions: Russian Orthodox, Sunni Islam, Shia Islam,
    RC
Currency: Russian Ruble

Rwanda

Area: 10,169 sq mi/26,338 sq km
Population: 8,648,000
Capital: Kigali
Other major city: Butare
Form of government: Republic
Religions: RC, Protestantism, Adventism,
    Islam
Currency: Rwandan Franc

St Kitts (St Christopher) and Nevis

Area: 101 sq mi/261 sq km
Population: 39,129
Capital: Basseterre
Other major city: Charlestown
Form of government: Parliamentary Democracy
Religions: Anglicanism, Methodism
Currency: East Caribbean Dollar

St Helena

Area: 47 sq mi/122 sq km
Population: 7,502
Capital: Jamestown
Form of government: British Overseas Territory
Religion: Anglicanism
Currency: St Helenian Pound

St Lucia

Area: 240 sq mi/622 sq km
Population: 168,458
Capital: Castries
Form of government: Parliamentary Democracy
Religion: Christianity
Currency: East Caribbean Dollar

St Pierre and Miquelon

Area: 93 sq mi/240 sq km
Population: 7,026
Capital: Saint Pierre
Form of government: Self-governing Territorial
    Collectivity of France
Religion: RC
Currency: Euro

St Vincent and the Grenadines

Area: 150 sq mi/388 sq km
Population: 117,848
Capital: Kingstown
Form of government: Parliamentary Democracy
Religion: Christianity
Currency: East Caribbean Dollar

Samoa (Western)

Area: 1,093 sq mi/2,831 sq km
Population: 176,908
Capital: Apia
Form of government: Constitutional Monarchy
Religion: Christianity
Currency: Tala

Samoa, American

Area: 77 sq mi/199 sq km
Population: 57,794
Capital: Pago Pago
Form of government: Unincorporated Territory of the
    USA
Religion: Christianity
Currency: US Dollar

San Marino

Area: 24 sq mi/61 sq km
Population: 29,251
Capital: San Marino
Other cities: Borgo Maggiore, Serravalle
Form of government: Republic
Religion: RC
Currency: Euro

São Tomé and Príncipe

Area: 372 sq mi/964 sq km
Population: 193,413
Capital: São Tomé
Form of government: Republic
Religion: RC
Currency: Dobra

Saudi Arabia

Area: 830,000 sq mi/2,149,690 sq km
Population: 27,019,000
Capital: Riyadh (Ar Riyād)
Other cities: Ad Dammam, Mecca, Jeddah, Medina
Form of government: Monarchy
Religions: Sunni Islam, Shia Islam
Currency: Saudi Riyal

Senegal

Area: 75,955 sq mi/196,722 sq km
Population: 11,987,000
Capital: Dakar
Other cities: Kaolack, Thiès, St Louis
Form of government: Republic
Religions: Sunni Islam, RC
Currency: CFA Franc

Serbia and Montenegro *see* **Montenegro, Serbia.**

Serbia *(as from 2006)*
Area: 34,107 sq mi/88,361sq km
Population: 9,396,000
Capital: Belgrade
Form of government: Republic
Religions: Serbian Orthodox, Islam,
  Christianity
Currency: New Yugoslav Dinar

Seychelles
Area: 175 sq mi/455 sq km
Population: 81,541
Capital: Victoria
Form of government: Republic
Religion: RC
Currency: Seychelles Rupee

Sierra Leone
Area: 27,699 sq mi/71,740 sq km
Population: 6,005,000
Capital: Freetown
Other city: Bo
Form of government: Republic
Religions: Sunni Islam, traditional beliefs,
  Christianity
Currency: Leone

Singapore
Area: 239 sq mi/618 sq km
Population: 4,492,000
Capital: Singapore
Form of government: Parliamentary Republic
Religions: Buddhism, Sunni Islam, Christianity,
  Hinduism
Currency: Singapore Dollar

Slovakia (Slovak Republic)
Area: 18,928 sq mi/49,035 sq km
Population: 5,439,000
Capital: Bratislava
Other cities: Kosice, Zilina, Nitra
Form of government: Parliamentary Democracy
Religion: RC
Currency: Slovak Koruna

Slovenia
Area: 7,821 sq mi/20,256 sq km
Population: 2,010,000
Capital: Ljubljana
Other cities: Maribor, Kranj
Form of government: Parliamentary Republic
Religions: RC, Orthodox, Islam
Currency: Tolar

Solomon Islands
Area: 11,157 sq mi/28,896 sq km
Population: 552,438
Capital: Honiara
Form of government: Parliamentary Democracy
Religion: Christianity
Currency: Solomon Islands Dollar

Somalia
Area: 246,201 sq mi/637,657 sq km
Population: 8,863,000
Capital: Mogadishu (Muqdisho)
Other major towns: Hargeysa, Burco
Form of government: Republic
Religion: Sunni Islam
Currency: Somali Shilling

South Africa
Area: 471,445 sq mi/1,221,037 sq km
Population: 44,187,000
Capital: (administrative) Pretoria (Tshwane),
  (legislative) Cape Town, (judicial) Bloemfontein
Other cities: Johannesburg, Durban, Port Elizabeth,
  Soweto
Form of government: Republic
Religions: Christianity, Islam
Currency: Rand

Spain
Area: 195,365 sq mi/505,992 sq km
Population: 40,397,400
Capital: Madrid
Other cities: Barcelona, Valencia, Seville, Zaragoza,
  Malaga, Bilbao
Form of government: Parliamentary Monarchy
Religion: RC
Currency: Euro

Sri Lanka
Area: 25,332 sq mi/65,610 sq km
Population: 20,222,000
Capital: Colombo
Other cities: Trincomalee, Jaffna, Kandy,
  Moratuwa
Form of government: Republic
Religions: Buddhism, Sunni Islam, Hinduism,
  Christianity
Currency: Sri Lankan Rupee

Sudan
Area: 967,500 sq mi/2,505,813 sq km
Population: 41,236,000
Capital: Khartoum (El Khartum)
Other cities: Omdurman, Khartoum North,
  Port Sudan
Form of government: Republic
Religions: Sunni Islam, traditional beliefs, Christianity
Currency: Sudanese Dinar

Suriname

Area: 63,037 sq mi/163,265 sq km
Population: 439,117
Capital: Paramaribo
Form of government: Republic
Religions: Hinduism, Protestant, RC, Sunni Islam,
  traditional beliefs
Currency: Surinam Dollar

Swaziland

Area: 6,704 sq mi/17,364 sq km
Population: 1,136,000
Capital: Mbabane
Other towns: Big Bend, Manzini, Mankayane,
  Lobamba
Form of government: Monarchy
Religions: Christianity, Islam, traditional beliefs
Currency: Lilangeni

Sweden

Area: 173,732 sq mi/449,964 sq km
Population: 9,016,000
Capital: Stockholm
Other cities: Göteborg, Malmö, Uppsala, Örebro,
  Linköping
Form of government: Constitutional Monarchy
Religion: Lutheranism
Currency: Swedish Krona

Switzerland

Area: 15,940 sq mi/41,284 sq km
Population: 7,523,000
Capital: Bern
Other cities: Zürich, Basle, Geneva,
  Lausanne
Form of government: Federal Republic
Religions: RC, Protestantism
Currency: Swiss Franc

Syria (Syrian Arab Republic)

Area: 71,498 sq mi/185,180 sq km
*Population*18,881,000
Capital: Damascus (Dimashq)
Other cities: Halab, Hims, Dar'a
Form of government: Republic
Religion: Sunni Islam
Currency: Syrian Pound

Taiwan

Area: 13,800 sq mi/35,742 sq km
Population: 23,036,270
Capital: T'ai-pei
Other cities: Kao-hsiung, T'ai-nan, Chang-hua,
  Chi-lung
Form of government: Multiparty Democracy
Religions: Taoism, Buddhism, Christianity
Currency: New Taiwan Dollar

Tajikistan

Area: 55,250 sq mi/143,100 sq km
Population: 7,320,000
Capital: Dushanbe
Other major city: Khujand
Form of government: Republic
Religions: Sunni Islam, Shia Islam
Currency: Tajikistani Somoni

Tanzania

Area: 362,162 sq mi/938,000 sq km
Population: 37,445,100
Capital: Dodoma
Other towns: Dar es Salaam, Zanzibar, Mwanza,
  Tanga
Form of government: Republic
Religions: Sunni Islam, RC, Anglicanism,
  Hinduism
Currency: Tanzanian Shilling

Thailand

Area: 198,115 sq mi/513,115 sq km
Population: 64,631,000
Capital: Bangkok (Krung Thep)
Other cities: Chiang Mai, Nakhon Ratchasima, Ubon
  Ratchathani
Form of government: Constitutional Monarchy
Religions: Buddhism, Sunni Islam
Currency: Baht

Togo

Area: 21,925 sq mi/56,785 sq km
Population: 5,548,000
Capital: Lomé
Other major city: Sokodé
Form of government: Republic
Religions: Traditional beliefs, Christianity, Sunni
  Islam
Currency: CFA Franc

Tonga

Area: 288 sq mi/747 sq km
Population: 114,689
Capital: Nuku'alofa
Form of government: Constitutional Monarchy
Religion: Christianity
Currency: Pa'anga

Trinidad and Tobago

Area: 1,981 sq mi/5,130 sq km
Population: 1,065,000
Capital: Port of Spain
Other towns: San Fernando, Arima
Form of government: Parliamentary Democracy
Religions: RC, Hinduism, Anglicanism, Sunni
  Islam
Currency: Trinidad and Tobago Dollar

Tunisia

Area: 62,592 sq mi/162,155 sq km
Population: 10,175,000
Capital: Tunis
Other cities: Sfax, Bizerte, Sousse
Form of government: Republic
Religion: Sunni Islam
Currency: Tunisian Dinar

Turkey

Area: 299,158 sq mi/774,815 sq km
Population: 70,413,000
Capital: Ankara
Other cities: Istanbul, Izmir, Adana, Bursa
Form of government: Republic
Religion: Sunni Islam
Currency: Turkish Lira

Turkmenistan

Area: 188,456 sq mi/488,100 sq km
Population: 5,042,000
Capital: Ashkhabad (Ashgabat)
Other cities: Chardzhou, Mary, Turkmenbashi
Form of government: Republic
Religions: Sunni Islam, Eastern Orthodox
Currency: Turkman Manat

Turks and Caicos Islands

Area: 166 sq mi/430 sq km
Population: 21,152
Capital: Grand Turk
Form of government: British Overseas Territory
Religion: Christianity
Currency: US Dollar

Tuvalu

Area: 10 sq mi/24 sq km
Population: 11,810
Capital: Funafuti
Form of government: Constitutional Monarchy
Religion: Christianity
Currency: Australian Dollar, Tuvaluan
   Dollar

Uganda

Area: 93,065 sq mi/241,038 sq km
Population: 28,195,000
Capital: Kampala
Other cities: Entebbe, Jinja, Soroti, Mbale
Form of government: Republic
Religions: RC, Protestantism, traditional beliefs, Sunni
   Islam
Currency: Ugandan Shilling

Ukraine

Area: 233,090 sq mi/603,700 sq km
Population: 51,094,000
Capital: Kiev (Kiyev)
Other cities: Dnepropetrovsk, Donetsk, Khar'kov,
   Odessa, Lugansk, Sevastopol
Form of government: Republic
Religions: Russian Orthodox, RC
Currency: Rouble

United Arab Emirates (UAE)

Area: 32,278 sq mi/83,600 sq km
Population: 2,602,000
Capital: Abu Zabi (Abu Dhabi)
Other cities: Dubai, Sharjh, Ras al Khaymah
Form of government: Federation
Religions: Sunni Islam, Shia Islam
Currency: Emirati Dirham

United Kingdom of Great Britain and Northern Ireland (UK)

Area: 94,248 sq mi/244,101 sq km
Population: 60,609,000
Capital: London
Other cities: Birmingham, Manchester, Glasgow,
   Liverpool, Edinburgh, Cardiff, Belfast
Form of government: Constitutional Monarchy
Religions: Christianity, Islam, Hinduism
Currency: Pound Sterling

United States of America (USA))

Area: 3,536,278 sq mi/9,158,960 sq km
Population: 298,444,000
Capital: Washington DC
Other cities: New York, Chicago, Detroit, Houston, Los
   Angeles, Philadelphia, San Diego, San Francisco
Form of government: Federal Republic
Religions: Protestantism, RC, Judaism,
   Islam
Currency: US Dollar

Uruguay

Area: 68,500 sq mi/177,414 sq km
Population: 3,431,000
Capital: Montevideo
Form of government: Republic
Religions: RC, Protestantism
Currency: Uruguayan Peso

Uzbekistan

Area: 172,742 sq mi/447,400 sq km
Population: 27,307,000
Capital: Tashkent
Other cities: Urgench, Nukus, Bukhara,
   Samarkand
Form of government: Republic
Religions: Sunni Islam, Eastern Orthodox
Currency: Uzbekistani Soum

Vanuatu

Area: 4,706 sq mi/12,189 sq km
Population: 208,869
Capital: Vila
Form of government: Republic
Religions: Christianity, traditional beliefs
Currency: Vatu

Vatican City State

Area: 0.2 sq mi/0.44 sq kilometre
Population: 1,000
Capital: Vatican City
Form of government: Papal Commission
Religion: RC
Currency: Euro

Venezuela

Area: 352,145 sq mi/912,050 sq km
Population: 25,730,000
Capital: Caracas
Other cities: Maracaibo, Valencia, Barquisimeto
Form of government: Federal Republic
Religion: RC
Currency: Bolivar

Vietnam

Area: 128,066 sq mi/331,689 sq km
Population: 84,402,000
Capital: Hanoi
Other cities: Ho Chi Minh City, Haiphong, Hué, Dà Nang
Form of government: Socialist Republic
Religions: Buddhism, RC , Taoism
Currency: Dong

Virgin Islands, British

Area: 58 sq mi/151 sq km
Population: 23,098
Capital: Road Town
Form of government: British Overseas Territory
Religions: Protestantism, RC
Currency: US Dollar

Virgin Islands, US

Area: 134 sq mi/347 sq km
Population: 108,605
Capital: Charlotte Amalie
Form of government: Self-governing Territory of the USA
Religions: Baptist, RC
Currency: US Dollar

Wallis and Futuna Islands

Area: 77 sq mi/200 sq km
Population: 16,025
Capital: Mata-Uru
Form of government: French Overseas Territory
Religion: RC
Currency: CFP Franc

Western Sahara

Area: 102,703 sq mi/266,000 sq km
Population: 273,008
Capital: Laâyoune (El Aaiún)
Form of government: Republic (*de facto* controlled by Morocco)
Religion: Sunni Islam
Currency: Moroccan Dirham

Western Samoa *see* Samoa.

Yemen

Area: 203,850 sq mi/527,978 sq km
Population: 21,456,000
Capital: San'a
Other cities: Aden, Al Hudaydah, Ta'izz
Form of government: Republic
Religions: Zaidism, Shia Islam, Sunni Islam
Currency: Yemeni Riyal

Zambia

Area: 290,587 sq mi/752,618 sq km
Population: 11,502,000
Capital: Lusaka
Other cities: Kitwe, Ndola, Mufulira
Form of government: Republic
Religions: Christianity, Islam, Hinduism
Currency: Zambian Kwacha

Zaire *see* Congo, Democratic Republic of the.

Zimbabwe

Area: 150,872 sq mi/390,757 sq km
Population: 12,236,000
Capital: Harare
Other cities: Bulawayo, Mutare, Gweru
Form of government: Republic
Religions: Christianity, traditional beliefs
Currency: Zimbabwean Dollar

Grammar

abstract noun a noun which is the name of a thing that cannot be touched but refers to a quality, concept or idea. Examples of abstract nouns include 'anger', 'beauty', 'courage', 'Christianity', 'danger', 'fear', 'greed', 'hospitality', 'ignorance', 'jealousy', 'kudos', 'loyalty', 'Marxism', 'need', 'obstinacy', 'pain', 'quality', 'resistance', 'safety', 'truth', 'unworthiness', 'vanity', 'wisdom', 'xenophobia', 'youth', 'zeal'. *See also* **concrete noun.**

active voice one of the two voices that verbs are divided into, the other being passive voice. In verbs in the active voice, commonly called **active verbs**, the subject of the verb performs the action described by the verb. Thus, in the sentence 'The boy threw the ball', 'throw' is in the active voice since the subject of the verb (the boy) is doing the throwing. Similarly, in the sentence 'Her mother was driving the car', 'driving' is in the active voice since it is the subject of the sentence (her mother) that is doing the driving. Similarly, in the sentence 'We saw the cows in the field', 'saw' is the active voice since it is the subject of the sentence (we) that is doing the seeing.

adjectival clause a kind of subordinate clause that describes or modifies a noun or pronoun. It is better known by the name relative clause.

adjective a word that describes or gives information about a noun or pronoun. It is said to qualify a noun or pronoun since it limits the word it describes in some way, by making it more specific. Thus, adding the adjective 'red' to 'book' limits 'book', since it means we can forget about books of any other colour. Similarly, adding 'large' to 'book' limits it, since it means we can forget about books of any other size.

Adjectives tell us something about the colour, size, number, quality or classification of a noun or pronoun, as in 'purple curtains', 'jet-black hair', 'bluish eyes'; 'tiny baby', 'large houses', 'biggish gardens', 'massive estates'; five children', 'twenty questions', 'seventy-five books'; 'sad people', 'joyful occasions', 'delicious food', 'civil engineering', 'nuclear physics', 'modern languages', 'Elizabethan drama'.

adverb a word that adds to our information about a verb, as in 'work rapidly'; about an adjective, as in 'an extremely beautiful young woman'; or about another adverb, as in 'sleeping very soundly'. Adverbs are said to modify the words to which they apply since they limit the words in some way and make them more specific. Thus, adding 'slowly' to 'walk', as in 'They walked slowly down the hill', limits the verb 'walk' since all other forms of 'walk', such as 'quickly', 'lazily', etc, have been discarded.

adverbial clause a subordinate clause that modifies the main or principal clause by adding information about time, place, concession, condition, manner, purpose and result, as in 'He left after the meal was over', 'They left it where they found it', 'Wherever I went I saw signs of poverty', 'I have to admire his speech, although I disagree with what he said', 'He does his best at school work even though he is not very good at it', 'Whilst I myself do not like him, I can understand why he is popular', 'We cannot go unless we get permission', 'He looked at her as if he hated her', 'They will have to work long hours in order to make that amount of money', 'They started to run so as to get home before it rained', and 'He fell awkwardly so that he broke his leg.' Adverbial clauses usually follow the main clause but most of them can be put in front of the main clause for reasons of emphasis or style.

agent noun a noun that refers to someone who is the 'doer' of the action of a verb. It is usually spelt ending in either *-er*, as 'enquirer', or in *-or*, as in 'investigator' and 'supervisor', but frequently either of these endings is acceptable, as 'adviser/advisor'.

agreement or **concord** the agreeing of two or more elements in a clause or sentence, i.e. they take the same number, person or gender. In English the most common form of agreement is that between subject and verb, and this usually involves **number agreement**. This means that singular nouns are usually accompanied by singular verbs, as in 'She looks well', 'He is working late' and 'The boy has passed the exam', and that plural nouns are usually accompanied by plural verbs, as in 'They look well', 'They are working late' and 'The boys have passed the exam'.

Problems arise when the noun in question can be either singular or plural, for example, 'audience', 'committee', 'crowd', 'family', 'government', 'group'. Such nouns take a singular verb if the user is regarding the people or items referred to by the noun as a group, as in 'The family is moving house', or as individuals, as in 'The family are quarrelling over where to go on holiday'.

Compound subjects, that is two or more nouns acting as the subject, whether singular or plural, joined with 'and', are used with a plural noun, as in 'My friend and I are going to the cinema tonight' and 'James and John are leaving today', unless the two nouns together represent a single concept, as 'brandy and soda', in which case the verb is in the singular, as in 'Brandy and soda is his favourite drink' and 'cheese and pickle' in 'Cheese and pickle is the only sandwich filling available'.

Indefinite pronouns such as 'anyone', 'everyone', 'no one', 'someone', 'either', 'neither' are singular and should be followed by a singular verb, as in 'Each of the flats is self-contained', 'Everyone is welcome', 'No one is allowed in without a ticket' and 'Neither is quite what I am looking for'.

Agreement with reference to both number and gender affects pronouns, as in 'She blames herself', 'He could have kicked himself' and 'They asked themselves why they had got involved'. Problems arise when the pronoun is indefinite and so the sex of the person is unspecified. Formerly in such cases the masculine pronouns were assumed to be neutral and so 'Each of the pupils was asked to hand in his work' was considered quite acceptable. The rise of feminism has led to a questioning of this assumption and alternatives have been put forward. These include 'Each of the pupils was asked to hand in his/her (or his or her) work', but some people feel that this is clumsy. Another alternative is 'Each of the pupils was asked to hand in their work'. Although it is ungrammatical, this convention is becoming quite acceptable in modern usage. To avoid both the clumsiness of the former and the ungrammatical nature of the latter, it is possible to cast the whole sentence in the plural, as in 'All the pupils were asked to hand in their work'.

also an adverb that should not be used as a conjunction instead of 'and'. Thus sentences such as 'Please send me some apples, also some pears' are grammatically incorrect.

although a conjunction that is used to introduce a subordinate adverbial clause of concession, as in 'They are very happy although they are poor', meaning 'Despite the fact they are poor they are happy'. 'Though' or 'even though' can be substituted for 'although', as in 'they are very happy even though they are poor'. *See* **adverbial clause** and **conjunction**.

and a conjunction that is called a coordinating conjunction because it joins elements of language that are of equal status. The elements may be words, as in 'cows and horses', 'John and James', 'provide wine and beer'; phrases, as in 'working hard and playing hard' and 'trying to look after her children and her elderly parents'; clauses, as in 'John has decided to emigrate and his brother has decided to join him' and 'He has lost his job and he now has no money'. When a coordinating conjunction is used, the subject of the second clause can sometimes be omitted if it is the same as the subject of the first clause, as in 'They have been forced to sell the house and are very sad about it'.

The use of and at the beginning of a sentence is disliked by many people. It should be used only for deliberate effect, as in 'And then he saw the monster', or in informal contexts.

Other coordinating conjunctions include 'but', 'or', 'yet', 'both. . . and', 'either. . . or', and 'neither. . . . nor', as in 'poor but honest' and 'the blue dress or the green one'.

antecedent a term that refers to the noun or noun phrase in a main clause to which a relative pronoun in a relative clause refers back. Thus in the sentence 'People who live dangerously frequently get hurt', 'people' is an antecedent. Similarly, in the sentence 'The child identified the old man who attacked her', 'the old man' is the antecedent. *See* **relative clause**.

any a pronoun that may take either a singular or plural verb, depending on the context. When a singular noun is used, a singular verb is used, as in 'Is any of the cloth still usable?' 'Are any of the children coming?' When a plural noun is used, either a plural or a singular verb can be used, the singular verb being more formal, as in 'Did you ask if any of his friends were/was there?'.

anyone a pronoun that should be used with a singular verb, as in 'Has anyone seen my book?' and 'Is anyone coming to the lecture?' To be grammatically correct, anyone should be followed, where relevant, by a singular, not plural, personal pronoun or possessive adjective, but, in order to avoid the sexist 'his', this involves sentences such as 'Has anyone left his/her book?' Because this construction is rather clumsy, there is a growing tendency to use 'their' and be ungrammatical.

apposition a term for a noun or a phrase that provides further information about another noun or phrase. Both nouns and phrases refer to the same person or thing. In the phrase 'Peter Jones, our managing director', ' Peter Jones' and 'our managing director' are said to be in apposition. Similarly, in the phrase 'his cousin, the chairman of the firm', 'his cousin' and 'the chairman of the firm' are in apposition.

as a conjunction that can introduce either a subordinate adverbial clause of time, as in 'I caught sight of him as I was leaving', a subordinate adverbial clause of manner, as in 'He acted as he promised', and a subordinate adverbial clause of reason, as in 'As it's Saturday he doesn't have to work'. it is also used in the as. . . . as construction, as in 'She doesn't play as well as her sister does'.

The construction may be followed by a subject pronoun or an object pronoun, according to sense. In the sentence 'He plays as well as she', which is a slightly shortened form of 'She plays as well as he does', 'he' is a subject pronoun. In informal English the subject pronoun often becomes an object pronoun, as in 'She plays as well as him'. In the sentence 'They hate their father as much as her', 'her' is an object and the sentence means 'They hate their father as much as they hate her', but in the sentence 'They hate their father as much as she', 'she' is a subject and the sentence means 'They hate their father as much as she does'. *See* **adverbial clause** and **conjunction**.

attributive adjective a term for an adjective that is placed immediately before the noun that it qualifies. In the phrases 'a red dress', 'the big house' and 'an enjoyable evening', 'red', 'big' and 'enjoyable' are attributive adjectives.

auxiliary verb a verb that is used in forming tenses, moods and voices of other verbs. These include 'be', 'do' and 'have'.

The verb 'to be' is used as an auxiliary verb with the -*ing* form of the main verb to form the continuous present tense, as in 'They are living abroad just now' and 'We were thinking of going on holiday but we changed our minds'.

The verb 'to be' is used as an auxiliary verb with the past participle of the main verb to form the passive voice, as in 'Her hands were covered in blood' and 'These toys are manufactured in China'.

The verb 'to have' is used as an auxiliary verb along with the past participle of the main verb to form the perfect tenses, as in 'They have filled the post', 'She had realized her mistake' and 'They wished that they had gone earlier'.

The verb 'to be' is used as an auxiliary verb along with the main verb to form negative sentences, as in 'She is not accepting the job'. The verb 'to do' is used as an auxiliary verb along with the main verb to form negative sentences, as in 'he does not believe her'. It is also used along with the main verb to form questions, as in 'Does he know that she's gone?' and to form sentences in which the verb is emphasized, as in 'She *does* want to go'. *See* **modal verb**.

base the basic uninflected form of a verb. It is found as the infinitive form, as in 'to go' and 'to take', and as the imperative form, as in 'Go away!' and 'Take it!' It is also the form that the verb in the present indicative tense takes, except for the third person singular, as in 'I always go there on a Sunday' and 'They go there regularly.'

be *see* **auxiliary verb**.

because a conjunction that introduces a subordinate adverbial clause of reason, as in 'They sold the house because they are going abroad' and 'Because she is shy she never goes to parties'. It is often used incorrectly in such constructions as 'The reason they went away is because they were bored'. This should be rephrased as either 'The reason that they went away is that they were bored' or 'They went away because they were bored'. *See* **adverbial clause**.

before a word that can either be a preposition, an adverb or a conjunction. As a preposition it means either 'coming or going in front of in time', as in 'He was the chairman before this one', or coming or going in front of in place, as in 'She went before him into the restaurant'. As an adverb it means 'at a time previously', as in 'I told you before' and 'He has been married before'. As a conjunction it introduces a subordinate adverbial clause of time, as in 'The guests arrived before she was ready for them' and 'Before I knew it they had arrived'. *See* **adverbial clause**.

both a word that can be used in several ways: as a determiner, as in 'He broke both his arms' and 'He lost both his sons in the war'; as a pronoun, as in 'I don't mind which house we rent, I like them both' and 'Neither of them work here. The boss sacked them both'; as a conjunction, as in 'He both likes and admires her' and 'She is both talented and honest'. Both can sometimes be followed by 'of'. 'Both their children are grown up' and 'Both of their children are grown up' are both acceptable. Care should be taken to avoid using both unnecessarily. In the sentence 'The two items are both identical', 'both' is redundant.

but a conjunction that connects two opposing ideas. It is a coordinating conjunction in that it connects two elements of equal status. The elements may be words, as in 'not James but John'; phrases, as in 'working hard but not getting anywhere' and 'trying to earn a living but not succeeding'; clauses, as in 'He has arrived but his sister is late', 'I know her but I have never met him' and 'He likes reading but she prefers to watch TV'. It should not be used when no element of contrast is present. Thus the following sentence should be rephrased, at least in formal English—'She is not professionally trained but taught herself'. The two clauses are in fact agreeing, not disagreeing, with each other and so, strictly speaking, but should not be used.

The use of but at the beginning of a sentence is disliked by many people. It should be used only for deliberate effect or in informal contexts.

case one of the forms in the declension of a noun, pronoun or adjective in a sentence.

clause a group of words containing a finite verb which forms part of a compound or complex sentence. *See* **main clause**, **subordinate clauses**, **adverbial clause**, **noun clause** and **relative clause**.

commands these are expressed in the imperative mood, as in 'Be quiet!', 'Stop crying!', 'Go away!'

common noun simply the name of an ordinary, everyday non-specific thing or person, as opposed to proper nouns, which refer to the names of particular individuals or specific places. Common nouns include 'baby', 'cat', 'girl', 'hat', 'park', 'sofa' and 'table'.

comparison of adjectives this is achieved in two different ways. Some adjectives form their comparative by adding -*er* to the positive or absolute form, as in 'braver', 'louder', 'madder', 'shorter' and 'taller'. Other adjectives form their comparative by using 'more' in conjunction with them, as in 'more beautiful', 'more realistic', 'more suitable' and 'more tactful'. Which is the correct form is largely a matter of length. One-syllable adjectives, such as 'loud', add -*er*, as 'louder'. Two-syllable adjectives sometimes have both forms as a possibility, as in 'gentler/more gentle', and 'cleverest/most clever'. Adjectives with three or more syllables usually form their comparatives with 'more', as in 'more comfortable', 'more gracious', 'more regular' and 'more understanding'. Some adjectives are irregular in their comparative forms, as in 'good/better', 'bad/worse', 'many/more'. Only if they begin with *un*- are they likely to end in -*er*, as in 'untrustworthier'.

Some adjectives by their very definitions do not normally have a comparative form, for example 'unique'.

complement the equivalent of the object in a clause with a linking verb. In the sentence 'Jack is a policeman', 'a policeman' is the complement. In the sentence 'Jane is a good mother', 'a good mother' is the complement', and in the sentence 'His son is an excellent football player', 'an excellent football player' is the complement.

complex sentence a type of sentence in which there is a main clause and one or more subordinate clauses. The sentence 'We went to visit him although he had been unfriendly to us' is a complex sentence since it is composed of a main clause and one subordinate clause ('although he had been unfriendly to us'). The sentence 'We wondered where he had gone and why he was upset' is a complex sentence since it has a main clause and two subordinate clauses ('where he had gone' and 'why he was upset').

compound sentence a type of sentence with more than one clause and linked by a coordinating conjunction, such as 'and' or 'but', as in 'He applied for a new job and got it' and 'I went to the cinema but I didn't enjoy the film'.

concrete noun the name of something that one can touch, as opposed to an abstract noun, which one cannot. Concrete nouns include 'bag', 'glass', 'plate', 'pot', 'clothes', 'field', 'garden', 'flower', 'potato', 'foot' and 'shoe'. *See* **abstract noun**.

conjunction a word that connects words, clauses or sentences. Conjunctions are of two types. A **coordinating conjunction** joins units of equal status, as in 'bread and butter', 'We asked for some food and we got it'. A **subordinating conjunction** joins a dependent or subordinating clause to main verbs: in 'We asked him why he was there', 'why he was there' is a subordinate clause and thus 'why' is a subordinating conjunction.

content words *see* **function word**.

continuous tenses *see* **tense**.

copula *see* **linking verb**.

copular verb *see* **equative** and **linking verb**.

count noun is the same as countable noun.

countable noun is one which can be preceded by 'a' and can take a plural, as in 'hat/hats', 'flower/flowers'. *See also* **uncountable noun**.

dangling participle a participle that has been misplaced in a sentence. A participle is often used to introduce a phrase that is attached to a subject mentioned later in a sentence, as in 'Worn out by the long walk, she fell to the ground in a faint'. 'Worn out' is the participle and 'she' the subject.

Another example is 'Laughing in glee at having won, she ordered some champagne'. In this sentence 'laughing' is the participle and 'she' is the subject. It is a common error for such a participle not to be related to any subject, as in 'Imprisoned in the dark basement, it seemed a long time since she had seen the sun'. This participle is said to be 'dangling'. Another example of a dangling participle is contained in 'Living alone, the days seemed long'.

It is also a common error for a participle to be related to the wrong subject in a sentence, as in 'Painting the ceiling, some of the plaster fell on his head', 'Painting' is the participle and should go with a subject 'he'. Instead it goes with 'some of the plaster'. Participles in this situation are more correctly known as **misrelated participles**, although they are also called dangling participles.

declarative mood the same as **indicative mood**.

declarative sentence a sentence that conveys information. The subject precedes the verb in it. Examples include 'They won the battle', 'He has moved to another town', 'Lots of people go there' and 'There is a new person in charge'.

declension the variation of the form of a noun, adjective or pronoun to show different cases, such as nominative and accusative. It also refers to the class into which such words are placed, as in first declension, second declension, etc. The term applies to languages such as Latin but is not applicable to English.

degree a level of comparison of gradable adjectives. The degrees of comparison comprise **absolute** or **positive**, as in 'big', 'calm', 'dark', 'fair', 'hot', 'late', 'short' and 'tall'; **comparative**, as in 'bigger', 'calmer', 'darker', 'fairest', 'hotter', 'late', 'shorter' and 'taller'; **superlative**, as in 'biggest', 'calmest', 'darkest', 'fairest', 'hottest', 'latest', 'shortest' and 'tallest'.

Degree can also refer to adverbs. Adverbs of degree include 'extremely', 'very', 'greatly', 'rather', 'really', 'remarkably', 'terribly', as in 'an extremely rare case', 'a very old man', 'He's remarkably brave' and 'We're terribly pleased'.

demonstrative determiner a determiner that is used to indicate things or people in relationship to the speaker or writer in space or time. 'This' and 'these' indicate nearness to the speaker, as in 'Will you take this book home?' and 'These flowers are for you'. 'That' and 'those' indicate distance from the speaker, as in 'Get that creature out of here!' and 'Aren't those flowers over there beautiful!'

demonstrative pronoun a pronoun that is similar to a demonstrative determiner except that it stands alone in place of a noun rather than preceding a noun, as in 'I'd like to give you this', 'What is that?', 'These are interesting books' and 'Those are not his shoes'.

dependent clause a clause that cannot stand alone and make sense, unlike an independent or main clause. Dependent clauses depend on the main clause. The term is the same as subordinate clause.

determiner a word that is used in front of a noun or pronoun to tell us something about it. Unlike an adjective, it does not, strictly speaking, 'describe' a noun or pronoun. Determiners are divided into the following categories: **articles** (a, an, the) as in 'a cat', 'an eagle', 'the book'; **demonstrative determiners** (this, that, these, those), as in 'this girl', 'that boy' and 'those people'; **possessive determiners** (my, your, his/her/its, our, their), as in 'my dog', 'her house', 'its colour', 'their responsibility'; **numbers** (one, two, three, four, etc, first, second, third, fourth, etc), as in 'two reasons', 'five ways', 'ten children'; and **indefinite** or **general determiners** (all, another, any, both, each, either, enough, every, few, fewer, less, little, many, most, much, neither, no, other, several, some), as in 'both parents', 'enough food', 'several issues'. Many words used as determiners are also pronouns. *See* **adjective; demonstrative determiner; number**.

direct object the noun, noun phrase, noun or nominal clause or pronoun that is acted upon by the action of a transitive verb. In the sentence 'She bought milk', 'bought' is a transitive verb and 'milk' is a noun which is the direct object. In the sentence 'She bought loads of clothes', 'bought' is a transitive verb and 'loads of clothes' is the direct object. In the sentence 'He knows what happened', 'knows' is a transitive verb and 'what happened' is a 'noun clause' or 'nominal clause'. A direct object is frequently known just as object. *See* **indirect object**.

direct speech the reporting of speech by repeating exactly the actual words used by the speaker, as in 'Peter said, "I am tired of this." '

distributive pronoun a pronoun that refers to individual members of a class or group. These include 'each', 'either', 'neither', 'none', 'everyone', 'no one'. Such pronouns, where relevant, should be accompanied by singular verbs and singular personal pronouns, as in 'All the men are to be considered for the new posts. Each is to send in his application'. Problems arise when the sex of the noun to which the distributive pronoun refers back is either unknown or unspecified. Formerly it was the convention to treat such nouns as masculine and so to make the distributive pronoun masculine, as in 'All pupils must obey the rule. Nowadays this convention is frequently considered to be unacceptably sexist and attempts have been made to get round this. One solution is to use 'him/her' (or 'him or her'), etc, as in 'The students have received a directive from the professor. Each is to produce his/her essay by tomorrow.' This convention is considered by many people to be clumsy. They prefer to be ungrammatical and use a plural personal pronoun, as in 'The pupils are being punished. Each is to inform their parents'. This use Is becomong increasingly common, even in textbooks. Where possible, it is preferable to rephrase sentences to avoid being either sexist or ungrammatical, as in 'All of the pupils must tell their parents.'

Each, either, etc, in such contexts is fairly formal. In less formal situations 'each of', 'either of', etc, is more usual, as in 'Each of the boys will have to train really hard to win' and 'Either of the dresses is perfectly suitable'.

do an auxiliary verb that is used to form negative forms, as in, 'I do not agree with you', 'They do not always win', 'He does not wish to go' and 'She did not approve of their behaviour'. It is also used to form interrogative forms, as in 'Do you agree?', 'Does she know about it?', 'Did you see that?' and 'I prefer to go by train. Don't you?' Do is also used for emphasis, as in 'I do believe you're right' and 'They do know, don't they?'

double passive a clause that contains two verbs in the passive, the second of which is an infinitive, as in 'The goods are expected to be despatched some time this week'. Some examples of double passives are clumsy or ungrammatical and should be avoided, as in 'Redundancy notices are proposed to be issued next week'.

dual gender a category of nouns in which there is no indication of gender. The nouns referred to include a range of words used for people, and occasionally animals, which can be of either gender. Unless the gender is specified we do not know the sex of the person referred to. Such words include 'artist', 'author', 'poet', 'singer', 'child', 'pupil', 'student', 'baby', 'parent', 'teacher', 'dog'. Such words give rise to problems with accompanying singular pronouns. *See* **each**.

dummy subject a subject that has no intrinsic meaning but is inserted to maintain a balanced grammatical structure. In the sentences 'It has started to rain' and 'It is nearly midnight', 'it' is a dummy subject. In the sentences 'There is nothing else to say' and 'There is no reason for his behaviour', 'there' is a dummy subject.

dynamic verb a verb with a meaning that indicates action, as 'work' in 'They work hard', 'play' in 'The boys play football at the weekend' and 'come' in 'The girls come here every Sunday'.

each a word that can be either a determiner or a distributive pronoun. Each as a determiner is used before a singular noun and is accompanied by a singular verb, as in 'Each candidate is to reapply', 'Each athlete has a place in the final', 'Each country is represented by a head of state' and 'Each chair was covered in chintz'.

Each of can sometimes be used instead of each, as in 'each of the candidates'. Again a singular verb is used. If the user wishes to emphasize the fact that something is true about every member of a group, **each one of** should be used and not 'every', as in 'Each one of them feels guilty', 'Each one of us has a part to play.

As a pronoun, each also takes a singular verb, as in 'They hate each other. Each is plotting revenge', 'These exercises are not a waste of time. Each provides valuable experience'.

Each, where relevant, should be accompanied by a singular personal pronoun, as in 'Each girl has to provide her own sports equipment', 'Each of the men is to take a turn at working night shift', 'The boys are all well off and each can afford the cost of the holiday' and 'There are to be no exceptions among the women staff. Each one has to work full time'.

Problems arise when the noun that each refers back to is of unknown or unspecified sex. Formerly nouns in such situations were assumed to be masculine, as in 'Each pupil was required to bring his own tennis racket' and 'Each of the students has to provide himself with a tape recorder'. Nowadays such a convention is regarded as being sexist and the use of 'he/her', 'his/her', etc, is proposed, as in 'Each pupil was required to bring his/her (or 'his or her') own tennis racket' and 'Each student has to provide himself/herself (or 'himself or herself') with a tape recorder'. Even in written English such a convention can be clumsy and it is even more so in spoken English. For this reason many people decide to be ungrammatical and opt for 'Each pupil was required to bring their own tennis racket' and 'Each student has to provide themselves with a tape recorder'. This Is becoming Increasingly acceptable, even In textbooks.

Both sexism and grammatical error can be avoided by rephrasing such sentences, as in 'All pupils are required to bring their own tennis rackets' and 'All students have to provide themselves with tape recorders'.

either a word that can be used as either a determiner or distributive pronoun. As a determiner it is used with a singular verb, as in 'Either hotel is expensive' and 'In principle they are both against the plan but is either likely to vote for it?'

Either of can be used instead of either. It is used before a plural noun, as in 'either of the applicants' and 'either of the houses'. It is accompanied by a singular verb, as in 'Either of the applicants is suitable' and 'Either of the houses is big enough for their family'.

Either can be used as a distributive pronoun and takes a singular verb, as in 'We have looked at both houses and either is suitable' and 'She cannot decide between the two dresses but either is appropriate for the occasion'. This use is rather formal.

In the **either . . . . or** construction, a singular verb is used if both subjects are singular, as in 'Either Mary or Jane knows what to do' and 'Either my mother or my father plans to be present'. A plural verb is used if both nouns involved are plural, as in 'Either men or women can play' and 'Either houses or flats are available'.

When a combination of singular and plural subjects is involved, the verb traditionally agrees with the subject that is nearer to it, as in 'Either his parents or his sister is going to come' and 'Either his grandmother or his parents are going to come'.

As a pronoun, either should be used only of two possibilities.

emphasizing adjective an adjective that is used for emphasis. 'Very' is an emphasizing adjective in the sentence 'His very mother dislikes him' and 'own' is an emphasizing adjective in 'He likes to think that he is his own master'.

emphasizing adverb an adverb used for emphasis. 'Really' is an emphasizing adverb in the sentence 'She really doesn't care whether she lives or dies', and 'positively' is an emphasizing adverb in the sentence 'He positively does not want to know anything about it'.

emphatic pronoun a reflexive pronoun that is used for emphasis, as in 'He knows himself that he is wrong', 'She admitted herself that she had made a mistake' and 'The teachers themselves say that the headmaster is too strict'.

ending the final part of a word consisting of an inflection that is added to a base or root word. The '-ren' part of 'children' is an ending, the '-er' of 'poorer' is an ending and the '-ing' of 'falling' is an ending.

equative a term that indicates that one thing is equal to, or the same as, another. The verb 'to be' is sometimes known as an **equative verb** because it links a subject and complement that are equal to each other, as in 'He is a rogue' ('he' and 'rogue' refer to the same person) and 'His wife is a journalist' ('his wife' and 'journalist' refer to the same person). Other equative verbs include 'appear', 'become', 'look', 'remain' and 'seem', as in 'She looks a nasty person' and 'He became a rich man'. Such verbs are more usually known as **copular verbs**.

every a word used with a singular noun to indicate that all the members of a group are being referred to. It takes a singular verb, as in 'Every soldier must report for duty', 'Every machine is to be inspected' and 'Every house has a different view'. Every should also be accompanied, where relevant, by a singular pronoun, as in 'Every boy has his job to do', 'Every girl is to wear a dress' and 'Every machine is to be replaced'. Problems arise when the sex of the noun to which every refers is unknown or unspecified. Formerly it was the custom to assume such a noun to be masculine and to use masculine pronouns, as in 'Every pupil is to behave himself properly'. This assumption is now regarded as sexist, and to avoid this 'he/she', 'him/her' and 'his/her' can be used. Many people feel that this convention can become clumsy and prefer to be ungrammatical by using 'they', 'them' and 'their', as in 'Every pupil is to behave themselves properly.' This use is becoming Increasingly common, even In textbooks. Many sentences of this kind can be rephrased to avoid being either sexist or ungrammatical, as in 'All pupils are to behave themselves properly'. *See* **each**.

everyone a pronoun that takes a singular verb, as in 'Everyone is welcome' and 'Everyone has the right to a decent standard of living'. In order to be grammatically correct, it should be accompanied, where relevant, by a singular personal pronoun but it is subject to the same kind of treatment as every.

feminine the term for the gender that indicates female persons or animals. It is the opposite of 'masculine'. The feminine gender demands the use of the appropriate pronoun, including 'she', 'her', 'hers' and 'herself', as in 'The girl tried to save the dog but *she* was unable to do so', 'The woman hurt *her* leg', 'Mary said that the book is *hers*', and 'The waitress cut *herself*'.

The feminine forms of words, formed by adding —*ess*, used to be common but many such forms are now thought to be sexist. Words such as 'author', 'sculptor', 'poet' are now considered to be neutral terms that can be used to refer to a man or a woman. Some -*ess* words are either still being used or are in a state of flux, as in 'actress'. *See* **-ess** in **Affixes** appendix.

finite clause a clause that contains a finite verb, as in 'when she sees him', 'after she had defeated him', and 'as they were sitting there'.

finite verb a verb that has a tense and has a subject with which it agrees in number and person. For example 'cries' is finite in the sentence 'The child cries most of the time', and 'looks' is finite in the sentence 'The old man looks ill'. However 'go' in the sentence 'He wants to go' is non-finite since it has no variation of tense and does not have a subject. Similarly in the sentence 'Sitting on the river-bank, he was lost in thought', 'sitting' is non-finite.

first person this refers to the person who is speaking or writing when referring to himself or herself. The **first person pronouns** are 'I', 'me', 'myself' and 'mine', with the plural forms being 'we', 'us', 'ourselves' and 'ours'. Examples include 'She said, "*I* am going home" ',

' "*I* am going shopping," he said', ' "*We* have very little money left," she said to her husband' and 'He said, "*We* shall have to leave now if we are to get there on time" '.

The **first person determiners** are 'my' and 'our', as in 'I have forgotten to bring *my* notebook' and 'We must remember to bring *our* books home.'

form word *see* **function word**.

fragmentary sentence *see* **major sentence**.

frequentative a term referring to a verb that expresses frequent repetition of an action. In English the verb endings *-le* and *-el* sometimes indicate the frequentative form, as in 'waddle' from 'wade', 'sparkle' from 'spark', 'crackle' from 'crack' and 'dazzle' from 'daze'. The ending *-er* can also indicate the frequentative form, as in 'stutter', 'spatter' and 'batter'.

function word a word that has very little meaning but is primarily of grammatical significance and merely performs a 'function' in a sentence. Function words include determiners, and prepositions such as in, on and up. Words that are not function words are sometimes known as **content words**.

Function word is also known as **form word** or **structure word**.

future perfect tense the tense of a verb that is formed by 'will' or 'shall' together with the perfect tense, as in 'They will have been married ten years next week', 'You will have finished work by this time tomorrow' and 'By the time Jane arrives here she will have been travelling non-stop for forty-eight hours'.

future tense the tense of a verb that describes actions or states that will occur at some future time. It is marked by 'will' and 'shall'. Traditionally 'shall' was used with subjects in the first person, as in 'I shall see you tomorrow' and 'We shall go there next week', and 'will' was used with subjects in the second and third person, as in 'You will find out next week', 'He will recognize her when he sees her' and 'They will be on the next train'. Formerly 'will' was used with the first person and 'shall' with the second and third person to indicate emphasis or insistence, as in 'I *will* go on my own' and 'We *will* be able to afford it'; 'You *shall* pay what you owe' and 'The children *shall* get a holiday'. In modern usage 'shall' is usually used only for emphasis or insistence, whether with the first, second or third person, except in formal contexts. Otherwise 'will' is used, as in 'I will go tomorrow', 'We will have to see', 'You will be surprised', and 'They will be on their way by now'.

The future tense can also be marked by 'be about to' plus the infinitive of the relevant verb or 'be going to' plus the infinitive of the relevant verb. Examples include 'We are about to leave for work', 'They are about to go on holiday', 'She is going to be late' and 'They are going to demolish the building'.

gemination the doubling of consonants before a suffix.

gender in the English language this usually refers to the natural distinctions of sex (or absence of sex) that exist, and nouns are classified according to these distinctions— masculine, feminine and neuter. Thus, 'man', 'boy', 'king', 'prince', 'emperor', 'duke', 'heir', 'son', 'brother', 'father', 'nephew', 'husband', 'bridegroom', 'widower', 'hero', 'cock', 'drake', 'fox' and 'lion' are masculine nouns. Similarly, 'girl', 'woman', 'queen', 'princess', 'empress', 'duchess', 'heiress', 'daughter', 'sister', 'mother', 'niece', 'wife', 'bride', 'widow', 'heroine', 'hen', 'duck', 'vixen' and 'lioness' are feminine nouns. Similarly, 'table', 'chair', 'desk', 'carpet', 'window', 'lamp', 'car', 'shop', 'dress', 'tie', 'newspaper', 'book', 'building' and 'town' are all neuter.

Some nouns in English can refer either to a man or a woman, unless the sex is indicated in the context. Such neutral nouns are sometimes said to have dual gender. Examples include 'author', 'singer', 'poet', 'sculptor', 'proprietor', 'teacher', 'parent', 'cousin', 'adult' and 'child'. Some words in this category were formerly automatically assumed to be masculine and several of them had feminine forms, such as 'authoress', 'poetess', 'sculptress' and 'proprietrix'. In modern times this was felt to be sexist and many of these feminine forms are now rarely used, for example, 'authoress' and 'poetess'. However some, such as actress and waitress, are still in common use.

genitive case a case that indicates possession or ownership. It is usually marked by *s* and an apostrophe. Many spelling errors centre on the position of the *s* in relation to the apostrophe.

gerund the *-ing* form of a verb when it functions as a noun. It is sometimes known as a **verbal noun**. It has the same form as the present participle but has a different function. For example, in the sentence 'He was jogging down the road', 'jogging' is the present participle in the verb phrase 'was jogging', but in the sentence 'Running is his idea of relaxation', 'running' is a gerund because it acts as a noun as the subject of the sentence.

Similarly, in the sentence 'We were smoking when the teacher found us', 'smoking' is the present participle in the verb phrase 'were smoking', but in the sentence 'We were told that smoking is bad for our health', 'smoking' is a gerund since it acts as a noun as the subject of the clause.

get this verb is sometimes used to form the passive voice instead of the verb 'to be'. The use of the verb 'to get' to form the passive, as in 'They get married tomorrow', 'Our team got beaten today' and 'We got swindled by the con man' is sometimes considered to be more informal than the use of 'be'. Often there is more action involved when the get construction is used than when be is used, since get is a more dynamic verb, as in 'She was late leaving the pub because she got involved in an argument' and in 'It was her own fault that she got arrested by the police. She hit one of the constables'.

Get is frequently overused. Such overuse should be avoided, particularly in formal contexts. Get can often be replaced by a synonym such as 'obtain', 'acquire', 'receive', 'get hold of', etc. Thus, 'If you are getting into money difficulties you should get some financial advice. Perhaps you could get a bank loan' could be rephrased as 'If you are in financial difficulty you should obtain some financial help. Perhaps you could receive a bank loan'.

got, the past tense of get, is often used unnecessarily, as in 'She has got red hair and freckles' and 'We have got enough food to last us the week'. In these sentences 'has' and 'have' are sufficient on their own.

goal this can be used to describe the recipient of the action of a verb, the opposite of 'agent' or 'actor'. Thus, in the sentence 'The boy hit the girl', 'boy' is the 'agent' or 'actor' and 'girl' is the goal. Similarly, in the sentence 'The dog bit the postman', 'dog' is the 'agent' or 'actor' and 'postman' is the goal.

govern a term that is used of a verb or preposition in relation to a noun or pronoun to indicate that the verb or preposition has a noun or pronoun depending on it. Thus, in the phrase 'on the table', 'on' is said to govern 'table'.

gradable a term that is used of adjectives and adverbs to mean that they can take degrees of comparison. Thus 'clean' is a gradable adjective since it has a comparative form (cleaner) and a superlative form (cleanest). 'Soon' is a gradable adverb since it has a comparative form (sooner) and a superlative form (soonest). Such words as 'supreme', which cannot normally have a comparative or superlative form, are called **non-gradable**.

habitual a term used to refer to the action of a verb that occurs regularly and repeatedly. The **habitual present** is found in such sentences as 'He goes to bed at ten every night', 'She always walks to work' and 'The old man sleeps all day'. This is in contrast to the **stative present**, which indicates the action of the verb that occurs at all times, as in 'Cows chew the cud', 'Water becomes ice when it freezes', 'Children grow up' and 'We all die'. Examples of the **habitual past** tense include; 'They travelled by train to work all their lives', 'We worked twelve hours a day on that project' and 'She studied night and day for the exams'.

hanging participle *see* **dangling participle**.

have a verb that has several functions. A major use is its part in forming the 'perfect tense' and 'past perfect tense', or 'pluperfect tense', of other verb tenses. It does this in conjunction with the 'past participle' of the verb in question.

The perfect tense of a verb is formed by the present tense of the verb have and the past participle of the verb. Examples include 'We have acted wisely', 'They have beaten the opposition', 'The police have caught the thieves', 'The old man has died', 'The child has eaten all the food', 'The baby has fallen downstairs', 'They have grabbed all the bargains', 'You have hated him for years' and 'He has indicated that he is going to retire'. The past perfect or pluperfect is formed by the past tense of the verb have and the past participle of the verb in question, as in 'He had jumped over the fence', 'They had kicked in the door', 'The boy had led the other children to safety', 'His mother had made the cake', 'The headmaster had punished the pupils' and 'They had rushed into buying a new house'. Both perfect tenses

and past perfect or pluperfect tenses are often contracted in speech or in informal written English, as in 'We've had enough for today', 'You've damaged the suitcase', 'You've missed the bus', 'He's lost his wallet', 'She's arrived too late', 'They'd left before the news came through', 'She'd married without telling her parents', 'He'd packed the goods himself' and 'You'd locked the door without realizing it'.

Have is often used in the phrase **have to** in the sense that something must be done. In the present tense have to can be used instead of 'must', as in 'You have to leave now', 'We have to clear this mess up', 'He has to get the next train' and 'The goods have to be sold today'. If the 'something that must be done' refers to the future the verb **will have to** is used', as in 'He will have to leave now to get there on time', 'The old man will have to go to hospital' and 'They'll have to move out of the house when her parents return'. If the 'something that must be done' refers to the past, **had to** is used, as in 'We had to take the injured man to hospital', 'They had to endure freezing conditions on the mountain', 'They'd to take a reduction in salary' and 'We'd to wait all day for the workman to appear'.

Have is also used in the sense of 'possess' or 'own', as in 'He has a swimming pool behind his house ', 'She has a huge wardrobe', 'We have enough food' and 'They have four cars'. In spoken or in informal English 'have got' is often used, as in 'They've got the largest house in the street', 'We've got problems now', 'They haven't got time'. This use should be avoided in formal English.

Have is also used to indicate suffering from an illness or disease, as in 'The child has measles', 'Her father has flu' and 'She has heart disease'. Have can also indicate that an activity is taking place, as in 'She's having a shower', 'We're having a party', 'She is having a baby' and 'They are having a dinner party'.

he a personal pronoun that is used as the subject of a sentence or clause to refer to a man, boy, etc. It is thus said to be a 'masculine' personal pronoun. Since he refers to a third party and does not refer to the speaker or the person being addressed, it is a third-person pronoun. Examples include 'James is quite nice but he can be boring', 'Bob has got a new job and he is very pleased' and 'He is rich now but his parents are still very poor'.

He traditionally was used not only to refer to nouns relating to the masculine sex but also to nouns that are now regarded as being neutral or of dual gender. Such nouns include 'architect', 'artist', 'athlete', 'doctor', 'passenger', 'parent', 'pupil', 'singer', 'student'. Without further information from the context it is impossible to know to which sex such nouns are referring. In modern usage it is regarded as sexist to assume such words to be masculine by using he to refer to one of them unless the context indicates that the noun in question refers to a man or boy. Formerly it was considered acceptable to write or say 'Send a message to the architect who designed the building that he is to attend the meeting' whether or not the writer or speaker knew that the architect was a man. Similarly it was considered acceptable to write or say 'Please tell the doctor that he is to come straight away' whether or not the speaker or writer knew that the doctor was in fact a man. Nowadays this convention is considered sexist. In order to avoid sexism it is possible to use the convention 'he/she', as in 'Every pupil was told that he/she was to be smartly dressed for the occasion', 'Each passenger was informed that he/she was to arrive ten minutes before the coach was due to leave' and 'Tell the doctor that he/she is required urgently'. However this convention is regarded by some people as being clumsy, particularly in spoken English or in informal written English. Some people prefer to be ungrammatical and use the plural personal pronoun 'they' instead of 'he/she' in certain situations, as in 'Every passenger was told that they had to arrive ten minutes before the coach was due to leave' and 'Every student was advised that they should apply for a college place by March' and this use is becoming increasingly common, even in textbooks. In some cases it may be possible to rephrase sentences and avoid being either sexist or ungrammatical, as in 'All the passengers were told that they should arrive ten minutes before the coach was due to leave' and 'All students were advised that they should apply for a college place by March'.

helping verb another name for **auxiliary verb**.

hendiadys a figure of speech in which two nouns joined by 'and' are used to express an idea that would normally be expressed by the use of an adjective and a noun, as in 'through storm and weather' instead of 'through stormy weather'.

her a personal pronoun. It is the third person singular, is feminine in gender and acts as the object in a sentence, as in 'We saw her yesterday', 'I don't know her', 'He hardly ever sees her', 'Please give this book to her', 'Our daughter sometimes plays with her' and 'We do not want her to come to the meeting'. *See* **he; she**.

hers a personal pronoun. It is the third person singular, feminine in gender and is in the poassessive case. 'The car is not hers', 'I have forgotten my book but I don't want to borrow hers', 'This is my seat and that is hers', and 'These clothes are hers'. *See* **his; her** and **possessive**.

him the third person masculine personal pronoun when used as the object of a sentence or clause, as in 'She shot him', 'When the police caught the thief they arrested him' and 'His parents punished him after the boy stole the money'. Traditionally him was used to apply not only to masculine nouns, such as 'man' and 'boy', but also to nouns that are said to be 'of dual gender'. These include 'architect', 'artist', 'parent', 'passenger', 'pupil' and 'student'. Without further information from the context, it is not possible for the speaker or writer to know the sex of the person referred to by one of these words. Formerly it was acceptable to write or say 'The artist must bring an easel with him' and 'Each pupil must bring food with

him'. In modern usage this convention is considered sexist and there is a modern convention that 'him/her' should be used instead to avoid sexism, as in 'The artist must bring an easel with him/her' and 'Each pupil must bring food with 'him/her'. This convention is felt by some people to be clumsy and some people prefer to be ungrammatical and use the plural personal pronoun 'them' instead, as in 'The artist must bring an easel with them' and 'Each pupil must bring food with them'. This use has become increasingly common, even in textbooks. In some situations it is possible to avoid being either sexist or ungrammatical by rephrasing the sentence, as in 'All artists must bring easels with them' and 'All pupils must bring food with them. *See* **he**.

him/her *see* **him**.

his the third personal masculine pronoun when used to indicate possession, as in 'He has hurt his leg', 'The boy has taken his books home' and 'Where has your father left his tools?' Traditionally his was used to refer not only to masculine nouns, such as 'man', 'boy', etc, but to what are known as nouns 'of dual gender'. These include 'architect', 'artist', 'parent', 'passenger', 'pupil' and 'student'. Without further information from the context it is not possible for the speaker or the writer to know the sex of the person referred to by one of these words. Formerly it was considered acceptable to use his in such situations, as in 'Every pupil has to supply his own sports equipment' and 'Every passenger is responsible for his own luggage'. In modern usage this is now considered sexist and there is a modern convention that 'his/her' should be used instead to avoid sexism, as in 'Every pupil has to supply his/her own sports equipment' and 'Every passenger is responsible for his/her own luggage'. This convention is felt by some people to be clumsy, particularly when used in spoken or informal written English. Some people prefer to be ungrammatical and use the plural personal pronoun 'their', as in 'Every pupil must supply their own sports equipment' and 'Every passenger is to be responsible for their own luggage' and this use has become increasingly common, even in textbooks. In some situations it is possible to avoid being sexist, clumsy and ungrammatical by rephrasing the sentence, as in 'All pupils must supply their own sports equipment' and 'All passengers are to be responsible for their own luggage.

his/her *see* **his**.

hybrid a word that is formed from words or elements derived from different languages, such as 'television'.

if a conjunction that is often used to introduce a subordinate adverbial clause of condition, as in 'If he is talking of leaving he must be unhappy', 'If you tease the dog it will bite you', 'If he had realized that the weather was going to be so bad he would not have gone on the expedition', 'If I had been in charge I would have sacked him' and 'If it were a better organized firm things like that would not happen'.

If can also introduce a 'nominal' or 'noun clause', as in 'He asked if we objected' and 'She inquired if we wanted to go'.

imperative mood the verb mood that expresses commands. The verbs in the following sentences are in the imperative mood: 'Go away!', 'Run faster!', 'Answer me!', 'Sit down!', 'Please get out of here!'. All of these expressions with verbs in the imperative mood sound rather imperious or dictatorial and usually end with an exclamation mark, but this is not true of all expressions with verbs in the imperative mood. For example, the following sentences all have verbs in the imperative mood: 'Have another helping of ice cream', 'Help yourself to more wine', 'Just follow the yellow arrows to the X-ray department', and 'Turn right at the roundabout'. Sentences with verbs in the imperative mood are known as **imperative sentences**.

imperfect a tense that denotes an action in progress but not complete. The term derives from the classification in Latin grammar and was traditionally applied to the 'past imperfect', as in 'They were standing there'. The imperfect has now been largely superseded by the progressive/continuous tense, which is marked by the use of 'be' plus the present participle. Continuous tenses are used when talking about temporary situations at a particular point in time, as in 'They were waiting for the bus'.

impersonal a verb that is used with a formal subject, usually 'it', as in 'It is raining' and 'They say it will snow tomorrow'.

indefinite pronouns these are used refer to people or things without being specific as to exactly who or what they are. They include 'everyone', 'everybody', 'everything', 'anyone', 'anybody', 'anything', 'somebody', 'someone', 'something' and 'nobody', 'no one', 'nothing', as in 'Everyone is to make a contribution', 'Anyone can enter', 'Something will turn up' and 'Nobody cares'.

independent clause a clause that can stand alone and make sense without being dependent on another clause, as in 'The children are safe'. Main clauses are independent clauses. Thus in the sentence 'She is tired and she wants to go home', there are two independent clauses joined by 'and'. In the sentence 'She will be able to rest when she gets home', 'She will be able to rest' is an independent clause and 'when she gets home' is a dependent clause. In the sentence 'Because she is intelligent she thinks for herself', 'she thinks for herself' is an independent clause and 'because she is intelligent' is a dependent clause.

indicative mood the mood of a verb which denotes making a statement. The following sentences have verbs in the indicative mood: 'We go on holiday tomorrow', 'He was waiting for her husband', 'They have lost the match' and 'She will arrive this afternoon'. The indicative mood is sometimes known as the **declarative mood**. The other moods are the imperative mood and subjunctive mood.

indirect object an object that can be preceded by 'to' or 'for'. The indirect object usually refers to the person who benefits from an action or receives something as the result of it. In the sentence 'Her father gave the boy food', 'boy' is the indirect object and 'food' is the direct object. The sentence could be rephrased as 'Her father gave food to the boy'. In the sentence 'He bought his mother flowers', 'his mother' is the indirect object and 'flowers' is the direct object. The sentence could have been rephrased as 'He bought flowers for his mother'. In the sentence 'They offered him a reward', 'him' is the indirect object and 'reward' is the direct object. The sentence could be rephrased as 'They offered a reward to him'.

indirect question a question that is reported in indirect speech, as in 'We asked them where they were going', 'They inquired why we had come' and 'They looked at us curiously and asked where we had come from'. Note that a question mark is not used.

indirect speech also known as **reported speech** a way of reporting what someone has said without using the actual words used by the speaker. There is usually an introductory verb and a subordinate 'that' clause, as in 'He said that he was going away', 'They announced that they were leaving next day' and 'She declared that she had seen him there before'. In direct speech these sentences would become 'He said, "I am going away" ', 'They announced, "We are leaving tomorrow" ' and 'She declared, "I have seen him there before" '. When the change is made from direct speech to indirect speech, the pronouns, adverbs of time and place and tenses are changed to accord with the viewpoint of the person doing the reporting.

infinitive the base form of a verb when used without any indication of person, number or tense. There are two forms of the infinitive. One is the **to infinitive** form, as in 'They wished to leave', 'I plan to go tomorrow', 'We aim to please' and 'They want to emigrate', 'To know all is to forgive all', 'To err is human', 'Pull the lever to open', 'You should bring a book to read', 'The child has nothing to do', 'She is not very nice to know' and 'It is hard to believe that it happened'. The other form of the infinitive is called the **bare infinitive**. This form consists of the base form of the verb without 'to', as in 'We saw him fall', 'She watched him go', 'They noticed him enter', 'She heard him sigh', 'They let him go', 'I had better leave' and 'Need we return' and 'we dare not go back'. See **split infinitive**.

inflect when applied to a word, this means to change form in order to indicate differences of tense, number, gender, case, etc. Nouns inflect for plural, as in 'ships', 'chairs', 'houses' and 'oxen'; nouns inflect for possessive, as in 'boys'', 'woman's', 'teachers'', and 'parents''; some adjectives inflect for the comparative form, as in 'brighter', 'clearer', 'shorter' and 'taller'; verbs inflect for the third person singular present tense, as in 'hears', 'joins', 'touches' and 'kicks'; verbs inflect for the present participle, as in 'hearing', 'joining', 'touching' and 'kicking'; verbs inflect for the past participle, as in 'heard', 'joined', 'touched' and 'kicked'.

inflection the act of inflecting—*see* **inflect**. It also refers to an inflected form of a word or a suffix or other element used to inflect a word.

-ing form this form of a verb can be either a present participle or a gerund. Present participles are used in the formation of the progressive or continuous tenses, as in

'We were looking at the pictures', 'Children were playing in the snow', 'They are waiting for the bus', 'Parents were showing their anger', 'He has been sitting there for hours'. Present participles can also be used in non-finite clauses or phrases, as in 'Walking along, she did not have a care in the world', 'Lying there, he thought about his life', 'Sighing, he left the room' and 'Smiling broadly he congratulated his friend'.

A large number of adjectives end in -ing. Many of these have the same form as the present participle of a transitive verb and are similar in meaning. Examples include 'an amazing spectacle', 'a boring show', 'an interesting idea', 'a tiring day', 'an exhausting climb' and 'aching limbs'. Some -ing adjectives are related to intransitive verbs, as 'existing problems', 'increasing responsibilities', 'dwindling resources', 'an ageing work force' and 'prevailing circumstances'. Some -ing adjectives are related to the forms of verbs but have different meanings from the verbs, as in 'becoming dress', 'an engaging personality', 'a dashing young man' and 'a retiring disposition'. Some -ing adjectives are not related to verbs at all. These include 'appetizing', 'enterprising', 'impending' and 'balding'. Some -ing adjectives are used informally for emphasis, as in 'a blithering idiot', 'a stinking cold' and 'a flaming cheek'.

Gerunds act as nouns and are sometimes known as **verbal nouns**. Examples include 'Smoking is bad for one's health', 'Cycling is forbidden in the park' and 'Swimming is his favourite sport'.

intensifier the term for an adverb that affects the degree of intensity of another word. Intensifiers include 'thoroughly' in 'We were thoroughly shocked by the news', 'scarcely' in 'We scarcely recognized them' and 'totally' in 'She was totally amazed'.

interjection a kind of exclamation. Sometimes they are formed by actual words and sometimes they simply consist of sounds indicating emotional noises. Examples of interjections include 'Oh! I am quite shocked', 'Gosh! I'm surprised to hear that!', 'Phew! It's hot!', 'Ouch! That was my foot!', 'Tut-tut! He shouldn't have done that!' and 'Alas! She is dead.'

interrogative adjective or **determiner** an adjective or determiner that asks for information in relation to the nouns which it qualifies, as in 'What dress did you choose in the end?', 'What kind of book are you looking for?', 'Which house do you like best?', 'Which pupil won the prize?', 'Whose bike was stolen?' and 'Whose dog is that?'

interrogative adverb an adverb that asks a question, as in 'When did they leave?', 'When does the meeting start?', 'Where do they live?', 'Where was the stolen car found?', 'Where did you last see her?', 'Why was she crying?', 'Why have they been asked to leave?', 'How is the invalid?', 'How do you know that she has gone?' and 'Wherever did you find that?'

interrogative pronoun a pronoun that asks a question, as in 'Who asked you to do that?', 'Who broke the vase?', 'What did he say?', 'What happened next?', 'Whose are those books?', 'Whose is that old car?', 'To whom was that remark addressed?' and 'To whom did you address the package?'

interrogative sentence a sentence that asks a question, as in 'Who is that?', 'Where is he?', 'Why have they appeared?', 'What did they take away?', 'Which do you prefer?' and 'Whose baby is that?'. Sentences that take the form of an interrogative question do not always seek information. Sometimes they are exclamations, as in 'Did you ever see anything so beautiful?', 'Isn't she sweet?' and 'Aren't they lovely?'. Sentences that take the form of questions may really be commands or directives, as in 'Could you turn down that radio?', 'Would you make less noise?' and 'Could you get her a chair?'. Sentences that take the form of questions may function as statements, as in 'Isn't there always a reason?' and 'Haven't we all experienced disappointment?'. Some interrogative sentences are what are known as rhetorical questions, which are asked purely for effect and require no answer, as in 'Do you think I am a fool?', 'What is the point of life?' and 'What is the world coming to?'.

intransitive verb a verb that does not take a direct object, as in 'Snow fell yesterday', 'The children played in the sand', 'The path climbed steeply', 'Time will tell', 'The situation worsened', 'Things improved' and 'Prices increased'. Many verbs can be either transitive or intransitive, according to the context. Thus 'play' is intransitive in the sentence 'The children played in the sand' but transitive in the sentence 'The boy plays the piano'. Similarly 'climb' is intransitive in the sentence 'The path climbs steeply' but transitive in the sentence 'The mountaineers climbed Everest'. Similarly 'tell' is intransitive in the sentence 'Time will tell' but transitive in the sentence 'He will tell his life story'.

introductory it the use of 'it' as the subject of a sentence in the absence of a meaningful subject. It is used particularly in sentences about time and the weather, as in 'It is midnight', 'It is dawn', 'It is five o'clock', 'It is twelve noon', 'It is raining', 'It was snowing', 'It was windy' and 'It was blowing a gale'.

invariable a word whose form does not vary by inflection. Such words include 'sheep' and 'but'.

inversion the reversal of the usual word order. It particularly refers to subjects and verbs. Inversion is used in questions, in some negative sentences, and for literary effect. In questions, an auxiliary verb is usually put in front of the subject and the rest of the verb group is put after the subject, as in 'Are you going to see her?' and 'Have they inspected the goods yet?'. The verb 'to do' is frequently used in inversion, as in 'Did he commit the crime?' and 'Do they still believe that?'. Examples of the use of inversion in negative sentences include 'Seldom have I witnessed such an act of selfishness', 'Never had she experienced such pain' and 'Rarely do we have time to admire the beauty of the countryside'. This use in negative sentences is rather formal.

Inversion frequently involves adverbial phrases of

place, as in 'Beyond the town stretched field after field', 'Above them soared the eagle' and 'Along the driveway grew multitudes of daffodils'.

Inversion is also found in conditional clauses that are not introduced by conjunction, as in 'Had you arrived earlier you would have got a meal' and 'Had we some more money we could do more for the refugees'.

irregular adjective an adjective that does not conform to the usual rules of forming the comparative and superlative (*see* **comparison of adjectives**). Many adjectives either add *-er* for the comparative and *-est* for the superlative, as in 'taller', 'shorter' and 'tallest', 'shortest' from 'tall' and 'short'. Some adjectives form their comparatives with 'more' and their superlatives with 'most', as in 'more beautiful', 'more practical' and 'most beautiful', 'most practical'. Irregular adjectives do not form their comparatives and superlatives in either of these ways. Irregular adjectives include:

positive	comparative	superlative
good	better	best
bad	worse	worst
little	less	least
many	more	most

irregular sentence *see* **major sentence**.

irregular verb a verb that does not conform to the usual pattern of verbs in that some of its forms deviate from what one would expect if the pattern of regular verbs was being followed. There are four main forms of a **regular verb**—the infinitive or base form, as in 'hint', 'halt', 'hate' and 'haul'; the third-person singular form, as 'hints', 'halts', 'hates' and 'hauls'; the -ing form or present participle, as 'hinting', halting', 'hating' and 'hauling'; the *-ed* form or 'past tense' or 'past participle', as 'hinted', halted', 'hated' and 'hauled.

Irregular verbs deviate in some way from that pattern, in particular from the pattern of adding *-ed* to the past tense and past participle. They fall into several categories.

One category concerns those that have the same form in the past tense and past participle forms as the infinitive and do not end in *-ed*, like regular verbs.

Some irregular verbs have two past tenses and two past participles which are the same.

Some irregular verbs have past tenses that do not end in *-ed* and have the same form as the past participle.

Some irregular verbs have regular past tense forms but two possible past participles, one of which is regular.

Some irregular verbs have past tenses and past participles that are different from each other and different from the infinitive.

jussive a type of clause or sentence that expresses a command, as in 'Do be quiet! I'm trying to study', 'Let's not bother going to the party. I'm too tired', 'Would you pass me that book' and 'Look at that everybody! The river has broken its banks'.

linking adverbs and **linking adverbials** words and phrases that indicate some kind of connection between one clause or sentence and another. Examples include 'however', as in 'The award had no effect on their financial situation. It did, however, have a marked effect on their morale'; 'moreover', as in 'He is an unruly pupil. Moreover, he is a bad influence on the other pupils'; 'then again', as in 'She does not have very good qualifications. Then again, most of the other candidates have even fewer'; 'in the meantime', as in 'We will not know the planning committee's decision until next week. In the meantime we can only hope'; 'instead', as in 'I thought he would have reigned. Instead he seems determined to stay'.

linking verb a verb that 'links' a subject with its complement. Unlike other verbs, linking verbs do not denote an action but indicate a state. Examples of linking verbs include 'He is a fool', 'She appears calm', 'He appeared a sensible man', 'You seemed to become anxious', 'They became Buddhists', 'The child feels unwell', 'It is getting rather warm', 'It is growing colder', 'You look well', 'She remained loyal to her friend', 'She lived in America but remained a British citizen' and 'You seem thoughtful' and 'She seems a nice person'. Linking verbs are also called **copula** or **copular verbs**.

main clause the principal clause in a sentence on which any subordinate clauses depend for their sense. The main clause can stand alone and make some sense but the subordinate clauses cannot. In the sentence 'I left early because I wanted to catch the 6 o'clock train', 'I left early' is the principal clause and 'because I wanted to catch the 6 o'clock train' is the subordinate clause. In the sentence 'When we saw the strange man we were afraid', the main clause is 'we were afraid' and the subordinate clause is 'when we saw the strange man'. In the sentence 'Because it was late we decided to start out for home as soon as we could', the main clause is 'we decided to start out for home' and the subordinate clauses are 'because it was late' and 'as soon as we could'. A main clause can also be known as a **principal clause** or an independent clause.

major sentence a sentence that contains at least one subject and a finite verb, as in 'We are going' and 'They won'. They frequently have more elements than this, as in 'They bought a car', 'We lost the match', 'They arrived yesterday' and 'We are going away next week'. They are sometimes described as **regular** because they divide into certain structural patterns: a subject, finite verb, adverb or adverbial clause, etc. The opposite of a major sentence is called a **minor sentence**, **irregular sentence** or **fragmentary sentence**. These include interjections such as 'Ouch!' and 'How terrible'; formula expressions, such as 'Good morning' and 'Well done'; and short forms of longer expressions, as in 'Traffic diverted', 'Shop closed', 'No dogs' and 'Flooding ahead'. Such short forms could be rephrased to become major sentences, as in 'Traffic has been diverted because of roadworks', 'The shop is closed on Sundays', 'The owner does not allow dogs in her shop' and 'There was flooding ahead on the motorway'.

masculine in grammatical terms, one of the genders that

nouns are divided into. Nouns in the masculine gender include words that obviously belong to the male sex, as in 'man', 'boy', 'king', 'prince' 'bridegroom', 'schoolboy' and 'salesman'. Many words now considered to be of dual gender formerly were assumed to be masculine. These include such words as 'author', 'sculptor' and 'engineer'. Gender also applies to personal pronouns, and the third personal singular pronoun masculine is 'he' (subject), 'him' (object) and 'his' (possessive). For further information *see* **he**; **she**.

mass noun the same as **uncountable noun**.

minor sentence *see* **major sentence**.

misrelated participle *see* **dangling participle**.

modal verb a type of auxiliary verb that 'helps' the main verb to express a range of meanings including, for example, such meanings as possibility, probability, wants, wishes, necessity, permission, suggestions, etc. The main modal verbs are 'can', 'could'; 'may', 'might'; 'will', 'would'; 'shall', 'should'; 'must'. Modal verbs have only one form. They have no -*s* form in the third person singular, no infinitive and no participles. Examples of modal verbs include 'He cannot read and write', 'She could go if she wanted to' (expressing ability); 'You can have another biscuit', 'You may answer the question' (expressing permission); 'We may see her on the way to the station', 'We might get there by nightfall' (expressing possibility); 'Will you have some wine?', 'Would you take a seat?' (expressing an offer or invitation); 'We should arrive by dawn', 'That must be a record' (expressing probability and certainty); 'You may prefer to wait', 'You might like to leave instructions' (expressing suggestion); 'Can you find the time to phone him for me?', 'Could you give him a message?' (expressing instructions and requests); 'They must leave at once', 'We must get there on time' (expressing necessity).

modifier a word, or group of words, that 'modifies' or affects the meaning of another word in some way, usually by adding more information about it. Modifiers are frequently used with nouns. They can be adjectives, as in 'He works in the *main* building' and 'They need a *larger* house'. Modifiers of nouns can be nouns themselves, as in 'the *theatre* profession', 'the *publishing* industry' and '*singing* tuition'. They can also be place names, as in 'the *Edinburgh* train', 'a *Paris* café' and 'the *London* underground', or adverbs of place and direction, as in 'a *downstairs* cloakroom' and 'an *upstairs* sitting room'.

Adverbs, adjectives and pronouns can be accompanied by modifiers. Examples of modifiers with adverbs include 'walking *amazingly* quickly' and 'stopping *incredibly* abruptly'. Examples of modifiers with adjectives include 'a *really* warm day' and 'a *deliriously* happy child'. Examples of modifiers with pronouns include '*almost* no one there' and '*practically* everyone present'.

The examples given above are all premodifiers. *See also* **postmodifier**.

mood one of the categories into which verbs are divided. The verb moods are indicative, imperative and subjunctive. The **indicative** makes a statement, as in 'He lives in France', 'They have two children' and 'It's starting to rain'. The **imperative** is used for giving orders or making requests, as in 'Shut that door!', 'Sit quietly until the teacher arrives' and 'Please bring me some coffee'. The **subjunctive** was originally a term in Latin grammar and expressed a wish, supposition, doubt, improbability or other non-factual statement. It is used in English for hypothetical statements and certain formal 'that' clauses, as in 'If I were you I would have nothing to do with it', 'If you were to go now you would arrive on time', 'Someone suggested that we ask for more money' and 'It was his solicitor who suggested that he sue the firm'. The word 'mood' arose because it was said to indicate the verb's attitude or viewpoint.

more an adverb that is added to some adjectives to make the comparative form (*see* **comparison of adjectives**). In general it is the longer adjectives that have more as part of their comparative form, as in 'more abundant', 'more beautiful', 'more catastrophic', 'more dangerous', 'more elegant', 'more frantic', 'more graceful', 'more handsome', 'more intelligent', 'more luxurious', 'more manageable', 'more opulent', 'more precious', 'more ravishing', 'more satisfactory', 'more talented', 'more unusual', 'more valuable'. Examples of adverbs with more in their comparative form include 'more elegantly', 'more gracefully', 'more energetically', 'more dangerously' and 'more determinedly'.

most an adverb added to some adjectives and adverbs to make the superlative form. In general it is the longer adjectives that have most as part of their superlative form, as in 'most abundant', 'most beautiful', 'most catastrophic', 'most dangerous', 'most elegant', 'most frantic', 'most graceful', 'most handsome', 'most intelligent', 'most luxurious', 'most manageable', 'most noteworthy', 'most opulent', 'most precious', most ravishing', 'most satisfactory', 'most talented', 'most unusual', 'most valuable'. Examples of adverbs with most in their superlative form include 'most elegantly', 'most gracefully', 'most energetically', 'most dangerously' and 'most determinedly'.

multi-sentence a sentence with more than one clause, as in 'She tripped over a rock and broke her ankle' and 'She was afraid when she saw the strange man'.

negative sentence a sentence that is the opposite of a **positive sentence**. 'She has a dog' is an example of a positive sentence. 'She does not have a dog' is an example of a negative sentence. The negative concept is expressed by an auxiliary verb accompanied by 'not' or 'n't'. Other words used in negative sentences include 'never', 'nothing' and 'by no means', as in 'She has never been here' and 'We heard nothing'.

neither an adjective or a pronoun that takes a singular verb, as in 'Neither parent will come' and 'Neither of them wishes to come'. In the **neither ... nor** construction, a singular verb is used if both parts of the construction are singular, as in 'Neither Jane nor Mary was present'. If both parts are plural the verb is plural, as in 'Neither their parents nor their grandparents are willing to look after them'. If the construction involves a mixture of singular and plural, the verb traditionally agrees with the subject that is nearest it, as in 'Neither her mother nor her grandparents are going to come' and 'Neither her grandparents nor her mother is going to come'. If pronouns are used, the nearer one governs the verb as in 'Neither they nor he is at fault' and 'Neither he nor they are at fault'.

neuter one of the grammatical genders. The other two grammatical genders are masculine and feminine. Inanimate objects are members of the neuter gender. Examples include 'table', 'desk', 'garden', 'spade', 'flower' and 'bottle'.

nominal clause *see* **noun clause**.

non-finite clause a clause which contains a non-finite verb. Thus in the sentence 'He works hard to earn a living', 'to earn a living' is a non-finite clause since 'to earn' is an infinitive and so a non-finite verb. Similarly in the sentence 'Getting there was a problem', 'getting there' is a non-finite clause, 'getting' being a present participle and so a non-finite verb.

non-finite verb a verb that shows no variation in tense and has no subject. The non-finite verb forms include the infinitive form, as in 'go', the present participle and gerund, as in 'going', and the past participle, as in 'gone'.

non-gradable *see* **gradable**.

noun the name of something or someone. Thus 'anchor', 'baker', 'cat', 'elephant', 'foot', 'gate', 'lake', 'pear', 'shoe', 'trunk' and 'wallet' are all nouns. There are various categories of nouns. *See* **abstract noun**, **common noun**, **concrete noun**, **countable noun**, **proper noun** and **uncountable noun**.

noun clause a subordinate clause that performs a function in a sentence similar to a noun or noun phrase. It can act as the subject, object or complement of a main clause. In the sentence 'Where he goes is his own business', 'where he goes' is a noun clause. In the sentence 'They asked why he objected', 'why he objected' is a noun clause. A noun clause is also known as a **nominal clause**.

noun phrase a group of words containing a noun as its main word and functioning like a noun in a sentence. Thus it can function as the subject, object or complement of a sentence. In the sentence 'The large black dog bit him', 'the large black dog' is a noun phrase, and in the sentence 'They bought a house with a garden', 'with a garden' is a noun phrase. In the sentence 'She is a complete fool', 'a complete fool' is a noun phrase.

noun, plurals *see* **Spelling** appendix.

number in grammar this is a classification consisting of 'singular' and 'plural'. Thus the number of the pronoun 'they' is 'plural' and the number of the verb 'carries' is singular. *See* **number agreement**.

number agreement or **concord** the agreement of grammatical units in terms of number. Thus a singular subject is followed by a singular verb, as in 'The girl likes flowers', 'He hates work' and 'She was carrying a suitcase'. Similarly a plural subject should be followed by a plural verb, as in 'They have many problems', 'The men work hard' and 'The girls are training hard'.

object the part of a sentence that is acted upon or is affected by the verb. It usually follows the verb to which it relates. There are two forms of object—the direct object and indirect object. A direct object can be a noun, and in the sentence 'The girl hit the ball', 'ball' is a noun and the object. In the sentence 'They bought a house', 'house' is a noun and the object. In the sentence 'They made an error', 'error' is a noun and the object. A direct object can be a noun phrase, and in the sentence 'He has bought a large house', 'a large house' is a noun phrase and the object. In the sentence 'She loves the little girl', 'the little girl' is a noun phrase and the object. In the sentence 'They both wear black clothes', 'black clothes' is a noun phrase and the object'. A direct object can be a noun clause, and in the sentence 'I know what he means', 'what he means' is a noun phrase and the object. In the sentence 'He denied that he had been involved', 'that he had been involved' is a noun phrase and the object. In the sentence 'I asked when he would return', 'when he would return' is a noun phrase and the object. A direct object can also be a pronoun, and in the sentence 'She hit him', 'him' is a pronoun and the object. In the sentence 'They had a car but they sold it', 'it' is a pronoun and the object. In the sentence 'She loves them', 'them' is a pronoun and the object.

objective case the case expressing the object. In Latin it is known as the accusative case.

part of speech each of the categories (e.g. verb, noun, adjective, etc) into which words are divided according to their grammatical and semantic functions.

participle a part of speech, so called because, although a verb, it has the character both of verb and adjective and is also used in the formation of some compound tenses. *See also* **-ing form** and **past participle**.

passive voice the voice of a verb whereby the subject is the recipient of the action of the verb. Thus, in the sentence 'Mary was kicked by her brother', 'Mary' is the receiver of the 'kick' and so 'kick' is in the passive voice. Had it been in the active voice it would have been 'Her brother kicked Mary'. Thus 'the brother' is the subject and not the receiver of the action.

past participle this is formed by adding -*ed* or -*d* to the base words of regular verbs, as in 'acted', ' alluded', 'boarded', 'dashed', 'flouted', 'handed', 'loathed', 'tended' and 'wanted', or in various other ways for irregular verbs.

past tense this tense of a verb is formed by adding -*ed* or -*d* to the base form of the verb in regular verbs, as in 'added', 'crashed', 'graded', 'smiled', 'rested' and 'yielded', and in various ways for irregular verbs.

perfect tense *see* **tense**.

personal pronoun a pronoun that is used to refer back to someone or something that has already been mentioned. The personal pronouns are divided into subject pronouns, object pronouns and possessive pronouns. They are also categorized according to 'person'. *See* **first person**, **second person** and **third person**.

phrasal verb a usually simple verb that combines with a preposition or adverb, or both, to convey a meaning more than the sum of its parts, e.g. to phase out, to come out, to look forward to.

phrase two or more words, usually not containing a finite verb, that form a complete expression by themselves or constitute a portion of a sentence.

positive sentence *see* **negative sentence**.

possessive *see* **genitive**.

possessive pronoun *see* **personal pronoun**, **first person**, **second person** and **third person**.

postmodifier a modifier that comes after the main word of a noun phrase, as in 'of stone' in 'tablets of stone'.

predicate all the parts of a clause or sentence that are not contained in the subject. Thus in the sentence 'The little girl was exhausted and hungry', 'exhausted and hungry' is the predicate. Similarly, in the sentence 'The tired old man slept like a top', 'slept like a top' is the predicate.

predicative adjective an adjective that helps to form the predicate and so comes after the verb, as 'tired' in 'She was very tired' and 'mournful' in 'The music was very mournful'.

premodifier a modifier that comes before the main word of a noun phrase, as 'green' in 'green dress' and 'pretty' in 'pretty houses'.

preposition a word that relates two elements of a sentence, clause or phrase together. Prepositions show how the elements relate in time or space and generally precede the words that they 'govern'. Words governed by prepositions are nouns or pronouns. Prepositions are often very short words, as 'at', 'in', 'on', 'to', 'before' and 'after'. Some complex prepositions consist of two words, as 'ahead of', 'instead of', 'apart from', and some consist of three, as 'with reference to', 'in accordance with' and 'in addition to'. Examples of prepositions in sentences include 'The cat sat on the mat', 'We were at a concert', 'They are in shock', 'We are going to France', 'She arrived before me', 'Apart from you she has no friends' and 'We acted in accordance with your instructions'.

present continuous *see* **tense**.

present participle *see* **-ing words**.

present tense *see* **tense**.

principal clause *see* **main clause**.

progressive present *see* **tense**.

pronoun a word that takes the place of a noun or a noun phrase. *See* **personal pronouns**, **he**, **her**, **him** and **his**, **reciprocal pronouns**, **reflexive pronouns**, **demonstrative pronouns**, **relative pronouns**, **distributive pronouns**, **indefinite pronouns** and **interrogative pronouns**.

proper noun a noun that refers to a particular individual or a specific thing. It is the 'name' of someone or something', as in Australia, Vesuvius, John Brown, River Thames, Rome and Atlantic Ocean.

question tag a phrase that is interrogative in form but is not really asking a question. It is added to a statement to seek agreement, etc. Examples include 'That was a lovely meal, wasn't it?', 'You will be able to go, won't you?', 'He's not going to move house, is he?' and 'She doesn't

drive, does she?' Sentences containing question tags have question marks at the end.

reciprocal pronoun a pronoun used to convey the idea of reciprocity or a two-way relationship. The reciprocal pronouns are 'each other' and 'one another'. Examples include 'They don't love each other any more', 'They seem to hate each other', 'We must try to help each other', 'The children were calling one another names', 'The two families were always criticizing one another' and 'The members of the family blame one another for their mother's death'.

reciprocal verb a verb such as 'consult', 'embrace', 'marry', 'meet', etc, that expresses a mutual relationship, as in 'They met at the conference', 'She married him in June'.

reflexive pronoun a pronoun that ends in '-self' or '-selves' and refers back to a noun or pronoun that has occurred earlier in the same sentence. The reflexive pronouns include 'myself', 'ourselves'; 'yourself', 'yourselves'; 'himself', 'herself', 'itself', 'themselves'. Examples include 'The children washed themselves', 'He cut himself shaving', 'Have you hurt yourself?' and 'She has cured herself of the habit'.

Reflexive pronouns are sometimes used for emphasis, as in 'The town itself was not very interesting' and 'The headmaster himself punished the boys'. They can also be used to indicate that something has been done by somebody by his/her own efforts without any help, as in 'He built the house himself', 'We converted the attic ourselves'. They can also indicate that someone or something is alone, as in 'She lives by herself' and 'The house stands by itself'.

reflexive verb a verb that has as its direct object a reflexive pronoun, e.g. 'They pride themselves on their skill as a team'.

regular sentence *see* **major sentence**.

regular verb *see* **irregular verb**.

relative clause a subordinate clause that has the function of an adjective. It is introduced by a relative pronoun.

relative pronoun a pronoun that introduces a relative clause. The relative pronouns are 'who', 'whom', 'whose', 'which' and 'that'. Examples of relative clauses introduced by relative pronouns include 'There is the man who stole the money', 'She is the person to whom I gave the money', 'This is the man whose wife won the prize', 'They criticized the work which he had done' and 'That's the house that I would like to buy'. Relative pronouns refer back to a noun or noun phrase in the main clause. These nouns and noun phrases are known as antecedents. The antecedents in the example sentences are respectively 'man', 'person', 'man', 'work' and 'house'.

Sometimes the relative clause divides the parts of the main clause, as in 'The woman whose daughter is ill is very upset', 'The people whom we met on holiday were French' and 'The house that we liked best was too expensive'.

reported speech *same as* **indirect speech**

rhetorical question a question that is asked to achieve

some kind of effect and requires no answer. Examples include 'What's this country coming to?', 'Did you ever see the like', 'Why do these things happen to me?', 'Where did youth go?', 'Death, where is thy sting?' and 'Where does time go?'. *See also* **interrogative sentence**.

second person the term used for the person or thing to whom one is talking. The term is applied to personal pronouns. The second person singular whether acting as the subject of a sentence is 'you', as in 'I told you so', 'We informed you of our decision' and 'They might have asked you sooner'. The second person personal pronoun does not alter its form in the plural in English, unlike in some languages. The possessive form of the second person pronoun is 'yours' whether singular or plural, as in 'These books are not yours'and 'This pen must be yours'.

sentence is at the head of the hierarchy of grammar. All the other elements, such as words, phrases and clauses, go to make up sentences. It is difficult to define a sentence. In terms of recognizing a sentence visually it can be described as beginning with a capital letter and ending with a full stop, or with an equivalent to the full stop, such as an exclamation mark. It is a unit of grammar that can stand alone and make sense and obeys certain grammatical rules, such as usually having a subject and a predicate, as in 'The girl banged the door', where 'the girl' is the subject and 'the door' is the predicate. *See* **major sentence**, **simple sentence**, **complex sentence**.

simple sentence a sentence that cannot be broken down into other clauses. It generally contains a finite verb. Simple sentences include 'The man stole the car', 'She nudged him' and 'He kicked the ball'. *See* **complex sentence** and **compound sentence**.

singular noun a noun that refers to 'one' rather than 'more than one', which is the plural form. *See also* **irregular plural**.

split infinitive an infinitive that has had another word in the form of an adverb placed between itself and 'to', as in 'to rudely push' and 'to quietly leave'. This was once considered a great grammatical sin but the split infinitive is becoming acceptable in modern usage. In any case it sometimes makes for a clumsy sentence if one slavishly adheres to the correct form.

stative present *see* **habitual** and **tense**.

strong verb the more common term for **irregular verb**.

structure word *see* **function word**.

subject that which is spoken of in a sentence or clause and is usually either a noun, as in 'Birds fly' (birds is the noun as subject); a noun phrase, as in 'The people in the town dislike him' (the people in the town' is the subject); a pronoun, as in 'She hit the child' (she is the pronoun as subject); a proper noun, as in 'Paris is the capital of France'. *See* **dummy subject**.

subjunctive *see* **mood**.

subordinate clause a clause that is dependent on another clause, namely the main clause. Unlike the main clause, it cannot stand alone and make sense. Subordinate clauses are introduced by conjunctions. Examples of conjunctions that introduce subordinate clauses include 'after', 'before', 'when', 'if', 'because' and 'since'. *See* **adverbial clause**; **noun clause**.

subordinating conjunction *see* **conjunction**.

superlative form the form of an adjective or adverb that expresses the highest or utmost degree of the quality or manner of the word. The superlative forms follow the same rules as comparative forms except that they end in -*est* instead of -*er* and the longer ones use 'most' instead of 'more'. *See also* **comparison of adjectives**.

tense the form of a verb that is used to show the time at which the action of the verb takes place. One of the tenses in English is the **present tense**. It is used to indicate an action now going on or a state now existing. A distinction can be made between the **habitual present**, which marks habitual or repeated actions or recurring events, and the **stative present**, which indicates something that is true at all times. Examples of habitual present include 'He works long hours' and 'She walks to work'. Examples of the stative tense include 'The world is round' and 'Everyone must die eventually'.

The **progressive present** or **continuous present** is formed with the verb 'to be' and the present participle, as in, 'He is walking to the next village', 'She was driving along the road when she saw him' and 'They were worrying about the state of the economy'.

The **past tense** refers to an action or state that has taken place before the present time. In the case of regular verbs it is formed by adding -*ed* to the base form of the verb, as in 'fear/feared', 'look/looked', and 'turn/turned'. *See also* **irregular verbs**.

The **future tense** refers to an action or state that will take place at some time in the future. It is formed with 'will' and 'shall'. Traditionally 'will' was used with the second and third person pronouns ('you', 'he/she/it', 'they') and 'shall' with the first person ('I' and 'we'), as in 'You will be bored', 'He will soon be home', 'They will leave tomorrow', 'I shall buy some bread' and 'We shall go by train'. Also traditionally 'shall' was used with the second and third persons to indicate emphasis, insistence, determination, refusal, etc, as in 'You shall go to the ball' and 'He shall not be admitted'. 'Will' was used with the first person in the same way, as in 'I will get even with him'.

In modern usage 'will' is generally used for the first person as well as for second and third, as in 'I will see you tomorrow' and 'We will be there soon' and 'shall' is used for emphasis, insistence, etc, for first, second and third persons.

The future tense can also be formed with the use of 'be about to' or 'be going to', as in 'We were about to leave' and 'They were going to look for a house'.

Other tenses include the **perfect tense**, which is formed using the verb 'to have' and the past participle. In the case of regular verbs the past participle is formed by adding *ed* to the base form of the verb. *See also* **irregular verbs**. Examples of the perfect tense include 'He has played his last match', 'We have travelled all day' and 'They have thought a lot about it'.

The **past perfect tense** or **pluperfect tense** is formed using the verb 'to have' and the past participle, as in 'She had no idea that he was dead' and 'They had felt unhappy about the situation'.

The **future perfect** is formed using the verb 'to have' and the past participle, as in 'He will have arrived by now'.

they *see* **him** and **third person**.

third person a third party, not the speaker or the person or thing being spoken to. Note that 'person' in this context can refer to things as well as people. 'Person' in this sense applies to personal pronouns. The third person singular forms are 'he', 'she' and 'it' when the subject of a sentence or clause, as in 'She will win' and 'It will be fine'. The third person singular forms are 'him', 'her','it' when the object, as in 'His behaviour hurt her' and 'She meant it'. The third person plural is 'they' when the subject, as in 'They have left' and 'They were angry' and 'them' when the object, as in 'His words made them angry' and 'We accompanied them'.

The possessive forms of the singular are 'his', 'hers' and 'its', as in 'he played his guitar' and 'The dog hurt its leg', and the possessive form of the plural is theirs, as in 'That car is theirs' and 'They say that the book is theirs'. *See* **he**.

to-infinitive the infinitive form of the verb when it is accompanied by 'to' rather than when it is the bare infinitive without 'to'. Examples of the to-infinitive include 'We were told to go', 'I didn't want to stay' and 'To get there on time we'll have to leave now'.

transitive verb a verb that takes a direct object. In the sentence 'The boy broke the window', 'window' is a direct object and so 'broke' (past tense of break) is a transitive verb. In the sentence 'She eats fruit', 'fruit' is a direct object and so 'eat' is a transitive verb. In the sentence 'They kill enemy soldiers' 'enemy soldiers' is a direct object and so 'kill' is a transitive verb. *See* **intransitive verb**.

uncountable noun or **uncount noun** a noun that is not usually pluralized or 'counted'. Such a noun is usually preceded by 'some', rather than 'a'. Uncountable nouns often refer to substances or commodities or qualities, processes and states. Examples of uncountable nouns include butter, china, luggage, petrol, sugar, heat, information, poverty, richness and warmth. In some situations it is possible to have a countable version of what is usually an uncountable noun. Thus 'sugar' is usually considered to be an uncountable noun but it can be used in a countable form in contexts such as 'I take two sugars in my coffee please'. Some nouns exist in an uncountable and countable form. Examples include 'cake', as in 'Have some cake' and 'She ate three cakes' and 'She could not paint for lack of light' and 'the lights went out'.

verb the part of speech often known as a 'doing' word. Although this is rather restrictive, since it tends to preclude auxiliary verbs, modal verbs, etc, the verb is the word in a sentence that is most concerned with the action and is usually essential to the structure of the sentence. Verbs 'inflect' and indicate tense, voice, mood, number, number and person. Most of the information on verbs has been placed under related entries. *See* **active voice, auxiliary verb, finite verb, -ing form, intransitive verb, irregular verbs, linking verb, modal verb, mood, non-finite verb, passive voice** and **transitive verb**.

verb phrase a group of verb forms that have the same function as a single verb. Examples include 'have been raining', 'must have been lying', 'should not have been doing' and 'has been seen doing'.

verbal noun *see* **gerund** and **-ing form**.

vocative case a case that is relevant mainly to languages such as Latin which are based on cases and inflections. In English the vocative is expressed by addressing someone, as 'John, could I see you for a minute', or by some form of greeting, endearment or exclamation.

voice one of the categories that describes verbs. It involves two ways of looking at the action of verbs. It is divided into active voice and passive voice.

weak verb a less common term for a regular verb, in which inflection is effected by adding a letter or syllable (dawn, dawned) rather than a change of vowel (rise, rose). *See* **irregular verb**.

Usage

-abled is a suffix meaning 'able-bodied'. It is most usually found in such phrases as 'differently abled', a 'politically correct', more positive way of referring to people with some form of disability, as in 'provide access to the club building for differently abled members'.

ableism or **ablism** means discrimination in favour of able-bodied people as in 'people in wheelchairs unable to get jobs because of ableism'. Note that the suffix '-ism' is often used to indicate discrimination against the group to which it refers, as in 'ageism'.

Aboriginal rather than **Aborigine** is now the preferred term for an original inhabitant of Australia, especially where the word is in the singular.

abuse and **misuse** both mean wrong or improper use or treatment. However, **abuse** tends to be a more condemnatory term, suggesting that the wrong use or treatment is morally wrong or illegal. Thus we find 'misuse of the equipment' or 'misuse of one's talents', but 'abuse of a privileged position' or 'abuse of children'. 'Child abuse' is usually used to indicate physical violence or sexual assault.

    Abuse is also frequently applied to the use of substances that are dangerous or injurious to health, as 'drug abuse', or 'alcohol abuse'. In addition, it is used to describe insulting or offensive language, as in 'shout abuse at the referee'.

academic is used to describe scholarly or educational matters, as 'a child with academic rather than sporting interests'. From this use it has come to mean theoretical rather than actual or practical, as in 'wasting time discussing matters of purely academic concern'. In modern use it is frequently used to mean irrelevant, as in 'Whether you vote for him or not is academic. He is certain of a majority of votes'.

access is usually a noun meaning 'entry or admission', as in 'try to gain access to the building', or 'the opportunity to use something', as in 'have access to confidential information'. It is also used to refer to the right of a parent to spend time with his or her children, as in 'Father was allowed access to the children at weekends'.

    However **access** can also be used as a verb. It is most commonly found in computing, meaning obtaining information from, as in 'accessing details from the computer file relating to the accounts'. In modern usage many technical words become used, and indeed overused, in the general language. Thus the verb **access** can now be found meaning to obtain information not on a computer, as in 'access the information in the filing cabinet'. It can also be found in the sense of gaining entry to a building, as in 'Their attempts to access the building at night were unsuccessful'.

accessory and **accessary** are interchangeable as regards only one meaning of **accessory**. A person who helps another person to commit a crime is known either as an **accessory** or an **accessary**, although the former is the more modern term. However, only **accessory** is used to describe a useful or decorative extra that is not strictly necessary, as in 'Seat covers are accessories that are included in the price of the car' and 'She wore a red dress with black accessories' ('accessories' in the second example being handbag, shoes and gloves).

accompany can be followed either by the preposition 'with' or 'by'. When it means 'to go somewhere with someone', 'by' is used, as in 'She was accompanied by her parents to church' Similarly, 'by' is used when **accompany** is used in a musical context, as in 'The singer was accompanied on the piano by her brother'. When **accompany** means 'to go along with something' or 'supplement something', either 'by' or 'with' may be used, as in 'The roast turkey was accompanied by all the trimmings', 'His words were accompanied by/with a gesture of dismissal', and 'The speaker accompanied his words with expressive gestures'.

acoustics can take either a singular or plural verb. When it is being thought of as a branch of science it is treated as being singular, as in 'Acoustics deals with the study of sound', but when it is used to describe the qualities of a hall, etc, with regard to its sound-carrying properties, it is treated as being plural, as in 'The acoustics in the school hall are very poor'.

activate and **actuate** both mean 'make active' but are commonly used in different senses. **Activate** refers to physical or chemical action, as in 'The terrorists activated the explosive device'. **Actuate** means 'to move to action' and 'to serve as a motive', as in 'The murderer was actuated by jealousy'.

actress is still widely used as a term for a woman who acts in plays or films, although many people prefer the term 'actor', regarding this as a neutral term rather than simply the masculine form. The **-ess** suffix, used to indicate the feminine form of a word, is generally becoming less common as these forms are regarded as sexist or belittling.

acute and **chronic** both refer to disease. **Acute** is used of a disease that is sudden in onset and lasts a relatively short time, as in 'flu is an acute illness'. **Chronic** is used of a disease that may be slow to develop and lasts a long time, possibly over several years, as in 'Asthma is a chronic condition'.

AD and **BC** are abbreviations that accompany year numbers. AD stands for 'Anno Domini', meaning 'in the year of our Lord' and indicates that the year concerned is one occurring after Jesus Christ was born. Traditionally AD is placed before the year number concerned, as in 'Their great-grandfather was born in AD 1801', but in modern usage it sometimes follows the year number, as in 'The house was built in 1780 AD.' BC stands for 'Before Christ' and indicates that the year concerned is one occurring before Jesus Christ was born. It follows the year number, as in 'The event took place in Rome in 55 BC'.

adapter and **adaptor** can be used interchangeably, but commonly **adapter** is used to refer to a person who adapts, as in 'the adapter of the stage play for television and **adaptor** is used to refer to a thing that adapts, specifically a type of electrical plug.

admission and **admittance** both mean 'permission or right to enter'. **Admission** is the more common term, as in 'They refused him admission to their house', and, unlike **admittance**, it can also mean 'the price or fee charged for entry' as in 'Admission to the football match is £3'. **Admittance** is largely used in formal or official situations, as in 'They ignored the notice saying "No Admittance"'. **Admission** also means 'confession' or 'acknowledgement of responsibility', as in 'On her own admission she was the thief'.

admit may be followed either by the preposition 'to' or the preposition 'of', depending on the sense. In the sense of 'to confess', **admit** is usually not followed by a preposition at all, as in 'He admitted his mistake' and 'She admitted stealing the brooch'. However, in this sense **admit** is sometimes followed by 'to', as in 'They have admitted to their error' and 'They have admitted to their part in the theft'.

In the sense of 'to allow to enter', **admit** is followed by 'to', as in 'The doorman admitted the guest to the club'. Also in the rather formal sense of 'give access or entrance to', **admit** is followed by 'to', as in 'the rear door admits straight to the garden'. In the sense of 'to be open to' or 'leave room for', **admit** is followed by 'of', as in 'The situation admits of no other explanation'.

admittance *see* **admission**.

adopted and **adoptive** are liable to be confused. **Adopted** is applied to children who have been adopted, as in 'The couple have two adopted daughters'. **Adoptive** is applied to a person or people who adopt a child, as in 'Her biological parents tried to get the girl back from her adoptive parents'.

aeroplane is commonly abbreviated to **plane** in modern usage. In American English **aeroplane** becomes **airplane**.

affinity may be followed by the preposition 'with' or 'between', and means 'close relationship', 'mutual attraction' or similarity, as in 'the affinity which twins have with each other' and 'There was an affinity between the two families who had lost children'. In modern usage it is sometimes followed by 'for' or 'towards', and means 'liking', as in 'She has an affinity for fair-haired men'.

ageism means discrimination on the grounds of age, as in 'By giving an age range in their job advert the firm were guilty of ageism'. Usually it refers to discrimination against older or elderly people, but it also refers to discrimination against young people.

agenda in modern usage is a singular noun having the plural **agendas**. It means 'a list of things to be attended to', as in 'The financial situation was the first item on the committee's agenda'. Originally it was a plural noun, derived from Latin, meaning 'things to be done'.

aggravate literally means 'to make worse', as in 'Her remarks simply aggravated the situation'. In modern usage it is frequently found meaning 'to irritate or annoy', as in 'The children were aggravating their mother when she was trying to read'. It is often labelled as 'informal' in dictionaries and is best avoided in formal situations.

agnostic and **atheist** are both words meaning 'disbeliever in God', but there are differences in sense between the two words. **Agnostics** believe that it is not possible to know whether God exists or not. **Atheists** believe that there is no God.

alcohol abuse is a modern term for alcoholism. *See* **abuse**.

alibi is derived from the Latin word for 'elsewhere'. It is used to refer to a legal plea that a person accused or under suspicion was somewhere other than the scene of the crime at the time the crime was committed. In modern usage **alibi** is frequently used to mean simply 'excuse' or 'pretext', as in 'He had the perfect alibi for not going to the party—he was ill in hospital'.

all together and **altogether** are not interchangeable. **All together** means 'at the same time' or 'in the same place', as in 'The guests arrived all together' and 'They kept their personal papers all together in a filing cabinet'. **Altogether** means 'in all, in total' or 'completely', as in 'We collected £500 altogether' and 'The work was altogether too much for him'.

alternate and **alternative** are liable to be confused. **Alternate** means 'every other' or 'occurring by turns', as in 'They visit her mother on alternate weekends' and 'between alternate layers of meat and cheese sauce'. **Alternative** means 'offering a choice' or 'being an alternative', as in 'If the motorway is busy there is an alternative route'. **Alternative** is found in some cases in modern usage to mean 'not conventional, not traditional', as in 'alternative medicine' and 'alternative comedy'.

Alternative as a noun refers to the choice between two possibilities, as in 'The alternatives are to go by train or by plane'. In modern usage, however, it is becoming common to use it to refer also to the choice among two or more possibilities, as in 'He has to use a college from five alternatives'.

although and **though** are largely interchangeable but **though** is slightly less formal, as in 'We arrived on time although/though we left late'.

amiable and **amicable** both refer to friendliness and goodwill. **Amiable** means 'friendly' or 'agreeable and pleasant', and is mostly used of people or their moods, as in 'amiable neighbours', 'amiable travelling companions', 'of an amiable temperament' and 'be in an amiable mood'. **Amicable** means 'characterized by friendliness and goodwill' and is applied mainly to relationships, agreements, documents, etc, as in 'an amicable working relationship', 'reach an amicable settlement at the end of the war' and 'send an amicable letter to his former rival'.

among and **amongst** are interchangeable, as in 'We searched among/amongst the bushes for the ball,' 'Divide the chocolate among/amongst you', and 'You must choose among/amongst the various possibilities'.

among and **between** may be used interchangeably in most contexts. Formerly **between** was used only when referring to the relationship of two things, as in 'Share the chocolate between you and your brother', and **among** was used when referring to the relationship of three or more things, as in 'Share the chocolate among all your friends'. In modern usage **between** may be used when referring to more than two things, as in 'There is agreement between all the countries of the EU' and 'Share the chocolate between all of you'. However, **among** is still used only to describe more than two things.

amoral and **immoral** are not interchangeable. **Amoral** means 'lacking moral standards, devoid of moral sense', indicating that the person so described has no concern with morals, as in 'The child was completely amoral and did not know the difference between right and wrong'. **Immoral** means 'against or breaking moral standards, bad'. 'He knows he's doing wrong but he goes on being completely immoral' and 'commit immoral acts'. Note the spelling of both words. **Amoral** has only one *m* but **immoral** has double *m*.

anaesthetic and **analgesic** are liable to be confused. As an adjective, **anaesthetic** means 'producing a loss of feeling', as in 'inject the patient with an anaesthetic substance', and as a noun it means 'a substance that produces a loss of feeling', as in 'administer an anaesthetic to the patient on the operating table'. A local anaesthetic produces a loss of feeling in only part of the body, as in 'remove the rotten tooth under local anaesthetic'. A **general anaesthetic** produces loss of feeling in the whole body and induces unconsciousness, as in 'The operation on his leg will have to be performed under general anaesthetic'. As an adjective **analgesic** means 'producing a lack of or reduction in, sensitivity to pain, pain-killing', as in 'aspirin has an analgesic effect'. As a noun **analgesic** means 'a substance that produces a lack of, or reduction in, sensitivity to pain', as in 'aspirin, paracetamol, and other analgesics'.

arbiter and **arbitrator**, although similar in meaning, are not totally interchangeable. **Arbiter** means 'a person who has absolute power to judge or make decisions', as in 'Parisian designers used to be total arbiters of fashion'. **Arbitrator** is 'a person appointed to settle differences in a dispute', as in 'act as arbitrator between management and workers in the wages dispute'. **Arbiter** is occasionally used with the latter meaning also.

artist and **artiste** are liable to be confused. **Artist** refers to 'a person who paints or draws,' as in 'Renoir was a great artist'. The word may also refer to 'a person who is skilled in something', as in 'The mechanic is a real artist

with an engine'. **Artiste** refers to 'an entertainer, such as a singer or a dancer', as in 'a list of the artistes in the musical performances'. The word is becoming a little old-fashioned.

at this moment in time is an overused phrase meaning simply 'now'. In modern usage there is a tendency to use what are thought to be grander-sounding alternatives for simple words. It is best to avoid such overworked phrases and use the simpler form.

atheist *see* **agnostic**.

au fait is French in origin but it is commonly used in English to mean 'familiar with' or 'informed about', as in 'not completely au fait with the new office system'. It is pronounced *o* fay.

authoress is not used in modern usage since it is considered sexist. **Author** is regarded as a neutral term to describe both male and female authors.

avoid *see* **evade**.

avoidance *see* **evasion**.

baited *see* **bated**.

barmaid is disliked by many people on the grounds that it sounds a belittling term and is thus sexist. It is also disliked by people who are interested in political correctness. However the word continues to be quite common, along with **barman**, and efforts to insist on **bar assistant** or **barperson** have not yet succeeded.

basically means literally 'referring to a base or basis, fundamentally', as in 'The scientist's theory is basically unsound', but it is frequently used almost meaninglessly as a fill-up word at the beginning of a sentence, as in 'Basically he just wants more money'. Overuse of this word should be avoided.

basis, meaning 'something on which something is founded', as in 'The cost of the project was the basis of his argument against it', has the plural form **bases** although it is not commonly used. It would be more usual to say 'arguments without a firm basis' than 'arguments without firm bases'.

bated as in 'with bated breath' meaning 'tense and anxious with excitement', is frequently misspelt **baited**. Care should be taken not to confuse the two words.

bathroom *see* **toilet**.

BC *see* AD.

because means 'for the reason that', as in 'He left because he was bored', and is sometimes misused. It is wrong to use it in a sentence that also contains 'the reason that', as in 'The reason she doesn't say much is that she is shy'. The correct form of this is 'She doesn't say much because she is shy' or 'The reason she doesn't say much is that she is shy'.

because of *see* **due to**.

beg the question is often used wrongly. It means 'to take for granted the very point that has to be proved', as in 'To say that God must exist because we can see all his wonderful creations in the world around us begs the question'. The statement assumes that these creations have been made by God although this has not been proved and yet this fact is being used as evidence that there is a God. **Beg the question** is often used wrongly to mean 'to evade the question', as in 'The police tried to get him to say where he had been but he begged the question and changed the subject'.

benign means 'kindly, well-disposed' when applied to people, as in 'fortunate enough to have a benign ruler'. This meaning may also be used of things, as in 'give a benign smile' and 'live in a benign climate'. As a medical term **benign** means 'nonmalignant, non-cancerous'. **Innocent** is another word for **benign** in this sense.

bête noire refers to 'something that one detests or fears', as in 'Loud pop music is her father's bête noire, although she sings with a pop group'. Note the spelling, particularly the accent (circumflex) on **bête** and the *e* at the end of **noire.** The phrase is French in origin and the plural form is **bêtes noires,** as in 'A bearded man is one of her many bêtes noires'.

better should be preceded by 'had' when it means 'ought to' or 'should', as in 'You had better leave now if you want to arrive there by nightfall' and 'We had better apologize for upsetting her'. In informal contexts, especially in informal speech as in 'Hey Joe, Mum says you better come now', the 'had' is often omitted but it should be retained in formal contexts. The negative form is 'had better not', as in 'He had better not try to deceive her'.

between is often found in the phrase 'between you and me' as in 'Between you and me I think he stole the money'. Note that 'me' is correct and that 'I' is wrong. This is because prepositions like 'between' are followed by an object, not a subject. 'I' acts as the subject of a sentence, as in 'I know her', and 'me' as the object, as in 'She knows me'.

between *see* **among.**

bi- of the words beginning with the prefix bi-, biannual and biennial are liable to be confused. **Biannual** means 'twice a year' and **biennial** means 'every two years'.

 Bicentenary and **bicentennial** both mean 'a 200th anniversary', as in 'celebrating the bicentenary/bicentennial of the firm'. **Bicentenary** is, however, the more common expression in British English, although **bicentennial** is more common in American English.

 Biweekly is a confusing word as it has two different meanings. It means both 'twice a week' and 'once every two weeks'. Thus there is no means of knowing without other information whether 'a bi-weekly publication' comes out once a week or every two weeks. The confusion arises because the prefix 'bi-', which means 'two', can refer both to doubling, as in 'bicycle', and halving, as in 'bisection'.

biannual *see* **bi-.**

bicentenary and **bicentennial** *see* **bi-.**

biennial *see* **bi-.**

billion traditionally meant 'one million million' in British English, but in modern usage it has increasingly taken on the American English meaning of 'one thousand million'. When the number of million pounds, etc, is specified, the number immediately precedes the word 'million' without the word 'of', as in 'The firm is worth five billion dollars', but if no number is present then

'of' precedes 'dollars, etc', ' as in 'The research project cost the country millions of dollars'. The word **billion** may also be used loosely to mean 'a great but unspecified number', as in 'Billions of people in the world live in poverty'.

birth name is a suggested alternative for **maiden name,** a woman's surname before she married and took the name of her husband. **Maiden name** is considered by some to be inappropriate since maiden in one of its senses is another name for 'virgin' and it is now not at all usual for women to be virgins when they marry. Another possible name alternative is **family name.**

biweekly *see* **bi-.**

blond and **blonde** are both used to mean 'a fair-haired person', but they are not interchangeable. **Blond** is used to describe a man or boy, **blonde** is used to describe a woman or girl. They are derived from the French adjective, which changes endings according to the gender of the noun.

boat and **ship** are often used interchangeably, but usually **boat** refers to a smaller vessel than a ship.

bona fide is an expression of Latin origin meaning literally 'of good faith'. It means 'genuine, sincere' or 'authentic', as in 'a bona fide member of the group', 'a bona fide excuse for not going', or 'a bona fide agreement'.

bottom line is an expression from accountancy that has become commonly used in the general language. In accountancy it refers to the final line of a set of company accounts, which indicates whether the company has made a profit or a loss, obviously a very important line. In general English, **bottom line** has a range of meanings, from 'the final outcome or result', as in 'The bottom line of their discussion was that they decided to sell the company', to 'the most important point of something', as in 'The bottom line was whether they could get there on time or not'.

can and **may** both mean in one of their senses 'to be permitted'. In this sense **can** is much less formal than **may** and is best restricted to informal contexts, as in ' "Can I go to the park now?" asked the child.' **May** is used in more formal contexts, as in 'May I please have your name?' Both **can** and **may** have other meanings. **Can** has the meaning 'to be able', as in 'They thought his legs were permanently damaged but he can still walk'. **May** has the additional meaning 'to be likely', as in 'You may well be right'.

 The past tense of **can** is **could,** as in 'The children asked if they could (= be permitted to) go to the park'. 'The old man could (= be unable to) not walk upstairs'. The past tense of **may** is **might,** as in 'The child asked if he might have a piece of cake (= be permitted to)'. 'They might (= be likely to) well get here tonight'.

cannot, can not, and **can't** all mean the same thing but they are used in different contexts. **Cannot** is the most usual form, as in 'The children have been told that they cannot go' and 'We cannot get there by public transport'. **Cannot** is written as two words only for emphasis, as in 'No, you can not have any more' and

'The invalid certainly can not walk to the ambulance'. **Can't** is used in less formal contexts and often in speech, as in 'I can't be bothered going out' and 'They can't bear to be apart'.

cardigan, jersey, jumper and **sweater** all refer to garments, often knitted, for the top part of the body. **Cardigan** refers to a jacket-like garment with buttons down the front. **Jersey, jumper** and **sweater** refer to a garment pulled over the head to get it on and off.

cardinal and **ordinal** numbers refer to different aspects of numbers. **Cardinal** is applied to those numbers that refer to quantity or value without referring to their place in the set, as in 'one', 'two', 'fifty' 'one hundred'. **Ordinal** is applied to numbers that refer to their order in a series, as in 'first', 'second', 'fortieth', 'hundredth'.

caster and **castor** are mainly interchangeable. Both forms can be applied to 'a swivelling wheel attached to the base of a piece of furniture to enable it to be moved easily' and 'a container with a perforated top from which sugar is sprinkled'. The kind of sugar known as **caster** can also be called **castor**, although this is less usual. The lubricating or medicinal oil known as **castor oil** is never spelt **caster**.

Catholic and **catholic** have different meanings. **Catholic** as an adjective refers to the Roman Catholic Church, as in 'The Pope is head of the Catholic Church', or to the universal body of Christians. As a noun it means 'a member of the Catholic Church', as in 'She is a Catholic but he is a Protestant'. Catholic with a lower-case initial letter means 'general, wide-ranging', as in 'a catholic selection of essays', and ' broad-minded, liberal', as in 'a catholic attitude to the tastes of others'.

celibate means 'unmarried' or 'remaining unmarried and chaste, especially for religious reasons', as in 'Roman Catholic priests have to be celibate'. In modern usage, because of its connection with chastity, **celibate** has come to mean 'abstaining from sexual intercourse', as in 'The threat of Aids has made many people celibate'. The word is frequently misspelt. Note the *i* after *l*.

Celsius, centigrade and **Fahrenheit** are all scales of temperature. **Celsius** and **centigrade** mean the same and refer to a scale on which water freezes at 0° and boils at 100°. This scale is now the principal unit of temperature. **Celsius** is now the more acceptable term. **Fahrenheit** refers to a scale on which water freezes at 32° and boils at 212°. It is still used, informally at least, of the weather, and statements such as 'The temperature reached the nineties today' are still common.

Note the initial capital letters in **Celsius** and **Fahrenheit**. This is because they are named after people, namely the scientists who devised them.

centenary and **centennial** are both used to refer to a 'one-hundredth anniversary'. **Centenary** is the more common term in British English, as in 'celebrate the town's centenary', whereas **centennial** is more common in American English. **Centennial** may be used as an adjective, as in 'organize the town's centennial celebrations'.

centigrade *see* **Celsius**.

centre and **middle** mean much the same, but **centre** is used more precisely than **middle** in some cases, as in 'a line through the centre of the circle' and 'She felt faint in the middle of the crowd'.

centre on and **centre around** are often used interchangeably, as in 'Her world centres on/around her children'. **Centre around** is objected to by some people on the grounds that **centre** is too specific to be used with something as vague as **around**. When it is used as a verb with place names, **centre** is used with 'at', as in 'Their business operation is centred at London'.

centuries are calculated from 1001, 1501, 1901, etc, not 1000, 1500, 1900, etc. This is because the years are counted from AD 1, there being no year 0.

chair is often used to mean 'a person in charge of a meeting, committee, etc', as in 'The committee has a new chair this year'. Formerly **chairman** was always used in this context, as in 'He was appointed chairman of the fund-raising committee' but this is disapproved of on the grounds that it is sexist. Formerly, **chairman** was sometimes used even if the person in charge of the meeting or committee was a woman, and sometimes **chairwoman** was used in this situation. **Chairperson**, which also avoids sexism, is frequently used instead of **chair**. **Chair** is also a verb meaning 'to be in charge of a meeting, committee, etc'.

-challenged is a modern suffix that is very much part of politically correct language. It is used to convey a disadvantage, problem or disorder in a more positive light. For example, 'visually challenged' is used in politically correct language instead of 'blind' or 'partially sighted', and 'aurally challenged' is used instead of 'deaf' or 'hard of hearing'. **-Challenged** is often used in humorous coinages, as in 'financially challenged', meaning 'penniless', and 'intellectually challenged', meaning 'stupid'.

charisma was formerly a theological word used to mean 'a spiritual gift', such as the gift of healing, etc. In modern usage it is used to describe 'a special quality or power that influences, inspires or stimulates other people, personal magnetism', as in 'The president was elected because of his charisma'. The adjective from **charisma** is **charismatic**, as in 'his charismatic style of leadership'.

chauvinism originally meant 'excessive patriotism', being derived from the name of Nicolas Chauvin, a soldier in the army of Napoleon Bonaparte, who was noted for his excessive patriotism. In modern usage **chauvinism** has come to mean 'excessive enthusiasm or devotion to a cause' or, more particularly, 'an irrational and prejudiced belief in the superiority of one's own cause'. When preceded by 'male', it refers specifically to attitudes and actions that assume the superiority of the male sex and thus the inferiority of women, as in 'accused of not giving her the job because of male chauvinism'. **Chauvinism** is frequently used to mean **male chauvinism**, as in 'He shows his chauvinism towards his female staff by never giving any of them senior jobs'. The adjective formed from **chauvinism** is **chauvinistic**.

chemist and **pharmacist** have the same meaning in one sense of **chemist** only. **Chemist** and **pharmacist** are both words for 'one who prepares drugs ordered by medical prescription'. **Chemist** has the additional meaning of 'a scientist who works in the field of chemistry', as in 'He works as an industrial chemist'.

childish and **childlike** both refer to someone being like a child but they are used in completely different contexts. **Childish** is used in a derogatory way about someone to indicate that he or she is acting like a child in an immature way, as in 'Even though she is 20 years old she has childish tantrums when she does not get her own way' and 'childish handwriting for an adult'. **Childlike** is a term of approval or a complimentary term used to describe something that has some of the attractive qualities of childhood, as in 'She has a childlike enthusiasm for picnics' and 'He has a childlike trust in others'.

Christian name is used to mean someone's first name as opposed to someone's **surname**. It is increasingly being replaced by **first name** or **forename** since Britain has become a multicultural society where there are several religions as well as Christianity.

chronic *see* **acute**.

city and **town** in modern usage are usually distinguished on grounds of size and status, a city being larger and more important than a town. Originally in Britain a **city** was a town which had special rights conferred on it by royal charter and which usually had a cathedral.

clean and **cleanse** as verbs both mean 'to clean', as in 'clean the house' and 'cleanse the wound'. However, **cleanse** tends to indicate a more thorough cleaning than **clean** and sometimes carries the suggestion of 'to purify', as in 'prayer cleansing the soul'.

client and **customer**, although closely related in meaning, are not interchangeable. **Client** refers to 'a person who pays for the advice or services of a professional person', as in 'They are both clients of the same lawyer', 'a client waiting to see the bank manager' and 'hairdressers who keep their clients waiting'. **Customer** refers to 'a person who purchases goods from a shop, etc', as in 'customers complaining to shopkeepers about faulty goods' and 'a regular customer at the local supermarket'. **Client** is used in the sense of 'customer' by shops who regard it as a more superior word, as in ' clients of an exclusive dress boutique'.

climate no longer refers just to weather, as in 'go to live in a hot climate', 'Britain has a temperate climate'. It has extended its meaning to refer to 'atmosphere', as in 'live in a climate of despair' and to 'the present situation', as in 'businessmen nervous about the financial climate'.

clone originally was a technical word meaning 'one of a group of offspring that are asexually produced and which are genetically identical to the parent and to other members of the group'. In modern usage **clone** is frequently used loosely to mean 'something that is very similar to something else', as in 'In the sixties there were many Beatles' clones', and 'grey-suited businessmen looking like clones of each other'.

collaborate and **cooperate** are not interchangeable in all contexts. They both mean 'to work together for a common purpose', as in 'The two scientists are collaborating/cooperating on cancer research' and 'The rival building firms are collaborating/cooperating on the new shopping complex'. When the work concerned is of an artistic or creative nature **collaborate** is the more commonly used word, as in 'The two directors are collaborating on the film' and 'The composers collaborated on the theme music'. **Collaborate** also has the meaning of 'to work with an enemy, especially an enemy that is occupying one's country', as in 'a Frenchman who collaborated with the Germans when they installed a German government in France'.

coloured *see* **black**.

commence, begin, and **start** mean the same, but **commence** is used in a more formal context than the other two words, as in 'The legal proceedings will commence tomorrow' and 'The memorial service will commence with a hymn'. **Begin** and **start** are used less formally, as 'The match begins at 2 p.m.' and 'The film has already started'.

commensurate is followed by 'with' to form a phrase meaning 'proportionate to, appropriate to', as in 'a salary commensurate with her qualifications' and 'a price commensurate with the quality of the goods'.

comparatively means 'relatively, in comparison with a standard', as in 'The house was comparatively inexpensive for that area of the city' and 'In an area of extreme poverty they are comparatively well off'. In modern usage it is often used loosely to mean 'rather' or 'fairly' without any suggestion of reference to a standard, as in 'She has comparatively few friends' and 'It is a comparatively quiet resort'.

compare may take either the preposition 'to' or 'with'. 'To' is used when two things or people are being likened to each other or being declared similar, as in 'He compared her hair to silk' and 'He compared his wife to Helen of Troy'. 'With' is used when two things or people are being considered from the point of view of both similarities and differences, as in 'If you compare the new pupil's work with that of the present class you will find it brilliant', and 'If you compare the prices in the two stores you will find that the local one is the cheaper'. In modern usage the distinction is becoming blurred because the difference is rather subtle.

comparison is usually followed by the preposition 'with', as in 'In comparison with hers his work is brilliant'. However, when it means 'the action of likening something or someone to something or someone else', it is followed by 'to', as in 'the comparison of her beauty to that of Garbo'.

complementary medicine is a term applied to the treatment of illness or disorders by techniques other than conventional medicine. These include homoeopathy, osteopathy, acupuncture, acupressure, iridology, etc. The word **complementary** suggests that the said techniques complement and work alongside conventional medical techniques. **Alternative medicine** means the same as **complementary medicine**, but the term suggests that they are used instead of the techniques of conventional medicine rather than alongside them.

compose, comprise and **constitute** are all similar in meaning but are used differently. **Compose** means 'to come together to make a whole, to make up'. It is most commonly found in the passive, as in 'The team was composed of young players' and 'The group was composed largely of elderly people'. It can be used in the active voice, as in 'the tribes which composed the nation' and 'the members which composed the committee', but this use is rarer. **Constitute** means the same as **compose** but it is usually used in the active voice, as in 'the foodstuffs that constitute a healthy diet' and 'the factors that constitute a healthy environment'. **Comprise** means 'to consist of, to be made up of'.

concave and **convex** are liable to be confused. **Concave** means 'curved inwards', as in 'The inside of a spoon would be described as concave'. **Convex** means 'curved outwards, bulging', as in 'The outside or bottom of a spoon would be described as convex'.

conducive, meaning 'leading to, contributing to', is followed by the preposition 'to', as in 'conditions conducive to health growth'.

conform may be followed by the preposition 'to' or the preposition 'with'. It is followed by 'to' when it means 'to keep to or comply with', as in 'conform to the conventions' and 'refuse to conform to the company regulations', and with 'with' when it means 'to agree with, to go along with', as in 'His ideas do not conform with those of the rest of the committee'.

connection and **connexion** are different forms of the same word, meaning 'a relationship between two things'. In modern usage **connection** is much the commoner spelling, as in 'no connection between the events' and 'a fire caused by a faulty connection'.

connote and **denote** are liable to be confused. **Connote** means 'to suggest something in addition to the main, basic meaning of something', as in 'the fear that the word cancer connotes' and 'The word 'home' connotes security and love'. **Denote** means 'to mean or indicate', as in 'The word cancer denotes a malignant illness' and 'The word "home" denotes the place where one lives'.

consist can be followed either by the preposition 'of' or by the preposition 'in', depending on the meaning. **Consist of** means 'to be made up of, to comprise', as in 'The team consists of eleven players and two reserve players'. **Consist in** means 'to have as the chief or only element or feature, to lie in', as in 'The charm of the village consists in its isolation' and 'The effectiveness of the plan consisted in its simplicity'.

constitute *see* **compose**.

contagious and **infectious** both refer to diseases that can

be passed on to other people but they do not mean the same. **Contagious** means 'passed on by physical contact', as in 'He caught a contagious skin disease while working in the clinic' and 'Venereal diseases are contagious'. **Infectious** means 'caused by airborne or waterborne microorganisms', as in 'The common cold is highly infectious and is spread by people sneezing and coughing'.

contemporary originally meant 'living or happening at the same time', as in 'Shakespeare and Marlowe were contemporary playwrights' and 'Marlowe was contemporary with Shakespeare'. Later it came to mean also 'happening at the present time, current', as in 'What is your impression of the contemporary literary scene?' and 'Contemporary moral values are often compared unfavourably with those of the past'. These two uses of **contemporary** can cause ambiguity. In modern usage it is also used to mean 'modern, up-to-date', as in 'extremely contemporary designs'.

convex *see* **concave**.

cooperate *see* **collaborate**.

co-respondent *see* **correspondent**.

correspondent and **co-respondent** are liable to be confused. **Correspondent** refers either to 'a person who communicates by letter', as in 'They were correspondents for years but had never met', or to 'a person who contributes news items to a newspaper or radio or television programme', as in 'the foreign correspondent of the *Times*'. A **co-respondent** is 'a person who has been cited in a divorce case as having committed adultery with one of the partners'.

cousin can cause confusion. The children of brothers and sisters are **first cousins** to each other. The children of **first cousins** are **second cousins** to each other. The child of one's **first cousin** and the **first cousin** of one's parents is one's **first cousin first removed**. The grandchild of one's **first cousin** or the **first cousin** of one's grandparent is one's **second cousin twice removed**.

crisis literally means 'turning point' and should be used to refer to 'a turning point in an illness', as in 'The fever reached a crisis and she survived' and 'a decisive or crucial moment in a situation, whose outcome will make a definite difference or change for better or worse', as in 'The financial situation has reached a crisis—the firm will either survive or go bankrupt'. In modern usage **crisis** is becoming increasingly used loosely for 'any worrying or troublesome situation', as in 'There's a crisis in the kitchen. The cooker's broken down'. The plural is **crises**.

criterion, meaning 'a standard by which something or someone is judged or evaluated', as 'What criterion is used for deciding which pupils will gain entrance to the school?' and 'The standard of play was the only criterion for entrance to the golf club'. It is a singular noun of which **criteria** is the plural, as in 'They must satisfy all the criteria for entrance to the club or they will be refused'.

critical has two main meanings. It means 'finding fault', as in 'His report on her work was very critical'. It also means 'at a crisis, at a decisive moment, crucial', as in 'It was a critical point in their relationship'. This meaning is often applied to the decisive stage of an illness, as in 'the critical hours after a serious operation', and is used also to describe an ill person who is at a crucial stage of an illness or dangerously ill. **Critical** also means 'involved in making judgements or assessments of artistic or creative works', as in 'give a critical evaluation of the author's latest novel'.

crucial means 'decisive, critical', as in 'His vote is crucial since the rest of the committee is split down the middle'. In modern usage it is used loosely to mean 'very important', as in 'It is crucial that you leave now'. **Crucial** is derived from crux, meaning 'a decisive point', as in 'the crux of the situation'.

curriculum is derived from Latin and originally took the plural form **curricula**, but in modern usage the plural form **curriculums** is becoming common.

curriculum vitae refers to 'a brief account of a person's qualifications and career to date'. It is often requested by an employer when a candidate is applying for a job. **Vitae** is pronounced *vee*-ti, the second syllable rhyming with my.

data was formerly used mainly in a scientific or technical context and was always treated as a plural noun, taking a plural verb, as in 'compare the data which were provided by the two research projects'. The singular form was **datum**, which is now rare. In modern usage the word **data** became used in computing as a collective noun meaning 'body of information' and is frequently used with a singular verb, as in 'The data is essential for our research'. This use has spread into the general language.

dates these are usually written in figures, as in 1956, rather than in words, as in nineteen fifty-six, except in formal contexts, such as legal documents. There are various ways of writing dates. The standard form in Britain is becoming day followed by month followed by year, as in '24 February 1970'. In North America the standard form of this is 'February 24, 1970', and that is a possibility in Britain also. Alternatively, some people write '24th February 1970'. Care should be taken with the writing of dates entirely in numbers, especially if one is corresponding with someone in North America. In Britain the day of the month is put first, the month second and the year third, as in '2/3/50', '2 March 1950'. In North America the month is put first, followed by the day of the month and the year. Thus in North America '2/3/50' would be '3 February 1950'.

Centuries may be written either in figures, as in 'the 19th century', or in words, as in 'the nineteenth century'

Decades and centuries are now usually written without apostrophes. as in '1980s' and '1990s'.

datum *see* **data**.

deadly and **deathly** both refer to death but they have different meanings. **Deadly** means 'likely to cause death, fatal', as in 'His enemy dealt him a deadly blow with his sword' and 'He contracted a deadly disease in the jungle'. **Deathly** means 'referring to death, resembling death', as in 'She was deathly pale with fear'.

decimate literally means 'to kill one in ten' and is derived from the practice in ancient Rome of killing every tenth soldier as a punishment for mutiny. In modern usage it has come to mean 'to kill or destroy a large part of', as in 'Disease has decimated the population'. It has also come to mean 'to reduce considerably', as in 'the recession has decimated the jobs in the area'.

defective and **deficient** are similar in meaning but are not interchangeable. **Defective** means 'having a fault, not working properly', as in 'return the defective vacuum cleaner to the shop', 'The second-hand car proved to be defective' and 'He cannot be a pilot as his eyesight is defective'. **Deficient** means 'having a lack, lacking in', as in 'The athlete is very fast but he is deficient in strength' and 'Her diet is deficient in vitamin C'.

deficient *see* **defective**.

definite article *see* **the**.

delusion and **illusion** in modern usage are often used interchangeably but they are not quite the same. **Delusion** means 'a false or mistaken idea or belief', as in 'He is under the delusion that he is brilliant' and 'suffer from delusions of grandeur'. It can be part of a mental disorder, as in 'He suffers from the delusion that he is Napoleon'. **Illusion** means 'a false or misleading impression', as in 'There was no well in the desert—it was an optical illusion', 'The conjurer's tricks were based on illusion' and 'the happy childhood illusions that everyone lived happy ever after'.

demise is a formal word for death, as in 'He never recovered from the demise of his wife'. In modern usage it applies to the ending of an activity, as in 'The last decade saw the demise of coal-mining in the area'. In modern usage it has come to mean also 'the decline or failure of an activity', as in 'the gradual demise of his business'.

dénouement means 'the final outcome', as in 'The novel had a unexpected dénouement'. It is pronounced day-*noo*-mon.

derisive and **derisory** are both adjectives connected with the noun 'derision' but they have different meanings. **Derisive** means 'expressing derision, scornful, mocking' as in 'give a derisive smile' and 'His efforts were met with derisive laughter'. Derisory means 'deserving derision, ridiculous' as in 'Their attempts at playing the game were derisory'. **Derisory** is frequently used to mean 'ridiculously small or inadequate', as in 'The salary offered was derisory'.

despatch and **dispatch** are interchangeable. It is most common as a verb meaning 'to send', as in 'despatch/dispatch an invitation'. It is rarer as a noun. It means 'a message or report, often official', as in 'receive a despatch/dispatch that the soldiers were to move on'. It also means 'rapidity, speed', as in 'carry out the orders with despatch/dispatch'.

dessert, pudding, sweet and **afters** all mean the same thing. They refer to the last and sweet course of a meal. **Dessert** has relatively recently become the most widespread of these terms. **Pudding** was previously regarded by the upper and middle classes as the most acceptable word of these, but it is now thought of by many as being rather old-fashioned or as being more suited to certain types of dessert than others—thus syrup sponge would be a pudding, but not fresh fruit salad. **Sweet** is a less formal word and is regarded by some people as being lower-class or regional. **Afters** is common only in very informal English.

devil's advocate is a phrase that is often misunderstood. It means 'someone who points out the possible flaws or faults in an argument etc', as in 'He played the devil's advocate and showed her the weakness in her argument so that she was able to perfect it before presenting it to the committee'. The phrase is sometimes wrongly thought of as meaning 'someone who defends an unpopular point of view or person'.

diagnosis and **prognosis** are liable to be confused. Both are used with reference to disease but have different meanings. **Diagnosis** refers to 'the identification of a disease or disorder', as in 'She had cancer but the doctor failed to make the correct diagnosis until it was too late'. **Prognosis** refers to 'the prediction of the likely course of a disease or disorder', as in 'According to the doctor's prognosis, the patient will be dead in six months'.

dice was originally the plural form of the singular noun **die**, but **die** is now rarely used. Instead, **dice** is used as both a singular and a plural noun, as in 'throw a wooden dice' and 'use three different dice in the same game'.

different is most usually followed by the preposition 'from', as in 'Their style of living is different from ours'. **Different from** is considered to be the most correct construction, particularly in formal English. **Different to** is used in informal situations, as in 'His idea of a good time is different to ours'. **Different than** is used in American English.

dilemma is frequently used wrongly. It refers to 'a situation in which one is faced with two or more equally undesirable possibilities', as in 'I can't decide which of the offers to accept. It's a real dilemma'.

dinner, lunch, supper and **tea** are terms that can cause confusion. Their use can vary according to class, region of the country and personal preference. Generally speaking, people who have their main meal in the evening call it **dinner**. However, people who have their main meal in the middle of the day frequently call this meal **dinner**. People who have **dinner** in the evening usually refer to their midday meal, usually a lighter meal, as **lunch**. A more formal version of this word is **luncheon**, which is now quite a rare word. **Supper** has two meanings, again partly dependent on class and region. It can refer either to the main meal of the day if it is eaten in the evening—when it is virtually a synonym for **dinner**. Alternatively, it can refer to a light snack, such as cocoa and toasted cheese, eaten late in the evening before going to bed. **Tea** again has two meanings when applied to a meal. It either means a light snack-type meal of tea, sandwiches and

cakes eaten in the late afternoon. Alternatively, it can refer to a cooked meal, sometimes taken with tea, and also referred to as **high tea**, eaten in the early evening, rather than **dinner** later in the evening.

disabled is objected to by some people on the grounds that it is a negative term, but it is difficult to find an acceptable alternative. In politically correct language **physically challenged** has been suggested as has **differently abled**, but neither of these has gained widespread use. It should be noted that the use of 'the disabled' should be avoided. 'Disabled people' should be used instead.

disablism and **disableism** mean 'discrimination against disabled people', as in 'He felt his failure to get a job was because of disablism'. **Disablist** and **disableist** are adjectives meaning 'showing or practising disablism', as in 'guilty of disablist attitudes'. They also refer to 'a person who discriminates on the grounds of disability', as in 'That employer is a disablist'.

disassociate and **dissociate** are used interchangeably, as in 'She wished to disassociate/dissociate herself from the statement issued by her colleagues', but **dissociate** is the more usual.

discover and **invent** are not interchangeable. **Discover** means 'to find something that is already in existence but is generally unknown', as in 'discover a new route to China' and 'discover the perfect place for a holiday'. **Invent** means 'to create something that has never before existed', as in 'invent the telephone' and 'invent a new form of heating system'.

disempowered in modern usage does not mean only 'having one's power removed', as in 'The king was disempowered by the invading general', but also means the same as 'powerless', as in 'We are disempowered to give you any more money'. **Disempowered** is seen in politically correct language as a more positive way of saying **powerless**.

disinterested and **uninterested** are often used interchangeably in modern usage to mean 'not interested, indifferent', as in 'pupils totally disinterested/uninterested in school work'. Many people dislike **disinterested** being used in this way and regard it as a wrong use, but it is becoming increasingly common. **Disinterested** also means 'impartial, unbiased', as in 'ask a disinterested party to settle the dispute between them'.

disorient and **disorientate** are used interchangeably. 'The town had changed so much since his last visit that he was completely disoriented/disorientated' and 'After the blow to her head she was slightly disoriented/disorientated'.

divorcee refers to 'a divorced person', as in 'a club for divorcees'. **Divorcé** refers to 'a divorced man', and **divorcée** to 'a divorced woman'.

double negative the occurrence of two negative words in a single sentence or clause, as in 'He didn't say nothing' and 'We never had no quarrel'. This is usually considered incorrect in standard English, although it is a feature of some social or regional dialects. The use of the double negative, if taken literally, often has the opposite meaning to the one intended. Thus 'He didn't say nothing' conveys the idea that 'He said something'.

Some double negatives are considered acceptable, as in 'I wouldn't be surprised if they don't turn up', although it is better to restrict such constructions to informal contexts. The sentence quoted conveys the impression that the speaker will be quite surprised if 'they' do 'turn up'. Another example of an acceptable double negative is 'I can't not worry about the children. Anything could have happened to them'. Again this type of construction is best restricted to informal contexts.

It is the semi-negative forms, such as 'hardly' and 'scarcely', that cause most problems with regard to double negatives, as in 'We didn't have hardly any money to buy food' and 'They didn't have barely enough time to catch the bus'. Such sentences are incorrect.

doubtful and **dubious** can be used interchangeably in the sense of 'giving rise to doubt, uncertain', as in 'The future of the project is dubious/doubtful', and in the sense of 'having doubts, unsure', as in 'I am doubtful/dubious about the wisdom of going'. **Dubious** also means 'possibly dishonest or bad', as in 'of dubious morals'.

draughtsman/woman and **draftsman/woman** are not the same. **Draughtsman/woman** refers to 'a person who draws detailed plans of a building, etc', as in 'study the plans of the bridge prepared by the draughtsman'. **Draftsman/woman** refers to 'a person who prepares a preliminary version of plans, etc', as in 'several draftswomen working on the draft parliamentary bills'.

drawing room *see* **sitting room**.

dreamed and **dreamt** are interchangeable both as the past tense and the past participle of the verb 'dream', as in 'She dreamed/dreamt about living in the country' and in 'He has dreamed/dreamt the same dream for several nights'.

drier and **dryer** can both be used to describe 'a machine or appliance that dries', as in 'hair-drier/hair-dryer' and 'tumbler drier/dryer'. As an adjective meaning 'more dry', **drier** is the usual word, as in 'a drier summer than last year'.

dubious *see* **doubtful**.

due to, owing to and **because of** should not be used interchangeably. Strictly speaking, **due to** should be used only adjectivally, as in 'His poor memory is due to brain damage' and 'cancellations due to bad weather'. When a prepositional use is required **owing to** and **because of** should be used, as in 'the firm was forced to close owing to a lack of capital' and 'The train was cancelled because of snow on the line'. In modern usage it is quite common for **due to** to be used instead of **owing to** or **because of** because the distinction is rather difficult to comprehend.

e.g. means 'for example' and is an abbreviation of the Latin phrase *exempli gratia*. It is used before examples of something just previously mentioned, as in 'He cannot eat dairy products, e.g. milk, butter and cream'. A comma is usually placed just before it and, unlike some abbreviations, it usually has full stops.

each other and **one another** used not to be used interchangeably. It was taught that **each other** should be used when only two people are involved and that **one another** should be used when more than two people are involved, as in 'John and Mary really love each other' and 'All the members of the family love one another'. In modern use this restriction is often ignored.

EC and **EEC** both refer to the same thing, but **EC**, the abbreviation for **Economic Community** replaced **EEC**, the abbreviation for **European Economic Community**.

Both have now been replaced by **EU**, for **European Union**.

effeminate *see* **female**.

egoist and **egotist** are frequently used interchangeably in modern usage. Although they are not, strictly speaking, the same, the differences between them are rather subtle. **Egoist** refers to 'a person intent on self-interest, a selfish person', as in 'an egoist who never gave a thought to the needs of others'. **Egotist** refers to 'a person who is totally self-centred and obsessed with his/her own concerns', as in 'a real egotist who was always talking about herself'.

eke out originally meant 'to make something more adequate by adding to it or supplementing it', as in 'The poor mother eked out the small amount of meat with a lot of vegetables to feed her large family'. It can now also mean 'to make something last longer by using it sparingly', as in 'try to eke out our water supply until we reach a town', and 'to succeed or make with a great deal of effort', as in 'eke out a meagre living from their small farm'.

elder and **older** are not interchangeable. **Elder** is used only of people, as in 'The smaller boy is the elder of the two'. It is frequently used of family relationships, as in 'His elder brother died before him'. **Older** can be used of things as well as people, as in 'The church looks ancient but the castle is the older of the buildings' and 'The smaller girl is the older of the two'. It also can be used of family relationships, as in 'It was his older brother who helped him'. **Elder** used as a noun suggests experience or worthiness as well as age, as in 'Important issues used to be decided by the village elders' and 'Children should respect their elders and betters'.

elderly, as well as meaning 'quite or rather old', as in 'a town full of middle-aged and elderly people', is a more polite term than 'old', no matter how old the person referred to is, as in 'a residential home for elderly people'. **Elderly** is used only of people, except when used humorously, as in 'this cheese is getting rather elderly'.

eldest and **oldest** follow the same pattern as **elder** and **older**, as in 'The smallest boy is the eldest of the three', 'His eldest brother lived longer than any of them', 'The castle is the oldest building in the town' and 'He has four brothers but the oldest one is dead'.

empathy and **sympathy** are liable to be confused although they are not interchangeable. **Empathy** means 'the ability to imagine and share another's feelings, experiences, etc', as in 'As a single parent herself, the journalist has a real empathy with women bringing up children on their own' and 'The writer felt a certain empathy with the subject of his biography since they both came from a poverty-stricken childhood'. **Sympathy** means 'a feeling of compassion, pity or sorrow towards someone', as in 'feel sympathy for homeless children' and 'show sympathy towards the widow'.

endemic is usually used to describe a disease and means 'occurring in a particular area', as in 'a disease endemic to the coastal areas of the country' and 'difficult to clear the area of endemic disease'.

enervate is a word that is frequently misused. It means 'to weaken, to lessen in vitality', as in 'she was enervated by the extreme heat' and 'Absence of funding had totally enervated the society'. It is often wrongly used as though it meant the opposite.

enquiry and **inquiry** are frequently used interchangeably, as in 'make enquiries/inquiries about her health'. However some people see a distinction between them and use **enquiry** for ordinary requests for information, as in 'make enquiries about the times of trains'. They use **inquiry** only for 'investigation', as in 'The police have begun a murder inquiry' and 'launch an inquiry into the hygiene standards of the food firm'.

equal can be followed either by the preposition 'with' or the preposition 'to', but the two constructions are not interchangeable. **Equal to** is used in such sentences as 'He wished to climb the hill but his strength was not equal to the task'. **Equal with** is used in such sentences as 'After many hours of playing the two players remained equal with each other' and 'The women in the factory are seeking a pay scale equal with that of men'.

equally should not be followed by 'as'. Examples of it used correctly include 'Her brother is an expert player but she is equally talented' and 'He is trying hard but his competitors are trying equally hard'. These should not read 'but she is equally as talented' nor 'but his competitors are trying equally as hard'.

Esq. a word that can be used instead of 'Mr' when addressing an envelope to a man, as in 'John Jones, Esq.'. It is mostly used in formal contexts. Note that Esq. is used instead of 'Mr', not as well as it. It is usually spelt with a full stop.

etc the abbreviation of a Latin phrase *et cetera*, meaning 'and the rest, and other things'. It is used at the end of lists to indicate that there exist other examples of the kind of thing that has just been named, as in 'He grows potatoes, carrots, turnips, etc', 'The girls can play tennis, hockey, squash, etc', 'The main branch of the bank can supply francs, marks, lire, kroner, etc'. Etc is preceded by a comma and can be spelt with or without a full stop.

ethnic is a word that causes some confusion. It means 'of a group of people classified according to race, nationality, culture, etc', as in 'a cosmopolitan country with a wide variety of ethnic groups'. It is frequently used loosely to mean 'relating to race', as in 'violent clashes thought to be ethnic in origin', or 'foreign' as in 'prefer ethnic foods to British foods'.

EU the abbreviation for European Union, the term which has replaced European Community and European Economic Community.

evade and **avoid** are similar in meaning but not identical. **Evade** means 'to keep away from by cunning or deceit', as in 'The criminal evaded the police by getting his friend to impersonate him'. **Avoid** means simply 'to keep away from', as in 'Women avoid that area of town at night'.

evasion and **avoidance** are frequently applied to the non-payment of income tax but they are not interchangeable. Tax **avoidance** refers to 'the legal nonpayment of tax by clever means'. Tax **evasion** refers to 'the illegal means of avoiding tax by cunning and dishonest means'.

even should be placed carefully in a sentence since its position can influence the meaning. Compare 'He didn't even acknowledge her' and 'He didn't acknowledge even her'. and 'He doesn't even like Jane, let alone love her' and 'He hates the whole family—he doesn't like even Jane'. This shows that **even** should be placed immediately before the word it refers to in order to avoid ambiguity. In spoken English people often place it where it feels most natural, before the verb as in 'He even finds it difficult to relax on holiday'. To be absolutely correct this should be 'He finds it difficult to relax even on holiday' or 'Even on holiday he finds it difficult to relax'.

except is commoner than **except for**. **Except** is used in such sentences as 'They are all dead except his father', 'He goes every day except Sunday'. **Except for** is used at the beginning of sentences, as in 'Except for Fred, all the workers were present', and where **except** applies to a longish phrase, as in 'There was no one present except for the maid cleaning the stairs' and 'The house was silent except for the occasional purring of the cat'. When followed by a pronoun, this should be in the accusative or objective, as in 'There was no one there except *him*' and 'Everyone stayed late except *me*'.

explicit and **implicit** are liable to be confused although they are virtually opposites. **Explicit** means 'direct, clear', as in 'The instructions were not explicit enough' and 'Give explicit reasons for your decision'. **Explicit** is often used in modern usage to mean 'with nothing hidden or implied', as in 'explicit sex scenes'. **Implicit** means 'implied, not directly expressed', as in 'There was an implicit threat in their warning' and 'an implicit criticism in his comments on their actions'. **Implicit** also means 'absolute and unquestioning', as in 'an implicit faith in his ability to succeed' and 'an implicit confidence in her talents'.

extrovert and **introvert** are liable to be confused although they are opposites. **Extrovert** refers to 'a person who is more interested in what is going on around him/her than in his/her own thoughts and feelings, such a person usually being outgoing and sociable', as in 'She is a real extrovert who loves to entertain the guests at parties'. **Introvert** refers to 'a person who is more concerned with his/her own thoughts and feelings than with what is going around him/her, such a person usually being shy and reserved', as in 'an introvert who hates having to speak in public' and 'introverts who prefer to stay at home than go to parties'. Both **extrovert** and **introvert** can be adjectives as well as nouns, as in 'extrovert behaviour' and 'introvert personality'. Note the spelling of **extrovert.** It was formerly spelt with an *a* instead of an *o*.

fahrenheit *see* **Celsius**.

family name is used in politically correct language instead of **maiden name** since this is thought to imply that all women are virgins before they are married. Thus 'Her family name was Jones' would be used instead of 'Her maiden name was Jones'. Another politically correct term is **birth name**, as in 'Her birth name was Jones'.

fantastic literally means 'relating to fantasy, fanciful, strange', as in 'fantastic dreams' and 'tales of fantastic events'. In modern usage it is often used informally to mean 'exceptionally good, excellent', as in 'have a fantastic holiday' and 'be a fantastic piano player'. It can also mean in informal usage 'very large', as in 'pay a fantastic sum of money'.

farther and **further** are not used interchangeably in all situations in modern usage. **Farther** is mainly restricted to sentences where physical distance is involved, as in 'It is farther to Glasgow from here than it is to Edinburgh'. **Further** can also be used in this sense, as in 'It is further to the sea than I thought'. When referring to time or extent, **further** is used, as in 'Further time is required to complete the task' and 'The police have ordered further investigations'. It can also mean 'additional', as in 'We shall require further supplies'. **Further,** unlike **farther,** can be used as a verb to mean 'to help the progress or development about', as in 'further the cause of freedom'.

faux pas is a French phrase that has been adopted into the English language. It means 'a social blunder, an indiscreet or embarrassing remark or deed', as in 'The hostess made a faux pas when she asked after her guest's wife, not knowing that they had divorced last year'. **Faux** is pronounced to rhyme with *foe*, and **pas** is pronounced *pa*.

fax is an abbreviation of 'facsimile' and refers to 'an electronic system for transmitting documents using telephone lines'. As a noun **fax** can refer to the machine transmitting the documents, as in 'the fax has broken down again'; to the system used in the transmission, as in 'send the report by fax'; and the document or documents so transmitted, as in 'He replied to my fax at once'.

female, feminine and **feminist** all relate to women but they are by no means interchangeable. **Female** refers to the sex of a person, animal or plant, as in 'the female members of the group', 'the female wolf and her cubs' and 'the female reproductive cells'. It refers to the childbearing sex and contrasts with 'male'. **Feminine** means 'having qualities that are considered typical of women or are traditionally associated with women', as in 'wear feminine clothes', 'take part in supposedly feminine

pursuits, such as cooking and sewing' and 'feminine hairstyles'. It is the opposite of 'masculine'. It can be used of men as well as women, when it is usually derogatory, as in 'He has a very feminine voice' and 'He walks in a very feminine way'. When applied in a derogatory way to a man, **feminine** means much the same as **effeminate**. **Feminine** also applies to the gender of words, as in 'Lioness is the feminine form of lion'. **Feminist** means 'referring to feminism', 'feminism' being 'a movement based on the belief that women should have the same rights, opportunities, etc', as in 'management trying to avoid appointing anyone with feminist ideas' and 'Equal opportunities is one of the aims of the feminist movement'.

ferment and **foment** can both mean 'to excite, to stir up', as in 'Troublemakers out to ferment discontent' and 'People out to foment trouble in the crowd'. Both words have other meanings that do not relate to each other. **Ferment** means 'to undergo the chemical process known as fermentation', as in 'home-made wine fermenting in the basement'. **Foment** means 'to apply warmth and moisture to in order to lessen pain or discomfort', as in 'foment the old man's injured hip'.

few and **a few** do not convey exactly the same meaning. **Few** is used to mean the opposite of 'many', as in 'We expected a good many people to come but few did' and 'Many people entered the competition but few won a prize'. The phrase **a few** is used to mean the opposite of 'none', as in 'We didn't expect anyone to turn up but a few did' and 'We thought that none of the students would get a job but a few did'.

fewer *see* **less**.

fictional and **fictitious** are both derived from the noun 'fiction' and are interchangeable in the sense of 'imagined, invented', as in 'a fictional character based on an old man whom he used to know' and 'The events in the novel are entirely fictitious'. However, **fictitious** only is used in the sense of 'invented, false', as in 'an entirely fictitious account of the accident' and 'think up fictitious reasons for being late'.

fill in and **fill out** are both used to mean 'to complete a form, etc, by adding the required details', as in 'fill in/fill out an application form for a passport'. In British English **fill in** is the more common term, although **fill out** is the accepted term in American English.

first and **firstly** are now both considered acceptable in lists, although formerly **firstly** was considered unacceptable. Originally the acceptable form of such a list was as in 'There are several reasons for staying here. First, we like the house, secondly we have pleasant neighbours, thirdly we hate moving house'. Some users now prefer to use the adjectival forms of 'second' and 'third' when using **first**, as in 'He has stated his reasons for going to another job. First, he has been offered a higher salary, second, he has more opportunities for promotion, third, he will have a company car'. As indicated, **firstly** is now quite acceptable and is the form preferred by many people, as in 'They have several reasons for not having a car. Firstly they have very little money, secondly, they live right next to the bus-stop, thirdly, they feel cars are not environmentally friendly'.

first name *see* **Christian name**.

fish and **fishes** are both found as plural forms of 'fish', but **fish** is by far the more widely used form, as in 'He keeps tropical fish', 'Some fish live in fresh water and some in the sea' and 'there are now only three fish in the tank'. **Fishes** is rarely used but when it is, it is usually used to refer to different species of fish, as in 'He is comparing the fishes of the Pacific Ocean with those of the Indian Ocean'. **Fish** can also be used in this case.

flak originally referred to 'gunfire aimed at enemy aircraft', as in 'Pilots returning across the English Channel encountered heavy flak'. In modern usage it is also applied to 'severe criticism', as in 'the government receiving flak for raising taxes'.

flammable and **inflammable** both mean 'easily set on fire, burning easily', as in 'Children's nightclothes should not be made of flammable/inflammable material' and 'The chemical is highly flammable/inflammable'. **Inflammable** is frequently misused because some people wrongly regard it as meaning 'not burning easily', thinking that it is like such words as 'incredible', 'inconceivable' and 'intolerant' where the prefix 'in' means 'not'.

flotsam and **jetsam** are often used together to refer to 'miscellaneous objects, odds and ends', as in 'We have moved most of the furniture to the new house—there's just the flotsam and jetsam left', and 'vagrants, tramps', as in 'people with no pity in their hearts for the flotsam and jetsam of society'. In the phrase **flotsam and jetsam** they are used as though they meant the same thing but this is not the case. Both words relate to the remains of a wrecked ship, but **flotsam** refers to 'the wreckage of the ship found floating in the water', as in 'The coastguards knew the ship must have broken up when they saw bits of flotsam near the rocks', while **jetsam** refers to 'goods and equipment thrown overboard from a ship in distress in order to lighten it', as in 'The coastguards were unable to find the ship although they found the jetsam'.

forbear and **forebear** are interchangeable in one meaning of **forbear** only. **Forbear** is a verb meaning 'to refrain from', as in 'I hope she can forbear from pointing out that she was right' and this cannot be spelt **forebear**. However, **forebear** meaning 'ancestor' can also be spelt **forbear**, as in 'One of his *forebears/forbears* received a gift of land from Henry VIII'.

The verb **forbear** is pronounced with the emphasis on the second syllable as for-*bair*. The nouns **forbear** and **forebear** are pronounced alike with the emphasis on the first syllable as *for*-bair. The past tense of the verb **forbear** is **forbore**, as in 'He forbore to mention that he was responsible for the mistake'.

forever can be spelt as two words when it means 'eternally, for all time', as in 'doomed to separate forever/for ever' and 'have faith in the fact that they would dwell forever/for ever with Christ'. In the sense of 'constantly

or persistently', only **forever** is used, as in 'His wife was forever nagging' and 'the child was forever asking for sweets'.

former and **latter** are opposites. **Former** refers to 'the first of two people or things mentioned' while **latter** refers to 'the second of two people or things mentioned', as in 'He was given two options, either to stay in his present post but accept less money or to be transferred to another branch of the company. He decided to accept the former/latter option'. **Former** also means 'previous, at an earlier time', as in 'He is a former chairman of the company' and 'She is a former holder of the championship title'.

further *see* **farther**.

gaol *see* **jail**.

gay originally meant 'merry, light-hearted', as in 'the gay laughter of children playing' and 'everyone feeling gay at the sight of the sunshine'. Although this meaning still exists in modern usage, it is rarely used since **gay** has come to be an accepted word for 'homosexual', as in 'gay rights' and 'gay bars'. Although the term can be applied to men or women it is most commonly applied to men, the corresponding word for women being **lesbian**. There is a growing tendency among homosexuals to describe themselves as **queer**, a term that was formerly regarded as being offensive.

geriatric is frequently found in medical contexts to mean 'elderly' or 'old', as in 'an ever-increasing number of geriatric patients' and 'a shortage of geriatric wards'. In such contexts **geriatric** is not used in a belittling or derogatory way, **geriatrics** being the name given to the branch of medicine concerned with the health and diseases of elderly people. However, **geriatric** is often used in the general language to refer to old people in a derogatory or scornful way, as in 'geriatric shoppers getting in the way' or 'geriatric drivers holding up the traffic'.

gibe and **jibe** both mean 'to jeer at, mock, make fun of', as in 'rich children gibing/jibing at the poor children for wearing out-of-date clothes'. **Gibe** and **jibe** are nouns as well as verbs as in 'politicians tired of the gibes/jibes of the press'.

Gipsy and **Gypsy** are both acceptable spellings, as in 'Gipsies/Gypsies travelling through the country in their caravans'. Some people object to the word **Gipsy** or **Gypsy**, preferring the word traveller, as in 'councils being asked to build sites for travellers'. The term **traveller** is used to apply to a wider range of people who travel the country, as in 'New Age travellers', and not just to Gipsies, who are Romany in origin.

girl means 'a female child or adolescent', as in 'separate schools for girls and boys' and 'Girls tend to mature more quickly than boys'. However it is often applied to a young woman, or indeed to a woman of any age, as in 'He asked his wife if she was going to have a night out with the girls from the office'. Many women object to this use, regarding it as patronizing, although the user of the term does not always intend to convey this impression.

gourmand and **gourmet** and **glutton** all have reference to food but they do not mean quite the same thing. **Gourmand** refers to 'a person who likes food and eats a lot of it', as in 'Gourmands tucking into huge helpings of the local food'. It means much the same as **glutton**, but **glutton** is a more condemnatory term, as in 'gluttons stuffing food into their mouths'. **Gourmet** is a more refined term, being used to refer to 'a person who enjoys food and who is discriminating and knowledgeable about it', as in 'gourmets who spend their holidays seeking out good local restaurants and produce'. In modern usage **gourmet** is often used as an adjective to mean 'high-class, elaborate, expensive', as in 'gourmet restaurants' and 'gourmet foods'.

graffiti Italian in origin and actually the plural form of **graffito**, meaning a single piece of writing or drawing, but this is now hardly ever used in English.

green is used to mean 'concerned with the conservation of the environment', as in 'a political party concerned with green issues' and 'buy as many green products as possible'. The word is derived from German *grün*, the political environmental lobby having started in West Germany, as it was then called.

grey and **gray** are both acceptable spellings. In British English, however, **grey** is the more common, as in 'different shades of grey' and 'grey hair', but **gray** is the standard form in American English.

Gypsy *see* **Gipsy**.

handicapped is disliked by some people because they feel it is too negative a term. There is as yet no widespread alternative apart from **disabled**, although various suggestions have been made as part of the politically correct language movement, such as **physically challenged** and **differently abled**.

hard and **soft** are both terms applied to drugs. **Hard drugs** refer to 'strong drugs that are likely to be addictive', as in 'Heroin and cocaine are hard drugs'. **Soft drugs** refer to 'drugs that are considered unlikely to cause addiction', as in 'cannabis and other soft drugs'.

hardly is used to indicate a negative idea. Therefore a sentence or clause containing it does not require another negative. Sentences, such as 'I couldn't hardly see him' and 'He left without hardly a word' are *wrong*. They should read 'I could hardly see him' and 'He left with hardly a word'. **Hardly** is followed by 'when', not 'than', as in 'Hardly had he entered the house when he collapsed', although the 'than' construction is very common.

he/she is a convention used to avoid sexism. Before the rise of feminism anyone referred to, whose sex was not specified, was assumed to be male, as in 'Each pupil must take his book home' and 'Every driver there parked his car illegally'. The only exception to this occurred in situations that were thought to be particularly appropriate to women, as in 'The cook should make her own stock' and 'The nurse has left her book behind'. In modern usage where attempts are made to avoid sexism either **he/she** or 'he or she' is frequently used, as in 'Each manager is responsible for his/her department' or 'It is a doctor's duty to explain the nature of the treatment to his or her patient'. People who regard this convention as being clumsy should consider restructuring the sentence or putting it in the plural, as in 'All managers are responsible for their departments'. Some users prefer to be ungrammatical and use a plural pronoun with a singular noun, as in 'Every pupil should take their books home' and this use is becoming increasingly common, even in textbooks.

heterosexism refers to discrimination and prejudice by a heterosexual person against a homosexual one, as in 'He was convinced that he had not got the job because he was gay—that the employer had been guilty of heterosexism'.

historic and **historical** are both adjectives formed from the noun 'history' but they are not interchangeable. **Historic** refers to events that are important enough to earn, or have earned, a place in history, as in 'Nelson's historic victory at Trafalgar' and 'the astronaut's historic landing on the moon'. It can be used loosely to mean 'extremely memorable', as in 'attend a historic party'. **Historical** means 'concerning past events', as in 'historical studies', or 'based on the study of history'.

hopefully has two meanings. The older meaning is 'with hope', as in 'The child looked hopefully at the sweet shop window' and 'It is better to travel hopefully than to arrive'. A more recent meaning, which is disliked by some people, means 'it is to be hoped that', as in 'Hopefully we shall soon be there'.

humanism and **humanitarianism** are liable to be confused. **Humanism** is a philosophy that values greatly human beings and their rôle, and rejects the need for religion, as in 'She was brought up as a Christian but she decided to embrace humanism in later life'. **Humanitarianism** refers to the philosophy and actions of people who wish to improve the lot of their fellow human beings and help them, as in 'humanitarians trying to help the refugees by taking them food and clothes'.

hyper- and **hypo-** are liable to be confused. They sound rather similar but they are opposites. **Hyper-** means 'above, excessively', as in 'hyperactive', 'hyperexcitable'. **Hypo-** means 'under, beneath', as in 'hypothermia'.

I and **me** are liable to be confused. I should be used as the subject of a sentence, as in 'You and I have both been invited', 'May Jane and I play?' and me as the object, as in 'The cake was made by Mary and me' and 'My brother and father played against my mother and me'. People often assume wrongly that me is less 'polite' than I. This is probably because they have been taught that in answer to such questions as 'Who is there?' the grammatically correct reply is 'It is I'. In fact, except in formal contexts, 'It is me' is frequently found in modern usage, especially in spoken contexts. Confusion arises as to whether to use I or me after 'between'. Since 'between' is followed by an object, me is the correct form. Thus it is correct to say 'Just between you and me, I think he is dishonest'.

i.e. is the abbreviation of a Latin phrase *id est*, meaning 'that is', as in 'He is a lexicographer, i.e. a person who edits dictionaries'. It is mostly used in written, rather than formal contexts, usually with full stops.

identical in modern usage can be followed by either 'with' or 'to'. Formerly only 'with' was considered correct, as in 'His new suit is identical with the one he bought last year'. Now 'to' is also considered acceptable, as in 'a brooch identical to one which he bought for his wife'.

illegible and **unreadable** are not totally interchangeable. **Illegible** refers to something that is impossible to make out or decipher, as in 'her handwriting is practically illegible'. **Unreadable** can also mean this, as in 'unreadable handwriting', but it can also mean 'unable to be read with understanding or enjoyment', as in 'His writing is so full of jargon that it is unreadable'.

imbroglio means 'a confused, complicated or embarrassing situation', as in 'politicians getting involved in an international imbroglio during the summit conference'. It is liable to be misspelt and mispronounced. Note the *g* which is liable to be omitted erroneously as it is not pronounced. It is pronounced im-*bro*-lio with emphasis on the second syllable which rhymes with 'foe'. **Imbroglio** is used only in formal or literary contexts.

impasse causes problems with reference to meaning, spelling and pronunciation. It means 'a difficult position or situation from which there is no way out, deadlock', as in 'The negotiations between management and workers have reached an impasse with neither side being willing to compromise'. Note the final *e* in the spelling. The first syllable can be pronounced 'am', or 'om' in an attempt at following the original French pronunciation, although in modern usage it is frequently totally anglicized as 'im'.

implicit *see* **explicit**.

imply and **infer** are often used interchangeably but they in fact are different in meaning. **Imply** means 'to suggest, to hint at', as in 'We felt that she was implying that he was lying' and 'She did not actually say that there was going to be a delay but she implied it'. **Infer** means 'to deduce, to conclude', as in 'From what the employer said we inferred that there would be some redundancies' and 'From the annual financial reports observers inferred the company was about to go bankrupt'. Note that **infer** doubles the *r* when adding '-ed' or '-ing' to form the past tense, past participle or present participle as **inferred** and **inferring**.

impracticable and **impractical** are liable to be confused. **Impracticable** means 'impossible to put into practice, not workable', as in 'In theory the plan is fine but it is impracticable in terms of costs'. **Impractical** means 'not sensible or realistic', as in 'It is impractical to think that you will get there and back in a day'; 'not skilled at doing or making things', as in 'He is a brilliant academic but he is hopelessly impractical'.

in lieu, which means 'instead of', as in 'receive extra pay in lieu of holidays', causes problems with pronunciation. It may be pronounced in lew or in loo.

indexes and **indices** are both plural forms of 'index'. In modern usage **indexes** is the more common form in general language, as in 'Indexes are essential in large reference books'. An **index** in this sense is 'an alphabetical list given at the back of a book as a guide to its contents'. The form **indices** is mostly restricted to technical contexts, such as mathematical information. **Indices** is pronounced in-dis-is and is the Latin form of the plural.

individual refers to 'a single person as opposed to a group', as in 'The rights of the community matter but so do the rights of the individual'. **Individual** is also sometimes used instead of 'person', but in such cases it is often used in a disapproving or belittling way, as in 'What an unpleasant individual she is!' and 'The individual who designed that building should be shot'.

indoor and **indoors** are not interchangeable. **Indoor** is an adjective, as in 'have an indoor match' and 'indoor games'. **Indoors** is an adverb, as in 'children playing outdoors instead of watching television indoors' and 'sleep outdoors on warm evenings instead of indoors'.

infer *see* **imply**.

infinite and **infinitesimal** are similar in meaning but are not interchangeable. **Infinite** means 'without limit', as in 'infinite space', or 'very great', as in 'have infinite patience' and 'He seems to have an infinite capacity for hard work'. **Infinitesimal** means 'very small, negligible', as in 'an infinitesimal difference in size' and 'an infinitesimal increase'. **Infinitesimal** is pronounced with the emphasis on the fourth syllable in-fin-it-*es*-im-il.

informer and **informant** both refer to 'a person who provides information' but they are used in different contexts. **Informer** is used to refer to 'a person who gives information to the police or authorities about a criminal, fugitive, etc', as in 'The local police have a group of informers who tell them what is going on in the criminal underworld' and 'The resistance worker was caught by the enemy soldier when an informer told them about his activities'. An **informant** provides more general information, as in 'My informant keeps me up-to-date with changes in personnel'.

in-law is usually found in compounds such as 'mother-in-law' and 'father-in-law'. When these compounds are in the plural the *s* should be added to the first word of the compound, not to **in-law**, as in 'mothers-in-law' and 'fathers-in-law'.

input used to be a technical term with particular application to computers. This meaning still exists and **input** can refer to the data, power, etc, put into a computer. As a verb it means 'to enter data into a computer', as in 'input the details of all the travel resorts in the area'. In modern usage it is frequently used in general language to mean 'contribution', as in 'Everyone is expected to provide some input for tomorrow's conference'. It is even found in this sense as a verb, as in 'input a great deal to the meeting'.

inquiry *see* **enquiry**.

install and **instal** are now both considered acceptable spellings. **Install** was formerly considered to be the only correct spelling and it is still the more common. The *l* is doubled in **instal** in the past participle, past tense and present participle as **installed, installing**. It means 'to put in', as in 'he installed a new television set'. The noun is spelt **instalment**.

instantaneously and **instantly** are interchangeable. Both mean 'immediately, at once', as in 'They obeyed instantaneously/instantly' and 'The accident victims were killed instantly/instantaneously'.

intense and **intensive** are not interchangeable. Intense means 'very strong, extreme', as in 'an intense desire to scream' and 'unable to tolerate the intense cold on the icy slopes'. **Intensive** means 'thorough', as in 'conduct an intensive search', and 'concentrated', as in 'an intensive course in first aid' and 'intensive bombing'.

invalid refers to two different words. If it is pronounced with the emphasis on the second syllable, as in-*val*-id it means 'not valid, no longer valid', as in 'This visa becomes invalid after six months'. If it is pronounced with the emphasis on the first syllable, as *in*-val-id, it means 'a person who is ill', as in 'The doctor has arrived to see the invalid'.

invent *see* **discover**.

inward and **inwards** are not used interchangeably. **Inward** is an adjective, as in 'an inward curve' and 'No one could guess her inward feelings'. **Inwards** is an adverb, as in 'toes turning inwards' and 'thoughts turning inwards'. **Inward** can be used as an adverb in the same way as **inwards**.

IQ is the abbreviation of 'intelligence quotient', as in 'He has a high IQ'. It is always written in capital letters and is sometimes written with full stops and sometimes not, according to preference.

irrespective is followed by the preposition 'of'. The phrase means 'not taking account of, not taking into consideration', as in 'All can go on the trip, irrespective of age'.

irrevocable is frequently misspelt and mispronounced. Note the double *r* and the *-able* ending. It is pronounced with the emphasis on the second syllable, as ir-*rev*-ok-ibl. When applied to legal judgements, etc, it is sometimes pronounced with the emphasis on the third syllable, as ir-rev-*ok*-ibl. The word means 'unable to be changed or revoked', as in 'Their decision to get divorced is irrevocable' and 'The jury's decision is irrevocable'.

its and **it's** are liable to be confused. **Its** is an adjective meaning 'belonging to it', as in 'The house has lost its charm' and 'The dog does not like its kennel'. **It's** means 'it is', as in 'Do you know if it's raining?' and 'It's not fair to expect her to do all the chores'.

jail and **gaol** are both acceptable spellings although jail is the more common. They mean 'prison' and can be both nouns and verbs, as in 'sent to jail/gaol for killing his wife' and 'jail/gaol him for his part in the bank robbery'.

jersey *see* **cardigan**.

jetsam *see* **flotsam**.

just is liable to be put in the wrong place in a sentence. It should be placed before the word it refers to, as in 'He has just one book left to sell', not 'He just has one book left to sell'. **Just** in the sense of 'in the very recent past' is used with the perfect tense, as in 'They have just finished the job', not 'They just finished the job'.

kind should be used with a singular noun, as 'This kind of accident can be avoided'. This should not read 'These kind of accidents can be avoided'. Similarly 'The children do not like that kind of film' is correct, not 'The children do not like those kind of films'. A plural noun can be used if the sentence is rephrased as 'Films of that kind are not liked by children'.

kindly can be either an adjective or adverb. The adjective means 'kind, friendly, sympathetic', as in 'A kindly lady took pity on the children and lent them some money to get home' and 'She gave them a kindly smile'. The adverb means 'in a kind manner', as in 'We were treated kindly by the local people' and 'They will not look kindly on his actions'.

kind of, meaning 'rather', as in 'That restaurant's kind of dear' and 'She's kind of tired of him', is informal and should be avoided in formal contexts.

knit in modern usage is becoming increasingly used as a noun to mean 'a knitted garment', as in 'a shop selling beautifully coloured knits'.

lady and **woman** cause controversy. **Lady** is objected to by many people when it is used instead of **woman**. Formerly, and still in some circles, it was regarded as a polite form of **woman**, as in '"Please get up and give that lady a seat", said the mother to her son'. Indeed, **woman** was thought to be rather insulting. For many people **woman** is now the preferred term and **lady** is seen as classist, because it is associated with nobility, privilege, etc, or condescending. However, **lady** is still quite commonly used, particularly when women are being addressed in a group, as in '"Ladies, I hope we can reach our sales target", said the manager' and 'Come along, ladies the bus is about to leave'. Phrases, such as **dinner lady** and **cleaning lady** are thought by some to be condescending but others still find **woman** rather insulting.

last is liable to cause confusion because it is not always clear which meaning is meant. **Last** as an adjective has several meanings. It can mean 'final', as in 'That was the musician's last public appearance—he died shortly after'; 'coming after all others in time or order', as in 'December is the last month in the year', 'The last of the runners reached the finishing tape'; 'latest, most recent', as in 'Her last novel is not as good as her earlier ones'; 'previous, preceding', as in 'This chapter is interesting but the last one was boring'. In order to avoid confusion it is best to use a word other than **last** where ambiguity is likely to arise. An example of a sentence which could cause confusion is 'I cannot remember the title of his last book', which could mean either 'his latest book' or 'his final book'.

latter *see* **former**.

lavatory *see* **toilet**.

lay and **lie** are liable to be confused. They are related but are used in different contexts. **Lay** means 'to put or place' and is a transitive verb, i.e. it takes an object. It is found in such sentences as 'Ask them to lay the books carefully on the table' and 'They are going to lay a new carpet in the bedroom'. **Lie**, meaning 'to rest in a horizontal position', is an intransitive verb, i.e. it does not take an object. It is found in such sentences as 'They were told to lie on the ground' and 'Snow is apt to lie on the mountain tops for a long time'. The confusion between the two words arises from the fact that **lay** is also the past tense of **lie**, as in 'He lay still on the ground' and 'Snow lay on the mountain tops'. The past tense of **lay** is **laid**, as in 'They laid the books on the table'. There is another verb **lie**, meaning 'to tell falsehoods, not to tell the truth', as in 'He was told to lie to the police'. The past tense of **lie** in this sense is **lied**, as in 'We suspect that he lied but we cannot prove it'.

leading question is often used wrongly. It should be used to mean 'a question that is so worded as to invite (or lead to) a particular answer desired by the questioner', as in 'The judge refused to allow the barrister to ask the witness the question on the grounds that it was a leading question'. However, it is often used wrongly to mean 'a question that is difficult, unfair or embarrassing'.

learn and **teach** are liable to be confused. **Learn** means 'to gain information or knowledge about', as in 'She learnt Spanish as a child', or 'to gain the skill of', as in 'She is learning to drive'. **Teach** means 'to give instruction in, to cause to know something or be able to do something', as in 'She taught her son French' and 'She taught her son to swim'. **Learn** is frequently used wrongly instead of **teach**, as in 'She learnt us to drive'.

learned and **learnt** are both acceptable forms of the past participle and past tense of the verb 'to learn', as in 'She has now learned/learnt to drive' and 'They learned/learnt French at school'. **Learned** in this sense can be pronounced either lernd or leant. However, **learned** can also be an adjective, meaning 'having much knowledge, erudite', as in 'an learned professor', or 'academic', as in 'learned journals'. It is pronounced *ler*-ned.

leave and **let** are not interchangeable. **Leave go** should not be substituted for **let go** in such sentences as 'Do not let go of the rope'. 'Do not leave go of the rope' is considered to be incorrect. However both **leave alone** and **let alone** can be used in the sense of 'to stop disturbing or interfering with', as in 'Leave/let the dog alone or it will bite you' and 'leave/let your mother alone—she is not feeling well'. **Leave alone** can also mean 'leave on one's own, cause to be alone', as in 'Her husband went away and left her alone', but **let alone** cannot be used in this sense. **Let alone** can also mean 'not to mention, without considering', as in 'They cannot afford proper food, let alone a holiday', but **leave alone** should not be used in this sense.

legible and **readable** are not interchangeable. **Legible** means 'able to be deciphered or made out', as in 'His writing is scarcely legible'. **Readable** can also be used in this sense, as in 'His handwriting is just not readable'. However **readable** is also used to mean 'able to be read with interest or enjoyment', as in 'He is an expert on the subject but I think his books are simply not readable' and 'I find her novels very readable but my friend does not like her style'.

lend and **loan** can cause confusion. **Lend** is used as a verb in British English to mean 'to allow someone the use of temporarily', as in 'Can you lend me a pen?' and 'His father refused to lend him any money'. **Loan** is a noun meaning 'something lent, the temporary use of', as in 'They thanked her for the loan of her car'. In American English **loan** is used as a verb to mean **lend**, and this use is becoming common in Britain although it is still regarded as not quite acceptable.

lengthways and **lengthwise** are used interchangeably, as in 'fold the tablecloth lengthways/lengthwise' and 'measure the room lengthwise/lengthways'.

lengthy and **long** are not interchangeable. **Lengthy** means 'excessively long', as in 'We had a lengthy wait before we saw the doctor' and 'It was such a lengthy speech that most of the audience got bored'. **Lengthy** is frequently misspelt. Note the *g*.

less and **fewer** are often confused. Less means 'a smaller amount or quantity of' and is the comparative form of 'little'. It is found in sentences such as 'less milk', 'less responsibility' and 'less noise'. **Fewer** means 'a smaller number of' and is the comparative of 'few'. It is found in sentences such as 'buy fewer bottles of milk', 'have fewer responsibilities', 'have fewer opportunities' and 'hear fewer noises'. **Less** is commonly wrongly used where **fewer** is correct. It is common but ungrammatical to say or write 'less bottles of milk' and 'less queues in the shops during the week'.

liable to and **likely to** both express probability. They mean much the same except that **liable to** suggests that the probability is based on past experience or habit. 'He is liable to lose his temper' suggests that he has been in the habit of doing so in the past. 'He is likely to lose his temper' suggests that he will probably lose his temper, given the situation, but that the probability is not based on how he has reacted in the past. This distinction is not always adhered to, and some people use the terms interchangeably.

libel and **slander** both refer to defamatory statements against someone but they are not interchangeable. **Libel** refers to defamation that is written down, printed or drawn, as in 'The politician sued the newspaper for libel when it falsely accused him of fraud'. **Slander** refers to defamation in spoken form, as in 'She heard that one of her neighbours was spreading slander about her'. Both **libel** and **slander** can act as verbs, as in 'bring a suit against the newspaper for libelling him' and 'think that one of her neighbours was slandering her'. Note that the verb **libel** doubles the *l* in the past participle, past tense and present participle, as **libelled** and **libelling**.

licence and **license** are liable to cause confusion in British English. **Licence** is a noun meaning 'an official document showing that permission has been given to do, use or own something', as in 'require a licence to have a stall in the market', 'have a licence to drive a car', and 'apply for a pilot's licence'. **License** is a verb meaning 'to provide someone with a licence', as in 'The council have licensed him as a street trader', 'The restaurant has been licensed to sell alcohol'. Note **licensed grocer** and **licensing laws** but **off-licence**. In American English both the noun and verb are spelt **license**.

lie *see* **lay**.

light years are a measure of distance, not time. A **light year** is the distance travelled by light in one year (about six million, million miles) and is a term used in astronomy. **Light years** are often referred to in an informal context when time, not distance, is involved, as in 'Owning their own house seemed light years away' and 'It seems light years since we had a holiday'.

like tends to cause confusion. It is a preposition meaning 'resembling, similar to', as in 'houses like castles', gardens like jungles', 'actors like Olivier', 'She looks like her mother', 'She plays like an expert', 'The child swims like a fish' and 'Like you, he cannot stand cruelty to animals'. To be grammatically correct **like** should not be used as a conjunction. Thus 'The house looks like it has been deserted' is incorrect. It should read 'The house looks as though/if it has been deserted'. Similarly, 'Like his mother said, he has had to go to hospital' should read 'As his mother said, he has had to go to hospital'.

likeable and **likable** are both acceptable spellings. The word means 'pleasant, agreeable, friendly', as in 'He is a likeable/likable young man'.

likely to *see* **liable to**.

literally is frequently used simply to add emphasis to an idea rather than to indicate that the word, phrase, etc, used is to be interpreted word for word. Thus, 'She was literally tearing her hair out' does not mean that she was pulling her hair out by the handful but that she was very angry, anxious, frustrated, etc.

livid and **lurid** are liable to be confused although they mean different things. **Livid** means 'discoloured, of a greyish tinge', as in 'a livid bruise on her face', and 'furious', as in 'When he saw his damaged car he was livid'. **Lurid** means 'sensational, shocking', as in 'give the lurid details about finding the body', and 'garish, glaringly bright', as in 'wear a lurid shade of green'.

living room *see* **sitting room**.

loan *see* **lend**.

loo *see* **toilet**.

lots of and **a lot of**, meaning 'many' and 'much', should be used only in informal contexts', as in '"I've got lots of toys," said the child' and 'You're talking a lot of rubbish'. They should be avoided in formal prose.

lounge *see* **sitting room**.

low and **lowly** are not interchangeable. **Low** means 'not high', as in 'a low fence', 'a low level of income', 'speak in a low voice' and 'her low status in the firm'. It can also mean 'despicable, contemptible', as in 'That was a low trick' or 'He's a low creature'. **Lowly** means 'humble', as in 'of lowly birth' and 'the peasant's lowly abode'.

lunch and **luncheon** both refer to a meal eaten in the middle of the day. **Lunch**, as in 'a business lunch' and 'have just a snack for lunch', is by far the more usual term. **Luncheon**, as in 'give a luncheon party for the visiting celebrity', is a very formal word and is becoming increasingly uncommon. *See also* **dinner**.

lurid *see* **livid**.

madam and **madame** are liable to be confused. **Madam** is the English-language form of the French **madame**. It is a form of formal of address for a woman, as in 'Please come this way, madam'. It is used in formal letters when the name of the woman being written to is not known, as in 'Dear Madam'. **Madam** can be written either with a capital letter or a lower-case letter. **Madam** is pronounced *mad*-am, with the emphasis on the first syllable. **Madame**, which is the French equivalent of 'Mrs', is occasionally found in English, as in Madame Tussaud's, and is pronounced in the same way as **madam**. In French **madame** is pronounced ma-*dam*.

majority and **minority** are opposites. **Majority** means 'more than half the total number of', as in 'The majority of the pupils live locally' and 'the younger candidate received the majority of the votes'. **Minority** means less than half the total number of', as in 'A small minority of the football fans caused trouble' and 'Only a minority of the committee voted against the motion'. **Majority** and **minority** should not be used to describe the greater or lesser part of a single thing. Thus it is wrong to say 'The majority of the book is uninteresting'.

male, masculine and **mannish** all refer to the sex that is not female but the words are used in different ways. **Male** is the opposite of 'female' and refers to the sex of a person or animal, as in 'no male person may enter', 'a male nurse', 'a male elephant' and 'the male reproductive system'. **Masculine** is the opposite of 'feminine' and refers to people or their characteristics. It refers to characteristics, etc, that are traditionally considered to be typically **male**. Examples of its use include 'a very masculine young man', 'a deep, masculine voice'. It can be used of women, as in 'She has a masculine walk' and 'She wears masculine clothes'. When used of women it is often derogatory and is sometimes replaced with **mannish**, which is derogatory, as in 'women with mannish haircuts'. **Male** can also be used as a noun, as in 'the male of the species' 'of the robins, the male is more colourful' and 'the title can be held only by males'.

man causes a great deal of controversy. To avoid being sexist it should be avoided when it really means 'person'. 'We must find the right man for the job' should read 'We must find the right person for the job'. Similarly, 'All men have a right to a reasonable standard of living' should read 'All people have a right to a reasonable standard of living' or 'Everyone has a right to a reasonable standard of living'. Problems also arise with compounds, such as 'chairman'. In such situations 'person' is often used, as in 'chairperson'. Man is also used to mean 'mankind, humankind', as in 'Man is mortal' and 'Man has the power of thought'. Some people also object to this usage and consider it sexist. They advocate using 'humankind' or 'the human race'.

many is used in more formal contexts rather than 'a lot of' or 'lots of', as in 'The judge said the accused had had many previous convictions'. **Many** is often used in the negative in both formal and informal contexts, as in 'They don't have many friends' and 'She won't find many apples on the trees now'.

masculine *see* **male**.

may *see* **can**.

maybe and **may be** are liable to be confused although they have different meanings. **Maybe** means 'perhaps', as in 'Maybe they lost their way' and 'He said, "Maybe" when I asked him if he was going'. It is used in more informal contexts than 'perhaps'. **May be** is used in such sentences as 'He may be poor but he is very generous' and 'They may be a little late'.

mayoress means 'the wife or partner of a male mayor', as in 'an official dinner for the mayor and mayoress'. A mayor who is a woman is called either 'mayor' or 'lady mayor'.

me *see* **I**.

meaningful originally meant 'full of meaning', as in 'make very few meaningful statements' and 'There was a meaningful silence'. In modern usage it has come to mean 'important, significant, serious', as in 'not interested in a meaningful relationship' and 'seeking a meaningful career'. The word now tends to be very much over-used.

means in the sense of 'way, method' can be either a singular or plural noun, as in 'The means of defeating them is in our hands' and 'Many different means of financing the project have been investigated'. **Means** in the sense of 'wealth' and 'resources' is plural, as in 'His means are not sufficient to support two families'.

media gives rise to confusion. In the form of **the media** it is commonly applied to the press, to newspapers, television and radio, as in 'The politician claimed that he was being harassed by the media'. **Media** is a plural form of 'medium', meaning 'means of communication', as in 'television is a powerful medium'. In modern usage **media** is beginning to be used as a singular noun, as in 'The politician blamed a hostile media for his misfortunes', but this is still regarded as being an incorrect use.

middle *see* **centre**.

mileage and **milage** are both acceptable spellings for 'the distance travelled or measured in miles', as in 'The car is a bargain, given the low mileage'. However **mileage** is much more common than **milage**. The word also means informally 'benefit, advantage', as in 'The politician got a lot of mileage from the scandal surrounding his opponent' and 'There's not much mileage in pursuing that particular line of inquiry'.

militate and **mitigate** are liable to be confused. **Militate** means 'to have or serve as a strong influence against', as in 'Their lack of facts militated against the success of their application' and 'His previous record will militate against his chances of going free'. **Mitigate** means 'to alleviate', as in 'try to mitigate the suffering of the refugees', or 'moderate', as in 'mitigate the severity of the punishment'.

millennium is liable to be misspelt. Note the double *n* which is frequently omitted in error. The plural form is **millennia**. **Millennium** refers to 'a period of 1000 years', as in 'rock changes taking place over several millennia'. In religious terms it refers to 'the thousand-year reign of Christ prophesied in the Bible'.

minority *see* **majority**.

Miss *see* **Ms**.

misuse *see* **abuse**.

mitigate *see* **militate**.

mnemonic refers to 'something that aids the memory'. For example, some people use a **mnemonic** in the form of a verse to remind them how to spell a word or to recall a date. The word is liable to be misspelt and mispronounced. Note the initial *m*, which is silent. **Mnemonic** is pronounced nim-*on*-ik, with the emphasis on the second syllable.

modern and **modernistic** are not quite the same. **Modern** means 'referring to the present time or recent times', as in 'the politics of modern times' and 'a production of Shakespeare's *Twelfth Night* in modern dress'. It also means 'using the newest techniques, equipment, buildings, etc, as in 'a modern shopping centre' and 'a modern office complex'. **Modernistic** means 'characteristic of modern ideas, fashions, etc', and is often used in a derogatory way, as in 'She says she hates that modernistic furniture'.

modus vivendi refers to 'a practical, sometimes temporary, arrangement or compromise by which people who are in conflict can live or work together', as in 'The two opposing parties on the committee will have to reach a modus vivendi if any progress is to be made'. It is a Latin phrase that literally means 'a way of living' and is pronounced *mo*-dus viv-*en*-di.

more is used to form the comparative of adjectives and adverbs that do not form the comparative by adding *-er*. This usually applies to longer adjectives, as in 'more beautiful', 'more gracious', 'more useful', and 'more flattering'. **More** should not be used with adjectives that have a comparative ending already. Thus it is wrong to write 'more happier'. **Most** is used in the same way to form the superlative of adjectives and adverbs, as in 'most beautiful', 'most gracious' etc.

Moslem *see* **Muslim**.

most *see* **more**.

movable and **moveable** are both possible spellings but **movable** is the more common, as in 'movable possessions' and 'machines with movable parts'.

Ms, Mrs and **Miss** are all used before the names of women in addressing them and in letter-writing. Formerly **Mrs** was used before the name of a married woman and **Miss** before the name of an unmarried woman or girl. In modern usage **Ms** is often used instead of **Miss** or **Mrs**. This is sometimes because the marital status of the woman is not known and sometimes from a personal preference. Many people feel that since no distinction is made between married and unmarried men when they are being addressed, no distinction should be made between married and unmarried women. On the other hand some people, particularly older women, object to the use of **Ms**.

much, except in negative sentences, is used mainly in rather formal contexts, as in 'They own much property'. 'A great deal of' is often used instead, as in 'They own a great deal of property'. In informal contexts 'a lot of' is often used instead of **much**, as in 'a lot of rubbish' not 'much rubbish'. **Much** is used in negative sentences, as in 'They do not have much money'.

Muslim and **Moslem** refer to 'a follower of the Islamic faith'. In modern usage **Muslim** is the preferred term rather than the older spelling **Moslem**.

naught and **nought** are not totally interchangeable. **Naught** means 'nothing', as in 'All his projects came to naught', and is rather a formal or literary word in this sense. **Naught** is also a less usual spelling of **nought**, which means 'zero' when it is regarded as a number, as in 'nought point one (0.1)'.

nearby and **near by** can cause problems. **Nearby** can be either an adjective, as in 'the nearby village', or an adverb, as in 'Her mother lives nearby'. **Near by** is an adverb, as in 'He doesn't have far to go—he lives near by'. In other words, the adverbial sense can be spelt either **nearby** or **near by**.

née is used to indicate the maiden or family name of a married woman, as in 'Jane Jones, née Smith'. It is derived from French, being the feminine form of the French word for 'born'. It can be spelt either with an acute accent or not—**née** or **nee**.

never in the sense of 'did not', as in 'He never saw the other car before he hit it', should be used in only very informal contexts. **Never** means 'at no time, on no occasion', as in 'He will never agree to their demands' and 'She has never been poor'. It is also used as a negative for the sake of emphasis, as in 'He never so much as smiled'.

nevertheless and **none the less** mean the same thing, as in 'He has very little money. Nevertheless/none the less he gives generously to charity'. **None the less** is usually written as three words but **nevertheless** is spelt as one word. In modern usage **none the less** is sometimes written as one word, as **nonetheless**.

next and **this** can cause confusion. **Next** in one of its senses is used to mean the day of the week, month of the year, season of the year, etc, that will follow next, as in 'They are coming next Tuesday', 'We are going on holiday next June' and 'They are to be married next summer'. **This** can also be used in this sense and so ambiguity can occur. Some people use **this** to refer to the very next Tuesday, June, summer, etc, and use **next** for the one after that. Thus someone might say on Sunday, 'I'll see you next Friday', meaning the first Friday to come, but someone else might take that to mean a week on from that because they would refer to the first Friday to come as 'this Friday'. The only solution is to make sure exactly which day, week, season, etc, the other person is referring to.

nice originally meant 'fine, subtle, requiring precision', as in 'There is rather a nice distinction between the two words', but it is widely used in the sense of 'pleasant, agreeable, etc', as in 'She is a nice person' and 'We had a nice time at the picnic'. It is overused and alternative adjectives should be found to avoid this, as in 'She is an amiable person' and 'We had an enjoyable time at the picnic'.

no one and **no-one** are interchangeable but the word is never written 'noone', unlike 'everyone'. **No one** and **no-one** are used with a singular verb, as in 'No one is allowed to leave' and 'No one is anxious to leave'. They are used by some people with a plural personal pronoun or possessive case when attempts are being made to avoid sexism, as in 'No one is expected to take their child away'. The singular form is grammatically correct, as in 'No one is expected to take his/her child away', but it is clumsy. 'No one is expected to take his child away' is sexist. Nobody is interchangeable with no one, as in 'You must tell no one/nobody about this'.

nobody *see* **no one**.

none can be used with either a singular verb or plural verb. Examples of sentences using a singular verb include 'There is none of the food left' and 'None of the work is good enough' and 'None of the coal is to be used today'. In sentences where none is used with a plural noun the verb was traditionally still singular, as in 'None of the books is suitable' and 'None of the parcels is undamaged'. This is still the case in formal contexts but, in the case of informal contexts, a plural verb is often used in modern usage, as in 'None of these things are any good'.

none the less *see* **nevertheless**.

not only is frequently used in a construction with 'but also', as in 'We have not only the best candidate but also the most efficient organization' and 'The organizers of the fête not only made a great deal of money for charity but also gave a great many people a great deal of pleasure'.

nought *see* **naught**.

noxious and **obnoxious** are liable to be confused. They both refer to unpleasantness or harmfulness but they are used in different contexts. **Noxious** is used of a substance, fumes, etc, and means 'harmful, poisonous', as in 'firemen overcome by noxious fumes' and 'delinquent children having a noxious influence on the rest of the class'. **Obnoxious** means 'unpleasant, nasty, offensive', as in 'He has the most obnoxious neighbours' and 'The child's parents let him off with the most obnoxious behaviour'. **Noxious** is used in formal and technical contexts rather than **obnoxious**.

nubile originally meant 'old enough to marry, marriageable' as in 'he has five nubile daughters'. In modern usage **nubile** is frequently used in the sense of 'sexually attractive', as in 'admiring the nubile girls sunbathing on the beach' and 'nubile models posing for magazine illustrations'.

numbers can be written in either figures or words. It is largely a matter of taste which method is adopted. As long as the method is consistent it does not really matter. Some establishments, such as a publishing house or a newspaper office, will have a house style. For example, some of them prefer to have numbers up to 10 written in words, as in 'They have two boys and three girls'. If this system is adopted, guidance should be sought as to whether a mixture of figures and words in the same sentence is acceptable, as in 'We have 12 cups but only six saucers', or whether the rule should be broken in such situations as 'We have twelve cups but only six saucers'.

nutritional and **nutritious** are liable to be confused. They both refer to 'nutrition, the process of giving and receiving nourishment' but mean different things. **Nutritional** means 'referring to nutrition', as in 'doubts about the nutritional value of some fast foods' and 'people who do not receive the minimum nutritional requirements'. **Nutritious** means 'nourishing, of high value as a food', as in 'nutritious homemade soups' and 'something slightly more nutrtious than a plate of chips'.

O and **Oh** are both forms of an exclamation made at the beginning of a sentence. **Oh** is the usual spelling, as in 'Oh well. It's Friday tomorrow' and 'Oh dear, the baby's crying again'.

objective and **subjective** are opposites. **Objective** means 'not influenced by personal feelings, attitudes, or prejudices', as in 'She is related to the person accused and so she cannot give an objective view of the situation' and 'It is important that all members of a jury are completely objective'. **Subjective** means 'influenced by personal feelings, attitudes and prejudices', as in 'It is only natural to be subjective in situations regarding one's children' and 'She wrote a very subjective report on the conference and did not stick to the facts'. **Objective** can also be a noun in the sense of 'aim, goal', as in 'Our objective was to make as much money as possible'. **Object** can also be used in this sense, as in 'Their main object is to have a good time'.

oblivious means 'unaware of, unconscious of, not noticing'. Traditionally it is followed by the preposition 'of', as in 'The lovers were oblivious of the rain' and 'When he is reading he is completely oblivious of his surroundings'. In modern usage its use with the preposition 'to' is also considered acceptable, as in 'They were oblivious to the fact that he was cheating them' and 'sleep soundly, oblivious to the noise'.

obnoxious *see* **noxious**.

obscene and **pornographic** are not interchangeable. **Obscene** means 'indecent, especially in a sexual way, offending against the accepted standards of decency', as in 'obscene drawings on the walls of the public toilet' and 'When his car was damaged he let out a stream of obscene language'. **Pornographic** means 'intended to arouse sexual excitement', as in 'pornographic videos' and 'magazines with women shown in pornographic poses'. **Obscene** is frequently misspelt. Note the *c* after the *s*.

oculist *see* **optician**.

of is sometimes wrongly used instead of the verb 'to have', as in 'He must of known she was lying' instead of 'He must have known she was lying'. The error arises because the two constructions sound alike when not emphasized.

Oh *see* **O**.

OK and **okay** are both acceptable spellings of an informal word indicating agreement or approval, as in 'OK/okay, I'll come with you', 'We've at last been given the OK/okay to begin building'. When the word is used as a verb it is more usually spelt **okay** because of the problem in adding endings, as in 'They've okayed our plans at last'. **OK** is sometimes written with full stops as **O.K.**

older *see* **elder**.

one is used in formal situations to indicate an indefinite person where 'you' would be used in informal situations, as in 'One should not believe all one hears' and 'One should be kind to animals'. This construction can sound rather affected. Examples of the informal 'you' include 'You would've thought he would've had more sense' and 'You wouldn't think anyone could be so stupid'. **One** when followed by 'of the' and a plural noun takes a singular verb, as in 'One of the soldiers was killed' and 'One of the three witnesses has died'. However, the constructions 'one of those … who' and 'one of the … that' take a plural verb, as in 'He is one of those people who will not take advice' and 'It is one of those houses that are impossible to heat'.

only must be carefully positioned in written sentences to avoid confusion. It should be placed before, or as close as possible before, the word to which it refers. Compare 'She drinks only wine at the weekend', 'She drinks wine only at the weekend' and 'Only she drinks wine at the weekend'. In spoken English, where the intonation of the voice will indicate which word **only** applies to it may be placed in whichever position sounds most natural, usually between the subject and the verb, as in 'She only drinks wine at the weekend'.

onto and **on to** are both acceptable forms in sentences such as 'The cat leapt onto/on to the table' and 'He jumped from the plane onto/on to the ground'. However, in sentences such as 'It is time to move on to another city' **onto** is not a possible alternative.

onward and **onwards** are not interchangeable. **Onward** is an adjective, as in 'onward motion' and 'onward progress'. **Onwards** is an adverb, as in 'march onwards' and 'proceed onwards'.

optician, ophthalmologist, optometrist and **oculist** all refer to 'a person who is concerned with disorders of the eyes' but they are not interchangeable. **Dispensing optician** refers to 'a person who makes and sells spectacles or contact lenses'. **Ophthalmic optician** refers to 'a person who tests eyesight and prescribes lenses'. **Optometrist** is another term for this. **Ophthalmologist** refers to 'a doctor who specializes in disorders of the eyes' and **oculist** is another name for this.

optimum means 'the most favourable or advantageous condition, situation, amount, degree, etc', as in 'A temperature of 20° is optimum for these plants'. It is mostly used as an adjective meaning 'most favourable or advantageous', as in 'the optimum speed to run the car at', 'the optimum time at which to pick the fruit' and 'the optimum amount of water to give the plants'. It should not be used simply as a synonym for 'best'.

optometrist *see* **optician**.

orientate and **orient** are both acceptable forms of the same word. **Orientate** is the more common in British English but the shorter form, **orient**, is preferred by some people and is the standard form in American English. They are verbs meaning 'to get one's bearings', as in 'difficult to orientate/orient themselves in the mist on the mountain'; 'to adjust to new surroundings', as in 'It takes some time to orientate/orient oneself in a new job'; 'to direct at', as in 'The course is orientated/oriented at older students'; 'to direct the interest of to', as in 'try to orientate/orient students towards the sciences'.

orthopaedic and **paediatric** are liable to be confused. They both apply to medical specialties but they are different. **Orthopaedic** means 'referring to the treatment of disorders of the bones', as in 'attend the orthopaedic clinic with an injured back'. **Paediatric** means 'referring to the treatment of disorders associated with children', as in 'Her little boy is receiving treatment from a paediatric consultant'. In American English these are respectively spelt **orthopedic** and **pediatric**.

other than can be used when **other** is an adjective or pronoun, as in 'There was no means of entry other than through a trap door' and 'He disapproves of the actions of anyone other than himself'. Traditionally, it should not be used as an adverbial phrase, as in 'It was impossible to get there other than by private car'. In such constructions **otherwise than** should be used, as in 'It is impossible to get there otherwise than by private car'. However, **other than** used adverbially is common in modern usage.

otherwise traditionally should not be used as an adjective or pronoun, as in 'Pack your clothes, clean or otherwise' and 'We are not discussing the advantages, or otherwise, of the scheme at this meeting'. It is an adverb, as in 'We

are in favour of the project but he obviously thinks otherwise' and 'The hours are rather long but otherwise the job is fine'. *See* **other than**.

owing to *see* **due to**.

p *see* **pence**.

paediatric *see* **orthopaedic**.

panacea and **placebo** are liable to be confused. **Panacea** means 'a universal remedy for all ills and troubles', as in 'The new government does not have a panacea for the country's problems'. It is often used loosely to mean any remedy for any problem, as in 'She thinks that a holiday will be a panacea for his unhappiness'. **Panacea** is pronounced pan-a-*see*-a. **Placebo** refers to 'a supposed medication that is just a harmless substance given to a patient as part of a drugs trial etc', as in 'She was convinced the pills were curing her headaches but the doctor has prescribed her a placebo'. It is pronounced pla-*see*-bo.

parameter is a mathematical term that is very loosely used in modern usage to mean 'limit, boundary, framework' or 'limiting feature or characteristic', as in 'work within the parameters of our budget and resources'. The word is over-used and should be avoided where possible. The emphasis is on the second syllable as par-*am*-it-er.

paranoid is an adjective meaning 'referring to a mental disorder, called **paranoia**, characterized by delusions of persecution and grandeur', as in 'a paranoid personality'. In modern usage it is used loosely to mean 'distrustful, suspicious of others, anxious etc', as in 'It is difficult to get to know him—he's so paranoid' and 'paranoid about people trying to get his job', when there is no question of actual mental disorder. **Paranoia** is pronounced par-a-*noy*-a.

paraphernalia means 'all the bits and pieces of equipment required for something', as in 'all the paraphernalia needed to take a baby on holiday', 'put his angling paraphernalia in the car'. Strictly speaking it is a plural noun but it is now frequently used with a singular verb, as in 'The artist's paraphernalia was lying all over the studio'. **Paraphernalia** is liable to be misspelt. Note the *er* before the *n*.

parlour *see* **sitting room**.

particular means 'special, exceptional', as in 'a matter of particular importance', or 'individual', as in 'Have you a particular person in mind?', and 'concerned over details, fastidious', as in 'very particular about personal hygiene'. **Particular** is often used almost meaninglessly, as in 'this particular dress' and 'this particular car', when **particular** does not add much to the meaning.

partner can be used to indicate one half of an established couple, whether the couple are married or living together, as in 'Her partner was present at the birth of the child'.

passed and **past** are liable to be confused. **Passed** is the past participle and past tense of the verb 'to pass', as in 'She has already passed the exam' and 'They passed an old man on the way'. **Past** is used as a noun, as in 'He was a difficult teenager but that is all in the past now' and 'He has a murky past'. It is also used as an adjective, as in 'I haven't seen him in the past few weeks' and 'Her past experiences affected her opinion of men'. **Past** can also be a preposition, as in 'We drove past their new house', 'It's past three o'clock' and 'He's past caring'. It can also be an adverb, as in 'He watched the athletes running past' and 'The boat drifted past'.

patent, in British English, is usually pronounced *pay*-tent, as in 'patent leather dancing shoes'. **Patent** in the sense of 'obvious', as in 'his patent dislike of the situation' and 'It was quite patent that she loved him' is also pronounced in that way. **Patent** in the sense of 'a legal document giving the holder the sole right to make or sell something and preventing others from imitating it', as in 'take out a patent for his new invention', can be pronounced either *pay*-tent or *pat*-ent. **Patent** in this last sense can also be a verb, as in 'He should patent his invention as soon as possible'.

peddler and **pedlar** are not interchangeable in British English. **Peddler** refers particularly to 'a person who peddles drugs', as in 'drug-peddlers convicted and sent to prison'. **Pedlar** refers to 'a person who sells small articles from house to house or from place to place', as in 'pedlars selling ribbons at the fair'.

pence, p and **pennies** are liable to be confused. **Pence** is the plural form of 'penny', as in 'There are a hundred pence in the pound'. It is commonly found in prices, as in 'apples costing 10 pence each'. **Pence** has become much more common than 'pennies', which tends to be associated with pre-decimalization money (the British currency was decimalized in 1972), as in 'There were twelve pennies in one shilling'. **Pence** is sometimes used as though it were singular, as in 'have no one-pence pieces'. In informal contexts **p** is often used, as in 'Have you got a 10p (pronounced ten pee) piece' and 'Those chocolate bars are fifteen p'. **Pence** in compounds is not pronounced in the same way as pence was pronounced in compounds before decimalization. Such words as 'ten pence' are now pronounced *ten pens*, with equal emphasis on each word. In pre-decimalization days it was pronounced *ten*-pens, with the emphasis on the first word.

pennies *see* **pence**.

people is usually a plural noun and so takes a plural verb, as in 'The local people were annoyed at the stranger's behaviour' and 'People were being asked to leave'. In the sense of 'nation', 'race' or 'tribe' it is sometimes treated as a singular noun, as in 'the nomadic peoples of the world'. **People** acts as the plural of 'person', as in 'There's room for only one more person in that car but there's room for three people in this one'. In formal or legal contexts **persons** is sometimes used as the plural of 'person', as in 'The lift had a notice saying "Room for six persons only"'.

per means 'for each' and is used to express rates, prices, etc, as in 'driving at 60 miles per hour', 'cloth costing £5 per square metre', 'The cost of the trip is £20 per person'

and 'The fees are £1000 a term per child'. It can also mean 'in each', as in 'The factory is inspected three times per year'.

per capita is a formal expression meaning 'for each person', as in 'The cost of the trip will be £300 per capita'. It is a Latin phrase which has been adopted into English and literally means 'by heads'. It is pronounced per *ka*-pi-ta.

per cent is usually written as two words. It is used adverbially in combination with a number in the sense of 'in or for each hundred', as in 'thirty per cent of the people are living below the poverty line'. The number is sometimes written in figures, as in '50 per cent of the staff are married'. The symbol % is often used instead of the words 'per cent', especially in technical contexts, as in 'make savings of up to 30%'. **Per cent** in modern usage is sometimes used as a noun, as in 'They have agreed to lower the price by half a per cent'.

percentage refers to 'the rate, number or amount in each hundred', as in 'the number of unemployed people expressed as a percentage of the adult population' and 'What percentage of his salary is free?'. It is also used to mean proportion, as in 'Only a small percentage of last year's students have found jobs' and 'A large percentage of the workers are in favour of a strike'. In modern usage it is sometimes used to mean 'a small amount' or 'a small part', as in 'Only a percentage of the students will find work'.

perquisite *see* **prerequisite**.

per se is a Latin phrase that has been adapted into English and means 'in itself', as in 'The substance is not per se harmful but it might be so if it interacts with other substances' and 'Television is not per se bad for children'. It should be used only in formal contexts.

person is now used in situations where 'man' was formerly used to avoid sexism in language. It is used when the sex of the person being referred to is either unknown or not specified, as in 'They are advertising for another person for the warehouse'. It often sounds more natural to use 'someone', as in 'They are looking for someone to help out in the warehouse'. **Person** is often used in compounds, as in **chairperson, spokesperson** and **salesperson**, although some people dislike this convention and some compounds, such as **craftsperson**, have not really caught on. **Person** has two possible plurals. *See* **people**. **Person with** and **people with** are phrases advocated in 'politically correct' language to avoid negative terms such as 'victim', 'sufferer', as in 'person with Aids'.

phenomenal means 'referring to a phenomenon'. It is often used to mean 'remarkable, extraordinary', as in 'a phenomenal atmospheric occurrence', and in modern usage it is also used loosely to mean 'very great', as in 'a phenomenal increase in the crime rate' and 'a phenomenal achievement'. This use is usually restricted to informal contexts.

phenomenon is a singular noun meaning 'a fact, object, occurrence, experience, etc, that can be perceived by the senses rather than by thought or intuition', as in

'She saw something coming out of the lake but it remained an unexplained phenomenon', and 'a strange, unusual or remarkable fact, event or person of some particular significance', as in 'Single parenthood is one of the phenomena of the 1990s'. The plural is **phenomena**, as in 'natural phenomena'. It is a common error to treat **phenomena** as a singular noun. Note the spelling of **phenomenon** as it is liable to be misspelt.

phone, which is a short form of 'telephone', is not regarded as being as informal as it once was. It is quite acceptable in sentences such as 'He is going to buy a mobile phone'. Note that **phone** is now spelt without an apostrophe.

phoney and **phony** are both acceptable spellings but **phoney** is the more common in British English. The word means 'pretending or claiming to be what one is not, fake', as in 'He has a phoney American accent' and 'There's something phoney about him'.

placebo *see* **panacea**.

plane and **aeroplane** mean the same thing, both referring to a 'a machine that can fly and is used to carry people and goods'. In modern usage **plane** is the usual term, as in 'The plane took off on time' and 'nearly miss the plane'. **Aeroplane** is slightly old-fashioned or unduly formal, as in 'Her elderly parents say that they refuse to travel by aeroplane'. The American English spelling is **airplane**. Note that **plane** is not spelt with an apostrophe although it is a shortened form.

pleaded and **pled** mean the same thing, both being the past tense and past participle of the verb 'to plead'. **Pleaded** is the usual form in British English, as in 'They pleaded with the tyrant to spare the child's life' and 'The accused pleaded guilty'. **Pled** is the usual American spelling.

plenty is used only informally in some contexts. It is acceptable in formal and informal contexts when it is followed by the preposition 'of', as in 'We have plenty of food', or when it is used as a pronoun without the 'of' construction, as in 'You can borrow some food from us—we have plenty'. Some people think its use as an adjective, as in 'Don't hurry—we have plenty time' and 'There's plenty food for all in the fridge', should be restricted to informal contexts. As an adverb it is a acceptable in both formal and informal contexts in such sentences as 'Help yourself—we have plenty more'. However, such sentences as 'The house is plenty big enough for them' is suitable only for very informal or slang contexts.

political correctness is a modern movement aiming to remove all forms of prejudice in language, such as sexism, racism and discrimination against disabled people. Its aims are admirable but in practice many of the words and phrases suggested by advocates of political correctness are rather contrived or, indeed, ludicrous. The adjective is **politically correct**.

practicable and **practical** should not be used interchangeably. **Practicable** means 'able to be done or carried out, able to be put into practice', as in 'His schemes seem fine in theory but they are never practicable'. **Practical** has several meanings, such as 'concerned with action and practice rather than with theory', as in 'He has studied the theory but has no practical experience of the job'; 'suitable for the purpose for which it was made', as in 'practical shoes for walking'; 'useful', as in 'a practical device with a wide range of uses'; 'clever at doing and making things', as in 'She's very practical when it comes to dealing with an emergency'; 'virtual', as in 'He's not the owner but he's in practical control of the firm'.

practically can mean 'in a practical way', as in 'Practically, the scheme is not really possible', but in modern usage it is usually used to mean 'virtually', as in 'He practically runs the firm although he is not the manager', and 'almost', as in 'The driver of that car practically ran me over'.

prefer is followed by the preposition 'to' not 'than', as in 'She prefers dogs to cats', 'They prefer Paris to London' and 'They prefer driving to walking'.

prerequisite and **perquisite** are liable to be confused although they are completely different in meaning. **Perquisite** means 'money or goods given as a right in addition to one's pay', as in 'various perquisites such as a company car'. It is frequently abbreviated to 'perks', as in 'The pay's not very much but the perks are good'. **Prerequisite** refers to 'something required as a condition for something to happen or exist', as in 'Passing the exam is a prerequisite for his getting the job' and 'A certain amount of studying is a prerequisite of passing the exam'.

prevaricate and **procrastinate** are liable to be confused although they have completely different meanings. **Prevaricate** means 'to try to avoid telling the truth by speaking in an evasive or misleading way', as in 'She prevaricated when the police asked her where she had been the previous evening'. **Procrastinate** means 'to delay or postpone action', as in 'The student has been procrastinating all term but now he has to get to grips with his essay'.

preventative and **preventive** both mean 'preventing or intended to prevent, precautionary', as in 'If you think the staff are stealing from the factory you should take preventative/preventive measures' and 'Preventative/preventive medicine seeks to prevent disease and disorders rather than cure them'. **Preventive** is the more frequently used of the two terms.

prima facie is a Latin phrase that has been adopted into English. It means 'at first sight, based on what seems to be so' and is mainly used in legal or very formal contexts, as in 'The police say they have prima facie evidence for arresting him but more investigation is required'. The phrase is pronounced *pri*-ma *fay*-shee.

prognosis *see* **diagnosis**.

programme and **program** are liable to cause confusion. In British English **programme** is the acceptable spelling in such senses as in 'a television programme', 'put on a varied programme of entertainment' 'buy a theatre programme' and 'launch an ambitious programme of expansion'. However, in the computing sense **program** is used. **Programme** can also be a verb meaning 'to plan, to schedule', as in 'programme the trip for tomorrow'; 'to cause something to conform to a particular set of instructions', as in 'programme the central heating system'; or 'to cause someone to behave in a particular way, especially to conform to particular instructions', as in 'Her parents have programmed her to obey them implicitly'. In the computing sense of 'to provide with a series of coded instructions', the verb is spelt **program** and the *m* is doubled to form the past participle, past tense and present participle, as **programmed** and **programming**. In American English **program** is the accepted spelling for all senses of both noun and verb.

protagonist was originally a term for 'the chief character in a drama', as in 'Hamlet is the protagonist in the play that bears his name'. It then came to mean also 'the leading person or paticipant in an event, dispute, etc', as in 'The protagonists on each side of the dispute had a meeting'. In modern usage it can now also mean 'a leading or notable supporter of a cause, movement, etc,' as in 'She was one of the protagonists of the feminist movement'.

provided and **providing** are used interchangeably, as in 'You may go, provided/providing that you have finished your work' and 'He can borrow the car provided/providing he pays for the petrol'. 'That' is optional. The phrases mean 'on the condition that'.

pudding *see* **dessert**.

pupil and **student** are not interchangeable. **Pupil** refers to 'a child or young person who is at school', as in 'primary school pupils and secondary school pupils'. **Student** refers to 'a person who is studying at a place of further education, at a university or college', as in 'students trying to find work during the vacations'. In modern usage senior **pupils** at secondary school are sometimes known as **students**. In American English student refers to people at school as well as to people in further education. **Pupil** can also refer to 'a person who is receiving instruction in something from an expert' as in 'The piano teacher has several adult pupils'. **Student** can also refer to 'a person who is studying a particular thing', as in 'In his leisure time he is a student of local history'.

quasi- is Latin in origin and means 'as if, as it were'. In English it is combined with adjectives in the sense of 'seemingly, apparently, but not really', as in 'He gave a quasi-scientific explanation of the occurrence which convinced many people but did not fool his colleagues', or 'partly, to a certain extent but not completely', as in 'It is a quasi-official body which does not have full powers'. **Quasi-** can also be combined with nouns to mean 'seeming, but not really', as in 'a quasi-socialist who is really a capitalist' and 'a quasi-Christian who will not give donations to charity'. **Quasi-** has several possible pronunciations. It can be pronounced *kway*-zi, *kway*-si or *kwah*-si.

queer in the sense of 'homosexual' was formerly used only in a slang and derogatory or offensive way. However, it is now used in a non-offensive way by homosexual people to describe themselves, as an alternative to 'gay'.

question *see* **beg the question**, **leading question**.

quick is an adjective meaning 'fast, rapid', as in 'a quick method', 'a quick route' and 'a quick walker'. It should not be used as an adverb, as in 'Come quick', in formal contexts since this is grammatically wrong.

quite has two possible meanings when used with adjectives. It can mean 'fairly, rather, somewhat', as in 'She's quite good at tennis but not good enough to play in the team' and 'The house is quite nice but it's not what we are looking for'. Where the indefinite article is used, **quite** precedes it, as in 'quite a good player' and 'quite a nice house'. **Quite** can also mean 'completely, totally' as in 'We were quite overwhelmed by their generosity' and 'It is quite impossible for him to attend the meeting'.

raison d'être is French in origin and is used in English to mean 'a reason, a justification for the existence of', as in 'Her children are her raison d'être' and 'His only raison d'être is his work'. The phrase is liable to be misspelt. Note the accent (^) on the first *e*. It is pronounced *ray*-zon detr.

rara avis is French in origin and means literally 'rare bird'. In English it is used to refer to 'a rare or unusual person or thing', as in 'a person with such dedication to a company is a rara avis'. It is pronounced *ray*-ra *ayv*-is or *ra*-ra *ay*-vis.

ravage and **ravish** are liable to be confused. They sound rather similar although they have different meanings. **Ravage** means 'to cause great damage to, to devastate', as in 'low-lying areas ravaged by floods' and 'a population ravaged by disease', or 'to plunder, to rob', as in 'neighbouring tribes ravaging their territory'. **Ravish** means either 'to delight greatly, to enchant', as in 'The audience were ravished by the singer's performance'. It also means 'to rape', as in 'The girl was ravished by her kidnappers', but this meaning is rather old-fashioned and is found only in formal or literary contexts.

re- is a common prefix, meaning 'again', in verbs. In most cases it is not followed by a hyphen, as in 'retrace one's footsteps', 'a retrial ordered by the judge' and 'reconsider his decision'. However, it should be followed by a hyphen if its absence is likely to lead to confusion with another word, as in 're-cover a chair'/'recover from an illness', 're-count the votes'/'recount a tale of woe', 'the re-creation of a 17th-century village for a film set'/'play tennis for recreation' and 're-form the group'/'reform the prison system'. In cases where the second element of a word begins with *e*, **re-** is traditionally followed by a hyphen, as in 're-educate', 're-entry' and 're-echo', but in modern usage the hyphen is frequently omitted.

re, meaning 'concerning, with reference to', as in 'Re your correspondence of 26 November', should be restricted to business or formal contexts.

readable *see* **legible**.

re-cover, recover *see* re-.

re-creation, recreation *see* re-.

referendum causes problems with regard to its plural form. It has two possible plural forms, **referendums** or **referenda**. In modern usage **referendums** is the more usual plural. **Referendum** means 'the referring of an issue of public importance to a general vote by all the people of a country', as in 'hold a referendum on whether to join the EC'.

re-form, reform *see* re-.

registry office and **register office** are interchangeable, although **registry office** is the more common term in general usage. The words refer to 'an office where civil marriage ceremonies are performed and where births, marriages and deaths are recorded', as in 'She wanted to be married in church but he preferred a registry office ceremony' and 'register the child's birth at the local registry office'.

rigour and **rigor** are liable to be confused. They look similar but they have completely different meanings. **Rigour** means 'severity, strictness', as in 'the rigour of the punishment', and 'harshness, unpleasantness', as in 'the rigour of the climate' (in this sense it is often in the plural, **rigours**), and 'strictness, detailedness', as in 'the rigour of the editing'. **Rigor** is a medical term meaning 'rigidity', as in 'muscles affected by rigor', or 'a feeling of chilliness often accompanied by feverishness', as in 'infectious diseases of which rigor is one of the symptoms'. **Rigor** is also short for **rigor mortis**, meaning 'the stiffening of the body that occurs after death'. The first syllable of **rigour** is pronounced to rhyme with 'big', but **rigor** can be pronounced either in this way or with the *i* pronounced as in 'ride'.

roof causes problems with regard to its plural form. The usual plural is **roofs**, which can be pronounced either as it is spelt, to rhyme with 'hoofs', or to rhyme with 'hooves'.

rout and **route** are liable to be confused. They look similar but are pronounced differently and have completely different meanings'. **Rout** as a noun means 'overwhelming defeat', as in 'the rout of the opposing army', and as a verb 'to defeat utterly', as in 'Their team routed ours last time'. **Route** refers to 'a way of getting somewhere', as in 'the quickest route' and 'the scenic route'. **Route** can also be a verb meaning 'to arrange a route for, to send by a certain route', as in 'route the visitors along the banks of the river'. **Rout** is pronounced to rhyme with 'shout'. **Route** is pronounced to rhyme with 'brute'.

scarfs and **scarves** are both acceptable spellings of the plural of 'scarf', meaning a piece of cloth worn around the neck or the head', as in 'a silk scarf at her neck' and 'wearing a head scarf'.

Scotch, Scots and **Scottish** are liable to be confused. **Scotch** is restricted to a few set phrases, such as 'Scotch whisky', 'Scotch broth' and 'Scotch mist'. As a noun **Scotch** refers to 'Scotch whisky', as in 'have a large Scotch with ice'. **Scots** as an adjective is used in such contexts as 'Scots accents', 'Scots people' and 'Scots attitudes'. As a noun **Scots** refers to the Scots language, as in 'He speaks standard English but he uses a few words of Scots.' The noun **Scot** is used to refer to 'a Scottish person', as in 'Scots living in London'. **Scottish** is found in such contexts as 'Scottish literature', 'Scottish history' and 'Scottish culture'.

sculpt and **sculpture** are interchangeable as verbs meaning 'to make sculptures, to practise sculpting', as in 'commissioned to sculpt/sculpture a bust of the chairman of the firm' and 'She both paints and sculpts/sculptures.

seize Note the *ei* combination, which is an exception to the '*i* before *e* except after *c*' rule.

sentiment and **sentimentality** are liable to be confused. They are related but have different shades of meaning. **Sentiment** means 'feeling, emotion', as in 'His actions were the result of sentiment not rationality'. It also means 'attitude, opinion', as in 'a speech full of anti-Christian sentiments'. **Sentimentality** is the noun from the adjective **sentimental** and means 'over-indulgence in tender feelings', as in 'dislike the sentimentality of the love songs' and 'She disliked her home town but now speaks about it with great sentimentality'.

sexism in language has been an issue for some time, and various attempts have been made to avoid it. For example, 'person' is often used where 'man' was traditionally used and 'he/she' substituted for 'he' in situations where the sex of the relevant person is unknown or unspecified.

ship *see* **boat**.

sine qua non is a Latin phrase that has been adopted into English and means 'essential condition, something that is absolutely necessary', as in 'It is a sine qua non of the agreement that the rent is paid on time'. It is used only in formal or legal contexts.

sitting room, living room, lounge and **drawing room** all refer to 'a room in a house used for relaxation and the receiving of guests'. Which word is used is largely a matter of choice. Some people object to the use of **lounge** as being pretentious but it is becoming increasingly common. **Drawing room** is a more formal word and applies to a room in rather a grand residence.

skilful, as in 'admire his skilful handling of the situation' is frequently misspelt. Note the single *l* before the *f*. In American English the word is spelt **skillful**.

slander *see* **libel**.

sometime and **some time** are liable to be confused. **Sometime** means 'at an unknown or unspecified time', as in 'We must get together sometime' and 'I saw her sometime last year'. There is a growing tendency in modern usage to spell this as **some time**. Originally **some time** was restricted to meaning 'a period of time', as in 'We need some time to think'.

spelled and **spelt** are both acceptable forms of the past tense and past participle of the verb 'to spell', as in 'They spelled/spelt the word wrongly' and 'He realized that he had spelled/spelt the word wrongly'.

stadium causes problems with regard to its plural form. **Stadiums** and **stadia** are both acceptable. **Stadium** is derived from Latin and the original plural form followed the Latin and was **stadia**. However, anglicized plural forms are becoming more and more common in foreign words adopted into English, and **stadiums** is now becoming the more usual form.

stanch and **staunch** are both acceptable spellings of the word meaning 'to stop the flow of', as in 'stanch/staunch the blood from the wound in his head' and 'try to stanch/staunch the tide of violence'. **Staunch** also means 'loyal, firm', as in 'the team's staunch supporters'.

start *see* **commence**.

stationary and **stationery** are liable to be confused. They sound alike but have completely different meanings. **Stationary** means 'not moving, standing still', as in 'stationary vehicles'. **Stationery** refers to 'writing materials', as in 'office stationery'. An easy way to differentiate between them is to remember that **stationery** is bought from a 'stationer', which, like 'baker' and 'butcher', ends in -*er*.

staunch *see* **stanch**.

stimulant and **stimulus** are liable to be confused. Formerly the distinction between them was quite clear but now the distinction is becoming blurred. Traditionally **stimulant** refers to 'a substance, such as a drug, that makes a person more alert or more active', as in 'Caffeine is a stimulant'. **Stimulus** traditionally refers to 'something that rouses or encourages a person to action or greater effort', as in 'The promise of more money acted as a stimulus to the work force and they finished the job in record time'. In modern usage the words are beginning to be used interchangeably. In particular, **stimulus** is used in the sense of **stimulant** as well as being used in its own original sense.

straight away and **straightaway** are both acceptable ways of spelling the expression for 'without delay, at once', as in 'attend to the matter straight away/straightaway'.

strata *see* **stratum**.

stratagem and **strategy** are liable to be confused. They look and sound similar but they have different meanings. **Stratagem** means 'a scheme or trick', as in 'think of a stratagem to mislead the enemy' and 'devise a stratagem to gain entry to the building'. **Strategy** refers to 'the art of planning a campaign', as in 'generals meeting to put together a battle strategy', and 'a plan or policy, particularly a clever one, designed for a particular purpose', as in 'admire the strategy which he used to win the game'.

stratum and **strata** are liable to be confused. **Stratum** is the singular form and **strata** is the plural form of a word meaning 'a layer or level', as in 'a stratum of rock' and 'different strata of society'. It is a common error to use **strata** as a singular noun.

student *see* **pupil**.

subconscious and **unconscious** are used in different contexts. **Subconscious** means 'concerning those areas or activities of the mind of which one is not fully aware', as in 'a subconscious hatred of her parents' and 'a subconscious desire to hurt her sister'. **Unconscious** means 'unaware', as in 'She was unconscious of his presence' and 'unconscious of the damage which he had caused', and 'unintentional', as in 'unconscious humour' and 'an unconscious slight'. **Unconscious** also means 'having lost consciousness, insensible', as in 'knocked unconscious by the blow to his head'.

subjective *see* **objective**.

such and **like** are liable to be confused. **Such** is used to introduce examples, as in 'herbs, such as chervil and parsley' and 'citrus fruits, such as oranges and lemons'. **Like** introduces comparisons. 'She hates horror films like *Silence of the Lambs*', and 'Very young children, like very old people, have to be kept warm.'

supper *see* **dinner**.

syndrome in its original meaning refers to 'a set of symptoms and signs that together indicate the presence of a physical or mental disorder', as in 'Down's syndrome'. In modern usage it is used loosely to indicate 'any set of events, actions, characteristics, attitudes that together make up, or are typical of, a situation', as in 'He suffers from the "I'm all right Jack" syndrome and doesn't care what happens to anyone else' and 'They seem to be caring people but they are opposing the building of an Aids hospice in their street—a definite case of "the not in my back yard" syndrome'.

tea *see* **dinner**.

teach *see* **learn**.

telephone *see* **phone**.

terminal and **terminus** in some contexts are interchangeable. They both refer to 'the end of a bus route, the last stop on a bus route, the building at the end of a bus route', as in 'The bus doesn't go any further—this is the terminus/terminal', but **terminus** is the more common term in this sense. They can also both mean 'the end of a railway line, the station at the end of a railway line', but **terminal** is the more common term in this sense. **Terminal** can refer to 'a building containing the arrival and departure areas for passengers at an airport' and 'a building in the centre of a town for the arrival and departure of air passengers'. **Terminal** also refers to 'a point of connection in an electric circuit', as in 'the positive and negative terminals', and 'apparatus, usually consisting of a keyboard and screen, for communicating with the central processor in a computing system', as in 'He has a dumb terminal so he can read information but not input it'. As an adjective **terminal** means 'of, or relating to, the last stage in a fatal illness', as in 'a terminal disease' and 'terminal patients'.

than is used to link two halves of comparisons or contrasts, as in 'Peter is considerably taller than John is', 'He is older than I am' and 'I am more informed about the situation than I was yesterday'. Problems arise when the relevant verb is omitted. In order to be grammatically correct, the word after 'than' should take the subject form if there is an implied verb, as in 'He is older than I (am)'. However this can sound stilted, as in 'She works harder than he (does)', and in informal contexts this usually becomes 'She works harder than him'. If there is no implied verb, the word after **than** is in the object form, as in 'rather you than me!'

the the definite article, which usually refers back to something already identified or to something specific, as in 'Where is the key?', 'What have you done with the book that I gave you?' and 'We have found the book that had we lost'. It is also used to denote someone or something as being the only one, as in 'the House of Lords', 'the King of Spain' and 'the President of Russia' and to indicate a class or group, as in 'the aristocracy', 'the cat family' and 'the teaching profession'. **The** is sometimes pronounced 'thee' when it is used to identify someone or something unique or important, as in 'Is that the John Frame over there?' and 'She is the fashion designer of the moment'.

their used in conjunction with 'anyone', everyone', 'no one' and 'someone', is becoming increasingly common, even in textbooks, although this use is ungrammatical. The reason for this is to avoid the sexism of using 'his' when the sex of the person being referred to is either unknown or unspecified, and to avoid the clumsiness of 'his/her' or 'his or her'. Examples of **their** being so used include 'Everyone must do their best' and 'No one is to take their work home'.

their and **there** are liable to be confused because they sound similar. **There** means 'in, to or at that place', as in 'place it there' and 'send it there'. **Their** is the possessive of 'they', meaning 'of them, belonging to them', as in 'their books' and 'their mistakes'.

their and **they're** are liable to be confused because they sound similar. **Their** is the possessive of 'they', meaning 'of them, belonging to them', as in 'their cars' and 'their attitudes'. **They're** is a shortened form of 'they are', as in 'They're not very happy' and 'They're bound to lose'.

this *see* **next.**

till and **until** are more or less interchangeable except that **until** is slightly more formal, as in 'They'll work till they drop' and 'Until we assess the damage we will not know how much the repairs will cost'.

toilet, **lavatory**, **loo** and **bathroom** all have the same meaning but the context in which they are used sometimes varies. **Toilet** is the most widely used of the words and is used on signs in public places. The informal **loo** is also very widely used. **Lavatory** is less common nowadays although it was formerly regarded by all but the working class and lower-middle class as the most acceptable term. **Bathroom** in British English usually refers to 'a room containing a bath', but in American English it is the usual word for **toilet**. **Ladies** and **gents** are terms for **toilet**, particularly in public places. **Powder room** also means this, as does the American English **rest room.**

town *see* **city.**

trade names should be written with a capital letter, as in 'Filofax' and 'Jacuzzi'. When trade names are used as verbs they are written with a lower case letter, as in 'hoover the carpet'.

try to and **try and** are interchangeable in modern usage. Formerly **try and** was considered suitable only in spoken and very informal contexts, but it is now considered acceptable in all but the most formal contexts, as in 'Try to/and do better' and 'They must try to/and put the past behind them'.

ultra is used as a prefix meaning 'going beyond', as in 'ultraviolet' and 'ultrasound', or 'extreme, very', as in 'ultra-sophisticated', 'ultra-modern', and 'ultra-conservative'. Compounds using it may be spelt with or without a hyphen. Words such as 'ultrasound' and 'ultraviolet' are usually spelt as one word, but words with the second sense of **ultra**, such as 'ultra-sophisticated', are often hyphenated.

unconscious *see* **subconscious.**

under way, meaning 'in progress', is traditionally spelt as two words, as in 'Preparations for the conference are under way'. In modern usage it is frequently spelt as one word, as in 'The expansion project is now underway'. It is a common error to write 'under weigh'.

underhand and **underhanded** are interchangeable in the sense of 'sly, deceitful', as in 'He used underhand/underhanded methods to get the job' and 'It was underhand/underhanded of him to not to tell her that he was leaving'. **Underhand** is the more common of the two terms.

uninterested *see* **disinterested.**

unique traditionally means 'being the only one of its kind', as in 'a unique work of art' and 'everyone's fingerprints are unique' and so cannot be modified by such words as 'very', 'rather', 'more', etc, although it can be modified by 'almost' and 'nearly'. In modern usage **unique** is often used to mean 'unrivalled, unparalleled, outstanding', as in 'a unique opportunity' and 'a unique performance'.

unreadable *see* **illegible.**

until *see* **till.**

up and **upon** mean the same and are virtually interchangeable, except that **upon** is slightly more formal. Examples include 'sitting on a bench', 'the carpet on the floor', 'the stamp on the letter', 'caught with the stolen goods on him' and 'something on his mind'; and 'She threw herself upon her dying mother's bed', 'a carpet of snow upon the ground' and 'Upon his arrival he went straight upstairs'.

upward and **upwards** are not interchangeable. **Upward** is used as an adjective, as in 'on an upward slope' and 'an upward trend in prices'. **Upwards** is an adverb, as in 'look upwards to see the plane'.

vacation, meaning 'holiday', in British English is mostly restricted to a university or college situation, as in 'students seeking paid employment during their vacation'. In American English it is the usual word for 'holiday'.

verbal and **oral** are liable to be confused. **Oral** means 'expressed in speech', as in 'an oral, rather than a written examination'. **Verbal** means 'expressed in words', as in

'He asked for an instruction diagram but he was given verbal instructions' and 'They were going to stage a protest match but they settled for a verbal protest'. It is also used to mean 'referring to the spoken word, expressed in speech', as in 'a verbal agreement'. Because of these two possible meanings, the use of **verbal** can lead to ambiguity. In order to clarify the situation, **oral** should be used when 'expressed in speech' is meant. **Verbal** can also mean referring to verbs, as in 'verbal endings'.

vice versa means 'the other way round, with the order reversed', as in 'He will do his friend's shift and vice versa' and 'Mary dislikes John and vice versa'. It is pronounced vis-e ver-sa, vi-si ver-sa or vis ver-sa and is derived from Latin.

vis-à-vis means 'in relation to', as in 'their performance vis-à-vis their ability' and 'the company's policy vis-à-vis early retirement'. It is pronounced vee-za-vee and is derived from French. Note the accent on the *a*.

-ways *see* **-wise**.

what ever and **whatever** are not interchangeable. **What ever** is used when 'ever' is used for emphasis, as in 'What ever does he think he's doing?' and 'What ever is she wearing'. **Whatever** means 'anything, regardless of what, no matter what', as in 'Help yourself to whatever you want' and 'Whatever he says I don't believe him'.

which and **what** can cause problems. In questions, **which** is used when a limited range of alternatives is suggested, as in 'Which book did you buy in the end?'. **What** is used in general situations, as in 'What book did you buy?'

whisky and **whiskey** both refer to a strong alcoholic drink distilled from grain. **Whisky** is made in Scotland and **whiskey** in Ireland and America. **Whisky** is the usual British English spelling.

who and **whom** cause problems. **Who** is the subject of a verb, as in 'Who told you?', 'It was you who told her' and 'the girls who took part in the play'. **Whom** is the object of a verb or preposition, as in 'Whom did he tell?', 'To whom did you speak?' and 'the people from whom he stole'. In modern usage **whom** is falling into disuse, especially in questions, except in formal contexts. **Who** is used instead even although it is ungrammatical, as in 'Who did you speak to?' **Whom** should be retained when it is a relative pronoun, as in 'the man whom you saw', 'the person to whom he spoke' and 'the girl to whom she gave the book'.

whose and **who's** are liable to be confused. They sound alike but have different meanings. **Whose** means 'of whom' or 'of which', as in 'the woman whose child won', 'the boy whose leg was broken', 'Whose bicycle is that?'

and 'the firm whose staff went on strike'. **Who's** is a shortened form of 'who is', as in 'Who's that?', 'Who's first in the queue?' and 'Who's coming to the cinema?'

-wise and **-ways** cause problems. Added to nouns, **-wise** can form adverbs of manner indicating either 'in such a position or direction', as in 'lengthwise' and 'clockwise', and 'in the manner of', as in 'crabwise'. In modern usage **-wise** is frequently used to mean 'with reference to', as in 'Weatherwise it was fine', 'Workwise all is well' and 'Moneywise they're not doing too well'. The suffix **-ways** has a more limited use. It means 'in such a way, direction or manner of', as in 'lengthways' and 'sideways'.

woman *see* **lady**.

Xmas is sometimes used as an alternative and shorter form of 'Christmas'. It is common only in a written informal context and is used mainly in commercial situations, as in 'Xmas cards on sale here' and 'Get your Xmas tree here'. When pronounced it is the same as 'Christmas'. The X derives from the Greek *chi*, the first letter of *Christos*, the Greek word for Christ.

X-ray is usually written with an initial capital letter when it is a noun meaning 'a photograph made by means of X-rays showing the bones or organs of the body', as in 'take an X-ray of the patient's chest'. Another term for the noun **X-ray** is 'radiograph'. As a verb it is also usually spelt with an initial capital, as in 'After the accident he had his leg X-rayed', but it is sometimes spelt with an initial lowercase letter, as in 'have his chest x-rayed'.

you is used in informal or less formal situations to indicate an indefinite person referred to as 'one' in formal situations. Examples include 'You learn a foreign language more quickly if you spend some time in the country where it is spoken', 'You would think that they would make sure that their staff are polite', 'You can get used to anything in time' and 'You have to experience the situation to believe it'. **You** in this sense must be distinguished from **you** meaning the second person singular', as in 'You have missed your bus', 'You must know where you left your bag' and 'You have to leave now'. *See* **one**.

your and **you're** are liable to be confused. **Your** is a possessive adjective meaning 'belonging to you, of you', as in 'That is your book and this is mine', 'Your attitude is surprising' and 'It is your own fault'. **You're** is a shortened form of 'you are', as in 'You're foolish to believe him', 'You're going to be sorry' and 'You're sure to do well'. Note the spelling of the pronoun **yours**, as in 'This book is yours' and 'Which car is yours?' It should not be spelt with an apostrophe as it is not a shortened form of anything.

Spelling

-able and -ible are both used to form adjectives. It is easy to confuse the spelling of words ending in these. *See* **Adjectives liable to be misspelt**.

accent refers to certain symbols used on some foreign words adopted into English. In modern usage, which has a tendency to punctuate less than was formerly the case, accents are frequently omitted. For example, an actor's part in a play is now usually spelt 'role' but originally it was spelt 'rôle', the accent on *o* being called a circumflex.

The accent is most likely to be retained if it affects the pronunciation. Thus 'cliché' and 'divorcé' usually retain the acute accent, as it is called, on the *e*. On the other hand, the accent known as the cedilla is frequently omitted from beneath the *c* in words such as 'façade/facade', although it is there to indicate that the *c* is soft, pronounced like an *s*, rather than a hard sound pronounced like a *k*.

apostrophe *see* **Punctuation** appendix.

book titles these can cause problems as to spelling and style. How they are treated in publications, business reports, etc, depends largely on the house style of the firm concerned. However, they are generally written in documents, letters, etc, as they appear on their title pages, that is with the first letter of the first word and of the following main words of the title in capital letters, and those of words of lesser importance, such as the articles, prepositions and coordinate conjunctions, in lowercase letters, as in The Guide to Yoga, Hope for the Best and In the Middle of Life.

Some people, and some house-style manuals, prefer to put the titles in italic, as in *A Room with a View* and *A Guide to Dental Health*. Others prefer to put book titles in quotation marks, as in 'Gardening for Beginners'. Such a convention can make use of either single or double quotation marks. Thus either 'Desserts for the Summer' or "Desserts for the Summer" is possible provided that the writer is consistent throughout any one piece of writing.

If the title of a book is mentioned in a piece of direct speech in quotation marks it goes within the opposite style of quotation marks from the piece in direct speech. Thus if the direct speech is within single quotation marks, the book title goes within double quotation marks, as in 'Have you read "Wuthering Heights" or are you not a Bronte fan?' If the direct speech is within double quotation marks, the book title goes between single quotation marks, as in "Would you say that 'Animal Farm' was your favourite Orwell novel?"

It is even quite common for book titles to appear in documents both in italic type and with quotation marks. To some extent the punctuation of book titles is a matter of choice as long as they are consistent, but there is a growing tendency to have as little punctuation as possible and to have as uncluttered a page as possible.

buildings can cause problems with regard to capital letters. The proper noun attached to the name of the building should have an initial capital letter, as should have the common noun that may be part of the name, as in The White House and The National Portrait Gallery.

businesses and **organizations** often cause problems with regard to their names or titles. In general the initial letters of the main words of the title should be in capital letters and the words of lesser importance, such as the articles, coordinating conjunctions and prepositions, should be in lower case, except when they are the first word of the title, as in 'The Indian Carpet Company', 'Kitchens for All' and 'Capital Industrial Cleaners'. Obviously, when the names of people are involved these should have initial capital letters, as in 'Jones and Brown'.

capital letters are used in a number of different situations.

The first word of a sentence or a direct quotation begins with a capital letter, as in 'They left early', 'Why have they gone?' and 'He said weakly, "I don't feel very well."'

The first letter of a name or proper noun is always a capital letter, as in 'Mary Brown', 'John Smith', 'South America', 'Rome', 'speak Italian', 'Buddhism', 'Marxism'.

Capital letters are also used in the titles of people, places or works of art, as in 'Uncle Fred', 'Professor Jones', 'Ely Cathedral', Edinburgh University', 'reading *Wuthering Heights*', 'watching *Guys and Dolls*', 'listen to Beethoven's Third Symphony' and 'a copy of *The Potato Eaters* by van Gogh'. They are also used in the titles of wars and historical, cultural and geological periods, as in 'the Wars of the Roses', 'the Renaissance', 'the Ice Age'.

Note that only the major words of titles, etc, are in capital letters, words, such as 'the', 'on', 'of', etc, being in lower-case letters.

A capital letter is used as the first letter of days of the week, months of the year, and religious festivals, as in 'Monday', 'October', 'Easter', 'Yom Kippur'. It is a matter of choice whether the seasons of the year are given capital letters or not, as in 'spring/Spring', 'autumn/Autumn'.

Apart from 'I', pronouns are lower-case except when they refer to God or Christ, when some people capitalize them, as in 'God asks us to trust in Him'.

Trade names should be spelt with an initial capital letter, as in 'Filofax', 'Jacuzzi', 'Xerox', 'Biro', 'Hoover'. When verbs are formed from these, they are spelt with an initial lower-case letter, as 'xerox the letter', 'hoover the carpet'.

doubling of consonants There are a few rules that can help you decide whether or not to double a consonant.

In words of one syllable ending in a single consonant

preceded by a single vowel, the consonant is doubled when an ending starting with a vowel is added, as in 'drop' and 'dropped', 'pat' and 'patting' and 'rub' and 'rubbing'.

In words of more than one syllable that end in a single consonant preceded by a single vowel, the consonant is doubled if the stress is on the last syllable, as in 'begin' and 'beginning', 'occur' and 'occurring', 'prefer' and 'preferred', 'refer' and 'referring' and 'commit' and 'committed'. In similar words where the stress is not on the last syllable, the consonant does not double, as in 'bigot' and 'bigoted' and 'develop' and 'developed'

Exceptions to this rule include words ending in 'l'. The 'l' doubles even in cases where the last syllable containing it is unstressed, as in 'travel' and 'travelled' and 'appal' and 'appalling'. 'Worship', in which the stress is on the first syllable, is also an exception, as in 'worshipped'.

geographical features these should be written with initial capital letters. They include the common nouns that are part of the name of the feature, as in Niagara Falls, Atlantic Ocean, River Thames, Mount Everest and Devil's Island.

hyphen *see* **Punctuation** appendix.

indefinite article a and an are the forms of the indefinite article.

The form a is used before words that begin with a consonant sound, as in *a* box, *a* garden, *a* road, *a* wall.

The form an is used before words that begin with a vowel sound, as in *an* apple, *an* easel, *an* ostrich, *an* uncle.

Note that it is the *sound* of the initial letter that matters and not the *spelling*. Thus a is used before words beginning with a *u* when they are pronounced with a *y* sound as though it were a consonant, as *a* unit, *a* usual occurrence. Similarly an is used, for example, before words beginning with the letter *h* where this is not pronounced, as in *an* heir, *an* hour, *an* honest man.

Formerly it was quite common to use an before words that begin with an *h* sound and also begin with an unstressed syllable, as *an* hotel, *an* historic occasion, but nowadays it is more usual to use *a* in such cases.

months of the year these are spelt with initial capital letters, as in January, February, March, April, May, June, July, August, September, October, November and December.

plural nouns singular nouns in English form plural forms in different ways. Most in add s to form the plural, as in 'cats', 'machines' and 'boots'.

Words ending in -s, -x, -z, -ch and -sh add es, as in 'buses', 'masses', 'foxes', 'fezzes or fezes', 'churches' and 'sashes'.

Nouns ending in a consonant followed by y have -ies in the plural, as 'fairies' and 'ladies', but note 'monkey', where the y is preceded by a vowel and becomes 'monkeys'. Proper nouns ending in y add s, as in 'the two Germanys'.

Some words ending in f have ves in the plural, as 'wives' and 'halves', but some simply add s to the singular form, as 'beliefs'. Some words ending in f can either add s or change to ves, as 'hoofs or hooves'.

Words ending in o cause problems as some end in *oes* in the plural, as 'potatoes' and 'tomatoes', and some end in s, as in 'pianos', while some can be spelt either way and have to be learned or looked up in a dictionary etc. Shortened forms, such as 'photo' and 'video', add simply s, as 'photos', 'videos'.

Some words have the same form in the plural as they do in the singular, such as 'sheep' and 'deer'. Some are plural in form already and so do not change. These include 'trousers' and 'scissors'.

Several words in English have irregular plural forms which just have to be learned or looked up in a dictionary, etc. These include 'men', 'mice' and 'feet'.

Some foreign words adopted into English used to retain the foreign plural form in English but this is becoming less common and, at the very least there is now often an English-formed alternative, as 'gateaux/gateaus', 'index/indices', 'formulae/formulas', 'appendixes/appendices'. However, several nouns of foreign extraction retain the foreign-style plural in English, such as 'criteria' and 'crises'.

Commonly misspelt words

All of us have problem words that cause spelling difficulties but there are some words that are generally misspelt. These include:

A

abbreviation	additional
abscess	address
absence	adequate
abysmal	adieu
accelerator	adjacent
accessible	admissible
accessories	admittance
accommodate	adolescence
accompaniment	adolescent
accumulate	advantageous
accurate	advertisement
accustomed	advice
achieve	advise
aching	aerate
acknowledge	aerial
acknowledgement/	aesthetic
acknowledgment	affect
acquaint	affiliation
acquaintance	afforestation
acquiesce	aggravate
acquiescence	aggravation
acquire	aggregate
acquit	aggression
acquittal	aggressive
acreage	aghast
across	agnosticism
actual	agoraphobia

agreeable
agreed
aisle
alcohol
alfresco
alibis
align
alignment
allege
allergic
alleys
alligator
allocate
allotment
allotted
almond
alms
alphabetically
already
although
aluminium
ambiguous
amethyst
ammunition
anachronism
anaesthetic
analyse
analysis
anarchist
ancestor
ancestry
anemone
angrily
anguish
annihilate
annihilation
anniversary
announcement
annulled
annulment
anonymous
anorak
answered
Antarctic
antibiotic
antithesis
anxiety
apartheid
apologize
appalling
apparently
appearance
appendicitis
appreciate
approval
aquarium
aquiline
arbiter

arbitrary
arbitration
archaeology
architectural
Arctic
arguably
arrangement
arrival
artichoke
ascend
ascent
asphalt
asphyxiate
asphyxiation
assassin
assassinate
assessment
assistance
associate
asthma
asthmatic
astrakhan
atheist
atrocious
attach
attendant
attitude
aubergine
auburn
auctioneer
audible
aural
automatic
autumn
awful
awkward

B

bachelor
bagatelle
baggage
bailiff
ballast
ballerina
banana
banister
bankruptcy
banquet
barbecue
barometer
barrister
basically
basis
bassoon
battalion
bazaar
beautiful
befriend
beguile

behaviour
beleaguer
belief
believe
belligerent
benefited
bequeath
berserk
besiege
bettered
bevelled
bewitch
bias
bicycle
biennial
bigamous
bigoted
bilingual
biscuit
bivouacked
blancmange
blasphemous
blasphemy
bleary
blitz
bodily
bonfire
bootee
borough
bouquet
bourgeois
boutique
bracketed
braille
brassiere
breadth
breathalyser
brief
broccoli
brochure
bronchitis
bruise
brusque
buccaneer
Buddhist
budding
budgerigar
budgeted
buffeted
bulletin
bumptious
bungalow
buoyancy
buoyant
bureau
bureaucracy
business
buttoned

C

cabbage
cafeteria
caffeine
camouflage
campaign
campaigned
cancelled
cancerous
candour
cannabis
cannibal
canvassing
capability
capillary
capitalist
caravan
carbohydrate
carburettor
career
caress
caries
carriage
cartoonist
cashier
cassette
castanets
casualty
catalogue
catarrh
catechism
catering
cauliflower
cautious
ceiling
cellophane
cemetery
centenary
centilitre
centimetre
certainty
champagne
championed
chancellor
changeable
channelled
characteristic
chasm
chauffeur
cheetah
cherish
chief
chilblain
chintz
chiropody
chisel
choreographer
choreography

chronically
chrysanthemum
cigarette
cinnamon
circuitous
cistern
civilian
claustrophobia
clientele
clique
coalesce
cocoa
coconut
coffee
cognac
coincidence
colander
collaborate
collapsible
colleague
colonel
colossal
comically
commandeer
commemorate
commentator
commercial
commiserate
commission
commissionaire
commitment
committal
committed
committee
communicate
commuter
companion
comparative
comparison
compatibility
compelled
competitive
computer
conceal
concealment
conceit
conceive
concession
concurrent
concussion
condemned
condescend
confectionery
conference
confetti
congeal
congratulations

conjunctivitis
conned
connoisseur
conscience
conscientious
conscious
consequently
consignment
consolation
conspicuous
constitute
consumer
contemptible
continent
continuous
contraception
contradictory
controlled
controller
controversial
convalesce
convenient
convertible
conveyed
convolvulus
coolly
cooperate
cooperative
coordinate
copying
coquette
corduroy
co-respondent
coronary
correspondence
correspondent
corridor
corroborate
corrugated
cosmopolitan
cosseted
councillor
counselling
counterfeit
courageous
courteous
crèche
credible
credited
crematorium
creosote
crescent
crisis
criterion
crocheted
crocodile
croupier

crucial
crucifixion
cruelly
cruise
cryptic
cubicle
cupful
curable
curiosity
curious
currency
curriculum vitae
customary
cynic
cynicism
cynosure
D
dachshund
daffodil
dahlia
dais
damage
dandruff
darkened
debatable
debauched
debility
deceased
deceit
deceive
deciduous
decipher
decoyed
decrease
decreed
defamatory
defeat
defendant
defied
definite
definitely
dehydrate
deign
deliberate
delicatessen
delicious
delinquent
delirious
demeanour
demonstrate
denouement
denunciation
dependence
depth
derailment
dermatitis
derogatory

descend
descendant
desiccate
desperate
detach
detachable
detergent
deterred
deterrent
deuce
develop
developed
development
diabetes
diagnosis
dialogue
diametrically
diaphragm
diarrhoea
difference
different
dilapidated
dilemma
dilettante
diminish
diminution
dinosaur
diphtheria
diphthong
disadvantageous
disagreeable
disagreed
disagreement
disappearance
disappeared
disappoint
disapproval
disastrous
disbelief
disbelieve
discipline
discotheque
discouraging
discourteous
discrepancy
discrimination
discussion
disease
disguise
dishevelled
dishonourable
disillusion
disinfectant
disinherited
dismissal
disobeyed
disparage

dispelled
disposal
dispossess
dissatisfaction
dissatisfy
dissect
disseminate
dissent
dissimilar
dissipated
dissipation
dissociate
dissolute
dissuade
distilled
distillery
distinguish
distraught
disuse
divisible
documentary
doggerel
domineering
donate
doubt
dragooned
drastically
draughty
drooled
drooped
drunkenness
dubious
dumbfounded
dungarees
duress
dutiful
dynamite
dysentery
dyspepsia

E

eccentric
ecclesiastic
ecologically
economically
ecstasy
eczema
effective
effervescence
efficacious
efficient
effrontery
eightieth
elaborate
electrician
elevenses
eligible
emancipate

embarrass
embarrassment
emergence
emergent
emolument
emotional
emphasize
employee
emptied
enable
encourage
encyclopedia
endeavour
endurance
energetically
enervate
engineer
enough
ensuing
entailed
enthusiasm
enumerate
epilepsy
equalize
equalled
equipped
erroneous
erudite
escalator
escapism
espionage
essence
essential
estranged
etiquette
euthanasia
eventually
evidently
exaggerate
exaggeration
exalt
exasperate
exceed
exceedingly
excellent
excessive
exchequer
excommunicate
exercise
exhaust
exhibit
exhilarate
exorcise
explanation
exquisite
extinguish
extraneous

extravagant

F

fabulous
facetious
faeces
Fahrenheit
fallacious
fanatic
farcical
fascinate
fatigue
fatuous
February
feeler
feign
ferocious
festooned
feud
feudal
fevered
fiasco
fibre
fictitious
fiend
fierce
fiery
filial
finesse
flabbergasted
flaccid
flammable
flannelette
fluent
fluoridate
fluoride
fluoridize
foliage
forcible
foreigner
forfeit
forthwith
fortieth
fortuitous
fortunately
frailty
frankincense
fraudulent
freedom
freight
frequency
friend
frolicked
fuchsia
fugitive
fulfil
fulfilled
fulfilment

fullness
fulsome
furious
furniture
furthered

G

gaiety
galloped
garrison
garrotted
gases
gateau
gauge
gazetteer
geisha
generator
genuine
gerbil
gesticulate
ghastly
ghetto
gigantic
gingham
giraffe
glamorous
glamour
glimpse
global
gluttonous
glycerine
gnarled
gnash
goitre
gossiped
government
graffiti
grammar
grandeur
gratefully
gratitude
gratuitous
greetings
gregarious
grief
grieve
grovelled
gruesome
guarantee
guarantor
guard
guardian
guest
guillotine
guinea
guise
guitar
gymkhana

gypsy/gipsy
H
haemoglobin
haemorrhage
halcyon
hallucination
hammered
handfuls
handicapped
handkerchief
happened
harangue
harass
harlequin
haughty
hazard
hearse
height
heightened
heinous
heir
herbaceous
hereditary
heroism
hesitate
hiccup, hiccough
hideous
hierarchy
hieroglyphics
hijack
hilarious
hindrance
hippopotamus
holiday
holocaust
homonym
honorary
honour
hooligan
horoscope
horrible
horticulture
hullabaloo
humorous
humour
hurricane
hurried
hygiene
hyphen
hypnosis
hypochondria
hypocrisy
hypotenuse
hypothesis
hypothetical
hysterical
I
icicle
ideological

idiosyncrasy
ignorance
illegible
illegitimate
illiberal
illiterate
imaginative
imitation
immaculate
immediate
immemorial
immoral
immovable
impasse
impeccable
imperative
imperceptible
imperious
impetuous
implacable
impresario
imprisoned
imprisonment
inaccessible
inadmissible
inappropriate
inaugural
incandescent
incessant
incipient
incognito
incommunicado
inconceivable
incongruous
incontrovertible
incorrigible
incredulous
incriminate
incubator
incurred
indefatigable
indefinable
indefinite
independence
independent
indescribable
indict
indictment
indigenous
indigestible
indomitable
indubitable
ineligible
inescapable
inexcusable
inexhaustible
infallible
infatuated
inferred

infinitive
inflamed
inflammable
inflationary
ingratiate
ingredient
inhabitant
inheritance
inhibition
iniquitous
initiate
initiative
innate
innocuous
innumerable
innumerate
inoculate
insecticide
inseparable
insincere
insistence
instalment
instantaneous
intercept
interference
interior
intermediate
intermittent
interpret
interpretation
interrogate
interrupt
interview
intrigue
intrinsically
intuition
intuitive
invariably
inveigle
inveterate
involuntary
involvement
irascible
irrelevant
irreparable
irreplaceable
irresistible
irresponsible
irrevocable
irritable
italicize
itinerant
itinerary
J
jackal
Jacuzzi
jeopardize
jettisoned
jewellery

jodhpurs
juggernaut
jugular
K
kaleidoscopic
karate
keenness
khaki
kidnapped
kilometre
kiosk
kitchenette
kleptomania
knick-knack
knowledgeable
kowtow
L
labelled
laboratory
labyrinth
lackadaisical
laddered
lager
language
languor
languorous
laryngitis
larynx
lassitude
latitude
laundered
launderette
layette
league
leanness
ledger
legendary
legible
legitimate
length
lengthened
leukaemia
levelled
liaise
liaison
lieu
lieutenant
lilac
limousine
lineage
linen
lingerie
linguist
liqueur
literature
litre
livelihood
loneliness
loosened

loquacious
lorgnette
lucrative
lucre
luggage
lugubrious
luminous
luscious
lustre
luxurious
lyric
M
macabre
maelstrom
magician
magnanimous
mahogany
maintenance
malaise
malaria
malignant
manageable
management
mannequin
manoeuvre
mantelpiece
manually
margarine
marijuana
marquee
martyr
marvellous
marzipan
masochist
massacre
matinee
mayonnaise
meagre
measurement
medallion
medieval
mediocre
melancholy
meningitis
meringue
messenger
meteorological
metropolitan
microphone
midday
migraine
mileage
milieu
millionaire
mimicked
mimicry
miniature
miraculous
mirrored

miscellaneous
mischief
mischievous
misogynist
misshapen
misspell
misspent
modelled
modelling
morgue
mortgage
mosquito
mountaineer
moustache
multitudinous
muscle
museum
mysterious
mythical
N
naive
narrative
naughty
nausea
nautical
necessary
necessity
negligence
negligible
negotiate
neighbourhood
neither
neurotic
neutral
niche
niece
ninetieth
ninth
nocturnal
nonentity
notably
noticeably
notoriety
nuance
numbered
numerate
numerous
nutrient
nutritious
O
obedient
obese
obituary
oblige
oblique
oblivious
obnoxious
obscene
obscenity

obsessive
obstetrician
occasion
occupancy
occupier
occupying
occurred
occurrence
octogenarian
odorous
odour
offence
offered
official
officious
ominous
omission
omitted
oneself
opaque
ophthalmic
opinion
opponent
opportunity
opposite
orchestra
ordinary
original
orthodox
orthopaedic
oscillate
ostracize
outlying
outrageous
overdraft
overrate
overreach
overwrought
oxygen
P
pacifist
pageant
pamphlet
panacea
panegyric
panicked
papered
parachute
paraffin
paragraph
paralyse
paralysis
paraphernalia
parcelled
parliament
paroxysm
parquet
partially
participant

particle
partner
passenger
passers-by
pastime
patterned
pavilion
peaceable
peculiar
pejorative
pencilled
penicillin
peppered
perceive
perennial
perilous
permissible
permitted
pernicious
perpetrate
persistence
personnel
persuasion
perusal
pessimism
pessimistically
pesticide
phantom
pharmacy
pharyngitis
pharynx
phenomenon
phial
phlegm
physician
physiotherapist
picketed
picnic
picnicked
picturesque
pioneered
pious
piteous
pitiful
plaintiff
plausible
pleurisy
pneumonia
poignant
politician
pollution
polythene
porridge
portrait
portray
positive
possession
possibility
posthumous

potatoes
precede
precedent
precinct
precipice
precocious
preference
preferred
prejudice
preliminary
prepossessing
prerequisite
prerogative
prescription
presence
preservative
prestige
prestigious
pretentious
prevalent
priest
primitive
procedure
proceed
procession
professional
profiteering
prohibit
promiscuous
pronunciation
propeller
proposal
proprietor
prosecute
protagonist
protein
provocation
prowess
psalm
psyche
psychiatric
psychic
publicly
pursuit
putative
pyjamas
Q
quarrelsome
questionnaire
queue
quintet
R
rabies
radioed
radios
railing
rancour
ransack

rapturous
reassurance
rebelled
rebellious
recalcitrant
receipt
receive
recommend
reconnaissance
reconnoitre
recruitment
recurrence
redundant
referee
reference
referred
regatta
regrettable
regretted
rehabilitation
reign
relevant
relief
relieve
reminisce
reminiscence
remuneration
rendezvous
repertoire
repetitive
reprieve
reprisal
requisite
rescind
resemblance
reservoir
resistance
resourceful
responsibility
restaurant
restaurateur
resurrection
resuscitate
retrieve
reunion
reveille
revelry
revenue
reversible
rhapsody
rheumatism
rhododendron
rhomboid
rhubarb
rhyme
rhythm
ricochet
righteous

rigorous
rigour
risotto
riveted
rogue
roughage
roulette
royalty
rucksack
ruinous
rummage
rumour
S
sabotage
sacrilege
saddened
salmon
salvage
sanctuary
sandwich
sanitary
sapphire
satellite
scaffolding
scandalous
scenic
sceptre
schedule
scheme
schizophrenic
schooner
sciatica
science
scissors
scruple
scrupulous
scurrilous
scythe
secretarial
secretary
sedative
sedentary
sensitive
separate
sergeant
serrated
serviceable
serviette
settee
shampooed
shattered
sheikh
sheriff
shield
shovelled
shuddered
siege
significant

silhouette
simply
simultaneous
sincerely
sixtieth
skeleton
skilful
slanderous
slaughter
sleigh
sleight of hand
sluice
smattering
smithereens
snivelled
soccer
solemn
solicitor
soliloquy
soloist
sombre
somersault
sophisticated
sovereign
spaghetti
spectre
spherical
sphinx
sponsor
spontaneity
spontaneous
squabble
squandered
squawk
staccato
staggered
stammered
statistics
statutory
stealth
stereophonic
stirrup
storage
strait-laced
straitjacket
strategic
strength
strenuous
stupor
suave
subpoena
subtle
succeed
successful
successor
succinct
succulent
succumb

suddenness
suede
sufficient
suffocate
suicide
sullenness
summoned
supercilious
superfluous
supersede
supervise
supervisor
supplementary
surgeon
surveillance
surveyor
susceptible
suspicious
sweetener
sycamore
symmetry
sympathize
symphony
synagogue
syndicate
synonym
syringe

T

tableau
taciturn
taffeta
tangerine
tangible
tattoo
technique
teenager
televise
temperature
tenuous
terrifically
terrifying
territory
terrorist
therapeutic
therefore
thief
thinness
thirtieth
thorough
thoroughfare
threshold
thrombosis
throughout
thwart
thyme
tightened
titivate
tobacconist

toboggan
toffee
tomatoes
tomorrow
tonsillitis
topsy turvy
tornadoes
torpedoes
torpor
tortoiseshell
tortuous
totalled
tourniquet
towelling
trafficked
tragedy
traitorous
tranquillity
tranquillizer
transcend
transferable
transferred
transparent
travelled
traveller
tremor
troublesome
trousseau
truism
trustee
tsetse
tuberculosis
tumour
tunnelled
tureen
turquoise
twelfth
typhoon
tyranny

U

unanimous
unconscious
undoubted
unduly
unequalled
unique
unnecessary
unremitting
unrequited
unrivalled
upheaval
uproarious

V

vaccinate
vacuum
vague
vanilla
variegate

vehement
vendetta
veneer
ventilator
verandah
vermilion
veterinary
vetoes
vice versa
vicissitude
vigorous
vigour
viscount
visibility
vivacious
vociferous
voluminous
volunteered
vulnerable

W

walkie-talkie
walloped
warrior
wastage
watered
weakened
wearisome
Wednesday

weight
weird
whereabouts
wherewithal
widened
width
wield
wintry
witticism
wizened
woebegone
wooden
woollen
worsened
worship
worshipped
wrapper
wrath
wreak
writhe

X

xylophone

Y

yield
yoghurt

Z

zealous
zigzagged

Adjectives liable to be misspelt

-able and -ible are both used to form adjectives. It is easy to confuse the spelling of words ending in these. The following adjectives are likely to be misspelt:

-able:
abominable
acceptable
adaptable
adorable
advisable
agreeable
amiable
approachable
available
bearable
beatable
believable
calculable
capable
changeable
comfortable
commendable
conceivable
definable
delectable
demonstrable
dependable
desirable

discreditable
disreputable
durable
enviable
excitable
excusable
expendable
foreseeable
forgettable
forgivable
healable
hearable
immovable
impassable
impeccable
implacable
impracticable
impressionable
indescribable
indispensable
inimitable
insufferable
lamentable
manageable

measurable
memorable
nameable
non-flammable
objectionable
operable
palpable
pleasurable
preferable
readable
recognizable
regrettable
renewable
reputable
sizeable
stoppable
tenable
tolerable

transferable
understandable
undoable
unmistakable
usable
variable
viable
washable
wearable
winnable
workable

ible:
accessible
admissible
audible
collapsible
combustible

compatible
comprehensible
contemptible
credible
defensible
destructible
digestible
discernible
divisible
edible
exhaustible
expressible
fallible
feasible
flexible
forcible
gullible

indelible
intelligible
irascible
negligible
perceptible
permissible
possible
repressible
reproducible
resistible
responsible
reversible
risible
sensible
susceptible
tangible
visible

Punctuation

Punctuation is the use of punctuation marks within a written text to enhance its meaning or fluency or to indicate aspects of pronunciation.

accent *see* **Spelling** appendix.

apostrophe a form of punctuation that is mainly used to indicate possession. Many spelling errors centre on the position of the apostrophe in relation to *s*.

Possessive nouns are usually formed by adding *'s* to the singular noun, as in 'the girl's mother', and 'Peter's car'; by adding an apostrophe to plural nouns that end in *s*, as in 'all the teachers' cars'; by adding *'s* to irregular plural nouns that do not end in *s*, as in 'women's shoes'.

In the possessive form of a name or singular noun that ends in *s*, *x* or *z*, the apostrophe may or may not be followed by *s*. In words of one syllable the final *s* is usually added, as in 'James's house', 'the fox's lair', 'Roz's dress'. The final *s* is most frequently omitted in names, particularly in names of three or more syllables, as in 'Euripides' plays'. In many cases the presence or absence of final *s* is a matter of convention.

The apostrophe is also used to indicate omitted letters in contracted forms of words, as in 'can't' and 'you've'. They are sometimes used to indicate missing century numbers in dates, as in 'the '60s and '70s', but are not used at the end of decades, etc, as in '1960s', not '1960's'.

Generally apostrophes are no longer used to indicate omitted letters in shortened forms that are in common use, as in 'phone' and 'flu'.

Apostrophes are often omitted wrongly in modern usage, particularly in the media and by advertisers, as in 'womens hairdressers', 'childrens helpings'. In addition, apostrophes are frequently added erroneously (as in 'potato's for sale' and 'Beware of the dog's'). This is partly because people are unsure about when and when not to use them and partly because of a modern tendency to punctuate as little as possible.

brackets are used to enclose information that is in some way additional to a main statement. The information so enclosed is called **parenthesis** and the pair of brackets enclosing it can be known as **parentheses**. The information that is enclosed in the brackets is purely supplementary or explanatory in nature and could be removed without changing the overall basic meaning or grammatical completeness of the statement. Brackets, like commas and dashes, interrupt the flow of the main statement but brackets indicate a more definite or clear-cut interruption. The fact that they are more visually obvious emphasizes this.

Material within brackets can be one word, as in 'In a local wine bar we had some delicious crepes (pancakes)' and 'They didn't have the chutzpah (nerve) to challenge her'. It can also take the form of dates, as in 'Robert Louis Stevenson (1850–94) wrote *Treasure Island*' and '*Animal Farm* was written by George Orwell (1903–50)'.

The material within brackets can also take the form of a phrase, as in 'They served lasagne (a kind of pasta) and some delicious veal' and 'They were drinking Calvados (a kind of brandy made from apples)' or in the form of a clause, as in 'We were to have supper (or so they called it) later in the evening' and 'They went for a walk round the loch (as a lake is called in Scotland) before taking their departure'.

It can also take the form of a complete sentence, as in 'He was determined (we don't know why) to tackle the problem alone' and 'She made it clear (nothing could be more clear) that she was not interested in the offer'. Sentences that appear in brackets in the middle of a sentence are not usually given an initial capital letter or a full stop, as in 'They very much desired (she had no idea why) to purchase her house'. If the material within brackets comes at the end of a sentence the full stop comes outside the second bracket, as in 'For some reason we agreed to visit her at home (we had no idea where she lived).'

If the material in the brackets is a sentence which comes between two other sentences it is treated like a normal sentence with an initial capital letter and a closing full stop, as in 'He never seems to do any studying. (He is always either asleep or watching television.) Yet he does brilliantly in his exams.' Punctuation of the main statement is unaffected by the presence of the brackets and their enclosed material except that any punctuation that would have followed the word before the first bracket follows the second bracket, as in 'He lives in a place (I am not sure exactly where), that is miles from anywhere.'

There are various shapes of brackets. Round brackets are the most common type. Square brackets are sometimes used to enclose information that is contained inside other information already in brackets, as in '(Christopher Marlowe [1564–93] was a contemporary of Shakespeare)' or in a piece of writing where round brackets have already been used for some other purpose. Thus in a dictionary if round brackets are used to separate off the pronunciation, square brackets are sometimes used to separate off the etymologies.

Square brackets are also used for editorial comments in a scholarly work where the material within brackets is more of an intrusion to the flow of the main statement than is normally the case with bracketed material. Angle brackets and brace brackets tend to be used in more scholarly or technical contexts.

capital letters *see* **Spelling** appendix.

colon a punctuation mark (**:**) that is used within a sentence to explain, interpret, clarify or amplify what has gone before it. 'The standard of school work here is extremely high: it is almost university standard', 'The fuel bills are giving cause for concern: they are almost double last year's'. 'We have some new information: the allies have landed'. A capital letter is not usually used after the colon in this context.

The colon is also used to introduce lists or long quotations, as in 'The recipe says we need: tomatoes, peppers, courgettes, garlic, oregano and basil', 'The boy has a huge list of things he needs for school: blazer, trousers, shirts, sweater, ties, shoes, tennis shoes, rugby boots, sports clothes and leisure wear' and 'One of his favourite quotations was: "If music be the food of love play on".

The colon is sometimes used in numerals, as in '7:30 a.m.', '22:11:72' and 'a ratio of 7:3'. It is used in the titles of some books, for example where there is a subtitle or explanatory title, as in 'The Dark Years: the Economy in the 1930s'. In informal writing, the dash is sometimes used instead of the colon, indeed the dash tends to be overused for this purpose.

comma a very common punctuation mark (**,**). In modern usage there is a tendency to adopt a system of minimal punctuation and the comma is one of the casualties of this new attitude. Most people use the comma considerably less frequently than was formerly the case.

However there are certain situations in which the comma is still commonly used. One of these concerns lists. The individual items in a series of three or more items are separated by commas. Whether a comma is put before the 'and' which follows the second-last item is now a matter of choice. Some people dislike the use of a comma before 'and' in this situation, and it was formerly considered wrong. Examples of lists include—'at the sports club we can play tennis, squash, badminton and table tennis', 'We need to buy bread, milk, fruit and sugar', and 'They are studying French, German, Spanish and Russian'. The individual items in a list can be quite long, as in 'We opened the door, let ourselves in, fed the cat and started to cook a meal' and 'They consulted the map, planned the trip, got some foreign currency and were gone before we realized it'. Confusion may arise if the last item in the list contains 'and' in its own right, as in 'In the pub they served ham salad, shepherd's pie, pie and chips and omelette'. In such cases it as well to put a comma before the final 'and'.

In cases where there is a list of adjectives before a noun, the use of commas is now optional although it was formerly standard practice. Thus both 'She wore a long, red, sequinned dress' and 'She wore a long red sequinned dress' are used. When the adjective immediately before the noun has a closer relationship with it than the other adjectives no comma should be used, as in 'a beautiful old Spanish village'.

The comma is used to separate clauses or phrases that are parenthetical or naturally cut off from the rest of a sentence, as in 'My mother, who was of Irish extraction, was very superstitious'. In such a sentence the clause within the commas can be removed without altering the basic meaning. Care should be taken to include both commas. Commas are not normally used to separate main clauses and relative clauses, as in 'The woman whom I met was my friend's sister'. Nor are they usually used to separate main clauses and subordinate clauses, as in 'He left when we arrived' and 'They came to the party although we didn't expect them to'. If the subordinate clause precedes the main clause, it is sometimes followed by a comma, especially if it is a reasonably long clause, as in 'Although we stopped and thought about it, we still made the wrong decision'. If the clause is quite short, or if it is a short phrase, a comma is not usually inserted, as in 'Although it rained we had a good holiday' and 'Although poor they were happy'. The use of commas to separate such words and expression from the rest of the sentence to which they are related is optional. Thus one can write 'However, he could be right' or 'However he could be right'. The longer the expression is, the more likely it is to have a comma after it, as in 'On the other hand, we may decide not to go'.

Commas are always used to separate terms of address, interjections or question tags from the rest of the sentence, as in 'Please come this way, Ms Brown, and make yourself at home', 'Now, ladies, what can I get you?' and 'It's cold today, isn't it?'

Commas may be used to separate main clauses joined by a coordinating conjunction, but this is not usual if the clauses have the same subject or object, as in 'She swept the floor and dusted the table'. In cases where the subjects are different and the clauses are fairly long, it is best to insert a comma, as in 'They took all the furniture with them, and she was left with nothing'.

A comma can be inserted to avoid repeating a verb in the second of two clause, as in 'he plays golf and tennis, his brother rugby'.

dash a punctuation mark in the form of a short line (**—**) that indicates a short break in the continuity of a sentence, as in 'He has never been any trouble at school—quite the reverse', 'I was amazed when he turned up—I thought he was still abroad'. In such situations it serves the same purpose as brackets, except that it is frequently considered more informal. The dash should be used sparingly. Depending on it too much can lead to careless writing with ideas set down at random rather than turned into a piece of coherent prose. The dash can be used to emphasize a word or phrase, as in 'They said goodbye then—forever'. It can also be used to add a remark to the end of a sentence, as in 'They had absolutely no money— a regular state of affairs towards the end of the month.'

The dash can also be used to introduce a statement that amplifies or explains what has been said, as in 'The burglars took everything of value—her jewellery, the silver, the TV set, her hi-fi and several hundred pounds.' It can be used to summarize what has gone before, as in 'Disease, poverty, ignorance—these are the problems facing us.

The dash is also used to introduce an afterthought, as in 'You can come with me—but you might not want to'. It can also introduce a sharp change of subject, as in 'I'm just making tea—what was that noise?' It can also be used to introduce some kind of balance in a sentence, as in 'It's going to take two of us to get this table out of here—one to move it and one to hold the door open.'

The dash is sometimes found in pairs. A pair of dashes acts in much the same way as a set of round brackets. A pair of dashes can be used to indicate a break in a sentence, as in 'We prayed—prayed as we had never prayed before—that the children would be safe', 'It was—on reflection—his best performance yet', and 'He introduced me to his wife—an attractive pleasant woman—before he left'.

Dashes are used to indicate hesitant speech, as in 'I don't—well—maybe—you could be right'. They can be used to indicate the omission of part of a word or name, as in 'It's none of your b— business', or 'He's having an affair with Mrs D—'.

They can also be used between points in time or space, as in 'Edinburgh–London' and '1750–1790.'

direct speech *see* **quotation marks**.

exclamation mark a punctuation mark (**!**) which occurs at the end of an exclamation, which is a word, phrase or sentence called out with strong feeling of some kind as in 'Get lost!', 'What a nerve!', 'Help!', 'Ouch!', 'Well I never!', 'What a disaster!', 'I'm tired of all this!' and 'Let me out of here!'

full stop a punctuation mark consisting of a small dot (**.**). Its principal use is to end a sentence that is not a question or an exclamation, as in 'They spent the money.', 'She is studying hard.', 'He has been declared redundant and is very upset.' and 'Because she is shy, she rarely goes to parties.'

The full stop is also used in decimal fractions, as in '4.5 metres', '6.3 miles' and '12.2 litres'. It can also be used in dates, as in '22.2.94', and in times, as in '3.15 tomorrow afternoon'.

In modern usage the tendency is to omit full stops from abbreviations. This is most true of abbreviations involving initial capital letters as in TUC, BBC, EEC and USA. In such cases full stops should definitely not be used if one or some of the initial letters do not belong to a full word. Thus, television is abbreviated to TV and educationally subnormal to ESN.

There are usually no full stops in abbreviations involving the first and last letters of a word (contractions) Dr, Mr, Rd, St, but this is a matter of taste.

Abbreviations involving the first few letters of a word, as in 'Prof' (Professor) are the most likely to have full stops, as in 'Feb.' (February), but again this is now a matter of taste.

For the use of the full stop in direct speech *see* **quotation marks**. The full stop can also be called **point** or **period**.

hyphen a small stroke (**-**) that is used to join two words together or to indicate that a word has been broken at the end of a line because of lack of space. It is used in a variety of situations.

The hyphen is used as the prefixed element in a proper noun, as in 'pre-Christian', 'post-Renaissance', 'anti-British', 'anti-Semitic', 'pro-French' and 'pro-Marxism'. It is also used before dates or numbers, as in 'pre-1914', 'pre-1066', 'post-1920', 'post-1745'. It is also used before abbreviations, as in 'pro-BBC', 'anti-EEC' and 'anti-TUC'.

The hyphen is used for clarification. Some words are ambiguous without the presence of a hyphen. For example, 're-cover', as in 're-cover a chair', is spelt with a hyphen to differentiate it from 'recover', as in 'The accident victim is likely to recover'. Similarly, it is used in 're-form', meaning 'to form again', as in 'They have decided to re-form the society which closed last year', to differentiate the word from 'reform', meaning 'to improve, to become better behaved', as in 'He was wild as a young man but he has reformed now'. Similarly 're-count' in the sense of 'count again', as in 're-count the number of votes cast', is spelt with a hyphen to differentiate it from 'recount' in the sense of 'tell', as in 'recount what happened on the night of the accident'.

The hyphen was formerly used to separate a prefix from the main element of a word if the main element begins with a vowel, as in 'pre-eminent', but there is a growing tendency in modern usage to omit the hyphen in such cases. At the moment both 'pre-eminent' and 'preeminent' are found. However, if the omission of the hyphen results in double *i*, the hyphen is usually retained, as in 'anti-inflationary' and 'semi-insulated'.

The hyphen was formerly used in words formed with the prefix *non-*, as in 'non-functional', 'non-political', 'non-flammable' and 'non-pollutant'. However there is a growing tendency to omit the hyphen in such cases, as in 'nonfunctional' and 'nonpollutant'. At the moment both forms of such words are common.

The hyphen is usually used with 'ex-' in the sense of 'former', as in 'ex-wife' and 'ex-president'.

The hyphen is usually used when 'self-' is prefixed to other words, as in 'self-styled', 'a self-starter', and 'self-evident'.

Use or non-use of the hyphen is often a matter of choice, house style or frequency of usage, as in 'drawing-room' or 'drawing room', and 'dining-room' or 'dining room'. There is a modern tendency to punctuate less frequently than was formerly the case and so in modern usage use of the hyphen in such expressions is less frequent. The length of compounds often affects the inclusion or omission of the hyphen. Compounds of two short elements that are well-established words tend not to be hyphenated, as in 'bedroom' and 'toothbrush'. Compound words with longer elements are more likely to be hyphenated, as in 'engine-driver' and 'carpet-layer'.

Some fixed compounds of two or three or more words are always hyphenated, as in 'son-in-law', 'good-for-nothing' and 'devil-may-care'.

Some compounds formed from phrasal verbs are

sometimes hyphenated and sometimes not. Thus both 'take-over' and 'takeover' are common, and 'run-down' and 'rundown' are both common. Again the use of the hyphen is a matter of choice. However some words formed from phrasal verbs are usually spelt without a hyphen, as in 'breakthrough'.

Compound adjectives consisting of two elements, the second of which ends in *-ed*, are usually hyphenated, as in 'heavy-hearted', 'fair-haired', 'fair-minded' and 'long-legged'.

Compound adjectives when they are used before nouns are usually hyphenated, as in 'gas-fired central heating', 'oil-based paints', 'solar-heated buildings' and 'chocolate-coated biscuits'.

Compounds containing some adverbs are usually hyphenated, sometimes to avoid ambiguity, as in 'his best-known opera', a 'well-known singer', 'an ill-considered venture' and 'a half-planned scheme'.

Generally adjectives and participles preceded by an adverb are not hyphenated if the adverb ends in *-ly*, as in 'a highly talented singer', 'neatly pressed clothes' and 'beautifully dressed young women'.

In the case of two or more compound hyphenated adjectives with the same second element qualifying the same noun, the common element need not be repeated but the hyphen should be, as in 'two- and three-bedroom houses' and 'long- and short-haired dogs'.

The hyphen is used in compound numerals from 21 to 99 when they are written in full, as in 'thirty-five gallons', 'forty-four years', 'sixty-seven miles' and 'two hundred and forty-five miles'. Compound numbers such as 'three hundred' and 'two thousand' are not hyphenated.

Hyphens are used in fractions, as in 'three-quarters', 'two-thirds', and 'seven-eighths'.

Hyphens are also used in such number phrases as 'a seventeenth-century play', 'a sixteenth-century church', 'a five-gallon pail', 'a five-year contract' and a 'third-year student'.

The other use of hyphens is to break words at the ends of lines. Formerly people were more careful about where they broke words. Previously, words were broken up according to etymological principles, but there is a growing tendency to break words according to how they are pronounced. Some dictionaries or spelling dictionaries give help with the division and hyphenation of individual words. General points are that one-syllable words should not be divided and words should not be broken after the first letter of a word or before the last letter. Care should be taken not to break up words, for example by forming elements that are words in their own right, in such a way as to mislead the reader. Thus divisions such as 'therapist' and 'mans-laughter' should be avoided.

inverted comma *see* **quotation marks.**

italic type a *sloping typeface* that is used for a variety of purposes. It is used to differentiate a piece of text from the main text, which is usually in Roman type. For example, it is used sometimes for the titles of books, newspapers, magazines, plays, films, musical works and works of art, as in 'he is a regular reader of *The Times*', 'She reads *Private Eye*', 'Have you read *Animal Farm* by George Orwell', 'He has never seen a production of Shakespeare's *Othello*', 'We went to hear Handel's *Messiah*', '*Mona Lisa* is a famous painting'. Sometimes such titles are put in quotation marks rather than in italics.

Italic type is also sometimes used for the names of ships, trains, etc, as in 'the launch of *The Queen Elizabeth II*', 'She once sailed in *The Queen Mary*' and 'Their train was called *The Flying Scotsman*'.

Italic type is also used for the Latin names of plants and animals, as in 'of the genus *Lilium*', 'trees of the genus *Pyrus*', '*Panthera pardus*' and '*Canis lupus*'.

Italic type is sometimes used for foreign words that have been adopted into the English language but have never been fully integrated. Examples include *bête noire*, *raison d'être*, *inter alia* and *Weltschmerz*.

Italic type can also sometimes be used to draw attention to a particular word, phrase or passage, as in 'How do you pronounce *formidable*?', or to emphasize a word or phrase, as in 'Is he *still* in the same job?'

ligature a printed character combining two letters in one, as in æ and œ. It is sometimes called a digraph.

line-break the division of a word at the end of a line for space purposes. This is marked by a hyphen.

lower-case letter the opposite of capital letter. It is also known informally as 'small letter'. Lower-case letters are used for most words in the language. It is capital letters that are exceptional in their use.

oblique a diagonal mark (**/**) that has various uses. Its principal use is to show alternatives, as in 'he/she', 'Dear Sir/Madam', 'two/three-room flat' and 'the budget for 1993/4'. The oblique is used in some abbreviations, as in 'c/o Smith' (meaning 'care of Smith'). The word 'per' is usually shown by means of an oblique, as in 60km/h (60 kilometres per hour).

paragraph a subdivision of a piece of prose. Many people find it difficult to divide their work into paragraphs. Learning to do so can be difficult but it is an area of style that improves with practice.

A paragraph should deal with one particular theme or point of the writer's writing or argument. When that has been dealt with, a new paragraph should be started.

However, there are other considerations to be taken into account. If the paragraph is very long it can appear offputting visually to the would-be reader and can be difficult to make one's way through. In such cases it is best to subdivide themes and shorten paragraphs. On the other hand, it is best not to make all one's paragraphs too short as this can create a disjointed effect. It is best to try to aim for a mixture of lengths to create some variety.

Traditionally it was frowned upon to have a one-sentence paragraph but there are no hard and fast rules about this. Usually it takes more than one sentence to develop the theme of the paragraph, unless one is a tabloid journalist or copywriter for an advertising firm, and it is best to avoid long, complex sentences.

The opening paragraph of a piece of writing should

introduce the topic about which one is writing. The closing paragraph should sum up what one has been writing about. New paragraphs begin on new lines and they are usually indented from the margin. In the case of dialogue in a work of fiction, each speaker's utterance usually begins on a new line for the clarification of the reader.

parentheses *see* **brackets**.

period *see* **full stop**.

point *see* **full stop**.

punctuation mark one of the standardized symbols used in punctuation, as the **full stop**, **comma**, **question mark**, etc.

question mark the punctuation mark (**?**) that is placed at the end of a question or interrogative sentence, as in 'Who is he?', 'Where are they?', 'Why have they gone?', 'Whereabouts are they?', 'When are you going?' and 'What did he say?'. The question mark is sometimes known as the **query**.

quotation marks *or* **inverted commas** are used to enclose material that is part of **direct speech**, which is the reporting of speech by repeating exactly the actual words used by the speaker. In the sentence:

Peter said, 'I am tired of this.'

'I am tired of this' is a piece of direct speech because it represents exactly what Peter said. Similarly, in the sentence:

Jane asked, 'Where are you going?'

'Where are you going' is a piece of direct speech since it represents what Jane said.

Quotation marks are used at the beginning and end of pieces of direct speech. Only the words actually spoken are placed within the quotation marks, as in:

'If I were you,' he said, 'I would refuse to go.'

The quotation marks involved can be either single or double, according to preference or house style.

If there is a statement such as 'he said' following the piece of direct speech, a comma is placed before the second inverted comma, as in:

'Come along,' he said.

If the piece of direct speech is a question or exclamation, a question mark or exclamation mark is put instead of the comma, as in:

'What are you doing?' asked John.
'Get away from me!' she screamed.

If a statement such as 'he said' is placed within a sentence in direct speech, a comma is placed after 'he said' and the second part of the piece of direct speech does not begin with a capital letter, as in:

'I know very well,' he said, 'that you do not like me.'

If the piece of direct speech includes a complete sentence, the sentence begins with a capital letter, as in:

'I am going away,' she said, 'and I am not coming back. I don't feel that I belong here anymore.'

Note that the full stop at the end of a piece of direct speech that is a sentence should go before the closing inverted comma.

If the piece of direct speech quoted takes up more than one paragraph, quotation marks are placed at the beginning of each new paragraph. However, quotation marks are not placed at the end of each paragraph, just at the end of the final one.

When writing a story, etc, that includes dialogue or conversation, each new piece of direct speech should begin on a new line or sometimes in a new paragraph.

Quotation marks are not used only to indicate direct speech. For example, they are sometimes used to indicate the title of a book or newspaper.

The quotation marks used in this way can be either single or double, according to preference or house style. If a piece of direct speech contains the title of a poem, song, etc, it should be put in the opposite type of quotation marks to those used to enclose the piece of direct speech. Thus, if single quotation marks have been used in the direct speech, then double quotation marks should be used for the title within the direct speech, as in:

'Have you read "Ode to a Nightingale" by Keats?' the teacher asked.

If double quotation marks have been used for the direct speech, single quotation marks should be used for the title, as in:

"Have you read 'Ode to a Nightingale' by Keats?" the teacher asked.

Roman type the normal upright type used in printing, not bold or italic type.

semicolon (;) a rather formal form of punctuation. It is mainly used between clauses that are not joined by any form of conjunction, as in 'We had a wonderful holiday; sadly they did not', 'She was my sister; she was also my best friend' and 'He was a marvellous friend; he is much missed'. A dash is sometimes used instead of a semicolon but this more informal.

The semicolon is also used to form subsets in a long list or series of names so that the said list seems less complex, as in 'The young man who wants to be a journalist has applied everywhere. He has applied to *The Times* in London; *The Globe and Mail* in Toronto; *The Age* in Melbourne; *The Tribune* in Chicago'.

The semicolon is also sometimes used before 'however', 'nevertheless' 'hence', etc, as in 'We have extra seats for the concert; however you must not feel obliged to come'.

Style

abbreviation a shortened form of words, usually used as a space-saving technique and becoming increasingly common in modern usage. Abbreviations cause problems with regard to punctuation. The common question asked is whether the letters of an abbreviation should be separated by full stops. In modern usage the tendency is to omit full stops from abbreviations. This is most true of abbreviations involving initial capital letters, as in TUC, BBC, EC and USA. In such cases full stops should definitely not be used if one or some of the initial letters do not belong to a full word. Thus 'television' is abbreviated to TV and 'educationally subnormal' to ESN.

There are usually no full stops in abbreviations involving the first and last letters of a word (contractions)—Dr, Mr, Rd, St—but this is a matter of taste.

An abbreviation involving the first few letters of a word, as in 'Prof' (Professor), is the most likely to a have full stop, as in 'Feb.' (February), but again this is now a matter of taste.

Plurals of abbreviations are mostly formed by adding lower-case *s*, as in Drs, JPs, TVs. Note the absence of apostrophes. *See also* **acronym**.

acronym a word that, like some abbreviations, is formed from the initial letters of several words. Unlike abbreviations, however, acronyms are pronounced as words rather than as just a series of letters. For example, OPEC (Organization of Petroleum Producing Countries) is pronounced *o-pek* and is thus an acronym, unlike USA (United States of America) which is pronounced as a series of letters and not as a word (*yoo-ess-ay,* not *yoo-say* or *oo-sa*) and is thus an abbreviation.

Acronyms are written without full stops, as in UNESCO (United Nations Educational, Scientific and Cultural Organization). Mostly acronyms are written in capital letters, as in NASA (National Aeronautics and Space Administration). However, very common acronyms, such as Aids (Acquired Immune Deficiency Syndrome), can be written with just an initial capital, the rest of the letters being lower case.

Acronyms that refer to a piece of scientific or technical equipment are written like ordinary words in lower-case letters, as laser (light amplification by simulated emission of radiation).

affix refers to an element that is added to the root or stem of a word to form another word. Affixes can be in the form of **prefixes** or **suffixes**. A prefix is added to the beginning of a word, as audio in audiovisual, an affix to the end, as -aholic in workaholic.

back formation the process of forming a new word by removing an element from an existing word. This is the reversal of the usual process since many words are formed by adding an element to a base or root word. Examples of

back formation include 'burgle' from 'burglary'; 'caretake' from 'caretaker'; 'donate' from 'donation; 'eavesdrop' from 'eavesdropper'; 'enthuse' from 'enthusiasm'; 'intuit' from 'intuition'; 'liaise' from 'liaison'; 'reminisce' from 'reminiscence'; 'televise' from 'television'.

base the basic element in word formation, also known as **root** or **stem**, e.g. in the word 'infectious' 'infect' is the base.

blend a word that is formed by the merging of two other words or elements, as in 'brunch' from 'breakfast' and 'lunch'; 'camcorder' from 'camera' and 'recorder'; 'chocoholic' from 'chocolate' and 'alcoholic'; 'motel' from 'motor' and 'hotel'; 'smog' from 'smoke' and 'fog'; 'televangelist' from 'television' and 'evangelist'.

book titles *see* **Spelling** appendix and **italic type** in **Punctuation** appendix.

borrowing the taking over into English of a word from a foreign language and also to the word so borrowed. Many words borrowed into English are totally assimilated as to spelling and pronunciation. Others remain obviously different and retain their own identity as to spelling or pronunciation, as *raison d'être,* borrowed from French. Many of them have been so long part of the English language, such as since the Norman Conquest, that they are no longer thought of as being foreign words. However the process goes on, and recent borrowings include *glasnost* and *perestroika* from Russian.

French, Latin and Greek have been the main sources of our borrowings over the centuries. However, we have borrowed extensively from other languages as well. These include Italian, from which we have borrowed many terms relating to music, art and architecture. These include *piano, libretto, opera, soprano, tempo, corridor, fresco, niche, parapet* and *grotto,* as well as many food terms, such as *macaroni, pasta, semolina* and *spaghetti.*

From the Dutch we have acquired many words relating to the sea and ships since they were a great sea-faring nation. These include *cruise, deck, skipper* and *yacht.* Through the Dutch/Afrikaans connection we have borrowed *apartheid, boss* and *trek.*

From German we have borrowed *dachshund, hamster, frankfurter, kindergarten* and *waltz,* as well as some words relating to World War II, for example, *blitz, flak* and *strafe.*

From Norse and the Scandinavian languages have come a wide variety of common words, such as *egg, dirt, glitter, kick, law, odd, skill, take, they, though,* as well as some more modern sporting terms such as *ski* and *slalom.*

From the Celtic languages have come *bannock, bog, brogue, cairn, clan, crag, slogan* and *whisky,* and from

Arabic have come *algebra, alkali, almanac, apricot, assassin, cypher, ghoul, hazard, mohair, safari, scarlet* and *talisman*.

The Indian languages have provided us with many words, originally from the significant British presence there in the days of the British Empire. They include *bungalow, chutney, dinghy, dungarees, gymkhana, jungle, pundit* and *shampoo*. In modern times there has been an increasing interest in Indian food and cookery, and words such as *pakora, poppadom, samosa,* etc, have come into the language.

From the South American languages have come *avocado, chocolate, chilli, potato, tobacco* and *tomato*. From Hebrew have come *alphabet, camel, cinnamon* and *maudlin*, as well as more modern borrowings from Yiddish such as *bagel, chutzpah, schmaltz* and *schmuck*.

From the native North American languages have come *anorak, kayak, raccoon* and *toboggan*, and from the Aboriginal language of Australia have come *boomerang* and *kangaroo*.

Judo, bonsai and *tycoon* have come from Japanese, *rattan* from Malay and *kung-fu, sampan* and *ginseng* from Chinese.

The borrowing process continues. With Britain becoming more of a cosmopolitan and multi-cultural nation the borrowing is increasing.

cliché a word or expression that has lost a lot of its impact through over use and overexposure. For example, 'accidents will happen' and 'across the board'. *See also* **Clichés** appendix.

coinage the invention of a new word or expression.

colloquialism a term used to describe an expression of the kind used in informal conversation.

derivative a word that has been formed from a simpler word or word element. For example, 'sweetly' is a derivative of 'sweet', 'peaceful' is a derivative from 'peace', 'clinging' is derived from 'cling' and 'shortest' is derived from 'short'.

dialect the language of a region or community with regard to vocabulary, structure, grammar and pronunciation.

doubles words that habitually go together, as in 'out and out', 'neck and neck', 'over and over', 'hale and hearty', 'rant and rave', 'fast and furious', 'hue and cry', 'stuff and nonsense', 'rough and ready', 'might and main', 'give and take', 'ups and downs', 'fair and square', 'high and dry' and 'wear and tear'. Doubles are also sometimes called **dyads**.

doublets pairs of words that have developed from the same original word but now differ somewhat in form and usually in meaning. Examples include 'human' and 'humane', 'shade' and 'shadow', 'hostel' and 'hotel', 'frail' and 'fragile', and 'fashion' and 'faction'.

dyads *see* **doubles**.

EFL English as a foreign language.

etymology the origin and history of a word; the study of the history of words.

euphemism is a term given to an expression that is a milder, more pleasant, less direct way of saying something that might be thought to be too harsh or direct. English has a great many euphemisms, many of these referring to specific areas of life, as in 'getting on a bit' for old and 'awaiting the patter of tiny feet' for pregnant. Euphemisms range from the high-flown to the coy, to slang.

figurative a term that refers to words that are not used literally. For example, 'mine' in the sense of 'excavation in the earth from which coal, tin, etc, is taken' is a literal use of the word. 'Mine' in the sense of 'He is a mine of information' is a figurative use of the word.

first language same as **mother tongue**.

formal the term used to refer to speech and writing that is characterized by more complicated and more difficult language and by more complicated grammatical structures. Short forms and contractions are avoided in formal speech and writing.

gobbledygook a noun that is used informally to refer to pretentious and convoluted language of the type that is found in official documents and reports. It is extremely difficult to understand and should be avoided and 'plain English' used instead.

hybrid a word that is formed from words or elements derived from different languages, such as 'television'.

idiolect a person's own style of language with regard to vocabulary, structure, etc, is known as ideolect, as in 'He is the son of academic parents and has rather a formal idiolect'.

homograph *see* **Homograph** appendix.

homonym *see* **Homonym** appendix.

homophone *see* **Homophone** appendix.

jargon refers to the technical or specialized language used by a particular group, e.g. doctors, computer engineers, sociologists, etc, to communicate with each other within their specialty. It should be avoided in the general language as it will not be clear to the ordinary person exactly what is meant.

journalese a derogatory name for the style of writing and choice of vocabulary supposedly found in newspapers. It is usually the style of writing in tabloid newspapers, such as widespread use of clichés, sensational language and short sentences, that is meant by the term.

language the means by which human beings communicate using words. Language can refer either to spoken or written communication. It can also refer to the variety of communication used by a particular nation or state, as in 'the French language'.

The term can also be used to refer to the style and vocabulary of a piece of writing, as in 'The language of his novels is very poetic'. It can also be used to denote the particular style and variety of language that is used in a particular profession or among a particular group of people with some common interest, as in 'legal language', 'technical language', etc. Such specialist language is sometimes referred to rather pejoratively as legalese, 'computerese', etc. *See* **jargon**.

lexicography the art and practice of defining words, selecting them and arranging them in dictionaries or glossaries.

lingua franca a language adopted as a common language by speakers whose mother tongues are different from each other. This enables people to have a common medium of communication for various purposes, such as trading. Examples include Swahili in East Africa, Hausa in West Africa and Tok Pisin in Papua New Guinea. The term historically referred to a language that was a mixture of Italian, French, Greek, Spanish and Arabic, used for trading and military purposes.

linguistics the systematic, scientific study of language. It describes language and seeks to establish general principles rather than to prescribe rules of correctness.

loanword a word that has been taken into one language from another. From the point of view of the language taking the word in, the word is known as a borrowing. Some loanwords become naturalized or fully integrated into the language and have a pronunciation and spelling reflecting the conventions of the language which has borrowed them. Other loanwords retain the spelling and pronunciation of the language from which they have been borrowed. These include 'Gastarbeiter', borrowed from German and meaning 'a foreign worker'.

localism a word or expression the use of which is restricted to a particular place or area. The area in question can be quite small, unlike dialect words or 'regionalism'.

malapropism the incorrect use of a word, often through confusion with a similar-sounding word. It often arises from someone's attempt to impress someone else with a knowledge of long words or of technical language.

mother tongue the language that one first learns, the language of which one is a native speaker.

native speaker *see* **mother tongue**.

neologism a word that has been newly coined or newly introduced into the language, as 'MP3 player', 'blog' and 'podcast'.

palindrome a word which reads the same backwards a forwards, such as 'level' or 'madam'. It can also apply to a phrase, as 'Able was I ere I saw Elba'.

pangram a phrase or sentence which contains all the letters of the alphabet. The ideal pangram contains each letter only once, but this is quite difficult to do, if the result is to be meaningful.

officialese a derogatory term for the vocabulary and style of writing often found in official reports and documents and thought of as being pretentious and difficult to understand. It is usually considered to be the prime example of gobbledegook.

orthography the study or science of how words are spelt.

philology the science, especially comparative, of languages and their history and structure.

prefix *see* **affix**.

redundancy same as **tautology**.

retronym a word or phrase that has had to be renamed slightly in the light of another invention, etc. For example, an ordinary guitar has become 'acoustic guitar' because of the existence of 'electric guitar'. Leather has sometimes become 'real leather' because of the existence of 'imitation leather'.

root same as **base**.

semantics the study of the historical development and change of word meaning

slang the name given to a set of highly colloquial words and phrases, often rapidly changing and ephemeral, which are regarded as being below the level of educated standard speech. The term is also used to refer to the language used by a particular group of people e.g. surfer's slang.

stem same as **base**.

stress emphasis placed on a particular sound or syllable of a word by pronouncing it with more force than those surrounding it.

suffix *see* **affix**.

synonym a word which has the same, or a similar, meaning to another word.

tautology unnecessary repetition, as in 'new innovations', 'a see-through transparent material' and 'one after the other in succession'. In these examples 'new', 'see-through' and 'in succession' are all unnecessary or **redundant** because the idea which they convey is conveyed by 'innovations', 'transparent' and 'one after the others respectively.

Pronunciation

accent commonly refers to a regional or individual way of speaking or pronouncing words, as in 'a Glasgow accent'.

cedilla the **diacritic** used in French to indicative a soft pronunciation, as 'façade'. *See also* **umlaut**.

consonant a speech sound which is produced by a closing movement, either partial or total, involving the vocal organs, such as the lips, teeth, tongue or the throat, which forms such a narrow constriction that the sound of air can be heard passing through. The term also applies to a letter of the alphabet sounded in this way. *See* **vowel**.

dental produced by the tip of the tongue positioned near the front teeth, as in the pronunciation of the letter 'd'.

diacritic a mark placed a either above or below a letter to indicate a certain emphasis or pronunciation.

diaeresis a mark that is placed over a vowel to indicate that it is sounded separately from a neighbouring vowel, as in 'naïve', 'Chloë'.

digraph a group of two letters representing one sound, as in 'ay' in 'hay', 'ey' in 'key', 'oy' in 'boy', 'ph' in 'phone' and 'th' in 'thin'. When the digraph consists of two letters physically joined together, as 'æ', it is called a 'ligature'.

diphthong a speech sound that changes its quality within the same single syllable. The sound begins as for one vowel and moves on as for another. Since the sound glides from one vowel into another, a diphthong is sometimes called a **gliding vowel**. Examples include the vowels sounds in 'rain', 'weigh', 'either', 'voice', 'height', 'aisle', 'road', 'soul', 'know', 'house', 'care', 'pure', 'during', 'here' and 'weird'.

disyllabic a term that describes a word with two syllables. For example, 'window' is disyllabic, since it consists of the syllable 'win' and the syllable 'dow'. Similarly 'curtain' is disyllabic since it consists of the syllable 'cur' and 'tain'.

elision the omission of a speech sound or syllable, as in the omission of 'd' in one of the possible pronunciations of 'Wednesday' and in the omission of 'ce' from the pronunciation of 'Gloucester'.

fricative a sound produced by forcing air through a partly closed passage, as in the pronunciation of 'th'.

gliding vowel same as **diphthong**.

hiatus a break in pronunciation between two vowels that come together in different syllables, as in 'Goyaesque' and 'cooperate'.

inflection a varying of tone or pitch.

International Phonetic Alphabet a system of written symbols designed to enable the speech sounds of any language to be consistently represented. Some of the symbols are the ordinary letters of the Roman alphabet but some have been specially invented. The alphabet was first published in 1889 and is commonly known as **IPA**.

intrusive r the pronunciation of the *r* sound between two words or syllables where the first of these ends in a vowel sound and the second begins with a vowel sound and where there is no 'r' in the spelling. It appears in such phrases as 'law and order', which is frequently pronounced as 'lawr and order'.

IPA *see* **International Phonetic Alphabet**.

labial formed by closing, or partially closing, the lips, as in the pronunciation of the letter 'm'.

labiodental produced by the lips and teeth together, as in the pronunciation of the letter 'v'.

length mark a mark used in phonetics in relation to a vowel to indicate that it is long. This can take the form of a 'macron', a small horizontal stroke placed above a letter, or a symbol resembling a colon placed after a vowel in the IPA pronunciation system.

macron *see* **length mark**.

phoneme the smallest unit of speech.

phonetics the science connected with pronunciation and the representation of speech sounds.

plosive denoting a burst of air, such as is produced when pronouncing the letter 'p'.

sibilant suggesting a hissing sound, as that produced when pronouncing the letter 's'.

umlaut the **diacritic** which indicates a change of vowel sound in German, as in *mädchen*.

spoonerism the accidental or deliberate transposition of the initial letters of two or more words when speaking, as in 'the queer old dean' instead of 'the dear old queen', 'a blushing crow' instead of a 'crushing blow' and 'a well-boiled icicle' instead of a 'well-oiled bicycle'. Spoonerisms are called after the Reverend William Archibald Spooner (1844–1930) of Oxford University.

velar produced by the back of the tongue on the soft palate, as in the pronunciation of the letter 'g' in the word 'grand', etc.

voiceless spoken without using the vocal cords, as in the pronunciation of the letter 'p'.

vowel a sound produced by the passage of air through the larynx, virtually unobstructed, no part of the mouth being closed and none of the vocal organs being so close together that the sound of air can be heard passing between them. The term is also applied to a letter of the alphabet sounded in this way. The vowels in the alphabet are a, e, i, o and u.

Words liable to be mispronounced

abdomen is now usually pronounced with the emphasis on the first syllable (*ab*-do-men).

acumen is now usually pronounced *ak*-yoo-men, with the emphasis on the first syllable, although formerly the stress was usually on the second syllable (yoo).

adult may be pronounced with the emphasis on either of

the two syllables. Thus *a*-dult and a-*dult* are both acceptable although the pronunciation with the emphasis on the first syllable (*a*-dult) is the more common.

adversary is commonly pronounced with the emphasis on the first syllable (*ad*-ver-sar-i) although in modern usage it is also found with the emphasis on the second syllable (ad-*ver*-sar-i).

aged has two possible pronunciations depending on the sense. When it means 'very old', as in 'aged men with white beards', it is pronounced *ay*-jid. When it means 'years of age', as in 'a girl aged nine', it is pronounced with one syllable, *ayjd*.

banal should rhyme with 'canal', with the emphasis on the second syllable (ba-*nal*).

blackguard, meaning 'a scoundrel', has an unusual pronunciation. It is pronounced *blagg*-ard.

brochure is usually pronounced *bro*-sher, despite the *ch* spelling, rather than bro-*shoor*, which is French-sounding.

Celtic is usually pronounced kel-tik.

cervical has two possible pronunciations. Both *ser*-vik-al, with the emphasis on the first syllable, and ser-*vik*-al, with the emphasis on the second syllable which has the same sound as in *Vik*ing in 'cervical cancer'.

chamois in the sense of 'a kind of cloth (made from the skin of the chamois antelope) used for polishing or cleaning' is pronounced *sham*-mi. In the sense of 'a kind of antelope', it is pronounced *sham*-wa.

chiropodist is usually pronounced kir-*op*-od-ist with an initial *k* sound, but the pronunciation shir-*op*-od-ist with an initial *sh* sound is also possible.

clandestine usually has the emphasis on the second syllable, as klan-*des*-tin', but it is acceptable to pronounce it with the emphasis on the first syllable, as *klan*-des-tin.

comparable is liable to be mispronounced. The emphasis should be on the first syllable, as in *kom*-par-able. It is often mispronounced with the emphasis on the second syllable.

contrary has two possible pronunciations. When it means 'opposite', as in 'On the contrary, I would like to go very much', it is pronounced with the emphasis on the first syllable (*kon*-trar-i). When it means 'perverse, stubborn', as in 'contrary children' it is pronounced with the emphasis on the second syllable, which is pronounced to rhyme with 'Mary'.

controversy is usually pronounced with the emphasis on the first syllable (*kon*-tro-ver-si). In modern usage there is a growing tendency to place the emphasis on the second syllable (kon-*tro*-ver-si).

dais meaning 'platform' or 'stage', is now usually pronounced as two syllables, as day-is. Formerly it was pronounced as one syllable, as days.

decade is pronounced with the emphasis on the first syllable as *dek*-ayd. An alternative but rare pronunciation is dek-*ayd*.

demonstrable is most commonly pronounced di-*mon*-strabl, with the emphasis on the second syllable, in mod-

ern usage. Previously the emphasis was on the first syllable as *dem*-on-strabl.

explicable is now usually pronounced with the emphasis on the second syllable (ex-*plik*-ibl). Formerly it was commonly pronounced with the emphasis on the first syllable (*ex*-plikibl).

exquisite has two possible pronunciations. It is most usually pronounced with the emphasis on the first syllable (*ex*-kwis-it) but some prefer to put the emphasis on the second syllable (iks-*kwis*-it).

finance can be pronounced in two ways. The commoner pronunciation has the emphasis on the second syllable and the first syllable pronounced like the fin of a fish (fin-*ans*). The alternative pronunciation has emphasis on the first syllable, which then is pronounced as fine (*fin*-ans).

formidable may be pronounced with the emphasis on the first syllable as *for*-mid-ibl or with the emphasis on the second syllable as for-*mid*-ibl.

forte the usual pronunciation is *for*-tay but it can also be pronounced as single syllable fort. The word means 'someone's strong point', as in 'Putting people at their ease is not her forte' and 'The chef's forte is desserts'. There is also a musical word **forte** meaning 'loud' or 'loudly'. It is of Italian origin and is pronounced either *for*-ti or *for*-tay.

foyer the most widely used pronunciation is foi-ay but it can also be pronounced fwah-yay following the original French pronunciation.

harass traditionally is pronounced with the stress on the first syllable, as *har*-as. However, in modern usage there is an increasing tendency to put the emphasis on the second syllable, as har-*as*, which is how the word is pronounced in America.

heinous is most commonly pronounced *hay*-nis, although *hee*-nis also exists.

hospitable can be pronounced in two ways. The more traditional pronunciation has the emphasis on the first syllable, as *hos*-pit-ibl. In modern usage it is sometimes pronounced with the emphasis on the second syllable, as hos-*pit*-ibl.

impious the emphasis should be on the first syllable as *im*-pi-us. This is unlike 'impiety' where the stress is on the second syllable.

incomparable the emphasis should be on the second syllable and not the third. It should be pronounced in-*kom*-pir-ibl.

inventory unlike the word 'invention', the emphasis is on the first syllable as *in*-ven-tri or *in*-ven-tor-i.

kilometre has two possible pronunciations in modern usage. It can be pronounced with the emphasis on the first syllable, as *kil*-o-meet-er, or with the emphasis on the second syllable, as kil-*om*-it-er. The first of these is the more traditional pronunciation but the second is becoming common.

laboratory should be pronounced with the emphasis on the second syllable, as lab-*or*-a-tor-i or lab-*or*-a-tri. In American English the emphasis is on the first syllable.

lamentable should be pronounced with the emphasis on the first syllable, as *lam*-en-tabl. However it is becoming common to place the emphasis on the second syllable in the same way that 'lament' does.

longevity should be pronounced lon-*jev*-iti. Some people pronounce it lon-*gev*-iti, but this is rarer.

machinations should be pronounced mak-in-*ay*-shunz but mash-in *ay*-shunz is becoming increasingly common in modern usage.

mandatory the emphasis should be on the first syllable, as *man*-da-tor-i.

margarine formerly the usual pronunciation was mar-ga-reen but now the most common pronunciation is mar-ja-reen.

migraine is pronounced *mee*-grayn in British English but the American pronunciation of *mi*-grayn, in which the first syllable rhymes with 'eye', is sometimes used in Britain.

motif is pronounced with the emphasis on the second syllable, as mo-*teef*.

naïve is pronounced ni-*eev*, with the emphasis on the second syllable, and the first syllable rhyming with 'my'. The accent on the *ï* (called a diaeresis) indicates that the two vowels *a* and *i* are to be pronounced separately.

necessarily is traditionally pronounced with the emphasis on the first syllable, but this is often very difficult to say except when one is speaking exceptionally carefully. Because of this difficulty it is often pronounced with the emphasis on the third syllable although this is considered by many people to be incorrect.

niche the most common pronunciation is *nitch*, but *neech*, following the French pronunciation, is also a possibility.

pejorative in modern usage it is pronounced with the emphasis on the second syllable, as in pi-*jor*-at-iv.

phlegm is pronounced *flem*.

prestige is pronounced prez-*teezh*.

primarily is traditionally pronounced with the emphasis on the first syllable, as *prim*-ar-el-i. Since this is difficult to say unless one is speaking very slowly and carefully, it is becoming increasingly common to pronounce it with the emphasis on the second syllable, as prim-*err*-el-i.

quay the spelling of the word does not suggest the pronunciation, which is *kee*.

questionnaire formerly the acceptable pronunciation was kes-tyon-*air*, but in modern usage kwes-chon-*air* is more common.

schedule is usually pronounced *shed*-yool in British English. However, the American English pronunciation *sked*-yool is now sometimes found in British usage.

subsidence has two acceptable pronunciations. It can be pronounced either sub-*sid*-ens, with the emphasis on the middle syllable which rhymes with 'hide', or *sub*-sid-ens, with the emphasis on the first syllable and with the middle syllable rhyming with 'hid'.

suit is pronounced *soot* or *syoot*.

suite is pronounced *sweet*.

swingeing is pronounced *swin*-jing, not like swinging.

trait is traditionally pronounced *tray* but *trayt* is also an acceptable pronunciation in modern usage

victuals is pronounced *vitlz*.

vitamin is pronounced vit-a-min, with the first syllable rhyming with 'lit' in British English. In American English the first syllable rhymes with 'light'.

Words liable to be confused

Some words with totally different meanings are liable to be confused, often, but not always, because they are pronounced in a similar way or have similar spellings. Below is a list of words which are often confused, together with short examples of usage to help you to differentiate them.

accept	accept a gift
except	everyone except Mary
access	access to the building; access to computer data
excess	an excess of food at the picnic
adapter	the adapter of the novel for TV
adaptor	an electrical adaptor
addition	an addition to the family
edition	a new edition of the book
adverse	an adverse reaction to the drug
averse	not averse to the idea
advice	seek legal advice
advise	we advise you to go
affect	badly affected by the news
effect	the effects of the drug
alley	a bowling alley
allay	allay the child's fears
allusion	make no allusion to recent events
delusion	under the delusion that he is immortal
illusion	an optical illusion
altar	praying at the altar
alter	alter the dress
alternately	feeling alternately hot and cold
alternatively	we could drive there – alternatively we could walk
amend	amend the law
emend	emend the text before printing
angel	heavenly angels
angle	a triangle has three angles; a new angle to the story
annex	annex a neighbouring country
annexe	build an annexe to the house

antiquated	antiquated attitudes
antique	valuable antique furniture
arisen	a problem has arisen
arose	a problem arose today
ascent	the ascent of Everest
assent	he gave his assent to the proposal
astrology	believers in astrology read horoscopes
astronomy	astronomy involves the scientific study of the stars and the planets
ate	we ate bread and cheese
eaten	we have eaten too much
aural	an aural impairment requiring a hearing aid; an aural comprehension test
oral	both oral and written language exams; oral hygiene recommended by the dentist
bad	bad men arrested by the police
bade	we bade him farewell
bail	the accused was granted bail
bale	a bale of cotton; bale out; bale out water; bale out of an aircraft
ballet	practising ballet steps
ballot	voting by means of a secret ballot
bare	bare feet
bear	bear the pain; bear children; bears looking for food
base	at the base of the pillar; base the argument on facts
bass	sing bass; fishermen catching bass
bath	lie soaking in the bath; bath the baby
bathe	bathe in the sea; bathe a wound
baton	the conductor's baton; a relay baton
batten	secure the broken door with wooden battens; batten down the hatches
beach	building sand castles on the beach
beech	beech and oak trees
been	having been famous
being	being poor scared her
beat	beat them at tennis; beat the dog with a stick
beet	sugar beet; soup made with beet
beat	we should beat them
beaten	we should have beaten them

became	she became famous
become	he wants to become a doctor
beer	a pint of beer
bier	a funeral bier
began	the child began to cry
begun	it had begun to rain
belief	he has belief in his son's abilities
believe	I believe that his son could succeed
beside	the bride stood beside the groom
besides	besides, he has no money; who, besides your mother, was there
bit	the dog bit the postman
bitten	he was bitten by a rat
blew	the wind blew; the hat blew away
blown	the wind had blown fiercely; the papers have been blown away
bloc	the African bloc of countries
block	a block of flats; a block of wood; block a pipe
boar	shooting wild boar
bore	the speaker is a bore
boast	boast about his achievements
boost	give a boost to the economy
bonny	a bonny little girl with beautiful hair
bony	the man's bony knees
born	babies born in hospital
borne	I could not have borne the pain; waterborne diseases
bouquet	a bouquet of roses
bookie	place a bet with a bookie
bow	take a bow after the performance; bow to the queen
bough	the bough of a tree is any one of its main branches
boy	boys and girls
buoy	a mooring buoy in the bay
breach	a breach of the peace; breach the enemy's defences
breech	the breech of a gun; a breech delivery of a baby
bread	bread and butter
bred	born and bred

break	break an arm	**chartered**	a chartered surveyor; a chartered boat
brake	failure of the car's brakes; he braked suddenly on seeing the dog in the road	**charted**	the charted areas of the region
breath	take a deep breath	**cheap**	buy cheap clothes at the market
breathe	breathe deeply	**cheep**	birds beginning to cheep
bridal	the bridal party going to the church	**check**	check the tyre pressure; act as a check on her extravagance
bridle	the horse's bridle	**cheque**	pay by cheque
broke	the watch fell and broke	**checked**	a checked tablecloth
broken	the watch was broken	**chequered**	a chequered career
brooch	wear a silver brooch	**choose**	you may choose a cake
broach	afraid to broach the subject	**chose**	she chose a peach from the fruit dish
		chosen	you have chosen well; the chosen few
buffet	[buffit] heavy waves regularly buffet the cliffs	**chord**	a musical chord; strike a chord
buffet	[boofay] serve a cold buffet at the party;	**cord**	the cord of a dressing gown; spinal cord; vocal cord
but	he was dead, but his family did not know	**coarse**	made of some coarse material; a coarse sense of humour
butt	butt in rudely to the conversation; the goat will butt you; a cigarette butt	**course**	taking a French course; a golf course; in due course
calf	a cow and her calf; the calf of the leg	**coma**	the patient is still in a coma
calve	hoping the cow would calve soon	**comma**	put a comma instead of the full stop
callous	a cruel, callous tyrant	**commissionaire**	the hotel commissionaire
callus	the callus on her finger	**commissioner**	a police commissioner
came	they came late	**compliment**	embarrassed at being paid a compliment
come	they promised to come	**complement**	a full complement of staff; the complement of a verb
cannon	soldiers firing cannons		
canon	the canons of the cathedral; the canons and principles of the Christian church	**complimentary**	complimentary remarks; complimentary tickets
canvas	a bag made of canvas; the canvas painted by a local artist	**complementary**	complementary medicine; a complementary amount; complementary angles
canvass	canvass for votes		
carton	a carton of milk	**compulsive**	a compulsive gambler
cartoon	children laughing at TV cartoons	**compulsory**	compulsory to wear school uniform
cast	the whole cast came on stage; cast a quick glance; a cast in the eye	**concert**	an orchestral concert
caste	the caste system in India	**consort**	the queen's consort
		confident	confident of success
censor	appoint a film censor; censor letters	**confidant**	he was the king's trusted confidant
censure	censure the child's unruly behaviour	**confidante**	she was the queen's closest confidante
cereal	cereal crops; breakfast cereal	**conscience**	suffering from a guilty conscience
serial	a magazine or radio serial	**conscious**	he was knocked out but is conscious now; a conscious decision
chafe	tight shoes will chafe your heels; chafe at the delay	**conservative**	a conservative, rather than radical, approach
chaff	separate the wheat from the chaff	**Conservative**	the Conservative Party in British politics

consul	he was British consul in Rome	**dependant**	trying to provide for his wife and other dependants
council	she was elected to the town council		
counsel	counsel for the defence; seeking professional counsel	**dependent**	dependent on her family for personal care
contemptible	a contemptible act of cowardice; a contemptible fellow	**deprecate**	strongly deprecate the behaviour of the gang of youths
contemptuous	contemptuous of the achievements of others; contemptuous of the law	**depreciate**	depreciate in value
continual	disturbed by continual interruptions; in continual pain	**desert**	camels in the desert; he deserted his wife and family
continuous	a continuous line of cars; a continuous roll of paper	**dessert**	have chocolate cake for dessert
coop	a chicken coop	**detract**	detract from his reputation as an actor
coup	a military coup	**distract**	try not to distract the driver
corps	an army corps; the corps de ballet	**device**	a device designed to save water
corpse	a corpse found in a shallow grave	**devise**	devise a rescue plan
councillor	a town councillor	**devolution**	the population voted for the devolution of power from the government to the assembly
counsellor	a bereavement counsellor	**evolution**	the theory of evolution was first proposed by Charles Darwin
courtesy	treat the visitors with courtesy	**dew**	the morning dew
curtsy	curtsy to the queen	**due**	payment is due now; in due course
credible	a credible story	**did**	you did enough; he did steal the money
creditable	a creditable performance	**done**	you have done enough
credulous	credulous enough to believe anything		
crevasse	a crevasse in the glacier	**die**	very ill and likely to die
crevice	a crevice in the rock	**dye**	about to dye her fair hair black
cue	a billiards cue; an actor famous for missing his cue	**died**	the poet died young
queue	the bus queue	**dyed**	he dyed his white shirt blue
curb	curb their extravagance	**dinghy**	a dinghy capsized in the storm
kerb	cars parked by the kerb	**dingy**	a dingy basement flat
currant	a currant bun	**disadvantageous**	disadvantageous to one of the teams; disadvantageous, rather than favourable, circumstances
current	unable to swim against the strong current; current affairs; electric current	**disadvantaged**	disadvantaged people in society
cygnet	a swan and her cygnets	**discomfit**	the question seemed to discomfit her
signet	a signet ring	**discomfort**	living in great discomfort
cymbal	banging the cymbals	**discriminating**	discriminating in their choice of wines
symbol	a symbol of purity; a mathematical symbol	**discriminatory**	discriminatory against women
		discus	throwing the discus
dairy	milk from the dairy	**discuss**	discuss the matter
diary	writing in her diary every night		
		distinct	see a distinct improvement; a style quite distinct from others
dear	dear friends; clothes which are too dear	**distinctive**	the distinctive markings of the zebra
deer	hunting deer		

draft	a first draft of a report
draught	there was a draught in the room from the open window; a draught of cold beer
dragon	a dragon breathing fire
dragoon	the dragoon guards; we dragooned her into helping us
drank	we drank some white wine
drunk	to have drunk too much; a drunk woman staggering down the street
drunken	a drunken, violent man; a drunken brawl
drew	the child drew a picture
drawn	he has drawn a picture of a house
driven	we were driven home by my father
drove	we drove home after midnight
dual	serve a dual purpose
duel	fight a duel
economic	a country facing economic disaster; charging an economic rent for the flat
economical	the economical use of resources; an economical car to run; economical with the truth
eerie	in the eerie atmosphere of a thick mist
eyrie	the eagle's eyrie
elder	Mary has two brothers and James is the elder
eldest	John has three sisters and Jill is the eldest
elicit	elicit information
illicit	an illicit love affair
eligible	eligible for promotion; an eligible bachelor
legible	scarcely legible handwriting
elude	elude capture by the police
allude	allude to facts which he had concealed
emigrant	emigrants leaving their native land
immigrant	illegal immigrants coming into a country
emigration	the poor standard of living led to mass emigration from the country
immigration	anxious to reduce the extent of immigration into the country
emission	the emission of poisonous gases
omission	the omission of her name from the invitation list

emotional	an emotional person; an emotional reaction
emotive	illegal immigration is an emotive subject
employee	hiring several new employees
employer	asking their employer for an increase in salary
enormity	the enormity of the crime
enormousness	the enormousness of the elephant
envelop	she wanted to envelop the child in her arms; mist began to envelop the mountains
envelope	a brown envelope
enviable	an enviable affluent lifestyle
envious	envious of other people's wealth
epitaph	carve an epitaph on a gravestone
epithet	King Alfred was given the epithet 'great'
equable	an equable climate; an equable temperament
equitable	an equitable system
erotic	erotic pictures of naked women
erratic	an erratic driver; impulsive, erratic behaviour
ewe	a ewe and her lambs
yew	the yew tree in the graveyard
exceedingly	exceedingly beautiful
excessively	excessively fond of alcohol
exceptional	a singer of exceptional talent; an exceptional amount of rain
exceptionable	find their behaviour exceptionable
executioner	bring the condemned man to the executioner
executor	an executor of a will
exercise	physical exercise; an English exercise
exorcise	exorcise evil spirits
exhausting	an exhausting climb
exhaustive	an exhaustive search
expand	expand the business; metals expanding in the heat
expend	expend a great deal of energy
expansive	his knowledge of literature was expansive
expensive	spending a lot of money on expensive meals

expedient	politically expedient	**flout**	flout the new school rule
expeditious	a parcel sent by the most expeditious method	**flaunt**	flaunt her long legs
		font	babies christened at the font
extant	old customs which are still extant in some areas	**fount**	printed in a small size of fount; the fount of all knowledge
extinct	an endangered species that is likely to be extinct soon; an extinct volcano	**forbade**	she forbade them to leave
		forbidden	she was forbidden to leave
faint	feel faint; a faint noise	**foresaw**	we foresaw trouble
feint	a feint in fencing	**foreseen**	the problem could not have been foreseen
fair	a fair result; fair hair; sideshows at a fair		
fare	bus fare; how did you fare in the exam?	**forgave**	we forgave them
		forgiven	we have forgiven them
fate	suffer a terrible fate; by a strange twist of fate	**forgot**	we forgot about the party
fête	a fête in aid of charity	**forgotten**	I had forgotten the event
fearful	fearful of being left behind; what a fearful smell	**formally**	formally dressed
fearsome	see a fearsome sight	**formerly**	formerly the president of the club
feat	perform a brave feat	**fort**	soldiers defending the fort
feet	sore feet	**forte**	tact is not his forte
fiancé	Jill and her fiancé	**foul**	commit a foul on the football pitch; a foul smell
fiancée	Jim and his fiancée	**fowl**	a chicken is a type of fowl
final	a final warning	**found**	they found the missing child
finale	all the cast took part in the final	**founded**	their grandfather founded the firm
flair	have a flair for languages	**freeze**	freeze the vegetables; freeze to death
flare	send up a flare as a signal for help; make the fire flare up; a skirt with a slight flare	**frieze**	a decorative frieze along the upper walls of a room
inflammable	highly inflammable substances such as petrol	**froze**	we froze the meat immediately
inflammatory	he made an inflammatory speech	**frozen**	frozen vegetables; half-frozen to death
flea	bitten by a flea	**funeral**	mourners at the funeral
flee	people began to flee from the burning building	**funereal**	solemn funereal music
		gaff	landing a fish with a gaff; blow the gaff
fleshy	fleshy upper arms; a fleshy fruit	**gaffe**	a social gaffe
fleshly	fleshly pleasures		
		gamble	he gambled on a horse in the next race
flu	suffering from flu	**gambol**	lambs beginning to gambol about
flue	cleaning the chimney flue		
flew	the bird flew away	**gate**	shut the gate
flown	the bird has flown away	**gait**	a shuffling gait
floe	an ice floe	**gave**	he gave money to the poor
flow	the flow of water	**given**	we weregiven some money
flour	flour to make bread	**gentle**	a gentle touch; a gentle breeze
flower	pick a flower from the garden	**genteel**	a genteel tea party

glacier	a glacier beginning to melt	**hoard**	a hoard of treasure
glazier	a glazier mending the window	**horde**	a horde of invaders
goal	score a goal	**honorable**	an honorable gentleman; honorable deeds
gaol	escape from gaol	**honorary**	the honorary post of secretary
gone	he has gone		
went	she went yesterday	**hoop**	jump through a hoop
		whoop	a whoop of delight
gorilla	a gorilla in the zoo		
guerrilla	guerrillas fighting in the mountains	**human**	a human being
		humane	the humane killing of the injured animal
grate	a fire burning in the grate		
great	a great improvement; a great man	**idle**	too idle to work
		idol	the pop star as teenage idol; worshipping an idol
grew	the plants grew well		
grown	the plant has grown tall		
grief	weeping from grief	**imaginary**	the child's imaginary friend
grieve	she needed time to grieve for her dead husband	**imaginative**	an imaginative story; an imaginative person
grill	put the meat under the grill	**immoral**	wicked and immoral
grille	a metal grille on the window	**immortal**	no one is immortal
grisly	the grisly sight of a decaying body	**inapt**	an inapt remark
grizzly	a grizzly bear	**inept**	an inept attempt
hail	a hail storm; a hail of bullets; hail a taxi	**incredible**	find the story incredible
hale	hale and hearty	**incredulous**	incredulous enough to believe anything
hair	the hairdresser cut off all her hair	**industrial**	an industrial estate
hare	a running hare in the field	**industrious**	studious and industrious
half	one half of the apple	**ingenious**	an ingenious plan
halve	halve the apple	**ingenuous**	an ingenuous young person
		its	a dog wagging its tail
hangar	an aeroplane hangar	**it's**	it's raining
hanger	a clothes hanger		
		jam	strawberry jam; a traffic jam; the machine seemed to jam
hanged	they hanged the murderer		
hung	they hung the pictures	**jamb**	a door jamb
heal	the wound began to heal	**jib**	jib at the high price; the jib of the crane
heel	a blister on the heel	**jibe (gibe)**	ignore the nasty jibe
hear	hear the news	**judicial**	a judicial enquiry into the accident
here	here and there	**judicious**	a judicious choice of words
hereditary	a hereditary title	**junction**	a road junction
heredity	part of his genetic heredity	**juncture**	at this juncture we went home
heron	a heron catching fish	**key**	a door key
herring	fishermen catching herring	**quay**	the boat tied to the quay
hid	we hid the treasure	**knead**	knead the bread dough
hidden	they have hidden the treasure	**kneed**	he kneed his attacker in the stomach

knew	we knew him slightly	**loot**	the thieves' loot
know	we did not know him	**lute**	playing the lute
known	if I had known		
		lumbar	lumbar pain
knight	a knight in shining armour	**lumber**	to lumber along awkwardly
night	a stormy night		
		luxuriant	luxuriant vegetation
laid	we laid the patient on the bed; they laid a new carpet	**luxurious**	a luxurious lifestyle
lain	he had lain injured for days	**magnate**	a shipping magnate
		magnet	a fridge magnet
lair	the animal's lair		
layer	a layer of dust	**mail**	deliver the mail
		male	male and female
laterally	moving laterally; thinking laterally		
latterly	latterly she was very ill	**main**	the main reason
		mane	the lion's mane
lath	a lath of wood is a thin strip of wood		
lathe	using a lathe in the factory	**maize**	the farmer grew maize
		maze	get lost in the maze
lead	pipes made of lead		
led	he led the group	**manner**	a friendly manner
		manor	a manor surrounded by beautiful gardens
leak	a leak in the pipe		
leek	a leek to make soup	**masterful**	she prefers masterful men
		masterly	a masterly performance
licence	he has a driving licence		
license	to license the sale of alcohol	**mat**	a door mat
		matt, matte	matt/matte paint
lifelong	a lifelong ambition		
livelong	the livelong day	**meat**	meat such as beef
		meet	I'm going to meet a friend
lighted	a lighted match		
lit	we lit the fire; we have lit the fire	**medal**	a gold medal
		meddle	meddle in the affairs of others
lightening	lightening the load		
lightning	struck by lightning; a lightning decision	**mediate**	mediate between the rival groups
		meditate	meditate to relax
liqueur	an after-dinner liqueur		
liquor	strong liquor such as whisky	**melted**	the ice cream melted; melted chocolate
		molten	molten lava
liquidate	liquidate a debt; liquidate an asset; liquidate an enemy	**metal**	chairs made of metal
liquidize	liquidize the soup	**mettle**	a test of the football team's mettle
literal	a literal translation	**meter**	read the gas meter
literary	literary and artistic tastes	**metre**	a metre of silk
literate	people who are scarcely literate		
		miner	a coal miner
loath/loth	loath/loth to join in	**minor**	a minor incident; legally still a minor
loathe	I loathe him		
		missal	members of the congregation carrying missals
local	the local shops; he enjoyed drinking at his local	**missile**	hit by a missile
locale	a perfect locale for a rock concert		
		mistaken	a case of mistaken identity; we were mistaken
loose	loose clothing	**mistook**	I mistook him for you in the dark
lose	lose your luggage; lose weight		

model	a model of a ship; a fashion model
module	a space module; a software module; a study module
momentary	a momentary lapse of memory
momentous	a momentous decision
moral	the moral of the story; a person with no morals
morale	staff morale was low in the firm
motif	decorated with a motif of roses
motive	a motive for murder
muscle	strain a muscle
mussel	eat fresh mussels
naturalist	a naturalist interested in local flowers
naturist	naked people on a naturist beach
naval	a naval cadet
navel	your navel is in the middle of your abdomen
negligent	negligent parents
negligible	a negligible amount of money
net	caught in a net
net, nett	net, nett profit
niceness	appreciate the old lady's niceness
nicety	the nicety of the distinction
notable	a notable figure in the town
noticeable	a noticeable improvement
nougat	nougat is a sweet
nugget	a nugget of gold; a nugget of information
oar	the boat's oars
ore	iron ore was taken from the mine
observance	the observance of school rules
observation	keep the patient under observation
of	made of gold; tired of working; a glass of wine
off	run off; switch off; badly off
official	an official report; official duties; council official
officious	upset at the officious manner of the hotel receptionist
organism	an organism found in the water supply
orgasm	to reach orgasm
outdoor	an outdoor sport
outdoors	playing outdoors

overcame	we overcame the enemy
overcome	an enemy difficult to overcome
overtaken	he was overtaken by the other runners
overtook	they overtook the car in front
pail	a pail of water
pale	looking pale; a pale colour
pain	suffering from pain
pane	a pane of glass
pair	a pair of gloves
pare	he began to pare his toenails
pear	an apple and a pear
palate	the soft palate
palette	an artist's palette
pallet	a straw pallet
passed	she passed the exam; we passed the other car; the feeling passed
past	past times; in the past; walking past the church; a mile past the village
pastel	pastel colours suit me
pastille	sucking a throat pastille
pâté	chicken liver pâté on toast
patty	a small meat patty
peace	warring nations now at peace
piece	a piece of cake
peak	a mountain peak; talent at its peak
peek	peek through the window
peal	the bells began to peal
peel	peel an orange
pearl	a pearl necklace
purl	knit two, purl two
pedal	pedal the bike
peddle	peddle their wares
pendant	wearing a silver pendant
pendent	pendent lights lit up the room
perceptible	a perceptible improvement
perceptive	a perceptive remark
perpetrate	perpetrate a crime
perpetuate	perpetuate the myth
persecute	he persecuted members of other religions
prosecute	prosecute thieves

personal	a personal letter; a personal assistant	**principal**	the college principal
personnel	the person in charge of office personnel	**principle**	a person of principle; the principle of the steam engine
phase	the next phase of the development; phase in the changes		
faze	nothing seems to faze her	**prise**	prise open the lid of the tin
		prize	win a prize
pigeon	a pigeon looking for food	**program**	a computer program
pidgin	pidgin English	**programme**	a theatre programme
place	a sunny place; get a place at university	**proof**	no proof of his guilt
plaice	plaice and chips	**prove**	able to prove her innocence
plain	a plain carpet; rather a plain girl; corn growing on the plain	**prophecy**	the gift of prophecy; her prophecy came true
plane	a plane taking off; the plane used by the joiner; writing on a different plane from other crime writers	**prophesy**	he was in a position to prophesy that there would be a war
plaintiff	evidence on behalf of the plaintiff	**prostate**	the prostate gland
plaintive	a plaintive cry	**prostrate**	lying prostrate on the ground
plate	the food on the plate	**purposely**	leave the book behind purposely
plait	wearing her hair in a plait	**purposefully**	walk purposefully into the room
plum	eating a plum	**quash**	quash a rebellion; quash a conviction
plumb	plumb straight; plumb in the middle; plumb the depths; plumb-in the bath	**squash**	squash the tomatoes; squash the insect with his foot; orange squash
politic	not politic to ask any questions	**quiet**	a quiet child; a quiet time of day
political	political parties	**quite**	quite good; quite right
pour	pour water	**racket**	the noisy children made quite a racket; a drugs racket; tennis racket
pore	pore over the book; a clogged pore	**racquet**	tennis racquet (variant spelling)
practice	go to football practice	**rain**	get wet in the rain
practise	to practise shooting at goal	**reign**	in the reign of the last king
		rein	a horse's reins
pray	pray to God	**raise**	raise one's arm; raise a family
prey	the fox's prey; prey on one's mind	**raze**	raze the whole street to the ground
precede	the leader who preceded the present one; precede them into the room	**ran**	they ran away
proceed	you may proceed; proceed to cause trouble	**run**	he started to run; she had run away
		rang	they rang the bell
precipitate	rash, precipitate action; precipitate economic panic	**rung**	the church bells were rung
precipitous	a precipitous slope	**rap**	rap at the window
		wrap	wrap the presents
premier	a meeting of European premiers; one of the country's premier actors	**rapt**	with rapt attention
première	the premiere of the film	**wrapped**	we wrapped the presents
premises	seek new office premises	**read**	I read the book last week
premise	based on a mistaken premise	**red**	a red dress
prescribe	prescribe antibiotics for the disease	**real**	made of real leather; a real friend
proscribe	proscribe the carrying of knives	**reel**	a reel of thread; dance a reel

refuge	seek refuge from the storm	**sail**	the sail of a boat; go for a sail
refugee	a political refugee	**sale**	an end-of-season sale
regal	a regal wave of the hand	**salon**	a hairdressing salon
regale	regale them with his adventures	**saloon**	a saloon car; a saloon bar
relief	bring relief from pain	**sang**	they sang a song
relieve	relieve the pain	**sung**	we had sung a song earlier
rest	rest after work	**sank**	the ship sank
wrest	wrest the knife from his hand	**sunk**	the ship has sunk
		sunken	a sunken wreck
retch	feel sick and begin to retch		
wretch	the poor wretch	**saviour**	the saviour of the organization; Christ the saviour
review	the review of the play; the annual salary review	**savour**	savour the delicious food
revue	a musical revue	**saw**	we saw him go
		seen	I have seen this film before
rhyme	children reciting a rhyme; cook rhymes with book	**sawed**	we sawed the wood
rime	rime on the grass on a cold morning	**sawn**	all the wood has been sawn
ridden	she had ridden the horse home	**scared**	scared of the dark
rode	he rode a fine stallion	**scarred**	scarred for life in the accident
right	the right person for the job; the right to be free; the right hand	**scene**	a scene in the play; the accident scene
rite	a religious rite	**seen**	he has seen the play
write	write in pencil	**scent**	the scent of roses
		sent	she sent a letter
risen	the sun had risen		
rose	the sun rose	**sceptic**	a sceptic arguing with the believers
		septic	a septic wound; a septic tank
road	the road through the town		
rode	the child rode her bicycle	**scraped**	he scraped the car on the gate
		scrapped	they scrapped their original plans
roe	cod roe		
row	a row of green beans; row a boat	**sculptor**	a statue by a famous sculptor
		sculpture	carve a piece of sculpture
role	play the role of Hamlet; the parental role	**seam**	sew the seam of a dress; a seam of coal
roll	a roll of carpet; a ham roll; roll a ball	**seem**	they seem familiar
rote	learn the answers by rote	**seasonal**	seasonal hotel work
wrote	he wrote a letter	**seasonable**	seasonable weather for spring
		seasoned	a seasoned dish of stew; seasoned travellers
rough	a rough material; rough weather		
ruff	a lace ruff at the neck		
rout	rout the enemy	**secret**	a secret hideout; their engagement was a secret
route	the shortest route to the town	**secrete**	secrete the money under the floorboards
rung	the bottom rung of the ladder; we had rung the bell	**see**	I see a light
wrung	she wrung her hands in grief	**sea**	boats sailing on the sea
rye	grow rye and barley	**sensual**	a sensual mouth
wry	a wry smile; a wry sense of humour	**sensuous**	the sensuous feel of the silk sheets

series	a series of disasters; a TV series	**soot**	soot falling down the chimney
serious	a serious matter; looking serious	**suit**	an evening suit
sew	sew new curtains	**sped**	the car sped away into the night
sow	sow seeds	**speeded**	we speeded up to pass the car in front
sewed	she sewed tiny stitches	**spoke**	she spoke with feeling
sewn	the dress which she had sewn	**spoken**	he has spoken to her parents
shaken	she was shaken by the accident	**sprang**	he sprang to his feet
shook	he shook the child angrily	**sprung**	the deer had sprung over the fence; the boat sprung a leak
shear	to shear sheep		
sheer	a sheer slope; sheer impertinence; sheer silk	**stair**	a stone stair
		stare	stare into space
shelf	put the book on the shelf	**stake**	a stake missing from the fence; stake a claim
shelve	shelve the plan	**steak**	eat a large steak
shoe	a leather shoe	**stalk**	the stalk of the flower
shoo	shoo the dog away	**stock**	a large stock of goods; stocks and shares
showed	we showed them the house	**stank**	he stank of beer
shown	he has shown me the book	**stunk**	the room had stunk for days
shrank	the child shrank back in fear; the dress shrank in the wash	**stationary**	the car was stationary not moving
shrunk	the child had shrunk from the angry man; the dress had shrunk	**stationery**	a shop stocking stationery
		statue	stone statues in the grounds of the house
sight	the sight of the woman crying	**statute**	pass a new statute
site	the battle site; a building site		
		steal	steal the money from the till
singeing	singeing a blouse with an iron	**steel**	tools made of steel
singing	singing a song		
		stile	climb over the stile
slay	slay an enemy in battle	**style**	dress with style; a style of writing
sleigh	a sleigh ride in the snow		
		stimulant	some athletes resort to taking illegal stimulants
slow	at a slow pace		
sloe	a ripe sloe	**stimulus**	the stimulus of a valuable prize
soar	soar up high	**storey**	the top storey of the house
sore	a sore finger	**story**	tell a story
solder	to solder metal	**straight**	a straight road; a straight answer
soldier	a soldier in the British army	**strait**	the Bering Strait
sole	the sole reason; the sole of the foot; a dish of sole	**straightened**	she had her teeth straightened
soul	he loved her body and soul; a poor old soul	**straitened**	in straitened circumstances
		strategy	the team's winning strategy; devise a strategy to counteract bullying
some	some people	**stratagem**	devise a stratagem to mislead the enemy
sum	the sum total		
son	a son and two daughters	**strewed**	they strewed flowers
sun	lie in the sun on the beach	**strewn**	flowers were strewn

strife	quarrelling and strife	**teeth**	have two teeth extracted
strive	strive to overcome the difficulty	**teethe**	the baby has begun to teethe
striven	we haven striven to succeed	**temporal**	temporal, not spiritual
strove	they strove to win	**temporary**	they could only offer him a temporary post
suede	a jacket made of real suede		
swede	cutting up a swede for dinner	**their**	their home
		there	stay there
suit	wearing a smart suit; a law suit; a suit of cards	**they're**	they're quarrelling again
suite	a three-piece suite; a suite of rooms; a ballet suite	**thorough**	a thorough cleaning
		through	he was just passing through
summary	a summary of the report; his summary dismissal	**thrash**	thrash the youth with a belt
summery	sunny, summery weather	**thresh**	thresh the corn
		threw	he threw the ball
sundae	an ice cream sundae	**through**	go through the door
Sunday	have a rest on Sunday		
		threw	he threw the ball
surplice	the priest's surplice	**thrown**	he had thrown the ball
surplus	a surplus of food at the party		
		throes	in the throes of studying for exams
swam	we swam in the river	**throws**	he throws the ball
swum	he has swum across the river		
		thyme	flavour the sauce with thyme
swingeing	a swingeing blow; swingeing cuts	**time**	not enough time; what time is it?
swinging	a swinging gate; the swinging sixties		
		tic	a nervous tic
swollen	her eye has swollen up; swollen glands	**tick**	the tick of the clock; the dog was bitten by a tick; in a tick; tick the correct answer
swelled	her injured ankle swelled		
swore	they swore they would find the killer	**timber**	a house made of timber
sworn	he has sworn to get revenge	**timbre**	the timbre of his voice
tail	the dog's tail	**tire**	runners beginning to tire
tale	tell a tale	**tyre**	change a car tyre
taken	she has taken the book	**to**	go to town
took	she took the book	**too**	she wants to go too
		two	two or three times
taper	a lighted taper; The road seems to taper there	**toe**	injure a toe
tapir	a tapir is a pig-like animal	**tow**	tow the broken-down car
taught	he taught us maths	**tomb**	the tomb of the Egyptian king
taut	a taut rope; a face taut with concentration	**tome**	struggling to read a legal tome
tea	a cup of tea	**topi**	wear a topi in the hot sun
tee	a golf tee	**toupee**	a bald man wearing a toupee
team	a football team	**tore**	she tore her dress
teem	soon the town will teem with tourists	**torn**	she has torn her dress; a torn dress
tear	wipe away a tear	**trait**	dishonesty is an unpleasant trait
tier	one tier of the wedding cake	**tray**	tea served on a tray

treaties	signing treaties to end the war	**wafer**	an ice cream wafer; a communion wafer
treatise	write a treatise on company law	**waver**	he began to waver about the decision
trod	she trod on the cat's tail	**waif**	a starving waif
trodden	a well-trodden path; she had trodden on a worm	**waive**	waive the extra charges
		wave	wave to their departing guests; a freak wave
troop	a troop of soldiers; troop out of school	**waist**	a leather belt round her waist
troupe	a troupe of actors	**waste**	liquid waste from the factory; a waste of food
turban	hair hidden by a turban		
turbine	a turbine engine	**want**	the workers want more money; for want of enough money
tycoon	a business tycoon	**wont**	she was wont to arrive late
typhoon	ships were damaged in the typhoon	**warden**	the warden of the hostel
unaware	unaware of what had happened	**warder**	a prison warder
unawares	taken unawares by the attack	**ware**	kitchenware; stallholders selling their wares
unconscionable	an unconscionable delay		
unconscious	knocked unconscious by the blow; unconscious of the recent event	**wear**	wear a skirt; show signs of wear
		way	the quickest way home; the correct way to do it
undid	they undid all the damage		
undone	the damage could not be undone	**weigh**	weigh the apples
unexceptional	a disappointing, unexceptional performance	**weak**	invalids too weak to get out of bed
unexceptionable	unnecessary complaints about unexceptionable behaviour	**week**	go to the supermarket every week
		weakly	the weakly old man did not survive
unwanted	unwanted guests	**weekly**	look forward to their weekly visit
unwonted	speak with unwonted enthusiasm		
		went	they went quite suddenly; she went pale
urban	prefer urban to rural life	**gone**	he has gone home; she had gone deaf
urbane	an urbane young man		
		wet	a wet day; wet the floor
vacation	the university students were on vacation till September	**whet**	whet the appetite
vocation	have a vocation to be a priest	**whit**	not care a whit
		wit	find his wit amusing; a person of wit and intelligence
vain	a vain young woman; a vain attempt		
vane	a weather vane	**whole**	the whole group went along
vein	inject the drug into a vein; a vein of gold	**hole**	dig a hole
vale	the Vale of Evesham		
veil	a hat with a veil; draw a veil over the incident	**withdrawn**	he has withdrawn from the election; a shy, withdrawn child
		withdrew	he withdrew from the election
veracity	he doubted the veracity of the account		
voracity	the voracity of the youth's appetite	**wittily**	he spoke wittily after dinner
		wittingly	she wittingly told a lie
vertex	the vertex of a cone		
vortex	the swimmer was caught in a vortex of water and drowned	**woe**	sadness and woe
		woo	woo her and marry her
vigilant	be vigilant because of pickpockets	**woke**	she woke early; he woke the baby
vigilante	the thief was caught by a vigilante	**woken**	she was woken early by the singing birds

wore	he wore the shoes	**wreath**	a holly wreath
worn	he had worn the shoes; an old, worn carpet	**wreathe**	mist had begun to wreathe the mountain peaks
would	we knew she would go	**wrote**	she wrote the letter
wood	a pine wood	**written**	she has written the letter
wove	he wove the material	**yoke**	the yoke of a dress; the yoke of a plough
woven	he has woven the material	**yolk**	egg yolk
weaved	the cyclist weaved in and out		
		yore	in days of yore
wreak	wreak vengeance; wreak havoc	**your**	your house
wreck	wreck the car; wreck their plans	**you're**	you're wrong, I'm right

Affixes

Affix refers to an element that is added to the root or stem of a word to form another word. Affixes can be in the form of **prefixes or suffixes**. A prefix is added to the beginning of a word, as with audio- in audiovisual, an affix to the end, as with -aholic in workaholic. Some common affixes are listed below:

a-, an- a prefix meaning 'without' or 'not', as in amoral, anonymous and atypical.

-able, -ible a suffix meaning 'that can be', as in laughable, washable, horrible and edible.

aero- a prefix meaning **1** 'air', as in aerobics and aeroplane, **2** 'aeroplane', as in aerodrome.

agro-, agri- a prefix meaning 'field', as in agriculture and agrochemicals.

-aholic a suffix indicating an 'addiction', formed on analogy with alcoholic, as in workaholic and shopaholic. It sometimes becomes **-oholic**, as in chocoholic.

ambi- a prefix meaning 'two' or 'both' as in ambivalent, having mixed or uncertain feelings about something, and ambidextrous, able to use both the right and left hand with equal skill.

-ana a suffix meaning 'things associated with', as in Americana.

ante- a prefix meaning 'before', as in antenatal, before birth.

anti- a prefix meaning 'against'. It is used in many words that have been established in English for a long time, as in antipathy, a feeling of hostility or dislike, but it has also been used to form many modern words, as in antifreeze, anti-nuclear and anti-warfare.

arch- a prefix meaning 'chief', as in archbishop, archduke and arch-enemy.

-arch a suffix meaning 'ruler' or 'leader', as in monarch and patriarch.

astro- a prefix meaning 'star', as in astrology, astronomy, astronaut, astrophysics.

-athon, -thon a suffix meaning 'large-scale' or 'long-lasting' as in marathon.

audio- a prefix referring to hearing. It is found in several words that have been established in the English language for some time, as in audition, but it is also used to form many modern words, as in audiotape and audiovisual.

auto- a prefix meaning 'of or by itself', as in autograph, autobiography and automatic, meaning working by itself.

bi- a prefix meaning 'two', as in bicycle, bifocal, bilingual and bisect. Bi- forms words in English in which it means half, and other words in which it means twice. This can give rise to confusion in such words as biweekly and bimonthly, where there are two possible sets of meanings. Biweekly can mean either every two weeks or twice a week so that one would not be able to be certain about the frequency of a biweekly publication. Similarly, a bimonthly publication might appear either twice a month or once every two months.

biblio- a prefix meaning 'book', as in bibliophile, a person who is fond of or collects books, and bibliography.

bio- a prefix meaning 'life' or 'living material', as in biography and biology.

-bound a suffix meaning **1** 'confined' or 'restricted', as in housebound and snowbound. **2** It can also mean 'obligated', as in duty-bound.

by- a prefix meaning **1** 'subordinate', 'secondary', as in by-product, **2** 'around', as in by-pass.

cardi- a prefix meaning 'heart', as in cardiology and cardiac.

cent-, centi- a prefix meaning 'hundred', as in centenary and centigrade.

chrono- a prefix meaning 'time', as in chronology.

-cide a suffix meaning 'killing', as in patricide and pesticide.

circum- a prefix meaning 'around', as in circumnavigate.

con-, com- a prefix meaning 'together with', as in connect, compare and compound.

contra- a prefix meaning 'opposite' or 'against', as in contrary, contradict and contraflow.

deca- a prefix meaning 'ten', as in decade and decathlon.

deci- a prefix meaning 'tenth', as in decibel and decimal

demi- a prefix meaning 'half', as in demigod.

di- a prefix meaning 'two' or 'double', as in dioxide, dilemma, diphthong and disyllabic.

dia- a prefix meaning **1** 'through', as in diaphanous, **2** 'apart', as in diacritical, diaphragm and dialysis, **3** and 'across', as in diameter.

dis- a prefix indicating 'opposite' or meaning 'not', as in disappear, disapprove, dislike, disobey, dispossess.

-dom a suffix meaning 'state' or 'condition', as in boredom, freedom, officialdom, martyrdom, **2** 'rank' or 'status', as in earldom, dukedom, **3** 'domain' or 'territory' as in kingdom.

dys- a prefix meaning, 'bad', 'impaired' or 'abnormal', as in dysfunctional and dyslexia, dyspepsia

eco- a prefix indicating 'ecology'. Following the increased awareness of the importance of the environment, there has been a growing interest in ecology. Many words beginning with eco- have been added to the English language. Some of these are scientific terms such as ecotype, ecosystem or ecospecies. Others are more general terms, such as ecocatastrophe and ecopolitics, and some are even slang terms, such as ecofreak and econut.

-ectomy a suffix that indicates 'surgical removal', as in hysterectomy, the surgical removal of the womb, mastectomy, the surgical removal of a breast, and appendicectomy, the surgical removal of the appendix.

-ed a suffix that forms the past tense and past participles of regular verbs, as in asked, caused, dropped and escaped.

-ee a suffix that is used as part of nouns that are the recipients of an action, as in deportee, a person who has been deported, employee and interviewee. The prefix can also be used as part of a noun indicating a person who acts or behaves in a particular way, as in absentee, a person who absents himself/herself, and escapee, a person who escapes.

electro- a prefix meaning 'electric' or 'electrical' as in electromagnetic.

-en a suffix with several functions. In one sense it indicates 'causing to be', as in broaden, darken, gladden, lighten and sweeten. It also indicates a diminutive or small version of something, as in chicken and maiden. It also indicates what something is made of, as in silken and wooden. It is also used to form the past participle of many irregular verbs, such as broken and fallen.

en- a prefix indicating 'causing to be', as in enrich and enlarge, and 'putting into', as in endanger and enrage.

equi- a prefix meaning 'equal', as in equidistant.

-er a suffix with several functions. It can indicate a person who does something, as in bearer, cleaner, employer, farmer, manager. Some words in this category can also end in '-or', as in adviser/advisor. It can also indicate a person who is engaged in something, as in lawyer. It also indicates a thing that does something, as in blender, cooker, mower, printer and strainer. It can also indicate the comparative form of an adjective, as in darker, fairer, older, shorter and younger. It can also indicate someone who comes from somewhere, as in Londoner.

-ese a suffix that indicates 'belonging to', 'coming from' and is used of people and languages, as in Chinese, Japanese and Portuguese. By extension it refers to words indicating some kind of jargon, as in computerese, journalese and legalese.

-esque a suffix of French origin that means 'in the style or fashion of', as in Junoesque, statuesque, Picassoesque, Ramboesque.

-ess a suffix that was formerly widely used to indicate the feminine form of a word, as in authoress from author, poetess from poet, editress from editor, and sculptress from sculptor. In many cases the supposed male form, such as author, is now considered a neutral form and so is used of both a woman and a man. Thus a woman as well as a man may be an author, a poet, an editor and a sculptor, etc. Some words ending in -ess remain, as in princess, duchess, heiress and hostess. Actress and waitress are still also fairly widespread.

-est a suffix that indicates the superlative forms of adjectives, as in biggest, smallest and ugliest.

-ette a suffix indicating **1** a diminutive or smaller version, as in cigarette and kitchenette; **2** imitation, as in flannelette and leatherette; **3** a female version, as in usherette, a female usher in a cinema. In this last sense it is sometimes used disparagingly, as in jockette, a derogatory word for a female jockey, and hackette, a derogatory word for a female journalist.

Euro- a prefix **1** referring to Europe, as in Eurovision; **2** more commonly now referring to the European Community, as in Euro-MP, Eurocrat and Eurocurrency.

ex- a prefix meaning 'former', as in ex-president, ex-wife.

extra- a prefix meaning 'beyond' or 'outside' as in extra-marital, meaning outside marriage, and extra-curricular, meaning outside the curriculum.

-fold a suffix meaning 'times' or 'multiplied by', as in fourfold, a hundredfold.

for- a prefix with several meanings. These include 'prohibition', as in forbid; 'abstention' as in forbear, forgo and forswear; 'neglect', as in forsake; 'excess' or 'intensity', as in forlorn; and 'away', 'off' or 'apart', as in forgive.

fore- a prefix meaning **1** 'before', as in forecast, foregoing and forefathers; **2** 'front', as in forehead, foreground.

-form a suffix meaning **1** 'having the form of', as in cruciform, meaning in the form of a cross; **2** 'having such a number of', as in uniform, multiform.

-ful a suffix indicating **1** the amount that fills something, as in handful, spoonful and bagful; **2** 'full of', as in beautiful, truthful and scornful; **3** 'having the qualities of', as in masterful; **4** 'apt to' or 'able to', as in forgetful and useful.

-free a suffix used to form adjectives indicating 'absence of' or 'freedom from', as in carefree, trouble-free, anxiety-free, tax-free, lead-free.

-friendly a modern suffix formed on analogy with user-friendly to mean 'helpful to' or 'supporting', as in child-friendly and environment-friendly.

-gate a modern suffix that is added to a noun to indicate something scandalous, often in politics. The suffix is derived from Watergate, and refers to a political scandal in the United States during President Richard Nixon's re-election campaign in 1972, when Republican agents were caught breaking into the headquarters of the Democratic Party in Washington, which were in a building called the Watergate Building. The uncovering of the attempts to cover up the break-in led to Richard Nixon's resignation.

geo- a prefix meaning 'earth', as in geography and geology.

-gram a suffix meaning **1** 'writing' or 'drawing', as in telegram, electrocardiogram and diagram; **2** used in modern usage to indicate a greeting or message, as in kissogram.

-graph a suffix meaning **1** 'written' or 'recorded', as in autograph, monograph, photograph; **2** 'an instrument that records', as in seismograph, tachograph and cardiograph.

gynaec-, gynaeco- a prefix meaning 'female' or 'woman', as in gynaecology.

-hand a suffix meaning **1** 'worker', as in deckhand, farmhand and cowhand; **2** 'position', as in right-hand.

haem-, haemo- a prefix meaning 'blood', as in haemorrhage and haematology.

hemi- a prefix meaning 'half', as in hemisphere.

hetero- a prefix meaning 'other', 'another' or 'different', as in heterosexual.

holo- a prefix meaning 'complete' or 'whole', as in holistic.

homo- a prefix meaning 'same', as in homogenous, homonym and homosexual.

-hood a suffix meaning 'state' or 'condition', as in babyhood, childhood, manhood, priesthood, womanhood and widowhood.

hydro- a prefix meaning 'water', as in hydro-electric and hydrophobia. It also means 'hydrogen', as in hydrochloride.

hyper- a prefix meaning 'over' or 'above', as in hyperactive, hypercritical and hypersensitive.

hypo- a prefix meaning 'under', as in hypothermia and hypodermic.

-ian a suffix indicating **1** a profession, job or pastime, as in comedian, musician, optician, physician; **2** proper names, as in Dickensian, Orwellian and Shakesperian.

-iana a suffix which is a form of form of **-ana** and indicates memorabilia or collections relating to people or places of note, as in Churchilliana.

-ible *see* **-able**.

-ics a suffix indicating 'science' or 'study', as in electronics, genetics, and politics.

-ify a suffix indicating 'making' or 'becoming', as in clarify, purify, satisfy and simplify.

infra- a prefix meaning 'below' or 'beneath', as in infrared and infrastructure.

-in a suffix meaning **1** 'in' or 'into', as in income, inside and invade; **2** 'not', as in incurable and incapable.

-ine a suffix indicating 'belonging to', as in canine, divine and feline.

-ing a suffix used to form the present participle of verbs, as in living, going and running.

inter- a prefix meaning 'between', as in intercity, intercontinental and interstate.

intra- a prefix meaning 'within', as in intravenous.

ise and **-ize** are both verb endings. In British English there are many verbs that can be spelt ending in either **-ise** or **-ize**, as in computerise/ize, economise/ize, finalise/ize, hospitalise/ize, modernise/ize, organise/ize, realise/ize, theorise/ize. There are a few verbs that cannot be spelt **-ize**. These include advertise, advise, comprise, despise, exercise, revise, supervise and televise.

-ish a suffix meaning **1** 'somewhat', as in baldish, smallish and youngish; **2** 'nationality', as in Spanish, Turkish and Polish.

-ism a suffix indicating **1** 'a state' or 'condition', as in conservatism, egotism and heroism, sometimes an 'abnormal state', as in alcoholism; **2** 'doctrine', 'theory' or 'system' of beliefs, as in Catholicism and Marxism; **3** 'discrimination' or 'prejudice', as in ageism, discrimination on the grounds of age, often against old or older people; classicism, discrimination on the grounds of social class; racism, discrimination on the grounds of race; and sexism, discrimination on the grounds of sex or gender, often against women.

iso- a prefix meaning 'equal', as in isobar and isosceles.

-ist a suffix indicating a believer, supporter or practitioner, as in atheist, fascist, feminist and Methodist.

-ite a suffix indicating a believer, supporter or practitioner, as in Thatcherite and Trotskyite.

-itis a suffix indicating an illness or disease, as in bronchitis, a disease of the chest and hepatitis, a disease of the liver.

-ize *see* **-ise**.

kilo- a prefix meaning 'a thousand', as in kilogram, kilohertz, kilolitre, kilometre and kilowatt.

-kin a suffix that indicates a diminutive or smaller version, as in lambkin and mannikin.

-kind a suffix indicating a group of people, as in humankind, mankind, womankind.

-less a suffix meaning **1** 'without' or 'lacking' added to nouns to form adjectives, as in expressionless, fearless, harmless, homeless and hopeless; **2** 'without being able to be measured', as in ageless, countless, priceless and timeless.

-let a suffix indicating a diminutive or smaller form of something, as in booklet, coverlet, droplet, islet, piglet, starlet and streamlet.

-like a suffix indicating similarity, as in childlike, dreamlike, lifelike and warlike.

-ling a suffix indicating a diminutive or smaller version of something, as in duckling, gosling and nestling.

-logue a suffix meaning 'conversation' or 'discussion', as in dialogue, monologue, prologue and travelogue.

-ly a common adverbial ending, as in hurriedly, sharply and tightly.

macro- a prefix meaning 'large in size or scope', as in macrobiotic, macrocosm and macrostructure.

-mania a suffix indicating abnormal or obsessive behaviour, as in kleptomania and pyromania.

mal- a prefix meaning **1** 'bad' or 'unpleasant', as in malodorous, having an unpleasant smell; **2** 'imperfect' or 'faulty', as in malformation and malfunctioning.

-man a suffix used with nouns to form nouns indicating someone's job, as in barman, chairman, policeman and salesman. Formerly, words ending in -man were often used whether or not the person referred to was definitely known to be a man. In modern usage, different ways have been found to avoid the sexism of -man; salesman has been changed in many cases to salesperson, chairman often becomes chairperson or chair; similarly, fireman has become fire-fighter and policeman frequently becomes police officer.

-mate a suffix referring to someone who shares something with someone, as in classmate, room, schoolmate, team-mate and workmate.

mega- a prefix meaning 'very large', as in megabucks and megastar. Many words using mega- in this way are modern and many are also informal or slang. In technical language mega- means 'a million times bigger than the unit to which it is attached', as in megabyte, megacycle, megahertz and megawatt.

meta- a prefix meaning 'alteration' or' transformation', as in metamorphosis.

-meter a suffix meaning 'a measuring instrument', as in altimeter, barometer, speedometer and thermometer.

-metre a suffix indicating metre, the unit of length, as in centimetre, kilometre and millimetre.

micro- a prefix meaning 'very small', as in microscope and microsurgery.

milli- a prefix meaning 'a thousand', as in millisecond and millennium.

mini- a prefix meaning 'very small' or 'least', as in minimum, minimal, and miniature. Mini- is frequently used to form modern words, as in minibus, minicab, mini-computer, mini-cruise and miniskirt. Modern words beginning with mini- can often be spelt either with a hyphen or without.

mis- a prefix meaning 'badly' or 'wrongly', as in misbehave, miscalculate, mistreat and misunderstanding.

-monger a suffix meaning 'dealer' or 'trader', as in fishmonger and ironmonger. As well as being used for occupations in which people sell things, it is used for people who 'trade' in less tangible things, as in gossipmonger, rumourmonger, scaremonger and warmonger.

mono- a prefix meaning 'one' or 'single', as in monochrome, monologue, monoplane and monosyllabic.

multi- a prefix meaning 'many', as in multiply and multitude. Multi- is frequently used to form new modern words, as in multi-media, multi-purpose, multi-storey and multi-talented.

-naut a suffix meaning 'navigator', as in astronaut.

neo- a prefix meaning 'new' or 'recent', as in neologism and neonatal.

neuro- a prefix meaning 'nerve', as in neurology, neuron and neurosurgery.

non- a prefix meaning 'not', as in nonsense and nonconformist.

-ock a suffix indicating a diminutive form, as in hillock and bullock.

-ocracy a suffix indicating a form of government, as in democracy, bureaucracy and meritocracy.

-ology a suffix meaning 'study of', as in biology and geology.

oholic *see* **-aholic**.

-ology a suffix meaning 'study o'f, as in biology, geology and technology.

omni- a prefix meaning 'all', as in omnipotent and omnivorous.

-osis a suffix indicating **1** a disease, as in tuberculosis; **2** a development or process, as in metamorphosis, a complete or major change.

para- a prefix meaning **1** 'beside', as in paramilitary, paramedic and paranormal; **2** '(defence) against', as in parasol and parapet.

pen- a prefix meaning 'almost', as in peninsula and penultimate.

per- a prefix meaning 'through', as in permit.

peri- a prefix meaning 'round', as in perimeter and periphery.

-phile a suffix indicating someone who loves or likes someone or something very much, as in Francophile, someone who loves France, and bibliophile, someone who loves books.

-phobe a suffix indicating someone who hates or fears someone or something very much, as in Europhobe and Francophobe. The condition has the suffix **-phobia**, as in Europhobia, and there is a whole range of conditions of this kind, as in claustrophobia, hatred or fear of enclosed spaces.

-phone a suffix meaning 'sound' or 'voice', as in megaphone, telephone and saxophone.

poly- a prefix meaning 'more than one' or 'many', as in polyandry, the practice of having more than one husband.

-person *see* **-man**.

post- a prefix meaning 'after', as in postpone, postscript and post-war.

pre- a prefix meaning 'before', as in precede, predict and preface.

pro- a prefix meaning **1** 'on' or 'forth', as in proceed and progress; **2** 'before', as in prologue and prophet; **3** 'in favour of', as in pro-British and pro-hunting.

pseudo- a prefix meaning 'false', 'spurious' or 'sham', as in pseudo-literary and pseudo-leather.

psych-, psycho- meaning 'mind', as in psychiatry and psychology.

re- a prefix meaning **1** 'back', as in return, resign and retract; **2** 'again', as in reconsider and retrial.

retro- a prefix meaning 'back' or 'backwards', as in retrograde, retrospect and retrorocket.

semi- a prefix meaning 'half', as in semicircle and semi-detached.

-ship a suffix indicating a state or quality, as in friendship, hardship and leadership

sub- a prefix meaning 'under', as in submarine, submerge and subconscious.

super- a prefix meaning 'over', as in supervise, supernatural and superfluous.

syn- a prefix meaning 'together', as in synthesis and synonym

techno- a prefix meaning 'craft' or 'skill', as in technical and technology.

tele- a prefix meaning 'distance', as in telephone, telescope and television.

-tor a prefix indicating a person, especially a person who does something, as in actor, sponsor and victor.

trans- a prefix meaning 'across', as in transaction, translate and trans-Atlantic.

-trix a prefix indicating a female equivalent, as in proprietrix of proprietor, now not very common.

un- a prefix indicating **1** not, as in unclean, untrue and unwise; **2** back or reversal, as in undo, unfasten and untie.

uni- a prefix meaning 'one', as in unicycle, unilateral and unity.

vice- a prefix meaning 'in place of', as in vice-president and vice-chancellor.

-ward, -wards a suffix indicating direction, as in homeward, seaward and outwards.

-ware a suffix meaning 'manufactured goods', as in glassware and silverware.

-ways a suffix indicating manner, way or direction, as in sideways.

-wise a suffix indicating **1** manner, way, or direction as in clockwise, lengthwise and otherwise; **2** with reference to, as in careerwise; **3** clever or sensible, as in streetwise.

-work a suffix indicating **1** material from which something is made, as in ironwork and woodwork; **2** a job or activity, as in farmwork, housework and needlework.

Homographs, Homonyms and Homophones

Homographs

A homograph is a word that is spelt the same as another word but has a different meaning and pronunciation. Some examples are:

bow, pronounced to rhyme with how, a verb meaning to bend the head or body as a sign of respect or in greeting, etc, as in 'The visitors bowed to the emperor' and 'The mourners bowed their heads as the coffin was lowered into the grave'.

bow, pronounced to rhyme with low, a noun meaning a looped knot, a ribbon tied in this way, as in 'She tied her hair in a bow' and 'She wears blue bows in her hair'.

lead, pronounced leed, a verb meaning to show the way, as in 'The guide will lead you down the mountain'.

lead, pronounced led, a noun meaning a type of greyish metal, as in 'They are going to remove any water pipes made from lead'.

row, pronounced to rhyme with low, a noun meaning a number of people or things arranged in a line, as in 'The princess sat in the front row'.

row, pronounced to rhyme with how, a noun meaning a quarrel, a disagreement, as in 'He has had a row with his neighbour over repairs to the garden wall'.

slough, pronounced to rhyme with rough, a verb meaning to cast off, as in 'The snake had sloughed off its old skin'.

slough, pronounced to rhyme with how, a noun meaning a swamp, as in 'get bogged down in a slough' and 'in the Slough of Despond'.

sow, pronounced to rhyme with low, a verb meaning to scatter seeds in the earth, as in 'In the spring, the gardener sowed some flower seeds in the front garden'.

sow, pronounced to rhyme with how, a noun meaning a female pig, as in 'The sow is in the pigsty with her piglets'.

Homonyms

A homonym is a word that has the same spelling and the same pronunciation as another word but has a different meaning from it. Examples include:

bill, a noun meaning a written statement of money owed, as in 'You must pay the bill for the conversion work immediately', or a written or printed advertisement, as in 'We were asked to deliver handbills advertising the play'.

bill, a noun meaning a bird's beak, as in 'The seagull has injured its bill'.

fair, an adjective meaning attractive, as in 'fair young women'; light in colour, as in 'She has fair hair'; fine, not raining, as in 'I hope it keeps fair'; just, free from prejudice, as in 'We felt that the referee came to a fair decision'.

fair, a noun meaning a market held regularly in the same place, often with stalls, entertainments and rides (now often simply applying to an event with entertainments and rides without the market), as in 'He won a coconut at the fair'; a trade exhibition, as in 'the Frankfurt Book Fair'.

pulse, a noun meaning the throbbing caused by the contractions of the heart, as in 'The patient has a weak pulse'.

pulse, a noun meaning the edible seeds of any of various crops of the pea family, as lentils, peas and beans, as in 'Vegetarians eat a lot of food made with pulses'.

row, a verb, pronounced to rhyme with low, meaning to propel a boat by means of oars, as in 'He plans to row across the Atlantic single-handed'.

row, a noun, pronounced to rhyme with low, meaning a number of people or things arranged in a line, as in 'We tried to get into the front row to watch the procession'.

Homophones

A homophone is a word that is pronounced in the same way as another but is spelt in a different way and has a different meaning. Examples include:

aisle, a noun meaning a passage between rows of seats in a church, theatre, cinema etc, as in 'The bride walked down the aisle on her father's arm'.

isle, a noun meaning an island, as in 'the Isle of Wight'.

alter, a verb meaning to change, as in 'They have had to alter their plans'.

altar, a noun meaning the table on which the bread and wine are consecrated for Communion in the Christian church, and which serves as the centre of worship, as in 'The priest moved to the altar, from where he dispensed Communion' and 'There is a holy painting above the altar'; or a raised structure on which sacrifices are made or incense burned in worship, as in 'The Druids made human sacrifices on the altar of their gods'.

ail, a verb meaning to be ill, as in 'The old woman is ailing'; or to be the matter, to be wrong, as in 'What ails you?'

ale, a noun meaning a kind of beer, as in 'a pint of foaming ale'.

blew, a verb, the past tense of the verb to blow, as in 'They blew the trumpets loudly'.

blue, a noun and adjective meaning a colour of the shade of a clear sky, as in 'She wore a blue dress'.

boar, a noun meaning a male pig, as in 'a dish made with wild boar'.

bore, a verb meaning to make tired and uninterested, as in 'The audience was obviously bored by the rather academic lecture'.

bore, a verb, the past tense of the verb to bear, as in 'They bore their troubles lightly'.

cereal, a noun meaning a plant yielding grain suitable for food, as in 'countries which grow cereal crops' and a prepared food made with grain, as in 'We often have cereal for breakfast'.

serial, a noun meaning a story or television play which is published or appears in regular parts, as in 'the final instalment of the magazine serial that she was following'.

cite, a verb meaning to quote or mention by way of example or proof, as in 'The lawyer cited a previous case to try and get his client off'.

sight, a noun meaning the act of seeing, as in 'They recognized him at first sight'.

site, a noun meaning a location, place, as in 'They have found a site for the new factory'.

feat, a noun meaning a notable act or deed, as in 'The old man received an award for his courageous feat'.

feet, a noun, the plural form of foot, as in 'The child got her feet wet from wading in the puddle'.

none, a pronoun meaning not any, as in 'They are demanding money but we have none'.

nun, a noun meaning a woman who joins a religious order and takes vows of poverty, chastity and obedience, as in 'She gave up the world to become a nun'.

know, a verb meaning to have understanding or knowledge of, as in 'He is the only one who knows the true facts of the situation', and to be acquainted with, as in 'I met her once but I don't really know her'.

no, an adjective meaning not any, as in 'We have no food left'.

rite, a noun meaning a ceremonial act or words, as in 'rites involving witchcraft'.

right, an adjective meaning correct, as in 'Very few people gave the right answer to the question'.

write a verb meaning to form readable characters, as in 'He writes regularly for the newspapers'.

stare, a verb meaning to look fixedly and a noun meaning a fixed gaze, as in 'She stared at him in disbelief when he told her the news' and 'He has the stare of a basilisk'.

stair, a noun meaning a series of flights of stairs, as in 'The old lady is too feeble to climb the stairs to her bedroom'.

Eponyms

An **eponym** is the name of a place or a thing that is called after a real or mythical person. It can also refer to the name of the person after whom something is named. English has many eponymous words, a selection of which is given below:

ampere the standard metric unit by which an electric current is measured, called after the French physicist André Marie Ampère, (1775–1836).

atlas a book of maps, called after Atlas, leader of the Titans in Greek mythology, who attempted to storm the heavens, and for this supreme treason was condemned by Zeus to hold up the vault of heaven on his head and hands for the rest of his life. The geographer, Gerardus Mercator (*see* **Mercator projection**), used the figure of Atlas bearing the globe as a frontispiece in his 16th-century collection of maps and charts.

aubrietia a trailing purple-flowered perennial plant, called after Claude Aubriet (1665–1742), a French painter of animals and flowers.

Bailey bridge a type of temporary military bridge that can be assembled very quickly, called after Sir Donald Bailey (1901–85), the English engineer who invented it.

baud a unit used in measuring telecommunications transmission speed denoting the number of discrete signal elements that can be transmitted per second, called after the French telecommunications pioneer, Jean M. Baudot (1845–1903).

Beaufort scale an international scale of wind velocities ranging from 0 (calm) to 12 (hurricane), called after Admiral Sir Francis Beaufort (1774–1857), the British surveyor who devised it.

becquerel the standard metric unit of radioactivity, defined as decay per second, called after the French physicist Antoine-Henri Becquerel (1852–1908), who began the study of radioactivity.

begonia a genus of tropical plants cultivated for their showy petalless flowers and ornamental lopsided succulent leaves, called after Michel Begon (1638–1710), a French patron of botany.

Belisha beacon a flashing light in an orange globe at the top of a post that marks a road crossing for pedestrians, called after the British politician, Leslie Hore-Belisha (1893–1957).

Biro™ a type of ball-point pen, called after its Hungarian-born inventor, Laszlo Jozsef Biro (1900–85).

bloomers a woman's underpants with full, loose legs gathered at the knee, called after the American social reformer, Amelia Jenks Bloomer (1818–94).

bougainvillea a genus of tropical plants with large rosy or purple bracts, called after the French navigator, Louis Antoine de Bougainville (1729–1811).

bowdlerize to remove what are considered to be indecent or indelicate words or passages from a book, called after the British doctor, Thomas Bowdler (1754–1825), who produced an expurgated edition of Shakespeare.

bowie knife a type of hunting knife with a long curving blade, called after the American soldier and adventurer, James Bowie (1799–1836), who made it popular.

boycott to refuse to deal or trade with a person, organization, etc, in order to punish or coerce them, called after the Irish land agent, Captain Charles Cunningham Boycott (1832–97), who was accorded such treatment after refusing to reduce rents.

Boyle's law the scientific principle that the pressure of a gas varies inversely with its volume at constant temperature, called after the Irish-born British physicist, Robert Boyle (1627–91), who formulated it.

Braille the system of printing for the blind using a system of raised dots that can be understood by touch, called after the blind French musician, Louis Braille (1809–52), who invented it.

Brownian motion the random movement of minute particles suspended in a fluid, caused by the bombardment of the particles by molecules of the fluid, called after the Scottish botanist Robert Brown (1773–1858), who first discovered the phenomenon in 1827.

buddleia a genus of shrubs and trees with lilac or yellowish-white flowers, called after Adam Buddle (d.1715), English clergyman and botanist.

Bunsen burner a burner with an adjustable air inlet that mixes gas and air to produce a smokeless flame of great heat, called after the German scientist, Robert Wilhelm Bunsen (1811–99), who invented it.

camellia a genus of oriental evergreen ornamental shrubs, called after the Moravian Jesuit missionary, George Joseph Kamel (1661–1706), who introduced it to Europe.

cardigan a knitted jacket fastened with buttons, called after James Thomas Brudenell, 7th Earl of Cardigan (1797–1868), who was fond of wearing such a garment. He was the British cavalry officer who led the Charge of the Light Brigade at Balaklava during the Crimean War (1854).

Celsius the scale of temperature in which 0° is the freezing point of water and 100° the boiling point, called after Anders Celsius (1701–44), the Swedish astronomer and scientist who invented it.

chauvinism an aggressive patriotism, called after Nicolas Chauvin of Rochefort, a 19th-century French soldier in Napoleon's army, and now used to apply to excessive devotion to a belief or case, especially a man's belief in the superiority of men over women.

clerihew a four-line verse consisting of two rhymed couplets of variable length, often encapsulating an unreliable biographical anecdote, called after the English writer, Edmund Clerihew Bentley (1875–1956), who invented it.

coulomb the standard metric unit for measuring electric charge, called after the French physicist, Charles Augustin de Coulomb (1736–1806).

dahlia a genus of half-hardy herbaceous perennial plants of the aster family grown for its colourful blooms, called after the Swedish botanist, Anders Dahl (1751–89).

daltonism colour blindness, especially the confusion between green and red, called after the British chemist and physicist, John Dalton (1766–1844), who first described it.

Darwinism the theory of evolution by natural selection, called after the British naturalist, Charles Robert Darwin (1809–82), who first described the theory.

Davy lamp a safety lamp used by miners to detect combustible gas, called after the English chemist, Sir Humphry Davy (1778–1829), who invented it.

degauss to neutralize or remove a magnetic field, called after the German mathematician, Karl Friedrich Gauss (1777–1855). *See also* **gauss**.

derrick now any crane-like apparatus but formerly a word for a gallows, called after a 17th-century English hangman at Tyburn with the surname of Derrick.

diesel an internal-combustion engine in which ignition is produced by the heat of highly compressed air, called after the German engineer, Rudolf Diesel (1858–1913), who invented it.

Doberman pinscher a breed of dog with a smooth glossy black and tan coat and docked tail, called after the German dog breeder, Ludwig Dobermann (1834–94), who first bred it.

Dolby™ an electronic noise-reduction system used in sound recording and playback systems, called after the American engineer, R. Dolby (1933–), who invented it.

Don Quixote a chivalrous or romantic person who tends to be carried away by his ideals and notions, called after Don Quixote, hero of the novel *Don Quixote de la Mancha* by the Spanish novelist Miguel de Cervantes Saavedra (1547–1616). *See also* **quixotic**.

Doppler effect *or* **Doppler shift** a change in the observed frequency of a wave as a result of the relative motion between the wave source and the detector, called after the Austrian physicist, Christian Johann Doppler (1803–53).

draconian an adjective meaning very cruel or severe, called after Draco, the 7th-century BC Athenian statesman who formulated extremely harsh laws.

dunce a person who is stupid or slow to learn, called after the Scottish theologian, John Duns Scotus (*c*.1265–1308).

Earl Grey a blend of Chinese teas flavoured with oil of bergamot, called after the British statesman, Charles, 2nd Earl Grey (1764–1845).

Eiffel Tower the tall tower in the centre of Paris, called after the French engineer, Alexandre Gustave Eiffel (1832–1923), who built it.

einsteinium an artificial radioactive chemical element, called after the German-born American physicist, Albert Einstein (1879–1955).

Everest the highest mountain in the world, called after Sir George Everest (1790–1866), Surveyor-General of India.

Fallopian tube either of the two tubes through which the egg cells pass from the ovary to the uterus in female mammals, called after the Italian anatomist, Gabriel Fallopius (1523–62), who first described them.

Fahrenheit the scale of temperatures in which 32° is the freezing point of water and 212° the boiling point, called after the German scientist, Gabriel Daniel Fahrenheit (1686–1736), who invented it.

farad the standard metric unit of capacitance, called after the English physicist and chemist, Michael Faraday (1791–1867), who discovered magnetic induction.

fermi a unit of length employed in nuclear physics, called after the Italian-born American physicist, Enrico Fermi (1901–54).

fermium an artificially produced radioactive element, also called after physicist, Enrico Fermi (1901–54).

forsythia a genus of widely cultivated yellow-flowered ornamental shrubs of the olive family, called after the English botanist, William Forsyth (1737–1804).

Fraunhofer lines dark lines that occur in the continuous spectrum of the sun, called after the German physicist and optician, Joseph von Fraunhofer (1787–1826).

freesia a type of sweet-smelling ornamental flower of the iris family, called after the German physician, Friedrich Heinrich Theodor Freese (d. 1876).

fuchsia a genus of decorative shrubs of Central and South America, called after the German botanist and physician, Leonhard Fuchs (1501–66).

Gallup Poll a sampling of public opinion, especially to help forecast the outcome of an election, called after the American statistician, George Horace Gallup (1901–84), who devised it.

galvanize to coat one type of metal with another more reactive metal, e.g. iron or steel coated with zinc, to protect the underlying metal; now also meaning to stimulate into action, called after the Italian physiologist, Luigi Galvani (1737–98).

gardenia a genus of ornamental tropical trees and shrubs with fragrant white or yellow flowers, called after the Scottish-born American botanist, Dr Alexander Garden (1730–91).

garibaldi a type of biscuit with a layer of currants in it, called after Giuseppe Garibaldi (1807–82), the Italian soldier patriot who is said to have enjoyed such biscuits.

gauss a standard unit for measuring magnetic flux density, called after the German mathematician, Karl Friedrich Gauss (1777–1855), who developed the theory of numbers and applied mathematics to electricity, magnetism and astronomy. *See also* **degauss**.

Geiger counter an electronic instrument that can detect and measure radiation, called after the German physicist, Hans Geiger (1882–1945), who developed it.

gerrymander to rearrange the boundaries of a voting district to favour a particular party or candidate, called after the American politician, Elbridge Gerry (1744–1814).

Granny Smith a variety of hard green apple, called after the Australian gardener, Maria Ann Smith or Granny Smith (d.1870), who first grew the apple in Sydney in the 1860s.

greengage a type of greenish plum, called after Sir William Gage (1777–1864), who introduced it into Britain from France.

guillotine an instrument for beheading people, called after Joseph Ignace Guillotin (1738–1814), French physician, who advocated its use in the French Revolution.

Halley's comet a periodic comet that appears about every 76 years, called after the British astronomer, Edmund Halley (1656–1742), who calculated its orbit.

Heath Robinson of or pertaining to an absurdly complicated design for a simple mechanism, called after the English artist, William Heath Robinson (1872–1944).

henry a metric unit of electric inductance, called after the American physicist, Joseph Henry (1797–1878), who discovered the principle of electromagnetic induction.

Herculean of extraordinary strength, size or difficulty, called after Hercules or Heracles, the son of Zeus in Greek mythology and best known for completing twelve difficult tasks known as the labours of Hercules.

Hoover™ a kind of vacuum cleaner, called after the American businessman, William Henry Hoover (1849–1932).

Jacuzzi™ a device that swirls water in a bath and massages the body, called after the Italian-born engineer, Candido Jacuzzi (*c*.1903–86).

JCB™ a mechanical digger that has a hydraulically powered shovel and an excavator arm, called after its English manufacturer, Joseph Cyril Bamford (1916–2001).

joule the metric unit of all energy measurements, called after the British physicist, James Prescott Joule (1818–89), who investigated the relationship between mechanical, electrical and heat energy.

kelvin the metric unit of thermodynamic temperature, called after the Scottish physicist, William Thomson, 1st Baron Kelvin (1824–1907).

Köchel number a number in a catalogue of the works of Mozart, called after the Austrian scientist, Ludwig Alois Friedrich von Köchel (1800–1877), a great admirer of Mozart, who compiled his catalogue in 1862.

leotard a one-piece, close-fitting garment worn by acrobats and dancers, called after the French acrobat, Jules Leotard (1842–70), who introduced the costume as a circus garment.

listeria a bacterium that causes a serious form of food poisoning, listeriosis, called after the British surgeon, Joseph Lister (1827–1912), who pioneered the use of antiseptics.

lobelia a genus of flowers that produce showy blue, red, yellow or white flowers, called after the Flemish botanist, Matthias de Lobel (1538–1616).

loganberry a hybrid plant developed from the blackberry and the red raspberry that produces large sweet purplish-red berries, called after the American lawyer and horticulturist, James Harvey Logan (1841–1928), who first grew it in 1881.

Luddite any opponent of industrial change and innovation, called after Ned Ludd, an 18th-century British labourer opposed to mechanization, who with others destroyed industrial machinery during riots between 1811 and 1816.

macadam a road surface composed of successive layers of small stones compacted into a solid mass, called after the Scottish engineer, John Loudon McAdam, (1756–1836), who invented it.

Machiavellian cunning, deceitful, double-dealing, using opportunist methods, called after the Florentine statesman and political theorist, Niccolò Machiavelli (1469–1527), author of *The Prince*.

Mach number the ratio of the speed of a body in a particular medium to the speed of sound in the same medium, called after the Austrian physicist and philosopher, Ernst Mach (1838–1916), who devised it.

mackintosh a type of raincoat, especially one made of rubberized cloth, called after the Scottish chemist, Charles Macintosh (1760–1843), who patented it in the early 1820s.

malapropism the unintentional misuse of a word by confusing it with another and so producing a ridiculous effect (e.g. "She is as headstrong as an allegory on the banks of the Nile"), called after Mrs Malaprop, a character in the play *The Rivals* (1775), by the Irish playwright Richard Brinsley Sheridan (1751–1816).

martinet a person who exerts strong discipline, called after Jean Martinet (d.1672), a French army drill master during the reign of Louis XIV.

maverick a stray animal or an independent-minded or unorthodox person, called after the American rancher in Texas, Samuel Augustus Maverick (1803–70), who refused to brand his cattle.

Melba sauce a sauce that is made from raspberries called after the Australian operatic singer Dame Nellie Melba [Helen Porter Mitchell] (1861–1931), for whom it was made. *See also* **Melba toast, peach melba**.

Melba toast bread that is thinly sliced and toasted, called after the Australian operatic singer Dame Nellie Melba [Helen Porter Mitchell] (1861–1931), for whom it was made. *See also* **Melba sauce, peach melba**.

Mercator projection a type of projection for the drawing of maps two-dimensionally, called after the Flemish geographer, Gerardus Mercator [Gerhard Kremer] (1512–94).

mesmerize to hypnotize or to fascinate or spellbind, called after the Austrian physician and pioneer of hypnotism, Franz Anton Mesmer (1734–1815).

Molotov cocktail a kind of crude incendiary weapon made by filling a bottle with petrol and inserting a short-delay wick or fuse, called after the Soviet statesman Vyacheslav Mikhailovich Molotov (1890–1986).

Montessori method a system of educating very young children through play, based on free discipline, with each child developing at his or her own pace, called after Maria Montessori (1870–1952), the Italian physicist and educator who developed it.

Moog synthesizer™ a type of synthesizer for producing music electronically, called after Robert Arthur Moog (1934–2005), the American physicist and engineer who developed it.

Morse code a code in which letters are represented by dots and dashes or long and short sounds and are transmitted by visual or audible signals, called after the American artist and inventor, Samuel Finley Breese Morse (1791–1872), who invented it.

narcissism excessive interest in one's own body or self, self-love, called after Narcissus, a handsome young man in Greek mythology who was punished for his coldness of heart (in not returning the love of Echo) by being made to fall in love with his own reflection in water and who pined away because he was unable to embrace himself.

newton the standard metric unit of force, called after the British physicist and mathematician, Sir Isaac Newton (1642–1727).

Nobel prizes prizes that are generally awarded annually and are given for outstanding contributions to physics, chemistry, physiology and medicine, economics, literature, and the promotion of peace, called after the Swedish chemist and engineer, Alfred Nobel (1833–96), whose will instituted the prizes.

ohm a metric unit of electrical resistance, called after the German physicist, Georg Simon Ohm (1787–1854).

Pareto principle an economic principle that 80% of the sales may come from 20% of the customers, called after the Italian economist and sociologist, Vilfredo Pareto (1848–1923).

Parkinson's disease a progressive nervous disease resulting in tremor, muscular rigidity, partial paralysis and weakness, called after the British surgeon, James Parkinson (1755–1824), who first described it.

Parkinson's law the law that states that work expands to fill the time available for its completion, called after the British historian and author, Cyril Northcote Parkinson (1909–93), who devised it.

pasteurize to sterilize drink or food by heat or radiation in order to destroy bacteria, called after the French chemist and bacteriologist, Louis Pasteur (1822–95).

pavlova a dessert of meringue cake with a topping of cream and fruit, called after the Russian ballerina, Anna Pavlova (1885–1931), for whom it was made.

peach melba a dessert of peaches, ice cream and Melba sauce, called after the Australian operatic soprano singer, Dame Nellie Melba [Helen Porter Mitchell] (1861–1931), for whom it was made. *See, also* **Melba sauce, Melba toast**.

Peter principle the principle that in a hierarchy every employee tends to rise to the level of his or her incompetence, called after the Canadian educator, Laurence J. Peter (1919–90), who formulated it.

Peter's projection a form of projection for depicting the countries of the world two-dimensionally, called after German historian, Dr Arno Peters (1916–), who devised it.

platonic of a close relationship between two people, spiritual and free from physical desire, called after the Greek philosopher, Plato (*c*.427–347 BC).

plimsoll a type of light rubber-soled canvas shoe, called after Samuel Plimsoll (*see* **Plimsoll line**) because the upper edge of the rubber was thought to resemble the Plimsoll line.

Plimsoll line the set of markings on the side of a ship that indicate the levels to which the ship may be safely be loaded, called after the English shipping reform leader, Samuel Plimsoll (1824–98).

poinsettia a South American evergreen plant, widely cultivated at Christmas for its red bracts, which resemble petals, called after the American diplomat, Joel Roberts Poinsett (1779–1851), who introduced it into the USA.

praline a type of confectionery made from nuts and sugar, called after Count Plessis-Praslin (1598–1675), a French field marshal, whose chef is said to have been the first person to make the sweet.

Pulitzer prizes a series of prizes that are awarded annually for outstanding achievement in American journalism, literature, and music, called after the Hungarian-born US newspaper publisher, Joseph Pulitzer (1847–1911).

Pullman a railway carriage that offers luxury accommodation, called after the American inventor, George Mortimer Pullman (1831–97), who first manufactured them.

quisling a traitor who aids an invading enemy to regularize its conquest of his or her country, called after the Norwegian politician, Vidkun Abraham Quisling (1887–1945), who collaborated with the Nazis in World War II.

quixotic, quixotical of a person, chivalrous or romantic to extravagance, unrealistically idealistic, called after Don Quixote, hero of the novel *Don Quixote de la Mancha* by the Spanish novelist, Miguel de Cervantes Saavedra (1547–1616).

rafflesia a genus of parasitic Asian leafless plants, called after the British colonial administrator, Sir Thomas Stamford Raffles (1781–1826), who discovered it.

raglan a type of loose sleeve cut in one piece with the shoulder of a garment, called after the British field marshal,, Fitzroy James Henry Somerset, 1st Baron Raglan (1788–1855).

Richter scale a scale ranging from 1 to 10 for measuring the intensity of an earthquake, called after the American seismologist, Charles Richter (1900–85), who devised it.

Romeo a romantic lover, called after Romeo, the hero of Shakespeare's tragedy *Romeo and Juliet*.

Rorschach test a personality test in which the subject has to interpret a series of unstructured ink blots, called after the Swiss psychiatrist, Hermann Rorschach (1884–1922), who devised it.

Rubik cube *or* **Rubik's cube** a puzzle that consists of a cube of six colours with each face divided into nine small squares, eight of which can rotate around a central square, called after the Hungarian designer, Erno Rubik (1944–), who invented it.

rutherford a unit of radioactivity, called after the British physicist, Ernest Rutherford, 1st Baron Rutherford (1871–1937).

sadism sexual pleasure obtained from inflicting cruelty upon another, called after the French soldier and writer, Count Donatien Alphonse François de Sade, known as the Marquis de Sade (1740–1814).

salmonella the bacteria that cause some diseases such as food poisoning, called after Daniel Elmer Salmon (1850–1914), the American veterinary surgeon who identified it.

sandwich a snack consisting of two pieces of buttered bread with a filling, called after John Montagu, 4th Earl of Sandwich (1718–92), who was such a compulsive gambler that he would not leave the gaming tables to eat but had some cold beef between two slices of bread brought to him.

saxophone a type of keyed brass instrument often used in jazz music, called after Adolphe Sax (1814–94), the Belgian instrument-maker who invented it.

sequoia one of two lofty coniferous Californian trees, called after the American Indian leader and scholar, Sequoya (*c*.1770–1843), also known as George Guess.

shrapnel an explosive projectile that contains bullets or fragments of metal and a charge that is exploded before impact, called after the British army officer, Henry Shrapnel (1761–1842), who invented it.

siemens the standard metric unit of electrical conductance, called after the German engineer and inventor, Ernst Werner von Siemens (1816–92).

silhouette the outline of a shape against light or a lighter background, called after the French politician, Étienne de Silhouette (1709–67).

simony the buying or selling of ecclesiastical benefits or offices, called after the sorcerer Simon Magnus, who lived in the 1st century AD.

sousaphone the large tuba that encircles the body of the player and has a forward-facing bell, called after the American bandmaster and composer, John Philip Sousa (1854–1932), who invented it.

spoonerism the accidental transposition of the initial letters or opening syllables of two or more words, often with an amusing effect (e.g. "queer old dean" for "dear old queen"), called after the British scholar and clergyman, William Archibald Spooner (1844–1930).

stetson a type of wide-brimmed, high-crowned felt hat, called after its designer, the American hat-maker, John Batterson Stetson (1830–1906).

tantalize to tease or torment by presenting something greatly desired but keeping it inaccessible, called after Tantalus, the mythical Greek king of Phrygia, who was punished in Hades for his misdeeds by being forced to stand in water that receded when he tried to drink and under fruit that moved away as he tried to eat.

tontine a financial arrangement in which a group of subscribers contribute equally to a prize that is eventually awarded to the last survivor, called after the Italian banker, Lorenzo Tonti (1635–90), who devised it.

tradescantia a genus of flowering plants cultivated for their foliage, called after the English botanist, gardener and plant hunter, John Tradescant (*c*.1570–1638).

trilby a type of soft felt hat with an indented crown, called after *Trilby*, the dramatized version of the novel by the English writer, George du Maurier. The heroine of the play, Trilby O'Ferral, wore such a hat.

Turing machine a hypothetical universal computing machine, called after the British mathematician, Alan Mathison Turing (1912–54), who conceived it.

Venn diagram a diagram in which overlapping circles are used to show the mathematical and logical relationships between sets, called after the British mathematician and logician, John Venn (1834–1923).

volt the metric unit of the force of an electrical current, called after the Italian physicist, Count Alessandro Volta (1745–1827).

Wankel engine a kind of four-stroke internal-combustion engine with a triangular-shaped rotating piston within an elliptical combustion chamber, called after the German engineer, Felix Wankel (1902–88), who invented it.

watt a metric unit of electrical power, called after the Scottish engineer and inventor, James Watt (1736–1819).

wellington a waterproof rubber boot with no fastenings that extends to the knee, called after Arthur Wellesley, 1st Duke of Wellington (1769–1852), the British soldier who defeated Napoleon at Waterloo (1815).

wisteria *or* **wistaria** a genus of purple-flowered climbing plants, called after the American anatomist, Caspar Wistar (1761–1818).

Zeppelin a rigid cigar-shaped airship, called after the German general and aeronautical pioneer, Count Ferdinand von Zeppelin (1838–1917), who designed and manufactured them.

Idioms

Idioms are English as it is spoken every day, and their conventions and phraseology have become established through use. An idiom can be defined as a form of expression peculiar to a language, especially one having a significance other than its literal meaning. The many examples of English idioms given below are presented under a variety of topic headings that have been alphabetized for easy access.

A

- **A1** first class, of the highest quality. <A1 is the highest rating given to the condition of ships for Lloyd's Register, Lloyds of London being a major insurance company>.
- **from A to Z** thoroughly, comprehensively.

above
- **above board** open, honest and without trickery. <Card cheats tend to keep their cards under the table, or board>.
- **above (someone's) head** too difficult to understand.
- **get a bit above oneself** to become very vain or conceited.

accident
- **accidents will happen** things go wrong at some time in everyone's life.
- **a chapter of accidents** a series of misfortunes.

account
- **give a good account of oneself** to do well.

ace
- **within an ace of** very close to. <From the game of dice, ace being the term for the side of a dice with one spot>.

Achilles
- **Achilles' heel** the one weak spot in a person. <Achilles, the legendary Greek hero, is said to have been dipped in the River Styx by his mother at birth to make him invulnerable but his heel, by which she was holding him, remained unprotected and he was killed by an arrow through his heel>.

acid
- **acid test** a test that will prove or disprove something conclusively. <From the use of nitric acid to ascertain whether a metal was gold or not. If it was not gold the acid decomposed it>.

across
- **across the board** applying to everyone or to all cases.

act
- **act of God** a happening, usually sudden and unexpected, for which no human can be held responsible.
- **get in on the act** to become involved in some profitable or advantageous activity, especially an activity related to someone else's success.
- **get one's act together** to get organized.

action
- **action stations** a state of preparedness for some activity. <From positions taken up by soldiers in readiness for battle>.
- **get a piece** *or* **slice of the action** to be involved in something, get a share of something.

ad
- **ad hoc** for a particular (usually exclusive) purpose. <Latin, 'to this'>.
- **ad-lib** to speak without preparation, to improvise. <Latin, 'according to pleasure'>.

Adam <Refers to the biblical Adam>.
- **Adam's ale** water.
- **not to know (someone) from Adam** not to recognize (someone).
- **the old Adam in us** the sin or evil that is in everyone.

add
- **add fuel to the fire** to make a difficult situation worse.
- **add insult to injury** to make matters worse.

Adonis
- **an Adonis** a very attractive young man. <In Greek legend Adonis was a beautiful young man who was loved by Aphrodite, the goddess of love, and who was killed by a boar while hunting>.

aegis
- **under the aegis of (someone)** with the support or backing of (someone). <In Greek legend Aegis was the shield of the god Zeus>.

after
- **after a fashion** in a manner that is barely adequate.
- **after (someone's) own heart** to one's liking; liked or admired by (someone).

against
- **against the clock** in a hurry to get something done before a certain time.
- **be up against it** to be in a difficult or dangerous situation.

age
- **a golden age** a time of great achievement.
- **a ripe old age** a very old age.
- **of a certain age** no longer young.

agony

- **agony aunt** *or* **uncle** a woman or man who gives advice on personal problems either in a newspaper or magazine column, or on television or radio.
- **agony column** a newspaper or magazine column in which readers write in with their problems, which are answered by the agony aunt or uncle. <Originally a newspaper column containing advertisements for missing relatives and friends>.

ahead

- **ahead of the game** in an advantageous position; in front of one's rivals.
- **streets ahead of (someone** *or* **something)** much better than (someone or something).

air

- **air** *or* **wash one's dirty linen in public** to discuss private or personal matters in public.
- **clear the air** to make a situation less tense by settling disagreements.
- **hot air** boasting; empty or meaningless words.
- **into thin air** seemingly into nowhere.
- **put on airs** to behave as though one were superior to others, to act in a conceited way.
- **up in the air** uncertain, undecided.
- **walk on air** to be very happy.

Aladdin

- **Aladdin's cave** a place full of valuable or desirable objects. <From the tale of Aladdin in the Arabian Nights who gained access to such a cave with the help of the genie from his magic lamp>.

alive

- **alive and kicking** in a good or healthy condition.

all

- **all and sundry** everybody, one and all.
- **all chiefs and no Indians** a surplus of people wishing to give orders or to administrate and a deficiency of people willing to carry orders out or to do the work.
- **all ears** listening intently.
- **all in** exhausted.
- **all in one piece** safely, undamaged.
- **all over bar the shouting** at an end to all intents and purposes.
- **all set** ready to go, prepared.

alley

- **alley cat** a wild or promiscuous person.

alliance

- **an unholy alliance** used of an association or partnership between two people or organizations that have nothing in common and would not normally work together, especially when this association has a bad purpose.

alma mater

- one's old university, college or school. <Latin, 'bountiful mother'>.

alpha

- **alpha and omega** the beginning and the end. <The first and last letters of the Greek alphabet>.

also

- **also-ran** an unsuccessful person. <A horse-racing term for a horse that is not one of the first three horses in a race>.

altar

- **be sacrificed on the altar of (something)** to be destroyed or suffer harm or damage so that something can be achieved or prosper.

alter

- alter ego a person who is very close or dear to someone. <Latin, 'other self'>.

altogether

- **in the altogether** in the nude.

Amazon

- a very strong or well-built woman. <In Greek legend the Amazons were a race of female warriors who had their right breasts removed in order to draw their bows better>.

American

- **as American as apple pie** typical of the traditional American way of life or culture.
- **the American dream** the hope of achieving success and prosperity through hard work, from the dreams which immigrants had when they landed in America to start a new life.

angel

- **an angel of mercy** a person who gives help and comfort, especially one who appears unexpectedly.
- **a fallen angel** a person who had formerly a good reputation for being virtuous or successful but no longer does so.

angry

- **angry young man** a person who expresses angry dissatisfaction with established social, political and intellectual values. <A term applied to British dramatist, John Osborne, author of the *play Look Back in Anger*>.

answer

- **the answer to a maiden's prayer** exactly what one desires and is looking for. <The answer to a maiden's prayer was thought to be an eligible bachelor>.

ant

- **have ants in one's pants** to be restless or agitated or impatient.

any

- **any old how** in an untidy and careless way.
- **anything goes** any kind of behaviour, dress, etc, is acceptable.

apart

- **be poles** *or* **worlds apart** to be completely different.

ape

- **go ape** to become extremely angry or excited

appearance

- **keep up appearances** to behave in public in such a way as to hide what is going on in private.

apple

- **in apple-pie order** with everything tidy and correctly arranged. <From French *nappe pliée*, 'folded linen', linen neatly laid out>.
- **rotten apple** a person who is bad or unsatisfactory and will have a bad influence on others.
- **the apple of (someone's) eye** a favourite, a person who is greatly loved by (someone). <Apple refers to the pupil of the eye>.
- **upset the apple-cart** to spoil plans or arrangements. <From the practice of selling fruit from carts in street markets>.

apron

- **tied to (someone's) apron-strings** completely dependent on a woman, especially one's mother or wife.

ark

- **like something out of the ark** very old-fashioned looking. <From Noah's ark in the Bible>.

arm

- **armed to the hilt** *or* **teeth** provided with all the equipment that one could possibly need.
- **be up in arms** to protest angrily.
- **chance one's arm** to take a risk.
- **cost an arm and a leg** to cost a great deal of money.
- **give one's right arm for (something)** to be willing to go to any lengths to get something.
- **keep (someone) at arm's length** to avoid becoming too close to or too friendly with someone.
- **the long arm of the law** the power or authority of the police.
- **right arm** chief source of help and support.
- **twist (someone's) arm** to force (someone) to do (something), to persuade (someone) to do (something).
- **with one arm tied behind one's back** very easily.
- **with open arms** welcomingly.

armour

- **chink in (someone's) armour** a weak or vulnerable spot in someone who is otherwise very strong and difficult to get through to or attack. <A knight in armour could be injured only through a flaw or opening in his protective armour>.
- **knight in shining armour** a person who it is hoped will save a situation or come to one's aid. <From medieval legends in which knights in armour came to the aid of damsels in distress>.

ashes

- **rake over the ashes** to discuss things that are passed, especially things that are best forgotten.
- **rise from the ashes** to develop and flourish out of ruin and destruction. <In Greek legend the phoenix, a mythical bird, who after a certain number of years of life set fire to itself and was then reborn from the ashes>.

attendance

- **dance attendance on (someone)** to stay close to (someone) in order to carry out all his or her wishes and so gain favour.

aunt

- **Aunt Sally** a person or thing that is being subjected to general abuse, mockery and criticism. <An Aunt Sally at a fair was a wooden model of a woman's head, mounted on a pole, at which people threw sticks or balls in order to win a prize>.

awakening

- **get/have a rude awakening** suddenly to become aware that a situation is not as good or pleasant as one thinks it is.

away

- **get away from it all** to escape from the problems of daily life, usually by taking a holiday.
- **the one that got away** a chance of success which one either did not or could not take advantage of at the time but which one always remembers. <Refers to a supposedly large fish which an angler fails to catch but about which he tells many stories>.

axe

- **get the axe** to be dismissed.
- **have an axe to grind** to have a personal, often selfish, reason for being involved in something. <From a story told by Benjamin Franklin, the American politician, about how a man had once asked him in his boyhood to demonstrate the working of his father's grindstone and had sharpened his own axe on it while it was working>.

baby

- **be left holding the baby** to be left to cope with a difficult situation that has been abandoned by the person who is really responsible for it.
- **throw out the baby with the bath water** accidentally to get rid of something desirable or essential when trying to get rid of undesirable or unnecessary things.

back

- **backhanded compliment** a supposed compliment that sounds more like criticism.
- **back number** a person or thing that is no longer of importance or of use. <Refers to an out-of-date or back copy of a newspaper or magazine>.

- **backseat driver 1** a passenger in a car who gives unasked-for and unwanted advice. **2** a person who is not directly involved in some activity but who offers unwanted advice.
- **back to the drawing board** to have to start again on a project or activity. <Refers to the board on which plans of buildings, etc, are drawn before being built>.
- **back to the grindstone** back to work.
- **bend over backwards** to go to great trouble.
- **get off (someone's) back** to stop harassing or bothering (someone).
- **have one's back to the wall**. to be in a very difficult or desperate situation. <Someone being pursued has to face his or her pursuers or be captured when a wall prevents retreat>.
- **know (something) backwards** *or* **like the back of one's hand** to know all there is to know about (something).
- **know (someone** *or* **something) like the back of one's hand** to know (someone or something) very well indeed.
- **put one's back into (something)** to put the greatest possible effort into (something).
- **put (someone's) back up** to annoy (someone). <A cat's back arches up when it is angry>.
- **see the back of (someone** *or* **something)** to get rid of (someone or something), not to see (someone or something) again.
- **take a back seat** to take an unimportant or minor role.
- **talk through the back of one's head** to talk nonsense.
- **the back of beyond** a very remote place.

bacon
- **bring home the bacon 1** to earn money to support one's family. **2** to succeed in doing (something). <Perhaps from the winning of a greased pig as a prize at a country fair>.
- **save (someone's) bacon** to save someone from a danger or difficulty.

bad
- **hit a bad patch** to encounter difficulties or a difficult period.
- **in (someone's) bad** *or* **black books** out of favour with (someone). <Refers to an account book where bad debts are noted>.
- **with a bad grace** in an unwilling and bad-tempered way.

bag
- **bag of bones** a person who is extremely thin.
- **bag of tricks** the equipment necessary to do something.
- **in the bag** certain to be obtained. <From the bag used in hunting to carry what one has shot or caught>.
- **mixed bag** a very varied mixture.

bait
- **rise to the bait** to do what someone has been trying to get one to do. <Refers to fish rising to the surface to get the bait on an angler's line>.

- **swallow the bait** to accept completely an offer, proposal, etc, that has been made purely to tempt one. <As above>.

baker
- **baker's dozen** thirteen. <From the former custom of bakers adding an extra bun or loaf to a dozen in order to be sure of not giving short weight>.

balance
- **in the balance** undecided, uncertain. <A balance is a pair of hanging scales>.
- **strike a balance** to reach an acceptable compromise.
- **tip the balance** to exert an influence which, although slight, is enough to alter the outcome of something.

bald
- **bald as a coot** extremely bald. <A coot is a bird with a spot of white feathers on its head>.

ball[1]
- **have a ball** to have a very enjoyable time.

ball[2]
- **a whole new ball game** used to emphasize how much a situation has changed.
- **be in the right ballpark** to be reasonably close to the amount which is required or wanted.
- **have the ball at one's feet** to be in a position to be successful. <From football>.
- **on the ball** alert, quick-witted, attentive to what is going on around one. <Referring to a football player who watches the ball carefully in order to be prepared if it comes to him>.
- **play ball** to act in accordance with someone else's wishes.
- **set** *or* **start the ball rolling** to start off an activity of some kind, often a discussion.

balloon
- **go down like a lead balloon** of a suggestion, idea, joke, etc, to be very badly received.
- **when the balloon goes up** when something serious, usually something that is expected and feared, happens. <From balloons sent up to undertake military observation in World War I, signifying that action was about to start>.

banana
- **go bananas** to go mad, to get extremely angry.

band
- **jump on the bandwagon** to show an interest in, or become involved in, something simply because it is fashionable or financially advantageous. <Refers to a brightly coloured wagon for carrying the band at the head of a procession>.
- **looking as though one has stepped out of a bandbox** looking very neat and elegant. <Refers to a lightweight box formerly used for holding small articles of clothing such as hats>.

bang
- **bang one's head against a brick wall** to do (something) in vain.
- **go with a bang** to be very successful.

bank
- **break the bank** to leave (oneself or someone) without any money. <In gambling terms, to win all the money that a casino is prepared to pay out in one night>.

baptism
- **baptism of fire** a first, usually difficult or unpleasant, experience of something. <From Christian baptism>.

bare
- **the bare bones of (something)** the essential and basic details of (something).

bargain
- **get more than one bargained for** to encounter more difficulty than one had expected or was prepared for.
- **drive a hard bargain** to try to get a deal that is very favourable to oneself.

barge
- **wouldn't touch (someone or something) with a bargepole** to wish to have absolutely no contact with (someone or something).

bark
- **bark up the wrong tree** to have the wrong idea or impression about (something), to approach (something) in the wrong way. <From raccoon-hunting, in which dogs were used to locate trees that had raccoons in them>.
- **(someone's) bark is worse than his or her bite** a person is not as dangerous or as harmful as he or she appears to be. <Refers to a barking dog that is often quite friendly>.

barrel
- **have (someone) over a barrel** to get (someone) into such a position that one can get him or her to do anything that one wants. <From holding someone over a barrel of boiling oil, etc, where the alternatives for the victim are to agree to demands or be dropped in the barrel>.
- **scrape the (bottom of the) barrel** to have to use someone or something of poor or inferior quality because that is all that is available. <Referring to the fact that people will only scrape out the bottom of an empty barrel if they have no more full ones>.

bat[1]
- **off one's own bat** by oneself, without the help or permission of any one else. <From the game of cricket>.

bat[2]
- **blind as a bat** having very poor eyesight. <Referring to the fact that bats live their lives in darkness>.
- **like a bat out of hell** very quickly.

battle
- **win the battle, but lose the war** to get some of the things which you wanted from an argument, discussion, etc, but to lose your most important goal.

bay
- **keep (someone or something) at bay** to keep (someone or something) from coming too close.

be
- **the be-all and end-all** the most important aim or purpose. <From Shakespeare's *Macbeth*, Act 1, scene VII>.

beam
- **off beam 1** on the wrong course. **2** inaccurate. <From the radio beam that is used to bring aircraft to land in poor visibility>.
- **on one's beam ends** very short of money. <Originally a nautical term used to describe a ship lying on its side and in danger of capsizing completely>.

bean
- **know how many beans make five** to be experienced in the ways of the world.
- **spill the beans** to reveal a secret or confidential information.

bear
- **bear garden** a noisy, rowdy place. <Originally referred to a public place used for bear-baiting, in which dogs were made to attack bears and get them angry, for public amusement>.
- **like a bear with a sore head** extremely bad-tempered.

beard
- **beard the lion in its den** to confront or face (someone) openly and boldly.

beat
- **beat about the bush** to approach (something) in an indirect way. <In game-bird hunting, bushes are beaten to make the birds appear>.
- **beat a (hasty) retreat** to run away. <Military orders used to be conveyed by a series of different drum signals>.
- **beat the drum** to try to attract public attention. <The noise of a drum makes people stop and listen>.
- **if you can't beat them (or 'em), join them (or 'em)** if you cannot persuade other people to think and act like you, the most sensible course of action is for you to begin to think and act like them.
- **off the beaten track** in an isolated position, away from towns or cities.

beauty
- **beauty is in the eye of the beholder** different people have different ideas of what is beautiful.
- **beauty is only skin deep** people have more important qualities than how they look.

beaver
- **eager beaver** a very enthusiastic and hard-working person.

- **work like a beaver** to work very industriously and enthusiastically. <Beavers are small animals that build dams, etc, with great speed and skill>.

beck
- **at (someone's) beck and call** having to be always available to carry out (someone's) orders or wishes. <Beck is a form of 'beckon'>.

bed
- **bed of roses** an easy, comfortable or happy situation.
- **get out of bed on the wrong side** to start the day in a very bad-tempered mood.

bee
- **have a bee in one's bonnet** to have an idea that one cannot stop thinking or talking about, to have an obsession. <A bee trapped under one's hat cannot escape>.
- **make a beeline for (someone *or* something)** to go directly and quickly to (someone or something). <Bees are reputed to fly back to their hives in straight lines>.

beer
- **not all beer and skittles** not consisting just of pleasant or enjoyable things.
- **small beer** something unimportant.

before
- **before one can say Jack Robinson** very rapidly, in an instant.

beg
- **beggar description** to be such that words cannot describe it. <From Shakespeare's *Antony and Cleopatra*, Act 2, scene II>.
- **beg the question** in an argument, to take for granted the very point that requires to be proved; to fail to deal effectively with the point being discussed.
- **going a-begging** unclaimed or unsold.

bell
- **bell the cat** to be the person in a group who undertakes something dangerous for the good of the group. <Refers to a story about some mice who wanted to put a bell on the neck of the cat so that they would hear it coming and who needed a volunteer to do it>.
- **ring a bell** to bring back vague memories.
- **saved by the bell** rescued from an unpleasant situation by something suddenly bringing that situation to an end. <From the bell that marks the end of a round in boxing>.

belt
- **below the belt** unfair. <In boxing, a blow below the belt is against the rules>.
- **belt and braces** used to describe extra precautions taken to make sure that all is well.
- **tighten one's belt** to reduce one's expenditure. <Belts have to be tightened if one loses weight in this case from having less to spend on food>.

bend
- **on bended knee** very humbly or earnestly.
- **round the bend** mad.

berth
- **give (someone) a wide berth** to keep well away from (someone). <Refers to a ship that keeps a good distance away from others>.

best
- **have the best of both worlds** to benefit from the advantages of two sets of circumstances.
- **put one's best foot forward** to make the best attempt possible.

bet
- **hedge one's bets** to try to protect oneself from possible loss, failure, disappointment, etc. <From betting the same amount on each side to make sure of not losing>.

better
- **have seen better days** to be no longer new or fresh.
- **the better part of (something)** a large part of (something), most of (something).
- **think better of (something)** to reconsider (something), to change one's mind about (something).

beyond
- **beyond the pale** beyond normal or acceptable limits. <The pale was an area of English government in Ireland in the 16th century>.

big
- **a big fish in a small pond** a person who seems better, more important, etc, than he or she is because he or she operates in a small, limited area.
- **the Big Apple** New York.
- **big guns** the most important people in an organization.
- **hit the big time** to be become extremely successful and famous
- **the Big Smoke** London.

bill
- **a clean bill of health** verification that someone is well and fit.
  <Ships were given clean bills of health and allowed to sail when it was certified that no one aboard had an infectious disease>.
- **fir or   fill the bill** to be exactly what is required. <Refers originally to a handbill or public notice>.
- **foot the bill** to pay for something, usually something expensive.

bird
- **a bird in the hand is worth two in the bush** something that one already has is much more valuable than things that one might or might not acquire. <A bird in the bush might fly away>.
- **a little bird told me** I found out by a means which I do not wish to reveal.

- **birds of a feather flock together** people who share the same interests, ideas, etc, usually form friendships.
- **give (someone) the bird** of an audience, to express its disapproval of a performer by hissing or booing so that he or she leaves the stage. <From the resemblance of the noise of the audience to the hissing of geese>.
- **kill two birds with one stone** to fulfil two purposes with one action.
- **the birds and the bees** the basic facts of human sexual behaviour and reproduction.
- **the early bird catches the worm** a person who arrives early or acts promptly is in a position to gain advantage over others.

biscuit
- **take the biscuit** to be much worse than anything that has happened so far.

bit
- **champing at the bit** very impatient. <A horse chews at its bit when it is impatient>.
- **take the bit between one's teeth** to act on one's own and cease to follow other people's instructions or advice. <Refers to a horse escaping from the control of its rider>.

bite
- **bite off more than one can chew** to try to do more than one can without too much difficulty.
- **bite the bullet** to do something unpleasant but unavoidable with courage.
- **bite the dust** to die or cease to operate or function.
- **bite the hand that feeds one** to treat badly someone who has helped one.
- **have more than one bite at the cherry** to have more than one opportunity to succeed at something.
- **the biter bit** used to indicate a situation in which someone who has tried to harm or do wrong to someone has suffered in some way as a consequence of this action.

bitter
- **a bitter pill to swallow** something unpleasant or difficult that one has to accept.

black
- **as black as one is painted** as bad as everyone says one is.
- **black sheep** a member of a family or group who is not up to the standard of the rest of the group.
- **in black and white** in writing or in print.
- **in (someone's) black books** *same as* **in (someone's) bad books** *see* **bad**.
- **in the black** showing a profit, not in debt. <From the use of black ink to make entries on the credit side of a ledger>.

blanket
- **on the wrong side of the blanket** illegitimate.
- **wet blanket** a dull person who makes other people feel depressed.

blessing
- **a blessing in disguise** something that turns out to advantage after first seeming unfortunate.

blind
- **the blind leading the blind** referring to a situation in which the person who is in charge of others knows as little as they do.

blood
- **in cold blood** deliberately and calmly.
- **like getting blood out of a stone** very difficult, almost impossible.

blow
- **blow hot and cold** to keep changing one's mind or attitude.
- **blow one's own trumpet** to boast about one's achievements.
- **blow the gaff** to tell something secret, often something illegal, to someone, often the police. <Perhaps from gaff, meaning mouth>.
- **blow the whistle on (someone)** to reveal or report someone's wrongdoing so that it will be stopped. <From the practice of blowing a whistle to indicate a foul in some ball games>.
- **see which way the wind blows** to wait and find out how a situation is developing before making a decision. <From sailing>.

blue
- **blue-eyed boy** a person who is someone's favourite.
- **bluestocking** an educated, intellectual woman. <From a group of women in the 18th century who met in London to discuss intellectual and philosophical issues and some of whom wore blue worsted stockings>.
- **once in a blue moon** hardly ever.
- **out of the blue** without warning.

bluff
- **call (someone's) bluff** to make (someone) prove that what he or she says is true is really genuine. <Refers to poker, the card game>.

board
- **go by the board** to be abandoned. <The board here is a ship's board or side, and to go by the board literally was to vanish overboard>.
- **sweep the board** to win all the prizes. <The board referred to is the surface on which card games are played and on which the bets are placed>.

boat
- **burn one's boats** to do something that makes it impossible to go back to one's previous position.
- **in the same boat** in the same situation.
- **miss the boat** to fail to take advantage of a opportunity.
- **push the boat out** to spend money in an extravagant way in order to celebrate something in a lavish way.
- **rock the boat** to do something to endanger or spoil a comfortable or happy situation.

bolt
- **a bolt from the blue** something very sudden and un-expected.
- **shoot one's bolt** to make one's final effort, have no other possible course of action.

bone
- **a bone of contention** a cause of dispute. <Dogs fight over bones>.
- **have a bone to pick with (someone)** to have a matter to disagree about with (someone). <From dogs fighting over a bone>.
- **make no bones about (something)** to have no hesitation or restraint about (saying or doing something openly). <Originally a reference to finding no bones in one's soup, which was therefore easier to eat>.
- **near the bone 1** referring too closely to something that should not be mentioned; tactless. **2** slightly indecent or crude.

boo
- **would not say boo to a goose** to be extremely timid.

book
- **bring (someone) to book** to make (someone) explain or be punished for his or her actions. <Perhaps referring to a book where a police officer keeps a note of crimes>.
- **by the book** strictly according to the rules.
- **cook the books** illegally to alter accounts or financial records.
- **throw the book at (someone)** to criticize or punish (someone) severely, to charge (someone) with several crimes at once. <Literally, to charge someone with every crime listed in a book>.

boot
- **get the boot** to be dismissed or discharged from one's job.
- **hang up one's boots** to retire from work, to cease doing an activity. <From hanging up football boots after a game>.
- **lick (someone's) boots** to flatter (someone) and do everything he or she wants.
- **pull oneself up by one's bootstraps** to become successful through one's own efforts.
- **put the boot in (someone) 1** to kick (someone) when he or she is already lying on the ground injured. **2** to treat (someone) cruelly or harshly after he or she has suffered already.
- **the boot is on the other foot** the situation has been completely turned round.
- **too big for one's boots** too conceited.

bottle
- **lose one's bottle** not to have the courage to do something or to go on with something.

bottom
- **bottom drawer** a collection of articles for the home, which a young woman gathered together before her marriage.

- **hit rock bottom** to reach the lowest possible level.
- **the bottom line 1** the most important point or part of something. **2** the result or outcome. <Refers to the bottom line in a financial statement which indicates the extent of the profit or loss>.

bow[1]
- **bow and scrape** to behave in a very humble and respectful way.
- **take a bow** to accept acknowledgement of one's achievements. <As above>.

bow[2]
- **draw the long bow** to exaggerate. <An archer carries a spare bow in case one breaks>.
- **have another/more than one string to one's bow** to have another possibility, plan, etc, available to one.

brain
- **cudgel** *or* **rack one's brains** to think very hard.
- **pick (someone's) brains** to find out (someone's) ideas and knowledge about a subject so that one can put them to one's own use.

brass
- **get down to brass tacks** to consider the basic facts or issues of something.

bread
- **know which side one's bread is buttered** to know the course of action that is to one's greatest advantage.
- **on the breadline** with scarcely enough money to live on.
- **the greatest thing since sliced bread** a person or thing that is greatly admired.

breath
- **hold one's breath** to wait anxiously for something.
- **take (someone's) breath away** to surprise (someone) greatly.
- **waste one's breath** to say something that is not taken heed of.

breathe
- **breathe down (someone's) neck 1** to be very close behind (someone). **2** to be waiting impatiently for something from (someone).

brick
- **like a cat on hot bricks** very nervous or restless.
- **try to make bricks without straw** to try to do something without the necessary materials or equipment. <A biblical reference, from Pharaoh's command concerning the Israelites in Exodus 5:7>.

bridge
- **build bridges** to do something to help people who are in some kind of opposition to each other to understand each other so that they ar eable to establish a relationship or co-operate with each other.
- **cross a bridge when one comes to it** to worry about or deal with a problem only when it actually arises.

bright
- **bright-eyed and bushy-tailed** very cheerful and lively.
- **look on the bright side** to be optimistic, to see the advantages of one's situation.

broad
- **have broad shoulders** to be able to accept a great deal of responsibility, criticism, etc.
- **in broad daylight** during the day.

brother
- **am I my brother's keeper?** the actions or affairs of other people are not my responsibility. <From the biblical story of Cain and Abel, Genesis 4:9>.
- **Big Brother** a powerful person or organization thought to be constantly monitoring and controlling people's actions. <From the dictator in George Orwell's novel *1984*>.

brown
- **in a brown study** deep in thought.

bucket
- **a drop in the bucket** a very small part of what is needed.
- **kick the bucket** to die. <Bucket here is perhaps a beam from which pigs were hung after being killed>.
- **weep buckets** to cry a great deal.

bull
- **hit the bull's eye** to do or say something that is very appropriate or relevant. <Refers to the exact centre of a dart board>.
- **like a bull at a gate** in a very unsubtle, unthinking way.
- **like a bull in a china shop** in a very clumsy way.
- **take the bull by the horns** to tackle (something) boldly.

bullet
- **get the bullet** to be dismissed or discharged.

burn
- **the burning question** a question of great interest to many people.

Burton
- **gone for a Burton** dead, ruined, broken, etc. <Originally a military term from Burton, a kind of ale>.

bus
- **busman's holiday** a holiday spent doing much the same as one does when one is at work. <Refers to a bus driver who drives a bus on holiday>.

bush
- **bush telegraph** the fast spreading of information by word of mouth. <A reference to the Australian bush>.

business
- **mean business** to be determined (to do something), to be serious.
- **mind one's own business** to concern oneself with one's own affairs and not interfere in those of other people.

butter
- **butterfingers** a person who often drops things.
- **look as though butter would not melt in one's mouth** to appear very innocent, respectable, etc.

butterfly
- **have butterflies in one's stomach** to have a fluttering sensation in one's stomach as a sign of nervousness.

cake
- **a piece of cake** something easy to do.
- **a slice** *or* **share of the cake** a share of something desirable or valuable.
- **have one's cake and eat it** *or* **eat one's cake and have it** to have the advantages of two things or situations when doing, possessing, etc, one of them would normally make the other one impossible.
- **sell** *or* **go like hot cakes** to sell very quickly.

cage
- **rattle (someone's) cage** to annoy or agitate (someone). <From visitors to a zoo rattling the cages of the animals to get them to react>.

calf
- **kill the fatted calf** to provide a lavish meal, especially to mark a celebration of someone's arrival or return. <From the parable of the prodigal son in the Bible, Luke 15:23>.

can
- **carry the can** to accept blame or responsibility, usually for something that someone else has done.

candle
- **burn the candle at both ends** to work and/or to play during too many hours of the day.
- **cannot hold a candle to (someone)** to be not nearly as good or as talented as (someone). <Literally, someone who is not good enough even to hold a light while someone else does the work>.
- **the game is not worth the candle** something that is not worth the effort that has to be spent on it. <From the translation of the French phrase *le jeu n'en vaut la chandelle*, referring to a gambling session in which the amount of money at stake was not enough to pay for the candles required to give light at the game>.

canoe
- **paddle one's own canoe** to control one's own affairs without help from anyone else.

cap
- **cap in hand** humbly. <Removing one's cap in someone's presence is a sign of respect>.
- **if the cap fits, wear it** if what has been said applies to you, then you should take note of it.
- **set one's cap at (someone)** to try to attract (someone of the opposite sex). <Perhaps a mistranslation of French *metter le cap*, to head towards>.

card

- **have a card up one's sleeve** to have an idea, plan of action, etc, in reserve to be used if necessary. <From cheating at cards>.
- **on the cards** likely. <From reading the cards in fortune-telling>.
- **play one's cards close to one's chest** to be secretive or non-communicative about one's plans or intentions. <From holding one's cards close to one in card-playing so that one's opponents will not see them>.
- **play one's cards right** to act in such a way as to take advantage of a situation.
- **put one's cards on the table** to make known one's plans or intentions. <In card-playing, to show one's opponent one's cards>.

carpet

- **sweep (something) under the carpet** to try to hide or forget about (something unpleasant).
- **the red carpet** special, respectful treatment. <Refers to the red carpet put down for a royal person to walk on during official visits>.

carrot

- **carrot and stick** reward as a method of persuasion.

carry

- **carry a torch for (someone)** to be in love with someone, especially with someone who does not return it. <A torch or a flame was regarded as symbolic of love>.

cart

- **put the cart before the horse** to do or say things in the wrong order.

Casanova

- **Casanova** a man who has relationships with many women. <From Giacomo Casanova, a famous 18th-century Italian lover and adventurer>.

Cassandra

- **Cassandra** a person who makes predictions about unpleasant future events but who is never believed. <In Greek legend, Cassandra, who was the daughter of Priam, king of Troy, had the gift of prophecy but was destined never to be believed. She predicted the fall of Troy>.

cast

- **cast pearls before swine** to offer something valuable or desirable to someone who does not appreciate it. <A biblical reference to Matthew 7:6>.

castle

- **castles in the air** *or* **castles in Spain** dreams or hopes that are unlikely ever to be realized.

cat

- **curiosity killed the cat** said as a warning not to pry into other people's affairs.
- **let the cat out of a bag** to reveal something secret or confidential, especially accidentally or at an inappropriate time. <Supposedly referring to a fairground trick in which a customer was offered a cat in a bag when he or she thought it was a piglet in the bag>.
- **like a scalded cat** in a rapid, excited way.
- **like something the cat brought** *or* **dragged in** very untidy or bedraggled.
- **not enough room to swing a cat** very little space.
- **not to have a cat's chance in hell** *or* **a cat's chance in hell** to have no chance at all.
- **play cat and mouse with (someone)** to treat (someone) in such a way that he or she does not know what is going to happen to them at any time. <A cat often plays with its prey, a mouse, before killing it>.
- **put** *or* **set the cat among the pigeons** to cause a disturbance, especially a sudden or unexpected one.
- **rain cats and dogs** to rain very heavily.
- **see which way the cat jumps** to wait and see what other people are going to do and how the situation is developing before deciding on one's course of action.
- **there's more than one way to kill** *or* **skin a cat** there's more than one way or method of doing things.
- **when the cat's away, the mice will play** when the person in charge or in control is not present the people whom he or she is in charge of will work less hard, misbehave, etc.

catch

- **catch (someone) napping** to surprise (someone) when he or she is unprepared or inattentive.
- **Catch 22** a situation in which one can never win or from which one can never escape, being constantly hindered by a rule or restriction that itself changes to block any change in one's plans; a difficulty that prevents one from escaping from an unpleasant or dangerous situation. <From the title of a novel by Joseph Heller>.
- **catch (someone) with his** *or* **her pants** *or* **trousers down** to surprise (someone) when he or she is unprepared or doing something wrong, especially when this causes embarrassment. <Refers to walking in on someone partially dressed>.

caviar

- **caviar to the general** something considered to be too sophisticated to be appreciated by ordinary people. <From Shakespeare's *Hamlet*, Act 2, scene II>.

ceiling

- **go through the ceiling** to rise very high, to soar.
- **hit the ceiling** *or* **roof** to lose one's temper completely.

chalice

- **hand/give (someone) a poisoned chalice** to be given something to do which seems an attractive proposition but which may well lead to failure or extreme difficulties.

chalk

- **as different as chalk and cheese** completely different.
- **chalk it up to experience** accept the inevitability of something.

- **not by a long chalk** not by a long way, by no means. <From the vertical chalk lines drawn to mark scores in a game, the longer lines representing the greater number of points>.

chance

- **have an eye to the main chance** to watch carefully for what will be advantageous or profitable to oneself.
- **not to have the ghost of a chance** not to have the slightest possibility of success.
- **change hands** to pass into different ownership.

change

- **change horses in mid-stream** to change one's opinions, plans, sides, etc, in the middle of something.
- **change one's tune** to change one's attitude or opinion.
- **ring the changes** to add variety by doing or arranging things in different ways.

chapter

- **chapter and verse** detailed sources for a piece of information. <From the method of referring to biblical texts>.

charity

- **charity begins at home** one must take care of oneself and one's family before concerning oneself with others.
- **cold as charity** extremely cold. <Charity is referred to as cold since it tends to be given to the poor and disadvantaged by organizations rather than by individual people and so lacks human feeling or warmth>.

charm

- **lead a charmed life** regularly to have good fortune and avoid misfortune, harm or danger.
- **work like a charm** to be very effective, to work very well.

chase

- **chase after rainbows** to spend time and effort in thinking about, or in trying to obtain, things that it is impossible for one to achieve.
- **cut to the chase** to start discussing or dealing with the most important part of something instead of wasting time on minor points. <Refers to the fact that in certain kinds of film a car chase is the most exciting part>.

cheek

- **cheek by jowl** side by side, very close together.
- **turn the other cheek** to take no action against someone who has harmed one, thereby giving him or her the opportunity to harm one again. <A biblical reference to Matthew 5:39, 'Whosoever shall smite thee on thy right cheek, turn to him the left one also'>.

cheese

- **hard cheese** bad luck, a sentiment usually expressed by someone who does not care about the misfortune.

Cheshire

- **grin like a Cheshire cat** to smile broadly so as to show one's teeth. <Refers to *Alice's Adventures in Wonderland* by Lewis Carroll, in which the Cheshire cat gradually disappears except for its smile>.

chest

- **get (something) off one's chest** to tell (someone) about something that is upsetting, worrying or annoying one.
- **old chestnut** an old joke, usually one no longer funny.
- **pull (someone's) chestnuts out of the fire** to rescue (someone) from a difficult or dangerous situation, often by putting oneself in difficulty or danger. <From a story by the 17th-century French writer La Fontaine, in which a monkey use a cat's paw to get hot nuts from a fire>.

chew

- **chew the cud** to think deeply about something.
- **chew the fat** to have a discussion or conversation.

chicken

- **chickens come home to roost** misdeeds, mistakes, etc, that come back with an unpleasant effect on the person who performed the misdeed, especially after a considerable time.
- **count one's chickens before they are hatched** to make plans which depend on something that is still uncertain.

child

- **child's play** something that is very easy to do.

chin

- **keep one's chin up** not to show feelings of depression, worry or fear.
- **take it on the chin** to accept or to suffer (something) with courage.

chip

- **a chip off the old block** a person who is very like one of his or her parents.
- **cash in one's chips** to die. <Refers to a gambler cashing in his or her chips or tokens in exchange for money at the end of a session>.
- **have a chip on one's shoulder** to have an aggressive attitude and act as if everyone is going to insult or ill-treat one, often because one feels inferior. <Refers to a former American custom by which a young man who wished to provoke a fight would place a piece of wood on his shoulder and dare someone to knock it off>.
- **have had one's chips** to have had, and failed at, all the chances of success one is likely to get. <Refers to gambling tokens>.
- **when the chips are down** when a situation has reached a critical stage. <A gambling terms indicating that the bets have been placed>.

choice

- **Hobson's choice** no choice at all; a choice between accepting what is offered or having nothing at all. <Refers to the practice of Tobias Hobson, an English stable-owner in the 17th century, of offering customers only the horse nearest the stable door>.

chop

- **chop and change** to keep altering (something), to keep changing (something).
- **get the chop 1** to be dismissed or discontinued. **2** to be killed.

chord
- **strike a chord** to be familiar in some way.
- **touch a chord** to arouse emotion or sympathy.

circle
- **come full circle** to return to the position or situation from which one started.
- **go round in circles** to keep going over the same ideas without reaching a satisfactory decision or answer.
- **run round in circles** to dash about and appear to be very busy without accomplishing anything.
- **vicious circle** an unfortunate or bad situation, the result of which produces the original cause of the situation or something similar. <In logic, the term for the fallacy of proving one statement by the evidence of another which is itself only valid if the first statement is valid>.

circus
- **a three-ring circus** a place where there is a lot of noise and a lot of confused activity going on.

clean
- **a clean slate** a record free of any discredit; an opportunity to make a fresh start. <Slates were formerly used for writing on in schools>.
- **come clean** to tell the truth about something, especially after lying about it.
- **keep one's nose clean** to keep out of trouble, to behave well or legally.
- **make a clean breast of (something)** to admit to (something), especially after having denied it.
- **make a clean sweep** to get rid of everything which is unnecessary or unwanted.
- **show a clean pair of heels** to run away very quickly.
- **squeaky clean** free of all guilt or blame. <Clean surfaces tend to squeak when wiped>.
- **take (someone) to the cleaners** to cause (someone) to spend or lose a great deal of money.

clear
- **clear as a bell** very easy to hear. <Bells, such as church bells, are very audible>.
- **clear as crystal** very easy to understand or grasp.
- **clear as mud** not at all easy to understand or grasp.
- **clear the decks** to tidy up, especially as a preparation for some activity or project. <Refers to getting a ship ready for battle>.
- **steer clear of (someone or something)** to keep away from or avoid (someone or something).
- **the coast is clear** the danger or difficulty has now passed. <Probably a military term indicating that there were no enemy forces near the coast and so an invasion was possible>.

cleft
- **in a cleft stick** unable to decide between two equally important or difficult courses of action.

clip
- **clip (someone's) wings** to limit the freedom, power or influence of (someone). <From the practice of clipping the wings of a bird to prevent it flying away>.

cloak
- **cloak-and-dagger** involving or relating to a great deal of plotting and scheming. <The combination of a cloak and a dagger suggests conspiracy>.

clock
- **like clockwork** very smoothly, without problems.
- **put back the clock** or **turn the clock back** to return to the conditions or situation of a former time.
- **round the clock** all the time; for twenty-four hours a day.

close¹
- **behind closed doors** in secret.

close²
- **a close shave** something that was only just avoided, especially an escape from danger, failure, etc.

cloud
- **cloud cuckoo land** an imaginary place, where everything is perfect; an unreal world.
- **every cloud has a silver lining** something good happens for every bad or unpleasant thing.
- **have one's head in the clouds** to be day-dreaming and not paying attention to what is going on around one.
- **on cloud nine** extremely happy.
- **under a cloud** under suspicion, in trouble.

coach
- **drive a coach and horses through (something)** to destroy (an argument etc) completely by detecting and making use of the weak points in it. <Refers to the fact that the defects (or holes) in the argument are so large as to let a coach and horses through them>.

coal
- **carry** or **take coals to Newcastle** to do something that is completely unnecessary, especially to take something to a place where there is already a great deal of it. <Refers to Newcastle in England which was a large coal-mining centre>.
- **haul (someone) over the coals** to scold (someone) very severely.

coat
- **cut one's coat according to one's cloth** to organize one's ideas and aims, particularly one's financial aims, so that they are within the limits of what one has or possesses.

cobweb
- **blow away the cobwebs** to make (someone) feel more energetic and alert after feeling rather tired and dull.

cock
- **a cock-and-bull story** an absurd story that is unlikely to be believed.
- **cock a snook at (someone)** to express one's defiance or contempt of (someone). <Originally referring to a rude gesture of contempt made by putting the end of

one's thumb on the end of one's nose and spreading out and moving one's fingers>.
- **go off at half cock** to be unsuccessful because of lack of preparation or because of a premature start. <Refers to a gun that fires too soon>.

coffee
- **wake up and smell the coffee** to become more aware of and more realistic about what is going on around one.

coin
- **pay (someone) back in his *or* her own coin** to get one's revenge on someone who has done harm to one by treating him or her in the same way.
- **the other side of the coin** the opposite argument, point of view, etc.

cold
- **get cold feet** to become nervous and change one's mind about being involved in (something).
- **give (someone) the cold shoulder** to act in an unfriendly way to (someone) by ignoring him or her.
- **in a cold sweat** in a state of great fear or anxiety. <From the fact that the skin tends to become cold and damp when one is very frightened>.
- **make (someone's) blood run cold** to cause terror or great distress in (someone).
- **pour *or* throw cold water on (something)** to discourage enthusiasm for (something).

colour
- **change colour** to become either very pale or else very red in the face through fear, distress, embarrassment, anger, guilt, etc.
- **nail one's colours to the mast** to commit oneself to a point of view or course of action in a very obvious and final way. <Refers to a ship's colours or flag. If this was nailed to the mast it could not be lowered, lowering the flag being a sign of surrender>.
- **show oneself in one's true colours** to reveal what one is really like after pretending to be otherwise. <Refers to a ship raising its colours or flag to indicate which country or side it was supporting>.
- **with flying colours** with great success. <Refers to a ship leaving a battle with its colours or flag still flying as opposed to lowering them in surrender>.

common
- **common-or-garden** completely ordinary.

conjure
- **a name to conjure with** the name of someone very important, influential or well known. <The suggestion is that such people have magical powers>.

contradiction
- **a contradiction in terms** a statement, idea, etc, that contains a contradiction.

convert
- **preach to the converted** to speak enthusiastically in favour of something to people who already admire it or are in favour of it.

cook
- **too many cooks spoil the broth** if there are a great many people involved in a project they are more likely to hinder it than help it.

cookie
- **that's the way the cookie crumbles** that is the situation and one must just accept it. <Cookie is American English for biscuit>.

cool
- **cool as a cucumber** very calm and unexcited.
- **cool *or* kick one's heels** to be kept waiting.
- **keep one's cool** to remain calm.
- **lose one's cool** to become angry, excited etc.

copy
- **blot one's copybook** to spoil a previously good record of behaviour, achievement, etc, by doing something wrong.

corn
- **tread on (someone's) corns** to offend (someone).

corner
- **cut corners** to use less money, materials, effort, time, etc, than is usually required or than is required to give a good result.
- **from all (four) corners of the earth** from every part of the world, from everywhere.
- **in a tight corner** in an awkward, difficult or dangerous situation.
- **paint oneself into a corner** to get oneself into a difficult situation from which there is only one method of escape or action.
- **turn the corner** to begin to get better or improve.

cost
- **cost a bomb *or* a packet** to cost a very great deal of money.
- **cost an arm and a leg** to cost an excessive amount of money.
- **cost the earth** to cost a very great deal of money.

cotton
- **wrap (someone) in cotton wool** to be over-protective of (someone).

count
- **out for the count** unconscious or deeply asleep. <Refers to boxing where a boxer who has been knocked down by his opponent has to get up again before the referee counts to ten in order to stay in the match>.

courage
- **have the courage of one's convictions** to be brave enough to do what one thinks one should.
- **pluck up *or* screw up courage** to force oneself to be brave.

court

- **laugh (someone *or* something) out of court** not to give serious consideration to (someone or something). <Refers to a trivial legal case>.
- **pay court to (someone)** to try to gain the love of (someone).
- **the ball is in (someone's) court** it is (someone's) turn to take action.
- **rule (something) out of court** to prevent (something) from being considered for (something). <Refers to a court of law where evidence, etc, ruled out of court has no effect on the case>.

Coventry

- **send (someone) to Coventry** collectively to refuse to associate with (someone). <Perhaps from an incident in the English Civil War when Royalists captured in Birmingham were sent to the stronghold of Coventry>.

cow

- **a sacred cow** something that is regarded with too much respect for people to be allowed to criticize it freely. <The cow is considered sacred by Hindus>.
- **till *or* until the cows come home** for an extremely long time. <Cows walk very slowly from the field to the milking sheds unless someone hurries them along>.

crack

- **a fair crack of the whip** a fair share, a fair chance of doing (something).
- **at (the) crack of dawn** very early in the morning.
- **crack the whip** to treat sternly or severely those under one's control or charge. <From the use of a whip to punish people>.
- **take a sledgehammer to crack a nut** to spend a great deal of effort on a small task or problem.

crest

- **be (riding) on the crest of a wave** to be going through a very successful period.

cricket

- **not cricket** not fair or honourable, unsportsmanlike. <The game of cricket is regarded as being played in a gentlemanly way>.

crocodile

- **crocodile tears** a pretended show of grief or sorrow. <Refers to an old belief that crocodiles weep while eating their prey>.

cross

- **cross the Rubicon** to do something that commits one completely to a course of action that cannot be undone. <Julius Caesar's crossing of the River Rubicon in 49 BC committed him to war with the Senate>.
- **have a cross to bear** to have to suffer or tolerate a responsibility, inconvenience or source of distress. <Refers to the fact that in the days of crucifixions, those being crucified had to carry their own crosses>.

- **talk at cross purposes** to be involved in a misunderstanding because of talking or thinking about different things without realizing it.

crow

- **eat crow** to have to admit or accept that one was wrong.

crunch

- **when it comes to the crunch** when a time of testing comes, when a decision has to be made.

cry

- **a far cry from (something)** a long way from (something), very different from (something).
- **cry over spilt milk** to waste time regretting a misfortune or accident that cannot be undone.
- **in full cry** enthusiastically and excitedly pursuing something. <Refers to the cry made by hunting dogs>.

cuckoo

- **a cuckoo in the nest** a person who gains some kind of advantage from a situation without contributing anything useful. <From the cuckoo's habit of laying their eggs in other birds' nests>.

cudgel

- **take up the cudgels on behalf of (someone *or* something)** to fight strongly on behalf of (someone or something), to support (someone or something) vigorously.

cue

- **take one's cue from (someone)** to use the actions or reactions of (someone) as a guide to one's own, to copy (someone's) actions. <A theatrical term, literally meaning to use the words of another actor as a signal for one to speak or move>.

cuff

- **off the cuff** without preparation. <Refers to the habit of some after-dinner speakers of making brief headings on the celluloid cuffs of their evening shirts as a reminder of what he or she wanted to say rather than preparing a formal speech>.

cup

- **not be one's cup of tea** not to be something which one likes or appreciates.

cupboard

- **cupboard love** pretended affection shown for a person because of the things he or she gives one. <From people and animals liking those who feed them, food being kept in cupboards>.
- **curry favour with (someone)** to try to gain the approval or favour of (someone) by insincere flattery or by being extremely nice to him or her all the time. <Originally curry favel, from Old French *estriller fauvel*, *fauvel* being a chestnut horse>.

curtain

- **be curtains for (someone *or* something)** to be the end of (someone or something). <Refers to curtains falling at the end of a stage performance>.

- **bring down the curtain on (something)** to cause (something) to come to an end. <See above>.
- **curtain lecture** a private scolding, especially one given by a wife to a husband. <From the curtains that formerly were hung round a bed>.

cut

- **a cut above (someone** *or* **something)** rather better than (someone or something).
- **cut a long story short** to give a brief account of something quite complicated or lengthy.
- **cut and dried** settled and definite. <Refers to wood that has been cut and dried and made ready for use>.
- **cut and thrust** methods and techniques of rivalry, argument or debate. <Refers to sword fighting>.
- **cut both ways** to have an equal or the same effect on both parts of a question or on both people involved in something.
- **cut it fine** to allow hardly enough time to do or get something.
- **not cut out for (something)** not naturally suited to.

cylinder

- **firing on all cylinders** working or operating at full strength. <Literally used of an internal combustion engine>.

dagger

- **at daggers drawn** feeling or showing great hostility towards each other.
- **look daggers at (someone)** to look with great dislike or hostility at (someone).

daisy

- **be pushing up the daisies** to be dead.
- **fresh as a daisy** not at all tired, lively.

damp

- **a damp squib** something which is expected to be exciting, effective, etc, but which fails to live up to its expectations. <Refers to a wet firework that fails to go off>.
- **put a damper on (something)** to reduce the enjoyment, optimism, happiness of (something).

dance

- **lead (someone) a (merry) dance** to cause (someone) a series of great, usually unnecessary, problems or irritations.

Darby

- **Darby and Joan** a devoted elderly couple. <From the names of such a couple in an 18th-century English ballad>.

dark

- **a shot in the dark** an attempt or guess based on very little information.
- **be whistling in the dark** to try to give the impression that one is more confident of, or less worried about, a situation than one actually is.
- **dark horse** a person or thing whose abilities, worth, etc, is unknown.

- **in the dark** lacking knowledge or awareness.
- **keep it** *or* **something dark** to keep it or something secret.

dash

- **cut a dash** to wear very smart or unusual clothes and so impress others.

Davy Jones

- **Davy Jones's locker** the bottom of the sea. <Davy Jones was a name given in the 18th century to the ruler of the evil spirits of the sea>.

dawn

- **a false dawn** an event which makes a situation look as though it is improving when it is not.

day

- **all in a day's work** all part of one's normal routine, not requiring extra or unusual effort.
- **any day of the week** whatever the circumstances.
- **call it a day** to put an end to (something); to stop doing (something), especially to stop working.
- **carry** *or* **win the day** to be successful, to gain a victory. <Originally a military term meaning to win a battle>.
- **daylight robbery** the charging of prices that are far too high.
- **(your, etc) days are numbered** you are about to be dismissed, be killed, etc.
- **every dog has his day** everyone will get an opportunity at some time.
- **have had one's** *or* **its day** to be past the most successful part of one's or its life.
- **live from day to day** to think only about the present without making any plans for the future.
- **make (someone's) day** to make (someone) very pleased or happy.
- **name the day** to announce the date of one's wedding.
- **not to be one's day** to be a day when nothing seems to go right for one.
- **one of these days** at some time in the future.
- **one of those days** a day when nothing seems to go right.
- **see daylight** to be coming to the end of a long task.
- **seize the day** to take advantage of any opportunities which occur now, rather than worry about the future.

dead

- **a dead duck** a person or thing that is very unlikely to survive or continue.
- **a dead loss** a person or thing that is completely useless or unprofitable.
- **cut (someone) dead** to ignore (someone) completely.
- **dead and buried** completely dead or extinct with no chance of being revived.
- **dead as a dodo** completely dead or out of fashion. <Refers to a flightless bird that has been extinct since 1700>.
- **dead beat** exhausted.
- **dead from the neck up** extremely stupid.

- **dead in the water** with no hope of success. <Refers to a dead fish which is no use to fishermen or anglers.>
- **Dead Sea fruit** a thing that appears to be, or is expected to be, of great value but proves to be valueless. <Refers to a fruit, the apple of Sodom, that was thought to grow on trees beside the shores of the Dead Sea. It was beautiful to look at but fell to ashes when touched or tasted>.
- **dead to the world** in a very deep sleep.
- **dead wood** a person or thing that is no longer necessary or useful.
- **enough to waken the dead** extremely loud.
- **let the dead bury their dead** past problems, quarrels, etc, are best forgotten. <A biblical reference to Matthew 8:22, in which Jesus said, 'Follow me and let the dead bury their dead'.>
- **over my dead body** in the face of my fierce opposition.
- **step into** *or* **fill dead men's shoes** to take over the position of someone who has died or left under unfortunate circumstances.
- **would not be seen dead in** *or* **with, etc**, extremely unlikely to be seen wearing something, accompanying someone, etc, because of an extreme dislike or aversion.

deaf
- **deaf as a post** completely deaf.
- **fall on deaf ears** not to be listened to, to go unnoticed or disregarded.
- **stone deaf** completely deaf.
- **turn a deaf ear to (something)** to refuse to listen to (something), to take no notice of (something).

deal
- **a raw deal** unfair treatment.

death
- **at death's door** extremely ill, dying.
- **be in at the death** to be present at the end or final stages of something. <Refers originally to being present at the death of the prey in a hunt>.
- **catch one's death (of cold)** to become infected with a very bad cold.
- **dice with death** to do something extremely risky and dangerous.
- **die the death** to be badly received. <Refers originally to an actor or performer getting a poor reception from the audience>.
- **sick** *or* **tired to death of (someone** *or* **something)** extremely weary or bored with (someone or something).
- **sign one's own death warrant** to bring about one's own downfall, ruin, etc.
- **will be the death of (someone) 1** to cause the death of (someone). **2** to make (someone) laugh a great deal.

deck
- **hit the deck** to fall to the ground.

deep
- **be thrown in at the deep end** to be put suddenly into a difficult situation of which one has no experience. <Refers to the deep end of a swimming pool>.
- **go off at the deep end** to lose one's temper.

degree
- **give (someone) the third degree** to subject (someone) to intense questioning, especially by using severe methods.
- **to the nth degree** to the greatest possible degree, extent or amount. <Refers to the use of n as a symbol to represent a number, especially a large number>.

dent
- **make a dent in (something)** to reduce (something) by a considerable amount.

depth
- **out of one's depth** in a situation which one cannot cope with. <Refers literally to being in water deeper than one can stand up in>.
- **plumb the depths of (something)** to reach the lowest level of unhappiness, misfortune, etc.

deserts
- **get one's just deserts** to be treated as one deserves, especially to receive deserved punishment.

design
- **have designs upon (someone** *or* **something)** to wish to possess (someone or something), usually belonging to someone else.

device
- **leave (someone) to his** *or* **her own devices** to leave (someone) to look after himself or herself, often after having tried unsuccessfully to help him or her.

devil
- **better the devil you know** it is preferable to have someone or something that one knows to be bad than take a chance with someone or something that might turn out even worse.
- **between the devil and the deep blue sea** faced with two possible courses of action each of which is as unacceptable as the other.
- **needs must when the devil drives** if it is absolutely necessary that something must be done then one must do it.
- **play the devil's advocate** to put forward objections to a plan, idea, etc, simply in order to test the strength of the arguments in its favour.
- **speak of the devil** here is the very person whom we have just been referring to. <Short for 'speak of the devil and he will appear' which refers to a superstition by which it was thought that talking about evil gave it the power to appear>.

diamond
- **rough diamond** a person who behaves in a rough manner but who has good or valuable qualities.

dice
- **load the dice against (someone)** to arrange things so that (someone) has no chance of success. <Refers to a method of cheating in gambling by putting lead or similar heavy material into a dice so that only certain numbers will come up>.

die[1]
- **be dying for (something)** to be longing for (something).
- **die with one's boots on** to die while still working. <Refers to soldiers dying in active service>.
- **never say die** never give up hope.

die[2]
- **the die is cast** a step has been taken which makes the course of future events inevitable. <A translation of the Latin *iacta alea est*, supposedly said by Julius Caesar when he crossed the Rubicon in 49 BC and so committed himself to a war with the Senate>.

differ
- **agree to differ** to agree not to argue about something any more since neither party is likely to change his or her opinion.
- **sink one's differences** to forget about past disagreements.
- **split the difference** to agree on an amount of money halfway between two amounts, especially between the amount that one person is charging for something and the amount that someone else is willing to pay for it.

dig
- **dig one's heels in** to show great determination, especially in order to get one's own wishes carried out.
- **dig one's own grave** to be the cause of one's own misfortune.

dilemma
- **on the horns of a dilemma** in a position where it is necessary to choose between two courses of action. <In medieval rhetoric a dilemma was likened to a two-horned animal on one of whose horns the person making the decision had to throw himself or herself>.

dim
- **take a dim view of (something)** to look with disapproval on (something).

dine
- **dine out on (something)** to be given social invitations because of information, gossip, etc, one can pass on.

dinner
- **like a dog's dinner** an untidy mess.
- **more of (something) than you have had hot dinners** a very great deal of (something).

dirt
- **dirty old man** an elderly man who shows a sexual interest in young girls or young boys.
- **(someone's) name is dirt** *or* **mud** (someone) is in great disfavour.

discretion
- **discretion is the better part of valour** it is wise not to take any unnecessary risks. <Refers to Shakespeare's *Henry IV Part 1*, Act 5, scene IV>.

distance
- **go the distance** to complete something successfully, to last until the end of something.
- **keep one's distance** not to come too close, not to be too friendly.
- **within striking distance** reasonably close.

dividend
- **pay dividends** to bring advantages at a later time. <Refers to dividends paid on money invested, as on stocks and shares>.

do
- **do one's bit** to do one's share of the work, etc.
- **do (someone) in** to kill (someone).
- **done for** without any hope of rescue, help or recovery.
- **do or die** to make the greatest effort possible at the risk of killing, injuring, ruining, etc, oneself.
- **do the honours** to act as host, to serve food or drink to one's guests.
- **do time** to serve a prison sentence.
- **not the done thing** not acceptable behaviour.
- **the do's and don'ts** what one should or should not do in a particular situation.

doctor
- **just what the doctor ordered** exactly what is required.

dog
- **a dog in the manger** a person who stops someone else from doing or having something which he himself or she herself does not want. <From one of Aesop's fables in which a dog prevents the horses from eating the hay in the feeding rack although he himself did not want to eat the hay>.
- **a dog's life** a miserable life.
- **dog eat dog** a ruthless struggle against one's rivals to survive or be successful.
- **go to the dogs** to be no longer good, moral, successful, etc.
- **give a dog a bad name** if bad things are said about a person's character they will stay with him or her for the rest of his or her life.
- **in the doghouse** in disfavour.
- **keep a dog and bark oneself** to employ someone to do a job and then do it oneself.
- **let sleeping dogs lie** do not look for trouble; if there is no trouble, do not cause any.
- **you can't teach an old dog new tricks** the older you get the more difficult it is to learn new skills or accept ideas or new fashions.

doggo
- **lie doggo** to remain in hiding, not to do anything that will draw attention to oneself.

donkey
- **donkey's ages** *or* **years** a very long time. <Perhaps from a pun on donkey's ears, which are very long>.
- **donkey work** the hard, often tiring or physical, part of any job.

- **talk the hind legs off a donkey** to talk too much or to talk for a very long time.

door

- **darken (someone's) door** to come or go into (someone's) house.
- **have a** *or* **one foot in the door** to start to gain entrance to somewhere or something when entrance is difficult. <Refers to someone putting a foot in a door to wedge it open in order to gain entrance>.
- **lay (something) at (someone's) door** to blame (someone) for (something).
- **open doors** to give someone an opportunity to improve his or her position, to improve someone's chances of success.
- **show (someone) the door** to make (someone) leave.

dose

- **a dose** *or* **taste of one's own medicine** something unpleasant done to a person who is in the habit of doing similar things to other people.

dot

- **dot the i's and cross the t's** to attend to details.
- **on the dot 1** exactly on time. **2** exactly at the time stated. <Refers to the dots on the face of a clock>.

double

- **at the double** very quickly. <A military term, literally at twice the normal marching speed>.
- **do a double take** to look at or think about (someone or something) a second time because one has not taken it in or understood it the first time.
- **double Dutch** unintelligible words or language. <Refers to the fact that Dutch sounds a very difficult language to those who are not native speakers of it>.

doubt

- **a doubting Thomas** a person who will not believe something without strong proof. <Refers to the biblical story Thomas, the disciple who doubted Christ, John 21:24–29>.

down

- **down in the dumps** *or* **down in the mouth** depressed, in low spirits.
- **down the drain** completely wasted.
- **down under** Australia.
- **get down to (something)** to begin to work at (something) in earnest.
- **go downhill** to get worse and worse, to deteriorate.
- **have a down on (someone** *or* **something)** to be very hostile or opposed to (someone or something).

drawer

- **out of the top drawer** from the upper classes or aristocracy.

dream

- **a dream ticket** used of two people who are expected to work very successfully together. <Originally used to refer to political elections>.

dress

- **dressed to kill** *or* **dressed to the nines** dressed in one's smartest clothes so as to attract attention.

drift

- **get the drift** to understand the general meaning of something.

drink

- **drink like a fish** to drink a great deal of alcoholic drinks.

drop

- **at the drop of a hat** immediately, requiring only the slightest excuse.
- **drop into (someone's) lap** to happen to (someone) without any effort.
- **let (something) drop** to let (something) be known accidentally.

drown

- **drown one's sorrows** to take alcoholic drink in order to forget one's unhappiness.

drum

- **drum (someone) out** to send (someone) away, to ask (someone) to leave. <Refers to the use of drums when an officer was being publicly dismissed from his regiment>.

dry

- **a dry run** a practice attempt, a rehearsal.
- **dry as a bone** extremely dry.
- **dry as dust** extremely dull or boring.
- **dry up** to forget what one was going to say.
- **keep one's powder dry** to remain calm and prepared for immediate action. <Refers to the fact that gunpowder must be kept dry to be effective>.

duck

- **a lame duck** a weak or inefficient person or organization.
- **a sitting duck** a person or thing that is very easy to attack. <Refers to the fact that a sitting duck is easier to shoot at than one flying in the air>.
- **be water off a duck's back** be totally ineffective. <Refers to the fact that water runs straight off the oily feathers on a duck's back>.
- **break one's duck** to have one's first success. <A cricketing term. No score in cricket is known as a duck>.
- **take to (something) like a duck to water.** to be able to do (something) right from the beginning naturally and without difficulty.
- **ugly duckling** an unattractive or uninteresting person or thing that develops in time into someone or something very attractive, interesting or successful. <Refers to the story by Hans Andersen about a baby swan that is brought up by ducks who consider it ugly by their standards until it grows into a beautiful swan>.

dust

- **let the dust settle** to give things time to calm down.

- **not see (someone) for dust** not to see (someone) again because he has run away. <Refers to clouds of dust left behind by horses or vehicles when they are moving fast>.
- **shake the dust from one's feet** to leave somewhere, usually gladly.
- **throw dust in (someone's eyes)** to attempt to confuse or deceive (someone). <Dust temporarily blinds people if it gets into their eyes>.

Dutch

- **Dutch auction** an auction in which the auctioneer starts with a high price and reduces it until someone puts in a bid.
- **Dutch courage** courage that is not real courage but induced by drinking alcohol. <Perhaps from a Dutch military custom of drinking alcohol before going into battle, perhaps from the fact that gin was introduced into England by the Dutch followers of William III>.
- **Dutch treat** a kind of entertainment or celebration where everyone concerned pays for himself or herself. <From Dutch lunch, to which all of the guests were expected to contribute some of the food>.
- **go Dutch** to share expenses.
- **talk to (someone) like a Dutch uncle** to scold (someone) or talk to (someone) for what is supposedly his or her own good. <Perhaps from the Dutch's reputation for strict family discipline>.

ear

- **go in one ear and out the other** not to make any lasting impression.
- **grin from ear to ear** to have a wide smile on your face.
- **have** *or* **keep one's ear to the ground** to keep oneself informed about what is happening around one. <Perhaps from a North American Indian method of tracking prey>.
- **(my, etc) ears are burning** someone somewhere is talking about (me, etc). <The belief that one's ears grow hot when someone is talking about one is mentioned by Pliny, the Roman writer>.
- **up to one's ears in (something)** deeply involved in (something). <A comparison with someone who is almost submerged by very deep water>.

earth

- **bring (someone) (back) down to earth** to make (someone) aware of the practicalities of life or of a situation.
- **run (someone** *or* **something) to earth** to find (someone or something) after a long search. <Refers to a hunting term for chasing a fox into its earth or hole>.

easy

- **easy as falling off a log** *or* **easy as pie** extremely easy.
- **easy on the eye** very attractive.

eat

- **have (someone) eating out of one's hand** to have (someone) doing everything that one wishes, because he or she likes or admires one. <Refers to an animal that is so tame that it will eat out of someone's hand>.

ebb

- **at a low ebb** in a poor or depressed state. <Refers to the tide when it has flowed away from the land>.

edge

- **be at the cutting edge of (something)** to be involved in the most modern, advanced development or stage of (something).
- **be on the edge of your seat** to be very excited and eager to know what happens next.
- **have the edge on (someone** *or* **something)** to have the advantage of (someone or something).
- **lose one's edge** to become less effective or less good at what you do. <Refers to a knife becoming blunt>.
- **push (someone) over the edge** to make someone unable to cope, mentally ill, etc.

egg

- **be left with egg on one's face** to be left looking foolish.
- **put all one's eggs in one basket** to rely entirely on the success of one project, etc.
- **teach one's grandmother to suck eggs** to try to tell someone how to do something when he or she is much more experienced than oneself at it.

eight

- **be** *or* **have one over the eight** to be or to have had too much to drink. <Refers to a former belief that one could have eight drinks before one is drunk>.

elbow

- **give (someone) the elbow** to get rid of (someone), to end a relationship with (someone).

element

- **in one's element** in a situation in which one is happy or at one's best. <Refers to the four elements of medieval science of fire, earth, air and water>.

elephant

- **a white elephant** something which is useless and troublesome to look after. <White elephants were given by the Kings of Siam followers who had displeased them since the cost of keeping such an elephant was such that it would ruin the follower>.
- **have a memory like an elephant** never to forget things.

eleventh

- **at the eleventh hour** at the last possible minute. <A biblical reference to the parable of the labourers in the vineyard in Matthew 20>.

empty

- **empty vessels make most noise** the most foolish or least informed people are most likely to voice their opinions.

end

- **at a loose end** with nothing to do, with no plans.
- **at the end of one's tether** at the end of one's patience, tolerance, etc. <Refers to a rope that will only extend a certain distance to let the animal attached to it graze>.

- **make ends meet** to live within the limits of one's income. <The ends referred to are the start and finish of one's annual accounts>.

enough
- **enough is as good as a feast** if you have enough of something you should be satisfied with that; you do not need any more.

eternal
- **eternal triangle** a sexual relationship between two men and one woman or between two women and one man.

even
- **get** *or* **keep on an even keel** to be or keep steady or calm with no sudden changes.

event
- **be wise after the event** to realize how a situation should have been dealt with after it is over.

evidence
- **turn Queen's** *or* **King's evidence** to give evidence against a fellow criminal in order to have one's own sentence reduced.

evil
- **the lesser of two evils** the less unpleasant of two fairly unpleasant choices.
- **put off the evil hour** *or* **day** to keep postponing something unpleasant.

ewe
- **(someone's) ewe lamb** (someone's) favourite. <A biblical reference to Samuel 12:3>.

exception
- **the exception that proves the rule** the fact that an exception has to be made for a particular example of something proves that the general rule is valid.

eye
- **an eye for an eye (and a tooth for a tooth)** a punishment to match the offence committed. <A biblical reference to Exodus 21:23>.
- **a sight for sore eyes** a pleasant or welcome sight.
- **be one in the eye for (someone)** to be something unpleasant that happens to someone who deserves it.
- **keep an eagle eye on (someone or something)** to watch (someone or something) extremely closely. <Refers to the fact that eagles are thought to have particularly keen vision>.
- **keep a weather eye open** *or* **keep one's eyes peeled** *or* **skinned** to keep a close watch, to be alert. <A nautical term for watching for changes in the weather>.
- **make eyes at (someone)** to look at (someone) with sexual interest.
- **not to bat an eyelid** not to show any surprise, distress, etc.
- **raise some/a few eyebrows** to surprise or shock some people.

- **see eye to eye with (someone)** to be in agreement with (someone).
- **there's more to (someone** *or* **something) than meets the eye** the true worth or state of (someone or something) is not immediately obvious.

face
- **be staring one in the face 1** to be very obvious, although one may not realize this at first. **2** to be likely to happen or to be about to happen.
- **face the music** to face and deal with a situation caused by one's actions. <Perhaps from a performer facing the musicians below the front of the stage as he or she makes an entrance on stage>.
- **fly in the face of (something)** to oppose or defy (something). <Refers to a dog attacking>.
- **get out of (someone's) face** to go away and stop annoying (someone).
- **have a long face** to look unhappy.
- **keep a straight face** to stop oneself from smiling or laughing.
- **lose face** to suffer a loss of respect or reputation.
- **make** *or* **pull a face** to twist one's face into a strange or funny expression.
- **put a brave face on it** to try to appear brave when one is feeling afraid, distressed, etc.
- **save (someone's) face** to prevent (someone) from appearing stupid or wrong.
- **show one's face** to put in an appearance, especially when one will not be welcome or when one will be embarrassed.

faint
- **faint heart never won fair lady** boldness is necessary to achieve what one desires.
- **not to have the faintest** not to have the slightest idea.

fair
- **by fair means or foul** by any method whatsoever.
- **fair game** a person or thing that it is considered quite reasonable to attack, make fun of, etc.
- **fair play** fairness and justice.
- **fairweather friends** people who are friendly towards one only when one is not in trouble.

fall
- **fall back on (someone** *or* **something)** to rely on (someone or something) if all else fails.
- **fall flat** to fail, to have no effect.
- **fall foul of (something** *or* **something)** to do something that arouses someone's anger or hostility.
- **fall from grace** to lose (someone's) favour.
- **fall over oneself to** to set about doing something with great willingness and eagerness.

false
- **under false pretences** by using deceit.

family
- **run in the family** to be a characteristic found in many members of the same family.

fancy

- **(footloose and) fancy free** not in love with anyone, not romantically attached.
- **take** *or* **tickle one's fancy** to attract one, to arouse a liking in one.

far

- **go far** to be very successful.
- **go too far** to do or say something that is beyond the limits of what is acceptable.

fast

- **play fast and loose with (something)** to act irresponsibly with (something).
- **pull a fast one on (someone)** to deceive (someone). <Refers to bowling a fast ball in cricket>.

fat

- **it isn't over till the fat lady sings** used to remind people that the result of a competition, etc. is not established until the end of the game, match, etc.
- **live off the fat of the land** to live in a luxurious fashion.
- **the fat is in the fire** trouble has been started and it cannot be stopped. <Fat causes a fire to flare up>.

fate

- **a fate worse than death** something terrible that happens to one, often rape.
- **seal (someone's) fate** to ensure that something, usually unpleasant, happens to (someone).
- **tempt fate** to act in a way that is likely to bring one ill luck or misfortune.

fear

- **there is no fear of (something)** it is not likely that (something) will happen.

feast

- **be feast or famine** to be a situation in which there is too much of something or too little.

feat

- **be no mean feat** used to emphasize the difficulty of a task or venture.

feather

- **a feather in one's cap** something of which one can be proud.
- **feather one's (own) nest** to make a profit for oneself, often at the expense of someone else.
- **make the feathers** *or* **fur fly** to cause trouble or a quarrel. <Refers to birds or animals fighting>.
- **ruffle (someone's) feathers** to annoy or upset (someone).
- **show the white feather** to show signs of cowardice. <A white feather in the tail of a fighting cock was a sign of inferior breeding>.

feel

- **feel in one's bones** to know (something) by instinct.
- **feel one's feet** to be becoming used to a situation.

feet

- **at (someone's) feet 1** easily within (someone's) reach or power. **2** greatly admiring of (someone).
- **drag one's feet** to take a long time to do something.
- **fall** *or* **land on one's feet** to be fortunate or successful, especially after a period of uncertainty or misfortune.
- **find one's feet** to become capable of coping with a situation.
- **have feet of clay** to have a surprising weakness, despite having been thought to be perfect. <A biblical reference to Daniel 2:31–34>.
- **have both feet on the ground** *or* **have one's feet on the ground** to be practical and sensible.
- **get under (someone's) feet** to hinder or get in (someone's) way.
- **put one's feet up** to take a rest.
- **stand on one's own feet** to be independent.
- **sweep (someone) off his** *or* **her feet** to affect (someone) with great enthusiasm or emotion; to influence (someone) to do as one wishes.

fence

- **mend fences** to put things right after a quarrel, etc.
- **sit on the fence** to refuse to take sides in a dispute, etc.

fiddle

- **fit as a fiddle** extremely fit.
- **play second fiddle to (someone)** to be in a subordinate or inferior position to (someone).

field

- **have a field day** to have a very busy, successful or enjoyable day.
- **play the field** to take advantage of many chances offered to one, especially to go out with several members of the opposite sex.

fight

- **fighting fit** extremely healthy and in good condition.
- **fight shy of (something)** to avoid (something).

fill

- **have had one's fill** to have had enough, to be unable to tolerate any more.

fine

- **get (something) down to a fine art** to have learned to do (something) extremely well.
- **go through (something) with a fine-tooth comb** to search (something) very carefully. <A fine-tooth comb is used to remove the nits (eggs) of head lice from hair>.

finger

- **be all fingers and thumbs** to be clumsy or awkward when using one's hands.
- **burn one's fingers** *or* **get one's fingers burnt** to suffer because of something that one has been involved in.
- **cross one's fingers** to hope for good fortune.

- **get** *or* **pull one's finger out** to stop wasting time and get on with something.
- **have a finger in every pie** to be involved in a large number of projects, organizations, etc.
- **have (something) at one's fingertips** to know all the information about (something).
- **let (something) slip through one's fingers** to lose (an advantage, opportunity, etc), often by one's inaction.
- **not to lift a finger** not to do anything at all.
- **point the finger at (someone)** to indicate who is to blame.
- **put one's finger on (something)** to identify (something) exactly.
- **twist** *or* **wrap (someone) round one's little finger** to be able to get (someone) to do exactly as one wishes.
- **work your fingers to the bone** to work extremely hard.

fire
- **get on like a house on fire** to get on very well.
- **hang fire** to wait or be delayed. <Refers to a gun in which there is a delay between the trigger being pulled and the gun being fired>.
- **in the firing line** in a situation in which you are likely to be blamed or criticized. <Refers to people who have been lined up in order to be shot dead.>
- **play with fire** to take tasks, to do something dangerous.
- **set the Thames** *or* **world on fire** to do something remarkable. <Refers to the River Thames, which it would be impossible to set alight>.
- **under fire** being attacked. <Refers literally to being shot at>.

first
- **first thing** early in the morning or in the working day.
- **in the first flush of (something)** in the early and vigorous stages of (something).

fish
- **have other fish to fry** to have something else to do, especially something that is more important or more profitable.
- **like a fish out of water** ill at ease and unaccustomed to a situation.
- **there are plenty more fish in the sea** many more opportunities will arise; many more members of the opposite sex are around.

fit
- **by fits and starts** irregularly, often stopping and starting.

fix
- **in a fix** in an awkward or difficult situation.

flag
- **hang** *or* **put the flags out** to celebrate something (a rare event).
- **run (something) up the flagpole** to put forward (a plan or idea) in order to gauge reactions to it.

flame
- **an old flame** a former boyfriend or girlfriend.
- **fan the flames** to make a difficult situation worse.

flash
- **a flash in the pan** a sudden, brief success. <Refers to a flintlock gun in which the spark from the flint ignited the gunpowder in the priming pan, the flash then travelling to the main barrel. If this failed to go off there was only a flash in the pan>.

flat
- **in a flat spin** in a state of confused excitement.

flavour
- **flavour of the month** a person or thing that is particularly popular at a particular time, although this is likely to be temporary.

flea
- **a flea in one's ear** a sharp scolding.

flesh
- **a thorn in (someone's) flesh** a permanent source of annoyance or irritation. <A biblical reference to II Corinthians 12:7>.
- **get** *or* **have one's pound of flesh** to obtain everything that one is entitled to, especially if this causes difficulties or suffering to those who have to give it. <Refers to Shakespeare's play *The Merchant of Venice*, in which Shylock tries to enforce an agreement by which he can cut a pound of flesh from Antonio>.

floodgates
- **open the floodgates** to make it possible for a great many people to do something, usually something considered undesirable, or make it likely that this will happen, perhaps by removing some kind of restriction.

floor
- **take the floor 1** to rise to make a public speech. **2** to begin to dance.
- **wipe the floor with (someone)** to defeat (someone) thoroughly.

fly[1]
- **a fly in the ointment** something that spoils something.
- **there are no flies on (someone)** there is no possibility of deceiving or cheating (someone), there is no lack of sense in (someone).
- **would like to be a fly on the wall** would like to be present and able to hear what is going on without being seen.

fly[2]
- **get off to a flying start** to have a very successful beginning.

foam
- **foam at the mouth** to be very angry. <Mad dogs foam at the mouth>.

follow

- **follow suit** to do just as someone else has done. <A reference to card-playing when a player plays the same suit as the previous player>.

fool

- **a fool's paradise** a state of happiness that is based on something that is not true or realistic.
- **be nobody's fool** to have a good deal of common sense.
- **fools rush in (where angels fear to tread)** an ignorant person can sometimes achieve what a warier person cannot. <From Alexander Pope's *An Essay on Criticism*>.
- **make a fool of (someone)** to make (someone) appear ridiculous or stupid.
- **not to suffer fools gladly** not to have any patience with foolish or stupid people.

foot

- **follow in (someone's) footsteps** to do the same as someone else has done before, particularly a relative.
- **get off on the wrong foot** to get off to a bad or unfortunate start.
- **have one foot in the grave** to be very old.
- **put one's foot down** to be firm about something, to forbid someone to do something.
- **put one's foot in it** to do or say something tactless.
- **shoot oneself in the foot** to make a mistake or do something stupid which causes problems for oneself or harms one's chances of success.

form

- **on form** in good condition, fit and in a good humour. <Form refers to the condition of a horse>.

fort

- **hold the fort** to take temporary charge of something.

forty

- **forty winks** a short nap.

frame

- **be in the frame 1** to be likely to get or win something. **2** to be suspected of being guilty of a crime.

free

- **free and easy** informal, casual.
- **give (someone) a free hand** give (someone) permission to do as he or she wishes.

French

- **take French leave** to stay away from work, etc, without permission. <Refers to an 18th-century French custom of leaving a party without saying goodbye to one's host or hostess>.

Freudian

- **a Freudian slip** the use of a wrong word while speaking that is supposed to indicate an unconscious thought. <Refers to the theories of the psychologist Sigmund Freud>.

Friday

- **man** *or* **girl Friday** an invaluable assistant. <Refers to Friday, a character in *Robinson Crusoe* by Daniel Defoe>.

friend

- **a friend in need is a friend indeed** a friend who helps when one is in trouble is truly a friend.

frog

- **have a frog in one's throat** to be hoarse.

fruit

- **forbidden fruit** something desirable that is made even more so because one is forbidden for some reason to obtain it. <Refers to the biblical tree in the Garden of Eden whose fruit Adam was forbidden by God to eat, Genesis 3>.

fry

- **out of the frying pan into the fire** free of a difficult or dangerous situation only to get into a worse one.

full

- **be full of oneself** to be very conceited.
- **in the fullness of time** when the proper time has arrived, eventually.

fuss

- **make a fuss of (someone)** to pay a lot of attention to (someone), to show (someone) a lot of affection.

gab

- **the gift of the gab** the ability to talk readily and easily.

gain

- **gain ground** to make progress, to become more generally acceptable or popular.

gallery

- **play to the gallery** to act in an amusing or showy way to the ordinary people in an organization, etc, in order to gain popularity or their support.

game

- **beat (someone) at his** *or* **her own game** to do better than (someone) at his or her activity, especially a cunning or dishonest one.
- **give the game away** to reveal a secret plan, trick, etc, usually accidentally.
- **play the game** to behave fairly and honourably.
- **the game is up** the plan, trick, crime, etc, has been discovered and so has failed.

garden

- **everything in the garden is lovely** everything is fine.
- **lead (someone) up the garden path** to mislead or deceive (someone).

gauntlet

- **run the gauntlet** to be exposed or subjected to blame, criticism or risk. <Gauntlet is a mistaken form of Swedish *gatlopp*. Running the *gatlopp* was a Swedish military punishment in which the culprit had to run between two lines of men with whips who struck him as he passed>.

- **take/pick up the gauntlet** to accept a challenge.
- **throw down the gauntlet** to issue a challenge. <Throwing down a gauntlet, a protective glove, was the traditional method of challenging someone to a fight in medieval times>.

ghost
- **give up the ghost** to die, stop working, etc. <Ghost refers to a person's spirit—a biblical reference to Job 14:10>.

gift
- **look a gift horse in the mouth** to criticize something that has been given to one. <Looking at a horse's teeth is a way of telling its age and so estimating its value>.

gild
- **gild the lily** to add unnecessary decoration or detail. <An adaptation of a speech from Shakespeare's *King John*, Act 4, scene II>.

gilt
- **take the gilt off the gingerbread** to take away what makes something attractive. <Gingerbread used to be sold in fancy shapes and decorated with gold leaf>.

gird
- **gird up one's loins** to prepare oneself for action. <A biblical phrase from the fact that robes had to be tied up with a girdle before men began work or they got in the way, Acts 12:8>.

give
- **give and take** willingness to compromise.

glad
- **glad rags** best clothes worn for special occasions.

glass
- **glass ceiling** an invisible barrier, established by tradition, personal discrimination, etc, which prevents women from achieving the top jobs in their companies, professions, etc.
- **people who live in glass houses should not throw stones** people with faults themselves should not criticize faults in others.

glove
- **fit like a glove** to fit perfectly.
- **take the gloves off** to begin to fight, argue, etc, in earnest. <Refers to boxers who wear protective gloves to soften their blows>.

gold
- **be sitting on a goldmine** to posses something very valuable or potentially profitable, often without realizing this.
- **like living in a goldfish bowl** in a situation where one has very little privacy.
- **strike gold** to do or find something that makes one very rich or very successful.

gnat
- **strain at a gnat (and swallow a camel)** to trouble oneself over a matter of no importance, something only slightly wrong, etc, (but be unconcerned about a matter of great importance, something very wrong, etc). <A biblical reference to Matthew 23:23–24>.

go
- **from the word go** right from the very start of something.
- **make a go of it** *or* **something** to make a success of something.
- **no go** impossible, not given approval.
- **on the go** continually active, busy.

goal
- **score an own goal** to do something which fails to achieve what you set out to do and, instead, harms your own interests.

goalpost
- **move the goalposts** to change the conditions, rules or aims applying to a project, etc, after it is under way so that it is disadvantageous to others but advantageous to oneself.

goat
- **act the goat** to behave in an intentionally silly way.
- **get (someone's) goat** to irritate (someone).

God, god
- **in the lap of the gods** uncertain, left to chance or fate.
- **there but for the grace of God go I** if I had not been fortunate the circumstances of another person could easily also have been mine.

gold
- **a gold mine** a source of wealth or profit.
- **be like gold dust** be very scarce.
- **golden boy** a young man who is popular or successful.
- **golden handshake** a large amount of money given to someone who is leaving a job, usually because he or she has been declared redundant.
- **good as gold** very well-behaved.
- **the crock** *or* **pot of gold at the end of the rainbow** wealth or good fortune that one will never achieve.
- **the golden rule** a principle or practice that it is vital to remember. <Originally the golden rule was that one should do to others as one would wish them to do to oneself>.
- **worth its** *or* **one's weight in gold** extremely valuable or useful.

good
- **be as good as one's word** to do what one has promised do.
- **be on to a good thing** *or* **have a good thing going** to be in a desirable or profitable situation.
- **be up to no good** to be planning something wrong or illegal.
- **give as good as one gets** to be as successful as one's opponent in an argument, contest, fight, etc.
- **good for nothing** worthless.

- **in (someone's) good books** in favour with (someone).
- **make good** to be successful in one's career or business.
- **take (something) in good part** to accept (something) without being offended or angry.

goods

- **deliver the goods** to do what one is required or expected to do.
- **goods and chattels** movable property. <An old legal term>.

goose

- **cook (someone's) goose** to ruin (someone's) chances of success.
- **kill the goose that lays the golden egg** to destroy something that is a source of profit. <Refers to one of Aesop's fables in which the owner of a goose that laid golden eggs killed it thinking to get all the eggs at once, only to discover that there were none>.
- **what's sauce for the goose is sauce for the gander** what applies to one person should apply to another, usually to a member of the opposite sex.

gooseberry

- **play gooseberry** to be the third person present with a couple who wish to be alone.

Gordian

- **cut the Gordian knot** to solve a problem or end a great difficulty by a vigorous or drastic method. <Refers to a legend in which whoever could untie a knot in a rope belonging to King Gordius of Phrygia, would be made ruler of all Asia. Alexander the Great severed the knot by cutting through it with a sword>.

gospel

- **take (something) as gospel** to accept (something) as absolutely true. <The gospel refers to the books of the Bible dealing with the life and teachings of Christ>.

grab

- **up for grabs** ready to be taken, bought, etc.

grace

- **saving grace** a good quality which prevents someone or something from being completely bad or worthless.
- **with a bad** *or* **good grace** in an unpleasant or pleasant and unwilling or willing way.

grade

- **make the grade** to succeed in what you are trying to achieve, often by reaching a required standard. <Originally referred to a train which succeeded in climbing a steep section of track>.

grain

- **go against the grain** to be against someone's inclinations, feelings or wishes. <Refers to the direction of the grain in wood, it being easier to cut or smooth wood with the grain rather than across or against it>.

grape

- **sour grapes** saying that something that one cannot have is not worth having. <Refers to one of Aesop's fables in which a fox that failed to reach a bunch of grapes growing above his head said that they were sour anyhow>.
- **the grapevine** an informal and unofficial way of passing news and information from person to person, gossip.

grass

- **grass widow** a woman whose husband is away from home for a short time for reasons of business or sport. <Originally the term referred to an unmarried woman who had sexual relations with a man or men, the origin being that such relations usually took place out of doors>.
- **let the grass grow under one's feet** to delay or waste time.
- **put** *or* **turn (someone) out to grass** to cause (someone) to retire. <Refers to turning out a horse into a field at the end of its working life>.
- **the grass is always greener on the other side of the fence** another set of circumstances or lifestyle always seems preferable to one's own. <Refers to the habit of grazing animals of grazing through the fence separating them from the next field>.
- **the grass roots** the ordinary people in an organization, etc.

grave

- **(someone) would turn in his** *or* **her grave** (someone) would be very annoyed or upset.

Greek

- **be all Greek to me, etc,** I, etc, don't understand any of it. <Refers to the fact that ancient Greek was considered a difficult language to learn>.

green

- **give the green light to (something)** give one's permission for (something).
- **have green fingers** to be good at growing plants.
- **the green-eyed monster** jealousy.

grief

- **come to grief** to suffer misfortune or failure.
- **give (someone) grief** to criticize or nag (someone).

grim

- **hang on** *or* **hold on like grim death** to take a firm, determined hold of something in difficult or dangerous circumstances.

grin

- **grin and bear it** to tolerate something without complaining.
- **wipe the grin off (someone's face)** to make (someone) stop feeling pleased or satisfied.

grind

- **grind to a halt** slowly begin to stop or cease working.

grip

- **get a grip (of** *or* **on something** *or* **oneself)** to take firm control (of something or oneself).

- **get** *or* **come to grips with (something)** to begin to deal with (something).

ground

- **cut the ground from under (someone's) feet** to cause (someone's) actions, arguments, etc, to be ineffective, often by acting before he or she does.
- **fall on stony ground** to have no attention paid to it. <Refers to seed falling on stony, infertile ground and so not being able to grow>.
- **get in on the ground floor** to be in at the very start of a project, business, etc.
- **get (something) off the ground** to get (a project) started. <Refers literally to a plane>.
- **hit the ground running** to start a new activity immediately with a great deal of energy and enthusiasm.
- **on one's own ground** dealing with a subject, situation, etc, with which one is familiar.
- **run oneself into the ground** to become exhausted from working too hard or trying to do too many things.
- **shift one's ground** to change one's opinions, attitude, etc.
- **stand one's ground** to remain firm, not to yield.
- **suit (someone) down to the ground** to suit someone perfectly.
- **thin** *or* **thick on the ground** scarce or plentiful.

guard

- **let your guard down/lower your guard/drop your guard** to stop being careful or alert.
- **on** *or* **off one's guard** prepared or unprepared for any situation, especially a dangerous or difficult one. <Refers to fencing>.

gum

- **gum up the works** to cause a machine, system, etc, to break down.

gun

- **be gunning for (someone)** to plan to harm (someone).
- **jump the gun** to start before the proper time. <Refers to athletes starting a race before the starting gun goes>.
- **spike (someone's) guns** to cause (someone's) plans or actions to be ineffective. <Refers historically to driving a metal spike into the touch-hole of a captured enemy gun which could not be moved away in order to render it useless>.
- **stick to one's guns** to remain firm in one's opinions, etc. <Refers to a soldier who keeps shooting at the enemy and does not run away>.

hackles

- **make (someone's) hackles rise** to make (someone) angry. <Hackles are the feathers on the necks of male birds which rise when the bird is angry>.

hair

- **a hair of the dog (that bit one)** an alcoholic drink taken as a supposed cure for having consumed too much alcohol the night before. <From an old belief that if you were bitten by a mad dog and got rabies you could be cured by having hairs of the dog laid on the wound>.

- **get in (someone's) hair** to irritate (someone).
- **keep one's hair on** to remain calm and not get angry.
- **let one's hair down** to behave in an informal, relaxed manner.
- **make (someone's) hair stand on end** to terrify or horrify (someone).
- **not to turn a hair** not to show any sign of fear, distress, etc.
- **split hairs** to argue about small unimportant details, to quibble.
- **tear one's hair (out)** to show frustration or irritation.

half

- **(someone's) better half** (someone's) wife or husband.
- **half a loaf is better than no bread** a little of something desirable is better than nothing.
- **meet (someone) halfway** to reach a compromise agreement with (someone).
- **not half** very much so.

hammer

- **go at it hammer and tongs** to fight or quarrel loudly and fiercely. <Refers to a blacksmith holding a piece of heated iron in his tongs and striking it loudly with his hammer>.

hand

- **be hand in glove with (someone)** to be closely associated with (someone) for a bad or illegal purpose.
- **force (someone's) hand** to force (someone) to do something that he or she may not want to do or be ready to do.
- **give** *or* **lend (someone) a (helping) hand** to help (someone).
- **go hand in hand** to be closely connected.
- **hand over fist** in large amounts, very rapidly. <Originally a nautical term meaning rapid progress such as can be made by hauling on a rope putting one hand after the other>.
- **have a hand in (something)** to be involved in (something), to have contributed to the cause of (something).
- **have one's hands full** to be very busy.
- **in good hands** well looked after.
- **keep one's hand in** to retain one's skill at something by doing it occasionally.
- **lend (someone) a hand** to help (someone).
- **live from hand to mouth** to have enough money only to pay for one's present needs without having any to save. <Whatever money comes into one's hand is used to put food in one's mouth>.
- **many hands make light work** a job is easier to do if there are several people doing it.
- **my, etc, hands are tied** something prevents me, etc, from acting as I, etc, might wish to.
- **not to do a hand's turn** to do nothing.
- **play into (someone's) hands** to do exactly what someone wants one to do because it is to his or her advantage. <Refers to playing one's hand at cards so as to benefit another player>.

- **show one's hand** to reveal to others one's plans or intentions, previously kept secret. <Refers to showing one's hand to other players in a card game>.
- **take (someone) in hand** to train or discipline (someone).
- **turn one's hand to (something)** to do, to be able to do.
- **wait on (someone) hand and foot** to look after (someone) to such an extent that he or she does not have to do anything for himself or herself.
- **wash one's hands of (someone *or* something)** to refuse to be involved any longer in (something) or to be responsible for (someone or something). <A biblical reference to the action of Pontius Pilate after the crucifixion of Jesus in Matthew 27:24>.
- **with one hand tied behind one's back** very easily.

handle
- **fly off the handle** to lose one's temper. <Refers to an axehead which flies off the handle when it is being used>.

hang
- **get the hang of (something)** to learn how to do (something) or begin to understand (something).
- **hung up on (someone *or* something)** obsessed with (someone or something).

happy
- **happy as a lark** *or* **sand-boy** extremely happy.
- **happy hunting ground** a place where someone finds what he or she desires or where he or she is successful.
- **the** *or* **a happy medium** a sensible middle course between two extremes.

hard
- **between a rock and a hard place** *see* **rock**.
- **hard as nails** lacking in pity, sympathy, softer feelings, etc.
- **hard cash** coins and bank-notes as opposed to cheques, etc.
- **hard facts** facts that cannot be disputed.
- **hard lines** bad luck. <Perhaps a reference to a ship's ropes being made hard by ice>.
- **hard of hearing** rather deaf.
- **hard up** not having much money.
- **take a hard line** to take strong, stern or unyielding action or have strong opinions about something.
- **the hard stuff** strong alcoholic drink, spirits.

hare
- **run with the hare and hunt with the hounds** to try to give one's support to two opposing sides at once.

hash
- **settle (someone's) hash** to deal with (someone) in such a way that he or she causes no more trouble or is prevented from doing what was intended.

hat
- **hats off to (someone)** (someone) should be praised and congratulated.

- **hat trick** any action done three times in a row. <Refers originally to a cricketer receiving a hat from his club for putting out three batsmen with three balls in a row>.
- **I'll eat my hat** an expression used to express total disbelief in a fact, statement, etc.
- **keep (something) under one's hat** to keep (something) secret.
- **knock (someone *or* something) into a cocked hat** to defeat or surpass (someone or something) completely. <A cocked hat was a three-cornered hat in the 18th-century made by folding the edges of a round hat into corners>.
- **pass the hat round** to ask for contributions of money.
- **take one's hat off to (someone)** to express or show one's admiration for someone).
- **talk through one's hat** to talk about something without any knowledge about it, to talk nonsense.
- **throw one's hat in the ring** to declare oneself a contender or candidate for something. <Refers to a method of making a challenge in prize boxing matches at fairgrounds, etc>.
- **wear a different** *or* **another hat** to speak as the holder of a different position.

hatch
- **batten down the hatches** to prepare for trouble. <Refers to preparations for a storm on a ship at sea>.
- **hatches, matches and despatches** the announcement of births, marriages and deaths in a newspaper.

hatchet
- **bury the hatchet** to agree to be friends again after a quarrel. <Refers to an American Indian custom of burying tomahawks when peace was made>.

have
- **have had it** to have no hope of survival, success, etc.
- **have it in for (someone)** to try to cause trouble for (someone).
- **have it out with (someone)** to discuss areas of disagreement or discontent with someone in order to settle them.
- **let (someone) have it** suddenly to attack (someone) either physically or verbally.

havoc
- **play havoc with (something)** to cause serious damage to (something).

hawk
- **watch (someone) like a hawk** to watch (someone) very carefully.

hay
- **go haywire** to go completely wrong, to go out of control. <Refers to wire that was used to bind hay. It very easily became twisted and therefore came to symbolize confusion>.
- **hit the hay** *or* **sack** to go to bed. <Beds were formerly filled with hay or made from the same material as sacks>.

- **like looking for a needle in a haystack** *see* **needle**.
- **make hay (while the sun shines)** to profit or take advantage of an opportunity while one has the chance. <Haymaking is only possible in fine weather>.

head

- **bite** *or* **eat** *or* **snap (someone's) head off** to speak very sharply and angrily to (someone).
- **bring (something) to a head** to bring something to a state where something must be done about it. <Refers to bringing a boil, etc, to a head>.
- **bury one's head in the sand** to deliberately ignore a situation so that one does not have to deal with it. <Refers to the old belief that ostriches hide their heads in the sand when they are in danger because they think that then they cannot be seen>.
- **cannot make head nor tail of (something)** cannot understand (something) at all.
- **give (someone) his or her head** to allow (someone) to do as he or she wishes. <Refers literally to slackening one's hold on the reins of a horse>.
- **go to (someone's) head I)** to make (someone) arrogant or conceited. **2** to make (someone) slightly drunk.
- **have a head for (something)** to have an ability or aptitude for (something).
- **have a (good) head on one's shoulders** to be clever or sensible.
- **have one's head screwed on the right way** to be sensible.
- **head over heels** completely.
- **hold one's head up (high)** not to feel ashamed or guilty, to remain dignified.
- **keep a level head** *or* **keep one's head** to remain calm and sensible, especially in a difficult situation.
- **keep one's head above water** to have enough money to keep out of debt.
- **knock (something) on the head** to put an end to (something).
- **laugh one's head off** to laugh very loudly.
- **lose one's head** to cease to remain calm, to act foolishly.
- **make headway** to make progress. <Refers originally to ships>.
- **off one's head** insane, not rational.
- **on (someone's) (own) head be it** (someone) must take responsibility or blame.
- **over (someone's) head** (I) too difficult for (someone) to understand. **2** when (someone) seems to have a better right. **3** beyond (someone) to a person of higher rank.
- **put** *or* **lay one's head on the block** to leave oneself open to blame, punishment, danger, etc. <Refers to laying one's head on the block before being beheaded>.
- **put our, etc, heads together** to discuss something together, to share thoughts on something.
- **rear its ugly head** to appear or happen.
- **scratch one's head** to be puzzled.
- **soft** *or* **weak in the head** not very intelligent, mentally retarded.
- **talk one's head off** to talk a great deal.
- **turn (someone's) head** to make (someone) conceited.

heart

- **cross one's heart (and hope to die)** this is said to emphasize the truth of what one is saying.
- **do (someone's) heart good** to give (someone) pleasure.
- **eat one's heart out** to be distressed because one cannot have someone or something which one is longing for.
- **from the bottom of one's heart** most sincerely, very much.
- **have one's heart in one's mouth** to feel afraid or anxious.
- **heart and soul** completely, with all one's energy.
- **(someone's) heart goes out to (someone)** (someone) feels sympathy or pity for (someone).
- **(someone's) heart is in the right place** (someone) is basically kind, sympathetic, etc, although not appearing to be so.
- **(someone's) heart is not in it** (someone) is not enthusiastic about something.
- **(someone's) heart sinks** (someone) feels depressed, disappointed, etc.
- **in good heart** cheerful and confident.
- **in (someone's) heart of hearts** in the deepest part of one's mind or feelings.
- **learn something by heart** to memorize (something) thoroughly.
- **lose heart** to grow discouraged.
- **not to have the heart (to do something)** not to be unkind, unsympathetic, etc, enough (to do something).
- **put new heart into (someone)** to make (someone) feel encouraged and more hopeful.
- **set one's heart on** *or* **have one's heart set on (something)** to desire (something) very much.
- **take heart** to become encouraged.
- **take (something) to heart 1** to be upset by (something). **2** to be influenced by and take notice of (something).
- **wear one's heart on one's sleeve** to let one's feelings be obvious.
- **with all one's heart** most sincerely.

heat

- **in the heat of the moment** while influenced by the excitement or emotion of the occasion.

heaven

- **in seventh heaven** extremely happy. <In Jewish literature the seventh heaven is the highest of all heavens and the one where God lives>.
- **manna from heaven** something advantageous which happens unexpectedly, especially in a time of trouble. <A biblical reference to Exodus 16:15>.
- **move heaven and earth** to make every effort possible.
- **smell** *or* **stink to high heaven** to have a strong and nasty smell.

heavy
- **make heavy weather of (something)** to make more effort to do something than should be required. <Refers originally to a ship which does not handle well in difficult conditions>.

hedge
- **look as though one has been dragged through a hedge backwards** to look very untidy.

heel
- **bring (someone) to heel** to bring (someone) under one's control. <Refers to making a dog walk to heel>.
- **take to one's heels** to run away.

helm
- **at the helm** in charge. <Refers to the helm of a ship>.

hen
- **like a hen on a hot girdle** very nervous and restless.

here
- **neither here nor there** of no importance.
- **the hereafter** life after death.

herring
- **a red herring** a piece of information which misleads (someone) or draws (someone's) attention away from the truth, often introduced deliberately. <A red herring is a strong-smelling fish whose scent could mislead hunting dogs if it were dragged across the path they were pursuing>.
- **neither fish nor fowl nor good red herring** neither one thing nor the other.
- **packed like herring in a barrel** very tightly packed.

hide[1]
- **neither hide nor hair of (someone *or* something)** no trace at all of (someone or something). <Hide is used in the sense of skin>.

hide[2]
- **on a hiding to nothing** in a situation where one cannot possibly win. <Perhaps a reference to boxing>.

high
- **a high flier** a person who is bound to be very successful or who has achieved great success.
- **be for the high jump** to be about to be punished or scolded.
- **be high time** be time something was done without delay.
- **be *or* get on one's high horse** to be or become offended in a haughty manner.
- **high and mighty** arrogant.
- **hunt *or* search high and low for (someone *or* something)** to search absolutely everywhere for (someone or something).
- **leave (someone) high and dry** to leave (someone) in a difficult or helpless state.
- **riding high** very successful. <Used literally of the moon being high in the sky>.

hill
- **over the hill** past one's youth or one's best.

history
- **the rest is history** used to indicate that no more need be said about something because the details of it are well known.

hit
- **be a hit with (someone)** to be popular with (someone).
- **hit-and-run accident** an accident involving a vehicle where the driver who caused it does not stop or report the accident.
- **hit it off** to get on well, to become friendly.

hog
- **go the whole hog** to do something completely and thoroughly. <Perhaps referring to buying a whole pig for meat rather than just parts of it>.

hold
- **have a hold over (someone)** to have power or influence over (someone).
- **hold good** to be valid or applicable.
- **no holds barred** no restrictions on what is permitted.

hole
- **hole-and-corner** secret and often dishonourable.
- **in a hole** in an awkward or difficult situation.
- **make a hole in (something)** to use a large part of (something).
- **need (something) like (someone) needs a hole in the head** to regard (something) as being completely unwelcome or undesirable.
- **pick holes in (something)** to find faults in (a theory, plan, etc).

holy
- **holier-than-thou** acting as though one is more moral, more pious, etc, than other people. <A biblical reference to Isaiah 65:5>.
- **the holy of holies** a private or special place inside a building. <A literal translation of the Hebrew name of the inner sanctuary in the Jewish Temple where the Ark of the Covenant was kept>.

home
- **a home from home** a place where one feels comfortable and relaxed.
- **bring *or* drive (something) home to (someone)** to cause someone fully to understand or believe (something).
- **do one's homework** to prepare thoroughly for a meeting, etc, by getting all the necessary information.
- **home and dry** having successfully completed an objective.
- **home truth** a plain, direct statement of something that is true but unpleasant or difficult for someone to accept.

run
- **run high** of feelings, tempers, etc, to be extremely angry, agitated, etc. <Refers to the sea when there is a strong current and high waves>.

- **make oneself at home** to make oneself comfortable and relaxed.
- **nothing to write home about** not very special, not remarkable.

hook

- **by hook or by crook** by any means possible.
- **off the hook** free from some difficulty, problem, etc, or something one does not want to do. <A reference to angling>.
- **sling one's hook** to go away.
- **swallow (something) hook, line and sinker** to believe (something) completely. <Refers to a fish that swallows not only the hook but the whole of the end section of the fishing line>.
- **the home stretch** *or* **straight** the last part of something, especially when this has been a particularly long or difficult process.

hoop

- **put (someone) through the hoop** to cause (someone) to experience something unpleasant or difficult. <Refers to circus performers who jump through hoops set on fire>.

hop

- **hopping mad** extremely angry.

hope

- **hope against hope** to continue to hope although there is little reason to be hopeful.
- **hope springs eternal (in the human breast)** it is in the nature of human beings to hope. <A quotation from Alexander Pope's *An Essay on Criticism*>.
- **pin one's hopes on (someone *or* something)** to rely on (someone or something) helping one in some way.

horn

- **draw in one's horns** to restrain one's actions, particularly the spending of money. <Refers to a snail drawing in its horns if it is in danger>.
- **lock horns** to argue or fight. <Refers to horned male animals who sometimes get their horns caught together when fighting>.

hornet

- **stir up a hornet's nest** to cause a great deal of trouble.

horse

- **eat like a horse** to eat a great deal.
- **flog a dead horse** to continue to try to arouse interest, enthusiasm, etc, in something which is obviously not, or no longer, of interest.
- **hold one's horses** not to move so fast.
- **horses for courses** certain people are better suited to certain tasks or situations. <Some horses run better on certain types of ground>.
- **straight from the horse's mouth** from someone closely connected with a situation and therefore knowledgeable about it. <It is as though a horse is giving a tip about a race in which it is running>.

- **wild horses would not drag (someone) to something *or* somewhere** nothing would persuade (someone) to attend something or go somewhere.
- **you can take a horse to the water but you cannot make it drink** you can encourage someone to do something but you cannot force him or her to do it.

hot

- **hot on (someone's) heels** close behind someone.

hour

- **the (wee) small hours** the hours immediately following midnight (1am, 2am, etc).
- **the witching hour** midnight. <Witches traditionally are supposed to be active at midnight>.

house

- **bring the house down** to cause great amusement or applause.
- **eat (someone) out of house and home**. to eat a great deal and so be expensive to feed.
- **keep open house** always to be ready and willing to welcome guests.
- **on the house** paid by the owner of shop, pub, etc.
- **safe as houses** completely safe.

hue

- **a hue and cry** a loud protest. <An old legal term meaning a summons for people to join in a hunt for a criminal>.

huff

- **in a** *or* **the huff** upset, offended or sulking.

humble

- **eat humble pie** to have to admit that one has been wrong. <Refers originally to a dish made from the umble or offal of a deer eaten by the lower classes>.

ice

- **break the ice** to ease the shyness or formality of a social occasion.
- **cut no ice** to have no effect.
- **icing on the cake** a desirable but unnecessary addition.
- **on ice** put aside for future use or attention.
- **(skate) on thin ice** (to be) in a risky or dangerous position.
- **the tip of the iceberg** a small sign of a much larger problem. <Refers to the fact that the bulk of an iceberg is hidden underwater>.

ill

- **it's an ill wind (that blows nobody any good)** in almost every misfortune there is something of benefit to someone.

imagination

- **a figment of one's imagination** something which has no reality.

immemorial

- **from time immemorial** from a time beyond anyone's memory, written records, etc; for an extremely long time. <In legal phraseology the expression means 'before the beginning of legal memory'>.

in

- **the ins and outs of (something)** the details of (something).

inch

- **be** *or* **come within an inch of (something)** to be or come very close to.
- **every inch a** *or* **the (something)** exactly the type of (something).
- **give (someone) an inch (and he** *or* **she will take a mile** *or* **an ell)** if one yields in any way to someone then the person in question will make even greater demands. <An ell is an old form of measurement>.

Indian

- **an Indian summer** a time of fine, warm weather in autumn. <Perhaps from a feature of the climate of North America whose original inhabitants were Indians>.

innings

- **have a good innings** to enjoy a considerable period of life, success etc. <Refers to cricket>.

interest

- **a vested interest in (something)** a personal and biased interest in (something).
- **with interest** to an even greater extent than something has been done, etc, to someone.

iron

- **have many** *or* **several irons in the fire** to be involved in several projects, etc, at the same time. < Refers to a blacksmith who heats pieces of iron before shaping them>.
- **rule (someone** *or* **something) with a rod of iron** to rule with sternness or ruthlessness.
- **strike while the iron is hot** to act at a point at which things are favourable to one. <Refers to a blacksmith's work>.
- **the iron hand in the velvet glove** sternness or ruthlessness hidden under an appearance of gentleness.

item

- **be an item** to be regarded as having a romantic relationship.

itch

- **be itching to (do something)** to want very much to (do something).
- **have an itching palm** to be greedy for money.

ivory

- **live in an ivory tower** to have a way of life protected from difficulty or unpleasantness. <*La toure d'ivoire*, French for 'ivory tower', was coined by the poet Charles Augustin Saint-Beuve in 1837>.
- **tickle the ivories** to play the piano. <The keys of a piano are made of ivory>.

jack, Jack

- **a jack of all trades (and master of none)** someone who can do several different kinds of job (but does not do any of them very well).

- **before you can say Jack Robinson** extremely rapidly.
- **every man jack** absolutely everyone. <Perhaps from the fact that Jack is a very common first name>.
- **I'm all right, Jack** my situation is satisfactory, the implication being that it does not matter about anyone else.

jackpot

- **hit the jackpot** to have a great success, often involving a large sum of money. <Refers to the pool of money in poker>.

jam

- **jam tomorrow** the promise of better things in the future. <From a statement by the Red Queen in *Alice Through the Looking-Glass* by Lewis Carroll>.
- **want jam on it** to want an even better situation, etc, than one has already. <Refers to asking for jam on bread when bread is quite sufficient>.

Jekyll

- **a Jekyll and Hyde** someone with two completely different sides to his or her personality <Refers to the character in *The Strange Case of Dr Jekyll and Mr Hyde*, a novel by Robert Louis Stevenson>.

Jeremiah

- **a Jeremiah** a pessimist. <A biblical reference to the Lamentations of Jeremiah>.

jet

- **the jet set** wealthy people who can afford to travel a great deal. <Refers to jet planes>.

jewel

- **the jewel in the crown** the must valuable or successful thing associated with someone or something.

job

- **a job lot** a mixed collection. <Refers to auctioneering>.
- **just the job** exactly what is required.
- **jobs for the boys** used to suggest that jobs are being given to friends and relatives of people in power or of authority, rather than to people who are qualified to get them. Sometimes such jobs are unnecessary and created especially for the friend or relative.
- **make the best of a bad job** to obtain the best results possible from something unsatisfactory.

Job

- **a Job's comforter** someone who brings no comfort at all but makes one feel worse. <A biblical reference to the friends of Job>.
- **enough to try the patience of Job** so irritating as to make the most patient of people angry. <A biblical reference to Job who had to suffer many misfortunes patiently>.

Joe

- **Joe Bloggs** *or* **Public** *or* **Soap** the ordinary, average person.

joint
- **case the joint** to inspect premises carefully, especially with a view to later burglary.

joker
- **the joker in the pack** someone in a group who is different from the rest in some way and may cause problems or have an effect on a situation. <Refers to a pack of playing cards>.

Jonah
- **a Jonah** someone who brings bad luck. <a biblical reference to the book of Jonah, Jonah 1:4–7>.

Jones
- **keep up with the Joneses** to make an effort to remain on the same social level as one's neighbours by buying what they have, etc.

joy
- **no joy** no success, no luck.

judge
- **sober as a judge** to be extremely sober, not to be at all drunk.

jury
- **the jury is still out** people have not yet reached a conclusion or made a decision about something.

justice
- **do (someone *or* something) justice 1** to show the true value of (someone or something). **2** to eat (a meal, etc) with a good appetite.

keep
- **for keeps** permanently.
- **keep one's own counsel** to keep one's opinions, problems, etc, secret.
- **keep oneself to oneself** not to seek the company of others much, to tell others very little about oneself.
- **keep (something) to oneself** to keep (something) secret.

ken
- **beyond one's ken** outside the range of one's knowledge or understanding. <Literally, ken used to mean range of vision>.

kettle
- **a different kettle of fish** a completely different set of circumstances.
- **a pretty kettle of fish** an awkward or difficult situation.

kibosh
- **put the kibosh on (something)** to spoil or ruin (something's) chances of success.

kick
- **for kicks** for thrills or fun.
- **get a kick out of** to get fun or a thrill out of something.
- **kick oneself** to be annoyed with oneself.
- **kick over the traces** to defy rules that control one's behaviour. <Refers to a horse drawing a cart which gets out of control of the driver>.

kick (someone) upstairs to appoint (someone) to a job which is more senior than the present one but which has less power.

kid[1]
- **handle (someone *or* something) with kid gloves** to deal with (someone or something) very tactfully or delicately.

kid[2]
- **the new kid on the block** the newest person in a place, activity, etc.

kill
- **be in at the kill** to be present when something important or decisive happens, often something that is unpleasant for someone. <Referring to the death of the fox in a foxhunt>.
- **kill (someone) with kindness** to spoil (someone) to the extent that it is a disadvantage to him or her.
- **make a killing** to make a large profit.
- **move in for the kill** to act decisively with a view to defeating one's opponent.

king
- **a king's ransom** a vast sum of money.

kingdom
- **till kingdom come** for a very long time. <Refers to the Lord's Prayer>.
- **to kingdom come** to death. <See above>.

kiss
- **kiss goodbye to (something)** to have to accept that you have lost (something) or that you are not going to get (something).
- **kiss of death** something which causes the end, ruin or death of something. <A biblical reference to the kiss by which Judas betrayed Jesus>.

kitchen
- **everything but the kitchen sink** used to emphasize how much luggage someone is taking, etc.

kite
- **fly a kite** to start a rumour about a new project to see how people would react if the project were put into operation. <Refers to the use of kites to discover the direction and strength of the wind>.
- **high as a kite** very excited.

kitten
- **have kittens** to get very agitated or angry.

knee
- **bring (someone) to his *or* her knees** to humble or ruin (someone). <Refers to going on one's knees to beg for something>.

knickers
- **get one's knickers in a twist** to become agitated.

knife
- **have one's knife in (someone)** to wish to harm (someone).

- **like a (hot) knife through butter** used to emphasize how easily someone has dealt with a difficult situation.
- **on a knife edge** in a very uncertain or risky state.
- **stick the knife in (someone)** to do something that will harm, upset or cause problems for (someone).
- **the knives are out for (someone)** used to describe a situation in which several people are planning to harm or cause problems for (someone).
- **the night of the long knives** a time when an act of great disloyalty is carried out, usually by the sudden removal of several people from power or employment. <Refers to 19 June 1934, when Adolf Hitler had a number of his Nazi colleagues imprisoned or killed>.

knot¹
- **at a rate of knots** extremely rapidly. <Refers to a method of measuring the speed of ships>.

knot²
- **tie the knot** to get married.

know
- **in the know** knowing facts, etc, that are known only to a small group of people.
- **know (something) inside out** to know and understand (something) very well indeed.
- **not to know one is born** to lead a trouble-free, protected life.
- **not to know whether one is coming or going** to be very confused, often because one is very busy.

knuckle
- **rap (someone) over the knuckles** to scold or criticize (someone).

labour
- **a labour of love** a long or difficult job done for one's own satisfaction or from affection for someone rather than for reward.

lamb
- **like a lamb to the slaughter** meekly, without arguing or resisting, often because unaware of danger or difficulty. <A biblical reference to Isaiah 53:7>.

land
- **a land of milk and honey** a place where life is pleasant, with plenty of food and possibilities of success. <A biblical reference to the Promised Land of the Israelites described in Exodus 3:8>.
- **see how the land lies** to look carefully at a situation before taking any action or decision. <Refers literally to sailors looking at the shore before landing>.

lane
- **it's a long lane that has no turning** every period of misfortune, unhappiness, etc, comes to an end or changes to happier circumstances eventually.
- **life in the fast lane** a life which is very busy and active and usually contains a lot of stress and pressure.

language
- **speak the same language** to have similar tastes and views.

lap
- **in the lap of luxury** in luxurious conditions.

large
- **large as life** in person, actually present. <From works of art, particularly sculptural, which are life-size>.
- **larger than life** extraordinary, behaving, etc, in an extravagant way.

last
- **on one's** *or* **its last legs** near to collapse.
- **the last word** the most fashionable or up-to-date example of something.

late
- **better late than never** better for something to arrive, happen, etc, late than never to do so at all.

laugh
- **have the last laugh** to be victorious or proved right in the end, especially after being scorned, criticized, etc. <From the saying he who laughs last laughs longest>.
- **laugh and the world laughs with you (weep and you weep alone)** when someone is cheerful or happy, other people share in his or her joy (but when he or she is sad or miserable, people tend to avoid him or her).
- **laugh on the other side of one's face** to suffer disappointment or misfortune after seeming to be successful or happy.
- **laugh up one's sleeve** to be secretly amused.
- **no laughing matter** a very serious matter.

laurel
- **look to one's laurels** to be careful not to lose one's position or reputation because of better performances by one's rivals. <A reference to the laurel wreath with which the ancient Greeks crowned their poets and victors>.
- **rest on one's laurels** to be content with past successes without trying for any more. <As above>.

law
- **be a law unto oneself** to behave as one wishes rather than obeying the usual rules and conventions.
- **lay down the law** to state one's opinions with great force, to give orders dictatorially.
- **the law of the jungle** the unofficial rules for survival or success in a dangerous or difficult situation where civilized laws are not effective.

lay
- **lay it on thick** *or* **lay it on with a trowel** to exaggerate greatly in one's praise, compliments, etc, to someone.

lead¹
- **a leading question** a question asked in such a way as to suggest the answer the questioner wants to hear.

- **leading light** an important person in a certain group, field, etc.

lead[2]
- **swing the lead** to avoid doing one's work usually by inventing deceitful excuses. <Originally naval slang>.

leaf
- **take a leaf out of (someone's) book** to use (someone) as an example.
- **turn over a new leaf** to change one's behaviour, etc, for the better.

league
- **not be in the same league as (someone)** not to be as able as (someone). <Refers to the grouping of clubs in soccer, etc, according to ability>.

leap
- **by leaps and bounds** very quickly or successfully.

lease
- **give (someone** or **something) a new lease of life** to cause (someone) to have a longer period of active life or usefulness or to have a happier or more interesting life.

least
- **least said soonest mended** the less one says in a difficult situation the less harm will be done.

leave
- **leave (someone) in the lurch** to leave (someone) in a difficult or dangerous situation without any help. <A lurch refers to a position at the end of certain games, such as cribbage, in which the loser has either lost by a huge margin or scored no points at all>.

leeway
- **make up leeway** to take action to recover from a setback or loss of advantage. <Leeway refers to the distance a sailing ship is blown sideways off its course by the wind>.

left
- **have two left feet** to be clumsy or awkward with one's feet, e.g. when dancing.
- **left, right and centre** everywhere, to an extreme degree.
- **(someone's) left hand does not know what his** or **her right hand is doing** (someone's) affairs are extremely complicated.

leg
- **break a leg** used as an interjection to an actor or other stage performer as a means of wishing him or her good luck. <In the theatre it is traditionally considered bad luck to wish an actor good luck in a direct way>.
- **give (someone) a leg up** to give (someone) some assistance to achieve advancement.
- **leg it** to run or go away quickly.
- **not to have a leg to stand on** to have no defence or justification for one's actions.

- **pull (someone's) leg** to try as a joke to make (someone) believe something that is not true.
- **stretch one's legs** to go for a walk.

legend
- **a legend in one's own lifetime** used to indicate that someone has become famous during his/her lifetime.

legion
- **their name is legion** there are a great many of them. <A biblical reference to Mark 5:9>.

length
- **go to great lengths** to take absolutely any action in order to achieve what one wants.

leopard
- **the leopard never changes its spots** a person's basic character does not change.

let
- **let oneself go 1** to enjoy oneself without restraint. **2** to stop taking trouble over one's appearance.

letter
- **the letter of the law** the exact wording of a law, rule, agreement clause. <A biblical reference to II Corinthians 3:6>.
- **to the letter** in every detail.

level
- **a level playing field** a situation which is completely fair to all involved and in which no one has any particular advantage.
- **find one's** or **its (own) level** to find out what situation, position, etc, one is naturally suited to.
- **on the level** honest, trustworthy.

lick
- **a lick and a promise** a quick, not thorough, wash or clean.
- **lick (someone** or **something) into shape** to improve (someone or something) greatly to bring up to standard. <Refers to an old belief that bear cubs are born shapeless and have to be licked into shape by their mothers>.

lid
- **blow** or **take the lid off (something)** to reveal the truth about (something).
- **keep the lid on (something)** to keep (something) secret or keep (something) under control so that it does not get any worse.
- **put the (tin) lid on (something)** to finish (something) off usually in an unpleasant way.

lie[1]
- **give the lie to (something)** to show that (something) is untrue.
- **lie in** or **through one's teeth** to tell lies obviously and unashamedly.

- **live a lie** to live a way of life about which there is something dishonest.

lie²

- **take (something) lying down** to accept an unpleasant situation without protesting or taking action against it.
- **the lie of the land** the nature and details of a situation. <Refers to sailors studying the nature of the coastline>.

life

- **breathe new life into (something)** to make (something) more lively, active or successful.
- **come to life** to become active or lively.
- **get a life** used to indicate to someone that you think that he/she has a boring, uninteresting life and should do something to change this.
- **life is just a bowl of cherries** used ironically to indicate that life can be difficult and unpleasant.
- **for dear life** or **for dear life's sake** to a very great extent, very rapidly, hard, etc.
- **lead** or **live the life of Riley** to lead a comfortable and trouble-free life.
- **not on your life** certainly not.
- **risk life and limb** to risk death or physical injury, to take extreme risks.
- **see life** to have wide experience, especially of varying conditions of life.
- **take one's life in one's hands** to take the risk of being killed, injured or harmed.
- **the facts of life** the facts about sex or reproduction.
- **the life and soul of the party** someone who is very lively and amusing on social occasions.
- **while** or **where there's life there's hope** one should not despair of a situation while there is still a possibility of improvement.

light¹

- **bring (something) to light** to reveal or uncover (something).
- **come to light** to be revealed or uncovered.
- **go out like a light** to go to sleep immediately.
- **hide one's light under a bushel** to be modest or silent about one's abilities or talents. <A biblical reference to Matthew 5:15, quoting Christ>.
- **in the cold light of day** when one looks at something practically and calmly.
- **light at the end of the tunnel** possibility of success, happiness, etc, after a long period of suffering, misery etc.
- **see the light**   l) to understand something after not doing so. **2** to agree with someone's opinions or beliefs after not doing so. **3** (also **see the light of day**) to come into existence.
- **shed** or **throw light on (something)** to make (something) clearer, e.g. by providing more information about it.

light²

- **be light-fingered** to be likely to steal.
- **light as a feather** extremely light.

- **make light of (something)** to treat (something) as unimportant.

lightning

- **lightning never strikes twice (in the same place)** the same misfortune is unlikely to occur more than once.
- **quick as lightning** or **like greased lightning** extremely rapidly.

lily

- **be lily-livered** to be cowardly. <Refers to an old belief that the liver had no blood in it>.

limb

- **out on a limb** in a risky and often lonely position; having ideas, opinions, etc, different from other people. <Refers to being stuck in an isolated position on the branch of a tree>.
- **tear (someone) from limb to limb** to attack (someone) in a fierce and aggressive way, either in deed or speech.

limbo

- **in limbo** in a forgotten or neglected position.

limelight

- **in the limelight** in a situation where one attracts a great deal of public attention.

limit

- **be the limit** to be as much as, or more than, one can tolerate.
- **off limits** beyond what is allowed.

line

- **all along the line** at every point in an action, process, etc.
- **along** or **on the lines of (something)** similar to (something).
- **be in line for (something)** to be likely to get (something).
- **be** or **come on line** to be ready for use, to be operating. <A computer reference>.
- **be (way) out of line** to behave in a way that is not acceptable.
- **bring (something) into line with (something)** to make (something) the same as or comparable with (something else).
- **down the line** some time in the future.
- **draw a line under (something)** to regard (something unpleasant) as being over and best forgotten so that people can move on.
- **fall into line** to behave according to the relevant rules, regulations or traditions.
- **lay it on the line** to make (something) absolutely clear to someone.
- **not one's line of country** not something which one knows a lot about or is interested in.
- **read between the lines** to understand or deduce something from a statement, situation, etc, although this has not actually been stated. <Refers to a method of writing secret messages by writing in invisible ink between the lines of other messages>.

- **step out of line** to behave differently from what is usually acceptable or expected. <Refers to a line of soldiers on parade>.
- **the line of least resistance** the course of action that will cause one least effort or trouble.
- **toe the line** to obey the rules or orders. <Refers to competitors having to stand with their toes to a line when starting a race, etc>.

lion
- **put one's head in the lion's mouth** to put oneself in a very dangerous or difficult position.
- **the lion's share** having a much larger share than anyone else. <Refers to one of Aesop's fables in which the lion, being a very fierce animal, claimed three quarters of the food which he and other animals had hunted for>.
- **throw (someone) to the lions** deliberately to put (someone) in a dangerous or difficult position, often to protect oneself. <Refers to a form of entertainment in ancient Rome in which prisoners were thrown to wild animals to be attacked and killed>.

lip
- **keep a stiff upper lip** to show no emotion, such as fear or disappointment when danger, trouble, etc, arises.
- **lick one's lips** to look forward to something with pleasure. <A reference to licking one's lips at the thought of appetizing food>.
- **(someone's) lips are sealed** (someone) will not reveal something secret.
- **pay lip-service to (something)** to say that one believes in or agrees with (something) without really doing so and without acting as if one did.
- **read my lips** used by someone to emphasize that people should believe or trust in what he/she is about to say.

litmus
- **a litmus test** something which assesses or demonstrates clearly what something is really like.

live[1]
- **beat** *or* **knock the living daylights out of (someone)** to give (someone) a severe beating.
- **live and let live** to get on with one's own life and let other people get on with theirs without one interfering.
- **live it up** to have an enjoyable and expensive time.

live[2]
- **a live wire** an energetic, enthusiastic person. <Refers to a live electrical wire>.

load
- **a loaded question** a question intended to lead someone into admitting to or agreeing with something when he or she does not wish to do so. <Refers to a dice loaded or weighted so that it tends always to show the same score>.

loaf
- **use one's loaf** to use one's brains, to think clearly.

lock
- **lock, stock and barrel** completely, with everything included. <Refers to the main components of a gun>.
- **under lock and key** in a place which is locked for security.

log
- **sleep like a log** to sleep very soundly.

lone
- **a lone wolf** someone who prefers to be alone.

long
- **in the long run** in the end, after everything has been considered.
- **the long and the short of it** the only thing that need be said, to sum the story up in a few words.

look
- **look askance at (someone** *or* **something)** to regard with disapproval or distrust.
- **look before you leap** give careful consideration before you act.
- **not to get a look-in** not to have a chance of winning, succeeding, being noticed, etc.

loose
- **cut loose** to free oneself from the influence of power of (someone or something).
- **on the loose** enjoying freedom and pleasure. <Refers originally to prisoners escaped from jail>.

lord
- **lord it over (someone)** to act in a proud and commanding manner to (someone).

lose
- **lose ground** to lose one's advantage or strong position.
- **play a losing game** to go on with something that is obviously going to be unsuccessful.

loss
- **cut one's losses** not to spend any more time, money or effort on something on which one has already spent a lot to little benefit.

love
- **not for love nor money** not in any way at all.
- **there's no love lost between them** they are hostile to each other.

low
- **keep a low profile** not to draw attention to oneself or one's actions or opinions.
- **lie low** to stay quiet or hidden.

luck
- **down on one's luck** experiencing misfortune.
- **push one's luck** to risk failure by trying to gain too much.
- **strike it lucky** to have good fortune.
- **thank one's lucky stars** to be grateful for one's good fortune.

lull

- **lull (someone) into a false sense of security** to lead (someone) into thinking that all is well in order to attack when he or she is not prepared.

mad

- **mad as a hatter** utterly insane, extremely foolish or eccentric. <Hat-making used to involve the use of nitrate of mercury, exposure to which could cause a nervous illness which people thought was a symptom of insanity>.
- **mad as a March hare** insane, silly, extremely eccentric. <Hares tend to leap around wildly in the fields during March, which is their breeding season>.

make

- **make a day** *or* **night of it** to spend a whole day or night enjoying oneself in some way.
- **make do with (something)** to use (something) as a poor or temporary substitute for something.
- **make it up** to become friendly again after a quarrel.
- **make-or-break** bringing either success or failure.
- **on the make** trying to make a profit for oneself.

man

- **a man of his word** someone who always does as he promises.
- **be one's own man** to be independent in one's actions, opinions, etc.
- **man of straw** a man who is considered to be of not much worth or substance.
- **man to man** frankly.
- **the man in the street** the ordinary, average person.
- **to a man** everyone without exception.

manner

- **to the manner born** as if accustomed since birth to a particular way of behaviour etc. <Refers to a quotation from Shakespeare's *Hamlet*>.

map

- **put (somewhere) on the map** to cause (somewhere) to become well known or important.

marble

- **have marbles in one's mouth** to speak with an upper-class accent.
- **lose one's marbles** to become insane or senile.

march

- **get one's marching orders** to be told to leave, to be dismissed. <Refers to a military term>.
- **steal a march on (someone)** to gain an advantage over (someone) by doing something earlier than expected. <Refers literally to moving an army unexpectedly while the enemy is resting>.

mark

- **be a marked man** *or* **woman** to be in danger or trouble because people are trying to harm one. 'Marked' means watched>.

- **beside** *or* **wide of the mark** off the target or subject. <Refers to hitting the target in archery>.
- **be up to the mark** to reach the required or normal standard.
- **get off one's mark** to get started quickly on an undertaking. <Refers to track events in athletics>.
- **hit the mark** to be correct or accurate. <Refers to the target in archery>.
- **leave one's mark on (someone** *or* **something)** to have an important and lasting effect on (someone or something).
- **make one's mark** to make oneself well known, to make a lasting impression.
- **overstep the mark** to do or say something which is unacceptable or offensive.
- **quick off the mark** quick to act. <Refers literally to a runner starting quickly in a race>.

marrow

- **chilled** *or* **frozen to the marrow** extremely cold.

mass

- **the masses** the ordinary people, taken as a whole.

match

- **a shouting match** a loud, angry discussion or argument about something.
- **meet one's match** to find oneself against someone who has the ability to defeat one in a contest, argument or activity.
- **a matter of life or death** something of great urgency, something that might involve loss of life.

meal

- **make a meal of (something)** to treat (something) as if it is more complicated or time-consuming than it is.

measure

- **for good measure** as something in addition to what is necessary.

meat

- **be meat and drink to (someone)** to be very important to (someone).
- **one man's meat is another man's poison** people have different tastes.

Mecca

- **a Mecca** a place that is important to a certain group of people and is visited by them. <Refers to the birthplace of Mohammed to which Muslims make pilgrimages>.

meet

- **meet one's Waterloo** to be finally defeated. <Napoleon was defeated for the last time at Waterloo by Wellington>.

melt

- **be in the melting-pot** to be in the process of changing. <Refers to melting down and reshaping metal>.

mercy

- **at the mercy of (someone** *or* **something)** wholly in the power or control of (someone or something).
- **be thankful for small mercies** to be grateful for minor benefits or advantages in an otherwise difficult situation.

merry

- **make merry** to have an enjoyable, entertaining time, to have a party.

message

- **get the message** to understand.

method

- **there is method in his madness** someone has a good, logical reason for acting as he does, although his actions seem strange or unreasonable. <A reference to Shakespeare's *Hamlet* Act 2, scene II>.

Midas

- **the Midas touch** the ability to make money or be successful easily. <Refers to a Greek legend about a king of Phrygia whose touch turned everything to gold>.

midnight

- **burn the midnight oil** to work or study until late at night.

mile

- **be miles away** to be thinking about something else and so not concentrating on what is being said to you or what is going on around you.
- **go the extra mile** to make a special effort and do more than you would usually do, more than you have been asked to do, etc in order to achieve something.
- **run a mile** used to indicate the lengths to which someone would go to avoid something.
- **stand** *or* **stick out a mile** to be extremely obvious.

mill

- **a millstone round one's neck** a heavy burden or responsibility.
- **calm as a millpond** extremely calm.
- **go through the mill** to experience a series of difficult or troublesome events, periods or tests. <From the grinding of corn in a mill>.
- **run-of-the-mill** usual, not special.

mince

- **make mincemeat of (someone** *or* **something)** to defeat (someone) soundly, to destroy (something).
- **not to mince matters** to speak completely frankly without trying to be too kind, etc.

mind

- **be** *or* **go out of one's mind** to be or become insane.
- **blow (someone's) mind** to amaze (someone), to excite (someone) greatly.
- **cross one's mind** to enter one's mind briefly.
- **give (someone) a piece of one's mind** to scold or criticize (someone) angrily.
- **great minds think alike** clever people tend to have the same ideas and opinions.

- **in one's right mind** sane, rational.
- **in two minds** undecided.
- **not to know one's own mind** not to know what one really wants to do.
- **put (someone) in mind of (someone** *or* **something)** to remind (someone) of (someone or something).
- **slip one's mind** to be temporarily forgotten.

mint

- **in mint condition** used but in extremely good condition. <Literally the unused condition of a newly minted coin>.

minute

- **up to the minute** modern or fashionable.

misery

- **put (someone) out of his** *or* **her misery** to end a time of worry, anxiety or suspense for (someone). <Originally a term for putting to death a wounded and suffering animal>.

miss

- **a miss is as good as a mile** if one fails at something it does not matter how close one came to succeeding.
- **give (something) a miss** not to go to or attend (something).

moment

- **have one's moments** to have times of success, happiness.
- **not for a moment** not at all.
- **the moment of truth** a crucial time, a time when one has to make an important decision, face up to a crisis, etc.

money

- **have money to burn** to have enough money to be able to spend it in ways considered foolish.
- **money for jam** *or* **old rope** money obtained in exchange for very little work, effort, etc. <Army slang>.
- **money talks** rich people have influence simply because they have money.
- **put one's money where one's mouth is** to give money for a cause or purpose which one claims to support.
- **spend money like water** to spend money very freely.
- **the smart money is on (something)** used to describe an event or situation which is very likely to take place. <Smart money is used to refer to people who know a lot about investment, business deals, etc>.
- **throw good money after bad** to spend money in an unsuccessful attempt to retrieve money which one has already lost.
- **you pays your money and you takes your choice** used to indicate the difficulty or impossibility of deciding which of two choices is the right one.

monkey

- **monkey business** action likely to cause trouble, illegal or unfair activities.

- **not to give a monkey's** not to care at all.
- **speak to the organ grinder, not his monkey** *see* **organ.**

month
- **a month of Sundays** an extremely long time.

Monty
- **the full Monty** used to indicate that something is absolutely complete or comprehensive or that it contains everything that is usually involved in such an activity or situation.

moon
- **ask** *or* **cry for the moon** to ask for something that it is impossible to get.
- **do a moonlight (flit)** to move away suddenly.
- **many moons ago** a very long time ago, sometimes used as a humorous exaggeration.
- **over the moon** extremely happy.
- **promise (someone) the moon** to make promises that have little hope of ever being realized.

more
- **the more the merrier** the more people that are involved the better.

morning
- **the morning after the night before** a morning when one is suffering from a hangover caused by drinking too much alcohol the night before.

moth
- **like a moth to a flame** used to describe someone who finds someone or something irresistibly attractive, even although the person or thing might cause harm or trouble.

motion
- **go through the motions** to make a show of doing something, to pretend to do something.

mould
- **break the mould** to do something in a completely new and better way.
- **cast in the same mould (as someone)** very similar (to someone). <Refers to iron-working>.
- **they broke the mould when they made (someone)** used to emphasize how special or exceptional someone is.

mountain
- **have a mountain to climb** used to emphasize how difficult it is going to be for someone to do or achieve something and how much effort will be needed.
- **if the mountain will not come to Mohammed, then Mohammed must go to the mountain** a saying which indicates that, if someone whom you want to see cannot or is unwilling to come to you, then you should make the effort to go to him or her. <Refers to a story about Mohammed in which he is asked to demonstrate

his power by getting Mount Sofa to come to him. When this did not happen, Mohammed is supposed to have said the words which form the saying>.
- **make a mountain out of a molehill** to greatly exaggerate the extent of a problem, etc.
- **move mountains** to achieve something that seems impossible or extremely difficult.

mouse
- **poor as a church mouse** extremely poor.
- **quiet as a mouse** extremely quiet.

mouth
- **be all mouth and trousers** to talk a lot about doing something but never actually do it.
- **have a big mouth** to talk a lot, especially about things, such as secrets, that one should not.
- **out of the mouths of babes and sucklings** used when a child says something that is surprisingly adult, true, wise, etc.
- **shoot one's mouth off** to talk in a loud and often boastful or threatening manner.
- **make one's mouth water** used to emphasize how delicious something smells or looks.
- **the movers and shakers** refers to people with power and influence. <Possibly derives from the poem 'Ode' by Arthur O'Shaughnessy (1844–81), 'We are the movers and shakers of the world forever'>.

much
- **much of a muchness** very similar.
- **not much of a (something)** not a very good (something).
- **not up to much** not very good.

mud
- **drag (someone/someone's reputation) through the mud** to damage (someone or someone's reputation) by saying bad things about him or her.
- **mud sticks** used to indicate that, if something bad is said about someone, some people are likely to believe this and to go on believing it, even if it is not at all true or if it has been disproved.
- **(someone's) name is mud** (someone) is in disfavour or is being criticized.
- **sling** *or* **throw mud at (someone *or* something)** to say bad or insulting things about (someone or something).

mule
- **stubborn as a mule** extremely stubborn.

multitude
- **cover a multitude of sins** to be able to apply or refer to a large number of different things. <A misquotation from the Bible, I Peter 4:8, 'Charity shall cover the multitude of sins'>.

mum
- **mum's the word** do not say anything.

murder

- **get away with murder** to do something bad, irresponsible, etc, without suffering punishment.
- **I could murder (something)** used to indicate that you would very much like to have (something) to eat or drink.
- **scream blue murder** to scream extremely loudly.

music

- **be music to one's ears** used to indicate that one is very pleased to hear something.

mustard

- **keen as mustard** very eager and enthusiastic.
- **not cut the mustard** not to be able to do or achieve something; not be good enough.

muster

- **pass muster** to be considered good enough. <Refers to the calling together of people in the armed services in order to make sure that their dress and equipment are in good order>.

mutton

- **mutton dressed as lamb** an older person, usually a woman, dressed in clothes suitable for young people.

nail

- **a nail in (someone's) coffin** something which helps to bring about (someone's) downfall or destruction.
- **hit the nail on the head** to be extremely accurate in one's description, judgement, etc, of someone or something.

name

- **be (someone's) middle name** used to emphasize how typical of someone something is.
- **call (someone) names** to apply insulting or rude names to (someone).
- **give (someone *or* something) a bad name** to damage the reputation of (someone or something).
- **make a name for oneself** to become famous or well known.
- **name names** to give the names of people, especially people who are guilty or accused of wrong-doing.
- **no names, no pack-drill** no names will be mentioned and so no one will get into trouble. <'Pack-drill' refers to a form of army punishment in which the soldiers being punished were forced to march up and down carrying all their equipment>.
- **the name of the game** the important or central thing.
- **to one's name** in one's possession or ownership.

nasty

- **a nasty piece of work** someone who is very unpleasant or behaves very unpleasantly.

navel

- **contemplate one's navel** to be too much concerned with oneself and one's own activities and problems rather than with other, often more important, problems.

near

- **a near miss** something unpleasant that very nearly happened, often the near collision of two planes in the sky.
- **a near thing** the act of just avoiding an accident, misfortune, etc.
- **one's nearest and dearest** one's close family.

neck

- **be in (something) up to one's neck** to be very much involved in something bad or illegal.
- **get it in the neck** to be severely scolded or punished.
- **have the brass neck to (do something)** to have the impertinence or brazenness to (do something).
- **neck and neck** exactly equal.
- **risk one's neck** to put one's life, job, etc, in danger.
- **stick one's neck out** to take a risk or do something that may cause trouble.
- **this *or* that, etc, neck of the woods** this or that, etc, part of the country. <Originally a term for a remote community in the woods of the early 19th-century American frontier>.

needle

- **like looking for a needle in a haystack** an impossible search.

nerve

- **get on (someone's) nerves** to irritate (someone).
- **have a nerve** to be impertinent or brazen.
- **live on one's nerves** to be worried and anxious all the time.
- **lose one's nerve** to become scared, and so be unable to continue with an activity or course of action.
- **touch a nerve** to refer to something about which someone feels particularly sensitive.
- **war of nerves** a situation in which two opponents or enemies use psychological meansagainst each other, for example by frightening or threatening the other side, rather than direct action.

nest

- **a nest-egg** savings for the future.
- **fly the nest** to leave one's parent home and go and live elsewhere.
- **foul your own nest** to do something which could have a bad effect on your own interests, activities or relationships.

net

- **cast one's net wide** to involve a large number of people or things or a large area.
- **slip through the net** not to be found or identified.

nettle

- **grasp the nettle** to set about an unpleasant or difficult task in a firm and determined manner.

never

- **never-never land** an imaginary land where conditions are ideal. <Refers to the idealized land in J.M. Barrie's play *Peter Pan*>.
- **on the never-never** by hire purchase.

new

- **new broom** someone who has just been appointed to a post and who is eager to be efficient, make changes, etc. <From the saying a new broom sweeps clean, a new broom being more effective than the old one>.

news

- **break the news to (someone)** to tell (someone) about something, usually something unpleasant or sad, that has happened.
- **no news is good news** if one has not received any information about someone or something then all is likely to be well since if something bad, such as an accident, had happened one would have heard.

next

- **next door to (something)** very nearly (something).
- **next to nothing** almost nothing, very little.

niche

- **carve a niche for oneself** to succeed in creating a secure job or position for oneself or for something.

nick

- **in good** or **poor nick** in good or poor condition.
- **in the nick of time** just in time, at the last possible minute.

nine

- **a nine days' wonder** something that arouses surprise and interest for a short time only. <Refers to a saying quoted by Chaucer—'where is no wonder so great that it lasts more than nine days'>.

ninepins

- **go down like ninepins** to become ill or damaged, or to be killed or destroyed rapidly, one after the other.

nip

- **nip (something) in the bud** to put a stop or end to (something) as soon as it develops.

nit

- **get down to the nitty-gritty** to begin to deal with the basic practical details, problems, etc.
- **nit-picking** the act of finding very minor faults in something, quibbling. <Refers to picking nits out of hair>.

no

- **no end of (something)** a great deal of (something).
- **no go** unsuccessful, in vain.
- **no way** under no circumstances.

nod

- **a nod is as good as a wink to a blind horse** a hint is often all that is necessary to communicate thoughts or feelings.
- **give/get the nod** to give/be given permission or approval for something.
- **have a nodding acquaintance with (someone** or **something)** to know (someone or something) slightly.

<Refers to knowing someone well enough to nod in greeting to him or her>.
- **nod off** to fall asleep, sometimes accidentally.

noise

- **big noise** an important person.
- **make all the right noises** to say things which are considered the right response to a particular situation or the things which someone wants to hear.

nook

- **every nook and cranny** absolutely everywhere. <Literally, in all the corners and cracks>.

nose

- **cut off one's nose to spite one's face** to do something that harms oneself, usually in order to harm someone else.
- **follow one's nose** to go straight forward.
- **get up (someone's) nose** to annoy or irritate (someone).
- **have a nose around** to have a good look round a place, usually out of curiosity and when one is not supposed to be doing so.
- **have a nose for (something)** to have a talent or ability for finding or noticing something.
- **keep (one's** or **someone's) nose to the grindstone** to keep (someone) working hard without stopping.
- **lead (someone) by the nose** to get (someone) to do whatever one wants. <Refers to the ring on a bull's nose>.
- **look down one's nose at (someone** or **something)** to regard or treat (someone or something) with disdain or contempt.
- **on the nose** exactly.
- **pay through the nose** to pay a great deal of money for something.
- **poke one's nose into (something)** to pry into or interfere in other people's affairs. <Refers literally to a dog>.
- **powder one's nose** a euphemism, sometimes used by women, meaning to go to the toilet.
- **put (someone's) nose out of joint** to make (someone) jealous or offended by taking a place usually held by him or her, e.g. in the affections of a person whom he or she loves. <Refers to a person whose nose has been broken by being hit in the face>.
- **rub (someone's) nose in it** to keep on reminding (someone) about something he or she has done wrong. <Refers literally to rubbing a dog's nose in its faeces with the intention of house-training it>.
- **see further than the end of one's nose** to be concerned with more than just what is happening in the immediate present and in the immediate vicinity.
- **thumb one's nose at (someone** or **something)** *see* **thumb.**
- **turn up one's nose at (something)** to treat (something) with dislike or disgust.
- **under (someone's) (very) nose 1** right in front of (someone) and so easily seen. **2** while (someone) is actually present.

note
- **strike the right note** to say or do something suitable for the occasion. <Refers to playing a musical instrument>.

nothing
- **come to nothing** to fail.
- **go for nothing** to be wasted or unsuccessful.
- **have nothing on (someone) 1** not to be nearly as good, skilful, bad, etc, as (someone). **2** to have no proof or evidence of (someone's) wrongdoing.
- **have nothing to do with (someone** *or* **something)** to avoid contact with (someone or something).
- **nothing ventured, nothing gained** one cannot achieve anything if one does not make an attempt or take a risk.
- **there is nothing to choose between (two people** *or* **things)** there is hardly any difference in quality, ability, etc, between (two people or things).
- **there's nothing to it** it is very easy.
- **think nothing of (something)** not to regard (something) as out of the ordinary, difficult, etc.

nowhere
- **be in the middle of nowhere** be in a place which is a long way away from a town or city, a lot of people, etc, often carrying the suggestion that the place is boring.
- **get nowhere** to make no progress, to have no success.

nudge
- **nudge, nudge, wink, wink** used to indicate that there is some form of sexual innuendo or hidden reference in something that has been said. <Came into common use influenced by a sketch by Eric Idle in the TV series *Monty Python's Flying Circus*>.

number
- **get** *or* **have (someone's) number** to find out or know what kind of person (someone) is and what he or she is likely to do.
- **(someone's) number is up** (someone) is about to suffer something unpleasant, such as dying, failing, being punished, being caught, etc.
- **number one** oneself.

nut[1]
- **a hard nut to crack** a difficult problem or person to deal with.
- **in a nutshell** briefly, to sum up.
- **the nuts and bolts of (something)** the basic details or practicalities of (something).

nut[2]
- **be nuts about (someone** *or* **something)** to like (someone or something) a very great deal, to be wildly enthusiastic about (someone or something).
- **do one's nut** to get very angry.
- **go nuts** to become extremely angry.

oak
- **great oaks from little acorns grow** a saying used to emphasize that even large and important things often begin a small way.

oar
- **put** *or* **stick one's oar in** to interfere in another's affairs, conversation, e.g. by offering unwanted opinions. <Perhaps refers to someone who is being rowed in a boat by others and who suddenly decides to take part in the rowing unasked>.
- **rest on one's oars** to take a rest after working very hard. <Refers literally to rowing>.

object
- **money, distance, etc, is no object** it does not matter how much money, distance, etc, is involved in the particular situation. <Originally 'money is no object' meant money or profits were not the main aim but it came to be misapplied>.

occasion
- **rise to the occasion** to be able to carry out whatever action is required in an important or urgent situation.

odd
- **against all the odds** in spite of major difficulties.
- **be at odds with (someone** *or* **something)** to be in disagreement with (someone or something), not to be in accordance with (something).
- **lay odds** to bet. <Refers to betting on horses>.
- **make no odds** to be of no importance, to make no difference.
- **odd man out** someone or something that is different from others. <Refers literally to someone left out of a game when the teams have been chosen>.
- **odds and ends** small objects of different kinds.
- **over the odds** more than one would usually expect to pay. <Refers originally to a horse-racing term>.

off
- **in the offing** about to or likely to happen, appear, etc. <A nautical term. Offing refers to the whole area of sea that can be seen from a particular point on shore>.
- **off and on** *or* **on and off** occasionally.

oil
- **be no oil painting** to be not at all attractive.
- **oil and water** used to emphasize how different two people or things are.
- **oil the wheels** to make something easier to do or obtain. <Wheels turn more easily if oil is applied to them>.
- **pour oil on troubled waters** to attempt to bring a state of calm and peace to a situation of disagreement or dispute. <Since oil floats on water it has the effect of making waves flat>.
- **strike oil** to obtain exactly what one wants, to be successful.

old
- **an old hand** someone who is very experienced (at doing something).
- **old as the hills** extremely old.
- **old hat** old-fashioned, no longer popular.
- **old master** (a work by) any great painter before the 19th century, especially of the 15th and 16th centuries.

- **the old-boy network** a system in which jobs and other advantages are obtained on the basis of knowing the right people rather than on ability. <The connection with such people is often that one was at school with them>.
- **the old country** the country from which an immigrant or his or her parents or grandparents originally came.
- **the old guard** the older members of a group who are old-fashioned in their opinions and tastes. <The translation of the name applied to the most experienced section of Napoleon's army>.

olive
- **olive branch** a sign of a wish for peace. <The olive branch was an ancient symbol of peace>.

omelette
- **you can't make an omelette without breaking eggs** a saying indicating that it is impossible to achieve something worthwhile without causing a few problems or difficulties.

on
- **be not on** used to indicate emphatic disapproval of or lack of acceptance of something.
- **be on to (someone)** having discovered some previously secret or unknown information about (someone) or his or her activities.

once
- **give (someone) the once-over** to look at or study (someone or something) quickly.

one
- **a one-horse race** a competition, contest, etc, in which one person or side is certain to win.
- **a one-night stand** a relationship, arrangement, etc, that lasts for one evening or night only. <Literally a single performance in one place given by a pop group, etc, on tour>.
- **get one over on (someone)** to gain a victory or advantage over (someone).
- **have a one-track mind** to think only of one subject all the time.
- **have had one too many** to have had too much to drink.
- **it takes one to know one** used to indicate that people who have faults of their own find it easy to spot such faults in others.
- **not be oneself** to be feeling slightly unwell, to be more depressed, etc, than usual.

onion
- **know one's onions** to know a subject, one's job, etc.

open
- **an open-and-shut case** free from uncertainty, having an obvious outcome.
- **an open secret** a supposed secret that is known to many people.
- **keep an open mind** to be willing to listen to other people's suggestions, ideas, etc, instead of just concentrating on one's own point of view.

- **lay oneself (wide) open to (something)** to put oneself in a position in which one is liable to be in receipt of (blame, criticism, accusations, attack, etc).

opposite
- **(someone's) opposite number** the person in another company, country, etc, whose job or role corresponds to someone's.

option
- **keep one's options open** to delay making a definite decision so that all choices are available as long as possible.

oracle
- **work the oracle** to produce the desired result, to obtain what one wants, especially by using cunning, influence or bribery. <Refers to the oracle at Delphi in Greek legend>.

order
- **the order of the day** something that should be done, worn, etc, because conventional, common, fashionable, etc. <Refers originally to a list of items to be discussed in the British parliament on a particular day>.

organ
- **speak to the organ grinder, not his monkey** used to emphasize that one wants to deal with someone in authority, not with someone associated with him or her who has no power. <An organ grinder was a person who played a kind of musical instrument on wheels, known as a barrel organ, in the street and he often had a monkey on the barrel organ to attract people or to collect gifts of money>.

other
- **look the other way** to ignore or disregard something wrong, illegal, etc.

out
- **come out** to make public the fact that one is a homosexual.
- **get (something) out of your system** *see* **system**.
- **out and about** going around outside, e.g. after an illness.

outside
- **at the outside** at the most.

over
- **be all over (someone)** to be extremely friendly and attentive to (someone).
- **over and done with** completely finished, at an end.

overboard
- **go overboard (about** *or* **for someone** *or* **something)** to be extremely enthusiastic about (someone or something).

overdrive
- **go into overdrive** to start to work extremely hard or to become extremely active.

owe

- **I owe you one** used to indicate that someone has done one some kind of favour and that one must return this some time.

own

- **come into one's own** to have the opportunity to show one's good qualities, talent, skill, etc.
- **hold one's own 1** to perform as well as one's opponents in a contest, an argument, etc. **2** to be surviving, to be holding on to life.

p

- **mind one's p's and q's** to be very careful, to be polite and well behaved. <Perhaps refers to a warning to a printer to be careful of the letters p and q so as not to confuse them>.

pace

- **put (someone *or* something) through its *or* his *or* her paces** to test the ability of (someone or something) by getting them to demonstrate what it, he or she is capable of. <Refers originally to assessing horses>.
- **show one's paces** to demonstrate one's abilities.
- **stay the pace** to maintain progress in an activity at the same rate as others.

pack

- **send (someone) packing** to send (someone) away firmly and frankly.

pain

- **a pain in the neck** someone or something that constantly irritates one.
- **no pain, no gain** a saying used to emphasize the fact that the acquiring of something advantageous or desirable often involves something difficult or unpleasant, but it is worth it.

paint

- **like watching paint dry** used to describe something extremely boring.
- **paint the town red** to go out and celebrate in a lively, noisy manner.

palm

- **grease (someone's) palm** to give (someone) money, to bribe (someone).
- **have (someone) in the palm of one's hand** to have (someone) in one's power and ready to do as one wishes.

paper

- **paper over the cracks** to try to hide faults, mistakes, difficulties, etc, in a hasty or careless way in order to pretend that there were no faults, mistakes, etc.
- **paper tiger** someone or something that has the outward appearance of being powerful and threatening but is in fact ineffective.

par

- **below *or* not up to par 1** not up to the usual or required standard. **2** not completely well.

- **on a par with (something)** of the same standard as (something), as good as (something).
- **par for the course** what might be expected, what usually happens. <Originally a golfing term meaning the number of strokes that would be made in a perfect round on the course>.

part

- **look the part** to have the appropriate appearance of a particular kind of person.
- **part and parcel (of something)** something that is naturally or basically part (of something).
- **take (something) in good part** to accept (something) without being angry or offended.
- **take (someone's) part** to support (someone) in an argument, debate, etc.
- **the parting of the ways** the point at which people must go different ways, take different courses of action, make different decisions, etc. <A biblical reference to Ezekiel 21:21>.

party

- **the party line** the official opinions, ideas, attitudes, etc, as set down by the leaders of a particular group.
- **the party's over** a pleasant or happy time has come to an end.

pass

- **make a pass at (someone)** to try to start a romantic or sexual relationship with (someone). <Originally a fencing term, meaning to thrust with a foil>.
- **pass away** to die.
- **pass by on the other side** to ignore someone in trouble and not help him or her. <A biblical reference to the parable of the Samaritan, Luke 10>.

past

- **I, etc, would not put it past (someone) to (do something)** I, etc, think (someone) is quite capable of (doing something bad).
- **past it** less good, etc, than when one or it was not so old.
- **past master** someone extremely talented or skilful.

pasture

- **pastures new *or* fresh fields and pastures new** used to indicate a new and different place or situation. <The longer version of the phrase is a misquotation of 'fresh woods and pastures new' from John Milton's poem 'Lycidas'.

pat

- **a pat on the back** an indication of praise or approval.

patch

- **not to be a patch on (someone *or* something)** not to be nearly as good as (someone or something).
- **patch it *or* things up** to become friends again after a quarrel.

path

- **beat a path to (someone's) door** to visit (someone) very frequently or in large numbers.

pave
- **pave the way for (something)** to make it possible or easier for (something to happen).

pay
- **put paid to (something)** to prevent (an action, plan, etc) from being carried out.

peace
- **keep the peace** to prevent disturbances, fighting, quarrelling, etc.
- **make one's peace with (someone)** to become, or try to become, friendly with (someone) again after a period of disagreement.

peacock
- **proud as a peacock** extremely proud.

pearl
- **pearls of wisdom** something wise or helpful, often used ironically.

pedestal
- **put (someone) on a pedestal** to treat (someone) with great respect and admiration. <Refers to the practice of putting statues of famous people on pedestals>.

peg
- **bring (someone) down a peg or two** to make (someone) more humble. <Refers to tuning musical instruments>.
- **off the peg** of clothes, ready to wear, not made for one specially.
- **a square peg in a round hole** used to describe someone who does not fit into a particular situation or environment and feels uncomfortable in it.

penny
- **a penny for them** *or* **your thoughts** what are you thinking about?
- **in for a penny, in for a pound** if one is going to do something one might as well do it boldly and thoroughly.
- **not to have a penny to one's name** to have no money at all.
- **penny wise and pound foolish** being careful with small items of expenditure and extravagant with large ones.
- **spend a penny** to urinate. <From the former price of admission to the cubicle of a public toilet>.
- **the penny drops** I, etc, suddenly understand. <Refers to a coin in a slot machine>.
- **turn up like a bad penny** to reappear or keep reappearing although not wanted or welcome.
- **two a penny** of little value because very common.

petard
- **hoist with one's own petard** to be the victim of one's own action which was intended to harm someone else. <Refers to Shakespeare's *Hamlet*, Act 3, scene IV. A petard was a device containing explosives used by military engineers>.

philistine
- **a philistine** someone who is not interested in artistic or intellectual pursuits. <The Philistines were a fierce race of people who fought against the Israelites in biblical times. The present meaning was influenced by German>.

phrase
- **to coin a phrase** literally, to say something new and inventive, but used usually to introduce a cliché or a common saying or expression.

pick
- **pick and choose** to choose very carefully from a range of things.

picnic
- **be no picnic** used to emphasize how difficult or unpleasant something is.

picture
- **be out of the picture** to be no longer involved in something.
- **the big picture** the whole situation, not just some details.
- **get the picture** to understand what is being explained or described.
- **put (someone) in the picture** to give (someone) all the information and detail about a situation.

pie
- **nice as a pie** exceptionally pleasant or friendly, often unexpectedly.
- **pie in the sky** something good expected or promised in the future which is unlikely to come about. <Refers to a quotation from a poem by the American poet Joe Hill>.

piece
- **go to pieces** to be unable to continue coping with a situation, life, etc.

pig
- **buy a pig in a poke** to buy (something) without examining it carefully or without knowing its worth. <Supposedly referring to a fairground trick in which a prospective customer was sold a cat in a bag thinking that it was a piglet>.
- **make a pig of oneself** to eat greedily, to eat a great deal.
- **make a pig's ear of (something)** to make a mess of (something), to do (something) very badly or clumsily.
- **pigs might fly** it is extremely unlikely that that will happen.

pikestaff
- **plain as a pikestaff** very obvious. <Pikestaff was originally packstaff, a staff for holding a traveller's pack and lacking any ornamentation. This sense of plain has been confused with that of plain meaning clear>.

pillar
- **from pillar to post** from one place to another, often repeatedly. <Refers originally to the game of real tennis>.

pilot

- **be on automatic pilot** to do something without thinking about what you are doing, because of tiredness, distress, etc., usually succeeding in doing it correctly because you have done it before.

pin

- **for two pins** given the least encouragement or reason.
- **on pins and needles** in a state of anxiety or suspense.
- **you could have heard a pin drop** there was silence.

pinch

- **at a pinch** if it is absolutely necessary.
- **feel the pinch** to have financial problems.

pink

- **in the pink** in good health. <Refers to the pink complexion of some healthy people>.
- **the pink of perfection** absolute perfection. <Refers to a quotation from Oliver Goldsmith's play, *She Stoops to Conquer*>.

pip

- **pipped at the post** beaten at the last minute. <Refers originally to horse-racing. A horse is pipped at the post if another horse passes it at the end of the race>.

pipe

- **in the pipeline** in preparation, happening soon. <Refers to crude oil being piped from the well to the refineries>.

piper

- **pay the piper** to provide the money for something and therefore be entitled to have a say in the organization of it. <Refers to the saying 'He who pays the piper calls the tune'>.
- **pipe dream** a wish or idea that can never be realized. <Refers to visions experienced by opium smokers>.

pistol

- **hold a pistol to (someone's) head** to use force or threats to get (someone) to do as one wishes.

place

- **fall into place** to become understood when seen in terms of its relationship to other things.
- **go places** to be successful in one's career.
- **know one's place** to accept the lowliness of one's position and act accordingly.
- **a place in the sun** a situation in which one will be happy, successful, well of, etc..
- **put (someone) in his** *or* **her place** to remind (someone) angrily of the lowliness of his or her position or of his or her lack of experience, knowledge, etc.

plague

- **avoid (someone** *or* **something) like the plague** used to emphasize how keen one is to keep away (from someone or something).

plain

- **plain sailing** easy progress. <Perhaps confused with plane sailing, a method of making navigational calculations at sea in which the earth's surface is treated as though it were flat>.

plate

- **have (something) handed to one on a plate** to get (something) without having to put any effort into it.

play

- **make a play for (someone** *or* **something)** to try to obtain (someone or something).
- **play hard to get** to make it difficult for someone to get to know one in order to make him or her more keen to do so.

plot

- **the plot thickens** the situation is getting more complicated and more interesting. <Refers to a quotation from George Villiers' play *The Rehearsal*>.

plug

- **pull the plug on (something)** to stop supporting (something), to stop (something) from continuing.

plum

- **have a plum in one's mouth** to speak with what is regarded as an upper-class accent.

plunge

- **take the plunge** to go ahead and do something, especially something difficult or risky, especially after having spent some considerable time thinking about it.

poacher

- **poacher turned gamekeeper** used to describe someone who has changed their job, attitude, opinion, etc, and now holds completely opposite views.

pocket

- **in (someone's) pocket** under the control or influence of (someone).
- **line one's pocket** to make money for oneself dishonestly.
- **out of pocket** having made a loss.

poetic

- **poetic justice** deserved but accidental punishment or reward.
- **poetic licence** the disregarding of established rules of form, grammar, fact, etc, by writers to achieve a desired effect.

point

- **the point of no return** the stage in a process, etc, when it becomes impossible either to stop or change one's mind. <Originally referred to the point in the flight of an aircraft after which it did not have enough fuel to return to its place of departure>.
- **up to a point** to some extent but not completely.

poison
- **poison-pen letter** an anonymous letter saying bad things about someone.

port
- **any port in a storm** any solution to a problem or difficulty will suffice.

possum
- **play possum** to pretend to be asleep, unconscious or dead. <The possum pretends to be dead when it is under threat of attack from another animal>.

post[1]
- **from pillar to post** from one place to another, often repeatedly.

post[2]
- **keep (someone) posted** to keep (someone) informed about developments in a situation.

pot
- **go to pot** to get into a bad or worse state. <Refers to meat being cut up and stewed in a pot).
- **keep the pot boiling** to keep something going or operating.
- **take pot-luck** to have a meal at someone's house, etc, without having anything specially prepared for one. <Literally to take whatever happens to be in the cooking-pot at the time>.
- **the pot calling the kettle black** someone criticizing (someone) for doing (something) that he or she does himself or herself.
- **the** *or* **a watched pot never boils** when one is waiting for something to happen, etc, the time taken seems longer if one is constantly thinking about it.

pour
- **it never rains but it pours** when something goes wrong it goes wrong very badly or other things go wrong too.

powder
- **be sitting on a powder keg** to be in a very risky or dangerous situation in which something could easily go wrong quite suddenly.

power
- **more power to (someone's) elbow** may (someone) be successful.
- **the power behind the throne** the person who is really in charge of or in control of an organization, etc, while giving the impression that it is someone else.
- **the powers that be** the people in charge, the authorities.

practice
- **practice makes perfect** if one practises doing something one will eventually be good at it.

practise
- **practise what one preaches** to act in the way that one recommends to others.

praise
- **sing (someone's** *or* **something's) praises** to praise (someone or something) with great enthusiasm.

premium
- **be at a premium** to be much in demand and, therefore, difficult to obtain. <A financial term meaning literally 'sold at more than the nominal value'>.

press
- **press-gang (someone) into (doing something)** to force (someone) or persuade (someone) against his or her will to (do something). <The press gang was a group of sailors in the 18th century who seized men and forced them to join the navy>.

pretty
- **come to a pretty pass** to get into a bad state.
- **cost a pretty penny** to cost a large amount of money.
- **sitting pretty** in a very comfortable or advantageous position.

prey
- **be a prey to (something)** regularly to suffer from (something).
- **prey on (someone's) mind** to cause constant worry or anxiety to (someone).

price
- **at a price** at a very high price.
- **a price on (someone's) head** a reward offered for the capture or killing of (someone).

pride
- **pride goes before a fall** being too conceited often leads to misfortune.
- **pride of place** the most important or privileged position.
- **swallow one's pride** to behave in a more humble way than one usually does or than one would wish to do.

prime
- **prime mover** someone or something that gets something started.

pro
- **the pros and cons** the arguments for and against. <Latin *pro*, 'for', and *contra*, 'against'>.

production
- **make a production of (something)** to make (something) appear to be much more complicated than it actually is.

proof
- **the proof of the pudding is in the eating** the real worth of something is only found out when it has been into practice or use.

proud
- **do (someone) proud** to treat (someone) exceptionally well or lavishly.

pull

- **pull the other one!** used to emphasize to someone that you do not believe him or her. Sometimes the phrase is extended to **pull the other one; it's got bells on!** <A reference to the phrase: pull (someone's) leg>.

pulse

- **keep one's finger on the pulse** to keep oneself informed about recent developments in a situation, organization, etc, or in the world. <Refers to a doctor checking the rate of someone's pulse for health reasons>.

Punch

- **pleased as Punch** extremely pleased or happy. <Refers to the puppet show character who is usually portrayed smiling gleefully>.

punch

- **pull one's punches** to be less forceful or harsh in one's attack or criticism than one is capable of. <Refers to striking blows in boxing without using one's full strength>.
- **roll with the punches** not to let difficulties or problems discourage one or have a bad or upsetting effect on one.

pup

- **sell (someone) a pup** to deceive (someone), often to sell or recommend something that turns out not to be as good as he or she thought.

purpose

- **at cross purposes** involved in a misunderstanding because of talking or thinking about different things without realizing it.

purse

- **hold the purse strings** to be in charge of financial matters.
- **you can't make a silk purse out of a sow's ear** see **silk**.

push

- **at a push** used to indicate that something can be done if it is absolutely necessary, but it will not be easy.
- **give (someone) the push** to dismiss (someone).

put

- **put it on** to feign, to pretend.
- **put-up job** something done to deceive or trick (someone).

putty

- **putty in (someone's) hands** easily influenced or manipulated by (someone). <Putty is a malleable substance>.

Pyrrhic

- **Pyrrhic victory** a success of some kind in which what it takes to achieve is not worth it. <From the costly victory of King Pyrrhus of Epirus, over the Romans at Heraclea in 280 BC>.

QT

- **on the QT** secretly. <An abbreviation of quiet>.

quantity

- **an unknown quantity** someone or something of which very little is known. <Refers literally to a mathematical term>.

queer

- **in Queer Street** in financial difficulties. <Perhaps changed from Carey Street in London where the bankruptcy courts were>.
- **queer (someone's) pitch** to upset (someone's) plans or arrangements. <Pitch here refers to the site of a market stall. Originally to queer someone's pitch was to set up a stall beside it selling the same kind of goods>.

question

- **a question mark over (something)** doubt or uncertainty in relation to (something).
- **out of the question** not possible.
- **pop the question** to ask (someone) to marry one.

queue

- **jump the queue** to go ahead of others in a queue without waiting for one's proper turn.

qui

- **on the qui vive** very alert. <From the challenge of a French sentry *Qui vive?* 'Long live who, whose side are you on?'>.

quick

- **cut (someone) to the quick** to hurt (someone's) feelings very badly. <The quick is the sensitive skin under the nail>.

quid

- **quids in** a fortunate position.

quit

- **call it quits** to agree that neither person owes the other one anything and that neither one has any kind of advantage over the other.

R

- **the three R's** reading, writing and arithmetic, thought of as the essential basics of education. <From *r*eading, *w*riting and a*r*ithmetic>.

rack

- **go to rack and ruin** to fall into a state of disrepair or into a worthless condition. <Rack means destruction>.

rage

- **all the rage** very fashionable or popular.

rail

- **off the rails** not sensible, disorganized, deranged. <Refers to a train leaving the track>.

rain

- **keep** *or* **put away** *or* **save (something) for a rainy day** to keep (something, especially money) until one really needs it. <Formerly most jobs, such as farm jobs, were dependent on the weather. Since they could not be carried out in rainy weather no money was earned then>.

- **rain or shine** whatever the weather.
- **take a rain check on (something)** used to indicate that you are unable to accept an invitation but would like to postpone it until a later date. <American in origin and a reference to the part of a ticket that you keep when a sports fixture cannot take place because of bad weather so that you can use it for entry to the fixture when it does take place>.

rake
- **thin as a rake** extremely thin.

rampage
- **be** *or* **go on the rampage** to rush about wildly or violently.

rank
- **close ranks** to act together and support each other as a defensive measure.
- **pull rank** to make unfair use of a position of authority to make someone else do as one wishes or to give one some kind of advantage.

rap
- **take the rap for (something)** to take the blame or punishment for (something).

rat
- **like a drowned rat** soaking wet.
- **smell a rat** to have a suspicion that something is wrong or that one is being deceived. <Refers to a terrier hunting>.
- **the rat race** the fierce competitive struggle for success in business, etc. <A nautical phrase for a fierce tidal current>.

raw
- **touch (someone) on the raw** to hurt or anger (someone).

razor
- **sharp as a razor** quick-witted and very intelligent.

read
- **take (something) as read** to assume (something).

real
- **the real McCoy** something genuine and very good as opposed to others like it which are not. <Perhaps from Kid McCoy, an American boxer who was called The Real McCoy to distinguish him from other boxers of the same name>.

reason
- **see reason** to be persuaded by someone's advice, etc, to act or think sensibly.
- **within reason** within sensible limits.

rebound
- **on the rebound** to start a new relationship while still suffering from the disappointment experienced at the end of the previous relationship.

record
- **for the record** so that it will be noted.
- **set the record straight** to put right a mistake or misunderstanding.

red
- **a red-letter day** a day remembered because something particularly pleasant or important happened or happens on it. <From the fact that important dates in the year are sometimes shown in red on calendars>.
- **catch (someone) red-handed** to find (someone) in the act of doing something wrong or unlawful. <Refers to finding a murderer with the blood of a victim on his or her hands>.
- **in the red** in debt, overdrawn. <From the use of red ink to make entries on the debit side of an account>.
- **like a red rag to a bull** certain to make (someone) angry. <From the widespread belief that bulls are angered by the sight of the colour red although they are in fact colour-blind>.
- **on red alert** ready for an an immediate danger. <Originally a military term for mobilizing civilians during an air-raid>.
- **red tape** the rules and regulations, official papers, etc, that are thought to characterize government departments. <From the reddish tape used by government offices to tie bundles of papers>.
- **see red** to get very angry.

reed
- **a broken reed** someone who is too weak or unreliable to be depended upon.

rest
- **lay (someone) to rest** to bury (someone).
- **rest assured** you can be quite certain.

return
- **return to the fold** to come or back to one's family, an organization, a set of principles or beliefs, etc, which one has previously left. <Refers to a sheep returning to the sheep-pen>.

rhetorical
- **rhetorical question** a question which does not require an answer.

rhyme
- **without rhyme or reason** without any logical or sensible reason or explanation.

rich
- **rich as Croesus** extremely rich. <Croesus was a ruler of the kingdom of Lydia who was very wealthy>.
- **strike it rich** to obtain wealth, often suddenly or unexpectedly.

riddance

- **good riddance to (someone *or* something)** I am glad to have got rid of (someone or something).

ride

- **be riding for a fall** to be on a course of action that is likely to lead to unpleasant results or disaster for oneself. <Refers originally to hunting>.
- **take (someone) for a ride** to deceive or trick (someone). <Originally American gangsters' slang for killing someone, from the practice of killing someone in a moving vehicle so as not to attract attention>.

rift

- **a rift in the lute** a slight disagreement or difficulty that might develop into a major one and ruin a project or relationship. <Refers to a quotation from Tennyson's *Idylls*>.

right

- **get *or* keep on the right side of (someone)** to act in such a way that (someone) feels or continues to feel friendly and well disposed towards one.
- **Mr *or* Miss Right** the perfect man or woman for one to marry.
- **right-hand man *or* woman** someone's most valuable and helpful assistant.
- **serve (someone) right** to be something unpleasant that (someone) deserves.
- **set (something) to rights** to bring (something) into a correct, organized, desired, etc, state.

ring

- **a dead ringer** someone who looks extremely like someone else. <Perhaps from the use of the phrase to mean a horse, similar to the original, illegally substituted in a race>.
- **have a ringside seat** to be in a position to observe clearly what is happening. <Originally refers to boxing>.

riot

- **read the riot act to (someone)** to scold (someone) severely and warn him or her to behave better. <The Riot Act of 1715 was read to unlawful gatherings of people to break the gathering up. If the people refused to disperse action could be taken against them>.

rise

- **rise and shine** to get out of bed and be lively and cheerful.
- **take a rise out of (someone)** to tease or make fun of (someone) so that he or she gets annoyed.

river

- **sell (someone) down the river** to betray or be disloyal to (someone). <Refers historically to selling slaves from the upper Mississippi states to buyers in Louisiana where working and living conditions were much harsher>.

road

- **hit the road** start out on a journey.
- **one for the road** one last drink before leaving.

roaring

- **do a roaring trade in (something)** to be selling a lot of (something).

rob

- **rob Peter to pay Paul** to pay (someone) with the money that should go to pay a debt owed to (someone else). <Refers to Saints Peter and Paul who share the same feast day, 29 July>.

rock

- **between a rock and a hard place** to be in a situation in which one is faced with a choice between two equally unpleasant or unacceptable alternatives.
- **steady as a rock** extremely steady, motionless.

rocket

- **not rocket science** used to indicate that something is quite easy and does not require much intellect or skill.

rod

- **make a rod for one's own back** to do something which is going to cause harm or problems for oneself in the future.
- **spare the rod and spoil the child** if a child is not punished for being naughty it will have a bad effect on his or her character.

rogue

- **a rogue's gallery** a police collection of photographs of known criminals.

roll

- **a rolling stone (gathers no moss)** a person who does not stay very long in one place (does not acquire very much in the way of possessions or responsibilities).
- **a roll in the hay** an informal way of describing having sex, especially when this is not part of a serious relationship.
- **be on a roll** used to indicate that things are going well and that good progress is being made.
- **be rolling in it *or* in money** to have a great deal of money.
- **be rolling in the aisles** to be laughing very heartily.

Rome

- **all roads lead to Rome** all ways of fulfilling an aim or intention end in the same result and so it does not does not matter which way one uses.
- **fiddle while Rome burns** to do nothing while something important is being ruined or destroyed. <The Emperor Nero was said to have played on a lyre while Rome was burning>.
- **Rome was not built in a day** a difficult task cannot be completed satisfactorily quickly.
- **when in Rome do as the Romans do** one should follow the customs, behaviour, etc, of the people one is visiting or living with. <A saying of St Ambrose>.

rooftop

- **shout (something) from the rooftops** to tell a great many people about (something).

roost

- **rule the roost** to be the person in charge whose wishes or orders are obeyed.

rope

- **give (someone) enough rope (and he will hang himself)** let (someone foolish) act as he or she pleases and he or she will bring about his or her own ruin, downfall, misfortune, etc.
- **know the ropes** to know the details and methods associated with a business, procedure, activity, etc.
- **on the ropes** used to describe a situation which is very close to failure or defeat.
- **rope (someone) in** to include (someone), to ask (someone) to join in, often against his or her will. <Refers to lassoing cattle in the American West>.
- **show (someone) the ropes** to teach (someone) the details and methods involved (in something).

rose

- **come up smelling of roses** to come out of a situation with some kind of advantage when it was expected to result in blame or harm for one.
- **everything's coming up roses** everything is turning out to be successful or happy.
- **look at (someone or something) through rose-coloured or rose-tinted spectacles or glasses** to view (someone or something) in an extremely optimistic light.

rough

- **give (someone) the rough edge of one's tongue** to scold or criticize (someone) severely.
- **ride roughshod over (someone)** to treat (someone) without any respect and without any regard for his or her views or feelings. <Horses are roughshod to give a better grip on icy, etc, roads>.
- **take the rough with the smooth** to accept the disadvantages as well as the advantages and benefits of a situation.

round

- **go the rounds** to be passed from person to person.
- **in round figures or numbers** to the nearest whole number, especially one that can be divided by ten.
- **round trip** the journey to somewhere plus the journey back.

rub

- **rub (something) in** to keep reminding someone about (something which he or she would rather forget).
- **rub off on (to) (someone)** to be passed to (someone), to affect (someone).
- **rub (someone) up the wrong way** to irritate (someone). <Refers to rubbing an animal's coat up the wrong way>.

- **there's the rub** that's the problem. <Refers to a quotation from Shakespeare's *Hamlet*, Act 3, scene I>.

rug

- **pull the rug (out) from under (someone)** suddenly to stop giving important help or support to (someone), to leave (someone) in a weak position.

rule

- **rule of thumb** a rough or inexact guide used for calculations of some kind.

run

- **a run for (someone's) money** a creditable or worthy performance or opposition. <A racing term indicating that the horse one has backed has actually raced although it has not won>.
- **(someone's) cup runneth over** someone feels very happy. <A biblical reference to Psalm 23:5>.
- **in the running** with a chance of success.
- **run its course** to continue to its natural end, to develop naturally.
- **run out on (someone or something)** to abandon (someone or something).
- **take a running jump** to go away.

rut

- **in a rut** in a routine, monotonous way of life. <Refers to the rut made by a cartwheel, etc>.

sabre

- **rattle one's sabre** to put on a show of anger or fierceness without resorting to physical force in order to frighten someone.

sack

- **sackcloth and ashes** sorrow or apology for what one has done or failed to do. <People in mourning used to wear sackcloth and throw ashes over their heads. The phrase has several biblical references, e.g. Matthew 11:21>.

safe

- **safe and sound** totally unharmed.
- **there's safety in numbers** it is safer to undertake a risky venture if there are several people involved.

sail

- **sail close to the wind** to come close to breaking the law or a rule.
- **sail under false colours** to pretend to be different in character, beliefs, status, work, etc, than is really the case. <Refers to a ship flying a flag other than its own, as pirate ships sometimes did>.

salad

- **(someone's) salad days** (someone's) carefree and inexperienced youth.

salt

- **below the salt** in a humble, lowly or despised position. <Formerly the salt container marked the division at a dinner table between the rich and important people and

the more lowly people, the important people being near the top and so above the salt>.
- **rub salt in the wound** to make someone feel worse. <Salt used to be used as an antiseptic but it was painful on raw wounds>.
- **take (something) with a grain** *or* **pinch of salt** to treat (something) with some disbelief.
- **the salt of the earth** someone very worthy or good. <A biblical reference to Matthew 5:13>.
- **worth one's salt** worth the money one is paid, of any worth. <Salt was once a valuable commodity and the reference is to that given to servants or workers>.

Samaritan
- **a good Samaritan** someone who helps people when they are in need. <A biblical reference to the parable in Luke 10>.

sand
- **build (something) on sand** to establish (something) without having enough support, money, likelihood of survival, etc, to make it secure or practicable. <A biblical reference to Matthew 7:26>.

sardine
- **packed like sardines** crowded very close together. <Sardines are sold tightly packed in tins>.

scarlet
- **scarlet woman** an immoral or promiscuous woman. <A biblical reference to the woman in scarlet in Revelation 17>.

scene
- **behind the scenes** out of sight of the public, etc. <Refers literally to people in a theatrical production who work behind the scenery offstage>.
- **come on the scene** to arrive or appear.
- **not (someone's) scene** not the kind of thing that (someone) likes.
- **set the scene for (something)** to prepare the way for (something), to be the forerunner of (something). <Refers originally to the preparation of the stage for theatrical action>.

scent
- **throw (someone) off the scent** to distract (someone) from a search for someone or something, e.g. by giving him or her wrong information. <Refers literally to dogs>.

scheme
- **the best-laid schemes of mice and men (gang aft agley)** the most carefully arranged plans (often go wrong). <Refers to a quotation from Robert Burns's poem, 'To a Mouse'>.

science
- **blind (someone) with science** to talk about something in such a complicated technical way that it is difficult for a layperson to understand.

score
- **know the score** to know exactly what is involved, to know all the facts of a situation. <Literally to know from the score in a game who is likely to win or lose>.
- **settle old scores** to get revenge for wrongs committed in the past.

scratch
- **start from scratch** to start from the very beginning, without any advantages. <Refers to the starting line (formerly scratched on the ground), from which runners start unless their handicap allows them to start further down the track>.
- **up to scratch** up to the required standard. <Refers originally to a scratch in the centre of a boxing ring to which boxers had to make their way unaided after being knocked down to prove that they were fit to continue>.

screw
- **have a screw loose** to be deranged, to be very foolish. <Refers literally to malfunctioning machinery>.

Scrooge
- **Scrooge** an extremely mean person. <Refers to a character in Charles Dickens's *A Christmas Carol*>.

Scylla
- **between Scylla and Charybdis** faced with having to choose between two equally undesirable choices. <Refers to Homer's *Odyssey* in which Odysseus had to sail down a narrow strait between Scylla, a monster on a rock, and Charybdis, an extremely dangerous whirlpool>.

sea
- **a sea change** a complete change in a situation, someone's opinion, attitude, etc.
- **all at sea** puzzled, bewildered.

seam
- **be bursting at the seams** to be extremely full.
- **come** *or* **fall apart at the seams** to be in a state of collapse or ruin. <From clothes coming to pieces>.

second
- **second nature** a firmly established habit.
- **second sight** the supposed power of seeing into the future.
- **second thoughts** a change of opinion, decision, etc.

seed
- **go to seed** to become shabby and uncared-for. <Refers literally to plants seeding after flowering and being no longer attractive or useful>.

separate
- **separate the sheep from the goats** *see* **sheep**.

sewn
- **(all) sewn up** completely settled or arranged.

shade

- **put (someone** *or* **something) in the shade** to be much better, etc, than (someone or something). <Refers to making someone seem dark by being so much brighter oneself>.
- **shades of (someone** *or* **something)** that reminds me of (someone or something). <It is as though the shade or ghost of someone or something were present>.

shadow

- **worn to a shadow** made exhausted and thin by over working.

shakes

- **in two shakes of a lamb's tail** in a very short time.

shape

- **knock (someone** *or* **something) into shape** to get (something) into the desired or good condition.
- **shape up or ship out** used to tell someone that he or she should start acting in a more responsible or appropriate way or get out.

sheep

- **might as well be hanged for a sheep as a lamb** if one is going to do something slightly wrong and have to pay a penalty one might as well do something really wrong and get more benefit. <Refers to the fact that stealing a lamb or a sheep used to be punishable by death>.
- **separate the sheep from the goats** to distinguish in some way the good, useful, talented, etc, people from the bad, useless or stupid, etc, ones. <A biblical reference to Matthew 25:32>.

shelf

- **on the shelf** unmarried and unlikely to get married because of being unattractive, old, etc. <Refers to goods that are not sold>.

shell

- **come out of one's shell** to become less shy. <Refers to a tortoise or crab, etc>.

ship

- **shipshape and Bristol fashion** neat, in good order. <Originally applied to ships. Bristol was formerly the largest port in Britain>.
- **ships that pass in the night** people who meet by chance and only on one occasion. <Refers to a quotation from 'Tales of a Wayside Inn' poem by Henry Wadsworth Longfellow>.
- **spoil the ship for a ha'porth of tar** to spoil something of value by not buying or doing something which would improve it but not cost very much. <Ship is dialect here for sheep—tar used to be used to prevent infections in sheep or to treat wounds>.
- **when (someone's) ship comes in** when (someone) becomes rich or successful. <Refers to merchants waiting for their ships to return with goods to sell>.

shoe

- **in (someone's) shoes** in (someone else's) place.
- **on a shoestring** using very little money.

shoot

- **shoot (something) down in flames** to destroy. <Refers literally to destroying aircraft by shooting at them>.

shop

- **talk shop** to talk about one's work.

short

- **by a short head** by a very small amount. <Refers to horse-racing>.
- **caught** *or* **taken short** having a sudden, urgent need to go to the toilet.
- **give (someone** *or* **something) short shrift** to spend very little time or thought on (someone or something). <Short shrift was the short time given to a criminal for confession before execution>.
- **make short work of (something)** to deal with or get rid of (something) very quickly.
- **sell (someone** *or* **something) short** not to do justice to, to belittle (someone or something). <Literally to give a customer less than the correct amount of something>.
- **short and sweet** short and to the point.

shot

- **a long shot** a guess or attempt unlikely to be accurate or successful, but worth trying.
- **a shot across the bows** something given as a warning. <From naval warfare>.
- **a shot in the arm** something that helps to revive (something). <Literally, an injection in the arm>.
- **big shot** an important person.
- **call the shots** to be in charge of events or a situation.
- **like a shot** very quickly or willingly.
- **shotgun wedding** a forced wedding, usually because the bride is pregnant. <From the idea that the groom was forced into the wedding by shotgun>.

shoulder

- **a shoulder to cry on** a sympathetic listener.
- **put one's shoulder to the wheel** to begin to work hard. <Refers to putting one's shoulder to the wheel of a cart, etc, to push it out of muddy ground, etc>.
- **rub shoulders with (someone)** to associate closely with (someone).
- **shoulder to shoulder** side by side.

shout

- **shout (something) from the rooftops** *see* **rooftop**.

show

- **get the show on the road** to get something started or put into operation. <Used originally of a theatre company going on tour>.
- **steal the show** to attract the most attention at an event. <Refers to someone getting most of the applause at a theatrical performance>.

sick

- **sick as a parrot** very disappointed.

side

- **let the side down** to hinder one's colleagues by not performing, etc, as well as they have.
- **on the side** in a way other than by means of one's ordinary occupation.
- **take sides** to support a particular person, group, etc, against another.

sieve

- **have a memory like a sieve** to be extremely forgetful.

sign

- **sign on the dotted line** to make a firm commitment to do something, often one that is legally binding. <Refers to the signing of a formal agreement or contract>.

sight

- **out of sight, out of mind** one ceases to think about someone who has gone away or about something which is no longer in front of one.

silence

- **silence is golden** it is better to say nothing in a particular situation.

silent

- **the silent majority** the people who make up most of the population but who rarely make their views known although these are thought to be moderate and reasonable.

silk

- **you can't make a silk purse out of a sow's ear** one cannot make something good or special out of poor materials.

silver

- **born with a silver spoon in one's mouth** to be born into an aristocratic or wealthy family. <Perhaps from the custom of giving a christening present of a silver teaspoon>.

sin

- **ugly as sin** extremely ugly.

sing

- **sing from the same hymn** or **song sheet** to be in agreement about something, often to show this agreement publicly.

six

- **a sixth sense** intuition, an ability to feel or realize something not perceived by the five senses.
- **at sixes and sevens** in a state of confusion and chaos.
- **knock (someone) for six** to take (someone) completely by surprise. <Refers to cricket—literally to score six runs off a bowl>.
- **six of one and half a dozen of another** so similar as to make no difference. <Half a dozen is six>.

sixty

- **the sixty-four (thousand) dollar question** the most important and/or difficult question. <From an American quiz game in which the contestant won one dollar for the first question, two for the second, four for the third, up to the last when he or she won sixty-four dollars or lost it all>.

size

- **cut (someone) down to size** to humble (someone), to reduce (someone's) sense of his or her own importance.

skeleton

- **have a skeleton in the cupboard** to have a closely kept secret about some cause of shame.

skin

- **by the skin of one's teeth** only just, very narrowly.
- **no skin off my, etc, nose** no difference to me, etc, of no concern to me, etc.
- **save one's skin** to save one's life or one's career.
- **skin and bone** extremely thin.

sky

- **praise (someone** or **something) to the skies** to praise (someone) extremely highly.
- **the sky's the limit** there is no upper limit.

slap

- **a slap in the face** a rebuff.
- **a slap on the wrist** a reprimand.

sleeve

- **have** or **keep (something) up one's sleeve** to keep (a plan, etc) in reserve or secret for possible use at a later time. <Refers to cheating at cards by having a card up one's sleeve>.

slip

- **a slip of the tongue** a word or phrase said in mistake for another.
- **give (someone) the slip** to succeed in escaping from or evading (someone).
- **let (something) slip** to say or reveal (something) accidentally.
- **there's many a slip 'twixt cup and lip** something can easily go wrong with a project, etc, before it is completed.

small

- **it's a small world** an expression used when one meets someone one knows somewhere unexpected.
- **small talk** light conversation about trivial matters.
- **the small print** the parts of a document where important information is given without being easily noticed.

smash

- **a smash-and-grab** a robbery in which a shop window is smashed and goods grabbed from behind it.
- **a smash hit** a great success. <Originally referred to a very successful popular song>.

smear

- **smear campaign** an attempt to blacken or damage someone's reputation by making accusations or spreading rumours about him or her.

smoke
- **go up in smoke** to end in nothing.
- **there's no smoke without fire** there is always some kind of basis to a rumour, however untrue it appears to be.

snail
- **at a snail's pace** extremely slowly.

snake
- **a snake in the grass** a treacherous person. <From Virgil's *Aeneid*>.

sneeze
- **not to be sneezed at** not to be ignored or disregarded.

sock
- **pull one's socks up** to make an effort to improve.
- **put a sock in it** to be quiet.

soft
- **have a soft spot for (someone)** to have a weakness, affection or exceptional liking for (someone).
- **a soft touch *or* mark** someone who is easily taken advantage of, deceived etc.

song
- **for a song** for very little money.
- **make a song and dance about (something)** to cause an unnecessary fuss about (something).

soon
- **speak too soon** to say something that takes for granted something not yet accomplished.

sore
- **a sore point** a subject which annoys or offends someone.
- **stick out like a sore thumb** to be very noticeable.

sort
- **it takes all sorts (to make a world)** one should be tolerant of everyone whatever they are like.
- **out of sorts** not feeling quite well, rather bad-tempered.

soul
- **the soul of (something)** a perfect example of (something).

soup
- **in the soup** in serious trouble.

spade
- **call a spade a spade** to speak bluntly and forthrightly.
- **do the spadework** to do the hard preparatory work at the beginning of a project. <Digging is the first stage of building houses, etc>.
- **in spades** used to emphasize the large amount of something.

spanner
- **throw a spanner in the works** to hinder or spoil (a project, plan, etc).

spar
- **sparring partner** someone with whom one often enjoys a lively argument. <Literally refers to someone with whom a boxer practises>.

spare
- **go spare** to become very angry or distressed.

speak
- **be on speaking terms** to be friendly towards someone and communicate with him or her.
- **speak for itself** to need no explanation.

spick
- **spick and span** clean and tidy.

spirit
- **the spirit is willing (but the flesh is weak)** one is not always physically able to do the things that one wishes do. <A biblical quotation, Matthew 26:40–41>.

spit
- **be the spitting image *or* the spit and image *or* the dead spit of (someone *or* something)** to be extremely like (someone or something).

spleen
- **vent one's spleen** to express one's anger and frustration. <The spleen was thought to be the source of spite and melancholy>.

split
- **a split second** a fraction of a second.

spoil
- **be spoiling for (something)** to be eager for (a fight, etc).

spoke
- **put a spoke in (someone's) wheel** to hinder (someone's) activity. <Spoke is from Dutch spoak, a bar formerly jammed under a cartwheel to act as a brake when going downhill>.

sponge
- **throw up the sponge** to give up a contest, struggle, argument, etc. <Refers originally to a method of conceding defeat in boxing>.

spot
- **hit the spot** used to indicate that something is just what is required or is completely satisfactory.
- **in a spot** in trouble, in difficulties.
- **knock spots off (someone)** to beat or surpass (someone) thoroughly.
- **put (someone) on the spot** to place (someone) in a difficult or awkward situation.
- **rooted to the spot** unable to move from fear, horror, etc.

sprat
- **a sprat to catch a mackerel** something minor or trivial given or conceded in order to obtain some major gain or advantage.

square
- **back to square one** back at the beginning. <Refers to an instruction in board games>.

squeak
- **a narrow squeak** a narrow escape.

stab
- **have a stab at (something)** to have a try at (something).
- **stab (someone) in the back** to behave treacherously towards (someone), to betray (someone).

stable
- **lock the stable door after the horse has bolted** to take precautions against something happening after it has already happened.

stage
- **a stage whisper** a loud whisper that is intended to be heard by people other than the person to whom it is directed. <From the fact that whispers on stage have to be audible to the audience>.
- **stage fright** the nervousness, sometimes leading to him or her forgetting words, felt by an actor when in front of an audience; often extended to that felt by anyone making a public appearance.

stamp
- **(someone's) stamping ground** a place where (someone) goes regularly. <Refers literally to animals>.

stand
- **know where one stands** to know the exact nature of one's position or situation.
- **make a stand against (something)** to oppose or resist (something one believes to be wrong, etc).
- **stand corrected** to accept that one has been wrong.
- **stand on ceremony** to be very formal.
- **stand up and be counted** to declare one's opinions publicly.

start
- **a false start** an unsuccessful beginning, resulting in one in having to start again. <From a start in a race which has to be repeated, e.g. because a runner has left the starting line before the signal has been given>.
- **be under starter's orders** to be ready to start doing something.
- **for starters** to begin with. <Starter refers literally to the first course of a meal>.

status
- **status quo** the situation as it is, or was, before a change. <Latin, literally 'the state in which'>.
- **status symbol** a possession which supposedly demonstrates high social position.

stay
- **stay the course** to continue to the end or completion of (something).

steady
- **go steady** to go out together regularly, to have a romantic attachment to each other.

steam
- **get all steamed up** to get angry or agitated.
- **get up steam** to gather energy and impetus to do (something). <Literally used of increasing the pressure of steam in an engine before it goes into operation>.
- **let off steam** to give free expression to one's feelings or energies. <Literally to release steam from a steam engine to in order to reduce pressure>.
- **run out of steam** to become exhausted, to lose enthusiasm. <Refers literally to the steam engine>.
- **under one's own steam** entirely through one's own efforts.

step
- **take steps** to take action of some kind.

stick
- **a stick to beat (someone) with** something which can be used to criticize or damage (someone).
- **get hold of the wrong end of the stick** to misunderstand a situation or something said or done.
- **give (someone) stick** to scold or criticize (someone). <Refers literally to beating someone with a stick>.

sticky
- **be on a sticky wicket** to be in a difficult or awkward situation that is difficult to defend. <Refers to cricket when the state of the ground or the weather make it difficult for the batsman to hit the ball>.
- **come to a sticky end** to meet some misfortune or an unpleasant death.

still
- **still waters run deep** quiet people often think very deeply or have strong emotions.

stitch
- **a stitch in time saves nine** prompt action at the first sign of trouble saves a lot of time and effort later.
- **have (someone) in stitches** to make (someone) laugh a great deal.
- **without a stitch on** completely naked.

stock
- **on the stocks** in preparation, in the process of being made or arranged. <Refers to the fact that a ship is supported on stocks, a wooden frame, while being built>.
- **take stock (of something)** to assess (a situation).

stomach
- **turn (someone's) stomach** to make (someone) feel sick, to disgust (someone).

stone
- **a stone's throw** a very short distance.
- **be set in stone** to be something that cannot be changed.
- **leave no stone unturned** to try every means possible.

stool

- **fall between two stools** to try to gain two aims and fail with regard to both of them, usually because of indecision.

stop

- **pull out all the stops** to put as much effort and energy into something as possible. <Refers to pulling out the stops of an organ so that it plays at full volume>.
- **stop dead** to stop suddenly and abruptly.
- **stop short of (something *or* doing something)** not to go as far as (something or doing something).

store

- **in cold storage** in reserve.
- **set great store by (something)** to consider (something) to be of great importance or value.

storm

- **a storm in a teacup** a great fuss made over a trivial matter. <Refers to the title of a farce written by William Bernard in 1854>.
- **take (someone *or* something) by storm** to make a very great and immediate impression (on someone or something). <Literally to capture a fort, etc, by a sudden violent military attack>.
- **weather the storm** to survive a difficult or troublesome situation or period of time. <Refers originally to ships>.

story

- **the same old story** a situation, etc, that occurs frequently.

straight

- **go straight** to start leading an honest life.
- **straight as a die** completely honest and fair.
- **straight talking** frank and honest statement or conversation.
- **the straight and narrow (path)** a good, virtuous way of life. <A variation on a biblical reference, 'Straight is the gate and narrow is the way which leadeth unto life', Matthew 7:4>.

stranger

- **be a stranger to (something)** to have no experience of (something).

straw

- **a straw in the wind** a small or minor incident, etc, that indicates what may happen in the future.
- **clutch at straws** to hope that something may happen to get one out of a difficulty or danger when this is extremely unlikely. <From the saying, 'A drowning man will clutch at a straw'>.
- **draw the short straw** to be the one in a group who has to perform an unpleasant or undesirable task. <Pulling out a straw from a collection of different lengths is a kind of lottery to decide who is to do something>.

the last straw *or* the straw that breaks the camel's back an event, etc, which, added to everything that has already happened, makes a situation impossible. <From the saying that it is the last straw added to its burden that breaks the camel's back>.

stream

- **come on stream** to begin to be used or to operate.

street

- **be right up one's street** to be exactly what one likes or what is suitable for one.

strength

- **go from strength to strength** to progress successfully from one achievement to another.
- **on the strength of (something)** relying on (something).

stretch

- **at full stretch** using all one's energy, abilities, powers, etc, as much as possible.
- **stretch a point** to go further than the rules or regulations allow in giving permission, etc, for something.

stride

- **get into one's stride** to become accustomed to doing something and so do it well and effectively. <A reference to running>.
- **make great strides** to make very good progress.
- **take (something) in one's stride** to cope with (something) without worrying about it. <Refers to a horse jumping an obstacle without altering its stride>.

string

- **have (someone) on a string** to have (someone) in one's control. <Refers to someone manipulating a puppet>.
- **how long is a piece of string?** used to emphasize how difficult or impossible it is to give a definite answer to a question.
- **pull strings** to use influence to gain an advantage or benefit of some kind. <As above>.
- **with no strings attached** without any conditions or provisos.

stroke

- **put (someone) off his *or* her stroke** to hinder or prevent (someone) from proceeding smoothly with an activity. <Refers to upsetting the rhythm of someone's rowing>.

strong

- **be (someone's) strong suit** be something at which (someone) is very good. <Refers to card-playing>.

stuff

- **a stuffed shirt** a pompous, over-formal person.
- **knock the stuffing out of (someone) 1** to beat (someone) severely. **2** to discourage (someone) completely, to deprive (someone) of vitality. <Refers to stuffed animals>.

strut one's stuff to do something which you know you do well, usually in a proud and confident way.

stumbling
- **a stumbling block** something that hinders or prevents progress. <A biblical reference to Romans 14:13>.

stump
- **stir one's stumps** to hurry up. <Stumps here means legs>.

style
- **cramp (someone's) style** to hinder (someone) from acting in the way that he or she would like or is accustomed to.

sugar
- **sugar daddy** an elderly man who has a young girlfriend or mistress to whom he gives expensive presents.
- **sugar the pill** to make something unpleasant more pleasant.

suit
- **men in (grey) suits** used to describe the powerful men who are in control of an organization, government, etc.
- **one's birthday suit** nakedness.

Sunday
- **(someone's) Sunday best** (someone's) smartest, formal clothes, of the kind worn to church on Sundays.

sure
- **sure as eggs is eggs** used to emphasize the certainty of something.

surface
- **scratch the surface of (something)** to deal with only a very small part of (something).

swallow
- **one swallow does not make a summer** a single success, etc, does not mean that a generally successful, etc, time is about to come. <Refers to the fact that swallows begin to come to Britain at the start of summer>.

swan
- **(someone's) swan song** the last work or performance by a musician, poet, playwright, actor, etc, before his or her death or retirement; by extension also applied to anyone who does anything for the last time. <Refers to an ancient legend that the swan sings as it is dying although it is otherwise silent>.

sweat
- **the sweat of one's brow** one's hard work.

sweet
- **be all sweetness and light** to seem to be pleasant and good-tempered.
- **have a sweet tooth** to like sweets, cakes and deserts.
- **sweet nothings** affectionate things said to someone with whom one is in love, endearments.

swim
- **be in the swim** be actively involved in social or business activities.

swing
- **get into the swing of things** to become accustomed to (something) and begin to understand and enjoy it. <Refers to the swing of a pendulum>.
- **go with a swing** to be very successful.
- **in full swing** at the most lively or busy part of something.
- **not enough room to swing a cat** see **cat**.
- **what you lose on the swings you gain on the roundabouts** disadvantages in one area of life are usually cancelled out by advantages in another.

swoop
- **at** or **in one fell swoop** in one single action or attempt, at the same time. <Refers to a quotation from Shakespeare's *Macbeth*, Act 4, scene III, the reference being to a hawk swooping on poultry>.

sword
- **a double-edged** or **two-edged sword** used to indicate that something has a bad and a good side.
- **cross swords with (someone)** to enter into a dispute with (someone).
- **the sword of Damocles** a threat of something bad that is likely to happen at any time. <Refers to a legend in which Damocles was forced by Dionysius of Syria to sit through a banquet with a sword hanging by a single hair over his head>.

T
- **to a T** exactly, very well. <Perhaps T stands for tittle, a small dot or point>.

tab
- **keep tabs on (someone** or **something)** to keep a check on (someone or something).
- **pick up the tab for (something)** to pay for (something). <Tab is an American term for bill>.

table
- **turn the tables on (someone)** to change a situation so that one gains the advantage (over someone) after having been at a disadvantage. <From the medieval game of tables, of which backgammon is a form, in which turning the board round would exactly reverse the position of the players>.

tail
- **chase one's tail** to spend a great deal of time and effort trying to do something but achieving very little.
- **have one's tail up** to be confident of success.
- **turn tail** to turn round and leave a difficult or dangerous situation.
- **with one's tail between one's legs** in an ashamed, miserable or defeated state. <From the behaviour of an unhappy dog>.

take

- **take after (someone)** to resemble.
- **take it out on (someone)** to treat (someone) in an angry or nasty way because one is disappointed, angry, etc, about something.

tale

- **live to tell the tale** to survive a dangerous or threatening situation, often used humorously.
- **tell tales** to report someone's wrong-doing.
- **thereby hangs a tale** there is a story associated with that. <A pun on tail, used by Shakespeare>.

talk

- **talk down to (someone)** to speak to (someone) in a condescending way as if he or she were inferior.
- **talk nineteen to the dozen** to talk a great deal and usually very rapidly.
- **the talk of the town** someone or something that is the subject of general conversation or gossip.

tall

- **a tall order** a difficult task.
- **a tall story** a story which is extremely unlikely.

tangent

- **go** or **fly off at a tangent** suddenly to leave the subject being discussed or the task being undertaken and move to a completely different subject or task.

tango

- **it takes two to tango** used to indicate a particular situation has to involve two people and that, therefore, both bear some responsibility.

tape

- **have** or **get (someone** or **something) taped** to have a full knowledge or understanding of (someone or something). <As if measured with a tape>.

tar

- **be tarred with the same brush** to have the same faults.

taste

- **leave a nasty taste in the mouth** to leave someone with unpleasant memories or associations.

tea

- **not for all the tea in China** not for anything at all, certainly not. <For a long time, China was the source of the world's tea>.

tear

- **tear a strip off (someone)** to scold (someone) severely.

teeth

- **by the skin of one's teeth** see skin.
- **cut one's teeth on (something)** to practise on or get early experience from (something). <Refers to children being given something to chew on to help their teeth come through>.

draw the teeth of (someone or **something)** to make (someone or something) no longer dangerous. <Refers to pulling out an animal's teeth.>

- **get one's teeth into (something)** to tackle (something) vigorously.
- **like pulling teeth** used to indicate how difficult something is to do.
- **kick (someone) in the teeth** to refuse to help or support (someone) when he or she is in need of it.
- **set one's teeth on edge** to irritate one.
- **teething troubles** problems occurring at the very beginning of a new project, etc. <From the pain experienced by babies when teeth are just coming through>.

tell

- **I told you so** I warned you and I was right to do so.

tender

- **leave (someone** or **something) to (someone's) tender mercies** to leave (someone or something) in the care of (someone nasty, inefficient, etc).

tenterhooks

- **be on tenterhooks** be very anxious or agitated waiting for something to happen. <Tenterhooks were hooks for stretching newly woven cloth>.

territory

- **it goes with the territory** used to indicate that something, usually some kind of problem or difficulty, usually occurs in connection with a particular, job, activity or situation and should be expected.

test

- **stand the test of time** to survive or still be in use or popular after a considerable period of time.

that

- **that's that** there is no more to be said or done.

thick

- **give (someone) a thick ear** to slap (someone) across the ear, to box (someone's) ears.
- **thick and fast** in great quantities and at a fast rate.
- **thick as thieves** extremely friendly.
- **thick as two short planks** extremely stupid.
- **through thick and thin** whatever difficulties arise.

thief

- **set a thief to catch a thief** the best way to catch or outwit a dishonest or deceitful person is to use the help of another who is dishonest as he or she knows the technique.

thin

- **be thin on top** to be balding.
- **spread oneself too thin** to try to do several different things at once, often with the result that none of them are done very well or properly.
- **thin as a rake** extremely thin.

thing

- **do one's (own) thing** to do what one likes to do or what one is good at doing.
- **have a thing about (someone *or* something) 1** to be very fond of or be particularly attracted to (someone or something). **2** to be scared of, to have a phobia about (someone or something).
- **one of those things** something that must be accepted.
- **see things** to see someone or something that is not there.
- **the thing is** the most important point or question is.

think

- **have another think coming** to be quite mistaken.

thread

- **hang by a thread** to be in a very precarious or uncertain state. <Probably a reference to the sword of Damocles>.
- **lose the thread** to cease to follow the course or development of an argument, conversation, etc.

throat

- **at each other's throats** quarrelling fiercely.
- **jump down (someone's) throat** to attack (someone) verbally or in an angry or violent manner.
- **ram (something) down (someone's) throat** to try forcefully to make (someone) accept ideas, opinions, etc.
- **stick in one's throat *or* gullet** to be difficult for one to accept or tolerate.

throw

- **throw up** to vomit.

thumb

- **thumb a lift** to ask for (and get) a lift in someone's vehicle by signalling with one's thumb.
- **thumb one's nose at (someone *or* something)** to express defiance or contempt at (someone or something), originally by making the rude gesture of putting one's thumb to one's nose.
- **thumbs down** rejection or disapproval. <From the method employed by the crowds in ancient Rome to indicate whether they thought the defeated gladiator should live or die after a fight between two gladiators. If the crowds turned their thumbs down the gladiator died. If they turned them up the gladiator lived.>
- **thumbs up** acceptance or approval. <See **thumbs down** above>.
- **twiddle one's thumbs** to do nothing, to be idle. <Literally to rotate one's thumbs round each other, indicating a state of boredom>.
- **under (someone's) thumb** under one's control or domination.

thunder

- **steal (someone's) thunder** to spoil (someone's) attempt at impressing people by doing what he or she intended to do before him or her. <John Dennis, a 17th/18th century playwright, invented a machine for simulating thunder in plays. When someone else used a similar device in a rival play Dennis said that he had stolen his thunder>.

ticket

- **just the ticket** exactly what is required.
- **meal ticket** someone who can be relied upon to support one, providing food and so on.

tickle

- **be tickled pink** to be delighted.

tide

- **swim against the tide** to do, say or believe things which are the opposite of what the majority of people are doing, saying or believing.
- **the tide is turning** used to indicate that a changing is occurring in people's attitudes, tastes, beliefs, etc.

tie

- **be tied up** to be busy or engaged.

tight

- **in a tight corner *or* spot** in a difficult or dangerous situation.
- **run a tight ship** to run an efficient, well-organized firm etc.
- **sit tight** to be unwilling to move or take action.

tightrope

- **walk a tightrope** to be in a very difficult situation, often one which involves opposing groups, which requires one to act with great caution and delicacy.

tile

- **a night on the tiles** a celebratory evening spent in a wild and unrestrained manner. <Refers to roof tiles and to cats sitting on them at night>.

tilt

- **at full tilt** at maximum speed. <Refers to knights tilting or jousting>.

time

- **ahead of one's time** with ideas in advance of one's contemporaries, often not understood.
- **all in good time** soon, when it is the right time.
- **behind the times** not up-to-date, old-fashioned.
- **do time** to be in prison.
- **have no time for (someone *or* something)** to have a very low opinion of someone or something and to wish not to associate with him, her or it.
- **have the time of one's life** to have a very enjoyable time.
- **have time on one's hands** to have more free time than one can usefully fill with work, etc.
- **in (someone's) own good time** when it is convenient for (someone), at whatever time or speed he or she chooses.
- **keep time 1** of a clock to show the time accurately. **2** to perform an action in the same rhythm as someone else.
- **kill time** to find something to do to pass some idle time, especially time spent waiting for someone or something.
- **mark time** to remain in one's present position without progressing or taking any action. <Refers to soldiers moving their feet as if marching but not actually moving forwards>.

- **not before time** not too soon, rather late.
- **no time at all** a very short time.
- **pass the time of day with (someone)** to greet (someone) and have a brief conversation, e.g. about the weather.
- **play for time** to act so as to delay an action, event, etc, until the time that conditions are better for oneself. <In games such as cricket it means to play in such a way as to avoid defeat by playing defensively until the close of the game>.
- **take time by the forelock** to act quickly and without delay. <Refers to the fact that time was often represented by an old man with no hair except for a forelock, a length of hair over his forehead>.
- **time and tide wait for no man** time moves on without regard for human beings and therefore opportunities should be grasped as they arise as they may not be there for very long.
- **time and time again** repeatedly.
- **time flies** time passes very quickly.

tip
- **be on the tip of one's tongue** to be about to be said.

tit
- **tit for tat** repayment of injury or harm for injury or harm. <Perhaps a variation on tip for tap, blow for blow>.

to
- **toing and froing** repeatedly going backwards and forwards.

toast
- **warm as toast** very warm and cosy.

tod
- **on one's tod** alone. <From Cockney rhyming slang 'on one's Tod Sloan', meaning 'on one's own', Tod Sloan having been a famous American jockey>.

toe
- **be on one's toes** to be alert and prepared for action.
- **make one's toes curl** to make one feel very uncomfortable or embarrassed.
- **put a toe in the water** to start doing something very slowly or gradually to see if one likes it, whether it will be successful, whether people will approve, etc.
- **tread on (someone's) toes** to offend (someone) by doing or saying (something) that is against his or her beliefs or opinions.

Tom
- **a peeping Tom** a man who gets sexual enjoyment from secretly watching women undress or women who are naked, especially by looking through the windows of their houses. <From the story of Lady Godiva who is said to have ridden naked through the streets of Coventry as part of a bargain made with her husband, Leofric, Earl of Mercia, to persuade him to lift a tax he had placed on his tenants. Everyone was to stay indoors so as not to see her

but a character, later called Peeping Tom, looked out to see her and was struck blind>.
- **every** or **any Tom, Dick and Harry** absolutely everyone or anyone, every ordinary person. <From the fact that all three are common English Christian names>.

tongue
- **have one's tongue in one's cheek** to say something that one does not mean seriously or literally, sometimes to say the opposite of what one means for a joke.
- **hold one's tongue** to remain silent or to stop talking.
- **set tongues wagging** to start people gossiping.

tooth
- **be** or **get long in the tooth** to be or become old.
- **fight tooth and nail** to fight, struggle or argue fiercely and determinedly.

top[1]
- **blow one's top** to lose one's temper.
- **get on top of one** used to indicate that someone is not coping with all the things that require to be done.
- **off the top of one's head** without much thought, without research or preparation.
- **over the top** too much, to too great an extent.
- **the top of the ladder** or **tree** the highest point in a profession, etc.

top[2]
- **sleep like a top** to sleep very soundly. <A pun on the fact that sleep used of a top means 'to spin steadily without wobbling'>.

toss
- **argue the toss** to dispute a decision. <Refers to arguing about the result of tossing a coin>.

touch
- **it's touch and go** it's very uncertain or precarious. <Perhaps refers to a ship that touches rocks or the ground but goes on past the danger without being damaged>.
- **lose one's touch** to lose one's usual skill or knack. <Probably refers to someone's touch on piano keys>.
- **the common touch** the ability to understand and get on with ordinary people.
- **the finishing touches** the final details which complete something.

tow
- **have (someone) in tow** to have someone following closely behind one.

towel
- **throw in the towel** to give up, to admit defeat. <From a method of conceding defeat in boxing>.

tower
- **a tower of strength** someone who is very helpful and supportive.

town
- **go to town** to act or behave without restraint, with great enthusiasm or with great expense.

track
- **cover one's tracks** to hide one's activities or movements.
- **from the wrong side of the tracks** used of someone who comes from a poor or less desirable area of town. <American in origin and refers to the fact that, when railways were built, they often divided an area into two sharply divided districts>.
- **keep** *or* **lose track of (someone** *or* **something)** to keep or fail to keep oneself informed about the whereabouts or progress of (someone or something).
- **make tracks (for)** to leave or set out (for).
- **on the right** *or* **wrong track** on the right or wrong course to get the correct answer or desired result.

trail
- **blaze a trail** to show or lead the way in some new activity or area of knowledge. <Refers to explorers going along a path and marking the way for those coming after them by stripping sections of bark from trees (blazing)>.

trial
- **trials and tribulations** difficulties and hardships.

trick
- **do the trick** to have the desired effect, to achieve the desired result.
- **never to miss a trick** never to fail to take advantage of a favourable situation or opportunity to bring advantage to oneself.
- **up to one's (old) tricks** acting in one's usual (wrong, dishonest or deceitful) way.

trooper
- **swear like a trooper** to swear very frequently or very strongly. <A trooper was an ordinary cavalry soldier>.

trot
- **on the trot 1** one after the other. **2** very active and busy.

trousers
- **wear the trousers** to make all the important decisions in a household.

trump
- **play one's trump card** to use something very advantageous to oneself that one has had in reserve for use when really necessary. <In card games a trump is a card of whichever suit has been declared to be higher-ranking than the others>.
- **turn up trumps** to do the right or required thing in a difficult situation, especially unexpectedly. <*See* above, refers to drawing a card from the trump suit>.

tune
- **call the tune** to be the person in control who gives the orders. <Refers to the saying 'He who pays the piper calls the tune'>.
- **in tune with (something)** in agreement with (something), compatible with (something).

- **to the tune of (something)** to the stated sum of money, usually high or higher than is expected or is reasonable.

turkey
- **cold turkey** a form of treatment for drug or alcohol abuse involving sudden and complete withdrawal as opposed to gradual withdrawal.
- **talk turkey** to talk plainly and honestly.

turn
- **a turn-up for the books** something favourable which happens unexpectedly. <Referred originally to a horse that unexpectedly won a race, the book meaning the total number of bets on a race>.
- **do (someone) a good turn** to help (someone) in some way.
- **done to a turn** cooked exactly right, cooked to perfection.
- **give (someone) quite a turn** to give (someone) a sudden shock or surprise.
- **turn turtle** to turn upside down, to capsize. <A turtle is helpless and easy to kill if it is turned over on its back>.

twice
- **think twice** to give careful consideration.

two
- **in two ticks** in a very short time. <Refers to the ticking of a cloak>.
- **put two and two together** to come to a (correct) conclusion from what one sees and hears.
- **two of a kind** two people of a very similar type or character.
- **two's company, (three's a crowd)** a third person who is with a couple is often unwanted as they want to be alone.

umbrage
- **take umbrage** to show that one is offended. <Originally meant to feel overshadowed, from Latin *umbra*, 'shade'>.

uncle
- **Uncle Sam** the United States of America. <Probably from the initials US which were stamped on government supplies, possibly because someone called Uncle Sam was employed in handling such supplies>.

under
- **under the influence** under the influence of alcohol, drunk.

up
- **be on the up-and-up** to be making successful progress.
- **be (well) up in** *or* **on (something)** to have an extensive knowledge of (something).
- **be up and running** to have started and be operating well.

- **be up to (someone)** it is (someone's) responsibility or duty.
- **be up to (something) 1** to be occupied with or in (something, often something dishonest, etc). **2** to be good enough, strong enough, etc, to do (something).
- **up and about** out of bed, after an illness.
- **up and doing** active and busy.
- **ups and downs** good fortune and bad fortune, successful periods and unsuccessful periods.
- **upstage (someone** *or* **something)** to take attention or interest away from (someone or something).

upshot

- **the upshot** the result or outcome. <Literally the last shot in an archery competition>.

upper

- **have** *or* **get the upper hand (of** *or* **over) (someone)** have or get an advantage or control (over someone).
- **on one's uppers** very poor. <Literally with no soles on one's shoes>.
- **upper-crust** of the upper class or aristocracy. <Refers literally to the upper part of the pastry of a pie above the filling>.

uptake

- **quick** *or* **slow on the uptake** quick or slow to understand.

Uriah

- **Uriah Heep** a sycophant, someone who always fawns over and toadies to others. <Refers to a character in Charles Dickens's novel *David Copperfield*>.

U-turn

- **do a U-turn** to change one's opinion, policy, etc, completely. <Refers originally to vehicle drivers making a turn in the shape of the letter U to reverse direction>.

vain

- **take (someone's) name in vain** to use (someone's) name disrespectfully, especially to swear using God's name. <A biblical reference to Exodus 20:7>.

variety

- **variety is the spice of life** the opportunity to do different things, experience different situations, etc, is what makes life interesting. <A quotation from a poem by William Cowper>.

veil

- **draw a veil over (something)** not to discuss (something), to keep (something) hidden or secret.

vengeance

- **with a vengeance** very strongly, much, etc.

vex

- **a vexed question** a difficult issue or problem that is much discussed without being resolved.

victory

- **landslide victory** a victory in an election by a very large number of votes.

view

- **a bird's-eye view of (something) 1** a view of (something) seen from high above. **2** a brief description, etc, of (something).

villain

- **the villain of the piece** the person responsible for an act of evil or wrongdoing. <Refers originally to the villain in a play>.

vine

- **a clinging vine** a possessive person, someone who likes always to be with someone else.
- **wither on the vine** to die to come to an end without being used, finished, etc. <Literally of grapes withering on the vine instead of being picked and eaten or made into wine>.

violet

- **a shrinking violet** a very timid, shy person.

voice

- **a voice crying in the wilderness** (someone) expressing an opinion or warning that no one takes any notice of. <A biblical reference to John the Baptist in Matthew 3:3>.
- **the still, small voice (of reason)** the expression of a calm, sensible point of view. <A biblical reference to I Kings 19:12>.

volume

- **speak volumes** to express a great deal of meaning without putting it into words.

vote

- **a vote of confidence** a vote taken to establish whether or not the government, a group of people, a person, etc, is still trusted and supported.
- **vote with one's feet** to leave.

wagon

- **circle the wagons** of a group of people, to work together to protect themselves against possible harm or danger. <In the American West pioneers used to form their wagons into a circle if they were under attack>.
- **on the wagon** not drinking alcohol. <Refers to a water wagon>.

wake

- **in the wake of (something)** immediately following, and often caused by (something). <Refers literally to the strip of water left by the passing of a ship>.

wall

- **be climbing the wall(s)** to feel frustrated, bored or impatient.
- **go to the wall** to suffer ruin. <Origin uncertain>.
- **off the wall** unconventional, strange.
- **up the wall** very annoyed, irritated, harassed, etc.

- **walls have ears** someone may be listening (to a secret conversation).

Walter
- **a Walter Mitty** someone who invents stories about himself to make his life seem more exciting. <Refers to a character in a James Thurber short story>.

war
- **have been in the wars** to have a slight injury.
- **on the warpath** very angry. <An American Indian expression>.

wart
- **warts and all** including all the faults, disadvantages. <Refers to the fact that Oliver Cromwell instructed his portrait painter, Sir Peter Lely, to paint him as he really was, including his warts, rather than try to make him look more handsome>.

wash
- **come out in the wash** to come to a satisfactory end. <Used literally of a stain on clothes, etc, that comes out when the article is washed>.
- **(something) won't wash** to be regarded as unacceptable or incredible.

water
- **blow (someone or something) out of the water** to destroy or defeat (someone or something) utterly.
- **hold water** to be accurate, to be able to be proved true. <From a vessel that is not broken>.
- **muddy the waters** to confuse a situation.
- **test the water/waters** to try to find out what the reaction is likely to be to a plan before one puts this into effect.
- **tread water** to take very little action. <Literally to keep oneself afloat in water by moving the legs (and arms)>.
- **water under the bridge** something that is past and cannot be changed and should be forgotten.

wave
- **make waves** to cause trouble.
- **on the same wavelength as (someone)** having the same opinions, attitudes, tastes, etc, as (someone).

way
- **be set in one's ways** to have a set routine in your life and to dislike having this disrupted.
- **get into the way of (something or doing something)** to become accustomed to (something or doing something).
- **get or have one's own way** to do or get what one wants.
- **go back a long way** used to indicate that people have known each other for a long time.
- **go out of one's way** to do more than is really necessary, to make a special effort.
- **go the way of all flesh** to die or come to an end.
- **have a way with (someone or something)** to have a special knack with (someone or something), to be good at handling (someone or something).

- **have everything one's own way** to get everything done according to one's wishes.
- **have it both ways** to have the advantages of two sets of situations, each of which usually excludes the possibility of the other.
- **lead the way** to go first, to be in front.
- **lose one's way** to cease to know where one is or which direction one is going in.
- **make way for (someone or something)** to stand aside to leave room for (someone or something).
- **mend one's ways** to improve one's behaviour.
- **not to know which way to turn** to be in trouble and to be too confused to be able to decide what to do for the best.
- **pay one's way** to pay one's expenses or one's share of expenses.
- **see one's way to (doing something)** to be able and willing to (do something).
- **there are no two ways about it** no other opinion, attitude, etc, is possible.
- **under way** in progress.
- **ways and means** methods, especially unofficial ones.
- **where's there's a will there's a way** a saying used to indicate that if one is determined to do something, then one will find a way to succeed in doing so.

wayside
- **fall by the wayside** to fail to continue to the end of something; to give up in the course of doing something. <A biblical reference to the parable of the sower in Luke 8:5>.

wear
- **be the worse for wear 1** to be in a bad state, looking tired, ill, untidy, etc. **2** to be drunk.

weather
- **under the weather** unwell.

web
- **a tangled web** used to describe a very complicate, confused situation.

wedge
- **drive a wedge between** to cause disagreement or ill will between two people or two groups, especially when they were formerly friendly.
- **the thin end of the wedge** a minor event or action which could be the first stage of something major and serious or harmful.

weight
- **a weight off one's mind** used to indicate that one no longer has to worry about something which has been worrying one for some time.
- **carry weight** to have influence, to be considered important.
- **pull one's weight** to do one's fair share of work, etc.
- **punch above one's weight** to try to do something which is thought to be beyond one's abilities.
- **take the weight off one's feet** to sit down.

- **throw one's weight about** *or* **around** to use one's power and influence in a bullying way.
- **throw one's weight behind (someone *or* something)** to support (someone or something).

west
- **go west** to be ruined, to be finished. <Airmen's slang from World War I>.

wet
- **wet behind the ears** to be young, inexperienced and naive.
- **have a whale of a time** to have an extremely enjoyable time.

what
- **give (someone) what for** to scold or punish (someone).
- **know what's what** to know the details of a situation, to know what is going on.
- **what have you** and similar things.

wheel
- **a fifth wheel** a person or thing that is not needed or is not wanted. <Refers to the fact that a vehicle needs only four wheels to keep running>.
- **reinvent the wheel** to do something which one considers new or innovative, but which is, in fact, very similar to something which has been done by someone else; to start a project from scratch without taking advantage of available information, research, etc.
- **set the wheels in motion** to start a process off.
- **wheeling and dealing** acting in an astute but sometimes dishonest or immoral way, especially in business.
- **wheels within wheels** used to indicate a very complicated situation with many different things involved, all influencing each other.

whip
- **have the whip hand** to have control or an advantage. <Refers to coach-driving>.
- **a whipping boy** someone who is blamed and punished for someone else's mistakes. <Refers literally to a boy who was punished for any misdeeds a royal prince made, since the tutor was not allowed to strike a member of the royal family>.

whisker
- **win by a whisker** to win by a very short amount.

whistle
- **wet one's whistle** to have a drink.
- **whistle for (something)** to ask for (something) with no hope of getting it. <Perhaps from an old sailors' superstition that when a ship is becalmed whistling can summon up a wind>.

white
- **a whited sepulchre** someone who pretends to be moral and virtuous but is in fact bad. <A biblical reference to Matthew 23:27>.
- **white lie** a not very serious lie.
- **whiter than white** extremely honest and moral.

wick
- **get on (someone's) wick** to annoy or irritate (someone) greatly.

wide
- **be wide open** used of a competition of some kind to indicate that it is very difficult to predict the winner as the competitors seem equally good.

wild
- **a wild goose chase** a search or hunt that cannot end in success.
- **sow one's wild oats** to enjoy oneself in a wild and sometimes promiscuous way when one is young.
- **spread like wildfire** to spread extremely rapidly. <Wildfire was probably a kind of fire started by lightning>.

will
- **with a will** enthusiastically and energetically.

wind
- **get one's second wind** to find renewed energy to go on doing something after a period of feeling tired and weak.
- **get wind of (something)** to receive information about (something) <Referring to the scent of an animal carried by the wind>.
- **in the wind** about to happen, being placed or prepared.
- **get the wind up** to become frightened or nervous.
- **raise the wind** to get enough money to do (something).
- **spit in the wind** to try to do something impossible and so waste time and effort.
- **take the wind out of (someone's) sails** to reduce (someone's) pride in his or her cleverness, abilities, etc. <Refers to the fact that a ship takes the wind out of another ship's sails if it passes close to it on the windward side>.
- **throw caution to the (four) winds** to begin to behave recklessly.
- **whistle in the wind** to make a statement or promise which is pointless since it is very unlikely to have any effect or produce any results.

windmill
- **tilt at windmills** to struggle against imaginary opposition. <Refers to an episode in Cervantes' novel *Don Quixote* in which the hero mistakes a row of windmills for giants and attacks them>.

window
- **go out the window** to disappear completely; to be ignore or forgotten about.
- **window-dressing** the presentation of something to show the most favourable parts and hide the rest. <Refers literally to the arranging of goods in a shop window to attract customers>.

wing
- **on a wing and a prayer** used to indicate that you hope to do something successfully even although you do not have the resources to do so.

- **spread one's wings 1** to leave home. **2** to try to put into practice one's own ideas, to make use of one's abilities. <Refers to young birds ready to try to fly and leave the nest for the first time>.
- **take (someone) under one's wing** to take (someone) under one's protection and guidance. <Refers to the practice of some birds of covering their young with their wings>.
- **try one's wings** to try to do something which one has never done before in order to see if one will be successful at it.
- **waiting in the wings** in a state of readiness to do something, especially to take over someone else's job. <Literally waiting in the wings of a theatre stage ready to go on>.
- **wing it** to do something without planning or preparation, to improvise.

wink
- **not sleep a wink** not to be able to sleep at all.
- **tip (someone) the wink** to give (someone) information secretly or privately.

wire
- **down to the wire** to the last possible minute.
- **get** *or* **have one's wires crossed** to be involved in a misunderstanding. <Refers to telephone wires>.

wise
- **none the wiser** knowing no more than one did before.
- **put (someone) wise to (something)** to give (someone) information about (something), make (someone) aware of (something).

wish
- **wishful thinking** believing that, or hoping that, something unlikely is true or will happen just because one wishes that it would.
- **wish (someone) joy of (something)** to wish that something will be a pleasure or benefit to someone (although one doesn't think it will).

wit
- **at one's wits' end** worried and desperate.
- **keep one's wits about one** to be alert and watchful.
- **live by one's wits** to live by cunning schemes rather than by working.
- **pit one's wits against (someone)** to use one's intelligence to try to defeat (someone).
- **scare (someone) out of his** *or* **her wits** to frighten (someone) very much.

witch
- **witch-hunt** a search for and persecution of people who are thought to have done something wrong or hold opinions which are thought to be dangerous etc. <Refers historically to organized hunts for people thought to be witches>.

wolf
- **a wolf in sheep's clothing** someone evil and dangerous who seems to be gentle and harmless. <A biblical reference to Matthew 7:15>.

- **cry wolf** to give a false warning of danger, to call unnecessarily for help. <Refers to one of Aesop's fables in which a shepherd boy used to amuse himself by calling out that a wolf was coming to attack his sheep and did this so many times when it was not true that no one believed when it was true, and all his sheep were killed>.
- **keep the wolf from the door** to prevent poverty and hunger.

wood
- **not to be able to see the wood for the trees** not to be able to consider the general nature of a situation, etc, because one is concentrating too much on details.
- **out of the woods** out of danger or difficulties.
- **touch wood** to touch something made of wood supposedly to keep away bad luck. <Refers to a well-known superstition>.

wool
- **pull the wool over (someone's) eyes** to deceive (someone).
- **wool-gathering** day-dreaming. <Refers to someone wandering around hedges gathering wool left by sheep>.

word
- **eat one's words** to admit that one was wrong in what one said.
- **get a word in edgeways** *or* **edgewise** to have difficulty in breaking into a conversation.
- **hang on (someone's) words** to listen carefully and eagerly to everything that someone says.
- **have a word in (someone's) ear** to tell (someone) something in private.
- **have words** to argue or quarrel.
- **keep one's word** to do as one promised to do.
- **put in a good word for (someone)** to say something favourable about (someone), to recommend (someone).
- **put words into (someone's) mouth** to say that someone has said something when he/she did not; to suggest that someone is going to say something when he/she has no intention of doing so.
- **say the word** say what you want and your wishes will be carried out.
- **take (someone's) word for it** to believe what someone says without question and without proof.
- **take the words out of (someone's) mouth** to say what (someone) was just about to say.

work
- **all work and no play makes Jack a dull boy** people should take some leisure time and not work all the time.
- **give (someone) the works** to give (someone) the complete treatment. <Originally slang for to kill someone>.
- **have one's work cut out** to face a very difficult task. <Literally to have a lot of work ready for on>.
- **worked up** agitated, annoyed.

world

- **a man of the world** a sophisticated and worldly man.
- **come down in the world** to be less well off, less successful etc. than formerly.
- **come up in the world** to be better off, more successful, etc. than formerly.
- **do (someone) the world of good** to have a very good effect on (someone); to be of great benefit or advantage to (someone).
- **for all the world like (someone or something)** exactly like (someone or something).
- **not the end of the world** used to make someone realize that things are not as bad as they think they are.
- **not to have long for this world** to be about to die.
- **on top of the world** very cheerful and happy.
- **out of this world** remarkably good.
- **think the world of (someone)** to be extremely fond of (someone).
- **the world is (someone's) oyster** (someone) has a great many possible opportunities or chances. <Refers to a quotation from Shakespeare's *The Merry Wives of Windsor*, Act 2, scene II>.

worm

- **a can of worms** an extremely complicated and difficult situation. <Refers to the fact that worms wriggle around a lot>.
- **(even) the worm turns** even the most humble or meek person will protest if treated badly enough.

worth

- **for all one is worth** using maximum effort.

wound

- **lick one's wounds** to try to recover from a situation in which one has been badly defeated or humiliated.
- **reopen old wounds** to remind people of past unpleasant experiences which they would prefer to forget about.

wrap

- **keep (something) under wraps** to keep (something) secret or hidden.

- **take the wraps off (something)** to reveal, or give details about, something that has been secret up till now.
- **wrapped up in (someone or something)** absorbed in, giving all one's attention to (someone or something).
- **wrap (something) up** to finish (something) completely.

writ

- **writ large** used to indicate that something is in its most extreme form.

write

- **the writing on the wall** something which indicates that something unpleasant, such as failure, unhappiness, disaster, etc, will happen. <A biblical reference to Daniel 5:5–31, in which the coming destruction of the Babylonian empire is made known to Belshazzar at a feast through mysterious writing on a wall>.

wrong

- **get on the wrong side of (someone)** to cause (someone) to dislike or be hostile to one.
- **not to put a foot wrong** not to make a mistake of any kind.

yarn

- **spin a yarn** to tell a long story, especially an untrue one that is given as an excuse. <Telling a story is compared to spinning a long thread>.

year

- **the year dot** a long time ago, the beginning of time.

yesterday

- **not born yesterday** not easily fooled.

young

- **you're only young once** one should take advantage of the opportunities that arise when one is young and has the energy, freedom, etc, to enjoy or exploit them.

zero

- **zero hour** the time at which something is due to begin. <Originally a military term>.

Appendix 12

Similes

A **simile** is a figure of speech in which a thing or person is, for the sake of comparison, said to be like another. The word 'simile' is derived from *similis*, the Latin word for 'like'. The words 'as' or 'like' usually appear in the simile, as in:

She was slim **as** a wand.
The fire spread **like** wildfire.

Some similes are extremely common. A list of these is given below:

agile as a monkey
alike as (like) two peas in a pod
bald as a coot
black as ebony
blind as a bat
bold as brass
brave as a lion
brown as a berry
calm as a millpond
changeable as the moon
cheerful as the day is long
clear as daylight
clear as mud (= not at all clear)
common as muck
cool as a cucumber
cunning as a fox
dead as a doornail
deaf as a post
drunk as a lord
dry as a bone
dry as dust (boring)
dull as ditchwater
easy as pie
easy as falling off a log
fit as a fiddle
flat as a pancake
frisky as a colt
good as gold
green as grass
happy as a pig in muck
happy as a sandboy
hard as nails
helpless as a babe in arms
hollow as a drum
hot as hell
innocent as a new-born babe
keen as mustard
light as a feather
lively as a cricket
mad as a hatter

merry as a lark
neat as a pin
old as the hills/Methuselah
patient as Job
plain as a pikestaff
playful as kitten
pleased as Punch
poor as a church mouse
pretty as a picture
proud as a peacock
quick as a flash
quiet as a mouse
rare as hen's teeth
rich as Croesus
safe as houses
sharp as a razor
sick as a dog
sick as a parrot (disappointed)
silent as the grave
simple as ABC
slow as a snail
sly as a fox
smart as paint
smooth as silk
sober as a judge
straight as a die
stubborn as a mule
sure as death
swift as an arrow
tall as a steeple
thick as thieves (friendly)
thick as two short planks (stupid)
thin as a rake
tight as a drum
tough as old boots
uncertain as the weather
weak as water
white as snow/a ghost
wily as a fox
wise as Solomon

Clichés

Clichés are an established feature of the English language, being particularly common in spoken English language and in informal written contexts. Some of them are hundreds of years old; others have taken only a short time to become popular.

People tend to use them unconsciously and most of us are unaware of quite how often we use them. There are many who claim to dislike clichés and regard them as somehow spoiling the language, but if they stopped to analyse what they say and write, even they would find that they use quite a lot of them.

People dislike clichés because they are overused. Many clichés start out as a particularly imaginative or clever way of saying something, but they become used so often by so many people that they lose their freshness and originality.

It would be almost impossible to rid our speech and writing entirely of clichés and, in any case, they often add a bit of colour to the language. Since they are such an established feature of English, it is important to learn how to use them correctly. However, particularly in fairly formal speech or writing, it is essential to try to avoid using them too frequently.

Some clichés are used in contexts in which they are virtually meaningless and act simply as conversational fillers. For example, there are people who use the expression 'at this moment in time' regularly when the word 'now' would be more appropriate. Likewise, many people use clichés such as 'the thing is', 'at the end of the day' or 'you know what I mean' in this way.

Below is a selection of common clichés which are particularly overused and so should be used sparingly.

A

accidents will happen things go wrong at some time in everyone's life

across the board applying to everyone or to all cases

actions speak louder than words how a person acts is more important than what they say

to add insult to injury to make matters worse

after due consideration after some thought

all things considered after some thought

an accident waiting to happen a dangerous situation

any port in a storm a welcome solution in a bad situation

as a matter of fact the following statement is true

at death's door an exaggeration to say someone is ill

at the drop of a hat without much of a reason at all

at the end of the day after everything has passed

at this juncture now

at this moment in time now

avoid like the plague to strenuously avoid

B

back to the drawing board back to the beginning

bag and baggage all your possessions

bag of tricks the equipment necessary to do something

batten down the hatches there's going to be trouble

beggars can't be choosers one needs a favour and has no other choice

be that as it may that may be so

better late than never an ironic way of saying something or someone is late

bite the bullet to get on with something despite unpleasantness

a blessing in disguise a bad situation from which may come good

blissful ignorance to be in the happy state of not knowing of an unpleasant situation

a blot on the landscape an ugly thing (usually a building) in a beautiful place

blushing bride an ironic description of a bride

bone of contention a cause of dispute

the bottom line the outcome or conclusion

bright-eyed and bushy-tailed alert and awake

by the same token using the same reasoning, or on the other side of the argument

C

call it a day give up and stop a venture

the calm before the storm a time before an unpleasant situation where everything seems fine

Catch 22 a situation in which one can never win or from which one can never escape

categorical denial strong denial

caught napping unprepared for a situation

chalk and cheese opposites

champing at the bit enthusiastic to get started at something

chapter and verse every detail

cheek by jowl very close together

a close shave an escape which was very nearly disastrous

chop and change alternate

to coin a phrase ironically, this is said when one is using a cliché

come full circle to return to the beginning of something

a commanding lead emphasis of lead

common or garden everyday

conspicuous by one's absence to deliberately boycott something

cool, calm and collected emphasis of calm

cover a multitude of sins a flattering surface on something, usually refers to clothing

at crack of dawn very early

cross that bridge when you come to it deal with matters in hand and think of other problems when they arise

to cut a long story short to summarise

cut and dried settled and definite

the cutting edge the latest technology

D

damn with faint praise to praise in a patronising or deliberately ironic way

a damp squib something which promises excitement but disappoints

a dark horse someone with a secret, usually an exciting or exotic one

day in, day out every day

dead as a dodo actually dead, or more metaphorically, out of favour

dead in the water has no chance of working

dead to the world fast asleep

a deafening silence a silence which is very prominent and embarrassing

dig one's own grave to be the cause of one's own misfortune

a dirty tricks campaign a campaign, usually political, uncovering, or possibly creating rumours of, a scandal regarding one's opponent

dog eat dog a ruthless struggle against one's rivals to survive or be successful.

donkey's years ago many years ago

don't count your chickens before they're hatched don't presume anything before it happens

doom and gloom pessimism

draw a blank no result

drown one's sorrows to get drunk to get over a disappointment

Dutch courage to get drunk to give the confidence to do something

E

each and every one of you everyone

eager for the fray looking for a fight

easier said than done more difficult than it appears to be

eat humble pie to admit that you are wrong

economical with the truth to leave out important facts

the end of an era the end of an important phase

enough is enough no more can be tolerated

the envy of the world enviable

every cloud has a silver lining bad situations can sometimes have consolations

every dog has his day everyone has their individual triumphs

every little helps a little help from a lot of different sources will eventually add up to create something more substantial

every man jack everyone

everything but the kitchen sink almost all your belongings

explore every avenue to look for all possibilities

F

face facts be honest with yourself

face the music face your responsibilities

the fact of the matter the truth of the situation

fair and square honestly

fall between two stools to try to gain two things at once and fail with regard to both of them

fall on deaf ears an explanation given to someone who doesn't want to listen

famous last words describing a statement about an event which is made directly before the exact opposite happens

far be it for me this something I would never do (usually said ironically)

a fate worse than death an exaggeration meaning death would be preferable

a feeding frenzy where many people are desperately after the same information (usually of the press)

few and far between very rare

a fighting chance a good chance of succeeding or surviving

fighting fit in good health

the finishing touches in the final stages

first and foremost first and most importantly

first things first most important things first

a flash in the pan a passing fashion or idea that will not last

the flavour of the month a person or fashion that is popular at the moment but may not last

flog a dead horse to pursue something that is not worth pursuing

the fly in the ointment an unpleasant feature that spoils something

food for thought something that makes you think

footloose and fancy free single and looking for a fun

forewarned is forearmed to be prepared so that you are able to cope with a possible event

a forlorn hope no hope

fresh fields and pastures new a new and different place or situation.

from the sublime to the ridiculous from a state of greatness to one of ridiculouness

from the word go from the start

from time immemorial a long time ago

G

gainful employment in work

gather ye rosebuds while ye may make the most of your youth

a general exodus everyone has left at once

generous to a fault extremely generous

a gentleman's agreement an agreement in word alone

get down to brass tacks to consider the basic facts

get more than one bargained for to encounter more difficulties than expected

the gift of the gab the ability to talk readily and easily

gild the lily to add unnecessary decoration

give up the ghost to die (person); to stop working (object)

a glowing tribute a flattering tribute

a glutton for punishment someone who has suffered but who goes back for more

go against the grain to act against your better judgement or wishes

go from strength to strength to get better and better

it goes without saying you should know what I'm talking about

a golden opportunity a great and unexpected opportunity that should be grasped

good as gold perfectly behaved

the gory details a description of the details of a situation (not necessarily a bad one)

grasp the nettle to set about a difficult task in a determined way

the greatest thing since sliced bread a very popular admired thing or person

green with envy very jealous

grin and bear it to suffer a bad situation without complaint

grind to a halt to stop suddenly

a guiding light someone who guides the way in a particular field

H

halcyon days a nostalgic (and idealistic) reference to a perfect time in one's life

hale and hearty healthy

half the battle the most difficult part of a situation is over with

hand over fist in large amounts; very rapidly

the happy couple newly married people

a hard act to follow someone who has previously been very successful at something

a helping hand help

high and dry left in a helpless state

hit the nail on the head to be extremely accurate in one's description

a hive of activity a very busy area

Hobson's choice no choice at all

the honest truth emphasis of the truth of statement

hope against hope to continue to hope although there is little reason to be hopeful

horses for courses certain people are better suited to certain tasks than others

how time flies time passes very quickly

I

if you can't beat 'em, join 'em if the majority disagree with you then why not just go along with them

if you can't stand the heat, get out of the kitchen if you can't cope with the job in hand then leave

ill-gotten gains possessions acquired dishonestly

in all conscience being completely fair and honest

in a nutshell briefly; to sum up

in any shape or form in any way at all

in less than no time in a very short time

in no uncertain terms in a very direct way

in splendid isolation standing out in a unique way

in the cold light of day when one looks at something rationally and calmly

in the dim and distant past something happened a long time ago (and should be forgotten)

in the fullness of time when the proper time has elapsed

in the nick of time just in time

in the pipeline in preparation

in the present climate in the present situation

in this day and age in these times

it'll all come out in the wash things will turn out for the best in the end

it never rains but it pours when something goes wrong other things go wrong too

it's a long story it is complicated

it's a small world said when coincidental meetings occur

it's early days it's too early to come to a conclusion

it takes two to tango it's not the fault of one person

J

jack of all trades someone who knows a little about a lot of things

jam tomorrow the (possibly false) promise of better thing in the future

the jewel in the crown the most valuable or successful thing associated with someone or something

jobs for the boys jobs give to friends rather than the most worthy of them

jump on the bandwagon to show interest because it's fashionable

just between you and me (and the gatepost) this is a secret

just deserts to get the punishment that is due to you

just for the record so that it will be noted

just one of those things something that has to be accepted

just what the doctor ordered just what is required

K

keep a low profile not to draw attention to oneself

keep oneself to oneself not to tell others very much about oneself or to mix with others very much

keep one's head above water to be just coping with a situation

keep one's nose to the grindstone to keep working hard

keep the wolf from the door to making just enough money to survive

kickstart to encourage something or to give, e.g., a project, an extra push

kill the fatted calf to provide a lavish meal for a celebration

kill two birds with one stone to complete two tasks at once

kill with kindness to be generous in some way to someone when it's not in his or her best interest

the kiss of death something which will cause the ruin of something

knee-jerk reaction an immediate (reflex) response to something

know all the answers to have all the information

know for a fact emphasising that ones knows something

know where one stands to know the nature of one's position

know which side one's bread is buttered on to know when one is in a fortunate position

L

a labour of love a difficult job done for the satisfaction of it

the lap of luxury in luxurious surroundings

large as life in person, actually present

last but not least although someone or something is last, it is not the least important thing

the last straw an event which makes a situation impossible

a leading light a leader, longstanding, in a certain area

leave in the lurch to abandon

leave no stone unturned to search everywhere

leave to someone's tender mercies to be left in the care of someone inefficient or dangerous

let bygones be bygones forget about past grievances

let's face it face the truth

level playing field a fair basis for something

the life and soul of the party a lively entertaining person

light at the end of the tunnel fortunate outcome following times of trouble

my lips are sealed it's a secret and I won't tell

a little bird told me I can't tell you my sources

lock, stock and barrel everything included

a lone wolf a loner

the long arm of the law the police

M

make an honest woman of marry

make ends meet to survive on little money

make the supreme sacrifice to die

make someone an offer they can't refuse an irresistible offer

make waves to get yourself noticed

man and boy as a child and an adult .

the man in the street ordinary person

manna from heaven something unexpectedly advantageous

man to man as equals, regardless of background etc.

many hands make light work the more helpers there are the quicker a job will be done

mark my words take note of what I'm saying

a matter of life or death a very grave situation

method in one's madness actions seem to be foolish but actually have a motive behind them

a millstone round one's neck a hindrance

the moment of truth when the result of something becomes apparent

a moot point a point of argument

more in sorrow than in anger more disappointed at someone's actions that angry

the more the merrier the more people involved the better

move heaven and earth to go to great lengths to achieve something

move the goalposts to change the aims of a project so that it disadvantageous to others but advantageous to oneself

the movers and shakers those with power

much of a muchness ordinary, indistinguishable from others

mutton dressed as lamb an older person (usually female) dressed in a way that is unflatteringly young

N

name names be specific in who it is that you are talking about

the name of the game the important or central thing behind something

nearest and dearest close family and close friends

needless to say something that it should be unnecessary to state

a new dawn a new opportunity or era

the nitty gritty basic practical details

no expense spared lots of money has been spent

no gain without pain (no pain, no gain) you have to experience bad things in order to progress

nothing to write home about not very interesting

no news is good news if you haven't heard anything then it's possible that nothing bad has happened

no peace for the wicked, no rest for the wicked ironic way of saying that a person is extremely busy and has to get on with their work

no show without Punch this person always seems to turn up (but is not really wanted)

no smoke without fire there's always some basis to a rumour

nothing venture, nothing gain if you don't at least try to do something you'll never know if you'll succeed

not just a pretty face intelligent as well as beautiful (often said in an ironic way by someone who knows that he or she is not beautiful)

not to put too fine a point on it not to get too detailed

nuts and bolts the basic details or practicalities of something

O

odds and ends objects of different kinds, perhaps that are left over and don't match

older and wiser to have got more wise with age

once bitten, twice shy to have experience an unfortunate situation and have learned from it

once in a blue moon very rarely

one in a million very rare

one of life's little ironies a situation that is the opposite of what one hoped would happen

one of those days a bad day

only time will tell you'll just have to wait and see what happens

on the back burner put to one side to be worked on later

on the dot exactly

opening gambit an opening move

an open secret not publicly discussed but is not a secret

or words to that effect something of the same meaning but said in a different way

out of sight, out of mind that which you don't see you are less likely to think about

over and done with finished

over my dead body I'll die before I let that happen

over the hill too old

P

pale into insignificance is overshadowed by something else

par for the course an expected experience in a certain situation

part and parcel an expected experience in a certain situation

the patter of tiny feet a baby

the picture of health very healthy

pie in the sky unrealistic expectations

plain sailing easy

pleased as Punch very pleased

the plot thickens a revelation makes a story more intriguing or complicated

the point of no return you've gone so far that going back is not a possible option

a poisoned chalice a seemingly attractive proposition that is actually dangerous

pound of flesh revenge

the powers that be people in charge

practice makes perfect to keep practising will aid perfection in a certain area

pride and joy something that makes one very proud

pride of place in a very prominent position

prime of life at an age where one is fit, healthy and mentally sharp

pull out all the stops to do everything possible

put one's best foot forward to make the best attempt possible

put two and two together to come to a conclusion about something

Q

quality of life an enjoyable fulfilling life

quality time time spent giving an individual lots of attention

quantum leap a sudden breakthrough

quite the reverse the opposite

R

a race against time time is running out

rain or shine whatever the weather

a rainy day an unspecified time in the future

the rat race the capitalist way of life

read my lips listen carefully to what I'm saying

red tape the rules and regulations of government office

reinvent the wheel wasting time doing work that's already been done

a reliable source a trustworthy basis for something

a resounding silence a meaningful silence

right as rain in full health

rings a bell sounds familiar

rising tide events that are about to take over

risk life and limb to put your life in danger

a rolling stone a person who never stays very long in one place

a rose between two thorns a beautiful or good person who has to decide between two unattractive choices

a rose by any other name whatever a beautiful thing happens to be named it remains beautiful

Rome wasn't built in a day a difficult task cannot be finished quickly

a rough diamond a person with a rough manner but who has great qualities

rule with a rod of iron to discipline in a strict manner

rumour has it I have heard rumours telling me this

S

safe and sound totally unharmed

a safe haven a place of safety

the salt of the earth a down to earth reliable person

saved by the bell saved from a bad situation by another event coming along

to say the least relates that this reaction/emotion is being described is being understated

search high and low to look everywhere

second to none the best

sell like hot cakes to be very popular

separate the sheep from the goats to distinguish the talented people from the stupid ones

a shadow of one's former self to be in some way diminished, either in physical size or in emotions

the shape of things to come how the future might be

share and share alike to be fair in one's dealings

ships that pass in the night strangers who meet once and never again

shoot oneself in the foot to say or do something that is to one's own detriment

short and sweet short and to the point

the show must go on despite misfortune an event will go ahead

signed, sealed and delivered finalised

a sign of the times something which indicates what society is like now

the silent majority the people who do not make their opinions known publicly

six of one and half-a-dozen of the other the same outcome

the sixty four thousand dollar question a key question that sums up a situation and the answer to which would be very valuable

slave over a hot stove to cook

slowly but surely to work in a slow but careful way

smell a rat to suspect something is wrong

the social whirl hectic social life

so far, so good at this point in the proceedings everything is fine

son and heir first-born son

so near and yet so far to have nearly accomplished something but near accomplishment is simply not good enough to get acclaim

sour grapes saying that something one cannot have is not worth having

spick and span very tidy

the spirit is willing not physically able to do something that one wishes to do

stand up and be counted make your opinions known publicly

a storm in a teacup a fuss over nothing

strange as it may seem this may look strange but it is actually true

suffer a sea change to have a complete change in attitude or opinion

suffer in silence to put up with something and not complain

the survival of the fittest to survive or flourish at the expense of those who are weaker

sweetness and light kind and friendly (usually just on the surface)

swings and roundabouts the same outcome

T

take the bull by the horns to tackle something boldly

take the rough with the smooth to accept that bad things can happen as well as good

talk of the devil said when someone or something you've just been talking about suddenly appears

tall, dark and handsome the clichéd idea of the perfect man

a tall order an unreasonable or very trying request

a (slight) technical hitch a mistake

teething troubles problems at the beginning of a project

tender loving care (TLC) to be looked after

terra firma to have one's feet safely on the ground

thankful for small mercies to be grateful for some small benefits in an otherwise unfortunate situation

that'll be the day that's not going to happen

that's for me to know and for you to find out it's a secret

that's life unexpected or difficult things can happen, you can't stop them

that's the way the cookie crumbles unexpected or difficult things can happen, you can't stop them

there but for the grace of God go I I could be in that situation

there's no fool like an old fool foolish behaviour in an older person always seems even more foolish than if a young person acted that way

these things happen unexpected or difficult things can happen, you can't stop them

through thick and thin through good times and bad

throw in the towel to give up

tie the knot to get married

tighten one's belt to be careful with your money

time flies time passes quickly

the tip of the iceberg there's a bigger problem that has still to surface or be dealt with

tired and emotional drunk

a tissue of lies a statement that is entirely dishonest in every way

tomorrow is another day you can try again another time

too good to be true so good that you can't believe it to be so

too little, too late not enough to solve a problem and too late in any case

too many chiefs and not enough Indians too many people want to be in charge and no one wants to listen to each other or do the work

too numerous to mention it would take too long to mention all the things I want to mention

touch and go a precarious situation

a tower of strength strong and reliable

trials and tribulations difficulties

turn over a new leaf to completely start over again in a new way

'twas ever thus it has always been like this

U

unaccustomed as I am to public speaking (usually said ironically) I'm not used speaking in public

unavoidable delay a delay caused by something you have no control over

under a cloud depressed

under the sun in the whole world

under the weather feeling run down

the university of life learning from real life experience

unsung hero someone who has not received the credit they deserve

an untimely end the death of someone who was very young and expected to make much of their life

untold wealth wealth of uncertain but probably very large amounts

the unvarnished truth a response that doesn't cover up any unpleasant facts

up in arms furious

up to the hilt thoroughly prepared

V

vanish into thin air to disappear without trace

variety is the spice of life lots of different things in your life make it more exciting

vested interest a motive (usually financial) for having an interest in something

a vexed question a difficult situation that is much discussed but still not solved

a vicious circle a bad situation, the result of which produces the original cause of the situation

vote with one's feet to show displeasure by leaving a situation

W

wait on hand and foot to do everything for someone

walls have ears people might be eavesdropping

warts and all good and bad

water under the bridge a situation that has passed and should be forgotten about

wedded bliss a (possibly ironic) way of describing marriage

the wee small hours after midnight

a well-earned rest a rest following hard work

what with one thing and another considering all the other things that have happened

wheels within wheels a complicated situation that has other thing involved

when all is said and done when all things have been considered and the argument is over

when in Rome join in with the customs of the people you are with

who/which shall remain nameless who need not be mentioned because we know who I am talking about

the whys and wherefores the reasoning behind an argument

without more ado without waiting much longer

the witching hour midnight

the world's your oyster the world is there for you to explore

with bated breath excitedly

wonders will never cease something has happened that has been long awaited but was not really expected to come about

a word to the wise a piece of advice

the writing is on the wall something is indicating that something bad is going to happen

Y

you can't make a silk purse out of a sow's ear you can't make something valuable out of something worthless

you can say that again what you've said is true and I agree

you can't teach an old dog new tricks there's no point in trying to make people change

you can't win 'em all bad things inevitably happen and you can't do anything about it

you know what I mean (added as emphasis to find out if listener empathises)

you must be joking I find what you've said ridiculous or unbelievable

your chariot awaits (ironic) said when someone is about to get into a vehicle

you're only young once make the most of your life

your guess is as good as mine neither of us know anything about this subject

Proverbs

A **proverb** is a short, memorable and often highly condensed saying that embodies a commonplace fact or experience.

Action

Actions speak louder than words
One good turn deserves another
Sooner begun, sooner done
The early bird catches the worm
It is the first step that is the most difficult

Age

A creaking door hangs long on its hinges
All would live long, but none would be old
An old fox is not easily snared
Crabbed age and youth cannot live together
Don't teach your grandmother to suck eggs
Life begins at forty
The best wine comes out of an old bottle
There's many a good tune played on an old
    fiddle
There's no fool like an old fool
They who live longest will see most
Years know more than books
You are only as old as you feel
You are never too old to learn
You can't teach an old dog new tricks
Youth and age will never agree

Anticipation

Do not halloo until you are out of the wood
Don't count your chickens until they are hatched
It is better to travel hopefully than to arrive
It isn't over until the fat lady sings
There's many a slip 'twixt cup and lip

Appearance

A fair face may hide a foul heart
All cats are grey in the dark
All that glitters is not gold
A monkey remains a monkey though dressed in silk
Appearances are deceptive
Beauty is in the eye of the beholder
Beauty is but skin deep
Beware the wolf in sheep's clothing
Be what you appear to be
Clothes make the man
Do not judge a book by its cover
Fine feathers make fine birds
First impressions are the most lasting
Handsome is as handsome does
Never judge from appearances
The eyes are the window of the soul
The fairest rose at last is withered
There is no making a good cloak of bad cloth
Things are not always what they seem
You can't tell a book from its cover
You must not hang a man by his looks

Caution

A stitch in time saves nine
Better safe than sorry
Better the devil you know than the devil you don't know
Curiosity killed the cat
Cut your coat according to the cloth
Don't count your chickens before they are hatched
Don't put all your eggs in one basket
Don't throw out the baby with the bathwater
Haste makes waste
Least said is soonest mended
Let sleeping dogs lie
Look before you leap
Marry in haste, repent at leisure
More haste, less speed
Once bitten, twice shy
One step at a time
Slow and steady wins the race
Slow but sure wins the race
The burnt child fears the fire
The less said the better
Think first and then speak
You must learn to walk before you can run

Change

A change is as good as a rest
A new broom sweeps clean
The rolling stone gathers no moss
Better the devil you know
Don't change horses in mid-stream
There is nothing new under the sun
You can't put back the clock
You can't put new wine in old bottles
Variety is the spice of life

Character

Blood will tell
Cut off a dog's tail and he will be a dog still
The apple never falls far from the tree
The leopard cannot change its spots
What's bred in the bone comes out in the flesh
You cannot make a silk purse out of a sow's ear

Choice

You cannot have it both ways
You cannot have your cake and eat it
You cannot serve god and Mammon
You cannot serve two masters
You pays your money and you takes your choice

Conduct

Ask no questions and you will be told no lies
Civility costs nothing
Cleanliness is next to godliness
Do as I say, not as I do

Do as you would be done by
Do not bite the hand that feeds you
Don't cut off your nose to spite your face
Don't hide your light under a bushel
If the cap fits, wear it
It is better to give than to receive
Least said soonest mended
Let sleeping dogs lie
Live and let live
Moderation in all thing
Never look a gift horse in the mouth
One good turn deserves another
People in glass houses should not throw stones
Practise what you preach
Pride goes before a fall
See no evil, hear no evil, speak no evil
Spare the rod and spoil the child
There is no use flogging a dead horse
The rolling stone gathers no moss
Travel broadens the mind
What you lose on the swings you gain on the roundabouts
When in Rome do as the Romans do
When the cat's away the mice will play
You cannot have your cake and eat it
You cannot make a silk purse out of a sow's ear

Courage and cowardice

A bully is always a coward
Attack is the best form of defence
Conscience makes cowards of us all
Discretion is the better part of valour
Faint heart never won fair lady
Fortune favours the bold
He that fights and runs away may live to fight another day
It is better to be a coward for a minute than dead for the
    rest of your life
Nothing ventured, nothing gained

Crime

All are not thieves whom the dogs bark at
An old poacher makes the best gamekeeper
It's an ill bird that fouls its own nest
Better to do nothing than to do ill
Caesar's wife must be above suspicion
Crime never pays
One rotten apple in the barrel infects all the rest
Poverty is the mother of crime
Set a thief to catch a thief
There are more thieves than are hanged
There is honour among thieves
To err is human, to forgive divine
Two wrongs do not make a right
You might as well be hanged for a sheep as a lamb

Death

All men must die
As a man lives so shall he die
Death is the great leveller
Dead men tell no tales
Death is a remedy for all ills
Death spares neither men nor beast
Fear of death is worse than death itself

It is as natural to die as to be born
Nothing is certain but death and taxes
One funeral makes many orphans
Shrouds have no pockets
The dead are soon forgotten
The good die young
We die as we live
When one is dead it is for a long time
Whom the gods love die young
You can only die once

Delay

Better late than never
He who hesitates is lost
Never put off till tomorrow what you can do today
Procrastination is the thief of time
Time lost cannot be recalled
Tomorrow never comes

Eating and drinking

Adam's ale is the best brew
An apple a day keeps the doctor away
An army marches on its stomach
Drink little that you may drink long
Eat to live, not live to eat
Example is better than precept
Good wine makes good blood
Hunger is the best sauce
In vino veritas (There is truth in wine)
Man cannot live by bread alone
The way to a man's heart is through his stomach
Thirst makes wine out of water
When the wine is in the wit is out

Folly

Empty vessels make the most sound
A fool and his money are soon parted
A fool's bolt is soon shot
Fools rush in where angels fear to tread
Fortune favours fools
He that is born a fool is never cured
Little things please little minds
There's no fool like an old fool
The world is full of fools
We have all been fools in our time

Friendship

A fair-weather friend changes with the wind
A favourite has no friends
A friend in need is a friend indeed
A man is known by the company he keeps
A trouble shared is a trouble halved
Birds of a feather flock together
Fish and guests stink after three days
He that lies down with dogs will get up with fleas
It is good to have friends in high places
Like will to like
One good turn deserves another
Save us from our friends
The best of friends must part

Happiness

A blithe heart makes a blooming visage
A happy heart is better than a full purse

All happiness is in the mind
Be happy when you can for you are a long time dead
Content is happiness
Happy is the country which has no history
It is a poor heart that never rejoices
Joy and sorrow are next-door neighbours
Laughter is the best medicine
No pleasure without pain

Health
A creaking gate lasts longest
An apple a day keeps the doctor away
Early to bed and early to rise makes a man healthy, wealthy
   and wise
Feed a cold and starve a fever
God heals, and the physician has the thanks
Health is better than wealth
The doctor is often more to be feared than the disease

Home
Dry bread at home is better than roast meat abroad
East west, home's best
Home is where the heart is
The hare always returns to her form
There's no place like home

Honesty
An honest man's word is as good as his bond
Better beg than steal
Confession is good for the soul
Honesty is the best policy
No honest man ever repented of his honesty
Plain dealing is best
Tell the truth and shame the devil
The truth will out

Hope and optimism
A drowning man clutches at straws
Every cloud has a silver lining
He that lives on hope has but a slender diet
Hope for the best and prepare for the worst
Hope keeps man alive
Hope springs eternal
It's an ill wind that blows nobody any good
Look on the bright side
The darkest hour is that before the dawn
The longest night will have an end
Where there's life, there's hope
Tomorrow is another day
Too much hope deceives

Law
Better no law than law not enforced
Every land has its own law
Every man is held to be innocent until he is proved guilty
Ignorance of the law excuses no man
Possession is nine points of the law
There's one law for the rich and another for the poor
The law is an ass
The more laws, the more offenders
You cannot make people honest by an act of parliament

Learning and knowledge
A little knowledge is a dangerous thing
A little learning is a dangerous thing

Experience is the best teacher
It is easy to be wise after the event
Knowledge is power
Much learning makes men mad
To know all is to forgive all
We must learn from our mistakes
What you don't know can't hurt you
Where ignorance is bliss, 'tis folly to be wise

Love
Absence makes the heart grow fonder
All's fair in love and war
All the world loves a lover
Better be an old man's darling than a young man's slave
Faint heart never won fair lady
It is best to be off with the old love before you are on with
   the new
Love begets love
Love comes in at the window and out at the door
Love conquers all
Love is blind
Love makes the world go round
Love sees no faults
Love will find a way
Lucky at cards, unlucky in love
Out of sight, out of mind
Pity is akin to love
The course of true love never did run smooth
The way to a man's heart is through his stomach
'Tis better to have loved and lost than never to have loved
Who would be loved, must love

Marriage
Marriage is a lottery
Marriages are made in heaven
Marry in haste, repent at leisure
Marry in Lent and you'll live to repent
Marry your son when you will, your daughter when you
   can
Men are April when they woo, December when they wed
Wedlock is a padlock

Miserliness
Don't spoil the ship for a hap'orth of tar
Grasp all, lose all
Greedy folks have long arms
Kill not the goose that lays the golden egg
The more you get, the more you want

Opportunity
A bird in the hand is worth two in the bush
Gather ye rosebuds while ye may
Make hay while the sun shines
Nothing ventured, nothing gained
Opportunity seldom knocks twice
Strike while the iron is hot
Take time by the forelock
There's no time like the present
The tide must be taken when it comes
Time and tide wait for no man

Patience
An oak is not felled at one stroke
A watched pot never boils

Everything comes to him who waits
Patience is a virtue
Rome was not built in a day
They also serve who only stand and wait
We must learn to walk before we can run

Power

A cat may look at a king
A house divided against itself cannot stand
All men cannot be masters
Attack is the best form of defence
Little is done where many command
Might is right
Money is power
No man can serve two masters
Power corrupts
The ballot is stronger than the bullet
The mightier they are, the harder they fall
The weakest go to the wall
United we stand, divided we fall
When Greek meets Greek then comes the tug of war
When two play one must lose
Why keep a dog and bark yourself?

Regret

It is easy to be wise after the event
It is too late to shut the stable door after the horse has
   bolted
Past cure, past care
There's no use in crying over spilt milk
Things past cannot be recalled
We never know the worth of the water till the well runs dry
What's done cannot be undone
You cannot make omelettes without breaking eggs

Responsibility

A bad workman blames his tools
As you make your bed, so you must lie on it
As you reap, so shall you sow
Every man is the architect of his own fortune
Paddle your own canoe
The absent party is always to blame

Silence

A closed mouth catches no flies
Silence is golden
Speech is silver, silence is golden
Still waters run deep
There is a time to speak and a time to be silent
When in doubt say nothing

Sleep

One hour's sleep before midnight is worth two after
Sleep is better than medicine
Sleep is the brother of death
There will be sleeping enough in the grave

Talking

Barking dogs seldom bite
Fine words butter no parsnips
The tongue is more venomous than a serpent's sting

Time

History repeats itself
There is a time and place for everything
Time and tide wait for no man

Time cures all things
Time flies
Time is a great healer
Time is money
Time lost cannot be recalled

Wealth and poverty

A fool and his money are soon parted
A light purse and a heavy heart
Enough is as good as a feast
God helps those who help themselves
Half a loaf is better than no bread
He that goes a-borrowing goes a-sorrowing
He who pays the piper may call the tune
It is better to be born lucky than rich
It is better to be poor and well than rich and ill
Lend your money and lose your friend
Money is not everything
Money is power
Money is a good servant but a bad master
Money makes money
Money talks
Neither a borrower nor a lender be
Penny wise and pound foolish
Poverty is no disgrace but it is a great inconvenience
Poverty is not a crime
Some people are born with a silver spoon in their mouth
Take care of the pennies and the pounds will take care of
   themselves
The art is not in making money but in keeping it
The poor you always have with you
Time is money
What you've never had, you never miss
When poverty comes in at the door, love flies out of the
   window
Who has nothing fears nothing

Weather

A cold April the barn will fill
After the storm comes a calm
A green Yule means a fat churchyard
April and May are the key of all the year
April showers bring forth May flowers
Lightning never strikes twice
Rain before seven, fine before eleven
Red sky at night, shepherd's delight, red sky in the
   morning, shepherd's warning
St Swithin's Day, if thou dost rain, for forty days it will
   remain

Work

A good beginning is half the work
A work done ill must be done twice
Business before pleasure
From small beginnings come great things
If a thing is worth doing it is worth doing well
Many hands make light work
No gain without pain
The devil finds work for idle hands to do
The work praises the workman
Too many cooks spoil the broth
You cannot make bricks without straw